The Editor desires to express his gratitude to readers for their criticisms and suggestions and to all those who in one way or another have contributed to this latest edition. Correspondence on editorial matters should be addressed to Dr Christopher Cook, Pears Cyclopaedia, Penguin Books Ltd, 27 Wrights Lane, Kensington, London W8 5TZ

PENGUIN BOOKS

Published by the Penguin Group
Penguin Books Ltd, 27 Wrights Lane, London W8 5TZ
Penguin Putnam Inc., 375 Hudson Street, New York, New York 10014, USA
Penguin Books Australia Ltd, Ringwood, Victoria, Australia
Penguin Books Canada Ltd, 10 Alcorn Avenue, Toronto, Ontario, Canada M4V 3B2
Penguin Books (NZ) Ltd, 182–190 Wairau Road, Auckland 10, New Zealand

Penguin Books Ltd, Registered Offices: Harmondsworth, Middlesex, England

First published 1897
108th edition published 1999
Copyright, © Penguin Books Ltd 1999

Pears is a trademark of Penguin Books Ltd

Printed in England by Clays Ltd., St Ives plc

A CIP catalogue record for this book is available from the British Library

0 140 28232 7

PEARS

CYCLOPAEDIA

1999–2000

A BOOK OF REFERENCE AND BACKGROUND
INFORMATION FOR ALL THE FAMILY

EDITED BY

CHRISTOPHER COOK

M.A. Cantab., D.Phil. Oxon., F.R. Hist. S.

*One Hundred and Eighth Edition
(Millennium Edition)*

CONTENTS

Sections are arranged alphabetically, or chronologically, or have
a detailed Table of Contents.

CONTENTS

THE STORY OF PEARS

Success stories in publishing, even in this closing year of the twentieth century, still abound. Success stories which go from strength to strength over 100 years are, by any standards, unique. Back in September 1991, the 100th edition of the world famous reference book took its familiar place on the shelves of bookshops across the world. This millennium edition (the 108th) is published more than one hundred years since *Pears* first appeared back in 1897.

The origins of *Pears Cyclopaedia* are no less fascinating than its phenomenal success—a success which produced sales of 3 million copies by the 1930s and at least as many again since. That success dates to 1865, when a young man of 24 joined the business of A&F Pears Ltd, soap makers to Queen Victoria. At a well-known Academy of Dancing and Deportment in the West End, Thomas J Barratt made the acquaintance of the eldest daughter of Mr Francis Pears. Miss Pears became Mrs Barratt, and Mr Barratt became the London Manager of Pears!

Thomas Barratt was an advertising genius. He declared that he would advertise as no soapmaker had ever advertised before. In the then relatively new profession of advertising, he made Pears Soap a world-wide name. Such advertisements as "Bubbles" and "Two years ago I used your soap, since when I have used no other" achieved lasting fame.

But perhaps the most original advertisement of all for Pears Soap was the little red *Pears Shilling Cyclopaedia*, first printed for A&F Pears by David Bryce and Son of Glasgow. It was published in December 1897, the year of Queen Victoria's Diamond Jubilee. This first edition contained an English dictionary, a medical dictionary, a gazetteer and atlas, desk information and a compendium of general knowledge entitled "A Mass of Curious and Useful Information about Things that everyone Ought to know in Commerce, History, Science, Religion, Literature and other Topics of Ordinary Conversation".

The idea was to keep the general public informed on the issues of the day, to equip them for social discourse, satisfy their curiosity and widen their learning. Topics ranged from hard facts to questions of etiquette, from why the Russians needed a port on the Mediterranean to the longevity of the clergy!

Although *Pears Cyclopaedia* slipped its connections with soap back in 1960 when the publishing rights were aquired by Pelham Books (and in turn passed to Penguin Books), there has been astonishing editorial continuity (only two editors since 1946, only three in the first 50 years). Now the price is rather more than the original shilling, but *Pears* still represents remarkable value for over 1,000 pages packed with information.

Many of the popular features of the first edition have been retained. The medical section, the gazetteer and atlas, the sections on Economics, Science, Literature, Ideas and Beliefs, Historical Events and General Information are all still there. Also there are topics of current social and political interest, specially commissioned for each edition. There are newer, equally-popular favourites in the present edition, including Classical Mythology, Sporting Records, the Biblical Glossary, Music and the World of Art. It is this blend of innovation and tradition—the tried and tested facts and figures alongside authoritative new articles in every edition that has made *Pears* so popular with generation after generation.

The single most important factor in the *Pears* success story, and the key to its truly unique publishing phenomenon, is that *it is the only book of its kind to be fully revised and updated by a team of experts every year*.

Schools and colleges, offices and libraries, students and researchers, newspapers, radio and TV stations—for all these, and many more, for whom readily accessible, reliable facts at their fingertips are needed, *Pears Cyclopaedia* remains an invaluable companion.

HISTORICAL
EVENTS

Historical events from the earliest times to the present day. For entries on specific historical topics, readers may wish to refer to Section L, General Information. Current political events are discussed in Section C, World Affairs. This edition continues the detailed chronicle of the dramatic events of the present decade that have seen great political and economic changes around the world as the century draws to its close.

CHRONICLE OF EVENTS

Note.—For classical history and for the past millennium most dates are well established. For other periods there is sometimes considerable uncertainty. Many of the dates in ancient history are either dubious or approximate, sometimes both.

B.C.   **PREHISTORY**

70,000,000   Earliest known primate (*Plesiadapis*).

35,000,000   *Aegyptopithecus*, ancestral ape from the Fayum.

20,000,000   *Proconsul*, possible ancestor of hominids in East Africa.

3,700,000   First hominids in East Africa – *Australopithecus*.

2,100,000   First hominid stone toolmaker – *Homo habilis*; present in Africa until 1,800,000 years ago.

1,600,000   Earliest *Homo erectus* in East Africa, present there and in Europe and Far East until 200,000 years ago.

500,000   Archaic modern man, *Homo sapiens*, present in Africa until 30,000 years ago.

100,000   Neanderthal Man, present in Europe until 35,000 years ago: Anatomically modern man, *Homo sapiens sapiens* present in Africa, dispersed worldwide.

70,000   Neanderthalers (Europe, Asia, N. Africa). Rhodesian Man (S. Africa). Solo Man (Java). Flake tools.

40,000   First cold phase ends. Neanderthal race becoming extinct. Second cold phase. *Homo sapiens* (modern man). Implements show significant advances: small knife-blades, engraving tools. Paintings and sculpture; magic rites and ceremonies. Cro-Magnons with Aurignacian culture.

18,000   Final culmination of last ice age.

     Aurignacian culture dying out to be replaced by Solutrean and then by the Magdalenian cultures. Great flowering of Palaeolithic art.

15,000   First immigrants from Asia to cross Bering Straits?

15,000   Last glaciers in Britain disappeared. Proto-Neolithic in Middle East. Agricultural settlements (*e.g.*, Jericho). Settled way of life leading to such skills as weaving, metallurgy; inventions such as ox-drawn plough, wheeled cart.

5,000   Britain becomes an island (land connection with continent severed by melting ice-sheets).

B.C. **CIVILISATION IN THE MIDDLE EAST**

4300–3100   Formation of urban settlements in S. Mesopotamia during the Uruk Period. Cuneiform writing developed.

3150   First Egyptian Dynasty; capital at Memphis. Hieratic writing already perfected. Early Minoan Age (Crete). Pictorial writing, copper, silver, gold in use. Early Mycenaean civilisation begins.

2900–2334   Early Dynastic Mesopotamia (Sumer & Akkad). Sumerian dominance; Royal Cemetery of Ur.

2870   First settlements at Troy.

2850   Golden Age of China begins (legendary).

B.C.

2700–2200   Old Kingdom (Pyramid Age) in Egypt.

2400   Aryan migrations.

2334–2279   Sargon of Agade; his Akkadian empire collapses soon after the death of his grandson Naram-Sin in 2218.

2205   Hsia Dynasty begins in China (legendary).

2200   Middle Minoan Age: pottery, linear writing in pen and ink.

1800–1400   Stonehenge built and rebuilt.

1792–1750   Hammurabi king of Babylon; law code.

1766–1122   Shang Dynasty in China.

1720–1550   Hyksos in Egypt. War chariots introduced. Hebrews entered Egypt (Joseph) *c.* 1600.

1552–1069   Egyptian New Kingdom: at zenith under XVIIIth Dynasty. Chronology more certain: Late Minoan Age; Linear B script.

1500   Powerful Mitanni (Aryan) kingdom in Asia Minor. Phoenicia thriving—trade with Egypt and Babylonia. Vedic literature in India.

1450   Zenith of Minoan civilisation.

1400   Ugarit (N. Syria) culture at its zenith. Cretan civilisation ends: Knossos burnt. Temple at Luxor built.

1352–1338   Amenhotep IV (Akhenaten), the "heretic" Pharaoh. Diplomatic archive of Tell el-Amarna.

1350   Zenith of Hittite civilisation.

1275   Israelite oppression (Rameses II); Exodus from Egypt (Moses). Phoenician settlements—Hellas and Spain (Cadiz). Tyre flourishing.

1250   Israelites invade Palestine (Joshua).

1200   Attacks on Egypt by "Peoples of the Sea". Downfall of Hittite kingdom. Siege of Troy (Homeric). Beginning of sea-power of independent Phoenician cities.

1122–256   Chou (Zhou) Dynasty in China.

1115   Magnetic needle reputed in China.

1005–925   Kingdom of David and Solomon: Jerusalem as Sanctuary.

1000   *Rig Veda* (India).

925–722   Israel and Judah divided.

893   Assyrian chronological records begin.

850   Foundation of Carthage (traditional).

781   Chinese record of an eclipse.

776   First Olympiad to be used for chronological purposes.

753   Foundation of Rome (traditional).

750   Greek colonists settling in Southern Italy.

745   Accession of Tiglath-Pileser III; Assyrian Power at its height.

722   Capture of Samaria by Sargon II: Israel deported to Nineveh.

700   Homer's poems probably written before this date. Spread of the iron-using Celtic Hallstatt culture about this time.

625   Neo-Babylonian (Chaldean) Empire (Nineveh destroyed 612).

621   Publication of Athenian laws by Draco.

610   Spartan constitution, made rigid after Messenian Wars: later attributed to Lycurgus.

B.C.
594 Athenian constitution reformed by Solon.

586 Capture of Jerusalem: Judah deported to Babylon (partial return 538).

561 Pisistratus tyrant of Athens.

560 Accession of Croesus—prosperity of Lydia.

538 Babylon taken by Persians: Empire founded by Cyrus, soon covers almost all of civilised Middle East.

509 Roman Republic founded (traditional).

508 Democratic constitution in Athens.

500 Etruscans at height of their power in Northern Italy.

GREAT AGE OF GREECE

499 Revolt of Ionian Greek cities against Persian king Darius.

494 Secession of Plebeians from Rome. Tribunes established.

490 Battle of Marathon: Athenian repulse of Persian attack.

480 Death of Buddha. Battle of Thermopylae: Spartans under Leonidas wiped out by Persians. Battle of Salamis: Persian fleet defeated by Athenians under Themistocles; Persian invasion of Greece halted.

479 Battles of Plataea and Mycale: Greek victories by land and sea respectively destroy Persian invasion force. Death of Confucius.

477 League of Delos founded by Athens for defence against Persia; soon becomes Athenian Empire. (467 Naxos kept in by force.)

461 Pericles comes to power in Athens.

458 Cincinnatus saves Rome (traditional).

456 Death of Aeschylus.

447 Building of Parthenon begun.

431 Death of Phidias. Outbreak of Great Peloponnesian War between Athens and Sparta. Pericles "Funeral Oration" (according to Thucydides).

425 Death of Herodotus.

416 Massacre of Melos by Athenians.

415 Sicilian Expedition: flight of Alcibiades from Athens to Sparta.

413 Loss of entire Athenian expeditionary force at Syracuse.

406 Death of Euripides and Sophocles.

405 Battle of Aegospotami: Athenian navy destroyed by Sparta.

404 Athenian surrender to Sparta: beginning of Spartan hegemony in Greece.

403 Beginning of epoch of Warring States in China.

400 Death of Thucydides, Greek historian (?).

399 Execution of Socrates.

390 Occupation of Rome by Gauls under Brennus.

371 Battle of Leuctra: Spartans defeated by Thebans: beginning of Theban hegemony in Greece.

370 Death of Hippocrates of Cos (?).

347 Death of Plato.

343 Last native Egyptian Dynasty ends; Persians reconquer Egypt.

338 Battle of Chaeronea: Greek city-states defeated by Philip II of Macedon, who becomes supreme in Greece.

336 Assassination of Philip of Macedon: accession of Alexander.

334 Alexander's invasion of Persian Empire. Battle of Granicus, first victory.

333 Battle of Issus: Alexander defeats Darius of Persia.

332 Alexander's siege and capture of Tyre, occupation of Egypt.

B.C.
331 Battle of Arbela (Gaugamela)—final defeat of Darius.

330 Death of Darius and end of Persian Empire. Alexander heir to civilisations of Middle East.

326 Battle of Hydaspes: Alexander conquers the Punjab.

323 Death of Alexander at Babylon. Beginning of Hellenistic Age in Middle East and Eastern Mediterranean. Ptolemy I founds dynasty in Egypt. Alexandria becomes intellectual centre of Hellenic world.

322 Death of Demosthenes.

321 Death of Aristotle. Maurya dynasty unites N. India.

312 Seleucus I founds dynasty in Asia.

300 Zeno the Stoic, Epicurus and Euclid flourishing.

ROME: CONQUESTS AND DECAY OF REPUBLICAN INSTITUTIONS

290 End of Third Samnite War. Rome dominates Central Italy.

280 Translation of Pentateuch into Greek.

275 Battle of Beneventum: Rome finally defeats Pyrrhus and the Greek cities of Southern Italy. Rome dominates all Italy.

274 Asoka becomes ruler of two-thirds of Indian sub-continent.

264 Beginning of First Punic War (Rome v. Carthage).

260 Battle of Mylae: first great Roman naval victory.

255 Defeat and capture of Regulus by Carthaginians.

250 Incursion of "La Tène" Iron Age people into Britain.

241 End of First Punic War. Sicily becomes first Province of Rome.

221 Kingdom of Ch'in (Qin) completes conquest of all Chinese states under Shih Huang-ti.

218 Outbreak of Second Punic War: Hannibal crosses Alps.

216 Battle of Cannae: Hannibal wipes out great Roman army.

214 Great Wall of China constructed (by linking existing walls).

213 Burning of Chinese classics.

212 Capture of Syracuse by Romans and death of Archimedes.

207 Battle of Metaurus: defeat and death of Hasdrubal. End of Hannibal's hopes of overcoming Rome.

205 Roman provinces organised in Spain.

202 Battle of Zama: Hannibal defeated by Scipio Africanus, 202–A.D. 220 Han Dynasty in China.

201 End of Second Punic War. Rome dominates Western Mediterranean.

196 After defeating Macedon, Rome proclaims independence of Greek city-states. Death of Eratosthenes the geographer (?).

160 Death in battle of Judas Maccabaeus: Jewish revolt against Seleucids continues successfully.

149 Outbreak of Third Punic War.

146 Carthage destroyed. Roman province of Africa formed. Roman provinces of Macedonia and Achaea formed, and most of remainder of Greece reduced to vassal status.

134 First Servile War; Revolt of slaves in Sicily under Eunus. Suppressed 132.

133 Siege and destruction of Numantia by Romans. Tiberius Gracchus Tribune. Attempted land reforms. Murdered 132.

129 Roman province of Asia formed from lands bequeathed by Attalus of Pergamum.

124 Chinese Grand College to train Civil Service officials.

123 Caius Gracchus Tribune. Attempted land reforms. Murdered 121.

110 Chinese expansion to include most of south-east of modern China, under Emperor Wu Ti. Commercial activity in Indian Ocean.

B.C.

106 Jugurtha captured by Marius and Sulla.

104 Second Servile War: revolt of slaves in Sicily under Tryphon and Athenion. Suppressed 101.

102 Chinese expedition to Ferghana and possible knowledge of West.

101 Battle of Vercellae: Marius ends threat of Cimbri to Rome.

91 Social War: revolt of Italian cities against Rome. Suppressed 88. Roman franchise granted to most Italians.

88 Civil Wars of Marius and Sulla begin.

87 Massacre in Rome by Marius.

82 Proscriptions in Rome by Sulla.

75 Belgic invasion of south-eastern Britain.

73 Third Servile War: revolt of slaves in southern Italy under Spartacus the gladiator. Suppressed 71.

63 Conspiracy of Catiline exposed by Cicero.

60 First Triumvirate: Pompey, Caesar, Crassus.

58 Beginning of Caesar's conquest of Gaul.

55 Caesar's first British expedition: second, 54.

53 Battle of Carrhae: destruction of Roman army under Crassus by Persians.

52 Revolt of Vercingetorix against Caesar.

50 Migration to Britain of Commius and his followers.

49 Caesar crosses the Rubicon. Beginning of war against Pompey and the Senate.

48 Battle of Pharsalus: defeat of Pompey by Caesar.

46 Caesar's calendar reforms.

44 Murder of Caesar.

43 Second Triumvirate: Antony, Octavian, Lepidus.

42 Battle of Philippi: defeat and death of Brutus and his associates.

31 Battle of Actium: naval victory of Octavian over Antony and Cleopatra. Octavian unchallenged master of the Roman world.

THE ROMAN EMPIRE

27 Octavian given the title of Augustus by the Senate.

19 Death of Virgil.

8 Death of Horace.

4 Birth of Jesus (date not certain).

A.D.

6 Civil Service Examination system in China.

9 Radical reforms by Wang Mang (short Hsin dynasty 9–23). Annihilation of Roman army under Varus by Teutonic tribesmen under Arminius.

10 Cunobelinus reigning over much of south-east Britain from Colchester.

14 Death of Augustus.

17 Death of Livy.

18 Death of Ovid.

30 Crucifixion of Jesus (date not certain).

43 Roman invasion of Britain under Aulus Plautius.

51 Caractacus taken to Rome as prisoner.

60 Revolt of Boudicca.

63 Great Fire of Rome.

64 Death of St. Paul (date not certain).

65 Death of Seneca.

66 Jews of Palestine rebelled against Roman rule.

68 Death of Nero—end of Julio-Claudian line of Roman Emperors.

70 Jerusalem taken and Jewish revolt suppressed by Titus.

79 Destruction of Pompeii and Herculaneum by eruption of Vesuvius.

A.D.

80 Completion of Colosseum (Flavian Amphitheatre).

83 Battle of Mons Graupius: Agricola crushes Caledonians.

96 Accession of Nerva: first of the "Five Good Emperors."

97 Chinese expedition under Kang Yin (lieutenant of Pan Ch'ao) penetrates to Persian Gulf.

117 Death of Trajan, accession of Hadrian. Roman Empire at its greatest extent.

122 Beginning of Hadrian's Wall (Tyne–Solway) by Aulus Platorius Nepos.

135 Suppression of Bar-Cochba's revolt and Dispersion of Jews.

142 Construction of Antonine Wall (Forth–Clyde) by Quintus Lollius Urbicus.

180 Death of Marcus Aurelius, last of the "Five Good Emperors." Beginning of the "Decline" of the Roman Empire (Gibbon).

193 Praetorian guards murder Emperor Pertinax, sell Empire to highest bidder (Didius Julianus).

196 Clodius Albinus, governor, withdraws forces from Britain to support his attempt to become Emperor. Northern Britain overrun by barbarians.

208 Septimius Severus visits Britain to punish Caledonians (death at York 211).

212 Edict of Caracalla. Roman citizenship conferred on all free inhabitants of Empire.

220 End of Han Dynasty: China divided and frequently invaded for next three centuries.

227 Sassanid Empire in Persia.

230 Emperor Sulin—Japanese history emerging from legendary stage.

251 Goths defeat and kill Emperor Decius.

259 Break-away "Gallic Empire" set up: suppressed 273.

273 Defeat of Zenobia and destruction of Palmyra by Emperor Aurelian.

284 Accession of Diocletian, who reorganises Roman Empire (293) with rigid social laws and heavy taxation.

287 Carausius attempts to found independent "Empire of Britain": suppressed 297.

306 Constantine proclaimed Emperor at York.

313 Edict of Milan. Christianity tolerated in Roman Empire.

320 Gupta dynasty reunites India.

325 Council of Nicaea: first general Council of the Church.

367 Successful attack on Britain by Picts, Scots, Saxons.

369 Restoration of Roman authority in Britain by Theodosius.

378 Battle of Adrianople: Goths defeat and kill Eastern Roman Emperor Valens.

383 Magnus Maximus withdraws forces from Britain to support his attempt to conquer north-western part of Empire.

388 Magnus Maximus defeated and killed in Italy.

395 Death of Emperor Theodosius the Great: the division of the Empire into East and West at his death proves eventually to be the final one.

406 Usurper Constantine III withdraws forces from Britain to support his claims: probable end of Roman military occupation of Britain.

410 Sack of Rome by Alaric the Goth. Emperor Honorius tells Britons to arrange for their own defence.

THE BARBARIAN INVASIONS

415 Visigoths begin conquest of Spain.

419 Visigothic kingdom of Toulouse recognised by Roman government.

429 Vandals begin conquest of North Africa.

432 St. Patrick begins mission in Ireland.

A.D.

446 "Groans of the Britons"—last appeal to Rome (traditional).

451 Châlons: Attila the Hun repelled from Gaul by mixed Roman–Barbarian forces.

452 Attila's raid into Italy: destruction of Aquilea and foundation of Venice by refugees.

455 Rome pillaged by Vandals.

476 Romulus Augustulus, last Western Roman Emperor, deposed by Odovacar: conventionally the end of the Western Roman Empire.

481 Clovis becomes King of the Franks, who eventually conquer Gaul (d. 511).

493 Theodoric founds Ostrogothic Kingdom in Italy (d. 526).

515 Battle of Mount Badon: West Saxon advance halted by Britons, perhaps led by Arthur (?).

BYZANTIUM AND ISLAM

527 Accession of Justinian I (d. 565).

529 Code of Civil Law published by Justinian. Rule of St. Benedict put into practice at Monte Cassino (traditional).

534 Byzantines under Belisarius reconquer North Africa from Vandals.

552 Byzantine reconquest of Italy complete.

563 St. Columba founds mission in Iona.

568 Lombard Kingdom founded in Italy.

570 Birth of Mohammed.

577 Battle of Deorham: West Saxon advance resumed.

581–618 Sui Dynasty in China.

590 Gregory the Great becomes Pope.

597 St. Augustine lands in Kent.

605 Grand Canal of China constructed.

618–907 T'ang Dynasty in China: their administrative system lasts in essentials for 1,300 years.

622 Hejira or flight from Mecca to Medina of Mohammed: beginning of Mohammedan era.

627 Battle of Nineveh: Persians crushed by Byzantines under Heraclius.

632 Death of Mohammed: all Arabia now Moslem. Accession of Abu Bakr, the first Caliph.

634 Battle of Heavenfield: Oswald becomes king of Northumbria, brings in Celtic Christianity.

638 Jerusalem captured by Moslems.

641 Battle of Mehawand: Persia conquered by Moslems.

643 Alexandria taken by Moslems.

645 Downfall of Soga clan in Japan, after establishing Buddhism: beginning of period of imitation of Chinese culture.

650 Slav occupation of Balkans now complete.

663 Synod of Whitby: Roman Christianity triumphs over Celtic Christianity in England.

685 Nectansmere: end of Northumbrian dominance in England.

698 Carthage taken by Moslems.

711 Tarik leads successful Moslem invasion of Spain.

718 Failure of second and greatest Moslem attack on Constantinople. Pelayo founds Christian kingdom of Asturias in Northern Spain.

726 Byzantine Emperor Leo III begins Iconoclast movement: opposed by Pope Gregory II, and an important cause of difference between Roman and Byzantine churches.

THE HOLY ROMAN EMPIRE AND THE TRIUMPH OF CHRISTIANITY IN EUROPE: NORSEMEN AND NORMANS

732 Poitiers: Moslem western advance halted by Charles Martel.

735 Death of Bede.

750 Beginning of Abbasid Caliphate (replacing Omayyads)

A.D.

751 Pepin King of the Franks: founds Carolingian dynasty. Ravenna taken by Lombards: end of Byzantine power in the West.

754 Pepin promises central Italy to Pope: beginning of temporal power of the Papacy.

778 Roncesvalles: defeat and death of Roland.

786 Accession of Haroun-al-Rashid in Baghdad.

793 Sack of Lindisfarne: Viking attacks on Britain begin.

795 Death of Offa: end of Mercian dominance in England.

800 Coronation of Charlemagne as Emperor by Pope Leo III in Rome.

814 Death of Charlemagne: division of empire.

825 Ellandun: Egbert defeats Mercians and Wessex becomes leading kingdom in England.

827 Moslem invasion of Sicily.

840 Moslems capture Bari and occupy much of Southern Italy.

843 Treaty of Verdun: final division of Carolingian Empire, and beginning of France and Germany as separate states.

844 Kenneth MacAlpin becomes king of Picts as well as Scots: the kingdom of Alban.

862 Rurik founds Viking state in Russia: first at Novgorod, later at Kiev.

866 Fujiwara period begins in Japan. Viking "Great Army" in England: Northumbria, East Anglia and Mercia subsequently overwhelmed.

868 Earliest dated printed book in China.

872 Harold Fairhair King of Norway.

874 Iceland settled by Norsemen.

885–6 Viking attack on Paris.

893 Simeon founds first Bulgar Empire in Balkans.

896 Arpad and the Magyars in Hungary.

899 Death of Alfred the Great.

900 Ghana at the height of its power in North West Africa.

907–960 Five Dynasties in China: partition.

910 Abbey of Cluny founded: monastic reforms spread from here.

911 Rolf (or Rollo) becomes ruler of Normandy.

912 Accession of Abderrahman III: the most splendid period of the Omayyad Caliphate of Cordova (d. 961).

928 Brandenburg taken from the Slavs by Henry the Fowler, King of Germany.

929 Death of Wenceslas, Christian King of Bohemia.

937 Battle of Brunanburh: crowning victory of Athelstan. West Saxon kings now masters of England.

955 Battle of Lechfeld: Magyars finally defeated by Otto the Great and settle in Hungary.

960–1279 Sung (Song) Dynasty in China.

965 Harold Bluetooth king of Denmark, accepts Christianity.

966 Mieszko I king of Poland, accepts Christianity.

968 Fatimids begin their rule in Egypt.

982 Discovery of Greenland by Norsemen.

987 Hugh Capet king of France: founder of Capetian dynasty.

988 Vladimir of Kiev accepts Christianity.

991 Battle of Maldon: defeat of Byrhtnoth of Essex by Vikings—renewed Viking raids on England.

993 Olof Skutkonung, king of Sweden, accepts Christianity.

1000 Leif Ericsson discovers North America.

1001 Coronation of St. Stephen of Hungary with crown sent by the Pope.

1002 Massacre of St. Brice's Day: attempt by Ethelred to exterminate Danes in England.

A.D.

1014 Battle of Clontarf: victory of Irish under Brian Boru over Vikings.

1016 Canute becomes king of England; builds short-lived Danish "empire."

1018 Byzantines under Basil 11 complete subjection of Bulgars.

1040 Attempts to implement Truce of God.

1046 Normans under Robert Guiscard in southern Italy.

1054 Beginning of Almoravid (Moslem) conquests in West Africa.

1060 Normans invade Sicily.

1066 Norman conquest of England under William I.

1069 Reforms of Wang An-Shih in China.

THE CRUSADES

1071 Manzikert: Seljuk Turks destroy Byzantine army and overrun Anatolia.

1073 Hildebrand (Gregory VII) becomes Pope. Church discipline and Papal authority enforced.

1075 Seljuk Turks capture Jerusalem.

1076 Kumbi, capital of Ghana, sacked by Almoravids: subsequent break-up of Ghana Empire.

1084 Carthusians founded by St. Bruno at Chartreuse.

1086 Compilation of Domesday Book.

1094 El Cid takes Valencia.

1095 Council of Clermont: Urban II preaches First Crusade.

1098 Cistercians founded by St. Robert at Citeaux.

1099 First Crusade under Godfrey of Bouillon takes Jerusalem.

1100 Death of William Rufus in the New Forest. Baldwin I: Latin Kingdom of Jerusalem founded.

1106 Tinchebrai: Henry I of England acquires Normandy, captures his brother Robert.

1115 Abelard teaching at Paris. St. Bernard founds monastery at Clairvaux.

1119 Order of Knights Templars founded.

1120 Loss of the White Ship and heir to English throne.

1122 Concordat of Worms: Pope and Emperor compromise on the Investiture Controversy, but continue to quarrel over other matters (Guelfs and Ghibellines).

1135 Stephen takes English crown: civil wars with Matilda and anarchy ensue.

1143 Alfonso Henriques proclaimed first king of Portugal.

1144 Moslems take Christian stronghold of Edessa.

1148 Second Crusade fails to capture Damascus.

1150 Carmelites founded about this time by Berthold.

1152 Accession of Emperor Frederick Barbarossa.

1154 Henry of Anjou succeeds Stephen: first of Plantagenet kings of England. Adrian IV (first English pope, Nicholas Breakspear).

1161 Explosives used in warfare in China.

1169 Strongbow invades Ireland: beginning of Anglo-Norman rule. Saladin ruling in Egypt.

1170 Murder of Thomas Becket in Canterbury cathedral.

1171 Spanish knightly Order of Santiago founded.

1176 Battle of Legnano: Frederick Barbarossa defeated by the Lombard League. Italian autonomy established.

1185 Kamakura Period in Japan: epoch of feudalism: until 1333.

1187 Hattin: destruction of Latin kingdom of Jerusalem by Saladin.

A.D.

1189 Third Crusade launched: leaders—Frederick Barbarossa, Philip Augustus of France, Richard Lionheart of England.

1191 Capture of Acre by Crusaders.

1192 End of Third Crusade without regaining Jerusalem. Richard I seized and held to ransom in Austria on return journey.

1198 Innocent III becomes Pope.

1202 Fourth Crusade, diverted by Venetians takes Zara from Byzantines.

1204 Fourth Crusade captures Constantinople, founds Latin Empire. King John of England loses Normandy to France.

1206 Temujin proclaimed Genghiz Khan (Very Mighty King) of all the Mongols: soon controls all of Central Asia.

1208 Albigensian Crusade launched: the first against Christians.

1212 Battle of Las Navas de Tolosa: decisive victory of Spaniards over Moors. The Children's Crusade.

THE CULMINATION OF THE MIDDLE AGES

1215 Fourth Lateran Council: the authority of the mediaeval Church and Papacy at its zenith. Dominicans recognised by the Pope. Magna Carta extorted by barons from John.

1223 Franciscans recognised by the Pope.

1229 Emperor Frederick II, through diplomacy, recognised by Moslems as King of Jerusalem.

1230 Teutonic Knights established in Prussia.

1237 Golden Horde (Mongols) begin subjugation of Russia.

1241 Mongol incursions into Central Europe.

1250 St. Louis of France captured on his Crusade in Egypt. Mamelukes become rulers of Egypt. Mandingo king declares his independence of Ghana and embraces Islam.

1256 Conference of Baltic ports; the first form of the Hanseatic League.

1258 Provisions of Oxford: barons under Simon de Montfort force reforms on Henry III of England. Baghdad destroyed by Mongols.

1264 Battle of Lewes: Montfort's party become rulers of England.

1265 Simon de Montfort's Parliament, Battle of Evesham: defeat and death of de Montfort.

1274 Death of Thomas Aquinas.

1279–1368 Mongol (Yuan) Dynasty in China (Kublai Khan).

1231 Repulse of Mongol attack on Japan.

1282 Sicilian Vespers: rising of Sicilians against French ruler.

1284 Completion of Edward I of England's conquest of Wales.

1290 Expulsion of Jews from England. Death of Maid of Norway: Edward I begins attempts to rule Scotland.

1291 Fall of Acre: end of Crusading in Holy Land. Everlasting League of Uri: beginnings of Swiss Confederation.

1294 Death of Roger Bacon, the founder of experimental science.

1295 "Model Parliament" of Edward I (anticipated in 1275).

1308 Death of Duns Scotus.

THE DECLINE OF THE MIDDLE AGES

1309 Papacy moves to Avignon: beginning of the Babylonish Captivity.

1312 Suppression of Templars by king of France and Pope.

1314 Battle of Bannockburn: victory of Robert Bruce secures Scottish independence.

1321 Death of Dante.

1325 Zenith of Mandingo Empire of Mali (North West Africa) under Mansa Musa; superseded at end of 15th century by Songhai empire.

1327 Deposition of Edward II; subsequently murdered.

A.D.
1336 Ashikaga Period in Japan: great feudal lords semi-independent of authority of Shogun.

1337 Death of Giotto.

1338 Beginning of Hundred Years' War between England and France.

1340 Battle of Sluys: English capture French fleet.

1344 Swabian League: weakness of Imperial authority in Germany obliges towns to form leagues for mutual protection.

1346 Battles of Crecy and Neville's Cross: spectacular English victories over French and Scots.

1347 Calais taken by Edward III of England. Cola di Rienzi attempts to reform government of Rome: killed 1354.

1348 Black Death reaches Europe (England 1349, Scotland 1350).

1351 Statute of Labourers: attempt by English Parliament to freeze wages.

1353 Statute of Praemunire: restraints placed on Papal intervention in England.

1354 Ottoman Turks make first settlement in Europe, at Gallipoli.

1355 Death of Stephen Dushan: collapse of Serbian Empire which he had built.

1356 Battle of Poitiers: capture of King John of France by Black Prince. "Golden Bull" regulates Imperial elections in such a way as to place power in the hands of the German princes: valid until 1806.

1358 The Jacquerie: rising of French peasants.

1360 Peace of Bretigny: Edward III makes great territorial gains in France.

1362 English becomes the official language in Parliament and the Law Courts.

1363 Timur (Tamerlane) begins his career of conquest in Asia.

1368–1644 Ming Dynasty in China.

1370 Bertrand du Guesclin Constable of France: regains much territory from the English. Peace of Stralsund: Hansa in complete control of Baltic Sea.

1377 Pope returns to Rome: End of Babylonish Captivity.

1378 Disputed Papal Election: Beginning of Western Schism.

1380 Battle of Chioggia: decisive victory of Venice over Genoa. Battle of Kulikovo: Dmitri Donskoi of Moscow wins first major Russian victory over Golden Horde.

1381 Peasants' Revolt in England under Wat Tyler.

1384 Death of John Wyclif.

1385 Battle of Aljubarotta: Portugal safeguards independence from Castile.

1386 Battle of Sempach: Swiss safeguard independence from Habsburgs. Jagiello (Vladislav V) unites Lithuania and Poland.

1389 Battle of Kossovo: crushing defeat of Serbs and neighbouring nations by Turks.

1396 Battle of Nicopolis: "the last crusade" annihilated by Turks.

1397 Union of Kalmar: Denmark, Norway and Sweden united under one crown: dissolved 1448.

1398 Timur invades and pillages Northern India.

1399 Richard II deposed by Henry IV: first of the Lancastrian kings of England.

1400 Owen Glendower revolts in Wales. Death of Chaucer.

1401 De Haeretico Comburendo: the burning of heretics made legal in England.

1410 Battle of Tannenberg: Poles and Lithuanians break power of Teutonic Knights.

1415 Battle of Agincourt: great success of Henry V of England in France. Council of Constance ends Western Schism, burns John Hus.

1420 Treaty of Troyes: English claims to French throne recognised. Hussite Wars begin: Bohemian heretics defend themselves successfully.

A.D.
1429 Relief of Orleans by Joan of Arc.

1431 Burning of Joan of Arc.

1433 Rounding of Cape Bojador: first great achievement in exploration ordered by Henry the Navigator.

1434 Cosimo die Medici begins his family's control of Florence.

1435 Congress of Arras: Burgundians withdraw support from England, in favour of France.

1438 Albert II became German king and began Hapsburg rule over Holy Roman Empire, 1438–1806.

1440 Death of Jan van Eyck.

1450 Rebellion of Jack Cade against government of Henry VI of England.

1453 Battle of Castillon: final English defeat and end of Hundred Years' War. Constantinople taken by Turks: end of Byzantine or Eastern Roman Empire.

RENAISSANCE, DISCOVERIES, "NEW MONARCHIES"

1454 First dated printing from movable types in Europe: Papal indulgence printed at Mainz.

1455 First battle of St. Albans: beginning of Wars of the Roses.

1458 Mathias Corvinus becomes king of Hungary. George of Podiebrad becomes king of Bohemia.

1461 Battle of Towton: Yorkist victory in a particularly bloody battle. Louis XI becomes king of France.

1467 Charles the Bold becomes Duke of Burgundy.

1469 Marriage of Ferdinand of Aragon with Isabella of Castile: union of the main kingdoms of Spain (1474). Lorenzo the Magnificent becomes ruler of Florence.

1470 Warwick ("The Kingmaker") turns Lancastrian, dethrones Edward IV.

1471 Return of Edward IV: Lancastrians crushed at Barnet and Tewkesbury. Ivan III of Moscow takes Novgorod: Muscovy rising to supremacy in Russia.

1476 Caxton sets up his press at Westminster.

1477 Battle of Nancy: defeat and death of Charles the Bold: end of the greatness of Burgundy.

1479 Pazzi conspiracy against the Medici in Florence.

1481 Inquisition becomes active in Castile (1484 in Aragon).

1485 Battle of Bosworth Field: beginning of Tudor period in England.

1487 Lambert Simnel's rising fails.

1488 Bartholomew Diaz rounds Cape of Good Hope.

1491 Brittany acquired by King of France (by marriage).

1492 Rodrigo Borgia becomes Pope Alexander VI. Granada, last Moorish foothold in Western Europe, conquered by Spain. Christopher Columbus discovers the West Indies.

1493 Sonni Ali brings Songhai Empire to height of its prestige: Timbuktu renowned centre of literary culture.

1494 Italy invaded by French led by Charles VIII: beginning of Italian Wars and "modern" European diplomacy and international relations. Treaty of Tordesillas: Spain and Portugal agree to divide unexplored part of world; subsequently approved by Pope.

1496 Hapsburg-Spanish marriages: foundation of later empires.

1497 Perkin Warbeck captured by Henry VII (hanged 1499). John Cabot discovers Newfoundland.

1498 Savonarola burned. Vasco da Gama at Calicut: the sea route to India found.

1499 Amerigo Vespucci charts part of the South American coast.

A.D.
1500 Brazil discovered by Pedro Cabral.

1503 Casa de Contratación established at Seville; beginnings of Spanish colonial government. Fall of Caesar Borgia.

1507 Alfonso de Albuquerque becomes Viceroy of Portuguese Empire in the East.

1513 Accession of Pope Leo X, zenith of Renaissance Papacy. Machiavelli writes *The Prince*. Balboa discovers the Pacific (South Sea). Battle of Flodden: James IV of Scotland defeated and killed by English.

1514 Battle of Chaldiran: Turkish victory begins long series of wars between Turkish and Persian Empires.

REFORMATION, HAPSBURG–VALOIS WARS

1515 Francis I becomes king of France: victory of Marignano ends legend of Swiss invincibility. Thomas Wolsey becomes Lord Chancellor of England and Cardinal.

1516 Algiers taken by Barbarossa; beginning of the Corsairs.

1517 Martin Luther nails up his Ninety-five Theses: beginning of the Reformation. Turks conquer Egypt.

1519 Charles V inherits Hapsburg lands and elected emperor. Magellan begins first circumnavigation of the world. Death of Leonardo da Vinci.

1520 Suleiman the Magnificent becomes Sultan; Turkish power at its height. Field of Cloth of Gold; celebrated diplomatic meeting, spectacular but with no results.

1521 Mexico conquered by Hernando Cortes. Belgrade taken by the Turks. Diet of Worms; Luther commits himself irrevocably. Charles V divides his dominions: Austrian and Spanish Hapsburgs.

1522 Rhodes taken by the Turks; Knights of St. John move to Malta. Election of Adrian VI, first non-Italian Pope since 1378.

1523 Swedes expel Danish overlords, elect Gustavus Vasa King.

1524 Peasants' War in Germany (suppressed 1525).

1525 Battle of Pavia: defeat and capture of Francis I by Imperialists.

1526 Battle of Mohács: Turkish victory ends Hungarian independence. Foundation of Danubian Hapsburg Monarchy (Hungarian and Bohemian crowns united with Austrian patrimony of Hapsburgs): Holy Roman Empire prolonged for 300 years. Battle of Panipat: Babar begins Moslem conquest of India, founds Mogul Empire.

1527 Sack of Rome by Imperialists. Italy under control of Charles V.

1529 Siege of Vienna by the Turks. Peace of Cambrai; pause in Hapsburg-Valois struggle, end of serious French intervention in Italy. Diet of Speyer: origin of the name Protestant.

1532 Peru conquered by Francisco Pizarro.

1533 Ivan IV (the Terrible) becomes Tsar. Marriage of Henry VIII and Catherine of Aragon declared null.

1534 Act of Supremacy: Henry VIII asserts control over English Church.

1535 Coverdale's English Bible printed. Execution of Thomas More and John Fisher.

1536 Execution of Anne Boleyn. Dissolution of smaller Monasteries by Henry VIII and Thomas Cromwell (remainder dissolved 1539). Pilgrimage of Grace: Northern rising because of religious grievances.

1538 Chibchas of Bogota conquered by Gonzalo de Quesada.

1540 Francisco de Coronado begins explorations in North America. Society of Jesus recognised by Pope.

1541 John Calvin regains authority in Geneva.

1542 First Portuguese reach Japan. New Laws of the Indies: first attempt to legislate for welfare of colonial natives, by Spanish government.

1543 Death of Copernicus.

1545 Opening of Council of Trent: the Counter Reformation.

A.D.
1547 Death of Henry VIII: Somerset Protector in the name of the boy king, Edward VI.

1549 First English Book of Common Prayer. Kett's Rebellion in Norfolk, because of economic grievances.

1550 Deposition of Protector Somerset: Northumberland rules England.

1553 Lady Jane Grey proclaimed Queen by Northumberland on death of Edward VI: Mary I succeeds. Servetus burned by Calvin.

1555 Latimer and Ridley burned by Mary. Religious Peace of Augsburg: policy of *cuius regio, eius religio* accepted in Germany.

1556 Charles V abdicated imperial powers in favour of brother Ferdinand. Cranmer burned. Akbar becomes Mogul Emperor (d. 1605).

1557 Macao becomes permanent Portuguese port in China.

1558 Calais lost by English to French. Elizabeth I becomes Queen of England.

1559 Peace of Cateau-Cambrésis: end of Hapsburg–Valois duel.

RELIGIOUS WARS

1561 Mary, Queen of Scots, returns to Scotland.

1562 First War of Religion in France: wars continue intermittently until 1598.

1563 Thirty-nine Articles define Elizabethan Church settlement.

1564 Birth of Shakespeare; death of Michelangelo.

1565 Malta beats off Turks.

1567 Deposition of Mary, Queen of Scots. Alva in the Netherlands: severe rule.

1568 Flight of Mary, Queen of Scots, to England: imprisonment. San Juan de Ulua: defeat of Hawkins, and end of his slave-trading voyages. Beginning of Anglo-Spanish maritime feud. Revolt of Moriscos of Granada (suppressed 1570).

1569 Rebellion of Northern Earls (Catholic) in England.

1570 Elizabeth I anathematised by Pope.

1571 Battle of Lepanto: spectacular defeat of Turkish sea-power by Don John of Austria. Bornu (or Kanem) in Central Sudan at its zenith under Idris III.

1572 Dutch "Sea Beggars" take Brill. Massacre of St. Bartholomew in France. Polish Crown elective again, on death of Sigismund II.

1576 Catholic League formed in France, led by Guise family.

1577 Drake begins voyage round world (returns 1580).

1578 Battle of Alcazar-Quivir: death of King Sebastian of Portugal. Parma re-establishes Spanish rule in Southern Netherlands.

1579 Union of Utrecht: seven northern provinces of Netherlands form what becomes Dutch Republic. Death of Grand Vizier Sokolli: decline of Turkish power begins.

1580 Philip II of Spain becomes king of Portugal.

1582 Gregorian Calendar (or New Style) introduced by Pope Gregory XIII.

1584 Assassination of William the Silent.

1585 Hidéyoshi Dictator of Japan: unification of the country. English intervention in Spanish–Dutch War.

1587 Execution of Mary, Queen of Scots. Drake "singes King of Spain's beard." Shah Abbas I (the Great) becomes ruler of Persia (d. 1629).

1588 Spanish Armada defeated.

1589 Death of Catherine de' Medici, Queen-Mother of France.

1592 Moorish conquest of African Songhai Empire.

1593 Henry IV of France becomes Catholic.

1598 Edict of Nantes: French Protestants guaranteed liberty of worship. End of French Wars of Religion.

1600 English East India Company founded. Tokugawa Period begins in Japan (Ieyasu takes title of Shogun, 1603): lasts until 1868.

A.D.

1601 Rebellion and execution of Earl of Essex. Elizabethan Poor Law.

1602 Dutch East India Company founded.

1603 Irish revolts finally suppressed by Mountjoy. Accession of James VI of Scotland as James I of England: Union of English and Scottish Crowns.

1604 Hampton Court Conference: James I disappoints Puritans.

1605 Gunpowder Plot.

1607 Virginia colonised by London company: Jamestown founded.

1608 Quebec founded by Champlain.

1609 Twelve Years' Truce between Spain and United Provinces: Dutch independence in fact secured. Expulsion of Moriscos from Spain.

1610 Assassination of Henry IV of France.

1611 Plantation of Ulster with English and Scottish colonists. Authorised Version of the Bible in England.

1613 Michael Romanov becomes Tsar: the first of the dynasty.

1614 Napier publishes his explanation of logarithms.

1616 Death of Shakespeare and Cervantes. Edict of Inquisition against Galileo's astronomy.

1618 "Defenestration of Prague": Bohemian assertion of independence begins Thirty Years' War.

1620 Pilgrim Fathers settle in New England.

1624 "Massacre of Amboina": English driven out of spice islands by Dutch. Richelieu becomes Chief Minister in France.

1628 Murder of Duke of Buckingham. Petition of Right by Commons to Charles I. Fall of La Rochelle: French Protestants lose political power. Harvey publishes his work on the circulation of blood.

1629 Charles I begins Personal Rule.

1630 Gustavus Adolphus of Sweden enters Thirty Years' War, turns tide against Imperialists.

1631 Sack of Magdeburg, one of the worst incidents of the Thirty Years' War.

1632 Battle of Lützen: death of Gustavus Adolphus.

1633 William Laud appointed Archbishop of Canterbury. Thomas Wentworth takes up his post as Lord Deputy of Ireland.

1634 Dismissal and murder of Imperialist general Wallenstein.

1635 John Hampden refuses to pay Ship Money.

1636 Japanese forbidden to go abroad.

1637 Russian pioneers reach shores of Pacific.

1638 Covenant widely signed in Scotland.

1639 First Bishops' War: Charles I comes to terms with Scots.

1640 Second Bishops' War: Charles I defeated by Scots. Long Parliament begins: abolition of Royal prerogatives. Great Elector (Frederick William) becomes ruler of Brandenburg. Revolt of Catalonia (finally suppressed 1659). Revolt of Portugal: Duke of Braganza proclaimed king.

1641 Japanese exclude all foreigners (except for small Dutch trading fleet). Massacre of Protestants in Ireland. Wentworth (Earl of Strafford) executed. Grand Remonstrance of Commons to Charles I.

1642 Charles I attempts to arrest the Five Members. Outbreak of English Civil War: first general engagement, Edgehill. Death of Richelieu.

1643 Mazarin becomes Chief Minister of France. Battle of Rocroi: French victory, end of Spanish reputation for invincibility. English Parliament agrees to Solemn League and Covenant, secures services of Scots army.

1644 Marston Moor: decisive battle of English Civil War. North lost to Charles I. Tippemuir: Montrose begins victorious Royalist

A.D.

campaign in Scotland. 1644–1911 Manchu (Qing) dynasty in China.

1645 Formation of New Model Army. Naseby: main Royalist army crushed. Battle of Philiphaugh: Montrose's army destroyed.

1646 Charles I surrenders to Scots.

1647 Charles I handed over to Parliament. Charles I seized by Army. Charles I flees to Carisbrooke Castle.

1648 Second Civil War: New Model Army defeats Scots and Royalists. "Pride's Purge": Parliament refashioned by Army. Peace of Westphalia ends Thirty Years' War.

ASCENDANCY OF FRANCE

1649 Charles I executed. England governed as Commonwealth. Cromwell in Ireland. New Code of Laws in Russia completes establishment of serfdom.

1651 Battle of Worcester: Cromwell's final victory, now master of all Britain. First English Navigation Act. Hobbes' *Leviathan* published.

1652 Foundation of Cape Colony by Dutch under Van Riebeek. First Anglo-Dutch War begins (ends 1654).

1653 Cromwell dissolves Rump, becomes Protector.

1655 Major-Generals appointed to supervise districts of England. Jamaica seized by English.

1656 Grand Vizier Kiuprili: revival of Turkish government.

1658 Death of Cromwell.

1659 Peace of the Pyrenees: France replaces Spain as greatest power in Western Europe.

1660 Restoration of monarch in Britain: Charles II. Royal Society founded.

1661 Death of Mazarin: Louis XIV now rules in person. "Clarendon Code"; beginning of persecution of Non-conformists in England.

1664 New York taken by English: Second Anglo-Dutch War ensues (ends 1667).

1665 Great Plague of London.

1666 Great Fire of London. Newton's discovery of law of gravitation.

1667 Dutch fleet in the Medway. War of Devolution begins: first of Louis XIV's aggressions.

1668 Portuguese Independence recognised by Spain.

1669 Death of Rembrandt.

1670 Secret Treaty of Dover between Charles II and Louis XIV. Revolt of peasants and Don Cossacks under Stenka Razin (suppressed 1671).

1672 Third Anglo-Dutch War begins (ends 1674). Murder of De Witt brothers: William of Orange becomes leader of Dutch against French invasion.

1673 Test Act deprives English Catholics and Non-conformists of public offices. Death of Molière.

1675 Battle of Fehrbellin: Swedes defeated by Great Elector; rise of Prussian military power. Greenwich Royal Observatory founded.

1678 "Popish Plot" of Titus Oates utilised by Shaftesbury and the Whigs to bring pressure on Charles II.

1679 Bothwell Brig: suppression of Scottish Covenanters. Habeas Corpus Act passed.

1680 Chambers of Reunion: Louis XIV uses legal arguments to complete annexation of Alsace.

1681 Oxford Parliament: Charles II overcomes his opponents, begins to rule without Parliament.

1683 Rye House Plot. Siege of Vienna by the Turks: last major Turkish attack on Europe.

1685 Sedgemoor: Monmouth's rebellion crushed by James II. Revocation of Edict of Nantes: persecution of French Protestants by Louis XIV.

A.D.

1688 Seven Bishops protest against James II's policy of toleration, and are acquitted. William of Orange lands in England: flight of James II. "The Glorious Revolution."

1689 Derry relieved: failure of James II to subdue Irish Protestants. Killiecrankie: death of Dundee and collapse of Highland rising. Bill of Rights defines liberties established by "Glorious Revolution."

1690 Locke's *Two Treatises on Government* published. Beachy Head: French victory over Anglo-Dutch fleet. Boyne: defeat of James II by William III.

1691 Capitulation of Limerick: surrender of Irish supporters of James II on conditions which are not fulfilled.

1692 Massacre of Glencoe: Government's "lesson" to Highlanders. La Hogue: Anglo-Dutch fleet regains command of the sea.

1693 National Debt of England begun.

1694 Bank of England founded.

1695 Press licensing abandoned: freedom of the press in England.

1696 Peter the Great sole Czar.

1697 Peace of Ryswyck between Louis XIV and William III. Peter journeys "incognito" to the West.

1699 Treaty of Karlowitz: great Turkish concessions to Austrians. Death of Racine.

1700 Great Northern War, involving all Baltic powers, begins (ends 1721). Battle of Narva: Russians defeated by Charles XII of Sweden. Death of Charles II of Spain: under French influence Louis XIV's grandson Philip of Anjou named successor.

1701 War of the Spanish Succession begins. Hungarian revolt led by Francis Rakoczi against Austrians. Elector of Brandenburg receives title of King of Prussia. Act of Settlement establishes Protestant Hanoverian Succession in England.

1703 Methuen Treaty between England and Portugal. St. Petersburg founded.

1704 Gibraltar taken by Rooke. Blenheim: Marlborough stops France from winning war.

1706 Ramillies: Marlborough's second great victory. Turin: Eugene defeats French in Italy.

1707 Almanza: Anglo-Austrian forces in Spain defeated by French under Berwick. Act of Union: English and Scottish Parliaments united. Death of Aurungzib, last powerful Mogul.

1708 Oudenarde: Marlborough's third great victory.

1709 Pultava: Charles XII's invasion of Russia smashed by Peter the Great. Malplaquet: Marlborough's fourth great victory—at great cost in lives.

1710 Tory government in England.

1711 Dismissal of Marlborough.

1713 Peace of Utrecht: England makes advantageous peace with Louis XIV. Bourbon king of Spain grants Asiento (monopoly of Spanish American slave trade) to England.

1714 Peace of Rastatt between France and Austria. Death of Queen Anne: accession of George I. Beginning of Hanoverian Dynasty in Britain. Whig oligarchy rules.

1715 Jacobite Rising defeated at Preston and Sheriffmuir. Death of Louis XIV. France under Regent Orleans.

ENLIGHTENED DESPOTS: FIRST BRITISH EMPIRE

1716 Septennial Act: English Parliament prolongs its life from three to seven years. Prince Eugene of Savoy defeated Turks at Petrovaradin (Yugoslavia).

1720 Collapse of Law's system of banking ("Mississippi Bubble") in France. "South Sea Bubble" in England.

A.D.

1721 Robert Walpole becomes first Prime Minister. Peace of Nystad: Sweden no longer a major power at end of Great Northern War. Russian gains.

1723 Death of Christopher Wren.

1727 First Indemnity Act for Non-conformists.

1729 Methodists begin at Oxford.

1730 Resignation from government of Townshend, who becomes agricultural pioneer.

1733 First Family Compact between Bourbon kings of France and Spain. Withdrawal of Walpole's Excise Bill. John Kay invents flying shuttle, first of the great textile inventions. Jethro Tull publishes *The Horse-Hoeing Husbandry*, advocating new agricultural methods.

1738 Lorraine ceded to France.

1739 Nadir Shah with Persian army sacks Delhi, ruins Mogul power. War of Jenkins' Ear begins between Spain and Britain.

1740 Frederick II (the Great) becomes king of Prussia. Maria Theresa succeeds to Austrian dominions. Frederick seizes Silesia, begins War of the Austrian Succession.

1742 Fall of Walpole.

1743 Dettingen: George II, last British king to command his army in the field, defeats French.

1745 Fontenoy: Duke of Cumberland defeated by Marshal Saxe. Jacobite Rebellion under Prince Charles Edward: initial success, victory of Prestonpans, march to Derby.

1746 Culloden: Jacobites destroyed by Cumberland.

1748 Treaty of Aix-la-Chapelle: Frederick retains Silesia, elsewhere status quo.

1750 Death of J. S. Bach.

1751 First volume of the *Encyclopédie* published in France. Clive takes and holds Arcot: checks plans of Dupleix in Southern India. Chinese conquest of Tibet.

1752 Britain adopts New Style calendar.

1753 British Museum begun by government purchase of Sloane's collection.

1755 Lisbon earthquake. Braddock's defeat and death at the hands of French and Indians.

1756 Diplomatic Revolution (alliance of Austria with France) achieved by Kaunitz; Britain and Prussia perforce became allies. Seven Years' War begins. Minorca taken from British by French (Byng executed 1757). Black Hole of Calcutta: suffocation of many British prisoners.

1757 Pitt Secretary of State, main influence in British government. Rossbach: one of Frederick II's numerous victories against heavy odds. Plassey: Clive conquers Bengal.

1759 "Year of Victories" for Britain: Quebec, Minden, Lagos, Quiberon Bay. James Brindley designs Worsley-Manchester Canal: the beginning of this form of transport in Britain. Voltaire publishes *Candide*. Death of Handel.

1760 Wandewash: decisive defeat of French in India, by Coote.

1761 Panipat: Mahrattas heavily defeated by Afghans. Fall of Pitt.

1762 Catherine II (the Great) becomes Czarina. Rousseau's *Social Contract* and *Emile* published.

1763 Peace of Paris: British colonial gains, First British Empire at its height. Peace of Hubertusburg: Frederick II retains his gains. Pontiac's Conspiracy: failure of Red Indian attempt to destroy British power.

1764 John Wilkes expelled from Commons. James Hargreaves invents spinning jenny.

1766 Henry Cavendish proves hydrogen to be an element.

1768 Royal Academy of Arts founded.

1769 Richard Arkwright erects spinning mill (invention of water frame).

1770 Struensee comes to power in Denmark (executed 1772). "Boston Massacre." James Cook discovers New South Wales.

1772 First Partition of Poland between Russia, Prussia and Austria.

A.D.

1773 Society of Jesus suppressed by Pope (restored 1814). Revolt led by Pugachov in Russia (suppressed 1775). "Boston Tea Party."

1774 Warren Hastings appointed first Governor-General of India. Treaty of Kutchuk Kainarji; great Turkish concessions to Russia. Karl Scheele discovers chlorine. Joseph Priestley's discovery of oxygen.

1775 Watt and Boulton in partnership at Soho Engineering Works, Birmingham. Lexington: first action in American War of Independence.

1776 American Declaration of Independence. Adam Smith's *Wealth of Nations* published.

1777 Saratoga: surrender of British army under Burgoyne to Americans.

1779 Beginning of great Franco-Spanish siege of Gibraltar (raised finally, 1783). Samuel Crompton invents spinning mule.

1780 Joseph II assumes sole power in Austria. Armed neutrality of maritime nations to restrain British interference with shipping.

1781 Joseph II introduces religious toleration, abolishes serfdom in Austria. Yorktown: surrender of British under Cornwallis.

1782 Battle of the Saints: Rodney's victory save British West Indies.

1783 Treaty of Versailles: American independence recognised. Pitt the Younger becomes Prime Minister of Britain. First flights in hot air (Montgolfier) and hydrogen (Charles) balloons.

1784 Death of Dr. Samuel Johnson.

1785 Edmund Cartwright invents the power loom.

1787 American Constitution drafted.

1788 Impeachment of Warren Hastings begins (ends 1795): English fleet commanded by Captain Arthur Phillip landed in Australia.

FRENCH REVOLUTION AND NAPOLEON

1789 Washington first President of U.S.A. French Revolution begins. Storming of the Bastille (July 14).

1790 Civil constitution of the Clergy in France.

1791 Flight of Louis XVI and Marie Antoinette to Varennes.

1792 Battle of Valmy: French Revolution saved from intervention of European kings. Denmark becomes first country to prohibit slave trade. France becomes a Republic.

1793 Louis XVI beheaded. Second partition of Poland.

1794 "Glorious First of June." Fall of Robespierre and end of Jacobin Republic. Negro revolt in Haiti led by Toussaint L'Ouverture.

1795 The Directory established. "Whiff of Grapeshot": Napoleon Bonaparte disperses Paris mob, Oct. 5. Batavian Republic set up by France.

1796 First Italian campaign of Bonaparte: victories of Lodi, Arcola.

1797 Treaty of Campo Formio: Bonaparte compels Austria to make peace. Britain left to fight France alone.

1798 Bonaparte goes to Egypt. Battle of the Nile. Vinegar Hill rebellion in Ireland suppressed.

1799 New coalition against France: Suvorov and Russians victorious in Italy. Bonaparte returns to France. *Coup d'état* of Brumaire, Nov. 9. Consulate set up.

1800 Parliamentary Union of Great Britain and Ireland.

1801 Treaty of Lunéville: Austria makes peace; great French gains in Germany.

1802 Peace of Amiens between Britain and France. *Charlotte Dundas*, first practical steamship, on Clyde.

1803 Insurrection in Ireland under Robert Emmet. Britain again at war with France.

A.D.

1804 Bonaparte becomes Emperor. Spain declares war against Great Britain. Serbian revolt against Turks under Kara George.

1805 Battle of Trafalgar, Nelson's great victory and death, Oct. 21. Battle of Austerlitz, Dec. 2.

1806 Death of Pitt, Jan. 23. Confederation of the Rhine: Napoleon's reorganisation of Germany, July 12. End of Holy Roman Empire, Aug. 6. Prussia overthrown at Jena. Napoleon declares Great Britain in a state of blockade—"Continental System."

1807 Slave trade abolished in British Empire. Treaty of Tilsit: with Alexander of Russia his friend, Napoleon controls all of Europe. Occupation of Portugal by French, to enforce Continental Blockade.

1808 Occupation of Spain by French. Spanish rising: guerilla warfare. Peninsular War begins. Battle of Vimeiro (defeat of French by Wellington), Aug. 21.

1809 Battle of Corunna and death of Sir John Moore, Jan. 16. Attempted risings in Germany against Napoleon: Austria renews war. Treaty of Schönbrunn, Oct. 14.

1810 Self-government established in Argentina: first South American state to become independent of Spain.

1811 Massacre of Mamelukes at Cairo. Luddite riots.

1812 Retreat from Moscow: destruction of Napoleon's Grand Army.

1813 War of Liberation starts in Germany. Defeat of French by Wellington at Vitoria, June 21

1814 Soult defeated by Wellington at Toulouse, April 10. Abdication of Napoleon, April 11; Louis XVIII king of France. Congress of Vienna (concluded June 1815) under guidance of Metternich. Resettlement of Europe, usually by restoration of kings. Germanic Confederation under Austrian supervision. Poland ruled by Czar. Kingdom of Netherlands to include Belgium.

THE OLD ORDER RESTORED

1815 Escape of Napoleon from Elba. Battle of Waterloo, June 18. Corn Law in Britain to safeguard agricultural interests by keeping up prices. Quadruple Alliance (Austria, Russia, Prussia, Britain) to maintain Vienna settlement and hold regular meetings ("Congress System") —frequently confused with Holy Alliance, which was simply a declaration of Christian principles. Napoleon sent to St. Helena, Oct. 16.

1818 Bernadotte made king of Sweden (Charles XIV), Feb. 6.

1819 Singapore founded by Stamford Raffles. Beginning of Zollverein (Customs Union) in Germany under Prussian influence. Parliamentary reform meeting at Manchester dispersed by military ("Peterloo"), Aug. 16.

1820 Death of George III, Jan. 29.

1821 Death of Napoleon at St. Helena, May 5.

1822 Congress of Verona: congress system breaks down with refusal of Britain (Canning) to intervene against revolutions.

1823 "Monroe Doctrine" announced by U.S.A. President. Dec. 2.

1824 Repeal of Combination Acts in Britain which had forbidden Trades Unions. Charles X king of France.

1825 Independence of all Spanish American mainland now achieved. Nicholas I Czar of Russia. First railway, Stockton to Darlington, opened.

1826 First crossing of Atlantic under steam by Dutch ship *Curaçao*. Menai suspension bridge opened.

1827 Battle of Navarino, Turkish and Egyptian fleet destroyed. Death of Beethoven.

1828 Death of Chaka, great Zulu conqueror.

1829 Greece independent. Catholic Emancipation Act in Britain. Metropolitan Police established.

A.D.

1830 Death of George IV, June 26. Louis Philippe ousts Charles X. Belgium breaks away from Holland. Russian Poland revolts.

1831 First Reform Bill introduced by Lord John Russell. Leopold of Saxe-Coburg becomes king of independent Belgium. British Association founded. Faraday discovers electromagnetic induction.

1832 Reform Bill passed, June 7. Walter Scott, Jeremy Bentham, and Goethe die. Electric telegraph invented by Morse.

1833 Beginning of "Oxford Movement" in English Church. First government grant made to English schools. First British Factory Act.

1834 Poor Law Amendment Act: tightening up of relief in Britain. "Tolpuddle Martyrs" victimised to discourage British working-class movement. Carlist wars begin in Spain.

1835 Municipal Reform Act revises British local government. The word "socialism" first used. "Tamworth Manifesto" of Peel defines aims of Conservative Party.

1836 People's Charter states programme of Chartists. Great Trek of Boers from British South African territory. Texas achieves independence of Mexico.

1837 Queen Victoria succeeds to the throne.

1838 National Gallery opened.

1839 First Afghan war begins. Chartist riots at Birmingham and Newport. Anti-Corn Law League founded. Aden annexed by Britain.

1840 Penny postage instituted. Queen Victoria marries Prince Albert of Saxe-Coburg-Gotha. "Opium War" with China begins. Union Act gives Canada responsible government. Last convicts landed in New South Wales.

1841 Hong Kong acquired by Britain.

1842 Chartists present second national petition and put themselves at the head of strikes. Great potato famine in Ireland begins.

1846 Repeal of the Corn Laws. Peel resigns.

1847 British Museum opened.

REVOLUTIONS AND NEW NATIONS

1848 Monster meeting of Chartists on Kennington Common, procession abandoned, Apr. 10. General revolutionary movement throughout the Continent. Louis Philippe abdicates: French Republic proclaimed. Swiss Federal Constitution established after defeat of Sonderbund (Catholic succession movement). Rising in Vienna: flight of Metternich, accession of Francis Joseph. Nationalist risings in Bohemia and Hungary. Frankfurt Parliament: attempt to unite Germany on liberal principles. Communist Manifesto produced by Marx and Engels. USA makes great territorial gains from Mexico. Gold discovered in California.

1849 Collapse of revolutionary movements. Rome republic besieged by French (June 3), defended by Garibaldi, holds out until July 2. Austrians take Venice, Aug. 22. Repeal of old Navigation Laws. Punjab annexed by Britain.

1850 Cavour becomes Prime Minister of Sardinia. Don Pacifico affair: privileges of British citizenship at their highest defended by Palmerston.

1851 Great Exhibition in Hyde Park. First satisfactory submarine telegraph cable between Dover and Calais laid. Gold in Australia.

1852 Independence of Transvaal recognised by Britain. Napoleon III Emperor of the French.

1853 U.S. Commodore Perry lands in Japan: beginning of Western influence. Russia and Turkey at war.

1854 War declared against Russia by France and Britain. Allied armies land in Crimea, Sept. 14 (Alma, Siege of Sevastopol, Balaklava, Inkerman). Orange Free State set up.

1855 Sardinia joins Britain and France against Russia. Fall of Sevastopol and end of Crimean War. Alexander II Czar of Russia.

A.D.

1856 Peace Treaty signed at Paris. Bessemer invents process for large-scale production of steel. Livingstone completes journey across Africa.

1857 Indian Mutiny. Relief of Lucknow. Canton captured by English and French.

1858 *Great Eastern* launched. Crown assumes government of India. Treaty of Aigun, by which China cedes Amur region to Russia.

1859 Darwin publishes *Origin of Species*. French support for Piedmont in war with Austria (Magenta, Solferino). Piedmont receives Lombardy. Harper's Ferry raid: John Brown hanged, Dec. 2.

1860 Garibaldi and the Thousand Redshirts in Sicily and Naples; most of Italy united to Piedmont. Vladivostok founded; Russia strongly established on N.W. Pacific.

1861 Abraham Lincoln takes office as Pres. of U.S. American Civil War commences with 11 states breaking away to form Southern Confederacy. Bull Run (July 21) Confederate success ends Federal hopes of easy victory. Victor Emmanuel proclaimed by first Italian Parliament as king of Italy. Emancipation of Serfs in Russia. Death of Prince Albert, Dec. 14.

1862 Bismarck becomes leading minister in Prussia. Garibaldi attempts to seize Rome but wounded at Aspromonte. Aug. 29. Cotton famine in Lancashire.

1863 Polish rising against Russia (suppressed 1864). French in Mexico. Battle of Gettysburg, July 1-3. Maximilian of Austria made emperor of Mexico.

1864 Cession of Schleswig-Holstein to Prussia and Austria. First Socialist International formed. Taiping rebellion in China ended. Federal army enters Atlanta, Sept. 2: General Sherman captures Savannah ("From Atlanta to the sea"). Dec. 22. Geneva Convention originated.

1865 Death of Cobden, Apr. 2. General Lee surrenders to Grant, Apr. 9. Lincoln assassinated, Apr. 14. Thirteenth Amendment to Constitution: slavery abolished in U.S. Death of Palmerston, Oct. 18. Lister introduces antiseptic surgery in Glasgow. Tashkent becomes centre of Russian expansion in Central Asia. Mendel experiments on heredity. William Booth founds Salvation Army.

1866 Austro-Prussian War over Schleswig-Holstein ("Seven Weeks War"). Prussian victory at Sadowa (July 3). Venice secured for Italy, who had, however, been defeated by Austrians at Custozza (June 24) and Lissa (July 20). Treaty of Prague, Aug. 23.

1867 North German Confederation founded. Emperor Maximilian of Mexico shot. Dominion of Canada established. Russia sells Alaska to America for $7 million. Garibaldi makes second attempt to seize Rome, but defeated by Pope with French support at Mentana, Nov. 3. Second Parliamentary Reform Bill passed (Disraeli "dished the Whigs").

1868 Shogunate abolished in Japan: Meiji period of rapid Westernisation under Imperial leadership begins. Ten Years' War (1868-78); struggle for Cuban independence from Spain. Impeachment of President Johnson (USA). Disraeli succeeds Derby as Prime Minister but defeated in general election by Gladstone, Nov.

1869 General Grant, Pres. of USA. Irish Church disestablished. Suez Canal formally opened.

1870 Napoleon III declares war against Prussia. French defeated at Woerth, Gravelotte, and Sedan. Paris besieged. Rome and Papal states annexed to kingdom of Italy. Irish Land Act passed. Forster's Education Act puts elementary education within reach of all children. Papal Infallibility announced.

1871 William I of Prussia proclaimed German emperor at Versailles, Jan. 18. Paris capitulates, Jan. 28. Commune of Paris proclaimed, Mar. 28. Peace signed at Frankfurt-on-Main, May 10. Government troops enter Paris and

A.D.

crush Communards, May 28. Thiers President of the Republic, Aug. 31. Mont Cenis tunnel opened. Trade Unions in Britain legalised.

RIVAL IMPERIAL POWERS

1872 Secret ballot introduced in Britain. Death of Mazzini, Mar. 10.

1873 Death of Livingstone, May 4. Ashanti war.

1874 Disraeli succeeds Gladstone as Prime Minister.

1875 England purchases Khedive's shares in Suez Canal, Nov.

1876 Bulgarian massacres. Serbo-Turkish war. Bell invents the telephone. Custer defeated and killed in last large-scale Red Indian success. Porfirio Diaz in power in Mexico (until 1911). Victoria declared Empress of India.

1877 Transvaal annexed to British Empire. War between Russia and Turkey. Satsuma rebellion in Japan: final unsuccessful attempt to halt new ideas.

1878 Congress of Berlin: general Balkan settlement. Cyprus leased to Britain (annexed 1914). Second war with Afghanistan (ended 1880). Edison and Swan produce first successful incandescent electric light.

1879 Dual control (Britain and France) in Egypt. Zulu War. Gladstone's Midlothian Campaign. Tay Bridge destroyed, Dec. 28.

1880 Beaconsfield ministry succeeded by second Gladstone ministry. Transvaal declared a republic.

1881 British defeat at Majuba: independence of Transvaal recognised. France occupies Tunis. Gambetta becomes Prime Minister of France. Revolt of the Mahdi in the Sudan. Pasteur's famous immunisation experiment to show that inoculated animals can survive anthrax.

1882 Lord Frederick Cavendish, Irish Secretary, assassinated in Phoenix Park, Dublin, May 6. Triple Alliance (Germany, Austria, Italy) first formed. Alexandria bombarded, July 11. Cairo occupied by British troops, Sept. 14.

1883 National Insurance begun in Germany. Death of Wagner.

1884 Wolseley heads expedition to Khartoum to rescue Gordon. French establish complete protectorate in Indo-China. Evelyn Baring takes over administration of Egypt. Russians capture Merv. Berlin Conference defines rights of European Powers in Africa. Third Parliamentary Reform Bill. Parsons invents his turbine. Greenwich meridian internationally recognised as prime meridian. Fabian Society founded.

1885 Khartoum captured; Gordon slain, Jan. 26.

1886 Upper Burma annexed by Britain. Home Rule Bill defeated in Commons. All Indians in U.S.A. now in Reservations. Daimler produces his first motor car. Completion of Canadian Pacific Railway. Gold discovered in the Transvaal.

1887 Queen Victoria's Jubilee celebration, June 21.

1888 William II German Emperor. County Councils set up in Britain.

1889 Mayerling: tragic death of Prince Rudolf of Austria, Jan. 30. Flight of General Boulanger, after attempting to become master of France. Second Socialist International set up. Great London dock strike, Aug. 15-Sept. 16. Parnell Commission concludes sittings, Nov. 23 (129th day).

1890 Parnell ruined by divorce case: Irish politicians split. Sherman Anti-Trust Law: first attempt in U.S.A. to break cartels. Opening of Forth Bridge, Mar. 4. Bismarck resigns, Mar. 17. Caprivi succeeds. Heligoland ceded to Germany.

1891 The United States of Brazil formed.

1892 Panama Canal financial scandals in France.

1893 Home Rule Bill passes third reading in Commons, Sept. 1: Lords reject Bill, Sept. 8.

1894 Opening of Manchester Ship Canal, Jan. 1.

A.D.

Gladstone resigns, Mar. 3, Lord Rosebery succeeds. Armenian massacres by Turks: repeated at intervals for next quarter of century. Japan declares war against China. Dreyfus convicted of treason.

1895 Opening of Kiel canal, June 21. Rosebery resigns, June 22; Salisbury Ministry succeeds. Treaty of Shimonoseki: Japan gets Formosa, free hand in Korea. New Cuban revolution breaks out against Spanish. Marconi sends message over a mile by wireless. Röntgen discovers X-rays. Freud publishes his first work on psycho-analysis. Jameson Raid, Dec. 29.

1896 Jameson raiders defeated by Boers, Jan. 1. Adowa: Italian disaster at hands of Abyssinians, the first major defeat of a white colonising power by "natives." Gold discovered in the Klondike.

1897 Cretan revolt leads to Greek-Turkish War. Hawaii annexed by U.S.A. Queen Victoria's Diamond Jubilee, June 22. Great Gold Rush began.

1898 Port Arthur ceded to Russia. Spanish-American War. *Maine*, U.S. warship blown up in Havana harbour. Treaty of Paris, Dec. 10: Cuba freed, Puerto Rico and Guam ceded to U.S.A., Phillipines surrendered for £20 million. Death of Gladstone, May 19. Battle of Omdurman, decisive defeat of Mahdists, Sept. 2. Empress of Austria assassinated, Sept. 10. The Curies discovered Radium.

1899 Boer War begins, Oct. 10.

1900 Boers attack Ladysmith, Jan. 6. Battle of Spion Kop, Buller repulsed with severe losses, Jan. 14. Relief of Kimberley, Feb. 15. Ladysmith relieved, Feb. 28. Mafeking relieved, May 17. Boxer outbreak in China, May. Annexation of Orange Free State, May 26. Roberts occupies Johannesburg, May 31. "Khaki Election." Annexation of the Transvaal, Oct. 25. Australian Commonwealth proclaimed, Dec. 30.

1901 Queen Victoria dies, Jan. 22. Trans-Siberian Railway opened for single-track traffic.

1902 Anglo-Japanese Alliance, Jan. 30. Death of Cecil Rhodes, Mar. 26. Treaty of Vereeniging ends Boer War, May 31.

1903 Congo scandal: celebrated case of misrule and exploitation. Royal family of Serbia assassinated, May 29. First controlled flight in heavier-than-air machine—Orville and Wilbur Wright at Kitty Hawk, U.S.A., Dec. 17.

1904 Russo-Japanese War begins, Feb. 8. Japanese victory at Yalu River, May 1. British forces under Younghusband reach Lhasa, Aug. 3. Treaty with Tibet signed at Lhasa, Sept. 7.

1905 Port Arthur falls to Japanese, Jan. 3. "Bloody Sunday" massacre at St. Petersburg, Jan. 22. Destruction of Russian fleet under Rozhdestvenski at Tsushima by Admiral Togo (May). Treaty of Portsmouth (U.S.A.) ends Russo-Japanese war. Separation of Church and State in France. Norway separates itself from Sweden.

1906 General strike in Russia. San Francisco destroyed by earthquake and fire, Apr. 18. Simplon tunnel opened for railway traffic, June 1. First Duma (Parliament with limited powers) in Russia. Liberal "landslide" majority in Britain: Labour M.P.s appear. Movement for Women's Suffrage becomes active in Britain. Algeciras Conference: Franco-German crises resolved in favour of France. Death of Ibsen. Vitamins discovered by F. G. Hopkins.

1907 New Zealand becomes a dominion.

1908 Annexation of Congo by Belgium. Young Turk revolution. Annexation of Bosnia and Herzegovina by Austria: severe rebuff for Russia. Asquith becomes Prime Minister of Britain.

1909 Old Age Pensions in Britain. Peary reaches North Pole. Blériot makes first cross-Channel flight. House of Lords rejects Lloyd George's budget. Union of South Africa formed. Henry Ford concentrates on producing Model T chassis: beginnings of cheap motors.

A.D.

1910 Accession of George V on death of Edward VII, May 6. Liberals win two General Elections. Labour Exchanges established in Britain. Death of Tolstoy and Florence Nightingale.

1911 Parliament Act: power of Lords decisively reduced. British M.P.s paid for first time. National Insurance in Britain. Great British rail strike. Tripoli taken from Turkey by Italy. Chinese Revolution. Amundsen reaches South Pole, Dec. 14.

1912 China becomes a Republic under Sun Yat Sen. *Titanic* disaster off Cape Race, Apr. 14–15. Great British coal strike. Scott's last expedition. Outbreak of Balkan Wars.

1913 Treaty of Bucharest: most of Turkey-in-Europe divided among Balkan states.

FIRST WORLD WAR

1914 Archduke Francis Ferdinand, heir to the Hapsburg thrones, assassinated at Sarajevo, June 28. Austria-Hungary declares war against Serbia, July 28. Germany declares war against Russia, Aug. 1. Germany declares war against France, Aug. 3. German invasion of Belgium: Great Britain declares war against Germany, Aug. 4. Great Britain declares war on Austria-Hungary, Aug. 12. British Expeditionary Force concentrated before Mauberge, Aug. 20. Battle of Mons; Japan declared war on Germany, Aug. 23. Battle of the Marne, Sept. 5–9. Trench warfare began on Aisne salient, Sept. 16. Three British cruisers (*Aboukir, Hogue,* and *Cressy*) sunk by one U-boat, Sept. 22. First Battle of Ypres, Oct. 12-Nov. 11. Raiding of German cruiser *Emden* until destroyed, Nov. 9. Battle of Coronel: German cruisers *Scharnhorst* and *Gneisenau* sink British cruisers *Good Hope* and *Monmouth,* Nov. 1. Great Britain declares war against Turkey, Nov. 5. Destruction of German squadron off Falkland Is., Dec. 8. British protectorate over Egypt proclaimed, Dec. 17. First Zeppelin appeared over British coast, Dec. 20.

1915 Turkish army defeated in Caucasus, Jan 5. Great Britain declared blockade of Germany, Mar. 1. Battle of Neuve Chapelle, Mar. 10–13. Naval attack on Dardanelles called off, Mar. 22. First landing of British, Australian, New Zealand troops on Gallipoli Peninsula, Apr. 25. Second Battle of Ypres, Apr. 22-May 25: Germans first used gas. Sinking of *Lusitania,* May 7. Battle of Aubers Ridge, May 9–25. Italy declares war on Austria, May 22. Italian Coalition Government formed, May 26. Italian army crosses Isonzo, June 2. Zeppelin destroyed by R. A. J. Warneford, June 7. Second landing of Allied troops at Suvla Bay. Italy declares war on Turkey, Aug. 20. Turks defeated at Kut-el-Amara, Sept 28. Serbia conquered by Austria and Bulgaria, Nov. 28. French and British troops occupy Salonika, Dec. 13. British troops withdraw from Anzac and Suvla, Dec. 20.

1916 Evacuation of Gallipoli completed, Jan 8. Opening of Battle of Verdun, Feb. 21. Republican rising in Ireland, Apr. 24. First Daylight Saving Bill passed. Fall of Kut, Apr. 29. Battle of Jutland, May 31. Brusilov's offensive in Galicia begins, June 4. Kitchener drowned when *Hampshire* struck mine, June 5. Battle of the Somme, July 1-Nov. 13: British losses: 420,000. Italians capture Gorizia, Aug. 10. Hindenburg and Ludendorff chiefs of German staff, Aug. 27. Rumania declares war against Austria and Germany, Aug. 27. Tanks first used by British, Sept. 15. Death of Francis Joseph of Austria, Nov. 21. Lloyd George forms War Cabinet, Dec. 6. Joffre replaced by Nivelle, early Dec.

1917 Unrestricted submarine warfare begins, Feb. 1. British troops occupy Baghdad, Mar. 11. Revolution in Russia, Mar. 12. U.S.A. declares war on Germany, April 6. Battle of Arras, Apr. 9-14: Vimy Ridge taken by Canadians, Apr. 10. Pétain replaced Nivelle, May 15. Messines Ridge taken by British, June 7. First American contingents arrive in France, June 26. Allenby assumes Palestine

A.D.

command, June 29. Third Battle of Ypres opened, July 31. Russia proclaimed a Republic, Sept. 15. British victory on Passchendaele Ridge, Oct. 4. French victory on the Aisne, Oct. 23. Caporetto: Italians severely defeated by Austrians. Oct. 24. Bolshevik Revolution, Nov. 7 (Oct. 25 O.S.). Passchendaele captured by British, Nov. 6. Balfour declaration recognised Palestine as "a national home" for the Jews, Nov. 8. Hindenburg Lines smashed on 10-mile front, Nov. 20. Fall of Jerusalem, Dec. 9. Russo-German armistice signed, Dec. 15.

1918 Treaty of Brest-Litovsk, Mar. 3. German offensive against British opened on Somme, Mar. 21. Battle of Arras, Mar. 21-Apr. 4. Second German offensive against British, Apr. 9-25. British naval raid on Zeebrugge and Ostend, Apr. 23. Foch appointed C.-in-C. Allied armies, Apr. 14. Peace signed between Rumania and Central Powers, May 7. *Vindictive* sunk in Ostend harbour, May 9. Last German offensive against French, July 15. British, Canadians, and Australians attack in front of Amiens, Aug. 8. Allenby destroyed last Turkish army at Megiddo, Sept. 19. Bulgarians signed armistice, Sept. 29. General Allied offensive in West began, Sept. 26. Germans accepted Wilson's Fourteen Points, Oct. 23. Great Italian advance, Oct. 24. Turkey surrenders, Oct 30. Austria accepts imposed terms, Nov. 3. Popular government in Poland (Lublin), Nov. 7. Revolutionary movement begins in Germany, Nov. 8. Kaiser abdicates and escapes to Holland, Nov. 9. Armistice signed by Germans, Nov. 11. Proclamation of Kingdom of Serbs, Croats and Slovenes in Belgrade, Dec. 1.

THE TWENTIES AND THIRTIES

1919 Peace Conference in Paris, Jan. 18. Einstein's theory of Relativity confirmed experimentally during solar eclipse, March 29. First direct flight across Atlantic by Sir J. Alcock and Sir A. W. Brown, June 15. Interned German fleet scuttled at Scapa Flow, June 19. Treaty of Peace with Germany signed at Versailles, June 28. Treaty of St. Germain: break-up of Austrian Empire, Sept. 10.

1920 Peace Treaty ratified in Paris. First meeting of League of Nations, from which Germany, Austria, Russia, and Turkey are excluded, and at which the U.S.A. is not represented. Prohibition in U.S.A. Peace Treaty with Turkey signed at Sèvres: Ottoman Empire broken up Aug. 10. Degrees first open to women at Oxford Univ., Oct. 14.

1921 Riots in Egypt, May 23. In complete disregard of the League of Nations, Greece makes war on Turkey. Heligoland fortresses demolished, Oct. 14. Irish Free State set up by Peace Treaty with Britain, Dec. 6.

1922 Four-Power Pacific Treaty ratified by U.S. Senate, Mar. 24. Heavy fighting in Dublin, the Four Courts blown up, July 2. Defeat of Greek armies by the Turks, Aug.-Sept. Mussolini's Fascist "March on Rome," Oct. 28.

1923 French troops despatched to Ruhr, Jan. 11. Treaty of Lausanne, July 24: Earthquake in Japan, Tokyo and Yokohama in ruins, Sept. 1. Rhine Republic proclaimed, Bavaria defies the Reich, Oct. 20. Turkish Republic proclaimed; Kemal Pasha, first President, Oct. 29.

1924 Lenin dies, Jan. 21. First Labour Ministry in Britain under MacDonald, Jan. 22; lasts 9 months. George II of Greece deposed and a Republic declared, Mar. 25. Dawes Plan accepted by London conference; Ruhr evacuation agreed to, Aug. 16.

1925 Hindenburg elected German President, Mar. 26. Treaty of Locarno signed in London, Dec. 1. Summer Time Act made permanent.

1926 Ibn Saud proclaimed king of the Hedjaz in Jeddah, Jan. 11. Evacuation of Cologne by British forces, Jan. 31. General strike in Britain.

1927 Lindbergh flies Atlantic alone, May 21.

1928 Earthquake in Greece, Corinth destroyed. Apr. 23. Capt. Kingsford-Smith flies the

A.D.

Pacific, June 9. General Nobile rescued by aeroplane from Arctic one month after disaster, June 24. Kellogg Pact accepted by Gt. Britain, July 18. German airship with 60 persons crosses Atlantic, Oct. 15. Women in Britain enfranchised on same basis as men.

1929 Second Labour Ministry under MacDonald. Graf Zeppelin makes numerous successful intercontinental flights. Commander Byrd flies over South Pole, Nov. 30. American slump and Wall Street crash.

1930 *R.101* destroyed in France on first flight to India, 48 lives lost, Oct. 5—end of British interest in airships.

1931 Great floods in China. Resignation of Labour Government and formation of Coalition under MacDonald. Invergordon naval mutiny.

1932 Manchuria erected into Japanese puppet state of Manchukuo, Feb. 18. Sydney Harbour Bridge opened, Mar. 19. Ottawa Imperial Conference.

1933 Hitler appointed Chancellor by Hindenburg, Jan. 30, and step by step gains supreme control. German Reichstag set on fire, Feb. 27.

1934 Dollfuss, Austrian Chancellor, murdered by Austrian Nazis, July 25. Death of Hindenburg, Aug. 2. Hitler becomes Dictator. Alexander of Yugoslavia assassinated in Marseilles, Oct. 9.

1935 Saar plebiscite for return to Germany, Jan. 13. Baldwin succeeds MacDonald as Prime Minister, June 7. War begins between Italy and Abyssinia, Oct. 3. Ineffectual economic "sanctions" by League of Nations against Italy, Nov. 18.

1936 Accession of King Edward VIII, Jan. 20. Repudiation of Locarno Treaty by Germany, Mar. 7. Remilitarisation of Rhineland, Mar. 8. Italian troops occupy Addis Ababa, May 5. Civil War breaks out in Spain, July 18. Inauguration of BBC high definition TV, Nov. 2. King Edward VIII abdicates after a reign of 325 days, Dec. 10. The Duke of York succeeds his brother as King George VI, Dec. 12.

1937 Coalition Ministry under Chamberlain, May 28. Japanese begin attempted conquest of China—"China incident," July 7.

1938 Austria annexed by Germany, Mar. 13. British navy mobilised, Sept. 28. Munich Agreement between Chamberlain, Daladier, Hitler, and Mussolini, Sept. 29.

1939

February 27 Great Britain recognises General Franco's Government.

March 16 Bohemia and Moravia annexed by Hitler and proclaimed a German Protectorate. **22** Memel ceded to Germany by Lithuania. **28** Anti-Polish press campaign begun by Germany.

April 1 Spanish War ends. **7** Italy seizes Albania. **14** First British talks with Russia. **27** Conscription introduced in Great Britain. **28** Hitler denounces Anglo-German Naval agreement and the Polish Non-Aggression Treaty.

May 12 Great Britain signs defensive agreement with Turkey. **22** Italy and Germany sign pact. **23** France and Turkey sign defensive agreement. **25** Anglo-Polish treaty signed in London.

July 10 Chamberlain re-affirms British pledge to Poland.

August 23 German-Soviet Pact signed by von Ribbentrop. **25** Japan breaks away from the Anti-Comintern Pact. **28** Holland mobilises. **31** British fleet mobilised.

SECOND WORLD WAR

September 1 Poland invaded by German forces. Great Britain and France mobilise. **1–4** Evacuation schemes put in motion in England and Wales: 1,200,000 persons moved. **2** Compulsory military service for all men in Britain aged 18 to 41. **3** War declared (11 a.m.) between Britain and Germany as from 5 p.m. **4** British liner *Athenia* sunk by submarine. R.A.F. raid the Kiel Canal entrance and bomb German warships. **6** First enemy air raid on Britain. **8** Russia mobilises. Russian troops on Polish border. **11** British troops on French soil. **17**

A.D.

Russian troops cross the Polish frontier along its entire length. Russian and German troops meet near Brest Litovsk: loss of *Courageous*. **27** Capitulation of Warsaw. **29** Nazi-Soviet pact signed in Moscow approving partition of Poland: Introduction of petrol rationing in Britain.

October 14 *Royal Oak* sunk in Scapa Flow with a loss of 810 lives.

November 8 Bomb explosion in the Bürgerbräukeller at Munich after Hitler's speech. Germans using magnetic mines. **29** Diplomatic relations between Russia and Finland severed. **30** Finland attacked by Russia.

December 11 Italy leaves the League of Nations. **13** Battle of the River Plate: engagement of German warship *Admiral Graf Spee* by H.M. cruisers *Exeter*, *Ajax*, and *Achilles*. **14** Rejection by Russia of the League of Nations' offer of mediation in the Russo-Finnish war. Russia expelled from the League of Nations. **17** *Admiral Graf Spee* scuttles herself in the entrance of Montevideo harbour.

1940

February 14 Finnish advanced posts captured by Russians. **16** 299 British prisoners taken off the German Naval Auxiliary *Altmark* in Norwegian waters. **26** Finns lose the island fortress of Kolvisto. Finns retreat from Petsamo.

March 12 British ships to be fitted with a protective device against magnetic mines. Finland concludes a peace treaty whereby she cedes to Russia the Karelian Isthmus, the town of Vipuri and a military base on Hango Peninsula.

April 9 Invasion of Denmark and Norway by Germany. **15** British troops arrive in Norway. **19** British soldiers land in the Faroes.

May 2 British troops withdrawn from Norway. **10** Holland, Belgium and Luxembourg invaded by German forces. Parachute troops landed near Rotterdam. British troops cross the Belgian border. British troops land in Iceland. Rotterdam bombed. **11** National Government formed under Churchill. **13** Queen Wilhelmina arrives in London. **14** Rotterdam captured. Holland ceases fighting. Allied troops land near Narvik. **17** Belgian Government moves to Ostend. **24** German forces enter Boulogne. **27** Belgian army capitulates on the order of King Leopold. British forces to be withdrawn from Flanders. Narvik captured by Allied forces. **29** Ostend, Ypres, Lille and other Belgian and French towns lost to the Germans.

June Evacuation of British army from Dunkirk (May 27–June 4): 299 British warships and 420 other vessels under constant attack evacuate 335,490 officers and men. **5** Hitler proclaims a war of total annihilation against his enemies. **8** German armoured forces penetrate French defences in the West near Rouen. **10** Italy declares war on Great Britain and France. **14** Paris captured by German forces. **15** Soviet troops occupy Lithuania, Latvia and Estonia. **22** French delegates accept terms for an Armistice. **25** Hostilities in France cease at 12.35 a.m.

July 1 Channel Islands occupied by Germany. **3** French naval squadron at Oran immobilised. **10** Battle of Britain began.

August 19 British withdrew from Somaliland. **25** British began night bombing of Germany.

September 6 King Carol of Rumania abdicates in favour of his son Michael. **7** London sustains severe damage in the largest aerial attack since war commenced. **15** Battle of Britain ends with British victory: German aeroplanes destroyed, 1,733; R.A.F. losses, 915. **23** Japanese troops enter Indo-China.

October 7 German troops enter Rumania. **28** Greece rejects an Italian ultimatum.

November 1 Greeks repel Italian attacks, **5** H.M.S. *Jervis Bay* lost defending Atlantic convoy from German warship *Admiral Scheer*. **11** Italian fleet at Taranto crippled by Fleet Air Arm. **14** Coventry heavily attacked, the Cathedral destroyed. **22** Albanian town of Koritza captured by the Greeks.

December 2 Bristol heavily bombed. **11** Sidi Barrani captured by British forces: beginning

A.D.

of Wavell's destruction of Italian forces in Cyrenaica. **29** City of London severely burned by incendiary bombs: Guildhall and eight Wren Churches destroyed.

1941

January 5 Bardia captured. **22** Tobruk captured by Australian troops.

February 7 Benghazi captured. **26** Mogadishu, capital of Italian Somaliland, occupied by Imperial troops. German mechanised troops in Libya.

March 4 British raid Lofoten Islands. **11** U.S. Lease and Lend Bill signed by Roosevelt. **27** Keren—main battle in British conquest of Abyssinia and Somaliland. **28** Cape Matapan: Italian fleet routed by British. **30** Rommel opens attack in N. Africa.

April 4 Addis Ababa entered by Imperial troops. **6** Greece and Yugoslavia invaded by German troops. **8** Massawa capitulates. **11** Belgrade occupied by German forces. **13** Bardia given up by British. Tobruk holds out. **24** Empire forces withdrawing from Greece. **27** Athens captured by the Germans.

May 2 Evacuation from Greece completed. **10** Rudolf Hess descends by parachute in Scotland. **20** Crete invaded by German air-borne troops. **24** H.M.S. *Hood* sunk. **27** German battleship *Bismark* sunk; British forces withdrawn from Crete.

June 2 Clothes rationing commences. **4** William II (ex-Kaiser of Germany) dies. **18** Treaty of friendship between Turkey and Germany signed. **22** Germany attacks Russia. **24** Russia loses Brest Litovsk.

July 3 Palmyra (Syria) surrenders to Allied forces. **7** U.S. forces arrive in Iceland. **9** General Dentz, the French High Commissioner in Syria, asks for Armistice terms. **25** Fighting round Smolensk.

August 25 British and Russian troops enter Persia. **27** The Dnepropetrovsk dam blown up by the Russians.

September 18 Crimea cut off from mainland. **19** Kiev entered by Germans.

October 6 German attack on Moscow. **16** Soviet Government leaves Moscow. Odessa occupied by German and Rumanian troops. **19** Taganrog on Sea of Azov captured by Germans. **26** Kharkov captured by the Germans.

November 14 *Ark Royal* sunk. **18** Libyan battle opens: Eighth Army's first offensive. **23** Bardia and Fort Capuzzo captured by British. **24** H.M.S. *Dunedin* torpedoed. **25** H.M.S. *Barham* sunk. **30** Russians re-take Rostov.

December 1 Points rationing scheme in force in Britain. **4** German attack on Moscow halted. **7** Japanese attack on Pearl Harbor. **8** Japanese forces land in Malaya. **9** British forces in Tobruk relieved. **10** H.M.S. *Repulse* and *Prince of Wales* sunk off Malaya by Japanese. Phillippines invaded by Japanese. **25** Hongkong surrenders to Japanese.

1942

January 2 Manila and Cavite taken by Japanese. **23** Japanese forces land in New Guinea and the Solomon Islands.

February 9 Soap rationed. **12** Escape through English Channel of German ships *Scharnhorst, Gneisenau,* and *Prinz Eugen*. **15** Singapore surrenders to Japanese. **27** Battle of Java Sea.

March 9 Surrender of Java to Japanese.

April 15 George Cross awarded to the island of Malta.

May 4–8 Battle of Coral Sea. **7** Madagascar invaded by British forces. **7** U.S. forces sink 11 Japanese warships off the Solomon islands. **30** Over 1,000 bombers raid Cologne. Canterbury bombed.

June 3–7 Midway Island: U.S. naval victory turns tide in Pacific. **20** Tobruk captured by the Germans.

July 16 R.A.F. make first daylight raid on the Ruhr.

August 6 Germans advancing towards the Caucasus. **10** American forces land in the Solomon

A.D.

Islands. **11** Malta convoy action (loss of H.M.S. *Eagle, Manchester, Cairo,* and one destroyer). **19** Raid on Dieppe. **23–25** Battle of Solomons.

September 6 Germans halted at Stalingrad.

October 23 El Alamein: Allied offensive opens in Egypt.

November 4 Rommel's army in full retreat. **5** Red Army holding firm at Stalingrad. **7** Allied invasion of N. Africa. **27** German forces enter Toulon. French Fleet scuttled.

December 2 First self-sustained, controlled nuclear chain reaction in uranium achieved by group working under Enrico Fermi at Chicago. **24** Admiral Darlan assassinated.

1943

January 6 German armies in the Caucasus and the Don elbow in retreat. **18** Leningrad 16-month siege ended. **23** Tripoli occupied by the Eighth Army. **27** American bombers make their first attack on Germany. **31** Remnants of the German army outside Stalingrad surrender.

February 9 Guadalcanal Island cleared of Japanese troops. **16** Kharkov retaken by the Russians.

March 1–3 Battle of Bismarck Sea. **23** 8th Army penetrates the Mareth Line.

May 7 Tunis and Bizerta captured by Allies. **12** All organised German resistance in Tunisia ceases. **16** Dams in the Ruhr breached by the R.A.F. **22** Moscow dissolves the Cominform.

June 3 French Committee for National Liberation formed in Algiers.

July 5 Battle of Kursk begins; largest tank battle in history ends in Russian victory; **10** Allied invasion of Sicily. **25** Mussolini overthrown. **28** Fascist Party in Italy dissolved.

August 17 Sicily in Allied hands.

September 3 Italian mainland invaded. **7** Italy surrenders. **9** British and American troops land near Naples. **10** Rome seized by the Germans. **14** Salamaua captured from the Japanese. **23** *Tirpitz* severely damaged (sunk Nov. 12, 1944). **25** Smolensk taken by the Russians.

October 1 Naples taken. **25** Russians capture Dnepropetrovsk and Dneprodzerzhinck.

November 6 Kiev taken by the Russians. **26** Second Battle of Solomons. **28** Churchill, Roosevelt, and Stalin meet in Teheran.

December 2 Men between 18 and 25 to be directed to the mining industry by ballot in Britain. **26** Sinking of German battleship *Scharnhorst*.

1944

January 22 Allied landings at Anzio. **28** Argentina breaks with the Axis Powers.

February 1 American forces land on the Marshall Islands. **2** Russians penetrate Estonia.

March 15 Cassino (Italy) destroyed by US bombers.

May 9 Sevastopol captured by Russians. **18** Capture of Cassino and Abbey by Allies. **19** 50 Allied officers shot after escaping from a German prison camp. **30** Battle for Rome commences.

June 4 Allied forces enter Rome. King of Italy signs decree transferring his powers to Prince Umberto, his son. **6** *D-Day*: invasion of Europe (over 4,000 ships in invasion fleet). **7** Defeat of Japanese thrust at India, outside Imphal. **9** Heavy fighting near Caen. **12** First V-1 falls on England. **18** Cherbourg peninsula cut by the Americans. Russians break through the Mannerheim Line.

July 3 Minsk captured by Russians. **9** Caen captured by Allies. **20** "Bomb plot" on Hitler's life. **21** Guam captured by Americans.

August 1 Uprising in Warsaw. **4** Myitkyina falls to Allied forces. **15** Allied forces land in southern France. Marseilles taken. Rumania surrenders. **25** Paris liberated. Rumania declares war on Germany.

September 3 Allies in Belgium. **4** Antwerp and Brussels taken by Allies. Holland entered. Finland "ceases fire." **6** Bulgaria asks for an armistice. **7** Boulogne entered by Allies. Bulgaria declares war on Germany. **8** First V-2 falls on England. **11** Allied forces fighting on

A.D.

Reich territory. **17** Allied airborne troops landed at Arnhem. **22** 1st Battle of Philippines.
October 3 Warsaw rising crushed by Germany. **14** Allies occupied Athens. **15** Hungary requested armistice. **20** US troops took Aachen. **25** Battle of Leyte Gulf: Japan's sea-power broken.
December 6 Civil war in Athens. **16** German counter-attack in Ardennes.

1945

January 5 Athens fighting ended. **9** US troops landed on Luzon. **13** Red Army occupied Budapest. **17** Red Army occupied Warsaw. **27** Red Army entered Auschwitz. **28** Burma Rd to China reopened.
February 4 Yalta Conference. **14** Dresden bombed. **19** US troops landed on Iwo Jima.
March 6 Allies took Cologne.
April 1 US invaded Okinawa. **11** Red Army entered Vienna. **12** Pres Roosevelt died. **27** Russian–US link-up in Germany. **28** Mussolini killed by Italian partisans. **29** German and Italian armies in Italy surrendered. **30** Suicide of Hitler.
May 2 Russians took Berlin. **3** British took Rangoon. **4** German forces in NW Germany, Holland and Denmark surrendered. **8** World War II ended; VE Day. **28** Air attacks on Japan.
June 26 World Security Charter to establish UN signed in San Francisco.
July 5 Allies recognised Polish government. **26** Labour won General Election: new PM Clement Attlee. **31** Potsdam Conference.
August 6 Atomic bomb destroyed Hiroshima. **9** Nagasaki atom bomb. **14** Unconditional surrender of Japan. **15** VJ Day.
September 5 Allies reoccupied Singapore.

"COLD WAR": AFRO-ASIAN INDEPENDENCE

October 15 Laval executed. **24** Quisling executed.
November 16 UNESCO founded in Paris. **20** Nuremberg trial opened.
December 27 IMF and World Bank established.

1946

February 1 Trygve Lie 1st UN Secretary-General.
March 5 Churchill's "Iron Curtain" speech.
April 18 League of Nations wound up.
May 25 Jordan independent.
June 30 US atom bomb test at Bikini.
July 13 £937m US loan to Britain. **22** King David Hotel, British HQ in Jerusalem, blown up.
August 1 Paris Peace Conference.
October 16 Nuremberg sentences carried out: Goering's suicide. **23** General Assembly of UN opened in New York.

1947

January 1 Coal nationalised. **14** Vincent Auriol 1st Pres of French IVth Republic.
February 20 Lord Mountbatten last Viceroy of India.
June 5 "Marshall Plan" inaugurated.
August 3 UN mediation ended Indonesia fighting. **15** India and Pakistan independent after partition.
October 6 International organisation of Communist Parties Cominform set up. **14** Sound barrier broken.
November 20 Princess Elizabeth married.
December 15 "Big 4" talks on Germany broke down.

1948

January 1 Railways nationalised. **4** Burma independent. **30** Gandhi assassinated.
February 1 Malayan federal constitution came into force. **27** Communists seized power in Czechoslovakia.
March 10 Czech Foreign Minister Jan Masaryk found dead.
April 1 Electricity nationalised. **16** OEEC set up.
May 14 British Mandate in Palestine ended: new State of Israel proclaimed.

A.D.

June 28 Cominform expelled Yugoslavia.
July 1 Berlin airlift. **5** NHS inaugurated.
August 1 Economic union of French, US and British zones in Germany.
September 4 Queen Wilhelmina of Netherlands abdicated. **9** N Korea independent, following S Korea. **17** UN mediator in Palestine assassinated.
November 3 Harry Truman elected US Pres. **14** Prince Charles born.
December 10 UN adopted Declaration of Human Rights.

1949

January 22 Chinese Communists took Peking.
April 1 Newfoundland became province of Canada. **4** 12 nations signed N Atlantic Treaty. **18** Republic of Ireland proclaimed.
May 1 Gas nationalised. **12** Berlin blockade lifted. **23** Federal Republic of Germany proclaimed.
August 8 1st meeting of Council of Europe.
September 14 Dr Adenauer 1st Chancellor of FDR. **21** Soviet atom bomb test.
October 1 People's Republic of China proclaimed under Chairman Mao Tse-tung. **12** German Democratic Republic proclaimed in Soviet sector.
December 8 Chinese Nationalist government set up in Formosa HQ. **27** Indonesia independent.

1950

January 26 Indian republic proclaimed under Pres Rajendra Prasad.
February 14 USSR–China alliance signed. **23** Labour won General Election.
June 25 N Korea invaded S Korea. **27** US air, naval, and later ground forces supported S Korea.
July 8 Gen MacArthur C-in-C of UN forces in Korea.
August 1 Chinese membership rejected by UN. **7** US offensive in Korea.
September 6 British troops in action in Korea.
October 19 UN forces took Pyongyang. **21** China invaded Tibet. **26** New Chamber of House of Commons opened.
November 26 Chinese offensive into N Korea.
December 4 Chinese took Pyongyang. **19** Gen Eisenhower appointed head of Nato forces.

1951

January 4 N Korean and Chinese troops captured Seoul. **17** French held back Viet Minh offensive in Tonkin.
March 19 Treaty of Paris signed to create European Coal & Steel Community.
April 11 Gen MacArthur replaced by Lt-Gen Ridgway.
May 2 Persian oil industry nationalised. **3** Festival of Britain opened.
June 7 British diplomats Burgess and Maclean vanished.
July 8 Korean ceasefire talks. **16** King Leopold of Belgians abdicated. **20** King Abdullah of Jordan assassinated.
September 1 Tripartite Security Treaty between US, Australia and New Zealand. **8** Japanese peace treaty.
October 16 Pakistan's PM Ali Khan assassinated. **19** British troops seized Suez Canal Zone. **25** Conservatives won General Election: Churchill PM.
December 24 Libya independent.

1952

February 6 George VI died: Accession of Queen Elizabeth II.
March 21 Kwame Nkrumah Gold Coast's 1st PM.
April 23 Japan regained sovereign and independent status.
May 27 European Defence Community Treaty signed.
June 23 US air attack on N Korea hydro-electric plants.
July 23 Military coup in Egypt: later King Faroukh abdicated. **30** Eva Peron died.

A.D.
August 1 Parliament ratified Bonn Agreement: W Germany again independent. **16** Lynmouth floods. **26** S African protests against racial laws.
September 8 Gen Neguib military Gov-Gen of Egypt.
October 3 Britain's 1st atomic bomb test in Monte Bello Is. **20** State of Emergency in Kenya over Mau Mau atrocities.
November 4 Republican Gen Eisenhower won US Presidental Election. **30** US hydrogen bomb test reported.

1953

February 3 E coast floods.
March 5 Stalin died. **14** Krushchev emerged as USSR leader. **24** Queen Mary died. **25** Polio vaccine announced. **31** New UN Sec-Gen Dag Hammarskjöld.
April 8 Mau Mau leader Jomo Kenyatta jailed.
May 29 Hillary and Tensing climbed Everest.
June 2 Elizabeth II crowned: ceremony televised. **17** E Berlin anti-Soviet riots. **18** Egyptian republic proclaimed.
July 27 Korean armistice signed.
August 14 Soviet hydrogen bomb test.
November 21 Piltdown skull exposed as hoax. **29** French took Dien Bien Phu.
December 23 Former KGB chief Beria executed.

1954

January 9 Sudan self-governing. **16** New French Pres René Coty.
February 3 1st Central African Federation parliament opened.
March 22 London gold market reopened.
April 18 Nasser took power as Egypt's PM. **21** USSR joined UNESCO.
May 4 Roger Bannister's 4-min mile. **8** Dien Bien Phu fell to Viet Minh. **17** Racial segregation banned in US state schools.
June 2 New Irish PM John Costello. **17** New French PM Pierre Mendès-France.
July 3 Food rationing ended. **21** Sino-French pact to end Indo-China war.
August 5 Persian oil dispute settled.
October 19 Anglo-Egyptian Suez Canal Agreement.
November 1 Algerian nationalist riots.
December 2 Senator McCarthy censured by Congress. **18** Cyprus riots for union with Greece.

1955

February 8 Marshall Bulganin Soviet PM and 1st Sec of Communist Party. **23** New French PM Edgar Fauré. **25** 1st meeting of SEATO.
April 5 Sir Winston Churchill resigned: new PM Sir Anthony Eden. **18** Hungarian PM Imre Nagy dismissed. **24** Afro-Asian Conference of 29 non-aligned nations. **29** Vietnam civil war.
May 5 W Germany attained full sovereignty; Western European Union established. **26** Conservatives won General Election.
June 2 Soviet-Yugoslav relations normalised. **15** UK-US nuclear cooperation agreed.
July 18 "Big 4" Geneva conference.
August 20 Riots in Algeria and Morocco.
September 15 EOKA guerrillas outlawed: British troops in Cyprus. **19** Gen Peron ousted. **22** ITV 1st broadcast.
October 6 New Greek PM Constantine Karamanlis. **20** Syria-Egypt mutual defence treaty. **26** S Vietnam declared independent republic.
November 2 New Israeli PM David Ben-Gurion.
December 7 Clement Attlee resigned. **14** New Labour Party leader Hugh Gaitskell.

1956

January 1 Sudan proclaimed independent republic.
February 25 Krushchev denounced Stalin. **29** Alabama race riots.
March 2 King Hussein of Jordan dismissed Lt-Gen Glubb, Commander of Arab Legion. **9** Archbishop Makarios deported to Seychelles. **23** Pakistan Islamic Republic within Commonwealth.
April 18 Krushchev and Bulganin in London.
June 13 British troops left Canal Zone. **23** Nasser elected Pres of Egypt unopposed. **29** Polish anti-Soviet riots.
July 26 Egypt seized Canal Zone.

A.D.
October 23 Hungarian uprising against Soviet domination. **25** Anti-Soviet Polish unrest. **29** Israel invaded Egypt seizing Sinai peninsula. **31** Anglo-French forces bombed Egyptian military targets.
November 1 Premium bonds launched. **4** Soviet tanks crushed Hungarian revolt. **5** Anglo-French troops seized Canal Zone. **6** Pres Eisenhower re-elected. **8** UN Canal Zone ceasefire. **16** Canal blocked. **21** UN troops controlled Canal Zone. **30** Flood of Hungarian refugees.
December 5 140 arrests in S Africa for alleged treason. **7** Anglo-French troops left Port Said.

1957

January 1 Egypt abrogated 1954 Anglo-Egyptian Treaty; Saarland returned to W Germany. **9** Sir Anthony Eden resigned: new PM Harold Macmillan.
February 15 New Soviet Foreign Minister Andrei Gromyko.
March 6 Ghana independent; De Valera won Irish General Election. **25** Treaty of Rome setting up EEC and EAEC (Euratom) signed by Benelux, France, Germany and Italy.
April 8 Suez Canal reopened. **17** Archbishop Makarios in Athens.
May 15 UK's 1st hydrogen bomb test.
June 11 Canada's new Convervative government under John Diefenbaker.
July 8 State of Emergency against IRA proclaimed in Republic of Ireland. **25** Tunisia became republic under Pres Bourguiba.
August 8 Myxomatosis rife. **30** Malaya independent.
September 4 Wolfenden Report published. **15** Chancellor Adenauer re-elected. **23** Asian flu epidemic. **25** National Guard sent in to enforce desegregation in Little Rock, Arkansas.
October 4 Soviet satellite launched. **11** Jodrell Bank radio telescope inaugurated.
November 3 Soviet satellite carrying dog in orbit.
December 19 NATO conference agreed US nuclear bases in Europe.

1958

January 1 Treaty of Rome came into force. **3** British W Indies Federation inaugurated. **28** Turkish Cypriot riots. **31** US satellite launched.
February 1 Syria and Egypt proclaimed United Arab Republic. **6** Munich plane crash: Manchester Utd lost 8 players. **14** Short-lived Jordan-Iraq union. **17** CND founded.
March 2 Dr Vivian Fuchs completed 1st crossing of Antarctica. **8** Yemen entered federation with UAR. **27** Bulganin ousted.
April 4 1st Aldermaston march. **17** Nationalists won S African General Election. **21** Maltese PM Dom Mintoff resigned.
May 13 Algerian French nationalists rebelled. **23** Hovercraft unveiled. **29** Gen de Gaulle returned to power.
June 9 Gatwick airport opened. **20** Greek Cypriots rejected British peace plan.
July 14 King Faisal of Iraq assassinated: republic established. **15** US marines in Lebanon. **17** British troops in Jordan. **24** 1st life peers announced. **26** Prince Charles named Prince of Wales.
August 5 US nuclear submarine passed under N Pole.
September 2 New S African PM Dr Verwoerd. **9** Notting Hill race riots. **28** French referendum approved Vth Republic.
October 2 EOKA campaign renewed. **9** Pope Pius XII died. **28** Angelo Roncalli elected Pope as John XXIII. **31** 1st heart pacemaker implanted.
December 8 Draft agreement at 3-power Geneva test ban talks. **21** De Gaulle 1st Pres of Vth Republic. **27** Soviet cooperation agreed with UAR on Aswan dam project. **31** Thalidomide implicated in birth defects.

1959

January 1 Cuba's Batista regime overthrown by Fidel Castro. **12** USSR *Lunik I* satellite 1st to escape Earth's gravity.
February 2 Indira Gandhi leader of India's Congress Party. **23** Archbishop Makarios returned to

A.D.

Cyprus. **26** State of Emergency in S Rhodesia: black nationalist parties dissolved.
March 4 Anti-British riots in Nyasaland: Hastings Banda arrested. **17** Lhasa uprising against Chinese rule: Dalai Lama fled.
May 6 "Cod war" with Iceland. **15** Jodrell Bank transmitted radio message to USA via moon.
June 17 Eamon de Valera voted Eire's Pres. **26** St Lawrence Seaway opened.
July 5 3 animals recovered safely after Soviet space flight. **18** Castro assumed Cuba's Presidency.
August 18 BMC launched Mini.
September 14 Soviet *Lunik II* landed on moon. **27** Ceylon's PM Bandaranaike assassinated.
October 8 Conservatives won General Election. **26** *Lunik III* sent back photos of dark side of moon.
November 1 Nationalist riots in Belgian Congo. **M1**, 1st UK motorway, opened. **20** EFTA agreement signed.
December 1 12 nations signed Antarctic Treaty. **3** Fréjus dam disaster. **14** Archbishop Makarios 1st Pres of Cyprus.

1960

January 1 French "new franc" introduced. **29** French settlers' revolt in Algeria.
February 2 De Gaulle granted emergency powers. **3** Harold Macmillan's "Wind of change" speech in Cape Town. **13** French atomic test in Sahara. **29** Agadir earthquake.
March 21 Sharpeville massacre in S Africa: 67 dead.
April 1 Hastings Banda freed. **9** Murder attempt on Dr Verwoerd. **19** Flood of E German refugees. **27** S Korean Pres Synghman Rhee resigned.
May 1 US U-2 military reconnaissance aircraft shot down over USSR. **7** Leonid Brezhnev new Soviet PM. **17** Paris "Big 4" Summit failed; Kariba Dam inaugurated. **25** Turkish military coup.
June 22 Krushchev attacked Mao and Chinese policies. **30** Belgian Congo became independent republic of Congo under PM Patrice Lumumba.
July 1 Ghana and Somalia became republics. **6** Congolese army mutiny: whites fled Leopoldville. **11** Katanga declared independence from Congo under Moise Tshombe. **21** Mrs Bandaranaike world's 1st woman PM.
August 8 Coup in Laos: new PM Prince Souvanna Phouma. **16** Cyprus declared republic.
September 14 Congolese army took power under Col Mobutu.
October 2 Talks to end "Cod war". **12** Disruptive behaviour from Krushchev at UN General Assembly. **20** *Lady Chatterley's Lover* trial.
November 9 Democrat John Kennedy elected US Pres. **21** Fighting between Congolese army and UN troops.
December 2 Lumumba arrested; Archbishop of Canterbury met Pope. **31** National Service ended; Farthing abolished.

1961

January 8 Referendum in France and Algeria backed de Gaulle; Portland spy ring arrests.
February 13 Lumumba dead.
March 21 US military aid to Laos. **26** French army rising in Algiers collapsed after 4 days.
April 12 Yuri Gagarin in 1st manned space flight. **19** Cuban exiles in Bay of Pigs invasion. **20** Angolan revolt.
May 1 1st betting shops opened. **5** Alan Shepherd made 1st US manned space flight. **17** S Korean military coup. **31** S Africa independent and left Commonwealth.
June 3 Kennedy-Krushchev Vienna talks. **27** Michael Ramsay enthroned as 100th Archbishop of Canterbury.
August 10 Britain formally applied to join EEC. **13** E Berlin border sealed: later Berlin Wall erected. **14** Kenyatta freed.
September 18 Dag Hammarskjöld killed in Congo plane crash. **30** Syria seceded from UAR.
October 10 Volcanic eruption on Tristan da Cunha: entire population evacuated. **23** 30 megaton Soviet atomic test. **24** Malta independent. **30** Stalin's body moved from Red Sq.
November 7 Adenauer elected Chancellor for 4th term. **28** UN condemned S African apartheid policy.

A.D.

December 15 Eichmann sentenced to death for crimes against Jewish people. **17** Indian troops invaded Goa and other Portuguese colonies.

1962

January 4 More US military aid for S Vietnam. **14** UK smallpox outbreak.
February 8 OAS bomb campaign in France and Algeria.
March 2 Nehru's Congress Party won Indian General Election. **14** Geneva disarmament talks reopened. **15** Liberals won Orpington by-election.
April 8 Algerian peace accord. **13** International agreement on marine pollution. **26** 1st UK satellite *Ariel* launched.
May 10 US troops in Laos. **13** New Indian Pres Dr Radhakrishnan. **25** Coventry cathedral consecrated.
July 1 Commonwealth Immigrants Act came into force. **3** Algeria independent. **10** 1st live tv US–Europe link-up via *Telstar*.
August 22 De Gaulle escaped 4th assassination attempt.
September 3 Trans-Canada highway opened. **27** Yemen proclaimed republic.
October 22 Cuban missile crisis. **28** Soviet missile sites in Cuba to be dismantled. **26** Fighting on China–India border.
November 7 Nelson Mandela jailed for incitement. **20** US Cuban blockade lifted. **21** Ceasefire in China–India border dispute. **26** US Turkish bases to be removed. **29** Anglo-French agreement on Concorde. **30** New UN Sec-Gen U Thant.
December 8 British troops clashed with Brunei rebels opposing Malaysian Federation. **9** Dr Julius Nyrere 1st Pres of Tanganyika. **15** Right-wing victory in S Rhodesian General Election.

1963

January 15 Moise Tshombe finally ended Katanga secession. **18** Hugh Gaitskell died. **22** Franco-German Treaty on political and military cooperation. **29** Britain refused EEC membership; "Kim" Philby disappeared from Beirut.
February 1 Nyasaland self-governing under PM Hastings Banda. **8** Military coup in Iraq: PM Kassim executed. **9** Joshua Nkomo jailed in S Rhodesia. **14** Harold Wilson new Labour leader; 1st successful kidney transplant.
March 8 Military coup in Syria. **27** Beeching Report axed railways. **29** Central African Federation collapsed.
April 6 US–UK Polaris agreement. **8** Liberals won Canadian General Election. **23** New German Chancellor Ludwig Erhart.
May 11 Greville Wynne in Moscow spy trial. **18** Federal troops sent to quell Alabama race riots. **20** Sukarno Life Pres of Indonesia. **25** OAU founded. **27** Kenyatta elected PM in Kenya's 1st General Election.
June 3 John XXIII died. **5** John Profumo, Secretary of State for War, resigned. **6** Martial law in Teheran after Ayatollah Khomeini arrested. **13** Buddhist riots in Saigon. **16** Valentina Tereshkova 1st woman in space. **21** Giovanni Battista Montini elected Pope as Paul VI. **26** Pres Kennedy in W Berlin.
July 22 Stephen Ward on trial in "Profumo affair" aftermath. **26** Skopje earthquake.
August 8 "Great Train Robbery": £2·6m. mailbags stolen. **8** US–UK–USSR test ban treaty. **28** Dr Martin Luther King's "Freedom March" on Washington. **30** Moscow–Washington "hot line" inaugurated.
September 16 Federation of Malaysia created: anti-British riots. **17** Fylingdales early warning missile system operational.
October 1 Nigeria declared republic within Commonwealth. **18** Harold Macmillan resigned: new PM Earl of Home, later Sir Alec Douglas-Home.
November 1 Military coup in S Vietnam. **22** Pres Kennedy assassinated: Vice-Pres Lyndon Johnson sworn in.
December 12 Kenya independent.

1964

January 4 Pope visited Holy Land. **29** Further S Vietnam military coup.
February 11 Turkish–Greek Cypriot fighting.

A.D.

March 19 UN peacekeeping troops in Cyprus.
April 9 Labour won 1st GLC elections. **13** New S Rhodesian PM Ian Smith. **21** BBC-2 on air. **22** Tanganyika and Zanzibar united as Tanzania.
May 27 Nehru died.
June 2 New Indian PM Lal Shastri; PLO founded. **4** Britain's *Blue Streak* rocket launched. **12** Life sentence on Nelson Mandela for treason. **14** Francois Duvallier Haitian Pres-for-Life.
July 2 US Civil Rights Act. **6** Nyasaland independent as Malawi. **10** Congo's new PM Moise Tshombe.
August 2 US destroyer attacked by N Vietnam in Gulf of Tonkin: US air raids in reprisal.
September 2 Indonesian troops landed in Malaysia. **21** Malta independent within Commonwealth.
October 15 Krushchev deposed: new Communist Party leader Leonid Brezhnev, new PM Kosygin; Labour won General Election: new PM Harold Wilson. **16** Chinese atomic test. **24** N Rhodesia independent as Zambia under Pres Kaunda.
November 1 Vietcong guerrillas attacked US S Vietnamese base. **2** King Saud of Saudi Arabia deposed by brother Faisal. **3** Pres Johnson won US Presidential Election. **17** Arms embargo on S Africa. **26** Belgian paratroopers rescued hostages from Congo rebels.
December 12 Kenya proclaimed republic under Pres Kenyatta.

1965

January 12 Indonesia left UN. **24** Churchill died.
February 7 US air raid on N Vietnam. **24** US bombed Vietcong in S Vietnam.
March 7 US marines in S Vietnam. **18** Soviet cosmonaut made 1st spacewalk. **25** Ceylon's new PM Senanayake. **28** Alabama civil rights protest. **30** US Saigon embassy bombed.
April 30 US marines in Dominica after military coup.
May 7 Rhodesia Front won Rhodesian General Election. **11** E Pakistan cyclone: 16,000 dead.
June 19 Algerian Pres Ben Bella ousted by Col Boumedienne. **29** US offensive against Vietcong.
July 29 Edward Heath new Conservative leader.
August 9 Singapore seceded from Malaysia. **11** Riots in Watts, Los Angeles.
September 8 India invaded Pakistan after Kashmir fighting: Pakistan air raids on New Delhi and later Bombay. **12** 50,000 more US troops in S Vietnam. **30** UK's 1st woman High Court judge.
October 7 Post Office Tower opened. **17** US and UK anti-Vietnam war protests. **22** India and Pakistan accepted UN ceasefire. **29** Rhodesia conciliation talks failed.
November 11 Rhodesian UDI: Britain declared regime illegal: sanctions imposed. **25** Gen Mobutu deposed Congo's Pres Kasavubu.
December 8 Vatican Council II closed. **17** Rhodesian oil embargo. **19** Pres de Gaulle re-elected.

1966

January 11 Indian PM Shastri died: new PM Indira Gandhi. **15** Army coup in Nigeria. **31** US bombing of N Vietnam resumed: UK Rhodesia trade ban.
February 24 Army coup in Ghana while Pres Nkrumah abroad.
March 31 Labour won General Election.
April 19 Australian troops in Vietnam.
June 30 France left NATO; US bombed Hanoi.
July 20 6-month pay and price freeze. **30** US bombed Vietnam demilitarised zone; England won World Cup. **31** US urban race riots.
Augst 11 Indonesia–Malaysia peace agreement. **13** Chinese cultural revolution began.
September 6 Dr Verwoerd assassinated: new S African PM John Vorster. **30** Bechuanaland became independent republic of Botswana; Ancient statues saved from waters of Aswan Dam.
October 3 Basutoland independent as Lesotho; Nigerian tribal fighting. **21** Aberfan coal tip disaster.
November 1 Vietcong shelled Saigon. **9** Florence floods; new Irish PM Jack Lynch.
December 1 Dr Kiesinger new W German Chancellor. **2** Harold Wilson and Ian Smith in inconclusive talks on HMS *Tiger*. **16** UN mandatory oil

A.D.

sanctions against Rhodesia. **22** Rhodesia left Commonwealth.

1967

January 18 New Liberal leader Jeremy Thorpe. **27** Flash fire killed 3 US astronauts during ground test.
February 22 Gen Suharto in power in Indonesia. **26** Major US offensive against Vietcong.
March 9 Stalin's daughter defected to West. **18** *Torrey Canyon* wrecked off Land's End: major pollution. **24** Army coup in Sierra Leone.
April 1 UK's 1st Ombudsman. **14** Conservatives won GLC elections. **21** Greek colonels seized power.
May 11 Britain applied to join EEC. **30** Biafra seceded from Nigeria.
June 5 6 Day War: Israel seized territory from Egypt, Jordan and Syria. **17** 1st Chinese H-bomb test.
July 1 Moise Tshombe arrested when plane hijacked to Algiers; BBC-2 began colour broadcasts. **7** Nigerian troops invaded Biafra. **15** De Gaulle in Quebec. **27** US urban race riots.
August 9 Biafran troops in Nigeria.
September 1 Majority verdicts allowed in UK criminal courts. **3** Swedish traffic switched to right. **20** *QEII* launched.
October 9 Che Guevara killed; New drink-driving laws. **22** Anti-Vietnam war demonstrations in US, UK and W Europe. **25** Abortion Bill passed. **31** Foot-and-mouth disease epidemic.
November 19 £ devalued. **29** Aden independent republic as S Yemen.
December 3 1st successful human heart transplant. **17** Australian PM Harold Holt drowned.

1968

January 5 Alexander Dubcek new moderate Czechoslovak PM. **9** New Australian PM John Gorton. **23** Intelligence ship *USS Pueblo* seized by N Korea. **31** Vietcong Tet offensive against S Vietnam cities: raid on US Saigon embassy.
February 24 US and S Vietnam troops recaptured Hue.
March 6 Black Rhodesians hanged in defiance of Queen's reprieve. **15** Foreign Secretary George Brown resigned. **17** Grosvenor Sq anti-Vietnam war demonstration.
April 4 Martin Luther King assassinated: riots throughout USA. **6** New Canadian Liberal PM Pierre Trudeau. **12** Student riots throughout Europe after shooting of W German student leader Rudi Dutschke. **21** Enoch Powell's immigration speech.
May 5 Student riots in Paris began. **9** Soviet troops on Czech border. **16** Ronan Point tower block collapsed. **19** French General Strike. **30** De Gaulle dissolved National Assembly and called General Election.
June 5 Robert Kennedy assassinated. **30** De Gaulle won landslide victory in French General Election.
July 1 Last EEC customs barriers removed; 36 nations signed Nuclear Non-Proliferation Treaty. **10** Couve de Murville succeeded Pompidou as French PM. **29** Papal encyclical against artificial contraception.
August 22 Warsaw Pact troops invaded Czechoslovakia.
September 11 Soviet tanks left Prague. **16** UK 2-tier postal system. **26** Theatre censorship abolished. **27** France vetoed UK EEC membership.
October 4 Warsaw Pact troops to remain in Czechoslovakia. **6** Londonderry riots against sectarian discrimination. **9** *HMS Fearless* Rhodesia talks failed.
November 1 US halted bombing of N Vietnam. **5** Republican Richard Nixon won US Presidential Election. **7** Prague anti-Soviet demonstrations.
December 27 3 US astronauts completed 10 orbits of moon.

1969

January 3 N Ireland sectarian violence. **19** Student Jan Palach set himself on fire in Wenceslas Sq in anti-Soviet protest.
February 3 Yasser Arafat PLO leader.
March 2 Soviet-China border clashes. **17** New Israeli PM Golda Meir. **19** British troops in

A.D.

Anguilla. **25** Pres Ayub Khan ousted by army coup under Gen Yahya Khan.

April 17 More troops sent to N Ireland; Dubcek replaced as Czech Communist Party leader by Gustav Husak. **18** Bernadette Devlin, civil rights worker, elected in Mid-Ulster by-election, UK's youngest MP. **23** Nigerian troops took Umuahia. **28** De Gaulle resigned after referendum defeat. **29** N Ireland PM Terence O'Neill resigned.

May 1 New N Ireland PM Maj James Chichester-Clark.

June 8 Spain closed Gibraltar border. **15** New French Pres Georges Pompidou: PM Jacques Chaban-Delmas.

July 1 Prince of Wales invested at Caernarvon. **21** Neil Armstrong and "Buzz" Aldrin 1st men on moon; Sen Edward Kennedy in court over Chappaquiddick drowning. **22** Gen Franco named Prince Juan Carlos as future Spanish King.

August 12 3 days of riots in Londonderry after Apprentice Boys' March. **15** British troops took over N Ireland security.

September 1 King Idris of Libya deposed by army revolutionaries under Muammar Gaddafi: republic proclaimed. **3** Ho Chi Minh died. **10** 7,000 troops in N Ireland. **24** Ton Duc Thang new N Vietnamese Pres. **28** Army erected Belfast "peace line": barricades dismantled: traffic curfew.

October 1 Olaf Palme Swedish PM. **10** N Ireland "B Specials" disbanded. **12** Troops used tear gas in N Ireland. **14** 50p coin issued. **15** "Vietnam moratorium" in USA. **21** New W German Chancellor Willi Brandt.

November 2 Starvation in Biafran refugee camps: Nigeria banned Red Cross aid.

December 18 UK death penalty permanently abolished.

1970

January 1 UK age of majority 18. **12** Biafra capitulated. **16** New Libyan PM Gaddafi; UK Hong Kong flu epidemic.

February 9 Equal Pay Bill passed in Commons. **11** Decentralisation of NHS announced.

March 1 US planes bombed "Ho Chi Minh trail" in E Laos. **2** Rhodesia declared republic. **18** Cambodia's Prince Sihanouk ousted. **19** 1st meeting between E and W German leaders.

April 2 Battle between Israeli and Syrian troops. **8** Israeli air raid on Nile delta village. **16** Clifford Dupont 1st Pres of Rhodesia. **17** *Apollo 13* crew rescued. **30** US troops in Cambodia.

May 4 4 student anti-war protesters shot dead at Kent State University, Ohio.

June 7 Jordan troops attempted to expel Palestinian guerrillas. **19** Conservatives won General Election: new PM Edward Heath. **26** Dubcek expelled from Communist Party. **30** UK, Denmark, Ireland and Norway opened talks on EEC entry.

August 2 1st use of rubber bullets in N Ireland. **30** Malayan PM Tengku Abdul Rahman resigned.

September 4 New Chilean Pres Socialist Salvador Allende. **12** Palestinian terrorists blew up 3 hijacked airliners in Jordan desert: 56 hostages held. **14** Palestinian guerrillas in control of N Jordan and Jordan's 2nd city Irbid. **22** New Malayan PM Abdul Razak. **27** Jordan–PLO truce signed in Cairo: PLO expelled from Jordan. **28** Nasser died. **30** All Western hostages freed in exchange for terrorists held by UK, W Germany and Switzerland.

October 5 New Egyptian Pres Anwar Sadat; Quebec separatists kidnapped British diplomat. **10** Quebec Minister Pierre Laporte kidnapped. **16** Trudeau outlawed FLQ and invoked emergency powers. **18** Laporte found dead. **19** Major oil find in N Sea by BP.

November 9 De Gaulle died. **13** Defence Minister Gen Assad seized power in Syria. **20** E Pakistan tidal wave: 150,000 dead.

December 3 Kidnapped British diplomat freed. **8** Pakistan's 1st free elections: Zulfikar Ali Bhutto victorious in W, Sheikh Mujibur Rahman in E.

December 14 Anti-government riots in Poland's Baltic ports: Communist Party leader Gomulka replaced by Gierek.

1971

January 1 Divorce Reform Act in force. **2** Ibrox Park football disaster. **3** Open University inaugu-

A.D.

rated. **8** British ambassador to Uruguay kidnapped by Tupamaros guerrillas. **15** Aswan High Dam inaugurated. **25** Ugandan Pres Obote ousted by army coup under Idi Amin.

February 4 Rolls-Royce bankrupt; Swiss women given vote in national elections. **9** 1st British soldier killed in N Ireland. **15** UK decimal day. **20** Idi Amin Uganda's self-appointed Pres.

March 23 New N Ireland PM Brian Faulkner. **26** Sheikh Mujibur Rahman declared E Pakistan independent as Bangladesh: civil war erupted: Rahman jailed. **29** Lt Calley found guilty of My Lai massacre.

April 5 Thousands dead in E Pakistan fighting. **10** Split between "official" and "provisional" IRA. **18** UAR, Syria and Libya formed Federation of Arab Republics. **22** Jean Claude Duvallier succeeded as Haitian Pres.

May 3 Erich Honeker Gen Sec of E German Communist Party. **13** Labour took over GLC. **14** 2m E Pakistan refugees in India. **28** Egypt–USSR friendship treaty.

June 6 Cholera epidemic in W Bengal: border with Bangladesh sealed. **15** Education Sec Mrs Thatcher announced end of free school milk. **30** 3 Soviet cosmonauts dead at end of space flight.

July 20 Anglo-Maltese defence talks collapsed.

August 10 Internment without trial in N Ireland: riots and firebomb attacks. **22** Right-wing coup in Bolivia.

September 9 British ambassador freed in Uruguay. **24** 90 Soviet diplomats expelled as spies. **27** Chequers talks on N Ireland between 3 PMs.

October 25 China admitted to UN. **27** Congo changed name to Zaire. **28** Parliament voted to join EEC. **31** IRA bomb at PO Tower.

November 23 India–Pakistan border fighting. **24** Rhodesia agreement signed.

December 3 Pakistan declared war on India. **6** India recognised Bangladesh. **7** Libya nationalised £80m BP assets. **17** Pakistan agreed ceasefire. **20** New Pakistan PM Zulfikar Ali Bhutto. **21** New UN Sec-Gen Kurt Waldheim. **26** US resumed N Vietnam bombing.

1972

January 9 Miners' strike. **12** Sheikh Mujibur Rhaman PM of Bangladesh. **13** Ghana coup led by Col Acheampong. **20** UK unemployment passed 1m. **22** Treaty of Brussels signed to admit UK, Denmark, Ireland and Norway to EEC. **30** "Bloody Sunday": army shot 13 Derry marchers dead; Pakistan left Commonwealth.

February 2 British embassy in Dublin burned down. **16** Widespread prolonged power cuts as miners' crisis deepened: State of Emergency declared. **22** IRA Aldershot bomb: 7 dead. **25** Miners ended strike.

March 4 2 killed, 146 injured by Belfast restaurant bomb. **21** 6 died in Belfast shops bombing. **30** Direct rule imposed in N Ireland; N Vietnamese offensive.

April 10 46 nations signed convention to ban biological warfare. **14** US retaliatory bombing of Hanoi and Haiphong. **18** Bangladesh joined Commonwealth.

May 3 Hue evacuated. **9** Israeli troops freed 92 hostages and killed Black September guerrillas at Lydda airport. **16** Segregationist Gov Wallace of Alabama crippled by gunman. **22** Ceylon became republic of Sri Lanka. **28** Duke of Windsor died. **29** Brezhnev–Nixon talks. **30** Tel Aviv airport massacre by PFLP; Official IRA agreed ceasefire.

June 16 5 burglars caught in Watergate building, Democrat campaign HQ; W German Red Army Faction guerrillas captured. **22** Provisional IRA ceasefire. **23** £ floated.

July 1 Pres Nixon's campaign manager resigned. **14** N Ireland ceasefire failed. **31** "Operation Motorman": army dismantled N Ireland barricades.

August 6 50,000 Ugandan Asians expelled to UK. **11** Last ground troops left Vietnam. **20** S Vietnamese troops retreated.

September 1 New Icelandic fishing limit 50 miles. **5** Black September guerrillas killed Israeli athletes at Munich Olympics, kidnapped others: hostages, 5 guerrillas and policeman killed in airport gun battle. **12** Icelandic gunboat sank 2 British trawlers.

October 5 United Reformed Church formed. **13** Bank rate abolished (new term MLR).

A.D.

November 6 Government froze prices, pay, rent and dividend increases for 90 days. **7** Pres Nixon re-elected. **19** Chancellor Brandt re-elected. **20** Silver Wedding of Queen and Prince Philip.

December 2 Gough Whitlam 1st Australian Labor PM since 1946. **18** US resumed bombing of N Vietnam. **21** Treaty between W and E Germany. **23** Nicaraguan earthquake devastated Managua.

1973

January 1 UK, Ireland and Denmark joined EEC. **27** Vietnam ceasefire signed.

February 1 EEC Common Agricultural Policy came into effect. **5** 1st Loyalists detained without trial in N Ireland. **12** 1st US prisoners released by N Vietnam. **21** Israeli fighters brought down Libyan Boeing 727: 104 dead.

March 1 Fine Gael and Labour coalition won Irish General Election: new PM Liam Cosgrave. **8** 2 bombs in central London. **9** N Ireland referendum: 591,820 in favour of retaining UK links. **11** French General Election: Gaullists and allies won absolute majority.

April 1 VAT introduced in UK.

May 7 Pres Nixon denied all knowledge of Watergate. **10** Elections for 36 new metropolitan district councils. **18** Royal Navy frigates sent to protect British trawlers in disputed 50-mile limit off Iceland. **31** Erskine Childers succeeded Pres de Valera of Eire.

June 1 Greece declared republic. **7** Skylab astronauts freed solar panels saving mission. **21** Mr Brezhnev and Pres Nixon signed arms limitation agreement.

July 31 1st sitting of N Ireland Assembly ended in chaos.

August 2 Summerland fire at Douglas, IOM. **19** George Papadopoulos 1st Pres of Greece.

September 3 Dr Henry Kissinger new US Secretary of State. **7** Len Murray new TUC General Secretary. **11** Allende government overthrown in Chile. **14** King Gustav of Sweden died. **20** Chelsea barracks bombed.

October 6 Arab–Israeli war began. **8** UK's 1st commercial radio station opened. **10** US Vice Pres Spiro Agnew resigned. **12** Gen Peron new Pres of Argentina with his wife as Vice Pres **16** Government embargo on arms sales to Middle East. **17** Arab oil producers cut supplies until Israel withdrew from occupied territories. **22** UN ceasefire agreed by Israel, Egypt and Jordan. **31** 3 Provisional IRA leaders freed from Mountjoy prison by hijacked helicopter.

November 8 UK–Iceland "cod war" ended. **12** Miners began overtime ban and ambulance drivers selective strikes. **14** Wedding of Princess Anne and Capt Mark Phillips. **25** Army coup in Greece.

December 5 50 mph speed limit imposed to conserve fuel. **6** Gerald Ford new US Vice Pres. **12** Rail drivers union ASLEF began overtime ban. **20** Spain's PM Admiral Carrero Blanco assassinated. **31** 3-day week imposed.

1974

January 1 Direct rule in N Ireland ended: new N Ireland Executive took office; Golda Meir won Israeli General Elections. **8** Lord Carrington Energy Secretary at head of new department. **9** Commons debate on energy crisis. **18** Israel and Egypt agreed withdrawal of forces. **22** Loyalists expelled from N Ireland Assembly.

February 10 Miners strike began. **28** UK General Election: no clear majority.

March 4 Edward Heath resigned: new minority Labour government. **9** UK resumed 5-day week. **11** Miners returned to work.

A.D.

April 10 Golda Meir and Cabinet resigned. **14** Fighting on Golan Heights and Mt Hermon. **24** S African General Election: Nationalist party won. **25** Army uprising in Portugal: regime in power since 1926 overthrown.

May 6 Chancellor Brandt resigned on discovery of E German spy in Chancellery. **15** Gen Spinola new Pres of Portugal; Israeli troops stormed village school in Ma'alot where children held hostage by Arab terrorists. **16** Herr Schmidt new W German Chancellor. **19** Giscard d'Estaing won French General Election. **28** N Ireland Executive collapsed: direct rule from Westminster resumed.

June 1 Flixborough chemical works explosion. **3** New Israeli PM Mr Rabin.

July 9 Pierre Trudeau won Canadian General Election. **13** Senate Watergate Committee Report. **15** Pres Makarios overthrown in Cyprus coup. **17** Bomb at Tower of London. **18** Statutory incomes policy ended. **20** Turkish invasion of Cyprus. **24** Supreme Court ordered surrender of 64 White House tape recordings. **26** Greek junta collapsed: Mr Karamanlis returned to power. **27** 3 articles of impeachment adopted by Judiciary Committee of House of Representatives against Pres Nixon.

August 6 Pres Nixon resigned. **9** Gerald Ford sworn in as US Pres.

September 8 Emperor Haile Selassie deposed. **30** New Portuguese Pres Gen da Costa Gomes.

October 5 Guildford pub bombings: 2 dead, 70 hurt. **10** Labour won UK General Election: overall majority of 3. **15** Riots at Maze prison.

November 2 Vladivostock Summit between Pres Ford and Mr Brezhnev. **7** Woolwich pub bombings: 2 dead. **17** Mr Karamanlis won 1st Greek General Election since 1967. **21** Birmingham pub bombings: 21 dead, 120 hurt. **29** Anti-Terrorism Act proscribing IRA.

December 3 Defence cuts announced. **7** Archbishop Makarios returned to Cyprus. **18** Wave of bombs in London. **25** Cyclone devastated Darwin, Australia.

1975

January 1 Watergate defendants found guilty. **24** Dr Coggan enthroned 101st Archbishop of Canterbury. **25** Shaikh Mujibur Rahman new Pres of single party state in Bangladesh.

February 11 Mrs Thatcher elected leader of Conservative Party. **13** Turkish Cypriots declared separate state.

March 13 Portugal's new Supreme Revolutionary Council took power. **25** King Faisal of Saudi Arabia assassinated. **26** S Vietnamese troops evacuated Hué and Da Nang.

April 17 Phnom Penh government surrendered to Khmer Rouge. **21** Pres Thieu resigned as N Vietnamese troops encircled Saigon. **25** 1st elections in Portugal for 50 years. **30** Vietnam War ended.

June 5 EEC referendum: UK in favour by 2:1 majority. **5** Suez Canal reopened. **12** Mrs Ghandi convicted of illegal use of government officials in 1971 campaign.

July 1 S S Ramphal new Commonwealth Secretary-General. **29** Military coup in Nigeria: new Head of State Brig Murtala Mohammed.

August 7 Hottest-ever August day in London. **15** Pres Rahman of Bangladesh assassinated. **27** Bombings in Caterham and London.

September 9 Prince Sihanouk returned to Cambodia. **24** Government steps to check unemployment.

October 3 Dutch industrialist kidnapped in Limerick. **15** Iceland extended fishing rights to 200

A.D.

miles. 21 UK unemployment over 1m. 26 Battles in Beirut between Christian Phalangists and left-wing Muslims.

November 3 Queen formally inaugurated North Sea oil. **11** Angolan independence; Australian Governor-General dismissed Labor government. **22** Prince Juan Carlos crowned King of Spain.

December 4 Detention without trial ended in N Ireland. **10** "Cod war" began. **11** IRA Balcombe St siege in London. **14** Liberal Country Party won Australian General Election. **18** Education Bill compelling comprehensive education published. **29** Sex Discrimination and Equal Pay Acts came into force.

1976

January 19 Commons Devolution debate.

February 11 MPLA recognised as Angola's legal government by OAU. **13** Nigerian Pres Murtala Mohammed assassinated.

March 5 Ulster Convention dissolved: direct rule continued. **16** Harold Wilson resigned. **24** Senora Peron of Argentina deposed. **25** Basil Hume enthroned as Archbishop of Westminster.

April 5 New PM James Callaghan.

May 10 Jeremy Thorpe resigned Liberal leadership. **28** Soviet–US treaty on underground nuclear explosions.

June 1 "Cod war" ended. **16** Riots in African township Soweto near Johannesburg. **24** Vietnam reunified.

July 2 Government emergency powers to control water shortage. **4** Israeli raid on Entebbe airport to free 100 hostages. **7** David Steel new Liberal leader. **10** Explosion at Hoffman-La Roche plant at Seveso: contamination over 7km radius. **14** Official handing-over to Tanzania and Zambia of Chinese-built Tanzam railway. **21** UK ambassador to Ireland assassinated. **28** Earthquake destroyed Tangshan, China.

August 25 PM Chirac of France resigned.

September 2 European Commission on Human Rights found Britain guilty of torture in N Ireland. **10** Zagreb air collision. **20** Sweden's Social Democratic Party ousted after 20 years. **24** Ian Smith accepted UK and US proposals for Rhodesian majority rule.

October 3 Bishop Muzorewa returned to Rhodesia from exile. **4** British Rail high-speed train entered service. **6** Military coup in Thailand. **25** National Theatre officially opened. **28** Geneva conference on Rhodesia's future.

November 1 Jimmy Carter elected Pres of USA. **15** Formal end of Lebanon's civil war: Syrian peacekeeping troops in Beirut.

December 16 Michael Manley won Jamaican General Election. **17** Vladimir Bukovsky, Soviet dissident, and Senor Corvalán, Chilean Communist veteran, exchanged.

1977

January 1 EEC extended fishing limits to 200 miles. **24** Rhodesia talks collapsed.

February 15 1976 deaths exceeded live births for 1st time. **17** Uganda's archbishop and 2 Cabinet ministers killed in mysterious circumstances.

March 1 James Callaghan's government went into minority. **7** Zulfikar Ali Bhutto won Pakistan election. **22** Mrs Gandhi resigned after election defeat. **23** Lib-Lab pact: no-confidence vote defeated. **24** New Indian PM Moraji Desai and Janata Party government sworn in. **27** Tenerife airport disaster.

April 21 Martial law in Pakistan. **22** Ekofisk Bravo oilfield disaster.

A.D.

May 13 N Ireland 11-day strike collapsed. **17** Menachem Begin's Likud Party won Israel election. **18** International Commission of Jurists reported Ugandan atrocities.

June 1 New UK road speed limits. **7** Silver Jubilee celebrations in London. **11** 11-day S Moluccan sieges ended in Holland. **15** 1st Spanish elections since 1936, won by PM Suarez's Union of Democratic Centre. **16** Fianna Fail won Irish General Election.

July 5 Pakistan army deposed PM Bhutto. **21** Mrs Bandaranaika's Sri Lanka Freedom Party defeated.

August 10 Panama Canal Agreement concluded. **13** Violence at Lewisham National Front march. **25** Scarman Report on Grunwick dispute.

October 31 Effective revaluation of £.

November 4 Mandatory UN arms embargo on S Africa. **14** Firemen's strike. **15** Son for Princess Anne. **19** Egyptian Pres Sadat and Israeli PM Begin met in Israel; Bay of Bengal cyclone killed 25,000. **30** National Party won S African General Election.

December 10 Malcolm Fraser's Conservative coalition won Australian General Election: Labor leader Gough Whitlam resigned. **21** OPEC froze oil prices.

1978

January 1 Air India plane crash off Bombay. **4** PLO London representative shot dead. **25** Government defeat on Scottish devolution. **29** Rhodesia talks in Malta with Joshua Nkomo and Robert Mugabe.

February 4 Ethiopian Ogaden offensive. **19** Egyptian commandos stormed hijacked plane at Larnaca.

March 3 Internal settlement agreed in Rhodesia between Ian Smith and 3 black Nationalist leaders. **8** New Italian PM Giulio Andreotti. **15** Israeli thrust into S Lebanon. **16** Aldo Moro, 5 times Italy's PM, kidnapped and murdered; *Amoco Cadiz* aground off Brittany: massive pollution.

April 3 1st regular radio broadcasts from Parliament. **10** Transkei, 1st tribal homeland to gain independence, cut diplomatic links with S Africa. **17.** No cases of smallpox anywhere during previous year. **26** Arab terrorist attack on bus on West Bank. **27** Afghanistan's Pres Daoud deposed in pro-Soviet coup.

May 1 1st UK May Day Bank Holiday. **24** Princess Margaret and Lord Snowdon divorced.

June 3 New Bangladeshi Pres Gen Zia ur-Rahman. **12** Provisional IRA leader Seamus Twomey sentenced in Dublin.

July 5 Ghanaian Pres Acheampong resigned. **9** Former Iraqi PM Gen Razzale al-Naif shot in London. **25** World's 1st "test tube" baby born. **31** Lib-Lab pact ended.

August 6 Pope Paul VI died. **13** Beirut PLO HQ bombed. **22** Gunmen held hundreds hostage in Nicaraguan parliament. **26** Cardinal Albino Luciani of Venice elected as Pope John Paul I.

September 8 Martial law in Tehran. **11** Martial law in Nicaragua. **16** Earthquake in Iran killed 11,000. **17** Camp David talks between Pres Sadat and PM Begin concluded framework for Middle East peace treaty. **28** Pope John Paul I died; New S African PM Pieter Botha.

October 10 New Kenyan Pres Daniel arap Moi. **15** Cardinal Karol Wojtyla of Cracow 1st non-Italian Pope for 450 years as John Paul II. **20** 4-week siege of Beirut lifted.

November 25 National Party won New Zealand

A.D.

General Election. 26 Clashes in Iran during 24-hour general strike. 27 Japanese PM Fukuda resigned. 30 Publication of *The Times* suspended until 13 Nov 1979.

December 17 OPEC announced oil price rise. 20 Israeli attack on Lebanese terrorist bases.

1979

January 1 New Iranian PM Dr. Bakhtiar. 4 Guadeloupe Summit between UK, US, W Germany and France. 7 Phnom Penh captured by Vietnamese and rebel troops. 15 Road haulage strike. 16 Shah left Iran. 17 UK admitted Vietnamese refugees. 30 Rhodesian whites-only referendum: 6:1 in favour of transfer to majority rule.

February 1 Ayatollah Khomeini returned to Iran from exile in Paris. 5 New Iranian PM Dr Bazargan. 14 "Concordat" between government and TUC. 15 Army take-over in Chad. 28 Final meeting of white Rhodesian House of Assembly.

March 1 Scots voting in favour of devolution failed to reach 40% requirement: Welsh voted overwhelmingly against devolution. 13 Government of Grenada overthrown. 26 Israel–Egypt peace treaty signed. 28 Radiation leak at Three Mile Island nuclear plant, Pennsylvania. 30 Shadow N Ireland Secretary Airey Neave assassinated. 31 Final withdrawal of British navy from Malta.

April 1 Islamic Republic in Iran. 2 1st visit of)Israeli PM to Egypt. 4 Former Pakistani PM Bhutto executed. 11 Kampala captured by Tanzanian troops and Ugandan exiles: new Ugandan leader Prof Yusofo Lule. 23 1 died, 300 arrested in clashes at Southall National Front march.

May 3 UK General Election: Margaret Thatcher 1st woman PM: Conservative overall majority 43. 16 Government removed legal obligation towards comprehensive education. 22 Joe Clark's Progressive Conservatives formed minority Canadian government. 29 Bishop Muzorewa Zimbabwe Rhodesia's 1st black MP.

June 4 S African Pres Vorster resigned after "Muldergate" scandal. 11 Conservatives won UK European elections. 18 Pres Carter and Pres Brezhnev signed SALT II treaty. 20 Ugandan Pres Lule deposed. 22 Jeremy Thorpe acquitted in Old Bailey conspiracy trial.

July 13 Abortion Law tightened. 17 Pres Somoza fled Nicaragua.

August 18 Heart transplant carried out at Papworth Hospital near Cambridge. 19 Former Cambodian leader Pol Pot convicted in his absence of murder of 3m people. 27 Earl Mountbatten killed by bomb on boat in Sligo.

September 10 London talks on Zimbabwe Rhodesia constitution. 19 3-party non-Socialist coalition won Swedish elections. 20 Emperor Bokassa of Central Africa Empire ousted. 26 UK compulsory metrication abandoned. 29 1st-ever Papal visit to Eire.

October 1 Civilian rule restored in Nigeria. 17 El Salvador colonels imposed martial law. 19 ITV strike ended. 23 Foreign exchange controls removed.

November 1 Military coup in Bolivia. 4 Iranian students occupied US embassy in Tehran. 9 US computer fault led to full-scale nuclear alert. 14 Iranian assets in US frozen.

December 5 Dutch Parliament rejected Nato's Cruise missile plan. 11 New Irish PM Charles Haughey. 12 Nato approved stationing of US missiles in Europe. 21 Rhodesian treaty signed. 27 Afghanistan's Pres Amin ousted in Soviet-backed coup.

1980

January 7 Mrs Gandhi's Congress Party won

A.D.

Indian General Election. 22 Dr Andrei Sakharov, winner of 1975 Nobel peace prize, sent into USSR internal exile. 27 Israel–Egypt border reopened.

February 12 Publication of Brandt Report "North South". 18 Pierre Trudeau won Canadian General Election.

March 4 Robert Mugabe's ZANU(PF) party formed government with absolute majority in Zimbabwe Rhodesia. 24 Archbishop Romero shot dead at altar in San Salvador. 25 Robert Runcie enthroned as Archbishop of Canterbury. 27 Oil accommodation rig overturned in North Sea.

April 2 Riots in St Pauls area of Bristol. 3 13-week steel strike ended. 9 Israeli troops moved into Lebanon. 13 US Olympic Committee voted to boycott Moscow Games. 18 Rhodesia became independent as Zimbabwe. 25 Unsuccessful attempt to free US hostages in Iran. 30 Queen Beatrix of the Netherlands invested.

May 5 SAS stormed besieged Iranian embassy in London. 18 Mount St Helens erupted.

June 22 Liberals won Japanese General Election. 23 Sanjay Ghandi, son of Indian PM, died in plane crash.

July 17 Military coup in Bolivia. 19 Moscow Olympics opened.

August 13 French fishermen blockaded Channel ports.

September 7 Hua Guofeng resigned as Chinese leader: replaced by Zhao Ziyang. 10 Libya and Syria to merge as unitary Arab state. 22 Outbreak of Iran–Iraq War.

October 5 Helmut Schmidt re-elected W German Chancellor. 10 Algerian earthquake: 4,000 dead. 15 James Callaghan resigned as Labour leader. 18 Liberal and Country coalition won Australian General Election. 23 Soviet PM Kosygin resigned. 24 Polish independent trade union Solidarity recognised by Polish authorities. 27 Hunger strike at Maze prison.

November 4 Ronald Reagan elected Pres of USA. 10 New Labour leader Michael Foot. 23 Earthquake in S Italy.

December 8 Dublin Summit between Mrs Thatcher and Charles Haughey; John Lennon shot dead in New York. 15 Dr Milton Obote sworn in as Ugandan Pres. 17 Prof Alan Walters appointed PM's personal economic adviser.

1981

January 1 Greece joined EEC. 20 US hostages left Iran. 21 Sir Norman Stronge and his son, former Stormont MPs, killed by IRA. 25 Roy Jenkins, Shirley Williams, William Rodgers and David Owen launched Council for Social Democracy; Mao's widow Jiang Qing convicted. 27 Joshua Nkomo appointed Minister without Portfolio in attempt to prevent Zimbabwe confrontation.

February 3 Norway's first woman PM Dr Gro Harlem Brundtland. 12 Rupert Murdoch bought *The Times*. 23 Failed military coup in Spain.

March 26 Social Democratic Party born. 30 Pres Reagan shot outside Hilton Hotel in Washington.

April 5 Pres Brezhnev in Czechoslovakia talks on Polish crisis. 11 Brixton riots.

May 9 Bomb exploded at Sullum Voe during Royal inauguration. 10 François Mitterrand won French Presidential Election. 13 Pope shot by Turkish gunman. 22 Peter Sutcliffe convicted of Yorkshire Ripper murders. 30 Bangladeshi Pres Zia ur-Rahman assassinated.

June 8 Israeli planes destroyed Iraqi nuclear reactor. 10 8 IRA prisoners escaped from Crumlin Rd jail. 13 Blanks fired at Queen during

A.D.

Trooping of Colour. **16** Liberal-SDP alliance announced. **21** Socialists won French General Election. **22** Ayatollah Khomeini dismissed Iran's Pres Bani-Sadr. **30** PM Begin secured continuation of Israeli coalition government; New Irish PM Dr Garret FitzGerald.

July 3 Southall race riots. **4** Toxteth riots. **15** Red Cross to mediate at Maze prison. **29** Wedding of Prince Charles and Lady Diana Spencer.

August 20 MLR suspended. **25** S African troops crossed into Angola. **30** Iran's Pres and PM killed by bomb.

September 1 Army take-over in Central African Republic. **18** France abolished capital punishment.

October 4 Maze hunger strike ended. **6** Pres Sadat assassinated. **10** IRA bomb in Chelsea: 2 dead. **14** New Egyptian Pres Hosni Mubarak. **18** Gen Jaruzelski new leader of Polish Communist Party. **26** Oxford St IRA bomb killed disposal expert.

November 6 Anglo-Irish Intergovernmental Council agreed. **14** Unionist MP Rev Robert Bradford shot dead.

December 8 Arthur Scargill new leader of National Union of Mineworkers. **11** Javier Perez de Cuellar new UN Secretary-General. **13** Martial law in Poland. **14** Israel annexed Golan Heights. **19** Penlee lifeboat lost during rescue attempt.

1982

January 4 EEC rejected USSR and Poland sanctions. **26** UK unemployment reached 3m.

February 5 Laker Airways collapsed. **19** De Lorean car company failed.

March 9 Charles Haughey new Irish PM. **16** Pres Brezhnev froze deployment of Soviet missiles in Europe. **18** Argentinians in S Georgia to dismantle whaling station raised Argentinian flag. **19** 3-year ban on England cricketers in unofficial S African tour. **24** Martial law in Bangladesh after coup.

April 2 Argentina invaded Falkland Is. **5** Lord Carrington and 2 Foreign Office ministers resigned: new Foreign Secretary Francis Pym. **25** British troops recaptured S Georgia; Israel handed over Sinai to Egypt.

May 2 Argentine cruiser *General Belgrano* sunk in British attack. **4** British destroyer HMS *Sheffield* hit by Exocet missile. **7** Britain extended total exclusion zone to within 12 miles of Argentine coast. **15** British commando raid on Argentine airstrip at Pebble I. **21** British troops established bridgehead at San Carlos. **28** Paratroops captured Goose Green and Darwin; Papal visit to UK.

June 3 Israeli ambassador shot in London. **4** Israel bombed Beirut's Palestinian quarter. **6** British took Bluff Cove and Fitzroy. **7** Argentine raid on *Sir Tristram* and *Sir Galahad* off Bluff Cove. **14** Falklands ceasefire. **17** Argentinan Pres Gen Galtieri ousted. **21** Prince William of Wales born. **23** Labour National Executive acted against Militant Tendency. **25** New US Secretary of State George Shultz.

July 1 New Argentinian Pres Gen Bignone. **2** Roy Jenkins new SDP leader. **20** IRA bombs in Hyde Park and Regent's Park.

August 4 Israeli tanks invaded W Beirut. **12** Ceasefire in Lebanon. **17** China and US agreed Taiwan policy. **21** PLO guerrillas left Beirut.

September 14 Princess Grace of Monaco died; Lebanese leader Bashire Gemayal killed by bomb. **17** Palestinian refugees killed in W Beirut camps. **19** Swedish Social Democrats won General Election.

October 1 New W German Chancellor Christian Democrat leader Helmut Kohl. **8** Polish govern-

A.D.

ment dissolved Solidarity. **11** Tudor warship *Mary Rose* raised. **21** SDLP and Sinn Fein refused to take seats won in Ulster Assembly election. **28** Socialists elected in Spain. **31** Thames barrier inaugurated.

November 1 Channel 4 tv opened. **10** Soviet leader Leonid Brezhnev died: new leader Yuri Andropov. **24** El Al went into liquidation. **25** Eire's new government formed by Fine Gael and Labour coalition.

December 6 Bomb at bar in Ballykelly killed 16. **12** 30,000 women ringed Greenham Common missile base in protest.

1983

January 25 EEC agreed common fishing policy. **31** New UK seat belt law.

February 9 Derby winner Shergar stolen in Co Kildare.

March 5 Labor Party won Australian General Election. **6** Christian Democrats won W German General Election. **22** New Israeli Pres Chaim Herzog.

April 18 US embassy in W Beirut bombed: many dead. **21** New UK £1 coin. **24** Austrian Chancellor Dr Bruno Kreisky resigned. **26** 8 famine relief workers kidnapped in Ethiopia by Tigré People's Liberation Front.

May 1 Demonstrations in 20 Polish cities. **16** 1st use of wheel clamps by London police. **17** Israel–Lebanon agreement on troop withdrawal. **18** State of Emergency in Sri Lanka. **23** S African raids on Maputo.

June 9 Conservative majority of 144 in UK General Election. **13** New SDP leader David Owen. **14** All-party Commons defence committee endorsed "Fortress Falklands" policy. **15** New Speaker of Commons Bernard Weatherill. **16** Mr Andropov elected Soviet Pres. **24** Syria expelled PLO leader Yasser Arafat.

July 3 Home of former Ulster MP Gerry Fitt burnt out by IRA. **15** 6 killed by bomb at Orly airport. **16** 20 killed in helicopter crash near Scilly Is.

August 4 Italy's 1st Socialist PM since 1946 Bettino Craxi. **5** Lebanese mosque explosion: 19 dead. **11** Chad town Faya- Largeau fell to Libyan troops. **14** French troops in NE Chad. **21** Philippine opposition leader shot dead at Manila airport. **31** S Korean airliner disappeared near Japan: USSR later admitted shooting it down.

September 4 Israeli army withdrew from Chouf mountains above Beirut. **15** Israeli PM Begin resigned. **23** Abu Dhabi air crash: 112 dead. **25** 38 IRA prisoners escaped from Maze prison: prison officer stabbed to death. **26** *Australia II* won America's Cup.

October 2 New Labour leader Neil Kinnock. **10** New Israeli government led by Yitzhak Shamir. **14** Cecil Parkinson resigned. **19** Grenada's PM Maurice Bishop shot by troops: Gen Hudson Austin in control. **23** Suicide bombers killed 229 US marines and 58 French paratroops in Beirut. **25** Troops from US and 6 Caribbean states invaded Grenada. **30** Radical Party leader Raul Alfonsin won Argentine General Election.

November 3 S African white minority voted to give limited representation to Asians and Coloureds. **12** New leader of Irish Republican movement Gerry Adams. **14** 1st Cruise missiles at Greenham Common. **15** Turkish Cypriot UDI under Rauf Denktash. **16** Yasser Arafat retreated to Tripoli. **21** Unionist Party withdrew from N Ireland Assembly in protest at Darkley Gospel Hall killings. **23** USSR quit Geneva disarmament talks. **26** £26m Heathrow bullion robbery. **27** Air crash near Madrid: 181 dead. **28** European space lab launched at Cape Canaveral.

December 6 1st UK heart–lung transplant. **7** Official Unionist Edgar Graham shot dead at

A.D.

Queen's University Belfast. **10** Bomb at Woolwich barracks. **15** NGA industrial action ended. **17** Harrods bomb: 6 dead, many injured. **31** Military coup in Nigeria: new leader Maj-Gen Mohammed Buhari.

1984

January 9 Share prices exceeded 800 on FT index. **20** £1m Christie's diamond robbery. **25** Government ban on union membership at GCHQ.

February 5 Lebanese Cabinet resigned. **8** British peacekeeping troops left Lebanon followed by French, Italians and US. **9** Soviet Pres Andropov died: succeeded by Konstantin Chernenko. **15** Druze and Shi'ite militiamen drove Lebanese army from S Beirut. **29** Canadian PM Pierre Trudeau resigned.

March 12 Miners strike against pit closures. **15** £5m Woburn Abbey silver robbery. **20** UK blamed for collapse of EEC Summit. **23** Foreign Office clerk jailed for leaking documents to *The Guardian*.

April 3 Coup in Guinea after death of Pres Sekou Touré. **17** WPC Yvonne Fletcher shot dead outside Libyan embassy: 10-day siege.

May 7 Christian Democrat Napoleon Duarté won Salvadorean Presidential election. **8** USSR and Warsaw Pact countries boycotted Olympics. **13** Angolan rebels freed 16 hostages. **18** IRA killed 4 members of security forces. **23** Lancs underground pumping station explosion: 15 dead.

June 1 Pres Reagan visited Ireland; Mrs Thatcher and PM Botha in Chequers talks. **5** US increased military role in Gulf. **6** Sikh fanatics in Golden Temple of Amritsar surrendered to Indian army: leader died. **14** UK European elections: Conservatives kept majority. **16** New Canadian Liberal Party leader and PM John Turner. **20** Education Secretary announced new GCSE examinations.

July 9 York Minster fire. **12** Robert Maxwell acquired Mirror Group newspapers. **13** Labour Party won New Zealand General Election. **17** French government resigned. **25** Soviet cosmonaut 1st woman to walk in space. **29** Los Angeles Olympics opened.

August 21 S African Coloured elections won by Labour Party: many arrests. **26** Wakefield salmonella outbreak. **31** TUC backed pit strike.

September 3 Riots in Transvaal townships. **4** Conservatives won Canadian General Election: new PM Brian Mulroney. **5** New Israeli government of national unity; TUC rejoined Neddy. **20** US Beirut embassy bombed. **26** Sino-British declaration on Hong Kong's future.

October 12 IRA bomb at Grand Hotel, Brighton. **23** Violence in S African townships. **30** Kidnapped Polish priest Fr Popieluszko found dead; Famine in Ethiopia. **31** Indian PM Mrs Gandhi assassinated by Sikh bodyguard: new PM her son Rajiv.

November 4 New Nicaraguan Pres Daniel Ortega. **6** Pres Reagan re-elected. **19** Mexico City gas explosion: 600 dead.

December 1 Labor Party won Australian General Election. **3** Leak of poison gas from pesticide factory in Bhopal, India: 2,500 dead, thousands blinded; Massive gains in 1st day's trading in British Telecom shares. **18** Local authorities told to cut capital spending by £1bn in 1985. **28** Rajiv Gandhi won Indian General Election

THE END OF THE COLD WAR

1985

January 3 12,000 Ethiopian Jews airlifted to Israel. **15** Civilian Pres for Brazil. **20** Tamil bomb on Sri Lankan train: 36 dead. **23** 1st House of Lords debate televised. **29** Oxford University refused PM honorary degree.

A.D.

February 4 Spain–Gibraltar border reopened. **18** Riots at Crossroads shanty town, S Africa. **19** S African anti-apartheid leaders arrested. **20** PM addressed joint session of US Congress. **25** £ at record low against $. **28** IRA bombed Newry police station.

March 3 Miners' strike ended. **4** New Zealand PM reaffirmed ban on nuclear weapons. **8** Beirut car bomb: 80 dead. **10** Pres Chernenko died: succeeded by Mikhail Gorbachev. **12** Geneva arms control talks. **5** Belgian government agreed to deploy Cruise missiles. **21** 19 blacks shot dead in Uitenhage on Sharpeville anniversary.

April 6 Sudanese Pres Numeiri deposed by army. **11** Tamil bomb killed 24 in Colombo just prior to Mrs Thatcher's arrival.

May 1 US trade ban on Nicaragua; Ethiopia's largest famine relief camp cleared by troops. **10** Pres Reagan froze defence spending. **11** Bradford City FC fire: 55 dead. **15** Sri Lankan Tamil terrorists killed 146. **22** Fighting in Beirut. **24** Tidal wave swamped Bangladesh islands: thousands dead. **29** 38 killed when wall collapsed at Heysel stadium, Brussels, before Liverpool v Juventus match.

June 10 Israel completed withdrawal from Lebanon. **12** Shi'ite gunmen blew up Jordanian aircraft after releasing hijack hostages.

July 2 New USSR Pres Andrei Gromyko: Foreign Minister Eduard Schevardnadze. **7** Robert Mugabe won Zimbabwe General Election. **10** Greenpeace ship *Rainbow Warrior* sunk in Auckland, NZ. **13** Live Aid concert for African famine relief. **19** Dam collapse at Stava, Italy: 260 dead. **21** S African State of Emergency. **27** Ugandan Pres Obote ousted.

August 12 Japanese Boeing 747 crashed near Tokyo: 524 dead. **17** E Beirut car bomb killed 54. **22** Manchester airport disaster: 54 dead. **27** Nigerian government ousted.

September 9 Riots in Handsworth, Birmingham. **11** S African citizenship restored to 8m blacks in tribal homelands. **17** Chancellor Kohl's secretary defected to E Berlin. **28** Brixton riots.

October 1 Israeli air raid on PLO's Tunisian HQ. **6** Policeman killed in riots on Broadwater Farm estate, Tottenham. **7** Italian cruise ship *Achille Lauro* hijacked by PLO. **20** Commonwealth leaders agreed measures against S Africa.

November 2 S African government controls on media riot coverage. **14** W Colombian volcano erupted: 20,000 dead. **15** N Ireland agreement signed by Mrs Thatcher and Dr Garret FitzGerald. **21** Reagan–Gorbachev Summit. **24** Egyptian commandos stormed hijacked Boeing in Malta.

December 5 UK to withdraw from UNESCO. **6** UK to participate in US Strategic Defence Initiative (SDI). **13** Westland helicopters in deal with US and Italian consortium. **27** Terrorist attacks on Israeli check-in desks at Rome and Vienna airports.

1986

January 7 Pres Reagan cut economic links with Libya. **9** Michael Heseltine and later Leon Brittan resigned over Westland affair: George Younger new Defence Secretary. **20** Anglo-French twin tunnel Channel rail link agreed. **24** N Ireland by-elections due to mass resignation of MPs. **26** *Sunday Times* and *News of the World* printed at Wapping despite print union action. **28** *Challenger* shuttle crashed on take-off.

February 7 Jean-Claude Duvalier left Haiti. **16** Mario Suares won Portuguese Presidential Election. **25** Mrs Corazon Aquino took power in Philippines. **28** Swedish PM Olof Palme assassinated.

March 2 Legal independence for Australia. **12** New Swedish PM Ingvar Carlsson. **16** New French PM

A.D.

Jacques Chirac. **24** US navy destroyed missile battery on Gulf of Sidra. **31** GLC and 6 Metropolitan councils abolished.

April 15 US bombed Benghazi and Tripoli in retaliation for Libyan terrorism. **17** 2 UK hostages killed in Lebanon. **26** Major accident at Chernobyl nuclear power plant, USSR: 19 deaths, radioactive cloud over Scandanavia. **30** Police invaded Golden Temple at Amritsar.

May 19 S African commando attacks on Zimbabwe, Zambia and Botswana.

June 6 Chief Constable of W Yorks to replace John Stalker in N Ireland "shoot-to-kill" inquiry. **8** New Austrian Pres Dr Kurt Waldheim. **12** Renewed State of Emergency in S Africa. **20** S Africa legalised 180-day detention without trial; Ban on sheep movement in Cumbria and N Wales due to radiation. **27** EEC Summit called for release of Mandela and recognition of ANC; International Court of Justice ruled US support for Nicaraguan Contras illegal.

July 6 Liberal Democratic Party won Japanese General Election. **22** Commons voted to ban corporal punishment in schools. **23** Prince Andrew named Duke of York on marriage to Sarah Ferguson. **25** Appeal Court banned publications by former MI5 officer Peter Wright.

August 5 Commonwealth sanctions against S Africa. **7** Ulster loyalist mob crossed border into Eire. **18** Mr Gorbachev announced unilateral freeze on nuclear testing. **25** Gas escape from volcanic crater in Cameroon: 1,500 dead.

September 1 Soviet cruise liner sank after collision: 400 dead. **5** Commandos stormed hijacked PanAm jet at Karachi. **16** Kinross goldmine fire in Transvaal: 177 dead.

October 2 US sanctions against S Africa. **7** *The Independent* newspaper launched; New state-funded city technology colleges announced. **12** Reagan–Gorbachev Summit collapsed over Star Wars programme; Queen visited China. **19** Pres Samora Michel of Mozambique killed in S Africa plane crash: new Pres Joaquim Chissano. **20** New Israeli PM Likud leader Yitzhak Shamir. **26** Conservative Party deputy chairman Jeffrey Archer resigned. **27** "Big Bang" day in City: computer failed. **29** Final section of M25 opened.

November 10 EEC (except Greece) backed sanctions against Syria. **13** Pres Reagan admitted arms sales to Iran. **24** Barclays Bank pulled out of S Africa. **25** John Poindexter and Col Oliver North dismissed over sale of arms to Contras.

December 1 DTI investigation into Guinness affair. **23** Dr Andrei Sakharov returned to Moscow.

1987

January 12 Rate Support Grant settlement: cuts of up to 30% imposed on 20 local authorities. **10** General Secretary of Chinese Communist Party Hu Yaobang resigned. **20** Archbishop of Canterbury's special envoy Terry Waite kidnapped in Beirut. **25** Chancellor Kohl's centre-right coalition won German election. **27** Mr Gorbachev offered Soviet people choice of election candidates: criticism of Brezhnev era.

February 10 140 political prisoners released in USSR. **12** Peaceful Moscow human rights demonstration dispersed violently. **22** 4,000 Syrian troops in W Beirut to enforce peace.

March 6 Zeebrugge ferry disaster: 193 dead. **10** Ireland's new PM Charles Haughey.

April 13 9 trains set alight in Soweto. **25** Lord Justice Gibson and Lady Gibson killed by N Ireland car bomb.

May 1 Government abandoned plan to dump nuclear waste. **5** Congressional hearing into Irangate affair. **6** National Party won S African whites-only election: 1m blacks on protest strike.

A.D.

14 Coup led by Lt-Col Sitiveni Rabuka in Fiji. **17** USS *Stark* hit by Iraqi Exocet: 37 dead. **26** US authorised Kuwaiti tankers in Gulf to fly US flag; Sri Lankan government offensive to recapture Jaffna Peninsula. **29** German Matthius Rust landed in Red Sq; S African commandos attacked Maputo targets.

June 1 Lebanese PM Rashid Karami murdered. **11** UK General Election: Conservatives won 3rd term with 101 majority. **12** Princess Anne created Princess Royal. **15** Christian Democrats won Italian General Election.

July 3 Former Gestapo chief Klaus Barbie found guilty of crimes against humanity. **13** Labor Party won Australian General Election. **17** France and Iran cut diplomatic relations. **20** Social Democrats won Portuguese General Election. **29** Indo-Sri Lankan peace accord signed: Colombo riots.

August 6 David Owen resigned as SDP leader after party voted to open merger talks with Liberals. **12** Pres Reagan accepted responsibility for Iran-Contra affair: no knowledge of diversion of funds. **17** Suicide of Rudolf Hess. **19** Hungerford massacre: 16 dead. **27** Pres Aquino crushed 5th coup in 18 months. **29** New SDP leader Robert Maclennan.

September 3 Bangladesh monsoon: 24m homeless. **4** UN Security Council endorsed Iran–Iraq peace plan. **5** Israeli air raid on Palestinian refugee camp: 40 dead. **7** Lebanese kidnappers released W German hostage. **9** Iraqi air raids on Iran. **23** Home Secretary ended sale of arms to Iran.

October 1 Los Angeles earthquake: 7 dead; 5 foreign tankers attacked in Gulf. **6** Fiji declared a republic. **15** Coup in Burkina Faso; US-protected supertanker hit by Iranian Silkworm missile. **16** Hurricane in S England: 19 dead. **17** Indian army crushed Jaffna rebels. **19** "Black Monday": London and NY shares crashed. **22** Iran attacked Kuwait oil loading terminal. **26** Lord Mackay succeeded Lord Havers as Lord Chancellor.

November 1 Deng Xiaoping resigned from Chinese Poliburo: replaced by Zhao Ziyang. **5** Former ANC chairman Govan Mbeki released after 23 years. **8** Enniskillen Remembrance Day bomb: 11 dead. **11** Moscow reformist leader Boris Yeltsin dismissed; Arab Summit declared support for Iraq. **18** King's Cross fire: 31 dead. **24** US and USSR agreed to scrap intermediate range nuclear weapons.

December 8 Pres Reagan and Mr Gorbachev signed INF agreement. **16** Roh Tae Woo won allegedly rigged S Korean Presidential Election. **17** Milos Jakes succeeded Czechoslovakian Pres Husak. **20** Manila ferry disaster: 2,000 drowned. **29** Space record of 11 months by Soviet cosmonaut. **31** Robert Mugabe executive Pres of Zimbabwe: Joshua Nkomo 1 of 2 Vice Pres.

1988

January 3 Mrs Thatcher longest-serving 20th century UK PM. **4** Purchases by W German and Japanese banks halted US ß slide. **8** Further Wall St crash. **11** Secret Belfast talks between SDLP and Sinn Fein. **17** Leslie Manigat won Haitian General Election amid protests.

February 2 3 women abseiled into Lords in Clause 28 protest. **5** 2 UN relief workers kidnapped in Lebanon. **7** W Bank and Gaza strip violence. **14** PLO officials killed by bomb in Limassol. **16** Prevention of Terrorism Act made permanent. **17** US Lt-Col William Higgins kidnapped in S Lebanon. **21** New Cyprus Pres George Vassiliou.

March 1 31 dead in riots in Azerbaijan city Sumga'it: Soviet tanks moved in. **3** Liberals and SDP formed Social & Liberal Democrats. **6** 3 IRA members shot dead in Gibraltar after bomb plan uncovered. **10** Prince Charles' friend Hugh Lindsay killed by avalanche: Prince escaped. **14** Gulf War flared; Israel imposed curfew in Gaza and W Bank. **16** Loyalist gunman killed 3 at IRA

A.D.

funeral. **17** US troops in Honduras. **18** State of Emergency in Panama. **19** 2 British soldiers lynched in vicinity of Republican funeral. **25** Government review of justice in N Ireland. **28** S African commandos killed 4 in Botswana.

April 4 3,000 Indian troops moved to Pakistan border. **5** Kuwait Airways 747 hijacked to Mashad, Larnaca, then Algiers. **7** ANC lawyer Albie Sachs injured by car bomb in Mozambique. **10** 80 killed in Islamabad and Rawalpindi arsenal fire. **14** Geneva accord on withdrawal from Afghanistan. **15** PLO military commander Abu Jihad murdered. **17** Iraq recaptured Faw peninsula. **18** John Demjanjuk found guilty on Treblinka charges. **22** Kanak militants rioted in New Caledonia.

May 1 IRA killed 3 British servicemen in Holland. **2** Israeli troops in Lebanon rounded up Palestinian guerrillas. **8** Pres Mitterrand re-elected: new French PM Michel Rocard. **10** Coalition re-elected in Denmark. **17** Commandos stormed Golden Temple. **22** Hungarian Communist Party leader ousted. **27** Syrian troops moved into Shi'ite S Beirut. **29** Moscow Summit: Pres Reagan and Mr Gorbachev signed INF treaty.

June 2 Mine disaster in Borken, W Germany. **10** Millenium of Christianity celebrated in USSR; S Africa extended press curbs. **15** IRA bomb killed 6 soldiers at Lisburn fun-run. **19** Haitian coup: civilian leader fled. **21** Toronto Economic Summit. **23** IRA shot down army helicopter at Crossmaglen; EEC agreed farm price freeze. **26** A320 airbus crash at French air show. **27** 57 dead in Gare de Lyon train crash.

July 1 Communist Party conference approved Gorbachev's democratising proposals. **3** USS *Vincennes* shot down Iranian airbus "by mistake": 200 dead. **5** Former priest held in Brussels over IRA arms procurement. **6** Explosion on North Sea oil rig Piper Alpha: 170 dead. **12** Nagorno-Karabakh's Armenian majority voted to leave Azerbaijan. **19** Soviet team at Greenham Common for missile check. **22** New EEC Commissioner Leon Brittan. **23** 3 killed by IRA landmine intended for Justice Higgins. **25** Ne Win retired as leader of Burma's ruling Socialist Party after 26 years; UN Gulf peace talks. **28** New SLD leader Paddy Ashdown.

August 1 Bomb at N London barracks killed soldier. **6** Train crash at Gare de l'Est: SNCF Chairman resigned. **8** Iran-Iraq ceasefire; Soviet troops withdrew from Kabul. **11** 6,000 North Sea seals died from canine distemper. **12** Burmese leader Sein Lwin resigned after week of violence: 1,000 dead. **17** Pakistan's Pres Zia killed in plane explosion. **21** 24,000 massacred in Burundi. **22** All-day opening in English and Welsh pubs. **25** Heart of Lisbon gutted by fire. **28** Ramstein air disaster. **31** Nelson Mandela suffering from TB.

September 3 Lee Kuan Yew won Singapore's General Election. **6** Kurdish leader's appeal to UN to intervene against genocide. **7** 2 stranded cosmonauts landed successfully. **12** W German hostage freed in Beirut. **14** Papal Mass pilgrims held hostage in Maseru: S African troops stormed bus. **17** Seoul Olympics opened. **18** Further coup in Burma. **19** Polish PM resigned. **20** New Pres of UN General Assembly Argentina's Dante Caputo. **22** Lebanon's Pres Gemayal appointed Christian PM. **31** Mr Gorbachev new Soviet Pres.

October 2 Estonian Popular Front founded. **6** State of Emergency in Algiers. **9** Serb protests in Yugoslavia. **10** Czechoslovakian PM resigned. **19** Ban on broadcast interviews with pro-violence groups in N Ireland. **20** Criminals' right to silence abolished in N Ireland. **28** Police crushed Prague rally.

November 8 George Bush won US Presidential Election. **10** Hungary legalised political opposition parties. **14** Agreement to end Sudan civil war. **21** Brian Mulroney won Canadian General Election. **22** State of Emergency in Azerbaijan. **23** "Sharpeville 6" reprieved. **24** Police clashed with students in Westminster student loans

A.D.

protest. **27** US banned PLO leader. **30** New Pakistani PM Benazir Bhutto.

December 4 Edwina Currie, junior Health Minister, in "salmonella in eggs" row. **7** Yasser Arafat voiced Palestinian recognition of Israel's existence; Disastrous Armenian earthquake: Pres Gorbachev abandoned US trip. **12** Clapham rail crash. **21** PanAm jumbo jet crashed on Lockerbie: 281 killed: caused by terrorist bomb. **22** Namibian independence accord signed by S Africa, Cuba and Angola. **29** Rajiv Gandhi on 1st working visit to Pakistan by Indian PM for 28 years.

1989

January 4 US jets shot down 2 Libyan MiGs. **7** Emperor Hirohito of Japan died. **8** Boeing 737 crashed on M1 embankment near Kegworth, Leics. **18** 1st steps towards legalisation of Solidarity. **20** Nagorno-Karabakh under Moscow's direct control. **31** White Paper proposed market-orientated NHS.

February 3 Alfredo Stroessner ousted in Paraguay after 35 years: replaced by Gen Rodriguez; Michael Manley won Jamaican General Election. **14** Ayatollah Khomeini ordered execution for blasphemy of Salman Rushdie, author of *The Satanic Verses*. **21** Leading Czech playwright Vaclav Havel jailed; 2 of Winnie Mandela's bodyguards charged with murder of young activist.

March 2 EC agreed to ban CFCs by 2000. **7** China imposed martial law in Lhasa. **24** *Exxon Valdez* aground off Alaska: 12m gallons oil spilt. **26** Soviet General Election: many senior officials defeated: Moscow victory for Boris Yeltsin.

April 14 Georgia's Communist leader, Pres and PM resigned. **15** 95 Liverpool supporters crushed to death in Hillsborough disaster; Death of Hu Yaobang sparked Beijing student riots.

May 13 Briton Jackie Mann kidnapped in Beirut. **14** Peronist Carlos Menem won Argentine General Election.

June 2 Tiananmen Sq massacre. **3** Ayatollah Khomeini died. **4** Solidarity won Polish elections. **15** Labour won UK European elections.

July 5 Pres Botha met Nelson Mandela. **19** Gen Jaruzelski executive Pres of Poland. **21** Burmese opposition leader Aung San Suu Kyi under house arrest. **24** Cabinet re-shuffle: Geoffrey Howe deputy PM and Leader of Commons, John Major Foreign Secretary.

August 1 1st Cruise missiles left Greenham Common. **14** Pres Botha resigned: acting S African Pres F W de Klerk. **23** Independence demonstration in Baltic states. **24** 1st non-communist Polish PM for 45 years.

September 6 Pres de Klerk's National Party won S African General Election. **11** Hungary opened border allowing E German refugees to escape. **13** Huge peaceful anti-apartheid protest in Cape Town. **18** Hungary announced transition to democracy. **19** Vietnamese army left Cambodia.

October 1 Thousands of E German refugees escaped through Warsaw and Prague embassies. **2** E Germany closed borders after demonstrations for reform. **4** Soviet workers given right to strike. **13** ANC's Walter Sisulu released after 25 years. **16** CITES banned ivory trade to save African elephant. **17** San Francisco earthquake. **18** E German leader Erich Honecker resigned: succeeded by Egon Krenz. **19** "Guildford 4" released. **26** Chancellor of Exchequer Nigel Lawson resigned: new Chancellor John Major, Douglas Hurd Foreign Secretary.

November 8 E German cabinet and politburo resigned. **9** E Germany opened borders to West: demolition of Berlin Wall began. **10** Bulgarian Communist leader Zhivkov ousted. **12** SWAPO won Namibian General Election. **17** Violent anti-government demonstration in Prague. **23** S African troops withdrew from Namibia after 74 years.

A.D.
24 Communist leader Milos Jakes and Czechoslovak politburo resigned. **28** Soviet parliament restored Azerbaijan's powers over Nagorno-Karabakh. **29** Indian PM Rajiv Gandhi resigned.

December 1 Czechoslovakia began demolition of Iron Curtain along Austrian border; E German Communist Party voted away monopoly of power. **3** Malta Summit: Pres Bush and Pres Gorbachev declared end of Cold War. **6** Egon Krenz resigned. **7** Lithuanian parliament abolished guarantee of Communist supremacy. **10** Czechoslovak Pres Husak resigned. **14** E German Stasi disbanded. **16** Huge violent demonstration against Romanian Pres Ceausescu in Timisoara. **20** US troops invaded Panama. **23** Fighting in Romania. **25** Ceausescus executed. **26** Ion Iliescu Pres of National Salvation Front government and Romania's provisional leader. **28** Alexander Dubcek Chairman of Czechoslovak Federal Assembly: Vaclav Havel, playwright and human rights activist, Pres until elections; Bulgarian demonstration for democracy; Lithuania launched USSR's 1st multiparty system; Latvia abolished Communist power monopoly.

THE CHANGING WORLD ORDER

1990

January 3 Manuel Noriega surrendered to US troops; KGB troop reinforcements in Azerbaijan. **11** Independence rally in Vilnius; Armenian parliament voted itself the right to veto Soviet laws. **14** Armenian nationalist leaders declared mobilisation against Azerbaijan. **15** Bulgaria abolished Communist monopoly rule. **20** Soviet troops took control of Baku. **22** Yugoslavia's Communist Party voted to abolish Party's monopoly of power. **25** Hurricane-force winds battered S of England: 46 died.

February 1 New coalition government in Bulgaria **2** 30-year ban on ANC lifted. **5** Temporary Government of National Responsibility in E Germany. **7** Soviet Communist Party abolished monopoly rule. **11** Nelson Mandela freed after 25 years. **13** Conference of World War II allies and E and W Germany ("4 + 2") agreed German reunification formula. **24** Pro-democracy demonstrations in Moscow, Belorussia and Ukraine.

March 6 Soviet parliament passed law sanctioning private property. **11** Lithuania's Supreme Council proclaimed independence. **18** Right-wing Alliance for Germany won E German General Election. **21** Soviet military presence increased in Lithuania; Namibian Independence celebrated. **23** Mongolia abolished Communist monopoly of power. **30** Estonian parliament proclaimed start of transition to independence. **31** Violence at massive anti-Community Charge demonstration in London.

April 11 Teesside Customs & Excise officers detained steel cylinders ("supergun") bound for Iraq. **15** Right-wing coalition formed Slovenian government. **19** Pres de Klerk rescinded 2 laws central to apartheid.

May 4 Latvia declared independence. **13** Baltic States Summit requested independence talks with Pres Gorbachev. **20** Romanian elections: NSF won huge victory. **27** First free elections in Poland for 50 years. **29** Boris Yeltsin elected Pres of Russian republic; Opposition League for Democracy, led by Aung San Suu Kyi, won Burmese elections.

June 1 Pres Bush and Pres Gorbachev signed accord on reduction of nuclear missiles. **7** Warsaw Pact Summit pledged radical transformation. **8** First free Czechoslovakian elections for 44 years: Russian parliament voted its laws to take precedence over those of USSR. **12** Russian Federation formally proclaimed sovereignty. **13** USSR eased Lithuanian blockade. **20** Chancellor of Exchequer John Major proposed new currency unit, the Ecu, backed by EMF. **22** Checkpoint Charlie in Berlin Wall removed.

July 6 NATO Summit agreed joint peace declaration with Warsaw Pact countries. **10** Pres Gorbachev

A.D.
re-elected Leader of Soviet Communist Party. **12** Boris Yeltsin resigned from Soviet Communist Party. **16** Ukraine issued declaration of sovereignty. **17** Solidarity split with formation of splinter groups. **20** IRA bomb at Stock Exchange. **23** Iraqi troops massed on Kuwaiti border. **27** Belorussia declared itself a sovereign state within USSR. **30** Ian Gow MP killed by IRA bomb. **31** Estonia seceded from USSR.

August 2 Iraqi forces invaded Kuwait. **6** Pretoria Minute: political prisoners freed, ANC hostilities suspended. **7** US ships, planes and troops in Gulf as part of multi- national defence force. **8** Iraq annexed Kuwait; Leader of Winnie Mandela's bodyguard sentenced to death for murder of teenage activist. **15** Pres Saddam Hussein offered Iran peace treaty. **20** Western hostages in Kuwait held at military bases and potential targets. **24** Irish hostage Brian Keenan released. **31** E and W Germany signed unification treaty.

September 1 Boris Yeltsin demanded resignation of Soviet government. **4** Prime Ministers of N and S Korea met for the first time. **10** All Cambodian factions accepted peace formula to end civil war. **12** 4 Allied Powers of World War II signed Treaty handing back full sovereignty to single united German state. **24** Soviet parliament granted Pres Gorbachev wide powers to rule by decree for 18 months. **26** Soviet parliament agreed bill on freedom of conscience and religious practice.

October 3 Germany celebrated reunification. **8** UK joined ERM. **24** Pakistan General Elections: Benazir Bhutto's PPP defeated. **25** Crash of Polly Peck International. **28** EC agreed 2nd stage of economic and monetary union: Britain alone in dissent. **30** Contact between French and British Channel Tunnel construction teams.

November 1 Sir Geoffrey Howe resigned from Cabinet; Communist Party swept from power in Soviet Georgia. **9** Mary Robinson Ireland's first woman and youngest-ever President. **17** Pres Gorbachev presented constitutional reforms giving him increased powers and reinforcing Federal Council. **21** CSCE conference closed with signing of Charter of Paris for a New Europe. **22** Mrs Thatcher resigned. **25** Nationalist parties in Bosnia-Herzegovina won first free elections for 52 years. **27** John Major won Conservative leadership. **28** New Cabinet included Norman Lamont as Chancellor of Exchequer, Michael Heseltine Environment Secretary. **29** UN resolution to use force against Iraq.

December 2 Chancellor Köhl won German elections. **6** Saddam Hussein announced immediate release of all foreign hostages. **9** Lech Walesa won Polish Presidential election. **13** Oliver Tambo, ANC President, in S Africa after 30-year exile. **15** Violent anti-Communist protests in Albania. **20** Soviet Foreign Minister Eduard Shevardnadze resigned. **24** Pres Gorbachev won greater powers from Soviet parliament.

1991

January 1 Fierce fighting in Mogadishu. **7** Soviet paratroopers in Baltic states. **8** Lithuanian PM Kasimiera Prunskiene resigned. **13** Soviet troops seized TV centre in Vilnius: 14 dead, thousands defended Parliament buildings: Boris Yeltsin and Baltic Presidents in UN appeal. **17** Huge air and missile attack on Iraq by US, British and Saudis, to liberate Kuwait in Operation Desert Storm. **18** Scud missile attacks on Israel. **19** Key Baghdad buildings damaged by missiles. **20** Scud missiles brought down by Patriot missiles. **25** Iraq released millions of gallons of Kuwait oil into Gulf. **29** Nelson Mandela and Chief Buthelezi made peace.

February 1 Repeal of remaining S African apartheid laws. **7** IRA attack on Downing St. **10** Lithuanian referendum in favour of independence. **13** US missiles destroyed Baghdad bunker: 300 civilians killed. **20** Statue of Enver Hoxha toppled in Tirana: Pres Alia announced new government. **22** Iraqis set fire to Kuwait's oil installations. **24** Ground war for liberation of Kuwait began.

A.D.

26 Kuwait City liberated. **27** Allied ceasefire in Gulf War.

March 3 Peace agreement between Allies and Iraq; Estonian and Latvian referendum in favour of independence. **4** S Iraq towns occupied by Shia Muslim resistance. **14** "Birmingham 6" released. **16** Kurdish guerrillas claimed control of Kurdistan. **17** Referendum on future of united USSR: minimal victory for Pres Gorbachev.

April 1 Kurdish revolt in N Iraq collapsed. **4** Refugee crisis on Turkish and Iranian borders; Russian parliament approved special powers for Boris Yeltsin to tackle economic crisis. **9** Soviet Georgia declared independence. **15** European Bank for Reconstruction & Development launched. **23** New Council Tax unveiled to replace Poll Tax. **26** Rebels advanced on Addis Ababa.

May 5 Virtual civil war between Serbs and Croats. **13** Winnie Mandela found guilty on kidnap and assault charges. **19** Croatian referendum in favour of independence. **21** Rajiv Gandhi assassinated; Pres Mengistu of Ethiopia fled. **26** First-ever Presidential elections in USSR held in Georgia. **29** Ethiopian People's Revolutionary Democratic Front in control in Addis Ababa.

June 5 Pres Bendjedid of Algeria postponed elections, and dismissed government. **9** Mt Pinatubo in Philippines erupted. **13** Boris Yeltsin elected Russian Pres. **17** Congress (I) Party won Indian General Election; S Africa formally abolished apartheid. **25** Slovenia and Croatia declared independence. **26** "Maguire 7" convictions overturned.

July 1 Warsaw Pact disbanded. **4** UK–China agreement on new Hong Kong airport. **5** Bank of Commerce & Credit International (BCCI) collapsed. **6** ANC's first National Congress ended with Nelson Mandela as new Pres and democratically-elected National Executive. **20** Boris Yeltsin banned Communist Party in factories, offices and local government. **22** John Major launched Citizens' Charter.

August 8 British hostage John McCarthy released. **19** Pres Gorbachev deposed in dawn coup: Emergency Committee of 8 hardliners in control: Yeltsin denounced coup. **21** Estonia and Latvia declared independence: 3 killed outside Russian parliament: coup collapsed. Yeltsin assumed control of Soviet troops: Pres Gorbachev reinstated: Soviet troops withdrew from Lithuania. **24** Pres Gorbachev resigned as Communist Party leader, and dissolved Party organisation: Ukraine declared independence. **25** Armenia, Georgia and Belorussia declared independence. **26** Vukovar in E Croatia besieged by Serbs and Yugoslav troops. **28** Central Committee of KGB dissolved. **29** Soviet Parliament voted to curtail Pres Gorbachev's power. **30** Azerbaijan, Kirghizia and Uzbekistan declared independence.

September 3 Nagorno-Karabakh declared independence from Armenia. **5** Pres Gorbachev made sweeping constitutional changes. **6** Leningrad formally reverted to former name, St Petersburg; Macedonian citizens voted for independence. **15** Pro-democracy party won Hong Kong's first election. **24** British hostage Jackie Mann released. **26** Romanian government resigned. **30** Military coup in Haiti: Pres Aristide fled.

October 2 Dubrovnik besieged. **13** Communists ousted in Bulgarian multi-party elections. **22** EC and EFTA agreed to form world's largest common market. **30** Middle East peace conference in Madrid. **31** Pres Kaunda defeated in Zambia's 1st multi-party presidential election by Victor Chiluba.

November 5 Body of Robert Maxwell found in sea off Canary Is. **8** EC sanctions on Yugoslavia; Forcible repatriation of Vietnamese boat people. **12** 100 civilians massacred by Indonesian army in E Timor. **18** Hostage Terry Waite released; Gen Aideed took control in Mogadishu. **25** "Tottenham 3" freed; Poland's 1st democratic Sejm for 50 years.

A.D.

December 1 Ukrainian referendum in favour of independence. **4** Hostage Terry Anderson released; £600m missing from Mirror Group pension fund. **6** Siege of Dubrovnik renewed. **8** Leaders of Russia, Ukraine and Belorussia agreed new Commonwealth of Independent States, and declared USSR defunct. **10** Maastricht Summit agreed Treaty of European Union: Britain obtained exclusive opt-out clauses on single currency and social charter. **19** Australian Labor Party voted to replace PM Bob Hawke with Paul Keating, former Treasurer. **20** Opening of Convention for a Democratic S Africa (CODESA). **21** 8 former Soviet republics joined CIS. **25** Pres Gorbachev resigned as Pres of USSR. **26** Soviet parliament met for last time. **27** 1st Algerian multi-party General Elections: victory for Muslim Fundamentalists in 1st stage.

1992

January 1 New UN Secretary-General Boutros Boutros Ghali. **12** Algerian Higher Security Council cancelled elections and introduced martial law. **16** Mohammed Boudiaf returned to Algiers as Leader of Council of State. **27** Maxwell pension funds wound up with loss of millions of pounds. **30** Taoiseach Charles Haughey resigned.

February 6 Croatian Pres Tudjman accepted plan for UN peacekeeping force. **11** Albert Reynolds new Taoiseach. **19** N and S Korea declared end to 40-year confrontation. **21** UN experts began destruction of Iraq's chemical weapons. **28** Iraq defied UN order to destroy missile equipment. **29** Bosnia-Herzegovina referendum in favour of independence.

March 4 Algeria banned Islamic Salvation Front. **5** Codesa agreed outline of power-sharing interim government. **10** Eduard Shevardnadze Pres of Interim State Council to rule Georgia. **17** S African referendum in favour of Pres de Klerk's moves to end apartheid; UN peacekeeping troops in Croatia. **31** UN arms embargo on Libya.

April 3 Pres Alia of Albania resigned. **6** Fierce fighting in and around Sarajevo between Muslims and Serbs; EC recognised Bosnia. **9** General Election: Conservative majority of 21 and record-breaking 4th term of office. **10** IRA bombs in London: 3 dead. **11** Cabinet re-shuffle: Kenneth Clarke Home Secretary, Michael Heseltine Trade & Industry Sec, Malcolm Rifkind Defence Sec. **13** Neil Kinnock resigned Labour leadership. **22** Serbs fought Muslims in Sarajevo. **27** Betty Boothroyd 1st-ever woman Speaker of Commons. **29** Los Angeles riots: 44 dead.

May 5 EC monitors withdrew from Sarajevo. **11** Azeris conceded last stronghold in Nagorno-Karabakh. **19** Serbian troops held 3,500 women and children hostage in Bosnia. **27** Mortar bombs in Sarajevo marketplace: 16 dead.

June 18 Kevin and Ian Maxwell charged with conspiracy to defraud. **20** UN Sarajevo peacekeeping activities suspended; Czech and Slovak political parties agreed to split Czechoslovakia into 2 separate states. **23** Yitzhak Rabin's Labour Party won Israeli General Election. **29** Pres Boudiaf of Algeria assassinated. **30** N Ireland Protestant leaders and Irish government met in 1st talks for 70 years.

July 9 Chris Patten sworn in as Governor of Hong Kong. **18** John Smith new Labour Party Leader. **19** Muslim refugees forced from homes by Serbs in "ethnic cleansing". **20** Czechoslovak Pres Vaclav Havel resigned. **30** UN peacekeeping forces sent to Somalia; **31** Marsh Arabs of S Iraq bombarded by Iraqi troops.

August 2 Israel to permit Arab police in occupied territories. **3** Confirmation of Serbian detention camps where torture and killings had occurred. **10** Ban on Protestant Ulster Defence Association. **18** British troops in Iraq and Bosnia to protect UN aid convoys. **25** Serb bombardment destroyed National Library in Sarajevo: 90 dead. **27** Iraq accepted exclusion zone; Lord Owen new EC peace negotiator. **28** 3,000th sectarian death in N Ireland.

A.D.
September 3 New Slovak constitution signed in Bratislava. **7** 28 ANC supporters shot dead by Ciskei troops as protest march crossed border. **9** Georgian forces and Abkhazia rebels agreed ceasefire. **11** £ close to ERM floor. **16** "Black Wednesday": £ withdrawn from ERM in *de facto* devaluation. **17** Khmer Rouge rejoined UN Cambodia talks. **20** French referendum on Maastricht Treaty: narrow majority in favour. **21** EC Foreign Ministers agreed ratification of Maastricht Treaty. **24** National Heritage Minister David Mellor resigned.

October 5 £ at record low. **7** Sweeping plans for Hong Kong democracy. **13** Government and British Coal announced closure of 31 collieries. **15** 1st British troops in Croatia to support UN. **16** Pres Babangida declared Nigerian primary Presidential election void. **26** Last Russian troops left Poland. **30** IRA bomb in Whitehall; Angolan war erupted.

November 3 Democrat Bill Clinton elected Pres of USA; GATT talks collapsed. **4** Government 3-vote majority in Maastricht debate. **11** Church of England General Synod voted narrowly in favour of ordination of women. **16** Formal alliance between Iran and Islamic Resistance Movement (Hamas) in occupied territories. **20** Windsor Castle fire. **26** Queen volunteered to pay income tax on private income.

December 2 German parliament won veto on EMU in Maastricht debate. **4** US troops in Somalia on food aid mission. **6** Swiss referendum against joining European Economic Area. **9** Prince and Princess of Wales separated. **12** EC Edinburgh Summit: deal saving Maastricht Treaty. **14** New Russian PM former Communist Viktor Chernomyrdin. **31** Bosnian leader Radovan Karadzic grounded aircraft indefinitely.

1993

January 1 Inauguration of single European market; 2 new states, Czech Republic and Slovakia, came into being. **5** EC report confirmed rape of 20,000 Bosnian Muslim women by Serb forces. **13** Allied aircraft bombed air defence centres in S Iraq. **19** Iraq declared unilateral ceasefire: UN nuclear inspectors given clearance. **24** Croat troops seized Maslenica bridge connecting N Croatia with Adriatic. **26** Vaclav Havel 1st President of new Czech state.

February 12 S African government and ANC agreed plans for elected black and white interim government. **14** Lithuania's 1st genuinely democratic Presidential Election won by Algirdas Brazauskas. **26** Terrorist bomb under World Trade Center, Manhattan.

March 5 S African multi-party talks resumed after 9 months. **8** Government defeated in Commons Maastricht debate. **13** Labor won record 5th term in Australian General Election. **16** VAT on domestic fuel in 2-stage plan announced in Budget. **20** IRA bombs in Warrington: 2 children dead. **23** Bosnian Serbs withdrew from UN peace talks. **25** Muslims and Croats signed full UN peace plan in New York. **26** UN Security Council voted to take over Somalia peacekeeping. **27** New Chinese Pres Jiang Zemin. **28** Right-wing landslide in French General Election. **29** New French PM Edouard Balladur.

April 2 State of Emergency in Azerbaijan. **4** Vancouver Summit: $1·6bn aid package to Russia. **8** UN admitted former Yugoslav republic Macedonia. **10** Chris Hani, Gen Sec of S African Communist Party and ANC leader, shot dead. **12** NATO enforced Bosnian "no fly" zone. **19** Waco siege ended: many dead. **24** IRA bomb in Bishopsgate. **25** Russian referendum: 58% backed Pres Yeltsin.

May 1 Sri Lankan Pres Premadasa assassinated. **4** Asil Nadir, former Chairman of Polly Peck, fled to N Cyprus. **18** Danish Maastricht Referendum: 56·8% in favour. **24** Eritrean independence. **27** Florence terrorist bomb: 6 dead, Uffizi museum damaged; Norman Lamont dismissed in Cabinet

A.D.
reshuffle: new Chancellor of Exchequer Kenneth Clarke.

June 6 1st democratic Latvian elections since 1931 won by centre-right alliance. **7** Bosnian government accepted "safe haven" plan. **11** US air strike against HQ of Gen Aideed. **13** 52 Bosnian Muslims killed in Serb rocket attack on Gorazde hospital. **15** Bosnia ceasefire agreed at Sarajevo airport.

July 3 Pres Clinton announced 1-year suspension of nuclear testing. **12** 16 Somalis killed in US helicopter attack on Gen Aideed's control centre. **22** Government defeated in Commons Maastricht vote. **29** ERM on verge of collapse.

August 2 Emergency meeting of EC Finance Ministers: *de facto* suspension of ERM. **4** Serb troops captured Mt Igman overlooking Sarajevo. **7** Buckingham Palace opened to public. **14** Serbs withdrew from Mt Igman. **18** Muslims, Serbs and Croats agreed to place Sarajevo under UN rule for 2 years, after 3-way division of Bosnia decided. **22** 55,000 Bosnian Muslims, including 30,000 refugees, trapped in E Mostar. **27** Muslims held UN convoy "hostage" in Mostar as protection against Croats. **29** Yasser Arafat won PLO executive committee support for radical peace plan giving Palestinians control of Gaza strip and Jericho.

September 9 PLO Chairman Yasser Arafat signed mutual recognition agreement with Israel. **13** Israel–PLO agreement signed at White House. **14** Jordan and Israel signed agreement. **21** Pres Yeltsin dissolved Russian parliament, and announced rule by decree: parliament swore in Speaker Alexander Rutskoi as Pres. **22** Pres Yeltsin supported by army, security forces, ministers, central bank and many world leaders. **24** US and Commonwealth lifted S African trade sanctions. **25** Russian Parliament (White House) telephones, power and hot water cut off. **29** Labour Party Conference passed John Smith's "One man one vote" motion.

October 4 Russian troops stormed White House: Alexander Rutskoi and other leaders surrendered: 170 dead. **12** Germany's highest court approved Maastricht Treaty. **19** Benazir Bhutto Pakistan's new PM. **25** Sinn Fein leader Gerry Adams banned from mainland Britain; Canadian General Election: landslide victory for Liberals.

November 1 European Union established as Maastricht Treaty came into force. **8** Pres Yeltsin approved final draft of new constitution. **9** Stari Most, Mostar's celebrated 16th century bridge, destroyed by Croats. **17** Pres de Klerk and Nelson Mandela ratified S Africa's 1st democratic constitution; US Congress endorsed N American Free Trade Agreement (NAFTA).

December 7 Transitional Executive Council (TEC) inaugurated in Cape Town. **12** Vladimir Zhirinovsky's ultra-nationalist Liberal Democratic Party won most seats in Russian Election. **15** Downing St Declaration by John Major and Taoiseach Albert Reynolds on future of N Ireland; GATT talks agreement. **19** Ruling Socialist Party won Serbian General Election. **21** Croats and Serbs agreed Muslim demand for one-third Bosnia–Herzegovina territory.

1994

January 5 Inkatha boycott of S African General Election. **9** Bosnia peace talks reopened with redrawn map. **13** District Auditor's inquiry charged Westminster City Council with gerrymandering. **17** Los Angeles earthquake; John Major revealed to have approved £234m aid to Malaysia for Pergau dam, linked to arms deal. **19** Serb-Croat pact to normalise relations. **30** US granted Gerry Adams visa for 2-day visit to New York conference. **31** Breakthrough in PLO–Israel talks.

February 5 Mortar attack on Sarajevo market: 68 dead. **7** Parliamentary Private Secretary Stephen Milligan found dead. **10** NATO 10-day deadline to

A.D.
Bosnian Serbs to withdraw weapons from Sarajevo area or risk air strikes. **20** All Serb heavy weapons withdrawn from Sarajevo exclusion zone or under UN control. **25** Jewish extremist settler shot dead 40 Arabs in Hebron mosque. **28** US jets shot down 4 Bosnian Serb aircraft after attacks on Muslim towns, NATO's first-ever aggressive intervention.

March 1 Bosnian Muslims and Croats signed US-brokered peace agreement. **4** Far-right white Afrikaner Volksfront, as well as Zulu Inkatha, registered for S African election. **9** IRA mortar attack on Heathrow airport. **22** PLO– Israel draft accord on armed presence to protect W Bank and Gaza Palestinians. **25** US troops left Somalia. **27** Italian General Election won by Silvio Berlusconi. **28** ANC security guards attacked Inkatha marchers carrying Zulu weapons: 30 dead. **31** State of Emergency in Natal and KwaZulu.

April 6 Presidents of Rwanda and Burundi died in rocket attack on plane. **7** Civil war in Rwanda: hundreds dead, including PM. **9** Thousands killed in Rwanda; 130 dead in Natal. **10** NATO air strike on Serbian troops advancing on Gorazde. **11** 2nd NATO air strike on Bosnian Serb troops. **12** RPF (Rwandan Patriotic Front) Tutsi rebels captured Kigali: government fled. **17** Bosnian army's defence of Gorazde failed: UN-Serb agreement to restore peace. **19** Agreement brought Inkatha Freedom Party into S African Elections. **23** Western allies' troops began Berlin withdrawal. **24** Bosnian Serbs withdrew from Gorazde after NATO ultimatum. **26** New S African constitution came into force: long queues to vote in Elections; Rwanda ceasefire.

May 2 Pres de Klerk conceded Election victory to Nelson Mandela: ANC won 63% vote. **3** 200,000 dead as Rwanda genocide continued. **4** Israel and PLO signed Agreement to end 27-year occupation of Gaza and W Bank, initiating Palestinian self-rule. **6** Channel Tunnel officially opened. **8** Former Communists won Hungarian Elections. **9** Nelson Mandela elected Pres of S Africa. **12** Labour leader John Smith died. **13** Jericho under Palestinian control. **19** 1st Channel Tunnel freight service. **23** S Yemen declared independence. **27** Alexander Solzhenitsyn returned to Russia.

June 1 S Africa rejoined Commonwealth. **2** Helicopter crash on Mull of Kintyre killed 29 anti- terrorism experts. **12** European Election: Labour won 62 seats with 44% vote; Austrian referendum in favour of EU membership. **24** EU Corfu Summit: Pres Yeltsin signed Partnership & Cooperation Agreement. **25** John Major vetoed appointment of Belgian PM Jean-Luc Dehaene as EC Pres. **28** Germany announced UK beef ban.

July 5 Yasser Arafat in Jericho: Palestine National Authority (PNA) sworn in; US, Russian and EU Foreign Ministers unveiled Bosnian peace plan in Geneva. **9** N Korean Pres Kim Il Sung died; G7 Naples Summit admitted Russia, effectively creating G8. **12** Commons inquiry into "cash for questions" and MPs' fees; Kim Jong Il to succeed father as N Korean Pres. **15** Emergency EU Summit endorsed Luxembourg PM Jacques Santer as new EC Pres. **16** 1st of 21 fragments of Comet Shoemaker-Levy 9 collided with Jupiter. **18** Hizbollah car bomb outside Jewish Centre in Buenos Aires: 100 dead; Israel-Jordan peace talks opened; EU brokered UK beef compromise with Germany. **20** Cabinet reshuffle: Michael Portillo Employment Sec, Jeremy Hanley Chairman of Conservative Party. **21** Tony Blair new Labour leader with 57% vote: John Prescott deputy leader. **25** King Hussein of Jordan and Israeli PM Rabin signed declaration ending 46-year conflict. **29** Neil Kinnock new British EC Commissioner.

August 8 New Israel-Jordan border crossing near Eilat inaugurated: Yitzhak Rabin 1st Israeli PM to visit Jordan. **12** "Cradle to grave" NHS ended with abandonment of guaranteed care of elderly. **15** Venezuelan terrorist Carlos "the Jackal" arrested. **16** Republican Senators' delay tactics effectively killed US Health Bill. **26** 1st British patient received mechanical heart. **28** Sunday Trading Act came into force. **31** IRA declared ceasefire: UK government demanded evidence of

A.D.
permanence. China to dismantle Hong Kong's democratic structure after 1997; Russian army left Latvia and Estonia.

September 12 Suicide pilot crashed light aircraft on White House lawn; Separatist PQ won control of Quebec provincial government. **16** Broadcasting ban on N Ireland extremists lifted. **21** Fossilised remains of oldest humans (*Australopithecus ramidus*) found in E Africa. **28** 910 drowned in Baltic ferry disaster.

October 3 Channel Tunnel car service began. **4** At Labour Party conference Tony Blair announced replacement of Clause IV: "common ownership of means of production". **6** Labour Party conference narrowly reasserted backing for Clause IV. **7** Iraqi troops massed on Kuwait border. **9** Build-up of US Gulf troops against Iraqi threat. **11** Saddam Hussein withdrew troops. **13** N Ireland Loyalist paramilitary groups announced ceasefire. **15** Pres Aristide returned to Haiti. **16** Chancellor Kohl narrowly won 4th term. **19** Tim Smith N Ireland Minister, and later Neil Hamilton Minister at DTI, resigned over "cash for questions" affair. **21** John Major opened way to talks with Sinn Fein: bans on leaders lifted, border roads opened. **25** New body established under Lord Nolan to oversee standards in public life. **26** Israel-Jordan peace treaty signed.

November 8 Republican landslide victory in US mid-term elections. **10** High Court ruled UK Pergau dam aid illegal; Saddam Hussein recognised Kuwait. **11** US abandoned Bosnia arms embargo. **14** UK National Lottery inaugurated. **17** Albert Reynolds resigned as Taoiseach. **18** Serb jets attacked UN "safe area" Bihac. **19** Bertie Aherne new Fianna Fail leader. **28** Government won Commons vote on European Finance Bill: Whip withdrawn from 8 Conservative abstainers; Serbs took Bihac; Norwegian referendum against EU membership. **29** Budget day: public spending cuts: VAT on fuel at 17·5% from April.

December 6 Government defeat on planned VAT increase on fuel; CSCE retitled Organisation for Security and Cooperation in Europe. **8** Chancellor of Exchequer's mini-budget to recoup £1bn lost by "VAT on fuel" defeat. **11** Russia invaded Chechnya. **13** Russian tanks blockaded Grozny. **15** New Irish Taoiseach John Bruton. **18** Russian troops attacked Grozny. **22** Italian PM Berlusconi resigned as coalition crumbled. **28** Grozny blitz.

1995

January 1 Austria, Finland and Sweden joined EU. **8** Sri Lankan government truce with Tamil guerrillas. **11** Pres Yeltsin assumed direct control of Russian armed forces. **12** Army to end Belfast daytime patrols. **17** Over 6,000 dead in Kobe earthquake. **18** Spanish Fishing Rights Bill narrowly passed after UK compensation doubled to £53m. **19** Grozny Presidential palace fell to Russians. **23** Portuguese PM Silva resigned.

February 6 US space shuttle Discovery and Russia's Mir space station rendezvous. **10** £267m compensation agreement for Maxwell pension funds. **18** UN Afghanistan peace plan under threat with emergence of Taliban Koranic student militia. **22** Joint Anglo-Irish document on N Ireland's future published. **26** 233-year-old Barings merchant bank collapsed.

March 2 Nick Leeson, Barings Bank financial trader involved in collapse, arrested in Frankfurt. **6** Spanish peseta and Portuguese escudo devalued after emergency meeting to realign ERM. **7** Dutch bank ING bought Barings in £1·6bn deal. **13** Tony Blair secured overwhelming National Executive support for new Clause IV. **17** Pres Clinton urged IRA to relinquish arms. **20** Sarin nerve gas attack on Tokyo subway; Turkish troops shelled N Iraq Kurd targets. **21** 35,000 Turkish troops with armoured support captured mountainous area of Iraqi Kurdistan. **24** Routine army patrols in Belfast to end. **27** Winnie Mandela dismissed from S. African government. **28** UN Global Warming Summit opened in Berlin.

A.D.

April 6 Scottish local elections result in the Conservatives failing to win control of any of the 29 new unitary authorities. **9** ZANU-PF win Zimbabwe general election. **19** Bomb outside a federal building in Oklahoma, USA kills 168; Gas attack in underground station in Yokohama, Japan. **20** Conservative MPs David Tredinnick and Graham Riddick suspended from House of Commons for taking money for questions. **21** FBI arrests Timothy McVeigh for the Oklahoma bombing. **23** Socialist candidate Lionel Jospin beats Gaullist Jacques Chirac in the first round of French Presidential elections. **24** Party whip restored to 8 Conservative Euro-rebels.

May 7 Chirac defeats Jospin in second round of French Presidential election. **11** Nolan Committee on Standards in Public Life publishes its first report. **13** Alison Hargreaves becomes the first woman to climb Mt Everest alone and without oxygen. **17** Chirac succeeds François Mitterrand as President of France; Alain Juppé new Prime Minister. **18** John Major refers the Nolan Committee recommendations to a House of Commons committee. **24** Former PM Lord Wilson of Rievaulx dies; UN ultimatum issued to Bosnia Serbs to surrender heavy weapons surrounding Sarajevo.

June 2 Bosnian Serbs released UN hostages including 11 British soldiers. **13** More UN hostages, including the remaining British ones, are released. **14** Chechen rebels seize hundreds of hostages in a hospital in Budyonnovsk in southern Russia. **17** Russian forces attack the hospital freeing 200 hostages. **18** All remaining UN hostages released by Bosnian Serbs. Chechen rebels escape taking 150 hostages into Chechnya. **19** All Russian hostages released by Chechens; EU Finance ministers set 1 Jan 1999 as date for single currency. **22** John Major resigns as leader of the Conservative Party. **23** Douglas Hurd resigns as Foreign Secretary, effective after the leadership contest.

July 4 John Major wins the leadership contest. **5** Cabinet reshuffle; Michael Heseltine the new Deputy Prime Minister. **10** Opposition leader Aung San Suu Kyi released after 6 years house arrest in Myanmar (Burma). **11** Bosnian Serbs capture Srebenica; USA restores full diplomatic relations with Vietnam. **13** All Muslims in Srebenica deported by Bosnian Serbs. **18** US Senate reopens the Whitewater investigative hearings. **25** Bosnian Serbs capture Zepa and deport all Muslims. **30** Military accord signed to end fighting in Chechnya.

August 4 Croatian offensive into Serb-held Krajina. 100,000 troops advance on 3 fronts. **7** 150,000 Serb refugees flee Krajina after Croat victory. **11** President Clinton vetoes legislation to lift unilaterally the Bosnian arms embargo. **17** Alison Hargreaves, 1st woman to climb Everest alone, dies in an avalanche on K2. **18** Driest summer since 1659. **22** Zaïre expels 11,000 refugees back to Rwanda. **27** Rugby Union turns professional. **28** Bosnian Serb shelling of Sarajevo kills 35 in city centre; James Molyneaux resigns as UUP leader.

September 5 French nuclear test at Mururoa atoll. **6** Riots in Tahiti, after nuclear test; Airport destroyed. **8** David Trimble elected new leader of UUP. **10** NATO uses cruise missiles against the Bosnian Serbs. **16** Bosnians and Croats advance across W. Bosnia. **17** Last Legislative Council elections in Hong Kong before 1997; Democratic Party beat Beijing-backed Democratic Alliance. **24** Israel and PLO agree to extend self-rule to most of West Bank. **27** European Court of Human Rights condemned killing of 3 IRA terrorists by SAS in Gibraltar in 1988. **28** Publishers' Association end the Net Book Agreement (NBA).

October 1 Metrication Day; All pre-packed food to be sold in metric units. **2** 2nd French nuclear test in Pacific. **3** OJ Simpson released after a unanimous not guilty verdict. **5** 60-day cease-fire in Bosnia agreed in US-brokered deal. **7** Alan Howarth, Tory MP for Stratford-on-Avon, defects to Labour. **9** Lord Home of the Hirsel, former PM, dies. **11** Bosnian cease-fire comes into

A.D.

effect. **18** Red Rum, winner of Grand National in 1973, 1974 and 1977, dies aged 30. **20** Secretary-General of NATO Willy Claes resigns. **30** Quebec independence referendum results in a No vote; Quebec Premier Jacques Parizeau steps down.

November 4 Israeli PM Yitzhak Rabin assassinated in Tel Aviv. **10** Ken Saro-Wiwa and 8 other human rights activists executed in Nigeria. **11** Nigeria suspended from the Commonwealth. **19** Lech Walesa defeated in Polish Presidential elections. **20** Princess of Wales gives interview on Panorama. **21** Bosnian peace deal agreed in Dayton, Ohio by the Presidents of Croatia, Serbia and Bosnia. **28** Northern Ireland peace process breakthrough; all-party talks to go ahead.

December 1 Nick Leeson sentenced to 6½ years in prison in Singapore. **8** International conference on reconstruction of Bosnia opens in London. **14** Bosnian peace agreement formally signed in Paris. **15** EU leaders agree to call the new single currency the Euro. **17** Communists come first in Russian parliamentary elections, winning 155 out of 450 seats. **19** Government loses the Fisheries vote in the House of Commons by 2 votes. **20** NATO takes over the UN role in Bosnia. **29** Tory MP Emma Nicholson defects to Liberal Democrats.

1996

January 6 Three tickets share biggest Lottery jackpot of £42 million. **7** Blizzards sweep across NE USA in worst storms for 70 years: over 100 die. **8** François Mitterrand dies of cancer aged 79. **18** Costas Simitis elected as new Greek Prime Minister. **19** Kevin and Ian Maxwell cleared of fraud. **21** Yasser Arafat elected as President of Palestine. **23** Trial of Yigal Amir, Yitzhak Rabin's assassin begins. **29** France announces the end of its Pacific nuclear tests.

February 4 Privatised trains run for the first time in 50 years. **9** IRA cease-fire expires as massive bomb explodes in South Quays, east London: 2 killed. **15** Scott Report on the Arms-to-Iraq Affair is published; Government ministers Nicholas Lyell and William Waldegrave refuse to resign. **16** Bosnian, Croatian and Serbian Presidents meet in Rome to cement the Dayton Accord. **18** IRA bus bomb in Aldwych. **22** Peter Clowes released after serving four years of a ten-year sentence for fraud. **23** Peter Thurnham, MP for Bolton NE, resigns from the Conservative party. **26** Government wins House of Commons' vote on the Scott Report by one vote. **28** Princess Diana formally agrees to a divorce.

March 2 John Howard becomes the new Australian PM as the Liberal-National Coalition wins a landslide victory in the general election. **3** José Maria Aznar wins the Spanish general election. **4** Northern Ireland proximity talks start at Stormont without Sinn Fein or the main Unionist parties. **6** Renewed fighting in the Chechen capital of Grozny. **13** Tom Hamilton kills 16 primary school children and their teacher in Dunblane, Scotland, before shooting himself. **14** Government orders an official inquiry into the Dunblane massacre. **17** The Queen and Princess Royal visit Dunblane; one minute's silence observed nationwide at 9.30am. **18** First of the funerals takes place in Dunblane. **19** President Nelson Mandela granted a divorce from Winnie; Bob Dole secures the Republican nomination. **20** The Government admits the possibility of a link between BSE in cows and CJD in humans. **21** France and 4 other EU countries suspend imports of British beef. **22** New Zealand, Germany and 12 other countries suspend British beef imports; Dunblane primary school reopens. **23** President Lee Teng-hui wins the first direct elections in Taiwan. **25** EU veterinary committee recommends a Europe-wide ban on British beef. **27** Yigal Amir sentenced to life imprisonment for the assassination of Yitzhak Rabin. **28** Government bans the use of beef products from cattle over 30 months old.

April 2 Cabinet agreement on a manifesto commitment to a referendum on a single European currency. **3** Government decides to slaughter 4

A.D.

million older cows. **10** US government orders the slaughter of all cattle imported from Britain. **11** Labour win Staffordshire SE by-election with a 22% swing from the Conservatives. **13** 400,000 refugees flee from southern Lebanon. **15** Israeli jets destroy a Beirut power station. **17** Decree nisi granted to the Duke and Duchess of York. **18** Israeli bombing of UN refugee centre in south Lebanon kills 101; Islamic fundamentalists shoot 18 tourists dead in Cairo. **21** Chechen rebel leader Gen. Dudayev killed in Russian attack. **22** Italian general election won by Olive Tree alliance: new PM Romano Prodi. **28** Gunman Martin Bryant killed 35 tourists in Port Arthur, Australia.

May 2 Conservatives suffered heavy losses in local council elections. **9** Dame Shirley Porter ordered to pay £31 million surcharge for gerrymandering; National Party withdrew from the Government of National Unity in South Africa. **10** Congress (I) party lost the Indian general election. **20** EU veterinary committee voted to continue British beef ban. **21** Britain decided to block all EU business until beef ban lifted. **28** President Clinton's former business partners in Arkansas found guilty of fraud and conspiracy. **30** Duke and Duchess of York granted a divorce. **31** Likud narrowly won the Israeli general election; Binyamin Netanyahu new PM.

June 1 New United Front coalition government in India. **5** European Commission authorised partial lifting of ban on British beef. **10** All-party talks began at Stormont Castle, but Sinn Fein excluded. **14** Irish peace forum opened in Belfast. **15** IRA bomb caused extensive damage and 200 injuries in central Manchester. **16** President Yeltsin won the first round of Russian Presidential election. **19** EU veterinary committee voted for lifting the British beef ban. **21** UK policy of non-cooperation with EU ended.

July 3 Yeltsin won the Russian Presidential election. **4** Prince of Wales proposed terms for divorce. **7** Loyalist march through Portadown blocked by RUC and army. **11** Portadown march allowed to progress: riots ensued in Belfast and across Northern Ireland. **12** Princess of Wales accepted the divorce deal: £15 million settlement, equal responsibility for the children and loss of HRH title. **15** Decree nisi granted to Prince and Princess of Wales. **16** Princess Diana resigned as patron of over 100 charities. **18** 228 killed as TWA jet exploded off Long Island, New York. **20** Centennial Olympic Games opened in Atlanta, Georgia. **22** David Heathcoat-Amory resigned as Paymaster-General. **25** Army coup in Burundi. **27** Nail bomb in Centennial Park, Atlanta, killed 2, injured over 100.

August 1 Somali warlord General Aideed died. **10** Bob Dole selected Jack Kemp as his running mate. **12** Republican Party convention opened in San Diego. **21** The Globe Theatre reopened with the first production of Shakespeare there since 1642. **26** Democratic Party convention opened in Chicago. **28** Prince and Princess of Wales granted a divorce. **29** Clinton adviser Dick Morris resigned after sex scandal. **31** Iraqi forces captured Kurdish capital of Arbil.

September 3 27 US cruise missiles fired on southern Iraq in Operation Desert Strike. **8** Thousands of Kurdish refugees fled to Iranian border. **9** Pro-Iraqi KDP forces captured PUK stronghold of Sulaimaniya. **10** Iraqis fired on US fighters. **19** Kevin Maxwell freed after judge blocked a second trial. **23** IRA terrorist suspect shot dead by police in west London. **24** Construction of a tunnel beneath Temple Mount precipitated protests in Jerusalem. **25** Unrest across the West Bank: 84 Palestinians killed in Ramallah. **26** Worst fighting in Israel for 30 years: 55 dead. **27** Taliban forces capture Kabul: ex-President Najibullah executed.

October 1 Israeli PM Netanyahu and Palestinian leader Arafat met in Washington DC; MP Neil Hamilton admitted taking cash for questions. **4** Ministry of Defence admitted Gulf War troops were exposed to harmful chemicals. **6** Lord McAlpine defected from the Tories to the Referendum Party. **12** Election in New Zealand

A.D.

resulted in a hung parliament; Tory MP for Bolton NE, Peter Thurnham, defected to the Liberal Democrats. **16** Cullen report on Dunblane published: all handguns except smallest calibre (.22) pistols to be banned. **17** President Yeltsin sacked National Security Adviser General Lebed. **25** Norwegian PM Gro Harlem Brundtland resigned. **26** Fighting engulfed eastern Zaïre.

November 5 President Clinton re-elected: Republicans retained both Houses of Congress; Benazir Bhutto dismissed as Pakistani PM. **13** Canadian-led UN force proposed for Zaïre: UK to contribute 3,500 troops. **15** Militia expelled from refugee camps in Zaïre: 400,000 refugees head back to Rwanda: UN resolution passed creating new force for Zaïre: 5,000 US troops committed. **17** President Milosevic annulled opposition victories in municipal elections: anti-government protests in Belgrade. **18** Fire in Channel Tunnel caused extensive damage. **26** Budget Day: 1p off basic rate of income tax. **27** First deaths from E-coli outbreak in Scotland.

December 2 Tory MP for Kensington and Chelsea, Sir Nicholas Scott, deselected by his local party. **6** Sir John Gorst, MP for Hendon North, resigned Tory party whip. **10** Government announced official inquiry into Gulf War syndrome; new coalition government in New Zealand: Jim Bolger remains PM. **11** Paymaster-General David Willetts resigned over cash for questions. **12** Labour win Barnsley East by-election: Government now in minority. **17** Tupac Amaru terrorists seized 430 hostages at Japanese embassy in Peru. **22** 225 hostages released in Peru. **24** One killed in clashes between rival protesters in Belgrade; two British nurses charged with murder in Saudi Arabia.

1997

January 1 Israeli soldier opened fire in Hebron marketplace. **3** President Milosevic admitted defeat in Serbian municipal elections. **5** Belgrade protests intensified. **14** Serbian opposition declared the winners of municipal elections by the Electoral Commission. **15** Israeli pull-out from Hebron agreed by Arafat and Netanyahu. **16** Iain Mills, Tory MP for Meriden, died. **17** Israeli troops withdrawn from Hebron. **20** President Clinton inaugurated; Labour pledge of no increase in personal income tax during first term. **26** Violent protests in Albania after the collapse of a pyramid investment scheme. **30** Sir George Gardiner deselected as Tory MP in Reigate.

February 3 Benazir Bhutto and Imran Khan defeated in Pakistani general election: Nawaz Sharif new PM. **4** 73 Israeli soldiers killed in helicopter crash. **5** O.J. Simpson found guilty in civil court case. **10** O.J. Simpson ordered to pay £15 million punitive damages. **15** Opposition protests in Albania intensified. **17** Government survived censure motion on BSE crisis. **19** Chinese Premier Deng Xiaoping died aged 92; 1st National Lottery draw on Wednesday. **21** Bridgewater Three freed after 18 years in jail. **22** Adult sheep (Dolly) successfully cloned by scientists.

March 2 Fighting in Vlore killed 12: state of emergency declared in Albania. **3** Rebels seized control of southern Albania. **5** Sweeping reforms of pensions announced. **8** Sir George Gardiner, Tory MP for Reigate, defected to the Referendum Party. **11** Albanian rebels closed in on Tirana. **13** Foreign nationals evacuated from Albania. **14** Fighting reached Tirana: foreigners evacuated under fire. **16** Albanian refugees flood into Italy. **17** John Major called general election for 1 May. **19** Political row erupted over publication of the Downey Report into cash-for-questions. **26** Tim Smith, Tory MP for Beaconsfield, resigned over the cash-for-questions affair. **30** Channel 5 started transmitting.

April 3 Tony Blair issued his 10-point contract with the people. **5** 150th Grand National abandoned after bomb scares. **6** BBC correspondent Martin Bell decided to stand on an anti-corruption ticket against Neil Hamilton in Tatton. **7** Grand National took place on a Monday for the first time. **14** Renewed EU row over fishing quotas;

A.D.

general strike in Kinshasa, Zaïre. 17 Major announced a free vote on single currency in House of Commons. 22 all hostages freed as embassy siege in Lima ended.

May 1 General election held in United Kingdom. Labour won landslide victory under Tony Blair, taking 419 seats. Conservatives reduced to 165 seats. The Liberal Democrats won 46 (their highest tally since 1929). 2 Gordon Brown became Chancellor of the Exchequer; Robin Cook new Foreign Secretary; John Prescott is Deputy Prime Minister. John Major resigned as leader of the Conservative Party. 4 New Labour Government announces its intention of joining EU Social Chapter. 6 Bank of England given control of interest rates. 7 Rebels closed in on Zaïrean capital of Kinshasa. 10 Earthquake in E. Iran left over 4,000 dead. 11 Government called 'drought summit' to discuss water crisis; chess computer Deep Blue defeated Gary Kasparov. 12 Russia and Chechnya signed peace treaty. 14 Author Laurie Lee died aged 82. 15 Trade union ban at GCHQ lifted. 16 President Mobutu fled Zaïre. 17 Rebels entered Kinshasa: Zaïre renamed Democratic Republic of Congo by new President, Laurent Kabila. 20 'Super' watchdog created to oversee City dealings. 25 Socialists won first round of French general election; coup in Sierra Leone. 26 French PM Juppé resigned. 27 NATO-Russian co-operation charter signed in Paris.

June 1 Socialists won the French general election: Lionel Jospin new PM. 2 Liberal Party won Canadian general election; Timothy McVeigh found guilty of Oklahoma bombing; row over Camelot directors' bonuses. 6 Fianna Fáil largest party after Irish general election: coalition government formed with Progressive Democrats. 10 Kenneth Clarke won first round of Tory leadership contest with 49 votes, Hague second with 41, Redwood third with 27; Lilley (24 votes) and Howard (23) withdrew. 11 MPs voted to ban all remaining handguns. 13 Timothy McVeigh sentenced to death. 17 In second round, Clarke won 64 votes, Hague 62, Redwood 38; Redwood eliminated. 18 Amsterdam Treaty signed by EU leaders. 19 Hague won final round (92 votes to 70) to become youngest Tory leader since 1783; 'McLibel' case ended after 313 days, the longest trial in English history: McDonald's awarded £60,000 libel damages. 25 Jacques Cousteau died. 26 Chances Peak in Montserrat erupted.

July 1 Hong Kong handed over to Chinese rule; UK rejoined UNESCO; actor Robert Mitchum died aged 79. 2 Labour's first Budget; actor James Stewart died aged 89. 3 Downey report into cash-for-questions published: 5 former Tory MPs, including Neil Hamilton, criticised. 6 Orangemen parade in Drumcree led to rioting across N. Ireland. 15 Slobodan Milosevic elected as Yugoslavian President. 17 Heavy rain across central Europe: River Oder burst its banks, severe flooding in Poland and Germany. 19 Politician Sir James Goldsmith died. 20 IRA reinstated its ceasefire. 28 Gordon McMaster, Labour MP for Paisley South, committed suicide.

August 2 Author William Burroughs died aged 83. 4 World's oldest person, Jeanne Caldwell, died aged 122 years, 5 months, 14 days. 5 Labour Lord Simon ended controversy over his BP shares by selling them. 7 Football's match-fixing trial ended with not guilty verdicts; fourth rise in interest rates to 7% since election. 8 Princess Diana arrived in Bosnia to campaign against landmines. 14 India and Pakistan celebrated 50th anniversary of independence. 17 Evacuation of Salem in Montserrat begun. 19 Tommy Graham, MP for Renfrewshire West, is suspended from Parliamentary Labour Party. 25 Former E. German leader Egon Krenz jailed for Berlin Wall deaths. 26 South African Vice-President F.W. de Klerk retired. 31 Diana, Princess of Wales killed in car crash in Paris: her companion Dodi Fayed and driver Henri Paul also died.

September 2 7 paparazzi charged with manslaughter. 3 Huge floral tributes at Royal palaces. 4 Royal Family returned to London from Balmoral; Jerusalem bomb blasts killed eight people. 5

A.D.

Queen addressed the nation in live TV broadcast; Kensington Gardens turned into impromptu shrine with thousands of bouquets and candles; Mother Teresa died aged 87. 6 Diana's funeral at Westminster Abbey: over 2 million lined the route, 31·5 million watched on TV – the biggest ever UK television audience; Sir Georg Solti died aged 84. 8 Over 400 died in ferry sinking off Haiti. 9 Actor Burgess Meredith died aged 89. 11 Scotland voted Yes-Yes in dual referendum on a Scottish Parliament and its tax-raising powers. 12 State funeral of Mother Teresa. 13 Elton John's tribute single to Diana, *Candle in the Wind*, sold 650,000 copies to become Number One. 16 Forest fires in Indonesia caused extensive smog across south-east Asia. 17 Draft landmines treaty rejected by the USA. 18 Referendum in Wales produced narrow vote (50·3% to 49·7%) in favour of Welsh Assembly; 7 tourists killed in bus bomb in Cairo. 19 6 killed in Southall rail crash. 20 Henri Paul buried in Brittany. 22 Former Speaker George Thomas (Viscount Tonypandy) died aged 88. 23 British nurse Lucille McLauchlan sentenced to 500 lashes. 26 Earthquakes in Italy damaged St Francis's Basilica, Assisi. 30 *Canberra* ended its last voyage.

October 1 Fiji readmitted to the Commonwealth. 7 Irish Foreign Minister Ray Burke resigned as all-party N. Ireland talks opened; Louise Woodward trial started; government announced free vote on gay age of consent. 9 Romani Prodi resigned as Italian PM; 250 killed as Hurricane Pauline hit Acapulco. 13 Singer John Denver died in plane crash. 14 Piers Merchant resigned as Tory MP for Beckenham; Arundhati Roy won the Booker Prize with *The God of Small Things*. 15 *Thrust* broke the sound barrier on land (766·109 mph); author Harold Robbins died; British nurse Deborah Parry spared the death penalty. 16 James A. Michener died aged 90. 21 *Candle in the Wind* bestselling record ever—31·8 million copies worldwide. 23 Hong Kong stock market fell 10%: FTSE dropped 157 points. 25 British Library Reading Room closed. 27 Dow Jones index fell 554 points; Chancellor committed UK to EMU after next election. 28 FTSE fell 458 points: Dow Jones recovered. 29 Ian Taylor resigned as Shadow N. Ireland spokesman over Tories' Euro policy. 30 Louise Woodward found guilty of second degree murder. 31 Woodward sentenced to life imprisonment; Mary McAleese elected new Irish President.

November 1 David Curry resigned from Shadow Cabinet over European policy. 2 Iraq turned back UN nuclear weapons inspectors. 3 Jenny Shipley new PM in New Zealand. 4 Government decided to exempt Formula 1 from ban on tobacco sponsorship. 5 Republicans won decisive victory in mid-term Congressional elections. 6 Labour hold Paisley South by-election; cash-for-questions inquiry failed to reach unanimous verdict on Neil Hamilton; Sir Isaiah Berlin died. 7 Spice Girls sacked their manager. 8 Controversy over donation to Labour by Formula 1 lobbyist Bernie Ecclestone. 9 BBC launched 24-hour news channel. 10 Louise Woodward's conviction reduced to involuntary manslaughter: she is set free; Labour returned Ecclestone's donation. 11 Government announced review of political party funding. 13 Iraq expelled 6 US weapons inspectors: UN pulls out inspection teams. 17 58 tourists killed in massacre at Luxor temple; Windsor Castle reopened. 19 World's first surviving septuplets born in Iowa. 20 Tories held Beckenham, Liberal-Democrats retained Winchester in by-elections; celebration of Queen's golden wedding anniversary. 21 Peter Temple-Morris resigned Tory whip to become Independent. 22 INXS singer Michael Hutchence hanged himself. 23 Japanese stockbrokers Yamaichi ceased trading. 26 Hastings Banda of Malawi died aged 99. 27 DTI report on Guinness take-over published. 28 Indian PM resigned; 260-vote majority in Commons for anti-hunting bill.

December 1 Stéphane Grappelli died aged 89. 2 Bushfires threatened Sydney. 3 Beef-on-the-bone ban announced by government; Earl and Countess Spencer divorced. 4 EU banned tobacco

A.D.

advertising. **6** Controversy over Paymaster-General Geoffrey Robinson's offshore trusts. **9** Internal market scrapped in NHS reforms. **10** 47 Labour MPs voted against the government in backbench revolt over lone parent benefit cutbacks: junior minister Malcolm Chisholm resigned. **11** Gerry Adams at Number 10 for talks; *Britannia* decommissioned. **15** Government banned EU meat imports not conforming to UK hygiene standards. **16** Beef-on-the-bone ban implemented; Glasgow Govan MP Mohammed Sarwar charged with election fraud. **18** Bill to create Scottish Parliament launched; Opposition leader Kim Dae-Jung won S. Korean presidential election. **25** Queen's Christmas message produced by ITV for the first time. **27** Loyalist terrorist leader Billy Wright murdered inside the Maze Prison: former IRA prisoner Seamus Dillon murdered in retaliation. **29** Inquiry launched into Maze killing.

1998

January 2 Frank Muir died, aged 77. **5** Singer Sonny Bono killed in skiing accident. **8** Currency crisis in Indonesia. **9** Mo Mowlam met with Loyalist leaders in Maze prison. **11** Ice storms in Canada left 3 million without power. **12** New British-Irish proposals for N. Ireland peace: cross-border council planned. **14** Sweeping reforms of Tory leader elections. **17** President Clinton questioned in Paula Jones harassment case. **21** Sex scandal erupted in Washington after allegations of Clinton's affair with Monica Lewinsky. **23** Lewinsky scandal deepended: Clinton accused of perjury. **26** Clinton denied any affair with Lewinsky; UDP quit N. Ireland peace talks. **27** Hillary Clinton in TV interviews to defend her husband.

February 3 Diana commemorative stamps went on sale. **8** Enoch Powell died aged 85. **9** Government defeated in Lords vote on newspaper pricing controls. **10** 2nd N. Ireland murder in 24 hours; peace talks threatened with collapse. **11** Monica Lewinsky's mother testified to grand jury. **13** Warmest February day on record (19·6C at Worcester). **16** Iraqi inspections crisis intensified; 204 killed in Taiwan jet crash. **19** UN Secretary-General Kofi Annan left on peace mission to Baghdad. **20** Sinn Fein suspended from N. Ireland peace talks: bomb blast in Moira. **22** Deal negotiated by Annan to end UN-Iraqi stand-off.

March 1 Countryside March in London attracted 250,000 demonstrators. **2** Princess Diana's will published; Albanian demonstrations in Kosovo province. **3** Two killed in Poyntzpass, N. Ireland. **5** Water discovered on the moon; Serb forces killed over 50 Albanians in Prekaz, Kosovo. **6** Louise Woodward's appeal began. **13** Private member's bill to ban hunting failed to get Government time in the Commons. **15** White House volunteer, Kathleen Willey, made new claims against Pres. Clinton. **16** Radio 4 revamp revealed; Dr Benjamin Spock died aged 94. **17** Budget day: record increase in child benefit, taxes on petrol and cigarettes up. **23** Pres Yeltsin sacked PM and cabinet; *Titanic* won 11 Oscars including Best Picture and Best Director. **24** Four girls and a teacher shot dead by two schoolboys in Jonesboro, Arkansas.

April 1 Paula Jones sex case against Pres. Clinton dismissed by federal judge. **6** Mitchell draft settlement on N. Ireland published; UK and France ratified Nuclear Test Ban Treaty. **7** Unionists rejected Mitchell blueprint: Blair flew to Belfast for crisis talks; singer Tammy Wynette died aged 55. **8** Intense negotiations on N. Ireland continued; Australian Senate rejected government's land rights' bill. **10** Peace agreement sealed in N. Ireland: new directly-elected assembly to be created; heavy rain caused widespread extensive flooding in central England. **15** Death of Pol Pot, Cambodian dictator. **17** Death of Linda McCartney (wife of Sir Paul McCartney). **18** Ulster Unionist Council supported David Trimble over peace deal. **20** Palestinian leader Yasser Arafat agreed to attend Middle East peace summit. **22** Controversy over shipment of nuclear material from Georgia to Britain. **30** End of wettest April for 180 years.

A.D.

May 2 Official birth of the 'Euro' at Brussels Summit; 11 EU countries have membership confirmed; Wim Duisenberg to take charge of European Central Bank. **4** Middle East peace talks in London. **6** Heavy flooding killed over 135 in southern Italy; independent inquiry into arms-to-Sierra Leone affair set up; Dutch coalition government won second term in elections. **7** Local elections in England; referendum in London approved creation of Mayor. **10** IRA prisoners temporarily released to attend Sinn Fein conference which voted for the Belfast Agreement. **11** India conducted three nuclear tests. **13** Frank Sinatra died aged 82. **15** LVF declared ceasefire. **16** Arsenal win FA Cup/League double. **18** US government launched anti-trust lawsuit against Microsoft. **19** Saudi death sentences on two British nurses commuted. **20** Congress announced investigations into President Clinton's campaign funding; crisis in Indonesia engulfed the country: hundreds killed after months of unrest. **21** President Suharto of Indonesia resigned. **22** Referenda on the Belfast Agreement in both parts of Ireland: 71% in Northern Ireland and 94% in the Republic in favour. **24** Pro-democracy parties won Hong Kong legislative elections; fighting in Kosovo escalated. **26** Veterans protested at state visit by Emperor of Japan; continuing heatwave in India: over 100 killed. **27** Share prices fell worldwide as Russian crisis intensified. **28** Pakistan conducted five nuclear tests: sanctions imposed on both India and Pakistan. **30** Rioting in Portadown. **31** Strong earthquake in north-east Afghanistan: 4,000 killed; Ginger Spice (Geri Halliwell) quit the Spice Girls.

June 1 Aid package for Russia announced. **2** Reports of Serbian massacres in Kosovo villages. **3** Train crash in Eschede, Germany, killed 96; border conflict between Ethiopia and Eritrea. **8** Nigerian President Abacha died. **10** World Cup opened in Paris; Sir David English, former editor of *Daily Mail*, and author Hammond Innes both died; European Commission called for resumption of British beef exports. **11** Dame Catherine Cookson died aged 91. **15** Yen at 8-year low against $. **18** Government announced introduction of minimum wage (£3·60ph) in April 1999; independent inquiry set up to look at deaths of babies at Bristol Royal Infirmary. **19** RAC members approved demutualisation of the rescue service. **21** Actress Maureen O'Sullivan died aged 87. **22** House of Commons voted for equal age of consent for gay men. **24** Car bomb exploded in Newtownhamilton, Armagh: no-one killed; James McArdle convicted of London Docklands bombing. **25** Northern Ireland assembly elections held under PR: UUP 28 seats, SDLP 24, DUP 20, Sinn Fein 18, Alliance Party 6, UK Unionist 5, others 7; the Queen opened the new British Library. **30** England knocked out of World Cup by Argentina on penalties: David Beckham sent off.

July 1 David Trimble elected First Minister of Northern Ireland, Seamus Mallon as Deputy; Diana museum at Althorp opened; Tim Henman became the first Briton in 25 years to reach Wimbledon men's semi-final: he lost. **5** Stand-off between Orange marchers and police at Drumcree began. **7** Nigerian pro-democracy leader Chief Abiola died in jail. **8** Heavy rioting in Nigeria; Australian Senate finally passed government's land rights' bill; first edition of Chaucer's Canterbury Tales sold for a record £4·6 million. **9** Violence continued across Northern Ireland. **12** Three boys burned to death in sectarian attack in Ballymoney, Antrim; Japanese PM Hashimoto resigned; France beat Brazil 3-0 to win World Cup. **13** IMF aid package for Russia agreed. **15** FTSE 100 index at record high (6,515·5 points). **16** Widespread floods in southern China: millions homeless. **17** Tidal wave killed 1,600 in Papua New Guinea; remains of last Russian Tsar reburied in St Petersburg; international conference agreed on creation of permanent international court for crimes against humanity. **22** House of Lords rejected gay age of consent clause: Government dropped it from bill. **24** Gunman killed two security guards on Capitol Hill; Tiny Rowland died aged 80. **26** President Clinton subpoenaed to appear before grand jury; renewed Serbian offensive in Kosovo. **27** Cabinet reshuffle: Peter Mandelson

A.D.

and Alistair Darling promoted, Harriet Harman and Gavin Strang sacked; former Pakistani PM Benazir Bhutto on trial for corruption. **28** Monica Lewinsky granted immunity from prosecution in return for testifying. **30** Court of Appeal overturned conviction of Derek Bentley, hanged in 1953. **31** UK ban on use of anti-personnel mines; Keizo Obuchi new Japanese PM; worldwide, July was the hottest month ever.

August 4 Big fall in Wall Street shares. **5** Iraq ended all co-operation with UN weapons inspectors. **6** Monica Lewinsky testified to grand jury; civil war in Democratic Republic of Congo re-erupted. **7** Bomb attacks on US embassies in Nairobi and Dar-es-Salaam: 240 dead. **8** Animal rights activists released 6,000 mink in Hampshire. **10** Taleban forces captured last opposition stronghold in Afghanistan; Nevis failed to gain independence from St Kitts. **13** Moscow share trading suspended; Swiss banks approved payment to Holocaust survivors. **15** Massive bomb in Omagh, Tyrone, killed 28. **17** President Clinton testified to grand jury; in live television address he admitted to an 'inappropriate relationship' with Ms Lewinsky; Russian rouble devalued. **18** Splinter group the Real IRA admitted responsibility for Omagh bomb; ruling coalition in New Zealand dissolved. **20** US missile attacks on Afghanistan and Sudan. **22** INLA announced ceasefire. **23** President Yeltsin sacked Russian cabinet: Victor Chernomyrdin new PM. **26** Rouble in free fall: European stock markets fell; perfume firm Yardley went into receivership; fighting around Congolese capital of Kinshasa. **27** Extensive flooding in Bangladesh. **31** Dow Jones index in second largest fall in history; Australian general election called.

September 3 Swissair plane crashed into sea off Halifax, Nova Scotia; 229 killed. President Clinton in Ireland. **4** Closure of Fujitsu computer chip factory on Tyneside announced. **6** Death of Akira Kurosawa, Japanese film director; Rupert Murdoch's BSkyB announced intention to acquire Manchester United. **7** 'Real IRA' declares total cease-fire; William Hague calls ballot of party members over EU single currency question. **10** Historic meeting of David Trimble and Gerry Adams; preliminary details of Starr Report on President Clinton leaked to media. **11** Starr Report released on Internet: Yevgeni Primakov chosen as new Russian Prime Minister. **12** Last routine army patrols carried out in Belfast. **13** Death of American politician George Wallace. **16** Microsoft becomes largest company in United States. **18** US Congressional Committee sanctions release of the 'Clinton Tapes'. **20** Release of 2 kidnapped Britons held in Chechnya; death of mother of Duchess of York in car crash in Argentina; death of actress Patricia Hayes. **21** Release of Clinton tapes; rioting in Malaysia as Queen closes Commonwealth Games. **24** Britain to resume diplomatic relations with Iran. **25** Frenchman Benoit Lecomte became first person to swim the Atlantic (coming ashore at Quiberon in Brittany). **27** German elections: Chancellor Kohl defeated by Social Democrats under Schröder (see **Section C** for details). **28** MCC voted to admit women members; collapse of Japan Leasing Company, biggest corporate collapse since World War II. **28** Albanian PM resigns.

October 4 Kidnapping of 3 British workers and a New Zealander in Chechnya. **5** Result of Conservative Party ballot on Europe confirmed William Hague's position on single currency. **7** Official visit to China by Tony Blair. **8** Bank of England reduced interest rates by ¼% to 7¼%; House of Representatives voted 258–176 to institute impeachment proceedings against President Clinton. **9** Italian PM Prodi loses confidence motion by 1 vote. **12** Serbian hard-line President Milosevic yields to Western pressure over Kosovo. **13** Neill Report revolutionises funding of political parties in the United Kingdom. **15** Channel 4 acquires rights to show Test Match cricket. **16** Nobel Peace Prize awarded jointly to John Hume and David Trimble. **17** Arrest of former dictator of Chile, General Pinochet, at a private London hospital; first international monitors arrive in Kosovo. **18** Death of actress Joan Hickson who played Agatha Christie's Miss Marple. **19** Terrorist

A.D.

bomb in Beersheba injured over 60; Middle East peace summit threatened. **23** Agreement reached at Maryland peace talks. **24** Torrential wind and rain sweeps British Isles. **27** Arrival of President Menem of Argentina on official visit; abrupt resignation of Ron Davies, the Secretary of State for Wales, after 'lapse of judgement' on Clapham Common; succeeded by Alun Michael. **28** Arrest of General Pinochet overturned in the High Court. **29** Publication of report of Jenkins Commission on electoral reform; death from cancer of Poet Laureate Ted Hughes. **30** Sixty teenagers (mainly foreigners) die in fire at Swedish discotheque.

November 4 Massive destruction by Hurricane Mitch in Central America. **5** Bank of England cuts interest rates by 0·5%. **8** Death of Lord Hunt (leader of 1953 Everest expedition). **9** Cricketer Geoffrey Boycott found guilty of assault. **11** 80th anniversary of ending of the First World War; details of proposed closer collaboration of Labour and Liberal Democrats revealed. **13** Final warnings sent to Saddam Hussein in renewed Gulf Crisis; Liberal Democrat groundswell of anger at closer collaboration plans with Labour. **14** ON Digital, second digital TV channel, launched; Iraq complies with Western demands for inspection of sites. **15** Death of US black leader Stokely Carmichael. **16** Firms agree to halt testing of cosmetic products on animals; Japanese government announces £115 bn aid package to rejuvenate ailing economy. **20** Furious reaction in Russia to assassination of opposition deputy Galina Staroyovoytova. **23** EU ban on exports of British beef lifted.

December 1 FTSE index fell over 200 points; wrestler Giant Haystacks died, aged 52. **2** William Hague sacked Lord Cranbourne as Tory leader in the Lords. **3** Four Tory peers resigned from front bench, two more leave the party. **7** Post Office privatisation ruled out by government. **8** Four Western hostages beheaded in Chechnya. **9** Home Secretary authorised Pinochet's extradition: Chile withdrew ambassador from UK. **10** Nobel peace prize presented to John Hume and David Trimble. **11** House of Representatives passed two articles of impeachment against Clinton; Pinochet extradition hearing started. **12** Two more impeachment articles passed by Congress; over 100 killed in Thai air crash. **13** Lord Grade died aged 91. **15** House of Lords defeated European elections bill for 6th time: Parliament Act invoked; FA chief Graham Kelly resigned; pensions reforms unveiled. **16** Anglo-American air strikes against Iraq. **17** Impeachment vote in Congress postponed; renewed bombing of Baghdad; Law Lords extradition ruling on Pinochet set aside. **19** Clinton impeached by House of Representatives on 2 counts: Speaker-elect Bob Livingstone resigned; bombing of Iraq halted. **20** Octuplets born in Texas; Spice Girls had Christmas Number One for third year in a row. **21** Row erupted over £373,000 loan from Paymaster-General Geoffrey Robinson to Trade Secretary Peter Mandelson. **23** Mandelson and Robinson both resigned from the Cabinet. **25** Richard Branson forced to abandon his round-the-world balloon trip. **26** Fighting resumed in Kosovo. **27** Five dead as storms hit UK. **28** 16 Westerners taken hostage in Yemen; 6 drown in Sydney-Hobart yacht race. **29** Four hostages killed during Yemeni rescue. **31** Tension in N. Iraq increased; Nigel Hawthorne knighted.

1999

January 2 Darren Gough became first English bowler to take an Ashes hat-trick since before 1900. **3** Heavy snowfalls paralysed eastern USA. **4** Charlie Whelan, Gordon Brown's Press Secretary, resigned. **5** Flu epidemic caused NHS crisis. **6** Prince Edward's engagement to Sophie Rhys-Jones announced; rebel forces entered Sierra Leone capital, Freetown; warmest January day in UK for 158 years (15·7°C). **7** US Senate sworn in for impeachment trial. **12** Freetown engulfed by flames and fighting. **13** Global shares downturn sparked by Brazilian devaluation. **14** Impeachment prosecution case started; MEPs voted not to sack the European Commission. **16** Serb massacre of ethnic Albanians in Kosovo: 45 dead. **18** England

A.D.

expelled from Five Nations rugby tournament. **19** President Clinton's defence began; Jonathan Aitken pleaded guilty to perjury; England readmitted to Five Nations. **20** Paddy Ashdown announced resignation as Liberal Democrat leader; Lords reform unveiled. **22** International Olympic Committee shamed by bribes scandal. **24** 6 IOC members suspended, 3 others resigned; Le Pen ousted as leader of French National Front. **25** Colombian earthquake killed over 1000; US missile attack on Basra; Commons voted for equal age of consent for gay men. **27** IRA informer Eamon Collins murdered; Senate voted to call 3 impeachment witnesses. **28** Prince Charles and Camilla Parker-Bowles appeared together in public for the first time. **29** Glenn Hoddle interview about reincarnation; renewed atrocities in Kosovo. **31** Tory MEP, Tom Spencer, not to seek re-election after drugs and pornography scandal.

February 1 Monica Lewinsky testified; first snow in Majorca for 94 years. **2** Glenn Hoddle sacked as England manager. **4** Mortgage rates at lowest level since 1965. **6** Video of Monica's testimony shown on TV. **7** King Hussein of Jordan died, aged 63. **8** Dame Iris Murdoch died, aged 79. **10** Heaviest snowfalls in 50 years across the Alps: avalanche in Chamonix killed 12. **11** Row over genetically modified (GM) foods. **12** Clinton acquitted by Senate on both charges: 55–45 against perjury, 50–50 on obstruction of justice. **15** Government pronounced GM foods to be safe. **16** Kurdish leader Abdullah Ocalan abducted by Turkish agents in Kenya: worldwide Kurdish protests, Greek embassy in London occupied. **17** 3 Kurds shot dead by Israeli Consulate guards in Berlin; Kevin Keegan made part-time, temporary England manager. **18** Greek embassy siege ended. **19** Scary Spice (Mel B) had baby girl, Phoenix. **20** Iraqi Shi'ite leader al-Sadr assassinated. **21** Extracts from report into death of Stephen Lawrence leaked. **23** Avalanche in Galtur killed 38; Kosovo peace talks ended in failure. **24** Lawrence Report published: Metropolitan Police criticised; Derek Nimmo died, aged 68. **25** Lawrence memorial vandalised: report revealed to have included informers' names; Juanita Broaddrick accused Clinton of rape in 1978. **27** General Obasanjo won Nigerian presidential election. **28** Israeli general murdered in S. Lebanon.

March 1 14 tourists kidnapped in Uganda. **2** 8 tourists, including 4 Britons, murdered in Uganda; Dusty Springfield died, aged 59. **3** Monica Lewinsky's TV interview broadcast. **4** US–EU trade war intensified; Posh Spice had a baby boy, Brooklyn. **5** Lord Denning died, aged 100; last *News at Ten* broadcast. **7** Stanley Kubrick died, aged 70. **8** Government announced 'Right to Roam' proposals; Joe DiMaggio died, aged 74. **9** Budget Day: basic rate of income tax down to 22p, starting rate of 10p introduced, Miras and married couple's allowances abolished; floods in N. Yorkshire. **10** Prince of Wales visited Argentina. **11** Oskar Lafontaine resigned as German Finance Minister; Private Lee Clegg acquitted of murder. **12** Poland, Hungary and the Czech Republic

A.D.

joined NATO; Yehudi Menuhin died, aged 82. **13** Renewed Serb attacks in Kosovo; bombs killed 13 in Istanbul. **15** Report on corruption in the EU Commission released; Kosovo peace talks reopened. **16** EU Commission resigned en masse; train crash killed 14 in Illinois. **17** 6 IOC members expelled; UK citizenship reinstated for remaining dependent territories; Rod Hull died, aged 63. **19** Fiona Jones, Labour MP for Newark, loses her seat after being found guilty of election fraud (later wins appeal). **21** *Shakespeare in Love* won 7 Oscars including Best Picture; Ernie Wise died, aged 73; round-the-world balloon trip ended successfully after 20 days; new Serb onslaughts. **22** Over 100 killed in ethnic clashes in Borneo. **24** NATO forces attacked Serbia; fire in Mont Blanc tunnel killed 40; Romani Prodi named EU President. **25** Renewed NATO missile attacks; Labour MP Mohammed Sarwar cleared of corruption. **26** Kosovar Albanians massacred by Serb forces. **27** US Stealth bomber crashed in Serbia. **29** Kosovar refugees fled to Albania, Macedonia and Montenegro; Paraguayan President Cubas resigned; Dow Jones Index closed over 10,000 points for the first time (10,006·78). **30** Ethnic cleansing forced thousands from Kosovo; NATO bombing continued. **31** Russia sent naval vessel to the Adriatic.

April 1 3 US soldiers captured by Serbs; N. Ireland disarmament talks ended in stalemate. **3** NATO attacks on Belgrade. **5** NATO created refugee sanctuaries in Macedonia; Lockerbie suspects flown to Holland. **6** NATO rejected Serb ceasefire offer; bombing continued; Lockerbie suspects charged. **7** Refugee camps in Kosovo cleared by Serb forces. **8** NATO sent 8,000 troops to Albania. **9** BSkyB bid for Manchester Utd blocked. **10** Renewed violence in E Timor. **13** Serb attacks across Albanian border; Lords rejected equal age of consent for gays. **14** 64 killed in NATO bombing of refugee convoy. **15** Home Secretary authorised extradition of Gen Pinochet; Benazir Bhutto convicted of corruption; sacked Labour MP Fiona Jones won her appeal. **16** Thousands more refugees fled Kosovo. **17** Nail bomb in Brixton injured 50. **18** Indian coalition government collapsed. **19** German Reichstag reopened; Turkish PM Ecevit resigned. **20** 15 killed in High School massacre in Littleton, Colorado; Kosovar refugee exodus continued. **22** Russia backed Serbian peace offer. **24** Nail bomb in Brick Lane injured 6. **25** First Kosovar refugees arrived in UK. **26** TV presenter Jill Dando murdered. **28** Serbian deputy PM Vuk Draskovic sacked; Sir Alf Ramsey died, aged 79. **30** Nail bomb at gay pub in Soho: 3 killed, 66 injured; Dame Shirley Porter cleared of gerrymandering.

May 3 Discovery of frozen body of mountaineer George Mallory (missing since 1924) near Everest summit. **6** Voting for first Scottish Parliament since 1707 and new Welsh Assembly leaves Labour short of an overall majority in both polls. In local elections, limited Conservative comeback (*see* **D13**).

PROMINENT PEOPLE

Glimpses of some of the famous people in the history of the world. See also Section C (under individual countries) for major figures in world affairs and Section D for leading British politicians; Section E for composers; Section M for prominent English novelists; Section S for figures from the biblical world; and also Section W for major figures in the history of the cinema.

PROMINENT PEOPLE

A

Abel, Sir Frederick (1826–1902). English military chemist, an authority on explosives. He and his friend James Dewar patented the propellant cordite (*see* **Section L**).

Abelard, Peter (1079–1142), one of the founders of scholastic moral theology, b. at Pallet (Palais) near Nantes. He lectured in Paris, where he was sought by students, though persecuted for alleged heresy. His main achievement was to discuss where others asserted. His love for Héloïse, a woman of learning, ended in tragic separation and in a famous correspondence.

Abercrombie, Sir Patrick (1879–1957), architect and town-planner. He was consulted on the re-planning of Plymouth, Hull, Bath and other cities and produced a plan for Greater London, 1943.

Acton, 1st Baron (John Emerich Edward Dalberg Acton) (1834–1902), English historian. He planned the *Cambridge Modern History.*

Adam, Robert (1728–92), architect, one of four Scottish brothers. He developed a character-istic style in planning and decoration and his achievements in interior design include Hare-wood House, Yorks.; Osterley Park, Middlesex; Syon House, Middlesex; Kedleston Hall, Derbyshire; Luton Hoo, Bedfordshire; and Kenwood. *See* **Neo-Classical Style, Section L.**

Adams, John (1735–1826), succeeded Washington as president of the USA. He was the first of the republic's ambassadors to England.

Adams, John Couch (1819–92), English mathematician and astronomer. He shared credit for the discovery of the planet Neptune (1846) with the French astronomer Leverrier, working independently.

Adams, Samuel (1722–1803), American revolutionary statesman, b. Boston. He advocated "no taxation without representation" as early as 1765; promoted the "Boston tea-party"; in 1776 signed the Declaration of Independence.

Adams, William (*c.* 1564–1620), navigator, b. Gillingham, Kent; the first Englishman to visit Japan. He found favour with the shogun Ieyasu, and an English and Dutch trading settlement was established till 1616.

Addams, Jane (1860–1935), American sociologist who founded Hull House, Chicago, in 1889.

Addison, Joseph (1672–1719), writer and Whig politician. He contributed to the *Tatler*, and was co-founder with Steele of the *Spectator.*

Adelard of Bath (*c.* 1090–*c.* 1150), English mathematician who translated into Latin the *Arithmetic* of Al-Kwarizmi and so introduced the Arabic numerals to the West (*see* **L8–9**).

Adenauer, Konrad (1876–1967), chancellor of the West German Federal Republic, 1949–63; founder and chairman of the Christian Democratic Party, 1945–66. To a defeated Germany he gave stable constitutional government and a place in the Western alliance. He promoted reconciliation with France but resisted accom-modation with Russia.

Adler, Alfred (1870–1937), Austrian psychiatrist, founder of the school of individual psychology. An earlier pupil of Freud, he broke away in 1911, rejecting the emphasis on sex, regarding man's main problem as a struggle for power to com-pensate for feelings of inferiority. *See* **Adlerian psychology, Section J.**

Adrian, 1st Baron (Edgar Douglas Adrian) (1889–1977), English physiologist. He shared with Sherrington the 1932 Nobel Prize for medicine for work on the electrical nature of the nerve impulse. O.M. 1942.

Adrian IV (Nicholas Breakspear) (d. 1159), pope 1154–59, the only English pope, b. near St. Albans. He crowned Frederick Barbarossa Holy Roman Emperor. Granted overlordship of Ireland to Henry II.

Aeschylus (524–456 B.C.), founder of Greek tragic drama. Of the many plays he wrote, only seven have come down to us, including *The Seven against Thebes, Prometheus Bound,* and a trilogy on Orestes.

Aesop (? 6th cent. B.C.), semi-legendary fabulist, originally a slave. The fables attributed to him probably have many origins.

Agassiz, Louis (1807–73), Swiss-American em-bryologist, author of *Lectures on Comparative Embryology,* intended for laymen, *Researches on Fossil Fishes,* and *Studies on Glaciers.* He was an opponent of Darwinian evolution.

Agricola, Gnaeus Julius (37–93), Roman governor of Britain, who subdued the country except for the Scottish highlands. His son-in-law Tacitus wrote his life.

Agrippa, Marcus Vipsanius (63–12 B.C.), Roman general.

Ahmad Khan, Sir Syed (1817–98), Indian educationist and social reformer who founded what is now the Aligarh Muslim University.

Airy, Sir George Biddell (1801–92), English mathematician who was astronomer royal for over 40 years, 1835–81. He set up a magnetic observatory at Greenwich.

Akbar, Jalal-ud-din Mohammed (1542–1605), Mogul emperor of India, son of Humayun. He extended the imperial power over much of India, stabilised the administration, promoted commerce and learning; and, though a Muslim, respected Hindu culture and tolerated Christian missions. His reign saw a flowering of culture.

Akhenaten, the name adopted by the heretic pharaoh **Amenhotep IV** (d. 1338 B.C.), who in-troduced a short-lived but influential religious and artistic reformation. He sought to convert his people from their polytheistic beliefs to a more compassionate religion based on the one supreme sun-god Aten (hence his name). His pacifism caused the temporary loss of most of Egypt's overseas territories. His wife was Nefertiti and he was succeeded by Tutankha-men, who gave in to the conservative forces of the priesthood.

Alanbrooke, 1st Viscount (Alan Francis Brooke) (1883–1963), British field-marshal; chief of the imperial general staff 1941–46. Sir Arthur Bryant's *The Turn of the Tide* and *Triumph in the West* are based on his war diaries.

Alarcón, Pedro Antonio de (1833–91), Spanish novelist. His short story, *El Sombrero de tres picos* (The Three-Cornered Hat) became the subject of Falla's ballet and of Hugo Wolf's opera *Der Corregidor.*

Alaric I (376–410), Visigothic chief who, as first auxiliary to the Roman emperor Theodosius, later attacked the empire, sacking Rome in 410.

Alban, St. (d. *c.* 303), proto-martyr of Britain, con-verted by a priest to whom he had given shelter. He suffered under Diocletian at Verulam (now St. Albans), where in the 8th cent. King Offa of Mercia founded the abbey of that name.

Albert, Prince Consort (1819–61), son of the Duke of Saxe-Coburg-Gotha, married Queen Victoria in 1840. He helped the queen with political duties, projected the international exhibition of 1851, and in 1861 in a dispute with the United States advised a conciliatory attitude which averted war. He died of typhoid fever and is commemorated by the Albert Memorial in Kensington Gardens.

Albertus Magnus (Albert the Great) (1206–80), Dominican scholastic philosopher, b. Swabia. His interest in nature as an independent obser-ver marked the awakening of the scientific spirit. Among his pupils was Thomas Aquinas.

Albright, Madeleine (b. 1937) American diplomat. Nominated first woman Secretary of State by President Clinton in December 1996. Born in Czechoslovakia, she served as US Ambassador to the United Nations, 1992–96.

Alcibiades (*c.* 450–404 B.C.), Athenian general and statesman. Pupil and friend of Socrates, he was an egoist whose career brought Athens disaster. He was murdered in Phrygia.

Alcott, Louisa May (1832–88), American author of

books for girls, notably *Little Women*.

Alcuin (735–804), English scholar, who settled on the Continent and helped Charlemagne with the promotion of education.

Aldred (d. 1069), Saxon archbishop of York who crowned William the Conqueror.

Aldrich, Henry (1647–1710), English composer of church music, theologian and architect. He designed Peckwater quadrangle at Christ Church, the chapel of Trinity College, and All Saints' Church, Oxford, and wrote the "Bonny Christ Church bells."

Alekhine, Alexander (1892–1946), world chess champion, 1927–35, 1937–46. He was born in Moscow but later became a French citizen.

Alembert, Jean le Rond d' (1717–83), French mathematician and philosopher, one of the encyclopaedists.

Alexander of Tunis, Earl (Harold Leofric George Alexander) (1891–1969), British field-marshal, b. Ireland. Directed retreat at Dunkirk 1940, and Burma 1942; C.-in-C. Allied Armies in Italy 1943–4; Supreme Allied Commander, Mediterranean 1944–5, Governor-general of Canada 1946–52.

Alexander II (1818–81), reforming Tsar of Russia, succeeded his father Nicholas in 1855. In 1861 he emancipated the serfs and in 1865 established provincial elective assemblies. Later his government became reactionary; he was assassinated by Nihilists; the pogroms followed.

Alexander the Great (356–323 B.C.), Greek conqueror. Educated by Aristotle, he succeeded his father Philip as king of Macedon in 336 B.C. He led the Greek states against Persia; and, crossing the Hellespont, he defeated Darius and sacked Persepolis. He captured Egypt and founded Alexandria. He penetrated to India. D. at Babylon.

Alexandra, Queen (1844–1925), daughter of Christian IX of Denmark, married the Prince of Wales (afterwards Edward VII) 1863.

Alfieri, Vittorio, Count (1749–1803), Italian poet and dramatist.

Alfonso the Wise (1221–84), king of León and Castile, known for his code of laws and his planetary tables. He caused the first general history of Spain to be written. Dethroned 1282.

Alfred the Great (849–99), king of Wessex who became a national figure. From the outset he had to repel Danish invaders. After years of effort he won the battle of Ethandun (Edington), and subsequently, probably in 886, made peace with Guthrum, leaving to the Danes the north and east. He built ships, was an able administrator, and promoted education, his own translations from the Latin being part of the earliest English literature.

Al-Kwarizimi (fl. *c.* 830), Persian mathematician said to have given algebra its name.

Allenby, 1st Viscount (Edmund Henry Hynman Allenby) (1861–1936), British general. He served on the Western front 1914–16, commanded in Palestine 1917–18, capturing Jerusalem on 9 December 1917.

Allende, Salvador (1908–73), Chilean radical leader, a Marxist democrat, who won the presidency 1970. He tried to bring social reform by democratic means but met his death resisting the military coup in 1973.

Alleyn, Edward (1566–1626), great early actor and founder of Dulwich College and Alleyn's School.

Al-Mamun (813–33), caliph of Baghdad, son of Harun-al-Rashid. He built an observatory at Baghdad.

Ambedkar, Bhimrao Ramji (1893–1956), Indian politician. A leader of the Untouchables (and champion of the poor) who helped frame the constitution at independence.

Amis, Sir Kingsley (1922–95), novelist, poet and critic, whose first novel, *Lucky Jim* (1954), is a classic of English comic fiction. He won the Booker Prize for *The Old Devils* (1986). He was appointed CBE in 1981 and knighted in 1990. See **M16**.

Ampère, André Marie (1775–1836), French physicist who propounded the theory that magnetism is the result of molecular electric currents. The unit of electric current is named after him.

Amundsen, Roald (1872–1928), Norwegian explorer, the first to navigate the north-west passage and to reach the south pole. Sailing in the fishing smack *Gjoa*, he made the north-west

passage in 3 years, 1903–6, and in 1911 sailed to the Antarctic in the *Fram*, reaching the pole on 14 December 1911, a month before his English rival Scott. His attempt to rescue Nobile after his crash in the airship *Italia* cost him his life.

Anacreon (*c.* 569–475 B.C.), Greek lyric poet.

Anaxagoras (488–428 B.C.), Ionian philosopher who came to Athens 464 B.C. and inspired Pericles and the poet Euripides with his love of science. His rational theories outraged religious opinion.

Anaximander (611–547 B.C.), Miletan philosopher, pupil of Thales, the first among the Greeks to make geographical maps, and to speculate on the origin of the heavenly bodies. He introduced the sundial from Babylon or Egypt.

Anaximenes (b. *c.* 570 B.C.), the last of the Miletan school founded by Thales. For him the primal substance was air. He was the first to see the differences between substances in quantitative terms.

Andersen, Hans Christian (1805–75), Danish writer, especially of fairy tales such as *The Little Mermaid* and *The Ugly Duckling*.

Anderson, Elizabeth Garrett (1836–1917), one of the first English women to enter the medical profession. She practised in London for many years and later became mayor of Aldeburgh, her native town, the first woman to hold the office of mayor. Sister of **Millicent Garrett Fawcett**.

Andrea del Sarto (1487–1531), Italian painter, b. Florence, the son of a tailor. Known as the "faultless painter," his chief works are the frescoes of the Annunziata at Florence and his Holy Families. He died of the plague.

Andrée, Salomon August (1854–97), Swedish explorer who attempted in 1897 to reach the north pole by balloon. In 1930 a Norwegian scientific expedition discovered the remains of the Andrée expedition on White Island.

Andrew, St., one of the apostles of Jesus, brother of Simon Peter, whose festival is observed on 30 November. He became the patron saint of Scotland in the 8th cent.

Andrewes, Sir Christopher (1896–1988), British medical researcher. Prominent virologist. Helped discover the common cold virus.

Andropov, Yuri Vladimirovich (1914–84), Russian statesman. General Secretary of CPSU, 1982; State President, 1983–84.

Angelico, Fra (1387–1455), Italian painter. An exquisite colourist, Fra Giovanni (his Dominican name) painted especially religious frescoes, mainly at Florence and Rome.

Ångström, Anders Jöns (1814–74), Swedish physicist who studied heat, magnetism, and spectroscopy; hence the ångström unit used for measuring the wavelength of light.

Annan, Kofi (b. 1938) Ghanaian international civil servant. Special envoy to former Yugoslavia, 1995–96. Succeeded as Secretary-General of the United Nations, January 1997.

Anne, Queen (1665–1714), Queen of Gt. Britain and Ireland. A daughter of James II, she succeeded William III in 1702. The act of union with Scotland was passed in 1707. A well-intentioned woman without marked ability, she was influenced by favourites, at first by the Duchess of Marlborough, but in the main she was guided by Tory and high church principles (she established Queen Anne's Bounty to improve church finances). Her reign was notable for literary output (Swift, Pope, Addison, Steele, Defoe), developments in science (Newton), architecture (Wren, Vanbrugh), and for the Duke of Marlborough's victories in war.

Anning, Mary (1799–1847), pioneering palaeontologist who discovered some of the most important early dinosaur fossils.

Anouilh, Jean (1910–87), French dramatist, whose plays include *Eurydice, Antigone, The Lark, Becket* and *The Fighting Cock*.

Anselm, St. (1033–1109), Italian scholar who succeeded Lanfranc as archbishop of Canterbury.

Anson, 1st Baron (George Anson) (1697–1762), English admiral who sailed round the world 1740–44, his squadron being reduced during the voyage from seven ships to one.

Antoninus Pius (86–161), Roman emperor, successor of Hadrian. In his reign, which was peaceful, the Antonine wall between the Forth and the Clyde was built to protect Britain from northern attack.

Antonius Marcus (Mark Antony) (*c.* 83–30 B.C.), Roman triumvir. He supported Caesar, and after the latter's death was opposed by Brutus and

Cassius, and defeated by Octavian; committed suicide. His association with the Egyptian queen Cleopatra is the subject of Shakespeare's play.

Antony, St. (c. 251–356), early promoter of the monastic life. B. in Upper Egypt, he retired into the desert, where he was tempted, but attracted disciples and founded a monastery. Took part in the Council of Nicaea 325. (From his supposed help against erysipelas derives its name of St. Antony's fire.)

Apelles, 4th cent. B.C., Greek painter whose chief paintings, which have not survived, were of Alexander the Great holding a thunderbolt and of Aphrodite rising from the sea.

Apollinaire, Guillaume (Wilhelm Apollinaris Kostrowitzi) (1880–1918), French poet representative of the restless and experimental period in the arts before the first world war. He invented the term *surrealism* (*see* **Section L**).

Apollonius of Perga (fl. 220 B.C.), Greek mathematician of the Alexandrian school, remembered for his conic sections; introduced the terms *ellipse, parabola,* and *hyperbola.*

Apollonius Rhodius (fl. 250 B.C.), scholar and poet of Alexandria and Rhodes, librarian at Alexandria. His epic *Argonautica* is about the Argonaut heroes.

Appert, Nicholas (1752–1841), sometimes known as François Appert, invented the method of preserving animal and vegetable foods by means of hermetically sealed cans or tins, and paved the way for the creation of a vast world industry.

Appleton, Sir Edward Victor (1892–1965), English physicist, best known as the discoverer of the ionised region of the upper atmosphere which became known as the Appleton layer. His researches led to the development of radar. Nobel prizewinner 1947.

Aquinas, Thomas, St. (c. 1225–74), scholastic philosopher and Dominican friar of Italian birth, whose philosophico-theological system (called Thomism) is still accepted by Catholic ecclesiastics. He understood Aristotle well and interpreted his thought in accord with Christian teaching. His most important works are *Summa contra Gentiles* and *Summa theologica.*

Arafat, Yasser (b. 1929), The leader of the PLO (Palestine Liberation Organization). Shared Nobel Peace Prize for his efforts to secure agreement with Israel (*see* **Section C**). Elected President, Palestine National Council, January 1996.

Arago, Dominique François Jean (1786–1853), French astronomer and physicist, remembered for discoveries in electromagnetism and optics.

Archimedes (287–212 B.C.), Greek mathematician, b. Syracuse, son of an astronomer; remembered for his contributions to pure mathematics, mechanics, and hydrostatics, notably the Archimedean screw for raising water, the conception of specific gravity, the doctrine of levers, and the measurement of curved areas. Not less than his scientific knowledge was his practical skill. He was killed by the Romans in the siege of Syracuse.

Argand, Aimé (1755–1803), Swiss physician, inventor of the lamp bearing his name, which was the first to admit a current of air to increase the power of flame.

Ariosto, Ludovico (1474–1533), Italian poet, author of *Orlando Furioso.*

Aristides (d. c. 468 B.C.), Athenian general and statesman, called "the just"; fought at Marathon.

Aristippus (c. 435–356 B.C.), founder of the Cyrenaic school of philosophy. He taught that man should aim at pleasure, but held that the pleasant was identical with the good.

Aristophanes (c. 444–c. 385 B.C.), Greek dramatist and comic poet, who satirised Athenian life. Among his plays are *The Clouds* and *The Birds.*

Aristotle (384–322 B.C.), Greek philosopher, pupil of Plato, after whose death in 347 he left Athens to become tutor to the young prince Alexander of Macedon. Subsequently at Athens he established his famous school in the garden known as the *Lyceum*, where he lectured in the *peripatos* (cloister) which gave his school of philosophy its name *Peripatetic.* He took the whole field of knowledge as his subject, giving it unity, and providing a philosophy which long held its own.

Arkwright, Sir Richard (1732–92), English inventor. A native of Preston, and originally a barber, he experimented with cotton-spinning machines. His "water frame" (run by water power),

patented in 1769, was an early step in the industrial revolution. In 1790 he made use of Boulton and Watt's steam-engine.

Armstrong, Neil (b. 1930), US astronaut, the first man to set foot on the moon, 21 July 1969.

Arne, Thomas Augustine (1710–78), English composer, remembered for *Rule, Britannia!* (from a masque called *Alfred*), and for Shakespearean songs such as *Where the Bee Sucks.* He also wrote operas (women singers appeared in *Judith* in 1761) and oratorios.

Arnold, Thomas (1795–1842), English headmaster, whose influence at Rugby (1828–42) gave it a high position among public schools. His son, **Matthew** (1822–88) was a poet, literary and social critic, and schools inspector. One of his famous poems is "Dover Beach," and his influential books include *Culture and Anarchy* (1869).

Arrhenius, Svante August (1859–1927), Swedish chemist, a founder of modern physical chemistry. Received 1903 Nobel prize for the theory of electrolytic dissociation (ionisation).

Artaxerxes, the name borne by several ancient Persian kings. The first Artaxerxes, son of Xerxes, reigned 464–424 B.C.; he was succeeded by Darius II 424–404 B.C., who was followed by Artaxerxes II, who reigned until 358 B.C. Artaxerxes III, the last to bear the name, was a treacherous man and was poisoned in 338 B.C.

Arthur (c. 500), fabled Celtic warrior, whose feats, although referred to in passing in early Celtic writings, were first narrated in Geoffrey of Monmouth's *Historia* (c. 1135). In mediaeval times his legend developed an extensive literature, woven together by Sir Thomas Malory in his *Morte d'Arthur*, printed in 1485.

Arundel, Thomas (1353–1414), archbishop of Canterbury 1396, and for a time lord chancellor. An enemy of heresy, he persecuted the Lollards.

Ashdown, Paddy (b. 1941), Leader of the Social and Liberal Democrats, 1988–99. M.P. Yeovil, 1983–.

Asimov, Isaac (1920–92), Russian-born American scientist and author, whose works include *The Intelligent Man's Guide to Science*, 1960; *Asimov's Guide to the Bible*, 1969–70.

Aske, Robert, (c. 1500–37), leader of the Pilgrimage of Grace 1536, directed against the Henrician Reformation; executed 1537.

Asoka (c. 269–232 B.C.), Indian emperor and upholder of Buddhism. At first he expanded his empire by conquest, but on being converted to Buddhism rejected war and aimed at the good of his people. He sent Buddhist missionaries as far as Sri Lanka and Syria. Art flourished.

Asquith, Herbert Henry, 1st Earl of Oxford and Asquith (1852–1928), Liberal prime minister 1908–16, having previously served under Gladstone. His government enacted social reforms including old-age pensions (1908) and unemployment insurance (1911), but as a war minister he had to give way to Lloyd George. He resigned leadership of his party in 1926.

Asser, a Welsh monk of the 9th cent., traditionally author of a life of King Alfred.

Astor, John Jacob (1763–1848), founder of the millionaire family. A native of Heidelberg, went to America, making a fortune in fur.

Astor, Viscountess (Nancy Witcher Astor, *née* Langhorne) (1879–1964), the first woman M.P. to take her seat in the Commons. An American by birth, wife of the 2nd Viscount Astor.

Atatürk, Kemal (1881–1938), builder of modern Turkey. A fine soldier, he defended the Dardanelles against the British in 1915 and drove the Greeks out of Turkey in 1922. President of the Turkish Republic, and virtually dictator, 1923–38.

Athanasius, St. (296–373), upholder of the doctrine of the Trinity against Arius, who denied the divinity of Christ. He was bishop of Alexandria. He is not now thought the author of the creed which bears his name.

Athelstan (895–940), grandson of Alfred the Great, was crowned king of England in 925, and was the first ruler of all England.

Attenborough, Sir David (b. 1926), British traveller and zoologist. Commentator in TV series *Life on Earth* (1979) and *The Living Planet* (1983). His latest TV series, *The Life of Birds* (1998) received great acclaim. Created Companion of Honour (1996). His brother **Lord Attenborough** (b. 1923) is an actor, film producer and director.

Attila (406–53), invading king of the Huns from Asia. He defeated the Roman Emperor

Theodosius, and entered Gaul, but was defeated in 451 near Châlons-sur-Marne.

Attlee, 1st Earl (Clement Richard Attlee) (1883–1967), Labour prime minister 1945–51, having served as deputy to Churchill 1942–5. Called to the Bar in 1905, he lectured at the London School of Economics 1913–23, was mayor of Stepney 1919, and parliamentary leader of his party 1935–55. His government helped to create a welfare society and granted independence to India.

Auchinleck, Sir Claude John Eyre (1884–1981), British field-marshal; G.O.C. North Norway 1940; C.-in-C. India 1941, 1943–7; Middle East 1941–2.

Auden, Wystan Hugh (1907–73), poet, b. in England and naturalised an American. Succeeded C. Day Lewis as professor of poetry at Oxford 1956–61.

Auer, Leopold (1845–1930), Hungarian violinist and teacher; Mischa Elman and Jascha Heifetz were among his pupils.

Augustine of Canterbury, St. (d. c. 605), first archbishop of Canterbury. He was sent from Rome in 597 by Gregory the Great to convert the English peoples.

Augustus, Caius Octavianus (63 B.C.–A.D. 14), first Roman emperor. Great-nephew of Julius Caesar, he was for 12 years triumvir with Mark Antony and Lepidus; then reigned alone. His reign was notable for peace, and for writers like Horace and Virgil; hence Augustan age for a great period in literature (the title Augustus was given him by the Senate).

Aurelius, Marcus Antonius. See **Marcus Aurelius Antoninus.**

Auriol, Vincent (1884–1966), French politician. President of the Fourth Republic 1947–54.

Aurangzeb (1618–1707), Mogul emperor of India. Son of Shah Jehan, he obtained power by acting against his father and brothers. In his long reign the Mogul empire reached its fullest extent; but he estranged Hindus and Sikhs; and when he died his authority was in dispute and the Mogul empire broke up.

Austen, Jane (1775–1817), author of *Emma, Mansfield Park, Northanger Abbey, Persuasion, Pride and Prejudice,* and *Sense and Sensibility.* Though confining herself to the personal relations of the English middle classes, she combined artistry, accuracy, imaginative power, satiric humour, sense, and genuine feeling with the ability to create a range of living characters. She spent the first 25 years of her life at her father's Hampshire rectory. She was unmarried.

Austin, 1st Baron (Herbert Austin) (1886–1941), English motor manufacturer, pioneer of the small car—the 7-horsepower car—which he put on the market in 1921.

Avenzoar (Ibn Zuhr) (c. 1090–1162), Arab physician, b. Seville. His chief work was the *Tasir.*

Averroës (Ibn Rushd) (1126–98), Arab philosopher, b. Córdova. He believed in the eternity of the world (not as a single act of creation as demanded by the current theology of Islam, Christianity and Judaism, but as a continuous process) and in the eternity of a universal intelligence, indivisible but shared in by all. He expounded Aristotle to his countrymen, but his teaching was modified by Neoplatonism.

Avicenna (Ali ibn-Sina) (980–1037), Arab philosopher and physician, of Bukhara, whose influence was through his *Canon of Medicine,* in which he attempted to systematise all medical knowledge up to his time.

Avogadro, Amedeo (1776–1856), Italian physicist, remembered for his hypothesis, since known as Avogadro's Law, that equal volumes of gases under identical conditions of temperature and pressure contain the same number of molecules.

Avon, Earl of. See **Eden, Anthony.**

Awdry, Reverend Wilbert Vere (1911–97), Anglican clergyman whose *Thomas the Tank Engine* railway stories gave pleasure to millions.

Ayrton, William Edward (1847–1908), English electrical engineer, inventor of a number of electrical measuring instruments. His first wife, **Matilda Chaplin Ayrton** (1846–83), was one of the first woman doctors, and his second wife, **Hertha Ayrton** (1854–1923), became known for her scientific work on the electric arc and sand ripples and for her work for woman suffrage.

Ayub Khan, Mohammed (1907–74), Pakistani military leader; president of Pakistan, 1958–69.

Azikiwe, Nnamdi (1904–96), Nigerian statesman; president of Nigeria, 1963–6.

B

Babbage, Charles (1801–71), British mathematician. He designed an analytical engine, the forerunner of the modern digital computer.

Baber, Babar or Babur (Zahir ud-din Mohammed) (1483–1530), founder of the Mogul dynasty which ruled northern India for nearly three centuries; a descendant of Tamerlane.

Bach, Johann Sebastian (1685–1750), composer. B. at Eisenach, Germany, he was successively violinist, church organist, and chief court musician. It was as organist at the Thomaskirche, Leipzig, that he composed the St. Matthew and the St. John Passion and the B minor Mass. His work was in the school of the contrapuntal style (especially the fugue and the chorale); after his day it lost favour, but this century it has gained ground continually.

Bach, Carl Philipp Emanuel (1714–88), 3rd son of the above, and one of the first experimenters in the symphonic and sonata forms.

Backhaus, Wilhelm (1884–1969), German pianist, gifted in interpreting classical and romantic concertos.

Bacon, Francis, Lord Verulam (1561–1626), English philosopher. He threw over Aristotelian deductive logic for the inductive method (*see* Baconian method, **Section J**); remembered for the impulse his writings gave to the foundation of the Royal Society (c. 1662). His chief work is the *Novum Organum.* His career as statesman under Elizabeth and James I was brought to an end by charges of corruption.

Bacon, Francis (1909–92), Dublin-born artist. A realist who depicted the complexity of human emotions (*e.g.* his *Study after Velazquez* of 1953).

Bacon, Roger (c. 1219/20–94), founder of English philosophy, advocate of the value of observation and experiment in science. He first studied arts at Oxford but when he returned from lecturing in Paris he devoted himself to experimental science, especially alchemy and optics. He became a Franciscan friar in 1257.

Baden-Powell, 1st Baron (Robert Stephenson Smyth Baden-Powell) (1857–1941), founder of Boy Scouts (1908) and Girl Guides (1910) to promote good citizenship in the rising generation; Chief Scout of the World 1921–41. As a young cavalry officer in the South African war he defended Mafeking.

Baer, Karl Ernst von (1792–1876), German naturalist, b. Estonia, founder of the science of embryology. He discovered the mammalian ovum (1827). An opponent of Darwin's theory.

Baffin, William (1584–1622), British navigator and explorer who in 1616 discovered the bay which separates the north-east coast of Canada from Greenland, which bears his name.

Bagehot, Walter (1826–77), English economist and journalist, editor of *The Economist.* Among his works are *The English Constitution.*

Baird, John Logie (1888–1946), Scottish TV pioneer, inventor of the televisor and the noctovisor.

Baker, Sir Benjamin (1840 1907), English civil engineer. With Sir John Fowler he built the Forth bridge and the London Metropolitan railway. He designed the vessel which brought Cleopatra's Needle to London. In Egypt he was consulting engineer for the Aswan dam.

Baker, Sir Herbert (1862–1946), English architect. Designed the Bank of England, Rhodes House, Oxford, and, with Sir E. Lutyens, New Delhi.

Bakst, Léon (1868–1924), Russian painter who designed scenery and costumes for Diaghilev's ballets.

Baldwin of Bewdley, 1st Earl (Stanley Baldwin) (1867–1947), Conservative prime minister, 1923–4, 1924–9, and 1935–7. His handling of the crisis over Edward VIII's proposed marriage ended with the king's abdication.

Balfour, 1st Earl (Arthur James Balfour) (1848–1930), statesman and writer. He was Conservative prime minister 1902–5. As foreign secretary under Lloyd George, he was responsible for a declaration on Palestine.

Ball, John (d. 1381), English priest and a leader of the Peasants' Revolt, after which he was executed. The couplet *When Adam delved, and Eve span, Who was then the gentleman?* is attributed to him.

Balliol, John de (d. 1269), founder of Balliol College, Oxford; a regent for Scotland; sided with Henry III against his barons.

Balliol, John de (1249–1315), king of Scotland. Son of the above, he claimed the throne against Robert Bruce and was chosen by the arbitrator, Edward I of England, whose overlordship he acknowledged. Later, on renouncing homage, he was taken captive and d. in retirement. His son **Edward Balliol** (d. 1363) obtained the kingdom for a time, acknowledging Edward III of England and surrendering Lothian; but retired on an annuity, 1356.

Balzac, Honoré de (1799–1850), French novelist of wide influence, and author of over eighty novels to which he gave the covering title of *La Comédie Humaine*, depicting the appetites and passions of the new social class born of the revolution and Napoleon.

Bancroft, Sir Squire (1841–1926), Victorian actor-manager.

Banda, Hastings (1898–1997), brutal dictator of Malawi who steered his country to independence.

Bandaranaike, Solomon West Ridgway Dias (1899–1959), socialist prime minister of Ceylon from 1956 until his assassination. His widow, **Mrs Sirimavo Bandaranaike**, became the world's first woman premier, 1960–5, 1970–7 and again after 1994, while his daughter, Chandrika Bandaranaike Kumaratunga, (b. 1945) has been president of Sri Lanka since 1994.

Banks, Sir Joseph (1743–1820), an amateur scientist of wealth who accompanied Captain Cook on his expedition to the Pacific 1768–76.

Banting, Sir Frederick Grant (1891–1941), Canadian physician who with C. H. Best discovered insulin.

Bantock, Sir Granville (1868–1946), composer of songs, orchestral and choral music.

Barbarossa (Ital. = red beard), surname of two brothers who were Barbary pirates: **Uruz** (*c.* 1474–1518), was killed by Spaniards, and **Khaireddin** (*c.* 1483–1546) conquered Tunis for the Turks and died in Constantinople.

Barbirolli, Sir John (1899–1970), conductor of the Hallé Orchestra 1943–70; succeeded Toscanini as conductor of the New York Philharmonic Symphony Orchestra 1937–42.

Barbusse, Henri (1874–1935), French writer, author of the war novel *Le Feu*, which portrays in a starkly vivid way the experience of the common soldier.

Barham, Richard Harris (1788–1845), English humorist, author of *The Ingoldsby Legends*, written under his pen-name of Thomas Ingoldsby. His best-known poem is *The Jackdaw of Rheims*.

Barnard, Christiaan Neethling (b. 1922), South African surgeon who has pioneered heart transplant surgery. His first heart transplant was carried out at Groote Schuur Hospital, Cape Town, in 1967.

Barnardo, Thomas John (1845–1905), founder of homes for orphan-waifs; devoted himself to the protection and care of destitute children.

Barrie, Sir James Matthew (1860–1937), Scottish author and dramatist. His novels include *A Window in Thrums*. Among his plays are *Dear Brutus*, *The Admirable Crichton*, and *Peter Pan* which gained great popularity with children.

Barrow, Isaac (1630–77), divine and mathematician, tutor of Sir Isaac Newton.

Barry, Sir Charles (1795–1860), architect of the houses of parliament at Westminster. The details were contributed by his assistant A. W. Pugin.

Barth, Karl (1886–1968), Swiss theologian, described by the late Pope John as a Protestant St. Thomas Aquinas.

Bartók, Bela (1881–1945), Hungarian composer. From an early age he was deeply interested in folk-song which inspired his researches into Hungarian and Rumanian peasant music. He left for America in 1940, where he lived precariously and apparently unhappily until the end of the war made a return possible, regrettably too late. *See* Section E.

Bartolommeo, Fra (di Paolo) (1475–1517), Italian painter. At first influenced by Savonarola. Some of his best work is at Lucca.

Bartolozzi, Francesco (1725–1815), Italian en-

graver, who settled in England and became a founder-member of the Royal Academy; noted for his stipple engravings.

Bashkirtseva, Maria Konstantinovna (1859–84), a Russian girl, achieved eminence as a painter in Paris, author of a famous diary.

Bassi, Agostino (1773–1856), Italian amateur microscopist who first suggested that infectious diseases might be caused by the invasion of the body by micro-organisms.

Batten, Jean Gardiner (1909–82), New Zealand airwoman who flew solo from England to Australia in 1934.

Baudelaire, Charles Pierre (1821–67), French poet of originality and sensitivity, best known for his *Les Fleurs du Mal*. His life was darkened by poverty and ill-health. He was also a talented draughtsman.

Bax, Sir Arnold (1883–1953), composer and Master of the King's Musick 1942–52. One of his best-known works is the poem, *Tintagel* (1917).

Baxter, Richard (1615–91), noncomformist divine, b. Shropshire; author of many books on theology; imprisoned after the Restoration by Judge Jeffreys.

Bayard, Pierre de Terrail, Seigneur de (*c.* 1474–1524), French knight, known as the "chevalier sans peur et sans reproche." He fought in campaigns against Italy and fell at the battle of Romagnano.

Bayle, Pierre (1647–1706), French philosopher, author of the *Dictionnaire historique et critique* (1697). His sceptical views influenced Voltaire and the encyclopedists of the 18th cent.

Baylis, Lilian Mary (1874–1937), manager of the Old Vic from 1898 and of Sadler's Wells from 1931.

Beardsley, Aubrey Vincent (1872–98), black-and-white artist, who published much work, some of it controversial (as in the *Yellow Book*).

Beatles, The (Sir Paul McCartney (b. 1942), John Lennon (1940–80), George Harrison (b. 1943), Ringo Starr (b. 1940)), a Liverpool pop group whose highly original and melodic songs held the attention of youth all over the world, especially during the period 1963–5 when they were in their prime. They parted in 1971 and went their separate ways. Lennon was shot dead in New York in 1980.

Beatty, 1st Earl (David Beatty) (1871–1936), British admiral; succeeded Jellicoe as commander of the Grand Fleet 1916–19. Commanding the British battlecruisers, he fought the German fleet on 28 August 1914 in the Heligoland Bight, and on 31 May 1916 off Jutland.

Beaufort, Sir Francis (1774–1857), hydrographer of the navy, who introduced the wind scale (1805) which bears his name. *See* Section Z.

Beaumont, Francis (1584–1616), and **Fletcher, John** (1579–1625), joint authors of many plays, including *The Maid's Tragedy* and *Philaster*.

Beaverbrook, 1st Baron (William Maxwell Aitken) (1879–1964), British newspaper owner and politician, a Canadian by birth. He gave energetic service as minister of aircraft production 1940–1. He controlled the *Daily Express*, *Sunday Express*, and *Evening Standard*.

Becket, Thomas (1118?–70), saint and martyr. An able chancellor, 1155–62, on becoming archbishop of Canterbury he made the position of the church his first care; and, coming into conflict with Henry II, was murdered in Canterbury cathedral. His shrine became a place of pilgrimage.

Beckett, Samuel (1906–89), Anglo-Irish dramatist and novelist, b. Dublin. Plays include *Waiting for Godot*, *Endgame*, *Krapp's Last Tape*, *Happy Days*, *Not I*; novels include *The Nouvelles* (3 stories), the trilogy: *Molloy*, *Malone Dies*, *The Unnamable*, and *How It Is*. His work expresses man's isolation, bewilderment and suffering. Nobel Prize for Literature, 1969.

Becquerel, Antoine Henri (1852–1908), French physicist who in 1896 discovered radioactivity in uranium. Shared with the Curies the 1903 Nobel prize in physics.

Bede, the Venerable (673–735), English historian and scholar; lived at Jarrow. His chief work is his *Ecclesiastical History* to 731.

Beebe, (Charles) William (1877–1962), pioneer oceanographer and biologist. Co-inventor of the bathysphere.

Beecham, Sir Thomas (1879–1961), English conductor and impresario. Founded the London Philharmonic Orchestra in 1931; introduced into England the operas of Richard Strauss, Russian operas, and the Diaghilev ballet;

championed the music of Delius.

Beecher, Henry Ward (1813–87), American preacher whose church was at Brooklyn.

Beerbohm, Sir Max (1872–1956), critic and caricaturist, master of irony and satire. His works include *Zuleika Dobson* and *A Christmas Garland*, and he contributed to the *Saturday Review*.

Beethoven, Ludwig van (1770–1827), composer. B. at Bonn (his father being a tenor singer at the Elector's court), at 17 he went to Vienna, was recognised by Mozart, and eventually settled there; he never married; gradually he became deaf. In the development from simplicity to complexity of musical treatment, he stands midway between Mozart and Wagner; but in him were uniquely combined the power to feel and the mastery of musical resources necessary to express his feelings. Between the years 1805 and 1808 he composed some of his greatest works: the oratorio *Mount of Olives*, the opera *Fidelio*, and the *Pastoral* and *Eroica* symphonies besides a number of concertos, sonatas, and songs. The symphonies, nine in number, rank as the greatest ever written. *See* **Section E**.

Begin, Menachem (1913–92), b. Poland; active in Zionist movement since youth; leader of Israeli *Likud* party; prime minister 1977–83. Made peace with Egypt (1979) but failed to solve Palestinian problem; took Israel into war in Lebanon (1982) which led to the end of his premiership and to renewed conflict in that country.

Behring, Emil von (1854–1917), German bacteriologist, founder of the science of immunology. Nobel prizewinner 1901.

Behring, Vitus (1680–1741), Danish navigator who entered the Russian service and in 1728 discovered the strait which bears his name.

Belisarius (505–65), Roman general under Justinian who fought against the Vandals.

Bell, Alexander Graham (1847–1922), inventor, b. Edinburgh, emigrated to Canada in 1870, later becoming an American citizen. In 1876 he exhibited an invention which was developed into the telephone. He devoted attention to the education of deaf-mutes.

Bell, Gertrude Margaret Lowthian (1868–1926), the "uncrowned queen of Arabia," was a traveller in the Middle East; her knowledge aided Britain in the first world war.

Bellini, family of Venetian painters: **Jacopo** (*c.* 1400–70) and his two sons, **Gentile** (1429–1507), whose works include the *Adoration of the Magi* (National Gallery); and **Giovanni** (*c.* 1429–1516), brother-in-law of Mantegna, and teacher of Giorgione and Titian.

Belloc, Hilaire (1870–1953), versatile writer whose works include *The Bad Child's Book of Beasts*, *The Path to Rome*, *Hills and the Sea*, *Cautionary Tales*, and historical studies of Danton, Robespierre, and Richelieu. B. in France, he became a British subject in 1902.

Bellow, Saul (b. 1915), American novelist and short-story writer, author of *Adventures of Augie March*, *Henderson the Rain King*, *Herzog*, *Mr. Sammler's Planet* and *Humboldt's Gift*. Nobel prize 1976.

Belzoni, Giovanni Battista (1778–1823), Egyptologist. B. at Padua, he settled in England in 1803. His first interest was in hydraulics, and for this purpose he went to Egypt to Mehemet Ali. There he explored Thebes, Abu Simbel, and one of the pyramids, sending some sculptures to the British Museum.

Benavente y Martinez, Jacinto (1866–1954), Spanish dramatist, whose plays include *Los Intereses Creados* (Bonds of Interest). Nobel prizewinner 1922.

Benedict, St. (*c.* 480–*c.* 550), patriarch of western monasticism. B. at Nursia, and at first a hermit at Subiaco, he attracted numerous followers and grouped them in twelve monasteries. Later he went to Monte Cassino, where he formulated the Benedictine rule, of wide application in Western Christendom.

Benes, Eduard (1884–1948), Czechoslovak statesman; co-founder with Thomas Masaryk of the Czech Republic after the break-up of the Austro-Hungarian monarchy (1918).

Ben Gurion, David (1886–1973), Zionist leader. He helped organise the Jewish Legion in 1918, and was prominently connected with the Labour movement in Palestine in between the world wars. Prime minister of Israel 1948–63.

Bennett, (Enoch) Arnold (1867–1931), English author, who wrote of the pottery towns where he was brought up. His novels include *The Old Wives' Tale* and *Clayhanger*.

Bennett, James Gordon (1841–1918), proprietor of the *New York Herald*. He sent out Stanley on an expedition to find Livingstone.

Bennett, Sir William Sterndale (1816–75), English composer, pianist and teacher, best known for his oratorio *The Woman of Samaria*, songs and piano pieces. Founded the Bach Society.

Bentham, Jeremy (1748–1832), utilitarian philosopher and writer on jurisprudence. His main works are *Government* and *Principles of Morals and Legislation*.

Bentley, Richard (1662–1742), classical scholar who did pioneer work in textual criticism.

Benz, Karl (1844–1929), German engineer whose motor car produced in 1885 was one of the first to be driven by an internal combustion engine.

Beresford, 1st Viscount (William Carr Beresford) (1768–1854), British general. He fought under Wellington in the Peninsular War and reorganised the Portuguese army.

Berg, Alban (1885–1935), Austrian composer whose best-known work is the three-act opera *Wozzeck*, based upon a drama by Büchner, which has become a modern classic.

Bergson, Henri Louis (1859–1941), French philosopher, exponent of the theory of creative evolution and the life force. Nobel prizewinner 1927. *See* **Vitalism, Section J**.

Bériot, Charles Auguste de (1802–70), Belgian violinist, whose wife was the operatic contralto Malibran. His son, **Charles Wilfrid de Bériot** (1833–1914) was a pianist who taught Ravel.

Berkeley, George (1685–1753), idealist philosopher and critic of Locke. His spiritual outlook led him to believe that reality exists only in the eye of God, that it is undiscoverable by science, though it can be revealed by religion. His chief works are *A New Theory of Vision* (1709) and *Principles of Human Knowledge* (1710). Of Irish birth, he became bishop of Cloyne.

Berlin, Irving (1888–1989), American composer of popular songs, b. Russia; pioneer of both ragtime and jazz music.

Berlin, Sir Isaiah (1909–97), British philosopher, b. Riga; Chichele Prof. of Social and Political Theory at Oxford 1957–67. His works include *Karl Marx*, *The Hedgehog and the Fox*, and *The Age of Enlightenment*. O.M. (1971). One of the foremost liberal thinkers of the 20th century.

Berlioz, Hector (1803–69), composer. B. near Grenoble, the son of a doctor, his romantic sensibility, taste for the grand (as in his *Requiem*), and response to literary influence made him a prime figure in the French romantic movement. His works include the *Symphonie Fantastique*, and the operas *Benvenuto Cellini* and *Beatrice and Benedict*. *See* **Section E**.

Bernadotte, Count Folke (1895–1948), nephew of King Gustav of Sweden. U.N. mediator for Palestine 1947. Assassinated by Jewish terrorists.

Bernadotte, Jean Baptiste (1764–1844), a French commander who served under Napoleon, and in 1810 was chosen heir to the throne of Sweden. In 1818 he succeeded as Charles XIV.

Bernal, John Desmond (1901–71), physicist, b. Ireland. Prof. of Physics, Birkbeck College, Univ. of London, 1937–63, Prof of Crystallography, 1963–8. Author of *The Social Functions of Science*, *Science in History*, *The Origin of Life*. Lenin peace prize 1953.

Bernard, Claude (1813–78), French physiologist whose discoveries eventually paved the way for the work of Pavlov and Hopkins.

Bernard of Menthon (923–1008), patron saint of mountaineers. He founded Alpine hospices in the passes that bear his name.

Bernard, St. (1090–1153), abbot of Clairvaux, which became a chief centre of the Cistercian order. This order aimed at seclusion and austerity, and practised manual work. His writings had wide influence in Europe.

Bernhardt, Sarah (1844–1923), French tragedienne, b. Paris, daughter of Dutch jewess. She became a member of the Comédie Française after the siege of Paris. Her first performance in London was in 1879. Her successes included *Phèdre*, *La Dame aux Camélias*, *Fédora*, *Théodora*, and *La Tosca*.

Bernini, Gian Lorenzo (1598–1680), Italian baroque sculptor. Born Naples. Did much work in Rome, designing the piazza for St. Peters.

Bernstein, Leonard (1918–90), Popular American composer, conductor and pianist. His scores included *Candide* (1956) and *West Side Story* (1957).

Berthelot, Marcellin Pierre Eugène (1827–1907), French chemist and politician. The first to produce organic compounds synthetically.

Berzelius, Jöns Jakob (1779–1848), Swedish chemist, founder of electrochemical theory. His work was mainly concerned with the exact determination of atomic and molecular weights and he devised the system of chemical symbols in use today.

Bessemer, Sir Henry (1813–98), inventor of the process of converting cast-iron direct into steel. This revolutionised steel manufacture, reducing the cost of production and extending its use.

Best, Charles Herbert (1899–1978), Canadian physiologist, who with F. G. Banting discovered the use of insulin in the treatment of diabetes.

Betjeman, Sir John (1906–84), English poet, author and broadcaster; Poet Laureate, 1972–84.

Bevan, Aneurin (1897–1960), British socialist politician, architect of the National Health Service which came into operation in 1948.

Beveridge, 1st Baron (William Henry Beveridge) (1879–1963), British economist who drew up the Beveridge Plan (1942), which formed the basis of the present social security services.

Bevin, Ernest (1881–1951), British trade union leader, who later became a forceful foreign secretary. He was assistant general secretary of the Dockers Union (his masterly advocacy of the London dockers' case in 1920 earned him the title of "the dockers' K.C."), later general secretary of the Transport and General Workers Union; Minister of Labour 1940–5, and Foreign Secretary 1945–51.

Beyle, Marie Henri. *See* Stendhal.

Bhave, Vinova (1895–1982), Indian reformer, leader of the Sarvodaya movement. A follower of Gandhi, in 1951 he began a walking mission to persuade landlords to help landless peasants.

Bhutto, Benazir (b. 1953) Pakistani politician. *See* Section C.

Bichat, Marie François Xavier (1771–1802), French physiologist whose study of tissues founded modern histology. His theory was that life is "the sum of the forces that restrict death."

Biddle, John (1615–62), unitarian. He taught in Gloucester: was several times imprisoned for his controversial writings; and died of fever contracted in prison.

Binyon, Laurence (1869–1943), poet, art critic, and orientalist, who worked at the British Museum 1893–1933.

Birch, Samuel John Lamorna (1869–1955), English landscape painter in watercolour, known for his Cornish and Australian studies.

Birkbeck, George (1776–1841), founder of mechanics' institutes, first at Glasgow, later in London (the Birkbeck Institution developed into Birkbeck College, London University).

Birkenhead, 1st Earl of (Frederick Edwin Smith) (1872–1930), English lawyer and politician; lord chancellor 1919–22; secretary for India 1924–8.

Bishop, Sir Henry Rowley (1786–1855), English composer who wrote *Home, sweet Home.*

Bismarck, Otto Eduard Leopold von, Prince Bismarck, Duke of Lauenburg (1815–98), Prusso-German diplomat and statesman, chief architect of the German empire. He was of Junker family. As Prussian ambassador at St. Petersburg (1859–62) and at Paris (1862), he learned to assess the European situation. He was recalled to Berlin by the king to become chief Prussian minister; and when the house of representatives would not pass a military bill he closed the house. He used a dispute over Schleswig-Holstein to bring about the defeat of Austria at Königgratz in 1866; and he provoked the Franco-Prussian war of 1870–1 when France was defeated at Sedan. Germany then became united under the military leadership of Prussia, with the king as emperor, instead of by the slower processes of democracy. He presided over the Berlin Congress of European powers in 1878. In 1884 he began a colonial policy. His authoritarian system, in spite of its inherent defects, was at least based on cautious and accurate assessment of power politics. This factor was not understood by

William II, who succeeded as emperor in 1888, and dismissed the "iron chancellor" in 1890.

Bizet, Georges (1838–75), properly **Alexandre César Léopold**, French composer, chiefly remembered for his opera *Carmen.*

Björnson, Björnstjerne (1832–1910), Norwegian poet, dramatist and novelist. His work provides an image of Norwegian life from the period of the sagas (*Kong Sverre*) to contemporary problems (*Over Aevne*).

Black, Sir James (b. 1924), Eminent British scientist. Discovered life-saving drug used to prevent heart attacks. Awarded Nobel Prize for Medicine, 1988.

Black, Joseph (1728–90), Scottish chemist. A professor first at Glasgow, later at Edinburgh, he was the first to undertake a detailed study of a chemical reaction. He laid the foundation of the quantitative science of heat and his dis-covery of latent heat was applied by Watt in improving his steam-engine.

Blackett of Chelsea, Baron (Patrick Maynard Stuart Blackett) (1897–1974), British physicist whose work on nuclear and cosmic ray physics gained him a Nobel prize in 1948; author of *Military and Political Consequences of Atomic Energy* (1948), *Lectures on Rock Magnetism* (1956), *Studies of War* (1962). Pres. British Assoc. 1956; Pres. Royal Society 1966–70; O.M. 1967.

Blackmore, Richard Doddridge (1825–1900), English novelist and author of *Lorna Doone.*

Blackstone, Sir William (1723–80), English judge. His *Commentaries on the Laws of England* is a classic.

Blackwood, Algernon (1869–1951), English novelist and writer of short stories.

Blackwood, William (1776–1834), originator of *Blackwood's Magazine.*

Blair, Anthony Charles Lynton (b. 1953), Prime Minister since May 1997. Leader of the Labour Party since 1994 (following the death of John Smith). M.P. for Sedgefield, 1983–. His 'New Labour' won a landslide victory in the 1997 general election. He became the youngest Prime Minister since 1812. *See* **Section C.**

Blair, Robert (1699–1746), Scottish poet, author of *The Grave.*

Blake, Robert (1599–1657), Parliamentary general and an admiral in the Cromwellian navy in the Dutch and Spanish wars.

Blake, William (1757–1827), English poet, mystic, and artist, son of a hosier in Carnaby market, Soho. A solitary and deeply religious man, he had a hatred of materialism. He produced his own books, engraving on copper plates both the text of his poems and the illustrations. His *Book of Job* is a masterpiece in line-engraving in metal, his poems range from the mystical and almost incomprehensible to the delightfully simple *Songs of Innocence.* He has been called "the great teacher of the modern western world." His art is in many ways reminiscent of that of the Spanish painter Goya.

Blanqui, Louis Auguste (1805–81), French revolutionary leader, master of insurrection. He invented the term "dictatorship of the proletariat," and his social theories, stressing the class struggle, influenced Marx.

Blériot, Louis (1872–1936), French airman; the first to fly the English Channel from Calais to Dover, on 25 July 1909.

Bligh, William (1754–1817), sailor, b. Plymouth. He accompanied Cook 1772–4, and discovered bread-fruit; but was in 1789 cast adrift from *The Bounty* by his mutinous crew. As governor of New South Wales (1806) he fought to suppress the rum traffic.

Blind, Karl (1826–1907), German agitator, b. Mannheim. He was active in the German risings of 1848, and imprisoned; but escaped and settled in England, remaining in touch with men like Mazzini and Louis Blanc.

Bliss, Sir Arthur (1891–1975), English composer; succeeded Sir Arnold Bax as Master of the Queen's Musick 1953.

Bloch, Ernest (1880–1959), composer, whose music is characterised by Jewish and oriental themes. B. in Geneva, he became a naturalised American.

Blondin, Charles (1824–97), French rope performer, who crossed the Niagara Falls on a tight-rope.

Blücher, Gebhard Leberecht von (1742–1819), Prussian general. He fought against Napoleon, especially at Lützen and Leipzig; and he completed Wellington's victory at Waterloo by his timely arrival.

Blum, Léon (1872–1950), French statesman, leader of the French Socialist Party. His efforts strengthened the growth of the Popular Front and the campaign against appeasement of Hitler. He held office only briefly and was interned in Germany 1940–5.

Blumlein, Alan Dower (1903–42), British electronics engineer and inventor, chiefly remembered for his fundamental work on stereophony.

Blunden, Edmund Charles (1896–1974), English poet and critic; professor of poetry at Oxford 1966–8.

Blunt, Wilfrid Scawen (1840–1922), English poet and political writer who championed Egyptian, Indian, and Irish independence; imprisoned in 1888 for activities in the Irish Land League.

Blyton, Enid (1897–1968), enduringly popular writer of more than 700 children's books. A teacher in South London, she is perhaps best remembered for the 'Famous Five' books, the 'Secret Seven' adventures and, of course, Noddy.

Boadicea (Boudicca), queen of the Iceni in eastern Britain, who fought against the Roman invaders, but was defeated in A.D. 61 and killed herself. Archaeologists tentatively identified her palace at Gallows Hill, Thetford, Norfolk.

Boccaccio, Giovanni (1313–75), Italian author, father of the novel. He is chiefly known for his *Decameron* (set in the neighbourhood of Florence during the plague), and for his life of Dante.

Boccherini, Luigi (1743–1805), Italian cellist and composer of chamber music.

Bode, Johann Ehlert (1747–1826), German astronomer remembered for his theoretical calculation (known as Bode's law) of the proportionate distances of the planets from the sun.

Boethius (480–524), Roman scientific writer who translated the logical works of Aristotle and provided the dark ages with some elementary mathematical treatises.

Bohr, Niels Henrik David (1885–1962), Danish nuclear physicist whose researches into the structure of the atom gave him great authority in the world of theoretical physics. With Rutherford he applied the quantum theory to the study of atomic processes. Nobel prize 1922.

Boieldieu, François Adrien (1775–1834), French composer especially of operas, including *La Dame blanche*.

Boileau-Despréaux, Nicolas (1636–1711), French literary critic and poet, best known for his *Satires*.

Boito, Arrigo (1842–1918), Italian poet and composer; he wrote the libretti of *Otello* and *Falstaff* for Verdi.

Boleyn, Anne (1507–36), queen of Henry VIII and mother of Queen Elizabeth. She was maid-in-waiting to Catherine of Aragon and her successor when Catherine's marriage was annulled. She failed to produce a male heir and was beheaded on a charge of adultery.

Bolivar, Simón (1783–1830), South American revolutionary, called the Liberator, b. Carácas. He led independence movements in the northwest of South America against Spanish rule, aiming at a South American federation. He founded Grand Colombia (now Venezuela, Colombia, Panama, Ecuador). Revered as a Latin-American hero.

Bonaventura, St. (1221–74), Franciscan theologian, b. Orvieto. His mystical theory of knowledge was in the Augustinian tradition.

Bondfield, Margaret Grace (1873–1953), as minister of Labour, 1929–31, she was the first woman to enter the cabinet and become a privy councillor.

Bondi, Sir Hermann (b. 1919), British mathematician and astronomer, b. Vienna: chief scientist to Min. of Defence, 1971–7.

Bone, Sir Muirhead (1876–1953), architectural draughtsman and etcher, b. Glasgow; excelled in dry-point and drawings of intricate scaffolding; official war artist in both world wars.

Bonhoeffer, Dietrich (1906–45), German Lutheran theologian who opposed Hitler. Executed by Nazis, 1945.

Boniface, St. (680–754), apostle of Germany. B. at Crediton, Devon, his name being Wynfrith, he became a Benedictine monk, and went as missionary to Friesland, securing papal approval. He founded Fulda Abbey and became archbishop of Mainz, but was martyred.

Bonnard, Pierre (1867–1947), French painter of landscapes, still life, and nudes.

Booth, Edwin Thomas (1833–93), American Shakespearean actor, brother of John Wilkes Booth who assassinated President Lincoln.

Booth, William (1829–1912), founder and first general of the Salvation Army, b. Nottingham. In 1865, with the help of his wife, Catherine Booth, he began mission work in the East End of London, which led to the creation in 1878 of the Salvation Army on military lines. It developed branches in many parts of the world. His son **Bramwell** (d. 1929) and his daughter **Evangeline** were among his successors. *See also* Salvation Army, Section J.

Boothroyd, Betty, *see* D16.

Borges, Jorge Luis (1899–1986), Argentine poet, critic, and short story writer. Some of his work has been translated into English, including *A Personal Anthology* and *Labyrinths.*

Borgia, Caesar (1476–1507), Italian general. The son of Pope Alexander VI, at 17 he was suspected of murdering his brother. He became captain-general of the church, and made himself master of Romagna, the Marches, and Umbria. Banished by Pope Julius II he met his death fighting in Spain.

Borlaug, Norman Ernest (b. 1914), American wheat scientist, responsible for the "green revolution" which transformed agriculture in less-developed countries. Awarded Nobel prize for peace 1970.

Borodin, Alexander Porfyrievich (1833–87), Russian composer who taught chemistry and founded a school of medicine for women. In a busy professional life he wrote two symphonies, two string quartets, the symphonic sketch *In the Steppes of Central Asia* and the opera *Prince Igor. See* Section E.

Borrow, George Henry (1803–81), English author, for many years agent for the British and Foreign Bible Society; he studied gypsy life and wrote of his experiences in *Lavengro, Romany Rye, Bible in Spain.*

Bose, Subhas Chandra (1897–1945), Indian nationalist leader; organised anti-British Indian National Army; killed in a plane crash.

Boswell, James (1740–95), Scottish author of *The Life of Dr. Johnson,* with whom he spent some years in intimacy. His own published journals and letters form an extensive literary collection.

Botha, Louis (1862–1919), South African soldier and statesman. In command of Transvaal forces 1899–1902 in the Boer war. Prime minister of the Transvaal in 1907, and first premier of the Union of South Africa in 1910.

Bottesini, Giovanni (1821–89), Italian double-bass player.

Botticelli, Sandro (c. 1445–1510), Italian painter. He worked under Fra Lippo Lippi, and was influenced by Savonarola. His art is delicate and poetic. His *Birth of Venus* is in the Uffizi Gallery, Florence, and his *Mars and Venus* in the National Gallery. He illustrated Dante's *Inferno.*

Bottomley, Horatio (1860–1933), English politician, journalist, and notorious financier, who died in poverty after imprisonment for fraud.

Botvinnik, Mikhail (1911–95), Russian chess player: world champion 1948–57, 1958–60, 1961–3.

Boughton, Rutland (1878–1960), English composer of the opera *The Immortal Hour,* and writer on the history and philosophy of music.

Boult, Sir Adrian (1889–1983), famous conductor of the London Philharmonic Orchestra 1950–7, and of the BBC Symphony Orchestra 1930–50. Musical Director BBC 1930–42.

Boulton, Matthew (1728–1809), engineer who in partnership with James Watt manufactured steam-engines at his Soho works near Birmingham. He also minted a new copper coinage for Great Britain.

Bowdler, Thomas (1754–1825), issued for family reading expurgated editions of Shakespeare and Gibbon, hence the term "bowdlerise."

Boyce, William (1710–79), London organist and composer, who also collected the works of English church composers. He was master of the orchestra of George III.

Boyd Orr, 1st Baron (John Boyd Orr) (1880–1971), British physiologist and nutritional expert. Director-general World Food and Agriculture Organisation 1945–8. Nobel prize 1949.

Boyle, Robert (1627–91), English scientist who with Robert Hooke laid the foundations of the modern sciences of chemistry and physics. He established the law which states that the volume of a gas varies inversely as the pressure upon it, provided temperature is constant. His chief work is the *Sceptical Chymist* (1661).

Bradley, Omar Nelson (1893–1981), American general. In the second world war he commanded in Tunis, Sicily, and Normandy.

Bradman, Sir Donald George (b. 1908), Australian cricketer who captained Australia in test matches against England 1936–48. One of the greatest batsmen of all time.

Bragg, Sir William Henry (1862–1942), English physicist. He held the chair of physics at Adelaide, Leeds, and London, and was professor of chemistry at the Royal Institution 1923–42. Pres. Royal Society 1935–40.

Bragg, Sir William Lawrence (1890–1971), son of the above. He succeeded Rutherford at the Cavendish laboratory, Cambridge, 1938–53. Dir. Royal Institution 1954–66. Shared with his father the 1915 Nobel prize for their fundamental work on X-rays and crystal structure.

Brahe, Tycho (1546–1601), Danish astronomer. At his island observatory at Uraniborg, provided by his sovereign, he carried out systematic observations which enabled Kepler to work out his planetary laws.

Brahms, Johannes (1833–97), composer. B. in Hamburg (son of a double-bass player). He was a friend of the Schumanns. See **Section E.**

Braille, Louis (1809–52), French educationist, who, as teacher of the blind, perfected his system of reading and writing for the blind. As the result of an accident when he was three years old he was himself blind.

Bramah, Joseph (1749–1814), English inventor of the safety-lock and hydraulic press which bear his name. He also invented the modern water-closet (1778) and a machine for printing the serial numbers on bank-notes.

Brandes, Georg Morris Cohen (1842–1927), Danish literary critic who exerted a vitalising influence on literature and art.

Brandt, Willy (1913–92), first social democratic chancellor of the Federal Republic of Germany, 1969–74. His main achievements were the Moscow and Warsaw treaties (1972) the treaty between E. and W. Germany (1973) which recognised their sovereign existence and the Brandt Report setting out a world development programme. Resigned party leadership, 1987.

Brangwyn, Sir Frank (1867–1956), artist of Welsh extraction, b. Bruges; first worked for William Morris making cartoons for textiles; he excelled in murals and in etching.

Breakspear, Nicholas. See **Adrian IV.**

Brecht, Bertolt (1898–1956), German dramatist and poet, b. Augsburg, whose brilliant experimental theatre was characteristic of the period in Germany between the two world wars. A Marxist, he left Nazi Germany in 1933 and returned after the war to direct the Berliner Ensemble in E. Berlin and develop his influential techniques of production. His plays include *The Threepenny Opera* (with music by Kurt Weill), *Mother Courage* and *The Caucasian Chalk Circle.* He may be regarded as the most original and vigorous dramatist and producer of this century.

Brennan, Louis (1853–1932), inventor, b. Ireland. His inventions include a gyro-directed torpedo and a mono-rail locomotive.

Breton, André (1896–1966), French poet, founder of the surrealist literary movement in France and a close friend of Apollinaire.

Brewster, Sir David (1781–1868), Scottish physicist, noted for his research into the polarisation of light; invented the kaleidoscope. He helped to found the British Association for the Advancement of Science.

Brezhnev, Leonid Ilyich (1906–82), succeeded Khrushchev as First Secretary of the Soviet Communist Party in 1964. Under his leadership the Soviet Union achieved strategic parity with the United States, society became more stable, education and living standards steadily improved, though the economy was put under strain with expectations not matching performance.

Bridges, Robert (1844–1930), poet laureate 1913–30. His *Testament of Beauty* (1929) has been called "a compendium of the wisdom, learning and experience of an artistic spirit."

Bridgewater, 3rd Duke of (Francis Egerton) (1736–1803), founder of British inland navigation by

his canal, to the design of James Brindley (*q.v.*) from Manchester to his coal mines at Worsley, later extended to join the Mersey at Runcorn.

Bridie, James (pseudonym of Osborne Henry Mavor) (1888–1951), Scottish author and dramatist. The first of his many successful plays was *The Anatomist*, produced in 1931. Other plays include *Tobias and the Angel, Jonah and the Whale, Mr. Bolfrey, Dr. Angelus.*

Bright, Sir Charles Tilston (1832–88), English telegraph engineer who supervised the laying of the British telegraph network and the Atlantic cables (1856–8).

Bright, John (1811–89), radical Quaker statesman and orator, b. Rochdale; friend of Cobden, with whom he promoted the movement for free trade.

Brindley, James (1716–72), English canal builder, b. Derbyshire, of poor parents, apprenticed as a millwright. He was employed by the Duke of Bridgewater (*q.v.*) and designed and constructed the Bridgewater canal, carrying it over the R. Irwell by an aqueduct, the first of its kind. He also built the Grand Trunk canal linking the Mersey with the Trent.

Britten, Baron (Edward Benjamin Britten) (1913–76), English composer, closely associated with the Aldeburgh festival. O.M. 1965. See **Section E.**

Broca, Paul (1824–80), French pathologist, anthropologist and pioneer in neuro-surgery. He localised the seat of speech in the brain and originated methods for measuring brain and skull ratios.

Broch, Hermann (1886–1951), Austrian novelist, author of the trilogy *The Sleepwalkers.* Lived in USA after 1938.

Broglie, prominent family of Piedmontese origin; **Victor Maurice** (1647–1727), and **François Marie** (1671–1745) were marshals of France; **Louis Victor, Prince de Broglie** (1892–1987) received the Nobel prize for his work on quantum mechanics, and his brother **Maurice, Duc de Broglie** (1875–1960), also a physicist, is noted for his work on the ionisation of gases, radioactivity, and X-rays.

Brontë, Charlotte (1816–55), forceful novelist, daughter of an Anglican clergyman of Irish descent, incumbent of Haworth, Yorkshire. She published under a pseudonym *Jane Eyre*, which was at once successful and was followed by *Shirley* and *Villette.* Her sister **Emily** (1818–48) wrote poetry and also *Wuthering Heights*; and **Anne** (1820–49) wrote *Agnes Grey.*

Brooke, Rupert (1887–1915), English poet who died during the first world war, whose works, though few, showed promise and include the poems *Grantchester* and *The Soldier.*

Brougham and Vaux, 1st Baron (Henry Peter Brougham) (1778–1868), English legal reformer; advocate of Queen Caroline against George IV; helped to found London university.

Brown, Sir Arthur Whitten (1886–1948), together with Sir John Alcock (d. 1919) in 1919 made the first transatlantic flight, crossing from Newfoundland to Ireland in 16 hr. 12 min.

Brown, Gordon. See **D16.**

Brown, John (1800–59), American abolitionist. His action in inciting black slaves to rebel in 1859 led to the civil war. He was hanged after failing to hold the U.S. arsenal at Harper's Ferry which he had captured. Known as "Old Brown of Osawatomie" and regarded as a martyr.

Browne, Charles Farrer (1834–67), American humorist (used pseudonym Artemus Ward).

Browne, Hablot Knight (1815–82), English artist, the "Phiz" of many book illustrations, including many of Dickens's novels.

Browne, Sir Thomas (1605–82), author of *Religio Medici* and *Urne-Buriall*, was born in London and practised in Norwich as a physician.

Browning, Elizabeth Barrett (1806–61), English poet. Owing to an injury in childhood, she spent her youth lying on her back, but her meeting with Robert Browning, whom she married, brought a remarkable recovery. In her lifetime her works were more read than those of her husband. They include *Cry of the Children, Sonnets from the Portuguese*, and *Aurora Leigh.*

Browning, Robert (1812–89), English poet. Because of his involved style his reputation grew only slowly. In *Strafford* and *The Blot on the 'Scutcheon* he attempted drama also. He married Elizabeth Barrett and lived mainly abroad. His works include *Dramatis Personae* and *The Ring and The Book*.

Bruce, Robert (1274–1329), Scottish national leader against Edward I and Edward II of England. Crowned king in 1306. He defeated Edward II at Bannockburn in 1314.

Bruce, William Spiers (1867–1921), Scottish polar explorer who led the Scottish national antarctic expedition in the *Scotia* 1902–4 and set up a meteorological station on the South Orkneys.

Bruch, Max (1838–1920), German composer and conductor, best known for his G minor violin concerto.

Bruckner, Anton (1824–96), Austrian composer and organist. *See* Section E.

Brummell, George Bryan (1778–1840), "Beau Brummell," fashion leader and friend of the Prince Regent (George IV).

Brunel, Isambard Kingdom (1806–59), English civil engineer, son of **Sir Marc Isambard Brunel** (1769–1849), whom he assisted in building the Thames (Rotherhithe) tunnel. He was engineer of the Great Western Railway and built the ocean liners, the *Great Western*, the *Great Britain* (brought back from the Falkland Is. to Bristol in 1970), and the *Great Eastern*. His other works include the Clifton suspension bridge over the R. Avon at Bristol and the Royal Albert bridge over the R. Tamar at Saltash.

Brunelleschi, Filippo (1377–1446), Italian architect, b. Florence; he adapted the ideals of the Roman period. His work in Florence includes the Pitti Palace, the churches of San Lorenzo and San Spirito, and the cathedral dome.

Bruno, Giordano (1548–1600), Italian philosopher. A Dominican friar, he came to favour the astronomical views of Copernicus and was burnt at the stake.

Bruno, St. (*c.* 1032–1101), German monk, founder in 1084 of the Carthusian order at La Grande Chartreuse in the French Alps.

Brutus, Marcus Junius (85–42 B.C.), conspirator against Julius Caesar; later committed suicide.

Buchanan, George (1506–82), Scottish humanist who spent most of his life in France lecturing and writing Latin poems, plays, and treatises.

Buchner, Eduard (1860–1917), German chemist, remembered for his work on the chemistry of fermentation. Nobel prizewinner 1907.

Büchner, Georg (1813–37), German dramatist. Dying at 24, his limited output (principally *Dantons Tod* and the fragment *Wozzeck*) is marked by power and maturity.

Buckle, Henry Thomas (1821–62), author of *The History of Civilisation in England*.

Buddha. *See* Gautama, Siddhartha.

Budge, Sir Ernest Alfred Wallis (1857–1934), archaeologist who conducted excavations in Mesopotamia and Egypt.

Buffon, Georges-Louis Leclerc, Comte de (1707–88), French naturalist, author of the *Histoire naturelle* (44 vols., 1749–1804).

Bulganin, Nikolai Alexandrovich (1895–1975), Soviet prime minister 1955–8; defence minister 1947–9, 1953–5. Retired 1960.

Bull, John (*c.* 1562–1628), English composer; possibly originator of *God save the Queen*.

Bülow, Hans Guido von (1830–94), German pianist and conductor. He married Liszt's daughter Cosima, who later left him to marry Wagner.

Bunsen, Robert Wilhelm (1811–99), German chemist, discoverer of the metals caesium and rubidium, and inventor of the Bunsen burner, battery, and pump. Made important observations in spectrum analysis.

Bunyan, John (1628–88), was originally a travelling tinker and is believed to have served in the Parliamentary army. He joined an Independent church in Bedford in 1655 and became a popular preacher. After the Restoration he was thrown into prison, and there wrote *The Pilgrim's Progress*. Of his 60 works, the best known after *Pilgrim's Progress* are *The Holy War*, *Grace Abounding*, and *Mr. Badman*.

Burckhardt, Jacob Christoph (1818–97), Swiss historian, author of *The Civilisation of the Renaissance in Italy*.

Burghley, 1st Baron (William Cecil) (1520–98), English statesman. After holding office under her two predecessors, he was Queen Elizabeth I's secretary of state, 1558–72, and lord high treasurer, 1572–98.

Burke, Edmund (1729–97), Whig writer and politi-

cal philosopher. B. in Dublin, he became secretary to Lord Rockingham and entered parliament in 1765. He advocated the emancipation (though not the independence) of the American colonies; and better administration in India; but was against the French revolution.

Burnett, Gilbert (1643–1715) bishop of Salisbury, b. Edinburgh. He wrote a *History of his Own Times*, which deals with many events of which he had personal knowledge.

Burnet, Sir John James (1859–1938), architect, b. Glasgow. The north front of the British Museum (King Edward's galleries) is his most important work in London.

Burney, Fanny (Madame D'Arblay) (1752–1840), originator of the simple novel of home life. Daughter of the organist, Dr. Burney, she published *Evelina* in 1778, and this brought her into court and literary society. She also wrote *Cecilia* and *Camilla*.

Burns, Robert (1759–96), Scottish poet. The son of a cottar, his first poems published in 1786 were at once successful, and he bought a farm. The farm failed, but he had a post as exciseman, and continued to write simply with tenderness and humour. Among his best-known songs are *Auld Lang Syne*, *Scots wa hae*, *Comin' through the rye*, and *The Banks of Doon*. *Auld Lang Syne* is sung all over the world at countless functions.

Burroughs, William (1914–97), novelist whose controversial work made him a cult figure.

Burton, Sir Richard Francis (1821–90), British explorer and orientalist, who made a pilgrimage to Mecca and Medina in 1853 disguised as a Moslem. He explored Central Africa and translated the *Arabian Nights* (16 vols.).

Burton, Robert (1577–1640), English cleric and scholar, author of *The Anatomy of Melancholy*.

Busby, Sir Matt (1909–94), legendary football manager who took Manchester United from tragedy to triumph.

Bush, George Herbert Walker (b. 1924). American politician. Vice-President of America, 1981–89. Elected 41st President, November 1988. Inaugurated, January 1989. First Vice-President to be elected President since Martin van Buren in 1836. His popularity soared in 1991 after the Gulf War, but quickly fell over domestic economic problems which contributed to his defeat in 1992.

Busoni, Ferruccio Benvenuto (1866–1920), pianist and composer of three operas (the last *Dr. Faust*, unfinished at his death), much orchestral and chamber music, and works for the piano. *See* Section E.

Butler, Joseph (1692–1752), English bishop, remembered for his *Analogy of Religion*, published in 1736 in reply to deistic attacks.

Butler, Nicholas Murray (1862–1947), American educationist who shared with the sociologist Jane Addams the 1931 Nobel peace prize.

Butler, Baron (Richard Austen Butler) (1902–82), Conservative M.P. for Saffron Walden 1929–65. Brought in Education Act 1944; helped secure Conservative acceptance of the welfare state; held high office 1951–64. "Butskellism" applied to Conservative social and economic policies of the '50s. Described as "the best prime minister we never had." Life peerage 1965.

Butler, Samuel (1612–80), English verse-satirist, author of the poem *Hudibras* against the Puritans.

Butler, Samuel (1835–1902), English novelist and satirist, author of *Erewhon* and its sequel *Erewhon Revisited*. Other works include *The Fair Haven*, *Life and Habit*, and *Evolution Old and New*, in which he attacked Darwinism. His autobiographical novel *The Way of All Flesh* and his *Notebooks* were published after his death.

Butt, Clara (1872–1936), English contralto; made her début in London in 1892.

Buxton, Sir Thomas Fowell (1786–1845), English social reformer; succeeded Wilberforce as leader of the anti-slavery group in parliament.

Buys Ballot, Christoph Henrich Diedrich (1817–90), Dutch meteorologist who formulated the law which bears his name (an observer with back to wind in northern hemisphere has lower pressure to left; in southern hemisphere to right).

Byrd, Richard Evelyn (1888–1957), American rear-admiral, explorer and aviator. He flew over the north pole, 1926; and in 1929 made the first flight over the south pole. He made other expeditions in 1925, 1933–5, 1939 and 1946.

Byrd, William (1543–1623), English composer of

church music, sacred choral music, string music, vocal and instrumental music; and a founder of the school of English madrigalists. He was organist of Lincoln cathedral at 20 and later of Queen Elizabeth's chapel royal. See **Section E.**

Byron, 6th Baron (George Gordon Byron) (1788–1824), English romantic poet who influenced European literature and thought. At 20 he published *Hours of Idleness*, which was violently attacked by the *Edinburgh Review*. This provoked his retaliatory *English Bards and Scotch Reviewers*, which caused a sensation. His *Childe Harold's Pilgrimage* appeared in 1812. His married life was unhappy. He went to help the Greeks in their struggle for independence and died at Missolonghi.

C

Cable, George Washington (1844–1925), American author and social critic, b. New Oreleans, whose writings reflect the colour problems of his day: *Ole Creol Days, The Silent South.*

Cabot, John (1425–c. 1500), Genoese explorer who settled in Bristol and sailed westwards under letters-patent from Henry VII of England in 1497. Discovered Newfoundland and Nova Scotia, believing them to be part of Asia, and may have reached the mainland of America before Columbus did. His son:

Cabot, Sebastian (1474–1557), was born in Venice, and in 1509 in search of a north-west passage to Asia sailed as far as Hudson Bay. Entered Spanish service in 1512, and spent several years exploring the Plate and Paraná rivers. Re-entered English service in 1548 and organised expedition to seek a north-east passage to India, which resulted in trade with Russia. English claim to North America is founded on the voyages of the Cabots.

Cabral, Pedro Alvarez (c. 1467–c. 1520), Portuguese navigator, friend of Vasco da Gama, discovered Brazil, which he named "Terra da Santa Cruz."

Cadbury, George (1839–1922), liberal Quaker philanthropist of Cadbury Bros., mainly responsible for the pioneer garden city of Bournville.

Cadogan, Sir Alexander (1884–1968), English diplomat. He helped to draft the charter of the United Nations organisation and became Gt. Britain's representative on the Security Council.

Caedmon, the first English Christian poet, lived in the 7th cent. and, according to Bede, was first a cowherd and later a monk at Whitby.

Caesar, Caius Julius (c. 101–44 B.C.), Roman general and writer. Under the declining republic, he was assigned in 61 the province of Gaul; in the course of pacifying it he invaded Britain (55 B.C.). Opposition in Rome to his career, mainly from Pompey, provoked him in 49 to the defiance of crossing the Rubicon with his army. He defeated Pompey, whom he pursued to Egypt, where he established Cleopatra as queen. At Rome he became dictator, and his reforms include the Julian calendar. He was murdered in 44. His career paved the way for Rome becoming an empire under his nephew Octavian.

Calderón de la Barca, Pedro (1600–81), Spanish dramatist, representative of contemporary Spanish thought, who also wrote court spectacles for Philip IV. Among his best-known works are *La Vida es Suenlt jo* and *El divino Orfeo.*

Callaghan, Lord (Sir James Callaghan) (b. 1912), Labour's fourth prime minister, 1976–9; parliamentary leader of the Labour Party, April 1976, following Sir Harold Wilson's resignation: elected for South Cardiff 1950–87; served as Chancellor of the Exchequer, Home Secretary, and Foreign Secretary in the Labour administrations, 1964–70, 1974–76. Succeeded by Foot as leader, 1980. Order of the Garter, 1987. His daughter, **Baroness Jay,** is a minister in the Labour Government.

Callas, Maria (1923–77). Born New York as Maria Kalogéropoulos. A great operatic singer.

Calvin, John (1509–64), French Protestant reformer and theologian. B. in Picardy, he broke with the Roman Catholic church about 1533, and subsequently settled in Geneva, where from 1541 he established a theocratic regime of strict morality. His theology was published in his *Institutes*; while, like Luther, he accepted justification by faith without works, he also

believed in predestination. His doctrines spread on the continent, in Scotland and to some extent in England. See **Section J.**

Camden, William (1551–1623), English antiquary and historian. His *Britannia* appeared in 1586.

Cameron, Sir David Young (1865–1945), Scottish etcher and landscape painter.

Cameron, Richard (1648–80), Scottish preacher who revolted in defence of the Solemn League and Covenant. Killed at Airds Moss (Ayrshire).

Cameron, Verney Lovett (1844–94), English explorer, the first to cross the African continent from east to west. He surveyed Lake Tanganyika. In 1872 went out to find Livingstone.

Camillus, Marcus Furius (4th cent. B.C.), Roman general. When the Gauls attacked in 387 B.C., he was made dictator and defeated them.

Camoltes, Luis Vaz de (1624–80), Portuguese poet, author of *Os Lusiadas*, an epic of Portuguese history and discovery.

Campbell, Colin, 1st Baron Clyde (1792–1863), Scottish general who was commander-in-chief in India during the Mutiny.

Campbell, Sir Malcolm (1885–1948), racing driver who held the land-speed record of 301 mile/h (1935) and water-speed record of 141·7 mile/h (1939). His son **Donald** held the water-speed record of 276·33 mile/h (1964); killed in 1967 at Coniston.

Campbell, Mrs. Patrick (Beatrice Stella Tanner) (1865–1940), English actress of beauty and wit, friend of G. B. Shaw.

Campbell, Thomas (1777–1844), Scottish poet, who at 22 published *The Pleasures of Hope*. His war poems include *Ye Mariners of England* and *The Battle of the Baltic*. He was one of the founders of University College, London.

Campbell-Bannerman, Sir Henry (1836–1908), Liberal statesman, prime minister 1905–8.

Camus, Albert (1913–60), French existentialist philosopher and writer, native of Algeria. Pre-occupied with the themes of the Stranger and the Absurd, the works for which he is particularly remembered are the philosophical essay *Le Mythe de Sisyphe*, the plays *Caligula* and *The Price of Justice*, and the novel *L'Etranger*. Nobel prize 1957. Killed in car crash.

Canaletto (**Antonio Canal**) (1697–1768), Italian artist. B. at Venice, he painted views of his city. From 1746 to 1756 he worked mainly in London. Some of his work is in the National Gallery, and there is a collection at Windsor.

Canning, George (1770–1827), English statesman. He was an advocate of Catholic emancipation, and was the first to recognise the free states of South America.

Cannizzaro, Stanislao (1826–1910), Italian chemist who carried forward the work of Avogadro in distinguishing between molecular and atomic weights.

Canova, Antonio (1757–1822), Italian sculptor. He infused grace into the classical style.

Canton, John (1718–72), English physicist and schoolmaster, the first to verify in England Franklin's experiments on the identity of lightning with electricity. He was the first to demonstrate that water is compressible and produced a new phosphorescent body (Canton's phosphorus) by calcining oyster shells with sulphur.

Canute (c. 994–1035), king of the English, Danes and Norwegians. The son of a Danish king, after some years of fighting he established himself as king of England and ruled with wisdom.

Capablanca, José Raoul (1888–1942), Cuban chess player, world champion from 1921 to 1927 when he was beaten by Alekhine.

Caractacus or **Caradoc,** a king in west Britain, who resisted the Romans in the first century. Captured, but freed by the emperor Claudius.

Carey, George Leonard (b. 1935), 103rd Archbishop of Canterbury, 1991–. Son of hospital porter. Bishop of Bath and Wells, 1987–91. He called in July 1996 for a national debate on current morality.

Carey, William (1761–1834), first Baptist missionary to India. Helped found Baptist Missionary Society (1792), whose bicentenary in 1992 celebrated the work of William Carey. An Oriental scholar, he published 24 translations of the scriptures as well as compiling Indian dictionaries.

Carissimi, Giacomo (1604–74), Italian composer, b. near Rome. He introduced more instrumental variety into the cantata and oratorio, and brought the recitative to perfection. His

Jephtha is still in print, and there are collections of his works at Paris and Oxford. *See* **Section E.**

Carlyle, Thomas (1795–1881), Scottish author. Of peasant stock, he went to Edinburgh university, but later lived mainly in England where he lectured. He married Jane Welsh. His individual views pervade his historical writing. His best-known works include *Sartor Resartus, Heroes and Hero Worship, Cromwell's Letters and Speeches,* and the *French Revolution.*

Carnegie, Andrew (1835–1919), philanthropist b. Dunfermline; emigrated to America 1848; after early struggles established the Carnegie iron works. He made munificent gifts to Free Libraries and other educational work.

Carnot, Lazare Nicolas Marguerite (1753–1823), French military engineer, prominent in the French revolutionary wars, 1792–1802. His son, **Sadi Carnot** (1796–1832), was a physicist and engineer who worked on the motive power of heat, establishing the principle that heat and work are reversible conditions.

Caroline, Queen (1768–1821), was married to George IV when he was Prince of Wales. They soon separated, but when he became king in 1820, she tried to assert her position. The question came before parliament. In spite of some public sympathy she was unsuccessful.

Carrel, Alexis (1873–1944), American surgeon who won the Nobel prize in 1912 for his success in suturing blood vessels in transfusion and in transplantation of organs. A Frenchman by birth, he returned to France in 1939.

Carroll, Lewis. *See* **Dodgson, Charles Lutwidge.**

Carson, Baron (Edward Henry Carson) (1854–1935), Irish barrister, solicitor-general for Ireland 1892; attorney general 1915; first lord of the admiralty 1916–17; member of the war cabinet 1917–18. He led a semi-militant organisation against Home Rule.

Carson, Rachel (1907–64), American biologist, remembered for *The Silent Spring.*

Carter, Howard (1873–1939), Egyptologist who was associated with Lord Carnarvon in discovering in 1922 the Tomb of Tutankhamun.

Carter, James Earl (b. 1924), American Democratic President 1977–81; former Governor of Georgia. His main achievements were the treaty between Israel and Egypt, the Panama Canal treaty, Salt II (though not ratified) and the settling of the release of American hostages held captive in Iran. More recently he has achieved successes as an international negotiator.

Cartier, Jacques (1494–1557), French navigator, b. St. Malo, who explored Canada, especially the gulf and river of St. Lawrence.

Cartwright, Edmund (1743–1823), English inventor of the power-loom, and also of a wool-combing machine, important steps in the weaving side of the textile revolution.

Cartwright, John (1740–1824), brother of the above; reformer and agitator against slavery.

Caruso, Enrico (1873–1921), Italian tenor, b. Naples.

Carver, George Washington (1864–1943), Black American agricultural chemist of world repute.

Casabianca, Louis de (c. 1752–98), captain of the French flagship *L'Orient* at the Battle of the Nile. He and his ten-year-old-son died together in the burning ship.

Casals, Pablo (1876–1973), Spanish cellist and conductor, son of an organist, b. Vendrell, Tarragona. He exiled himself from Spain in 1938.

Casanova de Seinfalt, Giacomo (1725–98), Italian scholar, diplomat and religious thinker whose reputation as a lover rests largely on his own heavily embroidered account.

Casement, Roger David (1864–1916), Irish nationalist. While in British consular service exposed abuses in Belgian Congo. Knighted 1911 (degraded 1916). Hanged after 1916 Easter Rising. His remains are in Glasnevin cemetary, Dublin.

Cassin, René (1887–1970), French jurist. Principal author, UN Declaration of Rights of Man. Nobel Peace Prize, 1968.

Cassini, French family of Italian origin, distinguished for work in astronomy and geography. Through four generations (1671–1793) they were heads of the Paris Observatory.

Cassius, Caius Longinus, Roman general who opposed the dictatorship of Julius Caesar, and took part in his murder. He died in 42 B.C. after being defeated by Mark Antony.

Castle, Baroness (Barbara Anne Castle) (b. 1910), Socialist politician who held high Cabinet office under Harold Wilson. As Transport Secretary (1965–68), she introduced the breath test. Later attempted to reform the trade unions with *In Place of Strife.* Campaigner for social justice.

Castlereagh, Viscount (Robert Stewart Castlereagh) (1769–1822), British minister of war and foreign secretary, who took a leading part in the Napoleonic wars. Committed suicide.

Castro, Fidel (b. 1927), Cuban revolutionary. After two unsuccessful attempts he succeeded in 1959 in overthrowing a police-state. He has initiated reforms in agriculture, industry, and education. His acceptance of Russian support led to the "missiles crisis" of 1962. The fall of Soviet communism has left his regime isolated.

Catherine, St. (4th cent.). Traditionally a virgin martyr in Alexandria, though not mentioned before the 10th cent. Legend represents her as tied to a wheel.

Catherine de' Medici (1519–89), Italian-born wife of Henry II and mother of three French kings (she was regent for Charles IX). Her antagonism to the Protestants may have led to the massacre of St. Bartholomew's day. She was able, and appreciated art and literature, but was unscrupulous and cruel.

Catherine of Aragon (1485–1536), first wife of Henry VIII of England, was daughter of Ferdinand and Isabella of Spain, and mother of Mary Tudor. After the Pope had refused to release Henry VIII from the marriage an English declaration of nullity was obtained (thus precipitating a movement towards the Reformation).

Catherine the Great (1729–96), Empress Catherine II of Russia. Daughter of a German prince, she married in 1745 the future Peter III, a weakling, later deposed and murdered. Intelligent, cultivated, autocratic, she proved a capable ruler for a time but was opposed by the landed interests and, despite plans for reform, her reign was marked by imperialist expansion and extension of serfdom.

Cato, Marcus Porcius (234–149 B.C.), Roman statesman and writer. His tenure of office as censor was characterised by austerity and conservatism. Advocated opposition to Carthage.

Catullus, Caius Valerius (c. 84–54 B.C.), Roman poet who wrote lyrics to Lesbia. His poems show sincere feeling and also Greek influence.

Cavell, Edith Louisa (1865–1915), English nurse who cared for friend and foe in Brussels in 1914–15, but was executed by the Germans for helping Allied fugitives to escape.

Cavendish, Henry (1731–1810), English scientist, a contemporary of Black, Priestley, Scheele, and Lavoisier, remembered for his investigations into the nature of gases. He discovered hydrogen and the chemical composition of water. The Cavendish Laboratory is named after him.

Cavour, Camilio Benso di (1810–61), Italian statesman, who, as premier of Sardinia, helped to bring about the unification of Italy.

Caxton, William (1422–91), the first English printer and publisher, a man of wide-ranging abilities. He probably learnt the art of printing at Cologne (1471–2), setting up his own printing press at Westminster (1476). He printed Chaucer's *Canterbury Tales,* Malory's *Le Morte d'Arthur* and Aesop's *Fables.*

Cecil of Chelwood, 1st Viscount (Robert Cecil) (1864–1958), English politician who helped draft the Charter of the League of Nations. Nobel prize for peace 1937.

Cecilia, St. (2nd or 3rd cent.), patron saint of music, often represented playing the organ.

Cellini, Benvenuto (1500–71), Italian sculptor and goldsmith. B. at Florence, he worked for some years in Rome. His bronze statue *Perseus with the head of Medusa* is at Florence. His life was adventurous and he wrote an *Autobiography* which is revealing of himself and his time.

Celsius, Anders (1701–44), Swedish physicist and astronomer. Invented centigrade thermometer.

Ceresole, Pierre (1879–1945), Swiss founder of International Voluntary Service. His pacifism led him to become a Quaker.

Cervantes, Saavedra Miguel de (1547–1616), Spanish novelist and dramatist, b. Alcalá de Henares. He was injured at the battle of Lepanto, and thereafter struggled to earn a livelihood from literature. His *Don Quixote* describes the adventures of a poor gentleman, con-fused in mind, who on his horse Rosinante with his squire Sancho Panza seeks adventures; it satirised chivalry, but is also a permanent criticism of life. Of his plays only two survive.

Cézanne, Paul (1839–1906), French painter, b. in Aix-en-Provence, the son of a wealthy banker and tradesman. He developed a highly original style, using colour and tone in such a way as to increase the impression of depth. He said that he wanted "to make of Impressionism something solid and durable, like the art of the Museums." Like Giotto, six hundred years before, he more than any other artist determined the course European painting was to take. *La Veille au Chapelet* and *Les Grandes Baigneuses* are in the National Gallery. He was a friend of Zola.

Chadwick, Sir Edwin (1800–90), English social re-former. Secretary of the Poor Law Board.

Chadwick, Sir James (1891–1974), English physicist, one of Rutherford's collaborators in the field of atomic research. Discovered the neutron in 1932, one of the main steps in the discovery of the fission process which led to the production of the atom bomb.

Chagall, Marc (1889–1985), Russian painter, b. at Vitebsk; the forerunner of surrealism.

Chamberlain, Joseph (1836–1914), English states-man. He began with municipal work in Birmingham. At first a Liberal under Glad-stone, he became Conservative. He opposed Home Rule for Ireland, and was the first ad-vocate of a partial return to protection.

Chamberlain, Neville (1869–1940), son of Joseph. He was prime minister 1937–40, when he ap-peased Hitler by the Munich agreement, 1938.

Chambers, Sir William (1726–96), British architect, b. Stockholm. He rebuilt Somerset House and designed the pagoda in Kew Gardens.

Champlain, Samuel de (1567–1635), French navi-gator who founded Quebec (1608), and discovered the lake known by his name.

Champollion, Jean François (1790–1832), French egyptologist, who found the key to the decipher-ment of hieroglyphics in the Rosetta stone (**L106**).

Chantrey, Sir Francis Legatt (1781–1841), English sculptor who left a fortune to the Royal Academy for the purchase of works of British art.

Chaplin, Sir Charles Spencer (1889–1977), first in-ternational screen star, with more than 50 years' achievement. B. in London, his mother was a music-hall singer and he made his début at five. In 1910 he went to the United States. *See* **Section W**.

Chapman, George (1559–1634), Elizabethan poet, dramatist, and translator of the *Iliad* and *Odys-sey*. His best-known play is *Bussy d'Ambois*.

Chapman, Sydney (1888–1970), English mathemati-cian and geophysicist, noted for his work on the kinetic theory of gases, geomagnetism, and solar and ionospheric physics. An upper layer of the atmosphere and a crater on the moon are named after him.

Charcot, Jean Baptiste (1867–1936), French ex-plorer, who in 1903–5 and 1908–10 commanded expeditions to the south polar regions. Charcot Island in the Antarctic is named after him.

Chardin, Jean Baptiste Siméon (1699–1779), French painter of still life and domestic scenes.

Chares (*c.* 300 B.C.), Greek worker in bronze from Rhodes, sculptor of the Colossus of Rhodes, one of the seven wonders of the world.

Charlemagne (742–814), Charles the Great. From being King of the Franks, he came to govern an empire comprising Gaul, Italy, and large parts of Spain and Germany, and was crowned Em-peror by the Pope in Rome on Christmas Day, A.D. 800. His revival of the Western Empire was the foundation of the Holy Roman Empirè (*q.v.*).

Charles, Jacques Alexandre César (1746–1823), French physicist, the first to use hydrogen gas in balloons and who anticipated Gay-Lussac's law on the expansion of gases.

Charles Edward (Stuart) (1720–88), the Young Pretender (*i.e.*, claimant of the English throne), grandson of James II, led an unsuccessful rising in 1745 and died in exile.

Charles (Philip Arthur George) (b. 1948), Prince of Wales, Duke of Cornwall and Rothesay, eldest son of Queen Elizabeth II; married Lady Diana Spencer, (*see* **B19**) daughter of 8th Earl Spencer, 1981. A decree nisi ending the marriage was granted on 15 July 1996. They had been separated officially since 1992. Their eldest son is Prince William (b. 1982).

Charles I (1600–49), King of England, Scotland, and Ireland, succeeded his father James I in 1625. Personally sincere, and having an appreciation of art, he was yet ill-fitted to cope with the political problems of his time. His marriage with the French princess Henrietta Maria was unpopular. He supported Arch-bishop Laud's strict Anglican-ism, and he also attempted to rule without parlia-ment. Defeated in the Civil War which broke out in 1642, he spun out negotiations for a settlement till he was beheaded in 1649.

Charles II (1630–85), King of England, Scotland, and Ireland, son of Charles I; after the Civil War escaped to France, and returned in 1660 when the monarchy was restored. His religious sympathies were Roman Catholic and his personal life was amorous; but in political matters he was shrewd and realistic, and contrived not to "go on his travels" again. He promoted the development of the navy, but had to accept the laws enforcing religious conformity imposed by parliament.

Charles V (1500–58), Hapsburg ruler, succeeded his grandfather, Maximilian I, as emperor of the Holy Roman Empire, and as heir to Ferdinand and Isa-bella succeeded to the Spanish crown. His rivalry with Francis I of France led to prolonged war. He crushed a revolt of peasants in 1525. He presided in 1521 at the Diet before which Luther appeared, after which religious struggle continued in Ger-many till the Augsburg settlement of 1555. In that year he retired to a monastery in Spain.

Charles XII of Sweden (1682–1718), a brave but rash and ambitious general. He repelled Russian attacks at Narva in 1700, but sub-sequntly pursuing military adventure he was defeated by Peter the Great at Poltava in 1709; and on invading Norway was killed.

Chateaubriand, François René, Vicomte de (1768–1848), French writer and diplomat. In a varied career he was at first an emigré, and later served as diplomat under both Napoleon and Louis XVIII. He was a friend of Mme. Recamier. His writings include *Mémoires d'outre-tombe*.

Chatham, 1st Earl of (William Pitt) (1708–78), English statesman and orator. His energetic con-duct of the Seven Years War was an important contribution to English victory and to acquisi-tions in Canada and India at the peace (1763), though by then he was out of office. In the dispute with the American colonies he upheld their right to resist imposed taxation, and collapsed while making a last speech on this dispute.

Chatterton, Thomas (1752–70), English poet who tried to pass off his writings as newly discovered ancient manuscripts. Killed himself at the age of 17.

Chaucer, Geoffrey (1340?–1400), English poet. His main work, *The Canterbury Tales*, gives a vivid picture of contemporary life.

Chaudhuri, Nirad Chandra (b. 1897), Indian author and broadcaster, who has been resident in England since 1970. His best-known book is *Autobiography of an Unknown Indian* (1951). His other works include *A Passage to England* (1959).

Chekhov, Anton (1860–1904), Russian dramatist and short-story writer, whose plays include *The Cherry Orchard*, *Uncle Vanya*, and *The Three Sisters*. His stories include *The Steppe*, *The Sleepyhead*, *The Post*, *The Student*, and *The Bishop*. He was of humble origin and while a student at Moscow supported his family by writing humorous sketches and tales.

Chernenko, Konstantin Ustinovich (1911–85) Soviet politician. Succeeded Andropov (*q.v.*) as General Secretary of the Communist Party, February 1984, but his ineffectual rule lasted a mere 13 months.

Cherubini, Luigi (1760–1842), Italian-born musi-cian, director of the Paris Conservatoire.

Cheshire, Lord (Group Captain Leonard Cheshire) (1917–92) War hero (most decorated World War II pilot) who founded the world-wide homes for the disabled.

Chesterfield, 4th Earl of (Philip Dormer Stanhope) (1694–1773), English statesman, whose *Letters* to his natural son, Philip Stanhope, are full of grace, wit, and worldly wisdom.

Chesterton, Gilbert Keith (1874–1936), English essayist, novelist and poet, who also wrote studies of Charles Dickens and Robert Browning. His works include *The Napoleon of Notting Hill* and *The Ballad of the White Horse*.

Chevalier, Albert (1861–1923), English music-hall comedian known for his coster sketches.

Chiang Kai-shek (1887–1975), Chinese general. He

at first fought for Sun Yat-sen. After the latter's death (1925), as commander of the Kuomintang army, he attempted to unite China; but he was more anxious to defeat the Communists than to repel the Japanese in Manchuria in 1931. In 1949 retreated to Taiwan (Formosa) after military defeat by the Communists.

Chichester, Sir Francis (1902–72), English seaman, who sailed his *Gipsy Moth IV* into Sydney harbour in 1966 after a 107-day voyage from Plymouth, and back again round the Horn.

Chippendale, Thomas (1718–79), designer of furniture, b. Otley, Yorks, son of a joiner. His designs are shown in *The Gentleman and Cabinet Maker's Director*, 1754.

Chirac, Jacques (b. 1932), French Gaullist politician, elected President of France, May 1995, Prime Minister, 1974–76 and 1986–88. *See* Section C.

Chirico, Giorgio de (1888–1978), painter associated with the surrealist school, born in Greece of Italian parents.

Chomsky, Noam (b. 1928), American theoretical linguist; inventor of transformational grammar.

Chopin, Frédéric François (1810–49). Polish pianist and composer, son of a French father and Polish mother. He has been called "the poet of the piano" because of the originality and delicacy of his playing. He enjoyed Paris intellectual and musical society, was a friend of George Sand, and played in numerous concerts all over Europe. He died of consumption. *See* Section E.

Chou En-lai (1898–1976), Chinese revolutionary statesman, administrator and diplomat. He organised revolt in Shanghai 1927, later formed close partnership with Mao Tse-tung, took part in the "long march" 1934–5, becoming prime minister of the new China in 1949.

Chrysostom, St. John (*c.* 347–407), preacher. Chrysostom means golden-mouthed. First at Antioch, and later as patriarch of Constantinople, he was an eloquent teacher; but by outspokenness he lost the Empress Eudoxia's favour and died from ill-treatment.

Churchill, Lord Randolph Henry Spencer (1849–95), Conservative politician, who held brief office only. He was father of Winston Churchill.

Churchill, Sir Winston Leonard Spencer (1874–1965), British statesman and author, son of the last-named. He entered parliament in 1900. He served as a junior officer with the British forces abroad; and during the Boer War he acted as war correspondent. He held the following ministerial posts; Under-Secretary for the Colonies 1905–8; President of the Board of Trade 1908–10; Home Secretary 1910–11; First Lord of the Admiralty 1911–15, 1939–40; Chancellor of the Duchy of Lancaster 1915; Minister of Munitions 1917; Minister of War 1918–21; Minister of Air 1919–21; Secretary of State for the Colonies 1921–2; Chancellor of the Exchequer 1924–9; Prime Minister and Minister of Defence 1940–5; Prime Minister 1951–5. Cast in the heroic mould, he lived a full life. His main achievement was as leader of the British people in the second world war. His writings include a biography of his ancestor, Marlborough, and histories of the first and second world wars. Hon. American citizenship conferred 1963.

Cibber, Colley (1671–1757), a London actor and dramatist. His best comedies are *The Careless Husband* and *Love's Last Shift*.

Cicero, Marcus Tullius (106–43 B.C.), Roman orator and philosopher, many of whose letters and speeches survive. He held political office but was killed by the troops of the triumvirate.

Cid (El Campeador) (*c.* 1035–99), name given to the Spanish knight Rodrigo Diaz, a soldier of fortune who fought against Moors and Christians alike. Myth made him a national hero.

Cierva, Juan de la (1895–1936), Spanish engineer who invented the autogiro.

Cimabue, Giovanni (Cenni di Pepo) (1240–1302), early Florentine painter. His only certain work is the St. John in Pisa cathedral.

Cimarosa, Domenico (1749–1801), Italian composer. His best-known opera is *Il Matrimonio Segreto*. He held revolutionary views.

Cimon (*c.* 512–449 B.C.), Athenian statesman and general, son of Miltiades. He defeated the Persian fleet at the mouth of the Eurymedon in 468. He worked for cooperation with other states, including Sparta.

Cipriani, Giambattista (1727–85), Italian painter of

historical subjects who worked in London; a founder member of the Royal Academy.

Clare, John (1793–1864), Northamptonshire labourer who became a poet. *Poems Descriptive of Rural Life and Scenery*, and *The Village Minstrel* were among his publications. He died in the county lunatic asylum.

Clarendon, 1st Earl of (Edward Hyde) (1609–74), English statesman and historian. He was chancellor to Charles II, and his daughter married the future James II, but he fell and died in exile. He wrote a *History of the Rebellion*.

Clark, Baron (Kenneth McKenzie Clark) (1903–83), English art historian. He was director of the National Gallery 1934–45, Slade professor of fine arts at Oxford 1946–50, and chairman of the Arts Council 1953–60. O.M. 1976.

Clarke, Sir Arthur C. (b. 1917), science fiction writer, author of *2001: A Space Odyssey* (1968) (with various sequels) and *The Garden of Rama* (1991).

Clarke, Kenneth, *see* D16.

Clarkson, Thomas (1760–1846) devoted his life to the abolition of slavery and shares with Wilberforce credit for the passing of the Act of 1807 abolishing the British slave trade.

Claude Lorrain (Gelée) (1600–82), French landscape painter. B. near Nancy, he settled in Rome. A close student of nature, he excelled in depicting sunrise or sunset.

Claudius (10 B.C.–A.D. 54), Roman emperor. After the murder of Caligula, he was proclaimed emperor almost accidentally by the Praetorian Guard. He was a sensible administrator. In his time the empire was extended to include Britain, Thrace, and Mauretania. He was probably poisoned by his wife Agrippina.

Clausewitz, Karl von (1780–1831), German military expert whose *Vom Kriege*, expounding his theories on war, dominated Prussia in the 19th cent.

Cleisthenes (6th cent. B.C.), Athenian constitutional reformer. Charged with redrawing the constitution of Athens after her occupation by Sparta in 510 B.C., he extended the work of Solon (*q.v.*). Henceforth all Athenians had equality of rights in the election of officials, regardless of wealth.

Clemenceau, Georges (1841–1929), French statesman of radical views; twice premier, 1906–9, 1917–20. He was a defender of Dreyfus.

Cleon (*c.* 495–429 B.C.) Athenian politician and demagogue, infamous for his extreme anti-Spartan position during the Peloponnesian War and his opposition to Pericles (*q.v.*).

Cleopatra (69–30 B.C.), daughter of Ptolemy XII, the seventh queen of Egypt by that name, a brilliant, ambitious woman. In 51 she became joint sovereign with her younger brother Ptolemy XIII. She was banished to Syria, but, obtaining the help of Caesar, regained the kingdom. She and Caesar became lovers, and in 47 she bore him a son Caesarion (later Ptolemy XV). After Caesar's murder she returned to Egypt. She met the triumvir Mark Antony and bore him twins; he deserted his wife and broke with his brother-in-law Octavian (later Augustus). Antony and Cleopatra were, however, defeated in 31 B.C.; Antony fell upon his sword, and Cleopatra killed herself with an asp bite. Her life inspired Shakespeare's *Antony and Cleopatra* and Shaw's *Caesar and Cleopatra*.

Clinton, Bill (William Jefferson) (b. 1946), 42nd President of the United States, defeating George Bush in November 1992. Inaugurated, January 1993. Born in Hope, Arkansas. A Rhodes Scholar at Oxford. Former Democrat governor of Arkansas. Became first Democrat since Roosevelt in 1936 to win reelection, but his second term beset by scandal allegations, leading to impeachment (which he survived). *See* Section C.

Clive, 1st Baron (Robert Clive) (1725–74), English general who helped to lay the foundations of English power in India. B. near Market Drayton, he entered the service of the East India Company. He contemplated suicide, but Anglo-French rivalry, culminating in the Seven Years War, gave scope for his military powers in the siege of Arcot and the battle of Plassey. As a governor he showed administrative capacity. His apparent suicide has been disputed by recent historians.

Clovis (*c.* 465–511), Merovingian king of the Franks and a convert to Christianity. He defeated the Burgundians and West Goths, and fixed his court at Paris.

Clyde, Lord. *See* Campbell, Colin.

Cobbett, William (1763–1835), English controversialist. He is known for his *Rural Rides*. Also published a weekly *Political Register* from 1802.

Cobden, Richard (1804–65), English advocate of free trade. The son of a Sussex farmer, he led agitation against the laws restricting import of corn, and they were repealed in 1846. He was impoverished by his public work and was helped by subscription.

Cochrane, Thomas, 10th Earl of Dundonald (1775–1860), British seaman, who crippled a French fleet in Biscay (1809), aided the liberation of Chile and Peru from Spanish rule (1819–22), of Brazil from Portuguese rule (1823–5), and assisted the Greeks in their struggle to throw off the Turkish yoke (1827).

Cockcroft, Sir John Douglas (1897–1967), Cambridge nuclear physicist who shared with E. T. S. Walton the 1951 Nobel prize. They had worked together at Cambridge in the historic "atom-splitting" experiments beginning with the transmutation of lithium into boron. He was directly involved in Britain's first nuclear power programmes.

Cockerell, Christopher (b. 1910), English inventor of the hovercraft, which works on the aircushioning principle. *See* Hovercraft, Section L.

Cocteau, Jean (1891–1963), French writer and artist in widely varied forms of art.

Cody, Samuel Franklin (1861–1913), American aviator, the first man to fly in Britain (1,390 ft. on 16 Oct. 1908). He became a British subject in 1909. Killed while flying.

Cody, William Frederick (1846–1917), American showman, known as "Buffalo Bill," whose Wild West Show toured America and Europe.

Coggan, Donald (b. 1909), 101st archbishop of Canterbury, 1975–80.

Cohn, Ferdinand Julius (1828–98), German botanist, founder of the science of bacteriology.

Coke, Sir Edward (1552–1634), English legal author, judge, and rival of Francis Bacon. His legal works are his *Reports* and *Institutes*.

Colbert, Jean Baptiste (1619–83), French statesman under Louis XIV, who fostered new industries, encouraged commerce, reformed the finances and established the navy on a sound basis. A patron of literature, science, and art.

Cole, George Douglas Howard (1889–1959), English economist and political journalist, professor of social and political theory at Oxford, 1944–57. Among his writings are *The Intelligent Man's Guide through World Chaos*, and *A History of Socialist Thought* (5 vols.).

Coleridge, Samuel Taylor (1772–1834), English poet, critic, and friend of Wordsworth, with whom he published *Lyrical Ballads*. His poems include *The Ancient Mariner*, *Christabel*, and *Kubla Khan*.

Coleridge-Taylor, Samuel (1875–1912), English composer, the son of a West African doctor practising in London and an Englishwoman. He is best known for his Hiawatha trilogy.

Colet, John (*c.* 1467–1519), English humanist and divine, founded St. Paul's School (1512). As scholar and friend of Erasmus he helped to bring the new learning to England.

Colette (Sidonie Gabrielle Claudine Colette) (1873–1954), French author of the *Claudine* stories, *Chéri* and *La Fin de Chéri*.

Collier, John (1850–1934), English painter noted for his "problem" pictures.

Collingwood, 1st Baron (Cuthbert Collingwood) (1750–1810), British admiral whose ship, the *Royal Sovereign*, led the fleet to battle at Trafalgar. On Nelson's death assumed command.

Collingwood, Robin George (1889–1943), English philosopher, historian, and archaeologist, associated with Oxford from 1908 to 1941. His philosophical thought is best studied in *Speculum Mentis*, *Essay on Philosophical Method*, *Idea of Nature*, and *Idea of History*.

Collins, Michael (1890–1922), Irish politician and Sinn Fein leader. He successfully organised guerrilla warfare, and mainly negotiated the treaty with Britain in 1921, but was killed in a Republican ambush on his return.

Collins, William (1788–1847), English landscape and figure painter.

Collins, William Wilkie (1824–89), son of the above; one of the first English novelists to deal with the detection of crime. *The Woman*

in White appeared in 1860.

Colt, Samuel (1814–62), of Hartford, Connecticut, invented the revolver in 1835. It was used in the war with Mexico.

Columba, St. (521–97), founder of the monastery of Iona, b. Ireland. From the island shrine he made missionary journeys to the Highlands of Scotland. The founder of Christianity in Scotland.

Columbanus, St. (*c.* 540–615), Irish abbot who founded a number of monasteries in continental Europe. *See* Monasticism, Section J.

Columbus, Christopher (*c.* 1451–1506), Italian navigator, b. Genoa, who, prevailing upon Ferdinand and Isabella of Spain to bear the expense of an expedition, in 1492 discovered the Bahamas, Cuba, and other West Indian islands. In 1498 he landed on the lowlands of S. America.

Comenius, John Amos (1592–1670), Czech educationist and pastor, advocate of the "direct" method of teaching languages, of the use of pictures in education, and of equality of educational opportunity for girls.

Compton, Arthur Holly (1892–1962), American physicist whose work on X-rays established what is known as the Compton effect (1923). While professor of physics at the university of Chicago (1923–45) he helped to develop the atomic bomb. Nobel prizewinner 1927.

Compton, Denis (1918–97), English cricketer. A postwar sporting idol and a most elegant batsman.

Compton, Karl Taylor (1887–1954), scientist-administrator, brother of the above.

Compton-Burnett, Dame Ivy (1884–1969), English novelist whose books deal with family relationships and include *Pastors and Masters*, *Men and Wives*, *A House and Its Head*, *Manservant and Maidservant*.

Comte, August (1798–1857), French philosopher, founder of positivism. *See* Positivism, Section J.

Condé, Louis, Prince de (1621–86), French general who defeated Spain at Rocroi in 1643.

Confucius or K'ung Fu-tse (*c.* 551–478 B.C.), the Chinese philosopher, founder of the system of cosmology, politics, and ethics known as Confucianism. *See* Confucianism, Section J.

Congreve, William (1670–1729). Restoration dramatist, whose witty plays include *The Way of the World* and *Love for Love*.

Conrad, Joseph (1857–1924), English novelist of Polish birth, whose parents were exiled to Russia for political reasons. He became master mariner in the British merchant service, and began to write novels after 1884. His novels include *Almayer's Folly*, *Lord Jim*, *Nostromo*.

Conscience, Hendrik Henri (1812–83), Flemish novelist who wrote *The Lion of Flanders*.

Constable, John (1776–1837), English landscape painter, b. East Bergholt, Suffolk. Unlike his contemporary Turner, who journeyed over the Continent with his sketchbook, he found his scenes within a few miles of his home. His work was more popular in France than in England at the time and affected the Barbizon school and Delacroix. Examples of his work are in the National Gallery (*The Hay Wain*, *Flatford Mill*, and *The Cornfield*), the Victoria and Albert, and the Tate (*The Valley Farm*).

Constant, Jean Joseph Benjamin (1845–1902), French painter of portraits and Oriental subjects.

Constantine (274–338), called "the Great," the first Christian Roman emperor. He was proclaimed at York by the army in 306. He stabilised the empire after a period of decline, and founded a new capital at Constantinople. A Christian council was held under his auspices at Nicaea in 325. Baptised on his death-bed.

Cook, James (1728–79), English navigator, son of an agricultural labourer. He entered the Royal Navy and gained a high reputation for his scientific skill. He made voyages of discovery to New Zealand and Australia in the ships under his command, *Endeavour*, *Resolution*, and *Adventure*. He anchored at Botany Bay in 1770 on his first voyage and gave it that name because of the interesting plants found on its shores. He also surveyed the Newfoundland coast. In an attempt to find the north-west passage he was murdered at Hawaii.

Cook, Robin. *See* D16.

Cook, Thomas (1808–92), pioneer of railway excursions and tourism. His first organised trip was from Leicester to Loughborough on 5 July 1841.

Cookson, Dame Catherine (1906–98), prolific authoress whose novels sold over 100 million copies. The illegitimate daughter of an alcoholic mother.

Cooper, Sir Astley Paston (1768–1841), English surgeon and author of medical textbooks.

Cooper, James Fenimore (1789–1851), American novelist, who produced stirring stories of adventure, among them *The Spy*, *The Last of the Mohicans*, *The Pathfinder*, and *The Deerslayer*.

Cooper, Samuel (1609–72), English miniaturist, represented with his brother Alexander (d. 1660) in the Victoria and Albert Museum. Among his miniatures is a portrait of Cromwell.

Copernicus, Nicolas (1478–1543), founder of modern astronomy, b. at Torun in Poland. He studied at Cracow and at a number of Italian universities before settling at Frauenburg in 1512 where he became canon of the cathedral. More of a student than a practical astronomer, he spent most of his private life seeking a new theory of the heavenly bodies. In his *On the Revolution of the Celestial Orbs*, he put forward the novel theory that the planets, including the earth, revolve round the sun.

Coppée, François Joachim (1842–1908), French poet, novelist and dramatist.

Coquelin, Benoît Constant (1841–1909), and **Coquelin, Ernest** (1848–1909), (Coquelin aîné et cadet), brothers, were leading lights of the French theatre.

Corelli, Arcangelo (1653–1713), Italian composer and violinist, who established the form of the concerto grosso. *See* Section E.

Corneille, Pierre (1606–84), French dramatist, who ranks with Racine as a master of classical tragedy. *Le Cid*, *Polyeucte*, and *Le Menteur* marked a new era in French dramatic production.

Cornwallis, 1st Marquess (Charles Cornwallis) (1738–1805), British general who commanded the British forces which surrendered to the Americans at Yorktown in 1781, thus ending the war of independence. He was twice governor-general of India.

Corot, Jean Baptiste (1796–1875), French landscape painter.

Correggio, Antonio Allegri da (1494–1534), Italian painter, b. Correggio. His style anticipates the baroque. His *Ecce Homo* is in the National Gallery.

Cortés, Hernando (1488–1547), Spanish adventurer, b. Medellin, Estremadura, who captured Mexico for Spain, crushing an ancient civilisation.

Coulton, George Gordon (1858–1947), scholar and historian of the Middle Ages. In his *Five Centuries of Religion* he sets forth his interpretation of monastic history in England.

Couperin, a family of French musicians who were organists at St. Gervais, Paris, from about 1650 till 1826. **François Couperin** (1668–1783), called "Couperin the Great," is the best known today for his harpsichord music.

Cousin, Victor (1792–1867), French educationist and philosopher, founder of the eclectic school.

Cousins, Samuel (1801–87), English mezzotint engraver of plates after Reynolds, Millais, Landseer, and Hogarth.

Cousteau, Jacques-Yves (1910–97), French underwater explorer, pioneer of aqualung diving. He opened up the oceans to exploration.

Couve de Murville, Maurice (b. 1907), French diplomat; de Gaulle's foreign minister 1958–68.

Coverdale, Miles (1488–1568), one of the early English reformers, b. Yorkshire, later to become bishop of Exeter. He assisted Tyndale in translating the Pentateuch and completed his own translation of the Bible in 1535. The Psalms still used in the Prayer Book and many of the phrases in the authorised version of 1611 are from his translation.

Coward, Sir Noël (1899–1973), British playwright, actor, director and composer. His first success (*The Young Idea*, 1923) was followed by a succession of witty plays and comedies. His popular songs included 'Mad Dogs and Englishmen'.

Cowdrey, Lord (Sir Colin Cowdrey) (b. 1932), English cricketer. Scored 42,719 runs in first-class cricket (and 107 centuries). First captained England, 1959. President of MCC, 1986–7.

Cowper, William (1731–1800), English religious poet. His work is characterised by simplicity and tenderness. His best-known poems are *John Gilpin* and *The Task*.

Cox, David (1783–1859), English landscape painter.

A collection of his works is in the Birmingham Gallery and the Tate Gallery.

Crabbe, George (1754–1832), English poet of grim humour; author of *The Village* and *The Borough*.

Craig, Edward Gordon (1872–1966), son of Ellen Terry, producer and author of books on stagecraft.

Cranmer, Thomas (1489–1556), archbishop of Canterbury under Henry VIII, and Edward VI; an ardent promoter of the Reformation. On Mary's accession he at first consented to return to the old faith, but when called upon to make public avowal of his recantation, refused, and was burnt at the stake. His contributions were the English Bible and Book of Common Prayer.

Crichton, James (1560–82), Scottish adventurer who for his scholarly accomplishments was called "the admirable Crichton." Killed in a brawl.

Crick, Francis Harry Compton (b. 1916), English molecular biologist. With James D. Watson discovered the structure of DNA (1953). Jointly (with Watson and Maurice H. Wilkins) awarded 1962 Nobel Prize for Medicine and Physiology. Author of *The Astonishing Hypothesis: the Scientific Search for the Soul* (1994).

Cripps, Sir Stafford (1889–1952), British Labour statesman. As chancellor of the exchequer in postwar Britain, his programme was one of austerity.

Crispi, Francesco (1819–1901), Italian statesman, who aided Garibaldi and was later premier.

Crispin, St. (c. 285), martyr with his brother. By tradition they were Roman and became shoemakers, hence patron saints of shoemaking.

Croce, Benedetto (1886–1952), Italian philosopher and critic. His philosophy is expounded in the four volumes of *Filosofia dello Spirito* (which has been translated into English). He founded and edited *La Critica* in 1908, a review of literature, history, and philosophy. He was strongly opposed to fascism.

Croesus (d. c. 546 B.C.), last king of Lydia, reputed to be of immense wealth. Conquered and condemned to death by Cyrus, he was reprieved when Cyrus heard him recall Solon's saying "Call no man happy till he is dead."

Crome, John (1769–1821), English landscape painter, b. Norwich.

Cromer, 1st Earl of (Evelyn Baring) (1841–1917), British diplomat who, as British comptroller-general in Egypt from 1883 to 1907, did much to maintain order, improve the finances and promote development.

Crompton, Samuel (1753–1827), English inventor of the spinning-mule (1779), which substituted machinery for hand work. He was b. near Bolton, a farmer's son, and benefited little by his invention.

Cromwell, Oliver (1599–1658), Protector of the commonwealth of England, Scotland, and Ireland. B. at Huntingdon, he represented Huntingdon in parliament. When civil war broke out, he served under the Earl of Essex; and then reorganised the parliamentary army, winning victories at Marston Moor and Naseby. Tortuous negotiations with Charles I could not be brought to an end, and he promoted the king's trial and execution in 1649. He defeated the Scots at Dunbar. When continued difficulties beset government he became Protector in 1653, but was soon obliged to govern by major-generals. His handling of Ireland enhanced the difficulties of that country. An able general and a strong character, he was personally tolerant (an Independent), sincere and devout; but he was in the revolutionary's dilemma—that there is no easy exit from a revolutionary situation.

Cromwell, Richard (1626–1712), son of the above, and his successor in the protectorate.

Cromwell, Thomas (1485–1540), English statesman, who succeeded Wolsey in the service of Henry VIII, and carried out the dissolution of the monasteries. Fell from favour and was executed.

Crookes, Sir William (1832–1919), English physicist who discovered the element thallium (1861) and invented the Crookes tube (1874) which was used by J. J. Thomson and others in their researches into the conduction of electricity in gases. He was also an authority on spiritualism.

Cruikshank, George (1792–1878), caricaturist and book illustrator, whose work includes illustrations to *Grimm's Fairy Tales*, and *Oliver Twist*.

Cuéllar, Javier Pérez de (b. 1920), Peruvian diplomat. UN Secretary-General, 1982–end of 1991. Succeeded in negotiating Iran-Iraq ceasefire

(1988) but failed to prevent Gulf War (1991).

Cummings, Bruce Frederick (1889–1919), English zoologist, better known however as the author of *Diary of a Disappointed Man* (1919) written under the pseudonym W. N. P. Barbellion.

Cunard, Sir Samuel (1787–1865), founder of the Cunard line of steam ships. He was born in Nova Scotia, of a Welsh family of Quakers.

Cunningham of Hyndhope, 1st Viscount (Andrew Browne Cunningham) (1883–1963). British admiral in two world wars, b. Edinburgh. He served as C.-in-C. Mediterranean, 1939–42 and Feb.–Oct. 1943; naval C.-in-C. for the assault on North Africa 1942; and first sea lord 1943–6.

Curie, Marie Sklodowska (1867–1934), first great woman scientist, b. Poland. Her father was a professor of physics at Warsaw. She came to Paris to study at the Sorbonne and married **Pierre Curie** (1859–1906), professor of physics. Thus began a fruitful collaborative career that led to the discovery of radium for which they shared the 1903 Nobel prize for physics. In 1911 Mme. Curie received the Nobel prize for chemistry. Pierre Curie was killed in an accident. *See also* Joliot-Curie.

Curzon of Kedleston, 1st Marquess (George Nathaniel Curzon) (1859–1925), statesman and administrator; viceroy of India 1898–1905; member of Lloyd George's war cabinet 1916–18; foreign secretary 1919–24.

Cuthbert, St. (*c.* 635–87), Celtic monk who became prior of Old Melrose (on the Tweed) and later of Lindisfarne. For a time he lived in seclusion on one of the Farne islands. The story of his life we owe to Bede.

Cuvier, Georges (1769–1832), French naturalist, noted for his system of classification of animals and his studies in comparative anatomy. His *La Règne Animal* (1819) became a standard work.

Cuyp, Albert (1620–91), Dutch landscape painter of sea and river views.

Cyprian, St. (d. 258), bishop of Carthage, and early Christian writer who was martyred.

Cyrus (559–529 B.C.), Persian emperor. He founded the Achaemenid line, having defeated the Medes. By conquering Lydia and Babylonia, he controlled Asia Minor. He was a wise ruler, allowing the Jews to rebuild their temple.

D

Daguerre, Louis Jacques Mandé (1789–1851), French photographic pioneer, who invented the daguerrotype process. *See* **Section L.**

Dahl, Roald (1916–90), British author of Norwegian parentage. He wrote macabre, ingenious stories, including those in *Kiss, Kiss* (1960), and highly popular books for children, such as *Charlie and the Chocolate Factory* (1964). Some of his stories were dramatised for the TV series, *Tales of the Unexpected.* Among popular recent film adaptations have been *James and the Giant Peach* and *Matilda.*

Daimler, Gottlieb (1834–1900), German inventor, with N. A. Otto of Cologne, of the Otto gas engine. The Mercédès car, exhibited at Paris in 1900, was named after the daughter of Emile Jellinek, Austrian banker and car enthusiast.

Dalai Lama, *see* Section L.

Dale, Sir Henry Hallett (1875–1968), English physiologist. He shared the 1936 Nobel prize for medicine for his work on the chemical transmission of nerve impulses.

Dalhousie, 1st Marquess of (James Andrew Broun Ramsay) (1812–60), governor-general of India. He annexed the Punjab, opened the civil service to Indians and acted against suttee.

Dalton, John (1766–1844), English chemist and mathematician, a Quaker teacher of Manchester. In 1808 in the first number of his *New System of Chemical Philosophy* (1808–27) the modern chemical atomic theory was first propounded by him. According to this the atoms of the chemical elements are qualitatively different from one another.

Damien, Father (1840–89), Belgian missionary priest, originally named Joseph de Veuster, who, witnessing the sufferings of the lepers confined on the Hawaiian island of Molokai, obtained permission to take charge, and remained there until he himself died of leprosy.

Damocles, 5th cent. B.C., Syracusan flatterer who pronounced the tyrant Dionysius the happiest of men. To illustrate the uncertainty of life, Dionysius invited him to a banquet, where a naked sword hung over his head by a hair. Hence the expression "Sword of Damocles" to mean impending danger or threat.

Damrosch, Walter Johannes (1862–1950), American conductor and composer, b. Breslau, Prussia. He promoted musical development in the U.S., when conductor of the New York Symphony Society which his father, Leopold Damrosch (1832–1885) had founded in 1878.

D'Annunzio, Gabriele (1863–1938), Italian poet, dramatist and nationalist. In 1919 he led a raid on Fiume and seized it, but was eventually forced to surrender. His bodyguard wore the black shirt, later the uniform of the Fascists.

Dante Alighieri (1265–1321), Italian poet, a figure of world literature. He was b. at Florence in a troubled period. Though he saw her but once or twice, he loved a lady whom he called Beatrice, who is believed to have been Bice Portinari who married Simone di Bardi; she died in 1290, after which Dante wrote his *Vita Nuova*. His next work *Convivio* was philosophical. He joined the party of the Bianchi, attained municipal office, but was imprisoned and in 1301 fled. His *Divina Commedia* is a description of hell, purgatory, and heaven, a work of moral edification, replete with symbolism. He d. at Ravenna.

Danton, Georges Jacques (1759–94), French revolutionary. To his eloquent lead in 1792 was largely due the defeat of the foreign forces attempting to quell the revolution. He was a member of the committee of public safety, and sought to modify the extremists, but was displaced by Robespierre and was executed.

D'Arblay. *See* Burney.

Darby, Abraham (1677–1717), member of the Quaker family of ironmasters of Coalbrookdale, Shropshire, who paved the way for the industrial revolution by developing iron metallurgy. His grandson **Abraham** (1750–91) built the first cast-iron bridge (1779) over the Severn at Coalbrookdale.

Darius I (548–486 B.C.), Persian king and founder of Persepolis. He extended the borders of the Persian empire beyond the Indus, and reorganised it into satrapies. He declared "God's plan for the earth is not turmoil but peace, prosperity and good government." On clashing with the Greeks, however, he was defeated at Marathon. **Darius II** was a natural son of Artaxerxes I and d. 405 B.C. **Darius III** (d. 331 B.C.) was the last of the Persian kings, and was defeated by Alexander and assassinated.

Darling, Grace Horsley (1815–42), English heroine who by putting off in a small boat from the lighthouse on one of the Farne islands, of which her father was keeper, saved the shipwrecked crew of the *Forfarshire.*

Darnley, Henry Stewart, Lord (1545–67), second husband of Mary, Queen of Scots (1565). He plotted the murder of her secretary Rizzio, and was subsequently himself murdered.

Darwin, Charles Robert (1809–82), English naturalist, b. Shrewsbury, one of the pioneers of experimental biology. After returning from his formative voyage round the world as naturalist on the *Beagle* (1831–6), he spent nearly twenty years building up evidence for his theory of evolution before publishing it in *The Origin of Species* (1859). In it he argued that the evolution of present-day morphology had been built up by the gradual and opportunistic mechanism of natural selection.

Daudet, Alphonse (1840–97), French writer who covered a wide range and whose works include *Lettres de mon Moulin, Robert Helmont,* and *Tartarin de Tarascon.*

David I (1084–1153), King of Scotland. As uncle of Matilda, daughter of Henry I of England, he supported her claim to the English crown, but was defeated. In Scotland he promoted unity.

David II (1324–71), King of Scotland. He was son of Robert Bruce. In invading England he was captured at Neville's Cross, 1346.

David, Sir Edgeworth (1848–1934), Australian geologist who accompanied Shackleton's antarctic expedition, 1907–9, leading the party that reached the south magnetic pole.

David, Jacques Louis (1748–1825), French painter of classical subjects and an ardent republican.

David, St., patron saint of Wales who lived in south Wales in the 6th cent.

Davidson, 1st Baron (Randall Thomas Davidson) (1848–1930), archbishop of Canterbury, 1903–28.

Davies, Sir Walford (1869–1941), English organist, composer, and broadcaster on music.

Davies, William Henry (1871–1940), Welsh poet. He spent some years tramping in both England and America, and his work shows knowledge of and love for nature. He wrote *Autobiography of a Super-tramp.*

Davies, William Robertson (1913–95), Canadian writer whose works included *Rebel Angels* (1981) and *What's Bred in the Bone* (1985).

Da Vinci. *See Leonardo.*

Davis, Jefferson (1808–89), American civil war leader. B. in Kentucky, he was made president of the Confederate States when the civil war broke out. After the war he was tried for treason, but discharged. He wrote *The Rise and Fall of the Confederate Government.*

Davis, John (*c.* 1550–1605), Elizabethan explorer and discoverer of Davis's Strait, the channel between the Atlantic and Arctic oceans on the west of Greenland. Invented the backstaff, or Davis's quadrant.

Davitt, Michael (1846–1906), Irish nationalist. The son of a peasant who later came to England, he joined the Fenians, and in 1870 was sentenced to penal servitude. On his release he helped to found the Land League in 1879; was again imprisoned; and wrote *Leaves from a Prison Diary.* He was subsequently returned to parliament.

Davy, Sir Humphry (1778–1829), English chemist, b. Penzance. Much of his work found practical application, *e.g.*, the miner's safety lamp which still bears his name. His *Elements of Agricultural Chemistry* (1813) contains the first use in English of the word "element." Michael Faraday was his assistant at the Royal Institution.

Dawkins, (Clinton) Richard (b. 1941), controversial Oxford biologist. Author of *The Selfish Gene* (1976), *The Blind Watchmaker* (1986), *Climbing Mount Improbable* (1996) and *Unweaving the Rainbow* (1998).

Day Lewis, Cecil (1904–72), poet and critic; professor of poetry at Oxford from 1951–6. He succeeded Masefield as poet laureate in 1968.

De Beauvoir, Simone (1908–86), feminist writer whose work *The Second Sex* is now the icon of feminism.

Debussy, Claude Achille (1862–1918), composer and leader of the French Impressionist school in music. Among his works are *Suite bergamasque*, containing the popular *Clair de lune*; *L'après-midi d'un Faune*, inspired by the poem of Mallarmé, and *La Mer*. He also wrote an opera *Pelléas et Mélisande.*

Defoe, Daniel (1660–1731), English political writer; also author of *Robinson Crusoe, Moll Flanders*, and a *Tour of Gt. Britain.* His *Shortest Way with Dissenters* brought him imprisonment.

De Forest, Lee (1873–1961), American inventor who was the first to use alternating-current transmission, and improved the thermionic valve detector by which wireless and sound films were made possible.

Degas, Edgar (1834–1917), French impressionist painter and sculptor, son of a banker. He painted subjects from everyday life—dancers, café life, the racecourse.

De Gasperi, Alcide (1881–1954), Italian politician who founded the Christian Democrat Party.

de Gaulle. *See Gaulle, Charles de.*

De Havilland, Sir Geoffrey (1882–1965), pioneer of civil and military aviation in Britain; designer of the famous Moth machines.

De Klerk, Frederik Willem (b. 1936), South African State President from 1989 to 1994. He launched a far-reaching reform process in South Africa. Shared Nobel Peace Prize, 1993, with Nelson Mandela. He retired from politics in 1997.

De Kooning, Willem (1904–97), one of the founding fathers of abstract expressionism in modern art.

Delacroix, Ferdinand Victor Eugène (1798–1863), French painter of the Romantic school.

De la Mare, Walter John (1873–1956), English poet and novelist whose work has a characteristic charm. Much of it was written for children.

Delane, John Thadeus (1817–79), editor of *The Times*, 1841–77, who did much to establish that paper's standing.

Delaroche, Paul (1797–1856), French historical painter.

Delibes, Clément Philibert Léo (1836–91), French composer of much graceful music, including operas, of which *Lakmé* is the best known, and ballets, among them *Coppélia.*

Delius, Frederick (1862–1934), English composer of German parentage. His music, highly idiosyncratic in idiom, was more readily received in Germany than in England until promoted by Sir Thomas Beecham. *See* **Section E.**

Delors, Jacques, (b. 1925), French socialist politician. President, European Commission, 1985–95.

Democritus (*c.* 470–*c.* 400 B.C.), one of the first scientific thinkers, pupil of Leucippus (fl. *c.* 440 B.C.). He took an atomic view of matter, denied the existence of mind as a separate entity, and counted happiness and inner tranquility as important moral principles. His attitude was not shared by his contemporary, Socrates, nor by Plato and Aristotle, but was accepted by Epicurus. The atomic theory thus passed into the background for many centuries.

Demosthenes (384–322 B.C.), Greek orator who, by his *Philippics*, roused the Athenians to resist the growing power of Philip of Macedon.

Deng Xiaoping (1904–97), Chinese politician, b. Szechwan; rehabilitated at Eleventh Party Congress (1977); effective leader of China in 1980s, target of May 1989 student revolt. Architect of the economic transformation of modern China, combining elements of capitalism with rigid Communist rule. His career began with the Long March and ended with the crushing of the democracy movement. *See* **Section C.**

Denning, Lord (Alfred Denning) (1899–1999), English judge. Master of the Rolls, 1962–82. Conducted Profumo affair enquiry, 1963. Outspoken defender of individual liberties. O.M. (1997).

De Quincey, Thomas (1785–1859), English essayist and critic; friend of Wordsworth and Southey. He wrote *Confessions of an English Opium-eater.*

De Reszke, Jean (1853–1925) and **De Reszke, Edouard** (1856–1917), Polish operatic singers, the first a tenor, the second a baritone.

Derrida, Jacques (b. 1930), controversial French writer and philosopher who bases his work on the analysis of language.

Derwentwater, 3rd Earl of (James Radcliffe) (1689–1716), leader of the English Jacobite movement. Defeated at Preston in 1715 and beheaded.

Descartes, René (1596–1650), French mathematician, pioneer of modern philosophy. Unconvinced by scholastic tradition and theological dogma, he sought to get back to why anything can be said to be true. The basis of his Cartesian philosophy is summed up in his own words, *Cogito, ergo sum* (I think, therefore I am).

Desmoulins, Camille (1760–94), French revolutionary. He represented Paris in the National Convention, and wrote witty and sarcastic pamphlets and periodicals. An ally of Danton.

Deutscher, Isaac (1907–67), Marxist historian, biographer of Stalin and Trotsky. B. in Poland. In 1939 he came to London.

De Valéra, Eamon (1882–1975), Irish statesman, b. New York, son of a Spanish father and an Irish mother. He was imprisoned for his part in the Easter rising of 1916. He opposed the treaty of 1921; and in 1926, when the republican Fianna Fáil was founded, he became its president. Prime minister, 1937–48, 1951–4, 1957–9; president of the republic, 1959–73.

de Valois, Dame Ninette (b. 1898), Irish-born ballet dancer and choreographer. She toured Europe with Diaghilev, 1923–5, and in 1931 founded the Sadler's Wells Ballet School (now Royal Ballet School), of which she became director. *Autobiography* (1957).

Dewar, Sir James (1842–1923), chemist and physicist, a native of Kincardine. He succeeded in liquefying hydrogen, and invented the vacuum flask. The explosive cordite was the joint invention of himself and Sir Frederick Abel.

Dewey, John (1859–1952), American philosopher, psychologist, and educationist. A follower of William James and an exponent of pragmatism.

De Witt, Jan (1625–72), Dutch republican statesman, who carried on war with England and later negotiated the Triple Alliance, but was overthrown by the Orange Party and murdered.

Diaghilev, Sergei Pavlovich (1872–1929), Russian ballet impresario and founder of the Russian ballet.

Diana, Princess of Wales (1961–97), born Diana Frances Spencer. Married **Charles**, Prince of Wales

(B14) in 1981. Divorced 1996. Tragic death in car crash, 31 August 1997.

Dickens, Charles (1812–70), popular English novelist of the 19th cent., with enormous output and capacity for vivid story-telling. Of humble origin, he was extremely successful. His best-known works are perhaps *Pickwick Papers*, *Oliver Twist*, *A Christmas Carol* (this influenced the observance of Christmas), *Dombey and Son*, *David Copperfield*, *Little Dor-rit*, and *Great Expectations*. His great-granddaughter, **Monica Dickens** (1915–92), wrote popular novels and light-hearted autobiographical books (*e.g.*, *One Pair of Hands*, 1939).

Dickinson, Emily (1830–86), American poet whose writing has a mystic quality. She lived a cloistered life.

Dickinson, Goldsworthy Lowes (1863–1932), English author, an interpreter and upholder of the Greek view of life.

Diderot, Denis (1713–84), French man of letters, critic of art and literature, and editor of the *Encyclopédie* (1713–84) to which many writers of the Enlightenment contributed.

Diemen, Anthony van (1593–1645), Dutch promoter of exploration. As governor-general in the Far East, he promoted Dutch trade and influence; and despatched Abel Tasman, who in 1642 discovered New Zealand and Van Diemen's Land (now Tasmania).

Diesel, Rudolf (1858–1913), German engineer, inventor of an internal combustion engine which he patented in 1893. *See also* **L34**.

DiMaggio, Joe (1914–99), US baseball legend known as Joltin' Joe and The Yankee Clipper.

Diocletian (245–313), Roman emperor and persecutor of Christianity. He divided the empire under a system of joint rule; later abdicated; and built a palace in Dalmatia.

Diogenes (412–322 B.C.), Greek cynic philosopher who lived in a tub and told Alexander to get out of his sunshine. He sought virtue and moral freedom in liberation from desire.

Dionysius the elder and younger, tyrants of Syracuse in the 4th cent. B.C.

Dirac, Paul Adrien Maurice (1902–84), English physicist who shared with Erwin Schrödinger the 1933 Nobel prize for their work on Heisenberg's theory of quantum mechanics. O.M. (1973).

Disney, Walter Elias (1901–66), American film cartoonist, creator of Mickey Mouse. He is known for his *Silly Symphonies*, *Snow White and the Seven Dwarfs*, and *Pinocchio*.

Disraeli, Benjamin, Earl of Beaconsfield (1804–81), British statesman and novelist who helped to form modern Conservatism in England. The son of Isaac (*q.v.*), he published his first novel at 21, and later *Coningsby* and *Sibyl*, which helped to rouse the social conscience. He entered parliament in 1837 and was prime minister 1868 and 1874–80, when he arranged the purchase of shares in the Suez canal. He was rival of Gladstone and friend of Queen Victoria.

D'Israeli, Isaac (1766–1848), father of Benjamin (*q.v.*) and author of *Curiosities of Literature*.

Dobson, Austin (1840–1921), English writer of light verse and of 18th cent. biography.

Dodgson, Charles Lutwidge (1832–98), English writer. Under the pseudonym Lewis Carroll, he wrote poems and books for children, including *Alice's Adventures in Wonderland*. In private life he was a lecturer in mathematics at Oxford.

Dolci, Carlo (1616–86), one of the last Florentine painters.

Dominic, St. (1170–1221), founder of the Friars Preachers or Black Friars. B. in Castile, he and his followers sought to teach the ignorant. In 1216 they were formed into an order and vowed to poverty. The order spread widely.

Domitian (**Titus Flavius Domitianus**) (A.D. 51–96), Roman emperor, son of Vespasian. Emperor from A.D. 81. He ruled despotically, aroused the hatred of the senate, and was assassinated as a result of a palace conspiracy.

Donatello (**Donato di Niccolò**) (*c.* 1386–1466), Italian sculptor, b. Florence, son of Niccolò di Betto di Bardo. He was the founder of modern sculpture, producing statues independent of a background, designed to stand in the open to be viewed from all angles. Among his masterpieces are the statues of *St. George* and *David* (in the Bargello, Florence) and his equestrian *Gattamelata* in Padua, the first bronze horse to be cast in the Renaissance.

Donizetti, Gaetano (1797–1848), Italian composer. The best known of his sixty operas are *Lucia di Lammermoor*, *La Fille du Régiment*, and *Don Pasquale*. *See* **Section E**.

Donne, John (1572–1631), English metaphysical poet and preacher (dean of St. Paul's). His poems and sermons marked by passion, wit, and profundity of thought have received full publicity only in the present century. His writings include *Elegies*, *Satires*, *Songs and Sonnets*, *Problems and Paradoxes* and the *Holy Sonnets*.

Doré, Gustave (1833–83), French artist who painted scriptural subjects and illustrated Dante, Milton, and Tennyson.

Dostoyevsky, Feodor Mikhailovich (1821–81), Russian novelist, b. Moscow. As a result of his revolutionary activity he was sent to hard labour in Siberia. In his books, which include *Crime and Punishment*, *The Brothers Karamazov*, *The Idiot*, and *The Possessed*, he explored the dark places of the human spirit to a degree not previously attempted.

Douglas of Kirtleside, 1st Baron (William Sholto Douglas) (1893–1969), British airman; commanded Fighter command, 1940–2, Coastal command, 1944–5. A Labour peer.

Douglas, Norman (1868–1952), novelist and travel writer. A Scot, born in Austria, he made his home on the Mediterranean. His works include *South Wind*.

Doulton, Sir Henry (1820–97), English potter and the inventor of Doulton ware.

Dowden, Edward (1843–1913), English literary critic and Shakespearean scholar.

Dowding, 1st Baron (Hugh Caswell Tremenheere Dowding) (1882–1970), British airman; commanded Fighter command during the Battle of Britain period (1940).

Dowland, John (*c.* 1563–1626), English composer of songs with lute accompaniment. His son Robert was later Court lutenist to Charles I.

Doyle, Sir Arthur Conan (1859–1930), British writer, b. Edinburgh, creator of the detective Sherlock Holmes and his friend and foil, Dr. Watson. He was trained as a doctor but gave up his medical practice in 1890 to devote himself to writing.

Doyle, Richard (1824–83), humorous artist on the staff of *Punch*.

D'Oyly Carte, Richard (1844–1901), noted English theatrical manager, who built the Savoy theatre and there produced Gilbert and Sullivan operas.

Draco (7th cent. B.C.), Athenian lawmaker who redrew the constitution of Athens in 621 B.C. and substantially increased the penalties for debt, thus giving his name to particularly severe laws.

Drake, Sir Francis (*c.* 1540–96), English seaman. In 1577–80 he sailed round the world in the *Golden Hind*. In 1587 he destroyed a number of Spanish ships in Cadiz harbour; and under Lord Howard he helped to defeat the Spanish Armada in 1588.

Draper, John William (1811–82), American chemist, b. near Liverpool. He was the first, using Daguerre's process, to take a successful photograph of the human face (1840), and the moon.

Dreiser, Theodore (1871–1935). American novelist of austere realism. Author of *An American Tragedy*.

Dreyfus, Alfred (1859–1935), French victim of injustice. Of Jewish parentage, in 1894 he was accused of divulging secrets to a foreign power, and was sentenced by a military secret tribunal to imprisonment for life on Devil's Island in French Guiana. At a new trial in 1899 he was again found guilty. Efforts continued to be made on his behalf, and in 1906 he was entirely exonerated, restored to his rank in the army, and made a Chevalier of the Legion of Honour.

Drinkwater, John (1882–1937), English poet and playwright. His plays include *Abraham Lincoln*, and *Oliver Cromwell*.

Drummond, William, (1585–1649), Scottish poet and Royalist pamphleteer. He was laird of Hawthornden.

Drury, Alfred (1857–1944), English sculptor, especially of statues of Queen Victoria at Bradford and Portsmouth.

Dryden, John (1631–1700), prolific English poet and dramatist, who also wrote political satire (*Absalom and Achitophel*). He was hostile to the revolution of 1688, and thereafter mainly translated classical writers, including Virgil.

Du Barry, Marie Jean Bécu, Comtesse (1746–

93), mistress of Louis XV of France and guillotined by the revolutionary tribunal.

Dubček, Alexander (1921–92), Czech political leader. First Secretary, Slovak Communist Party, 1968-69. His reform programme (the 'Prague Spring') prompted the Russian invasion of August 1968. Restored to public life, 1989.

Du Chaillu, Paul Belloni (1835–1903), traveller in Africa, who in 1861 and 1867 published accounts of his explorations. A French-American.

Dufferin and Ava, 1st Marquess of (Frederick Temple Hamilton-Temple Blackwood) (1826–1902), British diplomat, writer, and governorgeneral of Canada and viceroy of India.

Dulles, John Foster (1888–1959), U.S. Secretary of State in the Republican administration 1953-9. A staunch Cold War warrior.

Dumas, Alexandre (1802–70), French romantic novelist, among whose many works are The Three Musketeers, The Count of Monte Cristo, and The Black Tulip.

Dumas, Alexandre (1824–95), French dramatist, son of the above; author of La Dame aux Camélias.

Du Maurier, George (1834–96), contributor to Punch and author of Trilby.

Dummett, Professor Sir Michael (b. 1925), English philosopher. Succeeded Ayer as Wykeham Professor of Logic at Oxford University. Author of Logical Basis of Metaphysics (1990). Anti-racist.

Dundee, 1st Viscount (John Graham of Claverhouse), (1648-89), Scottish soldier ("Bonnie Dundee"). Employed to suppress the covenanters, he was defeated at Drumclog, but victorious at Bothwell Brig. At the revolution of 1688 he supported James II, and was killed in the (victorious) battle of Killiecrankie.

Dundonald, Earl of. See Cochrane, Thomas.

Duns Scotus, John (c. 1265–1308), Scottish scholastic philosopher, b. at Maxton near Roxburgh, opponent of Thomas Aquinas. He joined the Franciscans, studied and taught at Oxford and Paris, and probably d. at Cologne. He challenged the harmony of faith and reason.

Dunstable, John (c. 1380–1453), the earliest English composer known by name. He was a contemporary of the Netherlands composers Dufay and Binchois. See Section E.

Dunstan, St. (908-88), reforming archbishop of Canterbury. He lived through seven reigns from Athelstan to Ethelred, and was adviser especially to Edgar. Under him Glastonbury Abbey became a centre of religious teaching.

Dupleix, Joseph François (1697–1763), French governor in India. He extended French influence and power in the Carnatic, but his plans were frustrated by his English opponent, Clive. He was recalled in 1754 and died in poverty.

Dürer, Albrecht (1471–1528), German painter and engraver. B. at Nuremberg, he was (like his Italian contemporary, Leonardo) a man of intellectual curiosity and scientific insight. His best work is in his copper engravings, woodcuts, and drawings; the former include The Knight, Melancholia, and St. Jerome in his Study. He was the friend of Luther and Melanchthon.

Durham, Earl of (John George Lambton) (1792–1840), governor-general of Canada after the disturbances of 1837, and in 1839 presented to parliament the Durham Report, which laid down the principle of colonial self-government.

Durrell, Gerald (1925–95). Zoo pioneer, conservationist and writer on animals. Author of bestselling My Family and Other Animals. Founded Jersey Zoo, 1958. His story-telling ability reached a generation of conservationists.

Duse, Elenora (1861–1924), Italian tragedienne.

Duval, Claude (1643–70), notorious highwayman who came to England from Normandy and was eventually hanged at Tyburn.

Dvořák, Antonin (1841–1904), Czech composer whose music is rich in folk-song melodies of his native Bohemia. In 1884 he conducted his Stabat Mater in London. His New World symphony was composed in New York, where he was head of the National Conservatoire (1892-5). See Section E.

Dyson, Sir Frank Watson (1868–1939), English astronomer who was astronomer royal 1910–33, and astronomer royal for Scotland 1905–10.

Dyson, Sir George (1883–1964), English composer and writer. In The New Music he analysed the technique of modern schools of composition. He

composed several choral works such as The Canterbury Pilgrims and Nebuchadnezzar, which still remain popular.

E

Earhart, Amelia (1898–1937), American air pioneer. First woman to fly the Atlantic alone. Disappeared in 1937 during a Pacific flight.

Eastlake, Sir Charles Lock (1793–1865), English painter of historical and religious works.

Eastman, George (1854–1932), American inventor of the roll photographic film and Kodak camera.

Easton, Florence (Gertrude) (1882–1955), English operatic soprano of great versatility. Repertoire of 88 roles. Last woman to sing with Caruso in 1920.

Eck, Johann von (1486–1543), German Catholic theologian and opponent of Luther.

Eddington, Sir Arthur Stanley (1882–1944), English astronomer (Greenwich observatory 1906–13; Cambridge observatory 1914–44). His works include The Nature of the Physical World.

Eddy, Mrs Mary Baker (1821–1910), American founder of the Church of Christ Scientist. Her Science and Health with Key to the Scriptures was published in 1875. See Christian Science, Section J.

Edelinck, Gerard (1640–1707), Flemish engraver, b. Antwerp, the first to reproduce in print the colour, as well as the form, of a picture.

Eden, Robert Anthony, 1st Earl of Avon (1897–1977), British statesman. He entered parliament in 1923; became foreign secretary in 1935 (resigning in 1938 over Chamberlain's negotiation with Mussolini and rebuff to President Roosevelt); deputy prime minister in 1951; succeeded Sir Winston Churchill in 1955. His Suez policy divided the country. He resigned for health reasons in 1957. Earldom 1961.

Edgar (943–75), King of England 959–75. He was advised by Archbishop Dunstan.

Edgar Atheling (c. 1060–c. 1130), was the lawful heir of Edward the Confessor, but in the Norman invasion could not maintain his claim.

Edgeworth, Maria (1767–1849), Irish novelist, whose stories include Castle Rackrent, The Absentee, and Belinda.

Edinburgh, Duke of (Philip Mountbatten) (b. 1921), consort of Queen Elizabeth II. He relinquished his right of accession to the thrones of Greece and Denmark on his naturalisation in 1947 when he took the name of Mountbatten. He is the great-great-grandson of Queen Victoria, grandson of Admiral Prince Louis of Battenberg, and nephew of the late Earl Mountbatten of Burma.

Edison, Thomas Alva (1847–1931), American inventor of the transmitter and receiver for the automatic telegraph; the phonograph; the incandescent lamp (shared with the British inventor Swan); and many devices for the electrical distribution of light and power. From being a newsboy on the railway and later a telegraph clerk, he became a master at applying scientific principles to practical ends. He set up a laboratory at Menlo Park, New Jersey.

Edmund II (Ironside) (c 990–1016), the son of Ethelred, king of the English, made a compact with Canute to divide England, but soon afterwards died.

Edward the Confessor (c. 1004–1066), English king who preceded the Norman Conquest and founded Westminster Abbey. He was canonised in 1161.

Edward the Elder (c. 870–c. 924), son of Alfred, succeeded him as king of the West Saxons in 899. He overcame the Danes and reoccupied the northern counties.

Edward I (1239–1307), King of England, succeeded his father Henry in 1272. Able and energetic, his legislation influenced the development of the land law, and he summoned parliamentary assemblies. A soldier, he conquered Wales, building castles, but could not maintain his hold on Scotland.

Edward II (1284–1327), succeeded his father Edward I as king of England in 1307 and was defeated by the Scots at Bannockburn. Weak and inept, he was murdered in 1327.

Edward III (1312–77), succeeded his father Edward II as king of England in 1327. Popular and ambitious he began the Hundred Years

War with France. He fostered the woollen industry. Latterly he became senile.

Edward IV (1442–83), able but dissolute Yorkist leader whose reign (1461–70, 1471–83) brought about a revival in the power of the monarchy, in English sea power, and in foreign trade (in which he himself took part). Spent 1470–71, in exile. Began rebuilding of St. George's chapel, Windsor. Patron of Caxton.

Edward V (1470–83), succeeded his father Edward IV at the age of 12 and was a pawn in the quarrels of baronial relatives. He and his brother were shut up in the Tower by his uncle, Richard, Duke of Gloucester, and there probably murdered, though proof has not been established.

Edward VI (1537–53), succeeded his father, Henry VIII, as king of England when in his tenth year. He was delicate and studious, and his government was carried on successively by the Dukes of Somerset and Northumberland; while under Archbishop Cranmer the prayer book was issued. Named Lady Jane Grey his successor.

Edward VII (1841–1910), King of Great Britain and Ireland. The son of Queen Victoria, he married Princess Alexandra of Denmark in 1863, and succeeded his mother in 1901. Interested mainly in social life and in international contacts. He visited India in 1875.

Edward VIII (1894–1972), King of Great Britain, succeeded his father George V 1936, and abdicated later that year because of disagreement over his proposed marriage. He was created Duke of Windsor, and was governor of the Bahamas 1940–45. The Duchess of Windsor died in 1986.

Ehrlich, Paul (1854–1915), German bacteriologist, who at Frankfurt-on-Main carried out work in immunology. He discovered salvarsan for the treatment of syphilis. Nobel prizewinner 1908.

Eiffel, Alexandre Gustave (1832–1923), French engineer, one of the first to employ compressed air caissons in bridge building. Among his works are the Eiffel Tower (1887–9) and the Panama Canal locks.

Einstein, Albert (1879–1955), mathematical physicist whose theory of relativity superseded Newton's theory of gravitation. He was born in Ulm of Jewish parents, lived for many years in Switzerland, and held a succession of professorial chairs at Zurich, Prague, and Berlin. In 1921 he was awarded the Nobel prize for his work in quantum theory. He was driven by the Nazis to seek asylum in America and became professor at the Institute of Advanced Study at Princeton 1933–45. In August 1939 at the request of a group of scientists he wrote to President Roosevelt warning of the danger of uranium research in Germany and stressing the urgency of investigating the possible use of atomic energy in bombs. *See* Relativity, Section F, Part II.

Eisenhower, Dwight David (1890–1969), American general and statesman. He was C.-in-C. Allied Forces, N. Africa, 1942–3; and in the European theatre of operations, 1943–5; and was Republican President, 1953–61.

Eisenstein, Sergei Mikhailovich. *See* W8–9.

Eleanor (1246–90), Queen of Edward I. After her death in 1290 the king had memorial crosses erected at the twelve places where her body rested on its way from Grantham to Westminster.

Elgar, Sir Edward (1857–1934), English composer, specially of choral-orchestral works for festivals. His oratorios include *The Kingdom*, *The Apostles*, and *The Dream of Gerontius*; he also wrote the *Enigma Variations*, and the tone-poem *Falstaff. See* Section E.

Elgin, 7th Earl of (Thomas Bruce) (1766–1841), British diplomat who, with the object of saving them, conveyed some sculptures from the Parthenon in Athens to the British Museum.

Eliot, George (1819–80), pen-name of Mary Anne (later Marion) Evans, b. Warwickshire. Her novels include *Adam Bede*, *The Mill on the Floss*, *Silas Marner*, *Middlemarch*, and *Daniel Deronda*. Her works show deep insight. She lived with the writer George Lewes from 1854 until his death 25 years later. (Although Lewes had been deserted by his wife it was not then possible to obtain a divorce.) She brought up his three children.

Eliot, Thomas Stearns (1888–1965), poet and critic. He was born in St. Louis, Missouri, and became a British subject in 1927. His poems include *Prufrock and Other Observations*, *The Waste Land*, *The Hollow Men*, *Ash Wednes-*

day, *Four Quartets*; his verse dramas *Murder in the Cathedral* and *The Family Reunion*. He described himself as "classical in literature, royalist in politics, and Anglo-Catholic in religion". Nobel prizewinner 1948.

Elizabeth (b. 1900), Queen Consort of George VI, daughter of the 14th Earl of Strathmore. Before her marriage in 1923 she was Lady Elizabeth Angela Marguerite Bowes-Lyon.

Elizabeth I (1533–1603), Queen of England, daughter of Henry VIII, succeeded her sister Mary in 1558. Politically and intellectually able and firm, though personally vain and capricious, she chose to serve her able men such as William Cecil; and her long reign was one of stability, victory over the Spanish, and adventure in the New World; while the Church of England was established. It was however marred by the execution of Mary, Queen of Scots.

Elizabeth II (Elizabeth Alexandra Mary of Windsor) (b. 1926), Queen of Gt. Britain and N. Ireland, ascended the throne Feb. 1952 on the death of her father George VI. Her Consort, Prince Philip, Duke of Edinburgh, is the son of Prince Andrew of Greece and a descendant of the Danish royal family. They have four children: **Charles, Prince of Wales** (*see* B14), **Princess Anne** (b. 1950), **Prince Andrew** (b. 1960), and **Prince Edward** (b. 1964). Princess Anne was styled the Princess Royal in June 1987. She married Commander Tim Laurence in 1992, the first royal remarriage after a divorce since Henry VIII. Prince Charles and Princess Diana were divorced in 1996. In 1997 Diana was killed in a car crash. Prince Edward married Sophie Rhys-Jones in 1999.

Ellis, Havelock (1859–1939), English writer whose *Studies in the Psychology of Sex* was influential in changing the public attitude towards sex. His books were first published in America.

Emerson, Ralph Waldo (1803–82), American poet and essayist, b. Boston, member of the transcendentalist group of thinkers. Among his best-known poems are *Woodnotes*, *Threnody*, *Terminus*, *Brahma*, *The Problem*.

Emin Pasha, the name adopted by **Eduard Schnitzer** (1840–92), a German explorer associated with Gen. Charles Gordon in the Sudan as a medical officer; and governor of the Equatorial Province 1878–89, when he was menaced by the Mahdi and rescued by Stanley.

Emmet, Robert (1778–1803), Irish patriot, led the rising of 1803, was betrayed, and executed.

Empedocles (c. 500–c. 430 B.C.), Greek philosopher, b. Agrigentum in Sicily, founder of a school of medicine which regarded the heart as the seat of life, an idea which passed to Aristotle, as did his idea that all matter was composed of four elements: earth, air, fire, and water.

Engels, Friedrich (1820–95), German socialist, son of a wealthy textile manufacturer, lifelong friend of Karl Marx, with whom he collaborated in writing the *Communist Manifesto* of 1848. Through him Marx acquired his knowledge of English labour conditions.

Epaminondas (c. 418–362 B.C.), Theban general who led the Boeotian League against the attempt of Sparta to dominate Greece in the early 4th cent. B.C. and even defeated her army at the battle of Leuctra in 371 B.C.

Epicurus of Samos (342–270 B.C.), refounded the atomic view of matter put forward by Democritus, and held that peace of mind comes through freedom from fear, the two main sources of which he regarded as religion and fear of death. *See* Epicureanism, J17.

Epstein, Sir Jacob (1880–1959), sculptor, b. New York of Russian-Polish parents. His work includes *Rima*, in Hyde Park; *Day* and *Night* on the building of London Underground headquarters; *Genesis*, exhibited in 1931; *Lazarus*, in New College, Oxford; the *Madonna and Child* group in Cavendish Square, London; the figure of *Christ in Majesty* in aluminium in Llandaff cathedral; a sculpture for the TUC headquarters in London; and a bronze group for Coventry cathedral.

Erasmus, Desiderius (1466–1536), Dutch Renaissance humanist, who spent several years in England and was the friend of Dean Colet and Sir Thomas More. He aimed at ecclesiastical reform from within and scorned the old scholastic teaching. He thus prepared the way for Luther. His *Praise of Folly* is still widely read.

Erhard, Ludwig (1897–1977), German economist.

Chancellor (1963–7) after Adenauer.

Essex, 2nd Earl of (Robert Devereux) (1566–1601), favourite of Queen Elizabeth I in her old age. Unsuccessful as governor-general of Ireland, he returned to England against the Queen's wish; plotted; and was executed.

Ethelbert, King of Kent at the close of the 6th cent., accepted Christianity on the mission of St. Augustine.

Ethelred II (c. 968–1016), King of England. Unable to organise resistance against the Danish raids, he was called the Unready (from Old Eng. uraed = without counsel).

Etty, William (1787–1849), English artist of historical and classical subjects.

Eucken, Rudolf Christoph (1846–1926), German philosopher of activism, which puts personal ethical effort above intellectual idealism. Nobel prizewinner 1908.

Euclid, Greek mathematician of the 3rd cent. B.C. Famous for his *Elements*.

Euler, Leonhard (1707–83), Swiss mathematician, remembered especially for his work in optics and on the calculus of variations. He was called by Catherine I to St. Petersburg, where he was professor, 1730–41, and by Frederick the Great to Berlin, 1741–66. He became blind but continued his work.

Euripides (480–406 B.C.), Greek tragic dramatist, who is known to have written about 80 plays of which 18 are preserved, including *Alcestis, Medea, Iphigenia,* and *Orestes.* He displayed a sceptical attitude towards the myths.

Eusebius (264–340), ecclesiastical historian. His *Ecclesiastical History* gives the history of the Christian church to 324. He also wrote a general history, *Chronicon.*

Evans, Sir Arthur John (1851–1941), English archaeologist, known for his excavations at Knossos in Crete and his discovery of the pre-Phoenician script.

Evans, Dame Edith Mary (1888–1976), English actress, whose celebrated roles included Millamant in *The Way of the World,* and Lady Bracknell in *The Importance of Being Earnest.*

Evans, Sir Geraint Llewellyn (1922–92), much-loved Welsh opera singer. Principal Baritone, Royal Opera House, Covent Garden, 1948–84.

Evelyn, John (1620–1706), cultured English diarist who gives brilliant portraits of contemporaries. A book collector and librarian who wrote *Sylea,* a manual of arboriculture.

Eyck, Jan van (c. 1389–1441), Flemish painter, whose best-known work is the altarpiece in Ghent cathedral. His brother **Hubert** (c. 1370–1426) is associated with him.

Eysenck, Hans Jürgen (1916–97) was Professor of Psychology at the University of London Institute of Psychiatry. He was noted for his work on intelligence. His many publications include *Uses and Abuses of Psychology* (1953), *Know Your Own I.Q* (1962) and *Race, Intelligence and Education* (1971).

F

Fabius, the name of an ancient Roman family who over many generations played an important part in early Roman history. **Quintus Fabius Maximus Verrucosus** (d. 203 B.C.) saved Rome from Hannibal by strategic evasion of battle; hence his name *Cunctator* (delayer), and the term Fabian policy.

Fabre, Jean Henri Casimir (1823–1915), French naturalist, whose study of the habits of insects was recorded in his *Souvenirs entomologiques.*

Faed, name of two Scottish genre painters, **Thomas** (1826–1900), and **John** (1819–1902). A third brother, **James,** engraved their works.

Fahrenheit, Gabriel Daniel (1686–1736), German physicist, b. Danzig. He introduced c. 1715 the mercury thermometer and fixed thermometric standards.

Fairbairn, Sir William (1789–1874), Scottish engineer. In 1817 he took the lead in using iron in shipbuilding.

Fairfax, 3rd Baron (Thomas Fairfax) (1612–71), parliamentary general in the English civil war, and victor of Marston Moor. In 1650 he withdrew into private life.

Falconer, Hugh (1806–65), British botanist and

palaeontologist, b. Forres, Scot.; physician to East India Co.; introduced tea into India.

Falla de, Manuel (1876–1946), Spanish composer whose music is highly individual with a strong folk-song element. *See* **Section E.**

Fanon, Frantz (1925–61), West Indian psychoanalyst and revolutionary social philosopher.

Faraday, Michael (1791–1867), English experimental physicist, founder of the science of electromagnetism. He was the son of a Yorkshire blacksmith and at 13 became apprenticed to a bookseller in London. In 1813 he became laboratory assistant to Sir Humphry Davy at the Royal Institution, succeeding him as professor of chemistry in 1833. He set himself the problem of finding the connections between the forces of light, heat, electricity, and magnetism and his discoveries, translated by Maxwell (q.v.) into a single mathematical theory of electromagnetism, led to the modern developments in physics and electronics. He inaugurated the Christmas lectures for youngsters at the Royal Institution.

Farman, Henri (1874–1958), French aviator, one of the pioneers of aviation.

Farouk I (1920–65), King of Egypt, 1936–52. He was forced to abdicate after the 1952 coup.

Farrar, Frederick William (1831–1903), English clergyman, author of the schoolboy story *Eric.*

Faulkner, William (1897–1962), American novelist, whose series of novels, *The Sound and the Fury, As I Lay Dying, Light in August, Sanctuary,* depict the American South. Nobel prize 1949.

Fauré, Gabriel Urbain (1845–1924), French composer and teacher. His works include chamber music, nocturnes, and barcarolles for piano, an opera *Pénélope,* some exquisite songs, and *Requiem.* Ravel was among his pupils.

Fawcett, Millicent Garrett (1847–1929), educational reformer and leader of the movement for women's suffrage; one of the founders of Newnham College, Cambridge. Wife of the blind Liberal politician and economist, **Henry Fawcett** (1833–84) and sister of **Elizabeth Garrett Anderson.**

Fawkes, Guy (1570–1606), a Yorkshire catholic, who with Catesby and other conspirators planned the Gunpowder Plot. Though warned, he persisted and was captured and hanged.

Fénelon, François de Salignac de la Mothe (1651–1715), archbishop of Cambrai and author of *Telemachus.*

Ferdinand II of Aragon (1452–1516), who married Isabella of Castile, and with her reigned over Spain, saw the Moors expelled from Spain, equipped Columbus for the discoveries that led to Spain's vast colonial possessions, and instituted the Inquisition.

Ferguson, James (1710–76), Scottish astronomer who, from being a shepherd-boy, educated himself in astronomy, mathematics, and portrait painting.

Fermi, Enrico (1901–54), Italian nuclear physicist whose research contributed to the harnessing of atomic energy and the development of the atomic bomb. Nobel prizewinner 1938.

Feynman, Richard (Philips), (1918–88), American physicist, born of working-class Jewish parents. Helped develop the atomic bomb. Won Nobel Prize for Physics (1965) for work on quantum electrodynamics.

Fichte, Johann Gottlieb (1762–1814), German nationalist and Romantic philosopher who paved the way for modern totalitarianism.

Field, John (1782–1837), Irish composer of nocturnes, pupil of Clementi and teacher of Glinka. His work served as a model for Chopin.

Fielding, Henry (1707–54), English novelist, author of *Tom Jones, Joseph Andrews,* and *Amelia,* as well as plays.

Fildes, Sir Luke (1844–1927), English painter and woodcut-designer.

Finsen, Niels Ryberg (1860–1904), Danish physician who established an institute for light therapy and invented the Finsen ultra-violet lamp. Nobel prizewinner 1903.

Firdausi, *pen-name of* **Abu'l Kasim Mansur** (940–1020), Persian poet, author of the epic *Shah-Nama* or Book of Kings.

Fisher of Lambeth, Baron (Geoffrey Francis Fisher) (1887–1972), archbishop of Canterbury, 1945–61; Headmaster, Repton School, 1914–32.

Fisher, Herbert Albert Laurens (1865–1940), English historian and educational reformer.

Fisher, Sir Ronald Aylmer (1890–1962), British scientist who revolutionised both genetics and the philosophy of experimentation by founding the modern corpus of mathematical statistics.

FitzGerald, Edward (1809–83), English poet who translated the *Rubáiyát* of Omar Khayyám (1859).

Fitzroy, Robert (1805–65), British meteorologist, who introduced the system of storm warnings which were the beginning of weather forecasts.

Flammarion, Camille (1842–1925), French astronomer, noted for his popular lectures and books which include *L'Astronomie Populaire*.

Flamsteed, John (1646–1719), the first English astronomer royal, for whom Charles II built an observatory at Greenwich (1675) where he worked for 44 years.

Flaubert, Gustave (1821–80), French novelist, and creator of *Madame Bovary*. Other works were *Salammbô*, *L'Education sentimentale*, and *Bouvard et Pécuchet*.

Flaxman, John (1755–1826), English sculptor, b. York, employed as modeller by Josiah Wedgwood. He then took to monumental sculpture.

Flecker, James Elroy (1884–1915), English poet whose works include *Golden Journey to Samarkand*, *Hassan* (staged in London, 1923), and *Don Juan*, as well as many lyrics.

Fleming, Sir Alexander (1881–1955), Scottish bacteriologist who discovered the antibacterial enzyme lysozyme in 1922 and penicillin in 1928. Full recognition came during the war when Florey separated the drug now used from the original penicillin. Awarded Nobel prize jointly with Florey and Chain, 1945.

Fleming, Sir Ambrose (1849–1945), British scientist whose invention of the radio valve in 1904 revolutionised radio telegraphy and solved problems of radio-telephony. This eventually made possible high quality sound transmission, and thus led to broadcasting and television.

Fletcher, John (1579–1625), English dramatist who collaborated with Francis Beaumont (*q.v.*) in writing many pieces for the stage.

Flinders, Matthew (1774–1814), English navigator and explorer who made discoveries in and around Australia. He sailed through Bass Strait, so called in honour of his surgeon.

Florey, Baron (Howard Walter Florey) (1898–1968), British pathologist, b. Australia. Shared 1945 Nobel prize with Fleming and Chain for work on penicillin.

Fo, Dario (b. 1926), Italian playwright and performance artist, whose plays include *Accidental Death of an Anarchist* (1970) and *Can't Pay? Won't Pay!* (1974). Awarded Nobel Prize 1997.

Foch, Ferdinand (1851–1929), French general, b. Tarbes. In the first world war he halted the German advance at the Marne (1914), and was engaged in the battles of Ypres (1914 and 1915) and the Somme (1916). In 1918 he became supreme commander of the British, French, and American armies and dictated the terms of Allied victory.

Fokine, Michel (1880–1944), Russian dancer, choreographer to Diaghilev's company, and creator of *Les Sylphides*, *Prince Igor*, *Scheherazade*, *Firebird*, and *The Spectre of the Rose*.

Fokker, Anthony (1890–1939), Dutch aircraft engineer, b. Java. The Fokker factory in Germany made warplanes for the Germans in the first world war.

Fonteyn, Dame Margot (Mme. Roberto de Arias) (1919–91), prima ballerina of the Royal Ballet seen as the greatest ballerina of her age.

Foot, Michael (b. 1913), British journalist and politician; leader of the Labour Party 1980–83.

Ford, Gerald R. (b. 1913), American Republican President 1974–7; automatically succeeded Richard Nixon when he resigned.

Ford, Henry (1863–1947), founder of Ford Motor Company (1903), of which he was president until 1919, when he was succeeded by his son, **Edsel B. Ford** (1893–1943). He was the pioneer of the cheap motor car.

Forester, Cecil Scott (1899–1966), English novelist, author of the *Captain Hornblower* series.

Forster, Edward Morgan (1879–1970), English novelist, author of *The Longest Journey*, *A Room with a View*, *Howards End*, *A Passage to India*. O.M. 1969.

Foscari, Francesco (*c.* 1372–1457), Doge of Venice and victor over Milan.

Fourier, Charles (1772–1837), French socialist who propounded a system of associated enterprise which although utopian stimulated social reform.

Fourier, Jean Baptiste Joseph (1768–1830), French

mathematical physicist. He played an active part in politics, holding administrative posts in Egypt and Isère, yet finding time for his own research, especially on the flow of heat.

Fowler, Sir John (1817–98), was the engineer of the first underground railway (the London Metropolitan) and with his partner Sir Benjamin Baker, of the Forth bridge.

Fox, Charles James (1749–1806), English Whig statesman. Son of the 1st Lord Holland, he entered parliament at 19. He held office only for brief periods between 1770 and 1806, but he upheld the liberal causes of the day (American independence, the French revolution, and parliamentary reform), and was one of the impeachers of Warren Hastings.

Fox, George (1624–91), founder of the Society of Friends, son of a weaver of Fenny Drayton, Leicestershire.

Foxe, John (1516–87), English martyrologist, author of *History of the Acts and Monuments of the Church* (better known as *Foxe's Book of Martyrs*).

Frampton, Sir George James (1860–1928), English sculptor of the Peter Pan statue in Kensington Gardens and the Edith Cavell memorial.

France, Anatole (1844–1924), French writer, especially of short stories. Nobel prize 1921.

Francis I (1494–1547), King of France. Brilliant but ambitious and adventurous, he fostered learning and art, and met Henry VIII at the Field of the Cloth of Gold. His rivalry with the Emperor Charles V involved France in prolonged war, especially in Italy (he was captured at Pavia, 1525). He persecuted the Protestants.

Francis of Assisi, St. (1181/2–1226), founder of the Franciscan Order. Son of a wealthy cloth merchant, in 1208 he turned from a life of pleasure to poverty and the complete observance of Christ's teaching. He and his friars went about preaching the gospel by word and example, and the brotherhood increased rapidly. He was canonised in 1228.

Francis, Sir Philip (1740–1818), English politician, reputed author of the *Letters of Junius*.

Franck, César Auguste (1822–90), composer and organist, b. at Liège in Belgium. *See* **Section E.**

Franco, Francisco (1892–1975), Spanish general and dictator. He led the Fascist rebellion against the Republican government (1936) and with German and Italian help ended the civil war (1939). He ruled Spain as a dictator.

Franklin, Benjamin (1706–90), American statesman. B. at Boston, he was at first a printer and journalist. He then took an interest in electricity, explained lightning as of electrical origin, and invented the lightning conductor. He was active in promoting the Declaration of Independence in 1773; he negotiated French support; and helped to frame the U.S. constitution.

Franklin, Sir John (1786–1847), English Arctic explorer. His expedition in the *Erebus* and the *Terror* to find the north-west passage ended disastrously, and all attempts to find survivors failed.

Franks, Baron (Oliver Shewell Franks) (1905–92), British academic, diplomat and banker; British ambassador to U.S.A. 1948–52; provost of Worcester College, Oxford 1962–76; chosen to head Falklands inquiry 1982. O.M. 1977.

Fraunhofer, Joseph von (1787–1826), optical instrument-maker of Munich, the first to map the dark lines of the solar spectrum named after him.

Frazer, Sir James George (1854–1941), Scottish anthropologist, author of *The Golden Bough*.

Frederick I (*c.* 1123–90). Holy Roman Emperor, nicknamed Barbarossa. A strong personality, he sought to impose his will on the city-states of northern Italy and the papacy, and was defeated at Legnano in 1176 but was more successful with a conciliatory policy (1183). He had also to contend with opposition at home. He died on the third crusade.

Frederick II (1194–1250), Holy Roman Emperor, grandson of the above, and son of the heiress of Sicily. Brilliant and enlightened, he attracted to his court in Sicily Jewish, Mohammedan, and Christian scholars; founded the university of Naples; was a patron of the medical school of Salerno; wrote a treatise on falconry; and commissioned a code of laws. Politically he was less successful, having trouble with the Lombard cities, and being involved with the papacy especially as regards his delay in going on crusade; but after negotiations with the sultan of Egypt he actually was crowned king of Jerusalem.

Frederick II (the Great) (1712–86), King of Prussia. Having inherited from his father a well-drilled army, in 1740 he seized Silesia from Austria, and retained it through the resulting war and the Seven Years war. He also took part in the partition of Poland. An able administrator and and outstanding general he made Prussia powerful and strengthened its military tradition. He corresponded with Voltaire and he also played the flute.

French, Sir John, 1st Earl of Ypres (1852–1925), first British commander-in-chief in the first world war; replaced by Sir Douglas Haig in 1915.

Freud, Sigmund (1856–1939), psychiatrist and founder of psychoanalysis; b. Moravia, studied medicine in Vienna, where he lived until 1938 when the Nazi invasion of Austria sent him into exile in London where he died. His theories of the mind illumined the way we think about ourselves. His grandson, the artist **Lucien Freud** (b. 1911), was awarded the O.M. (1993).

Friedan, Betty (b. 1921), U.S. feminist who wrote *The Feminine Mystique* (1963). Founder of National Organisation of Women (NOW).

Friedman, Milton (b. 1912), American economist. Leading proponent of monetarism. Strongly influenced Thatcherite monetary policy.

Friese-Greene, William (1855–1921), English inventor of the cinematograph. His first film was shown in 1890. He died in poverty.

Frink, Elisabeth (1930–93), English sculptor whose figurative work made her a much-loved artist.

Frobisher, Sir Martin (1535–94), first British navigator to seek the north-west passage from the Atlantic to the Pacific through the Arctic seas. He is commemorated in Frobisher's Strait. He also fought against the Spanish Armada.

Froebel, Friedrich Wilhelm August (1782–1852), German educational reformer, founder of the Kindergarten system.

Froissart, Jean (1337–1410), French author of *Chronicles* covering the history of Western Europe from 1307 to 1400.

Frost, Robert (1874–1963), American poet, author of *Stopping by Woods on a Snowy Evening, Birches, The Death of the Hired Man, After Apple-Picking*.

Froude, James Anthony (1818–94), English historian and biographer of Carlyle.

Fry, Christopher (b. 1907), English poet and dramatist of Quaker family; author of *The Lady's Not for Burning, Venus Observed, The Dark is Light Enough, Curtmantle, A Yard of Sun* and the religious play *A Sleep of Prisoners*.

Fry, Elizabeth (1780–1845), English prison reformer. She lived at Norwich and belonged to the Society of Friends.

Fry, Roger (1866–1934), English art critic and painter; introduced the work of Cézanne and the post-impressionists into England; author of *Vision and Design.*

Fuchs, Leonhard (1501–66), German naturalist whose compendium of medicinal plants was for long a standard work. He was professor of medicine at Tübingen and the genus *Fuchsia* is named after him.

Fuchs, Sir Vivian Ernest (b. 1908), British geologist and explorer; leader of the British Commonwealth Trans-Antarctic Expedition 1957–8, the first to cross the Antarctic continent.

Fuller, Thomas (1608–61), English antiquarian and divine, author of *Worthies of England* and a *Church History of Britain.*

Fulton, Robert (1765–1815), American engineer who experimented in the application of steam to navigation, and in 1807 launched the *Clermont* on the Hudson.

Furniss, Harry (1854–1925), caricaturist, b. Wexford. He came to London as a young man, served on the staff of *Punch* and illustrated the works of Dickens and Thackeray.

G

Gade, Niels Vilhelm (1817–90), Danish composer. While studying at Leipzig he met Mendelssohn, whom he succeeded as conductor of the Gewand-

haus orchestra.

Gagarin, Yuri Alexeyevich (1934–68), Soviet cosmonaut, the first man to be launched into space and brought safely back (12 April 1961). Killed in an air crash.

Gainsborough, Thomas (1727–88), English landscape and portrait painter, b. at Sudbury in Suffolk. His portraits are marked by informality and grace.

Gaiseric or Genseric (c. 390–477), king of the Vandals, the ablest of the barbarian invaders of the Roman empire. He led his people from Spain into Africa, took Carthage, gained control of the Mediterranean and sacked Rome in 455.

Gaitskell, Hugh Todd Naylor (1906–63), Labour politician and economist. He was Chancellor of the Exchequer 1950–1; and leader of the Labour opposition 1955–63.

Galbraith, John Kenneth (b. 1908), American university professor of economics, b. Canada; author of *The Affluent Society* (1958), *The Liberal Hour* (1960), *The New Industrial State* (1967), *The Age of Uncertainty* (1977). He was ambassador to India 1961–3.

Galdós, Benito Pérez. *See* **Pérez Galdós.**

Galen, Claudius (131–201), physician, b. Pergamum (Asia Minor) of Greek parents. He systematised medical knowledge with his idea of purposive creation by the will of God; and thus discouraged original investigation. Many of his treatises survive, and his influence lasted for more than a thousand years.

Galileo (1564–1642), Italian scientist whose experimental-mathematical methods in the pursuit of scientific truth laid the foundations of modern science. He became professor of mathematics at Pisa university when he was 25 and lectured at Padua for 18 years. He made a number of fundamental discoveries, *e.g.*, in regard to the hydrostatic balance, thermometer, telescope, and foreshadowed Newton's laws of motion. He detected the four major satellites of Jupiter, the ring of Saturn, and the spots of the sun. He supported the superiority of the Copernican over the Ptolemaic theory, and was put under house arrest for so doing. He died the year Newton was born. Rehabilitated by Catholic Church, 1992.

Galsworthy, John (1867–1933), English novelist and playwright, author of *The Forsyte Saga*, a series of novels dealing with the history of an upper middle-class family. Nobel prize 1932.

Galton, Sir Francis (1822–1911), founder of eugenics, cousin of Darwin. His early work *Meteorographica* (1863), contains the basis of the modern weather chart. He was an early advocate of using finger-prints for rapid identification, and was one of the first to apply mathematics to biological problems.

Galvani, Luigi (1737–98), Italian physician and physiologist, whose experiments at Bologna demonstrated the principle of animal electricity.

Gama, Vasco da (c. 1460–1524), Portuguese navigator. Discovered the sea route to India in 1498 by rounding the Cape of Good Hope.

Gandhi, Indira (1917–84), daughter of Nehru, succeeded Shastri in 1966 to become India's first woman prime minister. She suffered a defeat at the polls in 1977 but was spectacularly successful in 1980. Assassinated 1984. Succeeded by her son, **Rajiv Gandhi**, who was assassinated in May 1991.

Gandhi, Mohandâs Karamchand (Mahatma) (1869–1948), Indian patriot, social reformer and moral teacher. From 1893 to 1914 he lived in South Africa opposing discrimination against Indians. In the movement for Indian independence after 1914 he dominated Congress, instituted civil disobedience, and advocated non-violence; and he sought to free India from caste. After independence he strove to promote the co-operation of all Indians but was assassinated on his way to a prayer meeting. His teaching of non-violence has had great influence.

Garbo, Greta (1905–90), Swedish film actress of poetical quality. Her films included *Queen Christina* and *Ninotchka*.

García, Manuel de Popolo Vincente (1775–1832), Spanish tenor, composer, and singing master. His son **Manuel Patricio Rodriguez** (1805–1906) was tutor to Jenny Lind. Both his daughters (Mme. Malibran and Mme. Viardot) were operatic singers.

Garcia Lorca, Federico. *See* **Lorca.**

Gardiner, Samuel Rawson (1890–1902), English

historian of the Stuart period.

Garibaldi, Giuseppe (1807–82), Italian soldier and patriot, who with Mazzini and Cavour created a united Italy. In 1834 he was condemned to death for helping in a republican plot to seize Genoa, but escaped to S. America. He returned in 1848 to fight for Mazzini but was again forced to flee. In 1851 he returned and gave his support to Cavour, taking part in the Austrian war of 1859. In 1860 with a thousand volunteers he freed Sicily, took Naples, and handed over the Two Sicilies to Victor Emmanuel who was proclaimed king.

Garrick, David (1717–79), English actor and theatrical manager. Brought up at Lichfield, he was taught by Samuel Johnson.

Garrison, William Lloyd (1805–79), American philanthropist who worked to end slavery.

Gaskell, Mrs. Elizabeth Cleghorn (1810–65), English novelist, author of *Mary Barton, Cranford*, and a *Life of Charlotte Brontë*. She was brought up by an aunt in the little Cheshire town of Knutsford.

Gaulle, Charles de (1890–1970), French general and statesman, son of a headmaster of a Jesuit school; first president of the Fifth Republic 1959–69. He fought in the first world war until his capture in 1916. In the second world war he refused to surrender (1940) and raised and led the Free French forces, with headquarters in England. He came to political power in 1958; allowed Algerian independence in 1962 in face of an army and civilian revolt, initiated closer ties with West Germany (Franco-German treaty 1963), recognised Communist China, withdrew from NATO, building his own nuclear force, vetoed Britain's entry into the Common Market (1963 and 1967); and based his government on personal prestige and use of the referendum in place of parliamentary approval. He was taken by surprise by the rising of students and workers in 1968 and resigned after losing the referendum in 1969.

Gauss, Karl Friedrich (1777–1855), German mathematician. He spent most of his life at the university of Göttingen where he set up the first special observatory for terrestrial magnetism. He made major contributions to astronomy, mathematics, and physics. The unit of magnetic induction is named after him.

Gautama, Siddhartha (Buddha, the enlightened) (c. 563–c.483 B.C.). B. near Benares, a rajah's son, he gave himself up to the religious life and attracted many disciples. Concerned with man's sorrow and suffering, he planned a movement which could be universally shared, in which kindness to others, including animals, took a leading part. His teaching is summarised in the "four noble truths" and the "eightfold path" (*see* **Buddhism, Section J**). After his death his teaching spread (with the help of the King Asoka) over much of India and through eastern Asia as far as Japan.

Gautier, Théophile (1811–72), French poet and novelist, author of *Mademoiselle de Maupin*.

Gay, John (1685–1732), English poet, author of *The Beggar's Opera* (set to music by Pepusch) and *Polly*.

Gay-Lussac, Joseph Louis (1778–1850), French chemist, who showed that when gases combine their relative volumes bear a simple numerical relation to each other and to the volume of their product, if gaseous (1808), *e.g.*, one volume of oxygen combines with two volumes of hydrogen to form two volumes of water vapour.

Ged, William (1690–1749), Scottish printer who patented stereotyping.

Geddes, Sir Patrick (1854–1932), Scottish biologist and a pioneer in town and regional planning, who invented the term conurbation.

Geikie, Sir Archibald (1835–1924), Scottish geologist. His brother **James** specialised in glacial geology.

Genghis Khan (1162–1227), Mongol conqueror. After years of struggle to make good his succession to his father, he overran much of Asia bringing devastation wherever he went.

Geoffrey of Monmouth (1100–54), chronicler, b. Monmouth, later bishop of St. Asaph. His chronicle drew on his creative imagination.

George I (1660–1727), became King of Great Britain in 1714 as descendant of James I. His chief minister was Sir Robert Walpole. Himself personally undistinguished, his reign saw

political development; and in spite of the Jacobite threat (rising in 1715) it began a period of dynastic stability.

George II (1683–1760), son of the above, succeeded in 1727, and survived a more serious Jacobite rising in 1745. His long reign helped the development of constitutional government, for he kept within the limitations of his powers and capacity; and it saw the extension of English power in India and North America.

George III (1738–1820), grandson of George II reigned 1760–1820. Sincere and well-intentioned, but not politically able, he suffered from mental illness due to intermittent porphyria. His reign saw a clash with John Wilkes, the rise of Methodism, and agrarian and industrial revolution; also the loss of the American colonies, the extension and the questioning of English power in India (Warren Hastings), and prolonged French wars.

George IV (1762–1830), eldest son of George III, reigned 1820–30, having become Prince Regent in 1812. Styled "the first gentleman of Europe," he is remembered for his interest in art and architecture. His married life was unfortunate, and the monarchy was at a low ebb; while his reign was a time of distress and of demand for reform.

George V (1865–1936), was the second son of Edward VII and Queen Alexandra. His elder brother died in 1892 and, in 1901, on his father's accession, he became heir to the throne. He joined the Navy as a cadet in 1877. In 1893 he married Princess Mary of Teck. He succeeded in 1910 and discharged his office conscientiously. In 1932 he began the royal broadcast on Christmas Day and in 1935 celebrated his silver jubilee.

George VI (1895–1952), second son of George V, was called to the throne in 1936 on the abdication of his elder brother, Edward VIII. His personal qualities gained wide respect.

George, Henry (1839–97), American political economist whose "single tax" on land values as a means of solving economic problems is expounded in his *Progress and Poverty* (1879).

George, St., patron saint of England, adopted by Edward III. He is believed to have been martyred by Diocletian at Nicomedia in 303 (and not, as believed by Gibbon, to be confused with George of Cappadocia). The story of his fight with the dragon is of late date.

Gershwin, George (1898–1937). American jazz pianist and song-writer, composer of *Rhapsody in Blue* and the Negro folk-opera *Porgy and Bess*.

Gesner, Conrad (1516–65), Swiss naturalist, b. Zurich. His magnificently illustrated volumes describe animal and vegetable kingdoms.

Ghali, Boutros Boutros (b. 1922), Egyptian politician. Secretary-General, United Nations, 1992–96.

Ghiberti, Lorenzo (1378–1455), Florentine sculptor whose bronze doors, beautifying the baptistry in Florence, were described by Michelangelo as fit for the gates of paradise.

Ghirlandaio, Domenico (1449–94), Florentine painter. Most of his frescoes are in Florence, including the cycle of the life of the Virgin and the Baptist in S. Maria Novella. Michelangelo began his apprenticeship in his workshop.

Giacometti, Alberto (1901–66), Swiss sculptor and painter, who worked mainly in Paris and produced abstract symbolic constructions.

Giap, Vo Nguyen (1912–86), Vietnamese general who defeated the French at Dien Bien Phu (1954) and withstood American intervention in the Vietnam war which followed. Replaced in 1980 as defence minister. Retired in 1982.

Gibbon, Edward (1737–94), English historian of the *Decline and Fall of the Roman Empire*.

Gibbons, Grinling (1648–1720), English woodcarver and sculptor, b. Rotterdam, was brought to the notice of Charles II by Evelyn, the diarist. The choir stalls of St. Paul's and the carving in the Wren library at Trinity College, Cambridge, are his work.

Gibbons, Orlando (1583–1625), English composer of church music. *See also* **Section E.**

Gibson, Sir Alexander Drummond (1926–95). Founder and music director of the Scottish Opera Company. One of the foremost Scottish musicians of the century.

Giddens, Anthony (b. 1938). Sociologist. Director, London School of Economics since 1997. Author, *The Third Way* (1998). Reith Lecturer, 1999.

Gide, André (1869–1951), French writer of many short novels in which he gives expression to his struggle to escape from his protestant upbringing (*Strait is the Gate*, *The Counterfeiters*). In his memoir *Si le grain ne meurt* he tells the story of his life up to his marriage.

Gielgud, Sir John (b. 1904), English actor and producer, grand-nephew of Ellen Terry, to whom, the Hamlet of his generation, the present popularity of Shakespeare is largely due. Order of Merit, 1996.

Gilbert, Sir Alfred (1854–1934). English sculptor and goldsmith. His sculptures include *Eros* in Piccadilly Circus.

Gilbert, Sir Humphrey (1537–83), English navigator. He was knighted by Queen Elizabeth for service in Ireland. In 1583 he discovered Newfoundland, but was drowned the same year.

Gilbert, William (1540–1603), English physician to Queen Elizabeth. His book *On the Magnet*, published in Latin in 1600, was the first major contribution to science published in England.

Gilbert, Sir William Schwenck (1836–1911), English humorist and librettist, of the Gilbert and Sullivan light operas. First known as author of the *Bab Ballads*, from 1871 he collaborated with Sir Arthur Sullivan, his wit and satire finding appropriate accompaniment in Sullivan's music. Their operas include *H.M.S. Pinafore*, *Patience*, *Iolanthe*, *The Mikado*, *The Gondoliers*, and *The Yeomen of the Guard.*

Giles, Carl Ronald (1916–95), newspaper cartoonist who discovered the comic genius in the family. His work appeared after 1943 in the *Daily Express.*

Gill, Eric (1882–1940), English sculptor and engraver, whose works include the *Stations of the Cross* (Westminster Cathedral), *Prospero and Ariel* (Broadcasting House), *Christ Driving the Money-changers from the Temple* (Leeds Univ.)

Gillray, James (1757–1815), English caricaturist who produced over a thousand political cartoons.

Giotto di Bondone (1267–1337), Florentine artist. A pupil of Cimabue, he continued the development away from Byzantine tradition towards greater naturalism. His frescoes survive in the churches of Assisi, Padua, and Florence. He designed the western front of the cathedral at Florence and the campanile.

Gissing, George Robert (1857–1903), English novelist whose works deal with the effect of poverty. The best known is *New Grub Street.*

Giulio Romano or **Giulio Pippi** (c. 1492–1546). Italian artist, was a pupil of Raphael. He was also an engineer and architect.

Gladstone, William Ewart (1809–98), English Liberal statesman. B. at Liverpool, he entered parliament in 1832 as a Tory and held office under Peel. From 1852 he served several terms as chancellor of the exchequer and was Liberal prime minister 1868–74, when his legislation included the education act of 1870, the ballot act, the disestablishment of the Church of Ireland and an Irish land act. In 1874 when Disraeli came to power, he temporarily withdrew, but made a come-back in 1879 with his Midlothian campaign. He was again prime minister 1880–5, 1886 and 1892–4; he carried a parliamentary reform act, and advocated home rule for Ireland but was unable to carry it.

Glazunov, Alexander Constantinovich (1865–1936), Russian composer, pupil of Rimsky-Korsakov. The first of his eight symphonies was composed when he was 16.

Glendower, Owen (c. 1350–c. 1416), Welsh chief, who conducted guerrilla warfare on the English border. He figures in Shakespeare's *Henry IV.*

Glinka, Mikhail Ivanovich (1804–57), Russian composer, first of the national school, best known for his operas, *A Life for the Tsar*, and *Russlan and Ludmilla*, based on a poem by Pushkin. *See* Section E.

Gluck, Christoph Wilibald (1714–87), German composer, important in the development of opera. He studied in Prague, Vienna and Italy, and his first operas were in the Italian tradition; but with *Orfeo ed Euridice* (1762) his style became more dramatic. There followed *Alceste*, *Armide*, and *Iphigénie en Tauride. See* Section E.

Goddard, Robert Hutchings (1882–1945), American pioneer of rocket development. He achieved (1926) the first rocket flight with a liquid-fuelled engine.

Gödel, Kurt (1906–78), American mathematician. Devised Gödel's proof, the vitally important proof of modern mathematics which declares that there will always exist statements that can be neither proven nor disproven in any mathematical system which has a finite number of axioms.

Godfrey of Bouillon (c. 1061–1100), Crusader on the first crusade. On capturing Jerusalem declined title of "king", preferring that of protector of the Holy Sepulchre.

Godiva, Lady (1040–80), English benefactress. According to tradition, she obtained from her husband Leofric, Earl of Chester, concessions for the people of Coventry by riding naked through the town.

Godwin, Earl of the West Saxons (d. 1053), was the father of Edith, wife of King Edward the Confessor, and of Harold, last Saxon king.

Godwin William (1756–1836), English political writer and philosopher, author of *Political Justice* (which criticised many contemporary institutions) and a novel *Caleb Williams*. He married **Mary Wollstonecraft** (1759–97), author of *A Vindication of the Rights of Women*; and their daughter, **Mary Wollstonecraft Godwin** (1797–1851) wrote *Frankenstein* and married Shelley.

Goethe, Johann Wolfgang von (1749–1832), German poet and thinker. B. at Frankfurt-on-Main, his first notable work was a romantic play, *Götz von Berlichingen*, followed by a novel *Werthers Leiden*. In 1776 he became privy councillor to the Duke of Weimar, whom he served for many years. He had wide-ranging interests, and made discoveries in anatomy and in botany. Among his later writings are the play *Iphigenie* and the novel *Wilhelm Meister.* His best-known work however is *Faust.*

Gogol, Nikolai Vasilievich (1809–52), Russian novelist and dramatist. His comedy, *The Government Inspector*, satirised provincial bureaucracy; and his novel, *Dead Souls*, deals with malpractice in the purchase of dead serfs.

Golding, Sir William (1911–93), novelist, whose imaginative and experimental fiction includes *Lord of the Flies* (1954) and *The Spire* (1964). Awarded the Nobel Prize for Literature (1983).

Goldsmith, Oliver (1728–74), Irish poet, dramatist and novelist. The son of a poor curate, he came to London in 1756, and eventually joined the circle of Dr. Johnson. Best known for his novel *The Vicar of Wakefield* and his play *She Stoops to Conquer.*

Golovine, Serge (1924–98), a supremely gifted French ballet dancer, equalled only by Nureyev.

Goncourt, Edmond Louis Antoine Huot de (1822–96) and **Jules Alfred Huot de** (1830–70), French brothers, remembered for their *Journal des Goncourts*, an intimate account of Parisian society.

Góngora y Argote, Luis de (1561–1627), Spanish poet, b. Córdova. In *Polifemo* and *Soledades* he attempted to express the core of poetry in new experimental forms.

Goodyear, Charles (1800–60), American inventor who discovered the art of vulcanising rubber.

Goossens, Sir Eugene (1893–1962), English conductor and composer of Belgian descent. His compositions include *Judith* and *Don Juan de Mañara*; brother of **Léon**, oboe virtuoso, and of **Sidonie** and **Marie Goossens**, harpists.

Gorbachev, Mikhail (b. 1931). Soviet politician. Succeeded Chernenko (*q.v.*) as General Secretary of the Communist Party, 1985. His accession marked the end of the "old-guard" leadership. Identified with policies of *glasnost* (openness) and *perestroika* (restructuring). President of the USSR from 1988 until his resignation on 25 December 1991. He presided over revolutionary changes both in Eastern Europe and Russia, but faced a growing crisis at home. The abortive coup in 1991 weakened his position, leading to the collapse of the USSR. Nobel Peace Prize, 1990.

Gordon, Charles George (1833–85), Scottish soldier. After service in the Crimea and China, in 1873 he was made governor of the Equatorial provinces of Egypt; and he was a notable governor of the Sudan, 1877–80. When a rising was led by the Mahdi, he was sent out in 1884 to the garrisons in rebel territory. Murdered by the Mahdi's forces on the palace staircase in Khartoum.

Gordon, Lord George (1751–93), agitator, led No-Popery riots in London in 1780.

Gore, Al (b. 1948), US Vice-President under Clinton. A Democratic contender for the presidential elections in 2000.

Gorky, Maxim (Alexey Maximovich Peshkov) 1868–1936), Russian writer. From the age of ten he worked at many trades from scullion on a Volga steamboat to railway guard, while learning to write: see *My Childhood*. His early work was romantic. He spent many years abroad, but returned in 1928, a supporter of the Soviet regime. His later work is marked by social realism.

Gosse, Sir Edmund (1849–1928), English poet and critic, known for his literary studies of the 17th and 18th centuries; and for his memoir *Father and Son*.

Gounod, Charles François (1818–93), French composer, known for his operas *Faust* and *Roméo et Juliette*. His lyrical gifts are shown in earlier works, such as *Le Médicin malgré lui* and *Mireille*.

Gower, John (1325–1408), English poet of the time of Chaucer, author of *Confessio Amantis*.

Goya y Lucientes, Francisco José (1746–1828), Spanish painter and etcher b. nr. Saragossa. He became court painter to Charles III in 1786. His portraits are painted with ruthless realism; his series of satirical etchings (*Los Caprichos* and the *Disasters of War*) expose man's inhumanity and express his hatred of the cruelty and reaction of his day.

Gracchi, the brothers **Tiberius** (163–133 B.C.) and **Gaius** (153–121 B.C.) who, as Tribunes of the People, tried to reform the system of public landholding and liberalise the franchise at Rome, but were both killed when the Senate suppressed their followers.

Grace, William Gilbert (1848–1915). English cricketer who scored 54,896 runs, including 126 centuries, and took 2,876 wickets.

Grahame, Kenneth (1859–1932), Scottish writer of books for children, including *The Golden Age*, *Dream Days*, and *Wind in the Willows*.

Grahame-White, Claude (1879–1959), the first Englishman to gain an aviator's certificate, 1909.

Grant, Ulysses Simpson (1822–85), American general of the civil war, and president of the United States from 1869 to 1876.

Granville-Barker, Harley (1877–1946), English dramatist, actor, and producer, who promoted the plays of Ibsen, Shaw, *etc*. His own works include *The Voysey Inheritance*.

Grass, Günter (b. 1927), German novelist and poet, whose most famous novel is *Die Blechtrommel* (1959; translated as *The Sin Drum*, 1961).

Grattan, Henry (1746–1820), Irish statesman, who struggled for Irish legislative independence and for Catholic emancipation (though himself a Protestant) and parliamentary reform; but unsuccessfully.

Graves, Robert Ranke (1895–1985), English writer, author of *Goodbye to All That*, written after the first world war; and of *I Claudius* and *Claudius the God*; besides poetry.

Gray, Thomas (1716–71), English poet, author of *Elegy written in a Country Churchyard* and *Ode on a Distant Prospect of Eton College*.

Greeley, Horace (1811–72), American newspaper editor, founder of the New York *Tribune* (1841).

Green, John Richard (1837–83), English historian, author of *Short History of the English People*.

Greenaway, Kate (1846–1901), English artist, who depicted children, especially in book illustrations.

Greene, Graham (1904–91), English novelist and journalist, whose novels (*The Power and the Glory*, *The Heart of the Matter*, *The End of the Affair*, *The Quiet American*, *Our Man in Havana*, *A Burnt-out Case*, *The Comedians*, *The Honorary Consul*), like his plays (*The Complaisant Lover*) and films (*Fallen Idol*, *The Third Man*) deal with moral problems in a modern setting. C.H. (1966), O.M. (1986). Widely regarded as the greatest English novelist of the second half of the century.

Greer, Germaine (b. 1939). Feminist and writer. Born in Melbourne, Australia. Her most famous work is *The Female Eunuch* (1970) which exposed the misrepresentation of female sexuality by a male-dominated society. Her most recent publication is *The Whole Woman* (1999).

Gregory, St. (*c*. 240–332), converted King Tiridates of Armenia, so founding the Armenian church.

Gregory I (the Great), St. (*c*. 540–604), Pope 590–604, was the last great Latin Father and the forerunner of scholasticism. The main founder of the temporal power and the political influence of the papacy, he also maintained the spiritual claims of Rome, enforcing discipline, encouraging monasticism, defining doctrine *etc*. He sent Augustine on a mission to England.

Gregory VII (Hildebrand) (*c*. 1020–85), Pope 1073–

85. He strove for papal omnipotence within the church and for a high standard in the priesthood (especially by stamping out simony and clerical marriage). He also upheld the papacy against the Holy Roman Empire, and the emperor Henry IV did penance for three days in the snow at Canossa.

Gregory XIII (1502–85), Pope 1572–85; introduced the Gregorian calendar.

Gregory, James (1638–75), Scottish mathematician. He invented a reflecting telescope and was the first to show how the distance of the sun could be deduced by observations of the passage of Venus across the disc of the sun. Successive generations of the family reached distinction.

Grenville, Sir Richard (1541–91), English sea captain, who with his one ship engaged a fleet of Spanish war vessels off Flores in 1591, an exploit celebrated in Tennyson's ballad *The Revenge*.

Gresham, Sir Thomas (1519–79), English financier and founder of the Royal Exchange. Son of a Lord Mayor of London, he was an astute moneyfinder for four successive sovereigns, including Queen Elizabeth I. "Gresham's Law" is the statement that bad money drives out good.

Greuze, Jean Baptiste (1725–1805), French artist, known especially for his studies of girls. His *Girl with Doves* is in the Wallace Collection.

Grey, 2nd Earl (Charles Grey) (1764–1845), British Whig statesman under whose premiership were passed the Reform Bill of 1832, a bill abolishing slavery throughout the Empire (1833), and the Poor Law Amendment Act, 1834.

Grey, Lady Jane (1537–54), Queen of England for a few days. The daughter of the Duke of Suffolk, she was put forward as queen by protestant leaders on the death of her cousin, Edward VI; but overcome by the legal claimant, Mary Tudor, and executed.

Grieg, Edvard Hagerup (1843–1907), Norwegian composer, b. Bergen. He presented the characteristics of his country's music with strong accentuation. He is best known for his incidental music to *Peer Gynt*.

Griffin, Bernard William (1899–1956), Roman catholic archbishop of Westminster, 1944–56.

Griffith, Arthur (1872–1922), the first president of the Irish Free State, 1921; founder of the *Sinn Fein* movement.

Griffith, David Wark (1880–1948), American film producer, who introduced the close-up, and the flash-back, and developed leading actors.

Grimaldi, Joseph (1779–1837), British clown, "the father of modern clowning", who won enormous acclaim at Covent Garden.

Grimm, the brothers **Jakob Ludwig Karl** (1785–1863), and **Wilhelm Karl** (1786–1859), German philologists and folk-lorists, best known for their *Fairy Tales*. Jakob published a notable philological dictionary, *Deutsche Grammatik*. The brothers also projected the vast *Deutsches Wörtebuch* which was completed by German scholars in 1961.

Grimond, Lord (Joseph) (1913–93), Leader of the Liberal Party, 1956–67.

Grimthorpe, 1st Baron (Edmund Beckett Denison) (1816–1905), horologist who invented the double three-legged escapement for the clock at Westminster, familiarly known as "Big Ben" (the name of the bell). Known as Sir Edmund Beckett.

Gromyko, Andrei Andreevich (1909–89), Russian diplomat and statesman. President, USSR, July 1985–88, Foreign Minister, 1957–85.

Grossmith, George (1847–1912), English actor. With his brother, **Weedon Grossmith**, he wrote *Diary of a Nobody*. His son, **George Grossmith** (1874–1935) was a comedian and introduced revue and cabaret entertainment into England.

Grote, George (1794–1871), English historian, author of a *History of Greece*.

Grotius (Huig van Groot) (1583–1645), Dutch jurist, the founder of international law. He was condemned to life imprisonment for religious reasons, but escaped to Paris, where he wrote *De Jure Belli et Pacis*.

Grouchy, Emmanuel, Marquis de (1766–1847), French general, who served under Napoleon; after Waterloo led defeated army back to Paris.

Grove, Sir George (1820–1900), English musicologist, author of *Dictionary of Music and Musicians*. By profession he was a civil engineer.

Guevara, Ernesto "Che" (1928–67), revolutionary hero, b. Argentina. He took part in the Cuban guerrilla war and became a minister in the Cuban government 1959–65. He was killed while leading a band of guerrillas against American-trained Bolivian troops. His remains were buried in Cuba in 1997.

Guido Reni (1575–1642), Italian painter of the Bolognese school whose works are characteristic of the Italian baroque of his period and include the *Aurora* fresco in the Rospigliosi palace at Rome, and *Crucifixion of St. Peter* (Vatican).

Guinness, Sir Alec (b. 1914), English actor of extraordinary versatility. Awarded an Oscar for *The Bridge on the River Kwai*. C.H. (1995).

Gustavus Adolphus (1594–1632), King of Sweden, the "Lion of the North." After a campaign in Poland he entered the Thirty Years' war in support of Swedish interests and Protestant distress, won the battle of Breitenfeld in 1631 and was killed in action the next year.

Gutenberg, Johann (*c.* 1400–68), German printer, b. Mainz, the first European to print with movable types cast in moulds. The earliest book printed by him was the Mazarin Bible (see **L76**).

Guy, Thomas (1644–1724), English philanthropist. A printer, he made money by speculation; and in 1722 founded Guy's Hospital in Southwark.

Gwyn, Nell (*c.* 1650–87), English actress and mistress of Charles II by whom she had two sons. Of Hereford origin, she sold oranges in London and became a comedienne at Drury Lane.

H

Hadley, George (1685–1768). He developed Halley's theory of the trade winds by taking into account the effect of the earth's rotation and the displacement of air by tropical heat (1735).

Hadrian (76–138), Roman emperor. An able general, he suppressed revolts, and he was also a lover of the arts. He visited Britain *c.* A.D. 121 and built a protective wall between Wallsend-on-Tyne and Bowness-on-Solway.

Hafiz, pseudonym of **Shams ad-Din Mohammed** (d. *c.* 1388), Persian lyrical poet. His principal work is the *Divan*, a collection of short sonnets called *ghazals*. The sobriquet *Hafiz*, meaning one who remembers, is applied to anyone who has learned the Koran by heart.

Hague, William. *See* **D17.**

Hahn, Otto (1879–1968), German chemist and physicist, chief discoverer of uranium fission.

Hahnemann, Samuel Christian Friedrich (1755–1843), German physician who founded homoeopathy (treatment of disease by small doses of drugs that in health produce similar symptoms).

Haig, Douglas, 1st Earl of Bermersyde (1861–1928), British field-marshal, b. Edinburgh. He replaced French as commander-in-chief in France, 1915–19, leading the offensive in August 1918; and after the war presided over the British Legion.

Haile Selassie I (1891–1975), Emperor of Ethiopia 1930–74. He spent the years of the Italian occupation 1936–41 in England. Deposed 1974.

Hakluyt, Richard (1553–1616), English writer on maritime discovery. B. in Herefordshire, he spent some time in Paris. From 1582 (when *Divers Voyages* appeared), he devoted his life to collecting and publishing accounts of English navigators, thus giving further impetus to discovery.

Haldane, John Burdon Sanderson (1892–1964), biologist and geneticist, noted not only for his work in mathematical evolutionary theory but for explaining science to the layman. He emigrated to India in 1957. He was the son of **John Scott Haldane** (1860–1936), b. Edinburgh, who studied the effect of industrial occupations upon health.

Haldane, 1st Viscount (Richard Burdon Haldane) (1856–1928). British Liberal statesman. As war minister in 1905 he reorganised the army and founded the Territorials.

Hale, George Ellery (1868–1935), American astronomer, after whom is named the 200-inch reflecting telescope on Mount Palomar.

Halévy, Ludovic (1834–1903), French playwright, who collaborated with Henri Meilhac in writing libretti for Offenbach and Bizet.

Halifax, 1st Earl of (Edward Frederick Lindley Wood) (1881–1959), British Conservative politician; foreign secretary during the period of appeasement of Germany; as Lord Irwin, viceroy of India 1926–31.

Halifax, 1st Marquess of (George Savile) (1633–95), English politician of changeable views, who wrote *Character of a Trimmer*.

Hall, Sir Peter (Reginald Frederick) (b. 1930). Leading director of plays, films and operas. Director, National Theatre, 1973–88.

Hallam, Henry (1777–1859), English historian, best known for his *Constitutional History*. He was father of Arthur Hallam, friend of Tennyson.

Hallé, Sir Charles (1819–95), German-born pianist and conductor, who settled in Manchester and organised an orchestra of high-class talent. He married the violinist Wilhelmine Neruda.

Halley, Edmond (1656–1742), English astronomer royal 1720–42. He published observations on the planets and comets, being the first to predict the return of a comet (*see* **Section L**). He furthered Newton's work on gravitation, setting aside his own researches. He made the first magnetic survey of the oceans from the naval vessel *Paramour*, 1698–1700. His meteorological observations led to his publication of the first map of the winds of the globe (1686).

Hals, Frans (*c.* 1580–1666), Dutch portrait painter, b. at Mechlin. He is best known for his *Laughing Cavalier* in the Wallace Collection, and for portraits in the Louvre and at Amsterdam.

Hamann, Johann Georg (1730–88), German philosopher. Friend of Kant. An important counter-Enlightenment thinker.

Hamilton, Alexander (1755–1804), American statesman and economist. With Madison and Jay he wrote the *Federalist* (1787). As secretary of the Treasury (1789–95) he put Washington's government on a firm financial footing and planned a national bank. He was the leader of the Federalists, a party hostile to Jefferson. He was killed in a duel.

Hamilton, Emma, Lady (*née* **Lyon**) (*c.* 1765–1815), a beauty of humble birth who, after several liaisons, was married in 1791 to Sir William Hamilton, British ambassador at Naples. There she met Nelson, and later bore him a child, Horatia.

Hammarskjöld, Dag (1905–61), Swedish Secretary-General of the United Nations, 1953–61. He was killed in an air crash while attempting to mediate in a dispute between Zaïre and the province of Katanga. Posthumous Nobel peace prize.

Hammond, John Lawrence (1872–1949), English historian of social and industrial history, whose works (with his wife Barbara) include *The Town Labourer* and *The Village Labourer*.

Hampden, John (1594–1643), English parliamentarian and civil war leader. He refused to pay Charles I's ship money in 1636. When civil war broke out, he raised a regiment and was killed on Chalgrove Field.

Hamsun, Knut, pen-name of Knut Pedersen (1859–1952), Norwegian author who in his youth struggled for existence, visited America twice and earned his living by casual labour. *The Growth of the Soil* won him the Nobel prize in 1920. Other great novels are *Hunger* and *Mysteries*.

Handel, George Frederick (1685–1759), German composer, son of a barber-surgeon to the Duke of Saxony; b. Halle, the same year as Bach; spent much of his life in England composing operas and oratorios. His operas, of which there are over 40, include *Atalanta, Berenice* and *Serse*, and his oratorios, of which there are 32, include *Saul, Israel in Egypt, Samson, Messiah, Judas Maccabaeus,* and *Jephtha*. Before he died he became blind and relied upon his old friend and copyist John Christopher Smith to commit his music to paper. *See* **Section E.**

Hannibal (247–182 B.C.), Carthaginian general. He fought two wars against Rome. In the first he conquered southern Spain. In the second he overran Gaul, crossed the Alps, and defeated the Romans in successive battles, especially at Cannae. Thereafter his forces were worn down by Roman delaying tactics; he was defeated by Scipio at Zama and later poisoned himself.

Harcourt, Sir William Vernon (1827–1904), Liberal politician who revised death duties.

Hardicanute (1019–42), son of Canute, and last Danish king of England.

Hardie, James Keir (1856–1915), Scottish Labour leader, one of the founders of the Labour party.

He first worked in a coal-pit; in 1882 became a journalist; and in 1892 was the first socialist to be elected to the House of Commons (for West Ham – South). He edited the *Labour Leader* 1887–1904. He was the first chairman of the parliamentary Labour party, 1906. A pacifist, he opposed the Boer war.

Hardy, Thomas (1840–1928), English novelist and poet, was trained as an architect and practised for some time, but became known in 1871 with *Desperate Remedies*. In 1874 his *Far from the Madding Crowd* was published. Following that came a series of novels, including *The Trumpet-Major*, *The Mayor of Casterbridge*, *Tess of the D'Urbervilles*, and *Jude the Obscure*. In 1908 he completed a dramatic poem, *The Dynasts*, whose central figure is Napoleon. His underlying theme is man's struggle against neutral forces, and he depicts the Wessex countryside.

Hargreaves, James (1720–78), English inventor, b. Blackburn. His spinning-jenny was invented in 1764 and became widely used, though his own was broken by spinners in 1768 and his invention brought him no profit.

Harkness, Edward Stephen (1874–1940), American banker and philanthropist, who in 1930 founded the Pilgrim Trust in Gt. Britain.

Harley, Robert, 1st Earl of Oxford and Mortimer (1661–1724), English statesman and collector of MSS. He held office under Queen Anne, and brought a European war to an end with the treaty of Utrecht. After the Hanoverian succession he lived in retirement, and formed the MSS. collection, now in the British Museum, which bears his name.

Harold II (1022–66), last Saxon king of England, was son of Earl Godwin. He was chosen king in succession to Edward the Confessor. He had at once to meet a dual invasion. He defeated the Norwegian king at Stamford Bridge; but was himself defeated by William of Normandy at the battle of Hastings (fought at Battle 1066).

Harriman, William Averell (1891–1986), American public official. He was adviser to President Roosevelt and later presidents especially on Marshall Aid and foreign affairs.

Harris, Joel Chandler (1848–1908), American author, creator of Uncle Remus and Brer Rabbit.

Harrison, Frederic (1831–1923), English philosopher and lawyer, author of *The Meaning of History* and *The Philosophy of Common Sense*. He was president of the Positivist Committee.

Harrison, John (1693–1776), "Longitude Harrison," English inventor of the chronometer, b. near Pontefract, Yorkshire, the son of a carpenter.

Harty, Sir Hamilton (1880–1941), composer and for some years conductor of the Hallé orchestra.

Harun al-Rashid (Aaron the Upright) (763–809), 5th Abbasid caliph of Baghdad. His court was a centre for art and learning, but he governed mainly through his vizier until the latter lost favour and was executed in 803. The *Arabian Nights* associated with him are stories collected several centuries later.

Harvey, William (1578–1657), English physician and discoverer of the circulation of the blood. B. at Folkestone, he studied at Padua while Galileo was there, and was physician to James I and Charles I. His treatise on circulation was published in Latin in 1628.

Hastings, Warren (1732–1818), English administrator in India. As governor-general of Bengal for the East India Company he revised the finances and administration and put down disorder. On his return to England he was impeached for alleged corruption, and, though acquitted, lost his fortune in his own defence. Later however he received a grant from the company.

Hauptmann, Gerhart (1862–1946), German dramatist and novelist. B. in Silesia. His play *The Weavers* deals with a revolt of 1844 and has a collective hero. Other works include *Die versunkene Glocke*, *Der arme Heinrich*, and *Rose Bernd*. Nobel prizewinner 1912.

Havel, Vaclav (b. 1936) Czech playwright, dissident and statesman. Imprisoned, 1979–83. President of Czechoslovakia, December 1989–92. President of new Czech Republic since January 1993.

Havelock, Sir Henry (1795–1857), British general who helped to put down the Indian mutiny.

Hawke, 1st Baron (Edward Hawke) (1705–81), English admiral, who in 1759 defeated the French at Quiberon in a tremendous storm.

Hawking, Stephen William (b. 1942), British theoretical physicist. Lucasian Professor of Mathematics, Cambridge University, since 1979. Author of *300 Years of Gravitation* (1987) and *A Brief History of Time* (1988). Companion of Honour (1989). Sufferer from motor neurone disease.

Hawkins, Sir John (1532–95), English sailor and slave-trader. Born at Plymouth. In 1562 he was the first Englishman to traffic in slaves. Treasurer of the Navy, 1585–88. He helped to defeat the Spanish Armada in 1588, commanding the *Victory*. Died at sea off Puerto Rico, 12 Nov. 1595.

Hawthorne, Nathaniel (1804–64), American author. His works include *The Marble Faun*, *The Scarlet Letter* and *The House of the Seven Gables*.

Haydn, Franz Joseph (1732–1809), Austrian composer, belongs to the classical period of Bach, Handel, and Mozart. He has been given the title "father of the symphony." Much of his life was spent as musical director to the princely Hungarian house of Esterhazy. In 1791 and again in 1794 he visited London, where he conducted his Salomon symphonies. His two great oratorios, *The Creation* and *The Seasons*, were written in old age. *See* **Section E**.

Hayek, Friedrich August (von) (1899–1992), Austrian economist. The 'father of monetarism.' Strongly influenced development of Thatcherite monetary policies. Shared Nobel Prize for Economics, 1974. C.H. (1984).

Hazlitt, William (1778–1830), English essayist and critic. His writings include *The Characters of Shakespeare's Plays*, *Table Talk*, and *The Spirit of the Age*. His grandson **William Carew Hazlitt** (1834–1913) was a bibliographer and writer.

Heaney, Seamus (b. 1939), Irish poet, whose works include *Death of a Naturalist* (1966) and *North* (1975). Professor of Poetry, Oxford University, 1989–94. Professor of Rhetoric and Oratory, Harvard University, USA. Awarded the Nobel Prize for Literature, 1995. His most recent book of poems is *The Spirit Level* (1996).

Heath, Sir Edward (b. 1916), British statesman, leader of the Conservative Party 1965–75; prime minister 1970–74; leader of the opposition 1965–70, 1974–75. In 1973 he took Britain into the EEC. Order of the Garter, 1992. "Father of the House" since 1992.

Hedin, Sven Anders (1865–1952), Swedish explorer of Central Asia; wrote *My Life as Explorer*.

Heenan, John Carmel (1905–76). English Roman Catholic Archbishop of Westminster 1963–76.

Hegel, Georg Wilhelm Friedrich (1770–1831), German idealist philosopher, b. Stuttgart, whose name is associated with the dialectic method of reasoning with its sequence of thesis —antithesis–synthesis. He studied theology at Tübingen with his friend Schelling. He taught philosophy at Jena, Nuremberg, Heidelberg, and Berlin. He produced an abstract philosophical system which was influenced by his early interest in mysticism and his Prussian patriotism. His doctrines were very influential in the 19th cent. and led to modern totalitarianism. *See* **Dialectical Materialism, Section J**.

Heidenstam, Verner von (1859–1940), Swedish author and poet, leader of a new romantic movement. Nobel prizewinner 1916.

Heine, Heinrich (1797–1856), German lyric poet, b. Düsseldorf. He lived mostly in Paris.

Heisenberg, Werner (1901–76), German physicist, noted for his theory of quantum mechanics and the Uncertainty Principle. Nobel Prize, 1932.

Heller, Joseph (b. 1923), U.S. novelist, whose celebrated novel is *Catch 22* (1961).

Helmholtz, Herman von (1821–94), German physicist and physiologist. He published his *Erhaltung der Kraft* (Conservation of Energy) in 1847, the same year that Joule gave the first clear exposition of the principle of energy. His pupil Heinrich Hertz discovered electromagnetic radiation in accordance with Maxwell's theory.

Heloïse (c. 1101–64), beloved of Abelard (*q.v.*). Her letters to him are extant.

Hemingway, Ernest (1898–1961), American novelist of new technique and wide influence. His works include *A Farewell to Arms*, *Death in the Afternoon*, *For Whom the Bell Tolls*, *The Old Man and the Sea*. He committed suicide. Nobel prizewinner 1954.

Henderson, Arthur (1863–1935), British Labour

politician, b. Glasgow. He worked mainly for disarmament. Nobel peace prize, 1934.

Henrietta Maria (1609–69), the daughter of Henry IV of France and wife of Charles I.

Henry, Joseph (1797–1878), American physicist and schoolteacher who independently of Faraday discovered the principle of the induced current. The weather-reporting system he set up at the Smithsonian Institution led to the creation of the U.S. Weather Bureau.

Henry I (1068–1135), King of England. The youngest son of William the Conqueror, he ascended the throne during the absence on crusade of his elder brother Robert of Normandy. His long reign brought order and progress, not entirely destroyed by the anarchy under his successor Stephen.

Henry II (1133–89), King of England. He was son of Matilda, daugher of Henry I, and Geoffrey Plantagenet, count of Anjou; and his lands stretched to the Pyrenees. He was a strong ruler to whom we largely owe the establishment of the common law system and permanent administrative reforms. His conflict with the Church led to the murder of archbishop Becket.

Henry III (1207–72), King of England, succeeded his father John in 1216. Himself devout and simple, his long reign was troubled by a partly factious baronial opposition.

Henry IV (1367–1413), grandson of Edward III and heir to the Duchy of Lancaster, became king of England in 1399. More solid and practical than his cousin Richard II, whom he had supplanted, he consolidated the government.

Henry V (1387–1422), son of Henry IV, succeeded his father as king of England in 1413. A successful commander, he renewed the French war and won the battle of Agincourt, but died young.

Henry VI (1421–71), son of Henry V, succeeded his father as king of England in 1422 as a baby. Gentle and retiring, he inherited a losing war with France. He founded Eton, and King's College, Cambridge. The Yorkist line claimed the crown from his (the Lancastrian) line, and the Wars of the Roses led to his deposition and death. Ruled 1422–61, 1470–71.

Henry VII (1457–1509) succeeded Richard III as king of England after defeating him in 1485. The first Tudor king, he was firm and shrewd, even avaricious; he built Henry VII's Chapel in Westminster Abbey, and encouraged John Cabot to sail to North America.

Henry VIII (1491–1547), King of England, succeeded his father Henry VII in 1509. A prince of the Renaissance, skilled in music and sports, he loved the sea and built up the navy. His minister Cardinal Wolsey fell when Henry, seeking divorce to obtain a legal heir, rejected papal supremacy and dissolved the monasteries. Ruthless and ostentatious, he executed Sir Thomas More and spent his father's wealth. The father of **Edward VI, Mary I** and **Elizabeth I**.

Henry IV of France (Henry of Navarre) (1553–1610). Prior to becoming king, he was the leader of the Huguenots; and although on being crowned he became a Catholic, he protected the Protestants by the Edict of Nantes. He then became a national king, but was later assassinated by Ravaillac, a religious fanatic.

Henry the Navigator (1394–1460), Portuguese promoter of discovery, son of John I. His sailors discovered Madeira and the Azores.

Henschel, Sir George (1850–1934), singer, composer, and conductor. B. in Breslau, he became a naturalised Englishman. Founder and conductor of the London Symphony Concerts (1886).

Hepplewhite, George (d. 1786), English cabinet-maker whose name is identified with the style which followed the Chippendale period.

Heraclitus of Ephesus (c. 540–475 B.C.), Greek philosopher. His discovery of a changing world (he lived in an age of social revolution when the ancient tribal aristocracy was beginning to give way to democracy) influenced the philosophies of Parmenides, Democritus, Plato, and Aristotle, and later, of Hegel.

Herbert, George (1593–1633), the most purely devotional of English poets.

Hereward the Wake, the last Saxon leader to hold out against the Normans. His base in the fens was captured in 1071 but he escaped. His exploits were written up by Kingsley.

Herod the Great (c. 73–4 B.C.). At first governor of Galilee under the Romans, he obtained the title of king of Judaea in 31 B.C. The massacre of the Innocents reported in St. Matthew (though not corroborated in any contemporary history) is in keeping with his historical character.

Herodotus (c. 485–425 B.C.), Greek historian, called by Cicero, the father of history. He travelled widely collecting historical evidence.

Herrick, Robert (1591–1674), English lyric poet. His poems include *Gather ye Rose Buds*, *Cherry Ripe*, and *Oberon's Feast*.

Herriot, Edouard (1872–1957), French Radical-Socialist statesman. A scholar, long-time mayor of Lyons. Three times prime minister. President of the National Assembly 1947–54.

Herschel, Sir John (1792–1871), British astronomer who continued his father's researches and also pioneered photography, a term introduced by him. One of his twelve children introduced fingerprints into criminology.

Herschel, Sir William (1738–1822), German-born astronomer who came to England from Hanover as a musician; father of the above. Unrivalled as an observer, and with telescopes of his own making he investigated the distribution of stars in the Milky Way and concluded that some of the nebulae he could see were separate star systems outside our own. He discovered the planet Uranus in 1781.

Hertz, Heinrich Rudolf (1857–95), German physicist, whose laboratory experiments confirmed Maxwell's electromagnetic theory of waves and yielded information about their behaviour.

Herzl, Theodor (1860–1904), founder of modern political Zionism, was b. Budapest. He convened a congress at Basle in 1897.

Heseltine, Michael. See **D17**.

Hesiod (fl. c. 735 B.C.), Greek poet, author of *Work and Days*, which tells of life in the country.

Hildegard von Bingen, St. (1098–1179), medieval Benedictine nun, visionary and writer. The 'Sibyl of the Rhine'.

Hill, Octavia (1838–1912), English social reformer concerned with the housing conditions of the poor, a pioneer in slum clearance in London; founder (with Sir Robert Hunter and Canon Rawnsley) of the National Trust.

Hill, Sir Rowland (1795–1879), originator of the penny postal system. He was secretary to the Postmaster-General 1846–54, then chief secretary to the Post Office until 1864.

Hillary, Sir Edmund (b.1919), New Zealand mountaineer and explorer. Won world-wide fame when he and Sherpa Tenzing were the first to reach the summit of Mt. Everest in 1953. Order of the Garter (1995).

Hindemith, Paul (1895–1963), German composer and viola player. He is associated with the movement in *Gebrauchsmusik*, which regarded music as a social expression. He incurred Nazi hostility and his later life was spent abroad. His numerous works include chamber works, songs, operas, ballet music, symphonies, and the oratorio *Das Umaufhörliche. See also* **Section E.**

Hindenburg, Paul von (1847–1934), German field-marshal. In 1914 he defeated the Russians at Tannenberg. In his old age a national hero, President of the German Reich, 1925–34.

Hinshelwood, Sir Cyril Norman (1897–1967), English chemist. He shared with Prof. Semenov of Russia the 1956 Nobel prize for chemistry for researches into the mechanism of chemical reactions. Pres. Royal Society, 1955–60.

Hinton of Bankside, Baron (Christopher Hinton) (1901–83), pioneer in nuclear energy.

Hippocrates of Chios (fl. c. 430 B.C.), Greek mathematician, the first to compile a work on the elements of geometry.

Hippocrates of Cos (fl. c. 430 B.C.), Greek physician, whose writings are lost, but who is believed to have established medical schools in Athens and elsewhere, and to have contributed towards a scientific separation of medicine from superstition. Seen as the ideal physician.

Hirohito, Emperor of Japan (1901–89), acceded to the throne in 1926. In 1946 he renounced his legendary divinity. Much controversy surrounds his role in Japanese aggression in the 1930s and his part in the Second World War.

Hitler, Adolf (1889–1945), German dictator, founder of National Socialism, b. in Austria, son of a customs official. He was in Vienna for 5 years with no regular work before going to Munich in

B32

1913; enlisted in Bavarian infantry at outbreak of the Kaiser's war. At the end of the war conditions in Germany favoured the growth of a fascist movement and under his leadership the National Socialist (Nazi) party climbed to power. He became Reich chancellor in 1933 and on the death of Hindenburg in 1934 Führer; and commander-in-chief Wehrmacht 1935. Under his regime working class movements were ruthlessly destroyed; all opponents—communists, socialists, Jews—were persecuted and murdered. By terrorism and propaganda the German state was welded into a powerful machine for aggression. There followed the occupation of the Rhineland (1936), the annexation of Austria and Czechoslovakia (1938–9), the invasion of Poland and declaration of war by Great Britain and France (1939), the invasion of Russia (1941). Final defeat came in 1945; on 30 April he committed suicide as the Russian troops closed in on Berlin.

Hobbes, Thomas (1588–1679), English philosopher who published *Leviathan* in 1651. He favoured strong government and supported the supremacy of the state, but his arguments aroused antagonism even among royalists. He was an enthusiast for scientific enquiry.

Hobhouse, Leonard Trelawney (1864–1929), English sociologist. His books include *The Theory of Knowledge*, *Morals in Evolution*, and *Development and Purpose*.

Ho Chi-minh (1892–1969), leader of the Vietnam revolutionary nationalist party of Indo-China, which struggled for independence from France during and after the second world war. His main purpose was to weld together the nationalistic and communistic elements in Vietnam. As president of North Vietnam he fought to extend his control over South Vietnam, defying the United States.

Hodgkin, Sir Alan (1914–98), British biophysicist working in the field of nerve impulse conduction. He was one of the world's most eminent biophysicists. Pres. Royal Society, 1970–75. Nobel prizewinner, 1970; O.M. 1973.

Hodgkin, Dorothy Crowfoot (1919–94), the third woman to win the Nobel prize in chemistry, awarded in 1964 for her X-ray analysis to elucidate the structure of complex molecules, notably penicillin and vitamin B-12. She and her team at the Department of Molecular Biophysics at Oxford succeeded in 1969 in determining the crystalline structure of insulin. O.M. (1965).

Hofbauer, Imre (d. 1990), Hungarian-born artist, whose brilliance was portrayed in his compassionate studies of the down-trodden.

Hogarth, William (1697–1764), English engraver and painter, who satirised his time with character, humour, and power, especially in his *Harlot's Progress*, *Rake's Progress*, *Marriage à la Mode*, *Industry and Idleness*, and *The March to Finchley*.

Hogg, Quintin (1845–1903), educationist and philanthropist who purchased the old Polytechnic Institution in 1882 and turned it into a popular college providing education at moderate rates. His grandson, **Lord Hailsham**, was Lord Chancellor 1970–4, 1979–83, 1983–87.

Hokusai, Katsushika (1760–1849), Japanese landscape artist of the Ukiyo-e (popular school).

Holbein, Hans, the elder (c. 1465–1524), German painter, b. Augsburg, father of:

Holbein, Hans, the younger (1497–1543), German painter, b. Augsburg; settled in London 1532. He won the favour of Henry VIII, for whom he painted many portraits. He is also known for his series *The Dance of Death*.

Holden, Charles (1875–1960), British architect, designer of public buildings, including British Medical Asscn. Building, London; Underground Head Offices; Senate House *etc.*

Holden, Sir Isaac (1807–97), British inventor of woolcombing machinery.

Hölderlin, Johann Christian Friedrich (1770–1843), German poet, friend of Hegel. His works include the novel *Hyperion* and the elegy *Menon's Laments for Diotima*. In his middle years his mind became unhinged.

Holford, Baron (William Graham Holford) (1907–75), British architect and town-planner; planned post-war redevelopment of London.

Holmes, Oliver Wendell (1809–94), American author. His writings include *Autocrat of the Breakfast Table*, *The Professor of the Breakfast*

Table, and *The Poet at the Breakfast Table.*

Holst, Gustave Theodore (1874–1934), British composer of Swedish descent whose compositions include *The Planets* suite, *The Hymn of Jesus*, an opera *The Perfect Fool*, and a choral symphony. An outstanding teacher. *See* **Section E.**

Holyoake, George Jacob (1817–1906), English social reformer and secularist. He wrote a history of the co-operative movement.

Holyoake, Keith Jacka (1904–83), New Zealand politician; prime minister 1960–72.

Home of the Hirsel, Lord (Alex Douglas-Home) (1903–95), British Prime Minister, 1963–64 (after renouncing his peerage as 14th Earl of Home). Foreign Secretary, 1960–63, 1970–74. Created Life Peer, 1974. His younger brother was the playwright **William Douglas-Home** (1912–92).

Homer (c. 700 B.C.), epic poet. He is supposed to have been a Greek who lived at Chios or Smyrna, and has been regarded as the author of the *Iliad* and the *Odyssey*, though this is tradition rather than ascertained fact.

Hood, 1st Viscount (Samuel Hood) (1724–1816), British admiral who in 1793 was in command of the Mediterranean fleet and occupied Toulon.

Hood, Thomas (1799–1845), English poet. His poems include *The Song of the Shirt*, *The Dream of Eugene Aram* and *The Bridge of Sighs*. He was also a humorist and punster.

Hooke, Robert (1635–1703), English physicist. His inventions include the balance spring of watches. He was also an architect and drew up a plan for rebuilding London after the Great Fire. His *Diary* is published.

Hooker, Richard (1554–1600), English theologian, author of *Ecclesiastical Polity*. He was Master of the Temple, 1585–91. For his choice of words he was known as "Judicious Hooker".

Hopkins, Sir Frederick Gowland (1861–1947), English biochemist, pioneer in biochemical and nutritional research. He first drew attention to the substances later known as vitamins. Pres. Royal Society 1930–5. Nobel prize 1929.

Hopkins, Gerard Manley (1844–89), English poet of religious experience and of a novel style.

Hopkins, Harry (1890–1946), Franklin Roosevelt's personal assistant at foreign conferences, and in the New Deal and Lend-Lease.

Hopkinson, John (1849–98), English engineer. By developing the theory of alternating current and of the magnetic current in dynamos he paved the way to the common use of electricity.

Hoppner, John (1758–1810), English portrait painter, b. Whitechapel, of German parents.

Horace (Quintus Horatius Flaccus) (65–8 B.C.), Roman satirist and poet, son of a Greek freedman. He wrote *Satires*, *Epodes*, *Odes*, and *Epistles*. He fought on the republican side at Philippi, but became poet laureate to Augustus.

Horniman, Annie Elizabeth Fredericka (1860–1937), founder of the modern repertory system in England. Her father F. J. Horniman founded the Horniman Museum.

Hosking, Eric (1909–91), bird photographer. A highly skilled ornithologist and tireless champion of the grace and beauty of birds.

Hoskins, William George (1908–92), the great local historian of England and the English. Author of *The Making of the English Landscape* (1955).

Houdini, Harry (Erich Weiss) (1874–1926), American illusionist, son of a Hungarian rabbi. Famed for his escapes from handcuffs.

Housman, Alfred Edward (1859–1936), English poet, author of *A Shropshire Lad*; he was also a classical scholar. His brother Laurence (1865–1959) was a playwright and wrote *Little Plays of St. Francis* and *Victoria Regina*.

Howard, John (1726–90), English prison reformer. Imprisoned in France in wartime, he subsequently investigated English prisons, securing reforms; and later also continental prisons, dying in Russia of gaol fever.

Howard of Effingham, 2nd Baron (Charles Howard) (1536–1624), afterwards Earl of Nottingham; commanded the fleet which defeated the Spanish Armada (1588), and took part in the capture of Cadiz (1596).

Howe, Elias (1819–67), American inventor of the sewing machine.

Howe, Julia Ward (1819–1910), American suffragette, author of *Mine eyes have seen the glory.*

Howe, 1st Earl (Richard Howe) (1726–99), British admiral whose victories over the French in two wars included that off Ushant on 1 June 1794 ("the glorious first of June").

Hua-Guofeng (b. 1922), b. Hunan, succeeded Mao Tse-tung as Communist Party Chairman, 1976–81.

Hubble, Edwin Powell (1889–1953), American astronomer, noted for his work on extragalactic nebulae. With the 100-inch telescope on Mount Wilson he detected the Cepheid variables. The Hubble space telescope is named after him.

Huddleston, Trevor (1913–98), Anglican archbishop who devoted his life to fighting apartheid.

Hudson, Henry (d. 1611), English navigator credited with the discovery of the Hudson river and Hudson Bay, where mutineers turned him adrift to die. He was on a voyage to find a passage by the north pole to Japan and China.

Hudson, William Henry (1841–1922), naturalist, b. Buenos Aires of American parents, naturalised in England (1900). His books include *The Purple Land, Green Mansions,* and *Far Away and Long Ago.* Hyde Park bird sanctuary was established in his memory.

Huggins, Sir William (1824–1910), astronomer who pioneered in spectroscopic photography.

Hughes, Ted (1930–98), English poet. Succeeded Sir John Betjeman as Poet Laureate (*see* **L97**) in 1984. His early, poignant poems observed the natural world (as in the collection *The Hawk in the Rain*). O.M. (1998).

Hughes, Thomas (1822–96), English novelist, author of *Tom Brown's Schooldays,* which is based on Rugby school.

Hugo, Victor Marie (1802–85), French poet, dramatist, and novelist, who headed the Romantic movement in France in the early 19th cent. His dramas include *Hernani, Lucrèce Borgia, Ruy Blas,* and *Le Roi s'amuse.* Of his novels *Notre Dame* belongs to his early period, *Les Misérables, Les Travailleurs de la mer,* and *L'Homme qui rit* were written in Guernsey.

Humboldt, Friedrich Heinrich Alexander, Baron von (1769–1859), German naturalist and explorer whose researches are recorded in *Voyage de Humboldt et Bonpland* (23 vols., 1805–34), and *Kosmos* (5 vols., 1845–62).

Hume, Cardinal (George) Basil (b. 1923), Catholic Benedictine monk. Abbot of Ampleforth, 1963–76, when he became Archbishop of Westminster.

Hume, David (1711–76), Scottish philosopher who developed the empiricism of Locke into the scepticism inherent in it. His main works are *Treatise of Human Nature* and *Dialogues Concerning Natural Religion.*

Hume, John, *see* **D17**.

Hunt, Holman (1827–1910), English artist, one of the founders of the Pre-Raphaelite movement. His pictures include *The Light of the World.*

Hunt, Baron (John Hunt) (1910–98), leader of the 1953 British Everest Expedition when Tenzing and Hillary reached the summit.

Hunt, Leigh (1784–1859), English poet and essayist. In 1813 he was fined and imprisoned for libelling the Prince Regent in *The Examiner.* He was a friend of Keats and Shelley.

Hurd, Lord, *see* **D17**.

Hus, Jan (1369–1415), Bohemian religious reformer. Strongly influenced by Wyclif, he urged reform both of abuses in the church and of doctrine. Sentenced to death or recantation, he suffered martyrdom on 6 July 1415. His death caused a civil war which lasted many years.

Hussein, King (1935–99), King of Jordan, 1952–99. A symbol of stability and the search for peace in the Middle East.

Hussein, Saddam (b. 1938), dictator of Iraq, 1979–. Launched the war with Iran in 1980 and the invasion of Kuwait, 1990. *See* **Section C**.

Hutton, James (1726–97), an Edinburgh doctor who founded modern geological theory.

Hutton, Sir Leonard (1916–90), foremost English cricketer. Captained England 23 times, scoring 364 in 1938 against Australia.

Huxley, Aldous (1894–1963), English novelist, author of *Brave New World.*

Huxley, Sir Julian (1887–1975), biologist and writer, grandson of T. H. Huxley and brother of Aldous; first director general of UNESCO 1946–8; a founder of the International Union for the Conservation of Nature and the World Wild Life Fund.

Huxley, Thomas Henry (1825–95), English biologist, b. Ealing. He started life as assistant-surgeon on H.M.S. *Rattlesnake* and during the voyage (1846–50) studied marine organisms.

After the publication of Darwin's *Origin of Species* he became an ardent evolutionist and gave the first recognisably modern lecture on the origin of life to the British Association in 1870. He coined the term "agnostic".

Huygens, Christian (1629–95), Dutch mathematician, physicist, and astronomer, son of the poet **Constantijn Huygens** (1596–1687); discovered the rings of Saturn, invented the pendulum clock, and developed the wave theory of light in opposition to Newton's corpuscular theory.

Hyde, Douglas (1860–1949), Irish scholar, historian, poet, and folk-lorist; first president of Ireland in the 1937 constitution, 1938–45.

Hypatia of Alexandria, the only woman mathematician of antiquity. She excited the enmity of Christian fanatics. Murdered in A.D. 415.

I

Ibsen, Henrik Johan (1828–1906), Norwegian playwright and poet, who dealt with social and psychological problems and revolutionised the European theatre. His chief works are *Ghosts, The Wild Duck, The Master Builder, A Doll's House, Hedda Gabler* and the poetic drama, *Peer Gynt.*

Ingres, Jean Auguste Dominique (1780–1867), French historical and classical painter. His paintings include *La grande odalisque* in the Louvre.

Innocent III (*c.* 1160–1216), Pope 1198–1216. He asserted the power and moral force of the papacy over the Emperor Otto IV, Philip II of France, and John of England. He launched the fourth crusade, encouraged the crusade against the Albigensian heretics, and held the 4th Lateran council. His pontificate marks the zenith of the mediaeval papacy.

Ionesco, Eugene (1912–94), French playwright of the Absurd, b. Romania, whose plays include *The Bald Prima Donna, The Chairs* and *Rhinoceros.*

Iqbal, Sir Muhammad (1877–1938), poet-philosopher, b. Sialkot (Pakistan). He wrote both poetry and prose in Urdu, Persian, and English, and his work is marked by mystic nationalism.

Ireland, John (1879–1962), English composer, popularly known for his setting of Masefield's *Sea Fever,* but also a composer of chamber music and sonatas for pianoforte and violin.

Irving, Sir Henry (1838–1905), English actor. At the Lyceum theatre from 1871, later with Ellen Terry, he gave notable Shakespearean performances, especially as Shylock and Malvolio.

Irving, Washington (1783–1859), American essayist, whose works include *Tales of a Traveller* and *The Sketch Book,* also biographies.

Isabella of Castile (1451–1504), reigned jointly with her husband, Ferdinand II of Aragon, over a united Spain, from which the Moors and the Jews were expelled. During their reign the New World was discovered.

Ismail Pasha (1830–95), grandson of Mehemet Ali, was Khedive of Egypt, and became virtually independent of the Sultan. Under him the Suez canal was made, but his financial recklessness led to Anglo-French control.

Ismay, 1st Baron (Hastings Lionel Ismay) (1887–1965), British general who was chief of staff to Sir Winston Churchill in the second world war.

Ito, Hirobumi, Prince (1841–1909), Japanese statesman, four times premier, who helped to modernise his country. He was assassinated.

Ivan the Great (1410–1505) brought the scattered provinces of Muscovy under one control and put an end to Tartar rule.

Ivan the Terrible (1530–84), crowned as first Tsar of Russia in 1547, was an autocratic ruler who consolidated and expanded Russia.

J

Jackson, Andrew (1767–1845), American general who was twice president of the United States.

Jackson, Reverend Jesse Louis (b. 1941). American clergyman and civil rights leader.

Jackson, Thomas Jonathan (1824–63), "Stonewall Jackson," was general on the Southern side in the American Civil War; killed at Chancellorsville.

Jacobs, William Wymark (1863–1943), English

novelist, b. London, author of humorous sea and other stories.

Jacquard, Joseph Marie (1752–1834), French inventor whose loom provided an effective method of weaving designs.

Jahangir (1569–1627), 3rd Mogul emperor and patron of art.

James I (1566–1625), King of England (1603–25) and, as James VI, King of Scotland (1567–1625). He was the son of Mary Stuart and succeeded to the English throne on the death of Elizabeth I. His reign saw the Gunpowder Plot of 1605 and the publication of the Authorised Version of the Bible, but it also marked an increasingly critical attitude of the Puritans towards the established church. Described as "the wisest fool in Christendom."

James II (1633–1701), King of England and, as James VII, King of Scotland (1685–8), was the younger son of Charles I. Personally honest, and an able admiral, he lacked political understanding; and when, having put down Monmouth's rebellion, he tried and failed to obtain better conditions for his fellow Roman Catholics, he was obliged in 1688 to flee the country.

James, Cyril Lionel Robert (1901–89), Trinidadian historian, literary critic, political theorist and cricket writer. Author of *Nkrumah and the Ghana Revolution* (1977) and *Spheres of Existence* (1980).

James, Henry (1843–1916), American novelist. He lived mainly in England. His work, noted for intellectual subtlety and characterisation, includes *The American, Daisy Miller, The Portrait of a Lady, What Maisie Knew*, and *The Spoils of Poynton*.

James, William (1842–1910), American psychologist and philosopher, brother of Henry. He was a protagonist of the theory of pragmatism developed by his friend C. S. Peirce, and invented "radical empiricism." His major works are *The Principles of Psychology, The Will to Believe*, and *The Meaning of Truth*.

Janáček, Leoš (1854–1928), Czech composer and conductor, and student of folk music, b. in Moravia, son of a village schoolmaster, creator of a national style. His best-known opera is *Jenůfa*. See **Section E.**

Jaurès, Jean (1859–1914), French socialist leader and writer. Assassinated by nationalist fanatic, 1914.

Jefferies, Richard (1848–87), English naturalist of poetic perception, b. in Wiltshire, author of *Gamekeeper at Home* and *The Life of the Fields.*

Jefferson, Thomas (1743–1826), American president, 1801–9. He created the Republican Party, by which the federalists, led by Hamilton, were overthrown, and helped to draft the Declaration of Independence. He tried unsuccessfully to bring an end to slavery. He negotiated the Louisiana Purchase of 1803.

Jeffreys, 1st Baron (George Jeffreys) (1648–89), English judge who held the "bloody assize" after Monmouth's unsuccessful rebellion. In 1686 he was sent to the Tower and there died.

Jellicoe, 1st Earl (John Rushworth Jellicoe) (1859–1935), British admiral. He fought the uncertain battle of Jutland in 1916, after which the German fleet remained in harbour.

Jenkins, Lord (Roy Jenkins) (b. 1920), British politician, b. Wales; Pres. EEC Commission 1977–80; served as Labour's Home Sec. 1965–7; Chanc. of Exchequer 1967–70. Elected M.P. for Glasgow Hillhead for Social Democrats, 1982–7. Leader, SDP 1982–June 1983. Order of Merit (1993). Chaired Commission on Voting System, 1997–8.

Jenner, Edward (1749–1823), English physician, b. in Gloucs., pupil of John Hunter. His discovery of vaccination against smallpox (1798) helped to lay the foundations of modern immunology.

Jerne, Niels Kai (1911–94), Danish microbiologist and Nobel laureate. The "Grand Old Man of Immunology".

Jerome, Jerome Klapka (1859–1927), English humorous writer. Author of *Three Men in a Boat.*

Jerome, St. (c. 331–420), scholar, whose translation of the Bible into Latin (the Vulgate) became for centuries the standard use.

Jesus Christ (c. 4 B.C.–A.D. 30), founder of Christianity, the son of Mary whose husband was Joseph, was born in a critical period of Jewish history. His home was at Nazareth in Galilee, but virtually nothing is known about his early life. When he was about 30 he began the mission which he believed to have been entrusted to him, proclaiming the Kingdom of God was at hand.

His teaching is summarised in the Sermon on the Mount, and its main theme is love, especially for the poor and downtrodden. He was later crucified. The main source of his life is the New Testament. The title "Christ" comes from the Greek word *christos* = anointed, which is the Greek translation of the Hebrew title *Messiah. See* **Section S.**

Jiang Zemin (b. 1926), Chinese politician. State President of China, 1993–. He has continued the economic policies of the late Deng Xiaoping.

Jiménez, Juan Ramón (1881–1958), Spanish lyric poet. Nobel prizewinner 1956.

Jinnah, Mohammed Ali (1876–1948), Pakistani statesman. B. at Karachi, he became president of the Muslim League, and succeeded in 1947 in establishing the Dominion of Pakistan, becoming its first governor-general.

Joachim, Joseph (1831–1907), Hungarian violinist and composer.

Joan of Arc, St. (Jeanne d'Arc) (1412–31), French patriot, called the Maid of Orleans; of peasant parentage (she was b. at Domrémy), she believed herself called to save France from English domination; and by her efforts Charles VII was crowned at Rheims in 1429. Captured by the Burgundians and sold to the English; burned as a heretic; canonised in 1920.

Joffre, Joseph Jacques Césaire (1852–1931), French general. He was commander-in-chief of the French army in the 1914–18 war.

John, St., the Baptist (executed A.D. 28). See **S15.**

John, St., the Evangelist, one of the twelve apostles of Jesus Christ. See **S15.**

John (1167–1216), youngest son of Henry II, was King of England from 1199. Able but erratic and arbitrary, he lost Normandy. Baronial opposition to him, under the influence of Archbishop Stephen Langton, acquired a national character, and in 1215 he was obliged to seal Magna Carta (*see* **Section L**).

John of Gaunt (1340–99). Duke of Lancaster, son of Edward III and father of Henry IV.

John XXIII (1881–1963), elected Pope in 1958, succeeding Pius XII, was formerly Cardinal Angelo Giuseppe Roncalli, patriarch of Venice. He sought to bring the Church closer to modern needs and to promote Christian unity.

John Paul II, (b. 1920), succeeded Pope John Paul I after his sudden death in 1978; formerly Cardinal Karol Wojtyla, archbishop of Cracow; first Pope to come from Poland. Assassination attempt made 1981. Presided over the Catholic Church during the fall of communism, but has grown increasingly conservative with age.

John, Augustus (1878–1961), British painter and etcher, b. in Wales: noted for his portraits.

John, Sir Elton (b. 1947), born Reginald Kenneth Dwight. Rock singer and pianist. Knighted (1998) after his rendering of *Candle in the Wind* at funeral of Princess Diana.

Johnson, Amy (1904–41), was the first woman aviator to fly solo from England to Australia.

Johnson, Lyndon Baines (1908–73), President of the United States, 1963–9. He became president on Kennedy's assassination and followed a progressive policy at home, but his achievements were clouded by the war in Vietnam.

Johnson, Samuel (1709–84), English lexicographer and man of letters, b. at Lichfield. His *Dictionary* was published in 1755, and was followed by *Rasselas, The Idler* (a periodical), and *Lives of the Poets.* He was a focus of London literary life of his day. His biographer was James Boswell.

Joliot-Curie, Jean Frédéric (1900–58), and his wife Irène (1896–1956), French scientists who discovered artificial radioactivity. Nobel prizewinners 1935. Joliot-Curie was one of the discoverers of nuclear fission. Irène was the daughter of Pierre and Marie Curie. Both were communists, and both died from cancer caused by their work.

Jones, Ernest Charles (1819–69), English Chartist leader and poet.

Jones, Sir Harold Spencer (1890–1960), British astronomer royal, 1935–55. His major research was to determine the mean distance of the earth from the sun, 93,004,000 miles.

Jones, Inigo (1573–1652), architect of the English renaissance who studied in Italy and inspired the use of Palladian forms in England. His buildings include the banqueting hall in Whitehall and the queen's house at Greenwich. He also designed furniture and introduced the proscenium arch and movable scenery on the English stage.

Jonson, Ben (1573–1637), English poet and dramatist. His plays include *Every Man in his Humour*, *Volpone*, and *The Alchemist*; and his poems *Drink to me only with thine Eyes*. He also produced court masques.

Josephine, Empress (1763–1814), wife of Napoleon I, *née* de la Pagerie, she was previously married to the Vicomte de Beauharnais. She was divorced from Napoleon in 1809.

Josephus, Flavius (38–*c*. 100), Jewish historian, author of *History of the Jewish War*.

Joule, James Prescott (1818–89), English physicist, pupil of Dalton, who researched on electromagnetism and determined the mechanical equivalent of heat. *See* **Section L.**

Jowett, Benjamin (1817–93), English scholar. He translated Plato's *Dialogues*, and he was an influential Master of Balliol College, Oxford.

Jowitt, Earl (William Allen Jowitt) (1885–1957), British Labour politician and Lord Chancellor. He wrote *The Strange Case of Alger Hiss*.

Joyce, James (1882–1941), Irish author, b. Dublin. His *Ulysses* gives a microscopic picture of a day in the life of two Irishmen, and flouted the conventions of his day. Other works include *Portrait of the Artist* and *Finnegans Wake*. He spent most of his life on the Continent.

Juin, Alphonse (1888–1967), French general who took part in the Allied invasion of Tunisia and the Italian campaign in the second world war.

Julian the Apostate (331–63), Roman emperor who tried to restore paganism in the empire. He was killed in war against Persia.

Jung, Carl Gustav (1875–1961), Swiss psychiatrist. A pupil of Freud, he later formulated his own system of analytical psychology. *See* **Section J.**

Junot, Andoche (1771–1813), French general defeated by Wellington in the Peninsular War.

Jusserand, Jean Jules (1855–1932), French author and diplomat, who wrote on English literature and wayfaring life in the Middle Ages.

Justinian I (483–565), Roman emperor in the East. He and his wife Theodora beautified Constantinople, and his general Belisarius was successful in war. He codified Roman law.

Juvenal (60–140), Roman poet and Stoic, remembered for his *Satires*.

K

Kafka, Franz (1883–1924), German-speaking Jewish writer, b. Prague, whose introspective work, the bulk of which was not published till after his early death from tuberculosis, has had a notable influence on later schools, especially the surrealists. It includes the three novels *The Trial*, *The Castle*, and *America*.

Kālidāsa (*c*. A.D. 400), chief figure in classic Sanskrit literature. No facts are known about his life and date, but certain evidence places him in the 5th cent. Seven of his works survive: two lyrics, *Ritu-samhara* (The Seasons), and *Megha-dūta* (Cloud Messenger); two epics, *Raghu-vamsa* (Dynasty of Raghu) and *Kumara-sambhava* (Birth of the Wargod); and three dramas, *Sakúntalā*, *Mālavikāg-nimitra*, and *Vikramorvaśīya*.

Kane, Bob (1915–98), American cartoonist who created Batman, the caped crusader.

Kant, Immanuel (1724–1804), German philosopher, author of *Critique of Pure Reason* (1781), *Critique of Practical Reason* (1788), and *Critique of Judgement* (1790). He came from a Pietist family of Königsberg, where he lectured, but the Prussian government forbade his lectures as anti-Lutheran. He was influenced by the writings of his neighbour Hamann (*see* **Romanticism, Section J**) and by Rousseau and Hume, and his own work was of immense influence in shaping future liberal thought. He believed in the freedom of man to make his own decisions and considered the exploitation of man as the worst evil.

Kapitza, Pyotr (1894–1984), Russian physicist who worked on atomic research with Rutherford at the Cavendish Laboratory, Cambridge, and returned to Russia in 1935. Member of the Soviet Academy of Sciences and Fellow of the Royal Society. Nobel Prize for Physics, 1978.

Kauffman, Angelica (1741–1807), Anglo-Swiss painter, a foundation member of the Royal Academy and the first woman R.A.

Kaulbach, Wilhelm von (1805–74), German pain-

ter who illustrated the works of Goethe and Schiller.

Kaunda, Kenneth (b. 1924), African leader of international standing, son of Christian missionaries. He was president of Zambia, 1964–91. His arrest in 1997 caused an outcry.

Kean, Charles John (1811–68), English actor-manager son of Edmund. He married Ellen Tree. In the 1850s played with her in spectacular revivals at the Princess's Theatre, London.

Kean, Edmund (1787–1833), English tragic actor. He made his name as Shylock.

Keats, John (1795–1821), English poet who in his short life produced poems notable for richness of imagination and beauty of thought. They include *Odes*, *Isabella*, and *The Eve of St. Agnes*.

Keble, John (1792–1866), English clergyman associated with the Tractarian movement (**J52**) and author of *The Christian Year*.

Keller, Helen Adams (1880–1968), American author and lecturer who overcame great physical handicaps (blind and deaf before the age of two) to live an active and useful life.

Kelvin of Largs, 1st Baron (William Thomson) (1824–1907), British mathematician and physicist, b. Belfast, known for his work on heat and thermodynamics, and contributions to electrical science and submarine telegraphy. In the domain of heat he stands to Joule as Maxwell stands to Faraday in the history of electrical science, both bringing pre-eminently mathematical minds to bear on the results of experimental discoveries. He introduced the Kelvin or Absolute scale of temperature and was one of the original members of the Order of Merit.

Kemble, Fanny (1809–93), English actress. She came of a noted theatrical family, her father and uncle respectively being the actors Charles Kemble and John Philip Kemble, and her aunt, Mrs. Siddons.

Kempenfelt, Richard (1718–82), English admiral, who sank with his ship the *Royal George* together with 600 of the ship's company off Spithead through a shifting of the guns which caused it to capsize.

Kempis, Thomas à (1380–1471), name by which the German mystic Thomas Hammerken was known, was a monk of the Augustinian order, whose life was mainly spent at a monastery near Zwolle. The author of *The Imitation of Christ*.

Kennedy, John Fitzgerald (1917–63), President of the USA, 1961–3, the youngest and the first Roman Catholic to be elected; son of a financier. He had world-wide pre-eminence and gave the American people a sense of purpose to meet the challenges of a scientific age. He opposed racial discrimination and initiated a new era of East–West relations; but his foreign policy sowed the seeds of the Vietnam war. He and his brother Robert (1925–68) were assassinated, the latter while campaigning for the presidency in 1968. Robert Kennedy was Attorney General, 1961–64 and promoted the Civil Rights Act.

Kent, William (1684–1748), English painter, furniture designer, landscape gardener, and architect, protégé of Lord Burlington, whose buildings include the great hall at Holkham and the Horse Guards, Whitehall.

Kenyatta, Jomo (1893–1978), African leader who became president of Kenya in 1964.

Kepler, Johann (1571–1630), German astronomer and mystic, for a short time assistant to Tycho Brahe whose measurements he used in working out his laws of planetary motion, which are: 1. Planets move round the sun not in circles, but in ellipses, the sun being one of the foci. 2. A planet moves not uniformly but in such a way that a line drawn from it to the sun sweeps out equal areas of the ellipse in equal times. 3. The squares of the period of revolution round the sun are proportional to the cubes of the distances. The explanation of these laws was given by Newton.

Kerensky, Alexander (1881–1970), Russian politician. Prime Minister of Provisional Government, July–November 1917. Rest of life in exile.

Keyes, 1st Baron (Roger John Brownlow Keyes) (1872–1945), British admiral who led the raid on Zeebrugge in 1918.

Keynes, 1st Baron (John Maynard Keynes) (1883–1946), British economist, who was a Treasury representative at the Versailles peace conference, and published his views in *The Economic Consequences of the Peace*. Author of *Treatise on Money* (1930) and *The General Theory of Employment, Interest and Money* (1936).

Khachaturian, Aram Ilich (1903–78), Armenian-born composer who wrote the popular *Sabre Dance* and *Spartacus* (from which the Love Song was used in T.V.'s Onedin Line.)

Khomeini, Ayatollah (1900–89), Iranian religious leader. After 16 years in exile, returned to Iran in 1979 after the overthrow of the Shah. Architect of Islamic Republic of Iran. Virulently anti-Western. Waged costly, futile war with Iraq.

Khrushchev, Nikita Sergeyevich (1894–1971), Russian statesman who became leader of the Soviet Union soon after the death of Stalin; first secretary of the Soviet Communist Party, 1953–64; prime minister, 1958–64. After the harsh years of the Stalinist régime he pursued a policy of relaxation in home and foreign affairs.

Kierkegaard, Sören (1813–55), Danish philosopher and religious thinker, whose views have influenced existentialism. His main work is *Either–Or*.

King, Mackenzie (1874–1950), prime minister of Canada, 1921–5, 1926–30, and 1935–48.

King, Martin Luther (1929–68), American clergyman and black civil rights leader; awarded the 1964 Nobel peace prize for his consistent support of the principle of non-violence in the black people's struggle for civil rights. Assassinated at Memphis, Tennessee.

Kingsley, Charles (1819–75), English clergyman and novelist, author of *Hypatia*, *Westward Ho!*, *Hereward the Wake* and *The Water Babies*.

Kinnock, Neil (b. 1942), Labour politician. Leader of the Labour Party 1983–92. Played a large part in reshaping the party for the 1992 election but resigned after Labour's fourth successive election defeat. EU Commissioner (with responsibility for Transport) since 1995.

Kinsey, Alfred (1894–1956). Sexologist. Founder, Institute of Sex Research at Indiana University. His work led to more liberal attitudes to homosexuality, more relaxed divorce laws *etc.*

Kipling, Rudyard (1865–1936), British writer, b. Bombay. His vivid work portrays contemporary British rule in India and includes *The Light that Failed*, *Stalky and Co.*, *Kim*, and the *Barrack Room Ballads*. Among his books for children are the *Just So Stories*, *Puck of Pook's Hill* and the *Jungle Books*. Nobel prize 1907.

Kirchhoff, Gustav Robert (1824–87), German mathematical physicist, who with R. W. Bunsen discovered that in the gaseous state each chemical substance emits its own characteristic spectrum (1859). He was able to explain Fraunhofer's map of the solar spectrum. Using the spectroscope, he and Bunsen discovered the elements caesium and rubidium.

Kissinger, Henry (b. 1923), American Secretary of State 1973–7; inventor of shuttle-service diplomacy. Shared Nobel peace prize for 1973 with Le Duc Tho.

Kitchener of Khartoum, 1st Earl (Horatio Herbert Kitchener) (1850–1916), English general. In 1898 he won back the Sudan for Egypt by his victory at Omdurman. He served in the South African war. Secretary of State for War, 1914–16. He was drowned on his way to Russia.

Klee, Paul (1879–1940), Swiss artist, whose paintings are delicate dream-world fantasies.

Klemperer, Otto (1885–1973), German-born conductor, renowned as interpreter of the Beethoven symphonies. Expelled by the Nazis he became an American citizen and returned to Europe in 1946. He had been principal conductor of the Philharmonic Orchestra since 1959.

Kneller, Sir Godfrey (1646–1723), portrait painter, b. at Lübeck, who settled in England and was patronised by successive English sovereigns.

Knox, John (1514–72), Scottish reformer, b. near Haddington. While in exile at Geneva he was influenced by Calvin. On return to Scotland he was a leader of the reforming party against Mary, Queen of Scots. He wrote a *History of the Reformation in Scotland*.

Koch, Robert (1843–1910), German bacteriologist who discovered the bacillus of tuberculosis, and worked on cholera and cattle diseases.

Kodály, Zoltán (1882–1967), Hungarian composer and teacher. He worked with Bartok in the collection of folk-tunes. See **Section E**.

Kohl, Helmut (b. 1930), Chancellor of the Federal Republic of Germany until defeated in 1998. First Chancellor of re-united Germany after 1990. One of the most powerful figures in contemporary European politics. Narrowly re-elected Chancellor, 1994. A Christian Democrat who in November 1996 became the longest-serving Chancellor in German history (except for Bismarck). See **Section C**.

Kokoschka, Oskar (1886–1980), Austrian portrait and landscape painter. Settled in England.

Korolyov, Sergei (1907–66), Russian space scientist, who designed the world's first earth satellite, the first manned spaceship and the first moon rocket.

Kosciusko, Tadeusz (1746–1817), Polish patriot. After experience gained in America in the War of Independence, he led his countrymen against Russia in 1792 and 1794 in opposition to the partition of Poland.

Kossuth, Louis (1802–94), Hungarian patriot, who in 1848 led a rising of his countrymen against the Hapsburg dynasty, but had to flee to Turkey and later to England.

Kosygin, Alexei Nikolayevich (1904–80), succeeded Khrushchev in 1964 as chairman of the Council of Ministers of the USSR (prime minister). A key technocrat.

Krebs, Sir Hans (1900–81), British biochemist, b. Germany. Taught at Cambridge and Sheffield and became Professor of Biology at Oxford in 1954. Nobel prize 1953.

Kreisler, Fritz (1875–1962), Austrian violinist, who composed violin music and an operetta. He became an American citizen in 1943.

Krenek, Ernst (1900–91), Austrian-American composer of partly Czech descent, whose compositions include the jazz opera *Jonny spielt auf*.

Kropotkin, Peter, Prince (1842–1921), Russian anarchist, geographer and explorer, who was imprisoned for favouring the political action of a working men's association, but escaped to England. He wrote on socialistic and geographical subjects. Returned to Russia, 1917.

Kruger, Stephanus Johannes Paulus (1825–1904), Boer leader, who in 1881 was appointed head of the provisional government against Britain, and later president. When the war of 1899–1902 turned against the Boers, he vainly sought help in Europe.

Krupp, Alfred (1812–87), founder of the German gun factories at Essen. He installed in a disused factory left him by his father a new steam-engine from England, began to make cast steel, and from 1844 specialised in armaments. The firm's factories made the Big Bertha guns which shelled Paris in 1918.

Krylov, Ivan Andreyevich (1768–1844), Russian writer of fables (the Russian La Fontaine.)

Kubelik, Jan (1880–1940), Czech violinist who at the age of 12 played in public.

Kublai Khan (1216–94), grandson of Genghis Khan, was the first Mongol emperor of China. He extended the Mongol empire by conquest, and lived in unparalleled splendour. His court was described by Marco Polo and is the subject of a poem by Coleridge.

Kubrick, Stanley. See **W11**.

L

La Fayette, Marie Joseph Paul Roch Yves Gilbert du Motier, Marquis de (1757–1834), French soldier and statesman. He fought for the colonists in the American War of Independence; and in the 1789 French revolution he proposed a declaration of rights and was commander of the National Guard till his moderation made him unpopular. When the monarchy was restored he was an opposition leader, and took part in the revolution of 1830.

La Fontaine, Jean de (1621–95), French poet and fabulist, b. in Champagne, a friend of Moliere, Boileau and Racine.

Lagerlöf, Selma (1858–1940), Swedish novelist and first woman member of the Swedish Academy. Nobel prizewinner 1909.

Lagrange, Joseph Louis, Comte (1736–1813), French mathematician, of Turin and Paris, whose interest in astronomy led him to distinguish two types of disturbance of members of the solar system, the periodic and the secular. He was called by Frederick the Great to Berlin to succeed Euler.

Lalande, Joseph Jerome LeFrançais de (1732–1807), French astronomer, author of *Traité d'astronomie*.

Lamarck, Jean Baptiste Pierre Antoine de Monet de (1744–1829), French biologist whose explanation of evolution was that new organs are brought into being by the needs of the organism in adapting to its environment and that the new characters acquired during its life-time can be passed on to the offspring through heredity, resulting in evolutionary change. See **F30**.

Lamb, Charles (1775–1834), English essayist, b. London. A clerk in the East India Office, he devoted his life to his sister Mary, who was of unstable mind. He is chiefly known for his *Essays of Elia*, and his letters, which have a blend of humour and tenderness.

Lambert, Constant (1905–51), English composer and critic, and conductor of Sadler's Wells ballet. His *Rio Grande* is in jazz idiom.

Landor, Walter Savage (1775–1864), English writer, b. Warwick, remembered for his *Imaginary Conversations* and poems.

Landseer, Sir Edwin (1802–73), English animal painter. He painted the *Monarch of the Glen* and designed the lions in Trafalgar Square.

Lane, Edward William (1801–76), English Arabic scholar, translator of the *Arabian Nights*.

Lanfranc (c. 1005–89), ecclesiastic. B. at Pavia, he became a prior in Normandy, and in 1070 an energetic archbishop of Canterbury.

Lang, Andrew (1844–1912), Scottish man of letters, whose output includes *Myth, Ritual and Religion*, poems, fairy-tales, and fiction.

Lang, 1st Baron (Cosmo Gordon Lang) (1864–1945), was archbishop of Canterbury, 1928–42.

Langland, William (1330?–1400?), English poet, probably educated at Malvern, author of *The Vision of Piers the Plowman*.

Langton, Stephen (1151–1228), archbishop of Canterbury. Adviser to the insurgent barons who induced King John to grant Magna Carta.

Lansbury, George (1859–1940), British Labour politician, founder of the *Daily Herald*. He improved London's amenities.

Lâo Tsze (old philosopher) (c. 600 B.C.), traditional founder of Taoism in China. See **Section J**.

Laplace, Pierre Simon, Marquis de (1749–1827), French mathematician and astronomer, author of *Celestial Mechanics* (1799–1825). He believed that the solar system had condensed out of a vast rotating gaseous nebula.

Lara, Brian Charles (b. 1969), West Indies cricketer. Born Trinidad. An accomplished batsman who made the highest-ever score in test cricket (375 against England at Antigua in April 1994). This was followed by 501 not out for Warwickshire against Durham at Edgbaston (also in 1994).

La Rochefoucauld, François, Duc de (1613–80), French writer, author of *Reflections and Moral Maxims*.

Larwood, Harold (1904–95), English cricketer, the most celebrated fast bowler of his time. At the centre of the 1932–3 'Bodyline' controversy.

Lasker, Emanuel (1868–1941), German chess player, world champion, 1894–1921.

Lassalle, Ferdinand (1825–64), German socialist who took part in the revolutionary movement of 1848 and organised workers movements.

Lassus, Orlandus (Lasso, Orlando di) (c. 1532–94), Flemish composer and choirmaster, contemporary of Palestrina, writer of *chansons*, madrigals, and sacred music. See **Section E**.

Latimer, Hugh (c. 1485–1555), English Protestant martyr, became bishop of Worcester in 1535, and was executed under Queen Mary.

Laud, William (1573–1645), archbishop of Canterbury and adviser to Charles I. His attempt to get conformity for his high church policy made him hated. He was impeached and beheaded.

Lauder, Sir Harry (1870–1950), Scottish comic singer of wide popularity. He also wrote *Roamin' in the Gloamin'*.

Laval, Pierre (1883–1945), French politician who collaborated with the Germans, 1940–45.

Lavoisier, Antoine Laurent (1743–94), French chemist, b. Paris, was the first to establish the fact that combustion is a form of chemical action. We owe the word *oxygen* to him.

Law, Andrew Bonar (1858–1923), Conservative politician, prime minister 1922–3.

Lawrence, David Herbert (1885–1930), English poet and novelist, b. Notts., a miner's son. He tried to interpret emotion on a deeper level of consciousness. His works, which have had wide influence, include *The White Peacock, Sons and Lovers, The Rainbow, Women in Love,* and *Lady Chatterley's Lover*; his plays had to wait half a century before coming to the stage in the 1960s.

Lawrence, Sir Thomas (1769–1830), English portrait painter.

Lawrence, Thomas Edward (1888–1935) (Lawrence of Arabia), British soldier who led the Arabs against the Turks in the war of 1914–18, and wrote *The Seven Pillars of Wisdom*.

Leacock, Stephen (1869–1944), Canadian humorist.

Leakey, Mary (1913–96), archaeological and palaeoanthropologist, the matriarch of a distinguished family of environmentalists and fossil hunters in East Africa.

Lean, Sir David. See **W11**.

Leavis, Frank Raymond (1895–1978), British critic, who edited *Scrutiny*, 1932–53, and whose works include *The Great Tradition, D. H. Lawrence, Novelist,* and *"Anna Karenina" and Other Essays*.

Lecky, William Edward Hartpole (1838–1903), Irish historian, author of *England in the Eighteenth Century*.

Leclerc, Jacques Philippe (Philippe, Comte de Hautecloque) (1902–47), French general. He led a Free French force in Africa in the second world war and liberated Paris in 1944.

Le Corbusier (1887–1965), pseudonym of Charles Edouard Jeanneret, Swiss architect, whose books and work (especially his Unité d'Habitation at Marseilles and the Punjab capital at Chandigarh) have influenced town-planning.

Le Duc Tho (1911–90), North Vietnamese politician. Chief negotiator at the Vietnam truce talks 1970–3. He would not accept the 1973 Nobel peace prize awarded jointly with Dr. Kissinger until peace had "really been restored in S. Vietnam."

Lee of Fareham, 1st Viscount (Arthur Hamilton Lee) (1868–1947), British politician who presented Chequers Court to the nation.

Lee Kuan Yew (b. 1923). First Prime Minister of Singapore, 1959–90. Helped establish prosperity of Singapore, but little opposition was tolerated.

Lee, Laurie (1914–97), poet and writer of autobiographical books about his Gloucestershire childhood and his experiences in Spain in the 1930s. *Cider with Rosie* (1959) has become a modern classic.

Lee, Robert Edward (1807–70), American Confederate general in the Civil War, who made the surrender at Appomattox.

Lee, Sir Sidney (1859–1926), English critic. Joint editor of the *Dictionary of National Biography*.

Leech, John (1817–64), Humorous artist and political cartoonist who contributed numerous drawings to *Punch*. He illustrated Surtees' novels and Dickens's *A Christmas Carol*.

Lehár, Franz (1870–1948), Hungarian composer. Among his most popular operettas are *The Merry Widow* and *The Count of Luxembourg*.

Leibnitz, Gottfried Wilhelm (1646–1716), German philosopher and mathematician, who invented the differential and integral calculus (1684) independently of Newton whose previous work on the same subject was not published until 1687. It was Leibnitz's nomenclature that was universally adopted.

Leicester, Earl of (Robert Dudley) (1533–88), English soldier, commanded English troops in the Netherlands, 1585–7, without much success, and in 1588 commanded forces assembled against the Armada. He was husband of Amy Robsart.

Leif Ericsson (fl. 1000), discoverer of Vinland on the north-east coast of America; b. Iceland, son of the Norse explorer, Eric the Red, who colonised Greenland.

Leighton, 1st Baron (Frederic Leighton) (1830–96), English painter whose works include *Paolo and Francesca*. He was also a sculptor.

Lely, Sir Peter (Pieter van der Faes) (1618–80), Dutch painter who settled in London and painted court portraits.

Lenin (Vladimir Ilyich Ulyanov) (1870–1924), Russian revolutionary leader and statesman. From 1893 to 1917 he worked underground in Russia and abroad for the revolutionary cause. During this time the Social-Democratic party was formed; within it developed an uncompromising revolutionary group, the Bolsheviks, and of this group Lenin was the leading spirit. In April 1917 he and his fellow exiles returned;

after the November revolution he headed the new government having to face both war and anarchy. In 1921 his "new economic policy" somewhat modified the intensive drive towards planned industrial development. He was born in Simbirsk (later Ulyanovsk) on the middle Volga.

Leonardo da Vinci (1452–1519), Italian artist and man of science, son of a Florentine lawyer and a peasant. He described himself (when applying to Lodovico Sforza, Duke of Milan, for the post of city planner) as painter, architect, philosopher, poet, composer, sculptor, athlete, mathematician, inventor, and anatomist. His artistic output is small in quantity, and he is best known for his *Last Supper* in the refectory of Santa Maria delle Grazie in Milan and his *Mona Lisa* in the Louvre. He recorded his scientific work in unpublished notebooks written from right to left in mirror writing. The anatomy of the body (himself carrying out dissections), the growth of the child in the womb, the laws of waves and currents, and the laws of flight, were all studied by him.

Leoncavallo, Ruggiero (1858–1919), Italian composer of the opera *Pagliacci*.

Leonidas was king of Sparta at the time of the invasion of Greece by Xerxes (480 B.C.), and led the defence of the pass of Thermopylae, where he fell.

Lermontov, Mikhail Yurevich (1814–41), Russian poet and novelist, exiled to the Caucasus for a revolutionary poem addressed to Tsar Nicholas I on the death of Pushkin. He has been called the poet of the Caucasus. His novel *A Hero of Our Time* was written at St. Petersburg. He lost his life in a duel.

Le Sage, Alain René (1668–1747), French author, b. in Brittany, who wrote *Gil Blas* and *Le Diable Boiteux*. He was also a dramatist and his plays include *Turcaret*.

Lesseps, Ferdinand, Vicomte de (1805–94), French engineer who while serving as vice-consul at Alexandria conceived a scheme for a canal across the Suez isthmus; the work was completed in 1869. He also projected the original Panama canal scheme, which failed.

Lessing, Gotthold Ephraim (1729–81), German philosopher, dramatist, and critic, noted for his work *Laokoon* and his play *Minna von Barnhelm*.

Leucippus (fl. 440 B.C.), Greek philosopher, founder with Democritus of atomism, a theory of matter more nearly that of modern science than any put forward in ancient times. One of his sayings survives: "Naught occurs at random, but everything for a reason and of necessity."

Leverhulme, 1st Viscount (William Hesketh Lever) (1851–1925), British industrialist and philanthropist. He founded Lever Bros. which later became Unilever Ltd., and was a practical exponent of industrial partnership. He gave Lancaster House to the nation.

Leverrier, Urbain Jean Joseph (1811–77), French astronomer who, working independently of J. C. Adams of Cambridge, anticipated the existence of the planet Neptune which was later revealed by telescopic search.

Lévi-Strauss, Claude (b. 1908), French social anthropologist, b. Belgium, exponent of the theory of symbolic structures. He has written works on anthropology, religion, myths and language. The final vol. of his *Introduction to a Science of Mythology* about the myths and rituals of American Indians was published in 1981.

Lewis, Sinclair (1885–1951), American writer of novels satirising small-town life and philistinism. His works include *Main Street*, *Babbitt* and *Elmer Gantry*. Nobel prizewinner 1931.

Liaquat Ali Khan (1895–1951), leader of the Moslem League (1946) and first premier of Pakistan in 1947. He was assassinated.

Lie, Trygve (1896–1968), Norwegian politician. Secretary-General of the United Nations, 1946–52.

Lilburne, John (1614–57), English agitator and pamphleteer, leader of the Levellers in Civil War.

Linacre, Thomas (c. 1460–1524), English humanist and physician, who translated Galen's works and founded the College of Physicians.

Lincoln, Abraham (1809–65), American president. Born in Kentucky, he became a lawyer and was returned to Congress from Illinois in 1846. He was a leader of the Republican party which was formed in 1856 to oppose slavery. He became president in 1861, in which year the Confederate States proposed to withdraw from the Union, and war broke out. The phrase "government of the people, by the people, for the people" comes from his Gettysburg speech of 1863. He was assassinated in 1865.

Lind, Jenny (1820–87), Swedish singer, popular in Europe, and known as the Swedish nightingale. She founded musical scholarships.

Linnaeus (1707–78), Swedish botanist, remembered for his system of defining living things by two Latin names, the first being its *genus*, and the second its *species*. His method is expounded in *Philosophia Botanica* (1751). In 1757 he was ennobled as Karl von Linné. He studied, taught and died at Uppsala.

Lippi, Fra Filippo (1406–69), Italian artist, b. Florence. Frescoes in Prato cathedral are his main work. His son **Filippino** (1457–1504) finished Masaccio's frescoes in the Carmine, Florence, and executed others, for instance in Santa Maria Novella.

Lippmann, Gabriel (1845–1921), French physicist who invented a capillary electrometer and was a pioneer in colour photography. Nobel prizewinner 1908.

Lippmann, Walter (1889–1974), American journalist of influence, writing for the New York *Herald Tribune*, 1931–62.

Lipton, Sir Thomas Johnstone (1850–1931), Scottish business man and philanthropist. B. Glasgow, he emigrated to America, but returned to Scotland and established extensive chainstores for groceries. He unsuccessfully competed in yachting for the America's Cup.

Lister, Baron (Joseph Lister) (1827–1912), English surgeon, son of **J. J. Lister** (1786–1869), an amateur microscopist. He founded antiseptic surgery (1865) which greatly reduced mortality in hospitals.

Liszt, Franz (1811–86), Hungarian pianist and composer. His daughter Cosima became the wife of Hans von Bülow and later of Wagner. *See* Section E.

Litvinov, Maxim (1876–1952), Russian diplomat, of revolutionary origin, who first as ambassador in London, then as commissar for foreign affairs, and 1941–3 ambassador to the U.S., gained respect and understanding for his country.

Livingstone, David (1813–73), Scottish explorer in Africa. He discovered the course of the Zambesi, the Victoria Falls and Lake Nyasa (now Lake Malawi), and roused opinion against the slave trade. At one time believed lost, he was found by Stanley (*q.v.*) on 10 Nov. 1871.

Lloyd-George of Dwyfor, 1st Earl (David Lloyd George) (1863–1945), Liberal statesman of Welsh origin. He was M.P. for Caernarvon, 1890–1944; and as chancellor of the exchequer he introduced social insurance, 1908–11. The war of 1914–18 obliged him to become a war premier (superseding Asquith), and he was subsequently one of the main figures at the peace conference. In 1921 he conceded the Irish Free State. His daughter, **Lady Megan Lloyd George**, was M.P. for many years.

Lloyd-Webber, Lord (Sir Andrew Lloyd-Webber) (b. 1948), British composer. His musicals include *Jesus Christ Superstar* (1970), *Evita* (1978), *Cats* (1981), *Starlight Express* (1983), *Phantom of the Opera* (1986), *Sunset Boulevard* (1993) and most recently *Whistle Down the Wind* (1998).

Locke, John (1632–1704), English liberal philosopher and founder of empiricism, the doctrine that all knowledge is derived from experience. His chief work in theoretical philosophy, *Essay Concerning Human Understanding*, was written just before the revolution of 1688 and published in 1690. Other writings include *Letters on Toleration*, *Treatises on Government*, and *Education*.

Lombroso, Cesare (1836–1909), Italian criminologist, whose *L'uomo delinquente* maintained the existence of a criminal type distinguishable from the normal.

Lomonosov, Mikhail Vasilievich (1711–65), Russian philologist and poet who systematised Russian grammar and orthography.

London, Jack (1876–1916), American author of adventure tales such as *Call of the Wild*.

Longfellow, Henry Wadsworth (1807–82), American poet, popular in his lifetime, author of *The Golden Legend* and *Hiawatha*.

Lope de Vega Carpio, Félix (1562–1635), Spanish writer of immense output. First a ballad-writer, he took to play-writing and founded the Spanish drama. The number of his plays is said to have been 1,500, the earlier ones historical, the later ones dealing with everyday life; but most are lost.

Lorca, Federico Garcia (1899–1936), Spanish poet and dramatist of Andalusia. Among his works are *Llanto por Ignacio Sánchez Mejías*, an unforgettable lament on the death of a bullfighter, and *Canción de Jinete* with its haunting refrain, "Cordoba, far away and alone." He was brutally murdered by Franco sympathisers at the outbreak of the civil war.

Louis IX (1214–70), St. Louis, King of France. Of saintly character (as described in Joinville's *Memoirs*), he also carried out practical reforms. He died on crusade.

Louis XIV (1638–1715), King of France. A despotic ruler, builder of Versailles, he also dominated the Europe of his day; but he sowed the seeds of future trouble for France by his exhausting wars. He revoked the Edict of Nantes which had given religious freedom to the Huguenots since 1598. His reign, however, was a great period for literature.

Louis XV (1710–74), King of France. Extravagant and self-indulgent, his reign marked a declining period for the monarchy, but produced some fine art.

Louis XVI (1754–93), King of France. Well-meaning but incapable, he saw the outbreak of the French revolution of 1789, in which he and his queen Marie Antoinette were executed.

Louis, Joe (Joseph Louis Barrow) (1914–81), American Black boxer, who became world heavyweight champion in 1937, successfully defending his title 26 times.

Low, Archibald Montgomery (1888–1956), British scientist who worked in varied fields, including wireless, television, and anti-aircraft and anti-tank apparatus.

Low, Sir David (1891–1963), British cartoonist, b. New Zealand, associated with the *Evening Standard* and later the *Guardian*; creator of Colonel Blimp.

Lowell, Robert (1917–77), American poet, author of the verse play *The Old Glory*, and *Life Studies*, an autobiographical volume in verse and prose.

Loyola, St. Ignatius (1491–1556), Spanish founder of the Jesuits, a missionary order working directly under the Pope.

Lucretius (99–55 B.C.), Roman poet, author of *De rerum natura*, a long philosophical poem advocating moral truth without religious belief.

Ludendorff, Erich (1865–1937), German general who directed German strategy in the first world war.

Lugard, 1st Baron (Frederick John Dealtry Lugard) (1858–1945), British colonial administrator in Africa, especially Nigeria, and exponent of the system of indirect rule through native chiefs.

Lukács, Georg (1885–1971), Hungarian writer, Marxist thinker and literary critic. His ideas are expounded in *History and Class Consciousness* (1923), *Studies in European Realism* (1946, Eng. tr. 1950), *The Historical Novel* (1955, Eng. tr. 1962).

Luther, Martin (1483–1546), German Protestant reformer. After spending time in a monastery, he was ordained priest (1507), and lectured at Wittenberg university. In 1517 he protested against the sale of indulgences; and when summoned before the Diet of Worms made a memorable defence. He was protected by the Elector of Saxony, and translated the Bible. German Protestantism culminated in the Augsburg confession (1530). *See* **Lutheranism (J29)**.

Luthuli, Albert (1899–1967), African non-violent resistance leader, an ex-Zulu chief. Killed in train accident. Nobel prize for peace 1960.

Lutyens, Sir Edwin Landseer (1869–1944), English architect both of country houses and public buildings; designed the cenotaph, Whitehall; city plan and viceroy's house, New Delhi, British Embassy, Washington and Liverpool Roman catholic cathedral.

Lyell, Sir Charles (1797–1875), Scottish geologist, whose *Principles of Geology* (1830–33) postulated gradual geological change and helped to shape Darwin's ideas. His terminology—Pliocene (*Greek* = more recent), Miocene (less recent) and Eocene (dawn)—is still in use.

Lynn, Dame Vera (b. 1917), immensely popular

singer, the 'Forces' sweetheart' immortalised in *We'll Meet Again* and *White Cliffs of Dover*.

Lysenko, Trofim (1898–1976), Russian biologist who maintained that environmental experiences can change heredity somewhat in the manner suggested by Lamarck.

Lytton, 1st Baron (Edward George Earle Lytton Bulwer-Lytton) (1803–73), English novelist and playwright, author of *The Last Days of Pompeii*.

M

Macadam, John Loudon (1756–1836), Scottish inventor of the "macadamising" system of road repair.

MacArthur, Douglas (1880–1964), American general. He defended the Philippines against the Japanese in the second world war, and was relieved of his command in 1951 in the Korean war.

Macaulay of Rothley, 1st Baron (Thomas Babington Macaulay) (1800–59), English historian, poet and Indian civil servant. His poems include *Lays of Ancient Rome*. In India he reformed the education system.

Macaulay, Zachary (1768–1838), anti-slavery agitator, father of the above.

Macbeth (d. 1057), Scottish king, married Gruoch, granddaughter of Kenneth, king of Alban. He was mormaer of Moray, succeeding Duncan in 1040 after killing him in fair fight. His reign of seventeen years was prosperous, but he was killed by Duncan's son, Malcolm, in 1057. Shakespeare's play is based on the inaccurate *Chronicle* of Holinshed.

MacDiarmid, Hugh (1892–1978), pseudonym of Christopher Murray Grieve, Scottish poet, leader of the Scottish literary renaissance; author of *A Drunk Man Looks at the Thistle*.

Macdonald, Flora (1722–90), Scottish Jacobite heroine who saved the life of Prince Charles Edward after the defeat at Culloden Moor in 1746.

Macdonald, Sir John Alexander (1815–91), Canadian statesman, first prime minister of the Dominion of Canada.

MacDonald, James Ramsay (1866–1937), Labour politician of Scottish origin, premier 1924 and 1929–31; also of a coalition 1931–5. His action over the financial crisis of 1931 divided his party.

MacDonald, Malcolm (1901–81), son of above, held positions overseas in the Commonwealth, the last as special representative in Africa.

Machiavelli, Niccolò (1467–1527), Florentine Renaissance diplomat and theorist of the modern state. His book *The Prince* (1513), dedicated to Lorenzo, Duke of Urbino, is concerned with the reality of politics—what rulers must do to retain power. His *Discourses* is more republican and liberal.

Mackail, John William (1859–1945), British classical scholar, translator of the *Odyssey*.

Mackenzie, Sir Compton (1883–1972), British writer, whose works include *Carnival, Sinister Street*, and a monumental autobiography.

MacLean, Sorley (Somhairle MacGill-Eain) (1911–96), Gaelic poet. His collected poems, *Choille gu Bearradh* (*From Wood to Ridge*), were published in 1989, and won the MacVitie Prize.

McLuhan, Herbert Marshall (1911–80), Canadian author of a number of books on contemporary communications, including *The Gutenberg Galaxy, The Mechanical Bride. See* **Section J.**

Macmillan, Harold (1894–1986), British Conservative statesman, prime minister 1957–63; During his premiership came the crises of the Berlin Wall and the Cuban missiles (in which his personal diplomacy played an influential role), de Gaulle's veto to our entry into Europe, the signing of the Partial Test-Ban Treaty and his "wind of change" speech which hailed African independence. Chancellor of Oxford University (1960–86), O.M. 1976. Created Earl of Stockton, 1984.

McMillan, Margaret (1860–1931), Scottish educational reformer, b. New York, and pioneer of open-air nursery schools.

Macneice, Louis (1907–63), British poet, playwright, and translator.

Macready, William Charles (1793–1873), British

actor and manager, especially associated with Shakespearean roles.

Maeterlinck, Maurice (1862–1949), Belgian man of letters, whose plays include *La Princesse Maleine, Pelléas et Mélisande*, and *L'Oiseau Bleu*. Nobel prizewinner 1911.

Magellan, Ferdinand (c. 1480–1521), Portuguese navigator, and commander of the first expedition (1519) to sail round the world.

Mahler, Gustav (1860–1911), Austrian composer and conductor; a writer of symphonies and songs, a classical romantic, much influenced by Anton Bruckner and Wagner. *See* **Section E.**

Mahavira, Vardhamana Jnatriputra (6th cent. B.C.), Indian historical (as opposed to legendary) founder of Jainism, which teaches the sacredness of all life. *See* **Jainism, Section J.**

Mailer, Norman (b. 1923), U.S. novelist, whose novels include *The Naked and the Dead* (1948) and *The Executioner's Song* (1979).

Maintenon, Françoise d'Aubigné, Marquise de (1635–1719), second wife of Louis XIV. Her first husband was the poet Scarron.

Major, John (b. 1943), Prime Minister from Nov. 1990 to 1997. Leader of the Conservative Party, 1990–97. M.P. (Con.) Huntingdon after 1979. Foreign Secretary, 1989. Chancellor of the Exchequer, 1989–90. His victory in the 1992 election heralded grave problems for his government over Europe and great electoral unpopularity. In 1995 he challenged his critics and won a leadership contest, but by late 1996 by-election losses (and defections) had produced a vulnerable administration. He was heavily defeated in the 1997 election. Created Companion of Honour (1999). *See* **Section C.**

Makarios III (1913–77), Greek Orthodox archbishop and Cypriot national leader. Deported by the British to the Seychelles in 1956, he returned in 1957. First President of Cyprus.

Malibran, Marie Félicité (1808–36), Spanish mezzo-soprano.

Malory, Sir Thomas (c. 1430–71), English writer. From earlier sources and legends of King Arthur and the Knights of the Round Table, he compiled the *Morte d'Arthur* printed by Caxton in 1485.

Malpighi, Marcello (1628–94), Italian physician and biologist. Founder of microscopic anatomy.

Malraux, André (1901–76), French novelist and politician. His works include *La Condition humaine, L'Espoir,* and *Psychologie de l'art* (tr. in 2 vols.), *Museum without Walls,* and *The Creative Act).* Served under de Gaulle.

Malthus, Thomas Robert (1766–1834), English clergyman and economist who in his gloomy essay *The Principle of Population* contended that population tends to increase faster than the means of subsistence and that its growth could only be checked by moral restraint or by disease and war. *See* **Malthusianism, Section J.**

Mandela, Nelson Rolihlahia (b. 1918), the President of South Africa, 1994–99, son of chief of Tembu tribe; imprisoned on political grounds 1964–90. His release from prison in February 1990 transformed the political scene in South Africa. Historic agreement (1993) with President De Klerk to form Government of National Unity after multi-party elections. Shared Nobel Peace Prize with De Klerk, 1993. The ANC victory in April 1994 paved the way for him to become President. Honorary Order of Merit, 1995. Stood down as ANC President, 1997. *See* **Section C.**

Manet, Edouard (1832–83), French painter. His impressionist pictures include *Olympia* and *Un bar aux Folies-Bergères* (the latter at the Courtauld).

Mann, Thomas (1875–1955), German writer who won world recognition at the age of 25 with his novel *Buddenbrooks*. His liberal humanistic outlook had developed sufficiently by 1930 for him to expose national socialism. He left Germany in 1933. Other works are *The Magic Mountain,* and the *Joseph* tetralogy. Nobel prizewinner 1929.

Mann, Tom (1856–1941), British Labour leader for more than fifty years.

Manning, Henry Edward (1808–92), English cardinal; archbishop of Westminster 1865–92. He was an Anglican churchman before he entered the church of Rome.

Mansfield, Katherine (Kathleen Beauchamp) (1890–1923), short-story writer, b. Wellington, New Zealand, whose work was influenced by the short stories of Chekhov. Her second husband was **John Middleton Murry,** literary critic.

Manson, Sir Patrick (1844–1922), Scottish physician, the first to propose that the malarial parasite was transmitted by the mosquito.

Manuzio, Aldo Pio (1450–1515), Italian printer, founder of the Aldine press in Venice which issued books famed for their type and bindings.

Manzoni, Alessandro (1785–1873), Italian novelist and poet, b. Milan. Author of historical novel *I Promessi Sposi* (The Betrothed).

Mao Tse-tung (1893–1976), Chinese national and Communist leader. B. in Hunan, of rural origin. As a young man he worked as assistant librarian at Peking University. He understood how to win peasant support for a national and progressive movement. Attacked by Chiang Kai-shek, he led his followers by the "long march" to N.W. China, whence later they issued to defeat both Japanese and Chiang and proclaim a People's Republic in 1949, and later to promote the "great leap forward" of 1958–9 the commune movement). He stood for an egalitarian democratic society, unbureaucratic, with revolutionary momentum. He promoted the "cultural revolution" (1965–9). *See* **Maoism, Section J.**

Marat, Jean Paul (1743–93), French revolution leader, largely responsible for the reign of terror, and assassinated by Charlotte Corday.

Marconi, Guglielmo Marchese (1874–1937), Italian inventor and electrical engineer who developed the use of radio waves. In 1895 he sent long-wave signals over a distance of a mile, and in 1901 received in Newfoundland the first transatlantic signals sent out by his station in Cornwall, thus making the discovery that radio waves can bend around the spherically-shaped earth. Nobel prizewinner 1909.

Marcus Aurelius Antoninus (121–180 A.D.), Roman emperor and Stoic philosopher of lofty character, whose *Meditations* are still read.

Marcuse, Herbert (1898–1979), political philosopher. B. Berlin, he emigrated to the U.S. during the Nazi regime. A critic of Western industrial society, he saw the international student protest movement as the catalyst of revolutionary change.

Maria Theresa (1717–80), Empress, daughter of the Hapsburg Charles VI. Able and of strong character, she fought unsuccessfully to save Silesia from Prussian annexation. She promoted reforms in her dominions. She married the Duke of Lorraine and had 16 children.

Marie Antoinette (1755–93), Queen of France, was daughter of the above and wife of Louis XVI; accused of treason, she and her husband were beheaded in the French revolution.

Marie Louise (1791–1847), daughter of Francis I of Austria, became the wife of Napoleon and bore him a son (Napoleon II).

Marius, Caius (157–86 B.C.), Roman general who defended Gaul from invasion; later civil war forced him to flee from Rome, and on his return he took terrible revenge.

Mark Antony. *See* Antonius, **Marcus.**

Marlborough, 1st Duke of (John Churchill) (1650–1722), English general, victor of Blenheim, Ramillies, Oudenarde and Malplaquet. His wife, Sarah Jennings, was a favourite of Queen Anne.

Marlowe, Christopher (1564–93), English dramatist and precursor of Shakespeare. His plays include *Dr. Faustus, Tamburlaine the Great, Edward II,* and *The Jew of Malta.* His early death was due to a tavern brawl.

Marryat, Frederick (1792–1848), English author of sea and adventure stories, including *Peter Simple, Mr. Midshipman Easy,* and *Masterman Ready.* A captain in the Royal Navy.

Marshall, George Catlett (1880–1959), American general. U.S. chief of staff 1939–45; originated the Marshall Aid plan. Nobel prize for peace 1953.

Martial, Marcus Valerius (c. 40–104), Roman poet, b. in Spain, remembered for his epigrams.

Marvell, Andrew (1620–78), English poet and political writer. He was Milton's assistant.

Marx, Karl (1818–83), German founder of modern international communism, b. Trier of Jewish parentage. He studied law, philosophy and history at the universities of Bonn and Berlin, and later took up the study of economics. In conjunction with his friend Engels he wrote the *Communist Manifesto* of 1848 for the Communist League of which he was the leader. Because of his revolutionary activities he was forced to leave the continent and in 1849 settled in London. Here, mainly while living at 28 Dean Street, Soho, he wrote *Das Kapital*, a deep analysis of the economic laws that govern modern society. In 1864 he helped to found the first International. He ranks as one of the most original and influential thinkers of modern times. He was buried in Highgate cemetery. *See* **Marxism, Section J.**

Mary I (1516–58), Queen of England, was daughter of Henry VIII and Catherine of Aragon. A Roman Catholic, she reversed the religious changes made by her father and brother, and about 300 Protestants were put to death. She married Philip of Spain.

Mary II (1662–94), Queen of England with her husband the Dutch William III. As daughter of James II, she was invited to succeed after the revolution of 1688 and expelled her father.

Mary Stuart, Queen of Scots (1542–87), daughter of James V of Scotland and Mary of Guise, she laid claim to the English succession. She was imprisoned in England by Elizabeth and beheaded. Her husbands were the dauphin of France (d. 1560), Lord Henry Stewart Darnley (murdered 1567) and Bothwell.

Masaryk, Jan Garrigue (1886–1948), Czech diplomat. The son of Thomas, he was Czech minister in London 1925–38, and foreign secretary while his government was in exile in London and after it returned to Prague, 1940–8.

Masaryk, Thomas Garrigue (1850–1937), Czech statesman and independence leader. He was the first president of Czechoslovakia, 1918–35.

Mascagni, Pietro (1863–1945), Italian composer of *Cavalleria Rusticana.*

Masefield, John (1878–1967), English poet. His best-known works are *Salt-Water Ballads* (as a boy he ran away to sea), and *Reynard the Fox.* He became poet laureate in 1930.

Maskelyne, John Nevil (1839–1917), English illusionist. He also exposed spiritualistic frauds.

Massenet, Jules Emile Frédéric (1842–1912), French composer of songs, orchestral suites, oratorios, and operas, among them *Manon* and *Thaïs.*

Massine, Léonide (1896–1979), Russian dancer, one of Diaghilev's choreographers.

Masters, Edgar Lee (1869–1950), American poet remembered for his *Spoon River Anthology.*

Matisse, Henri (1869–1954), French painter, member of a group known as *Les Fauves* (the wild beasts) for their use of violent colour and colour variation to express form and relief.

Matsys (Massys), Quentin (1466–1530), Flemish painter, b. Louvain, settled Antwerp; he worked at a time when Italian influence was gaining ground. His *Money-changer, and his Wife* is in the Louvre.

Matthews, Sir Stanley (b. 1915), first footballer to be knighted. He made 880 first-class appearances, 54 for England. Played in the legendary 1953 Cup Final (when Blackpool beat Bolton Wanderers 4–3).

Maugham, William Somerset (1874–1965), British writer, b. Paris. He practised as a doctor till the success of *Liza of Lambeth* (1897) followed by *Of Human Bondage.* He was a master of the short story and his work reflects his travels in the East. In both world wars he served as a British agent.

Maupassant, Guy de (1850–93), French writer whose novels and short stories show penetrating realism. His stories include *Boule de Suif, Le Maison Tellier,* and *La Parure.*

Mauriac, François (1885–1970), French writer whose novels deal with moral problems and include *Le Baiser au Lépreux* and the play *Asmodée.* Nobel prizewinner 1952.

Maurois, André (Emile Herzog) (1885–1967), French writer whose works include lives of Shelley and Disraeli.

Maxim, Sir Hiram Stevens (1840–1916), American inventor of the automatic quick-firing gun.

Maxton, James (1885–1946), Scottish Labour politician and pacifist; entered parliament 1922; chairman of I.L.P. 1926–31, 1934–9.

Maxwell, James Clerk (1831–79), Scottish physicist. He wrote his first scientific paper at 15, and after teaching in Aberdeen and London became first Cavendish professor of experimental physics at Cambridge. His mathematical mind, working on the discoveries of Faraday and others, gave physics a celebrated set of equations

for the basic laws of electricity and magnetism. His work revolutionised the understanding of fundamental physics.

May, Peter (Barker Howard) (1929–94). English cricketer. The finest post-war batsman produced in Britain. A long-serving and successful captain.

Mazarin, Jules (1602–61), cardinal and minister of France was b. in Italy. In spite of opposition from the nobles, he continued Richelieu's work of building up a strong monarchy.

Mazeppa, Ivan Stepanovich (1644–1709), Cossack nobleman, b. Ukraine (then part of Poland, before E. Ukraine passed to Russia, 1667). He fought unsuccessfully for independence allying himself with Charles XII of Sweden against Peter I of Russia (Poltava, 1709). Byron wrote a poem about him.

Mazzini, Giuseppe (1805–72), Italian patriot. B. Genoa, he advocated a free and united Italy, and from Marseilles he published a journal, *Young Italy.* Expelled from the Continent, he took refuge in London in 1837. In 1848 he returned to Italy, and became dictator of the short-lived Roman republic, which was put down by French forces. His contribution to Italian unity was that of preparing the way.

Mechnikov, Ilya (1845–1916), Russian biologist who discovered that by "phagocytosis" certain white blood cells are capable of ingesting harmful substances such as bacteria (*see* **Diseases of the Blood, Section P**). For his work on immunity he shared the 1908 Nobel prize for medicine.

Medawar, Sir Peter Brien (1915–87), British zoologist, author of *The Art of the Soluble* and *The Future of Man;* president of the British Association 1969. Nobel prizewinner 1960. O.M. 1981.

Medici, Florentine family of merchants and bankers who were politically powerful and who patronised the arts. **Cosimo the Elder** (1389–1464) was for over 30 years virtual ruler of Florence. His grandson, **Lorenzo the Magnificent** (1449–92), poet, friend of artists and scholars, governed with munificence. His grandson, **Lorenzo,** was father of **Catherine de' Medici,** Queen of France (*q.v.*). A later **Cosimo** (1519–74) was an able Duke of Florence and then Grand-Duke of Tuscany, which title the Medicis held until 1737.

Méhul, Etienne Nicolas (1763–1817), French operatic composer. *Joseph* is his masterpiece.

Meir, Golda (1898–1978), leading member of the Israeli Labour Party, her premiership included the Six Day and Yom Kippur wars.

Meitner, Lise (1878–1969), co-worker of Otto Hahn (*q.v.*) who interpreted his results (1939) as a fission process.

Melanchthon, Philip (1497–1560), German religious reformer, who assisted Luther, and wrote the first Protestant theological work, *Loci communes.* He drew up the Augsburg confession (1530).

Melba, Nellie (Helen Porter Mitchell) (1861–1931), Australian soprano of international repute.

Melbourne, 2nd Viscount (William Lamb) (1779–1848), English Whig statesman, was premier at the accession of Queen Victoria.

Mendel, Gregor Johann (1822–84), Austrian botanist. After entering the Augustinian monastery at Brünn he became abbot and taught natural history in the school. His main interest was the study of inheritance, and his elaborate observations of the common garden pea resulted in the law of heredity which bears his name. His hypothesis was published in 1866 but no real attention was given to it until 1900.

Mendeleyev, Dmitri Ivanovich (1834–1907), Russian chemist, first to discover the critical temperatures. He formulated the periodic law of atomic weights (1869) and drew up the periodic table (*see* **Section F**), predicting the properties of elements which might fill the gaps. Element 101 is named after him.

Mendelssohn-Bartholdy, Felix (1809–47), German composer, grandson of Moses Mendelssohn, philosopher. He belongs with Chopin and Schumann to the early 19th cent. classic-romantic school, and his music has delicacy and melodic beauty. He was conductor of the Gewandhaus concerts at Leipzig for a time and often visited England. *See* **Section E.**

Menuhin, Lord (Yehudi Menuhin) (1916–99), famous violinist, b. New York of Russian Jewish parentage.

He first appeared as soloist at the age of seven. He went on to become the greatest violinist of his age. Founded a School for musically gifted children. Order of Merit, 1987.

Menzies, Sir Robert Gordon (1894–1978), Australian Liberal statesman, P.M. 1939–41, 1949–66.

Mercator, Gerhardus (Gerhard Kremer) (1512–94), Flemish geographer who pioneered the making of accurate navigational maps. He worked out the map which bears his name in which meridians and parallels of latitude cross each other at right angles, enabling compass bearings to be drawn as straight lines.

Meredith, George (1828–1909), English writer, b. Portsmouth. His novels include *The Ordeal of Richard Feverel*, *The Egoist*, *Evan Harrington*, *Diana of the Crossways*, and *The Amazing Marriage*. His poetry includes *Modern Love* and *Poems and Lyrics of the Joy of Earth*.

Mesmer, Friedrich Anton (1733–1815), Austrian founder of mesmerism (*see* **J32**).

Mestrovič, Ivan (1883–1962), Yugoslav sculptor of international repute. He designed the temple at Kossovo. He later lived in England, and examples of his work are in London museums.

Metastasio, Pietro (Pietro Bonaventura Trapassi) (1698–1782), Italian librettist who lived in Vienna and provided texts for Gluck, Handel, Haydn, and Mozart.

Metternich, Clemens (1773–1859), Austrian statesman and diplomat. Foreign Minister, 1809–48. Chancellor, 1812–48.

Michelangelo (Michelagniolo Buonarroti) (1475–1564), Italian painter, sculptor and poet. Of a poor but genteel Tuscan family, his first interest in sculpture came through his nurse, wife of a stone-cutter. He was apprenticed to Domenico Ghirlandaio. Like Leonardo, he studied anatomy, but instead of spreading his talents over a wide field, he became obsessed with the problem of how to represent the human body. In him, classical idealism, mediaeval religious belief, and renaissance energy met. Perhaps his most impressive work is the ceiling of the Sistine Chapel (a surface of about 6,000 square feet), the *Last Judgement* behind the chapel altar, his marble *Pietà* (St. Peter's) the statue of *David* (Academy, Florence), the great figure of *Moses* (San Pietro in Vincoli, Rome), and the four allegorical figures *Day*, *Night*, *Dawn*, *Twilight* (intended for the tombs of the Medici family at San Lorenzo, Florence).

Michelet, Jules (1798–1874), French historian who wrote a history of France in 24 vols. and of the revolution in 7 vols.

Michelson, Albert Abraham (1852–1931), American physicist, b. Poland. He collaborated with E. W. Morley in an experiment to determine ether drift, the negative result of which was important for Einstein. Nobel prizewinner 1907.

Mickiewicz, Adam (1798–1855), Polish revolutionary poet, author of *The Ancestors* and *Pan Tadeusz*.

Mill, John Stuart (1806–73), English philosopher. A member of Bentham's utilitarian school, he later modified some of its tenets. His main work is *On Liberty*, which advocates social as well as political freedom and warns against the tyranny of the majority. *The Subjection of Women* supported women's rights. He also wrote *Principles of Political Economy*. He was godfather to Bertrand Russell.

Millais, Sir John Everett (1829–96), English artist, b. Southampton; in his earlier years a pre-Raphaelite (*Ophelia*). Later works include *The Boyhood of Raleigh* and *Bubbles*. He married Mrs. Ruskin after the annulment of her marriage.

Millet, Jean François (1814–75), French painter of rural life, sometimes in sombre mood; his works include *The Angelus*.

Millikan, Robert Andrews (1868–1954), American physicist, who determined the charge on the electron and discovered cosmic rays. Nobel prizewinner 1923.

Milne, Alan Alexander (1882–1956), English humorist and poet whose work for children is still widely read.

Milner, 1st Viscount (Alfred Milner) (1854–1925), British administrator, especially in South Africa; author of *England in Egypt*.

Milošević, Slobodan. *See* **C**.

Milstein, César (b. 1927) Argentinian-born molecular biologist. Joint Nobel Prize for Medicine, 1984.

Miltiades (d. 489 B.C.), one of the leaders of the

Athenian army against the Persians at Marathon.

Milton, John (1608–74), English poet, author of *Paradise Lost*. B. in London, he wrote while still at Cambridge *L'Allegro*, *Il Penseroso*, *Comus*, and *Lycidas*. The Civil War diverted his energies for years to the parliamentary and political struggle, but during this period he defended in *Aereopagitica* the freedom of the press. After he had become blind he wrote *Paradise Lost* and a sonnet *On His Blindness*.

Minot, George Richards (1885–1950), who with W. P. Murphy discovered the curative properties of liver in pernicious anaemia. Shared Nobel prize 1934.

Mirabeau, Gabriel, Honoré Victor Riquetti, Comte de (1749–91), French revolutionary leader. His writings and speeches contributed to the revolution of 1789.

Mirrlees, Sir James Alexander (b. 1936), Professor of Political Economy at Cambridge since 1995. Shared 1996 Nobel Prize for Economics.

Mistral, Frédéric (1830–1914), French poet, and founder of a Provençal renaissance. His works include *Lou Trésor dóu Félibrige* and a Provençal dictionary. Nobel prizewinner 1904.

Mitchell, Reginald Joseph (1895–1937), British aircraft designer. Famous for developing the *Spitfire*.

Mithridates (c. 132–63 B.C.), King of Pontus, in Asia Minor; after early successes against the Romans was defeated by Pompey.

Mitterrand, François Maurice Marie (1916–96), French socialist politician, proclaimed fourth president of the Fifth Republic, 21 May 1981. Re-elected May 1988 for second 7-year term until 1995. The longest serving President of the Fifth Republic. He died of cancer in 1996.

Mobutu Sese Seko (1930–97), brutal and corrupt dictator of Zaire (now Dem. Rep. of Congo), 1965–97. He impoverished his country.

Modigliani, Amedeo (1884–1920), Italian painter and sculptor, b. Livorno. His portraits and figure studies tend to elongation and simplification. He lived mainly in Paris.

Moffatt, James (1870–1944), Scottish divine who translated the Bible into modern English.

Mohammed (570–632), the founder of Islam, the religion of the Moslems, received the revelation of the Koran (their sacred book), and the command to preach, at the age of 40. By his constant proclamation that there was only One God he gathered around him a loyal following, but aroused the hostility of other Meccans. The Moslems were forced to flee to Medina in 622, but grew sufficiently to return to Mecca eight years later, and establish the Kaaba as the goal of the pilgrimage in Islam. *See* **Islam, Section J**.

Molière (Jean Baptiste Poquelin) (1622–73), French playwright. B. in Paris, he gained experience as a strolling player, and subsequently in Paris, partly in the king's service; he wrote an unsurpassed series of plays varying from farce as in *Les Précieuses ridicules* to high comedy. Among his plays are *Tartuffe*, *Le Misanthrope*, and *Le Bourgeois gentilhomme*.

Molotov, Vyacheslav Mikhailovich (1890–1986), Russian diplomat. He succeeded Litvinov as commissar for foreign affairs, 1939–49.

Moltke, Helmuth, Count von (1800–91), Prussian general and chief of staff (1858–88) during the period when Prussia successfully united Germany.

Mond, Ludwig (1838–1909), German chemist who in 1867 settled in England as an alkali manufacturer and in partnership with John Brunner successfully manufactured soda by the Solvay process.

Monet, Claude (1840–1926), French painter, leader of the Impressionists, the term being derived in 1874 from his landscape *Impression soleil levant*. He liked painting a subject in the open air at different times of day to show variation in light.

Monk, George, 1st Duke of Albemarle (1608–69), English general and admiral, whose reputation and moderation were mainly responsible for the return of Charles II in 1660.

Monmouth, Duke of (James Scott) (1649–85), English pretender, natural son of Charles II; centre of anti-Catholic feeling against succession of Duke of York (later James II). His troops, mostly peasants, were routed at Sedgemoor (1685) by John Churchill (later Duke of Marlborough). Beheaded on Tower Hill.

Monnet, Jean (1888–1979), French political economist, "father of the Common Market." He drafted the Monnet plan for French economic recovery

(1947) and the plan to establish the European Coal and Steel Community.

Monroe, James (1758–1831), president of the U.S. He propounded the doctrine that the American continent should not be colonised by a European power.

Montagu, Lady Mary Wortley (1689–1762), English writer. From Constantinople where her husband was ambassador she wrote *Letters* of which a complete edition was published 1965–7. She introduced England to the idea of inoculation against smallpox.

Montaigne, Michel de (1533–92), French essayist of enquiring, sceptical and tolerant mind.

Montcalm, Louis Joseph, Marquis de (1712–59), French general, who unsuccessfully commanded the French at Quebec against Wolfe.

Montesquieu, Charles-Louis de Secondat, Baron de la Brède et de (1689–1755), French philosopher. His works include *Lettres persanes*, a satire on contemporary life; and *De l'esprit des lois* giving his political philosophy. The latter was based largely, but to some extent mistakenly, on English practice, and its influence led the U.S. constitution to separate the executive (President) from the legislature (Congress).

Montessori, Maria (1870–1952), Italian educationist, who developed an educational system based on spontaneity.

Monteverdi, Claudio (1567–1643), Italian composer who pioneered in opera. His chief dramatic work is *Orfeo* (1607). *See* **Section E.**

Montezuma II (1466–1520), Aztec emperor of Mexico when the Spanish under Cortés invaded.

Montfort, Simon de, Earl of Leicester (*c.* 1208–65), English statesman. He led the barons in revolt against the ineffective rule of Henry III, but he differed from other rebels in that he summoned a parliamentary assembly to which for the first time representatives came from the towns. He was killed at Evesham.

Montgolfier, the name of two brothers, **Joseph Michel** (1740–1810) and **Jacques Etienne** (1745–99), French aeronauts who constructed the first practical balloon, which flew 6 miles.

Montgomery of Alamein, 1st Viscount (Bernard Law Montgomery) (1887–1976), British field-marshal; commanded 8th Army in North Africa, Sicily, and Italy, 1942–4; commander-in-chief, British Group of Armies and Allied Armies in Northern France, 1944.

Montrose, Marquess of (James Graham) (1612–50), Scottish general. In the Civil War he raised the Highland clansmen for Charles I and won the battles of Tippermuir, Inverlochy, and Kilsyth; but was finally defeated and executed.

Moody, Dwight Lyman (1837–99), American revivalist preacher, associated with Ira D. Sankey, the "American singing pilgrim."

Moore, George (1852–1933), Irish novelist, author of *Confessions of a Young Man, Esther Waters,* and *Evelyn Innes.*

Moore, Henry (1898–1986), English sculptor in semi-abstract style, son of a Yorkshire coalminer. Examples of his work are to be seen all over the world, in the Tate Gallery, St. Matthew's Church, Northampton, the Unesco building in Paris, in Kensington Gardens, *etc.*

Moore, Sir John (1761–1809), British general, who trained the infantry for the Spanish Peninsular campaigns and conducted a brilliant retreat to Corunna, where he was mortally wounded after defeating the French under Soult.

Moore, Thomas (1779–1852), Irish poet, author of *Irish Melodies, Lalla Rookh,* and *The Epicurean* (novel). He also wrote a life of Byron.

More, Sir Thomas (1478–1535), English writer and statesman. In 1529 he succeeded Wolsey as lord chancellor, but on his refusal to recognise Henry VIII as head of the church he was executed. His *Utopia* describes an ideal state. He was canonised 1935.

Morgan, Sir Henry (*c.* 1635–88), Welsh buccaneer who operated in the Caribbean against the Spaniards, capturing and plundering Panama in 1671. Knighted by Charles II and made deputy-governor of Jamaica.

Morgan, John Pierpont (1837–1913), American financier who built the family fortunes into a vast industrial empire.

Morland, George (1763–1804), English painter of rural life.

Morley, 1st Viscount (John Morley) (1838–1923), English biographer and Liberal politician. He held political office, but is mainly remembered for his lives of Gladstone, Cobden *etc.*

Morley, Thomas (*c.* 1557–1603), English composer of madrigals, noted also for his settings of some of Shakespeare's songs. He was a pupil of Byrd, organist of St. Paul's cathedral, and wrote *Plaine and Easie Introduction to Practicall Music* (1597) which was used for 200 years.

Morris, William (1834–96), English poet and craftsman. His hatred of 19th-cent. ugliness, his belief in human equality, and in freedom and happiness for all, combined to make him a socialist, and he accomplished much for the improvement of domestic decoration. He was a popular lecturer, founded the Socialist League and the Kelmscott Press.

Morrison of Lambeth, Baron (Herbert Morrison) (1888–1965), British Labour statesman. From being an errand-boy, he rose to become leader of the London County Council. During the war he was Home Secretary, and he was deputy prime minister, 1945–51.

Morse, Samuel Finley Breese (1791–1872), American pioneer in electromagnetic telegraphy and inventor of the dot-and-dash code that bears his name. He was originally an artist.

Moulin, Jean (1899–1943) French resistance leader who died under Nazi torture.

Mountbatten of Burma, 1st Earl (Louis Mountbatten) (1900–79), British admiral and statesman. In the second world war he became chief of combined operations in 1942. As last viceroy of India, he carried through the transfer of power to Indian hands in 1947 and was the first governor-general of the dominion. His assassination by Irish extremists evoked horror.

Mozart, Wolfgang Amadeus (1756–91), Austrian composer. B. Salzburg, he began his career at four and toured Europe at six. In 1781 he settled in Vienna, where he became a friend of Haydn and where his best music was written. His genius lies in the effortless outpouring of all forms of music, in the ever-flowing melodies, in the consistent beauty and symmetry of his compositions, and in the exactness of his method. Among the loveliest and grandest works in instrumental music are his three great symphonies in E. flat, G minor, and C (called the "Jupiter"), all written in six weeks in 1788. Three of the greatest operas in musical history are his *Marriage of Figaro* (1786), *Don Giovanni* (1787), and *The Magic Flute* (1791). His last composition, written under the shadow of death, was the *Requiem Mass,* a work of tragic beauty. *See* **Section E.**

Mugabe, Robert Gabriel (b. 1924), first prime minister of independent Zimbabwe after his election victory in March 1980.

Muggeridge, Malcolm (1903–90), broadcaster and journalist who became an ardent Christian.

Müller, Sir Ferdinand (1825–96), German-born botanist who emigrated to Australia, where he was director of the Melbourne Botanical Gardens, 1857–73, and whence he introduced the eucalyptus into Europe.

Müller, Friedrich Max (1823–1900), Philologist and orientalist. Born Dessau. A professor at Oxford.

Mulroney, (Martin) Brian (b. 1939), Prime Minister of Canada, 1984–93. Elected leader of the Progressive Conservative Party, 1983. First Conservative leader from Quebec in nearly 100 years.

Mumford, Lewis (1895–1990), American writer on town-planning and social problems. His works include a tetralogy: *Technics and Civilisation, The Culture of Cities, The Condition of Man,* and *The Conduct of Life; The Myth of the Machine,* and *The Urban Prospect.*

Munnings, Sir Alfred (1878–1959), English painter, especially of horses and sporting subjects.

Murdoch, Iris (1919–99), British novelist. *See* **M17.**

Murdock, William (1754–1839), Scottish engineer and inventor, the first to make practical use of coal gas as an iluminating agent (introduced at the Soho works, Birmingham, 1800).

Murillo, Bartolomé Esteban (1617–82), Spanish painter, b. Seville, where he founded an Academy. His early works, such as *Two Peasant Boys* (Dulwich) show peasant and street life; his later paintings are religious, *e.g.,* the *Immaculate Conception* in the Prado.

Murray, Gilbert (1866–1957), classical scholar of Australian birth who settled in England. A teacher of Greek at the universities of Glasgow and Oxford, he translated Greek drama so as to bring it within the reach of a wide public.

Mussolini, Benito (1883–1945), Fascist dictator of Italy 1922–43. From 1935 an aggressive foreign policy (Abyssinia and Spain) was at first successful, and in June 1940 he entered the war on the side of Hitler. Defeat in North Africa and the invasion of Sicily caused the collapse of his government. He was shot dead by partisans while trying to escape to Switzerland.

Mussorgsky, Modest Petrovich (1839–81), Russian composer whose masterpiece is the opera *Boris Godunov* after the play by Pushkin. His piano suite *Pictures at an Exhibition* was orchestrated by Ravel. *See* **Section E.**

N

Naipaul, Sir Vidiadhur Surajprasad (b. 1932), Trinidadian novelist and writer, whose novels include *A House for Mr Biswas* (1961). Awarded the Booker Prize for *In a Free State* (1971).

Nanak (1469–1538), Indian guru or teacher, who tried to put an end to religious strife, teaching that "God is one, whether he be Allah or Rama." *See* **Sikhism, Section J.**

Nansen, Fridtjof (1861–1930), Norwegian explorer. In 1893 his north polar expedition reached the highest latitude till then attained—86° 14'. He published an account called *Farthest North.* He was active in Russian famine relief, 1921. Nobel peace prize 1922.

Napier, John (1550–1617), Scottish mathematician, b. Edinburgh, invented logarithms (published 1614) and the modern notation of fractions, improvements in the methods of mathematical expression which helped to advance cosmology and physics.

Napoleon I (Bonaparte) (1769–1821), French emperor and general, of Corsican birth (Ajaccio). Trained in French military schools, he became prominent in the early years of the revolution, with uncertainty at home and war abroad. In 1796 he became commander of the army in Italy and defeated the Austrians, so that France obtained control of Lombardy. He then led an expedition to Egypt but Nelson destroyed his fleet. After further Italian victories, he made a *coup d'état* in 1799, and in 1804 became emperor. Against continuing European opposition, he defeated the Austrians at Austerlitz, and his power in Europe was such that he made his brothers Joseph, Louis, and Jerome kings of Naples, Holland, and Westphalia; but in Spain he provoked the Peninsular War, and his armies were gradually driven back by the Spanish, helped by Wellington; while his invasion of Russia in 1812 ended in a disastrous retreat from Moscow; and in 1814 the Allies forced him to abdicate and retire to Elba. He emerged again in 1815 to be defeated at Waterloo and exiled to St. Helena. His government at home was firm and promoted some reforms (*e.g.*, legal codification), but the country was weakened by his wars. In Europe, in spite of the suffering caused by war, there was some spread of French revolutionary ideas, and equally a reaction against them on the part of authority. The imperial idea lingered in France, and Napoleon's remains were brought to Paris in 1840. He married first Josephine Beauharnais and second Marie Louise of Austria. Marie Louise was the mother of **Napoleon II** (1811–32).

Napoleon III (1808–73), son of Napoleon I's brother Louis. He returned to France in the revolution of 1848, and in 1851 came to power by a *coup d'état.* In his reign Paris was remodelled. His foreign policy was adventurous (the Crimean war, intervention in Mexico, war against Austria and Italy); but when he was manoeuvred by Bismarck into the Franco-Prussian war and defeated at Sedan he lost his throne and retired to England. His wife was Eugénie de Montijo.

Nash, John (1752–1835), English architect who planned Regent Street, laid out Regent's Park, enlarged Buckingham Palace, and designed Marble Arch and the Brighton Pavilion.

Nash, Paul (1889–1946), English painter and designer, official war artist in both world wars. Best-known pictures are *The Menin Road* of 1918 and *Totes Meer* of 1941.

Nash, Walter (1882–1968), New Zealand Labour politician; prime minister 1957–60.

Nasmyth, James (1808–90), Scottish inventor of the steam-hammer, which became indispensable in all large iron and engineering works.

Nasser, Gamal Abdel (1918–70), leader of modern Egypt and of the Arab world. He led the 1954 coup that deposed General Neguib. He became president of the Egyptian Republic in 1956 and of the United Arab Republic in 1958. His nationalisation of the Suez Canal in 1956 precipitated a short-lived attack by Britain and France, Israeli–Arab hostility led to the June war of 1967. He carried out reforms to bring his people out of near-feudalism, including the building (with Russian help) of the Aswan High Dam.

Navratilova, Martina (b. 1956) Czech-born tennis player of outstanding ability. She won 18 Grand Slam singles, 37 Grand Slam doubles and 149 other championship singles titles.

Needham, Joseph (1900–95), British biochemist, historian of science and orientalist. Author of the monumental *Science and Civilisation in China.*

Nehru, Pandit Jawaharlal (1889–1964), Indian national leader and statesman, first prime minister and minister of foreign affairs when India became independent in 1947. A leading member of the Congress Party, during which time he was frequently imprisoned for political activity. He played a part in the final negotiations for independence. Under his leadership India made major advances. In world affairs his influence was for peace and non-alignment. His daughter was **Indira Gandhi**, *(see* **B25**).

Nelson, 1st Viscount (Horatio Nelson) (1758–1805), English admiral. Son of a Norfolk clergyman, he went to sea at 12 and became a captain in 1793. In the French revolutionary wars he lost his right eye in 1794 and his right arm in 1797. Rear-admiral in 1797, he defeated the French at Aboukir Bay in 1798. He was also at the bombardment of Copenhagen in 1801. In 1805 he destroyed the French fleet at Trafalgar, in which battle he was killed. His daring and decision made him a notable commander. He loved Emma Hamilton.

Nernst, Walther Hermann (1864–1941), German scientist who established the third law of thermodynamics that dealt with the behaviour of matter at temperatures approaching absolute zero. Nobel prizewinner 1920.

Nero, Claudius Caesar (A.D. 37–68), Roman emperor, the adopted son of Claudius. He was weak and licentious and persecuted Christians. In his reign occurred the fire of Rome.

Newcomen, Thomas (1663–1729), English inventor, one of the first to put a steam-engine into practical operation. In 1705 he patented his invention, the pumping-engine used in Cornish mines until the adoption of Watt's engine.

Newman, Ernest (1868–1959), English music critic, whose chief work is the *Life of Richard Wagner.*

Newman, John Henry (1801–90), English priest and writer, who became a cardinal of the Roman church in 1879, and was a founder of the Oxford Movement. (*See* **J52**) He is best remembered by his *Apologia pro Vita Sua* in which he described the development of his religious thought. He wrote *Lead, kindly Light,* set to music 30 years later by J. B. Dykes, and *The Dream of Gerontius,* set to music of Elgar.

Newton, Sir Isaac (1642–1727), English scientist, b. Woolsthorpe, Lincs. (the year Galileo died). He studied at Cambridge but was at home during the plague years 1665 and 1666 when he busied himself with problems concerned with optics and gravitation. Through his tutor Isaac Barrow he was appointed to the Lucasian chair of mathematics at Cambridge in 1669 and remained there until 1696 when he was appointed Warden, and later Master of the Mint. He was a secret Unitarian and did not marry. His three great discoveries were to show that white light could be separated into a sequence of coloured components forming the visible spectrum; to use the calculus (invented by him independently of Leibnitz) to investigate the forces of nature in a quantitative way; and to show by his theory of gravitation (for which Copernicus, Kepler and Galileo had prepared the way) that the universe was regulated by simple mathematical laws. His vision was set forth in the *Philosophiae Naturalis Principia Mathematica* of 1687, usually called the *Principia*. It was not until 200 years later that Einstein showed there could be another theory of celestial mechanics.

Ney, Michel (1769–1815), French general who served under Napoleon, especially at Jena, Borodino, and Waterloo.

Nicholas II (1868–1918), last emperor and Tsar of Russia, son of Alexander III. His reign was marked by an unsuccessful war with Japan (1904–5), and by the 1914–18 war. Ineffective and lacking ability, he set up a Duma in 1906 too late for real reform. Revolution broke out in 1917. He and his family were shot in July 1918.

Nicholson, Sir William (1872–1949), English artist known for his portraits and woodcuts. His son, **Ben Nicholson**, O.M., (1894–1981) was a giant of English painting, with styles from Cornish landscapes to his controversial white minimalism.

Nicolson, Sir Harold (1886–1968), English diplomat, author, and critic. His works include *King George V* and *Diaries and Letters*. His wife was **Victoria Sackville-West** (1892–1962).

Niemeyer, Oscar (b. 1907), visionary modernist architect who designed Brasilia (capital of Brazil).

Niemöller, Martin (1892–1984), German Lutheran pastor who opposed the Nazi regime and was confined in a concentration camp. He was president of the World Council of Churches in 1961.

Nietzsche, Friedrich Wilhelm (1844–1900), German philosopher, in his younger years influenced by Wagner and Schopenhauer. His teaching that only the strong ought to survive and his doctrine of the superman are expounded in *Thus spake Zarathustra*, *Beyond Good and Evil* and *The Will to Power*.

Nightingale, Florence (1820–1910), English nurse and pioneer of hospital reform, who during the Crimean war organised in face of considerable official opposition a nursing service to relieve the sufferings of the British soldiers, who called her "the lady with the lamp." Her system was adopted and developed in all parts of the world.

Nijinsky, Vaslav (1892–1950), Russian dancer, one of the company which included Pavlova, Karsavina and Fokine, brought by Diaghilev to Paris and London before the 1914–18 war. In *Les Sylphides*, *Spectre de la Rose* and *L'Après-midi d'un Faune* he won a supreme place among male dancers.

Nikisch, Arthur (1855–1922), Hungarian conductor of the Boston Symphony Orchestra, 1889–93. He was piano-accompanist to the Lieder singer, Elena Gerhardt.

Nimitz, Chester William (1885–1966), American admiral, commanded in the Pacific 1941–5.

Nixon, Richard Milhous (1913–94), Republican president (for two terms) of the U.S., 1969–74. In foreign affairs he negotiated the withdrawal of American troops from S. Vietnam and began a process of reconciliation with China and détente with the Soviet Union. But at home the Watergate conspiracies brought disgrace and an end to his presidency. His resignation in August 1974 rendered the impeachment process unnecessary; he accepted the pardon offered by his successor, President Ford.

Nkrumah, Kwame (1909–72), Ghanaian leader, first premier of Ghana when his country achieved independence in 1957. Promoted the Pan-African movement; but unsound finance and dictatorial methods led to his overthrow in 1966.

Nobel, Alfred Bernhard (1833–96), Swedish inventor and philanthropist. An engineer and chemist who discovered dynamite, he amassed a fortune from the manufacture of explosives; and bequeathed a fund for annual prizes to those who had contributed most to the benefit of mankind in the fields of physics, chemistry, medicine, literature and peace.

Nolan, Sir Sidney Robert (1917–92), foremost Australian artist and set designer. Best known for his works depicting 19th cent. outlaw Ned Kelly. O.M. 1983.

North, Frederick (1732–92), favourite minister of George III who held the premiership from 1770 to 1782. (He held the courtesy title of Lord North from 1752.) The stubborn policies of George III led to the American war of independence.

Northcliffe, 1st Viscount (Alfred Charles Harmsworth) (1865–1922), British journalist and news-

paper proprietor, b. near Dublin. He began *Answers* in 1888 with his brother Harold, (later Lord Rothermere). In 1894 they bought the *Evening News*, and in 1896 the *Daily Mail*. In 1908 he took over *The Times*.

Northumberland, John Dudley, Duke of (1502–53), English politician who attempted to secure for his daughter-in-law Lady Jane Grey the succession to the throne after Edward VI.

Nostradamus or **Michel de Notre Dame** (1503–66), French astrologer and physician, known for his prophecies in *Centuries*.

Novalis, the pseudonym of Baron Friedrich von Hardenberg (1772–1801), German romantic poet and novelist, whose chief work is the unfinished *Heinrich von Ofterdingen*.

Nuffield, 1st Viscount (William Richard Morris) (1877–1963), British motor-car manufacturer and philanthropist, and until he retired in 1952 chairman of Morris Motors Ltd. He provided large sums for the advancement of medicine in the university of Oxford, for Nuffield College, and in 1943 established the Nuffield Foundation, endowing it with £10 million.

Nureyev, Rudolf Hametovich (1938–93), the most celebrated ballet dancer of modern times. Born nr. Lake Baikal. Soloist, Kirov Ballet, Leningrad, 1958–61. Naturalised Austrian citizen, 1982. Ballet Director, Paris Opéra, 1983–89, Principal Choreographer, 1989–92.

Nyerere, Julius (b. 1922), Tanzanian leader. He became first premier of Tanganyika when it became independent in 1961; and president. In 1964 he negotiated its union with Zanzibar.

O

Oates, Lawrence Edward (1880–1912), English antarctic explorer. He joined Scott's expedition of 1910, and was one of the five to reach the south pole; but on the return journey, being crippled by frost-bite, he walked out into the blizzard to die.

Oates, Titus (1649–1705), English informer and agitator against Roman catholics.

O'Casey, Sean (1880–1964), Irish dramatist whose plays include *Juno and the Paycock*, *The Silver Tassie*, *Red Roses for Me*, and *Oak Leaves and Lavender*.

Occam (**Ockham**), **William of** (c. 1270–1349), English scholar and philosopher and one of the most original thinkers of all time. He belonged to the Order of Franciscans, violently opposed the temporal power of the Pope, espoused the cause of nominalism and laid the foundations of modern theories of government and theological scepticism. *See* Occam's razor, Section J.

O'Connell, Daniel (1775–1847), Irish national leader. A barrister, he formed the Catholic Association in 1823 to fight elections; his followers aimed at the repeal of the Act of Union with England, and formed a Repeal Association in 1840; but the formation of the Young Ireland party, the potato famine, and ill-health undermined his position and he died in exile.

O'Connor, Feargus (1794–1855), working-class leader in England, of Irish birth. He presented the Chartist petition in 1848.

O'Connor, Thomas Power (1848–1929), Irish nationalist and journalist, sat in parliament 1880–1929 and founded the *Star*.

Oersted, Hans Christian (1777–1851), Danish physicist who discovered the connection between electricity and magnetism.

Offa (d. 796), king of Mercia (mid-England), was the leading English king of his day, and built a defensive dyke (**L90**) from the Dee to the Wye.

Offenbach, Jacques (1819–80), German-Jewish composer, b. Cologne, settled at Paris, and is mainly known for his light operas, especially *Tales of Hoffmann*.

Ohm, Georg Simon (1787–1854), German physicist, professor at Munich, who in 1826 formulated the law of electric current–Ohm's law, (**L90**).

Olivier, Baron (Laurence Kerr Olivier) (1907–89), British actor and director, especially in Shakespearean roles. He also produced, directed, and played in films, including *Henry V*, *Hamlet*, and *Richard III*, and in television drama. In 1962 he was appointed director of the National

Theatre (which opened in 1976) and in 1970 received a life peerage. O.M. 1981.

Oman, Sir Charles William (1860–1946), English historian, especially of mediaeval warfare and of the Peninsular War. He also wrote memoirs.

Omar ibn al Khattab (581–644), adviser to Mahomet, succeeded Abu Bakr as 2nd caliph. In his reign Islam became an imperial power. He died at the hands of a foreign slave.

Omar Khayyám (c. 1050–1123), Persian poet and mathematician, called Khayyám (tent-maker) because of his father's occupation. His fame as a scientist has been eclipsed by his *Rubaiyat*, made known to English readers by Edward FitzGerald in 1859.

O'Neill, Eugene Gladstone (1888–1953), American playwright who won success in 1914 with the one-act play, *Thirst*. His later plays include *Anna Christie, Strange Interlude, Mourning Becomes Electra, The Iceman Cometh*. Nobel prize, 1936.

Oppenheimer, J. Robert (1904–67), American physicist who was director of atomic-energy research at Los Alamos, New Mexico, 1942–5, when the atomic bomb was developed but in 1949 he opposed work on the hydrogen bomb on moral grounds.

Orchardson, Sir William Quiller (1835–1910), Scottish painter, b. Edinburgh, best known for his *Napoleon I on board H.M.S. Bellerophon* and *Ophelia*.

Origen (c. 185–254), Christian philosopher and Biblical scholar, who taught at Alexandria and Caesarea, and was imprisoned and tortured in the persecution of Decius, 250

Orpen, Sir William (1878–1931), British painter of portraits, conversation pieces, and pictures of the 1914–18 war.

Ortega y Gasset, José (1883–1955), Spanish philosopher and essayist, known for his *Tema de Nuestro Tiempo* and *La Rebelión de Las Masas*.

Orwell, George (Eric Arthur Blair) (1903–50), English satirist, b. India, author of *Animal Farm* and *Nineteen Eighty-Four*.

Osborne, John (1929–94), playwright, was one of the "Angry Young Men" of the 1950s. His play *Look Back In Anger* (1956) marked a revolution in English theatre. His other plays include *The Entertainer* (1957), *Luther* (1961) and *Inadmissible Evidence* (1965).

Osler, Sir William (1849–1919), Canadian physician and medical historian, authority on diseases of the blood and spleen.

Ossietzky, Carl von (1889–1938), German pacifist leader after the first world war; sent by Hitler to a concentration camp. Nobel peace prize 1935.

Oswald, St (c. 605–42), won the Northumbrian throne by battle in 633 and introduced Christianity there.

Otto I (the Great) (912–73), founder of the Holy Roman Empire (he was crowned king of the Germans in 936 and emperor at Rome in 962). The son of Henry I of Germany, he built up a strong position in Italy (as regards the papacy) and in Germany where he established the East Mark (Austria).

Otto, Nikolaus August (1832–91), German engineer who built a gas engine (1878) using the four-stroke cycle that bears his name.

Ouida (Maria Louise Ramée) (1839–1908), English novelist of French extraction, whose romantic stories include *Under Two Flags*.

Ovid (43 B.C.–A.D. 18), Latin poet (Publius Ovidius Naso), chiefly remembered for his *Art of Love* and *Metamorphoses*. He died in exile.

Owen, Lord (David Owen). *See* D17.

Owen, Robert (1771–1858), Welsh pioneer socialist, b. Montgomeryshire. As manager, and later owner, of New Lanark cotton mills he tried to put his philanthropic views into effect; other communities on co-operative lines were founded in Hampshire and in America (New Harmony, Indiana) but although unsuccessful they were influential in many directions. He inaugurated socialism and the co-operative movement.

Owens, Jesse (1913–80), American black athlete whose 1936 Olympic triumph infuriated Hitler.

P

Pachmann, Vladimir de (1848–1933), Russian pianist gifted in the playing of Chopin.

Paderewski, Ignace Jan (1860–1941), Polish pianist and nationalist. He represented his country at Versailles and was the first premier of a reconstituted Poland. He died in exile.

Paganini, Niccolò (1782–1840), Italian violinist and virtuoso who revolutionised violin technique.

Pahlevi, Mohammed Riza Shah (1919–80), last Shah of Iran. Pro-Western ruler of Iran whose ruthless suppression of opposition helped precipitate an Islamic revolution. Went into exile, January 1979.

Paine, Thomas (1737–1809), political writer, b. Norfolk, son of a Quaker. Spent 1774–87 in America supporting the revolutionary cause. On his return to England wrote *The Rights of Man* in reply to Burke's *Reflections* on the French revolution which led to his prosecution and flight to France where he entered French politics and wrote *The Age of Reason*, advocating deism. His last years were spent in America but this time in obscurity.

Palestrina, Giovanni Pierluigi da (c. 1525–94), Italian composer of unaccompanied church music and madrigals. *See* Section E.

Palgrave, Sir Francis (1788–1861), English historian and archivist, an early editor of record series. His son **Francis Turner Palgrave** (1824–97) was a poet and critic and edited *The Golden Treasury*; another son, **William Gifford Palgrave** (1826–88) was a traveller and diplomat.

Palissy, Bernard (c. 1510–89), French potter who discovered the art of producing white enamel, after which he set up a porcelain factory in Paris which was patronised by royalty.

Palladio, Andrea (1508–80), Italian architect, b. Padua, whose style was modelled on ancient Roman architecture (symmetrical planning and harmonic proportions) and had wide influence; author of *I Quattro Libri dell' Architettura*.

Palmer, Samuel (1805–81), English landscape painter and etcher, follower of Blake whom he met in 1824. *Bright Cloud* and *In a Shoreham Garden* are in the Victoria and Albert Museum.

Palmerston, 3rd Viscount (Henry John Temple) (1784–1865), English Whig statesman. At first a Tory, he was later Whig foreign secretary for many years, and prime minister 1855 and 1859–65. His vigorous foreign policy wherever possible took the lead and bluntly asserted English rights.

Pancras, St. (d. 304), patron saint of children, was (according to tradition) baptised in Rome where he was put to death at the age of fourteen in the persecution under Diocletian.

Panizzi, Sir Anthony (1797–1879), Italian bibliographer and nationalist. Taking refuge in England after 1821, he became in 1856 chief librarian of the British Museum, undertook a new catalogue and designed the reading room.

Pankhurst, Emmeline (1858–1928), English suffragette who, with her daughters Christabel and Sylvia, worked for women's suffrage, organising the Women's Social and Political Union.

Panufnik, Sir Andrzej (1914–91), Polish-born composer. His first major work, the *Graduation Concert* was performed in 1935. The first Pole to be knighted.

Papin, Denis (1647–1714), French physicist and inventor. He invented the condensing pump, and was a pioneer in the development of the steam-engine. Not being a mechanic, he made all his experiments by means of models.

Paracelsus (Theophrastus Bombastus von Hohenhelm) (1493–1541), Swiss physician whose speculations though muddled served to reform medical thought. He criticised the established authorities, Galen and Aristotle, and experimented and made new chemical compounds. His earliest printed work was *Practica* (1529).

Park, Mungo (1771–1806), Scottish explorer in west Africa, where he lost his life. He wrote *Travels in the Interior of Africa* (1799).

Parker of Waddington, Baron (Hubert Lister Parker) (1900–72) Lord Chief Justice, 1958–70.

Parker, Joseph (1830–1902), English Congregational preacher, especially at what later became the City Temple.

Parnell, Charles Stewart (1846–91), Irish national leader. To draw attention to Ireland's problems, he used obstruction in parliament. He was president of the Land League but was not implicated in crimes committed by some members. His party supported Gladstone, who became converted to Home Rule. His citation in divorce proceedings brought his political career to an end.

Parry, Sir William Edward (1790–1855), English explorer and naval commander in the Arctic, where he was sent to protect fisheries and also tried to reach the north pole.

Parsons, Sir Charles Algernon (1854–1931), English inventor of the steam-turbine, who built *Turbinia*, the first turbine-driven steamship in 1894.

Pascal, Blaise (1623–62), Frenchman of varied gifts, b. at Clermont-Ferrand. At first a mathematician, he patented a calculating machine. His *Lettres provinciales* influenced Voltaire. In 1654 he turned to religion. See Jansenism, Section J.

Pasternak, Boris Leonidovich (1890–1960), Russian poet and writer. B. Moscow, he published his first poems in 1931. For some years his time was spent in translating foreign literature, but in 1958 his novel *Dr. Zhivago*, which describes the Russian revolution and is in the Russian narrative tradition, was published abroad, though banned in the Soviet Union. He was awarded a Nobel prize but obliged to decline it.

Pasteur, Louis (1822–95), French chemist, b. at Dôle in the Jura, whose work was inspired by an interest in the chemistry of life. His researches on fermentation led to the science of bacteriology and his investigations into infectious diseases and their prevention to the science of immunology. The pathological-bacteriological import of his researches came about mainly through his disciples (Lister, Roux, and others) and not directly, though all founded on his early non-medical investigations on organisms of fermentation, *etc.*, which were of great importance in industry, and fundamentally. He spent most of his life as director of scientific studies at the Ecole Normale at Paris. The Institute Pasteur was founded in 1888.

Patmore, Coventry (1823–96), English poet. *The Angel in the House* deals with domesticity. Later became a Roman catholic, and *The Unknown Eros* is characterised by erotic mysticism.

Patrick, St. (*c.* 389–*c.* 461), apostle of Ireland, was born in Britain or Gaul, and after some time on the continent (taken thither after his capture by pirates) went as missionary to Ireland, where after years of teaching and a visit to Rome he fixed his see at Armagh. He wrote *Confessions.*

Patten, Chris. See D17.

Patti, Adelina (1843–1919), famous coloratura soprano, b. in Madrid of Italian parents.

Paul, St. See Section S.

Paul VI (Giovanni Battista Montini) (1897–1978), elected Pope in 1963. His encyclical *Humanae Vitae* (1968) condemned contraception.

Pauli, Wolfgang (1900–58), Austrian-born physicist who first predicted theoretically the existence of neutrinos. Nobel prize 1945.

Pauling, Linus Carl (1901–94), American scientist. Won 1954 Nobel Prize for Chemistry (for work on molecular structure). Won 1963 Nobel Prize for Peace (the only person to receive two Nobel Prizes outright).

Pavarotti, Luciano (b. 1935), Italian operatic tenor. Acclaimed for such roles as Rodolfo in *La Bohème*, the Duke of Mantua in *Rigoletto etc.*

Pavlov, Ivan Petrovich (1849–1936), Russian physiologist, known for his scientific experimental work on animal behaviour, particularly conditioned reflexes and the relation between psychological stress and brain function. Nobel prizewinner 1904.

Pavlova, Anna (1882–1931), Russian ballerina, b. St. Petersburg, excelling in the roles of *Giselle* and the *Dying Swan.*

Peabody, George (1795–1869), American philanthropist, a successful merchant who lived mainly in London. He gave large sums to promote education and slum clearance.

Peacock, Thomas Love (1785–1866), English novelist, b. Weymouth. His works included *Headlong Hall* and *Nightmare Abbey.*

Pearson, Lester Bowles (1897–1972), Canadian politician who served as minister for external affairs 1948–57, and prime minister 1963–8.

Peary, Robert Edwin (1856–1920), American arctic explorer, discoverer of the north pole (1909).

Peel, Sir Robert (1788–1850), English Conservative statesman, b. in Lancashire, son of a manufacturer. He first held office in 1811. With Wellington he enacted toleration for Roman catholics in 1829. As home secretary he reorganised London police. He developed a new policy of Conservatism, and in 1846, largely as a result of the Irish famine, he repealed the corn laws.

Peierls, Sir Rudolf (1907–95), Wykeham Professor of Physics at Oxford, 1963–74. A founding father of the atomic age.

Peirce, Charles Sanders (1839–1914), American physicist and philosopher, founder of the theory of pragmatism. See **J49**.

Pele (b. 1940), legendary Brazilian footballer. Real name Edson Arantes do Nascimento.

Penfield, Wilder Graves (1891–1976), Canadian brain surgeon, author of *The Cerebral Cortex of Man, Epilepsy and the Functional Anatomy of the Human Brain.* O.M.

Penn, William (1644–1718), English Quaker and founder of Pennsylvania. The son of Admiral William Penn, he persisted in becoming a Quaker, and on receiving for his father's services a crown grant in America he founded Pennsylvania. He wrote *No Cross, No Crown.*

Penney, Baron (William George Penney) (1909–91), British scientist. His nuclear research team developed the advanced gas-cooled reactor.

Pepys, Samuel (1633–1703), English diarist and naval administrator. His diary, 1660–69, was kept in cipher and not deciphered till 1825. It gives vivid personal details and covers the plague and fire of London. (The first complete version of the diary was issued in 1970.)

Perceval, Spencer (1762–1812), Prime Minister, 1809–12. He was assassinated by a deranged bankrupt.

Pereda, José Maria de (1833–1906), Spanish regional novelist (around his native Santander).

Pérez Galdós, Benito (1843–1920), Spanish novelist and dramatist, who has been compared to Balzac for his close study and portrayal of all social classes, especially in the series of 46 short historical novels *Episodios nacionales.* His longer novels, *Novelas españolas contemporáneas,* some of which are translated, number 31.

Pergolesi, Giovanni Battista (1710–36), Italian composer, best known for his humorous opera *La Serva Padrona* and his *Stabat Mater.*

Pericles (*c.* 490–429 B.C.), Athenian statesman, general, and orator, who raised Athens to the point of its fullest prosperity, and greatest beauty, with the Parthenon, Erechtheum, and other buildings; but he died of plague following the outbreak of the Peloponnesian war.

Perkin, Sir William Henry (1838–1907), English chemist, b. London, who while seeking to make a substitute for quinine discovered in 1856 the first artificial aniline dye, mauve.

Perón, Juan (**Domingo**) (1895–1974), Argentinian populist politician. President, 1946–55. Returned in triumph from exile (1973). His third wife **Isabelita Péron,** succeeded him as President on his death in 1974.

Perry, Frederick John (1909–95), the greatest player in the history of British lawn tennis. Last British player to win singles titles at Wimbledon (1934, 1935 and 1936).

Persius Flaccus Aulus (A.D. 34–62), Roman satirist and Stoic philosopher.

Perugino, Pietro (1446–1524), Italian artist. He worked in the Sistine Chapel at Rome and he taught Raphael.

Perutz, Max Ferdinand (b. 1914), British chemist. Nobel Prize, 1962 (with Sir John Kendrew). Founding father of the world-renowned Laboratory of Molecular Biology at Cambridge.

Pestalozzi, Johann Heinrich (1746–1827), Swiss educational reformer whose theories laid the foundation of modern primary education. His teaching methods were advanced for his time. He wrote *How Gertrude Educates Her Children.*

Pétain, Henri Philippe (1856–1951), French general and later collaborator. In the first world war he was in command at Verdun. Headed the pro-German Vichy regime in World War II.

Peter, St. See S21.

Peter I, the Great (1672–1725), emperor of Russia. Son of **Alexei,** he succeeded his brother after some difficulty. He reorganised the army, and, after coming to Deptford to learn shipbuilding, he created a navy. To some extent he westernised Russian social life, and created a new capital at St. Petersburg (1703). In war with Charles XII of Sweden he was at first defeated, but later victorious at Poltava (1709). He married a peasant, Catherine, who succeeded him.

Peter the Hermit (*c.* 1050–1115), French monk who preached the First Crusade, originated by pope Urban II at the council of Clermont. He went on the crusade himself, but gave up at Antioch.

Petrarch, Francesco (1304–78), Italian poet, son of a Florentine exile. He is chiefly remembered for his poems *To Laura*, but he was also a scholar who paved the way for the Renaissance.

Petrie, Sir Flinders (1853–1942), British egyptologist. He excavated in Britain (1875–90), Egypt (1880–1924), and Palestine (1927–38). See his *Seventy Years of Archaeology*.

Pevsner, Sir Nikolaus (1902–83), German-born architectural historian. Author of *The Buildings of England* (46 vols., 1951–74).

Phidias (5th cent. B.C.), Greek sculptor especially in gold, ivory and bronze, worked at Athens for Pericles. No certain examples of his work are extant, but the Elgin marbles in the British Museum may be from his designs.

Philip II of France (1165–1223), son of Louis VII. He went on the Third Crusade with Richard I of England, but in France is mainly remembered for firm government, the recovery of Normandy from England, and the beautifying of Paris.

Philip II of Macedonia (382–336 B.C.), a successful commander, made his leading military kingdom in Greece. Father of Alexander the Great.

Philip II of Spain (1527–98), succeeded his father Charles V in Spain and the Netherlands, also in Spanish interests overseas. In the Netherlands his strict Roman catholic policy provoked a revolt which ended in 1579 in the independence of the United Provinces. He married Mary Tudor of England; and after her death sent the ill-fated Armada against Elizabeth in 1588.

Philip V of Spain (1683–1746), first Bourbon king, succeeded his great-uncle Charles II and was grandson of Louis XIV. His accession provoked European war.

Phillip, Arthur (1738–1814), first governor of New South Wales. Under his command the first fleet of 717 convicts set sail from Britain to Australia, and with the founding of Sydney in 1788 colonisation of the whole country began.

Phillips, Stephen (1868–1915), English poet who wrote verse dramas, *e.g. Paolo and Francesca*.

Piaf, Edith (1915–63), French singer and actress, renowned for her interpretation of the *Chanson*. Her real name was Edith Giovanna Gassion.

Piast, first Polish dynasty in Poland until the 14th cent. and until the 17th cent. in Silesia.

Piazzi, Giuseppe (1746–1826), Italian astronomer who discovered Ceres, the first of the asteroids to be seen by man.

Picasso, Pablo Ruiz (1881–1973) Spanish painter, b. Málaga; received his early training in Catalonia and settled in Paris in 1903. He and Braque were the originators of Cubism (*c.* 1909). His influence over contemporary art is comparable with that exercised by Cézanne (*q.v.*) over the artists of his time. Perhaps the best-known single work is his mural *Guernica*, painted at the time of the Spanish civil war, expressing the artist's loathing of fascism and the horrors of war. His genius also found scope in sculpture, ceramics, the graphic arts, *etc.*

Piccard, Auguste (1884–1962), Swiss physicist, noted for balloon ascents into the stratosphere and for submarine research. In 1960 his son **Jacques** made a descent of over 7 miles in the Marianas trench in the western Pacific in a bathyscaphe designed and built by his father.

Piggott, Lester (Keith) (b. 1935), outstanding popular long-time jockey. Won the Derby 9 times, champion jockey 11 times. Rode 4,000th winner in Britain, 14 August 1982.

Pilsudski, Joseph (1867–1935), Polish soldier and statesman who in 1919 attempted by force to restore Poland's 1772 frontiers but was driven back. From 1926 he was dictator.

Pindar (522–443 B.C.), Greek lyric poet.

Pinero, Sir Arthur Wing (1855–1934), English dramatist whose plays include *Dandy Dick*, *The Second Mrs. Tanqueray* and *Mid-Channel*.

Pinochet, Augusto (b. 1915), Chilean dictator who led 1973 coup and presided over a regime of brutality and murder.

Pirandello, Luigi (1867–1936), Italian dramatist and novelist whose plays include *Six Characters in Search of an Author*. Nobel prize 1934.

Pissarro, Camille (1830–1903), French impressionist painter of landscapes; studied under Corot.

Pitman, Sir Isaac (1813–97), b. Trowbridge. Inventor of a system of phonographic shorthand.

Pitt, William (1759–1806), English statesman. Younger son of the Earl of Chatham, (*q.v.*) he

entered parliament at 21 and became prime minister at 24 in 1783 when parties were divided and the American war had been lost. He rose to the position, and held office with scarcely a break till his death. An able finance minister, he introduced reforms, and would have gone further, but Napoleon's meteoric rise obliged him to lead European allies in a long struggle against France. He died worn out by his efforts.

Pius XII (1876–1958), elected pope 1939. As Eugenio Pacelli, he was papal nuncio in Germany and later papal secretary of state. It has been argued that he could have taken a stronger line against Nazi war crimes.

Pizarro, Francisco (c. 1478–1541), Spanish adventurer, b. Trujillo. After Columbus's discoveries, he conquered Peru for Spain, ending the Inca empire. He was murdered by his men.

Planck, Max (1857–1947), German mathematical physicist, b. Kiel, whose main work was on thermodynamics. In 1900 he invented a mathematical formula to account for some properties of the thermal radiation from a hot body which has since played an important role in physics. Nobel prize 1918. See **Quantum theory, Section L.**

Plato (427–347 B.C.), Athenian philosopher, pupil of Socrates, teacher of Aristotle. He founded a school at Athens under the name of the Academy, where he taught philosophy and mathematics. His great work is his *Dialogues*, which includes the *Republic*, the longest and most celebrated. His known writings have come down to us and constitute one of the most influential bodies of work in history. *See also* **Mind and Matter, Section J.**

Playfair, 1st Baron (Lyon Playfair) (1818–98), a far-sighted Victorian who stood for the greater recognition of science in national life. He forsook his profession as professor of chemistry at Edinburgh to enter parliament.

Plimsoll, Samuel (1824–98), English social reformer, b. Bristol. He realised the evil of overloading unseaworthy ships, and as M.P. for Derby he procured the passing of the Merchant Shipping Act, 1876 which imposed a line (the Plimsoll Mark) above which no ship must sink while loading.

Pliny the Elder (A.D. 23–79), Roman naturalist, author of a *Natural History*. He died of fumes and exhaustion while investigating the eruption of Vesuvius. His nephew, **Pliny the Younger** (A.D. 62–113), wrote *Letters* notable for the insight they give into Roman life.

Plotinus (c. 203–c. 262), Greek philosopher, was the founder of Neoplatonism, which had considerable influence on early Christian thought.

Plutarch (c. 46–120), Greek biographer, whose *Lives* portray 46 leading historical figures (in pairs, a Greek and a Roman whose careers were similar). Although based on myth his *Life of Lycurgus* about life in Sparta had a profound influence on later writers, *e.g.*, Rousseau and the romantic philosophers. He was educated at Athens but visited Rome.

Poe, Edgar Allan (1809–49), American poet and story-writer, b. Boston, Mass. His poems include *The Raven*, *To Helen*, and *Annabel Lee*, and his stories, often weird and fantastic, include *Tales of the Grotesque and Arabesque*.

Poincaré, Raymond Nicolas (1860–1934), French statesman. He was president 1913–20, and as prime minister occupied the Ruhr in 1923.

Pol Pot (1926–98) Evil dictator of Kampuchea (now Cambodia) and mass murderer.

Pole, Reginald (1500–58), archbishop of Canterbury, cardinal of the Roman church and antagonist of the reformation. He opposed Henry VIII's divorce and went abroad in 1532, writing *De Unitate Ecclesiastica*; as a result of which his mother, Countess of Salisbury, and other relatives were executed. Under Mary he became archbishop and died the year she did.

Pollard, Albert Frederick (1869–1948), English historian, especially of the Tudors; first director of the Institute of Historical Research.

Polo, Marco (1256–1323), Venetian traveller, who claimed to have made journeys through China, India, *etc.*, visiting the court of Kubla Khan, and leaving an account of his travels.

Pompadour, Jeanne Antoine Poisson, Marquise de (1721–64), mistress of Louis XV of France. She exercised disastrous political influence.

Pompey (106–48 B.C.), Roman commander, who

cleared the Mediterranean of pirates, and became triumvir with Caesar and Crassus.

Pompidou, Georges Jean Raymond (1911–74), French administrator and politician who succeeded de Gaulle as president 1969.

Pope, Alexander (1688–1744), English poet, b. London, of a Roman catholic family, and largely self-educated. His brilliant satire was frequently directed against his contemporaries. He is remembered for *The Rape of the Lock*, *The Dunciad*, *Essay on Criticism*, and *Essay on Man*.

Popper, Sir Karl Raimund (1902–94), British philosopher of science, b. Vienna; author of *The Open Society and Its Enemies* (1945), *Conjectures and Refutations* (1963), *Objective Knowledge* (1972). He rejects the doctrine that all knowledge starts from perception or sensation and holds that it grows through conjecture and refutation. One of the most influential modern philosophers.

Potter, Dennis (1935–94), television dramatist, wrote many innovative and stimulating plays. These included three six-part serials: *Pennies from Heaven* (1978), *The Singing Detective* (1986) and *Lipstick on your Collar* (1993).

Potter, Mary (1847–1913), only Englishwoman to found a religious nursing order, the Little Company of Mary (known as the "Blue Nuns").

Pound, Ezra Loomis (1885–1972), American poet and writer on varied subjects, a controversial figure. Noted for his translations of Provençal, Latin, Chinese, French, and Italian poets.

Poussin, Nicolas (1593–1665), French painter. He lived in Rome 1624–40, 1642–65. His *Golden Calf* is in the National Gallery.

Powell, (John) Enoch (1912–98), English politician, at first Conservative, later Ulster Unionist. A great parliamentarian and renowned orator, his right-wing views on immigration were unacceptable to the party leadership. He was also a Greek scholar.

Powys, John Cowper (1872–1964), English writer, best known for his novel *Wolf Solent* and his essays *The Meaning of Culture* and *A Philosophy of Solitude*. His brothers, **Theodore Francis** (1875–1953) and **Llewelyn** (1884–1939) were also original writers.

Prasad, Rajendra (1884–1963), Indian statesman, first president of the Republic of India, 1950–62.

Praxiteles (4th cent. B.C.), Greek sculptor, whose main surviving work is *Hermes carrying Dionysus*.

Preece, Sir William Henry (1834–1913), Welsh electrical engineer, associated with the expansion of wireless telegraphy and telephony.

Prescott, John. *See* **D18.**

Presley, Elvis (Aron) (1935–77). Legendary rock singer whose songs (Hound Dog, Love Me Tender *etc.*) sold millions. Buried at Gracelands, Memphis.

Prichard, James Cowles (1786–1848), English ethnologist who perceived that people should be studied as a whole. His works include *Researches into the Physical History of Mankind* and *The Natural History of Man*. He practised medicine.

Priestley, John Boynton (1894–1984), English critic, novelist, and playwright, b. Bradford. His works include the novels *The Good Companions*, *Angel Pavement*, and the plays *Dangerous Corner*, *Time and the Conways*, *I Have Been Here Before*, and *The Linden Tree*, O.M. 1977. He married the writer and archaeologist **Jacquetta Hawkes** (d. 1996) in 1953.

Priestley, Joseph (1733–1804), English chemist who worked on gases, and shared with Scheele the discovery of oxygen. A presbyterian minister, he was for his time an advanced thinker. In 1794 he settled in America.

Prior, Matthew (1664–1721), English poet. In early life he was a diplomat. He was a neat epigrammatist and writer of occasional pieces. His works include *The City Mouse and Country Mouse* and *Four Dialogues of the Dead*.

Pritchett, Sir Victor Sawdon, (1900–97) accomplished novelist, short-story writer and critic. His *Complete Short Stories* were published in 1990 and his *Complete Essays* in 1992. C.H., 1993.

Prokofiev, Sergei Sergeyevich (1891–1953), Russian composer, whose music has a strong folk-song element, rich in melody and invention. He has written operas; *The Love of Three Oranges*, *The Betrothal in a Nunnery*, *War and Peace*; ballets: *Romeo and Juliet*, *Cinderella*; symphonies, chamber music, and the music for Eisenstein's films *Alexander Nevsky*, *Ivan the Terrible*.

Protagoras (c. 480–411 B.C.), Greek philosopher, chief of the Sophists, noted for his scepticism and disbelief in objective truth, and for his doctrine that "man is the measure of all things."

Proudhon, Pierre Joseph (1809–65), French socialist. In 1840 he propounded the view that property is theft. His main work is *Système des contradictions économiques* (1846).

Proust, Marcel (1871–1922), French psychological novelist, author of a series of novels known under the title of *A la recherche du temps perdu*. His works have been translated into English.

Ptolemy of Alexandria (Claudius Ptolemaeus) (fl. A.D. 140), astronomer and founder of scientific cartography. In the *Almagest* he attempted a mathematical presentation of the paths along which the planets appear to move in the heavens. His other great work was his *Geographical Outline*.

Puccini, Giacomo (1858–1924), Italian composer, b. Lucca, whose operas include *Manon Lescaut*, *La Bohème*, *Tosca*, *Madam Butterfly*, and *Turandot* (completed by a friend).

Pupin, Michael Idvorsky (1858–1935), physicist and inventor (telephony and X-rays).

Purcell, Henry (1659–95), English composer, b. Westminster, son of a court musician. He became organist of the chapel royal and composer to Charles II. His best works are vocal and choral. *See* **Section E.**

Pusey, Edward Bouverie (1800–82), English theologian, a leader of the Oxford or Tractarian movement with Keble and at first also with Newman, till the latter became Roman catholic.

Pushkin, Alexander (1799–1837), Russian writer, b. Moscow, whose place in Russian literature ranks with Shakespeare's in English. He wrote in many forms—lyrical poetry and narrative verse, drama, folk-tales and short stories. Musicians have used his works as plots for operas—the fairy romance *Russlan and Ludmilla* was dramatised by Glinka; the verse novel *Eugene Onegin* and the short story *The Queen of Spades* were adapted by Tchaikovsky, and the tragic drama *Boris Godunov* formed the subject of Mussorgsky's opera. He was inspired by the wild beauty of the Caucasus. He was killed in a duel defending his wife's honour.

Pym, John (1584–1643), English parliamentary leader in opposition to Charles I. He promoted the impeachment of Strafford and Laud.

Pythagoras (c. 582–500 B.C.), Greek philosopher, b. on the island of Samos, off the Turkish mainland, which he left c. 530 to settle at Croton, a Greek city in southern Italy. He was a mystic and mathematician, and founded a brotherhood who saw in numbers the key to the understanding of the universe.

Q

Quasimodo, Salvatore (1901–68), Italian poet of humanity and liberal views whose works include *La vita non e sogno*. Nobel prizewinner 1959.

Quesnay, François (1694–1774), French economist, founder of the physiocratic school. *See* **Section J.**

Quiller-Couch, Sir Arthur Thomas (1863–1944), English man of letters, b. Bodmin, known as "Q." He edited the *Oxford Book of English Verse*. King Edward VII Professor of English, Cambridge University, 1912–44.

R

Rabelais, François (c. 1495–1553), French satirist. At first in religious orders, he later studied medicine and practised at Lyons. His works, mainly published under a pseudonym, are full of riotous mirth, wit and wisdom. The main ones are *Gargantua* and *Pantagruel*.

Rabin, Yitzhak (1922–95) Israeli defence chief and statesman. He was first Prime-Minister from 1974–77. Again as Prime Minister he was an architect of the peace process. Assassinated in 1995.

Rachel, Elisa (Elisa Felix) (1821–58), Alsatian Jewish tragic actress. Her chief triumph was in Racine's *Phèdre*.

Rachmaninov, Sergey Vasilyevich (1873–1943), Russian composer and pianist, b. Nijni-Novgorod (now Gorki), best known for his *Prelude*. After 1917 he settled in America. *See* **Section E.**

Racine, Jean (1639–99), French tragic poet whose dramas include *Andromaque*, *Iphigénie* and *Phèdre*. An orphan, he was brought up by grandparents who sent him to Port Royal school where he acquired a love of the classics. In Paris he became a friend of Molière, whose company acted his first play, and of Boileau, with whom he became joint historiographer to Louis XIV. *Esther* and *Athalie* were written for Madame de Maintenon's schoolgirls.

Rackham, Arthur (1867–1939), English artist and book-illustrator, especially of fairy tales.

Radhakrishnan, Sir Sarvepalli (1888–1975), Indian philosopher and statesman, vice-president of India 1952–62, president 1962–7. He was at one time a professor at Oxford.

Raffles, Sir Thomas Stamford (1781–1826), English colonial administrator who founded a settlement at Singapore in 1819. He was also a naturalist, and founded the London Zoo.

Raikes, Robert (1735–1811), English educational pioneer, whose lead in the teaching of children at Gloucester on Sundays led to an extensive Sunday School movement.

Raleigh, Sir Walter (1552–1618), adventurer and writer. He found favour at the court of Elizabeth I, helped to put down the Irish rebellion of 1580, and in 1584 began the colonisation of Virginia, introducing potatoes and tobacco to the British Isles. At the accession of James I he lost favour and was sent to the Tower, where he wrote his *History of the World*. Released in 1615 to lead an expedition to the Orinoco, he was executed when it failed.

Raman, Sir Chandrasekhara Venkata (1888–1970), Indian physicist whose main work has been in spectroscopy. For his research on the diffusion of light and discovery of the "Raman effect" he was awarded the 1930 Nobel prize.

Ramanuja (*fl.* A.D. 1125) Indian philosopher, the most revered teacher of the Vaishnava Hindus of south India.

Rameau, Jean Philippe (1683–1764), French composer and church organist whose works on musical theory influenced musical development.

Ramkrishna Paramahamsa (1834–86), one of the great spiritual Hindu teachers of modern India.

Ramón y Cajal, Santiago (1852–1934), Spanish histologist who made discoveries in the structure of the nervous system. Shared 1906 Nobel prize.

Ramphal, Sir Shridath 'Sonny' (b. 1928), Guyanese statesman. Secretary-General of the Commonwealth, 1975 to 1990. Foreign Minister, Guyana, 1972 to 1975. First black Chancellor of a British university.

Ramsay, Sir William (1852–1916), Scottish chemist, and discoverer with Lord Rayleigh of argon. Later he discovered helium and other inert gases, which he called neon, krypton, and xenon. Nobel prizewinner 1904.

Ramsey, Arthur Michael (1904–88), archbishop of Canterbury, 1961–74. Widely travelled, he worked hard for church unity.

Ranke, Leopold von (1795–1886), German historian, one of the first to base his work on methodical research. Author of a *History of the Popes*.

Raphael (Raffaello Santi) (1483–1520) of Urbino was the youngest of the three great artists of the High Renaissance. He was taught at Perugia by Perugino, and then at Florence he came under the influence of Leonardo and Michelangelo. Raphael's Madonnas, remarkable for their simplicity and grace, include the *Madonna of the Grand Duke* (Palazzo Pitti), the *Sistine Madonna* (Dresden) the *Madonna with the Goldfinch* (Uffizi), the *Madonna of Foligno* (Vatican), and the *Ansidei Madonna* (National Gallery). He painted the frescoes on the walls of the Stanza della Segnatura in the Vatican, and designed 10 cartoons for tapestries for the Sistine Chapel. After the death of Bramante, appointed architect for the rebuilding of St. Peter's.

Rasputin, Grigori Yefimovich (1869–1916), Russian peasant from Siberia, a cunning adventurer who at the court of Nicholas II exerted a malign influence over the Tsarina through his apparent ability to improve the health of the sickly Tsarevich Alexis. He was murdered by a group of nobles.

Rathbone, Eleanor (1872–1946), social reformer who championed women's pensions and in her book *The Disinherited Family* set out the case for family allowances.

Rattle, Sir Simon (b. 1955), foremost conductor. Music Director, City of Birmingham Symphony Orchestra, 1991–8.

Ravel, Maurice (1875–1937), French composer, pupil of Fauré, one of the leaders of the impressionist movement.

Rawlinson, Sir Henry Creswicke (1810–95), English diplomat and archaeologist. He made Assyrian collections now in the British Museum and translated the Behistun inscription of the Persian king Darius. He also wrote on cuneiform inscriptions and on Assyrian history.

Ray, John (1627–1705), English naturalist. A blacksmith's son, he went to Cambridge, travelled in Europe, and produced a classification of plants. He also wrote on zoology.

Rayleigh, 3rd Baron (John William Strutt) (1842–1919), English mathematician and physicist. He studied sound and the wave theory of light; and with Sir William Ramsay discovered argon. Nobel prizewinner 1904.

Read, Sir Herbert (1893–1968), English poet and art critic. His writings include *Collected Poems*, *The Meaning of Art*, and an autobiography, *Annals of Innocence and Experience*.

Reade, Charles (1814–84), English novelist. His chief work is *The Cloister and the Hearth*. He also wrote *Peg Woffington*, *It is Never too Late to Mend*, and *Griffith Gaunt*, aimed at social abuses.

Reagan, Ronald (b. 1911). U.S. President, 1981–89; former T.V. and film star, 1937–66. Governor of California, 1967–74. Won Republican victory, 1980. Re-elected in landslide victory, 1984. His popularity remained, helping ensure the election of George Bush (*q.v.*) as his successor.

Réaumur, René Antoine Ferchault de (1683–1757), French naturalist who invented a thermometer of eighty degrees, using alcohol.

Récamier, Jeanne Françoise (*née* Bernard) (1777–1849), French beauty and holder of a noted salon. Her husband was a banker.

Regnault, Henry Victor (1810–78), French chemist and physicist, who worked on gases, latent heat, and steam-engines.

Reith, 1st Baron (John Charles Walsham Reith) (1889–1971), Scottish civil engineer, first director-general of the B.B.C. 1927–38

Rembrandt (Rembrandt Harmenszoon van Rijn) (1606–69), Dutch painter and etcher, b. Leiden, a miller's son, one of the most individual and prolific artists of any period. His output includes portraits, landscapes, large groups, etchings, and drawings. He settled in Amsterdam establishing his reputation with *The Anatomy Lesson*, painted in 1632. In 1634 he married Saskia, a burgomaster's daughter. *The Night Watch* was painted in 1642; it was not well received and Saskia died the same year, leaving the infant Titus. The path from relative wealth to lonely old age is depicted in his self-portraits. Caring little for convention or formal beauty, his work is characterised by bold realism and spiritual beauty, by vitality and simplicity. His understanding of the play of colour and the effects of light can give his pictures a mystical beauty, as in the atmospheric painting *The Mill*. His figures, even for religious pictures, were taken from real life, the Jews in the etching *Christ Healing* from the Jewish quarter where he lived. He met the misfortunes of later life by withdrawing from society, but it was then that he produced his greatest works.

Renan, Ernest (1823–92), French writer who, though not accepting the orthodox viewpoint, wrote on religious themes, especially a *Life of Jesus*.

Reni, Guido. See **Guido Reni.**

Rennie, John (1761–1821), Scottish civil engineer who built the old Waterloo and Southwark bridges. He also designed docks at London, Liverpool, Leith, Dublin, and Hull; constructed Plymouth breakwater; made canals and drained fens.

Renoir, Pierre Auguste (1841–1919), French impressionist painter, b. Limoges. His works include portraits, still-life, landscapes, and groups, including *La Loge*, *Les Parapluies*, *La première Sortie*, *La Place Pigalle*. He was later crippled with arthritis.

Reuter, Paul Julius, Freiherr von (1816–99), German pioneer of telegraphic press service, who in 1851 fixed his headquarters in London.

Reymont, Vladislav Stanislav (1868–1925), Polish novelist, author of *The Peasants*. Nobel prize, 1924.

Reynolds, Sir Joshua (1723–92), English portrait painter, b. Plympton, Devon. His portraits, which include *Mrs. Siddons*, are remarkable for expressiveness and colour and he was a sympathetic painter of children. He was first president of the R.A. from 1768 till his death.

Rhodes, Cecil John (1853–1902), English empire-builder. B. at Bishop's Stortford, he went to South Africa for health reasons and there prospered at the diamond mines. He became prime minister of what was then Cape Colony and secured British power in what is now Zimbabwe and Zambia. He withdrew from politics after the failure of the Jameson Raid of 1895. He founded scholarships at Oxford for overseas students.

Ricardo, David (1772–1823), English political economist of Jewish descent. By occupation a London stockbroker, he wrote a useful work, *Principles of Political Economy*.

Richard I (1157–99), succeeded his father Henry II as king of England in 1189. A patron of troubadours and a soldier (Lion-heart), he went on the third Crusade and took Acre, but could not recover Jerusalem from Saladin. On his return journey across Europe he was imprisoned and ransomed. He was killed in war with France.

Richard II (1367–1400), son of the Black Prince, succeeded his grandfather Edward III as king of England in 1377. Artistic and able, but erratic and egocentric, he personally at the age of fourteen met the Peasants' Revolt in 1381, making untenable promises. Latterly his rule became increasingly arbitrary, and he was deposed and imprisoned in 1399.

Richard III (1452–85), King of England (1483–5), younger brother of the Yorkist, Edward IV, is believed to have murdered his two nephews in the Tower. He was defeated and killed at Bosworth by the invading Earl of Richmond, who as Henry VII brought to an end the Wars of the Roses. Richard's character is disputed, but he was able and might have been a good ruler.

Richard, Sir Cliff (b. 1940) English singer, 'the first Knight of Pop'. Born Harry Webb in Lucknow, India. His first hit was '*Move It*' in 1958. He has had a number one hit in each of the last four decades.

Richards, Sir Gordon (1904–86), foremost English jockey who rode 4,870 winners. Knighted in 1953 after he won the Epsom Derby on *Pinza*.

Richardson, Sir Albert Edward (1880–1964), British architect, author of *Georgian Architecture*.

Richardson, Sir Owen Willans (1879–1959), English physicist who worked on thermionics, or emission of electricity from hot bodies. Nobel prizewinner 1928.

Richardson, Sir Ralph David (1902–83), English actor who worked at the Old Vic, on the West End stage, and at Stratford-on-Avon, and appeared in films, including *South Riding*, *Anna Karenina*, and *The Fallen Idol*.

Richardson, Samuel (1689–1761), English author of *Pamela*, *Clarissa*, and *The History of Sir Charles Grandison*, exercised considerable influence on the development of the novel.

Richelieu, Armand Jean du Plessis, Duc de (1585–1642), French statesman, cardinal of the Roman church. As minister to Louis XIII from 1624 till his death, he built up the power of the French crown at home in central government, and by his military preparedness and active foreign policy gave France a lead in Europe.

Ridley, Nicholas (1500–55), English Protestant martyr, bishop of Rochester and later of London. He was burnt with Latimer.

Rienzi, Cola di (1313–54), Italian patriot, b. Rome, led a popular rising in 1347 and for seven months reigned as tribune, but had to flee, was imprisoned, and eventually murdered.

Rilke, Rainer Maria (1872–1926), German lyric poet, b. Prague. His work, marked by beauty of style, culminated in the *Duino Elegies* and *Sonnets to Orpheus*, both written in 1922, which gave a new musicality to German verse. His visits to Russia in 1899 and 1900 and his admiration for Rodin (who had been his wife's teacher) influenced his artistic career.

Rimbaud, Jean Nicolas Arthur (1854–91), French poet, b. Charleville, on the Meuse. In his brief poetic career (4 years from about the age of 16) he prepared the way for symbolism (*Bateau* *ivre*, *Les Illuminations*) and anticipated Freud (*Les déserts de l'amour*). He became intimate with Verlaine and at 18 had completed his memoirs. *Une saison en enfer*.

Rimsky-Korsakov, Nikolai Andreyevich (1844–1908), Russian composer whose works include the operas *The Maid of Pskov*, *The Snow Maiden*, *Le Coq d'or*, and the symphonic suite *Scheherezade*. He was a brilliant orchestrator and re-scored many works, e.g. Borodin's *Prince Igor*.

Rizzio, David (1533?–66), Italian musician and secretary of Mary, Queen of Scots. He was murdered in her presence at Holyrood by her jealous husband, Darnley.

Robbia, Luca Della (1400–82), Florentine sculptor who introduced enamelled terra-cotta work.

Roberts of Kandahar, 1st Earl (Frederick Sleigh Roberts) (1832–1914), British general. He took part in the suppression of the Indian Mutiny, in the Afghan war (relieving Kandahar), and when in command in South Africa in the Boer War he relieved Kimberley and advanced to Pretoria.

Robertson, Sir William (1860–1933), the first British soldier to rise from private to fieldmarshal. His son, **Brian Hubert, 1st Baron** (1896–1974) was chairman of the British Transport Commission, 1953–61.

Robeson, Paul (1898–1976), American Negro singer, b. Princeton, especially remembered for his singing of Negro spirituals, and his appearance in works ranging from *Showboat* to *Othello*.

Robespierre, Maximilien Marie Isidoire de (1758–94), French revolutionary. A country advocate, b. Arras, he was in 1789 elected to the States General and in 1792 to the Convention. He became a leader of the Jacobins, the more extreme party which came to power under stress of war and after the king's execution in 1793. In this crisis, the Committee of Public Safety, of which he was a member and which used his reputation as a cloak, sent many to the guillotine. He opposed the cult of Reason and inaugurated the worship of the Supreme Being. In the reaction from the reign of terror he was denounced, tried to escape, but was guillotined.

Robinson, Mary (b. 1944), President of Republic of Ireland, 1990–97 (1st woman President). Labour politician, lawyer and campaigner for women's rights. Appointed UN High Commissioner for Human Rights, 1997.

Robinson, William Heath (1872–1944), English cartoonist and book-illustrator, especially known for his humorous drawings of machines.

Rob Roy (Robert McGregor) (1671–1734), Scottish freebooter who helped the poor at the expense of the rich, and played a lone hand in the troubled times of the Jacobite rising of 1715.

Robsart, Amy (1532–60), English victim (it is believed) of murder. The wife of Robert Dudley, Earl of Leicester, she was found dead at Cumnor Place. Her death was used by Scott in *Kenilworth*.

Rockefeller, John Davison (1839–1937), American philanthropist, b. Richford, N.Y. He settled in Cleveland, Ohio, and with his brother William founded the Standard Oil Company, making a fortune. His philanthropic enterprises are carried on by the Rockefeller Foundation. **Nelson Rockefeller** (1908–79), Vice-Pres. of the United States 1974–7, was his grandson.

Rodin, Auguste (1841–1917), French sculptor, b. Paris. His best-known works include *Le Penseur*, *Les Bourgeois de Calais*, the statues of Balzac and Victor Hugo, and *La Porte d'Enfer*, a huge bronze door for the Musée des Arts Décoratifs, which was unfinished at his death.

Rodney, 1st Baron (George Rodney) (1719–92), English admiral, who served in the Seven Years War and the War of American Independence; in the latter war he defeated the French fleet under de Grasse.

Rogers, Sir Richard (George) (b. 1933), Architect of international repute. His creations include Lloyd's Building in London, the Pompidou Centre in Paris and the European Court of Human Rights building in Strasbourg.

Roland de la Platière, Manon Jeanne (1754–93), a leading figure in the French revolution. Her husband **Jean Marie** (1734–93), belonged to the more moderate or Girondist party, and when threatened escaped; but she was imprisoned and executed. She wrote *Letters* and *Memoirs*.

Rolland, Romain (1866–1944), French author,

whose main work is a ten-volume novel, *Jean Christophe*, the biography of a German musician, based on the life of Beethoven, and a study of contemporary French and German civilisation. Nobel prizewinner 1915.

Rolls, Charles Stewart (1877–1910), with **Henry Royce** (1863–1933) the co-founders of Rolls-Royce car manufacturers (at Derby in 1907).

Romero y Galdames, Oscar (1917–80), Roman Catholic Archbishop of San Salvador. His courageous criticism of the regime led to his murder in 1980 while preaching. Nobel Prizewinner.

Romilly, Sir Samuel (1757–1818), English lawyer and law-reformer, who aimed at mitigating the severity of the criminal law.

Rommel, Erwin (1891–1944), German Field-Marshal. He took part in the 1940 invasion of France, and was later successful in commanding the Afrika Korps till 1944. He committed suicide.

Romney, George (1734–1802), English artist, b. in Lancashire. He painted chiefly portraits, especially of Lady Hamilton, and lived mainly in London, but returned to Kendal to die.

Röntgen, Wilhelm Konrad von (1845–1923), German scientist who in 1895 discovered X-rays. Nobel prizewinner 1901.

Roosevelt, Franklin Delano (1882–1945), American statesman, a distant cousin of Theodore Roosevelt. During the first world war he held office under Wilson, and though stricken with poliomyelitis in 1921 continued his political career, becoming governor of New York in 1929 and U.S. president in 1933 (the first to hold office for more than two terms), till his death. A Democrat, he met the economic crisis of 1933 with a policy for a "New Deal" (*see* Section L). He strove in vain to ward off war. Towards other American countries his attitude was that of "good neighbour." After Pearl Harbor, he energetically prosecuted the war, holding meetings with Churchill and Stalin, and adopting a "lend-lease" policy for arms. He kept contact with his people by "fireside talks." His wife **Eleanor** (1884–1962) was a public figure in her own right.

Roosevelt, Theodore (1858–1919), American president. Popular because of his exploits in the Spanish-American war, he was appointed Republican vice-president in 1900, becoming president when McKinley was assassinated. Re-elected 1905. He promoted the regulation of trusts; and his promotion of peace between Russia and Japan gained the Nobel prize, 1906.

Rops, Félicien (1833–98), Belgian artist, known for his often satirical lithographs and etchings.

Ross, Sir James Clark (1800–62), Scottish explorer of polar regions, who accompanied his uncle Sir John, and himself discovered the north magnetic pole in 1831. He commanded the *Erebus* and *Terror* to the antarctic (1839–43). His discoveries included the Ross ice barrier.

Ross, Sir John (1777–1856), Scottish explorer of polar regions, uncle of the above. He searched for the north-west passage and discovered Boothia peninsula.

Ross, Sir Ronald (1857–1932), British physician, b. India, who discovered the malaria parasite. Nobel prizewinner 1902.

Rossetti, Dante Gabriel (1828–82), English poet and painter, son of **Gabriele** (1783–1852), an exiled Italian author who settled in London in 1842. With Millais, Holman Hunt and others he formed the Pre-Raphaelite brotherhood which returned to pre-Renaissance art forms. His model was often his wife, Elizabeth Siddal. His poems include *The Blessed Damozel*. His sister **Christina Georgina** (1830–94) wrote poetry, including *Goblin Market*.

Rossini, Gioacchino Antonio (1792–1868), Italian operatic composer. *See* Section E.

Rostand, Edmond (1868–1918), French dramatist, whose *Cyrano de Bergerac* made a sensation in 1898.

Rotblat, Sir Joseph (b. 1908), Polish-born British physicist. Shared 1995 Nobel Prize for Peace.

Rothenstein, Sir William (1872–1945), English portrait painter. His son, **Sir John** (1901–92), was an art historian and director of the Tate.

Rothschild, Meyer Amschel (1743–1812), German financier, founder of a banking family, b. Frankfurt. His five sons controlled branches at Frankfurt, Vienna, Naples, Paris and London (**Nathan Meyer**, 1777–1836). Nathan's son, **Lionel** (1808–79), was the first Jewish member of the House of Commons.

Roubiliac, Louis François (1695–1762), French sculptor who settled in London and carved a statue of Handel for Vauxhall gardens and one of Newton for Trinity College, Cambridge.

Rouget de Lisle, Claude Joseph (1760–1836), French poet, author of words and music of the *Marseillaise*, revolutionary and national anthem.

Rousseau, Henri (1844–1910), influential French "Sunday" painter, called "Le Douanier" because he was a customs official; self-taught, he was for long unrecognised as an artist of considerable talent and originality; he used the botanical gardens for his jungle scenes.

Rousseau, Jean-Jacques (1712–78), French political philosopher and educationist, b. Geneva, herald of the romantic movement. After a hard childhood he met Mme. de Warens who for some years befriended him. In 1741 he went to Paris where he met Diderot and contributed articles on music and political economy to the *Encyclo-pédie*. *La Nouvelle Héloïse* appeared in 1760, *Emile*, and *Le Contrat Social* in 1762. *Emile* is a treatise on education according to "natural" principles and *Le Contrat Social*, his main work, sets forth his political theory. It begins, "Man is born free and everywhere he is in chains." Both books offended the authorities and he had to flee, spending some time in England. Later he was able to return to France. His views on government did much to stimulate the movement which culminated in the French Revolution.

Royce, Henry, *see under* Rolls, Charles Stewart.

Rubens, Sir Peter Paul (1577–1640), Flemish painter. B. in exile, his family returned to Antwerp in 1587. He studied in Italy and visited Spain. His range was wide, his compositions vigorous, and he was a remarkable colourist. *Peace and War, The Rape of the Sabines,* and *The Felt Hat* are in the National Gallery.

Rubinstein, Anton Grigorovich (1829–94), Russian pianist and composer, who helped to found the conservatoire at St. Petersburg (Leningrad); as did his brother **Nicholas** (1835–81) at Moscow.

Rücker, Sir Arthur (1848–1915), English physicist, who made two magnetic surveys of the British Isles, 1886, and 1891.

Ruisdael, Jacob van (*c.* 1628–82), Dutch painter of landscapes, b. Haarlem. Several of his works are in the National Gallery, including *Coast of Scheveningen* and *Landscape with ruins*.

Rupert, Prince (1619–82), general, son of Frederick of Bohemia and his wife Elizabeth, daughter of James I of England. He commanded the Royalist cavalry in the English civil war, but was too impetuous for lasting success.

Rushdie, (Ahmed) Salman (b. 1947), controversial author of *The Satanic Verses* (1988 Whitbread Novel Award). Under death sentence (*fatwa*) by ayatollahs until lifted in 1998. He has also published *The Moor's Last Sigh* (set in his native Bombay) and, in 1994, *East, West* (a book of short stories). His latest book, *The Ground Beneath Her Feet*, was published in 1999.

Ruskin, John (1819–1900), English author and art critic, b. London. His *Modern Painters* in 5 volumes was issued over a period of years, the first volume having a strong defence of Turner. He helped to establish the Pre-Raphaelites. Other notable works include *The Seven Lamps of Architecture, The Stones of Venice* and *Praeterita. Unto this Last* develops his views on social problems, and he tried to use his wealth for education and for non-profitmaking enterprises. Ruskin College at Oxford is named after him. In 1848 he married Euphemia Gray, but in 1854 she obtained a decree of nullity and later married Millais.

Russell, 3rd Earl (Bertrand Arthur William Russell) (1872–1970), English philosopher, mathematician, and essayist, celebrated for his work in the field of logic and the theory of knowledge, and remembered for his moral courage, belief in human reason and his championship of liberal ideas. He published more than 60 books, including *The Principles of Mathematics* (1903). *Principia Mathematica* (in collaboration with A. N. Whitehead; 3 vols., 1910–13), *The Problem of Philosophy* (1912), *Mysticism and Logic* (1918), *The Analysis of Mind* (1921), *An Inquiry into Meaning and Truth* (1940) and *History of Western Philosophy* (1945). His *Autobiography* (3 vols.) appeared 1967–9. He was the grandson of Lord John Russell. John Stuart Mill was his godfather. Nobel prize for literature 1950; O.M. 1949.

Russell, 1st Earl (John Russell), (1792–1878), English statesman, third son of the 6th Duke of Bedford. He had a large share in carrying the parliamentary reform bill of 1832. He was Whig prime minister 1846–52 and 1865–6. He was also a historian and biographer.

Russell of Killowen, 1st Baron (Charles Russell), (1832–1900) British lawyer, b. Ireland; lord chief justice 1894–1900. He defended Parnell.

Rutherford, 1st Baron (Ernest Rutherford) (1871–1937), British physicist, b. New Zealand, eminent in the field of atomic research. His experiments were conducted at Manchester and Cambridge and attracted young scientists from all over the world. In 1911 he announced his nuclear theory of the atom and in 1918 succeeded in splitting the atom.

Ruysdael, Jacob van. See Ruisdale.

Ruyter, Michiel Adrianszoon de (1607–76), Dutch admiral who ranks with Nelson. He fought against England and in 1667 caused alarm by sailing up the Medway as far as Rochester and up the Thames as far as Gravesend. He was mortally wounded at Messina.

S

Sachs, Hans (1494–1576), German poet, b. Nuremberg. A shoemaker, he wrote over 6,000 pieces, some dealing with everyday life, many (including *Die Wittenbergische Nachtigall*) inspired by the Reformation.

Sachs, Julius von (1832–97), German botanist, founder of experimental plant physiology. He demonstrated that chlorophyll is formed in chloroplasts only in light.

Sadat, Mohammed Anwar El (1919–81), Egyptian statesman, President of Egypt 1970–81. His visit to Israel in Nov. 1977 was a bold and courageous move which led to the Camp David peace treaty with Israel. Assassinated 1981.

Sádi or **Saadi** (Muslih Addin) (c. 1184–1292), Persian poet, b. Shiraz, best known for his *Gulistan* (Flower Garden).

Sainte-Beuve, Charles Augustin (1804–69), French critic, b. Boulogne. He studied medicine, abandoning it for journalism, and after attempting to write poetry, turned to literary criticism. His work reveals the wide range of his intellectual experience and includes *Causeries du lundi* and *Histoire de Port-Royal*.

Saint-Just, Antoine (1767–94), French revolutionary, a follower of Robespierre.

St. Laurent, Louis Stephen (1882–1973), Canadian politician, prime minister 1948–57.

Saint-Saëns, Charles Camille (1835–1921), French composer, for 20 years organist at the Madeleine. His compositions include symphonic and chamber music and the opera *Samson et Dalila*, which was produced by Liszt at Weimar in 1877. See Section E.

Saint-Simon, Claude, Comte de (1760–1825), French socialist, who in his *L'Industrie* and *Nouveau christianisme* prepared the way for much later thought.

Saintsbury, George (1845–1933), literary historian and critic. Professor of Rhetoric and English Literature, Edinburgh University (1895–1915). His many books include *A Short History of English Literature* (1898) and *A History of Criticism* (1900–04).

Sakharov, Andrei Dimitrievich (1921–89), Soviet nuclear physicist and human rights campaigner. Nobel prizewinner 1975.

Sala, George Augustus (1828–95), English journalist who contributed to *Household Words* and was a notable foreign correspondent.

Saladin (el Melik an-Nasir Salah ed-Din) (1137–93), sultan of Egypt and Syria and founder of a dynasty, who in 1187 defeated the Christians near Tiberias and took Jerusalem. This gave rise to the unsuccessful Third Crusade, in which Richard I of England joined. His great qualities were admired by his opponents.

Salam, Abdus (1926–96), theoretical physicist and mathematician of world stature. Pakistan's first Nobel Laureate.

Salazar, Antonio d'Oliveira (1889–1970), Portuguese dictator, having first been premier in 1932, a new constitution being adopted in 1933. He gave Portugal stability, but refused to bow to nationalism in Portuguese Africa and India.

Salimbene de Adamo (1221–c. 1228), mediaeval chronicler, b. Parma, whose vivid description of life is embodied in his *Cronica*.

Salisbury, 3rd Marquess (Robert Arthur Talbot Gascoyne-Cecil (1830–1903), English Conservative statesman, prime minister 1885–6, 1886–92, 1895–1902, mainly remembered for his conduct of foreign affairs during a critical period.

Salk, Jonas (1914–95), developer of the first effective vaccine against poliomyelitis.

Samuel, 1st Viscount (Herbert Samuel) (1870–1963), British Liberal statesman of Jewish parentage.

Sand, George (1804–76), pseudonym of the French writer Aurore Dupin Dudevant. Her publications are extensive and varied, and include the novel *Mauprat*, rural studies, and an autobiography *Histoire de ma vie*. She was associated with Alfred de Musset and Chopin.

Sanger, Frederick (b. 1918), British scientist noted for his work on the chemical structure of the protein insulin. Nobel prizewinner 1958, and 1980.

Sankey, Ira David (1840–1908), American evangelist and composer, associated with Moody.

San Martin, José de (1778–1850), South American national leader in securing independence from Spanish rule to his native Argentina, Chile and Peru.

Santayana, George (1863–1952), American philosopher and poet, b. Madrid, of Spanish parentage. Professor of philosophy at Harvard, 1907–12. His books include *The Sense of Beauty, The Life of Reason*, and *The Realms of Being*.

Santos-Dumont, Alberto (1873–1932), Brazilian aeronaut who in 1898 flew a cylindrical balloon with a gasoline engine. In 1909 he built a monoplane.

Sappho of Lesbos (fl. early 6th cent. B.C.), Greek poetess, of whose love poems few remain.

Sardou, Victorien (1831–1908), French dramatist popular in his day. Sarah Bernhardt created famous parts in *Fédora, Théodora* and *La Tosca*; *Robespierre* and *Dante* were written for Irving.

Sargent, John Singer (1856–1922), American painter, b. Florence, who worked mainly in England, especially on portraits.

Sargent, Sir Malcolm (1895–1967), popular British conductor, who conducted the Promenade Concerts from 1950 till his death, and succeeded Sir Adrian Boult as conductor of the BBC Symphony Orchestra, 1950–7.

Sartre, Jean-Paul (1905–80), French existentialist philosopher, left-wing intellectual, dramatist, essayist and novelist. His major philosophical work is *L'Etre et le Néant* and his plays include *Les Mouches, Huis Clos, Crime passionel, La Putain respectueuse*, and *Les Séquestrés d'Altona*. He was awarded (though he declined it) the 1964 Nobel prize.

Sassoon, Siegfried (1886–1967), English poet and writer with a hatred of war. He is mainly known for *The Memoirs of a Foxhunting Man*, the first part of the *Memoirs of George Sherston*.

Savonarola, Girolamo (1452–98), Florentine preacher and reformer, a Dominican friar, who denounced vice and corruption not only in society but also in the Church itself, especially attacking Pope Alexander VI. He was excommunicated, imprisoned, and with two of his companions, hanged and burned. His passion for reform made him impatient of opposition and incapable of compromise, yet he was a notable figure and commands the respect of later ages. George Eliot's *Romola* portrays him.

Scarlatti, Alessandro (1659–1725), Italian musician who founded the Neapolitan school of opera. He composed over 100 operas, 200 masses, and over 700 cantatas and oratorios. His son **Domenico** (1685–1757) was a harpsichord virtuoso whose work influenced the evolution of the sonata. The chief years of his life were spent at the Spanish court in Madrid. See Section E.

Scheele, Carl Wilhelm (1742–86), Swedish chemist, discoverer of many chemical substances, including oxygen (c. 1773—but published in 1777 after the publication of Priestley's studies).

Schiaparelli, Giovanni Virginio (1835–1910), Italian astronomer, noted for having observed certain dark markings on the surface of the planet Mars which he called canals (recent close-range photographs show none).

Schiller, Johann Christoph Friedrich von (1759–1805), German dramatist and poet, b. Marbach in Württemberg, began life as a military surgeon. His play *The Robbers* with a revolutionary theme was successful in 1782 in Mannheim. After a stay at Dresden, where he wrote *Don Carlos*, and at Jena, where he wrote a history of the Thirty Years War, he became the friend of Goethe and removed to Weimar, where he wrote *Wallenstein, Mary Stuart, The Maid of Orleans* and *William Tell*. He is a leading figure in the European romantic movement.

Schirrmann, Richard (1874–1961), German originator of youth hostels. A schoolmaster, in 1907 he converted his schoolroom during holidays to a dormitory. The Verband für deutsche Jugendherbergen was founded in 1913, and the International Youth Hostels Federation in 1932, with Schirrmann as first president.

Schlegel, Friedrich von (1772–1829), German critic, b. Hanover, prominent among the founders of German Romanticism, whose revolutionary and germinating ideas influenced early 19th-cent. thought. His brother, **August Wilhelm** (1767–1845), made remarkable translations of Shakespeare (which established Shakespeare in Germany), Dante, Calderón, and Camões.

Schliemann, Heinrich (1822–90), German archaeologist, who conducted excavations at Troy and Mycenae. The subject of numerous biographies mostly based on his own writings which are now viewed with some scepticism.

Schmidt, Helmuth (b. 1918), German social democrat (SPD) statesman; succeeded Brandt as Chancellor of West Germany 1974–83.

Schnabel, Artur (1882–1951), American pianist of Austrian birth, regarded as a leading exponent of Beethoven's pianoforte sonatas.

Schoenberg, Arnold (1874–1951), Austrian composer of Jewish parentage who in 1933 was exiled by the Nazi regime and settled in America, teaching at Boston and Los Angeles. Among his works are the choral orchestral *Gurre-Lieder* and *Pierrot Lunaire. See* **Section E.**

Schopenhauer, Arthur (1788–1860), German philosopher, b. Danzig, important historically for his pessimism, and his doctrine that will is superior to knowledge. His chief work is *The World as Will and Idea*. He regarded his contemporary Hegel as a charlatan.

Schröder, Gerhard. *See* **Germany, Section C.**

Schubert, Franz Peter (1797–1828), Austrian composer, b. Vienna, the son of a schoolmaster, and a contemporary of Beethoven. He wrote not only symphonies, sonatas, string quartets, choral music and masses, but also over 600 songs of unsurpassed lyrical beauty.

Schumann, Robert Alexander (1810–56), composer of the early 19th cent. German romantic school. He wrote much chamber music, four symphonies, a piano concerto, and choral music, but it is his early piano pieces and songs that give constant delight. His wife **Clara** (1819–96) was one of the outstanding pianists of her time.

Schweitzer, Albert (1875–1965), Alsatian medical missionary, theologian, musician and philosopher, b. at Kaysersberg. After publishing learned works, he resigned a promising European career to found at Lambaréné in French Equatorial Africa a hospital to fight leprosy and sleeping sickness and made it a centre of service to Africans. His motivation was atonement. Nobel peace prize 1952. O.M. 1955.

Scipio, Publius Cornelius (237–183 B.C.), Roman general in the second Punic War, known as Scipio Africanus the elder. **Scipio Africanus the younger** (185–129 B.C.) was an adoptive relative and an implacable opponent of Carthage (destroyed 146).

Scott, Charles Prestwich (1846–1931), English newspaper editor. Under his editorship (1872–1929) the *Manchester Guardian* (now *The Guardian*) became a leading journal.

Scott, Sir George Gilbert (1811–78), English architect in the Gothic revival. He restored many churches and designed the Albert Memorial and the Martyrs' Memorial at Oxford.

Scott, Sir Giles Gilbert (1880–1960), English architect, grandson of above, designed the Anglican cathedral at Liverpool and planned the new Waterloo Bridge.

Scott, Robert Falcon (1868–1912), English antarctic explorer. He led two expeditions; one 1901–4 which discovered King Edward VII Land; and another 1910–12 which reached the south pole and found the Amundsen records; but while returning the party was overtaken by blizzards and perished 11 miles from their base. *See also* **Antarctic exploration, L7.** His son, Sir Peter Scott (1909–89), was an artist, ornithologist and pioneer conservationist.

Scott, Sir Walter (1771–1832), Scottish novelist and poet, b. Edinburgh. He was educated for the law, but came to know and love the Border country and his interests were literary; and in 1802–3 he issued a collection of ballads, *Border Minstrelsy*. Poems such as *Marmion* and *The Lady of the Lake* followed. His novels appeared anonymously, beginning with *Waverley* in 1814; and continuing with *Guy Mannering, The Antiquary, Old Mortality, Rob Roy*, and *The Heart of Midlothian*. From 1819 he turned also to English history, with *Ivanhoe* and *Kenilworth*. In 1826 he became bankrupt, largely as the fault of his publishing partner.

Scriabin, Alexander (1872–1915), Russian composer and pianist, who relied to some extent on extra-musical factors such as religion, and in *Prometheus* tried to unite music and philosophy.

Seacole, Mary (1805–81), Jamaican businesswoman and nurse. Famous for her nursing of British soldiers in the Crimean War (1854–6), even though the War Office had rejected her help.

Seeley, Sir John Robert (1834–95), English historian, author of a life of Christ, *Ecce Homo*.

Segovia, Andrés (1894–1987), Spanish concert-guitarist. He adapted works by Bach, Haydn, Mozart *etc.* to the guitar.

Selfridge, Harry Gordon (1858–1947), American-born merchant who in 1909 opened a new style of department store in Oxford Street.

Semmelweis, Ignaz Philipp (1818–65), Hungarian obstetrician, a pioneer in the use of antiseptic methods, thus reducing the incidence of puerperal fever.

Sen, Amartya (b. 1933), Indian-born economist. Awarded 1998 Nobel Prize for Economics. Author of *Poverty and Famines* (1981). Master of Trinity College, Cambridge since 1998 (the first non-white head of an Oxbridge College).

Seneca, Lucius Annaeus (c. 4 B.C.–A.D. 65), Roman stoic philosopher who was a tutor to Nero, but lost favour and was sentenced to take his own life.

Senefelder, Alois (1772–1834), Bavarian inventor of lithography about 1796.

Senna, Ayrton (1960–94), Brazilian motor racing champion. The leading driver of his generation, he died in the 1994 San Marino Grand Prix at Imola.

Severus, Lucius Septimius (146–211), Roman emperor, and a successful general. On a visit to Britain he suppressed a revolt, repaired Hadrian's Wall, and died at York.

Sévigné, Marie de Rabutin-Chantai, Marquise de (1626–96), French woman of letters. Her letters to her daughter Françoise written in an unaffected elegance of style give a moving picture of fashionable French society.

Sgambati, Giovanni (1841–1914), Italian pianist (pupil of Liszt), composer and teacher, who revived interest in classical instrumental music.

Shackleton, Sir Ernest Henry (1874–1922), British explorer, who made four antarctic expeditions; that of 1909 reached within 100 miles of the south pole. He died on his last expedition.

Shaftesbury, 7th Earl of (Anthony Ashley Cooper) (1801–85), English philanthropist largely responsible for legislation reducing the misery of the industrial revolution. He was for 40 years chairman of the Ragged Schools Union.

Shakespeare, William (1564–1616), England's greatest poet and dramatist, b. Stratford-on-Avon. Little is known of his career up to his eighteenth year, when he married Anne Hathaway. He came to London at the height of the English renaissance and soon became connected with the Globe theatre as actor and playwright. Thirty-eight plays comprise the Shakespeare canon. Thirty-six were printed in the First Folio of 1623 (the first collected edition of his dramatic works), of which eighteen had been published during his lifetime in the so-called Quartos. *Henry VI* (3 parts), *The Two Gentlemen of Verona, The Comedy of Errors, The Taming of the Shrew, Richard III, Titus Andronicus* and *Love's Labour's Lost* seem to have been the earliest, followed by *Romeo and Juliet, A Midsummer Night's Dream, Richard II* and *King John*. Then followed *The Merchant of Venice, Henry IV*

(2 parts), *Henry V, Much Ado About Nothing, The Merry Wives of Windsor,* and *As You Like It.* Then came some of his greatest plays: *Julius Caesar, Troilus and Cressida, Hamlet, Twelfth Night, Measure for Measure, All's Well that Ends Well, Othello, King Lear, Macbeth, Timon of Athens, Antony and Cleopatra* and *Coriolanus.* Shakespeare's career ended with *Pericles, Cymbeline, The Winter's Tale, The Tempest, King Henry VIII* and *The Two Noble Kinsmen* (often ascribed to him). In mastery of language, in understanding of character, in dramatic perception, and in skill in the use of ritual he has never been surpassed.

Sharp, Granville (1735–1813), English abolitionist of slavery. Founder of colony of Sierra Leone.

Shastri, Shri Lal Bahadur (1904–66), Indian politician who became prime minister of India after the death of Nehru in 1964. He died of a heart attack at the end of the Soviet-sponsored Tashkent talks.

Shaw, George Bernard (1856–1950), Irish dramatist who conquered England by his wit and exposure of hypocrisy, cant, and national weaknesses, and whose individual opinions found expression in musical criticism, socialist pamphlets and plays. His plays include *Man and Superman, Heartbreak House, Back to Methuselah, Saint Joan, The Apple Cart,* and *Buoyant Billions,* and most have important prefaces. In 1884 he joined the newly-born Fabian Society. Nobel prizewinner 1925.

Shelley, Percy Bysshe (1792–1822), English poet, b. Horsham. He was a master of language and of literary form, and a passionate advocate of freedom and of new thought. Sent down from Oxford for his pamphlet *The Necessity of Atheism,* he came under the influence of William Godwin; and, after his first marriage came to an unhappy end, married the latter's daughter, Mary Wollstonecraft, herself a writer. In the same year began his friendship with Byron. His works include *The Revolt of Islam, The Masque of Anarchy* (an indictment of Castlereagh), *The Cenci* (a play on evil), and *Prometheus Unbound,* besides lyrics such as *To a Skylark* and *Ode to the West Wind.* He was accidentally drowned while sailing near Spezzia.

Shepard, Alan (1923–98), American astronaut. The first American (and the second man) to fly in space in 1961.

Sheppard, Hugh Richard (Dick) (1880–1937), Anglican clergyman and pacifist. He made St. Martin-in-the-Fields a centre of social service and also founded the Peace Pledge Union.

Sheraton, Thomas (1751–1806), English cabinetmaker, b. Stockton, whose *Cabinetmaker's Book* promoted neo-classical designs.

Sheridan, Richard Brinsley (1751–1816), British dramatist, b. Dublin. He was a brilliant writer of comedies, especially *The Rivals, The Duenna, The School for Scandal,* and *The Critic.* He acquired and rebuilt Drury Lane theatre, which reopened in 1794, but was burnt down in 1809; and this, with his lack of business sense, brought him to poverty, in spite of his friends' efforts to help him. He was also in parliament.

Sherman, William Tecumseh (1820–91), American general, who served especially in the Civil War. He took part in the battles of Bull Run and Shiloh, was appointed in 1864 to the command of the southwest, and with 65,000 men marched across Georgia to the sea. In 1865 he accepted Johnston's surrender.

Sherrington, Sir Charles Scott (1857–1952), English scientist, an authority on the physiology of the nervous system. His research led to advances in brain surgery. His principal work is *Integration Action of the Nervous System* (1906). Shared with E. D. Adrian the 1932 Nobel prize.

Shirley, James (1596–1666), English dramatist. His tragedies include *The Traitor,* and his comedies *Hyde Park.* His death was hastened by the Great Fire.

Sholokhov, Mikhail Aleksandrovich (1905–84), Russian novelist, author of *And Quiet Flows the Don.* Nobel prizewinner 1965.

Shostakovich, Dimitri (1906–75), Russian composer whose music is complex, profound, and deeply significant of the Soviet age in which he lived. His works include operas, ballets, symphonies, chamber music, *etc. See* **Section E.**

Sibelius, Jean (1865–1957), Finnish composer imbued with national feeling. His works in-

clude seven symphonies, a violin concerto, and several tone poems, notably *Finlandia,* and some based on the Finnish poem *Kalevala. See* **Section E.**

Sickert, Walter Richard (1860–1942), British artist, b. Munich. He was influenced by Degas, and has himself influenced later painters. His *Ennui* is in the Tate Gallery.

Siddons, Sarah (1755–1831), English actress especially in tragic parts. She was daughter of the manager Roger Kemble.

Sidgwick, Henry (1838–1900), English philosopher who wrote *Methods of Ethics,* and who also promoted women's education, with the foundation of Newnham and Girton colleges at Cambridge.

Sidney, Sir Philip (1554–86), English poet and writer, best remembered for his *Arcadia, Apologie for Poetrie,* and *Astrophel and Stella,* all published after his death. He was killed at the battle of Zutphen, where he passed a cup of water to another, saying "Thy necessity is greater than mine."

Siemens, Sir William (1823–83), German-born electrical engineer who settled in England and constructed many overland and submarine telegraphs. He was brother of **Werner von Siemens,** founder of the firm of Siemens-Halske.

Sienkiewicz, Henryk (1846–1916), Polish novelist and short-story writer; best known of his historical novels is *Quo Vadis?* Nobel prize, 1905.

Sikorski, Vladislav (1881–1943), Polish general and statesman, prime minister of the Polish government in exile (1939) and commander-in-chief of the Polish forces. Killed in an aircraft accident at Gibraltar.

Simpson, Sir James Young (1811–70), Scottish obstetrician who initiated the use of chloroform in childbirth.

Sinatra, Frank (1915–98), legendary singer and actor, a pre-eminent entertainment figure.

Sinclair, Upton (1878–1968), American novelist whose documentary novel *The Jungle* (1906) on the Chicago slaughter yards caused a sensation.

Singer, Isaac Merritt (1811–75), American mechanical engineer who improved early forms of the sewing-machine and patented a single-thread and chain-stitch machine.

Sisley, Alfred (1839–99), French impressionist painter of English origin, who painted some enchanting landscapes, such as *Meadows in Spring* in the Tate Gallery. He was influenced by Corot and Manet.

Sitwell, Edith (1887–1964), English poet, a great experimenter in verse forms. *Gold Coast Customs, Façade* (set to music by William Walton) and *Still Falls the Rain* are probably best known. She had two brothers, **Osbert** (1892–1969) and **Sacheverell** (1897–1988), both poets and critics.

Slessor, Mary (1848–1915), Scottish missionary (the 'Great Mother') in Calabar, Nigeria.

Slim, 1st Viscount (William Slim) (1891–1970), British soldier who rose from private to field-marshal. He commanded the 14th Army in Burma, was chief of the Imperial General Staff 1948–52, and governor-general of Australia 1953–60.

Sloane, Sir Hans (1660–1753), British collector, b. Ireland. He practised in London as a physician. His library of 50,000 volumes and his collection of MSS. and botanical specimens were offered under his will to the nation and formed the beginning of the British Museum.

Slowacki, Julius (1809–49), Polish romantic poet, a revolutionary, he lived in exile in Paris. His work includes the poetic dramas *Kordian, Balladyna* and *Lilli Weneda,* written in the style of Shakespeare; and the unfinished poem *King Spirit* which reveals his later mystical tendencies.

Smeaton, John (1724–92), English engineer; he rebuilt Eddystone lighthouse (1756–59), improved Newcomen's steam-engine, and did important work on bridges, harbours, and canals. He also invented an improved blowing apparatus for iron-smelting.

Smetana, Bedřich (1824–84), Czech composer, creator of a national style. He was principal conductor of the Prague National Theatre, for which he wrote most of his operas, including *The Bartered Bride* and *The Kiss.* Best known of his other compositions are the cycle of symphonic poems *My Country* and the string quartets *From My Life.* He became totally deaf in 1874, suffered a mental breakdown, and died in an asylum. *See* **Section E.**

Smiles, Samuel (1812–1904), Scottish writer, *b.* Haddington, in early life a medical practitioner, remembered for *Self Help* (1859), and his biographies of engineers of the industrial revolution.

Smith, Adam (1723–90), Scottish economist, *b.* Kirkcaldy. In Edinburgh he published *Moral Sentiments*. Later he moved to London, and his *Wealth of Nations* (1776) is the first serious work in political economy.

Smith, Sir Grafton Eliot (1871–1937), Australian anatomist who did research on the structure of the mammalian brain. His works include *The Evolution of Man*.

Smith, John (1580–1631), English adventurer who in 1605 went on a colonising expedition to Virginia and was saved from death by the Red Indian Pocahontas.

Smith, John (1938–94), leader of the Labour Party, 1992-94. His much-respected, modernising leadership was ended by his untimely death. He is buried on the island of Iona.

Smith, Joseph (1805–44), American founder of the Mormons. He claimed that the *Book of Mormon* was revealed to him. In 1838 feeling against the Mormons culminated in a rising and Smith was murdered. He was succeeded by Brigham Young. *See* **Mormonism, Section J.**

Smith, Sydney (1771–1845), Anglican divine and journalist, who founded the *Edinburgh Review* and supported Catholic emancipation.

Smith, William (1760–1839), English surveyor and canal-maker, the first to map the rock strata of England and to identify the fossils peculiar to each layer.

Smith, Sir William Alexander (1854–1914), Scottish founder of the Boys' Brigade (1883), the oldest national organisation for boys in Britain.

Smith, William Robertson (1846–94), Scottish biblical scholar whose "Bible" contribution to the 9th edition of *The Encyclopaedia Britannica* resulted in an unsuccessful prosecution for heresy.

Smollett, Tobias George (1721–71), Scottish novelist whose work is noted for satire and coarse humour. His main novels are *Roderick Random*, *Peregrine Pickle*, and *Humphrey Clinker*.

Smuts, Jan Christian (1870–1950), South African statesman and soldier. B. in Cape Colony, during the Boer War he fought on the Boer side. He was premier of the Union 1919–24, 1939–48, and worked for cooperation within the Commonwealth and in the world, but his party was defeated in 1948 by Malan's Nationalists.

Smyth, Ethel Mary (1858–1944), English composer and suffragette. Her main works are operas (*The Wreckers* and *The Boatswain's Mate*) and a *Mass in D*. She studied at the Leipzig Conservatory.

Snow, Baron (Charles Percy Snow) (1905–80), English physicist and novelist, author of the essay *The Two Cultures and the Scientific Revolution*, and *Strangers and Brothers* (11 vols.).

Snyders, Frans (1597–1657), Flemish still-life and animal painter who studied under Breughel.

Soane, Sir John (1753–1837), English architect who designed the Bank of England. He left the nation his house and library in Lincoln's Inn Fields (Soane Museum).

Sobers, Sir Garfield (b. 1936), West Indies and Nottinghamshire cricketer who ranks as one of the greatest all-rounders. Knighted 1975.

Socinus or **Sozzini Laelius** (1525–62), Italian founder of the sect of Socinians, with his nephew **Faustus** (1539–1604). Their teachings resemble those of Unitarians.

Socrates (470–399 B.C.), Greek philosopher and intellectual leader, was the son of a sculptor of Athens. He distinguished himself in three campaigns (Potidaea, Delium, and Amphipolis). Returning to Athens, he devoted himself to study and intellectual enquiry, attracting many followers; through these, especially Xenophon and Plato, we know of his teachings, for he wrote nothing. In 399 B.C. he was charged with impiety and with corrupting the young, found guilty, and accordingly died by drinking hemlock; *see* Plato's *Apology*, *Crito*, and *Phaedo*.

Soddy, Frederick (1877–1956), English chemist, who in Glasgow about 1912 laid the foundation of the isotope theory. Nobel prizewinner 1921.

Solon (638–558 B.C.), Athenian lawgiver, who in a time of economic distress cancelled outstanding debts, and introduced some democratic changes.

Solti, Sir Georg (1912–97), one of the great conductors of his time. Music director of Covent Garden and Chicago Symphony Orchestra.

Solzhenitsyn, Alexander Isayevich (b. 1918), Russian novelist, b. Rostov-on-Don; author of *One Day in the Life of Ivan Denisovich*, a documentary novel depicting life in one of Stalin's prison camps where he spent many years of his life. He was expelled from the Soviet Writers' Union in 1969, and from his country in 1974, returning in 1994. Nobel prize 1970. Elected to Russian Academy of Sciences, 1997. His recent publication, *Russia in the Abyss* (1998) lays bare the evils of Russia in the 1990s.

Somerset, Duke of (**Edward Seymour**) (1506–52), lord protector of England in the time of the young Edward VI, but he fell from power and was executed.

Soper, Lord (Donald Soper) (1903–98), Methodist preacher and campaigner for socialism. Known as 'soapbox Soper'.

Sophocles (495–406 B.C.), Athenian dramatist, who was awarded the prize over Aeschylus in 468. Of over a hundred plays of his, the only extant ones are *Oedipus the King*, *Oedipus at Colonus Antigone*, *Electra*, *Trachiniae*, *Ajax*, *Philoctetes*.

Sopwith, Sir Thomas (1888–1989), British designer of 'Sopwith Camel' biplane.

Sorel, Georges (1847–1922), French advocate of revolutionary syndicalism, author of *Reflections on Violence* (1905). The irrational aspects of his philosophy (derived from Bergson) appealed to Mussolini and the Fascists.

Soult, Nicolas Jean de Dieu (1769–1851), French general who fought under Napoleon in Switzerland and Italy, at Austerlitz, and in Spain.

Sousa, John Philip (1854–1932), American bandmaster and composer of some stirring marches.

Southey, Robert (1774–1843), English poet and historian. In 1803 he settled near Coleridge at Keswick, and in 1813 became poet laureate. His best work was in prose: histories of Brazil and of the Peninsular War; lives of Nelson, Wesley, *etc.*

Southwell, Robert (1561–95), English poet and Jesuit martyr, beatified 1920. His poems include *The Burning Babe*.

Spaak, Paul Henri (1899–1972), Belgian statesman and advocate of European Union. Secretary-general of NATO, 1957–61.

Spark, Muriel (b. 1918), British novelist and writer of short stories. *See* **M17(1)**.

Spartacus (d. 71 B.C.), Thracian rebel. A Roman slave and gladiator in Capua, he escaped and headed a slave insurrection, routing several Roman armies, but was defeated and killed by Crassus.

Speke, John Hanning (1827–64), British explorer. In 1858 he discovered the Victoria Nyanza; in 1860 with J. A. Grant traced the Nile flowing out of it.

Spence, Sir Basil Urwin (1907–76), Scottish architect, mainly known for the new Coventry cathedral, for Hampstead civic centre and for university architecture. O.M. 1962.

Spencer, Herbert (1820–1903), English philosopher. B. Derby, he was at first a civil engineer, then a journalist (sub-editor of the *Economist*), when he wrote *Social Statics*. He coined the phrase (1852) "the survival of the fittest" and his *Principles of Psychology* (1855), published four years before Darwin's *Origin of Species*, expounded doctrines of evolution. Author of the ten-volume *Synthetic Philosophy*.

Spencer, Sir Stanley (1891–1959), English artist of visionary power. His two pictures of the *Resurrection* are in the Tate Gallery. He also painted Cookham regatta.

Spender, Sir Stephen (1909–95), poet and critic, first made his name as one of the politically committed poets of the 1930s. He was co-editor of *Encounter* 1953–67 and Professor of English, University College, London 1970–77.

Spengler, Oswald (1880–1936), German historicist who held that every culture is destined to a waxing and waning life cycle and that the West European culture was entering its period of decline. His principal work is *The Decline of the West*. His views prepared the way for national socialism.

Spenser, Edmund (1552–99), English poet, b. London and educated at Cambridge. His *Shepheards Calendar* appeared in 1579. In 1580 he went to Ireland as the lord deputy's secretary, and later acquired Kilcolman castle, where he wrote most of his main work, *The Faerie Queene*. His castle was burnt in an insurrection in 1598, when he returned to London. He is called "the poet's poet."

Spinoza, Baruch (1632–77), Dutch philosopher, b. Amsterdam, whose parents came to Holland from Portugal to escape the Inquisition. An independent thinker, his criticism of the Scriptures led to his being excommunicated from the synagogue. He supported himself by grinding and polishing lenses. He owed much to Descartes but was mainly concerned with religion and virtue. His philosophical theories are set out in the *Ethics* (published posthumously).

Spock, Dr Benjamin (1903–98). Paediatrician and child psychologist. Author of *Baby and Child Care* (1946).

Spofforth, Reginald (1770–1827), English writer of glees, including *Hail, Smiling Morn.*

Spurgeon, Charles Haddon (1834–92), English Baptist who preached at the vast Metropolitan Tabernacle, London, from 1861 (burnt down 1898).

Staël, Anne Louise, Baronne de Staël-Holstein (1766–1817), French writer. Daughter of the finance minister, Necker, she married the Swedish ambassador, and kept a salon. Her *Lettres sur Rousseau* appeared in 1788. After the revolution she lived partly abroad, partly in France, and after a visit to Italy wrote her novel *Corinne* (1807).

Stalin (Joseph Vissarionovich Djugashvili) (1879–1953), Soviet dictator who for nearly 30 years was leader of the Russian people. He originally studied at Tiflis for the priesthood, but became an active revolutionary and took part in the civil war after 1917. After Lenin's death, he ousted Trotsky and became the outstanding figure. He modernised agriculture on socialist lines by ruthless means, and his series of five-year plans from 1929 made Russia an industrial power. On the German invasion in 1941 he assumed military leadership; and later attended Allied war conferences. After his death a gradual process of 'de-Stalinisation' began.

Stanford, Sir Charles Villiers (1852–1924), Irish composer of instrumental, choral, operatic, and other music.

Stanley, Sir Henry Morton (1841–1904), British explorer, b. Denbigh. He fought for the Confederates in the American Civil War. He then became a correspondent for the *New York Herald*, was commissioned to find Livingstone, and did so in 1871 at Ujiji, and with him explored Lake Tanganyika. In 1879 he founded the Congo Free State. His works include *Through the Dark Continent* and an *Autobiography*.

Stark, Freya Madeline (1893–1993), British writer and explorer of the Arab world.

Stead, William Thomas (1849–1912), editor of *Pall Mall Gazette*. Campaigned against child prostitution.

Steel, Lord (Sir David Steel) (b. 1938), Liberal (Lib. Dem.) MP, 1965–97. Leader, Liberal Party, 1976–88.

Steele, Sir Richard (1672–1729), British essayist, b. Dublin. He founded the *Tatler* (1709–11), to which Addison also contributed, and later the *Spectator* (1711–12) and the *Guardian* (1713).

Steen, Jan (1626–79), Dutch genre painter, b. Leiden, son of a brewer. *The Music Lesson* and *Skittle Alley* are in the National Gallery, the *Lute Player* in the Wallace collection.

Steer, Philip Wilson (1860–1942), English painter, especially of landscapes and of portraits.

Stefansson, Vilhjalmur (1879–1962), Canadian arctic explorer of Icelandic parentage; author of *Unsolved Mysteries of the Arctic.*

Stein, Sir Aurel (1862–1943), British archaeologist, b. Budapest. He explored Chinese Turkestan.

Steiner, Rudolf (1861–1925), founder of anthroposophy. *See* **Section J.**

Stendhal, pseudonym of Marie Henri Beyle (1783–1842), French novelist, b. Grenoble. He was with Napoleon's army in the Russian campaign of 1812, spent several years in Italy, and after the revolution of 1830 was appointed consul at Trieste, and afterwards at Civitavecchia. In his plots he recreates historical and social events with imaginative realism and delineates character with searching psychological insight. His main works are *Le Rouge et le Noir*, and *La Chartreuse de Parme.*

Stephen (1105–54), usurped the crown of England from Henry I's daughter in 1135; and, after anarchy, retained it till his death.

Stephen, Sir Leslie (1832–1904), English writer, critic, and biographer. He edited the *Cornhill*

Magazine (1871–82), and the *Dictionary of National Biography* (1882–91), and was the father of Virginia Woolf.

Stephenson, George (1781–1848), English engineer; a locomotive designer, b. at Wylam near Newcastle, a colliery fireman's son. As enginewright at Killingworth colliery he made his first locomotive in 1814 to haul coal from mines. He and his son Robert built the *Locomotion* for the Stockton and Darlington Railway (1825), the first locomotive for a public railway. His *Rocket* at 30 miles an hour won the prize of £500 in 1829 offered by the Liverpool and Manchester Railway. He also discovered the principle on which the miners' safety lamp was based. First president of the Institution of Mechanical Engineers.

Stephenson, Robert (1803–59), English engineer, son of the above, engineered railway lines in England and abroad, and built many bridges including the Menai and Conway tubular bridges.

Sterne, Laurence (1713–68), English novelist and humorist. His main works are *Tristram Shandy* and *A Sentimental Journey*. He led a wandering and unconventional life, dying in poverty.

Stevenson, Adlai (1900–65), American politician, an efficient governor of Illinois, 1949–53; ambassador to the UN, 1960–5, and unsuccessful presidential challenger to Eisenhower 1952 and 1956.

Stevenson, Robert (1772–1850), Scottish engineer and builder of lighthouses, who invented "intermittent" and "flashing" lights.

Stevenson, Robert Louis (1850–94), Scottish author, b. Edinburgh. He suffered from ill-health and eventually settled in Samoa. His main works are *Travels with a Donkey, Treasure Island, Kidnapped, Dr. Jekyll and Mr. Hyde,* and *The Master of Ballantrae.*

Stinnes, Hugo (1870–1924), German industrialist who built up a huge coalmining, iron and steel, and transport business, and later entered politics.

Stockton, Earl of. *See* **Macmillan, Harold**

Stoker, Bram (Abraham Stoker) (1847–1912), Irish author of the horror story *Dracula* and *Personal Reminiscences of Henry Irving.*

Stokes, Sir George Gabriel (1819–1903), Irish mathematician and physicist to whom is due the modern theory of viscous fluids and the discovery that rays beyond the violet end of the spectrum (the ultra-violet rays) produce fluorescence in certain substances.

Stopes, Marie Carmichael (1880–1958), English pioneer advocate of birth control. Her *Married Love* appeared in 1918, and she pioneered birth control clinics.

Stoppard, Sir Tom (b. 1937), playwright, whose witty and linguistically inventive plays deal with intellectual themes. His plays include *Rosencrantz and Guildenstern Are Dead* (1966), *Jumpers* (1972), *Arcadia* (1993) and *The Invention of Love* (1997).

Stowe, Harriet Beecher (1811–96), American author of *Uncle Tom's Cabin* (1852), written to expose slavery.

Strachey, John St. Loe (1901–63), English Labour politician and writer. He held office 1945–51.

Stradivari, Antonio (1644–1737), Italian maker of violins, b. Cremona, first in his art.

Strafford, 1st Earl of (Thomas Wentworth) (1593–1641), English statesman. He supported Charles I with a "thorough" policy, both as president of the north and as lord deputy in Ireland, where he introduced flax. His efficiency made him a special target when parliament met, and he was impeached and executed.

Strauss, David Friedrich (1808–74), German theologian, whose *Life of Jesus* attempted to prove that the gospels are based on myths.

Strauss, family of Viennese musicians. **Johann Strauss** (1804–49), the elder, was a composer of dance music, who with Joseph Lanner established the Viennese waltz tradition. His son, **Johann Strauss** (1825–99), the younger, although not so good a violinist or conductor as his father, was the composer of over 400 waltzes, which include *The Blue Danube* and *Tales from the Vienna Woods*. Two of his brothers, **Josef Strauss** (1827–70) and **Eduard Strauss** (1835–1916) were also composers and conductors.

Strauss, Richard (1864–1949), German composer and conductor, the son of a horn player in the opera orchestra at Munich. He succeeded von Bülow as court musical director at Meiningen. His works include the operas *Salome, Elektra,* and *Der Rosenkavalier,* the symphonic poems *Don Juan, Till Eulenspiegel*, and *Don Quixote*, and many songs. *See* **Section E.**

Stravinsky, Igor (1882–1971), Russian composer and conductor, pupil of Rimsky-Korsakov. His ballets. *The Fire Bird* (1910). *Petrushka* (1911), representative of his early romantic style, and the revolutionary *The Rite of Spring*, which caused a furore in 1913, were written for the ballet impresario Diaghilev. He adopted a neo-classical style in later works, for example, in the ballets *Pulcinella* and *Apollo Musagetes* and the opera-oratorio *Oedipus Rex.* He brought new vigour and freedom to rhythm and younger composers have been much influenced by his music. He became a French citizen in 1934 and a U.S. citizen in 1945. *See* **Section E.**

Strindberg, Johan August (1840–1912), Swedish writer of intense creative energy. His work is subjective and reflects his personal conflicts. He produced some 55 plays as well as novels, stories, poems, and critical essays. *Lucky Peter, Gustav Adolf, Till Damascus, The Father, Miss Julie* are some of his plays.

Suckling, Sir John (1609–42), English poet, author of *Why so pale and wan?* He invented cribbage.

Sudermann, Hermann (1857–1928), German writer of plays and novels, including *Frau Sorge* (translated as Dame Care).

Suharto, General (b. 1921). Authoritarian president of Indonesia from 1968 to 1998. *See* **Section C.**

Sukarno, Ahmed (1901–70). The founding father of Indonesia. An authoritarian president, 1950–68.

Sulaiman the Magnificent (1494–1566), sultan of Turkey, conqueror, and patron of art and learning, who dominated the eastern Mediterranean but failed to capture Malta.

Sulla (138–78 B.C.) Roman general, he supported the oligarchy of the Senate against the demagogues Marius (Julius Caesar's uncle) and Cinna and established himself dictator in 82 B.C.

Sullivan, Sir Arthur Seymour (1842–1900), famous composer, mainly known for the music he wrote for light operas with W. S. Gilbert as librettist, especially *The Pirates of Penzance, Patience, The Mikado, The Yeomen of the Guard* and *The Gondoliers.* He also wrote sacred music, some of which remains very popular. He and George Grove discovered Schubert's lost *Rosamunde* music.

Sully, Maximilien de Béthune, Duc de (1560–1641), French statesman, finance minister to Henry IV.

Summerson, Sir John (1904–92), the most distinguished British architectural historian of his generation. Recipient of Royal Gold Medal for Architecture (1976). Most often associated with John Nash and the Georgian period. Longest-serving Curator of Sir John Soane's Museum.

Sumner, Mary (1828–1921), founder of the Mothers' Union to help promote the virtues of family life.

Sun Yat Sen (1867–1925), Chinese revolutionary, idealist and humanitarian. He graduated in medicine at Hong Kong, but after a rising failed in 1895 he lived abroad, planning further attempts, which succeeded in 1911 when the Manchus were ousted and he became president.

Sutherland, Graham Vivian (1903–80), British artist. He painted the 80th birthday portrait of Winston Churchill for parliament, and designed the tapestry for Coventry cathedral. O.M. 1960.

Suu Kyi, Aung San (b. *c.* 1945), Opposition leader in Myanmar (Burma). Nobel Peace Prize, 1991.

Swan, Sir Joseph Wilson (1829–1914), British scientist who shares with Edison the invention of the incandescent electric lamp.

Swedenborg, Emanuel (1689–1772), Swedish author of *Arcana Coelestia, The Apocalypse Revealed, Four Preliminary Doctrines*, and *The True Christian Religion.* He claimed that his soul had been permitted to travel into hell, purgatory, and heaven. His works became the scriptures of his followers, the Swedenborgians.

Sweelinck, Jan Pieterszoon (1562–1621), Dutch organist and composer of sacred music. In his fugues he made independent use of the pedals, and prepared the way for Bach. *See* **Section E.**

Swift, Jonathan (1667–1745), English satirist, b. Dublin of English parents. He crossed to England in 1688 to become secretary to Sir William Temple, and took Anglican orders, but did not obtain promotion. His *Tale of a Tub* and *The Battle of the Books* appeared in 1704. At first active in Whig politics, he became Tory in 1710, writing powerful tracts such as *Conduct of the Allies* (1711). In 1714 he

retired to Ireland as Dean of St. Patrick's. His devoted women friends followed him—Hester Johnson (d. 1728), the Stella of his *Journal*, and Esther Vanhomrigh (d. 1723), the Vanessa of his poetry. Here he wrote *Gulliver's Travels* (1726) and *The Drapier's Letters.*

Swinburne, Algernon Charles (1837–1909), English poet and critic. He first won attention with a play, *Atalanta in Calydon*, in 1865, followed by *Poems and Ballads.* Later followed *Songs before Sunrise, Bothwell*, and *Mary Stuart.*

Swithin, St. (d. 862), English saint, bishop of Winchester. Violent rain for 40 days fell in 971 when his body was to be removed to the new cathedral; hence the superstition as to rain on 15 July.

Symonds, John Addington (1840–93), English author who wrote on the Italian Renaissance.

Synge, John Millington (1871–1909), Irish poet and playwright, author of *Riders to the Sea* and *The Playboy of the Western World.*

T

Tacitus, Gaius Cornelius (*c.* 55–120), Roman historian. His chief works are a life of his father-in-law Agricola, and his *Histories* and *Annals.*

Tagore, Rabindranath (1861–1941), Indian poet and philosopher who tried to blend east and west. His works include the book of poems *Chita.* Nobel prize 1913 (first Asian recipient).

Talbot, William Henry Fox (1800–77), English pioneer of photography which he developed independently of Daguerre. He also deciphered the cuneiform inscriptions at Nineveh.

Talleyrand-Périgord, Charles Maurice de (1754–1838), French politician and diplomat, led a mission to England in 1792 and was foreign minister from 1797 until 1807. He represented France at the Congress of Vienna.

Tallis, Thomas (*c.* 1510–85), English musician, with Byrd joint organist to the chapel royal under Elizabeth. He composed some of the finest of our church music.

Tamerlane (Timur the Lame) (1336–1405), Mongol conqueror. Ruler of Samarkand, he conquered Iran, Transcaucasia, Iraq, Armenia, and Georgia, and invaded India and Syria. He defeated the Turks at Angora, but died marching towards China. A ruthless conqueror, he was also a patron of literature and the arts. The line of rulers descended from him are the Timurids. He is the subject of a play by Marlowe.

Tarquinius: two kings of Rome came from this Etruscan family; **Lucius the Elder** (d. 578 B.C.); and **Lucius Superbus**, or the proud, (d. 510 B.C.) whose tyranny provoked a successful rising and brought an end to the monarchy.

Tartini, Giuseppe (1692–1770), Italian violinist, who wrote *Trillo del Diavolo.* He discovered the "third sound" resulting from two notes sounded together, a scientific explanation of which was later given by Helmholtz.

Tasman, Abel Janszoon (1603–59), Dutch navigator despatched by Van Diemen. He discovered Tasmania or Van Diemen's Land, and New Zealand, in 1642.

Tasso, Torquato (1544–95), Italian epic poet, b. Sorrento, author of *Gerusalemme Liberata.* He also wrote plays, *Aminta* and *Torrismondo.*

Tawney, Richard Henry (1880–1962), British historian, b. Calcutta, pioneer of adult education, and leader of socialist thought—the first critic of the affluent society.

Taylor, Alan John Percivale (1906–90), English historian. Broadcaster, lecturer and radical. Author of such works as *English History, 1914–45.*

Taylor, Sir Geoffrey Ingram (1886–1975), British scientist, noted for his work on aerodynamics, hydrodynamics, *etc.* O.M. 1969.

Taylor, Jeremy (1613–67), English divine, b. Cambridge, author of many religious works, of which the chief are *Holy Living* and *Holy Dying.*

Tchaikovsky, Peter Ilyich (1840–93), Russian composer. His music is melodious and emotional and he excelled in several branches of composition. Among his works are the operas *Eugene Onegin* and *The Queen of Spades* (both from stories by Pushkin), symphonies, including the *Little Russian* and the *Pathétique*, ballets, including *Swan Lake, The Sleeping*

Beauty, and *The Nutcracker*, the fantasies *Romeo and Juliet*, and *Francesca da Rimini*, the piano concerto in B flat minor, the violin concerto in D, and numerous songs. *See* Section E.

Tedder, 1st Baron (Arthur William Tedder) (1890–1967), British air marshal. From 1940 he reorganised the Middle East Air Force and later became deputy supreme commander under Eisenhower for the invasion of Europe.

Teilhard de Chardin, Pierre (1881–1955), French palæontologist and religious philosopher. He went on palæontological expeditions in Asia, but his research did not conform to Jesuit orthodoxy, and his main works were published posthumously, *The Phenomenon of Man* and *Le Milieu Divin.*

Telemann, Georg Philipp (1681–1767), German composer, b. Magdeburg. His vitality and originality of form are appreciated today after a long period of neglect. His works include church music, 46 passions and over 40 operas, oratorios *etc.*

Telford, Thomas (1757–1834), Scottish engineer, originally a stonemason. He built bridges (two over the Severn and the Menai suspension bridge), canals (the Ellesmere and Caledonian canals), roads, and docks.

Tell, William, legendary Swiss patriot, reputedly required by the Austrian governor Gessler to shoot an apple from his son's head, and the subject of a play by Schiller. The story is late, but the Swiss confederation did first arise in the 14th cent. with Schwyz, Uri, and Unterwalden.

Temple, Frederick (1821–1902), English divine. He was headmaster of Rugby, 1857–69, and archbishop of Canterbury, 1897–1902.

Temple, William (1881–1944), English ecclesiastic, son of above, was a leading moral force in social matters and a worker for ecumenism. He was headmaster of Repton, 1910–14, and became archbishop of Canterbury in 1942.

Temple, Sir William (1628–99), English diplomat and writer, was instrumental in bringing about the marriage of Princess Mary with William of Orange. Swift was his secretary.

Templewood, 1st Viscount (Samuel John Gurney Hoare) (1880–1959), British Conservative politician. He piloted the India Act through the Commons while secretary for India, 1931–5; and as foreign secretary he negotiated an abortive pact with Laval.

Teniers, David, the elder (1582–1649), and **the younger** (1610–94), Flemish painters of rural life and landscape. The elder lived at Antwerp and the younger at Brussels.

Tenniel, Sir John (1820–1914), English artist, principal cartoonist for *Punch* 1864–1901 and illustrator of Lewis Carroll's *Alice* books.

Tennyson, 1st Baron (Alfred Tennyson) (1809–92), English poet-laureate, b. Somersby, Lincs. A master of language, his publications extended over 60 years, mirroring much of his age. *In Memoriam* reflects his grief for his friend Arthur Hallam. Apart from his lyrics, his longer works include *The Princess*, *Maud*, *Idylls of the King*, and *Enoch Arden.*

Terence, Publius Terentius Afer (c. 184–159 B.C.), a Latin poet and dramatist, an African (Berber), who rose from the position of a slave.

Teresa, Mother (1910–97), Albanian-born Catholic whose work in the Calcutta slums won world-wide acclaim.

Teresa, St. (1515–82), influential Spanish religious reformer and writer, b. Avila, a woman of boundless energy and spiritual strength. She entered the Carmelite order about 1534, established a reformed order in 1562 (St. Joseph's, Avila), and also founded, with the help of St. John of the Cross, houses for friars. Her writings include *The Way of Perfection* and *The Interior Castle.*

Terry, Ellen Alice (Mrs. James Carew) (1848–1928), English actress, especially in Shakespearean parts with Sir Henry Irving, and in the plays of her friend Bernard Shaw.

Tertullian Quintus (c. 160–220), Carthaginian theologian whose works, especially *Apologeticum*, have profoundly influenced Christian thought.

Tesla, Nikolai (1856–1943), Yugoslav physicist and inventor; went to America 1883; pioneer in high-tension electricity.

Tettrazzini, Luisa (1871–1940), Italian soprano, especially successful in *Lucia di Lammermoor.*

Tetzel, John (c. 1465–1519), German Dominican preacher, whose sale of indulgences for St. Peter's building fund provoked Luther.

Thackeray, William Makepeace (1811–63), English novelist, b. Calcutta, author of *Vanity Fair*, *Pendennis*, *Esmond*, *The Newcomes*, *The Virginians*, *Philip*, and *Lovel the Widower.* He edited the *Cornhill Magazine* from the first number in 1860, his most notable contributions being *Roundabout Papers.* He also wrote *Yellowplush Papers* and *The Book of Snobs* and lectured on *The English Humorists* and *The Four Georges.*

Thales of Miletus (c. 624–565 B.C.), earliest of the Greek scientists; he created a sensation by his prediction of an eclipse of the sun, which was visible at Miletus in 585 B.C. He looked upon water as the basis of all material things, and in his mathematical work was the first to enunciate natural laws.

Thant, Sithu U (1909–74), Burmese diplomat; secretary-general of the UN 1962–72.

Thatcher, Baroness (Margaret Hilda Thatcher) (b. 1925), leader of the Conservative Party 1975–90; prime minister, 1979–90; first woman to lead a western democracy; secured landslide victory, June 1983; M.P. (Finchley), 1959–92. Historic third successive election victory, June 1987. On 3 Jan 1988 became longest serving P.M. since Asquith. By 1990 she faced increasing unpopularity, reflected in a challenge to her leadership. Deserted by many in her party, she resigned on 28 November 1990. Created Baroness Thatcher of Kesteven, 1992. Order of the Garter (1995).

Themistocles (c. 523–458 B.C.), Athenian soldier and statesman. He fortified the harbour of Piraeus and created a navy, defeating the Persians at Salamis in 480 B.C. He prepared the way for later greatness, but fell from power and died in exile.

Theocritus (c. 310–250 B.C.), Greek poet, especially of pastoral subjects. His short poems came to be called *Idylls.*

Theodoric the Great (455–526), King of the East Goths, who conquered Italy. Himself an Arian, he practised toleration, and his long reign was peaceful and prosperous.

Theodosius the Great (346–95), Roman emperor of the East (the Empire being divided in 364). He was baptised as a Trinitarian, issuing edicts against the Arians, and after a judicial massacre at Thessalonica he did penance to (St.) Ambrose.

Theophrastus (c. 372–287 B.C.), Greek philosopher, who succeeded Aristotle as teacher at Athens and inherited his library. He is best known for his botanical works and his *Characters* (moral studies).

Thierry, Augustin (1795–1856), French historian, known for his *History of the Norman Conquest.*

Thiers, Louis Adolphe (1797–1877), French statesman and historian. After a varied political career, he became president in 1871, helping to revive France after defeat. He wrote a history of the Revolution.

Thomas, Dylan (1914–53), Welsh poet, whose highly individual *Eighteen Poems* (1934) brought him instant recognition. There followed *Twenty-five Poems* and *Deaths and Entrances. Under Milk Wood*, a play for voices, has more general appeal.

Thompson, Sir D'Arcy Wentworth (1860–1948), Scottish zoologist whose *On Growth and Form* (1917) has influenced biological science.

Thomson, Sir George Paget (1892–1975), English physicist, son of Sir J. J. Thomson; author of *The Atom*, *Theory and Practice of Electron Diffraction*, *The Inspiration of Science.* Nobel prizewinner 1937.

Thomson, James (1700–48), Scottish poet who wrote *The Seasons* and *The Castle of Indolence.*

Thomson, James (1834–82), poet and essayist, b. near Glasgow. Wrote *The City Of Dreadful Night.*

Thomson, Sir Joseph John (1856–1940), English physicist and mathematician, leader of a group of researchers at the Cavendish laboratory, Cambridge. He established in 1897 that cathode-rays were moving particles whose speed and specific charge could be measured. He called them corpuscles but the name was changed to electrons. This work was followed up by the study of positive rays which led to the discovery of isotopes, whose existence had earlier been suggested by Soddy. Nobel prize 1906.

Thoreau, Henry David (1817–62), American essayist and nature-lover, who rebelled against society and lived for a time in a solitary hut. His chief work is *Walden*. He was a friend of Emerson.

Thorez, Maurice (1900–64), French communist leader from 1930 and after the second world war.

Thorndike, Dame Sybil (1882–1976), English actress. She made her début in 1904, and played in Greek tragedies, in the plays of Shakespeare and Shaw, and in Grand Guignol. Her husband was Sir Lewis Casson.

Thornycroft, Sir William Hamo (1850–1925), English sculptor, whose works include a statue of General Gordon in Trafalgar Square.

Thorpe, Sir Thomas Edward (1845–1925), English chemist who researched in inorganic chemistry and with his friend Arthur Rücker made a magnetic survey of the British Isles.

Thorwaldsen, Bertel (1770–1844), Danish sculptor whose works include the Cambridge statue of Byron.

Thucydides (c. 460–399 B.C.), Greek historian, especially of the Peloponnesian War in which he himself fought. He was not merely a chronicler, but saw the significance of events and tried to give an impartial account. The speeches attributed by him to leaders include the beautiful funeral oration of Pericles.

Tiberius, Claudius (42 B.C.–A.D. 37), Roman emperor who succeeded Augustus. His early reign was successful but his later years were marked by tragedy and perhaps insanity. He is the Tiberius of Luke 3.1.

Tillett, Benjamin (1860–1943), English trade-union leader, especially of a dockers' strike in 1889 and a transport-workers' strike in 1911.

Tillotson, John (1630–94), English divine, a noted preacher. Archbishop of Canterbury, 1691–94.

Tindal, Matthew (1655–1733), English deist, author of *Christianity as old as the Creation*.

Tintoretto (1518–94), Venetian painter whose aim it was to unite the colouring of Titian with the drawing of Michelangelo. His numerous paintings, mostly of religious subjects, were executed with great speed, some of them on enormous canvases. His *Origin of the Milky Way* is in the National Gallery. His name was Jacopo Robusti, and he was called Il Tintoretto (little dyer) after his father's trade.

Tippett, Sir Michael Kemp (1905–98), English composer whose works include the operas *The Midsummer Marriage*, *King Priam*, and *Knot Garden*, and the song-cycles *Boyhood's End* and *The Heart's Assurance*. O.M. 1983. *See* **Section E.**

Titian (Tiziano Vecelli) (c. 1487–1576), Venetian painter. He studied under the Bellinis and was influenced by Giorgione, for example, in his frescoes at Padua. His mature style is one of dynamic composition and full colour, as in his *Bacchus and Ariadne* (National Gallery). Among his principal works are *Sacred and Profane Love* (Borghese Gallery, Rome), and some in the Prado, Madrid.

Tito (Josip Broz) (1892–1980), Yugoslav leader, b. Kumrovec. In 1941 he organised partisan forces against the Axis invaders, liberated his country, and carried through a communist revolution. In 1945 he became the first communist prime minister and in 1953 president. He successfully pursued an independent line .

Titus (A.D. 39–81), Roman emperor, son of Vespasian, ended the Jewish war with the capture of Jerusalem. He completed the Colosseum.

Tizard, Sir Henry Thomas (1885–1959), English scientist and administrator. He was chairman of the Scientific Survey of Air Defence (later known as the Tizard Committee) that encouraged the birth of radar before the second world war. He was chief scientific adviser to the government, 1947–52.

Tocqueville, Alexis, Comte de (1805–59), French liberal politician and historian, author of *Democracy in America*, still relevant reading.

Todd, 1st Baron (Alexander Robertus Todd) (1907–97), Scottish biochemist, noted for his work on the structure of DNA. Nobel prizewinner 1957; Pres. Royal Society 1975. O.M. (1977).

Tolkien, John Ronald Reuel (1892–1973). Academic and writer. Professor of English language and literature at Oxford, 1945–59. Famous as creator of *The Hobbit* (1937), *The Lord of the Rings* (3 vols, 1954–5) and *The Silmarillion* (1977).

Tolstoy, Leo Nikolayevich, Count (1828–1910), Russian writer and philosopher, b. Yasnaya Polyana. Of noble family, he entered the army

and fought in the Crimean War. Beginning with simple, natural accounts of his early life (*Childhood* and *Boyhood*), he proceeded to articles on the war, and so eventually to perhaps his best work, the long novel *War and Peace*, followed by *Anna Karenina*. Increasingly preoccupied with social problems, he freed his serfs before this was done officially, and refused to take advantage of his wealth. His later works include *The Kreutzer Sonata* and *Resurrection*.

Tonypandy, Viscount (George Thomas) (1909–97), Speaker of the House of Commons, 1976–83.

Tooke, John Horne (1736–1812), English politician and pamphleteer, was a supporter of Wilkes and later of Pitt. He was tried for high treason, but was acquitted.

Torquemada, Tomas de (1420–98), first inquisitor-general of Spain.

Torricelli, Evangelista (1608–47), Italian physicist, pupil of Galileo. He invented the barometer and improved both microscope and telescope.

Toscanini, Arturo (1867–1957), Italian conductor, b. Parma. He had a remarkable musical memory, and was at the same time exacting and self-effacing.

Toulouse-Lautrec, Henri de (1864–1901), French painter, whose pictures portray with stark realism certain aspects of Parisian life in the nineties, especially the *Moulin Rouge* series. Many are in the Musée Lautrec at Albi.

Tovey, Sir Donald Francis (1875–1940), English pianist and composer. His compositions include chamber music, a piano concerto, and an opera *The Bride of Dionysus*; and his writings *Essays in Musical Analysis*.

Toynbee, Arnold (1852–83), English historian and social reformer. The settlement Toynbee Hall was founded in his memory.

Toynbee, Arnold Joseph (1889–1975), nephew of above, English historian, known mainly for his 10-volume *A Study of History*, an analysis of many civilisations. He was for 30 years director of the Institute of International Affairs.

Traherne, Thomas (c. 1636–74), English religious poet, b. Hereford; author also of *Centuries of Meditations*.

Trajan (c. 53–117), Roman emperor, was a successful general and administrator. Born in Spain.

Tree, Sir Herbert Beerbohm (1853–1917), English actor-manager of the Haymarket theatre until 1897 when he built His Majesty's theatre. Sir Max Beerbohm was his half-brother.

Trenchard, 1st Viscount (Hugh Montague Trenchard) (1873–1956), British air-marshal. He served with the Royal Flying Corps in the first world war. The first air marshal of the R.A.F.

Trent, 1st Baron (Jesse Boot) (1850–1931), British drug manufacturer, b. Nottingham. He built up the largest pharmaceutical retail trade in the world, and was a benefactor of Nottingham.

Trevelyan, George Macaulay (1876–1962), English historian, known for his *History of England* and *English Social History*.

Trevelyan, Sir George Otto (1838–1928), English liberal politician, father of above. He wrote a life of his uncle Lord Macaulay.

Trevithick, Richard (1771–1833), English mining engineer and inventor, b. near Redruth, Cornwall. His most important invention was a high-pressure steam-engine (1801) and he is commonly (and rightly) acknowledged as the inventor of the steam locomotive for railways.

Trimble, David. *See* **D18.**

Trollope, Anthony (1815–82), English novelist. His early life was a struggle, the family being supported by his mother's writings. His own career was in the post office, but by strict industry he produced many novels especially portraying clerical life (the *Barchester* series) and political life (the Palliser Novels).

Trotsky, Leo (Lev Davidovich Bronstein) (1879–1940), Russian revolutionary, b. of Jewish parents in the Ukraine, one of the leaders of the Bolshevik revolution. As commissar of foreign affairs under Lenin he led the Russian delegation at the Brest-Litovsk conference. He differed from Stalin on policy, believing in "permanent revolution," according to which socialism could not be achieved in Russia without revolutions elsewhere, and was dismissed from office in 1925 and expelled from the Communist party in 1927. In 1929 he took up exile in Mexico where he was assassinated.

Trudeau, Pierre Eliott (b. 1919), Liberal prime minister of Canada 1968–79, 1980–84.

Truman, Harry S. (1884–1972), U.S. President, 1945–53. He inherited the presidency on Roosevelt's death in 1945 when he took the decision to drop the first atom bomb, and he won the election of 1948. He intervened in Korea and dismissed General MacArthur.

Tulsi Das (1532–1623), Indian poet whose master piece *Ram-Charit-Mānas* (popularly known as the *Ramayana* and based on the Sanskrit epic of *Vālmīki*) is venerated by all Hindus.

Turenne, Henri de la Tour d'Auvergne, Vicomte de (1611–75), French commander who was successful in the Thirty Years' War.

Turgenev, Ivan Sergeyvich (1818–83), Russian novelist, friend of Gogol and Tolstoy, who spent part of his life in exile. His works include *Fathers and Children, Smoke,* and *Virgin Soil.*

Turing, Alan Mathison (1912–54), computer genius. Developed concept (1936) of Turing machine. Deeply unhappy personal life.

Turner, Joseph Mallord William (1775–1851), English landscape painter, b. London, a barber's son. He entered the Royal Academy and was at first a topographical watercolourist. Later he turned to oil and became a master of light and colour, achieving magical effects, especially in depicting the reflection of light in water. His works include *Crossing the Brook, Dido building Carthage, The Fighting Temeraire, Rain, Steam and Speed.* He also made thousands of colour studies. He encountered violent criticism as his style became more abstract which led to Ruskin's passionate defence of him in *Modern Painters.* He bequeathed his work to the nation.

Tussaud, Marie (1761–1850), Swiss modeller in wax who learnt from her uncle in Paris, married a Frenchman, and later came to England where she set up a permanent exhibition.

Tutankhamen (d. *c.* 1327 B.C.), Egyptian pharaoh of the 18th dynasty, son-in-law of Akhenaten, whose tomb was discovered by Howard Carter in 1922, with the mummy and gold sarcophagus intact. He died when he was 18. Recent X-ray evidence has suggested he may have been murdered in his sleep.

Tutu, Desmond Mpilo (b. 1931), South African churchman. Archbishop of Cape Town, 1986–96. Nobel Peace Prize, 1984. Outstanding opponent of apartheid.

Twain, Mark (Samuel Langhorne Clemens) (1835–1910), American humorist. His *Innocents Abroad* was the result of a trip to Europe. His works include *A Tramp Abroad, Tom Sawyer, Huckleberry Finn,* and *Pudd'nhead Wilson.*

Tweedsmuir, 1st Baron (John Buchan) (1875–1940), Scottish author of biographies, historical novels, and adventure stories, including *Montrose* and *Thirty-nine Steps.* He was governor-general of Canada 1935–40.

Tyler, Wat (d. 1381), English peasant leader. He was chosen leader of the Peasants' Revolt of 1381 (due to various causes), and parleyed at Smithfield with the young king Richard II, but was killed.

Tyndale, William (*c.* 1494–1536), English religious reformer, translator of the Bible. He had to go abroad, where he visited Luther and his New Testament was printed at Worms. When copies entered England they were suppressed by the bishops (1526). His Pentateuch was printed at Antwerp, but he did not complete the Old Testament. He was betrayed, arrested, and executed. Unlike Wyclif, who worked from Latin texts, he translated mainly from the original Hebrew and Greek and his work was later to become the basis of the Authorised Version of the Bible.

Tyndall, John (1829–93), Irish physicist whose wide interests led him to research on heat, light, and sound, and on bacteria-free air and sterilisation. He discovered why the sky is blue (Tyndall effect) and pioneered popular scientific writing, *e.g., Heat as a Mode of Motion.*

U

Unamuno, Miguel de (1864–1936), Spanish philosopher, poet, essayist, and novelist, author of *El Sentimiento Trágico de la Vida* (The Tragic Sense of Life).

Undset, Sigrid (1882–1949), Norwegian novelist, daughter of an antiquary, author of *Jenny, Kristin Lavransdatter,* and *Olav Audunsson.* Nobel prizewinner 1928.

Unwin, Sir Raymond (1863–1940), English architect of the first garden city at Letchworth.

Ursula, St., said in late legend to have been killed by Huns at Cologne with many companions while on pilgrimage. It took rise from a 4th cent. inscription which simply referred to virgin martyrs.

Usher or **Ussher, James** (1581–1656), Irish divine who in 1625 became archbishop of Armagh, and whose writings include a long-accepted chronology, placing the creation at 4004 B.C.

V

Valentine, St., was a christian martyr of the reign of the emperor Claudius II (d. A.D. 270). The custom of sending valentines may be connected with the pagan festival of Lupercalia.

Valéry, Paul (1871–1945), French poet and essayist, strongly influenced by the symbolist leader, Mallarmé. His poems include *La jeune Parque, Charmes,* and *Le cimetière marin.*

Vanbrugh, Sir John (1664–1726), English architect and playwright. His buildings include Blenheim Palace and his plays *The Provok'd Wife.*

Vancouver, George (1758–98), British navigator who served under Captain Cook, also doing survey work, and who sailed round Vancouver island.

Vanderbilt, Cornelius (1794–1877), American merchant and railway speculator who amassed a fortune and founded a university at Nashville. His son, **William Henry Vanderbilt** (1821–85), inherited and added to it.

Van Dyck, Sir Anthony (1599–1641), Flemish painter, b. Antwerp. He studied under Rubens, travelled in Italy, and then settled in England with an annuity from Charles I. He excelled in portraits, especially of Charles I and Henrietta Maria, and of their court.

Vane, Sir Henry (1613–62), English parliamentary leader during the civil war period, though not involved in the execution of Charles I. He was executed in 1662.

Van Gogh, Vincent (1853–90), Dutch painter of some of the most colourful pictures ever created. With passionate intensity of feeling he painted without pause whatever he found around him—landscapes, still life, portraits; his was a truly personal art. His life was one of pain, sorrow, and often despair, and in the end he committed suicide.

Vauban, Sebastien de Prestre de (1633–1707), French military engineer, whose skill in siege works (*e.g.,* at Maestricht 1673) was a factor in the expansive wars of Louis XIV. He protected France with fortresses and also invented the socket bayonet.

Vaughan Williams, Ralph (1872–1958), English composer, b. Gloucestershire. After Charterhouse and Cambridge he studied music in Berlin under Max Bruch and, later, in Paris, under Ravel. He wrote nine symphonies besides a number of choral and orchestral works, operas (including *Hugh the Drover, Riders to the Sea*), ballets, chamber music, and songs. He showed great interest in folk tunes. *See* Section E.

Velasquez, Diego (*c.* 1460–1524), Spanish conquistador, first governor of Cuba.

Velasquez, Diego Rodriguez de Silva y (1599–1660), Spanish painter, b. Seville, especially of portraits at the court of Philip IV, and also of classical and historical subjects. He made two visits to Italy (1629–31, 1649–51), studying the Venetian painters, especially Titian, which hastened the development of his style. Among his masterpieces are *The Maids of Honour, The Tapestry Weavers* (both in the Prado), the Rokeby Venus and a portrait of Philip IV (both in the National Gallery), the landscape views from the Villa Medici (Prado) and *Juan de Pareja* (sold in London in 1970 for £2·25 million).

Venizelos, Eleutherios (1864–1936), Greek statesman, b. Crete. He became prime minister in 1910 and held this office intermittently. He promoted the Balkan League (1912), forced the king's abdication (1917), and brought Greece into the war on the Allied side, securing territorial concessions at the peace conference, but his expansionist policy in Turkish Asia failed.

Verdi, Giuseppe (1813–1901), Italian composer, b. near Busseto in the province of Parma. His early works include *Nabucco, Ernani, I Due Foscari,* and *Macbeth*; a middle period is represented by *Rigoletto, Il Trovatore, La Traviata, Un Ballo in Maschera,* and *Don Carlos*; to the last period of his life belong *Aida, Otello,* and *Falstaff* (produced when he was 80). See **Section E.**

Verlaine, Paul (1844–96), French poet, one of the first of the symbolists, also known for his memoirs and confessions. His works include *Poèmes saturniens, Fêtes galantes, Sagesse,* and *Romances sans paroles.* He was imprisoned for two years in Belgium for shooting and wounding his friend Rimbaud. He died in poverty in Paris.

Vermeer, Jan (1632–75), Dutch painter, b. Delft. His main paintings are of domestic interiors, which he makes into works of art, as in *Lady at the Virginals* (National Gallery). His reputation has grown during the last century.

Verne, Jules (1828–1905), French writer of science fiction, including *Five Weeks in a Balloon, Twenty Thousand Leagues Under the Sea, Round the World in Eighty Days.*

Vernier, Pierre (1580–1637), French inventor of the small sliding scale which enables readings on a graduated scale to be taken to a fraction of a division.

Veronese, Paolo (1528–88), Italian painter of the Venetian school, whose works include *Marriage Feast at Cana in Galilee, The Feast in the House of Simon,* and *The Presentation of the Family of Darius to Alexander, His Adoration of the Magi* is in the National Gallery.

Veronica, St., legendary woman who was said to hand her kerchief to Christ on the way to Calvary, to wipe his brow, and his impression was left on the kerchief. In its present form her legend dates from the 14th cent.

Verwoerd, Hendrik Frensch (1901–66), South African politician, b. Amsterdam, exponent of the policy of apartheid; prime minister 1958–66. He was assassinated.

Vespasian, Titus Flavius (A.D. 9–79), Roman emperor. He was sent by Nero to put down the Jews and was proclaimed by the legions. He began the Colosseum.

Vespucci, Amerigo (1451–1512), Florentine explorer, naturalised in Spain, contractor at Seville for Columbus. He later explored Venezuela. The use of his name for the continent arose through a mistake.

Vico, Giambattista (1688–1744), Italian philosopher of history and of culture, b. Naples. His ideas were developed in his *Scienza nuova* (science of history) but it was not until our own day that his originality as a thinker was fully recognised.

Victor Emmanuel II (1820–78), first king of Italy. King of Sardinia, he was proclaimed king of Italy in 1861 after the Austrians had been defeated and Garibaldi had succeeded in the south. Rome was added in 1870.

Victoria (1819–1901), Queen of the United Kingdom of Gt. Britain and Ireland and Empress of India, was granddaughter of George III and succeeded her uncle, William IV, in 1837. In 1840 she married Prince Albert of Saxe-Coburg-Gotha, who died in 1861. Conscientious, hard-working, and of strict moral standards, she had by the end of a long life (jubilees 1887 and 1897) won the affection and respect of her subjects in a unique degree. Her reign saw industrial expansion, growing humanitarianism, literary output, and in the main prolonged peace.

Villeneuve, Pierre de (1763–1806), French admiral defeated by Nelson at Trafalgar and captured along with his ship, the *Bucentaure.*

Villon, François (1431–?1463), French poet, b. Paris, who lived at a turbulent time at the close of the Hundred Years War. After fatally stabbing a man in 1455 he joined the *Conquillards,* a criminal organisation. They had a secret language (the *jargon*) and it was for them that he composed his ballads. His extant works consist of the *Petit Testament* (1456), originally called *Le Lais,* and the *Grand Testament* (1461), masterpieces of mediaeval verse.

Virgil (Publius Vergilius Maro) (70–19 B.C.), Roman epic poet, b. at Andes near Mantua, he went to Rome to obtain redress for the military confiscation of his farm. He was patronised by Maecenas, and wrote his pastoral *Eclogues,* followed by his *Georgics.* His best-known work, the *Aeneid,* deals with the wanderings of Aeneas after the fall of Troy till his establishment of a kingdom in Italy.

Vivaldi, Antonio (c. 1675–1743), Venetian composer, violin master at the Ospedale della Pieta. His output of orchestral works was prolific and Bach arranged some of his violin pieces for the harpsichord. See **Section E.**

Volta, Alessandro (1745–1827), Italian physicist of Pavia, who, working on the results of Galvani, invented the voltaic pile, the first instrument for producing an electric current. It provided a new means for the decomposition of certain substances. His name was given to the volt, the unit of electrical potential difference.

Voltaire (François Marie Arouet) (1694–1778), French philosopher and writer. His first essays offended the authorities, and he spent the years 1726–9 in England, where he wrote some of his dramas. Returning to France, he published his *Philosophical Letters,* which aroused the enmity of the priesthood. At this juncture, the Marquise du Châtelet offered him the asylum of her castle of Cirey, and for the next 15 years he made this his home, writing there his *Discourses of Man, Essay on the Morals and Spirit of Nations, Age of Louis XIV,* etc. His most celebrated book was *Candide,* in which he attacked the theory of Optimism. Its observations include *"pour encourager les autres"* (about Admiral Byng's execution) and its final message: *"il faut cultiver notre jardin."*

Vondel, Joost van don (1587–1679), Dutch poet who lived at Amsterdam. Most of his dramas are on biblical subjects, and the two most famous are *Jephtha* and *Lucifer.*

Voroshilov, Klimenty Efremovich (1881–1969), Soviet general who commanded the Leningrad defences in 1941. USSR president, 1953–60.

Vyshinsky, Andrei Yanuarievich (1883–1954), Soviet jurist and diplomat; conducted the prosecution of the Moscow treason trials, 1936–8.

W

Wade, George (1673–1748), English general and military engineer who, after the rising of 1715, pacified the Scottish highlands, constructing military roads and bridges. In the 1745 rising Prince Charles' forces evaded him.

Wagner, Richard (1813–83), German composer, b. Leipzig. He achieved a new type of musical expression in his operas by the complete union of music and drama. He made use of the *Leit-motif* and was his own librettist. His originality and modernism aroused a good deal of opposition, and he was exiled for some years. But he was supported by loyal friends, including Liszt, the young King Ludwig of Bavaria, and the philosopher Nietzsche. He began the music of the *Ring des Nibelungen* in 1853, but it was not until 1876 that the whole of the drama (Rheingold, Valkyrie, Siegfried, Götterdämmerung) was performed at Bayreuth under the conductor Hans Richter. Other operas are *The Flying Dutchman, Rienzi, Tannhäuser, Lohengrin, Tristan und Isolde, Die Meistersinger von Nürnberg,* and *Parsifal,* a religious drama. He married Liszt's daughter Cosima.

Walcott, Derek (b. 1930), West Indian poet and playwright, whose works include *Collected Poems 1948–1984* (1986) and *Omeros* (1990). He won the Queen's Gold Medal for Poetry (1988), the W. H. Smith Literary Award (1991), and the Nobel Prize for Literature (1992).

Waldheim, Kurt (b. 1918), Austrian diplomat; succeeded U Thant as secretary-general of the UN, 1972–81. President of Austria, 1986–92.

Walesa, Lech (b. 1943), Polish trade unionist. Shipyard worker in Gdansk. Leader of *Solidarity.* Awarded 1983 Nobel Peace Prize. President of Poland from 1990 until his defeat in the 1995 presidential election.

Waley, Arthur (1889–1966), English orientalist, known for his translations of Chinese and Japanese poetry and prose. The first to bring the literature of those countries to the western world.

Walker, George (1618–90), hero of the siege of Londonderry in 1688, who kept the besiegers at bay for 105 days.

Wallace, Alfred Russel (1823–1913), British naturalist, b. Usk, Monmouth, joint author with Darwin of the theory of natural selection. In 1858, while down with illness in the Moluccas, he sent a draft of his theory to Darwin in England who was amazed to find that it closely agreed with his own theory of evolution which he was on the point of publishing. The result was a reading of a joint paper to the Linnean Society.

Wallace, Edgar (1875–1932), English novelist and playwright, known for his detective thrillers.

Wallace, Sir Richard (1818–90), English art collector and philanthropist. His adopted son's wife bequeathed his collection to the nation (Wallace Collection, Manchester Square, London).

Wallace, Sir William (c. 1274–1305), Scottish patriot. He withstood Edward I, at first successfully, but was defeated at Falkirk, taken to London and brutally murdered.

Wallenstein, Albrecht von (1583–1634), German soldier and statesman during the Thirty Years War. An able administrator of his own estates, he sought the unity of Germany, but was distrusted and eventually assassinated.

Waller, Edmund (1606–87), English poet of polished simplicity, author of *Go, lovely rose*. He was able to agree with both parliamentarians and royalists.

Wallis, Sir Barnes Neville (1887–1979), British scientist and inventor whose many designs include the R100 airship, the Wellington bomber, the swing-wing aircraft, and the "bouncing bomb" that breached the Ruhr dams in 1943.

Walpole, Horace, 4th Earl of Orford (1717–97), younger son of Sir Robert Walpole, English writer, chiefly remembered for his *Letters*, his *Castle of Otranto*, and his "Gothic" house at Strawberry Hill.

Walpole, Sir Hugh Seymour (1884–1941), English novelist, b. New Zealand. His works include *Fortitude*, *The Dark Forest*, and *The Herries Chronicle*.

Walpole, Sir Robert, 1st Earl of Orford (1676–1745), English Whig statesman, who came to office soon after the Hanoverian succession and is considered the first prime minister—a good finance minister, a peace minister, and a "house of commons man."

Walter, Bruno (1876–1962), German-American conductor, especially of Haydn, Mozart, and Mahler.

Walter, John (1776–1847), English newspaper editor. Under him *The Times*, founded by his father **John Walter** (1739–1812), attained a leading position.

Walton, Izaak (1593–1683), English writer, especially remembered for *The Compleat Angler*. He also wrote biographies of Donne, Hooker, and George Herbert.

Walton, Sir William Turner (1902–83), English composer, whose works include concertos for string instruments, two symphonies, two coronation marches, *Façade* (setting to Edith Sitwell's poem), and an oratorio, *Belshazzar's Feast*. O.M. 1967.

Warbeck, Perkin (1474–99), Flemish impostor, b. Tournai, who claimed to be the younger son of Edward IV with French and Scottish backing, but failed and was executed.

Warwick, Earl of (Richard Neville) (c. 1428–71), "the kingmaker." At first on the Yorkist side in the Wars of the Roses, he proclaimed Edward IV king; but later changed sides and restored the Lancastrian Henry VI. He was killed at Barnet.

Washington, Booker Taliaferro (1858–1915), American black educationist, author of *Up from Slavery*.

Washington, George (1732–99), first U.S. president. B. in Virginia, of a family which originated from Sulgrave, Northants., he served against the French in the Seven Years War. When the dispute between the British government and the Americans over taxation came to a head, he proved a successful general, and Cornwallis's surrender to him at Yorktown in 1781 virtually ended the war. In 1787 he presided over the Philadelphia convention which formulated the constitution, and was president 1789–97.

Watson, John Broadus (1878–1958), American psychologist, an exponent of behaviourism. *See* Behaviourism, Section J.

Watson-Watt, Sir Robert (1892–1973), Scottish physicist, who played a major part in the development of radar.

Watt, James (1736–1819), Scottish engineer and inventor, b. Greenock. He made important improvements to Newcomen's steam-engine by inventing a separate condenser (applying Black's discoveries (1761–4) on latent heat) and other devices based on scientific knowledge of the properties of steam. He was given support by Matthew Boulton, a capitalist, and settled down in Birmingham with him. He defined one horse-power as the rate at which work is done when 33,000 lb are raised one foot in one minute. He also constructed a press for copying manuscripts. The watt as a unit of power is named after him.

Watteau, Jean Antoine (1684–1721), French painter. He painted pastoral idylls in court dress. His works include *Embarquement pour Cythère* in the Louvre.

Watts, Isaac (1674–1748), English hymn-writer, author of *O God, our help in ages past*.

Watts-Dunton, Walter Theodore (1836–1914), English poet and critic, friend of Swinburne whom he looked after until his death in 1909.

Waugh, Evelyn (1902–66), English satirical writer, author of *Vile Bodies*, *The Loved One*, *Brideshead Revisited*, *Life of Edmund Campion*, *The Ordeal of Gilbert Pinfold*, and an autobiography, *A Little Learning*.

Wavell, 1st Earl (Archibald Percival Wavell) (1883–1950), British field marshal. He served in the first great war on Allenby's staff and in the second he commanded in the Middle East 1939–41, defeating the Italians; and in India 1941–3. He was viceroy of India 1943–7.

Webb, Matthew (1848–83), English swimmer, the first to swim the English Channel (1875).

Webb, Sidney James, Baron Passfield (1859–1947), and his wife **Beatrice**, *née* Potter (1858–1943), English social reformers and historians. They combined careful investigation of social problems (their books include *History of Trade Unionism* and *English Local Government*) with work for the future; they were members of the Fabian Society, launched the *New Statesman*, and helped to set up the London School of Economics. He held office under Labour.

Weber, Carl Maria Friedrich Ernst von (1786–1826), German composer, who laid the foundation of German romantic opera. His reputation rests principally on his three operas, *Der Freischütz*, *Euryanthe*, and *Oberon*. He was also an able pianist, conductor, and musical director. *See* Section E.

Webster, Daniel (1782–1852), American statesman and orator. He held office more than once and negotiated the Ashburton Treaty which settled the Maine–Canada boundary.

Webster, Noah (1758–1843), American lexicographer, who published an *American dictionary of the English language*.

Wedgwood, Dame Cicely Veronica (1910–97), English historian, author of *William the Silent*, *Thomas Wentworth*, *The Thirty Years' War*, *The King's Peace*, *The Trial of Charles I*; a member of the Staffordshire pottery family. O.M. 1969.

Wedgwood, Josiah (1730–95), English potter, who at his Etruria works near Hanley produced from a new ware (patented 1763) pottery to classical designs by Flaxman, and gave pottery a new impetus.

Wei Jingsheng (b. 1951), Chinese human rights campaigner. Imprisoned, 1979–93, for his political beliefs. Imprisoned again, 1995, then exiled.

Weill, Kurt (1900–50), German composer of satirical, surrealist operas, including *Die Dreigroschenoper* and *Mahagonny* (librettist Brecht). His wife, the Viennese actress **Lotte Lenya** (d. 1981) will be remembered for her singing of the Brecht songs and the interpretation of her husband's works. They left Europe for the United States in 1935.

Weingartner, Felix (1863–1942), Austrian conductor, also a composer and writer of a text book on conducting.

Weismann, August (1834–1914), German biologist. He worked on the question of individual variability in evolution, stressing the continuity of the germ plasm and rejecting the idea of inheritance of acquired characteristics.

Weizmann, Chaim (1874–1952), Israeli leader, b. Pinsk. He came to England in 1903 and taught biochemistry at Manchester. He helped to secure the Balfour Declaration (1917). In 1948 he became first president of Israel.

Wellesley, Marquess (Richard Colley Wellesley) (1760–1842), British administrator. He was a successful governor-general of India, and was brother of the Duke of Wellington.

Wellington, 1st Duke of (Arthur Wellesley) (1769–1852), British general. B. in Ireland, he joined the army and gained experience in India. In the Peninsular War he successfully wore down and drove out the invading French. When Napoleon escaped from Elba, Wellington defeated him at Waterloo. Thereafter he took some part in politics as a Tory, but in the last resort was capable of accepting change.

Wells, Herbert George (1866–1946), English author. B. London, he was at first a teacher. He believed in progress through science, and became one of the most influential writers of his time. His long series of books includes romances of the Jules Verne variety (*The Time Machine*, *The Island of Dr. Moreau*, *The Invisible Man*), sociological autobiography (*Love and Mr. Lewisham*, *Kipps*, *Tono-Bungay*, *The History of Mr. Polly*, *Mr. Britling Sees it Through*), and popular education (*Outline of History*, *The Science of Life*, *The Work*, *Wealth and Happiness of Mankind*, *The Shape of Things to Come*, *The Fate of Homo Sapiens*). He was a founder member of the Fabian Society.

Wenceslaus, St. (907–929), Patron saint of Czechoslovakia. A Christian ruler, murdered by his brother Boleslav on his way to Mass. The 'Good King' of the Christmas carol.

Wesley, Charles (1707–88), English hymnwriter. He was the companion of his brother John, and wrote over 5,500 hymns, including *Love divine* and *Jesu, lover of my soul*.

Wesley, John (1703–91), English evangelist and founder of Methodism (at first a nickname applied to friends of himself and his brother), b. at Epworth. After a trip to Georgia and after encountering Moravian influence, he began to teach on tour, covering in over 50 years more than 200,000 miles and preaching over 40,000 sermons. He made religion a live force to many ignorant folk of humble station who could only be reached by a new and direct challenge. He made a feature of the Sunday school and increased the use of music (the brothers' first hymnbook appeared in 1739). He did not plan separation from the Anglican church, though it was implicit in his ordination of a missionary, and it took place after his death. *See also* Methodism, Section J.

Westermarck, Edward Alexander (1862–1939), Finnish sociologist. His works include *History of Human Marriage*, *Origin and Development of the Moral Ideas*, and *The Oedipus Complex*.

Westinghouse, George (1846–1914), American engineer who invented an air-brake for railways (1868) called by his name, and pioneered the use of high tension alternating current for the transmission of electric power.

Westmacott, Sir Richard (1775–1856), English sculptor of Achilles in Hyde Park.

Wharton, Edith (1862–1937), American novelist and friend of Henry James. Her works include *House of Mirth* and *Custom of the Country*.

Whately, Richard (1787–1863), English archbishop of Dublin. He wrote treatises on *Rhetoric* and *Logic*.

Wheatstone, Sir Charles (1802–75), English physicist, one of the first to recognise Ohm's law. In 1837 he (with W. F. Cooke) patented an electric telegraph. He also introduced the microphone.

Wheeler, Sir Charles (1892–1974), English sculptor, especially on buildings. His autobiography is *High Relief*. President, R.A., 1956–66.

Whistler, James Abbott McNeill (1834–1903), American artist. B. at Lowell, he studied in Paris and settled in England. He reacted against the conventions of his day, and Ruskin's uncomprehending criticism of his work resulted in a lawsuit. Among his main works are

studies of the Thames, and a portrait of his mother, now in the Louvre.

White, Sir George Stuart (1835–1912), British general. Defended Ladysmith in the Boer War.

White, Gilbert (1720–93), a father of English ecology. His book *The Natural History and Antiquities of Selborne*, published in 1789, became the bible of the ecology movement.

White, Patrick (1912–90), Australian novelist whose books include *The Aunt's Story*, *Riders in the Chariot*, *The Solid Mandala* and *The Eye of the Storm*. Nobel prize 1973.

Whitefield, George (1714–70), English evangelist, b. Gloucester. He was at first associated with the Wesleys, but differed from them on predestination. His supporters built him a "Tabernacle" in London, and he had other chapels elsewhere. However, he founded no lasting sect.

Whitgift, John (1530–1604), archbishop of Canterbury in the time of Elizabeth I (from 1583). His policy helped to strengthen Anglicanism.

Whitman, Walt (1819–92), American poet, b. Long Island. He led a wandering life and did hospital work in the Civil War. He aimed at forming a new and free American outlook. His works include *Leaves of Grass*, *Drum Taps*, and *Democratic Vistas*.

Whittier, John Greenleaf (1807–92), American Quaker poet, b. Haverhill, Mass. He wrote against slavery (*Justice and Expediency*), turning to poetry after the Civil War, especially remembered for *Snow-bound*.

Whittington, Richard (c. 1358–1423), English merchant. Son of a Gloucestershire knight, he became a London mercer and was mayor of London 1398, 1406, 1419. The cat legend is part of European folklore.

Whittle, Sir Frank (1907–96), 'the father of jet flight'. The first flights of Gloster jet propelled aeroplanes with Whittle engines took place in May 1941. O.M. (1986).

Whymper, Edward (1840–1911), English wood-engraver and mountaineer. He was the first to climb the Matterhorn.

Wilberforce, William (1759–1833), English philanthropist, b. Hull. He was the parliamentary leader of the campaign against the slave trade, abolished in 1807. He then worked against slavery itself, but that further step was only taken in the year of his death.

Wilcox, Ella Wheeler (1855–1919), American writer of romantic sentimental verse.

Wilde, Oscar Fingall (1854–1900), Irish author and dramatist, son of a Dublin surgeon and leader of the cult of art for art's sake. His works include poems, fairy-tales, short stories, and witty plays—*Lady Windermere's Fan*, *A Woman of No Importance*, *An Ideal Husband*, and *The Importance of Being Earnest*. In a libel action he was convicted of homosexual practices and imprisoned for two years, when he wrote *The Ballad of Reading Gaol*.

Wilder, Thornton Niven (1897–1975), American author and playwright. Among his books are *The Bridge of San Luis Rey* and *Ides of March*.

Wilkes, John (1727–97), English politician. A Whig, he violently attacked George III in his paper the *North Briton*, and as a result of unsuccessful proceedings against him, general warrants were determined illegal. He was again in trouble for obscene libel; his defiance of authority brought him popularity, and he was four times re-elected to parliament but refused his seat, until his opponents gave way. He helped to establish freedom of the press.

Willcocks, Sir William (1852–1932), British engineer, b. India, who carried out irrigation works in India *etc*. He built the Aswan dam (1898–1902).

Willett, William (1856–1915), English advocate of "daylight savings," adopted after his death.

William I of England (1027–87), the "Conqueror," Duke of Normandy, claimed the English throne as successor to Edward the Confessor, and defeated Harold II at Hastings in 1066. An able commander and a firm ruler, he crushed Saxon resistance, especially in the north, transferred most of the land to his Norman followers, and drew England into closer relations with the continent, as did his archbishop Lanfranc. He ordered the Domesday survey.

William II of England (1056–1100), the Conqueror's son, surnamed Rufus, succeeded in

1087. Capricious and self-indulgent, his reign was troubled, and he was shot (by accident or design) while hunting in the New Forest.

William III of England (1650–1702), King of England, Scotland, and Ireland (1689–1702), son of William II of Orange and Mary, daughter of Charles I. He married Mary, daughter of the Duke of York (later James II) while stadtholder of Holland. In 1688, when James had fled the country, he was invited to succeed and he and Mary became joint king and queen. The revolution of 1688 brought to England tolerance of Protestant worship, but William was mainly concerned with war against France, ended in 1697.

William IV of England (1765–1837), third son of George III, succeeded his brother George IV in 1830; called the "sailor king." The reform bill of 1832 and other reform measures were carried without obstruction from him.

William I of Germany (1797–1888), King of Prussia and first German emperor. He succeeded to the throne in 1861 and continued resistance to reform, appointing Bismarck as chief minister, and supporting him through the Austro-Prussian and Franco-Prussian wars. His personal character was simple and unassuming.

William II of Germany, the Kaiser (1859–1941), King of Prussia and German emperor from 1888, was grandson of William I and of Queen Victoria. He was intelligent but impetuous, and believed in military power. He dismissed Bismarck. In 1914 his support of Austria helped to precipitate European war, and the resulting defeat brought his abdication, after which he lived in retirement at Doorn in Holland.

William the Silent (1533–84), Dutch national leader. Prince of Orange, he led the revolt of the Protestant Netherlands against the rule of the Spanish Philip II. The union of the northern provinces was accomplished in 1579, and Spanish rule was renounced by 1584, in which year William was assassinated.

Williams, Sir George (1821–1905), founder of the Young Men's Christian Association.

Williamson, Malcolm (b. 1931), Australian composer, pianist and organist; succeeded Sir Arthur Bliss as Master of the Queen's Musick.

Willis, Ted (Lord Willis) (1914–92), socialist politician and playwright. His best-known play was *Woman in a Dressing Gown* (1962), and he created the TV series, *Dixon of Dock Green* (1953–75).

Wilson, Sir Angus (1913–91), British novelist and man of letters. See **M16**.

Wilson, Edmund (1895–1972), American critic, author of *Axel's Castle* (1931), *The Triple Thinkers* (1938), *The Wound and the Bow* (1941), *To the Finland Station* (1940), *The Shores of Light* (1952), *The Dead Sea Scrolls* (1955).

Wilson of Rievaulx, Lord (Sir Harold Wilson) (1916–95), British statesman, leader parl. Labour Party 1963–76; prime minister 1964–6, 1966–70, 1974–6. Entered parliament 1945 as member for Ormskirk; elected for Huyton 1950–83. Returned as Prime Minister on four occasions. Resigned March 1976. Founder of the Open University.

Wilson, Richard (1714–82), British landscape painter, b. Montgomeryshire. Admired by Turner and Constable.

Wilson, Thomas Woodrow (1856–1924), American statesman. He was U.S. president 1913–21, brought America into the first world war and advocated the League of Nations, but was not a successful negotiator at the peace conference and could not carry his country into the League. He introduced prohibition and women's suffrage.

Wingate, Orde Charles (1903–44), leader of the Chindit forces engaged behind the Japanese lines in Burma during the second world war.

Winifred, St., the 7th cent. patron saint of North Wales, said in late legend to have been killed by her rejected suitor, Prince Caradoc, but restored by her uncle.

Wiseman, Nicholas Patrick (1802–65), cardinal, b. in Spain of an Irish family. In 1850 on the restoration in England of the Catholic hierarchy he became first archbishop of Westminster.

Wittgenstein, Ludwig Josef Johann (1889–1951), Austrian linguistic philosopher whose main works were the *Tractatus Logico-Philosophicus* of his early period, much admired by Russell, and the *Philosophical Investigations*.

Wodehouse, Pelham Grenville (1881–1975), English humorist, creator of Jeeves in the Bertie Wooster stories. He became a U.S. citizen.

Wolf, Friedrich August (1759–1824), German scholar, a founder of scientific classical philology.

Wolf, Hugo (1860–1903), Austrian song-writer. In his settings of over 300 German lyrics, including many of Mörike and Goethe, he achieved union of poetry and music. See **Section E**.

Wolfe, James (1727–59), British general, b. Westerham. He showed early promise in the Seven Years' War, and was given command of the expedition against Quebec, which in spite of its strong position he captured, but lost his life.

Wolsey, Thomas (c. 1475–1530), English cardinal. A butcher's son at Ipswich, he entered the church, becoming archbishop of York and cardinal, while in the same year (1515) he became Henry VIII's lord chancellor. But in spite of his ability he was unable to secure papal sanction for the king's divorce from Catherine of Aragon, and fell from power and died.

Wood, Sir Henry Joseph (1869–1944), English conductor, founder of the Promenade Concerts which he conducted from 1895 till his death.

Woodcock, George (1904–79), trade union leader. TUC general secretary 1960–69; first chairman, Commission on Industrial Relations, 1969–71.

Woodsworth, James Shaver (1874–1942), Canadian politician, parliamentary leader of the Co-operative Commonwealth Federation.

Woodville, Elizabeth (1437–91), wife of Edward IV. Her daughter Elizabeth married Henry VII.

Woolf, Virginia (1882–1941), English writer, daughter of Sir Leslie Stephen and wife of Leonard Woolf with whom she founded the Hogarth Press. Her works include *To the Lighthouse, Mrs. Dalloway, The Waves, A Room of One's Own*.

Wollstonecraft, Mary (1759–97), feminist and writer. She was most famous for her work *A Vindication of the Rights of Women* (1792), a seminal protest against the limited opportunities open to women. See **Feminism, J20**.

Wootton of Abinger, Baroness (Barbara Frances Wootton) (1897–1988), English social scientist. Her works include *Social Science and Social Pathology, Crime and the Criminal Law*.

Wordsworth, William (1770–1850), English poet, b. Cockermouth. He went to Cambridge, and in 1798 with Coleridge issued *Lyrical Ballads*, a return to simplicity in English poetry. He settled at Grasmere with his sister Dorothy (1771–1855), to whose insight his poems owe much. Among his best works are his sonnets and his *Ode on the Intimations of Immortality*, besides his *Prelude*.

Wren, Sir Christopher (1632–1723), English architect, b. Wiltshire. After the great fire (1666) he prepared an abortive plan for rebuilding London, but did in fact rebuild St. Paul's and more than fifty other city churches, including St. Stephen, Walbrook, and St. Mary-le-Bow. Other works include Chelsea Hospital, portions of Greenwich Hospital, the Sheldonian theatre, Oxford, and Queen's College library, Oxford. He had wide scientific interests (he was professor of mathematics at Gresham College, London, and professor of astronomy at Oxford) and helped to found the Royal Society.

Wright, (William Ambrose) Billy (1924–94), the golden-boy of post-war English football. A former captain of Wolves and England, he won 105 caps for England, captaining his country 90 times.

Wright, Frank Lloyd (1869–1959), American architect, initiator of horizontal strip and all-glass design. Buildings include the Imperial Hotel, Tokyo, and the Guggenheim Museum, New York.

Wright, Orville (1871–1948), American airman who with his brother **Wilbur** (1867–1912) in 1903 was the first to make a controlled sustained flight in a powered heavier-than-air machine, flying a length of 852 ft. at Kitty Hawk, N.C.

Wright, Richard (1908–60), black American novelist. Author of *Native Son* (1940) a pioneering novel of black revolt. A later work *The God That Failed* reflects his disillusion with communism.

Wyatt, James (1746–1813), English architect who built Fonthill Abbey.

Wyatt, Sir Thomas (1503–42), English poet (and diplomat) who introduced the sonnet from Italy.

Wyatt, Sir Thomas the younger (c. 1520–54), son of above, unsuccessfully led a revolt against Queen Mary on behalf of Lady Jane Grey.

Wycherley, William (1640–1715), English dramatist of the Restoration period. A master of satiric comedy, his plays include *Love in a Wood*, *The Plain Dealer* and *The Country Wife*.

Wyclif, John (*c*. 1320–84), English religious reformer. He taught at Oxford, later becoming rector of Lutterworth. He insisted on inward religion and attacked those practices which he thought had become mechanical. His followers, called Lollards, were suppressed, partly for political reasons. The Wyclif Bible, the first translation of the Latin Vulgate into English, was mainly the work of his followers at Oxford.

Wykeham, William of (1324–1404), English churchman. He held office under Edward III and became bishop of Winchester in 1367. He founded New College, Oxford, and Winchester School, and improved Winchester cathedral.

Wyllie, William Lionel (1851–1931), English marine painter of *The Thames Below London Bridge*.

Wyspianski, Stanislav (1869–1907), Polish poet, dramatist and painter. His plays *The Wedding*, *Liberation*, and *November Night* treat of national themes.

X

Xavier, St. Francis (1506–52), "apostle of the Indies," b. at Xavero in the Basque country. He was associated with Loyola in founding the Jesuits, and undertook missionary journeys to Goa, Ceylon, and Japan.

Xenophon (444–359 B.C.), Athenian general and historian. He commanded Greek mercenaries under the Persian Cyrus, and on the latter's death safely marched the Ten Thousand home through hostile country. His chief works are the *Anabasis*, the *Hellenica*, and *Cyropaedia*.

Xerxes (*c*. 519–465 B.C.), King of Persia, was son of the first Darius. In 481 B.C. he started on an expedition against Greece when, according to Herodotus, he had a combined army and navy of over two and a half million men. He defeated the Spartans at Thermopylae, but his fleet was overcome at Salamis. He reigned from 485 to 465 B.C. and met his death by assassination.

Ximénes de Cisneros, Francisco (1436–1517), Spanish statesman and churchman. He became cardinal in 1507; carried out monastic reforms; and directed preparation of a polyglot bible, the *Complutensian*; but as inquisitorgeneral he was fanatical against heresy. He was adviser to Queen Isabella; in 1506 regent for Queen Juana; and himself directed an expedition to conquer Oran and extirpate piracy.

Y

Yeats, William Butler (1865–1939), Irish lyric poet and playwright, b. near Dublin, a leader of the Irish literary revival. His plays were performed in the Abbey Theatre (which with **Lady Gregory** (1852–1932) he helped to found), and include *Cathleen Ni Houlihan*, *The Hour Glass*, and *Deidre*. A complete edition of the *Collected Poems* appeared in 1950.

Yeltsin, Boris Nikolayevich (b. 1931), Russian politician. President, since May 1990, of the Russian Federation. At first an ally of Gorbachev (*q.v.*) then a rival. Yeltsin's role in opposing the August 1991 coup greatly strengthened his power and undermined the old Soviet Union. Architect of the Commonwealth of Independent States. He successfully overcame the 1993 communist rising in Moscow. Re-elected President 1996, despite grave economic problems, a resurgence of nationalism and communism, the Chechnya war and serious health problems. *See* **Section C.**

Yonge, Charlotte Mary (1823–1901), English novelist. Influenced by Keble, she wrote novels which faithfully reflect some aspects of Victorian life; one such is *The Daisy Chain*. She also wrote historical fiction *e.g. The Dove in the Eagle's Nest*.

Young, Brigham (1801–77), American Mormon leader, and president in 1844 after the founder's death. He was a main founder of Salt Lake City. He practised polygamy. *See* **Section J.**

Young, Francis Brett (1884–1954), English novelist, author of *My Brother Jonathan* and *Dr. Bradley remembers*.

Young, James (1811–83), Scottish chemist, b. Glasgow, whose experiments led to the manufacture of paraffin oil and solid paraffin on a large scale.

Young, Thomas (1773–1829), English physicist, physician and Egyptologist, b. Somerset, of Quaker family. He established the wave theory of light and its essential principle of interference, put forward a theory of colour vision, and was the first to describe astigmatism of the eye. He was largely responsible for deciphering the inscriptions on the Rosetta stone.

Younghusband, Sir Francis Edward (1863–1942), English explorer and religious leader. He explored Manchuria and Tibet, and wrote on India and Central Asia. He founded the World Congress of Faiths in 1936 (*see* **Section J**).

Ypres, 1st Earl of. *See* **French.**

Ysaÿe, Eugène (1858–1929), Belgian violinist and conductor, noted chiefly for his playing of the works of Bach and César Franck.

Yukawa, Hideki (1907–81), Japanese physicist, who received the 1949 Nobel prize for predicting (1935) the existence of the meson.

Z

Zadkiel (angel in rabbinical lore), pseudonym of two astrologers: **William Lilly** (1602–81) and **Richard James Morrison** (1794–1874).

Zadkine, Ossip (1890–1967), Russian-born sculptor who made play with light on concave surfaces.

Zaharoff, Sir Basil (1849–1936), armaments magnate and financier, b. Anatolia of Greek parents. He was influential in the first world war.

Zamenhof, Ludwig Lazarus (1859–1917), Polish-Jew who invented Esperanto. He was by profession an oculist.

Zeno of Citium (?342–270 B.C.), philosopher, founder of the Stoic system. He left Cyprus to teach in Athens.

Zeppelin, Ferdinand, Count von (1838–1917), German inventor of the dirigible airship, 1897–1900. It was used in the first world war.

Zeromski, Stefan (1864–1925), Polish novelist, author of *The Homeless*, *The Ashes*, *The Fight with Satan*.

Zhukov, Georgi Konstantinovich (1896–1974), Soviet general, who led the defence of Moscow and Stalingrad and lifted the siege of Leningrad in the second world war. He accepted the German surrender in 1945.

Zhukovsky, Vasily Andreyevich (1783–1852), Russian poet and translator of German and English poets. For many years he was tutor to the future Tsar Alexander II.

Zola, Emile Edouard (1840–1902), French novelist, b. Paris, of Italian descent. His series, *Les Rougon-Macquart*, portrays in a score of volumes (the best known of which are perhaps *L'Assommoir*, *Nana* and *Germinal*) the fortunes of one family in many aspects and in realistic manner. He had the moral courage to champion Dreyfus.

Zorn, Anders Leonhard (1860–1920), Swedish sculptor, etcher, and painter.

Zoroaster (**Zarathustra**) (fl. 6th cent. B.C.), Persian founder of the Parsee religion. He was a monotheist, and saw the world as a struggle between good (Ahura Mazda) and evil (Ahriman). *See* **Zoroastrianism, Section J.**

Zoshchenko, Mikhail (1895–1958), Russian writer of humorous short stories, which include *The Woman who could not Read and other Tales* and *The Wonderful Dog and other Stories*.

Zosimus (fl. *c*. 300), the first known alchemist. He lived in Alexandria.

Zuccarelli, Francesco (1702–88), Italian artist of fanciful landscapes. He spent many years in London and was elected a founder member of the R.A. (1768).

Zuckermann, Baron (Solly Zuckermann) (1904–93), British biologist; chief scientific adviser to British governments; 1940–71. Author of *Scientists and War* and *The Frontiers of Public and Private Science*. O.M. 1968.

Zwingli, Ulrich (1484–1531), Swiss religious reformer. He taught mainly at Zurich, where he issued a list of reformed doctrines, less extreme than those of Calvin.

Zwirner, Ernst Friedrich (1802–61), German architect who restored Cologne cathedral.

BACKGROUND TO WORLD AFFAIRS

This section is in three parts. The first provides an up-to-date chronicle of political developments in Britain over the last decade, concluding with a survey of the record of the new Labour Government. The second part provides a wide-ranging guide to events in important areas elsewhere in the world. The third part consists of a series of special topics. This edition includes articles on the war in the Balkans, the changing fortunes of the Clinton presidency, the Yeltsin era in Russia, and the search for peace in the Middle East.

TABLE OF CONTENTS

BACKGROUND TO WORLD AFFAIRS

This section is in three parts. The first outlines the political history of the United Kingdom since 1989. The second part provides a wide-ranging guide to events elsewhere in the world and takes stock of the changing patterns in international relations. The third section contains special topics on particular themes. The reader is invited to turn to **Section D** for further key facts and figures relating to the British political system.

I. SURVEY OF THE BRITISH POLITICAL SCENE

BRITISH POLITICAL EVENTS 1989–99

Background Note.

In the decade after 1979, Margaret Thatcher (see **B59**) dominated British politics. However, by 1989 discontent within her party and opposition to her policies within the country brought a challenge to her leadership. After a first ballot of Conservative MPs, it was clear Margaret Thatcher was wounded. She declared within minutes of the announcement of the result that she would stand again. The following day, however, she was persuaded to consult her colleagues. After interviewing each of her Cabinet, she came reluctantly to the conclusion that her position was untenable, and announced her withdrawal. This opened the field to two further candidates: Douglas Hurd and John Major. A week later John Major topped the poll and, to avoid a third ballot, both his rivals stood down. On 28 November, Mrs Thatcher left Downing Street for the last time as Prime Minister, technically undefeated but having lost the confidence of her colleagues, and at the end of the longest premiership this century.

The Advent of John Major.

Although he was Mrs Thatcher's preferred choice as successor, John Major started to distance himself from her, immediately in the style of his Government and increasingly in policy as well. His Cabinet contained more changes than predicted. Norman Lamont, his campaign manager, was promoted to Chancellor of the Exchequer; Chris Patten succeeded Kenneth Baker as Party Chairman; and in a tactically astute move, Michael Heseltine was appointed to the Department of the Environment with the crucial task of finding a way out of the poll tax crisis. The new Prime Minister declared his intention of establishing a less presidential style. He sought to capitalise on his reputation as a "man in the street", and he began to talk of the social impact of policies and of the need for close collaboration with Europe in a manner little heard from his predecessor. However, before he had much opportunity to make his mark, he faced the exceptional challenge of war.

Gulf War.

In August 1990 Iraq invaded and annexed Kuwait. President Bush, with the active encouragement of Mrs Thatcher, pressed the UN Security Council first to impose economic sanctions and then to set a deadline for withdrawal. Meanwhile, a multinational coalition of forces was assembled in Saudi Arabia under American leadership and including a significant British contingent. Despite repeated efforts to find a diplomatic solution, the Iraqi President, Saddam Hussein, refused to withdraw. Shortly after the expiry of the UN deadline in January 1991, the coalition forces commenced an air attack, of unprecedented intensity and accuracy, on strategic targets in Iraq and Kuwait. This was followed by a land war in which heavy coalition casualties had been feared. However, Iraqi resistance had been worn down by weeks of air bombardment. The occupying troops surrendered or fled with only minimal force such that Kuwait was retaken and a ceasefire declared in a matter of days and with almost no coalition casualties. The war quickly established Mr Major on the international stage and – although British involvement was supported by Neil Kinnock and Paddy Ashdown – it gave the Prime Minister early opportunities to project himself as a national leader which, it was thought, would result in substantial political dividends for the Conservatives.

Conservative fortunes were indeed revived by the war and by the honeymoon enjoyed by any new leader. However, their impact was more short-lived than had been expected. British politics reverted very quickly to domestic issues, in particular the economic recession and the poll tax. Rather than riding on the crest of a victory wave of popularity, the Government was rebuffed in one of the biggest electoral upsets ever when it lost Ribble Valley in March 1991, again to the Liberal Democrats. Without question, the poll tax had been the cause of its defeat. Finding a solution was, however, proving more elusive than Ministers had hoped. In the Budget, the Chancellor sought to limit the damage caused by the tax by announcing a rebate of £140 per person, recouped by a 2½% increase in VAT. Two days later, Michael Heseltine announced that in 1993 the poll tax would be replaced by a new local tax based on property but also including a personal element. The details, which would establish whether this was to be the "son of poll tax" or a return to the rates, had still to be worked out, and proved to be difficult for a Government torn between loyalty towards the underlying principles of the poll tax – once described by Mrs Thatcher as her flagship – and recognition of its apparently fatal unpopularity in the minds of a majority of the electorate. To ease the burden of local government finance, Mr Heseltine also heralded a reform of local government to create a single-tier structure throughout the country.

A New Political Scene.

Perversely, after being attacked under Mrs Thatcher for being dictatorial, the Government was now accused of dithering. In the early Spring the opinion polls showed the Conservatives and Labour to be level-pegging, and a marked improvement in the fortunes of the Liberal Democrats, now unchallenged as the third party following the decision in June 1990 to wind up the SDP. Party politics were also transformed by the disappearance of one towering personality. The three major parties were led by individuals – John Major, Neil Kinnock and Paddy Ashdown – of similar age and standing. On policy too there was a convergence towards the centre. Labour had already moved in this direction as a result of its policy reviews and new image. Now the Conservatives were muting their radical stance and discarding the Thatcherite rhetoric. The prospects for the General Election, due before June 1992, seemed therefore wide open. Following a poor Conservative showing in the May local elections (with widespread Labour and Liberal Democrat gains), speculation concerning an early election was dampened. The loss of the Monmouth by-election (on 16 May) to Labour dealt any lingering expectations of an early election a final blow. On a swing of over 12 %, in the second safest Conservative seat in Wales, Labour swept to victory with a 2,406 majority. Against this electoral background, with unemployment rising swiftly and interest rates still worryingly high, the country was set for a long and protracted battle in the run-up to the General Election.

Politics in the second half of 1991 and the first months of 1992 were shaped, firstly, by the knowledge that the General Election would have to take place by July of 1992, and secondly, that the economic setting within which the election would take place would be unpropitious for the government.

The Major Administration.

John Major devoted the first fifteen months before the election to establishing a distinctive image for himself and the government he led. He was constrained by some opinion within his own party from distancing himself too greatly from Margaret Thatcher in policy towards public spending, the economy in general, and European integration but spurred on by the knowledge that he had to set a course for the Conservative Party and the country different from that of his predecessor. In practice, Mr. Major's administration set a course for public policy sharply at variance with that which he had inherited. Willing as Mrs. Thatcher had been to modify principle for political advantage, Mr. Major effectively reinstated the politics of pragmatism as the first article of governing faith. This development was evident in five respects:

* The Government announced that the Poll Tax was to be abandoned and replaced by a "Council Tax" based on the value of property.

* Policy towards Europe was refashioned. Negotiations over European integration leading up to the Maastricht summit in December 1991 resulted in Britain securing a clause enabling it to opt out of Community agreements on social policy, and to stand back from monetary union. The Prime Minister took pains to commit himself rhetorically to the defence of Britain's national interests and sovereignty, and opposed any movement towards a federal European state in which sovereignty would be formally and legally divided between the Community and the member states. However, the agreement he secured was much closer in content to that which (for example) Douglas Hurd sought than that with which Margaret Thatcher would have been content. In practice, Major's diplomacy was almost as skilful as his marginalisation of right-wing dissenters within the Conservative Party. Mrs. Thatcher eventually supported him in a formal Commons vote on the outcome of Maastricht.

* The "Citizens' Charter" was launched in the summer of 1991 and relaunched six months later to underline the government's determination to promote the rights enjoyed by consumers of public services, including central and local government. Although its provisions did not extend to private industry and commerce, it showed Major's shrewdness in identifying widespread dissatisfaction at the quality of service received from public bodies with a belief that some public services could be held accountable without necessarily privatising them thoroughly. The programme assisted the government's aim to portray itself as mindful of the needs of consumers.

* Under Mr. Major, the government was on several occasions to show tactical flexibility and a willingness to spend money in order to defuse damaging issues. The compensation of haemophiliacs infected by the AIDS virus through being given contaminated blood was but one instance which marked a change of style at No. 10 Downing Street, and a shift towards the image of a caring government.

* Monetary policy, which since the entry into the Exchange Rate Mechanism had been effectively set in Germany rather than London, remained tight throughout the pre-election period. Although nominal rates fell, real rates remained very high as the rate of inflation also dropped. Faced with a persisting recession, weak confidence among business people about commercial prospects, and the imminence of the General Election,

fiscal policy was dramatically loosened. The Public Expenditure proposals in the autumn of 1991 heralded a fiscal loosening with a Public Sector Borrowing Requirement (PSBR) of £10·5 billion. This was furthered by the Budget of 10 March 1992 which saw a fiscal stimulus of some £5 billion in the form of lower taxes, and a surge in the expected Public Sector Borrowing Requirement to £27 billion.

The Election Background.

On 9 April 1992, Britain went to the polls in one of the most keenly-contested and closely fought contests of the post-war period. The election ended many months of "phoney" electioneering and was held against a background of claims and counterclaims concerning the state of the British economy. Repeated forecasts by Treasury ministers in the autumn and winter of 1991/2 of imminent recovery from recession reflected their genuine expectations that a Spring election would be called with interest rates drifting down, inflation under firm control, and the first stirrings of economic growth apparent. The election was actually called in less propitious circumstances when the Prime Minister had lost almost all room for tactical manoeuvre. The economy remained in deep and prolonged recession, public spending was rising rapidly (resulting in a Public Sector Borrowing Requirement of £28 billion), the politically-sensitive reforms of the National Health Service were in troubled mid-course, and the final Poll Tax bills were about to arrive. There remained the potentially damaging constitutional question of Scotland's increasingly uncertain relationship with the rest of the Kingdom.

The April 1992 Election.

Against the published indications of every major polling organisation and the large exit polls conducted on the day of the election, the Conservatives were returned with an overall majority. The results were as follows:

		Votes	
Con	Lab	Lib Dem	Nat/other
41·9	34·4	17·8	5·9

		Seats	
Con	Lab	Lib Dem	Nat/other
336	271	20	24

The new parliament has a different appearance from the old. Several senior members of the Labour and Conservative Parties retired: Denis Healey, Michael Foot, Norman Tebbit, David Owen, Cecil Parkinson, and most notably of all, Margaret Thatcher, did not seek re-election. Others were defeated: both Chris Patten (Chairman of the Conservative Party) and Lynda Chalker (the Overseas Development Minister) lost their seats in Bath and Wallasey respectively. Mr Major's new administration is also very different from the old: Kenneth Baker, the former Home Secretary, left the government as did Tom King, the former Defence Secretary, and (briefly) Peter Brooke, the former Northern Ireland Secretary. Two women joined the Cabinet: Gillian Shephard, at Employment, and Virginia Bottomley, at Health. John Wakeham, former Leader of the House of Commons, was appointed Leader of the House of Lords, whilst Michael Heseltine, who had a characteristically vigorous and energetic campaign, won the post he had long coveted: Secretary of State for Trade and Industry, whilst Kenneth Clarke became the new Home Secretary.

The remarkable achievement of a fourth successive term of office for the Conservatives brought a further round of internal dissension within the Labour Party, but only a brief respite for the Prime Minister, John Major, from the three, linked problems of ratification of the Maastricht Treaty, Britain's membership of the Exchange Rate Mechanism and the country's continuing economic recession.

Advent of John Smith.

Neil Kinnock, under whom the Labour Party had largely shed its electorally lethal image of unfitness for government, announced shortly after his party's election defeat that he would resign the Leadership. John Smith, a conservative Scots advocate who had previously held the position of Shadow Chancellor, was overwhelmingly elected to succeed him over the challenge of Bryan Gould. Mr Smith was the sole member of the Shadow Cabinet elected by the Parliamentary Labour Party in 1993 himself to have been a member of a Labour Cabinet. Cautious by instinct, and forensic by legal training, Smith set in train a Commission under the Chairmanship of Sir Gordon Borrie to review the nature, purposes, and structure of the Welfare State as a prelude to establishing new policies for welfare and (by implication) for taxation. To the evident frustration of some colleagues, not all of them on the left of the party, the assumption which underlay Smith's approach in his first six months as leader was that the Conservative majority in the Commons would hold, whatever the outcome of the debate on Maastricht, for the full term of the Parliament.

During the autumn of 1992, Mr Smith's apparent assumption appeared open to doubt when, following consistent, vigorous, assertions of the centrality of ERM membership to the government's anti-inflation strategy, the markets' doubts about its credibility overwhelmed the Treasury's capacity to resist. Britain's withdrawal from the mechanism provoked a wider crisis within the mechanism and widened divisions between pro- and anti-Europeans within the Conservative Party. Freed of the need to maintain the value of sterling within its ERM bands, however, the government began to cut short-term interest rates aggressively and frequently in order to stem the fall in output and (which marked a significant shift in government rhetoric) to improve prospects for employment.

A Sea of Troubles.

The economy nonetheless continued to contract, albeit at a slower rate than for most of 1991, and unemployment grew rapidly, reaching a total of 3 million in January 1993. Confidence showed signs of fragile recovery in early 1993, but house prices continued to weaken, and the rate of business failures remained high. Under these circumstances, British Coal's proposal in the autumn of 1992 to close thirty of the remaining coal mines following the privatised electricity companies' decisions to buy much less coal from British suppliers in the future than they had done in the past, provoked a storm of protest from opposition and government benches which the government headed off only at the price of an expensive and humiliating retreat. Whilst inflation was brought down to levels comparable with major European competitors, the recession damaged not only the industrial base, but greatly harmed public sector finances. So rapidly did the Public Sector Borrowing Requirement (PSBR) grow, that many in the Conservative Party (who had campaigned in the April 1992 General Election on a platform of implacable opposition to tax increases) were by the spring of 1993 agreeing that increases in taxation and reductions in public spending were required in order to close the rapidly growing gap between income and expenditure.

Conservatives in Disarray.

A damaging by-election defeat at the previously safe Conservative seat of Newbury, Berkshire, precipitated the dismissal of the Chancellor of the Exchequer, Mr. Norman Lamont, from his post in the summer of 1993. The Chancellor was scarcely solely to blame for the deterioration in public finances, the sluggish recovery, or the Conservatives Government's deep unpopularity (not least among its core voters in the South of England). Nevertheless, his lack of empathy and finesse in dealing with a public bruised by a long recession and very high real interest rates, had long been a source of grumbling discontent for the government. Defeat at Newbury intensified it, and precipitated the Chancellor's departure from the government led by the man whose close political ally he had been.

For the remainder of 1993 and in the first months of 1994, morale on the Conservative backbenches and, more tellingly, in local Conservative Associations, remained low; exceptionally poor public opinion poll ratings, though of little moment in the middle of a parliament, added to the discomfiture of government and party. Disunity within the parliamentary party posed considerable difficulties for government whips and business managers,

despite the removal of the single greatest focus of anti-EC discontent within the Party by the final ratification of the Maastricht Treaty. The right-wing faction which had caused such turmoil within the Parliamentary Party in the eighteen months following the 1992 election victory on the European Question, remained unreconciled to the weakening of the tone and substance of policy under Mrs. Thatcher's successor.

Some of the government's misfortunes were self-inflicted, reflecting a combination of poor staff work and (more especially) uncertainty and fitfulness in direction from the Prime Minister himself. The clearest example was that of a strange, misconceived, attempt at the Party Conference in the autumn of 1993 to launch a campaign of "Back to Basics", the content of which was differently defined by different politicians and groups in the party, but part of which was originally intended by some in the Party to have a morally cleansing effect upon politics. The campaign collapsed in the first weeks of 1993 amidst sundry scandalous revelations about the private lives of certain government ministers.

Crisis for the Prime Minister.

The prospects for the premiership of John Major deteriorated rapidly in the spring of 1994. Partly this was due to his position over British voting rights in an enlarged Europe (he suddenly adopted an unrealistic tough stance, only to abandon it with equal speed). But it was the electoral trough in which the party found itself which proved even more problematic. In the opinion polls, the party was at rock bottom. In the May local elections, the electoral day of reckoning arrived.

The outcome of the local elections was a disaster for the Conservatives. Across the length and breadth of the country, normally loyal towns deserted the Conservatives. The litany of losses included Kingston, Colchester and Winchester. The resurgent Liberal Democrats made a net gain of 388 seats, Labour a gain of 88 and the Conservatives a loss of 429. Not only did these results increase speculation on John Major's ability to survive, but they appeared to herald heavy losses in the European elections.

The Death of John Smith.

The sudden death of Mr Smith on 12 May 1994 forced a labour leadership contest and threw the party's future direction into question. Campaigning for the forthcoming European Parliamentary elections was suspended until after Mr Smith's funeral on 20 May. The delay gave an increasingly buffeted Mr Major a short breathing space. But failure in May's local elections was followed by disaster in the 9 June European elections. The Tories took 18 seats with 28% of the vote, their lowest share in any 20th century election. Labour won 62 seats with 44% of the vote, while the Liberal Democrats' 17% gained them only two seats. In the Eastleigh by-election on the same day, a Tory majority of almost 18,000 was turned into a Liberal lead of over 9,000 votes.

The Advent of Tony Blair

Mr Smith's deputy, Mrs Beckett, took over as acting leader and proved effective in the role. However, on 21 July, Labour turned to its centrist 41-year-old home affairs spokesman, Tony Blair, electing him leader with 57% of the vote. The more traditionalist John Prescott, who had also stood for the leadership, was elected as his deputy.

Although described by one commentator as a politician apparently "almost wholly lacking in ideological ballast", Mr. Blair had, as a shadow minister, effectively destroyed the Tory party monopoly on law and order with the slogan that Labour would be "tough on crime, tough on the causes of crime".

In his leadership campaign Mr. Blair accepted the principle of a minimum wage, but would give no figure; he favoured full employment, but was unwilling to provide a target or a timetable. He advocated changes to Labour's commitment to public ownership and would make no promises about taking the privatised utilities back into public ownership. Like Mr. Smith before him, Mr. Blair would increasingly face criticism for the imprecision of Labour's intentions. However,

Labour maintained, and improved upon, its lead in the opinion polls. Mr. Blair was also subject to remarkably flattering media coverage.

Mr. Blair faced his first test as leader when, despite pressure from union leaders, he refused to back the rail signallers' industrial action on the eve of the annual TUC congress. Denying he was sitting on the fence, Mr. Blair said it was "not the function of politicians to start barging into industrial disputes".

The July 1994 Cabinet Reshuffle.

Against a background of growing unpopularity, Mr Major reshuffled his Cabinet on 20 July, replacing four senior ministers. The changes coincided with the release of the Pergau Dam report which criticised linking aid funding with arms purchases and called the conduct of former defence minister Lord Younger "reprehensible". Even prolonged industrial action by railway signal staff through the summer gave the government no comfort, as public opinion appeared sympathetic to the strikers' case.

Although, as ministers argued, there were distinctly improving economic indicators, the government could not translate this to a "feel good factor" in the public mind. Instead, its reputation was further threatened by the emergence of a "sleaze factor". In August Lord Archer, a political confidant of Mr Major, was exonerated following accusations that he had used insider knowledge in share dealings. At the end of October two junior ministers resigned after admitting they had asked Parliamentary questions for payment while they were backbenchers. Mr Major moved quickly to establish a standing committee under Lord Nolan, a senior judge, to investigate and make recommendations on office holders' conduct. The public mood was not improved by reports of directors of privatised utilities awarding themselves massive pay increases.

At the Labour Party conference there were calls, particularly during the economic debate on 3 October, for what GMB leader John Edmonds described as some "concrete" to be mixed with the rhetoric, particularly on full employment and the minimum wage. But on television Mr. Blair, though he pledged a future Labour government to introduce a minimum wage "sensibly and effectively", would not be drawn on a figure.

In his conference speech on 4 October, Mr. Blair promised full employment as a goal, that Britain would sign the European Social Chapter on workers' rights, a Bill of Rights and Freedom of Information Bill, a Scottish Parliament and a Welsh Assembly, and a reduction in the powers of the House of Lords. But his call for a revision of the party constitution's Clause Four, Part IV—the section setting out Labour's objective of public ownership—caused inner party turmoil. Since Mr. Gaitskell's thwarted attempt to abandon Clause Four in 1960, no Labour leader (whatever his private feelings) had attempted such a move.

The NEC Elections.

In elections to the 29-strong National Executive Committee on 2 October there had been a small, but nonetheless remarkable, resurgence of the left. The previous year's conference had seen an eradication of the left on the NEC. With one member one vote being used for the first time in 1994, two Campaign Group members—Dennis Skinner and Diane Abbott—were surprisingly elected to the NEC by the party's constituency section. Their election demonstrated suspicions about the direction in which Mr. Blair hoped to take what he called "New Labour". A potentially humiliating defeat for Mr. Blair on Clause Four seemed imminent. In the event, on 5 October the conference voted to retain the clause only by the narrowest of margins—50·9 to 49·1%.

A New General Secretary.

Mr. Blair now moved to confirm his hold on the party. On 17 October Larry Whitty, Labour general secretary for the past nine years, was replaced by Tom Sawyer, a leading trade union ally of Mr. Blair. It was thought his appointment would help influence union leaders in Mr. Blair's Clause Four campaign. A week later Mr. Blair completed a sweeping reshuffle of his front bench

and the whips' office. There were, however, some surprises, including the appointment of Campaign Group member "Red Dawn" Primarolo to the Treasury team.

Widening Conservative Divisions.

Conservative divisions became more openly intense in the autumn. There was no reference to Post Office privatisation in the Queen's Speech on 16 November because backbench Tory resistance (echoing the policy's unpopularity in the country) made the Cabinet doubt the likelihood of passing the legislation proposed. Even more dangerous for the government's survival were fundamental disagreements within the party over Britain's future in Europe.

Mr Major announced on 16 November that he would treat the European Community (Finance) Bill as a vote of confidence. This was aimed at "Eurosceptic" backbenchers reluctant to see Britain's contribution to Europe increase from 1·2 to 1·7% as the Bill proposed.

The "Eurosceptics".

On the European Bill's second reading on 27 November, the government won two crucial votes comfortably. But the Tory whip was withdrawn from eight backbench "Eurosceptics" who abstained on one or both. When a ninth voluntarily relinquished the party whip, Mr Major was theoretically at the head of a minority government. Further humiliation followed when, on 6 December, the government suffered defeat in its attempts to impose the full rate of VAT on household fuel and heating. The measure was rejected by 319 votes to 311 as 17 Tory backbenchers voted against the government. A week later at Dudley West the Tories suffered their worst by-election defeat at the hands of Labour for 50 years.

Mr Major attempted to unite his divided party, and to preserve his own position, by attacking Labour's proposals on home rule for Scotland and Wales. Playing the union card had worked effectively in the 1992 general election but the situation was now more problematic because, paradoxically, of the apparent success of his Northern Ireland policy.

Opinion Poll Popularity.

Mr. Blair was clearly proving an asset, consolidating the popularity for the party achieved by Mr. Smith. The party's position in the opinion polls remained strong and party membership was increasing. A leaked report to the prime minister from Tory vice-chairman John Maples revealed in November how much the new leader's attractiveness to the public was feared. It was Mr. Blair's turn to be embarrassed when it was revealed early in December that he intended to send his son to a grant maintained secondary school when party policy was to discontinue them on taking office.

The Clause Four Campaign.

The Clause Four campaign cleared its first hurdle when the NEC agreed by 20–4 on 30 November that a revision of the party's constitution was necessary. There were, however, criticisms—and not only from the left of the party—that this was an unnecessary diversion when Labour should be concentrating its energies on attacking an increasingly vulnerable government.

On 14 December the NEC accepted Mr. Blair's proposal to put a new version of the party's aims to a special conference on 29 April. His intention was clearly to ensure the question was resolved before Clause Four supporters could rally support at the summer trades union conferences and the party conference in October. When 32 Labour European Parliament members challenged Mr. Blair by placing an advertisement in *The Guardian* on 9 January 1995 supporting Clause Four, he accused them of "not learning from our history, but merely living in it."

Mr. Blair faced two sets of problems in his campaign. The first was the resistance to the proposed change from some trade union leaders. There were reports early in the New Year that some were offering a trade-off: they would support him in return for pledges to renationalise the privatised public utilities, particularly the railways. The second problem was that many constituency party members were staunch supporters of Clause Four as it stood.

Mr. Blair insisted on 25 January that it was essential that the majority of constituency parties supported the change. To win this support, he and deputy leader Mr. Prescott planned a programme of rallies in ten towns and cities from 26 January to 2 March. Early reports suggested opinion was moving Mr. Blair's way and on 4 February Labour's youth conference voted 68 % for change to 17 % against.

Further support for change came at the party's Scottish conference on 10 March when trade unions and constituency activists backed Mr. Blair's proposals by 58·3 % to 41·6 %

Mr. Blair and his deputy formally introduced their revised Clause 4 to the party's National Executive Committee (NEC) on 13 March. In 350 words, they pledged Labour to a "dynamic" mixed economy in a society where "power, wealth and opportunity are in the hands of the many, not the few." Labour, to the approval of traditionalists, was described as a "democratic socialist party". The NEC overwhelmingly endorsed the new wording by 23 to 3 (with five trade union abstentions). As Labour's lead in the opinion polls over the Conservatives continued—by mid-March it stood at over 30 %—Mr. Blair took his party deeper into Tory ideological territory in a speech on 22 March in which he attacked truancy, anti-social council tenants and reminded voters that they had duties as well as rights.

Blair Triumphant.

In the event, the April party conference gave overwhelming support to the reform of Clause 4. The final votes were 65·23 % in favour of change, 34·77 % against. The constituencies (with 30 % of the total vote) voted 90 % for change. The unions, with 70 % of the vote, voted only 54·6 % for change, with such unions as the TGWU, Unison, RMT and the NUM voting against.

Following victory over Clause 4, Mr. Blair suffered a setback in June when the influential Transport and General Workers' Union re-elected "old Labour" Bill Morris as its leader rather than Mr. Blair's preferred candidate Jack Dromey. Mr. Dromey was, coincidentally, the partner of Labour front bench spokeswoman Harriet Harman. There were more difficulties for Mr. Blair through the summer. On 10 August a Labour backbencher attacked Mr. Blair's "inner sanctum" of advisers. GMB union leader John Edmonds expressed what he said was a common concern at the speed of Mr. Blair's reforming revolution. But former deputy leader Roy Hattersley went to the heart of the problem by suggesting that Mr. Blair should not forget the interests of the poor in his quest for middle class votes.

The Northern Ireland Peace Process.

If there was one bright spot for the government – and one for which opposition parties gave Mr Major ungrudging praise – it was in the events following the December 1993 Downing Street Declaration.

Sinn Fein delayed a formal response and asked for clarification on the Unionist community's veto. But on 31 August 1994, the IRA announced a ceasefire. In the previous 25 years 3,169 people had been killed, 38,680 injured, and there had been 10, 001 bombings. Mr Major welcomed the ceasefire but, aware of Unionist fears, said there had been no "secret deals" with the IRA. On 13 October the loyalist para-militaries announced an end to violence.

As the ceasefire continued, Mr Major announced the possibility of talks involving Sinn Fein before Christmas. But the Ulster Unionists remained concerned about their long-term position in any agreement reached between London and Dublin.

On 18 January 1995 Unionist members at Westminster threatened withdrawal of support from what was now, in effect, a minority government. The threats became more pronounced with the leak on 1 February of a draft document on cross border bodies proposing a voice for Dublin in Northern Ireland affairs. The future of the peace process became unclear.

A further attempt by Mr Major to reunite his party came over Europe. Having taken the whip

from the more determined Eurosceptics, he moved towards them in the New Year. There was an increasing emphasis on nationalism and British participation in a single European currency was rejected, at least until "the time was right". But divisions within the Cabinet (reportedly 17–5 pro-Europe) were thrust into the open when chancellor of the exchequer Mr Clarke derided Eurosceptic fears that monetary union implied political union on 9 February. He was contradicted the next day by employment secretary Michael Portillo. It appeared the two wings of the party were positioning themselves for a future leadership contest.

The Government suffered further humiliation when the Tory candidate lost his deposit at the Islwyn by-election on 17 February, pushed from second to fourth place with 3·9% of the vote. The atmosphere of collapse continued when Britain's oldest merchant bank, Barings, went into receivership on 26 February after making estimated losses of £750 million on the derivatives market and the failure of a last-minute Bank of England rescue attempt.

The one bright spot for the government was Northern Ireland, where the ceasefire held. But even here there was disappointment at slow progress towards a settlement, largely due to disagreement over the Provisional IRA giving up its weapons. A joint Anglo-Irish Framework Document unveiled on 22 February aroused much disapproval from Ulster Unionists. The document proposed an assembly for Northern Ireland, a charter of rights, an end to the Irish territorial claim, and a joint parliamentary forum of representatives from the south and the north. The right of the people of Northern Ireland to decide their own future would be given legislative backing. By mid-April preparations were under way for discussions on the proposals by the province's main political parties. Sinn Fein continued to be excluded because of the continuing impasse over paramilitary weapons.

The government's European policies brought it close to parliamentary defeat once again on 1 March as a number of Tory backbenchers abstained and former chancellor of the exchequer Norman Lamont voted with the opposition. Mr Major appeared increasingly unfortunate in his friends when his chancellor, Kenneth Clarke, admitted on 16 March that voters were not giving the government credit for economic recovery and suggested that the "feel bad factor" might last for much longer. Former party treasurer Lord McAlpine declared that a period in opposition could be healthy. The government's majority fell further with the death on 20 March of the only Ulster Unionist backbencher to consistently support the prime minister.

The 1995 Local Elections.

Mr Major attempted to regain the political initiative from an increasingly confident Labour Party on 2 April by offering voters a package of future legislation which included more nursery places, a harder line on asylum seekers, a charter for victims of crime and a reduction in income tax to 20p. But four days later the Tories were humiliated at the hands of Labour and Nationalists in local authority elections in Scotland. They took only 11% of the vote and won in only 82 of the 1,161 seats contested, losing control of six councils.

The municipal elections of 4 May 1995 were a disaster for the Conservatives and a triumph for both Labour and the Liberal Democrats. Voters were electing over 11,700 councillors in 324 English authorities and the entire councils in the 22 new unitary Welsh authorities. The Conservatives finished with a net loss of over 2,000 seats, Labour with some 1,800 net gains and the Liberal Democrats 495 net gains. Labour were estimated to have polled 48% of the vote, the Conservatives 25% and the Liberal Democrats 23%. Coming on top of Tony Blair's easy victory in modernising Clause 4 at the special Party Conference, the political landscape had now been greatly changed.

The Nolan Report.

There was a reminder of the sleaze issue which had so dogged the government with the publication on 11 May of Lord Nolan's report "Standards in Public Life". There were disputes among Conservatives about how far the recommendations on MPs financial interests outside Parliament should be accepted. Inner-party sniping against Mr Major continued. Extracts in May from Lady Thatcher's second volume of memoirs condemned the government's "lack of purpose" and implied that Mr Major should be replaced as party leader. To underline the problem, the Conservatives lost the Perth and Kinross by-election to the Scottish Nationalists on an 11·5% swing on 25 May.

The Conservative Leadership Contest.

Mr Major's response to an apparently permanent stream of troubles was his shock resignation as Conservative leader on 22 June. He challenged his critics to "put up or shut up." Only John Redwood, a right-wing Eurosceptic, took up the challenge, resigning as Welsh Secretary on 26 June. Others, it appeared, were awaiting the result of the first ballot before declaring themselves. In the event, Mr Major secured an apparently easy victory on 4 July, taking 218 votes to Mr Redwood's 89. This meant, however, that including abstentions and spoilt ballots a third of Conservative MPs had failed to support Mr Major.

The July 1995 Cabinet Reshuffle.

Mr Major's victory was followed by a Cabinet reshuffle. Mr Heseltine became First Secretary of State and deputy Prime Minister with extensive powers, a reward it was suggested for his agreement not to stand against Mr Major. Malcolm Rifkind replaced Douglas Hurd as Foreign Secretary and Michael Portillo was appointed Defence Secretary. Mr Major had hoped to impose his authority on the party, but through the summer there appeared to be a further shift to the right, particularly over Britain's future in Europe. The loss of Little-borough and Saddleworth to the Liberal Democrats on 27 July (with the Conservatives forced into third place) reduced the government's majority to nine. In September a former Tory MP defected to Labour, declaring that Mr Major was the "most incompetent, purposeless prime minister in living memory." This was to prove only a foretaste of disasters to come.

On 7 October, the eve of the Conservative Party conference, former junior minister Alan Howarth announced that he was seeking the Labour whip in the House of Commons, reducing the government's majority to five. Mr Howarth said that he could not remain a member of a party which exhibited the "arrogance of power". The notable event of the conference itself was an intemperate speech by Mr Portillo which, though well received by delegates and applauded by Mr Major, was seen as weakening his claim to future party leadership.

Relations with the Trade Unions.

Mr. Blair's concern, however, was the continuing Conservative charge that Labour government threatened restoration of trade union power. He set out the relationship between the unions and a future Labour government at the Trades Union Congress on 11 September. Government had an obligation to listen to the unions, as it did employers. "But the decisions must rest with us. We will be the government and we will govern for the whole country, not any vested interest within it." However, a leaked party document, "The Unfinished Revolution", drawn up by one of Mr. Blair's closest advisers, stated plainly, "Labour is not ready for government." The party lacked a sustainable political project and, the paper said, required a more centralised leadership to give it the necessary coherence.

Mr. Blair's speech at the Labour Party conference in October gave the party's aim as placing "power, wealth and opportunity in the hands of the many, not the few." He promised an "information super-highway" deal with BT, smaller class sizes, increased nursery provision, more police on the beat, a publicly accountable railway, legislation for a Scottish Parliament and a Welsh Assembly, and an end to hereditary peerages as the initial step towards an elected second chamber.

But Labour remained vulnerable to questions about how it would pay for change if, as it declared, it was no longer a tax and spend party. Resolutions passed at the conference gave few clues. Training and job creation for young people would be funded by a windfall tax on private utility profits. The NHS internal market and GP fundholding would be replaced by a health-led rather than financial ethic. The leadership were, however, able to avoid making a commitment on the amount of a minimum wage and an attempt to restore Clause 4 was overwhelmingly defeated.

Continuing Problems.

Mr Major suffered a further personal rebuff on 6 November on the Nolan recommendations. Voting on, among other issues, a ban on paid advocacy by MPs and a requirement to disclose earnings from outside consultancies, 73 Conservatives voted with the Opposition and 31 abstained. Two days later the newly appointed Conservative Central Office communications director resigned, criticising what he called the government's "siege mentality" and the party's plans to fight a highly personalised election campaign. It was clear, however, from the cautious tone of the budget at the end of the month that Mr Major had every intention of waiting until 1997 to call an election. The Chancellor, Mr Clarke, reduced income tax by only a penny rather than the sweeping cut demanded by many in his party. If there were to be tax cuts to promote the still elusive "feel good factor" they would not come until the autumn of 1996. There were, however, curbs in welfare benefits for lone parents and the under 25s.

The government suffered defeat once more on a Common Fisheries Policy debate as Conservative Eurosceptics joined forces with the Opposition on 19 December. But the year ended with a devastating blow on 29 December when Emma Nicholson, a former Conservative vice-chairman, defected to the Liberal Democrats. She accused the government of indecision, weak leadership on Europe and of neglecting the interests of the British people by its lurch to the right. The Conservative majority, 21 at the 1992 general election, now fell to three.

Division in the party was now intense. Mr Major called a crisis meeting of Cabinet friends at Chequers on 1 January. Mr Portillo, a leading right-winger, denied the party had moved to the right under Mr Major and said that Eurofederalists like Ms Nicholson should leave the party. Lady Thatcher warned Mr Major of the dangers of returning to "One Nation" policies. One Nation Conservatives in the 50-strong Macleod Group, stung by this, were only dissuaded from issuing their own manifesto by calls for party unity. On 12 January Mr Major rejected Lady Thatcher's call, denied he had shifted to the left as leader and insisted he would fight the general election on the centre ground. Nonetheless, the Cabinet appeared to have capitulated to Euro-sceptic demands for a tougher stance on Europe with an announcement on 18 January that it would produce a white paper on its general objectives before the forthcoming Maastricht review conference in March.

A Stakeholder Society.

What remained missing was Labour's "big idea", the project that would pose an alternative to Conservatism rather than simply its replacement. The end of 1995 had seen Labour attempting, not unsuccessfully, to take the "One Nation" mantle from the Conservatives. The concept was further developed during Mr. Blair's tour of the Asian "tiger economies" in January 1996. In Singapore he announced that Labour intended to build a "stake-holder society" or "stakeholder economy". Vague as it remained (the idea sought to strike a new balance between individualism and community), stakeholding opened up a genuine debate which appeared to favour Labour. "Empowering the individual in a strong and cohesive society is what the stakeholder economy is about," Mr. Blair declared. Conservative charges that it was simply a return to the discredited corporatism of the 1970s, or that Thatcherism was the stakeholder society, rang hollow.

Divisions over Education.

At the centre of stakeholding was educational opportunity. This had emerged as a major issue in political debate between Labour, the Conservative government and the Liberal Democrats. It was education that was to bring about what Mr. Blair himself said was his worst period for his leadership since taking over the party and to give the Conservatives what they hoped was the key to a restoration of their fortunes. On 20 January it was revealed that Labour front bench spokeswoman Harriet Harman was to send her son to a selective, grant maintained grammar school. It was Labour policy to end selection. The Conservative Education Secretary intensified the embarrassment by praising Ms. Harman for exercising choice. Mr. Blair was faced not only by charges of hypocrisy but also by demands within the Labour Party for Ms. Harman's resignation. He saved Ms. Harman with a call for unity although the furore demonstrated the divisions that might emerge if Labour formed a government. In addition, the issue of apparent double standards gave the Conservatives a valuable campaigning weapon.

The Irish Peace Setback.

The survival of the government now appeared to become linked with the Irish peace process. In January 1996 the newly elected Ulster Unionist leader David Trimble warned that the government could not count on automatic support. There were fears of the impact this might have on the peace process that had begun so optimistically in 1994. Throughout 1995 negotiations were at a standstill over the government's insistence that all-party talks could not begin until the IRA had made serious moves towards decommissioning its weapons. Sinn Fein interpreted this as a demand for surrender. Irish premier John Bruton attempted to end the impasse in July by proposing that Sinn Fein could attend all-party talks with negotiations on arms running in parallel. With no progress on this, a planned Anglo-Irish summit on 6 September was postponed.

Relations with Dublin remained sour and in November only an imminent visit to Ireland by US President Bill Clinton forced a compromise—the appointment of an international body under US Senator George Mitchell to consider a way over the arms obstacle. Meanwhile, the British and Irish governments were to undertake negotiations leading to round table talks at the end of February 1996. Sinn Fein and the IRA nonetheless declared that any proposal for arms to be surrendered was "ludicrous". The Mitchell Commission report on 24 January 1996 accepted that the IRA would not begin to disarm before all-party negotiations began and attempted a compromise. The report also mentioned the possibility of an elected assembly in Northern Ireland to encourage confidence, something the Ulster Unionists had proposed. Mr Major's immediate acceptance of this was criticised by Dublin and denounced by John Hume of the SDLP as evidence of the government "trying to buy votes in the House to keep itself together."

The Liberal Democrats.

As the government's majority had fallen through 1995, bringing the possible collapse of the government closer, Liberal Democrat leader Paddy Ashdown effectively abandoned his party's policy of "equidistance" between the Conservatives and Labour on 26 May. He declared that if the government lost its majority and sought Liberal Democrat support to remain in office, he would not give it. The defeat of the government, he said, was the "precondition of Britain's future success." Mr Ashdown went on at his party's conference in September to criticise Labour's timidity at revealing its policies, particularly on constitutional reform. The Liberal Democrats reaffirmed their commitment to additional spending on education and to Europe. By January 1996 a senior adviser to Mr Ashdown was raising the prospect of a post-election coalition with Labour, although both parties remained wary of any formal agreement. Mr Ashdown himself said on 20 January 1996 that he saw the Liberal Democrats' relationship with a future Labour government as the "cayenne pepper for an otherwise pretty bland repast."

Developments in 1996.

How long the government could survive, with further by-elections in the offing, was problematic for Mr Major. His government faced a series of debilitating crises. Sir Richard Scott's report on arms sales to Iraq was published on 15 February.

He charged ministers with repeatedly and deliberately misleading Parliament about the change in government policy at the end of the Iran-Iraq war in 1988. His particular criticism of Mr William Waldegrave and Attorney General Sir Nicholas Lyell led to demands for their resignations. The government, in the event, survived by 320-319 votes in a debate on the report on 26 February.

The already stalled Ireland peace process suffered a further setback when the IRA ended its ceasefire on 9 February, exploding a bomb in London Docklands which killed two people. The Irish premier, John Bruton, appeared on 13 February to soften his objections to Mr Major's proposal for elections in Northern Ireland to resolve the impasse over IRA arms decommissioning. The IRA mounted a further terrorist attack in London three days later, killing three people. Mr Major declared that he intended to continue with the peace process. On 28 February both he and Mr Bruton met Sinn Fein's demand for a firm date for all-party talks. The date was set for 10 June and talks would follow elections to be held in Northern Ireland. There were reports of significant divisions within the IRA over the wisdom of renewing violence. At Sinn Fein's conference on 23 March, the party's leader Gerry Adams, said that Sinn Fein would participate in the elections. There were, however, criticisms from possible participants over the form the elections were to take.

Divisions within the Conservative Party over Europe showed no signs of abating as the March Inter-Governmental Conference (IGC) on the reform of the European Union approached. On 14 February Eurosceptics pressed Mr Major to argue for an enlarged but less centralised European Union. Meanwhile, Conservative members of the European Movement urged support for the principle of moves towards a single currency and a modification of Britain's veto powers. The government issued a White Paper on 12 March setting out its approach to the IGC. The paper called for curbs on the authority of the European Court of Justice (which had made a number of decisions embarrassing to the government) and the retention of national sovereignty in foreign, defence and immigration policies. It rejected moves towards ending the national veto on European policy-making. A debate on the White Paper on 21 March served only to confirm the depth of division within the party. Mr Benn, however, pointed out that it would be misleading to suggest that the Labour Party was not equally divided.

Whichever party formed a government after the election faced protracted and difficult negotiations at the IGC which opened in Turin on 29 March. The enlargement of the European Union by entry of the former Communist countries of Eastern and Central Europe raised many questions about the functioning of the EU's basic institutions. Developing democracy within the EU demanded more power for the European Parliament, with an inevitable weakening of national parliaments. There were important questions to be answered about a common European foreign and defence policy and about common policies to solve the problem of the 20 million unemployed.

A Vulnerable Government.

Following the loss to Labour of the Staffordshire South-East by-election on 11 April, the government's majority was reduced to 1. Widespread losses in the May local elections confirmed the government's unpopularity. It now faced a difficult road to recovery. Dissension over Britain's relations with the European Union—and more particularly moves towards a single currency—continued to dominate Mr Major's increasingly vulnerable government. The Labour Party, though apparently more committed to co-operation with Europe than the Conservatives, preserved its unity by avoiding detailed public discussion of the wider issues. On 11 June 74 Conservative backbenchers supported a bill introduced by Tory Eurosceptic MP Bill Cash calling for an early referendum on the government's European policy. Revelations that Mr Cash's European Foundation had received donations from not only Sir James Goldsmith (founder in October 1995 of the Referendum Party) but also from Baroness Thatcher, led Mr Major to express his anger at the debilitating effect of inner-party wrangling. Goldsmith's intention to field candidates in the coming general election threatened up to 20 Conservative seats. The depth of division became starker when, on 23 July, a junior Treasury minister resigned, complaining about what he called a "relentless" drive towards political union with Europe.

The New Labour Agenda.

Labour announced revised plans on 26 June for Scottish and Welsh devolution, a central part of proposed constitutional change. Both Wales and Scotland were promised a referendum on the issue within six months of a Labour government coming to office. A new departure was that Scotland would be asked to decide whether its assembly should have tax-raising powers. This change led to the resignation of Labour's Scottish affairs spokesman. The government took the announcement as an opportunity to present Labour policy as a threat to the union. In July, Mr Blair toured Britain to win party support for the "Road to the Manifesto". He denied criticisms of a lack of radicalism in the party's programme, declaring that Labour took a path "between and ahead of the old left and the new right." The word "new" appeared 107 times in the draft, the word "socialism" only once. The party leadership faced complaints in August about the allegedly excessive influence in policymaking of what had come to be known as "spin doctors".

Further evidence of the remodelling of New Labour came at the Blackpool TUC conference in September, with senior Labour figures eager to demonstrate the distance between the party and the trades unions. A junior opposition employment spokesman suggested that a post-election Labour Party would sever links with its industrial wing.

Continuing Government Difficulties.

What had become known as the "sleaze factor" continued to undermine the government's position. On 14 October the House of Commons Standards and Privileges Committee opened its enquiry into "cash for questions" allegations against Tory former junior minister Neil Hamilton. Later charges against a junior minister that he had attempted to exert undue influence on how the allegations were to be dealt with forced his resignation. In June the ninth junior minister since 1992 had been forced to resign following allegations about his private life.

There was increasing disappointment—and bitter mutual recrimination—over what had initially been seen as a step towards a settlement in Northern Ireland. All-party negotiations opened at Stormont on 10 June, with representatives from the British and Irish governments and nine of the ten groups elected to the 110 member Constitutional Forum in May. Sinn Fein was excluded because of the failure of the Irish Republican Army (IRA) to renew the ceasefire. Discussion soon degenerated into procedural arguments. Sinn Fein boycotted the first meeting of the Constitutional Forum on 14 June and on the following day the IRA exploded two bombs in Manchester, injuring over 200 people and causing an estimated £1 billion damage. There were renewed sectarian clashes in Northern Ireland as Protestants mounted traditional marches over the summer. The IRA carried out its first major terrorist operation in Northern Ireland on 7 October, exploding two bombs at the British Army headquarters. The attack prompted fears that loyalist paramilitaries would break their two year ceasefire.

Pre-Election Tactics.

Through the autumn and winter, government and opposition manoeuvred to take the high ground on education and law and order, with shadow home affairs minister Mr Straw determined not to be exposed as weak on crime by Michael Howard. It was clear, however, that the Tories intended to base their appeal on the strength of the economy (which, to their disappointment, delivered no opinion poll dividends) and on Labour's past record and present inexperience. Mr Clarke's budget on 26 November provided little comfort to the Conservatives. Within an overall £1·9 billion public spending reduction, Mr Clarke increased provision for health and education but targeted social security – and lone parents in particular – for savings. He reduced basic rate income tax to 23%, with balancing increases in indirect taxation.

Draft Labour Manifesto.

Labour's draft manifesto, *New Labour, New Britain*, was overwhelmingly endorsed by the party membership on 4 December. There were, however, complaints from some members of the "take it or leave it" nature of the leadership's consultation. Labour easily held Barnsley East in a by-election on 12 December as the Liberal Democrats pushed the Tory candidate into third place. Mr Major – once again leading a minority administration – warned Eurosceptics that challenging his "wait and see" policy over the single currency (by now a code for European integration) could provoke the party's worst split for a century and usher in a Labour government. As the New Year opened, Mr Major attempted to bridge party divisions by declaring it was unlikely that Britain's European partners would launch the single currency as planned on 1 January 1999. If they did, Britain would remain outside unless there had been genuine economic convergence.

Mr Blair concentrated his attention on defusing Conservative charges that New Labour contained an old Labour core. On 29 December he rejected the corporatism implicit in a senior union leader's call for a "social partnership" between government, employers and the TUC. A week later he advocated "zero tolerance" of crime, further hardening Labour's law and order stance. But the most decisive move came from shadow chancellor Gordon Brown on 20 January, the culmination of Labour's project to counter Conservative "tax and spend" attacks. A Labour government, he said, would not increase income tax rates and would commit itself to Mr Clarke's spending plans for the first two years of a new administration.

The Vote of Confidence.

As scares over food safety continued, the government survived a vote on the issue on 17 February. Abstention by the Ulster Unionists gave the government a majority. But Mr Major's attempts to hold his party together were weakened by the support former Tory prime minister Edward Heath gave to Labour positions on devolution, the Social Chapter and the minimum wage on 23 February. Tensions within the Cabinet were revealed by foreign secretary Malcolm Rifkind's declaration that the government was "hostile" to monetary union and Health Secretary Stephen Dorrell's statement – hurriedly withdrawn – that Britain would not join the single currency on 1 January 1999. A further blow came with the defection of Sir George Gardiner, a deselected backbencher, to the Referendum Party.

The government's fate appeared settled by a 17·2% swing to Labour in the Wirral South by-election on 27 February. No government had ever recovered from a defeat of this magnitude so close to a general election.

The Election Campaign.

Mr Major announced a 1 May election on 17 March. Rarely had Labour entered a contest so apparently united, and never had the Conservatives been so clearly divided. A largely uneventful and uninspiring campaign culminated in one of the most dramatic results of any 20th century general election. Denied the opportunity to attack Labour with the "tax and spend" charges of 1992, the Conservatives were weakened by critical in-fighting over Europe and seemed incapable of turning Britain's relatively strong economic position to their advantage. For almost two weeks the campaign effectively slipped from the Conservatives' grasp as the "sleaze" issue dominated media coverage. Labour—wary of losing a commanding lead in the opinion polls—fought a tightly disciplined and controlled battle. The Liberal Democrats effectively seized the ground between a cautious Labour Party and the divided Conservatives, concentrating their efforts in 50 key constituencies.

The Outcome.

The result was a catastrophe for the Conservatives and a triumph for Labour with an overall swing of 10%. Mr Blair became prime minister with a landslide 179 seat majority, a record in the party's history, greater even than in 1945. The Liberal Democrat performance, putting Mr

Ashdown at the head of the largest third party presence since 1929, was almost as significant. Tactical voting played a crucial part in the Conservatives' defeat. But with 71 % of the electorate voting there was a 7 % fall in turnout compared with 1992. The final results were as follows:

Votes

Lab	Cons	Lib Dem	Nats/Others
43·1 %	30·6 %	16·7 %	9·6 %

Seats

Lab	Cons	Lib Dem	Nats/Others
418	165	46	30

The Scale of Labour's Victory.

Labour succeeded not only in regaining support lost since 1979 in the South and Midlands but also in occupying hitherto safe Conservative territory. The result represented the Conservatives' lowest share of the vote since 1832. So extensive was the Conservative defeat that the party emerged with no MPs in Scotland and Wales and lost its last remaining strongholds in the English cities. Among the leading Conservative casualties were Michael Portillo, Malcolm Rifkind, Michael Forsyth, Roger Freeman, Tony Newton and William Waldegrave (all ejected by Labour) and Ian Lang (who fell to the SNP). Former Chancellor Norman Lamont was removed by a Liberal Democrat while Labour ousted David Mellor, 1922 Committee chairman Sir Marcus Fox and Edwina Currie.

A notable feature of the new House of Commons is the increased presence of women, with a doubling in their numbers from 60 to 120, 101 of whom are Labour MPs. The ethnic minority presence increased marginally. Among the smaller parties, the SNP increased its tally to six MPs (although its vote hardly shifted), while Plaid Cymru remained at four. In Northern Ireland, Sinn Fein won two seats, threatening the SDLP's position as the leading nationalist party. The Referendum Party lost most of its deposits but was credited with assisting in the removal of a number of Conservatives. A remarkable result was the ejection of the Conservative Neil Hamilton by Martin Bell, a television reporter standing as an Independent.

The Blair Administration.

Mr Blair's initial appointments to the new government were predictable, with John Prescott becoming deputy prime minister (with responsibility for transport, the environment and the regions) while Gordon Brown was given the Treasury. Robin Cook was appointed Foreign Secretary, Jack Straw took the Home Office, David Blunkett was given responsibility for education and employment and Lord Irvine became Lord Chancellor. Margaret Beckett, the only appointee with previous ministerial experience, was appointed President of the Board of Trade. Marjorie Mowlam was given the Northern Ireland Office, Donald Dewar the Scottish Office, while Harriet Harman went to Social Security.

Conceding that 18 years of Conservative government had ended, Mr Major announced on 2 May his intention of resigning the party leadership, opening up the certainty of further debilitating divisions in his party over the succession.

Labour in Power: The First Months.

Britain's first Labour government for 18 years began with an unexpected move on 6 May as the Chancellor gave up his power to set interest rates, handing operational control over monetary policy to the Bank of England. Less surprising, but nonetheless a sign of the changed atmosphere—and a transformed attitude towards co-operation with Europe (Mr Blair was soon to speak of his ambitions for a "People's Europe")—was the announcement by the Foreign Secretary, Mr Cook, that Britain would sign up to the European social chapter on employees' rights. Mr Cook promised, too, an "ethical dimension" to Britain's conduct of foreign policy. A small but symbolic mark of a new beginning came on 16 May with the restoration of rights of trade union membership at the Government Communication Headquarters.

The Queen's Speech on 14 May stuck closely to Labour's election manifesto, with proposals for 26 Bills including legislation on raising educational standards and reducing class sizes, establishing a Low Pay Commission to recommend a minimum wage figure, abolishing the NHS internal market, taking sterner measures against youth crime and banning the private possession of all handguns. The government also set out its plans for referenda on devolved assemblies in Scotland and Wales and a new strategic authority for London (see **D21–2**).

Conservative Leadership Contest.

The Conservatives, still in shock from the extent of their defeat, passed over the figures from the past (including former Chancellor Kenneth Clarke, whom Labour could thank for a relatively healthy economy) in selecting their new leader, but clung to an ideology that pre-dated Mr Major. William Hague, who defeated Mr Clarke by 92 votes to 70 on a third ballot on 19 June, was, at 36, the party's youngest leader for 200 years. Mr Hague came from the party's Eurosceptic Thatcherite wing and his Shadow Cabinet appointments—Mr Lilley as Shadow Chancellor, Mr Howard at foreign affairs, and Mr Redwood shadowing Trade and Industry—consolidated the right's grip. However, Mr Clarke's refusal to accept a post highlighted divisions, particularly over Europe.

The Liberal Democrats, numerically at their strongest in Parliament for over 70 years, appeared to find it difficult to know how to best wield their strength. On 22 July Mr Blair invited their leader, Mr Ashdown, and four senior colleagues to join a Cabinet committee to discuss constitutional and electoral reform "and other mutual interests". Both denied this represented a return to the Lib-Lab Pact of the 1970s and, clearly, Mr Blair needed no such support. Mr Ashdown declared that his party would continue to press its views on taxation and public spending, areas in which policy differed radically from that of the government. But what remained of Labour's left expressed concern that while Liberal Democrat co-operation was welcome, the trade unions and the wider party were being, in their view, ostentatiously marginalised.

The July 1997 Budget.

In the election campaign Labour had promised to maintain the Conservative government's overall spending totals and not to increase direct taxation. Mr Brown's July budget—"a people's budget for Britain's future"—found some room for extra spending on education and health, and imposed a £5·2 billion "windfall" tax on the privatised utilities to fund employment and training for young people, the long-term unemployed and lone parents. Corporation tax was reduced by 2 % and VAT on domestic fuel cut from 8 % to 5 %. The budget was broadly welcomed but the announcement on 23 July that the student maintenance grant was to be abolished and that students in higher education were to pay tuition fees—effectively ending universal free full-time higher education—caused disquiet.

The Northern Ireland Question.

Within days of taking office Mr Blair and the Northern Ireland Secretary, Dr Mowlam, sought to break the deadlock in the Irish peace process by re-opening official meetings with Sinn Fein. On 25 June Mr Blair announced that full negotiations between all parties to the process would begin in September, reach a conclusion in May 1998 and that proposals would then be put to a referendum. Sinn Fein could participate if it committed itself to the principle of non-violence. On 19 July the IRA announced an "unequivocal restoration" of the ceasefire abandoned in February 1996. Mr Blair surmounted the arms decommissioning issue, which had been partly responsible for the stall in the process, by accepting that the IRA would relinquish its weapons during rather than before negotiations. As planned, talks opened in September, and full-scale negotiations including Republican and Loyalist representatives, began in October. There was a private, but symbolically significant, handshake at Stormont between Mr Blair and Sinn Fein's Gerry Adams. Despite a spate of sectarian murders over the winter of 1997–98 following the killing of a Loyalist terrorist in the Maze Prison, what appeared to be a genuine desire for peace allowed negotiations to continue. For the Good Friday Agreement of April 1998, see **D21–2**.

The Death of Princess Diana.

Mr Blair's sure touch, and feeling for the public mood, was in evidence following the death of Diana, Princess of Wales, and her companion in a car accident in Paris on 31 August. What one commentator described as a "carnival of grief" in Britain between her death and burial brought the long-running crisis of the monarchy to a head. There was criticism of the Royal Family's response. The Queen, for example, made no statement of any kind for a week. Mr Blair seized the opportunity, dubbed Diana "The People's Princess" and reputedly encouraged the Royal Family to open up to popular feeling.

The End of Labour's Honeymoon?

Labour now encountered a period of awkwardness, one that suggested the talents of its media manipulators, so impressive in opposing the Conservative government, were less effective when Labour itself was in office. When Mr Blair was on holiday in the summer, there was an almost open jockeying for position between his deputy, Mr Prescott, and the manipulator-in-chief, Minister without Portfolio Mr Mandelson. In October confusion over Labour's position on entry to European monetary union was compounded by over-enthusiastic "spin doctors" operating on behalf of the Chancellor. At the autumn conference Mr Blair was given a small warning about the pace of change in the party when left-winger Mr Ken Livingstone was elected to the National Executive Committee and Mr Mandelson failed to gain a place. In November Labour's credibility was seriously damaged by the government's decision to seek exemption for Formula One motor racing from a European ban on tobacco advertising in sport. A suspicion was raised that a million pound donation to party funds had bought, if not influence, then at least access to influence. In December a significant section of the Parliamentary party revolted over benefits reductions and within days a Treasury minister—responsible for taxation—was found to be the beneficiary of a multi-million pound offshore trust fund.

The Government and Europe.

After successfully surmounting the hurdles of the Scottish and Welsh devolution referenda in September (both Wales and Scotland voted in favour, *see* **D21**), the government finally clarified its position on European monetary union at the end of October. Britain would join eventually, but not before the end of the current Parliament in 2002, and then only if certain criteria were met and entry was approved in a referendum. Britain would, however, take steps to prepare for entry. The Conservative leadership hardened Mr Major's "wait and see" approach, committing itself to campaign against entry in the next general election and possibly beyond. Serious divisions now became apparent. The pro-Europeans lined up behind Mr Clarke and Mr Heseltine, the former deputy prime minister. Mr Clarke spoke of the possibility of a cross-party alliance in favour of monetary union and in January 1998 he, Mr Heseltine and Lord Howe warned Mr Hague of the dangers involved in further concessions to the party's Eurosceptics.

The Welfare State Debate.

Mr Brown's November financial statement unveiled a plan for the most drastic reform of the Welfare State since its inception. This lay at the centre of the government's policy but also threatened to provoke serious dissent in the party. Ministers denied reform was "Treasury led" but there could be no denying that the prime objective was to reduce a bill that now approached £100 billion annually. On 10 December 47 Labour MPs defied a three-line whip and 14 abstained to show their disapproval of a reduction in lone parent benefits. Others voted with reluctance for what had been a Conservative proposal that Labour in opposition had condemned. The responsible minister, Ms Harriet Harman, emerged from the events significantly weakened. There was further discontent when plans to curb disability benefits were leaked. Mr Blair warned that the future would bring greater demands for discipline and unity in the party. He also announced that he would chair a new ministerial group on welfare reform and that a Social Exclusion Unit was being established to oversee policy aimed at disadvantaged groups. In January 1998 the government began piloting its promised "Welfare to work" scheme in which the young and long-term unemployed would be required to choose between a subsidised private sector job, voluntary work or education and training. The aim, Mr Brown said, was to eliminate unemployment in the 21st century, though he could not say how far below the present 5% it would fall.

The New Conservatives?

Mr Hague, meanwhile, continued his task of reinventing the Conservatives, one he had begun at the 1997 conference. In February 1998 he presented a document entitled *The Fresh Future* which proposed the most drastic internal party reforms for over a century. Party leaders were to be elected by one member-one vote, though MPs would retain the power of removing leaders and would select leadership candidates. There was to be a drive to recruit a million new members (particularly young members), an enlargement of party democracy, and greater openness on funding (with a ban on foreign donations). These reforms were duly approved in March 1998.

The March 1998 Budget.

Mr Brown's March 1998 budget increased child benefit, proposed tax credits to improve the incomes of working families and disabled people, and gave an extra £500 million to health, a similar sum to public transport, and £250 million for education. The pattern continued with his three-year Comprehensive Spending Review in July.

In July the government became embroiled in a 'cash for access' scandal, with allegations that lobbyists linked to senior figures in the Labour Party were securing preferential access to ministers. The Cabinet Office warded off threats to the government's reputation by issuing a new code of conduct.

July also saw Mr Blair's first Cabinet reshuffle. Harriet Harman—with the benefits review stalled—was replaced at Social Security by Alistair Darling. Mr Mandelson took over Trade and Industry. Margaret Beckett became Leader of the House and Ann Taylor was moved to Chief Whip. Chancellor of the Duchy of Lancaster David Clark gave way to Jack Cunningham, with the unofficial title of 'Cabinet enforcer'.

There was a mild tremor for the leadership in September when the leftish 'Grassroots Alliance' captured four of the six places in a ballot for the constituency section of the National Executive Committee (NEC). However, loyalists swept the board in elections to the MP and MEP section, with veteran Dennis Skinner losing his place amidst allegations of Millbank interference and intimidation. Mr Blair denied in his party conference speech that the government were simply moderate Tories, acknowledging a growing sense of disappointment among some supporters.

Cracks in the Labour Image.

Further fractures began to appear in the government's facade from the autumn. As lists of job losses grew and growth forecasts were reduced from 2% to 1%, Mr Brown insisted his strategy was working and denied Conservative charges of a £36 billion 'black hole' in the government's spending plans. But October showed manufacturing output falling and the Chancellor—having relinquished control over interest rates—could only hint that he hoped the Bank of England would soften its position. In his annual pre-budget report in November, Mr Brown denied Britain was being drawn into a deepening world recession.

Having rejected the invitation to become a founder member of the single European currency in January 1999, Mr Blair faced charges that Britain was marginalising itself. At an informal summit of European leaders at the end of October he attempted to ward this off by committing Britain to deeper integration, urging common defence and foreign policies and a closer co-ordination of economic and employment policies. But with the electorate still wary of the European adventure, he was later to attack a move towards integrated tax policies.

On 27 October Welsh Secretary Ron Davies

resigned following a mugging incident about which he could give only a garbled and contradictory explanation. What appeared to be a sexual element led to the conclusion that Labour was as prone to bizarre scandal as the Conservatives. Mr Davies was replaced by the unexciting but loyal Alun Michael.

The next stage of the Labour crisis came in November when Mr Blair and Liberal Democrat leader Mr Ashdown announced an extension in cross-party co-operation. Their intention, they said, was to end the 'destructive tribalism' of British politics. The inference drawn by many Labour and Liberal MPs—to whom the announcement came as a surprise—was that a coalition or even merger was being contemplated. The deputy Labour leader, Mr Prescott, was reportedly furious at Mr Blair's failure to consult him. Mr Blair made his ambitions more explicit in a speech on 15 December. Labour was to become like the Gladstonian Liberals—a 'broad coalition of those who believe in progress and justice'.

The Queen's Speech on 24 November revealed few surprises: reforms of the House of Lords, the legal aid system and disability benefits; a bill to extend trade union rights, the establishment of an author-ity for London, and proportional representation for the 1999 European Parliamentary elections. What was missing was the long-promised Freedom of Information Bill. (For progress on constitutional reform, see **Special Topic D21–2**).

The Mandelson Resignation.

The crisis entered its final stage on 23 December with the resignation of Mr Mandelson after only 150 days in the Cabinet. He was revealed to have been the beneficiary of a £373,000 loan from Paymaster General Geoffrey Robinson while in opposition to enable him to buy a house way out of the reach of a backbench MP. Mr Robinson—already harried by the Conservatives for allegedly using offshore accounts to avoid tax—resigned shortly after. The loss of Mr Mandelson—Mr Blair's ally in refashion-ing the party—appeared to put the whole project at risk. Rumours that Mr Mandelson's Cabinet rivals had leaked the information—Mr Brown's press sec-retary resigned in January 1999—suggested a gov-ernment riven by ambitious jealousies. Mr Prescott took the opportunity at the end of the month to make a coded call to move away from spin to substance.

Although the December events had no impact on Labour's lead in the polls, January 1999 saw a relaunch with co-ordinated ministerial appearances attempting to renew the government's appeal to Middle England. But there was some slight redress-ing of the past. On 25 January the Commons voted 313–130 to lower the age of gay consent to 16. The Employment Relations Bill introduced on 28 January promised to ease union recognition and to increase compensation for unfair dismissal.

Problems for Hague.

It was perhaps inevitable—given Mr Blair's success at being all things to all voters—that Mr Hague should find difficulty in shaking off charges that his party was irrelevant. Over Europe, the Conservatives presented a picture of total disarray. Mr Hague attempted to assert his Eurosceptic stance by reach-ing over the heads of the divided Parliamentary party to the (increasingly elderly) grassroots. He was rewarded on the eve of the party conference in October 1998 with a predictable 84·4 % support on 58·9 % turnout. But the defection of a Conservative MEP to the Liberal Democrats was followed by hints from pro-Europeans grouped around Michael Heseltine, Kenneth Clarke and Chris Patten that there was always the possibility of establishing a breakaway party.

There were also threats from the right. Mr Hague's conference speech on the 'British Way' was seen as an attempt to counter a future leadership challenge from Michael Portillo. In November Mr Portillo—out of the Commons since May 1997 but positioning himself for a return—launched a thinly camouflaged attack on Mr Hague's leadership in the *Daily Telegraph*.

November revealed the gulf between business and the party as the Confederation of British Industry contradicted Conservative attacks on the govern-ment's economic stance and supported Labour spending plans. Mr Hague's dismissal of the party's leader in the House of Lords in December for a com-promise deal with the government over reform of the upper house, while justified, showed a certain

unsureness of touch. Mr Hague's supporters claimed that his firmness against the party's traditional elite demonstrated his credentials as a modernising leader. A speech in which Mr Hague called for a 'huge cultural change' among Conservatives—followed by a flight in February to the United States to learn lessons from the Republicans—highlighted the obstacles he faced in presenting his party as an alternative to an all-embracing New Labour.

The End of the Ashdown Era.

For the Liberal Democrats, there were increasing strains over Mr Ashdown's 'constructive opposition' and—though he denied it—these were at least in part the reason for the sudden announcement of his resignation as leader in January 1999. The Liberal conference in September 1998 demonstrated the dif-ficulties Mr Ashdown faced leading a party in which some members felt he was too timid in pushing for redistribution. The conference voted in favour of taxing child benefit for the better off, 50 % taxation on incomes over £100,000, and a full minimum wage at 16 rather than 21.

Following party criticisms over his November agreement with Mr Blair on cross-party co-operation, Mr Ashdown suffered a humiliating 2–1 defeat at the hands of his parliamentary colleagues on the issue of support for the Queen's Speech. Admitting there was plotting to depose him, he hinted at a ballot to test support for his co-operation with Labour. But on 20 January 1999 Mr Ashdown stunned his party by announcing his intention to stand down as leader following the spring local and European Parliamentary elections.

The Lawrence Report.

The most significant examination of race relations in Britain since the 1980s—Sir William Macpherson's report into police failures over the racist murder in 1993 of Stephen Lawrence—was published on 24 February. Sir William criticised the Metropolitan Police's investigation into the murder for revealing 'professional incompetence, institutional racism and a failure of leadership by senior officers.' He made over 70 recommendations on confronting police racism but it was widely acknowledged that the problem was not confined to this one public body. The government's dilemma, as far as the immediate issue was concerned, was how to satisfy ethnic minority hopes that the report marked a turning point while at the same time preventing a backlash from an embittered police service.

War in the Balkans.

Mr Blair took Britain a step closer to membership of the European single currency with a statement to the Commons on 23 February and opened the way to a cross-party alliance of supporters which, with the obvious inclusion of Mr Clarke and Mr Heseltine, threatened to intensify tensions within the Conservatives. The preparations set in train by Mr Blair, his critics claimed, made membership almost a foregone conclusion, despite the require-ment for popular ratification by referendum. The whole question of the EU, however, was put into the melting pot with the crisis following the resigna-tion *en bloc* of the EU Commissioners (*see* **C67**). This, in turn, was overshadowed by the outbreak of war in the Balkans over the Kosovo question (*see* **C68**).

Historic Election Outcome.

Voting took place on 6 May 1999 for elections to the first Scottish Parliament since 1707, the new Welsh Assembly and for around 13,000 local councillors. Labour emerged as easily the largest party in the Scottish Parliament (*see* **D13**) but, short of an overall majority. The Nationalists were somewhat disap-pointed. A deal between Labour and the Liberal Democrats seemed likely. In Wales, Labour took 28 of the 60 seats in the Assembly, with Plaid Cymru polling well above the expectation of many analysts.

In the local council elections, Labour lost some ground from its high-point of 1995 and the Conservatives made a limited recovery (giving, it seemed, some temporary much-needed relief to Mr Hague's embattled leadership). The Liberal Democrats lost seats to the Conservatives (mainly in the South) but made inroads from Labour in parts of the North. *See also* **D13**.

II. THE CHANGING WORLD SCENE

WESTERN EUROPE

FRANCE.

The presidential elections of May 1988 brought to an end two years of "cohabitation' between the Socialist President, Francois Mitterrand and the neo-Gaullist Prime Minister, Jacques Chirac. Of the nine candidates who stood in the first round on 24 April only the two best-placed candidates, Mitterrand and Chirac, went through to the run-off ballot a fortnight later. In this second poll the outgoing Socialist President defeated his right-wing rival by 54·02 to 45·98 per cent of the votes cast thereby becoming the first French President to be re-elected for a second seven year term of office by popular vote. Mitterrand's re-election was not a decisive victory for socialism. His election programme contained few left-wing proposals; his success reflected his ability to attract centrist votes. This fact, together with the continued decline of the Communist Party vote and the impressive performance of the neo-fascist candidate, Jean-Marie Le Pen confirmed the extent to which French politics had shifted to the Right since 1981.

A Woman Prime Minister.

The difficulties facing Mitterrand after his 1988 victory soon mounted. Indeed, the resignation of Prime Minister Michel Rocard in May 1991 and his replacement by Edith Cresson presaged a year of extreme difficulty for President Mitterrand and for the government. Between the time of her appointment and the regional elections of March 1992, politics were notable primarily for the weakness of the government, for the disruptive effects of the issue of immigration upon the public agenda and the extraordinary erosion in support for the Socialist Party. In times of economic prosperity, the impact of immigration as an issue would be slight but in circumstances of persistently high unemployment, its salience is higher and its significance altogether greater. Support for the National Front as measured by opinion polls was at 15 % in early 1992, but support for the Front's policy on immigration is twice as great. The significance of this difference was not lost on politicians in other parties: Jacques Chirac and Giscard d'Estaing have both attempted to woo those who favour stricter limits on immigration with thinly disguised appeals to racial prejudice.

Background to Electoral Disaster.

A hint of the electoral disaster which awaited the Socialist Party in the Spring regional elections was apparent in a by-election near Lille on 26 January 1992: having polled 31 % in the first round of voting there in the general election in 1988, the Socialist candidate took a mere 13 % in 1992. Faced with parliamentary elections in 1993, the pressure upon Mitterrand to revive both his own and his party's prospects was great.

Regional elections held on 22 March, and cantonal polls on 29 March, resulted in heavy defeats for the ruling Socialist Party. Faced with a deepening of the government's unpopularity, President Mitterrand replaced Edith Cresson with Pierre Bérégovoy, who had held the post of Finance Minister since 1984.

Difficulties of Bérégovoy.

France's establishment of credibility for its policy of a strong Franc within the Exchange Rate Mechanism (ERM) came under fierce pressure in 1992 and early 1993. The primary cause of the difficulty was the policy of the Bundesbank to keep German interest rates high in order to choke off German inflation. Since the franc was linked to the Deutschmark within the ERM, the French government was obliged to maintain French interest rates at much higher levels than were consistent with the need to stimulate French domestic demand. President Mitterrand's popularity suffered as unemployment rose relentlessly, and the Socialist government

of M. Bérégovoy slid towards defeat in the parliamentary elections of March 1993.

The right-wing RPR of Jacques Chirac, and the centre-right UDF of Giscard d'Estaing, fought the legislative elections under the allied banner of the Union for France (UPF). The alliance declared that a new government of the right would seek to reduce unemployment by stimulating economic growth, extend the privatisation programme begun under Chirac's Prime Ministership between 1986 and 1988 to the remainder of the large state-run enterprises, create an independent Bank of France, and persist with a broadly pro-European policy.

Landslide for the Right.

The elections resulted in a landslide victory for the right-wing coalition, the crushing of the Socialist Party and its allies, the resistance of the Communist Party to final elimination, and the failure of the two Ecologist parties and the National Front to gain any seats in the Assembly. The final results were as follows:

Party	Percentage of National Vote	Seats
RPR	28·27	247
UDF	25·84	213
FN (National Front)	5·66	—
Other right-wing parties	3·56	24
Radical Left ⎱	3·32	6
Other left-wing parties ⎰		10
Socialists	28·25	54
Communists	4·61	23

The result marked a complete transformation from the old party balance in the Assembly where the left had enjoyed a slender majority in coalition with their allies, and the Communists. Legislatively and politically devastated, the Socialists were now too marginal to pose any significant threat to the huge right-wing majority.

Although it was organised as a single party, divisions on monetary and European policies within the RPR were apparent even in the flush of election victory, fuelled by the contending ambitions of senior figures within it. A federation of five parties, the UDF was even less cohesive: two of its constituent parts (the Republican Party, and the CDS) enjoyed considerable autonomy in the Assembly between 1988 and 1993 and might now be tempted to break away from the UDF entirely not least because it would take little for opposition within the UDF to Giscard's leadership to break through the surface. Imposing discipline upon such an unwieldy and unstable base as the RPR and UDF now presented in the Assembly would be exceptionally difficult.

Balladur as Prime Minister.

Nevertheless, there was for Mitterrand little prospect that his sytematic outmanoeuvring of the RPR Prime Minister Jacques Chirac under the earlier cohabitation between 1986 and 1988 would be repeated with Edouard Balladur in the remaining two years of his Presidency. Their internal fissures notwithstanding, the position of the two large right-wing parties was altogether stronger than it was then, and Mitterrand himself would not be a candidate for re-election in 1995. Moreover, Michel Rocard, the politician regarded as the Socialists' likeliest candidate in 1995, was defeated in his attempt to retain his seat in the Assembly; his Presidential prospects were, accordingly, damaged and those of his rivals, Jacques Delors and Laurent Fabius, somewhat enhanced. Having chosen to stay out of the government and to remain as Mayor of Paris, Jacques Chirac presented a powerful obstacle to the ambitions of any and all candidates on the left. Their party, created by Francois Mitterrand in 1971, was now demoralised and discredited, and the centre of French partisan gravity had shifted.

The 1995 Election Background.

High unemployment, pervasive political corruption, and Mitterrand's distinctive variant upon General de Gaulle's theme of *grandeur*, realised in the building of hugely expensive public monuments in Paris, dominated the campaign for the 1995 election.

Having begun 1995 trailing Prime Minister Edouard Balladur by a significant margin in the opinion polls, Jacques Chirac recovered, partly by reason of the Prime Minister's errors of judgement, to a point where, by mid-April, he enjoyed a clear lead. Not only did his victory in the first round over Balladur, and the Socialist candidate, Lionel Jospin, seem assured, but all polls also gave Chirac a majority in the second round. Chirac's strength derived from his authority over the Gaullist RPR, and his success in establishing a distinctive image. In contrast to Balladur, whose chilly aloofness made political recovery yet more difficult, Chirac gave every indication of relishing the campaign. Balladur gave the appearance of accepting the inevitability of high unemployment; Chirac, reviving old Gaullist memories of the activist and interventionist state, did not.

Chirac versus Balladur.

In fact, neither Chirac nor Balladur nor even Jospin provided any clear policy for reducing unemployment, restoring some measure of social cohesion to a divided France or of public faith in the democratic legitimacy of political institutions. Nor would a President Chirac or Balladur, both quintessential members of the Fifth Republic's governing elite, be likely fundamentally to wish to occupy an office whose grandeur was conspicuously diminished. The reason for the weakness of political debate lay partly in the substantive difficulty of the questions involved, but partly also in the lines of fracture which lay just beneath the surface both of Chirac's and of Balladur's support: Chirac's coalition among the political elite extended to free-market neo-liberals, old-style Gaullists of a newly-hostile anti-European kind, and social conservatives. His own platform, notably that on Europe, reflected the tensions which this variegated coalition implied: on the one hand, he committed himself to implementation of European Monetary Union whilst on the other declining to give a date by which such union might be achieved. His insistence upon the primacy of the Franco-German axis in foreign and monetary policy was, similarly, in tension not only with his quasi-Gaullist insistence upon the nation-state as the building-block of an expanded European Union, but also with laxer fiscal and more generous welfare policies than Balladur's.

Outcome of the First Round.

The first round of voting surprised observers, and confounded all pollsters, by giving Lionel Jospin a plurality victory over Chirac, and pushing Balladur to third place, as the table shows.

Candidate	Party	Votes (mill.)	%
Jospin	Socialist	7·10	23·3
Chirac	RPR	6·35	20·8
Balladur	RPR	5·66	18·6
Le Pen	National Front	4·57	15·0
Hue	Communist	2·63	8·6
Laguiller	Trotskyist	1·62	5·3
de Villiers	Movement for France	1·44	4·7
Voynet	Greens	1·01	3·3
Cheminade	New Solidarity	0·09	0·3

Jospin and Chirac each entered the second round with the customary task of expanding their small plurality coalitions into winning majority ones, and faced unusual difficulties in doing so. The pattern of the vote revealed unusually complicated political divisions: indeed, the proportion of the first-round vote won by the two leading candidates was the smallest in the history of the Fifth Republic. Whilst the combined right-wing vote of 60% presented Jospin with a more difficult task than Chirac of coalition-building, Le Pen's heavy support gave the extreme right leverage over Chirac which gave him little freedom of manoeuvre in making his political calculations.

Narrow Chirac Victory.

In the event, after a lacklustre campaign in which Jospin emerged as a strong challenger, Chirac won a narrow victory by 52% to 48%, becoming the fifth president of the Fifth Republic. On his third attempt, he had secured the presidency. However, his numerous electoral pledges, during the campaign, on unemployment and social affairs, together with his somewhat Byzantine policy statements on Europe, all suggested his presidency might be a difficult one.

Chirac in Power.

Chirac's first six months in office proved turbulent. Firstly, to the intense and public opposition of many traditional Asian and Pacific allies, he ordered the resumption of French nuclear testing in the Pacific from 1 October. Secondly, Prime Minister Juppé became entangled in a minor corruption scandal following an opinion delivered by the Central Corruption Prevention Service that he acted illegally when Assistant Mayor of Paris in letting an apartment owned by the city to his son at a rent below the market rate. Thirdly, Juppé's extraordinarily early reshuffle of his government in November 1995, forced by a combination of ministerial incompetence and the rapid fall both of his own and of the President's popularity, proved insufficient to avert an acute bout of industrial action by public sector workers which drew considerable public sympathy. Union discontent was kindled by Chirac's abandonment of reflation (which he had trumpeted during the May election campaign as a means of alleviating high unemployment) and his embrace of economic austerity in order to reduce the fiscal deficit by two percentage points so that France might meet the criteria for monetary union. In the short-term, the strikes cut industrial production and increased international pressure on the French currency. Since consumer spending had already weakened following increases in taxation of Fr45 billion announced by the government in its June budget, anxiety both about the government's capacity to sustain growth (and, hence, its own revenue) and to convince the markets of its determination to defend the Franc's value grew towards the end of the year.

Aftermath of the Strikes.

Damaged by deepening public unpopularity, Juppé spent much of 1996 attempting to establish a political recovery on the back of renewed economic activity. The key problem remained that of unemployment which rose remorselessly throughout the year to a record of nearly 13%. Joblessness was especially high among the young, whilst the number of long-term unemployed rose by the year's end to more than one million.

The 1997 Elections.

In a political gamble that proved to be a major miscalculation, President Chirac called snap elections for 25 May and 1 June. The outcome, far from seeing the return of a right-wing government, paved the way for a Socialist victory under Jospin.

The Left secured victory for several reasons. Particularly, Socialist leader Lionel Jospin had shrewdly built up electoral alliances with several other groups on the Left: the Communist Party, which in the event gained 14 seats, allowing its parliamentary presence to rise from 24 to 38, the Green Party and other small groupings on the Left such as the Radical Socialists. On the other side of the spectrum, the ostracised right-wing Front National split the Right's vote, taking 15% at the first round. The Right lost 200 of its previous 464 seats in the 577-member parliament: 29% of voters abstained from the second round, after 32% had from the first.

This highlights the potentially destabilizing influence of Jean-Marie Le Pen's extreme-right Front National on the French Right. This is due in large part to the party's refusal to cooperate with the other parties of the Right. The Communists, on the other hand, were instrumental in sweeping the Left to victory through electoral alliances. Had the FN done the same with the RPR and UDF, the electoral outcome might have been different. Indeed some parts of the moderate Right's election manifesto were explicit attempts to pander to the Front National's electorate. Recent measures such as the "Lois Pasqua" restricting immigration and access to French citizenship were destined to woo those who had in the past voted for the FN on xenophobic grounds.

Composition of the New Government.

Lionel Jospin's government, named on 4 June, reflected his electoral alliances. It was also composed of a third of women. In it were three Communist ministers including Jean-Claude Gayssot in charge of transport and housing. Other ministers with more traditionally socialist credentials include Dominique Strauss-Kahn, who was named to the Finance Ministry. Hubert Vedrine, who became Foreign Minister, had been diplomatic advisor to François Mitterrand during his whole Presidency.

First Months in Power.

Against the expectations of most observers, Lionel Jospin enjoyed remarkable success in his first nine months as Prime Minister (not least in sustaining strong public opinion poll support). At the outset of his Premiership, he faced the major obstacles of reconciling the programme on which he ran for election (including a commitment to introduce a 35-hour working week without loss of wages, and an ambitious scheme for the creation of 150,000 jobs in the public sector; and the objective of reducing taxes on income and spending), with the harsh realities which his country's strategic commitment to EMU membership imposed. He was further constrained both by his need to hold together his governing coalition of Socialists and Communists, and by his own ambition to run for the Presidency in 2002.

The new government's prospects were powerfully assisted by Jospin's politically adroit handling of the major challenges. He enjoyed remarkable sway over the Socialist Party by the end of 1997, as his imposition of his own candidate (François Hollande) as leader of the Socialist Party demonstrated. In matters of policy, he effected an extraordinary U-turn by undertaking the largest privatisation (selling off a quarter of France Telecom) in French history; remarkably, too, he defused labour disputes which might have undermined less able politicians.

Economic Buoyancy.

Jospin was, critically, assisted by the economy growing more sharply (at about 2·4%) in 1997 than it had for some years, and by the popularity among French voters (not to mention his Communist allies in government) for increases in taxation being imposed upon business rather than upon individuals. In consequence, unemployment stopped rising, and rising tax receipts offered an improved prospect that, in the event that the improvement were sustained through 1998, France would achieve a public sector deficit of 3·0% of GDP or less, thereby meeting one of the key criteria for EMU membership. Having miscalculated so grievously in holding early Parliamentary elections in 1997, President Chirac found himself politically discredited and hence at a grave disadvantage. Chirac had little room for manoeuvre: under the Fifth Republic's Constitution, the President cannot call new Parliamentary elections for at least a year after the last ones. That was the formal position. Informally, the political reality in 1997 and early 1998 was that Chirac was himself faced with a Prime Minister who succeeded in drawing more power to the Premiership than any of his Fifth Republic predecessors in the office had done under conditions of cohabitation; a continuing struggle to assert his authority over the fragmented and frequently quarrelsome parties of the democratic right; and the electoral threat of the extreme right-wing National Front. For the Front, the desperate weakness of the democratic right presented an unprecedented opportunity which the squabbles of ambitious pretenders to the Presidency in the RPR and UDF did nothing to lessen.

Jospin's Continuing Success.

Lionel Jospin's success as Prime Minister continued throughout 1998: remarkably, his public opinion approval ratings remained at above 60%. At the beginning of 1999, he nevertheless faced growing difficulties. The first was that of economic anxieties: the annual rate of economic growth, which had fallen in nearly every quarter during 1997 and 1998, was widely forecast to fall further in 1999. The second was that the French right's credibility, which had been so heavily damaged by electoral defeat in 1997 and turmoil in 1998, was boosted by the formal split of the National Front which offered the attractive possibility to democratic right-wing parties of winning additional support from disillusioned National Front voters (though the terms upon which such support might be gained were likely to prove controversial). One opinion poll in December 1998 showed that, despite approval of Jospin's performance as Prime Minister, a majority of voters would support Chirac in a Presidential election.

Fragmentation of the Right.

Tensions within the left notwithstanding, the fissiparousness of the right was of greater political salience: right-wing parties found themselves in an unusually fluid state. The creation of The Alliance in May 1998 was no more than a loose confederation, divided by personal ambitions and policy differences (not least over Europe). The UDF, itself a confederation of the non-Gaullist right since its foundation by Giscard d'Estaing in 1978, split after the April 1998 regional elections. The split was caused by the expulsion of Charles Millon, a senior UDF politician, who had won election as President of the Rhônes-Alpes region with National Front support. Millon then founded his own party entitled *La Droite*. A month after the Regional elections, Alain Madelin took the Liberal Democrats (a freemarket, pro-European grouping) out of the UDF into the newly-formed Alliance. The UDF was, accordingly, left as a Christian Democratic rump led by its leader since 1995, François Bayrou.

GERMANY.

The Road to Reunification.

From 1990, discussion of German politics can no longer be easily divided into East and West. The East German Communist regime collapsed in late 1989, as waves of East Germans took advantage of the ending of travel restrictions between Hungary and Austria to leave their crumbling country. As the regime disappeared by Christmas 1989, the East German state had begun its own process of disappearance by Easter 1990. The official celebrations attending the 40th anniversary of the East German state were marked by the attendance of Mikhail Gorbachev whose policies had done so much to undermine Communist rule in eastern Europe, and by mass unrest in Leipzig, Dresden, and East Berlin. In the space of a few weeks, the remaining shreds of legitimacy attaching to Herr Honecker's administration fell away. His successor was Egon Krenz, who had the distinct political disadvantage of having had responsibility for internal security and of rigging the municipal elections in May 1989. He lasted but a few weeks until his replacement by Hans Modrow, the reformist Mayor of Dresden.

The End of the Berlin Wall.

On 9 November, the Berlin Wall was breached. In the ten months preceding that momentous event, 200,000 East Germans had left for the West; in the week that followed it, 3 million East Germans followed (most of them simply to visit and return). The regime fell away from beneath its leaders; on 3 December, the Politburo and Central Committee resigned. Politicians who had only weeks before exercised absolute power now found themselves under investigation for corruption and abuse of power.

Formation of New Parties.

New parties sprang up, and old ones which for forty years had been quiescent allies of the ruling Communist Party now broke free, finding independent voices. Elections were set for 18 March 1990. In the three months between the effective collapse of Communism and the elections, West and East German politics became inextricably linked. Two states, with two economic systems, remained. But the one nation now looked to a fusing of its nationhood with statehood, and the calculations of German voters on both sides of the disappearing border were made with unity in mind. As the elections approached, so the timetable for unity shortened. Foreign politicians gradually accommodated themselves to the prospect of unity. Where Mikhail Gorbachev and Margaret Thatcher had as late as December 1989 been powerfully antipathetic to German unity, they were forced by the extraordinary speed of events to acquiesce in its inevitability. From early 1990 onwards, discussion proceeded not about whether unity would take place but about the circumstances under which it would occur, and with what speed.

The March 1990 Elections.

The election on 18 March took place between three main groupings: the Alliance for Germany which was a coalition of three conservative parties favouring rapid reunification, immediate introduction of the Deutschmark to the east on the basis of a one-for-one exchange rate, and a free-market economy; the Social Democratic Party which favoured a more gradual approach to unity and a social market economy; and the Democratic Socialist Party, the successor to the discredited Communist Party. The campaign was dominated by West German political parties and the leading West German politicians, and resulted in a landslide victory for the conservative Alliance for Germany. This result had not seemed remotely likely as recently as two weeks before polling day but the East German CDU's commitment to rapid reunification and a market economy swung the day. The new East German Prime Minister, Lothar de Maizière, was faced with the remarkable task of overseeing the process of the elimination of the East German state and its absorption into a new Federal Republic.

Rapid Political Development.

The rest of 1990 continued to be a year of breathless political development in Germany: on 1 July, the East German monetary system was merged with the West's, and the soft-currency Ostmark was replaced by Europe's most important currency, the Deutschmark. On 3 October, the two states became one country. Two months later, on 2 December, a united Germany voted in the first nation-wide elections since 1932.

The West German party system was reproduced in the eastern *lander*. There were nonetheless differences between parties in the west and those in the east: the PDS won almost no support in the west but retained some in the east, whilst the CDU nominally had merely an ally in the east in the shape of the German Social Union (DSU). In fact, the electoral rule which permitted the formation of joint lists in those cases where parties were not competitors enabled the CDU to run alongside the DSU. The PDS, with a regionally-skewed voter base, was disadvantaged for the same reason. For this election only, the east was treated as a separate voting area: if a party achieved 5% of the vote there, it would qualify for representation in the Bundestag.

Kohl Returns to Power.

The architect of the process of unification, Helmut Kohl, was returned to power at the head of CDU/CSU/FDP coalition. The conservative part of that coalition, the CDU/CSU, won just 43·8% of the vote – its poorest performance since 1949. The FDP won 11·0%. This thoroughly creditable performance reflected the popularity of the Foreign Minister, Hans Dietrich-Genscher, in the eastern *lander*, and the

success of the FDP's plea to voters that they receive sufficient support to enable them to act as a counterweight to Herr Kohl's conservatives. The SDP won 33·5%, giving them their worst result since the heavy defeat of 1957 when Chancellor Adenauer won an overall victory; the Greens won just 3·9% (which, because they fell below the 5% barrier, caused them to be excluded from the Bundestag). Green representation was not eliminated, however, because the coalition in the eastern *lander* between Alliance '90 and the Greens brought them 5·9% of the regional vote. Extreme right-wing Republicans, feeding off the discontent among some conservatives at Herr Kohl's decision to recognise the Oder-Neisse line as Poland's western border, won 2·1% of the vote (and hence no seats).

The Aftermath of Victory.

The task facing Herr Kohl in the aftermath of electoral victory was huge. At home, it amounted to nothing less than the complete reconstruction of what had once been East Germany. The former Communist state's soft-currency markets in the Soviet Union had been lost; its goods were hopelessly outdated and hence uncompetitive in West European markets. The most obvious consequence was that the cost of unification would be enormous. The eastern *lander* would inevitably make huge demands for capital reconstruction on the west, and substantial rises in public spending for unemployment and social security.

These pressures were reflected in significant rises in German interest rates in the six months following monetary unification in July. The risk that private investment might as a result be "crowded out" was not insignificant. Tax rises, which Kohl resisted in the latter half of 1990 in order to preserve his political position ahead of the December elections, were eventually implemented (though nominally to finance Germany's financial contribution to the allied efforts in the Gulf crisis).

Foreign Policy Problems.

Abroad, Germany struggled with the problem encapsulated by the Gulf crisis – that of reconciling her post-war democratic, consensualist traditions at home with diplomatic and even military involvement abroad. It seemed more likely than not that Kohl would seek to entrench Germany ever more firmly in the European Community. In addressing these questions, Kohl found himself more heavily constrained politically than he would have wished by the new-found weight of the FDP, especially by Genscher. Having played so spectacular a part in the theatre of reunification, Kohl found himself with a more difficult role in the expensive task of reconstructing a nation whose two parts had, in thirty years of enforced division grown further apart than many Germans had believed. The dragging weight of the collapse of East German industry was also very much greater than had been generally anticipated and placed additional strains upon the coalition in Bonn.

Chancellor Kohl suffered a humiliating reverse in elections on 21 April 1991 in the south-western state of Rhineland-Palatinate. In the first test of Kohl's diminishing popularity since the national elections of December 1990, the conservative Christian Democrats lost office after 44 years on a swing of 7% to the Social Democrats. It was a reflection of disenchantment at the economic problems brought about by unification.

The Rebuilding of East Germany.

Chancellor Kohl's government continued in 1991 and early 1992 to struggle with the immense task of rebuilding the East German economy in the face of a gently rising inflation rate, tight monetary policy, an economy which hovered on the edge of recession, and increasing wage pressures. Taxes were increased in July 1991 in an attempt to finance some of the costs of unification, but government borrowing nonetheless grew sharply.

As her exposed position during the Gulf War indicated, the collapse of the Soviet Union and the associated political order in eastern Europe gave Germany a greatly enhanced importance in continental and world politics which the diplomacy surrounding preparations for the European summit at Maastricht confirmed. In the short-term, Maastricht did nothing to alter the dominance which the Bundesbank, the German central bank, exercised over European monetary policy. Both Britain and France found during 1991 that their sovereignty over monetary conditions was severely circumscribed by the need to maintain the positions of their currencies within the European Exchange Rate Mechanism, and that German interest rates set the bench-mark for all others. These were high in an attempt to force inflation down; they would be kept high even at the price of the economy drifting into recession.

Strains on Kohl.

Under such extraordinary strains, Helmut Kohl's CDU performed remarkably strongly, drawing roughly equal support to the SPD as measured by opinion polls. However, the calculations of the FDP remained pivotal to politics in Bonn as they did in the *Länder*. The possibility existed that the FDP could seek to join the SPD in a coalition after the next elections in 1994. In early 1992, the SPD was still to address convincingly the question with which it had struggled during the 1980s: who should face Kohl for the Chancellorship. Two candidates suggested themselves: Björn Engholm, the Prime Minister of Schleswig-Holstein who was elected Party Chairman in the early summer of 1991, and Hans-Ulrich Klose who was the new SPD Floor Leader in the Bundestag.

In April 1992, the pressure on Kohl intensified with the resignation of the long-serving Foreign Minister, Genscher, and the outbreak of public sector strikes.

Gathering Economic Recession.

Germany slid rapidly into economic recession in the autumn of 1992, with industrial production falling by an annual rate of 20 % in the final quarter. Some sectors, such as vehicles and machine tools, two vertebrae of the German economy, faced much more dramatic falls in demand and output. Demand at home fell as cyclical recession was intensified by the Bundesbank's action in sustaining exceptionally high real interest rates in order to choke off what its ruling Council rightly regarded as an unacceptably high rate of inflation of more than 4 %. At the same time, export markets were weak because of recession elsewhere in western Europe, sluggish demand in Eastern Europe because of a shortage of foreign exchange, rising labour costs which made German products increasingly uncompetitive, and a Deutschmark which the chaos of September 1992 had left significantly overvalued. For eastern Germany, the problems were yet more serious, primarily because labour costs there began to close on those in west Germany, so rendering the east's lack of competitiveness yet more serious. The costs to western Germany of unification remained punishingly high, adding greatly to public spending and to the underlying fiscal imbalance.

Opposition Weakness.

The opposition SPD failed completely to exploit the economic disorder over which the CDU/FDP coalition presided, not least because there exists no obvious policy response to the combination of stubbornly high inflation, deepening recession, fiscal disorder, and (which is novel for Germany) a balance of payments deficit. One of the few polls to take place in the twelve months up to March 1993 was municipal elections in Hesse at the end of the period for which, significantly, turnout fell. The SPD's support fell by more than 8 percentage points, and the CDU's by 2·3 percentage points but the Greens recovered their share by nearly 2 percentage points leaving the FDP unchanged. The most remarkable aspect of the result, however, was the surge of extreme right-wing parties. The largest of them, the Republican Party (whose leader was a former SS officer) gained 8·3 % of the total vote.

Rise of the Right.

The rise of the extreme right was fed in 1992 and early 1993 by the large influx of refugees from eastern Europe, especially those fleeing civil war in Bosnia: by the end of 1992, Germany's foreign-born population stood at approximately 5·5 million. The

problem was further exacerbated by internal migration from the eastern *länder*. During the summer and autumn of 1992, attacks (some of them murderous) upon immigrants intensified debate within Germany about the country's condition and direction. The government's problems in dealing with levels of immigration more than 50 % higher than in 1991 were compounded both by Germany's carrying a significantly higher share of the total refugee burden than her EU partners and by high rates of unemployment.

Economic Pressures.

Linked demographic and economic pressures arising from reunification continued to make life difficult for German politicians and people in 1993 and early 1994. The establishment of structures and values conducive to democratic stability was overwhelmingly the dominant consideration in German politics for the first forty years of its existence. Under the extraordinary strains of integrating an economic and ecological disaster zone of the eastern *länder* into the west, the structures and values which served Germany well between 1949 and 1989 are now being found wanting. Unemployment grew to more than 8 % by the end of 1993;

Adjustment would be easier were German political leaders of greater stature. However, skilled as he had proved in keeping his own party reasonably united, and in maintaining a coalition with the FDP since 1982, Federal Chancellor Helmut Kohl had yet to convince the German population of the necessity for fiscal stringency if reunification was to succeed, and the German economy's competitiveness to be improved. The major opposition force, the Social Democratic Party (SPD) was in little better condition than the governing coalition. Although it was boosted by local elections in Brandenburg in December 1993, its new leader, Rudolf Scharping, was even less charismatic than the Chancellor himself.

The 1994 Elections.

Despite securing its second lowest vote since the establishment of the Federal Republic in 1949, the CDU emerged from the elections on 16 October 1994 as the largest party in the Bundestag. The results of the election, in which the turnout was 79 %, were:

	Percentage share of the vote	Change	Seats	Change
CDU/CSU	41·5	−2·3 %	294	−25
SPD	36·4	+2·9 %	252	+13
FDP	6·9	−4·1 %	47	−32
The Greens	7·3	+3·4 %	49	+49
PDS	4·4	+2·0 %	30	+13

The CDU/CSU's continuation in office in coalition with the FDP (which squeaked back into the Bundestag, thanks largely to CDU/CSU supporters voting tactically to boost the centrist party's vote as a means of increasing the prospects of the CDU/CSU forming the government) owed much to Chancellor Kohl. Exploiting the strong economic recovery evident throughout 1994, Kohl's dominating personality reassured a plurality of German voters as he had done (albeit with more conviction) following reunification in 1990. A month after the election, the Bundestag reelected Kohl, by the narrowest of margins, as Chancellor.

Although the election's outcome did not alter the Chancellor's formal position, it changed his political circumstances considerably. Not only was the CDU/CSU's position in the Bundestag weaker but his FDP partners emerged from the election damaged and in some disarray, and the SPD remained in control of the upper house (the Blundesrat). The medium-term significance of the elections was the heightened possibility that the FDP would be disabled by internal party wrangling, obliging the CDU/CSU to look to the SPD as a new partner in government.

The Advent of Lafontaine.

At its party congress held in Mannheim in mid-November 1995, the SPD elected Oskar Lafontaine, Prime Minister of Saarland and the SPD's candidate for Chancellor in the first unified German election held in 1990, as its chairman in succession to Rudolf Scharping whose tenure had been marked by the party's continuing failure to convince the public of its purposes and political grip. Rather than close its deficit of 5 percentage points on the governing CDU, the SPD endured the galling experience of seeing the gap widen despite a weakening economy and a rapid rise in unemployment. Discontent within the party grew over the course of 1995 to the point where the November party congress was marked by a mixture of despair and disarray.

Developments in 1996.

Electoral unpopularity also increased political tensions within the FDP, the CDU/CSU's tiny, declining and factionalised coalition partners. The party's general secretary was replaced during 1995, whilst the Federal Justice Minister, an FDP member, was forced to resign in December 1995 following her adoption of anti-crime measures which many of her liberal party colleagues denounced. The FDP's weakness, to be tested anew by three *Land* elections in March, posed a problem for Chancellor Kohl whose government depends upon the FDP regaining its balance and overcoming its internal tensions. The Chancellor already faced enormous difficulties in realising his objectives of monetary union by 1999, and extending EU membership to Poland, Hungary, and the Czech Republic. As in France, so in Germany: the combination of an economy growing less strongly in 1995 and early 1996 than in 1994, and of undiminished pressure to meet the Maastricht convergence criteria left politicians with little room for manoeuvre. In an attempt to increase employment, and to reduce the incentive for German companies to invest abroad rather than at home, the government proposed measures in February 1996 to reduce social security costs, taxes, and subsidies, and to liberalise retail, telecommunications, energy, and labour markets.

In March 1996, Chancellor Kohl received a welcome boost from a strong showing by the Christian Democrats (and an uplift in support for the struggling Free Democrats) in regional elections in Baden-Württemberg, Rhineland-Palatinate and Schleswig-Holstein. The results were a bad setback for the SPD.

Kohl and EMU.

Chancellor Kohl's commitment to EMU continued undiminished through 1997, despite growing discontent among German voters not only with the project's cost in unemployment (particularly in the eastern *Länder*), but with the risk that EMU would provide a weaker currency than the Deutschmark which it replaced. Kohl's determination to implement EMU on terms as favourable to Germany as possible (and which were least irritating to German voters) led him to declare that he would seek a fifth term of office in the federal elections to be held on 27 September 1998. German voters' doubts about EMU have not been assuaged, but the Chancellor's commitment was grounded in what he declared to be grand strategy. For him, upon EMU's success hung the prospects for continuing peace in Europe. If Germany's domestic economic circumstances were more robust, his political problems at home and abroad would be fewer. As it was, Germany's economic growth remained sluggish and heavily dependent upon exports to neighbouring European countries. Recovery from the recession of 1993 and the punishing fiscal pressures arising from reunification remained far from complete.

The 1998 Election Background.

Although relations with the CSU (the CDU's sister conservative party in Bavaria) were both awkward and diverting, Kohl's authority over the CDU in the short term was solid, having been reestablished by his commanding performance at the annual party conference in October 1997.

Early in 1998 the victory of Gerhard Schröder in elections in Lower Saxony established him as the most potent opposition challenger to Chancellor Kohl for many years. The growing difficulties facing Kohl were to be seen in elections in Saxony-Anhalt in April, when the far right German People's Party took

12·7% of the vote and Christian Democrat support slumped.

The Ousting of Kohl.

The election held on 27 September turned in large part on German voters' judgements of Chancellor Helmut Kohl. That judgement was a resounding rejection of Kohl's attempt to win a fifth successive term: the CDU/CSU's share of the vote fell from 41·4% to 35·2% of the vote, its lowest share since the foundation of the Federal Republic in 1949. In the eastern *länder*, the CDU/CSU vote fell by no less than 11 percentage points. The SPD were the major beneficiaries of the CDU/CSU collapse (the largest percentage fall suffered by any German party in its post-war democratic history): the SPD's share of the vote rose from 36·4% in 1994 to 40·9% in 1998. The PDS, dependent for almost all of its electoral strength on its vote in the eastern *länder*, gained 5·1% of the vote nationally and hence just succeeded in surmounting the 5% barrier required for representation in the Bundestag. Despite seeing their vote fall by 0·7 percentage points, the FDP retained their own representation with 6·2% of the national vote. So, too, did *Die Grünen* with 6·7%; their prize was enhanced with Gerhard Schröder's decision to include them in his governing coalition.

Party	Seats in Bundestag	Percentage of votes
	(1994 totals in parenthesis)	
SPD	298 (252)	40·9 (36·4)
CDU/CSU	245 (294)	35·2 (41·4)
FDP	44 (47)	6·2 (6·9)
Die Grünen	47 (49)	6·7 (7·3)
PDS	35 (30)	5·1 (4·4)
Others	– –	– –

Schröder in Power.

The Schröder government's first six months in office were marked by much turbulence, attributable in part to the problems of adjustment to the unfamiliarities of government. Disagreement between the Chancellor and the (Green) Minister for the Environment over the thorny question of the speed with which nuclear power was to be phased out broke out into the open. Quarrels over reform of taxation also became public knowledge.

A Troubled Coalition.

These differences reached a climax in March 1999 with the dramatic resignation of Oskar Lafontaine, the Finance Minister (and also Chairman of the ruling SPD). Although Schröder moved quickly to limit the damage (and the financial markets celebrated) it seemed likely that the Schröder government would not escape the affair quite so easily, particularly as the NATO air attack on Serbia (*see* **C**68) provoked new divisions within the coalition.

ITALY.

In 1993, Italy was convulsed by reform so rapid as might justify the term "revolutionary". In advance of parliamentary elections in March 1994, the entire party system changed. Mainstays of the old regime, especially the Christian Democrats and the Socialists, effectively imploded under the devastating impact of continuing revelations about the depth and breadth of the systematic corruption of public life. Coupled with deep regional divisions, electoral volatility, and public opinion polls which gave no party more than one-fifth of the vote, the risks to Italy's stability and coherence from elections fought under new rules by new parties were great. Proportional representation was not completely ended: one-quarter of the seats would continue to be allocated by proportional representation. Accordingly, many voters would continue to vote as they previously did: for the party they support rather than the tactically rational option of voting for the party best placed to defeat the party to which they were most intensely opposed. With three groupings in most constituencies, individual calculations about the party for which it was most rational to vote were rendered exceptionally difficult.

The new system, therefore, offered no guarantee that threats to the country's stability could be overcome: in the months leading up to the elections, parties congregated in three loose coalitions, none of which were internally stable and some of which were greatly weakened by serious fault lines (especially of region) running through them. The three main groupings were:

* *The Centre* parties formed loose groupings around the "Pact for Italy", dominated by former Christian Democrats.

* *The Left* formed a broad alliance under the banner of the "Progressives"—the first occasion since 1948 that left-wing parties in Italy had overcome the differences between them for electoral purposes. The grouping included the Greens, the former Communist PDS, the remnants of the discredited Socialists, the Network movement, Liberals, Catholic radicals, the Marxist Communist Refoundation Party, and free-enterprise centrists.

* *The Right* was more deeply divided. Little common ground existed between the neo-fascist National Alliance and the Northern League on the one hand, and Silvio Berlusconi's *Forza Italia* on the other. The National Alliance, a remarketed version of the neo-fascist MSI, had its greatest strength in the south; the Northern League, a populist movement built around the charismatic leadership of Umberto Bossi on a programme of protest against the large state subsidies to the south, espoused a federalist programme which the National Alliance explicitly rejected. *Forza Italia* was unencumbered by principle, and fuelled by novelty. The three parties nevertheless found it expedient to campaign on the same platform.

The Outcome.

The electoral campaign of the political novitiate Berlusconi was powerfully assisted by his ownership of half of Italy's media outlets. By dint of the collapse of the centre parties, and his energetic campaigning exploitation of his electronic media ownership, Berlusconi's *Forza Italia* emerged from the elections as the single largest party. The election resulted in the right-wing alliance winning an absolute majority in the Chamber of Deputies, with 366 seats out of the total of 630, but just failing to win a majority of the 315 seats in the Senate. Given that neither Bossi nor Fini possessed the political stature necessary to make a plausible bid for the Premiership, Berlusconi was in a powerful position to assume the office, the delaying and bargaining tactics of his erstwhile colleagues in the other two right-wing parties notwithstanding. In the space of little more than two months, Berlusconi had propelled himself from magnate to Prime-Minister designate. On 28 April Berlusconi was finally invited to try to form a Cabinet.

The Berlusconi Administration.

The election of a new government led by media magnate Silvio Berlusconi following the elections of March 1994 heightened expectations of an end to the politics of stagnation and corruption. In fact, Berlusconi made little progress in gaining control of public finances. Moreover, in his tenacious grip upon his vast media interests, he represented in his own person and politics the ills which he had set out to right. Nor did the realigned political system which resulted in the formation of the centre-right grouping of the Northern League, the neo-fascist National Alliance, and Berlusconi's own party vehicle, *Forza Italia*, establish a firm basis for government.

Berlusconi's government fell in December 1994 following the Northern League's departure from the coalition in an attempt to force the creation of a new parliamentary commission to reform the franchising of television. The issue of media ownership concentration had weakened Berlusconi, and prompted the creation of an exceptionally weak new, technocratic, government under the leadership of Lamberto Dini, a former Director-General of the Bank of Italy.

The Fall of Dini.

Under the pressure of sustaining majorities for a new budget, Prime Minister Dini's government lost

cohesion in the latter part of 1995: the former Communist PDS's enthusiasm for the Prime Minister's fiscal austerity waned as the impact of cuts to the social welfare budget and public sector employment upon the Party's core constituency deepened. With the budget finally approved, and having lost the support of the Northern League and the PDS, Dini did what he had undertaken to do and resigned. In early February 1996, President Antonio Scalfaro nominated Antonio Maccanico to form a new government and with a brief to engineer significant constitutional reform, support for which among the political elite is lacking. The attempt by Maccanico to form a broad-based government came to an abrupt end in mid-February.

With the failure of Maccanico, Italy was plunged into renewed crisis as fresh elections were called for April 1996.

The 1996 Election.

The result of the General Election held on 21 April was that the centre-left Olive Tree coalition of six parties achieved a clear victory with 319 of the 630 seats at stake in the Chamber of Deputies over the centre-right Freedom Alliance coalition under Silvio Berlusconi. Much the largest party in the disparate Olive Tree coalition was the Democratic Left (PDS) with 172 of the 319 seats, but it was led by Romano Prodi, a technocratic centrist. Duly appointed Prime Minister, Prodi assembled a government in his own image, providing continuity with the two previous governments. A clear indication of the new government's technocratic cast was that Massimo D'Alema, the PDS leader, chose to remain outside the government with the implication that his support for the government would prove contingent. At the outset, however, the greatest threat to the government's stability was thought to be that of the timing and cause of any withdrawal of support for Prodi, the likelihood of which would increase as the new government strained to meet the demanding budgetary conditions for EMU membership.

Developments in 1997.

Italian politics in 1997 were played out against the backcloth of the government's drive to ensure that Italy qualified for EMU membership. Aided by a moderate rise in the rate of economic growth during 1997, and a special 'Tax for Europe' amounting to 1·8 million lire for the average middle-class family, the government's revenues were boosted sufficiently to make Italy's qualification for EMU probable. With a public sector deficit of approximately 2·8 % by mid-1998, Germany was in a weak position to deny Italy membership of EMU's first wave since her own fiscal position (not to mention that of France) was weaker than Italy's. That was not how Chancellor Kohl had imagined at Maastricht that events would turn out; his room for manoeuvre on the matter had by early 1998 almost vanished.

Amidst such unaccustomed fiscal prudence, Italian politics were nevertheless not without their theatrical qualities. Having in October come close to overturning Mr Prodi's government over the Prime Minister's budget cuts, Mr D'Alema, leader of the (ex-Communist) Democratic Party of the Left, presented the report of the parliamentary commission, charged with consideration of the reform of the Italian Constitution, which he had chaired. The report recommended the formal establishment of Italy as a federal entity; for the election of the President by direct popular vote rather than by parliamentary vote as at present; and for significant parliamentary and judicial reform. The proposals can be implemented only if parliament and voters themselves (via a referendum) approve them. Coupled with modest reforms to the extraordinarily generous pensions system, 1997 was a strikingly good year for consensual government.

Moreover, voters appeared to approve: local and direct mayoral elections across Italy in 1997 resulted in a surge of support for candidates supportive of Mr Prodi's Olive Tree coalition and defeats for right-wing candidates running under the banner of Mr Berlusconi's Freedom Alliance.

The Resignation of Prodi.

Defeated in a Parliamentary vote of confidence on 9 October 1998, Romano Prodi resigned as Prime

Minister. The vote arose from the opposition of certain members of Communist Refoundation (RC) to the government's budget for 1999; the division within the RC led to the party formally splitting into two—the rump of the RC, and the new Party of Italian Communists, led by Armando Cossutta. Without full support from the RC, Prodi's hopes of constructing a Parliamentary coalition sufficiently large to win the confidence vote rested on support from the centre UDR party. Since such support was not forthcoming on terms acceptable to Prodi (broadly, that any government which he led should first win the electorate's approval), the government fell.

The D'Alema Coalition.

The majority that eventually formed was led by the former Communist, Massimo D'Alema, leader of the Democratic Left (DS). A coalition of seven parties, it was based upon a core of left-wing backing including the DS itself; Cossata's new party; much of the rest of the Olive Tree coalition; and centrist support from the UDR. Despite the proximate cause of Prodi's administration being dissent over the budget, Prime Minister D'Alema pledged to continue Prodi's fiscal and financial policies in order to reassure the markets. Despite the new government's intention to continue the process of federalising Italy, and its limited room for manoeuvre over the small centrist parties' self-interested opposition to the reduction of the proportionality of the electoral system, it is upon its economic achievements and failures that it will be judged. The support lent by the drive to meet the terms of EMU entry had greatly assisted Prime Minister Prodi's policy of imposing discipline upon the public finances; without that incentive, the pressures to relax policy will grow. That in turn would make it difficult for D'Alema to sustain the fragile coalition that supported his administration.

SPAIN.

Political Crisis in Spain.

As problems of public finance, falling business confidence, and rising inflation crowded in upon the government in 1994, Spanish politics were thrown into crisis by the alleged involvement of the government's Anti-Terrorist Liberation Groups (GAL) in the illegal killing of twenty-three suspected members of the Basque separatist ETA movement in the 1980s. The charges came after a rash of corruption allegations: one concerned the UGT trade union (whose links with the PSOE are close), and another the alleged preferential government treatment of the Prime Minister's brother-in-law. The GAL case was more damaging than either. It reached high into the Spanish government, entangling the former security chief and, possibly, both the Interior Minister and Gonzalez himself. Were the judicial investigation actually to inculpate the Prime Minister, the government's prospects of survival would be slender because the Catalan CiU party would be bound to withdraw its support. Even if Gonzalez were to escape embroilment in the scandal, the government was bound to be weakened by the revelations.

Background to the 1996 Elections.

Effectively prevented from resigning as Prime Minister by Spain's presidency of the European Union during the second half of 1995, Felipe Gonzalez entered 1996 prepared to lead the PSOE into an early general election on 3 March. His authority was diminished by accusations of corruption, a phone tapping scandal which prompted the resignation of former deputy prime minister Narcis Serra, and of government involvement in the killings of ETA suspects. The government also failed to make significant progress in reducing an exceptionally high rate of unemployment. Gonzalez nevertheless remained the Socialists' greatest single electoral asset.

The Advent of Aznar.

In the general election held on 3 March, the People's Party (PP) won 156 seats out of a total of 350 in the Congress of Deputies. José Maria Aznar, leader of the People's Party, then spent some weeks building an understanding with other parties sufficiently large and stable to grant him an overall majority on most issues. The agreement turned upon Aznar's success in reaching an accord with the CiU, the Catalan Nationalist Party. Despite winning only 16 seats, the CiU again demonstrated its remarkable capacity to exact a heavy price for supporting the plurality winner. At the behest of the CiU's leader, Jordi Pujol, the PP agreed that income tax receipts should be split between the national government and the regions (thereby reducing the power of the national government to control public expenditure); that compulsory national military service be ended by 2001; and that the office of civil governor (Madrid's representative in the regions) be abolished. Like other European governments, the new Spanish administration found itself obliged to adopt stringent public expenditure policies in order to have any prospect of achieving the Maastricht criteria for EMU membership in 1999: the government imposed a freeze on public sector salaries with the object of saving approximately £1 billion, and accelerated the privatisation programme. Although the CiU supported the PP government's policy of EMU membership (to which end it supported the PP in the parliamentary vote on the draft budget), differences between the two parties emerged within months of the agreement between them being signed. The CiU's determination to advance the cause of Catalan autonomy, whilst not immediately imperilling the party's understanding with the PP, left many in the PP and the PSOE uneasy about the threat to national cohesion.

Spain and Monetary Union.

Spain's progress towards meeting the criteria set for joining the European Single Currency continued unabated during 1997: the public sector deficit appeared set to fall below 3·0%, whilst the rate of inflation fell to 2·0% by the end, the economy grew by 3·4%, and the stockmarket reached a record high early in 1998 (having gained more than 50% in value in twelve months). With a fall in unemployment (though only to the comparatively high level of approximately 20%), and a steady opinion poll lead over the divided opposition PSOE, José Aznar had cause for some satisfaction at the end of 1997. Unsurprisingly in the light of the concessions made to the Catalans by Madrid under Mr Aznar's leadership, Mr Jordi Pujol, Catalan Regional President, undertook in January 1998 that his Catalan Party would continue its support of Aznar's government to the end of the current Parliament in 2000, thereby affording the Prime Minister the prospect of continuing political stability as a base for EMU entry.

The ETA Ceasefire.

Attempting to forge closer links with other Basque nationalist organizations, but also reflecting its increased political marginalisation, ETA (the terrorist Basque separatist movement) began an indefinite ceasefire on 18 September. PNV, the main Basque nationalist party, was itself drawn in 1998 into closer contacts with ETA's political wing, Herri Batasuna, by reason of the collapse of the PNV's alliance with PSOE in the Basque regional government. In the event that a further understanding between PNV and Herri Batasuna were to develop, the pressures for greater decentralization in the Basque country, and probably in Catalonia, would grow. In the event, the regional election results left the PNV with one fewer seat, but the coalition led by Herri Batasuna with three more seats, in the Basque assembly. Whilst the Partido Popular (PP) gained five seats to become the second largest group, Herri Batasuna's leaders concluded that the results vindicated their new political strategy.

It became plain in 1998 that the PP's leadership regarded the fact of the Party's dependence upon Basque and Catalan nationalists for its Parliamentary majority with unease. Prime Minister Aznar's developing strategy to enable his party to extract itself from that uncomfortable political position was one of repositioning the PP as a party of the centre. His purpose in doing so was to draw support from the PSOE in an attempt to win an overall majority. With elections due by the Spring, the strategy was prudent but not one assured of success.

RUSSIA AND EASTERN EUROPE

RUSSIA.

Note: For the continuing political and economic convulsions in Russia under the beleaguered presidency of Boris Yeltsin, *see* **Special Topic, C64–5.**

POLAND.

Poland's first free parliamentary elections for more than half a century were held in late October 1991 but most voters chose not to participate, and no clear result emerged from the confusion of 125 parties competing for seats. Of these, more than twenty parties won representation in the Sejm, with no single party exercising dominance. After the election, three unstable groupings of parties existed within the Sejm. These groups were what had been Solidarity and its successors, then the Christian Democrats, and finally the successors to the former Communists.

Formation of a stable government from such a multiply-divided Sejm proved exceptionally difficult. Divisions of opinion about how the Communist past should be confronted ran deep, while the social and political costs of compliance with western bankers' (and especially the IMF's) agendas for economic reform exacerbated discontents. Unemployment grew rapidly.

These tensions dominated Poland in the 1990s. Governments, under Olszewski, Suchoka *etc.*, came and went. The transition to a market economy was painful. By February 1995 the Pawlak government was in crisis.

The Crisis of February 1995.

Growing tensions between the two parties of the governing coalition, the Democratic Left Alliance (SLD) and the Polish Peasant Party (PSL) in 1994 led to Prime Minister Waldemar Pawlak, a member of the PSL, being replaced in February 1995 with Jozef Oleksy, a member of the SLD, Speaker of the Sejm, opponent of President Walesa, and a man with a reputation for being an astute bargainer and conciliator.

The crisis and its disposition was intimately connected to the contest for the Presidency in mid-1995, the prospect of which proved sufficient to stifle creative governance. Walesa constantly staked out positions in opposition to the government during 1994. As part of an attempt to remove his most powerful potential opponent for the Presidency, Walesa had sought to manoeuvre Alexander Kwasniewski, leader of the SLD, into the Premiership. The move having failed, Kwasniewski's long-term prospects were good – whether he opted to stand for the Presidency against Walesa, or to seek the Premiership under a reformed constitution in which the President's role was greatly reduced.

The 1995 Presidential Election.

The second round run-off in the presidential election resulted in a victory for Aleksander Kwasniewski, leader of the former communist Democratic Left Alliance (SLD) and a member of Poland's last communist administration, over the incumbent President Lech Walesa by 51·7% to 48·3%. Kwasniewski won majority support from, among other groups, men, the unemployed, and younger voters. Walesa also won the support of three-quarters of those who had backed the right-wing candidate and former Prime Minister Jan Olszewski; he would have secured a higher proportion had Olszewski given Walesa more enthusiastic support.

For Poland's large anti-communist forces, electoral defeat for Solidarity's founder was both devastating and dispiriting. Kwasniewski was sensitive to the need to extend his support base into and beyond the centre-ground but constrained in doing so by the depth and bitterness of the divide between former Communists and the right. In an attempt to present himself as a national President bent on healing division rather than a sectional one exploiting it, Kwasniewski resigned from the SLD after the election.

The government which Jerzy Buzek formed at the end of October was a coalition of two party organizations of contrasting types and ideologies:

* The first, Election Action Solidarity (AWS) was itself a coalition of interests rather than a coherent party. It drew its strength from the Solidarity Trade Union, from sundry church-based organizations, and from a collection of groups on the right and centre-right of Polish politics.

* The second, the Freedom Union, was a pro-business party dedicated to the establishment of free markets.

As a result, the various forces within AWS did not easily or naturally cohere, especially given the much clearer ideology within the Freedom Union. Decisions on matters such as wage restraint, and a closure programme for loss-making coal mines, were especially problematic given the strength of trade union links with AWS. There were also likely to be difficulties within the AWS over implementation of the government's radical plans for devolution of power (and of a substantial fraction of tax revenue) from the centre to new regional governments since the plans cut across established interests.

EU Prospects.

Otherwise, the new government inherited a problem with which some of its neighbours would be delighted to be faced: that of exceptionally rapid economic growth. Recognizing that growth rates of more than 5·0% are fraught with inflationary risk, the new government has continued the policy of its predecessor in seeking to restrain demand by budgetary tightening. The central bank has assisted the policy of restraint by running a tight monetary policy. Achievement of economic stability, particularly with regard to further progress in reducing the inflation rate, will assist Poland's negotiations for accession to the EU, formal sessions for which began in March 1998. Questions of agricultural support and tariff reduction in industrial products, not least in steel, are nevertheless likely to ensure that the negotiations are not without difficulty.

Recent Economic Problems.

Despite losing approximately one-fifth of its export business to Russia, Poland survived Russia's financial crisis in August 1998 with remarkable equanimity. Whilst the short-term losses on its equity markets were heavy, and the zloty underwent an effective devaluation against the dollar of approximately 5% between early August and late September, both the government and the central bank kept a steady nerve. By the end of the year, the central bank was faced with a problem of the zloty's appreciation: that gave the bank room to cut interest rates both in order to prevent the problems for Polish exporters arising from a highly-valued currency and to stimulate a domestic economy which by early 1999 was growing less rapidly than the government wished.

THE FORMER CZECHOSLOVAKIA.

In October 1989, Vaclav Havel was a prisoner of a Communist-run Czechoslovakia; on 29 December, he was sworn in as the newly-democratic Czechoslovakia's President. Alexander Dubcek, the country's leader during the "Prague Spring" of 1968 which was ended by the Soviet invasion in the August of that year and who lived in internal exile for most of the twenty-two years that followed, was elected chairman of the federal assembly in Prague on 27 December 1989.

Democratic Revolution.

Czechoslovakia's democratic revolution was slow to arrive. A large demonstration in Prague on 17 November 1989, brutally treated by police in baton-charges, spawned others on succeeding nights in other Czech and Slovak cities. Too late for their own good, the Prime Minister, Ladislav Adamec and the Communist Party secretary, Milos Jakes, made small concessions to those demonstrating for Czechoslovakian reforms as far-reaching as those in Poland and Hungary. Within a fortnight, Communist power in Czechoslovakia collapsed and Civic Forum, the opposition peacefully led by the inspirational Vaclav Havel, emerged as the dominant political force. On 10 December, what was left of the Communist leadership accepted the formation of a government in which they were a minority. The new foreign minister was Jiri Dienstbier, a founder of Charter 77, the human rights group and spokesman for Civic Forum. Other ministers were also drawn from the ranks of dissidents, until recently marginalised (many of them imprisoned) by the old communist regime.

The process of economic adjustment grew more painful during 1991: industrial production fell to approximately three-quarters of 1990 levels, whilst GDP fell by a fifth and continued to fall further (albeit at a slower rate) in the early months of 1992. Under the austere policies of Finance Minister Vaclav Klaus, the prize of virtually zero inflation was achieved by the summer of 1991. The second phase of the government's privatisation plan attracted substantial public support.

Wide variations in economic activity were apparent within the Federation: Slovakia's economy was hampered by the Republic being mired in the old anxieties and fears of anti-semitism, the narrowest nationalism, and persisting public support for Communist officials and attachment to Communist norms. The Czech Republic, less dependent than Slovakia upon trade with former Comecon countries, stood to benefit disproportionately from the lowering of tariff barriers with the European Community.

THE CZECH REPUBLIC AND SLOVAKIA.

On 1 January 1993, Czechoslovakia split into its two constituent republics, the Czech Republic and Slovakia. From the time of elections in June 1992 to the Federal Assembly and the two National Councils, the outcome had appeared likely because the two parties which had emerged the strongest from the polls were plainly unwilling to create a federal government. Czechoslovakia polarised by party along the boundary between the two republics, making a federal accommodation improbable.

The 1996 Election.

The first general election to be held in the Czech Republic since the "velvet divorce" with Slovakia was held in 1996.

The results of the election resulted in a surge in support for the Social Democrats (CSSD) to a little more than one-quarter of the vote and 61 seats in parliament. Accordingly, the three-party governing coalition fell just short of an overall majority in the 200 seat parliament. Vaclav Klaus formed a new government, but found himself dependent upon the KDU-CSL which, whilst winning only 8·1% of the vote and 18 seats in parliament, showed itself willing to contemplate throwing its support to the CSSD. By early 1997, the government's weakness was such that an early election appeared a distinct possibility.

The Fall of Klaus.

Following a large devaluation of the koruna, and its survival of a Parliamentary confidence vote on its package of spending cuts by only two votes in June 1997, Prime Minister Vaclav Klaus's fractious government stumbled on, enmired in gathering scandals over party financing, and allegations of insider dealing over privatisation receipts. The damaging drift was ended when Finance Minister Pilip (Vice-Chairman of Klaus's ODS Party) precipitated the government's fall with a call for the Prime Minister's resignation at the end of November. Klaus's resistance to Pilip's demand led to the withdrawal of the KDU-CSL party grouping from the governing coalition. When the Civic Democratic Alliance (ODA) then itself withdrew from the cabinet, President Havel publicly demanded that the government resign.

The 1998 Elections.

The right-wing government did not fall until November 1997. The elections which followed seven months later, just two years after the previous poll, resulted in a growth of support for centre parties and a fall in support for the racist right-wing Republican Party which failed to surmount the 5% hurdle for Parliamentary representation. The results were as follows:

Party	Parliamentary Seats	Share of vote
CSSD (Social Democrats)	74	32·3%
ODS (Civic Democratic Party)	63	27·7%
US (Freedom Union)	19	8·6%
KDU-CSL (Christian Democrats)	20	9·0%
KSCM (Communist Party)	24	11·0%

After three weeks of negotiations, no agreement on coalition emerged. Instead, Vaclav Klaus, leader of the ODS, agreed to support a minority single-party government led by Milos Zeman of the CSSD. The details of the agreement provided that there should be consultation about policy questions prior to their submission to Parliament, and that neither party should support a vote of no-confidence in the other.

The election provided clear evidence of a change of government leading to a change of policy: fiscal policy became decidedly looser under Zeman's administration which, given the economy's sluggish condition and the equally sluggish tax-revenue growth accompanying it, resulted in the government resorting to increased borrowing on capital markets.

HUNGARY.

The Death of Antall.

Prime Minister Jozsef Antall died in mid-December 1993, and was succeeded by Peter Boross, Minister of the Interior in Antall's administration. With only six months before elections fell due, Boross conspicuously lacked the moderate Antall's appeal to those beyond the Hungarian Democratic Forum Party (MDF). Whereas Antall sought wide support, Boross's career suggested that his politics were more narrowly right-wing; moreover, Boross lacked a firm base in the party (which he had joined only in 1992).

Foreign Policy Developments.

In foreign policy, Hungary's relations with its neighbours in Slovakia, Serbia and (in particular) Romania continued to be made difficult by conflicting views about the status of Hungarian minorities in those countries. Hungary's anxieties were heightened by an agreement between Slovakia and Romania to adopt an agreed policy towards ethnic minorities within their two states. The problem presented by the Hungarian minority in the Romanian province of Transylvania was especially severe and not easily susceptible of solution, not least because nationalist parties in both Hungary and Romania were content to exploit the question for factional ends. The domestic political support lent to the Romanian government by extreme nationalist parties limited Bucharest's capacity to adopt a more enlightened policy towards the Hungarian minority within its borders. The visit to Bucharest of the Hungarian Foreign Minister in September 1993 drew no concessions from his hosts, an outcome which, in turn, enabled right-wing nationalist opinion in Hungary to use the issue to put pressure on the administration in Budapest.

The May 1994 Elections.

The Hungarian Socialist Party (MSZP), led by Gyula Horn, emerged from the elections of May 1994 with an overall majority in parliament. Seeking to broaden support within Hungary and reassure opinion among western governments and investors about his determination to marginalise the left-wing of his party and its trade union allies. Horn nonetheless chose to form a coalition with the Alliance of Free Democrats (SZDSZ). The new government's programme included policies to reform parliament (including election law), the media, education, and local government. Its first eight months in office revealed that the major strains within the government lay within the MSZP, not within the SZDSZ. However, to the extent that the Prime Minister was tempted to accommodate the political pressures to his left, he risked the coalition's stability. Given that the bulk of government debt in Hungary is short-term, and that foreign investors lacked confidence, Horn's freedom of manoeuvre was slight.

The 1998 Elections.

Elections held in May and June 1998 resulted in the FIDESZ-Hungarian Civic Party (FIDESZ-MPP) gaining a plurality of votes and seats. In order to gain a majority of seats in the 386 parliament, FIDESZ-MPP formed a coalition with the Hungarian Democratic Forum (MDF) with which it had allied itself in the elections, and with the rural Independent Smallholders' Party (FKGP) giving it an overall majority of 19. The rewards to FIDESZ-MPP's coalition partners were the granting of one ministry to MDF and four (reflecting noteworthy success in the coalition negotiations) to the FKGP. With the exception of Agriculture (headed by the FKGP's eccentric leader Josef Torgyan), the major ministries are in the hands of FIDESZ-MPP members. More importantly, Prime Minister Viktor Orban intends that the government's strategic direction will come from his own (expanded and strengthened) office.

ROMANIA.

Having watched the rapid progress of the democratic revolutions in Eastern Europe with as much horror as others experienced exhilaration, President Ceausescu's own brutal Stalinist regime collapsed within the space of a few days in December 1989. Within five weeks of the opening of the choreographed Communist Party Congress in Bucharest, Ceausescu was overthrown. After a "trial" by a kangaroo court, he and his wife were shot on Christmas Day.

The revolution began with demonstrations in Timisoara which were ended bloodily by troops on 17 December. Attempting to bolster his support by a rally in Bucharest on 21 December, troops again opened fire—but this time on demonstrators who defied Ceausescu by openly denouncing him. The army's loyalty to Ceausescu quickly evaporated, and he was obliged to leave the headquarters of the Communist Party by helicopter in order to escape the wrath of the crowds at its doors.

The revolution was bloody. During the three days between the capture of Ceausescu and his wife Elena and their execution, the *Securitate* secret police fought a rearguard action against the army and the people. The number of persons killed is unknown, but probably not more than 2,000. Unsurprisingly, politics in Romania has been unsettled afterwards.

FORMER YUGOSLAVIA.

Civil War and Ethnic Cleansing.

Declarations of independence by the former Yugoslav Republics of Slovenia and Croatia led to clashes on the borders of Slovenia from July 1991, followed by heavy fighting on Croatian territory between Croatian militia and Serbian irregulars (chetniks) backed by the Yugoslav Federal Army. Main centres of fighting were eastern and central Croatia and the Adriatic coast around Dubrovnik. Yugoslavia officially ceased to exist in January 1992 and Slovenia and Croatia were recognized as independent states.

On 29 February 1992 Muslim leaders in Bosnia-Herzegovina declared independence. Bosnian Serbs and the Serbian leadership in Belgrade rejected this, and war began on 6 April with the opening of the siege of the capital Sarajevo. Serbs were accused of 'ethnic cleansing' to secure territorial domination, and a UN trade embargo was imposed on Serbia on 31 May. Peace talks in Geneva, mediated by Lord Owen and Cyrus Vance, began on 26 August. On 16 November a UN naval blockade was mounted against Serbia and Montenegro. Fighting continued as a further peace conference was held in Geneva on 22–23 January 1993. Serbs attacked Muslim enclaves at Srebenica and Goradze. Numerous peace talks collapsed.

The Dayton Peace Agreement.

Following a summer's military operations which left the Bosnian Serbs politically and militarily weakened and under insistent American pressure, the Presidents of Bosnia, Serbia, and Croatia initialled a peace agreement at Dayton, Ohio on 21 November 1995. The deal provided for:

(i) Bosnia to be a single state but to comprise two entities: a Muslim-Croat Federation, and a Serb Republic.

(ii) Sarajevo to be a unified city.

(iii) The central Bosnian government to have jurisdiction over foreign affairs, trade, and monetary policy.

(iv) The institutions of the central Bosnian state to comprise a legislature, constitutional court, presidency, and a central bank.

(v) Individuals charged with war crimes to be banned from public office.

The arrangement's durability is open to serious question. To different degrees and for different reasons, the agreement is resented by all parties.

Serbia under Milosevic.

Tactically, Milosevic has shown himself an astute leader of the rump Yugoslavia (*i.e.* Serbia and Montenegro): in the mid-1990s, he insulated Serbia from direct conflict even as he conspired with Croatian leaders to divide Bosnia. He has repeatedly shown himself an inflexible negotiator save on those (rare) occasions such as the Dayton Peace Agreement in 1995 (*see above*) when he became convinced that NATO would take direct military action against him if he were not to compromise. He has stirred Serbian nationalism at devastating human cost throughout Croatia, Bosnia and, in the late 1990s, Kosovo. Whilst the Dayton Accord brought Bosnia a measure of stability, it did so only as a result of its being governed under an international supervisory arrangement; its medium-term prospects for a resettlement of refugees and a wider peace rested upon the establishment of a government in Croatia led by a party which understood a brokered Bosnian peace to be in Croatia's interests as well as Bosnia's. That is not the view taken by the governing HDZ under the leadership of President Franjo Tudjman: the HDZ's position allows for no such settlement.

The Origins of the Kosovo Crisis.

Milosevic has successfully exploited even the economic privations of ordinary Serbs which have resulted from the imposition of trade sanctions to his own advantage, stigmatising potential opponents as traitors to the Serbian cause. Milosevic's own survival has nevertheless come at punishing cost. Powerfully though it assisted the entrenching of his power over Serbia and the former Communist elite, Milosevic's rescinding in 1989 of the autonomous status accorded Kosovo by President Tito and his subsequent belligerence in the province have gravely threatened wider Balkan political stability. A brutal Serb offensive in Kosovo in 1998 ended only when Milosevic judged that President Clinton and NATO colleagues were on the point of sanctioning air attacks on Serbian forces. A resumption of Serbian attacks in December was itself ended by credible American threats of NATO air strikes, and American-sponsored proximity talks in Paris which began in

February 1999 under a strict timetable.

Failure of Peace Talks.

The Paris Peace Talks, adjourned later in February 1999, resumed in mid-March. Serbia had taken the opportunity to renew its military offensive against Kosovan villages. Meanwhile, the UCK appeared ready to accept a compromise autonomy deal, leaving Serbia isolated. By late March NATO was on the verge of launching an air assault as Serb defiance continued. With the failure of the Holbrooke mission, NATO attacks began on 24 March.

War in the Balkans.

For the onset of war in the Balkans, the refugee tragedy and the wider implications, *see* **C68**.

THE MIDDLE EAST

ISRAEL.

The June 1992 Elections.

Israel held elections on 23 June, with Labour under the leadership of Yitzhak Rabin who had ousted Shimon Peres on 19 February. Labour representation in the Knesset increased from 39 to 44, while Likud's fell from 41 to 32. Mr. Rabin was confirmed as prime minister on 13 July. Israel cancelled projected settlement plans in the occupied territories and, in a meeting between Mr. Rabin and President Bush on 11 August, the $10 billion loan guarantee was restored. Peace talks with Arab negotiators re-commenced on 21 October, though they were hampered by uncertainty over the forthcoming US presidential elections. But the talks were halted on 17 December when Israel seized over 400 alleged members of the outlawed fundamentalist Islamic Resistance Movement (Hamas) following the murder of a police officer and attempted to deport them to Lebanon. Lebanon refused to accept them and the deportees were stranded in the border area in harsh conditions, arousing international criticism and the threat of UN sanctions.

Easing of PLO Restrictions.

However, on 19 January 1993 the Israeli parliament lifted the ban on political contacts with the PLO. Mr. Rabin reduced the Hamas deportees' two-year term of exile in March, opening the way for the resumption of Arab-Israeli peace talks. On 24 March Ezer Weizman was elected president by parliament to replace Chaim Herzog. The following day Benjamin Netanyahu replaced Yitzhak Shamir as leader of the right-wing opposition Likud party. Increasing violence—15 Israelis and 25 Palestinians were killed in March alone—prompted the government to seal off Gaza and the West Bank at the end of March, preventing 120,000 Palestinians entering Israel to work.

The Gaza Strip/Jericho Proposals.

In secret talks with PLO representatives in May, Israeli negotiators suggested a possible withdrawal of troops from the Gaza Strip and Jericho. A meeting between a cabinet minister and PLO chairman Yasir Arafat on 5 August in effect ended the ban on official contacts. On 13 August foreign minister Shimon Peres said Israel would continue to negotiate with Palestinian representatives despite its awareness that some were PLO officials. The Israeli cabinet accepted a draft accord with the Palestinians—negotiated in parallel discussions with the official talks—on 31 August.

Recognition of the PLO.

As agreement neared, Israel recognised the PLO on 9 September. A peace accord was signed by Mr. Rabin and Mr. Arafat in Washington on 13 September by which Israeli troops would withdraw from the Gaza Strip and Jericho on the West Bank on 13 December. Parliament ratified the agreement on 23 September and detailed negotiations on the withdrawal opened on 11 October. However, on 14

November discussions stalled over Israel's demand to control border crossings and protect settlers. Meanwhile, violence continued and by mid-December 38 Palestinians and 18 Israelis had been killed since the September agreement. The detailed negotiations over the Washington settlement which continued into 1994 raised obstacles which prevented Israel's withdrawal from the agreed areas.

Progress in 1994.

During 1994 the US-sponsored peace talks between Israel and her Arab neighbours made significant progress but at the same time led to outbreaks of violence which bode ill for the future stability of the region. In the course of the year Israel made peace with Jordan, advanced on the implementation of the 1993 accords with the Palestinians and saw a slight thaw in relations with Syria. The prospects for economic integration throughout the region also looked rosier at the end of the year than at the start. The year however also saw the first violent clashes between Yasser Arafat's security forces and the Islamist opposition groups and a rise in disillusionment among Palestinians as to the benefits of the peace process. Hardline Israeli settlers also intensified their often violent activities against the talks.

The year opened with mixed, but largely negative, portents. On 9 January Yasser Arafat concluded talks in Cairo with Israeli Foreign Minister Shimon Peres, agreeing on a framework for implementation of the September Declaration of Principles (DoP) signed in Washington. Although an agreement was necessary to keep the process going, critics soon charged that Arafat had given too much away and had in fact largely accepted Israel's conditions for the interim period, which will last until talks begin on the final status of the occupied territories. In particular, Arafat accepted Israel's insistence on *de facto* control over the border crossings into Gaza and Jericho, the territories to be initially transferred to Palestinian control according to the DoP; he also agreed to postpone discussion of the fate of Israeli settlements on Palestinian territory, and agreed to allow Israeli troops to continue to be responsible for the security of these enclaves.

The Hebron Massacre.

Implementation of these measures was brought to an abrupt halt on 25 February when an Israeli settler and army officer, Baruch Goldstein, perpetrated a massacre at the Ibrahimi mosque in Hebron, gunning down 48 Palestinian worshippers. The massacre brought to the fore the question of Israeli settlements and the vulnerability of Palestinians under occupation to acts of Jewish terrorism as well as repression by the army. In the weeks following the massacre it was revealed that Israeli soldiers had no orders to fire on settlers attacking Palestinians and the occupation forces clamped a curfew on the Palestinian residents of Hebron, allowing settlers to move freely and, in some cases, applaud Goldstein. In the course of riots that erupted throughout Israel and the occupied territories after the attack, the Israeli Defence Forces (IDF) killed at least another 27 Palestinians.

The massacre was "avenged" on 6 April by *Hamas*, the main Palestinian Islamist movement, when it killed seven Israeli civilians with a car-bomb in Afula. The peace process nonetheless resumed as both Rabin and Arafat had invested too much to be able to retreat from their positions.

The talks resulted in the 4 May signing between Arafat and Rabin of what became known as the Cairo Agreement. This settled the details left hanging in February and paved the way for the redeployment of the IDF and their replacement by a newly-constituted Palestinian police force. This police force gradually deployed in the liberated areas of Gaza and Jericho and was welcomed by the population. Arafat himself set up his headquarters in Gaza on 1 July where he was greeted with some joy and hopes that he would soon improve the economic and political lot of the Strip's residents.

The Assassination of Yitzhak Rabin.

The sense of shock that reverberated inside Israel following the assassination of Prime Minister Yitzhak Rabin on 4 November 1995, by a right-wing Jewish extremist, was immense. Two issues immediately came to the fore. The first revolved around the future of the Middle East peace process and the future of the ruling Labour coalition in the forthcoming Israeli elections without the trusted Rabin at the helm. The second was that a fellow Jew had perpetrated the act. This began a process of Israeli self assessment and the dawning realisation that Israeli society was not as cohesive as many inside the country had imagined. These fears were exacerbated when it was discovered that the assailant, Yigal Amir, was not acting alone and in the period following the murder, numerous supporters of right-wing Jewish organisations were arrested. Rabin's funeral was a remarkable testimony to a politician who had moved from being a warrior towards the need to embrace peace. Leaders and representatives from Arab nations were among the mourners, including Egyptian leader Hosni Mubarrak and King Hussein of Jordan, who paid a moving tribute.

Netanyahu's Victory.

Rabin's assassination produced a wave of sympathy for the Labour Party and his successor Shimon Peres. Sensing this, Peres took the decision to bring forward the date of the Israeli elections in order to secure a mandate for the continuation of the peace process. Elections were scheduled for 29 May 1996. In the intervening period however, the Palestinian organisation *Hamas* launched a series of suicide bombs in Jerusalem, Ashqelon and Tel Aviv which left over 60 people dead. The bombings rapidly eroded Peres's popular support and left the Labour leader open to old charges that he was incapable of maintaining Israeli security. In part reaction to this claim, and in an attempt to bolster his position in the run up to the elections, Peres sanctioned operation "Grapes of Wrath" in April 1996 against *Hizbollah* positions deep inside Lebanon. The deaths of 105 Palestinian refugees in a UN camp at Qana further undermined his position. On 29 May Benyamin Netanyahu, leader of the Likud Party, emerged as the new Prime Minister of Israel in a close election. Netanyahu secured 50·4%; Peres 49·5%. Netanyahu took a much tougher stance on the peace process, promising the Israelis security before negotiations could proceed. Further, his government consisted of a coalition of hard-line and religious orthodox groupings. His refusal to meet with Palestinian leader, Yasser Arafat, and the continued closure of the West Bank and Gaza Strip lead to rising discontent among the Palestinians.

The Jerusalem Issue.

Netanyahu's policy towards the Palestinians appeared contradictory. Promising to continue with the peace process, he also maintained there could be no independent Palestinian state or room for compromise over the sovereignty of Jerusalem. This general sense of frustration found expression in violence when, in September 1996, Israeli authorities opened a 488-metre tourist tunnel in Jerusalem that runs adjacent to the al-Aqsa Mosque and exits onto the Via Dolorosa. President Arafat used the opening of the tunnel to rally support behind the Palestinian National Authority (PNA), citing the tunnel as an infringement on Muslim holy sites. Israeli refusal to close the tunnel (to have done so would have implied some Palestinian control over the City) resulted in the worst violence seen in the territories since the Israeli occupation of 1967. Many Israelis and Palestinians were killed and hundreds wounded in bitter fighting. In an attempt to salvage the peace process, US President Bill Clinton convened a peace summit at the White House with President Arafat, Prime Minister Netanyahu and King Hussein of Jordan. Egyptian President Hosni Mubarrak refused to attend. The talks proved inconclusive although they did produce a short-term objective of stabilising the violence. By the end of 1996 the Israelis and Palestinians resumed negotiations though without any major breakthrough. The Netanyahu government sought a partial re-negotiation of the peace agreement signed by the Labour Party and Palestinian officials, particularly with regard to the proposed Israeli troop withdrawal from Hebron which remained an unresolved issue.

New Tensions.

Although a deal on Hebron was finally concluded on 15 January 1997, Israeli intransigence on starting work on a new settlement for 32,000 Jews in occupied East Jerusalem (on the hill known as Har Homa) caused a further deterioration in relations. The massacre of 7 Israeli girls by a deranged Jordanian soldier on 13 March raised tensions to new heights. Following a *Hamas* suicide bombing on 21 March the future of the peace process looked increasingly fragile.

Corruption Allegations.

The political scene in Israel was thrown into turmoil in April 1997 when Benjamin Netanyahu only narrowly escaped prosecution over an appointment tainted with corruption. Police had recommended he be charged for fraud and breach of trust over the failed nomination of Roni Bar-On, a little known criminal lawyer and Likud party official, for the top legal post of Attorney General. Opposition politicians challenged the decision not to prosecute as yet more divisions in Israel's political system emerged in the wake of its most serious political scandal.

Volatile Domestic Politics.

However, Netanyahu survived the storm, with enough strength remaining in June 1997 to engineer the resignation of one of his main opponents. Finance Minister Dan Meridor, who had not supported him during the Bar-On affair. This created friction within Likud when Infrastructure Minister Ariel Sharon was rumoured to be Meridor's replacement, as Sharon's promotion to a major cabinet position would have indicated his rehabilitation from his involvement in the Sabra-Chatila massacres of Palestinians in Lebanon in 1982. He also seemed to be positioning himself as a possible challenger to Netanyahu, and another possible leadership contender, Foreign Minister David Levy, by meeting with former Labour Prime Minister Shimon Peres to discuss modification of the legislation allowing direct election of the Prime Minister, to reduce the number of Knesset members needed to dismiss the Prime Minister from 80 to 61, and by meeting Palestinian officials to discuss the stalemated peace process. Netanyahu also avoided a crisis in June with the influential American Jewish community by creating a committee to examine the question of a "conversion law" which would have allowed Orthodox Jewish clerics to vet conversions carried out by the more modernist Conservative and Reform movements. Also in June, Ehud Barak won the Labour leadership with a majority of slightly more than 50 per cent. Although seen as a candidate who could pose a threat to Netanyahu from the opposition benches, in the media, and eventually at the polls, his performance to date has not been as successful as expected, and internal opposition remains within the Labour party.

More Suicide Bombs.

With the peace process already stalemated, a double suicide bomb hit a market in Jerusalem on 30 July, killing 13 Israelis and two bombers, and was subsequently claimed by *Hamas*. The bombing seemed to be in response to the Israeli determination to continue with the Har Homa settlement and to American vetoes of UN resolutions regarding the matter which would otherwise have condemned Israel. Only two days before the incident Benjamin Netanyahu had boasted on Israeli television that he had successfully fulfilled his election pledge to bring Israelis "peace with security". However, public opinion seemed to harden behind the government, with the opposition voiceless in criticising the policies which may have helped provoke the bloody reaction. The government immediately renewed its closure of Palestinian areas, froze the PNA's assets in Israel and suspended transfers of customs duties to it, claiming that the authority must act against its "terrorist infrastructure". The IDF also arrested 150 Palestinians from villages in the West Bank still under Israeli control. However, the PNA did not carry out large-scale arrests of Islamists and in fact participated with *Hamas* in a National Unity Forum in Gaza. It was also unclear if the bombers had actually come from Palestinian territory.

New US Secretary of State Arrives.

Hamas' response came on 4 September immediately prior to the visit of US Secretary of State Madeleine Albright to Israel in an attempt to give new life to the Oslo process—three more suicide bombers detonated themselves on a crowded street in Jerusalem, killing four Israelis. Albright's visit was generally regarded as unsuccessful. She left the region stating that she would only return once Israelis and Palestinians had themselves moved the process forward. However, immediately following her visit, Israeli settlers seized a number of houses in the Palestinian village of Ras al-Amud on the outskirts of the Old City of Jerusalem.

The suicide bombings combined with events in Lebanon created a new sense of dread in Israel, as well as a humbling of military pride. On 5 September the IDF suffered one of its most humiliating defeats ever, during an incursion into Lebanon. 12 IDF soldiers from a prestigious naval commando unit were killed in an *Hizbollah* ambush, during which elements of the Lebanese Army and the Shiite militia Amal also engaged the Israelis. By October, some 39 Israeli troops had been killed in combat in Lebanon in 1997.

New Peace Initiative.

For recent developments towards attempting to secure a breakthrough in the peace talks stalemate, *see* **C67**.

EGYPT.

Escalating Violence.

During 1994 the government managed to make headway against the violent fundamentalist groups opposing it. An energetic programme of mass arrests, shoot to kill policies, extraditions from abroad and police infiltration of groups pushed the rebels on the defensive and forced them largely to limit their activities to their Upper Egyptian strongholds around Assiut.

During 1995 however, violence again intensified. In January alone the death toll from political violence stood at 80. In response the government re-doubled its efforts to crush the three year armed insurgency by the militants. Increasingly, the government began to blame events upon the Muslim Brotherhood, which although it had been outlawed for over 20 years, still operated from its headquarters in Cairo. In November 1995, just prior to parliamentary elections, 54 Brotherhood leaders were controversially found guilty of crimes against the state and given jail sentences by military judges. This sparked off huge controversy and placed the Egyptian judicial system under immense scrutiny.

The 1995 Elections.

Egypt held elections to its new 444-seat Parliament in late November 1995, but the process was immediately overshadowed by accusations from opposition movements that the elections were fixed. Allegations of cheating focused on irregularities in the electoral registers preventing many individuals from voting and more seriously the fact that hundreds of opposition supporters and some candidates (mainly Islamists), were detained prior to and during the election.

The high turn out of the electorate was used by Hosni Mubarak to justify the results. The President's ruling National Democratic Party won a landslide victory and Mubarak immediately indicated there was no need to make significant changes to the government as a result of the parliamentary elections. There were some suggestions however that the Egyptian authorities were prepared to arrange for some opposition figures to win parliamentary seats provided they distance themselves from extremist movements.

Counter-Terrorism Efforts.

On 13 March 1996, Egypt hosted the "Summit of the Peace-Makers" at Sharm al-Shaikh. The meeting was very rapidly convened in the light of the *Hamas* bombings inside Israel that threatened the Middle East peace process. Intense American diplomacy persuaded leaders and officials of 27 nations and representatives from the UN and EU to attend. Iran, Iraq, Libya and Sudan were not invited while Syria and Lebanon declined their invitations. The four-hour gathering did not result in any concrete measures, although all the leaders pledged, by all political and economic means possible, to clamp down on terrorism. One month later four armed Islamists machine gunned a crowd of elderly female Greek tourists in Cairo killing 17, mistakenly believing them to be Israelis. In August 1996 the UN Security Council voted to impose an air embargo on Sudan in an attempt to press the Sudanese authorities to extradite three Egyptians accused in a plot to assassinate Hosni Mubarak in June 1991 in Addis Ababa. The sanctions followed diplomatic and travel restrictions imposed the previous May.

The Luxor Massacre.

In spring 1997 some 30 Coptic Christians were killed in southern Egypt in two separate attacks on their villages. In September, an attack by a "mentally-ill" individual with no known affiliation with Islamist organisations killed 9 German tourists and an Egyptian in Cairo's central Tahrir Square, supposed to be one of the most secure areas of the capital. Showing their disdain for their imprisoned leaders call for an end to violence, on 13 October Islamists killed 9 policemen and two others on a train, and on 17 November the Islamic Group undertook the worst-ever terrorist attack in Egypt, killing some 60 tourists and 3 Egyptians at the Temple of Hapshetsut on the West Bank of the Nile in Luxor. The slaughter prompted many tourists to immediately leave the country and others to cancel bookings, doing inestimable damage to the estimated \$8 billion a year industry which comprises 8 per cent of GDP, which had finally recovered from earlier campaigns of violence, surpassing pre-Gulf war levels in 1997. The attack prompted the resignation of Interior Minister Hassan al-Alfi.

Middle East Peace Initiatives.

For recent developments, *see* **C67**.

JORDAN.

Peace with Israel.

In contrast with the chaotic Palestinian scene, Jordan's King Hussein moved swiftly and relatively easily in 1994 to achieve peace with Israel. At the beginning of the year it had been unclear how willing he would be to move out ahead of either the PLO or of Syria, both of which were unenthusiastic to a rapid Jordanian deal with Israel. King Hussein nonetheless concluded that the benefits of rapid establishment of relations were worth the risks. On 25 July Hussein and Rabin signed a declaration in Washington, vowing to end their state of war. Despite hiccups, this was followed on 26 October by a formal peace treaty signed on the Israeli–Jordanian border.

An Israeli–Jordanian peace had never been predicted to pose too many problems since the ostensible issues of contention, Jordanian claims over territory and water rights, were never regarded by either country as of great strategic moment. The two countries had been "best of enemies" for many years and had long covertly co-operated. Israel nonetheless regarded the treaty as of historic significance as, from November onwards, Israelis could now cross another of their land borders and the two countries could work together openly on development, trade and tourism projects. In addition, Israel proved adept at using Jordan to apply pressure on Arafat. Israeli negotiators agreed on a "special role" for Hussein in relation to the Jerusalem holy places, a move which infuriated the Palestinian leadership. A low-key struggle for control of the West Bank subsequently resumed with the PNA banning a pro-Jordanian newspaper.

For King Hussein the treaty was more of a gamble. His signature provoked opposition in parliament, especially from Islamist deputies who opposed the peace and claimed that Jordan had sold out the Palestinians due to US pressure. The extent of pressure became evident over the summer and autumn as Washington took a series of steps which encouraged Hussein to go along. These included easing the UN-mandated inspection regime for ships entering Aqaba port, forgiving much of Jordan's debt to the US and offering military aid to the country.

Violence in Karak.

In August 1996, the southern city of Karak erupted in violence following the government's decision to raise the price of bread by 200%, in addition to other food commodities. Rioters were also demanding greater political freedom, although King Hussein took the step to dissolve the 80-seat parliament's summer session and quelled the disturbances with the use of force. The Jordanian government also accused Iraq of inciting the rioters.

Death of King Hussein.

The death of the ailing King Hussein (*see* **B33**) in February 1999 brought a wealth of tributes to his major role over so many years in the Middle East. He was succeeded by King Abdullah.

THE PALESTINIANS.

The Peace Accord, 1993.

A peace accord signed by Mr. Arafat and Mr. Rabin in Washington on 13 September proposed an Israeli withdrawal from the Gaza Strip and Jericho on the West Bank beginning on 13 December. The areas would come under Palestinian self-government. The PLO central council, at a meeting boycotted by its most radical elements, ratified the agreement on 12 October by 63 votes to eight but criticisms of Mr. Arafat's autocratic style continued. Detailed negotiations with Israel over the withdrawal ran into obstacles when Israel demanded the right to protect Jewish settlers, to control border crossings and on the exact extent of Jericho. On 13 December the PLO and Israel agreed to postpone the deadline for implementation a further ten days.

Israeli-Palestinian Breakthrough.

During late 1994 and the majority of 1995, the Israeli-Palestinian negotiations teetered on the edge of collapse. The Israelis were demanding that Yasser Arafat take firm action to address the problem of Palestinian extremism, in particular against *Hamas* following the Beit Lid suicide attack on 22 January 1995 which left 20 Israeli soldiers dead and 68 civilians injured. In return the PLO demanded the Israeli government begin to redeploy its troops from the West Bank. This stalemate dragged on throughout the year until a breakthrough was reached with the Taba agreement signed at the White House on 28 September 1995.

Although radical elements on both sides were opposed to the deal, the PLO proclaimed the document the first real step towards an autonomous Palestinian state. Under the agreement the Palestinian National Authority (PNA) gained full control of the six main West Bank towns of Jenin, Tulkarm, Nablus, Qalgiliya, Ramallah and Bethlehem and authority over 440 smaller villages. Partial autonomy was granted over Hebron where the situation was complicated by the fate of 415 Jewish settlers whose security was still protected by the Israeli Defence Forces (IDF). The agreement gave the PNA jurisdiction over an estimated population of 1·3 million. Furthermore, the PNA was also given responsibility for public order and the right to establish an executive with legislative powers. Throughout the latter part of 1995, the IDF rapidly withdrew from a large area of the West Bank.

The Taba Agreement.

During 1995, the efforts made by Yasser Arafat to establish an independent Palestinian homeland bore fruit. The Taba agreement of September 1995 extended the authority of the Palestinian National Authority over most of the West Bank. Furthermore, throughout the year a rapprochement developed between the radical Hamas organisation and the PNA which seemed to lesson the likelihood of a Palestinian civil war. Not all Arab leaders

warmed to the attitude taken by Arafat. Libya's Colonel Gaddafi in particular reacted angrily to the peace talks by expelling 30,000 Palestinian refugees working inside his country. Gaddafi argued the Palestinians were no longer refugees since the PLO had established its own autonomous entity. However, the Palestinians were refused entry into Gaza and the West Bank by the Israelis who feared they would stay permanently. As a result tens of thousands of Palestinians were placed into a make-shift refugee camp on the edge of the Egyptian-Gaza Strip border.

Palestinian Elections.

A significant event took place on 20 January 1996 when Palestinians voted in their first ever election. Around 750,000 of a potential electorate of just over 1 million awarded Yasser Arafat 88% of the votes cast in the Presidential elections. Arafat declared the election the first step in the creation of an independent Palestinian state. The election also determined the balance of the newly created 88-member Palestinian Council. Fifty seats were captured by Arafat's Fatah movement with the remaining seats going to "independents", the majority of whom were sympathetic towards Fatah policies. Critics however, pointed out that power overwhelmingly resided with the President and indeed the Council did not directly participate in the on-going Palestinian-Israeli peace dialogue.

Moreover, concerns were expressed that the elections favoured the Israelis with the Council merely acting as a "pressure valve" to regulate Palestinian frustrations rather than as a forum with real powers over an independent jurisdiction. Nevertheless, they were important for several reasons. Firstly, they laid the foundations for a Palestinian political culture as distinct from the operations of the old Palestine National Council, largely based on patrimony and factional quotas. Secondly, the elections gave Arafat real legitimacy in his negotiations with the Israelis as the unquestioned representative of the Palestinian people. Despite these advances, the PNA was continually accused of human rights abuses.

Growing Discontent.

There was growing discontent with the leadership of Yasser Arafat in the PNA in 1997. Part is no doubt due to the deadlocked peace process, as many Palestinians have come to realise the reality of the Oslo Accords may not match the rhetoric of their politicians, but there are other causes. With unemployment and underemployment estimated at 30 per cent, and 25 per cent of the population living below the poverty line of $500-600 per year, anger is increasingly directed at the PNA. Many Palestinians view the PNA administration as corrupt, nepotistic and oppressive, and its heavy-handed security forces have cracked down on a number of occasions against domestic discontent and are involved in enforcing the unpopular and non-transparent tax system.

Developments in 1997.

In 1997, it appeared, as US negotiator Dennis Ross stated, that the Israeli-Palestinian peace process was surviving only because "there is no acceptable alternative". The US negotiators and their administration came under growing criticism from the PNA and Arab states for their perceived bias towards Israel, with growing calls for EU or other mediation. The main sticking points remained delays in the scheduled Israeli withdrawal from Zone B and C areas of the West Bank and continuing settlement activity, particularly in Jerusalem. Clashes also continued with settlers in Hebron and at Gush Qatif in Gaza, with the former only ending in July when the IDF surrounded the area in preparation for what appeared to be a reoccupation, and after 2 Palestinians had died and some 500 were injured. The Israeli objective in Jerusalem was seen by the PNA as an attempt to merge mainly Arab East Jerusalem and West Bank areas of "Greater Jerusalem" into Israeli territory demographically before final status negotiations got underway. The PNA reacted by raising money for their own real estate investment and drawing attention to the Israeli activity of seizing the identification of Palestinians who could not "prove" that they lived inside Jerusalem's municipal boundaries. A Palestinian estate agent was killed after a statement by PNA Justice Minister Furayh Abu Middayn that Palestinians selling land to Israelis could face the death penalty. After the visit of US Secretary of State Madeleine Albright in September, the two sides met in Washington on 29 September where nine joint committees were established to address issues still pending from the Oslo and Hebron agreements. One, on security issues, is chaired by the CIA station chief in Israel to verify PNA action against *Hamas* and Islamic Jihad extremists on its territory. Discussions continued in November with little progress being made.

Yasser Arafat's Health.

There was as well growing international concern regarding the health of President Arafat, opening up the question of possible successors. Arafat has suffered from health problems since a plane crash in Libya in 1992, and has appeared ill in public on a number of occasions in 1997, passing out in two meetings. Some believe that he may be in the early stages of Parkinson's disease, or simply suffering from overwork and despair at the state of the peace process. The main concern regarding his health relates to his possible successors, as there does not appear to be one sure candidate. The PNA's unratified Basic Law stipulates that this should be the Speaker of the Palestinian Legislative Council, Ahmed Quray. A more feasible candidate is that of Mahmoud Abbas, a moderate and the PLO's chief negotiator and specialist in foreign affairs. Less likely are the various heads of the PNA security organs, most of whom are relatively young and inexperienced in politics, and being won over by Abbas. As all are loyal to Arafat, there is unlikely to be political unrest until such a time as the President steps down or his illness worsens, by which point Abbas may have solidified his position. The growing political force of *Hamas* may also provide a challenge to the PNA's succession process.

Release of Yasin.

The outcome of the Mash'al Affair (the bungled Israeli spy episode) resulted in the homecoming to Gaza of the *Hamas* spiritual leader, the 61-year old paralysed Sheikh Ahmed Yasin, from an Israeli jail where he had spent the last eight years. 22 other political prisoners were also released by Israel, which was a major boost to Palestinian morale in a year when there was not much to cheer about. However, Yasin has refused to pledge to renounce terrorism, and has added to the increasing domestic political profile of *Hamas*, giving them a leader with the stature of Yasser Arafat and posing more domestic political problems, as well as possible opportunities, for the PNA leader.

The Peace Deadlock.

For recent developments, *see* **C67**.

IRAN.

The 1992 Election.

The first elections to the 270 seat *Majlis*, Iran's parliament, since the death of Ayatollah Khomeini in 1989 were held on 10 April and 8 May 1992 and resulted in a setback for Islamic radicals who had previously held 60% of seats. Although there were no formal political parties, the results were seen as a victory for the moderate supporters of President Rafsanjani's Society of Combatant Clergymen. Mr Rafsanjani sought to attract foreign investment by moving towards a free market economy. The radicals, who were increasingly blamed for Iran's economic stagnation, favoured retaining a centralised economy. On 5 May the Supreme Council of Investment removed limits on the share foreign owners could have in Iranian businesses. But poverty in Iran had led to the growth of squatter communities in urban areas and in April and May there was serious rioting in five major cities. President Rafsanjani's attempts to rebuild relations with the west suffered a setback when, on 2 November, a government-backed religious charity announced an increase in the $2 million reward for the assassination of *Satanic Verses* author Salman

Rushdie. President Rafsanjani survived an assassination attempt on 10 February 1993.

On 25 May 1993 Iranian aircraft bombed bases in Iraq sheltering opposition People's Mujahedeen guerrillas. The guerrillas had attacked oil pipelines in Iran and claimed to have killed hundreds of government troops. In elections on 11 June President Rafsanjani was elected to a second four-year term in a four man contest. His opponents were selected by the Council of Guardians, a body of conservative Islamic clerics. President Rafsanjani took 63% of the votes cast and his nearest opponent, former labour minister Ahmed Tavakoli, won 24%. The low turn-out, 56% as opposed to 70% four years earlier, was attributed to apathy caused by economic hardship and dissatisfaction with clerical rule.

Radicals versus Moderates.

During 1994 the radical-moderate struggle continued to swing back and forth. A fall in oil prices was a severe blow to the economy and to Rafsanjani's reform plans. Although he claimed that the five year development plan completed in 1994 was a success, it had built up foreign debts of $20–$30 billion. The reform programme provoked discontent as it involved cutting subsidies and grants to religious institutions and major riots took place in several cities, including Qazvin. Terrorist violence also swept the country with bombs in Shia shrines, including Mashhad, and the murder of several Christian clergymen. The government blamed these on opposition Mujahidin guerillas but it is likely that they were attempts by the regime to create a state of siege and make people rally round the regime. Attempts to attract foreign investors were set back by the government's inability to reform the exchange rate system and a resistance to allowing foreign investment. The exiled opposition claimed during the year that the end of the regime was nigh and elected a President in exile. The government responded by bombing Mujahidin bases in Iraq in November.

US Trade Sanctions.

Economic difficulties were set to prevail during 1995 when the American administration enforced its own trading sanctions on the Islamic Republic.

On 5 August 1996, President Clinton signed a bill imposing sanctions against US and foreign companies doing major business with Iran or Libya. The European Union and Japan reacted strongly to these measures, with France in particular affirming that it would retaliate if any sanctions were imposed on French firms. Earlier in the year, Iran held parliamentary elections to the 270-member *Majlis*. The elections heralded the official establishment of four political factions in the Republic although the results themselves strongly favoured the ruling moderate elite under President Rafsanjani. Right-wing 'traditionalists' were the biggest losers who saw their number reduced in the new forum from 150 to around 100.

Presidential Elections.

In May 1997 Mohammad Khatami defeated his conservative rival and *Majlis* speaker Ali Akbar Nateq-Nouri in presidential elections to replace Rafsanjani. Although Nateq-Nouri, the establishment candidate, was favoured to win, Khatami was elected with 69% of the 29·1 million ballots cast. Khatami's cabinet was a mix of reformers and conservatives, while his policies concentrated on social and domestic reform, especially the economy. Khatami has proposed removing much of the restrictive legislation passed by the previous government, particularly in the fields of media, arts and culture, as well as civil rights, especially for women. Foreign policy has been re-energised with the creation of a team headed by former UN representative Dr. Kamal Kharrazi as foreign minister.

Foreign Relations.

Kharazzi was quite successful in 1997 at improving Iran's relations with Arab neighbours and Europe, but less so with the US. Khatami's election has been cautiously welcomed in Washington, but no substantive change in the American "containment" policy has occurred.

The Montazeri Affair.

The former heir to Ayatollah Khomeini demonstrated in November 1997 the difficulties President Khatami would have with some of his more liberal initiatives. The 75-year old Ayatollah Hussein Ali Montazeri, a leading dissident cleric, publicly challenged the regime and its system of *velayat-e faqih*, or rule of Islamic jurisprudence, which provided Supreme Leader Ayatollah Khamenei with authority and legitimacy. Montazeri implied in his statement that political power should be based on a mandate from the people, and not religion. The reaction was almost instantaneous—on 19 November Revolutionary Guards and *Hizbollahis* attacked Montazeri's home and religious school in the holy city of Qom, physically assaulting the cleric and his family. National protests broke out across Iran, with protest marches and strikes in several cities in support of Khamenei. The incidents demonstrated the careful path President Khatami would have to tread in carrying out his reforms.

Tension with Afghanistan.

In the summer of 1998 there was growing hostility between Iran and Afghanistan following the killing of nine Iranians in a Taliban attack. Ayatollah Ali Khamenei warned that the Taliban movement represented a threat to the entire Islamic world. In September over 200,000 Iranian troops were deployed on the border with Afghanistan and an invasion appeared imminent. Although the immediate crisis waned, antagonism between the two states remained.

Anniversary of the Revolution.

As the 20th anniversary of the revolution approached in 1999, there appeared to be increasing moves towards democratisation under President Khatami. In mid-1998 the mayor of Tehran, Gholamhossein Karbaschi, was suspended from office following a conviction for corruption. Mr Karbaschi, a prominent supporter of President Khatami, went on to form the first post-revolutionary political party, the Servants of Construction. The party—based around technocrats—advocated neo-Thatcherite economic and social policies. In December President Khatami and his followers attempted to institutionalise his reform movement by establishing the Islamic Iron Participation Front. The move followed growing conservative protests at President Khatami's programme. In November terrorists attacked a bus carrying American businessmen, clearly attempting to damage improving Iran-US relations.

IRAQ.

The Invasion of Kuwait.

During the spring and summer of 1990 Iraq came under increasing Western criticism as a result of its burgeoning non-conventional weapons programme. On 15 March the execution of a British journalist raised a storm, and on 2 April Saddam threatened to devastate Israel if it attacked Iraq's weapons programme.

In July Saddam Hussein accused Kuwait of stealing £1·3 billion worth of oil from disputed border territory and claimed that Kuwait was conspiring to undermine Iraq's economy by excessive oil production. He demanded compensation and moved troops towards the frontier. Iraq agreed to a Kuwaiti proposal for discussions but these broke down on 1 August. The following day Iraq invaded Kuwait, claiming to have been invited to support a popular uprising. The Emir, Sheikh Jabir Ahmed al-Sabah, fled to Saudi Arabia. Iraq installed a puppet government but at the end of August annexed Kuwait as Iraq's 19th province.

Operation Desert Shield.

The build-up of coalition forces—Operation Desert Shield—ran parallel with peace moves. A UN deadline expired at 5.00 GMT on 16 January 1991. Shortly before midnight the war between the coalition and Iraq—Operation Desert Storm—began. Over the next six weeks Iraq and Kuwait suffered almost continual air bombardment. The attacks were met with anti-aircraft fire but there was limited reaction from Iraq's 700-strong air force, 132 of its best aircraft fleeing to Iran for sanctuary.

Retaliation by Iraq.

Iraq's main military response was to launch Scud missiles against Israel and Saudi Arabia. Israel was hit by 39 missiles. The missile attacks' importance lay in their potential political effects rather than their military impact. If Israel retaliated, Arab support for the coalition might weaken. President Bush urged restraint on Israel, backing this with the deployment of anti-Scud Patriot missiles in Israel.

At the same time Iraq released a large oil slick from Kuwait, apparently in an attempt to pollute the Gulf. The firing of Kuwaiti oil wells followed with serious environmental consequences.

The impact of continual bombing on civilians raised international concern. On 13 February two bombs hit what the coalition claimed was a military command bunker in Baghdad. The bunker was sheltering 400 civilians, mainly women and children. Hundreds were killed. On 24 February the allied land offensive opened.

The Allied Land Offensive.

Iraq fielded the world's fourth largest army, with 555,000 regular and 480,000 reserve troops. An estimated 545,000 were deployed in or near Kuwait with a further quarter of a million in northern Iraq. The army included 2,595 tanks, 1,625 artillery pieces and 1,945 armoured personnel carriers. As the land battle began 1,300 tanks, 800 armoured vehicles and 1,100 artillery pieces had reportedly been destroyed by bombing. The largest allied force—commanded by General Norman Schwarzkopf—was the American, with 527,000 combat and support troops, 3,400 tanks and armoured vehicles, and almost a thousand aircraft. The British force, the second strongest, was led by Lt.-Gen. Sir Peter de la Billière.

The 100-Hour War.

The battle for Kuwait lasted 100 hours. The main allied attack was directed towards the Euphrates Valley, while a French Rapid Action Force went to the west, encircling an estimated 500,000 Iraqi troops. Iraqi forces—including the elite Republican Guard—offered minor resistance, and allied casualties were light. Iraq's casualties were estimated at between 50 and 150,000 and 175,000 troops were taken prisoner. On 25 February Baghdad Radio reported that the withdrawal from Kuwait had begun. Allied air forces bombed the retreating army on the road to Basra, turning it into what one press report described as a "slaughterhouse". On 26 February President Saddam conceded that Kuwait was no longer part of Iraq. As US marines and local resistance fighters took control of Kuwait City the exiled Emir declared martial law.

The Kurdish Rebellion.

Taking advantage of Iraq's preoccupation with Kuwait, Kurdish rebels launched a major offensive, taking a string of towns including Zakho, Dahuk, and Kirkuk. (*See* C67 for the background to the Kurdish question). After the Gulf War ceasefire, however, Saddam Hussein turned his army loose on them. The flight of the Kurdish people to bleak mountain refuges awakened the conscience of the world. Allied forces moved into northern Iraq to establish "safe havens" for the Kurds. In May, UN personnel also moved in.

These safe havens enabled the Kurds to return to their towns and Kurdish guerrillas replaced Iraqi security forces in much of northern Iraq. At the same time a major uprising broke out in the south of the country as disaffected soldiers and the Shia population followed President Bush's advice to rise up and remove Saddam. These rebels received aid from Iran but none from the West and were rapidly crushed by Saddam's forces. Kurdish leaders however, emboldened by Western support, began to negotiate an autonomy agreement with Saddam. The negotiations progressed slowly as Saddam waited for the West to lose interest and Kurdish leaders disagreed among themselves.

Having failed to support the Kurdish and Shia rebellions when they were strong enough to threaten Saddam, the US set out to keep him weak by arranging for the UN to supervise the dismantling of Iraq's arsenal of non-conventional weapons. UN investigations revealed that Iraq had a far more sophisticated and extensive nuclear programme than originally believed. Trade sanctions were also maintained as a way of encouraging Iraqis to remove their leader, but a succession of coup attempts took place in vain.

Punitive Air Strikes.

The UN Security Council repeated its charges on 11 January 1993 that Iraq was continuing to violate the cease fire terms by obstructing UN weapons investigators and making two incursions into Kuwait. US and British aircraft mounted punitive attacks on Iraq on 13, 17 and 18 January, destroying missile batteries and attacking an industrial complex north of Baghdad which had formerly been a nuclear plant. President Saddam ordered his forces to cease fire in what had been an undeclared war on 19 January and conceded entry to UN inspectors. Forty civilians were killed in the air attacks.

Extension of Economic Sanctions.

The UN voted to extend economic sanctions on 29 March 1993 because of continuing repression of Kurds in the north and Shi'ite Moslems in the south, and refusal to co-operate with the commission setting the border with Kuwait. Sanctions imposed in the wake of the Gulf War had been intended to heighten dissatisfaction among the Iraqi people with President Saddam. But his position appeared as secure as ever, while the suffering caused to the most vulnerable sections of the people was intense.

From 7–14 July Iraq discussed with UN officials its appeal to allow the sale of $1·6 billion of oil to buy essential food and medicines. While no decision was made, Iraq announced on 19 July its willingness to allow long-term UN monitoring of its weapons production. But accusations in November that Iraq had recently used chemical weapons against Shi'ites in the south made the lifting of sanctions unlikely.

Throughout 1994 the US and Britain continued to insist on the continuation of sanctions even through Turkey, Russia and France, were keen to restore ties with Iraq in order to restore trade relations. The sanctions were crippling the economy and impoverishing Iraqis even further, leading Saddam himself to assume the prime-ministership and impose draconian anti-profiteering measures. In a desperate attempt to force the UN to reconsider he moved Republican Guard divisions towards Kuwait, leading the Western allies to deploy troops to the region. There was however no indication that he wanted to fight, especially since the army was plagued by desertion and lack of supplies. The UN weapons inspectors announced on 10 October that they had destroyed the bulk of Iraq's weapons of mass destruction and installed a monitoring regime. This was to remain in place for at least six months before the embargo on oil sales could begin to be lifted but it appeared likely that the US and Britain would seek to retain sanctions until Saddam fell. Even Iraq's acceptance of the existence of Kuwait and the UN-drawn border in November failed to convince Washington and London to soften their stance, despite signs that they were becoming increasingly isolated in the international community.

The opposition meanwhile showed little sign of being able to topple the regime. In the south the army continued to drain the marshes and evict villagers while in the north, Kurdish groups fought among themselves and the Iraqi National Congress took a lower profile. The intra-Kurdish clashes led to widespread human rights abuses and to a Turkish invasion aimed at the Kurdish Workers Party (PKK) on the grounds that the Turkish border was no longer secure.

Pressure meanwhile intensified on Saddam Hussein as his troops clashed with Shia fighters in the south and Kurds in the north even as reports emerged of a coup attempt in which his son Udai was wounded.

Saddam's Referendum.

On 15 October 1995, Iraqi citizens endorsed the leadership of Saddam Hussein for another 7 years. The Iraqi dictator amassed 99·96% of the vote, though the election could hardly have been termed free or fair. The referendum was called in an attempt to shore up his position following the defection of his son-in-law and cabinet member, Lt. General Hussein Kamel, to Jordan on 8 August 1995. This defection was thought to seriously weaken the position of Saddam since General Kamel was regarded as a close confidant and his flight only served to highlight the feuding that had occurred within the ruling regime.

The referendum was used by Saddam to counter the growing speculation that his grip on power was fast weakening, whilst at the same time enabling him to restore some of his personal prestige. Furthermore, the election was portrayed as a break with the past. The international community was told that the administration had been purged and that it was Hussein Kamel who had been behind Iraqi recalcitrance in relation to the concealment of its arms programme from UN inspectors. For his part, Hussein Kamel began a concerted effort to portray himself as a replacement for his father-in-law. Yet he made little impact while in exile. He was deeply mistrusted by Iraqi opposition movements in the Arab world and was denied asylum in Saudi Arabia, Syria and the United States. After outstaying their welcome in Amman, Hussein Kamel and his brother Saddam Kamel announced their intention to return to Baghdad in February 1996. Within days both were dead, the result of a shoot out with younger family members who accused them of bringing dishonour onto the al-Majid clan. Throughout 1996, Iraq continued to be the thorn in the side of American foreign policy, often refusing to allow UN weapon inspectors entry into sites they wished to investigate. Nevertheless, in May 1996 Iraq and the UN reached an agreement (UN Resolution 986) on the resumption of limited Iraqi oil exports to pay for vital food and medical supplies. Later in the year, resolution 986 was suspended by the Iraqis who disputed the number of UN monitors to be allowed into the country. During November 1996 however, Iraqi authorities reached a "full agreement" on its implementation. Although an important development in Iraqi relations with the UN, the overall sanctions regime remained intact.

Turmoil in Kurdistan.

Following two years of stalemate in the factional Kurdistan war, events moved rapidly when the Iranian-backed Patriotic Union of Kurdistan (PUK) launched an offensive against the Kurdistan Democratic Party (KDP) in July 1996. Sensing the opportunity to extract political gain, Saddam Hussein entered into an informal alliance with the KDP to overthrow the PUK. On 31 August Iraqi troops backed the KDP to occupy the regional capital of Arbil, subsequently taking the strategic town of Suleimaniya and most of northern Iraq. The KDP was installed as the new government before Iraqi forces withdrew. The offensive effectively ended the "democratic experiment" inside Kurdistan following the elections of 1991. More significantly it highlighted Saddam Hussein's willingness to disregard the will of the international community to maintain a Kurdish safe haven in the north of the country. In an attempt to remedy this the Clinton administration sanctioned cruise missile strikes against the Baghdad regime and extended the 'no-fly' zone to 20 miles south of the Iraqi capital. Aside from inflicting physical punishment, the strike failed to destabilise the existing regime or guarantee the Kurds safety from potential Iraqi incursions. Indeed, the US attack was widely condemned inside the Arab world with only Kuwait offering its unanimous support. By October the US had managed to broker a cease-fire between the two sides but only after the PUK, rearmed by Iran, launched a counter-offensive in which they retook Suleimaniya.

Relations with the UN.

Saddam Hussein continued to toy with the inspectors of the UN arms inspection team dismantling his weapons of mass destruction programmes in 1997. Incidents occurred in June, with inspectors denied access to suspected sites containing weapons information and in some cases their physical security was threatened. This resulted in calls for new sanctions against Baghdad in October, which would have included a travel ban on senior Iraqi officials. However, these were essentially abandoned in early November when it became clear that Russia, France and China did not support them. Emboldened by this open split in the coalition against him, Saddam subsequently refused on 3 November to admit US members of the inspection team into Iraq and threatened to shoot down the U-2 reconnaissance aircraft supporting the mission. The American response was strong and forceful, with the deployment of 15 warships, including an aircraft carrier, to the Gulf, with another carrier deployed on 20 November, and accompanying calls for full Iraqi compliance with UN resolutions. However, a compromise agreement mediated by Russia was reached in Geneva as it was again clear that the coalition against Iraq had disintegrated, with Britain the only major member backing US calls for the use of force and no Arab support whatsoever for such action, even from Kuwait—mainly due to US inaction against Israel in the Arab-Israeli peace process. UN inspectors returned to work on 22 November and U-2 flights resumed on 24 November under an agreement which would allow re-examination of the personnel establishment of inspection teams to allow for more non-American inspectors, as well as granting access to presidential sites which had previously been out of bounds to arms inspectors. More importantly for Baghdad, there were hints that economic sanctions could be removed with Saddam Hussein still in power, provided inspectors were satisfied with the disposition of Iraq's weapons of mass destruction. The crisis also demonstrated the failure of the US "containment" policy and provided a domestic boost for Saddam following the American climb-down.

Renewed Confrontation.

Early in 1998, the crisis of late 1997 was repeated. Once again, Saddam Hussein threatened to block the work of the UN inspectors. Once again, America rushed military reinforcements to the Gulf. In Britain, the Labour Government very openly supported America. But the Arab states held back.

Following Mr Annan's apparent defusing of the crisis in February 1998 the UN Security Council warned Iraq of the 'fatal consequences' of failing to honour the agreement. On 26 March, UN weapons experts began inspections at eight sites, culminating with President Saddam's main palace in Baghdad. Inspectors were soon claiming, however, that information about germ warfare was being held back and that they had been able to make no progress in determing whether Iraq had destroyed its weapons of mass destruction.

As the Iraqi foreign minister called for the setting of a time limit on inspections, the UN renewed sanctions for a further six months. At the end of May inspectors resumed their search for chemical warheads and the United States announced a new agreement on 15 June on disarmament verification as a preliminary to the lifting of sanctions. However, on 24 June chief weapons inspector Richard Butler confirmed reports that traces of nerve gas had been found in Iraqi missile fragments. A week later, an American fighter fired on an Iraqi missile site.

Threats and Responses.

At the end of July Iraq demanded an end to the UN trade embargo and as August opened Butler left Baghdad, alleging that Iraq was failing to meet its commitment to destroy weapons of mass destruction. By the end of October the Iraqi government said it had withdrawn all co-operation with weapons monitors. On 10 November the United States warned that Iraq's capability could be rapidly restored without preventative action and UN personnel were withdrawn as an attack appeared imminent. In a letter to UN secretary general Kofi Annan, Iraq offered to renew co-operation and inspections were resumed on 17 November. But on 16 December inspectors were withdrawn as Mr Butler again alleged the Iraqi authorities were failing to co-operate. From 16–19 December US and British forces fired hundreds of Cruise missiles at Iraqi targets as a punishment for this failure.

Recent Events.

Clashes and bombing attacks continued into 1999. It remained unclear how far the intention was to provoke President Saddam's overthrow or—as US President Clinton had maintained in December 1998—simply to contain him. Opposition to President Saddam within Iraq remained weak and divided. The Iraqi National Congress, with a base in the north of the country, called for democracy but its dependence on US funds suggested it would win little internal backing. The Supreme Council for Islamic Revolution in Iraq, supported by neighbouring Iran, seemed equally unlikely to gain widespread support. The ousting of President Saddam by his own Republican Guard—in which there had allegedly been plans for a coup—was unlikely to guarantee future stability, let alone democratic government.

SYRIA.

Assad's Fourth Term.

On 12 March 1992 President Assad inaugurated his fourth term by accusing the United States of mounting an arms blockade against the Arab states while allowing Israel to build up its arsenal. The US had attempted to intercept a ship allegedly transporting Scud missiles to Syria. However, President Assad told the US Secretary of State on 21 February 1993 that he was anxious to resume Arab-Israeli peace talks suspended on 17 December 1992.

The talks (which resumed on 27 April) were threatened when, on 25 July 1993, Syrian soldiers in Lebanon's Bekaa Valley were killed in Israeli air attacks on guerrilla villages. But Syrian forces refrained from retaliatory action and, while condemning Israel, did not withdraw from the peace negotiations. Syria was involved in negotiating a ceasefire with Israel, Lebanon and Hizbollah forces and appeared to take steps to prevent further Iranian weapons reaching the guerrillas. In talks on 16 January 1994 President Assad told US President Clinton that Syria wanted "normal" relations with Israel.

On the domestic front, Assad's plans for a smooth succession were blown off course by the death of his son and anointed successor Basil in a car crash on 21 January.

Syria-Israel Negotiations.

Throughout the year the Syrian–Israeli track of negotiations moved with glacial slowness, if at all. President Hafiz al-Asad seemed ready to make a deal with Israel, in exchange for the return of all of the Golan Heights. He was, however, wary of being pressured by Israel and the US into accepting a deal which would not give him what he wanted. He was intensely annoyed by King Hussein's separate agreement and watched cautiously as Arafat's deal teetered on the brink of disaster. During frequent meetings with US Secretary of State Warren Christopher, who shuttled between Middle Eastern capitals throughout the year, he followed a two track strategy. On the one hand, he made clear his willingness to talk. Foreign Minister Farouq al-Sharaa, in a conciliatory gesture, addressed the Israeli public on Israeli TV. On the other hand, he continued to support the Islamist movement *Hizbollah* which mounted attacks on the IDF in South Lebanon.

Strong diplomatic pressure from the Americans aimed at kick-starting the peace negotiations between the Syrians and the Israelis made little headway despite the concerted efforts of the Clinton administration. Negotiations were resumed early in 1995 after their curtailment the previous December, but progress was, at best, slow. Implementation of a "land for peace" accord was complicated by a number of factors. Syria's continued close relationship with Iran caused most concern for the Israelis, since the Islamic Republic is the main sponsor of *Hizbollah* in Lebanon. US diplomatic efforts, aimed at calming these fears, took the form of aid inducements to persuade the Syrians to revoke their strategic alliance with Iran. However Syria has not moved ground on this issue.

The diplomatic offensive towards Israel was weakened following the Republican landslide in the US congressional elections of December 1994.

President Clinton and his Secretary of State, Warren Christopher, found it increasingly difficult to apply economic pressure on the Israelis to give ground. The Israeli government itself also had to respond to the domestic political situation where the electorate was increasingly sceptical about Syrian intentions. Furthermore, the majority of voters seemed to be supportive of the highly vocal campaigns by the 13,000 Jewish settlers inside the Golan. The Israeli attitude of insisting on retaining the right to station observation posts on the Heights, a position Syria rejects, was intended to allay public suspicions. The real longer term pre-occupation however, was the issue surrounding control of water resources from this region. Syria has hinted about a possible water sharing deal but only if the Israelis withdraw.

Relations with Israel.

Syria's frosty relationship with Israel continued in 1996. Despite intense diplomatic efforts from the Americans, which in late 1995 and early 1996 resulted in "talks about talks", little progress was made between the two sides. In December 1995, Washington attempted to kick-start negotiations by secluding both Israeli and Syrian negotiators at Wye Plantation, Maryland, in a similar strategy which brought tangible results between the warring factions in the former Yugoslavia. Despite successive rounds of intensive negotiations the two sides could not agree on the extent of peace nor on specific issues such as the fate of the Golan Heights and the supply of water in the region. Talks were suspended in March 1996. The election of hard-line Israeli Premier Benyamin Netanyahu in May led to a further deterioration in relations between the two sides. Assad's frustration with Netanyahu, who ruled out a return of the Golan Heights in exchange for a comprehensive peace treaty, led the Syrians to threaten the use of force to reclaim the territory. In late August, Assad moved his 14th Division, an elite commando force, from Beirut to "defensive positions" further south, although none of these troops crossed the Litani "red-line" established inside Lebanon by the Israelis in 1976. Although Israel was alarmed by these movements, and began preparing its troops in response, neither side was eager for a direct conflict and the battle became one of rhetoric.

Recent Developments.

Perhaps the most surprising event in recent Syrian foreign relations has been the beginning of a warming in relations with their Ba'athist rivals in Baghdad. In June, the border between the two states was re-opened for the first time in 17 years, when diplomatic relations were broken over Syria's support for Iran in the war with Iraq. Syria also took advantage of the stalemate in the Arab-Israeli peace process (both multilaterally and in its bilateral track) to attempt to build an informal "rejectionist" front of Arab states including Iran, Iraq, Saudi Arabia and the other Gulf States.

KUWAIT.

Kuwait was occupied by Iraq for seven months from 2 August 1990, the emir going into exile in Saudi Arabia. For details of the Iraqi invasion, and the subsequent military confrontation, see **C30**.

SOUTH ASIA

INDIA.

Assassination of Rajiv Gandhi.

The 1991 elections, held against a backcloth of rising Hindu militancy, became increasingly violent. On 21 May, addressing an election rally 30 miles from Madras, Rajiv Gandhi was assassinated by a terrorist bomb. India (and the world) was stunned. The remaining elections were postponed. After unsuccessfully attempting to instal Rajiv's widow as his successor, the party chose veteran Congressman and former Foreign Secretary P. V. Narasimha Rao as party leader. The Gandhi dynasty was

ended and India entered a new and uncertain political future.

India under Rao.

The next round of the delayed elections took place on 15–16 June. Congress (I) failed to win an independent parliamentary majority, taking 218 seats and having the support of a further 17 members. The BJP increased its representation from 88 to 120 seats. On 20 June Mr. Rao defeated an attempt to oust him from the party leadership and was sworn in as prime minister. Echoing Mr. Gandhi's pre-election speeches, Mr. Rao proposed a free market, austerity and the encouragement of foreign investment as the solution to the country's economic problems. In November his government shored up its precarious minority hold on power with a number of by-election successes. Mr. Rao's government also made a number of radical foreign policy moves, ending 30 years of diplomatic coldness with China on 13 December, and recognising Israel. Congress (I) was successful in state assembly and parliamentary elections held in Punjab on 19 February 1992, the first since 1985. But this was largely because the Sikh Akali Dal party boycotted the elections and separatist terrorists kept the turnout down to 28% by intimidation. Mr. Rao's government faced increasing united opposition criticism of the inflation and unemployment brought on by its economic policies.

On 9 March 1992 the prime minister Narasimha Rao won an important vote on his economic programme which amounted to a vote of confidence forced by the opposition Bharatiya Janata Party (BJP). But on 31 March his foreign minister was forced to resign following allegations of involvement in the long-running Bofors corruption scandal. India was rocked by intense violence following the destruction of a mosque in the northern town of Ayodhya by Hindu extremists on 6 December. By 13 December over 1,200 people had been killed and an estimated 5,000 injured in clashes between Hindus, Moslems and the security forces throughout India. The government reacted by banning three Hindu and two Moslem extremist organisations. On 16 December three state governments run by the opposition BJP were dismissed on the orders of the cabinet because of alleged BJP involvement in the destruction of the mosque. The rioting intensified popular discontent with the government, and this was not defused by a cabinet reshuffle undertaken by Mr. Rao on 17 January 1993 in which 14 ministers were dismissed. Violence struck again when, on 12 March, the Bombay business quarter was hit by terrorist bombs which killed over 300 people and wounded more than 1,000.

Claims against Pakistan.

On 21 April the government announced it had evidence linking Pakistan's intelligence services to the bombings. Inter-communal clashes continued and on 3–4 May over 100 people were killed in the north-eastern state of Manipur. Premier Rao's alleged indecisiveness in the face of communal strife was at the centre of a no confidence motion in parliament on 28 July. A unified challenge by the normally fragmented opposition also accused his government of encouraging corruption. Earlier, on 16 June, a stockbroker involved in a securities scandal alleged he had paid Mr. Rao $300,000 in November 1991 for future political favours, an allegation Mr. Rao denied. Mr. Rao's government narrowly won the vote by 265 to 251.

Mr. Rao's Congress (I) did creditably in regional elections held in November while the BJP failed to build on what it hoped would be a "Hindu wave". The elections had been seen as a mid-term verdict on the central government. But Mr. Rao faced a further crisis when his finance minister Manmohan Singh, the driving force behind India's move to a market economy, was accused in a parliamentary report of "constructive responsibility" for a £860 million financial scandal. Mr. Rao's government finally secured an absolute majority in parliament when, on 30 December, ten members of a faction of Janata Dal joined Congress.

Strikes, Demonstrations and Electoral Defeats.

A strike called by the opposition BJP on 10 February 1994 against price rises in essential commodities won wide support. In his 1994–95 budget proposals on 28 February, finance minister Manmohan Singh remained committed to growth despite concern over the level of public borrowing. But on 4 March the ruling Congress (I) suffered a serious setback at the hands of the BJP in elections for four upper house seats in Gujarat, taking two instead of the expected three.

Economic developments had further repercussions when there were violent demonstrations in New Delhi on 5–6 April against India's accession to the Uruguay Round of the General Agreement on Tariffs and Trade, which the opposition claimed weakened national sovereignty. Strikes brought large areas of the country to a halt on 15 April.

Mr Rao's position was threatened by his party's disastrous results in state elections held in December. Congress (I) lost three of the four crucial southern states, including Mr Rao's home state of Andhra Pradesh. He responded by threatening a party purge, blaming the losses on infighting. A leading rival, Arjun Singh, resigned from the cabinet, declaring his "disillusion with the leadership." Mr Singh was suspended from the party on 24 January 1995 for "indulging in anti-party activities." As Congress (I) faced another round of state elections in February, it appeared that Mr Rao might face serious revolt from within his party.

The position of Mr Rao's government was further undermined by defeat in state elections in March 1995. In the economically crucial state of Maharashtra, a right wing alliance of the BJP and Shiv Sena ejected Congress from power for the first time in 44 years. In neighbouring Gujarat the BJP succeeded in winning sole power. In both states poorer voters were protesting against the impact of the central government's economic liberalisation programme.

Despite this series of electoral setbacks, Mr Rao was able to retain the support of fellow party leaders for his economic programme. But in early April Congress (I) dissidents threatened to vote against his 1995/96 budget unless their amendments were accepted. The continuing crisis in Kashmir—over 50 Muslims were killed in clashes with Indian security forces on 27 April—prompted an opposition motion of censure against Mr Rao's handling of the situation. His government defeated this by 221 to 186 votes.

Background to 1996 Election.

But divisions within the ruling party remained. A dissident faction elected former minister Nairain Dutt Tiwari as Congress (I) president on 19 May and called for a return to what they claimed was the traditional Congress concern for poor and lower caste Indians. Mr Tiwari was immediately expelled from Congress for "anti-party activity." On 23 May the annual budget passed successfully through parliament. In an upsurge of Sikh separatist terrorism in August, the Chief Minister of the Punjab was killed with 12 other people in a car bomb explosion outside the state government offices in Chandigarh.

Mr Rao attempted to strengthen his political authority by enlarging and shuffling his cabinet in mid-September. Many of the new ministers came from states in which Mr Rao's Congress (I) had performed particularly badly in elections. However, 1996 opened with renewed violence. On 3 January there were serious casualties when the latest of a series of bombs exploded in the capital. Responsibility was claimed by a Kashmiri separatist group. Political upheaval followed when seven leading figures from the governing Congress (I) and opposition BJP, including six former ministers, were charged with receiving bribes in an £11 million corruption scandal on 16 January. Two days later three serving ministers implicated in the scandal resigned. The scandal broadened when, on 23 January, the leader of the BJP accused Mr Rao himself of having accepted bribes to help finance the election campaign that had brought him to power. It was against this background that Mr Rao decided to call a general election.

The Congress Humiliation.

Congress (I) suffered a humiliating defeat in the elections fought in April and May 1996, being pushed into third place by the Hindu nationalist Bharatiya Jawata Party (BJP) and the National Front-Left Front (NF-LF) alliance. Congress and its allies emerged with 139 seats, the BJP and its allies with 194 and the NF-LF with 179. A short-lived BJP government under Atal Behari Vajpayee was replaced on 1 June by a fragile NF-LF United Front administration led by the relatively unknown H. D. Deve Gowda. The coalition of over a dozen left-wing and regional parties, including the Communist Party of India, won a confidence vote on 12 June. The new government's budget proposed to address the concerns of the poor while maintaining fiscal prudence. Meanwhile, Mr Rao was accused on 12 June with four other former ministers of attempting to survive a confidence motion in 1993 by bribery. Mr Rao maintained his innocence but resigned the Congress (I) leadership on 21 September to be replaced by Sitram Kesri as provisional party president.

In September, the first state elections for nine years were held in the disputed Kashmir against the background of continuing separatist violence. Dr Farooq Abdullah's National Conference Party, which advocated greater Kashmiri autonomy, took 54 seats in the 87 seat house. The elections were boycotted by separatist supporters and there were criticisms of the heavy Indian military presence. Dr Abdullah's election did nothing to end militant violence and in the three months following his election over 15 people were killed.

Following an unprecedented vote by Congress deputies for his resignation in the interests of party unity, Mr Rao stood down as Congress (I) parliamentary delegation leader on 19 December. He was succeeded on 3 January 1997 by party president Sitram Kesri.

The Advent of Gujral.

India was thrown into crisis at the end of March 1997 when Congress (I) withdrew its support from the coalition, accusing the government of drifting. There, were, however, suggestions that Congress was concerned at the government's determined investigations into corruption. On 11 April, Mr Gowda stood down as prime minister after losing a confidence motion. The governing coalition, to the disappointment of Congress, remained united and on 22 April the foreign minister, Mr Inder Kumar Gujral, emerged at its head.

K. R. Narayanan—vice president since 1992—was overwhelmingly chosen as President by the electoral college in July as the first Dalit ("untouchable") to hold the post. In September, in an attempt to meet a budget deficit provoked by public service pay increases, the government introduced a package of spending cuts and tax increases. But the atmosphere of vacillation and weakness surrounding Mr Gujral's United Front coalition intensified in October when the cabinet first agreed and then disagreed with a request by President Narayanan to dismiss the Bharatiya Janata Party (BJP) government in Uttar Pradesh state.

Resignation of Gujral.

In November, Congress—clearly seeking to break the coalition—demanded the resignation of three ministers attached to a Tamil party allegedly linked with the assassination of Rajiv Gandhi. Although his government's survival would be in doubt if Congress withdrew, Mr Gujral refused. Congress—hoping that by forcing a crisis and by persuading Mr Gandhi's widow, Sonia, to enter public life, it could revive its political fortunes—left the coalition at the end of the month. Mr Gujral resigned immediately, ending a term that had lasted only seven months. The Hindu nationalist BJP attempted to construct a viable coalition but on 3 December admitted its failure and on the following day President Narayanan dissolved parliament and called early elections. Congress's hopes were renewed when Mrs Gandhi announced on 29 December that she would campaign for the party in the forthcoming general election, although she refused to become a candidate.

The 1998 Elections.

The electorate delivered an ambiguous verdict out of which the Bharatiya Janata Party (BJP) attempted to form India's first avowedly Hindu government in coalition with 12 smaller parties and a number of independent MPs. BJP leader Atal

Bihari Vajpayee was sworn in as prime minister on 19 March 1998 but it appeared from the start that his administration would be riven by political and personal differences. As Congress absorbed another electoral defeat, Mrs Gandhi accepted the post of party president, replacing the octogenarian Sitaram Kesri in the hope of regaining the support of a younger generation.

Mr Vajpayee's newly-elected BJP-led coalition suffered an early blow with the resignation in April of a minister following corruption charges. There were calls for the sacking of three more. But it was the international situation—with the growing regional economic crisis as a background—which proved the more threatening. Pakistan's successful testing on 6 April of a missile capable of penetrating deep into India prompted an accusation by the Indian defence minister on 3 May that China was providing Pakistan with nuclear technology. Heading a weak coalition, the BJP appeared to be preparing to display its nationalist credentials. India detonated five underground nuclear devices on 11 and 13 May, becoming the world's sixth nuclear power.

When Pakistan threatened to respond, Indian deputy prime minister Lal Krishna Advani criticised Pakistan's continuing role in the disputed Kashmir region. However, Mr Vajpayee took a more conciliatory line on 27 May, offering a 'no first use' deal. Pakistan conducted test explosions the following day, followed by a further round on 30 May. As international criticism mounted, there were public celebrations of the Hindu nationalist BJP government's increasingly aggressive stance towards its neighbour. Opposition Congress president Sonia Gandhi backed the government.

With fears of an arms race throughout South Asia, the United States government suspended official aid, stopped defence sales and barred commercial loans. Japan announced an immediate freezing of $25 million grant aid and other states—though not Britain, France or Russia—followed suit. India's finance ministry now announced its response to the growing regional economic crisis. While military spending was to rise by 14 % (with a 68 % increase in atomic energy expenditure), import tariffs were to be raised to 8 %.

But on 24 June a new anti-BJP alliance was formed, the National Democratic Front (NDF). The NDF's leaders accused the BJP of leading India into crisis and called on all secular parties to unite against the governing coalition. This, combined with international pressure, prompted an attempt to repair relations with Pakistan. On 23 September Mr Vajpayee and the Pakistan premier Mr Sharif agreed in New York on the need to restrain an arms race. Talks on 18 October concluded with a pledge to meet again to discuss the 50-year dispute over Kashmir.

Kashmir remained a source of difficulty when Mr Vajpayee and Pakistani prime minister Nawaz Sharif issued a Lahore Declaration on 21 February 1999 in which they promised to share information on their nuclear activities. Mr Vajpayee admitted that this step towards improved relations would arouse criticism from hardliners in his party.

The 1999 Political Crisis.

India was plunged into renewed political turmoil in April 1999 with the defeat of the BJP government by 1 vote in a parliamentary vote of confidence. At first, it seemed Sonia Gandhi might muster a coalition, but a third election in three years became the only option.

SRI LANKA.

Origins of the Civil War.

Tension between the Tamil minority and the Sinhalese majority in Sri Lanka led to rioting in the northern town of Jaffna, beginning on 14 August 1977, in which 125 people died. The situation grew even more serious in the 1980s. Acts of terrorism by Tamil Liberation Tigers provoked violence by the army against the Tamil community. A state of emergency was declared on 4 June 1981. Two soldiers, the first military victims, were killed in an ambush in Jaffna in October 1981. Talks between President Jayawardene and the Tamil United Liberation Front failed to find a political solution. In 1987 Indian troops were requested

to assist the Sri Lankan government and a force of 100,000 Indian troops attacked Tamil positions in the Jaffna peninsula. Guerrilla war continued and in 1989 Indian troops began to withdraw. In the south the ultra-left JVP movement active from 1971 conducted an increasingly bitter terror campaign after 1987. During the 1990s violence continued. President Ranasinghe Premadasa was assassinated on 1 May 1993, but a ceasefire with Tamils was signed in January 1995. It did not hold and violence continued.

As 1998 opened there seemed, despite peace efforts, no end to the violence. On 25 January Liberation Tigers were blamed for the bombing of a Buddhist shrine in Kandy in which 11 were killed. Clashes continued between government forces and rebels in the north of the country. The opposition United National Party (UNP), which had rejected President Kumaratunga's 'union of the regions' proposals, unveiled its own power-sharing package on 31 January. Fiftieth anniversary celebrations of Sri Lanka's independence on 4 February were held under intense security in the capital Colombo.

The 1998 State of Emergency.

The government attempted to symbolise its control over the city of Jaffna—a Tiger stronghold until its capture in 1995—by appointing a Tamil mayor on 26 March. She was murdered in her home on 17 May following her refusal to obey a Tiger request to resign. In June, the government attempted to ban reporting of military operations following bloody clashes around the northern town of Kilonochchi in which hundreds died. As the situation deteriorated, the government declared a state of emergency, extending powers to arrest and detain without trial on 4 August. The cancellation of provincial elections in the south due at the end of the month promped UNP accusations that the government feared an electoral test.

As hundreds more died in fighting for control of towns along the northern highway, LTTE leader Velupillai Prabhakaran called on 6 September for the appointment of a mediator to broker a re-opening of peace talks. The government responded by announcing it was considering trying him in his absence. But the LTTE inflicted a heavy blow on the government by capturing Kilonochchi on 1 October after a three day battle.

The ruling People's Alliance captured a western province from the opposition United National Party in January 1999 in elections marked by violence and accusations of massive vote rigging.

PAKISTAN.

As opposition to Ms Bhutto mounted, police broke up a demonstration organised in Rawalpindi by the opposition party Jamaat-i-Islami on 27 October 1996. There were further demonstrations in Islamabad and Rawalpindi the following day. The country's generals were reported on 1 November to have drawn up a list of allegedly corrupt politicians and officials, including Ms Bhutto and opposition Pakistan Muslim League (PML) leader Nawaz Sharif. Ms Bhutto's dismissal by President Leghari on 4 November seemed inevitable. Interim prime minister Meraj Khalid dissolved the national and provincial assemblies and called elections for 3 February 1997. Ms Bhutto's husband, former investment minister Asif Ali Zardari, was placed under house arrest and later charged with complicity in the murder of Ms Bhutto's brother.

Continuing military influence was underlined on 6 January 1997 with the establishment of a 10-member national security council giving the armed forces a formal advisory role in government. Ms Bhutto condemned this and said that, although the PPP would participate in the February elections, she would not accept the result. A bomb explosion outside a court in Lahore on 18 January killed over 20 people, including the leader of Sipah-e-Sahaba, an extremist Sunni Muslim group.

Triumph of Nawaz Sharif.

The outcome of the election was a triumph for the Pakistan Muslim League headed by Nawaz Sharif. Benazir Bhutto's Pakistan People's Party was decimated whilst Imran Khan made no impact at all. In a sense, though, the real victors were the forces of disillusion. Turnout was very low and faith in the politicians even lower.

The government announced an economic reform programme on 28 March 1997 intended to reduce prices, increase imports and generate employment. At the same time, the prime minister, Mr Sharif, promised to combat widespread tax evasion and corruption. Significant constitutional change came when, on 1 April, the National Assembly stripped the President of his power to dissolve parliament. This had led to the ousting of three governments since its introduction in 1985. In addition, authority to appoint armed forces chiefs and provincial governors was transferred to the prime minister. The changes were welcomed by opposition leader Ms Bhutto. Mr Sharif immediately dismissed the chief of naval staff following corruption allegations. Less welcome to the Pakistan People's Party (PPP) was anti-terrorist legislation introduced in August giving the police sweeping powers to combat violence between Sunni and Shia Muslims. The PPP accused the government of violating human rights.

Accusations of Corruption.

Ms Bhutto's husband, Asif Ali Zardari, was formally indicted with 18 others on 5 July on murder and conspiracy charges in connection with the death of Ms Bhutto's estranged brother in 1996. In September accusations of corruption over government contracts by Ms Bhutto and her family came to a head when Swiss banks froze accounts estimated to be worth £8.4 million. The government claimed indisputable evidence but made no move to prosecute. Ms Bhutto strenuously denied the charges.

Constitutional Crisis.

A serious constitutional crisis now threatened Pakistan with a return to military rule. On 12 November Mr Sharif, in conflict with the chief justice, Mr Sajjad Ali Shah, over judicial appointments, was charged with contempt of court and faced possible disqualification from office. The army chief of staff cancelled a visit overseas at the request of President Leghari, a prominent member of the PPP, prompting Mr Sharif to threaten to impeach the President. Mr Sharif's trial was thrown into chaos on 28 November as supporters of his Pakistan Muslim League stormed the court, forcing an adjournment. Mr Shah's position weakened on 1 December as it became clear he had lost the backing of the majority of the supreme court judges. Unwilling to dismiss Mr Shah, President Leghari resigned the following day. Mr Sharif appeared to have won this round of the crisis and he was strengthened by the overwhelming election on 31 December of his presidential nominee, Pakistan Muslim League senator Rafiq Tarar.

Signs of Destabilisation.

As 1998 opened, the prospects for regional relations seemed optimistic. At a summit, the prime ministers of Pakistan, Bangladesh and India agreed on regular foreign minister meetings and pledged to create a South Asia free trade area by 2001. At home, however, the ethnic violence and Islamic factional fighting that had plagued the country continued. The government soon accused Indian intelligence of acting as a force for destabilisation. On 6 April Pakistan successfully tested a surface-to-surface missile capable of penetrating deep into India, provoking the Indian government into a declaration that it would draw the 'appropriate' conclusion.

Meanwhile, the government's campaign against former prime minister Benazir Bhutto continued and at the end of March the Sind High Court issued an arrest warrant against her for misuse of power. On 28 April the Lahore High Court ordered the freezing of the entire Bhutto family's assets until she appeared in court to answer corruption charges.

The Nuclear Arms Race.

Relations with India reached a new low in 1998 when India detonated five underground nuclear devices on 11 and 13 May. There were immediate demands from politicians, military officers and religious leaders to follow suit. Despite an offer by the Indian prime minister on 27 May of a 'no first use'

deal and an appeal from President Clinton, Pakistan tested five underground nuclear devices on 28 and 30 May. The United States imposed immediate economic sanctions. International concern prompted Mr Sharif and Indian premier Mr Vajpayee to agree at a meeting in New York to restrain what threatened to be a serious arms race.

Popular though flexing of Pakistan's nuclear muscle had been, Mr Sharif was politically vulnerable. In September the police reported to President Muhammad Rafique Tarar that Mr Sharif had amassed a personal fortune in offshore bank accounts. As the government wrestled with severe economic difficulties compounded by sanctions imposed in response to the nuclear tests, there were fears that the allegations could trigger a long-threatened declaration of martial law by chief of staff General Jehangir Karamat. However, on 7 October General Karamat took early retirement.

Mr Sharif moved to consolidate his position with the Islamic right. On 8 October he won Cabinet approval for the introduction of Islamic law (Sharia)—something the army (and elements of Mr Sharif's Muslim League) had opposed. Despite criticisms from human rights activists and fears for the position of women, the proposals passed through the lower house of the legislature by 115–16 on 9 October. Religious violence in Karachi continued, with over 100 killed in gun battles over the summer.

Pakistan and India gave the impression of attempting to resolve the looming arms race. Talks on 18 October concluded with a pledge to discuss the 50-year dispute over Kashmir. Negotiations were resumed on 5 November—as both states sought an end to the sanctions imposed following the May nuclear tests—but the Kashmir question appeared as insoluble as ever. When, on 3 January 1999, Mr Sharif escaped an assassination attempt—four people were killed in a bombing—police blamed the Indian government and the Muttahida Quami Movement (MQM).

Mr Sharif and Indian prime minister Mr Vajpayee took a step towards improving relations when they issued a Lahore Declaration on 21 February. Both promised to share information on nuclear activities. However, at a joint press conference Mr Sharif and Mr Vajpayee avoided discussion of renewed fighting in the disputed Kashmir region.

BANGLADESH.

As 1995 opened, the government was confronted by a series of violent strikes. There were serious clashes during a three day general strike in Dhaka from 2–4 January and two people were killed in a textile workers' strike in Chittagong on 22 January. Seven people were killed and over a hundred injured in a strike from 12–15 February. A general strike called by the three main opposition parties paralysed Dhaka and other major towns on 12–13 March. This was followed by a blockade of all road, rail and waterway communications and a siege of Dhaka on 28 March. There were more anti-government strikes in early April. Opposition parties organised a three day general strike beginning on 16 September which paralysed all major towns and cities. Mrs Zia offered talks but insisted she would not hand over power to a caretaker administration in the run-up to elections in February 1996. There were serious clashes between supporters of the ruling Bangladesh National Party and opposition groups during a general strike mounted from 16–19 October.

As pressure intensified, Mrs Zia attempted to break the political impasse and end continuing violent confrontation by advising President Abdur Rahman Biswas on 24 November to call early elections. However, this did not satisfy the opposition parties which continued to demand elections under a neutral caretaker government.

The 1996 Election.

The general election on 15 February 1996 was marked by a massive opposition boycott as only 15% of the electorate participated. Fifteen people died in street clashes between political rivals. Mrs Zia nonetheless claimed a renewed mandate and rejected calls for her resignation when the new parliament opened on 19 March. However, as senior civil servants warned that the country was virtually ungovernable, she yielded to opposition demands on 26 March. A caretaker government was formed by Muhammad Habibur Rahman.

The caretaker government was sworn in on 3 April, with Muhammad Rahman as "Chief Adviser". On 20 May, an attempted military coup by Awami League supporter General Abu Saleh Muhammad Nasim was foiled by troops loyal to President Biswas. In elections held on 12 June the Awami League won 146 seats but failed to gain an overall majority. The Bangladesh National Party (BNP) took 116 seats, Jatiya Dal (led by imprisoned former President Ershad) 32, and Jamaat-i-Islami three. Awami League leader Shaikh Hasina Wajed—daughter of the country's first President, Shaikh Mujibur Rahman—was appointed prime minister, supported by Jatiya Dal. Her position was strengthened in July with the allocation of 27 of the 30 nominated women's seats in the country's parliament, the Jatiya Sangsad, and a number of by-election victories. The Awami Party's nominee, Shahabuddin Ahmed, replaced President Biswas on 8 October.

There were criticisms when former president General Mohammed Ershad was granted bail in January 1997 as he faced further charges of corruption and misuse of power during his period in office. Critics claimed this resulted from a deal between the ruling Awami League and Jatiya Dal (JD), which General Ershad had led from prison. JD had played a crucial role in the appointment of prime minister Shaikh Hasina Wajed's government in June 1996. However, on 30 June JD split following General Ershad's expulsion from the leadership.

Confrontation on the Streets.

The opposition Bangladesh Nationalist Party (BNP) was, meanwhile, confronting the government on the streets. A general strike mounted by the BNP on 3 July against increased taxes ended in violent clashes between government and opposition supporters. There was further violence during a one day nationwide general strike at the end of September protesting against police harassment of BNP rallies. Three BNP leaders were arrested in October following a gun battle with police during a transport blockade organised by the party. Intent on embarrassing the government during negotiations for foreign aid, the BNP boycotted the new session of the legislature on 2 November while its supporters clashed with police. However, on 5 November overseas aid donors promised $1·9 billion for 1998.

Over 20 years of insurgency ended in early December when the government signed a peace treaty with Shanti Bahini rebels operating in the Chittagong Hill Tracts. The violence had cost over 8,000 lives and forced 50,000 refugees into neighbouring India.

The South Asia Summit.

As the Asian financial crisis showed no signs of abating, prime minister Sheikh Hasina Wajed hosted a summit with the Indian and Pakistan premiers on 15 January 1998. The three pledged to reduce tariffs and trade restrictions to create a South Asia free trade area by 2001. At the start of February the Shanti Bahini rebels who had been fighting for Chittagong Hill Tracts autonomy for over 20 years formally surrendered following the granting of an amnesty. The opposition Bangladesh National Party (BNP) ended its four month boycott of the legislature on 9 March. A week later, Jatiya Dal—led by former President Ershad—left the government. This, however, had no effect on the prime minister's position as Awami League by-election victories since the 1996 general election enabled it to govern alone. The government moved against the BNP on 21 April, with the levelling by the prime minister of corruption charges against her predecessor Begum Khaleda Zia, members of her family and former ministers. Zia denied the charges, which she said were politically motivated.

Recent Events.

There were violent clashes in the capital Dhaka between government and opposition supporters as a seven party opposition alliance led by the BNP mounted a general strike against the treaty with the Shanti Bahini rebels. In July BNP leader Begum Khaleda Zia was charged with abuse of power for having packed the police force with her supporters while in office from 1991 to 1996. In August she was charged with corruption, including profiting from

an aircraft purchase deal along with five other ministers.

The BNP continued with its attempt at undermining the government through a series of general strikes during October and November. There were a number of deaths and 500 injuries in fighting between rival political groups during a three day strike mounted from 9–11 November.

THE FAR EAST

CHINA.

In the spring of 1989 the Communist government faced a serious challenge to its authority, triggered by the death on 15 April of Hu Yaobang, the disgraced former party general-secretary. Beijing University students demanding his rehabilitation staged a sit-in outside the Great Hall of the People. On the day of his funeral, 22 April, there were demonstrations in a dozen major cities. Deng Xiaoping warned of possible bloodshed. But on 27 April a march by 100,000 students in Beijing calling for democracy and attacking party corruption passed off peacefully. On 4 May 300,000 demonstrators filled Tiananmen Square, signifying growing popular support. Students began a hunger strike in the square on 13 May, demanding political reforms of the kind being enacted in the Soviet Union, their presence disrupting a visit by Mr Gorbachev on 15 May.

The hunger strikers called for a televised dialogue with the government as, on 17 May, a million people marched in Beijing, others demonstrated in 20 cities, and workers announced they would strike in support of the students. Divisions opened in the party hierarchy, with Zhao Ziyang apparently favouring dialogue while the Prime Minister, Li Peng, announced that martial law would come into force on 20 May. The people of Beijing massed in the square to prevent the troops entering.

Massacre in Tiananmen Square.

As the students in the square perceptibly tired hardliners within the party prevailed. On 4 June thousands of troops and scores of tanks moved in, staging a bloody massacre in which 2,500 were initially reported killed. With the world watching the carnage on television, China appeared on the brink of chaos. Sporadic clashes continued in Beijing and in cities throughout China over the next two days. There were reports that the 38th Army, which had refused to enforce the martial law decree, was facing the 27th Army and a clash seemed possible.

But on 8 June Li Peng appeared on television and praised the troops who had put down the protesters. The following day the party leadership, minus Zhao Ziyang, presented a united front on television. The official government media called on citizens to inform on "counter-revolutionary" dissidents. Arrests of activists now began alongside a government propaganda campaign to minimise the extent of casualties in the Tiananmen Square massacre. By 21 June 1,500 activists had been arrested, including Guo Haifong, a prominent student leader. All independent student and workers organisations were ordered to disband. As the arrests continued protesters received harsh punishment.

Purge of Student Sympathisers.

The party now began a purge of what it saw as its own unreliable elements. Several leading officials were ousted at a Central Committee meeting on 24 June, including Zhao Ziyang, who was dismissed for "counter-revolutionary rebellion" and replaced by Jiang Zemin. Many lower level party members were expelled for having supported the democracy movement.

By July unofficial reports claimed 10,000 had been arrested and the government itself admitted 2,500. Through the summer arrests, prison sentences and executions continued. The party did, however, acknowledge the legitimacy of some of the protesters' complaints. The party Politburo announced a programme to combat corruption on 28 July.

Background of Economic Discontent.

Although the dramatic events of the summer had passed and resistance crushed, the government faced economic problems that might provoke a renewal of discontent and unrest. An austerity programme introduced in September 1988 to combat inflation of over 30 % had resulted in falling living standards and rising unemployment. Articles in the party and army press implied that troops would be used again if the party felt itself to be in danger. With unconfirmed reports that 1,500 officers and soldiers faced courts martial for mutiny in the protests, the party conducted a campaign of ideological indoctrination to guarantee the army's loyalty.

Rise of Jiang Zemin.

At the meeting of China's parliament, the National People's Congress, in March 1990, there was an easing of the austerity programme. Deng Xiaoping resigned on 22 March as chairman of the State Military Commission, handing its leadership to Jiang Zemin. Although the party leadership appeared to be attempting to distance itself from the Tiananmen Square massacre, Li Peng declared on 20 March that "socialist China will stand firm as a rock" and dissent would be punished. The party was determined that China would not follow the path of the Soviet Union and Eastern Europe.

On 24 April Li Peng met President Gorbachev in Moscow, the first such high-level visit for 26 years. The two leaders signed a 10-year economic and scientific co-operation treaty and agreed on troop cuts along the Sino-Soviet border.

On 3–4 June Beijing University students mounted demonstrations to commemorate the first anniversary of the crushing of the pro-democracy movement. Students were injured in clashes with police and the authorities sealed off Tiananmen Square to prevent demonstrators entering.

Economy in Recession.

China's economy remained in recession, largely as a result of the 1988 austerity measures. In March 1990 the Finance Minister had admitted that the economic situation was "grim". Reports in June put unemployment at its highest for ten years, with foreign investment slowing dramatically. A Party Central Committee meeting in December attempted to reconcile divisions between reformist and conservative factions and approve a new five-year economic plan. A vaguely worded compromise emerged, combining a recognition of the need to encourage Western investment with a determination to resist dramatic reform.

The Dissident Trials.

The need not to offend potential foreign investors—together with government hopes of minimising the significance of the 1989 pro-democracy demonstrations—appeared to influence the treatment of dissidents. The trials began in December 1990 of individuals involved in the 1989 Beijing protests including student leaders Guo Haifeng and Wang Dan, both of whom received—as did other students—relatively lenient sentences. But an unknown number of workers were more harshly dealt with.

Moves towards eventual unity with Nationalist Taiwan continued. Since 1983 mainland China had favoured a "one country, two systems" solution. In December 1990 Taiwan president Lee Teng-hui announced the ending of the "state of war" with China that had existed for over 40 years and advocated a peaceful reunification. Economic ties had already been strengthened but Chinese proposals in December for talks between the Communist and Nationalist parties were rejected by Taiwan.

At the opening of China's parliament, the National People's Congress, on 23 March 1991, prime minister Li Peng acknowledged the role market forces could play in developing the economy. But he stressed that China would remain a socialist society. Despite a worsening budget deficit, increased military spending was announced. Conflicts between reformists and anti-reformists continued. The appointment of Deng Zhu, the mayor of Shanghai, as a vice premier with responsibility for developing the eastern coastal area and promoting links with the West, appeared to represent a victory for the reformist line of Deng Xiaoping.

Death of Mao's Widow.

On 14 May Jiang Qing, Mao's widow and a member of the 1970s "gang of four", committed suicide. The official announcement of her death was delayed until the second anniversary of the Tiananmen Square massacre on 4 June had passed. In Beijing there were limited student demonstrations to commemorate the 1989 events.

On 10 August China agreed in principle to sign the 1968 Nuclear Non-proliferation Treaty. But on 13 November, as Beijing prepared for what was seen as a diplomatically significant visit by US Secretary of State James Baker, an internal government document was leaked which alleged the United States was seeking the collapse of communism in China. The document appeared to represent the view of many senior government officials. Mr Baker left Beijing on 17 November declaring that a gulf in relations remained. There was, however, a distinct improvement in relations with offshore Taiwan, with proposals in February 1992 for China and Taiwan to open liaison offices in each other's capitals.

Economic Liberalisation in China.

China's parliament, the National People's Congress, met from 12 March to 3 April 1992. The meeting closed with some embarrassment for China's premier, Li Peng, as his final statement was strengthened by the Congress to emphasise the free market reforms advocated by Deng Xiaoping. Li was known to prefer a greater element of state planning. China's economic liberation bore fruit with the renewal of relations with South Korea on 24 August. In September China's central bank announced plans to create a stock exchange regulatory body modelled on the US Securities and Exchange Commission.

At the opening session of the National People's Congress on 15 March 1993 Mr. Li, despite his identification with conservative forces in the Communist Party, outlined a sweeping programme of economic change aimed at strengthening market reforms and re-structuring the state sector by reducing the number of government departments and cutting the bureaucracy by 25 %.

The Congress continued with the election on 27 March of Jiang Zemin—the party general secretary and chairman of the central military commission—as state president to succeed Yang Shangkun. On 29 March a new constitution was approved, China's fifth since 1949. China's economic reforms were formally enshrined in the constitution as a move to a "socialist market economy". Closer relations with Taiwan appeared to be developing following meetings in Singapore between two organisations representing the respective governments. Agreement was reached on 29 April on educational, cultural and scientific co-operation.

Unrest in Sichuang.

Resentment among China's 800 million peasants that their incomes were lagging behind those of factory workers and entrepreneurs expressed itself in riots in early June in Sichuang province. China's cabinet, the State Council, responded by ordering local officials to reduce taxes previously imposed. There were also clashes in Qinghai province on 7 October between thousands of Moslem demonstrators and Chinese troops. The demonstrations followed increasingly violent incidents over the previous five years.

In the long-delayed Communist Party central committee plenary session which opened on 11 November, reformists attempted to push through tax reforms favouring central government. A final communique issued on 14 November announced sweeping reforms in state industries, banking, taxation, social security, foreign trade and investment, and officially abandoned communism. But on 21 December the government reimposed price controls on 27 basic commodities because of fears that rising prices might provoke popular unrest.

An Inflationary Economy.

Currency and taxation reforms announced in December 1993 increased inflationary pressures in the economy. By January 1994, inflation reached 30% in some urban areas. Premier Li Peng instituted price controls on 20 basic commodities in mid-March in recognition of widespread concerns about inflation. Economic development became entangled with human rights issues when US Secretary of State Warren Christopher visited China in March and suggested that concessions on "most favoured nation" trading status depended on China's human rights record. Mr Li said China would never accept American "human rights concepts".

Crackdown on Dissidents.

A crackdown on dissidents came in April – an open show of defiance to the United States. As the anniversary of the 1989 Tiananmen Square massacre approached, the government extended its powers to detain and restrict dissidents. Nevertheless, on 26 May President Clinton announced his decision to renew "most favoured nation" status and abandoned any linkage with human rights. China introduced further laws against dissidents on 4 June. However, on 5 July the National People's Congress approved a new labour law which included an eight-hour day, a minimum wage and improved conditions. The law, which came into effect on 1 January 1995, ended the guarantee of a job for life.

Nine dissidents who had called for trade union rights and political reforms were imprisoned on 16 December. Several were prominent members of the Free Labour Union of China, a group set up in 1991.

The Succession to Deng.

As Mr Deng's health was rumoured to be declining, Communist Party leader Jiang Zemin consolidated his authority and prepared the framework for an orderly transition. In March 1995, he succeeded in appointing two supporters as vice premiers, despite some opposition from delegates to the National People's Congress. Mr Jiang had also succeeded in creating a power base through a series of promotions. A former mayor of Shanghai, Mr Jiang took over running the party after the 1989 Tiananmen Square massacre. The resignation of Chen Xitong, Secretary of the Beijing Party Committee, was further evidence of the power struggle beginning in China in early summer 1995.

Relations with Taiwan.

Relations with Taiwan had appeared to be improving. But the decision on 16 June by the Clinton administration to grant a visa for a visit to the United States to Taiwanese President Lee Teng-hui prompted China to withdraw its ambassador to Washington for "consultations". Discussions between "unofficial" Chinese and Taiwanese groups which had, in the past, promised greater friendliness between the two states, were postponed by China. Tension intensified when China carried out missile tests close to Taiwan from 21–26 July, following similarly threatening military exercises. There were further missile tests in August.

However, Jiang Zemin's proposal in October for a China-Taiwan summit conference was immediately welcomed by the Taiwanese premier Lien Chan. But at a meeting with President Clinton on 24 October, Jiang Zemin declared that China would tolerate no interference in its desire to reunite with Taiwan. Further military manoeuvres held on an island facing Taiwan in November were clearly designed to influence the coming Taiwanese elections and particularly to dissuade voters from supporting pro-independence parties.

In elections held on 3 December, the ruling Nationalist Party (KMT) gained less than half the total vote for the first time. The pro-independence Democratic Progressive Party, China's real target, took 54 seats in Taiwan's 164 seat parliament.

Human Rights Record.

China's attitude towards human rights continued to be a source of concern internationally, although the leading industrial powers remained reluctant to lose what was becoming an increasingly attractive market. Harry Wu Honda, a prominent civil liberties activist and a naturalised US citizen, was arrested on 19 June. After admitting espionage he was expelled from China on 24 August. There were protests when, on 28 December, the country's fore-

most dissident, Wei Jingsheng, was sent to a labour camp for 14 years for his human rights activities.

The rapid advances in China's economy continued. A five year plan for the year 1996–2000 announced by the Communist Party's Central Committee in September envisaged a doubling of the gross national product by the year 2000 and an annual growth rate of 8%–9%. The party also announced pro-Jiang Zemin appointments to the Central Military Commission on 12 October, clearly designed to weaken the influence of Deng Xiaoping in the People's Liberation Army (PLA). The PLA would play a significant role in the post-Deng succession.

Renewed Tension over Taiwan.

Tension over Taiwan increased with Chinese warnings in January 1996 to the United States that it was preparing to make missile attacks on the island following Taiwanese President Lee Teng-hui's expected victory in the March presidential elections.

On 7 March China renewed its missile tests in the Taiwan Straits, prompting the United States to warn of possible "grave consequences". As 150,000 Chinese troops prepared for military exercises on the mainland opposite the Taiwanese island of Quemoy, the United States deployed a second naval task force. However, on 14 March the Chinese government gave a private assurance that it had no intention of invading. In the Taiwanese elections on 23 March, President Lee Teng-hui was returned to office with 54% of the vote. The candidate advocating outright independence, Peng Ming-hui, came second with 21%.

Relations with Russia.

Relations with Russia showed signs of distinct improvement and economic and security agreements were concluded between Russian president Boris Yeltsin and Jiang Zemin in April 1996. Following China's attempted intimidation of Taiwan, Lee Teng-hui was sworn in as Taiwanese president on 20 May and adopted a conciliatory tone in his references to China. On 29 July China carried out an underground nuclear test but announced a moratorium on future nuclear testing the following day.

The Health of Deng.

Speculation continued over the health of elder statesman Deng Xiaoping, who had not been seen in public since 1994 and was confined to hospital in May. The resignation of his son-in-law from a senior position suggested a waning in Deng's influence. It was against this background that Communist Party leaders met in July and August, with the 92-year-old Deng absent but with a significant attendance by military commanders. The meeting recommended stronger measures to combat crime and to maintain social stability. President (and party general secretary) Jiang Zemin appeared strengthened by proposals for a new leadership structure. This was confirmed at the annual meeting of the party's central committee in October. There was a clear call by the leadership for firm ideological control, despite the rapid pace of economic reform the country was undergoing. The party's leaders were positioning themselves for the inevitable power struggle that would follow Deng's death.

Developments in 1996.

China responded cautiously to a possible threat to relations with Japan that emerged in 1996. The uninhabited Diaoyus islands north east of Taiwan were given to Japan by the United States in 1972. In July 1996 Japanese nationalists hoisted their country's flag over the islands to assert sovereignty. The government discouraged displays of national sentiment on the mainland, fearing that demonstrators might run out of control.

Repression in Tibet continued throughout 1996. Chinese troops were deployed around the capital Lhasa after clashes which followed the banning of displays of images of the exiled spiritual leader, the Dalai Lama. On 25 June the government accused the Dalai Lama of acting as a "puppet of international forces" and declared that Tibet could never become independent. In September, the Dalai Lama suggested relations would improve under a post-Deng leadership.

The Return of Hong Kong.

As 1 July 1997 approached, China prepared to resume sovereignty over Hong Kong. In 1842 Hong Kong had been ceded by China to Britain under the Treaty of Nanking. Britain acquired Kowloon Peninsula in 1860 and in 1898 leased the New Territories from China for 99 years. Under the 1984 Sino-British Declaration, Britain agreed that on the expiry of the lease, sovereignty over the whole of Hong Kong would revert to China. China guaranteed that Hong Kong would retain a capitalist economy following handover. However, China declared it would overturn democratic reforms extended by Chris Patten following his appointment as governor in 1992.

As handover approached, Britain appealed to China not to dissolve the democratically elected Legislative Council. But China appointed a 400-member committee to select Mr Patten's replacement and, on 11 December, the committee named a Hong Kong businessman, Mr Tung Chee-hwa, an opponent of Mr Patten's reforms, as chief executive designate. China said a provisional council (from which members of Hong Kong's Democratic Party would be barred) would replace the Legislative Council. Despite protests from Britain and the United States, Mr Tung confirmed in January 1997 that he supported China's proposed curb on civil rights after handover in July.

The Legacy of Deng.

Deng Xiaoping's death on 19 February 1997 opened the question of how successful his designated successor, Jiang Zemin, would be at riding the economic tiger Deng had nurtured since his return to power in 1979. The last of the veterans of 1949, Deng had suffered in the Cultural Revolution of 1966–76. After Mao's death, Deng used the pro-democracy movement to oust his rivals but a decade later unleashed tanks against a new generation of democrats. His 'market-Leninist' revolution was economic rather than political and the party remained supreme. With the peasants freed from the communes, and international investment welcomed, China's economy grew by 9% a year from 1978. Many prospered and much of the population saw life transformed. But the country also experienced inflation, high crime, widespread corruption and growing unemployment. As Deng died it appeared that China's stability was threatened less by demands for political liberalisation than by stark contrasts in prosperity between the country's regions.

Acceleration of Economic Reforms.

At the National People's Congress in March 1997, premier Li Peng announced plans to speed reform in state-owned enterprises. The process of cementing China's international relations continued with a visit to Beijing by US Vice President Gore in March and a visit to Moscow by President Jiang in April. China also signed border agreements with the governments of neighbouring former Soviet republics. The visit of French President Chirac in May ended a period of strained relations over France's criticisms of China's human rights abuses. On 19 May, US President Clinton renewed China's "most favoured nation" trading status.

Growing Internal Tension.

There were, however, signs of growing domestic tension. A bomb explosion in Beijing in May—following a similar incident in March—was claimed by exiled ethnic Uighurs pressing for an independent state in Xinjiang. Although the government claimed the incidents were insignificant, eight Uighurs were executed for terrorism in Xinjiang at the end of May. In March there had been reports of the worst labour unrest since 1949 in Sichuan province over low wages and in June two activists were imprisoned in Shenzhen for attempting to establish an independent trade union. Throughout the summer there were almost daily reports of demonstrations against unemployment and party corruption. Political liberalisation remained problematic. The official position was that there could be no democratisation until the country's physical needs had been satisfied. But in September, the influential Chinese Academy of Social Sciences warned that political reform was essential.

The 15th Party Congress.

The 15th Party Congress which opened on 12 September set the scene for China's economic advance into the 21st century and, in effect, the removal of the last pillar of socialism. State owned industries already accounted for only 30% of China's gross domestic product. President Jiang announced sweeping proposals to privatise over 100,000 state industries, leaving only the strategic defence and transport sectors in government hands. He admitted that the programme would cause "temporary difficulties" to workers. However, the contradiction of a liberalised market system functioning alongside rigid political control remained unresolved. The dangers of corruption were highlighted by a report that over 120,000 party members had been expelled since 1992.

Entrenchment of Jiang.

The congress ended with President Jiang firmly entrenched as China's leader. Elections to the 193-member party central committee removed potential critics and rivals while the new Politburo was notable for the absence of army representatives. Vice-premier Zho Rongji's responsibility for the economic programme effectively confirmed him as Li Peng's successor as premier when the latter retired in March 1998.

President Jiang then moved to raise China's international profile with a visit to Washington in late October. Although successful in terms of trade negotiations, there was public disagreement between President Jiang and President Clinton over China's attitude to human rights. In November, Russian President Yeltsin and President Jiang gave at least the appearance of resolving longstanding border disagreements.

Asian Financial Crisis.

As financial crisis swept South Asia the government announced drastic reforms of the banking system on 16 January 1998, with an emphasis on increasing competition and easing credit for agriculture and small business. The National People's Congress (NPC) which met from 5–14 March to ratify decisions already taken by the Communist Party emphasized a massive pruning of the state bureaucracy. On 5 March outgoing Premier Li Peng pointed to structural problems and uneven regional development. The number of ministries was to be reduced from 40 to 29 and the civil service from eight to four million. Zhu Rongji—the government's chief economic planner for the previous five years—was appointed prime minister and President Jiang Zemin returned as head of state for a second term.

Growing economic links between China and the West were symbolised by the first China-European Union summit on 2 April. With China's response to the growing South Asian economic crisis a central concern, China was praised for not devaluing its currency. In June President Clinton announced the renewal of China's most-favoured-nation trading status shortly before an official visit. But on 4 June officials expressed fears that devaluation might become necessary in face of the effect on China's exports of the continuing decline of the Japanese yen. Little emerged from President Clinton's visit—the first since the 1989 Tiananmen Square massacre—but there were frank exchanges with President Jiang Zemin over human rights at a press conference.

Corruption and Human Rights Issues.

The government's commitment to tackling the serious problem of corruption was demonstrated on 31 July when former party secretary and Beijing mayor Chen Xitong (unpopular for his role in the 1989 massacre) was imprisoned for 16 years for financial irregularities. On 10 September the government announced the demobilisation of 100,000 troops, the start of a reduction in the three million strong army by 500,000. But a series of currency curbs and price controls raised a question over whether the government would continue an open-door policy on investment. In light of the deteriorating economic situation—and attacks on the Hong Kong currency—China's development minister left the possibility of devaluation in 1999 open.

On an official visit in October 1998, British prime minister Tony Blair referred to differences over human rights and raised the issue of Tibet but also compared developments in China to his own Third Way. Less successful were talks between President Jiang and a representative from Taiwan in December. Rejecting an offer of autonomy of the kind accorded to Hong Kong, Taiwan refused even to consider reunification until China had introduced political democracy.

Anti-NATO Ferment.

The calamitous attack by NATO on the Chinese Embassy in Belgrade during the Kosovo conflict (see **C68**) unleashed a wave of protest. The American and British embassies in Beijing were besieged. It remained to be seen if this marked a new anti-Western nationalism in China.

JAPAN.

The governing coalition of Tomiichi Murayama proved increasingly fragile throughout 1995. February had seen opposition from Liberal Democratic Party (LDP) members to Mr Murayama's proposal to apologise to Asian countries for Japan's conduct in World War Two. A faction within Mr Murayama's Social Democratic Party of Japan (SDPJ) threatened to break away to form a new centrist party. In addition, a new opposition party—Shinshinto, or New Frontier—won a surprising gubernatorial election victory in February. Local elections on 9 April confirmed this general dissatisfaction with the main parties, with dramatic victories by independents in Tokyo and Osaka.

Mr Murayama negotiated a compromise on 6 June over the issue of how to deal with the forthcoming 50th anniversary of the end of the war in Asia by threatening to call a general election if there was no agreement. While expressing regret, the government would not go as far as many Asian countries wanted. The government went on to win a no confidence vote comfortably on 12 June.

A further shift in political feeling came in elections on 23 July to the House of Councillors, Japan's upper chamber. On a low turn-out, the SDPJ lost almost two thirds of the seats in which it was standing. The LDP fared better but the surprise came in the strong showing of the small Communist Party and of Shinshinto. Mr Murayama reshuffled his cabinet. SDPJ general secretary Wataru Kubo's refusal to take a portfolio highlighted the growing tensions within the Socialists. It had been Mr Kubo who had threatened to create a new centrist party. On 21 September, the SDPJ voted at a national convention to accept a leadership proposal to disband the party and to establish a new "democratic and liberal" party. There were changes within the LDP the following day when Ryutaro Hashimoto became the new leader.

The Advent of Hashimoto.

Following a year of uncertainty, Mr Murayama resigned as prime minister on 5 January 1996. He was succeeded—with a parliamentary vote of 282 to 167 on 11 January—by the LDP leader Ryutaro Hashimoto, restoring power to the party whose 38-year rule had ended only 19 months previously. Mr Hashimoto favoured traditional Japanese politics—government carried out by links between politicians, state officials and businessmen. The opposition Shinshinto attempted to fracture the government coalition by blocking business of the Diet committee considering the annual budget in protest against plans to allocate funds to bail out seven insolvent mortgage companies. But a by-election victory on 24 March strengthened the coalition's position. However, political fragmentation continued and on 3 March the New Socialist Party (NSP) was formed by left-wing defectors from the SDPJ.

Tension over Okinawa.

A visit by US President Clinton in April culminated in the signing of a Joint Declaration on Security which emphasised Japan's role in regional security. However, the US military bases on Okinawa—the lease of which was due to expire in May 1997—remained a source of tension. In March three American soldiers were imprisoned for a rape committed in 1995. In a referendum called by Okinawa's governor on 8 September 1996 a

majority voted for allowing the bases to remain but to reduce the numbers of troops deployed.

Mr Hashimoto dissolved the Diet on 27 September and called an election for 20 October, the first to be held under a new combined single seat and proportional representation system. Political realignment continued with the formation on 28 September by Yukio Hatoyama, previously a leading Sakigake figure, of the liberal Democratic Party of Japan (DPJ). The DPJ included 57 Diet members—35 from the Social Democratic Party (the renamed SDPJ) and 15 from Sakigake—making it the third largest party. His position further weakened by this new configuration, Mr Murayama resigned as SDP leader and was replaced by Takako Doi.

The election result represented a victory for traditional machine politics, with an attempted reassertion by the LDP of its hold on the country. On a much reduced turnout (58 % as against 67 % in 1993), the LDP took 239 of the 500 Diet seats, short of a clear majority. The SDP saw its representation halved from 30 to 15 seats and was replaced as the dominant party of the left by the Communists, who took 26 seats. Ichiro Ozawa's New Frontier Party took 156 seats and the Democratic Party 52. Mr Hashimoto formed a minority government on 7 November with a cabinet dominated by party elders, none of whom was under the age of 50 and only one of whom was a woman.

A Vulnerable Administration?

The vulnerability of Mr Hashimoto's government was revealed at the opening of the Diet on 20 January 1997. He was heckled by the opposition and received little support from his Liberal Democratic Party (LDP) colleagues as he promised an overhaul of the country's economy and warned of sacrifices being necessary to reduce the budget deficit. The long drawn out crisis over corruption continued as the authorities appeared to be making serious efforts to clean the slate. In January, an independent member of the Diet's upper house was arrested on fraud charges. The Recruit scandal—which had shaken the country's political establishment and forced the resignation of prime minister Takeshita in 1989—continued to reverberate. On 23 March, former LDP Chief Cabinet Secretary Takao Fujinami was given a suspended prison sentence for his involvement in the affair. A former minister admitted bribery charges on 26 March and in April police raided three leading brokerage companies seeking evidence of links with organised crime.

Economic and Financial Problems.

In February, Japan's problems were international. Alleging that its trade with Japan was facing obstacles by restrictive practices at the country's ports, the United States threatened to impose surcharges on Japanese ships in American ports. However, following the Japanese government's success in maintaining facilities for the US military presence in Okinawa, imposition of the surcharges was postponed until September. Final agreement on the shipping problem was reached in October, but not before there were threats to detain Japanese vessels in US ports.

In an attempt to reduce Japan's mounting deficit, the cabinet imposed public spending reductions. Government expenditure was to be reduced by 200 million yuan in 1998, with the largest cuts in defence, development assistance and public works. In September the LDP regained its majority in the Diet's lower house following defections from the opposition Shinshinto. However, a cabinet reshuffle on 11 September in which Mr Hashimoto appointed Koko Sato—a former minister convicted of accepting bribes in the 1976 Lockheed scandal—aroused widespread criticism. Mr Sato resigned two weeks later and Mr Hashimoto apologised for being insensitive to public opinion.

The Asian Financial Crisis.

As financial crisis spread through south-east Asia—and the long-term scandal over business relationships with corporate criminals continued—the LDP announced emergency measures on 21 October to stimulate the economy, including deregulation of the property market, a reduction in corporate taxation and increased assistance to small and medium-sized businesses. However, in November a major security house and a bank collapsed as a result of over-extended debts. As the Nikkei stock market index slumped, the Economic Planning Agency announced on 14 November that the economy had come to a standstill. The Nikkei index rose on reports of a controversial government plan to prop up vulnerable financial institutions by buying shares in them. As the country's fourth largest securities house collapsed on 24 November, the yen fell to a five-year low against the dollar. On 17 December the government announced a surprise £9·5 billion tax reduction programme, but concern over a Japanese economic crash mounted in 1998.

Continuing Financial Scandal.

Financial scandal continued into 1998. In January charges of corruption in the Finance Ministry were broadened to include major banks and a Liberal Democratic Party (LDP) MP committed suicide. In March, the Central Bank governor resigned following bribery allegations against an official. As unemployment reached 3·6%—the highest for 45 years—the government attempted stimulation of the ailing economy with increased public works. The budget announced on 8 April included more pump-priming, with income tax cuts and public spending increases. Despite a supplementary budget in May, the Economic Planning Agency (EPA) reported that the economy remained stagnant and was worsening.

Japan in Recession.

As unemployment reached over 4% and the yen fell significantly against the dollar, the Social Democratic Party and the New Party Sakigake ended their alliance with the ruling LDP on 30 May. Both parties criticised the weakness of the government's anti-corruption measures. There was further bad news for the government on 12 June with an EPA report that GDP had fallen during 1997, exports were falling and consumer spending stagnant. As the yen fell further—triggering fears of the impact on Asian economies—Mr Hashimoto survived a no confidence motion in the Diet by 273 votes to 207. But in July, LDP losses in elections to the Upper House threatened Mr Hashimoto's ability to pass legislation. He resigned as prime minister and was succeeded on 30 July by Keizo Obuchi.

The IMF—reporting that GDP threatened to decline further—urged a restructuring of the financial sector as an essential preliminary to revival. Having finally secured support from opposition parties, the LDP responded in October by taking powers to nationalise weakened banks. On 16 November the government presented a further stimulus package of $122 billion, including income and corporate tax cuts, public works to create a million jobs, and the distribution of vouchers to encourage consumption. Mr Obuchi strengthened his position in January 1999 by appointing a member of the opposition Liberal Party to his cabinet, an essential move to push further budget measures (and controversial changes in Japan's defence stance) through the Diet. Ironically, the establishment of the Liberals by an LDP defector in 1993 had opened the country's long-running political crisis.

KOREA.

In 1997 South Korea stood on the brink of the crisis sweeping through south-east Asia's "tiger" economies. On 25 July a major conglomerate and car manufacturer, the Kia Group, defaulted on loans and within a month the government was forced to announce an aid package of $3·9 billion to banks threatened as collapsing *chaebols* (conglomerates) were unable to meet their debts. It was the *chaebols* that, with cheap government credit, had pushed through South Korea's economic miracle. On 13 October the Finance Ministry announced a package of measures to boost the Seoul stock exchange, which had reached an all-time low. But there was no respite and by the end of October five *chaebols* had gone into liquidation. As the Finance Minister resigned on 19 November there were fears that the currency would collapse.

Election Background.

Political uncertainty added to the atmosphere of panic. Elections were imminent and in July the ruling New Korea Party (NKP) nominated Lee Hoi Chang as its presidential candidate to face the opposition National Congress for New Politics (NCNP) nominee, Kim Dae Jung, a prominent former dissident and political prisoner. In November the centre-left NCNP and the conservative Liberal Democrats (LD) formed an alliance to contest the December elections.

A package of measures intended to stabilise the situation met with little success and, following the failure of Japan and the United States to provide support, South Korea turned to the International Monetary Fund on 21 November to seek standby credit to avoid defaulting on overseas debts. This was described in the media as a "national shame". However, both the stock market and the currency continued their decline. In return for a £30 billion aid package, the government was forced to agree to IMF demands for an opening of capital markets, higher interest rates, increased privatisation and a reduction in government spending and economic growth. The trade unions prepared for a repetition of events earlier in the year to meet the inevitable redundancies this would provoke. By mid-December the South Korean currency, the won, had fallen by 40% against the dollar.

Famine in North Korea.

Meanwhile, in North Korea, Kim Jong Il was confirmed as successor in October 1997 to his father, Kim Il Sung, who had died in 1994. This came against the background of continuing famine, intensified by a drought that wrecked the harvest. United Nations aid officials doubted that food stocks would last into 1998 and while both China and the United States promised aid, Red Cross organisations in the south and north of the country reached agreement on distribution of supplies. In June the North Korean government had said it was prepared for war with both the south and the United States following an exchange of fire between northern and southern naval vessels. But throughout August and September progress was reported in preparations for peace talks involving the South, North, China and the United States and the first substantive discussions began in New York in December.

Advent of Kim Dae Jung.

In the presidential elections held on 18 December, the governing party was ejected for the first time in half a century as Kim Dae Jung was narrowly elected. His programme of cutting unemployment and taxation did not appear feasible given the constraints forced on the South Korean economy by the IMF. Mr Kim—who was inaugurated in February 1998—confirmed this on the day following his election when he declared that he would implement the IMF conditions and stated that "reform without pain is not possible."

Meanwhile, as the North Korean population suffered increasing malnutrition and, in some areas, outright starvation through famine, the governing Korean Workers' Party appeared to be acknowledging the necessity for an economic restructuring proposed by the United Nations Development Programme in co-operation with Pyongyang officials. At the centre lay an encouragement of individual agriculture and a reform of the 1,200 state farms.

Growing Economic Turmoil.

As 1998 opened, both parts of Korea were suffering economic turmoil. In the north, as famine continued, the United Nations organised massive food supplies to feed the starving population. While less dire in extent, the south faced the fallout of the Asian financial crisis and in February the newly-elected President Kim Dae Jung prepared to implement economic reforms demanded by the International Monetary Fund (IMF) in return for the $21 billion stand-by credit which had been negotiated in December 1997.

There was faltering progress in the developing relations between north and south. On 19 February North Korea issued a conciliatory statement expressing a willingness to open dialogue with South Korean political groups. There was a further session of the four-party talks between the north, south, the United States and China aimed at creating a permanent peace agreement to replace the 1953 armistice from 16–21 March. In April North Korean leader Kim Jong Il issued an open letter calling for a seminar on reunification.

There were violent protests in the southern capital Seoul on May Day against growing unemployment and in June the Korean Federation of Trade Unions mounted a general strike. A second strike was averted as the union agreed on tri-partite discussions with the government and employers. As it became clear that 1998 GDP growth would fall to 4 %, the IMF permitted a relaxation in fiscal policy, with increased support for the unemployed. But there were further strikes on 14–15 July in protest against rising unemployment and privatisation.

North Korean Nuclear Programme.

Fears continued over North Korea's nuclear programme, together with its testing of ballistic missiles. In August, President Kim's offer of direct dialogue with the north was rejected. The test firing of a missile over Japan received an angry reaction, including the imposition of economic sanctions by Japan. Despite increasing concern over the apparent irrationality of North Korean policy, the United States and the north announced progress in talks in September and agreed to re-open the four-party discussions on the peninsula's future. But in November the north refused to allow access to a suspected nuclear weapon site to US inspectors. As tension heightened, US President Clinton warned there would be a firm response to any military action by the north. On 18 December a North Korean submarine intruding into southern waters was sunk.

CAMBODIA (KAMPUCHEA).

The Japanese Peace Plan.

Under international pressure, Prime Minister Hun Sen agreed in February 1998 to accept a Japanese peace plan allowing First Prime Minister Norodom Ranriddh (ousted by Hun Sen in July 1997) to return to Cambodia to take part in the July 1998 elections. Ranriddh was to be tried for his links with the Khmer Rouge with a guaranteed pardon. Seven months' fighting ended with the announcement of a ceasefire by Ranriddh's supporters on 27 February. Ranriddh was tried in his absence on 4 March, sentenced to five years imprisonment and immediately pardoned. He returned from exile at the end of the month.

There were continuing divisions in the by now severely depleted Khmer Rouge. A faction led by Sam Rainsy announced it would participate in the July elections. On 15 April the death was reported of notorious Khmer Rouge leader Pol Pot, a prisoner of his former followers. As head of the country's government from 1975–79, Pol Pot was responsible for the deaths of two million people. Mutinies in the Khmer Rouge forces had already reduced the movement to a rump and at the end of May the government claimed to have captured the movement's last border camp. However, peace talks between the government and Ranriddh faltered and his FUNCINPEC—together with its allies in the National United Front—threatened to boycott the July elections.

The 1998 Elections.

In what proved to be a relatively peaceful election to the 122-seat Constituent Assembly on 26 July, FUNCINPEC took 31·7 % of the vote and 43 seats, the Sam Rainsy Party 41·4 % and 64 seats. The CPP's offer of a coalition government was rejected by both parties and throughout August and September relations deteriorated, with Hun Sen accusing his opponents of mounting an assassination attempt as the Constituent Assembly opened on 24 September. But in November a deal was brokered in which Hun Sen would remain Prime Minister with Ranriddh as Assembly chairman. A cabinet was sworn in at the end of the month with 12 CPP ministers and 11 from FUNCINPEC.

Final Khmer Rouge Surrender.

The surrender of the remnants of the Khmer Rouge in December—with an amnesty for their leaders, despite international calls for their prosecution—brought an end to over 30 years of civil war. However, King Norodom Sihanouk declared in January 1999 that he was willing to face trial for his collaboration with the Khmer Rouge in the mid-1970s.

BURMA (MYANMAR).

In September 1988 student-led protests brought down the 28-year regime of General Ne Win. But at least 5,000 pro-democracy activists were killed by the military junta—the State Law and Order Restoration Council (SLORC)—which succeeded him. SLORC promised free elections and an early return to civilian rule. However, in June 1989 Aung San Suu Kyi, leader of the National League for Democracy (NLD), the main opposition grouping, was placed under house arrest. In January 1990 she, and other leading opposition figures, were banned from standing in elections to be held in May, the first for 30 years.

The NLD won 397 of the 485 National Assembly seats in elections held on 27 May 1990. Since these elections, repression continued in Burma throughout the 1990s. Although Aung San Suu Kyi was released from prison, it was only to be kept under house arrest. Meanwhile military offensives were waged against ethnic rebels.

Human Rights Abuses.

On 29 January 1997, 14 people—five members of the main opposition party, the National League for Democracy (NLD)—were imprisoned for involvement in the December 1996 student protests. Burma's human rights record had repercussions as the last major US company in the country, PepsiCo, announced that it would withdraw by the end of May. European Union foreign ministers expressed concern to the Association of South East Asian Nations (ASEAN) at Burma's forthcoming membership of the organisation and trade sanctions were reimposed in April.

Forces of the ruling State Law and Order Restoration Council (SLORC) renewed their offensive against Karen National Union (KNU) guerrillas on 31 January following a breakdown in peace talks. As fighting continued through February and March and refugees fled into neighbouring northern Thailand, the KNU abandoned its headquarters. Responsibility for a bomb explosion at the home of SLORC's second secretary—army Chief of Staff Lieutenant General Tin Oo—on 6 April was denied by the KNU and by the opposition National Coalition Government of the Union of Burma (NCGUB). There were suggestions that the action was part of a power struggle within SLORC.

From SLORC to SPDC.

SLORC—in power since 1988—dissolved itself on 15 November, re-appearing as a 19-member State Peace and Development Council (SPDC). Comprising mainly younger regional military commanders, the SPDC continued to be led by the country's top four generals, with Than Shwe as chairman and Khin Nyant as first secretary. In a cabinet shuffle that followed, General Than Shwe took the posts of Prime Minister and Minister of Defence. The SPDC—threatened by the financial crisis sweeping south-east Asia—now launched an anti-corruption campaign in an effort to revive an ailing economy and encourage support from Western aid donors. At the end of December five ministers were dismissed and placed under house arrest. However, the home affairs minister made it clear in a meeting with NLD leaders that the SPDC had no plans to introduce greater democracy.

Developments since 1998.

The ruling junta's repression of the opposition continued with a 25-year prison sentence imposed in April 1998 on prominent National League for Democracy (NLD) activist Daw San San after an interview in which she had criticised the military government. In March 40 people were arrested for plotting a campaign of bombings and assassinations and on 30 April the SDLC announced that six people (including four members of the exiled All Burma Democratic Front) had been sentenced to death for possessing explosives. In May, there were reports that 80-year old Thakin Ohn Min—a veteran independence campaigner and adviser to NLD leader Aung San Suu Kyi—had been imprisoned for seven years. This followed a 15-year sentence imposed on an opposition activist for writing a history of the Burma student movement.

Continued International Concerns.

The SDLC appeared to have made a conciliatory move by allowing the NLD to hold a congress on 27–28 May to celebrate the eighth anniversary of the annulled 1990 elections. The NLD called on the military government to open a dialogue on the restoration of democracy. But in July there were clashes with government forces as NLD leader Aung San Suu Kyi made three attempts to leave the capital Rangoon to meet opposition activists. The extent of international concern was demonstrated by US Secretary of state Albright's warning that the SDLC was directly responsible for Aung San Suu Kyi's welfare. The largest anti-regime demonstrations for a number of years took place at Rangoon University on 2–3 September. Troops struggled to prevent the protests spilling over on to the streets of the capital.

The opposition now attempted to convene a 'People's Parliament' made up of those who would have taken their seats following the 1990 elections. The SDLC responded by arresting 800 opposition activists, prompting protests from Britain, the US and the European Union. Pressure on the regime was increased when on 5 September the World Bank refused to make further loans on the grounds that the government had defaulted on payments. A ten-member committee, including Aung San Suu Kyi, asserted that the SDLC laws had no authority. In October and November the SDLC released 300 NLD activists, but 500 (including 200 elected representatives) remained in custody.

INDONESIA.

Indonesia's independence from the Netherlands—proclaimed in August 1945—was formally recognised on 27 December 1949. Dr Sukarno became president. In 1957 he introduced "guided democracy", replacing the elected parliament with an appointed legislature. Following an attempted coup in 1965, the Indonesian Communist Party was banned and thousands of its supporters killed. In March 1966 the army assumed emergency powers under General Suharto. He was elected president by the People's Consultative Assembly in March 1968 and went on to be re-elected in 1973, 1978 and 1983.

President Suharto's "New Order" gave the army a pivotal place in Indonesian politics, attempting a balance between the communists on the left and Islamic fundamentalists on the right. The army was also involved in counter-insurgency operations in East Timor—which was integrated into Indonesia in July 1976 following Portugal's withdrawal in 1975—and in Irian Jaya, which Indonesia had occupied in 1963. Politics was dominated by the official party, Golkar.

A Repressive Regime.

By the 1990s Indonesia's human rights record was arousing increasing international criticism, particularly in occupied East Timor, where the government faced resistance from guerrillas of the separatist Revolutionary Front for the Independence of East Timor (Fretelin). In November 1991 there was particular condemnation following a massacre by Indonesian troops at a demonstration in East Timor. Golkar retained power with a reduced majority in elections held in 1992 and President Suharto was unanimously elected for a sixth consecutive five-year term by the puppet People's Consultative Assembly in March 1993. But he soon faced resistance from a newly-formed Indonesian Prosperous Labour Union (SBSI) which called a successful one-hour national strike. In an effort to ward off political opposition, the government moved against the Indonesian Democratic Party (PDI) which was led by Megawati Sukarnoputri,

daughter of former President Sukarno (ousted by Suharto in the 1960s). Although Fretelin guerrilla resistance weakened, Indonesia faced growing criticism.

In March 1997, the Indonesian Institute of Sciences issued a controversial report—commissioned by President Suharto in 1995—calling for a reduction in the military's involvement in politics and for an improvement in the government's attitude towards human rights. There was growing anti-Suharto activity but in May 1996 Golkar was returned to power with an increased majority. However, over 250 people were killed during the campaign and, while the elections were taking place, East Timor separatists launched attacks on police and polling stations.

The Asian Financial Crisis.

Indonesia's economic weakness was now intensified by the general financial crisis spreading through much of Asia during 1997. In November, President Suharto reluctantly agreed to seek International Monetary Fund (IMF) assistance. The IMF granted a stand-by credit of $10 billion. In return, Indonesia was to encourage competitiveness by dismantling state and private monopolies, reducing subsidies, and ending concessions to businesses operated by the President's family. As in previous periods of political tension, Chinese-owned businesses were attacked. President Suharto was re-elected unopposed for a seventh five-year term in March. But student protests continued. As President Suharto rejected IMF calls for a liberalised economy, demonstrations increased in intensity.

The Fall of Suharto.

A broadcast by President Suharto on 19 May offering reform was greeted with cynicism. Two days later he resigned, naming as his successor his vice-president, B. J. Habibie. President Habibie pledged economic, political and legal reform but retained prominent Suharto supporters in his cabinet. He outlined proposals for the legalisation of political parties, legislative elections in May 1999 and the election of a new president in December 1999. Following riots in East Timor demanding a referendum on separation from Indonesia, President Habibie offered the territory 'special status' and announced the withdrawal of a thousand troops in July.

Anti-Chinese Violence.

At a special party congress held in July, the ruling Golkar attempted to adapt itself to the new situation by promising a break with its authoritarian past. As the economic crisis that had forced Suharto from power deepened, anti-Chinese violence continued, particularly in Sumatra, prompting China to freeze food aid in protest. Early September saw the first major demonstrations against the new government as students in Jakarta demanded a reduction in food prices and President Habibie's resignation.

A 12-party anti-Golkar alliance formed on 12 September challenged the continuing dominance of pancasila, the official state ideology. Mass demonstrations in Jakarta and five other cities in October raised new economic and political demands and repeated calls for President Habibie's resignation.

As the newly appointed People's Consultative Assembly met to prepare the ground for transition to democracy in mid-November, thousands of anti-government protesters took to the streets. Habibie appealed for calm but ordered the army to act sternly against what he claimed was an attempt to topple the government. At the end of the month there was serious violence between Muslims and Christians in the capital and in January 1999 45 people were killed in religious rioting in the eastern islands.

Autonomy for East Timor?

The foreign minister, Ali Alatas, announced on 27 January that the government was willing to grant independence to East Timor if the territory rejected autonomy proposals. But as anti-independence terrorism intensified, there were fears that the civilian government's concession would face resistance from the military. In the event, a UN-backed plan for a plebiscite on 8 August to decide Timor's future was agreed.

AFRICA

ETHIOPIA AND ERITREA.

A new constitution adopted on 8 December 1994 provided for a federal government and nine states. Any area had a guaranteed right to secede. The trial opened three days later of former President Mengistu (in exile in Zimbabwe) and 72 members of Ethiopia's former ruling Dergue on charges of crimes against humanity.

The 1995 Elections.

Elections were held in May in 545 of the country's 548 constituencies. The Ethiopian People's Revolutionary Democratic Front (EPRDF) emerged the overall winner with 438 seats in the Council of People's Representatives, other parties shared 81 seats and eight independents were elected. The new constitution was formally instituted on 22 August, a Republic of Ethiopia was proclaimed, and the Council elected Negaso Gidada as President of the Republic. Interim head of state Meles Zenawi was elected Prime Minister by the Council.

Meanwhile, Ethiopia had concluded an economic agreement with Eritrea, which had seceded in 1993, on 5 April. The agreement was intended to lay the basis for the creation of an economic and customs union in the longer term. However, relations with Sudan continued to deteriorate. On 1 September Sudan was accused of harbouring terrorists and the fundamentalist National Islamic Front (NIF) of deliberately fomenting bad relations between the two countries. Restrictions were placed on Sudanese activities in Ethiopia to "protect and safeguard" security.

Police announced the arrest on 21 June of members of the Ethiopian National Patriotic Front. The Front was alleged to be planning a campaign of terrorism, including the assassination of state officials and foreigners. In August 1996 Ethiopian troops were deployed against Ogaden separatist guerrillas based in Somalia. The government claimed to have killed over 200 members of the Islamic Union in an attack mounted in reprisal for a bombing in Addis Ababa on 5 August and the attempted assassination of a minister in July.

The Trial of Mengistu.

Further charges of genocide and war crimes were laid on 13 February 1997 against former head of state Mengistu Haile Mariam and over 5,000 members of the Dergue. Mengistu, overthrown in May 1991, had been on trial since December 1994 but remained in exile in Zimbabwe. There were further terrorist incidents in the east of the country in February. In August, the National Disaster Prevention Commission reported that over three million people faced starvation because of the effect of continuing low rainfall. A million required immediate aid.

War with Eritrea.

In January 1998, the Ethiopian-Somali Democratic League announced its intention to merge with the Ogaden National Liberation Front to form a joint regional government under the title of the Somali Democratic Party. The fusion formally took place in June. Meanwhile, at the end of the month the government ordered the arrest of the editors of 14 independent newspapers without charge, forcing at least four out of business. Despite hitherto cordial relations with its neighbour, on 13 May the Council of Ministers accused Eritrea of invading the north east of Ethiopia. Eritrea, claiming 100 had been killed in clashes, accused Ethiopia of being the aggressor. At talks convened by the Organisation of African Unity (OAU) in Burkina Faso in August there were mutual accusations of maltreatment of nationals. As fighting escalated—by November there were clashes on three fronts—

OAU peace efforts continued. But in February 1999 there were fears that full-scale war was about to erupt.

ALGERIA.

Rise of Fundamentalism.

The dominant feature of recent Algerian politics has been the fall from power of the FLN and the rise of the growing fundamentalist Islamic movement, the Islamic Salvation Front (FIS). The result has been a continuing political crisis and bitter civil war in the 1990s.

A Catalogue of Slaughter.

Between 1992 and 1997, the estimated death toll from the civil war climbed to some 80,000. On 5 June 1997, legislative elections (which excluded the banned FIS) were won by the newly formed National Democratic Rally (RND), widely regarded as the political instrument of the military-backed government. In a surprise move on 15 July, Abbassi Madani, the founder and leader of the outlawed FIS, was freed on parole, one week after the release of the organisation's provisional leader, Abdelkader Hachani.

Atrocities reached new heights in 1997 with entire villages in effect eradicated by "terrorist" attacks, with perhaps the worst attack occurring on 24 September at Bentalha, where more than 250 men, women and children had their throats slit, were hacked to death, or were burnt alive. Such slaughter often occurred within earshot of government security forces.

Attempts at Mediation.

In December 1997 and early 1998 first Canada and then the EU sent special envoys to Algeria to press the government to allow outside investigation of the situation, with little success—the EU mission being hampered by its own internal divisions. However, violence continued unabated with at least 100 (and perhaps as many as 400) villagers slaughtered on the first night of the holy month of Ramadan, 31 December.

The escalation in violence that had begun at Ramadan continued into 1998 as almost 2,000 civilians were killed in attacks mounted by the Armed Islamic Group (GIA). In a National People's Assembly Debate on the security situation on 6 February, prime minister Ahmed Ouyahia denied opposition charges that government forces were involved in the massacres in an attempt to eradicate Islamicism and rejected calls for international intervention in a war in which over 80,000 had now died. In March the government claimed successes in attacks on GIA bases west of the capital and in April—despite the earlier denials—arrested officials allegedly involved in violence.

The UN Mission.

A United Nations mission arrived in the country at the government's invitation on 22 July to report on the conduct of the war. As the mission left in August, the government said it would continue to reject any demand for foreign intervention. There was widespread surprise when, on 11 September, President Zeroual announced his intention to stand down in February 1999, almost two years before his term was due to expire. There were reports that his resignation had been encouraged by generals who rejected his compromises with moderate Islamic parties.

Background to Elections.

It was the turn of the prime minister, Ahmed Ouyahia, to resign on 14 December, partly due to criticisms of his controversial austerity policies. Mr Ouyahia—who was replaced by Ismail Hamdani—was expected to be the ruling National Democratic Rally's presidential candidate in elections planned for 1999. The moderate Islamic Social Movement for Peace (MSP) named its candidate, Sheikh Mahfoud Nahnah, on 19 December. In February 1999, veteran opposition leader Hocine Ait Ahmed was declared candidate for the Socialist Forces Front (FFS).

LIBYA.

In November 1990, British and American investigators charged Libyan intelligence agents with responsibility for the bombing of an American airliner that crashed over Lockerbie, Scotland in December 1988 and France accused Libya of masterminding the bombing of a French airliner over Niger in September 1989. The US and Britain demanded the extradition of the Libyan suspects, but Gaddafi denied responsibility. He announced an internal investigation into the affair and launched an intense diplomatic campaign to resist US and British pressure. He promised to halt his support for terrorist groups such as the Provisional Irish Republican Army.

UN Sanctions.

As allegations of Libyan involvement in international terrorism continued, the UN Security Council agreed to impose limited sanctions—a ban on air travel and arms sales to Libya—unless two agents suspected of responsibility were handed over for trial by 15 April. President Gaddafi suggested he would hand over the agents to an Arab government.

A visit by Libyan pilgrims to Islamic holy places in Israel on 31 May was interpreted as an attempted diplomatic overture by President Gaddafi and bitterly criticised by the PLO. The pilgrimage ended abruptly on 2 June when the group's spokesman called for the overthrow of Israel's "Zionist occupation". On 11 November the UN security council voted to impose tighter economic sanctions against Libya from 1 December unless two men suspected of involvement in the December 1988 Lockerbie bombing were handed over for trial. The stand-off continued from 1994 to 1997 with Gaddafi declaring his willingness to have the two suspects tried by the International Court of Justice (ICJ) but the UK and France rejected this proposal.

Recent Developments.

Libya's international relations continued to be dominated by the 1988 Lockerbie terrorist bombing. In March 1998 the United Nations renewed sanctions first imposed in 1992 following Libya's refusal to hand over two men suspected of mounting the action. President Gaddafi agreed in April that the men could be tried in a neutral country, a proposal accepted by Britain and the United States in August. The government denied in June that President Gaddafi had been shot and wounded in an assassination attempt. In October—apparently disappointed by the failure of the Arab League to support Libya's campaign against UN sanctions—the state external radio service began to describe itself as the 'Voice of Africa' rather than the 'Voice of the Greater Arab Homeland' and President Gaddafi implied that his country's future lay with Africa rather than the Arab world. Although Libya had agreed that the two suspects should face trial in the Netherlands, it was not until April 1999 that the handing over took place. The two defendants faced trial (under Scottish law) at Camp Zeist in the Netherlands. Sanctions were duly ended.

NIGERIA.

Background to Crisis.

Following the military coup which brought him to power in 1993, General Sani Abacha had crushed virtually all organised political opposition, imprisoned the man whom many believed to be Nigeria's elected President, and broken the trade union movement. In 1995 his prevarication over a return to civilian rule, together with the imprisonment and execution of human rights activists, led Nigeria into deeper international isolation. The year opened with renewed suspicions that

General Abacha was determined to prolong the transition to civilian rule and extend his own power. Meetings of the National Constitutional Conference (NCC)—the body established to prepare the transition—were adjourned for three months. This was followed by the arrest on 10 March of 29 civilians and army personnel for allegedly plotting the overthrow of General Abacha. Unofficial reports put the numbers arrested at over 600. Among them were the country's former military leader, General Olusegen Obasanjo, a prominent campaigner for a speedy return to democracy. As fears for their fate grew, the government was forced to deny in April that 60 members of the armed forces had been summarily executed.

Further evidence of General Abacha's delaying tactics came on 25 April when the NCC withdrew its previous recommendation that military rule should end on 1 January 1996 and issued constitutional proposals extending the deadline into the future. An appeal by South African Archbishop Desmond Tutu for the release of the man many believed to be the rightful Nigerian President—Moshood Abiola—and of General Obasanjo (the only Nigerian military ruler ever to have relinquished power voluntarily) was ignored by General Abacha. Instead, the trial of the alleged coup plotters before a military tribunal opened on 5 June.

Formation of the National Liberation Council.

With the internal opposition cowed, Nigerian intellectuals—among them the Nobel laureate writer Wole Soyinka—announced the formation in New York of a National Liberation Council on 18 June. The Council's objective was to establish a government in exile. The Council refused to name the majority of its members, some of whom it claimed were living in Nigeria itself.

Despite General Abacha's continual denials that he planned to hold on to power, the long drawn out crisis was provoking Nigeria's international isolation. The British government warned him on 6 July that Nigeria was unlikely to be welcome at the November Commonwealth Conference unless there were clear signs of a rapid return to democracy. This had little effect. The Nigerian Defence Ministry confirmed on 14 July that 42 people, including General Obasanjo, had been convicted and that 14 had been sentenced to death for planning a coup. There was immediate denunciation from the United States, France, Canada, the European Union and the Commonwealth and appeals for clemency from Nelson Mandela, Jerry Rawlings of Ghana and Idriss Déry of Chad. South Africa imposed a ban on arms sales on 1 August.

Harassment of what little internal opposition remained continued. On 1 August, two editors were sentenced to life imprisonment for publishing stories about the alleged coup attempt. In September two journalists were imprisoned for speculating about Abacha's health. General Abacha accused "certain Western countries" of working with local dissidents to destabilise Nigeria. He threatened unspecified retaliation.

General Abacha was more specific about a timetable for the return to civilian rule on 1 October. He intended to remain in power until 1 October 1998, by which date reforms would be in place to enable elections to take place. The remaining bans on political activity were to be lifted and a national electoral commission appointed by the end of the year. Local elections would be held at the end of 1996 and presidential elections at the end of 1998. Clearly hoping to ward off the growing threat of international sanctions and of suspension from the Commonwealth, General Abacha commuted the July death sentences and reduced the terms of imprisonment.

The Trial of Saro-Wiwa.

But whatever beneficial effect General Abacha's statement may have had was immediately undone when, on 31 October, a military tribunal imposed the death sentence on nine human rights activists, including the writer Ken Saro-Wiwa, for alleged complicity in murder. The nine were members of the Movement for the Survival of the Ogoni People (MOSOP), an organisation seeking redress for the environmental devastation caused by oil companies in the Niger delta. Over 2,000 Ogonis had been killed by Nigerian security forces during protests.

Despite a widespread international outcry against the sentences, the nine were hanged on 10 November. There were immediate demands for stringent sanctions to be imposed and for the expulsion of Nigeria from the Commonwealth. However, Commonwealth leaders meeting in New Zealand held back, instead insisting that General Abacha should hand over to civilian government in two years rather than the three he proposed. In a speech on the second anniversary of his coup on 17 November, General Abacha dismissed international outrage at the executions and refused to compromise on his transition programme. Three days later the European Union imposed a range of sanctions including a ban on arms sales, froze all but humanitarian aid, but held back from an oil embargo at the insistence of Britain and the Netherlands. Nevertheless, repression in Ogoniland continued and 19 further activists were arrested.

By the end of November there had still been no approval of the draft constitution, the electoral commission had not been appointed and there were no signs of machinery to arrange the transition. President Mandela described Nigeria as an "illegitimate, barbaric, arrogant military dictatorship" and he was joined in his attack by President Mugabe of Zimbabwe. However, General Abacha was not without support in Africa. On 6 December, the secretary general of the Organisation of African Unity expressed the body's support for General Abacha and made clear its opposition to the international campaign against him.

Events in 1996.

Events took a potentially more disturbing turn when, on 17 January 1996, General Abacha's eldest son was killed in an aircraft crash in northern Nigeria. A group claiming to represent opponents of the regime, the United Liberation Front for Nigeria's Liberation, claimed responsibility for the crash. Although pro-democracy organisations denounced the use of violence it remained to be seen whether Nigeria was entering a more dramatic phase in the crisis.

In February 1996, General Abacha accused foreign governments of assisting his exiled opponents. Pro-democracy groups in exile formed a new umbrella organisation, the United Democratic Front of Nigeria (UDFN), on 1 April. General Abacha's refusal to allow entry to a Commonwealth mission to discuss human rights violations and progress towards a restoration of democracy prompted the imposition of an arms embargo on 23 April. But internal divisions were revealed when General Abacha dismissed the army and air force commanders in March and conducted a further purge of senior officers in May. This was seen as an attempt by General Abacha to remove potential rivals for power.

The Murder of Kudirat Abiola.

The country's internal political crisis continued with the murder by unidentified gunmen on 4 June of Kudirat Abiola, wife of Chief Abiola, the winner of the quashed 1993 presidential elections. The authorities closed Ibadan University the following day after students had led thousands of demonstrators in protests against her death. The government denied involvement in her murder and offered a reward for information leading to arrests. In an effort to avert threatened economic sanctions, foreign minister Tom Ikimi led a delegation to London in June to meet the Commonwealth Ministerial Action Group (CMAG). Mr Ikimi's proposed three year transition to civilian rule was rejected as inadequate.

Riots in Kaduna.

In September the government faced protests from Shia Muslims in the northern city of Kaduna. Over 50 people were killed in clashes with troops when 10,000 demonstrated on 18 September against the arrest of Muslim Brotherhood leader Ibrahim Yakub el-Zagzaki. A Brotherhood spokesman declared that the movement's object was to overthrow what it described as the corrupt Abacha government. Another anti-Abacha group, the Liberation Organisation of Nigeria (LON), claimed responsibility for bomb explosions in December 1996 and January 1997. Two soldiers were killed in

an attack mounted in Lagos on 7 January. LON, which claimed to have support among army officers, declared that violence would be necessary to remove General Abacha.

The military government moved against those whom it held responsible for the explosions on 12 March, charging 12 dissidents – including Nobel laureate Wole Soyinka – with treason. Among those accused and facing the death penalty were leaders of the opposition grouping Nadeco. Mr Soyinka, living in exile in the United States, accused the international community of collaborating with General Abacha's dictatorship. During largely peaceful multi-party municipal elections on 15 March, demonstrators called for the release of opposition leader Moshood Abiola.

Harassment of Opposition.

The government made a further move against its opponents in March 1997 when 15 people—including exiled Nobel prize winner Wole Soyinka—were accused of waging a terrorist campaign against General Abacha's regime. Four bomb explosions outside army barracks during May in which four people were killed were blamed by the government on supporters of Soyinka's National Democratic Coalition (NADECO). The south of the country also faced ethnic clashes in April which led to serious losses in oil production. Troops were deployed on 27 April as warring groups took oil workers hostage, forcing the Shell oil company to reduce production. The shortages disrupted economic activity and troops guarded petrol stations to maintain order. Meanwhile, in neighbouring Sierra Leone, Nigerian soldiers serving as part of a West African peacekeeping force, unsuccessfully attempted to restore civilian government following a military coup in May.

The military government announced a timetable for elections leading to civilian government on 2 July. State assembly elections would take place on 6 December, parliamentary elections on 25 April 1998 and gubernatorial elections on 1 August 1998. As the October 1997 Commonwealth summit approached, opposition groups renewed pressure for Nigeria's expulsion—the country's membership had been suspended in 1995—and for the imposition of economic sanctions. General Abacha was accused of making no effort to keep his promise to restore civilian rule by October 1998. No new draft constitution had been produced and leading political prisoners remained in custody.

Foiled Coup Attempt.

The government responded to criticism in November by calling on Britain to pay compensation for the years of colonial exploitation. General Abacha repeated his claim that civilian government would be restored in 1998 and on 17 November he dismissed his cabinet to enable members to prepare themselves for civilian rule. But on 21 December the government announced it had foiled a coup attempt. General Abacha's deputy, Lieutenant General Oladipo Diya, and a number of other senior officers were arrested. General Diya had, however, narrowly escaped an assassination attempt days previously and the opposition suggested General Abacha was conducting a purge. Further arrests followed.

The elections of April 1998 gave hope to the opposition. There was a widespread boycott by many millions of voters. The elections were followed by protests against the Abacha regime. On 1 May seven protesters were killed by police in a demonstration in Ibadan in the south west of the country calling for General Abacha's resignation. Over 140 detainees were released a week later in fulfilment of Abacha's November 1997 pledge to free political prisoners. However, human rights activists denied that those freed were genuine political activists.

The Death of Abacha.

The situation was dramatically transformed with the death on 8 June of General Abacha following a heart attack. The event was so fortuitous that murder was suspected. Chief of Staff General Abdusalem Abubakar was sworn in as the country's leader the following day. His pledge to restore civilian rule in October 1998 was followed by the release of prominent political prisoners, including General Obasanjo. There was further drama with the death on 7 July of Moshood Abiola who had been imprisoned following what was believed to be his victory in the annulled 1993 presidential elections. Again there were suggestions that he had been murdered and 60 people were killed in protests in the Yoruba heartland.

Background to 1999 Elections.

General Abubakar announced a revised programme for the transition to civilian rule on 20 July. Following the restoration of rights to political activity, an elected civilian president would be sworn in on 29 May 1999. Fifteen members of a 23-strong cabinet appointed in August were civilians. A newly-formed Independent National Electoral Commission (INEC) set out a rolling programme of local, state and federal elections to take place in December 1998–January 1999. New political parties emerging included the People's Democratic Party (PDP) and the All People's Party (APP), both of which included the bulk of the leading civilian political activists.

There were further releases of political detainees—including 19 ethnic Ogoni activists imprisoned in 1994—in September and on 14 October the Nobel prize winning writer and prominent opponent of military rule Wole Soyinka returned to Nigeria. At the end of the month General Obasanjo—the only military ruler to have voluntarily relinquished power to a civilian government—announced he had joined the PDP.

In elections held on 20 February, Olesugun Obasanjo's PDP emerged as the leading party in the House of Representatives and Senate. General Obasanjo went on to victory in the presidential elections held a week later, taking 18 million votes to the 11 million won by his only opponent, former finance minister Olu Falae. There was, however, evidence of widespread fraud and manipulation and Mr Falae declared he would challenge the result. As handover to civilian rule on 29 May approached it seemed that Nigeria would be re-admitted to the Commonwealth.

KENYA.

There were clashes in Kibera, a slum area in the capital Nairobi in October 1996 between members of the Nubian and Luo groups. In Kenya's highly ethnically divided politics, Nubians supported the ruling KANU while Luos backed the opposition FORD-Kenya. The area's FORD-Kenya MP accused the authorities of encouraging divisions for their own political purposes.

Leading opposition figure Koigi wa Wamwere was imprisoned for four years on 2 October for allegedly attempting to steal weapons from the police. Wamwere, who had been in custody since 1993, had been influential in the formation of Safina. The government's opponents sought to unite their forces in an Opposition Alliance, the establishment of which was announced on 30 November. Leakey was named as chief co-ordinator.

President Moi's accusation in September against neighbouring Uganda of training a guerrilla force to invade Kenya was followed by a bomb explosion in Nairobi. His opponents suggested this and the allegations were part of President Moi's attempt to divert public attention from demands for constitutional reform. A leading dissident, Koigi wa Wamwere was convicted of armed robbery in October following a trial condemned by human rights groups and opposition politicians. However, in December Mr Wamwere was released on bail and allowed abroad for specialist medical treatment.

Developments in 1997.

President Moi's opponents expressed concern when, on 15 January 1997, he restored his close political ally Nicholas Biwott to the cabinet. He had dismissed Mr Biwott in 1991 following allegations of his involvement in the murder of foreign minister Robert Ouko. Four days of violent protests took place in the capital Nairobi on 23–26 February following the death of a student leader. Police denied claims that he had been murdered. On 24 February the government closed the university indefinitely. Following police attacks on opposition rallies in April, 14 ambassadors in Kenya issued a joint condemnation of police brutality and called on

the government to restore freedom of speech and assembly to its opponents. The government reacted angrily and warned opposition leaders against seeking foreign support.

Registration of voters for forthcoming elections opened on 16 May but President Moi rejected opposition and church calls for constitutional reform before the elections, pointing to the problems reform had caused in other African states. The leaders of the main opposition groupings—Raila Odinga of the National Development Party, Kenneth Matiba of FORD-Asili, Michael Wamawala of FORD-Kenya, and Paul Muite of Safina—were placed under house arrest on 31 May following the breaking up by police of an opposition rally.

Growth of Popular Protest.

But it was the fall of his former Zaïrean ally, President Mobutu in May, that appeared to threaten President Moi's position. Demonstrations against his regime won greater popular support as the country's economy continued its decline. As one, youths chanted "Mobutu has gone and Moi is next". Following pro-democracy demonstrations on 10 July in which ten people were killed, and under pressure from the National Convention Executive Committee (NCEC), President Moi offered a reform package. But in August the International Monetary Fund delivered a further blow by withholding a £130 million loan because of continuing corruption.

A Chaotic Election.

During thinly-attended celebrations on 10 October commemorating the 19th anniversary of President Moi's accession to power, police broke up opposition demonstrations, arresting several MPs. Deputy opposition leader James Opengo called for the presidential and parliamentary elections to be postponed pending the establishment of an independent electoral committee. However, the elections went ahead against a background of violence, with charges from the opposition of widespread corruption. Chaotic organisation of the ballot forced voting to be extended into a second day. On 4 January 1998 the country's electoral commission declared that President Moi had been returned to office. However, his opponents in the contest—Mwai Kibaki, Raila Odinga and Charity Ngilu—rejected the result, claiming that the poll had been rigged.

The newly-elected President Moi was heckled by opposition MPs when he arrived at the National Assembly's first session on 3 February 1998. They were protesting at the death of 100 people in clashes between Kikuyu supporters of President Moi's main rival, Mwai Kihanki, and Mr Moi's Kalenjin tribe. In persistent Kalenjin violence against Kikuyus over 200 were killed in February and 300,000 driven from their homes. Human rights activists warned of the danger of civil war in the Rift Valley.

Recent Developments.

President Moi and his ruling Kenya African National Union (KANU) faced a major challenge when on 22 February 1998 12,000 bank workers struck over finance ministry proposals to tax concessionary loans they received. Threats of mass sackings on 3 March provoked the Central Organisation of Trade Unions (COTU) to declare a general strike, which was called off when the tax was suspended. However, a policy of austerity was clearly the government's intention. On 5 March finance minister Simeon Nyachae announced public spending cuts and tax increases to curb the 1997–98 budget deficit. Five days later the World Bank promised a $100 million loan. In April the government declared the need for a 20% reduction in public sector salaries.

In late April, finance minister Nyachae described the economy's parlous state at a conference in Mombassa attended by 82 KANU MPs, 80 opposition MPs, and representatives of the World Bank and donor countries. He condemned corruption among senior figures, a charge endorsed by KANU MPs. President Moi described the statements as 'of no consequence' but called a one-day economic conference on 6 May. Here he announced a spending review affecting 25 government departments, with threats that it would be necessary to reduce the civil service and the number of teachers.

Mr Moi ordered troops into the Rift Valley on 9 May to seize illegal weapons. The following day the long-promised review forum convened, including MPs, together with members of non-governmental organisations, religious groups and critics of the government. On 19 June there were student riots in the capital Nairobi.

CONGO (ZAÏRE until 1997).

The Democratic Republic of the Congo became independent from Belgium in 1960 and following major upheavals General Joseph-Désiré Mobutu seized power in 1965. In 1971 he renamed the country Zaïre. His regime faced a number of rebellions and was consistently criticised for human rights abuses. Under international pressure, President Mobutu agreed in 1990 to allow the establishment of a multi-party democracy. The obstacles he placed in the way of this provoked widespread opposition. The crisis which erupted throughout Central Africa in 1996—triggered by the 1994 Rwandan civil war—set the scene for President Mobutu's overthrow.

Revolt against Mobutu.

In October 1996, President Mobutu accused Rwanda of backing a Tutsi militia against him in the east of the country and his army moved against the militia with Hutu support. As Rwanda invaded to support the Tutsis, the Alliance of Democratic Forces for the Liberation of Congo-Zaïre (AFDL), led by the long-term anti-Mobutu rebel Laurent Kabila, opened what would prove to be a decisive offensive against President Mobutu's army in the east. President Mobutu returned from convalescence in France in November following surgery to find his army in full retreat. In December the Alliance called for his resignation following the capture of his main base in central Zaïre. President Mobutu left the country once more in January 1997, leaving his army commanders to attempt to save the regime with the assistance of white mercenaries. After rapid rebel advances, Zaïre's second largest city Lubumbashi fell to the rebels in April.

Triumph of Kabila.

President Mobutu fled into exile on 16 May. He died in Morocco in September. On 17 May ADLF troops occupied the capital Kinshasa. The country was renamed and Mr Kabila became President, ruling by decree at the head of a predominantly ADLF administration. Political activity was suspended but a new constitution was promised by December 1998, with elections following in April 1999. President Kabila had declared that he had abandoned Marxism-Leninism and favoured a free market, democracy and human rights. The new government moved rapidly to end the extortion and looting that had marked the previous regime and restored a sense of security to the urban centres. But six months after Mr Kabila's seizure of power he still could not claim total control over the country. His unwillingness to allow a UN investigation of massacres of Tutsi refugees by his Rwandan allies in eastern Congo provoked the US and the European Union into threatening to withhold essential aid. But with the Rwandan troops who had helped him to power still occupying the area, Mr Kabila had little choice. In October 1997 President Kabila appointed a constitutional commission, instructing it to present a draft constitution in May 1998.

Under pressure from foreign aid donors, on 26 November President Kabila—after months of obstruction—gave permission to the UN to investigate alleged massacres of Rwandan Tutsis. As well as seeking sympathetic treatment of the country's £8·3 billion international debt, the Congo sought £300 million in aid to begin economic reconstruction. The new government had, however, proved effective in reducing the inflation rate from several thousand to 8% by November and was beginning crucial infrastructural improvements.

Developments in 1998.

A foretaste of what 1998 would bring came in February when the government reported it had defeated rebel forces near the eastern town of Bunia. But in April serious ethnic and political clashes were continuing and President Kabila visited the region. All party political activity had been banned in May 1997 and there were arrests of opposition figures. In February 1998 Léon Kengo wa Dondo—a prime minister under former President Mobutu's regime—announced the formation of a government in exile in Belgium. President Kabila signed a decree in May establishing a 300-member constituent and legislative assembly to exercise power in the run-up to elections promised for mid-1999. He attempted to ward off complaints of political exclusion from Tutsis by appointing a prominent Tutsi to his cabinet in June.

However, in August a serious rebellion began in the east, close to the border with Rwanda. Military commanders in Goma and Bukavu withdrew support from President Kabila on 2 August and a second rebel front opened in the west of the country two days later. The rising's leader, Arthur Z'Ahdi Ngoma, announced the formation of a Congolese Democratic Rally (RDC) on 4 August. At the heart of the rebellion were the Banyamulenge Tutsis, whose support had placed President Kabila in power. They were joined by thousands of former Mobutu soldiers and a range of ethnic and political dissidents united by their enmity to the new government. There were rapid rebel advances, with the country's third largest town, Kisangani, falling on 26 August.

Failure of Mediation Attempts.

Mediation attempts by the Organisation of African Unity (OAU) and the Southern African Development Community (SADC) met with failure as the war became internationalised. At a meeting in Zimbabwe on 18–19 August, President Kabila was promised the support of Zimbabwe, Angola, Namibia and Kenya. By the end of the month thousands of troops from Angola—whose government accused the rebels of assisting UNITA in the renewed Angolan civil war—were fighting alongside President Kabila's forces. They were joined by a contingent from Zimbabwe. Political and logistical support came from Egypt, Eritrea and Libya. The RDC gained the support of Rwanda and Uganda.

The military situation appeared to have reached stalemate in September as President Kabila's army stemmed RDC advances. But with an increase in aid from Rwanda and Uganda, RDC forces overran more territory in the east and south in October and claimed control over 45% of the Congo. The Congolese bombing of Uganda threatened a dangerous escalation of the war, with fears that the whole of Central Africa would become embroiled. A renewed attempt at mediation led by President Mandela of South Africa collapsed and at a meeting on 21 October, President Kabila's allies promised to launch an anti-rebel offensive. The war was, however, creating pressure in Zimbabwe—where President Mugabe faced mutiny from troops being sent to the Congo—and Angola—where the government faced growing UNITA attacks.

An Unresolved Conflict.

By the end of November, with the rebels holding the majority of key towns and river ports in the east, pressure was mounting on President Kabila to open negotiations. Following his pledge to allow the legalisation of political parties from 1 January, the RDC—militarily successful but politically divided—appeared willing to consider a ceasefire. But a conference of the six countries involved convened by UN Secretary General Kofi Annan came to nothing. As 1999 opened, Congolese aircraft bombed rebel-held Kisangani and the government claimed to have recaptured two towns.

SOUTH AFRICA.

The Background.

The old era of apartheid (see **Section J**) and white supremacy came to an end in the early 1990s. Mandela (see **B40**) was released from prison and work on a new political system began. Against a background of violence and apprehension, the first test came with the 1994 elections.

Despite right-wing bomb outrages, there was a heavy turnout in the elections. The ANC won a sweeping victory with 63% of the vote, the National Party retained a considerable following, and Inkatha (with 10% of the vote) won in its KwaZulu homeland. On 2 May Mr de Klerk conceded defeat. The way was clear for Mr Mandela to be formally inaugurated as president on 10 May. ANC deputy chair Thabo Mbeki became first deputy president, with Mr de Klerk as second deputy president.

The New South Africa.

A multi-racial cabinet was appointed on 11 May. Among the leading appointments were Chief Buthelezi as Home Affairs Minister and Joe Modise (formerly commander of the ANC armed wing) as Defence Minister. Joe Slovo, the Communist Party leader, became Housing Minister, while Derek Keys remained Finance Minister. In a statement welcomed by the white business community, President Mandela promised on 24 May that he would limit government spending, reduce the budget deficit and avoid tax increases. But on 5 July Mr Keys resigned as Finance Minister, although he agreed to remain in office until October.

Problems of the Government.

Of even more concern to the government was evidence of growing frustration and disappointment at slow progress in reform. It faced a wave of industrial unrest and demonstrations for increased wages and to an end to racial discrimination in employment. By the end of July, 48 separate strikes were taking place and the union federation COSATU warned the government to balance its concern with the interest of employers with those of its supporters. Police fired rubber bullets at demonstrators protesting in Johannesburg against a 500% increase in water and electricity prices. Clashes continued between ANC and Inkatha supporters but, despite almost 50 deaths in the last week of August in KwaZulu, the state of emergency imposed in March was lifted. Inkatha itself was riven by a power struggle between Chief Buthelezi and King Goodwill Zwelithini, forcing Chief Buthelezi to concede on 25 September that an independant Zulu kingdom was unlikely.

President Mandela's government's introduction of the Land Rights Act on 11 November represented the first legislation aimed at reversing the effects of apartheid since the election. The Act – which created a land claims court and an arbitration commission – was intended to redress the grievances of people dispossessed by white land confiscation.

The popular housing minister, Joe Slovo, died in the New Year and was given a full state funeral on 15 January 1995.

The 'Fresh Start' Initiative.

In January 1995 there were fears that the National Party (NP) would withdraw from the government following bitter disputes with the ANC over an indemnity from prosecution granted to police and former government members in 1994.

President Mandela and Mr de Klerk announced on 20 January that they were determined on a "fresh start". But in February the Inkatha Freedom Party announced a boycott of both chambers of parliament on the grounds that both the ANC and the NP had reneged on an agreement for international mediation on Inkatha's demand for the establishment of a federal state. The boycott ended on 5 March.

There were problems, too, within the ANC. The party instituted a code of conduct on 15 February in an attempt to meet criticisms of corruption amongst its members. There were continuing allegations against Mrs Mandela and she was dismissed from her junior ministerial post on 27 March. The government was also faced by a two week campaign of industrial action by the country's three main trade union federations from 6 June. The unions opposed government moves towards privatisation and were concerned at elements of proposed labour relations legislation.

The fragile coalition government was further threatened when murder charges were laid against the former defence minister, General Magnus Malan, and also ten other retired senior military officers for their alleged complicity in a massacre

that had taken place in 1987. The case went to the heart of the so-called "Third Force" conspiracy involving elements of the security forces and white politicians under the apartheid regime. Mr de Klerk criticised the arrests.

Local Elections.

There was more satisfying news for the ANC, however, in local elections held on 1 November. There had been a belief that black support for the ANC might collapse because of the government's slowness in delivering its promises. Instead it was the white vote that fragmented. The ANC easily matched its 1994 general election performance, taking two thirds of the popular vote. Many white voters shifted from the National Party to independents or the separatist Freedom Front. Voting was unable to take place in KwaZulu, where many people had died in political violence since January, or in Cape Town.

The first draft of the new constitution was published on 22 November 1995. But communal violence continued with the killing of 19 ANC supporters by Inkatha members in Shobashobane on 25 December. Fears of an escalation prompted meetings between President Mandela, Zulu King Goodwill Zwelithni and Inkatha leader Chief Buthelezi in January 1996.

Trial of Malan.

On 11 March, the trial opened of former defence minister General Magnus Malan and 15 co-defendants on murder and conspiracy charges connected with the killing of ANC supporters in 1987. They were acquitted on 20 October, the court ruling that they had planned a military operation against anti-apartheid activists and had not intended the use of murder squads. The Truth and Reconciliation Commission, chaired by Archbishop Tutu, represented a further attempt to come to terms with South Africa's recent past. However, the Commission's attempt to encourage reconciliation aroused controversy. Some families, including that of murdered black consciousness leader Steve Biko, took court action in May 1996 to prevent the Commission granting an amnesty to those who had killed their relatives.

The New Constitution Debate.

The Constituent Assembly formally approved the new constitution on 7 May, with only the small African Christian Democratic Party voting against. The white right-wing Freedom Front abstained, while Inkatha Freedom Party members refused to attend. The National Party (NP) had only agreed to accept the proposed constitution following President Mandela's threat of a referendum. On 9 May Mr de Klerk announced that the NP would withdraw from the government of national unity at the end of June on the grounds that a genuine multi-party democracy demanded a strong opposition party. Meanwhile, on 12 May Cyril Ramaphosa—the main rival to Thabo Mbeki to succeed President Mandela—resigned as ANC secretary-general.

The Constitutional Court rejected the proposed constitution on 6 September, criticising inadequate devolution to provincial governments and an overemphasis on the workers' rights as opposed to those of employers. The Constituent Assembly was given 90 days to rectify these and what the Court identified as other faults. President Mandela welcomed the rejection as an opportunity to clarify the constitution, as did the National Party leadership.

Charges of corruption within the governing ANC threatened party unity. Major-General Bantu Holomisa—a popular junior minister—declared he intended to form a new party following his dismissal and expulsion from the ANC for alleging that the ANC and a cabinet minister had accepted payments from a casino owner. Among Major-General Holomisa's allies were President Mandela's former wife, Winnie. The ANC's problems were compounded by criticisms of President Mandela's growing autocracy and dislike of his designated successor Thabo Mbeki.

President Mandela signed South Africa's Constitution, the product of six years of negotiations, in Sharpeville (scene of a massacre of anti-apartheid demonstrators in 1960) on 10 December. National Party leader F. W. de Klerk was absent.

The Truth and Reconciliation Commission.

The Truth and Reconciliation Commission announced in January 1997 that five former security officers had sought amnesty for their killing in 1977 of black activist Steve Biko. In 1996 Biko's family had been among those demanding that the Commission should be stripped of its powers to grant amnesties. The request for amnesty of former law and order minister Adriaan Vlok in February represented the first admission by an apartheid era minister that he had been responsible for political crimes. As the deadline for applications approached in May, the ANC instructed all national executive committee members since 1961—apart from President Mandela himself—to approach the Commission. However, former state presidents Botha and de Klerk, together with Inkatha leader Chief Mangosuthu Buthelezi, declined the opportunity.

Riots in Johannesburg.

February 1997 saw the most serious rioting in the country since the 1994 elections. Coloured residents of townships in Johannesburg protesting at what they saw as more favourable treatment for the black population over employment policies and the writing off of rent arrears, clashed with police and four demonstrators were killed and 200 injured. At the opening of Parliament on 7 February, President Mandela announced that combating the escalating crime wave would be a priority. He promised also to act against corruption in the civil service and to speed the country's privatisation programme. In presenting the 1997–98 budget on 12 March, the finance minister declared that his austerity measures were intended to achieve greater social justice while maintaining fiscal responsibility. The Confederation of South African Trade Unions (COSATU) criticised him for failing to use the budget as a springboard for sweeping development.

There were, meanwhile, further developments in white politics. On 17 May Roelf Meyer, the moderate National Party (NP) representative in the 1992–94 constitutional talks, left the NP to form a party which, he said, would challenge both the ANC and the NP at the 1999 elections. In September he announced, with former ANC minister Bantu Holomisa, the establishment of the United Democratic Movement (UDM). On 26 August Mr de Klerk announced his retirement from the NP leadership. He was succeeded in September by the relatively unknown Marthinus van Schalkwyk.

Developments in 1997.

Riots in a township outside Johannesburg in September over the local authority's attempt to enforce taxation demonstrated continuing tensions. The ANC's shift to the right left a vacuum which there were suggestions Mrs Mandela—still popular with the grass roots—could fill. In April she had been overwhelmingly re-elected president of the ANC Women's League, despite strenuous ANC leadership support for her opponent. In November she began a campaign for the party's deputy presidency, attacking the ANC leadership for its failure to deliver its promises to the black majority and for its record on crime. But on 24 November, Mrs Mandela began a nine-day appearance before the Truth and Reconciliation Commission, where her position was weakened by further allegations of her involvement in seven murders.

The ANC conference which opened on 18 December was the last at which Mr Mandela appeared as party president. He was succeeded by Thabo Mbeki. The conference was remarkable for Mr Mandela's opening address in which he attacked whites who, he claimed, were refusing to recognise the reality of majority rule, and fellow ANC members, whom he accused of corruption and careerism.

President Mandela opened a new session of parliament on 6 February 1998 with a defence of affirmative action in redressing racial imbalances in employment, despite criticisms from the liberal Democratic Party. He also announced plans to reduce the one-million strong civil service. He ordered an official inquiry on 27 March into allegations that dissident left-wing ANC members, including his former wife, had conspired to over-

throw him. Although dismissing the charges, he feared they were an attempt to destabilise his government.

A Changing Political Scene.

The National Party—which had governed the country during the apartheid era from 1948–94—appeared on the point of extinction as it was trounced in municipal by-elections by the liberal Democratic Party in May. White voters appeared to be abandoning the National Party because of its links with apartheid and the effectiveness of Democratic Party attacks on ANC authoritarianism and government corruption.

It was the ANC itself which faced problems at the end of June. After several years of economic austerity and high interest rates aimed at curbing inflation and reducing the budget deficit, the rand remained weak. Against the background of the Asian financial crisis, the currency tumbled further, forcing a further rise in interest rates. This threatened the alliance with the Confederation of South African Trade Unions which had already blamed rising unemployment—and the consequent social problems, including a growth in crime—on the government's policies.

Military Intervention in Lesotho.

There were further problems for the government following military intervention in Lesotho in September. Following charges that elections in May in neighbouring Lesotho had been rigged, there were violent demonstrations in August and September and reports of an attempted military coup. After a request for support from Lesotho's prime minister, South African Home Affairs Minister Mangosuthu Buthelezi, in the absence abroad of President Mandela and his deputy, despatched 600 troops to the capital, Maseru. They faced an unexpected level of resistance from the army and civilians angry at invasion by a foreign state. In two days of fighting, nine South African soldiers, 58 members of the Lesotho army and 47 civilians died. Maseru remained in chaos and the events—combined with President Mandela's failure to secure mediation in the Congo civil war—raised questions about South Africa's foreign policy competence.

Truth and Reconciliation Commission Report.

The Truth and Reconciliation Commission published its report on 29 October after sitting for over two years, hearing 21,000 witnesses and considering 7,000 amnesty requests. The Commission's chair, the Rev. Desmond Tutu, claimed the body had acted as an effective force for reconciliation but in opinion polls over 80% thought it had intensified racial antagonism. The report condemned apartheid as a crime against humanity and criticised the National Party. The Commission also criticised Chief Buthelezi's Inkhata Freedom Party and the part played by business, the judiciary, the churches and the media. The ANC and its armed wing were accused—although it was acknowledged they had been involved in a 'legitimate struggle'—of human rights violations.

The End of an Era.

President Mandela called in his last state of the nation speech on 5 February for national unity in the elections planned for 2 June 1999. These elections, and the end of Mandela's term as President, would mark the end of an era for South Africa.

ZIMBABWE.

In elections to the 150 seat parliament held on 8/9 April 1995, Mr Mugabe's ruling Zanu-PF emerged with 118 seats against two for the opposition, due largely to an apathetic 50% turnout and a lack of opposition candidates. Zanu-PF was unopposed in 55 seats. A further 20 seats were filled by presidential appointees and ten allocated to traditional chiefs.

President Mugabe announced his new cabinet on 20 April, making new appointments to the Industry and Commerce Ministry and to Finance. Presenting his budget on 27 July, Finance Minister Ariston Chambati warned that economic growth was expected to fall from 5·2% in 1994 to a maximum of 2% in 1995, principally as a result of the effect of drought on agriculture and manufacturing. There was more disappointing economic news on 14 September when the International Monetary Fund delayed a loan for balance of payments support for six months because the government had failed to curb public expenditure sufficiently.

The Arrest of Sithole.

Three men, reportedly members of an armed dissident group known as Chimwenje, were arrested on 8 October accused of plotting to assassinate President Mugabe. The Rev. Ndabaningi Sithole, leader of the right-wing opposition ZANU-Ngonga was accused of complicity in the plot and was arrested five days later. Mr Sithole's supporters claimed this was an attempt to discredit his candidacy in the 1996 presidential elections. It was also apparently intended to distract attention from 50% unemployment, falling wages, deteriorating public services and widespread corruption. For criticising the latter, Margaret Dongo had been expelled from ZANU-PF in 1994. How far her views seemed to be supported was confirmed when, in November 1995, she won a surprise by-election victory in the capital Harare against the ZANU-PF candidate. With Presidential elections due to be held on 17–18 March 1996, Mrs Dongo urged opposition candidates Bishop Abel Muzorewa and Mr Sithole to withdraw, so denying President Mugabe electoral credibility. Mr Sithole stood down a week before polling, alleging persistent harassment by the state security force. Bishop Muzorewa followed suit the day before the elections after failing to secure a postponement on the grounds that the electoral laws were unfair. Mr Mugabe went on to secure a hollow victory in an election marked by a thin turn-out.

Following his election victory, President Mugabe reiterated his determination to continue the government's land redistribution policy. He warned Britain in June 1996 that unless aid was increased the government would confiscate white owned land without compensation.

Trade Union Militancy.

In August the government was confronted by a national strike among public sector workers claiming wage increases. Public Service and Labour Minister Florence Chitauro declared the action illegal and threatened mass arrests. On 23 August the strikers were dismissed and recruitment began to replace them. The Zimbabwe Congress of Trade Unions threatened an all-out general strike on 28 August. The government backed down and announced that 60% wage increases would be phased in over three years. Strikes continued on the issue of reinstatement of dismissed workers and on 21 October 12,000 nurses and doctors struck on the grounds that promised wage increases had not been paid. Once more, the government threatened dismissals.

A peaceful demonstration mounted by the strikers in Harare was broken up with tear gas and two leaders of the Zimbabwe Congress of Trade Unions were arrested. The strikers, despite deaths among children and the elderly, nonetheless appeared to have considerable public support. President Mugabe himself came under criticism in November. Against the background of a stagnant economy, 50% unemployment and growing urban poverty, he had spent much time touring Africa and Europe. An independent newspaper denounced what it called the "arrogance" of a "virtual one-party dictatorship."

In November the government attempted to meet criticisms of its slowness in providing settlement for the landless by announcing that it would not renew leases on state-owned farms held by whites when they expired.

Rise of Popular Discontent.

President Mugabe—who had made virulent attacks on homosexuality—faced embarrassment in February 1997 when his close political ally, Canaan Banana (president from 1980–87), faced serious sexual charges. Further charges of sexual harassment followed in May. Throughout the summer, as popular discontent rose, Zimbabwe was faced by a wave of strikes from civil servants, construction workers, bank staff and nurses. In October large

numbers of the country's 350,000 labourers on predominantly white-owned farms struck for higher wages. Although there was no violence, strikers rejected calls by the Agricultural and Plantation Workers' Union for a return to work to enable negotiations to begin. It was the issue of white ownership, and the position of landless black workers, to which President Mugabe turned in an attempt to bolster his position.

Land Confiscation, October 1997.

On the eve of the Commonwealth Conference in October, President Mugabe announced his intention to confiscate 12·3 million acres of white-owned land. As Britain had originally stolen the land from Africans, he declared, then compensation was Britain's responsibility. Since independence in 1980, 60,000 people had been resettled on previously white-owned land. There were allegations, however, that ruling ZANU-PF politicians were among the beneficiaries of land redistribution. The 4,500 largest farms in Zimbabwe accounted for 14% of the country's gross domestic product and 40% of total exports. In November, the British government refused to fund resettlement of land that was not voluntarily relinquished. But in December agriculture minister Kumbirai Kangai said that the first 1,500 farmers would be expected to vacate the land by August 1998.

Tax Increases and Strikes.

There was, however, growing popular dissatisfaction with President Mugabe, with the Zimbabwe Confederation of Trade Unions (ZCTU) leading the opposition of the urban poor. In mid-December ZCTU led a two-day general strike ostensibly against tax increases but in reality in protest against unemployment and general economic despair. The taxes had been levied to buy off threats to the government from discontented former liberation fighters. The bulk of the increases were withdrawn but the ZCTU secretary general, Morgan Tswangirai, was attacked in his office two days later. ZCTU announced it would open a campaign for constitutional reform. On 18 December, veteran opposition leader the Rev. Ndabaningi Sithole was imprisoned for two years.

Rioting in Harare.

There was serious rioting in the capital Harare in January 1998 following a 20% increase in the price of maize meal, the staple food. As protests spread through the country—and were as much directed at President Mugabe as the increase itself—the rise was withdrawn. In February students demonstrating for higher grants were attacked by police and from 3–4 March the Zimbabwe Congress of Trade Unions (ZCTU) brought the country to a standstill with a successful general strike, despite a government warning that the action was illegal. An increasingly unpopular President Mugabe accused dissidents in the ruling ZANU-PF of plotting his overthrow in March. A student was killed in clashes in Harare in April and as protests continued into May, students called for Mugabe's resignation and—referring to the overthrow of President Suharto—threatened 'another Indonesia'. A new opposition party formed in June—the General Confederation of Patriots—threatened to lead protests of the unemployed and students to oust the president.

Growing Unpopularity of Mugabe.

The threatened takeover of white-owned farms remained a useful political symbol for an increasingly unpopular President Mugabe. In January 1998 the government had agreed to postpone seizure of over 1,500 farms in return for promises of World Bank and European Union loans. A government announcement on 6 March suggested no productive land would be seized and that full compensation would be paid. But in June squatters occupied rich farming lands east of Harare and defied government appeals for them to withdraw.

In July the government outlined plans to resettle 100,000 families over the next five years on land purchased from white farmers and at the end of August President Mugabe handed plots to 40 families. However, the government modified its proposals following international aid donors' criticisms in September that they were over-ambitious. But in November President Mugabe ordered the immediate seizure of 840 farms. The International Monetary Fund (IMF) responded by withholding £32 million aid intended to bolster a collapsing currency. The aid was released in January 1999 as Zimbabwe once again agreed to reduce the pace of land reform.

Zimbabwe's Vietnam?

President Mugabe also faced growing concern at the country's involvement in the Congo civil war, which was costing the country a million dollars a day and in which hundreds of Zimbabwean troops had allegedly been killed. There were reports of desertions among troops being sent to fight and independent MP Margaret Dongo—who was joined in her criticisms of involvement by the ZCTU—called the war 'Zimbabwe's Vietnam'. President Mugabe—shortly before leaving for a five-country overseas tour—banned strikes following a week of stoppages led by the ZCTU in protests against further price increases.

Human Rights Abuses.

The ZCTU—led by Morgan Tsvangirai—was emerging as the leading opposition force but it was the army that appeared to pose the most immediate threat to President Mugabe. On 16 December 23 officers—motivated by discontent with his management of the economy and the war in the Congo—were arrested for allegedly plotting his overthrow. No move was made against a cabinet minister and an MP also said to be involved. But in January 1999 two journalists who were arrested for reporting the attempt were tortured while in custody. There were widespread protests at what was seen as further evidence of the decline in human rights under President Mugabe and trade union leaders called for international aid to be withheld. On 26 January a protest outside parliament by lawyers was broken up by riot police. Fears grew as Mr Mugabe rejected criticisms over the breakdown in civil rights that the country was moving closer to becoming a police state.

ZAMBIA.

In November 1991 Zambia held its first multi-party elections for 23 years. President Kaunda's United National Independence Party (UNIP) had ruled Zambia (formerly Northern Rhodesia) since independence in 1964. Following elections in 1968 President Kaunda intensified a programme of nationalisation and moved towards a one-party state, which was imposed in 1972. But the nationalisation of copper mining, and the attempt to provide extensive social services, proved expensive. Zambia had been among Africa's richest countries in 1964 but by the 1980s living standards had fallen dramatically as copper reserves declined and agriculture failed. UNIP's rule became more oppressive.

Formation of the MMP.

Against this background of economic failure, President Kaunda was forced in July to recognise the formation of an opposition Movement for Multi-Party Democracy (MMP). The MMP leader, Frederick Chiluba, had been chairman of the 300,000 strong Zambia Congress of Trade Unions since 1974 and was a longstanding opponent of one-party rule. The MMP, which advocated a market economy, an end to agricultural subsidies, and the encouragement of foreign investment through the privatisation of mining, had broad support among unions, business, and students.

The combined presidential and National Assembly elections saw an overwhelming defeat for the UNIP. The MMD won 135 assembly seats and UNIP the remaining 15. In the presidential election Mr. Chiluba took 62% of the vote. President Chiluba called for respect to be shown to Dr. Kaunda, whom he called "the father of the nation". Mr. Levy Mwanawasa was appointed vice-president and Zambia began a programme of economic reform.

Despite an apparently smooth transition to parliamentary democracy with elections in November 1991 President Chiluba declared a state of emergency on 4 March 1993. Ten people were detained, including the son of former President Kaunda. The foreign minister, Vernon Mwaanga, accused the opposition UNIP of receiving funds from Iran and Iraq to seize power.

The Cabinet Restructuring.

On 11 February 1994 President Chiluba was forced to restructure his cabinet following allegations that two ministers were involved in corruption and drug trafficking. The Zambia Congress of Trade Unions (ZCTU), President Chiluba's former power base, had called on him to carry out a drastic purge of the cabinet. ZCTU remained unsatisfied, accusing seven of the remaining ministers of involvement in the scandal. Western aid donors forced the resignation of the foreign minister, community affairs minister and deputy speaker of parliament. In July President Chiluba dismissed his legal affairs minister and in the same month vice-president Levy Mwanawasa resigned, accusing the government of condoning greed. He was replaced by Brigadier-General Godfrey Miyanda.

Growing Political Tensions.

As allegations of corruption in government circles mounted, Lands Minister Chuulou Kalima was dismissed on 25 January 1995 for "gross indiscipline and irresponsibility." President Chiluba ordered all ministers and members of parliament to declare their assets and liabilities within 48 hours on 9 February. The governor of the Bank of Zambia was replaced a fortnight later.

Former President Kaunda's return to politics led to his arrest on 20 February for holding an illegal meeting. There were also growing tensions within the ruling Movement for Multiparty Democracy (MMD). Two MMD MPs were expelled on 24 June for allegedly bringing the party into disrepute. On 2 July, party vice-president Levy Mwanawasa said the MMD had lost direction and announced he would stand against President Chiluba at the next party convention. President Chiluba attempted to strengthen his position by reshuffling his cabinet on 17 July. However, one of the expelled MPs, Dean Mung'omba, announced the formation of the Zambia Democratic Congress (ZDC) on 30 July, claiming to have won the support of many disaffected MMD members.

Mr Kaunda was elected president of the United National Independence Party (UNIP) on 28 June, taking the post from the incumbent by an almost five to one margin. Mr Kaunda was threatened with arrest by the Home Affairs minister on 10 July for allegedly inciting civil disobedience in his campaign for early elections. UNIP parliamentary leader Dingiswago Banda defected to the ruling MMD on 11 August, having initially refused to step down from his post in favour of a Kaunda nominee.

As antagonism between the government and Mr Kaunda intensified, the Home Affairs minister announced on 16 October that Mr Kaunda could face deportation for having failed to register as a Zambian citizen on independence in 1964 and for retaining citizenship of Malawi (his birthplace) until 1970. Mr Kaunda had, the minister said, ruled Zambia illegally during this period. The threat of deportation was withdrawn three days later, but the draft of a new constitution now included a clause making it mandatory for presidential candidates to be Zambian by birth.

Constitutional Amendments.

President Chiluba signed a controversial constitutional amendment on 28 May clearly aimed at former President Kaunda, leader of the opposition United National Independence Party (UNIP). The amendment stipulated that all presidential candidates must be second generation Zambians, a device to prevent Mr Kaunda—whose parents were Malawian immigrants—from standing in future elections. Western aid donors responded by suspending further assistance. On 3 June six leading UNIP members, including the party's vice-president, were arrested and accused of membership of "Black Maria", a group allegedly responsible for terrorist bombings. The six were acquitted in November.

Closure of Lusaka University.

President Chiluba's actions provoked violent demonstrations by students demanding postponement of the elections and negotiations with the opposition. On 11 November 1996 the government ordered the closure of Lusaka University. The student's demands were supported on 14 November by President Mandela of South Africa. However, the elections went ahead on 18 November and were boycotted by UNIP and the majority of opposition parties. President Chiluba was overwhelmingly elected. Following his swearing in three opposition leaders went into hiding after hearing police were preparing treason charges against them. Police also raided the offices of observer groups, which had criticised the conduct of the elections.

Events in 1997.

On 1 February 1997, finance minister Ronald Penza presented a budget intended to encourage a reduction in dependence on foreign aid and to ensure rapid moves towards the privatisation of the country's copper mining industry, a policy insisted on by aid donors. However, on 15 June the International Monetary Fund warned the government that failure to achieve a budget surplus would prevent the provision of further assistance.

Former President Kenneth Kaunda was slightly wounded when police fired on an opposition rally in Kapwe on 23 August. President Chiluba denied Mr Kaunda's allegation that it was an assassination attempt.

One officer was killed in an coup attempt by what the government originally described as drunken army officers on 28 October. The rebels, who seized the national broadcasting station, were rapidly quelled. In spite of Chiluba's growing unpopularity, the attempt aroused no civilian or military support. Five weeks later the attempt appeared to have been more serious when President Chiluba demoted his vice president and defence minister, retired the air force commander and moved the army commander into the foreign service.

The Arrest of Kaunda.

Former President Kaunda's United National Independence Party (UNIP) accused President Chiluba of staging the coup to justify attacks on the opposition. There were reports, too, that the opportunity was being taken to purge potential opponents in President Chiluba's own Movement for Multiparty Democracy (MMD). On 25 December, five days after returning to the country from South Africa, Mr Kaunda was arrested for alleged complicity in the October coup attempt. An estimated 90 opposition politicians and army officers were also placed in custody. Mr Kaunda, who denied any involvement, and immediately began a hunger strike, was released from custody on 31 December but placed under house arrest.

On 10 January 1998, former President Kenneth Kaunda was charged with actively supporting the October 1997 coup attempt but this was reduced in February to knowing of the plot but failing to report it. On 17 March, President Chiluba—hoping to appease Western aid donors—lifted the state of emergency imposed following the attempted overthrow. Over 90 people had been arrested for alleged complicity. The World Bank emphasised when it announced the provision of $350 million aid in May that this was linked to an improvement in human rights as well as economic reform, including privatisation of copper mining.

Developments in 1998.

A growing disappointment with President Chiluba was demonstrated on 9 April when a breakaway from the ruling Zambia Democratic Congress (ZDC) formed a new party—the Zambia Democratic Congress-Popular Front (ZDC-PF)—and accused the ZDC leadership of having lost its democratic credentials. Former President Kaunda was released from house arrest on 1 June following the withdrawal of all charges against him as part of an agreement brokered by President Mandela. In return, Mr Kaunda announced his retirement from active politics and in July stood down as leader of the United National Independence Party (UNIP), a post he had held since 1960. The resignation of his deputy

on 19 October intensified the leadership crisis in UNIP.

Former finance minister Ronald Penza was murdered in his home on 6 November. Mr Penza—who had been dismissed from his post in March following disagreements with President Chiluba—had been a potential opposition candidate at presidential elections due in 2000. Five members of the six-strong gang responsible for the murder were killed in a gun battle with police.

THE UNITED STATES

The 1992 Election.

The election in November 1992 of Governor William J. (Bill) Clinton of Arkansas as the 42nd President of the United States was unsurprising given the prominent lead that the Democrats had in the opinion polls throughout the campaign. However the manner of his election was unusual in that the general election of 1992 (in which the whole of the House of Representatives and one-third of the Senate was also up for election) was dominated by the participation of an independent candidate, Ross Perot of Texas. Clinton handsomely beat the incumbent Republican President George Bush by 370 votes to 168 in the electoral college, but his share of the popular vote (43%) was actually *less* than that achieved by the losing Democratic challenger in 1988, Michael Dukakis. The difference between the election of 1992 and the previous contest was the dramatic fall in the national Republican vote; George Bush's share fell an unprecedented 16%, the worst performance by an incumbent president since the Great Depression. Ross Perot claimed the vote of very nearly one American in five—the best result for a third party candidate since 1912; had he not been in the race the final result would have been much closer. Nonetheless Clinton's success should not be underestimated—even in circumstances in which the total vote was divided among three candidates, he nearly succeeded in achieving the average Democratic share of the past 20 years.

A Disappointing Start.

As he completed his first year in office in January 1994, the only thing about Bill Clinton's presidency which the majority of his fellow Americans could agree upon was that he had failed to fulfil the mandate for "change" for which he had campaigned so effectively before the presidential election fourteen months earlier. If most voters have remained ambivalent and confused about President Clinton's intentions, allegiances and political competence, so has official Washington; his first year in office was marked both by signal legislative triumphs and by a series of mistakes which, if none amounted to a full-blown crisis, at least together suggested an Administration prone to lurching from one avoidable issue to another. The president seemed fated to be unable to maintain public confidence in his direction for more than a few weeks at a time and as a result was subject to violent swings in the public estimation of his ability.

The Legislative Record.

These misfortunes stood in stark contrast to President Clinton's actual record of achievement, particularly in his relationship with Congress, which public opinion somehow contrived to overlook or at least discount. With Congress Clinton managed a better first year record even than the popular Eisenhower, being supported by the legislature in nine out of ten votes; neither was he obliged to resort to the power of presidential veto to block legislation with which he disagreed, in stark contrast to his predecessor who used the veto 21 times during his last year in office. Clinton proved particularly adept at persuading Congress to enact his legislative agenda—during his first year he was able to pass bills which had been languishing for years (such as the Brady bill on gun-control), though a number of these were partisan measures which had been blocked by President Bush and which were simply awaiting the election of a Democratic president.

Clinton's most important achievements were to

secure the passage of his budget in August and then three months later to win congressional ratification of the North American Free Trade Agreement (NAFTA) with Canada and Mexico. Failure to win either could have undermined his presidency in its first year. The budget was the closer of the two, passing the Senate only on the casting vote of Vice President Al Gore. Although at the time this was seen as indicative of Clinton's difficulties in maintaining support for his programme within his own party, in retrospect the tortured passage of the budget was part of a wider institutional and sectorial conflict in American politics. Seeking the largest reduction in the federal budget deficit in history—$500 billion over five years—the president was dependent upon legislators of both parties who wished to hold out for a deeper cut and yet who refused to accept the abolition of specific programmes or services which benefited their own constituents. This problem was not unique to the Clinton presidency and undoubtedly it will resurface in the future, but the consequences were likely to be diminished in the medium term by the robust growth (c. 3%) which the United States enjoyed during 1993 as the economy finally moved out of the longest recession since the war. The spectre of unemployment which so damaged President Bush during the 1992 election and upon which Clinton campaigned so effectively seemed to be diminishing.

The Ratification of NAFTA.

Securing the ratification of NAFTA was arguably the more important congressional victory. In origin this was a Republican measure and in supporting it the president was obliged to build a coalition with the minority Republicans and to disappoint both the bulk of his own party in Congress, which remained ambivalent about free trade, and particularly the trades unions (a bold move given that these supply most of the party's campaign funds). In the end Clinton's margin of victory in the November vote was more comfortable than for the budget, despite the fact that he had come to support NAFTA rather late in the day. The political consequences of this episode were particularly important because it marked a signal victory over the anti-free trade platform of the maverick 1992 presidential candidate Ross Perot, who had led the opposition to NAFTA but whose star was seen to wane during the year. However success was achieved partly at the expense of the most vigorous round of political horse-trading seen in Washington for years, as the president struck individual deals with numerous members of Congress.

Problems of Political Management.

Unfortunately for Clinton the benefits of such achievements were undermined by his political management of the Administration, which during the first year seemed unfocused or on occasion inept. Charges of a failure of presidential leadership were given weight by the successes of the Republican party, which won six of the year's most important state and mayoral elections (including New York City); however it could fairly be maintained that this was simply a continuation of the anti-incumbent feeling which had brought Clinton himself to the White House and was likely to hurt the Democrats more because they held the majority of federal and state offices. More importantly the transition from the Bush Administration was accomplished with agonising slowness, such that by the end of the first year only half of the one thousand presidential appointments requiring Senate confirmation had actually been made. This problem was compounded by the nature and fate of individual candidates for office. Critics claimed that initial cabinet appointments were an attempt to placate as many interests as possible, in pursuit of a campaign pledge to name a cabinet which reflected America's ethnic and social diversity. Many nominations were bungled—most seriously Clinton required three attempts to appoint an Attorney-General—perhaps reflecting a new Administration's lack of understanding both of Washington politics and of its candidates' credentials. However a concerted attempt to counter the impression of inexperienced management was made in the early summer with the appointment as White House director of

communications of the veteran David Gergen, who had served under President Reagan; the extent to which Clinton has subsequently appeared more "presidential" indicates that this has been at least partly successful.

Foreign Policy Failures.

The sphere in which Clinton's weaknesses were most apparent was foreign policy. The record was not distinguished. Even before his election Clinton was calling for bolder action by the United States on a host of international issues—Bosnia, Somalia, Russia, or nuclear weapons proliferation—but in office he proved singularly unable either to carry his foreign allies with him on most occasions or to provide a concrete statement of what US policy should be in a post-Cold War world. The new concept of the "enlargement" of democratic market relations and institutions remained quite vague. Clinton's Secretary of State Warren Christopher, who served under President Carter, proved pragmatic but often discreet to the point of invisibility; and opposition from established interests at home or abroad frequently resulted in the Administration quickly backing down. This was most clearly visible during the first year in Clinton's relationship with the US military. The first weeks of his presidency were occupied by an avoidable confrontation over the issue of privacy of homosexuals serving in the armed forces and the year ended with the enforced resignation of the Secretary of Defense Les Aspin, who never in fact fully established his own team at the Pentagon. The primary responsibility for this must lie with the president, who persistently gave the impression that he considered foreign policy to be largely an intrusion onto his domestic agenda.

The Failure of Health Care Reform.

The problems of political management which had bedevilled the Administration since its inception were made obvious during the course of 1994 by the fate of health care reform. This had been only a minor theme in Clinton's campaign in 1992, but once elected he seized on the issue as one which could show him off as a "New Democrat". Action was needed to control the spiralling costs of Medicare, the government-subsidised programme of health care for the elderly.

In September 1993 the president proposed to Congress a bill to achieve universal national health insurance coverage within five years, by requiring compulsory employer-funded insurance for the working population. The Clinton plan rejected the so-called "single payer" model operated by Canada (in which the government would arrange insurance directly), in favour of encouraging "managed competition" through so-called Health Maintenance Organisations. However the plan quickly attracted considerable political opposition; this was partly motivated by the fact that the plan had been produced by a White House task force chaired by Mrs Hillary Clinton, who was seen by cultural conservatives as a symbol of the very interventionist, 1960s-style liberalism which President Clinton claimed to have rejected. More importantly, the plan had been devised independently of the Democratic leadership in Congress and with little attempt to seek the bipartisan support of the Republican opposition. In retrospect this was seen to be a serious oversight.

President Clinton received a significant boost in the opinion polls when he unveiled his plan—declaring dramatically that he would veto any final version which did not provide universal coverage—and the Senate minority leader Robert Dole was moved to agree that there was a "crisis" in the American health system. However, as the bill passed through numerous congressional committees it emerged that there was little support for many of its features. In particular voters disliked the fact that employers and employees were obliged to purchase health care cover from only a limited number of providers, or that the plan restricted one's choice of doctor. The already insured middle class criticised the plan as too bureaucratic. The Democratic and Republican leaderships in Congress both proposed their own versions, promising more limited coverage by a later date; but even these could not gain sufficient support, and the House and the Senate recessed in the summer of 1994 without having taken any final vote on the reform bill. In September the retiring Democratic Senate majority leader George Mitchell was obliged to tell the president that the issue was effectively dead.

The Mid-Term Elections.

The loss of health care reform was perhaps made inevitable by the imminence of the mid-term congressional elections in November, when all of the House and one-third of the Senate would be re-elected. The Republican landslide—having agreed that health care was in crisis when that interpretation was popular—quickly recognised that the majority of Americans would not yet welcome fundamental change particularly if it raised taxes or led to job losses by increasing employers' costs. Clinton's reform proposals allowed Republicans to depict him as a traditional "big government" Democrat, one out of touch with the concerns of ordinary Americans. The election campaign of 1994 was remarkable for the vicious personal attacks on the President; great efforts were made by the Republicans nationally to associate moderate or liberal congressional Democrats with the Clinton style and philosophy. In part this strategy was an attempt to build upon increasing public dissatisfaction with 'politics as usual' and in particular with the image of the federal government and of Congress itself. Indeed the campaign was marked in several states by popular movements to amend the state constitutions by referendums limiting the number of terms which an individual might serve in Congress.

The Republican Landslide.

The outcome of the elections themselves on 9 November was truly extraordinary. The Republican strategy succeeded beyond all expectation, as congressional Democrats suffered devastating losses across the country. Many liberal and moderate grandees of the party were swept from office, such as the Speaker of the House of Representatives Thomas Foley (the first incumbent Speaker to fall since 1860), or Governors Mario Cuomo of New York and Ann Richards of Texas in state races. The Democrats lost 53 seats in the House and the Republicans none, which gave the latter control of the House for the first time since 1954 and thus of the whole Congress. Much of the credit for the victory was owed to the vigorous national campaign waged by the Republican whip in the House, Newt Gingrich, who was to become Speaker of the House when Congress reconvened in January 1995.

The Contract with America.

Gingrich was able to unite Republican candidates behind a ten-point manifesto which he dubbed a "Contract with America", many of whose provisions such as welfare reform, increased defence spending and tax cuts for the middle class harked back to the Reagan era. These proved extremely popular among voters, especially in the more conservative South which in this election now completed its transition from being the bedrock of the Democratic Party to being an almost exclusively Republican region.

The Republican seizure of Congress opened up the prospect of two very difficult years for President Clinton ahead of the presidential election in November 1996. He recognised the extent of the damage in his State of the Union address in January 1995 when he explicitly tried to align himself with middle class concerns, promising action on welfare and crime and seeking limited tax cuts. However the President's fortunes were greatly enhanced by the difficulties which the Republicans had in implementing their agenda. The new majority in Congress was divided between the radical New Right in the House under Speaker Gingrich and the more moderate Republicans in the Senate led by Majority Leader Bob Dole. The election of 1994 had returned a large "freshman" class of representatives (numbering 73) who represented conservative suburban communities in the South and West of the United States and who owed little allegiance to the traditional Republican party leadership.

Seeing themselves as having been sent to Washington to cut the federal government down to size, they largely refused to compromise on the principles of the Contract and the House leadership achieved its goal of passing within the first 100 days of the new Congress measures designed to end "politics as usual". These included making the Congress itself subject to any relevant laws it might pass (such as health and safety in the workplace); ending so-called "unfunded mandates", by which Congress might oblige the states to implement a federal law but not compensate them financially for doing so; and reducing the number of federal regulations, which were seen to hamper business. But certain major proposals were not enacted, in particular the radical proposal to limit the number of terms any member of Congress might serve; nor did the Republican leadership seem willing to address the fundamental question of the financing of election campaigns, which had long attracted criticism in the United States for the influence it supposedly gives to corporate contributors.

Disagreements with the Senate.

However it was not plain sailing for the House Republicans. The Contract with America was not especially popular with the voters. A low turnout of some 40 per cent of voters in the mid-term election meant that it had in fact been endorsed by only one-fifth of the potential electorate; and, as the first year of the Republican Congress unfolded, it seemed clear that fundamental reform of the welfare state would require deep cuts in programmes which the middle class supported, such as Medicare and Social Security (old age pensions). Such cuts were politically impossible to achieve and the Senate Republicans watered down many of the Contract's provisions or refused to pass them at all (such as the proposal to amend the Constitution to require a balanced budget).

The Battle Over The Budget.

As the first year of Republican majority progressed, President Clinton was best able to resist the New Right on issues on which the Democrats had middle class support, especially the federal budget. Battles over the budget had been a hallmark of the contest in the Reagan years between the Democratic Congress and the Republican White House; now the roles were reversed. The budget for next fiscal year (beginning in October 1995) was due to be authorised over the summer. The Republicans' initial position was to demand deep cuts in welfare programmes in conjunction with a $245 billion tax cut. Welfare in particular was to be "decentralised" by turning responsibility for it over to the states. Clinton claimed that such moves would not only harm the poor but that reductions in federal money for education, job training and Medicare would hurt the middle class as well. As the start of the new fiscal year approached it proved impossible for the Congress to pass the significant number of bills necessary to implement a budget and it was forced to adopt several "continuing resolutions" to extend existing authorisations temporarily. President Clinton accepted these initially, but in November he dramatically vetoed a second set of resolutions—claiming that congressional Republicans had attached certain unacceptable provisions—and the federal government was forced to close down certain of its "non-vital" operations and lay off or leave without pay three-quarters of a million workers. A further veto in December resulted in another shutdown over the holiday period which was not ended until early January 1996.

Democratic Gains, 1995.

The confrontation with the Republicans over the budget seemed to raise President Clinton's popularity with the voters, since a majority of Americans blamed the Congress for the impasse. The president had gone part way towards accepting Republican demands by agreeing that the federal budget should be brought into balance within the next seven years, and in return Speaker Gingrich had reduced the amount which the House Republicans planned to trim from Medicare to $168 billion from $270 billion the month before. Republican flexibility perhaps resulted from growing evidence that the Democratic position had significant popular support: in late 1995 the Democrats won state elections in Virginia, Maine and Kentucky; and in January 1996 they gained their first US senator from Oregon for 29 years in an election which was notable for being conducted entirely by postal ballot. Hence President Bill Clinton entered 1996 in surprisingly robust form. It was clear that in the year since the Republican takeover of Congress he had been able to rebuild the image of his presidency and project himself to the voters as a moderate who would restrain the radicals of the New Right.

Successes in Foreign Policy.

Clinton's revived popularity was due in part to his successes in foreign policy, an area where he had previously been criticised for either personal disinterest or his failure to develop any "grand strategy" for the United States in the aftermath of the Cold War. During the latter part of 1995 however the Democratic Administration was able to claim some important achievements. Clinton's timely personal intervention in the Northern Ireland peace process was instrumental in getting it restarted and his triumphant visit to the province in late November confirmed the enduring importance of the United States in European affairs. Perhaps more importantly American military intervention (through NATO) in the conflict in the former Yugoslavia—effectively on the side of the beleaguered Bosnian government—finally brought the warring parties to the negotiating table, which the European states had failed to achieve. In November a comprehensive peace agreement was signed in Dayton, Ohio and the following month President Clinton committed the first American troops to Bosnia as part of the newly formed IFOR. This action was not universally popular in the United States (the House Republicans having initially declined to vote funds for the mobilisation) and there remained the possibility that any resumption of war in Yugoslavia which caused heavy American casualties would cost the president the 1996 election.

The Climate of Domestic Opinion, 1996.

The approach of the 1996 presidential election saw the United States afflicted with widespread alienation from politics and pessimism about the future of the country, in perhaps greater measure than had been the case before Clinton's own election. This was so despite his Administration's relatively creditable domestic record, particularly in economic management. In his State of the Union address in January the president was able to claim eight million jobs created during his term of office and the lowest combined rate of unemployment and inflation (the so-called "misery index") in nearly three decades. But during the previous year the public had been disturbed by growing evidence of polarisation in American society. In April 1995 the United States suffered its worst ever domestic terrorist attack, when the Federal Building in Oklahoma City was destroyed by a bomb which killed 167, including children. Initially thought to be the work of Islamic radicals, the bombing was later revealed to have been caused by disaffected right-wing extremists who sought to mark the anniversary of the FBI's assault in 1993 on the Branch Davidians' compound in Waco, Texas. Newt Gingrich, Republican Speaker of the House of Representatives, caused political controversy when he suggested in connection with this and other episodes that such actions were understandable (if not justifiable) given the "anti-American" policies and agenda of the Clinton Administration. Furthermore the verdict of acquittal in the murder trial of former football star O.J. Simpson—announced in October after televised proceedings which had lasted over a year—produced another national outpouring of self-examination and recrimination, because the conclusion was seen by many to have been racially motivated.

Clinton's Second Term.

For details of the 1996 presidential election and the scandals that at one stage threatened to engulf President Clinton, see Special Topic, C65–6.

CANADA

The 1995 Referendum.

During 1995 political life was dominated by the approaching referendum on the future of Quebec. The narrowness of the federalists' victory (by one percentage point on a turnout of 94%) in the referendum of 30 October 1995 weakened Prime Minister Chrétien: federalist victory strengthened the separatists' resolve. Those aspects of Chrétien's personality which had previously appeared as the virtues of consensualism and reassurance now appeared as the vices of irresolution and incredibility. Yet his personal political dilemma was Canada's also: his difficulty in simultaneously addressing both the unquenched demand in Quebec for greater autonomy, if not for full sovereignty, whilst retaining the support of resentful and sceptical anglophone opinion elsewhere was one which any Canadian premier would have had to face. In Quebec, Jacques Parizeau resigned as leader of the Parti Quebecois to be replaced by the galvanic Lucien Bouchard whose first task is to prepare for provincial elections in 1996, and whose second is to use the elections as a springboard for a further referendum (probably in 1997) on Quebec's future. As Premier of Quebec, Bouchard will strain mightily to hold a referendum only when convinced that the separatist cause will triumph.

Developments in 1996.

In an attempt to regain the political initiative and deflect public attention from Bouchard's assumption of office on the following day, Chrétien made wide-ranging changes to his Cabinet in late January 1996, allocating four posts to Quebecois politicians. Heeding calls from western provinces for fuller account to be paid to their preferences and priorities, he strengthened western representation in the Cabinet through the allocation of a new Cabinet position to a politician from British Columbia, and the granting of chairmanships of two important Cabinet Committees to westerners. The central thrust of government policy remains unaltered: the reduction of the fiscal deficit; the creation of new jobs; privatisation; and the establishment of a workable relationship with Quebec within a federal structure of a kind that the western provinces would tolerate. It is an exceedingly demanding set of objectives.

The Economic Background.

Chrétien's government lost some ground both to the Conservatives and to the New Democrats in the second half of 1996, but retained its dominance (partly because it faced challenges from different parties in different provinces). Much of the Liberal political advantage stemmed from the vigour of Canada's export economy. Viewed from the perspective of that buoyant export performance, the economy enjoyed remarkable success in 1996: the rate of price inflation continued at its low levels of approximately 1·5%; the federal government seemed likely to succeed in eliminating the annual budget deficit before the end of the decade; and the surplus on foreign trade in 1996 was a record high.

The 1997 Election.

Taking advantage of these good economic indicators, and with the opinion polls in his favour (and obvious divisions amongst the opposition) an early election was called for 2 June 1997. In the election, the Liberal Party was returned to power, albeit with a reduced majority. The outcome was as follows:

Party	Seats	% vote
Liberals	155	39%
Reform	60	19%
Bloc Quebecois	44	11%*
Progressive Conservatives	20	19%
NDP	21	11%

*(39% in Quebec)

The Voting Analysed.

The regional distribution of the vote in the election was even more highly skewed than it had been in 1993. The Bloc's vote, of course, was drawn entirely from Quebec. The Liberals' support was now heavily dependent upon Ontario (where the party won all but two of the 103 constituencies) and weakening both in the Maritime provinces (where it lost 21 seats over dissatisfaction with the government's fiscal prudence), and in the west. The Conservatives had almost no strength in Ontario (where the party won only one constituency) but two areas of support in Quebec (where its leader, Jean Charest, attracted some nationalist support with a proposal for enhanced autonomy for Quebec within Canada) and the Maritimes. The Reform Party drew its strength entirely from the western provinces, where there was strong opposition to granting Quebec the status of a 'distinct society' within Canada. The gradual alignment of party with region would make the bargained resolution of the Quebec question exceedingly hard.

Recent Political Developments.

In a major advisory opinion, issued on 20 August 1998 in response to questions put to it by the federal government, the Canadian Supreme Court intervened, with caution and not without ambiguity, in the question of Quebec's right to secede from Canada. The outcome satisfied neither side: the Court held that even were a majority of the province to support the option of secession in a referendum, Quebec would enjoy no right of secession: it would be obliged to negotiate a secession with the federal and provincial governments. A unilateral declaration of independence would be impermissible. There would, however, be a balancing obligation upon the federal and provincial governments to negotiate with Quebec in good faith if a referendum result yielded a "clear majority" on an "unambiguous question" (neither of which terms the Court defined).

The Quebec Elections.

In a provincial election in November, the Parti Quebecois (PQ) won a majority of Assembly seats, but gained a smaller proportion of the vote than the Quebec Liberal Party. That disappointing result for the PQ indicated that Prime Minister Bouchard was unlikely to call a referendum on independence in 1999. The Province's relationship with Ottawa remains an issue of the first importance, but the politics of the question in 1999 are being expressed more in bread and butter issues of public spending and the nature and extent of Federal support for Provincial public programmes than in the fundamental question of sovereignty. Other Provinces which also find themselves under fiscal pressures at home (not least Ontario) are also pressing the Federal government for greater, unconditional, financial support. There is also considerable public pressure for higher spending on health care, and resistance to Finance Minister Paul Martin's policy of attaching priority to fiscal restraint: neither Martin nor Prime Minister Chrétien have significant room for political manoeuvre.

LATIN AMERICA

ARGENTINA.

The 1995 Presidential Elections.

President Menem's centre-right Justicialist Party comfortably won the presidential and congressional elections on 14 May. President Menem was returned with almost 50% of the vote, defeating the centre-left Front for a Country in Solidarity (Frepaso) candidate who won almost 30%. Frepaso had been formed as a coalition of socialists, Communists and Christian Democrats at the end of 1994. The results overall appeared to confirm popular rejection of the traditional parties.

The country's second city, Córdoba, suffered serious rioting on 22–23 June after the financially pressed provincial government introduced salary cuts and tax increases. The Radical Civic Union governor blamed the federal government for the province's problems. President Menem offered to despatch troops to quell disorder but did not offer financial assistance.

Unemployment, which officially increased from 12·5% in April to 18·6% in July, remained a crucial issue. On 2 August President Menem introduced measures to create 350,000 jobs including publicly funded infrastructure projects and concessions for private employers taking on labour. However, demonstrations against unemployment continued, notably in Córdoba on 10 August. On 6 September there was a 12 hour protest general strike in Tucumán and Córdoba provinces.

The Budget Crisis.

In November 1995 President Menem called on Congress to declare a state of economic emergency to empower him to raise taxes, dissolve government agencies and privatise state-owned enterprises. On 10 January 1996 a presidential decree cut the 1996 budget by $200 million. The reduction was made to meet International Monetary Fund (IMF) demands for curbs in public expenditure as a condition of further loans. President Menem further increased his executive powers through an Administrative Reform Act passed by the Chamber of Deputies on 7 February and the Senate on 22 February. He said his new powers would enable him to "slash" government spending.

Dissatisfaction with Austerity.

But there was growing evidence of public dissatisfaction with President Menem's austerity policies. On 30 June the candidate of the ruling Justicialist Party was pushed into third place in the elections for the mayor of the capital Buenos Aires. The centre-right Radical Party (UCR) candidate emerged as victor with almost 40% of the vote, the centre-left Front for a Country and Solidarity (Frepaso) coming second with 26%. The Justicialist Party suffered further humiliation over the resignation of three ministers in July. One resigned following charges that he had been a member of a neo-Nazi group, a second as a result of an arms scandal, and the Economy minister—Domingo Cavallo, the leading force behind economic restructuring—went following months of open disagreement with President Menem.

The new Economy minister, Roque Fernández, announced a package of measures on 12 August, including large tax increases. Agreeing to some modifications, President Menem declared he would use emergency powers to force the remainder through. But the crisis was growing. On 8 August three trade union federations—including the General Confederation of Labour (CGT), an ally of the ruling Justicialist Party—had mounted a 24 hour general strike against wage cuts and reductions in family allowances. The new package provoked a 36 hour general strike on 26–27 September. The stoppage was backed not only by the union federations but by the UCR, Frepaso and a number of deputies and senators from the Justicialist Party. President Menem was called on by a union leader to "govern for the people and not for the IMF".

Human Rights Issues.

March brought a reminder of the "dirty war" waged against political dissidents by the 1976–83 military dictatorship. Human rights groups welcomed a Spanish judge's issuing of an international warrant for the arrest of Leopoldo Galtieri, military president from 1981–82 and beneficiary of an amnesty from President Menem in 1989, for his alleged role in the murder of three Spanish nationals. The country's present violence came into focus on 14 April with demands for the resignation of the Interior and Education ministers following the killing of a woman during a teachers' demonstration. This was followed two weeks later by a Press Workers' Union protest against the murder of a journalist, allegedly sanctioned by a "political mafia" of businessmen, criminals, politicians and police. Congress itself was suspended on 29 April following fighting between Peronist and opposition deputies during a debate on privatisation of the country's largest bank. The opposition accused the government of intending to use the proceeds to finance public works schemes to win support in the October elections.

Popular Unrest.

The combination of free market policies—with resulting unemployment and growing poverty—and proposed reforms to weaken organised labour provoked widespread unrest in May. The government declared that it would continue with IMF-approved policies and blamed left-wing groups and the media for exploiting legitimate grievances to provoke unrest. However, on 22 May the government announced that a $600 million World Bank loan would be used to combat unemployment.

The 1997 Mid-Term Elections.

In August, the centrist Radical Civic Union (UDR) and the centre-left Front for a Country in Solidarity (Frepaso) formed an Alliance to contest the October mid-term elections to the Congress lower house. The Alliance accepted President Menem's free-market reforms but attacked his apparent indifference to judicial and police corruption. Despite President Menem's charge that the Alliance would return to a state-controlled economy and hyper-inflation, the Alliance took 45·6 % of the vote against 36·1 % for the ruling Justicialist Party (PJ), inflicting the Peronists' first electoral defeat for a decade. Though remaining the largest party, PJ now depended on smaller provincial parties to retain legislative control. In the key Peronist base of Buenos Aires, the Alliance candidate Graciela Fernàndez Meijide, defeated her rival by 48 % to 41 %.

Economic Reform Attempts.

President Menem's attempts at economic reform won Supreme Court support in January 1998 with authorisation of his decree to privatise the country's airports. On 4 February the International Monetary Fund (IMF) approved a further three-year credit package to underpin the government's 1998–2000 economic reform programme. There were, however, conditions. On 23 March President Menem authorised tax measures which were central to structural reform. The proposals—which the Treasury Secretary said were intended to halve the country's 14 % unemployment and to combat widespread tax evasion—were criticised by business and industrial leaders. But on 6 April the IMF urged restraint on Argentina's annual growth rate of 8 % and a reduction in the trade deficit. The IMF criticised proposed labour reforms (a watered-down version of which was passed in September) and called for the postponement of public works programmes.

Recent Developments.

At the end of March the Chamber of Deputies and the Senate approved the repeal of the 'dirty war' legislation by substantial majorities. The effect, however, was not to be retroactive and individuals already amnestied would not face charges. The repeal legislation was the work of the centre-left Front for a Country in Solidarity (Frpasco), the opposition partner of the Radical Civil Union (UCR), under whom the amnesty legislation had originally been passed. On 9 June Jorgé Rafael Videla (military leader from 1976–81) was charged with illegally placing children of detainees for adoption during his period in power. Videla had been sentenced to life imprisonment in 1985 for crimes against humanity but was released under amnesty in 1990. A similar charge was laid against a former admiral in November. In October the Supreme Court had supported the right of families of the 'disappeared' (opposition activists kidnapped and murdered by the former miliary regime) to obtain information about their relatives' fate.

President Menem's hopes of a third term appeared thwarted when, on 1 June, the electoral appeals court ruled he could not stand in the 1999 presidential elections. President Menem—elected in 1989 and 1994—initially rejected the ruling but on 21 July announced he would not seek a further term in office. At the end of October he made a five-day official visit to Britain to improve relations and encourage trade. President Menem restated Argentina's claim to the Malvinas (the Falklands) and Britain re-asserted that sovereignty was not negotiable. President Menem wrote a conciliatory open letter to the islands' population in November.

BRAZIL.

Constitutional reforms in May 1994 reduced the presidential term from five to four years. In presidential elections on 3 October, Mr Cardoso took 45 % of the vote in an eight candidate race. His closest challenger, Luis Inacio Lula da Silva of the Workers' Party, polled 25 %.

President Cardoso, whose term began in January 1995, had promised to concentrate on the fight against poverty. But as the effects of the Mexican crisis spread through Latin America, he abandoned promises to spend up to $20 billion on Brazil's infrastructure, putting stabilization and economic growth before immediate measures to help the poor. On 3 February presidential plans for constitutional reform were hampered by his decision to veto a 42 % rise in the minimum wage. At the same time he announced that he and his ministers would take a 25 % cut in salary. Opinion polls showed a slip in his popularity among the electorate from 70 % at the start of his term to 36 %.

An exchange rate crisis forced devaluation of the *real* on 6 March, threatening the government's anti-inflation policy. As interest rates and the minimum wage were increased, Roman Catholic bishops questioned the government's claim that it could combine free market reforms with welfare improvements for the poor.

The government's privatisation programme met with a series of public sector protests. On 3 May a general strike halted all railways, telecommunications and social security offices. Troops seized four state owned oil refineries on 24 May to end a month long strike by 45,000 oil workers. Privatisation nevertheless went ahead, although complaints about the slow progress in privatisation, in particular from the Liberal Front Party, were to force the resignation on 10 October of National Bank for Economic and Social Development president Edmar Bacha. The Chamber of Deputies voted in June to end the state monopoly in the oil industry and telecommunications. The government announced a four year plan on 6 September aimed at achieving 4–5 % annual economic growth by the end of the century.

The Land Question.

A decree issued by President Cardoso on 8 January 1996 allowing regional governments and individuals access to land previously allocated to indigenous Indians aroused protests that the government had submitted to business interests. On 20 January 1,500 landless peasants occupied a private estate west of São Paulo. Government claims to have resettled 40,000 landless families during 1995 were disputed by activists who suggested that five million families remained landless.

The government's main concern continued to be the country's finances. On 9 February, in an attempt to counter inflation, the government took measures to discourage inflows of foreign capital attracted by the country's 30 % interest rate. It was faced, however, by the weakening in the Chamber of Deputies on 21 March of a bill intended to end special pensions for privileged groups, among them senior officials and some deputies. The government failed to reverse the amendments on 22 May, despite declaring that its efforts to reduce the budget deficit were being threatened.

Slow Pace of Reform.

On 17 April 19 people were killed by troops deployed to end road blockades erected by the landless workers' movement, the MST, in protest against the slowness of agrarian reform. President Cardoso's own Brazilian Social Democratic Party (PSDP) expressed concern at the government's social reform record. With 37,000 families occupying 168 estates, President Cardoso requested Congress on 24 April to make legislation for the expropriation of uncultivated land a priority. On 23 June, however, he warned the MST that if land seizures continued the army would be used to assist police in evictions. As alarming for public order was the relaunch in September of the Rural Democratic Union (UDR), a hardline landowners' organisation which had disbanded in 1995. The UDR said it would recruit four million landowners to counter MST activities.

Moves towards privatisation were accelerated on 2 July when the government announced that it had abandoned plans to retain state control of tele-communications. President Cardoso followed this in August by agreeing to over two billion *reals* in federal spending cuts in an attempt to reduce the deficit.

Anti-Government Protests.

There was unaccustomed unanimity between the militant Landless Workers' Movement (MST) and the relaunched landowners' association, the Rural Democratic Union (UDR), when the leaders of both organisations warned in January 1997 that the country faced unprecedented rural violence. The MST had recently begun occupying land close to the cities as a tactical move to encourage urban working class support. April saw one of the largest ever anti-government protests when the 25,000 MST demonstrators, supported by liberal Catholic bishops and trade union and left-wing leaders, con-demned the effect of free market reforms. The gov-ernment responded on 17 April by offering to expand its land reform programme and to grant credit to recently settled families. On 11 June, fol-lowing denunciation by Catholic bishops of the trial and imprisonment of an MST leader for murdering a landowner, President Cardoso issued a decree speeding up land redistribution. However, following a six month lull in occupations, 200 landless families seized two ranches in the south of the country in August to place pressure on the government to accelerate its programme.

Failure of Civil Service Reform.

Government attempts to reform the civil service—60% of state expenditure went on official salaries—met with less success. The Chamber of Deputies approved, with a narrow majority, a proposal to allow redundancies in the civil service. The Senate rejected the proposal on 10 June but the reform finally passed in the autumn. The Senate did, how-ever, bring President Cardoso's ambition to remain in office a step nearer by approving a constitutional amendment allowing him to seek election for a second term. But there were signs of instability in the ruling Brazilian Social Democratic Party (PSDB) which threatened President Cardoso's ambitions. In August former finance minister Ciro Gomes—a possible rival in the 1998 elections—deserted the PSDB for the Social Progress Party (PPS) and former President Itamar Franco returned to political activity.

Nevertheless, on 9 October the Brazilian Democratic Movement Party (PMDB)—the largest member of the governing coalition—announced support for President Zedillo's re-election in return for electoral agreements with the PSDB and the Liberal Front Party (PDT) while the Communist Party of Brazil (PCdoB) failed to persuade the Brazilian Socialist Party (PSB) to back a PT candidate.

The Austerity Package.

In the wake of the Asian financial crisis, the gov-ernment introduced an austerity package on 10 November in an attempt to maintain its three-year economic stabilisation programme. The measures were combined with a doubling of interest rates to 40%. The package included cuts in the civil service, reductions in state budgets, increased income tax and duties, together with measures to encourage exports and small and medium-sized businesses.

Impact of Global Problems.

The year 1998 was dominated by the effects of the world financial crisis on Brazil and by attempts to avoid a devaluation that would have further inter-national repercussions. On 13 March President Cardoso presented the Cabinet with a 12-point plan to combat unemployment, rising under the impact of his November 1997 austerity measures. The pro-gramme included labour reforms to increase flexibil-ity in contracts and encourage part-time work.

There were continuing problems over the land issue. On 17 March 10,000 members of the Landless Workers' Movement (MST) occupied government buildings in 15 states to force the government to release funds for land reform. The occupations ended when the finance minister agreed to resume negotiations. In May there was serious unrest in the north east of the country which had been stricken with drought in March, with outbreaks of looting among the ten million people in the eight states affected.

Privatisation of 20% of the government's hold-ings in the telecommunications system in July raised an unexpectedly high $19·1 billion. The sale was followed by allegations of corruption among officials involved in the deal.

The Financial Crisis.

The world international crisis now began its most serious impact on Brazil. Against the background of growing debt, stock exchange prices tumbled on 3 September and trading was temporarily suspended. On 5 September the central bank raised the interest rate to over 10% in an attempt to stem capital out-flows. In August and September there was a total capital outflow of over $3·5 billion, with estimated reserves down to $50 billion. There were persistent denials by the government that it intended to devalue as debts threatened to move beyond the ability to meet them. As the largest economy in Latin America the knock-on effects threatened to be drastic. The International Monetary Fund (IMF), World Bank and the United States promised support. With presidential elections approaching, President Cardoso's pledge to impose further eco-nomic austerity was welcomed by the IMF.

President Cardoso won a second term in the 4 October elections, taking a slightly reduced 53·1% to the Workers' Party's increased 31·7%.

Despite left-wing gains in legislative elections, the five party coalition backing President Cardoso cap-tured 377 of the 513 Chamber of Deputies seats. As he had promised during his campaign, President Cardoso announced a stringent three year Fiscal Stability Programme on 28 October, including large cuts in public expenditure and tax increases. The programme was intended to secure further IMF/World Bank support. On 4 November the Chamber of Deputies approved reform of the massively indebted public pensions sector. The IMF agreed to provide a $41·5 million rescue package a week later.

Devaluation and After.

But hopes of a respite were short-lived. On 3 December the stock exchange fell 10% as the Chamber of Deputies rejected $2·2 billion social security cuts aimed at reducing the $64 billion bud-get deficit. With the economy—the world's ninth largest—contracting by an annual 6%, there were fears of a domino effect on Latin America. As 1999 opened, the resignation of the governor of the central bank provoked a 10% fall in the real. The final crisis came with the decision of the governor of one of Brazil's largest states to stop repaying money owed to the central government. On 13 January the cen-tral bank was forced to devalue the real by 8%, defying a pledge made to the IMF in return for the November 1998 rescue package. A week later—with the real having fallen 22% against the dollar—finance minister Pedro Malan attempted to regain confidence by promising Brazil would meet its $70 billion short-term debt commitments to interna-tional banks. Congress passed the unpopular social security cuts and President Cardoso announced the establishment of an anti-inflation committee. In February the government began seeking new cuts in spending after agreeing with the IMF to further reduce the budget deficit.

MEXICO.

The 1997 Elections.

The ruling Institutional Revolutionary Party (PRI) suffered its worst electoral defeat in 70 years in July's mid-term congressional, gubernatorial and local elections. For the first time, the PRI (with 38·5% of the vote) lost control of the 500-seat

Chamber of Deputies, though it remained the largest party. The PRI would depend on the support of either the centre-left Party of the Democratic Revolution (PRD)—which had taken 25·8% of the vote—or the centre-right National Action Party (PAN), with 26·9%. But PRI fragmentation came into the open with the formation of a dissident grouping of senators intent on rejecting any attempts by the president to use party control of the Senate to block legislation from the lower house. As the first opposition-dominated Congress convened on 1 September, President Zedillo warned of the need to adhere to the government's stringent economic policies.

Developments in Chiapas.

In August, the army was reported to be reducing its presence in three areas controlled by the Zapatista Liberation Army (EZLN) in the southern state of Chiapas. But on 22 December 45 pro-Zapatista refugees were killed by paramilitary gunmen in the worst violence since the 1994 uprising. The government claimed initially that the deaths were the result of a feud but the EZLN accused the government itself of complicity. On 28 December the mayor of the local municipality was charged with organising the massacre and over 40 alleged participants were arrested. As 5,000 troops moved into the area, the EZLN accused the government of preparing renewed violence against Zapatista supporters.

Following the massacre of 45 people in Chiapas in December 1997, the Interior Minister and state police chief were forced to resign. Demonstrations in Mexico and abroad demanded the withdrawal of troops from the region and compliance with the San Andreas peace accord negotiated by President Zedillo's representatives in February 1996. The Zapatista National Liberation Army (EZLN) rejected a government offer to resume talks in February 1998, declaring that the government had failed to respect previous agreements. Despite arrests in connection with the December massacre in April, negotiations seemed further away than ever when Bishop Samuel Ruiz, a leading mediator between the government and EZLN, resigned. In November 1997 he survived an assassination attempt by paramilitaries allegedly financed by the ruling Institutional Revolutionary Party (PRI). Bishop Ruiz accused the government of conspiring against a settlement.

Recent Developments.

Politically, however, the PRI appeared to be reviving. In August the party retained two governorships in state elections, although it lost one to the conservative opposition National Action Party (PAN). The PRI took most of the town councils and the majority of seats in legislative elections in Chiapas and Otaxaca in October. As the turn-out fell to 30% in some areas the EZLN accused the PRI of intimidating voters by deploying extra troops in Chiapas. However, on 18 October the EZLN offered to re-open negotiations through a multi-party commission. On 21–22 November 29 EZLN delegates accused the government of mounting a war of extermination against indigenous people at preliminary meetings with the commission. The delegates also met representatives of 300 popular organisations to plan an unofficial national referendum in 1999 to force the government to ratify the 1996 agreement.

As the stalemate continued, the government introduced a potentially unpopular austerity budget on 13 November, including tax increases and public spending cuts of $2·5 billion. Inflation targets were set at 13% in 1999, falling to 10% in 2,000, with annual growth set to decline to 3%.

AUSTRALASIA

AUSTRALIA.

Post-War Background.

Post-war electoral domination by the Liberal-Country coalition ended with the 1972 victory of Labour under Gough Whitlam. In 1975 Whitlam was dramatically dismissed by the Governor-General, pre-cipitating a constitutional crisis and ushering in eight years of Liberal-Country government. Labour was swept back into power in 1983 under Bob Hawke, who went on to lead the party to election victories in 1984, 1987, and 1990. Although emotional ties with Britain and Europe remain strong, the economic and strategic importance of Asia has increased, with Japan rapidly becoming Australia's largest trading partner. By 1993 East Asia accounted for 58% of Australian exports compared to only 21% in 1957.

The Keating Administration.

Paul Keating became Labour leader and Prime Minister in December 1991. Despite a deepening recession, Labour scored a surprise victory in the March 1993 General Election, capitalising on popular opposition to the Liberal–National coalition plan for a goods and services tax. Labour won 45% of the vote and 80 seats to the coalition's 44% and 65 seats, with Independents gaining 2 seats. Following the removal of trade barriers with New Zealand in 1990, Keating continued to promote regional economic co-operation with an Asia-Pacific free trade area planned by 2020.

The fragile economic recovery was threatened by the prolonged drought in Eastern Australia in 1994–5. The Coalition, with a majority of State governments and John Howard re-elected as leader, continued to maintain a slight lead in the polls when Keating called an election in January 1996.

The March 1996 Election.

On 2 March John Howard became Australia's twenty-fifth Prime Minister as the Liberal-National Coalition won a landslide victory, ending 13 years of Labour government and the political career of Paul Keating. One third of the Cabinet lost their seats as a 6% national swing against Labour left the Liberals with enough MPs to govern alone. In Labour's old heartland of New South Wales the swing was 9%, sealing Labour's defeat. The final result was: Liberal–National Coalition 48% of the vote and 94 seats compared to Labour's 39% and 48 seats. Independents won 5 seats. The republican issue was overshadowed by the economy, especially youth unemployment, and Keating's abrasive style.

The Immigration Backlash.

Until 1946 when mass immigration from war-torn Europe began, the population was predominantly of Anglo-Celtic origin. By 1993, 23% of the population were born outside Australia, and non-Europeans, largely excluded until the White Australia policy was abandoned in 1973, now constitute the majority of immigrants. "Multiculturalism" replaced "assimilation" as official policy towards immigrant communities, achieving a fairly harmonious accommodation of ethnic diversity. However, concern over jobs during the recession led to increasing antipathy towards Asian communities. The debate intensified after the election of the former chip-shop owner turned independent MP, Pauline Hanson, founder of the One Nation party. Her strong stance against Asian immigration and Aborigines found favour with some but prompted an equally forceful response. Anti-racism protesters frequently clashed with Hanson supporters, and her views dominated the headlines. In June 1998, One Nation won 11 seats and 23% of the vote in the Queensland state elections, and nationally was at 13% in opinion polls. Its popularity was crucial to the outcome of the general election.

The October 1998 Election.

A very close election resulted in a slim victory for the coalition government, despite a 5% swing to Labour and the unpopularity of the proposed goods and services tax. The Liberal-National coalition won 39·5% of the vote and 80 seats, compared to Labour's 40% and 67 seats, and one independent. Pauline Hanson lost her seat as One Nation polled 8·5% nationally, winning only one Queensland Senate seat, but it was that party's racist policies that provided the flashpoints. The anti-racist Unity Party was launched to counter One Nation, four ex-Prime Ministers urged voters to reject racism and Hanson declared a media blackout in the final week. Throughout a rather lacklustre campaign, both main parties remained level in the polls, and it became obvious that the vagaries of the Australian PR system would determine the outcome. Voters list the candidates in order of preference, and if no-one wins 50% initially, votes are re-allocated until one candidate reaches a majority. The 2nd preferences of One Nation and Democrat supporters effectively decided the results in many marginal seats.

The Wik Bill.

Comprising only 1·5% of the population, Aborigines remain a disadvantaged minority with higher infant mortality, lower life expectancy and living standards below average. The historic High Court decision in 1992 to recognise land rights existing before European settlement in 1788 (the Mabo ruling) led to the then Labour government introducing the Native Title Act 1993. This outlined procedures for establishing native title, including those over expired mining leases, as well as the right to negotiate over future use of native title land. The new Coalition government responded with the Native Title Amendment Bill, aiming to limit many of the original powers. This itself was overtaken by the Wik case of December 1996, in which the High Court ruled that native title was not automatically permanently extinguished by pastoral leases. The government had based its bill on the supremacy of pastoral leases, the system where land is rented from the Crown for pastoral use. Such leases, covering about 40% of Australia, would negate many native title claims.

The government was prompted to incorporate a '10-point plan' into its bill to take account of the Wik ruling. It confirmed both that any pre-Wik lease granting 'exclusive' tenure would extinguish native title, and that the right to negotiate over land use, especially mining, was further restricted. In late 1997 the Labour-controlled Senate passed several controversial amendments, reducing the effects of the 10-point plan. These amendments were rejected by the House of Representatives, producing a political stalemate and prospects of early elections. But in July 1998 the Senate finally passed the bill, ending the stand-off.

A New Cultural Identity.

The choice of Sydney for the 2000 Olympics reflects the Australian influence on world sport and its importance domestically. Cricket, rugby and the Melbourne Cup horse race remain national pastimes. In the arts, the era of 'cultural cringe' typified by Dame Edna Everage and Sir Les Patterson has been replaced by a new self-confidence. Growing international recognition of Australian cinema has recently been matched by popular success at the box office with films such as *Strictly Ballroom*, *Muriel's Wedding* and *Priscilla*.

A Resident for President?

Tentative moves in the 1970s towards a republic, with a new national anthem and the scrapping of royal patronage, were given fresh impetus by the Whitlam crisis. By 1986 the Australia Act had established the independence of Australian law, abolishing Westminster's residual legislative and judicial controls. Public opinion on the future of the monarchy remained fairly evenly divided, despite Keating's open commitment to a republic by 2001. Overshadowed during the 1996 election, the debate moved centre stage again in February 1998 as the constitutional convention met and agreed a way forward. The 152 delegates, half appointed, half elected, voted to call a referendum in 1999 on whether or not Australia should become a republic. The two-week convention was held against a background of increasing support for a republic—67% of voters favour scrapping the monarchy. It was clear that the republicans would win the day, but it was less certain which model for a new constitution would succeed. Many republicans want a directly-elected president, the most popular option with the public. But the preferred option of the Australian Republican Movement narrowly won and will form the basis of the referendum question. It allows for a candidate to be chosen by the Prime Minister and Leader of the Opposition from a list of public and state nominations. The final decision then rests with the federal parliament which must elect the president by a two-thirds majority. The president would have the same powers as the

Governor-General and the term of office would be five years.

To succeed, the proposal must win an overall majority nationally as well as a majority in most states. Further tensions remain over a new national flag and over the timing of any changes—some want to see an Australian president open the Sydney Olympics in 2000. It seems more likely that a new President of the Commonwealth of Australia will be inaugurated in time to celebrate the centenary of Federation on 1 January 2001.

NEW ZEALAND.

The October 1996 Election.

The National Party under Jim Bolger, having won the 1990 election, introduced an austerity package to reduce the budget deficit. Pensions, benefits, the health and education services were all deeply affected, as was National's popularity, but inflation and unemployment did finally start to fall and Bolger narrowly won again in November 1993 with a majority of 1. An election was called on 12 October 1996, and fought under the new mixed-member proportional system (MMP), which introduced a degree of proportional representation. 65 seats, including 5 Maori seats, were fought under the first-past-the-post system, with the remaining 55 seats apportioned to party lists, reflecting the overall support for the parties. A party had to win 5% of the national vote, or a directly-elected seat, in order to qualify for a party list seat. The new system precipitated new parties and coalitions, resulting in a hung Parliament: National 44 seats, Labour 37, New Zealand First 17, Alliance 13, Act NZ 8, United 1. With no party able to govern alone. NZ First's leader Winston Peters entered into protracted coalition talks with both the main parties. Although NZ First had won many votes, especially from Maoris and the elderly by campaigning against National, a new coalition between these two was formed on 10 December. Bolger remained as Prime Minister, with Peters as Treasurer and Deputy Prime Minister. The announcement of a NZ$5 billion programme of health and education spending was overshadowed by dissatisfaction amongst some NZ First supporters. Peters' limousine was set alight as polls showed that two-thirds of NZ First voters had wanted a coalition with Labour. Republicanism was not a major election issue. Although Bolger was pushing for a republic by 2000, opinion polls consistently put support at below 30%.

Domestic and Foreign Friction.

Relations with the Maori population, 10% of the total, had started to improve with the creation of a Ministry of Maori Development in 1991 and proposals for compensation for confiscated lands, first outlined in December 1994. A "fiscal envelope", with a limit of NZ$1 billion, was proposed by the government for this purpose, but rejected by most Maori tribes as insufficient. Maori protesters disrupted Waitangi Day celebrations in February 1995, fighting with police and spitting at the Governor-General. Only the Tainui tribe has assented, receiving NZ$170 million, and assured 17% share of any further settlements and a royal apology from the Queen in November 1995. Labour's 1985 declaration of a nuclear-free zone, enforced by legislation in 1987, put the future of the ANZUS pact in doubt, although relations with the USA have improved since US warships no longer carry tactical nuclear weapons. The resumption of French nuclear testing under the Pacific atoll of Muroroa in 1995 caused outrage. French products were boycotted, diplomatic relations collapsed and New Zealand resumed its court case against France at the International Court of Justice.

A Troubled Government.

On 3 November 1997, following Bolger's resignation, Jenny Shipley was elected as the new leader of the National Party, and so became New Zealand's first woman Prime Minister. She had risen to prominence as a tough reformer of the country's health and social services. One of her first actions was to rule out any moves towards a republic. Of more immediate concern were the Coalition's abysmal poll ratings: over 80% of voters disapproved of the government. By August 1998, internal tension between the Coalition partners had reached a peak, with Shipley's call for a referendum on the future of the MMP system causing further friction with Winston Peters. The decisive issue was the proposed sale of the government's majority share of Wellington airport. On 12 August, NZ First ministers objected to the sale and walked out of the Cabinet. Within a week, Peters was sacked as Deputy Prime Minister. The Coalition had imploded completely, leaving National as a minority governing party, and NZ First disintegrated as a political party. Seven MPs left to support Shipley as independents, meaning that the government survived a no confidence vote.

THE SOUTH PACIFIC.

A handful of island states, many of them tiny in terms of land and population size, stretch across the world's largest ocean. Most achieved independence in the last 30 years, though some are French Overseas Territories (New Caledonia and Tahiti) and others still have the Queen as their official head of state (Papua New Guinea, Solomon Islands and Tuvalu).

Fiji.

Ceded to Britain in 1874, Fiji finally achieved independence in October 1970. A military coup in 1987 ousted the government and a republic was declared. The racist policies of the new regime led to international ostracism. A new constitution was implemented in 1998 and Fiji was readmitted to the Commonwealth.

Kiribati.

Formerly the Gilbert Islands, they were annexed by Britain during World War I, and were the site of heavy fighting in World War II. Independence was granted in July 1979. In 1995 Kiribati officially, but controversially, moved the International Date Line eastwards so that it would be the first country to see the new millennium.

New Caledonia.

French overseas territory. Continuing conflict, often violent, between independence movement and government.

Papua New Guinea (PNG).

Comprising the eastern half of New Guinea plus the offshore islands of New Britain, New Ireland and Bougainville. Germany and Britain divided the area between them in 1884. German New Guinea was invaded during World War I, becoming a League of Nations mandate afterwards. Japanese invasion in World War II led to liberation and a UN trusteeship by Australia. Independence followed in September 1975. Since 1989 a secessionist movement in Bougainville has campaigned for independence, resulting in continued sporadic fighting. A tidal wave hit the north coast of PNG in July 1998, killing over 1,500 people.

Samoa.

In 1899, the Samoan islands were divided between the USA and Germany. The German half, known as Western Samoa, was occupied by New Zealand in 1914, later becoming a UN trust territory. January 1962 saw independence and in 1997 the country's name was shortened to Samoa. American Samoa remains a US-administered territory.

Solomon Islands.

Divided between Germany and Britain until 1899, when British rule was extended to the whole archipelago. The islands, particularly Guadalcanal, were the scene of intense fighting during World War II. Independence was achieved in July 1978. Tension remains with neighbouring Papua New Guinea over the conflict in Bougainville.

Tahiti.

Main island of French Polynesia. French nuclear testing on the Mururoa atoll started in 1966. The resumption of testing in October 1995 resulted in worldwide condemnation and riots in Tahiti's capital, Papeete. The tests were abandoned in January 1996.

Tonga.

A constitutional monarchy which was a British protectorate from 1900 until full independence in June 1970.

Tuvalu.

Formerly the Ellice Islands, they were annexed by Britain during World War I, and granted independence in September 1978.

Vanuatu.

Previously known as the New Hebrides, they were administered by a joint Anglo-French condominium from 1906 until independence in July 1980.

III. SPECIAL TOPICS

RUSSIA: THE YELTSIN ERA

The chronology below sets out the key dates from the disintegration of the former Soviet Union and the ending of communist rule until the presidential elections of 1996. A detailed discussion of more recent events follows.

1991

Aug. Attempted hard-line coup in Moscow while Gorbachev on holiday in Crimea. Russian premier Boris Yeltsin defies coup and prepares to defend Russian parliament building with aid of loyal troops and populace. Coup collapses in face of popular resistance and declarations of independence by Republics. The leading plotters are arrested. Gorbachev returns to Moscow. Under pressure from Yeltsin, adopts sweeping reforms. Baltic states become independent states of Latvia, Estonia and Lithuania; Communist Party of Soviet Union dissolved, ending 74-year rule; Gorbachev resigns as General Secretary, retaining office of executive President of rapidly dissolving Soviet Union. Negotiates an association with ten Republics for a looser union with a common foreign and defence policy.
Dec. Leaders of Belorussia, Russian Federation and Ukraine declare that the Soviet Union is dead; in the Declaration of Minsk they proclaim new 'Commonwealth of Independent States' (CIS) with headquarters at Minsk in Belorussia. Formal resignation of Mikhail Gorbachev as President of the now defunct Soviet Union; the Russian flag replaces the Hammer and Sickle above the Kremlin; key EC states (and America) recognize independence of Russian Federation.

1992

Jun. Yegor Gaidar becomes premier of Russia.
Sept. Lithuania signs agreement with Russia for withdrawal of former Soviet troops.
Dec. Russian Congress blocks President Yeltsin's plans for a referendum on the powers of the President; also removes Yegor Gaidar as premier and replaces him with Viktor Chernomyrdin.

1993

Mar. President Yeltsin announces rule by decree and plan to hold a national referendum on 25 April. Move to impeach the President by Congress defeated.
Apr. Russian referendum gives vote of confidence to President Yeltsin and his economic policy.
Sept. President Yeltsin suspends parliament and calls for elections.
Oct. Suppression of rising against President Yeltsin's suspension of parliament.

1994

Jan. Reformers Gaidar and Fedorov leave Yeltsin government.
Dec. Russia gives ultimatum to breakaway Chechen Republic to disband army and free all prisoners; failure to reach agreement leads to major military assault on Chechen Republic.

1995

Jun. Russia and Ukraine finally settle dispute over Black Sea fleet.
Nov. President Yeltsin forced to relinquish control of four key ministries after second heart attack.
Dec. Yeltsin resumes powers.

1996

Jan. Resignation of liberal Russian foreign minister Andrei Kozyrev.
Feb. President Yeltsin announces intention of seeking second term.

RECENT EVENTS

Background to the 1996 Presidential Election.

Weakened by his own poor health, his and his armed forces' mishandling of the Chechnya problem, and his deep unpopularity, Yeltsin's prospects of winning the Presidency did not seem all that good. However, the first round in the Presidential election on 16 June 1996 resulted in Yeltsin winning 35 % of the vote, Zyuganov 32 %, and General Lebed 14·7 %. Yavlinsky, leader of Yabloko, won only 7·4 %, and the extreme nationalist Zhirinovsky, polling much less well than his party had done in the December 1995 parliamentary elections, only 5·8 %.

Buoyed by excellent organisation which boosted the turnout figure to approximately two-thirds of the eligible electorate, highly tendentious television coverage of the election, and his own campaigning skills, Yeltsin secured victory against Zyuganov in the second round by 53·7 % to 40·4 %. The President's decisive achievement was to frame the terms of the debate to his own advantage: he presented the choice before Russians as being between the option of reasoned progress under his own leadership, and that of reactionary communist danger under Zyuganov. Given that he had himself risen to power within the completely undemocratic system of communism, it was no small achievement for Yeltsin to paint himself as Russia's best anti-communist hope. And, assisted by Zyuganov's own leaden-footed campaign, he succeeded despite his poor health. More was at stake for Russia than a single election campaign: the ageing of the Communist cohort of voters meant that Zyuganov's bid for the Presidency was likely to be the last made by a defender of the old regime.

Events in 1997.

Russian politics during the remainder of 1996 were dominated by Yeltsin's evident physical incapacity. Although his recovery from heart by-pass surgery in November appeared sound, his weakened condition continued to prevent him from exercising power. Power-seekers accordingly gathered around the Presidential office. Anatoly Chubais, the President's Chief of Staff, came to exercise much power himself and introduced into the administration numerous businessmen. Such significant political challenges to the President and Prime Minister as there were came from beyond Moscow, as the disastrous and bloody failure of Russia's attempt to prevent Chechnya from asserting its autonomy vividly showed. Elsewhere, a rash of gubernatorial elections in the regions during the winter of 1996/7 resulted in victories for candidates whose interests and purposes, fuelled by their electorates' frequently hostile attitudes to Moscow, diverged from Yeltsin's own.

Under the circumstances, however, Russia's political condition was remarkably stable: far from seeking to perpetuate their opposition to Yeltsin, Zyuganov and his communist allies worked constructively with Prime Minister Chernomyrdin in the Duma. The neutralisation of the Communist threat, coupled with the effective marginalising of other opponents, left Yeltsin beyond immediate challenge at the centre. The President was, nevertheless, desperately enfeebled physically: although no opponent could strike against him in the short term, his potential successors such as Yuri Luzhkov, the Mayor of Moscow, busily but discreetly courted likely supporters during the winter of 1996 and the early months of 1997.

A Fragile Democracy.

Transition to democracy and economic stability in Russia continued to be deeply problematic in 1997: democracy's structural and legal foundations in Russia were skeletal, a culture of democracy was evanescent, and economic success confined to a minority of Russian citizens. Many Russians, especially the elderly and dependent, continued to become poorer; most government employees (including most soldiers) could not rely upon receiving their salaries; suppliers of goods and services to government were fortunate to be paid on time; the elderly often did not receive their pensions; successful business people were almost always engaged in paying protection money. The state's failure to pay its bills was in part attributable to the parallel failure of many citizens and companies to pay their taxes. Without privatisation receipts, the government's financial circumstances would be much worse than they are; they are in any case sufficiently difficult for the IMF to have suspended payments to Russia under its Extended Fund Facility programme. Under such circumstances, the state's budget-making was close to the heart of continuing struggles between Yeltsin himself, the government, and the Duma.

Partly in an attempt to maintain a balance of forces within the government, Yeltsin dismissed three of its members in mid-November and within a week replaced Chubais (who had unwisely become embroiled in a minor scandal over a book royalty deal) as Finance Minister with Mikhail Zadornov, head of the Duma's Budget Committee.

The Fall of Chernomyrdin.

Fearing that Prime Minister Chernomyrdin had acquired too independent a power base, President Yeltsin dismissed him in March 1998. However, Yeltsin's attempt to compensate for his inability to exercise Presidential control over policy by asserting Presidential authority over the Prime Minister failed. Whilst he eventually succeeded in installing his choice of the technocrat Sergei Kiriyenko as Chernomyrdin's successor, the experiment was short-lived. Kiriyenko fell victim to the political fall-out from a rapid deepening of Russia's crisis: in the late summer of 1998, the crisis was dramatically symbolised by the double shock of the rouble's devaluation and the government's default on $40 billion worth of rouble-denominated bonds.

Six days after the rouble's devaluation, Yeltsin sought to saddle Kiriyenko with responsibility for the dramatic policy failure by dismissing his government and attempting to replace him with Chernomyrdin. Whilst Yeltsin's naming of Chernomyrdin was itself an implicit admission of his grave political weakness, the Duma rebuffed him by rejecting his choice. Chernomyrdin could find support only among his own political party. Yeltsin eventually nominated Yevgeny Primakov, the acting Foreign Minister in Chernomyrdin's caretaker administration, as Prime Minister.

The Rise and Fall of Primakov.

In his first six months in office, Primakov gave the impression of restoring a measure of stability to the country. Yet his achievement was more apparent than real: the output of the Russian economy continued to fall in 1998, albeit at a slower rate than previously; the rouble commanded little confidence among investors; in large part as a result of the partial default in August 1998, the government was effectively denied access to international capital markets; the banking system remained chronically sick; and new investment from abroad collapsed. Few foreign investors would lend to Russia in its current or prospective condition since they were most unlikely to see a return. Neither holders of Russian debt run up since 1991, nor holders of Soviet-era debt incurred before that date, could be confident of their interest payments arriving in 1999. The combination of circumstances undermined Russia's international trade which, since imports supplied so high a proportion of much Russian industry's components and services, further weakened domestic production. Yeltsin had become a political cipher: any thoughts he may have had in early 1998 of running for a third term had entirely disappeared twelve months later. In the early months of 1999 Primakov, though scarcely young, and anything but a vigorous reformer, seemed the only plausible source of leadership in Russia. However, the sudden dismissal of Primakov and the entire Cabinet on 12 May emphasised once again the unpredictability of Russian politics.

CLINTON: THE SECOND TERM

Note: For the background to this article, *see* C54–7.

The 1996 Election Campaign.

Clinton's opinion poll lead was maintained throughout the campaign, though there was always the question of how many voters would follow the candidate of the Reform Party, Ross Perot, now making his second independent presidential bid. Perot's candidacy was probably more of an impediment to the Republicans, as it had been in 1992, and during October the Dole campaign appeared to show signs of disorganisation. In particular its candidate was unable to articulate to the voters a clear set of priorities for government, relying instead upon his personal record as a distinguished legislator and war hero. The Clinton camp by comparison was much better organised and financed, although this was less significant now that, with the commencement of the formal campaign, Dole had become eligible for a federal subsidy. Dole was personally well regarded and one-on-one was a capable speaker (as was clear in two TV debates with Clinton in October), but he never seriously challenged the president's popularity.

The Result.

What did hurt the Democrats badly in the final week of the campaign were allegations about illegal campaign contributions from foreign donors which suggested that the White House had been engaged in unethical activities. This caused a more serious dip in Clinton's ratings than had attacks on his personal morality in the 1992 campaign or the enforced resignation during the Democratic convention of his campaign director because of an affair. Nonetheless the president's lead was sufficient to carry him through to polling day on 5 November. The outcome of the election was predictable: Clinton won 47 million votes (49% of the total), Dole 39 million (41%) and Perot some 8 million (8%), thus becoming the first incumbent Democrat since Franklin Roosevelt to win re-election, a significant personal triumph. More sweeping was the margin in the vote by state: Clinton took 379 votes in the electoral college, Dole 159. Once again Perot, having failed to win the popular vote in any individual state, did not win any electoral votes. That the result was a foregone conclusion seemed confirmed by the fact that voter turnout slumped a 72-year low, only 49%. The result in the congressional election was much closer. The Republicans just managed to keep control of the House of Representatives, but their hold on the Senate increased to 55 seats. Although House Speaker Gingrich began the new year embroiled in ethics charges, the congressional party under the direction of Senate Majority Leader Trent Lott seemed to promise four years of determined if pragmatic opposition to President Clinton.

Second Term Inauguration.

Bill Clinton's inauguration to his second term in January 1997 was widely seen as an opportunity for the U.S. President to articulate a clear vision of his administration's course over the next four years. His convincing victory over his Republican challenger Bob Dole and the simultaneous loss of Republican seats in Congress, suggested that it would be Clinton who would now be setting the legislative agenda. But within twelve months there were to be very grave doubts about whether the President could survive in office at all, as his administration and even Clinton himself became mired in the biggest political scandal since the Iran-Contra affair. Commentators were divided over whether his presidency was fatally weakened, but all agreed that its failings were ultimately Clinton's own.

A Robust Economy.

The most important political development in the United States in 1997 could not, however, be attributed to the federal government at all—though Clinton still sought credit for it. The continuing strength of the domestic economy, as it entered its sixth straight year of growth, was the country's biggest asset. The President had been able to claim in his re-election campaign that 13 million jobs had been created since 1992, but it was a combination of orthodox macroeconomic policies and rising domestic demand which was responsible for this situation rather than the federal government. Economic growth contributed to a rapid decline in the budget deficit—to the point where in January 1998 Clinton could announce a balanced budget for the next fiscal year—and the President largely abandoned the interventionist policies which had marked the earlier part of his first term in office.

However economic strength was not matched by political consensus about domestic or social policy. The President seemed inclined to follow the Republican agenda (as on welfare reform) and he failed to offer concerted or consistent leadership to his own party in Congress, which led to several high-profile revolts by congressional Democrats. Particularly embarrassing was the White House's failure in November to lobby hard enough or soon enough for a reauthorisation of the President's power to negotiate trade deals without congressional amendment. The loss of this authority indicated a President without a clear strategy or a united party. Only in the sphere of foreign relations did Clinton gain much respect in Washington. His appointment of a former Republican senator as Defense Secretary showed his desire to fashion a bipartisan policy; and furthermore the administration demonstrated it was prepared to use the United States' status as the world's remaining superpower to advance American interests when in July it endorsed the expansion of NATO in Europe against Russian wishes. The President also took a hard line against Iraq in October, and again in January 1998, over its refusal to allow U.N. weapons inspectors access to secret sites, so proving that he was broadly in favour of following the Middle East policy laid down by his Republican predecessor despite the international unpopularity this incurred.

A Series of Scandals.

The lack of strategic direction which seemed to afflict the Clinton presidency throughout 1997 was encapsulated in a series of scandals which erupted firstly during the summer over campaign finance and later in the year over the President's personal behaviour. Allegations that both Clinton and Vice-President Gore had broken federal law by making telephone calls from the White House to solicit campaign contributions resulted in high-profile congressional investigations, although in the end the attorney general decided that there was not enough evidence to warrant appointing an independent counsel.

However, it was the work of another independent counsel, Kenneth Starr, examining the Whitewater affair, which provoked the greatest crisis of the Clinton presidency, the Monica Lewinsky affair.

In the United States the events of 1998 ensured that the presidency of Bill Clinton would forever be remembered for his impeachment. The scandal of the President's affair with Monica Lewinsky, which had surfaced in the January of that year, could not be suppressed. The investigation of the independent counsel Kenneth Starr came to its conclusion in September and three months later the House of Representatives voted to impeach Clinton, the first time in American history that such action had been taken against an elected President. (Andrew Johnson, impeached in 1868, had been the Vice-President who succeeded the assassinated Abraham Lincoln. Richard Nixon in 1974 resigned before he could be impeached.)

The Lewinsky Affair.

Although President Clinton had weathered the first months of the scandal and appeared to win an important point when in April a federal judge dismissed the suit of Paula Jones (who claimed Clinton when governor of Arkansas had sexually harassed her), his case was severely weakened in July when Kenneth Starr obtained Ms Lewinsky's testimony by granting her immunity from prosecution. Immediately Clinton acknowledged a subpoena to appear before the grand jury, the first time a sitting President had been obliged to testify in a criminal case. Three weeks later, in a harrowing performance which was later shown on television at the instruction of the House judiciary committee, he argued that his own definition of 'sexual relations' did not

cover the acts described by Ms. Lewinsky and so he could not be guilty of perjury in his previous testimony in the Paula Jones case. Broadcasting to the nation that evening the President admitted his affair with Lewinsky and profoundly apologised; nevertheless he argued that there had never been any attempt by the White House to obstruct justice and that the matter should be closed.

So far the American public appeared remarkably tolerant of Clinton's behaviour. Many sought to distinguish between his private behaviour, of which they disapproved, and his leadership in office, which they resoundingly endorsed. The United States was enjoying a sustained period of economic prosperity and polls indicated that Clinton's approval ratings actually rose after his confession to stand near 70 per cent. However the President's opponents in the Congress were determined to press charges of illegal behaviour. Thus in September Starr submitted a lengthy report to the House Judiciary committee suggesting perjury and obstruction of justice, complete with embarrassing details of Clinton's conduct with Lewinsky. The Congress voted to release it immediately via the Internet and for weeks thereafter the political process in the United States was overtaken by speculation about whether the President would be impeached and, if convicted, removed from office.

The Elections of 1998.

National attention was focussed on the midterm elections in November for the Congress and numerous state offices, which were expected to produce significant Republican gains. However in a remarkable turnaround the Democrats managed not only to hold up their popular vote but even to win additional seats in the House of Representatives—a feat not achieved by the President's party in midterm since 1934. The important state of California chose a Democrat for governor, though the emerging Republican standard bearer George W. Bush (son of the former President) was comfortably re-elected in Texas and his brother Jeb won Florida. Although analysts immediately began examining these results for clues about the next presidential contest, the most important result was that the public had convincingly rejected Republican attempts to make the elections a referendum on Bill Clinton. The first casualty was the Speaker of the House Newt Gingrich, who announced he would not seek re-election in the forthcoming Congress, and his expected successor Bob Livingstone was likewise soon forced to step down after admitting to an affair of his own.

President Clinton's fortunes momentarily seemed to have revived, but congressional Republicans were deeply angered by his defiant answers to the Judiciary Committee's ongoing investigation and in December the committee voted for four articles of impeachment alleging perjury and obstruction of justice. Before these could go to a vote of the full House an international crisis over the expulsion of UN weapons inspectors from Iraq led to US and British military attacks against the Iraqis and the House leadership was obliged to postpone consideration. Unfortunately for Clinton many critics saw this as a cynical attempt to 'wave the flag' and two days later the House voted to impeach him, thus sending him for trial in the Senate.

Trial in the Senate.

Events moved to their final phase in January 1999 when the Senate convened as a court of impeachment under the Chief Justice of the United States and began hearing the case for the prosecution from Republican members of the House. Although the trial was a severe embarrassment for Clinton, it was doubtful even from the outset that there would be a two-thirds majority of Senators to convict as required by the Constitution. Democrats and moderate Republicans seemed to prefer halting the process and instead voting to censure the President, which Clinton indicated he would accept. It was clear by the end of January that the President would survive and would serve in office, "to the last hour of the last day", as he had previously declared. With the vote on 12 February 1999 when the Senate decisively acquitted him of high crimes and misdemeanours, Clinton achieved a great triumph—but at the expense of a deeply tarnished presidency.

MIDDLE EAST SPOTLIGHT

MIDDLE EAST PEACE PROCESS.

Note: For the background to this article, *see* C25–33 under individual countries.

The peace process continued to stagnate through 1998. In September Mr Arafat, blaming Mr Netanyahu for delaying a settlement, raised the stakes by threatening to announce his intention to declare a Palestinian state in May 1999. Mr Netanyahu in turn accused Mr Arafat of failing to crack down decisively on Islamic terrorists. US President Clinton attempted to salvage the position by calling both leaders to Washington and, following nine days of negotiations, the Wye Accord was sealed on 23 October.

The 1998 Wye Accord.

Under the terms of the agreement, Israeli troops were to be withdrawn from 13% of the West Bank and a further 14% of the territory under joint Israel-Palestinian authority was to come under full Palestinian control. The phased troop withdrawal would be contingent on Palestinian co-operation in suppressing Islamic extremists. The Palestinian authorities were to arrest 30 suspected terrorists while Israel guaranteed to release 750 Palestinian prisoners. Finally, Palestine was to withdraw its demand for the elimination of Israel as a state. On 2 November, Mr Arafat accepted an appeal for a delay in implementation to allow Mr Netanyahu to win ratification from his cabinet and the Knesset.

Divisions in Israel.

The intensity of divisions in Mr Netanyahu's coalition now became clear. On 11 November his cabinet accepted the Wye Accord by 8–4 with five abstentions. Five days later—as Foreign Minister Ariel Sharon urged increased Jewish settlement in the West Bank—Mr Netanyahu suspended troop withdrawals on the grounds that Mr Arafat was not moving firmly enough against extremists. Withdrawals began on 19 November and the following day 250 Palestinian prisoners were released, although the Palestinians complained that the majority were criminals rather than political prisoners. There was further pressure on a wavering Mr Netanyahu (whose sympathies appeared to be with the rejectionists)—when *Hizbollah* guerrillas killed seven Israeli soldiers in Lebanon.

Renewed West Bank Violence.

December saw renewed West Bank violence, together with a hunger strike by 2,500 Palestinian prisoners in protest against the delay in further releases. President Clinton appealed for Israel to adhere to the Wye timetable on 13 December as the Palestinian National Council voted to overturn the long-term demand for Israel's destruction. Mr Netanyahu's position was becoming increasingly untenable and on 21 December—apparently unable to sustain support in the coalition for his hardline approach—he asked the Knesset for authority to call a general election. The Knesset voted 81–30 for elections in six months. Within days Mr Netanyahu's Likud party was fracturing, with both moderates and far-right members threatening to resing.

The 1999 Election Background.

On 4 January 1999 elections were called for May. Israel faced a four-month campaign in which a major casualty would be the peace process. The death in February of King Hussein of Jordan—a pivotal figure over many years in the quest for a settlement—cast a further shadow.

THE KURDISH QUESTION.

The arrest in Kenya and return to Turkey of rebel Kurd leader Abdullah Ocalan in February 1999 brought the longstanding Kurdish Question to renewed prominence. Mr Ocalan's Kurdistan Workers' Party (PKK) had been fighting for inde-

pendence in the south east of Turkey for 14 years in a war in which over 20,000 had died. Mr Ocalan was charged with treason and attempting to divide the country. The majority of Kurds live in four countries—Turkey (13 million), Iran (5·7 million), Iraq (4·2 million) and Syria (one million)—and the more militant lay claim to an independent Kurdistan straddling all four. This has ensured the enmity of governments in the region for the Kurds.

The Position in Turkey.

In Turkey the Kurds have been denied a separate ethnic identity as the government has attempted to enforce assimilation since the 1920s. A border guerrilla campaign conducted by the Syrian-based Marxist PKK has met with a ruthless response from the Turkish authorities and a million Kurds have become refugees. However, support for the PKK is by no means total among Kurds, despite the Turkish government's policy of making Kurdish political organisation illegal.

The Iranian authorities have historically attempted to encourage rather than enforce Kurdish assimilation. However, the Islamic Revolution of 1979 was followed by a declaration of holy war against the Kurds following their attempts to create an autonomous Kurdish region. During the 1980-88 Iran-Iraq war, Kurds in Iran were able to seize and hold significant areas of the country. Repression was been most extreme in Iraq, where 17% of the Kurds live. Since the end of the 1991 Gulf War, the Western allies have envorced a 'no-fly' zone in the north of the country in an attempt to protect the Kurds from government atrocities. It is only in Syria that the Kurds' separate identity is not actively discouraged. Syria provides a base for the PKK and the government allows training facilities for guerrillas. This is, however, a political tactic on the part of the Syrian government in a diplomatic campaign against Turkey. Demonstrations throughout Europe by Kurds in protest against Mr Ocalan's arrest revealed the potential dangers of failing to find an international solution to the Kurdish Question.

THE EU TURMOIL

Background to Berlin Summit.

Britain's prime objective at the March 1999 European Union (EU) summit in Berlin was to prevent any reduction in the £2 billion annual rebate secured by Mrs Thatcher in 1984 while at the same time maintaining the Labour government's reputation as a committed supporter of the European project. The rebate represents two thirds of the difference between Britain's contribution to the EU's annual £60 billion budget and what it receives. Mr Blair arrived in Berlin pledging "not a Euro more, not a Euro less". A second objective was a cut in the Common Agricultural Policy (CAP) subsidy to small farmers (the largest proportion of whom were French), which accounted for half the EU budget. In the event, the result was the fudge that Europe has come to expect.

Resignation of EU Commissioners.

The Berlin summit—mounted to overcome apparent deadlock over the European budget—was overshadowed by two crises going beyond the purely economic. On 15 March all 20 European Commission members—including president Jacques Santer—resigned following a scathing report accusing the Commission of mismanagement, corruption and nepotism. At the same time, North Atlantic Treaty Organisation (NATO) forces were preparing to launch an air attack on Serbia (*see* **C68** for events in the Balkans), with no certainty that Europe would remain united over the action.

The first issue dealt with was a new Commission president. With little argument, and with Britain and Germany as his leading supporters, former Italian prime minister Romano Prodi was offered the post. In return, Italy was to show co-operation on an increase in its budget contribution. Following ratification of Mr Prodi's appointment by the European Parliament after the June elections, member states were to nominate replacements for the other 19 Commissioners, though it was assumed many of the former office holders would be returned to their posts.

Financial Questions.

The EU's financial future proved more problematical and a resolution was only achieved after 20 hours of non-stop discussions. On the CAP—to the particular satisfaction of France and despite the Commission's original proposal for sharp cuts—the summit agreed on phased reductions in subsidies for cereal, beef and dairy producers. Nonetheless, this promised to be to the advantage of European consumers, who would benefit from a gradual fall in prices. Germany was disappointed in its attempt to win a significant reduction in its £7·3 billion annual contribution to the EU budget. However, under new rules to be introduced in two years, contributions to the budget were to be based on each country's Gross Domestic Product rather than VAT receipts. This ensured that Italy would make a contribution more in line with its economic strength, a concession ensured by Mr Prodi's appointment as Commission president, with Germany and Britain as gainers.

Britain and the Summit.

Mr Blair won an undertaking that Britain's rebate would remain, with its cost distributed among the other 14 members. But in return he made a concession on a potential windfall payment expected as the EU was enlarged. It was estimated that this could cost Britain up to £154 annually by 2006.

Britain's achievements on regional aid were mixed. In 1994–99, the Scottish Highlands and Islands had received £247 million. Under a new programme, the area would receive £210 million in 2000–2006. Northern Ireland had benefited from £1·2 billion in 1994–99. This was lost, but the blow was cushioned with a "peace programme fund" guaranteeing £280 million over the next five years. In England, Merseyside retained its special aid status and was joined by West Wales, South Yorkshire and Cornwall, with an extra £70 million promised in 2000–2006.

But the European crisis remained. Backing down over the CAP issue demonstrated the EU's inability to grasp the nettle of market liberalisation for fear of offending French susceptibilities. The EU's long term financing remained unresolved. Finally, a lame duck Commission faced conflict in the Balkans and a looming trade war with the United States, with no real authority.

WAR IN THE BALKANS

The Start of NATO Air Strikes.

As hopes that a settlement could be reached at Rambouillet collapsed in March (see **C25**) a renewed Serb offensive against ethnic Albanians in Kosovo followed the withdrawal of international monitors. The North Atlantic Treaty Organisation (NATO) responded by launching air strikes on Serbia intended to achieve the demands made at Rambouillet—a withdrawal of Serb forces from Kosovo and the return of ethnic Albanian refugees under the protection of an international force. NATO leaders—apparently confident that Cruise missiles would have the desired effect—ruled out a land attack on Serbia.

By late April it was clear that President Milosevic had won the first round. Despite increased NATO bombing—with action extended from military to economic and industrial targets—the position of the ethnic Albanians significantly worsened as over half

a million were driven from their Kosovo homeland by the Serbs. President Milosevic took advantage of the Western attack to re-assert his control over Serbia and to extend his influence over not only Kosovo but also neighbouring Montenegro, Macedonia and Bosnia. His apparent propaganda success was consolidated as civilian casualties mounted in Serbia.

Pressure of Public Opinion.

However, as reports of Serb atrocities in Kosovo continued, public opinion in Britain and the United States appeared willing to support the use of ground forces. NATO leaders maintained that the preferred option was the deployment of a peace-keeping force after a Serb surrender rather than mounting a direct attack. The political fear was that once NATO troops suffered casualties, public support (particularly in the United States, with memories of disaster in Vietnam still potent) would fade.

For NATO, maintaining unity was as necessary as success if the 50-year old organisation was to retain credibility in the post-Cold War world. Yet there were divisions from the outset with Italy and, more seriously, Greece (where public opinion felt an affinity for Serbia) uneasy about the bombing. As the possibility of land action increased, the fears of fragmentation intensified. Serbia attempted to play on the divisions with a series of peace proposals.

The impact of events on the Balkans was equally difficult. Montenegro—despite being yoked with Serbia in the Yugoslav Federal Republic—was democratic, pro-Western and opposed the excesses of Serb 'ethnic cleansing'. But as Serb pressure intensified preservation of Montenegro's integrity remained uncertain. Macedonia, with a culturally diverse population, came under particular pressure from a flood of Albanian Kosovan refugees which threatened to shatter the fragile ethnic balance maintained by the democratic government.

The Albanian Question.

The situation for Albania was more ambiguous. Though clearly suffering from an influx of refugees, the country now enjoyed unquestioned Western support and—should Kosovo be detached from Serbia—the possibility of an eventual enlargement into a Greater Albania or, at the very least, increased Western interest and aid. But a short-term resolution of the Kosovan question could lead to wider ethnic demands which would threaten the stability of Greece, Croatia, Bulgaria, Bosnia and Romania.

Alienation of Russia.

Russia—a longstanding supporter of Serbia—remained central to any hope of peace. The Western powers humiliated Russia by opening the bombing campaign without consultation. Unwilling to countenance NATO ground action and under nationalist pressure, there were threats from the Kremlin of a wider European conflict. But Russia would have to play an essential role in any settlement with Serbia and was a factor that NATO could not afford to neglect. Indeed, one suggestion for a peacekeeping division of Kosovo acceptable to all sides involved Russian troops in the Serb areas and NATO troops in the Albanian areas.

Whatever the immediate outcome—a compromise settlement as outlined by the Group of 8 meeting in May or an occupation of Kosovo following success in the bombing campaign—the West had made a commitment to a long-term involvement in Balkan affairs. An unsatisfactory compromise would represent not the end of the story but a new and possibly even more problematic beginning. Meanwhile the diplomatic dangers of the Balkan War were highlighted in May with the missile attack on the Chinese embassy in Belgrade.

POLITICAL COMPENDIUM

This compendium provides a compact reference work of key facts and figures for an understanding of modern British politics. It is fully revised each year to take account of the latest political events. Readers will also find that the preceding section, *Background to World Affairs*, provides a detailed record of the Labour Government up to the elections of May 1999 for the Scottish Parliament and Welsh Assembly.

TABLE OF CONTENTS

POLITICAL COMPENDIUM

A. THE MONARCHY

The Queen is a constitutional monarch. In law she is the head of the executive, an integral part of the legislature, head of the judiciary, commander-in-chief of the armed forces and temporal head of the Church of England. In practice, the Queen's role is purely formal; she reigns, but she does not rule. In all important respects she acts only on the advice of her ministers. However, she still plays an important role symbolically as Head of State and Head of the Commonwealth.

Monarchs since 1900

1837–1901	Victoria
1901–1910	Edward VII
1910–1936	George V
1936	Edward VIII
1936–1952	George VI
1952	Elizabeth II

B. GENERAL ELECTIONS

For electoral purposes the United Kingdom is divided into 659 constituencies (651 before the 1997 General Election) each returning one MP to the House of Commons. All British subjects and citizens of the Irish Republic are entitled to vote provided they are 18 years old and over and are included on the electoral register which is compiled annually. The only exceptions are members of the House of Lords and those incapacitated through insanity or imprisonment. Anyone who is entitled to vote and aged at least 21 may stand as a candidate, the only exceptions being undischarged bankrupts, clergymen in the established church and the holders of certain other public offices. All candidates have to pay a deposit of £500, which is forfeited unless they receive 5% of the votes cast. In each constituency the winning candidate has (under the present voting system) only to obtain a simple majority.

General Elections, 1918–97

VOTES CAST (thousands)

	Conservative	Labour	Liberal*	Communist	Plaid Cymru	SNP	Others
1918	4,166	2,546	2,753	—	—	—	1,296
1922	5,500	4,241	4,189	34	—	—	462
1923	5,538	4,438	4,311	39	—	—	260
1924	8,039	5,489	2,928	55	—	—	126
1929	8,656	8,390	5,309	51	1	—	243
1931	12,320	6,991	1,509	75	2	21	293
1935	11,810	8,465	1,422	27	3	30	273
1945	9,988	11,995	2,248	103	16	31	752
1950	12,503	13,267	2,622	92	18	10	290
1951	13,745	13,949	731	22	11	7	177
1955	13,312	12,405	722	33	45	12	313
1959	13,750	12,216	1,639	31	78	22	125
1964	12,023	12,206	3,093	46	70	64	168
1966	11,418	13,095	2,328	62	61	128	171
1970	13,145	12,198	2,117	38	175	307	384
1974 (Feb.)	11,910	11,646	6,059	33	171	632	958
1974 (Oct.)	10,501	11,457	5,347	17	166	840	897
1979	13,698	11,532	4,314	17	133	504	1,024
1983	12,991	8,437	7,775	12	125	331	952
1987	13,761	10,030	7,340	6	124	417	859
1992	14,092	11,563	6,003	–	154	630	1,178
1997	9,590	13,550	5,240	–	160	620	2,440

* 1983 and 1987 figures for Liberals include the SDP total. Recent figures are for Lib Dems.

The Speaker has been regarded as a candidate of the party he represented before appointment.

SEATS WON

	Conservative	Labour	Liberal*	Communist	Plaid Cymru	SNP	Others (GB)	Others (NI)	Total
1918	383	73	161	0	0	0	9	81	707
1922	344	142	115	1	0	0	10	3	615
1923	258	191	158	0	0	0	5	3	615
1924	412	151	40	1	0	0	10	1	615
1929	260	287	59	0	0	0	6	3	615
1931	521	52	37	0	0	0	3	2	615
1935	429	154	21	1	0	0	8	2	615
1945	213	393	12	2	0	0	16	4	640
1950	299	315	9	0	0	0	0	2	625
1951	321	295	6	0	0	0	0	3	625
1955	345	277	6	0	0	0	0	2	630
1959	365	258	6	0	0	0	1	0	630
1964	304	317	9	0	0	0	0	0	630
1966	253	364	12	0	0	0	0	1	630
1970	330	288	6	0	0	1	1	4	630
1974 (Feb.)	297	301	14	0	2	7	2	12	635
1974 (Oct.)	277	319	13	0	3	11	0	12	635
1979	339	269	11	0	2	2	0	12	635
1983	397	209	23	0	2	2	0	17	650
1987	376	229	22	0	3	3	0	17	650
1992	336	271	20	0	4	3	0	17	651
1997	165	419	46	0	4	6	1	18	659

Others (NI): Ireland in 1918, Northern Ireland only 1922–79. Ulster Unionists regarded as Conservatives 1922–70.

The Speaker has been regarded as an MP of the party he or she represented before appointment.

* 1983 and 1987 figures for Liberals include SDP MPs. Since 1992 figures are for the Liberal Democrats.

By-Elections 1945–May 1999

Parliament	Government	No. of By-elections	Changes	Con. +	Con. -	Lab. +	Lab. -	Lib./All.* +	Lib./All.* -	Others +	Others -
1945–50	Lab.	52	3	3	—	—	—	—	—	—	3
1950–51	Lab.	16	0	—	—	—	—	—	—	—	—
1951–55	Con.	48	1	1	—	—	1	—	—	—	—
1955–59	Con.	52	6	1	4	4	—	1	1	—	1
1959–64	Con.	62	9	2	7	6	2	1	—	—	—
1964–66	Lab.	13	2	1	1	—	1	1	—	—	—
1966–70	Lab.	38	16	12	1	—	15	1	—	3	—
1970–74	Con.	30	8	—	5	1	3	5	—	2	—
1974	Lab.	1	0	—	—	—	—	—	—	—	—
1974–79	Lab.	30	7	6	—	—	7	1	—	—	—
1979–83	Con.	20	6	1	4	1	1	4	1	—	—
1983–87	Con.	31†	6	—	—	—	4	4	—	1	1
1987–92	Con.	24	8	—	—	—	7	4	—	1	—
1992–97	Con.	18	9	—	—	—	8	3	—	2	1
1997–	Lab.	4	0	—	—	—	—	—	—	—	—

* Liberal 1945–79; Alliance (Liberal and SDP) 1979–89, Liberal Democrat after 1990.
† Includes 15 by-elections held in Northern Ireland in January 1986 following Unionist resignations in protest at Anglo-Irish Agreement.

Composition of the House of Commons (May 1999)

Labour, 417; Conservative, 165; Liberal Democrat, 46; Ulster Unionist, 10; SNP, 6; Plaid Cymru, 4; Social Democrat Labour Party, 3; Sinn Fein, 2; Democratic Unionist Party, 2; United Kingdom Unionist Party 1; Independent, 1; the Speaker, 1; Vacant (Leeds Central).

As yet (May 1999) no seats have changed hands at by-elections.

General elections must be held every five years, but may occur more frequently either because no government can command a majority in the House of Commons or at the request of the Prime Minister. If a seat falls vacant between general elections a by-election is, held on a date usually chosen by the party which previously held the seat. Elections are generally held on Thursdays.

Electoral Reform

The Labour Government elected in May 1997 appointed a Commission on Voting Systems (chaired by Lord Jenkins) to examine changes to the electoral system. The recommendations of the Jenkins Commission, and the changes to the voting system already implemented for the European elections, and for the Scottish Parliament and Welsh Assembly, are discussed on **D21–2**.

TURNOUT AND PARTY SHARE OF VOTES CAST

Turnout (%)		Share of Poll (%)		
		Conservative	Labour	Liberal
1918	59	39	24	26
1922	71	38	30	29
1923	71	38	31	30
1924	77	48	33	18
1929	76	38	37	23
1931	76	59	32	7
1935	71	54	39	6
1945	.73	40	48	9
1950	.84	44	46	9
1951	83	48	49	3
1955	77	50	46	3
1959	79	49	44	6
1964	77	43	44	11
1966	76	42	48	9
1970	72	46	43	8
1974 (Feb.)	78	38	37	19
1974 (Oct.)	73	36	39	18
1979	76	44	37	14
1983	73	42	28	26*
1987	75	42	31	23*
1992	78	42	34	18**
1997	73	31	43	17

* includes SDP figures.
** Liberal Democrats

C. POLITICAL PARTIES

For their background, see Conservatism (**J12**), Liberalism (**J29**) and Socialism (**J48**).

Party Leaders

The Conservative Party leader is elected by the members of its parliamentary party. In 1993, Labour adopted a new democratic system for electing future leaders. This system was used to elect Tony Blair in 1994 after the death of John Smith. The Social and Liberal Democrat leader is elected by party members nationally. Changes to the method of electing a Conservative leader were proposed after the 1997 defeat.

Leaders (as at May 1999)

Labour	Mr Tony Blair
Conservative	Mr William Hague
Liberal Democrat	Mr Paddy Ashdown*
Plaid Cymru	Mr Ieuann Wyn Jones
SNP	Mrs Margaret Ewing
Ulster Unionist	Mr David Trimble

*Retired as party leader, summer 1999.

Conservative Party Leaders since 1900

1900–2	Marquis of Salisbury
1902–11	A Balfour
1911–21	A Bonar Law
1921–22	A Chamberlain
1922–23	A Bonar Law
1923–37	S Baldwin
1937–40	N Chamberlain
1940–55	(Sir) W Churchill
1955–57	Sir A Eden
1957–63	H Macmillan
1963–65	Sir A Douglas-Home
1965–75	(Sir) E Heath
1975–90	Mrs M Thatcher
1990–97	J Major
1997–	W Hague

Labour Party Leaders

1906–8	J K Hardie
1908–10	A Henderson
1910–11	G Barnes
1911–14	J R MacDonald
1914–17	A Henderson
1917–21	W Adamson
1921–22	J Clynes

1922–31	J R MacDonald
1931–32	A Henderson
1932–35	G Lansbury
1935–55	C Attlee
1955–63	H Gaitskell
1963–76	H Wilson
1976–80	J Callaghan
1980–83	M Foot
1983–92	N Kinnock
1992–94	J Smith
1994–	A Blair

Liberal Party Leaders

1900–8	Sir H Campbell-Bannerman
1908–26	H Asquith
1926–31	D Lloyd George
1931–35	Sir H Samuel
1935–45	Sir A Sinclair
1945–56	C Davies
1956–67	J Grimond
1967–76	J Thorpe
1976–88	D Steel

Social and Liberal Democratic Party Leader

1988–99	P Ashdown

Party Officers

Conservative Party

Chairman of the Party Organisation
(appointed by the Leader of the Party)

1959–61	R Butler
1961–63	I Macleod
1963	I Macleod
	Lord Poole
1963–65	Viscount Blakenham
1965–67	E du Cann
1967–70	A Barber
1970–72	P Thomas
1972–74	Lord Carrington
1974–75	W Whitelaw
1975–81	Lord Thorneycroft
1981–83	C Parkinson
1983–85	J Selwyn Gummer
1985–87	N Tebbit
1987–89	P Brooke
1989–90	K Baker
1990–92	C Patten
1992–94	Sir N Fowler
1994–95	J Hanley
1995–97	Dr B Mawhinney
1997–98	Lord Parkinson
1998–	M Ancram

Chairman of Conservative (Private) Members'
Committee (or the 1922 Committee)

1955–64	J Morrison
1964–66	Sir W Anstruther-Gray
1966–70	Sir A Harvey
1970–72	Sir H Legge-Bourke
1972–84	E du Cann
1984–92	Sir C Onslow
1992–97	Sir M Fox
1997–	Sir A Hamilton

Labour Party

General Secretary

1944–62	M Phillips
1962–68	A Williams
1968–72	Sir H Nicholas
1972–82	R Hayward
1982–85	J Mortimer
1985–94	L Whitty
1994–98	T Sawyer
1998–	Ms M McDonagh

Chairman of the Parliamentary Labour Party

1970–74	D Houghton
1974	I Mikardo
1974–79	C Hughes
1979–81	F Willey
1981–87	J Dormand
1988–92	S Orme
1992–97	D Hoyle
1997–	C Soley

Social and Liberal Democratic Party

President
(election by Party members)

1988–90	I Wrigglesworth
1990–94	C Kennedy
1994–98	R Maclennan
1998–	Baroness Maddock

Plaid Cymru—Chief Executive: K Davies

Scottish National Party—Chief Executive: M Russell

D. PARLIAMENT

Parliament consists of the Queen, the House of Lords and the House of Commons. Over the centuries the balance between the three parts of the legislature has changed such that the Queen's role is now only formal and the House of Commons has established paramountcy over the House of Lords. Because of the party system the initiative in government lies not in Parliament but in the Cabinet. But Parliament, and especially the Commons, has important functions to play not only as the assembly to which the government is ultimately responsible but also in legitimising legislation, voting money and in acting as a body in which complaints may be raised.

House of Lords

Composition. The House of Lords comprised *c.* 1,240 peers in early 1999. These consisted of 26 bishops and archbishops, 10 Lords of Appeal, over 400 Life Peers and more than 760 hereditary peers. No new hereditary peers were created between 1964 and 1983. Since then, there have been 3: Viscounts Tonypandy (George Thomas) and Whitelaw, and the Earl of Stockton (Harold Macmillan who died in December 1986). Less than 300 peers attend more than one-third of the Lords' proceedings, although 621 peers voted in the debate over Maastricht. Figures of party strengths in the Lords are not easy to obtain, but one source identified 476 Conservatives, 176 Labour and 70 Social and Liberal Democrats in early 1999. The current Labour Government has introduced plans for major reform of the House of Lords, including legislation to strip hereditary peers of their voting rights. *See* **D21–2**.

Functions.

(1) Legislation. Some bills on subjects which are not matters of partisan controversy are initiated in the Lords. It also examines in detail many bills which originated in the Commons, but its part is limited by the Parliament Acts, under which it cannot require the Commons to agree to amendments nor delay a bill indefinitely.

(2) Debate. The Lords provides a forum for men and women, distinguished in most fields of national life, to discuss issues of importance free from the reins of party discipline.

(3) Court of appeal. The Lords is the highest court of appeal. Only the law lords take part in its legal proceedings.

House of Commons

Composition. The size of the House of Commons is gradually increasing. At the last election (held in May 1997) there were 659 MPs elected to represent single-member constituencies (529 in England, 72 in Scotland, 40 in Wales and 18 in Northern Ireland). Its proceedings are presided over by the Speaker, who is elected by MPs, at the beginning of each session. The present (May 1999) Speaker, Miss Betty Boothroyd (the first woman Speaker) was elected to the office in 1992.

MPs sit on parallel rows of seats, known as benches, with those who support the government on one side of the chamber and the rest on the other side. Members of the government and the spokesmen of the Opposition are known as "frontbenchers"; other MPs are "backbenchers".

Functions.

(1) Legislation. There are two types of legislation—*public acts*, most of which are introduced by

the government, but which can also be introduced by individual MPs, and *private acts*, which confer special powers on bodies such as local authorities in excess of the general law and which are subject to special procedures.

All public legislation must pass through the following stages before becoming law:

First Reading. The bill is formally introduced.

Second Reading. The general principles of the bill are debated and voted.

Committee Stage. Each clause of the bill is debated and voted.

Report Stage. The bill is considered as it was reported by the committee, and it is decided whether to make further changes in individual clauses.

Third Reading. The bill, as amended, is debated and a final vote taken.

The Other House. The bill has to pass through the same stages in the other House of Parliament.

Royal Assent. The Queen gives her assent to the bill which becomes law as an Act of Parliament.

(2) Scrutiny of government activities. There are a number of opportunities for the opposition and the government's own back-benchers to criticise government policy. They can question ministers on the floor of the House; they can table motions for debate and speak in debates initiated by the government; and they can take part in one of the select committees set up to scrutinise government activity.

Committees. The House of Commons uses committees to assist it in its work in various ways. They are of two types:

Standing Committees. A standing committee is a miniature of the House itself, reflecting its party composition, and consists of between 20 and 50 MPs. Its function is to examine the Committee Stage of legislation. Usually seven or eight such committees are needed.

Select Committees. A select committee is a body with special powers and privileges to which the House has delegated its authority for the purpose of discovering information, examining witnesses, sifting evidence and drawing up conclusions which are then reported to the House. A few select committees are established *ad hoc*, but the majority are semi-permanent.

E. HER MAJESTY'S GOVERNMENT
The Labour Cabinet (as at May 1999)

Prime Minister, First Lord of the Treasury and Minister for the Civil Service	Mr Tony Blair
Deputy Prime Minister and Secretary of State for the Environment, Transport and the Regions	Mr John Prescott
Chancellor of the Exchequer	Mr Gordon Brown
Secretary of State for Foreign and Commonwealth Affairs	Mr Robin Cook
Lord Chancellor	Lord Irvine of Lairg
Secretary of State for the Home Department	Mr Jack Straw
Secretary of State for Education and Employment	Mr David Blunkett
Secretary of State for Trade and Industry	Mr Stephen Byers
President of the Council and Leader of the House of Commons	Ms Margaret Beckett
Secretary of State for Scotland	Mr Donald Dewar
Secretary of State for Defence	Mr George Robertson
Secretary of State for Health	Mr Frank Dobson
Secretary of State for Social Security	Mr Alistair Darling
Secretary of State for Culture, Media and Sport	Mr Chris Smith
Secretary of State for Northern Ireland	Ms Marjorie Mowlam
Secretary of State for Wales	Mr Alun Michael
Secretary of State for International Development	Ms Clare Short
Minister of Agriculture, Fisheries and Food	Mr Nick Brown
Leader of the House of Lords and Minister for Women	Baroness Jay
Chancellor of the Duchy of Lancaster and Minister for the Cabinet Office	Mr Jack Cunningham
Chief Secretary to the Treasury	Mr Alan Milburn
Chief Whip	Ms Ann Taylor

Ministers not in the Cabinet

(this list excludes some more junior appointments and the legal officers)

Agriculture, Fisheries and Food, Minister of State	Mr Jeffrey Rooker
Cabinet Office, Minister of State without Portfolio	Lord Falconer
Defence, Ministers of State	Mr Doug Henderson
	Lord Gilbert
Education and Employment, Ministers of State	Mr Andrew Smith
	Ms Estelle Morris
Minister for Higher Education	Baroness Blackstone
Environment and Transport, Ministers of State	Mr Richard Caborn
	Ms Hilary Armstrong
	Mr Michael Meacher
Foreign and Commonwealth Office, Ministers of State	Mr Derek Fatchett*
	Mr Tony Lloyd
Minister for Europe	Ms Joyce Quin
Health, Ministers of State	Ms Tessa Jowell
	Mr John Denham
Home Office, Ministers of State	Mr Paul Boateng
	Lord Williams of Mostyn
Northern Ireland Office, Ministers of State	Mr Paul Murphy
	Mr Adam Ingram
Scottish Office, Ministers of State	Mr Henry McLeish
	Ms Helen Liddell
Social Security, Minister of State	Mr John Murphy
Trade and Industry, Ministers of State	Mr Brian Wilson
	Mr Ian McCartney
	Mr John Battle
Minister for Trade and Competitiveness in Europe	Lord Simon
Transport, Minister for	Mr John Reid
Treasury, Financial Secretary	Ms Barbara Roche
Paymaster General	Ms Dawn Primarolo
Economic Secretary	Ms Patricia Hewitt

*The death of Derek Fatchett on 9 May 1999 left a vacancy at the Foreign Office.

Principal Ministers 1900–1945

	Prime Minister	Chancellor of the Exchequer	Foreign Secretary	Home Secretary	Leader of the House of Commons
1900–2	Marquis of Salisbury	Sir M Hicks-Beach	Marquis of Salisbury Marquis of Lansdowne	Sir M White-Ridley C Ritchie	A Balfour
1902–5	A Balfour	C Ritchie A Chamberlain	Marquis of Lansdowne	A Akers-Douglas	A Balfour
1905–8	Sir H Campbell-Bannerman	H Asquith	Sir E Grey	H Gladstone	Sir H Campbell-Bannerman
1908–16	H Asquith	D Lloyd George R McKenna	Sir E Grey	H Gladstone W Churchill R McKenna Sir J Simon Sir H Samuel	H Asquith
1916–22	D Lloyd George	A Bonar Law A Chamberlain Sir R Horne	A Balfour Earl Curzon	Sir G Cave E Shortt	A Bonar Law A Chamberlain
1922–23	A Bonar Law	S Baldwin	Earl Curzon	W Bridgeman	A Bonar Law
1923–24	S Baldwin	S Baldwin N Chamberlain	Earl Curzon	W Bridgeman	S Baldwin
1924	J R MacDonald	P Snowden	J R MacDonald	A Henderson	J R MacDonald
1924–29	S Baldwin	W Churchill	(Sir) A Chamberlain	Sir W Joynson-Hicks	S Baldwin
1929–35	J R MacDonald	P Snowden N Chamberlain	A Henderson Marquis of Reading Sir J Simon	J Clynes Sir H Samuel Sir J Gilmour	J R MacDonald
1935–37	S Baldwin	N Chamberlain	Sir S Hoare A Eden	Sir J Simon	S Baldwin
1937–40	N Chamberlain	Sir J Simon	A Eden Viscount Halifax	Sir S Hoare Sir J Anderson	N Chamberlain
1940–45	W Churchill	Sir K Wood Sir J Anderson	Viscount Halifax A Eden	H Morrison Sir D Somervell	C Attlee * Sir S Cripps A Eden

* Churchill deputed day to day business to Attlee.

Principal Ministers 1945– May 1999

	Prime Minister	Chancellor of the Exchequer	Foreign Secretary	Home Secretary	Leader of the House of Commons
1945–51	C Attlee	H Dalton Sir S Cripps H Gaitskell	E Bevin H Morrison	C Ede	H Morrison C Ede
1951–55	Sir W Churchill	R Butler	Sir A Eden	Sir D Maxwell-Fyfe G Lloyd George	H Crookshank
1955–57	Sir A Eden	R Butler H Macmillan	H Macmillan S Lloyd	G Lloyd George	R Butler
1957–63	H Macmillan	P Thorneycroft D Heathcoat Amory S Lloyd R Maudling	S Lloyd Earl of Home	R Butler H Brooke	R Butler I Macleod
1963–64	Sir A Douglas-Home	R Maudling	R Butler	H Brooke	S Lloyd
1964–70	H Wilson	J Callaghan R Jenkins	P Gordon Walker M Stewart G Brown M Stewart	Sir F Soskice R Jenkins J Callaghan	H Bowden R Crossman F Peart
1970–74	E Heath	I Macleod A Barber	Sir A Douglas-Home	R Maudling R Carr	W Whitelaw R Carr J Prior
1974–76	H Wilson	D Healey	J Callaghan	R Jenkins	E Short
1976–79	J Callaghan	D Healey	A Crosland D Owen	R Jenkins M Rees	M Foot
1979–90	Mrs M Thatcher	Sir G Howe N Lawson J Major	Lord Carrington F Pym Sir G Howe J Major D Hurd	W Whitelaw L Brittan D Hurd D Waddington	N St John-Stevas F Pym J Biffen J Wakeham Sir G Howe J MacGregor
1990–97	J Major	N Lamont K Clarke	D Hurd M Rifkind	K Baker K Clarke M Howard	J MacGregor A Newton
1997–	A Blair	G Brown	R Cook	J Straw	A Taylor M Beckett

Since 1979, there have been 13 or 14 select committees, each one scrutinising the work of one or two government departments (e.g. Agriculture, Foreign Affairs, Treasury and Civil Service); and various others including the following: European Legislation, Members' Interests, Parliamentary Commissioner for Administration, Privileges, Public Accounts, and Statutory Instruments.

Central Government

The executive work of central government is performed by the Prime Minister and the other ministers of the Crown. The power of executive action is not given to a government department as a corporate body but to the minister individually, who is responsible for the exercise of his duties legally to the Queen and politically to Parliament. For this reason, all ministers must be members of either the Commons or the Lords.

At the head of the government structure is the Cabinet, which consists of the leading members of the majority party in the Commons, selected by the Prime Minister. Most Cabinet ministers are the heads of government departments, which are staffed by civil servants, but there are usually some without departmental responsibilities. Although legally ministers are individually responsible for the exercise of government powers, politically it is accepted that the Cabinet is collectively responsible for government policy. It thus acts as one man, and a minister who disagrees with the Cabinet must either resign or remain silent.

Size of the Government since 1945

	Cabinet Ministers	Non-Cabinet Ministers	Junior Ministers	Total
1945	20	20	49	89
1950	18	22	44	84
1960	20	23	45	88
1965	23	33	55	111
1970	17	26	41	84
1975	24	31	54	109
1993	22	28	46	96

F. HER MAJESTY'S OPPOSITION

The leader of the largest party opposed to the government is designated Leader of Her Majesty's Opposition and receives an official salary. The leading spokesmen of the Opposition meet together as a committee and are generally known as the Shadow Cabinet. A Conservative Shadow Cabinet, officially known as the Leader's Consultative Committee, is selected by the leader of the party. Labour Shadow Cabinets, officially known as the Parliamentary Committee, are elected by the Parliamentary Labour Party, but the leader retains the right to invite members to take charge of particular subjects.

G. OTHER EXECUTIVE BODIES

A large number of semi-autonomous agencies have been established to carry out functions on behalf of the government, usually because a particular function is considered to be unsuitable for a normal government department. In this category are bodies such as the British Broadcasting Corporation and the Commission for Racial Equality which need to be insulated from the political process, and the former nationalised industries, most of which were managed by public corporations so as to secure managerial flexibility. Some public control over these bodies was maintained by means of various powers which ministers possessed.

H. THE CIVIL SERVICE

The civil service is the body of permanent officials who, working in the various departments, administer the policy of central government. It consists of some 490,000 people. Of these, 75% are now employed in 140 government agencies.

Over 80% of the civil service work outside Greater London, mainly in the regional and local offices of departments such as Health, Social Security, Education and Employment, Inland Revenue etc.

The political head of each department is a minister, but, as he often has no previous experience of the field to which he is appointed and his tenure of office may be fairly short-lived, great

Major Public Bodies	Chairman/Chief Executive
Arts Council	Mr Gerry Robinson
Bank of England	Mr Eddie George**
British Broadcasting Corporation	Sir Christopher Bland
Civil Aviation Authority	Sir Malcolm Field
Commission for Racial Equality	Sir Herman Ouseley
Competition Commission*	Dr Derek Morris
Council for the Protection of Rural England	Ms Kate Parminter
Equal Opportunities Commission	Ms Kamlesh Bahl
Financial Services Authority	Mr Howard Davies
Higher Education Funding Council for England	Lord Dearing
Independent Television Commission	Sir George Russell
London Transport	Mr Denis Tunnicliffe
National Consumer Council	Mr David Hatch
Post Office	Mr Neville Bain
Radio Authority	Sir Peter Gibbings
Strategic Rail Authority	Sir Alastair Morton

*Formerly the Monopolies and Mergers Commission   **Until 2003

responsibility falls on the shoulders of the permanent civil servants in his department. Civil servants remain largely anonymous and their relationship with their minister is a confidential one. They are non-political in the sense that they serve all political parties impartially.

Civil Service Numbers

	Total		Total
1970	702,000	1993	567,000
1979	732,000	1998	490,000

Senior Civil Servants

Head of the Home Civil Service

1945–56	Sir E Bridges
1956–63	Sir N Brook
1963–68	Sir L Helsby
1968–74	Sir W Armstrong
1974–78	Sir D Allen
1978–81	Sir I Bancroft
1981–83	Sir R Armstrong / Sir D Wass
1983–88	Sir R Armstrong
1988–98	Sir R Butler
1998–	Sir R Wilson

Head of the Diplomatic Service

1945–46	Sir A Cadogan
1946–49	Sir O Sargent
1949–53	Sir W Strang
1953–57	Sir I Kirkpatrick
1957–62	Sir F Hoyer Millar
1962–65	Sir H Caccia
1965–68	Sir S Garner
1968–69	Sir P Gore-Booth
1969–73	Sir D Greenhill
1973–75	Sir T Brimelow
1975–82	Sir M Palliser
1982–86	Sir A Acland
1986–91	Sir P Wright
1991–94	Sir D Gillmore
1994–97	Sir J Coles
1997–	Sir J Kerr

Permanent Secretary to the Treasury

1945–56	Sir E Bridges
1956–60	Sir N Brook / Sir R Makins
1960–62	Sir N Brook / Sir F Lee
1962–63	Sir N Brook / Sir W Armstrong
1963–68	Sir L Helsby / (Sir) W Armstrong

1968	Sir W Armstrong / Sir D Allen
1968–74	Sir D Allen
1974–83	Sir D Wass
1983–91	Sir P Middleton
1991–98	Sir T Burns
1998–	Sir N Wicks

Secretary to the Cabinet

1938–47	Sir E Bridges
1947–63	Sir N Brook
1963–73	Sir B Trend
1973–79	Sir J Hunt
1979–88	Sir R Armstrong
1988–98	Sir R Butler
1998–	Sir R Wilson

I. LOCAL GOVERNMENT

Local government in the United Kingdom is the creation of Parliament. Its structure is laid down by Parliament, and local authorities may only exercise those powers which Parliament either commands or permits them to exercise. Their functions include responsibility for all education services, except further and higher education, most personal welfare services, housing, public health, environmental planning, traffic management and transport, in each case subject to some central government control. Draft legislation in 1999 heralded a major shake-up of the running of town halls, opening up the prospect of directly-elected mayors with wide-ranging executive powers. The government was also pledged to attack corruption in local government.

The structure of local government varies in different parts of the country.

In London and the six metropolitan areas there has been, since April 1986 (when the Greater London Council and the metropolitan county councils were abolished), a single-tier system with a few special bodies undertaking county-wide functions.

A referendum on the future government of London was held on 7 May 1998 when voters decided they wanted a new Greater London Assembly and a directly elected Mayor. Londoners choose their first directly-elected Mayor on 4 May 2000.

Following the earlier review of local government proposed by the Conservative Government in 1991, many old councils have disappeared. Among authorities now abolished are Avon, Humberside and Cleveland, all created in 1974. Berkshire has become the only old shire authority to be abolished under the review.

In Wales, 22 all-purpose councils replaced the 8 counties and 37 district councils in 1996. Elections to these "shadow" councils first took place in May 1995.

In Scotland, 29 single-tier authorities replaced the existing 2-tier structure after April 1996. These new authorities were first elected in April 1996. There are single-tier island councils in Orkney, Shetland and the Western Isles.

For a summary of seats gained and lost in recent local elections, *see* **D13**. *See also* **D12** for current control of metropolitan councils.

First-tier Authorities (as at May 1999)

This list excludes Avon, Cleveland and Humberside which were abolished in April 1996. Since April 1995 the Isle of Wight has been a unitary authority, whilst Hereford and Worcester has been reorganised and Berkshire has lost its old status.

ENGLAND	Name	Political control in 1999	Number of districts	Administrative capital
Non-Metropolitan Counties	Bedfordshire	Con.	4	Bedford
	Buckinghamshire	Con.	5	Aylesbury
	Cambridgeshire	Con.	6	Cambridge
	Cheshire	Lab.	8	Chester
	Cornwall	NOM.	6	Truro
	Cumbria	Lab.	6	Carlisle
	Derbyshire	Lab.	9	Matlock
	Devon	NOM.	10	Exeter
	Dorset	NOM.	8	Dorchester
	Durham	Lab.	8	Durham
	East Sussex	NOM.	7	Lewes
	Essex	NOM.	14	Chelmsford
	Gloucestershire	NOM.	6	Gloucester
	Hampshire	Con.	13	Winchester
	Hertfordshire	NOM.	10	Hertford
	Kent	Con.	14	Maidstone
	Lancashire	Lab.	14	Preston
	Leicestershire	NOM.	9	Leicester
	Lincolnshire	Con.	7	Lincoln
	Norfolk	NOM.	7	Norwich
	Northamptonshire	Lab.	7	Northampton
	Northumberland	Lab.	6	Morpeth
	North Yorkshire	NOM.	8	Northallerton*
	Nottinghamshire	Lab.	8	Nottingham
	Oxfordshire	NOM.	5	Oxford
	Shropshire	NOM.	6	Shrewsbury
	Somerset	SLD.	5	Taunton
	Staffordshire	Lab.	9	Stafford
	Suffolk	NOM.	7	Ipswich
	Surrey	Con.	11	Kingston-on-Thames
	Warwickshire	NOM.	5	Warwick
	West Sussex	Con.	7	Chichester
	Wiltshire	NOM.	5	Trowbridge

NOM.—No overall majority.
* In North Yorkshire, the York City Council area was extended in April 1996 and the council became a unitary authority.

WALES

The following 22 new unitary authorities took up their duties on 1 April 1996.

Aberconwy and Colwyn	Merthyr Tydfil
Anglesey	Monmouthshire
Blaenau Gwent	Neath and Port Talbot
Bridgend	Newport
Caernarfonshire and Merionethshire	Pembrokeshire
Caerphilly	Powys
Cardiff	Rhondda, Cynon, Taff
Cardiganshire	Swansea
Carmarthenshire	Torfaen
Denbighshire	Vale of Glamorgan
Flintshire	Wrexham

SCOTLAND

The following 32 new unitary authorities took up their duties on 1 April 1996.

Aberdeenshire	Fife
Angus	Highland
Argyll and Bute	Inverclyde
Borders	Midlothian
City of Aberdeen	Moray
City of Dundee	North Ayrshire
City of Edinburgh	North Lanarkshire
City of Glasgow	Orkney Islands Council
Clackmannan	Perthshire and Kinross
Dumbarton and Clydebank	Renfrewshire
Dumfries and Galloway	Shetland Islands Council
East Ayrshire	South Ayrshire
East Dumbartonshire	South Lanarkshire
East Lothian	Stirling
East Renfrewshire	Western Isles Islands Council
Falkirk	West Lothian

Metropolitan Councils in England

	Name	Population	Political control (May 1999)
London	Barking & Dagenham	153,700	Lab.
	Barnet	319,400	NOM.
	Bexley	220,000	NOM.
	Brent	248,000	Lab.
	Bromley	295,600	NOM.
	Camden	189,100	Lab.
	Croydon	333,800	Lab.
	Ealing	297,000	Lab.
	Enfield	262,600	Lab.
	Greenwich	212,100	Lab.
	Hackney	193,800	NOM.
	Hammersmith and Fulham	156,000	Lab.
	Haringey	216,000	Lab.
	Harrow	210,700	Lab.
	Havering	230,900	NOM.
	Hillingdon	247,700	NOM.
	Hounslow	206,000	Lab.
	Islington	176,000	NOM.
	Kensington and Chelsea	159,000	Con.
	Kingston-on-Thames	141,800	NOM.
	Lambeth	264,700	Lab.
	Lewisham	241,500	Lab.
	Merton	182,300	Lab.
	Newham	228,900	Lab.
	Redbridge	230,600	NOM.
	Richmond-on-Thames	179,900	Lib Dem.
	Southwark	229,000	Lab.
	Sutton	175,500	Lib Dem.
	Tower Hamlets	176,600	Lab.
	Waltham Forest	220,000	Lab.
	Wandsworth	266,000	Con.
	Westminster	204,000	Con.
Greater Manchester	Bolton	265,000	Lab.
	Bury	181,000	Lab.
	Manchester	432,000	Lab.
	Oldham	221,000	Lab.
	Rochdale	207,000	Lab.
	Salford	229,000	Lab.
	Stockport	291,000	Lib Dem.
	Tameside	222,000	Lab.
	Trafford	218,000	Lab.
	Wigan	313,000	Lab.
Merseyside	Knowsley	155,000	Lab.
	Liverpool	477,000	Lib Dem.
	St. Helens	180,000	Lab.
	Sefton	294,000	NOM.
	Wirral	334,000	Lab.
South Yorkshire	Barnsley	226,000	Lab.
	Doncaster	293,000	Lab.
	Rotherham	256,000	Lab.
	Sheffield	532,000	Lib Dem.
Tyne & Wear	Gateshead	203,000	Lab.
	Newcastle-upon-Tyne	285,000	Lab.
	North Tyneside	195,000	Lab.
	South Tyneside	157,000	Lab.
	Sunderland	298,000	Lab.
West Midlands	Birmingham	1,012,000	Lab.
	Coventry	304,000	Lab.
	Dudley	312,000	Lab.
	Sandwell	294,000	Lab.
	Solihull	200,000	NOM.
	Walsall	265,000	Lab.
	Wolverhampton	246,000	Lab.
West Yorkshire	Bradford	480,000	Lab.
	Calderdale	194,000	NOM.
	Kirklees	386,000	NOM.
	Leeds	725,000	Lab.
	Wakefield	317,000	Lab.

THE SCOTTISH PARLIAMENT
AND WELSH ASSEMBLY

Voting took place on 6 May 1999 for the first elections to the new Scottish Parliament and Welsh Assembly. In both Scotland and Wales, Labour had a commanding position at the 1997 General Election (neither Scotland nor Wales had returned a single Conservative). Much attention was centred in 1999 on the performance of the Nationalists. The outcome was as follows:

SCOTTISH PARLIAMENT

Party	Seats (1)*	Seats (2)**	Total
Labour	53	3	56
SNP	7	28	35
Cons	–	18	18
Lib Dems	12	5	17
Others	1	2	3

WELSH ASSEMBLY

Party	Seats (1)*	Seats (2)**	Total
Labour	27	1	28
PC	9	8	17
Cons	1	8	9
Lib Dem	3	3	6

*(1) Constituency seats won on 'First Past the Post' system.
**(2) 'Top-up' seats won under Proportional Representation.

THE MAY 1999 LOCAL ELECTIONS

The Background.

The local elections of 6 May 1999 (held the same day as the first elections for the Scottish Parliament and Welsh Assembly) provided a major nation-wide test of the electoral popularity of the Labour Government. Labour found itself on the defensive needing to retain the record number of council seats won 4 years earlier in 1995 (when the Conservatives had lost 1,885 seats and Labour had won 42 councils). Although London was not voting, the elections were seen as a test of the relative popularity of Labour and the Conservatives (and the strength of the Liberal Democrats at grassroots level). No less than 12,000 seats across 360 councils were being contested.

The Outcome.

Although Labour lost some ground captured in 1995, the Conservative recovery was uneven. Conservatives took some seats back from the Liberal Democrats. They in turn took Sheffield from Labour and captured Stockport. The tally of councils controlled and lost was:

	Councils Controlled	Councils +/−
Labour	132	−27
Cons	61	+48
Lib Dem	20	−11
NOC	112	− 6

J. REDRESS OF GRIEVANCES

In the first instance most citizens who are aggrieved by the decision of a public body take up their complaint with the body concerned, either personally or in writing. If this does not satisfy them they have a number of options which vary according to the type of body and the nature of their complaint.

Central Government

1. *MPs.* MPs may be contacted by letter, and many of them hold regular surgeries in their constituencies. On receipt of a complaint they can write to the minister in charge of the department concerned or ask a question in Parliament. If the complainant alleges maladministration (*e.g.*, arbitrary action, undue delay) this can be referred to the *Parliamentary Commissioner for Administration* (usually known as the Ombudsman). His powers and responsibilities are set out in the Parliamentary Commissioner Act 1967. In 1994 they were extended to include complaints arising from the Code of Practice on Access to Government Information.

Parliamentary Commissioner for Administration

(and Health Service Commissioner since 1973)

1967–71	Sir Edmund Compton
1971–76	Sir Alan Marre
1976–78	Sir Idwal Pugh
1979–85	Sir Cecil Clothier
1985–90	Sir Anthony Barrowclough
1990–96	Sir William Reid
1997–	Mr Michael Buckley

Parliamentary Commissioner for Standards

(established in 1995 after the Nolan Report)

1995–98	Sir Gordon Downey
1998–	Ms Elizabeth Filkin

2. *Tribunals and inquiries.* In certain areas of government (*e.g.*, social security), special tribunals exist to adjudicate on disputes between citizens and government. In others (*e.g.*, planning) an inquiry can be set up. In both cases the machinery is less formal and more flexible than the ordinary courts.

3. *Courts of law.* On certain restricted matters (*e.g.*, that a public body has acted outside its lawful powers), citizens have recourse to ordinary courts.

Local Government

1. *Councillors.* Local councillors can be contacted in the same way as MPs. They can also refer complaints of maladministration to a *Commissioner for Local Administration* (or local Ombudsman). There are five commissioners, three in England and one each in Scotland and Wales, each investigating complaints in a particular part of the country.
2. *Tribunals and inquiries* (as above).
3. *Courts of law* (as above).

Other Bodies

1. *National Health Service.* Each health authority has its own complaints procedure subject to a national code of practice. Complaints, other than those involving the exercise of clinical judgement, may be taken to the *Health Service Commissioner*. Special procedures exist for complaints against doctors.

2. *Privatised Industries.* In former nationalised industries, independent regulatory bodies have been created. Some of these are listed below.

Office of Gas Supply (OFGAS)

Mr C McCarthy

Office of the Rail Regulator

Mr John Swift

Office for Standards in Education (OFSTED)

Mr Chris Woodhead

Office of Telecommunications (OFTEL)

Mr D Edmonds (Director-General)

Office of Water Services

Mr I C R Byatt (Director-General)

Office of Electricity Regulation
Professor S Littlechild (Director-General)

Office of Fair Trading
Mr John Bridgeman

K. PRESSURE GROUPS

Large numbers of groups exist to exert pressure on government by direct consultation with ministers and civil servants, lobbying Parliament and general publicity campaigns. Some exist to defend interests such as labour, business or consumers; others promote particular causes such as the prevention of cruelty to children or the banning of blood sports. Of great importance in contemporary politics are the groups representing labour and business.

Trade Unions

In 1979, 57% of workers belonged to a trade union. Now (1999) only about 30% (some 6·8 million) are members of a trade union or staff association. For a further discussion of the role of trade unions, see **Section G Part I**.

Among the largest unions are:

UNISON *
Transport and General Workers' Union
Amalgamated Electrical and Engineering Union
General, Municipal, Boilermakers' and Allied
   Trades Union
Manufacturing, Science, Finance Union
Union of Shop, Distributive and Allied Workers

* Formed in 1993 by the merger of NALGO, NUPE and COHSE.

The following unions have over 500,000 members.

Union	Principal Officer	Members
UNISON	R Bickerstaffe	1,400,000
TGWU	W Morris	897,000
GMB	J Edmonds	740,000
AEEU	P Gallagher	726,000

The major unions, representing over 80% of total union membership, are affiliated to the *Trades Union Congress*, which is the federal body of the trade union movement, representing its views to government and others, and giving assistance on questions relating to particular industries.

TUC General Secretaries since 1946

1946–60	(Sir) V Tewson
1960–70	G Woodcock
1970–74	V Feather
1974–84	L Murray
1984–93	N Willis
1993–	J Monks

Business

The peak organisation representing British business is the *Confederation of British Industry*, formed in 1965. Its members now comprise over 11,000 individual enterprises and over 200 representative organisations (employers' organisations, trade associations *etc.*).

Director-Generals of the CBI

1965–69	J Davies
1969–76	(Sir) C Adamson
1976–80	(Sir) J Methven
1980–87	(Sir) T Beckett
1987–92	(Sir) J Banham
1992–95	H Davies
1995–	J Adair Turner

Business is also represented by large numbers of associations which promote the interests of individual industries and sectors.

L. THE MEDIA

1. Principal Newspapers

The British are more committed to the reading of newspapers than any other country in Europe. Some 66% of the population read a national daily regularly. However, in the last few years this figure has been gradually declining, as the press faces increasing competition from the Internet, as well as television. For recent circulation figures of individual papers, see **D15**.

Ownership

The largest grouping is News International with 35% of the UK newspaper market. Owned by Rupert Murdoch it possesses *The Sun, The Times*, the *Sunday Times*, and the *News of the World*. It also owns 40% of BSkyB, as well as extensive interests in the US and Australia. The Mirror Group has 26% from *The Mirror*, the *Sunday Mirror*, the *People* and the *Daily Record* (published in Scotland). It has recently sold its interest in the company that runs *The Independent* and *Independent on Sunday*. United News and Media has 13% from *The Express, Express on Sunday*, and *Daily Star*. It also owns over 80 local newspapers. Associated Newspapers (12%) owns the *Daily Mail, Mail on Sunday*, and large regional holdings, including the *Evening Standard* in London. Smaller holdings are the Telegraph (7% from the *Daily Telegraph* and *Sunday Telegraph*); the Guardian (3% from *The Guardian, The Observer* and local newspapers); and Pearson (1% from the *Financial Times*).

2. Broadcasting

British Broadcasting Corporation

Established in 1926 as a public service body and financed by licence fees paid by all owners of TV sets. It is directed by a board of governors appointed by the government.

    Services: Radio—5 national networks; 36 local radio stations. TV—2 channels.

    Chairman of the Board of Governors, 1996–
    Sir Christopher Bland

    Director-General, 1993–*   Sir John Birt

* until April 2000

Independent Television Commission

Established in 1991, as successor to Independent Broadcasting Authority to license programme contracting companies and to regulate their output. Independent broadcasting is financed by advertising revenue.

    Services:—One channel, operated by 15 regional companies, and a second (Channel 4) run by two organisations (one for England and Scotland, the other for Wales). A common news service is provided for all the companies by Independent Television News Ltd.

    Chairman, 1991–   Sir George Russell

Radio Authority

In 1991 it inherited the Independent Broadcasting Authority's responsibilities for radio.

    Chairman, 1995–   Sir Peter Gibbings

Editorially all broadcasting authorities are expected to show political balance.

Broadcasting Standards Commission – formed in 1997 from a merger of the old Broadcasting Standards Council and the Broadcasting Complaints Commission. Its future is currently (1999) uncertain.

Paper	Proprietors	Circulation 1998/99 (millions)	General political stance
National Dailies			
The Express	United News & Media	1·1	Right
Daily Mail	Associated Newspapers	2·3	Right
The Mirror	Mirror Group	2·3	Left
Daily Star	United News & Media	0·6	Right
Daily Telegraph	The Telegraph plc	1·1	Right
Financial Times	Pearson	0·3	Right
Guardian	Guardian Media Group	0·4	Centre
Independent	Independent Newspapers	0·2	Ind.
Sun	News International	3·8	Right
The Times	News International	0·7	Right
*National Sundays**			
Independent on Sunday	Independent Newspapers	0·3	Ind.
Mail on Sunday	Associated Newspapers	2·2	Right
News of the World	News International	4·3	Right
Observer	Guardian Media Group	0·4	Centre
Express on Sunday	United News & Media	1·1	Right
Sunday Mirror	Mirror Group	2·0	Left
Sunday People	Mirror Group	1·8	Left
Sunday Telegraph	The Telegraph plc	0·8	Right
Sunday Times	News International	1·3	Right

*A new Scottish newspaper, the *Sunday Herald*, was launched in February 1999.

M. SCOTLAND, WALES AND NORTHERN IRELAND

The structure of government in Scotland, Wales and Northern Ireland differs from that in England.

Scotland

Most central government functions here have been the responsibility of a single department, the Scottish Office, based in Edinburgh and represented in the Cabinet by the Secretary of State for Scotland. On many matters special Scottish legislation is enacted by Parliament and administrative structure (*e.g.* the local government system) and practice (*e.g.* the educational system) differ from that in England.

The Labour Government elected in May 1997 has established a 129-member Scottish Parliament (following a 'Yes' vote on the issue on 11 September). Of those voting 74·3 % voted in favour of a Scottish Parliament while 63·5 % backed tax raising powers.

The Parliament, elected on 6 May 1999, has devolved powers over such areas as education, health, law and local government. Foreign, defence, security and constitutional issues will remain at Westminster. The Scottish Parliament is able to increase or decrease tax by 3p. Some of the MPs were elected from a party list (*see also* D13).

Wales

The Welsh Office, based in Cardiff and represented in the Cabinet by the Secretary of State for Wales, performs many central government functions in Wales but its responsibilities are narrower than its Scottish counterpart. In other respects too government in Wales resembles more closely that in England.

The Labour Government elected in May 1997 created a Welsh Assembly, following a very close referendum vote in favour. Of the 22 voting areas, 11 voted in favour, 11 voted against in the referendum on 18 September 1997 (the final figures were 'Yes', 559,419; 'No', 552,698; majority, 6,721). On a turnout of 50·1 %, 50·3 % had voted in favour. A massive 'yes' vote in Carmarthenshire decided the outcome. For details of the new Assembly, *See* D21.

Northern Ireland

From 1921 until 1972 Northern Ireland was governed under the scheme of devolution embodied in the Government of Northern Ireland Act 1920. This created the Northern Ireland Parliament, generally known as Stormont after its eventual location. Executive powers were formally vested in the Governor of Northern Ireland, but were in effect performed by a Prime Minister and small cabinet, responsible to Stormont.

The onset of troubles in the province led the UK Government in 1972 to suspend the Government of Northern Ireland Act. Since then, apart from a period of four months in 1974, Northern Ireland has been ruled direct from Westminster, the powers of government being vested in the Secretary of State for Northern Ireland. Most local government functions in the province are performed either by the Secretary of State or by special boards. There are, however, 26 elected district councils with limited functions, mainly in the environmental field. Under the terms of the Anglo-Irish agreement, signed in November 1985, the Republic of Ireland has been granted consultative status on certain issues. Following the Downing Street Declaration, extensive consultations took place on a framework document for the future government structure in Northern Ireland. For details of the 1998 peace proposals, *see* D22.

N. BRITAIN IN EUROPE

Since joining the European Economic Community (now the European Union) in 1973, the United Kingdom has participated in the principal institutions of the European Union as follows:

Council of Ministers and Commission

The Council of Ministers is the main decision-making body within the Union, consisting of representatives of the 15 member states (12 before 1995), each government delegating one of its ministers according to the business under discussion. The principal UK delegate is the Secretary of State for Foreign and Commonwealth Affairs.

The Commission heads a large bureaucracy in Brussels which submits proposals to the Council of Ministers, implements its decisions, and has powers of its own to promote the Community's interests. Its members are appointed by agreement among the member states for 4-year renewable terms. Members are pledged to independence of national interests.

President of the Commission (1999): Romano Prodi (Italy)

UK Commissioners (1999):
Sir Leon Brittan
Mr Neil Kinnock

Former Presidents of the Commission

1958–66	Walter Hallstein (West Germany)
1966–70	Jean Rey (Belgium)
1970–72	Franco Malfatti (Italy)
1972–73	Sicco Mansholt (Netherlands)
1973–77	Francois-Xavier Ortoli (France)
1977–81	Roy Jenkins (UK)
1981–85	Gaston Thorn (Luxembourg)
1985–95	Jacques Delors (France)
1995–99	Jacques Santer (Luxembourg)

European Parliament

Apart from general powers of supervision and consultation, the Parliament, which meets in Luxembourg and Strasbourg, can dismiss the Commission and has some control over the Community Budget. Until 1979 it consisted of members nominated by the national parliaments of the member states. The first direct elections were held in June 1979, the second in June 1984, and the third in June 1989. The fourth elections were held in June 1994, when Britain elected 87 MEPs, 6 more than in 1989. Five extra seats were given to England and one to Wales.

For the elections in June 1999 the European Parliament constituencies, which used to elect one member, were replaced by large multi-member constituencies (or regions). London, for example, became one constituency instead of the former ten. Electors voted not for an individual candidate but for a party list of candidates. These elections represented the first time proportional representation had been used nationwide.

UK Seats Won, 1979-94

	1979	1984	1989	1994
Conservative	60	45	32	18
Labour	17	32	45	62
Liberals (Lib Dems)	0	0	0	2
Scottish Nationalist	1	1	1	2
Democratic Unionist	1	1	1	1
Official Unionist	1	1	1	1
Social Democratic and Labour	1	1	1	1

UK Party Leaders:

Conservative	Mr Edward McMillan-Scott
Labour	Mr Alan Donnelly

European Court of Justice

The European Court is responsible for interpreting and applying the Community treaties. Its decisions are binding in the member countries. It consists of thirteen judges and six advocates-general, appointed by the member governments.

O. BRITAIN AND THE UN

Britain was one of the founding members of the United Nations Organization which was created in 1945. The UN (May 1999) has 185 member states. Its principal organs, with headquarters in New York, are:

the General Assembly in which each member state has one vote and which normally meets once a year in September;
the Security Council which has five permanent members (China, France, Russia, UK, USA) and ten non-permanent members elected for a two-year term.

Also linked with the UN are various international organizations, including the International Court of Justice (based in the Hague), the International Labour Organization (based in Geneva), the Food and Agriculture Organization (based in Rome), the UN Educational, Scientific and Cultural Organization (based in Paris) and the World Health Organization (based in Geneva).

UN Secretary-General: Mr Kofi Annan (Ghana).

UK Permanent Representative to the UN and Representative on the Security Council: Sir Jeremy Greenstock.

P. WHO'S WHO IN BRITISH POLITICS 1979-99
(for MPs, present constituency only is indicated)

Ancram, Michael, b. 1945; MP (Con) Devizes since 1992 (MP earlier in Scotland); Minister of State, Northern Ireland Office, 1994-7; Shadow Constitutional Affairs Spokesman, 1997-8; Succeeded Lord Parkinson as Conservative Party Chairman, 1998.

Ashdown, Paddy, b. 1941; MP (Lib) 1983-8, (SLD)

since 1988 (Yeovil); Leader, Social and Liberal Democratic Party from 1988 to 1999.

Baker, Lord, b. 1934; MP (Con) 1968-97 (Mole Valley); Secretary of State for the Environment 1985-6, for Education and Science 1986-9, Chancellor of Duchy of Lancaster and Chairman of the Conservative Party 1989-90; Home Secretary 1990-92.

Beckett, Margaret, b. 1943; MP (Lab) 1974-9 and since 1983 (Derby South); joined Treasury frontbench team, 1989; close ally of John Smith; Deputy Leader 1992-4; Shadow Health Secretary, 1994-5; Trade and Industry, 1995-7. President of the Board of Trade and Secretary of State for Trade and Industry, 1997-8. Currently (1999) Leader of the House of Commons.

Beith, Alan, b. 1943; MP (Lib) 1973-88, (SLD) since 1988 (Berwick); Deputy Leader, Liberal Party 1985-8; contender for leadership of SLD, 1988.

Benn, Anthony Wedgwood, b. 1925; MP (Lab) 1950-83 (except for short period between father's death and renunciation of the family peerage) and since 1984 (Chesterfield); Minister of Technology 1966-70, Secretary of State for Industry 1974-5 and for Energy 1975-9; Member Labour Party NEC 1959-60 and 1962-93.

Blair, Tony, see **B8**.

Blunkett, David, b. 1947; MP (Lab) since 1987 (Sheffield Brightside). Shadow spokesman on environment (with local government and poll tax issues), 1988-92. Shadow Health spokesman 1992-5. Shadow Education and Employment spokesman, 1995-7. Appointed Secretary of State for Education and Employment, May 1997.

Boothroyd, Betty, b. 1929; MP (Lab) since 1973 (West Bromwich until 1974, then West Bromwich West). Speaker of the House of Commons since May 1992 (the first woman to be elected to the Speakership).

Bottomley, Virginia, b. 1948; MP (Con) Surrey South-West, May 1984-. Secretary of State for Health, 1992-5; Secretary of State for National Heritage, 1995-7.

Brittan, Sir Leon, b. 1939; MP (Con) 1974-89; Chief Secretary to the Treasury 1981-3, Secretary of State for Home Department 1983-5, and for Trade and Industry 1985-6; EEC Commissioner since 1989. Appointed Vice-President, 1995.

Brown, Gordon, b. 1951; MP (Lab) since 1983 (Dunfermline East); Shadow spokesman on trade 1989-92; Shadow Chancellor, 1992-7. Appointed Chancellor of the Exchequer, May 1997.

Butler, Lord, b. 1938; entered civil service in 1961, Treasury 1961-9, 1975-82 and 1985-7, Principal Private Secretary to Prime Minister 1982-5, Secretary to the Cabinet and Head of the Home Civil Service, 1988-98.

Callaghan, Lord, see **B12**.

Carrington, Lord, b. 1919; Member of House of Lords since 1938; Leader of Opposition in the Lords 1964-70 and 1974-9; Secretary of State for Defence 1970-4, for Energy 1974, and for Foreign and Commonwealth Affairs, 1979-82; Secretary-General of NATO 1984-8; Chairman Conservative Party Organisation 1972-4.

Clarke, Kenneth, b. 1940; MP (Con) since 1970 (Rushcliffe); Paymaster General 1985-7, Chancellor of the Duchy of Lancaster 1987-8, Secretary of State for Health 1988-90, for Education 1990-92. Home Secretary 1992-3, Chancellor of the Exchequer 1993-7. Defeated by William Hague for Conservative leadership, 1997. Leading pro-European.

Cook, Robin, b. 1946; MP (Lab) since 1974 (Livingston); Shadow spokesman on Health 1987-92; Shadow Trade and Industry spokesman, 1992-4. Shadow Foreign Secretary, 1994-7. Appointed Foreign Secretary, May 1997.

Cunningham, Jack, b. 1939; MP (Lab) since 1970 (Copeland); Shadow Leader of the House of Commons 1989-92; Shadow Foreign Secretary, 1992-4. Shadow Trade and Industry Secretary, 1994-5; National Heritage, 1995-7. Minister of Agriculture, Fisheries and Food, 1997-8. Minister for the Cabinet Office and Chancellor of the Duchy of Lancaster, 1998-.

Davies, Ron, b. 1946; MP (Lab) since 1983 (Caerphilly); Shadow Secretary of State for Wales, 1992–7; Secretary of State for Wales, 1997–8. Resigned from the Cabinet, 1998.

Dewar, Donald, b. 1937; MP (Lab) 1966–70 and since 1978 (Glasgow Garscadden). Elected to Shadow Cabinet 1984–; Opposition Chief Whip 1995–7. Secretary of State for Scotland since 1997; Chosen to lead Labour in Scottish Assembly, 1998. The 1999 elections left him poised to become Scotland's First Minister.

Dobson, Frank, b. 1940; MP (Lab) since 1979 (Holborn and St. Pancras); Shadow spokesman on Transport and London, 1993–4. Shadow Environment spokesman, 1994–7. Appointed Secretary of State for Health, May 1997.

Donaldson, Lord, b. 1920; Barrister since 1946, QC 1961; High Court Judge 1966–79, President, National Industrial Relations Court 1971–4; Lord Justice of Appeal 1979–82; Master of the Rolls, 1982–92.

Dorrell, Stephen, b. 1952; MP (Con) since 1979, (Loughborough, then Charnwood since 1997); Secretary of State for National Heritage, 1994–5; Secretary of State for Health, 1995–7.

Edmonds, John, b. 1944; National Industrial Officer, General and Municipal Workers Union (later General, Municipal, Boilermakers and Allied Trades Union) 1972–85, General Secretary since 1985.

Field, Frank, b. 1942; MP (Lab) since 1979 (Birkenhead). Expert on social security. Director, Child Poverty Action Group, 1969–79. Appointed Minister of State in charge of Welfare Reform, 1997. Resigned, 1998.

Foot, Michael, b. 1913; MP (Lab) 1945–55 and 1960–92 (Blaenau Gwent); Secretary of State for Employment 1974–6, Lord President of the Council and Leader of the Commons 1976–9; Member Labour Party NEC 1971–83, Deputy Leader 1976–80, Leader, 1980–3.

Fowler, Sir Norman, b. 1938; MP (Con) since 1970 (Sutton Coldfield); Secretary of State for Transport 1979–81, for Social Services 1981–7 and for Employment 1987–90. Chairman, Conservative Party, 1992–4.

Gould, Bryan, b. 1939; MP (Lab) 1974–9 and 1983–94 (Dagenham); Shadow spokesman on the environment 1989–92; Member, Labour Party NEC 1988–92. Unsuccessfully contested leadership, 1992. Returned to New Zealand, 1994.

Hague, William, b. 1961; MP (Con) since 1989 (Richmond, Yorks); Secretary of State for Wales, 1995–7. Became Leader of the Conservative Party, 1997, following election defeat of John Major.

Harman, Harriet, b. 1950; MP (Lab) since 1982 (Camberwell & Peckham); Shadow Health Secretary under Tony Blair. Secretary of State for Social Security, 1997–8.

Hattersley, Lord, b. 1932; MP (Lab) 1964–97 (Birmingham Sparkbrook); Secretary of State for Prices and Consumer Protection 1976–9; Shadow Home Secretary 1987–92; Deputy Leader 1983–92.

Healey, Lord, b. 1917; MP (Lab) 1952–92 (Leeds East); Secretary of State for Defence 1964–70, Chancellor of the Exchequer 1974–9; Member Labour Party NEC 1970–5 and 1980–3, Deputy Leader 1980–3.

Heath, Sir Edward, see **B**30.

Heseltine, Michael, b. 1933; MP (Con) since 1966 (Henley); Secretary of State for the Environment 1979–83; for Defence 1983–6; for the Environment 1990–92. Secretary of State for Trade and Industry 1992–5; Deputy Prime Minister 1995–7.

Howard, Michael, b. 1941; MP (Con) since 1983 (Folkestone and Hythe); Secretary of State for Employment 1990–92, for the Enviroment, 1992–3. Home Secretary, 1993–7. Shadow Foreign Secretary 1997–9.

Howe, Lord, b. 1926; MP (Con) 1964–6 and 1970–92 (Surrey East); Solicitor-General 1970–2, Minister for Trade and Consumer Affairs 1972–4, Chancellor of the Exchequer 1979–83, Secretary of State for

Foreign and Commonwealth Affairs 1983–9, and Leader of the House of Commons (and Deputy Prime Minister) 1989–90. Companion of Honour.

Hume, John, b. 1937; MP (SDLP) Foyle, 1983–. Leader, Social Democratic and Labour Party, since 1979. MP (SDLP) Northern Ireland, 1979–. Declined to stand for Irish Presidency, 1997. Shared 1998 Nobel Peace Prize (with David Trimble).

Hurd, Lord, b. 1930; MP (Con) 1974–97 (Witney); Minister of State, Foreign Office 1979–83, Home Office 1983–4, Secretary of State for Northern Ireland 1984–5, for Home Department 1985–9, and for Foreign and Commonwealth Affairs, 1989–95.

Irvine, Lord, b. 1940; Created Life Peer, 1987. Shadow Lord Chancellor, 1992–7. Lord Chancellor since 1997. Friend and mentor of Tony Blair.

Jenkins, Lord, see **B**34.

Joseph, Lord (Sir Keith Joseph), (1918–94). MP (Con) 1956–87 (Leeds South-East). Secretary of State for Social Services, 1970–4; for Industry, 1979–81; for Education and Science, 1981–6. Leading 'guru' of the Thatcherite right-wing.

Kaufman, Gerald, b. 1930; MP (Lab) since 1970 (Manchester Gorton); Minister of State, Department of Industry 1975–9; Shadow Foreign Secretary, 1987–92.

King, Tom, b. 1933; MP (Con) since 1970 (Bridgwater); Minister for Local Government 1979–83, Secretary of State for the Environment Jan.–June 1983, for Transport June–Oct. 1983, for Employment 1983–5, for Northern Ireland 1985–9, and for Defence, 1989–92.

Kinnock, Neil, see **B**36.

Lamont, Lord, b. 1942; MP (Con) 1972–97 (Kingston-upon-Thames); Financial Secretary, Treasury 1986–9, Chief Secretary 1989–90, Chancellor of the Exchequer, 1990–3.

Lawson, Lord, b. 1932; MP (Con) (Feb.) 1974–92 (Blaby); Editor, *The Spectator,* 1966–70; Financial Secretary to the Treasury 1979–81, Secretary of State for Energy 1981–3, Chancellor of the Exchequer 1983–9.

Lilley, Peter, b. 1943; MP (Con) since 1983 (St Albans, 1983–97, Hitchin and Harpenden since 1997). Trade and Industry Secretary, 1990–92; Secretary of State for Social Security, 1992–7. Leadership candidate, 1997; Deputy Leader of the Conservative Party since 1998.

Mackay, Lord, b. 1927; Member of House of Lords since 1979; Advocate since 1955, QC 1965; Lord Advocate 1979–84; Lord of Appeal 1985–7; Lord Chancellor, 1987–97.

Major, John, see **B**40.

Mandelson, Peter, b. 1953; MP (Lab) Hartlepool, 1992–. Opposition Whip, 1994–7. Widely seen as an architect of 1997 election victory. Minister of State, Cabinet Office, 1997–8; Secretary of State for Trade and Industry, 1998. Resigned December 1998.

Maude, Francis, b. 1953; MP (Con) since 1997 (Horsham) (earlier MP for Warwickshire North, 1983–92); Financial Secretary to the Treasury, 1990–92; Chairman, Deregulation Task Force, 1994–7; Shadow Culture Secretary, 1997–8; appointed (1998) Shadow Chancellor of the Exchequer.

Mawhinney, Sir Brian, b. 1940; MP (Con) since 1979 (Peterborough, then Cambridgeshire NW). Secretary of State for Transport, 1994–5. Chairman of the Conservative Party, 1995–7. Shadow Home Secretary, 1997–8.

Mayhew, Lord, b. 1929; MP (Con) 1974–97 (Tunbridge Wells). Solicitor General, 1983–7; Attorney General, 1987–92. Secretary of State for Northern Ireland, 1992–. A key figure in the search for a peaceful settlement in Northern Ireland.

Michael, Alun, b. 1943; MP (Lab) Cardiff South and Penarth since 1987. Minister of State, Home Office, 1997–8. Secretary of State for Wales, 1998–. Chosen to lead Labour in Welsh Assembly.

Monks, John, b. 1945; official of Trades Union Congress. Deputy General Secretary, 1987–93, General Secretary since 1993.

Mowlam, Marjorie, b. 1949; MP (Lab) since 1987 (Redcar); Shadow Northern Ireland Secretary under Tony Blair. Appointed Secretary of State for Northern Ireland, May 1997.

Owen, Lord, b. 1938; MP (Lab) 1966–81, (SDP, Ind. Soc. Dem. after 1990) 1981–92 (Plymouth Devonport); Secretary of State for Foreign and Commonwealth Affairs 1977–9; co-founder of Social Democratic Party 1981 and Leader 1983–7 and from 1988 until its dissolution in 1990. Co-Chairman, Peace Conference on ex-Yugoslavia, 1992–5. Created Companion of Honour, 1995.

Paisley, Rev. Ian, b. 1926; MP (Protestant Unionist 1970–4, Democratic Unionist since 1974) since 1970 (Antrim North); MEP since 1979; member of Stormont 1970–2, NI Assembly 1973–5, NI Constitutional Convention 1975–6, NI Assembly after 1982.

Patten, Christopher, b. 1944; MP (Con) 1979–92 (Bath); Secretary of State for the Environment 1989–90; Chancellor of the Duchy of Lancaster, 1990–92; Chairman of the Conservative Party, 1990–92. Governor of Hong Kong, 1992–7. Created Companion of Honour, 1998.

Portillo, Michael Denzil Xavier b. 1953; MP (Con) Dec, 1984–97 (Southgate). Chief Secretary to the Treasury, 1992–5. Secretary of State for Defence, 1995–7. Defeated in 1997 election.

Prescott, John, b. 1938; MP (Lab) since 1970 (Hull East); Shadow spokesman on Transport, 1988–93; on Employment, 1993–4. Deputy Leader of the Labour Party, 1994–7. Appointed Deputy Prime Minister, and Secretary of State for the Environment, Transport and the Regions, May 1997.

Prout, Lord, b. 1942; MEP (Con) 1979–94 (Shropshire and Stafford); Chief Whip, European Democratic Group 1983–7, Leader, 1987–94.

Redwood, John, b. 1951; MP (Con) since 1987 (Wokingham). Secretary of State for Wales, 1993–5. Resigned to contest (unsuccessfully) the leadership against John Major (July 1995). Shadow Trade and Industry Secretary after 1997.

Ridley, Lord, 1929–93; MP (Con) 1959–92 (Cirencester and Tewkesbury); Secretary of State for Transport 1983–6, for the Environment 1986–9, and for Trade and Industry 1989–90.

Rifkind, Sir Malcolm, b. 1946; MP (Con) Edinburgh Pentlands, Feb 1974–97. Secretary of State for Scotland, 1986–90; for Transport, 1990–92; for Defence, 1992–5; Foreign Secretary, 1995–7.

Robertson, George, b. 1949; MP (Lab) since 1978 (Hamilton South); Shadow Scottish Secretary under Tony Blair. Appointed Secretary of State for Defence, May 1997.

Salmond, Alex, b. 1954; MP (SNP) since 1987 (Banff and Buchan); Leader of SNP since 1990. On left of party.

Shephard, Gillian, b. 1940; MP (Con) Norfolk South-West, 1987–. Secretary of State for Employment, 1992–3; Minister of Agriculture, Fisheries and Food, 1993–4. Secretary of State for Education 1994–7 (Education and Employment after 1995). Shadow Secretary of State for Environment, Transport and the Regions (until 1999).

Short, Clare, b. 1946; MP (Lab) since 1983 (Birmingham Ladywood). Various Shadow Cabinet posts. Appointed Secretary of State for International Development, 1997.

Smith, Chris, b. 1951; MP (Lab) since 1983 (Islington South and Finsbury); Shadow Social Security Secretary. Appointed National Heritage Secretary, May 1997. Office now renamed Department of Culture, Media and Sport.

Smith, John, see **B56**.

Steel, Lord, see **B57**.

Straw, Jack, b. 1946; MP (Lab) since 1979 (Blackburn); Shadow Home Secretary under Tony Blair. Appointed Home Secretary, May 1997.

Taylor, Ann, b. 1947; MP (Lab) since 1974 (Dewsbury); Shadow Leader of the Commons under Tony Blair. President of the Council and Leader of the House of Commons, 1997–8; Labour Chief Whip since 1998.

Tebbit, Lord, b. 1931; MP (Con) 1970–92 (Chingford); Secretary of State for Employment 1981–3, for

Trade and Industry 1983–5, Chancellor of the Duchy of Lancaster 1985–7; Chairman, Conservative Party Organisation 1985–7.

Thatcher, Baroness, see **B59**.

Trimble, David, b. 1944; MP (Ulster Unionist) since 1990 by-election (Upper Bann). Leader of the Ulster Unionists since 1995. Chief Minister in Northern Ireland Assembly since 1998. Shared 1998 Nobel Peace Prize (with John Hume).

Waddington, Lord, b. 1929; MP (Con) 1979–90 (Ribble Valley); Government Chief Whip 1987–9, Home Secretary 1989–90; Leader, House of Lords 1990–92. Subsequently Governor of Bermuda.

Walker, Lord, b. 1932; MP (Con) 1961–92 (Worcester); Secretary of State for the Environment 1970–2 and for Trade and Industry 1972–4, Minister of Agriculture 1979–83, Secretary of State for Energy 1983–7 and for Wales 1987–90.

Weatherill, Lord, b. 1920; MP (Con) 1964–92 (Croydon North East); Conservative Whip 1970–9; Deputy Speaker 1979–83, Speaker, 1983–92.

Whitelaw, Viscount, b. 1918; MP (Con) 1955–83; Lord President of the Council and Leader of the Commons 1970–2, Secretary of State for Northern Ireland 1972–3, for Employment 1973–4 and Home Secretary 1979–83, Lord President of the Council and Leader of the House of Lords 1983–8; Chairman Conservative Party Organisation 1974–5.

Widdecombe, Ann, b. 1956; MP (Con) since 1997 (Maidstone and the Weald) (earlier MP for Maidstone, 1987–97); Minister of State, Employment, 1994–5; Minister of State, Home Office, 1995–7. Appointed Shadow Secretary of State for Health in 1998.

Willetts, David, b. 1956; MP (Con) since 1992 (Havant); Paymaster-General, 1996; currently (1999) Shadow Secretary of State for Education and Employment.

Williams, Baroness, b. 1930; MP (Lab) 1964–79, (SDP) 1981–3; Secretary of State for Prices and Consumer Protection 1974–6 and for Education and Science 1976–9; Member Labour Party NEC 1970–81; co-founder of Social Democratic Party 1981 and President 1982–8; joined SLDP, 1988.

Willis, Norman, b. 1933; official of Trades Union Congress since 1959. Deputy General Secretary 1977–84, General Secretary, 1984–93.

Wright, Lord, b. 1931; entered Diplomatic Service in 1955, Deputy Under Secretary, Foreign and Commonwealth Office 1982–4, Ambassador to Saudi Arabia 1984–6, Permanent Under Secretary 1986–94.

Q. GLOSSARY OF RECENT POLITICS

Anglo-Irish Agreement Agreement on Northern Ireland reached by Mrs Thatcher and the Irish premier Garret Fitzgerald on 15 November 1985. The Agreement recognised the right of the Northern Irish people to decide their own destiny but gave the Irish government a consultative role in the province's affairs through an Intergovernmental Conference where political, legal and security matters would be discussed. The Agreement was angrily received by the Protestant community and Unionist MPs boycotted the Commons in protest.

Back to Basics Attempt by Mr Major at the 1993 Conservative party conference to give an ideological thrust to his apparently drifting government. The slogan was open to many interpretations, although it involved a return to "old standards". An element of personal morality, with attacks, for example, on single mothers, led to the policy's collapse in ridicule when there were revelations of adultery and other sexual activities of ministers.

Black Wednesday Heavy selling of the pound on the money markets in 1992 prompted the raising of the base rate twice on 16 September to 15%. When this failed to preserve sterling's value relative to the Deutschmark, Chancellor of the Exchequer Norman Lamont withdrew Britain from the Exchange Rate Mechanism (ERM) and effectively devalued the pound. Despite the longer term beneficial effect on the British economy, the crisis with its underlying impression of drift and weak leadership undermined the position of John Major and led to Norman Lamont's eventual resignation.

Brighton bombing On 12 October 1984 a Provisional IRA bomb exploded at the Grand Hotel, Brighton, during the Conservative party conference, killing five people (including a Conservative MP), and seriously injuring Norman Tebbit and his wife. Mrs Thatcher was among those who narrowly escaped death.

Brixton riots Rioting broke out on 11 April 1981 following an incident in the week-long "Operation Swamp" mounted by police against street crime but which the local black population saw as unnecessarily provocative. During three days of rioting black and white youths fought the police, burnt buildings and vehicles and looted the central shopping area. Further riots broke out in Toxteth, Southall, Handsworth, Manchester and a wide range of towns in July. There was further rioting in Brixton on 28 September 1985 (following the accidental shooting of a black woman by police) and again in 1995 after the death of a young black man in custody.

Broadwater Farm A local authority housing estate in Tottenham, North London, the scene of rioting on 6 October 1985 following the death of a black woman during a police raid. A police officer was killed during the clashes. Three black youths imprisoned for his murder were released in 1991 following successful appeals, one of many contemporary cases which called the police and judicial system into serious question.

Bruges Group Group formed following a speech in Bruges by Mrs Thatcher on 20 September 1988. The group supported her view set out in the speech that European co-operation should be restricted to an economic relationship between separate sovereign states rather than a thoroughgoing European union.

Citizens Charter An attempt to make public services more responsive to consumers' wishes, announced by Mr Major on 22 July 1991.

Clause 28 A Section of the 1988 Local Government Act inserted by Tory backbenchers which banned local authorities from promoting the acceptability of homosexuality in schools. The clause was seen by many lesbians and gay men as the beginning of an attack on their legal rights.

Delors Plan Proposal for European political and monetary union drawn up under Jacques Delors, President of the European Commission from 1985. The plan envisaged the creation of a European Monetary System, a central bank to exert greater influence and eventually control over national monetary policies. The plan was accepted in 1989 as the basis for future moves towards European Monetary Union but the plan's apparently inevitable progress towards European unity aroused resistance from Mrs Thatcher's government.

Downing Street Declaration Agreement on 15 December 1993 between Mr Major and Irish prime minister Albert Reynolds offering Provisional Sinn Fein participation in multi-party talks on the future of Ireland within three months of a permanent end to IRA terrorism. Although unification could not take place without Unionist agreement, the British government took a near-neutral stance on its possibility. The Declaration followed meetings between Sinn Fein president Gerry Adams and SDLP leader John Hume (and the revelation of previous secret contacts between the government and Sinn Fein). Hopes of immediate peace were disappointed but Provisional IRA announced a ceasefire on 31 August 1994. This ended in February 1996.

Dries Conservative Party members (and supporters of Mrs Thatcher) who favoured an economic policy of strict monetarism, reduced public expenditure, lower taxation, increased privatisation of state and local authority enterprises, and a curtailing of trade union power.

Essex Man Stereotypal South of England Conservative voter and Thatcher supporter in the 1980s, seen as a vulgar materialist racist. The expression (together with the sexist Essex Girl)—although first coined by Conservative journalist Simon Heffer—was used with superior disdain by the liberal middle classes.

Falklands Factor Britain's success in the Falklands War and her undoubted determination to win at all costs helped Mrs Thatcher—hitherto one of the most deeply unpopular of 20th century prime ministers—win an overwhelming victory in the 1983 general election and consolidated her power in the Conservative Party until 1990.

Falklands War Fought to restore the 2,000 population on the Falklands (Malvinas) Islands to British control following invasion by Argentine forces on 2 April 1982. A 6,000 strong military and naval task force crossed the Atlantic, landed on 21 May and captured the capital Port Stanley on 14 June, forcing the Argentine surrender.

GCHQ Government Communications Headquarters in Cheltenham which collected signals intelligence through a worldwide network of listening posts. The government banned GCHQ workers from union membership on 25 January 1984 following the allegedly disruptive effects of a civil service strike in 1981. Workers who refused to leave their union were dismissed. This ban was lifted in 1997 by the newly-elected Labour Government.

Good Friday Agreement See **D22**(2).

Greenham Common Base where Cruise missiles were deployed in 1983. Women protesting at their planned deployment began a vigil at the base perimeter on 12 December 1982 and a "peace camp" of protesters remained there until the missiles were withdrawn in 1989. The camp became a symbol internationally of anti-nuclear protest and growing feminist consciousness.

Iron Lady Title bestowed on Mrs Thatcher while she was opposition leader by the Soviet Army newspaper *Red Star* on 23 January 1976 because of her uncompromising position on defence and international relations. Mrs Thatcher took the title proudly.

Jenkins Commission See **D21**.

Lawrence Inquiry Report See **C13**.

Maastricht Treaty signed on 10 December 1991 following a summit of European leaders setting out agreements reached on the Treaty of European Union. Leading a party deeply divided on Europe, Mr Major negotiated clauses allowing Britain to opt out of a single currency and the Social Chapter. The treaty was ratified by Parliament, despite a vigorous campaign for a referendum on the issue led in the House of Lords by Lady Thatcher.

Matrix-Churchill A Coventry machine tool company, three of whose executives were charged with breaking an embargo on selling arms to Iraq imposed in the 1980–88 Iran–Iraq War. The evidence of former minister Alan Clark revealed that the government had unofficially abandoned the policy and documents which ministers sought to prevent the court seeing showed the three had acted with government approval. The three were acquitted in November 1992. Mr Major appointed an inquiry under Lord Justice Scott to investigate the affair.

Miners' strike A bitter dispute in 1984–85, seen in part as the Conservative party's revenge for the 1974 strike which led to the fall of the Heath government. The NUM led by Arthur Scargill took action against what he claimed was a plan for massive pit closures. The NUM refused to hold a national ballot and this lost the support of the wider trade union leadership, as well as opening the way for a breakaway Union of Democratic Miners to continue working. Tactically, the miners suffered from opening their strike in the spring when coal stocks were high. The dispute was harshly fought, with much hardship among miners' families. Labour, led by Mr Kinnock, though sympathetic to the miners, distanced itself for fear of the impact on its electoral prospects. The miners' eventual defeat was followed by a closure programme far worse than that Mr Scargill had warned of.

Nolan Committee The Committee on Standards in Public Life set up in 1994 under the chairmanship of Lord Nolan following a series of "sleaze" events. One of its recommendations was the establishment of the office of Parliamentary Commissioner for Standards (*see* **D13**(1)).

Opting out Right of a school to leave local education authority control if a majority of parents and governors vote to do so, introduced in the 1988 Education Reform Act. The school is directly funded by central government and the governing body is responsible for spending and performance.

Orgreave Scene of one of the most crucial confrontations of the 1984–85 miners' strike. Thousands of Yorkshire miners attempted to force the closure of a British Steel coking plant by picketing in May and June 1984. There were large numbers of arrests and injuries and complaints of excessive police violence

Parkinson Scandal After a long affair with Trade & Industry Secretary Cecil Parkinson, his mistress Sara Keays became pregnant in 1983. Parkinson, as party chairman, had played a large part in the May general election Conservative landslide victory. With Mrs Thatcher's support, Mr Parkinson attempted to retain office but further revelations by Miss Keays forced his resignation at the party conference in October. Mr Parkinson returned to office as Energy Secretary in 1987.

Ponting Case Defence Ministry civil servant Clive Ponting was acquitted at the Old Bailey in March 1985 of breaching the Official Secrets Act by leaking classified information suggesting ministers had lied to Parliament about the sinking of the Argentine battleship *General Belgrano* in 1982. Mr Ponting leaked the information in protest against the government's persistence in saying the battleship had posed an immediate danger to the British task force. His acquittal challenged the previous assumption that the interests of the state and of the government were synonymous.

Privatisation See **L99**.

Public Order Act 1986 The Act, which aroused criticism from civil liberties groups, created a new range of public order offences by extending police powers over marches and demonstrations, and creating for the first time statutory controls over open-air meetings and picketing. The Act made trespass a criminal offence.

Scarman Report Lord Scarman was appointed to investigate the causes of the April 1981 Brixton riots and other disturbances. His report defended the measures police had taken but pointed to the need for more ethnic minority police officers, for the screening of recruits for racist attitudes and the dismissal of proven racist officers, greater consultation with local communities, more police on the beat, and the regulation of police search powers. Scarman also stressed the need to confront underlying social issues such as the regeneration of the inner cities and the prevention of racial discrimination.

Scott Report The Report of Sir Richard Scott, published in 1996, into the 'Arms-to-Iraq' affair. The government narrowly survived a Commons vote on the Scott Report.

Sinn Fein Ban Order issued by Home Secretary Douglas Hurd on 19 October 1988 preventing the broadcasting of direct statements by representatives of Sinn Fein, the Ulster Defence Association and other organisations linked with terrorism. Actors were allowed to read transcripts of their comments, weakening the ban's effectiveness. The ban was lifted in September 1994 following the Provisional IRA ceasefire.

Social Chapter Section of the Treaty on European Union rejected by the Thatcher and Major governments. The seven Articles of the Chapter include: the improvement of living standards within a context of economic competitiveness; encouragement of health and safety at work, equality for women, and consultation of workers by employers; promotion of management-worker consultation by the European Commission; and European co-ordination of social policy. In May 1997 the new Labour Government took the first steps to join the Social Chapter.

Spycatcher Title of the autobiography of former MI5 operative Peter Wright which contained details of abuses by the agency, including a plan to overthrow the Labour government in the 1970s. Mrs Thatcher attempted to ban its publication and the government fought a case in New South Wales, where Wright was living. During the trial Cabinet Secretary Sir Robert Armstrong admitted he had been "economical with the truth". The government lost the case on 2 June 1988 but publication was prevented in Britain until 13 October 1988

when the House of Lords ruled against the government.

Trafalgar Square Riot Violent demonstration against the widely unpopular poll tax (community charge) on 31 March 1990, the culmination of prolonged nationwide protests. Over 130 were injured, including 57 police, and 341 arrested in fighting and looting which spread through the centre of London. Mrs Thatcher, who was deeply committed to the tax, was replaced as leader in the autumn and plans to abolish the tax were later announced.

Two Nations Phrase, originally from the novel *Sybil* by 19th century Conservative politician Benjamin Disraeli, describing a society with a gulf between rich and poor. Used in the 1980s to encapsulate the division between the depressed North, with collapsing industries and unemployment, and the more prosperous South, and also more widely to describe the divisions created by unemployment.

Wandsworth Conservative-controlled local authority in south west London which provided a model for Tory boroughs in the 1980s by pioneering the reduction and contracting-out of council services. Known as the "flagship" authority because of its exemplary Thatcherite policies, Wandsworth was also unique in setting a nil level of poll tax, thanks to substantial central government grants. The borough was always compared favourably with neighbouring Lambeth, controlled by the Labour "loony left".

Westland Affair A government crisis which almost forced Mrs Thatcher's resignation as prime minister in 1986. On 13 November 1985 the ailing Westland Helicopters announced a rescue deal involving a US–Italian consortium. Defence Secretary Michael Heseltine favoured a deal with a European company. On 6 January 1986 a letter to Mr Heseltine from the Solicitor General Sir Patrick Mayhew warning him about his position was leaked to the press. Mr Heseltine resigned dramatically by walking out of a Cabinet meeting on 9 January. On 24 January Trade & Industry Secretary Leon Brittain resigned after allegations of his involvement in the leak. Only mishandling of a Commons debate by opposition leader Neil Kinnock prevented responsibility being attached to Mrs Thatcher.

Wets Conservative Party members who were less than fervent supporters of Mrs Thatcher's more radical policies, used as a term of abuse by her followers, the "dries". Wets favoured a more centrist economic line and were concerned about the social effects of many of her policies, particularly those leading to mass unemployment. Mrs Thatcher inherited a large number of wets from her predecessor Edward Heath but had removed most of them from her Cabinet by 1983.

SPECIAL TOPIC

LABOUR'S CONSTITUTIONAL REVOLUTION

The Agenda.

Labour's programme of constitutional reform, an essential part, Mr Blair declared, of his programme for the modernisation of Britain, aroused varying responses. For one commentator, Scottish and Welsh devolution represented the most dramatic constitutional change since the partition of Ireland in 1922. But another denied that anything more than moderate tinkering could be expected from such a socially and politically conservative leader. For example, Mr Blair's astute management of the events surrounding the death in August 1997 of Diana, Princess of Wales, revealed him to be far from republican in his sympathies. But what justification could there be for an hereditary head of state when the right of hereditary lords to legislate was to be abolished? There were criticisms too that the individual elements of constitutional reform outlined in Labour's manifesto—devolved assemblies in Scotland and Wales (but not in the English regions) a London-wide authority, reform of the House of

Lords, a new electoral system, an end to the culture of secrecy in national and local government, and incorporation of the European Convention on Human Rights into British law—lacked any consistent linkage.

Scotland and Wales.

The 1974–79 Labour government had attempted and failed to secure devolution for Scotland and Wales. Referenda in 1979 resulted in outright rejection in Wales and an insufficient majority in favour in Scotland. But in the Queen's Speech in May 1997, the government promised referenda for devolved assemblies in Scotland and Wales and for a new strategic authority, together with a mayor, for London.

From the year 2000, Scotland was to have a parliament in Edinburgh for the first time since the Act of Union in 1707. The parliament, with an annual block grant of £14 billion, was to deal with matters now devolved to the Scottish Office, including education, health, law and order, local government, economic development, roads, the environment and the arts. Westminster would retain responsibility for defence, foreign policy, social security and macro-economic and fiscal policy. If the Scots voted in their referendum for tax-raising powers, the Scottish Parliament would have the authority to increase or lower the United Kingdom income tax rate by up to 3%.

The Scottish Parliament was to have 129 members (MSPs), 73 of whom would be elected for the existing Westminster constituencies (but with Orkney and Shetland divided into two seats) by the first past the post system. The remaining 56 MPs were to be elected from party lists in the eight European Parliament constituencies by proportional representation. Scotland would continue to send 72 members to Westminster, though this was expected to reduce over time. The "West Lothian" question of 1979 remained unanswered—why should Scottish MPs be allowed to debate and vote on what were essentially English affairs while English MPs would have no equivalent right to involve themselves in Scottish affairs? In addition, there was still to be a Secretary of State for Scotland in the Cabinet.

In May 1998 it was announced that the opening of the Scottish Parliament was to be in July 1999—two months after the elections—rather than, as originally planned, in January 2000. For details of the elections, *see* D13.

The Devolution Referenda.

Scottish voters were asked two questions in the referendum held on 11 September: whether they were in favour of a parliament and whether this parliament should have tax-raising powers. Labour, the SNP and the Liberal Democrats campaigned for a Yes-Yes vote, while the Conservatives favoured No-No, arguing that devolution would lead inevitably to a break up of the Union. On a 60% turnout, the Scots voted in favour of a parliament by 74·3% to 25·7% and in favour of tax-raising powers by 63·5% to 36·5%.

Wales voted a week after the Scots. The Welsh were offered a representative assembly in Cardiff with fewer powers than the Scottish Parliament on the grounds that, in a country under English rule for 700 years, there appeared to be less popular pressure for the full trappings of statehood. The Welsh assembly would deal with issues currently the responsibility of the Welsh Office, including education, health, agriculture, roads and planning. As well as defence, foreign policy, social security and macro-economic and fiscal policy, Westminster would retain control over home affairs and the judicial system. The assembly was to have 60 members, 40 elected in existing Westminster constituencies under the first past the post system and the remaining 20 from party lists by proportional representation. Labour, the Liberal Democrats and Plaid Cymru campaigned in support of the proposed assembly while the Conservatives led the opposition. In Wales the referendum vote was markedly closer than in Scotland, with 50·3% voting for an assembly to 49·7% against on a 50% turnout.

New London Authority.

Attention then moved to London which, since the abolition of the Greater London Council by the Conservatives in 1986, had been without a strategic city-wide authority. Labour proposed the establishment of a Greater London Authority—though its powers were left unclear—and the institution of an office of mayor. The Conservatives criticised suggestions made by the deputy prime minister, Mr Prescott, in October 1997 as adding another layer of bureaucracy to London. There were also criticisms that in the referendum on the issue promised for May 1998 Londoners were not to be allowed to choose to have a GLA with or without a mayor but would have to accept or reject the package in its entirety. Despite a low turnout, 72% of those voting supported Labour's proposals. There seemed no early prospect of devolution to the English regions, despite growing demands in the north east and in Yorkshire.

The 270-clause Greater London Authority Bill was introduced in the Commons in January 1999 and provided for an elected mayor and a 25-member GLA with an annual budget of £3·3 billion. The GLA was to be given powers to raise money from motorists earmarked for spending on public transport. The main consideration for the government appeared to be constructing a selection procedure that would prevent former Greater London Council leader Ken Livingstone from becoming the Labour candidate. Elections for the mayor and new authority were set for May 2000.

Reform of the Voting System.

Although Mr Blair appeared not to be absolutely persuaded of a need to reform the voting system, on 30 October he announced the appointment of a five-strong Electoral Reform Commission chaired by Lord Jenkins, the veteran Liberal Democrat (and former Labour deputy leader), to devise a proportional voting system for Westminster within a year. This, too, would be tested in a referendum.

On proportional representation—an issue that divided the country and the Labour Party itself—there was more movement. Lord Jenkins's Electoral Reform Commission issued its report on 29 October 1998. Under the Alternative Vote Top-Up proposals—which Lord Jenkins envisaged would take eight years to implement—the House of Commons was to be reduced in size from 659 members to a maximum of 560. Electors would have two votes, with one going to constituency candidates in order of preference and the other to Top-Up candidates to ensure a fairer representation of votes won by the parties. A constituency candidate winning half the vote would take the seat but if no candidate reached 50% the votes won by the least popular candidate would be redistributed until a victor emerged. The new House of Commons was to consist of 80–85% constituency MPs and 15–20% Top-Up MPs.

The Jenkins proposals were given a low-key government response, attacked by the Conservatives and welcomed—despite some disappointment—by the Liberals. Divisions within the Labour Party came into the open as a 130-strong Labour First Past the Post Group of MPs promised to campaign against proportional representation, while a similar number of Make Votes Count members pledged support. However, it was agreed that elections to the European Parliament in 1999, together with those to the Scottish Parliament and Welsh Assembly, would be held under proportional representation.

The House of Lords.

On the House of Lords, Labour's manifesto had pledged the removal of hereditary peers' speaking and voting rights. However, when a Cabinet committee under the Lord Chancellor, Lord Irvine, was established on 21 December to prepare the reforms it became clear that the government's intention was the outright abolition of hereditary peerages by 1999. The justification was the manifest unfairness and undemocratic nature of the present system. The Lords comprised 499 Tories (326 hereditary, 173 life peers), 160 Labour (15 of whom were hereditary), and 66 Liberal Democrats (23 of whom were hereditary). There were, in addition, 325 cross-benchers. What caused concern was that the shape of a future second chamber remained unclear. With the Conservatives pledged to resist abolition, there was also the possibility of a damaging struggle with

Tory peers who could use their strength to block other Labour legislation.

Protracted resistance by the House of Lords to the European Parliamentary Elections Bill in November 1998 underlined the government's determination to reform the upper house. In January 1999 the government issued a White Paper setting out interim proposals and appointed a Royal Commission to consider the final shape of a reformed second chamber. Mr Blair said in the White Paper that abolition of the hereditary principle represented a 'radical and historical task.'

Stage one of the reform was a bill to abolish the hereditary peers' sitting and voting rights, though a small number were likely to remain in an interim upper house. If the Lords resisted, the Parliament Act would be invoked to ensure removal of the hereditary peers by the year 2000. The parliamentary aspects of the Royal Commission's report—which was expected by the end of 1999—would be considered by both Houses. The government would then ensure that the second stage was approved by Parliament by the next general election. There were criticisms of the vagueness of what would replace the second chamber and accusations that if members were not to be directly elected they would be little more than creatures of the government that appointed them. It was clear, however, that the House of Commons could not contemplate the existence of a rival clothed with the authority of direct election. Mr Blair attempted to counter criticism by promising appointments would be controlled by an independent commission.

Freedom of Information Act.

A further crucial plank in the reform platform was a Freedom of Information Act intended, as a White Paper issued on 11 December said, to end the "entrenched culture of secrecy" in government. There was to be a "presumption of openness", with a legal right to see official documents and other data held by Whitehall, local authorities, quangos, the NHS, the armed forces and privatised utilities. The security and intelligence agencies were to be exempt from the proposed Act's provisions, as was information touching on defence and international relations, personal privacy, commercial confidentiality and the advice given to ministers by civil servants. An Independent Information Commissioner was to be appointed to intervene where disclosure was refused. An organisation which refused, without legitimate grounds, to disclose information would face a contempt of court charge. Early legislation to bring in the Act was promised.

Supporters of constitutional reform had their first disappointment over the Freedom of Information Bill. Despite the drawing up of a draft bill, progress faltered following the dismissal of the minister responsible in July 1998. There were reports of resistance in the civil service and—now they were in office—among ministers. Following the Queen's Speech in November 1998, Home Secretary Jack Straw promised a draft bill for consultation in 1999. Without firm commitment on the part of the government, there seemed little likelihood of a bill appearing in the 1999 Queen's Speech.

Human Rights Bill.

The government made an early announcement that it would present a Human Rights Bill to incorporate the European Convention on Human Rights into United Kingdom law. The UK had ratified the Convention in 1951 but British citizens seeking a remedy under it were forced to go to the European Court of Human Rights. The Bill introduced a fast track procedure to adapt existing UK legislation to make it compatible with the Convention and rights under the Convention were to be taken into account when developing new policies and legislation. The Bill proposed that it would be unlawful for public bodies to act in a way that was incompatible with rights under the Convention.Citizens would be able to invoke these rights in any civil or criminal proceedings brought against them by a public body, or in any proceedings which they brought against a public body. Although a court would not be able to set aside existing primary legislation, higher courts would be able to issue a formal declaration of incompatibility with the Convention to alert government to the need to change the relevant laws. As debate on the Bill, which was expected to come into force by late 1998, began there were suggestions that one effect would be to bring in a privacy law by the back door.

The Human Rights Act received Royal Assent in November 1998 but, because it was necessary to ensure members of judicial and government bodies affected were trained in the legislation's implications, would not come into effect until early 2000.

Northern Ireland.

A further important constitutional development came with what appeared to be a successful stage in the movement towards peace in Ireland. On 10 April eight parties—ranging from the Ulster Unionists to Sinn Fein—reached the Good Friday Agreement following 22 months of negotiations. The document provided for a 108-member Northern Ireland Assembly, run by a 12-member executive committee. Elections were to take place in June following acceptance by a referendum in May. A North-South Council of Ministers from Belfast and Dublin would promote joint policies. A Council of the Isles—with representatives from London, Dublin, Belfast, the Scottish Parliament and the Welsh Assembly—was to meet twice a year to discuss issues of mutual interest. Following a referendum, Ireland would withdraw its long-standing constitutional claim to Northern Ireland. The release of Republican and Loyalist paramilitary prisoners and the decommissioning of weapons remained open to negotiation.

On 25 June 1998 elections to the 108-member Northern Ireland Assembly were marked by successes for the nationalists and republicans as the SDLP took 24 seats and Sinn Fein 18. The Ulster Unionist Party (UUP) emerged as the strongest single party with 28 seats and on 1 July UUP leader David Trimble was named First Minister. Outrage at a republican splinter group bombing in Omagh on 25 August in which 28 people died united all sections of the community. But the refusal of the Provisional IRA to decommission its weapons threatened to stall the peace process as the UUP declared it would not take its seats alongside Sinn Fein members. There was also growing concern about the growth in so-called punishment beatings inflicted by members of republican and loyalist groups.

By April 1999, one year after the Good Friday Agreement, these issues remained unresolved as an atmosphere of pessimism surrounded the peace process.

THE WORLD OF MUSIC

The art of music as it has developed in the Western world, with an outline historical narrative, a glossary of musical terms and an index to composers. The period covered runs from early secular music to the vibrant new music forms of the late twentieth century. A Special Topic in this edition surveys the world of the musical stage, with its popular musicals, light opera and musical comedy.

TABLE OF CONTENTS

THE WORLD OF MUSIC

In writing this section no special knowledge on the part of the reader is assumed; it is for those who want to know about the history of music, how different styles evolved, and how one composer influenced another. It is a background to music as the science section is a background to science, and just as the latter cannot show the reader the colours of the spectrum but only tell of Newton's experiments and of the relationship between colour and wavelength, so in this section we can only describe human achievements in the world of sound. But knowing something about a composer, his work, and when he lived can help to bring fuller understanding and enjoyment when listening to his music.

The section is in four parts:

I. Historical Narrative and Discussion
II. Glossary of Musical Terms
III. Index to Composers
IV. Special Topic

I. HISTORICAL NARRATIVE AND DISCUSSION

The history of music, like that of any people or art, is not one of uninterrupted progress towards some ideal perfection. For five centuries or more music in the West has achieved peaks of accomplishment in one style or another before society has dictated or composers have felt the need for something new and different. Thus Wagner's music-drama *Parsifal*, lasting five hours, is not necessarily a more rewarding work than what Monteverdi achieved in *Orfeo* 250 years earlier. More complex yes, more rewarding—well, that is for the listener to judge.

We must keep this in mind when considering the development of music from a starting point of, say, Gregorian chant down to the complicated structures of a Schoenberg in our own day. In this development there is no true dividing line between one period and another, nor must simplifying terms such as "classical" or "romantic" be taken too literally.

The earliest history of Western music as we know it today is closely bound up with the Church, for music had to be provided for services. The earliest Christian music was influenced by Greek songs, few of which unfortunately have survived, and by the music of synagogues, where the art of chanting originated. The modal system of the ancient Greeks was highly organised. The earliest Greek scale was from A to A and the four descending notes A,G,F,E became the basis of their musical theory, and it is from them that Western music learned to call notes after the letters of the alphabet. A scale can begin on any note and always includes two semitones upon which much of the character of a melody depends.

The Greek modes were based on the white notes only; the Dorian, Phrygian, Lydian, and Mixolydian began respectively on E,D,C, and B. Their character was thus decided by the position of the semitones, and they formed the basis, often corrupted, of the mediaeval modes. This system was transmitted through Latin writers such as Boethius and Cassiodorus, and through Arabic writers. The eight Church modes were not established until the 8th or 9th cent. Their four plagal modes, as they are called, started in each case, for technical reasons, a fourth below the authentic modes.

By the end of the 6th cent. Gregorian chant had developed so far that some sort of permanent record was required. *Neumes*, signs placed over the Latin text, were the earliest attempt at musical notation. Gradually lines came into use until a four-line stave was established, probably in the 11th and 12th cent., and with them clef signs, although the treble clef as we know it today did not appear until the 13th cent.

And what is this music—plainchant—like? It is an unaccompanied, single line of melody, which, when we have become used to its "antique" flavour is heard to have a wide range of spiritual and emotional expression, not excluding word painting. The texts used came from the Liturgy. These beautiful, extended lines of flowing, flexible melody can still be heard on Sundays in Roman Catholic cathedrals and churches.

Polyphony is Born.

The 10th cent. saw the appearance of a book called *Musica Enchiriadis* (whose authorship is disputed) which introduced theories about unison singing in which the melody is doubled at the fourth or fifth. Organum, or diaphony, is used to describe this method of writing, a term which confusingly could also be used for a kind of singing where melismatic melody was heard over a drone note on the organ. Rules came into fashion defining which intervals were allowed and which parts of the church services could be sung in more than one part. By the time of Guido d'Arezzo (c. 990–1050), a Benedictine monk who helped advance notation, contrary motion was permitted as the cadence was approached, another technical advance. Gradually the voices became more and more independent, and the third, so long considered a discord, came into use. Pérotin, of Notre Dame, was the first composer to write for three and four voices, and he and his great predecessor Léonin were the great masters of early polyphony. The proximity and spikiness of Pérotin's harmony is almost modern-sounding, and as with Gregorian chant, once we have adjusted ourselves to the sound, this music can be a rewarding experience.

Early Secular Music.

In mediaeval France, towards the end of the 11th cent., there developed what has become known as the age of the troubadours, poet-musicians. They were the successors to the *jongleurs*, or jugglers, and minstrels about whom we know little as practically none of their music has survived. The troubadours hymned the beauty of spring and of ladies. Contemporary with them in Germany were the Minnesingers. Their songs were mostly set in three modes. Adam de la Halle (d. 1287), because so much of his music survives, is perhaps the best known of the troubadours. He was a notable composer of *rondels*, an early form of round, of which the English *Sumer is icumen in*, written by a monk of Reading c. 1226, is a fine example. In that modes were used, the troubadours' music remained definitely akin to that of ecclesiastical hymns, although there is an undoubted feeling of our modern major scale in some of the songs.

Ars Nova and Early Renaissance.

The term *ars nova* derives partly from writings of Philippe de Vitry (1291–1361) who codified the rules of the old and the new music in a valuable treatise. This *new art* represented a freeing of music from organum and rhythmic modes, and an increase in the shape and form of melodic line. France was the centre of music during the 14th cent. and apart from Philippe de Vitry the leading composer was Guillaume de Machaut (1300–77), who wrote many secular works as well as a polyphonic setting of the Mass. His music is notable for its vigour and tenderness as well as for its technical expertise. Meanwhile in 14th-cent. Italy a quite separate branch of *ars nova* was developing. Imitation and canon were to be noted in the music of Italian composers, and vocal forms such as the Ballata, Madrigal (which often included instrumental accompaniment) and Caccia (a two-voice hunting song in canon) were common. The greatest Italian composer of this period was the blind organist and lutenist Francesco di Landini (*c.* 1325–97). Italian pieces of the time, as compared with their French counterparts, are notable for their sensual rather than their intellectual qualities, a difference—it has been noted—between The Southern and The Northern New Art.

England was less affected by *ars nova*, but surviving music shows the influence of the Continent. Not until the 15th cent. did she begin to make a significant contribution to the history of music. Both John Dunstable (*c.* 1380–1453), who was no less eminent as a mathematician and an astronomer than as a musician, and his contemporary Lional Power advanced the technique of music by their method of composition (use of the triad, for instance) and mellifluous style. Their musicianship was much appreciated on the Continent. Dunstable depended less upon the use of *cantus firmus*—a fixed melody—and increased the use of free composition.

After Dunstable the next great figure in European music was Guillaume Dufay (*c.* 1400–74), the most celebrated composer of the Burgundian school. His music is distinguished for its blend of flowing melody, cleverly wrought counterpoint and tender expressiveness. Much travelled, Dufay was a man of catholic outlook. Together with Dunstable and the Burgundian Gilles Binchois he bridged the gap between 14th cent. *ars nova* and the fully developed polyphony of the 15th cent.

Composers of the 14th and 15th cents. also showed an interest in secular music, and many of their songs (those of Binchois particularly) have been preserved.

The results of Dufay's good work can be heard in the flowering of the Franco-Netherland school later in the 15th cent. Its two most notable representatives are Ockeghem (*c.* 1420–95) and his pupil Josquin des Prés (*c.* 1450–1521), who carried musical expressiveness even further than Dufay; their work can also be grand and majestic. Indeed Josquin's wide range, from the humorous to the dignified, partially accounts for his justly deserved high reputation. He was a master of counterpoint but tempered his mechanical ingenuity with imaginative insight.

Throughout the Renaissance choral music was breaking away, as we have seen, from its earlier bonds. The mediaeval tradition of having the *cantus firmus* in the tenor went by the board; the use of dissonance, when only two voices were used in mediaeval times, was abandoned in favour of euphony; and all the voices, democratically, came to share the musical lines. Composers also began to respect their texts; where words were previously fitted to the music, the reverse was now the case. In Josquin's music, indeed, we have the first attempts at symbolism: matching verbal ideas with musical ones. The importance of this musical renaissance has been realised only over the past thirty years. At last the Renaissance composers are coming to be seen not merely as historical figures relevant only in so far as their work culminated in the great classical composers,

but as masters in their own right, whose music should be nearly as familiar to us as is that of a Mozart or a Beethoven.

With the exception of Dufay, little is known of the lives of the musicians so far mentioned. Most of them were in the service of royal or ducal households where they were in charge of the chapel choir, or else they worked in or around the great cathedrals, teaching at choir-schools. They were well rewarded for their services and their social position was probably high.

During recent years there has been an appreciable revival of interest in mediaeval music. Numerous ensembles have emerged with their own ideas about how it should be performed—an indication that it is alive and not just part of the history of music. It can communicate just as well as the music of later eras.

The Sixteenth Century.

By the 16th cent. music in England was a steadily expanding art and much encouraged. Music-making in the home was becoming quite the fashion in social circles. The Chapels Royal remained the chief musical centres but the music was changing with the development of new secular forms so that it was not so much religious as a part of life. Composers began their lives as choirboys and received a thoroughgoing education, both theoretical and practical.

Carrying on from where Josquin and his contemporaries left off, Palestrina in Italy, Victoria in Spain, Lassus in the Netherlands, and Byrd in England brought the polyphonic style to its zenith. At the same time came the rise of the madrigalists, first in Italy, then in the Netherlands; and then the beginnings of instrumental music as it came to be known in the succeeding centuries.

The vocal composers began to use chordal (homophonic) as well as contrapuntal (polyphonic) methods of writing—examples are Victoria's *Ave Verum Corpus* and Palestrina's *Stabat Mater*—but polyphony was still the fullest most magnificent instrument of composition, as for instance in Byrd's *O Quam Gloriosum* which shows an eager response to the mood and to the inflection of the words in a kind of vocal orchestration. A feature of all these composers' music, but more especially that of Victoria (*c.* 1535–1611) and Palestrina (1525–94), is its serene simplicity and fervour of utterance. Palestrina was perhaps more spacious in his effects, Victoria the more passionate. How well we can imagine—and sometimes hear—their music resounding down the naves of the great cathedrals of Europe.

The music of Lassus (*c.* 1532–94) is distinguished both in sheer amount and in vitality. His mastery in the field of motets was unrivalled, encompassing a wide range of subject and mood. He and his fellow Flemish composers, Willaert, de Monte and Arcadelt, were also expert in the Madrigal, a form popular in Italy and England as well. The Madrigal was a contrapuntal setting of a poem, usually not longer than twelve lines, in five or six parts. The subject (of the poetry) was usually amorous or pastoral. It was a short-lived, but highly prolific vogue. Orlando Gibbons (1583–1625), Thomas Weelkes (*c.* 1573–1623), and John Wilbye (1574–1638) were the most prominent English exponents.

Instrumental Music.

By the end of the 14th cent. instrumental music began to become something more than mere anonymous dance tunes or primitive organ music. Instruments often accompanied voices, or even replaced them, so that the recorder, lute, viol, and spinet indoors, and sackbuts and shawms outdoors, had already been developed by the time instrumental music came to be written down. Gradually a distinction grew up between what was appropriate to the voice and what was suitable for instruments, Byrd, Gibbons, and Giles Farnaby in England, the great blind keyboard player, Cabezón (1510–66) in Spain, and Fresco-baldi (1583–1643) in Italy produced valuable instrumental works. Perhaps the *Parthenia* and the *Fitzwilliam Virginal Book*, collections of Early English Keyboard music, give as fair a representa-tive idea as any of the development of instrumen-tal form at this time.

In chamber music musicians often played collections of dance tunes strung together to make a whole; or they chose fantasies (or "fancies"), where a composer altered a tune as he wished. Then there were sets of variations on a ground, that is a simple tune played over and over again on a bass viol.

As far as brass instruments are concerned, they were often used on festive occasions in spacious halls or in cathedrals. The Venetian composer Andrea Gabrieli (*c.* 1510–86) was the first to com-bine voice and instruments and his nephew Giovanni Gabrieli (1557–1612) carried the process further to produce sacred symphonies, often using antiphonal effects.

Drama in Music.

Not until the end of the 16th cent. did anyone begin to think about combining drama and music, and so "invent" the new art we know today as opera. A group of artistic intelligentsia met to-gether in Florence and conceived the idea of re-viving the ancient declamation of Greek tragedy. They took Greek mythological subjects, cast them in dramatic form, and set them to music, not in the choral polyphonic style of the Madrigal, but with single voices declaiming dialogue in music. The earliest examples of what was called *Dramma per Musica* were Peri's *Dafne* in 1597 (now lost) and his *Euridice*, in which he co-operated with Caccini. The new style came to its full flowering with the appearance of Monteverdi (1567–1643), whose genius would surely have shone in any age.

Monteverdi's first opera, *Orfeo*, produced in 1607, is a landmark of dramatic expression, and it is nothing less than a catastrophe that so many of his later operas have been lost. His *Orfeo* pro-vides the basic ground work for the operas of the next two centuries: recitative, accompanied re-citative, and aria. His last opera *L'Incoronazione di Poppea*, written when he was at the great age (for those days) of 75, succeeds in its aim of creat-ing a free, fluid form, slipping easily from recitative to arioso and even aria without the strict, closed forms that were to be used in the 17th and 18th cent. He focuses attention to an almost unbe-lievable extent on character rather than situation. He creates real people with all their faults and foibles—the kittenish, sexually attractive Poppaea, the power-drunk, infatuated Nero, the noble Seneca, and the dignified, rejected empress Octavia. As recent productions have shown these characters leap from the musical page as if they had just been created, each unerringly delineated in musical terms. Only the vocal line, the continuo, and the very incomplete instrumen-tal ritornelli parts have been preserved, but in sen-sitive, knowledgeable hands tonal variety in the shape of wind and string parts can be added, as we know certain instruments were available to the composer.

Monteverdi's successors were Cavalli (1602–76), Cesti (1623–69) and Stradella (1642–82), who gave the solo voice more and more prominence en-couraged by the advent of the castrati's brilliant voices. These artificially created singers had a vogue and popularity similar to "pop" singers of today, fêted wherever they appeared. The aria became more extended and ornate, and dramatic verisimilitude gradually but inexorably took second place to vocal display. An aria was nearly always in *da capo* form, the first section being repeated after a contrasting middle one.

Sixteenth- and Seventeenth-century Church Music.

Of course, the invention of a new dramatic style affected church music too. The concentration on

the vertical aspect of music (homophony) as opposed to the horizontal (polyphony) led to the increasing importance of the voice in religious music. In Italy, it is true, there was the late-flowering, great madrigalist Carlo Gesualdo (1560–1614), whose harmonic daring still astonishes us today, but by 1600 the cantata was coming to replace older forms in church music. In its simplest form this was a story told in accompanied recitative, Giacomo Carissimi (*c.* 1604–74) was one of the first significant composers of this new form. He too was in on the birth of the oratorio, whose forerunner was the *sacra rappresentazione* (mystery or miracle play) of early 16th-cent. Florence. Then in the mid-16th cent. St. Philip Neri brought in elements from popular plays on sacred subjects in his services in Rome, designed to hold the attention of youth—rather as certain parsons have tried with "pop" services today. Emilio del Cavalieri (*c.* 1550–1602) and Carissimi developed the form adding arias and choral move-ments, omitting actual representation. Alessan-dro Scarlatti (1660–1725), whose oratorios bear a close resemblance to his operas, brought oratorio to its zenith in Italy.

Heinrich Schütz (1585–1672), Bach's great predecessor, was the founder of German church music. His historical place has never been called into question but only in recent times have the intrinsic merits of his own music come to be re-cognised. He studied with Giovanni Gabrieli in his youth and later came under the influence of Monteverdi, so it was not surprising that he brought Italian ideas across the Alps to Germany and wrote the first German opera *Daphne*, now sadly lost. He also introduced his country to the Italian declamatory style and to the new kind of concertato instrumental writing. But his drama-tic religious works were his greatest contribution to musical development. He wrote with a devout intensity, bringing to life the scriptural texts by closely allying his urgent music to the words. His three settings of the Passions—Matthew, Luke, and John—paved the way for Bach's even more remarkable works in this genre. Two contem-poraries of Schütz, Johann Herman Schein (1586–1630) and Samuel Scheidt (1587–1654), were both important figures in German Reformation music.

Lully, Purcell, and Seventeenth-century Opera.

France resisted the tide of Italian opera, al-though paradoxically it was an Italian, Jean-Baptiste Lully (*c.* 1632–87), who charted the different course of French opera which was from the beginning associated with the court ballet. His musical monopoly during the reign of Louis XIV was put to good use. In his thirteen operas the libretto, usually on classical, allegorical themes, plays a vital part in the composition, which is therefore less clearly divided between recitative and aria than in Italian opera. The orchestration and the ballets assume greater importance than in the traditional Italian form. It was, in short, a more realistic, less stylised art.

In England, opera developed out of the enter-tainment known as the Masque, a succession of dances, accompanied by voices and instruments and often incorporated in a drama or spectacle. Henry Lawes's (1596–1662) setting of Milton's *Comus* is probably the most famous of these en-tertainments. The *Venus and Adonis* of John Blow (1649–1708) can be called the first English opera because here the music is gradually gaining the ascendancy over the spoken word. However, it was Purcell (*c.* 1659–95), Blow's pupil, with *Dido and Aeneas*, who really gave dramatic life to the new medium by giving his characters a true musical personality that was subtler than any-thing the mere spoken word could achieve. The grief-laden lament of the dying Dido "When I am laid in earth" has an expressive power, achieved by extraordinarily bold harmonic effects, never before and seldom since achieved. The opera was in fact written for a young ladies' boarding school. Purcell followed it with several outstand-ing semi-operas—such as *The Fairy Queen* (to Dryden's text). His untimely death at the age of 36 probably robbed us of several full-length operas—and perhaps a consequence of this was that English music after him did not develop as it should have done.

His verse anthems and much of his instrumental music, especially the Fantasias, are also rich in imaginative mastery through his original use of harmony and counterpoint. However, a large number of his pieces were written for a specific occasion and many of the odes are set to impossibly trite texts. At least his genius was partly acknowledged in his own day, and he was appointed organist in Westminster Abbey where he was buried with due pomp. He is said to have died through catching cold when locked out of his own house at night.

Vivaldi and the Rise of Instrumental Music.

Out of the dance suites popular in the 16th cent. and the beginning of the 17th (known in Italy as the *Sonata da Camera*) developed the concerto. This began as two groups of instrumentalists compared and contrasted with each other as in Giovanni Gabrieli's *Sonata piano e forte*. With Arcangelo Corelli (1653–1713) the concerto grosso took a more definite shape, alternating a solo group of instruments with the main body of strings in three or more contrasting movements. Giuseppe Torelli (1658–1709), Francesco Geminiani (1687–1762) and Tommaso Albinoni (1671–1750) were other notable contributors to the form, but none of the composers so far mentioned has today achieved the popularity of the priest Antonio Vivaldi (*c.* 1678–1741), himself a violinist, who had at his disposal the orchestra at the Ospedale della Pieta in Venice. The young women at this music school also contributed the vocal side of the concerts there of which there are many descriptions. One says: "They sing like angels, play the violin, flute, organ, oboe, cello, bassoon—in short no instrument is large enough to frighten them . . . I swear nothing is so charming than to see a young and pretty nun, dressed in white, a sprig of pomegranate blossom behind one ear, leading the orchestra, and beating time with all the grace and precision imaginable." For this body, Vivaldi wrote about 500 concertos which maintain a remarkably even quality, but "The Four Seasons" are perhaps the most felicitous.

Meanwhile organ music was advancing rapidly in technique. Girolamo Frescobaldi (1583–1643) and Jan Pieterszoon Sweelinck (1562–1621) wrote works that provided the foundation of the Italian and Northern German schools of organ music. Their ricercares gradually developed into the fugue, a vein so richly mined by Bach. Among their successors the most notable figure before Bach was Johann Pachelbel (1653–1706).

Other keyboard music, especially for the harpsichord, was the particular province of France; and Jean-Philippe Rameau (1683–1764) and François Couperin (1668–1733) were both masters of keyboard style and harmonic invention. They wrote many pieces of subtle charm and exquisite craftsmanship.

Bach (1685–1750).

The two giant figures of Bach and Handel bestride the first half of the 18th cent. Their differences are perhaps greater than their similarities. Bach wrote essentially for himself (although of course, he had to satisfy his employers at Cöthen and Leipzig) while Handel was composing to please his wide public. Bach was a provincial, always remaining in central Germany; Handel was widely travelled. Bach was devoutly religious, almost ascetic; Handel was more a man of the world. They never met.

To summarise Bach's vast output in a short space is virtually impossible. One can only try to distil the flavour of his music. He brought the art of polyphony to the highest pitch of mastery that has ever been achieved or is ever likely to be achieved. In his famous "Forty-Eight" and "the Art of the Fugue" he explored all the fugal permutations of the major and minor keys. At the same time his music rose above technical brilliance to achieve, especially in his organ music,

the two Passions, many of the church cantatas, and the B minor Mass, intense emotional and expressive power. The cantatas, from his Leipzig appointment (1723) onwards, were integrated into the services. They consisted usually of a chorus based on a Lutheran hymn tune, recitatives, several extended arias, and a concluding chorus usually a straightforward version of the hymn tune in which the congregation joined. There are some two hundred of these works and they contain a wealth of comparatively unknown and sometimes even unrecognised beauties. The St. John and the St. Matthew Passion extend these procedures to a grand scale, an Evangelist telling the new Testament story in vivid recitative, the chorus taking the part of the crowd, soloists pondering in arias on the meaning of the Gospel, and Jesus's words being sung by a bass. Anyone who has heard either of these works well performed cannot help but dismiss from his mind any idea of Bach as a mere dry-as-dust musical mathematician. In the St. Matthew Passion, every suggestion in the text that can possibly be illustrated by a musical equivalent is so illustrated. The Old Testament Pharasaic law is represented by strict musical forms such as the canon; Christ's sayings are given noble arioso life; and the arias reflect truly the New Testament's compassionate message. Technically the work is a marvel; expressively it is eloquent. The B minor Mass, although it contains borrowings from many of his own works, still stands as a satisfying monumental whole in which Bach's choral writing achieved a new richness, the adaptations being in accord with their new setting.

Bach's instrumental music, especially the violin concertos and the unaccompanied works for violin and cello, not only show the immense range of his powers but also contain many of his deeper thoughts, whereas the orchestral suites and the Brandenburg concertos are more extrovert, particularly the rhythmically exuberant fast movements.

Bach closes an era—that of the later contrapuntalists—by achieving the *ne plus ultra* in fugal composition; his last, incomplete work, The Art of the Fugue, is evidence of that. In recent years there has been a trend towards playing Bach's music on original instruments of his time (or replicas) and singing it with appropriately sized, sometimes all-male choirs.

Handel (1685–1759).

During his lifetime Handel was far more widely recognised as a great composer than Bach, and his music, unlike Bach's, maintained its place in popular esteem until the re-discovery of Bach and the dominance of the symphony placed Handel somewhat in the background.

During the latter part of the 19th cent. Handel's name was mainly associated with mammoth, anachronistic performances of a small sample of his oratorios at the Crystal Palace and elsewhere in England. In his lifetime these works, and all his other pieces in the genre, were sung by a small choir who were outnumbered by the instrumental players. Over the past few years authentic-sized performances of his oratorios and a revival of interest in his operas have revealed the real Handel, unknown to our grandparents.

The operas were neglected partly because the vocal prowess they required—and which the castrati so brilliantly supplied—was no longer available and because their dramatic life, at least according to 19th- and early 20th-cent. tenets, hardly existed. Now it is realised that this neglect has deprived us of an unending stream of glorious melody and of much daring harmony. But perhaps it is in the hitherto disregarded oratorios, such as *Semele*, that Handel's innate dramatic sense and musical range are to be heard gloriously fulfilled, and the pastoral serenade *Acis and Galatea* is surely one of the most delightful scores ever composed.

Handel was a colourful, imaginative orchestrator, and this can be heard both in his accompaniment to vocal music and in his concerti grossi, op. 3 and 6, the earlier set exploiting a diversity of interesting string and wind combination. In his writing he was at home in a polyphonic or homophonic style as his superb choruses show. His organ concertos, of which he was the "inventor" (to quote a contemporary source), were often played between the acts of his oratorios. They are alternately expressive and exuberant pieces calling for some virtuosity from the player. His occasional works, such as the Water Music and Fireworks Music show his ingenuity in extending the range of the typical 17th cent. suite to serve a particular occasion.

Handel's working life was mostly spent in England where his Italian operas were acclaimed. In the years between his arrival here in 1711 and 1729 he wrote nearly thirty operas. It was only when the public tired of these and his reputation slumped that he turned to oratorio with equal success.

Bach and Handel between them crowned the age of polyphony that had lasted for two hundred years or more. After them, it is hardly surprising that composers began looking for a new style, already anticipated in the music of Rameau and particularly Dominico Scarlatti (1685–1737), whose harpsichord sonatas foreshadowed the classical sonata form that was to dominate music for the next two hundred years. The change in musical style about 1750 was partly the result of a change in musical patronage. Bach was the last great composer to earn his living through being employed by the church. The new patrons were the nobility who liked to have a composer on hand to write for the various evening entertainments of the time. For this purpose the princes and dukes had their own orchestras and their own small opera houses. The music required had to be elegant, formal, *galant*. Haydn was exceptionally fortunate in having an employer, Prince Nicholas of Esterhazy, who allowed him to write more or less as he wished so that he was able to develop symphonic form into something more than a pleasing way of passing an evening.

The early symphonists, culminating in Haydn, broke away from Bach's contrapuntal treatment of the orchestra. Instruments now came to be treated in a more colourful manner according to their particular timbre. The court of Mannheim had an orchestra of a standard unheard hitherto, and Johann Stamitz (1717–57) and his son Karl (1745–1801) influenced the great composers who were to follow in their footsteps. The composition of their orchestra was flexible, oboes, flutes, and horns often being added to the standard string section. Bach's son Carl Philipp Emanuel (1714–88) added to and developed symphonic and sonata form, especially as regards keys and subjects.

Haydn and Mozart.

These two figures dominate the second half of the 18th cent. as Bach and Handel do the first. In a brief space only a general picture can be presented of their huge output and influence. Of Haydn's 104 symphonies (there may even be others) nearly all are worthy of study and hearing. The craftsmanship is always remarkable, the invention ever new. Indeed without Haydn's harmonic daring or his melodic ingenuity, the even greater symphonic thought of Beethoven would have been impossible: Haydn laid the groundwork on which his successor built towering edifices. A work such as the 93rd symphony in D is typical of his mature style with its searching introduction, powerfully wrought, earnestly argued first movement, beautiful *Largo* and resourceful bustling finale. Haydn did not fight shy of contrapuntal writing: the development section of this symphony's first movement and the finale are evidence of that, but it was only as an integral part of a predominantly homophonic technique.

Mozart's symphonies are not so different in form from Haydn's but—and this must be a subjective judgment—he put more emotional feeling into his. Nobody could listen to the heart-

searching first movement of his 40th symphony without being deeply moved. It was in his final three works in the medium that Mozart brought his symphonic art to perfection, and these obviously had an effect on Haydn's later symphonies written after them. For passion and tenderness contained within a classical form these late symphonies, and many other of Mozart's works, have yet to be surpassed.

Haydn, who has been rightly termed "the Father of the Symphony", was also the founder of the string quartet—perhaps the most perfect, because the most exactly balanced, form of musical expression. The four instruments—two violins, viola, and cello—discuss, argue, commune with each other over the whole gamut of feeling. In his quartets Haydn's mastery of structure is even more amazing than in his symphonies. Mozart's quartets (especially the six devoted to Haydn) and even more his quintets achieve miracles of beauty in sound, nowhere more so than in the first movement of the G minor (his most personal key) quintet. The two late piano quartets show how the piano *can* be ideally combined with strings. His clarinet quintet is also a masterly work.

Haydn did not leave any concertos of consequence. Mozart's, especially those for piano, are among his greatest works. As a brilliant clavier player himself, he showed a consummate skill in writing for the keyboard. Although the instrument he knew was slightly less advanced than the piano today, his concertos call for virtuosity in execution, yet they are as searching in emotional content as the late symphonies and quartets. Indeed the C major concerto (K. 467) and the C minor (K. 491) may be said to hold the quintessential Mozart. As well as twenty (mature) piano concertos, Mozart wrote six for the violin, four for the horn, and eighteen others, but none of these, delightful as they are, can be placed in quite the same class.

Of their church music, Haydn's sixteen masses and his oratorios—*The Creation* and *The Seasons* (both late works)—are perhaps more worthy of attention than Mozart's various masses, but we must not forget Mozart's final work—the Requiem or the serene late Motet *Ave Verum Corpus*.

Eighteenth-century Opera.

Mozart—for many the first great opera composer—did not, of course, create his masterpieces out of nothing. In France, Lully was followed by Rameau (1683–1764), who carried on his tradition of using classical themes but developed a more flexible style of recitative and greatly increased vividness of expression. But it was Gluck (1714–87) who more than anyone broke out of the straitjacket of the now ossified Italian form of opera—dominated by the singer—and showed just what could be achieved in moving human terms. Drama in music really came of age with his *Orfeo e Euridice* (1762), *Alceste* (1767) and *Iphigénie en Tauride* (1779). His simplicity and poignancy of expression were not lost on Mozart.

Meanwhile in Germany a kind of opera called *Singspiel* appeared during the 18th cent. Breaking away from classical themes, mundane stories were told in dialogue and music.

Until quite recently Haydn's operas were dismissed as unworthy representations of his genius but, chiefly through the enlightening efforts of the Haydn scholar, H. C. Robbins Landon, some of his fifteen surviving works in the medium have been successfully revived. They have proved to be perfectly viable for the stage and, especially in the ensembles, full of that delightful invention to be found in the rest of his opus, if on a less fully developed scale. Still as musical drama they inevitably fall far short of Mozart's achievements, for the younger composer seems to have had an instinctive feeling for the stage. Into his operas he poured his most intense, personal music. He vividly portrays the foibles, desires, loves, and aspirations of mankind.

The earlier, immature stage pieces of his youth led to such works as *Lucio Silla* (1772) and *La*

Finta Giardiniera (1775) with their first glimpses of the glories to come. His first indubitably great opera is *Idomeneo* (1781). Despite its unpromisingly static plot, *Idomeneo* reveals Mozart's stature through its ability to breathe new life into a conventional *opera seria* form. Though influenced by Gluck it is yet more human and touching in its musical expression. To succeed this Mozart wrote a much more frivolous piece *Die Entführung aus dem Serail*. Stemming from the *Singspiel* tradition, it none the less creates real-life characters who have much charming music to sing.

After three lesser pieces Mozart embarked on his four masterpieces—*Le Nozze di Figaro* (1786), *Don Giovanni* (1787), *Cosi fan tutte* (1790), and *Die Zauberflöte* (1791).

Figaro, as well as being a delightful comedy, explores more fully than any previous opera situation and character, which find expression in beautiful arias and in two finales of symphonic proportion. In *Don Giovanni*, less satisfactory as a dramatic structure, the range of musical characterisation and insight into human motives is widened still further. *Cosi* lyrically but humorously expresses the follies of love. Mozart could not help but love his characters and his music for them is at one and the same time amusing and heartfelt, *Die Zauberflöte*—The Magic Flute—displays Mozart's deep-felt concern for his fellow men and for truth in an opera of great spiritual strength. Nor has opera any more loveable personality than the birdcatcher Papageno. Mozart's final opera *La Clemenza di Tito*, extolling imperial magnanimity, has never achieved the success or popularity of his other maturer stage works, though it contains much excellent music, and has recently been revived with honour in several opera houses.

Beethoven.

Mozart was the last major composer to depend, to any large extent, on private patronage for his living, and even he left the service of the Archbishop of Salzburg because he could not stand the restrictions imposed on his freedom. Henceforth composers would have to stand on their own two feet with all the advantages (liberty) and disadvantages (lack of security) that implied. Beethoven (1770–1827) was the first such composer of importance.

Although his work is usually divided into three periods, that division is somewhat too arbitrary, for no other composer in history, with the possible exception of Wagner, has shown such a continual development of his genius. Coming at just the right moment in musical history, he crowned the achievements of Haydn and Mozart with music of the utmost profundity of thought and feeling that looks back to its classical heritage and forward to the romantic movement of the 19th cent. His influence on musical thinking and writing is incalculable.

His first period shows his strong melodic gifts and the beginning of his individuality in developing form and structure to suit his own ends and match his particular genius. Unusual keys are explored, unusual harmonic procedures employed. With the "Eroica" (his third symphony) he established his position as a great composer. The unity of purpose he here achieved within a long and diverse structure is truly staggering, even today. In the first movement alone the formal invention and cogency went far beyond what even Mozart had achieved in his "Jupiter" symphony, and the second movement—a vast funeral March—has an overwhelmingly tragic emotional content. But the "Eroica" was followed by six equally great symphonies, each one as varied, as inventive, as unified as the others. The ninth symphony is significant both for its length and its finale. Here Beethoven crowns three superb instrumental movements with a choral movement that, as well as summing up all that has gone before, expresses in music the joy in existence more ecstatically than any other work.

The burning intensity of Beethoven's genius is just as evident in his chamber music. His quartets are the product of a revolutionary age in which the social graces and formal restraint of the 18th cent. were thrown off in a search for a more personal mode of expression. The early op. 18 set, and the Razoumovsky quartets, op. 59, go even beyond the range of Haydn's and Mozart's works in the medium but it was in his late quartets, his final musical testament, that Beethoven refined and distilled his art for posterity. No words can possibly describe their unique quality, but any and every chance should be taken to make their acquaintance; the effort required will be more than amply rewarded.

The early piano concertos do not reach quite that level of attainment, but the last three, together with the violin concerto, are on a par with the finest of the symphonies and quartets, as well as being considerable tests of the performers' technique. The Triple Concerto for piano, violin, and cello is an unusual and rewarding work.

Beethoven's grandest choral work—and one of the most noble in existence—is the Mass in D (*Missa Solemnis*). Its vast scale and sublime utterance often defeat performers, but when it is successfully done there is no more spiritually uplifting experience for the listener, except perhaps Beethoven's only opera, *Fidelio*. This simple escape story was transformed by Beethoven's creative fire into a universal symbol of liberty, the composer identifying himself with the struggle for freedom from tyranny and release from darkness.

Beethoven lived in a period of war and revolution. A passionate believer in the brotherhood of man and in liberty, he was shocked to find his ideals thrown over by revolutionaries-turned-dictators. His own tragedy of deafness, which came upon him at the moment of his triumph, nearly submerged him, but in the end he won through and produced the string of masterpieces from the "Eroica" onwards. Hope springing from despair, love from hatred, victory over defeat, these are the unquenchable legacies left by Beethoven.

The Romantic Movement.

Inevitably, the Romantic movement in literature that burst forth about 1800 was bound to have its counterpart in music. And so it was. Breaking the classical bonds, composers such as Schubert, Schumann, Liszt, and Berlioz sought a new freedom in musical expression. Form became of less importance than content; and that content often had literary connections. For their purposes a larger orchestra was needed and supplied, but the miniature, the song especially, because of its very personal connotation, was also a favourite form.

Schubert (1797–1828)—described by Liszt as "the most poetic of musicians"—is perhaps the greatest lyrical genius in musical history. In him the Viennese tradition and influence of Haydn, Mozart, and Beethoven reached its zenith. The song was always Schubert's starting point, so it is hardly surprising that his reputation as a song writer has never been impaired but in his symphonic and instrumental works too it is always his inexhaustible fund of melody that first calls for attention. Nobody could listen to his "Trout" quintet, for piano and strings, his octet, his fifth symphony, or his song cycle *Die Schöne Müllerin* without being enchanted and invigorated by the sheer tunefulness of the music. But there is much more to Schubert than this: his understanding of the possibilities of harmonic change, his grasp of orchestral coloration (in the great C major symphony, for instance), his free use of sonata structure.

Although Mozart, Haydn, and Beethoven had all contributed to the song as an art form, it was with Schubert that it achieved its first full flowering. If he had written nothing but his songs, his place in the musical firmament would be assured. With his *Erlkönig* in 1815 the German *Lied* came of age and from then until the end of his life he wrote more than six hundred songs, hardly a dud among them. Whether it is the charm of *Heiden-röslein*, the drama of *Der Doppelgänger* or the numbed intensity of the *Winterreise* cycle, Schubert unerringly went to the heart of a poet's meaning; indeed he often raised poor verses to an inspired level by his settings.

There is only room to mention one or two other composers, some of them wrongly neglected, who were roughly contemporaries of Beethoven and Schubert: the Czech Dussek (1760–1812), who like Beethoven bridges the classical–romantic gulf, Boccherini (1743–1805), the two Italian opera composers Cimarosa (1749–1801) and Paisiello (1740–1816), the Frenchman Méhul (1763–1817) and the German Hummel (1778–1837).

Weber (1786–1826) lacked Beethoven's energy and constructive powers and Schubert's sheer lyrical profundity, but he is an important figure, especially in the field of opera, where his *Der Freischütz* and *Oberon* led the way to a more flexible, dramatically realistic form of opera. His vivid imagination exactly fitted the new romantic mood abroad. The sheer beauty in the melodic shape of his music is also not to be denied. His instrumental works are attractive but insubstantial.

Mendelssohn and Schumann.

Mendelssohn (1809–47) was the civilised craftsman among the Romantic composers. A boy genius—many of his finest works were written before he was twenty—he maintained the importance of classical form while imbuing it with his own affectionate brand of poetic sensibility. His third and fourth symphonies—the "Scottish" and "The Italian"—(and possibly the fifth "The Reformation"), his string quartets (some of which go deeper than the rest of his music), octet, violin concerto, first piano concerto, and of course, the incidental music to "A Midsummer Night's Dream" represent his tidy yet effervescent style at its most winning.

Schumann (1810–56) is less easy to categorise. His early romantic flame was burnt out by some flaw in his intellectual and/or emotional make-up, and his inspiration seems to have declined in later years. No matter, by then he had given us the marvellous song cycles of 1840, an ever fresh piano concerto, many fine piano solos, including the mercurial, popular *Carnaval* and four symphonies, which, if not structurally perfect, contain much lovely music. The joys and sorrows of love and the feeling for natural beauty are all perfectly mirrored in these charming, lyrical works, and in the genial piano quintet.

Romantic Giants.

Berlioz (1803–69) and Liszt (1811–86) are the two most typical representative composers of the Romantic era. Both have always been controversial figures, with ardent advocates and opponents either unduly enthusiastic or unfairly derogatory. Berlioz might be termed the perfect painter in music. With an uncanny mastery of orchestral sound he could conjure up the countryside, the supernatural and the historical with the utmost ease. He based his music on the "direct reaction to feeling" and a desire to illustrate literature by musical means. That his technical expertise was not always the equal of his undoubted genius, can be heard in many of his larger works such as the dramatic cantata *The Damnation of Faust* and the dramatic symphony *Romeo and Juliet*, yet most people are willing to overlook the occasional vulgarity for the ineffable beauty of his many fine pages, but brutal cuts in his music, such as are often made in, for instance, his epic opera *The Trojans* only have the effect of reducing the stature of his works. We must accept him, warts and all. Anyone who has seen the two parts of *The Trojans*, presented complete in one evening at Covent Garden, will realise that Berlioz knew what he was about.

His output is not quantitatively large but includes several monumental works, as well as *The Trojans*, The *Requiem* ("Grand Messe des Morts") requires a tenor solo, huge chorus and orchestra, and brass bands, although Berlioz uses these forces fastidiously. The *Symphonie funèbre et triomphale* calls in its original form, for choir brass, and strings. But Berlioz was just as happy writing on a smaller scale as his exquisite song cycle, to words of Théophile Gautier, *Nuits d'Été*, shows. Gautier perhaps summed up better than anyone Berlioz's singular talent: "In that renaissance of the 1830s Berlioz represents the romantic musical idea, the breaking up of old moulds, the substitution of new forms for unvaried square rhythms, a complex and competent richness of orchestration, truth of local colour, unexpected effects in sound, tumultuous and Shakespearian depth of passion, amorous or melancholy dreaminess, longings and questionings of the soul, infinite and mysterious sentiments not to be rendered in words, and that something more than all which escapes language but may be divined in music."

During his lifetime Liszt was fêted and honoured not only by his musical colleagues but by the world at large, which idolised him and his piano. Then his reputation took a plunge from which it has only recently recovered. To be sure much of his early music is glitter and gloss, but his symphonies and tone poems—especially the Faust Symphony, the Dante Symphony (both, of course, inspired by literature), and *Orpheus* and *Prometheus*—and his late piano works show that he was an extraordinary harmonic innovator. The piano sonata in B minor brings his romantic, wilful temperament within a reasonably stable, pianistic form, and as such is a landmark in the repertory of the instrument. Liszt's output was prodigious, but the inquiring listener should explore the more original of his compositions already mentioned to form a true picture of his fertile genius.

Chopin.

Chopin (1810–49) was the master of the keyboard, par excellence. His development of the technical and expressive capabilities of the piano is unique in musical history. His inventive powers were poured out with nervous passionate energy and in a highly individual style through twenty astonishing, possibly agonised years of creative activity before his early death. A Chopin melody, limpid, transparent, singing, can be recognised easily by anyone, but his style gradually developed into something more subtle, more satisfying than pure melody. He took the greatest care of every detail so that any alteration, however small, upsets the perfect balance of his work. His poetic sensibility can be found in any of his works; for his constructive ability we must turn to the Ballades, the B minor Sonata, and the Barcarolle, while the Preludes and Studies blend technical powers and emotional expressiveness in ideal proportions.

Nineteenth-century Opera.

After Mozart's operas and Beethoven's *Fidelio* the medium might have been expected to decline. Instead it took on a new, if different, lease of life that culminated in Verdi's extraordinary output.

Rossini (1792–1868) created a world of exuberant high spirits in his operatic works that are as cheerful and heart-warming today as they were when they were first performed.

He always worked in and around the lyric theatres of Italy and between 1810 and 1830 poured out a stream of works, not all of which can be expected to be masterpieces. However, *Il Barbiere di Siviglia*, *L'Italiana in Algieri*, *La Cenerentola* and *Le Comte Ory* will always delight audiences as long as opera houses exist. Although these works are difficult to sing really well, their vitality and charm can never be submerged even by poor voices or indifferent staging.

His German contemporaries were critical of his confidence and frivolity, but his works show a consistency of invention and an irresistible tunefulness that anyone might envy. In recent years, there has also been a renewed interest in his more serious operas—*Otello* (1816), *La Gazza Ladra* (1817), *Semiramide* (1823), *La Siège de Corinthe* (1820), and *Guillaume Tell* (1829)—which were certainly surpassed in dramatic power by his successors but which nevertheless are not to be despised or neglected.

William Tell, to give it its most popular title, was his last work for the stage although he lived on for nearly forty years in retirement in Paris, scene of many of his greatest successes. There he enjoyed good living, dispensing *bons mots*, and occasionally composing trifles. An exception is the unpretentious *Petite Messe Solennelle*, written originally for soloists, chorus, a harmonium, and two pianos. Rossini later orchestrated it, but he would not allow it to be performed during his lifetime. The first public performance was on 28 February 1869, as near as possible to the 78th anniversary of the composer's birth on Leap Year Day 1792.

In contrast to the mercurial Rossini, Vincenzo Bellini (1801–85) was an exquisite, romantic figure dealing with exquisite, romantic stories, an operatic equivalent to Chopin, who much admired him. His delicate, sinuous vocal line (in the arias) and brilliant acrobatics in the final sections (cabalettas) require singers of the utmost accomplishment to do them justice, although his music is never as florid as Rossini's. His most typical and popular works are probably *La Sonnambula* (1831), *Norma* (1831) and *I Puritani* (1835). The first is a tender, homely country story, the second an almost heroic lyrical drama of sacrifice, and the third a rather unsatisfactory historical story redeemed by its appealing music. In our own day singers of the calibre of Maria Callas, Joan Sutherland, Giuletta Simionato, and Marilyn Horne have brought Bellini's operas a popularity almost equal to that they enjoyed at the time they were written.

Gaetano Donizetti (1797–1848) was an even more prolific operatic composer than Rossini. He wrote at least 75 works, mostly for the Italian stage, several of which, such as *Alfredo il Grande* or *Emilia di Liverpool*, are never likely to be revived, but during the past few years, with the renewed interest in what are called the *Ottocento* operas, many of his serious operas have been resuscitated and found as enjoyable in performance as his more frequently heard comedies.

He was a well-grounded musician and although his invention is often criticised for being too tied to the conventions of his day performances often belie this reputation, his dramatic instinct proving sure. *Lucia di Lammermoor*, because of the chances it offers to a coloratura soprano with tragic pretensions, has always held the stage and of late, *Lucrezia Borgia*, *Anna Bolena*, *La Favorita*, and *Poliuto* have all been successfully revived. Of his lighter works, the comedies *L'Elizir d'Amore* and *Don Pasquale* have never declined in popularity. One of his last works was *Linda di Chamounix* (1842) which he wrote for Vienna where it aroused such enthusiasm that the Emperor appointed him Court Composer and Master of the Imperial Chapel.

French Opera.

The taste in Paris was for more and more lavish productions. Following Spontini (1774–1851), whose works were comparatively austere, came Halévy (1799–1862) and Giacomo Meyerbeer (1791–1864) whose operas contain all the ingredients that came to be expected of "Grand Opera"—spectacle, huge ensembles, showpieces for the soloists, and extended, if superfluous ballet. Drawing from Italian, German, and French traditions Meyerbeer's works contained everything the public wanted, yet today they are seldom revived, perhaps because his creative powers were essentially derivative, yet when they *are* given, operas like *Les Huguenots*, *Le Prophète*, and *L'Africaine* still have the power to fascinate and his influence on his successors, notably Wagner, was considerable.

Verdi.

Italian opera in the 19th cent. culminated in the works of Giuseppe Verdi (1813–1901), who rose from a peasant background to become his country's most noted composer, as well as something of a natural hero during the period of the Risorgimento. His earliest works, indeed, often roused his hearers to patriotic fervour. For instance, *Nabucco* (1841), with its theme of an oppressed people seeking deliverance, was treated as a symbol of the Italians' fight for freedom.

Musically, Verdi developed out of all recognition during the course of his long career. The continuously flowing structure of his last two operas *Otello* and *Falstaff* is very far removed from the start–stop formulas, inherited from his predecessors, of his first works, yet even they are touched, in harmonic subtleties, orchestral felicities, and a sense of drama, by a spark of genius, a burning inspiration that sets him apart from all other operatic composers. *Ernani* (1844), *I due Foscari* (1844), and *Luisa Miller* (1849) all have foretastes of glories to come even if as a whole they are flawed dramas, and these "galley years", as Verdi himself later described them, gave him the essential know-how to produce his later, greater operas, as well as establishing him incontrovertibly as the most popular Italian composer of the time.

However, it was with *Rigoletto* (1851), *Il Trovatore* (1853), and *La Traviata* (1853) that Verdi first really staked his claim to immortality. In these pieces his increasing dramatic mastery is married to a wonderful flow of lyrical melody, at the same time controlled by a fine musical sensibility. They were followed by four operas—*Simon Boccanegra* (1857), *Un Ballo in Maschera* (1858), *La Forza del Destino* (1862), and *Macbeth* (revised version, 1865)—in which Verdi overcame complexities of story line by his continually developing musical powers. This period is crowned by *Don Carlos* (written for the Paris Opéra, 1867) a masterly exercise in combining private and public situations in a single, grand, and characterful work. In some respects Verdi never surpassed the subtlety of his writing in this opera. *Aïda* (1871) carried on the process but the characterisation in this ever-popular piece is less refined than in *Don Carlos*, if the grandeur of the design is more spectacular.

The success of *Otello* (1887) owes nearly as much to the skill of Boito whose literary ability combined with musical knowledge (he was himself a composer) presented Verdi with an ideal libretto for his seamless music in which the drama moves inevitably to its tragic end. Recitative, aria, ensemble are fused in a single, swiftly moving music-drama, which in its very different way equals that of Wagner. *Falstaff* (1893) achieves the same success in the field of comic opera, a brilliant, mercurial ending to a distinguished career. If Verdi had written only these two final masterpieces his place in musical history would have been assured.

Brahms.

Brahms (1833–97) has justly been described as "a romantic spirit controlled by a classical intellect," for while complying with most of the formal regulations of sonata form he imbued them with an emotional content that accorded with his time. Indeed Schumann declared that he was the "one man who would be singled out to make articulate in an ideal way the highest expression of our time."

Perhaps in his chamber music will be found the quintessence of his art. The piano and clarinet quintets, the two string sextets, the horn trio, and the violin sonatas all are designed on a large scale yet the expression remains intimate, the design and structure clear.

The symphonies and concertos, though, remain his most popular works; they are part of the solid repertory of every orchestra and most piano and violin players in the world. Their high seriousness, constant lyrical beauty, and control of form are deeply satisfying. They do not provide the extremes of passion and excitement provided by his contemporaries, but their study provides continuous absorption and delight. The double concerto for violin and cello deserves a mention as a unique work in music.

Brahms wrote more than two hundred songs in which the desire for melodic beauty takes precedence over the words and meaning. Many are set to poor poetry, but hidden away are still some unexplored treasures, and the Four Serious Songs, at least, are tragic masterpieces. In a lighter vein the two sets of *Liebeslieder Walzer* for four voices are irresistible. The choral Requiem, too, is a fine work.

Bruckner.

In recent years Bruckner's reputation *vis-à-vis* his great contemporary Brahms has been enhanced in England. The old conception of him as a naïve Austrian unable to grasp the fundamentals of symphonic architecture has died hard, and the prevailing popularity of his grandest works is at last gaining him his rightful place in the 19th-cent. firmament. The nine symphonies and the masses are his chief claim to immortality. They contain melodies of unforgettable beauty, symphonic paragraphs of unparalleled grandeur, and an appreciation of formal development that, though different, is equally as valid as that of Brahms. The movements of his symphonies are long and he often pauses, as if for breath and to admire the scenery, before he reaches the climactic peak of his musical journey. His idiom is best approached by a newcomer to his work through the fourth and seventh symphonies as they are perhaps the easiest to understand, but the fifth, sixth, eighth, and ninth (unfinished) are just as beautiful—and cogently argued—once one has acquired the knack, so to speak, of listening to his music. Most of these works are now to be heard in their original form, stripped of the veneer of "improvements" suggested to the diffident composer by his friends.

The masses, which translate Bruckner's symphonic ideas to the choral plain, and Bruckner's delightful string quintet are worth investigating.

Wagner.

Praised only this side of idolatry by his admirers, unmercifully criticised by his detractors, Richard Wagner (1813–83) is perhaps the most controversial composer in musical history. And so it was bound to be with such a revolutionary figure, whose writings, other than his music, contain, to say the least, dubious theories and whose operas, composed to his own libretti, broke the bonds of the form as known until his time. He regarded music-drama as a fusion of all the arts—music, literature, painting—in one unity. With *The Ring of the Nibelungs* he achieved his purpose; no other work of art has ever tried to encompass the whole of existence. Today, and surely forever, musicians, philosophers, and writers will argue over its meaning, and each age will reinterpret it according to its own lights.

But before he reached this pinnacle of achievement, Wagner gradually transformed opera—through *Rienzi*, *The Flying Dutchman*, *Tannhäuser*, and *Lohengrin*—so that a new mould was fashioned to take what he wanted to pour into it. He introduced the *Leitmotiv*, a musical theme that could be associated with a particular person, situation, or idea, each time it occurred. Slowly he developed the musical form so that the drama could unfold continuously without breaks for arias. By the time he began to write *Tristan and Isolde* and *Die Meistersinger*, he had perfected his methods and had he never undertaken *The Ring* that tragedy and that comedy would have assured him his place in the musical firmament. Indeed, *Die Meistersinger* is considered a masterpiece even by those who are not willing or prepared to accept the rest of the Wagnerian ethos.

The length and complexity of these operas, and of *Parsifal*, a work of unique beauty in spite of

certain *longueurs*, means that it is almost essential to prepare oneself by homework, with libretti and records, before attempting to assimilate them in the opera house. The added effort is well worth while for the ultimate musical satisfaction they bring because Wagner was more than an operatic reformer; he opened up a new harmonic language (especially in the use of chromaticism) that was logically to develop into the atonality of the 20th cent.

Wolf.

As Wagner was the culmination of the 19th cent. symphonic and operatic tradition, so Hugo Wolf (1860–1903) summed up, if he did not surpass, the achievements in song-writing of Schubert, Schumann, and Loewe (1796–1869).

Wolf was a lonely, pathetic man. He lived much of his life in poverty, and eventually lost his reason and died of an incurable disease. These circumstances account perhaps for his almost feverish bursts of creative activity, which were also the outward sign of his burning genius. His greatest contributions to the art of *Lieder* were his extraordinary insight into the poet's meaning and the harmonic means by which he heightened the expression of the words. He raised the importance of the piano part even higher than had Schumann, and in some of his songs the vocal part takes the form of a free declamation over a repeated idea in the piano. However, in the main the vocal and piano parts are interweaved with great subtlety, and he unerringly matched the very varied moods of the poems he chose to set. His greatest creative period was between early 1888 and early 1890 when songs poured from his pen daily—more than 50 settings of the German poet Mörike, 20 of Eichendorff, more than 50 of Goethe, and more than 40 of Heyse and Geibel (the Spanish Song-book). Later he composed songs from Heyse's Italian Song-book and the three Michelangelo sonnets. And the range of his creative understanding was wide, taking in the almost wild passion of the Spanish songs, the humanity and humour of the Italian love-songs, the titanic power of *Prometheus* (Goethe), the varying moods of the Mörike book, and the intangible power of the Michelangelo sonnets. There are almost inexhaustible riches here for the inquiring mind to discover. Outside *Lieder*, Wolf 's output is small, but it includes a sadly neglected opera, *Der Corregidor*, the Italian Serenade for string quartet (alternatively for small orchestra) and a tone poem *Penthesilea*.

Ernest Newman, his greatest champion, summed up his work most aptly: "Wolf practically never repeats himself in the songs; every character is drawn from the living model. It is a positively Shakespearian imagination that is at work—Protean in its creativeness, inexhaustibly fecund and always functioning from the inside of the character or the scene, not merely making an inventory from the outside."

National Movements.

During the course of the 19th cent., alongside the emergence of national political identity, came the rise of nationalism in music, fertilising traditional Western—that is basically German—musical forms with folk material. Of these groups the Russian is certainly the most important, if not the most vital.

Glinka (1804–57) was the first important Russian composer of the national school and, although his two operas *A Life for the Tsar* (sometimes called *Ivan Susanin*) and *Russlan and Ludmilla* are strongly influenced by Italian models, they do introduce Russian song and harmony into the texture. He undoubtedly influenced Borodin (1833–87), Cui (1835–1918), Balakireff (1837–1910), Mussorgsky (1839–81) and Rimsky-Korsakov (1844–1908)—the so-called "Five" of 19th-cent. Russian music. However, each was very much of an individualist too. Borodin was a lecturer in chemistry who wrote in his spare time. His two symphonies, two string quartets led up to his most notable work, the opera *Prince Igor*, left incomplete at his death. Balakireff, friend and adviser to the rest of the group, wrote little himself, but his orchestral works and the piano fantasia, *Islamey*, are worthy of investigation.

Modest Mussorgsky (1839–81) is today seen as the most important and inspired of "The Five." More than the others he used Russian song and Russian speech as the basis of his operas in which he portrayed the lives and destinies of his own people. Although his capacities were seriously impaired by an uncongenial job, poverty, and drinking, he produced two great operas, *Boris Godunov* and *Khovanshchina*, and another *Sorochintsy Fair* that is immensely enjoyable. *Boris* should be given in its original, with spare orchestration, but more often than not it is heard in Rimsky-Korsakov's more elaborate revision. In any case the opera exists in various versions, none of them necessarily the right one; what is important is to hear it in one or the other because of its great portrayal of Boris's personality set against the background of the Russian people, unforgettably presented in choral outbursts. *Khovanshchina* was completed by Rimsky-Korsakov, *Sorochintsy Fair* by Tcherepnin (although other versions also exist). Mussorgsky's songs explore a new vein of naturalistic vocal declamation. Each of the four *Songs and Dances of Death* is a miniature drama worthy of Wolf, although of course in a quite other idiom. The *Nursery* songs miraculously conjure up a child's world as seen from a child's point of view. Many of the individual songs, the *Sunless* cycle too, should be investigated.

Rimsky-Korsakov (1844–1908) is perhaps a less attractive figure because so much of his music seems heartless or merely decorative, but this judgment is probably made on the strength of hearing *Shéhérazade* and the *Capriccio Espagnol* a few too many times. Such of his 15 operas as are played evince a (literally) fantastic mind and lyrical vein, and it is a pity that *Sadko*, *The Snow Maiden*, and *The Tsar's Bride*, at least, are not heard more often.

Tchaikovsky.

Peter Ilyich Tchaikovsky (1840–93) is a more universally admired figure than any of "The Five" and his music is indubitably closer to the mainstream than theirs in that it adheres more nearly to Western European forms. His popularity is due to his unhesitating appeal to the emotions and to his tender, often pathetic melodic expression. His lyrical gift is stronger than his sense of architecture, as he himself admitted. Yet his later symphonies—the fourth, fifth, and sixth (the *Pathétique*)—are all cogently enough argued and invigorating, as can be heard in the hands of a conductor willing to emphasise their formal power rather than their tendency towards sentimentality; the orchestral craftsmanship is also superb. The three piano concertos and the violin concerto offer rare opportunities for virtuoso display within a reasonably dramatic structure and his various overtures are always exciting to hear.

The three ballets—*The Sleeping Beauty*, *Swan Lake*, and *Nutcracker* show Tchaikovsky's skill on a smaller and perhaps more congenial scale, but only two of his operas—*Eugene Onegin* and *The Queen of Spades*—survive in regular performance. They demonstrate his ability to delineate character and his always eloquent melodic invention. His songs often felicitously capture a passing mood or emotion.

Smetana and Dvořák.

The Czech national school is dominated by two composers—Smetana (1824–84) and Dvořák (1841–1904). In his own country Smetana holds a unique position as the father of his country's music—which is remarkable when you consider that he lived in a country that was then under Austrian rule and never spoke the Czech language perfectly. Yet his music is filled with the spirit of Czech history and national life, and many of his operas, his most important contribution, deal purely with national subjects. The reawakening of interest in things national, after Austria's defeat by Italy in 1859, led to the establishment of a Provisional Theatre in 1862 and Smetana's first opera *The Brandenburgers in Bohemia* was produced there in 1866, but its success was eclipsed by the enormous popularity of *The Bartered Bride*, which appeared the same year. Its melodic charm, lively characterisation and cosy humour have carried it round the world and it is the one Smetana opera to be in the repertory of most opera houses. However, his next opera *Dalibor* (1868) is considered by some authorities as his masterpiece. It is conceived on a heroic scale, and frequently rises to great dramatic heights. His later operas include *Libuse* (1872) a solemn festival tableau, *The Two Widows* (1874), a delightful comedy, *The Kiss* (1876), *The Secret* (1878), and *The Devil's Wall* (1882).

His main orchestral work *Má Vlast* (My Country), written between 1874 and 1879, is a cycle of six symphonic poems nobly depicting the life and legends of his country. He composed only three mature chamber works—an elegiac piano trio, written in 1855 in memory of the death of his eldest daughter, and two string quartets, both autobiographical. The first in E minor (1876)—"From My Life"—tells of his youth and aspirations until a terrible, screeching E in *altissimo* describes the onset of deafness; the second in D minor, sadly neglected, was described by the composer as an attempt to explain the "whirlwind of music in the head of one, who has lost his hearing," and was probably influenced by Beethoven's later music.

Dvořák combined a fecund melodic gift with an intelligent grasp of structure. His symphonies and chamber music are mostly written in classical form, yet the works are imbued with a spontaneity and freshness that have not lost one whit of their charm over the years.

He wrote nine symphonies and, although only the last three or four are regularly performed, they are mostly mature works, several of which, for instance No. 7 in D minor (formerly known as No. 2) reach a tragic grandeur at times. They are all orchestrated in a masterly way and are full of delightful detail. Dvořák wanted to show that a Brahms could come out of Bohemia—and he succeeded in doing so while maintaining a definitely individual flavour, strongly influenced by natural rhythms.

He wrote three concertos, one each for piano, violin, and cello. The earlier ones are interesting without being quite in the first flight of the composer's output, but the cello concerto of 1895 is perhaps the composer's crowning achievement—warm, mellifluous, romantic.

He wrote chamber music throughout his long creative life. Some of the early works are weak and derivative, but the later string quartets, the "Dumky" trio, and the piano quartet and quintet are expressive and full of unforced invention. Dvořák felt himself somewhat hampered when setting words, nevertheless his *Stabat Mater* and *Te Deum* are both deeply felt choral works and he wrote songs throughout his career, many of them very fine indeed. He wrote ten operas, but only *Rusalka* (1901) has gained a foothold outside Czechoslovakia.

Janáček.

The Moravian composer Leos Janáček (1858–1928) spent most of his life in Brno as a working musician. His music has recently come to be recognised as some of the most original written in the past hundred years. His operas, in which he closely followed the inflection of the speech of his native land, are his finest works. Over the score of his last opera, *From the House of the Dead*, he wrote the words "In every human being there is a divine spark", and it is this deep love of humanity that permeates all his works. Of his operas *Kátya Kabanová* (1921) and *The Cunning Little Vixen*

(1924), the *Makropoulos Affair* (1926), and *From the House of the Dead* (adapted from a Dostoyevsky novel, 1928) are the most important and they have all been produced in Britain in recent years. His original genius is self-evident in all of them.

Among his orchestral works *Taras Bulba* and *Sinfonietta* should be noted, and his two string quartets, very difficult to play, should be better known. The song cycle, *Diary of one who has disappeared*, for tenor, contralto, and three female voices with piano, and the Glagolithic Mass contain music of much expressive beauty.

Hungary.

The Hungarian musical outburst came somewhat later than that of other countries. Its great figure is Bela Bartók (1881–1945) who, as well as being a national figure, has proved an influential composer in the whole of 20th-cent. music. His mind was full of folk music, but it was transmuted by his strongly personal style and powerful intellect into something highly original. His music is tense and volatile but this restlessness is sometimes relieved by a kind of other-wordly, ethereal lyricism, as in the lovely slow movements of his quartets.

Bartók was affected as much by the musical innovations of Debussy and Stravinsky (see below) as by East European, notably Magyar, folk music and many of his works are an attempt to meld the two.

The most important part of his output is undoubtedly his string quartets which cover most of his creative life. To this intimate form he confided his personal innermost thoughts and in it conducted his most far-reaching musical experiments, thereby extending its boundaries beyond anything previously known. As with Beethoven's late quartets many of Bartok's rely on organic or cyclic development while remaining just within the laws of classical form. As Mosco Carner puts it, "For profundity of thought, imaginative power, logic of structure, diversity of formal details, and enlargement of the technical scope, they stand unrivalled in the field of modern chamber music."

The most important of his orchestral works are the three piano concertos, of which the first two are harsh and uncompromising, and fiendishly difficult to play, while the third, written in 1945, is mellower and more diatonic. The second violin concerto (1937–8) shows the various elements of Bartók's style in full flower, by turns exuberant, passionate, and brilliant. The *Music for Strings, Percussion and Celesta* (1937) is remarkable for its strange sonorities and its fascinating texture. The *Concerto for Orchestra* (1944) is more immediately appealing and again shows the composer in complete command of a large canvas. Of the piano works *Mikrokosmos* (1935) and the sonata for two pianos and percussion (1937) are worth investigating.

His chief stage pieces are *The Miraculous Mandarin* (1919), a harsh, cruel ballet which drew appropriately dramatic music from the composer, and the opera *Duke Bluebeard's Castle* (1911), a luscious, original score that makes one regret that he wrote no more operas later in his career.

Kodály (1882–1967) was from early years closely associated with Bartók and with him collected Hungarian folk melodies using many of them in his music. He worked in many forms and the more important of his works are the *Peacock Variations* for orchestra, and the choral *Psalmus Hungaricus* and *Te Deum*, The *Dances of Galánta*, and the opera *Háry János*, and the sonatas for cello and for unaccompanied cello.

Sibelius, Nielsen and Grieg.

Among Scandinavian composers the Finn Jean Sibelius (1865–1957) and the Dane Carl Nielsen (1865–1931) are outstanding. Sibelius is a lone northern figure ploughing his own furrow oblivious or, at any rate, ignoring the unusual developments that were taking place in Central Europe, yet his seven symphonies are strong as granite, honest, rugged works that will undoubtedly stand the test of time. They are not by any means all similar in mood, or even form. The first is very much influenced by Tchaikovsky and Borodin, the second and third show a more personal style developing, the fourth is terse and tragic, the fifth lyrical, bright, and lucid; the sixth is perhaps most typically Sibelian in its evocation of primeval nature, and the seventh—in one continuous movement—is a more purely abstract piece, notable for its structural logic and the grandness of its themes. The violin concerto is the most easily understood of the composer's main works and has a grateful part for the soloist.

The tone poems *The Swan of Tuonela, Pohjola's Daughter, En Saga, Night Ride and Sunrise, The Bard,* and *Tapiola* uncannily evoke the icy words of the legends of the far north, and the primeval forces of nature. Sibelius's one string quartet *Voces Intimae* and many of his songs are worth hearing too. His music, reviled in some quarters during the 1950s, has since been restored to favour, and seems to be enjoyed again by critics and the general public alike.

Carl Nielsen (1965–1931) is another individualist. His six symphonies, like Sibelius's seven, are the most important part of his output, but whereas Sibelius was dealing with a huge, uninhabited northern landscape, Nielsen is more friendly and serene in his music, which is seldom forbidding, always inventive, throwing a new light, through unusual ideas about harmony, structure and tonality, on traditional forms. He also wrote highly individual concertos for the flute and clarinet, four string quartets and two operas—the dramatic, rather Brahmsian *Saul and David* (1902) and a delightful comedy, *Maskarade* (1906), full of lyrical music.

The Norwegian composer Edvard Grieg (1843–1907) was essentially a miniaturist whose range of feeling was not wide but whose music is always gentle and appealing. His most notable works are the romantic piano concerto, the atmospheric incidental music to Ibsen's play *Peer Gynt*, the charming Lyric Suite, and the small piano pieces. Not an important composer, then, but always an attractive one.

Elgar and the English Revival.

After the death of Purcell there is hardly a name in English music worth speaking of until the 19th cent. when Hubert Parry (1848–1918) and Charles Villiers Stanford (1852–1924), actually an Irishman, led a revival. Their music is seldom heard today, but their pioneer work paved the way for Edward Elgar (1857–1934). Although all were influenced by Brahms they nevertheless managed to establish a new English tradition that has been carried on in our own day. Elgar's symphonies are laid out on a grand, leisurely scale and they are both eloquent and exhilarating. His violin concerto has an elegiac slow movement as has the glorious cello concerto and both contain many fine opportunities for the soloist. His cello concerto is as appealing a work as any by Elgar expressing his innermost thoughts. His *Enigma Variations* are a series of portraits in sound of his friends, but there is another overall theme to go with them that has never been identified. This has not prevented the work from becoming Elgar's most popular, not surprisingly when one considers its charm and melodiousness. Three other orchestral pieces that should not be neglected are his symphonic study *Falstaff*, a many-sided musical picture of the Fat Knight, and the overtures *Cockaigne*, a happy evocation of London, and *In the South*, inspired by a visit to Italy. His three late chamber works, written when he was 61, are reticent, economic pieces that remove any misconception of Elgar as a bombastic composer. His songs are mostly feeble, but the oratorios, notably *The Dream of Gerontius*, show the composer's ability to control a large canvas. The composer himself wrote over the score of *Gerontius*,

"This is the best of me"—a verdict with which we can readily agree.

French Music.

The Belgian César Franck (1822–90) was the main figure in mid-19th-cent. France. His influence spread even wider than his music of which only the D minor Symphony, the Symphonic Variations for piano and orchestra, the piano quintet, and the violin sonata are likely to be encountered today. The leading French piano composers of that time were Gounod (1818–93), Bizet (1838–75) and Massenet (1842–1912). Gounod's *Faust*, Bizet's *Carmen* (composed just before his untimely death when he caught cold after a swim) and Massenet's *Manon* all retain a deserved place in the repertory; each is a well-judged mini-drama unafraid of romantic ardour and forceful, histrionic strokes. Some of Massenet's other numerous operas, such as *Werther* and *Don Quichotte*, have enjoyed a revival in recent years.

Concurrently with similar movements in French painting and poetry came the French Impressionist composers at the end of the 19th cent. Their leader—and one of the great seminal forces of modern music—was Claude Debussy (1862–1918). His aim was to capture a mood or sensation, and he did that by more or less inventing a fresh system of harmony using a whole-tone scale, unusual chords, and by creating in the orchestra new, highly personal textures—there is no mistaking the Debussy idiom once you have heard at least one piece by him. His impressionistic style did not lead him, however, to abandon form as some have suggested, and his main works are just as closely organised as those by classical German composers. His music is sensuous and poetic yet nearly always structurally satisfying as well.

His reputation, at least with the general musical public, rests largely on his orchestral music, a few piano pieces and his only opera *Pelléas et Mélisande*. *La Mer* is a scintillating evocation of the sea in all its moods; *Nocturnes*, *Images*, and *Prélude à l'Après-midi d'un Faune* exactly suggest different places, times, moods—the "Iberia" and "Gigues" sections of *Images*, calling to mind respectively the spirit of Spain and the flickering light of a rainy English night. *Pelléas*, based on a Symbolist drama by Maeterlinck, tells a story of love, jealousy, and murder in predominantly restrained yet emotionally loaded terms. It is an elusive original work that has no predecessor or successor. Intensely atmospheric, rivetingly beautiful, it weaves an irresistible spell over the listener.

Debussy's chamber music is unjustly neglected. His string quartet (1893) was one of the first works in which he displayed his new and strange world of sound, and the three late sonatas, one for violin, one for cello, and the third for flute, viola, and harp are elliptical, compressed pieces which seem to be questing disjointedly into new regions of sound. His songs too, are worthy of investigation, and his piano music, especially the twenty-four Preludes and some of the shorter pieces, contain some of his most imaginative and original ideas and thoughts.

Gabriel Fauré (1845–1924) is a difficult figure to place. He lived through all kinds of musical revolutions yet they seemed to affect the character of his work very little. He has never been, and is never likely to be, a widely known or popular composer, yet his music has a reticence and delicacy that is very appealing. Despite his dreamy, retiring art he was not a recluse, but a very sociable man.

He was content with forms as he found them, but he imbued them with a very personal, human style. Perhaps his art is best heard in his songs. They are not overtly passionate or dramatic but the long, sinuous melodies and subtle harmonies are exquisitely wrought. Of the song-cycles, *La Bonne Chanson*, *Cinq Mélodies* (Verlaine), *Le Chanson d'Eve*, and *L'Horizon Chimérique* are best known. The last written in 1922, when the composer was seventy-seven, is a beautiful setting

of words by a soldier killed in the first World War. There are also many remarkable single songs, many of them settings of poems by Verlaine. His opera *Pénélope*, based on the classical heroine, is unjustly neglected.

He wrote few orchestral pieces, but the *Ballade* for piano and orchestra and the *Pavane* are among his most typical, and delicate compositions, and his outstanding piano music, modelled on Chopin's, includes Nocturnes, Impromptus, and Barcarolles. His chamber music covers more than half a century from the violin sonata of 1876 to the string quartet written the year he died. In that period he composed two piano quartets, two piano quintets, another violin sonata and two cello sonatas, the later works failing to show quite the unforced lyrical grace of the earlier ones. Perhaps Fauré is best approached with the first piano quartet, a charming, easily assimilated work, and the beautiful choral *Requiem*.

Saint-Saëns (1835–1921), an accomplished, cultivated musician, has had a "bad press" but his craftsmanship, as displayed in his symphonies, concertos, and *Samson et Dalila* (one among his 12 operas) is not to be despised.

Henri Duparc (1844–1933), despite a very long life, is known today only for a group of songs he wrote before he was forty. They are among the most emotionally direct yet tasteful melodies ever written. Paul Dukas (1865–1935) is another figure off the beaten track, as it were. He, too, is known only for a handful of compositions. He was strongly influenced by Vincent d'Indy (1851–1931) and the school who strongly opposed Debussy's new ideas, yet he could not help but come under Debussy's spell. Dukas's one great work is his opera *Ariane et Barbe-Bleue*, the text adapted from a Maeterlinck play written with the composer in mind.

Maurice Ravel (1875–1937), a pupil of Fauré, followed in Debussy's footsteps, although his later pieces were more ascetic. Indeed, he was one of the most fastidious of composers, always seeking, and often finding, artistic perfection. The works he wrote before 1918 are definitely of the Impressionist School and it would be difficult to imagine more beautiful sounds than are to be found in the ballet *Daphnis el Chloé*, in the song-cycle *Shéhérazade*, and the piano fantasy *Gaspard de la Nuit*. His first style was summed up in the A minor piano trio (1915). In his later music Ravel was struggling, not always successfully, to keep up with new developments such as jazz and atonality. The piano concerto, for instance, shows very strongly the influence of jazz.

Outstanding orchestral works of his, other than *Daphnis* are *Rapsodie espagnole* (1907), *La Valse* (1920), a sumptuous evocation of the Vienna waltz, and the ever-popular *Boléro*. Two chamber works, besides the trio, are masterpieces—the string quartet (1902–3) and the Introduction and Allegro for Harp, String Quartet, Flute, and Clarinet. This Septet composed in 1906, ravishes the senses with magical sound.

Ravel's piano pieces are perhaps his most notable contribution to music, combining an extraordinary feeling for the instrument's technical possibilities with the sensibility of a Chopin, and in this field *Jeux d'eau*, *Miroirs*, and *Ma Mère l'Oye*, all written just after the turn of the century, come very close to the perfection of *Gaspard de la Nuit*. His songs show his unusual appreciation of the need to fuse poetic and musical values, and he set exotic poems for preference. His output in this field includes the cycle *Histoires naturelles* (1906), acutely observed settings of five poems about birds and animals; *Cinq Mélodies populaires grecques* (1907), charming settings of Greek folk songs; *Trois Poèmes de Mallarmé* (1913); and *Chansons madécasses* (1926), suitably exotic settings of three poems by an 18th-cent. Creole poet called Parny. Finally in 1932 came *Don Quichotte à Dulcinée*, three poems by Paul Morand, Ravel's last composition.

Ravel wrote two operas—the slight but moderately amusing *L'Heure espagnole* (1907), nicely orchestrated in a faintly and appropriately Spanish style and *L'Enfant et les Sortilèges* (1925) to a story by Colette, a delicious fantasy about a naughty child who gets his due punishment for tormenting animals and destroying furniture.

French music after Debussy and Ravel was dominated by the slighter composers known as *Les Six*, the most important of whom were Arthur Honegger (1892–1955, Swiss born), Darius Milhaud (1892–1974) and Francis Poulenc (1890–1963). Each has contributed music of some wit and charm to the repertory. They were influenced by Erik Satie (1866–1925), an eccentric but interesting figure who wrote works with odd titles such as *Three Pear Shaped Pieces*. His music is entirely unsentimental, often ironic.

Spain.

Felipe Pedrell (1841–1922) has been aptly described as the midwife of Spanish nationalist music. As a musicologist and teacher he strongly influenced the two main composers of the school, Manuel de Falla (1876–1946) and Enrique Granados (1867–1916). Falla's output was not large and most of it was written around the years of the first world war. The pre-war years were spent in Paris where Falla came under the influence of Debussy. However his style is individual and evokes all the passion and gaiety of his native land. Perhaps his most typical works are in two ballets *Love the Magician* (1915) and *The Three-Cornered Hat* (1919). The opera *La Vida Breve* (1905) despite its weak libretto also has much appeal. The vivacity and smouldering passion at the heart of the country's character is conjured up by the *Seven Popular Songs* (1914) and the *Nights in the Gardens of Spain* (1916) for piano and orchestra. His later works, especially the harpsichord concerto of 1926, show Falla tending towards a less ebullient, more restrained style. The second opera, *Master Peter's Puppet Show* (1923) is a miniaturist work, refined and intense. His third opera *Atlantida*, left unfinished at his death, was completed by his pupil Ernesto Halffter and first staged in 1962.

Granados was perhaps a more restrictedly Spanish composer than Falla, but his music is unfailingly attractive and deserves to be better known. The opera *Goyescas* (1916) is most famous for the second interlude and opening of Act III—*La Maja y el Ruiseñor* (The Lover and the Nightingale), a haunting, sinuous melody for soprano, generally heard in its original form as a piano solo.

The chief claim to fame of Albéniz (1860–1909) is *Ibéria*, masterly descriptive pieces for piano. Many of his other piano works are now more well known in the form of very effective guitar arrangements. Turina (1882–1949), attempted a more cosmopolitan style, but his most often heard music is typically Spanish.

The Late German Romantics.

While composers such as Debussy, Sibelius, Stravinsky and Schoenberg (see below for the latter pair) were striking out along new paths, Richard Strauss (1864–1949) continued in the trend of 19th-cent. German composers; he was the tradition's last great figure. At least two of his operas—*Salome* and *Elektra*—were considered shocking at the time, but today we can hear that they are essentially big-scale, romantic works—natural successors to Wagner's—however startling the harmonies may once have seemed.

If Strauss did not achieve the granite intellectual greatness of Beethoven or Wagner, there is no denying his melodic genius and powers of fertile invention which overlaid the streak of vulgarity and inflation in his musical make-up. His first outstanding achievement was in the field of the symphonic poem, where he carried the work of composers such as Liszt and Berlioz to its logical conclusion. Starting with *Don Juan* in 1888 and ending with *Sinfonia Domestica* in 1903 he wrote a series of kaleidoscopic works, full of enormous vitality, endless melody, and fascinating orchestration. The most easily assimilated—and the most popular—are *Don Juan* and *Till Eulenspiegel* but some of the longer works, notably *Also Sprach Zarathustra* (based on Nietzsche's

prose poem) and *Don Quixote* (based, of course, on Cervantes's great work) will reward the persistent, inquiring mind with long hours of enthralled listening. Other works sound somewhat dated in their bombastic over-confidence, though Strauss's skill in composition seldom flagged at this stage of his long creative career. The symphonic poems all tell something of a story usually based on a literary source, but it is not essential to the enjoyment of the music to know what this is, although it may be helpful.

Strauss's reputation is even more solidly based on his fifteen operas, the earliest of which *Guntram* was first performed in 1894, the last, *Capriccio*, in 1942. During these years the essentials of Strauss's style changed little, though it became very much more refined as the years passed. His first operatic period ended with the violent, sensual tragedies *Salome* (1905) and *Elektra* (1909), the latter being his first collaboration with his chief librettist, Hugo von Hofmannsthal. Then came their unique *Der Rosenkavalier* (1911), which filters the charm and the decadence of 18th-cent. Vienna through early 20th-cent. eyes. This was followed by *Ariadne auf Naxos* (1912). Originally intended to be given after Molière's *Le Bourgeois Gentilhomme*, it was later presented (1916) without the play but with an amusing Prologue, written by von Hofmannsthal. *Die Frau ohne Schatten* is the most grandiose result of the Strauss–Hofmannsthal partnership. It is a complex psychological allegory, but Strauss's contribution is not on as consistently lofty a level as is his librettist's. *Intermezzo* (1924), which has a libretto by Strauss himself, is a largely autobiographical domestic comedy, which has lately gained in reputation as a compact, charming piece. With *Die Aegyptische Helena* (1928), an opera on a mythical theme, and *Arabella* (1933), another sensuous Viennese comedy, the Strauss–Hofmannsthal collaboration ended on account of the librettist's death. Strauss then wrote *Die Schweigsame Frau* (1935) to a libretto by Stefan Zweig, based on a play by Ben Jonson, and *Friedenstag* (1938), *Daphne* (1938)—a beautiful opera—and *Die Liebe der Danae* (written 1938–40) with Josef Gregor as librettist. His swan-song was *Capriccio*, a dramatisation of the old argument about the relative importance of words and music in opera. The libretto is by the conductor Clemens Krauss and the opera, a serene, melodious work, was a fit end to a great operatic career.

However, Strauss went on composing till nearly the end of his life, adding a group of late orchestral pieces to his already large catalogue of works. The *Metamorphosen* for 23 solo string instruments, is probably the best of these. During his long creative career he wrote numerous songs, many of them, such as *Morgen*, *Wiegenlied* and *Ruhe, meine Seele* of surpassing beauty.

Other notable figures in German music at this time were Max Reger (1873–1916), a somewhat ponderous but highly accomplished composer who, in a quarter of a century of creative life, wrote more than 150 works, of which his sets of variations, his piano concerto, and chamber music are probably the most impressive. Hans Pfitzner (1869–1949), another German traditionalist, is chiefly remembered today for his opera *Palestrina*, about events, now known to be spurious, in the life of the 16th-cent. Italian composer.

Twentieth-century Music.

Gustav Mahler (1860–1911), the Austrian Jewish composer, is one of the most important figures in 20th-cent. music. In a sense he bridges the gulf between the late Romantics, who were tending more and more towards chromaticism and away from established key relationships, and the atonalists, who abandoned the key system entirely. His detractors maintain that his inflation of allegedly banal Viennese beer-house music to unheard-of lengths rules him out of court as a serious writer. His admirers would claim that his music encompasses the whole of life in enormous, valid structures. The truth, if truth there be, perhaps lies somewhere in between: if his material does not always justify the length of his symphonies, and if there are occasional imperfections and *longueurs*, these shortcomings are worth enduring for the sake of the depth of utterance, the humanity and the poetry of the great pages. He admitted himself that "I cannot do without trivialities," but it is out of these impurities that he forged his titanic victories.

His music is undoubtedly best approached through his songs, where the words force him to discipline his wide-ranging vision. *Lieder eines fahrenden Gesellen* (1884), to his own words, *Kindertotenlieder* (1901–4), to poems by Rückert, and some individual songs perfectly relate words to music, and are all of a poignant loveliness. Similarly *Das Lied von der Erde* (1908), especially the last of the six songs, is a touching farewell to the world, nobly expressed.

The ten symphonies, however, are Mahler's most impressive legacy to posterity. They are almost impossible to characterise briefly so vast are they in terms of both length and variety. The first, fourth and ninth are probably the easiest to grasp but the fifth, sixth and seventh, despite flaws, contain some of his most awe-inspiring conceptions. The second and third, both of which use soloists and chorus, are revolutionary in orchestration and structure; they both try, inevitably without complete success, to carry out the composer's dictum, "a symphony should be like the world—it must contain everything." The eighth is even more gargantuan, but as in all Mahler's work size does not mean loss of clarity or an overloading of the structure. Part one—a mighty choral invocation—is a visionary setting of the mediaeval hymn *Veni Creator Spiritus.* Part two, which incorporates adagio, scherzo, and finale in one, is a setting of the final scene of Goethe's *Faust.* Until recently all of Mahler's unfinished tenth symphony that was ever performed was the Adagio, but the musicologist and Mahler scholar, the late Deryck Cooke, provided a performing version of the symphony to critical and popular acclaim during the 1960s and thus added a noble, and also optimistic epilogue to the Mahler opus. The debate over the quality of Mahler's music is likely to continue; one fact, however, that cannot be gain-said is his popularity with an ever-increasing audience, largely made up of young people. There must be something in his uncertainty and intense self-inquiry that accords with the mood of the youthful mind.

Schoenberg and the Second Viennese School.

Arnold Schoenberg (1874–1951) revolutionised Western music by his twelve-note method—a system which uses all the notes of the chromatic scale "and denies the supremacy of a tonal centre," as Schoenberg himself puts it. This serial technique of composition, as it is commonly called, naturally sounds strange to an ear acclimatised to music written, as it were, with a home base, but Schoenberg and his disciples Berg and Webern showed that the system could produce works that were something more than mere intellectual exercises. None of the more recent advances in music would have been possible, even thinkable, without Schoenberg's pioneer work.

Schoenberg always considered himself as much as a composer as a theorist or teacher, and his works are supposed to appeal as much to the emotions as to the intellect, although to be understood they do, of course, require the listener's concentrated attention. To appreciate how his ideas developed it is necessary to hear first his pre-atonal music, such as the *Gurrelieder* (1900–1) and *Verklärte Nacht* (1899), in which he carried Wagnerian chromaticism to extreme lengths. The *Gurrelieder*, in particular, is a luxuriant, overblown work that shows the Wagnerian idiom in an advanced stage of decay, in spite of many beautiful pages of music. In his succeeding works the feeling of tonality began to disappear until in the Three Piano Pieces (opus 11), of 1909, he finally rejected tonality, although the new 12-note scheme is not yet evident; traces of the old order can still be heard. The succeeding works were mostly short, highly compressed, and very expressive. Schoenberg was reaching out for a new system,

which would "justify the dissonant character of these harmonies and determine their successions." By 1923 he had formulated his 12-note system and the Five Piano Pieces (opus 23), and the Serenade (opus 24) of that year, can thus be considered the first works that used a note-row as the fundamental basis of their composition. Between 1910 and 1915, however, the Russian composer Alexander Skryabin (1872–1915) had attempted to define a new method of composition of his own employing the "mystic chord" of ascending fourths, but his scheme proved comparatively abortive when compared with Schoenberg's. Josef Hauer (1883–1959) also developed a 12-note system which he propounded in 1919 and he always considered himself, rather than Schoenberg, as the true founder of the system. He later worked out a system of tropes (*i.e.,* half-series of six notes).

To return to Schoenberg, in later works he shows much more freedom and assurance in the use of his system. The wind quintet (1924), the Variations for Orchestra, opus 31 (1927–8), the third (1926), and fourth (1936) string quartets, and the string trio (1946) are modern classics of their kind; they require concentrated listening and a degree of understanding of the unfamiliar style of composition. The set of songs with piano *Das Buch der hängenden Gärten* (opus 15), written in 1908, *Pierrot Lunaire*, opus 21 (1912) and the Four Songs, opus 22 (1913–14) provide a kind of bridge between tonality and atonality that the adventurous mind should cross. The monodrama *Erwartung* (1909) is another fascinating work, but perhaps the unfinished *Moses and Aaron* (1932) is Schoenberg's masterpiece as its production at Covent Garden in 1965 showed. Here, for certain, the composer matched his obvious intellectual capacities with an evident emotional content and managed to combine *Sprechgesang* (speech-song) and singing with a real degree of success.

It is only in recent years that Schoenberg's music has had a real chance to make its mark through the essential prerequisite of frequent performance. If his idiom now seems approachable, and a reasonably natural outcome of late 19th-cent. developments, it is perhaps because other, more recent composers have extended the boundaries of sound much further.

Schoenberg's two most respected disciples were Anton Webern (1883–1945) and Alban Berg (1885–1935). Webern's output is small, reaching only to opus 31, and many of his works are very brief. They are exquisitely precise, and delicate almost to a fault. He was trying to distil the essence of each note and in so doing carried the 12-note system to its most extreme and cerebral limit. His music has often been described as pointillist in the sense that one note is entirely separated from the next, there being little discernible melody. Beyond Webern's music, there is indeed the sound of nothingness, and he was rightly described during his lifetime as the "composer of the *pianissimo espressivo*". In his later works, Webern tended towards a strict, and often ingenious use of form and the Variations for Orchestra of 1940 are a good example of this and of his delicacy of orchestration. Webern's influence has perhaps been greater than the impact of his own music, even though he has had no direct successor.

Berg's music is much more accessible. Like Webern his total output was not large, but nearly all his works are substantial additions to the repertory. He is also the directest link between Mahler and the second Viennese School, as Mahler's music influenced him strongly. He studied with Schoenberg from 1904 to 1910. His music is more intense, more lyrical, and less attenuated in sound than Schoenberg's or Webern's. His humanity and abiding compassion can be heard most strongly in his finest opera *Wozzeck* (1925) and his violin concerto (1935), written as an elegy on the death of Manon Gropius, a beautiful 18-year-old girl. Both works are very carefully designed yet formal considerations are never allowed to submerge feeling, and the note-row is fully integrated into the structure.

Both *Wozzeck* and the unfinished but rewarding

Lulu are concerned with society's outcasts who are treated with great tenderness in both operas. The later work is entirely dodecaphonic, all the opera's episodes being based on a theme associated with Lulu. Between these operas Berg wrote the highly complex Chamber Concerto for piano, violin, and thirteen wind instruments (1925) and the expressive Lyric Suite (1926). Among his other works the Seven Early Songs (1908–9) and the concert aria *Der Wein* (1929) are notable.

Stravinsky.

Igor Stravinsky (1882–1971) was another vital figure in 20th-cent. music. If his influence has been in quite another and perhaps less drastic direction than Schoenberg's it is hardly less important. Indeed, future musical historians may consider his achievement the more significant. He has been compared with the painter Picasso in his almost hectic desire to keep up with the times, yet, although he wrote in a number of very different styles over a period of fifty years, every work of his is stamped with his own definitive musical personality. His most revolutionary and seminal work is undoubtedly *The Rite of Spring* (written for the ballet impresario Diaghilev), which caused a furore when it first appeared in 1913, and although it no longer shocks, the rhythmical energy, the fierce angular thematic material, and the sheer virtuosity of the orchestration will always have the power to excite new audiences. Before *The Rite* Stravinsky had written two ballets for Diaghilev—*The Firebird* and *Petrushka*—that are no less filled with vitality and new, albeit not so violent, sounds. During the next thirty years Stravinsky wrote a series of ballet works, gradually becoming more austere and refined in composition. *Apollo* (1928) and *Orpheus* (1947) belong among his most attractive scores.

Stravinsky did not confine himself in stage works to the ballet. *The Nightingale* (1914) is a charming, early opera; *The Soldiers Tale* (1918) is a witty combination of narration, mime, and dance; *Les Noces* (1923) is a concise, original choreographic cantata for soloists and chorus; *Oedipus Rex* (1927) is a dignified version of the Sophocles play, which can be staged or given on the concert platform; either way it is a moving experience. *Perséphone* (1934), a melodrama for reciter, tenor, chorus, and orchestra is an appealling, lucid score. After the war his most important stage work by far was *The Rake's Progress* (1951), with a libretto by W. H. Auden and Chester Kallman. This fascinating opera is deliberately based on 18th-cent. forms and the music itself is neo-classical, always attractive, sometimes haunting.

Stravinsky was no laggard in writing for the concert-platform either. The finest of his orchestral pieces are probably the fervent choral *Symphony of Psalms* (1930), the violin concerto (1931) and the aggressive compact Symphony in Three Movements (1945). Of his chamber music the octet (1923), a duo concertant (1932), and septet (1952) are probably the most important, but no piece, even the dryest and most pedantic, is without redeeming features.

Stravinsky is often thought of as an aloof, detached figure. He has been castigated for his lack of lyrical warmth. But in spite of his own professed desire to drain his music of specific emotion, craftsmanship and originality, often with a strange other-worldly beauty added, are unmistakably there throughout his many scores. Quirky and annoying he may be, dull never.

Busoni and Puccini.

Italian music in the early part of the century was dominated by two very different composers—Ferruccio Busoni (1866–1924) and Giacomo Puccini (1858–1924). Busoni is a difficult figure to place. His austere, intellectual power is never called in question, but he seldom, if ever, succeeded in translating his technical prowess into altogether successful compositions. We can admire the strength, honesty, and often beauty of such works as his huge piano concerto (1903–4), *Fantasia Contrappuntistica* (1912)—for piano solo—and his unfinished opera *Doktor Faust* without ever capitulating to them entirely. None the less, it has to be admitted that those who have studied his music closely have always fallen completely under his spell. In style his music is anti-Romantic and often neo-Classical yet he was an ardent admirer of Liszt and more especially of Liszt's realisation of the possibilities of the pianoforte. Busoni, himself a great pianist, carried on where Liszt had left off in his own piano music, in which form and expression often find their perfect balance. *Doktor Faust* is undoubtedly his most important opera but *Die Brautwahl* (1908–10) and *Turandot* (1917) have many points of interest too.

Puccini's *Turandot*—his last opera—is a much grander version of the same Gozzi fable and the culmination of this great opera composer's work. His achievement is at an almost directly opposite pole to Busoni's. Not for him the severity or intellectuality of his contemporary. He sought and found an almost ideal fusion of straight-forward lyricism and dramatic truth. His music unerringly follows the pathos and passion of the stories he sets and all his characters "live" as human beings. That, and his abundant flow of easy, soaring melody, are the reasons for his immense popular success, unequalled by any other 20th-cent. composer. Whether it is the pathetic Mimi (*La Bohème*—1896) and Cio-Cio-San, (*Madam Butterfly*—1904), the evil Scarpia (*Tosca* —1900), the cunning Schicchi (*Gianni Schicchi*— 1918), the ardent Rodolfo (*La Bohème*) and Cavaradossi (*Tosca*), or the ice-cold Turandot (*Turandot*—1926). Puccini's musical characterisation is unfailing. And he backs his *verismo* vocal writing with an orchestral tissue that faithfully reflects the milieu of each opera, for instance, Japanese for *Butterfly*, Chinese for *Turandot*, while never losing his particular brand of Italian warmth. His orchestration is always subtle and luminous.

Other Italian composers who wrote operas in the *versimo* style of Puccini were Leoncavallo (1858–1919), Mascagni (1865–1945), and Giordano (1867–1948). Mascagni's *Cavalleria Rusticana* and Leoncavallo's *Pagliacci* have formed an inseparable bill and a regular part of the repertory in most opera houses.

Prokofiev, Shostakovich, and Rachmaninov.

Sergey Prokofiev (1891–1953) spent part of his creative life in his native Russia, part of it (1918–34) abroad, mostly in Paris. His early music, apart from the popular Classical Symphony (1916–17) tended to be acid and harsh, but on his return to Russia his style, though still frequently satirical, became warmer, more Romantic. The third piano concerto (1917) and the second symphony (1924) are good examples of the former period, the ballets *Romeo and Juliet* (1935) and *Cinderella* (1941–4) and the fifth (1944) and sixth (1946) symphonies of the latter. His music gives the impression of immense rhythmical energy, as in the outer movements of several of his nine piano sonatas, but this fierce drive is often leavened by the soft, wistful lights of his slow movements. His second string quartet (1941), perhaps, presents all the elements of his music in the kindest light.

His strong leaning towards fantasy and mordant parody is felt in his earlier operas *The Love of the Three Oranges* (1921) and *The Fiery Angel* (1922–5). Towards the end of his life much of Prokofiev's music fell into official disfavour.

Dmitri Shostakovich (1906–75) also suffered from attacks on his style. He had to conform to Stalin's requirements for writing music, but he survived and continued to produce music of universal appeal, as, for example, his later string quartets. Like Prokofiev, his music falls into two very distinct styles: one humorous and spiky, the other intense, very personal and often large-scale in its implications. Not all his symphonies reach the expressive depths of numbers one, five, six, eight, ten and fourteen, but they all have rewarding passages, and his violin and cello concertos are of high quality. He also wrote fifteen string quartets, a piano quintet (an attractive piece) and two operas: the satirical *The Nose* (1930) and *Katrina Ismailova* (1934, revised 1959), originally known as "Lady Macbeth of Mtsensk."

Although Sergey Rachmaninov (1873–1943) was born in Russia, he left his home country in 1918, disliking the Soviet régime, and lived mostly in Switzerland and the United States. His music is chiefly notable for its Romanticism, nostalgic melody, nervous energy and, in the piano works, its opportunities for displays of virtuosity. The first three piano concertos, the third symphony, the piano preludes, and the Rhapsody on a theme of Paganini, are his most typical and attractive works, and many of his songs are touching and beautiful. He wrote three operas.

Weill and Hindemith.

Kurt Weill (1900–50) is chiefly known for his socio-politically pointed operas, such as *Die Dreigroschenoper* (1929), *Mahagonny* (1929), *Der Jasager* (1930) and *Happy End* (1929), all effective works on the stage, and for his particular brand of brittle, yet fundamentally romantic music. His influence on later composers has been considerable.

Paul Hindemith (1895–1963) in his later years wrote in a strictly tonal, often neo-classical idiom, after being one of the most advanced intellectuals of his time. As well as many chamber and orchestral works, he wrote three formidable operas: *Die Harmonie der Welt*, *Cardillac* and *Mathis der Maler*.

Ives and Copland.

Charles Ives (1874–1954) is generally recognised as the first American composer of major stature. Most of his works were composed before about 1920, while he was pursuing a successful career in insurance. Ives' music is noted for its thorough-going electicism and his refusal to be bound by rules and conventions. His work anticipates many 20th century techniques, such as polytonality and polyrhythm, which he seems to have arrived at independently of others. Folk song, hymn tunes, dance music and the sound of the brass band all appear in his compositions, many of which are evocative of his New England background (*e.g. Three Places in New England*, the *Holidays Symphony*, the *Concord* Sonata). It was not until the 1930s that Ives began to achieve recognition, but his influence on later American composers can hardly be exaggerated.

Aaron Copland (1900–90) was a composer who had absorbed a variety of influences—from his Jewish background, contemporary Europe, American folk music and jazz, Latin American music—while writing music which is instantly recognisable as his own in its clean textures and taut rhythms. Early works such as the Piano Concerto (1927) show the use of jazz styles, while the Piano Variations (1930) combine inventiveness and technical discipline in a tough, concentrated and highly dissonant piece. A move towards a simpler, more immediately appealing idiom is evident in pieces like *El Salón México* (1936), and the ballets *Billy the Kid* (1938), *Rodeo* (1938) and *Appalachian Spring* (1944) and the Third Symphony (1946). These works remain Copland's most popular and frequently performed pieces. A number of works from the 1950s and 1960s experiment with serial techniques, while retaining his individual voice.

Vaughan Williams, Holst and Delius.

The twentieth century revival of music in England owes much to Ralph Vaughan Williams (1872–1958) and Gustav Holst (1874–1934). The English folk song revival, associated with Cecil Sharp, was in full swing during their formative years, and both composers produced arrangements of folk songs as well as assimilating the folk idiom into their own styles. The influence of 16th century polyphony is also strong in Vaughan Williams' music, the most obvious example being the *Fantasia on a Theme by Thomas Tallis* (1909). Vaughan Williams' strongest works (*e.g.* the first, fourth, fifth and sixth sym-

phonies, the ballet *Job*, the choral *Dona Nobis Pacem*) show his characteristic alternation of the forceful and the contemplative.

Holst was a more enigmatic figure. Only his suite *The Planets* and the choral work *The Hymn of Jesus* have established themselves in the regular repertory, but his bold harmonic experiments and the austerity, even mysticism, of his style as heard in the opera *Savitri* and the orchestral piece *Egdon Heath* are perhaps more typical of this meditative, original composer.

Frederick Delius (1862–1934) was the major English composer to fall under the sway of French impressionism, though his English (north country) background, his friendship with Grieg, and the time he spent in America all contributed to the formation of his musical style. He lived in France from 1888 onwards. His most important works are the atmospheric tone-poems for orchestra, such as *Brigg Fair*, the vocal and orchestral *A Mass of Life*, *Sea Drift* and *Appalachia*, and the opera *A Village Romeo and Juliet*.

Walton, Britten and Tippett.

Sir William Walton (1902–83) became known as an *enfant terrible* with the witty and irreverent *Façade* (1923) for speaker and chamber orchestra (with words by Edith Sitwell). The poetic Viola Concerto (1929) shows another side of his musical character. His First Symphony (1934–5) is an arresting, dramatic score and the colourful oratorio *Belshazzar's Feast* (1931) is a landmark in choral music. Walton's rhythms show the influence of jazz and of Stravinsky but he is generally felt to be a quintessentially English composer. An Elgarian element is clear in such occasional pieces as the coronation marches *Crown Imperial* (1937) and *Orb and Sceptre* (1953).

Benjamin Britten (1913–76) did as much as anyone to establish English music on the forefront of the international stage. Much of his music seems to have an immediate appeal to large audiences and certainly his many stage works earned him quite exceptional prestige both at home and abroad. *Peter Grimes* (1945), *Billy Budd* (1951), *Gloriana* (1953), *A Midsummer Night's Dream* (1960) all show his mastery of stage technique and the first two are also moving human documents. On a smaller scale he has achieved as much with his chamber operas—*The Rape of Lucretia* (1946), *Albert Herring* (1947), *The Turn of the Screw* (1954)—and the three Parables for Church Performance—*Curlew River* (1964), *The Burning Fiery Furnace* (1966) and *The Prodigal Son* (1968). His operatic output was crowned by *Death in Venice* (1973). If he had written nothing else, these dramatic works would have marked him out as a composer of outstanding imaginative gifts. In addition to these, however, the choral works culminating in the *War Requiem* (1962), the various song cycles written, like so much else, for his friend Peter Pears, the *Serenade* for tenor, horn and strings, *Nocturne* for tenor and orchestra, the three *Canticles*, and the *Spring Symphony* are further evidence of both his intense emotional commitment and his technical skill. Despite the strong influence of such composers as Purcell, Schubert, Verdi, Mahler and Berg, his style is entirely his own; his musical personality combines, it has been said, "a deep nostalgia for the innocence of childhood, a mercurial sense of humour and a passionate sympathy with the victims of prejudice and misunderstanding."

This last quality was also evident in the emotional make up of Sir Michael Tippett (1905–98), as expressed in such works as the oratorio *A Child of our Time* (1941) one of his earliest successes, which shows both his compassion and his ability to write on a large scale. This and the Concerto for Double String Orchestra (1939) remain his most popular works. Tippett was open to a wide range of influences, both musical (from English Madrigals, Monteverdi and Beethoven to Negro spirituals and jazz) and non-musical (*e.g.* the ideas of Jung). His early style—often richly lyrical and affirmative of the continued power of tonality—reached its culmination in his allegorical opera *The Midsummer Marriage* (1952), the Piano Concerto (1955) and the Second Symphony (1957). A new style, spare and incisive, with structure arising from the juxtaposition of contrasting ideas rather than from a process of development, was evident in his second opera, *King Priam* (1961) and its offshoots, the Second Piano Sonata (1962) and the Concerto for Orchestra (1963). The mystical, ecstatic *The Vision of St. Augustine* (1965), a complex, difficult but rewarding work, is one of his finest from this period. The opera *The Knot Garden* (1970) exemplifies again Tippett's concern with human relationships and the need for self-knowledge. Tippett never ceased to explore and experiment; his inspiration still seems as fresh as ever. His most recent works, *The Mask of Time*— a huge choral piece—and the Fourth Piano Sonata (1984) have something of the quality of summarising statements about the musical and non-musical concerns of a lifetime.

Olivier Messiaen and Elliott Carter.

Amongst the many schools and groups of composers in the twentieth century, two major figures stand apart, Olivier Messiaen (1908–92) and Elliott Carter. Both born in 1908, each is an individualist of great influence and stature who has pursued his own path to a personal style of composition.

A devout Catholic, Messiaen viewed himself as a theological composer and music as a medium for a profound communication, celebration and contemplation of the love and mystery of God. Few of his works are liturgical but most have religious and doctrinal themes, for example *La Nativité du Seigneur* (1935) for organ and *Vingt Regards sur l'Enfant-Jésus* (1944) for piano. Messiaen was inspired to compose by hearing the music of Debussy. This influence can be particularly seen in Messiaen's flexible rhythms, sensitive scoring and use of timbre. Indeed, he identifies sounds with colours and views composition as painting. The other major early influence was that of the East, particularly Indian music. Messiaen often uses Hindu rhythmic patterns alongside Greek poetic metres, plainsong and other medieval techniques and Stravinskian devices. The sum of these can be seen in *Quatuor pour le fin du temps* for violin, clarinet, cello and piano which he composed in a prisoner of war camp in 1940. A very complex work, it reflects the primacy Messiaen gives to rhythmic control. Its overwhelming impression however is of lush and exotic sounds and textures. Similarly, the vibrant colours and rhythms of the massive *Turangalila-symphonie* (1946–8) for orchestra effectively realise the ideas of life and vitality embodied in the Sanskrit title.

After *Turangalila*, Messiaen adopted a less luxurious style. It was works such as the *Livre d'orgue* (1951) which profoundly influenced many young composers of post-war years in the use of systematic transformations of rhythm and dynamics using a system of modes in a quasi-serial fashion. For Messiaen it is the seven harmonic modes, inspired by Debussy, Liszt and the Russian "Five", which are perhaps more important because they give his music its unique sound quality.

The 1950s saw the integration of the final element crucial to Messiaen's music; birdsong. A keen ornithologist, he collected and accurately notated the songs of many birds for incorporation into compositions. *Catalogue d'oiseaux* (1951–8) is a collection of thirteen piano pieces featuring French bird songs. For Messiaen birdsong represented, "the true lost face of music", and it provided a source of inspiration for many of his major post-war works. Since 1960, his style has become simpler and less complex to the ear. To encounter the many elements of his music one can do little better than to listen to *La Transfiguration de Notre Seigneur Jésus-Christ* (1963–9) for one hundred voices, seven instrumental soloists and a large orchestra. Its subject is the mystery of God, his relationship with man and nature as a revelation of God. Messiaen draws upon all his compositional techniques in a spellbinding and overwhelming work that is a profound affirmation of faith. It is fitting that his most recent work is a vast opera (1973–83), *St François d'Assise* about the saint who is best known for his great spirituality and for gaining inspiration and insight from nature.

Carter's reputation is based on a small number of works. He has concentrated on problems of language and structure in a dramatic context unlike Messiaen's preoccupations with colour and the communication of religious truths. Carter's early works reflect a variety of influences: Stravinsky, Hindemith and the English Virginalists. He con-

sciously aimed at a simple, lyrical, accessible style, for example, in the ballet, *Pocahontas* (1938–9) and *Holiday Overture* (1944). During those war years however there occurred a change of direction. The Piano Sonata (1945–6) saw the start of a compositional style where instruments were endowed with personalities who act as protagonists in a drama. His ideas crystallised in the *String Quartet No. 1* (1950–1) after an absorbing study of the music of Ives, Cowell and African and Oriental music. It led to the use of very complex rhythmic relationships and a very tightly-knit pitch structure that could be traced back to a simple and small source, in this case a four-note chord. After this Carter refined his portrayal of his dramatis personae such that in *String Quartet No. 2* (1959) his players each have a separate personality defined by melodic material, gestures and rhythms. They converse, argue and enact that work's dramatic programme. *String Quartet No. 3* (1971) marked a shift in approach. Although the players were still "personalities", the work relied heavily on the use of contrast between strict and flexible writing between members of two duos. The *Symphony of Three Orchestras* (1975–7) and *Triple Duo* (1983) continue to explore the possibilities of simultaneous presentation of independent and sometimes unrelated processes. Carter's music makes rewarding, though not always easy, listening.

THE AVANT GARDE SINCE 1945

Serialism.

The early post-war years saw a renewed interest in "twelve-note techniques" otherwise known as "serialism". Composers like Stravinsky and Dallapiccola (1904–75), who had shunned serialism in earlier years, began to experiment and absorb serial techniques into their musical style. Stravinsky, for example, in works such as *Threni* (1957–8) explored ideas of varied repetition both of small ideas and large sections, in a serial context. A clear example to listen to is the fifteen-minute *Requiem Canticles* (1964–6). During the progression from its Prelude to Postlude, one can hear the piece subtly develop. The succeeding movements, and phrases within movements, slightly alter that which has gone before, evolving into something fresh.

This period also saw the emergence of a new generation of composers, keen to jettison the past and begin anew. Serialism was a favoured tool, its revival stemming from Paris, where Webern's pupil René Leibowitz was teaching, and the USA where Schoenberg had fled from Nazi Germany. The American Milton Babbitt (b. 1916) was much concerned with codifying serial techniques. His younger European contemporaries Pierre Boulez (b. 1925) and Karlheinz Stockhausen (b. 1928) sought to increase the number of musical elements that could be controlled by a predetermined method. They sought to emulate the rigorous methods of Webern, hoping to control not only pitch, but also rhythm, timbre and intensity of attack. In doing so they hoped to create an impersonal, emotionally restrained music.

Attention went first to controlling rhythm. Forerunners of this control can be seen in movement three of Berg's *Lyric Suite* and in Webern's Op.30 Variations. However, the catalyst came from Messiaen. He inspired his pupil Boulez to explore the possibilities of rhythmic and dynamic serialism in his Second Piano Sonata (1951). The performance of Messiaen's *Modes de valeurs et d'intensités* (1949) at the Darmstadt Summer School proved decisive for Stockhausen. Although not serial, the piece established scales of pitch, length of note (duration), loudness and attack. The 1950s were to see this potential for serialism taken to extremes. Boulez reached "total serialism" in *Structures 1a* for piano. However, having attained it he soon became frustrated with its restrictions. Some of the more fantastic and exotic elements of earlier works were allowed to reappear. *Le Marteau sans Maitre* (1952–4) for mezzo-soprano and six instruments is a masterly setting of three surreal poems by René Char, with instrumental interludes. For the listener it is the contrasts of timbres, of flexible and regular pulsing rhythms, of sound and silence that are spellbinding. The virtuosic serial workings are hidden.

Stockhausen reached total serialism in *Kreuzspiel* (1951) for oboe, bass clarinet, piano and percussion. Each note's pitch, length, dynamic and timbre are part of a predetermined plan. All are concerned with "Kreuzspiel" or "crossplay". Its various processes reverse or change over throughout so that at the end we have returned full circle. The effect is of clear-cut lines where each note is weighted. However, despite the intention of the composer, the effect is not unemotional, especially with the insistent throbbing of the percussion, and the piece builds to a series of climaxes before dying away. *Punkte* (points) (1952) for orchestra finds each note being treated as an isolated point of sound. It illustrates some of the problems of total serialism; often very difficult to play, it can be monotonous or lack focal points, appearing to be random rather than rigorously controlled. Stockhausen therefore transferred his attention to using not points but bursts of sound and moved towards possibly his most significant contribution to music, "moment form". There, different aspects of a note, chord or sound are suspended in eternity for contemplation and re-examination. Works became longer, slower and had a greater emphasis on colour and the effects of spatial separation, both between sounds and between their sources. *Carré* (1959–60) uses four orchestras between which chords move and evolve. Stockhausen wrote "you can confidently stop listening for a moment . . . each moment can stand on its own and at the same time is related to all the other moments". Although unifying principles in pitch content *etc.* might be present, "strict" serialism had been gently left behind, until *Mantra* (1970). This work for two pianos, percussion and two electronic ring modulators is totally based on a thirteen-note row, the mantra, with a different duration, mode of attack and dynamic for each note. These permeate the whole piece. For example, each of the thirteen sections is dominated by one of the thirteen types of attack. The work's climax is the coda where the 156 versions of the mantra used are rushed through in a few minutes. The work is important, not only as marking a return to serialism and notated music, but also in its rediscovery of melody—something unthinkable twenty years earlier.

Since the 1960s serialism and integral serialism have had less of an influence in Europe, although they have continued to hold a fascination for American composers such as Milton Babbit (b. 1916). Composers have used the underlying concept of serialism (*i.e.* using a systematic approach to detailed structuring) without using the technique in any strict sense. Examples of this include Maxwell Davies's use of magic number squares (*see below*), and Harrison Birtwistle's use of random numbers to generate rhythmic and melodic elements. The Hungarian composer György Ligeti (b. 1923) uses very tightly controlled canonic music which he describes as 'micropolyphony' which, though not serial, has a similarly organised and systematic approach. One of the reasons for the use of systems is to take some of the decision-making out of the compositional process. Birtwistle has said that he would seize up if he had to make all the decisions in his music.

Mathematics and Music.

The younger generation of composers have often used mathematical systems for composing which are not necessarily serial. A good example is Sir Peter Maxwell Davies (b. 1934). Use of durational ratios, ciphers and magic squares features prominently in his work, partly reflecting his interest in medieval music. A magic square is a number square where the sum of any line is the same. This becomes the basis for a composition by assigning notes to the numbers—a technique that Davies has often used since the mid-1970s. For example, in *Ave Maris Stella* (1975), each of the nine movements uses a different transformation of the square and follows a characteristic route through the square. The work is governed by the square at all levels: it even determines the precise length of each movement. Far from being a mathematical exercise however the piece shows masterly control which is particularly revealed in its drama and the beauty of its colours.

Mathematical processes of a different type have been taken up by the Greek, Xenakis (b. 1922), possibly because of his original training as an en-gineer and architect in France. His rejection of serialism led to the use of "stochastic" principles, derived from the mathematical laws governing probability. He also applied mathematical set theory to composition. The use of these ideas however is not audible. In *Nomos Alpha* (1965) for solo cello, for example, it is the use of contrasts, of texture, dynamic, register and timbre which give shape and form for the listener.

Chance.

Although for many serialism represented the way of reviving music after the excesses of romanticism, some looked beyond Europe to the East. John Cage (1912–92) found inspiration there, studying Zen Buddhism in the early 1950s. By using the "chance operations" of the Chinese *I Ching* (Book of Changes) Cage brought a new radical approach to Western music. *Music of Changes* (1951) for piano is fully notated but its content is the result of operations where chance has a role. The use of "indeterminacy" or "chance" gave the performer an active role in determining the course of a piece. This might come about by providing "graphic notation"—an artist's impression of what the piece might sound like. Thus Earle Brown's *December 1952* is a visual design to be realised on any instrument as the performer sees fit. Alternatively the composer could give the performer control over the order of sections or their content. *Twenty-five pages* (1953) by Brown is for one to twenty-five pianos. Each person has twenty-five pages and may arrange them in any order before commencing. Thus music was no longer to be necessarily a progression of fixed and immutable steps to an endpoint. This and other traditional assumptions about music were challenged in Cage's most well-known outrage, *4' 33"*. The performer does not play any notes at all. The music consists of the sounds in the environment that occur during a period of four minutes and thirty-three seconds.

In 1957, both Stockhausen and Boulez took to chance having realised that total control was an impossibility. The more rigorous the control of musical elements, the more impossible it became to realise it accurately. Stockhausen's first experiment with chance techniques was Piano Piece XI which is a single page with nineteen fragments of music. They may be played in any order but the tempo, dynamic and attack must be that shown at the end of the previous fragment. After one fragment has been played three times the work ends. Boulez's Third Piano Sonata was less free. There the choices are in the nature of varying routes through the piece. Boulez saw his music as using a form of control that is not random but akin to throwing a dice. Limited choices in the combination of instruments and their choice of lines form the basis of *Pli selon pli* (1957–65) for soprano and orchestra, offering Boulez a way "to fix the infinite".

For Stockhausen, chance has been a way to encourage performer participation and the development of "intuitive music-making". In *Prozession* (1967) for example, performers react to what is going on guided by plus or minus signs in the score which denote whether the response should be positive or negative. It has worked well in combination with the ideas behind moment form. *Stimmung* (1968) is a 45 minute meditation on one chord whose parts and overtones emerge and merge into the whole, punctuated by erotic poems, magic numbers and words which are delivered in response to chance operations. The culmination of these ideas may be seen in *Aus den Sieben Tagen* (1968) where the score for each of the seven movements is a short poem.

Use of indeterminacy does not necessarily have to be so extreme. For Witold Lutoslawski (1913–93) use of controlled chance techniques has provided a way for composing atonal music without embracing serialism. During 1955–60 Lutoslawski evolved a harmonic language which used twelve-note chords for expression and colour. In 1960 he heard a performance of Cage's Piano Concerto and realised that he could use chance techniques to add a rhythmic freedom and new types of texture to his music. The exact combination of sounds at any given moment is often a matter of chance but the overall effect is planned. Textures are created by the constant repetition of small melodic ideas and simple rhythms in different parts, creating a kaleidoscope of sound, and by lines of counterpoint set off against each other, often sliding from one note to another blurring the transition between chords. The music of Lutoslawski is a fine example of the use of chance as a tool in compositions which still have strong links to tradition. The direction and drama of works such as *Mi-Parti* (1976) and his Third Symphony (1983) are firmly in the composer's hands, relying heavily on his skilful sense of harmonic movement, use of colour and proportion. Only small rhythmic details are left to chance.

Ligeti's music often sounds as if it were chance-like but in fact his massive textural structures of the 1960s are controlled by highly organised arhythmic canons. Each instrument or voice follows the same line of notes but with different rhythmic values. The listener hears a kaleidoscopic and ever-changing background cluster. Significant works from this period include: *Atmosphères* for orchestra (1961), *Requiem* (1963–5), and *Lux Aeterna* for voices (1966).

Ligeti's music was made famous when the above works were used (without the composer's permission) by Stanley Kubrick in his film *2001: a Space Odyssey*. Ligeti's music since the 1970s shows a rediscovery of elements that he had previously shunned such as melody, harmony and even tonality/modality. Typical examples include Horn Trio (1982), Piano Concerto (1988) and Violin Concerto (1992) which show influences from African music, fractal geometry and the piano music of the American Conlon Nancarrow (b. 1912). The redis-covery of previously rejected elements can also be seen in the music of the Polish composer Krzysztof Penderecki (b. 1933) and Luciano Berio (b. 1924), and can be seen as a symptom of the existence of Post-Modernism in music.

Electronic Music.

An important part of the post-war struggle with musical language has been the development of elec-tronic means to generate, manipulate and record sounds. Its pioneer was the Frenchman Edgard Varèse (1883–1965). Before the war he had been an independent and radical composer much concerned with the exploration of new sounds. This had led to an emphasis on the exploitation of percussion effects in works such as *Intégrales* (1924–5) and *Ionisation* (1933). The following work *Ecuatorial* (1934) explored further, using primitive electrically gen-erated sounds produced by two Ondes Martenot. However the catalyst for further development was the invention of the tape recorder which provided an easy means to store sounds that could then be rearranged by cutting and rejoining the tape in dif-ferent ways. Varèse explored these possibilities in *Déserts* (1949–54) which alternated recorded and instrumental sounds in an atmospheric work which really seems to conjure up the aridity and emptiness of the desert. Recorded sound offered the possibility of creating illusions of aural space by technical manipulation and by judicious positioning and con-trol of loudspeakers. This is a fundamental part of Varèse's great masterpiece, *Poème Electronique* (1958) which used soprano, chorus, bells, organs and artificial sounds. Its spatial effects were achieved by using many loudspeakers positioned around a specially designed pavilion at the 1958 Brussels Exhibition.

Generally, electronic music-making required a studio and the 1950s saw the setting up of important studios in Paris and Cologne. In Paris Pierre Schaeffer (b. 1910) pioneered "musique concrète" which used altered and rearranged natural sounds, for example, the sound of a steam train, to create a musical piece. At Cologne where Stockhausen worked, the emphasis was on creating new synthetic sounds.

Electronic music had the potential to generate complex, accurate serial structures through precise electronic operations. Boulez's studies in this how-ever did not satisfy him and he neglected the medium until 1970 when he became Director of IRCAM (*Institut de Recherche et de Coordination Acoustique/Musique*). Stockhausen however found electronic music an ideal medium to create a musical unity far beyond that of serialism; pitch, timbre, rhythm and form could be seen as different aspects of the same thing—vibration. He did not restrict himself to pure synthetic sounds and in 1955–6 created perhaps his most well-known electronic work, *Gesang der Jünglinge*. This combines synthetic sounds with a recorded boy's voice to portray the three boys in the fiery furnace from the Book of Daniel.

With *Kontakte* (1958–60) for piano, percussion and tape, Stockhausen began an exploration of the interplay between live performers and electronic sound which still preoccupies him today. The work explores "contact" between real and artificial sounds and between the elements of music. Compared to pure electronic music, the presence of the live performers made it easier to listen to, pro-viding a visual focus and making each performance unique. The next step was to create "live" electronic music where performers created their electronic sounds on stage. Cage had already begun this in 1960 with *Cartridge Music*. Stockhausen's first attempt, *Mikrophonie I* (1964–5), *Cartridge Music* gives much freedom to the performer in creating the electronic effects. A desire to create a world music led to one of the most vast electronic works to date, *Hymnen* (1966–7), a two-hour work for quadraphonic tape or tapes, soloists and optional symphony orchestra. Stockhausen constructed it out of national anthems from all over the world. Inspired by the occult *Urantian Book*, he became more ambitious still, seeking a galactic music. *Sirius* (1977) for four soloists and electronic music deals with the arrival on earth of four visitors from the star Sirius.

In America, developments have followed a differ-ent course. There, the use of computer synthesised sounds has been the main interest because of the computer's superior control and accuracy. It has allowed the continuation of abstract composition where complicated operations are achieved simply and effectively. Computer synthesis can also be applied to existing material. For example, *Chrono-meter* (1971) by Harrison Birtwistle (b. 1934).

Minimalism.

The transformation of existing material on tape has been a crucial part of an American movement dating from the 1960s known as "Minimalism'. Its chief exponents are Steve Reich (b. 1936), Philip Glass (b. 1937), Terry Riley (b. 1935) and La Monte Young (b. 1935). Minimal music uses material which is limited in pitch, rhythm and timbres; the ele-ments are subjected to simple transformations rely-ing heavily on repetition. Of great importance are the subtle evolution from one idea to another as repetitions are modified, and the use of "phasing" techniques. Phasing is the effect of altering the rate of repetition between parts repeating the same material so that it is no longer synchronised. The effect of works such as *Drumming* (1971) by Reich may appear long and non-dramatic. However, the listener is not expected to concentrate all the time but to become aware of a piece's various elements and processes. The music's patterns will change as the listener's attention shifts from one aspect to an-other. As in moment form, minimalist works owe much to Indian concepts of time as a circular rather than linear phenomenon. In recent years, the minim-alists have developed their style and there are greater differences between the four. Philip Glass has written several operas, *Einstein on the Beach* (1975), *Satyagraha* (1980), *Akhnaten* (1983), *The Making of the Representative for Planet 8* (1986), *The Fall of the House of Usher* (1988), *1000 Airplanes on the Roof* (1988) and *The Voyage* (1992). Recent works by Reich include *Different Trains* (1988) for String Quartet and tape, *The Cave* (1993) a multi-media extravaganza and *The Four Sections* (1987) for full orchestra.

Music Theatre.

During the early post-war years many composers were grappling with the tools of composition. Only more "traditional" writers such as Britten, Tippett and Hans Werner Henze (b. 1926) were engaged in writing opera. By 1970 however, most composers were including elements of theatre in their work even if they were not necessarily engaged in writing full-scale operas.

One of the major composers of "traditional" opera has been Henze. His first three operas draw heavily on the past. For example, *Boulevard Solitude* (1952) updates the story of Manon, a nineteenth-century favourite. After moving to Italy in 1953, Henze's stance appeared more traditional still as lyrical ele-ments became more dominant in contrast to the abstract athematic style of contemporaries such as Stockhausen. Increasingly Henze's operas began to reflect his preoccupation with socialism. The *Bassarids* (1966), for example, examines through a mythological guise the precipitation of social upheaval and disruption. The oratorio *Das Floss der "Medusa"* (1968) is dedicated to Che Guevara and provoked such struggles between police and left-wing students at its premiere that Henze went to Cuba for a year. There he was inspired to write *El Cimarrón* (1969–70), a vocal monologue portraying a Cuban runaway slave accompanied by flute, guitar and percussion. For a while, Henze continued to reject the traditional opera format because of its bourgeois overtones, preferring a more intimate, chamber style. But in 1976 Henze returned to opera with *We come to the River*. It reflected a renewal of Italianate lyricism, the exploitation of opera's full potential and a less overt political message.

Exponents of Music Theatre.

Luigi Nono (1924–90) also exploited theatre for political ends, beginning with *Intolleranza* (1960). However he found greater resource than Henze in contemporary developments, taking full advantage of the opportunities offered by electronics. *Contrappunto dialettico della mente* (1967–8) includes the sounds of political demonstrations. Like Henze, Nono also returned to the opera house after a long break from large-scale opera with *Al gran sole carico d'amore* (1972–4), which consolidated the techniques he had developed in the previous decade.

"Theatre" became a dominant characteristic in the works of Luciano Berio (b. 1925). One of his most famous works is *Circles* (1960) for female voice, harp and percussion. The virtuosic technique used there and in other works was inspired by the phenomenal vocal elasticity of his then wife, Cathy Berberian. "Circles' are depicted at many different levels in the work's structure and content. More importantly, these are underlined by the singer moving about the stage during the performance. Berio's next few works became overtly political, culminating in *Laborintus II* (1965) which was intended as an attack on capitalism via a musical collage and extracts from Dante's *Inferno*. Many of Berio's larger scale works since *Laborintus II* have been theatrical in their virtuosity and instrumental technique. For example, *Sequenza IV* (1965) demands a pianist with very agile feet. This type of dramatic gesture is much seen in Stockhausen's work, particularly those written for his own music ensemble, for example, *Solo* (1966). Since *Alphabet für Liege* (1972) his work has become increasingly theatrical and from 1978, Stockhausen has been working on an opera project *Licht*. Twenty years earlier, such a project would have been unthinkable.

Davies and Birtwhistle.

The small-scale synthesis of text, music and gesture characteristic of Berio has greatly influenced British work in music theatre, notably the work of Sir Peter Maxwell Davies and Sir Harrison Birtwistle. Davies' work is very powerful particularly through its use of parody and wild use of outrageous gesture. *Vesalii Icones* (1969) uses a naked male dancer portraying parts of the Stations of the Cross and scenes from the anatomy text by Vesalius. It is a good example of parody, particularly of what Davies views as nineteenth-century grossness—it includes a vile distortion of a Victorian hymn tune which turns into a foxtrot, both played on a honky-tonk piano. Many of his works feature a single vocal soloist, with instrumental back up, who plays the part of a crazed, obsessive individual. For example, *Eight Songs for a Mad King* (1969) features the instrumentalists in giant bird cages who must suffer the mad ravings of George III played by the singer.

Davies has written two full-scale operas to date, *Taverner* (1962–8) and *The Martyrdom of St. Magnus* (1976) and is currently working on a third, *Resurrection*. *Taverner* deals with two fundamental preoccupations of Davies—the nature of faith and betrayal—and uses both musical and dramatic parody to convey its message. *St. Magnus* was written after Davies moved to Orkney. It reflects a change in style, uses only a small orchestra and is for production "in the round".

Birtwhistle's first major dramatic work was a chamber opera, *Punch and Judy* (1966) which uses grotesque and violent gestures. However, while Davies' roots may lie with early Schoenberg, Birt-

wistle has found inspiration in the clear-cut lines and ritualism of Stravinsky. Possibly his most significant work to date is *The Mask of Orpheus* (1973–5 and 1981–3). He has written two new operas, *Gawain* (1981–91) and *The Second Mrs. Kong* (1994).

MUSIC OF THE 1990s

It is difficult to stand back from the music of the present, but the following brief survey provides a guide for readers.

Brian Ferneyhough (b. 1943) is continuing to expand the chamber music repertoire using traditional structures as a framework for music in which micro-tones play an increasingly important part. He is currently working on a seven-part cycle of chamber works of which three are complete; *Superscriptio* for solo piccolo (1981), *Carceri d'Invenzione I* (1982) and *Carceri d'Invenzione II* (1985) for chamber orchestra (II with solo flute). Robin Holloway (b. 1943) has also been active in composing smaller scale works, often lyrical, of which recent examples are his *Viola Concerto* (1985) and the bleak *Ballad* for harp and chamber orchestra (1985). Nigel Osborne (b. 1948) has used electronic and non-Western music in his work, gravitating recently towards vocal works. 1986 saw the premiere of his theatre piece, *Hells Angels*. Other recent operas are *Where the Wild Things Are* (1984) and *Higglety, Pigglety Pop!* (1985) by Oliver Knussen (b. 1952) which attracted acclaim for a young composer already noted for his symphonies, vocal and chamber work. Tim Souster (1943–94) has been active in composing and promoting electronic music of all types, some influenced by rock music. A recent example is his *Quartet with Tape* (1985). Meanwhile choral music is flourishing with new works by Paul Patterson (b. 1947) which often involve new types of notation and vocal technique, and several ritualistic works by John Tavener (b. 1948), inspired by his Eastern Orthodox faith. For example *Doxa* (1982) sets a single word from the Eastern liturgy. A meteoric rise to fame has been achieved by George Benjamin (b. 1960) starting with *Ringed by the Flat Horizon* (1980) written while still at Cambridge.

Diversity of Approach.

The emerging British composers of the 1980s and 1990s are diverse in their compositional approaches and interests. One feature they do have in common is an eclecticism drawing from a wide range of sources such as football chants (Turnage), jazz (Butler) and Celtic culture (MacMillan and Weir). There is also a trend towards greater approachability in the style and language of their music. There has been a realisation that audiences have been alienated in the past, and composers have attempted to make their music more communicative. One manifestation of this is the apparent 'rediscovery' of tonality or modality by several composers discussed below.

Mark-Anthony Turnage (b. 1960) is one of the most characteristic and popular composers of his generation. He uses material from popular culture in his music (like Martland and MacMillan) including rhythmic and melodic elements, which can be most clearly seen in his controversial opera *Greek* (1990), a setting of Steven Berkoff's play. His rich and colourful orchestration can be heard in his orchestral works such as *Three Screaming Popes* (1989), *Momentum* (1990–1) and *Drowned Out* (1993).

James MacMillan (b. 1959) is a part of the general rebirth of the arts in Scotland and shows something of his Celtic heritage in such works as *The Confessions of Isobel Gowrie* (1990) which explores a wide range of Scottish traditional music. His music since *Litanies of Iron and Stone* (1987) shows an increase in rhythmic drive, perhaps influenced by his interest in rock music, and also an increasing approachability. His major compositions since *Litanies* have mostly used external political or religious subjects as inspiration, for example *The Exorcism of Rio Sumpul* (1989) which is based on a helicopter raid on a village in El Salvador. His musical language is characterised by colourful instrumentation, a powerful rhythmic drive and an eloquent lyricism, which can be seen clearly in his popular *Veni Veni Emmanuel* (1993) written for the percussionist Evelyn Glennie. His most recent work is *Seven Last*

Words from the Cross (1994). It shows an austere, restrained and fundamentally tonal language.

Judith Weir (b. 1954) also makes reference to her Celtic heritage in her music. Her main compositional output is in the area of opera and music drama. *A Night at the Chinese Opera* (1987) is perhaps her best known work to date and is evidence of her interest in Chinese Yuan dramas. Her two later operas use magical stories: *The Vanishing Bridegroom* (1990) is based on 3 linked Scottish folktales, and *Blond Eckbert* (1994, for the English National Opera) on a fairytale by the German Romantic writer Ludwig Tieck. Her musical language shows influences from folk music, tonality and composers such as Stravinsky, Janacek and Peter Maxwell Davies.

Martin Butler (b. 1960) like MacMillan has shown a shift in his musical language from a Modernist approach to one which is more eclectic and expressive. As he states: "Recent pieces of mine have drawn, more or less directly, on Irish and bluegrass fiddle music, Latin salsa and dance music, and various types of jazz." Examples showing these influences include *Jazz Machines* (1990) for chamber ensemble, *Bluegrass Variations* (1988) for violin, and *Tin Pan Ballet* (1986) for ensemble and DX7 synthesiser. His most substantial work to date is his opera *Craig's Progress* (1994) which uses the "twin inheritances of opera and comic books".

Steve Martland (b. 1959) is a key figure of radical minimalism in Britain and owes much of his musical development to his studies with Louis Andriessen at the Royal Conservatory in The Hague. His music, like that of MacMillan, is strongly shaped by his socialist politics and is characterised by uncompromising aggression and bold sonorities. Like Andriessen he explores hocketing techniques in works like *Drill* (1987) and *Birthday Hocket* (1989), both for 2 pianos. His larger scale works include *Babi Yar* (1983) for large orchestra in 3 groups and *Crossing the Border* (1990–91) for String Orchestra.

It can be seen that there are several intersecting lines of development in British contemporary music, but most of the younger generation are united by the rejection of old Modernist ideals and the attempt to build stronger relationships with the concert-going and compact disc-buying audience.

The New Millennium.

With the advent of the new millennium it is tempting to identify the direction that contemporary music is taking, and who might be the composers to watch. It is, however, easier and less hazardous to identify broader trends than to pick out particular individuals. The major shift in contemporary music over the last 20 years is towards a more tonal/modal music with a parallel shift towards greater comprehensibility. It is likely that successful composers in the future will be those who communicate directly with their audience. Some of the British composers discussed earlier, such as Weir and Turnage, show this characteristic, although this is not to suggest that their music is without depth or artistic richness.

There will also be a continued interest of composers into popular idioms and an exploration of the grey areas in between genres. Minimalism and Post-Minimalism, which explore the interesting area of contemporary music, popular music and world music, will continue to thrive and evolve into more sophisticated and varied forms. It would be wrong to suggest that the tougher, more modernist style of music will disappear in the next millennium; diversity of style and pluralism will continue to be a defining characteristic of New Music. Some of the most innovative current composers and stylistic groupings will be outlined below.

Popular Minimalism: Michael Nyman.

The British composer Michael Nyman (b. 1944) is an example of a composer who writes music which cannot be easily categorised, as it consists of an amalgam of Minimalism, Baroque Ground Bass and Popular rhythms. Nyman's most characteristic works have been those written for Peter Greenaway's films such as *The Draughtsman's Contract* (1982), *A Zed and Two Noughts* (1985) and *The Cook, The Thief, His Wife, and Her Lover* (1989) which show a powerful and distinctive style. Nyman's music for *The Piano* (1992), directed by Jane Campion, is less hard-edged and original than his earlier works, but it does suit the film and has brought him much

popularity. His non-film music includes: the chamber opera *The Man Who Mistook His Wife for a Hat* (1987) based on the case study by the psychiatrist Oliver Sacks and the music of Schumann; The Piano Concerto (1993) based on the music from *The Piano*; and three string quartets (1985, 1988 & 1990).

Post-Minimalism: John Adams.

The American composer John Adams is considered to be a significant innovator in the Minimalist genre. His recent style could be better classified as Post-Modernist or perhaps Post-Minimalist as he avoids the austere Minimalism of Steve Rich or Philip Glass, in favour of a richer and more backward looking style. *Grand Pianola Music* (1981) for chamber orchestra, 3 sopranos and 2 solo pianos is an example of this more eclectic approach using jazz-like harmony and a banal tune at the end which is alarmingly reminiscent of Beethoven's *Ode to Joy*. Adams describes it as "the most thorough piece I've ever written about who I am musically. It has a real streak of vulgarity in it, full of the vernacular of American musical experience."

Adams, like Glass, has latterly explored the larger canvas of opera using relatively recent historical events for the plots. Examples include: *Nixon in China* (1987) which outlines the historic meeting between President Nixon and Chairman Mao; and *The Death of Klinghoffer* (1991) which highlights the eternal clash of the Arabs and the Jews. What Adams's music shows above all is the increasing pluralism in the styles of contemporary music which include popular idioms and also the raiding of past musical genres to create a fascinating blend of disparate materials.

The Modernists: Birtwistle, Stockhausen, Boulez.

Modernist composers, who reject the notion that there are 'easy answers' in art, will continue to have a significant role in contemporary music. The leading 'Modernists' include Stockhausen, Boulez, Birtwistle, Xenakis, Ligeti, and Ferneyhough. Their music is very diverse in style but they have a common commitment to atonal music, the use of systems in their music and an avoidance of the approachability of the Post-Modernists like Holloway or the American David Del Tredici (b 1937), or the Mystics such as Pärt, Tavener or Górecki.

Harrison Birtwistle is a British composer who has continued to use an uncompromising, non-tonal and often very aggressive musical language. He is also a figure who is seen as the most original and distinctive voice of his generation. His musical development can be seen as the gradual evolution of one basic approach which shows increasing refinement of technique, but without changing his main focus on the issue of the structuring time. His most recent works include: *Earth Dances* for large orchestra (1985–6) which shows a complex layering of strata, like the earth's crust; *Gawain* (1991), an opera based on a Middle English Romance about courtly chivalry among knights; and *The Second Mrs Kong* (1994) which explores a confusing plethora of film and mythic characters.

In the 1995 last night of the Proms, John Drummond, the controller of Radio 3, had the audacity to commission Birtwistle to write *Panic* for John Harle, the saxophonist. The result was a wild and virtuoso work which sounds almost like free jazz. It caused uproar in the press as it brought an example of modernist violence into what is usually a cosy, musically mediocre and blatantly jingoistic event. Birtwistle shows that it is still possible to write attractive, and challenging music, and still get an audience.

Other Modernists have perhaps fared less well in the 1980s and 1990s. Boulez, the archetypal Modernist, seems to be rewriting old works such as the orchestral *Notations* (1977–) or continuations of existing works such as the recent reworking of *explosante-fix* (1993).

Stockhausen has continued with his seven opera project *Licht* which he began in 1977 and has become increasingly isolated, working with a very close-knit group of players, including several of his family members. All his compositional work is focused on *Licht* which has much in common with Wagner's *The Ring* – however *Licht* seems to lack the unity and perhaps the consistency of *The Ring*.

It would appear that Stockhausen is no longer the innovator of the 1960s and 1970s, and has perhaps lost his direction.

Mystics and the New Simplicity: Arvo Pärt.

As part of the shift towards a greater comprehensibility in music, a number of composers have written music imbued with mysticism, usually allied to an increased religious devotion. Arvo Pärt (b. 1935), the Estonian, is an example of a composer whose earlier works are in the Modernist serial tradition but who had a change of heart in the late 1960s. At this time he made an intensive study of Gregorian Chant, 13th Century Notre Dame Organum, and Renaissance Polyphony. "Gregorian Chant has taught me what a cosmic secret is hidden in the art of combining two or three notes," he said in 1988.

He managed to incur the wrath of the old communist authorities throughout his career, firstly as a serial composer, then as a composer using religious texts, and finally, when Western Serialism was becoming accepted in the 1970s, he shifted to a new simplicity in his music. His most significant works in the later style include: *Tabula Rasa*, a double concerto for two violins (1977); *Passio* for voices and instruments (1982); *Stabat Mater* for Soprano, Alto and strings (1985); and *Litany* for soloist, choir and orchestra (1994).

Other composers who have embraced a mystical and simple approach in their music include: John Tavener (b. 1944) the British composer who rediscovered his Greek Orthodox roots; Henryk Górecki (b. 1933), the Polish composer whose Symphony No. 3 (1976) was a chart hit; and the Georgian symphonic composer Giya Kancheli (b. 1935).

It is unlikely that at the beginning of the next millennium there will be any one dominating style or composer. The present pluralistic scene, where there is a richness and variety of style, will probably continue for the foreseeable future.

POPULAR MUSIC AND JAZZ

Introduction.

The evolution of popular music and jazz is arguably the most far-reaching musical development of recent times. Many of the world's population have heard of Michael Jackson, or The Beatles, but few will have heard of such significant musical figures as Arnold Schönberg or Pierre Boulez. The audience for contemporary classical or 'art' music is an ever-shrinking one, and only styles which have links with popular music, such as minimalism, (*see* E21), or look to the past, such as post-Modernist/neo-Romantic music, have any significant audience. Therefore popular music could be considered by future musicologists as the most significant musical genre of the twentieth century.

The term 'popular music' is problematic as not all popular music is actually that popular or commercial, but it has come to mean music which has its roots in the blues. Popular music is aimed at the whole spectrum of the population, whereas classical or 'art' music has always had a following among the educated middle classes, and therefore could be considered elitist. The roots of present day popular music include folk song, African music, ballads, blues, jazz, and ragtime as well as elements of Western classical music. The development of blues, jazz and popular music will be outlined below.

The Blues: Origins.

The origins of the blues are a mixture of African influences brought by the slaves to North America, work songs used on the plantations, and Western musical elements. The work songs were sung by the slaves as they worked and had a call and response pattern. One man would sing the verse and the rest of the workers would reply with a chorus. The style of singing was different from the Western approach

as it included growls, cries, and falsetto avoiding a pure tone. Rhythm is also a more developed feature in African music and the blues and jazz show traces of this.

The field holler was a variety of work song which was sung by a lone worker and consisted of a long, tremulous one or two line call, often in falsetto, and comparatively free in form. This type of call has been recorded in the savannah parts of West Africa. Other elements contributing to the origins of the blues include reels, dances, and jigs of Anglo-Scottish-Irish origin with African rhythmic elements and tuning, played on banjos (a descendant of the African *bania*) and fiddles. European-influenced song forms were also adopted by the Black Americans in the nineteenth century.

The Structure of the Blues.

The structure of the blues may have been heavily influenced by ballads such as *Railroad Bill* which was popular among black vocalists of the nineteenth century. This had the form of a couplet with a rhyming third line as a chorus. In blues the couplet was replaced with a repeated line:

See, see rider, see what you have done,
See, see rider, see what you have done,
You've made me love you, now my man done come.

The basic blues structure consisted of three lines within a 12 bar stanza and the rhyme schemes included *aaa, abb, abc* but *aab* predominated. The chord sequence, which was usually played by the guitar, can be described as follows (one chord per bar in the key of C major):

I (CEG), I, I, I, IV (FAC), IV, I, I, V⁷ (GBDF),
IV, I, V⁷ (last line I).

This is the most simple form and there are many variants.

The scale used by blues vocalists and instrumentalists is called the blues scale, because of the flattened or 'blue' notes. In the key of C major, the simplest scale consists of C E♭ F G B♭ which is also a pentatonic scale found in much folk music. The 'blue' notes are the E♭ and B♭ although a vocalist may not bend the notes exactly to these pitches.

The rhythmic language of the blues is also significant and includes syncopation; a displacement of the beat, and 'swung' quavers, consisting of the first quaver of a pair being longer and heavier than the second, rather than being equal as in classical music. Many of the above technical features, such as the 12 bar blues sequence, the blues scale, and the rhythmic style, can be observed in jazz and popular music.

The term 'blues' relating to song probably did not emerge until after 1900, but the original sixteenth century meaning was 'a condition of melancholy or depression' which describes the nature of many blues lyrics. The early blues singers, based in the South of the United States, worked in 'medicine shows' to attract buyers for dubious patent medicines. Wandering blues singers, rather like the French medieval troubadours, sang and played for their living, and helped to disseminate the blues in the early years of the present century. By 1910 white folk song collectors had noted the existence of the blues and in 1912 *Dallas Blues* by Hart Wand and Lloyd Garret was published – the first published example.

It is unlikely that the large number of published blues songs had a major effect on blues singers as few could read music. Probably the blues were passed on orally, and later, through recordings. The blues originated in the South, known as the Delta Blues, but in the 1920s blues singers moved North to record, along with the jazz musicians.

Classic Blues.

Mamie Smith (1883–1946) was the first black singer whose records were sold to the black public. *Crazy Blues*, which was recorded in 1920 and sold 75,000 copies in one month, made her a fortune and encouraged other black singers to follow her example, recording specifically for black listeners on what were dubbed 'race records'.

The term 'Classic Blues' refers to the songs of women singers based in New York and Chicago, particularly the larger-voiced contraltos who focused on blues and were backed by jazz musicians. Gertrude 'Ma' Rainey (1886–1939) was a significant example who was closest to the folk tradition. She was known as the 'Mother of the Blues', worked with Louis Armstrong on *Jelly Bean Blues* (1924), and made over 100 records in five years.

Bessie Smith (1894–1937) is probably the best known blues singer and her recording of *Down Hearted Blues* (1923) established her as the most successful black artist of the time. Her singing showed a powerful, emotional involvement, particularly noticeable in her slow blues songs.

Blues in the 1930s.

The poor conditions of the Depression may have partly triggered a more aggressive and powerful blues sound in the 1930s, with larger bands and the introduction of drummers and electrical amplification. This style of blues has been described as 'Urban Blues' and the guitarist Big Bill Broonzy (1893–1958) was an important exponent. In the early 1930s he added a trumpet, clarinet, a second guitar and a bass to make his Memphis Five Band, later adding a drummer. This created a music which had the drive needed for dancing. Other pioneers of Urban Blues include Tampa Red with his Chicago Five.

Postwar Blues.

The evolution of blues into an ensemble-based genre continued after the war with singers like Muddy Waters (1915–83) and B.B. King (b. 1925). King, while remaining true to the blues form, explored aspects of jazz, gospel, and soul, with an innovative and expressive guitar technique. The blues have continued to have a significant role in music, but the genre has been largely absorbed into popular music.

Jazz: Origins.

It is difficult to give a comprehensive definition of jazz because of the variety of different styles within the genre. Generally, jazz shows a heightened preoccupation with rhythm, an emphasis on free improvisation, and usually a tonal/modal basis. Jazz emerged around the same time as the blues, and shares some of the latter's origins. Jazz has also had a significant influence on 'classical' composers, examples including Milhaud's *Le Creation du Monde* and Stravinsky's *Ragtime*.

Jazz originated in New Orleans around 1900, although the precise nature of the music played at that time is unclear because the earliest recording was made in 1917 by the white Original Dixieland Jazz Band. New Orleans jazz consisted of dense counterpoint from the front line wind instruments: saxophone, cornet, clarinet, and trombone, using material from the blues, marches or ragtime. The melody was usually embellished on the cornet with a higher counter-melody on the clarinet or saxophone. The rhythm section consisted of a piano, guitar or banjo playing the harmony, the drummer playing syncopated march rhythms, and a tuba or bass saxophone playing the bass line. There were short breaks for improvised solos from the wind players.

In the 1920s and 1930s the most innovative jazz musicians worked in Chicago and New York, and there was a musical shift towards more complex harmony, with a more subtle approach to improvisation. This can be seen in Bix Beiderbecke's (1903–31) cornet playing, for example *Davenport Blues* (1925) which shows a more expanded and imaginative approach to the improvised solo. Louis Armstrong (1901–71) with his Hot Five and Hot Seven had a more aggressive and rhythmically adventurous approach, which had a greater impact on the style. Other significant bands that moved to Chicago in the 1920s include King Oliver's Creole Jazz Band and Jelly Roll Morton's band.

Swing and Bebop.

In the 1920s another strand emerged known as orchestral jazz which can be seen in Fletcher Henderson's (1897–1952) band, partly due to the work of his arranger Don Redman. His approach to arranging was to use the sections: saxophones, brass (trumpets and trombones), and a rhythm section of banjo, tuba, piano and drums. Henderson created a combination of arranged big band sound with swinging jazz solos by such players as Louis

Armstrong. The term 'swing' describes the bands of the 1930s onwards, and also refers to the rhythmic approach where all quavers were 'swung' in a triplet rhythm. The difference between the 'swing' bands and their precursors is that the former had a greater control of the arrangement, and a tighter and more unified rhythm.

Duke Ellington (1899–1974) and his Orchestra had a major impact on the development of big band composition, exploring a new range of expression. His compositions include miniature tone-poems such as *Daybreak Express* (1933), recompositions such as *Ebony Rhapsody* (1934) based on Liszt's *Hungarian Rhapsody No. 2* and solo concertos like *Clarinet Lament* (1936).

Benny Goodman (1909–86) was the significant white band leader of the period and succeeded in transforming Fletcher Henderson's approach with a more classically-based accuracy. He kept the swing element but removed the more adventurous approach to expression and note bending of the black bands.

In the 1940s a new style appeared called 'Bebop' or 'Bop' which consisted of complex, jagged, and stabbing harmonies, combined with free flowing scalic improvisation. The finest exponent of bebop was the alto saxophonist Charlie Parker (1920–55). He generally worked in small ensembles and played breathtaking improvisations of chromatic and irregular melodies, using rhythms which contradicted the underlaying pulse. Other important bebop players include the trumpeters Dizzy Gillespie and Miles Davis, and the pianist Thelonious Monk, all of whom played with Parker. Bebop marked a radical shift in the development of jazz as it allowed a much freer mode of expression, comparable with contemporary 'art' music.

Cool, Free Jazz and Fusion.

Miles Davis (1926–91) is unusual among jazz musicians as he successfully transformed his style several times, including swing, bebop, cool, modal jazz, fusion and funk. *The Birth of the Cool* (1949–50) with his own 9-piece band created a new sound which eschewed the frenetic activity of bebop for a drier, mellower, and 'cooler' sound. Other musicians working in this almost classical chamber of music style included Lennie Tristano and Gill Evans. In *A Kind of Blue* (1959) Davis continued his development into modal jazz where long stretches of music are based on one chord, with the improvised solos on a compatible mode.

The next step entailed removing the chord progressions completely, which Ornette Coleman (b. 1930) did in his 'free jazz' by removing harmony instruments from his groups. In addition, tempo and the time signature are variable in his work, giving his music a very fluid rhythmic flow. *Free Jazz* (1960) is Coleman's seminal recording, and his work was continued by the pianist Cecil Taylor and the trumpeter Don Cherry.

In the 1960s 'pop music' dominated the musical scene and in this period the use of electronics and musical elements from rock 'n' roll can be observed. Miles Davis' *Bitches Brew* (1969) is a good example of the fusion of jazz and rock. From 1970 to the present day the jazz scene has similar characteristics to that of contemporary 'art' music in the multiplicity of coexisting styles. This makes it difficult to identify a clear direction of development. The most innovative current jazz performers include the pianist Keith Jarrett, George Russell, Anthony Braxton and Evan Parker.

Popular Music: Origins.

Popular Music can be defined as music which is aimed at the populace rather than an elite. Its abbreviated form 'pop', has been used since the 1950s, although one early use of this word was for a popular concert – first recorded in 1862. Popular music of the eighteenth and nineteenth centuries was briefer, simpler, and lighter than contemporaneous classical music.

In the early twentieth century, song writers such as Jerome Kern, Irving Berlin, George Gershwin, and Cole Porter, continued to develop the popular song often using 32 bar ballad form. This consisted of an introductory verse of 16 or 32 bars followed by a more memorable and lyrical chorus of 32 bars constructed of 4×8 bar sections: AABA. The songs were more imaginative than the above formula suggests and used sophisticated harmony influenced by both jazz and classical music. Tin Pan Alley was the area in New York City where many popular songs from the 1920s to 1950s were composed and published. 'Popular music' is now generally used for music since the 1950s with roots in rock 'n' roll, covering music as diverse as 'The Sex Pistols' and Cliff Richard.

Rock 'n' Roll and Rock.

Rock 'n' roll is a form of rhythmicised blues, evolving from rhythm and blues, and was meant for dancing. Its tempo was fast and furious, the words were largely sexually based, the dynamic was loud, and the vocal style aggressive and semi-shouted. The instrumentation was dominated by electric guitars, saxophones, and a powerful rhythm section of drums, piano and bass, with a strong emphasis on the first beat of each bar. Successful American performers include Bill Haley and his Comets, Jerry Lee Lewis, Elvis Presley, Chuck Berry and Little Richard.

In the early 1960s rock 'n' roll was revitalised by the emergence of new bands including the Beach Boys in the US and British groups such as the Beatles, the Rolling Stones, and the Who. These groups helped to transform the genre into a more varied and sophisticated form which became 'rock'.

The main features of 'rock' were developed in California by the Byrds and other bands in San Francisco. Rock had the flexibility and potential to create more varied and complex structures. The Beatles illustrated this greater sophistication in albums such as *Revolver* (1966) and *Sgt. Pepper's Lonely Hearts Club Band* (1967). Their contribution to the development of popular music was immense through the unfolding of a varied and distinctive musical language, and also their evolution of studio techniques, including multi-tracking and sound processing. They disengaged their music from the 'live performance' which would have been impossible for many of their best recorded songs. The basic characteristics of rock are an instrumentation of electric guitars, bass guitar, keyboard and drums; a fast, pounding rhythm from the bass and drums; and rather egocentric performances.

Heavy Metal, Punk and Reggae.

Heavy metal was developed from the blues progressions of the late 1960s by 'power trios' like Cream and the Jimi Hendrix Experience. It consisted of guitar-based rock with highly amplified and virtuosic guitar and bass, creating a 'wall of sound'. In the 1970s heavy metal bands included Deep Purple, Steppenwolf and Black Sabbath who were followed by the new wave of British bands such as Def Leppard and Iron Maiden. Live performance is very important for heavy metal, as fans enjoy interacting with the performers.

Punk was a term originally given to garage-based US rock of the 1960s, but was more famously used for music in 1976 played by the British bands, Sex Pistols, Clash, and Buzzcocks, who had been influenced by Richard Hell, and Patti Smith playing in New York City. Punk attempted to make rock 'dangerous' again, consisting of aggressive, anti-establishment lyrics, very basic guitar-based rock played at great speed. Punk evolved into New Wave which has similar energy but with more finesse and musical technique. Examples include Blondie and Talking Heads.

Reggae also emerged in the 1970s consisting of a Jamaican pop style developed from Ska (a shuffling hybrid of rhythm and blues) and Mento. The music is much slower and more sensuous than other popular genres and has a hypnotic, bass-dominated sound, a 'chopped off' beat, and often a lyrical and expressive vocal line. Bob Marley was the most impressive performer, along with Desmond Dekker and Jimmy Cliff.

Disco, House and Techno.

In the last 20 years music for dancing has become prevalent through the Discotheque and latterly the 'Rave'. Disco consists of a thumping bass drum on each beat of the music and is considered a debased form of pop music. It was promoted by the film *Saturday Night Fever* (1977) and is a relatively simple style, making use of drum machines and synthesisers which give it an anonymous quality.

House is based on Disco and consists of the warm, feel-good music of the late 1980s. The term comes from the use of warehouses for performance, and it originated in Chicago with Frankie Knuckles.

Techno, originating in Detroit, was also a development of the 1980s. It is a percussion-based electronic dance music, with stripped-down drum beats and bass lines. UK labels include Rising High and Warp and successful groups are Prodigy, Orbital, and L.F.O.. Most techno uses a 'groove' or movement by repetition, which builds up an evolving musical texture in a similar way to minimalist music.

Grunge.

Originating in Seattle during the mid-1980s, the grunge movement has largely usurped traditional heavy metal to become one of the most influential rock sounds of the 1990s. Essentially a mixture of blues-based chord progressions, punk-like energy levels and nihilistic lyrical content, the typical grunge song contrasts quieter, contemplative verses against raging, aggressive choruses. To achieve the deep and sinister sound at the heart of the music, grunge performers often de-tune their guitars and basses from standard concert pitch by up to two whole tones.

Since the movement came to world-wide prominence in 1992, grunge's most commercially successful acts have included Pearl Jam, Soundgarden and Alice In Chains. But by far the most important band to emerge from the genre was Seattle-based group Nirvana, whose second album, *Nevermind*, encapsulated much of grunge's intrinsic appeal. Unfortunately, Nirvana's singer/songwriter Kurt Cobain reacted badly to the demands of fame and subsequently took his own life in 1994. He has since become a cultural icon to disaffected teenagers everywhere. Though its forward momentum was temporarily checked by Cobain's death, grunge continues to grow with newer groups such as Live, Bush, Ash and Korn all expanding on the form's more dominant musical themes.

Brit-Pop.

After a particularly uneventful period in the history of British pop, a slew of similarlly themed bands emerged in 1993 and commercially re-invigorated the domestic music scene. Taking their blueprint from the sounds and styles of the 1960s—with the music of The Beatles and The Kinks a clear reference point—groups such as Manchester's Oasis, London's Blur and Sheffield's Pulp all but dominated the UK charts in the 1990s. In direct opposition to America's grunge movement, the lyrical content of much of Brit-Pop is optimistic in nature, with images of casual hedonism and wry social commentary well to the fore.

Conversely, as the genre continues to evolve, emergent acts such as Radiohead and The Verve are directly challenging the more formulaic aspects of the Brit-Pop sound. More 'rock' than 'pop', these groups employ odd time signatures, thicker orchestral textures and lyrical themes of paranoia and rigorous self-examination to inform their music. The result of such experimentation has meant that original Brit-Pop acts have been forced to re-evaluate their position and explore wider musical themes in an effort to compete.

Boy Bands and Girl Bands.

One of the more interesting developments to come out of the popular music scene in recent years has been the increasing proliferation of boy/girl bands. Unlike most pop acts that hone their musical craft in rehearsal rooms and concert halls over a period of years, the majority of boy/girl bands are 'manufactured', with group members brought together by prospective managers through the process of audition.

As record producers and professional song-writers often provide these acts with their material, the skills required of the average boy/girl band member differ greatly from more traditional groups. In place of instrumental prowess, they must be youthful in appearance, able dancers and reasonably proficient singers. When marketed properly, these acts have achieved huge chart success, finding a dedicated fanbase consisting not only of teenagers, but also children as young as five or six.

A sterling example of a successful boy band was Take That, who enjoyed an almost Beatles-like public profile until their break-up at the start of 1996. (After his departure from Take That, Robbie Williams went on to achieve great acclaim as a soloist, reaching a pinnacle of his career in 1999). Interestingly, a 'Samaritans Hotline' was established to help fans deal with their dissolution. Nonetheless, within months, Take That had been replaced in the public's affections by two more boy bands, Boyzone and the Backstreet Boys. By far the most commercially profitable of the all girl groups has been the Spice Girls, who continue to dominate both the UK and US charts with their easy blend of soulful melodies and appealing dance routines. Their simple mantra of 'Girl Power' has also become a catchphrase for many teenagers.

Though boy and girl bands offer little in developmental terms to the course of popular music, their continued success indicates a trend towards a more generalised form of entertainment within the pop scene, where the ability to dance well is as highly prized as a fine singing voice.

Jungle/Drum and Bass/Ambient.

Jungle is a loose term used to describe a frenetically paced form of dance music that originated in the UK 'rave/club' scene in the early 1990s. Like Techno music, jungle is percussion based and reliant on the use of drum machines and synthesisers to provide its centralised core. Yet, where it differs from techno and house music is in the profound absence of mid-range frequencies, with virtually no vocals or guitar used to enhance melody. Instead, both bass and treble frequencies are heavily compressed, creating a thunderous, filtered sound. To add to the sense of musical drama, jungle moves at a pace of approximately 156–180 BPM (beats per minute), almost double the speed of the average pop song. Some of jungle music's more notable performers include Tricky and Goldie.

Drum and bass is similar to jungle music in that it relies heavily on rhythm to enforce its point. However, in stark contrast to jungle's more repetitive approach, drum and bass often manipulates time signatures, speeding the beat up and down at irregular intervals to create a jarring musical effect. Because it compresses and stretches four bar progressions, drum and bass is often compared to jazz/bebop in terms of musical sensibility and performance. Roni Size is considered to be Great Britain's leading exponent of the drum and bass style.

Ambient is one of the most recent musical genres to emerge from the UK club scene. Effectively, it is a music of texture, where minimalist drum machine patterns and pulsating synthesisers are employed to invoke a sense of atmosphere and general relaxation. Less frenetic than either jungle or drum and bass, ambient is often played in smaller rooms within clubs, enabling the 'raver' a much needed opportunity to relax after an energetic night's dancing. Leading ambient acts include Black Dog, Plaid and Future Sound of London.

II. GLOSSARY OF MUSICAL TERMS

A. Note of scale, commonly used for tuning instruments.

Absolute Music. Music without any literary descriptive or other kind of reference.

A Capella. Literally "in the church style." Unaccompanied.

Accelerando. Quickening of the pace.

Accidental. The sign which alters the pitch of a note; ♯ (sharp) raises and a ♭ (flat) lowers note by one semitone, ✗ (double sharp) and ♮ (double flat) alter by two semitones.

Ad lib. (L. *ad libitum*). Direction on music that strict time need not be observed.

Adagio. A slow movement or piece.

Aeolian mode. One of the scales in mediaeval music, represented by the white keys of the piano from A to A.

Air. A simple tune for voice or instrument.

Alberti Bass. Characteristic 18th century keyboard figuration derived by splitting chord(s) of an accompanying part. Tradition credits Alberti as its inventor.

Allegretto. Not quite so fast as *Allegro*.

Allegro. Fast, but not too fast.

Alto. An unusually high type of male voice; also the vocal part sung by women and boys with a low range.

Ambrosian Chant. Plainsong introduced into church music by St. Ambrose, bishop of Milan (d. 397), and differing from Gregorian chant.

Andante. At a walking pace, not so slow as *Adagio* nor as fast as *Allegretto*.

Animato. Lively.

Answer. Entry in a fugue or invention which imitates or "answers" the theme at a different pitch.

Anthem. Composition for use in church during a service by a choir with or without soloists.

Antiphonal. Using groups of instruments or singers placed apart.

Appoggiatura. An ornament consisting of a short note just above or below a note forming part of a chord.

Arabesque. Usually a short piece, highly decorated.

Arco. Direction for string instruments to play with bow.

Aria. Vocal solo, usually in opera or oratorio, often in three sections with the third part being a repeat of the first. An *Arietta* is a shorter, lighter kind of aria.

Arioso. In the style of an aria; halfway between aria and recitative.

Arpeggio. Notes of a chord played in a broken, spread-out manner, as on a harp.

Ars antiqua. The old mediaeval music, based on organum and plainsong, before the introduction of *Ars nova* in 14th cent.

Ars Nova. New style of composition in 14th century France and Italy. It has greater variety in rhythm and independence in part-writing.

Atonal. Not in any key; hence *Atonality*.

Aubade. Morning song.

Augmentation. The enlargement of a melody by lengthening the musical value of its notes.

Ayre. Old spelling of *air*.

B. Note of scale, represented in Germany by H.

Bagatelle. A short, generally light piece of music. Beethoven wrote 26 Bagatelles.

Ballad. Either a narrative song or an 18th-cent. drawing-room song.

Ballade. A substantial and dramatic work, often for piano. Notable examples are by Chopin and Brahms.

Ballet. Stage entertainment requiring intrumental accompaniment; originated at French court in 16th and 17th cent.

Bar. A metrical division of music; the perpendicular line in musical notation to indicate this.

Barcarolle. A boating-song, in particular one associated with Venetian gondoliers.

Baritone. A male voice, between tenor and bass.

Baroque. A term applied, loosely, to music written in the 17th and 18th cent., roughly corresponding to baroque in architecture.

Bass. The lowest male voice; lowest part of a composition.

Bass Drum. Largest of the drum family, placed upright and struck on the side.

Bassoon. The lowest of the woodwind instruments, uses double reed.

Beat. Music's rhythmic pulse.

Bel canto. Literally "beautiful singing"—in the old Italian style with pure tone and exact phrasing.

Berceuse. Cradle song.

Binary. A piece in two sections is said to be binary in form. The balance is obtained by a second phrase (or section) answering the first.

Bitonality. Use of two keys at once.

Bow. Stick with horsehair stretched across it for playing string instruments.

Brass. Used as a collective noun for all brass or metal instruments.

Breve. Note, rarely used nowadays, with time value of two semibreves.

Bridge. Wood support over which strings are stretched on a violin, cello, guitar, etc.

Buffo(a). Comic, as in *buffo bass* or *opera buffa*.

C. Note of scale.

Cabaletta. Final, quick section of an aria or duet.

Cadence. A closing phrase of a composition or a passage, coming to rest on tonic (key note).

Cadenza. Solo vocal or instrumental passage, either written or improvised, giving soloist chance to display technical skill to audience.

Calando. Becoming quieter and slower.

Canon. A piece or section of music resulting from one line of music being repeated imitatively in the other parts which enter in succession.

Cantabile. Song-like, therefore flowing and expressive.

Cantata. Vocal work for chorus and/or choir.

Cantilena. Sustained, smooth melodic line.

Cantus firmus. Literally "fixed song." Basic melody from 14th to 17th cent., around which other voices wove contrapuntal parts.

Canzonet. Light songs written in England *c.* 1600.

Carillon. A set of bells in tower of church, played from a keyboard below.

Carol. Christmas song.

Castrato. Artificially-created male soprano and alto, fashionable in 17th and 18th cent. (The castration of vocally gifted boys prevailed in Italy until the 19th cent.)

Catch. A part-song like a round, in vogue in England from 16th to 19th cent.

Cavatina. An operatic song in one section, or a slow song-like instrumental movement.

Celesta. Keyboard instrument with metal bars struck by hammers.

Cello. Four-stringed instrument, played with bow, with a bass range. Comes between viola and double bass in string family.

Cembalo. Originally the Italian name for the dulcimer, but sometimes applied to the harpsichord.

Chaconne. Vocal or instrumental piece with unvaried bass.

Chamber Music. Music originally intended to be played in a room for three or more players.

Chanson. Type of part-song current in France from 14th to 16th cent.

Chant. Singing of psalms, masses, etc., in plainsong to Latin words in church.

Choir. Body of singers, used either in church or at concerts.

Chorales. German hymn tunes, often made up of by Bach.

Chord. Any combination of notes heard together. *See also* Triad.

Chording. Spacing of intervals in a chord.

Chorus. Substantial body of singers, usually singing in four parts.

Chromatic. Using a scale of nothing but semitones.

Clarinet. Woodwind instrument with single reed in use since mid-18th cent.

Clavichord. Keyboard instrument having strings struck by metal tangents, much in use during 17th and 18th cent. as solo instrument.

Clavier. Used in German (*Klavier*) for piano, in England for any stringed keyboard instrument.

Clef. Sign in stave that fixes place of each note.

Coda. Closing section of movement in Sonata form.

Coloratura. Term to denote florid singing.

Common chord. *See* Triad.

Common Time. Four crotchets to the bar, 4/4 time.

Compass. Range of notes covered by voice or instruments.

Composition. Piece of music, originated by a composer's own imagination; act of writing such a piece.

Compound Time. Metre where beats are subdivided into threes rather than twos.

Con Brio. With dash.

Concert. Public performance of any music.

Concertato. Writing for several solo instruments to be played together.

Concerto. Work for one or more solo instruments and orchestra.

Concerto grosso. Orchestral work common in 17th and 18th cent. with prominent parts for small groups of instruments.

Concord. Opposite of discord, *i.e.*, notes that when sounded together satisfy the ear. (Conventional term in that its application varies according to the age in which one lives.)

Conduct. To direct a concert with a baton.

Consecutive. Progression of harmonic intervals of like kind.

Consonance. Like Concord.

Continuo. Bass line in 17th and 18th century music. Played by a bass instrument and keyboard, the latter improvising on the indicated harmonies.

Contralto. A woman's voice with a low range.

Counterpoint. Simultaneous combination of two or more melodies to create a satisfying musical texture. Where one melody is added to another, one is called the other's counterpoint. The adjective of counterpoint is contrapuntal.

Counter-tenor. Another name for male alto.

Courante. A dance in triple time.

Crescendo. Getting louder.

Crook. Detachable section of tubing on brass instruments that change the tuning.

Crotchet. Note that equals two quavers in time value.

Cycle. Set of works, especially songs, intended to be sung as group.

Cyclic form. Form of work in two or more movements in which the same musical themes recur.

Cymbal. Percussion instrument; two plates struck against each other.

D. Note of scale.

Da Capo (abbr. D.C.). A *Da Capo* aria is one in which the whole first section is repeated after a contrasting middle section.

Descant. Additional part (sometimes improvised) sung against a melody.

Development. Working-out section of movement in sonata form. *See* Sonata.

Diatonic. Opposite of chromatic; using proper notes of a major or minor scale.

Diminished. Lessened version of perfect interval, e.g., semitone less than a perfect fifth is a diminished fifth.

Diminuendo. Lessening.

Diminution. Reducing a phrase of melody by shortening time value of notes.

Discord. Opposite of concord, *i.e.*, notes that sounded together produce a clash of harmonies.

Dissonance. Like discord.

Divertimento. A piece, usually orchestral, in several movements; like a suite.

Dodecaphonic. Pertaining to 12-note method of composition.

Dominant. Fifth note of major or minor scale above tonic (key) note.

Dorian Mode. One of the scales in mediaeval music, represented by the white keys on the piano from D to D.

Dot. Placed over note indicates staccato; placed after note indicates time value to be increased by half.

Double bar. Two upright lines marking the end of a composition or a section of it.

Double bass. Largest and lowest instrument of violin family; played with bow.

Drone bass. Unvarying sustained bass, similar to the permanent bass note of a bagpipe.

Drum. Variety of percussion instruments on which sound is produced by hitting a skin stretched tightly over a hollow cylinder or hemisphere.

Duet. Combination of two performers; composition for such a combination.

Duple Time. Metre in which there are two beats to a bar.

Dynamics. Gradations of loudness or softness in music.

E. Note of scale.

Electronic. Term used to describe use of electronic sounds in music.

Encore. Request from audience for repeat of work, or extra item in a programme.

English horn (*Cor anglais*). Woodwind instrument with double reed of oboe family.

Enharmonic. Refers to use of different letter names for the same note, *e.g.* F and E♯. Often exploited to achieve modulation between distantly related keys.

Ensemble. Teamwork in performance; item in opera for several singers with or without chorus; a group of performers of no fixed number.

Episode. Section in composition usually divorced from main argument.

Exposition. Setting out of thematic material in a sonata-form composition.

Expression marks. Indication by composer of how he wants his music performed.

F. Note of scale.

False relation. A clash of harmony produced when two notes, such as A natural and A flat, are played simultaneously or immediately following one another.

Falsetto. The kind of singing by male voices above normal register and sounding like an unbroken voice.

Fanfare. Flourish of trumpets.

Fantasy. A piece suggesting free play of composer's imagination, or a piece based on known tunes (folk, operatic, etc.).

Fermata. Pause indicated by sign ⌢ prolonging note beyond its normal length.

Fifth. Interval taking five steps in the scale. A perfect fifth (say, C to G) includes three whole tones and a semitone; a diminished fifth is a semitone less, an augmented fifth a semitone more.

Figure. A short phrase, especially one that is repeated.

Fingering. Use of fingers to play instrument, or the indication above notes to show what fingers should be used.

Flat. Term indicating a lowering of pitch by a semitone, or to describe a performer playing under the note.

Florid. Term used to describe decorative passages.

Flute. Woodwind instrument, blown sideways. It is played through a hole, not a reed. Nowadays, sometimes made of metal.

Folksong. Traditional tune, often in different versions, handed down aurally from generation to generation.

Form. Course or layout of a composition, especially when in various sections.

Fourth. Interval taking four steps in scale. A perfect fourth (say, C to F) includes two whole tones and a semitone. If either note is sharpened or flattened the result is an augmented or a diminished fourth.

Fugato. In the manner of a fugue.

Fugue. Contrapuntal composition for various parts based on one or more subjects treated imitatively but not strictly.

G. Note of scale.

Galant. Used to designate elegant style of 18th-cent. music.

Galliard. Lively dance dating back to 15th cent. or before.

Gavotte. Dance in 4/4 time, beginning on third beat in bar.

Giusto. Strict, proper.

Glee. Short part-song.

Glissando. Rapid sliding scales up and down piano or other instruments.

Glockenspiel. Percussion instrument consisting of tuned steel bars and played with two hammers or keyboard.

Grace note. *See* Ornament.

Grave. In slow tempo.

Grazioso. Gracefully.

Gregorian Chant. Plainsong collected and supervised mainly by Pope Gregory (d. 604).

Ground Bass. A bass part that is repeated throughout a piece with varying material on top.

Guitar. Plucked string instrument of Spanish origin, having six strings of three-octave compass.

H. German note-symbol for *B.*

Harmony. Simultaneous sounding of notes so as to make musical sense.

Harp. Plucked string instrument of ancient origin, the strings stretched parallel across its frame. The basic scale of C flat major is altered by a set of pedals.

Harpsichord. Keyboard stringed instrument played by means of keyboard similar to a piano but producing its notes by a plucking, rather than a striking action.

Homophonic. Opposite of polyphonic, *i.e.*, indicated parts move together in a composition, a single melody being accompanied by block chords, as distinct from the contrapuntal movement of different melodies.

Horn. Brass instrument with coiled tubes. Valves introduced in 19th cent. made full chromatic use of instrument possible.

Hymn. Song of praise, especially in church.

Imitation. Repetition, exactly, or at least recognisably, of a previously heard figure.

Impromptu. A short, seemingly improvised piece of music, especially by Schubert or Chopin.

Improvise. To perform according to fancy or imagination, sometimes on a given theme.

In alt. The octave above the treble clef; *in altissimo*, octave above that.

Instrumentation. Writing music for particular instruments, using the composer's knowledge of what sounds well on different instruments.

Interlude. Piece played between two sections of a composition.

Intermezzo. Formerly meant interlude, now often used for pieces played between acts of operas.

Interval. Distance in pitch between notes.

Ionian mode. One of the scales in mediaeval music, represented on piano by white keys between C and C, identical therefore to modern C major scale.

Isorhythmic. Medieval technique using repetitions of a rhythm but with different notes. Much used in 15th century motets.

Jig. Old dance usually in 6/8 or 12/8 time.

Kettledrum (It. pl. *Timpani*). Drum with skin drawn over a cauldron-shaped receptacle, can be tuned to definite pitch by turning handles on rim, thus tightening or relaxing skin.

Key. Lever by means of which piano, organ, etc., produces note; classification, in relatively modern times, of notes of a scale. Any piece of music in major or minor is in the *key* of its tonic or keynote.

Keyboard. Term used to describe instruments with a continuous row of keys.

Key-signature. Indication on written music, usually at the beginning of each line, of the number of flats or sharps in the key of a composition.

Kitchen Department. Humorous term for percussion section of an orchestra.

Lament. Musical piece of sad or deathly significance.

Largamente. Spaciously.

Largo. Slow.

Leading-motive (Ger. *Leitmotiv*). Short theme, suggesting person, idea, or image, quoted throughout composition to indicate that person, etc.

Legato. In a smooth style (of performance, etc.).

Lento. Slow.

Libretto. Text of an opera.

Lied (pl. *Lieder*). Song, with special reference to songs by Schubert, Schumann, Brahms, and Wolf.

Lute. String instrument plucked with fingers, used in 15th- and 16th-cent. music especially.

Lydian mode. One of the scales in mediaeval music, represented by white keys of piano between F and F.

Lyre. Ancient Greek plucked string instrument.

Madrigal. Contrapuntal composition for several voices, especially prominent from 15th to 17th cent.

Maestoso. Stately.

Major. One of the two main scales of the tonal system with semitones between the third and fourth, and the seventh and eighth notes. Identical with 16th-cent. Ionian mode.

Mandolin(e). Plucked string instrument of Italian origin.

Manual. A keyboard for the hands, used mostly in connection with the organ.

Master of the King's (or Queen's) Musick. Title of British court appointment, with no precise duties.

Melisma. Group of notes sung to a single syllable.

Mélodie. Literally a melody or tune; has come to mean a French song (cf. German *Lied*).

Metronome. Small machine in use since the beginning of the 18th cent., to determine the pace of any composition by the beats of the music, *e.g.*, =60 at the head of the music indicates sixty crotchets to the minute.

Mezzo, Mezza. (It. = "half") *Mezza voce* means using the half voice (a tone between normal singing and whispering). *Mezzo-soprano*, voice between soprano and contralto.

Minim. Note that equals two crotchets in time value.

Minor. One of the two main scales of the tonal system (cf. major), identical with 16th-cent. Aeolian mode. It has two forms—the harmonic and melodic, the former having a sharpened seventh note, the latter having the sixth and seventh note sharpened.

Minuet. Originally French 18th-cent. dance in triple time, then the usual third movement in symphonic form (with a contrasting trio section) until succeeded by scherzo.

Mixolydian mode. One of the mediaeval scales represented by the white keys on the piano from G to G.

Modes. Scales prevalent in the Middle Ages. *See* Aeolian, Dorian, Ionian, Lydian, Mixolydian, Phrygian.

Modulate. Changing from key to key in a composition, not directly but according to musical "grammar".

Molto. Much, very; thus *allegro molto*.

Motet. Sacred, polyphonic vocal composition. More loosely, any choral composition for use in church but not set to words of the liturgy.

Motive, motif. Short, easily recognised melodic figure.

Motto. Short, well-defined theme recurring throughout a composition, cf. *Idée fixe* in Berlioz's *Symphonie Fantastique*.

Movement. Separate sections of a large-scale composition, each in its own form.

Music drama. Term used to describe Wagner's, and sometimes other large-scale operas.

Mutes. Devices used to damp the sound of various instruments.

Natural (of a note or key). Not sharp or flat.

Neoclassical. Clear-cut style, originating during 1920s, that uses 17th and 18th century forms and styles. It constituted a reaction to the excesses of romanticism.

Ninth. Interval taking nine steps, *e.g.*, from C upwards an octave and a whole tone to D.

Nocturne. Literally a "night-piece" hence usually of lyrical character.

Nonet. Composition for nine instruments.

Notation. Act of writing down music.

Note. Single sound of specified pitch and duration; symbol to represent this.

Obbligato. Instrumental part having a special or essential rôle in a piece.

Oboe. Woodwind instrument with double reed, descended from hautboy; as such, in use since 16th cent., in modern form since 18th cent.

Octave. Interval taking eight steps of scale, with top and bottom notes having same "name"; C to C is an octave.

Octet. Composition for eight instruments or voices.

Ondes Martenol. Belongs to a class of melodic instruments in which the tone is produced by electrical vibrations controlled by the movement of the hands not touching the instrument.

Opera. Musical work for the stage with singing characters, originated *c.* 1600 in Italy.

Opera buffa (It.), *Opéra bouffe* (Fr.). Comic opera (in the English sense), *not* to be confused with *Opéra comique* (Fr.) which is opera with spoken dialogue and need not be humorous.

Opera seria. Chief operatic form of 17th and 18th cent., usually set to very formal librettos, concerning gods or heroes of ancient history.

Operetta. Lighter type of opera.

Opus (abbr. *Op.*). With number following *opus* indicates order of a composer's composition.

Oratorio. Vocal work, usually for soloists and choir with instrumental accompaniment, generally with setting of a religious text.

Orchestra. Term to designate large, or largish, body of instrumentalists originated in 17th cent.

Orchestration. Art of setting out work for instruments of an orchestra. To be distinguished from *Instrumentation (q.v.)*.

Organ. Elaborate keyboard instrument in which air is blown through pipes by bellows to sound notes. Tone is altered by selection of various stops and, since the 16th cent., a pedal keyboard has also been incorporated.

Organum. In mediaeval music a part sung as an accompaniment below or above the melody of plainsong, usually at the interval of a fourth or fifth; also, loosely, this method of singing in parts.

Ornament. Notes that are added to a given melody by composer or performer as an embellishment.

Overture. Instrumental introduction or prelude to larger work, usually opera. Concert overtures are simply that: *i.e.*, work to be played at start of a concert.

Part. Music of one performer in an ensemble; single strand in a composition.

Part-song. Vocal composition in several parts.

Passacaglia. Composition in which a tune is constantly repeated, usually in the bass.

Passage. Section of a composition.

Passion. Musical setting of the New Testament story of Christ's trial and crucifixion.

Pastiche. Piece deliberately written in another composer's style.

Pavan(e). Moderately paced dance dating from 16th cent. or earlier.

Pedal. Held note in bass of composition.

Pentatonic. Scale of five consecutive notes, *e.g.*, the black keys of the piano.

Percussion. Collective title for instruments of the orchestra that are sounded by being struck by hand or stick.

Phrygian Mode. One of the scales of mediaeval music, represented by the white keys on piano from E to E.

Piano. Soft, abbr. *p*; *pp=pianissimo*, very soft; instrument, invented in 18th cent., having strings struck by hammer, as opposed to the earlier harpsichord where they are plucked. The modern piano has 88 keys and can be either "upright" (vertical) or "grand" (horizontal).

Pianoforte. Almost obsolete full Italian name for the piano.

Pitch. Exact height or depth of a particular musical sound or note.

Pizzicato. Direction for stringed instruments, that the strings should be plucked instead of bowed.

Plainchant, Plainsong. Mediaeval church music consisting of single line of melody without harmony or definite rhythm.

Polka. Dance in 2/4 time originating in 19th cent. Bohemia.

Polonaise. Polish dance generally in 3/4 time.

Polyphony. Combination of two or more musical lines as in *counterpoint*.

Polytonality. Simultaneous use of several keys.

Postlude. Closing piece, opposite of Prelude.

Prelude. Introductory piece.

Presto. Very fast. *Prestissimo.* Still faster.

Progression. Movement from one chord to next to make musical sense.

Quartet. Work written for four instruments or voices; group to play or sing such a work.

Quaver. Note that equals two semiquavers or half a crotchet.

Quintet. Work written for five instruments or voices; group to play or sing such a work.

Rallentando. Slowing down.

Recapitulation. Section of composition that repeats original material in something like its original form.

Recitative. Term used for declamation in singing written in ordinary notation but allowing rhythmical licence.

Recorder. Woodwind instrument, forerunner of flute.

Reed. Vibrating tongue of woodwind instruments.

Register. Set of organ pipes controlled by a particular stop; used in reference to different ranges of instrument or voice (*e.g.*, chest register).

Relative. Term used to indicate common key signature of a major and minor key.

Répétiteur. Member of opera house's musical staff who coaches singers in their parts.

Rest. Notation of pauses for instrument in composition, having a definite length like a note.

Retrograde. Term used to describe a melody played backwards.

Rhapsody. Work of no definite kind with a degree of romantic content.

Rhythm. Everything concerned with the time of music (*i.e.*, beats, accent, metre, etc.) as opposed to the pitch side.

Ritornello. Passage, usually instrumental, that recurs in a piece.

Romance, Romanza. Title for piece of vague song-like character.

Romantic. Term used vaguely to describe music of 19th cent. that has other than purely musical source of inspiration.

Rondo. Form in which one section keeps on recurring.

Rubato. Manner of performing a piece without keeping strictly to time.

Sackbut. Early English name for trombone.

Saxophone. Classified as wind instrument, although made of brass, because it uses a reed.

Scale. Progression of adjoining notes upwards or downwards.

Scherzo. Literally "a joke". Often used as a light movement in the middle of a sonata type work.

Score. Copy of any music written in several parts.

Second. Interval taking two steps in scale, *e.g.*, C to D flat, or to D.

Semibreve. Note that equals two minims or half a breve.

Semiquaver. Note that equals half a quaver.

Semitone. Smallest interval commonly used in Western music.

Septet. Composition for seven instruments or voices.

Sequence. Repetition of phrase at a higher or lower pitch.

Serenade. Usually an evening song or instrumental work.

Seventh. Interval taking seven steps in the scale.

Sextet. Composition for six instruments or voices.

Sharp. Term indicating a raising of pitch by a semitone.

Shawm. Primitive woodwind instrument, forerunner of oboe.

Simple time. Division of music into two or four beats.

Sinfonietta. Small symphony.

Sixth. Interval taking six steps in the scale.

Solo. Piece or part of a piece for one performer playing or singing alone.

Sonata. Term to denote a musical form and a type of composition. In *sonata form* a composition is divided into exposition, development and recapitulation. A *sonata* is a piece, usually for one or more players following that form.

Song. Any short vocal composition.

Soprano. Highest female voice.

Sostenuto. Sustained, broadly.

Sotto voce. Whispered, scarcely audible, applied to vocal as well as instrumental music.

Spinet. A small keyboard instrument belonging to the harpsichord (*q.v.*) family.

Sprechgesang. (Ger. Speech-song.) Vocal utterance somewhere between speech and song.

Staccato. Perform music in short, detached manner.

Staff. Horizontal lines on which music is usually written.

Stop. Lever by which organ registration can be altered.

String(s). Strands of gut or metal set in vibration to produce musical sounds on string or keyboard instruments. Plural refers to violins, violas, cellos, and basses of orchestra.

Study. Instrumental piece, usually one used for technical exercise or to display technical skills, but often having artistic merits as well (*e.g.*, Chopin's).

Subject(s). Theme or group of notes that forms principal idea or ideas in composition.

Suite. Common name for piece in several movements.

Symphony. Orchestral work of serious purpose usually in four movements, occasionally given name (*e.g.*, Beethoven's "Choral" symphony).

Syncopation. Displacement of musical accent.

Tempo. Pace, speed of music.

Tenor. Highest normal male voice.

Ternary. A piece in three sections is said to be in ternary form. The balance is obtained by repeating the first phrase or section (though it need not be exact or complete) after a second of equal importance.

Tessitura. Compass into which voice or instrument comfortably falls.

Theme. Same as *subject* but can also be used for a whole musical statement as in "theme and variations."

Third. Interval taking three steps in scale.

Time. Rhythmical division of music.

Timpani. See Kettledrum.

Toccata. Instrumental piece usually needing rapid, brilliant execution.

Tonality. Key, or feeling for a definite key.

Tone. Quality of musical sound; interval of two semitones.

Tonic Sol-fa. System of musical notation to simplify sight-reading.

Transcribe. Arrange piece for different medium, instrument, or voice than that originally intended.

Transition. Passage that joins two themes or sections of a composition.

Transpose. To move a musical idea, theme or piece to a different key from its original.

Treble. Highest part in vocal composition; high boy's voice.

Triad. Three note chord. Usually consists of a note and those a third and fifth above.

Trio. Work written for three instruments or voices; group to play or sing such a work.

Trombone. Brass instrument with slide adjusting length of tube.

Trumpet. Metal instrument of considerable antiquity; modern version has three valves to make it into a chromatic instrument.

Tuba. Deepest-toned brass instrument with three or four valves.

Twelve-note. Technique of composition using full chromatic scale with each note having equal importance. Notes are placed in particular order as the thematic basis of works.

Unison. Two notes sung or played together at same pitch.

Valve. Mechanism, invented in early 19th cent. to add to brass instruments allowing them to play full chromatic scale.

Variation. Varied passage of original theme. Such variations may be closely allied to or depart widely from the theme.

Verismo. Term to describe Italian operas written in "realist" style at the turn of this century.

Vibrato. Rapid fluctuation in pitch of voice or instrument. Exaggerated it is referred to as a "wobble" (of singers) or tremolo.

Viol. String instrument of various sizes in vogue until end of 17th cent.

Viola. Tenor instrument of violin family.

Violin. Musical four-string instrument, played with bow, of violin family, which superseded viol at beginning of 18th cent.

Virginals. English keyboard instrument, similar to harpsichord of 17th and 18th cent.

Vivace. Lively.

Voluntary. Organ piece for church use, but not during service.

Waltz. Dance in triple time, fashionable in 19th cent.

Whole-tone scale. Scale progressing by whole tones. Only two are possible, one beginning on C, the other on C sharp.

Xylophone. Percussion instrument with series of wood bars tuned in a chromatic scale and played with sticks.

Zither. String instrument laid on knees and plucked. Common in Central-European folk music.

III. INDEX TO COMPOSERS

IV. SPECIAL TOPIC

THE MUSICAL STAGE

The history of 'light', 'popular' works for the musical stage is probably as long as that of their more serious counterpart, opera. However, it is in the last century-and-a-half that a definite genre, or group of genres, can be identified. Definitions are always problematic, but the combination of spoken dialogue and song is common to most of the works in question. The role of the music, its style and the extent of its use and integration into the drama are all matters of importance for the composer and librettist. Subject-matter is varied: if 'romantic love' and 'sentimental comedy' characterise much of this repertoire, it has also been used frequently for purposes of satire and parody as well as for material of a perfectly serious nature—and of course many of the best examples combine all these.

Operetta: Paris.

The first operetta so-called was *Madame Mascarille* by Jules Bovery (1856), but the real founder of operetta in the modern sense, and its first musical genius, was Jacques Offenbach (1819–80). Between 1855 and 1879 he wrote about 90 operettas; the most famous are *Orpheus in the Underworld* (1858, revised and expanded 1874), *La Belle Hélène* (1864)—both parodies of the world of classical Greek mythology which had long been a staple of operatic plots; *La Vie Parisienne* (1867), *La Grande Duchesse de Gerolstein* (1867), and *La Périchole* (1868), works of more direct contemporary application. With their polkas, can-cans and waltzes, Offenbach's works conjure up the brilliance and superficiality of the Second Empire; his music was not only popular but was appreciated by fellow-musicians both in France and elsewhere.

Of Offenbach's successors, two should be mentioned. Charles Lecocq (1832–1918) made a deliberate attempt to create a clear, singing, *French* style appropriate for the changed culture of the bourgeois republic that had emerged from the disasters of 1870–71—*La Fille de Madame Angot*, produced in Brussels in 1872 and in the French capital the following year was said to have 'awakened Paris from the torpor in which its theatre lived since the dark days of the Commune'. André Messager (1853–1929) (*Véronique* 1898) is known for the tender, refined and youthful quality of his music.

Operetta: Vienna.

If Paris can be considered the birthplace of operetta, Vienna is the city which came to seem its natural home, and the rhythm of the Viennese waltz underlies its most memorable and characteristic examples (although marches, polkas and the Hungarian Gypsy style also play an important role). The success of Offenbach's works in Vienna in the 1850s, and his own visits in 1858 and 1864 gave the impetus to the development of the genre there, with Franz von Suppé (1819–95) a prominent figure: Suppé's *Das Pensionat* (1860) is often considered to be the first Viennese operetta; *Die schone Galathée* (1865), influenced by *La Belle Hélène*, was perhaps the first to establish itself in the repertory.

Johann Strauss.

The acknowledged master of Viennese operetta, simply in terms of the quality of his achievement, was Johann Strauss II (1825–99). A leading composer of dance music, Strauss seems to have been initially unwilling to try his hand at an operetta—by some accounts Offenbach finally persuaded him; it was not until 1874, after various works with unsatisfactory libretti and too obvious an imitation of Offenbach's style, that he created, in *Die Fledermaus*, the work that can justly be considered the greatest Viennese operetta, and perhaps the high point of the whole genre. The brilliant libretto, with its gentle mockery of manners and society and its varied cast of characters, gave Strauss the opportunity to produce memorable, beautiful and lively music of substance and sophistication in a popular style; psychological insight is also not lacking.

Strauss always had problems finding suitable libretti (unlike Offenbach he did not have a regular collaborator), and although his output of operettas is quite large, it is only in *Der Zigeunerbaron* (*The Gypsy Baron*) that he found a libretto which enabled him to produce another work approaching the stature of *Die Fledermaus*.

Other successful operetta composers in Vienna in the latter part of the nineteenth century were Karl Millöcker (*Gräfin Dubarry*, 1879; *Der Bettelstudent*, 1882), Karl Zeller (*Der Vogelhändler*, 1891) and Richard Heuberger (*Der Opernball*, 1898).

Franz Lehár.

A libretto turned down by Heuberger was accepted by Franz Lehár (1870–1948), formerly a bandmaster in the Imperial Army, who had achieved success as a composer by his *Gold and Silver Waltz*. *The Merry Widow* (*Die lustige Witwe*) was produced in Vienna in December 1905; it was an overnight success, and productions soon followed throughout Europe, and in the USA and Australia. (Its success was commercial as well as artistic—'Merry Widow' merchandise of various kinds became all the rage.) The plot has a fair degree of frivolity, but there is genuine dramatic tension in the relationship of the two main characters; Lehár's music, while firmly in the Viennese tradition, has a distinctive and individual voice. Lehár was the outstanding operetta composer of his time, with the same kind of classic status as Strauss. *The Count of Luxembourg* (1909) is another delightful work, with again the dramatic interest heightened by Lehár's haunting music. In later works Lehár broadened his range, taking in elements of the emerging popular styles of the century (including *e.g.* the tango and the fox-trot) and showing the influences of contemporary operatic composers like Richard Strauss and Puccini; the orientalism and the unhappy ending of *The Land of Smiles* (1923) contrast strikingly with his earlier works; *Frasquita* (1922) and *Giuditta* (1934) are described as 'comic operas' rather than operettas.

Of the many other composers of Viennese operetta in this period, two should be mentioned as having made lasting contributions. Oscar Straus with *A Waltz Dream* (1907) and *The Chocolate Soldier* (1909, based on Bernard Shaw's *Arms and the Man*), and Emmerich Kalman with *The Gypsy Princess* (1915) and *Countess Maritza* (1924).

England: Gilbert and Sullivan and after.

The 1860s saw the beginning of operetta, under French and Viennese influence, in England, but the major English contribution to the nineteenth-century operetta tradition was made in the 1870s and 1880s by Sir Arthur Sullivan (1842–1900) and Sir William S. Gilbert (1836–1911). Like Offenbach and unlike Strauss, Sullivan was fortunate in having a regular collaborator—indeed, the fact that they are invariably referred to as Gilbert and Sullivan (in that order) indicates how important Gilbert's libretti were to the success of their works, and the extent to which they formed a genuine partnership. From *Trial by Jury* (1875)—a one-act comic opera with no spoken dialogue—to *The Gondoliers* (1889) they produced a succession of comic masterpieces. *The Yeomen of the Guard* has pretensions to greater seriousness, and there are passages in other works (*e.g. Iolanthe*, 1882) which explore character and emotion in some depth, but it is primarily the combination of tunefulness and humour which has kept the Gilbert and Sullivan operas alive. Sullivan's music often parodies the styles and conventions of nineteenth-century opera, while Gilbert's libretti offer satirical commentary on topics of contemporary interest—indeed, to gain an insight into the political, social and cultural atmosphere of the period one could do much worse than study these texts. The law (*Trial by Jury*), the 'Aesthetic' movement (*Patience*, 1881) the police force (*The Pirates of Penzance*, 1879), women's emancipation (*Princess Ida*, 1884), orientalism (*The Mikado*, 1885) are some targets of Gilbert's good-natured but sharp wit.

A brief account of the British repertoire after Gilbert and Sullivan should include the 'musical comedies' (so called) of the 1890s and later by such composers as Sidney Jones (*A Gaiety Girl*, 1893; *The Geisha*, 1896) and Lionel Monckton (*The Arcadians*, 1909; *The Quaker Girl*, 1910), and the light operas of Sir Edward German (*Merrie England*, 1902).

The operetta tradition continued between the wars and into the mid-century with Noël Coward (*Bitter Sweet*, 1929; *Conversation Piece*, 1934) and Ivor Novello (*Glamorous Night*, 1935; *Careless Rapture*, 1936; *The Dancing Years*, 1939; *Perchance to Dream*, 1945; *Kings Rhapsody*, 1949). In the 1950s, nostalgia and charm are evident in the works of Julian Slade (*Salad Days*, 1954, and *Free as Air*, 1957) and Sandy Wilson (*The Boy Friend*, 1953—described on the title-page as 'A new musical comedy of the 1920s').

The USA.

In the USA the French and Viennese repertoire and the works of Gilbert and Sullivan created an audience for operetta, and eventually gave the impetus for work by American composers. The Irish-American cellist and conductor Victor Herbert (1859–1924) was perhaps the most significant composer for the musical stage in the early years of the twentieth century, with works such as *Babes in Toyland* (1903) and *Naughty Marietta* (1910). Immigrants of a younger generation such as Rudolf Friml (1879–1972) and Sigmund Romberg (1887–1951) continued to write in a recognisably Viennese-influenced style, as in Friml's *Rose-Marie* (1924) and *The Vagabond King* (1925) and Romberg's *Blossom Time* (1921—based on the music and life of Schubert), *The Student Prince* (1924), *The Desert Song* (1926) and *The New Moon* (1928).

Both English musical comedy and the specifically American traditions of the vaudeville and the minstrel show are also important in the late nineteenth and early twentieth centuries. The influence of ragtime and early jazz, with their characteristic syncopations, contributed in the 1910s and 1920s to the developing style of the musical (as it came to be called).

The Musical: Show Boat and after.

It is generally recognised that a turning-point came in December 1927 with the production of *Show Boat* by Jerome Kern (1885–1945) and Oscar Hammerstein II (1895–1960). Kern, a classically-trained musician with many years' experience of work in the theatre (and who, in collaboration with the English writers P.G. Wodehouse and Guy Bolton had done much to establish a musical comedy tradition in America), was one of the most highly respected light-music composers of the time, and had great success in the 1920s with shows such as *Sally* (1920) and *Sunny* (1925). *Show Boat* impresses by its epic scale, its inclusion of serious subject-matter (notably race relations) and the use of music to create atmosphere, drama and character. Most of all, Kern's songs remain fresh, with their combination of memorable melody and sophisticated harmony. One is struck also by their range, from the waltz-song 'You are Love', with its roots firmly in Viennese operetta, to the quasi-Spiritual 'Ol' Man River' and the blues-influenced 'Can't Help Lovin' Dat Man'. Stylistically, Kern was one of the most important figures in the transition from the European-based musical language of operetta and musical comedy to the genuinely American idiom of the musical; and *Show Boat* revealed that the Broadway musical, at a quite early stage in its development, had the potential to be a genuine, unified work of art without losing its entertainment value.

Kern's later musicals, such as *The Cat and the Fiddle* (1931), *Music in the Air* (1932) and *Roberta* (1933), while containing many fine and well-loved songs, retreat in subject-matter and treatment to the musical comedy tradition.

Kern and his contemporaries Irving Berlin (1888–1989), George Gershwin (1898–1937), Cole Porter (1891–1964) and Richard Rodgers (1902–79) created the central classic repertoire of American popular song, largely in the contexts of the Broadway show and the Hollywood film. The genre of the Broadway musical in the 1920s and 1930s

is sometimes described as the 'song and dance musical' in which the plot is fairly trivial and the 'book' (libretto) is largely an excuse for a series of tuneful songs and dances. This tended to give way in the 1940s and later to the 'integrated' musical, in which all elements—plot, dialogue, music, dance—are essentially directed towards the single aim of putting over a convincing drama to the audience. This is not to say that the book is not sometimes important in the earlier period—one might mention for example Gershwin's political satire *Of Thee I Sing* (1931), influenced by Gilbert and Sullivan and dealing with the ever-topical subject of an American presidential election. The songs of the period are noted both for their musical sophistication and for the wit and verbal dexterity shown by the lyricists (*e.g.* Ira Gershwin, who worked with his brother George and others; Lorenz Hart who collaborated with Rodgers; Porter who wrote his own lyrics).

When Rodgers's partnership with Hart was brought to an end by the latter's alcohol-related decline, Rodgers embarked upon a collaboration with Oscar Hammerstein II which produced a series of popular successes (with varied and often serious subject-matter and literary sources) which dominated the musical stage for years, from *Oklahoma!* (1943) to *The Sound of Music* (1959). These works depend for their quality on both Rodgers's outstanding melodic gift and Hammerstein's verbal facility; equally important is the unified conception whereby speech, music and dance all contribute to the drama. Atmospheric effects such as the off-stage voice beginning 'O What a Beautiful Morning' at the start of Act I of *Oklahoma!*; the extensive use of underscoring (music accompanying spoken dialogue); and operatic passages such as the eight-minute Soliloquy in *Carousel*—these all indicate an approach to the musical which is both assured and genuinely creative and imaginative.

West Side Story.

If nevertheless the musical always ran the risk of lapsing into a slightly complacent, comfortable tunefulness, it was again given a jolt by Leonard Bernstein's *West Side Story* (1957). This adaptation of the Romeo and Juliet story set among New York gangs is demanding on performers and musically uncompromising. While it contains memorable songs in ballad style ('Maria', 'Somewhere') and catchy dance numbers ('America'), Bernstein (1918–90), as befits a musician of formidable ability in many fields, wrote a score which is influenced both by modern European and American 'classical' composers (*e.g.* Stravinsky and Copland) and by progressive developments in jazz. The symphonic approach and the use of a sophisticated motivic and thematic technique put Bernstein's score on a par with many works on the other side of the 'classical/popular' divide; indeed, it is arguable that *West Side Story* is more genuinely original in musical terms than many of Bernstein's overtly 'classical' works.

Subsequent Developments.

The history of the musical in the USA and the UK over the last forty years cannot be adequately summarised here. Suffice it to note both the work of those who have stayed in the mainstream (Lerner and Loewe: *My Fair Lady*, 1956; *Camelot*, 1960), and that of the experimenters like Stephen Sondheim (who wrote the lyrics for *West Side Story* and moved on to become an important composer of musicals in his own right: *Follies*, 1971; *A Little Night Music*, 1973; *Pacific Overtures*, 1976; *Sunday in the Park with George*, 1984). A willingness to explore all kinds of subject-matter is evident in, for example, the musicals of Sir Andrew Lloyd Webber (*Jesus Christ, Superstar*, 1971; *Evita*, 1978; *Cats*, 1981; *Phantom of the Opera*, 1986) and of Claude-Michel Schönberg (*Les Misérables*, 1980; *Miss Saigon*, 1989). Since the idea of a totally sung musical is also evident in a number of recent works, we may conclude that the only real difference now between opera and the musical is that of style and musical language. Whether the popular style of the late twentieth century is strong enough to succeed in the challenge it has taken on is, perhaps, too early to say.

THE WORLD OF SCIENCE

A contemporary picture of scientific discovery, designed to explain some of the most important ideas in astronomy, physics, chemistry, biology, physical and social anthropology, and to give some account of current research in various fields, including in this edition special topics on molecular biology, plate tectonics, the search for extraterrestrial life and recent advances in nanotechnology. Also included is a variety of useful scientific tables. Readers will also find many definitions of scientific terms in the General Information section.

TABLE OF CONTENTS

THE WORLD OF SCIENCE

In Parts I, II, and III the inanimate universe is described. This is the domain of cosmology, astronomy, geology, physics, and chemistry. There are already many interesting links which join this realm to that of the living and make it difficult to say where the boundary lies. Nevertheless it is still convenient to accord to the biological and social sciences two separate chapters, IV and V. Part VI provides some useful scientific tables. Part VII consists of specialist articles on topics of current scientific interest.

I. ASTRONOMY AND COSMOLOGY—THE NATURE OF THE UNIVERSE

The universe includes everything from the smallest sub-atomic particle to the mightiest supercluster of galaxies. The scientific view of the universe (not the only view but the one we are concerned with here) is a remarkable achievement of the human mind, and it is worth considering at the outset what a "scientific view" is, and what is remarkable about it.

A scientific view of something is always an intimate mixture of theories and observed facts, and not an inert mixture but a seething and growing one. The theories are broad general ideas together with arguments based on them. The arguments are designed to show that, if the general ideas are accepted, then this, or the other thing ought to be observed. If this, that, or the other actually are observed, then the theory is a good one; if not, then the theoreticians have to think again. Thus theoretical ideas and arguments are continually subjected to the severe test of comparison with the facts, and scientists are proud of the rigour with which this is done. On the other hand, theories often suggest new things to look for, i.e., theories lead to predictions. These predictions are frequently successful, and scientists are entitled to be proud of that too. But it follows that no theory is immutable; any scientific view of any subject may, in principle, be invalidated at any time by the discovery of new facts, though some theories are so soundly based that overthrow does not seem imminent.

A remarkable aspect of the scientific view of the universe is that the same principles are supposed to operate throughout the whole vastness of space. Thus the matter and radiation in stars are not different from the matter and radiation on earth, and their laws of behaviour are the same. Therefore theories hard won by studies in terrestrial physics and chemistry laboratories are applied at once to the whole cosmos. Astronomy and cosmology are spectacular extensions of ordinary mechanics and physics.

LOOKING AT THE UNIVERSE

The universe is observable because signals from it reach us and some manage to penetrate our atmosphere.

First, there are waves of visible light together with invisible rays of somewhat longer (infra-red) and somewhat shorter (ultra-violet) wavelengths. These waves show us the bright astronomical objects and, to make use of them, astronomers have constructed telescopes of great power and precision backed up with cameras, spectroscopes, and numerous auxiliaries. The biggest telescope in the world is the 10 m reflector based at Mauna Kea in the United States. The earth's atmosphere acts as a distorting and only partially transparent curtain and the erection of telescopes on satellites is beginning to extend optical telescope performance significantly. Indeed, the Hubble Space Telescope, launched in 1990, has already dramatically expanded our knowledge of the universe.

Secondly, there are radio waves of much longer wavelength than light. Radiotelescopes are sensitive radio receivers with specialised aerial systems. The scientific stature of modern radioastronomy was emphasised by the award in 1974 of the Nobel Physics Prize to two Cambridge radio astronomers, Ryle and Hewish.

Other types of radiation reach the earth from outer space but do not necessarily penetrate the atmosphere. Cosmic radiation consists of fundamental particles, including protons (**F16**) of extremely high energy, moving at velocities very close to that of light. These particles are commonly detected using vast tanks of water surrounded by electronic equipment. X-rays and neutrinos (**F16**) are also generated by certain interesting classes of astronomical objects (**F5**). With the advent of satellite-borne detectors and apparatus buried in deep mines, new facets of cosmic-ray astronomy, X-ray astronomy, and neutrino astronomy are now rapidly deepening our knowledge of the nature of the universe and of the violent processes by which galaxies as well as individual stars and planetary systems evolve.

Great Distances and Large Numbers

To visualise the immense scale of the universe is almost as much a problem for the scientist as for the layman. The conventional shorthand is to express 1,000 as 10^3; 1,000,000 as 10^6. On this scale the earth is $1\cdot496 \times 10^8$ km away from the sun. Concorde, for example, the world's fastest airliner, took about $3\frac{1}{2}$ hours to travel 5,000 km from London to New York. The "Viking" spacecraft in 1976 took just over a year to travel the 200 million km to Mars. These distances, however, are minute by comparison with the distance even to the nearest star, Proxima Centauri, some 4×10^{13} km away. This distance is more conveniently expressed in terms of the travel time of light itself. With a velocity of nearly 300,000 km per second, in a year light travels about $9\cdot46 \times 10^{12}$ km. The distance to Proxima Centauri is therefore $4\cdot2$ light years. Even this distance, enormous on our terrestrial scale, is a small cosmic distance. The diameter of our Galaxy is about 10^5 light years, while the most distant objects yet observed lie over $1\cdot3 \times 10^{10}$ light years away.

PLANETS, STARS AND GALAXIES

The Solar System

The earth is the third, counting outward, of nine planets revolving in nearly circular orbits round the sun. Some of their particulars are given in the Table (**F8**). The sun and its planets are the main bodies of the solar system. Mainly between the orbits of Mars and Jupiter revolve numerous small bodies—the minor planets or asteroids, the largest of which, Ceres, is only 947 km in diameter. Apart from these, the solar system is tenuously populated with particles varying in size from about a micron (10^{-6} m) to hundreds of metres in diameter. Some of these objects collide with the earth's atmosphere. The smaller particles (micrometeoroids) are too small to be visible. Larger particles (meteoroids) cause the phenomenon known as meteors (commonly referred to as 'shooting stars') when they burn up at around 100 km altitude. The particle collides with air molecules. This causes frictional heating which usually results in complete vapourisation of the particle. Even larger chunks, of rocky or iron composition, cause the rare and brilliant fireballs, some of which survive their high-speed flight through the earth's atmosphere and may later be recovered. Such objects (meteorites) are very important, providing examples of extraterrestrial rocks, and thus giving the composition of some of the most primitive material left in the solar system. Collisions with very large meteorites (or small asteroids) are now, fortunately, very rare. However, the large meteorite crater in Arizona is one recent reminder that such collisions still occur, although much less frequently now than earlier in the history of the planetary system. The surfaces of Mercury, the Moon, Mars, and Venus together with those of many other planetary satellites still show the scars from collisions with a multitude of objects of up to tens of km in diameter.

Comets are fascinating objects which, from time to time, provide a spectacular sight. More than 700 comets have been observed so far, and about six new ones are discovered each year. At the heart of every comet is a small nucleus. In 1986 the Giotto space probe revealed that Halley's comet has a potato-shaped nucleus measuring 15 km by 10 km. This nucleus consists of ices of various gases, chiefly water, interspersed with dust particles. In their highly elliptical orbits comets spend most of their life at great distances from the sun, where the temperature is very low because of the feeble solar radiation, so that all the "icy" materials are solid. Periodically, when each comet returns to the inner parts of the solar system, the increasing solar radiation heats the surface layers, evaporating the volatile ices, which carry the surface dust away from the comet nucleus. Solar-radiation pressure, acting on the dust constituents, and the solar wind acting on the ionised constituents, form the gigantic cometary tails which may reach 2×10^8 km in length—larger than the radius of the earth's orbit. The dramatic impact of the fragments of Comet Shoemaker-Levy 9 on the dark side of Jupiter in 1994 created spots on the planet's surface that were as big as the earth's diameter and that lasted for seven weeks. See also L28.

The sun itself is a dense, roughly spherical mass of glowing matter, 1,392,000 km across. Its heat is so intense that the atoms are split into separated electrons and nuclei (F11) and matter in such a state is called plasma. At the sun's centre the temperature has the unimaginable value of about 15 million degrees Centigrade (a coal fire is about 800°C). Under such conditions the atomic nuclei frequently collide with one another at great speeds and reactions occur between them. The sun consists largely of hydrogen and, in the very hot plasma, the nuclei of hydrogen atoms interact by a series of reactions whose net result is to turn hydrogen into helium. This is a process which releases energy just as burning does, only these nuclear processes are incomparably more energetic than ordinary burning. In fact, the energy released is great enough to be the source of all the light and heat which the sun has been pouring into space for thousands of millions of years.

Emerging from the sun and streaming past the earth is a "solar wind" of fast-moving electrons and protons (F11) whose motion is closely linked with the behaviour of an extensive magnetic field based on the sun. In fact, the region round the sun and extending far into space past the earth is full of complex, fluctuating particle streams and magnetic fields which interact with planetary atmospheres causing, among other things, auroras and magnetic storms.

Stars

In colour, brightness, age, and size the sun is typical of vast numbers of other stars. Only from the human point of view is there anything special about the sun—it is near enough to give us life.

Even the possession of a system of revolving planets is routinely observed in other stars (see Special Topic, F78).

No star can radiate energy at the rate the sun does without undergoing internal changes in the course of time. Consequently stars evolve and old processes in them give rise to new. The exact nature of stellar evolution—so far as it is at present understood—would be too complex to describe here in any detail. It involves expansion and contraction, changes of temperature, changes of colour, and changes in chemical compositon as the nuclear processes gradually generate new chemical elements by reactions such as the conversion of hydrogen to helium, helium to neon, neon to magnesium, and so on. The speed of evolution changes from time to time, but is in any case very slow compared with the pace of terrestrial life; nothing very dramatic may occur for hundreds of millions of years. Evidence for the various phases of evolution is therefore obtained by studying many stars, each at a different stage of its life. Thus astronomers recognise many types with charmingly descriptive names, such as supergiants, blue giants, sub-giants, red, white and brown dwarfs.

The path of stellar evolution may be marked by various explosive events. One of these, which occurs in sufficiently large stars, is an enormous explosion in which a substantial amount of the star is blown away into space in the form of high-speed streams of gas. For about a fortnight, such an exploding star will radiate energy 200 million times as fast as the sun. Japanese and Chinese (but not Western) astronomers recorded such an occurrence in A.D. 1054, and the exploding gases, now called the Crab nebula, can still be seen in powerful telescopes and form a cloud six or seven light-years across. While it lasts, the explosion shows up as an abnormally bright star and is called a *supernova*. In late February 1987 a spectacular supernova was observed in our nearby galaxy the Large Magellanic Cloud. At a distance of only 1.7×10^5 light years this supernova was the closest to the Earth for over 400 years. Many theories have been confirmed by the findings.

Groups of Stars

It is not surprising that ancient peoples saw pictures in the sky. The constellations, however, are not physically connected groups of stars but just happen to be patterns visible from earth. A conspicuous exception to this is the Milky Way, which a telescope resolves into many millions of separate stars. If we could view the Milky Way from a vast distance and see it as a whole we should observe a rather flat wheel of stars with spiral arms something like the sparks of a rotating Catherine wheel. This system of stars is physically connected by gravitational forces and moves through space as a whole; it is called a *galaxy*.

The Galaxy is about 10^5 light-years across and contains roughly 10^{11} stars. An inconspicuous one of these stars near the edge of the wheel is our sun; the prominent stars in our night sky are members of the galaxy that happen to be rather near us. Sirius, the brightest, is only 8.6 light-years away, a trivial distance, astronomically speaking.

The galaxy does not contain stars only, there are also clouds of gas and dust, particularly in the plane of the galaxy. Much of the gas is hydrogen, and its detection is difficult. However, gaseous hydrogen gives out radio waves with a wavelength of 21 cm. Radio telescopes are just the instruments to receive these, and workers in Holland, America, and Australia detected the gas clouds by this means. In 1952 they found that the hydrogen clouds lie in the spiral arms of the galaxy, and this is some of the strongest evidence for the spiral form.

Another important feature of the galactic scene is the weak but enormously extensive magnetic field. This is believed to have an intimate connection with the spiral structure.

Around the spiral arms, and forming part of the galaxy, are numerous globular clusters of stars. These are roughly spherical, abnormally densely packed, collections of stars with many thousands of members. Because of its form and density, a globular cluster may be assumed to have been formed in one process, not star by star. Thus all its stars are the same age. This is of great interest to astronomers, because they can study differences between stars of similar age but different sizes.

Galaxies

One might be forgiven for assuming that such a vast system as the galaxy is in fact the universe; but this is not so. In the constellation of Andromeda is a famous object which, on close examination, turns out to be another galaxy of size and structure similar to our own. Its distance is given in the table (**F8**). The Andromeda galaxy is the same basic structure as our own, but roughly half as big again. The Milky Way, the Andromeda nebula, and about two dozen other galaxies form a cluster of galaxies called the Local Group. It is indeed a fact that the universe is populated with *groups, clusters* and *superclusters*, of *galaxies*. A cluster may contain two or three galaxies, but some contain thousands.

By about 1920 it was known that there were at least half a million galaxies, and with the advent of the 2·54 m. Mt. Wilson telescope this number rose to 10^8 and has now been increased further by larger telescopes which can see out to distances greater than 10^{10} light years. Through the powerful telescopes the nearer galaxies reveal their inner structures. Photographs of galaxies are among the most beautiful and fascinating photographs ever taken, and readers who have never seen one should hasten to the nearest illustrated astronomy book. Most galaxies have a spiral or elliptical structure but about 2 per cent have peculiar wisps and appendages. Some galaxies are strong emitters of radio waves. A recently discovered type of galaxy is the starburst galaxy. This is an otherwise normal galaxy in which huge numbers of stars are forming in a small volume at its centre.

The Expanding Universe

Two discoveries about galaxies are of the utmost importance. One is that, by and large, clusters of galaxies are uniformly distributed through the universe. The other is that the distant galaxies are receding from us.

How is this known? Many readers may be familiar with the Doppler effect first discovered in 1842. Suppose a stationary body emits waves of any kind and we measure their wavelength, finding it to be L cm. Now suppose the body approaches us; the waves are thereby crowded together in the intervening space and the wavelength appears less than L; if the body recedes the wavelength appears greater than L. The Austrian physicist, J. Doppler (1803–53), discovered the well-known change of pitch of a train whistle as it approaches and passes us. The same principle applies to the light. Every atom emits light of definite wavelengths which appear in a spectroscope as a series of coloured lines—a different series for each atom. If the atom is in a receding body all the lines have slightly longer wavelengths than usual, and the amount of the change depends uniquely on the speed. Longer wavelengths mean that the light is redder than usual, so that a light from a receding body shows what is called a "red shift." The speed of recession can be calculated from the amount of red shift.

It was the American astronomer, V. M. Slipher, who first showed (in 1914) that some galaxies emitted light with a red shift. In the 1920s and 1930s the famous astronomer E. Hubble (1889–1953) measured both the distances and red shift of many galaxies and proved what is now known as Hubble's Law about which there is now some controversy. This states that the speed of recession of galaxies is proportional to their distance from us. This does not apply to our neighbours in the Local Group, we and they are keeping together. Hubble's Law has been tested and found to hold for the farthest detectable galaxies; they are about 7×10^9 light-years away and are receding with a speed approaching that of light.

The expansion of the universe does not imply that the Local Group is the centre of the universe —from any other viewpoint in the universe Hubble's Law would also be valid, and the distant galaxies would, similarly, all appear to be rapidly receding.

One possible implication of this most exciting scientific discovery is that, if the galaxies have always been receding, at an early time they must have been closer together. We can calculate that about 10^{10} years ago all the matter of the universe could have been densely packed. The truth or otherwise of this hypothesis is the most fundamental question of cosmology, and its testing still drives the quest to explore the universe, by larger and more sensitive telescopes, to the greatest possible distances.

Quasars, Pulsars and Black Holes

In November 1962 Australian radio astronomers located a strong radio emitter with sufficient precision for the Mt. Palomar optical astronomers to identify it on photographs and examine the nature of its light. The red shift was so great that the object must be exceedingly distant; on the other hand it looked star-like, much smaller than a galaxy. By the beginning of 1967 over a hundred of these objects had been discovered and other characteristics established, such as strong ultra-violet radiation and inconstancy, in some cases, of the rate at which radiation is emitted. Not all of these so-called quasars are strong radio emitters; some show all the other characteristics except radio emission. It has been estimated that the "quiet" kind are about a hundred times more numerous than the radio kind. One great problem here is: how can such relatively small objects generate such inconceivably great amounts of energy that they appear bright at such huge distances? Recent observations suggest that quasars are only the central visible part of an otherwise undetected galaxy. There may also be a massive black hole near the quasar centre.

Late in 1967, while investigating quasars, Cambridge radio astronomers discovered pulsars, a new type of heavenly body. Their characteristic is the emission of regular pulses of radio waves every second or so. A pulsar in the Crab nebula has a repetition rate even faster—about 1/30 sec— and it follows that pulsars must be very small bodies little if at all bigger than the Earth.

The existence of such small bodies raises again the problem of the ultimate fate of evolving stars. Much depends on their mass because this determines how strong the inward pull of gravity is. For a star to be at least temporarily stable the inward pull must be balanced by an outward pressure. In the sun this is the pressure of the burning hydrogen and the resulting average density is about 1·4 times that of water (**Table, F8**). In some stars the inward pressure is so great that collapse proceeds until it is balanced by a different type of outward pressure that sets in when electrons and atomic nuclei are forced into proximity. Stars so formed are the "white dwarfs". They are millions of times denser than the sun—"a matchbox of their matter would weigh a ton"— and they are very small though not small enough to be pulsars. The latter are now generally thought to be a million times denser even than white dwarfs and to consist largely of tightly packed neutrons. Such bodies are called neutron stars.

Could the tendency of a massive star to fall inwards ever be so great that no outward pressure known to physics would suffice to balance it? Apparently it could! Many astrophysicists now hold on theoretical grounds that such a gravitational collapse could create a high density object whose gravitational field would be too strong to allow anything—including light waves—ever to leave the body. Such hypothetical objects are called "black holes" because, light and other signals being unable to emerge from them, their matter has literally disappeared from view. Black holes could be detected by the disturbance their gravitational attraction causes to neighbouring visible stars and also because atoms attracted by the black hole should emit intense X-rays before falling so far in that they too disappear into the black hole. Both of these detection methods led some astronomers to conjecture that there is a black hole in the constellation of Cygnus. There is another promising candidate for a black hole in the Large Magellanic Cloud. The theory of gravitational collapse raises profound and unresolved problems about our physical concepts.

Very recently, it has been conjectured that black holes, formed by the "death" of individual stars, and perhaps even on a massive scale at the centre of large and dense galaxies, have been responsible for "devouring" a very significant proportion of the total mass of the universe. Since this "devoured" mass is invisible by direct observation, we may have considerably underestimated the average density, and thus the total gravitational field of the universe.

In 1995 scientists discovered compelling evidence of the existence of the biggest black hole ever found, with a mass equivalent to 40 million of our suns.

THE ORIGIN AND DEVELOPMENT OF THE UNIVERSE

Scientists can only attempt to explain the universe by relating its observable structure to the features predicted by alternative theories of its origin and development. The time span of all our observations of the Cosmos is so small by comparison with the lifetime of the universe (more than 10^{10} years). Also, contrary to many other scientific disciplines, it is impossible to repeat the "experiment", under controlled conditions. We must, therefore, explore the evolution of the universe by using the fact that light from the most distant galaxies has taken about 10^{10} years to reach us, thus providing us with a crucial, if tantalisingly remote and thus indistinct, view of the universe at a much earlier epoch.

Several models of the universe have been based on Einstein's theory of General Relativity (F17). Einstein's equations may be solved to predict the evolution of the universe. However, there is a spectrum of solutions which vary from a continuous and indefinite expansion at the present rate to an eventual slowing and subsequent contraction to a dense state, again in the distant future, which hints at a "pulsating" universe.

As an alternative to the Evolutionary theory, Bondi, Gold, and Hoyle (1948) suggested the so-called "Steady-State" theory. This theory has no initial dense state or "origin" and, on a large scale, the density of galaxies and stars is always as at present.

The Formation of Galaxies and Stars

On any theory of the universe, some explanation has to be found for the existence of clusters of galaxies. In all theories galaxies condense out from dispersed masses of gas, principally hydrogen.

It is believed on theoretical grounds each galaxy could not condense into one enormous star but must form many fragments which shrink separately into clusters of stars. In these clusters many stars, perhaps hundreds or thousands or even millions, are born. A small cluster, visible to the naked eye, is the Pleiades. The Orion nebula, visible as a hazy blob of glowing gas in the sword of Orion, is the scene of much star-forming activity at present. However, the best evidence yet for witnessing the birth of a star comes from observations by the Infrared Astronomical Satellite (IRAS). Deep within a gas and dust cloud called the Ophiuchus dark nebula, matter is falling inward in a manner predicted by contemporary theories of star formation. At the centre of this collapsing cloud there seems to be an embryonic star perhaps only 30,000 years old.

According to the Evolutionary theory the "initial dense state" consisted of very hot plasma in a state of overall expansion. The expanding plasma was both cooling and swirling about. The random swirling produces irregularities in the distribution of the hot gas—here it would be rather denser, there rather less dense. If a sufficiently large mass of denser gas happened to occur, then the gravitational attraction between its own particles would hold it together and maintain its permanent identity, even though the rest of the gas continued to swirl and expand. Such a large mass would gradually condense into fragments to become a cluster of galaxies.

Revolutionary Discoveries

The 1960s witnessed revolutionary developments in both observational and theoretical astronomy. For example, it now seems agreed that remote sources of radio waves are more abundant the weaker their intensity. This strongly suggests that they are more abundant at greater distances. Thus the universe is not *uniform* as the original steady-state theory prescribed. Since greater distances correspond to earlier times, any extra abundance of objects observed at the greater distance means that the universe was denser in its younger days than now. This favours an evolutionary theory of the universe.

The same theory requires that the initial dense state of the universe—aptly christened "the primaeval fireball"—should contain intense electromagnetic radiation with a distribution of wavelengths characteristic of the high temperature. As the fireball, *i.e.*, the universe, expanded over a period of about 10^{10} years it cooled, and one feature of this process is that the wavelengths of the radiation increase and their distribution becomes characteristic of a much lower temperature. In fact, the wavelengths should now be concentrated round about 1 mm to 1 cm (corresponding to about $-270°C$) and the radiation should approach the earth uniformly from all directions. Radiation just like this was detected in the 1960s by extremely sensitive instruments both at ground-based observatories and flown from balloon payloads high in the earth's atmosphere—above most of the water vapour and other constituents which interfere with such delicate observations. This "microwave background" radiation appears to be "cosmological", and thus supports strongly the evolutionary or "Big Bang" theory as opposed to the "Steady-State" theory, which cannot rationally explain the radiation.

In 1992 data from the Cosmic Background Explorer (COBE) satellite strengthened the Big Bang theory still further. Minute variations in the temperature of the background radiation across the sky help to show that the distribution of matter in the early universe could act as a blueprint for the future large-scale structures we can observe today.

The Formation of the Chemical Elements

A stable nucleus is one that lasts indefinitely because it is not radioactive. There are 274 known kinds of stable atomic nuclei and little likelihood of any more being found. These nuclei are the isotopes (F12) of 81 different chemical elements; the other elements, including, for example, uranium and radium are always radioactive. Some elements are rare, others abundant. The most common ones on earth are oxygen, silicon, aluminium, and iron. However, the earth is rather atypical. It is especially deficient in hydrogen, because the gravitational attraction of our small planet was not strong enough to prevent this very light gas from escaping into space.

It is possible to examine the chemical constituents of meteorites and to infer the composition of the sun and other stars from the spectrum of the light they emit. By such means, the conclusion has been reached that 93% of the atoms in our galaxy are hydrogen, 7% are helium; all the other elements together account for about one in a thousand atoms. A glance at the Table of Elements (*see* end of Sec.) will show that hydrogen and helium are two of the lightest elements: they are in fact the two simplest. The problem is to explain how the heavier chemical elements appear in the universe at all. It is here that a fascinating combination of astronomy and nuclear physics is required.

We have already referred to the fact that the energy radiated from the sun originates in nuclear reactions which turn hydrogen into helium. Why is energy given out? To answer this question we note that nuclei are made up of protons and neutrons (F11). These particles attract one another strongly—that is why a nucleus holds together. To separate the particles, energy would have to be supplied to overcome the attractive forces. This amount of energy is called *binding energy* and is a definite quantity for every kind of nucleus. Conversely, when the particles are brought together to form a nucleus the binding energy is *released* in the form of radiations and heat. Different nuclei consist of different numbers of particles, therefore the relevant quantity to consider is the *binding energy per particle*. Let us call this B. Then if elements of *high* B are formed out of those of *low* B there is a *release* of energy. *See also* **Nuclear Energy, L88.**

Now B is small (relatively) for light elements like lithium, helium, and carbon; it rises to a maximum for elements of middling atomic weight like iron; it falls again for really heavy elements like lead, bismuth, and uranium. Consequently, energy is released by forming middleweight elements either by splitting up heavy nuclei ("nuclear fission") or by joining up light ones ("nuclear fusion"). *See also* **L88.**

It is the latter process, fusion, that is going on in stars. The fusion processes can be studied in physics laboratories by using large accelerating machines to hurl nuclei at one another to make them coalesce. In stars the necessary high velocity of impact occurs because the plasma is so hot. Gradually the hydrogen is turned into helium, and helium into heavier and heavier elements. This supplies the energy that the stars radiate and simultaneously generates the chemical elements.

The Heaviest Elements

The very heavy elements present a problem. To form them from middleweight elements, energy has to be *supplied*. Since there is plenty of energy inside a star, a certain small number of heavy nuclei will indeed form, but they will continually undergo fission again under the prevailing intense conditions. How do they ever get away to form cool ordinary elements, like lead and bismuth, in the earth? One view links them with the highly explosive supernovae, to which we have already referred earlier. If the heavy elements occur in these stars the force of the explosion disperses them into cool outer space before they have time to undergo the fission that would otherwise have been their fate. The heavy elements are thus seen as the dust and debris of stellar catastrophes. The view is in line with the steady-state theory, because supernovae are always occurring and keeping up the supply of heavy elements. In the evolutionary theory some of the generation of elements is supposed to go on in the very early stages of the initial dense state and to continue in the stars that evolve in the fullness of time. It cannot be claimed that the origin of the chemical elements is completely known, but we have said enough to show that there are plausible theories. Time and more facts will choose between them.

The Formation of the Planets

Precisely how the planetary system was formed is still not understood in detail. From extremely precise observations of the movements of some nearby stars, it seems certain that other planetary systems occur among our stellar neighbours. By inference, it is thus probable that among certain classes of stars, planetary systems are very common throughout the universe.

Two other facts are crucial for any theory of planetary system formation. First, all the planetary orbits lie nearly in the plane perpendicular to the axis of rotation of the sun. The planets' rotations about the sun are all in the same direction and their axes of rotation, with two exceptions (Venus and Uranus), are close to the polar axis of their orbit planes, and in the same sense as their orbital rotation about the sun. Secondly, there is a very strong inverse correlation between planetary distance from the star and the planet's mean density, particularly if the correct allowance is made for the effects of gravitional compression in the deep interiors of planets (greater in large than in small planets).

Rather than theories which would place planetary formation as either the random collection of pre-formed planets by the sun in its path through the galaxy or as the consequence of a very near encounter between our sun and another star, it is now generally believed that the origin of the planetary system (and most of the satellites, etc.) was a direct consequence of the process which originally formed the sun.

As the primaeval solar nebula contracted, to conserve angular momentum, its rotation rate increased, and a diffuse equatorial disk of dust and gas formed. In the cold outer region (10–20° K) of this disk, all materials except helium and possibly hydrogen could readily condense on dust particles. Near the centre the temperature was higher, increasingly so as the proto-sun heated up, initially by the energy released by its gravitational contraction and, later, by the thermonuclear processes (**F4(1)**).

The Process of Accretion

Within this rotating and swirling disk of gas and dust, the process of accretion proceeded. Low-velocity collision between dust particles from time to time allowed larger particles to be created, composed of a mixture of the heavier elements and also the "icy" materials, particularly so in the colder outer regions where more of the "ices" were in a frozen state. Virtually our only information on the composition of such particles comes from detailed study of meteorites and from spectroscopic observation of comets. Eventually rocks of the size of centimetres, metres, and even kilometres were built up in this way. The build-up, controlled by low-velocity collisions, particularly of "sticky" materials, and also by electrostatic charges, was, at all times, however, moderated by occasional destructive high-velocity collisions. The relatively high viscosity of the dust and gas mixture throughout the disk must have been very important in producing a relatively uniform, rotational motion throughout the disk.

When "rocks" a few kilometres in size had been created new factors became important. Gravitational forces firstly increased the capacity of the larger "rocks" to accrete additional dust and smaller particles and, secondly, allowed some retention of material after even high-velocity collisions which would have destroyed smaller pieces.

The next stage is possibly the most difficult to model. Within a relatively uniform disk containing large numbers of rocks up to a few kilometres in diameter mixed within the residual dust and a large amount of gas, and extending to well outside Pluto's orbit, a small number of massive planets were formed. Some debris now remains as the comets and asteroids; however this debris and all the major planets, including the massive Jupiter, represent in total only a very small percentage of the original material of the solar nebula which was not condensed to form the sun.

It would appear that relatively quickly, during a period of 10^7 or 10^8 years, the large numbers of kilometre-sized objects, by collision and mutual gravitational attraction, formed the nuclei of the present planets and probably, in most cases, their major satellites also, in orbits relatively similar to their present ones. The planet-building process was most efficient at distances from the sun corresponding to the present orbits of Jupiter or Saturn, a compromise between temperature decreasing with distance from the sun, allowing a greater percentage of the total material to be solid and thus available for accretion, and density of material being greater closer to the sun.

The Jovian Planets

The outer or "Jovian" planets must have grown quickly, sweeping up hydrogen and helium gas as well as solid particles. Closer to the sun, the "icy" materials, still mainly in gaseous form, could not contribute very significantly to the initial accretion process, so that only smaller planets could form. Owing to their smaller mass, gravitational field and thus lower "escape velocity," they were only able to accrete a small proportion of the heavier gas present within the inner part of the solar system. Thus, at present, these

THE SOLAR SYSTEM

	Mean distance from Sun (millions of km)	Diameter km	Period of Revolution	Average density (water = 1)	Number of Satellites
Sun	—	1,392,000			—
Mercury	57·9	4,880	88 days	5·4	0
Venus	108·2	12,104	224·7 days	5·2	0
Earth	149·6	12,756	365·26 days	5·5	1
Mars	227·9	6,787	687 days	3·9	2
Jupiter	778·3	142,800	11·86 years	1·3	16
Saturn	1,427	120,000	29·46 years	0·7	18
Uranus	2,869·6	51,118	84·01 years	1·2	17
Neptune	4,496·6	49,528	164·8 years	1·7	8
Pluto	5,900	c. 2,250	247·7 years	0·6	1

Note: Chiron, an object recently discovered orbiting the sun between Saturn and Uranus has not been given "planet" status due to its small size.

"terrestrial" planets are much denser than the outer "Jovian" planets, much smaller in size, and contain very little hydrogen or helium. The planet-building process was probably ended by two factors: the gravitational disruptive effect of the planets already formed and the enhanced "solar wind" of the young sun, which swept much of the residual dust and gas out of the solar system.

Before the process was complete, however, the gravitational energy released by the material falling onto the proto-planets plus the radioactive heating of short-lived isotopes present at the time of planetary formation were responsible for melting most of the bodies of the planets and probably all the larger satellites and asteroids. This process allowed gravitational segregation of denser and lighter materials within the planets, and the production of the core, mantle and crustal regions of each of the terrestrial planets. Long after the dust and gas were driven from the solar system and the planet surfaces cooled and solidified, the residual larger rocks and asteroids, of which enormous numbers were originally still present, continued to be swept up by each of the planets. The record of this violent stage of the solar system's development can still be seen in the saturation cratering observed on the Moon, Mercury, and Mars.

Recent Discoveries

In the past three decades, direct space exploration, using automated space probes (and manned spacecraft in the case of the Moon) has enormously increased our knowledge of the solar system. Notable have been the Viking, Pioneer and Voyager projects. The five space probes to Halley's comet in 1986 were also a huge success. Important discoveries have continued to be made by ground-based telescopes such as a new ring system of Uranus, the object Chiron, and the radar investigation of the terrain of Venus. More recently, the Mars Pathfinder mission, the Galileo trip to Jupiter, the Ulysses probe investigation of the sun and the repaired Hubble Space Telescope have all generated great quantities of exciting new scientific data.

THE EARTH

Structure

The earth has the shape of a slightly flattened sphere, with an equatorial radius of 6,378 km and a polar radius 21 km less. Its mass can be calculated from Newton's Law of Gravitation and from measurements of the acceleration due to gravity, and is $5·97 \times 10^{24}$ kg. The average density follows from these two figures and is about 5·5 grams per cubic centimetre. This is nearly twice the density of typical rocks at the surface, so there must be very much denser material somewhere inside, and the earth must have a definite internal structure.

This structure can be investigated using shock waves from earthquakes or large explosions. These are received at recording stations at different distances from their source, having penetrated to varying depths within the earth, and their relative times of arrival and characteristic forms enable the deep structure to be worked out. This consists of three main units, a core at the centre with a radius about half that of the earth, the mantle outside this, and the thin crust, about 35 km thick under the continents and 5 km thick under the oceans, forming a skin surrounding the mantle.

The composition of these three units can be deduced by observation and inference. For example, meteorites which arrive at the earth's surface from other parts of the solar system consist of three main types, composed of iron-nickel alloy, stony silicates, and a mixture of iron and silicates. Could these have originated from the break-up of some planet like the earth? If so, then perhaps the core of the earth is made up of iron-nickel alloy and the mantle of magnesium-rich silicates. Experiments on the physical properties of these materials at high pressures show strong similarities with the measured properties of the earth's interior. In addition, rocks composed of magnesium-rich silicates are found at the earth's surface in places where material seems to have come from great depth, such as in the debris from volcanic explosions. These may be direct samples of the earth's mantle.

SOME ASTRONOMICAL DISTANCES

(1 light-year = $9·46 \times 10^{12}$ km).

Object	Distance from Earth (light-years)	Velocity of recession (km per second)	Object	Distance from Earth (light-years)	Velocity of recession (km per second)
Sun	$1·6 \times 10^{-5}$	—	Andromeda Galaxy	$2·2 \times 10^{6}$	—
Nearest star (Proxima Centauri)	4·2	—	Galaxy in Virgo	$7·5 \times 10^{7}$	1,200
Brightest star (Sirius)	8·6	—	Galaxy in Gt. Bear	10^{9}	14,900
Pleiades	410	—	Galaxy in Corona Borealis	$1·3 \times 10^{9}$	21,600
Centre of Milky Way	$3·0 \times 10^{4}$	—	Galaxy in Bootes	$4·5 \times 10^{9}$	39,300
Magellanic clouds (the nearest galaxies)	$1·6 \times 10^{5}$	—	Very remote quasi stellar object	$~1·2 \times 10^{10}$	~280,000

Core, Mantle and Crust

By these arguments, and by many others, a picture can be built up of the internal structure of the earth. The core is composed of iron–nickel alloy. It is liquid at the outside, but contains a solid inner core of radius about one-fifth of that of the earth. For a further discussion, *see* **Geology, F47–8.**

Rocks

Rocks are naturally occurring pieces of the solid earth. If you take a rock and break it up into grains, then separate the grains into different heaps of like grains, each heap will consist of grains of the same *mineral*. For example, the kind of rock called granite can be divided into glassy grains of the mineral quartz, milky white or pink grains of the mineral feldspar, shiny black flakes of the mineral biotite, and shiny colourless flakes of the mineral muscovite. Both biotite and muscovite belong to the mica group of minerals. Each different mineral has a well-defined composition or range of composition, and a definite and characteristic arrangement of the atoms that compose it. There are several thousand known kinds of minerals, but only fifty or so are at all common. Rocks are discussed in more detail later (*see* **F47–8**).

Age of Rocks

There are two distinct ways of estimating the age of rocks. The first gives the *relative age*. It is based on the principle that in a sequence of sediments, older rocks lie underneath and younger ones above, that igneous rocks are younger than the rocks they intrude, and that folded rocks are formed earlier than the earth movements that fold them. Correlation of a sequence of rocks in one place with those in another is made by fossil faunas and floras. Thus a complete scale of relative ages can be built up, stretching back to the first rocks containing fossils. The *age in years* can, on the other hand, be measured by using radioactive elements contained in rocks. If the amount of a radioactive element present is measured, and the amount of the product of radioactive decay can also be found, then, using the known rates of decay, the time since the product started to accumulate (defined for this purpose as the age in years) can be measured. This method is particu-larly useful for studying rocks that do not contain fossils (igneous and metamorphic rocks, or those too old to contain fossils). By similar methods, the *age of the earth* can be obtained. This turns out to be about 4.6×10^9 years. The rocks containing the first fossils are 2.5–3×10^9 years old, while organised life in abundance first appeared about 0.6×10^9 years ago.

The Continents and the Ocean Floor

The outer part of the earth, namely, the *asthenosphere* and the solid mantle and crust overlying it, the *lithosphere*, is in a state of restless movement, and it is this movement that gives rise to the formation of oceans, continents, and mountain belts. The study of this movement, the science of *plate tectonics*, is discussed in the **Special Topic, F77**.

The Rest

There is a lot more to the study of the earth than has been possible to set down here. The oceans, the atmosphere, and the rocks of the crust all interact with one another in their development in a complex way. The surface of the earth has gradually changed as life has evolved over thousands of millions of years and ice ages have come and gone, changing the surface again and again. Just as important is the economic potential of the earth, on which we depend for all of our energy and all raw materials. This section has given the basic framework within which such further investigations are carried out, to help the reader understand as he reads more widely.

II. PHYSICS—THE FUNDAMENTAL SCIENCE OF MATTER

WHAT PHYSICS IS ABOUT

Introduction

Anyone compelled by curiosity or professional interest to look into contemporary journals of pure physics research is soon struck by the fact that the old test-book division of physics into "heat, light, sound, electricity, and magnetism" has become very blurred.

Two different, though complementary, sections can be distinguished. First, there is the physics concerned with the properties of matter in bulk, with solids, liquids, and gases, and with those odd but very important substances, such as paints, plastic solutions, and jelly-like material, which are neither properly solid nor liquid. In this vast domain of physics questions like this are asked: Why is iron magnetic, copper not? What happens when solids melt? Why do some liquids flow more easily than others? Why do some things conduct electricity well, others badly, some not at all? During the last century, particularly the last few decades, it has become clear that such questions can be answered only by raising and solving others first. In particular, we must ask: (i) Of what nature are the invisible particles of which matter is composed? and (ii) How are those particles arranged in bulk matter?

The first of these two questions has generated the second major category of modern physics: this is the physics of particles and of the forces that particles exert on each other. In this field which represents science at its most fundamental questions like this are asked: If matter is composed of small units or particles, what are they like? How many kinds of particle are there? Do the particles possess mass? electric charge? magnetism? How do the particles influence each other? How can their motion be described and predicted?

The discussion which follows has been divided into two main parts (1) Particles and Forces, and (2) The Properties of Matter in Bulk, with part (1) describing the microscopic structure of matter and part (2) its macroscopic properties.

PARTICLES AND FORCES

Aristotle to Newton

The inference that matter should be composed of small particles or atoms originated, it is true, in classical times. The atomic idea was an attempt to solve the age-old problem of matter and its peculiar properties. The ancients had provided themselves with two solutions to the problem of matter:

(i) The theory of the four elements (earth, water, fire, air), from which all different forms of matter were composed by selecting different ratios of the four ingredients. This approach had been used by traditional philosophy and was adopted by Aristotle.
(ii) The theory of atomism which postulated the existence of atoms and empty space.

Atomism remained very much in the background in the development of Western Science and persisted even longer in the Arab world. The idea that matter is composed of "small units" was in reality forced into the mental development of mankind by the repeated application of the process of dimension halving. By the time of Newton atomism had come to the fore and Newton considered that God had made the Universe from "small indivisible grains" of matter. Neverthe-

less, the search for the "philosopher's stone" was still, in the seventeenth century, the main pursuit of many scientists, but the new chemistry of the seventeenth century made use of atomistic concepts. Newton's physics was a mechanics concerning particles in a vacuum and when Boyle described his gas law (*i.e.*, Pressure × Volume is constant at a fixed temperature) he visualised matter as composed of particles with specific qualitative properties. It was, of course, the advance of experimental techniques which enabled scientists to test ideas and theories on the nature of matter.

Dalton and Atomic Theory

The modern view of atomism need be traced no farther than the beginning of the nineteenth century when Dalton and his contemporaries were studying the laws of chemical combination using precise weighing techniques. By that time the distinctions between elements, compounds, and mixtures were already made. Compounds and mixtures are substances which can be separated into smaller amounts of chemically distinguishable constituents. Elements (see end of Sec.) cannot be so divided. In a mixture the components may be mixed in any proportion and sorted out again by non-chemical means. In a compound the elements are combined in fixed proportions by weight. This last fact gives the clue to atomic theory.

Dalton pointed out that the fixed combining weights of elements could easily be explained if the elements consisted of atoms which combined in simple numerical ratios, *e.g.*, 1 atom of element A with one of B, or one of B with two of C, and so on. For instance, 35·5 g of chlorine combine with 23·0 g of sodium to make 58·5 g of ordinary salt. If we assume one atom of chlorine links with one of sodium, then the atoms themselves must have weights in the ratio 35·5 to 23·0. This turns out to be consistent with the combining weights of chlorine and sodium in all other compounds in which they both take part. Sometimes two elements combine in several different proportions by weight. But this is easily explained by assuming that the atoms link up in a variety of ways *e.g.*, one iron atom with one oxygen, or two irons with three oxygens, or three irons with four oxygens. Then the three different combining proportions arise from the three different numbers of atoms, *using in each case the same ratio of oxygen atom weight to iron atom weight.*

Atomic Weight

Over the century and a half since Dalton, these ideas have been repeatedly tested by chemical experiments No. one now doubts that every chemical element has atoms of characteristic weight. The atomic weight or more properly the relative atomic mass, of an element is by international agreement expressed relative to one isotope (*see* below) of carbon, namely carbon-12 which is given the relative mass of twelve. These numbers are only ratios; the real weight of one single oxygen atom is $2·7 \times 10^{-23}$ g.

Valency

That the combinations of atoms in definite proportions was necessary to produce compounds, or more correctly molecules, was known from 1808. The reason why only one atom of sodium and one of chlorine was required to produce one molecule of salt was unknown. Further the seemingly odd combinations of two atoms of hydrogen (H) with one of oxygen (O) to give water (H_2O), while only one atom of hydrogen could combine with chlorine to give hydrogen chloride (HCl) could not be explained. This situation was not resolved until around 1860, when the chemical formulae of many molecules were known. It was then discovered that homologies existed in the elements, for example the series Na, K, Rb, Cs, or Fl, Cl, Br, I, and this culminated in the Periodic Table of the elements (see end Sec.). The valency of an atom was determined by its position in the periodic table and determined by the number of electrons (see below) which the atom has orbiting its nucleus. Atoms combined to form molecules in a manner which maintained the number of "valence" electrons in a stable grouping of 2, 8, or 18 (*see* **F24**). For example, sodium has one valence electron and chlorine seven, therefore the combination NaCl gives the stable grouping of eight; hydrogen has one and oxygen six, hence it requires two atoms of hydrogen and one of oxygen to give one stable molecule, H_2O. Other more complicated molecular structures and types of bonding between atoms are dealt with in the chemistry section. This discovery of particles smaller than the atom itself was necessary to fully comprehend the nature of valency in atomic combinations.

J. J. Thomson and the Electron

Matter is electrically uncharged in its normal state, but there exist many well-known ways of producing electric charges and currents—rubbing amber, or rotating dynamos, for example. It is therefore necessary to have some theory of electricity linked to the theory of matter. The fundamental experiment in this field was made by J. J. Thomson when, in 1897, he discovered the electron.

If you take two metal electrodes sealed inside a glass vessel and if the pressure of the air is reduced from atmospheric pressure, 76 cm of mercury, to 1 mm of mercury by mechanical pumping and then a high voltage, several kilo-volts, is applied to the electrodes, the negative electrode emits a "radiation" which causes the walls of the tube to glow. The rays are called *cathode rays*. The discovery of the electron was essentially a clarification of the nature of cathode rays. Thomson showed that they were streams of particles with mass and negative electric charge and a general behaviour unlike any other atomic particle known at that time. The importance of this discovery for the world of science cannot be overestimated, and its technical progeny are in every home and factory in X-ray machines, television tubes, and all electronic devices.

Rutherford–Bohr Atom

Since the electrons emerge from matter, they are presumably parts of atoms. The relation between the negative electrons and the positively charged constituents of matter was elucidated by the great experimenter Rutherford and the great theoretician Bohr. Their work, just before the First World War, showed that the positive charge, together with almost all the mass, is concentrated in the central core or nucleus of the atom about which the very light-weight electrons revolve. The diameter of an atom is about 10^{-8} cm, roughly one three-hundred-millionth part of an inch. The central nucleus has a diameter about 10,000 times smaller still. The nucleus and the electrons hold together because of the electric attraction between them.

The positive charge of the nucleus is responsible for holding the electron in the region of space around the nucleus. The electrostatic Coulomb force, if left on its own would quickly attract the electrons into the nucleus but since the electrons move in orbits, circular and elliptical, they experience an outward centrifugal force which balances the inward electrostatic force. The mechanism is similar to that which holds the earth in orbit around the sun, only here a gravitational force replaces the effect of the Coulomb force. Modern theories of the electronic structure of atoms are quantum mechanical (*see* below).

At this stage work could, and did, go on separately along several different lines:

(i) Electrons could be studied on their own. Nowadays the handling of beams of electrons of all sizes and intensities has become a major branch of technology.

(ii) The nucleus could be treated as a special problem, and this led to the mid century flowering of nuclear physics, to the atomic bomb, and to nuclear power.

(iii) The behaviour of electrons in the atom could be analysed; this is the great domain of atomic physics which spreads into many other sciences as well.

Volumes have been written about these three fields, but we can spare only a few lines for each.

The Electron

Electrons are expelled from solids by light, heat, electric fields, and other influences. It has therefore been possible to study beams of electrons on their own *in vacuo*. Electrons inside matter, either as constituents, or temporarily in transit, can also be observed by their innumerable effects. These observations all show the particles to be indistinguishable one from another; all electrons are the same wherever they come from. They have a definite mass (9.11×10^{-28} g), a negative electric charge, a magnetic moment, and a "spin" (intrinsic rotatory motion). No one has ever subdivided an electron or obtained an electric charge smaller than that on one electron. The electronic charge is therefore used as a basic unit of charge in atomic physics. The electron has come to be the best known of all the "fundamental particles." It is now used in research as probe for studying the structure of matter, for which it is ideally suited, since it is very much smaller than an atom. A whole field of electron-scattering research which studies the nature and structure of solids, liquids, and gases is being actively conducted in many laboratories.

The Nucleus

The early research programmes in nuclear physics were greatly facilitated by the occurrence in nature of certain unstable (radioactive) nuclei which emit fast-moving fragments. The latter can be used as projectiles to aim at other nuclei as targets; the resulting impacts yield much valuable information. This technique still dominates nuclear physics, though nowadays the projectiles are artificially accelerated by one or other of the large costly machines designed for the purpose.

The First Discovery

The most important early discovery was that the nucleus consists of two types of fundamental particle—the positively charged *proton* and the electrically neutral *neutron*. These two are of nearly equal mass (about 1,800 times that of the electron), and like electrons, have a magnetic moment and spin. The proton charge is equal to the electron charge, though opposite in sign. Consider a moderately complex nucleus like that of iron. This usually has 30 neutrons and 26 protons. Its atomic weight therefore depends on the total number of neutrons plus protons, but the total charge depends only on the number of protons—called the *atomic number*. The latter is denoted by Z while the total number of neutrons plus protons is called the *mass number* and denoted by M. A species of nucleus with given values of Z and M is called a *nuclide*. Z is also the number of electrons in the atom, since the atom as a whole is electrically neutral. The atomic number determines the chemical nature of the atom (*see below*), so that by altering the number of *neutrons* in a nucleus we do not change the chemical species. It is therefore possible to find—and nowadays to make—nuclei of the same element which nevertheless differ slightly in weight because they have different numbers of neutrons. These are called *isotopes*. Iron isotopes are known with anything from 25 to 36 neutrons, but all have 26 protons. Thus a set of isotopes consists of the various nuclides that have the same Z but different M's.

When the atomic properties of isotopes are measured it is found that small, hyperfine differences in the motions of the electrons around the respective nuclei exist. These result from the different total spin of the isotopes and its effect on the orbiting electrons. This influence of atomic properties by nuclear effects is important in that it provides a link between different fields of research.

Stable Nuclides

The protons and neutrons in a nucleus are bound together by strong forces called *nuclear forces*. In many cases, the forces are so strong that no particles ever escape and the nucleus preserves its identity. There are two hundred and seventy-four different combinations of neutrons and protons of this kind, and they are called the *stable nuclides*. The earth is largely composed of such stable nuclides, because any unstable ones have, in the course of time, spontaneously broken up into stable residues.

Nevertheless, there are some unstable nuclei left on earth. They give rise to the phenomenon of radioactivity which was discovered by Becquerel in 1893.

Unstable Nuclides: Radioactivity

Becquerel found that certain chemicals containing uranium gave off rays capable of blackening a photographic plate, and shortly afterwards Marie and Pierre Curie discovered more substances, including radium, which produce similar but stronger effects. By now, about fifty chemical elements having radioactive properties are known to exist on earth, some, like radium, being strongly radioactive, others, like potassium, being so weak that the radiations are difficult to detect. These are called the *natural radioactive nuclides*.

The main facts about radioactivity are as follows: it is a *nuclear* phenomenon and (with minor exceptions) proceeds quite independently of whatever the electrons in the atom may be doing. Thus, the radioactivity of an atom is not affected by the chemical combination of the atom with other atoms, nor by ordinary physical influences like temperature and pressure. The radioactivity consists of the emission by the substance of certain kinds of rays. The early workers, Rutherford being the giant among them, distinguished three kinds of rays labelled α, β, and γ. These are described below. Whatever kind of ray is examined, it is found that the radiation from a given sample decreases gradually with time according to a definite law which states that the intensity of radiation decreases by half every T seconds. The number T, called the half-life, is constant for each radioactive material, but varies enormously from substance to substance. For instance, radium decreases its activity by a half every 1,602 years, whereas the half-life of one of the astatine isotopes is about $0 \cdot 1 \times 10^{-6}$ sec.

α-, β-, and γ-rays

The three most well-known types of radioactive emission are quite distinct from one another.

(i) α-rays or α-particles consist of two protons and two neutrons bound together. They are ejected from the radioactive nucleus with one of several well-defined speeds. These speeds are high, often of the order 10^9 cm per sec. Two protons and two neutrons are the constituents of the nucleus of helium, and α-particles are thus fast-moving helium nuclei.

(ii) β-rays are moving electrons. They may emerge from their parent nucleus with any speed from zero to a definite maximum. The maximum speed often approaches that of light, and is different for each isotope. The electron has a positively charged counterpart, the positron (see below), and β-rays are sometimes positrons. To distinguish the two cases, the symbols β^- and β^+ are used. The naturally occurring β-radiations are almost all β^-.

(iii) γ-rays travel with the speed of light because they are in fact electromagnetic waves differing from light only in the extreme shortness of their wavelength. They have no electric charge.

It is unusual, though not unheard of, for the same radioactive substance to emit both α- and β-rays. On the other hand, γ-rays frequently accompany either α- or β-rays.

γ-rays pass through matter easily; in fact, they are extra penetrating X-rays. α-rays can be stopped by thin sheets of tissue paper. α-rays brought to rest pick up a pair of electrons from the surrounding matter and become neutral helium atoms, and helium gas from this source is consequently found imprisoned in certain radioactive rocks. β-rays are intermediate in penetrating power between α- and γ-rays.

We must now try to interpret these observations.

Radioactive Disintegration

A nucleus is a collection of neutrons and protons interacting with each other and possessing collectively a certain amount of energy. Just as some human organisations lose their coherence if they accept too many members, so nuclei can remain stable only if (i) the total number of particles is not too great, and (ii) neutrons and protons are there in suitable proportions. Radioactive nuclei are the ones for which either or both these conditions do not hold. Sooner or later such nuclei eject a fragment, thus getting rid of some energy they cannot contain. This is called a *radioactive disintegration*, and the fragments are the α-, β-, and γ-rays. α-emission relieves a nucleus of two neutrons and two protons and some energy; γ-emission simply carries off excess energy without altering the number or kind of particles left behind. β-emission is more complicated. There are no electrons normally present in a nucleus, but they are suddenly created and explosively emitted if a neutron changes into a proton; positive electrons are similarly generated if a proton changes into a neutron. β-emission is therefore a mechanism for changing the ratio of protons to neutrons without altering the total number of particles.

Both α- and β-emission change the Z of a nucleus, and the product, or daughter nucleus, is a different chemical element. α-emission also changes the M. It might happen that the daughter nucleus is unstable, in which case it too will disintegrate. Successive generations are produced until a stable one is reached. Part of such a family tree is shown below. The symbols above the arrows show the kind of rays emitted at each stage, the figures are the mass numbers, M, and the names and symbols of chemical elements can be found on **F64–5**.

$$\text{U}^{238} \xrightarrow{\alpha} \text{Th}^{234} \xrightarrow{\beta} \text{Pa}^{234} \xrightarrow{\beta} \text{U}^{234} \xrightarrow{\alpha} \text{Th}^{230} \xrightarrow{\alpha}$$

$$\text{Ra}^{226} \xrightarrow{\alpha} \text{Rn}^{222} \xrightarrow{\alpha} \text{Po}^{218} \xrightarrow{\alpha} \text{Pb}^{214} \xrightarrow{\beta} \text{Bi}^{214} \xrightarrow{\beta}$$

$$\text{Po}^{214} \xrightarrow{\alpha} \text{Pb}^{210} \xrightarrow{\beta} \text{Bi}^{210} \xrightarrow{\beta} \text{Po}^{210} \xrightarrow{\alpha} \text{Pb}^{206}$$
(Pb^{206} is stable lead).

This family exists naturally on earth, because the head of the family, U^{238}, has so long a half-life (4.5×10^9 years) that there has not yet been time enough since its formation for it to have disappeared.

Artificial Radioactivity

Nowadays many new radioactive isotopes can be man-made. All that is required is to alter the M or Z (or both) of a stable isotope to a value which is incompatible with stability. The means for doing this is *bombardment*, *i.e.*, stable nuclei are exposed to the impacts of atomic particles such as streams of protons from an accelerator, the neutrons in an atomic reactor, or simply the α-particles from another radioactive substance.

The new material is called an *artificially radio-active isotope.* Artificial radioactivity is not different in kind from that of the naturally radio-active substances, but the half-lives are usually on the short side. Indeed, the isotopes in question would exist in nature but for the fact that their short half-lives ensured their disappearance from the earth long ago.

Suppose a piece of copper is exposed to the intense neutron radiation in an atomic reactor at Lucas Heights, Australia.

The more abundant of the two stable isotopes of ordinary copper has thirty-four neutrons and twenty-nine protons (*i.e.,* $Z = 29$, $M = 63$). In the reactor many (not all) of these nuclei absorb a neutron, giving an unstable copper nucleus with $Z = 29$, $M = 64$. When removed from the reactor the specimen is observed to be radioactive with a half-life of 12.8 hours. It is somewhat unusual in that it gives out both β^- and β^+ rays. Some nuclei emit electrons, leaving a daughter nucleus with one more positive charge than copper, *i.e.,* a zinc nucleus ($Z = 30$, $M = 64$). One neutron has become a proton, and the re-sulting zinc nucleus is stable. The others emit positrons, leaving behind a nucleus in which a proton has been turned into a neutron ($Z = 28$, $M = 64$); this is a stable nickel nucleus. The overall process is one example of the artificial transmutation of the chemical elements which is now a commonplace of nuclear physics. It was first discovered by Irene and Frederick Joliot-Curie in 1934.

Lack of a Complete Theory

Consider now a collection of, say, one million radioactive nuclei of the same kind. It is im-possible to tell exactly when any one of them will disintegrate; it is a matter of chance which ones break up first. All we know is that, after a time equal to the half-life, only a half a million will survive unchanged. In general, the more excess energy a nucleus has, the more likely it is to break up, and therefore the shorter the half-life of that particular nuclear species. In principle, to cal-culate the half-life theoretically, one would have to have a reliable theory of nuclear forces and energies. This is still being sought after, so it is probably fair to say that while the laws of behaviour of radioactive isotopes are well and accurately known, the *explanation* of this behaviour in terms of the properties of protons and neutrons is by no means complete.

Nuclear Fission—Chain Reaction

A discovery important not just for nuclear physics but for the whole of mankind was made by Hahn and Strassman in 1939. This was the dis-covery of nuclear fission in uranium. One of the natural isotopes of uranium is an unstable one, $U235$, with 143 neutrons and 92 protons. It norm-ally shows its instability by emitting α- and γ-rays. If uranium is bombarded with neutrons, some $U235$ nuclei temporarily gain an extra neutron, which makes them even less stable. This they show by splitting into two roughly equal parts, called fission fragments, together with two or three neutrons. There are two highly important things about this disintegration. One is that the two or three neutrons can promote further disintegrations in other uranium nuclei, and the process can therefore be self-propagating: it is then called a *chain re-action.* The other is that the total mass of the fission products is less than that of the original nucleus. This mass difference does not disappear without trace; it turns into energy according to a formula referred to in a paragraph below (**F18(1)**).

Nuclear Fusion

The ability of two light nuclei to combine and form a heavier nucleus is called fusion. A reac-tion of this nature does not form a chain process but proceeds in singly induced reactions. A typical fusion reaction is the formation of a helium nucleus (mass 3) from two deuterium nuclei which are made to collide at an energy of 60 keV (speed of 2.4×10^6 m/s)

i.e., $^2D_1 + {}^2D_1 \rightarrow {}^3He_2$ (0·82 meV) + n(2·45 meV)

where the $^3He_2$ particle has kinetic energy of 0·82 meV and the free neutron has free kinetic energy of 2·45 meV. This type of reaction is exo-energetic, the additional kinetic energy coming from the tighter binding of the nucleus in ^3He than in the two separate deuterium nuclei. The energy released in this form of nuclear reaction is much more than that in a fission process and is respon-sible for the emitted energy of the sun which burns hydrogen to form helium.

Applications of Nuclear Reactions

The world has two uses for the energy released in nuclear reactions:

(1) nuclear weapons;
(2) nuclear power plants.

The only nuclear bombs to be used in anger employed the fission chain reaction proceeding at a rapid rate which quickly becomes uncontrollable and produces a tremendous explosion. The second generation of nuclear warhead uses the fusion reaction, which is initiated by a fission-reacting detonator to produce an even more des-tructive blast. The third generation of nuclear warhead uses the large flux of very energetic neutrons to kill biological material, but the blast effect is essentially zero, hence attacks with neutron bombs leave most non-biological material and structures intact.

In the second application the nuclear fission process is controlled to provide a constant source of energy to drive turbines which produce elec-tricity.

Both uses represent epoch-making technical achievements, but mankind has yet to show itself capable of bearing sanely the burden of respon-sibility which nuclear physicists have laid upon it. One thing is certain: the discoveries will not cease. Already, other fissionable elements have been made and used; new chemical elements have been created; nuclear plants ("atomic piles") have stimulated great demands for new materials that will stand the heat and radiation inside the reactor, and this promotes research in other fields of science; irradiation inside an atomic pile gives new, and potentially useful properties to old materials; nuclear power drives ships and submarines. It is difficult to write even briefly about contemporary nuclear physics without feel-ing keenly the ambiguity of its powerful promises.

Atoms

A nucleus surrounded by its full complement of electrons is an electrically neutral system called an atom. Neither the atom as a whole, nor its nucleus, counts as a "fundamental particle" because either can be subdivided into more elementary parts, thus:

atom → electrons + nucleus → electrons + neutrons + protons

The chemical identity of the atoms of a given element, which was Dalton's key idea, depends entirely on the number and motion of the elec-trons. For example, the simplest element, hydrogen, has one proton for a nucleus, and one electron. The latter is comparatively easily detached or disturbed by the electric forces exerted by neighbouring atoms, consequently hydrogen is reactive chemically, *i.e.,* it readily lends its electron to build chemical structures with other equally co-operative elements. The second element, helium, has a nucleus of two protons and two neutrons; outside are two electrons in a particularly stable arrangement. Both electrons orbit the nucleus in the same spacial orbit, but with their spin directions oppo-site and at 90° to the plane through the nucleus and the electrons. This pair of electrons is so difficult to disarrange that the special name of closed shells has been coined to cover such cases. The fact that two electrons can be present in the same orbit is only possible if their spins are anti-parallel (Pauli Exclusion Principle). In the case of a stable group of eight electrons they arrange themselves in groups of two and their spins antiparallel. Helium with its closed shell will not react chemically, whereas hydrogen, which has an open shell of only one electron, will react very quickly with other atoms.

As the nuclear charge increases, different electron arrangements of greater or lesser stability succeed one another, with every so often a closed shell corresponding to one of the chemically inert gases neon, argon, xenon, krypton.

Such considerations, pursued in sufficient detail, enable atomic physics to account for all the differences and similarities among the chemical elements and, in principle at least, for all other facts of chemistry as well.

Ions

Changes in the atomic properties of an atom are accomplished by altering the position of any electron from one orbit to another. In the limit when an electron is completely removed from the atom, leaving it positively charged, the atom is said to be ionised and is called a positive ion. An atom can be singly or multiply ionised up to a level equal to the number of electrons existing in the neutral atom. In addition, atoms can, through distortion of the existing electrons, accept an additional electron and become negative ions. These can be formed in a resonance scattering process and exist only for life-times of only 10^{-14}s or be formed by chemical reactions. The roles played by negative and positive ions in the upper atmosphere of the earth and stellar atmospheres have been of special interest to atomic physicists since the 1930s.

Maxwell and Electromagnetic Waves

Atoms are held together by the electric attraction of the nucleus for the electrons. Finer details of atomic behaviour depend on the magnetic moments of the particles. Any moving charged particle gives rise to magnetic effects, and in the dynamo a coil moving in a magnet produces an electric current. It can be seen therefore that electric and magnetic phenomena are intimately linked. Any region of space subject to electric and magnetic influences is called an *electromagnetic field*.

In 1862, before the discovery of the electron, Maxwell, while still in his twenties, had perfected a general theory of the electro-magnetic field. This theory today still describes correctly almost all electro-magnetic phenomena. The elegance of this theory is difficult to appreciate, but it alone was the only theory of pre-twentieth century physics which satisfied the prerequisites of Einstein's relativity theory (1905), *i.e.*, inherent in its structure was the concept of relativistic invariance. *Inter alia*, he proved that disturbances in the electric and magnetic conditions at one place could be propagated to another place through empty space, with a definite velocity, just as sound waves are propagated through air. Such electromagnetic disturbances in transit are called *electromagnetic waves*, and their velocity turned out experimentally to be the same as that of light and radio waves—which was a decisive argument to show that both of these phenomena are themselves electro-magnetic waves.

Einstein and Photons

In the years between about 1900 and 1920 this view was upset by Planck, Einstein, Millikan, and others, who focused attention on phenomena (radiant heat, photoelectricity) in which light behaves like a stream of particles and not at all like waves. A wave and a particle are two quite different things, as anyone will admit after a moment's contemplation of, say, the ripples on a pond and a floating tennis ball. The acute question was: is light like waves or particles?

Theoretical physicists have devised means of having it both ways. To say that light behaves as particles means that the waves of the electromagnetic field cannot have their energy subdivided indefinitely. For waves of a given frequency, there is a certain irreducible quantity of energy that must be involved whenever light interacts with anything. This quantity is the product hv where v is the frequency and h is a constant named after Planck. Each such unit

is called a *quantum of the electromagnetic field* or a *photon* and is counted as one of the fundamental particles. Frequencies and wavelengths vary widely. Typical wavelengths are: radio—hundreds or thousands of metres; radar—a few centimetres; visible light—5×10^{-5} cm; X-rays—10^{-8} cm.

De Broglie and Particles

Since it seemed possible to attribute particle properties to electro-magnetic waves, then why not associate wave properties with particles. If an electron (mass m) is travelling with a velocity of v cm/s, then De Broglie (1923) suggested that its characteristic wavelength would be given by the relation $mv \lambda = h$; for example if $v = 10^3$ m/s, $m = 9 \times 10^{-31}$ kg, $h = 6 \cdot 626^{-34}$ joules-seconds, then $\lambda = 7 \cdot 36 \times 10^{-7}$ m, which is the same wavelength as red light. This proposal was confirmed in 1927 by Davisson and Germer when they showed that electrons could produce diffraction, a property until then only associated with light. These wave-like properties are now known to exist for all particles, and we now consider a particle with momentum mv to behave like a wave of wavelength $\lambda = h/mv$.

De Broglie made his revolutionary assertion in his doctoral thesis, and his examiners were so uneasy about the validity of the hypothesis that they were prepared to fail the young man in his examination. Happily for De Broglie, Einstein was visiting that particular university and he was asked his opinion of the idea; his reply ensured success for De Broglie and saved the examiners from future embarrassment.

Molecules

Electrical attractions and interactions of various kinds can cause atoms to combine with each other or themselves to form molecules. Two similar atoms, say hydrogen, combining to form the homonuclear diatomic molecule H_2, while two different atoms, hydrogen and chlorine, will form a heteronuclear diatomic molecule HCl. Molecules have a wide range of complexity, from simple pairs of atoms to highly intricate spirals and chains composed of thousands of atoms. The biological basis of all life is, of course, molecular in both origin and function.

Excited Atoms

Like nuclei, atoms, when given excess energy (insufficient to ionise them), will absorb the energy in one of the electrons, which is then displaced from its equilibrium state to a state (or orbit) of higher energy. It will remain there for typically 10^{-8} seconds before returning to its equilibrium position with the excess energy being emitted as light. The time an atom remains in its excited state can exceed 10^{-8} seconds; lifetimes of $0 \cdot 1$ second are known, and these metastable states are prevented by the atomic properties of the atom from decaying quickly to their equilibrium states. The colour of the light emitted is characteristic of the atom involved, with the more energetic transitions giving blue light while the less energetic transitions give red light. Hence the emitted colour (or wavelength) of the light can be used as a tool for chemical identification and study of the various transition probabilities in atoms.

Herein lies the explanation of innumerable natural and technical phenomena, such as the colours of glowing gases whether they exist in the sun and stars, in aurora, or in street-lamps and neon signs. Herein also lies the reason for the importance of spectroscopy, which is the study of the characteristic radiation from excited states for spectroscopy is not only a useful tool for the chemical identification of substances ("spectroscopic analysis") but was one of the main routes along which twentieth-century physicists broke through to a knowledge of the inner nature of the atom.

Forces in Nature

Nature uses four, at high energies three, different forces to make one particle interact with another. The weakest force is **gravity** which although present at all particle interactions, is insignificant in atomic and nuclear interactions. Gravity controls the mass distribution in the universe and the force has an infinite range of interaction.

The **electric force** which also has an infinite range of interaction is much stronger than the gravitational force and is responsible for the binding forces inside atoms by the attraction of nuclei for electrons.

Inside the nucleus two types of interaction take place which require different forces for their existence:

(1) the forces which hold neutrons and protons together in the nucleus and this is the **strong force**, and

(2) the **weak force** which controls the changes in charge state of nucleons, e.g., the β-decay process when a neutron in a nucleus changes into a proton with the ejection of an electron is controlled by the weak force.

Both these nuclear forces are short-range with their radius of influence approximately 10^{-13} cm, with the weak force acting on all matter and the strong force acting on quarks only. In today's parlance, gravity will act on any particle with mass, the electric force on any particle with charge, the strong nuclear on quarks and the weak nuclear on quarks and leptons (*see below*).

Quarks appear to experience short-range freedom of movement combined with a long-range binding, explained by one new theory called the **bag model**. The proton, i.e., the nucleus of atomic hydrogen, is composed of three quarks which move about freely within the shell of the proton; only when one quark tries to escape across the boundary of the proton does it experience a force which rebinds into the proton. Before we discuss further the interactions of these forces we must describe the range of particles which exist in physics.

Elementary Particles

When considering the word elementary in this context the reader should be wary of thinking that it implies some degree of absoluteness. The elementary mass of any particlular particle is always highly qualified and subject to change. When a particle is discovered physicists measure its properties, i.e., mass, electric charge, and spin, and determine which of the four forces to which it is subject. In addition, its life-time must be determined to see if the particle is stable or only a transient particle which will break up into other particles. The life-times of unstable particles are extremely short, ranging from 10^{-17}s to 10^{-21}s, and it is debatable if a particle which lasts only for 10^{-21}s should be called a particle. Generally now such short-lived particles are called resonances which are produced in an interaction which is only a step to the final product.

The rudimentary classification of particles is into four groups:

(1) gauge bosons
(2) leptons
(3) mesons
(4) baryons

All particles have an anti-particle which has the same mass but opposite charge as the real particle, the only exception being the photon, which is its own anti-particle and forms a group on its own. The leptons (electron, muon, and neutrino) form a stable group of particles and do not react to the strong nuclear force. This group of particles, and the photon, are perhaps the most fundamental of all particles. The mesons are unstable particles and (as will be seen later) exist only to act as a means which enables nucleons to interact with each other. They are subjected to the strong nuclear force. All particles heavier than the proton are called baryons, every one of them, except the proton, is unstable in some degree, and a vast number of them are known. Only a few are listed in the Table on page **F16.**

Mesons and baryons are collectively called hadrons. All of these unstable particles have been detected either in the cosmic flux falling on the earth or produced in the very high energy accelerating machines in Europe, the USA, and the former USSR.

Strangeness

Some particles have long life-times ~10^{-9} s, which is much larger than that encountered normally. Particles which possessed these long life-times were called "strange". Strangeness describes not a new property of matter but a different quality of matter which persists long enough to enable that particle to engage in strong nuclear-force interactions. Hence strangeness does not persist indefinitely. The decay of a strange particle into other particles with the abolition of strangeness proceeds via the weak nuclear force. The strange (and doubly strange) particles form highly symmetrised shapes when combined with non-strange particles. The pattern itself does not explain anything, but the underlying theory, known as Group Theory, does indicate by symmetry arguments which particle should be necessary to form a complete group. This mathematical procedure had a resounding success in 1964 when it predicted the existence of a triply strange particle known as "omega minus". The organisation of particles according to their properties of mass, spin, and strangeness in groups is now only an organisation exercise, and it will not tell us anything about the composition of nucleons.

Interactions of Particles

The method by which atomic, nuclear, and subnuclear particles interact is via the exchange of energy which can be considered as a particle exchange. The interaction between electric charges proceeds by the exchange of photons. For example, two charges feel each other by one charge emitting a photon which interacts with the second charge. Since the electric force has infinite range, its force-carrying particle has zero mass. The same criteria apply in the gravitational force, where the graviton is the particle which carries the force effect between particles of matter. Since the weak and strong forces are short-range, then their force-carrying particles have finite masses. The weak force is transmitted by W and Z particles and the strong force can be considered as transmitted by mesons. The quarks also interact via the strong force, here carried by gluons (mass at present unknown), which also feel the force themselves. Strangeness is conserved in strong nuclear reactions but not in weak ones.

A theory which combines the electric and weak forces into a single interaction has predicted the masses of the W and Z particles to be around 82 and 93 GeV respectively. In early 1983 experimental evidence was found by international groups at CERN for the existence of the W particle with the predicted mass thereby giving considerable support to this theory. A long term aim is to unify all the known forces of nature into a single interaction.

Quarks

The stability of the leptons contrasts sharply with the instability of the hadrons (excepting the proton), and this as well as other things had led physicists to consider that all hadrons were composed from different combinations of yet undiscovered particles. Gell-Mann first postulated the existence of three particles from which the nucleons, mesons, and hence all hadrons are composed. These "new" particles are attributed with fractional electric charges of $+\frac{2}{3}$, $-\frac{1}{3}$, and $-\frac{1}{3}$ of the electron charge. The particles were called quarks. The name quark was taken from the novel *Finnegans Wake* by James Joyce, the meaning of which is obscure, which is perhaps appropriate, but as students of Joyce will know, quark means "non sense", and other interpretations as to its meaning, such as the "sound of seagulls" or "quarts" are wrong. The three

SOME MEMBERS OF THE ATOMIC FAMILY

The numbers in brackets after the name denote first the electric charge and second, the mass. The charge on an electron is counted as −1 unit and the electron mass as +1 unit. Thus (+1,207) means the particle has a positive charge of 1 unit and a mass 207 times that of the electron.

The mass energy of an electron is 0·51 MeV, hence conversion to mass energies can be made by multiplying the given mass by 0·51. Thus the muon has a mass energy of 106 MeV. Note: the letter M is used to denote quantities of millions and the letter G to denote quantities of thousand of millions.

Photon (0, 0)	A quantum of electromagnetic radiation, *e.g.*, light, X-rays, γ-rays. The concept was introduced by M. Planck in 1900 when he described the emission of light as taking place in "packets" rather than in a steady stream. The energy of a photon is proportional to the frequency of the radiation and inversely proportional to the wavelength.

Leptons

Electron (−1, 1)	Discovered by J. J. Thomson in 1897. The number of orbital electrons in an atom determines its chemical properties. Actual rest mass = $9 \cdot 1 \times 10^{-28}$ g. Emitted as β-rays by some radioactive nuclei. A stable particle.
Positron (+1, 1)	Positive counterpart or, "anti-particle", to the electron. Predicted theoretically by P. A. M. Dirac in 1928 and first discovered in cosmic rays by C. D. Anderson in 1932. Emitted as β-rays by some radioactive nuclei. When positrons and electrons collide they usually annihilate each other and turn into γ-rays; consequently, positrons only last about 10^{-10} sec. within ordinary matter, but are stable in isolation.
Neutrino (0, 0) and Anti-neutrino (0, 0)	These particles travel with the speed of light and are distinguished from one another by the relation of their spin to their direction of motion. A neutrino is emitted with the positron during positive β-decay; and an anti-neutrino with the electron during negative β-decay. Their interaction with matter is extremely slight. First postulated by Pauli in 1933 and detected in 1956. π-meson decay also produces neutrinos and anti-neutrinos but in 1962 it was proved experimentally that these are a different species. Thus there are two kinds of neutrino each with an anti-neutrino. All these particles are distinguished from photons by having different spin.
Muon (±1, 207)	Similar to, but heavier than, the electron and positron; disintegrates into electron (or positron if positive) + neutrino + anti-neutrino.

Mesons

Pion (±1, 273) or (0, 264)	The π-meson. Charged pions decay either into muons and neutrinos or into electrons and neutrinos. Neutral pions decay into γ-rays, into "positron-electron pairs", or both. Pions are intimately connected with nuclear forces, *i.e.*, with the "strong" interaction.
Kaon (±1, 966) or (0, 974)	The K-mesons. These decay in many different ways producing other mesons, electrons, and neutrinos.

Baryons

Proton (+1, 1836·1)	The positively-charged constituent of nuclei; the hydrogen nucleus is one proton. Fast-moving protons occur in cosmic rays. Does not spontaneously disintegrate.
Anti-proton (−1, 1836·1)	Negative anti-particle of the proton. Its existence was long suspected. Artificially produced and detected for the first time in 1955. Will react with the proton to produce pions or kaons.
Neutron (0, 1838·6)	Discovered by J. Chadwick in 1932. The neutral constituent of nuclei. When free it spontaneously disintegrates into a proton, an electron, and an anti-neutrino, after an average lifetime of about 18 minutes. Passes through matter much more easily than charged particles.
Anti-neutron (0, 1838·6)	The anti-particle of the neutron from which it is distinguished by properties connected with its magnetic moment and spin. Will react with neutron to produce pions or kaons.
Lambda Particle (0, 2183)	Discovered in 1947. Decays into proton plus pion.
Sigma Particle (0 or ±1; about 2330)	Various modes of disintegration, producing neutrons, protons, mesons and lambda particles.
Omega Particle (±1, 3272)	Predicted by scientists and duly discovered at Brookhaven, New York, in 1964.
Psi Particle (0, about 6100)	Discovered independently by two laboratories in the USA 1974. Still under intensive study.

quarks were called up, down, and strange and have the properties given in the Table below:

Name	charge	spin	mass-energy (MeV)
up	$+\frac{2}{3}$	$\frac{1}{2}$	336
down	$-\frac{1}{3}$	$\frac{1}{2}$	338
strange	$-\frac{1}{3}$	$\frac{1}{2}$	540

These particles interact with each other via the strong force. Hence it can be seen that by taking different combinations of quarks, different hadrons can be built up. For example, the proton is two up quarks and one down, the neutron is two down and one up. The simplicity of this system can be appreciated, but the only experimental evidence to support the existence of quarks is indirect. No one has yet isolated a single quark! Many scientists are seeking ways to produce and detect them, but as yet (1999) no claims have stood the test of scrutiny. Further theoretical and experimental evidence has proved the existence of three more quarks, known as top, bottom and charmed (*see below*). These six elementary particles are complimented by six equivalent anti-matter particles, each with the opposite charge of its mate.

The K-mesons, for example, are composed of a quark and an anti-quark either with the spins of the two quarks aligned parallel to give a net spin of one, or aligned antiparallel to give a net spin of zero. The charges +1, −1, and 0 are simply determined by selecting the correct combination of up and down quarks.

Charm

In the quest to unite the weak and electric forces, theoreticians were forced to introduce yet another new particle into the quark family. This was a charmed quark with charge $+\frac{2}{3}$. The four members of the quark family had seemed then to be symmetrical with the four members of the lepton group (electron, muon, and two neutrinos). Since the charmed quark had charge $+\frac{2}{3}$ and mass of 1,500 MeV, it could simply replace the up quark as a building brick in nucleons to produce charmed matter. For example, by replacing the up quark with a proton and a meson by a charmed quark we get a charmed proton and a charmed meson. The first experimental evidence of the existence of charm was obtained by the high-energy physics group at University College, London, working at CERN laboratory, when they established the existence of "a neutral current interaction" in neutrino scattering experiments. Although "naked" charm has never been detected, charmed mesons (masses of 1,865 and 2,020) have been detected by the SPEAR laboratory in USA and charmed anti-protons have also been detected with masses of 2,260 MeV. The experimentally determined masses are in sufficient agreement with theory to confirm the existence of the charmed quark. Theoretical proof for the existence of two more quarks, top and bottom, soon followed and by 1995 both had been discovered by experimentalists. As a whole, this theory of elementary particles is called the standard model and has become generally accepted. Scientists are not happy to rest with this, however, because the number of unspecified parameters involved (the standard model has about 20 of these) seems too many for a fundamental theory. The search is on for deeper patterns and symmetries to explain matter.

The Higgs Particle

Since the discovery of the top quark, physicists have concentrated their efforts on tracking down an even rarer particle called the Higgs. Finding it would not only continue to validate the standard model, but would also help theorists explain the existence of mass. Since the US government decided to stop funding its expensive Superconducting Supercollider project, the search is wholly in the hands of the Europeans at CERN (**L24**).

QUANTUM THEORY AND RELATIVITY

Quantum Theory

In our discussion of the nature of the various particles in physics we have alluded to them as being classified with well-defined sizes and weights. Of course, once we consider the physics of matter on a scale which is smaller than that of our everyday comprehension, then the classical physics of Newton is insufficient and we must use quantum physics. In the atomic region of reality we are again faced with the problem of indivisibility where the Greeks stopped their thinking and called the smallest particles of the universe atoms. Today we know that each separate particle is composed of a definite amount of energy, and the larger the particle, *i.e.*, the more energy it is composed of, the easier it is to detect. We also know that the exchange of force between nucleons is carried by particles and that this inchangeability between mass and energy is a reality of quantum theory. To see this more fully we must realise that quantum theory rests on the theory of measurement! If a particle, of any type or structure, is composed of an amount of energy ΔE, then it is necessary to make measurements on it for a certain minimum time before it is detected. This minimum time Δt is given by the equation $\Delta E \times \Delta t \geq \hbar$, where $\hbar$ is Planck's constant divided by 2π; hence it can be seen that the smaller ΔE, then the longer a measurement must be made to detect the particle. Correspondingly, the time of measurement itself introduces an uncertainty, ΔE, in the energy of the particle. As well as the parameters ΔE and Δt, a particular physical event can be expressed in terms of its momentum p and position q, and these can also be expressed in a relationship as $\Delta p \times \Delta q \geq \hbar$. Hence one can ask at what position in space, q, is a particular particle with momentum p? Or what exactly is the wavelength of a wave? It may be thought that the first question cannot reasonably be asked of a wave nor the second of a particle, but bearing in mind the dual roles of particles and waves discussed earlier, then these questions can be interchanged. We know that electrons behave both as particles and waves. Since electrons have something in common with both, one question cannot be answered precisely for electrons without ignoring the other; alternatively, both questions can be given an imprecise answer. As the wavelength of electrons is intimately connected with their speed, one has to accept an accurate knowledge of the speed (wavelength) and ignorance of position, or the converse, or *inaccurate* knowledge of both. This is the famous Heisenberg Uncertainty Principle. Quantum theory is a set of mathematical rules for calculating the behaviour of fundamental particles in accordance with the Uncertainty Principle. In spite of its equivocal-sounding name, the principle has led to an enormous increase in the accuracy with which physical phenomena can be described and predicted. Quantum theory includes all that previous theories did and more.

Quantum theory grew up in the same epoch as the Theory of Relativity. Heroic attempts have been made to combine the two, but with only partial success so far. Relativity is concerned with all motion and all physical laws, but its characteristic manifestations occur only when something is moving with nearly the velocity of light. Quantum theory is likewise all-embracing, but its typical phenomena almost always occur when something on the minute atomic scale is in question. Consequently, the vast majority of everyday mechanics needs no more than the classical theory laid down by Newton, which is neither relativistic nor quantum.

Relativity

Historically, relativity grew out of attempts to measure the speed with which the earth moved through that hypothetical medium called the ether, which was supposed at that time to be the bearer of light waves. To take a simple analogy: sound waves travel through still air with a certain definite speed, v. If you move through the air with speed v' towards oncoming sound waves, they will pass you at the speed $v + v'$. Michelson and Morley, in their celebrated experiment of 1887, failed to find the corresponding behaviour on the part of light. This is so important an experiment that it has been repeated, and repeatedly discussed ever since. In October 1958 the latest and most accurate confirmation of the Michelson–Morley result was announced. It seems as if light always travels with the same speed relative to an observer, however fast he moves relative to anything else. Einstein put it this way: two observers moving with any constant velocity relative to each other will always agree that light travels past them at the same speed; this speed is denoted by *c*, and is approximately 186,000 miles per second.

It should be remembered that the limiting value of the velocity of light in relativity is a postulate introduced by Einstein not a conclusion which the theory provides. There may exist forms of matter which can travel faster than light!

Nevertheless, the postulate that the maximum velocity encountered in the universe is *c*, logically developed, leads to remarkable conclusions. For instance: if you walk from tail to nose of an aircraft at 4 m.p.h. and the plane is receding from me at 300 m.p.h., then you recede from me at 304 m.p.h. "Common sense", Newton, and Einstein would all agree on this. But if you could walk at 0·25*c* and the plane moved at 0·5*c*, the Newtonian mechanics would give your recession speed as 0·75*c*, whereas Einsteinian relativity would give about 0·67*c*. Although at the everyday speed of 300 m.p.h., the disagreement, though present in principle, is absolutely negligible, at speeds near that of light it becomes very pronounced. Many experiments show that the relativity answer is right.

Equivalence of Mass and Energy

The most famous consequence of relativity theory from which we derive benefit is the knowledge that mass can be converted into energy. The amount of energy, E, which can be derived from a given mass, m, of any type of material is given by the celebrated equation $E = mc^2$. If we take one gram of ash and convert it into the free energy of which it is composed we would get 10^8 kilowatts of power, sufficient to heat 15 houses for a year. The heat provided by the material which produced the ash is equivalent to that obtained from burning a single match. The massive energy released by $E = mc^2$ has been demonstrated in the power of nuclear weapons, but this energy has also been put to peaceful uses in nuclear-powered electricity generating stations.

In fundamental particle physics the masses of particles were always expressed in units of mass energy using $E = mc^2$ as the conversion equation. This is a matter of convenience from the realisation that mass is simply a condensed form of energy. The mesons which are the force-exchanging particles in the strong interaction have a mass energy of approximately 130 MeV, which is equivalent to a real mass of only 210^{-26} grams. The energy of the sun is provided by the conversion of real mass into light energy through thermonuclear fusion processes.

Mass and Rest Mass

The concept of mass is not a simple idea to grasp, for as we have seen, the mass of a body which is at rest is equivalent to its inherent latent energy. Further complications and interpretations arise when the body starts moving and its mass is no longer necessarily a constant quantity.

A stationary body can be observed to have a mass called its *rest mass*. If the body moves, it has energy of motion and therefore, according to Einstein's mass–energy equation, it increases its mass. Mass thus depends on speed, but in such a way that there is very little change unless the speed approaches that of light. Many experiments on atomic particles demonstrate this. The interesting question now arises: do all fundamental particles have rest mass? or do some have mass derived solely from their energy? The answer appears to be that photons and neutrinos have no rest mass; all other particles have. The Table on **F16** gives their rest masses.

Special Theory of Relativity

The mathematical development of Einstein's ideas, leading to the conclusions just referred to, constitutes the Special Theory of Relativity.

Stated more generally, the theory raises the question whether two observers in uniform relative motion could ever detect, as a result of their relative speed, any difference in the physical laws governing matter, motion, and light. To this, Special Relativity answers: No. The detailed theory involves special consideration of the results the two observers would obtain when measuring (i) the spatial distance, and (ii) the time interval, between the same two events. It turns out that they would not agree on these two points. They would agree, however, on the value of a certain quantity made up jointly of the spatial distance and the time interval in a somewhat complex combination. The intimate mixture of space and time in this quantity has led to the treatment of the three space dimensions and time on an equivalent footing. Hence the frequent references to time as the "fourth dimension". Minkowski devised an extremely elegant presentation of relativity theory by using an extension of ordinary geometry to four dimensions. A line drawn in his four-dimensional space represents the path of a particle in space and time, *i.e.*, the whole history of the particle. Thus the movement of particles in the ordinary world is turned into the geometry of lines in Minkowski's four-dimensional world of "space–time".

General Relativity and Gravitation

In 1915, 10 years after the publication of the Special Theory of Relativity, Einstein published his theory of General Relativity. This apparently innocuous extension of the ideas of special relativity to include accelerated relative motion opened up new and difficult fields of mathematical complexity which, when solved, enabled Einstein to include gravitation in the theory. In discussing the physics of atomic, nuclear, and subnuclear particles, we did not include the effect of the gravitational force, since in relation to the Electric, Weak, Strong, and Colour forces it is extremely small and can be neglected in the discussion of the structure of matter but not in the discussion of astronomical problems and the movements of large-scale electrically uncharged bodies.

It has been usual, ever since Newton, to say that two bodies of mass m_1 and m_2, separated by a distance r attract one another with a force proportional to $m_1 m_2 / r^2$. This is Newton's inverse square law of gravitation which explains the movements of planets and comets and the falling to earth of an apple from a tree.

The apple's fall is accelerated, and we observe this by noting its position relative to certain marks fixed with respect to us, and by timing it with some sort of clock. This system of location in space and time may be called our "frame of reference". We therefore assert that, in our frame of reference, the apple falls down with an acceleration which Newton saw no alternative but to attribute to a thing called gravitational attraction. Galileo had shown that *all* bodies fall with the same acceleration at all points, and we can now rephrase this by saying that in our frame of reference there is a constant gravitational attraction or *uniform gravitational field*. (This last statement and Galileo's demonstration only refer strictly to points fairly near the earth's surface; at greater distances the gravitational field decreases and is therefore not uniform.)

Now suppose a collection of falling bodies is observed by us and an intelligent creature, designated C, inhabits one of them. C has his own frame of reference fixed relative to him and we have ours fixed relative to us. In C's frame neither his own body, nor any of the others, is accelerated, and therefore he has no reason to suppose a gravitational force is acting on them. We have, therefore, the following situation:

(i) in our frame, fixed relative to us, we find all the bodies falling subject to a gravitational pull;

(ii) in C's frame, undergoing accelerated fall relative to us, no gravitational field is apparent to C.

It looks, therefore, as if one has only to choose the correct frame of reference for the measurements in order to remove the need for any assumptions about the existence of gravitational fields. This is a simple illustration of the connection between gravitation and frames of reference for the measurement of space and time. Einstein's General Theory of Relativity extends this to cover non-uniform gravitational fields and shows that what Newton taught us to call the gravitational field of material bodies is better thought of as a peculiarity of the space and time in the neighbourhood of such bodies. Since space-time, as we mentioned above, can be expressed in geometrical terms, Einstein has transformed the theory of gravitation into an exercise (a difficult one) in the geometry of space-time. Other physicists, in Einstein's tradition, are trying to turn *all* physics into geometry, but no one knows whether this is really feasible.

All this abstruse work is much more than a demonstration of mathematical power and elegance. Observable phenomena which fall outside the scope of Newton's theory of gravitation are accounted for by relativity. One is the small but definite discrepancy between the actual orbit of the planet Mercury and the predictions of Newton's theory. Another is the effect of a gravitational field on the wavelength of light emitted by atoms. Similar atoms in different places in a gravitational field emit radiations with slightly different wavelengths. For example, the light from an atom in the intense field of a star should have slightly longer wavelength than the corresponding light from an atom on earth. This effect has always proved very difficult to detect with certainty. However, Einstein's prediction was verified in 1960 by a very subtle method which was purely terrestrial in its operation. The atoms being compared were placed at the top and bottom of a water tower and the difference in their emission was detected by means that belong rather to nuclear physics than to astronomy.

Quantum Theory and Relativity Combined

The atomic family table refers to "antiparticles". The theory which first introduced such things in 1934 is due to the Cambridge physicist Dirac and was epoch-making. Dirac conceived an equation to describe the motion of electrons subject to the laws of both quantum theory and relativity. His achievement was thus to synthesise these two great ideas. The spin of the electron was originally a supposition that helped to make sense of spectroscopic observations of light emitted from atoms. Dirac's equation made spin a logical consequence of the union of relativity and quantum theory. Perhaps even more important was the brilliant inference that the equation for the electron implied the existence of another particle having the same mass and spin but with a positive instead of a negative electric charge. This object is called the electron's anti-particle and is now well known as a positron.

Every particle is now believed to imply an anti-particle, so it is conceivable that the universe could have been (but isn't) an anti-universe, i.e., all the electrons and protons might have been positrons and antiprotons and so on. The laws of physics would still have been applicable, however.

The gravitational force has an infinite range and therefore its force-carrying particles must travel at the speed of light. The graviton is the name of the particle which transmits the gravitational force between bodies with mass. To date (1999) no experiment has detected the existence of gravitons which are the postulated quanta of gravitational waves. There is an exact analogy between photons, the quanta of electro-magnetic radiation, and gravitons.

Conservation Laws

If charged particles interact, then it is found that the amount of electric charge existing after the reaction is the same as that which existed before the event. This is called the law of the conservation of charge. Many other conservation laws exist in physics, e.g., conservation of mass energy, angular momentum, linear momentum, and other more abstruse conservation laws exist in particle physics, e.g., conservation of baryons, leptons, strangeness, isotopic spin, and parity. The last three conservation laws listed have been found to have a limited jurisdiction, and the violation of parity in the weak interaction was a great surprise to physicists.

Any reader who looks in a mirror knows that the left- and right-hand sides of his face are interchanged in the image. Fortunately mirrors do not also turn the image upside down, but, if they did, the face would then have undergone what is called "a parity transformation". A screwdriver driving a right-handed screw downwards becomes, on parity transformation, a screwdriver driving a left-handed screw upwards. The law of conservation of parity is a way of asserting that any physical process that goes on in the world could equally well go on—obeying the same laws—in a parity transformed world. There is nothing left-handed that does not in principle have a right-handed counterpart.

For many years this belief was strongly held. It came as something of a shock when, in 1957, after theoretical proposals by Lee and Yang in America, Wu and co-workers proved that parity was not always conserved. To understand Wu's experiment, we must recall that nuclei can have intrinsic spin. Suppose the axis of spin were downwards into the page and the rotation were suitable for driving an ordinary screw into the page. Then Wu showed that beta-rays from such a nucleus are emitted *preferentially upwards, i.e.,* against the direction of travel of the screw. The parity transformed version of this would have the beta-rays preferentially emitted in the same direction as the travel of the screw and, if parity is conserved, this process would happen too. But it does not. If the beta-rays in the experiment had been emitted in equal numbers up and down, then the parity transformed version would have had this feature too, and thus parity would have been conserved.

A reprieve for the standard model came when P symmetry was combined with a transformation of charge. But when this new CP symmetry was also found to break down, scientists were forced back to their accelerators to search for either another patch to, or an alternative for, the standard model.

Conclusion

Over a century's development of the atomic ideas has brought a progressive, if jerky, increase in the mathematical precision of the theories. In some fields of particle physics, observations to one part in a million, or even better, can be explained, to that level of accuracy, by the existing theories. At the same time, however, the theories have lost visual definition. An atom as an invisible but none the less solid billiard ball was easy enough; so was a light wave conceived like a sound wave in air. Even after Rutherford, an atom consisting of a miniature solar system merely exchanged the solid billiard ball for a system of revolving billiard balls and was no great obstacle to visualisation. But since quantum theory and the Uncertainty Principle, every unambiguous visualisation of fundamental wave-particles leaves out half the picture, and although the electrons are in the atom, we can no longer represent them in definite orbits. The moral seems to be that visualisation is unnecessary, or at best a partial aid to thought.

THE PROPERTIES OF MATTER IN BULK

One of the most obvious and at the same time most wonderful things about the properties of matter is their great variety. Think of air, diamond, mercury, rubber, snow, gold, pitch, asbestos. . . . Even the differences of state of the same chemical substance are remarkable enough, ice, water, and steam, for example. One of the aims of physics is to reach an understanding of all these different properties by explaining them in terms of the behaviour of the particles discussed in the previous section (**F10–19**). The widespread success with which this imposing programme has been carried out indicates the maturity of physics. It is difficult to think of any major property of matter in bulk for which there is not some attempted theoretical explanation, though future physicists will no doubt regard some present-day theories as rudimentary or incorrect.

Physics, Statistics, and Thermodynamics

Take a number equal to the population of London, multiply it by itself, and multiply the product by another million. The answer is about the number of molecules in 1 cubic centimetre of ordinary air. They are constantly moving about and colliding with one another. Even if the nature of the molecules and their laws of motion were perfectly understood, it would clearly be impracticable to calculate the exact paths described by each particle of so vast an assembly. This difficulty brought into being a whole branch of physics concerned with calculating the overall or average properties of large numbers of particles. Just as statisticians will provide the average height, income, expectation of life, and so on, of the population of London, without knowing everything about every individual, so statistical physicists can work out average properties of molecules or atoms in large groups. This important branch of physics is called *Statistical Mechanics*. It was founded in the nineteenth century by Maxwell, Boltzmann, and Gibbs and is still being actively developed.

Consider now all the molecules in 1 cubic centimetre of air contained in a small box. They are continually bombarding the walls of the box and bouncing off. This hail of impacts (it is actually about 10^{23} impacts per square centimetre per second) is the cause of the pressure which the gas exerts against the walls of the box. Now suppose we pump air in until there is twice as much as before, though the box is still the same size and at the same temperature. This means that the density of the gas (*i.e.*, the mass of 1 unit of volume) has doubled. We should now expect twice as many impacts per second on the walls as before, and consequently twice the pressure. We therefore arrive at a conclusion that, if the volume and temperature are constant, the pressure of a gas is proportional to its density. This is one of the simplest statistical arguments that can be checked against observation; in fact, it stands the test very well.

Heat, Temperature, and Energy

The proviso about the temperature remaining the same is an important one for the following reason. In the nineteenth century there was much discussion about the nature of heat. To Joule we owe the now well-established view that heat is equivalent to mechanical work. In one of his experiments, in the 1840s, the work necessary to rotate paddle wheels against the resistance of water in a tank generated heat that caused a slight rise in the temperature of the water. Joule found out exactly how much work was equivalent to a given quantity of heat. However, one can do other things with work besides generate heat; in particular, work creates motion, as when one pushes a car. Bodies in motion possess a special form of energy, called kinetic energy, which is equal to the work done in accelerating them from a state of rest. We have, then, three closely connected ideas: work, heat, and kinetic energy. Now according to the views of the nineteenth century, which are still accepted, any heat given to a gas simply increases the kinetic energy of its molecules; the hotter the gas, the faster its molecules are moving. If, therefore, the gas in our box is allowed to get hotter, there is an increase in molecular speed, and the impacts on the walls become correspondingly more violent. But this means the pressure increases, so we have another law: if the density remains the same, the pressure increases if the temperature does.

Laws of Thermodynamics

Such considerations as these have been pursued with great elaboration and subtlety. The notions of heat, temperature, energy, and work—familiar but vague in everyday life—have been given precise definitions, and the relations between them have been enshrined in the Laws of Thermodynamics. Enshrined is perhaps a suitable word, because these laws are so soundly and widely based on experimental results that they have greater prestige than any others in physics. If any proposed physical law comes in conflict with thermodynamics then so much the worse for that law—it has to be revised. It is sometimes asserted that no one is properly educated who does not understand the Second Law of thermodynamics. We cannot, therefore, leave this section without at least stating the two best known thermodynamic laws:

First Law: *If any physical system is given a quantity of heat, and if the system performs some work, then the energy of the system increases by an amount equal to the excess of heat given over work done.* This law asserts that heat, energy, and work are convertible one into the other, and that all such transactions balance exactly. This is one form of a principle accepted as fundamental in all science, *viz.*, the Principle of the Conservation of Energy, according to which energy can never be created or destroyed, but only changed from one form to another.

Second Law: *It is impossible to make an engine which will continuously take heat from a heat source and, by itself, turn it all into an equivalent amount of mechanical work.* In fact, all engines which produce work from heat—steam engines for example—always use only a fraction of the heat they take in and give up the rest to some relatively cool part of the machine. The Second Law makes this obligatory on all work-from-heat devices. This statement of the Second Law has an engineering ring about and, indeed, it arose from the work of the nineteenth-century French engineer Carnot. Nevertheless, it can be rephrased in terms of the concept of entropy, and has been applied with unbroken success to all fields of science involving the transfer of heat and allied matters. It sets a definite limit to the kinds of physical and chemical process that can be conceived to take place. Nothing has been known to contravene it.

The States of Matter

The molecular motion in gases has been referred to in the previous section. Tacitly it was assumed that each molecule acted independently of all others, except that collisions occurred between them. In reality, molecules exert attractive forces on one another and, if a gas is cooled so that molecular movements become relatively sluggish, a time comes when the attractive forces succeed in drawing the molecules close together to form a liquid. This process is called condensation.

The molecules in a liquid are packed tightly together and they impede each other's movements. On the other hand, movement still persists, and the molecules struggle about like people in a milling crowd. Besides wandering about, the molecules vibrate. These motions represent the energy contained in the liquid.

The fact that the molecules, though irregularly packed, can still slip past one another and move from place to place, explains the essential property of liquids that distinguishes them from solids—ability to flow. As a matter of fact, although the rather vague assertion that in a liquid molecules are irregularly packed would be generally accepted, there is no agreed opinion on what the irregularity is actually like. Indeed, not only the precise structure of liquids, but the theory of liquids in general, is fraught with such considerable mathematical difficulties that the liquid state is much less well understood than the solid or gaseous.

Most solids are crystals. The popular idea of a crystal is of something which has a more or less regular geometrical form with faces that shut in the light—like snowflakes or gems. However, crystallinity really depends on a regular inner pattern of the atoms, and may or may not show itself on the visible surface. A lump of lead, for example, is crystalline, despite its appearance.

The actual arrangement of the atoms in a crystal can be extremely complex. Some are

F21

quite simple, however. The largest model of a crystal structure must surely be the 400-ft. "Atomium" building in the 1958 Brussels Exhibition. This consisted of eight balls, representing atoms, situated at the corners of a cube, and one more ball exactly in the middle. Imagine this repeated in all directions so that every ball is the centre of a cube whose corners are the eight neighbouring balls. This is known to crystallographers and physicists as the "body-centred cubic structure"; it is the actual arrangement of atoms in iron, sodium, chromium, and some other metals. If every ball, instead of being the centre of a cube, were the centre of a regular tetrahedron (a solid figure with four equal triangular faces), and had its four neighbours at the corners of the tetrahedron, then we should have the "diamond structure". This is how the carbon atoms are arranged in diamonds.

In crystals the atoms are locked into a regular ordered structure by attractive forces which give the solid its rigidity and prevent it from flowing. The atoms are so close together that any attempt to press them closer involves crushing or distorting the atoms—a process they resist strongly. This explains why solids (and liquids too) are so difficult to compress. Gases can easily be compressed because there is so much space between the molecules.

The distinction between solid and liquid is not so sharp as is commonly supposed. A lump of dough will not bounce, but is plastic; a steel ball-bearing is very elastic and bounces excellently, but one cannot mould it in the fingers. Neither dough nor steel qualifies for description as a liquid. There are, however, substances which can be moulded like plasticine into a ball that will then bounce very well on the floor like an elastic solid, and finally, if left on a flat table, will spread into a pool and drip off the edge like a liquid. There is no point in trying to force such things into rigid categories. One may say instead that for short, sharp impacts the material behaves like an elastic solid, but under long-sustained forces it flows like a liquid. The properties of these, and many other anomalous materials, are increasingly engaging the attention of those who study the science of flow—*rheology*. It is interesting to see how many familiar and important materials exhibit peculiar rheological behaviour—paint, dough, ball-pen ink, cheese, unset cement, and solutions of nylon and other plastics are only a few examples.

Inside a Crystalline Solid

We now return to our wallpaper analogy of crystal structure and give some free play to our visual imagination.

Suppose we have walls papered with a regular pattern of, say, roses, fuchsias, and green leaves. These represent the different kinds of atoms in the solid. Careful observation shows that the whole pattern is shimmering. The flowers and leaves are not stationary, but are undergoing slight random oscillations about their proper positions. In a crystal these movements are called thermal vibrations, and are never absent. The hotter the crystal, the more the vibration, and at a high enough temperature the vibrations become so great that the atoms get right out of position and the pattern disappears altogether, *i.e.*, the crystal melts. Thermal vibrations are essential to the theory of solids, and are responsible for numerous physical properties.

Next we note something extraordinary about some of the papered walls. On these the paper has been hung in irregular patches fitted together like a not very well-made jig-saw puzzle. Lines of roses which should be vertical are horizontal in some patches, oblique in others. This represents the situation in most ordinary solids, for they consist of many small pieces of crystal irregularly packed together. Such material is called *poly-crystalline*, and the small pieces are *crystal grains*. Crystal grains may be almost any size, sometimes visible to the naked eye, as often on galvanised iron.

However, on one wall, we see excellent regularity and no obvious patches at all. The physicist would call this a *single crystal*, and several techniques exist for preparing them. Natural single crystals can be found, and there are some beautiful large single crystals of rock salt. But on examining the single crystal wall closely, we find a number of places where the paperhanger has failed to make adjacent pieces register perfectly—there is a slight disjointedness. This occurs in real single crystals, and the line along which the structure fails to register is called a *dislocation*. These are much studied by physicists because of their bearing on the mechanical properties of solids, on the yielding of metals under strong stress, for instance.

This by no means exhausts the possibilities of the wallpaper analogy; several other phenomena can be found. For example, in a place where there should be a fuchsia there is actually a daffodil—something completely foreign to the pattern. Or perhaps a small wrongly shaped leaf is jammed between the proper leaves in a place that should really be blank. These represent chemical impurity atoms. The first is called *substitutional*, because it occupies the position of an atom that should be there, the second is called *interstitial*, because it does not. Substitutional impurities of indium metal, deliberately added to the semi-conductor silicon, make possible the manufacture of transistors (*see* **Section L**). Some steels derive their valuable properties from interstitial carbon atoms within the iron pattern.

What physicists call a vacancy would occur if a flower or leaf were simply missing. Remembering that all the atoms are vibrating, we should not be surprised if occasionally an atom jumps into a neighbouring vacancy if there happens to be one, *i.e.*, the atom and the vacancy change places. Later this may occur again. In the course of time, a rose which was near the ceiling may make its way to the floor by jumping into vacant rose positions when they occur near enough. This process, which the physicist calls *diffusion*, is also analogous to the game in which numbers or letters can be moved about in a flat box because there is one vacant space to permit adjustment. The more vacancies there are in a crystal, the faster diffusion occurs. It is, in fact, very slow in solids, but is nevertheless evidence that apparently quiescent materials are really internally active.

Metals, Electricity, and Heat

There is ample evidence that inside metals there are large numbers of free electrons. To illuminate this statement let us take sodium metal as an example. One single sodium atom has a nucleus with eleven protons; there are therefore eleven electrons in the atom. The outermost one is easily detached, leaving a positively charged sodium ion behind. We may think of these ions arranged in the three-dimensional pattern characteristic of sodium crystals. It is the same as the iron structure previously described. The detached electrons, one per atom, occupy the spaces in between. The usual metaphor is that the structure of ions is permeated by a "gas" of electrons. Like all visualisations of fundamental particles, this must be taken as a rough approximation. The important point is that the electrons in the gas are not bound to individual atoms but may wander freely about the crystal, hindered only by the collisions they make with the vibrating ions.

This is the picture as it appeared to physicists of the first decade of this century, and we can explain many properties of metals with it. Naturally the theory has developed greatly since then, thanks to the great work of Lorentz, Sommerfeld, and Bloch; it now relies heavily on quantum theory, but it is surprising how little violence is done to modern ideas by the simple picture we are using.

The free electrons move randomly in all directions at thousands of miles per hour. If the metal is connected across a battery it experiences an electric field. Electrons are negatively charged particles, and are therefore attracted to the electrically positive end of the metal. They can move through the metal because they are free; this flow is not possible to those electrons which remain bound to the ions. The function of the battery is to keep the flow going and, for as long as it is going, it is the electric current.

The flow of electrons is not unimpeded. They

constantly collide with the ions and are deflected from the path of flow. This hindrance is what the electrician calls *electrical resistance*. The electric force, due to the battery or a dynamo, accelerates the electrons, thus giving them extra energy; but they lose this to the ions at collisions because the ions recoil and vibrate more than before. The net effect of innumerable collisions is to increase the thermal vibrations of the ions, *i.e.*, to make the metal hotter. This is the explanation of the fact well known to every user of electric irons; that electric current heats the conductor. If a strong current is passed through a wire, the heating is so great the wire glows, as in electric-light bulbs, or melts and breaks, as in blown fuses.

If one end of a metal rod is heated we soon feel the heat at the other end; metals are excellent thermal conductors. This is because the mobile free electrons carry the heat energy down the rod, passing it on to the ions by colliding with them. Substances without free electrons cannot do this, nor can they conduct electricity well; we have, in the free electrons, an explanation of the fact that the good electrical conductors are the good heat conductors. For technical purposes, it would be useful to have electrical insulators that would conduct heat well, and *vice versa*; but this is almost a contradiction in terms, and one can only compromise.

Non-conductors and Semi-conductors

There are some elements, and numerous compounds in which all the electrons are so tightly bound to their parent atoms that free electron flow is impossible. These materials are electrical and thermal insulators.

Let us return to our sodium atom. It readily loses its outer electron, forming a positive ion. The ion is very stable; indeed, its electron arrangement resembles the "closed shell" belonging to the inert gas neon. The chlorine atom, on the other hand, would have a very stable structure, resembling the inert gas argon, if only it could be given one extra electron to complete the closed shell. If the outer sodium electron were given to a chlorine atom we should have two stable ions, one positive and one negative. These would then attract each other and form a compound. This is just how common salt, sodium chloride, is formed, and its crystals consist of a regular network of alternate sodium and chlorine ions. As all the electrons are bound to ions, it is not surprising that salt will not conduct electricity or heat to any appreciable extent. Not all insulating compounds are built on this pattern, but all have structures which bind the electrons tightly.

We have seen (**F20**) that Nature does not permit a hard-and-fast distinction between solids and liquids; nor does she between conductors and insulators. Over a hundred years ago, Faraday knew of substances which would conduct electricity, but rather badly. A common one is the graphite in pencils. Others are the elements selenium, germanium, and silicon, and a considerable number of compounds. Such substances are called semi-conductors.

Semi-conductors conduct badly because they have so few free electrons, many thousands of times fewer than metals. In very cold germanium—say, 200 degrees below freezing—all the electrons are tightly bound to atoms and the substance is an insulator. It differs from normal insulators in that, on warming it, the gradually increasing thermal vibration of the crystal detaches some of the electrons, for they are only moderately tightly bound. The warmer the crystal becomes, the more of its electrons become detached and the better it conducts electricity. By about the temperature of boiling water, there are so many freed electrons that conduction is moderately good, though less good than in metals. This is basic semi-conductor behaviour. Because transistors were made of germanium, and because they are of such great technical importance, more knowledge has accumulated about germanium than about any other material. *See also* **Transistor, Section L.**

Magnetism

The most important thing about magnetism is that it is inseparably connected with electricity. Oersted showed this in July 1820, when he deflected a magnetic compass needle by passing an electric current through a wire near it. Since then, many experiments have shown that wherever a current flows there will certainly be a magnetic field in the surrounding space. The laws of this are very well known now—they are the Maxwell equations previously referred to (**F14**). However, most people first meet magnetism when, as children, they pick up pins with a magnet. Where is the electricity here? and what is a magnet?

The explanation of magnetism exemplifies beautifully the technique of explaining the bulk properties of matter in terms of fundamental particles. In the atoms the electrons are moving, and a moving electric charge constitutes an electric current. Therefore each moving electron is a tiny source of magnetism. It does not immediately follow that every atom is a source of magnetism because it might—and often does—happen that the magnetic effect of different electrons in the atom cancel out. In helium atoms, for example, the two electrons have equal but opposed magnetic effects. Nevertheless, some atoms and ions have a net effect called their *magnetic moment*. This simply means they behave like tiny magnets. Crystals containing such atoms will be magnetic, though the magnetism is much weaker than in ordinary magnets because the different atoms largely annul one another's effects. In a very limited number of crystals, however, the magnetic ions act on one another in a special way which forces all the atomic magnets to point in the same direction. The total effect of many co-operating atoms is very strong and the crystal becomes what we normally call a magnet. Iron acts like this, so do cobalt and nickel, the rarer elements gadolinium and dysprosium, and a fair number of alloys. On the whole, this behaviour, which is called *ferromagnetism*, is very rare. The reason for the co-operation of all the atomic magnets is not explained to everyone's satisfaction yet, though the key idea was given by Heisenberg in 1928.

In the section dealing with the electron it was pointed out that every electron has an *intrinsic* magnetic moment. This is in addition to any effect simply due to the electron's motion round a nucleus. The net effects of ions are therefore partly due to the intrinsic magnetism of electrons. In the ferromagnetic metals the latter is by far the most important contribution. Thus we pick up pins and, benefit from magnets in other ways, because innumerable fundamental particles act in co-operation for reasons that are still somewhat obscure. It is interesting to ask whether the electrons responsible for magnetism are the same free electrons that allow the metals to conduct electricity. It is thought not.

We are accustomed to think of magnets as metallic. Actually the magnet originally discovered by the Chinese was the mineral lodestone, which is a non-metallic oxide of iron. Nowadays a number of non-metallic magnets are made. They are called *ferrites*, and some are insulators and some are semi-conductors. The combination of magnetism and insulation is technically very valuable in radio, radar, and other applications. The explanation of ferrite behaviour is related to that of metallic ferromagnetism, but is not the same.

Conclusion

The aim of the second part of this account of physics is to show how our conception of fundamental particles allows us to build theories of the properties of matter. This very aim shows that the two "major divisions" of physics referred to at the beginning (**F10**) are divided only in the way that labour is divided by co-operating workers to lighten the task. For the task of physics is a very great one—no less than to explain the behaviour of matter; and since the universe, living and inanimate, is made of matter, physics must necessarily underlie all the other sciences.

III. THE WORLD OF THE CHEMISTS

WHAT CHEMISTRY IS ABOUT

Chemistry is the scientific study of the preparation, composition and architecture of chemical compounds, and of the modes and mechanisms of their transformations or reactions. Natural (and other) processes can be classified as *physical*, in which no chemical reactions occur, for example water running down a hill, and *chemical* if changes occur in the chemical compounds involved. Common examples are the burning of fuel, whether in a biological cell, an internal combustion engine, or a lowly domestic grate. Biological changes at the molecular level in plants and animals generally consist of many chemical reactions, as do some geological changes in rocks and deposits. Chemistry therefore is rooted in physics and interpenetrates biology (biochemistry) and geology (geochemistry). Some of the main sub-divisions of chemistry are delineated in the Table. Chemists not only aim to discover new reactions by trial and error, but by seeking to understand chemical change aspire to design new compounds and reactions. New reactions can be used to produce useful physical *effects* in new ways—like light from the cold chemical candle (chemiluminescence) as the firefly does, and electricity from more efficient batteries and from fuel cells—or to produce new *synthetic products*. These can be faithful copies of compounds like penicillin which have been discovered first in nature, or completely new, invented, compounds like the sulphonamide drugs.

This research activity, which is mainly centred in the Universities, is the basis of a large chemical industry, one of the major manufacturing industries. Other branches which deal with more restrictive topics or use combinations of the above for specific goals have names which are self-explanatory, for example:—analytical chemistry, colloid chemistry, pharmaceutical chemistry, chemistry of dyes, petroleum chemistry, polymer chemistry, environmental chemistry, medicinal chemistry.

Main Divisions of Chemistry

	Elements, Compounds and reactions involved	Examples
Organic Chemistry	Carbon in combination mainly with H, O, N.	Natural products Carbohydrates Steroids Proteins
Inorganic Chemistry	All elements and compounds not covered in organic chemistry. Minerals and salts.	Inorganic polymers (e.g., silicones) Transition metal complexes Organometallic compounds
Physical Chemistry	Mathematical and physical descriptions of organic and inorganic compounds and reactions.	Electrochemistry Chemical thermodynamics Molecular spectroscopy Photochemistry
Biochemistry	The chemistry of biological systems	Enzymes Biosynthesis.

ELEMENTS AND COMPOUNDS

Elements

The reader will find a description of the formation of chemical elements in Part I (**F6**). They are listed alphabetically in the Table of Elements (with their chemical symbols) and in order of atomic number (*see* **F11**) in the Periodic Table. Other details may be found in Section L. They vary widely in natural abundance terrestrially. In the earth's crust the most abundant elements are oxygen (O), silicon (Si), aluminium (Al), and iron (Fe). Our familiarity with them varies too, not only because of the rarity of some (thulium, Tm, and radium, Ra) and the artificiality of a few (plutonium, Pu) but because we meet some only in combination with other elements and not in their elemental state, for example, fluorine (F) in fluorides. The most familiar non-metallic elements besides oxygen and nitrogen are probably gaseous molecular states (O_2 and N_2) are probably carbon (C), as graphite (or diamond!) and sulphur (S). Among the metallic elements most people know aluminium (Al), tin (Sn) and lead (Pb) from the main groups of the Periodic Table, and the transition metals: iron (Fe), chromium (Cr), nickel (Ni) as well as copper (Cu) and the precious metals silver (Ag), gold (Au) and platinum (Pt). Increasingly familiar because of their use in semi-conductors are the metalloids silicon (Si) and germanium (Ge).

Compounds

Most terrestrial matter as we know it can be classified in terms of the chemical compounds it contains, *i.e.*, is a mixture of compounds. Each compound consists of chemical elements in combination, the relative amount of each being characteristic and definite (Law of Constant Composition). Compounds vary not only in the number of elements combined but also in their proportions: carbon dioxide has twice as much oxygen per carbon as carbon monoxide (*see* atoms and molecules).

The properties of a compound can be, and normally are, very different from the properties of the elements it contains, a fact not commonly recognised in the popular imagination, witness phrases like—"it's good for you, it's got iron in it". This does not mean that elemental metallic iron is present but rather that some seemingly beneficial compound of iron is present. The ambiguity is that although iron is essential to human life in the form of haemoglobin in the blood, it also can form highly poisonous compounds. Similarly arsenic (As), although notoriously poisonous as the element and in some of its compounds, was nevertheless contained in one of the first chemotherapeutic drugs ever produced, salvarsan. The point can be further illustrated with sodium chloride, a water-soluble white crystalline solid, which is a compound of the very reactive metal sodium (capable of reacting violently with water), and of chlorine (known as a poisonous green gas). Similarly diamond (a particular elemental form, or allotrope, of carbon) is one of the hardest known substances but may be combined with hydrogen (the highly inflammable gas which can combine with oxygen gas to give water), to give thousands of different derivatives which include benzene (a liquid), methane (a gas) and various hydrocarbon waxes and polishes.

ATOMS AND MOLECULES

Atoms vary in weight, structure and size from one element to the next (*see* **Part II, F10**). Molecules are made from whole numbers of atoms in combination. A particular molecule is characterised by the number of atoms of each of its constituent elements. It has a characteristic weight called its *molecular weight* (the sum of the weights of the atoms in it), and a characteristic three dimensional structure (*see below*).

An aggregate of molecules of the same type is a chemical compound, so that the molecule is to a compound as the atom is to an element.

The Mole

It is frequently very useful to know when the amounts of two compounds are the same, not in terms of their masses but in terms of the number of molecules each contains, since chemical reactions occur at the molecular level and involve small relative numbers of molecules of the reacting species at each step. Avogadro (*see* **B5**) suggested that equal volumes of gases under identical conditions contained equal molecular numbers (*see* **L12**) and it followed that if the weights of two substances were in the ratio of their relative molecular masses (molecular weights) then they too contained equal numbers of molecules. The approximate molecular weights of water (H_2O) and ethanol or ethylalcohol (C_2H_5OH) are 18 and 46 respectively and so 18 g of water for example contain the same number of molecules as 46 g of ethanol.

The amount of substance referred to in each case is called 1 mole. For any compound the weight of 1 mole is equal to the gramme molecular weight. Molecular weights (or relative molecular masses) are now referred to the carbon-12 atomic scale (*see* **F10**). The modern definition of the mole therefore is that it is the amount of substance which contains the same number of elementary particles as there are atoms in twelve grammes of carbon-12. This number, called Avogadro's number, is $6.022\,169 \times 10^{23}$.

Molecular Structure and Isomers

Modern spectroscopic and diffraction methods have enabled the details of molecular structures to be accurately determined not only with respect to the distances between atoms (normally in the range 1–5 Å", *i.e.*, 100–150 pm for adjacent atoms) and the angles which define the structure, but also with respect to the various internal motions (vibrations and rotations).

Sometimes two (or more) different compounds have the same molecular weight (and are called, therefore, *isomers*) but have different molecular structures in which the same atoms are arranged in different relative positions, and hence have different properties. If two isomeric structures are related as left and right hands are related, the isomers are stereoisomers of a particular class called enantiomers. An example is glucose. Even such subtle variation as this produces differences in properties which can be crucial in biological function or drug metabolism.

A familiar simple example of *structural* isomers are ethylalcohol (or ethanol) and dimethyl ether of formula C_2H_6O. They each can be represented by the structural formulae

$$CH_3-CH_2-OH \text{ and } \begin{matrix} CH_3 \\ O \\ CH_3 \end{matrix}$$

in which the lines represent some of the *covalent chemical bonds* (*see below*). It is these interatomic forces which hold the atoms in specific spatial arrangements. Some examples are shown in Fig. 1.

CHEMICAL BONDING

The number of possible arrangements of a given set of atoms is limited since each type of atom (each element) is capable of forming only a limited number of bonds, equal to its *valency*. The valency varies from element to element; hydrogen has a valency of one (exceptionally two); oxygen, two; nitrogen, three; and carbon four (hence the molecular formulae H_2, H_2O, NH_3 and CH_4 for hydrogen, water, ammonia and methane respectively).

In some compounds two atoms may be joined by a *multiple bond* so that the valency number may be reached. Examples are the double and triple bonds in ethylene (ethene) and acetylene (ethyne) respectively:

$$CH_2 = CH_2 \text{ and } CH \equiv CH$$

The modern theory of chemical bonding is electronic. Bonds are formed:

(i) by the sharing of electrons in pairs between two bonded atoms (*covalent* bonding); or

(ii) by the transfer of an electron from one atom to another to form oppositely charged ions (*ionic* bonding).

The ionic situation is electrically *polar* whereas pure covalent bonds have no polarity. If, however, the shared electrons are not shared equally between the bound atoms some effective electron transfer occurs and the bond has some polar character. Covalent bonds between *dissimilar* atoms are generally polar. If one of the two atoms provides *both* the shared electrons, the polarity is particularly high and the bond is called *dative covalent*.

VALENCIES OF THE ELEMENTS

Electronic Theory of Valency

These ideas of the chemical bond lead to a ready explanation of the valencies of the elements (which are periodic if the elements are arranged in order of atomic number) when combined with knowledge of the electronic structure of atoms.

In the original Bohr theory the electrons of atoms move in well defined orbits arranged in shells. The known elements use seven shells, and each element has its unique number of electrons equal to the atomic number, Z ranging from 1 in hydrogen to 103 in lawrencium. Each element also has its unique arrangement of its electrons in these shells. The build-up of electrons in the above sequence follows well-defined rules. The resulting electron configuration of the elements is an important starting point for a discussion of valency. The shells each have a limited capacity and the numbers of electrons that can be accommodated in the first four labelled 1, 2, 3, 4 (or sometimes K, L, M, N) are 2, 8, 18, 32 respectively. Each of these shells has sub-shells of which there are four main types designated s, p, d and f which can contain 2, 6, 10 and 14 electrons respectively. If all the orbits in a shell have electrons actually present in them the shell is filled or closed and this confers on the shell an unusual stability or inertness. Conversely, unfilled shells lead to activity and the electrons in the incompletely filled shells largely determine the chemical and physical properties of the element and are responsible for the combination of atoms to form molecules. These electrons are referred to as *valence electrons*. The inner shell, *i.e.*, the one nearest the nucleus, can accommodate only two electrons (the element helium has just that number) and the next two shells can hold eight each. Large atoms, *e.g.*, lead, radium, have many filled shells and, subject to special exceptions, the general rule is that the inner shells are the filled ones and the outer shell may be incomplete. Elements which have equal numbers of electrons in their outer shell resemble each other and come in the same Group of the Periodic Table. Thus the elements with complete electronic shells are chemically unreactive gases, *e.g.*, argon and neon (minor constituents of the atmosphere). Elements with just one electron in the outer shell are highly reactive metals, *e.g.*, sodium and potassium which lose this electron readily to give monopositive ions, *e.g.*, Na^-. These elements are called electropositive. Contrariwise elements with just one electron too few are electronegative and readily gain one electron either by sharing, or by capture (to form anions, *e.g.*, Cl^-).

More generally, at least for the light elements of Periods 2 and 3 of the Periodic Table, the valence of an element is given by the Group Number, N, *i.e.*, the number of valence electrons which must be lost by the electropositive metals, or by $8-N$, the number of electrons which electronegative elements need to gain.

The covalence of an electronegative element is increased by one if it loses one electron to form a positive ion, and decreased by one if it gains an electron. Thus nitrogen with a covalence 3 can give either N^- which can form 4 covalent bonds (in the ammonium ion, NH_4^-) or the N^- ion with

Valence Electrons (N) and Valency (V)

N = 1	2	3	4	5	6	7	8
V = 1	2	3	4	3	2	1	0
Hydrogen Sodium Potassium	Magnesium Calcium Barium	Aluminium Gallium	Carbon Silicon Germanium Tin Lead	Nitrogen Phosphorus Arsenic	Oxygen Sulphur	Fluorine Chlorine Bromine Iodine	Helium Neon Argon

$\longleftarrow$——Metals——$\longrightarrow$ $\longleftarrow$——————$\longrightarrow$ Non-metals:
  Positive ions   Covalent   Negative ions
                            compounds   or covalent compounds

a covalency of 2 (*e.g.*, NH_2^-). Similarly oxygen can give H_3O^-, the hydroxonium ion (the acid principle in water), H_2O (water itself), and OH^- (the hydroxyl ion).

IONIC BONDS, SALTS AND ACIDS

These bonds are normally formed between electropositive elements (at the left of the Periodic Table, *e.g.*, sodium and potassium) and electronegative elements (at the right of the Periodic Table, *e.g.*, oxygen, fluorine, chlorine). The ionic charge may be determined from the valency: Na^+, Mg^{++}, Al^{+++}; O^-, Cl^-.

Ions may contain a number of atoms, as shown by many of the common anions: hydroxyl, OH^-; nitrate, NO_3^-; sulphate, SO_4^-; carbonate CO_3^-. Ionic solids formed from a metal ion and one of these anions are called *salts* and are derived from the parent *acid* in which the anion is bound to a *hydrogen ion* (or ions): HNO_3, nitric acid; H_2SO_4, sulphuric acid. Sulphuric acid can form two series of salts, one called *normal* based upon the SO_4^{--} ion and a second (called acid salts since they contain a hydrogen) based upon the HSO_4^- ion. Phosphoric acid, H_3PO_4, has three series of salts. A substance which reacts with an acid to form a salt and water as the only products is called a *base*. An example is sodium hydroxide, NaOH (caustic soda). The Lewis definitions of acid and base are given below.

The ionic forces are less directional in character than covalent bonds are, but in solids the ions are in regular fixed arrangements (*see* **Part II**). Each anion is surrounded by cations and is attracted to them by electrostatic Coulomb forces. These are of long range and so the anion is attracted not only to the closest cations. Additionally each cation is surrounded by anions so that the bonding is not localised. The whole solid therefore is like a giant molecule and is not easily broken down by melting. This contrasts with covalent compounds in which the forces between molecules are small, the main attractions being within the molecule.

The structures adopted depend upon the relative numbers of the anions and cations (which are determined by ionic charges) and by the relative ionic sizes, which have been deduced from X-ray diffraction measurements.

COVALENT BONDS

In the simple theory the shared electron pairs are localised between two atoms. Multiple bonds result when there are more pairs shared. The multiplicity (or *bond order*) is then integral. The theory may be extended by admitting that an electron pair may be shared between more than two atoms in *delocalised bonding* which can then give rise to fractional bond orders. The best example is benzene (and graphite) where nine pairs of electrons are shared between six carbon-carbon bonds giving a bond order of 1·5.

Modern Theories

Modern theories of valency make use of the concepts of quantum mechanics (*see* **F17**) in which each of the well-defined electron orbits of the s, p, d and f electrons in the Bohr theory is replaced by the idea of the electron cloud with a spatial electron density and distribution. Each of these electron clouds (now called an orbital) has a definite shape depending upon the type of electrons. The orbitals of s electrons are of spherical shape with a density that falls off with the distance from the nucleus. The peak density occurs at the old Bohr radius. Electrons of the p type have orbitals with double lobes giving the figure of eight or dumbell shape. There are three such orbitals in every shell except the first and they are arranged mutually at right angles. Each one can contain two electrons giving a total of six. The d orbitals are five in number. Each again can contain two electrons giving a total of ten. Four of these d orbitals have shapes like four-leaf clovers, whereas the fifth has two lobes, rather like the p orbitals but with the addition of a torus or doughnut. The shapes of the f orbitals are even more complicated. It is the shape of these orbitals and their relative spatial arrangement which gives the covalent bond its directional character. The idea of electron sharing between two atoms becomes the result of overlap of an orbital on one atom with an orbital on another to give a bonding *molecular orbital* which can contain the pair of shared electrons. The bond energy is a maximum when this overlap is optimum and this occurs when the atoms are in certain definite positions thus giving the molecule its own characteristic shape.

Molecular shape

For elements from the second row of the Periodic Table the number of electrons in the valence shell can be eight arranged in four pairs of orbitals (one 2s and three 2p orbitals). These orbitals can be combined or *hybridised* to give the basic tetrahedral shape (*see* Fig. 1). Each of these can overlap with say an orbital of a hydrogen atom (the 1s) to give a bonding orbital which can accommodate two electrons. Alternatively each orbital can, if the atom has enough electrons, contain two non-bonding electrons called a *lone pair*. The basic molecular shapes of methane (CH_4), ammonia (NH_3), and water (H_2O) may then be rationalised as in Fig. 1.

The bond angle in methane is the tetrahedral angle (109° 28'). The angles in ammonia (107° 18') and water (104° 30') are smaller probably because the lone pair orbital is slightly more repulsive than the bonding orbital is. This closes down the angles between the bonds.

The lone pairs may be used to bind the hydrogen ions from acids to give tetrahedral NH_4^- and pyramidal H_3O^-. It is the lone pairs therefore which give ammonia and water their basicity. In the modern concept of acids and bases due to Lewis, a base is an electron donor and an acid becomes an electron acceptor. This definition of an acid includes the older idea of it as a hydrogen ion producer in that the hydrogen ion is an electron acceptor but it is more general—a Lewis acid need not be a protic acid.

Bond Lengths

Many covalent bond distances have been measured

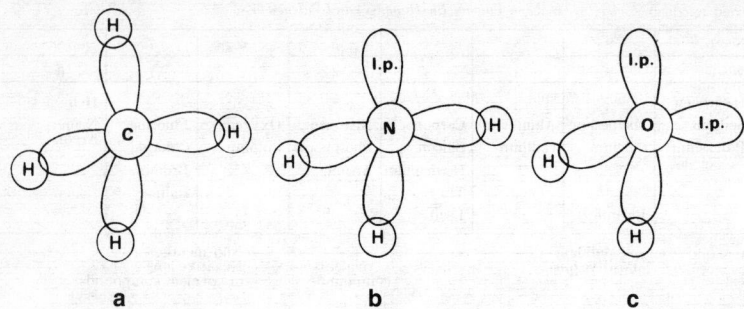

Fig. 1. The spatial arrangements of the atoms and orbitals in (a) methane (CH_4), (b) ammonia (NH_3) and (c) water (H_2O). The basic shape is tetrahedral and the hybridised orbitals are lone pair orbitals (l.p.) and bonding orbitals.

and each may be apportioned between the bound atoms to give a self-consistent set of covalent bond-radii for each element which can be used in predictions of molecular structures. These radii vary inversely with the bond order involved. Thus the carbon-carbon bond length varies from 154 pm (*i.e.*, 10^{12}m) for C–C to 135 pm for C=C.

Bond Energies

Bonds differ in their strength depending upon the atoms and the bond order. A double bond between two given atoms is stronger than a single bond but generally not as strong as two single bonds. Thus "unsaturated" compounds, which contain multiple bonds, will tend to form "saturated" compounds containing only single bonds since the energetics are favourable.

Functional Groups

Compounds may be further classified according to certain persistent groups of atoms which have a residual valency and can combine with other groups. Thus the methyl group (CH_3) related to methane (CH_4) by the removal of a hydrogen atom can combine with other atoms or groups of valency one: methyl chloride (chloromathane), CH_3Cl; methyl alcohol (methanol), CH_3OH; dimethyl ether, CH_3OCH_3. Common functional groups are shown in the table.

CHEMICAL ENERGETICS

Chemical reactions are accompanied by energy changes which can be utilised as heat (in fires) or mechanical work (in explosions or rockets), or to produce electric current in batteries. Chemical compounds can therefore be said to store energy and to possess "internal energy." The energy can be thought of as being stored in the chemical bonds. The energy change (at constant volume) in a reaction is then a result of changes (denoted ΔU) in the nett internal energy of the reactants and products by the law of the conservation of energy. If the conditions are those of constant pressure, the energy change is due to overall changes in a closely related properly called enthalpy (ΔH).

It was at one time thought that reactions would proceed only if energy was given out (*exothermic* processes). Although this is now known to be true at the lowest temperature, in other cases a second consideration, the entropy term, needs to be considered, as the existence of *endothermic* changes confirms. A new "energy" term defined to contain the entropy consideration and called the Gibbs Free Energy, G, may then be used. Natural or "spontaneous" processes are accompanied by a decrease in the nett value of G, and systems tend to assume whichever state has the lowest value of G.

Chemical Equilibrium

Certain chemical changes, like physical changes

Some Classes of Simple Organic Compounds

Name	General Description and Formula	Examples
Alkanes (or paraffins)	"Saturated" hydrocarbons of the general formula C_nH_{2n+2} Contain single bonds only	methane (CH_4) butane (C_4H_{10})
Alkenes (olefins)	"Unsaturated" hydrocarbons of general formula C_nH_{2n} Contain double bonds	ethylene (C_2H_4) styrene ($C_6H_5.C_2H_3$)
Alkynes (acetylenes)	"Unsaturated" hydrocarbon of general formula C_nH_{2n-2} Contain triple bonds	acetylene (C_2H_2)
Enols (alcohols)	Contain the OH group, bound for example to an alkyl group $C_nH_{2n+1}OH$	methylalcohol (CH_3OH) ethylalcohol (C_2H_5OH)
Ketones	Contain the C=O group $C_nH_{2n+1}C{=}O$	acetone ($CH_3)_2CO$
Aldehydes	Contain the CHO group	formaldehyde (HCHO) acetaldehyde (CH_3CHO)
Aromatic hydrocarbons	Ring compounds with reactions similiar to the proto type, benzene (C_6H_6)	napthalene ($C_{10}H_8$) anthracene ($C_{14}H_{10}$)
Phenyl compounds	Derivatives of the phenyl group, C_6H_5	phenol (C_6H_5OH) aniline ($C_6H_5NH_2$)
Heterocyclic compounds	Ring compounds containing mainly carbon atoms and one or more other atoms, *e.g.*, nitrogen	pyridine (C_5H_5N) thiophene (C_4H_4S)

such as raising and lowering weights, or freezing and melting water, may be easily reversed. The forward and backward reactions which are proceeding continuously can then be made to balance out, given enough time, and the system is said to be in equilibrium.

Suppose that X and Y when mixed are partially converted to Z and an equilibrium mixture is obtained under certain defined conditions. The relative amounts $[X]$, $[Y]$, etc., are then definite and governed by the equilibrium constant defined as

$$K = \frac{[Z]}{[X][Y]}$$

Putting it in another way, if we know K we can predict the relative amounts of products and reactants, i.e., the extent to which the reaction proceeds. K in turn depends upon the change in Gibbs Free Energy for the reaction:

$$\Delta G = -RT \ln K$$

where R is the gas constant, and T the absolute temperature, and ln denotes the natural logarithm.

The efficiency of a reaction therefore can be predicted theoretically since values for ΔG can frequently be calculated from tabulated values of ΔH and ΔS. Such studies constitute *chemical thermodynamics*, the branch of thermodynamics (see **F20**) applied to chemical reactions. It is an essential consideration in industrial processes.

Bond Enthalpies

The enthalpy (**L40**) of a molecule can be thought of as the sum of the enthalpies associated with each covalent bond, for each of which there is a characteristic value. Determination and tabulation of these bond energies helps in the prediction of enthalpy changes in new reactions involving covalent molecules. Similarly for ionic solids.

THE SPEED OF REACTIONS—CATALYSIS

A good analogy to illustrate the difference between chemical thermodynamics and kinetics is the downhill flow of water. The water will seek the lowest point where it has the lowest potential energy, and in an analogous way a reaction will try to proceed to the state with the lowest Gibbs Free Energy. However, the speed of both water flow and reaction will depend upon a large number of factors, particularly the available *pathway* (or reaction mechanism). Indeed water at the top of a mountain or in a domestic bath may not flow down at all if a suitable path is blocked say by a hillock (or bath plug). The unblocking may involve the expenditure of energy, for example to lift the water over the dam (or pull out the plug). In reactions this type of energy is called the *activation energy*. It can be supplied in a number of ways (see below) such as heating. Sometimes it is small and (thankfully) at other times it is large enough that thermodynamically feasible reactions do not occur at all quickly. Each of us is, in fact, *thermodynamically* unstable with respect to our combustion products, mainly CO_2 and H_2O, i.e., we should burn (!), but fortunately we are *kinetically stable*.

A *catalyst* is a substance which will provide an alternative reaction pathway of low activation energy, i.e., it can speed up a reaction, without itself being consumed in the process. The analogy for the water flow would be a tunnel through the hillock. Catalysts are very important industrially, for example, in the manufacture of sulphuric acid (using platinised asbestos or vanadium pentoxide), in the Haber process for ammonia used for fertilisers (iron derivatives), and in the "cracking" of crude oil to give lighter oils (aluminium oxide). Natural catalysts are called *enzymes* (see **F31–2**).

CLASSIFICATION OF REACTIONS

Chemical change can be brought about by a variety of techniques used separately or together:

mixing of single substances
heating single substances or mixtures
electrolysing solutions
exposure to light or radiation
addition of catalysts.

The changes can be classified according to the results produced:

Dissociation—breakdown into simpler substances or ions
Addition—in which one type of molecule or ion is added to another
Polymerisation—reaction of a substance (monomer) with itself to produce larger molecules of the same composition (polymer)
Substitution—in which one particular group in a molecule is replaced by another
Elimination—in which one particular group in a molecule is lost
Exchange—in which two groups are mutually substituted one by the other
Oxidation—removal of electrons (increase of oxidation number), e.g., Fe^{++} ferrous ion is oxidised to ferric, Fe^{+++}
Reduction—the converse of oxidation

More significantly modern classifications are based upon the precise *molecular mechanism* employed. Examples are

Nucleophilic attack—where an electron-rich reagent attacks a position of low electron density in a molecule
Electrophilic attack—where an electron-depleted reagent—an electrophile (for example, a positive ion)—attacks a position of high electron density
Bimolecular reaction—one which involves two molecules unlike a monomolecular reaction which involves only one in each step

Precise descriptions can be built up: substitution, nucleophilic, bimolecular.

ELECTROLYTES, ELECTROLYSIS AND ELECTROCHEMICAL CELLS

Electrolytic Solutions

Ionic solids can dissolve in some solvents especially if each has a high dielectric constant to cut down the force of attraction between oppositely charged ions. The process can be assisted by solvation of the ions and also by the entropy changes which favour the less ordered state of affairs—the liquid rather than the ordered solid.

Electrolysis

The oppositely charged ions are capable of independent movement and the application of an electric potential from an external battery or source of direct current to electrodes in the solution will cause the ions to move. The positive ions (cations) will move to the negatively charged electrode (the cathode) and the negatively charged ions (anions) to the positively charged anode. At the electrodes chemical changes occur and ions may be converted to uncharged species and deposited: for example, sodium ions (Na^+) to sodium metal, Na. This process is referred to as electrolysis. Faraday discovered two laws of electrolysis: (i) the amount of any substance deposited (or dissolved) is proportional to the amount of electricity used; (ii) the relative amounts of substances deposited by the same quantity of electricity are in the ratio of their *equivalent weights*.

For any ion discharged below a certain value of the applied voltage the *discharge voltage* is small. In an electrolyte containing many different ionic species therefore, each ionic discharge will occur only as the appropriate potential is reached. For solutions of acids, hydrogen (formed from H^+ ions) is discharged at the cathode, and oxygen (formed from OH^- ions) at the anode. Electrolysis is important commercially for the refining of metals, electroplating, and in the production of many basic chemicals.

Electrochemical Cells

Ever since 1800 when Volta produced an electric battery consisting of alternate plates of silver and zinc separated by cloth impregnated with salt, the search for new batteries has been continuous. In each new battery a different chemical process is harnessed to produce electrical energy. The battery must not only be feasible according to the laws of thermodynamics, but must be practicable and cheap for widespread consumer use.

The voltages developed in any battery can be predicted from a knowledge of the two processes occurring: one at the cathode and the other at the anode. Voltages can be ascribed to each of these "half cells" according to the chemical reaction which occurs and the condition used, for example concentrations of the reactants (the so-called "standard electrode potentials"). The voltage of any combination of two half cells is the sum of the half-cell voltages. Furthermore each of these voltages is related to the change in the Gibbs Free Energy for its reaction and can, in theory, therefore be predicted thermodynamically.

CHEMISTRY IN MODERN LIFE

Chemistry plays a crucial role in modern life, not least in the third world, as well as in the more developed nations. In the UK chemistry has been studied, developed and put to practical use as well as anywhere in the world in modern times. It is no accident that the largest specialised scientific society in the UK is the Royal Society of Chemistry (RSC) and that its forerunner, The Chemical Society, lays claim to being the oldest in the world. The high quality of chemical science at the crucial level of basic research is indicated by the remarkable frequency with which the Nobel Prize in Chemistry has come to the UK The success is not confined to academic activity but, surely as a consequence, it extends to the economic life of the nation.

The UK chemical industry is among the largest in the world and one of the most successful. In national statistics it is included in the manufacturing sector alongside other sectors which have a high chemical component such as petroleum and petroleum products. Its output covers a very wide range. Firstly there are the so called "basic chemicals", such as sulphuric acid, which are utilised in the manufacturing processes of other sectors.

In agriculture chemicals are not only important in the form of bulk products such as fertilizer, without which modern agriculture could not operate efficiently, but also for the 'finer' chemicals such as herbicides and insecticides. Manufactured synthetic polymers and plastics are omnipresent in modern life, for example in architecture and building as well as in many familiar household products and uses. The list here is long and includes moulded casings for televisions and other electronic and electrical products, kitchen utensils, all forms of coverings from paints and varnishes to fabrics. Then there are the "fine" chemicals: cosmetics and pharmaceuticals, ranging from vanity products to the birth control pill and life-saving synthetic drugs. Petroleum products from oil cover an extremely wide range. Petroleum is a most valuable "feed stock" for other products and in this use it is arguably more unique and precious than as a fuel or energy source.

Nevertheless, chemistry has had as bad a press recently as other basic physical sciences have had, with the consequence that young people turned away at the turn of the decade from studying the sciences. In the popular mind, chemistry has become associated with pollution resulting from the manufacturing, use and misuse of synthetic chemicals, as well as industrial accidents. Indeed, the word "chemical" has been used increasingly in a pejorative way, even in informed broadcasting and reportage. Thus chemical fertilizers (meaning synthetic fertilizers) are distinguished falsely from organic fertilizers. This sort of practice ignores the fact that we ourselves consist of, use, rely on, are surrounded by naturally occurring chemicals, organic and inorganic, as well as the useful man-made synthetics.

The word *chemist* fares no better. Whereas the terms physicist, biologist, mathematician and scientist are generally used unambiguously, the word chemist is commonly used for the pharmacist or apothecary, at least in the UK if not generally in the rest of the world.

IV. BIOLOGY—THE SCIENCE OF LIFE

WHAT BIOLOGY IS ABOUT

Biology embraces the study of all living things which exist on earth at the present time and also the recognisable remains of those that are extinct. Living things or organisms range from the apparently simple micro-organisms such as viruses and bacteria to the largest animals and plants.

Living Processes

The enormous variation and complexity of living processes make the task of understanding and defining life a very difficult one. Every living organism undergoes continual physical and chemical changes which, in spite of their diversity, are referred to as the metabolism of the organism. Metabolism involves the processing of food materials, the production of waste products, and all the intermediate stages between these whereby energy and matter are provided for the operation, maintenance, and growth of the organism. These reactions are under very exact chemical or nervous control at every stage and can be slowed down or speeded up as the need arises. Thus the organism can react to changes in the environment in which it lives, adjusting its activities in relation to the external changes. Finally, organisms can reproduce either in an identical or very slightly modified form. In this process new individuals are produced and the species continues to survive. Differences between offspring and parents can, under certain circumstances, act cumulatively over many generations and so form the basis of evolutionary change in which new species of organism are ultimately formed. Viruses occupy a middle ground between biology and chemistry, as do the more recently discovered transposons, which are organisms in the genetic sense of undergoing replication but are so simple that they are amenable to chemical analysis. However, since these are intimately dependent on cellular organisms, they are included in the study of biology rather than chemistry.

Molecular Biology

It has been evident for many years that the most fundamental aspects of these living processes occur in basic structural units known as cells. The study of living processes at the molecular and cell level has been given a tremendous impetus in recent years by the advent of new techniques which enable microscopic and submicroscopic parts of cells to be examined. Physicists, chemists, and mathematicians have found themselves working alongside biologists in this field and several of the very notable advances have been made by physical scientists. Molecular biology is a term frequently used in describing this rapidly expanding and fascinating field of research.

EVOLUTION

Introduction.—The idea that species of living organisms could change over long periods of time was considered by some Greek writers and, much later, by the Frenchmen Buffon and Lamarck at the end of the 18th cent. Further, the work of the 18th cent. geologists such as James Hutton and William Smith provided a basis without which the major contribution of Darwin, the great 19th cent. naturalist, would have been impossible. Hutton showed that the earth's surface had undergone prolonged upheavals and volcanic eruptions with consequent changes in sea level. This implied that the earth was much older than had previously been supposed. Smith developed a method of dating the geological strata by means of the fossils found in them and demonstrated that widely different types of animals and plants existed at different periods of the earth's history. Later in this section (**F47–8**) a general picture is presented of the evolution of organisms from the simple to the complex and from the aquatic to the terrestrial environment. These discoveries were in conflict with the Biblical account in the book of Genesis and, although various attempts were made to explain them away or discredit them, it became abundantly clear that through millions of years life has been continually changing, with new species constantly arising and many dying out.

The Evidence for Evolution

1. *The Geological Record.*—It has already been pointed out that successively younger rocks contain fossil remains of different and relatively more complex organisms. The spore-bearing plants preceded the gymnosperms and the angiosperms arose much later. Similarly in the vertebrate series the fish appeared before the amphibia which were followed by the reptiles and later by the air breathing, warm-blooded birds and mammals. On a more restricted level the evolution of the horse has been worked out in great detail from the small *Eohippus* which was about a foot high and had four digits on the forefeet and three on the hind-feet to the large one-toed animal living today. However, such complete series are rare and the geological record is very incomplete. There are a number of gaps, particularly between the major groups of organisms. No satisfactory fossil evidence is known of the ancestors of the angiosperms (**F42**(2)) so perhaps they did not grow in conditions which favoured their preservation as fossils. On the other hand, *Archæopteryx* provides an indisputable link between the reptiles and the birds.

Although we talk about the age of fishes, the age of reptiles and so on it must be emphasised that these are the periods during which particular groups were abundant or even dominant. Each group probably originated many millions of years before it became widespread. Further, some groups, such as the giant reptiles and the seed-ferns, died out completely whereas others, the fishes and true ferns for example, are still common today although many fishes and ferns that exist today are very different from those of the Devonian and Carboniferous periods (**F48**). On the other hand some species, for example the maidenhair tree, have remained unaltered for many millions of years.

2. *Geographical Distribution.*—Nearly all the marsupials or pouched mammals are found in the Australian continent which was cut off from the mainland about 60 million years ago. All the fossil evidence indicates that at that time the eutherian or placental mammals did not yet exist. The marsupials are the only naturally occurring mammals in Australia (**F37**(1)) but since the isolation of the continent the group has given rise to a large number of species very similar in appearance to those which evolved elsewhere in the world among the eutherian mammals. There are marsupials which look like wolves, dogs, cats and squirrels; yet they have no close biological relationships to these animals. Further, some marsupials such as the kangaroos have evolved which are unlike any other creatures in the rest of the world. Quite clearly the isolation of Australia so long ago has resulted in the evolution of these distinct types, just as Darwin found in the Galapagos islands where each has its own distinct flora and fauna which differ also from those of the S. American mainland.

3. *Anatomy.*—The comparative study of the development and mature structure of the mammalian body provides much evidence that all the species have evolved from a single ancestral stock.

Although the arm of an ape, the leg of a dog, the flipper of a whale and the wing of a a bat appear very different externally they are all built on the same skeletal plan. It would be difficult to explain such similarities unless they had all evolved from a common type. There is also evidence that the early development of an animal recapitulates its biological history to a certain extent. For example, the gill slits found in fish are formed during the early stages in the development of a mammal although later they disappear. Finally, apparently useless vestigial structures sometimes occur which would be inexplicable unless regarded in the light of an evolutionary history. In man a small appendix and vestiges of a third eyelid occur but these are functionless although in other animals such structures are well developed and functional, e.g., the appendix in the rabbit.

4. *Human Selection.*—During his brief history on earth modern man has continually selected and bred animals and plants for his own use. We have only to look at the various breeds of dogs which have been developed from a single wild type to see that under certain circumstances great structural divergence can occur in a species even in a relatively short time. The advent of genetic engineering may represent a qualitatively new form of evolution: many can now bypass the slow process of natural selection for small beneficial alterations in a species by rapid laboratory screening for dramatic changes selected to his advantage.

The Darwinian Theory of Evolution.

—Darwin amassed a great deal of information such as that outlined above which convinced him that evolution of life had taken place over millions of years. His was the first real attempt to collect all the evidence scientifically and no other satisfactory alternative explanation of all the facts he presented has been proposed. Perhaps even more important was his attempt to explain *how* evolution had actually occurred. He published his theory after many years of work in his book *The Origin of Species by Means of Natural Selection* in 1859. Some of his ideas have since been modified owing to our increased knowledge of genetics but they are so important that it is worth-while recounting his theory.

1. *The Struggle for Existence.*—It is clear that in nature there is a severe struggle for existence in all animals and plants. Over a period of time the number of individuals of a species in a given community does not vary greatly. This implies that the number of progeny which survive to become mature breeding individuals more or less replaces the number of mature ones that die. Generally speaking the reproductive output of a species is much greater than this. For example, a single large foxglove plant may produce half a million seeds each one of which is potentially capable of giving rise to a new individual. Obviously nearly all the progeny die before reaching maturity and the chance of any single one surviving is very remote.

2. *Variation.*—The individuals of any generation of human beings obviously differ from one another and such differences are found in other organisms. It is clear that they vary considerably in structure, colour, activity and so on. Darwin also pointed out that generally these variations were passed on from one generation to the next, for example, the children of tall parents tend to grow tall.

3. *Survival of the Fittest.*—If there is an intense struggle for existence in their natural environment among individuals of a species having different characteristics, those which are best "fitted" to a given set of conditions are most likely to survive to maturity. These will reproduce and the features which enabled them to survive will be passed on to their offspring. This process is liable to continue and a species will become better adapted to its environment.

4. *Natural Selection.*—Over a long period of time the environment of a given species is never stable but will change in various ways. As it does so the characters which best fit the individuals to the changed environment will be selected. If an environmental change affects only part of the range occupied by a species, the populations living in different parts may adapt and come to differ so much that they are no longer able to interbreed, with the result that the original species has now become two distinct species.

Darwin and Lamarck.

—Darwin pictured evolution as a slow continuous process with natural selection operating on the small inheritable variations found between the individuals of a species which were undergoing intense competition. This neglects the important effect of the environment on the growth and structure of the individual. It is obvious that external conditions will affect the development of an organism, for example the effect of various soil conditions on the growth of a plant or the amount of food material available to an animal. Lamarck maintained that the characters acquired by an individual owing to the effect of its environment could be passed on to its offspring. Undoubtedly characters are acquired by the individual during its growth but in spite of many attempts to prove otherwise no experiments have been done which prove conclusively that these are inherited by the offspring. Thus Lamarck's theory that evolution has occurred by the inheritance of acquired characters is not widely acceptable today.

Neodarwinism

Darwinism received something of a setback during the early years of modern genetics. There did not seem to be much in common between the large mutations studied by geneticists and the small continuous variations which Darwin thought were the basic material upon which selection acted. With time, it became evident that not all mutations are large in their effects and that much of the continuous variation which occurs does indeed have a genetic basis. Mathematicians such as J. B. S. Haldane and Sewall Wright showed that even very small selective advantages would cause genes to spread throughout populations as the generations passed by. Further development of this idea has led to the 'selfish gene' model, in which the struggle for existence, variation and survival of the fittest operate at the level of genes rather than whole animals, which are relegated to the role of mere vehicles allowing the expression of genes and, thus, the struggle between them. Experiments and observations on natural populations showed that evolution—seen as progressive, adaptive genetic change—does indeed occur today. For example, the proportion of dark-coloured moths has greatly increased in many areas where smoke pollution occurs, as a result of predation by birds on the now more obvious light forms. Again, many pest insects have evolved genetic resistance to the insecticides used to attack them. Increases in the available fossil information suggest that evolution occurs in fits and starts, with long periods of stability alternating with short periods of rapid change. This is called the punctuated equilibrium model, and the 'punctuations' may be associated with sudden changes in climatic conditions.

GENETICS

Mendelism

Genetics is the study of the mechanisms of the hereditary process. Modern genetics began with the experiments of Gregor Mendel, an Austrian monk in 1865. He studied the inheritance of different factors in peas by crossing different strains and counting the numbers of plants with different characters in the succeeding generations.

In one experiment Mendel crossed peas with round seeds with peas having wrinkled seeds. All of the offspring (known as the "first filial" or F1 generation) had round seeds. Mendel allowed these plants to pollinate themselves, and then measured the characteristics of their offspring (the F2 generation). There were 5,474 round-seeded plants and 1,850 wrinkled-seeded plants in the F2 generation, a ratio of very nearly three to one. The character of roundness can be described as being "dominant" over the "recessive" character of wrinkledness.

In order to explain his results Mendel suggested that the characters of roundness and wrinkledness were determined by particulate factors (now called *genes*), and that each plant possessed two genes for each feature. Suppose the gene for roundness is *A* and that for wrinkledness is *a*. Then the parental plants in Mendel's experiment will be represented by *AA* (round seeds) and *aa* (wrinkled seeds). The gametes (the ovules and the sperm nuclei of the pollen grains) will be *A* and *a* respectively. When these combine to form the F1 generation they will produce plants with the genetic constitution *Aa*. Both male and female gametes of the F1 generation are then of the two types *A* and *a*, and these can combine, on self-pollination, in four different ways:

F1	male gamete	female gamete	F2
	A	*A*	*AA*
Aa	*A*	*a*	*Aa*
	a	*A*	*aa*
	a	*a*	

The individuals of the F2 generation will thus have genetic constitutions of *AA*, *Aa* and *aa* in the approximate proportions 1 : 2 : 1. Since both *AA* and *Aa* individuals have round seeds, the ratio of round-seeded plants to wrinkled-seeded plants will be about three to one, which indeed it is.

Mendel's results were ignored for many years until their rediscovery at the beginning of this century. Mendelian ratios were then found to govern inheritance in a large number of other cases, such as coat colour in rabbits and cattle, and white eyes and other characteristics in the fruit fly *Drosophila*. In other cases characteristics are governed by more than one set of genes so the simple mathematical relationships are obscured. This occurs in quantitative features, such as yield in crop plants and weight in animals.

Application of modern statistical methods to Mendel's results suggest that they were subjected to certain 'massaging'—they are in fact simply too good to be true. However, many repeats of his experiments have shown that his conclusions are indeed statistically valid.

Chromosome Theory

The chromosomes are dark-staining filaments which, as we shall see later, can be observed in the nucleus at cell division. Their behaviour was described in the nineteenth century, but it was not clear what their function was. After the rediscovery of Mendel's work, Sutton suggested that the genes are carried on chromosomes, since the observed behaviour of the chromosomes corresponded very well with the theoretical behaviour of Mendel's factors.

Further evidence for the chromosome theory of inheritance came from study of the phenomenon known as sex-linkage, in which the expression of a gene depends upon the sex of the individual in which it is found. Haemophilia in man, for example, is a hereditary disease which is normally found only in males, although it is clear that females can act as carriers (Queen Victoria was one, since one of her sons, three of her grandsons and seven of her greatgrandsons were haemophiliacs). Cytological study shows that there is one pair of chromosomes which differ in the two sexes. In the female (in man and most animals) the two chromosomes of this pair are similar and are known as the X chromosomes. In the male one of these is replaced by a much smaller Y chromosome. Hence recessive genes which are found on only one X chromosome are expressed in the male, since there is no other dominant gene present. A female haemophiliac would have haemophilia genes on both X chromosomes; this could only arise from a carrier mother and a haemophiliac father, a very rare occurrence.

In recent years it has become clear that chromosomes are composed largely of the DNA molecules of the cell nucleus, to be discussed later (**F33–4**). And since it has become evident that genes are DNA molecules, we now have a firm chemical basis for the assumption that genes are carried on chromosomes. Genetics has thus to some extent become a branch of molecular biology.

Mutations

Sometimes a DNA molecule may not replicate itself exactly during the process of cell division. When this happens the gene which it constitutes has changed its character so as to produce a difference effect when expressed in the individual organism. Such a change is known as a gene mutation. It seems likely, for example, that Queen Victoria's haemophilia gene arose as a mutation in herself or in her mother. Mutations, as we shall see, are of vital importance in providing the genetic variation upon which evolutionary selection can act.

The frequency with which mutations occur is increased by certain chemicals and by ionising radiation. Hence the need for caution in exposing the body to X-rays and to radioactive materials, and the concern over the possible genetic effects of radioactive waste from power stations and from military testing programmes.

THE CELL

Cells were first seen in 1665 by Robert Hooke when he looked at a piece of cork under his primitive microscope. It was not until 1839, however, that Schlieden and Schwann produced the cell doctrine which visualised the cell as both the structural and functional unit of living organisation. Viruses constitute a difficulty since in many ways they are intermediate between living and dead matter. They are absolutely dependent on cells of other organisms for their continued existence. Outside living cells they are inert molecules which may take a crystalline form. Inside a host cell, however, they become disease-producing parasites which multiply and show many of the other properties of living organisms. They are minute and lack the complex organisation usually associated with cells. Notwithstanding their somewhat ambiguous position, the viruses are often treated as though they were single cells or parts of cells and their extreme simplicity has made them ideal material for many types of research at this level.

Structure and Function of Cells

Though the constituent cells of a multicellular organism are usually specialised to perform particular functions, they have a great many features in common. The cell is often said to be made up of a substance called protoplasm, a term for the fundamental material of life which dates from the 19th cent. Protoplasm has two main constituents, the cytoplasm and the nucleus, and is bounded on the outside by a cell or plasma membrane. Plant cells generally have an additional wall composed primarily of cellulose and used for support. The nucleus is the controlling centre of the cell and has rather limited metabolic capabilities. The cytoplasm contains various organelles which operate to produce energy and new cell structure during the normal metabolism of the cell.

Cells take up the raw materials for metabolism through the cell membrane from extracellular fluid which surrounds them. The nutrients include carbohydrates, fats, proteins, minerals, vitamins, and water. Fats and carbohydrates are important principally as sources of energy, though both types of compound are found in permanent cell structure. Proteins are complex substances of high molecular weight which contain nitrogen in addition to the carbon, hydrogen, and oxygen found in the other compounds. They are of fundamental importance in the structure and function of the cell and are built up of a number of simple nitrogen-containing organic molecules called amino acids. There are twenty amino acids occurring commonly in nature so that the number of possible combinations in large protein molecules is quite clearly enormous. A group of proteins whose significance is well established are the enzymes which are the catalysts of chemical reactions in living cells. Each enzyme will control and speed up a specific reaction even though it is present in very small amounts and is usually unchanged at the end of the process. A large number of inorganic mineral salts are essential for cells to function normally. Some, such as sodium, potassium, and calcium salts, are needed in considerable quantity; others are required only in trace amounts and these include iron, copper, and manganese. The trace elements are usually important constituents of enzyme systems. Vitamins are also necessary in very small amounts and many act as 'co-enzymes', *i.e.* molecules which must bind to an enzyme before the enzyme is able to catalyse its specific reaction.

I. CYTOPLASM

For a long time cytoplasm was thought to be a homogeneous and structureless substrate in which enzymes occurred as part of a general colloidal system. With the refinement of techniques such as electron microscopy and ultracentrifugation, more and more identifiable components have been found within the cytoplasm. It now seems certain that the material other than these recognisable particles is not a structureless matrix but a highly organised and variable complex, organised around a network of protein filaments called the cytoskeleton, which is responsible for maintaining the internal distribution of organelles and also for cell movements, as in amoebae.

Mitochondria and Oxidation

Mitochondria vary in shape from cylindrical rods to spheres and in size from 0·2 to 3·0 μm. When seen in the living cell they are in constant motion. The whole structure is enclosed within a thin double membrane, the inner layer of which is thrown into folds extending across the central cavity of the mitochondrion and dividing it into small chambers. The function of mitochondria is to provide energy for the reactions of the rest of the cell. Almost the whole machinery for the oxidation of foodstuffs is to be found in the mitochondria. Slight damage to the mitochondrion will render it unable to carry out a complete cycle of oxidative processes. Destruction of parts of the double membrane system prevents the production of energy-rich phosphate bonds in adenosine triphosphate (ATP) in which energy is stored and transported about the cell.

Chloroplasts and Photosynthesis

Chloroplasts are particles found in cells in the green parts of plants, in fact they contain the green pigment called chlorophyll. They are involved in the process known as photosynthesis in which energy absorbed from light is used to synthesise carbohydrates from carbon dioxide and water, oxygen being formed as a byproduct.

Chloroplasts are disc-shaped or flat ellipsoids from 2 to 20 μm across, possessing a complex structure which in many ways is reminiscent of that found in mitochondria. A typical double membrane surrounds the structure and the inside is made up very largely of a stack of discs consisting of paired membranes connected at their ends to form closed systems. This seems to be a further development of the type of lamellated structure seen dividing the central cavity of a mitochondrion. The chlorophylls and other pigments, such as the orange yellow carotenoids, seem to be arranged in layers a single molecule thick in the chloroplast discs so that they are maximally exposed to light.

Photosynthesis is probably the most important of all biological reactions, and can be regarded as the basis of all higher life, and is responsible for producing the oxygen required for efficient metabolism. The whole animal population of the world, including man, is dependent on plants for food since even the meat-eating carnivores prey upon herbivores. Although scientists continue to make efforts to produce adequate food materials from simple compounds, there is still no better machinery known for doing this than the plant cell. Man is dependent on photosynthesis not only for his supplies of food but also for much of his fuel, since much of the combustible material removed from the earth is of plant origin.

Endoplasmic Reticulum, Ribosomes, and Protein Synthesis.

Ribosomes, which are tiny granules composed of protein and RNA, are found in the cytoplasm, both free and attached to the surface of a system of membrane tubules called the endoplasmic reticulum, which permeates most of the cell. Ribosomes are responsible for the synthesis of proteins, which are bound to the endoplasmic reticulum and inject their proteins into the system of tubules as they are synthesised. The proteins can then be folded into the correct three-dimensional structure, modified by addition of sugar units, and transported to other parts of the cell. Some proteins accumulate in a special part of the endoplasmic reticulum, the Golgi apparatus, which lacks attached ribosomes and from which small vesicles bud off and later fuse with the plasma membrane to release their contents to the outside of the cell.

Nucleic Acids

The term nucleic acid covers a class of substances, usually of great complexity, built up from smaller units called nucleotides. Each nucleotide consists of a base, united to a sugar, in turn united to phosphoric acid. Nucleotides are joined together in a linear fashion by means of the phosphoric acid residues to form a chain from which the bases project at right angles into the centre of the double helix formed by two DNA molecules. Two types of sugar are found in naturally occurring nucleic acids and these are the ribose of RNA and the deoxyribose of deoxyribonucleic acids (DNA). We shall return to the latter when the nucleus is considered. Four nitrogen-containing bases occur in nucleic acids and in RNA—adenine, cytosine, guanine, and uracil. In DNA the uracil is replaced by thymine.

Protein Synthesis

RNA is predominantly manufactured in the nucleus and subsequently moves out into the cytoplasm. There are three major types of RNA, and all are involved in synthesising proteins. Ribosomal RNA, or rRNA, combines with a number of proteins to form the ribosomes, which act as the assembly line for proteins. Messenger RNA, or mRNA, carries a copy of the structural information encoded by a particular gene and, once in the cytoplasm, associates temporarily with ribosomes to have this information 'translated' into the structure of the protein. Transfer RNA, or tRNA, has a characteristic 'clover-leaf' structure, and picks up amino acids from the cytoplasm and carries them to the ribosome for addition to a growing protein chain. The information in genes and hence in the mRNA molecule is encoded as sequences of three of the nucleotide bases; each such *codon* tells the ribosome to add a particular amino acid to the protein it is making. Thus, as the ribosomes slide along the mRNA molecule, it stops at each codon, waits for the correct tRNA to arrive with the required amino acid, transfers the amino acid from the tRNA molecule to the growing protein, releases the used tRNA, and moves along to the next codon. mRNA molecules contain a number of special 'signal sequences' to tell the ribosome where to start and stop reading its instructions.

Nucleic acids are composed of four different nucleotide bases, while proteins are made using 20 different amino acids; mRNA molecules also need at least one codon as a 'start here' sign and another as a 'stop' sign. Clearly, a code of one base per amino acid would only be able to make proteins with four amino acids; a code of two bases per amino acid would be able to encode 16 amino acids, which is still insufficient. A code using three bases per amino acid can encode 64 amino acids, which is far more than enough, but is nonetheless the minimum that can be used. The genetic code is thus 'redundant', and most amino acids can be specified by more than one codon. Examination of the genetic code showed that redundancy is organised in such a way as to minimise the effects of changes in DNA nucleotides (mutation); thus, the amino acid valine has four codons, GUA, GUU, GUC and GUG, and changes in the last base will have no effect on the protein synthesised. Changes in the first position also have relatively minor effects, because all codons with U in the second position code for amino acids with only slightly different physical and chemical properties. Thus, evolution has taken great care to develop and maintain an optimal system for its own operating.

Cell Membrane

Though the cell membrane plays a most vital part in regulating what can enter and leave the cell, it remains rather poorly understood. It consists of two layers of lipid molecules with protein and other large molecules embedded within it. These protein molecules have many functions, including attachment of cells to each other, signalling the occurrence of extracellular events to the inside of the cell, and transport of water and other molecules into and out of cells. The first of these depends on the proteins and other molecules of different cells recognising each other and having the ability to join together; other adhesion molecules fix cells to various surfaces. Changes in cell recognition proteins are thought to be important in the spread of cancer cells through the body. Signalling functions involve proteins that pass right through the cell membrane and have, on the part exposed outside the cell, the ability to bind specific chemical compounds, such as hormones and neurotransmitters. When this occurs, the physical structure of the transmembrane protein changes, and this change is recognised by other proteins attached to the inner surface of the membrane. This induces an alteration in catalytic activity, for example increasing the production of cyclic adenosine mononucleotide (cAMP), which then diffuses to other parts of the cell to initiate changes in the activity of the cell. Such changes include increases in membrane permeability for sodium or potassium (as in nerve cells), increases in corticosteroid synthesis (as in adrenal cells), and many others. The intermediate molecules such as cAMP in the example above are termed 'second messengers'. Transport of many substances, particularly metal ions (sodium, potassium, calcium) and sugars is mediated by membrane proteins which form pores through the membrane. These pores are of different sizes and chemical properties, which allows each pore type to be specific for a given chemical compound; this allows cells to regulate the composition of their contents very precisely. In many cases, regulation is by processes more complex than simple diffusion through a pore that can open and close; some pore proteins can actively pump ions across membranes, to give higher or lower concentrations inside the cell than outside. Such processes can be monitored by impaling cells with microscopic glass electrodes and measuring the voltages across their membranes; manipulation of the external conditions (e.g. removing calcium ions and adding substances known to open or close particular types of pore) can be used to determine which pores are active in a given type of cell and see how pore activity changes during biochemical and physiological processes such as conduction of nerve impulses.

II. NUCLEUS

The main regions of the nucleus are the surrounding nuclear membrane, a mass of material known as chromatin, and a small sphere called the nucleolus. The nuclear membrane is a double structure very much like the membranes of the cell surface and endoplasmic reticulum. Suggestions have been made that these membranes are continuous at some regions within the cell. The status of chromatin was in doubt for many years. Light microscope studies reveal very little structure in the nucleus until the time when the cell is preparing for, and undergoing, division or mitosis. At this time a number of discrete double strands, the chromosomes, are revealed by virtue of their chromatin content—the material stains heavily with special dyes.

The nucleolus is a specialised region containing copies of the genes encoding ribosomal RNA, and are sites of intensive production of the latter. Thus, cells engaged in high levels of protein synthesis have a more developed nucleolar apparatus.

Cell Division

During division of body cells (mitosis) the chromosomes behave in regular and recognisable sequence. In the first stage called prophase they appear and at the same time the nuclear membrane breaks down. Next, in metaphase, the chromosomes become arranged across the equator of a spindle-shaped collection of fibrils which appears in the area formerly outlined by the nucleus. Then follows anaphase in which the two threads of each chromosome, the chromatids, move to opposite poles of the spindle. Finally in the last stage, telophase, nuclear membranes are formed round the two separate collections of chromosome material and the cytoplasm itself divides into two. These two cells are formed each containing the same number of chromosomes as the parent and the cells enter a period of rest, or interphase, between divisions. During interphase the chromatin material disappears as the DNA spreads through the nucleus, the high level of organisation observed during cell division no longer being needed.

Division of germ cells (oocytes, sperm cells) is more complex, and occurs by the process of meiosis. This will not be described in detail here, but the essential point is that the parent cell has two sets of chromosomes, one inherited from the mother and one from the father. During meiosis, these are cut and rejoined to each other to produce 'mosaic' chromosomes, and one set is distributed to each of the two daughter cells. A new organism is formed when a sperm cell delivers its one set of chromosomes to complement the one set present in an egg cell to produce a new cell with two sets, from which the new organism develops.

Genes

These are the elements which contain all hereditary information and the medium whereby hereditary features are transmitted from one cell to the next, either in the same organism or from parents to offspring via the fertilised egg. Experiments indicated that the same genes always occupy the same position on chromosomes and this really demands a structural continuity through the life of the cell. Thus, the DNA which is loosely packed during interphase, is 'condensed' into chromosomes for cell division by attachment of the necessary proteins; after division, the chromosomes are decondensed to allow the DNA to return to its normal function of specifying the metabolic activity of the cell.

One of the most fundamental problems in biology since the discovery of inheritance by means of genes has been the chemical nature of the genes and how genes are passed from generation to generation in such a way as to explain Mendelian inheritance. Genes have been shown to consist, at the chemical level, of DNA, and the structure of the DNA molecule was established by Watson and Crick. For an introduction to the structure of this molecule, see **F70**. This will inform the reader that DNA molecules are usually double-stranded, i.e. composed of two linear molecules arranged side by side. This is the explanation for a number of studies which showed that the proportions of the four nucleotide bases in DNA molecules from most sources follow a certain ratio, which results from pairing of A bases in one strand with T bases in the other and vice versa, and C bases in one strand pairing with G bases in the other and, again, vice versa. The contribution of Watson and Crick, along with their under-known colleague Rosalind Franklin, was to show that two linear DNA molecules joined together to form a double helix. FIG. 1 (see **F34**) illustrates the complementary nature of the DNA molecule; the A-T and G-C pairs have different 'lock-and-key' structures which are responsible for the specificity of base pairing.

The importance of these discoveries is that they provided the structural basis for our understanding of the mechanisms by which a long molecule, about 1 m of DNA in every human cell, can carry out its functions of transcription, replication and repair. These are all copying operations, involving the transmission of genetic information: organisms are the expression of information and DNA is the store of that information. The information is copied to make RNA (transcription, for making proteins and thus bodies), to make DNA (replication, to make offspring), and to correct errors in one of the two strands (repair, to protect against mutation).

This molecular theory of genetics has received extensive support, much of it in the form of com-plex and often subtle laboratory investigations. More dramatic support was provided by Khorana and his group when they started from simple chemicals bought in bottles and used a limited number of enzymes to assemble a bacterial tRNA gene; the artificial gene was found able to carry out many of the functions of the natural gene. Similar studies have resulted in the construction and manipulation of synthetic genes encoding a number of other mol-ecules, particularly hormones. However, these are not generally used methods, because it is usually easier to take a ready-assembled gene from an organism which has built it for us.

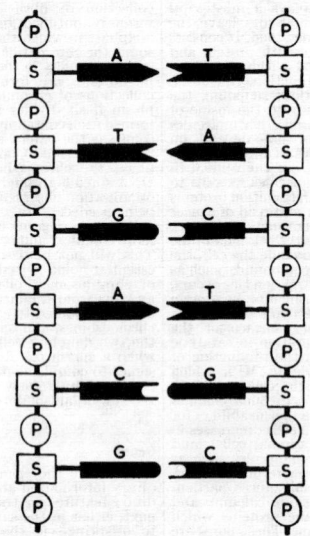

FIG. 1. A portion of a DNA molecule showing how it is made up of two strands of nucleotides. Each nucleotide consists of a base, which may be Adenine (A), Thymine (T), Guanine (G), or Cytosine (C), united to the Pentose Sugar, Deoxyribose (S), in turn joined to Phosphoric Acid (P). The nucleotides are linked through the phosphoric acid groups. The two strands are held together by hydrogen bonds between bases, adenine linking only with thymine, and guanine only with cytosine. They are twisted round each other so that the molecule is in the form of a double helix.

Note: Readers may wish to refer to **F70–76** for a Special Topic devoted to recent developments in the field of modern molecular biology. There is also a glossary of terms on **F74** which may provide help for readers new to this important area of modern biology.

MULTICELLULAR ORGANISATION

It is axiomatic, if evolutionary theory is accepted, that in the course of very long periods of time there has been a general change in multicellular organisation from the simple aggregation of cells with little individual differentiation, to the highly specialised and differentiated cells and tissues seen in complex animals and plants.

Furthermore the complex organisation must be built up in the lifetime of each animal or plant from the single-celled stage of the fertilised egg. The essential problems in development are: (1) how is the smooth succession of shape changes produced during cell division so that an appropriate and recognisable end product is reached?; (2) how do the cells *differentiate* during this temporal sequence so that those which form part of the eye, say, are different from those of liver and blood?

Method of Development

There are some important differences in the method of development in animals and plants. In animals there tends to be a relatively short period during which the basic structure is produced and after which growth, repair, and replacement may cause adjustment rather than major change. In higher plants, on the other hand, the apical regions of both roots and shoots remain in a permanently embryonic state and add material, which then differentiates, in a continuous process throughout the life of the plant. In spite of these differences—and in any case there are many exceptions—the two main problems in development are essentially similar in both animals and plants.

A great deal of work has been done on animal development since this takes place in a fairly stereotyped way during a short period of time. The fertilised egg of an animal divides in such a way as to form a hollow ball of cells, the blastula, which folds in on itself to produce a two-layered sac, the gastrula. A third layer, the mesoderm, is now added between the two layers, known as ectoderm on the outside, and endoderm on the inside. At this stage much of the animal's basic structure is established. Many aspects of this orderly sequence can be explained in terms of specific adhesive properties of cells, so that a cell will stick to others of the same type but not to unrelated types. Other mechanical properties such as elasticity, particularly in surface layers, are important in maintaining shape and producing appropriate changes during processes when one layer is folded in on another. Why cells should have the different physical properties necessary to produce an integrated whole embryo is not known, but certainly it cannot be thought that every cell has an absolutely fixed constitution and therefore a predetermined role in development. Large parts of developing embryos can be removed in early stages and their places taken by remaining cells so that intact organisms are still produced.

Formation of Specialised Tissues

This is essentially a problem in the regulation of gene activity since each cell division generally produces daughter cells which are genetically identical. It seems likely therefore that instructions are carried on the chromosomes to cope with all requirements of the organism, but that in specialised cells only a small fraction of this full potential is realised. For a long time embryologists have known that egg cytoplasm shows regional differences which make identical nuclei behave differently, and it is thought that regional cytoplasm can in some way control gene activity. Techniques for the transplantation of nuclei in developing frog embryos have been perfected and it has been possible to put a nucleus from an intestinal cell of a tadpole into an enucleate egg. The egg will go on to develop normally even though its nucleus came from a fully specialised cell derived from endoderm. The embryo will form blood and muscle from the mesodermal layer and all the other components of an organism, under the influence of a nucleus which normally would have produced none of these things. One can conclude that all the genes are present, even in the nuclei of specialised cells, but that they have to be placed in a suitable cytoplasmic environment in order to be activated. Similar nuclear transplantation experiments indicate that genes can be "turned off" as well as "turned on" by an appropriate cytoplasmic environment, even though the nuclei come from cells which are so specialised as to stop dividing. Chemical signals secreted by cells in particular parts of the embryo are known to play a major role in directing the differentiation of nearby cells to form a variety of body structures. The cells receiving these signals respond differently to the local concentrations of these chemicals.

A study of cell differentiation and the development of multicellular organisation leads us to the view that, important though the nucleus and its genes are in controlling cell activity, an integrated organism is the result of complex interactions between its constituent cells and between the cytoplasm of those cells and their nuclei.

THE CLASSIFICATION OF ORGANISMS

It was clear to the biologists of the 17th cent. that animals and plants could be fitted into different groups or species. John Ray, a leading biologist of the day, defined a species as a group of individuals capable of interbreeding within the group. This criterion, with its corollary that a species is reproductively isolated from organisms outside the group, has survived more or less unchanged to the present day. The early workers also saw that some species were very similar to one another while others were obviously dissimilar. Systems of classification based on the similarities and differences were drawn up so that all organisms could be fitted into an orderly scheme and species could be given names in accordance with the scheme. The most famous collector and classifier was the Swede, Linnaeus, who established his reputation in the 1730s. A very large number of animals and plants are known by the names given to them by Linnaeus.

Systematics, as this type of study is called, acquired a new significance after Darwin and the theory of evolution. The most satisfactory classification became one which reflected the evolution of the organisms classified, a so-called natural classification. It is not always easy to produce because ancestral types tend to become extinct and the problem then becomes one of reconstructing a whole branching system when only the ends of the branches are known. A great deal of the work on systematics has, of necessity, to be done on museum specimens which may be fossils or material preserved in some way by the collectors. The biological criterion of reproductive isolation cannot be used to define a species when the only available representatives are in a preserved state. In this case the scientist must resort to an assessment of structural differences in an attempt to decide whether two organisms are of different species. Other fossil evidence found at the same site as the fossil being classified is often important, in that it can provide evidence of biological and behavioural characteristics such as the type of food consumed and nest-building activity. In recent years computer techniques have been used to compare large numbers of structural differences between groups of animals or plants, as well as physiological and biochemical characteristics. All these techniques have led to the realisation that even the species cannot be regarded as a static point in an evolutionary pattern. Some species die out and others arise as conditions in the environment slowly change.

When the systematist shifts his attention to the higher levels of classification the problems are just as great as at the species level. Different species having features in common can be grouped together into genera, genera into families, families into orders, orders into classes, and classes into phyla. The dividing lines between different groups at all levels is always difficult and in the final analysis somewhat arbitrary since at these levels we do not have any biological criterion such as exists for the species. The evolutionary status of the larger groups is also poorly defined. Many are now recognised to be polyphyletic, which is to say that there are several main evolutionary lines running right through the group.

THE ANIMAL KINGDOM

The animal kingdom is divided into about 24 large groups or phyla though the number varies between different classifications. Ten of the more important phyla are listed below.

1. Protozoa.—Microscopic, unicellular forms of great variety. Some may have more than one nucleus and others form colonies. Many are able to swim by waving hair-like flagella or cilia. Others move by putting out extensions of the body or pseudopodia into which the rest of the body then flows. Protozoa are found in the sea, in fresh water and in the soil. Some are parasitic and cause important diseases in animals and man such as sleeping sickness and malaria.

2. Porifera.—Sponges. Very primitive, multi-cellular animals whose cells display considerable independence of one another. Largely marine. The body which may become branched and plant-like is supported by a framework of spicules and fibres. The bath sponge is the fibrous skeleton of certain species.

3. Coelenterates.—Hydra, jellyfish, sea anemones, corals. Simple animals which have a body only two cells thick surrounding a gut cavity with a single opening to the outside. Largely marine. Many are colonial. Coral reefs are formed from the calcareous skeletons of these animals.

4. Platyhelminths.—Flatworms, which are free living in water, and liver flukes and tapeworms, which are parasitic. A third, solid block of cells, the mesoderm, has been developed between the two layers of cells seen in the coelenterates. A simple gut may be developed and the reproductive system is complex especially in the parasitic forms.

5. Nematodes.—Roundworms. The body is smooth and pointed at each end. Some of the most numerous and widespread of all animals. Free living in all environments and parasitic in practically all groups of plants and animals. At the same level of complexity as the Platyhelminths.

6. Annelids.—Segmented worms such as earthworms, marine worms and leeches. A system of spaces, the body cavity, is developed in the mesoderm so that movements of the main body of the animal and movements of the gut become more or less independent. Digestive, excretory, circulatory, nervous and reproductive systems are all well developed.

7. Arthropods.—A very large, diverse and important group of animals which includes crustaceans such as crabs, shrimps and water fleas; myriapods, such as centipedes and millepedes; insects; and arachnids, such as spiders and scorpions. The arthropods show many of the developments seen in annelids and in addition they possess a jointed, hard exoskeleton. Paired appendages grow out from the segments of the body and form antennae, mouth parts, walking legs, etc. The muscles within the skeleton are able to exert a fine control over the movement of the appendage. In order to grow these animals have to shed the exoskeleton periodically.

8. Molluscs.—Mussels, clams, oysters, squids, octopods and snails. Complex body form but somewhat different from annelid-arthropod type. Unsegmented body protected by shell which is variously developed in different types. It forms two valves in mussels and oysters, a spiral structure in snails, is reduced and internal in squids and completely lost in octopods.

9. Echinoderms.—Starfish, brittle stars, sea cucumbers, sea urchins, and sea lilies. All marine and all radially symmetrical, usually with five radii. Completely unlike the other advanced, major groups. Circulatory, excretory and nervous systems differently developed. Locomotion and feeding by means of hundreds of tube feet projecting from under surface.

10. Chordates.—Sea squirts, Amphioxus, fish, amphibia, reptiles, birds and mammals. Segmented animals which at some stage in their life have gill slits leading from pharynx to the outside and a supporting notochord from which, in all chordates except sea squirts and Amphioxus, is developed a vertebral column or backbone. Those animals with a backbone are commonly referred to as vertebrates, *all* those without as invertebrates. These are obviously names of convenience having no phylogenetic significance since they lump together totally unrelated phyla in one case and align these with a part of a single phylum in the other. The vertebrates have been investigated more completely than any other animals because of their direct structural and functional relationship with man himself. There are five well defined classes which are listed below. The first vertebrates were the fish and from them came the amphibia. The amphibia gave rise to the reptiles and both birds and mammals evolved from different reptilian stock.

(a) Fish

Cold blooded, aquatic animals breathing by means of gills. Sharks, rays and dogfish belong to a group known as the elasmobranchs characterised by a skeleton made of cartilage. Bony fish, most of them in a group called the teleosts, include almost all the fresh water fish and the common marine fish such as cod, mackerel, plaice, herring, etc.

(b) Amphibia

Cold blooded, more or less terrestrial animals which have to return to water to breed. Five-fingered limbs are developed in place of the fins of fish. The egg hatches into a tadpole larva which is aquatic and breathes by gills. At metamorphosis the larva changes into the terrestrial adult which possesses lungs. Some amphibia such as the axolotl may become sexually mature as a larva and so never metamorphose into the adult. The class includes newts, salamanders, frogs and toads.

(c) Reptiles

Cold blooded and terrestrial. These animals do not return to water to breed because they have an egg with a relatively impermeable shell containing the food and water requirements of the developing embryo. There is no larval stage. Present day reptiles such as lizards, snakes and crocodiles are all that remains of a tremendous radiation of dinosaur-like creatures which occurred in the Mesozoic (**F48**).

(d) Birds

Warm blooded and adapted for aerial life. The characteristic feathers are both to insulate the body against heat loss and to provide the airfoil surfaces necessary for flight. The birds are an astonishingly uniform group and show less diversity of structure than much lower classification categories (*e.g.*, the teleosts) in other classes. The relationships of the 8,000 or more species of bird are difficult to establish because of this uniformity. It is clear that the flightless forms such as the ostrich are primitive and that the penguins are also in a separate category but the typical modern birds are classified in a large number of rather arbitrary orders. About half of all the known species are placed in one enormous order called the Passeriformes or perching birds.

(e) Mammals

Warm blooded animals which have been successful in a tremendous variety of habitats. Mammals are insulated from the environment by the characteristically hairy and waterproofed skin. They are, with two exceptions, viviparous which means that their young are born alive and in typical mammals at an advanced stage of development. In the marsupials of Australia the young are born at an early stage and transferred to a pouch where they develop further. The two exceptions referred to are primitive monotreme mammals known as the duck-billed platypus and spiny ant-eater and these animals lay eggs. The young of mammals are suckled by means of the milk-producing mammary glands. The mammals include aquatic whales and dolphins, hoofed ungulates, flesh eating carnivores, rodents and insectivores, the aerial bats, and the tree-climbing primates to which man himself belongs.

THE PHYSIOLOGY OF ANIMALS

In multicellular animals cells are of various types, constituting distinct tissues and organs which perform special functions in the body. Although each cell has its own complex metabolism there must be coordination between cells forming special tissues and between the tissues which form the whole organism in order for the body to function efficiently. The study of these functional interrelationships at the tissue and organism level of organisation is the province of the physiologist.

1. Movement, Fibrils and Skeletons

(a) **Muscles.**—The prime movers in almost all animal movement are large protein molecules in the form of microscopic fibrillar threads. These fibrils convert the chemical energy stored in the high energy phosphate bonds of ATP into mechanical energy. In the long, thin cells forming the muscles of animals, it has been discovered that there are two sets of fibrils, one formed of a protein called myosin, the other of actin, arranged in a regular, interdigitating fashion. When the muscle contracts the fibrils slide past one another so that, although the fibrils themselves do not change in length, the muscle as a whole develops tension and shortens. Fine bridges extend from the myosin fibrils to attach on to the actin and it is here that the conversion of chemical to mechanical energy goes on.

(b) **Skeletons.**—In order for muscles to work effectively it is necessary for them to operate in some sort of skeletal system. Contraction but not relaxation is an active process; muscles are usually arranged in antagonistic pairs so that one muscle can extend the other. A skeleton also provides a system of levers so that the muscles can do work against the environment in an efficient manner. A simple type of skeleton found in fairly primitive animals is the hydrostatic system of coelenterates and worms. Here the animal can be thought of as a fluid-filled bag or tube which can change shape but whose volume remains constant. By contraction of circular muscles the tube will become long and thin and conversely contraction of longitudinal muscles makes the tube short and fat. Examination of an earthworm will demonstrate how alternating waves of activity of this type passing from head to tail can move the animal over the ground. The earthworm shows an advance over the simplest systems because the hydrostatic tube

is broken up into small units by the segmentation of the body. This makes local responses possible. The next advance to be seen is the development in animals such as arthropods and vertebrates of a firm skeleton to which muscles are directly attached. The skeleton can then be used to support the body and to engage the environment. It seems to matter little whether an endoskeleton (vertebrates) or exoskeleton (arthropods) is developed since in both cases a tremendous radiation of fins for swimming, legs for walking and wings for flying can be seen. However in other respects these two types of skeleton show significant differences. The exoskeleton for example offers more protection than the endoskeleton while apparently setting an upper size limit. All the really big animals have endoskeletons.

(c) **Cilia.**—Fibrillar systems are also seen in the hair-like cilia which project from the surface of some cells. Cilia are important in a number of ways. They are the organelles of movement in many protozoa, they are used to produce water currents past the bodies of some aquatic animals, and they are of great importance in moving fluid within the body where they are used. They beat in a regular fashion, the effective stroke being accomplished with the cilium held straight out from the surface and the recovery stroke with the cilium flexed at the base.

2. Feeding

All animals require complex organic substances, proteins, fats and carbohydrates, together with small amounts of salts and vitamins. These materials are obtained by eating the dead bodies of plants and other animals. They are taken into the alimentary canal and there broken down or digested by enzymes into simpler, soluble amino acids, sugars and fatty acids. These substances are absorbed and distributed to various parts of the body where they are used in cell metabolism (**F31–2**) or stored for future use.

Many animals, called macrophagous feeders, take in relatively large masses of food. Some such as frogs and snakes swallow their food whole, but many break it up first. Arthropods have modified appendages arranged round the mouth for cutting, some molluscs have a rasp-like radula with which to scrape off particles, and many mammals break up their food with jaws and teeth. The teeth are usually well adapted to the type of food. Carnivores have large, sharp canines, premolars and molars with which to tear the flesh of the prey, fish-eating seals have small peg-like teeth to grip the fish and herbivorous ungulates have flat grinding teeth with which they break up hard plant material.

In contrast, microphagous feeders collect small particles of food material from the environment by continuous filtration. In bivalve molluscs and many marine worms water currents are produced by beating cilia. Food is trapped within the confined space through which the water flows by means of a plentiful supply of sticky mucus in the filtering region. Some crustacea use fine hairs to sieve off food material, often from water currents created by the swimming movements. The most startling of filter feeders is the whalebone whale. As the whale swims forward a stream of water flows in at the front of the mouth and out at the sides via sheets of whalebone which filter off the organisms on which the animal feeds. Though macrophagy seems to favour the attainment of larger size there are exceptions! Another type of particulate feeding is seen in those animals which eat deposits of detritus as do many worms. Finally some animals take in only soluble food materials. These fluid feeders include internal parasites like the tapeworm which absorb substances over the surface of the body, and insects such as the aphid with sucking mouth parts.

3. Respiration. Gills, Lungs and Tracheae

All living cells respire and remain alive only if supplied with oxygen. In a multicellular body, however, many cells are remote from the oxygen of the environment and the need arises for an efficient respiratory system by which oxygen can be taken up and carbon dioxide released. In addition a circulatory system is necessary to transport the oxygen to and from the respiring cells.

(a) Simple Gas Exchange Systems

Animals such as protozoa do not need special structure for gas exchange. Diffusion over the whole body surface ensures an adequate supply of oxygen. Much larger animals such as earthworms also find it possible to rely on diffusion alone, partly because their consumption of oxygen is fairly low, and partly because their bodies are permeable all over. For various reasons most animals restrict the permeability of the outer layers of the body and under these conditions special respiratory areas have to be developed.

(b) Gas Exchange in Water

Aquatic animals, except those such as whales breathing at the surface, have to obtain their oxygen from the supplies which are dissolved in the water. This presents several problems because water is a dense medium, there is not a lot of oxygen in solution, and its diffusion rate is low. For these reasons there is a surprising functional uniformity in gill systems and they are very different from lungs. Gills are fine, finger-like processes with a good blood supply which are held out in a water stream. The water current is brought very close to the gill filaments so that the length of diffusion pathway for oxygen is minimal. There is a "counter current" flow of water and blood so that the water containing most oxygen comes into contact with the blood just leaving the gill. This ensures that most of the oxygen can be transferred from water to blood through the thin gill cells. The efficiency of "counter current" systems is well known to the engineer but they were invented by aquatic animals long before they were by man. These features can be seen in the gills of molluscs, crustacea and fish. The pumping devices which maintain the water currents also operate economically. Flow is maintained in crustacea by appendages modified to form beating paddles, in many molluscs by ciliary movement, and in fish by the operation of a double pump in mouth and opercular cavities. In almost all cases there is a continuous current over the gills, the water coming in one way and going out another. Thus the animal avoids reversing the flow with the consequent waste of energy in accelerating and decelerating a large mass of water. Fish, for example, take water in at the mouth and force it out through the gill slits (sharks) or operculum (teleosts).

(c) Gas Exchange in Air

Air breathing animals do not encounter these problems since the medium is less dense, contains a great deal (21%) of oxygen and diffusion rates are high. Lungs are therefore in the form of sacs whose walls are well supplied with blood. The area of the walls may be increased by folding so that the lung becomes spongy and full of minute air spaces called alveoli where the gas exchange goes on. Only the main airways receive fresh air as the lung expands; oxygen is renewed in the alveoli by diffusion. Ventilation of the lung is accomplished by a tidal flow of air in and out of the same tubular opening known as the trachea. The actual ventilating mechanism varies in different animals. In the amphibia for example air is forced into the lungs when the floor of the mouth is raised with the mouth and nostrils shut. The lungs are emptied by elastic recoil and by lowering the floor of the mouth. Higher vertebrates use a costal pump which changes the volume of chest and lungs by movements of the ribs. This change in volume is further assisted in mammals by the diaphragm, a sheet of muscle which lies beneath the lungs and separates thorax and abdomen. In many animals sound producing organs are associated with the lungs and trachea. The larynx is a vocal organ in frogs, some lizards, and most notably mammals. In birds voice production takes place in the syrinx situated further down at the base of the trachea.

A completely different gas exchanging system is seen in insects. Branching tubes, known as tracheae, run throughout the body and carry oxygen directly to the cells without the intervention of a blood system. The tracheae communicate with the outside world via a series of holes called spiracles. Although the main tubes may be actively ventilated, diffusion in the system accounts for a large part of the movement of oxygen between the outside world and cells.

4. Circulation

In the larger animals a transport system is necessary to convey materials about the body and in many, but not all, it is in the form of a blood system. Blood systems are of two types, closed and open.

(a) Open Systems

In an open circulatory system blood is pumped from the heart into a few major arteries but these very quickly give way to large tissue spaces or sinuses so that the tissues and organs of the body are directly bathed in blood. Blood flows slowly from the sinuses back to the heart. Both mollusc and arthropods possess an open system.

(b) Closed Systems

In a closed system blood is pumped round the body in a branching network of arteries and comes into contact with tissues and cells via very thin walled vessels called capillaries. Substances diffuse into and out of the blood through capillary walls. From capillaries, blood enters the veins and so returns to the heart. Blood flow in the tubes of a closed system is much more brisk and blood pressures tend to be higher than in an open system. In annelids the closed system is fairly simple with a vessel above the gut in which blood moves forward connecting to one below in which blood moves backwards. The blood is pumped by peristaltic contraction of the vessels and this system must be regarded as the precursor of a localised pump. Simple hearts are in fact seen in some annelids.

In vertebrates a well defined heart is always present, situated ventrally at the level of the forelimbs. In fish there is a single auricle and ventricle and the latter pumps blood directly to the gills. From the gills the blood is collected into a dorsal aorta which then branches to serve the rest of the body. Associated with the development of lungs and loss of gills in the tetrapods, we see a progressive modification of this simple pattern. The most posterior gill vessel is taken over as the lung or pulmonary artery and slowly a completely separate circuit evolves. This involves the division of the single heart into right and left sides, the former pumping blood to the lungs and the latter to the body. In the birds and mammals where the division is complete the system can be seen to be functionally satisfactory. Blood flows along the following route: left auricle to left ventricle, to body, to right auricle, to right ventricle, to lungs, to left auricle, and so on. Thus blood charged with oxygen in the lungs returns to the heart before being pumped to the body.

(c) Function of the Blood

Most of the materials transported by the blood such as nutrients, waste materials and hormones are carried in solution in the plasma. The respiratory gases, oxygen and carbon dioxide, are present in greater quantity than would be possible if they were in simple solution. Carbon dioxide is carried in the form of bicarbonate and oxygen combines with blood pigment. The best known blood pigment is haemoglobin which is found in a variety of animals and gives the red colour to blood. When oxygen is present in high concentration, as it is in the lungs, combination occurs to give oxyhaemoglobin. If the concentration of oxygen is low, as it is in the tissues, dissociation occurs and oxygen is given off leaving reduced haemoglobin. Carbon monoxide will combine more readily than oxygen with haemoglobin so that in carbon monoxide poisoning the blood cannot transport oxygen. The haemoglobin of vertebrates is contained in high concentration in red blood corpuscles. The amount of haemoglobin and, hence, oxygen carried is greater than if the pigment is not in corpuscles. In mammals the oxygen carrying capacity of blood is thirty times that of a similar quantity of water. Other blood pigments are the blue haemocyanin found in crustacea and molluscs, and the violet haemerythrin found in some worms. Also present in the blood are various types of white corpuscle which are part of the defence mechanism of the body and ingest invading bacteria. Special blood proteins such as fibrinogen, causing clot formation, and antibodies effective against foreign substances occur in the plasma.

5. Excretion, Ionic Regulation and Kidney Tubules

As the chemical reactions included under the term metabolism proceed, so numerous waste products accumulate. The most important of these are compounds containing nitrogen, such as ammonia, urea and uric acid, arising from the use of protein as an energy source. In terrestrial animals they are removed from the blood by the kidney. The basic unit of a kidney is the tubule; in worms these tubules are not concentrated into a solid kidney but occur, a pair in every segment, right down the body. The kidney tubule begins with an end sac, corpuscle or funnel which is closely associated with the body cavity or the blood system. Fluid is filtered from the body cavity or blood into the corpuscle whence it passes to the tubule proper. During passage down the tubule, useful materials are reabsorbed through the tubule cells into the blood whereas unwanted materials remain and pass to the outside world.

Although it is usual to think of kidney function being primarily one of nitrogenous excretion, it is quite common to find that in aquatic animals the kidneys are hardly used for this purpose. In these animals the tubules are primarily concerned in regulating the salt and water levels in the body, nitrogenous wastes being eliminated by diffusion through any permeable surface. In fresh water for example all animals have osmotic problems since the body fluids have a much greater osmotic pressure than the environment. Water tends to enter the body and salts tend to leave. Fresh water animals produce large quantities of very dilute urine, filtering off a lot of blood plasma into the tubules but reabsorbing all wanted materials including the invaluable salts. Fresh water crustacea, molluscs and fish all possess tubules of different morphology which show very similar functional properties.

Different environmental conditions impose different demands on the osmotic and ionic regulating machinery. In very dry conditions, such as in deserts, it is obviously of advantage to reabsorb as much water from the tubule as possible. All animals do this but it is interesting that only birds and mammals have discovered the secret of so concentrating the urine that its salt concentration is higher than that in the blood. This is done by means of a hairpin-like loop in the tubule called the Loop of Henle, another example of a counter current device.

6. Co-ordinating Systems

Overall co-ordination of the animal's body, so that it functions as a whole and reacts appropriately to environmental changes, is largely the province of two systems, one chemical or hormonal, the other nervous. In one respect these are systems for homeostasis, that is for preserving the *status quo*, in spite of considerable environmental fluctuation. Paradoxically they can also initiate change as, for example, one can see in the daily repertoire of complicated behaviour patterns produced by almost any animal.

(a) Nervous Systems

(i) Sensory Information

Before appropriate reactions can be produced to any stimulus it is necessary to measure its intensity, position, duration and, most important, character. This is done by sense organs which are usually specialised to receive stimuli of a single modality or character. Thus photoreceptors detect light, mechanoreceptors detect mechanical disturbance and chemoreceptors detect specific chemicals. In all cases the sense organs produce a message about the stimulus in the form of nerve impulses which travel up the nerve from the sense organ to the rest of the nervous system. Change of stimulus intensity is usually signalled as a change in frequency of nerve impulses. The position of the sense organ which is active indicates the position of the stimulus within or without the body. The duration of the repeated discharge of nerve impulses indicates the duration of the stimulus.

(ii) Simple Networks

The simplest type of nervous system is the network of interconnected nerve cells (neurones) found in the coelenterates. Branching processes of the nerve cells communicate with neighbouring processes at special regions called synapses. Quite complicated behaviour is possible even with this relatively simple system. If a sea anemone is prodded violently it will close up equally violently, showing that activity has spread throughout the network. If it is tickled gently it will respond with local contractions around the site of stimulation. The movements of feeding and locomotion are very delicately performed at appropriate times.

(iii) Central Nervous Systems

In the majority of animals all the nerve cells tend to become collected into a solid mass of tissue referred to as a central nervous system (CNS). Within the mass the nerve cells are interconnected via synapses in the same way as in a nerve net. The connexions with sense organs and muscles are made via long processes called axons. Numbers of axons are usually bound together with connective tissue to form a nerve trunk. In annelids and arthropods the CNS is seen as a ventral cord lying beneath the gut with a swelling or ganglion in each segment of the body. In molluscs, the ganglia are usually more closely grouped around the oesophagus, with the possible provision of a pair of ganglia further back in the viscera. Vertebrates possess a dorsal nerve cord which is uniform in diameter and not ganglionated, though nerves emerge from it in a segmental fashion. The segmental nerves arise in two separate bundles or roots. The dorsal root is made up entirely of sensory nerves conveying information to the CNS. The ventral root consists of motor nerves which convey nerve impulses to the muscles of limbs and alimentary canal together with other effector organs such as glands.

(iv) Reflexes

A reflex, in which stimulation of a sense organ or sensory nerve results in the almost immediate contraction of a muscle, is the simplest type of CNS activity. Reflexes have been studied in all animals but the best known ones can be seen in frogs, cats, dogs, and sometimes humans. The very simplest is the stretch reflex, in which a stretched muscle is made to contract by activity coming into the CNS from stretch receptors in the muscle. The activity is relayed directly to the motor neurones of the muscle concerned, making them active and thus causing the muscle to contract. This reflex is monosynaptic, *i.e.* there is only the single synaptic connexion between sensory nerve and motor neurone. The knee jerk in humans is a stretch reflex, the stretch being caused by hitting the muscle tendon as it passes over the knee. Much of the recent work on reflexes has been done on this simple system, notably by Eccles. The flexor reflex, which is seen as the sudden withdrawal of a limb from any painful stimulus, is more complicated. Although the stimuli may vary, the withdrawal response is always accomplished by contraction of flexor muscles which bring the limb in towards the body. The reflex is polysynaptic, *i.e.* several intermediate neurones connect the sensory nerves through to the motor neurones. More complicated still is the scratch reflex in which an animal is made to scratch its flank in response to an irritation or tickling in that region. This reflex demonstrates some of the more involved properties of the CNS For example a dog will continue to scratch for a time after the tickling has stopped, so that the CNS must continue to be active in the absence of sensory stimulation. This has been called after-discharge.

(c) The Brain

The CNS functions in a more complicated way than is suggested by study of the reflexes and most of these higher activities are co-ordinated by the brain. A greater condensation of neurones is seen at the front end of the CNS of all animals because of the larger numbers of sense organs in that region. Brains, which become the dominant part of the CNS, can be seen in arthropods, molluscs and vertebrates. The close association with sense organs is illustrated by the vertebrate brain which is divided into three regions: (a) forebrain (nose), (b) midbrain (eye) and (c) hindbrain (ear and taste). However, the brain is much more than a relay station for these stimulus modalities and it receives information from other parts of the body via the spinal cord. All this information is correlated and activity patterns initiated and transmitted to appropriate regions. In lower vertebrates, the roof of the midbrain (the optic tectum) is the important correlation centre and its effectiveness has been well established in studies on instinct and learning in fish. Another region of the brain of importance in all vertebrates is a dorsal upgrowth of the hindbrain called the cerebellum. This is a motor co-ordinating centre which ensures that all activities are performed in a smooth and well balanced way by the muscles and limbs of the body. In reptiles, the forebrain begins to take over the correlation role and in mammals this development reaches its peak in the cerebral cortex. In man the cortex overshadows the rest of the brain and contains some 1,000,000,000 neurones. It is easy to see the magnitude of the problem of understanding a system of this complexity. The bee's brain with far, far fewer cells can initiate complicated behaviour such as the hive dances. The possibilities offered by the human cortex seem vastly greater, though they are often realised in ways which give cause for concern. At the moment it would be quite impossible to build a computer with the properties of the human brain, though the first steps have been taken with the development of 'neural networks' of computers, which display a limited amount of learning and integration skills.

(b) Hormonal Regulation

Many aspects of an animal's metabolism are regulated, not by the nervous system, but by specific chemical signals known as hormones which are circulated in the blood stream. Growth, carbohydrate metabolism, salt balance, activity of ovaries and testes and their associated structures, and colour change are all regulated in some way by hormones. The substances are secreted by endocrine glands or ductless glands as they are often called. The important endocrine glands in vertebrates are the thyroid, parathyroid, adrenal, pancreas, the sex glands, and the pituitary.

In the past the endocrine and nervous systems were regarded as exerting an independent control in slightly different functional areas of the body. It is clear now that the integration of the two systems is much greater than was formerly envisaged and in vertebrates is accomplished through the pituitary gland. Secretions of this gland regulate almost all other endocrine glands and the secretions of the pituitary are either produced in the CNS with which it is directly connected or are controlled by CNS secretions. An astonishing, parallel development of other neurosecretory systems, such as those of the pituitary, has been found in a variety of animals and in all types the neurosecretory organ complex is the dominant endocrine gland of the body. In crustacea the so-

called X organ complex found within the eyestalk, and in insects neurosecretory cells connecting to the corpora cardiaca glands, occupy the functional position of the vertebrate pituitary. They all regulate growth, metabolism and reproductive physiology, either directly or through the medication of other endocrine glands.

7. Animal Behaviour

In discussing the nervous system we have already dealt with simple mechanisms such as the reflex. Very much more complicated are the instinctive and learned patterns of behaviour which are studied by animal psychologists and ethologists such as Lorenz and Tinbergen.

(a) Instinct

Instinct is inborn behaviour which does not have to be learnt and is usually performed in a stereotyped way. For example a gull will retrieve an egg taken out of its nest by shovelling it back with the underside of its beak. The gull will never replace an egg in its nest in any other way, for example by using a wing or leg, and once it has begun a retrieval it will usually continue the movements back to the nest even though the egg is taken away. An instinctive behaviour pattern is triggered off by a particular stimulus or "releaser" which may be a very small part of the total environment. A male stickleback will attack a very crude model with a red belly but will not attack an exact model without it. The red underside appears to be a much more important stimulus than general shape. A particular instinctive pattern cannot always be elicited and the reaction of an animal very largely depends on when the behaviour was last produced. The longer the time that elapses, the easier it is to trigger off the instinctive pattern until eventually it may appear in the absence of an appropriate set of environmental circumstances.

(b) Learning

Learning is that behaviour acquired during the organism's lifetime as a result of experience. Evidence of learning has been seen in many animals from worms upwards though, as might be expected, the more complicated types of learning are found only in those animals with elaborate nervous systems. A simple type of learning is seen when an animal, upon repeated exposure to a stimulus, gradually decreases the normal response which is usually one of flight, until eventually the response may disappear completely. This process is called habituation. More complex are the conditioned reflexes, which were first discovered by Pavlov. In these an animal can in some way connect a conditioned stimulus such as a bell, with an unconditioned stimulus such as meat, so that eventually it salivates when the bell is rung. Trial and error learning of the type needed to be successful in running a maze is more complicated still. In this there is a retrospective element because the reward at the end of the maze comes after all the responses. Many animals can run mazes but the white rat has been extensively used in experiments of this nature and there is a huge literature on this one animal. A final category of learning can be called insight learning; in this an animal shows evidence of resolving a new problem without trial and error. This type of learning involves the perception of relations between different parts of the environment and though there may be examples in arthropods and molluscs the clearest evidence of it is seen in the behaviour of birds and mammals.

8. Reproduction

A single animal may live for a short or long time, but eventually it dies, and the continuance of the species is dependent upon reproduction. Some protozoa, such as *Amoeba*, reproduce asexually by the simple division of the cell to produce two new individuals. Asexual reproduction also occurs in some coelenterates, such as jelly-fish, in which there is an alternation of sexual and asexual generations. However, the vast majority of animals only reproduce sexually.

This involves the fusion of two cells, the gametes, produced by adult individuals, and each zygote thus formed develops into an individual of the next generation. The gametes are of two kinds, the large, spherical, immobile ova produced by the female gonad or ovary and the much smaller motile sperms produced by the male gonad or testis. The motility of the sperms helps them to reach the passive ovum, which contains food reserves to support the early development of the embryo.

Worms.—The flat worms, particularly parasitic forms, have complicated life cycles, and many are hermaphrodite, *i.e.*, each individual has both male and female organs. Cross-fertilisation usually occurs, the sperms from one worm being introduced into the female duct of another. The round worms are unisexual, and internal fertilisation also occurs. Of the annelids the polychaete worms are unisexual, but the ova and sperms are shed into the sea, where fertilisation takes place. However, *Lumbricus* and the leeches are hermaphrodite, cross-fertilisation takes place and the eggs are laid in cocoons.

Arthropods.—Many crustacea are unisexual, though the sedentary barnacles are hermaphrodite. Internal fertilisation may occur, but in the crabs and crayfish pairing takes place and the sperms are deposited on the tail of the female. When the eggs are shed they become fertilised and remain attached to the abdominal appendages. Most crustacea have motile larval stages into which the eggs first develop. In *Daphnia*, the water-flea, parthenogenesis sometimes occurs, *i.e.*, the eggs develop without being fertilised. The sexes are separate in the arachnida and there are usually no larval stages except in the primitive king-crabs. The insects are also unisexual, and the fertilised eggs are laid after copulation. In some, *e.g.*, dragon-flies, an immature nymph similar to the adult is formed, but in flies, beetles, moths, and many others the egg hatches into a larval form. This then develops into a pupa, from which the final adult or imago is produced. In the social ant's nest the workers are sterile females with large heads, reduced eyes, and no wings. The males and queens are winged, and insemination of the latter occurs during the "nuptial" flight.

Molluscs and Echinoderms.—Most lamellibranchs are unisexual, although some species of scallops and oysters are hermaphrodite. There are motile larval forms, and in the swan mussel, *Anodonta*, the larvae develop in the mantle cavity of the parent and when liberated become attached to the gills or fins of fish, where they remain parasitic for some time. Some gastropods are unisexual, but the slugs and snails are hermaphrodite. In the latter cross-fertilisation occurs, the two approaching snails being stimulated to copulate by firing small sharp darts of calcium carbonate into each other. The echinoderms are unisexual, and fertilisation takes place in the sea. The egg first develops into a ciliated larval form.

Vertebrates.—The sexes are always separate in the vertebrates. In some cartilaginous fish, *e.g.*, dogfish, internal fertilisation occurs and the eggs are laid in protective sacs. In contrast, the bony fish shed ova and sperms into the water, where fertilisation takes place. Although pairing may take place in amphibia, fertilisation occurs in water, and there is usually an aquatic larval stage. The reptiles, birds, and mammals are independent of water for fertilisation, as copulation takes place and the sperms from the male are introduced directly into the female. Most reptiles and all birds lay eggs with hard shells. Development of the embryo in marsupial mammals begins in the female uterus, but is continued in a ventral pouch which surrounds the teat of the mammary gland. In the two living species of monotreme mammals the eggs are incubated in a similar pouch. Finally, in the eutherian mammals the embryo develops in the female uterus and is born at an advanced stage.

Diversity of Sexual Reproduction.—This brief survey will give some idea of the diversity of sexual reproduction in animals. External fertilisation is very much a matter of chance, and large numbers of gametes are produced which offset the great losses of gametes and embryos that this method involves. Internal fertilisation is more certain, and is also independent of external water—an important factor in land animals. In vertebrates particularly there is increase in the care of the young by the parents, involving the development of characters of behaviour as well as those of structure. Some fish lay their eggs in holes or nests which are protected by the male. Similarly, a few frogs build nests, while others carry the eggs about. The eggs of birds require a constant high temperature for their development, and they are usually incubated by the parents. After hatching the young are fed and guarded by the parents until they can leave the nest and fend for themselves. In the eutherian mammals the embryos are attached to the uterus wall by the placenta, *via* which food materials pass from the mother. The period of gestation is long, and after birth the young are supplied with milk from the mother until they are weaned and can feed themselves. Another feature in mammals is the period of "childhood" during which they play and learn and are protected and fed by their parents. The internal fertilisation, internal development, and care and protection of the young after birth which is so conspicuous in the higher vertebrates results in the reduction of losses during the vulnerable embryonic and young stages, and in consequence relatively few progeny are produced by a pair of individuals.

THE PLANT KINGDOM

There are various ways in which the main classes of the plant kingdom can be grouped, but a simple, up-to-date arrangement is given in the chart. Vascular plants are often known as the *Tracheophyta* because they all possess woody conducting elements. These are absent in non-vascular plants, and the, fungi and algæ are often called *Thallophyta*, *i.e.*, they have a relatively simple plant body or thallus. Many of the bryophytes also possess a thallus, but in some there is a stem bearing leaves, although a true vascular system is absent. Many thallophytes are aquatic, whereas the tracheophytes are mostly land plants in which the development of woody tissues can be related to the attainment of the land habit as the plant kingdom evolved. However, the chart should not be taken as indicating the evolutionary relationships of the various groups. It is more a convenient arrangement which reflects the relative complexity of the plant body.

1. Bryophyta.—These are the liverworts (Hepaticae) and the mosses (Muscineae). They are all small plants characterised by a sharply defined life-cycle. This consists of an alternation of generations, the "plant" being a gametophyte bearing sex organs. The latter are multicellular, the female archegonium containing a single stationary ovum and the male antheridium producing many motile sperms. The latter are released and swim in water to the archegonium, where fertilisation takes place. After this a sporophyte is formed which is always dependent on the gametophyte and never becomes free living. The sporophyte usually consists of an absorbing foot buried in the tissue of the gametophyte and a stalk or seta bearing at the top a single sporangium. In many mosses this is a complex structure with hygroscopic teeth which move apart only when dry, thus releasing the minute spores only when conditions are suitable for their dissemination in the air. The bryophytes are of little economic importance, and may be looked upon as an evolutionary sideline. However, they occupy suitable "niches" in many plant communities, and species of the bog-moss *Sphagnum* cover large areas where rainfall is high.

2. Psilopsida.—This is a small group of primitive, vascular, spore-bearing plants. Its only living representatives are two rare genera of the southern hemisphere. However, a number of fossil forms are known from the Devonian period. The best known are those found in the chert at Rhynie in Scotland. The plants are excellently preserved, and their internal structure can be easily seen.

They were probably marsh plants with prostrate and erect leafless stems, although *Asteroxylon* had simple leaves.

3. Sphenopsida.—The only living members of this group are about twenty-five species of horsetails (*Equisetum*). In the Carboniferous period many tree forms existed (*e.g.*, *Calamites*), the remains of which are very common in coal deposits.

4. Lycopsida.—In the Carboniferous period the tree clubmosses were also prominent members of the forests (*e.g.*, *Lepidodendron*). They often reached 30m in height, were branched or unbranched, and had large simple leaves. They also had extensive root systems. The only living members belong to a few genera of small herbaceous clubmosses, such as *Lycopodium* and *Selaginella*. Like the true mosses, they have an alternation of generations, but the elaborate plant with stem, leaves, and roots is the sporophyte, and the gametophyte is very small. In *Lycopodium* only one kind of spore is produced, and the resultant gametophyte is bisexual. *Selaginella* produces numerous small microspores which give rise to the very reduced male gametophytes and motile sperms and the few large megaspores which produce the female gametophytes. The latter are formed within the megaspore wall, which splits to allow the sperms to reach the small archegonia.

5. Filicinae.—These are the true ferns, which in some classifications are put with the horsetails and clubmosses in the Pteridophyta or vascular cryptogams (*i.e.*, vascular plants without seeds). The ferns have a long fossil history, and remains very similar to the living Royal ferns (*Osmunda*) are known from the Carboniferous. The ferns are widespread and particularly abundant in tropical forests. The majority are herbaceous perennial plants, but a few are aquatic, and there are some tree ferns, which may reach 6 m in height. Most ferns possess a stem bearing roots and large leaves or fronds. The plant is the sporophyte and produces numerous spores in sporangia borne on the fronds. Each spore gives rise to a minute green free-living gametophyte known as the prothallus, which bears the archegonia and antheridia. After fertilisation a young sporophyte develops, which at first draws nourishment from the prothallus. Thus, as in the Bryophyta, external water is essential for the motile sperms to swim in, and there is a clearly defined alternation of generations, but the sporophyte is a complex independent plant, and the gametophyte is reduced though free-living.

6. Gymnospermae.—These were the dominant land plants in the Mesozoic era, although fossil remains are found as far back as the Devonian. The living members still form large forests in the north temperate regions. They are mostly tall evergreen trees with roots, stems, and small leaves. The conifers include the pines (*Pinus*), larches (*Larix*), and yews (*Taxus*). The cycads are a relic group of tropical plants with thick, unbranched trunks and large fern-like leaves. The maiden-hair tree of Japan (*Ginkgo biloba*) has also had a long geological history. Another interesting gymnosperm is *Metasequoia*, a genus well known to palaeobotanists. In 1948 a few living specimens were found in a remote area of China. Seeds were collected and plants are now being grown in botanical gardens all over the

world. The gymnosperms are characterised by the production of "naked" seeds, which are usually born on cones. The male pollen grains, which are equivalent to the microspores of *Selaginella*, are carried by wind to the ovule of the female cone. The pollen germinates and the pollen tube carries the male gametes to the reduced archegonia borne on the female prothallus, which, unlike those of the ferns, is retained within the ovule on the parent plant. After fertilisation an embryo is formed, the prothallus becomes the food store or endosperm, and the outer part of the ovule becomes the seed coat. The cycads and *Ginkgo* retain a primitive feature in that the male gametes are motile and they swim to the archegonia from the pollen tube.

7. Angiospermae.—The apparent sudden rise of the angiosperms in the Cretaceous period is still the "abominable mystery" it was to Darwin. Various suggestions have been put forward, but nothing definite is known about the origin of the group. The angiosperms or flowering plants are now the dominant group over most of the land surface of the earth, and at least 250,000 species are known. Apart from the natural vegetation, the majority of our crop and garden plants are angiosperms. They occur in every type of habitat and range in form from gigantic trees to minute plants, such as the duck-weeds. Some are climbers, others succulents, and a number have reverted to the aquatic habit. Although most possess chlorophyll, a few are partial (*e.g.*, mistletoe) or complete parasites (*e.g.*, dodder).

Flower, Fruit and Seeds.—The diagnostic feature of the group is the production of seeds, which are completely enclosed within the female part of the flower, the ovary. Basically a flower is a short reproductive shoot which bears several whorls of lateral organs. At the base are several, often green, protective sepals forming the calyx, and above this are the often brightly coloured petals of the corolla. Within this are the stamens of the androecium or male part of the flower. Centrally is the female gynoecium of one or more carpels containing the ovules. The parts of the flower may be free, as in the buttercup, or fused together. In many species the petals are fused (sympetalous), the stamens are borne on the corolla (epipetalous), and the carpels are fused to form a compound gynoecium (syncarpous). The stamens possess anthers, which produce pollen grains. These are shed and carried by insects or wind to the receptive stigmas of the carpels. Each produces a tube which grows down the style to the ovary and enters an ovule. The ovule is a complex structure containing an ovum and a primary endosperm nucleus. Two male nuclei are discharged from the pollen tube, one fuses with the ovum and the other fuses with the primary endosperm nucleus. After this "double fertilisation" an embryo is formed which is embedded in the nutritive endosperm and the outer tissues of the ovule form the seed coat or testa. The ovary of the carpel develops into the fruit containing the seeds. Fruits are of various kinds, being either dehiscent and opening when mature to release the seeds or indehiscent, with a succulent or dry wall. The indehiscent fruits are shed as a whole, and often contain only a single seed. Seeds and fruits show great variation in structure, and often have adaptations assisting dispersal. Some have hairs or wings which aid wind dispersal, whereas others have hooks or are sticky and are transported by animals. Some have flotation devices and may be carried a great distance from the parent plant by water. Seeds vary in size from the microscopic seeds of orchids to those of the double coconut, which may weigh 18 kg. Only about 10% of the weight of a seed is water, and the embryo, although alive, is dormant. The bulk of a seed consists of stored food material, commonly fats or starch and proteins, which may be contained in the endosperm surrounding the embryo, although in some species the endosperm is absorbed during seed development and the food is stored in the one or two swollen seed leaves or cotyledons of the embryo.

Classification of Flowering Plants.—John Ray (1627–1705) was the first botanist to recognise the two great divisions of the angiosperms—the dicotyledons with two seed leaves and the monocotyledons with only one. This primary division of the flowering plants is still recognised. Other differences are also found between the two groups. The dicotyledons usually have net-veined leaves and the floral parts are in fours or fives, whereas the monocotyledons usually have leaves with parallel veins and the floral parts are in threes.

Note: The present classification of plants will soon be revolutionised by a new classification according to DNA. This reclassification is currently (1999) underway.

THE PHYSIOLOGY OF PLANTS

Some of the fundamental differences between animals and plants can be ascribed to the ways in which the two groups of living organisms satisfy their requirements for food material. In a simple way at least, an animal can be thought of as a mobile gastro-intestinal tract which is highly specialised to search out and receive food in convenient, concentrated packets. In typical land plants, however, a quite different organisation exists because the organic nutrition is based on the process of photosynthesis in which carbon dioxide from the air is combined with water from the soil to form simple carbohydrates. An expanded foliage system is necessary to absorb carbon dioxide and to expose the photosynthetic pigment, chlorophyll, to sunlight. Similarly, an expanded root system is needed to absorb the other ingredients of nutrition, water and mineral salts, from the soil. The work of the plant physiologist is devoted to understanding the functional relationships between these two expanded systems of root and shoot.

The Spread of Roots

In addition, the physiologist is concerned with the progressive elaboration of root and shoot as the plant grows. Plants show much less specialisation of their cells into discrete tissues and organs than do animals and they also retain special areas, at root and shoot tips for example, where new cells are added to the structure throughout the life of the plant. In some cases whole plants can be regenerated from very few cells taken almost anywhere from a growing plant body. The orderly regulation of growth and differentiation is thus a basic property of much plant tissue.

1. Movement of Solutes and Water

The movement of water and inorganic solutes in a plant is primarily upwards from the roots where they are absorbed, to the leaves or growing regions where evaporation of water or the use of both water and salts occurs. Water and inorganic ions permeate freely through the cell walls and air spaces of the more peripheral cells of the roots. Equilibrium is established between the insides of cells in this region and the water and salts outside, water tending to enter by osmosis and the salts by diffusion or active transport. Increase in cell volume which would be caused by continual influx of materials is, of course, restricted by the inextensible cell wall. In the centre of the root is a region packed with the specialised conducting tissues called xylem and phloem. These form continuous channels through the root and into the shoot and clearly serve for the conduction of water and substances

in solution. In the root this central region is separated from the more peripheral tissue by a single layer of cells, the endodermis. The endodermal layer can actively pump water and salts from the outer regions through into the longitudinal conducting strands of, in this case, the xylem. Evidence for this pumping activity can be seen in the exudation of liquid from the base of a plant stem cut close to ground level. In some cases pressures of 8 to 10 atmospheres have been generated in roots as a result of the pumping action of the endodermal cells.

Water is also moved up a plant by forces generated in the leaves. Constant evaporation from the walls of leaf cells, both on the surface and within the substance of the leaf, causes loss of water from the plant. The process is called transpiration and, within limits, the plant can control transpiration rate by regulating the ease with which water-saturated air passes to the exterior through perforations in the leaf surface called stomata. The diameter of these apertures can be regulated by movements of guard cells surrounding the stomatal openings. Loss of water from the leaf cells is made good by withdrawing more water from the xylem elements within the leaves and stem of the plant. Cohesive forces between water molecules prevent the continuous water columns within the xylem from breaking. The net result is that water is drawn up the stem as transpiration occurs in the leaves. Considerable suction pressures have been measured by suitable manometer systems attached to the cut stems of actively transpiring plants. In addition materials such as dyes or radioactive isotopes have been followed as they move up the conducting xylem vessels at rates which can usually be related to the rate of transpiration.

2. Movement of Organic Substances

The organic substances, whose site of manufacture is primarily in the leaves, have to be distributed to the rest of the plant body. It is thought that a second conducting tissue, the phloem, is mainly responsible for the distribution of these materials in solution. Ploem is found as a layer of tissue to the outside of the xylem vessels in a plant stem. It consists of conducting cells which are rather different from those of the xylem, which serve, as we have seen, mainly in the transport of water and salts. Whereas xylem tissues are composed of dead cells whose cell walls form effective longitudinal conducting channels, phloem is made up mainly of living cells. Elements called sieve tubes are the most important conducting cells in phloem and, during the initial stages of differentiation, a sieve tube has a full complement of cytoplasm and cell organelles. Later differentiation sees the protoplasmic structures break down, but even in mature sieve tubes protoplasmic strands join through the perforated ends of adjacent cells and may extend longitudinally through the conducting elements.

Ringing experiments in which a complete ring of phloem is cut from the outside of a plant, provide evidence of the tissue's function in longitudinal conduction of carbohydrates. Sugars accumulate above such a ring but not below it. Samples of fluid taken from sieve tubes have also revealed high concentrations of carbohydrates in the sap. The method used to obtain such samples is very ingenious. Several aphids (insects such as green fly) are known which parasitise the phloem translocation channels of plants. The aphid is allowed to insert its stylet tip into the phloem vessels and is then anaesthetised and cut off the inserted stylet. Sap exudes from the stylet stump and can be collected and analysed.

3. Growth

Growth is usually, but not always, thought of as involving increase of size as measured by length, volume, or weight. In these terms any unit in a plant, whether root, shoot or fruit would follow a sigmoid growth curve with growth starting slowly, then speeding up, before finally slowing down at maturity leading on to death. Growth may also be considered as an increase in the number of cells, an increase in substances such as water, protein or DNA in the growing system, or an increase in complexity of organisation.

The organisation of growth, no matter how it is measured, presents a number of interesting problems. In the first divisions of a fertilised egg, all cells divide. Very soon this property becomes localised, polarity is established, and the young embryo develops a shoot tip and a root tip. These have then become discrete regions of cell division. The cells behind them cease active division, enlarge by developing large vacuoles and form mature plant tissue. A circular strand of dividing tissue, called the cambium, is left in the stem between differentiated xylem and phloem. The cambium is responsible for growth in girth. The acquisition of polarity has far-reaching consequences, for the behaviour of a shoot tip is very different from that of a root. The shoot tip, for example, gives rise to leaf cells with photosynthesising chloroplasts and it grows upwards away from gravity and towards light. The root tip gives rise to cells which absorb salt and water, and it grows towards gravity and away from light.

Quite a lot is known about the mechanisms which regulate growth by cell enlargement in the regions behind the actively dividing tips. Cell enlargement is achieved by the secretion of water and solutes to form a substantial vacuole within the cell, thus causing an overall increase of volume and expansion of the cell wall. The degree of enlargement is affected by external stimuli such as light and gravity, producing the differential growth patterns seen when plants orientate to these stimuli. Substances, called plant hormones or auxins, are now known to be produced at the growing apex and to move back causing vacuole formation in the actively elongating region. The distribution of auxin is affected by light or gravity so that the plant will turn towards or away from the stimulus. Indoleacetic acid is the active growth substance occurring naturally in many plants. Several man-made substances are also effective and are widely used as weedkillers. Evidence is also accumulating to show that a group of substances exists in plants to control cell division, just as auxins regulate cell enlargement.

Monera, Protista and Fungi

Monera

Monera are simple single-celled organisms lacking a clearly defined nucleus and membrane-bound subcellular organelles such as mitochondria and chloroplasts; they constitute the prokaryotes, or bacteria, archebacteria and blue-green algae. Many authors believe that the archebacteria should be placed in a kingdom of their own. This is a vast group of minute organisms of very simple structure. They are spherical or rod shaped and may exist as separate cells, some species being motile, or as long chains or irregular masses. There is a wall of complex composition, and cytoplasm which contains glycogen and fat. Electron-microscope studies have revealed the presence of structures which appear to consist of nuclear material. Multiplication is by simple division, which may take place very rapidly. For example, *Bacillus subtilis* can divide every 20 minutes, so that in 8 hours a single cell may give rise to 16 millions. Limited sexual processes also occur. Bacteria can survive unfavourable conditions by producing a resistant spore within the cell. They do not possess chlorophyll, though a few are pigmented. Most obtain their food already formed, and are thus either saprophytes or parasites. The saprophytic bacteria occupy a vital position in the living world. They are responsible for most of the decay of dead organic matter, and it has been truly said that without them the surface of the earth would soon become completely covered with the dead bodies of animals and plants. Bacteria also play a vital part in the circulation of nitrogen in nature. By breaking down organic material, ammonia is released and ammonium carbonate is formed in the soil. This is oxidised by other bacteria to form nitrates, which can be absorbed by plants again. Yet other bacteria can "fix" atmospheric nitrogen, and one species, *Rhizobium leguminosum*, occurs in the root nodules

of the pea plant. Such plants are often grown on poor soils and ploughed in, thus improving the fertility of the soil. The parasitic bacteria are also of great importance, as they are responsible for many diseases of plants, animals, and man.

Protista

This kingdom consists of algae other than the blue-gree algae, along with protozoa and slime moulds. They are mostly unicellular, microscopic, non-vascular organisms; many are motile by virtue of flagella, cilia and pseudopodia.

These are essentially aquatic organisms which contain chlorophyll. They range from microscopic forms to the large seaweeds. The green algae (Chlorophyceae) live mostly in fresh water and may be unicellular, motile or non-motile, or filamentous, though a few found in tropical seas are more complex. The brown algae (Phaeophyceae) are mostly seaweeds which possess a brown pigment, fucoxanthin, which masks the green chlorophyll. They include the bladder-wracks (*Fucus*) and kelps (*Laminaria*) of our coasts and the seaweeds which form dense floating masses over hundreds of square miles of the Sargasso Sea. Another group is the red algae (Rhodophyceae), mostly seaweeds of delicate form, the unicellular motile diatoms (Bacillariophyceae). All algae possess unicellular reproductive organs. Various types of life cycle occur, the most complex is found in the red algae.

Fungi

These are multicellular non-vascular organisms, (forming mycelia with low levels of differentiation into tissues, and more highly differentiated replicative bodies (*e.g.* mushrooms). None contains chlorophyll. Hence, like the bacteria, they are either parasites on other living plants and animals or saprophytes which live on dead organic matter. Some are unicellular aquatic plants, but many have a body called a mycelium composed of many branched threads or hyphæ. In the higher fungi (*e.g.*, toadstools, bracket fungi, and puff-balls) complex reproductive structures are formed which produce spores. In the aquatic species these may be motile, but the majority form minute, airborne spores. The spore output is often very great, and a single mushroom may produce 1,800 million spores. Some fungi are serious diseases of crop plants, such as potato blight and wheat rust.

ECOLOGY

The important branch of biology which deals with the relationship between living organisms and their environment must now be considered. Living organisms and the physical environment in which they exist form what is termed an ecosystem. Obviously it would be possible to regard the whole world as a giant ecosystem, though for purposes of study it would be extremely unrewarding and impractical. A pond, a rocky or sandy shore, a forest, and a peat bog are examples of ecosystems on a somewhat smaller scale, possessing different properties and containing populations of animals and plants that are different both in number of individuals and in species represented. The ecologist seeks to understand why a particular species is present in certain numbers in an ecosystem in terms of that species' interaction with all other living organisms (biotic factors) and with the physical (abiotic) factors of the ecosystem.

1. Abiotic Factors

All living organisms will show ranges of tolerance for abiotic factors such as temperature, humidity, salinity, oxygen levels, amount of light, etc. Clearly, if any factor in the environment moves outside the range of tolerance of a species, it becomes limiting for that particular species which is then excluded from the environment. Within the range of tolerance there will be an optimum value for each abiotic factor at which a species will survive best.

There is not a firm line separating suitable and unsuitable environments, but rather a steady shift from optimum values into conditions in which an organism finds it more and more difficult to survive.

One of the most important abiotic factors in an environment is the nature of the substrate upon or within which an organism moves and settles.

(a) **The Terrestrial Environment.**—Soil is the commonest substrate for terrestrial organisms. Particle sizes, ranging from the coarsest gravel soils, through sands and silts to the finely textured clays, have extensive effects on the flora and fauna of any area. Coarsely textured soils are obviously penetrated most easily both by roots and by soil animals. Soils of this type also allow the rapid movement of water and soil gases, but they have the serious disadvantage of poor water retention. The level at which water saturation occurs is known as the water table and is an important abiotic factor. The terrestrial environment tends on the whole to dehydrate organisms and there is always a marked dependence on water supplies.

Soil characteristics also vary with depth. A vertical section through any soil is referred to as its profile and has considerable bearing on the ecosystems in which the soil is involved. The layers, or horizons, of a soil profile vary enormously from one soil to another. Below a surface layer of organic debris one can, in general terms, distinguish a layer of soil from which substances have been leached (A horizon), soil containing the leached-out substances from the layer above (B horizon), the weathered parent material (C horizon), and finally the parent rock or some other stratum beneath the soil (D horizon).

Humus

Humus, which is formed from animal and plant remains and is located in the lower parts of the A profile, is of great importance in providing food for soil organisms and chemical elements such as nitrogen, phosphorus, and calcium for plant growth. It is also important in maintaining good soil structure and, though inorganic fertilisers can supply chemical elements, they have little or no effect on structure. Soil requires careful cultivation, and structure is easily disturbed by such things as heavy farm machinery, which can lead to the creation of impermeable layers with the disastrous exclusion of oxygen and oxygen-consuming organisms.

(b) **The Aquatic Environments.**—Marine and freshwater environments together cover more than 75 per cent of the earth's surface and, since they can be occupied throughout their entire depth, offer a much greater volume of living space than does the land. There is only a slight difference between the density of water and of living tissues, so that the bodies of aquatic organisms are very largely supported by the environment and do not need strong woody stems or powerfully muscled limbs to hold them up. Water has a high specific heat, which means that large amounts of heat are needed to raise its temperature. The result is that aquatic environments tend to show much smaller fluctuations in temperature than the terrestrial ones. In general, the larger the volume of water the smaller are the fluctuations in temperature, and so the fauna and flora of the oceans will not show wide temperature tolerance, whereas that of small pools will, but in neither case will the tolerance be so great as that shown by many terrestrial forms. Oxygen and carbon dioxide concentrations are very different in water and in air and are also variable from one aquatic environment to another, making them suitable for the support of different fauna and flora.

An important difference between the sea and freshwater is seen when their salt concentrations are determined.

Osmotic and ionic regulation

Organisms living in fresh or in sea water face quite dissimilar problems in osmotic and ionic regulation. Life evolved originally in the sea and the salt concentration in the blood of marine molluscs, crustaceans, and echinoderms, for example, is about the same as in sea water itself. Marine organisms have, on several occasions in the course of their evolution, moved into freshwater. Representatives of the worms, crustaceans, molluscs, and vertebrates have all independently invaded this very dilute habitat. What is more, all these animals show approximately the same types of modification to cope with the change. Their outer layers, in the main, become impermeable and the salt concentration of their blood is reduced considerably and to a spectacularly low level in the freshwater mussel. The kidneys become enlarged and produce a large volume of dilute urine. By these means freshwater animals can cut down loss of their salts. It is interesting that all terrestrial vertebrates, including the mammals have retained a salt concentration in their blood of about half the seawater level and this is partly attributable to their freshwater ancestry. The ultimate development of salinity tolerance is seen in such animals as the salmon and eel which move from fresh to salt water and back again during their life cycle.

2. Biotic Factors

(a) **Associations between Organisms.**—No organism can be considered to be independent of any other organism in an ecosystem but in some cases close associations of various types can be developed between different species or different members of the same species.

Commensalism is an association which benefits one member but has little effect on the other. Small organisms can live within the protective covering offered by a larger individual, as, for example, commensal crabs living within the shell of some species of oyster.

Symbiosis is a somewhat closer association in which both members benefit, as do certain species of green algae and the coelenterates in whose body tissues they live. The algae are protected and the coelenterates benefit from the food produced by the photosynthetic plant. Some symbiotic organisms are unable to survive outside the association. The lichens which are associations of algae and fungi, are examples of this type of symbiosis, as are some of the food-processing micro-organisms together with the animals in whose intestinal tracts they live.

Social animals. In some cases animals of the same species form social groups in which co-operative effort and division of labour makes them more successful in exploiting a particular environment. Social development is most obvious among certain insects such as termites, ants, wasps, and bees, and among the vertebrates. Social organisation in these groups may lead to the development of different behaviour patterns and ultimately, as in ants and bees, for example, to the evolution of a variety of structural modifications so that different castes are recognisable.

Parasitism. Not all associations are of mutual benefit and when one organism becomes sufficiently specialised so that it can live successfully on materials extracted from another, the latter is always adversely affected. Parasites, by causing disease in, and sometimes the death of, the host, can influence population growth and size. Important groups are bacteria, protozoa, fungi, nematodes (roundworms), and platyhelminths (tapeworms and liver flukes). Viruses are also important disease-producing agents which are incapable of an independent existence outside the cells of the host and utilise the host cell's metabolic pathways directly to synthesise new virus material.

Control of Parasites

Many parasites (and other pests which may disturb the comfort and health of man) can now be controlled to some extent, and, for a variety of reasons, such control procedures have extensive effects on the ecosystems involved. The regulation of some bacterial parasites by means of antibiotics, and control of the insect vectors of organisms such as the malaria parasite by means of insecticides, have both been important factors in the increase in human population. Though the beneficial effects of pest control of all types are clear, the process is not without its difficulties and dangers. Indiscriminate use of many chemical agents has led to the development of resistant strains. In any group of organisms, some will naturally be more resistant to a pesticide or antibiotic than others and these will be the survivors of any treatment that is less than totally effective. They will form the breeding stock for subsequent generations and so progressively more and more resistant types will evolve. Thus, there are now many strains of bacteria resistant to penicillin and other antibiotics. Even more alarming is the recent discovery that this resistance can be transferred in an infective way between bacteria of different species. Another complication associated with chemical control is that the agent concerned frequently affects a wide spectrum of organisms, including those that are in no sense injurious to man or his crops. Thus DDT kills bees and other pollinating insects unless its application to a crop is very precisely timed. In addition, the accumulation of quantities of chlorinated hydrocarbons such as DDT in the environment is known to have an injurious effect on organisms other than insects. Because these chemicals are broken down very slowly they now form a serious problem in environmental pollution.

New Methods of Control

Agents such as DDT are now being replaced with much more specific pesticides which inhibit particular stages of development of particular species of pests, *i.e.* growth regulators. Biological control is also becoming much more widely used, and is based on introduction of species which are specific predators of local pest populations.

(*b*) **The Food Factor.**—Plants are the ultimate source of organic food for all animals. The most important food plants are those capable of photosynthesis in which organic material is synthesised from carbon dioxide and water, using radiant energy from the sun to drive the reaction.

Food Chains. Plants are eaten by herbivores which in turn are eaten by carnivores. It is possible to see many such sequences, called food chains, in all ecosystems. For example, in the open sea, green algae are the important photosynthetic organisms; these are eaten by a small crustacean, *Calanus*, which in turn forms a large part of the diet of the herring. Feeding relationships are usually of much greater complexity than is suggested by a simple food chain. Thus, *Calanus* represents about 20 per cent of the herring's diet but it is also eaten by many other marine animals as well. For example, it forms about 70 per cent of the total diet of larval sand eels. The larval eels are eaten in turn by the herring and may form 40 per cent of its diet. Because an animal's diet is usually quite varied and one species of animal may be part of the food of a wide range of different animals, interactions are set up which are referred to as food webs. However, for general comparative purposes it is possible to disregard the detail of species and to group together all organisms with similar food habits. When this is done a relationship known as pyramid of numbers often appears in which organisms at the base of a food chain (the primary producers) are extremely abundant, while those at the apex (the final consumers) are relatively few in number.

Productivity. The validity of using numbers of individuals in such an analysis is often open to question, especially when ecosystems are to be compared. For example, a comparison between numbers of herring and numbers of whales as final consumers in two pyramidal systems is not very informative. This difficulty is partially overcome by using estimates of the total weight (biomass) of organisms at each level rather than their number. Even this has disadvantages because determinations of biomass give a measure of the amount of material present at any one time (the standing crop) but give no indication of the amount of material being produced or the rate of its production (the productivity). In some parts of the sea, for example, the biomass of small animals forming the zooplankton is greater than that of the plant life or phytoplankton on which it depends for food. This seems to contravene the pyramid concept. However, the rate of production of new material by the phytoplankton is very much greater than by the zooplankton so that, if taken over a year, the total amount of plant material produced would far exceed the total production of animal material. Productivity is a concept of great practical and theoretical importance. It may be determined in terms of the actual organic material produced in an area over a set period of time or, more usefully, in terms of the amounts of energy transferred and stored at each food level, again over a set period of time.

Photosynthetic efficiency

Under natural conditions only 1 to 5 per cent of the light falling on a plant is converted by its photosynthetic system into chemical energy contained in the material of its tissues. Similarly herbivores which consume plants will pass on to their predators only some 10 per cent of the energy contained in the plant material they eat. These low values for photosynthetic efficiency and ecological efficiency respectively are due to the fact that most of the energy appears as heat during the metabolic reactions needed to sustain life and only a small amount is incorporated into new tissue. It is easy to see that the form of a pyramid of numbers can be explained in terms of low ecological efficiency, as can the observation that a food chain rarely has more than five links. The loss of energy at each stage must mean that each succeeding stage becomes smaller and smaller in number and that the number of stages is severely limited.

Human Population and Food. The present very large increase in human population (*see* **World Population, L130**) has led to a pressing need for the controlled exploitation of food resources in the world. Consideration of the processes of energy transfer suggests that man should be mainly herbivorous. They also suggest that present agricultural crops, with the possible exception of sugar cane, do not achieve as high a primary productivity as that encountered in some natural ecosystems. Crops rarely achieve complete plant cover of the land throughout the growing season so as to trap the maximum amount of sunlight. It would be necessary to mix crops to do this effectively and there would then be complicated harvesting problems.

If man remains an omnivore, as he almost certainly will, then his domestic food animals will continue to be herbivorous as they are at present, though whether they will be the same hervibores is less easy to predict. Beef cattle raised on grassland convert only 4 per cent of the energy in the plants of their environment into similar chemical energy in their tissues. At the present time intensive farming practices are being employed to improve conversion, usually by harvesting plant material, processing it, and bringing it to the animals which are housed in special buildings. This cuts down on the wastage of plant food because it can be grown under better conditions and less of it is consumed by animals other than the cattle. Careful breeding and the limitation of the period over which livestock is raised to that of maximum growth efficiency have also contributed to conversions of some 35 per cent, achieved in the case of broiler chickens and calves. The moral problems raised by these methods and the circumstances which make them necessary give rise to widespread concern.

Fish are also an important part of man's diet. Many populations have been overfished so that returns have gone down in spite of intensified fishing effort. The fisheries scientist is concerned to discover the limit at which the maximum number of fish can be taken without depleting the population year by year.

Population Dynamics

Study of the numbers of organisms in a population, together with their change and regulation, forms a branch of the subject of considerable practical importance known as population dynamics.

Numbers of animals and plants tend to increase up to the capacity of the environment. The rate of increase will be determined by the balance between reproduction rate and mortality. As Malthus appreciated, adults of any organism tend to replace themselves by a greater number of progeny and, in the absence of losses by mortality and other factors, there is a vast potential for increase in all populations. If an organism doubles its number in a year, there will be a 1,000-fold increase in 10 years, and a 10 million-fold increase in 20 years. Increase of this type soon leads to shortages and overcrowding so that mortality goes up, the net rate of increase diminishes, and finally an equilibrium is reached with no further increase in number. The change with the passage of time follows and S-shaped curve. At equilibrium, the numbers are kept at a steady level by factors such as competition for food, refuge, or space.

Human population is increasing rapidly at the present time, mainly because of the fall in deathrate. Food production is also increasing, but in some areas the world supply and requirement are so evenly matched that drought or war are inevitably followed by a famine. Though the human population has not yet reached the stage of equilibrium, it is clear that ultimately it must be subject to forces of regulation similar to those that control populations of other organisms. Birthrate cannot exceed death-rate indefinitely in any living organism. By limiting the size of families it is possible for man to achieve a population equilibrium at levels lower than those at which regulative factors such as famine or aggression must begin to operate. Rational control of birth-rate seems to offer the best chance of averting a global population disaster.

GEOLOGY

The Science of Geology

Geology deals with the composition and structure of the Earth, the physical processes which act upon that composition and structure, and the history of change and development the planet has undergone since its formation, 4·6 billion years ago. The science embraces a number of specialist disciplines which are beyond the scope of this introductory article, but a sense of the fascination of geology as a subject of scientific enquiry and popular interest may be found in a single observation: the summit of Mount Everest, standing 8854 m above sea level, is composed of limestone that was formed on the ocean floor, hundreds – perhaps even thousands – of metres below sea level.

Early Geological Explanations

Attempts to explain the puzzles of the Earth's structure and dynamic processes go back to the very beginnings of scientific endeavour. Long before the marine origin of the Himalayas came to the attention of science, for example, classical scholars were attempting to explain similar evidence of marine origin in European mountains. In the 6th century B.C. Xenophanes of Colophon concluded that since seashells (fossil seashells, that is, though not then known as such) were embedded in the rocks of mountain ranges far from the coast, the Earth and the sea must once have been mixed up together. With regard to earthquakes and volcanoes, Aristotle (384–322 B.C.) concluded that they were caused by hot winds that forced their way through fractured rocks deep underground and occasionally burst through weak spots in the Earth's surface.

For many centuries, the true explanations of geological phenomena were simply beyond the reach of human enquiry. Cataclysmic earthquakes, volcanic fire and brimstone remained principally the sobering evidence of a hellish underworld upon which religion and popular mythologies were founded. On a practical note, Chinese administrators had kept a detailed record of earthquakes since 780 B.C. and, in the early decades of the 2nd century A.D., their technicians had even invented a device enabling them to detect distant earthquakes – the first seismograph – but direct knowledge of the Earth's geology remained meagre until the 20th century.

Modern Geological Knowledge

The fundamental aspects of the dynamic processes that raise mountains from the sea, cause volcanoes to erupt and earthquakes to fracture the landscape have only become known since the 1960s.

The problem has always been access. The Earth's terrestrial surface is a tiny fraction of its total mass (if the Earth was reduced to the size of a globe 50 cm in diameter, the portion accessible to direct observation through even the deepest mines and boreholes would be less than 1 millimetre thick). But, although scientists cannot examine the interior of the Earth directly, the seismograph (much developed from its Chinese progenitor) and associated instrumentation ultimately has enabled them to describe its internal structure with some certainty: seismic waves are bent to varying degrees by the varying density of material as they pass through the Earth, and analysis of these variations defines the type of materials present and the depths at which they occur.

The Earth's structure. The Earth is an almost spherical body with an equatorial radius of 6371km, and slightly less along its polar axis (due to the flattening of the poles). Seismic investigations have shown that the Earth is made up of three layers which are distinguished one from another by their composition and density. The central *core* of the planet is the densest of the three; the surrounding *mantle* is a thick shell of less dense rocky material, and above the mantle lies the thinnest, least dense and outermost layer, the *crust*.

The Core. This is a spherical mass (radius 3488km), composed predominantly of metallic iron, but also containing small amounts of nickel and other elements. Pressure in the central mass of the core (extending more than 5140km below the Earth's surface to its centre) is so great that despite the extremely high temperatures at those depths the inner portion of the core (radius 1231km) is solid metal, while in the outer core (2257km thick) the temperature and pressure regime is such that the iron is molten and remains in liquid form. The Earth's magnetic field is generated by circulation movements in the liquid outer core.

The Mantle is a shell of rocky material nearly 3000km thick which surrounds the core. As with the core, the composition of the mantle is the same throughout, and its physical state also varies with the prevailing temperature and pressure regimes. In the lower part of the mantle the rock is so highly compressed that it remains solid despite extremely high temperatures. This zone, extending from the core-mantle boundary (2883km from the Earth's surface) to a depth of about 350km, is called the *mesosphere* ('middle sphere').

In the upper part of the mantle, from 350 to between 200 and 100km below the Earth's surface, the temperature and pressure regimes are such that rocks melt and remain in a form more akin to butter or warm tar than solid rock. This zone is known as the *asthenosphere* ('weak sphere').

Above the asthenosphere lies a zone in which the rocks are cooler and more solid than those in the plastic asthenosphere below. This hard outer zone, which includes the uppermost mantle and all of the *crust* is called the *lithosphere* ('rock sphere'). The lithosphere extends to depths of from 10 to 200km below the Earth's surface.

The Crust. This wraps the Earth in a thin layer of material in which life has evolved. Oceans, mountains, meadows, forest, rivers, every living organism – and even the atmosphere which breathes life into the system – is a product of the Earth's thin crust and subject to the geological processes it undergoes. Unlike the core and the mantle, which are of nearly constant thickness, the thickness of the crust varies considerably. These are two main divisions, distinguished by their density: the more dense oceanic crust, which has an average thickness of about 8km, and the less dense continental crust, which has an average thickness of 45km and is up to 70km thick under high mountain chains and less than 30km under some low-lying plains.

As their names imply, the two crust types constitute the oceanic and continental portions of the Earth's surface, but both are an integral part of the lithosphere which, in effect, is floating on the molten asthenosphere. But the lithosphere is not a fixed and seamless layer, it is broken into a number of huge plates – like ice on a lake during a thaw – which are moved about by convection currents in the asthenosphere below.

Plate Tectonics. See **Special Topic, F77.**

The Composition of the Earth's Crust. The many different kinds of *rock* found in the Earth's crust are each an assemblage of two or more minerals, bonded together. A mineral, in its turn, is a discrete solid substance consisting of chemical elements, with a specific chemical composition and a characteristic crystal structure. Iron, for instance, is an element (Fe); iron oxide is a mineral (Fe_3O_4); iron ore is a rock composed of iron and other minerals. More than 3500 minerals have been identified, but of these about 20 make up more than 95 per cent of the Earth's crust. And of the elements, 12 comprise 99.23 per cent of the total crust mass. Thus the crust consists of a limited number of minerals in which one or more of the 12 abundant elements is an ingredient. Oxygen is the most abundant element, comprising 45.20 per cent by weight of the crust, followed by silicon (27.20 per cent), aluminium (8.00 per cent) and iron (5.80 per cent).

The Rocks. The rocks of which the Earth's crust is composed, though numerous in their different mineral composition, can be grouped in just three families, distinguished one from the other by the manner in which they were formed.

Igneous rocks (from the Latin *igneous,* meaning fire). Igneous rocks are those which were formed from the cooling and consolidation of *magma,* the molten rock which erupts from volcanoes. Basalt is the most common igneous rock, comprising about 80 per cent of all magma erupted by volcanoes. Igneous rocks are the initial source of all the various (and some valuable) minerals that are known. Though constituting a tiny fraction of the total amount of magma that is brought to the surface these minerals may settle out in distinct bands, or

may be concentrated together as the parent rock erodes and its particles accumulate in sedimentary deposits.

Sedimentary rocks. Those rocks which are formed by the settling and consolidation of materials that had previously existed in some other form. Most originated as loose particles that were weathered from their parent material and transported in suspension by wind, water or ice to some other location, where they were deposited and subsequently consolidated into sedimentary rock – sandstone is a typical example, shale is another. Others were originally organic material, which as it died and decomposed formed beds of sedimentary rock. Limestone, for example, was originally the shells and remains of marine animals; coal is a combustible sedimentary rock, more than 50 per cent of which is decomposed plant matter.

Metamorphic rocks. From the Greek *meta* (meaning change, and *morphe,* meaning form: thus, change of form) are those rocks which have been changed from their original form (either igneous or sedimentary) into something else by the effects of high temperature, high pressure, or both. The process is analogous to that which occurs when a clay pot is fired in the kiln. The high temperatures trigger a series of chemical reactions in the tiny mineral grains that make up the clay. New compounds form, and the soft malleable clay becomes hard and rigid. Marble is a metamorphic rock, transformed by heat and pressure from the irregularities of sedimentary limestone into a glistening mass of uniformly sized, interlocking grains of soft calcite.

Earth History. Of the Earth's crust as a whole (which of course includes the oceanic as well as the continental crust), 95 per cent consists of igneous rock, the remaining 5 per cent being sedimentary (in this classification metamorphic rocks are considered to be either igneous or sedimentary, depending on their origin). But at the surface, where material is constantly being eroded from one place, transported and deposited in another, sediments and sedimentary rocks are found nearly everywhere. In fact, 75 per cent of all rock at the surface is sedimentary, and only 25 per cent igneous.

Sedimentary rocks have been accumulating for millions of years. They have built up in layers, or *strata* (singular *stratum*) which in places are thousands of metres thick. Each environment where sediments accumulate leaves a distinctive imprint in the rock, so that the form and content of each layer and the sequence in which they occur reveal a history of changing landscapes, climate, plant and animal life on Earth. The age of the sedimentary rocks (determined by *geochronology*) dates the sequence of changes in the landscape through time, while the fossil remains of plants and animals found within sedimentary rocks enable *paleontologists* to follow the evolution of lifeforms which populated that landscape. Most of what we know about the dinosaurs who ruled the Earth from about 200 million to 65 million years ago, has been deduced from the evidence of fossils. Likewise, fossils tell us that the evolutionary history of the animal which currently rules the Earth, *Homo sapiens sapiens,* extends back a mere 5 million years or so.

V. SCIENCES OF MAN

PHYSICAL ANTHROPOLOGY

In the broadest terms of scientific classification, humans are part of the *animal kingdom*—that is to say they are multicellular organisms which feed by ingesting complex organic substances and are capable of independent movement. More than one million animal species have been described (and the actual number may be nearer 10 million). Each belongs to one of the many phyla (singular *phylum*, meaning tribe or stock) into which the animal kingdom is divided. Humans belong to the phylum chordata, *subphylum* vertebrata, which includes all animals with a spinal cord enclosed within a vertebral column, and a skull enclosing the brain.

Each phylum is divided into a number of *classes*, among which humans are classified as four-limbed vertebrates of the class mammalia: warmblooded animals with mammary glands which secrete milk for the nourishment of young, skin with hair or fur, a body cavity divided by a muscular diaphragm which assists respiration, three ear bones and seven neck vertebrae.

Sub-classes of Mammals

There are about 4,500 species of mammal, classified in three *subclasses*: the *prototheria*, which is a group of oviparous (egg-laying) mammals consisting solely of the duckbill platypus and spiny anteaters of Australia and New Guinea; the *metatheria*, represented by about 260 species of viviparous (live-bearing) marsupials whose young are born in a very immature state and carried by their mother in an external pouch for some time after birth; and the *eutheria*, which are mammals with a placenta permitting substantial development of the young before birth.

The great majority of mammals belong to the eutheria—including humans. The subclass itself is divided into *orders*, numbering 16 in all, which range from the insectivora (shrews, moles, hedgehogs *etc*) and pholidota (pangolins), to the proboscidea (elephants) and cetacea (whales). Lemurs, monkeys, apes and humans are grouped together in the primate order; all are tree-dwellers (or descendants thereof) whose distinctive similarities are their fingers, flat nails, and reduced sense of smell.

The primate order is split into three *suborders*: the prosimii, represented by the living lemurs, lorises and galagos; the tarsoidea (the living tarsiers); and the anthropoidea (monkeys, apes and humans). The anthropoidea order is divided into two *infraorders*: the platyrrhini, meaning flat-nosed and comprising the New World monkeys of central and south America; and the catarrhini (thin-nosed), which are the Old World monkeys, the gibbons, the apes, and humans.

The catarrhini infraorder divides into two *superfamilies*: the cercopithecoidea (Old World monkeys), and the hominoidea (gibbons, apes and humans); and the hominoid superfamily splits into three *families*: the hylobatiae (gibbons); the pongidae (apes), and the hominidae (humans). The hylobatids and pongids are distinguished by long arms and short legs, reflecting a predominantly arboreal way of life, while the principal distinguishing features of the hominid family are an habitual upright posture and bipedal gait, and a large brain.

Each zoological family is a group of related genera (sing. *genus*, meaning race, origin); a genus is a collection of closely related *species* (meaning kind, or sort), and a species is a group of individuals who are capable of breeding among themselves. There are several genera and numerous species of the hylobatid and pongid primate families alive today, but only one living species of hominid: modern humans—*Homo sapiens*.

It will be seen from the above that the relationships which form the basic structure of zoological classification set every species in the context of a greater whole—genus, family, order, and so on. *Homo sapiens* is no exception. Man is not the end-product of the entire evolutionary process, as is commonly supposed. On the contrary, man's place in nature is at the end of a relatively short line radiating from among the millions which have evolved since life on Earth began.

The origin of the primates

The primates are essentially tropical animals. With the exception of humans, virtually all living species are arboreal, and 80 per cent of them are found in the tropical rain forests. Their most distinctive characteristic is the very general and unspecialised nature of their anatomical structure, and the highly specialised and adaptable nature of their behaviour. While other mammals evolved specialised physical characteristics (the giraffe's long neck, for example), the primates have retained the basic structure of the ancestral mammalian form and have instead adapted their behaviour to suit prevailing circumstances. The human hand is a case in point—it has the same number of bones operated by the same arrangement of muscles as the arboreal primates possessed 45 million years ago, yet the human hand serves a much greater variety of uses.

The fossil evidence indicates that primates have existed for at least 70 million years. They were one of the groups of placental mammals which survived the mass-extinction event which closed the Cretaceous period of geological time, about 65 million years ago. The dinosaurs were among those which disappeared with that event, and their passing marks the end of the epoch known as the age of the reptiles. Some reptiles survived, of course, but with the declining prominence of the dinosaurs the mammals flourished, heralding the age of the mammals with a burst of adaptive radiation which eventually took them into every ecological niche which the dinosaurs had previously occupied.

The early mammals had lived in the shadow of the dinosaurs for more than 100 million years before the Age of the Reptiles came to a close. They were small (typically about 10 cm long), and occupied parts of the environment that the large reptiles could not reach—the nocturnal world, for instance, (a temporal dimension in which the cold-blooded reptiles could not function), and rocky crags, holes and forest undergrowth. Here they evolved a high degree of sensory perception. Sight, sound, touch and smell assisted their capture of the invertebrate prey upon which they largely subsisted; integration of cerebral and physical equipment was crucial, and while the later evolution of the dinosaurs was concerned primarily with physical structure, that of the early mammals was concerned with the development of brain and behaviour. This equipped them well for the radiation which followed.

Of the various habitats available to the mammals as the age of the reptiles drew to a close, the ancestors of the primates took to the trees. Here they found a rich and varied diet—leaves, buds, fruit, insects, birds' eggs and nestlings—but also a suite of new demands. Life in the trees called for a shift in the emphasis of the mammals' environmental awareness. While the nose had probably been the most important organ of ground-dwelling mammals, the eyes were more crucial in the trees.

Because a tree is a spatially restricted environment, an arboreal animal needs to be particularly aware of its whereabouts. It must know if a potential predator is in the same tree, and if a fruit is at the end of a safe branch. It must be able to see clearly and judge distances accurately as it moves through the branches. These requirements favoured the evolution of stereoscopic vision, which was further enhanced by the advent of colour vision.

Life in the branches also called for greater agility. An ability to flex the paws and grasp things was advantageous; digits evolved into fingers, claws into fingernails. Front limbs became principally a means of holding on, while the rear limbs served as a means of propulsion and also of static support.

Thus the animals could leap safely about the trees, and also could sit with the spine erect, the head turning with a perceptive eye, the ears twitching.

It can be supposed that the attributes favouring an arboreal existence also promoted yet more cerebral development. A large brain relative to body size evolved; accommodating a larger brain required some restructuring of the skull, which in turn was affected by the masticatory demands of the foods which the animals ate—fruit, leaves, insects, meat. Such an omnivorous diet calls for neither the specialised canines and slicing teeth of the carnivores, nor the grinding molars of the herbivores. The ancestral set of general all-purpose teeth was retained. The jaws broadened and shortened, the face flattened, the eyes looked forward and the expanding brain took up more and more room at the back of the skull. These interactive and interdependent features evolved over millions of years, a mosaic of cause and effect from which evolved the order of mammals known as the primates.

In basic zoological terms, the primates which evolved from the early arboreal mammals are distinguished from all other placental mammals by the fact that they have retained the four kinds of teeth found in ancestral mammals (incisors, canines, premolars and molars); they can hold things between finger and thumb, they have frontally directed eyes and have a large brain, relative to body size. They are represented today by 193 living species, all but one of which are covered with hair.

Hominid ancestry

The broadest categories of the primate order were also the earliest to have existed in evolutionary time, and the divisions were created principally by the geographic isolation resulting from the breakup of Gondwanaland, the supercontinent on which the primates had originated. Thus, the tarsier suborder became confined to the islands of Indonesia and the Philippines, and the prosimian suborder is best represented today by the lemurs of Madagascar, where the infraorder has been isolated for close on 60 million years. Another infraorder of prosimian, represented by the pottos, lorises and bushbabies, remained on continental Africa and Asia, and has found isolation in a nocturnal way of life as other primates adopted a diurnal lifestyle.

Isolation similarly split the anthropoid suborder when the landmass of South America broke away from Gondwanaland about 40 million years ago, carrying with it the primate stock which evolved into the platyrrhines—the New World monkeys. Subsequently, the catarrhine stock left on Gondwanaland split into its two main groups, probably along the lines of diverging dietary preferences. One group adopted a mainly herbivorous diet and gave rise to the Old World monkeys or cercopithecoids (represented today by the baboons and the colobines), while the other retained a more omnivorous diet and produced the hominoids (gibbons, apes and humans).

The precise dates at which these splits occurred are uncertain, but the fossil evidence suggests that the hominoid line is at least 25 million years old. A putative ancestor from that time has been found in the Fayum, south west of Cairo. The land is arid desert now, but 25 million years ago it was tropical rain forest and swampland, laced with broad meandering rivers. Scientists excavating fossil beds in the region have recovered the remains of a creature which is described formally as *Aegyptopithecus zeuxis*, though it is more colloquially known as the "dawn ape". Jaws and teeth, a skull and the skeletal parts of several individuals suggest that *Aegyptopithecus* was diverse and very generalised in its physical form. Experts have reconstructed from the fossil evidence a picture of a small arboreal primate, about the size of a domestic cat, with a sinuous back, long limbs, and all four feet capable of both grasping branches and conveying food to the mouth. The eyes looked forward, indicating stereoscopic vision, and the brain was larger in proportion to bodyweight than that of any other mammal then alive.

The descendants of *Aegyptopithecus* and its kind appear to have been very successful in evolutionary terms. More than 50 species are known from the fossil record, and hence palaeoanthropologists are inclined to refer to the Miocene (the geological period extending from 26 million to 8 million years ago) as the age of the ape. One of these species, *Proconsul africanus*, is believed to represent the evolutionary line which led to the modern apes and humans.

First described from a nearly complete face and partial skull discovered by Mary Leakey on Kenya's Rusinga Island, Lake Victoria, in 1948, *Proconsul* was a tree-dwelling animal about the size of a baboon which roamed East Africa about 18 million years ago, sometime after the monkey and ape lines had diverged. More remains were recovered during the 1970s, enabling scientists to reconstruct a skeleton that was essentially 75 percent complete. The result showed an unexpected mixture of characteristics. *Proconsul* had a backbone resembling that of the gibbon, shoulder and elbow joints like those of the chimpanzee, and the wrists of a monkey. Overall, *Proconsul* is quite unlike any living ape, but could be ancestral.

Around 17 million years ago, the African continental plate butted up against Europe, raising high mountains and creating a landbridge across which many African animals migrated into Eurasia for the first time. Among them were apes whose fossil remains have also been proposed as candidates for the ancestry of the ape and human lines. *Dryopithecus* was found in Greece, *Ramapithecus* and *Sivapithecus* in the Siwalik Hills of northern Pakistan. The fossil evidence was fragmentary, but for many years *Ramapithecus*, dating from 14 million to 7 million years ago, was almost universally accepted as the earliest known ancestor of the human line. During the early 1980s, however, the discovery of more complete ramapithecine remains showed that it and the sivapithecines are more likely to represent ancestors of the orang-utan on their evolutionary and migratory journey to the south-east Asian islands where they are found today. Consensus opinion now rates the dryopithecines as close cousins headed for extinction, and regards Africa as the cradle of mankind.

The emergence of mankind

The question of human origins has intrigued every generation. Charles Darwin (*see* **B18**) added a biological dimension with the publication of *The origin of species* in 1859. The controversy aroused by Darwin centred very largely around the mistaken idea that the theory of evolution implied that humans were descendants of the apes. This mistake is still encountered with surprising frequency, even though Darwin's original work and the many studies conducted since then all make the evolutionary proposition quite clear: humans are not descended from the apes, the two branches evolved simultaneously from a common ancestor which existed sometime in the past.

Among evolutionists, the question of human origins is basically a question of when the divergence of the ape and human lines occurred, and what the common ancestor looked like. For the greater part of the time since Darwin's day it has been assumed that the answers to these questions would be supplied by the fossil remains of the ancestral forms which might be recovered from geological deposits of ever-greater antiquity—if only those fossils could be found. Thus began the search for the missing link, as it became popularly known. By the 1960s the results of these fossil hunts had provided the basis for a widely-accepted scenario in which humans had evolved from *Ramapithecus* on a line which had split from the apes some 30 million years ago. Since the 1960s, however, this fossil-based scenario has been displaced by one based on biochemistry which puts the human/ape split at just 5 million years ago.

Instead of studying fossil bones, biochemists have used the genetic material (DNA—deoxyribonucleic acid) of related living species to measure the amount of time which has passed since they diverged from a common ancestor. This work is based on three findings: first, DNA accumulates random mutations and changes over time which are evident in the protein structure of all individuals of a species. Second, as two lineages diverge from a common ancestor, each lineage accumulates changes in its DNA which are different from those of the other. Third, the accumulation of changes tends to occur at a regular, almost clocklike rate through time. Clearly, the greater the differences, the longer the divergence, and biochemists have thus been able to put a timescale on the divergence of the apes and humans. The orang-utan split away from the African hominoid stock about 12 million years ago, and the gorilla lineage diverged from the common ancestor of apes and humans about 8 million years ago. The chimpanzee and human lineages were the most recent to diverge from the common ancestor, their split having occurred about 5 million years ago.

Origin of the hominid lineage

In one sense the facts of human origins can be reduced to a series of dates at which humans and related species diverged from their common ancestors. But an intriguing question remains even then: what caused the splits; why did the species diverge from their common ancestor?

A species is the result of reproductive isolation. If the individual members of a viable breeding population reproduce only among themselves for any length of time, the genetic changes which accumulate with each generation will eventually produce a closely-related population which is significantly different from both its ancestral stock and the other descendants of that stock. If the process continues long enough a discrete species will have evolved, one which can only produce fertile offspring among its own kind. It can be supposed with some certainty that the reasons for the isolation which provoked speciation lay in the prevailing ecological circumstances of the time. Food supply would have been a primary factor, and this would have been susceptible to other factors such as climatic variation, the incursion of competing animals, climatic changes, or simply the pressures of a growing population.

Any one or a combination of these ecological factors could have moved a viable breeding population of individuals into reproduction isolation where they might evolve into a discrete species. Migration is the most obvious course by which such isolation could have been achieved—but not the only one. Exploiting an alternative food resource, or adopting different social strategies could have achieved a similar degree of isolation even in close proximity with the ancestral population.

Precisely why the gorilla, chimpanzee and human lineages diverged between 8 million and 5 million years ago is not known. It may have been a consequence of the major climatic fluctuations which occurred during that time, when the overall pattern ranged from hot and dry to wet and very cold. The tropical forests retreated to the equatorial region, woodlands became dominant and grasslands proliferated. And with the changes in vegetation the composition of resident animal populations changed too. Many species became extinct, particularly among the browsers, while the grazers became more numerous. Doubtless the common ancestor of apes and humans was also affected by these developments, but the only certainties are that divergence and speciation occurred during that time, and that the distinctive characteristics of the living species can be considered as adaptations which proved advantageous to a reproductively isolated population.

Distinctive Human Characteristics

The distinctive characteristics of humans are the adaptation to a terrestrial way of life and bipedal locomotion; the much reduced face and jaws, and the greatly enlarged brain. In evolutionary terms, bipedalism was the crucial movement, and it has been suggested that this was a consequence of the climatic changes which reduced the forest area and thereby increased competition for its resources. Under pressure from other arboreal primates, the human ancestor found a niche on the savannah. Whatever the case, bipedalism offered extensive evolutionary advantages. This was not because bipedalism itself is a particularly effective means of locomotion but rather because it freed forelimbs from locomotor functions and made them available for other purposes. One of the most important of these was the use of tools, and subsequently toolmaking. When the ancestral hominids first colonised the terrestrial habitat they had few inbuilt defence mechanisms and the ability to use stones, sticks and bones to ward off predators must have been of considerable survival value (as has been observed among present-day chimpanzees when they take to the ground). Initially used for defence, tools eventually were used in attack, heralding the adoption of a hunting mode of life. Toolmaking is also thought to have been one of the practices which favoured the development of language, and, since toolmaking called for fine manipulative skills, hand and brain evolved together; particularly those parts of the brain concerned with precise motor control and tactile sensation.

Another consequence of freeing the forelimbs through bipedalism was that carrying became so much easier. Thus food and other items could be carried over considerable distances and this facilitated the establishment of a home base. Perhaps even more important, the human infant could be carried in its mother's arms and held close to her body, allowing a much closer and more intimate relationship between mother and child than is possible in other animals. In terms of its physical development, the human infant is born in a very immature state; in part because of the limitations to the size of the birth canal imposed by the demands of bipedalism, but especially because of the large brain size of adult humans. It is therefore long dependent on parental care. This raises problems in a society where pregnant women and nursing mothers become dependent upon the group for food. Social bonds were forged in response, and it has been argued that the evolution of the particular form of reproductive cycle found in humans, in which the female is receptive to the male throughout most of her menstrual cycle should be seen as a means of ensuring that a male will be willing to assume responsibility for females and offspring.

FOSSIL EVIDENCE OF HUMAN EVOLUTION

A fundamental premise of palaeoanthropology (the study of man in times past) rests on the contention that unequivocal evidence of human evolution would be found in fossils of known antiquity linking modern man to extinct ancestor. Ideally, the fossils should comprise a series of complete skeletons from a precisely dated sequence of time: this would enable scientists to trace the evolutionary development of humans with complete certainty. But the arbitrary nature of the fossilization process virtually eliminates all chance that such an ideal could ever be achieved or even approached. Far from ideal, palaeoanthropology has had to work with a slowly accumulating collection of diverse and often very fragmentary specimens ever since it became an established discipline in the mid-19th century. In the first fifty years only five specimens were discovered; another twenty-five years passed before a dozen were known, and even today the significant specimens could all be accommodated on a billiard table. The fossils have come from Europe, the Far East and Africa; they span over 3 million years, but as clues to the process of human evolution during that time they represent a minute fraction of mankind's potential ancestry. It has been calculated that ten skulls from East Turkana in Kenya (an exceptional collection covering 1 million years), for example, represent only one individual in every 100 million.

Problems of Evidence

The shortage of evidence is compounded by other problems. Uncertainties concerning age, for instance, mean that differing features which may represent evolutionary change over time cannot be placed in chronological order. And many fossils are so broken, distorted or incomplete that unequivocal interpretation of their significance is rarely possible. In such cases, different authorities may emphasize the importance of different features with equal validity, and the points distinguishing their interpretations may be so slight that each depends as much upon the proponent's beliefs about the course of human evolution as upon the evidence presented.

Beliefs have always been an important component of palaeoanthropological debate, and for many years they centred around the question of the order in which humans had acquired the characteristics which distinguish them from other primates. Which came first—the restructuring of the jaw and speech?

The erect posture and bipedal gait? The enlargement of the brain? Two broad groupings developed in the science—one believing that enlargement of the brain had been the prime mover; the other contending that bipedalism had led the way—and as each new fossil was discovered it was immediately assessed according to those propositions. Neanderthal Man (1857) was initially dismissed as non-human on the basis of the shape and proportions of its brain; Java Man (1891) was promoted as small-brained but bipedal and dubbed *Homo erectus* because a thighbone was found in the same deposit as the skull; Piltdown Man (1912) was a forgery which found widespread acceptance because its large brain and apelike jaw confirmed the beliefs of prominent authorities; *Australopithecus* (1925) was rejected as a candidate for human ancestry because its small brain did not match the expectations of the day.

Subsequent discoveries, including fossils and a trail of fossilized footprints, have shown that hominids were fully bipedal more than 3.6 million years ago, though the configuration of skull and jaw remained distinctly apelike for some time thereafter, while brainsize did not begin to approach modern proportions until 1.5 million years ago.

Finding the fossils

Fossils (from the latin *fossilis*, meaning dug up) are the end products of a process in which organisms are buried and infiltrated by minerals which replace them, molecule by molecule, until, where organic material existed before, stone remains, exactly preserving the form of the original. Fossils have been the source of virtually all that is known about the evolution of life—from the oldest known forms (microscopic fossil algae dating back to 3.5 billion years) to modern times.

For an organism to become fossilized it must first of all be entrapped in a suitable material, away from the attention of scavengers and decomposers. Aquatic organisms comprise by far the greatest number of fossils, not only because they have been more numerous throughout the history of life, but also because the seabed or lake bottom favours fossilization. Terrestrial organisms are less commonly found as fossils (most are consumed or decomposed by other creatures soon after death), and hominid fossils are among the rarest of all.

Palaeoanthropologists wishing to find the fossil remains of early humans are limited by two major factors. First, humans evolved in the comparatively recent past and were not numerous until recent times—which means that the total number available for fossilization must always have been relatively small. Second, their way of life and the terrain they occupied were unlikely to favour the fossilization of their remains, and there are few places in the world where fossil beds of a suitable age and composition are exposed.

Early European Sites

In scouring the world for potential fossil deposits, palaeoanthropologists have found ancient caves to be a most productive source of fossils (and not only of hominids). Whether originally used as shelters, or as dens to which predators such as leopards or hyenas may have retreated with their victims, bones left in the cave did not decay, but were fossilized as debris and rockfalls filled the caves. The first hominid fossils ever known to science were discovered at cave sites in Europe—Cannstadt in Germany (*c*.1700); Koestritz, Upper Saxony (1820); Kent's Cavern, Devon (1829); Engis in Belgium (1833), Gibraltar (before 1848), Neanderthal in Germany (1857). Several of the discoveries made before Darwin published his theory of evolution in 1859 received little notice at the time of discovery; some were lost. Investigations moved to the Far East at the end of the 19th century, where *Homo erectus* was recovered from riverbed deposits in Java (1891), and again in cave deposits near Peking during the 1920s.

Fossil Discoveries in Africa

Cave sites in South Africa have also proved to be a good source of hominid fossils. Alerted in the 1920s by quarrymen exploiting the lime-rich infills of ancient cave systems in the dolomitic hills, palaeoanthropologists have since recovered a number of important fossils from these sites.

The famed fossil sites of East Africa are predominantly volcanic in origin; the ash settling from eruptions associated with the formation of the Rift Valley having created conditions that were particularly suitable for the fossilization of bone. At Olduvai Gorge in Tanzania, where an ancient lake basin was inundated by successive eruptions of ash and subsequently drained by geological faulting, a river has sliced through the deposits to reveal much evidence of the hominids who frequented the area from at least 2 million years ago. Volcanic eruptions similarly preserved the 3.6 million year old footprint trail at Laetoli, near Olduvai.

As at Olduvai, volcanic activity and a lakeside environment were also responsible for the preservation of hominid fossils dating from 3.1 million years ago which have been found in the Afar depression of Ethiopia, and those dating from 1.8 million years ago found in the Koobi Fora region of the Lake Turkana basin, northern Kenya.

Hominid fossil sites may be discovered by chance or by a geological survey which deliberately sets out to locate cave sites or sedimentary beds of an age and situation which renders them likely to contain hominid remains. In cave sites the fossils are nearly always embedded in a hard calcrete matrix from which they are removed by careful preparation after the rock has been removed from the cave. Open sedimentary beds often extend over many hundreds of square kilometres and specific sites worthy of excavation are usually identified by foot surveys leading to the discovery of fossil bone eroding from the side of a watercourse, or a steep slope cutting into the fossil deposits.

Assessing the age of hominid fossils

The age of a fossil is of paramount importance to the palaeoanthropologist in the assessment of its evolutionary significance. Until the late 1950s scientists could do no more than assess the age of their finds in *relative* terms, that is according to the kinds of other fossil animals found in the same deposit or sequence of deposits. The fossil record as a whole gives a broad picture of the order in which various animal forms have evolved and become extinct through the course of geological time. Hominid fossils are not found among the remains of dinosaurs, for instance, so must be younger; on the other hand, they must be older than any extinct animals (such as hyenas and pigs) which may be found in deposits overlaying the hominid beds.

Relative dating was always of limited use to palaeoanthropologists since human evolution occurred in a recent and extremely brief period of geological time (if the whole of Earth history was condensed into 24 hours, man would have existed for little more than one minute). Estimates of the fossils' age in years were made from time to time, but they were rough estimates based on guesses of how fast evolution proceeds, and of the rate at which sedimentary deposits accumulate. Most underestimated the actual ages which were given when developments during the 1950s, enabled geochronologists to give an *absolute* date for hominid fossil deposits.

Methods of Dating

Several methods of absolute dating have been applied to the study of fossil man:

Radiometric dating is based on the principle that a radioactive "parent" element decays into a stable "daughter" element at a constant rate. Once the rate of decay is known, the age of a sample can be calculated from the ratio of parent to daughter elements which it contains. It should be noted that it is not the fossils themselves that are dated, but the deposits in which they are found. The cave sites of South Africa and elsewhere are devoid of materials suitable for radiometric dating, but the volcanic beds of East Africa have proved especially informative in this respect because they contain the minerals necessary for the *potassium-argon* dating method, which measures the ratio of the radioactive isotope of potassium, K-40, to its decay product, the gas argon 40. Potassium-argon is used for the absolute dating of deposits between 230,000 and 26 million years old, which makes it particularly suited to the needs of palaeoanthropologists.

Fission-track dating is a method in which the age of a specimen is assessed from the tracks made by the fission of uranium atoms within them. The density and number of tracks already present in the specimen are compared with those produced when the specimen is exposed to neutron radiation in the laboratory. This comparison provides the basis for an estimate of age.

Radiocarbon dating: the radioisotope carbon-14 accumulates in living tissue, but begins to decay after death. The rate of decay is known, and so the proportion of carbon-14 remaining in a specimen is a measure of the time which has passed since the organism ceased to live. After about 50,000 years, however, so little carbon-14 remains that dating becomes impossible. This limited timespan makes the methods of little use to palaeoanthropologists, but it has proved immensely useful to archaeologists in the dating of wood and other organic materials.

Thermoluminescence: with the passage of time, certain substances accumulate energy in the form of electrons trapped at defects in the crystal lattice of their constituent minerals. When the materials are heated this energy is given off as a "puff" of light (thermoluminescence, or TL); the intensity of that light is a measure of how long the energy had been accumulating in the material, and this can be set against a known timescale to give an estimate of the material's age. The method has been particularly useful in dating archaeological finds such as pottery, where it is certain that the firing process reset the material's TL clock to zero when the pot was made, but it has also been used to date flints that were dropped in early man's campfires. These go back to 100,000 years ago.

Geomagnetic dating (also known as *palaeomagnetic dating*): makes use of the fact that the Earth's magnetic field has changed direction many times in its history. When metals are deposited in sediments they align with the prevailing magnetic field, which is then effectively "fossilized" as the sediments harden. The record of these directional changes through geological time establishes a sequence of broad time-segments which can be used for dating deposits directly, or as a check of other methods.

THE FOSSIL LINEAGE

From the earliest days of palaeoanthropological research, investigators have tended to consider the fossils in chronological order (on either the relative or the absolute timescale), from oldest to youngest, and to describe the differences between them as progressive evolutionary changes which have led, ultimately, to modern man. So long as the number of hominid fossils remained small, and the temporal distance between them large, this attractively simple scheme remained valid, inculcating a general readiness to believe that human evolution had been a straightforward single-line affair, unwaveringly directed towards its ultimate expression: *Homo sapiens sapiens* and contentious only in the matter of which human attributes were acquired first—restructuring of the jaw, the bipedal gait, or the large brain?

Straightforward and attractive, yes, but contradicting the evidence of evolution in many other mammalian lineages. The fossil remains of pigs, horses, and antelopes, for example, display a tremendous amount of variation, not only through the geological sequence, but also at any given point on it, indicating that their evolution had been more of a radiation than a single line, with extinctions and proliferations of species occurring at many points in their evolutionary histories. Indeed, the frequency of extinction and speciation found in the fossil record of most organisms whose remains have been found suggests that such patterns are the rule. Why should humans be the exception?

The answer emerging from the tremendous advances made in palaeoanthropological research over the past twenty years is that they are not. Though the total number of fossil hominids is small (as was the total number of hominids available to be fossilized, especially when compared with the size of living pig, antelope and horse populations), it shows that there have been extinctions and speciations during the course of human evolution too.

The fossil hominids discovered so far date from over 3.5 million years ago to less than 30,000. This survey presents them in a series of broad groupings which represents both a chronological sequence and a presumed evolutionary progression, but it should be noted that the relationship of one fossil to another is not always a matter of universal agreement. A brief account of the discovery and initial description of each is given, together with some discussion of evolutionary status and affinities.

The australopithecines

The oldest known group of hominids, dating from 3.7 to 1.6 million years ago. Most authorities now accept four species—*Australopithecus afarensis, A. africanus, A. boisei* and *A. robustus*. The taxon was created in 1925 by Raymond Dart (1893–1988), professor of anatomy at the Witwatersrand University in South Africa, to accommodate a fossil skull which had been sent to him following its discovery during blasting activities at a lime quarry near Taung, in the northern Cape Province. The specimen comprised the greater part of a juvenile skull, together with a endocast of the right half of the brain (formed by the petrification of sediments which had filled the cranium after death). The face was complete and undistorted, with large rounded orbits, flattened nasal bones and a forward jutting jaw. Though the overall configuration of the specimen was essentially apelike, Dart noted several features which in his view made it more likely to represent the hominid lineage. The dental arcade was parabolic (it is more U-shaped in the apes); the erupting permanent teeth had a hominid cusp pattern; the braincast displayed certain hominid characteristics, and the foramen magnum (the hole in the base of the skull through which the spinal cord joins the brain) was set well forward beneath the skull, indicating that the head had been held erect at the top of the spine as in humans, and implying that the creature had been bipedal. In apes the foramen magnum is more to the rear of the skull and the head is slung forward, as befits their quadrupedal gait.

When Dart published his conclusions he claimed that his *Australopithecus africanus* (the southern ape of Africa) represented an early stage of human evolution. The claim was rejected, principally because it contradicted prevailing views. No evidence of early man had been found in Africa until then, and consensus opinion held that man had evolved in Asia or Europe, where the known fossils had been found. Furthermore, *A. africanus* had a small brain and a jaw of hominid configuration, which directly contradicted the faked Piltdown skull then still reinforcing the contention that a large brain and ape-like jaw would have characterised the earliest human ancestors. The leading authorities of the day dismissed *Australopithecus* as an ape, and therefore nothing to do with human evolution.

More than a decade later, in 1936, a retired Scots medical doctor and palaeontologist, Robert Broom (1866–1951), decided to look for more specimens of *Australopithecus* and re-investigate the matter of its relationship to human evolution. Broom was then 69. By the time he died in 1951 at the age of 84, he and his associates had recovered numerous australopithecine fossils from cave sites at Sterkfontein, Swartkrans and Kromdraai near Pretoria, in the Transvaal. Broom's findings confirmed Dart's assertion that the australopithecines were good candidates for the ancestry of man. Though Broom tended to create a new taxon for each of his finds, it soon emerged that two species were represented: the lightly-built *A. africanus*, which includes the Taung specimen and is often referred to as the *gracile* australopithecine; and the heavily-built *A. robustus*, the *robust* australopithecines. Mean brain size is estimated to have been 450 cc for *A. africanus*; 500 cc for *A. robustus*.

Dating the South African fossils has always been a problem, due to the confused geology of the infills and a lack of materials suitable for dating. The current consensus view suggests a date of about one million years ago, though some authorities claim that two million could be nearer the mark.

The Work of the Leakey Family

In 1959 Louis Leakey (1903–72) and his wife, Mary (1913–96), recovered an almost complete skull, lacking the mandible, from deposits at Olduvai Gorge in Tanzania subsequently dated at 1.7 million years by the potassium-argon method. Though the skull showed definite affinities with the robust australopithecines from South Africa, it was thought to differ sufficiently to merit the creation of a new genus: *Zinjanthropus* (East African man), with the species name *boisei* honouring a benefactor. Subsequently the generic distinction has been dismissed and the specimen is now known as *Australopitheus boisei*.

Since 1969 teams under the direction of National Museums of Kenya Director, Richard Leakey (1944–), have recovered numerous australopithecine fossils with both gracile and robust affinities from 1.4 to 1.8 million year old deposits at East Turkana, northern Kenya. In 1985, the same team recovered a robust australopithecine skull from 2.5 million year old deposits on the west shore of Lake Turkana.

Between 1973 and 1977 joint French and American expeditions recovered large numbers of gracile australopithecine fossils from deposits dated at 2·6 to 3·3 million years ago in the Afar depression region of north-eastern Ethiopia. The fossils proved to be remarkably similar to others found at Laetoli, near Olduvai Gorge, by Mary Leakey in 1974–5 which were dated at 3.6 million years. In publishing the Afar findings, Donald Johanson, (1943–) and his co-authors concluded that the Afar and Laetoli material represented a single species which was sufficiently distinct from existing species to merit the creation of a new taxon: *Australopithecus afarensis*. Mary Leakey objected to this conclusion.

The fossil hominids discovered at Laetoli came from the same age deposit as a trail of fossilised footprints, and this circumstantial evidence invites the inference that the trail was made by those same hominids—*A. afarensis*. Evidence has been adduced for and against, but the issue remains contentious.

The affinities of the australopithecines

The South African discoveries established the australopithecines as viable candidates for the early ancestry of man, while fossils from East Africa and Ethiopia have shown that the species were widely dispersed through Africa between 3·7 and 1·6 million years ago. The distinction between the robust and gracile species is considered to represent differences in diet, the heavier teeth and facial build of the robust australopithecines reflecting the masticatory demands of an herbivorous diet while the lightly-built gracile australopithecines were adapted to a less demanding omnivorous diet. This distinction is presumed to represent a dietary specialization which led the robust australopithecines away from the ancestral australopithecine stock and ultimately to extinction, while the gracile line continued and thus represents the earliest known stage of hominid evolution.

Several schemes of australopithecine phylogeny (the evolutionary history of the group) have been proposed, their suggestions as to the manner by which the australopithecines evolved among themselves and ultimately into *Homo* differing principally on the questions of whether or not *A. afarensis* is accepted as a valid species, and whether the Afar and Laetoli fossils represent a single species or two distinct species. But despite their differences, no scheme denies that the australopithecines represent a pre-human phase of hominid evolution during which considerable advances were made in the development of the upright stance and bipedalism, and in the modification of the dentition, while expansion of the brain proceeded slowly; and all agree that the next stage of human evolution is presently understood to be represented by *Homo habilis*.

HOMO HABILIS

The taxon was created by Louis Leakey and his co-authors in a 1964 *Nature* paper describing hominid remains excavated at Olduvai Gorge in 1961 from deposits dated at 1.7 million years by the potassium-argon method. The fossils comprised a lower mandible, skull fragments, and a group of handbones. They were found in association with stone tools, and this was a persuasive factor in the authors' decision to assign the fossils to the genus *Homo*, since no tools had ever been found incontrovertibly associated with the australopithecines and it was generally considered that man by definition was a toolmaker. Hence the name, *Homo habilis*, colloquially translated as "handy man".

Further remains of *Homo habilis* were found at Olduvai in succeeding years, including teeth, limb bones and a badly crushed and distorted skull. Richard Leakey's team at East Turkana discovered the skull known as 1470 (from its museum accession number KNM-ER 1470), which is informally described as *Homo habilis*, as are sundry other finds from East Turkana. Remains assigned to *Homo habilis* have also been recovered from excavations at the Swartkrans and Sterkfontein cave sites in South Africa, and at deposits in the Omo river basin in southern Ethiopia. In 1986, a new survey of the Olduvai Gorge deposits (led by Donald Johanson), recovered numerous fragments of skull, jaw and limb representing a single individual, which was subsequently assigned to *Homo habilis*.

The fossil evidence of *Homo habilis* recovered to date gives the species wide distribution through Africa, and a timespan dating from 2.1 to 1.8 million years ago. The species' mean brainsize is estimated to have been 750 cc.

The affinities of *Homo habilis*

Though the significance of the fossils was widely acknowledged, and the association of stone tools as a definition of man not questioned, *Homo habilis* did not find universal acceptance when the species was first proposed in 1964. All agreed that stone tools and an enlarged brain represented a significant step in the human direction, but some critics felt that the Olduvai material was insufficient evidence upon which to found a new species; others felt that if the material were to be assigned to a new species it should be within the genus *Australopithecus*, not *Homo*. The specimen certainly possessed a blend of gracile australopithecine and *Homo* characteristics which might be supposed to present an intermediatory stage between the two, but critics observed that in the then prevailing state of knowledge there was insufficient temporal and morphological space for a new species between *Australopithecus* and *Homo erectus* (the latter is generally accepted as the immediate antecedent of modern humans, *see below*). Louis Leakey, however, firmly believed that both *Australopithecus* and *Homo erectus* were aberrant offshoots from the hominid line which became extinct, and his promotion of *Homo habilis* as the oldest representative of the human line must be seen in the light of this belief.

The status of *Homo habilis* itself has not been much clarified in the quarter century since it was first described. Two main issues have arisen: First, the discovery of *Homo erectus* fossils from 1.6 million year deposits at East Turkana indicates that *Homo habilis* was one of at least three hominid species alive at that time (the other was *A. robustus*), which questions its status as an ancestor of *H. erectus*. Second, the *Homo habilis* fossils discovered at Olduvai in 1986 by Johanson and his team show a considerable degree of affinity with the *Australopithecus afarensis* material dating from more than 3.5 million years ago, which suggests that the ancestral form remained unchanged for a very long time, and that the *Homo* characteristics evident in later specimens of *H. habilis* must have evolved very quickly.

The evidence suggests that *Homo habilis* is still more of an idea in an evolutionary scheme than a well-defined example of anatomical fact linking one species to another. Only more evidence and rigorous analysis of early hominid variation will resolve the question of its status.

HOMO ERECTUS

The most widespread and longest-surviving of the fossil hominids. Remains have been found in north and east Africa, Europe, Indonesia and China. The fossils date from 1.6 million years ago (West

Turkana) to less than 300,000 years (China). Mean brain size ranges from 900 cc in early specimens to 1100 cc in late specimens.

The first known specimens were described by Eugene Dubois (1858–1940) in 1894 and included a calotte (the cranial vault) and a complete femur (thighbone) excavated from sedimentary deposits comprising freshwater sandstones, conglomerates and volcanic material at a bend of the Solo river in Central Java, Indonesia. The cranial capacity was relatively small (900 cc) while the femur was entirely human, and this combination led Dubois to assign the fossils to a new species: *Pithecanthropus erectus*, meaning erect ape-man, while the specimen became popularly known as Java Man. When fossils of similar configuration were found in China (Peking Man) both the Java and Peking material was assigned to the taxon *Homo* with sub-specific distinctions made for the Java (*Homo erectus javensis*) and Peking material (*Homo erectus pekinensis*). Subsequently, sub-specific distinctions were dropped and the taxon became known as *Homo erectus*.

Remains displaying *Homo erectus* characteristics have been recovered in Europe from sites in Germany (both East and West), Hungary, Greece, and France, and in 1960 a skull found at Olduvai Gorge extended the range of the species to Africa. Subsequently, further remains were found in Morocco and Algeria, in the Omo river basin of Ethiopia, and the Lake Turkana basin, northern Kenya.

In 1985 a virtually complete *Homo erectus* skeleton was found in deposits on the western side of Lake Turkana dated at 1.6 million years old. The remarkable preservation of the specimen is thought to be the result of the body having sunk quickly into lake silts after death. The skeleton is immature, its development matching that of a modern 12 year old. Estimates based on its limb size and modern growth rates suggest that the individual would have stood 1.68 m tall as an adult. Cranial capacity is as yet undetermined, but clearly relatively low. The forehead is low and recedes, as does the chin.

The affinities of *Homo erectus*

Though *Homo erectus* is well positioned in time to be both a descendent of earlier hominid forms and an ancestor of modern humans, several questions arise from its distribution and physical characteristics. Some authorities argue that the Asian and African forms are so distinct that the latter should not be assigned to *Homo erectus*. Others have suggested that the species represents a side branch of human evolution which became extinct, and its co-existence with *Homo habilis* at East Turkana indeed could be seen as reason for dismissing it from the human line.

There is also continuing debate on whether the relatively incomplete material from Europe represents the "true" *Homo erectus* or a group that should be more closely aligned to modern humans. This in turn raises the question of the *Homo erectus/Homo sapiens* transition: was this a gradual change, as some authorities see demonstrated in the Omo material? Or was there a long period of stasis followed by abrupt change?

ARCHAIC HOMO SAPIENS

A term applied to specimens which might be said to exemplify the *Homo erectus/Homo sapiens* transition mentioned above, and also integral to the proposition that modern man evolved in Africa in the relatively recent past. The definitive specimen (Rhodesia Man) was discovered in the course of mining operations at Kabwe, Zambia in 1921, and comprises a complete cranium, teeth and skeletal fragments. Recent appraisal of the site and associated finds has suggested that the remains date from at least 125,000 years ago. Cranial capacity is 1280 cc, indicating an enlarged brain. Numerous other specimens assigned to the group have come from more than 30 sites spanning Africa from north to south and covering a timespan ranging from 500,000 to 30,000 years ago. Some display features characteristic of the ancestral hominids, others are entirely modern. An age of about 100,000 years has been given to comparable forms known from Qafzeh in Israel, but all other evidence of anatomically modern man known from outside Africa is significantly younger. This is seen as indicating that modern man originated in Africa and migrated from the continent to populate the rest of the world not more than 200,000 years ago.

NEANDERTHAL MAN

The first specimen was discovered by quarrymen clearing a cave in the Neander valley, near Dusseldorf in 1857. Following its classification as a distinct species in 1864, *Homo neanderthalensis* soon became symbolic of the popular view of early man as an inferior and degenerate version of modern man. Based at first on a shortage of evidence and a determination to believe in the purity of the human line, this misconception was later reinforced by the distinguished palaeontologist Marcellin Boule (1861–1942) in a series of reports on Neanderthal remains found in cave sites at La Chapelle-aux-Saints and La Ferrassie between 1908–1912. Boule interpreted skeletal deformities as indicative of an habitual slouching gait and concluded that Neanderthal Man was every bit as degenerate as had been popularly supposed. Subsequent studies have shown that the deformities were the result of arthritis and that the Neanderthals were a sturdy and successful race, well-adapted to the environmental conditions of their time.

Discoveries of Neanderthal fossils at Engis in Belgium (1832), and Gibraltar (before 1848) predated the original find, and further remains have been found in Europe, Iraq and Israel. Bone structure and stout muscular attachments indicate that the Neanderthals were generally short and thick-set, with large feet and hands and a body form similar to that of modern cold-adapted people. Average brain size was over 1400 cc (some 10 percent larger than modern human, relative to body size) and exceeded 1700 cc in some large males. Dating of the fossil sites indicates that the Neanderthals lived from about 130,000 to 35,000 years ago. Thus they appear to have been a well-adapted and successful group of hunters and gatherers who ranged across Europe with the advance and retreat of the Ice Age.

The affinities of *Homo neanderthalensis*

Anatomical characteristics evident in both the Neanderthals and *Homo erectus* indicate that the two shared a common ancestry and possibly even a direct line of descent, but their relationship to modern man is far less clear. There are common characteristics, but much more that is different between the two forms. Moreover, it is generally felt that the proximity of the dates at which the Neanderthals disappeared and the modern humans became prevalent leave too little time for evolution to have effected the change from one to the other. After 100,000 years of unchallenged existence, the Neanderthals disappeared between 35,000 and 30,000 years ago. Only the remains of people anatomically indistinguishable from modern humans have been recovered from more recent sites.

This transition from Neanderthal to anatomically modern man poses what has become known as the "Neanderthal Problem": what happened to the Neanderthals in Europe? Only one of three explanations could apply: either the Neanderthals themselves were transformed into modern humans by a very rapid process of evolution, or they were overrun and replaced by modern humans who moved into Europe from some other point of origination, or they interbred with modern human immigrants and their distinctive characteristics were lost in the process. All three explanations have had their advocates. Argument and counter-argument have been pursued at length since the turn of the century, but genetic research (see below) indicating that modern humans originated in Africa and left the continent relatively recently strongly suggests that replacement was probably responsible for the disappearance of the Neanderthals. This need not have been a violent process. Some interbreeding also could have been involved, and the principal factor could have been better adaptation, perhaps of a behavioural or social nature. It has been suggested, for instance, that speech and enhanced social communication could have given the modern humans adaptive advantages in the changing, post-Ice Age climate of Europe which increased their reproductive rate and population growth while Neanderthal numbers declined to the point of extinction.

HOMO SAPIENS SAPIENS

Fossil remains of anatomically modern humans are known from sites in Europe, Africa, the Near East, Asia and Australia. The first and most famous to be found was Cro-Magnon Man, unearthed in the Dordogne region of France in 1868 and dating from about 40,000 years ago. Fragmentary fossils of a wholly modern form recovered from a cave at the Klasie's river mouth in South Africa date back to more than 100,000 years ago, while those from the Mungo site in Australia are from 32,000 years ago. On present knowledge, these two finds represent the greatest time-depth and geographic dispersal of early modern humans.

The dispersal of modern humans appears to have been rapid between 30,000 and 20,000 became especially so with the domestication of animals and crop plants from about 10,000 years ago. Migration into the Americas was delayed until a landbridge across the Bering Straits opened through glacial ice about 18,000 years ago, but excavations have shown that modern humans were well-established in north America soon thereafter and had spread as far south as the Chilean Andes by 12,000 years ago.

The spread and proliferation of anatomically modern humans is inextricably linked with the development of technological skills, art, and circumstantial evidence of social interaction. While the Neandertals employed a stone tool technology little improved from earlier forms, the anatomically modern humans introduced the flint-flaking techniques by which a greater variety of tools were made. Personal adornment and careful burial of the dead were features of their lifestyle not evident among the Neandertals, and cave paintings speak eloquently of their perceptive talents.

More recent studies of mitochondrial DNA, which is inherited strictly through the maternal line because the sperm does not contribute mitochondria to the fertilised egg cell, show that modern humans can trace their ancestry to a single female, commonly referred to as Eve, a member of a population living in Africa some 150,000 years ago.

THE STUDY OF SOCIAL ANTHROPOLOGY

Social anthropology is concerned with the way men live as members of ordered societies. It has been described as a branch of sociology, or as the sociology of the simpler peoples. Neither description is wholly correct. A social anthropologist seeks to identify the *structure* of the society he studies and the *processes* of social interaction within it. His method is direct contact—what has been called "participant observation." Therefore he must deal with a unit small enough to be manageable with this technique. Nation-states, such as sociologists commonly work among, are too large. Most social anthropologists have done their work in what we call "small-scale" societies; that is, peoples who lacked such media of communication as writing or money, let alone mechanical means of transport, until these were brought to them from Europe. A social anthropologist may choose to work in some section of a society that possesses those techniques—in the ancient countries of the East or in Europe or America. In that case he confines himself to a microcosm such as a village or a factory. When he is writing of societies alien to his own and that of most of his readers he is obliged to describe their *culture* as well as their social relationships, since without such a description his readers would not be able to picture, or even understand, the social rules that are his main subject of study; this would be superfluous for a sociologist taking modern machine society for granted. Culture has been called the raw material out of which the anthropologist makes his analysis of social structure. It is the sum total of standardised ways of behaving, of lore and technique, of belief and symbolism, characteristic of any given society. The founders of social anthropology in Britain were B. Malinowski and A. R. Radcliffe-Brown.

The Notion of Roles

All the world, as Shakespeare said, is a stage, and this is a key metaphor for social anthropologists. Every individual does indeed play many parts, not consecutively but all together; for every social relationship carries with it the expectation of society that the parties to it will behave in approved ways. Father and children, ruler and subject, buyer and seller, husband and wife; every one of these words is the name of a *role* to be played by the person it describes. The playing of roles involves the recognition of claims and obligations as well as appropriate modes of behaviour in personal contacts. All these rules are called *norms*; when they are concerned with rights and obligations they are *jural norms*. A social norm is what people think ought to happen; unlike a statistical norm, it may or may not be what happens in the majority of cases.

Kinship and Marriage

In societies of simple technology most roles are *ascribed*; that is, the parts people will play in life are given them at birth by the fact of their parentage and of the group of which this makes them members. In other words, the most important principle of organisation is *kinship*. W. H. R. Rivers called this "the social recognition of biological ties." The ties in question can be called genealogical; they all derive from the recognition of common ancestry. Such ties may be fictitious, as when a child is adopted. But in the vast majority of cases the relationships that are recognised are actually biological.

No man can recognise for social purposes all the individuals with whom he has a common ancestor somewhere in the past, or even know of their existence; their number increases with every generation. In every society a selection is made, from the whole universe of genealogically related persons, of certain categories towards which an individual recognises specific obligations and on whom he can make specific claims. Such *corporate groups* of kin have a permanent existence; they recruit new members in each generation in accordance with recognised rules. Kin groups are concerned largely with the transmission of property, and for this and other purposes they recognise the common authority of a senior man; they are also religious groups.

The common patrimony of a kin group normally consists in land or livestock; in societies of more advanced technology it may be a boat, as in Hong Kong, or even, as in Japan, a family business. It may have non-material resources too, such as the right to supply chiefs or priests for the society as a whole; this may be put conversely as the right to hold political or religious office. Those who share a common patrimony have a common interest in preserving and increasing it. Wrongs done by their members to outsiders are compensated from their collective resources, and they have joint responsibility for seeking compensation if one of their own members is injured or killed.

Descent

Kin groups may be recruited according to a number of principles. A principle widely followed in small-scale societies is that of *unilineal descent*; that is, group membership is derived from one parent only, either the father (*patrilineal* or *agnatic*) or the mother (*matrilineal*). Property is *administered* by men in either system, but in the matrilineal system it is *inherited* from the mother; hence its control passes from a man to the sons of his sisters. In a unilineal system every individual recognises kin linked to him through the parent from whom he does not trace his descent; this is the principle of *complementary filiation*. The complementary kin are *matrilateral* where the descent rule is patrilineal, *patrilateral* where it is matrilineal. A unilineal descent group is called a *lineage*.

Descent can also be traced *cognatically*; that is, all descendants of a common ancestral pair may be recognised as forming one *kindred*. In such a system there is no permanent group patrimony; people inherit a share of the property of both their parents, and this is often conferred upon them when they marry, while their parents are still living. Or all the inhabitants of a village may share rights in its rice-fields or fishing ponds; a man chooses among what kin he will live, but he can have rights in one village only. In such a system there are no continuing groups defined by descent; the permanent group is territorial, consisting of the inhabitants of the village.

Marriage

Kinship status is defined by legitimate birth, and this in its turn by legal marriage. There are always rules against marriage with specified categories of kin, though these are not necessarily near kin. Some societies consider that the ideal marriage is that between the children of a brother and a sister; if such marriages are repeated through the generations they create a permanent link between two lineages. Marriage between members of the same lineage is nearly always forbidden; this is expressed in the term *lineage exogamy*. The general effect of the prohibitions is to spread widely through a society the links created by marriage, links that impose an obligation of friendship on groups that without them would be mutually hostile.

In a matrilineal system women bear children for their own lineage; it is expected that they should be fathered by a man who has married their mother according to the approval procedure, but a child's lineage membership is not affected by the marriage of its mother. But in a patrilineal society wives must be brought from outside to bear children for the group. Associated with this fact is the payment of *bridewealth*, which used to be mistakenly interpreted as the purchase of wives. This payment is what fixes the status of a woman's children; all those she bears while the bridewealth is with her lineage are reckoned as the children of the man on whose behalf it was paid, even if he is dead and she is living with another partner. In a matrilineal society the making of gifts is part of the marriage procedure, but they are of slight economic value in comparison with bridewealth. The difference is correlated with the difference in what the husband acquires by the marriage; in both cases he gains the right to his wife's domestic services and sexual fidelity, but where bridewealth is paid he can also count her children as his descendants and call on their labour when he needs it.

In societies where most roles are ascribed by the fact of birth, marriage is the most important field in which there is freedom of choice. But the choice is commonly exercised not by the couple but by their lineage seniors. *Polygamy*, or the simultaneous marriage of a man to more than one woman, is permitted in lineage-based societies; indeed it is the ideal, though only a minority of men attain it.

Authority Systems

Every society has some arrangements for the maintenance of order, in the sense that force may be used against those who infringe legitimate rights. In every society theft, adultery, and homicide are treated as offences. Where no individual has authority to punish these on behalf of the community, *self-help* is the approved course. Lineage membership is significant here; a man who is wronged will go with his kin to seek redress (for a theft or adultery) or vengeance (for the homicide of a kinsman). Vengeance can be bought off by the payment of compensation; but because the taking of life is a serious matter in the most turbulent of societies, there must also be a solemn reconciliation, with a sacrifice to the ancestral spirits, between the lineages of killer and victim. The recognition of an appropriate method of dealing with injuries has been described as "the rule of law" in its simplest form.

Within a lineage the senior man is expected to settle quarrels, and the ancestral spirits are believed to punish with sickness juniors who do not listen to him. When quarrels break out between members of different lineages, their elders may meet and seek a solution. Where there is no hereditary authority individuals may attain positions of leadership in virtue of their powers of mediation by persuasion.

In addition to the maintenance of rights, most societies require at some time arrangements for the organisation of collective activities. It is possible for there to be no ascribed role of organiser; in such a case leadership is a matter of competition. Competitive leadership in economic activities is characteristic particularly of the very small societies of New Guinea. What is needed here is not only powers of persuasion but resources to reward the participants. The very important principle, to be discussed later, that every gift ought at some time to be returned, is the basis of their position. A man who can put others in his debt can call upon their labour. It may take a long time to build up the necessary resources for acknowledged leadership, and leadership may be lost to a rival and is not necessarily passed to an heir.

Responsibility both for law and order and for collective activities may be shared on recognised principles among the whole adult male population. This is done where society is organised on the basis of *age*, a system widely found in east and west Africa. In such a system all adult men pass through a series of stages at each of which appropriate tasks are allotted to them. In its simplest form the division is made into "warriors" and "elders". This principle may be complicated in various ways, but the essence of it is that men in their prime are responsible for activities requiring physical strength, impetuosity, and courage, while their elders have the task of mediating in disputes, discussing public affairs, and performing sacrifices to the ancestors. Men in the warrior grade are the fighting force, and may also have the police functions of summoning disputants and witnesses before the elders, and seizing property from a man who has been adjudged to pay compensation and does not do so voluntarily. Sometimes specific public works are allotted to them, such as rounding up stray cattle or clearing weeds from paths or springs. It is also possible for community responsibilities to be shared in more complicated ways, as for example among the Yakö of Nigeria, where the adherents of particular religious cults are believed to call on the spirit which they worship to punish persons guilty of particular offences.

Hereditary Chiefs

Where there are hereditary chiefs, both public works and the maintenance of law and order are the responsibility of the chief and his subordinate officials. Resources are accumulated for public purposes by the collection of tribute, and labour is obtained for public works by the recognition of the principle that persons in authority can claim the labour of those subject to them. Expectations are attached to the role of chief as to any other. Chiefs are expected to dispense justice fairly, to be generous to the poor, to reward loyalty, and to be successful in war, and they are reminded of these expectations in the course of the elaborate rituals performed at their accession. The prosperity of the whole land is commonly held to be bound up with the health of the chief and the favourable attitude towards him of supernatural beings. He may be obliged to obey all kinds of ritual restrictions to this end; for example it was believed of the ruler of Ruanda, in east Africa, that he must not bend his knee lest the country be conquered. Chiefs are either themselves responsible for the performance of ritual on behalf of the whole populace or must maintain priests to do this.

Social anthropologists have recently turned their attention to the process of competition for the commanding roles which any society offers. Some would claim to have discarded the idea of structure altogether in favour of that of process; yet the structure must be taken into account as the set of rules in accordance with which the game is played. There are societies where it is the rule that on the death of a chief his sons must fight for the succession, to test who is the strongest and has the largest following. There are others where the rule of succession may seem to be clear, and yet there can always be dispute as to who fits it best. Sometimes people pursue the struggle for power by accusing their rivals of witchcraft; sometimes by massing their followers behind them in a show of strength before which their adversaries retire; the first is the method of the Ndembu in western Zambia, the second that of the Pathans in the Swat Valley in Pakistan. Such confrontations occur at moments of crisis, but the process of building up support is going on all the time. The study of these processes is among the most interesting new developments in social anthropology.

Economic Systems

The typical methods of subsistence in societies of simple technology are food-gathering (hunting and collecting roots and berries), herding, and agriculture. The domestication of animals and plants came relatively late in man's history; without it there could have been no permanent settlement, no cities, no civilisation. But the life of those food-gatherers who still exist is not a hard one; they can get an adequate diet in a very short working week. The three modes of subsistence should not be thought of as forming a historical series; moreover, there are many varieties of each, depending on the nature of the environment and the techniques used.

We shall never know what brought about the "agricultural revolution" or why the greater number of our ancestors chose the harder, but more productive, life of cultivators. This may have been somehow made necessary by the pressure of population in certain areas. Nor shall we know when and how trade and exchange began. We can reject the argument of Adam Smith that people first provided themselves with enough to eat and then began to exchange the products of specialists for surplus food. Exchanges are made among and between peoples who suffer from periodic famines, and the objects which are most valued are not exchanged for food.

These exchanges are not conducted, however, through the medium of a currency which enables people to calculate the relative value of goods of different kinds, as does money in a commercial society. Certain goods can be exchanged only for certain others—in the highlands of New Guinea, for example, shells and the plumes of rare birds. This has led to much controversy on the question whether primitive peoples can be said to have money. Of course, if money is defined as a universal medium of exchange, they do not. But some modern anthropologists find that too strict a definition, and prefer to say that, whereas modern currencies are "general-purpose money," societies of simple technology have different kinds of "special-purpose money"—strings of shells, hoe-blades, iron bars and the like, which are used only in a limited range of transactions.

It is certainly true, however, that money of this kind cannot be made the means of very exact calculations of profit and loss. It is often assumed that where there is no such common medium of exchange people do not make any economic calculations, and dispose of their property in ways that are the reverse of business-like. The principal reason why this assumption is made is the great importance attached to societies of simple technology to the making of gifts. The essential difference between a gift and a commercial exchange is that no return is stipulated. In the commercial world goods are sold, services hired, at a price, and anyone who fails to pay has broken a contract and is liable to be punished. The obligation to return a gift is a moral one. Moreover, to compete in the giving of gifts seems at first sight the very opposite of competition in the acquisition of wealth. But in most societies people who have a surplus of wealth like to have a reputation for generosity; only in the affluent world of machine production people feel the need to have many more material possessions before they begin to think in terms of surplus.

The Exchange of Gifts

The exchange of gifts plays a particularly large part in the societies of Melanesia, where men form partnerships for the express purpose of giving and receiving valuable objects, and earn prestige at least as much by giving as by receiving. This exchange of valuables, mostly shell ornaments, is so important that it has a name in the language of each society. The first such exchange system to be described by an anthropologist was the *kula* of the Trobriand Islands, observed by Malinowski. An important man had a partner in an island on either side of his own home; from one he received armbands and returned necklaces, from the other he received necklaces and returned armbands. These objects did not become part of a store of wealth for any man; nobody could hold one long before it was time to pass it on to his partner. To receive his gift a man sailed by canoe to his partner's home; he was there welcomed peaceably, and while he was making his formal visit the crew were bartering their goods on the shore with the local populace. Thus the *kula* partnership had the nature of a political alliance; it was a means of maintaining peaceful relations between populations which would otherwise have been hostile.

In the highland area of New Guinea identical objects are exchanged, so that the relative value of amounts given and received can be calculated. In some parts the ideal is that a return gift should be twice the original one. Naturally it is no small achievement to carry on a prolonged series of exchanges at such a rate. Very few men manage it, and those who do are the acknowledged leaders of their community. For each large gift he has made a man wears a little bamboo stick hung round his neck; thus his munificence is publicly proclaimed. A new partnership is initiated by making the minimum gift. Men make these partnerships with others not bound to them by kinship, notably with their relatives by marriage. Each partnership extends the range within which a man can count on friendly treatment. So widespread is the idea that gifts should be repaid, and services rewarded, after some delay, and at the discretion of the man making the return, that where the highland people have taken to growing coffee for sale, the large-scale planters do not pay wages but employ young men for planting who get their return by coming to them later for help in difficulties. Of course the young men would stop giving their work if they judged that the return was not adequate.

Significance of Gifts

Gift-giving, then, is an investment, but not one that produces a direct material return. One anthropologist, R. F. Salisbury, has called it an investment in power. The second classic example of the uneconomic use of goods is the *potlatch* practised by the Kwakiutl and kindred tribes of the northwest coast of America. This was a public distribution of goods at which the recipients had to be given their gifts in strict order of rank. The giver earned prestige and power by the scale of his gifts, by his knowledge of the correct rank order, and by the famous deeds (*potlatches* and others) which he was able to claim as feats of himself and his ancestors. Rivals for precedence would assert their claim by vying with each other in the amounts they distributed. The Kwakiutl way of avenging an insult was what has been called the "rivalry gesture." The man who thought he had been insulted actually destroyed valuable property by throwing it on a fire, or into the sea, and his enemy had to match him in destruction or be humiliated.

Certainly this is not turning resources to material advantage. Equally, it is not done without calculation. In the affluent society people display their superior affluence because this demonstrates their prestige rating, just as in the *potlatch*; and they keep on good terms, through the hospitality they offer, with people from whom they may later seek a return in professional dealings, rather as in the Melanesian gift-exchanges. In fact a substantial proportion of the incomes of people in European societies who are by no means affluent goes into the making of gifts—to parents, to kin, to friends, to persons who have helped one or given one hospitality; gifts which are given as a matter of moral obligation. The difference between the uses to which resources are put in societies of simple and of complex technology is one only of degree. The proportion that is devoted to securing non-material advantages is higher in the small-scale societies, and so is the proportion of gift-giving to commercial exchange. In gift-giving there is no bargaining, but there is a clear expectation of return. The initiation of new social relationships by the making of gifts is not by any means confined to New Guinea. Bridewealth which legitimises children is the most widespread example. Pastoral peoples in East Africa also make gifts of stock to selected friends in distant parts. The friend on his home ground is a sponsor for his partner, and he is expected to make return gifts from time to time, and may be asked for a beast if his partner is in difficulties.

A small number of social anthropologists have specialised in the study of the economic systems of small-scale societies, and have asked whether the concepts devised for the analysis of monetary economies—such notions, for example, as capital and credit—can be applied to people who gain their livelihood directly from the resources of their immediate environment. Starting from the assumption that there is always some choice in the allocation of resources, they have observed how these choices are actually made in the societies where they have worked. They have asked how the value of such goods as are obtained by barter is measured; how labour is obtained, how directed and how rewarded for such enterprises as the building of a canoe or a temple, which call for the co-operation of large numbers. They have examined the use of media of exchange, asking how far any of these fulfil the functions that we associate with money.

The general conclusion of these studies is that peoples of simple technology are perfectly capable of rational calculation in the allocation of their resources, even though their calculations are rough by comparison with those of the entrepreneur in an industrial society. They know what to regard as an adequate return when they are bartering goods. They withhold goods from consumption when they are planning an enterprise; that is to say, a man who proposes to initiate such an activity as canoe-building, arranges to be able to feed his labour force.

Religion

All societies of simple technology have beliefs, and think that unseen personalised beings influence the course of nature by direct intervention, causing rain to fall if they are pleased with the actions of men and withholding it if they are angry, sending sickness as a punishment and so forth. In the great majority of such societies the most important spirits to be worshipped are those of dead ancestors. But there may also be a belief in gods responsible for particular aspects of the world, to whom offerings are made for protection or success in their special fields. Many preliterate peoples believe in a "high god" from whom all other spirits derive their power, and one school of anthropology sees this as evidence of an original state of higher religious consciousness from which man has declined; but this view is not widely held.

Rituals involving groups of people are commonly performed on occasions when changes of status are to be signalised. A child becomes a member of society not by being born, but at a naming or showing ceremony. A youth or girl becomes adult at initiation. Marriage, which makes a couple into potential parents and links their kin groups, is another such ritual.

In funerary rites the dead person is made into an ancestor, and his heir adopts his social personality and his responsibilities. The accession of a man to political office is surrounded by ritual, and chiefs frequently observe annual rites at the time of harvest, when it is the season, not the person, that is changing. These are *confirmatory* rituals, designed to keep society and the world on an even course. When something goes wrong, a drought or epidemic or an individual sickness, *piacular* rituals are performed to make peace with the spirits responsible for the disaster.

An essential aspect of many of these religions is the belief in witchcraft—that is that it is possible for humans to harm others merely by hating them. Witchcraft supplies an explanation of an undeserved misfortune. Diviners employ a multitude of techniques (which anthropologists rather inaccurately call oracles) to detect whether a disaster is a merited punishment or is due to witchcraft.

Myths

Every small-scale society has its myths—stories which tell how the word as people know it came to be. Sometimes their ritual re-enacts the myth; often the myth tells how the ritual was first performed and thereby gives a reason for its continuance. Then there are myths telling how death and evil came into the world. Some myths lend authority to the existing social order, and particularly to the claims of ruling groups, by telling how the social structure was divinely ordained. Under the influence of the French anthropologist Lévi-Strauss, many anthropologists are beginning to see both myths and the symbolism of ritual as man's earliest attempt to order intellectually the world of his experience.

The existence of ultra-human beings on whom the affairs of men depended was universally taken for granted until a very short time ago. As long as this belief was held, the established order in any society was supported by the tenets of religion. But there are also revolutionary religions. In recent years anthropologists have been inspired by the many new religions that have arisen in developing territories to give more attention to this side of the subject. Notably in Melanesia, a succession of prophets have appeared with a message announcing the imminent coming of an ideal world from which all hardships would be banished, including the subjection of the indigenous peoples to colonial rulers. These events turned the attention of anthropologists, along with sociologists and historians, to the study of similar movements in the past, and we now have a considerable body of literature on such subjects as "the religions of the oppressed."

Closer study of traditional religions from this point of view has shown that they also often include symbolic reversals as part of their regular ritual. The high are brought low and the humble exalted. In his ritual installation a chief may be beaten and abused by his subjects, or a rite that confirms his authority may include a simulated rebellion. Women may assume for a day the garb and authority of men. There is a temporary suspension of the rules and cultural forms which differentiate the members of the ritual congregation. This may go as far as "ritual licence", in which actions that at other times are offences liable to punishment, notably sexual promiscuity, are permitted and must not be made a reason for quarrels. Or it may be simply that the participants are masked, stripped naked, or dressed identically. Such rituals affirm their common membership, or communitas, as it has been called, and where they express not merely unity and equality, but the reversal of high and low, they remind the powerful that they must not abuse their power. Rites of this kind form a phase in complex rituals. They are followed by a re-affirmation of the accepted order in its ideal form, where hierarchical relations maintain order without promoting injustice. This theory would interpret the new "subversive" religions as the response to situations in which the injustices of the powerful have gone too far for the re-assertion of communitas to be possible.

Social Change

No doubt all the societies that anthropologists have studied have been gradually changing throughout the centuries when their history was not recorded. But they experienced nothing like the rapidity of the changes that came to them when they were brought under the rule of European nations and introduced to mass production and a money economy. The effect of this has been in essence to widen the range of choice in the relationships that people can form. A man may choose to be dependent on an employer rather than on work in co-operation with his kin or village mates. He is more likely to rise in the world by going to school and getting a city job than by earning the respect of the villagers or the approval of a chief. Small-scale societies are now becoming merged in larger ones and the close ties of the isolated village are loosened. In the newly created industrial areas new specialised associations are formed to pursue professional and other interests. The social insurance that kinship provided is lacking, and it has not as yet been replaced by what the state offers in the highly industrialised societies. The minority that has whole-heartedly adopted the values of the industrialised world now produces the political rulers of new states. They are impatient to carry the majority along the same road, but there are profound conflicts of value between them and the still largely illiterate masses.

The first studies of this type of social change

were mainly interested in the effects of intrusive influence on traditional institutions in rural areas. Later, attention was turned to social relationships in the cities which have come into being, or greatly increased in size and population, as a result of the development of commerce and industry. Recent work is largely concerned with the extent to which immigrants to the cities preserve their sense of a distinctive home origin. Immigrant populations which have abandoned all their traditional customs often preserve a strong sense of a common identity which differentiates them from their neighbours, and sometimes they even create a myth of the possession of "special customs" that has no foundation in fact. This sense of a particularly close relationship between people from the same place of origin is called *ethnicity*. It has been argued that when the members of an *ethnic group* are in a privileged position they appeal to the sense of ethnicity to close the ranks against outsiders. The less fortunate might be more likely to unite on a non-ethnic basis to improve their position. Divisions based on ethnicity cut across those based on social class. This is a field in which the interests of social anthropologists and sociologists overlap. The conclusions drawn from studies in African cities could be, and no doubt will be, tested against work among immigrant populations in Europe and America.

Recent Trends in Social Anthropology

Structural Anthropology, as it has been developed in France by Lévi-Strauss, has the aim of establishing the universal characteristics of cultural, that is rule-governed, human behaviour, as opposed to the natural, instinctive behaviour of non-human species. Lévi-Strauss finds the distinguishing feature of man in communication by symbols, and holds that the way in which symbols are constructed reflects the structure of the human brain. As he uses the term social structure, it means the system of symbols by which a given society comprehends the world of its experience.

According to Lévi-Strauss communication is an exchange, and for him all exchange is communication. The prohibition of incest, which represents to him man's first move from natural to cultural life, obliges men to exchange their sisters, giving them to other men as wives. Then they exchange goods for goods or services. But for Lévi-Strauss the most important exchange is that of messages, and his central interest is in the codes in which the messages are embodied. Every code is an arbitrary set of symbols, the meaning of which depends on the way in which they are related. A code is based on a logical structure, so that social structure is the structure of a socially accepted code. It should be noted that the existence of the structure is not demonstrated independently of the code, but deduced from it, while the nature of the code is deduced from the supposed nature of the structure.

For the principles of structure Lévi-Strauss turns to the linguists, notably Roman Jakobson, according to whom all speech-sounds can be analysed into pairs of opposites; it is by recognising these opposites that children learn to speak and to distinguish meaning. Lévi-Strauss argues that the structure of the human brain leads men to classify the objects of their experience into opposites, then finding mediating terms to link the opposites. The recognition of differences is in his view the basis of classification, more important than the recognition of similarities. In totemism, a phenomenon which many anthropologists have tried to explain, awareness of differences between social groups is expressed by associating them with different animals. Exogamous descent groups, the groups which exchange sisters, are commonly called by the names of animal species. Each group has its totem animal, and they often believe that they must not eat this animal. The rules attached to these animal names form a code which can be decoded as: "We, Elephants, are different from them, Lions", not because either group is *like* elephants or lions, but because the groups differ as species differ. Any contrasting species would do; there is no intrinsic relation between Elephants and elephants just as there is none between the sounds of a word and its

meaning. Totemism, then, is an arbitrary code to express the principles on which a society is organised.

Lévi-Strauss' most massive work is devoted to the interpretation of myth. In his view the material of myth comes from the unconscious. He has made an extensive study of the myths of Amerindian peoples, and has found that stories in which the incidents are superficially dissimilar lead to the same conclusion (convey the same message), and on the way deal with oppositions (or contradictions) between rules or necessary facts of life and human wishes. The episodes of myths are the symbols of the code, and they can be combined in many different ways, but always according to an underlying, unconscious logic (structure). To explain this logic he draws comparisons with music and with mathematics. A musical note has no meaning in itself, only as an element in a melody or a chord. A musical composition plays with modifications or transformations of themes or harmonies, and just as a theme can be transposed into a different key, so a message can be conveyed in images that may refer to the objects of all the different senses; sight (light and darkness), taste (cooking—the first volume of his great book on myths is called *The Raw and the Cooked*), hearing (noise and silence) and so on. Note that all these codes are concerned with contrasts. From mathematics Lévi-Strauss takes the idea of a system of algebraic signs which can be combined in many permutations. Ultimately the theory of myth tells us that the important socially prescribed relations between persons of different status can be represented as relations between animal species, between kinds of food, between kinds of sound and silence, smells and tastes, aspects of landscape or any of these in combination.

According to Lévi-Strauss, although the deep structure of thought is unconscious, the classification of observed phenomena is conscious, and is the first activity of the human mind. Hence he rejects the view that peoples of simple technology are interested in natural phenomena only in so far as these have practical uses.

Cognitive Anthropology was first taken up as a special field in America, where its pioneers were Ward Goodenough, Charles E. Frake and Harold Conklin. It has much in common with the structuralism of Lévi-Strauss, but its practitioners are not interested in myths, and the majority make less extensive claims than he does. Some of them do believe that studies of the way in which different peoples classify the objects of their experience should lead to the discovery of universal cognitive principles, but they do not seek to reduce all categories to binary oppositions; rather they talk of *contrast sets*.

Studies in cognitive anthropology began with the examination of kinship terms by the method known as *componential analysis*. Instead of asking what relatives were grouped together under a designation found in English kinship, such as "father" or "brother", cognitive anthropologists looked for the essential *components* of any kin term, and found these to be sex, generation, and lineal or non-lineal relationship to the speaker or the person referred to by the term. This method was considered to give a truer picture of the principles according to which people group their relatives.

Cognitive anthropology has also been directed to other *domains* of experience, that is fields to which a distinguishable vocabulary is observed to apply; for example, to the classification of colours or of disease, but most of all to that of flora and fauna, or folk taxonomy, as this is called. These studies elucidate not only the principles according to which people group and distinguish the objects of their environment but also the factual knowledge they have of them.

Marxist anthropology developed along with the general revival of interest in Marxist theory largely inspired by the new interpretation of Marxism introduced by the French writer Louis Althusser, not himself an anthropologist. The leading anthropological theorist in this field was Maurice Godelier, also in France. Like Lévi-Strauss, Marxists look for the unperceived structural laws on which all society rests, but they look in another direction. They find their answer in the *relations of production*, that is in the manner in which production is organised, and in particular the distribution of the resources which make production possible. They apply to the study of pre-capitalist societies the analysis which Marx himself made of capitalism, and seek to place the primitive and peasant societies of today, and also some vanished societies of which there are records, in their place in a line of developing social formations, each a transformation of its predecessor. Thus Marxist anthropology is in a sense an historical study, and can be contrasted with functional analysis in which societies are taken as they are when the observer sees them and treated, as Malinowski put it, as "going concerns". A functionalist study asks what keeps a society going; hence Marxists regard such studies as essentially conservative.

For Marxists a *social formation* is a combination of the forces of production and the relations of production. The forces of production consist in labour power and technical knowledge, and in the way production is organised. The relations of production are the relations between those who control the means of production—land or machines —and those who supply their labour power. Those who control the means of production are able to determine what share of the product shall go to the workers, and invariably they take more than a fair share. The state exists to practise this *extraction of surplus value*, as it is technically called. Accepted religious beliefs and other systems of ideas are not, as Lévi-Strauss and the cognitive anthropologists would have it, attempts to organise experience; they are delusions which conceal from the workers the way in which they are exploited. One social formation gives way to another when its *internal contradictions*—conflicts, incompatibilities—become too acute to be contained within the existing system. All aspects of a society are linked to the relations of production. Hence Marxist anthropologists do not admit the validity of cross-cultural comparisons between different institutions, such as kinship, economics, politics or religion, and argue that only social formations can be compared.

Thus they have given much more attention than earlier anthropologists to societies of hunters and gatherers, where nobody is dependent on others for the weapons that are the sole means of production. As soon as the means of production are appropriated by one section of society, the opposition of classes is observed. This change took place in the Neolithic period, when the invention of agriculture led to the recognition of rights in land. Even in those systems in which land is regarded as the common property of a group, the senior man or men who control its use are in a position to exploit their juniors, so that there are class divisions among kinsmen. It is also sometimes argued that where people believe that specialists in magic can influence the weather, or promote the growth of crops as the Trobriand magicians observed by Malinowski do, their knowledge is indispensable to production, and so they, too, make the workers dependent on them and can exploit them.

Marxist anthropologists make use of the ethnographic work of Malinowski and his pupils, who looked, as Malinowski had taught them, for the importance of reciprocity in exchange. Lévi-Strauss also discusses this in his theory of the exchange of women as the basis of kinship systems. But Marxists are concerned with inequalities rather than reciprocities in exchange, inequalities that those who own the means of production can impose. Thus they would not agree with Malinowski's followers, that there is any reciprocity in a state between rulers and ruled, that subjects pay tribute and rulers make their return both by maintaining order and in direct economic terms by the redistribution of wealth.

The study of **ecology** combines the work of anthropologists with that of human geographers and many natural scientists. It is associated with the name of the American anthropologist Julian Steward. Ecologists study the relations between society, technology and environment. They differ from the biologists who invented the term "ecology" in that they examine man's modification of his environment as well as his adaptation to it. Early ecological work concentrated on food-gathering populations who modify their environment very little, but it was soon extended to societies of pastoralists and cultivators.

Ecological studies have practical implications in various directions. They throw light on the success or failure of policies that are intended to raise standards of living, for example by persuading or compelling nomad pastoralists to become settled cultivators. A type of enforced change which has become widespread is the resettlement of populations whose homes have been flooded by the damming of rivers for hydro-electric projects; here the alteration in the environment is sudden and dramatic, quite unlike the effects of the unplanned changes of the past. It is usually accompanied by attempts to create a new environment that will make higher standards of living available, through housing schemes, new educational facilities, the introduction of new crops or farming methods, and so on. The proliferation of such schemes has been said to provide the anthropologist with a "laboratory situation" in which both policies and reactions can be compared. By combining ecological with medical studies it is possible to consider the prevalence of malnutrition or parasitic diseases in relation not only to the non-human environment but also to social groupings and norms which render certain populations, and particular categories within such populations, more vulnerable than others to these health hazards.

Another meeting-ground between anthropology and the natural sciences is in the new interest of sociologists in **ethology**, the study of the evolution of social behaviour. The classical exponents of this study have been Tinbergen in Holland and Lorenz in Austria. Close observation of the interaction between individuals and groups among non-human species has led many ethologists to conclude that animal populations may appropriately be regarded as societies. They hope to learn what tendencies among humans are genetically determined and so may not be amenable to deliberate attempts at social change. A subdivision of this study, human ethology, concentrates on minute details of behaviour with the aim of identifying gestures, facial expressions and the like that are found in all cultures, and so may be supposed to spring from affective systems common to all humanity. Yet a narrower subdivision is child ethology. Some anthropologists believe that these studies offer the key to the question What is Man? What are the characteristics that distinguish him from other animals, and how in fact did natural selection enable him to develop them?

These studies are still in their infancy, and in their present state they are vulnerable to some dangers. It is difficult, perhaps impossible, to use in the description of behaviour language which does not assume that what is described is social, the very question that the ethologists are asking. The assumption may be made unconsciously, but if it is consciously recognised it is possible to guard against it. The language used may also lead to the attribution to non-human animals of reactions that are specifically human (*anthropomorphism*). Zoologists may too readily assume that all human behaviour can be reduced to those reactions which are transmitted in our evolutionary heredity, forgetting that the processes of social conditioning are much more elaborate in man than in other animals. Anthropologists on their side may be too ready to seek the kind of interpretation of non-human behaviour that supports their *a priori* idea of the nature of man, *e.g.*, whether he is essentially aggressive or pacific, competitive or co-operative.

DEVELOPMENT ANTHROPOLOGY

Introduction

The word development became a technical term in colonial administration with the implementation in the British territories of the Colonial

Development and Welfare Act of 1940. With the passing of this measure Britain abandoned the principle that colonial territories should be self-supporting, and made available from British revenues grants for projects expected to improve the standard of living of the local populations. "Welfare" implied the expansion of social services: "development" was investment calculated to increase productivity. After the Second World War a similar policy was introduced in France, and as former colonial territories became independent the United States and the United Nations also contributed funds for their development; the United Nations proclaimed a "development decade" in 1960. The motives behind these policies were various; governments sought to extend their political influence, their trading relations and opportunities for their nationals, but a humanitarian element was also present. The development of resources had always been the aim of colonial powers, but now the emphasis was on the development of peoples.

The Problems of Development

In a sense anthropologists have been interested in problems of development from the time when, under the influence of Malinowski, British anthropologists turned from the reconstruction of the past to what he called "the anthropology of the changing African". African was taken as the type because it was the International African Institute, supported by large American grants, which supplied the bulk of the funds made available for research in anthropology in the period between the two world wars. Malinowski's pupils observed the effects that European penetration had had on African and other populations, and tended to concentrate on those which had been adverse. For a time they deplored economic development altogether, but they came to realise that the changes introduced by colonial rule were irreversible. They also had to recognise the fact that Western science and technology could and should be used for the benefit of non-Western peoples, particularly to raise standards of health and nutrition. Their attention was now focused on small-scale innovations with these aims, such as had of course always been attempted under colonial rule. The "community development" projects which had some vogue in West Africa in the period just before independence aimed at making much improvements through the efforts of the people expected to benefit from them, with some assistance from governments. Independent India adopted a community development policy which involved the division of the whole country into development areas under officials of the central government. Since the improvements sought were of a kind that any anthropologist would approve, it now became our task to explain the indifference or resistance which they so often encountered. Some also looked critically at the explanations in terms of "peasant conservatism" that were offered by people who were interested in development but not versed in anthropological theory.

The Awareness of Poverty

The interest in development which was manifested after the Second World War arose from a new awareness of the poverty of many millions of people in those newly independent countries that began to be called "under-developed", and later from the recognition that population was increasing faster than natural resources. These poorer countries were contrasted with the highly industrialised ones, which were assumed to be "developed", and it was further assumed that their problem was simply that too little capital had been invested in industry. Hence external finance was offered for development programmes which aimed at rapid industrialisation, and the next assumption was that this would increase national productivity, as it often did, and thus would automatically raise standards of living. It proved, however, to do little to alleviate the poverty of the peasant majorities of the populations concerned.

Food Production

Attention then turned to the possibility of increasing food production and peasant incomes along with it, by introducing more efficient methods of farming. Since most anthropologists have worked among rural populations, it is here that they might be expected to have something to contribute, and that their advice has in fact sometimes been sought. An anthropologist may, for example, be appointed as a member of a UN development team; or a private company may engage one as consultant, as was done when copper was discovered on the island of Bougainville and the inhabitants were not satisfied with the compensation they were offered for the expropriation of their land. Sometimes one has been asked to comment on an elaborate multiple project such as the damming of a river for a hydro-electric scheme and the resettlement of the people whose homes would be flooded, and has been able to indicate situations that would have to be taken into account and persuade the planners to work to a slower timetable.

But more often anthropologists have come to the scene after a plan has been carried through, have been able to see the various ways in which the results have differed from what was expected, and sometimes reasons why it has failed altogether—if, for example, a farm project does not attract or hold settlers.

The Colson–Scudder Survey

A well-known example of a study which was begun before the change that was planned and continued after it, is that made by Elizabeth Colson and the ecologist Thayer Scudder of the 56,000 Gwembe Tonga who were moved from their homes when the Kariba Dam was built on the Zambezi River. They made a detailed study of the Gwembe social organisation and adaptation to the environment in their traditional homes, and returned when the move was still a recent drama in most people's lives, and at intervals in later years. Their final study contrasted the adaptation to the move made by two village communities whose home environments had been very different and who had been moved to new sites only a few miles apart.

In their study of the resettlement process they called attention to the hardships that had been caused by requirements of technicians which were allowed to override consideration for human values. The height of the dam was raised after the preparations for resettlement had begun, so that the area to which many people had agreed to move was flooded and they had to be sent elsewhere. Those who had furthest to go had to be moved *en bloc* in a single day because the Public Works Department could only release the number of lorries needed for one day. New sites were not provided with water in time for the move, as had been promised.

This list of grievances illustrates both a failure to co-ordinate the activities of different technical departments of government and a lack of imaginative sympathy. But it also indicates that the agents of change must work within the limits of their technical resources. It would have been quite impracticable in this case, for example, for Public Works to transport several thousand people over 100 miles by a shuttle service, picking up families or even whole villages as and when they were ready to move. After all, the Kariba Dam had not been conceived as an operation to benefit the Gwembe Tonga. Anyone who is convinced that a project must go through can argue that the people who are affected will settle down after a temporary upset; and in a sense they do, as they come to take their new circumstances for granted.

Nevertheless, if those in authority think it important not to impose unnecessary hardships on those who are subject to their decisions, this detailed account of an exercise which is likely to be repeated in some form where dams are built, populations moved from disaster areas, refugees settled and so on, is a record to which they can look to see what mistakes they might avoid.

The Weinrich Study

A comparable study is that made by Dr. A. H. K. Weinrich (Sister Mary Aquina) of the African response to the various policies pursued by the government of Rhodesia (before independence) with the aim of improving African farming. Certain areas of land were earmarked for purchase by Africans who were required to show that they were efficient farmers. Others were irrigated and offered on lease to farmers who had to follow a closely controlled programme of work. The largest proportion of the area of land allotted to African occupation was "tribal trust land", where, after an attempt to enforce fixed standards of cultivation, the authorities fell back on the educational work of missionaries and extension officers. Dr. Weinrich investigated communities holding land in each of these three ways, and concluded that no great improvement in cultivation could be observed in any, except in the case of a minority of men and women who had followed courses of training to qualify as "master farmers". Her own conclusions were drastic: that *all* rights to agricultural land, including those of Europeans, should be conditional on efficient cultivation, and that every African cultivator should be held individually responsible for a specified area of land. Much more attention should be given to the education of peasant farmers in place of attempts at coercion, and farming communities should be given a say in the management of their own affairs. At the time when her findings were published, Zimbabwe had not achieved independence but whatever the type of government, it will have to deal with the problems that she has analysed.

These two examples of action taken in territories where policy was dominated by European settler interests. Few such territories remain today, and it is the professed aim of the rulers of all the new states to seek the welfare of the indigenous populations. In such a context an anthropologist could be in a stronger position. If his views were asked in advance, he might be able to say that an apparently beneficial scheme would not really be so; or that it would need to overcome specific difficulties arising from existing power structures or modes of co-operation; or that the benefits would be lost if they were not accompanied by technical instruction (for instance, in the control of irrigated water supplies or the maintenance of pumps).

A difficulty in organising co-operation between anthropologists and development agents lies in the different time-scales with which they work. An anthropologist does not expect to speak with confidence about the people he studies until he has worked with them for at least a year. No doubt a development plan takes a year to complete, but once it has been adopted it is expected to be put into operation as soon as possible. Time-tables are drawn up, and even if deadlines are seldom met, there must be an attempt to meet them. In any event, decisions have to be taken at the moment when problems arise. Occasionally an anthropologist has actually been put in charge of a small-scale project and has had to face this dilemma.

Some would say, then, that the studies made after the event to explain failure or disappointment form the most valuable contribution of social anthropology; they are there as warnings or lessons for future planners, provided the planners will read them—but this is a risky assumption. Others would say that development agents should learn the elements of social anthropology as part of their training, and if they did, "village level" or "rural development" workers would certainly be more sensitive to the reception of their activities by villagers.

Intermediate Technology

Where there are the best prospects for fruitful co-operation is in the introduction of small-scale improvements such as are sometimes called "intermediate technology". Such improvements can sometimes be made by people who have made no academic study of anthropology at all, if they have enough local knowledge. It was an anthropologist working with a WHO team who pointed out that apparently simple additions to children's diet were far beyond the means of urban workers in Jakarta, but it was a doctor in India who discovered how to make existing food sources far more nutritious.

A field that anthropologists are only now beginning to enter is that of the traditional contribution of women to the farm and household economy. The exhortations and demonstrations of agronomists have commonly been directed to men, and men have been persuaded—sometimes—that methods involving harder work will bring in higher returns; it is not often noticed that the women may be doing the harder work while the men get the price of the crop. A move is now being made to train women for anthropological fieldwork among their own compatriots. They will have the general knowledge of social structure that must be the basis of any research, but they will concentrate their attention on women and on those aspects of co-operation in the household that have generally been taken for granted in the past. What are the chores that occupy a woman's day and how could they be lightened by the adoption of simple labour-saving devices? What are their ideas on the health and feeding of children and on the treatment, or recourse for aid, in sickness? How much independence of decision do they have, and in what contexts? One outcome of these studies is expected to be a fuller understanding of women's attitudes towards child-bearing and their receptiveness or resistance to the idea of family planning which is now beginning to be considered so urgently important in heavily populated countries.

The Anthropology of Development

A distinction has been drawn between "development anthropology", that is anthropology in the service of development and "the anthropology of development", or the study of interactions between all persons concerned in development, those who intend to bring benefits as well as the supposed beneficiaries. Studies of the latter type would depart from that focus on the reaction of intended beneficiaries which has been the main interest of anthropologists up to now, and would examine not only the motives of development planners but the interactions between the representatives of different interests engaged in planning. In the two African examples cited here, the benefit of the peasant cultivators was not the primary aim; the Kariba Dam was intended to provide electric power for industry, the various Rhodesian land policies, as Dr. Weinrich repeatedly emphasises, to enable an African population to subsist within limits set by the interests of a European one. Other plans are forced on governments by one crisis or another. But in addition, closer analysis would show how the competing interests of different technical agencies may influence the content of any development scheme and will certainly influence the allocation of resources within it. Governments are not the only empire-builders; divisions within them also seek to extend their power, and every expert thinks the most important benefits are those that depend on his own expertise (anthropologists are no exception). The most effective study of this kind that has been made is the work not of an anthropologist but of a political scientist, Robert Chambers, who followed in detail the history of the Mwea land settlement that was initiated in Kenya just before independence. He, however, was not solely interested in description as opposed to prescription; he travelled through Africa looking at settlement schemes, and concluded that the most important prerequisite for success was to keep government provision to the minimum and rely on self-help. But, brilliant as his analysis of the planning process is, it does not tell anyone how to plan better. It just throws light on human weakness and suggests the impossibility of making a perfect plan. A good many anthropologists would hope to offer more, even if they had to confine themselves to limited aspects of a plan.

VI.   SCIENTIFIC TABLES
TABLE OF ELEMENTS

Element (Symbol)	Atomic Number	Atomic Weight	Valency	Element (Symbol)	Atomic Number	Atomic Weight	Valency
actinium (Ac)* ...	89	227		molybdenum (Mo)		42	95.94
aluminium (Al) ..	13	26.9815	3				
americium (Am)* ..	95	243	3, 4, 5, 6	neodymium (Nd)	60	144.24	3
antimony (Sb) ...	51	121.75	3, 5	neon (Ne)	10	20.17	0
argon (Ar)......	18	39.944	0	neptunium (Np)*	93	237	4, 5, 6
			4, 5, 6	nickel (Ni)...	28	58.71	2, 3
arsenic (As).....	33	74.9216	3, 5	niobium (Nb)....	41	92.906	3, 5
astatine (At)* ...	85	210	1, 3, 5, 7	nitrogen (N) ...	7	14.0067	3, 5
				nobelium (No)* ..	102	254	
barium (Ba)	56	137.34	2				
berkelium (Bk)* ..	97	247	3, 4	osmium (Os)	76	190.2	2, 3, 4, 8
beryllium (Be) ...	4	9.0122	2	oxygen (O)	8	15.9994	2
bismuth (Bi)	83	208.980	3, 5				
boron (B)	5	10.811	3	palladium (Pd)...	46	106.4	2, 4, 6
bromine (Br)	35	79.904	1	phosphorus (P)...	15	30.9378	3,5
				platinum (Pt) ...	78	195.09	2, 4
cadmium (Cd) ...	48	112.40	2	plutonium (Pu)*..	94	244	3, 4, 5, 6
				polonium (Po)* ..	84	210	
calcium (Ca)	20	40.08	2	potassium (K) ...	19	39.102	1
californium (Cf)* .	98	251		praseodymium (Pr)	59	140.907	3
carbon (C).......	6	12.0111	2, 4	promethium (Pm)*	61	145	3
cerium (Ce)	58	140.12	3, 4	protactinium (Pa)*	91	231	
caesium (Cs)	55	132.905	1				
chlorine (Cl).....	17	35.453	1, 3, 5, 7	radium (Ra)*....	88	226	2
chromium (Cr)..	24	51.996	2, 3, 6	radon (Rn)*....	86	222	0
cobalt (Co)	27	58.9332	2, 3	rhenium (Re)....	75	186.2	
copper (Cu)	29	63.546	1, 2	rhodium (Rh) ...	45	102.905	3
curium (Cm)*....	96	247	3	rubidium (Rb)...	37	85.47	1
				ruthenium (Ru) ..	44	101.07	3, 4, 6, 8
dysprosium (Dy) .	66	162.50					
				samarium (Sm) ...	62	150.35	2, 3
einsteinium (Es)* .	99	254		scandium (Sc) ...	21	44.956	3
erbium (Er).....	68	167.26	3	selenium (Se)....	34	78.96	2, 4, 6
europium (Eu)...	63	151.96	2, 3	silicon (Si)......	14	28.086	4
				silver (Ag)......	47	107.870	1
fermium (Fm)*...	100	253		sodium (Na)	11	22.9898	1
fluorine (F)	9	18.9984	1	strontium (Sr) ..	38	87.62	2
francium (Fr)*...	87	223	1	sulphur (S)	16	32.064	2, 4, 6
gadolinium (Gd)..	64	157.25	3	tantalum (Ta) ...	73	180.947	5
gallium (Ga)	31	69.72	2, 3	technetium (Tc)* .	43	99	6, 7
germanium (Ge)..	32	72.59	4	tellurium (Te) ...	52	127.60	2, 4, 6
gold (Au)	79	196.967	1, 3	terbium (Tb)	65	158.925	3
				thallium (Tl)	81	204.37	1, 3
hafnium (Hf)....	72	178.49	4	thorium (Th)	90	232.038	4
helium (He).....	2	4.0026	0	thulium (Tm)...	69	168.934	3
holmium (Ho) ...	67	164.930	3	tin (Sn).......	50	118.69	2, 4
hydrogen (H)....	1	1.00797	1	titanium (Ti) ...	22	47.90	3, 4
				tungsten (see wolfram)			
indium (In)	49	114.82	3				
iodine (I)	53	126.904	1, 3, 5, 7	uranium (U)	92	238.03	4, 6
iridium (Ir).....	77	192.2	3, 4				
iron (Fe).......	26	55.847	2, 3	vanadium (V) ...	23	50.942	3, 5
krypton (Kr)....	36	83.8	0	wolfram (W)	74	183.85	6
lanthanum (La) ..	57	138.01	3	xenon (Xe)	54	131.30	0
lawrencium (Lr)* .	103	257					
lead (Pb).......	82	207.19	2, 4	ytterbium (Yb) ..	70	173.04	2, 3
lithium (Li).....	3	6.941	1	yttrium (Y).....	39	88.905	3
lutetium (Lu)....	71	174.97	3				
				zinc (Zn).......	30	65.37	2
magnesium (Mg)..	12	24.305	2	zirconium (Zr) ...	40	91.22	4
manganese (Mn)..	25	54.9380	2,3,4,6,7				
mendeleevium (Md)*	101	256					
mercury (Hg)...	80	200.59	1, 2				

* In the cases of these elements, which are very rare or not found in nature, but have been artificially prepared, atomic weight in the chemical sense is meaningless; the integral mass of the most stable isotope known is given

Note: In 1961 the isotope of carbon-12 replaced oxygen as a standard, the weight of its atom being taken as 12This change of standard has meant a slight adjustment in atomic weights from the old chemical scale

The new elements with an atomic number higher than that of uranium 238 (element 92) are termed Transuranics

GAS LAWS

The Perfect or Ideal Gas Law: $pV = nRT$

where n is the number of moles in volume V at pressure p and absolute temperature T, and R is a universal constant

Van der Waals' equation: $\left(p + \dfrac{a}{V^2}\right)(V - b) = nRT$

where a and b are constants, different for each gas.

PERIODIC TABLE

PERIODIC TABLE OF THE ELEMENTS

Key to Chart

Atomic Number → 1 B
Symbol →
Atomic Weight → 10.811

Transition metals

Noble metals

GROUP	1A	2A	3B	4B	5B	6B	7B	8	8	8	1B	2B	3A	4A	5A	6A	7A	0
Period	Alkali metals	Alkaline earth metals																Inert gases
1	1 H 1·00797																	2 He 4·0026
2	3 Li 6.941	4 Be 9·0122											5 B 10·811	6 C 12·0111	7 N 14·0067	8 O 15·9994	9 F 18·9984	10 Ne 20·179
3	11 Na 22·9898	12 Mg 24·305											13 Al 26·9815	14 Si 28.086	15 P 30·9738	16 S 32·064	17 Cl 35·453	18 Ar 39·948
4	19 K 39·103	20 Ca 40·08	21 Sc 44·9559	22 Tl 47·90	23 V 50·942	24 Cr 51·996	25 Mn 54·938	26 Fe 55·847	27 Co 58·933	28 Ni 58·71	29 Cu 63·546	30 Zn 65·37	31 Ga 69·72	32 Ge 72·59	33 As 74·9216	34 Se 78·96	35 Br 79·904	36 Kr 83·80
5	37 Rb 85·4678	38 Sr 87·62	39 Y 88·9059	40 Zr 91·22	41 Nb 92·9064	42 Mo 95·94	43 Tc 99	44 Ru 101·07	45 Rh 102·905	46 Pd 106·4	47 Ag 107·870	48 Cd 112·40	49 In 114·82	50 Sn 118·69	51 Sb 121·75	52 Te 127·60	53 I 126·904	54 Xe 131·30
6	55 Cs 132·905	56 Ba 137·34	57 La* 138·91	72 Hf 178·49	73 Ta 180·947	74 W 183·85	75 Re 186·2	76 Os 190·09	77 Ir 192·2	78 Pt 195·09	79 Au 196·967	80 Hg 200·59	81 Tl 204·37	82 Pb 207·19	83 Bi 208·980	84 Po 210	85 At 210	86 Rn 222
7	87 Fr 223	88 Ra 226	89 Ac† 227															

* Lanthanides (see L72)

58 Ce 140·12	59 Pr 140·907	60 Nd 144·24	61 Pm 145	62 Sm 150·96	63 Eu 151·96	64 Gd 157·25	65 Tb 158·925	66 Dy 162·50	67 Ho 164·930	68 Er 167·26	69 Tm 168·934	70 Yb 173·04	71 Lu 174·97

† Actinides (see L3)

90 Th 232·038	91 Pa 231	92 U 238·03	93 Np 237	94 Pu 244	95 Am 243	96 Cm 247	97 Bk 247	98 Cf 251	99 Es 254	100 Fm 253	101 Md 256	102 No 254	103 Lr 257

Roman type—metals

Italic type—semiconductors } These designations refer to the normal materials usually at room temperature. Processes like heating or compressing can turn metals into insulators and vice versa.

Bold type—non-metals }

Note: It may be possible by artificial methods such as bombardment by other nuclei to produce elements with atomic numbers greater than 103. However all the very heavy elements are unstable and decay spontaneously into lighter elements. Because the lifetime of such elements is short no element with an atomic number greater than Uranium (92) occurs naturally on earth.

MEASURES, UNITS AND METROLOGY

Before any quantity can be measured one must decide on the *units* used for measurement. For example, a 2 lb loaf of bread when weighed in ounces will give 32, *i.e.* 2×16. This is because there are 16 oz in a pound. It would be incorrect to say the weight of the loaf is 2 or 32. We say it is 2 lb or 32 oz and we can convert from one unit to another by knowing the ratio of their sizes.

If a standard pound is kept somewhere this can be used to calibrate other standard weights using accurate scales. These in turn can be used to calibrate other weights which in turn can be compared with the loaf with scales in order to weigh the bread. Nowadays, for scientific purposes, weights are compared with that of the *international prototype kilogram* (**L70**), kept at Sèvres in France. For a long time the length of an object was obtained by making a comparison, direct or indirect, with the standard metre if using the metric system or the standard yard if using the Imperial system. The standard metre was the length between two notches on a metal rod, kept at a controlled temperature, at Sèvres. Time is measured in seconds, which at one time was defined as a certain fraction of the tropical year.

Definitions of this kind are unsatisfactory for two reasons. First, the tropical year is not constant and even the most carefully kept metal rods are liable to change their dimensions over a long period of time. Secondly, it is not always convenient to do a comparison with an object kept in France. Nowadays every effort is made to define units in terms of some fundamental property of matter which is reproducible everywhere and does not require comparison with one particular object. The second is now defined using an atomic clock and can be measured to an accuracy of 1 part in 10^{12}. Variations in the rotation of the earth are far greater than this. The metre is nowadays defined in terms of the distance light travels in one second (**L82**). Although the kilogram could likewise be defined in terms of some fundamental quantity of matter, such as insisting the mass of an electron is 9.1083×10^{-31} kilogram, this quantity is only known to about 2 parts in 10^5. Comparisons with the standard kilogram can lead to an accuracy of the order 10^{-9}, so at present this definition of the kilogram stands.

The scientist nowadays mainly uses the S.I. system of units. SI is short for "Système International d'Unités" and it is a system of metric units now coming into international use through the agency of such bodies as the General Conference of the International Bureau of Weights and Measures and the International Organisation for Standardisation (ISO) in whose work Britain participates. Information about SI units is available in booklets published by the British Standards Institution, 389 Chiswick High Road, London W4 4AL.

Definitions of the Base Units

The system uses the seven *base quantities* listed below:

Quantity	Name of unit	Symbol of unit
Length	metre	m
Mass	kilogram	kg
Time	second	s
Electric current	ampere	A
Thermodynamic temperature	kelvin	K
Luminous intensity	candela	cd
Amount of substance	mole	mol

The seven S.I. base units are defined as follows:

The *metre* is the length travelled by light in a vacuum in $1/299\ 792\ 458$ sec (**L82**).

The *kilogram* is the mass of the international prototype of the kilogram (**L70**). Scientists use the word 'mass' where the layman would say "weight". Strictly speaking, weight is not a base quantity and is a measure of *force*.

The *second* is the duration of $9\ 192\ 631\ 770$ periods of the radiation corresponding to the transition between the two hyperfine levels of the ground state of the caesium-133 atom (*see* **Clock L26**).

The *ampère* is that constant current which, if maintained in two straight parallel conductors of infinite length, of negligible circular cross-section, and placed 1 metre apart in vacuum, would produce between these conductors a force equal to 2×10^{-7} newton per metre of length.

The *Kelvin*, unit of thermodynamic temperature, is $1/273.16$ of the thermodynamic temperature of the triple point of water (*see* **Absolute Temperature L3**).

The *Candela* is the luminous intensity, in the perpendicular direction, of a surface of $1/600\ 000$ square metre of a black body at the temperature of freezing plantinum under a pressure of $101\ 325$ newtons per square metre. Luminous intensity is a property of a *source* and is the amount of luminous flux (light) it throws out per steradian.

TABLE I

Quantity	Name of SI unit	Symbol	SI unit in terms of base units or derived units
frequency	hertz	Hz	$1\ \mathrm{Hz} = 1\ \mathrm{s}^{-1}$
volume	stere	st	$1\ \mathrm{st} = 1\ \mathrm{m}^3$
density	kilogram per cubic metre		$\mathrm{kg\ m}^{-3}$
velocity	metre per second		$\mathrm{m\ s}^{-1}$
force	newton	N	$1\ \mathrm{N} = 1\ \mathrm{kg\ m\ s}^{-2}$
pressure, stress	pascal	Pa	$1\ \mathrm{Pa} = 1\ \mathrm{N\ m}^{-2}$
viscosity (dynamic)	pascal second		$\mathrm{Pa\ s}$
work, energy, quantityof heat	joule	J	$1\ \mathrm{J} = 1\ \mathrm{N\ m}$
power	watt	W	$1\ \mathrm{W} = 1\ \mathrm{J\ s}^{-1}$
quantity of electricity	coulomb	C	$1\ \mathrm{C} = 1\ \mathrm{A\ s}$
electric potential, EMF	volt	V	$1\ \mathrm{V} = 1\ \mathrm{W\ A}^{-1}$
electric field	volt per metre		$\mathrm{V\ m}^{-1}$
electric capacitance	farad	F	$1\ \mathrm{F} = 1\ \mathrm{C\ V}^{-1}$
electric resistance	ohm	Ω	$1\ \Omega = 1\ \mathrm{V\ A}^{-1}$
electric conductance	siemens	S	$1\ \mathrm{S} = 1\ \Omega^{-1}$
magnetic flux	weber	Wb	$1\ \mathrm{Wb} = 1\ \mathrm{V\ s}$
magnetic flux density	tesla	T	$1\ \mathrm{T} = 1\ \mathrm{Wb\ m}^{-2}$
inductance	henry	H	$1\ \mathrm{H} = 1\ \mathrm{V\ s\ A}^{-1}$
magnetic field	ampère per metre		$\mathrm{A\ m}^{-1}$
luminous flux	lumen	lm	$1\ \mathrm{lm} = 1\ \mathrm{cd\ sr}$
luminance	candela per square metre		$\mathrm{cd\ m}^{-2}$
illuminance	lux	lx	$1\ \mathrm{lx} = 1\ \mathrm{lm\ m}^{-2}$
heat flux density, irradiance	watt per square metre		$\mathrm{W\ m}^{-2}$
heat capacity	joule per kelvin		$\mathrm{J\ K}^{-1}$
specific heat capacity	joule per kelvin per kilogram		$\mathrm{J\ kg}^{-1}\ \mathrm{K}^{-1}$
thermal conductivity	watt per metre per kelvin		$\mathrm{W\ m}^{-1}\ \mathrm{K}^{-1}$

The *mole* is the amount of substance of a system which contains as many elementary entities as there are atoms in 0·012 kilogram of carbon 12. Since this number is approximately 6·022 17 × 10²³ a mole of hydrogen molecules, for example, is approximately this number of hydrogen molecules.

In addition to the base units, two SI *supplementary units* are listed below:

Quantity	Name of unit	Symbol of unit
Plane angle	radian	rad
Solid angle	steradian	sr

They are defined as follows:

The *radian* is the plane angle between two radii of a circle which cut off on the circumference an arc equal in length to the radius.

The *steradian* is the solid angle which, having its vertex in the centre of a sphere, cuts off an area of the surface of the sphere equal to that of a square with sides of length equal to the radius of the sphere.

Derived Units

Most quantities that occur in nature are *derived quantities* and are measured in *derived units*. Speed is a derived quantity which can be measured in metres/sec, so that the units of speed involve the definition of two base units, *i.e.* metres and seconds. It is said that speed has the dimensions of [length]/[time], also written $[L][T]^{-1}$, since the metre is a measure of length and the second is a measure of time. In any equation in science the dimensions of both sides must always be the same and this is often a useful check of whether the equation is correct. If a mile = 1609·3 metre and an hour = 3600 sec, one mile/hr = 1609·3/3600 m s⁻¹. Conversions between any unit and any other unit which measures the same quantity can be similarly obtained.

Table I gives a list of some important derived quantities that occur in nature and in the fourth column the SI unit that is used to measure it. Some of these derived units have a name (usually that of a famous scientist) and a symbol which are given in the second and third columns. Thus for example, the SI unit of force is a kilogram metre sec⁻², but this unit is also given the name of a newton. A force of 5 kg m s⁻² is 5 newton, which is sometimes written "5N".

Multiples and Fractions of Units

Within the SI system there are special prefixes for forming multiples and sub-multiples of its units.

Factor by which the unit is multiplied	Prefix	Symbol
10¹²	tera	T
10⁹	giga	G
10⁶	mega	M
10³	kilo	k
10²	hecto	h
10	deca	da
10⁻¹	deci	d
10⁻²	centi	c
10⁻³	milli	m
10⁻⁶	micro	m
10⁻⁹	nano	n
10⁻¹²	pico	p
10⁻¹⁵	femto	f
10⁻¹⁸	atto	a

Examples: one thousandth of a metre is one millimetre (1 mm); one million volts is one megavolt (1 MV). These prefixes are *recommended* but other multiples and sub-multiples will be used when convenient, *e.g.*, the centimetre (cm), the cubic decimetre (dm³).

The following is a selection of special points to note:

(i) The name litre now means 1 cubic decimetre or 10⁻³m³ and is a measure of volume.

(ii) Days, hours, and minutes are still used to measure time, though some scientists may prefer to use kiloseconds, etc.

(iii) The SI unit of plane angle is the radian (rad), but degrees, minutes and seconds are still used as well. $1° = \frac{\pi}{180}$ rad.; 1 rad $= 57·295\ 78° = 57°\ 7'\ 44·81''$

(iv) A Celsius temperature, say 15 degrees, is written 15°C; note that 15C would mean 15 coulombs.

The Imperial System of Units

The SI system is not the only system of units in use today, although it is the one most favoured by scientists. The Imperial system is widely used in the UK and other English speaking countries and some Imperial weights and measures are given below:

Length

1 nail	= 2¼ in
1 link	= 7·92 in
12 in	= 1 ft
3 ft	= 1 yd
22 yd	= 1 chain
10 chains	= 1 furlong
8 furlongs	= 1 mile = 1760 yd = 5280 ft

Area

1210 yd²	= 1 rood
4 roods	= 1 acre = 4840 yd²
640 acres	= 1 mile²

Volume

$$1728\ in^3 = 1\ ft^3$$
$$27\ ft^3 = 1\ yd^3$$

Capacity

4 gills	= 1 pint
2 pints	= 1 quart
4 quarts	= 1 gallon
2 gallons	= 1 peck
4 pecks	= 1 bushel
8 bushels	= 1 quarter
36 bushels	= 1 chaldron
1 gal	= 277·274 in³

Weight (Avoirdupois)

(System used in commerce)

1 dram	= 27·343 75 grains
16 drams	= 1 oz = 437·5 grains
16 oz	= 1 lb = 7000 grains
14 lb	= 1 stone
28 lb	= 1 quarter
4 quarters	= 1 cwt = 112 lb
20 cwt	= 1 ton = 2240 lb

Troy Weight

1 pennyweight	= 24 grains
480 grains	= 1 ounce

The only unit of troy weight which is legal for use in trade in Britain is the ounce Troy, and weighings of precious metal are made in multiples and decimals of this unit.

The term *carat* is not a unit of weight for precious metals, but is used to denote the quality of gold plate, and is a figure indicating the number of 24ths of pure gold in the alloy, *e.g.*, a 9 carat gold ring consists of nine parts of pure gold and fifteen parts of base metals.

Nautical Measures

1 nautical mile = 6080 ft = 1853·18 m
1 knot = 1 nautical mile per hour = 1·151 mile/h

Note.—In future the international nautical mile of 1852 m will be used.

Note.—The British Pharmaceutical Code and the

British National Formulary—the official works of medicinal reference—no longer contain the apothecaries' units of measurement since medicine is now measured in metric units. Prescriptions are in 5 millilitre (*ml*) units; medicine bottles are in six sizes from 50 to 500 *ml*.

Selected Conversions between Units

Length

1 inch	= 2·54 cm
1 foot	= 30·48 cm
1 yard	= 0·9144 m
1 mile	= 1609·344 m
1 fathom	= 6 feet
1 nautical mile	= 1852 m

1 fermi	= 1 fm (femtometre)
1 X unit	= 0·1002 pm (picometre)
1 angstrom	= 100 pm
1 micron	= 1 μ m
1 astronomical unit	= 149·6 Gm
1 light year	= 9460·70 Tm
1 parsec	= 30,857 Tm
	= 3·26 light years

For Angstrom, Light year, Parsec, Astronomical Unit *see* **Section L**.

Area

1 hectare (ha)	= 10^4 m2 = 2·471 acre
1 acre	= 0·404686 ha
1 acre	= 4840 yd² which is approximately 70 yards square
1 mile²	= 258·999 ha = 2·58999 km²
1 barn	= 100^{28} m² (measure of nuclear cross-section)

Volume

1 litre (l)	= 0·001 m³
1 gallon UK	= 4·546 092 1

1 gallon UK is the volume of 10 lb water at 62° F

1 pint	= 0·568 l which is approximately 4/7 l
1 gallon US	= 0·8327 gallon UK

Mass and Weight

1 oz	= 0·02835 kg
1 lb	= 0·453 592 37 kg
1 cwt	= 50·80 kg
1 ton	= 2240 lb = 1016 kg = 1·016 tonne
1 tonne	= 1000 kg

Angle

	degree	minute	second	radian	revolution
1 degree	= 1	60	3600	$1·745 \times 10^{-2}$	$2·778 \times 10^{-3}$
1 minute	= $1·667 \times 10^{-2}$	1	60	$2·909 \times 10^{-4}$	$4·630 \times 10^{-5}$
1 second	= $2·778 \times 10^{-4}$	$1·667 \times 10^{-2}$	1	$4·848 \times 10^{-6}$	$7·716 \times 10^{-7}$
1 radian	= 57·30	3438	$2·063 \times 10^5$	1	0·1592
1 revolution	= 360	$2·16 \times 10^4$	$1·296 \times 10^6$	6·283	1

1 rt angle = 90°   1 grade = 0·01 rt angle

Time

	second	minute	hour	solar day	year
1 second	= 1	$1·667 \times 10^{-2}$	$2·778 \times 10^{-4}$	$1·157 \times 10^{-5}$	$3·169 \times 10^{-8}$
1 minute	= 60	1	$1·667 \times 10^{-2}$	$6·944 \times 10^{-4}$	$1·901 \times 10^{-6}$
1 hour	= 3600	60	1	$4·167 \times 10^{-2}$	$1·141 \times 10^{-4}$
1 solar day	= 86400	1440	24	1	$2·738 \times 10^{-3}$
1 year	= $3·156 \times 10^7$	525,900	8766	365·24	1

Force

	newton	dyne	poundal	kg force	pound force
1 newton	= 1	10^5	7·233	0·1020	0·2248
1 dyne	= 10^{-5}	1	$7·233 \times 10^{-5}$	$1·020 \times 10^{-6}$	$2·248 \times 10^{-6}$
1 poundal	= 0·1383	13830	1	0·01410	0·03108
1 kg force	= 9·807	980700	70·93	1	2·205
1 lb force	= 4·448	$4·448 \times 10^5$	32·17	0·4536	1

Energy, Work, Heat

	joule	kW. hr	ft lb	calory	B.t.u
1 joule	= 1	$2·778 \times 10^{-7}$	0·7376	0·2389	$9·478 \times 10^{-4}$
1 kW. hr	= $3·600 \times 10^6$	1	$2·655 \times 10^6$	$8·598 \times 10^5$	3412
1 ft lb	= 1·356	$3·766 \times 10^{-7}$	1	0·3238	$1·285 \times 10^{-3}$
1 calory	= 4·187	$1·163 \times 10^{-6}$	3·088	1	$3·968 \times 10^{-3}$
1 B.t.u.	= 1055	$2·931 \times 10^{-4}$	778·2	252	1

1 kW. hr (kilowatt hour) is 1 unit (Board of Trade unit) as measured by the electricity meter.
1 B.t.u. is a British thermal unit and is the amount of heat required to raise the temperature of 1 lb of water by 1° Fahrenheit.
1 Therm is 100 000 B.t.u. and is equivalent to the heat generated by 29·3 units of electricity.
1 calorie is the heat required to raise the temperature of 1 gm of water by 1° C. The calorie as used by weightwatchers is actually 1000 calories as defined above.
1 erg is 10^{-7} joule.
1 electron volt (eV) is $1·6 \times 10^{-19}$ joule.

Pressure

	pascal	millibar	atmosphere	torr	lb/sq in
1 pascal	= 1	0·01	$9·869 \times 10^{-6}$	$7·501 \times 10^{-3}$	$1·450 \times 10^{-4}$
1 millibar	= 100	1	$9·869 \times 10^{-4}$	0·7501	0·01450
1 atmosphere	= 101 300	1013	1	760	14·7
1 torr	= 133·3	1·333	$1·316 \times 10^{-3}$	1	0·01934
1 lb/sq in	= 6895	68·95	0·06805	51·72	1

1 pascal = 1 newton/sq metre = 10 dyne/sq cm
1 torr is the pressure due to 1 mm of mercury.
By atmosphere is meant "standard atmosphere" which is 760 mm or 29·92 inches of mercury.

Temperature

The Celsius scale is the same as the Centigrade scale. To convert from degrees Fahrenheit (°F) to degrees Celsius (°C), subtract 32 from the temperature in Fahrenheit and multiply by 5/9. To convert from Celsius to Fahrenheit multiply the temperature in Celsius by 9/5 and add 32. Applying this rule we obtain:

$$0° C = 32° F \quad 20° C = 68° F$$
$$5° C = 41° F \quad 25° C = 77° F$$
$$10° C = 50° F \quad 30° C = 86° F$$
$$15° C = 59° F \quad 35° C = 95° F$$

37° C (normal body temperature) is 98·6 ° F, −40° C = −40° F.

The absolute zero temperature (lowest possible temperature) is −273·15° C.
To convert from ° C to degrees Kelvin (° K) add 273·15 to the temperature in Celsius so that the absolute zero is 0° K.
To obtain the temperature according to the Rankine scale add 459·69 to the temperature in Fahrenheit. 0° Rankine is the absolute zero.

The c.g.s System in Electromagnetism

The centimetre gram second (c.g.s.) system of units is favoured by some scientists (notably theoretical physicists). There are in fact two sets of c.g.s. units: electrostatic units (e.s.u.) and electromagnetic units (e.m.u.). Electrostatic units are sometimes given the prefix *stat* and electromagnetic units sometimes given the prefix *ab*. Thus voltage can be measured in statvolts (e.s.u.) or abvolts (e.m.u.) as well as in volts (S.I.).

These two systems do not normally treat charge or current as base quantities as the S.I. system does but as derived quantities. In the electrostatic system the unit of electric charge, the statcoulomb is defined so that one statcoulomb of charge placed at a distance of 1 cm from another statcoulomb of electric charge in a vacuum repels it with a force of 1 dyne. In the electromagnetic system the abampere is such that if two parallel wires in a vacuum 1 cm apart both carry a current of 1 abampere the force between them is 2 dynes per cm length of wire. Also the force between two magnetic poles of unit strength one centimetre apart in a vacuum is one dyne. These two systems usually treat permittivity and permeability as dimensionless quantities, unlike the S.I. system.

In the table below c = $2·997\ 925 \times 10^{10}$ and is the speed of light in cm s^{-1}.
The symbol "≏" means "is approximately equal to".
Thus c ≏ 3×10^{10} cm s^{-1}.

Quantity	S.I. Unit			e.m.u.	e.s.u.
Current	ampere	A	1 abampere = 10A	1 statampere = 1 abamp/c	
				1 amp ≏ 3×10^9 statamp	
Charge	coulomb	C	1 abcoulomb = 10 C	1 statcoulomb = 1 abcoulomb/c	
EMF	volt	V	1 abvolt = 10^{-8} V	1 statvolt = c abvolt ≏ 300 V	
Capacitance	farad	F	1 abfarad = 10^9 F	1 statfarad = 1 abfarad $\times c^{-2}$	
				1 F ≏ 9×10^{11} statfarad	
Permittivity	F m^{-1}			1 e.s.u./1 S.I.U. = $10^{11}/(4\pi c^2)$.	
				Since the permittivity of a vacuum in e.s.u. is 1 this is equivalent to saying the permittivity of a vacuum in S.I. units = $10^{11}/(4\pi c^2)$ ≏ $1/36\pi \times 10^9$.	
Magnetic field	A m^{-1}			1 oersted (e.m.u.) = $10^3/(4\pi)$ Am^{-1}	
Magnetic flux density	tesla	T	1 gauss (e.m.u.) = 10^{-4} tesla. 1 gauss is equivalent to a magnetic field of 1 oersted in a vacuum		
Magnetic flux	weber	Wb	1 maxwell (e.m.u.) = 10^{-8} Wb		
Inductance (self or mutual)	henry	H	1 abhenry = 10^{-9}H		
Permeability	H m^{-1}			1 e.m.u./1 S.I.U. = $4\pi \times 10^{-7}$. Since the permeability of a vacuum in e.m.u. is 1, this equivalent to saying the permeability of a vacuum in SI units = $4\pi \times 10^{-7}$.	

Units Related To Radioactivity

Radioactivity is the spontaneous disintegration of atomic nuclei to form lighter nuclei and to simultaneously emit fast moving particles. These particles are usually either α particles, electrons, neutrons, X rays or γ rays, the latter two being photons. These particles constitute radiation and can have a profound effect on the materials through which they pass, *e.g.* causing cancer in humans. Units are required to define the amount of radioactivity, exposure to radiation, absorbed dose of radiation and effective absorbed dose of radiation by human tissue.

The SI unit of radioactivity is the *bequerel* (Bq), which is the number of disintegrations per second. It is a measure of the amount of radioactive material present.

The emitted particles cause ionisation in a substance through which they pass. If this substance is a gas an electric field can be used to collect the ionised particles at electrodes before they recombine and enable the amount of ionisation produced to be measured. The number of SI units of exposure to radiation is the number of coulombs of electricity that would be produced in a kilogram of dry air by the radiation. The SI unit of exposure to radiation is the *coulomb* per kilogram.

Since the particles are fast moving they have energy. If they are absorbed by the medium through which they pass this energy is transmitted to the medium. The number of SI units of absorbed dose of radiation is the number of joules produced in a kilogram of this medium. The SI unit of absorbed dose of radiation is the *gray* (Gy).

Some of the absorbed particles have more effect on human tissue than others. Each type of particle has a factor and the effective absorbed dose of radiation is the absorbed dose times the quality factor (g.v.) which is a weighted sum of the quality factors for each of the component particles. For α particles q.v. = 20, for neutrons q.v. = 10, for electrons, X rays and γ rays q.v. = 1. The SI unit of effective absorbed radiation dose is called the Sievert (Sv).

Number of Sv = Number of Gy × q.v.

Non SI units are also used to measure these quantities. The conversions are as follows:

1 Curie (Ci) = 3.7×10^{10} Bq,
1 Roentgen (R) = 2.58×10^{-4} C kg^{-1}
1 rad = 10^{-2} Gy
1 Roentgen Equivalent Man (REM) = 10^{-2} Sv

Quantity units	Name of SI unit	Symbol	SI unit in terms of base or derived
Radioactivity, disintegrations per second	becquerel	Bq	s^{-1}
Exposure to radiation	coulomb/kilogram		C kg^{-1}
Absorbed dose of radiation, joule/kilogram	gray	Gy	J kg^{-1}
Effective radiation dose absorbed by tissue	sievert	Sv	J kg^{-1}

VII. SPECIAL TOPICS

MODERN MOLECULAR BIOLOGY

Editor's Note.

This article, written by Dr. James Howard Pringle of Leicester University, summarises the landmark steps in the history of molecular biology, from the discovery of nucleic acids in the nineteenth century to the first successful treatment of a human disease by means of recombinant DNA technology. For those not familiar with the terms used in molecular biology, a concise glossary of the main terms is given (**F74–76**). A knowledge of the current revolution in genetics is fundamental to an understanding of modern biology.

All the structures and functions of living organisms are determined by their genes. Changes in genes lead to changes in structure and/or function, which can result directly in a variety of diseases, including inherited diseases and cancer. Genes are also important in infectious disease, because the properties of the bacteria and viruses that cause disease are determined by their genes. The new science of molecular biology, which has arisen in the last few years, allows scientists to study individual genes and the effects of changes within them. Studies of genes have given us a greater understanding of many diseases, as well as new methods for their diagnosis and treatment, and have also allowed us to start manipulating organisms ranging from viruses to animals to improve our ability to exploit them in biotechnology. Other areas in which molecular biology is important include the understanding of body development and of the evolutionary relationships between different organisms.

The Historical Background.

The technology to investigate our genes has been developed over the last 50 years to the extent that we can now manipulate human genes in vitro and use them to treat genetic disease. This achievement is a result of advances in molecular biology which allows complicated biological systems to be investigated by studying their genes. The spin off will

enable mankind to understand the genetic basis of disease, to synthesise gene products commercially using biotechnology, to investigate the genetic diversity of living systems and to determine the evolutionary links between organisms. What follows is a historic account of the events leading to the establishment of modern molecular biology and the subsequent use of this technology to diagnose and eventually treat human genetic disease. The table highlights the milestones in the development of recombinant DNA technology, the "tools of the trade".

Although nucleic acids were discovered in the 19th century by Miescher, the development of modern molecular biology starts in 1944 when Avery and co-workers at the Rockefeller Institute in New York demonstrated for the first time that genetic information is held in nucleic acid not protein as previously believed. Nucleic acids, deoxyribonucleic acid (DNA) and ribonucleic acid (RNA) are information molecules allowing the genetic identity of an organism to be stored, retrieved and copied. DNA is the gene store found mainly in the chromosomes within the nucleus and is duplicated during cell division. RNA occurs mainly in the nucleolus, a structure within the nucleus as well as in the cytoplasm. Its main role in the cell is to aid the transfer of genetic information from genomic DNA to the synthesis of functional proteins, a process called gene expression.

The Work of Watson and Crick.

In 1953 Watson and Crick, working in Cambridge, proposed the double helical structure of DNA based on their interpretation of X-ray diffraction studies of Wilkins and Rosalind Franklin. The attraction of the proposed structure was that it accounted for the ability of the molecule to reproduce itself in such a manner that an identical replica of itself would be formed at each cell division.

DNA is composed of long chains of molecules called nucleotides which form each strand. The nucleotides are composed of a base (adenine, thymine, guanine and cytosine), a sugar (deoxyribose) and a phosphate molecule. The arrangement

MILESTONES IN THE DEVELOPMENT OF RECOMBINANT TECHNOLOGY

1869	Miescher isolated DNA for the first time.
1944	Avery proved that genetic information is carried by DNA rather than protein.
1953	Watson and Crick demonstrated the double-helical structure of DNA based on X-ray results of Franklin and Wilkins.
1957	Kornberg discovered DNA polymerase, the enzyme that copies strands of DNA (DNA replication).
1961	Marmur and Doty discovered that DNA single strands can reform the double-helical structure, establishing that nucleic acids can be specifically identified by renaturation reactions.
1966	Nirenberg, Ochoa, and Khorana elucidated the genetic code.
1967	Gellert discovered DNA ligase, the enzyme used to join DNA fragments together.
1970	Khorana synthesis of the first gene.
1970	Temin and Baltimore reverse transcriptase discovered RNA to DNA.
1970	Nathans and Hamilton Smith characterisation of DNA restriction nucleases, leading to their later purification and use of DNA sequence.
1972	Jackson first recombinant DNA molecules generated.
1972–1973	DNA cloning techniques were developed by the laboratories of Boyer, Cohen, Berg and their colleagues at Stanford University and the University of California at San Francisco.
1975	Southern developed gel-transfer hybridisation for the detection of specific DNA sequences.
1976	Kan, Golbus and Dozy first prenatal diagnosis using a gene specific probe.
1975–1977	Sanger and Barrell and Maxam and Gilbert developed rapid DNA-sequencing methods.
1977	Jeffries and Flavell discovery of gene splicing.
1977	Itakura somatostatin synthesised using recombinant DNA.
1978	Maniatis and colleagues construct human gene libraries.
1979	Burrell first recombinant vaccines.
1981–1982	Palmiter and Brinster produced transgenic mice.
1985	Mullis and co-workers invented the polymerase chain reaction (PCR).
1985	Development of DNA fingerprinting.
1986	Start of the genome project.
1990	Gene therapy for the adenine deaminase gene.
1990–1998	Intense development of modified organisms including plants with resistance to viruses, insects, and herbicides, with modified storage properties, modified protein and oil contents, and expressing animal proteins. Development of transgenic animals secreting therapeutic proteins in milk. Development of recombinant vaccines using different host bacteria and viruses, some for multiple immunising properties. Cloning of a sheep from a somatic cell and development to adulthood (cloning performed in 1990). First reproducible cloning of a mammal from adult cells (of mice) by scientists at University of Hawaii (1998). Entire genetic blueprint of the nematode worm decoded (1998).

of bases in the DNA is not random: guanine in one strand pairs with the cytosine in the other strand and adenine always pairs with thymine. At nuclear division the two strands of DNA molecules separate and each chain is then copied using specific base pairing to generate a complementary strand. In 1957 Kornberg discovered DNA polymerase, the enzyme that copies strands of DNA during DNA replication.

The Composition of the Human Genome.

The human genome is made up of 23 pairs of chromosomes. Each chromosome contains a single molecule of DNA between 50–250 million nucleotide base pairs long. Therefore the human haploid genome is 3 thousand million base pairs long. What is the link between nucleotide and amino acid sequence and how many genes can such a large genome code for? The first successful attempt to break the genetic code was made by Nirenberg and Matthaei in 1961 while working in the National Institute of Health in the United States. Later it was shown that the genetic information in DNA molecules was stored in the form of triplet codes; a sequence of three nucleotide bases determines the identity of one amino acid; by 1966 a complete genetic code for all twenty amino acids was established. In 1970 Khorana and his colleagues succeeded in synthesising a gene in vitro for the first time by assembling its constituent base pairs or sequence using DNA polymerase. Another important discovery was the Marmur and Doty (1961) was the denaturation and renaturation properties of nucleic acids. High temperature can be used to separate DNA strands and when allowed to cool the DNA helix reforms by complementary base pair alignment. Therefore the information retained in the order of the nucleotide bases controls the specific identity of genes. Analysis of human DNA using renaturation experiments showed that a large proportion of the DNA is made up of repetitive sequences that do not code for genes. Thus although the genome is very large and could code for millions of genes the actual number is likely to be nearer thousands.

Recombinant DNA Techniques.

During the 1970s recombinant DNA techniques emerged as further analysis of nucleic acids and associated enzymes expanded. In 1970 Nathans and Hamilton Smith discovered a group of enzymes which occur in micro-organisms and they are now referred to as Class II restriction endonucleases. These enzymes were found to cleave the DNA molecule at sequence specific sites. It meant that DNA fragments of reproducible size could be produced and that DNA fragments containing a particular gene, for example, could be cut out from the rest of the DNA molecule.

The discovery of another enzyme which was subsequently proved to be of immense value in cloning genes was made by Temin and independently by Baltimore (1970). Genetic information is usually transferred from DNA to RNA by a process referred to as transcription and then the messenger RNA(mRNA) migrates into the cytoplasm where this genetic information is translated into protein. However, Temin and Baltimore and their colleagues showed that in retroviruses genetic information could flow in the reverse direction from RNA to DNA. This is referred to as RNA-directed DNA synthesis and the enzyme responsible is called reverse transcriptase. This enzyme provides a method of making a complementary copy of a gene referred to as complementary DNA(cDNA) and mRNA is converted to cDNA by the enzyme. For example, red blood cells contain only globin mRNA and therefore if this mRNA is reverse transcribed it is possible to make a globin cDNA copy. Other examples include using mRNA from the pancreas to clone the insulin gene. Globin cDNA is now used extensively to diagnose various haemoglobin abnormalities in the foetus and recombinant insulin is now used to treat insulin-dependent diabetes. Many other cDNAs have since been synthesised and sequenced and these find wide applications in the biotechnology industry.

Cloning Human Genes.

Cloning of the cDNA for genes was developed

from the experiments joining recombinant DNA fragments using the "sticky" or cohesive ends produced by some of the restriction enzymes to produce biologically functional hybrid DNA molecules. The two molecules are joined together by DNA ligase, an enzyme discovered by Gellert in 1967 which bonds the sugar phosphate molecules together. The first successful recombinant experiments were achieved in Edinburgh by Jackson in 1972. They were followed by the introduction of plasmid vectors to carry fragments of foreign DNA. Plasmids are naturally occurring small circular pieces of DNA found in the cytoplasm of bacteria. They are extrachromosomal and replicate independently of the host bacterial genomic DNA. By using a restriction endonuclease that cuts the plasmid DNA at a single site, the plasmid can be opened up and a foreign piece of DNA with the same restriction endonuclease sites inserted. Once ligated together the new recombinant plasmid can be introduced into a bacterial host and cloned. This is in fact the actual recombinant part of the process. In 1973 Boyer, Cohen and Berg constructed the first plasmid using a recombinant DNA technique, this plasmid is referred to as pSC101; p for plasmid, SC after its originator Stanley Cohen. Later, other plasmids were developed, perhaps the most important being pBR322, BR after the originators Bolivar and Rodriguez. If cDNA sequences are inserted into a plasmid designed or engineered to express the cDNA then recombinant protein can be produced and purified. To date a large variety of vectors have been constructed to clone and express genes in different organisms including bacteria, yeast, mammalian cells and plant cells. In order to clone large fragments of DNA, vectors have been designed from viruses and chromosomes. For example, yeast artificial chromosomes (YACs) have been used to clone large pieces of human DNA millions of nucleotides long.

The Work of Southern.

In 1975 Southern in Edinburgh pioneered a technique which proved essential for the subsequent developments in this field. If DNA is extracted from human tissues or cells, this DNA contains thousands of genes of the host organism. These genes must be selected or identified from the millions of fragments of DNA digested by restriction enzymes. How can a particular gene or nucleic acid sequence be identified among all this DNA? The first step is to separate the restricted fragments of DNA on an agarose gel, which results in the fragments separating under an electric current according to their size, smaller fragments migrating further than larger fragments. Among these fragments will be the ones containing the genes of interest. Southern's technique was to transfer the DNA fragments from the gel with an alkali buffer onto a nitrocellulose filter. This allows the fragments to be permanently fixed to the filter. The specific fragments can then be identified by hybridising a radiolabelled probe of nucleic acid fragments to the filter, where they will form double stranded molecules with their complementary strands. These hybrids are then displayed by autoradiography by exposing the filter to an X-ray film in the dark, radiolabelled bands on the X-ray film demonstrate the presence of DNA homologous to the probe. Modifications of this method can be used to identify mRNAs from total RNA extracted from cells or tissues using solvents. Hybridisation of probes to RNA filters is called Northern blotting and is used to assess which genes are expressed in different cells or tissues.

The methods developed for identifying genetic change using Southern blotting were the forerunner for prenatal diagnosis of genetic disease whereby certain genetic disorders in the foetus can be detected early in pregnancy. If the foetus proves to be affected with the genetic defect the parents may opt to have the pregnancy terminated. On the other hand, if the foetus proves to be unaffected the pregnancy is allowed to continue. In this way the parents can be sure that the child they will have will not be affected with an inherited genetic disorder. The usual procedure is to remove a small amount of amniotic fluid which surrounds the foetus by transabdominal amniocentesis or alternatively a small sample of the placenta called chorionic villi. Both procedures are safe in competent hands and

carry very little risk to the foetus. By looking for chromosomal changes in the foetal DNA it is possible to diagnose a variety of genetic diseases. Also, by making DNA from the foetal or placental sample it is possible to detect genetic change. This was first described in 1976 by Kan, Golbus and Dozy. They were able to show if the foetus was affected by α thalassaemia, a disorder in which the α-globin genes are deleted. This was observed by reduced hybridisation with the appropriate α-globin cDNA probe prepared from reticulocyte mRNA using reverse transcriptase.

This represented a major step forward in the field of prenatal diagnosis. It is now possible not only to identify a variety of genetic defects but also to give prenatal counselling giving parents the risk of having a genetically abnormal child and with the choices that incurs. In 1977, a year after Kan's report, there appeared two new and relatively simple methods for rapidly sequencing the bases in a DNA molecule. One of the methods was developed in the MRC Laboratory of Molecular Biology at Cambridge by Sanger and Barrell and the other at Harvard University by Maxam and Gilbert. The DNA sequencing methods evolved by these workers meant that given a piece of DNA it was now possible to analyse its nucleotide base sequence. This was to have far-reaching consequences.

Gene Structure Discoveries.

It was also at this time that recombinant DNA technology led to major discoveries concerning gene structure. It had always been assumed that genes were discrete and contiguous structures of DNA which coded for particular enzymes or peptides. However, in 1977 Jeffries and Flavell published the first report on the structure of a gene from a higher organism, *i.e.* the rabbit globin gene. It was found that the genes were in fact rarely contiguous stretches of DNA. It turned out that at least in higher organisms, almost all the genes are interrupted by so-called intervening sequences or introns, the remaining parts of the genes separated by introns being called exons. This led to the concept of gene splicing, subsequently it has been shown that during transcription the precursor RNA derived from introns is excised and the precursor RNA from non contiguous exons are spliced together to form functional mRNA. Thus exons and not introns specify the primary structure of the gene product. This finding was to have far reaching consequences particularly with regard for the use of DNA technology in biosynthesis.

Biosynthesis of Human Protein.

At the same time as the fine details of gene structure were beginning to be revealed the first biosynthesis of a human protein using DNA technology was reported by Itakura in 1977 and the first genetic engineering firm Genentech Incorporated in the United States was founded specifically to develop recombinant DNA methods for making medically important drugs. Itakura and his colleagues successfully obtained the bacterial expression of a cloned gene for somatostatin, a peptide hormone which among other things inhibits growth hormone and is used for the treatment of children with excessive growth. From knowing the amino acid structure of somatostatin they were able to infer the nucleotide base composition of its gene. This was relatively easy because somatostatin contains only 14 amino acids. The assembled synthetic gene, along with various regulators, was then inserted into the plasmid pBR322 and cloned in bacterium *Escherichia coli*. Since the first step many other valuable hormones and proteins have been synthesised using DNA technology. For example, Goeddel and his colleagues at Genentech published details of their successful synthesis of human insulin in 1979. Subsequently marketing approval for the genetically engineered insulin was obtained by the Eli Lilly Corporation in 1982 and is now available for the treatment of diabetes.

Factor VIII is another medically important gene essential for the treatment of haemophilia. This gene has also been cloned and expressed as a recombinant protein. The gene presented major cloning difficulties because the full length cDNA could not be synthesised so the gene had to be assembled from genomic DNA by cloning the many exon fragments into the vector in the correct order, a feat which took 8 man years.

Further Advances: The DNA Library.

As more experience was gained in cloning DNA sequences and confidence in the techniques grew the feasibility of possibly cloning DNA sequences from the entire human genome began to be entertained. The fragments produced by restriction enzymes and cloned into appropriate vectors could be stored and in this way a so-called library of individual genome could be produced. The pioneers in this regard were Maniatis and his colleagues in California, who reported the first successful construction of a gene library in 1978 and this was to prove extremely valuable for subsequent research. Currently DNA libraries are available for many organisms. In humans DNA libraries for each chromosome and cDNA libraries representing mRNA from different tissues and cells are available. The human genome project has the aim of identifying and sequencing all DNA libraries. This project became feasible with the development of automated DNA sequencing and computer analysis of the very large sequence database.

The Identification of Genetic Disorders.

Recombinant DNA technology had been so far used to detect defined genetic disorders in the foetus by demonstrating an abnormality in amniotic fluid cell DNA using gene specific probes. However, in many genetic disorders the identity of the basic biochemical defect is unknown and therefore a specific gene probe cannot be produced. Kan and Dozy in 1978 showed that an entirely different approach was feasible. The new approach depended on demonstrating that the disease producing gene is very closely linked to a particular restriction enzyme recognition site. It is known that variations in DNA sequence occur randomly throughout the entire genome and are apparently without any ill effects. These variations result in a loss of existing restriction sites or acquisition of new restriction sites. Such changes in DNA sequence mean that fragments produced by a particular restriction enzyme will be of different lengths in different people and they can be recognised by different mobilities on electrophoresis. They are referred to as restriction fragment length polymorphisms and are inherited as simple genetic traits obeying Mendelian laws of inheritance. If a disease producing gene could be shown from family studies to be closely linked to a restriction fragment length polymorphism then it would provide a method of detecting the disease without actually knowing anything about the gene itself. Kan and Dozy found that restriction enzyme DNA fragments incorporating the β globin gene were of different sizes depending on whether the chromosome carried the normal gene or the gene for sickle cell anaemia. Much work is currently directed towards finding such linkages using a variety of genetic markers. The repetitive DNA found throughout the genome has proven useful in this respect as micro-satellite DNA repeats show extensive variation and can be used to map most genetic traits.

Successful Gene Cloning.

By the late 1970s reports of successful gene cloning were becoming almost an everyday occurrence. One of particular importance was a report in early spring of 1979 by Burrell and his colleagues, then working in Edinburgh, of a successful cloning of the hepatitis B viral antigen. This was followed shortly afterwards by similar reports in the Pasteur Institute in Paris and Stanford Medical School in California. The importance of this work was that it opened up the possibility of producing an effective and safe vaccine against a relatively common disease which on occasions can lead to chronic ill health and even death. Following these reports DNA technology also began to be used to produce other viral antigens for use in developing vaccines as well as important biologically active proteins such as interferon. The production of vaccines and cellular proteins is a major commercial use for

recombinant DNA technology. Though the emphasis has been so far largely on DNA in relation to medicine, at the same time significant developments were also taking place in relation to agriculture and animal husbandry, for example the successful cloning of viral antigens of the foot and mouth disease by Clyde and his colleagues.

Advances with Cancer Genes.

The year 1982 saw the publication of the first attempts to isolate, clone and characterise human cancer genes, in this case a gene associated with bladder cancer. DNA was extracted from cancer cells, fragmented with restriction enzymes and then applied to a special line of cultured mouse fibroblasts referred to as NIH3T3. In tissue culture these cells became transformed and formed clumps rather than a flat single layer of cells when exposed to the whole tumour cell DNA from the cancer tissues. When the specific fragments of DNA capable of transforming NIH3T3 cells were identified the genes they contained were termed cancer genes or oncogenes. We all carry such genes and there is much speculation and interest at present in trying to find out how they may become activated. Another type of gene associated with cancer has been identified recently from cancers which show a hereditary form. These genes are called tumour suppressor genes as they normally prevent the development of cancer. Studies of hereditary cancers (such as retinoblastoma, Wilm's tumour and familial adenomatous polyposis) have identified the genes by linkage analysis providing a screening method to detect individuals at risk of developing these forms of cancer. Many problems still remain to be answered, in particular how oncogenes and tumour suppressor genes can lead to the development of cancer.

Transgenes.

One way of investigating an abnormal gene or cancer associated gene is to test its function by reinserting it into an organism and see what effect it has. By replacing the normal gene with the altered gene the function of the mutant protein can be tested. Palmiter and Brinster in 1982 injected linear DNA containing the gene of interest into fertilised mouse eggs which developed into mice with the foreign gene in many of their cells. Animals with the foreign gene in the germ line cells were then used to pass the foreign gene on to their progeny, creating permanently altered animals called transgenic organisms. The foreign genes are called transgenes. This approach can also be used to target and inactivate genes of interest producing "knockout" experiments which answer questions about the importance of a specific gene to normal growth and development.

Advances in DNA Technology.

By 1985 the availability of purified DNA polymerases and chemically synthesised DNA oligonucleotides has made it possible to amplify and clone specific DNA sequences rapidly without the need for living cells. The technique, called polymerase chain reaction (PCR) was invented by Mullis and co-workers in 1985 and allows the DNA from a selected gene or region of the genome to be amplified a thousand million fold provided that part of the nucleotide sequence is known. The principle of the technique is to double the amount of DNA in reaction cycles. Each cycle heat denatures the DNA producing single strands, followed by the oligonucleotide primers hybridising with the target complementary sequences as the DNA solution cools, followed by the synthesis of complementary DNA from the primer using the single strand as a template. By repeating the cycle 20–30 times and by using an enzyme which is able to withstand the high denaturation temperatures the DNA is amplified exponentially. Therefore the PCR is very sensitive so even DNA from single cells can be amplified and visualised using this method. The method has replaced many of the original DNA techniques for cloning specific genes and detecting genetic mutations, and it can be used to amplify RNA by first transcribing them into DNA with reverse transcriptase. It can be applied to the diagnosis of genetic diseases and to the detection of low levels of microbial infection. It can also be used to amplify genes from single cells taken at the first stages in the development of the embryo, improving early detection of genetic abnormalities. It has great promise in forensic medicine as a means of analysing minute traces of blood or other tissues and identifying the person from whom they came by their genetic "DNA fingerprint" using mini and micro satellite sequences.

The Future.

The most important medical application for this technology is its eventual use to treat genetic and other disease directly by gene therapy. Human genetic engineering raises unique safety, social, and ethical concerns. The first successful therapy was carried out in the National Institute of Health in the United States in 1990 on a 4-year-old girl suffering from adenosine deaminase (ADA) deficiency. Patients with ADA deficiency have a defect in DNA metabolism which affects growth of their immune system. By infecting the patients cultured lymphocytes with a retrovirus containing the normal recombinant ADA gene the defect was treated and the healthy cells were returned to the patient's blood. In future gene therapy will be used to treat cancer and acquired immune deficiency syndrome as well as a variety of genetically inherited diseases.

This brief history of the developments which have led to the establishment of modern molecular biology has only outlined some of the principal techniques and applications. The ability to manipulate our own genes will have far reaching consequences which we are only just realising. Although the human genome is genetically complicated the tools are now available to clone, sequence and investigate the function of every gene. The genetic revolution has arrived.

GLOSSARY OF GENETIC TERMS

Biotechnology A set of methods for using living organisms to make a variety of products, including alcoholic drinks, bread, enzymes used in washing powders, and medical drugs.

Blotting A method of detecting specific nucleic acid sequences. A mixture of molecules is separated by size on a gel made of agarose, and a filter made of nylon or nitrocellulose is then placed on the gel, so that the nucleic acid molecules bind irreversibly to the filter. A nucleic acid of known sequence, which has been radioactively labelled, is then incubated with the filter so that the labelled nucleic acid sticks ("hybridises") with molecules of complementary sequence attached to the filter, so that the latter can be detected and the size can be measured. When DNA is attached to the filter, the procedure is called Southern blotting after its inventor; when RNA is attached to the filter, it is called Northern blotting. A similar method exists for proteins, using antibodies to detect specific proteins, which is called Western blotting.

cDNA An abbreviation for complementary DNA, which is a DNA "copy" of an mRNA molecule extracted from a cell; this is often the first step in cloning a gene, and is carried out using reverse transcriptase.

Chromosomes Chromosomes are structures found in the nuclei of plant and animal cells and consist of the cell's DNA, along with a number of specialised proteins. The functions of the chromosome are to minimise the space occupied by the DNA—in mammalian cells, up to 2 m of DNA has to be packed into a nucleus only 4–10 μm in diameter—and to distribute newly synthesised DNA to the daughter cells after cell division. Somatic cells (i.e. cells not specialising in reproduction) of different species contain different numbers of chromosomes, e.g. man (46), cat (38), mouse (40), honey bee (16),

Drosophila fruit fly (8), and potato (8). The chromosomes in each case consist of 2 sets of paired chromosomes; reproductive cells contain only 1 set of chromosomes, and are thus described as haploid. Bacteria contain a single chromosome, which is much simpler than the chromosomes of higher organisms, and is circular.

Cloning The production of genetically identical copies of a biological material, for example starting from a single cell. In recombinant DNA technology, cloning consists of joining a DNA molecule to a vector (q.v.) and putting the resulting recombinant molecule into a bacterium, where the vector then allows large quantities of the DNA molecule to be made.

Cytoplasm The contents of a cell apart from its nucleus and other intracellular organelles (mitochondria, etc.).

Denaturation In general, the breakup of the higher structure of a biological polymer. For example, egg white becomes opaque on cooking because of denaturation of the protein albumin, caused by heat. In nucleic acids, denaturation refers to the breakage of the hydrogen bonds between the nucleotide bases that hold the two strands of a double-stranded DNA molecule together: heating a double-stranded molecule causes the two strands to separate (this is also called "melting"). If a solution of denatured DNA molecules is allowed to cool slowly enough for the separated strands to bump into each other, the double helix re-forms; this is called renaturation, and only occurs when the base sequences of two DNA molecules are complementary to each other (see **Nucleic acids**). Double-stranded molecules consisting of one DNA strand and one RNA strand ("heteroduplexes") can also be formed by this method.

Deoxyribonucleic acid (DNA) See **Nucleic acid, F75.**

DNA Fingerprinting DNA fingerprinting consists of examining repetitive DNA in the genome for variations in the lengths of restriction fragments. The DNA from the genome is cut with a restriction enzyme known to cut repetitive sequences into short pieces and is then used in blotting experiments using probes that hybridise to the repetitive sequences. Every individual has his own pattern, so that fingerprinting can match blood to a particular person, and patterns are inherited from parent to child, allowing the method to identify relationships between individuals.

Exon See **Intron, F75.**

Gene A unit of genetic information, i.e. the DNA sequence encoding one protein or RNA gene product.

Gene expression The process of making a product (protein or RNA) from a gene. Regardless of the gene product, the first step consists of transcribing the DNA to make an RNA copy; this can be the final product, or it can be translated to make a protein molecule.

Gene product When the information in a gene is copied, the final product is either a protein or an RNA molecule. The term gene product includes both of these. It does not usually include messenger RNA (mRNA), which is an intermediate between the DNA of the gene and the final protein.

Genetic code Sequence information in genes is used to specify amino acid sequences in proteins. There are four bases in nucleic acids and 20 amino acids in proteins, so a direct one-to-one correspondence is not possible. Groups of two bases could only store information about eight amino acids. Three bases (a "codon") can store information about 64 amino acids; this is the code that is used. Since there are only 20 amino acids in proteins, the code is quite redundant, most amino acids being represented by 2, 3 or 4 different codons, though these codons are generally related, e.g. GGA, GGT, GGC, and GGG all encode the amino acid glycine. Three of the 64 codons have the special function of telling ribosomes that the protein it is making has come to an end; these are called "stop codons".

Genetic disease A disease caused by a defect in a gene (*i.e.* a mutation) or in a chromosome. A well known example of a genetic disease caused by a point mutation is cystic fibrosis. Some types of leukaemia are associated with a chromosomal defect, where the long arms of chromosome 21 are shorter than normal (this is called the Philadelphia chromosome).

Genetic diversity The number of different *alleles* in a population. An *allele* is an individual's version of a particular gene, so the larger and more varied a population, the more different versions of a given gene it will contain, and the greater will be its genetic diversity. The importance of genetic diversity is that a larger allele pool makes a species better able to adapt to changing conditions.

Genome The total set of genetic information in an organism. Physically, the genome corresponds to the sum of all the chromosomes in a cell, *i.e.* all the DNA that the cell contains. The genome thus consists of all the genes encoding proteins and RNA molecules, as well as large amounts of non-coding or silent DNA. Much of this is made of repeated DNA sequences, which can be classified into a number of families.

Haploid Most animal cells contain two pairs of chromosomes—one from the father and one from the mother, and are called *diploid*. Reproductive cells (spermatozoa and oocytes) contain only one set of chromosomes and are called *haploid*. When a spermatozoon and an oocyte fuse, the resulting cell becomes diploid and develops into a new animal. A similar process occurs in plants.

Human genome project A large international collaborative project whose aim is to determine the nucleotide sequence of the entire human genome.

In vitro Used of an experiment that is not carried out in a living body.

In vivo Used of an experiment carried out in a living body.

Intron The nucleic acid sequence of a gene is often much longer than needed to encode the protein or RNA product of that gene. The part of the gene containing protein-encoding information is found to be split up into sometimes numerous small pieces called exons, which are separated by non-coding pieces called introns. Transcription produces an RNA copy (a pre-mRNA) containing both exon and intron sequences. Before the mRNA migrates out of the nucleus, the parts of the pre-mRNA corresponding to the introns are removed, a process called splicing.

Ligase An enzyme that is used in recombinant DNA technology for joining the ends of two DNA molecules together, usually after renaturation of sticky ends. Ligase is involved in the replication and repair of DNA.

mRNA An RNA molecule that is a copy of the base sequence of a gene, and carries that sequence from the nucleus to the cytoplasm to instruct the ribosomes to make a protein of the correct amino acid sequence.

Mutation A change in the sequence of bases in a gene. This can be a change from one base to another (point mutation), or loss or addition of one or more bases from or to a gene sequence (deletions and insertions respectively). Changes which do not alter the structure of the gene product, *e.g.* mutations in exons and mutations in codons that do not alter the amino acid encoded by those codons, are called silent mutations.

Nucleic acids Biological polymers consisting of a chain of sugars joined by phosphate groups, where each sugar carries a nucleotide base. There are two important nucleic acids, deoxyribonucleic acid (DNA), which is the chemical of which genes are made in most organisms, and ribonucleic acid (RNA), of which three types (mRNA, rRNA and tRNA) are involved in protein synthesis; some viruses carry their genes in the form of RNA. Nucleic acids store information in the sequence of chemical bases attached to the sugars; the bases in DNA are adenine (A), thymine (T), cytosine (C) and guanine (G), while those in RNA are the same except that uracil (U) replaces thymine. The two ends of a nucleic acid molecule are different; one is called the 5'-end and the other is called the 3'-end. DNA is usually double-stranded; that is, two DNA molecules are linked together side by side and pointing in opposite directions as a double helix, joined by hydrogen bonds between the bases, each point towards the centre of the helix. Because of the chemical structures of the bases, C can only form hydrogen bonds with G and vice versa, T and U can only form bonds with A, while A forms hydrogen bonds with T in DNA and with U in RNA. Thus, if the sequence of bases in one of the two strands in a double-stranded DNA molecule is 5'-CATTG-3', the "complementary" sequence in the other strand will be 3'-GTAAC-5'. The RNA sequence complementary to this DNA sequence will be 3'-GUAAC-5'. Two molecules that have similar sequences are said to be homologous.

Nucleolus A structure within the nucleus, consisting of copies of the cell's ribosomal RNA genes, which are sometimes needed in larger numbers than can be provided within the chromosomes, *i.e.* when cells have to synthesise large quantities of protein and thus need large numbers of ribosomes.

Nucleotides Nitrogen-containing bases attached to a sugar phosphate. *See* **Nucleic acids.**

Oligonucleotides Very short nucleic acid molecules. Oligonucleotides are often used as the probes in blotting studies and other recombinant DNA techniques because oligonucleotides of known sequences can easily be made in the laboratory.

Oncogenes A number of cancers have been found to be caused by viruses. The ability of a virus to cause cancer is conferred upon it by special genes, which are called oncogenes. Oncogenes are usually related to normal cellular genes involved in regulation of cell growth, and cancer due to oncogenes can be thought of as resulting from the abnormal expression of a normal gene.

Peptides Very short proteins.

Plasmid A small circular DNA molecule containing a replication origin (it is thus a replicon) commonly found in bacteria. Plasmids are widely used in recombinant DNA technology as vectors for cloning DNA fragments because of their small size. In nature, plasmids are responsible for a considerable proportion of bacterial antibiotic resistance—moving from cell to cell, they carry antibiotic resistance genes with them.

Polymerase chain reaction (PCR) A method for synthesizing relatively large amounts of a nucleic acid of known sequence, using polymerase enzymes and oligonucleotides.

Proteins Biological polymers made of amino acids, of which 20 are used in living organisms. The properties of a particular protein depend on the sequence of amino acids of which it is made, and this sequence is determined by the sequence of nucleotide bases in the gene corresponding to the protein. Proteins can be structural (*e.g.* collagen) or they can be enzymes, which catalyse chemical reactions. Some proteins, such as haemoglobin, have the special function of transporting other chemicals around the body.

Recombinant DNA technology A more precise term for genetic engineering.

Repetitive sequences Much of the DNA in the genome of a higher organism does not contain genes, but consists of apparently functionless sequences, some of which are repeated head-to-tail. Genomes contain a number of families of related repeats, and up to 20% of the genome can consist of sequences present at up to 1,000,000 repeated copies.

Replicon A DNA molecule that is able to replicate in a cell. In order to do this, the molecule needs to carry a special sequence called a replication origin, which is the point at which synthesis of new copies of the DNA begins.

Restriction endonucleases Enzymes found in bacteria that cut DNA molecules; their function is to protect bacteria against infection from viruses. Class II restriction enzymes, the group which is important in recombinant DNA techniques, bind to a short (usually 4 or 6 bases) sequence and cut the DNA in or close to the recognition sequence.

Bacteria protect themselves against their own restriction enzymes by chemically modifying their DNA. Restriction enzymes allow DNA molecules whose sequences are known to be cut at predetermined positions. Many enzymes cut the two strands of a DNA molecule in slightly different places, to leave single-stranded overhangs ("sticky ends"); these can be renatured to join pieces of DNA together in a specific way.

Retrovirus A virus which stores its genetic information in the form of RNA instead of DNA; several are tumour-inducing viruses, and the viruses associated with AIDS are retroviruses. Replication of these viruses starts with making a DNA copy of the RNA genome, using the enzyme reverse transcriptase.

Reverse transcriptase A viral enzyme found in some viruses that use RNA instead of DNA for their genomes. This is an RNA-dependent DNA polymerase, and makes a DNA copy of the viral RNA, which is the first step in the replication of such viruses.

Ribonucleic acid (RNA) *See* Nucleic acids.

Splicing *See* Intron.

Transcription The process of copying a DNA molecule to make a complementary RNA copy of a gene. Transcription occurs in the nucleus of higher organism cells, and is carried out by enzymes called DNA-dependent RNA polymerases.

Transgene A foreign gene inserted into a higher organism (animal or plant). This is done by inserting the gene into the organism at an early stage of embryonic development; since all the cells of the adult come from these early embryo cells, all adult cells will contain the inserted gene. Such organisms are called transgenic animals or plants.

Translation The process of converting a gene sequence in the form of mRNA into a protein sequence. Translation is carried out by ribosomes.

Vector In recombinant DNA technology, a replicon that is used for cloning DNA sequences. Vectors are usually small and simple replicons, *i.e.* plasmids and bacteriophages.

NANOTECHNOLOGY

Introduction.

Nanotechnology, or the technology of the very small, is an exciting if still mostly theoretical branch of engineering. To understand the implications of the mass of speculation surrounding the topic, it helps to get a sense of the scale the planned devices might be built on and an idea of the special role individual molecules have to play. The prefix nano simply means 'a billionth part of'; a 'nanometre' is a billionth part of a metre. 'Nanotechnology' is the sort of engineering that happens on this tiny scale. Since the concept was first mooted in 1959 by the physicist Richard Feynman, speculators have said that these developments will one day eclipse all previous technical advances, end the scarcity of resources and solve all the world's problems.

To see why people are so optimistic about such tiny things, think about the history of working with smaller and smaller devices. The millimetre is a thousand times smaller than the metre and is handy when designing and building the parts of a clock or a simple motor. A thousand times smaller again is the micrometre, a unit commonly used in the production of computer chips and jet engines. A thousand times smaller still, at a thousand-

thousand-thousandth of a metre, is the nanometre. Many scientific speculators expect the things built with this degree of precision to supply an equivalent leap in utility.

Nano-machines.

Molecules are typically measured in nanometres and these are the building blocks that nanotechnologists wish to use. They plan to arrange them not in chunks of billions at a time (as do our most exacting engineering tools) but *individually*. A machine on this scale might be built from a million separate molecules, take its orders from coded sequences similar to DNA and be programmed to grab the constituents of rock and air and rearrange them to make food. This is expected to be possible because we can see precedents in nature. Proteins made in cells create all the different kinds of living tissue we see in the world around us. Nature's own nano-machines operate on the legacy of millions of years of trial and error. Scientists now want to add sophisticated designs to this process.

Applications range from the seemingly miraculous, such as the manufacture of an unlimited supply of food and energy, to the sort of consumer goods we never knew we wanted: paint that changes colour, clothes that re-tailor themselves each time they are worn. Unlike many other projected scientific utopias, none of this depends on some undiscovered phenomena. The individual properties of the constituent molecules are all very well known. The problem we have is our inability to handle such a tiny construction set.

Nanotechnology Engineering.

Molecular engineers hope to set a thief to catch a thief by using nanomachines called 'assemblers' to build other machines according to coded instructions. Of course the first assemblers need to come from somewhere, but it is hoped we can hijack natural mechanisms to bring the first one together. Even at the incredible speed that these machines will be able to work at, their tiny size means that it would take a single assembler decades to make a morsel of food. The true power of nanotechnology will only be harnessed when the assembler is programmed to make copies of itself. An hour later you would have two assemblers. In another hour, four. Exponential growth would give you billions of assemblers in a few days. These could then be programmed together to manufacture a car in hours, perhaps using far lighter and stronger materials than any currently available.

Not all of nanotechnology is mere speculation. We are already dealing with the world on a finer scale than ever before. In 1990 scientists at an IBM research laboratory positioned 35 xenon atoms on a nickel crystal, spelling out that company's initials. A new breed of microscope, called scanning tunnelling microscopes, has allowed us to observe down to the resolution of individual molecules and atoms. Also, chemists and biologists have been busy rearranging molecules for a long time. Genetic engineering has taught us a lot about how we can fiddle with the tools evolution has given us. Tiny natural factories called ribosomes are regularly exploited to produce a range of useful proteins.

Latest Developments.

Before 1985, it was believed that pure carbon only appeared in two forms, diamond and graphite. The discovery of a third form, the *buckminsterfullerene* (60 carbon atoms arranged in the shape of a football) stunned the scientific community and set imaginations racing for possible nanotechnological uses. There followed the discovery of the nanotube: pipe-shaped arrangements of carbon atoms of theoretically unlimited length which could be capped at each end by half a buckminsterfullerene. Because these molecules are hollow, they are incredible light and strong. Several tubes strung together could make a thread strong enough to suspend a grand piano. In 1997 a group of Dutch technologists found a way of forcing a nano-tube to carry an electrical current, something which could revolutionise computers and electronics.

A separate development at the Massachusetts Institute of Technology has been dubbed the 'atom laser'. This machine, which can only work under strictly controlled conditions, has been able to manipulate groups of atoms with unprecedented precision. Just a million atoms at a time are emitted from the device, all tuned to the same quantum state (much as photons of light in a laser have their wavelengths exactly in step). This means that the atoms have stopped behaving individually and act as one. This is another important achievement that brings us closer to getting individual atoms to do what we want.

Conclusions.

There have been many technological revolutions that have shaped our world. Most take a long time to establish themselves. Some, like the power of nuclear explosions, are discovered and put into practise almost immediately. Nanotechnology is held back solely by our inability to grasp matter with the finesse we desire. Once we find a way to do so, life will probably change very quickly. Engineers are already coming up with designs for nano-machines. The advent of the first assemblers will be followed by a fascinating period as the backlog of plans are put into action.

PLATE TECTONICS

Introduction.

Plate tectonics is the branch of geological science which ascribes the structural complexities of the Earth's crust to the interactions of the lithosphere plates as they move about on the asthenosphere. Though the first intimations of the theory of plate tectonics were published only in 1963, the idea that the continents might have moved across the surface of the globe has a long history. In a book published in 1838 a Scots clergyman, Thomas Dick, noted that the east coast of South America neatly matched the west coast of Africa and suggested that the continents had once been joined and were subsequently rent asunder by some tremendous force. Sundry others made the same observation, and in the early 20th century an Austrian meteorologist, Alfred Wegener (1880–1930), gathered together the evidence that transformed observation into a theory of 'Die Verschiebung der Kontinente'. The terms means 'the displacement of continents' but became known in English as *continental drift*.

Wegener proposed that all the continents had once been joined in a single mass, which he called Pangaea (meaning all lands), until about 200 million years ago, when it split in two, with the section he called Laurasia (including north America and Eurasia) drifting northward, and Gondwanaland (south America, Africa, Antarctica, India and Australia) drifting south. Subsequently, the two masses split further and the continents drifted to their present positions.

Wegener's theory of continental drift was persuasive, but failed to provide one crucial explanation: what manner of forces had driven the continents apart? The answer came in the 1960s, when it was found that the age of the ocean floor increased with distance from the mid-ocean ridges (and to an equal extent on both sides). The phenomenon was described as *seafloor spreading*, and it shows that the active volcanic fissures which run down the length of the Atlantic (and above sea-level in Iceland), for instance, mark the points from which the South American and the African portions of the lithosphere are being pushed apart by forces in the asthenosphere below. Further investigations have shown that seafloor spreading occurs in all the oceans.

Six large plates and several smaller ones make up the lithosphere which enwraps the Earth, each a single unit of continental crust and associated oceanic crust. The six major plates are: the African Plate, the Antarctic Plate, the Australian-Indian Plate, the Eurasian Plate, the North American Plate, and the South American Plate. The smaller Nazca, Caribbean, Arabian, Philippine and others are situated at the interstices of the larger plates. The plates flex slightly in response to movements in the asthenosphere below, which causes some local lifting or sinking of the crust, but intense deformation occurs only at the edges, where plates are in contact. These plate margins are known as *active zones*.

The Active Zones.

There are three kinds of active zone: divergent margins, along which plates are moving apart; convergent margins, along which plates are moving towards each other, and transform fault margins, where two plates are sliding past each other. Each type of margin creates a distinctive topography in its vicinity and each is associated with a particular kind of earthquake and volcanic activity. California's San Andreas Fault, for example, is situated where the Pacific and North American plates are sliding past each other – a transform fault margin. The volcanoes of the western Pacific rim mark the convergent margins of the Pacific Plate and its neighbours. The Mid-Atlantic Ridge is a divergent margin, as described above, and similar features are found in all the ocean basins.

The plates move at rates averaging up to 12 cm per year – slowly but inexorably. Thus the Earth's surface is constantly changing. Almost all the earthquake, volcanic and mountain-building activity which marks the active zones of the Earth's crust occurs in the vicinity of plate boundaries and is related to their movements. Features that seem changeless are merely transient wrinkles in the scale of geological time. The Himalayas and Mount Everest, for instance, began to form about 45 million years ago, as the Australian-Indian Plate converged on its northern neighbour, the Eurasian Plate. Limestone that had formed on the ocean floor was heaved up into the sky.

Collision Zones and Subduction Zones.

The Himalayas represent a *collision zone*, where the convergent margins of the plates are surmounted by continental crust, which as crumpled and risen. The Alps and the Atlas mountains are similarly related to collision zones involving only continental crust. Along convergent margins where oceanic crust is involved, *subduction zones* are created. Here the margin of one plate is driven beneath the other, down into the mantle where it melts (at depths of between 100 and 300km beneath the surface). Being less dense than the mantle, the molten material then rises and erupts through the crust above. Around the western Pacific rim, where portions of oceanic crust converge on each other, these eruptions have built chains of volcanic islands, *island arcs*, on the margin of the overriding plate. The Aleutians, Kurile, Japanese and Marianas islands are examples of these island arcs. On the west coast of south America, however, where the Nazca Plate converges on the South American Plate, oceanic and continental crust meet. Here (as elsewhere in similar circumstances) the spreading oceanic crust is consumed beneath the continental crust, and molten material from the subduction zone had built a chain of volcanoes and a high mountain range on the continental margin – the Andes.

THE COMMUNICATIONS REVOLUTION

Introduction.

The obituary for the printed word has been predicted many times, most frequently in print. The type of books most usually responsible, books about computers and the new electronic media, have proliferated. Ten years ago there were just a few slim volumes. These days the average high street book shop has high stacks of text books and teach-yourself guides to the Internet and the World Wide Web. Most of these books communicate their part of the message – that the revolution is here and the printed page is finally done for – over something in the region of a thousand printed pages.

From the printing press (see **L99**) to desktop publishing (see **V5**) we have seen many miracles in the way words are stored, processed and distributed. No one would say that the developments of the past few years were not just as miraculous as any in recent history. To go further and claim that a revolution had occurred in the way we communicate would require evidence of a complete change of method.

Electronic Mail.

The simplest method of distant communication is to send a letter. The innovations of postal service, telegraphy, telephony and facsimile transmission have been followed neatly by the system of E-mail (*see* **V5**). The convention for communication directly from computer terminal to computer terminal was established in 1972. For twenty years it steadily grew in popularity, but in the 1990s the number of E-mails sent has increased astronomically. The Electronic Messaging Association estimated that, in 1997, 2·7 *trillion* E-mails were sent.

Most messages are pure text, encoded using a convention called the American Standard Code for Information Interchange, or ASCII (*see* **V2**). The existing network can easily cope with as many of these text messages as we are likely to want to send. It has also become possible to attach diagrams, digitized photographs, sound recordings and even video footage to these electronic messages. The only limit to this sort of multi-media communication is the time it takes. Most E-mails have to struggle down a telephone line on their way to their destination. This means that even a simple picture can take prohibitively long to send or receive.

The Internet.

The Internet was originally developed by American military planners to help their nuclear weapons control systems survive attack. It differed in the topology of its design from any previous network of computers, rejecting the 'hub and spokes' arrangement that could be wiped out by a single strike at the system's core. Instead, a variable number of machines supplied and received information to and from each other. This way, even if all but two of the participants were destroyed, there would always be a network.

What the military did for the system's robustness, academia then did for its accessibility. The universities and colleges of the world took on the same protocols as a method for sharing the results of their research. A paper or document on the Internet can be linked to any other such document through a system called 'hyper-text'. Here certain words, phrases or pictures are declared to be 'hyperlinks'. These are analogous to the footnotes in a paper-based system. A note at the bottom of the page might tell you where to look up a particular reference. On the Internet, activating a hyper-link brings the referenced document immediately on to your screen, even if the referring and the referred to documents are stored on machines on different sides of the planet. If *Pears Cyclopaedia* were a hyper-text document, merely pointing at one of the bold references would cause the book to spring open at the correct page.

Entrepreneurs became involved around 1988, when the first Interop trade show was organized. After this, commercial use of the Internet ballooned. For a more detailed look "inside" the Net, *see* **V16–18**.

Digital Television.

For the same reason that a compact disc is smaller than a long-playing record, a digitized television channel occupies much less space than its analogue cousin. In the UK we are already close to capacity with the number of analogue television channels we have. The advent of digital terrestrial broadcasting in 1998 has facilitated nearly thirty separate channels. Parallel developments in satellite television may give subscribers up to three hundred channels. This sounds like a lot, but it is still inadequate for the things some in the industry hope will be possible. At the 1997 Edinburgh Television Festival one speculator spoke about the domestic TV becoming more like a telephone or super-store or banking facility in the home. This sort of full interaction, with the consumer shaping the medium, is only feasible with digital cable systems. The reasons why this is unlikely to happen, even in those parts of the country where the roads have already been dug up and the cables laid, is mostly to do with the politics of the television industry.

Networks.

Television's desire to offer interactivity is the mirror of the Internet's desire to distribute high quality sounds and pictures. Commentators from both sides have said that the world's computer networks and television companies are struggling towards the same goal from opposite starting points. The only limiting factor is the network or distribution channel. The obvious answer of laying the best cables to every home and office (fiber optics, *see* **V6**) has proved to be too expensive to happen in the short term. It may also prove to be unnecessary. In October 1997 the UK companies Norweb Communication and Northern Telecom announced the development of a new technology that, they claim, would enable them to use the existing power lines infrastructure as information access networks. Further, the companies pointed out that the data transmission rates are ten-times faster than anything currently possible. A month later British Telecom announced its own new innovation to transform existing telephone lines into rapid multimedia connections using "digital access technology". It is likely that, at the end of the day, only one network will be used. So far neither technology has significantly established itself.

LIFE IN THE UNIVERSE

The Background.

Throughout human history we have gazed at the heavens and mused if, out there in the night sky, there are other beings who contemplate the cosmos as we do. Are humans some fluke of Darwinian luck destined to appear only once in a universe otherwise teeming with unintelligent life? Or, other than Earth, is the universe completely sterile? Serious research is taking place to try and answer some of these questions. Broadly it is split into three areas.

1) Establishing whether life of any sort exists in our solar system. Currently the main focus is on Mars and the largest of Jupiter's satellites, Europa.

2) Discovering signs of life around extra-solar planets. Over a dozen planets have so far (1999) been discovered around stars. Billions of dollars have been set aside for European and American researchers to build satellites aimed at directly seeing Earth type planets.

3) Radio searches listening for biological signals across the entire sky. The Search for Extra-Terrestrial Intelligence (SETI) project has recently been given a serious mandate in America and Britain to search the heavens for signs of life.

Life on Mars.

At the dawn of the century US astronomer Percival Lowell insisted he could see canals on Mars constructed, he supposed, by an advanced civilisation. Spacecraft sent to the planet (**F8**) in the 1960s and 1970s found no evidence for life in any form. For several decades the story seemed to end there. However, in August 1996 scientists from the National Aeronautics and Space Administration (NASA) announced they had detected possible signs of microbial life on Mars. The alleged evidence was found in a lump of rock little bigger than a potato. The rock was ejected from Mars by a powerful impact which sent it hurtling through space for 16 million years until it finally landed in Antarctica.

The rock appears to contain carbonate globules that have structures resembling ones produced by bacteria on Earth. There are also particular chemical compounds known as polycyclic aromatic hydrocarbons (PAHs) (**F26**) that are indicative of decaying microbes. Currently many scientists are sceptical of these claims, suggesting instead that the PAHs were picked up during the thousands of years the rock sat in Antarctica. The debate continues between scientists. Currently the sceptics are holding sway as they claim that the possibility for life on Mars is so extraordinary that there will need to be much more evidence than a singular rock before it is accepted as fact.

Life in the Solar System.

Beyond Earth, the only other system that shows any evidence of life is the largest of Jupiter's satellites, Europa. At first glance Europa seems an unlikely place for life. It has a surface covered with nearly pure ice. Recent data from NASA's Galileo satellite reveals Europa may have a subterranean ocean of water below the ice caused by radioactive decay and tidal warming. In addition, volcanism in the core would help produce enough energy and minerals to start life. The Galileo satellite has also detected organic molecules and frozen water on two other moons in the solar system, although it is thought they both lack the energy sources that life is thought to require. Mars and Europa stand alone as being the only places outside Earth that can be identified as having (or had) all the ingredients necessary to spawn life.

Extra-Solar Planets.

For years astronomers searched without success for evidence of planets around other stars. The difficulty lay in the fact that unlike stars, which are fuelled by nuclear reactions, planets only faintly reflect light. For example, the sun outshines its planets by about a billion times in visible light and about a million times in the infra red. Astronomers had to devise special ways to detect planets around their parent star. On 6 October, 1995 two Swiss astronomers stunned the world with the announcement that they had detected a planet around the star 51 Pegasi.

This is how they did it. It is well known that our sun exerts a gravitational force on the Earth. Since gravitational force increases with mass, and the sun is much more massive than the Earth, it seems to us as though the Earth is in orbit aroound our Sun and the Sun remains absolutely stationary. This is not the whole story. The Earth also exerts a gravitational force (**F18**) on the sun, a force that pulls the sun around in a tiny circular or oval path. In short, the Earth causes the sun to wobble slightly. It is from this wobble (called the Doppler planet-detection technique) that the Swiss astronomers detected a planet around 51 Pegasi. This works by looking at the to-and-fro oscillation of the star's light which is caused by the wobble. Astronomers use a machine called a spectrometer—which works like a prism—that strips the light arriving from the star into wavelengths which they measure over time for tiny changes that occur due to the wobble.

Using the Doppler technique over the past four years over a dozen extra-solar planets have been found. Could they harbour life? It seems not as the planets discovered so far are similar in size and mass to that of Jupiter, suggesting they are huge gassy giants that would be unable to host life as we understand it. This is not particularly disheartening news as one would expect to find the giant planets first. However, the newly discovered planets have two other odd characteristics. Firstly, unlike the solar system planets two of the planets are in oval, rather than circular, orbits near their stars and secondly, five planets orbit extremely close to their stars, closer than Mercury is to the sun.

Searching for Earth-type Planets.

The race is on to find earth sized planets. Already researchers have claimed to have detected one earth sized planet around a star using the indirect Doppler method discussed above. However, the current instrumentation is insufficient to see the planets directly. This may be about to change. A NASA space telescope mission called the *Terrestrial Planet Finder*, and a European Space Agency mission called *The Darwin Project* both aim to locate and directly image earth type planets and search for evidence of life within the next ten years. Both projects will operate deep in the solar system, millions of miles away from earth and comprise about 6 telescopes separated by about 60 metres. They will send infra red light to a central station using a technique called interferometry. This method, already used by astronomers on the ground, enables a group of small telescopes to work effectively as a much larger one.

The Search for Extra-Terrestrial Intelligence (SETI).

The SETI project assumes that intelligent life has developed radio telescopes and advanced computers for processing signals. Despite these requirements it is a branch of research that is beginning to be taken seriously. British researchers at Jodrell Bank and American researchers at Arecibo in Puerto Rico are about to take part in the most sensitive and comprehensive search to date for radio communications. They aim to detect signals from extraterrestrial civilisations beyond our solar system. These methods will be particularly interesting when coupled with any suspected earth-like extra solar objects.

Conclusions.

Scientists are scouring the solar system and distant star systems for signs of life. An all sky survey has commenced listening for technological activity in the form of radio signals. All three research areas have made important advances in recent years. Billions of pounds will be spent in the next few decades on serious research to try to answer the question: is there anybody out there?

NEW RESEARCH ON ELECTRONS

Introduction.

By the early 1880s it was commonly believed that, using Newton's laws of mechanics, Maxwell's equations of electromagnetism and the laws of thermodynamics, all physical phenomena would soon be understood. Scientists generally thought that the few experimental facts which did not seem to fit these laws would soon be reconciled. Physics was seen to be exhausted. The discovery of the electron, one hundred years ago in 1897, marked a renaissance in physics that has continued to the present day. Scientific advances are rarely made in a technological and cultural vacuum. They are dependent on the scientific climate, the cultural background and important social and economic factors which can provide the will, manpower and, of course, the funding for scientific research. The Great Exhibition of 1851, the Franco-Prussian war of 1870 and reforms in British universities focused attention on the importance of science and technology in the new industrialised society.

The Discovery of the Electron.

In the 1880s there was controversy over the nature of peculiar rays emitted from a cathode (**F11**) in a vacuum. There were two schools of thought. A predominantly German approach held that the rays were an unusual form of electromagnetic (e.m.) waves (**F14**) whilst British researchers thought that they were negatively charged particles. The dispute provides a classic case history of a scientific debate in which two quite different models explain most, but not all, of the observable facts. The British camp point out the e.m. rays are not bent by magnetic fields, and the Germans were influenced by the fact that the rays could go through thin films. Since atoms, the smallest known particles, could not penetrate these films it seemed to them unlikely that the cathode rays were made of particles. Over the next few decades many innovative experiments were performed, designed to resolve the argument. In 1877 J.J. Thompson reported a series of brilliant experiments modified and extended from work by Hertz and Schuster that led to the general acceptance of the charged particle model for cathode rays. The electron had been discovered. The way was clear to begin thinking about possible constituents and structures of the atom; it was no longer a fundamental particle. The era of modern physics had begun.

The research into cathode rays unexpectedly led to the discovery of X-rays and radioactivity. Both were powerful and important tools, useful throughout physics. Both were used to discover more about the physical nature of the electron (**F11**). By 1923, De Broglie (**F14**) suggested that any particle has an associated wavelength by virtue of its motion. In other words, the electron behaves like a particle when interacting with matter and a wave when it is moving through space, a phenomena known as wave-particle duality. In this way, in the great scientific debate that led up to the discovery of the electron, both the English and German camps were in some sense correct.

Modern Applications.

The discovery of the electron enabled scientists to investigate the physical nature of crystal structures (**F21**). The de Broglie wavelengths of atoms were simply too small to investigate the structure of such solids. By virtue of the extremely short wavelength associated with electrons it is possible to resolve tiny objects using an electron microscope, making it far more powerful than a standard optical device. An electron microscope works by focusing a stream of electrons onto an object, such as an AIDS virus. The electrons are emitted from a cathode and focused using suitable magnetic and electrostic fields. A vastly enlarged image can be observed on a photographic plate. A modern high-resolution scanning-transmission electron microscope can resolve objects down to 2×10^{-10} meters.

The flow of electrons in conductors forms the basis of the science of electronics, the applications of which have a profound impact on our lives. Electrons themselves are used to engrave the chips in which they flow using a process called electron beam lithography. The electrons are accelerated and focused in an intense beam to engrave precise circuit patterns on suitable substances, such as silicon.

Electronic devices depend on the fact that the force exerted on an electron by the voltage applied is great compared to the mass of these charge carriers. As a consequence the carrier is subject to a very great acceleration and reaches a maximum velocity in 10^{-9} seconds or less. This rapid reaction is crucial to the fast operation of components and provides an upper-limit to the speed of integrated circuits. This permits the device to amplify or generate currents at frequencies up to 10^{10} Hertz or to respond to electric stimuli in less than 10^{-10} seconds.

The flow of current in integrated circuits is pivotal to the operation of computers. The computer has been established as the base of the information revolution, the impact of which may yet exceed that of the industrial revolution. It is impossible to predict how the tiny electron will be used to change our lives as it enters its second century of service.

As if to emphasise this, physicists working in 1997 in the same laboratory in Cambridge as J. J. Thomson one hundred years ago, finally managed to isolate a single electron, play with it, and go on to measure its tiny charge with an accuracy never before achieved. It is a breakthrough with major applications for the future of electronics.

BACKGROUND TO ECONOMIC EVENTS

The aim of this section is to help the ordinary reader (as well as the student) to follow economic events as they happen, and to understand the controversies that accompany them. The section looks not only at central problems of economic policy but also at recent developments in Britain under the Labour Government. It also examines the many topical issues elsewhere in the world, including the debt burden in Africa, prolonged stagnation in Japan and the birth of the euro.

TABLE OF CONTENTS

BACKGROUND TO
ECONOMIC EVENTS

This section is divided into four parts. Part I gives a brief description of the most important problems of economic policy. Part II is concerned with a more detailed survey of the British economy and the way in which it operates. In the course of this survey, the specialised terms used by economists are explained, and the attempt is made to present an intelligible summary of the information, facts and figures relevant to an understanding of economic events. There are five main sub-sections: International Trade and Payments; Employment, Production, and Industry; Incomes, Wages, and Prices; Money, Banking, and Finance; and Economic Aspects of the Public Services. Part III outlines the main economic problems faced by the less developed countries, and the economic policies of Britain and other developed countries towards the less developed world. Some suggestions for further reading are given at the end of Parts II and III. Part IV is written as shortly before publication as possible, and contains a survey of recent developments in the British economy.

I. CENTRAL PROBLEMS OF ECONOMIC POLICY

Why Economists Disagree.

On many of the most important issues Economics is in a state of disarray. Economic problems are in general as serious as they have ever been, yet the economics profession is no less divided now than in the past on the diagnosis of the problems and on the prescriptions for economic policy. Why is this the case?

It is important to distinguish between *positive* and *normative* economics, *i.e.*, between consideration of how the economy actually works and of how it ought to be made to work. Even if economists were unanimous in their understanding of the economy, different economists might nevertheless prescribe conflicting policies because they made different moral or political judgements. For instance, macroeconomic policy prescriptions might depend crucially on the relative strength of one's dislike for the two evils, inflation and unemployment. But disagreement among economists is not only about goals and objectives. In macroeconomics, the "Keynesian consensus" which held sway in the 1950s and 1960s gave way in the 1970s and 1980s to a variety of different schools of thought. This development reflected changes in the economy and the emergence of new and more pressing economic problems: a rise in the rates of inflation and unemployment and a fall in the rate of economic growth. The accepted analysis and prescriptions were found wanting. At the simplest level, the disputing schools divided into the *New Keynesians*, on the one hand, and the *Monetarists*, or *New Classical* school, on the other.

The two major political parties in Britain were, in the 1980s, committed to extreme and radically different approaches to the solution of Britain's economic problems. The Conservative Government, in office 1979–97, placed its faith in *laissez faire* economics, in the efficient operation of market forces, and in Monetarist policies. The Labour Party did not accept that the uncontrolled play of market forces would be beneficial, and it favoured Keynesian reflation and an expansion of state activity and state control. In part, these different approaches were based on differences in economic analysis. However, much of the disagreement was really based on differences in objectives, or on ideological considerations. Policies based on ideology or slogans can be dangerous. A great disservice is done by those who claim to have simple answers to what in reality are complex problems. The May 1997 General Election was unusual in that the two main contending parties did not offer distinctly different economic policies to the electorate.

Economic relationships are complicated and changeable, and normally difficult to measure. Economists cannot conduct rigorous experiments in the way that natural scientists do. Everything is happening at once in an economy, and the influence of any one variable is not easy to isolate, even with the use of sophisticated statistical techniques. This is another reason why economists disagree, and why they should always bear in mind the limitations of their knowledge.

Are Economists Useful?

Given their disagreements and the limitations of their knowledge, can economists perform a useful function? In the 1985 Reith Lectures, concerned with the influence of economic ideas on economic policy, David Henderson complained about the influence of what he called *do-it-yourself economics*. Over wide areas of policy the judgements of politicians and their officials, as also public opinion in general, are guided by beliefs and perceptions about the workings of the economy which owe little or nothing to the economics profession. The amateurs have not been driven from the field, and they are often in control of policy.

According to Henderson, do-it-yourself economics is based on peoples' intuitions and tends to be interventionist: politicians like to be active and to be seen to be active. These intuitions rarely extend beyond the immediate effects of the intervention, whereas professional economists analyse the less obvious, indirect and often unintended effects of interventions, which take place through the response of market forces. To give a simple example, rent controls appear to tackle the ill-effects of housing shortage but, by deterring investment in housing, they may exacerbate the shortage. Or mortgage interest tax relief may be electorally popular, but the economist's approach is to trace its consequences through to the end of the chain—higher house prices, losers as well as gainers, and less resources for non-housing. The professional approach is generally more quantitative than that of the amateur. Economists *can* often be useful, but their advice is ignored more frequently by policy-makers than that of, say, lawyers or engineers.

The Objectives of Policy: Avoiding Unemployment.

The central issues of economic policy concern certain desirable objectives. One important objective is the avoidance of unemployment. Between the wars, mass unemployment was Britain's most urgent problem: unemployment caused waste, hardship and poverty. For a long time after 1945, the maintenance of full employment was accepted as a primary objective of economic policy by all political parties. Until the late 1960s less than 2 per cent of the labour force was unemployed.

Unemployment can be either *cyclical* or *structural*. Cyclical unemployment, arising from a lack of demand in the economy, can be tackled by Government measures to increase total spending in the economy. Structural unemployment arises from a misallocation of resources. In the 1970s and 1980s it grew as redundancies rocketed in the increasingly uncompetitive manufacturing sector, *e.g.*, motor and engineering industries, and in declining industries such as steel and coal.

With the emergence during the last 25 years of new and greater problems of inflation, the commitment to full employment first faltered and then was withdrawn. The concern that has daunted Governments in recent years is that expansionary policies to eliminate cyclical unemployment might fuel a spiral of inflation. Between 1983 and 1986, and again in 1993, unemployment exceeded the figure of 3 million, or 10 per cent of the labour force.

The Objectives of Policy: Controlling Inflation.

A second objective of economic policy has been the cure of inflation. In the 1960s retail prices increased on average by 4·4 per cent per annum; in the 1970s by no less than 14 per cent per annum; in the 1990s by 6·6 per cent per annum; and between 1990 and 1997 by 3·2 per cent per annum. Inflation can be harmful in various ways. It is associated with an arbitrary redistribution of purchasing power. Prices rise for everyone but some groups in society are better able to protect themselves against inflation. The feeling that particular groups are falling behind is a source of much unrest and discontent. Moreover, the general economic uncertainty that inflation brings can become a threat to economic prosperity.

Two main explanations have been advanced to account for inflation. The first stresses the role of excess demand or spending power in the economy—of too much money chasing too few goods. Such *demand-pull* theories are put forward by Monetarists, who point to increases in the money supply in generating demand, and by Keynesians who recommend restrictive monetary and fiscal policies to curb excess demand, when it arises. The second explanation stresses the role of excessive increases in costs, *e.g.*, wage costs or imported raw material costs, in raising prices. Such *cost-push* theories imply, for instance, that policies are needed to restrain the power of trade unions to raise wages. Neither explanation precludes the other: both demand-pull and cost-push factors are likely to have contributed—with different strengths at different times—to inflation. Moreover, adherents of both views recognise that, once expectations of continued inflation become entrenched, these expectations themselves sustain and fuel the inflation.

The Objectives of Policy: Promoting Growth.

A third objective of economic policy is the fostering of economic growth. Successive British Governments in the post-war period have tried to raise the growth rate—the most important long run determinant of the standard of living. Britain's living standards have risen gradually in the post-war period, but more rapidly prior to the first oil shock (by 2·5 per cent per annum over the period 1948–73) than after it (by 1·6 per cent per annum over the period 1973–97). The long run British growth rate compares unfavourably with that achieved by most other industrial countries.

The determinants of economic growth are not well understood, but most economists would agree that in order to raise the growth rate it is necessary to encourage the community to save, and businesses to invest, a higher proportion of the national income. In a fully employed economy the source of increased output is higher productivity, *i.e.*, output per worker. There is a danger, however, that higher productivity growth will be achieved at the expense of employment, as has partly been the case in Britain since 1980: reported employment fell over the 1980s and barely rose over the 1990s.

A constraint on the achievement of the above objectives has been the need to maintain balance in international payments. The British balance of payments position has been precarious, so that unfavourable turns of events have precipitated economic crises. Indeed, concern about the balance of payments so dominated economic policy-making at times during the post-war period that improvement in the balance of payments was a major objective of policy. The expansion in the late 1970s of North Sea oil production, and the resulting confidence of foreign investors, transformed the British balance of payments. But this created new problems, particularly the adverse effect of the ensuing high exchange rate on manufacturing, our traditional export sector and an important employer of labour. The emergence of vast flows of funds in the 1980s and 1990s meant that the balance of payments could be increasingly regulated by means of interest rate policy. But this in turn subordinated domestic monetary policy to the foreign balances.

The Inter-relationship of Economic Problems.

The achievement of each of the objectives briefly described above is extremely complex. The difficulties are further aggravated by the fact that the problems are inter-related in such a way that measures which are helpful for one objective can make others more difficult to achieve. For example, a reduction of purchasing power might be considered helpful in the control of inflation. But it could also lead to an increase in unemployment, and to a slowing down in the rate of growth of the economy. Many economic commentators now hold that it is no longer possible to keep unemployment down to the levels of the 1950s and 1960s without unleashing cumulative inflation, and that the control of inflation must now have the highest priority. This must be the rationale for the economic policies of the Conservative Government in office after 1979, as it paid little heed to the short run effects of its policies on unemployment and economic growth. In 1980 the Government faced an inflation rate of 18 per cent and an unemployment rate of 6 per cent. By 1987 it had got inflation down, to below 4 per cent, but unemployment had risen to 10 per cent. In 1998 the figures were 6·1 and 2·8 per cent respectively

There are other examples of a conflict in policy objectives. For instance, while the advent in the 1970s of a floating exchange rate can help to correct the balance of payments, a depreciating pound can in turn fuel inflation. The defence of a fixed exchange rate can force interest rates higher and higher, with unhelpful deflationary effects on the economy - as happened in the early 1990s.

The Worsened Economic Climate.

In the mid-1970s, after 30 years of rapid growth and unprecedented prosperity for the major Western economies, the prospects for continued growth became much less favourable. This resulted partly from the acceleration of inflation in many countries, bringing with it insecurity and loss of confidence. However, the main cause was the remarkable increase in the price of oil in 1973 and again in 1979, a fuel on which the Western economies had become heavily dependent. This produced a strong burst of inflation and gave rise to an unprecedented balance of payments problem and world recession. The international infectiousness of high interest rates, economic recession and rapid inflation made it hard for any one country to avoid these ills. The 1980s and 1990s were a period of relatively slow world economic growth for the major economies.

II. SURVEY OF THE BRITISH ECONOMY

1. INTERNATIONAL TRADE AND PAYMENTS

International Trade.

(i) Imports and Exports.

In 1995 the United Kingdom bought from abroad goods to the value of £168 billion (thousand million), or about £2,870 per head. Food accounted for 10 per cent of this total, and basic materials, fuels and chemicals for 18 per cent. The great majority of imports (72 per cent) were manufactures. The most important manufacturing imports were machinery and transport equipment: electrical machinery represented no less than 19 per cent of the total imports and road vehicles another 11 per cent. All this can be seen in the table. The table also shows the remarkable similarity in the composition of exports and imports. This pattern is in sharp contrast to the traditional pattern of trade, in which Britain imported food and raw materials and exported finished manufactures.

There are three main determinants of the level of British imports. One is the competitiveness of British with foreign producers. Britain imports those commodities which—at the ruling exchange rate between the pound and foreign currencies—can be bought more cheaply from foreign than from home producers. Secondly, the level of imports depends on the extent to which free trade is prevented by tariffs on imported goods or by other devices. Thirdly, as total incomes in the economy expand, there is a general increase in the demand for goods and services including imports. Therefore imports can be expected to vary with the total incomes in the country, known as the *national income*.

UNITED KINGDOM IMPORTS AND EXPORTS, 1995

Imports of goods	£ million	Percentage of total
Food, drink, and tobacco .	16,012	9·5
Basic materials .	6,351	3·8
Fuels .	5,875	3·5
Chemicals, oils and fats	18,438	11·0
Manufactures of materials .	28,205	16·8
Machinery and transport equipment .	69,047	41·0
Miscellaneous manufactures .	23,057	13·7
Other .	1,359	0·8
TOTAL IMPORTS .	168,335	100·0
Exports of goods		
Food, drink, and tobacco .	11,237	7·3
Basic materials .	2,731	1·8
Fuels .	9,295	6·0
Chemicals, oils and fats .	21,370	13·9
Manufactures of materials .	22,569	14·7
Machinery and transport equipment .	65,823	42·8
Miscellaneous manufactures .	18,992	12·4
Other .	1,756	1·1
TOTAL EXPORTS .	153,761	100·0

Whereas in 1968 imports amounted to 23 per cent of national income, in 1995 the proportion was 31 per cent. The main reason for this rise is the liberal-isation of trade among countries during the postwar period. An example is the formation of the *European Economic Community* in 1956 and Britain's entry to it in 1973.

Since the exports of one country must be the imports of another, the same factors in reverse—foreign competitiveness, access to foreign markets, and the level of foreign incomes—determine the level of British exports. In 1995 these amounted to over £154 billion of which 70 per cent were manufactures.

In the past, Britain gained from trade by exporting manufactures, in which she had a *comparative advantage*, in return for food and raw materials, which she was not suited to produce. Increasingly—with the growth of trade and specialisation among the major economies—Britain gains from trade by exporting those manufactures in which her producers specialise and importing other manufactures. Among the main manufacturing exports are cars and commercial vehicles, tractors, aircraft and aircraft engines, finished steel, various forms of machinery, woollen fabrics, man-made fibres, and chemicals; among the main manufactured imports are wood products, aluminium, newsprint, cars, and aircraft.

(ii) The Terms of Trade and the Volume of Trade.

The value of trade can be separated into two components, price and volume. The ratio of the average price of exports to that of imports is known as the *terms of trade*; and a rise in the price of exports relative to imports indicates an improvement in the terms of trade.

Superficially it would appear that any improvement in the terms of trade raises the value of British exports relative to imports. However, faster inflation in Britain, leading to a more rapid increase in export prices, would harm rather than help the balance of payments. Similarly, inflation in Britain makes it more difficult to compete with imports. The relevant concept that economists use is the *price elasticity of demand, i.e.* the percentage fall in demand for a product in response to a percentage rise in its price. If this elasticity is less than one, the value (price times volume) of exports falls as their price rises.

(iii) Trade Competitiveness.

The main determinant of trading success is competitiveness: a country's costs of production in relation to its competitors' costs. A country's competitiveness is harmed by domestic inflation of costs and prices, and helped by depreciation of the external value of its currency, *i.e.* of its *exchange rate*. There are various measures of trade competitiveness. One is the *index of relative export prices* (UK export prices divided by a weighted average of competitors' export prices, all expressed in United States dollars). Another is the *index of import price competitiveness* (the ratio of an import-weighted index of UK producer prices of domestic sales of manufactures to the average price of imports of manufactures).

The table (**G7**) shows these measures of trade competitiveness in manufactures over the period 1975–96, with 1990 set equal to 100. We see that export competitiveness has worsened since 1975, when sterling was low, but has improved since 1980, when sterling was high. Import competitiveness has improved over the years.

The Balance of Payments.

A detailed examination of recent movements in the British *balance of payments* is made in **Part IV**. Here we explain the underlying concepts and the terms used.

UK COMPETITIVENESS IN TRADE IN
MANUFACTURES, 1975–96, 1990=100

	Relative export prices	Relative import prices
1975	90·5	—
1980	111·6	124·7
1985	102·0	109·3
1990	100·0	100·0
1996	106·4	96·9

THE PATTERN OF BRITISH TRADE, 1995

£ billion	Exports to	Imports from	Trade balance
European Union	89·1	93·2	−4·1
of which:			
France	15·2	16·3	−1·1
Belgium	8·3	8·0	0·3
Netherlands	12·3	11·4	0·9
Germany	20·2	26·1	−5·9
Ireland	7·7	7·0	0·7
Spain	6·1	4·5	1·6
Italy	7·9	8·2	−0·3
United States	18·0	20·3	−2·3
Canada	1·8	2·4	−0·6
Japan	3·8	9·6	−5·8
Australia	2·1	1·1	1·0
Eastern Europe	3·8	3·4	0·4
Oil exporting countries	6·3	3·3	3·0
India	1·7	1·4	0·3
South Africa	1·8	1·1	0·7
Newly industrialising Asia	9·7	13·5	−3·8
of which:			
Hong Kong	2·7	3·5	−0·8
Singapore	2·1	2·2	−0·1
South Korea	1·2	1·6	−0·4
China	0·8	1·9	−1·1
TOTAL	**153·8**	**168·3**	**−14·5**

(i) The Balance of Visible Trade.

The *balance of (visible) trade* is the difference
between exports and imports of goods. It is said to
be in *surplus* if exports exceed imports and in *deficit*
if imports exceed exports.

The table shows the geographical pattern of
British trade in 1995. There is a trade surplus with
some countries and a deficit with others. However,
these are unimportant: all that counts is the ability
to finance an overall net deficit. The European
Union accounts for no less than 57 per cent of total
UK trade (exports plus imports). Within the EU,
Britain's main trading partners are Germany (14
per cent), France (10 per cent), the Netherlands,
Belgium and Italy, in that order. The United States
accounts for 12 per cent of British trade. A growing
source of trade, particularly of imports, are the
newly industrialising countries of Asia (7 per cent),
including Hong Kong, Singapore, South Korea and
China.

(ii) The Balance on Current Account.

The chronic deficit in the balance of visible
trade has in normal years been offset by a surplus
in the *balance of invisible trade*. This relates to international transactions in services as opposed to
goods. The main components are: net receipts from
non-residents for services such as shipping, civil aviation, tourism, insurance, and financial services; net
receipts of gifts and grants made to this country;
net receipts of interest, dividends, and profits
earned on overseas investment.

(iii) Capital Flow.

The capital account of the balance of payments
contains net private investment abroad (being the
difference between investment abroad by United
Kingdom residents and investment by foreigners in
the United Kingdom). There are also large, short-
term capital flows, sometimes referred to as
monetary movements. These include bank lending
and borrowing—trade credits, changes in sterling
reserves held by foreign governments, and Euro-
dollar transactions. Such funds can be highly volatile, moving out of a currency if there is a risk of its
depreciation and into it if there is a chance of
appreciation or if other currencies are suspect.

Therefore, monetary movements often accentuate a
surplus or deficit in the other items of the balance of
payments. They are also dependent on relative
rates of interest at home and abroad, being
attracted to financial centres which offer high
interest rates.

(iv) Foreign Exchange Reserves.

A deficit on current plus capital account can be
financed through an increase in liabilities, *i.e.* by
government borrowing from abroad, or by a reduction in assets, *e.g.*, a depletion of the official
foreign-exchange reserves. The official reserves are
used to finance payments abroad which cannot be
financed in any other way: they are a last line of
defence in international trade.

The book-keeping identity of international payments and receipts requires that the flow of goods
and services on current account should be precisely
offset by the total *net transactions in assets and liabilities*. However, not all such transactions can be
accurately recorded. There is generally an unre-
corded capital flow, known as the *balancing item*. In
some years the balancing item is so large that it
actually exceeds the current account balance.

Correcting a Deficit.

If an imbalance in international payments
persists, the deficit cannot be met indefinitely
from official financing. At some stage the
Government must take action to remove the
deficit. What action can it take? There are
a number of alternatives available, each with its
advantages and disadvantages, and economic
opinion is by no means unanimous on the choice
of policy. Let us consider each of these alternatives in turn.

(i) Variation of the Exchange Rate.

The *exchange rate* is the ruling rate of exchange of
pounds for dollars or other currencies. It determines the value of British goods in relation to
foreign goods. Under the post-war Bretton Woods
arrangements (*see* **G9**), Britain and other countries maintained a constant value of their currencies in terms of gold, permitting only very
minor fluctuations of the exchange rate about
its par value. However, persistent balance of
payments deficits or surpluses caused occasional
adjustments of the official exchange rate, the
response to persistent deficit being *devaluation*
and to persistent surplus *upvaluation*.

In 1972 the major countries adopted a system of
fluctuating exchange rates. However, exchange
rates are not permitted to fluctuate entirely freely,
i.e., so that the market supply and demand for
foreign exchange are continuously equated. While
the monetary authorities permit the foreign-
exchange market to influence the exchange rate,
they are prepared in the national interest to intervene in the market (by buying or selling their currency) and so to keep the exchange rate within
bounds. Given some flexibility in the exchange rate,
a tendency for a deficit to arise is thus met by a
depreciation of sterling, and an incipient surplus by
appreciation.

If the pound depreciates in terms of other
currencies, British exports (which are paid for
in pounds) become cheaper to foreigners and British
imports (paid for by purchasing foreign currency)

THE PATTERN OF WORLD TRADE, 1995

Exports from/to	Developed countries	Developing countries	Ex-communist countries	World total
Developed countries	49·4	16·6	1·8	68·6
Developing countries	16·2	11·1	0·5	27·9
Ex-communist countries	1·8	0·7	0·9	3·5
World total	67·4	28·4	3·2	100·0

become more expensive to holders of pounds. In this way a fall in the value of the pound can improve the British balance of payments position by encouraging exports and discouraging imports.

But there are certain disadvantages attached to depreciation. The prospect of depreciation results in a speculative outflow of capital funds: and one fall may be taken as a sign that there will be a further fall in the future. Moreover, the rise in the price of imports of raw materials and consumption goods results in higher costs and prices and then in wage demands to maintain the British standard of living. It is possible that inflation will in this way neutralise the beneficial effects of depreciation.

The probable effect of a depreciation in Britain is initially to *worsen* the balance of trade, because the sterling price of imports is likely to be raised by more than that of exports. After about six months the effect of the depreciation on quantities —curbing imports and expanding the volume of exports—dominates, and the balance of trade improves. However, the improvement is maintained only if fiscal and monetary policies can prevent the fall in sterling from feeding through to domestic prices and costs and so both neutralising the gain in competitiveness and exacerbating inflation.

The Fortunes of Sterling.

The pound was devalued from £1 = $4·0 in 1949, when an official exchange rate of £1 = $2·8 was established, and again in 1967, to a rate of £1 = $2·4. In 1972 the value of sterling in relation to other currencies was allowed to *float*. With widespread floating, an *effective exchange rate* is now calculated, which shows the value of sterling in relation to a bundle of other currencies, with each currency receiving a weight according to the extent of trade with Britain. This rate followed a strong downward trend in the face of rapid inflation until 1977, and then recovered until 1980 due mainly to the advent of North Sea oil. Thereafter, the value of sterling has tended to decline, reflecting the generally faster rate of inflation in Britain than in most of her trading partners. By 1997 sterling had depreciated by a third of its 1980 value.

Britain became a member of the *Exchange Rate Mechanism* (ERM) from October 1990 until sterling was forced out by speculation in September 1992. Membership of the ERM required effectively fixing sterling (within narrow bands) to the *European Currency Unit* (ECU), so relinquishing the exchange rate as a policy variable. At the start of 1999 exchange rates of most currencies within the European Union were fixed irreversibly against a single currency, the *Euro*. Whether Britain should join this monetary union will be a major issue in the coming years (*see* **G53–4**).

(ii) Currency Convertibility.

A currency is fully *convertible* if it can be freely exchanged for any other currency at the ruling rates of exchange. Exchange controls impose restrictions on convertibility. In the early post-war period there was a world-wide shortage of dollars: if sterling had been convertible, there would have been a rush to obtain dollars, with the consequence that Britain's reserves would soon have been exhausted.

Foreign exchange control has become a less feasible policy as a result of the revolution in information technology. The explosion in the way in which funds can be transferred and intermediation of all kinds can take place makes such controls increasingly impractical for any reasonably sophisticated economy (*see* **Part IV**).

(iii) Import Controls and Tariffs.

Import controls impose limitations on the quantity or value of goods which are permitted to enter a country; tariffs are duties levied on imported goods so that the price of those goods to consumers in a country is higher than the price received by the foreigners supplying the goods. In the early post-war years, Britain maintained strict import controls over a wide range of goods.

All countries impose tariffs. However, their rights to do so are closely circumscribed by the rules of the *World Trade Organisation* (WTO), which works towards free trade in goods and services, especially through a reduction in tariffs. The disadvantage of introducing import controls or tariffs to correct a deficit in the balance of payments is that the benefits of free trade are lost. Moreover, there is always the possibility of retaliation by trading partners.

Britain's powers to impose tariffs and quotas on imports are greatly restricted by membership of the European Union, since this requires free trade within the Union and a common external tariff.

(iv) Deflation.

For much of the post-war period, the UK balance of payments was far from secure. As a result, domestic economic policies were much influenced by balance of payments considerations. By ruling out devaluation and trade restrictions, the authorities had to fall back on *deflation* of the economy to correct periodic deficits. In other words, the Government took measures to discourage demand and so cut back incomes and employment. In this way, the authorities secured a fall in demand for imports. Deflation is a painful method of correcting a deficit: not only does it have a direct effect on the level of incomes and employment, but it is also liable to slow down the rate of growth of the economy. This can happen because deflation can weaken the incentive to expand productive capacity by investing.

Deflation need not be the conscious policy. When inflation is high and the balance of payments weak, deflation may result from policies to raise domestic interest rates in order to protect sterling against speculative outflows of capital. This is a good description of British economic policy in the early 1990s.

International Trade Flows.

We can divide the world into three trading groups: the industrial countries (mainly OECD), the developing countries and the ex-communist countries. The matrix of the world exports presented in the table above shows that the industrial countries accounted for no less than 69 per cent of world exports, 49 per cent being exports to countries within that group. Trade within the European Union represented 25 per cent of the world total. No less than 80 per cent of industrial countries' exports were manufactured goods. The developing countries exported 28 per cent of the world total. Trade between the developed and the developing countries amounted to 28 per cent of the total. The ex-communist countries were still not much integrated into the world economy.

A breakdown of world exports by commodity in 1995 shows the predominance of manufactures—accounting for 77 per cent of the total. Machinery and transport equipment made up the majority of manufactures. Agricultural food and raw materials accounted for 12 per cent of world exports and minerals for 11 per cent, most of which was oil.

The International Monetary System.

(i) The International Monetary Fund.

The *International Monetary Fund* (IMF) was set up at Bretton Woods in 1944 with the object of working towards free trade at stable exchange rates. Under the original agreement establishing the Fund, members agreed to make their currencies convertible into other currencies and gold at fixed rates of exchange, and agreed not to impose exchange or import controls without the permission of the Fund.

The function of the Fund is to make foreign-exchange resources available to members which run into balance of payments difficulties. Each member country has a deposit (called its quota), paid partly in foreign exchange and partly in its own currency, with the Fund. In return, it is granted certain automatic drawing rights, which entitle it to borrow foreign currencies from the Fund. The Fund has power to make larger loans, and to grant standby credits to be drawn on if required. Before the Fund will make such loans and credits available it has to be satisfied that the borrowing country is taking appropriate action to correct the balance-of-payments disequilibrium. The relations between the IMF and the developing countries are examined on **G**46.

(ii) International Money.

Gold played a central role in the international monetary system during the 1950s and 1960s. Central banks were prepared to buy and sell gold at a fixed price in terms of their currencies, and gold was exchanged among them in settlement of imbalances. The price of gold was held for many years at $35 per fine ounce. However, this fixed price in the face of rising costs of gold production meant that gold supply could not increase rapidly enough to provide the international liquidity needed to finance expanding world trade, and gold gradually lost its monetary role.

The domestic currency of the United Kingdom is not backed by gold: on a ten-pound note the Governor of the Bank of England promises to pay the bearer on demand the sum of ten pounds—merely another note! Yet, within Britain, there is complete confidence in the currency, because it is generally acceptable and so convertible into goods and services. Just as gold no longer backs the domestic currency, there is no need for gold in settlement of international payments. All we need is a generally acceptable international currency, *i.e.*, one in which all countries have confidence. Only very limited steps towards the creation of an international currency—the issue by the IMF of small quantities of *special drawing rights* (SDRs)—have been made.

(iii) Foreign Exchange Reserves.

Surplus countries are prepared to hold short-term debt in foreign currencies—so earning a rate of interest—confident that their future trading deficits can be financed by payment of these currencies. They can perform their function only if there is confidence that they can be converted into other currencies and hence into goods and services at current exchange rates.

After World War Two the dollar replaced the pound as the main reserve currency, used in settlement of international payments. The United States ran a large and persistent payments deficit during the 1950s and 1960s, made possible by the willingness of the creditor countries to build up their dollar balances. But there is necessarily a limit to such a process. The deficits produced periodic fears that the dollar would be devalued; and this resulted in speculation against the dollar, and contributed to the breakdown of the Bretton Woods system. In recent years the deutschmark has come to rival the dollar as a reserve currency.

(iv) International Capital Markets.

There are now vast sums of money that are moved between international financial centres

according to which centre offers the greatest safety and the highest rate of interest. For instance, foreign governments, corporations and individuals hold balances in sterling (*e.g.* Treasury bills, short term loans and bank accounts). The size of the funds held in sterling will depend on the rate of interest in London in relation to other financial centres and on expectations about the exchange rate between sterling and other currencies.

The sensitivity of capital flows to the rate of interest means the Government has the power to protect the balance of payments against an adverse balance of trade. For instance, high interest rates protected the huge current account deficit in the early 1990s. However, that episode also reveals the limitations of this policy variable. Eventually, in September 1992, speculators expected that the pound would have to fall and, through capital flight, precipitated its collapse (*see* **G**49).

London and Tokyo are the largest international banking centres in the world, each accounting for nearly a quarter of the lending market. The external liabilities of UK banks can create problems for the regulation of economic activity. Movements in the market affect interest rates, credit and exchange rates in different countries, and they can thwart domestic monetary policies.

2. EMPLOYMENT, PRODUCTION, AND INDUSTRY

Population.

In 1997 the population of the United Kingdom was estimated to be 59·0 million—52·2 m. in England and Wales, 5·1 m. in Scotland, and 1·7 m. in Northern Ireland. Since 1971 the population has increased by only 5½ per cent. This slow increase is accounted for by the birth rate (the number of live births per 100 people) exceeding the crude death rate. In 1997 the former was 1·25 and the latter was 1·1. The size of population is also affected by the net migration rate. Since the early 1980s there has been a small positive net inflow into the UK. Between 1995 and 1997, 267,000 people per annum migrated into the UK and 211,000 per annum left.

The official estimate of the population of the United Kingdom in the year 2021 is 62·2 million. But prediction of future trends is difficult. For instance, it depends on immigration and emigration policies, the effect of improving medical services on the average length of life, trends in the age at which people marry, advances in techniques of birth control, and attitudes towards desirable family size. This projection is based on the belief that the birth rate will slightly exceed the death rate. It is also projected that the birth rate will continue to gradually fall as the large generation born in the 1960s pass beyond their child-bearing years.

The Labour Force.

Of the total population only some are of *working age, i.e.*, between the minimum school leaving age of 16 (15 before 1973) and retiring age—65 years for men and 60 for women. Of course, not all those of working age do work and not all those above working age have retired. In 1998 the labour force was 27·9 million. Of males aged 16 and over, 85 per cent were in the labour force compared with 72 per cent of females. The labour force is defined to include not only those who are gainfully employed (as employees or self-employed) but also the unemployed who are looking for work and those on work related government training programmes. Students and housewives are excluded unless they do some work for cash. One feature of the past decade or so has been a fall in the proportion of adult males going out to work, a fall which is expected to continue. It is caused by an increasing number of students and others undergoing full-time training and by more people retiring early. Those factors also affected the proportion of women going out to work, but they have been more than offset by a rising participation of married women, particularly in part-time work. This trend is again expected to continue.

Most of the labour force work for wages and salaries as employees. Of the total for the United Kingdom in 1998 of 27·9 million, 3·1 m. were employers or self-employed. 22·9 were employees,

0·3 m. were on work-related government training programmes or in unpaid family work, and 1·7 m. were recorded as unemployed. There has been an increase in the porportion of the workforce who are self-employed. So less than half the population who are at work have to produce not only for themselves but also for the rest of the population who are either not in the labour force or who are unemployed.

The table (**G11**) shows the industries in which people work. As an economy develops there is a tendency for employment in the primary sector to decline as the production industries expand. As an economy gets richer still, the proportion of income spent on services increases, and employment in the service sector consequently rises whilst the proportion of the workforce in production industries declines. Thus, in the early 1950s services accounted for only about one third of total employment; whereas by 1998 the proportion had risen to over 75 per cent.

Employment and Unemployment.

In 1998 an average of 1·4 m persons—4·7 per cent of the working population—were unemployed in the UK This figure excludes school-leavers. In most post-war years until the late 1960s the average was lower than 1·5 per cent. This contrasts with an average figure in 1937, the best year of the 1930s, of 11 per cent, and with a figure of 22 per cent at the bottom of the slump in 1932. The low unemployment of the post-war years was not maintained from the late 1960s. Unemployment grew to reach almost one million in early 1972. It then started to fall back with the general economic recovery, only to start rising again from late 1974 as the economy moved back into recession. Unemployment peaked in 1986 but fell sharply between then and the first half of 1990. The figures then began to rise sharply once again as the economy entered recession, topping 2 million by Spring 1991 and continuing to rise until early 1993, since when there has been a dramatic fall.

Until the late 1960s 1–1·5 per cent unemployment was somewhere near the practicable minimum. Some unemployment is more or less inevitable. A seasonal rise in unemployment in the winter must be expected, e.g., in seaside towns, and for this reason unemployment in January is higher than in June. Moreover, some unemployment is bound to be involved in job-changing and as the demands of industries change. Finally there is a core of people who are simply unemployable. "Full employment" means that there should be about as many jobs vacant as there are workers looking for jobs. A large excess of vacancies is evidence of inflationary pressure in the labour market, for it means that the employers needing workers to meet the demands for their products will have to compete with each other by bidding up wages.

Most commentators feel that the practicable minimum level of unemployment has increased since the late 1960s. By minimum they mean that any attempt to reduce unemployment below it, by injecting monetary demand, would be likely to cause increasing inflation or a deteriorating balance of trade. Many possible reasons have been advanced for the increase in this "equilibrium rate of unemployment"—that rate of unemployment consistent with stable inflation and balanced trade. One explanation is that as the fixed costs (like National Insurance) of employing workers went up, so employers were more careful to economise on labour. Another possible explanation was that the level of social security benefits as a whole was too high, causing people to demand an unrealistically high wage before accepting a job. Whilst the above factors, particularly the burden of National Insurance contributions, may well have played a role at times, it is unlikely that they have been persistently important.

Many of the unemployed have skills which are redundant in an economy where the structure of industry is changing. Hence there may be an excess demand for some skills even when many people are without work—indeed this is the case at present. As well as skill mismatch of this sort, there may be geographical mismatch—that is the distribution of the population may not coincide with the distribution of job vacancies. This is one interpretation of Mr. Tebbit's famous exhortation: "Get on your bike!" However, there is grave disagreement amongst observers about the importance of such mismatch explanations. No-one denies that there is a severe degree of mismatch in the British economy; the doubt concerns the extent to which it has increased. Similar disagreement attends the claim that technological advance, reducing the need for labour, is a major factor. Interestingly many industrialists would put this as a prime explanation. Most economists would be inclined to disagree with them. They would put greater stress on a too rapid growth of real wages (that is wages compared to prices), causing employers to try to produce a given amount of output with smaller quantities of labour. Many used to put a large share of the blame for this on the shoulders of trade unions. If trade unions push up wages, employers may respond by putting up prices; unions then push up wages again in an attempt to obtain an increase in their living standards. Thus a wage-price spiral may cause increasing inflation. Governments concerned about inflation may therefore be forced to run the economy at lower levels of demand.

The experience of the late 1980s when a surge in output growth and a sharp drop in unemployment contributed to a renewed increase in inflation and to a dramatic worsening of the balance of trade suggests that the equilibrium rate of unemployment had not fallen despite the supply-side reforms of the 1980s. Though unions were weaker, competition between employers for a limited stock of suitable workers, as well as a pervasive belief that rising real wages are important for motivating staff, may be amongst the more important explanations of why the real wage and the equilibrium rate of unemployment remained high. Also of importance was the UK's failure to much improve its relatively inadequate performance (by international standards) in vocational education and training. Recently some commentators have laid stress on two other structural characteristics: the lack of coordinated wage bargaining and the lack of a time limit on social security benefit for the unemployed. Also prominent in contemporary debate is the contention that demand for unskilled labour is threatened by cheap labour in the Third World competing effectively in the production of standardised products. Some also argue that the increased use of high technology by many firms is destroying the demand for less skilled workers.

Causes of Unemployment.

Whatever the relative importance of these explanations, there is little doubt that the major cause of the rise in unemployment in the early 1980s was deficiency of aggregate demand for British goods. This in turn is was partly the consequence of restrictive government policies, and partly of our loss of international competitiveness. There is, however, dispute as to how much of this reduction in demand was necessary to stabilise inflation. Indeed there were some who thought that much of the fall in inflation rates in the early 1980s was the consequence of a massive slowdown in the rate of increase in world commodity prices and the consequentially slower growth of import prices. Equally there are those who believe that even if it was necessary in the above sense, it contributed to increasing the rate of equilibrium unemployment—because some of the workers who lost their jobs became hard to re-employ. Partly this was because of the effect of joblessness on their own attitudes and skills, and partly because of the perceptions of employers as to their worth. It may also have been difficult for the unemployed to "compete" with the employed by "bidding down" wages, since the latter may have great bargaining power vis a vis their employers for whom their departure would represent a major waste of training expenditure.

To some extent official unemployment figures are misleading, in that certain individuals may not record themselves as being out of work and will thus appear to drop out of the working population. Until 1982 the official unemployment figure was calculated on the number registered as available for work. Registration was a prerequisite for claiming unemployment benefit. Individuals not eligible for such benefits—particularly married women—often did not register as unemployed even if they still wished to work. Their only incentive for doing so was if they felt that the authorities would help them find a job. Further, the count did not include those who were temporarily stopped or working short time. Since late 1982 the official unemployment figures have been calculated according to the number actually claiming benefit, for which registering as available for work is no longer essential. Those under 18 are now not included in the unemployment figures, as they are assumed to be on a training scheme, to have a job, or to have remained in full-time education. The above are not the only changes that have been introduced in the last few years in the way that unemployment is measured. For example, older workers tend not to get included in the count, whilst many believe that the special employment and training measures (*see* **G15–16**) artificially deflate the unemployment figure. So much concern has been expressed about the quality of the claimant count figures that the Government has introduced an alternative set of unemployment figures derived from the Labour Force Survey. A combination of the changes in the way unemployment has been calculated, and the rapid expansion of demand in the second half of the decade, meant that recorded unemployment fell steadily between early 1986 and mid 1990. Thereafter, the emerging recession in the UK economy pushed unemployment back up, and at an accelerating rate. By the first quarter of 1991, seasonally adjusted unemployment was increasing by about 80,000 per month. Much to the surprise of many, unemployment started to fall slowly from early 1993. This came much earlier than had happened in the aftermath of earlier recessions. Though much of the increase in employment came in the form of part-time work, it is probably the case that the labour market was also witnessing the counterpart of a more thorough shedding of labour during the recession. By early 1999 unemployment had fallen to less than 1·3 million. This has caused some commentators to speculate that at last the equilibrium rate of unemployment has started to fall significantly. This is because wage inflation has remained pretty stable and the

balance of trade reasonably healthy. However, it will take another year or so before the truth of this speculation can be put to the test.

Regional Unemployment.

Extreme variations in regional unemployment were not a general feature of the post-war period: only in Northern Ireland was unemployment persistently very high. Nevertheless, regional inequalities existed and were magnified in absolute terms in the 1980s.

In 1998 the proportion of all workers unemployed in the UK was 4·8 per cent. Even within the more fortunate regions there are pockets of high unemployment. These are concentrated particularly in the inner areas of large cities, but also elsewhere. For example, in East Anglia, Great Yarmouth had an unemployment rate of 10·1 per cent in early 1999, whilst in the South West, Newquay had 12·0 per cent.

One of the main reasons for the traditional regional pattern of unemployment used to be that certain industries and services, in which big changes had been taking place, tended to be grouped in specific regions. Most of our early industrial centres had to be established close to coal, iron ore, and adequate water supplies. But employment in many long-established industries has been declining. Such industries include textiles, mining and quarrying, shipbuilding, and agriculture. On the other hand new and growing industries, and their related head offices, were concentrated in Greater London, the South East, and the Midlands. The growth of services, too, centred on the areas where industry was booming and population is increasing. In the absence of government intervention, it was thought that the process would tend to become cumulative, and regional inequalities would grow rather than diminish. The 1970s saw an interesting change. The West Midlands, traditionally after the South-East, the most prosperous area of the country, was severely hit by the particular impact of the recession on engineering, and appeared as one of the regions with higher than average unemployment. This remained the case until recently despite the fact that in the mid 1980s the West Midlands began to benefit from the ripple effect of the boom in the South East and as firms began to relocate some of their activities from the crowded South-East to areas where the labour market was less tight. Other areas of high unemployment saw little or no improvement in their relative position during the period of strong economic growth 1986–1988, the worst affected regions remaining Northern Ireland, Scotland, the North and North-West. This may have been linked to an additional factor—the relative concentration of unemployment in inner city areas in particular regions. Unemployment in the inner cities has grown more rapidly than elsewhere since the 1960s, and seems to be the result of limited growth of firms there together with only a slow emergence of new enterprise. When the economy slowed down in 1989 and entered recession in 1990 and 1991, a different pattern of regional unemployment started to emerge. In contrast to the recession of the early 1980s, the downturn affected service industries before manufacturing, so the initial rise in unemployment was heavily concen-

---

DISTRIBUTION OF EMPLOYEES BY INDUSTRY, UNITED KINGDOM
JUNE 1998
(Percentages of all employees)

	Males	Females
Distribution, hotels, catering and repairs	20	26
Manufacturing	25	10
Financial and business services	16	19
Transport and communication	9	3
Construction	8	1
Agriculture	2	1
Energy and water supply	1	
Other services	19	40

UNEMPLOYMENT AND VACANCIES
(United Kingdom, thousands)

	Unemployment.† (Annual Average)	Vacancies. (Annual Average)	Unemployment as a percentage of total labour force
1972	876	147	2·9
1974	618	298	2·0
1976	1,359	122	4·1
1978	1,383	210	4·4
1980	1,665	143	4·8
1982	2,917	111	9·4
1984	3,160	157	10·6
1986	3,293	188	11·1
1988	2,370	248	8·2
1990	1,665	173	5·4
1992	2,779	117	9·6
1994	2,636	157	9·4
1996	2,122	225	7·4
1998	1,381	296	4·8

† Prior to October 1982 the unemployment count consisted of those people registered at Jobcentres who were unemployed (the registrant count). From October 1982 the unemployment count consisted of those claiming unemployment-related benefits.

PERCENTAGE OF WORKERS UNEMPLOYED, BY REGIONS

	Annual average* 1965	Late 1998*
North	2·4	7·3
Yorkshire and Humberside	1·0	5·6
East Midlands	0·8	4·1
East Anglia	1·2	3·3
South East	0·8	2·6
South West	1·5	3·4
Wales	2·5	5·4
West Midlands	0·6	4·7
North West	1·5	4·2
Scotland	2·8	5·5
N. Ireland	5·9	7·2

* Excluding school-leavers.

trated in the South East and in other regions where service industries predominate, such as East Anglia. Some commentators christened this the "yuppie recession". This had the effect of substantially narrowing regional variations in unemployment. A noteworthy aspect of these recent developments concerns Scotland and Wales. Traditionally both countries exhibited higher unemployment than the UK average. However the latest recession hit them less badly than many other areas of the UK. This was true even more strongly of Northern Ireland. For a while unemployment in Scotland and Wales was little different from the national average. However, recently unemployment there crept above it.

The Table shows that in late 1998 Yorkshire and Humberside, the North and Northern Ireland were also experiencing above average unemployment. What the future holds for regional employment is uncertain. But it is clear that there are presently still discrepancies between regions in disposable income per head. For example in 1994–95, average gross household income was 54 per cent. higher in the South East (the richest area) than in Wales (the poorest).

Regional Planning.

There are essentially two ways of tackling the problem of regional imbalances; taking jobs to the people or bringing people to the jobs. In so far as the latter alternative is chosen, the Government should encourage the mobility of labour, *e.g.*, through retraining schemes or rehousing subsidies. However, the migration of population may damage community life in the denuded areas, and cause congestion, housing shortages, and overcrowding in the booming regions. The Government can create employment opportunities in the relatively depressed regions in various ways. It can try to induce expanding industries to set up new plants in these regions by offering tax incentives or grants; it can authorise additional expenditure on public works—*e.g.*, by accelerating road-building programmes—to provide additional employment; it can place orders for the goods it needs—*e.g.*, defence contracts—where work is required. It can also use physical controls on expansion in the better-off areas; between 1947 and 1981 factory building over a particular size, which was changed from time to time, required the granting of an *Industrial Development Certificate*.

(i) Labour's Policy in the 1960s.

On taking office in October 1964, the Labour Government made regional planning the responsibility of its Department of Economic Affairs. Britain was divided into eight regions, with the intention of producing a plan for each region.

Fiscal incentives to locate industry in the depressed regions were given, *e.g.*, the cash grants provided in 1966 for new plant and machinery in manufacturing were at twice the national rate in the Development Areas. Buildings also received cash grants in Development Areas, in Intermediate Areas (where regional depression existed but in not such an acute form), and in Special Development Areas (where depression was most acute). By contrast, office building in London and some other cities was strictly limited. To encourage the mobility of labour, the Government introduced redundancy compensation and achieved some expansion in both public and private training facilities. In 1967 regional differentials in the selective employment tax were also introduced. This was known as the Regional Employment Premium (REP).

(ii) Policy in the 1970s.

In 1970 the incentive to invest in the Development Areas was affected by the Conservative Government's replacement of cash grants (except on buildings) by a system of initial allowances against tax. Whereas cash grants had been 40 per cent of investment in plant and machinery in Development Areas and 20 per cent in other areas, there was now a 100 per cent initial allowance in Development Areas and 60 per cent initial allowances in other areas. The system of initial allowances is explained on **G14**.

In 1972 the Government introduced 100 per cent allowances throughout the country on all investment in plant and machinery; the preferential treatment of investment in Development Areas was therefore ended. Instead *regional development grants*, in the form of cash payments towards investment in plant, machinery and buildings, were introduced. The Government also proposed in four years to triple expenditure on retraining facilities, and to pay a worker who had undergone retraining a housing grant if he moved house to take a new job; and also a grant to any worker in an assisted area who moved house to take a new job. It should be remembered, however, that strong measures were necessary merely to replace the Labour Government's system of cash grants, and the REP which it was planned to phase out in 1974. Though, in the event, REP was retained by the incoming Labour Government, it was finally replaced by more selective measures in 1977.

(iii) Conservative Policy in the 1980s and 1990s.

In July 1979, the new Conservative Government announced some changes to be introduced over the 1979–83 period. The extent of the assisted areas would be gradually reduced, so as to cover 25 per cent instead of 40 per cent of the employed population and some areas were "down-graded". Industrial Development Certificate procedures were abolished in 1981.

It was also felt that in a slack labour market, regional policy was more likely to re-allocate a given number of jobs rather than increase them in net terms. Alongside regional policy, therefore, were introduced measures on inner city decay (a problem even in non-assisted areas such as the South East), rural development and derelict land. In his March 1980 Budget the Chancellor announced proposals to establish about half a dozen "Enterprise Zones". These were small sites (of no more than 500 acres) with problems of economic and physical decay. The Zones were an experiment to test how far industrial and commercial activity could be encouraged by the removal of certain fiscal burdens, and by the removal or streamlined administration of statutory or administrative controls. In January 1996 there were 7 such zones. Although the government did not envisage extending the scheme massively, enterprise zones were seen to be an effective way of tackling particular local problems. Simplified Planning Zones were also designed to assist urban development. An additional measure, announced in the 1983 Budget, was the establishment of a number of "freeports" which would enjoy similar relief from fiscal burdens, in particular local authority rates. By early 1985 there were 6 of these. However, the experiment with freeports proved to be unsuccessful. Of the six established only Southampton and Liverpool ever lived up to their initial expectations. The abolition of fiscal barriers within the EU after 1992 in any case removed much of the rationale for freeports.

In 1981 the Government set up two Urban Development Corporations (UDCs), one in London's Docklands and the other in Merseyside. The aim of the UDCs was to reclaim and develop derelict land for housing, commercial and recreational purposes. By early 1992 the London Docklands UDC had received over £1,300 million in Government aid and had obtained over £9 billion in private sector funding commitments. The London Docklands is the site for one of the largest single office developments in Europe, although progress was affected by the downturn in the UK commercial property market in the period 1989–92. From 1987 ten more UDCs were established in Birmingham, the West Midlands, Bristol, Leeds, Central Manchester, Greater Manchester, Sheffield, Teesside, Tyne and Wear, and Plymouth. All the UDCs were abolished in 1998. In 1988 the Government also announced an Action For Cities programme to improve co-operation between Government departments, private enterprise and local authorities in order to rejuvenate derelict inner city areas. Task Forces operate under this regeneration banner. City Grant (introduced in 1981) encouraged private sector initiatives in the inner cities. In 1991 the Government launched a further scheme—"City Challenge" Abolished in 1998, this had provided Government funding for 'particularly imaginative' local authority schemes.

In 1983 the Government introduced a Green Paper on regional policy. The suggestion was for a tighter and more selective approach, with aid being directed more at job creation, at small firms and at the services. But even this non-interventionist Government concluded that "wage adjustments and labour mobility cannot be relied upon to correct regional imbalance in employment opportunities". By the end of 1984 there were only two types of assisted areas in Britain—development and intermediate. In 1993 the development and intermediate areas were re-defined—they now cover about 35 per cent of the working population. Throughout the assisted areas help is available mainly through Regional Selective Assistance (RSA). This is available for help to "create and safeguard jobs; help attract international investment; improve regional and local competitiveness; and help areas adversely affected by the impact of economic change". In England policy and help is delivered through English Partnerships and the Rural Development Commission. Similar roles are played in Scotland by Scottish Enterprise and Highlands and Islands Enterprise; in Wales by the Welsh Development Agency; and in Northern Ireland by the Department of Economic Development. Help is available from the European Union through its Structural Funds, especially the European Regional Development Fund.

The Conservative Government's distrust of general regional assistance was confirmed by its decision in 1988 to abolish automatic regional grants. All assistance for the regions is now selective. The new philosophy was that the "market" would eventually erode the disparity in regional performance, as regional variations in pay encouraged a redistribution in regional employment.

The new Labour Government has announced its intention to establish 8 Regional Development Agencies and a strategic authority for London. The RDAs were due to start operations in April 1999. They will take over the work of English Partnerships, the Rural Development Commission and the Government Offices for the Regions.

National Income.

Gross domestic income (GDI) is the sum total of incomes received for the services of labour, land, or capital in a country. Gross domestic product (GDP) is the money value of all the goods and services produced in the country. So as to avoid double-counting, only the *value added* at each stage of production is included: firms' purchases of goods and services from other firms are excluded. The revenue from selling the GDP is either paid out to the hired factors of production—labour, land, and capital—or retained in the form of profits. Therefore, provided it is calculated net of taxes on goods produced, GDP must equal GDI. To estimate gross national income (GNI) from GDI it is necessary to add the net income—such as profits and interest—received from abroad. If an allowance is made for wear and tear of the nation's capital equipment, *i.e.*, for *capital consumption*, we arrive at net national income, better known as the *national income.*

In 1997 the gross national income of the United Kingdom was £811,535 million, implying a national income per head of over £13,000. In 1955 the corresponding figure had been about £330 per head. However, only part of the increase in value was due to an increase in the quantity of goods and services produced; some of the increase simply reflected a rise in prices. It is important to calculate changes in the volume of output—known as *real output*—as well as changes in its value. Real output is calculated by the statistical device of constructing an index number. This is done by calculating the volume of goods and services provided in each year and then valuing these goods and services at the prices found in one particular year. Thus between 1955 and 1997 the money value of gross national product per head rose by over 3,600 per cent, whereas real per capita incomes little more than doubled, and the difference represented a rise in prices.

The Quality of Life.

In real terms national income per head rather more than doubled between 1955 and 1997.

National income per head is an indicator of the standard of living. However, this measure is necessarily a crude one. For instance, it cannot take into account new and better products; nor does it indicate changes in the distribution of income between rich and poor; nor in the length of the working week or year.

Data of national income per head may also conceal important changes in the "quality of life", *e.g.*, in our physical environment. This is affected by such things as traffic congestion, noise, water- and air-pollution. Between 1961 and 1997 the number of car miles travelled on British roads quadrupled. Movement of civil aircraft over Britain increased even more. The air in our cities became less polluted by smoke, sulphur dioxide, carbon monoxide and lead. However, concern about other emissions from motor vehicles has increased, whilst the number of our rivers, canals and estuaries which were polluted remained significant. Complaints about noise were noticeably higher in the 1980s than before, and were even higher by the late 1990s.

In recent years environmental concerns have moved increasingly from the national to the international level. In particular the issue of global warming has become important. This is in part the consequence of emissions of carbon dioxide and carbon monoxide destroying the ozone layer. Noteworthy is that consumption—cars and aerosols, for example—as well as production contributes to this problem. Government anti-pollution policy is set out in the 1990 and 1995 Environment Protection Acts. There had been growing public concern with environmental issues, and an awareness that the Conservative government's "laissez faire" approach to industrial policy might have prevented progress being made on issues such as carbon dioxide emissions from power stations. In answer to its critics, the government pointed to co-operation with international bodies such as the EC and the OECD in developing laws on pollution control. It also published a White Paper in September 1990 entitled "This Common Inheritance" which set out a policy framework for the 1990s. The paper was widely criticised by environmentalists as lacking substance, since it failed to support measures such as a carbon tax. Meanwhile the Environmental Protection Act of 1990 announced the phasing in of a so-called integrated system of pollution control. Various agencies in this process (*e.g.* the National Rivers Authority and Her Majesty's Inspectorate of Pollution) were merged to form the Environment Agency in 1996. There were similar bodies for Scotland and Northern Ireland. At the beginning of 1994, BS7750 was published. This was described by the Government as "the world's first standard for environmental management systems".

In 1997 the new Labour Government merged the Departments of Environment and Transport, in the hope that this would enable a more integrated approach to environmental issues. Britain remains committed to a strategy of sustainable development, phraseology first arising from the "earth summit" in Rio de Janeiro in 1992.

Industrial Production.

It is fairly easy to measure output in the main manufacturing industries, and in many of the other industries producing goods. It is much more difficult to do so for the service industries: the output of a doctor or a teacher is not easily measured. So each month the Office for National Statistics calculates the *index of industrial production* covering the main production industries. Industrial production is thus an early indicator of economic trends (*see* **Part IV**), but historically it is prone to fluctuate more than the other components of GDP.

Manufacturing industry accounts for most industrial production. Within manufacturing the following industries have expanded rapidly since World War II—chemicals, including drugs, plastics, cosmetics and detergents, coal and petroleum products, including oil refining, and instrument and electrical engineering. The slowest growing manufacturing industries are textiles, clothing, leather and shipbuilding, which are losing their markets to cheaper competitors. Those industries in which demand has stagnated tend to be the industries in which output per employee, *i.e.*, productivity, has stagnated.

International Comparisons.

In the 1960s and 1970s Britain's GDP grew less rapidly than that of almost any other major Western country. The British economy was also characterised by a relatively slow growth of output per head, *i.e.*, productivity. Britain fell behind many of the European countries in terms of income per head.

Many explanations of Britain's poor performance were suggested, and there is by no means agreement on this matter among economists. However, until recently there was general consensus that relatively slow productivity growth was the main culprit rather than an inadequate growth of capital and labour. The factors most often blamed were poor management, an inadequate and inefficient industrial relations system and low investment in training and research. Commentators differed in the relative importance they assigned to these different explanations, but agreed that low investment in physical plant and machinery was likely to have been the consequence rather than the primary cause of low growth. However in the last few years some economists have started to put renewed stress on the importance of capital and labour inputs. They argue that traditional analysis has under-estimated the effect of investment in either capital or labour. This is because new investment embodies technical progress which increases productivity, and there are knock-on effects on the rest of the economy which are hard to measure but nevertheless very real. For example, if a business spends money on developing a new product, the very existence of this new product creates opportunities for others. Think of the peripheral products and services which have relied on the development of cheap home computers.

Economists who argue in this manner have developed so-called endogenous growth theories. They have argued that, when a business invests in physical equipment or in training or in research and development, it creates potential opportunities not just for itself but for others. By this mechanism investment can have a substantial impact on productivity.

The performance of the British economy in the mid- to late 1980s was much better relative to other countries than was the case in the 1970s. Growth in total output averaged about 2·5 per cent per annum in the period 1980–88, compared to a European average of less than 2·0 per cent in the same period. **Part IV** includes a discussion of possible reasons for the UK's relatively better economic performance in the mid to late 1980s. Sceptics who believed that there had been no real underlying improvement were proved at least partly correct. The period of rapid growth in 1986–88 finally ended because it met the UK's traditional constraints of inflation and balance of payments weakness. The policy tightening invoked to cope with these depressed the UK economy and kept growth well below the European average in the period 1989–94. *See* **Part IV** for later developments.

Investment.

In 1997 gross investment in capital assets amounted to £133,710 million in the United Kingdom. This was 16·5 per cent of GNP. The net addition to the nation's stock of capital assets was only 30 per cent of total investment, the rest being needed to offset the wastage of assets already in use, *i.e.*, to make good the *capital consumption*.

There are five main kinds of investment: plant and machinery, vehicles, dwellings, other new buildings and works and intangible fixed assets. In 1997 the five categories accounted for 40·2, 10·8, 18·0, 27·7 and 3·3 per cent respectively. Investment may also be analysed by the purpose for which it is used. Social services such as education and health take a small proportion of total investment. Distribution and other service industries take a large proportion: investment in electricity, gas and water alone accounts for over 5 per cent of total non-dwelling investment. It is clear that some sectors of the economy are more capital-intensive than others. Manufacturing investment is low in relation to the contribution of manufacturing to output. There is evidence that the quality of investment undertaken has shown a marked improvement in recent years. The net real return on capital employed by all non-oil industrial and commercial companies stood at 9 per cent in the mid-1990s.

Increasing Investment.

Historically, the proportion of total output invested—the *investment ratio*—has been lower in Britain than in other countries with faster growth rates of output and productivity; and there is reason to believe that a higher proportion would have improved the growth rate to a certain extent. This was seen in the mid 1980s when a sharp acceleration in productivity growth was associated with a recovery of investment (particularly in manufacturing) from the very depressed levels of the early 1980s. But in a fully employed economy it is not possible to increase investment expenditures without curtailing other forms of expenditure, notably private and public consumption. This curtailment would have to be brought about by increasing taxation or encouraging people to save or by pruning public services. Yet the very act of restricting private consumption may induce private firms to *reduce* their investment expenditures. For society as a whole, increasing investment involves a choice between the loss of current consumption and the ensuing gain of future consumption.

In 1997 91·1 per cent of total investment in the United Kingdom was carried out in the private sector, 7·6 per cent by public authorities and 1·25 per cent by the public corporations. The Government has more control over investment in the public sector than in the private sector. Governments do possess various policy measures by which to influence private investment (*see also* **Part IV**) but private investment is volatile and highly dependent on businessmen's expectations, es-pecially their expectations about the future growth of their markets. It is no easy matter to raise the British investment ratio. Even in the sustained growth of the mid and late 1980s, investment rates were particularly high only for two or three years.

The Finance of Investment.

Any business is allowed to charge as a cost the depreciation of its assets. Normal depreciation allowances used to be based on the original cost of the asset and on its expected useful life. In a time of price inflation depreciation allowances calculated in this way will not provide sufficient finance to permit the replacement of assets at higher prices, and accountants have been slowly moving towards the concept of depreciation allowances being based on replacement costs.

Governments have adopted certain fiscal devices to encourage replacement and net investment. Soon after the war initial allowances were introduced. Under this system firms were permitted to charge against profits in the first year of its life 20, or at times 40, per cent of the cost of any new equipment, and the system amounted to a loan of the tax saved in the first year, repaid over the life of the asset. In 1954 initial allowances for machinery were replaced by a system of investment allowances, under which a firm could charge against profits 20 per cent of the cost of any new machine, with the difference that all ordinary depreciation allowances were still chargeable. So the investment allowance was a grant, not a loan, of the saved tax. In 1966, initial and investment allowances on new plant and machinery in three sectors—manufacturing, mining, and shipping—were replaced by cash grants. Other plant and machinery and industrial building received higher initial allowances. In 1970 the Conservative Government reintroduced initial allowances in place of investment grants but in 1972 tried to encourage investment by granting free depreciation; *i.e.* 100 per cent allowance in the first year. The details of capital allowances changed from time to time over the following decade, but in the 1984 Budget a more radical change was announced. By 1986 first year allowances were scrapped, to be replaced by an annual allowance of 25 per cent and lower rates of Corporation Tax. In 1988–89 the Corporation Tax rate was reduced to 35 per cent, with a lower rate for small companies.

In response to the serious recession, the March 1991 Budget made a retrospective reduction in the Corporation Tax rate of 1% for the financial year 1990–91, and cut Corporation Tax by a further 1% to 33% for 1991–92 and beyond. The Spring 1998 Budget cut the rate to 30 per cent, and to 20 per cent for small companies. This leaves British rates of company taxation well below the European norm. In 2000 a new rate of 10 per cent will be introduced for profits up to £10,000.

Apart from Government help, companies rely mainly on retained profits, which are often larger, taking companies as a whole, than their net investment. Other sources of company finance are borrowing in financial markets and the issue of company shares. As compared to many other countries, in Britain a relatively high proportion of external investment funds are raised by equity issue rather than by direct borrowing. Much public investment must be financed by the Treasury, except for relatively small amounts raised by public corporations on the financial markets. The 1979 Conservative Government announced its intention to seek private capital for some public investment projects, e.g. roadbuilding. The Government also maintained a new stress on helping small firms. This had been given particular impetus by the report of the Wilson Committee and by differentially favourable tax treatment in recent Budgets. The 1989 Enterprise Initiative continued this theme of assistance to small firms—by, for example, state-funded consultancy help. Some 10,400 consultancy projects were completed in 1993–94. Traditionally, investment measures are concerned with reducing the cost of capital. Many people believe that investment could be increased more effectively if more steps were taken to encourage a high and stable demand for output.

Labour Subsidies.

Initially Government subsidies were employed primarily as incentives for investment, particularly in a regional context. A 1972 Act, however, gave wide powers to the Government to offer financial assistance in almost any form to almost any enterprise, provided the assistance was "in the public interest". The Labour Government in 1974 greatly increased subsidisation, aimed chiefly at maintaining employment. These subsidies consisted chiefly of direct assistance to industries both within and outside the assisted areas and labour subsidies in the form of temporary employment and job creation schemes, aimed particularly at young people. Thus there was a new emphasis on subsidies which cheapened the cost of labour. Some of the schemes, like the Temporary Employment Subsidy, were pure subsidies in this sense. Others combined the subsidy element with measures to increase either the mobility or training of workers, the Youth Opportunities Programme for instance. The new Conservative Government cut back on such schemes soon after its election in 1979, but did continue an emphasis on training, particularly with the Youth Training Scheme (later, Youth Training), which was significantly extended in 1986.

Two other major subsidies were introduced. The Community Programme encouraged sponsoring agencies or individuals to set up projects of community value to utilise unemployed labour. The Government provided a cash grant for each person employed, and paid their wage which was supposed to be equivalent to the going rate for the job in the area. A second subsidy was the Enterprise Allowance Scheme, which provided a small weekly payment to help the unemployed set up their own business. Subsequently, this was effectively replaced by the Business Start-Up Scheme. Until 1985 the Government had a fourth scheme called the Young Workers' Scheme, which paid employers to take on youths for them to gain work experience.

In 1986 and 1987 the Government shifted to more overt job subsidies, including the Job Start Scheme whereby a worker taking a job paying less than a specified minimum was paid the balance by the State. Other schemes were however phased out, including the New Workers Scheme (designed to encourage the young to accept low-paid employment) and the Job Release Scheme (which subsidised early retirement). Job-Sharing schemes however remained in place for longer.

By 1989 all training schemes for unemployed adults had been amalgamated under an umbrella Employment Training Scheme (later, Employment Training) which offered full-time training with an employer for all those who had been unemployed for at least six months. Job Restart interviews were provided for the long term unemployed, whilst

help continued to be given via Employment Action.

Training.

An emphasis on training is now a major part of the Government's supply strategy for the labour market. There had long been criticism of the British training effort. It was said that the school system was ill attuned to the needs of industry, that not enough young people continued with education or full-time training after the minimum school-leaving age. The old apprenticeship system was justly accused of being too rigid and of forming skills often inappropriate to changing technology. Financing of industrial training was thought to be insufficient. There was inadequate provision for the retraining of adults—so necessary if sufficient occupational flexibility was to be assured in a changing world.

In some respects matters had been getting worse. The recession of the early 1980s, for example, decimated training recruitment. As a consequence of Government policy, most of the old Industrial Training Boards were disappearing, without adequate substitutes being found. Yet at the same time, official thinking on training became more sophisticated after the mid 1970s.

Although training was the focus of much attention, the main outcomes—Youth Training and Employment Training—were regarded by many as merely cosmetic devices to hide unemployment. The main criticisms of recent training programmes include lack of finance and a failure to address the key problem that arises under private sector provision of training, namely that unless an employer can guarantee that an employee stays in the firm for a considerable period of time, then the employer's return from the training investment is less than society's. The consequence is that if left to their own devices private employers will "underinvest". Rather than endorsing greater Government involvement to overcome this problem, a 1992 White Paper outlined arrangements whereby employers who lost workers whom they had trained might receive compensation either from the departing workers themselves or from their new employers. However, little came of this suggestion. Meanwhile there has been some progress in the area of youth training and vocational education. The school curriculum has been made more vocationally directed. The 1988 Education Act introduced a National Curriculum which, along with the switch from "O" Levels to GCSE, was intended to improve the vocational orientation of secondary education. More generally, the National Council for Vocational Qualifications is introducing a standard set of national qualifications to replace the myriad previously available. Some YT schemes were excellent whilst some industries were developing better alternatives to the old apprenticeship system.

The 1988 Employment Act.

The 1988 Employment Act incorporated all the employment training schemes for adults under the Employment Training Initiative. This was workplace-based and was supported by a significant number of large employers. The scheme was designed to provide job-specific training over twelve months. Despite support from many employers, the scheme was criticised widely in the Trade Union movement where it was regarded as another means of attracting cheap labour and artificially reducing the official unemployment register. More generally there was some doubt about the quality of training being offered by some of the firms participating in the scheme.

As well as introducing the Employment Training Scheme, the 1988 Employment Act also brought substantial changes in structure of responsibility for training. At the local level, training is overseen by a network of Training and Enterprise Councils (TECs). Each TEC is an independent company, with two-thirds of its board being comprised of local employers. The reason for majority representation for businesses in TECs was said by the Government to be that local industry had the best insight into local skills needs. One difficulty is that the government laid down fairly rigid rules about the seniority of the businessmen serving on TECs and this has caused recruitment difficulties in some areas. It is doubtful whether increased employer involvement in TECs will, in itself, make any difference to Britain's poor record in the area of skills training compared to other countries. A deficiency in education and training is now widely blamed for the UK's bad industrial record and for the emergence of skills shortages at relatively high levels of unemployment. Meanwhile tentative steps were taken to encourage individuals to take more responsibility for their own training decisions. Pilot schemes of Training Credits were introduced which were meant to give people the power to shop around for good training, whilst the 1991 Budget introduced tax relief for personal training expenditures. These credits were intended to provide access to a new Modern Apprenticeship scheme. Meanwhile in 1993 Employment Training and Employment Action were replaced by two new schemes—Training for Work and Jobplan Workshops. Much progress has been made. More people are undergoing training and achieving qualifications, but the general view is that the UK still lags behind. Much of the training that is taking place is at a relatively low level.

The Conservative Government had a set of official targets both for foundation and lifelong learning. At the same time increasing stress was placed on helping and encouraging firms to become Investors in People (IIP). This involves not only developing a proper training strategy but also integrating it into the company's planning and operating procedures. Those who achieve IIP status obtain a "kitemark" which is intended to signal quality to potential customers. Official schemes for adults are now directed largely at bringing the long term unemployed back into contact with the world of work. Emphasis on younger people continued via Youth Training and Modern Apprenticeships, with the stress moving towards training fewer people to a higher standard.

The new Labour Government put, if anything, even greater stress on education and training. The term 'the learning society' became the common currency of public discussion. Yet the substance of policy changed little. Youth training continued to be subsidised via Modern Apprenticeships and, at a lower level, via National Traineeships. Adult training was subsidised via Training for Adults, which had replaced Training for Work. Two new initiatives were announced—Individual Learning Accounts and the University of Industry. Both initiatives emphasised the role of individuals rather than of the employer, and to an extent placed government subsidy and decision taking into their hands. However, a more fundamental question remains unanswered. The thrust of policy continues to be to solve the UK's VET problems by increasing the *supply* of skills. But it may be that the problem is that employers do not demand skill. Many commentators believe that too many British producers are producing low specification goods (the basic version of a good) with low-skill production methods. In other words the country is getting the VET performance that its employers want. Only if substantial numbers of them change their product strategies will VET improve.

Monopoly and Competition.

A trend to increasing size and increasing capitalisation has been going on now for many decades, and in the process it has changed the face of British industry. In the early 19th century the typical firm was the owner-managed textile mill. Then in the 1860s and 1870s came the discovery of cheap methods of making steel, with the consequential immense growth in the engineering industries. Most of the chemical industry is still newer, and there are many entirely 20th century industries such as aircraft, electronics and bio-technology.

In the capital-intensive industries the big firm predominates. In some it has become almost a monopoly; in others the pattern is of a few firms, all large. In 1999 the top British companies included oil firms (British Petroleum and Shell), tobacco firms (British American Tobacco), pharmaceutical firms (Glaxo Wellcome and SmithKline Beecham), defence conglomerates such as British Aerospace.

The extent of *concentration* of British industry—according to measures such as the proportion of the output of an industry produced by the largest three firms—has increased since 1945. For example, in 1995 only 475 of over 130,000 businesses in manufacturing had more than 1,000 employees. Concentration increased particularly rapidly in the 1960s. There are two possible reasons for such an increase.

The first is the natural growth of already large firms; the second is because of merger activity. This latter factor has been the more important in Britain. Although evidence is scanty, there is some suggestion that for a while in the mid 1970s, concentration stopped increasing, and it may even have fallen a little. From the late 1980s there was a massive increase in merger activity.

Competition goes on, but it has changed its form. Competition used to be largely by price. Now it is also by advertising and by variations in the quality and other features of the product—detergents and motor cars being good examples. In many industries, groups of firms producing similar products entered into agreements which had the effect of restricting competition, for example through schemes for price-fixing. The effect was to increase the price to the consumer and to reduce the amount of output available. Some authorities have estimated that the total "welfare" loss because of this was relatively small, and have argued that our major concern should be over the dangers of large corporations having substantial political power because of their size, and over their using this power to force the Government into unwise decisions about, for example, subsidising inefficient management.

Domestic monopolies are also limited by foreign competition, and by the discipline of "potential cross entry"—that is, the possibility that a powerful firm may be attracted into a new sector by the sight of very high profits. The British industrial scene has nevertheless changed substantially, not only with the emergence of very large and powerful domestic firms, but also with the extensive presence of foreign-owned multinationals. Finally, however, it is worth remembering the words of the Nobel Prize winning economist, Sir John Hicks, that the greatest return to a monopolistic existence is a quiet life. In other words, firms will try not to make "too large" profits for fear of attracting new competition. An interesting question, however, is how far the stock market "disciplines" firms into maximising their profits. If they do not, the argument goes, dividends will be low, investors will sell their shares whose price will go down, thus rendering the firm liable to be taken over.

Regulation of Competition and Monopoly.

(i) Restrictive Practices Court.

The Restrictive Trade Practices Acts of 1956 and 1968 outlawed many of the main forms of restrictive agreements preventing competition. Collective price-fixing was declared to be illegal unless an industry could show that the practice brought substantial benefit to the public. Collective price-fixing was the system under which a central association for the industry laid down minimum prices at which members might sell. Usually such a system was backed by arrangements for collective boycotts, under which members of the association would refuse to sell goods to wholesalers or retailers who broke the rules. Collective boycotts were also found in industries without collective price-fixing, one common purpose being to make sure that retailers did not sell a manufacturer's products below his recommended price. This form of collective resale price maintenance was also outlawed by the Acts.

Under the Acts any restrictive agreements of several specified kinds had to be registered with the Registrar of Restrictive Practices. He then had to decide whether there was a *prima facie* case for the discontinuation of the agreement, and, if he thought there was, the case was referred to a Restrictive Practices Court, containing both judicial and lay members. For an agreement to be upheld, the agreeing parties had to prove to the Court that the agreement conferred some substantial benefit on the public which out-weighed any injury it did to the public. A 1976 Act extended this legislation to cover service agreements.

In 1989 the government announced its intention to amend the existing legislation on Restrictive Trade Practices. It was intended that this would prohibit agreements which have the effect of preventing, restricting or distorting competition unless exemptions were given on the grounds of offsetting economic benefits. Many professional groups have voluntarily relaxed restrictive practices—for example, accountants, solicitors, stockbrokers, dentists and doctors. There has also been some legislation covering, for instance, the provision of legal services.

(ii) Resale Prices Act.

The Act of 1956 permitted individual manufacturers to enforce *resale price maintenance* (r.p.m.) for their own products. Few suppliers would want the publicity of enforcing r.p.m. through the courts, but they could still put some commercial pressure on price-cutters, *e.g.*, by offering less favourable terms or by refusing them supplies. The Resale Prices Act of 1964 prohibited all methods of enforcing minimum resale prices. However, goods which had been registered in due time with the Registrar of Restrictive Practices or had been approved by the Restrictive Practices Court, were exempted, temporarily in the former case and permanently in the latter. For r.p.m. to be approved by the Court, it had to be shown that some ensuing benefit to customers (*e.g.*, of increased quality or more retail outlets) outweighed any detriment. With the exception of books and some pharmaceuticals, where r.p.m. is still not unlawful, r.p.m. has largely been replaced by "recommended" retail prices, which are in effect maximum prices. This practice has been investigated by the Monopolies Commission, which found that it was not always against the public interest.

(iii) The Monopolies Commission.

The Restrictive Practices Acts left untouched those industries in which one firm is dominant: these remained the responsibility of the Monopolies Commission. This is an independent administrative tribunal, established in 1948, with powers to investigate and decide whether a monopoly (defined in terms of market share) is contrary to the "public interest."

The Monopolies and Mergers Act of 1965 strengthened control over monopolies and mergers. With regard to monopolies, the Government wished to provide itself with legal powers of enforcement: previously monopolies had been expected to comply voluntarily with the findings of the Monopolies Commission. The Act also permitted the Government to refer a merger or a proposed merger to the Monopolies Commission in cases where the merger would lead to monopoly (defined as control of at least one third of the market) or would increase the power of an existing monopoly, or where the value of the assets taken over exceeded £5 million (now £70 million). The 1965 Act was repealed in 1973 and replaced by the Fair Trading Act. The rules governing referral to the Monopolies Commission were changed in this later Act. Since 1989, the decision to refer a merger to the Monopolies Commission, and the criteria by which the commission examines the public interest, have become less rigidly defined. Considerations of formal market share are probably less important than for example, the existence of barriers to entry. The Companies Act of 1989 also introduced a number of changes aimed at improving procedures for merger control: a voluntary procedure for pre-notification of proposed mergers which would allow rapid approval; provision for the companies involved to accept statutory undertakings which might obviate the need for a full investigation by the Commission; and the temporary prohibition on dealing in one another's shares in the case of a merger referred to the Commission. The Act also strengthened powers given to the Secretary of State for Industry under the 1980 Competition Act to refer questions concerning the efficiency, cost or monopoly position of public sector bodies to the Commission.

In interpreting the public interest, the Monopolies Commission has to weigh up the negative aspects (of large size, high prices, reduced product choice and restricted entry for new firms into the market) against the benefits of greater resources for product innovation and lower costs due to synergy. More recently, emphasis has been placed upon the importance of international competition and it is argued that British firms need to be large to compete effectively.

(iv) The Fair Trading Act.

The 1973 Fair Trading Act placed the previously dispersed responsibilities for overseeing competition policies in the hands of a civil servant—the Director General of Fair Trading. The Monopolies Acts of 1948 and 1965 were repealed and replaced by rather more comprehensive rules. Monopoly was now defined as control of one quarter of the market instead of one third. For the first time local monopolies were made subject to control. Also "complex monopolies" were made subject to investigation—that is situations where no one firm had 25 per cent of the market, but where several of them collaborated to restrict competition. The Director General of Fair Trading—as well as the Department of Trade and Industry—was enabled to refer monopoly situations to the Monopolies Commission; though it was still only the Department which could make references on mergers. Additionally the Director General took over the functions of the Registrar of Restrictive Practices and responsibility for general consumer protection, and set up a new body to assist in that aim—the Consumer Protection Advisory Committee.

In 1978 the Labour Government published a review of its general policy which recommended a more neutral policy towards mergers and that greater stress should be put on competition.

In 1980 the new Conservative Government introduced a Competition Act which strengthened the powers of the authorities to deal with practices which limited competition in both the public and private sectors. Procedures were also speeded up considerably. There was a new power to refer nationalised industries and other public bodies for investigation of their efficiency, costs, services to consumers, and possible abuse of monopoly position. Perhaps the most celebrated case of applying the authorities' new legislation involves the UK Stock Exchange. In return for a pledge from the Government not to prosecute, the Stock Exchange abolished the restrictive practices which governed entry into the stockbroking profession, and separate the broking from the market-making functions in the stock market—the so-called "Big Bang" in the City of London. Self-regulation for the City was enshrined in the Financial Services Act of 1986. Of increasing importance are EC provisions, Articles 85 and 86, which relate to anti-competitive practices which affect trade between member states.

(v) The Enterprise Initiative and Companies Act, 1989.

A 1988 Enterprise White Paper proposed changes to competition policy, some of which were enacted in the course of 1989. Thereafter the main reason for referring mergers was their likely effect on competition (*see* (iii) above). Though "public interest" referrals remain, the Government will intervene only rarely. Generally, it was claimed, the "market" would look after the public interest. When judging the impact of a merger on competition, due regard is given to foreign competition and also to potential entrants. The latter represents a particular fashion among modern industrial economists, who argue that many apparently monopolistic or oligopolistic industries may in fact be constrained to behave in a relatively competitive manner by the possibility that other firms might be attracted into their sector by high profits. Accordingly Monopolies Commission hearings are increasingly concerned with the existence or otherwise of "barriers to entry". Mergers policy is not, however, without its critics, many of whom believe that the criteria for referral are now too lax, particularly compared to general practice in Europe. In 1993 the Government announced that it intended to take tougher measures against anti-competitive practices. In 1992 the Cadbury Committee, on the management of companies, provided a code of best practice for company boards. The new Labour Government intends to introduce a Competition Bill which "will be based closely on EC competition rules".

(vi) Industrial Structure.

Mergers may lead to monopoly and to the abuse of monopoly power. But it would be wrong to presume that mergers are always bad: mergers—by facilitating research and other economies of large-scale production—may increase industrial efficiency. For this reason the *Industrial Reorganisation Corporation* (IRC) was set up in 1966 under Government auspices. Its functions were to promote industrial reorganisation in the interests of industrial efficiency, *e.g.*, by enabling industries to achieve economies of scale or by reorganising inefficiently managed firms. It assisted firms in agreed regroupings and could intervene to encourage a particular takeover which, in its estimation, was in the public interest. However its objective in making loans was to "prod" and not to "prop" inefficient firms. It supported mergers in electronics, trawling, nuclear power, mechanical engineering, and other industries. In 1970 the Conservative Government decided to wind up the IRC. However, some of the proposed functions of the National Enterprise Board, set up in 1975, were similar to those performed by the IRC (*see* **Part IV**). The 1979 Conservative Government initially streamlined the NEB, and subsequently amalgamated it with the National Research and Development Corporation to form the British Technology Group.

(vii) The Competition Bill.

New legislation is expected to come into effect in 2000. It is concerned with anti-competitive agreements and the abuse of dominant positions. The main enforcer will be the Director General of Fair Trading. The new law will be more closely aligned with EU legislation. A new Competition Commission will be established, and will replace the Monopolies and Mergers Commission. The regulation of mergers will be relatively unchanged.

Nationalised Industries.

After the extensive privatisation of industries and utilities undertaken during the last decade, the Nationalised Industries now account for less than 1 per cent of GDP. The Post Office, London Transport, British Nuclear Fuels and the Civil Aviation Authority are the most significant concerns which remain in public ownership.

Nationalisation was a central feature of the policies of the post-Second World War Labour Government. With the exception of steel—denationalised 1951–53 and re-nationalised in 1967—nationalisation was for a long time not extended into manufacturing industry. The post-1974 Labour Government nationalised the shipbuilding and aerospace industries, and established the British national Oil Corporation and the National Enterprise Board with wide powers to take holdings in private industry. Under the 1979 Conservative Government the post-war trend towards greater public ownership of industry was reversed (*see* **Part IV**).

A 1967 White Paper, amended in 1978, dictated that as well as achieving specified financial targets, nationalised industries should earn a target rate of return on their investments and price according to the marginal cost of a service.

With respect to pricing, it was government policy that subsidies could be made for some services which were justified on social grounds, *e.g.*, grants to British Rail to continue unremunerative rail services. The 1979 Conservative Government was much more vigorously reluctant to continue this approach. Cross-subsidisation of non-commercial services by commercial services within a nationalised industry is now actively discouraged.

The post-1979 Government challenged the whole concept of running publicly-owned industries even where a natural monopoly quite clearly exists. Industries remaining under state control have also been unable to raise sufficient outside investment capital because of the imposition of strict External Financing Limits. Public sector monopolies such as British Telecom and British Gas have been returned to the private sector and have remained largely monopolies. Prices are regulated to ensure that they reflect general inflation adjusted for changes in the industry's underlying cost structure. One difficulty is that prices may nevertheless be set too high because the regulator (for example, OFTEL for British Telecom) relies heavily on information which is provided by the monopolist. Restructuring of the industry may help overcome this difficulty, since this makes available several sources of information from the component firms and thus allows sensible comparisons to be made. This was one of the motives behind privatising electricity and water as area boards. The Government has also

sought to introduce competition in the provision of public services. For example, local authorities are now obliged to put services such as refuse collection out to public tender. Many traditional civil service functions have been put out to Agencies. Following the 1988 Education Act schools can effectively compete for pupils and as of April 1991 hospitals are essentially competing for patients referred through general practitioners. The new Labour Government has announced its intention to abolish many aspects of the NHS internal market, and to alter the administrative arrangements for schools.

3. INCOMES, WAGES, AND PRICES

Personal Income.

National income is a measure of the total income accruing to the residents in a country in return for services rendered (*see* **G13**). It therefore consists of the sum of wages, salaries, profits, and rents having allowed for depreciation. But not all this income accrues to persons, *e.g.*, companies do not distribute all their profits to shareholders and some nationalised industries earn profits. This is part of national income but not of *personal income*. On the other hand, some personal incomes are not payments for services rendered. Such incomes are called *transfer incomes* to emphasise that their payment does not add to the national income, but only transfers income from one agent to another. Included in this category are retirement pensions, child benefit and student grants.

Personal Disposable Income.

Not all personal income is available for spending. In 1997 the State took 12 per cent of household income in *income taxation*, and 16 per cent went as Social Security contributions, which being compulsory are in effect a form of tax, and in contributions to pension schemes, council tax and other deductions. The remaining 72 per cent of income—called *personal disposable income*—was available for spending. However, not all disposable income need be spent on consumer goods and services; income can instead be saved. There are many possible motives for saving, *e.g.*, to meet future contingencies, for a future purchase such as a house or car, for retirement, or for the income to be derived from saving. Saving as a fraction of personal disposable income fluctuated from 7 to 10 per cent between 1960 and 1971. By 1975 it had reached about 13 per cent. It remained high thereafter, and peaked at about 15 per cent in 1980. It then fell and was only 5·6 per cent in 1988 although it recovered rapidly to a level of 12·5 per cent in 1992. By the end of 1993 it was 11·8 per cent and fell to 9·5 per cent in 1994. It then recovered again to stand at 11·3 in 1996 and at 11·0 in 1997, only to fall slightly in 1998. Many explanations of this varying savings ratio have been advanced—historically it has often been higher, the higher the rate of inflation. In the mid-1980s the fall in savings was related to rapid growth in the value of personal sector wealth, particularly in housing. Finally it has often been related to the perceptions of economic security prevalent at any given time.

The recovery of the ratio in the early 1990s seems to be closely linked to the high level of uncertainty generated by the recession, and also with the fall in the real value of the personal sector's assets relative to its debt. This latter phenomenon is intimately linked to the decline in house prices.

Types of Personal Income.

The table (**G19**) shows the sources of household income. In 1997, the share of income from employment was 56 per cent. This rose considerably in the post-Second World War period. The share of salaries grew relative to that of wages, not because average salaries rose faster than average wages but because the number of salaried workers expanded rapidly. With the development of the Welfare State there was an increase in the percentage of incomes derived from public grants—pensions, social security payments, student grants, *etc*.

Over the post-war period as a whole, the share of self-employment income and incomes from property fell while that from wages and salaries and from social security benefits tended to rise. Over the

SOURCES OF HOUSEHOLD INCOME
1987 AND 1997

(As percentage of total)

	1987	1997
Wages and salaries . .	61	56
Operating income . .	11	11
Net property income .	8	10
Social benefits . .	19	21
Other transfers . .	1	1

past 15 years or so, however, income from self-employment has begun to increase a little, in line with a larger share of the self-employed in the labour force. The share of income from annuities and pensions is also tending to grow along with the expansion of privately-funded occupational pension schemes.

Inequality of Income.

In 1996–97 the top 20 per cent of income receivers (defined as households rather than individuals) received over twice as much original income as that received by the average household. Thus Britain is far from being an egalitarian society. For the first three decades after the Second World War, inequality diminished. But from the mid 1970s and through the 1980s, there was a very strong increase in inequality. The picture stabilised in the 1990s.

Taxes on income are of course progressive, rising as income increases. This progressivity was reduced through the 1980s as higher rates of income tax were lowered. By the beginning of 1992 there was a standard rate of 25 per cent and just one higher rate of 40 per cent. The Budget of that year introduced an additional lower band of 20 per cent. Subsequent Budgets lowered the standard rate to 24 and then 23 per cent. In 1999 the lower band of 20 per cent was abolished, and replaced by one of 10 per cent in the case of earned income. The 20 per cent rate remains for income from savings.

The table below shows the shares of disposable income. This is original income minus direct taxes and plus cash benefits. We can see that the effect is redistributive. In 1996–97 the top 20 per cent received slightly more than twice what the average household received. Allowing for the effects of indirect taxation and benefits in kind produces final income. As the table shows the net effects of these adjustments is for further redistribution to the less well-off households.

Thus the direct tax burden somewhat squeezes the distribution of incomes. But until the mid 1970s the narrowing dispersion of incomes before tax was of greater importance in making Britain rather more egalitarian than taxation policy. Between the mid-1970s and the early 1990s, however, inequality of pre-tax incomes increased, whilst the tax benefit system as a whole became less redistributive. As with original income this trend appears to have halted in the last few years.

Income and Spending Power.

In various ways figures for incomes alone under-estimate the degree of inequality in British society. First, incomes are defined as income for tax purposes. Any allowed expenses are excluded; and for the self-employed and the higher ranks of management the expense allowance now adds substan-

tially to spending power. Second, if one buys an asset which then rises in value one gains extra spending power. Such capital gains can be very important to the wealthy in periods of boom in ordinary share prices, land prices and house prices. Yet only in 1965 did capital gains become taxable and even then the rate of tax on capital gains was low in relation to the rate on additional income. From 1988, capital gains have been taxed at the individual's or corporation's higher rate of tax, although there is a larger tax-free allowance. The 1998 Budget introduced lower rates for long-term gains. In 1999 the rates were 20 per cent and 40 per cent, depending on the level of income and gains.

Inequality of Wealth.

Spending power depends not only on income and capital gains but also on the sheer amount of capital owned. Data on the ownership of capital in Britain have to be estimated indirectly from information arising in connection with the payment of death duties, supplemented by information from capital transfer tax (from 1986 inheritance tax) returns and therefore cannot always be relied upon. An alternative method is to estimate the stock of wealth by working back from information on investment income, but this approach is also prone to error. It appears from the table that the most wealthy 1 per cent of the population own 19 per cent of all wealth, whilst 51 per cent of all wealth is owned by the richest 10 per cent. Even more strikingly, the poorer half of the population own only 7 per cent of total wealth.

WEALTH OF INDIVIDUALS IN BRITAIN,
1995

Percentage of wealth owned by:	
Most wealthy 1 per cent of population	19
,, ,, 5 ,, ,, ,, ,,	38
,, ,, 10 ,, ,, ,, ,,	51
,, ,, 25 ,, ,, ,, ,,	73
,, ,, 50 ,, ,, ,, ,,	93

It should be emphasised, however, that the data refer to *individuals* rather than to *households*: this can give a misleading impression if, for example, the assets of married couples are generally registered in the name of one of the marriage partners rather than as jointly-owned assets. Nevertheless, it is fair to conclude from the data that the disparity of wealth is considerably greater than that of income. Moreover, there is a natural tendency for the inequality of wealth to grow because the higher income groups tend to save a higher proportion of their income and so to accumulate capital more readily. The Government by capital transfer tax tried but largely failed to neutralise this tendency.

Capital transfer tax (CTT) was introduced in 1974. Until then only transfers of wealth on death or shortly before death were taxable. The CTT had many loopholes, but did something to redistribute wealth. The 1986 Budget effectively abolished CTT for gifts *inter vivos*, the tax (renamed inheritance tax) applying on death or transfers made in the 7 years preceding death.

Wages and Salaries.

In 1997 56 per cent of personal income was paid in the form of wages and salaries.

DISTRIBUTION OF ORIGINAL, DISPOSABLE AND FINAL HOUSEHOLD INCOME, 1996–97
(As a percentage of the average income of all households)

	Quintile groups of households				
	Bottom Fifth	Next Fifth	Middle Fifth	Next Fifth	Top Fifth
Original Income	12	35	80	131	242
Disposable Income	37	56	86	119	202
Final Income	49	63	86	113	189

GROSS WEEKLY EARNINGS,
GREAT BRITAIN

(Average earnings, adults, April 1997)

	Manual	Non-Manual
Men . . .	£314·3	£483·5
Women . . .	£201·1	£317·0

AVERAGE GROSS WEEKLY EARNINGS
OF FULL-TIME ADULT MALE
EMPLOYEES, BY SELECTED
OCCUPATIONS, APRIL 1997

	£ per week
National government senior administrators . . .	1069·2
Treasurers and company financial managers	1029·4
Medical practitioner . . .	912·2
Legal professional . . .	774·5
University teacher . . .	614·4
Production manager . . .	572·1
Accountant . . .	565·3
Engineer, civil or structural .	541·0
Scientist	532·8
Policeman (sergeant and below) .	478·8
Primary teacher . . .	470·1
Telephone fitter . . .	413·1
Electrician . . .	391·0
Tool maker and fitter . .	388·6
Coach and vehicle body builder .	328·2
Postal worker and mail sorter .	312·1
Unskilled building worker . .	306·5
Heavy goods driver . .	294·9
Bricklayer . . .	294·0
Painter and decorator . .	287·4
Dustman . . .	273·5
General clerk . . .	270·3
General farm worker . .	249·1
Butcher . . .	240·9
Hospital porter . . .	225·3
Total workers . . .	408·7
of which: Manual . . .	314·3
Non-manual . .	483·5

Earnings by Occupation.

Different occupations command different pay, as the table shows. The figures are of average earnings. The structure of pay reflects in part the amount of responsibility which the different jobs entail. The differentials reflect also the ease of entry into various occupations. This in turn depends on the degree of specialised knowledge, skill or talent required, and in a few cases it depends on the extent to which artificial barriers to entry have created scarcity. The structure of pay is also influenced, of course, by the degree of organisation and bargaining strength of workers in different occupations. Finally, the relative strengths of demand for different types of worker is important, as is the force of custom.

Within the manual occupations the difference between skilled, semi-skilled and unskilled pay narrowed over the post-war years. This was most marked during the war, in the years immediately after the war and between 1970 and 1976 when skilled workers were often granted the same flat rate advances as unskilled. The last few years have seen a reversal of such narrowing and indeed further widening. Recent years have also seen a widening of the gap between manual and non-manual pay.

Earnings by Industry.

Even within the manual occupations there are significant differences in earnings among industries. These are associated with the bargaining strength of different groups of workers, with the prosperity of the industry, and with the average skill levels required in production. Manufacturing industries as a whole pay relatively well. Public administration (including local government) is a low-wage sector.

Earnings by Sex.

There are very significant earnings differences within each industry between men and women. There are two possible reasons why women are paid less than men. One is that they are crowded into lower-paying occupations. The second is that they may have lower pay than men within the same occupation. Either form of disadvantage could be the result of discrimination or of women possessing inferior productive characteristics. In practice it is a very difficult distinction to make. Equal opportunities and equal pay legislation attempts to reduce discrimination. The Equal Pay Act (1970) obliged a firm to pay men and women, who are doing the same job, the same wage by the end of 1975. In 1972 women in manual occupations had median earnings which were about half those of men. By 1978 this figure had risen to over 60 per cent, though by the early 1980s this improvement had slowed down, and by 1997 was 71 per cent. Women in non-manual occupations had median earnings which were 70·6 per cent of their male counterparts. These changes are explained by the impact of the Act, by flat rate general increases agreed under incomes policies, and by trade union bargaining policy under inflation. There have been renewed initiatives against sexual discrimination. In particular, in 1984 an amendment to the Equal Pay Act insisted that as well as paying men and women doing the same job the same rate of pay, parity of pay should also apply to jobs of equal value. The Equal Opportunities Commission has issued a Code of Practice which suggests positive actions which employers might take to improve the lot of women in employment. Recently this has contributed to a catch-up for women in areas of the retail trade. A number of "equal pay for work of equal value" claims have been made under the 1984 Act and taken to the European Court of Human Rights. Recent examples of such claims include those filed by women upholsterers in the car industry and by clerks in the banking industry. As yet, such claims have been quite rare and have had at most a marginal impact on pay differentials.

Overtime and short-time.

The earnings of any individual worker depend on many factors, and are usually well above the basic wage rate payable for a *standard working week*. They include overtime earnings; and overtime working is common for men. In most weeks in the 1970s 1–2 million operatives in manufacturing—about a third of the total—worked overtime to the extent of 8 to 9 hours. In 1996 930,000 operatives worked an average of 9·7 hours of overtime each. Nor is overtime confined to male manual employment; it is found, for example, in office work and even in some of the professions like medicine and accountancy. The working week is composed of standard hours and overtime hours. Its length has diminished since before the war, although the standard week has been more significantly reduced.

In most industries, for manual workers it was cut from 48 to 44 hours soon after the war. A 42-hour week was introduced between 1960 and 1962, and there was a movement towards a 40-hour standard working-week in the late 1960s. Subsequently there were pressures from unions, notably in engineering industries, to reduce the standard week below 40 hours, and indeed this has happened in many sectors. In much of the chemical industry, for example, it is often as low as 35 hours. The standard working week tends to be slightly less for white collar workers than for manual workers. Notwithstanding these developments total hours worked have increased for many people since the early 1980s. The consequence is that working hours are now longer in the UK than in continental Europe.

Short-time, the working of less than the standard week, has not been common since the war. It has been important in particular industries at particular times: during 1994 it was far smaller than overtime. In September 1996 12,000 operatives in manufacturing were on an average short-time of 11·2 hours a week—a total 134,000 hours lost as against the substantially greater amount of overtime in the same month. When the economy was growing very rapidly in the period 1986–88 it was disappointing that higher output was in many instances met through increased overtime rather than higher employment. This may have reflected natural caution on the part of employers about the durability of Britain's economic recovery at that time—a caution which appears justified in the light of the subsequent recession.

Earnings and Rates.

Overtime is not, however, the main reason why earnings exceed basic wage-rates; for most workers earn more than the minimum in the standard working-week. One reason is payment by results, the system of payment under which the worker's wage depends partly on output or performance. A common form is still the piecework system, under which pieceworkers are paid a fixed low rate per hour for each hour worked plus a fixed piecework price for each operation performed; but some employers tend to prefer schemes under which the bonus payment is related to the output or some other measure of the performance of a larger group or to that of a whole factory. Individual merit-related pay is becoming increasingly fashionable, particularly in white-collar work. An example of such a scheme would be that each employee is given a cost of living increase each year plus an additional amount based on merit, as judged by an annual assessment. This principle has been extended further in some large firms, where employees receive performance-related bonuses according to whether or not they have met pre-determined objectives or targets. Some trade unionists regard this as a potentially severe threat to collective negotiations about pay.

Wage Determination.

In Britain there were 7·1 million trade union members in 245 unions in 1997. Most of these unions are very small, 143 of them having less than 2,500 members. But 17 have memberships over 100,000. Union membership has fallen from its peak of 13·3 million in 1979, and today is at its lowest level since the war. The proportion of employees who are union members is nowadays only about 30 per cent. The main job of unions is collective bargaining with employers. The structure and scope of collective bargaining changed significantly in the 1980s. Until the beginning of that decade in most industries most employers belonged to associations which bargained collectively on their behalf. Some big firms, however, preferred to remain outside the associations, and strike their own bargain with the unions. Before the war many firms tried to encourage the formation of Company Unions, i.e., of unions confined to employees of a single firm; but this became very uncommon. In some lowly paid trades minimum wages were fixed by Wages Councils set up by the Department of Employment: and representatives of the workers and employers, and independent members, met together to reach agreement on the settlement to be recommended to the Minister. But over most of industry the aim of collective bargaining was to reach voluntary agreement, and the Department of Employment intervened only when no agreement is reached. In 1974 the Labour Government set up the *Advisory Conciliation and Arbitration Service* (ACAS) to provide independent mediation and arbitration services.

Development of Plant Bargaining.

After the Second World War plant bargaining developed as an increasingly important supplement to industry-wide bargaining in many sectors of the economy. Initially this was largely informal bargaining, with shop-stewards (unpaid lay trade union officials at the plant level) negotiating with management about, for example, special rates for working new machines. It is this which to a large degree was responsible for the growing gap between wage rates and earnings. The Donovan Commission, which was set up to inquire into the state of industrial relations and which reported in 1968, also saw it as a major cause of many of Britain's industrial relations problems, such as a high level of strike activity. Realising that it was impossible to put the clock back, the Commission recommended that plant bargaining procedures should be formalised, giving, for instance, proper channels for the resolution of wage disputes. In the 1970s there was indeed an increase in *formal* plant negotiations, with many plants setting their own wage rates and

using national agreements purely as a minimum benchmark. This development probably improved the climate of industrial relations. In the mid 1970s some companies, especially in manufacturing, which had been concerned about the administrative cost as well as about the leapfrogging effects of plant agreements, had moved to single company bargains.

Thus in the years up to the 1980s there had been increasing decentralisation of bargaining. This continued apace during the 1980s with active Government encouragement. The national multi-employer bargain declined considerably in significance and in many cases disappeared altogether. Thus the proportion of the workforce covered by such agreements fell from 60 per cent in 1978 to 35 per cent in 1989. At the same time pay setting in many companies was becoming more decentralised to profit and cost centres. Simultaneously the range of issues over which bargaining took place diminished, whilst even pay setting became more individualised.

It has always been the case, and still is, that more people are covered by collective bargaining than are union members. Nevertheless such has been the decline of unionism that increasingly large numbers of workers find that a collective bargain has little, if any, role to play in the determination of their pay. This is particularly true in the growing service sector and in small firms. The traditional heartlands of union influence are the public sector and the declining manufacturing industries. Although instances of formal de-recognition have been relatively few, even in these areas the influence of collective bargaining has waned. There has been a deliberate move to "individualise" the determining of pay; and here new fashions in payments systems, like merit pay, have played a large role.

Strikes.

The strike has alwasy been the unions' weapon of last resort. Most unions maintain strike funds in order to support their members when they call them out on strike; but these funds are small, and strike pay is usually very much below normal wages. So unions cannot afford to call strikes irresponsibly, and major official strikes are relatively uncommon. Nevertheless, the big strikes are important; for the success or failure of one big strike can affect the results of all the other collective bargaining under way at the time.

Before the 1980s most strikes were neither large nor official. An official strike is one called by a union, usually by decision of the national executive, and is typically the result of collective bargaining about wages. But unofficial strikes called by local leaders were often about other matters. Few of the big unofficial strikes which plagued the docks were about wages; rather they reflected job insecurity and the poor state of labour relations in that industry. Much the same may be said about the continual strikes in shipbuilding, many of them caused by demarcation disputes concerning which jobs should be done by which type of skilled worker. Other strike-prone industries were mining and vehicles. In most industries there have always been very few strikes, and they have tended to be concentrated in the larger plants.

From the mid-1950s the number of strikes in Britain increased, except in coal mining. In 1969 and 1970 there was a huge jump in both the number of stoppages and working days lost. After that industrial disputes fell to a more normal level, and indeed by the early 1980s were at an historically very low intensity. Partly this reflected the impact of high unemployment, but may also have represented a more permanent improvement in Britain's strike record. When unemployment fell sharply in 1988 and 1989, the number of strikes did not increase disturbingly. In spite of a succession of transport strikes in the summer of 1989, and an ambulance dispute later in the year, working days lost in 1989 numbered just over 4 million, only a little above the average of the previous four years. Thereafter there was a further reduction in strike activity, only for 1996 to show a slight resurgence. In that year there were 223 stoppages and 1,299,000 working days lost. By 1998 activity had fallen back to 155 stoppages involving 90,000 workers.

WAGES AND PRICES, 1960–98
(1955 = 100)

	Weekly earnings	Index of retail prices	Real earnings
1960	130	114	114
1965	175	136	129
1970	250	169	148
1975	540	313	173
1980	997	611	163
1985	1,537	865	178
1990	2,321	1,154	201
1995	2,957	1,364	217
1996	3,057	1,397	219
1997	3,201	1,440	222
1998	3,358	1,490	225

In its Industrial Relations Act of 1971 the Conservative Government laid down new laws for the regulation of industrial relations and for the curbing of strikes. However, the Act was repealed by the incoming Labour Government in 1974, which itself brought in several new pieces of legislation, including the Trade Unions and Labour Relations Act, the Employment Protection Act, and the Trade Unions and Labour Relations (Amendment) Act. As well as increasing legal protection for the individual employee and extending trade union immunities and rights, this legislation was concerned to improve industrial relations practice. The belief behind the legislation was that this could be done by machinery which ensured, for example, that employers formally recognised unions for collective bargaining purposes and that unions had greater access to information to enable them to negotiate about issues (such as a firm's investment plans) which previously ignorance had precluded them from doing.

With the election of a Conservative Government in 1979, the direction of legislation altered again. The 1980 Employment Act introduced measures to moderate the closed shop, provide funds for secret union ballots about important issues such as industrial action, and to limit picketing to only the establishments at which strikes were taking place. A further Act in 1982 intensified pressure on the unions. In particular it introduced further measures against existing closed shops and increased the liability of unions for the actions of their members. In 1984 came the Trade Union Act concerned with union democracy. In this context unions were denied immunity if strikes took place without ballots, voting members of union executives had to be elected, and periodic ballots on the political use of union funds were required. In 1988 a further piece of legislation was passed by Parliament, which, inter alia, made it illegal for unions to discipline members who refused to obey a strike call, even a legal one. Such legislative developments were likely to reduce unions' ability to call and prosecute strikes, and possibly also will diminish the scope for local union leaders to have a decisive impact on strike decisions. The legislative process continues. A new Employment Act, passed in the final months of 1990, made further reforms to the closed shop and to the rules governing both secondary and unofficial industrial action. It removed Trade Union immunity for acts in contemplation or furtherance of trade disputes when there had been secondary action (redefined to include those working or performing services under contract) other than in the course of peaceful picketing. The Act also amended the Employment Act of 1980, making unions liable for the actions of all their officials, including their workplace representatives, during an industrial dispute. The 1990 Act also effectively outlawed the pre-entry closed shop by making it unlawful to refuse to employ someone on the grounds of union membership or lack of it. Much of the Conservative legislation was consolidated in the Trade Union and Labour Relations (Consolidation) Act of 1992.

The 1993 Act.

In 1993 the Trade Union Reform and Employment Rights Act was enacted. It finally abolished Wages Councils, whose scope had been much reduced by legislation in 1986. Strike ballots had to be postal, and industrial action was only legal after a period of notice had been given. Two other provisions were of greater significance. First, henceforth workers would be able to decide for themselves which union to join. This provision could massively diminish the ability of the TUC to regulate competition amongst its member unions, and weaken its power still further. Second, workers would have to periodically re-affirm their willingness to have their subscriptions automatically deducted from their pay. This would eliminate any tendency for people to remain members of a union through inertia. The new Labour Government intends to make some changes to the legislative framework, the main one of which is likely to involve provisions for enforcing the recognition of unions.

Fairness at Work.

In a 1998 White Paper, *Fairness at Work*, the Labour Government proposed to 'soften' various aspects of the Conservative legislation. Amongst its proposals on individual rights was one to reduce the qualifying period for protection against unfair dismissal. Amongst its proposals on collective rights was one to introduce procedures whereby unions would be able to compel employers to recognise them for bargaining purposes.

Prices and Real Incomes.

Prices rose very rapidly (by over 30 per cent) between 1949 and 1953, and earnings only just kept ahead in this period. But after that *real earnings* (*i.e.*, the command which money earnings have over goods and services) rose quite steadily until the early 1970s. Since then real earnings have increased more spasmodically (*see* Part IV).

Price Changes.

In the calculation of real wages it is usual to make use of the *index of retail prices*, commonly called the cost-of-living index. The index is calculated monthly by the Department of Employment, and it naturally has an influence on the course of wage negotiations.

Over the last forty years or so the allocation of consumers' expenditure amongst different items has altered substantially. Of growing importance in household budgets were housing and transport and vehicles, whilst of diminishing importance was food. As people grow richer they spend a smaller proportion of their income on food. Nor have price changes been the same for all types of goods and services. For example, during the same long period, prices of fuel and light went up by more than the average whilst those for clothing, drink and durable household goods rose by less.

The general retail price index is calculated by weighting each of the commodity price indexes by the proportionate importance of that commodity in total expenditure in a particular year, and then summing all the indexes, *i.e.*, the general index is a *weighted average* of its constituent indexes. A different pattern of expenditure would mean a different set of weights, and hence a different cost-of-living index. For instance, the poor—and particularly pensioners—spend a higher proportion on the basic necessities; food, fuel and light, and housing. It is possible that the cost-of-living rose more for the poor than for t he rich over these years.

The cost-of-living index has not risen evenly in Britain. There were spurts of rapid inflation in the periods 1950-52 and 1954-56, followed by a decade of relatively little inflation (averaging under 3 per cent per annum). After 1967, however, the rate of inflation accelerated, rising progressively from 2·5 per cent per annum between 1966 and 1967 to 7·0 per cent between 1971 and 1972. For more recent developments *see* **Part IV**.

The Causes of Inflation.

(i) Import Prices.

Prices charged in the shops are determined by a great many factors, over many of which the Government has little or no control. First among these is the price of imports. Prices of imported food and raw materials are determined in the world markets, in which Britain is only one of many purchasers. Prices in raw material and food markets can fluctuate wildly. Big increases in commodity prices occurred during the Korean war, in the early 1970s and in 1979 (*see* **Part IV**). The sharp increases in the prices of primary commodities contributed to British inflation at these and other times, but for most of the post-war period the rise in import prices has been less rapid than domestic inflation even allowing for unfavourable exchange rate movements which push up the price of imports in sterling terms.

The source of domestic inflation has to be looked for in the tendency for the incomes of factors of production (wages, profits and other incomes) to rise faster than real output; and this has happened in almost every year since the war.

(ii) The Influence of Demand.

An explanation of domestically generated inflation is that it arises not so much from increased costs as from demand pressures increasing prices and profits. If there is an increase in aggregate demand for goods and services in the economy, how does the economy respond? If it is operating at less than full employment, producers are able to expand their production to meet the additional demand. But if full employment has already been achieved, it is the price level and not production which rises. Given an excess demand for goods and services, there is competitive bidding for the limited supplies and producers are able to sell at higher prices. A more sophisticated version of this argument recognises that full employment cannot be precisely defined: rather, there are degrees of less or more unemployment. Bottlenecks appear in different firms and industries at different stages; so that any increase in demand is met by an increase in both prices and production. But the lower the rate of unemployment, the more the responses take the form of price increases.

A variant of this approach is the so-called *quantity theory of money*, in which inflation is seen as a response to an increase in the supply of money; there is too much money chasing too few goods. The theory dates back at least to David Hume, but it was generally discredited as a result of the writings of Maynard Keynes in the 1930s. However, it was revived by Milton Friedman and has received some measure of acceptance among economists, especially in the United States.

The great shortages during and immediately after the war would no doubt have generated rapid demand inflation had it not been for rationing and price controls; and the spurt of inflation between 1954 and 1956 was associated with a very high pressure of demand. On the other hand, inflation has occurred even in periods of relatively high unemployment. Moreover, the method by which most firms price their products is on the basis of their costs; so that most prices are not directly sensitive to the pressure of demand. A more plausible mechanism by which demand might influence prices indirectly is through its effect on wages. In fact, there has been a lively debate as to

the extent to which wages are influenced by the pressure of demand as opposed to being relatively independent of it. There is, however, general agreement that wages are the main driving force behind prices.

(iii) Wages and Inflation.

When employers grant a wage increase, they will immediately consider whether they should increase their prices to cover their increased wage-costs. As it is common practice for firms to fix the selling prices of their products by first calculating the direct cost of labour and of materials, and then adding on a percentage to cover overhead costs and profits, they will tend to want to raise their prices not only to cover the cost of the wage advance, but also to cover their percentage addition. Moreover, in deciding whether or not their customers will stand for such increases, firms will be influenced by the knowledge that their competitors have to pay the increased wages too, and will probably therefore be raising their prices. So industry-wide wage advances—and changes in costs of materials—are particularly likely to be passed on to the consumer; and, as wage-earners are also consumers, to generate further demands for wage advances to cover the increased prices.

Once this spiral gets going, it is very hard to stop it. In general, the requirement is that wage earnings should not rise faster than productivity (output per man). But as in some industries productivity is very slow to rise, and as it would often be unfair and impracticable to exclude their workers from participating in any general rise in the standard of living, this requirement means that in industries with a rapid growth of productivity wage advances should be kept well below the rate of rise of productivity. For two reasons this is rather difficult. First, rising productivity often raises the wages of some workers in these industries automatically, because they are paid by results or through some incentive scheme. The rise of wages from this source takes the form of a tendency on the part of earnings in these industries to rise faster than basic wages. Second, employers in the rapidly-growing industries have far less reason to resist demands for wage increases than those in slowly-growing industries. Indeed, they are quite likely to bid up wages in order to obtain and motivate labour rather than to try to hold down wages.

There are therefore major problems in preventing a faster rise in wages than in productivity, with its consequence of rising prices. And once a wage-price spiral has started, the problems become more acute because workers and employers become accustomed to substantial annual advances in money wages. A main source of continuing price inflation has been the tendency of money wages to continue to advance at a rate that was appropriate when the cost-of-living was going up sharply, but ceased to be appropriate in later years.

(iv) The Phillips Curve.

Even if wage behaviour is primarily responsible for inflation, the pressure of demand may still be important. If unemployment is low or falling rapidly, and unfilled vacancies high, there is competitive bidding among employers to obtain or retain their workers. Moreover, with the economy booming the bargaining strength of trade unions increases: employers are more willing to concede wage demands. These possibilities have led economists to postulate—and indeed to measure—the so-called *Phillips Curve* relationship: the lower the level of unemployment, the faster the rate of increase in money wages. Such a relationship has been found to exist in the British economy over some periods. But it is dangerous to postulate "general laws" in economics: in the 1970s inflation increased despite high and growing unemployment and governments in most Western countries were confronted with a phenomenon known as stagflation. Clearly, changes in the cost-of-living, expectations for the future, Government policies and the degree of militancy of trade unionists can all have a significant influence on wage behaviour; and the level of demand may at times be relatively unimportant.

There are many schools of thought attempting to explain developments from the late 1960s, but it is possible to discern two general approaches. The first is that trade unions behaved reactively. In other words, they responded in their wage demands to their expectations about prices and Government policies. A restrictive monetary policy might help moderate inflation, in that it might directly reduce prices and it might affect expectations. The second school of thought was that unions, as well as responding to their perception of the events they faced, acted in a more initiatory way—to fulfil, for example, aspirations (developed perhaps over a long period of time) about what their real earnings, and therefore their share of the national cake, should be. In striving to realise these aspirations, they might be relatively unaffected by concern over rising unemployment. A likely explanation was that unions felt unconcerned about relatively minor variations in the unemployment rate, safe in the knowledge that Government was committed to the maintenance of full employment. In the mid-1970s such a commitment was quite explicitly abandoned. That, together with the experience of very high unemployment in the 1980s might, it was argued, tighten the demand constraint in more prosperous future times. No longer, it was argued, would unions or workers be able to count on being "protected from the consequences of their own actions". Many economists, therefore, were surprised at the persistence of quite high wage inflation during the very high unemployment of the mid-1980s. Their attempts to explain this are described in **Part IV**.

Modern Approaches to Inflation.

Modern approaches to inflation suggest that workers (or unions) have a "target" real wage and at the same time there is a "feasible" real wage which the economy can afford. Only when the two are equal will inflation be stable. At any given time there is a unique level of unemployment (or economic activity) at which the two will be consistent. If the Government attempts to run the economy at lower levels of unemployment, there will be a wage-price spiral of the sort already described, and as a consequence increasing inflation. Both the target wage and the feasible wage are determined by the underlying structures of the labour and product markets (e.g. the power of the unions, or the effectiveness of training, or basic productivity performance) as well as by the attitudes of workers and employers. Thus it is the supply-side which determines the level of unemployment at which it is safe to run the economy. The more unhealthy the supply-side, the higher this level of unemployment will be. Hence the modern stress on supply-side reform.

The Effects of Inflation.

British Governments have been concerned about inflation mainly because of its effects on British competitiveness, and hence on the balance of payments. If our costs rise relative to competitors' costs, British exporters find it more difficult to compete in foreign markets if they raise their prices; and if they keep prices down in order to compete, this implies their having to accept lower profit margins on exports than on sales in the home market, and so discourages exporting. Alternatively, this lack of competitiveness might be reflected in falling exchange rates, although membership of the ERM from the autumn of 1990 until the autumn of 1992 limited the scope for currency changes. Depreciation by itself is not necessarily a bad thing, but the danger is that it can start a spiral. An initial depreciation causes price inflation to increase at home, which causes further wage increases, which leads to further depreciation, and so on. The result could be hyper-inflation. This clearly has a major efficiency cost, since it will cause people to economise on the use of money in conducting their transactions.

Inflation can have other harmful consequences. It often produces a redistribution of income, with the strong gaining at the expense of the weak, i.e., the poorly organised workers and the pensioners. In inflationary conditions income gains can appear to result not so much from work or sacrifice as from ingenuity and speculation and the exercise of economic and political power. Inflation can breed insecurity and industrial unrest. Among businessmen it increases uncertainty, reduces investment and hence growth. Finally, it causes a redistribution of income away from lenders to borrowers unless interest rates remain positive in real terms, as they are at present. What is clear is that the costs of inflation are significantly greater the more unanticipated it is. It is also clear that its interaction with the tax system can have real consequences—particularly for the corporate sector.

Government Policy against Inflation.

There are several possible methods of attack on the inflationary spiral of wages and prices. Their usefulness will depend on the causes of the inflation.

One policy appropriate to most inflations, and also helpful to other objectives of economic policy, is to achieve a faster rate of productivity growth. The faster the growth of average productivity the faster can average incomes rise without an increase in average prices. Comprehensive and detailed government control of wages, except as an emergency policy, was thought for a long time to be impractical for political and institutional reasons, as was comprehensive and detailed control of prices. Experience suggested that such detailed policy, except as a temporary general "freeze", would be very difficult to operate and, if successful, would involve a major loss of flexibility in the economy. At the other extreme, general exhortations to unions to exercise restraint on wages, and to manufacturers to exercise restraint on prices, were thought to have little effect. After 1974 more people began to think that a semi-permanent incomes policy might in fact be a viable policy tool. This is discussed in **Part IV**.

The Government can attempt to regulate inflation by controlling purchasing power through its monetary and fiscal policies, the nature of which will be examined below. There is a danger that curbing demand also curbs the growth of output and productivity in the economy; so conflicting with other objectives of economic policy. Moreover, there is no certainty that inflation is sensitive to the rate of unemployment over the politically acceptable range of unemployment.

A final option is to try to impose an external inflationary discipline by linking the exchange rate to that of a low-inflation currency, removing the option of devaluation and thereby imposing a constraint upon employers' ability to pass on cost increases without loss of external competitiveness. By entering the ERM in October 1990 the Government effectively chose this option. Since leaving the ERM in the autumn of 1992, the Government has had to search for an alternative strategy. The policy which has emerged is based on the belief that inflation is influenced by monetary policy. However this influence takes time. Therefore a 12 or 24 month view of underlying inflation is taken and interest rates are set accordingly. Interest rates control the demand for and therefore the supply of money—on the assumption that the financial system produces more or less the quantity of money demanded. This interest rate policy is made an open one through the mechanism of reported monthly meetings between the Bank of England and the Treasury. It is believed that this openness is an important indicator to the general public of the government's determination to maintain inflation at very low levels. The Government's target is 2·5 per cent per annum.

4. MONEY, BANKING AND FINANCE

Economic Objectives and Demand Management.

The various economic objectives—full employment, balance of payments equilibrium, the control of inflation, etc.—which, as mentioned in **Part I**, have been shared by all post-war British Governments, are all to a greater or a lesser extent dependent for their attainment upon the type of *demand management* policy pursued by the government. By this is meant the policy, or set of policies, with which the government seeks to regulate the total level of expenditure on goods and services. The latter is the sum of consumption and investment expenditure by both the private sector (firms and consumers) and the public sector (the government and the nationalised industries). If the resulting level of aggregate demand for output is greater than the amount which can be produced with the economy's resources the result will be shortages leading to inflation and/or an increased demand for imports. If the level of demand is not high enough, on the other hand, the result will be a waste of resources, *i.e.*, workers will be unemployed and capital equipment will be underutilised. Hence it is crucial for the government to keep the pressure of demand at an appropriate level by regulating the various types of expenditure making up the total.

Fiscal and Monetary Policy.

One way in which the government can attempt to regulate demand is by fiscal policy, *i.e.*, the regulation of taxes and public expenditure (*see* **Part IV**). If the government believes, for example, that the level of demand is too high, it may seek to reduce it by raising taxes whilst leaving public expenditure unchanged, thereby reducing its *budget deficit* (*i.e.*, the excess of public spending over tax revenue). Since the private sector's expenditure plans are financed partly out of its after-tax income and partly out of borrowing, an increase in taxes will generally reduce private sector expenditure, so that total expenditure then falls if public expenditure is held constant. Conversely, the government can cut taxes or increase public spending if it wants to expand the economy by increasing total expenditure.

However, fiscal policy of this type is not independent of *monetary policy*, *i.e.*, the regulation of interest rates or the stock of money in the economy. For example, if the government increases public spending it has to pay for the various resources which this involves. The finance may come from additional taxes, but if the government does not raise taxes the extra expenditure then has to be paid for in one of two ways: either the government increases its borrowing from the private sector by issuing government stock in return for money to pay for public expenditure; or the government prints new money for this purpose. In the latter case the supply of money is increased; in the former case interest rates will generally be increased, since the private sector will probably require higher interest rates if it is to be induced to lend extra funds to the government.

Economic Controversies.

The operation of monetary and fiscal policies has been a long-standing area of controversy among economists, although the nature of the disagreements has tended to alter somewhat over time. One traditional controversy has been between "Keynesian" and "monetarist" economists. The former take their lead from the English economist J. M. Keynes, whose most well-known work was published in the 1930s, whilst the pioneer of monetarism, in a series of books and articles in the 1950s and 1960s, was Milton Friedman of Chicago University. Keynesian ideas dominated economic policy making in Britain and elsewhere from the end of the second world war up to the late 1960s. Since the mid-1970s policy making has been predominantly monetarist, though by the mid-1980s some Keynesian elements appeared to be re-surfacing. These various phases of policy making are described in more detail later, after the main principles of monetary and fiscal policies, and the sources of economic controversy, have been considered.

The Keynesian approach had a clear view about both the aims and the methods of macroeconomic policy making. The main aim was to achieve and maintain high levels of output and employment—Keynes's ideas were developed primarily in reaction to the mass unemployment of the inter-war period—and the main policy instrument for this purpose was fiscal policy. Keynesians argued that suitable choices of tax rates and of levels of public spending could maintain demand at a level high enough to secure continuous full employment. They also advocated that fiscal policy should be *fine tuned*, *i.e.* that tax and spending decisions should be frequently reviewed and amended in the light of short term changes in economic conditions.

From the mid-1950s onwards, Milton Friedman and others began to dispute both the aims and the methods of Keynesian policy makers. They had several important criticisms. First, they argued that

on the basis of evidence from America, Britain, and elsewhere, the money supply was the main determinant of the level of economic activity, contrary to Keynesian ideas. Secondly, they were suspicious of fine tuning, arguing that frequent policy changes could destabilise rather than stabilise the economy. Thirdly, they questioned the policy aim of giving over-riding priority to the level of employment, arguing that this potentially conflicted with other aims such as the balance of payments and the control of inflation. Monetarists therefore urged governments to pay much more attention to controlling the money supply, and to a wider range of policy objectives.

From the mid-1970s to the mid-1980s monetarist prescriptions were broadly followed. The experience led to modifications in the traditional attitudes of both groups of economists.

Not many economists would now advocate an unqualified return to the sort of Keynesian policy-making practised in the 1950s and 1960s, and to this extent "Keynesianism" could be said to be discredited. However, experience of monetarism has suggested that some of its ideas are misleading or over-simplified as guides to policy-making, and some of its early advocates have modified or extended their policy prescriptions as a result. Equally, however, some of its ideas have won a measure of acceptance from former sceptics. In addition, new economic issues emerged in the 1980s, whose policy implications defy straightforward classification in either "Keynesian" or "monetarist" terms. As a result, many professional economists would now find it difficult to classify themselves as either "Keynesian" or "monetarist", even though these labels continue to be widely used in popular discussions of policy-making.

The Ricardian Approach.

Both monetarists and Keynesians agree that changes in the size of the government's budget deficit have significant effects on the economy—their disagreements concern the nature of the effects. A third school of thought, often called "Ricardian", argues in contrast that budget deficit changes may have little impact—in some circumstances no impact at all—upon economic activity. This approach gained many adherents in the 1970s and 1980s. It concentrates on the future effects, as well as the immediate impact, of a change in the budget deficit. If the government reduces taxes while holding its spending level constant, and increases its borrowing in order to replace the lost tax revenue, this new borrowing will have to be repaid, with interest, some time in the future. For example, new borrowing in 1999 using government bonds with a 5-year redemption period will have to be repaid in 2004. The Ricardian approach argues that when the repayment falls due this will require taxes to be raised. The Ricardian approach goes on to argue that the prospect of future tax increases is foreseen by consumers at the time when the cut in taxes takes effect, and that consumers save the resulting increase in their current disposable incomes in order to be able to meet the anticipated extra tax bill in the future. Consequently, Ricardians argue, tax cuts do not stimulate economic activity because they do not generate increases in demand. The same argument applies in reverse.

The Ricardian approach thus argues that changes in budget deficits have little or no impact on economic activity, because they induce offsetting changes in savings, whereas both Keynesian and monetarist theories predict that the main impact is on current spending. The difference reflects the Ricardian assumption that consumers are willing, and able, to work out the future implications of current policy changes and to take account of both present and future effects in deciding on their current behaviour. Some economists argue that, in practice, most people are not sufficiently well informed nor sophisticated to pay much attention to the future implications of current tax changes. Other economists argue that, even if people are able to make sophisticated calculations, there is so much uncertainty about the future course of events that people are likely to discount them very heavily. Yet another complication is that if the repayment of current borrowing is sufficiently delayed, the burden may fall on future generations rather than on current tax payers.

Whilst all these arguments suggest reasons why

changes in the size of the budget deficit are likely to lead at least to some change in the pressure of demand, and not simply to changes in savings, the Ricardian view has nonetheless become quite influential. This is partly because studies in many countries, but especially America, suggest that the impact of budgetary changes on demand pressure is often less strong than would be predicted by simple Keynesian ideas. In addition, Ricardian ideas have become quite influential in financial markets, which now routinely assess the longer term prospects for fiscal policy, as well as its immediate impact.

The Definition of "Money".

Money plays a central role in any modern economy: without it, all but the simplest buying and selling transactions would become difficult or impossible, since people would then have to use barter. In a barter economy goods are traded directly, so that anyone wishing to obtain, say, food has to pay for it by providing the food producer with some good or service which he requires. The obvious difficulty is that this relies on a "double coincidence" of wants: if the prospective food purchaser cannot supply anything which the food producer wants, the transaction cannot take place. Hence barter only works well in very simple economies with a limited range of goods and with a high degree of self sufficiency. It cannot operate in an economy with a significant range of goods and services, and with specialisation of production. In these circumstances money is the essential oil which lubricates the economic process: an individual can buy a range of goods with the money earned from his job, instead of having to trade products directly.

Although most people probably have a clear idea of what they understand by "money", it is in fact an extremely difficult concept to define with precision. Economists tend to define it as anything which is readily acceptable as a means of payment. Evidently "money" in this sense constitutes "cash"—banknotes and coins—and also current account bank deposits, since possession of the latter allows the drawing of cheques which, normally, are a universally acceptable means of payment.

The total of cash and current account deposits at any given time is one possible definition of the supply of money existing at that time: in Britain it is known as "M1". However, it is by no means the only possible measure. The problem is that there are many other financial assets which are nearly as good as money in the sense that, although not themselves a means of payment, they can be converted quickly into money. These assets are often called "near money". An example of "near money" is *time deposits* at banks. These are accounts which pay interest and for which (as the name suggests) notice may have to be given if funds are to be withdrawn. They cannot automatically be used to draw cheques, and for this reason do not quite satisfy the economist's definition of "money", since they are not, in principle, a means of payment. In practice, however, funds can be transferred from them into current accounts—and then used for payment—with virtually no effort or delay. Indeed, banks will often honour cheques which are drawn on the strength of a time deposit account. For these reasons, such accounts are "nearly" as good as money, and might legitimately be included in a working definition. This sort of argument led to the development of a wider operational definition of money, known as "M3". M3 was defined as M1, plus time deposits, and also foreign currency accounts and public sector accounts. A variant on this, called *sterling M3* (*i.e.* excluding the foreign currency components of M3) was used as the main indicator of monetary policy in Britain for several years in the early 1980s, and indeed in 1984 M1 was abandoned as a formal policy target. It was replaced by M0, the so-called "monetary base", defined as notes and coins in circulation plus banks' deposits held at the Bank of England. The argument in favour of M0 was that a growing proportion of M1 was made up of interest-bearing deposits and that it therefore increasingly represented peoples' savings decisions; hence it no longer provided a good guide to the amount of money available to finance current demands for goods and services.

Whatever the merits of M0 as an indicator of demand pressure, it should be noted that it does not correspond to the definition of "money" as a means of payment because it excludes all current and deposit bank accounts, essentially on the grounds that holders of such accounts might choose to regard them as vehicles for savings rather than for financing current spending. It therefore narrows the definition of money beyond M1 by including only those elements for which there is no plausible demand other than as a means of payment.

Liquidity.

In contrast, many people criticised even the "wide" definition of money, M3, on the grounds that it excluded accounts at institutions other than banks. This is potentially important since total deposits with the banks are less than total deposits with non-bank institutions. If the government controls M1 (or M3) as a means of controlling aggregate demand, its policy may be circumvented if, say, people run down building society accounts in order to increase their current expenditure. Another way of putting this is to say that the range of "near money" assets extends beyond time deposits to include building society accounts, and perhaps even wider collections of assets. This has been recognised by the development of correspondingly wider working definitions of money, "M4" and "M5". M4 equals M3 plus building society accounts, and M5 equals M4 plus money market instruments such as Treasury Bills.

The traditional argument for concentrating on measures like M1 or M3 rather than on wider measures of liquidity was that building society accounts, and similar assets, could not be used directly as means of payment: it was necessary first to withdraw cash from a building society account before making a purchase. However, during the 1980s this changed rapidly, as the banks and the building societies began to compete much more closely. On the one hand, the banks moved increasingly into the home loans business in an attempt to capture some of the traditional business of the building societies. Conversely, by the end of the 1980s most of the main building societies were issuing cheque books to account holders, and such cheques had become widely acceptable as a means of payment.

The Trend in Building Societies.

The building societies altered in other ways, widening their range of financial and housing services to the point at which the larger societies were more appropriately viewed as financial conglomerates—firms offering a full range of financial services—than in terms of their traditional role as lenders for house purchase. This trend was accentuated in 1989 when the second largest society, the Abbey National, took steps to convert itself from a mutual society—the traditional arrangement for building societies, whereby they are owned by their members—to a public company, quoted on the Stock Market, and so owned by shareholders. Members voted in favour of the proposal, making the Abbey National much more like a bank and much less like a traditional building society.

This brought to a head the question of whether or not building society accounts should be included in official definitions of "money". The Abbey National's deposits were included in M4 but not in M3, reflecting its previous role but not its new status. Faced with such confusion, and with the prospect that other building societies might make the same change, the monetary authorities decided to abandon M3 as a measure of "money", let alone as an active target of policy. Since then, therefore, M0 and M4 have been used as the main monetary indicators.

An "intermediate" measure, M2, has also been given more emphasis. Whereas M4 includes all private sector deposits in all banks and building societies, M2 includes only "retail" deposits, which mainly comprise deposits which pay no interest, together with cheque-bearing sight and time deposits. Hence, whilst M4 continues to provide a measure of "broad" money, M2 attempts to measure those parts of the total money stock which are likely to be used mainly for regular transactions rather than as a way of saving for the future. Hence M2 corresponds rather more closely than does M4 to the notion of money as a "means of payment", whilst M4 attempts to take account of the fact that many other financial assets can easily be turned into means of payment.

Building Society Conversions.

Initially other building societies did not choose to follow the Abbey National's lead. Subsequently, however, the largest building society, the Halifax, and two other large societies, the Woolwich and the Alliance and Leicester, also converted into banks. Conversely, several large societies, including the Nationwide, announced that they had decided against conversion and would remain as building societies. Those making the change argued that it would give them greater commercial freedom, in terms both of the ability to extend their range of activities beyond the housing market, and of the ability to borrow from a wider range of sources. Some sceptics argued that the Abbey National's activities still closely resembled those of a traditional building society some six years after its conversion. Those building societies deciding against conversion also argued that there were advantages in remaining as mutual societies. Their argument was that they did not need to generate profits to pay shareholders; instead all the benefits of their operations could be given directly to their members.

This argument was given practical effect early in 1996 when the Nationwide announced a significant reduction in its standard mortgage rate. This seemed to be aimed mainly at competing with those lenders who had converted, or planned to convert, into banks. The Nationwide argued that the latter would not be able to match its lower rates, because to do so would reduce their profits too far to be able to pay acceptable dividends to their shareholders. There was uncertainty about how these emerging issues would be resolved, but it seemed possible that the end-result would be somewhat lower profit margins, and thus better terms for those borrowing for house purchase. If so, financial restructuring in the housing finance market would have been beneficial, at least in this respect.

The Choice of Targets.

The fact that "money" can be defined in so many different ways, each having some plausible justification, poses an obvious problem: if it is important to control the money supply, which measure is the one to be controlled? This is of some practical importance since the various monetary aggregates often grow at very different rates. Over the longer term M1 has been steadily falling in size relative to M3. Such variations in the growth of different monetary aggregates were one reason why monetary targets lost favour with the British government in the mid-1980s (*see* **G31**).

The Liquidity Spectrum.

By definition "money" is completely liquid. Building society accounts are clearly highly liquid assets. Other types of financial assets—*e.g.*, long-dated government stock, known as *gilt-edged securities*—are less liquid, since although the owner of such assets can easily exchange them for money, he cannot confidently predict the *price* at which he can do so. For example, he may have to sell at a time when the market price of government stock is unusually low, so that he realises relatively little money from the sale. Thus "liquidity" refers not only to the speed with which assets can be sold, but also to the predictability of the amount of money which the sale will realise. In practice, there is a *liquidity spectrum*, i.e., a whole range of different types of asset, each possessing a different degree of liquidity. The spectrum includes not only financial assets but also real assets—houses, capital equipment, etc.—the latter being highly illiquid, *e.g.*, selling a house takes a long time, involves high transactions costs, and the sale price is unpredictable.

Liquidity and Expenditure.

Assets towards the illiquid end of the spectrum are obviously not "near money" and could never plausibly become so. However, the precise point at which the boundary should be drawn between "near money" assets and other, less liquid ones, is

not clear. Indeed, many economists would argue that it is not sensible to try to define such a boundary. This is partly because its position is not objectively defined at any particular time, but more fundamentally because it cannot be regarded as fixed and immutable over time. The gradual change in the status of the building societies and their deposits illustrates the tendency for the boundary to shift.

The existence of a large spectrum of financial assets, and the tendency for the "near money" boundary to shift over time, emphasises the practical difficulty of controlling the money supply. If "money" and various forms of "near money" are in practice very close substitutes for one another, attempts by the government to control the money supply may be self defeating, because whatever the precise definition of "money" which is used, some liquid assets will be excluded, and the financial sector may then negate the effects of the controls by shifting towards greater use of other assets, not included in the definition and therefore not subject to control. This problem is often known as "Goodhart's Law", named after Charles Goodhart, formerly an economic adviser at the Bank of England. Goodhart's Law states that as soon as the government attempts to regulate any particular set of financial assets, these become unreliable as indicators of economic trends. The basic reason is that financial institutions can relatively easily devise new types of financial assets, and this allows them to negate the effects of controls on particular types of assets, based on particular definitions of the money supply. There is very little which the government can do to prevent it.

Indirect Control of Money Supply.

One response by policy-makers during the 1980s was to try to control the money supply indirectly, by fixing interest rates, instead of attempting to control it directly. The principle behind this idea is that the demand for money varies inversely with interest rates. Higher interest rates tend to reduce the demand for money because they increase the *opportunity cost* of holding money, i.e. the amount of interest income which is sacrificed by keeping funds in money (which traditionally does not pay interest) instead of in some other financial asset on which interest is paid. If the monetary authorities reduce the money supply, the resulting shortage of money will tend to drive interest rates upwards as people try to sell other financial assets (so driving the price of these assets down, and driving up the interest rates payable on them) in order to build up their money balances. Faced with difficulties in controlling the money supply, however, the monetary authorities in the UK tended during the 1980s to reverse this procedure, pushing interest rates up in the expectation that this would reduce the demand for money and that the supply of money would then fall in line. The difficulty with this approach was similar to that with direct control of the money supply. Rapid changes in the financial sector tended to make the relationship between interest rates and money demand difficult to predict. For example, most banks in the UK started to offer interest payments on current accounts during the 1980s. By thus reducing the opportunity cost of holding money, this had the effect of increasing the demand for money at each level of interest rates.

More generally, attempting to control the money supply by using interest rates is an indirect procedure which relies to a considerable extent upon factors beyond the government's control. The largest component of the money supply is deposits at the main banks. If interest rates are to be used to control the money supply, changes in interest rates have to be able to induce changes in the level of bank deposits. The mechanism involved is as follows. If interest rates rise, this will tend to reduce the demand for bank loans and overdrafts, since the cost of servicing these debts is increased. The resulting fall in bank borrowing reduces the pressure of demand for goods and services—since some of this is financed by borrowing—and this in turn reduces sales and sales receipts. This fall in receipts means that less money is deposited with banks; at this point the objective of reducing money supply by reducing bank deposits is achieved. However, whilst this mechanism is clear in principle, in practice its weak link is the relationship between interest rates and the demand for bank loans. In the early 1980s, for example, when interest rates were raised to what were then record levels, the demand for bank loans proved surprisingly resilient. One reason for this may have been the problems experienced by many individual companies, which found their cash flow positions squeezed between depressed sales revenue and relatively buoyant labour costs. For many firms, bank loans represented a possible way of easing these cash flow problems. The demand for loans remained relatively strong, even in the face of high interest rates.

In practice, if interest rates are kept sufficiently high for a sufficiently long period of time, the demand for loans is likely to fall eventually, with consequent downward pressure on the money supply and on aggregate demand. The problem for policy-makers in judging the appropriate level of interest rates in the context of such delayed reactions. If initial increases in rates have little or no immediate effect, there is a strong temptation to raise rates further—indeed, to continue raising them until the money markets respond. However, the danger is that rates will be raised much too far, so that the market response, when it comes, will be far stronger than planned or desired. Economists sometimes illustrate this by the analogy of someone pulling one end of a piece of elastic, in order to pull towards them a heavy weight which is attached to the other end. Initial gentle tugging does not move the weight, and there is a temptation to pull harder and harder. The end-result is that the person doing the pulling is likely to be hit in the face when the pressure reaches the point at which the weight is catapulted forwards.

Consider the British government's policy in 1989, when it raised interest rates to very high levels to reduce demand pressure. During 1989 the effect was very limited, but the subsequent recession proved to be far deeper and more prolonged than expected. The same problem can occur in reverse. In 1992 the government made a series of reductions in interest rates to stimulate economic activity. When these failed to have any immediate significant impact, the government came under pressure to make still further cuts, despite the danger that these would eventually produce an excessive response. Such pressures provide another illustration of the potential difficulties caused by politicians' desires to be seen to respond actively to current problems—even if, sometimes, it would be better in the longer run not to respond.

The National Debt and Government Borrowing.

The *National Debt* is a measure of the total indebtedness of the government, excluding local authorities. The table below shows how it has varied over time. Although the absolute size of the National Debt has risen steadily, this simply reflects inflation: as a proportion of national income the National Debt has fluctuated, rising sharply after each of the two World Wars—both of which saw borrowing on a massive scale by the government to finance the war effort—but falling slowly but steadily for 20 years up to 1975. From 1975 to the mid-1980s the proportion altered little; in the second half of the 1980s, it fell sharply; in the early 1990s it rose again.

THE NATIONAL DEBT IN SELECTED YEARS

	The National Debt (£bn.)	The National Debt as a percentage of national income
1900	0·6	31·9
1914	0·7	25·6
1921	7·6	147·7
1938	7·8	150·6
1946	23·0	259·6
1975	46·4	49·0
1988	171·0	38·0
1992	180·4	33·6
1994	269·2	47·2
1996	402·6	54·8
1998	432·0	51·0

The government borrows in several different ways. First, the issue of new bank-notes is a form of borrowing: as seen above it can be used to finance a budget deficit. Second, it borrows from foreign governments (*see* **G**9). Third, it borrows from companies through tax reserve certificates, whereby-company taxes are paid at the later date when the taxes become legally due. Fourth, it borrows from private individuals through the various forms of national savings, *e.g.*, Post Office accounts.

These four types of borrowing result in *non-marketable debt*, *i.e.*, an individual who has a Post Office account cannot sell it in the market to another individual. Two other types of borrowing—gilt-edged securities and Treasury Bills—result in *marketable debt*, *i.e.*, an individual who owns gilt-edged securities can sell them in the market to someone else. In practice, most gilt-edged and all Treasury Bills are held by institutions—banks, discount houses, etc.—rather than by private individuals. However, whereas Treasury Bills, representing short-term (usually three months) loans to the government are liquid assets (*i.e.*, they can quickly be cashed at a predictable price), gilt-edged are illiquid. They represent promises to repay a certain sum of money at a specified date, *e.g.*, government stock outstanding in 1995 had an average remaining life of approximately 10 years, with significant redemptions due in each of the next five years. Occasionally stock is issued without a repayment date. Owners of such stock are in effect promised a fixed annual interest payment for ever. At any time prior to the repayment gilt-edged can be traded, and there is a large market for such trading in which the market price (as opposed to the fixed repayment price) varies widely.

Interest Rates and Debt Financing.

As already seen, such variations in gilt-edged market prices cause changes in interest rates on all financial assets. Aside from the effects on aggregate demand, interest rate changes themselves have a large impact upon the financing of the National Debt, and hence upon overall public expenditure. For example, if restrictions on the growth of the money supply cause interest rates to rise, this increases the interest charges which the government has to pay on its existing debts. Furthermore, the accompanying fall in the market price of government stock may cause potential buyers of new issues of stock to anticipate further falls (*i.e.*, further increases in interest rates), in which case they will be reluctant to purchase the stock—and the government will be unable to finance its budget deficit—unless and until these further changes occur. When they do, the interest charges on the National Debt are further increased; and the market may still be unsettled, expecting yet further changes.

It is problems of this sort which at one time led many Keynesians to advocate a policy of promoting stable (or at least slowly changing) interest rates—an "orderly market" for financial assets—rather than a predetermined growth rate of the money supply. Monetarists object on the grounds that the government cannot in practice stabilise interest rates in this manner. They argue that although the government may be able to stabilise or even reduce interest rates in the short run by a rapid expansion of the money supply, this expansion will itself *increase* interest rates in the longer run. This is because, on the monetarist approach, the monetary expansion increases demand for real output, which in turn generally increases the rate of inflation. If this causes people to expect a higher future rate of inflation, gilt-edged stock then becomes less attractive to investors because of the associated decline in the anticipated real value of its fixed interest payments. The demand for gilt-edged stock therefore falls, which pushes its price down and thus its effective interest rate up. This continues until the effective interest rate has risen sufficiently to offset the higher expected inflation. Interest rates elsewhere tend to get bid up at the same time, since banks, building societies, *etc.*, have to protect their own reserves.

Monetarists therefore distinguish between the *nominal* interest rate, *i.e.*, the current money value of the interest rate, and the *real* interest rate, *i.e.*, the nominal rate minus the expected rate of price inflation on real output. They argue that firms and consumers are concerned about the real, not the nominal, interest rate; in this case nominal rates must inevitably rise if inflation increases—which it will do, on the monetarist argument, if the government, in pursuing a Keynesian policy of stabilising interest rates, over-expands the money supply. Hence the monetarists produce a paradox; a monetary policy which seeks to hold interest rates down may instead cause them to rise.

The Trend of Interest Rates in Britain.

It is difficult to deny that some element of the monetarist view of interest rates has operated in the post-war period, especially in more recent years. For example, rates on most financial assets showed a trend increase until the early 1980s. Since inflation and therefore, in all probability, inflationary expectations showed a similar trend, the rise in nominal interest rates was broadly consistent with the monetarist position.

For much of the 1980s the trends of the 1970s were reversed, with nominal interest rates gradually declining from their peak levels of 1979–81, albeit with some fluctuations. This is again broadly consistent with the monetarist viewpoint. Inflation in the UK fell quite sharply after 1981, stabilising at 3–5 per cent in the mid-1980s. Inflation expectations almost certainly fell in a similar fashion, as the Thatcher government's determination to eliminate high inflation gradually gained credibility in financial markets and among the wider public, so helping to break the "inflation psychology" which had built up during the 1970s. Hence nominal interest rates would be expected to fall. However, in 1988 and 1989 inflation started to rise once again. Partly for this reason, nominal interest rates also began rising again after the middle of 1988. By early 1990 they had returned to even higher levels than at the beginning of the 1980s.

One point to note is that *nominal* interest rates can be very misleading as a guide to *real* interest rates which, as explained above, are equal to nominal rates minus the expected rate of inflation. In the 1970s nominal rates were very high but for most of the time the rate of inflation was even higher, so that real interest rates were negative. This was particularly marked in 1975–76, when nominal rates reached a then record high level of around 16 per cent. At the time, however, inflation was running at around 25 per cent, implying real interest rates of around minus 9 per cent—a record *low* level. The same has applied in reverse in the 1980s. Nominal interest rates fell to lower levels than in the 1970s, but inflation fell faster, so that by 1986 nominal interest rates of around 12 per cent coexisted with inflation of around 5 per cent, implying real interest rates of plus 7 per cent—a record *high* level. Thus changes in nominal interest rates cannot be taken as a good guide to changes in the real cost of borrowing.

Inflation and National Debt Financing.

The distinction between real and nominal interest rates also substantially qualifies the earlier point about the effect of inflation on the financing of the National Debt. The latter consists mainly of debts which are fixed in money value. Hence, persistent inflation erodes their real value in terms of purchasing power. This substantially offsets the increased burden of interest payments when higher inflation raises nominal interest rates. In effect, the government loses through higher inflation in terms of interest payments, but gains in terms of the erosion of the real burden of its debts. Another way of making this point is that the burden of the National Debt really depends on real rather than nominal interest rates, and the latter are by no means a reliable guide to the former. For example, in the mid-1970s the official measure of the budget deficit was equivalent to over 6 per cent of national income, but after adjusting for inflation this was actually equivalent to a small surplus. The public sector's debt was being eroded by inflation by more than enough to offset its interest payments.

International Influences on Interest Rates.

Another substantial complication in considering interest rates concerns the relationship between interest rates in Britain and in other countries. The removal of exchange controls in 1979, and the much greater degrees of competition and openness in foreign exchange markets which emerged in the 1980s, mean that changes in interest rates in other countries, especially Germany, have come to play a major role in determining British rates. Institutions such as pension funds, insurance companies, and large industrial companies which have substantial amounts of money to invest are now easily able to move money between alternative assets in different currencies. Consequently, if interest rates in Germany rise above those in Britain there will normally be a large movement of funds out of assets such as British government bonds, denominated in sterling, and into German marks in order to take advantage of the higher rates of return. The same applies if interest rates rise in other important financial centres such as Tokyo. Since selling of sterling assets implies a reduced demand for sterling and increased demand for other currencies, this tends to push down the exchange rate of sterling against other currencies. If the British government is reluctant to see a fall in the exchange rate it will then be forced to allow a rise in British interest rates in order to prevent it.

These international linkages became even more important when, in October 1990, the government finally decided that the UK should join the Exchange Rate Mechanism (the ERM) of the European Monetary System (*see* **G**54). This involved a commitment to hold the pound within an agreed band of values against all other ERM currencies. This meant that interest rate policies became subordinate to the exchange rate. If, for example, the sterling exchange rate moved close to the bottom of its band, the UK government would be required to take offsetting action, the most likely such action being an increase in interest rates.

The German mark is normally the strongest currency in the ERM, so that Britain's entry was interpreted by many commentators as effectively fixing the pound's value to that of the mark. This still further emphasised the importance of international influences on domestic UK interest rates. Indeed, some people opposed Britain's entry into the ERM on precisely these grounds.

This argument was put increasingly strongly as the UK plunged into a very severe recession in 1991 and 1992. Critics argued that it was illogical to keep real interest rates at record high levels—as was the case for almost the whole of 1991—during a deep recession. In effect, they argued, Britain's interest rates were being decided according to the needs of the German rather than the British economy. Many of the critics felt vindicated when, after Britain left the ERM in September 1992, rates were rapidly reduced by 3 percentage points. On the other side of the argument, however, it was pointed out that, whether inside or outside the ERM, Britain was inescapably part of a highly integrated world economy, and that cuts in British interest rates would depress the exchange rate and so generate inflationary pressures.

The Commercial Banks.

If the government does adopt monetary targets, its main need is to find ways of influencing the behaviour of the commercial banks, known in England as the clearing banks. For as seen above, the main component of the money supply is the deposits of the clearing banks.

In Britain there are four main banks with one or more branches in every town. Each of them earns profits by borrowing at low or zero rates of interest—anyone holding a bank account is in effect making a loan to his bank—and lending out part of the resulting funds at higher interest rates. In normal circumstances—*i.e.*, unless there is a run on the banks—not all deposits will be withdrawn at once; therefore the banks need keep only a small proportion of their deposits in the form of cash. This proportion is known as the *cash ratio* and until 1971 the Bank of England required it to be at least 8 per cent. Also, between 1951 and 1971 the Bank of England requested that the banks held liquid assets—Treasury Bills, commercial bills, and money at call and short notice as well as cash—equal to at least 30 per cent of deposits. This was known as the *liquidity ratio*.

The commercial banks can "create" money because of their ability to accept deposits far in excess of their cash and liquid asset holdings; as economists would say, because they operate under a *fractional reserve system.* If a bank provides an overdraft facility to a customer who then draws cheques on the facility, the recipients of these cheques pay the proceeds into their bank accounts which are thereby enlarged; and this represents an increase in the money supply, since the enlarged accounts can be used to finance additional transactions. Thus any increase in the banks' cash and liquid asset holdings allows them to expand loans, overdrafts, etc.—and thereby the money supply—by a multiple amount.

The government can control the money supply by controlling the components of banks' cash and liquid asset holdings. A reduction in the latter can be engineered by *open market operations,* which involve the Bank of England's selling more gilt-edged than it otherwise would; this reduces the banks' liquidity, since, as already seen, gilt-edged are not regarded as liquid assets, so that their purchase involves a drain of liquidity from the banks. At the same time, as already seen, it will generally involve a rise in interest rates.

Financial Deregulation.

When the Thatcher government took office in 1979 it embarked on a series of measures to reduce the degree of government control over and regulation of the financial sector of the economy. Its general philosophy here, as in other economic contexts, was to increase the importance of market forces and reduce the role of the government. The first, and in some ways the most dramatic change was the removal, in October 1979, of all the remaining foreign exchange controls. Further deregulation followed in stages. In June 1980 the government ended the Supplementary Special Deposits Scheme, which had required the banks to place zero interest deposits at the Bank of England to prevent the assets concerned from being used instead as a base for monetary expansion. In 1981 further changes in monetary control techniques were made. The reserve assets ratio was abolished. Instead, the banks undertook to keep an average of 6 per cent, and never normally less than 4 per cent, of their eligible liabilities as secured money with members of the London Discount Market Association and/or with money brokers and gilt-edged jobbers. They were also required to keep cash balances equal to ½ per cent of eligible liabilities in non-interest bearing accounts at the Bank of England. At the same time the Government abolished *Minimum Lending Rate.* It intended instead to set short term interest rates within an undisclosed band, thus abandoning its previous ability to influence the general level of interest rates by announcing a change in MLR. The main idea behind these changes was to attempt to introduce a greater role for market forces in the determination of interest rates.

Two further changes proved to have very important effects. In October 1983 the Building Societies Association ended its previous practice of recommending a common mortgage rate for all mortgage lenders. In future each lending institution was left free to choose its own rate. The main effect was to encourage new institutions to enter the housing finance market. The latter was also significantly affected when, in December 1986, the Bank of England withdrew its "guidance" on mortgage lending by financial institutions, thus leaving the market entirely unregulated. The main consequence was that the supply of credit, especially for housing finance, was sharply increased during the mid-1980s. This in turn contributed to an excessively rapid growth of demand, and the resurgence of inflation and balance of payments problems, during 1988 and 1989 (*see* **G**48).

The Stock Exchange.

Whilst short-term credit is mostly provided by banks and Finance Houses, long-term borrowing by companies is undertaken through the Stock Exchange. Firms in the private sector of the economy issue three main types of security on the Stock Exchange. *Debenture Stock* is simply a fixed-interest loan. *Preference Stock* is a fixed-interest loan with provisions for waiving the interest if no profits are earned. The most important type, representing the great majority of holdings, are *Ordinary Shares.* The owner of an Ordinary Share is, legally, a part-owner of the company concerned, with a right to participate in any net profits which it makes (though he has no legal right to any particular level of dividend or interest payment).

In contrast to government stock, a significant proportion of Ordinary Shares is owned by private individuals. However, an increasing proportion is owned by insurance companies and pension funds, which have grown in importance as private superannuation schemes have become more widespread. It is likely that the market for Ordinary Shares, like that for government stock, will eventually be completely dominated by such large institutional investors.

The attraction of Ordinary Shares to the investor wanting an outlet for his savings is that because they represent a part ownership of the firm concerned, their prices and dividends are likely to rise as the value of the firm increases. This is so whether the firm's value increases in real terms, because it is expanding, or simply in money terms, because of general inflation. Thus Ordinary Shares generally represent a reasonable "hedge" against inflation—unlike fixed-interest securities such as gilt-edged. It is for this reason that the dividend yield on Ordinary Shares does not tend to rise with inflation: the demand for Ordinary Shares does not necessarily fall if inflation increases, so that their prices and yields are not affected in the same way as those of gilt-edged and other fixed-interest securities by changes in inflation rates.

The Big Bang.

In October 1986 several major changes occurred in the organisation of the Stock Exchange. These had been under active discussion and planning for several years, but because they were all formally introduced simultaneously, they became known as the *Big Bang.* The main changes consisted of alterations in the structure and ownership of firms operating in the stock market, removal of restrictions on charging for financial services, and new forms of regulation of activity.

Traditionally, stock market firms had been divided into "jobbers" and "brokers". The former were responsible for the trading of shares on the floor of the stock market, whilst the latter dealt with clients and provided business for the jobbing firms—clients wishing to buy or sell shares were not allowed to deal directly with jobbers. The market imposed what was known as the "single capacity" restriction: no firm was allowed to be both a jobber and a broker. It also imposed strict limits on the ownership of all member firms: they were required either to be partnerships, or to be limited companies with a maximum limit on the amount of capital which could be owned by non-member firms (*i.e.* firms not actually operating in the market). In addition, the market operated fixed minimum commission rates on share deals.

Although this structure had worked well in earlier years, during the 1970s and 1980s it started to become increasingly inappropriate. The main catalyst for change was the growing *internationalisation of financial markets.* This was itself the result of several forces. Technological developments were making it very easy for financial firms to obtain virtually instant information, at very low cost, about assets in any currency and any country. Simultaneously, firms needing finance, especially the large multinationals operating throughout the world, were becoming increasingly willing to consider finance from any source. In addition, the abolition of UK exchange controls in 1979 meant that UK financial institutions rapidly acquired a much more diversified range of assets and interests, and needed to deal regularly in markets throughout the world, and also to compete within the UK against foreign based financial firms. Their ability to do so was heavily constrained by the traditional arrangements: minimum commission requirements restricted competition, the single capacity arrangement was unwieldy, and the limits on outside capital ownership meant that most of the firms were undercapitalised in terms of the scale of risks which they needed to run in global operations.

Consequences of Big Bang.

The Big Bang swept away most of the old restrictions. It allowed "single capacity" firms to operate, ended minimum commission rates, and removed restrictions on the entry and the ownership of firms. The main result was a series of mergers between and takeovers of old-established stock market firms. After Big Bang, most of the firms operating in the market were merely parts of, or subsidiaries of, much larger financial conglomerates, many of them foreign owned. These large firms felt that they could raise their overall profitability by operating in the UK stock market, though for many of them this was only one part of a large range of financial activities. Big Bang effectively recognised that the London stock market, like other stock exchanges around the world, could no longer be organised so as to supply finance for solely UK-based firms: instead, it was now a part of a global market for finance.

It was recognised that these new arrangements would need *regulation*, to protect the interests, and retain the confidence, of clients. The 1986 Financial Services Act provided the framework. This gave the Trade and Industry Minister the power to authorise firms as "fit and proper" to operate in the stock market, and in other financial contexts such as insurance services. In practice this power was largely delegated, in the first instance to the *Securities and Investments Board* (SIB), whose members were appointed by the Bank of England and the government. Concern about financial regulation persisted, however, and an early priority for the Labour Government, elected in 1997, was to initiate a tougher regulatory regime.

Monetary Policy in Britain.

Keynesian ideas were to come under increasingly strong intellectual challenge from monetarists in the 1960s, and by the second half of the 1970s monetarist ideas had become the dominant influence upon policy making. This happened in two stages. The first occurred in the autumn of 1976 when Britain applied to the IMF for large credit facilities. One of the requirements which the IMF imposed as a condition of granting these facilities was that the Government should lay down, and stick to annual *monetary targets, i.e.,* target annual growth rates in sterling M3. Successive governments adopted this approach for the next ten years.

The adoption of monetary targets in turn meant that the *public sector borrowing requirement* (p.s.b.r.) became a target, rather than a consequence, of policy. The p.s.b.r. is the combined deficit of central government, local authorities and public corporations. It has to be financed by a combination of borrowing (from the private sector or from abroad) and increasing the money supply. Since domestic borrowing will push up interest rates, any government which has a monetary target and which is also unwilling to tolerate rises beyond a certain point in interest rates, will be compelled to limit the size of the p.s.b.r. This has to be done by a combination of tax rises and cuts in public spending. Thus targets for monetary growth carry implications for the government's tax and expenditure policies.

The second, and decisive, stage in the growth of monetarist influence was the election of a Conservative government in May 1979. The new government came into office committed to a monetarist approach to economic policy; several of its leading members declared themselves converts, to a greater or lesser extent, to the teachings of Professor Friedman, and rejected the Keynesianism of earlier post-war years. Early in its term of office, therefore, the new government published its medium-term financial strategy, designed to operate over the period 1980–84. It aimed to secure steady cuts from year to year over this period in both the monetary growth rate, and the p.s.b.r. as a proportion of national income. The government took the view that the scale of past government borrowing had contributed a great deal to the rapid inflation rates of the 1970s.

Doubts about Monetarism.

By the end of 1981 the experience since 1976, and more especially since 1979, had begun to erode support for monetarist ideas, at least in their simple form. One area of doubt concerned the actual ability of the government to control money supply, however defined; this led to the 1981 changes in monetary control techniques mentioned above. A second argument revived the traditional Keynesian emphasis upon wider measures of liquidity: some economists, led by Nobel prize winner Professor James Meade, argued that the govern-

ment should abandon monetary targets and instead set targets for the growth of *money national income*—the volume of output multiplied by its average price level—and should use a variety of fiscal instruments for this purpose, with monetary policy being used mainly to influence interest rates and the exchange rate.

The Demise of Monetary Targeting.

In the course of the 1980s these criticisms gathered force. Despite its clear commitment to steady reductions in the growth rate of the money supply as a central part of its anti-inflation policy, Mrs. Thatcher's government persistently failed to achieve its monetary targets. Moreover its main target—£M3—became very volatile and, apparently, increasingly unreliable as a guide to underlying economic trends. By the middle of the 1980s it was clear that the government was attaching steadily less weight to formal monetary targets, and the 1987 Budget announced the end of £M3 as a target. This was certainly a substantial change from the period 1979–83, when £M3 was overwhelmingly the main policy instrument of macroeconomic policy.

New Controversies.

This modification of the Government's views was matched by changes in the views of many Keynesian economists. The traditional Keynesian view that money does not matter, which as discussed above dominated policy making for some twenty years after 1945, had been discarded by almost all the government's critics (some of whom pointed out that Keynes himself had never argued that money was unimportant). Most economists accepted that there was sufficient evidence from the experience of the British economy in recent years to indicate that excessive expansion of the money supply was bound to lead to rises in inflation and nominal interest rates and was therefore harmful. In a sense, therefore, some of the traditional disputes between monetarists and Keynesians, which had persisted to the end of the 1970s, seemed to be coming to an end. Many monetarists accepted that simple monetary targeting was not sufficient; nearly all Keynesians accepted the need to prevent excessive monetary expansion.

New areas of controversy had partly replaced some of these traditional disagreements. For example, as the public sector borrowing requirement was reduced and eventually eliminated, giving way to a budget surplus during the 1987–8 financial year, there was much discussion on how this surplus should be used. Options included cutting tax rates, raising public spending, or repaying some of the accumulated National Debt. The Government, and many erstwhile monetarists, tended to favour the tax cutting option; many erstwhile Keynesians favoured increased public spending. However, this disagreement had little to do with traditional disputes about fiscal and monetary policies, and much more to do with alternative views about how best to stimulate the supply side of the economy. Hence traditional arguments about how best to regulate the *demand* side of the economy were increasingly being replaced by disputes about how to regulate the *supply* side—though many of the protagonists remained the same.

Confusion in Policy-Making.

The abandonment of monetary targetting in the second half of the 1980s coincided with what, in retrospect, appears to have been a considerable loss of cohesion in economic policy-making. Up to the mid-1980s the Thatcher governments, despite the various criticisms mentioned, had maintained a consistent approach to policy, with the defeat of inflation always the main priority and the use of monetary targets within the Medium Term Financial Strategy the main policy instrument. In the second half of the decade neither of these features was so clear cut. Whilst the Government continued to maintain that control of inflation was still the main priority, its actions suggested some modification. Similarly, whilst it continued to argue that monetary control was vital, in practice it seemed relatively unconcerned at evidence that various monetary indicators suggested a danger of rapidly rising inflation.

Two episodes of policy making in particular illustrated these apparent changes. In 1986, £M3 exceeded its target by a large amount. The Government's response, as already mentioned, was to abandon £M3 as a target in the following year, thus ignoring the potential inflationary implications. This policy was justified by the Chancellor at the time on the grounds that £M3 had become too volatile to be a useful policy indicator. In effect Mr. Lawson was invoking Goodhart's Law. Whilst this had some intellectual justification, it is difficult to believe that the Government would have responded in the same way in the early 1980s. A second, similar policy episode occurred in 1988. By this time the Government was using M0 as its only formal monetary indicator. However, at the same time the Government had become increasingly preoccupied with exchange rate targets, and at the time the Chancellor was seeking to prevent the exchange rate of the pound from rising above three D-marks. To achieve this aim he was prepared to accept increases in M0 above the target range. Hence the Government in effect abandoned its monetary target in favour of an exchange rate target.

This emphasis on exchange rate targetting had emerged partly in response to pressure from companies engaged in large amounts of international trade, for whom volatile and unpredictable exchange rates had become an increasingly important problem. These firms argued in favour of policies aimed at stabilising exchange rates so as to make trading conditions more predictable. Many economists and policy makers were sympathetic to this view. However, economists emphasised that a policy of fixing or controlling the exchange rate was incompatible with one of monetary targetting. If the Government fixes the exchange rate it then has to allow the money supply to vary by whatever amounts are required to maintain the exchange rate target. However, it seemed that this point was not clearly grasped by the British Government, with the result that the clarity which had characterised policy making in the early 1980s was lost. After 1987 it became increasingly difficult to be sure about either the aims or the methods of policy making. This perception of confusion caused a gradual erosion of confidence in the Government by the financial markets.

When the Government took the decision to enter the Exchange Rate Mechanism of the European Monetary System in October 1990, it seemed that the confusion in policy-making had been resolved. Once again the Government had a clear strategy: all other policies were now subordinate to the requirement to maintain the sterling exchange rate within its agreed ERM bands, and this in turn was designed to re-emphasise the central importance of controlling inflation. However, the financial markets gradually lost confidence in the willingness or ability of the government to maintain the agreed exchange rate, and the resulting speculative pressure forced the pound out of the ERM again in September 1992. For the next few months, confusion about policy re-emerged in an even sharper form. The Government appeared to have no clear view about either the ultimate objectives of policy-making, or the appropriate policy tools. Gradually, however, a new view emerged which gave greater weight to encouraging growth in economic activity, whilst still stressing the importance of the inflation objective. The new emphasis on growth reflected the seriousness of the recession in which the economy had been trapped for the previous two years. The Government committed itself to adjusting taxes, public spending and interest rates in ways designed to give the economy the best possible chance of recovery. This marked a considerable shift of emphasis from policy-making in the 1980s.

The New Labour Government.

As the Government's economic policy evolved in the 1990s, the Labour opposition was also altering its stance. Following its fourth successive general election defeat in 1992, many of its traditional commitments to high levels of public expenditure, and associated tax rates, were modified or abandoned. This was especially the case following the sudden death of the Labour leader, John Smith, and his replacement by Tony Blair. With Mr. Blair as the new leader, and Gordon Brown as the Shadow Chancellor, the Labour Party was now firmly under the control of its "modernising" wing, and the result was a sharp shift in its economic policy stance. The reduced emphasis on taxes and public spending was matched by an abandonment of its traditional commitment to nationalisation, and a new commitment to private enterprise and market forces.

The Monetary Policy Committee.

These changes narrowed the gap between Labour and the Conservatives, and probably helped to achieve the large Labour majority in the May 1997 election. Within a few days of the election, however, the new Chancellor, Mr. Brown, produced a major surprise—and a fundamental change in the operation of monetary policy—when he announced that he proposed to give the Bank of England independent control of interest rates. For the previous 50 years such decisions had been made by elected politicians. Under the Chancellor's proposals the decisions would in future be made by a newly constituted *Monetary Policy Committee* (MPC) of the Bank of England. The MPC would consist of the Governor of the Bank, three other Bank officials, and four independent economists to be appointed by the Chancellor. The Committee was to meet monthly and to decide on interest rates at each such meeting by majority vote, with the Governor having a casting vote, with its minutes subsequently being published. Under the proposals the government specified an inflation target, and the MPC's duty was then to choose interest rates in a way which it judged would be consistent with achieving the target over time.

Bank of England Independence.

Many economists had long advocated giving the Bank independent control of interest rates, and the new Chancellor's move was widely welcomed in economic and financial circles. The basic justification underlying the idea was that it would be likely to increase the *credibility* of the Government's commitment to low inflation and to sound financial policies. This was because if politicians have control of interest rates, they face temptations to use this control for electoral purposes to over-expand the economy, especially in the run-up to elections, regardless of the adverse longer term implications for the inflation rate. Bank officials, by contrast, face no similar temptations because they do not need to secure re-election. International comparisons of countries suggest a clear tendency for those countries with relatively independent central banks to have relatively low inflation rates.

Although the Chancellor's move was generally welcomed, there were also some criticisms. One argument was that the new approach might prolong recessions by removing the ability to respond to adverse shocks by relaxing monetary policy. A second criticism was that the details of the policy might generate instability. The Chancellor announced an inflation target, with narrow bands of a single percentage point on either side. The fear of some critics was that the Bank would have to make very frequent adjustments of interest rates to prevent the economy from moving outside such narrow bands.

A third criticism was that the MPC might exercise an initial bias in favour of unduly high interest rates in an effort to establish its anti-inflation credibility. In the event this criticism did not appear justified. In its first six months the MPC made a series of small, quarter-point, upward adjustments of interest rates, but it resisted calls from some economists for much larger increases, just as it ignored calls for cuts in rates by others, who were concerned about the strong exchange rate.

5. ECONOMIC ASPECTS OF THE PUBLIC SERVICES

The Cost of Public Services.

In 1997, total public expenditure was £315,471 million, about £5,000 per head. Of this the bulk (over 80 per cent) was spent by central government, and the remainder by local authorities and public corporations. Total public expenditure has increased more than twentyfold since 1960, and rose as a proportion of GNP from 34 per cent to a peak of more than 50 per cent in 1983, before declining to 44 per cent in the period 1983–88.

In 1991, public spending's share in national income rose quite sharply as the recession and higher levels of unemployment pushed up expenditure on social security. After Mr. Major became Prime Minister there was also greater emphasis on public spending programmes such as health. Nevertheless, from 1993 government current spending as a proportion of GDP declined slightly.

Central Government collects in revenue considerably more than it spends itself, but transfers funds to the local authorities, to the National Insurance Fund, and to the public corporations. The expenditure of the public sector as a whole has generally exceeded its revenue, the difference being met by net borrowing. However, the buoyancy of privatisation receipts and the process of "real fiscal drag"— where tax allowances keep pace with inflation but not the rise in earnings so that tax payments as a percentage of earned incomes go up—provided some offset. There was a financial deficit in each year of the 1980s until 1988 when there was a surplus of £8 billion. There was also a surplus in the following year, but then the Government started to move back into deficit as the recession pushed up spending, depressed tax revenues and curbed the Government's scope for further privatisations. In 1996 the public sector borrowing requirement was £24·8 billion, or 4·7 per cent of GDP. The PSBR fell dramatically in 1997 (to £6 bn), rising to £10 bn in 1998. Even so the ratio of government debt to GDP will remain high. The problem the Government faces is clear. The welfare state is expensive. Good economic climes remove some of this expense in that unemployment falls and private incomes rise. But the country remains with a large dependent population, partly because of the increase in poverty and partly because of demographic forces increasing the retired as a proportion of the population. Add to that the expenditure burden of servicing existing public debt, and it is easy to see that the problem is an intractable one.

Not all categories of public expenditure have expanded at the same rate. Over the period from 1984, for example, expenditure on public order and safety, social security, health and education increased faster than the total; expenditure on agriculture and on housing and community amenities fell behind the total.

Public Housing.

Expenditure on public housing (net of sales) amounted to less than 1 per cent of public expenditure in 1998. Housing expenditure consists of two quite different items. There is the capital cost of building new houses or of improvement grants and the like. There is also a recurrent cost, in the form of subsidies. April 1990 saw new financial arrangements for public sector housing, and a number of Government subsidies were consolidated into a Housing Revenue Account Subsidy of £3·8 bn in 1998–99. Direct subsidies to rents have fallen sharply in the past few years; and the new system, by "ringfencing" local authorities housing revenue accounts, is intended to put housing services on a more "businesslike footing". As a general rule, the Government's aim is to divert subsidies from the property to the person, via the housing benefit system. A 1995 White Paper in general terms confirmed the direction of government policy.

For most of the post-war period governments provided a substantial subsidy to public sector housing, either in the form of help for new building, or as a direct subsidy to rents. The mix depended very much on the priorities of the day. From 1972 to 1975 there was a "fair rent" system, which then gave way to a system designed to subsidise the construction of new dwellings and improvements to the existing housing stock. The whole direction of policy for public sector housing was altered by the Housing Act of 1980. Since then subsidies have been substantially reduced. Central government now calculates the amount by which it will finance housing subsidies on the assumption that local authorities charge council house tenants a "fair" or "market" rent. The result is that council rents have risen substantially in real terms. At the same time, private ownership has been encouraged e.g. through the sale of council houses. Between 1979 and 1997, 2·1 million council houses are estimated to have been sold. The Housing Act of 1988 further eroded the

role of local authorities in the provision of housing by allowing public sector tenants to change their landlord if the authority in question was deemed to be unsatisfactory, and housing associations and other registered social landlords are becoming significant providers of new housing in the subsidised rented sector. Such organisations now own and manage over one million homes in England. If registered with the Housing Corporation or equivalent bodies in Scotland and Wales, they can qualify for Social Housing Grants. There have been a variety of initiatives (not least in the 1996 Housing Act) to enable/encourage Housing Associations and also private sector concerns to take over responsibility for local authority housing, although in many instances public sector tenants have been unwilling to risk a change of landlord even if dissatisfied with the standard of service provided by local authorities. An Act of 1993 was designed to add further impetus to tenant purchases.

The Housing Market.

Government housing policy must be seen in terms of the housing market as a whole. In 1997 there were 24·6 million dwellings in the United Kingdom, 67 per cent being owner-occupied, 23 per cent council or housing association houses, and the other 10 per cent privately rented. The importance of owner-occupation has grown and that of private renting has declined: in 1960 they had accounted for 42 per cent and 32 per cent of the total respectively. One of the main aims of the 1988 Housing Act was to stimulate the private rented sector by deregulating rents on new private sector lettings. On an international comparison, the private rented sector in 1994, as a percentage of total housing stock, was 22 per cent in the EU as a whole. In Germany it was as high as 41, whilst in Portugal it was 24 and in France 20. Only Ireland and the Netherlands had a smaller rental sector than the UK. It should also be noted that the pattern of tenure varies quite significantly across different parts of the UK—owner occupation ranges from 46 per cent in Scotland to 73 per cent in South-West England.

The switch to owner-occupation in the UK is largely the result of Government policy. Rent controls meant that there was little incentive to build houses for renting, nor even to maintain existing rented houses, although the 1988 and 1996 Housing Acts were intended to remove some of the disincentives to private rental. On the other hand, Government has given considerable tax advantages to owner-occupiers. Owner-occupied houses are exempt from the capital gains tax introduced in 1964, and owner-occupiers can also obtain tax relief on mortgage-interest payments on a principal of up to £30,000. In 1990, mortgage interest relief represented a direct subsidy to owner-occupiers worth some £6·2bn, a more than ten-fold increase since the early 1960s. The real cost of mortgage interest relief more than doubled during the 1980s alone. It is therefore unsurprising that steps have been taken to reduce this subsidy, even though mortgage interest relief is something of a political "sacred cow". The £30,000 limit for relief has been unchanged since March 1983, in spite of very rapid house price inflation since that date. Until August 1988 unmarried owner-occupiers could claim tax relief on multiples of £30,000, depending on the number sharing. Relief is now restricted to £30,000 per property. In the March 1991 Budget mortgage interest relief was restricted to the basic rate of income tax; previously higher rate tax payers could claim relief on interest payments at their highest marginal rate of income tax. Since the abolition of the Schedule A tax in 1961—whereby owner-occupiers paid tax on the rental income imputed to their houses—this tax relief on interest payments must be justified as an inducement to home-ownership; but it is also a considerable subsidy to owner-occupiers, who tend to be the relatively well-off. From 1994 mortgage interest relief was limited to 20 per cent. From April 1995 it was further limited to 15 per cent and from April 1998 to 10 per cent. The 1999 Budget announced the complete abolition of mortgage interest relief from 2000.

The year 1953 was a peak for public sector housebuilding in the United Kingdom when 256,000 council dwellings were completed. There was a trough in 1961 (119,000), a peak in 1967 (204,000) and a subsequent fall to 108,000 in 1973. Since the mid 1970s there has been a steady decline in the construction of public dwellings. In 1993 only about 30,000 new houses were completed by Housing Associations. By contrast, the number of private dwellings completed rose steadily from 63,000 in 1953 to a peak of 222,000 in 1968. Thereafter the number fell back to an annual average of slightly less than 200,000 in the early 1970s, and still further to an average of about 130,000 in the early 1980s, rising again in 1983 to about 148,000, and to a peak of 200,000 in 1988 before falling to 180,000 in 1989, 161,000 in 1990 and 154,000 in 1991. In 1996 about 150,000 new private dwellings were completed. The total number of dwellings completed reached a peak of 414,000 in 1968, and fell to 270,000 in 1974. Since then, the best year has been 1976 (315,000), the worst 1992 (171,000), while 190,000 dwellings were completed in 1997.

House Price Inflation.

Over the 15 years 1955–70 the rate of inflation in the price of modern existing houses averaged 5 per cent per annum: somewhat faster than the rise in the cost of living. After 1970 there was a great surge in house prices: between December 1970 and December 1972 the average rise was no less than 30 per cent per annum. There are various reasons for this remarkable inflation. Partly it reflected the rapid acceleration of general inflation; in such times it is sensible to hold one's wealth in the form of assets which will appreciate in value. It also reflected the decline in house-building after 1968, and a slowing-down in the rate at which building land became available. The precise timing of the inflation resulted from the sudden and large increase in the availability of building society mortgages. And as the inflation grew, so optimistic expectations helped to raise house prices still further. By 1974 the rate of increase had slowed down considerably. It slowed even further in 1975 and 1976. In 1978 and 1979 prices started to accelerate again, slackening off in 1980, only to start accelerating again at the end of 1982. This rise was sustained through to 1988, but 1989 through to early 1991 saw sharp falls in house prices, particularly in areas such as the South East and East Anglia where house price inflation had accelerated rapidly in the previous two years. By 1990 the housing market slowdown was evident in all regions, and nationally house prices fell by 5 per cent. Further declines were registered in 1991 and 1992, but the pattern varied from region to region. In particular there were early signs of a recovery of the market in Northern England, Wales, Scotland and Northern Ireland. By 1996 a slow, but general recovery in house prices was underway. By and large this has continued since then.

Current Housing Needs.

At the beginning of the 1990s the number of dwellings exceeded the number of households by just under one million. Yet the picture is not as rosy as this implies. The regional distribution of supply and demand was not equally spread. The measured number of households understates the number of "units" needing accommodation—a married couple, for example, living in someone else's house. Such concealed units are thought to number 800,000. Much accommodation is substandard in some way or other—a 1986 survey of dwellings in England and Wales indicated that about 2·9 million homes or more than 12 per cent of the housing stock was unfit for habitation. In 1990 housing renewal areas were established in England and Wales to cover, inter alia, renovation and redevelopment of substandard housing. These complement housing action areas in Scotland and Northern Ireland, which have authority to channel funds for redevelopment where at least half the housing stock does not meet "statutory tolerable" standards. In spite of such initiatives, the above factors, together with personal financial and social problems, mean that a worrying number of people are homeless. Thus by 1997 103,340 households were accepted as homeless by the local authorities. The problem was particularly acute in London. The 1996 Housing Act was in part designed to help the homeless by creating easier and more rapid access to council housing.

Education.

Educational expenditure accounted for about 12 per cent of public expenditure in 1998. It had increased over the previous 25 years for two reasons. First the number of full-time pupils had grown. Second the more expensive sectors—secondary schools and universities—expanded most rapidly. For example, in 1996–97 there were 3·7 million students in state secondary schools as opposed to 3·2 million in 1961, although the 1996–97 figure was well below the comparable total for 1981 of 4·6 million. This reflects changing demographics. Falling birth rates meant that the secondary school population reached a peak in the mid-to-late 1970s, after which it fell. Higher education subsequently started to see the impact of these declining birth rates. Even so, there were about 1·2 million full-time students in higher education in 1996–97, compared with a total of 456,800 in 1970–71. In 1996–97 a further 697,000 part-timers were in higher education and 2,435,000 students in further education. The proportion of young people entering higher education rose from one in eight to one in five by 1990. The Government's target had been for the total to rise to one in three by 2000. The autumn of 1993 saw a record entry which effectively met that target.

In December 1972 the Conservative Government published a White Paper setting out plans for the expansion of education over the following decade. More emphasis was to be placed on nursery schooling for the 3- and 4-year-olds: within 10 years it would be available to all children whose parents wanted them to attend. There would be a school building programme to replace old school buildings. Teacher training would be expanded to reduce pupil-teacher ratios further. Higher education would be expanded less rapidly than in the previous decade, and the emphasis would be placed on polytechnics and other non-university colleges. Unfortunately many of these plans were thwarted, largely as a result of cut-backs in total public expenditure. It was, however, generally recognised that education can be an economic investment for the future just as much as capital formation in, say, machinery or roads. There is a "private return" on "investment in education", which takes the form of higher earnings over the lifetime of the person educated; and there is a "social return" on public resources devoted to education being the greater contribution to the national product which trained and educated people can make. Although many of the 1972 White Paper plans were not implemented, both the 1974 Labour and 1979 Conservative Governments considered longer term policies for education. The key theme of a consultative White Paper in 1977 was the need to attune school curricula to the employment needs of school-leavers, and to encourage stronger ties between schools and industry. This has been a recurrent theme. Questions about longer term educational requirements were initially subsumed under the post-1979 Conservative Government by debate on the relative merits of private and public sector education. There was also a renewed emphasis on making the later years of school education more directly related to labour market requirements, represented, for example, by the increased involvement in the mid-1980s of the Manpower Services Commission, and later the Training Commission, in school programmes, such as the Technical and Vocational Education Initiative.

The Introduction of Markets into Education.

In 1985 in a White Paper entitled "The Development of Higher Education into the 1990s", the Government also considered ways of improving the contribution of higher education to economic performance. Thus the links between full-time education and job training are being intensified. The system of National Vocational Qualifications (and their school counterparts, GNVQs) is intended to unify academic and vocational credentials.

Such themes were continued in the Education Reform Act, passed in the 1988 Parliamentary session. It proposed the introduction of a National Curriculum, the establishment of City Technical Colleges and giving business greater representation on the new University Funding Council than it had had on the University Grants Committee. Many of the provisions of the 1988 Education Reform Act remain highly controversial, particularly those which relate to the National Curriculum and what is perceived to be over-rigid prescription of its content. Many commentators saw the Act as increasing central government's control over education—for example, LEAs lost control of the Colleges of Further Education and of the former Polytechnics, while schools could choose to opt out of Local Authority control in favour of administration by central government if a majority of parents and governors so desired. At the same time the Act emphasised the theme of intensified competition in the provision of education. Schools now had to compete for pupils and universities for funding. In schools this was known as the policy of "open enrolment". The theme of greater competition was also evident in the higher education sector, where the "binary divide" between universities and polytechnics was ended. All such establishments are now funded by the Higher Education Funding Council.

The Dearing Committee reported on the future of higher education in 1997. Amongst the matters it considered was the size of the university sector. The problem is that the number of graduates being produced is increasing faster than the number of traditional graduate jobs. The question has to be asked, therefore, as to how productively some of our graduates are being used; and whether resources might not, with social profit, be diverted to other elements of the education system. Unfortunately, Dearing failed to consider adequately this important issue. In 1998 the new Labour Government announced a new framework for the organisation of schools. Essentially this continues the theme of markets, but in part restores the position of LEAs.

Social Security.

In 1988 the Social Security system underwent considerable change and there have been further changes since then. In what follows we first describe the old system, before turning to the new.

There were two forms of social security: *National Insurance* and *Supplementary Benefits*. The former was non-means tested. They were designed to be exactly what the name indicated—insurance for when an individual met circumstances implying a loss of income, be that circumstance old age, unemployment or sickness. By contrast the latter were means tested, and were designed to keep people out of poverty. As such under the original Beveridge scheme, they were meant to be a safety net for the unfortunate few. The majority were to be covered by the insurance element. Formidable financing difficulties meant that this ideal was never achieved, and supplementary benefits attained an unwanted prominence in the British social security system.

(i) National Insurance.

Under this scheme employees received rights to unemployment benefit, sickness benefit, retirement pensions, widows' benefits, injury and disablement benefits, *etc*. Ten million pensioners receive National Insurance pensions. For those below pensionable age, the major national insurance benefit available was unemployment benefit. Weekly rates are laid down for each benefit, *e.g.* in October 1998 a rate of £50·35 was paid to a single person receiving Jobseeker's Allowance (the successor to unemployment benefit). The basic rate was increased according to the number of dependants. In 1966 an earnings-related supplement was introduced for unemployment benefits paid to persons between 18 and 65 (men) or 60 (women): the supplement being related to earnings in the previous tax year. The maximum total benefit, including increases for dependants, amounted to 85 per cent of earnings. This, together with tax rebates, meant a higher income out of work for a very few people. In 1982 the earnings-related unemployment supplement was withdrawn, whilst unemployment benefit became taxable.

By far the most important benefit was and is the retirement pension, paid as of right to contributors on retirement. Individuals may increase their rate of pension by staying on at work after the minimum retiring age of 65 for men and 60 for women. In October 1998 basic retirement pensions were £64·70 per week for single persons and £103·40 for a married couple. In accordance with European legislation, measures have been introduced to make the state pension age 65 for both men and women. The change will be phased in over ten years, starting from 2010.

Social Security benefits used to be up-dated in November each year, to account for inflation in the year to the previous May. Under the Government's social security reforms (*see* **G**36), in 1986 the uprating took place in July, and in subsequent years in April.

(ii) The Financing of National Insurance.

Many benefits are conditional upon the payment of National Insurance contributions which most of the adult population have to pay. For employees, both employer and employee pay a contribution. The self-employed also pay contributions of smaller size than the sum of the employer's and employee's contribution, but they were not entitled to unemployment benefit. As a result of the 1985 and 1989 Budgets, employers' and employees' national insurance contributions were cut for the lowest paid workers, in order to increase the incentives to work and to hire more labour. At the same time, while a maximum earnings limit for employees' contributions remains, the upper-earnings limit on employer's contributions has been abolished. In the 1989 Budget the structure of National Insurance payments was altered. Previously, the rate went from zero to more than 9 per cent once an individual hit the lower earnings limit. This meant that someone moving just above the lower limit for National Insurance contributions could face a marginal tax rate in excess of more than 100 per cent which was clearly a major disincentive. Although such traps have by no means been eradicated, National Insurance contributions are now charged at 2 per cent on earnings below the lower earnings limit once that limit has been reached, and thereafter at 10 per cent until the upper earnings limit. From April 1999 there will be further reforms. Individuals will no longer have to pay contributions on earnings below the lower limit, whilst the system for employer contributions will be much simplified and their liability to pay contributions at all for lower paid workers will be removed.

The National Insurance Scheme is an odd mixture of insurance and tax. The levels of contributions, when the scheme started in 1948, were fixed on the actuarial principle that contributions by or on behalf of an individual plus a specified State contribution should on average suffice to pay for the benefits to which he was entitled. But the scheme did not allow for inflation and a rising standard of living. In particular a succession of increases granted in the rate of pensions has put an end to this actuarial probity. Instead the principle became established that the rate of contributions in each year, together with a transfer from the Government, should equal the total benefits paid out in that year. Expenditure on non-contributory benefits is covered by general revenues.

(iii) Reform of Pensions.

There are about ten million pensioners in Britain. At least a quarter of these are kept out of poverty only by receiving income support and other benefits. Many of the remainder find their living standards considerably reduced from when they were working. This is because the existing state retirement pension is inadequate. There are some occupational pension schemes which offer a better income. Over 9 million people are now members of schemes. Many other individuals now also contribute to personal pensions. However, like personal savings, many of the schemes tend to have only limited safeguards against inflation unless they are index-linked. There are also often substantial losses involved in changing jobs.

A scheme for graduated pensions was introduced for employees in 1961. Under the scheme there were two kinds of employees—*ordinary* and *contracted-out*. In the case of contracted-out workers, their employer (on whom the decision whether to contract out rested) had to institute a private superannuation scheme that gave at least as favourable terms as the new State scheme, including the provision that rights under the scheme should be transferable up to the limits of the State scheme. Transferability was the guarantee that the individual did not lose his pension rights when he changed his job. In practise transferability was never really achieved.

In 1969 the Labour Government made proposals in a White Paper to replace the National Insurance Scheme by a new scheme of superannuation and social insurance, in which both contributions and benefits would be related to the earnings of the individual. It argued that the existing scheme failed to provide security in old age. The new earnings-related contributions would be mostly higher than contributions under the existing scheme, especially among higher earners; and in return higher pensions and other benefits would be paid.

An important feature of the proposed scheme was that benefits were to take into account both changes in prices and in general living standards. Thus, for instance, a contributor who received earnings equal to the national average throughout his working life would receive a pension calculated on the national average earnings at the time he reached pension age, not on the money he received over his working life. Some two-thirds of employed men were contracted-out, *i.e.*, in occupational pensions schemes, in 1970. The Government intended that these schemes should continue to exist together with the State scheme, and it proposed to allow for partial contracting out of the State scheme.

These plans lapsed with the change of Government in 1970. The Conservative Government announced its proposals for reform in a White Paper published in 1971. It considered that the costs of earnings-related benefits would be too great; instead it favoured earnings-related contributions for basically flat-rate pensions. In addition it wished to encourage contracting out, so that almost all employees would also be members of a private occupational pension scheme, in which pensions would be related to past contributions. The Government recognised that it would have to ensure that occupational pension rights were transferable between jobs. Like the previous Government, it envisaged a legal guarantee that State pensions would be revised every two years.

Meanwhile the Government had become aware of the need for a frequent adjustment of pension rates in an era of high inflation. In early 1975 the full pension entitlement was £10 for a single person and £16 for a married couple. In October 1998 the rates stood at £64·70 for a single person and £103·40 for a married couple. The difficulty of funding an adequate state pension when the number of pensioners is rising relative to the size of the workforce has led to a withdrawal from the goals for pensions laid down in the 1970s. These goals were for a two-tier pension. The bottom tier was a common flat-rate for everyone. The top tier was earnings-related—that is, a fixed proportion of the pensioner's previous earnings. Because of the flat-rate element, a low earner would be able to expect a pension which was a higher percentage of his working income than that obtained by a higher earner. Contributions to the scheme would be earnings related. The pensions would be fully protected against inflation, and women would enter the scheme on the same footing as men. There was an obvious emphasis on the need to protect women from poverty in retirement, after the death of the husband. There would be a maximum pension entitlement and a maximum contribution. For this reason among others, the Government planned to encourage new and improved occupational schemes, to exist alongside the state scheme. It was hoped that the scheme would come to full maturity by 1998, this long delay reflecting the formidable difficulties in financing the plan. In the meantime fully earnings-related contributions started in 1975, and minor earnings-related benefit in 1979. These replaced flat-rate National Insurance payments and graduated pension contributions. In the event, funding problems meant that the earnings-related component had less impact than originally intended.

A renewed concern in the early 1980s was with a particular aspect of occupational pensions—their transferability from job to job. Someone who left an occupational scheme had the choice of either leaving his pension rights at his old employer, and receiving a deferred pension at retirement age, usually unadjusted for inflation between his departure and retirement; or, if his old and new employers both agreed, transferring the fund, from which effectively the pension is paid, to his new employer, usually at great loss to himself. Government has attempted to introduce the full transferability of pension rights from job to job—at least for those who have been with an employer for more than two years. In changes introduced in 1988, employees were given the right to opt out of SERPS or of an employer's own scheme, and set up their own priv-

ate pension plan. At the same time, a worker who left for another job after 2 years (instead as previously after 5 years) would be able to preserve his pension rights (with some protection for inflation) or have them transferred to a new scheme if the scheme was willing to accept them. Over 8 million people have now taken out personal pensions. The Social Security Act of 1990 contained provisions specifically designed to improve protection for occupational and personal pension schemes, including the appointment of a Pensions Ombudsman. The Social Security Act of 1993 introduced a 1 per cent additional rebate for personal pension holders aged 30 and over, and provided for a Treasury grant to be paid into the National Insurance Fund.

The advantage to the government of a shift into private pension schemes is that it will reduce the impact of demographic change, namely the cost of supporting a larger retired population relative to that of working age. Both private and state schemes are now operating on a fully funded basis *i.e.* the individual pays for his or her future pension entitlement, which contrasts with the "pay as you go" system in operation in many countries where pension payments are funded by current contributions.

Intense concern has started to be expressed about whether the State can continue to maintain the present pension system. The essential problem increasingly was seen to be the non-means tested component. Many commentators were starting to argue that eventually the bulk of pension payments would have to be means-tested.

(iv) Poverty in Britain.

Despite the existence of National Insurance there are many people in Britain whose income falls below that which the Government regarded as adequate. These people are supported from Government revenues by means of *income support*, formerly *supplementary benefits*, and before 1966 known as *National Assistance*. It was a fault of the National Insurance Scheme that so many have required this assistance. In 1998 about 1·5 million pensioners received income support, with many more getting extra help with rent. Of families whose head was in work, 831,000 received Family Credit, whilst well over half of the unemployed were wholly dependent on additional state support. A Treasury Report, published in 1999, concluded that 12 million people in the UK were in poverty.

Until recently anyone who was out of work for more than a year lost entitlement to unemployment benefit and became reliant on supplementary payments through what was the supplementary benefit system and is now income support (*see* (v) *below*). From 1996 all unemployed benefit recipients were transferred a single benefit (the Jobseeker's Allowance), regardless of duration of unemployment. A major fault with the earlier supplementary benefits scheme was that they could not be paid to those in employment whose earnings were below the benefit level, and if such persons became unemployed they could claim benefits only up to their normal earnings level. The *Family Income Supplement* was introduced in 1971 to alleviate hardship amongst low earners, but it has been estimated that only half of those eligible claimed F.I.S. The take-up of the new Family Credit payment was initially even lower.

(v) The Reform of Social Security.

In 1985 the Government issued a White Paper detailing reforms of the whole social security system. The basis of dissatisfaction was three-fold. First, the system was a complex and costly one to run. Second, it worked in such a way as to help some who, on official definitions of poverty, did not need assistance; whilst, conversely, it failed to provide it for some who did. Third, it created unemployment benefit traps, supplementary benefit traps and poverty traps. These imply that people who are unemployed or employed on low pay might be deterred from taking employment or taking jobs with higher pay, because the combined effects of the tax and benefit system mean that the consequential increase in their net income is negligible. Behind their proposed reforms was the concern about future financing difficulties, and a wish to make the system simpler. The main elements of the new system were introduced in April 1988.

On pensions, it was originally proposed to retain basic pensions, but to abolish earnings related pensions (SERPS). Instead, greater stress was to be placed on occupational pension schemes. Substantial political pressures caused a change of mind, and SERPS was retained, albeit in a modified form (see (iii) on **G36**). Universal child benefit was retained. But for low earnings families, FIS was replaced by *Family Credit*, paid through the pay packet. As compared to FIS it allows a smoother tapering of payments as original income increases. For those not in work, supplementary benefits were replaced by "*income support*", which is intended to be simpler and to involve a smaller range of payments. Benefits were at a lower rate for the under-25s and at a higher rate for pensioners. An additional sum is paid for each dependent child, as it is for single parents and the long-term sick and disabled. Beyond these, there are no additional payments. There was also a new simplified scheme for housing benefits. Unemployment benefit, the maternity allowance (in revised form) and sickness benefit survived the 1988 review, but maternity and death grants were abolished. Substantial changes were made in provisions for widowhood.

The Government's catchphrase for these reforms was "the twin pillars": state help combined with encouragement for private provision. Returning to the three major complaints about the previous system, certainly the revised one was cheaper to administer. It probably directed the benefits more accurately. It may also have alleviated the worst traps, but in substantially improving the lot of some in this respect, it worsened it for more. Indeed, the scheme was not a major departure, and fell far short of more radical proposals for a combined tax and benefit credit system.

In 1996 benefits for the unemployed were replaced by the Jobseekers' Allowance. In the previous year Invalidity Benefit and Sickness Benefit were replaced by the much more strictly tested Incapacity Benefit. In October 1999, Family Credit will be replaced by the Working Families' Tax Credit, which will provide more generous work incentives.

Public Revenue.

In the table we show government revenue and expenditure. No less than 40 per cent of the total public revenue in 1997 came from social security contributions and taxes on income and wealth. Taxes on expenditure accounted for rather less of the total. Two commodities in particular were heavily taxed: alcoholic drink and tobacco. These commodities are singled out partly for social reasons and partly because—in economists' jargon—the demand for them is *inelastic*; *i.e.*, the public reduces its consumption of drink and tobacco only slightly in response to a rise in their price. Indirect taxation—taking the form of excise duties and purchase taxes (value added tax after 1973)—used to be spread very unevenly over different sorts of expenditure. The introduction of Value Added Tax in 1973 tended to even out the incidence of indirect taxes on different goods and services, though tobacco, drink and motoring continued to be hit.

Until 1989 in Scotland, and 1990 in England and Wales, the major method of collecting local taxes was through rates. A rateable value was assessed for each commercial or domestic property, corresponding roughly to its size, imputed rental value, and amenities. Each year, the appropriate local authority decided at what rate in the pound to tax this rateable value. On the dates mentioned above, the government substantially altered the local tax system in an ostensible effort to broaden the tax base for the domestic element. Instead of local taxes being paid on the basis of property ownership, each adult paid a flat rate charge or poll tax. Although some minor adjustment was made for personal circumstances, the tax was highly regressive and its introduction was very controversial. Part but not all of the objections related to the government's under-estimate of the burden of local government revenue which could fall on the personal sector. Local authorities were no longer allowed to levy rates on the business sector—these were charged uniformly by central government and the proceeds were then distributed to local authorities on some notional calculation of need. The large burden of local authority taxation falling on persons, particularly in previously low-rated areas, was tackled by an increasingly bureaucratic system of rebates. The first year of the poll tax in England and Wales merely served to demonstrate its unpopularity and its inefficiency in high collection costs. In order to defray the political consequences of the poll tax, the March 1991 Budget included a provision to reduce poll tax bills in 1991–92 and beyond, financed by a rise in the VAT rate from 15% to 17·5%. Even this failed to overcome objections to a tax which created far more losers than gainers, and in April 1991 the government announced plans to revert to a property-based system of local taxation, retaining only vestigial elements of the poll tax principle that all should contribute something to the cost of local services. The Government proposed that the new "Council Tax" would be a property tax banded according to the size of dwelling, thus reintroducing an element of progressivity. The Council Tax came into existence in 1993–94.

The Budget.

Each year the Chancellor of the Exchequer announces his Budget for the coming fiscal year. The most important and most difficult task in drawing up the Budget is to decide on the size of deficit to aim for. The deficit is the excess of public expenditure over public revenue; and it has to be financed by borrowing or by printing money. A large deficit is normally reflationary; sometimes that may be required to get the economy out of recession. A small deficit—and even more, a surplus—is deflationary, and is a means of holding a demand-pull inflation in check.

In 1970 there was a small surplus, and thus the net borrowing requirement was negative. After that the borrowing requirement became large and positive, peaking in the recessionary years 1979–82. In the 1980s more favourable economic circumstances and the one-off receipts from major privatisations enabled the public sector accounts to swing into surplus. In 1988 this surplus or Public

PUBLIC REVENUE AND EXPENDITURE

	1995	1996	1997
EXPENDITURE			
Current	284,307	295,359	302,173
Capital	22,246	17,692	15,695
Financial	−2,529	−7,650	−2,397
Total	304,024	305,401	315,471
RECEIPTS			
Operating Surplus	10,901	11,656	12,195
Taxes on production	94,010	100,653	109,987
Taxes on income and wealth	106,982	112,087	121,636
Taxes on capital	1,441	1,637	1,687
National insurance	44,371	46,400	50,657
Property income	7,172	7,280	6,611
Miscellaneous	469	429	428
Total	265,346	280,142	303,201
Deficit	38,678	25,259	12,270

Sector Debt Repayment (PSDR) was £12·4 billion (about 3 per cent of GDP) but it then fell to £9·6 billion in 1989 and only £1·9 billion in 1990. By 1991 the public finances had once again deteriorated markedly and were in deficit by some £8·8 billion. The reason for the elimination of the PSDR was a combination of much slower economic growth, difficulties with the privatisation programme, and a significant increase in government expenditure. The last of these was largely due to much higher public sector pay awards. A surplus is not itself indicative of a very tight fiscal policy, any more than a deficit automatically implies an expansionary stance. To assess the true fiscal stance, one must adjust the surplus/deficit for the effects of inflation, privatisation receipts, and the stage of the economic cycle, *i.e.* the level of unemployment. Therefore it was particularly worrying that from 1991 the PSBR continued to increase, to £30bn in 1992 and £43bn in 1993, despite the recovery in the domestic economy. Thereafter it started to fall back, initially slowly and then more rapidly to stand at £10bn in 1998.

The calculation of the precise deficit or surplus needed is a chancy business; for the level that is required depends on the amount of sav-ing and on the amount of spending out of credit that people intend to do—and this is not easily predictable. It also depends on the change in the foreign balance. Nor can the Chancellor be sure his figures are right: estimating next year's revenue, and even next year's expenditure by the Government is difficult enough, but he needs to estimate also the likely trends of private income and expenditure, without really reliable information as to what they were in the past year. This has been particularly evident in recent years, when official economic statistics have been subject to massive error and subsequent re-vision, and the Chancellor's Budget forecasts for the year ahead have proved wildly inaccurate. One good example is provided by his 1988 Budget fore-cast for the balance of payments. In March 1988 the official forecast for the current account deficit in the year ahead was £4 billion—in the event the deficit was almost four times larger.

Advance Cash Limits.

The introduction of advance *cash limits* on a large proportion of expenditure in 1976 was meant to give the Government greater control over projected spending. Prior to that the general rule had been to estimate public expenditure for the following year on the basis of its volume. If inflation was higher than predicted, then the tendency was to preserve volume by increasing the value of expenditure. Cash limits altered this, and in 1982 cash planning institutionalised this change. A large proportion of government spending was fixed in value terms, and if inflation exceeded the predicted rate, then volume suffered. From 1993 there was a major change in budgetary arrangements. For many years spending plans had been announced in the Autumn, and full budget proposals and tax changes the following Spring. From 1993 there was a unified Budget.

In spite of such problems, fiscal policy—running large deficits when economic activity is low, and small ones or surpluses when it seems to be excessively high—is the most important action through which the economy can be kept on an even keel. Monetary policy may help; but the Budget decision of the Chancellor on changes in taxation and public expenditure is the key one. Indeed, it can be argued that the role of fiscal policy was enhanced by membership of the EMS Exchange Rate Mechanism (ERM). Even after withdrawal from ERM, the level of interest rates is now largely determined by the need to preserve sterling's value on the foreign exchanges, meaning that the only domestic policy tool over which the government has any direct control is the fiscal stance.

6. SOURCES OF STATISTICS: SOME SUGGESTIONS FOR FURTHER READING

The non-specialist will find that most of the sta-tistics he needs are given in the *Annual Abstract of Statistics*, published every year by The Stationery Office. This comprehensive document includes figures on population, social conditions, education, labour, production, trade and balance of payments, national income and expenditure, wages and prices, and many other topics. For more up-to- date infor-mation, reference should be made to the *Monthly Digest of Statistics* which has a similar coverage and gives month-by-month figures. A selection of the more important series, presented in a manner which can more easily be understood by the layman, is given in another Stationery Office publication, *Economic Trends*, also issued monthly.

Fuller information on labour problems is given in *Labour Market Trends* (incorporating the *Depart-ment of Employment Gazette*) and on financial matters in the *Bank of England Quarterly Bulletin*. These two periodicals include discussions on the statistics presented. *Social Trends* contains articles and detailed statistics on social, cultural and economic conditions in Britain. A sourcebook on the EU is *Basic Statistics of the Community*, annual (Eurostat).

For an analysis of developments in the economy see the *National Institute Economic Review*, a private publication issued by the National Institute for Economic and Social Research. The quarterly *Oxford Review of Economic Policy* (Oxford Univer-sity Press) contains up-to-date articles on aspects of the economy.

For a comprehensive and systematic introduc-tion to the British economy the reader is referred to Peter Curwen, *Understanding the UK Economy* (Macmillan). Other introductory texts include N.F.R. Crafts and N. Woodward, *The British Economy since 1945* (Oxford), Tony Buxton et al., *Britain's Economic Performance* (Routledge), and D. Morris (ed), *The Economic System in the UK* (Oxford).

Interesting books on particular topics include J. Vickers et al., *Regulatory Reform* (MIT), N. Crafts and G. Toniolo, *Economic Growth in Europe since 1945* (Cambridge). and A. B. Atkinson, *The Economics of Inequality* (Oxford).

III. THE LESS DEVELOPED ECONOMIES

Income Levels.

Two-thirds of the world's population live in dire poverty—a poverty which can scarcely be imagined by those accustomed to the standards of living attained in the relatively few developed countries of the world. The orders of world in-equality may be seen from the table comparing annual gross national products per capita by region, converted into pounds sterling at official exchange rates. These figures are only very approximate be-cause exchange rates are misleading indicators of purchasing power and because the averages conceal considerable income inequalities within some re-gions and countries. Nevertheless, it is clear that poverty is widespread in the world. The alleviation of this poverty is widely recognised as the most important economic—and indeed political—task for

the world community. The 50 low-income devel-oping countries referred to in the table have average income per capita of £250 per annum, and contain 3,180 million people; over 2,400 million in 9 Asian countries and 440 million in 27 African countries.

According to a World Bank estimate, a third of the population of all developing countries in 1980 had a calorie intake below 90 per cent of the requirement laid down by the Food and Agricul-tural Organisation and the World Health Organisa-tion; this meant that they did not get enough calories for an active working life. A sixth (340 million) had a calorie intake below 80 per cent: they did not get enough calories to prevent stunted growth and serious health risks. The areas particularly affected were South Asia and sub-Saharan Africa.

What is a Less Developed Country?

There are no less than 140 countries comprising the so-called "Third World," known variously as "less developed" or "developing" or "poor" countries. There is a great diversity among them, and yet they have a number of features in common. Foremost is their poverty, but even poverty is not universal: some of the oil-producing countries such as Saudi Arabia, Kuwait and Libya have achieved very high levels of income per capita while retaining many of the other characteristics of less developed countries.

GROSS NATIONAL PRODUCT PER CAPITA
BY GROUPS OF COUNTRY AND SELECTED
COUNTRIES, 1997

	(£ p.a.)
Low-income developing countries	213
of which: Bangladesh	130
India	238
Sri Lanka	488
Tanzania	128
China	524
Middle-income developing countries	1,152
of which: Turkey	1,909
Thailand	1,707
Brazil	2,878
Mexico	2,244
Industrialised countries	15,671
of which: Spain	8,848
UK	12,628
Germany	17,232
USA	17,524
Japan	23,079

Most of the developing countries are primarily agricultural economies, with the bulk of the population engaged in *subsistence agriculture*. For many millions of peasant farmers the primary objective is to produce enough food for their family to subsist. India is a classic example, with no less than 64 per cent of its 900 million people dependent on agriculture for a living. Most less developed countries have only a small industrial sector as yet: it is rare for the output of the manufacturing sector to exceed 25 per cent of the gross domestic product. The main exceptions to this rule are the successful exporters of labour-intensive manufacturing goods, such as Hong Kong, Singapore, Taiwan and South Korea. Many of the less developed countries lack the necessary ingredients for successful industrialisation—capital, skills and entrepreneurship.

The developing countries vary enormously in size—from the teeming masses of India and China to scores of countries with less than a million people. The development problems and possibilities facing large and small countries are very different. The small size of most developing economies forces them to concentrate on the production of one or two primary products for world markets. Their high degree of specialisation and heavy dependence on exports and imports makes these economies dangerously vulnerable to the vagaries of world trade and the world economy.

Apart from their poverty, the less developed countries have other economic characteristics and problems in common. However, it is dangerous to generalise because there are also important differences. In particular, they vary in their degree of development and in their potential for development. A semi-industrialised, urbanised country such as Argentina has little in common with an utterly backward country such as Chad, and the economic prospects for an oil-rich country such as Venezuela are far brighter than for a country with few natural resources such as Tanzania.

Population Growth.

Many developing countries are experiencing an unprecedented population explosion: annual rates of increase of between 2 and 3 per cent—which double population in as little as 35 and 24 years

respectively—are experienced. This is a phenomenon of the last five decades. Death rates have fallen sharply in response to improved health services and modern methods of control, *e.g.*, immunization programmes and the eradication of malaria through DDT spraying. On the other hand, birth rates have been kept up by such factors as tradition, social prestige, religion, the need for security in old age, and a lack of facilities for family planning.

The table (**G40**) indicates that over half the world's population lives in Asia, and that the developed regions account for under a quarter of the total. Apart from Australasia (into which immigration is high) the developed countries show slower rates of population growth than Africa, Latin America and Asia. The figures of population density may easily be misleading, since they take no account of the nature of the area, *e.g.*, deserts are included. But it is clear that Asia is more densely populated than Africa or Latin America.

Life Expectancy.

Although death rates have fallen in the developing countries, especially infant mortality, life expectancy is generally low in the poorest countries. Thus, for instance, the expectation of life at birth in 1994 was below 50 years in many countries of Africa, including Malawi, Ethiopia, Niger and Sierra Leone, and some in Asia, including Afghanistan and Bhutan. Life in these countries is all too short.

Life expectancy is related to income per head. In most of the developed countries life expectancy at birth is about 77 years, being 76 in the United Kingdom, Germany and the United States and 79 in Japan in 1994. However, the average length of life depends also on the quantity and quality of medical provision and the degree of income inequality about the mean: life expectancy reached 70 years in some of the poorest countries, including China and Sri Lanka. Life expectancy is an important but neglected indicator of the "quality of life".

The Population Problem.

In many developing countries there is population pressure on the land, and many people want more land for farming. Population density is a hindrance in agricultural economies, but not necessarily in industrial economies: because it is industrialised and has accumulated much capital, Western Europe can support at a high standard of living a population more concentrated even than that of Asia.

As a result of rapid population growth the pressure of population on the land has increased. The consequences have been far more serious in countries such as Bangladesh (with a population density of 818 people per square kilometre in 1994) or India (279 per sq km) than in Zambia (12 per sq km) or Brazil (18 per sq km). In those countries with abundant land the expanding population can spread into unused areas; but as land becomes increasingly scarce, less and less productive land must be brought into cultivation and soil erosion and loss of fertility become major problems. A substantial increase in output is required to prevent a fall in per capita income as population grows, and an even greater increase is required if living standards are to be improved. Between 1979–81 and 1994–96 food production in the developing countries as a group increased by 69 per cent and per capita food production rose by 28 per cent.

Even in those countries with plenty of land a rapid increase in population can have harmful effects. For instance, it diverts scarce investment resources away from directly productive investments such as factories and irrigation projects so as to meet the needs of the expanding population for more schools, hospitals, housing, cities and other public services.

Family Planning Programmes.

In many African and the poorer Latin American countries the rate of population growth appears to be constant, but in the more developed parts of Latin America and much of Asia there are signs that the growth rate has peaked and is now declining. The annual rate of growth of population in the early 1990s averaged 2·4 per cent in the low-income developing countries (excluding India and China) and 1·4 per cent in the middle-income developing countries; it was as high as 2·6 per cent in sub-Saharan Africa.

The different experiences may reflect differences in government policies: in 1980 a quarter of less developed countries had no official family planning programme. The success stories include India, where in about 1990, 43 per cent of married women used contraceptives and the birth rate fell from 3·9 to 2·9 per cent per annum between 1970 and 1993, China (83 per cent contraceptive use and a fall from 3·3 to 1·9 per cent) Colombia (66 per cent contraceptive use and a fall from 3·6 to 2·4 per cent) and South Korea (77 per cent contraceptive use and a fall from 3·0 to 1·6 per cent).

The successful cases show what can be done, but private incentives and attitudes still favour large families in many poor societies: simply providing facilities for family planning may not be enough. In Pakistan, for instance, contraceptive use was only 14 per cent and the birth rate, which had barely fallen over the 23 years, was still over 4·0 per cent.

Problems of Agriculture.

There are many millions of peasant farmers throughout the Third World eking out a subsistence from the soil. The margin between what can be produced and what is required to support life is narrow: the failure of crops because of drought, floods or pests can lead to famine unless food is quickly supplied from outside the area affected.

Agricultural production may be held back by a shortage of land, or by the use of primitive tools and methods of cultivation (which may in turn be due to a lack of farming knowledge and skills or to a lack of funds for investment in land improvement or equipment), or by an unjust system of land tenure which deprives the farmer of incentive to raise production. Perhaps all these problems must be tackled simultaneously.

The Green Revolution.

A technology is being introduced which can increase the yields from foodgrains by 50 per cent or more in tropical areas. This new technology is commonly thought to have caused a *green revolution*. It consists of new high-yielding seeds, largely for wheat and rice. Not only are the yields per acre higher but also shorter cropping cycles permit multiple cropping. The new technology economises on land and, being labour-intensive, provides more farm employment. The introduction of high-yielding cereals is important in the emergence of India and Pakistan into the ranks of solid economic achievers.

However, we cannot assume that it is going to solve the problem of foodgrain shortage in the poorer countries. As yet, the new seeds are less resistant to drought, floods and disease. To be effective, they require substantial inputs of fertiliser and of water; in many areas expensive irrigation is important to their success. Moreover, the fact that fertiliser and water are complementary inputs has meant that the green revolution has caught on—and been encouraged by governments—among the larger, more prosperous farmers in the better-

watered, more prosperous regions. This is true of, *e.g.*, Mexico, Pakistan and the Philippines. Unless governments ensure that the benefits of the green revolution are widely spread, the net effect might even be to harm small peasant farmers by increasing the competition from large farmers.

Land Reform.

There are many forms of land tenure in less developed countries. In black Africa communal or tribal ownership of land is common, with members of the community or tribe receiving rights to use the land individually. In parts of Asia and Latin America, there is private ownership of land, which—particularly where the land is densely populated—has often led to great inequality of land ownership. In some cases land tenure is characterised by absentee landlords and share-cropping tenants. The development of large estates produces a class of landless labourers.

The need for land reform varies according to the circumstances. In most cases the main argument is for greater social justice. In some cases it may be possible also to expand production by redistributing land more evenly or by giving land to share-cropping tenants and so improving their incentives. On the other hand, large farmers may have access to technology, skills and capital which small farmers lack: there is a danger that greater equity will be achieved only at the expense of efficiency. Hence the need to ensure that land reform is accompanied by a package of measures, *e.g.*, education, training and advice, and credit for fertiliser, tools and land improvements. Few governments have succeeded in implementing serious land reform programmes. The main reason is that the system of land tenure in a country often reflects the balance of political power: land reform invariably faces political opposition from entrenched interests. By the same token, a successful land reform may alter the balance of political power so as to facilitate broad-based development.

Exports of Primary Products.

Most developing countries export primary products (foodstuffs, industrial raw materials or minerals) and import manufactured goods, especially the capital goods (plant, machinery and vehicles) required for development. This international division of labour has operated to the disadvantage of the developing countries in recent decades. The world demand for their primary products has increased only slowly. This is because people spend just a small part of their additional income on food (*e.g.*, tea, coffee, cocoa), because synthetic substitutes have been developed for many raw materials (*e.g.*, rubber, cotton, jute), because developed countries protect their own agriculture (*e.g.*, sugar) and because demand in the developed countries has moved towards commodities with low raw material content (*e.g.*, from heavy industries to services).

In consequence, the general trend has been for the prices of primary products to fall in relation to those of manufactured goods. Oil is a special case (*see* **G50**). The terms of trade of the developing countries worsened by 16 per cent between 1985 and 1995 (*see* **G6**). Unsatisfactory prices of primary commodities have contributed to the shortage of foreign exchange which restricts investment expenditure in many poor countries.

Economic Instability.

The prices of various primary products tend to fluctuate violently from one year to another. Many developing economies depend heavily on the exports of one or two commodities. For instance, coffee is the most important product in Brazil, cotton in Egypt, copper in Zambia, sugar in Cuba, cocoa in Ghana, tin in Bolivia and diamonds in Botswana. Fluctuations in the world price of its main export cause instability in the export revenues of a country, and this in turn can produce fluctuations in income throughout its domestic economy.

Even the oil-producing developing countries, whose problems are in many ways quite different, have faced problems of economic instability. The governments of these countries have had to decide how best to use their oil revenues to promote economic and social development without overturning their societies. The political events in Iran

POPULATION SIZE, GROWTH AND
DENSITY BY REGION

	Population 1994 (m)	Growth rate 1990–95 (% p.a.)	Density 1994 (per sq km)
North America	290	1·0	13
Europe	726	0·2	32
Oceania	28	1·5	3
Africa	708	2·8	23
Latin America	474	1·8	23
Asia	3,403	1·6	107
of which:			
India	919	2·4	279
China	1,209	1·1	126
World Total	5,530	1·6	42

during the 1980s were closely related to the economic boom which oil produced.

Problems of Industrialisation.

In those underdeveloped countries where there is population pressure on the land, alternative employment has to be created in industry or services. Even in countries with a surplus of land, if there is heavy dependence on one or two primary products, industrialisation provides a means of diversifying the economy.

But industrialisation is not an easy course. Because the margin between agricultural production and food consumption is narrow, the surplus from the agricultural sector exchangeable for the products of other sectors e.g., industry and services—is small; i.e., the demand for the goods and services produced by other sectors is low. A second constraint on industrialisation is imposed by competition from abroad; new industries in an unindustrialised country have to compete with established industries in industrial countries, which have the advantage of experience, a trained labour force and markets big enough for them to reap all the potential economies of large-scale production.

Industrialisation Strategies.

One means of overcoming the small size of market is to export manufactures to the developed countries. Developing countries with cheap labour are likely to have a comparative advantage in the manufacture of relatively labour-intensive commodities. A number of less developed countries have had remarkable success in following this strategy. Among their successful activities are textiles, clothing and labour-intensive components of electronic equipment.

A means of overcoming competition from the industries of the developed countries is by nurturing an infant industrial sector behind tariff walls—which is how the United States and Germany developed their industries in the face of British competition in the nineteenth century. A number of developing countries have adopted this strategy. However, it has its drawbacks. Sometimes the "infants" never grow up, and vested interests press for continued protection. Import-substituted industrialisation often means that raw materials or semi-processed goods are imported for local production. There is a danger that fluctuations in export proceeds will periodically curtail imports of necessary intermediate goods. The under-utilisation of capital in the manufacturing sector because of foreign exchange shortages has frequently occurred in countries such as India, Pakistan, Tanzania and Ghana.

The Newly Industrialising Countries.

The remarkable success of a handful of developing countries—the *newly industrialising countries* (NICs)—in exporting manufactured goods raises the questions: why were they successful, and can others do the same?

South Korea is perhaps the most successful of the NICs. After a period in which government pursued a policy of industrialisation through import substitution, the policy was changed in the 1960s to one of promoting exports of labour intensive manufactures. This was achieved by devaluing the currency in order to encourage export industries in which the country would have a comparative advantage, and liberalising imports to discourage inefficient industrial production. In 1962 South Korea exported manufactures worth $10 million; in 1990 their value was $64,000 million. Between 1962 and 1990 the proportion of the labour force employed in industry rose from 10 to 30 per cent, manufacturing production rose by 17 per cent per annum, and GNP per capita rose by 7 per cent per annum. The labour-intensive nature of industrialisation, as well as its speed, helped to alleviate poverty through the market: first employment and later, as labour became scarce, also real wages rose rapidly.

South Korea benefited from its trading relationships with Japan and its close ties with the United States in finding markets for its products. It has a well educated labour force: 87 per cent of the relevant age group in 1990 were enrolled in secondary school, which is higher than any other developing country. Industrialisation may also have benefited from stable autocratic government and a beleaguered sense of national purpose. In part the Korean success represents the harnessing of cheap labour in almost free trade conditions for exporters. However, the government also played an active role, e.g. it both generated high savings and successfully directed savings into the favoured sectors. It will take much more than policies of *laissez faire* for other developing countries to be able to emulate South Korea. In 1997 financial crisis brought an abrupt halt to Korean economic success (see **G**46(2)).

The most successful NICs—known as the "Gang of Four"—are Hong Kong, South Korea, Taiwan and Singapore. As a group they exported manufactures equal to 8 per cent of world exports of manufactures in 1990.

Outward-Oriented Industrialisation Policies.

The success of the NICs has led many policy advisers to press for more outward-oriented industrialisation policies. The policy advice is gradually to dismantle the system of protection of import-substituting industries and to devalue the currency in order to provide incentives to export manufactures. It is argued that competition in world markets will act as a spur to domestic efficiency and help to divorce economic activities from domestic political processes.

The traditional view has been that few developing countries could succeed in breaking into world markets for manufactures. However, potential access to the markets of industrialised countries is far better than it used to be, and broadly-based progress has been made. In 1970 manufactures accounted for 27 per cent of the exports of the developing countries, but in 1992 for 52 per cent. If the NICs constitute the "first division", a "second division" of countries has expanded manufacturing exports rapidly, including India, China, Pakistan, Thailand, Turkey, Malaysia, Colombia, Brazil and Mexico. In 1992 manufacturing accounted for 39 per cent of the exports of low-income developing countries (excluding China and India), for over two-thirds in the case of China and India, and for 49 per cent of the total in the case of the middle-income developing countries.

Unemployment and Underemployment.

Unemployment and underemployment occur on a very considerable scale in both the rural and the urban areas of developing countries. Consider first the rural case. Because farm work is normally shared, underemployment—disguised unemployment—is more common than open unemployment. People work for only a part of the day or year. Where land is scarce, underemployment is chronic: people would like to work more if only they had more land. Unless the yield from the land can be raised, growth in population causes greater underemployment and reduces income per head on the land. Where land is abundant, underemployment is a seasonal phenomenon. People are fully employed in the busy season—harvesting and planting—but underemployed at other times of the year.

In the towns open unemployment is common with people queueing for *modern sector* jobs at the job centres and at the factory gates. Rates of urban open unemployment well in excess of 10 per cent are frequently recorded, e.g., in Ghana, Colombia, Zimbabwe, Trinidad, South Africa and the Philippines. Few developing countries can afford unemployment benefits, so that job-seekers remain openly unemployed only until their savings are used up or support by their relations is withdrawn. Then they have to scrape out a subsistence in the urban *informal sector* while waiting and hoping for something better. Underemployment is rife in the easily entered traditional sector activities such as petty trading, hawking, beer brewing, fetching and carrying. A shoeshiner may be on the streets for ten hours a day but have only a couple of customers. The more people enter these activities, the further average income per worker is depressed. In many less developed countries this self-employment in the traditional sector accounts for the majority of urban workers.

Migration to the Cities.

Urbanisation is proceeding at an unprecedented pace in much of the Third World. Over the decade 1970–80 the total urban population of the developing countries as a whole grew by 50 per cent and over the period 1980–90 by 50 per cent again. The table illustrates the pace of urbanisation in a number of developing countries.

URBAN POPULATION AS A PERCENTAGE
OF TOTAL POPULATION IN SELECTED
DEVELOPING COUNTRIES, 1980 AND 1995

	1980	1995
50 low-income developing countries	21	29
of which: Ethiopia	11	13
Uganda	9	12
Kenya	16	28
Nigeria	27	39
India	23	27
China	19	30
Zimbabwe	22	32
58 middle-income developing countries	52	60
of which: Philippines	38	53
Colombia	64	73
Turkey	44	70
Brazil	66	78
Malaysia	42	54
South Korea	57	81
Saudi Arabia	67	79
24 high-income countries	75	75

Rural people are often drawn to the cities at a rate well in excess of the capacity of the cities to absorb them productively. The reason for this migration might be economic or social. The economic explanation runs in terms of an income differential between the urban and the rural areas. Relatively unskilled wages in the modern sector of the economy—often governed by minimum wage legislation or trade union bargaining—can be well above the incomes to be derived from peasant agriculture. People go to the town in search of modern sector wage jobs, although they may actually end up underemployed in the low-income traditional sector. Rural-urban migration may be a social phenomenon: rural people are attracted by the facilities and "bright lights" of the cities. The recent expansion of education in many countries may also play a part, since a high proportion of the migrants are school leavers.

Whatever the reasons, the consequences are socially harmful and politically explosive. Shanty towns and slums proliferate in the cities and their outskirts; poverty, disease and crime flourish.

In 1950 there were only two urban agglomerations in the world with more than 10 million inhabitants, New York and London. On present trends, there will by the year 2000 be 25 such cities, of which 20 will be in the third world and the largest will be Mexico City with a forecast population of 31 million.

Employment Creation.

In many developing countries, the objective of creating productive employment has received growing priority. For various reasons the growth of modern sector employment has been tardy and has lagged behind the growth of output. One reason is that the modern sector normally uses capital equipment and technology which is imported from the developed countries. This means that, even in countries with cheap and abundant labour, the most profitable techniques of production are often capital-intensive, so that the amount of scarce investment funds required to equip a worker is high.

There is some danger that the establishment of capital-intensive factories may actually harm existing labour-intensive production. For instance, sandals can be made by small cobblers using local leather (or old car tyres) or by a large plant using imported plastic materials: a new factory employing a few machine operators might displace many more traditional craftsmen who have no alternative employment opportunities.

Governments, by encouraging or discouraging particular forms and areas of investment, have the power to influence the growth of employment. In the rural areas the encouragment and organisation of labour-intensive developmental or community projects can assist in harnessing the one abundant resource which almost all developing countries possess: unskilled labour.

Educated Labour.

Many developing countries are faced with the dual problem of unskilled labour surpluses and scarcities of skilled and educated labour. The problem is particularly acute in some of the previously colonised countries of Africa. To give an extreme example: at the time of its independence in 1964, Zambia had only 100 Zambian university graduates and 1,200 secondary school graduates in a population of 3·5 million. In such countries the great shortage of educated and skilled people enabled them to earn high incomes— with the result that there was a very unequal distribution of income. And even in countries where surpluses have developed, the existence of an international market for professional people such as doctors and engineers helps to keep up their earnings: these countries suffer from a "brain drain" to the developed world.

Economic development is not just a matter of physical capital accumulation: it requires also an increase in *human capital, i.e.* in skilled and educated labour. Not only more knowledge but also new habits and attitudes—*e.g.*, attitudes towards risk-taking, hard work and thrift. Education—of the right sort and with suitable content—is generally acknowledged to be important for development, although the benefits of education cannot be quantified at all precisely.

Educational Policy.

The table shows enrolment ratios (the percentage of children in the relevant age-group who are enrolled in education) at the primary, secondary and higher educational levels for selected developing countries in 1993. There is a strong tendency for enrolment ratios to increase with the income per head of a country. Educational provision remains extremely low in most of the low-income developing countries, particularly beyond the primary level. On the other hand, there are developing countries whose problem is now surplus rather than shortage of educated labour. Such cases are common in Asia, *e.g.* India and the Philippines.

By no means all countries had achieved universal primary education by 1993. The primary enrolment ratio was as low as 20 per cent in Ethiopia, 22 per cent in Mali, 25 per cent in Niger and 39 per cent in Pakistan. In some countries this was due to financial costs and constraints, and in others to lack of parental demand, especially in the case of female education.

The table also shows that enrolment ratios increased rapidly in most countries between 1980 and 1993. The high financial returns accruing to the educated have generated powerful pressures for the expansion of state education, to which governments have often acceded. Rapid expansion in quantity has frequently been accompanied by a decline in quality of education. In the Philippines, for instance, where the same proportion are in tertiary education as in Britain (28 per cent), most are in institutions of poor quality.

Some governments have found that it is easier to expand an educational system than it is to expand an economy, and shortages have given way to surpluses. The response to surplus may take various forms: unemployment of the educated, or displacement of the less educated from their jobs, so pushing the unemployment down the educational ladder, or pressures on government to create unnecessary jobs for the educated in the public service. In this last case—previously true of Egypt, for example—scarce resources are doubly wasted.

Economic Aid.

The main industrial countries—organised as a 21-member *Development Assistance Committee* (DAC)—have provided economic aid to the developing countries. The total net flow of economic assistance to the developing countries was $197 billion in

1996. Roughly $130 billion of this was net private investment and $55 billion official aid from governments. One sixth each of the net *official development assistance* (ODA) was contributed by Japan and the United States; the other principal donors were Germany, France, the Netherlands and Britain, in that order. Net private investment is volatile and cannot be relied upon.

The DAC nations have accepted three aid targets. One is that the net flow of private and official resources combined should exceed 1 per cent of each country's gross national product. In 1995, 4 out of 21 countries achieved this percentage, including Britain. The second target is that net ODA should exceed 0·7 per cent of GNP; 4 countries managed this in 1995. The third target, more generally achieved, concerns the "grant element"—the extent to which ODA contains an element of grant as opposed to commercial loans.

The flow of resources from the DAC countries to the developing countries grew in real terms but, expressed as a proportion of GNP, it was the same, at about 0·75 per cent, in 1985 and 1995. Net ODA fell, from 0·35 to 0·27 per cent, over the decade.

EDUCATIONAL ENROLMENT RATIOS IN DEVELOPING COUNTRIES, 1980 AND 1993

	Primary		Secondary		Tertiary	
	1980	1993	1980	1993	1980	1993
China	112	118	45	56	1	4
India	83	102	20	25	5	9
48 other low-income countries	75	75	21	26	4	5
of which:						
Zimbabwe	70	118	6	45	1	6
Tanzania	93	70	3	6	0	0
Pakistan	39	65	14	21	2	3
Sri Lanka	102	106	54	75	3	6
Egypt	73	97	50	75	16	17
54 middle-income countries	104	104	50	64	20	23
of which:						
Philippines	112	109	65	74	25	28
Brazil	99	106	33	39	11	12
South Korea	110	101	78	92	15	48
Thailand	99	98	29	38	13	19

Note: A figure of zero indicates that it is closer to 0 than to 1 per cent, and a figure greater than 100 is possible because of under-age and over-age pupils.

Forms of Aid.

Aid to the developing countries takes many forms, it serves many purposes and it is given for many reasons. Less developed countries need aid to provide finance for development projects; to provide foreign exchange with which imports for development purposes can be bought; and to provide the trained manpower and technical knowledge they lack. The motives of the donor are not always humanitarian. "Aid" can take a military form; it can be used to prop up an incompetent or unjust government, or to buy political support. Nor is aid always beneficial to the recipient country. It may be wasted on ill-conceived or prestige projects, or cause the government simply to relax its own efforts. Concern over donors' motives and instances of waste have led some people to react against aid-giving. However, the correct remedy is not to cut off aid but rather to prevent its misuse.

Financial aid is not always enough. Many developing countries need technical assistance in planning their development, to ensure that development possibilities are exploited and that scarce resources are used to best advantage. Hence the many schemes for providing experts by individual countries and by the technical agencies of the United Nations, such as the Food and Agriculture Organisation (FAO), the World Health Organisation (WHO), the International Labour Organisation (ILO), the United Nations Educational, Scientific and Cultural Organisation (UNESCO), and so on. Hence also the schemes for educating and training people from the developing countries.

Foreign Private Investment.

One possible form of assistance is private investment by firms from developed countries. These investments—setting up branch factories, for example—are concentrated in those projects which appear profitable to the investor. However, it has been questioned whether private investment constitutes aid to less developed countries. Its opponents argue that the benefits can be weak: foreign owned firms repatriate high profits and avoid tax by means of royalty payments to the parent company or unrealistic pricing of their transactions with the parent company; and these firms deter local enterprise. Supporters of foreign investment point to the high political risks which necessitate high profits in order to attract investors to developing countries, and question whether resources are available for any alternative path to development. A form of compromise which has become common in the Third World is a partnership arrangement between multinational companies and government or private firms in the host country.

British Aid.

In 1996 Britain's total ODA was £2,286 million, equal to £40 per head of population. In real terms this official aid had risen by 20 per cent over the previous decade.

Government aid may be divided into multilateral and bilateral aid. Multilateral aid (half the total in 1996) is given through the medium of the international development institutions: bilateral aid is given directly to the developing countries. Almost all British ODA takes the form of grants, and the rest is loans. Roughly half of bilateral financial aid is formally tied to the purchase of British goods and services. Other aid is not tied formally, and may be used directly to finance local expenditure; but when it is used to finance imports directly, it has to be spent on British goods if these are available on competitive terms. Most multilateral aid is untied. The tying of aid tends to raise the costs to developing countries; but it also encourages countries to be more generous.

Aid takes the form not only of financial but also of technical assistance. Government expenditure on technical assistance amounted to 60 per cent of bilateral aid in 1996–97. 34 per cent of British ODA went to the 50 poorest countries of the world in 1995, and 46 per cent to sub-Saharan Africa. The countries receiving most UK aid in 1996–97 were India, Tanzania, the states of ex-Yugoslavia and Bangladesh. However, it is the micro-states which often fare best in per capita terms.

All British official aid is channelled and co-ordinated by the *Department for International Development* (DFID). In addition there are various private associations concerned with promoting development, such as Oxfam, War on Want and World Development Movement.

The World Bank.

The International Bank for Reconstruction and Development (IBRD) known as the *International Bank* or as the *World Bank*, is an agency of the United Nations established in 1945. It has the primary function of making funds available to assist developing countries. Member nations agreed to subscribe quotas—fixed in much the same way as the quotas for the IMF—to the Bank. In fact, only a small proportion of the quotas has been called up by the Bank; the major part of the Bank's resources are borrowed—on the security of the remainder of the quotas—in financial centres.

Loans are made to finance specific projects and the Bank will normally make a loan only if it is satisfied that the investment will yield a revenue sufficient to enable the payment of interest on the loan, and the repayment of the sum lent. It is clear that some projects of great benefit cannot be financed in this way, because they would not yield returns quickly or large enough to meet the Bank's requirements for interest and repayment. Accordingly, the *International Development Association* has the power to make loans at low rates of interest and with more generous repayment conditions. The IDA contributes towards the development of education and agriculture (net $4·9 billion in 1995). In 1995 the World Bank made additional commitments but, because of repayments of loans, its net contribution was actually negative (−80·5 billion).

Trade Reform.

An important development in recent decades that has benefited the world economy in general and the developing economies in particular, is the negotiated move towards greater freedom of trade. In 1947, when the *General Agreement on Tariffs and Trade* (GATT) was born, average tariff levels were 38 per cent. In 1962, they stood at 17 per cent. After seven successive rounds of trade negotiations— the most important of which were the Tokyo Round and the Uruguay Round—by 1995 tariffs were down to only 4 per cent on average.

The Uruguay Round.

The *Uruguay Round* was a long drawn-out series of trade negotiations within the GATT, originally begun in Uruguay in 1986. After seven years a far-reaching trade agreement was finally concluded in December 1993. There was agreement to cut tariffs, on average, by 40 per cent. There was also agreement to extend the GATT disciplines to many services and to agriculture. The agreement committed the European Union to substantial liberalisation of its farm policies.

It was inevitable that progress on trade policies would be difficult because of perceived conflicts of interest. Even though the world as a whole might gain from freer world trade, any individual country might suffer. Many developing countries fear that greater competition from imports will threaten their protected industries, often born behind tariff barriers; and some developed countries fear that greater competition from low-wage countries producing labour-intensive manufactures will threaten their own production and employment in manufacturing. In that context, the Uruguay Round appeared to have reached a successful conclusion.

The World Trade Organisation.

The *World Trade Organisation* (WTO) is the international body, based in Geneva, that arranges and promotes trade among countries. It was established in 1995, as a successor to the GATT, initially to implement the Uruguay Round agreement. It administers multilateral trade agreements, acts as a forum for trade negotiations, and seeks to resolve trade disputes. It promotes trade without discrimination—the only notable exception being free trade areas and customs unions. It is as much concerned with trade in services and in ideas (intellectual property) as with trade in goods.

The three most sensitive trade issues facing the WTO are agriculture, textiles and clothing, and dumping. In the case of agricultural products, which are subject to heavy *non-tariff barriers* (NTBs), quotas were converted into equivalent tariffs, which would in turn be reduced over six years of implementing the Uruguay Round. The Multifibre Arrangement is a method of protecting industrial countries against the textiles and clothing exports of developing countries by means of NTBs. These restrictions are to be phased out over ten years. The most serious omission of the Uruguay Round was its failure to tighten discipline over anti-dumping laws, the favourite instrument for NTBs.

Inequality Within Countries.

In some less developed countries economic growth has been achieved without any apparent improvement in the lot of the masses. The majority of the people are engaged in agriculture in the rural areas, whereas much of the development has taken place in industry and services in the urban areas. A minority of people have benefited—industrialists, bureaucrats, educated and skilled workers, organised labour in the modern sector of the economy—but the poor living in the urban slums, often in open or disguised unemployment, and the enormous numbers in the rural areas have been little affected by development. In many countries the fruits of development have not been widely spread. It is a widespread criticism that development policies have been biased towards industry and towards the cities, and that rural people in agriculture have

been neglected. This outcome may be a reflection of the uneven distribution of political power within a developing country.

The growth of GNP per capita as a goal of development has been questioned. Governments have shown a greater concern for poverty, employment creation and social equity. Many donors have modified their aid policies to try to reach the poor. The DFID attempts to classify its aid according to its main purpose (economic reform, good government, environment, *etc*). In 1996–97, 27 per cent of UK aid was classified as direct assistance to poor people within the recipient countries.

Basic Needs.

A direction in which international thinking has moved is towards the acceptance of a *Basic Needs* strategy of development. Essentially the aim is to alleviate absolute poverty, *i.e.*, to meet minimum standards of food, shelter, clothing and safe drinking water, and to satisfy certain other basic human needs. It is proposed that these standards be reached not so much by means of welfare transfers as by enabling the poor to help themselves through productive employment. The minimum standards are inevitably subjective, there are economic and political obstacles to the fulfilment of basic needs, and the approach does not translate easily into specific policies. Nevertheless, the basic needs strategy has an impact on the priorities both of aid agencies and of recipient governments.

Human Development.

There is a growing emphasis in developing countries and in the donor community on *human development, i.e.* the notion that development of peoples' *capabilities* to improve and control their lives is an important end in itself. For instance, in addition to helping people to raise their incomes, being better informed, in better health and having a greater say in local affairs are regarded as good in themselves. This had led to greater emphasis on basic health and basic education services, as ways of improving peoples's lives. The DFID classified 64 per cent of its aid programme in 1996–97 as being at least partly for human development objectives.

The Causes of Famine.

In the last couple of decades food production in the developing countries has done little more than keep pace with the growth of population. Many developing countries have become net food importers, and this trend is likely to continue.

Famine is by no means always simply the result of a fall in food production which affects all people in the area uniformly. In the 1974 Bangladesh famine and the terrible Ethiopian famines, those who suffered most were respectively the landless, who normally exchange labour for food, and pastoralists, who normally exchange cattle for food grains. The landless, losing their source of earnings because farmers no longer hired labourers, and pastoralists, seeing the prices of their emaciated beasts fall as more and more were marketed, could no longer buy food: these were the people who starved.

Inequality Among Countries.

Not all less developed countries have fared equally well in recent years. In particular there appears to be a tendency for disparities among less developed countries to widen. The countries which have performed well tend to be semi-industrialised and able to respond to opportunities for exporting manufactures to the developed countries, or to be well endowed with mineral or oil resources. Growth success stories include Turkey, Chile, Botswana, Thailand, China, South Korea, Taiwan, Malaysia and Singapore. Some of these are on the way to becoming self-reliant economically: they are known as the *newly industrialising countries* (NICs). The poorest countries—42 of which were designated the *least developed countries* (LLDCs)—are experiencing the greatest difficulty in escaping from the vicious circle of poverty. A growing recognition of their problem has led the DAC countries to reallocate aid in favour of the least developed countries, and to offer aid on more concessionary terms to these countries.

Between 1985 and 1995 the annual rate of economic growth of income per capita varied greatly among regions: from −1·1 per cent in Sub-Saharan Africa, to −0·3 per cent in the Middle East and North Africa, 0·3 per cent in Latin America, 2·9 per cent in South Asia, and to 7·2 per cent in East Asia.

The East Asian Economic Miracle?

East Asia has a remarkable record of high and sustained economic growth over the last quarter-century. Much of this is due to the performance of Japan, the "Gang of Four" (Hong Kong, Korea, Singapore and Taiwan) and three other successful economies, Indonesia, Malaysia and Thailand. What are the reasons for their success? What can other countries learn from their experience?

Most of them share a number of characteristics which point to the explanation. First, most have extremely high ratios of investment in physical capital to GDP, assisted by high saving rates. Rapid capital accumulation, then, is a necessary condition for rapid economic growth, but it may not be a sufficient condition. It, too, needs to be explained. A second common feature was rapid accumulation of human capital: educational participation rates were high even in the 1960s, and subsequently rose. Economic growth was probably also assisted by a sharp decline in population growth rates. Fourth, these countries have created a business-friendly environment, and have generally sought foreign technology and investment.

A fifth general feature was good economic management, which tended to be in the hands of bureaucrats, insulated from political influence and interest groups. It would be wrong to claim that these are free market economies: in several, government interventions to accelerate the pace of development have been pervasive. In particular, they have promoted exports in various ways: they have all adopted outward-orientated industrialisation policies.

Successful Economic Reform in China.

China is another country in East Asia that has performed remarkably well in recent years. The average annual growth rate of real income per capita in China over the period 1985–96 was no less than 8 per cent. The reasons for its success are rather different from those for other East Asian countries. In 1976, when Mao died, it was a communist country with central planning and in which politics, rather than economics, was in command. Today it is in many respects a market economy in which the role of the state, previously all-pervasive, is rapidly diminishing. The economic reforms in China proceeded steadily in a way which brought greater prosperity to almost everyone. The successful reforms in China are to be contrasted with the current policy problems in Eastern Europe and the former USSR. The Chinese experience is worth examining.

Reforming Chinese Agriculture.

China contains no fewer than 1,200 million people, of whom 860 million (72 per cent) live in rural areas. The economic reforms began in the rural areas. Under Mao agriculture was collectivised and the peasants lacked incentives: farm production stagnated. The new leadership permitted the peasants to disband their communes and restore household production on family farms. Farm production grew by 8 per cent per annum between 1978 and 1984, as peasants responded to new opportunities and higher prices for their products.

There was a second transformation of the Chinese countryside: the growth of rural industry, owned collectively by villages or privately. By 1996 rural industry employed 130 million people. It contributed greatly to the absorption of surplus labour on the land.

Reforming Urban China.

The urban reforms began in 1984. Although it had grown rapidly, industry—mainly state-owned—in urban China was inefficient. Enterprises had no autonomy within the centralised planning system. Prices and production were determined by the state, all output was sold to the state and all profits handed over to the state. The reforms took the form of decentralising decisions and introducing

market sales and market prices alongside the state plan: gradually the market came to dominate the plan, and far more consumer goods were produced as the market for them expanded. By 1996, 70 per cent of urban households had a refrigerator, 93 per cent a colour television set, and 90 per cent a washing machine. Assisted by foreign investment and technology and by low labour costs, both rural and urban industry were increasingly able to export manufactures to the developed economies.

Prospects for the Chinese Economy.

If recent trends were to continue, China would become the largest economy in the world by 2015. However, various obstacles may slow down future economic growth. One is a shortage of highly educated workers, the result of giving priority to basic rather than higher education. Second, land is currently leased to households: without property rights, long term investments in agriculture could be deterred. Third, there is a problem of inefficient, loss-making enterprises which, together with fiscal decentralisation, has contributed to a growing budgetary problem for the state. Fourth, some people have got rich very quickly, and some regions—in particular, the coastal provinces—have prospered more than others. The rise in these income inequalities could contribute to social and political unrest, and so threaten economic progress. There is little sign as yet of political change to match the economic transformation.

Economic Stagnation in Africa.

Africa has become the area that presents the greatest economic problem. Income per head in Sub-Saharan Africa has fallen since 1980. There are various reasons not associated with natural phenomena. First, population growth has continued to rise and now stands at 2·8 per cent per annum. Second, the terms of trade of the region deteriorated by 36 per cent between 1980 and 1995. Third, Africa's external debt is now 54 per cent of its GNP, making the region the most heavily indebted of all. Debt service obligations were 12 per cent of export revenues in 1998, but not all were actually paid, so that arrears accumulated. Both the level and the efficiency of investment have fallen. Fourth, drought has hit many countries of Africa in the 1980s and 1990s, including the Sahel, Eastern Africa and Southern Africa. This has not only produced great human suffering but it has also created problems of economic recovery and development.

With the World Bank forecasting a further fall in living standards, Africa is the focus of aid donors' attention. Some of Africa's problems are within the control of their governments, and aid agencies have increasingly made their aid to African countries conditional on the reform of economic policies. This involves a strategy requiring less government intervention, more reliance on market forces and more grass-roots development, and emphasising the development of institutional and human capacities to provide the enabling environment for growth.

Growing Indebtedness.

The external indebtedness of the developing countries grew rapidly in the 1970s and 1980s. Many developing countries failed to adjust fully to the worsened economic and trading conditions after the oil crisis of 1973, preferring instead to borrow heavily. After the second oil crisis in 1979–80, the world economy went into prolonged recession. Many developing countries were squeezed between stagnating foreign exchange earnings and heavy foreign exchange commitments. This precipitated two problems: a *debt crisis* for certain heavily indebted developing countries and the need for *stabilization policies* among a broader group of developing countries.

The Debt Crisis.

It was the more successful developing countries which attracted lending: Brazil and Mexico together accounted for 40 per cent of the private debt. A measure of the strain on developing countries is provided by the ratio of debt and of debt servicing (annual interest and amortisation payments) to annual foreign exchange earnings from exports. These ratios had reached 133 per cent and 18 per cent respectively in 1983. This precipitated the debt crisis, in which a general default on debts was widely feared.

Countries became increasingly dependent on new loans to service the old, and private banks were reluctant to provide these. In all the major cases a rescheduling of debt repayments was arranged, usually in conjunction with IMF programmes. However, the formal procedures for managing debt problems were overtaken by informal actions, such as the suspension of debt servicing. The mounting arrears caused Western banks to raise their balance sheet provisions against loans to the problem debtors, writing the cost off against profits.

The debt crisis peaked in 1986, and thereafter it was eased by the acceleration of world economic growth, by debt reduction initiatives for the poorest countries, and by debt write-offs. For debtors, the problem represented economic hardship, a dampening of investment, and social and political discontent. In 1998 interest on debt still took 9 per cent of the export proceeds of developing countries.

Accelerating Inflation.

The serious macroeconomic strains which most developing countries experienced in the 1980s gave rise to accelerating inflation in many cases. Whereas the annual rate of inflation over the period 1980–93 in OECD countries averaged 4·3 per cent, in developing countries it averaged 73 per cent. This average was of course much influenced by the hyperinflations in a few countries (Bolivia 187 per cent per annum, Brazil 423 per cent, Argentina 374 per cent, Israel 70 per cent and Nicaragua 664 per cent) but high inflation was a pervasive phenomenon. It was a response—sometimes acting as a safety valve—to such problems as foreign exchange shortage, loss of government revenue, food shortage, debt servicing, and tardy growth of or fall in real incomes. Once established, inflation could feed on itself by changing expectations and behaviour, and it became very difficult to eliminate.

The IMF and Stabilization Policies.

Many developing countries ran into serious balance of payments problems in the 1980s. The current account deficit of the developing countries taken as a whole, at $48 billion in 1986 – the worst year of the 1980s – was equivalent to 8 per cent of exports. Many sought temporary financial assistance from the International Monetary Fund (*see* **G9**).

As a condition of its larger loans the IMF generally requires a country to accept a series of *stabilization* measures. The typical stabilization package contains the following policies: a devaluation to assist the balance of payments, monetary and credit restrictions and reduced government budget deficits to reduce demand and curb inflation, and, more generally, the elimination of restrictions such as import controls and interest rate regulations in order to harness market forces.

The wisdom of such a package in a developing country is much disputed among economists. It is most obviously the correct remedy when the problem is one of general excess demand in the economy. However, when the problem arises from an extraneous shock, such as a fall in the world price of a major export or a financial crisis, the IMF's remedies may prove to be inappropriate. Credit restrictions and cuts in government spending may depress the economy, reducing output and employment. This may temporarily alleviate the immediate problems of inflation and balance of payments deficit, but the effect on long run economic growth may be negative.

It is for these reasons that critics accuse the IMF of doctrinairely and narrowly focussing on monetary variables and ignoring structural problems and developmental objectives. The IMF, on the other hand, often sees itself as a handy scapegoat for unpopular measures made inescapable by domestic economic mismanagement.

Globalization of Financial Markets.

One of the policy reforms pressed for by the IMF and the World Bank, and eagerly adopted by many developing country governments, was the liberalization of financial markets. There was a substantial increase in private capital flows to developing countries in the 1990s, reflecting financial liberaliza-

tion and the welcoming stance of host governments. Capital inflows into developing countries as a group increased from $76 billion in 1990 to $224 billion in 1996. Roughly half of the 1996 total was official and bank lending (creating debt), and half direct investment. Asia received half of the total and Latin America a third. *Emergent stock markets* flourished in such countries as Argentina, Chile, Thailand, Malaysia, Taiwan and China.

In principle, capital inflows are good for the developing countries, encouraging investment and accelerating economic growth. However, they also carry dangers, as the examples of Mexico in 1994 and East Asia in 1997–98 show.

The Mexican Crisis, 1994–95.

From 1988 Mexico followed a policy of macroeconomic stabilization and adjustment. Until December 1994 the policy seemed to work—inflation was curbed, the public sector deficit became a surplus, and Mexico's foreign debt problems were eased. The creation of the *North American Free Trade Area* (NAFTA) in 1994 meant that, with investors' confidence high, vast funds were attracted into Mexico. The inflow of funds appreciated the peso, and this in turn created a large current account deficit in the balance of payments. Noting the fiscal relaxation before the election, the financial markets began to doubt whether the economic strategy was sustainable. In December 1994 there was a capital flight from the peso; its value collapsed by 40 per cent and the foreign exchange reserves dwindled.

The United States and the IMF provided a $53 billion international rescue plan. The object of this emergency package was to provide sufficient liquidity to Mexico for holders of Mexican assets not to abandon the peso. The austerity programme then introduced by the Mexican government deflated the economy and raised unemployment. The drastic devaluation of the peso, with time, corrected the balance of payments and restored Mexico's credibility. This episode illustrates how large flows of international capital can wreak havoc on a vulnerable economy.

The East Asian Financial Crisis.

Many of the East Asian countries suffered a serious financial crisis in 1997 and 1998. The crisis began in Thailand but it spread rapidly to engulf South Korea, Malaysia, Indonesia, and the Philippines. Other major developing economies of the region—China, Taiwan and Singapore—were shaken but relatively unscathed.

There were common roots to the crisis, although the reversal of market sentiment became infectious. Financial liberalization produced a wave of investment in the region, funded from both local and foreign sources. Some of the investment was ill-conceived, and some politically influenced (hence the term "crony capitalism"). The investment boom in turn contributed to worsening current accounts on the balance of payments, which were anyway suffering from the tying of currencies to the appreciating US dollar. By 1997 there was sufficient concern to set off a capital flight, which in turn fed on itself. Currencies depreciated very sharply. For instance, between July 1997 and February 1998 the Indonesian rupiah fell by three-quarters of its value against the US dollar, and the Thai baht, the South Korean won, and the Malaysian ringgit by 40 per cent or more. This increased the burden of debt, and of debt servicing, denominated in terms of foreign currency, and so further destroyed confidence.

The countries in crisis received support from the IMF and the World Bank, on condition that they introduced policies of monetary and fiscal restraint to stabilize their economies. The hope was that these policies, together with their depreciated currencies, would restore their export competitiveness in world markets. However, it would take time to repair the damage. The "East Asian miracle" (*see* **G45(1)**) was over, at least for the time being.

The State versus the Market.

The role that the state should play in economic development has become a major issue. In past decades the governments of most developing countries have been extremely interventionist. The presumption was that markets do not work well in underdeveloped economies and that the state can improve on the market outcome by directly allocating resources. However, many countries lacked the skilled manpower required to make the economic bureaucracy efficient, and the economic powers taken by the state were often an invitation to corruption. By the end of the 1980s there was a widespread feeling that the pendulum had swung too far in favour of the state.

The 1990s have seen a move towards greater reliance on the market in many developing countries. In the words of John Maynard Keynes, "the important thing for government is not to do things which individuals are doing already, and to do them a little better or a little worse; but to do those things which at present are not done at all." In many developing countries there is a case for privatising state-owned enterprises and for doing away with price controls, import quotas, high tariffs, heavy production subsidies and the like. At the same time, governments need to do more in those areas where markets alone cannot be relied upon, such as investing in health, nutrition, education, family planning and poverty alleviation, and building an efficient infrastructure within which private enterprises can flourish.

Structural Adjustment Policies.

The process whereby developing economies are redirected towards improved balance of payments, debt reduction, more openness to the world economy, less government intervention and greater use of markets, has come to be known as *structural adjustment*. It is being promoted by international donors and resisted by domestic vested interests. Many governments have accepted the need for structural adjustment; time will tell whether rhetoric becomes reality.

Much of the World Bank's lending now takes the form of *Structural Adjustment Loans*, providing funds to the government of a developing country on condition that it implements agreed structural adjustment policies (*see* **G43**). Supporters seek to justify such lending in terms of its results; opponents see it as an infringement of national sovereignty.

Environmental Issues.

To be economically sustainable development must also be environmentally sustainable. Much of the population increase in the 1990s is occurring in environmentally fragile regions of the world. Desertification, deforestation, soil depletion through over-use of fragile land, and pollution are issues of growing concern.

Environmental degradation can contribute to famine (as in Ethiopia) and to devastating flooding (as in Bangladesh). Population pressures, poverty, inadequate systems of land tenure and the growing need for fuelwood lead to the cutting or burning of forests and the clearing of new land. This can be a problem of global as well as national dimensions on account of its effects on the global climate. Problems of pollution have become critical in many of the large urban agglomerations of the Third World. Sanitation, clean water and clean air are important aspects of the quality of life, and these require that government plays an active role.

Environmental Policies.

Environmental dangers are greater in poor countries which can little afford to invest in environmental protection and resource management. Their governments often find it difficult to monitor, regulate and control environmental pollution. Rather than attempt to regulate, it may be better to levy taxes on polluting equipment (*e.g.* combustion machinery) or fuels (*e.g.* petrol) according to the expected level of pollution. If, as in large cities, household use of energy is a major contributor to pollution, the types of fuel and equipment which reduce pollution might be subsidised and those that increase it might be taxed.

In 1989 the OECD nations agreed to give greater emphasis to environmental improvements in their aid policies. A *Global Environmental Facility* was established by donors to assist developing countries to undertake investment projects which would protect the global environment. These would include protection of the ozone layer, affected by *chlorofluorocarbon* (CFC) and other gas emissions, limiting "greenhouse" gas emissions (such as carbon dioxide and methane) that contribute to global warming, protecting biological species against extinction and protecting international waters against pollution (*e.g.* waste pollution and oil spills). Recognising the global advantages of such projects, the international donors are willing to offer this aid on concessional terms.

The United Nations Conference on Environment and Development, otherwise known as the *Earth Summit*, was held in Rio de Janeiro in June 1992. It failed to produce specific commitments concerning the environment, but it helped to change attitudes and emphasis. For instance, principles were agreed on forest conservation and the control of greenhouse gases. *See also* **L132**.

Some Suggestions for Further Reading.

For an introduction to the subject the reader is referred to Michael Todaro, *Economic Development* (Longman). Ian Little, in *Economic Development* (Basic Books) assesses the development record and the way in which ideas and policies have evolved. The Department for International Development has compiled a handbook of *British Aid Statistics*.

The World Bank produces an annual *World Development Report*; each edition has a theme, the theme in the 1997 edition being *The State in a Changing World* and in the 1998 edition *Knowledge for Development*. The Organisation for Economic Cooperation and Development, comprising all the major developed countries, publishes an annual review of aid and development entitled *Development Cooperation* (OECD).

An interesting quarterly publication of the IMF and the World Bank, *Finance and Development*, is available free of charge: applications should be sent to *Finance and Development*, IMF Building, Washington, DC 20431, USA.

IV. RECENT DEVELOPMENTS IN THE BRITISH ECONOMY

1. INTERNATIONAL DEVELOPMENTS

The Balance of Payments.

The balance of payments problem has dominated events in the British economy until recent years and may do so again. It is therefore important to analyse the balance of payments in some detail; to understand why the balance of payments has been a problem; and to see its effects on economic policy. The balance of payments and its components are explained on **G6–8**. The balance of payments in the period 1995–98 is shown in the table on **G48**.

The Early 1970s.

In the face of a sterling crisis in 1972, the pound was allowed to float downwards (from the previously fixed rate of \$2·60 = £1) for the first time since a period in the 1930s. The current account deteriorated sharply in 1973. The most important reason was the higher price of imports: this period witnessed a remarkable inflation in the prices of various primary products in world markets. This unprecedented jump in primary commodity prices stemmed from the sharp and well-synchronised expansion of the major industrial economies during 1972 and 1973.

Oil: Crisis and Response.

An event of great importance was the decision of the Arab oil-producing states, taken in October 1973, to restrict oil supplies and to raise oil prices. The restriction of supplies was initiated as a short-run political weapon in the Arab–Israeli conflict; but it revealed a potential for obtaining higher

THE UK BALANCE OF PAYMENTS 1995–98
(£ BILLION)

	1995	1996	1997	1998
Export of goods	153·7	167·4	171·8	163·7
Import of goods	165·4	180·5	183·7	184·3
Visible balance	−11·7	−13·1	−11·9	−20·6
Invisible balance	8·0	12·5	18·0	18·1
Current balance	−3·7	−0·6	6·1	−2·5
Net direct investment	−15·2	−6·0	−16·3	..
Net portfolio investment	−2·1	−15·6	−23·4	..
Other investment	18·1	22·9	30·8	..
Official reserves*	0·2	0·5	2·4	..
Net capital transactions	0·9	1·8	−6·5	..
Balancing item	2·8	−1·2	0·4	..

.. = not available   * a positive sign denotes drawings on the reserves

prices which had not previously been exploited by the *Organisation of Petroleum Exporting Countries* (OPEC). Alternative sources of energy could not be developed—and thus the demand for oil could not be curtailed or even its growth retarded—for some years. However, maintenance of high prices depended on the ability of the OPEC group to restrict oil supplies to the market despite the incentive of each individual country to take advantage of the high prices by expanding its sales. Comparing 1974 with 1973, the price of oil imported into Britain almost trebled.

In the wake of the oil crisis the world economy duly moved into severe recession. To this the British economy was no exception: real GDP stagnated in 1974 and fell in 1975. During 1975 the rate of inflation in Britain was some 15 per cent above the average for the OECD countries: it became clear that sterling would have to be depreciated further.

The exchange rate slid to a low point of $1·57 in October 1976, and the Bank of England's minimum lending rate was hurriedly raised to the unprecedented level of 15 per cent. The Government applied to the IMF to draw on the United Kingdom's credit tranche of $3·9 billion. The successful conclusion of these negotiations in January 1977, and the borrowing of more than £1 billion from the IMF, helped to restore confidence.

The "oil deficit" in the balance of payments, huge in the mid-1970s, slowly declined as North Sea oil production expanded, and was transformed into an "oil surplus", becoming as large as £5·5 billion in the mid-1980s, and then declining. The sharp build-up in production from almost nil in 1975 had arrived at about 100 million tonnes in 1980, roughly equal to UK net consumption of oil. British production of petroleum and natural gas amounted to 7 per cent of GDP in the peak year, 1984.

The exploitation of North Sea oil was a mixed blessing. Through its strengthening of the balance of payments and consequent raising of the exchange rate, it harmed the manufacturing sector. The problems of structural adjustment, of which rising unemployment was a symptom, brought a social cost.

The Balance of Payments in the 1980s.

Increased demand for sterling beginning in 1977 was met in part by the willingness of the monetary authorities to let the exchange rate rise. It rose steadily to reach a peak of $2·44 in October 1980. This was partly due to North Sea oil production, its direct effect on the balance of payments and its indirect effect on foreign confidence in the British economy. Also important were the high interest rates engendered by the government's restrictive monetary policy and the low level of demand for imports caused by the recession in the domestic economy. With the economy slumping, the trade balance moved into surplus for the first time in many years.

The appreciation of sterling helped to curb domestic inflation by keeping down the sterling price of imports (an imported good selling for $1 could now be bought for fewer pence). However, it also had a harmful effect on the manufacturing sector and on competitiveness (an exported good costing £1 would now have to be sold at a higher dollar price to cover costs). The current account surplus fell after 1982, reflecting a lagged adjustment to the unfavourable competitiveness of British products, and it deteriorated sharply from 1986 onwards. The main reason for this was an upswing in the economy—the so-called "Lawson boom". The overall balance of payments was protected by relatively high interest rates in London.

Policy Dilemmas.

The policy dilemma which this posed led to a remarkable public conflict between the Prime Minister and the Chancellor of the Exchequer at the time of the 1988 budget: the former favoured a free market outcome and the latter stabilisation of the pound through official intervention. The Prime Minister was right in the sense that the authorities now have limited power to control the exchange rate in the face of huge capital flows. The Chancellor was right in the sense that the market, left to itself, is unlikely to produce the outcome that the balance of trade and the economy require. British interest rates were raised in order to curb demand and reduce inflation. This posed a policy contradiction. On the one hand, a higher interest rate was needed to curb inflation; on the other hand, it had the effect of curbing trade competitiveness.

The Effects of Entry to the EMS.

In October 1990 the decision was finally taken to make Britain a fuller member of the *European Monetary System* (EMS) by entering the *Exchange Rate Mechanism* (ERM) (*see* **G53**(2)). This had important implications for the conduct of economic policy. Greater co-ordination of monetary policy with the rest of Europe was now required. The Bank of England would have to be given more independent responsibility and the setting of interest rates would be less subject to political control. There was less scope for exchange rate realignment.

In the long run the wage and price inflation rate and the interest rate in Britain would have to be brought into line with those of Europe. However, the tendency for the British economy to generate excessive wage pressure remained firmly-rooted. There was a danger that the process of economic alignment would be a painful one, in which inflation was curbed by holding back demand in the economy. The difficulties facing the economy were compounded by the relatively high level of the exchange rate at which sterling entered the ERM. Maintaining the entry exchange rate might require a long and deep economic recession. The need to maintain sterling within the permitted ERM band required the authorities to keep interest rates above German levels. German rates were rising and this prevented the government from reducing interest rates by as much as the recession warranted.

Black Wednesday.

German interest rates rose further in 1992, reflecting Bundesbank concern about inflation. Despite the severity of the economic recession in Britain (GDP fell by 3 per cent between 1990 and 1992), the current account remained in deficit (£10 billion in 1992). The markets lost confidence in the ability and commitment of the British Government, faced with weak international competitiveness and a depressed economy, to defend the pound within the EMS. Speculation fed on itself and, despite heavy (and costly) financial support by the Bank of England and the Bundesbank, the Government was defeated by the markets on *Black Wednesday*, 16 September. The pound dropped sharply, depreciating by some 16 per cent.

The old policy had failed, mainly because the government had joined the EMS at an over-valued rate for sterling. The government hastened to invent a new policy regime. Unemployment had reached 10 per cent and was still rising: it was decided to place greater emphasis on overcoming the recession. Indeed, some commentators regarded Black Wednesday as heaven-sent: the markets had saved the government from its self-imposed straitjacket.

Response to Devaluation.

The pound was worth 2·82 deutschmarks in August 1992 and 2·36 deutschmarks in February 1993. The Treasury bill rate fell from 9·9 to 5·5 per cent over the same period, and other interest rates came down as well. The improved competitiveness provided a boost for producers, and lower interest rates eased the burden on mortgage-holders and encouraged investors. At last there was the prospect of an end to economic contraction.

In the four quarters after the devaluation there was an 11 per cent improvement in British competitiveness: the inflationary impact of the devaluation was very limited because of the extremely depressed state of the economy. With a lag, exports began to rise rapidly: by 3 per cent in 1993 and by no less than 11 per cent in 1994. The economy also began to recover, growing by 2 per cent in 1993 and by 4 per cent in 1994. There was an improvement in the current account, the deficit falling to £2 billion in 1994. Britain was benefitting from export-led growth in the wake of the enforced devaluation of sterling.

During 1996 the value of sterling began to appreciate sharply: by 10 per cent against a basket of currencies from April to November. This reflected confidence in the British economy relative to its European partners, together with higher interest rates in Britain and their expected rise, as pressed for by the Bank of England. The appreciation helped to keep down the rate of inflation but the pound—nearly back to its level before the 1992 enforced devaluation— was now overvalued.

The Prospects for Sterling.

In 1998, at the time of the March budget, speculation pushed sterling to a nine-year peak. The financial markets judged that the Chancellor had not exercised sufficient fiscal restraint in his budget, and that interest rates would therefore have to be raised to curb demand in the economy, so appreciating sterling.

The balance of payments on current account moved from surplus to deficit in 1998, and the deficit was predicted to rise no less than £7 billion in 1999. This deterioration reflected the overvaluation of the pound, caused by the policy of maintaining higher interest rates in Britain than in its main trading partners. Interest rates are determined by the Bank of England's *Monetary Policy Committee* (MPC), whose brief is to control the rate of inflation (*see* **G32** and **G56**). From mid-year the MPC made a series of interest rate reductions as the economy appeared to falter, and sterling depreciated somewhat as a result. Nevertheless, when the euro was created at the start of 1999, the pound remained too high: a tying to the euro at the rate that then prevailed (£1 = 1·41 euros) would have threatened British growth and prosperity.

The NICs and British Wages.

One of the most remarkable changes in the world economy has been the rise of the *newly industrialis-* ing countries (NICs) (*see* **G41**). They have greatly expanded their exports to the industrialised economies. Their success is based mainly on their efficient use of low-wage labour to produce labour-intensive manufactures.

Economic theory predicts that when there is an increase in trade between two regions with different endowments, and different prices, of capital and labour, these prices will tend to equalise. Thus as a result of the increase in British imports from low-wage countries, unskilled wages should tend to fall in relative terms. This is precisely what has happened in Britain over recent years. The ratio of non-manual to manual wages rose from 1·2 in 1979 to 1·5 in 1994. The increase in imports from the NICs may also have contributed to the growth of unemployment among relatively unskilled manual workers. Expressed as a percentage rate, this is considerably higher than that for the labour force as a whole.

We should recognise, however, that increased imports from low-wage countries are not the only likely influence on unskilled wages. New technology often substitutes capital and skilled labour for less skilled labour. The demise of incomes policy and the decline in trade union membership may also have helped to widen the distribution of wages in Britain.

International Investment.

One of the more successful items in the UK balance of payments has been net interest, profit, and dividends from private sources. After the freeing of controls on direct investment abroad in 1979, UK investment overseas rose sharply, from £6 billion in 1979 to £90 billion in 1997. This was accompanied by corresponding increases in interest, dividends and profit from abroad (£95 billion gross, £10 billion net, in 1996), which contributed to the surplus on invisibles in the current account.

The remarkable expansion of international investment, both by foreign companies in the United Kingdom and by British companies abroad, reflects the growing importance of *multinational (or transnational) companies* in the world economy. Some 165 multinationals account for 80 per cent of British private investment abroad. The multinationals tend to dominate the world markets for technologically advanced products. They account for no less than 60 per cent of trade in manufactures in the developed world. Their financial and market power, their global investment strategies, and their ability to avoid national taxation pose a challenge to the economic sovereignty of national governments.

Multinationals in Britain.

Just as many British companies operate abroad, so many foreign companies have subsidiaries and affiliates in Britain. Some household names— including the oil companies Exxon and Mobil, the motor companies Ford, Vauxhall and Nissan, the electrical companies Phillips and Hoover, and new technology companies such as IBM, Kodak and Rank Xerox—are foreign-based. In the 1990s Britain has attracted more foreign direct investment than any other European Union country (averaging a quarter of the total in 1990–95). This may have been assisted by the lack of labour market regulation in Britain and the advantage of English as the language of business. Similarly, the total stock of UK inward investment (£155 billion in 1995) exceeded that in other European Union countries and indeed all countries except the United States.

Events such as the purchase of Rover by BMW in 1994 brought the issue of foreign ownership into public debate. Opponents of foreign takeovers may be motivated by crude nationalism or by a concern that production would become internationally more footloose. Although particular cases may require scrutiny, the liberal policies which British Governments have adopted towards both inward and outward foreign investment make sense. Countries which cut themselves off from the technological and other skills of multinational companies would find it difficult to compete internationally in the long run.

Foreign-owned companies accounted for 18 per cent of employment in UK manufacturing in 1992, and they produced some 40 per cent of total manufacturing exports. For instance, Britain now has export surpluses of computers and colour televisions, sectors dominated by foreign-owned companies. The productivity per worker in foreign companies was 30 per cent above the UK average in 1992. This is partly because some invested at "green field" sites, where the plant would be entirely new and it would be easy to introduce new working practices. It is also because some of the most productive companies in the world have been attracted to Britain. For instance, in Sunderland Nissan was able to select just 10 per cent of its many applicants, to train these workers to very high standards, and to achieve quality control and productivity levels which equal those in the Nissan plants in Japan.

The International Economic System.

The international monetary system is explained on **G9**. The main problems facing the international economic system in the 1970s were world inflation and the international imbalance caused by the increased price of oil, and the resultant threat to economic growth. In the 1980s and 1990s the main problems were international debt, world recession and tardy economic growth. We trace the issues and events as they unfolded.

Introduction of Flexible Exchange Rates.

The United States ran a large and persistent payments deficit in the 1950s and 1960s. This was initially financed through the willingness of foreigners to run up dollar balances. However, distrust of the dollar grew. Massive speculation against the dollar forced the United States government to suspend the convertibility of dollars into gold. The dollar was devalued in 1973 and the EC countries agreed that their currencies would float against the dollar.

The international monetary system had entered a new era of flexible exchange rates. The Bretton Woods system, which had operated throughout the post-war period, had come to an end. No longer would countries be required to maintain fixed exchange rates subject only to periodic realignment in response to fundamental disequilibrium in their balance of payments.

The system had broken down because it could no longer perform its function. The imbalance between the United States and the other major countries was the immediate cause of the breakdown. Perhaps the more basic reasons, however, were the growing shortage of international reserves, the growing volume of internationally mobile short-term funds, and the more rapid and divergent national rates of inflation.

The First Oil Crisis.

The price of oil rose from $3·5 to $9·3 a barrel between 1973 and 1974. The oil-producing countries ran a vast current account surplus in 1974, which meant a corresponding deficit for the oil-importing countries as a group. Such a transformation in the international balance of payments was unprecedented in its scale and speed. It involved a massive transfer of purchasing power from consumers to producers of oil. Since only a small part of the additional oil revenue was spent, this had a severe deflationary effect on the world economy.

The less developed countries sustained large deficits in the wake of the oil price increase. The deposits made by oil-producers in western banks gave these banks an opportunity to lend on a much enlarged scale. Private lending to developing countries increased greatly; this sowed the seeds of the debt crisis of the 1980s (see **G45**(2)).

The Second Oil Crisis.

The price of oil doubled over the course of 1979, rising from $13 to $25 a barrel. This was due to the halving of Iranian oil production after the revolution in Iran, and to a scramble for oil stocks by the consuming countries. In 1980, assisted by the outbreak of war between Iran and Iraq, the OPEC oil price averaged $32 a barrel.

These factors combined to cause economic stagnation in the OECD countries during 1980. The higher oil price led again to higher inflation (13 per cent in 1980) and an increased balance of payments deficit in the industrial countries. Both the restrictive

monetary policies which were then introduced and the high interest rates which they generated had a depressing effect on the major economies.

The Oil Market.

The table shows how average world prices of oil have moved since 1973, both in nominal terms and in real terms (nominal prices being deflated by the price of world exports of manufactures). The two great increases occurred in 1973–74 and 1979–80.

World production of crude oil in 1985 was at the same level (21 billion barrels)as it had been in 1974. However, OPEC production was down to below 6 billion barrels. Saudi Arabia was unwilling to continue withholding production so that other members— such as expansionist Libya, war-torn Iran and Iraq and heavily indebted Nigeria—could exceed their quotas: Saudi production expanded rapidly. Market forces took over. The spot price of oil collapsed, from just under $30 a barrel at the beginning of December 1985 to $10 a barrel at the beginning of April 1986. The cartel had fallen apart.

The OPEC members agreed to new quotas which, if adhered to, would keep up the price of oil, but the strains within the organization proved to be too great and in October 1988 the OPEC price fell short of $12 a barrel. The fall reflected high world stocks and excess production of crude oil. The oil market could now be best characterised as a free-for-all. Early in 1999 the average OPEC price was $11 a barrel, but with the onset of war in the Balkans it rose rapidly.

Crisis in the Banking System.

During the second oil crisis the non-oil developing countries were in general not prepared to take the harsh measures needed to control their deficits, so long as they could obtain finance from somewhere. Although this response of the poor countries was understandable, it contributed to the growing problem of international indebtedness (see **G45**).

The difficulties experienced by the international banks were partly beyond their control, being due, for instance, to the rise in interest rates produced by restrictive monetary policies, and partly to their own lack of caution. Perhaps they were too much swayed by the competitive pressures to make loans from the additional deposits coming from the OPEC surplus, and complacently confident that "the authorities" would rescue banks in trouble.

The Mexican debt crisis of late 1982 brought out the precariousness of the international banking system. After that, one substantial debtor country after another sought debt rescheduling or a standstill on repayments of principal. Stop-gap credits had to be cobbled together, and in addition the IMF emergency lending facility was enlarged, and agreement was reached to expand the IMF quota resources by about half.

The Rise and Fall of the Dollar.

The dollar appreciated very rapidly - by some 20 per cent - in 1984. This was mainly a consequence of developments in financial markets. Interest rates in the United States were high, due to the strength of economic expansion and the consequent demand for funds, and to the vast Federal Government budget

WORLD PRICE AND PRODUCTION OF OIL, 1973–98

| | Price (OPEC average) | | Production (billion barrels) | |
	Nominal ($ per barrel)	Real (1973 = 100)	OPEC	World
1973	3·5	100	11·3	21·2
1974	9·6	228	11·2	21·2
1978	13·1	222	10·9	23·1
1979	19·0	283	11·3	24·0
1980	31·9	428	9·8	23·1
1985	28·0	442	5·8	20·8
1986	15·6	220	6·7	21·9
1994	15·9	165	9·5	24·0
1996	20·4	200	9·7	24·7
1997	19·3	212	9·9	26·3
1998	13·0	..	9·9	26·8

deficit which, on account of the restrictive monetary policy, was financed by debt issue. These high rates of interest, together with the anticipated profitability of the booming economy and the widespread sentiment that the dollar would continue to rise, attracted funds from abroad. The long-expected depreciation of the dollar eventually came in March 1985: it had fallen 20 per cent against other currencies by the end of the year.

World Financial Crisis, 1987.

A global financial crisis occurred in October 1987. The most fundamental cause was a loss of confidence in the economic policies of the US Government. No significant action had been taken to reduce the Federal budget deficit—action which would be needed to eliminate the trade deficit.

The budget deficit and tight monetary policy increased US interest rates. This posed a threat to equity prices, which had risen during the year on a speculative wave. Market operators became increasingly sceptical that the dollar could be supported in the face of the US trade deficit.In October the markets panicked, share prices plummeted and, as funds left the US, the dollar depreciated sharply. Stock exchanges around the world followed the New York lead.

The financial crisis led to fears that it would cause world-wide economic recession if business confidence was shaken and investment dried up. As a precaution, governments in various countries responded to the deflationary impetus by adopting more expansionary fiscal and monetary policies, hoping thereby to lower interest rates. In other respects, conditions in 1988 were favourable for faster world economic growth: world inflation was lower than it had been for many years, and oil and primary commodity prices were low. These propitious factors prevailed: the OECD economy grew rapidly.

World Recession, 1990–93.

It was the prospect of inflation accelerating which caused most governments—including those of the United States and the United Kingdom—to raise interest rates during 1988. When inflationary pressure built up, economic growth was reined in. The United States and various EU countries moved into recession, and the economies of Eastern Europe contracted as planning and direction were dismantled without being replaced by markets and incentives. The table shows that 1991 was a year of serious recession in the advanced economies, as were 1992 and 1993. However, growth picked up in 1994, led by the United States, and tardy economic recovery continued in 1996 and 1997. Nevertheless, growth of output and living standards over the 1990s is likely to fall well short of post-war achievements in most countries of the OECD.

ANNUAL AVERAGE GROWTH RATES OF REAL GDP IN THE ADVANCED ECONOMIES, 1980–98

1980–89	1990–98	1990	1991	1992	1993
2·9	2·3	2·7	1·2	1·9	1·2

1994	1995	1996	1997	1998
3·2	2·5	3·0	3·1	2·0

The Economic Performance of Japan.

Japan's economy outpaced all the major industrial economies until the 1990s. Over the period 1965–89 annual growth of real income per head was no less than 4·3 per cent. Even in the 1980s it was 3·2 per cent, whereas inflation was only 1·4 per cent per annum. The current account surplus was consistently above 2 per cent of GNP, partly offset by an outflow of long term capital, and the yen continued to appreciate in value. The Tokyo stock market rose inexorably—by over fourfold between 1982 and 1989.

By 1990 Japan's national income per capita (expressed in purchasing power parity) was 10 per cent higher than Britain's, and its total GNP was 55 per cent that of the United States. Japan, with its population of 124 million, had become an economic superpower. Its success is bound up with the hard work and thriftiness of its people.

In 1990 signs emerged that Japanese economic confidence and expectations were faltering. Despite a continuing current account surplus, the yen depreciated. The Nikkei share index fell sharply and interest rates were raised. Speculative buying of shares and land was probably the culprit. The high level of share prices in relation to company profits strengthened the incentive to move capital abroad, and this realisation triggered the fall in the yen and in shares.

While the yen recovered, asset prices did not. Between the end of 1989 and the end of 1992 share prices were halved. The fall in the prices of their assets placed the Japanese banks in financial jeopardy. The economy slowed down from a growth rate of 5 per cent in 1990 to 1 per cent in 1992 to less than 1 per cent in the years 1993–95. The fear of a financial crisis sapped the economy, and in 1992 and again in 1993 the Japanese Government resorted to fiscal expansion as a means of stimulating the economy. Recorded unemployment remained low but this was because excess labour was retained by firms. The inexorable rise of the yen – by a quarter in real terms in the years 1993 and 1994 – was a brake on economic recovery.Only in 1995 did it begin to fall—by a quarter in the next two years.

The Japanese economy stagnated in 1997 and actually declined (by 2·5 per cent) in 1998. Business confidence remained low and was further depressed by the Asian financial crisis (see **G**46). The banking system remained vulnerable. A fiscal stimulus by government was urgently needed to bolster flagging demand and avoid a stock market collapse.

Exchange Rate Arrangements.

In late 1998 the following exchange rate arrangements were in operation. 45 currencies, including the pound, the dollar and the yen, were independently floating. Another 56 currencies had "managed floats", *i.e.*, floating subject to a policy of periodic government intervention. 13 members of the EU, but not including Britain, maintained a co-operative arrangement to float together under the European Monetary System. Most developing countries pegged their currencies to those of major trading partners, 20 to the dollar, 15 to the French franc, 4 to the SDR, and 13 to some currency composite of their own choice.

It is not clear from recent experience that greater exchange-rate flexibility can produce equilibrium in international payments. It seems that the balance of payments takes a long time—perhaps two or three years—to adjust to a depreciation of the exchange rate. In the meantime there might be wage increases to compensate for the increase in the cost of living brought about by the depreciation. which in turn tend to neutralise the depreciation.

The table below shows both recent exchange rates against sterling and the movement of the *real effective exchange rate* of the major currencies since 1990. Each is measured against a basket of other currencies and adjusted for changes in costs to obtain a measure of competitiveness. We see that, between 1990 and 1998, the pound appreciated in real terms by 19 per cent, the dollar by 9 per cent, the mark by 4 per cent and the yen by 13 per cent: smaller economies gained in competitiveness. Over a period of several years, movements in exchange rates and in prices tend to offset each other. This long run tendency is known as *purchasing power parity*. However, it is only a weak tendency when there are large flows of short term funds.

EXCHANGE RATES, DECEMBER 1998

	Exchange rate against sterling, (£1 =)	Index of effective exchange rate, (1990 = 100)
Sterling	1·00	119
US dollars	1·66	109
Deutschmark	2·78	104
Japanese yen	192·30	113

The Integration of Financial Markets.

There is a growing worldwide integration of financial markets. Financial intermediation has become a footloose industry with only limited ties to particular national markets or stock exchanges. Borrowers and lenders in different countries are brought together often by intermediaries based in a third country. The major currencies are traded in most financial centres and dealing continues around the clock. There are now over 250 companies whose equity is traded around the world.

Much of this change is due to technological innovations in communications. The declining cost of communication has meant that arbitrage is now possible at only very small price differentials, and companies throughout the world are alive to the advantages of scanning money and currency markets on a worldwide basis to meet their requirements at least cost. The consequent competitive pressures have meant that those markets have become more integrated.

Markets for Risk.

Economic life is full of uncertainties and risks. Some individuals or companies dislike taking risks and are willing to pay to avoid them; others are willing to take risks in search of gain. Markets therefore develop in which risk is bought and sold like any other commodity. The most well-known are insurance markets. For instance, by pooling the risks of many customers, insurance companies can offer house insurance on terms that are attractive to most house-owners.

If the insurers are not as well informed as their customers, insurance markets may not work. For instance, if companies selling private health insurance cannot know about the health of individual customers and they therefore charge everyone the average premium, this can drive the healthy out of the market and push up the premiums. The healthiest of the remaining customers always have an incentive to withdraw, and so the market can collapse. This is an argument for having a national health service without permitting anyone to opt out of paying contributions.

Markets for Derivatives.

The explosive growth of *derivatives* since the 1980s has been one of the most profound innovations in financial markets since the introduction of limited liability equity markets early in the nineteenth century. For a price, the amount and type of market risk associated with almost any combination of assets and liabilities can now be tailored to suit the needs of market participants.

A *derivative* market is a particular form of market for risk. A derivative is a tradable contract based on (or derived from) something which is actually marketed, such as a commodity (*e.g.* wheat, oil) or a financial asset (*e.g.* a currency, a share, or a share index). Instead of buying or selling the commodity or financial asset itself, the derivative is traded.

The most common derivatives are *futures* and *options*. A future obliges each party to the contract to fulfil it in the future. It is an obligation to buy, or to sell, (say) cocoa at some future date. An option is a similar contract to trade in the future, but it allows the choice of fulfilling the contract or letting the option to do so lapse.

Both futures and options provide ways of avoiding risk. If an exporter will need to sell its dollar proceeds in three months' time, it can sell dollars forward at a fixed price, so transferring the risk of a fall in the dollar to the market. Alternatively, it can, for a premium, take out an option to sell dollars forward. If the dollar falls, the option is used; if it rises, the producer can take advantage of the price rise by selling the dollars in the *spot* (*i.e.* actual) market.

Derivative markets have expanded greatly in recent years. Trading takes place by computer link, or on a trading floor at exchanges such as the London International Financial Futures Exchange (*Liffe*), or over-the-counter (*e.g.* at a bank).

The Dangers of Derivatives.

Professional investment managers use derivatives to hedge against risk, *i.e.* to sell risk in the sense of buying risk protection. A derivative can offer the same exposure to a market as the underlying commodity or share, but more quickly and at much lower initial outlay and cost. There is no need to own the commodity or asset. Herein lies a danger: derivatives can also be used to buy risk, *i.e.* to speculate in pursuit of big but risky profits.

It was precisely speculation of this sort that caused the collapse of Barings, Britain's oldest bank, in February 1995. An employee of Barings – a trader in the Singapore derivatives market – speculated on a future rise in the Japanese share market (the Nikkei share price index). Partly because of the Kobe earthquake, the index fell, and Barings incurred overwhelming losses of over £850 million.

Volatility of the Foreign Exchanges.

The movements in the 1970s towards greater flexibility of exchange rates helped to correct international imbalances. The early 1980s was a period in which governments made a virtue out of their reduced control over financial markets, and appeared to throw themselves on the mercies of the market. It also coincided with a world-wide shift in the political climate away from a belief in the efficiency of central control towards a greater reliance on the allocative forces of competition. Fairly "clean" floating of currencies (with little central bank intervention) was adopted, and exchange rate policies were not pursued.

The burgeoning and integration of financial markets make control of short term capital flows very difficult and give rise to the possibility of exaggerated and destabilising movements in international exchange rates. Exchange rates became more responsive to expectations about currency revaluation and to interest rate arbitrage than to underlying current account imbalances. By the 1990s, the inadequacies of this system—the volatility and economic irrationality of the behaviour of currencies—were more apparent, and the threat it poses to the international economy more appreciated. Examples of the havoc that short term capital flows can cause are provided by the experiences of Mexico in 1994 and the East Asian financial crisis of 1997 and 1998 (*see* **G46**).

The European Union.

The *European Community* (EC), now called the *European Union* (EU), was set up by the Treaty of Rome, ratified in 1958. It consisted of six full members—Belgium, France, Holland, Italy, Luxembourg, and Western Germany. Britain had participated in the negotiations which led up to its formation, and had argued in favour of a looser "free trade area" without a common external tariff, and excluding trade in agricultural products. No compromise acceptable to the Six was found, and Britain joined with six other European countries—Austria, Denmark, Norway, Portugal, Sweden, and Switzerland—in forming the *European Free Trade Area* (EFTA).

POPULATION AND GNP PER
HEAD OF EUROPEAN UNION
COUNTRIES, 1995

	Population	GNP per head*
Austria	8·0	112
Belgium	10·1	112
Denmark	5·2	116
Finland	5·1	96
France	58·0	107
Germany	81·5	110
Greece	10·4	66
Ireland	3·6	93
Italy	57·3	103
Luxembourg	0·4	169
Netherlands	15·4	107
Portugal	9·9	67
Spain	39·2	77
Sweden	8·8	101
United Kingdom	58·4	96
Total	371·6	100

* Comparisons are based on purchasing power parities.

The United Kingdom acceded as a full member of the EC on 1 January 1973. Two of Britain's EFTA partners—Ireland and Denmark—joined on the same date, so forming an expanded Community of nine countries. Economic ties with the Community strengthened. Excluding trade with the oil-exporting countries, British trade with the original EC countries rose from 25 per cent of the total in 1972 to 30 per cent in 1974. In 1994 no less than 60 per cent of British trade was with the EU.

The table (**G52**) shows the population and relative incomes of the EU members, which numbered 15 in 1999.

Economic Arrangements of the EU.

The EU forms a common market with no tariffs or trade controls within it and a Common External Tariff (CET). There is a Common Agricultural Policy (CAP), which is maintained by a system of variable import levies setting *threshold prices* on imports of agricultural products from outside the Union, and by means of *intervention prices* at which agricultural products of the EU are purchased. The EU has a large Budget required mainly for supporting the CAP, *i.e.*, for subsidising farmers. There is free movement of both goods and labour within the Union, and a certain degree of fiscal harmonisation.

It is in the British interest that the CAP—with its heavy support of farmers—be reformed. EU funds are available to protect farmers by buying excess food and building up stocks of food if the free market price falls below the intervention price. As a result "food mountains" have developed. Various attempts have been made by the group of farm ministers and by the European Commission to cut the subsidy by gradually reducing the prices paid to farmers. However, reform of the CAP runs up against vested interests: progress is slow.

Towards Economic Integration.

In 1970 the Commission of the EC published the *Werner Plan*, which aimed at transferring the principal economic decisions from the national to the Community level, and at establishing within the Community complete freedom of movement of goods, services, persons and capital, with fixed and constant rates of exchange between national currencies or, preferably, a common currency. However, these ideas proved too radical for the time.

The *Single European Act* was introduced in 1986 to establish a free internal market in the Community. This was defined as an area without frontiers in which the free movement of goods, persons, services and capital is ensured. The single market involves the end of exchange controls, common financial services and technical standards, and mutual recognition of professional qualifications.

The Act circumscribed the powers of member countries to impose a veto in all but sensitive issues. It also made provision for what is called "cohesion", which means reducing the gap between rich and poor regions of the Community. The Act should be seen as a small step in the direction of a federal Europe.

The European Monetary System.

The *European Monetary System* (EMS) was introduced in 1979. A currency was permitted to float within a 2¼ per cent band on either side of the par rate between the currency and any other member's currency. Central bank intervention was required to keep the currency within the band. The participating currencies were defined in *European Currency Units* (ECUs), issued against the deposit of 20 per cent of national gold and foreign exchange reserves and used to settle intervention debts.

The difference in inflation rates among countries in the EMS necessitated periodic currency realignments. In each case the deutschmark was upvalued relative to the French franc.

The Debate over the EMS.

Initially Britain resisted the blandishments of EMS members to join them. This was partly because of the large and unpredictable flows of funds in and out of sterling on account of London's role as a financial centre. However, another reason was that, Britain being a net oil exporter, the British balance of payments is likely to move inversely to that of other EU countries as the world price of oil fluctuates.

Nevertheless, events were pushing Britain towards full membership of the EMS, involving entry to the *Exchange Rate Mechanism* (ERM). The ERM requires member countries to keep their exchange rates fixed within narrow bands and to adopt domestic monetary policies to achieve this target. Entry to the ERM was supported by most industrialists because exchange rate stability would reduce the uncertainty they faced in exporting and importing. In April 1989 a cabinet division emerged over entry to the ERM. The Chancellor of the Exchequer was in favour, mainly because it would impose an external constraint on Britain's inflation rate. However, the Prime Minister was against, mainly because it would involve loss of control over monetary policy.

British Entry to the ERM.

In October 1990 John Major, then Chancellor of the Exchequer, announced that Britain would join the ERM. The exchange rate was set at a rate of £1 = 2·95 deutschmarks. However, the rate could be varied within a band of 6 per cent—considerably wider than the 2·25 per cent band applying to other EMS currencies.

It is interesting to note that the disagreement between the Prime Minister, Margaret Thatcher, her Chancellor of the Exchequer, Nigel Lawson, and her Deputy Prime Minister, Sir Geoffrey Howe, which led eventually to the resignation of all three of them, was related to the dispute over entry to the EMS. To many members of the public this seemed an obscure technical issue, but underlying the technicalities were important points of substance, relating to the most effective policies to control inflation and to maintain national sovereignty.

The subsequent emergence of John Major as the new Prime Minister did not remove doubt about policy towards permanently fixed exchange rates and, a single European currency. However, the issue cut across party lines with all the major parties containing both supporters and opponents. The arguments involved the basic question: how much control over economic policy should be surrendered by national governments?

The Treaty of European Union.

At a summit meeting held in Maastricht in December 1991, leaders of the Community member states—the *European Council*—agreed on a draft Treaty of European Union (the *Maastricht Treaty*). European economic and monetary union was now a gradual but irreversible commitment. It was agreed to establish a single currency by 1999, administered by a single independent central bank.

John Major signed the Treaty but secured important concessions: Britain would not be required to participate in a social policy agreement, intended to provide a charter of social rights for workers. Federal goals were dropped from the draft Treaty, allegedly in return for concessions on other matters made by the British government. Britain's opposition to the Social Charter was based on grounds of cost and of ideology, *e.g.* it would "restore trade union practices that the government had spent much of the last twelve years eliminating".

Difficulties arose over the Maastricht Treaty as it required ratification by each one of the member countries. Some countries held a referendum. Only in Denmark was there a "no" vote, but this and the French referendum (narrowly in favour) cast doubt on the extent of popular support for closer union within the Community. Concessions were made to Denmark in the hope that these would pave the way to a successful referendum; and this proved to be the case. The British Government eschewed a referendum but managed to secure ratification of the Treaty in Parliament. The Community became the *European Union* on 1 November 1993.

Crisis in the Community, 1992.

Another reason for disquiet about the achievement of economic and monetary union according to the Maastricht timetable was the upheaval in the EMS in 1992. High interest rates in Germany posed problems for the countries with weak currencies and depressed economies. In particular, there was speculation against the lira and the pound. On 13 September, the lira was devalued 7 per cent by agreement, and on 17 September the pound was forced out of the EMS by speculation, despite massive supportive intervention (*see* G49). The lira was also then floated. The French franc came under speculative pressure but survived owing to Bundesbank support. The credibility of commitments to EMU was damaged by these shocks to the system.

In the light of the 1992 crisis and subsequent strains on the system, the problems of restricting exchange rate fluctuations within the EMS were more widely acknowledged. In August 1993 it was agreed that all ERM currencies except the guilder and the mark would have wider bands of 15 per cent. However, Britain chose not to rejoin the ERM.

EMU 1999.

At Maastricht in 1991 certain *convergence criteria* were laid down as a condition for *European Monetary Union* (EMU) in 1999. They concerned inflation, the fiscal situation, interest rates and exchange rates. Each joining country's inflation rate should not be greater than those of the three lowest-inflation countries by more than 1·5 per cent per annum. The ratio of the budget deficit to GDP should not exceed 3 per cent, and the ratio of government debt to GDP should not exceed 60 per cent. Long term interest rates should be within two percentage points of those in the three lowest-inflation countries. Finally, each joining country must have maintained ERM parity within the normal margins for at least two years. The argument was that, unless these conditions were satisfied, the tensions among divergent economies would be too great to withstand the permanent locking of exchange rates that is implicit in the creation of the new currency, the *Euro*. The European Council confirmed that stage 3 of EMU would start on 1 January 1999, with the Euro replacing national currencies no later than 1 July 2002.

The Future of EMU.

Perhaps the greatest obstacle to EMU was the need to reduce the budget deficits of the 15 EU countries. Having been 5·2 per cent of GDP in 1992, the ratio averaged 4·5 per cent in 1995 and 4·0 per cent in 1996. A further fall was required—and indeed the figure fell to 2·8 per cent in 1997. The danger was that governments, in attempting to curb inflation and cut their budget deficits, would raise taxes and lower their expenditures in such a way that their economies stagnate. Moreover, the effect would be contagious within this integrated bloc: a fall in the demand for imports by one country implies a fall in demand for exports by another.

The economic growth rate of the European Union, which had averaged 3·2 per cent per annum in the 1970s and 2·2 per cent per annum in the 1980s, averaged under 2·0 per cent per annum in the 1990s up to 1998.

The danger remained that countries would enter EMU without having achieved adequate convergence. If this proved to be the case, it would generate serious economic and political strains within the monetary union. The choice would then have to be made between less economic integration and closer political integration in order to solve the problems.

The Stability and Growth Pact.

Member states, led by Germany, were concerned that countries within EMU would lack fiscal discipline. As a safeguard against this danger, a *Stability and Growth Pact* was concluded in June 1997. It prescribed sanctions against countries that breach the Maastricht budget deficit ceiling (3 per cent of GDP). Such penalties would also assist fiscal policy coordination among member states. There is a counterargument, however. It is that governments will need more, not less, fiscal autonomy in pursuing their macroeconomic objectives once they cede power over monetary policy to the *European Central Bank* (ECB). The fiscal rules might thus be put to the test by governments held responsible by their electorates for achieving national prosperity and growth.

Expansion of the Union.

Greece joined the Community in 1981, and Spain and Portugal in 1986. East Germany was incorporated in 1990. In 1994 the electorates of Austria, Finland and Sweden voted to join, and the Norwegians voted narrowly against. The three countries entered the Union in 1995. The Treaty on Economic Union provides that any European state whose system of government is democratic may apply to become a member of the Union. Turkey, Cyprus and Malta submitted applications.

Ten countries of central and eastern Europe could also be expected to apply in the future. They would add another 105 million people to the Union. However, their incomes per head are considerably lower than those of the existing members, ranging in 1995 from 18 per cent of the mean in Latvia to 59 per cent in Slovenia. Their entry would bring the political benefit of greater stability in Europe, but there would be economic costs for the existing members. Unless the CAP were reformed, its cost would be greatly increased. Expansion would also widen economic inequality among member states and so require larger regional budgetary transfers, and it would probably retard economic and monetary integration within the Union.

The North American Free Trade Area.

The *North American Free Trade Area* (NAFTA) was established in 1994. It is a free trade area of the United States, Canada and Mexico, creating a common market with roughly the same population and income as the European Union.

The moves towards NAFTA began in the mid-1980s, partly as a response to the success of the European Community. The goals of NAFTA are to eliminate barriers to trade and investment and to improve regional co-operation. The United States favours the expansion of NAFTA to include other countries in the Americas; a likely contender being Chile.

Economic Reform in Eastern Europe.

Over 40 years of centrally planned economic systems have left a legacy of stagnating economies with major structural and macroeconomic problems. Output per head remains well below that of the EU countries. The remarkable political revolution that took place in almost all of Eastern Europe in 1989 and 1990 provided the opportunity and the challenge to introduce an economic revolution, with the dismantling of central planning and the introduction of market economies.

The problems of transition are considerable, as the new governments have inherited large fiscal deficits, rapid inflation, polluted environments and heavy external indebtedness. For instance, in 1989 debt exceeded $1,000 per capita in Bulgaria, the GDR, Hungary and Poland. The new electorates have high expectations of rapid economic improvement, but the move to market prices involves large price changes and associated changes in incomes and vast transfers of resources, including the closing down of unprofitable activities.

Between 1990 and 1994, total GDP in the transition economies of Eastern Europe and the former Soviet Union fell by no less than 38 per cent. Over the same period prices rose by a remarkable 1800 per cent! However, by 1997 those economies that had advanced furthest to a market economy—including Poland, the Czech and Slovak Republics, Hungary and Slovenia—had turned the corner and were enjoying strong economic growth.

2. INTERNAL DEVELOPMENTS

The Post-1945 Era.

Since the end of World War Two, the British economy has experienced mixed fortunes. Throughout the 1950s and 1960s, economic growth was relatively rapid by historic standards, and unemployment very low. The Prime Minister in the late 1950s, Harold Macmillan, won a General Election in 1959 with the slogan "you've never had it so good". There were also problems, however. Inflation persisted, and gradually increased to levels which, by the mid-1970s, had become unacceptable. Balance of payments crises periodically forced governments to deflate the economy. The share of public spending in total national income rose, and with it the share of incomes paid in taxes; there was continued argument about whether or not this was acceptable. A further cause for concern was that Britain's growth rate was less than that of many competitor countries. Over time, therefore, the country's relative position gradually worsened.

Thatcherism.

In the 1970s economic growth dried up, and the problems of inflation, balance of payments deficits and rising government expenditure all intensified. There was a widespread feeling in the country that a change of emphasis was needed, and this led to the election of Margaret Thatcher as Prime Minister in 1979. Mrs. Thatcher promised, and delivered, many changes. She broke the inflationary psychology which had taken hold in the 1970s, though at the cost of a large and prolonged rise in unemployment. She reduced the powers of trade unions, whose aggressive bargaining had contributed to the country's inflationary problems and had also seemingly held back productivity advances. She privatised many previously state-owned industries, and in this and other ways sought to reduce the share of public spending in national income.

Mrs. Thatcher's changes were initially highly controversial but many of them subsequently won wider acceptance within the country. There were problems, however. The sharp rise in unemployment put pressure on the public finances, with the result that Mrs. Thatcher made little headway with her aim of cutting the share of public spending in national income. This aim was itself a source of some problems, producing a squeeze on resources for essential public services such as health and education. Over the years of Mrs. Thatcher's leadership, the feeling also grew that her policies were in some respects unnecessarily divisive. The sharp widening of income inequality during the 1980s typified the problem: whilst average incomes grew quite fast, those on relatively low incomes experienced virtually no rise at all. These problems gradually eroded Mrs. Thatcher's support, and in 1990 she was removed as Prime Minister and replaced by John Major.

The 1990s.

At the start of the 1990s the economy was plunged into a steep recession, as the government was forced to deflate the economy in order to remove the effects of what, with hindsight, had been the over-expansionary policies of the late 1980s. The government also had to raise taxes in order to remove a substantial deficit in the public finances, itself partly a product of the recession but also of over-optimistic cuts in taxes in the late 1980s.

Not surprisingly, the combination of tax increases and a steep recession made Mr. Major's government very unpopular, especially since the government had won the 1992 General Election on promises of steady economic growth and tax cuts. Further unpopularity resulted when, in September 1992, the government was forced to pull the pound out of the European Exchange Rate Mechanism into which it had entered two years previously. The government had made ERM membership the centrepiece of its economic policy. When it was forced to abandon the policy, it lost its reputation for economic competence. Mr. Major's government never recovered from this.

Britain's Relative Performance.

As the 1997 election approached, there was naturally much debate about the government's economic record, after nearly 18 years in power. The government claimed to have transformed the economy; its critics argued that economic performance had been poor, with the country losing ground internationally. The statistical table on G59 shows that extreme judgements on either side of the argument are difficult to justify. In terms of income and productivity growth, the country's performance, compared with other industrial economies, improved somewhat during the 1980s and 1990s compared with earlier decades. However, critics could argue that there was still much ground to make up, with average productivity levels in the mid-1990s still some 20 per cent below those in

Germany. The country's unemployment and inflation performance remained poor. To some extent this reflected poor performance in the European Union generally, but both the U.S.A. and Japan could point to a better performance over those 18 years. Overall, such international comparisons pointed to a slight strengthening of the British economy in relation to its competitors, but there remained a gap between Britain and the strongest economies.

The 1997 General Election

As usual, economic issues played a big role in the campaign. The Government argued that its policies had generated a strong and sustainable recovery from the recession of the early 1990s. It pointed to a relatively rapid growth in average real income since 1993, and to a sustained fall in unemployment over the same period. The Government also argued that future projections were favourable. Its forecasts for the public finances suggested that the public sector borrowing requirement would continue to fall as a proportion of national income, and that it would be entirely eliminated by the year 2000. Critics argued that these projections were unrealistically optimistic, for example because they incorporated implausibly small increases in spending on basic public services. The Government's critics also pointed to other potential dangers. For example, in the run-up to the election there were signs of growing inflationary pressure, suggesting that the level of unemployment might have fallen to an unsustainably low level.

Many of the arguments between the political parties about taxes and spending which had dominated the 1992 general election played a much less prominent role in the 1997 campaign. This reflected a substantial narrowing of the gap in policy between the two main parties. In the 1992 campaign Labour had committed itself to increased expenditure on pensions and child benefit, among other things, potentially to be paid for by higher taxes. By contrast, early in 1997 the Shadow Chancellor, Gordon Brown, committed Labour, if elected, to stick to the Conservative spending plans for its first two years in office. He also committed a future Labour Government not to raise the basic, or higher, rates of income tax. The Liberal Democrats continued to make the case for higher tax rates in order to finance extra spending on, especially, education.

The First Labour Budget.

In the event, Labour won the election with a large majority, and at the beginning of July the new Chancellor, Gordon Brown, introduced his first Budget. The Chancellor confirmed the pre-election commitment to unchanged income tax rates and overall public spending levels, but responded to the danger of economic over-heating by a net increase in tax revenue from other sources. The total increase in tax revenue, compared with the previous Government's plans, was about £3·4 bn in the current tax year and nearly £4 bn in the following year. The biggest single source of extra tax revenue came from the abolition of dividend tax credits, a move whose main impact was expected to be on pension funds. Other sources of extra revenue included higher stamp duty, reductions in tax relief on mortgage interest payments, and additional excise duties.

The Windfall Tax.

The centrepiece of the budget was a once-off windfall tax on the excess profits of the privatised utilities. The revenue from this tax, which was expected to be around £5 bn, was not included as part of the Government's overall macroeconomic plans, because it was earmarked to pay for the new Welfare-to-Work strategy, aimed at getting unemployed individuals back into work. Under the plan the Government would pay a subsidy to any employer who gave a job to a previously long term unemployed individual. The scheme would also support education and training schemes designed to increase unemployed people's chances of finding work. The policy had been strongly advocated by Labour while in opposition. Critics argued that it provided a very expensive way of creating perhaps only temporary jobs, and were also concerned about the usefulness of the proposed training schemes. Another initiative announced in the Budget was the enactment of Labour's long-standing promise to reduce VAT on domestic fuel.

As economic events unfolded during 1997, the need for the Chancellor's decision to raise taxes became clear. The economy grew rapidly, unemployment continued to fall, and there were signs of inflationary pressure in the labour market. However, simultaneously the pound rose strongly against other European currencies (though not against the dollar). The combination of a strong exchange rate and buoyant economic growth posed an awkward policy dilemma. The government had made a commitment not to raise income taxes, and felt politically constrained in the extent to which other taxes could be increased. Hence its main weapon in combating over-heating in the economy was higher interest rates. However, the latter tended to raise the exchange rate still further by making sterling investments increasingly attractive. Higher exchange rates, in turn, threatened to damage the trading sector of the economy. Hence the political difficulty of raising taxes threatened to constrain the Government's ability to operate a balanced policy.

The 1998 Budget.

The Chancellor presented the 1998 Budget in March. The main emphasis was on a series of measures designed to help families with children, and to improve work incentives for those on relatively low incomes. Mr. Brown raised Child Benefits in line with the inflation rate, but also gave an additional boost of £2·50 per week in the rate payable for the eldest child in each family. Simultaneously he announced the intention of taxing Child Benefit for those at the top end of the income scale and additional help for children in lower income households (through extra payments for children aged under 11 with parents on income support).

New Work Incentives.

Work incentives were addressed in a series of measures. Support for child care costs was designed to encourage more mothers from lower-income households to seek work. Families were to receive up to 70 per cent of child care costs, subject to a maximum of £100 per week for the first child and £150 per week for two or more children. The payments were to be made in full for one-child families with incomes of less than £14,000 per year, and for larger families with incomes of up to £17,000. Thereafter the benefit payable would taper off as incomes rose, reaching zero for those earning more than £22,000 for one-child families and £25,000 for larger families.

The measure aimed to provide significant assistance to potential working mothers in lower-income families, while leaving those in better-off families to continue to meet the costs themselves. This reflected evidence that child care costs were a particularly severe work deterrent to those on lower incomes, because such costs represented a higher proportion of their potential earnings than for those with greater earning power. It also helped to bring the country more into line with many European countries, where governments typically provide much more support for child care. Perhaps because of this difference, lone mothers in the UK had some of the lowest employment rates in Europe. Critics generally welcomed the plans but argued that they did not go far enough, for example because the tapered withdrawal of the benefit left many on relatively low incomes with little or no help.

Working Families Tax Credit.

Another measure aimed at helping lower-income households was the replacement of Family Credit with a new *Working Families Tax Credit* (WFTC). The WFTC was planned to be more extensive than Family Credit, potentially helping around 1·5 million—rather than around 700,000—families. Its intention was to improve work incentives for families with children if their incomes were below £300 per week, by giving tax credits conditional on specified minimum hours worked per week. Critics noted that the WFTC would still generate high marginal tax rates, and they also argued that it might involve a trans-

fer of income from women to men within families, since Family Credit went to women whereas the WFTC could go to either parent.

National Insurance Changes.

Encouragement for lower-paid employees also came in the form of a reorganisation of National Insurance contributions. Employees on relatively low incomes would henceforth pay less contributions on the first slice of their income, and simultaneously employers' contributions on higher-paid employees were raised. The overall objective was to encourage employers to offer more jobs to those with relatively low earning power, among whom unemployment problems were concentrated.

The overall impact of such measures was to achieve some shift in the distribution of income in favour of lower-income households, and also in favour of those with children at the expense of those without.

The British Economy in 1998.

During 1998 economic growth slowed down, the main reason being a worsening of the balance of payments: export growth slowed sharply, whilst import growth continued largely unchanged. This reflected the continuing effects of what most commentators judged to be an overvalued exchange rate, especially against other European currencies, which made it difficult for British-based firms to compete.

Aside from the worsening of the balance of payments, 1998 saw few major problems for the British economy. Unemployment continued to fall, inflation stabilised at around 2·5 per cent, and the public sector finances appeared to be soundly based. Among different sectors of the economy, manufacturing fared relatively badly—being particularly affected by the high exchange rate—and the construction sector was weak, but this was compensated by rapid growth in business services, transport, and telecommunications. Productivity growth slowed somewhat, but this almost certainly reflected a short run cyclical effect, as firms held on to employees in the face of what they judged would be a short-lived slowdown in growth and sales.

During the year the *Monetary Policy Committee* (MPC) of the Bank of England caused some controversy with its monthly decisions on interest rates. In the first half of the year it held interest rates constant, whereas some of its critics argued that, with the economy slowing down, cuts in interest rates were essential in order to stimulate demand. The MPC's view was that caution was justified, since the data did not all point in the same direction. With hindsight the critics seemed to be justified. This episode showed the difficulty of short run decision-making in this and related spheres: judgements on interest rates have to take account of many pieces of evidence, and only rarely do all the indicators point unambiguously in the same direction. In the event, the MPC changed tack in the middle of the year, and a series of monthly reductions in interest rates followed. Whilst this might be thought a somewhat delayed response, it had the incidental advantage of strengthening the credibility of the Committee's resolve not to risk any resurgence of inflationary pressures.

The 1999 Budget.

In March the Chancellor presented his annual Budget. In the run-up to the Budget, most independent observers had predicted that it would be broadly neutral. In the event Mr. Brown produced a mildly expansionary Budget. This reflected higher tax receipts during the 1998–99 tax year than had been predicted. It also reflected the effect of the significant falls in interest rates during the previous year, which had reduced the burden of public sector debt repayments. A third factor was the cumulative effect of a series of tax increases over the previous five years, some introduced by Labour and some by the previous Conservative government. The overall effect of the policy announcements was to give away some £6 billion over the next three years, partly in lower taxes and partly in higher public expenditure.

The main source of tax cuts was income tax. The Chancellor surprised almost everyone with a reduction in the basic rate of income tax from 23 to 22 per cent. A second change was the introduction of a new lower rate of 10 per cent, to be charged on the first £1500 of taxable income. The latter was to apply immediately, and the former from the following tax year. These were the most visible parts of a package of reforms to income tax and National Insurance. Some of the other changes partly offset the effects of lower income tax rates. Thus, the previous 20 per cent lower income tax band was abolished. It had covered the first £4,300 of taxable income. Hence the initial rate of tax was lowered, from 20 to 10 per cent, but simultaneously the basic rate of tax would in future start at a lower level of income than previously. The Chancellor acted to remove what some had seen as an anomaly in the National Insurance system whereby anyone earning less than the lower limit of £64 per week made no payments, but someone earning fractionally more than £64 had to pay 2 per cent on the entire earnings, rather than simply the excess. This "entry fee" into work was abolished, and simultaneously the lower limit for payments was itself raised to £66 per week. At the other end of the scale, the Chancellor raised the upper limit for National Insurance, beyond which payments are not required, to £500 per week.

Redistribution towards Poor Families and Children.

The overall effect of the tax and National Insurance changes was intended to provide a modest amount of redistribution in favour of lower income individuals and families, who would be helped by a lower initial rate, lower National Insurance payments, and also by higher personal tax allowances. Conversely, for higher earners some of the gains from the lower basic tax rate would be offset by higher National Insurance payments, reflecting the increase in the upper limit for payments.

The Chancellor also set himself the aim of helping families with dependent children, and indeed presented this as one of the themes of his Budget. He announced sizeable increases in Child Benefit, with a new weekly rate of £14.60 for the first child and £9.60 for each subsequent child, rising to £15 and £10 respectively the following year. He also announced a significant structural reform of the tax system, in which the married couple's tax allowance would be scrapped, and simultaneously a new children's tax credit would be introduced in 2001. These changes were intended to reverse trends over the previous two decades, in which the tax system had been tilted against families with children. Mr. Brown also aimed to direct help especially towards lower income families, by tapering the child credit for those families with at least one parent earning enough to pay tax at the higher rate. The combined effect of these changes was a significant redistribution of after-tax income in favour of lower income families with children.

These changes were welcomed by some of the pressure groups which had campaigned for priority to be given to combatting child poverty. There were qualifications, however. In particular it was pointed out that much child poverty was concentrated in households, especially single parent households, where there was no-one in work and earning. For these families the Chancellor's changes would have little or no effect. Child tax credit would only benefit those in work and earning enough to be tax payers; and means-tested benefits would be at least partly reduced to take account of higher income from Child Benefit.

Abolition of MIRAS.

Another change which affected personal income tax payments was the Chancellor's abolition of tax relief for mortgage interest payments. The value of this relief had been gradually reduced by previous Chancellors, who had limited relief first to basic, and then to lower, tax rates, and had also reduced the size of loans to which it applied. The Chancellor's decision finally ended an element of the tax system which many economists and others had long since come to view as a counterproductive anomaly, directing help towards people who did not necessarily need it, and artificially increasing demand for housing compared with other things. The Chancellor's decision had been made easier by the sharp falls in interest rates over the previous twelve months.

Tax Incentives.

Other tax changes which directly affected individuals and families included increases in duty on tobacco and petrol. Mr. Brown continued the established policy of increasing these duties by more than the annual rate of inflation. In the case of tobacco, taxes were raised by 5 percentage points more than the inflation rate. This reflected the view that smoking, as a major cause of illness and premature death, should be firmly discouraged. Health campaigners welcomed the continuation of this policy, though the tobacco industry pointed out that British tobacco taxes were now significantly higher than those in the rest of the EU, risking an increase in smuggling. In the case of petrol, duties were raised by 6 per cent, some 3 points higher than the inflation rate. This reflected the government's continued commitment to discouraging the use of private transport, in an attempt to reduce carbon dioxide emissions from car exhausts, and so to play a part in the world-wide effort to combat global warming and the greenhouse effect.

Environmental Initiatives.

The structure of Vehicle Excise Duty was altered. Previously the same annual tax had been levied on all private cars, but in future a two-tier tax would operate: cars with small engines, which produce less exhaust emissions, would be subject to a lower rate of duty. Mr. Brown also announced that, from 2000 onwards, the rate of Vehicle Excise Duty on new cars would be determined primarily by their carbon dioxide emission rate. Environmental campaigners broadly welcomed these measures, though economists pointed out that they were not ideally designed to combat carbon emissions, since Vehicle Excise Duty is a tax on the ownership, rather than the use, of cars. The ideal tax system would tax car users according to their rate of use, and also according to their pattern of use (for instance, imposing higher taxes for use of cars in heavily congested urban areas during peak commuting times than for use in sparsely populated rural areas).

The Chancellor announced other measures aimed at reducing greenhouse gas emissions. Under the Kyoto Treaty of 1997—an international agreement aimed at combatting global warming—the British government was committed to cutting emissions of a basket of carbon dioxide and other greenhouse gases to 12·5 per cent below their 1990 levels by the target date of 2010. The government was itself committed to an even tougher target—a 20 per cent reduction in carbon dioxide emissions by 2010—under the terms of its 1997 election manifesto. To meet these aims, Mr. Brown announced a new tax on industrial energy use, to come into operation in 2001. The money raised by the new tax would all be rebated to industry by means of reductions in the rates of employers' National Insurance contributions. The tax would thus be "revenue neutral", its aim being not to raise income but to alter the incentives facing firms, making them keener to use less energy, and also to find ways of using energy in more environmentally-friendly ways.

The Chancellor announced various measures aimed at improving incentives for industrial innovation, especially in small firms. Tax credits for research and development expenditure in start-up and small firms, to take effect in 2000, would underwrite up to one third of such expenditures. Small firms were also helped by a reduction in their corporation tax rate from the standard 30 per cent rate to a lower, 20 per cent, rate; and an even lower starting rate of 10 per cent was also introduced, matching the new low starting rate for personal income tax. Yet another measure aimed at helping small firms was the proposal to allow them to offer tax-free equity options to newly-recruited managers; this was intended to make it easier for small firms to compete with larger firms when hiring key personnel.

Fiscal Loosening.

Some of the Chancellor's fiscal loosening came in the form of increased public expenditure rather than lower taxes. Thus, Mr. Brown announced additional money for schools, aimed in particular at helping with purchases of books; for universities, in the form of extra spending on refurbishing scientific laboratories; for the National Health Service, with new money for hospital rebuilding and for improvements in doctors' surgeries; and for law and order, with extra spending on surveillance equipment aimed at reducing the amount of crime. Some critics argued that the Chancellor should not have cut the standard rate of income tax, but should instead have used that money to increase further the amount of public health and education spending.

The redistribution in favour of people on relatively low incomes was achieved not by significantly increased taxes on higher income earners but instead by some fiscal loosening. In support of this policy, Mr. Brown pointed to Treasury projections that the public sector net borrowing requirement would be almost zero in 1998–99, and would turn into a surplus in 1999–2000. Critics pointed out that these forecasts were dependent upon the Treasury's forecasts for economic growth. The growth projections were for a slowdown—to annual growth of 1·1·5 per cent during 1999, but then a recovery to annual growth of 2·25–2·75 per cent in 2000, and a further improvement to 2·75–3·25 per cent in 2001. If these forecasts turned out to be too optimistic, it would then be difficult or impossible to achieve the public borrowing targets. There was room for doubt about the growth forecasts. The sharp falls in interest rates during 1998, and evidence of a recovery in manufacturing output, were consistent with Mr. Brown's optimism. On the other hand, the predictions implied that the economy would grow at a rate some way above its long-term growth rate.

Prospects for Economic Growth.

The post-war economy has seen boom-periods and recessions, but generally speaking, the UK has tended to lag behind most other industrial countries in terms of economic growth (see **G14**). Various governments have adopted policies aimed at stimulating growth. Prior to Mrs Thatcher's Conservative government, which came to power in 1979, most of these measures were based on demand management policies. An early example of such policies was the National Plan introduced by the Labour government in 1965. The plan aimed for a growth rate of 4 per cent per annum but was abandoned after only a year when the economy was faced with a balance of payments crisis. Most policies aimed at expanding growth through stimulating demand have failed because of supply-side bottlenecks. Mrs Thatcher's Government made a major reversal in political judgement by persuading voters to reward government for long-term supply-side economic policies, although, given the problems encountered in the period 1989–92, the evidence that the UK underwent a "supply-side" revolution under Mrs. Thatcher's stewardship is mixed. Though growth has been relatively rapid in recent years, this has gone only part of the way to restoring the relative losses of the past.

(i) Pressures on the Industrial Sector.

In common with other industrialised economies, the UK has seen a major shift in the structure or composition of the economy. This has involved a significant reduction in its productive base, specifically the manufacturing sector, and a greater dependence on the service sector. This process is known as de-industrialisation. To illustrate the shift it is useful to look at the structure of the labour force. Between 1960 and 1998 the total number of employees in employment in the UK hardly changed. Within this total, however, employment in manufacturing halved. This larger non-industrial sector imposes extra demands on industrial production. Capital goods for investment in services have to be provided from the output of the industrial sector, whilst industrial production is also needed for consumers employed in the services and elsewhere. Thus less is left over for investment in industry itself and for industrial exports. This has meant an inadequate growth of industrial capacity. Consequently when governments have attempted to stimulate the economy, bottlenecks quickly develop and imports of consumer goods increase rapidly. The result is balance of payments difficulties, which are only partially alleviated by increasing exports of services like insurance, and force the government into taking deflationary action. This vicious circle could only be broken by an upsurge in industrial investment, which until the last few years was prevented by declining

profitability, or by a healthy growth of net exports of services which would both alleviate the balance of payments constraint and provide the funds for investment.

Some commentators have argued that the problem was a direct result of the growth in public sector employment in the 1960s and 1970s. This had to be paid for either by workers or private employers, and trade unions made sure that it was the employers; if, for example, income tax was raised, this was passed on in successful wage demands. The result was declining profitability. This analysis is at best speculative. It is not, for example, at all evident that public sector employment grew nearly as rapidly as implied. In certain activities such as local government there was a very rapid growth, but overall the ratio of general government to total employment increased only modestly—from 15 per cent in 1961 to 19·6 per cent in 1974. The ratio was 19 per cent in 1996. There was a rather more significant increase in public sector current spending on goods and services as a percentage of GDP; from 16·5 per cent in 1960 to 22·1 per cent by 1975 In 1989 it was 19·3, but because of the recession had risen to 20·7 by 1991 and was still 20·0 in 1994. By 1997, it had fallen back to 18·4 per cent. It was argued that such figures understated the true change. They exclude transfers from people who produce to those who do not, such as pensioners, though this may be justifiable since such *transfer payments* do not represent final claims on resources by the public sector. It was argued that the claim of the public sector on output which could be sold increased by almost 50 per cent between 1961 and 1974 thus reducing the resources available for industrial investment. The Conservative government, subscribing to this view, was committed to reducing the share of public expenditure in GDP, believing that this was necessary to reduce taxes on both persons and companies. This, they believed, would restore work and profit incentives, although there is scant evidence in support of this view. Between 1979 and 1986 the share of public expenditure fell only slightly, mainly because of much greater demands on the social security system; thereafter some progress was made largely due to rapid economic growth only for this progress to be halted by the recession at the end of the decade.

This is only one school of thought among those economists who are concerned that Britain is becoming *de-industrialised*. Another group of economists, also concerned with de-industrialisation, rejects the argument that it is the consequence of the expansion of the public sector. They stress the inability of British industry to maintain its share of world trade in manufactures, a share which fell in volume terms from almost 9 per cent in the early 1970s to less than 6 per cent by the mid-1980s, though there was subsequently a slight recovery. The forces causing this failure cannot be arrested by a once-and-for-all devaluation. On the demand side the conditions for an expansion of British exports are unfavourable; an important reason for this being that Britain tends to specialise in products for which demand tends to rise relatively slowly in response to increases in the standard of living. On the supply side, it is argued, there is a vicious circle of declining market share, declining profits and investment and declining competitive power. Some members of this group then point to the need for demand expansion, in order to stimulate output growth, and ultimately, higher productivity growth, which is the key to international competitiveness. The problem in Britain, though, appears to be in stimulating supply in an effective manner.

Yet other economists have argued that Britain's industrial structure, similar as it is to that of Germany, cannot account for our problems. Rather it is that Britain has narrowed the technological gap between herself and the US—for a long time the technical leader—more slowly than have her major competitors, thus failing to exploit the opportunities for unusually rapid growth. Recently particular stress has been put on Britain's supply-side faults leading to non-price competitiveness. Particularly emphasised are flaws in education and training at all levels—often dubbed as low quality-low skill equilibrium. By low quality is meant low specification. Too many British firms, it is argued, have got used to operating with relatively unskilled labour, and as a consequence tend to operate at the low specification end of product ranges. Therefore they can compete only on cost, and as is shown elsewhere

TRENDS IN ECONOMIC PERFORMANCE

	National income growth	Productivity growth	Unemployment rate	Inflation rate
		(annual percentages)		
United Kingdom				
1960–73	3·4	2·9	2·5	4·8
1973–79	2·4	1·8	3·4	14·9
1979–89	2·5	2·0	9·0	8·2
1989–96	1·7	1·6	7·9	3·9
European Union				
1960–73	4·8	4·5	2·2	5·2
1973–79	2·5	2·3	4·2	11·8
1979–89	2·3	1·8	8·7	7·1
1989–96	1·9	1·4	10·7	3·2
United States				
1960–73	4·3	2·3	4·9	3·3
1973–79	2·9	0·3	6·8	7·7
1979–89	2·7	1·0	7·3	5·0
1989–96	1·9	0·8	6·1	2·7
Japan				
1960–73	9·4	8·1	1·3	6·2
1973–79	3·5	2·8	1·9	8·2
1979–89	3·9	2·6	2·4	2·3
1989–96	1·6	1·0	2·9	0·4

Britain's record in this respect is not impressive. Even more worrying is that it is not countries like Germany and France with whom in the medium term we shall have to compete on cost, it is low wage emergent economies like Korea and Thailand. Countries which can move to the high end of a product range will find that their sales are much less dependent on price.

Whatever disagreement exists about causes, there is basic agreement that Britain does have an industrial problem. Not least is the question of which new activities—be they in industry and services—will replace those activities in which we were once strong but no longer are. A 1985 House of Lords Select Committee documented the decline of manufacturing, accelerated as it was by the general recession after 1979. To many it was too messianic in tone, both in regard to its view of the inevitability of manufacturing's demise and the lack of new activities to take its place. Be that as it may, it is worrying that Britain still lags in fundamental international competitiveness.

(ii) The National Enterprise Board.

In 1975 the Labour Government introduced an *Industry Act*. Underlying this Act was the feeling that private enterprise, on its own, had not done enough to stimulate a high rate of growth. The Act aimed to remedy this by setting up the *National Enterprise Board*. Its functions were to assist the establishment, development or maintenance of any industrial enterprise or industry, to extend public ownership into profitable areas of manufacturing, to promote industrial democracy in undertakings controlled by it, and to hold and manage the securities of any other property in public ownership. The Board's borrowing capability was very modest in relation to the market value of the share capital of major British firms. Funds for aid could also be dispensed by the Board. Both the Minister for Industry and the Treasury had a responsibility to ensure that the Board earned an "adequate" return on capital employed.

Critics argued both that the Act was doctrinaire socialism and that it was not proved that such state intervention would have more favourable effects than the workings of free private enterprise.

Even before the NEB was effectively operational, state acquisitions in the private sector had proceeded apace. Normally the Government had provided help to ailing companies on condition of taking a shareholding, under the provisions of the Conservatives' 1972 Industry Act. State holdings in eight companies were handed over to the NEB at its inception. These companies were British Leyland, Rolls-Royce, Cambridge Instruments, Ferranti, Herbert, Brown-Boveri-Kent, Dunford

and Elliott, and ICL. The NEB acquired shareholdings in another twenty-eight companies by early 1978.

When the Conservatives won the 1979 General Election there was some expectation that the National Enterprise Board would be abolished. Though this did not happen immediately, it soon became plain that the new Government did not intend to allow the Board any role other than that of overseeing a limited number of companies in need of temporary assistance. Subsequently the NEB was merged with the National Research and Development Corporation to form the British Technology Group. BTG's aims were noticeably different from those of the NEB. The aim of BTG, which was privatized, was primarily to promote the development of new technology, often from the universities, into important commercial products. In order to assist the transfer of technology BTG could also provide finance, either through equity or project finance.

(iii) Privatisation.

Soon after taking office, the Conservative Government announced its intention to sell off a portion of official holdings in several sectors—British Airways, British Aerospace, shipbuilding, freight and British Petroleum. The Government believed that reform of the nationalised industries was a key element in providing the framework for economic recovery, arguing that exposure to market forces through privatisation and competition was the best way to improve industrial performance. Companies that have now been privatised include British Gas, British Telecom, British Steel Corporation, Cable and Wireless, the National Freight Consortium, Amersham International, The Rover Group, Jaguar, Enterprise Oil, Britoil, Associated British Ports, Rolls-Royce, Royal Ordnance, BAA, nearly all the National Bus Company subsidiaries, the British Shipbuilders' warship-building yards, the regional water and sewage companies in England and Wales, and, most recently, the electricity distribution and generating industries, as well as British Coal, British Rail, Scottish Nuclear and Nuclear Electric. A major problem is that, to the extent that privatised industries retain monopoly power, there is a need for close regulation to force their managers to behave competitively. It is generally believed that the regulatory devices used are often imperfect.

One major effect of the privatisation program was an increase in share ownership. In 1979 only 7 per cent of the population were shareholders; by 1998 this had increased to 20 per cent, although many individuals hold shares in only one or two companies. There has also been a fashion for privatisation abroad, but the process has been more intense in Britain than in any other country. Going alongside this programme, were programmes of "liberalisation" and of "franchising". By the former is meant the policy of allowing and encouraging competition in previously uncompetitive or regulated markets—for example, telecommunications and road passenger transport. By the latter is meant the process by which state establishments (*e.g.* hospitals) "put out" certain functions, which had previously been performed "in-house", to private companies (*e.g.* catering). This spread of sub-contracting, however, extends far beyond publicly provided activities.

(iv) An Approach to Industrial Strategy.

In 1975 a White Paper, entitled *An Approach to Industrial Strategy*, set out the Government's general views on planning for growth. The strategy was based on the fact that despite Britain's overall poor performance, some sectors had done very well. There was therefore a need to identify specific problems which had held back particular industries as well as a need to identify general problems. Some 40 sectoral working parties were established under the auspices of the National Economic Development Council, and were composed of representatives of management, workers and the Government. Their task was to analyse their own industry in detail and to agree a programme of action designed to improve competitive performance, and to make Britain a high-output, high-wage economy. Specifically they were asked to consider the following: how to get more out of existing investment and manpower in order to improve productivity; how to increase the level and quality of investment; how to improve non-price competitiveness; how to ensure that their sectors concentrate on the "correct" export markets; how to provide a sufficient supply of skilled workers. In 1978 the working parties presented their first reports. The planning provisions of the 1975 Industry Act were abandoned by the Conservative Government, but the NEDC Sector Working Parties continue to operate, albeit under a series of different titles. It is difficult to quantify their precise effects upon sectoral performance.

One area where the 1975 Industry Act had practical consequences was in the introduction of schemes of financial assistance to industry. The assistance was directed towards increases in productivity (*e.g.* by re-equipment), or to increases in product relevance to export markets, to improving non-price competitiveness and to improving marketing. In addition there was an export market entry guarantee scheme to cover the risks of entering new markets. Nevertheless, the crucial question remained not just whether the performance of particular sectors could be improved, but whether it could be ensured that Britain produced the right mix of products to meet the threats to employment and to our trading balance of both technological change and foreign competition. On these issues, the Conservative Government believed firmly that if Britain is to succeed, the impetus is most likely to come from risk-taking individual entrepreneurs and companies. In January 1988 the Department of Trade and Industry launched its Enterprise Initiative specifically to help small and medium-sized businesses. Great stress was put on the role of a network of Business Links to help small firms. Further measures were announced in a succession of White Papers on Competitiveness from 1994.

(v) British Oil Production.

The discovery of oil and gas in the UK Continental Shelf in the 1960s had major implications for the UK's long-term growth prospects. Arguably the main benefit has been to "cushion" our trade deficit as revenues from oil exports and a reduced dependence on imported oil have helped to offset a gradual deterioration in the balance on non-oil goods. The other side of the coin, however, is that after the first oil price shock in 1973 many oil producers' exchange rates became overvalued as the price of oil rose and also more volatile as exchange rates were influenced by expectations of future oil price movements. The UK, along with other oil producing nations suffered as a higher exchange rate eroded competitiveness and exacerbated the deterioration in the trade balance. Linked to this is the idea of Dutch disease which suggests that the loss of competitiveness resulting from petrocurrency status accelerates the process of de-industrialisation. Problems such as these were specific to the oil producing countries, but the repercussions of two oil price hikes, in 1973 and 1979, were felt world-wide.

The UK became self-sufficient in oil in 1981 and production of gas and oil reached a peak in 1996. In 1997 Britain was the world's ninth largest producer of crude oil and natural gas liquids, with an output of 351,250 tonnes a day. The UK will remain self-sufficient for some time. However, the viability of producing oil from offshore reserves depends on many economic factors, not least of which is the price of oil itself. Following the oil price collapse in 1986, the prospects for future production weakened, since the incentive for further exploration and development diminished. The subsequent recovery of prices in 1987 diminished but did not fully allay the concern, although the upturn in the world oil market following Iraq's invasion of Kuwait in August 1990 produced the first conclusive evidence of a recovery in Britain's oil exploration industry.

Meanwhile the Government tried to ensure that the state got a substantial share of the returns from offshore oil extraction. A major worry was the large degree of foreign ownership of the oil companies involved in the operations. A specific oil tax was initially proposed in the 1974 Oil Taxation Bill and implemented, in a modified form, in the 1975 Oil Taxation Act. Petroleum Revenue Tax (PRT) was introduced at 45 per cent and royalties at 12·5 per cent. Corporation tax was to be deducted from the residue at the standard rate. It was envisaged that this would allow the oil companies an adequate return on capital. A ring fence around a company's oil extraction activities prohibited losses made outside the North Sea being used to offset North Sea profits for corporation tax purposes. Concern had been expressed that such a tax system would discourage exploitation of the "marginal fields", that is the smaller oil-fields which might not justify the huge initial expenditure needed to make them productive. Several safeguards were, therefore, proposed. No petroleum revenue tax would be levied until a field had earned back 135 per cent of its capital outlay. Fields returning less than 30 per cent on investment after paying p.r.t. would have the tax refunded. There was also to be discretionary provision to return all or part of the 12· per cent royalties. The Government reiterated its intention to press for 51 per cent state participation in the oil-fields, which it proceeded to do through the agency of the British National Oil Corporation.

Since its inception in 1975 the UK offshore taxation system has undergone many modifications. In August 1978 the rate of PRT was increased to 30 per cent while the PRT capital uplift was raised to 175 per cent from 135 per cent. In 1980 the PRT rate was once again increased, this time to 70 per cent. In March 1981, a fourth tax—Supplementary Petroleum Duty (SPD)—was introduced and was charged at 20 per cent of the landed value of gross revenues less an allowance equivalent to 0·5 million tonnes of oil per six-month period. In March 1982 SPD was replaced by Advance Petroleum Revenue Tax, identical to SPD save for the time of charges. The taxation system was becoming increasingly onerous for the oil companies and, as concern grew about the viability of developing marginal North Sea fields, modifications to the tax regime had to be made to ease the fiscal burden on oil. The main change was that a distinction was made between the tax treatment of the established Southern Basin fields and newer higher cost fields granted development approval after April 1982. For the latter group the PRT allowance was doubled to 1 million tonnes and royalty payments were abolished. In addition, Advance PRT was abolished from January 1987. In March 1988 the PRT allowance for the more profitable Southern Basin fields was reduced to 100,000 tonnes. In the Spring 1993 Budget the Chancellor announced his intention to reduce PRT from 75 per cent to 50 per cent for existing oilfields, and to eliminate it altogether for new fields. At the same time costs of new exploration and development ceased to be capable of being offset against tax. Fields approved after 1993 are charged only Corporation Tax.

The 1978 White Paper.

In March 1978 the Government published a White Paper, *The Challenge of North Sea Oil*. In this it was estimated that by the mid-1980s North Sea Oil would increase national income by £6 billion per year and improve the balance of payments to the tune of £8 billion per year. Perhaps a more crucial aspect of the White Paper was that the annual benefit to government revenue was expected to be £4 billion. This estimate has, however, on occasions proved wide of the mark, largely because of fluctuations in the exchange rate and in the dollar price of oil. Revenues tailed off at the end of the decade, in part because of the disruption to North Sea activity caused by the Piper Alpha disaster in 1989. They were £2·0 billion in 1990–91 and turned negative in 1992.

The most crucial issue was how the extra revenue was to be used. The 1978 White Paper designated four priorities: more resources for industrial investment; funds for energy conservation and new energy investment; the reduction of the level of personal taxation; the improvement of certain essential services. It was clear that the Government believed that North Sea oil provided it with an opportunity to stimulate sustained growth, and the first two of the four priorities were obviously designed with this in mind. However, the election of a Conservative Government in 1979 signalled a change of emphasis.

In the 1980 Budget it was implied that henceforth the oil tax revenue would be used almost exclusively to reduce the size of the public sector borrowing requirement and the scale of personal and corporate taxation. In the previous year proposals were published to reduce BNOC's role. Its preferential position in future licensing was ended, as were special access to official finance through the National Oil Account and its statutory role as adviser to the Government. Effectively its role in exploration and production activities was abandoned. In early 1985, the Conservative government announced that BNOC was to be abolished, and that oil prices would be much more closely related to market developments. The authorities' other main worry was the fast rate of extraction of North Sea gas.

(vi) A Productivity Breakthrough?

The main cause of our poor relative growth rates in the post-war period was lower productivity increases than achieved in other countries: and as in other countries this growth slowed down in the 1970s. Between 1963 and 1973, the average annual growth of output per person employed was 2·9 per cent in the whole economy and 4·2 per cent in manufacturing. Productivity fell between 1973 and 1975, in the wake of the first oil-price shock. Between then and 1979, it grew at an average of 2·5 per cent per annum in the economy as a whole and at 2·1 per cent in manufacturing. Indeed but for North Sea oil, this performance would have looked even worse. Capital scrapping appears to have been an important contributory factor. With the second oil crisis and recession productivity declined in 1980. Between 1980 and 1989 productivity growth averaged 5·2 per cent in manufacturing and 2·4 per cent in the economy as a whole. In the recession after 1989 productivity growth slowed. However in 1992 it resumed a healthy growth, particularly in manufacturing. In 1994 productivity growth in manufacturing was 5·0 per cent and in 1995 was 1·6 per cent. The corresponding figures for the whole economy were 3·3 per cent and 2·0 per cent. Slow productivity growth continued in the subsequent three years.

Many commentators described the experience of the mid-1980s as a "productivity breakthrough". Certainly the UK's performance improved significantly relative to that of its major competitors, at least in manufacturing. A number of possible explanations have been advanced for this. An initial boost was undoubtedly given by a very rapid shedding of labour. Some argue that much of the improvement was a statistical illusion caused by the "batting average effect". By this they mean the following. In the early 1980s there were what were then record levels of company liquidations and bankruptcies. If it was generally the least efficient companies which went to the wall, then their departure from the scene would have increased average measured productivity, without the performance of the surviving companies necessarily having improved one jot. However this explanation is probably a minor one, since it was by no means only weak firms which were driven out of business. The impact of new technology is cited by

RETAIL PRICES, AVERAGE EARNINGS, REAL AVERAGE EARNINGS AND REAL DISPOSABLE INCOMES
1971 = 100

	Retail prices	Average earnings	Real average earnings	Real disposable incomes
1973	117·3	127·2	108·4	115·4
1974	136·0	150·0	110·3	114·4
1975	168·7	189·7	112·4	114·9
1976	196·7	220·5	112·1	114·5
1977	228·0	240·3	105·4	112·0
1978	246·7	271·2	109·9	120·6
1979	279·9	313·1	111·9	127·6
1980	330·4	378·2	114·5	129·6
1981	369·6	426·5	115·4	128·7
1982	401·4	466·7	116·3	128·0
1983	419·6	506·2	120·6	131·4
1984	440·7	536·5	121·7	134·8
1985	467·3	581·9	124·5	138·5
1986	483·2	627·9	129·9	144·9
1987	503·3	676·7	134·5	150·0
1988	528·0	735·5	139·3	158·6
1989	569·2	802·4	141·0	167·2
1990	622·9	880·4	141·3	172·0
1991	659·5	950·8	144·2	171·9
1992	684·2	1,008·9	147·5	176·6
1993	695·1	1,042·4	150·0	176·2
1994	712·5	1,084·6	152·2	176·8
1995	736·7	1,124·7	152·7	182·3
1996	754·3	1,162·9	154·2	188·1
1997	777·7	1,215·2	156·3	194·7
1998	804·1	1,274·7	158·5	198·4

some writers as significant. Again it is probably only a minor factor, since other countries should have been affected in the same way, and yet the majority of them showed little improvement in productivity performance as compared to the 1970s. Almost certainly the major explanations lie in the changed attitudes and practices of management, unions and individual workers. People were frightened as they had never been before by the recession of the early 1980s. What is more the Government's anti-inflationary stance appeared credible—after all who had believed that any government would allow unemployment to rise so rapidly to 3 million? As a consequence management became more determined than ever before to achieve cost-cutting, flexible use of labour and efficiency. Workers and unions were more compliant, not least in the case of the unions because of massively reduced bargaining power.

Which mixture of explanations is correct is important for deciding whether the productivity breakthrough of the mid-1980s was a once-and-for-all phenomenon or whether it presaged a longer run improvement in our productivity performance. Despite evidence that working practices and management techniques continue to improve, an abrupt deterioration in productivity performance as the economy entered the difficult period 1989–91 made many commentators more sceptical about the durability of the improved productivity performance in the medium term. Such scepticism was increased by recent experience.

On balance, in the medium term it seems reasonable to hope for the productivity performance of the late 1960s. Changed management and worker attitudes should be a continuing source of productivity gain if these more realistic attitudes enable them to meet and react more effectively than formerly to the rapid pace of change in the modern world.

Inflation.

(i) Wages and Prices.

Between 1971 and 1999 earnings increased by 1174 per cent. Only part of this increase represented a rise in the purchasing power of workers, since prices increased by over 700 per cent. Thus real earnings increased by only 58·5 per cent—less than 2 per cent per annum. Purchasing power is also affected by changes in direct taxation. Allowing for tax effects, real personal disposable income went up by nearly 100 per cent. The table shows annual average prices, earnings, real earnings and also real disposable income (*i.e.* the purchasing power of total personal incomes after income tax), all as indices based on 1971 =100.

(ii) The Attack on Inflation.

Between the late 1960s and the mid 1970s there was growing price and earnings inflation. The reasons for this were complex, but significant were the growing aspirations for higher living standards expressed by workers in high pay claims. Employers were able to absorb only a fraction of their higher labour costs in their profit margins and passed the remainder on in higher prices, which caused the workers to make even greater pay demands. This behaviour was to a degree "validated" by relatively slack demand management policies. There were signs that governments in a number of Western countries were becoming increasingly concerned by such developments, a concern which became critical as they faced the inflationary implications of the oil crisis of 1973 in the aftermath of which there was a major spurt in inflation in 1974.

1975 saw an even higher rate of inflation. Average weekly earnings rose by over 26 per cent. Productivity fell and prices rose by about 24 per cent. Import prices made a smaller contribution to inflation than in the previous two years. Real earnings rose by 2 per cent, implying a further drop in the share of profits in domestic income. But through 1975 inflation moderated.

Domestic inflation moderated still further in 1976. The main contributor to this was the deceleration in the rate of increase in labour costs. Average weekly earnings were 16 per cent higher than in 1975. Real earnings were therefore slightly lower than in the previous year, implying some recovery in the share of profits in domestic income. By far the largest influence on the de-celeration of wage inflation was the voluntary incomes policy, first the £6 limit and from August its successor, which aimed at a 4· per cent increase in basic wage rates. However, in the last few months of the year price inflation showed a small increase. This upturn is explained by the sharp fall in the value of the pound during the year putting up the cost of raw materials and fuel purchased by British industry.

Retail prices were nearly 16 per cent higher in 1977 than in 1976, whilst earnings were less than 10 per cent higher. Real earnings, therefore, fell by nearly 6 per cent, and this meant some further recovery in the share of profits in national income. Real disposable income fell by the smaller amount of 2· per cent, because of the reduction of taxes in the April and October budgets. Productivity improved hardly at all during the year, and so the earnings increases meant a similar increase in labour costs per unit of output, these costs feeding through to prices.

There was a considerable contrast between the two halves of 1977. In the year to July 1977 prices rose at the rate of about 17 per cent, inflation being exacerbated by the depreciation of sterling in 1976, and further fed by the delayed impact of earnings increases of 14 per cent during Stage I of incomes policy, which ended in July 1976. Since by early 1977 Stage II of the incomes policy was holding earnings increases down to 10 per cent, real personal income was badly squeezed in the first half of the year. These lower increases in earnings together with the appreciation of sterling had their effect on retail prices in the second half of the year. By early 1978 price inflation had fallen below 10 per cent. At the same time earnings had begun to increase at the rate of about 15 per cent per annum. This, together with the 1977 tax cuts, meant an appreciable recovery in real personal income.

Thus by early 1978 price inflation had fallen back into single figures, and it continued to fall steadily until the middle of the year. From then inflation started to increase again, so that by the spring of 1979 was going back into double figures.

Stage III of the incomes policy, which ran for the year ending July 1978, was looser than Stage II, and was accompanied by earnings increases of nearly 15 per cent. This was beginning to feed through to prices by the middle of 1978, and was the cause of the acceleration of inflation. By early 1979 earnings were rising at an annual rate of 14 per cent, and this despite continued low rates of increase of import prices and a renewed squeeze on profits, implied a likely further increase in price inflation. Real personal disposable income continued its recovery of late 1977. With earnings rising faster than prices and with only a modest increase in direct tax payments, r.p.d.i. improved substantially during 1978.

Falling Inflation.

In early 1979, then, price inflation was starting to increase slowly but was still within single figures (at annual rates). Two important wage settlements following strikes—the lorry drivers and local authority manual workers—set the pace for a higher rate of increase of earnings. By the end of 1979 they were rising at nearly 20 per cent per annum compared to about 14 per cent a year earlier. In December 1979 retail prices were going up at a rate of 17 per cent per annum. An increase in indirect taxation contributed 3 per cent to price inflation. But pay remained the main force driving prices. The Conservative Government was elected in May 1979 with the defeat of inflation a central plank of its economic policy. Despite a de-flationary fiscal and monetary policy, retail prices continued to rise, reaching a year on year increase of over 20 per cent in the second quarter of 1980. Much of this was due to the effects of higher indirect taxes and continued wage pressure, and was despite an appreciation in the value of sterling. Towards the end of 1980 the rate of inflation began to fall. This was partly a consequence of the recession, both at home and abroad, making it difficult for firms to mark up over costs. Real wages rose, albeit slowly, implying a further squeeze on profits.

Inflation continued to fall in 1981, as pressure on wages eased and the recession became deeper. The year on year increase in retail prices was 12 per cent. Real personal disposable income fell by 1 per cent mainly because of the Chancellor's failure to index income tax allowances and bands in the 1981 Budget. The squeeze on disposable incomes continued into 1982 as taxation rose further.

The fall in inflation continued in 1982 and into 1983, when the annual rates were 8½ per cent and 4½ per cent respectively. This was despite a declining effective exchange rate. The recession and international competition were important influences making British industrialists very wary of putting up prices. At the same time earnings inflation was falling, being 9·4 per cent in 1982 and 8·5 per cent in 1983, whilst productivity was still increasing strongly.

After 1983 price inflation remained low, successive year-on-year figures until 1987 being 5·0 per cent, 6·0 per cent, 3·4 per cent and 4·2 per cent. The main cause of these slight variations was the course of oil prices. During 1987 inflation altered little. A strong pound, low world inflation and a resurgence of strong productivity growth all played their part.

RISE IN CONSUMER PRICES, PER CENT PER ANNUM

	1959–92*	1992–93	1993–94	1994–95	1995–96	1996–97	1997–98
USA	4·9	2·6	2·5	2·3	2·1	1·8	0·9
Japan	5·3	1·1	0·8	−0·5	0·1	1·6	0·5
France	6·1	2·2	2·1	1·6	1·8	1·1	0·9
Germany	3·5	4·1	3·0	1·8	2·0	1·8	1·0
Italy	8·8	5·1	4·6	5·7	4·4	2·4	1·7
UK	7·4	3·5	2·2	2·9	3·1	2·5	1·8

* Annual average.

Inflation reached a low point at the beginning of 1988, helped by a strong exchange rate. However, it soon became clear that inflationary pressures were emerging in the economy, largely as a result of excessive demand, but the trend was exacerbated by rising interest rates and sustained earnings growth. In early 1989, inflation averaged nearly 8 per cent and concerns over accelerating growth in labour costs forced the Government to maintain a tight monetary stance.

Ironically, higher interest rates feed through into higher retail prices via their effect on mortgage rates. This effect was seen clearly in 1989, when interest rate rises early in the year pushed inflation to a peak of over 8 per cent in the spring. A period of unchanged interest rate levels allowed retail price inflation to fall back to 7 per cent in the early autumn, before another interest rate rise in October (this time to defend a weak pound) pushed inflation back to above 8 per cent. Wage bargainers base their assessment of changed living costs on movements in retail prices, so an anti- inflationary policy based solely on the use of high interest rates may, perversely, create just the right conditions for a wage-price spiral.

More seriously, 1989 also saw a steady rise in underlying inflation. If one strips out the effect of mortgage interest rate changes, retail price inflation accelerated from under 5 per cent in early 1989 to nearly 6· per cent in March 1990. This shows that inflationary pressures were building up quite independently of interest rate rises. One source of pressure was higher unit labour costs as earnings growth increased and productivity performance deteriorated. A second source was the exchange rate; between February 1989 and the end of the year the pound fell by around 15 per cent against the deutschemark and by 10 per cent against the US dollar. This clearly put up import prices.

Inflation and the Poll Tax.

The introduction of the poll tax was to raise retail price inflation (both "headline' and underlying) still further. Combined with excise duty changes announced in the March 1990 Budget, the poll tax forced inflation up above 10 per cent in the autumn of 1990. At its peak in September and October 1990, retail price inflation reached around 11 per cent. Excluding mortgage interest payments, underlying inflation rose well above 9 per cent in the final months of the year. Although underlying inflation remained stubbornly high, a succession of interest rate cuts in late 1990 and early 1991, combined with the unwinding of the effect of the poll tax on the index, brought headline inflation down to 6· per cent in April 1991, to around 4 per cent by the end of 1991 and down still further by early 1993. But the fall in underlying inflation was smaller, though the deep recession greatly constrained the ability of domestic producers to raise their prices. As the economy emerged from the recession it was thought that inflation would start to increase again. Inflation reached 1·2 per cent in June 1993. This was the lowest rate since February 1964. Thereafter it crept up to 2·5 per cent per annum in 1994 and to 3·4 per cent in 1995. Then it fell back to 2·5 per cent during 1996. There was little pressure on prices from the cost side. Though earnings growth had increased to around 4 per cent by 1995, this was more than offset by weak world prices and in 1996 by a rise in sterling. In 1997 average earnings grew by 4·7 per cent—faster than in any year since 1992. This was the consequence of high demand in the economy. Productivity grew by significantly less and therefore unit labour costs grew by 2·5 per cent. Though some of this increase was absorbed in profit margins, it applied pressure on prices. Higher interest rates added more and thus retail prices went up by 3·1 per cent. However, since the Government's target of 2·5 inflation excludes the effects of mortgages, this target was met. Commentators initially perceived earnings growth to be getting stronger early in 1998. However, it transpired that official earnings figures were being calculated on a misleading basis, and indeed the Government temporarily suspended their publication. By the end of the year, it was clear that earnings pressures were in fact modest. Consequently the Government's underlying price inflation targets were being met. But, since pro-

ductivity growth was slow, unit labour costs were increasing relatively rapidly.

Growth in Earnings.

Over the years the growth in earnings had been a particular cause for concern: between 1980 and the end of the decade, our earnings were rising faster than those of most other OECD countries. Thus, despite improved productivity performance, wage costs per unit of output increased faster than those of our major competitors. In other words, they did even better on these critical variables than we did.

In this context, a remarkable fact is that throughout the early 1980s, when unemployment was rising, the real earnings of those in work continued to increase, as did real personal disposable income, which also incorporates the income of those not working. As the economy went into boom in 1987 and 1988 earnings inflation picked up. As late as 1990 earnings inflation showed little sign of slowing down, running at 9·5 per cent. By early 1991 it was still as high as 9·25 per cent. The unemployed did little to bid down pay. Rather it was forced up by high company profits, skill shortages, and the needs of employers—to attract good workers and to motivate their existing employees. During the course of 1991 earnings inflation started to moderate. By 1994 it was down to about 3·8 per cent per annum. It has remained low only, as we have seen, to rise somewhat in 1997. By early 1999 it was modest.

As a result of the above developments, inflation in Britain fell more into line with the rates prevailing in major competitor countries than had been the case in earlier years. However some commentators doubt whether this represents a permanent improvement in our relative inflation performance. Only time will tell; but it is noteworthy that in 1995–98 Britain was exhibiting slightly higher inflation than the other countries listed in the table on **G62**.

Inflation Policy.

Britain's cost competitive position in world trade has deteriorated over the medium term in relation to that of her main rivals; this is one major reason for her recurrent deficits on the current account of the balance of payments. The British share in total world exports of manufactures fell from the late 1950s until the mid-1970s. Thereafter there was some recovery. Nevertheless the recovery was small in relation to the losses of earlier years. There are essentially two methods of improving competitiveness. There could be a depreciation of the pound in terms of other currencies, although this option was severely circumscribed by membership of the ERM. Alternatively, there must be policies to limit the increase in British costs; either by increasing productivity growth or by limiting pay rises. Up to 1967 the Government concentrated on the latter alternative, either by restrictive budgetary policies or by *incomes policy*. In 1967 the pound was devalued, and from 1972 to October 1990 it was allowed to float, though the Government from time to time stepped in to prevent it floating freely. Since the UK's exit from ERM in 1992, there has again been a "managed" float. Most commentators believe that the pound is now over-valued because of our relatively high interest rates. However, for many years it was generally believed that an incomes policy was still needed if any depreciation was to be successful, and if harshly restrictive monetary and fiscal policies were to be avoided. Other harmful effects of inflation are discussed in **Part II**.

(i) Incomes Policy under Labour.

In October 1964 the Labour Government's new Department of Economic Affairs was made responsible for achieving an incomes policy. A "Joint Statement of Intent on Productivity, Prices and Incomes" was signed in December 1964. In this document the TUC and the employers' organisations undertook to co-operate with the Government in producing an effective machinery for the implementing of an incomes policy.

It was declared that growth in earnings per employee should equal the planned growth in national output per employee. Thus, in those industries (e.g., engineering) in which productivity growth exceeded this "norm", earnings should rise less rapidly than productivity, and in those industries in which productivity growth fell short of the norm, earnings could rise more rapidly than productivity. Growth in earnings per employee should exceed the norm only in exceptional cases; i.e., as a reward for increasing productivity by eliminating restrictive working practices; if necessary to transfer labour from one industry to another; if earnings were too low to maintain a reasonable standard of living; or if a group of workers had fallen seriously out of line with earnings for similar work.

To make specific recommendations on the basis of this policy, the Government set up a *National Board for Prices and Incomes*. The Board produced over 150 reports. There was no statutory authority to enforce its recommendations: reliance was placed on voluntary methods and the power of persuasion and public opinion. However, in late 1965 the Government introduced a compulsory "Early Warning" system, whereby it was notified in advance of any intended increase in incomes or in certain prices. As a result, the Government and the Board had time to consider increases before they were put into effect.

(ii) The Prices and Incomes Standstill.

This approach met with little success. A voluntary incomes policy is very difficult to implement, since it depends on co-operation among Government, workers, and employers; moreover, co-operation among representatives at the top may be undermined by "wage-drift" at the factory level.

Therefore, as part of the July measures taken to deal with the balance of payments problem, the Government introduced a "prices and incomes standstill." Increases in prices and incomes were as far as possible to be avoided altogether until the end of 1966. Increases already negotiated but not yet implemented were deferred for 6 months. The first half of 1967 was a period of "severe restraint." Any price increases were carefully examined, and the norm for income increases was zero. Any increase in earnings had to be justified by one of the four conditions for exception, referred to above. To enforce its "freeze" the Government took the unprecedented step of asking Parliament for reserve powers (including penalties for offenders), which were to be used only if the need should arise. For the most part, there was a voluntary observation of the standstill; but from October 1966 the Government found it necessary to exercise its powers of compulsion in a few cases. These powers lapsed in August 1967.

There then followed a year in which there was to be a "nil norm" except where increases in incomes could be justified by one of the four exceptional criteria. The Government could no longer legally prevent pay and price increases, but it did retain the power to delay them. Whereas the Government succeeded in slowing down the rise in wages and prices during the year in which it took compulsory powers, in the second half of 1967 weekly wage rates rose at an annual rate of 6 per cent. The advantage gained from the previous restraint was diminished but not entirely lost.

(iii) Incomes Policy after Devaluation.

Incomes policy was made both more difficult and more important by the devaluation of the pound: more difficult in that devaluation involved a cut in the standard of living, and more important in that it was important that the trading benefit from devaluation should not be neutralised by inflation.

In April 1968 the Government published a White Paper outlining its policy for the period until the end of 1969. Wage increases had still to be justified by the four criteria, and there was a "ceiling" of 3 per cent per annum except for "productivity agreements" and low-paid workers. Price increases were permitted only to meet unavoidable increases in costs per unit of output, and price reductions were required when these fell. The Government intended to rely on the voluntary cooperation of unions and employers over pay; but

it decided to lengthen its delaying powers for pay and price increases up to 12 months, and take powers to enforce price reductions recommended by the Board.

Between November 1967 and November 1968 the retail price index rose by over 5 per cent, mainly due to the effect of devaluation on import prices. In the face of this rise in the cost of living the incomes policy met with firm resistance. In practice the ceiling of 3 per cent per annum rapidly became the normal increase. In the first year after devaluation average earnings rose by 7·5 per cent. Workers were thus able to protect themselves against price inflation and to increase slightly their real incomes.

During 1969 wage and price inflation accelerated. In December the Government published a White Paper on its incomes policy for the period after 1969. It laid down a norm for wage increases of 2·5 to 4·5 per cent per annum: increases were to exceed the upper limit only in exceptional circumstances. Comparisons with other workers were not to be used, except in the case of public servants (e.g., teachers and nurses) whose productivity could not easily be measured. The Government's powers to delay the implementation of proposed wage and price increases were reduced. However, the incomes policy laid down in the White Paper was tempered by the imminence of a General Election and the recent cost of living increases; and it did not prevent a "wage explosion" occurring in 1970.

(iv) Conservative Policy.

On taking office in June 1970 the Conservative Government eschewed its predecessor's approach to incomes policy and disbanded the National Board for Prices and Incomes. To curb the inflation it maintained the economy in recession and squeezed company liquidity, hoping in this way to weaken wage pressures and strengthen the resistances of employers. In addition it attempted to resist demands for wage increases in the public sector, at the cost of prolonged strikes, e.g., in electricity supply, postal services and coal mining. In the former two cases it met with some success; in the case of the coal miners' strike early in 1972 the Government was unable to hold the line. In any event this form of incomes policy—like the "pay pause" of 1961—was both partial and discriminatory. The Government also intervened to curb price rises in the nationalised industries, e.g., postal charges and steel prices. The main initiative on prices came from the Confederation of British Industry (CBI): in July 1971, it asked its members to avoid price increases over the next twelve months or to limit them to 5 per cent or less in unavoidable cases. Over 170 leading British companies agreed to comply.

The Government measures were by no means a sure remedy for the inflation spiral. Moreover, even its apparent strategy of deterring wage demands by maintaining high unemployment was dropped in the reflationary budget of 1972. The Government appeared to place its faith in its Industrial Relations Act to solve wage inflation in the long run, by, as it saw matters, redressing the balance of power between unions and employers.

(v) The Pay and Price Standstill.

In 1972 wage demands became more difficult to contain because of the increase in the cost-of-living resulting from the effective devaluation of the pound in June and the rise in world food prices during the year. There was a marked increase in the number and seriousness of strikes (see **G21**). In the six months between the first and third quarters of 1972 average weekly earnings rose by no less than 7 per cent. It was inevitable that the Government would intervene. The expectation of an impending freeze encouraged further wage and price increases, especially after the CBI's period of voluntary restraint had elapsed.

The Government first tried to achieve a tri-partite voluntary agreement with the CBI and the TUC. After this attempt had failed, in November the Conservative Government reversed its previous policy and introduced a statutory Prices and Pay standstill. In effect there was a standstill on all prices of goods and services other than imports and fresh foods, a standstill on rents, on dividends, and on all wages and salaries including those previously negotiated but not yet in operation. Offenders were liable to be fined.

(vi) The Price Commission and the Pay Board.

In early 1973 the Government formulated its policy for after the standstill in a series of documents, culminating in a Price and Pay Code. Two new agencies—a *Price Commission* and a *Pay Board*—were established to regulate prices, dividends, rent, and pay in accordance with the Price and Pay Code.

In Stage Two of the policy—lasting from the end of the pay standstill on 31 March until the autumn—the following criteria on pay applied. The total annual pay increase for any group of employees should not exceed £1 a week plus 4 per cent of the current pay bill excluding overtime. There was flexibility for negotiation of increases within a group: emphasis was to be on the lower paid and the maximum allowable increase was £250 a year. Exceptions to the limit were made for, *e.g.*, movement towards equal pay between the sexes, personal increments and promotion, and some improved pension benefits. The Pay Board had to be notified of all settlements involving less than 1,000 employees but settlements involving more than 1,000 employees required its prior approval. It became an offence to strike or threaten to strike to force an employer to contravene an order of the Pay Board.

Prices in Stage Two could be increased only to take account of *allowable* cost increases. Moreover to allow for productivity growth, firms were permitted to pass on as price increases only a fraction of the increase in the wage costs allowed by the Code. Prices were also limited by the requirement that net profit margins should not exceed the average percentage level of the best two of the last five years. Exceptions were made for companies which could show that without higher profits their investment would be held back. Large firms had to give prior notice of price increases to the Price Commission, medium sized firms had to report regularly on prices, and small firms had to keep price records. Imports, fresh foods, auctioned goods, secondhand goods and interest charges were among the exemptions from the controls. Dividends could not be raised by more than 5 per cent over the previous year.

One of the problems facing the policy was the continued sharp rise in world food prices after the standstill was declared. This made public acceptance of the Government policy more difficult to achieve.

(vii) Stage Three.

Stage Three of the counter-inflation policy was introduced in October 1973. Price controls were similar to those under Stage Two. Wage increases negotiated for any group of workers were statutorily limited to an average of either £2·25 a week per head, or if preferred, 7 per cent per head, with a limit of £350 a year on the amount to be received by any one individual. However, further increases were permitted beyond these limits, to deal with certain specific matters: changes in pay structures, better use of manpower, efficiency schemes, "unsocial" hours, and progress towards equal pay for women. A novel aspect of the pay policy was the *threshold agreement* to safeguard against increases in the cost of living. It was possible for wage negotiators to bargain for a pay increase of up to 40p a week, payable if the retail price index reached 7 per cent above its level at the beginning of Stage Three, with up to another 40p a week for each percentage point it rose thereafter until the end of Stage Three in November 1974. It was claimed that these agreements were responsible for a large part of the wage and price inflation of 1974. Indeed in a purely statistical sense this was correct. The threshold was triggered eleven times, which meant an extra £4.40 per week for anyone under the scheme. It was estimated that 10 million workers were covered by such arrangements by October 1974. The idea behind thresholds was that unions, when negotiating wage increases, might have unduly pessimistic expectations about inflation. By introducing automatic compensation, such expectations would be taken out of the bargaining situation.

Without this compensation, it might be argued, many groups would have refused to settle under Stage Three terms, and their pay increases would have been just as large or even larger than the ones which they actually obtained.

(viii) The Miners' Strike.

Over 6 million workers had settled under the Stage Three provisions by the end of February 1974. The National Union of Mine-workers, however, feeling strongly that their relative pay had fallen and recognising their new bargaining powers resulting from the oil crisis, refused to settle under Stage Three. A national overtime ban was begun in November which in January 1974 became a national strike. In November the Government declared a State of Emergency and in January introduced a three-day week for industry in order to conserve coal and electricity (which depended on coal). It was unwilling to waive the Stage Three legislation in the miners' case, despite a declaration by the Trade Union Congress that its member unions would not invoke a settlement of the miners' dispute in support of their own claims. The Government referred the NUM claim to the Pay Board, for the Board to determine whether the miners constituted a special case which justified a further increase in their relative pay. The Government then called a General Election. The Pay Board reported just after the election, and recommended that an additional increase be paid, on the grounds that the long-run contraction of the industry would in future be reversed and that higher relative pay would be necessary to recruit and retain sufficient mineworkers. The incoming Labour Government settled with the miners on terms very similar to those recommended by the Pay Board.

(ix) The Social Contract.

The Labour Party came to power pledged to deal firmly with prices but to abandon statutory wage controls. It took early action on house rents and food prices, by means of controls and subsidies. The Pay Board was abolished and the policy of compulsory wage restraint thus finally ended in July 1974. The Price Code and the Price Commission were, however, retained.

During the February 1974 general election campaign an agreement between the TUC and the Labour Party was announced. This became known as the *social contract*, and formed the backbone of the Labour Government's attempts to stem wage inflation. The idea was that, in return for the repeal of the Industrial Relations Act, the introduction of a measure of industrial democracy and various other concessions, the TUC would be able to persuade its members to co-operate in a programme of voluntary wage restraint. In this way it was hoped to avoid the strains caused by formal incomes policies, which had always appeared to trade unionists to leave them without any role to play. Under a voluntary system they could still do their job—that is bargain about wage rates. The terms of the contract were that there should be a twelve-month interval between wage settlements; and that negotiated increases should be confined either to compensating for price increases since the last settlement, or for anticipated future price increases before the next settlement. It is hardly surprising that most negotiators took the latter option. An attempt by the TUC to exclude this had failed.

(x) Voluntary Restraint.

By early 1975 it was evident that this policy had failed. Some wage settlements were of the order of 30 per cent. In July 1975 the Government announced that there would be a limit of £6 per week on pay increases, £6 representing 10% of average earnings. There were to be no exceptions to this, and those earning more than £8,500 a year were to get nothing at all. The Government had the prior agreement of the TUC, which agreed to try to persuade its members to comply. The policy was voluntary to the extent that there were no legal sanctions against individual unions, but in another sense there were very powerful sanctions. These operated through the Price Code. No firms could pass on in prices any part of a pay settlement above the limit.

The £6 limit was due to lapse in July 1976, and the April 1976 Budget gave the first indications of a possible successor. The Chancellor announced that he would make cuts in the effective amount of tax paid by private individuals, if he could secure trade union agreement to a second year of pay restraint. This would allow an increase in take-home pay with the employers bearing less than half the cost. Therefore prices would rise more slowly and our competitive position deteriorate more slowly than if the whole increase had been achieved by putting up money wages. Agreement was reached with the TUC. From August 1976 more severe limits on pay operated than under the £6 limit. For those earning less than £50 a week, wage increases were limited to £2.50; for those earning between £50 and £80 the limit was 5 per cent, whilst those earning more than £80 could get no more than a £4 per week increase. Average earnings at that time were about £75 per week, and the implied overall limit was about 4· per cent.

Success of Policy.

There is no doubt that this pay policy was successful in holding down earnings. During the £6 policy, earnings rose by 14 per cent—a dramatic fall from the 30 per cent rise in the previous year. An all-round increase of £6 would have meant a 10 per cent rise. Another 2 per cent can be explained by the implementation of agreements made before August 1975, by moves towards equal pay, and by increased overtime earnings. This leaves only 2 per cent unaccounted for. Some of this "slippage" was no doubt evasion of the limits. There is no reason to think that there was any greater slippage from the 4½ per cent policy, and during the year of its operation (until August 1977) earnings rose by only 9 per cent. It is unclear whether the success of the policy was due as much to the threat of Price Code sanctions and to the recession in the economy as to the voluntary co-operation of the trade unions.

The 4½ per cent policy was due to lapse at the end of July 1977, and in the March 1977 Budget the Chancellor again offered the prospect of tax cuts if trade union agreement to a new stage could be reached. In the event the TUC agreed to continue its support for the 12-month rule, whereby no union should attempt more than one settlement in a year. It could not, however, agree to a limit of a specific amount. In return the Government gave a modest reduction in income tax, and introduced a "voluntary" policy of its own. This new Stage III policy was to last until the end of July 1978 and aimed for a national earnings increase of no more than 10 per cent during this time. No specific limit was to be put on individual negotiations, but the Government reserved the right to impose sanctions on firms whose settlements appeared inconsistent with the national target. These sanctions might be exercised through the Price Commission's controls on profit margins, through public purchasing policy and the placing of contracts, and through consideration of industrial assistance. The Government did stress, however, the possibility that larger increases could be obtained by self-financing productivity deals.

By the spring of 1978 it seemed that earnings increases during this stage of policy would turn out to be as high as 14 per cent. The Government was reasonably successful in holding the public sector down to near 10 per cent, though there were some costly productivity deals, particularly in coal mining. But the main problem was in the private sector. Though the majority of wage-rate increases were at about 10 per cent, earnings drift together with consolidation of the previous two years' increases in rates worked out for overtime, piece rates or shiftwork were pushing earnings increases way above 10 per cent. In addition, productivity deals were incorporated in about 30 per cent of agreements, in each case adding between 6 per cent and 10 per cent to pay. It is unclear how many of these deals involved genuine cost saving.

In the early summer the Government announced its plans for the 1978–79 pay round. Its objective was to limit the growth in national earnings to around 5 per cent, and it was soon clear that its tactics were very similar to those it had employed in support of its 10 per cent target during the 1977–78 pay round: seeking to keep as many groups of workers as possible to settlements at or very near to the target figure by direct negotiations in the public sector and by the renewed threat of sanctions in the private sector; allowing additional increases for self-financing productivity deals; and using promises of additional increases in subsequent pay rounds in order to induce groups regarding themselves as "special cases" to settle for 5 per cent in the current round.

(xi) Conflict with the Unions.

A serious problem, however, was the TUC's hostility to the policy. Although the TUC had not supported the Government's 10 per cent target of the previous year, it had in practice helped the Government by putting pressure on unions to settle for increases which were not too obviously out of line with its policy. This time the TUC was not prepared to do this. Its reluctance stemmed mainly from concern that the frustration apparently felt by many workers after three years of pay controls would lead to widespread unofficial strikes which would undermine union leaders' authority.

The Government therefore had to enforce its policy without TUC help. In the early autumn of 1978 it seemed to be having some success as several groups settled for not much more than the limit, but the policy was severely undermined by a two-month strike at Ford's which ended with a settlement of around 17 per cent. Subsequently Parliament refused to support the Government's proposed use of sanctions against Ford and other firms breaching the guidelines, so that the Government was left without any effective incomes policy in the private sector. As a result other groups of workers felt free to ignore the guidelines: the most spectacular breach of the policy being an increase of over 20 per cent for road haulage drivers after a disruptive strike in January 1979.

Such settlements in the private sector naturally made public sector workers unwilling to accept 5 per cent increases. The Government therefore offered 9 per cent more to most groups. However, this did not satisfy some of the lower-paid, public sector employees, particularly ambulance drivers and manual workers in hospitals and local authorities. They mounted a series of strikes, some of which—withdrawal of emergency ambulance services and disruption of hospitals—caused widespread concern and led to a growing public debate about the extent and the use of trade union power.

To deal with these problems the Government set up a new body, the Comparability Commission, to review the pay of those public sector workers who claimed that they had fallen behind comparable groups in the private sector: health and local authority workers were among the first to have their pay referred to the Commission.

(xii) Reluctant Union Acquiescence.

The new Conservative Government, which took office in May 1979, allowed the work of the Comparability Commission to continue until the end of 1980. Otherwise it eschewed a formal incomes policy. Its strategy to control earnings inflation consisted of two strands. The first was to use cash limits in the public sector and a tight monetary policy in the private. This was intended to moderate settlements. If it did not, it was argued, it would at least make unions aware that high settlements had an unemployment cost. The second strand of policy was to reform the structure of bargaining, so as to redistribute the balance of power between union and employer. By the early autumn of 1980, the Government had moved in the direction of declaring specific limits in the public sector. Whilst they were managing to keep their settlements low in public services, they were less successful in nationalised industries. It was certainly hard to argue that pay inflation in the public sector as a whole was noticeably less than in the recession-hit private sector.

There was a muted union reaction to this policy. Though 1979 saw the largest number of working days lost through strikes in any year since 1926, by early 1981 working days lost, like the number of stoppages, were at a very low level, and thereafter on both measures, industrial strife remained very low. By early 1982 the Government's policies were having some measure of success. In the nationalised industries even the miners were held to just over 9 per cent. In the civil service, the government launched a sustained attack on automatic comparability-based pay determination, arguing that market forces should play a role. Thus grades—like computer staff—for whom demand was high were offered greater pay increases than others, whilst new entrants—of whom there was excess supply—were offered no pay increases at all. In the weaker tax-dependent sections of the public sector—e.g. teachers—the Government was ruthless in enforcing very low pay settlements.

Meanwhile the recession kept settlements in the private sector at low levels. Through 1982 and into 1983 there was a further gradual reduction in pay inflation. In 1984 the policy was under some—albeit not serious—threat. There was evidence that the Government was finding it more difficult to hold the line in the public sector—a number of comparability deals were threatening. In the private sector, better economic fortunes were starting to result in some pay pressures. 1985 saw a continuation of these tensions in the public sector. Apart from the miners' strike, the Government faced severe difficulties from the civil servants and teachers. Yet, though it failed to hold public sector pay down to the 3 per cent cash limit, it was still managing to impose significantly lower settlements than in the private sector. In 1986 and 1987, however, pay in the public sector rose as rapidly as in private employment—by about 7 and 8 per cent respectively. In the period 1988–late 1990 earnings inflation started to edge up again as strong corporate profits and expectations of higher price inflation encouraged high pay demands. The Government was very eager to limit the extent of earnings increases and tried through high interest rates and a strong exchange rate to dissuade employers from conceding to what it considered to be excessive pay awards. In the public sector the Government faced severe opposition from several sectors. During the summer of 1989, British Rail and London Underground workers staged a series of one day strikes causing considerable disruption to businesses in central London. This was followed by a prolonged strike by the Ambulance service, who withdrew all but emergency services. The Government's policy throughout these disputes was to keep its distance from the negotiations and leave the discussions to the management and unions, presumably in an attempt to deflect criticism away from the Government at a time of increasing dissatisfaction with the Conservative Government and Mrs. Thatcher.

As earnings inflation threatened to take off during the boom, and was slow to come down at least in the early stages of the recession, many commentators began to doubt just how fundamentally the labour market had been reformed.

(xiii) Membership of the ERM.

After many years of debate the UK finally acceded to the Exchange Rate Mechanism of the EMS in October 1990. By accepting the discipline of linking the pound to a low-inflation currency (the deutschmark) the government effectively decided to make the exchange rate the main instrument of anti-inflation policy. Domestic interest rates were now largely determined by the need to keep sterling within its prescribed band; they could not therefore be used to target growth in the domestic money supply. Although the pound's value could still change if other members of the ERM agreed, it was largely the case that loss of competitiveness occasioned by higher-than-average wage inflation could not be accommodated by exchange rate depreciation. This was particularly serious given that most commentators believed that the pound joined at an overvalued level—sterling's purchasing power parity was generally estimated to be closer to DM2·40 than the DM2·95 central rate at which the UK entered. The hope was that wage bargainers in the UK reacted to the exchange rate discipline

by accepting smaller pay rises and bringing competitiveness more into line with European competitors. If this did not happen, the UK would suffer much slower growth and higher levels of unemployment than would otherwise have been the case. When France and Italy joined the ERM it took many years for wage inflation to drop to German levels. Adjusting to the ERM would have been much easier if the government either had accepted the need for some form of incomes policy, or made genuine attempts to improve the supply side of the labour market e.g. through better education and training. ERM membership was only likely to be a relatively painless anti-inflation policy if accompanied by domestic measures designed to make the labour market work. The UK's withdrawal from the ERM in 1992 relieved the situation. But the ERM episode revealed the continuing need for fundamental reform.

(xiv) Making the Labour Market Work.

Incomes policies were often criticised on two grounds. The first was that, at best, they work for only a short time. The second was that they cause distortions in relative pay and prices. Hindsight might tell us that their success is no more short-run than is the impact of savage budgetary policies. It might also tell us that whatever allocative inefficiencies are involved, such inefficiencies are minor when compared with the vast waste of resources and personal anguish caused by very high levels of unemployment.

The Conservative Government seemed to believe that structural reform of the labour market was the only real alternative to incomes policies of the conventional kind. If there were features of the labour market which tended to produce inflationary pressures, better, it was argued, to root these out at source rather than tinker with them as an incomes policy would do. Thus the emphasis on trade union reform and on refusing to use demand injections to attack problems of unemployment. This concern also explains the emphasis on reducing the real value of social security benefits as a percentage of income in work. Thereby people would have a greater incentive to work and to accept reasonable wage settlements. This approach was confirmed in the 1985 White Paper, *The Challenge to the Nation*. Three desiderata were mentioned: individuals pricing themselves into jobs; flexibility in the face of change; freedom from regulation. In this spirit, the Government reformed Wages Councils in 1986, in particular totally removing juveniles from their orbit. Wages Councils were finally abolished in 1993. The Government further weakened employment protection legislation. The Government also encouraged employers to engage in more decentralised pay setting, in particular to break away from multi- employer industry wide agreements, and to concentrate more on paying according to their own specific needs. The extent to which this "strategy" has worked is a vital, but undecided, question. Certainly the UK's failure to improve more significantly its relative unit labour cost performance casts some shadows of doubt. Yet many who are sceptical, now accept that our labour market problems are so deep-seated as to require structural action.

Welfare to Work.

The new Government is placing much faith in its Welfare to Work programme. This involves offering subsidised job opportunities to the young and the long-term unemployed. The 'New Deal' for the young who have been unemployed for more than six months involves four options: a subsidised job for 6 months; a placement with a voluntary organisation; a placement with an Environmental Task Force; and a place on a full-time education and training course.

In the case of a job, the young person is meant to be paid the market wage. Enhanced benefits are given to those with a voluntary organisation or task force, and benefits to those in education. The long-term adult unemployed are offered subsidised jobs. There are a number of underlying themes. These include: bringing the disadvantaged back into the world of work, enhancing their prospects by this and by training; and making benefits conditional upon a willingness to work. Critics point out that such schemes may simply cause others (who are not subsidised) to lose their jobs. The response appears to be that such 'churning' of unemployment would help the macroeconomy, in the sense that the proportion of any given stock of unemployed who are short-term will increase, and that this will cause greater wage restraint in the labour market. Some commentators argued that the National Minimum Wage, introduced at £3·60 per hour for adults in April 1999, would also improve the supply side. They believed that it would encourage employers to improve the skills of their workers, thus enhancing the nation's competitiveness. This theme of education and training was shot through the Government's 1998 White Paper on Competitiveness, with its stress on the 'learning society' and 'the knowledge-driven economy'. More novel was its emphasis on the need for collaboration and 'networking' among firms.

MONEY MATTERS

This popular section provides a concise yet authoritative introduction to the complex problems of money, investment and taxation. There is help and guidance on such matters as house-buying, self-assessment, savings and insurance, as well as details of the tax changes set out in the March 1999 Budget and an introduction to the world of electronic commerce.

TABLE OF CONTENTS

MONEY MATTERS

I. MONEY

1. SPENDING

Planning a Budget.

Most of us need some form of financial planning. Wages and salaries are usually paid in regular weekly or monthly instalments. The flow of expenditure, on the other hand, is normally much less even. Bills often seem to get lonely and like to arrive in batches. The way to deal with this problem is to work out an annual budget consisting of your major expenditures. An example is given in Table 1 though, of course, the actual figures will depend on your circumstances.

TABLE 1. *An Example of an Annual Budget*

	£
Council Tax	700
Mortgage or rent	2,000
House and contents insurance	200
Gas	200
Electricity	200
Telephone	200
Road tax	155
Car insurance	200
Television rental and licence	200
Life assurance	100
Holidays	1,000
Christmas expenses	500
Annual subscriptions	45
Clothing	400
Season ticket	—
	6,100
Allowance for price increases (say 5 % of 6,100)	305
Estimated total bills	6,405
Monthly average	533·75

List the amounts you spent last year under each of the headings. As prices are likely to continue to rise, it is worth adding on a little extra to be on the safe side. In the example, average price increases of 5 per cent are allowed for. It is also sensible to add a small amount for unforeseen expenditure. Having calculated your estimated total bills for the forthcoming year, you can then calculate how much money has to be reserved each month or each week for these items. In the example, this works out at £533·75 per month, or £123·17 per week on average.

Preparing a budget like this has a number of advantages. First of all, by planning in this way you can save money. For example, it is cheaper to pay car tax once a year rather than every six months. Annual season tickets are cheaper than monthly or quarterly ones. Also, it is usually cheaper to pay your insurance premiums in one go, rather than by instalments. A second advantage is that you have a clear idea of your major expenses, so you know how much money there is left over for day-to-day expenses. Thirdly, because the money can be put aside when you are paid, the cash is usually ready when the bills come in.

It is also possible to arrange this through a bank with a budget account. What happens is that you calculate your monthly expenses as above. The bank then transfers that amount each month from your current account (more on this below) to a separate budget account. A separate cheque book is provided for this account. When the bills come in, you simply write out a cheque for them. Using a bank in this way does have an advantage in that you can overdraw on the budget account if a lot of bills come in early in the year. The bank will, however, expect the account to run mainly in credit. There is also a charge for this service.

2. SPENDING ECONOMICALLY

Many forms of expenditure are almost unavoidable. Thus the council tax and rent or mortgage payments cannot usually be altered unless you move home. Nevertheless, in many other areas savings can be made.

As a general guide, the Consumers' Association publishes a monthly magazine *Which?* This provides a great deal of information about the price and quality of different products. Information about subscriptions to this magazine can be obtained from *Which?*, Subscription Department, PO Box 44, Hertford, SG14 1SH. Alternatively, it is available at libraries.

Food.

There are several points to remember when buying food. First of all, larger shops often sell goods at lower prices than smaller shops. As most people know, supermarkets often sell their own brands of many products. "Own brands" are, on average, cheaper than the brands of leading manufacturers. For example, on items such as peas, baked beans, soup and soap powder, own brands can be up to 15 per cent cheaper. On some lines, such as washing-up liquid, the savings can be even greater. There is no reason to suppose that own brands are inferior. They are commonly produced in the same place as the branded products. Often, the only difference is the packaging—and the price.

Other savings can be made with stores' special offers. Things like washing powder and toothpaste will be needed sooner or later; so it can make sense to buy these items when an offer is on, rather than waiting until you have run out.

When comparing prices, it is worth bearing in mind that the quantity varies as well. It is, therefore, better to compare the *unit cost* of products. This is the cost per gram or ounce. Packaging can easily make something look larger than it actually is.

Domestic Appliances.

Like food, the price of domestic appliances varies. Much of the variation depends on the number of extras. For example, a basic gas or electric cooker costs something in the region of £300. Such a cooker would serve a family quite adequately. If, however, you want a model with extras, then the cost can be £800 or more. A second important factor is where the appliance is sold. The price of the same model can vary considerably from place to place, so it is very worthwhile shopping around. There may also be a delivery charge. Discount warehouses are usually the cheapest place to buy appliances. The sales can also make a substantial difference to the price. Most appliances are likely to be cheaper in both winter and summer sales. Fridges are often particularly good bargains in winter sales, for obvious reasons. There is nothing inferior about domestic appliances sold in sales. Traders usually want to clear their premises for new lines. They also realise that January and the summer would otherwise be very lean times.

A particular question often arises as to whether to rent or to buy a television set. The advantages of renting are that repairs and service calls are included in the rent. If the set breaks down it is also likely to be repaired more quickly than if you owned a set. And if it cannot be fixed straightaway the rental company will provide a substitute until the original is repaired. On the other hand, it is generally true that it is cheaper to buy in the long run. This is true even if you buy the set on hire purchase. And if you decide to dispose of the set, you can always sell it. (Provided, of course, that any HP payments have been completed.)

Cars.

Cars are very expensive to buy and to run. It is quite common for the annual cost of running a car (including the drop in its secondhand value) to exceed £3,000. So it is worth thinking carefully about whether or not to buy a car. It may be cheaper to use taxis. They also have the advantage of removing any worries about parking, maintenance and drunken driving.

If you do decide to buy a car, the initial investment can be greatly reduced by buying a secondhand car. The value of most cars drops considerably in their first year. There are other advantages in buying second hand. A used car will have been run in and the teething troubles ironed out. However, if the car is more than three years old it must have an MOT (Ministry of Transport) test every year. The test is now very tough, so cars should be checked carefully before purchase.

If you do not get a guarantee from a reputable dealer you should consider having it examined by the AA or the RAC. They charge a fee for the service, but it may avoid a purchase you later regret. Alternatively, if faults are discovered it may enable you to negotiate a lower price.

Before setting out to buy a secondhand car it is sensible to study the market. Car price guides are widely available. They provide useful information on cars of different ages and condition. The two major sources of secondhand cars are professional dealers and private sellers. You are unlikely to get a bargain if you buy from a dealer, since they are very familiar with the value of used cars. If you buy privately you avoid the mark-up of the dealer, and so can expect to pay less. Even if you buy a new car, it can pay to ask for a discount, especially if you are paying cash. Dealers receive a sizeable discount on new cars. You may be able to persuade one to pass some of it on to you. Whatever sort of car you buy, new or old, you should give it a test drive. Even new cars are not immune from faults.

3. BORROWING

Under certain circumstances, it can be advantageous to borrow money. The biggest example in many peoples' lives is buying a house with the aid of a mortgage (see **H**11). On a much smaller scale most goods can be bought with the aid of credit. This does enable you to enjoy something without having to wait while you accumulate the cash to buy it outright. As prices rise, you may also be able to buy goods more cheaply through buying straightaway. And you save money buying things like season tickets annually. But there are some disadvantages with borrowing. Some people might find easy credit too much of a temptation and spend more than they can afford.

In addition, borrowing usually costs money. How much it costs depends on where the loan comes from. At the cheapest end of the scale are first mortgages. At the beginning of 1999 mortgage interest rates varied around 7 per cent and overdraft rates varied from 14 to around 20 per cent. The interest rate on personal loans was usually around 16 per cent. At the other end of the scale are second mortgages, some hire-purchase arrangements and check trading. The rates of interest at the top end can be 30 per cent per year or even more. There are many sources of credit, so only the main ones will be discussed here.

Banks.

A flexible way of borrowing from a bank is to arrange an overdraft. This allows you to overdraw your current account up to a limit agreed with the bank manager. Overdrafts can be a relatively cheap way of borrowing since interest is charged only on the outstanding balance, but by being overdrawn you might incur higher bank charges. If you wish to overdraw regularly it may be worth comparing different banks' charges for overdrawn accounts. Unauthorised overdrafts should be avoided as they usually lead to higher interest and other charges.

With a personal loan you receive a lump sum and pay it back in regular instalments. This can make it easier to manage the repayments. Often the rate of interest will be fixed for the period of the loan. This is advantageous if interest rates rise during this time but not, of course, if interest rates fall. As with overdrafts, it may be worth shopping around to find the most favourable terms, and some building societies now offer personal loans as well.

Credit Cards.

Credit cards can be a convenient way of spreading the cost of purchases over a short period. They are also easy to use. When you buy something on credit the retailer produces a sales voucher which you check and sign. The retailer then gives you a copy. You can also draw cash from a bank displaying the appropriate sign. Every month you are sent a statement showing how much you owe. You then have to repay a certain minimum amount. If you wish to pay more, or clear all the debt, you can.

Credit cards can be cheap if you only need the borrowing facility for a short time, or if you normally pay all your bills in one go. For longer term loans it is usually cheaper to borrow the money in a different way, such as with a bank loan. It is also now possible for sellers to charge a higher price for credit card transactions. At the time of writing (1999) few retailers actually imposed higher charges, but if this becomes common practice it might be worth considering another form of payment.

Credit cards are now issued by a wide range of financial institutions. Originally cards were issued free of charge but many now have an annual fee. The rates of interest vary between cards and have fluctuated in recent years between 1·5 and 2·25 per cent per month but recently some credit cards have been offering cheaper rates. Some of the equivalent annual rates are as follows:

Rate per month	Equivalent rate per year
%	%
1·50	19·5
1·75	23·1
2·00	26·8
2·25	30·6

Normally no interest is charged if the statement is paid off in full. For most cards, if only a part repayment is made, or if the payment arrives after the due date, there is no interest free credit period. On this basis, if you make a purchase just before the statement date and subsequently repaid the balance in full, you may get about 20 to 35 days free credit. If, however, the purchase was made, say, three weeks before the statement, you could get up to 56 days free credit. For this reason, it can be useful to have two credit cards. If your statement dates differ, you can then use the card with the statement date furthest away. Credit cards can also be used overseas.

Other Cards.

There are several other cards. Affinity cards are credit cards which allow you to donate money to a worthy cause—for example 25p for every £100 spent. Store cards are operated in the same way as credit cards and sometimes offer special concessions. However the rate of interest charged is often higher than for credit cards and, of course, you can only use them in the issuer's shops. Charge cards, such as *American Express*, normally have no spending limits, but they do not offer extended credit and there is a charge for the card itself.

Hire Purchase.

Hire purchase is a form of credit but the rates of interest on hire-purchase agreements are generally higher than those charged on bank or credit-card loans. Salesmen sometimes quote "flat" rates of interest. This refers to the difference between the cash price and the cost if bought on credit. For example, suppose you could buy a cooker for £500 cash, or £625 payable in monthly instalments for one year. The extra cost of buying on credit is £125. This gives an annual flat rate of interest of 25 per cent on the £500 borrowed. But this is not the real rate of interest. The reason is that from the first month some of the capital has been repaid. In fact, the average amount borrowed throughout the year is just over £250. The true rate of interest on the balance outstanding (rather than the original loan) is over 40 per cent in this example. This calculation is known as the APR or annual percentage rate.

Insurance Companies.

If you have an insurance policy you may be able to borrow money from the insurance company on the strength of it. The policy would have to have a cash-in, or surrender value. The interest charged on such loans is often lower than other rates.

Second Mortgages.

These are loans that are secured on your home. As a result rates of interest may be lower than on some other forms of borrowing but your home is at risk if you fail to keep up the repayments.

4. SAVING

There are several reasons why people save. They include the need to meet unforeseen expenditures, to provide for retirement or simply to buy large items such as a car. It is normally cheaper to pay cash rather than to buy on hire purchase. Although many people save only when they have money left over from their various outgoings, it is better to plan savings. That is, budget your income and expenditure and to regard savings as part of your regular outgoings. This allows capital to be built up on a regular basis.

Before deciding where to invest these savings there are factors that you should consider. The first is whether to invest for short or long periods of time. It is generally true that long-term savings attract a higher rate of interest. However, there are usually financial penalties or constraints that will restrict your ability to draw on the money when required. This loss of *liquidity* is important, since you may require money immediately to meet unforeseen expenditures.

Another consideration is the rate at which prices are increasing; that is the rate of inflation. The saver is particularly concerned with what goods or services money will buy in the future. The important rate of return of an investment is not the nominal or money rate of interest but the real rate of interest. If, for example, an investment offers a return of 7 per cent per annum and the rate of inflation is 5 per cent per annum, the real rate of interest is 2 per cent per annum. The individual requires 5 per cent per annum merely to maintain the purchasing power of his capital.

The real rate of interest is very important during periods of inflation because it may well be negative. For example, if the nominal rate of interest is 7 per cent per annum and the rate of inflation rises again, to say, 10 per cent per annum the real rate of interest is minus 3 per cent per annum. This means that when the saver withdraws money in the future, it will not buy the same quantity of goods or services it would have when the investments were made.

Having considered these general points, we can now look at specific forms of investment.

National Savings.

These are schemes provided by the Government. A summary of National Savings and their features is shown in Table 2.

TABLE 2. *A Summary of National Savings Investments*

Investment	Features
Ordinary Account	Instant access to savings
Investment Account	One month's notice required
Fixed Interest Savings Certificates	Can invest for five years
Index-linked Savings Certificates	Tax-free and inflation-proof
Premium Savings Bonds	Chance to win a prize
Capital Bonds	Guaranteed interest
FIRST Option Bonds	Can invest for a year
Income Bonds	Regular income
Pensioners' Income Bonds	For those 60 and over
Children's Bonus Bonds	For children

The National Savings Bank.

This was formerly known as the Post Office Savings Bank. There are over 20,000 post offices in the UK where you can deposit or withdraw money. There are two types of account available:

Ordinary accounts can be opened with as little as £10. They can also be opened for young children, but withdrawals are not normally allowed until the child reaches seven years of age.

Interest is calculated on each complete £1 deposited for a full calendar month. The money begins to earn interest from the first day of the month after it is deposited. It does not earn interest on the month in which it is withdrawn. You should therefore try to deposit money towards the end of the month and withdraw at the beginning of the month. There are two rates of interest. In 1999 these were 1·00 per cent and 1·20 per cent. The higher rate applies to balances of £500 or more, provided the account has been kept open for the whole calendar year. The lower rate applies to other balances. The interest is added on 31 December of each year, and the first £70 is tax free. The maximum amount normally allowed in an account is £10,000.

Up to £100 a day can be drawn on demand from your account. The bank book will be retained for checking if the withdrawal exceeds £50. If you require more than £100 you will have to allow a few days before you get your money. This is because you must apply in writing. Greater flexibility in withdrawing money can be achieved by having more than one account. For example, if you have two accounts you can draw up to £200 on demand. If you have a "Regular Customer Account', you can withdraw up to £250 a day at your chosen post office and still retain your bank book. A person qualifies for a Regular Customer Account if he or she has used the chosen post office for at least six months.

The advantage of the system is its accessibility, since there are post offices in almost every town and village, and they are open six days a week. It is cheap, since there are no bank charges and money earns interest. Also, money is available on demand.

So, National Savings ordinary accounts are a good place to keep small amounts of money to meet unforeseen expenditures. On the other hand, the services offered are still limited and the rates of interest are relatively low.

Investment Accounts.

Like ordinary accounts, anyone over the age of seven can open an account. Children under seven can have one opened on their behalf. The minimum sum required to open an account is £20 and the maximum holding is £100,000. The rate of interest is higher than an ordinary account and is liable to tax, but tax is not withheld at source. Interest is calculated on a daily basis. This means that interest is earned on each whole pound for every day it is in the account. The interest is automatically credited on 31 December each year. The rate of interest increases with the size of the balance and the maximum rate applies to £50,000 or more.

There is no limit on the amount of money that can be withdrawn. However, notice of one month is required. Investment accounts are better than ordinary accounts for long-term savers, although higher rates of interest can be obtained elsewhere.

Savings Certificates.

There have now (1999) been many issues of fixed interest Savings Certificates, but only one is on sale at any given time. At the time of writing, the 50th Issue was on sale. The minimum investment is £100, and an individual can invest up to £10,000. However there are special facilities for people cashing in earlier Issues of Certificates, which they have held for at least five years, and are reinvesting in the 50th Issue. If they do this, they may hold "Reinvestment Certificates' of the 50th Issue without restriction in addition to any purchases made within the general £10,000 limit. This £10,000 (or the reinvested amounts) may be held in addition to any holdings of other National Savings Certificates. Instead of earning interest in the usual way, the value of the Certificates rises at an accelerating rate. The 50th Issue offers a guaranteed return of 3.50% p.a. compound when held for five years.

This is free of both income tax and capital gains tax. Interest is earned for each completed period of three months. No interest is earned on Certificates cashed in the first year except for the 50th Issue Reinvestment Certificates mentioned above.

You need not cash in Certificates when they reach maturity. In most cases, however, it will pay to do so. The General Extension Rate, the rate of interest currently paid on matured Certificates, is now well below most interest rates. Again anyone can hold certificates, including children under seven.

Tax-free Savings Certificates can be held in addition to Individual Savings Accounts (ISAs).

Index-linked Savings Certificates.

These were originally known as "granny bonds' because when index-linked certificates were first issued they were only available to people over a certain age but this restriction no longer applies. The 15th issue was available in 1999 and earns extra interest for each year of the five year term. The repayments are also tax free.

The certificates are available in units of £100. You may buy up to £10,000 of the current issue in addition to any holdings you may have from previous issues. You may also reinvest from mature Savings Certificates and mature Yearly Plan Certificates over the £10,000 limit without any restriction.

The Yearly Plan.

This scheme was designed for regular investment but was withdrawn for new savers from early 1995.

Premium Bonds.

Premium Bonds are one of the most popular forms of national savings. No interest is earned as such on the bonds. Instead, you have a regular chance to win a cash prize each week and month.

All the prizes are tax free. However, before a bond is included in the draw it has to be held for three calendar months following the month in which it was bought. The winning numbers are generated by ERNIE (Electronic Random Number Indicator Equipment). The winning numbers are drawn entirely at random so that each bond has an equal chance of winning.

The size of the prizes varies from £50 to £100,000 and, from April 1994, there has been a monthly prize of £1,000,000. Prizewinners are notified by post, so it is important to notify the Bonds and Stock Office of any change of address. The numbers of prize-winning bonds and a complete list of unclaimed prizes can be consulted at major post offices. In addition most daily newspapers publish the numbers of bonds which have won the larger prizes. If you fail to claim a prize at the time of the draw, this can be done later.

Premium Bonds can be bought at post offices, and banks. Any person over the age of 16 can buy bonds. A parent, grandparent or guardian can buy bonds on behalf of their children. For individuals aged 16 or over the mimimum initial purchase is now £100 and the maximum holding is £20,000.

Capital Bonds.

Capital bonds are for people who wish to put some money away for a period of five years. They are available in multiples of £100 and the maximum amount held for all issues of capital bonds (except Series A) is £250,000. On each anniversary of the purchase interest is added and the rate of interest increases each year. The amount of interest is guaranteed over the period. At current rates (May 1999), the return is equal to 4.65 per cent compound. The bonds are repayable in full at the end of this period with all the interest due.

Although the interest is paid at the end of the five years, for income tax payers the interest is taxable each year. No further interest is earned after five years. Early repayment can be made after three months' notice is given but no interest is payable for repayments made in the first year.

FIRST Option Bonds.

FIRST stands for Fixed Interest Rate Savings Tax-Paid. This bond is for savings of at least £1,000 which are to be invested for at least a year or more. It is called an option bond because each year the investor has the option of either cashing in the bond without penalty or leaving it invested at a fixed rate of interest. No interest is payable if the bond is repaid before the first anniversary of purchase. If the bond is repaid between anniversary dates a lower rate of interest applies to the period between the most recent anniversary and the date of repayment. Investors may hold any amount between £1,000 and £250,000. Income tax is deducted but higher rate taxpayers have some further tax to pay.

Income Bonds.

These bonds provide a regular income from capital. The minimum investment is £2,000. Extra amounts can be invested in multiples of £1,000. The maximum holding is £250,000. The interest is paid on the fifth of each month and is taxable but tax is not withheld at source. In May 1999 the rate of interest was 4.80 per cent for holdings under £25,000 and 5.05 per cent for holdings of £25,000 or more. Repayments may be obtained by giving three months' notice, but if repayment is made in the first year the bond will earn only half the published rate of interest. The interest rate is adjusted from time to time and full details are available at post offices.

Pensioners' Bonds.

The Pensioners' Guaranteed Income Bonds are designed for people of 60 and over who want a monthly income from their capital. The minimum investment is £500 and the maximum £50,000. The interest rate is fixed and guaranteed for the first five years the bond is held. For the ninth series the rate of interest is 4.65 per cent. The interest is paid on the 19th of each month directly into the investor's bank or building society account. Withdrawals can be made after 60 days notice and no interest is payable during this period.

Children's Bonus Bonds.

These are designed to be suitable gifts for children. They can be bought in units of £25 up to a maximum of £1,000 per child in the current issue. Before making such a gift, therefore, it is worth checking that it would not take the child's holding over the maximum. The bonds can be bought for any child under 16 and will continue earning interest until the child is 21. A bonus is added every five years. As nothing further is earned after the 21st birthday they should then be cashed in. All interest and bonuses are tax-free. The current (May 1999) bonds (Series N) offer a guaranteed and tax-free return of 4.65 per cent per annum compound when held for the first five years.

Building Societies.

There are many building societies in the United Kingdom. Some of these are national, others local. All building societies are "mutual' organisations set up for the benefit of their investing and borrowing members. However, some of the former building societies such as the Abbey National and the Halifax have converted themselves into banks. There is no difference in the security of your money as between the small and large societies. If you want to be absolutely sure, you should choose one that has Trustee Status and is a member of the Building Societies Association.

For many years the interest rates quoted by building societies have been tax paid at the basic rate but non-taxpayers have not been allowed to claim the tax back. However the system was changed so that from 6 April 1991 non-taxpayers no longer have to suffer tax on the interest. Interest rates are higher for regular savings and the longer you are prepared to commit your money.

Banks.

Banks offer two main types of account, current and deposit. Current accounts are for everyday transactions and are discussed later (**H8**). Deposit accounts are more suitable for savings.

The rates of interest offered on deposit accounts do tend to change more quickly than those offered by other schemes. This is because the deposit rate is based on each bank's base rate which change as interest rates generally change. The deposit rate is usually between $4\frac{1}{2}$ and 3 per cent below the base rate. The current rate offered by the various banks is usually on display at the bank branches. Interest is calculated on a daily basis. The interest is taxable, but in the past tax has not been deducted at source. However, from 6 April 1985, bank interest has been paid in the same way as building society interest. There is no minimum or maximum amount that can be deposited. If you want ready access to your savings, deposit accounts can be attractive for small amounts of money. But you should look at the rates offered by National Savings and Building Societies before choosing a bank deposit account.

Tax Exempt Special Savings Schemes (TESSAs).

Tax Exempt Special Savings Schemes (TESSAs) were introduced in January 1991 and investors could open new accounts until April 1999. The accounts run for five years.

At the end of the five years the saver receives a bonus consisting of the money which would otherwise have gone in tax, provided that the capital has remained untouched. Capital can be withdrawn at any time but this leads to the loss of all tax advantages.

Personal Equity Plans.

Personal equity plans (PEPs) were introduced on 1 January 1987 to provide a tax incentive for investing in shares. They were available for new investment until April 1999 when they were replaced by Individual Savings Accounts (ISAs).

Individual Savings Accounts (ISAs).

The Individual Savings Accounts (ISAs) are a new tax-free way of saving. They became available from April 1999 and replace the previous TESSAs and PEPs. Existing TESSAs at April 1999 continue to run their course and when they mature the capital can be transferred into an ISA. Any continuing subscriptions and the maturing capital from a TESSA will not count against the annual subscription limit for a person's ISA account. Similarly PEPs in place in April 1999 can continue to be held outside ISAs but with the tax advantages.

Anyone who is 18 or over and a UK resident for tax purposes may open an ISA. In the first year (that is the tax year 1999/2000) a person may invest up to a maximum of £7,000 in an ISA, of which up to £3,000 may be a cash component. After the first year the annual investment limit is £5,000, of which up to £1,000 may be in cash and £1,000 in life insurance. There will be no lifetime contributions limit and the Government has said that the scheme will run initially for ten years.

The cash component of ISAs can be invested in cash accounts at banks and building societies or National Savings. For life insurance policies, up to £1,000 may be invested in a single premium policy. The rest can be invested in stocks and shares which qualified for TESSAs and PEPs, but not unlisted shares or those quoted on the Alternative Investment Market (AIM) since the ownership of such shares might already attract tax relief.

ISAs have to be run by authorised managers. Each person will be able to take out one ISA a year but can invest with a different manager the following year. Also, it is possible to move ISAs from one manager to another. Each year there is also a choice. The whole ISA can be placed with one manager. Alternatively separate managers may be chosen for the different components of the ISA—the £3,000 in stocks and shares, £1,000 in cash and £1,000 in life assurance.

Gilt Edged Securities.

As well as raising taxes to finance its expenditure, the Government borrows from the general public. It does this by issuing gilt-edged stock. There are basically two types of stock, redeemable and irredeemable. Redeemable or dated stocks are those that the Government has agreed to repurchase on a certain date. Usually, two dates are given. This means that the Government cannot redeem them before the first date, but it must redeem them on or before the last date. Each stock has a *par* or face value of £100. This is the amount that will be repaid on redemption. An example of a redeemable stock is the 8 per cent Treasury Stock 2000–2006. Stocks that the Government is not committed to redeem are called irredeemable or undated stocks. The $2\frac{1}{2}$ per cent consol introduced after the Second World War is an example.

The cost of buying or selling securities will depend on whether you go through a stockbroker or through the Department for National Savings, Bonds and Stock Office. It is cheaper to use the National Savings Stock Office, although you can only deal in stocks that are on the National Stock Register. There is no limit to the total amount you may hold. Application forms may be obtained from Post Offices.

The interest or *coupon rate* on a stock is normally paid half-yearly. Some pay quarterly, which is particularly useful for old-age pensioners, for example. This is based on the nominal or par value. For example, the 8 per cent Treasury Stock pays £8·00 per year. However, the price that you pay for the stock will probably be less than par. The effective rate of interest or *running yield* will therefore be greater than 8 per cent.

Prices of stocks fluctuate so that their yield keeps in line with interest rates generally. This presents the possibility of a capital gain or loss. However, it is generally true that as the stock approaches redemption, the closer the price will be to par, and the smaller the capital gain. The further away redemption is, the lower the price of the stock, and hence the greater will be the capital gain if the stock is held to redemption. Government securities are a very marketable investment. They can be sold quickly if need be. Also, stocks are free of capital-gains tax if in your possession for more than one year.

Shares.

For the more adventurous, there is the possibility of investing in shares on the stock market. Since share prices can fall as well as rise, it is advisable to "spread your risk." This means that you must have a varied and balanced collection of shares in your portfolio. To do this will require a lot of capital and knowledge of the market. So it is best to seek professional advice from a stockbroker or your bank manager. People with more limited means will be better advised to participate indirectly in the stock market by holding units in a unit trust.

Unit Trusts and Investment Trusts.

Unit trusts sell "units" to investors and use the proceeds to buy shares. This allows the investor to spread the risk of his or her investment over all the shares the trust owns. Unit trusts are run by professional managers who can be expected to know more than many investors about the merits of different securities. The value of the units of a trust is worked out each day in line with the value of the fund's stock market investments. Two prices are quoted. The "offer' price is the price at which investors can buy units. The "bid' price is the price at which the managers will repurchase units. The offer price is higher than the bid price and the difference contributes towards the cost of running the trust. In addition, there is usually a small half-yearly or yearly charge. Units can be bought and sold directly from the managers.

Investment trusts are companies which invest in securities. Like unit trusts they enable investors to spread their investment risk. However, unlike unit trusts they have a fixed share capital. The shares in investment trusts are bought and sold in the same way as those of other companies, but some investment trusts also have savings schemes which can be taken out directly with the managers.

Life Assurance as Saving.

Life assurance policies provide an alternative method of saving regular amounts for long periods of time. The various policies are considered in the section on insurance. However one version which should be considered under the heading of saving is the tax-exempt life insurance policies sold by Friendly Societies.

Friendly Societies: Tax Exempt Policies.

Friendly Societies are allowed limited tax relief on life insurance and endowment business and can therefore offer tax-free savings plans. In 1995 the general limit on a person's premiums was increased from £200 to £270 a year.

5. BANKS

Most people are familiar with the high street banks. These are the clearing banks and are known as the Big Four. They are the National Westminster, Midland, Barclays and Lloyds. In addition, there are a number of smaller banks, such as the Royal Bank of Scotland and the Co-operative Bank. There is also the Girobank. Banks offer a variety of services, and we begin by considering current accounts.

Current Accounts.

A current account is a safe and easy way of making and receiving payments and is now offered by some building societies as well as banks. Many current accounts are operated free of charge if you stay in credit. If you go overdrawn or require additional services the charges vary considerably so it can be worth shopping around. To open an account you will have to supply samples of your signature, proof of identity and probably the names of two referees. These could be your employer and a friend with a bank account. To pay further amounts into your account, you simply fill in a paying-in slip provided by the bank. Some current accounts now attract interest but the rates are often very low indeed.

Making Payments.

With a current account you will receive a cheque book. This is used in making cash withdrawals from the bank or in making payments without using cash. A cheque is not money. It is merely a written instruction to the bank to pay an amount out of your account, to the person(s) named on the cheque. Cash can be obtained from your local branch. If you require cash from another you must make special arrangements or use a cheque card.

Cheque Cards.

Most retailers are reluctant to accept an unsupported cheque. This is because they do not know if you have sufficient money in your account for the bank to honour the cheque. And, of course, the cheque book may have been stolen. This problem is overcome by a cheque card. The card guarantees that the bank will honour cheques up to £50 or sometimes more regardless of the state of the customer's account. You have to be a reliable

and well-established customer before your bank will give you a cheque card. A cheque drawn on a cheque card cannot be stopped or cancelled.

Cash Cards.

Increasingly these cards can be used for more than just simply withdrawing cash from cash machines, for example checking the balance of the account or ordering statements. They are operated using your Personal Identification Number (PIN). This should be kept secret at all times and never written down where a thief could see it.

Debit Cards (Switch Cards, Connect Cards).

These are sometimes known as switch or connect cards and are the electronic version of cheques. Your card is swiped through a machine, you are asked to sign a voucher and the amount is then debited from your current account.

Standing Orders.

There are other ways of making payments apart from cheques. If asked, the bank will automatically make regular payments from your account. These "standing orders" are useful for paying such things as insurance premiums, subscriptions and mortgage repayments.

Direct Debiting.

Direct debits are slightly different from standing orders. In both cases you give your bank a written instruction to meet payments as they fall due. However, with direct debiting the recipient approaches your bank which then deducts the payment from your account. This can be convenient where the amount varies. The recipient has to tell you beforehand of the date and amount of payment. If you wish to cancel a direct debit instruction you should write to both your bank and the recipient.

Bankers' Drafts.

These are cheques which are payable by a bank itself and are therefore a very acceptable means of payment. They can be useful in buying expensive items when a personal cheque may not be so acceptable. Once a bankers' draft has been used to pay for something, it cannot then be cancelled through the bank.

Telephone Banking.

The first full telephone banking service was set up in 1989 and this facility has since been introduced by other high-street banks. It has the convenience of operating a bank account by telephone from home or elsewhere and some banks charge calls at the local rate. The main banking services are normally accessible in this way.

Other Services.

In addition to the services mentioned, banks provide a whole range of other services. These include lending (considered in the section on Borrowing), deposit accounts (considered in the section on Saving), travel facilities, advice on investment, insurance and taxation, safe custody of items and many more. For further information on the additional services banks offer, contact your nearest branch.

Girobank.

The National Giro was set up by the Government to provide a low-cost current-account bank service. When Giro started it was considerably cheaper to run compared with a current account at a bank. However, the difference is now small. Giro can be opened via the post or through the 20,000 Post Offices in the UK. These are generally open six days a week. You therefore have access to your account for more days and for longer hours than you do with the commercial banks.

6. INSURANCE

Insurance is a contract to pay a premium in return for which the insurer will pay compensation in certain eventualities, for example, fire or theft. In effect, insurance is a means of sharing certain risks. The traditional forms of insurance are general insurance and life assurance. The latter is usually called "assurance" because the cover is given against the occurrence of an event which is inevitable.

Life Assurance.

Life assurance provides a capital sum to your estate in the event of your death. Some policies also combine a savings element so that you receive a lump sum if you survive the period. These are called endowment policies. As a general point, it is just as important that you do not overburden yourself with life assurance as it is to have some form of cover. If you have to give up or surrender your policy before it matures there are usually severe financial penalties. There are three basic types of life assurance: term assurance, whole-life assurance and endowment assurance. All forms of life assurance used to attract tax relief. However, this was changed in the Budget of 13 March 1984 so that the tax relief does not apply to policies taken out after that date.

Term Assurance.

This type of policy provides life assurance for a fixed period of time. Should you die during the term of the policy your estate will receive the sum assured. However, if you survive the period you receive nothing. There are variations on the basic type of term policy. A *decreasing term* policy, for example, is often necessary if you have a mortgage. The sum assured decreases as you pay off the mortgage.

Other types of policies include level and convertible term policies. With *level term* policies the sum assured remains fixed throughout the term of the policy A *convertible term* policy has the additional benefit of being able to convert it to another kind of policy later on, if you so desire. Term policies provide the cheapest form of life cover.

Whole-Life Assurance.

With this type of policy you are normally required to pay the premiums for the whole of your life-time. Like term assurance, the sum assured is paid out to your estate only on your death. Whole-life policies can either be with or without profits. A with-profits policy will be more expensive, since the sum received on your death will be the sum assured plus a share in the profits made by the company. Having to keep up the premiums after your retirement can be a problem, so *limited payment* policies are available. Premiums are paid until you reach a specific age, although life cover continues until your death. The premiums will be higher than for a straight whole-life policy.

Endowment Assurance.

Both whole-life and term policies normally provide benefit only on your death. With an endowment policy, benefit is still provided should you die before the maturity date of the policy. But if you survive this period you will receive the sum assured. Like whole-life policies, these policies can be with or without profits. Although the more expensive, with-profits endowment policies are the most popular form of life assurance in this country. However, the proportion of the premium used to provide death cover is small. This is because the chances of dying before the maturity date are usually low. Thus, the bulk of the premiums is used by the company to build up the capital sum on maturity.

Endowment policies are often used in conjunction with loans for house purchase, school fees and for providing for retirement. As well as with-profits investment policies, life assurance companies offer other investment policies. These include equity linked contracts, property bonds and policies linked to building societies. With unit-linked contracts the bulk of the premium is used to purchase units in a unit trust. Property bonds are very similar, except the investment is in property.

General Insurance.

As mentioned earlier, this provides cover for an eventuality that may never happen. The types of general insurance considered here are for house and possessions, motor vehicles, sickness and medical insurance.

Insuring your House and Possessions.

If you are buying a house on a mortgage the bank or building society will insist that it is insured. The sum that you will have to insure your house for may be more than what you paid for it. This is because the insurance value will be related to the cost of rebuilding the house. It is therefore important to adjust the amount for which the house is insured periodically to keep pace with inflation. Alternatively, you can take out policies which are "index-linked." Although most policies give the same kind of cover, there is no standard house insurance. So you should check to see if your policy covers all eventualities. This is particularly important if your area is prone to such events as flooding or subsidence.

Unless you have a combined policy, the contents of your home and other possessions will not be covered by your house insurance. In the past insurance companies have reimbursed the purchase cost of articles, less a charge for wear-and-tear. However, you can get policies that do not make this deduction.

House and Possessions.

If you are a tenant living in rented accommodation you should only buy policies that cover the contents of the house and leave the landlord to buy insurance for the buildings. For owner-occupiers, it is best to buy a combined policy of house and possessions. This has the advantage that it will be generally cheaper than buying two separate policies.

Motor Insurance.

Motor insurance is compulsory by law. However, only a basic minimum is compulsory, and many people prefer to take out more comprehensive policies. Insurance companies offer two main types of policy; third party and comprehensive insurance.

Third-Party Motor Insurance.

The additional cover provided by this type of policy is the cost of repairing the other driver's car. Also, if you incur legal costs in dealing with a claim, these will be reimbursed if your insurer approves your actions. Since third-party insurance does not cover damage to your car, it is only suitable if your car is fairly old. "Third party, fire and theft" will cover you if your car is burnt out or stolen, but not if it is damaged in an accident.

Comprehensive Motor Insurance.

If your car is relatively new and hence more valuable, then you should consider a comprehensive policy. The most important additional benefit of such a policy is cover for loss or accidental damage to your car.

Sickness and Medical Insurance.

If you consider the benefits provided by the National Insurance schemes and the National Health Service to be inadequate, you can take out insurance that provides for you when ill. There are several schemes. *Hospital risk insurance* provides a sum only for the period you are in hospital. You may consider it best to have a *permanent health insurance*. This provides cover for the total period you are ill. In addition to providing an income for yourself when ill, there are schemes that provide for private medical treatment. The most well-known is the British United Provident Association (BUPA).

Buying Insurance.

Because of the bewildering variety of policies available it is often best to seek professional advice when buying insurance. This can be obtained from an insurance broker or your bank.

7. BUYING A HOUSE

Buying a house is very often preferable to renting a home. Your own house provides you and your family with a secure home. A house is also one of the soundest investments available to most people. In addition, a house can be a useful asset. For example, if you wish to move elsewhere the house can always be sold and the proceeds used to buy a home elsewhere. A house can be particularly valuable on retirement. With the mortgage paid off the retired owner can choose from a number of possible courses of action. He or she could continue living in it rent free. If the house proved too large for retirement part of it could always be let out to provide some additional income. Alternatively, the owner could move to a smaller home and the difference in the value of the two houses would provide a useful capital sum.

For many people there is no satisfactory alternative to buying a home. Most people are unlikely to be offered council accommodation. Furthermore, a home owner is likely to find it much easier to move than a council tenant. Councils are often reluctant or unable to offer new accommodation when their tenants wish to move; whereas an owner occupier can always sell his house and buy another elsewhere.

Accommodation rented privately also has its disadvantages. Reasonably priced rented accommodation is often difficult to find. Tenants sometimes pay nearly as much, or even more, in rent than they would have to pay for a mortgage on property. Finally, rents are likely to rise as inflation continues. Mortgage repayments on the other hand, although they fluctuate from time to time, are related to the original loan and not to the current value of the property.

The Costs.

The basic drawback of buying a house is the cost of buying and selling. The costs can include solicitor's and surveyor's fees and (in the case of selling) an estate agent's fee. If the mortgage is a high proportion of the value of the house, the lender may make an additional charge. Normally there will be the costs of fitting out a new home—the cost of curtains is one example. These costs clearly mean that it is not advantageous to buy a home if you expect to move in the near future.

An obstacle for many people is cash. One hundred per cent mortgages are uncommon, and the buyer has to find the difference between the mortgage offered and the price of the house. There are also the other fees mentioned above. The position may be illustrated with an example. Mr. and Mrs. Smith agree to buy a house for £80,000. The Smiths' building society is prepared to lend them 95 per cent of the value of the property. In this case, the loan would be £76,000 which leaves the Smiths £4,000 to find. On top of the £4,000, the Smiths have to pay a valuation fee to the bank or building society. The valuation fee is related to the value of the property so that the higher the value, the higher the fee. It may be possible to arrange for the surveyor making the valuation for the lender also to produce a house buyer's report for the buyer. A combined fee of £350 is shown in the example but it is possible, of course, to have a more detailed survey done if you wish. If the price of the house exceeds £60,000 stamp duty also has to be paid. The rate of the stamp duty is currently 1 per cent of the value of the house. Note that duty is levied on the total price of the house, and not just the excess over £60,000. So, for example, the stamp duty on a £80,000 house would be £800. Finally, the Smiths receive a solicitor's bill for £600. The solicitor's charge will depend partly on the value of the house, and partly on how much work the solicitor has to do to transfer the house from the seller to the buyer.

In this example, therefore, the Smiths need at least £5,750 of their own money. Frequently the amount of money needed will be greater than this. For example, if the Smiths' mortgage were limited to 90 per cent of the value of the house they may have had to find at least £9,750.

Cost of the house	£80,000
Mortgage	£76,000
	4,000
Valuation and survey fees	350
Solicitor's fee	600
Stamp duty	800
	£5,750

It should also be borne in mind that more money is needed to furnish the house. A first-time buyer needs almost everything from curtains to a cooker, and from doormats to a dinner service. Not all of these things need to be bought straight away of course. Nevertheless, some items, such as something to sleep on, and to eat off, will be needed almost immediately.

So it can be seen that, unless one is likely to move in the near future, buying a house can be a sensible decision. The key thing is to save up a reasonable sum of money towards these costs.

Choosing a House.

Given the price of houses, selecting your future home is clearly not a decision to be rushed. Possibly the first thing to do is to work out how much you can afford to pay. If you need a mortgage, building societies and other lenders will give you a rough indication of the maximum amount they will lend. They cannot give a precise figure, however, because the amount a society will lend depends not only on your income but also the house itself. There is more on this below. The next stage is to decide where you would like to live. If you are not familiar with the area it pays to spend time studying a map in detail. That way you soon get an idea of the proximity of each area to your work, to the nearest shopping centre and so on. It is also worth thinking carefully about the type of house you want. You may, of course, be influenced by what is available. Nevertheless, if you have a fairly clear idea of what you want a lot of time can be saved by eliminating houses that are obviously unsuitable. Features to think about include whether you want a house, bungalow or flat; the number of bedrooms you require and whether you want a large, medium or small garden.

The next move is to find out as much as possible about the current state of the home market. Estate agents are always delighted to deluge prospective home buyers with details of many properties. Many of them might be unsuitable for you, but they will begin to give you an idea of the value of different houses. You may also change your mind about the sort of house you want. Estate agents are not the only source of information about houses for sale. Houses are often advertised privately, usually in the local newspaper. And because the seller will be saving hundreds of pounds in estate agent's fees, you might be able to buy a house advertised privately for less than one handled by an agent.

There are several other considerations that should be borne in mind. For example, if you are likely to have to move within a few years you may wish to buy a house which is relatively easy to resell. Such a house might be a fairly modern three-bedroomed semi-detached house which is close to shops and schools: rather than a "character" property in a remote area.

Buying a House.

The process of buying a house should not be rushed either. In fact, at this stage it is well to have two or three properties in mind. This reduces the disappointment should you fail to get your first choice. It also puts you in a better bargaining position over the price of the house. There is nothing sacred about the asking price. Sellers will often ask for a bit more than they think they will probably get. So, depending on the state of the market, it can often pay to offer less than the advertised price.

When a price is agreed, make it "subject to contract." Neither party is formally bound to the agreement until the contracts are actually exchanged. Before that happens there are a number of things to be done. First of all you will probably want a solicitor. It is not absolutely necessary to use a solicitor, but unless you are familiar with the procedure it is usually advisable to do so. If you need a mortgage the next thing to do is to give full details of the house you intend to buy to your building society or bank manager. He or she will then arrange to have the property surveyed and valued. The purpose of this is to safeguard the building society's money by making sure that the house is a good investment. When the building society is ready it will inform you how much it is prepared to lend on the house. Your solicitor should then be instructed to complete the remaining formalities.

As soon as the solicitors are satisfied about the technicalities of the purchase the next stage is the signing and exchange of contracts. The contract is usually prepared in duplicate with one copy to be signed by the buyer and one by the seller. The buyer is normally expected to pay a deposit of 10 per cent of the purchase price when contracts are exchanged. The exchange of contracts legally commits both parties to the purchase. This commitment stands regardless of what happens thereafter. This is why it is important for you or your solicitor or both to find out as much as possible about the property before the contract is signed. The contract will contain a number of details, including the date on which the deal will be completed. The date is usually a few weeks ahead and allows both parties to make final arrangements before the house is actually handed over. On the completion date the balance of the purchase money is paid, and the purchaser can take possession of the house.

The length of time between finding a home of your choice and taking possession can vary considerably. It depends on the number of complications involved. If everything goes well it would probably take between eight and ten weeks to buy the house. Such is the process of buying a home. However for many people the major consideration is the mortgage. It is therefore worth describing mortgages in greater detail.

Mortgages.

A "mortgage" is a technical term meaning that certain rights over one's property are given to someone else as security for a loan. In other words, if you buy a house with a loan you give a mortgage as security. In everyday usage, however, a mortgage refers just to the loan, even though the property is still used as security. Even if you can afford to pay cash, it is often worthwhile buying a house with the aid of a mortgage. As inflation continues the value of money declines, and so the real value of the mortgage also declines. As a result, the mortgage repayments will not tend to rise in line with inflation.

It is true that interest rates fluctuate and that when they rise your mortgage repayments will rise as well. But sooner or later the rate of interest will fall again. In addition, when interest rates rise it is sometimes possible to extend the repayment period, rather than increase the monthly repayments. The most common types of mortgage are repayment mortgages and endowment mortgages. In recent years many lenders have been offering attractive discounts to new borrowers. These can be very advantageous but you should be aware of any conditions such as penalties for repaying the mortgage early.

Repayment Mortgages.

Repayment mortgages are usually the most straightforward. They are repaid in equal monthly instalments. Each payment consists partly of interest and partly of a repayment of capital. In the early years the repayments consist almost entirely of interest. As the loan is paid off, the interest element declines.

There has been some tax relief on mortgage interest. It is normally given directly by the Inland Revenue to the lender through a scheme called MIRAS (Mortgage Interest Relief At Source).

However, the tax relief has been reduced in recent years and will be removed completely from April 2000.

Endowment Mortgages.

An "endowment mortgage" is a mortgage linked to an insurance policy. When the policy matures there should be sufficient funds to pay off the mortgage but this is not guaranteed. In the meantime you only pay interest on the loan. If you die before the end of the agreement the insurance policy would pay off the mortgage. Endowment mortgages usually cost more than repayment mortgages because of the premium for the insurance policy. However, there is the advantage that as with other insurance policies, it is possible to have a "with-profits" element in an endowment policy. This costs more, but it means that the insurance company not only guarantees to provide a minimum sum but also adds "bonuses" each year. The size of the bonus depends on the investment position of the company. When the policy matures the pay-out (including bonuses) should cover the mortgage and leave you with a substantial sum as well. It should be noted however, that there has been a recent trend towards reduced bonus rates and repayment mortgages might be more suitable for many people. Endowment policies should be regarded as a long-term arrangement.

If you surrender an endowment policy early you may receive little or nothing back.

Personal Equity Plan Mortgage.

A PEP mortgage is similar to an endowment mortgage, but monthly payments were originally made into a personal equity plan (*see* **H**7) rather than an insurance policy. Interest is still payable on the outstanding mortgages. PEPs were replaced with ISAs (*see* **H**7) in April 1999. However PEP mortgages can continue through an ISA.

Getting a Mortgage.

The majority of mortgages have been supplied by building societies but in recent years banks have become an important source of mortgages. Some insurance companies also provide mortgages, but this is only a minor source of loans. Some employers, such as banks and building societies, will provide their employees with loans at favourable rates.

The first thing to do is to plan ahead. As we have seen, you will probably need to put up a substantial sum of money of your own, so you should start saving as soon as possible. It can be advantageous to save by investing in a building society. When mortgage funds are in short supply societies are likely to consider their own investors before casual applicants. Building societies have fairly strong preferences about the sort of property they are prepared to lend on. For example, they are often very reluctant to lend on older property. Many building societies are also reluctant to lend on flats. Nevertheless, the lending policies of building societies differ, so if you are turned down by one society, try another. It can also help to ask people who are likely to have close contacts with building societies. Estate agents, your solicitor or bank may each be able to suggest a possible source.

How Much Can Be Borrowed?

The final question to be dealt with in this section is how much an individual will be allowed to borrow. As stated above, this partly depends on the value of the house concerned. But it also depends on the financial status of the borrower. Building societies have to safeguard their investors' money. Societies are careful not to lend more to anyone than they are likely to be able to repay. A person with a secure career may therefore be treated more favourably than a person whose future earnings are uncertain. Again, different societies have different policies. None the less, it is very rare for building societies to lend more than two and a half or three times your annual income. Most building societies will also take a spouse's income into account, but for a smaller proportion.

For example, suppose you went to a lender which was prepared to lend up to two and a half times your annual earnings plus an amount equal to your spouse's annual income. If you earn £20,000 and your spouse £10,000, the lender would then be prepared to lend you up to £60,000:

Your income	£20,000	Maximum loan	£50,000
Spouse's income	£10,000	Maximum loan	£10,000
		Combined Limit	£60,000

The extent to which your spouse's income is taken into account depends on the lender.

II. TAXES

Taxation permeates almost every aspect of financial life. In addition, the entire subject is exceedingly complex, and the tax system is altered or amended at least once a year. All that will be attempted here, therefore, is a description of some of the most common situations faced by taxpayers. If your circumstances are more complicated you should consult your tax office, or take professional advice, or both.

For reasons which are largely historical, taxes are often divided into *direct* and *indirect* taxes. Direct taxes are paid to the Inland Revenue. There are four main types of direct taxation:

1. Income tax
2. Capital gains tax
3. Inheritance tax (formerly Capital transfer tax)
4. Corporation tax

It could also be argued that National Insurance Contributions are a form of tax and they are also described below.

Indirect taxes are collected mainly by the Customs and Excise. They include:

1. Value added tax
2. Customs and excise duties
3. Car tax
4. Stamp duties

Stamp duties are, however, the responsibility of the Inland Revenue.

In terms of the amount of revenue raised, income tax is by far the most important tax. It is also the tax most likely to affect the average taxpayer directly.

8. INCOME TAX

If you are resident in the United Kingdom tax is levied on your income whether it originates in the UK or from overseas. Even if you are not resident, tax is still levied on any income you have which originates in the UK. Tax is charged for each year of assessment; that is the year from 6 April to the following 5 April.

Income Subject to Tax.

Most types of income are taxable, including the following:

Income from employment. This includes wages, bonuses, commission. tips and benefits in kind, such as the private use of the company's car.

Income from self-employment, business, professions and vocations.

Interest, dividends and annuities.

Rent.

Pensions.

Income not Subject to Tax.

A few types of income are not subject to tax. The main groups are:

The first £70 of interest per person received from ordinary deposit accounts in the National Savings Bank.

Interest on National Savings Certificates and increases in the value of Index-Linked National Insurance Certificates. Also, interest from the Save-As-You-Earn scheme is exempt.

Sickness benefit (but not statutory sick pay), family credit, attendance allowance, maternity benefit, child benefit, housing benefit, invalidity benefit and non-contributory invalidity pension.

Educational grants and awards.

Compensation for loss of employment—up to £30,000.

War widows' pensions.

Wound and disability pensions.

Any wins from gambling, including Premium Bond prizes.

The capital element of annuity payments.

Profit-related pay, within certain limits.

Personal Allowances and Rates of Tax.

Almost everyone is entitled to at least one personal allowance which may be deducted before tax is levied on the remainder of a person's income. The allowances for 1998/99 and 1999/2000 are shown in Table 3.

The basic personal allowance is available to individuals generally and there are two levels of higher personal allowances for those aged 65 and over and 75 and over. These higher personal allowances are reduced if total income exceeds a certain limit (£16,200 in 1998/99 and £16,800 in 1999/2000). The allowance is reduced by £1 for every £2 that limit is exceeded until it reaches the normal single or married allowance. The married couple's allowance is normally given to the husband though since April 1993 it is possible to choose to split the allowance between spouses. Also, the wife may claim the whole of the married couple's allowance if the husband agrees. Although the married couple's

TABLE 3. *Personal Allowances Against Gross Income in 1998/99 and 1999/2000*

	1998/99	1999/2000
	£	£
Personal allowance	4,195	4,335
Personal allowance age 65–74	5,410	5,720
Personal allowance age 75 and over	5,600	5,980
Married couple's allowance	1,900	1,970
Married couple's allowance age 65–74	4,965	5,125
Married couple's allowance age 75 and over	5,025	5,195
Additional personal allowance	1,900	1,970
Widow's bereavement allowance	1,900	1,970
Blind person's allowance	1,330	1,380

allowance used to be granted at the full basic rate of tax, it has been restricted to 20 per cent from April 1994, 15 per cent from 1995 and 10 per cent from April 1999. The married couple's allowance will be abolished altogether from 5 April 2000 for couples who are both aged less than 65 on that date.

The additional personal allowance may be claimed by a person who is single, separated, divorced or widowed and has a child living with him or her for at least part of the year. The widow's bereavement allowance is granted only for the tax year in which the husband died, and the tax year following the bereavement unless the widow remarries. Like the married couple's allowance, the additional personal allowance and the widow's bereavement allowance have been restricted to 20 per cent from 1994, 15 per cent from 1995 and 10 per cent from 1999. After these personal allowances (and any allowable expenses) have been deducted from gross income, the remaining taxable income is subject to the rates shown in Table 4. These reliefs will also be abolished from April 2000. Instead a new Childrens Tax Credit will be introduced from April 2001.

TABLE 4. *The Rates of Income Tax in 1998/99 and 1999/2000*

| | Taxable Income | |
	1998/99	1999/2000
	£	£
Lower rate of 20% (10% in 1999/2000)	1–4,300	1–1,500
Basic rate of 23% (22% for 2000/2001)	4,301–27,100	1,501–28,000
Higher rate of 40%	over 27,100	over 28,000

Income from savings is taxed at 20 per cent and 40 per cent when income exceeds the basic rate limit.

9. ASSESSMENT AND COLLECTION

The administration of income tax is the responsibility of the Inland Revenue. In practice, the job is divided into two parts: assessment and collection. The "assessments" for tax are the responsibility of inspectors of taxes in over 700 tax offices spread throughout the country. When an individual's tax has been assessed the information is then passed to a collector of taxes who actually sends out the bill. If you receive a tax bill which you think is wrong you should contact the inspector. The collector has no power to amend the bill, his or her job is to collect the amounts decided between you and the inspector.

For historical reasons, income is divided into six groups known as "schedules." These are:

1. *Schedule A:* Income from property.

2. *Schedule B:* Income from commercial woodlands. Schedule B was finally abolished in 1988.

3. *Schedule C:* Certain interest and annuities paid out of public revenue.

4. *Schedule D:* Income from trades, businesses and professions. Also included are interest, rents and income not covered by other schedules.

5. *Schedule E:* This is the schedule that affects most people as it covers wages and salaries. It also deals with pensions.

6. *Schedule F:* Dividends and other distributions made by companies.

Pay-As-You-Earn.

By far the largest schedule is Schedule E. Nearly all Schedule E income is taxed through the Pay-As-You-Earn (PAYE) system. PAYE is the method used to deduct tax from wages, salaries and some pensions. In order to keep the deductions as accurate as possible, PAYE is operated on a cumulative basis. This means that your earnings, tax paid and so on are accumulated throughout the tax year. This is how it works. At the beginning, or before the start of the tax year, your tax-free allowances are added up. The total is then converted into a code number. For example, if your allowances came to £4,000 and you are married, then your code number would be 400H. The H suffix denotes that you are entitled to the married couple's allowance. If you are single or a working wife the suffix would be L (representing the "lower" single person's allowance). If there are special circumstances, for example if you had a second job, the suffix would probably be T. There are also special suffixes for pensioners. The main ones are P for single people, and V for married pensioners. The new code K is used where the value of the perks from your job are greater than your personal allowances. This enables the excess to be collected through the PAYE system. If your current code number is different from the previous one the tax office will send you a "Notice of Coding." This will show the allowances the tax office has taken into account and how your code number has been calculated. If you do not receive a notice of coding you may request one. You should always check to see that you have received your full entitlement to allowances. Your code number is also sent to your employer so he knows how much tax to deduct from your earnings. It is worth noting that the higher your code, the lower the tax deducted from your pay.

A Typical Example.

It may be of interest to work through a simple example of PAYE operating. Suppose that a person's allowances for the year amount to £5,200, and the appropriate code is issued to his employer. The principle is that the annual allowances are divided by the number of pay periods in the year. If an individual is paid weekly, therefore, his allowances are divided by 52. In our example the individual would be granted £100 worth of allowances each week. This weekly allowance is then accumulated as the tax year progresses. Hence in, say, week 26 of the tax year the individual would be entitled to £2,600 worth of allowances. At the same time, the PAYE system accumulates the amount of earnings received. This enables the amount of tax to be deducted to be calculated accurately. Suppose the individual in our example earned £140 in Week 1 of the tax year. The employer knows from the code number that the person's allowances for that week amount to £100. The employer then deducts this £100 from the £140 gross pay, which leaves £40 of "taxable pay." The next stage is to calculate the tax due on £40.

To assist him or her in this process, the employer has two sets of tax tables. The first table converts code numbers into weekly or monthly allowances. After these allowances have been deducted from gross pay the second set of tables is used to calculate the tax due on the remaining pay. In the example, there is £40 of taxable pay, so with a tax rate of, say, 30 per cent, £12 would be deducted in tax. Suppose that the wage in the second week was also £140. Because of the cumulative feature, the value of the allowances would now be £200. (£100 for the second week, plus £100 for the first week). Cumulative pay would now be £280. After deducting the allowances, taxable pay is now £80. The second set of tables would now show a total of £24 due in tax. However, £12 ("cumulative tax paid") was deducted in week 1. The amount of tax due in week 2, therefore, is a further £12 (£24 minus the £12 deducted in week 1). This process then continues for the rest of the tax year.

PAYE has a number of advantages. These include accurate deductions of tax. The system can also repay tax during the year if the employee's pay falls substantially. Repayments occur when the value of the allowances accumulates faster than gross pay. The system does not always work in this way. For example, suppose you fail to send your tax return back to the tax office. You may find that you are then put on the Emergency Code (E). This code only gives you allowances equal to the single person's allowance, so if you are entitled to more you will have too much tax deducted. This, of course, provides you with an incentive to sort out your tax affairs with the Inland Revenue. In addition, a taxpayer who becomes unemployed will not normally receive any rebate due until after either he or she ceases to claim unemployment or supplementary benefit, or the end of the tax year. Also, rebates cannot usually be paid if a person is on strike.

Sometimes you may find that you have been put on what is known as a "week 1" basis. This means that tax is being deducted from your pay on a *non-cumulative* basis. In other words, every week is treated as though it were the first week of the tax year. One of the main results of the "week 1" basis is that it prevents tax repayments being made automatically if, say, your income falls through unemployment.

How to Check your Code Number.

As you can see from the above explanation, your code number is the factor that determines the amount of tax that is deducted from your pay. You can check your code number by examining your Notice of Coding. You should compare the allowances and expenses you claimed on your tax return with the ones listed on the Notice. One item which might appear on the Notice of Coding is "Tax unpaid for earlier years." This is to enable the tax office to collect outstanding tax by lowering the value of your code. The tax will then be collected slowly over the tax year rather than in one lump sum.

Appeals.

When your tax for the year is assessed you will be sent a Notice of Assessment. This is often not considered necessary if you are taxed under PAYE and your tax situation is straightforward, though you can still ask for one.

If you receive a Notice of Assessment which you think is wrong you must appeal within 30 days of the date appearing on the Notice. Appeals made after 30 days are normally allowed only if you can provide a satisfactory explanation such as being in hospital or abroad, and can show that the appeal was made without unreasonable delay. Most appeals are settled directly with the inspector. If you and the inspector cannot agree, then the case goes before the Commissioners of Income Tax. There are two types of Commissioners: the General Commissioners and the Special Commissioners. The General Commissioners are unpaid and recruited from members of the public. They sit with a clerk who provides advice on tax law. The Special Commissioners are professional civil servants who are experts in tax matters. It is often said that if your appeal is based on common sense, rather than the intricacies of tax law, you may do better to go to the General Commissioners. Each party pays its own costs for hearings before the Commissioners. If, however, the case is taken on to the High Court, or further, the loser usually pays the costs.

10. SELF-ASSESSMENT

Self-assessment was introduced for those receiving income tax returns from 1997. It is a different way of calculating and paying tax which has been used in many other countries for some time. The main difference with the previous system is that a greater responsibility is placed on taxpayers to keep records, to complete their tax returns properly and to send them back on time. For taxpayers who are late there are penalties.

Self-assessment tax returns contain different schedules which apply to different sorts of income received by taxpayers. They are designed to allow taxpayers to be able to work out their own tax. There is also a guide which should be read carefully before completing the return.

With self-assessment, the process is stricter than before. Not all taxpayers are required to complete a tax return but they should all keep the necessary records to enable them to do so if required. If taxpayers receive income or capital gains which should be taxed and have not been, they are required to inform the Inland Revenue within six months of the end of the tax year, that is by 5 October. Most tax returns are sent out in April each year. If taxpayers wish the Inland Revenue to calculate their tax for them they should submit their returns by 30 September. If the taxpayer does the calculation

then the return does not have to be submitted until 31 January. All outstanding tax should also be paid by 31 January.

If the tax return is not submitted by 31 January then a fixed penalty of £100 is applied. If the return is still outstanding six months later a further penalty of £100 becomes due. The Inland Revenue is able to ask the Commissioners of Income Tax to apply further penalties of up to £60 a day where they feel it is necessary. Interest is charged on overdue tax and there is also a 5 per cent penalty for tax outstanding at the end of February.

Some Basic Advice.

It is very worthwhile keeping a tax file containing all the information relevant to your tax affairs. The whole process of completing a tax return is much simpler if you keep all the relevant documents close together. These documents include items such as: P60 (from your employer); dividend advice slips; receipts for expenses. You may also be asked by the inspector to submit detailed records supporting expense claims. A second point is to keep a copy of your return. A photocopy is perhaps the best method of doing this. Alternatively, you can keep a separate record of what you put in the return as you go along.

Keeping a copy of your return has two advantages. First of all it will help you deal with any questions the inspector may have about your return. Secondly, it will enable you to complete your next return more easily. The tax office usually compares your latest tax return with your previous one to see if you have forgotten something. So it is better if you spot any omissions first. If you get into difficulties with your return, you can always telephone or write to the tax office whose address appears on the front of the form. If you wish to call personally, most tax offices are open for public enquiries between 10 am and 4 pm. But remember to take your tax file with you. It does not matter if you wish to make a personal call and your tax office is hundreds of miles away. This is often the case with Londoners and people who work for large nationwide companies. You can always call at a local office and in London there are special PAYE enquiry offices. (Their addresses are in the telephone directory.) Most enquiries can be handled without recourse to your official file. If the file is needed, the Inland Revenue can arrange to have it sent to a local office.

Completing the Return.

All taxpayers are required to complete the summary sheet which indicates which supplementary pages are required. If you have income under any of the headings then you are directed to the relevant supplementary pages.

Employment Income.

If you are an employee you should receive a form P60 from your employer after 5 April each year. The P60 will show your total earnings and tax deducted under PAYE. You should also give other income from employment such as tips which are not shown on your P60. Other information needed includes benefits and expenses. These are shown on form P11D which is supplied by employers when appropriate. You will also need details of lump sums and compensation payments and, if relevant, details of dates working abroad.

Expenses in Employment.

The basic rule covering claims for employment expenses is that they must be incurred wholly, exclusively and necessarily in the performance of the duties of that employment. The rule is usually applied quite strictly. Thus, for example, travel expenses to and from work are not normally allowable because they are not incurred *in the performance* of the duties of the employment. Travelling expenses may be allowed, but only if incurred in the course of the employment.

Nevertheless, there are several types of expenditure which may be claimed. They include subscriptions to professional bodies, tools and some types of industrial clothing. Trade Unions often agree a fixed allowance with the tax office, but you can still claim for actual expenses if they exceed the agreed figure.

Share Schemes.

Many share schemes are not taxable but those which should be entered. Remember that when shares are sold there may also be some liability to capital gains tax.

Self-employment.

Self-employment includes running your own business. It is possible to be both an employee and self-employed and payments received without deduction of tax—for example, working on a free-lance basis—may be counted as self-employment income. If you make money from your hobby it is likely to be considered as a trade and treated as self-employment income.

Partnership.

This applies if at any time during the tax year you were entitled to a share of the profits, losses or income from a business which you carried out in partnership. You must complete this part even if you did not actually draw any money from the business.

Land and Property.

Land and property includes immobile caravans and houseboats. You need details of rents and other incomes received and allowable expenses. Income from land and property belonging to a partnership should be entered under the partnership pages of the return.

Foreign.

This covers income from abroad and you need information on the gross amounts of income, which country it came from and any foreign or UK tax already paid. This part of the return also covers holiday homes abroad which you let out.

Trusts etc.

If you have income from trusts you should receive a form giving details from the trustees.

Capital Gains.

This requires details of assets sold or disposed of and the amount for which they were originally purchased and the date they were acquired. Further information is given below.

11. CAPITAL GAINS TAX

When you dispose of an asset or possession you may make a capital gain or a capital loss. An asset is property of any kind. It includes both property in the United Kingdom and property overseas. You are considered to have disposed of an asset if you sell it, lose it, exchange it or give it away. However, the transfer of a possession between a husband and wife who are not separated is not considered to be a disposal.

Tax-free Gains.

The following assets are exempt from the tax:

Your home (but see below).

Personal possessions, household goods and other chattels, provided that each item is worth £6,000 or less at the time of the disposal. A set of goods, for example a pair of vases, is counted as one item. (*Chattels* means tangible, movable property.)

Animals, private cars, caravans and boats. Also other chattels which are wasting assets; that is assets expected to last 50 years or less.

Life assurance policies.

National Savings Certificates, British Savings Bonds and Save-As-You-Earn.

British government stocks if owned for more than one year or inherited. This exemption has been extended to corporate bonds (*e.g.* debentures) which are issued after 13 March 1984 and which are held for at least twelve months.

British money.

Foreign currency obtained for personal or family expenditure.

Winnings from betting or from Premium Bonds.

Gifts to charities.

Gifts to certain institutions such as the National Trust and the British Museum.

Your Own Home.

When you sell your house any capital gains you make will normally be exempt from tax. From 1980/81 onwards this exemption has applied (within certain limits) if you let part of your home. However, there are a number of circumstances in which you may get only partial exemption. For example, if you use part of your home for business you may not be allowed full exemption from capital gains tax. These circumstances are described in more detail in the Inland Revenue leaflet CGT4, *Capital Gains Tax—Owner-occupied houses*. You should enter any gains from the disposal of your house on your tax return in case they are not wholly exempt.

Capital Losses.

Your capital gains can be reduced by deducting allowable losses. An allowable capital loss is usually one which would have been taxable if it had been a gain. For example, a loss on an item which is exempt, such as your car, would *not* be considered an allowable loss. If your losses exceed your gains in the tax year you can carry the balance forward to set against gains in future years. You can also deduct allowable expenditure from your capital gains (or add them to your capital losses). Allowable expenditure includes the costs of acquiring or disposing of an asset; for example, commission, conveyancing costs and advertising. It also includes expenditure which increases the value of the asset, such as improvements to property.

Working Out Your Gain.

Normally your capital gain (or loss) is the amount you receive when disposing of the asset *minus* the original amount you paid for it. If you give the asset away, the market value at the time of disposal is used instead. The same method is used if you were originally given the asset, or if you inherited it.

Shares.

If you buy batches of the same share at different prices the cost of each share is considered to be the average cost. For example, suppose you purchase 100 shares in a company for £200. Three months later you buy a further 100 of the same shares for £300. You would then have a total of 200 shares which cost you £500. The average cost is, therefore, £2·50 per share. When you sell all or some of these shares the calculation of your gain or loss will be based on this average cost.

The Rates of Capital Gains Tax.

From its introduction in 1965 to 1988, capital gains tax was levied at a flat rate of 30 per cent. From 6 April 1999 capital gains have been charged at an individual's income tax rate for savings income, currently 20 per cent (or 40 per cent). However the tax is only applied to an individual's gains over, £6,300 for 1996/97, £6,500 for 1997/98, £6,800 for 1998/99 and £7,100 for 1999/2000. Gains accruing prior to April 1982 are exempt.

12. INHERITANCE TAX

Inheritance tax emerged from the remains of the previous capital transfer tax in March 1986. Capital transfer tax applied to transfers of capital made both during life and on a person's death.

Capital transfer tax had replaced the old estate duty which was imposed on property passing at death, and gifts made within 7 years before death. The position has now turned full circle because, essentially, inheritance tax, like the old estate duty, is levied on transfers between individuals made on the death of the donor, or up to 7 years before death.

The Tax.

Inheritance tax is payable on transfers made on or after 18 March 1986 on transfers made at death or in the years preceding death. Certain gifts, most of which are listed below, are exempt from tax. All other gifts which are not exempt and which are made within 7 years of death are taxable as soon as the total amount of taxable transfers exceeds the threshold for tax. For 1999/2000 the threshold for tax is £231,000.

Furthermore, there are rules, similar to those operated under estate duty, which apply where the donor continues to enjoy some benefit from a gift even after it has been "given away". For example, this might apply where a person gives his or her home to the children, but continues to live in it. If this happens, for the purpose of inheritance tax, the gift will normally be treated as if it had been given on the date such enjoyment finally ceases.

The method of valuing assets largely continues on from the previous capital transfer tax and estate duty. Assets are usually valued at the price they would fetch on the open market at the time of the transfer.

The value of the estate on death will be taxed as the top slice of cumulative transfers in the 7 years before death. (For capital transfer tax the cumulation period was 10 years.)

From 1999/2000 the tax is levied at a single rate of 40 per cent on transfers over the £231,000 threshold. However, where gifts are made between individuals more than 3 years before the death of the donor the rate of tax is reduced by the relevant percentage given in Table 5. Different rules apply to gifts into and out of trust, discretionary trust charges and gifts involving companies.

TABLE 5. *Relief for Lifetime Transfers*

Years between gift and death	Percentage of full charge
0–3	100
3–4	80
4–5	60
5–6	40
6–7	20
Over 7	0

Exempt Transfers.

Certain transfers are eligible for exemption in much the same way as they were under capital transfer tax, including the following:

Transfers up to £3,000 in any one year (unused relief may be carried forward for one year only).

Small gifts of up to £250 to any one recipient in any tax year.

Gifts made as part of normal expenditure.

Marriage gifts as follows:

Parents	£5,000 each
Grandparents	£2,500 each
Bride and groom	£2,500 to each other
Other people	£1,000 each

Transfers between husband and wife if the recipient is domiciled in the United Kingdom.

Gifts to charities and political parties. A "political party" is defined for this purpose as one with two M.P.s, or one M.P. and not less than 150,000 votes for its candidates at the last general election.

Gifts for national purposes, *etc.* For example, gifts to the National Trust, National Gallery, universities and museums are exempt.

Other Relief.

There is also some relief for business assets, agricultural land and shares which represent a controlling interest in a company. In addition, a certain amount of relief is available for minority shareholdings in unquoted companies.

Administration and Collection.

The responsibility for the administration of inheritance tax lies with the Inland Revenue, and the procedures for assessment, appeals and penalties are similar to those for income tax. As with the previous capital transfer tax, the responsibility for dealing with Inland Revenue enquiries about transfers made before death lies with the personal representatives of the deceased. Where a person's death creates tax liability on gifts previously made, the main responsibility for the tax falls on the recipient, but with recourse to the donor's estate if necessary.

13. VALUE ADDED TAX

Value Added Tax (VAT) was introduced in the United Kingdom on 1 April 1973, and replaced the old Purchase Tax and Selective Employment Tax. One of the main reasons for changing the system was to harmonise the UK's indirect tax system with those of the other members of the European Union, each of which now has some kind of value added tax.

As its name suggests, VAT is levied on the goods and services you buy. In the budget of June 1979, the standard and higher rates of VAT were amalgamated into a single rate of 15 per cent and this was increased to 17.5 per cent in April 1991. The government, however, has the power to vary the rates of VAT by up to a quarter during the year in the interests of economic management. Some goods and services are "zero-rated" and others are "exempted" from VAT, a distinction which is explained shortly.

Anyone who has a business with a turnover of £51,000 per year or more must register with the Customs and Excise. In some circumstances it can be advantageous to register even if you have a business with a turnover below this (*see* "Registration" on **H**17).

How VAT Works.

VAT is payable at every stage of production when goods and services are supplied either to another business or to the final consumer. VAT is also payable on imported goods (and some imported services). The tax is charged by the supplier, who then pays it over to the Customs and Excise. For example, a simple VAT invoice for a good would show:

	£
Goods supplied	100·00
VAT at 17·5%	17·50
Total payable	£117·50

When a business calculates how much VAT is payable to the Customs and Excise it can deduct any VAT it has been *charged* on the goods and services it has purchased itself. For instance, suppose a firm buys some wood for £100 (plus £17·50 VAT) which it turns into furniture and sells for £200 (plus £35 VAT). The tax position would then be as follows:

	£	£
Receipts for furniture	200	
VAT charged to customer		35·00
Cost of wood	100	
VAT charged by supplier		17·50
VAT payable to Customs & Excise		£17·50

The final customer is charged £35 VAT and the Customs and Excise receives £35 in VAT (£17·50 from the furniture maker and £17·50 from the wood supplier).

In principle, each business pays tax on only the *value* it has *added* to its output. In our example above, the firm took £100 worth of wood and turned it into £200 worth of furniture. It could be said, therefore, that the firm has increased the value of the wood by £100. Accordingly, £17.50 VAT is payable to the Customs and Excise. Since each firm is taxed on its "value added," and charges the tax to its customer, the eventual VAT bill is related to the final value of the product and is paid by the final customer.

The way VAT is operated can be further illustrated by tracing the production of a good from the raw material stage through to the sale to the final customer. *See* Table on **H**18.

Zero-rated Supplies.

Goods and services that are "zero-rated" are in principle subject to VAT, but the rate applying to them is zero. This means that while VAT is not charged on these goods, businesses can still recover VAT paid on their own purchases. The effect of this arrangement is that zero-rated goods and services should be entirely free of VAT. For example, exports are relieved of VAT in this way.

Goods and services which are zero-rated may be summarised as follows:

Food—but not items such as pet foods, ice cream, soft drinks, alcoholic drinks, "meals out," and hot takeaway food and drink.
Water—except distilled water and bottled water.
Books—including newspapers, periodicals, music and maps (stationery is taxable).
Talking books and wireless sets for the blind.
News services. News services supplied to newspapers.
Fuel and Power—but not petrol and petrol substitutes. However VAT has been charged on domestic fuel and power since 1 April 1994. The rate was cut to 5% from September 1997.
Construction—of buildings.
Transport—except taxis, hired cars and boats and aircraft used for recreation.
Caravans—provided they are too large to be used as trailers on the roads. Houseboats are also zero-rated.
Gold and banknotes—but not gold coins or jewellery.
Drugs, medicines, medical and surgical appliances—provided they are purchased on a prescription.
Exports.
Charities.
Clothing and Footwear—for young children, industrial protective clothing and crash helmets.

Exempt Supplies.

Exempt goods and services are not subject to VAT, even in principle. A business cannot take any credit for VAT paid on the supplies used to produce exempt goods. Exemption is therefore less advantageous than zero-rating, but if a good falls into both categories it is zero-rated. Exempt items include:

Land.
Insurance including brokers' services.
Postal services, but not telephones and telex.
Betting, gaming and lotteries.
Finance such as banking.
Education—including incidental services.
Health.
Burial and cremation services.
Trade Unions and Professional Bodies
Sports Competitions.

The Tax Point.

The tax point is the date on which liability to VAT arises. There are rigid rules for fixing the tax point. This is to prevent businesses from gaining an unfair advantage from manipulating the date of transactions, either to delay the payment of VAT, or to take advantage of changes in the rates of tax.

Basically the tax point is the date when goods are despatched or made available to the customer. There are, however, two main exceptions to this. First, if an invoice is issued within 14 days of this time, the date of the invoice becomes the tax point. Secondly, if payment is made in advance, the date of payment becomes the tax point. It is also possible for particular businesses to make special arrangements with the Customs and Excise regarding the tax point.

Registration.

As already stated, anyone who has a business which has a taxable turnover of £51,000 or more a year must register with the Customs and Excise. For this purpose a "business" means any trade, profession or vocation. This includes partnerships, one-man businesses and free-lance work. It also includes clubs and associations such as sports clubs, but it does not include trade unions.

Businesses with a turnover of less than £51,000 a year are not liable to register, but it might be in their interests to do so. Where a trader pays more VAT for his supplies than he receives from his customers, he may be entitled to a rebate. This is most likely to happen where a business makes or supplies mainly items that are zero-rated or exported, but it may also happen with a new business. Rebates can be claimed only by registered traders.

To register for VAT, you simply contact the local VAT office (the address will be in the local telephone directory under "Customs and Excise"). You will then be sent form VAT 1, which you will have to complete and return. If a person wishes to de-register he may do so if he can satisfy the Customs and Excise that his taxable turnover (including the VAT) of all his business activities in the next 12 months will have fallen sufficiently. You can also, of course, deregister if you sell, cease trading or retire from your business.

VAT Records.

Businesses which are not exempt from VAT are required to keep certain records of their purchases and sales and the VAT relating to them. Furthermore, a *tax account* must be kept. This should contain a summary of the VAT totals from the main records and also VAT payments made to the Customs, or any repayments received.

Most businesses also have to issue *tax invoices* when making sales. Exceptions are retail businesses and sales of zero-rated goods and services. A tax invoice has to include the business's VAT registration number, the invoice number, the tax point and the tax charged.

Returns and Payment.

Traders registered for VAT have to make a return every three months whilst large VAT payers are required to make monthly payments on account. Some traders who are likely to receive rebates may also be allowed to submit returns every month. The return must be made within 30 days of the end of the period to which it relates, and any VAT due should normally be paid at the same time.

Essentially, the return requires the trader to calculate the value of his sales and the VAT charged thereon. He must also add up all the purchases of his business and the VAT paid on these inputs. The basic calculation will then look something like this:

Total sales for the period	£10,000	
VAT received		£1,750
Total inputs (purchases) for the period	£8,000	
VAT paid		£1,400
Balance payable to the Customs & Excise		£350

Appeals.

There are independent VAT tribunals to deal with appeals over a wide range of issues. This includes whether or not a trader should be registered and, if so, what the effective date of registration is; the amount of VAT payable; the amount of credit that can be taken for VAT paid on a business's purchases; and the value of goods and services supplied. From the tribunal there is an appeal to the High Court and from there to the Court of Appeal on a point of law (but not ques-

	Basic Price £	VAT £	Amount Received by Customs and Excise (C & E) £
Manufacturer imports raw materials	1,000	175	
Manufacturer pays VAT to C & E			+175
Manufacturer sells goods to wholesaler	2,000	350	
Manufacturer pays VAT to C & E			+175 (£350 minus £175)
Wholesaler sells goods to retailers	3,000	525	
Wholesaler pays VAT to C & E			+175 (£525 minus £350)
Retailers sell goods to customers	5,000	875	
Retailers pay VAT to C & E			+350 (£875 minus £525)
Customers pay	5,000 plus 875 VAT		
Customs and Excise receive total			£875

tions of fact). In Scotland such appeals go to the Court of Session. There are time limits for submitting appeals, and the procedure for appealing to the VAT Tribunals is described in a booklet available from the local VAT office.

Retailers.

Retailers are in a special position because they are usually unable to record each sale separately. Retailers are not required to issue tax invoices unless asked by customers, and there are several special schemes for calculating the amount of VAT payable. Retailers usually charge a price which is inclusive of VAT, and the amount of VAT can be calculated by using the appropriate fractions. With the rate of 17.5 per cent the relevant fraction is 7/47ths of the gross price. For example, the amount of VAT payable on an article with a gross price of £117.50 would be £117.50 × 7/47 = £17.50.

Further Information.

The Customs and Excise provide a series of detailed leaflets which cover all aspects of VAT, and which are available free of charge from any VAT office.

14. NATIONAL INSURANCE CONTRIBUTIONS

In the March 1999 Budget the Chancellor announced significant changes to National Insurance contributions to bring the system into closer alignment with income tax.

There are four classes of National Insurance contribution. Class 1 relates to employees, Classes 2 and 4 to the self-employed and Class 3 is voluntary.

The Class 1 contribution is paid partly by the employee and partly by the employer. Employees pay a contribution based on their earnings between the 'lower earnings limit' and the 'upper earnings limit'. These are being increased substantially. The lower earnings limit is rising from £64 a week in 1998/99, to £81 in 1999/2000 and £87 from April 2000. The upper earnings limit is being increased from £485 in 1998/99 to £535 a week in 1999/2000 and to £500 a week from April 2001. Also, the employers' National Insurance contributions on benefits in kind will be extended to cover not just cars and fuel but other benefits which are already subject to income tax.

Class 2 contributions are levied at a flat rate on the self-employed and this has been reduced from £6.35 a week in 1998/99 to £2 a week. The self-employed are also liable to Class 4 contributions which are related to the level of their profits. There is some further discussion of the highly complex subject of National Insurance contributions in **Section G**.

III. MISCELLANY

THE COUNCIL TAX

The council tax was introduced in April 1993. The new tax is based on property but there is also a personal element. The property element is assessed using a new system of banding which is constructed around average property values. Every home in Britain is allocated to one of eight bands according to its value. Properties in the same band in a local authority area are assessed to tax on the same basis. The tax levied on homes in the highest band is limited to two and a half times the amount levied on homes in the lowest band.

The assessment to tax begins with the assumption that each home contains two adults, but households of three or more adults are not charged extra. However a personal element remains in that single adult households receive a discount of 25 per cent of the basic charge. Discounts are also extended to students. If the first or second adult in a household is a student, a student nurse or Youth Training trainee, he or she is entitled to a personal discount. So, for example, in a household of students and no other adults, two 25 per cent discounts are available.

For individuals with a second home, the tax should be reduced by two personal discounts so that only half the usual charge would apply.

People on low incomes may be entitled to Council Tax Benefit. The claim form for Income Support also includes a claim form for Council Tax Benefit. For those not claiming Income Support a claim form should be available from the Council, or Regional Council in Scotland.

Valuations for Council Tax.

The value of each home for the purposes of council tax is the value on 1 April 1991. This is worked out on the basis of the amount the home could have been sold for on the open market if it had been sold on 1 April 1991. Each home is put in one of the eight bands shown in Table A. The amount of council tax payable is then calculated on the basis of the band in which your home is placed.

TABLE A

COUNCIL TAX VALUATION BANDS

Band	£
A	Up to 40,000
B	40,001–52,000
C	52,001–68,000
D	68,001–88,000
E	88,001–120,000
F	120,001–160,000
G	160,001–320,000
H	Over 320,000

Appeals.

It is not possible, of course, to appeal against the amount of council tax your council decides to raise. However, there are some grounds for appeal. One of these is where there has been a *material change* in the value of the home. This may arise, for example, because part of the dwelling has been demolished. There is no appeal on the grounds that there has been a general movement in house prices. A leaflet entitled "Council Tax—How to Appeal" should be available from your local council.

Granny Annexes.

The Government announced proposals that where an annex or similar self contained part of a property is occupied by an elderly or disabled relative of the residents living in the rest of it, then it should not be regarded as a separate dwelling for council tax purposes. These proposals were to come into force on 1 April 1997.

CHILD SUPPORT AGENCY

The Child Support Agency (CSA) came into operation as an arm of the Department of Social Security on 5 April 1993. The principle underlying the 1991 Child Support Act is that "absent parents" should pay maintenance for their children living with former partners ("parents with care"), the majority of whom depend on social security benefits. Fewer than a third of the 1,500,000 lone parents caring for two million children in 1993 received child maintenance. The CSA will eventually take over responsibility for all child maintenance and this power will be removed from the courts.

The CSA concentrated initially on lone parents making new claims for Income Support, Family Credit or Disability Working Allowance. They were asked to authorise the CSA to pursue absent parents for child maintenance. Parents already on these benefits were to be approached by the CSA between 1993–96, although administrative difficulties delayed this. If a lone parent "unreasonably refuses to co-operate" with the CSA her benefit can be reduced for 18 months. Refusal to co-operate is only accepted where there is a risk that pursuing the absent parent could cause the lone parent or a child living with her to suffer "harm or undue distress". Since January 1996, the benefit penalty is also not imposed if there is a disabled person living in the household.

The Formula for Calculations.

Child support maintenance is calculated by the CSA according to a rigid formula. It is argued that the amounts are more consistent than those imposed in court settlements. Critics of the Act, though often agreeing with it in principle, object to the punitive nature of the "reduced benefit direction". They also complain that since whatever child maintenance a parent receives is deducted from her benefit she usually ends up no better off. Indeed, it was claimed when the CSA came into operation that the purpose of the scheme was primarily to reduce benefits expenditure, with savings originally estimated at £530 million annually. The CSA service will become available to parents not on benefit in the future and they will be asked to pay a fee.

By 1994 the operation of the CSA was attracting increasing criticism—not just from fathers but from the women and children whom the Act had been designed to help. The difficulties facing the Agency were highlighted in December 1994 when it was decided, because of a backlog of 350,000 cases, to suspend pursuing one third of absent fathers on its books.

Recent Changes to the CSA.

In January 1995, after continuing criticism over the working of the Agency, the Social Security Secretary, Peter Lilley, announced several important changes. These included a new limit on how much an absent parent should pay (30% maximum of his net income) and greater discretionary powers for the CSA. Clean break settlements, where both partners had agreed to a division of their capital before April 1993, were now to be taken into account, as would the housing costs of second families. As a result, payments particularly by better-off absent parents were reduced sub-

stantially. There is now a limited right of appeal on assessments. The deadline of 1996 for separated parents not on benefit to begin using the CSA was deferred indefinitely.

Administrative chaos in the CSA caused the replacement of its first chief executive by a career civil servant. The National Audit Office reported in 1995 that over half of the maintenance assessments made by the Agency were incorrect and the Ombudsman declared that he did not have enough staff to investigate all the cases of CSA maladministration referred to him.

A major change made to the scheme from autumn 1996 (with pilot testing in some areas from April) was provision for "departure" from the standard formula in cases where the absent parent had particularly expensive travel to work costs, high travel costs to maintain contact with his children, expenses arising from disability, debts from the former relationship and the costs of caring for stepchildren. In addition, since April 1997 Income Support claimants receiving child maintenance have had up to £5 credited each week with the Benefits Agency, up to a maximum of £1000. This is payable as a lump sum if the parent leaves benefit to take up 16 hours or more work a week.

An important change was made in October 1996 in the treatment of parents with care who refused, without good cause, to provide information to enable the CSA to trace an absent parent to pay maintenance. Previously benefit was reduced for 18 months. The period is now three years, with provision for reduction for a further three years. In addition, the parent with care may also be asked to attend a social security fraud interview. The change was made because of suspicion that some parents with care on benefit were colluding with absent parents and receiving maintenance which they did not declare.

Current Developments.

With the election of the Labour government in May 1997, the future of the almost totally discredited Child Support Agency remained uncertain. A number of changes were made in 1998 in an attempt to make administration more effective, including an expansion in home interviews of lone parents claiming social security benefits and a seven days a week telephone service. However, in March 1998 the House of Commons Public Accounts Committee issued a report confirming continuing chaos in the functioning of the CSA. There remained a backlog of over 400,000 cases unprocessed since March 1997, while child maintenance uncollected by the Agency now totalled £1·1 billion, over 70% of which appeared to be unrecoverable. The Committee condemned the CSA's decision not to attempt to rectify errors in hundreds of thousands of assessments. Whether the CSA would survive and, if so, in what form, now depended on a review and consultation process instituted by the government.

ELECTRONIC COMMERCE

Electronic commerce is sometimes known as 'e-commerce' and exploits the development of the Internet (*see* **Section V**). This is the world wide network of computers which enables individuals and companies with computers to communicate with each other often using existing telephone lines. The 'World Wide Web' is the part of the Internet that incorporates images, videos and audio elements as well as text. Individuals and companies can use the Internet and World Wide Web to provide information about themselves and their products and can access such information from others at the touch of a few buttons. Electronic commerce simply describes using computers to do business—buying and selling goods and services or undertaking financial transactions.

Recent Rapid Growth.

Electronic commerce has been present for some years. However, it is beginning to develop rapidly as computers become more widely used by both individuals and companies. It is already possible to buy a very wide range of items over the Internet.

Many commercial items are themselves suitable for trading over the Internet—such as computer software and recorded entertainment. On-line information includes research databases. Periodicals and some encyclopaedias are available as are consulting and similar services. Financial transactions and stock trading now take place electronically around the world and it is even possible to gamble using the Internet.

To help guide the newcomer through the electronic commerce jargon, here is a glossary of terms.

Glossary of Electronic Commerce.

AIS. Automated Information Systems.

Authentication. Electronic identification of people and businesses.

DES. Data Encryption Standard.

Digital cash. Sometimes known as 'e-cash' or electronic cash.

Digital signatures. Electronic identification of the sender of a message or document.

E-cash. Electronic cash.

E-mail. Messages sent electronically.

EDI. Electronic Data Interchange—transferring data in a standard format from one computer application to another either within a business or between businesses.

Electronic cash. Electronic currency which may be used to make payment electronically.

Electronic coins. Sometimes called electronic tokens, they represent an electronic system for making small payments.

EFT. Electronic Funds Transfer, the transfer of funds and related information electronically.

Electronic purse or *wallet.* Software that allows electronic money to be stored and payments to be made.

Electronic signature. The electronic version of a handwritten signature.

Encryption. Changing data into a form which is more secure.

Home page. The reception page or main page of a web site.

Modem. A device for converting computer data into a form which can be transmitted over a telephone network.

Online storefront. A trader's website.

PAN. Primary Account Number.

POS. Point of Sale.

Protocol. The rules relating to the transmission of electronic information.

SET. Secure Electronic Transaction—a method of securing credit card transactions over the Internet.

Smart card. Plastic card containing a microchip which can 'store' money. This can then be used as a means of payment with a device that can read the information on the card.

VAN. Value Added Network—used to send data, often between companies.

Virtual wallet. An electronic purse.

Web page. A document on the World Wide Web.

Web site. A location on the World Wide Web containing information relating to a person or organisation.

MYTHS AND LEGENDS

This popular section gives a brief introduction to the myths and legends of Greece and Rome in an easily referable form. Great artists and writers throughout the ages have enriched their work by reference to these ancient tales of the classical world and some knowledge of them is indispensable to the full appreciation of our art and literature.

I. CLASSICAL MYTHOLOGY

A

Abas. In Greek mythology either (1) the son of Celeus and Metanira. His mockery of Demeter (q.v.) as she drank resulted in his being turned into a lizard, or

(2) the twelfth king of Argolis who owned a magic shield from which he derived authority. He was the father of Acrisius (q.v.) and Proetus (q.v.).

Abderus. The friend of Heracles (q.v.) in whose care Heracles left the mares of Diomedes (q.v.). The horses ate him and Heracles founded Abdera, a coastal town in Thrace, in his honour.

Absyrtus (or **Apsyrtus**). Half brother of the sorceress Medea (q.v.). When Aëtes pursued Jason (q.v.) and Medea, in order to recover the golden fleece, Medea slew the boy, cut his corpse into pieces and tossed the pieces into the sea. Because Aëtes stopped his ship to collect the pieces of his son for burial Jason and Medea were able to escape.

Abyla. See **"Pillars of Hercules"**.

Acamas. Son of Theseus (q.v.) and Phaedra (q.v.), brother of Demophon (q.v.). He went to Troy (q.v.) with Diomedes (q.v.) to demand the return of Helen (q.v.). He and his brother also rescued their grandmother Aethra, who had been Helen's slave, when Troy fell.

Acastus. Son of Pelias King of Iolcos and one of the Argonauts (q.v.). When Medea (q.v.) caused his father's death he banished her and Jason (q.v.). Showed hospitality to Peleus (q.v.) but suspecting him of advances towards his wife he left Peleus to die at the hands of the Centaurs (q.v.). Later Peleus returned to slay the couple. Acastus was the father of Laodamia (q.v.).

Acestes. In Roman mythology a chieftain of Trojan descent who had settled in Sicily prior to the arrival of Aeneas (q.v.).

Achelous. A great river god, the son of Oceanus (q.v.) and Tethys (q.v.). By defeating Achelous Heracles (q.v.) won the hand of Deianeira (q.v.) daughter of Oeneus (q.v.).

Acheron. A real river of Epirus flowing into the Ionian Sea. Part of it runs underground which may account for its position in Greek mythology. Here it is the "river of grief" which flows in the underworld of the dead.

Achilles. A Greek warrior who is the principal character of the *Iliad*. The son of Peleus (q.v.) King of the Myrmidones at Phthia in Thessaly and Thetis (q.v.) one of the Nereides (q.v.). As a baby his mother dipped him in the Styx (q.v.) making him invulnerable save for his heel, by which she held him. He was educated in the arts of war and hunting, and in morality, by Cheiron (q.v.). His mother, knowing that he would die at Troy (q.v.) tried to prevent him joining the Greek expedition there by disguising him as a girl and sending him to the court of Lycomedes, King of Scyros. Here Lycomedes' daughter Deidamia, bore him a son, Neoptolemus (q.v.). Odysseus (q.v.) learned of this subterfuge and visited Lycomedes' court disguised as a merchant. While the king's daughters and the disguised Achilles were surveying his wares he suddenly produced swords which Achilles eagerly clasped, thus revealing himself. Achilles proved himself the most formidable warrior at Troy. At Tenedos on the way to Troy he killed Tenes and his father Cyncus and by raiding Aeneas' (q.v.) cattle prompted him to join the Trojan forces. In the tenth year of the war Achilles quarrelled with Agamemnon (q.v.) over the captive girl Briseis and withdrew from the fighting. However he loaned his armour to Patroclus, his cousin and friend who was slain by Hector (q.v.). His death prompted Achilles to cease sulking in his tent and to return to the fray. Thetis gave him new armour made by Hephaestus (q.v.) and wearing this he slew Hector. He also killed Penthesilea (q.v.) and the

Greek Thersites (q.v.). After killing Memnon (q.v.) Achilles was shot in his vulnerable ankle at a battle near the Scaean gate (q.v.) Odysseus and Ajax (q.v.) recovered his body and argued over his armour.

Acis. In later Greek legend the young son of Faunus (q.v.) and a river nymph. He loved the sea-nymph Galatea (q.v.) and was killed by his jealous rival Polyphemus (q.v.). According to Sicilian tradition he was then turned into the river of the same name which runs at the foot of Mount Etna. This tradition first appears in the writing of Theocritus (q.v.) and later in Ovid's (q.v.) "Metamorphoses". It inspired paintings by Poussin and Claude and the opera *Acis and Galatea* by Handel.

Acrisius. Son of Abas (q.v.), twin brother of Proetus (q.v.) and King of Argos. Warned by an oracle that the son of his daughter Danaë (q.v.) would kill him he had her locked up in a brazen tower. But this was to no avail because Zeus (q.v.) visited her and fathered Perseus (q.v.), Acrisius then cast mother and son adrift on the sea, locked in a chest. Years later Perseus returned to Argos causing Acrisius to flee to Larissa. However Perseus, visiting Larissa to take part in the games, accidentally killed him with a discus.

Acropolis. In general terms a high citadel found in all Greek cities. The best known acropolis is that at Athens which was first inhabited around 2000 B.C. From time immemorial it was dedicated to Athene (q.v.).

Actaeon. Mythical huntsman and grandson of Cadmus (q.v.) of Thebes. Artemis (q.v.) turned him into a stag, torn to pieces by his own hounds because he inadvertently spied her bathing. The story is recounted in Ovid's (q.v.) "Metamorphoses" and recalled in the works of Titian, Veronese, Poussin, Rembrandt, Gainsborough and Parmigiano.

Admetus. King of Pherae in Thessaly and husband of the beautiful Alcestis (q.v.). Apollo (q.v.) offered to allow Admetus to avoid death if one of his family would die in his place. Alcestis offered herself but according to legend either Persephone (q.v.) refused the self-sacrifice or Heracles (q.v.) rescued Alcestis from Hades (q.v.). This forms the theme of one of Euripedes' best known plays and Gluck's opera *Alceste* (in which Apollo not Heracles saves her).

Adonis. A Syrian deity associated with the mystery of vegetation. He was a beautiful Cypriot youth, the son of Myrrha and her father. For this incest Myrrha was turned into a tree. Nine months later Adonis was born from the bark of the tree, taken up by Aphrodite (q.v.) and placed in the care of Persephone (q.v.). He spent alternate parts of the year with Persephone and Aphrodite who loved him. He was killed by a boar sent by Artemis (q.v.). Shakespeare's *Venus and Adonis* is based on Ovid's (q.v.) version of the tale while Shelley's elegy on the death of Keats, *Adonais*, derives its title from Bion's *Lament for Adonis*. Adonis was painted by Titian, Veronese and Poussin.

Adrastus. Son of Talaus and King of Argos. An oracle told him that his offspring would be a lion and a boar and in accordance with this he gave his daughter Argia to Polynices (q.v.) and her sister to Tydeus (q.v.) who bore images of these animals on their shields. He attempted to restore Polynices to his throne at Thebes (see **Seven against Thebes**). He survived this adventure—some say due to his magic horse Arion (q.v.)—and led a second expedition of the Epigoni, (q.v.) against Thebes, dying of grief when he heard that his son Aegialeus had fallen in the attack.

Aeacides. The descendants of Aeacus (q.v.).

Aeacus. Son of Zeus and Aegina and King of the Myrmidones. The Myrmidones were originally ants, transformed into men by Zeus at the request of Aeacus. He aided Poseidon (q.v.) and Apollo (q.v.) in the construction of the walls of Troy. He had two sons, Peleus (q.v.) and Telamon (q.v.) by his wife Endeis. He was also the father of Phocus (q.v.) by a Nereid. Aeacus later exiled Peleus (future father of Achilles) for the murder of Phocus. A model of virtue and piety, Aeacus was made one of the three judges of the Underworld.

Aeaea. In the Odyssey the island home of Circe (q.v.).

Aedon. In Greek mythology the wife of Zethus, king of Thebes. She was jealous of Niobe, wife of Zethus' brother Amphion (q.v.). In trying to murder Niobe's son she killed her own son Itylus by mistake. In pity Zeus (q.v.) turned her into a nightingale whose song still mourns Itylus.

Aegaeon. Alternative name for Briareus (q.v.).

Aegeus. King of Athens and father of Theseus (q.v.) by Aethra (q.v.) daughter of Pittheus king of Troezen. She brought Theseus up secretly at her father's court, during which time Aegeus married Medea (q.v.). When Theseus finally returned to his father's court Medea fled. Before Theseus went to slay the Minotaur (q.v.) he and Aegeus agreed that he would hoist a white sail when returning to Athens to signal his success. On returning Theseus forgot to do this and Aegeus seeing a black sail on his son's ship supposed him dead and, in grief threw himself into the sea, henceforth called the Aegean.

Aegisthus. The son of Thyestes (q.v.) by his daughter Pelopia. Pelopia exposed the baby but it was rescued by her husband Atreus (q.v.) who believed it to be his own son. Atreus was king of Mycenae and when Thyestes, an enemy, returned in later years he ordered Aegisthus to kill him. But father and son recognised each other and Aegisthus killed Atreus. Thyestes became king of Mycenae but Atreus had had two sons by Aerope, Menelaus (q.v.) and Agamemnon (q.v.). Agamemnon expelled Thyestes and reclaimed his father's throne. While Agamemnon was at Troy (q.v.) Aegisthus seduced his wife Clytemnestra (q.v.) and helped her murder him on his return. These two murderers of Agamemnon now ruled Mycenae. But at the urging of his sister Electra (q.v.) (whom Aegisthus would have liked to kill and whom he forced to marry a peasant) Agamemnon's son Orestes (q.v.) and his friend Pylades (q.v.) returned from exile in Phocis and with Electra's help avenged their father, slaying Aegisthus and Clytemnestra.

Aeneas. The Trojan hero regarded by the Romans as their ancestor. The son of Anchises (q.v.) and Aphrodite (q.v.). Led the survivors of the Trojan War to Italy. The lover of Dido. See under **Aeneid**.

Aeneid. Virgil's (q.v.) unfinished epic poem. In 12 volumes, it is written to honour Rome, to increase the prestige of Augustus (by recalling the deeds of his supposed ancestor) and to foretell prosperity to come. It describes Aeneas' (q.v.) wanderings after Troy fell, recounting his stay in Carthage and love for Dido (q.v.) the funeral games of his father Anchises (q.v.) in Sicily, a journey to the Underworld to visit his dead father's spirit and his arrival at the mouth of the Tiber where he landed on the Latin shore. Here he fought wars with the Latins and their allies before finally defeating Turnus the Rutulian prince and uniting the races by marrying Lavinia the Latin princess. He founded Lavinium, named in her honour.

Aeolian Isles. The present Aeolian Isles are off the North East of Sicily, forming part of the Liparia group. They are mentioned in the Odyssey.

Aeolus. In Greek mythology (1) the son of Helen and ruler of Thessaly, believed to be the brother of Dorus and Xuthus (q.v.) and the ancestor of the Aeolians or Aeolic Greeks, i.e. those inhabiting Aeolis.

(2) The son of Poseidon (q.v.) and ruler of the Aeolian isles (q.v.). Zeus (q.v.) made him guardian of the winds. He gave Odysseus (q.v.) a bag of winds which his men let loose and which blew the ship off course.

Aeschylus. See **B2**.

Aetolus. Legendary conqueror of Aetolia. The son of Endymion (q.v.) king of Elis, he was banished across the Corinthian Gulf after accidentally killing Apis in a chariot race.

Agamemnon. Son of Atreus (q.v.) and Aerope, brother of Menelaus (q.v.) and king of Mycenae. He married Helen's (q.v.) half-sister Clytemnestra (q.v.) and commanded the Greek forces at Troy (q.v.). Before the Greek fleet could leave Aulis to sail for Troy he had to sacrifice his daughter Iphigenia (q.v.). At Troy he quarrelled with Achilles (q.v.) when he seized Briseis from Achilles. He did this because Apollo (q.v.) had forced him to return Chryseis to her father, the Trojan Chryses (q.v.).

On his return to Mycenae he was murdered by Aegisthus (q.v.) and Clytemnestra. Clytemnestra attacked him with an axe while he was bathing. This occurred despite the warning given to Agamemnon by Cassandra (q.v.) whom he had brought back from Troy as his mistress. He was avenged by his children Orestes (q.v.) and Electra (q.v.). The story inspired Aeschylus' (q.v.) trilogy Orestia.

Aganippe. A fountain at the foot of Mt. Helicon, sacred to the Muses (q.v.) who are sometimes called Aganippides. It inspired those who drank from it. The fountain of Hippocrene, also sacred to the Muses, was known as Aganippis.

Agathyrsans. In the Aeneid (q.v.) a tribe in Thrace.

Aglaia. "The bright one": one of the Graces (q.v.).

Aides or **Aidoneus.** Hades (q.v.).

Ajax. (Greek Aias) In Greek legend two Ajaxes appear. The first was the son of King Telamon of Salamis. He killed Teuthras King of Teuthrania, an ally of Troy (q.v.) and took his daughter Tecmessa. At Troy he fought all day with Hector (q.v.) and at the end of the duel they exchanged gifts, Hector giving him a sword. With Menelaus (q.v.) he rescued the body of Patroclus (q.v.) and with Odysseus (q.v.) killed Glaucus and rescued the body of Achilles. Homer (q.v.) says the pair quarrelled over the armour and that Odysseus killed him. Later, when Odysseus summoned the spirits of the dead Ajax held aloof. But Sophocles (q.v.) in his Ajax calls on another tradition in which Ajax, disappointed at not being given the Palladium (q.v.) of Troy when the city fell, went mad, killing the Greek sheep under the delusion they were his rivals before impaling himself on the sword Hector had given him. The other Ajax was the son of Oileus, king of the Locrians. He was courageous but blasphemous. When Troy was sacked he dragged Cassandra (q.v.) from the altar of Athene (q.v.) where she sought refuge and gave her to Agamemnon (q.v.). On his return to Greece Poseidon (q.v.) saved him from shipwreck in a storm sent by Athene. Taking shelter on a rock he boasted himself more powerful than the goddess. She commanded Poseidon to crack the reef with his trident and Ajax drowned.

Alba Longa. The Latin city founded by Ascanius (q.v.) in the Alban Hills. In fact, as well as legend, Alba was the mother city of Rome which was probably founded as one of her western outposts. Alba was capital of the Latin League, a confederation of Latin states, but was eventually supplanted by Rome.

Alcaeus. See **Alcmene**.

Alcestis. Daughter of Pelias (q.v.) and the only one of his daughters not to follow Medea's (q.v.) advice and boil him alive. Married Admetus (q.v.) and was devoted to him.

Alcides. Another name for Heracles (q.v.) whose grandfather was reputed to be Alcaeus.

Alcinous. King of the mythical Phaeacians of the isle of Scheria. A grandson of Poseidon (q.v.), he married Arete his own sister. Father of the beautiful Nausicaa (q.v.). He entertained Odysseus and gave him a ship. He was also said to have entertained the Argonauts and refused to return Medea to her father. Scheria has been identified with Corfu.

Alcmaeon. In myth the son of Amphiaraus (q.v.) and Eriphyle (q.v.). One of the Epigoni (q.v.).

Alcmene. The wife of Amphitrion (q.v.) son of Alcaeus. Her brothers had been slain by the Taphians and she would not consummate her marriage until Amphitrion avenged them. While he was away warring with the Taphians Zeus (q.v.) appeared in his likeness and fathered Heracles (q.v.) upon her. Hermes (q.v.) was ordered to delay the dawn in order that Zeus might take his time—an amusing situation which has appealed to Plautus, Molière and Dryden. Later that night the real Amphitrion returned and fathered Iphicles (q.v.). In his Amphitryon 38 Jean Giraudoux claims 37 versions of the tale have preceded him. On the death of Amphitrion Alcmene married Rhadamanthus (q.v.).

Alcyone or **Halcyone**. (1) Leader of the Pleiades (q.v.), daughter of Atlas (q.v.) and Pleione.

(2) The daughter of Aeolus (q.v.) and wife of Ceyx. When Ceyx was lost at sea she drowned herself in sorrow. The sympathetic gods turned the pair to kingfishers which supposedly bred during the winter solstice. Then Aeolus forbids the wind to blow leaving the Aegean calm while they build and sit on their nest. This is the time of year

called the "Halcyon days". The story is told in Ovid's (*q.v.*) "Metamorphoses" and Chaucer's "Book of the Duchess".

Alecto. One of the Erinnyes (*q.v.*).

Alexander the Great. *See* **B3**

Amalthea. The she-goat which nursed the infant Zeus in the Dictaean cave in Crete. As a reward she was placed among the stars as Capricorn while one of her horns which had broken off became the Cornucopia, or horn of plenty.

Amazons. Mythical race of female warriors at one time believed by the Greeks to live in Thrace or Asia Minor. As the Greeks' knowledge of the world grew, so the homeland of the Amazons was held to be more distant. In the *Iliad* (*q.v.*) Priam (*q.v.*) is said to have warred with them, though they came to the aid of Troy (*q.v.*). Achilles (*q.v.*) slew their queen Penthesilea (*q.v.*). Heracles (*q.v.*) fought with them and seized the girdle of the queen Hippolyte (*q.v.*) while Theseus (*q.v.*) carried off either Hippolyte or Antiope (*q.v.*). Theseus' act caused the Amazons to invade Attica but Theseus defeated them in the streets of Athens. In antiquity it was thought they amputated their right breast (Greek *mazos*) in order to hold a bow better.

Ambrosia. The food of the Olympians which gave immortality.

Ammon. The Egyptian god Amun was known to the Greeks from the 7th century B.C. when they came into contact with his cult at the Siwa oasis. They identified him with Zeus. Alexander the Great consulted the oracle of Zeus and Ammon was recognised as the son of Zeus by the priests of the oracle. A legend grew up that Alexander was begotten by Ammon in the form of a snake.

Amphiaraus. *See* **Seven Against Thebes.**

Amphion. Twin brother of Zethus, sons of Zeus (*q.v.*) and Antiope (*q.v.*). Antiope was married to Lycus King of Thebes who divorced her. She was cruelly treated by his second wife Dirce. The twins were raised by herdsmen on Mt. Cithaeron. When they reached manhood they avenged their mother by killing Zethus and tying Dirce to the horns of a wild bull. The fountain into which her body was thrown henceforth bore her name. The twins now took possession of Thebes and built the fortifications below the Cadmea. Amphion, who had been given a lyre by Hermes (*q.v.*) played so skilfully that the stones moved into place of their own accord. They ruled jointly, Zethus marrying Thebe who gave her name to the city, and Amphion marrying Niobe (*q.v.*).

Amphitrion. Son of Alcaeus, husband of Alcmene (*q.v.*) and father of Iphicles (*q.v.*). Foster father of Heracles (*q.v.*). When Heracles killed his teacher Linus with Linus' own lyre, Amphitrion sent him away to keep cattle. Later Amphitrion was killed helping Heracles defeat the Minyans.

Amphitrite. The daughter of Nereus (*q.v.*) leader of the Nereids (*q.v.*). Persuaded by Delphinos to accept Poseidon (*q.v.*) (Delphinos was rewarded by having his image placed amongst the stars as the Dolphin). By Poseidon she was mother of Triton (*q.v.*). Her hatred of Scylla (*q.v.*), Poseidon's daughter by another, led her to turn Scylla into a monster with six barking heads and twelve feet.

Amphitroniades. Another name for Heracles (*q.v.*) whose putative father was Amphitrion (*q.v.*).

Amyclae. One of the most sacred sites in the Peloponnese, a sanctuary a few miles from Sparta consecrated to Hyacinthus (*q.v.*).

Anchises. A cousin of Priam (*q.v.*). For his piety he was allowed to sleep with Aphrodite (*q.v.*) who bore him Aeneas. When Troy (*q.v.*) fell Aeneas carried his father (now blind) to safety through the Dardanian gate of the city. He died in Sicily and was buried at Eryx. In the *Aeneid* (*q.v.*) he appears among the blessed spirits of the dead to foretell Rome's greatness. *Aeneas carrying his Father* is an early work of Bernini.

Ancus Martius. The legendary fourth king of Rome who succeeded Tullus Hostilius. A grandson of Numa Pompilius (*q.v.*) he ruled from 640 to 616 B.C. He was very religious but also succeeded in defeating the Latins. He was succeeded by Tarquin the Elder.

Andromache. A Trojan princess, wife of Hector (*q.v.*) and by him mother of Astyanax. When Troy fell her son was thrown from the city walls, despite her spirited defence of him with a pestle. She was carried off to Epirus by Neoptolemus (*q.v.*) and here married his brother in law Hellenus and

became joint ruler. She also had a son by Neoptolemus and was threatened by his jealous wife Hermione (*see* Racine's *Andromaque*). Her days were ended at Pergamum, the city founded by her and Neoptolemus' son, Molossus. In historic times the Molossi claimed descent from Molossus and Neoptolemus.

Andromeda. *See* **Cassiopeia**.

Antaeus. A Libyan giant, son of Poseidon (*q.v.*) and Ge (*q.v.*). An invincible wrestler until Heracles (*q.v.*), realising he drew his strength from his mother, held him in the air and squeezed him to death. He is featured in a painting by Pollaiuolo in Florence.

Antenor. The wisest of the Trojans. Priam (*q.v.*) sent him to reclaim Hesione from Telamon after Heracles (*q.v.*) sacked Troy (*q.v.*). He advised the Trojans to return Helen (*q.v.*) to Menelaus (*q.v.*) but they refused. His hatred for Deiphobus (*q.v.*) led him to help the Greeks steal the Palladium (*q.v.*). The husband of Theano and father of Laocoön (*q.v.*). After Troy fell he and his wife went to Italy and founded either Venice or Padua.

Antigone. Daughter of Oedipus (*q.v.*) and Jocasta (*q.v.*) she accompanied her father into exile (recalled in Sophocles' *Oedipus at Colonus*). After his death she returned to Thebes where her brother Eteocles (*q.v.*) and Polynices (*q.v.*) were warring on each other. Both perished in battle and her uncle Creon (*q.v.*) seized power. Because Polynices had fought against his own country Creon refused him burial. Antigone defied Creon and buried her brother with full rites and was imprisoned in a cave for doing so. Here she hung herself, and her betrothed, Creon's son Haemon, committed suicide in despair. The story and the ethical principles it raises are the basis of Sophocles' *Antigone*. In his work of the same name Anouilh reconsiders the arguments involved.

Antilochus. Son of Nestor (*q.v.*) a valiant Greek warrior at Troy (*q.v.*). Too young to sail from Aulis when the expedition began he arrived later. Slain by Memnon (*q.v.*) while defending his father.

Antinous. *See* **Odysseus.**

Antiope. (1) An Amazon, sister of Hippolyte (*q.v.*). According to some legends she was carried off by Theseus (*q.v.*), perhaps with the aid of Heracles (*q.v.*) and bore him Hippolytus (*q.v.*).

(2) A Theban princess who bore Amphion (*q.v.*) and Zethus to Zeus (*q.v.*) who visited her in the form of a satyr (*q.v.*). Her father exposed the children on Mt. Cithaeron. She was badly treated and imprisoned by Lycus and his wife Dirce (Lycus was either her husband, who divorced her to marry Dirce, or her uncle). She was later freed and avenged by her twin sons. Titian, Correggio and Watteau have all painted Zeus visiting Antiope as a satyr.

Aphaia. A goddess worshipped in Aegina and identified with the Cretan Britomartis.

Aphrodite. The goddess of love, desire and procreation, known to the Romans as Venus. She sprang from the seed of Uranus (*q.v.*), rising naked from the sea at Paphos in Cyprus. However, Homer (*q.v.*) holds her to be the daughter of Zeus (*q.v.*) and Dione, and makes her the wife of Hephaestus (*q.v.*). She was not faithful to Hephaestus, but bore children by Ares (*q.v.*), Poseidon (*q.v.*), Dionysus (*q.v.*), and Hermes (*q.v.*), She loved the mortals Adonis (*q.v.*) and Anchises (*q.v.*) by whom she bore Aeneas (*q.v.*), and tempted Paris (*q.v.*) to desert Oenone. It was to her that Paris gave the golden apple of discord, she being the "fairest" goddess. In return she promised him the most beautiful woman in the world. Around her waist she wore a magic girdle which made her beautiful and irresistibly desirable.

Apis. The sacred bull of Memphis which the Egyptians worshipped as a god.

Apollo. Son of Zeus (*q.v.*) and the mortal Leto; twin brother of Artemis (*q.v.*). As a child he killed the she-dragon Python on Mt. Parnassus and took over her role as the oracle at Delphi. Hence he was sometimes known as the Pythian or as Loxias "the Ambiguous". He was also a symbol of light and was known as Phoebus or "shining". Apart from being god of prophecy he was a god of song and music, having been given the lyre by Hermes (*q.v.*). He was the leader of the Muses (*q.v.*) and was sometimes called Musagetes. He could be a destroyer (he is always portrayed with bow and arrows) and sent plagues amongst the Greeks at Troy, but was also protective against evil and was father of Asclepius (*q.v.*). When Zeus slew Asclepius he retaliated by slaying the Cyclopes (*q.v.*)

15

and was punished by being sent as a servant to Admetus (q.v.) of Pherae in Thessaly. Prior to this Zeus had sent him as a bondsman to King Laomedan whom he helped to build the walls of Troy. This was punishment for his part in a conspiracy (led by Hera, Poseidon and himself) against Zeus. He loved Hestia (q.v.) but also seduced the nymph Dryope and attempted to seduce Daphne. When Daphne protested she was turned into a laurel tree. Amongst mortal women he at one time loved Cassandra (q.v.). With his sister Artemis he shot the giant Tityus, whom the jealous Hera sent to violate Leto; it was he who shot the vulture which tormented Prometheus and he also helped Paris (q.v.) shoot Achilles (q.v.). He was identified with the sun-god by later writers but in Homer (q.v.) he and Helios (q.v.) are quite distinct.

Arachne. A Lydian maiden who competed with Athene (q.v.) at a weaving contest. When she won the angry goddess forced her to hang herself before turning her into a spider and her weaving into a cobweb.

Arcadia. Green but mountainous region, isolated in the centre of the Peloponnese. Its inhabitants were primitive shepherds and peasants.

Arcas. The son of Zeus (q.v.) and Callisto (q.v.) who gave his name to Arcadia (q.v.).

Ares. The son of Zeus (q.v.) and Hera (q.v.) and the god of war. Associated with Mars, by the Romans. He was disliked by all the gods save Hades (q.v.) and Eris (q.v.) because of his love of battle for its own sake. He loved Aphrodite (q.v.), and Hephaestus (q.v.) once caught the pair in an invisible net exposing them to the ridicule of the other gods. The father of Penthesilea (q.v.) by Otrere. He was once defeated by Heracles (q.v.), was wounded by Diomedes (q.v.) and imprisoned for 13 months (till Hermes (q.v.) released him) in a brazen vessel by the Aloeidae (q.v.). Athene (q.v.) got the better of him on several occasions. He once stood trial on the site of the Areopagus.

Arethusa. A river and a river goddess of southern Greece. She was pursued under the sea to Sicily by the river god Alpheus. In Sicily she was identified with Artemis and a cult of Artemis Arethusa flourished at Syracuse.

Argo. A fifty-oared ship built for Jason (q.v.) by Argus. In its prow Athene (q.v.) fitted an oracular beam.

Argonauts. The heroes who sailed with Jason (q.v.) in the Argo (q.v.) to fetch the golden fleece from Colchis. Their ranks included Heracles (q.v.), Orpheus (q.v.) Castor and Polydeuces (q.v.) Echion, Idas (q.v.) and Lynceus (q.v.). The voyage was an adventurous one and after dallying at Lemnos they passed through the Hellespont and reached Mysia. Here Hylas (q.v.) was lost and Heracles stayed to look for him. At some point the Sirens (q.v.) were passed with the help of Orpheus (q.v.) and at Bebrycos Polydeuces (see **Castor**) slew Amycus. In Thrace they rid Phineus (q.v.) of the Harpies (q.v.) and in return were told how to navigate the Symplegades (q.v.).

Argus. (1) The builder of the Argo (q.v.).

(2) A hundred-eyed giant set by Hera (q.v.) to watch Io (q.v.).

(3) The faithful hound of Odysseus (q.v.).

Ariadne. The daughter of Minos (q.v.) and Pasiphae (q.v.). She helped Theseus (q.v.) but he abandoned her at Naxos when Dionysus (q.v.) fell in love with her. He married her and gave her a crown of seven stars which became a constellation after her death.

Arimaspi. A mythical people of the Scythian steppes said to be neighbours of the Hyperboreans. They had one eye and constantly fought a group of griffins for the gold they guarded. Herodotus (q.v.) tells of a poem by Aristeas, a priest of Hyperborean Apollo, about them. Aristeas is clearly a *shaman*, able to separate body and soul and to be in two places at once. Aeschylus (q.v.) refers to them when describing Io's (q.v.) wanderings.

Arion. A fabulous horse, the offspring of Demeter (q.v.) and Zeus (q.v.). Demeter had taken the form of a mare and Zeus raped her in the form of a horse. She also gave birth to the nymph Despoena and possibly Persephone (q.v.) at the same time as Arion. It saved Adrastus (q.v.) at the siege of Thebes.

Aristaeus. The son of Apollo (q.v.) and a Lapith (see Lapithae) girl Cyrene. A minor deity, the protector of cattle, fruit trees and bee-keepers. Virgil (q.v.) makes Cyrene a nymph and says that Aristaeus fell in love with Eurydice who died of a snake bite she received while fleeing from him. In punishment all his bees were killed. Cyrene sought the advice of Proteus (q.v.) and Aristaeus made sacrifices of cattle to placate the nymphs. Nine days later he found fresh swarms in the carcasses.

Aristophanes. See **B4.**

Artemis. The daughter of Zeus (q.v.) and Leto (q.v.) twin sister of Apollo (q.v.). Her Roman counterpart was Diana. She was often conflated with Hecate (q.v.) and Selene (q.v.), the moon goddess. A goddess of the chase and protectoress of children and young animals. She was also treated as a mother or earth goddess in the Asian tradition and was worshipped orgiastically at Ephesus. She was generally portrayed with a bow and arrow, made by Hephaestus (q.v.) and like Apollo could spread the plague and death. With her arrows she punished impiety (e.g. Niobe). A virgin who sternly protected her own chastity, she was known to punish unchastity in others e.g. Callisto (q.v.).

Ascanius. The son of Aeneas (q.v.) and Creusa, who escaped from Troy (q.v.) with his father. Another tradition makes his mother the Latin princess Lavinia. He succeeded his father as king and made Alba Longa (q.v.) his capital.

Asclepius or **Aesculapius.** The son of Apollo (q.v.) and Coronis, a god of healing whose worship spread to Rome after a plague in 293 B.C. He was taught healing by Cheiron the centaur (q.v.). Once he brought a dead man back to life and Zeus (q.v.) punished him, killing him with a thunderbolt. At Apollo's request he was placed among the stars.

Asopus. A river god, the son of Oceanus (q.v.) and Tethys (q.v.). The father of Evadne, Euboea and Aegina.

Astraeus. A Titan (q.v.) and by Eos the father of the beneficent winds. According to other traditions he also fathered the stars.

Astyanax. The son of Hector (q.v.) and Andromache (q.v.). He was a sensitive child frightened by the plume of his father's helmet. When Troy (q.v.) fell Andromache struggled to protect him but Neoptolemus (q.v.) threw him from the city walls. Another tradition says she took him to Neoptolemus' court in Epirus.

Atalanta. The Boeotian Atalanta was the daughter of Schoeneus and wife of Hippomenes, the Arcadian Atalanta, the daughter of Iasus and Clymene and wife of Milanion. Similar tales were told of her in both traditions. She was exposed by her father and suckled by a bear sent by Artemis (q.v.) with whom she was sometimes identified. She became a famous huntress and hunted the Calydonian Boar (q.v.). Though vowed to virginity she bore Meleager (q.v.) a son. She refused to marry any suitor except he who beat her in a foot race. Hippomenes (or Milanion) did this by placing three golden apples, gifts from Aphrodite (q.v.) in her path, causing her to stop and collect them.

Athamas. The son of Aeolus and king of Orchomenus in Boeotia. He loved Ino (q.v.) who bore him Learchus and Melicertes, but Hera (q.v.) forced him to marry Nephele who bore him Phrixus and Helle (q.v.). Hera drove him mad because he sheltered Dionysus (q.v.) and he killed Learchus. Ino flung herself into the sea with Melicertes and both became sea deities. Ino became Leucothea and Melicertes became Palaemon. Athamas fled to Thessaly.

Athene or **Athena.** Identified with Minerva by the Romans. The daughter of Zeus (q.v.) and Metis (q.v.). Though it was foretold she would be a girl, an oracle said that if Metis bore another child it would be a son who would depose Zeus. He then swallowed Metis and later suffered a terrible headache near Lake Triton. Hermes (q.v.) knew the cause and persuaded Hephaestus (q.v.) to cleave Zeus' skull. Out sprang Athene fully armed. She was the goddess of wisdom and patron of arts and crafts, a protectress of agriculture and also a warrior. Moreover, she was a virgin (see Pallas). She disputed possession of Athens with Poseidon (q.v.): he offered the city the horse, Athene the olive which was judged to be the better gift. Henceforth she was patron of the city which was a centre of her cult. Her epithet 'glaucopis' meant "bright-eyed" or "owl-faced" and in the Odyssey (q.v.) she assumed the form of a bird. Athenian coins bore an owl and the saying "Owls to Athens" meant the same as "Coals to Newcastle". She was worshipped on the Acropolis. A defender of all heroes who worked for the good of mankind, e.g. Heracles (q.v.).

Atlantiades. Another name for Hermes (q.v.) whose mother Maia was the daughter of Atlas (q.v.).

Atlantis. A legendary island said to be to the west of the Pillars of Hercules (q.v.). Its inhabitants, once powerful and virtuous, became wealthy and degenerate and were conquered by the Athenians. Later the island sank beneath the ocean in a day and a night. It may be that the island Plato speaks of in *Timaeus* was part of Crete or some other island which suffered when a volcano on Suntorini (ancient Thera) erupted.

Atlas. A Titan (q.v.) the son of Iapetus and Clymene and brother of Prometheus (q.v.) and Epimetheus. For his part in the Titanomachia (q.v.) he was condemned to carry the sky on his shoulders and stood holding it far to the west of the Pillars of Hercules (q.v.). For a brief time Heracles (q.v.) shouldered his burden. It is said Perseus (q.v.) turned him to stone with Medusa's (q.v.) head and he was identified with Mt. Atlas in North-West Africa. The father of Calypso (q.v.) and the Pleiades (q.v.).

Atreus. *See* **Thyestes.**

Attis. A god of vegetation whose cult originated in Phrygia and involved a festival of death and resurrection in the Spring. A consort of Cybele (q.v.) according to one tradition he castrated himself in a religious frenzy and became head of her college of eunuch priests.

Augeas. A king of Elis with more sheep and cattle than any other man. Heracles (q.v.) was given the task of cleansing his filthy stables (the Augean stables) which had not been cleared for many years. Heracles promised to cleanse them in a day in return for one tenth of the cattle. He did so by diverting the rivers Peneius and Alphaeus through them but Augeas refused to pay him. Heracles later invaded Elis, killed Augeas, his sons and their allies the Moliones and destroyed the city of Pylus which had also helped Augeas. One tradition says he spared Augeas.

Aurora. The Roman goddess of the dawn, associated with the Greek Eos (q.v.).

Antolycus. The son of Hermes (q.v.) and Chione, father of Anticleia and thus grandfather of Odysseus (q.v.). Also grandfather of Sinon (q.v.). He was renowned for trickery, cunning and theft.

Aventine. One of the hills of Rome and the southernmost. It was close to the Tiber, was outside the pomerium and was associated with the "plebians".

Avernus, Lake. The modern Lago di Averno near Naples, thought to be an entrance to the Underworld. This is how Aeneas (q.v.) was told to enter Hades (q.v.). Agrippa linked it with the Lucrine Lake while building the harbour of Portus Julius.

B

Bacchae. The female followers of the cult of Bacchus or Dionysus whose worship was characterised by wine-induced frenzies of a mystic nature. At the height of such frenzies they believed themselves to be at one with the god. Also known as Bacchantes, Maenads and Thyiads.

Bacchoi. Male equivalent of the Bacchae.

Bacchus. Latin name for Dionysus (q.v.).

Bassaris. A Bacchante (*See* **Bacchae**).

Baucis. *See* **Philemon.**

Bellerophon. Son of Glaucus (q.v.) King of Corinth. He killed one Bellerus and fled to Tiryns where Anteia, wife of the King Proetus falsely accused him of trying to seduce her. Proetus sent him to his father-in-law Iobates with a letter requesting Iobates to kill the bearer of it. Reluctant to kill a guest Iobates sent him to kill the Chimaera (q.v.). Capturing Pegasus (q.v.) with a golden bridle given to him by Athene (q.v.) he was able to accomplish the task. He was then sent to fight the Amazons (q.v.) and again triumphed. On his return to Tiryus he survived an ambush set by Iobates and finally persuaded the king of his innocence. Iobates made him his heir. One tradition says Bellerophon presumed to rise to Olympus on Pegasus but Zeus sent a gadfly which stung the horse. Pegasus threw Bellerophon to earth but itself entered Olympus.

Belus. One of Poseidon's (q.v.) sons and father of Danaus (q.v.), Cepheus (q.v.) and Aegyptus.

Biton and Cleobis. Sons of a priestess of Hera (q.v.) in Argos who drew their mother's chariot several miles to the goddess's temple when no oxen could be found. Their mother asked Hera to bestow on them the best of gifts for mortals, and they died in their sleep in the temple.

Boeotia. Region of northern Greece; the capital city was Thebes.

Bona Dea. A Roman fertility goddess. Only women worshipped her. Cicero (q.v.) recounts an occasion when his opponent Clodius (q.v.), disguised as a woman, entered an annual nocturnal ceremony of her worshippers over which the chief magistrate's wife presided.

Boreas. The Roman Aquilo; the north wind in Greek mythology. Son of Astraeus (q.v.) and Eos (q.v.) and brother of the other beneficent winds Zephyrus (q.v.), Notus (q.v.) and Eurus (q.v.). A friend of Athens who destroyed Xerxes' (q.v.) fleet. He carried off Oreithyia, daughter of Erechtheus king of Athens who bore him two sons Zetes (q.v.) and Calais (q.v.) and two daughters, Chione and Cleopatra, wife of Phineus.

Brauron. Site on the east coast of Attica. Centre of a cult of Artemis (q.v.). It was believed the locals had killed a she-bear, an animal sacred to the goddess, and that she demanded they worship her on the site, and that girls between the ages of 7 and 11 serve her and live in her temple. Also believed to be the burial place of Iphigenia (q.v.) after her sacrifice at Aulis.

Briareus or **Aegaeon.** One of the Hecatoncheires (q.v.).

Briseis. *See* **Achilles.**

Brontes. One of the Cyclopes (q.v.).

Brutus, Lucius Junius. According to a Roman tradition accepted by Livy (q.v.) the liberator of Rome from the Etruscan kings following the rape of Lucretia (q.v.). Also the first Roman consul in 509 B.C. He ordered the execution of his own sons when they became involved in a conspiracy to restore the monarchy.

C

Cacus. In Roman tradition this fire-breathing giant and his sister Caca were children of Vulcan (q.v.) who lived on the Palatine hill (q.v.), although Virgil in book 8 of the *Aeneid* (q.v.) makes it the Aventine (q.v.). Virgil tells how Cacus stole the cattle of Geryon (q.v.) from Hercules (q.v.) who pursued Cacus back to his cave, tracking him by the cattle's mooing. There he slew Cacus. This event has been portrayed in a painting by Poussin and a statue by Bandinelli in the Signoria, Florence.

Cadmus. Son of Agenor, king of Phoenicia and grandson of Poseidon (q.v.). When Zeus (q.v.) carried off his sister Europa (q.v.) he went to look for her but was told by the Delphic oracle (*see* Apollo) to relinquish the search and to follow a magical cow. Where the cow lay down he was to found a city. The place where it sank became the site of the Cadmea, the citadel of Thebes. Here Cadmus slew the dragon guarding the spring of Ares and on her advice sowed its teeth. The Sparti (q.v.) sprang up. Cadmus married Harmonia (q.v.) and their wedding was attended by the gods. Their children included Autonoe, Ino, Semele (q.v.) Agave Polydoros (q.v.) and Illyrius. In old age Cadmus, who had introduced the use of letters to Greece from Phoenicia, gave up his throne to his grandson Pentheus at Troy and went to reign in Illyria. Later he and Harmonia were received into Elysium (q.v.) in the form of serpents.

Caeneus. Originally the nymph Caenis turned into a man at her own request by Poseidon (q.v.). Accompanied the Argonauts (q.v.) and hunted the Calydonian Boar (q.v.). Invulnerable to normal blows he was killed by the Centaurs (q.v.) in their battle with the Lapithae (q.v.) when they buried him beneath a pile of trees. His soul left the body as a bird and in the Underworld again became female.

Calais. Twin brother of Zetes. Winged sons of Boreas (q.v.) and Oreithyia, they accompanied the Argonauts (q.v.) and drove off the Harpies (q.v.), tormenting Phineus (q.v.) husband of their sister Cleopatra.

Calchas. A renegade Trojan seer who helped the Greeks at Troy (q.v.). He foretold that Troy would not fall without Achilles' (q.v.) presence and that the sacrifice of Iphigenia (q.v.) was necessary to secure a favourable wind. It was he who advised Agamemnon to return the girl Chryseis to her father the Trojan priest Chryses. This caused Agamemnon to seize Briseis and sparked the quarrel with Achilles. Calchas later died of grief when surpassed in prophecy by Mopsus, a mysterious mythical figure who was also said to have sailed with the Argonauts (*q.v.*).

Calipe. *See* **Pillars of Hercules**.

Calliope. *See* **Muses**.

Callirhoë. Daughter of the river god Achelous (*q.v.*) and wife of Alcmaeon (*q.v.*). Alcmaeon gave her the necklace and robe of Harmonia (*q.v.*).

Callisto. Daughter of Lycaon (*q.v.*). One of Artemis' (*q.v.*) huntresses. She bore Arcas (*q.v.*) to Zeus (*q.v.*) who sought to conceal their affair from Hera (*q.v.*) by turning Callisto into a bear. Realising the ruse Hera had the bear hunted down but Zeus saved her and placed her amongst the stars as Arctos. Others say that Artemis turned her into a bear and Arcas hunted her. In this version Callisto became the Great Bear constellation and Arcas the Little Bear.

Calydonian Boar. A savage boar which Artemis (*q.v.*) sent to ravage Calydon because its king, Oeneus (*q.v.*) had not offered her proper sacrifice (*see also* Atalanta and Meleager). Pausanias (*q.v.*) tells of a story of long tusks found at Tegea, seen by Augustus and taken to Rome.

Calypso. A nymph of Ogygia who tended Odysseus (*q.v.*) there for eight years until Zeus (*q.v.*) ordered her to send him home to Ithaca. The name means "hidden" and she may have been a death goddess. At one point she offers the hero eternal youth, but he refuses, preferring real life. She bore him two sons.

Camilla. The Roman equivalent of an Amazon (*q.v.*) —a female warrior.

Capaneus. *See* **"Seven Against Thebes"**.

Capricorn. *See* **Amalthea**.

Cassandra. Daughter of Priam (*q.v.*) and Hecuba and twin of Helenus. She was given the gift of prophecy by Apollo (*q.v.*) but when she disappointed him he decreed that no one would ever believe her prophecies. Several times her important warnings went unheeded, *e.g.* against Paris (*q.v.*) going to Sparta, and against the wooden horse (*q.v.*). She was taken as a slave by Agamemnon (*q.v.*) when Troy (*q.v.*) fell and became his mistress. She was murdered with him by Clytemnestra (*q.v.*).

Cassiopeia. The wife of Cepheus and mother of Andromeda. Her boast that Andromeda was more beautiful than the Nereids (*q.v.*) caused Poseidon (*q.v.*) to send a monster to ravage the kingdom. Only the sacrifice of Andromeda could prevent this. Perseus (*q.v.*), who found her chained naked to a rock by the sea, offered to save her if she would become his wife. Cepheus and Cassiopeia agreed to this and Perseus slew the beast. Her parents then attempted to renege on their promise, claiming Andromeda was promised to another. At her wedding to Perseus the other suitor and his followers attempted to seize the bride but Perseus turned them all to stone with the head of Medusa (*q.v.*). The images of Cepheus and Cassiopeia were set amongst the stars by Poseidon.

Castalian Spring. Sacred spring on Mt. Parnassus, near the site of the Delphic oracle. Here the young girl Castalia drowned herself to avoid Apollo's (*q.v.*) advances.

Castalides. A name for the Muses (*q.v.*).

Castor and Polydeuces. (*Latin* **"Pollux"**) The "Dioscuri". The twin "Sons of Zeus", brothers of Helen (*q.v.*) and the sons of Leda (*q.v.*) the wife of Tyndareus of Sparta. One tradition says that they were born from an egg, like Helen, after Zeus had visited Leda in the form of a swan. Others say only Polydeuces was Zeus' son and that Castor being the son of Tyndareus was a mere mortal. Castor was a famous horse tamer and Polydeuces a great boxer. Sailing with the Argonauts (*q.v.*) Polydeuces slew Amycus son of Poseidon (*q.v.*) who lived on the isle of Bebrycos. Amycus was a renowned boxer who killed travellers by challenging them to a boxing match. They also hunted the Calydonian boar (*q.v.*). The Dioscuri fought a mortal battle with their cousins the twins Idas and Lynceus Zeus then killed Idas but Polydeuces begged to die with his brother. However Zeus decided they should live alternate days with the gods and under the earth. Their image was placed amongst the stars as Gemini. Poseidon gave them power over the wind and waves and they became protectors of seafarers. They were said to have appeared on horseback to help the Romans against the Latins in the battle of Lake Regillus in 484 B.C., after which their cult was adopted at Rome.

Centaurs. A race of savage creatures, half-man, half-horse which inhabited the woodlands and mountains, particularly those of Thessaly. They were the offspring of Ixion and a cloud. In Homer (*q.v.*) the centaurs appear as representatives of primitive desires, fighting, drinking and womanising, but later they are only portrayed as turning to violence when drunk. When they tried to abduct Deidamia (*q.v.*) from her wedding, they became involved in a famous battle with their neighbours the Lapithae (*q.v.*).

Centimani. *See* **Hecatoncheires**.

Cephalus. Husband of Procris who was carried off by Eos (*q.v.*). Eos released him but Procris, suspicious of the time he spent hunting, followed him into the woods. Hearing him praying for a breeze she supposed it to be his mistress (the Roman equivalent of Eos was Aurora, the Latin for breeze aura). Moving closer she was struck by his spear, which never missed, and killed. The story is told by Hesiod and Ovid and inspired paintings by Poussin and Claude.

Cepheus. King of Tegea and one of the Argonauts (*q.v.*). He and most of his 20 sons were killed helping Heracles (*q.v.*) fight Hippocoon.

Cerberus. A huge and savage dog, the offspring of Echidne (*q.v.*) and Typhon (*q.v.*) which guarded the entrance to Hades (*q.v.*). He is usually said to have had three heads, but Hesiod gives him fifty. His back was covered with serpents' heads and he had a snake for a tail. Heracles (*q.v.*) dragged him from the Underworld; Orpheus (*q.v.*) charmed him with music when seeking Eurydice while Aeneas (*q.v.*) drugged him with a cake of honey and narcotics, hence "a sop to Cerberus".

Cercyon. A son of Hephaestus (*q.v.*) reigning near Eleusis. Here he challenged all travellers to a wrestling match and killed them, until he challenged Theseus (*q.v.*) and was killed himself.

Ceres. Ancient Italian corn-goddess worshipped in a temple on the Aventine. Games and a spring festival, the Ceriala, were held in her honour. She was associated with Demeter (*q.v.*) from an early date and her daughter Proserpina with Persephone (*q.v.*).

Ceryneian Hind. A creature with brazen feet and golden antlers. One of Heracles' (*q.v.*) tasks was to catch it alive. He pursued it for a year and caught it without shedding blood by pinning its forelegs together with an arrow.

Chalybes. Mythical inhabitants of north Asia Minor said by some traditions to have invented iron working.

Chaos. In Greek creation myth Chaos was the infinite space existing before creation. From Chaos sprang Ge (*q.v.*), the Earth.

Charities. Also called the Gratiae or Graces by the Romans. They were originally divinities of nature. In the *Iliad* (*q.v.*) only one Charity is personified, Charis, wife of Hephaestus (*q.v.*). Later the three Graces appear, Aglaia, Thalia and Euphrosyne, friends of the Muses (*q.v.*) with whom they inhabited Mt. Olympus.

Charon. The surly ferryman who transported the dead across the Styx (*q.v.*) to Hades (*q.v.*). He only transported them if they had received the correct funeral rite and if their relatives had placed a small coin, his fare, under the tongues. However Heracles (*q.v.*) forced his passage and Orpheus (*q.v.*) charmed his with his lyre. Amongst the Etruscans (*q.v.*), as in modern Greek folklore, he was regarded as a synonym or figure of death. Virgil (*q.v.*) portrays him with unkempt white hair and eyes of fire in the 6th book of the *Aeneid*.

Charybdis and Scylla. Two monsters guarding the Straits of Messina. Charybdis swallowed the sea and vessels on it, three times a day, regurgitating what she swallowed each time. Opposite was Scylla, the daughter of Poseidon (*q.v.*) by a mortal, whom the jealous Amphitrite (*q.v.*) turned into a monster with six barking heads and twelve feet. Odysseus (*q.v.*) was forced to pass between the two evils and the equally undesirable choice between the pair has become proverbial.

Cheiron. Also called Chiron. A centaur (*q.v.*). A son of Cronus (*q.v.*) and Philyra, hence he is sometimes referred to as Philyrides. Unlike his fellow centaurs a wise and kindly being who learnt music, medicine, hunting and prophecy from Apollo (*q.v.*) and Artemis (*q.v.*). This learning he imparted to numerous heroes including Achilles (*q.v.*), the Dioscuri (*q.v.*), Jason (*q.v.*) and Peleus (*q.v.*). An immortal, he was accidentally wounded by the poisoned arrow of his friend Heracles (q.v.). In pain he longed for death. By surrendering his immortality he was relieved of life and suffering and placed among the stars as Sagittarius.

Chimeira. A monster with a lion's head, goat's body and a serpent for a tail. It could breathe fire. The offspring of Echidne (q.v.) and Typhon (q.v.), though some say it was begot by the Sphinx (q.v.) and Orthrus (q.v.). It was killed by Bellerophon (q.v.) while ravaging Lycia. The beast gave us the word "chimera" or fanciful notion.

Chryseis. (Cressida) Daughter of the Trojan seer and priest of Apollo (q.v.). Chryseis was captured by Agamemnon (q.v.) who refused to ransom her. Apollo then sent a plague on the Greek camp and when Calchas (q.v.) explained the cause Agamemnon released her. He then seized Briseis thus causing the quarrel with Achilles (q.v.). The medieval *Roman de Troie* tells how Troilus loved her, but she left him for Diomedes (q.v.). This is the basis of Chaucer's *Troilus and Criseyde* and Shakespeare's *Troilus and Cressida*.

Chrysippus. The son of Pelops (q.v.), murdered by his half-brother Atreus (q.v.) and Thyestes (q.v.) at the instigation of his step-mother Hippodameia (q.v.).

Chthonius. See Spartii.

Claros. Site of a shrine and oracle of Apollo (q.v.) to the south of Smyrna.

Circe The daughter of Helios (q.v.) and Perse. A sorceress living on the island of Aeaea (Virgil (q.v.) identifies it with Circeii in Campania (q.v.)). She turned Odysseus' (q.v.) men into swine but he resisted by use of the herb "moly" given to him by Hermes (q.v.). Having forced her to restore his men he stayed a year with her and she advised him on his trip to the Underworld and return to Ithaca. She had a son, Telegonus by him and later married his son by Penelope (q.v.), Telemachus (q.v.). In the *Argonautica* of Apollonius of Rhodes she purifies Jason (q.v.) and Medea (q.v.) of murder on their return from Colchis. She was worshipped in Campania in the form of Feronia.

Cisseus. Father of Hecabe (q.v.).

Cleobis. See Biton.

Clio. See Muses.

Cloacina. Ancient Roman divinity of "purification", later identified with Venus.

Cloelia. A Roman girl, legendary for having escaped from Porsenna (q.v.) when taken hostage and swimming back to Rome across the Tiber.

Clotho. One of the Fates (q.v.). She pulled the Limbs of Pelops (q.v.) from the cauldron in which they were to be boiled, thus enabling his restoration to life.

Clytemnestra. Daughter of Tyndareus (q.v.) and a half-sister of Helen (q.v.) and Castor and Polydeuces (q.v.). Wife of Agamemnon (q.v.) by whom she bore Orestes (q.v.), Iphigenia (q.v.) and Electra (q.v.). While Agamemnon was at Troy (q.v.) she began an affair with Aegisthus (q.v.) and on his return the pair murdered him. She was killed by Orestes. Her murder of Agamemnon should be seen in the context of his infidelity with Cassandra (q.v.) and others and his sacrifice of Iphigenia. This is how Strauss views the matter in his opera *Elektra*.

Cocles. The "one-eyed", a nickname of Horatius (q.v.) who kept the bridge across the Tiber.

Cocytus. The river of wailing in Hades (q.v.).

Coeus. One of the Titans (q.v.).

Cornelia. Mother of the "Gracchi", daughter of Scipio Africanus and a model of what Romans of the Republic thought a matron should be. On the deaths of her sons she withdrew to Misenum and her home became a centre of culture. She appears in Plutarch's (q.v.) *Lives* of her sons and he tells us that when a visitor asked to see her jewels she presented her sons saying "These are my jewels".

Coronis. Thessalian princess made pregnant by Apollo (q.v.) but who fell in love with an Arcadian youth. Learning of this from a crow, Apollo sent Artemis (q.v.) to kill her. The unborn child was snatched from her and given to Cheiron (q.v.) to rear. The child was Asclepius (q.v.).

Corybantes. Priests of Rhea (q.v.) or Cybele (q.v.) in Phrygia and Asia Minor. Known for their dancing and performance of wild rites to the sound of drums and cymbals.

Corydon. Common Arcadian shepherd's name but in Virgil's (q.v.) second *Eclogue* the shepherd Corydon laments his "faithless Alexis". From this Corydon has become a symbol of homosexual love.

Creon. A "ruler" or "prince" and the name often given to subsidiary characters in Greek legend, e.g. the brother of Jocasta (q.v.) who succeeds Oedipus (q.v.). See also **Jason.**

Cretan Bull. A magnificent white bull sent by Poseidon (q.v.) to Minos (q.v.) for sacrifice. Minos' wife Pasiphaë (q.v.) so admired the bull she had Daedalus (q.v.) construct a hollow cow for her to get inside. She then mated with the bull and later bore the Minotaur (q.v.). Minos also admired the bull and rather than sacrifice it, substituted another bull. The original bull escaped to ravage Crete until captured by Heracles (q.v.) and taken to Eurystheus (q.v.). Eurystheus freed it and it ravaged Greece until captured by Theseus (q.v.) at Marathon (q.v.) and sacrificed to Athene (q.v.).

Creusa. Feminine equivalent of Creon. The most famous is the daughter of Priam (q.v.), first wife of Aeneas (q.v.) and mother of Ascanius. She was lost in the escape from Troy (q.v.) when the city fell. When Aeneas looked for her he met only her ghost who bid him go forward to meet his destiny.

Croesus. Last king of Lydia who in the mid-6th century B.C. amassed a great fortune. His wealth is proverbial. Regarded as a model of piety for his gold offerings to Apollo (q.v.) at Delphi (q.v.). He met Solon and tried to persuade him to admit that Croesus was the happiest of men. Solon refused, saying that no man could be considered happy till his life had ended. The Delphic oracle told him that a great empire would fall if he invaded Persia. His own did. The Persian king Cyrus ordered him to be burnt alive but he called on Solon's name and told Cyrus of Solon's sayings. Cyrus pardoned him and made him an adviser. A later tradition says Apollo saved him and carried him to the land of the Hyperboreans.

Crommyum, Sow of. Wild sow slain by Theseus (q.v.).

Cronus. The son of Uranus (q.v.) and Ge (q.v.). The youngest of the twelve Titans (q.v.). When Ge stirred the Titans to revolt against Uranus she gave Cronus a flint sickle with which he castrated his father. Having deposed Uranus, Cronus reigned supreme and consigned the Cyclopes (q.v.) and the Hecatoncheires (q.v.) to Tartarus (q.v.). He married his sister Rhea (q.v.) and by her was father of Hestia (q.v.), Demeter (q.v.), Hera (q.v.), Poseidon (q.v.), Hades (q.v.) and Zeus (q.v.). Mindful of a curse by Uranus and Ge that he too be deposed by his own son, he swallowed each child at birth. But Rhea gave him a stone to swallow instead of Zeus and later gave him an emetic forcing him to regurgitate his other children. They now joined Zeus in a war on Cronus and the Titans. The Cyclopes aided them and gave Zeus the thunderbolt, Poseidon the trident and Hades a helmet of darkness or invisibility. Cronus was defeated and the Titans were consigned to Tartarus.

Cupid or **Amor.** Roman god of love, identified with the Greek Eros (q.v.).

Curetes. Priests of Rhea (q.v.) who drowned the cries of the infant Zeus (q.v.) as he lay in the Dictaean Cave by the clashing of their weapons. This prevented Cronus (q.v.) finding and devouring him. They were half-divine and in later times were conflated with the Corybantes (q.v.) who were also believed to be half-divine. All became part of Dionysus' ritual.

Cybele. The mother goddess of Phrygia where she and her lover Attis (q.v.) were worshipped in orgiastic rites and purification ceremonies including bathing in the blood of a sacrificed bull. Her symbol was a black stone and this was brought to Rome from Pessinus in 204 B.C. However it was only during the reign of Claudius that Roman citizens were allowed to serve as her priests and the oriental eunuchs serving her cult were always frowned upon. Her worship is described by Lucretius (q.v.) in book 2 and Catullus in his *Attis.* The artists of the classical world portray her with a crown of towers, a libation dish and tambourine, flanked by lions to show her control of wild nature.

Cyclops. Generally known to the Greeks as one-eyed giants living in a distant country, perhaps Sicily. In Homer (q.v.) the Cyclops Polyphemus is a man-eating son of Poseidon (q.v.), made drunk and blinded by Odysseus (q.v.) and his men whom he had captured and meant to eat. Hesiod (q.v.) refers to three Cyclops but describes them as Titans (q.v.). The three (Brontes, Steropes and Arges) were sons of Ge (q.v.) and Uranus (q.v.) who made weapons for Zeus (q.v.), Poseidon and Hades (q.v.) (see **Cronus**). Other traditions make them skilled craftsmen helping Hephaestus (q.v.) at his Sicilian forge. They were also builders of cities including Athens and the walls of Tiryns.

Cyllenius. Another name for Hermes (q.v.) who was said to have been born on Mt. Cyllene in southern Greece.

Cyncus. "The Swan", a mythical king of Liguria who loved Phaeton (q.v.) and was turned into a swan.

Cynthia. A name given to Artemis (q.v.). She and Apollo (q.v.) were thought to have been born on Mt. Cynthus in Delos and were thus referred to as Cynthia and Cynthus.

Cyrene. In myth the mother of Aristaeus (q.v.) by Apollo (q.v.) who carried her to Libya where she gave her name to the city of Cyrene.

Cythera. An island off the south-east coast of Greece noted for its sanctuary of Aphrodite (q.v.). She was thus referred to as "the Cytherean".

D

Dactyli. Greek equivalent of the Roman Chalybes (q.v.) the mythical beings who lived on Mt. Ida in northern Asia Minor and invented iron-working.

Daedalus. Mythical Athenian craftsman. His jealousy of his nephew Perdix of Talos, who was said to have invented the saw, caused him to throw Perdix from Athene's (q.v.) temple on the Acropolis (q.v.). Having thus committed murder he fled to Crete. Here he arranged the liaison between Pasiphaë (q.v.) and the Cretan Bull (q.v.) which produced the Minotaur (q.v.). Then, to conceal what had transpired from Minos (q.v.) he built the famous labyrinth to hide the Minotaur. When Minos discovered the truth he imprisoned Daedalus and his son Icarus in the labyrinth. Pasiphaë released them and Daedalus invented wings which, when attached to their shoulders by wax, enabled him and his son to fly. However Icarus flew too near to the sun, the wax melted, and he fell to his doom in the Icarian sea. Daedalus reached Cumae and then went to Sicily. Here King Cocalus welcomed him and when Minos arrived in pursuit Cocalus' daughters helped Daedalus kill him. In Sicily Daedalus was credited with many wonderful buildings including a honeycomb of gold for Aphrodite's (q.v.) temple on Mt. Eryx. His name has become synonymous with ingenuity and skill, hence "Daedal" and "daedalian" in the English language.

Damocles. Member of the court of Dionysius I, tyrant of Syracuse. Cicero tells how the tyrant had him eat a sumptuous dinner while a sword was suspended by a hair over his head. This illustrated the luxurious but precarious life style of the tyrant and "the sword of Damocles" has become proverbial.

Danaë. A princess of Argos, daughter of King Acrisius (q.v.). An oracle told the king that Danaë's son would kill him so he imprisoned her in a brazen tower. Zeus (q.v.) visited her in a shower of gold and fathered Perseus (q.v.). Acrisius cast them adrift in a box and they came to Seriphos. They were found by the fisherman Dictys and taken to the king Polydectes. He wished to marry Danaë and so, to get Perseus out of the way, sent him to fetch the head of Medusa (q.v.). Danaë was saved from Polydectes' advances when Perseus returned and, showing the head, turned him to stone.

Danai. A general name used by Homer for the Greeks assembled at Troy. It was meant to perpetuate the memory of a common ancestor, Danaus (q.v.).

Danaus. A king of Libya and the father of 50 daughters, the "Danaides". His brother Aegyptus, who had 50 sons, wanted a mass marriage, but Danaus fled with his daughters to Argos where he became king. Eventually Aegyptus' sons followed and demanded the "Danaides". Danaus agreed but gave each daughter a weapon with which they slew their husbands on the wedding night. All, that is, save Hypermestra who spared Lynceus. Lynceus killed Danaus and became king of Argos. In the Underworld the Danaides were condemned to carry water in sieves for ever. The story is told by Pindar (q.v.) and the Danaides form the chorus in Aeschylos' (q.v.) *Suppliants*.

Daphne. The daughter of the river god Peneus or Ladon. A nymph pursued by Apollo (q.v.). To escape him she prayed either to her father or to the Earth to be turned into a laurel tree, which she was. Apollo made himself a laurel wreath as consolation and it became the prize at the Pythian Games held in his honour.

Daphnis. The son of Hermes (q.v.) and a nymph. She abandoned the infant but he was raised by Sicilian shepherds. Pan (q.v.) taught him the pipes and he was the originator of pastoral poetry. Later he was unfaithful to a nymph who loved him and in revenge she blinded him. His father ordered forth the fountain of Daphnis near Syracuse in his honour.

Dardanus. The son of Zeus (q.v.) and the Pleiad (q.v.) Electra. He founded Dardania on land given to him by Teucer. He was grandfather of Tros, great grandfather of Ilus (q.v.) and Ganymede (q.v.). Hence an ancestor of the Trojans who were sometimes called Dardanids, Dardans or Dardonians. Roman legend sometimes envisages him migrating to Dardania from Italy.

Deianeira. The daughter of Oeneus, king of Calydon and the wife of Heracles (q.v.) who won her hand by defeating the river god Achelous (q.v.). She bore him a son Hyllus. After accidentally killing Eunomus, Heracles took her and Hyllus into voluntary exile. When they came to cross the River Evenus the centaur (q.v.) Nessus offered to transport her on his back. However he tried to rape her and was killed by Heracles. As he lay dying he told her to take his blood as it was a charm which would keep Heracles in love with her. Later Heracles won Iole, daughter of Eurytus King of Oechalia, in an archery contest. When Eurytus refused to surrender Iole Heracles invaded Oechalia and defeated him. He then ordered Deianeira to send him a white shirt which he was to wear at a thanksgiving sacrifice to Zeus (q.v.). Deianeira, jealous of Iole, dipped the shirt in the blood of Nessus. But the blood was poisonous and when Heracles donned the shirt it burned his body and attempts to pull it off tore pieces of flesh from the hero. In agony he ordered Hyllus to build a funeral pyre on which he would find quick death and release from the pain. He also had Hyllus marry Iola. Deianeira, horrified at the result of her action, hanged herself. The story forms the plot of Sophocles' *Women of Trachis*.

Deidamia. The maiden who fell in love with Achilles (q.v.) and bore him Neoptolemus (q.v.).

Deiphobus. *See* **Helen** and **Helenus.**

Delis, Delius. Epithets of Artemis (q.v.) and Apollo (q.v.) who were born on Delos (q.v.).

Delos. Site of the important Ionian shrine of Apollo (q.v.). Here he was known as Phoebus ("the shining") or Lycius. When the jealous Hera (q.v.) pursued Leto (q.v.) she sought asylum where she could give birth to Apollo, her son by Zeus (q.v.). Delos, which was so poor it could lose nothing to Hera's wrath, accepted her.

Delphi. Site of Apollo's (q.v.) Dorian shrine and the most famous centre of his worship. Here he took his prophetic role having replaced Python. The oracle, located near the Castalian spring, was supposed to contain the omphalos or navel store of the Earth. A priestess, the Pythia, sat on a tripod chewing the intoxicating laurel leaf and voicing his utterances. Intoxicating vapours also issued from a chasm in the shrine. In this role Apollo was known as Loxias "the Ambiguous". (*See* **Croesus**). The priests of the shrine were not incorruptible and were known to take sides, e.g. with Sparta against Athens and with Philip of Macedon against Greece. The oracle had greatest influence during the period of overseas colonisation when its advice on location of colonies was always sought. The oracle encouraged Rome to defy Hannibal but was looted by Sulla. Nero visited it and Hadrian tried in vain to revive its prestige. Its decline came with the advance of Christianity and the growing interest in astrology as a means of prophecy. The temples at Delphi were sacked by Alaric in A.D. 396. Apollo's temple with its inscribed maxims "Know thyself" and "Nothing in excess" had stood on the highest point of Mt. Parnassus and had housed the sepulchre of Bacchus (q.v.) who was also worshipped at Delphi.

Demeter. The counterpart of the Roman Ceres, a

Greek corn-goddess responsible for the fertility of the earth. The daughter of Cronus (q.v.) and Rhea (q.v.) she became mother of Persephone (q.v.) or Kore ("the maiden") by her brother Zeus (q.v.). A 7th century B.C. Homeric *Hymn to Demeter* tells how Hades (q.v.) carried off Persephone from Eleusis twelve miles from Athens (Ovid says she was taken while gathering poppies in Sicily). Demeter scoured the earth for her until Helios (q.v.) told her what had occurred. She then shunned Olympus (q.v.) and wandered the earth, forbidding it to bring forth fruit and therefore threatening famine. Zeus finally agreed that Persephone could leave Hades provided she had not eaten in the Underworld. Hades agreed to let her go but tempted her into eating a pomegranate. She thus had to spend half a year with him in the Underworld and half with Demeter. Demeter again made the earth fertile but turned Ascalaphus, who had seen and reported Persephone eating the pomegranate, into an owl. She punished those who had been unkind to her during her wandering (*see* **Abas**) but rewarded those who had treated her hospitably. She taught Triptolemus, another son of Celeus (q.v.) the art of agriculture and gave him an ear of corn whose virtues he revealed to his fellow men. The Eleusian Festival was held in Demeter's honour from the 6th century B.C. and there was an annual procession from Eleusis to Athens. Those who spoke Greek were initiated into the mysteries of her cult. The Thesmophoria, a celebration of the foundation of laws, was held in her honour in many cities.

Demophon (1) The son of Theseus (q.v.) and Phaedra (q.v.) brother of Acamas (q.v.). He helped rescue his grandmother Aethra who had been Helen's (q.v.) slave, when Troy (q.v.) fell. Phyllis, a Thracian princess, loved him and committed suicide when he left her to visit Athens. She was then transformed into a tree.

(2) The son of Celeus and Metaneira. Demeter (q.v.) tried to reward the pair for their kindness to her by making Demophon immortal. To achieve this he had to be suspended above a fire, but Metaneira cried out thus breaking the spell and he perished.

Deucalion. The son of Prometheus (q.v.), husband of Pyrrha and father of Hellen. He was thus the ancestor of the Greeks. When Zeus (q.v.) decided to flood the earth in order to destroy mankind they escaped in an ark which finally made land on Mt. Parnassus. The couple prayed to Themis (q.v.) that mankind be restored and were told to scatter their mother's bones behind them. They took this to mean stones, the skeleton of Mother Earth. The rocks Deucalion scattered became men; those Pyrrha scattered became women.

Diana. Italian goddess of woods, women, childbirth and later, by association with the Greek Artemis (q.v.), the moon. Her cult was originally centred on the volcanic Lake Nemi at Aricia. The lake was known as Diana's mirror. The priest here, known as the rex, was always a runaway slave who had murdered his predecessor. A temple of Diana, said to have been founded by Servius Tullius also stood on the Aventine.

Dictaean Cave. A cave on Mt. Dicte in Crete, the reputed childhood home of Zeus (q.v.). Hence he was known as Dictaeus.

Dictys. (1) The sailor who found Perseus (q.v.) and his mother Danaë (q.v.) adrift at sea in a chest.

(2) A Cretan said to have accompanied Idomeneus (q.v.) to the Trojan war. His diary of the war was supposedly buried near Cnossos and found in the reign of Nero.

Dido. A daughter of the king of Tyre originally called Elissa. Her husband Sychaeus was murdered but with a few followers she escaped to Libya and founded Carthage (**K31**). Local legend said she burnt herself on a funeral pyre to avoid marrying Iarbas, a native king. The Roman version, given in the *Aeneid* takes Aeneas (q.v.) to Carthage where Dido's unrequited love for him results in her death. Aeneas abandons her to fulfil his destiny as ancestor of Rome.

Didyma. A great sanctuary of Apollo (q.v.) at Miletus.

Dindyma. Mountain in Asia Minor and a centre of the Cybele's (q.v.) cult.

Diomedes. (1) A king of the Bistones in Thrace who possessed man-eating mares. A labour of Heracles (q.v.) was to bring them to Eurystheus (q.v.). This he did by stealing them and beating off

his pursuers. But while he was busy fighting, the mares devoured his friend Abderus. Heracles founded the city of Abdera in his honour. Eurystheus freed the horses on Mt. Olympus (q.v.) where wild beasts devoured them.

(2) The son of Tydeus, king of Argos. One of the Epigoni (q.v.). He also went to Troy (q.v.) and was a companion of Odysseus (q.v.). With Odysseus he sailed to fetch Achilles (q.v.) and later Neoptolemus (q.v.). He encouraged Agamemnon (q.v.) to sacrifice Iphigenia (q.v.) and helped Odysseus capture the Trojan spy Dolon. He wounded Aeneas (q.v.) and Aphrodite (q.v.) as she saved the Trojan. He also wounded Ares. He returned from Troy to find his wife had been unfaithful and went to settle in Daunia in Italy. Here he married Euippe, daughter of king Daunus. He was buried on one of the Diomedan islands.

Dionysus. The Roman Bacchus. Also called Bromius "the Boisterous". The son of Zeus (q.v.) and Semele, a mortal, Zeus visited her in the guise of a mortal but when she was six months pregnant the jealous Hera (q.v.) came to her as an old woman. She advised Semele to demand her lover appear in his true form. Zeus unwillingly agreed to do so and Semele was consumed by fire. The unborn child was sewn up in Zeus' thigh to be born as Dionysus. The child was given into the care of Athamas and Ino. He was disguised as a girl but Hera learned the truth and drove Athamas mad, causing him to kill his own son. Hermes (q.v.) then took Dionysus to Mt. Nysa in India where he was raised by nymphs. Zeus placed their images in the stars as the Hyades. Here he was taught the use of the vine by his tutor Silenus and his satyrs and here he invented wine. As an adult he journeyed through India, Egypt, Syria and Asia accompanied by a wild following of Maenads or Bacchae and Satyrs. As he went he founded cities and taught cultivation of the vine. When he reached Thrace, Lycurgus, king of the Edones, opposed him but was driven mad by Rhea (q.v.) and slew his own son. His people then had him torn apart by horses. King Pentheus of Thebes also opposed Dionysus and was torn apart by crazed Bacchae whose ranks included his mother and sisters. Entranced they took him for a wild animal. Sailing to Naxos Dionysus was captured by pirates for sale as a slave. He became a lion and turned the oars to serpents. Ivy grew on the mast. The terrified pirates jumped overboard and became dolphins. At Naxos he married Ariadne (q.v.) whom Theseus (q.v.) had deserted. He was eventually received into Olympus as a god, replacing Hestia (q.v.). He fetched his mother to Olympus from the Underworld and she was henceforth known as Thyone. Dionysus was the god of wine and intoxicating herbs like ivy and laurel. He was also the god of tillage and law giving. He was worshipped at Delphi (q.v.) and in the spring festival, the Great Dionysia. In Rome the mysteries of his cult were a closely guarded secret. His followers worshipped him in communal wine-induced frenzies and the ritual involved sacrifice of animals, flagellation and a mystical marriage of novices with the god.

Dioscuri. *See* **Castor and Polydeuces.**

Dirce. *See* **Antiope.**

Dis or **Orcus.** Hades (q.v.).

Dodona. Site of an oracle of Zeus (q.v.) in north west Greece near modern Janina. It was associated with the union of Zeus and Dione, a minor goddess. The oracle centred on an oak and messages were transmitted by the rustling branches and cooing of pigeons nesting in it. The priests were "Selloi" who slept on the ground and walked barefoot. It was visited by Croesus (q.v.) and Alexander the Great offered the sanctuary a large sum of money.

Dryope. The daughter of King Dryops. Apollo (q.v.) seduced her and she was carried off by the Hamadryads (nymphs of trees).

E

Echidne. A mythical creature, half-woman, half-serpent. Mother by Typhon (q.v.) of the Chimaera (q.v.), Sphinx (q.v.), Cerberus (q.v.), Hydra (q.v.), Nemean Lion, Orthrus (q.v.), and Ladon. Slain by Argus.

Echion. A son of Hermes (*q.v.*). An Argonaut (*q.v.*) who took part in the hunt of the Calydonian boar (*q.v.*).

Echo. A nymph who occupied Hera's (*q.v.*) attention by incessant talk while Zeus (*q.v.*) enjoyed himself with the other nymphs. In punishment Hera deprived her of the power of speech except to repeat the words of others. Echo loved Narcissus who refused her. Heart-broken she pined away to nothing, only her voice remaining. Artemis (*q.v.*) punished Narcissus for his heartlessness by making him fall in love with his own reflection. Despairingly he committed suicide and was turned into a flower.

Egeria. An Italian goddess or nymph whose worship was connected with that of Diana (*q.v.*). She was associated with water. It was believed she advised Numa Pompilius (*q.v.*) especially on religious matters and Livy tells us they met in a sacred grove near Rome.

Eileithyia. A goddess of childbirth whom the Greeks associated with Artemis (*q.v.*) and the Romans with Juno (*q.v.*).

Elatus. The father of Caeneus and one of the Lapithae (*q.v.*).

Electra. (1) A Pleiad (*q.v.*).
(2) The daughter of Agamemnon (*q.v.*) and Clytemnestra (*q.v.*). Treated as a slave by her mother and Aegisthus (*q.v.*) she later helped her brother Orestes (*q.v.*) and his friend Pylades (*q.v.*) avenge their father and married Pylades. This is the basis of Euripides' *Electra* and Strauss's *Elektra*. Freud gave the name "Electra complex" to female fixation on the father, the opposite of the "Oedipus complex".

Electryon. The son of Perseus (*q.v.*) and Andromeda (*q.v.*). King of Mycenae and father of Alcmene (*q.v.*) wife of Amphitrion (*q.v.*).

Eleusis. A sacred site twelve miles west of Athens facing Salamis. Here Celeus received Demeter (*q.v.*). Games and an oracle were found there. A cult involving "Mysteries" was centred there and administered by two families, the Eumolpidae and Kerykes. Ceremonies were held twice a year in Spring and Autumn and initiation to the mysteries, of which we know little, was open to all men, Greek or not, free or slave, who had not committed murder.

Elissa. *See* Dido.

Elpenor. One of Odysseus' (*q.v.*) crew who fell off the roof of Circe's (*q.v.*) palace while sleep-walking and broke his neck. When Odysseus visited the Underworld his shade begged for cremation and a burial mound in which his ear was to be planted.

Elysium. A blessed abode of the dead, placed by Homer near the Underworld but not in Hades (*q.v.*). The virtuous went here after death. It was a land of warmth never knowing cold or snow. Later it was associated with "Fortunate Isles" holding "Elysian Fields" which were believed to be far to the west, beyond the Pillars of Hercules (*q.v.*).

Empusae. Daughters of Hecate (*q.v.*). They were demons with the haunches of an ass who wore brazen slippers. Able to turn themselves into cows, bitches or young maidens, as the latter they lay with young men and sucked their blood as they slept.

Enceladus. A son of Ge (*q.v.*). One of 24 giants (*q.v.*) with serpents' tails whom Alcyoneus led in an assault on Olympus (*q.v.*). Buried under Mt. Etna in Sicily as a punishment.

Endymion. Either a shepherd of Caria or an Aeolian youth who became king of Elis. As he slept in a cave Selene (*q.v.*) the moon saw him and descended to kiss him. Captivated by his looks she made him fall into a dreamless everlasting sleep so that she could always gaze upon him. His son Aetolus conquered Aetolia.

Enipeus. A river god, beloved of Tyro (*q.v.*).

Eos. The goddess of the dawn, the Romans identified her with Aurora (*q.v.*). The daughter of Hyperion (*q.v.*) and Theira and sister of Helios (*q.v.*). She drove the chariot of Helios each morning to announce his arrival and traversed the sky with him as Hemera before landing in the west as Hespera. The wife of Astraeus and by him mother of the stars and all the winds save the east. She carried off several handsome youths including Orion (*q.v.*) Cephalus (*q.v.*), and Tithonus to whom she bore Memnon (*q.v.*). She requested Zeus (*q.v.*) to make Tithonus immortal but forgot to ask for eternal youth and as he aged he shrank to a cicada.

Epaphus. The son of Zeus (*q.v.*) and Io who ruled

Egypt and was said by some to be the sacred bull of Egypt, Apis (*q.v.*).

Epeius. A cowardly son of Panopeus who built the Trojan Horse.

Ephialtes. One of the 24 giants (*q.v.*) led by Alcyoneus. (*See also* Otus).

Epidaurus. Site of a famous sanctuary of Asclepius (*q.v.*) built in the 6th century B.C. Here pilgrims could see the tomb of the god.

Epigoni. Descendants of the "Seven against Thebes" (*q.v.*) who also attacked the city ten years after their fathers had done so. They were assembled by Adrastus (*q.v.*) and their ranks included his own son Aegialeus, Diomedes son of Tydeus, Sthenelus son of Capaneus and Eradne and Therseander. Like his father Polynices (*q.v.*) Therseander bribed Eriphyle (*q.v.*) into persuading Alcmaeon into joining the assault on Thebes. Aegialeus died at the walls of the city but the Theban prophet Teiresias advised the citizens to leave the city at night as he had foreseen the Argives (*i.e.* the Epigoni), capturing an empty city. He died next morning drinking from the well of Tilphussa. Adrastus died of grief hearing of his son's death while the remaining Epigoni were left holding an empty city. Alcmaeon went home to take revenge on Eriphyle (*q.v.*).

Erebos. A deep chasm in the Underworld.

Erebus. "Darkness", the son of Chaos (*q.v.*) and father of Aether and Hemera by "Night", his sister. Some traditions hold that the Fates (*q.v.*) were daughters of Erebus and Night and that they held sway even over Zeus (*q.v.*).

Erechtheus. Son of Pandion and grandson of Erichthonius (*q.v.*) with whom he is sometimes confused or identified. Both were reared by Athene (*q.v.*) and were associated with serpents. Both were mythical kings of Athens. When the Eleusians led by Eumolpus, a son of Poseidon (*q.v.*), invaded Athens, Erechtheus was told by an oracle to sacrifice his daughter Otonia. He did so and her sisters Protogonia and Panora also sacrificed themselves. He slew Eumolpus and was slain by lightning from either Poseidon or Zeus (*q.v.*).

Erichthonius. A son of Hephaestus (*q.v.*) by Athene (*q.v.*). The child was concealed in a chest by the normally chaste Athene and entrusted to the daughters of Cecrops of Athens who were forbidden to open it. However they did so and finding a serpent inside went mad and leaped to their death from the Acropolis (*q.v.*). Erichthonius eventually succeeded Cecrops as King of Athens and was grandfather of Erechtheus. It was said Erichthonius was the founder of the Panathenaean games in honour of Athene and that he was the first man to harness a team of four horses to a single chariot.

Eridanus. An Italian river god, later thought to be the River Po.

Erigone. The daughter of Icarius. Led to her father's grave by his faithful pet hound Maera, she hanged herself from the tree beneath which he lay.

Erinnyes. Three daughters of Mother Earth whom she conceived by the blood of Uranus (*q.v.*) when Cronus (*q.v.*) castrated him. They personified the conscience and were powerful divinities who punished crimes of sacrilege, especially matricide. They pursued Alcmaeon (*q.v.*) and drove Orestes (*q.v.*) mad and into exile. These winged creatures had serpent hair and lived in the Underworld. Their names were Alecto, Magaera and Tisiphone. Orestes was acquitted by Athene (*q.v.*) of matricide following his defence by Apollo (*q.v.*). To pacify the Erinnyes Athene gave them a grotto at Athens where they received libations and sacrifices. Henceforth they were euphemistically referred to as the Eumenides or "kindly ones".

Eriphyle. The sister of Adrastus (*q.v.*) and wife of the seer Amphiarus. Mother of Alcmaeon (*q.v.*). Polynices (*q.v.*) bribed her into persuading Amphiarus into joining the Seven Against Thebes (*q.v.*) despite the seer's prophecy that only Adrastus would survive their expedition. She received the necklace of Harmonia (*q.v.*) for this. Later Thersander bribed her with the magic robe of Harmonia into persuading Alcmaeon to join the Epigoni (*q.v.*). On returning from Thebes Alcmaeon slew her for her sixfold deceit.

Eris. A female divinity personifying Quarrels and Strife for the Greeks.

Eros. The Greek god of love, identified with the Roman Cupid (*q.v.*) or Amor. A son of Aphrodite (*q.v.*), whom he often accompanied, by either her father Zeus (q.v.) or Hermes (q.v.). His half-brother was Anteros, son of Aphrodite and Ares (q.v.) who personified mutual love. It was only from the 4th century B.C. onwards that he came to be represented as a winged boy firing arrows of love which could wound both men and gods. (See **Psyche**).

Erymanthian Boar. A giant wild boar from Mt. Erymanthus which was ravaging the region of Psophis until captured by Heracles (q.v.). Whilst performing this task he was given wine made by Dionysus (q.v.) by the centaur Pholus. A dispute broke out with other centaurs, eager as ever for their share of the drink, and in the resulting battle Heracles accidentally wounded his friend Cheiron (q.v.). He caught and chained the boar in a snow drift and delivered it to Eurystheus (q.v.) before going to join the Argonauts (q.v.).

Erysichthon. Son of Triopas. He was punished with an insatiable hunger by the goddess Demeter (q.v.) for felling trees in one of her sacred groves.

Eryx. Mythical Sicilian hero. A son of Venus (q.v.) and a renowned boxer. The mountain near modern Trapani is named after him.

Eteocles. See **Seven Against Thebes**.

Etruscans. See **L41**.

Eumneus. Born of royal birth but given to Phoenician slave traders, Eumneus' story is told in Book 15 of the *Odyssey*. He became Odysseus' (q.v.) faithful swineherd.

Eumolpus. "The good singer", son of Poseidon (q.v.) and Chione. Chione threw him into the sea at birth but Poseidon saved him and he was raised at the court of King Tegyrius of Thrace before becoming a priest of Demeter (q.v.) and Persephone (q.v.) at Eleusis. Here he initiated Heracles (q.v.) into the mysteries and taught the hero the lyre. He later made war on Athens and was slain by Erechtheus (q.v.). His descendants became hereditary priests of the Eleusian mysteries.

Euphorbus. Son of Panthous, a Trojan who wounded Patroclus (q.v.) before he was slain by Hector (q.v.).

Euphrosyne. One of the Charities or Graces (q.v.).

Euripides. See **B23**.

Europa. Daughter of Agenor and Telephassa and a grand-daughter of Poseidon (q.v.). While she was on the sea-shore Zeus (q.v.) appeared in the form of a white bull and when she jumped on his back carried her off to Crete where he fathered three sons on her, Minos (q.v.), Rhadamanthus (q.v.) and Sarpedon (q.v.). The Cretan king married her and adopted the children. Zeus gave her a necklace fashioned by Hephaestus (q.v.) which rendered the wearer irresistibly beautiful.

Eurystheus. A grandson of Perseus (q.v.). He was conceived shortly after Heracles (q.v.) but when Zeus (q.v.) boasted that Heracles would rule the House of Perseus, Hera (q.v.) in her jealousy extracted a promise from Zeus that the next son born to the House of Perseus would be its ruler. She then delayed the birth of Heracles until after that of Eurystheus. Later, after Heracles had slain his children in a fit of madness he was told by the oracle to serve Eurystheus in order to be cleansed of guilt. Eurystheus, a cowardly and contemptible creature, set him twelve labours. After Heracles' death he decided to expel the Heracleidae (q.v.) or descendants of Heracles from Greece but they sheltered at Athens. Eurystheus attacked the city but was resisted by Theseus (q.v.), Iolaus (q.v.) and Hyllus (q.v.). An oracle demanded the sacrifice of one of Heracles' children and Macaria slew herself. Eurystheus was then defeated and slain by Alcmene.

Eurus. The South-East wind, son of Astraeus (q.v.) and Eos.

Euryale. One of the Gorgons (q.v.).

Eurydice. The wife of Orpheus (q.v.). She died from a snake bite and Orpheus followed her to the Underworld. Hades (q.v.) delighted by Orpheus' lyre playing allowed him to take her back to life provided he did not look back. Unfortunately at the gates of the Underworld the anxious Orpheus could no longer resist the temptation to gaze on her beauty nor acquiesce in her accusations of indifference. He turned round to see her and she was lost to him.

Eurytus. See **Deianeira**.

Euterpe. Muse of music and lyric poetry.

Evadne. The daughter of Iphis and wife of Capaneus

who killed herself on the funeral pyre of the Seven against Thebes (q.v.).

Evander. A mythical king of Arcadia who settled in Italy on the future site of Rome.

Evenus. The father of Marpessa. When Idas carried her off he drowned himself in the river which henceforth bore his name.

F

Fates. The personifications of impersonal destiny who sometimes seem to control even Zeus (q.v.), at others merely to perform his will. The concept developed of three Moirae (*Latin* Parcae) daughters of Zeus and Themis (q.v.), or of Erebus (q.v.) and Night. The first, Clotho, spins the thread of life, Lachesis measures it, and Atropus cuts it. With Hermes (q.v.) they composed the Alphabet.

Faunus. An Italian god of the flocks, herds and wild countryside, later identified with Pan (q.v.). In this context he was half-human, half-goat and lived in Arcadia (q.v.). He had a shrine on the Palatine Hill. He is sometimes regarded not as one god but as numerous spirits of the woods or "fauns".

Faustulus. A kindly shepherd who, with his wife Acca Larentia, raised Romulus (q.v.) and Remus (q.v.). His name relates to Faunus (q.v.) and his wife's to Lares (q.v.) respectively the pastoral god of Latium and the tutelary deities of the Roman home. Up to Cicero's time Romans proudly pointed to a hut on the Palatine which was said to be that where Faustulus raised Romulus but, embarrassingly, a hut with similar claims also stood on the Capitol.

Fidius. Dius Fidius was a name for Jupiter (q.v.) as guarantor of Good Faith.

Flora. Italian goddess of flowers and the spring, worshipped at Rome from the mid 3rd century B.C. Ovid tells us the April festival in her honour, "Ludi Florales" was one of drunken boisterousness. As an earth nymph called Chloris she was pursued by Zephyr (q.v.) and changed into Flora whose breath spread flowers across the fields. The scene has been a subject for Botticelli, Titian and Poussin.

Fortuna. Roman goddess identified with Tyche (q.v.).

Fortunate Isles. See **Elysium**.

G

Gaea or Ge. The "Earth" who sprang from Chaos (q.v.). She was mother of Uranus (q.v.), the heavens, and Pontus the sea. By Uranus she was mother of the Hecatoncheires (q.v.), the Cyclopes (q.v.), the Titans (q.v.) and Themis (q.v.). When Uranus condemned the Cyclopes to Tartarus (q.v.) she instigated rebellion by the Titans and gave Cronus (q.v.) the flint sickle with which he castrated Uranus. From the blood which fell on her she bore Erinnyes (q.v.) and from the blood which fell into the sea came Aphrodite (q.v.). By Tartarus she was mother of Typhon (q.v.). She gave Hera (q.v.) a tree of golden apples which was guarded by the Hesperides (q.v.). The Romans identified her with their own earth goddess Tellus.

Gaetulians. A mythical savage tribe which the Romans placed in North Africa.

Galatea. (1) A sea nymph who loved the Sicilian shepherd Acis (q.v.). She was pursued by the Cyclops Polyphemus and to escape him threw herself into the sea off Sicily. She turned Acis into a river.

(2) See **Pygmalion**.

Ganymede. The most handsome of youths, the son of Tros (q.v.) and Callirhoë. Zeus (q.v.) loved the youth and taking the form of an eagle carried him off to become cup-bearer of the gods, leaving Tros two white horses in compensation. A subject for Correggio, Rubens, and Rembrandt.

Garamantians. Mythical North African tribe appearing in the *Aenead* (q.v.).

Ge. See **Gaea**.

Geryon. A three-bodied monster living on the island of Erythia far to the west of the known world.

Here he kept cattle guarded by Eurytion, son of Ares (q.v.) and Orthrus (q.v.). Heracles (q.v.) was sent to steal the cattle by Eurystheus (q.v.) and on his way to Erythia erected the "Pillars of Hercules" (q.v.), before sailing, on a boat provided by Helios (q.v.), to the island. He overcame Eurytion, Orthrus and Geryon and fetched the cattle to Eurystheus.

Giants (Gigantes). (1) The sons of Ge (q.v.) and Uranus (q.v.), twenty-four giants with serpents' tails who, to avenge the imprisonment of their brothers the Titans (q.v.), attacked the gods on Mt. Olympus (q.v.). Their leader was Alcyoneus and their ranks included Porphyrion, Ephialtes, Pallas, Minas, Enceladus and Polybotes. The gods finally triumphed due to the help of Heracles (q.v.) and the giants were buried under various volcanoes in punishment.

(2) In another version two giants, Ephialtes and Otus, the sons of Iphimedeia and Poseidon (q.v.), but called the Aloeidae after the name of Iphimedeia's husband Aloeus, attacked Olympus. At an early age the two imprisoned Ares (q.v.), then swearing to rape Hera (q.v.) and Artemis (q.v.) they stacked Mt. Pelion on top of Mt. Ossa in order to climb to the heavens. But Artemis lured them to Naxos and disguised as a doe leapt between them and they slew each other by accident. In Hades (q.v.) they were tied by vipers to a pillar back to back.

Glauce. Or Creusa, daughter of Creon. For her Jason (q.v.) forsook Medea (q.v.) and in revenge the sorceress sent Glauce a garment which enveloped her in flames and also killed Creon.

Glaucus. (1) King of Corinth, son of Sisyphus and Merope and father of Bellerophon (q.v.). He fed his horses on human flesh but Aphrodite (q.v.) caused them to devour Glaucus himself because he mocked her.

(2) His great-grandson, the grandson of Bellerophon who fought for the Trojans and was slain by Ajax (q.v.).

(3) The son of Minos (q.v.) and Pasiphaë (q.v.) who was drowned in a barrel of honey. The seer Polyides found the corpse and was entombed with the boy for failing to restore him. Both were saved when a serpent revealed a magic herb which resurrected Glaucus.

(4) A Boeotian fisherman who pursued Scylla (q.v.) and was turned into a sea god on eating a magic herb.

Golden Age. A concept of Hesiod's who lists four ages of man in his *Works and Days*: golden, silver, bronze and iron. Horace, Virgil, and Ovid also refer to it. A tranquil time when Cronus (q.v.) ruled as the ideal king.

Golden Bough. A gift Aeneas (q.v.) had to take to Proserpina (q.v.) before he could enter the Underworld. Also associated with the cult of Diana (q.v.) at Aricia where a runaway slave had to break the bough from a sacred tree before killing the priest and taking his place. Subject of a painting by J. W. M. Turner.

Gordian Knot. Gordius was a peasant who was acclaimed king of Phrygia by the inhabitants when he appeared in a wagon. An oracle had prophesied that the new king would appear thus. In thanksgiving he dedicated the cart to Zeus (q.v.) in the acropolis of Gordium. An oracle prophesied that he who untied the complex knot joining the yoke and pole would rule all Asia. It was eventually severed by Alexander the Great.

Gorgons or **Gorgones.** Three beautiful sisters, Medusa (q.v.), Stheno and Euryale, daughters of Phorcys and Ceto. Medusa slept with Poseidon (q.v.) in a temple of Athene (q.v.) and was transformed into a winged monster with serpent hair and brazen claws by the goddess as punishment. She could turn those who looked on her to stone. The Gorgons were sisters of the Graeae (q.v.). *See also* Perseus.

Graces (also **Gratiae).** *See* **Charities.**

Graeae. Sisters of the Gorgons (q.v.) who lived on Mt. Atlas. The three old women possessed only one eye and one tooth which they shared, passing them from one to the other. Perseus (q.v.) stole the eye and thus forced them to reveal the whereabouts of Medusa (q.v.) and also of the Stygian nymphs who gave him the winged sandals, magic wallet and helmet of Hades which Hermes (q.v.) said he needed in order to slay Medusa.

Gyes or **Gyges.** One of the Hecatoncheires (q.v.).

H

Hades. (1) The son of Cronus (q.v.) and Rhea (q.v.) brother of Zeus (q.v.) and Poseidon (q.v.). The Cyclopes (q.v.) gave him a helmet of darkness which made him invisible. When he and his brothers threw lots for their kingdoms Hades won the Underworld, home of the dead. His name was later extended to his realm itself. He was one of the few gods to like Ares (q.v.) and Hermes (q.v.) was his herald, conducting the shades of the dead to the Underworld. Because his name was too dread to mention he was often called "Pluto" (q.v.). No favours were expected of him so no temples were dedicated to him. He abducted Persephone (q.v.) and also chased the nymph Minthe (whom the jealous Persephone turned into a mint plant) and Leuce, who was turned into the white poplar.

(2) His realm, the Underworld, land of the dead. Its deepest reaches were called Tartarus (q.v.). Hades and Persephone ruled over it. Persephone was accompanied by Hecate (q.v.). There were five rivers in Hades, the Styx, Acheron, river of woe, Phlegethon, river of flame, Lethe, river of forgetfulness and Cocytus river of wailing. Three judges Minos (q.v.), Aeacus (q.v.) and Rhadamanthus (q.v.) decided on what would happen to souls, sending the evil for punishment, the virtuous to Elysium (q.v.) and those who had led indifferent lives to the drab asphodel fields.

Harmonia. The daughter of Ares (q.v.) and Aphrodite (q.v.) and the wife of Cadmus (q.v.). The gods attended their wedding and Aphrodite gave her the necklace which Zeus (q.v.) had given to Europa (q.v.). It had been made by Hephaestus (q.v.) and conferred irresistible beauty on the wearer. Athene (q.v.) gave her a robe which conferred divine dignity on its possessor. The couple had three children, Autonoe, Ino and Semele (q.v.). After Cadmus had resigned his throne to Pentheus (q.v.) the couple left Thebes and were eventually, in the form of serpents, received in Elysia (q.v.). The necklace and robe were later used to bribe Eriphyle.

Harpalyce. A mythical princess of Thrace, a fierce warrior and huntress.

Harpies (Greek "snatchers"). Originally spirits of the wind, in Homer they appear to carry people off to their death. Later they are portrayed as winged monsters with women's heads and claws, sent by the gods to torment mortals. They snatched and carried off people for their food.

Hebe. A personification of the Greek word for youth, the daughter of Zeus (q.v.) and Hera (q.v.). She was cupbearer to the gods until replaced by Ganymede (q.v.). Her Roman counterpart was Juventas. She married Heracles (q.v.) after his apotheosis.

Hecabe or **Hecuba.** The second wife of Priam (q.v.) who bore him 19 sons including Hector (q.v.) and Paris (q.v.). By Apollo (q.v.) the mother of Troilus (q.v.). Taken as a slave by Odysseus (q.v.) when Troy (q.v.) fell. Priam had entrusted their youngest son Polydorus, plus much gold, to Polymester, king of the Thracian Chersonese. He had murdered Polydorus and thrown his body into the sea. When Odysseus took her to the Thracian Chersonese she found the body, killed Polymester and his two sons, and escaped in the form of a bitch, Maera.

Hecate. An ancient goddess, later closely associated with Artemis (q.v.). Originally she was venerated by women, she was powerful in Heaven, Earth and the Underworld. But primarily she was seen as a goddess of the Underworld and companion of Persephone (q.v.). She was represented holding torches and accompanied by wolves. She was most formidable at the full moon with which she was associated. A practitioner of sorcery her image was worshipped at crossroads where she was portrayed with three heads or three bodies.

Hecatoncheires. The sons of Ge (q.v.) and Uranus (q.v.), three 100-handed giants called Cottus, Gyes or Gyges and Briareus or Aegaeon.

Hector. The eldest son of Priam (q.v.), Trojan hero of the Trojan War. Husband of Andromache (q.v.) and father of Astynax. He fought the great Ajax (q.v.) until nightfall when the two exchanged gifts. He slew Patroclus and in turn was slain by Achilles (q.v.) who dragged his body round the walls of Troy (q.v.). Priam begged for the corpse and his funeral is the closing scene of Homer's *Iliad*. A chivalrous warrior.

Helen. The daughter of Leda (*q.v.*) by Zeus (*q.v.*), hatched from an egg, and the sister of Clytemnestra (*q.v.*), Castor and Polydeuces (*q.v.*) (known as the Dioscuri). She was raised at the court of Leda's husband, Tyndareus of Sparta. As a child she was abducted by Theseus (*q.v.*) and Pirithous (*q.v.*) but being too young to marry, was left with Theseus' mother Aethra. The Dioscuri rescued her and Aethra became her slave. The most beautiful of women she had many suitors who swore to defend her chosen husband, Menelaus (*q.v.*). She was taken by Paris (*q.v.*) to Troy (*q.v.*) thus causing the Trojan war (*q.v.*) and "launching a thousand ships" (of the Greeks who went to reclaim her). When Paris died Helenus (*q.v.*) and Deiphobus quarrelled for her, the latter forcibly marrying her. By then she was homesick for Sparta and when Odysseus (*q.v.*) entered Troy in disguise told him so and gave him information useful to the Greek cause. When Troy fell Deiphobus was killed and mangled by Odysseus and Menelaus, but when Menelaus chased her, sword drawn, to punish her, she calmed him by baring her breast. In the *Odyssey* she was reconciled to Menelaus and became a domesticated and faithful wife. She bore him a daughter, Hermione. It appears that Helen may have been a pre-Greek goddess associated with birds and trees. Various tales are told of her. Stesichorus says that only her phantom went to Troy: the real Helen went to Egypt. Another legend says that at her death she was carried off to live eternally with Achilles (*q.v.*) on a "white isle". Others suggest that her mother was not Leda but Nemesis (*q.v.*).

Helenus. The son of Priam (*q.v.*) and Hecabe (*q.v.*), twin of Cassandra (*q.v.*) and a prophet. He quarrelled with his brother Deiphobus over Helen (*q.v.*) and when the latter forcibly married her fled Troy (*q.v.*) and was captured by Odysseus (*q.v.*). Calchas (*q.v.*) had said that only Helenus knew the secret oracles of how Troy would fall. He told Odysseus that the city would be taken in the summer if a bone of Pelops (*q.v.*) were brought to the Greeks, if Neoptolemus (*q.v.*) joined them, and if the Palladium (*q.v.*) were stolen. These things were done. After the war he was taken by Neoptolemus and prophesied a safe home for him. When Neoptolemus settled in Epirus he gave part of the kingdom to Helenus who married Andromache (*q.v.*).

Helicon. A mountain in Boeotia (*q.v.*) sacred to Apollo (*q.v.*) and inhabited by the Muses (*q.v.*) who were thus called respectively Heliconiades and Heliconides.

Helios. Equates to the Roman "Sol". A Titan later identified with Hyperion and Apollo (*q.v.*), though some traditions make him the son of Hyperion and Theia. A sun-god, his chariot was drawn across the sky each day by four horses and at night he returned to the east floating on the stream of Ocean, which surrounded the earth, in a large cup. The husband of Rhode by whom he had seven sons and a daughter, Pasiphaë. He was father of Phaeton (*q.v.*) by Clymene and of Circe (*q.v.*) by Perse. He reputedly saw all, but missed Odysseus' (*q.v.*) men stealing his cattle. When he shone too brightly Odysseus (*q.v.*) fired an arrow at him. Admiring the hero's boldness he lent him his cup or boat with which to travel to Erythia. It was he who told Demeter (*q.v.*) that Hades (*q.v.*) had abducted Persephone (*q.v.*).

Hellas, Hellenes, Hellenism. The Greeks of the classical period termed themselves Hellenes and their country Hellas (in contrast to Homer's "Achaeans"). They traced their common descent from Hellen (*q.v.*) an eponymous hero. In modern times Hellenism refers to the culture flourishing in Greece, the Aegean isles, the Ionian coast of Asia Minor and Magna Graecia between the first Olympiad in 776 B.C. and the death of Alexander the Great in 323 B.C.

Hellen. Eponymous ancestor of the Greeks or Hellenes (*q.v.*), the son of Pyrrha and Deucalion (*q.v.*). His sons were Aeolus, Dorus and Xuthus.

Hephaestus. One of the Olympian gods, the son of Zeus (*q.v.*) and Hera (*q.v.*). The god of fire and metal work, known to the Romans as Vulcan (*q.v.*). He was hated by Hera because he was lame and she threw him down from Olympus and he landed in the sea where Thetis (*q.v.*) and Eurynome cared for him. Nine years later Hera

accepted him back but Zeus, angry with him for taking Hera's side in a quarrel, again cast him down. He was a day falling and landed on Lemnos. On returning to Olympus he sought to keep the peace between Zeus and Hera. The other gods always laughed at his lameness. His workshop was said to be on Olympus or else in Sicily, where the Cyclopes (*q.v.*) helped him in his labours. He made palaces for all the gods, the necklace of Harmonia (*q.v.*), the armour of Achilles (*q.v.*) and a wide variety of other wonderful articles. He was married either to Charis or to Aphrodite (*q.v.*) who deceived him with Ares (*q.v.*).

Hera. The Roman Juno, daughter of Cronus (*q.v.*) and Rhea (*q.v.*), sister and wife of Zeus (*q.v.*). A pre-Hellenic goddess, originally having power over all living things and vegetable life, she gradually lost these functions and eventually was only the goddess of marriage and childbirth. She was the mother of Ares (*q.v.*), Hephaestus (*q.v.*), Hebe (*q.v.*) and Ilythia (*q.v.*) by Zeus. Her virginity was renewed annually by bathing in a magical spring near Argos. Though she was the goddess of marital fidelity she had difficulty controlling the amorous adventures of her own husband (who had wooed her in the form of a cuckoo) and was violently jealous of his many affairs and cruel to her rivals and their offspring, *e.g.* Semele, Leto, Alcmene and Heracles. She once led a conspiracy against Zeus in which Poseidon (*q.v.*) and Apollo (*q.v.*) participated. Zeus was enchained and when he was freed he punished her by suspending her from the sky by the wrists with an anvil on each ankle. She helped Jason (*q.v.*) but was opposed to the Trojans because Paris (*q.v.*) did not give her the apple of discord. Her name means simply "lady".

Heracleidae. The children of Heracles (*q.v.*). Eurystheus (*q.v.*) attempted to expel them from Greece but failed.

Heracles. A hero who later became a god, a figure popular all over Greece and in Italy where the Romans knew him as Hercules. The son of Alcmene (*q.v.*) and Zeus (*q.v.*) and half-brother of Iphicles (*q.v.*). Alcmene fearing Hera's (*q.v.*) jealousy exposed him but by mistake Hera nursed him. After he had been returned to his mother Hera sent two snakes to kill him in his cradle, but he strangled them. He was taught to fight by Castor (*q.v.*), to play the lyre by Eumalpus, to wrestle by Autolycus (*q.v.*) and the art of archery by Eurytus. Linus also tried to teach him to play the lyre but, when he censured his awkward pupil, Heracles killed him with his own instrument. Amphitryon (*q.v.*) then sent him to keep cattle. At the age of 18, after a 50-day chase, he killed a huge lion on Mt. Cithaeron because it had been ravaging the herds of Amphitrion and Thespius. He did this with a wild olive club and later wore the pelt everywhere, though some other sources say he wore the pelt of the Nemean lion. In reward Thespius gave him his 50 daughters. At Thebes he defeated the Minyan heralds of Orchomenus who had come to demand tribute. Creon, king of Thebes, rewarded him by giving him his daughter Megara or Megera who bore him several children. His half-brother Iphicles married Creon's youngest daughter. Hera now made him mad and he killed his own children and two of Iphicles'. At Delphi the Pythia (*q.v.*), calling him Heracles for the first time, sent him to serve, for 12 years, his wretched cousin Eurystheus (*q.v.*) in order to purify himself of the murder. At the end of that time he would become immortal. With his nephew Iolaus (*q.v.*) as companion he embarked on 12 labours set by Eurystheus. These were to fetch the pelt of the Nemean lion, to kill the Hydra of Lerna (*q.v.*), to capture alive the Ceryneian Hind (*q.v.*), to capture alive the Erymanthian Boar (*q.v.*), to cleanse the stables of Augeas (*q.v.*), to drive off the Stymphalian Birds (*q.v.*), to capture the Cretan Bull (*q.v.*), to fetch the horses of Diomedes (*q.v.*), to fetch the girdle of Hippolyte (*q.v.*), to steal the cattle of Geryon (*q.v.*), to fetch the golden apples of the Hesperides (*q.v.*) and to bring back Cerberus (*q.v.*). After capturing the Erymanthian Boar he had joined the Argonauts (*q.v.*) but his squire Hylas was spirited off by the Naiads (*q.v.*) while fetching water at Cios in Mysia and Heracles left the expedition to search for him. Having completed his service for Eurystheus he returned to Thebes and here gave Megara to Iolaus. But Hera again drove him mad and he killed Megara and her children. Some traditions say he also killed himself and his family. He now desired to marry Iole daughter of his friend Eurytus of Oechalia and won her in an archery contest. But Eurytus refused to surrender her because Heracles had slain his own children. The incident ended in Heracles killing Iphitus (q.v.) but he later seized Iole. To purify himself of this murder he went to serve Omphale (q.v.). After serving her he and Telamon saved Hesione, daughter of Laomedon (q.v.) and sacked Troy (q.v.). Heracles gave Hesione to Telamon and ransomed Priam (q.v.). Next he made war on Augias and Neleus (q.v.) and then on Hippocoon who had helped Neleus. In this he was assisted by Cepheus (q.v.) and he restored Tyndareus (q.v.). At this time he seduced the priestess Auge, daughter of Aleus king of Tegea, who bore him a son, Telephus. Now he married Deianeira (q.v.) who inadvertently caused his death. As Heracles ascended his funeral pyre, to be burned alive he gave his bow and quiver to Philoctetes (q.v.) who kindled the flame but thunderbolts demolished the pyre and he was carried on a cloud to Olympus. Here he was reconciled to Hera and married Hebe (q.v.), himself becoming an immortal. Numerous other legends concerning Heracles exist. We are told he rescued Alcestis (q.v.), helped the gods defeat the Giants (q.v.), defeated Antaeus (q.v.) and, when the Delphic Oracle would not give him an answer seized the sacred tripod and struggled with Apollo (q.v.) for it. Xenophon tells us that before beginning his adventures Heracles was confronted by two beautiful women, one offering a life of ease, the other of service to mankind and he had to choose between the two. Other writers tell of him having to choose between two roads offering similar alternatives to the women. From a mighty and boisterous hero the picture of Heracles gradually developed into a morality tale of selfless service and fortitude eventually rewarded and for this reason the Stoic philosophers of Rome idealised him.

Hercules. See **Heracles**.

Hermaphroditus. The son of Hermes (q.v.) and Aphrodite (q.v.) who refused the advances of the nymph Salmacis. Her request that their bodies be joined in one was then granted by the gods. The name gives us the word "hermaphrodite", a being with the characteristics of both sexes.

Hermes. The Roman Mercury. Originally a god of fertility. The son of Zeus (q.v.) and Maia, daughter of Atlas (q.v.). He was born on Mt. Cyllene (hence he was sometimes referred to as Cyllenius). While still hours old he left the cradle and stole Apollo's (q.v.) cattle. He invented the lyre by stringing a tortoise shell with cow-gut and gave it to Apollo. This calmed Apollo's wrath and the two became friends. Zeus made him messenger of the gods and gave him his winged sandals (the Alipes), broadbrimmed hat (the Petasus) and herald's staff (caduceus) originally entwined with two white ribbons, later represented as entwined snakes. He conducted the souls of the dead to Hades (q.v.) and in this role was known as Psychopompus. The patron of travellers, traders and thieves and the father of Autolycus the thief, by Chione, and of Echion herald of the Argonauts (q.v.). He was the father of Pan (q.v.) by Penelope (q.v.) and a companion of the Muses (q.v.). He helped the Fates compose the alphabet, invented the musical scale, weights and measures and olive cultivation. A god of dice games. As herald he was eloquent and in *Acts* ch. XIV St. Paul, who spoke in tongues more than any man, is mistaken for him.

Hermione. The daughter of Helen (q.v.) and Menelaus (q.v.). Betrothed by Tyndareus (q.v.) to Orestes (q.v.) but given to Neoptolemus (q.v.) by Menelaus.

Hero. A priestess of Aphrodite (q.v.) at Sestos. Her lover Leander (q.v.) used to swim the Hellespont each night to see her but drowned when a storm extinguished the light she used to guide him. She then drowned herself. The subject of a play by Marlowe and paintings by Rubens and Turner.

Herodotus. See **B31**.

Heroes. To the Greeks a hero was the son of a mortal or divinity who was essentially superior to other men. They were venerated and received sacrifices because they were believed to help the living. Thus Theseus (q.v.) was supposed to have helped the Athenians at Marathon. "Heroic poetry" was epic poetry, telling of their deeds.

Hesiod. See **B31**.

Hesperides. "The daughters of evening" who lived in a land at the end of the world, far to the west. These maidens guarded a tree belonging to Hera (q.v.) which bore golden apples. They were assisted by a dragon, Ladon. Ge (q.v.) had given the tree to Hera on her wedding day. On the advice of Prometheus (q.v.) Heracles (q.v.) (who had been sent to get the apples by Eurystheus (q.v.)) persuaded Atlas (q.v.) to fetch three apples while he shouldered Atlas' burden. Atlas then refused to take the sky back on his shoulders but Heracles tricked him into doing so. On his return journey Heracles slew Antaeus (q.v.). Eurystheus gave the apples back to Heracles and he passed them to Athene to return to the Hesperides.

Hesperus. The evening star, the Greek form of the Latin vesper or evening.

Hestia. The sister of Zeus (q.v.) and Hera (q.v.), the goddess of the hearth worshipped by every family. Though Poseidon (q.v.) and Apollo (q.v.) tried to seduce her she swore to Zeus always to remain a virgin. The Romans worshipped her counterpart, the goddess Vesta (q.v.).

Hippodamia. (1) The daughter of Oenomaus, king of Elis. An oracle said he would die at the hands of his son-in-law so he challenged all her suitors to a chariot race. Victory meant they could marry Hippodamia, defeat meant death. His horses were the gifts of his father Ares (q.v.). However Pelops (q.v.) engineered his death and married Hippodamia.
(2) The wife of Pirithous (q.v.). When a drunken centaur (q.v.) abducted her on her wedding day the battle between the Lapithae (q.v.) and Centaurs occurred.

Hippolyte. A queen of the Amazons (q.v.) and sister of Antiope. Heracles (q.v.) had to fetch her golden girdle for Eurystheus. At first he was well received but Hera (q.v.) stirred the Amazons against him and in the fight he slew Hippolyte and took the girdle. Returning home he saved Laomedon's (q.v.) daughter Hesione. Another legend says Theseus (q.v.) abducted Hippolyte who bore him the son Hippolytus (q.v.).

Hippolytus. The son of Theseus (q.v.) and the Amazon Hippolyte (q.v.) or her sister Antiope (q.v.). When Theseus married again to Phaedra (q.v.), sister of Ariadne (q.v.), Phaedra fell in love with her stepson and committed suicide when he refused her. She left a note falsely accusing Hippolytus. Theseus prayed to Poseidon (q.v.) who was under an obligation to him, that Hippolytus would die the same day. Poseidon then sent a sea-monster which scared the youth's horses and he was dragged to death behind his chariot.

Homer. See **B32**.

Horae. The "hours", three daughters of Zeus (q.v.) and Themis (q.v.) and tutelary goddesses of nature and the seasons. They were bound to the soil and promoted fertility. Thus they were important and are involved in solemn oaths. However they rarely appear except in attendance on other gods and have no "adventures".

Horatii. Three Roman brothers whose tale is told by Livy. In the mid 7th century B.C. while Rome was ruled by Tullus Hostilius the city of Alba Longa (q.v.) was destroyed and its population transferred to Rome. According to legend the Horatii challenged the three Alban champions, the Curatii, to a sword battle. Two Horatii were killed but the third slew all the Curatii. On returning to Rome he met his sister, who had been engaged to one of the Curatii, weeping. He stabbed her to death. After ceremonies of expiation Tullus acquitted him of murder.

Horatius Cocles. Another of the Horatii family, the "one-eyed" (Cocles). In the 6th century B.C. he held the Etruscans at bay on the wooden Sublican bridge into Rome until it was pulled down beneath him. He then swam the Tiber to safety. The subject of a *Lay* by Macaulay.

Hyacinthus. A Peloponnesian youth loved by Apollo (q.v.) who was killed when the jealous Zephyrus (q.v.) diverted a discus to hit him. From his blood sprang the "hyacinth" flower. He had a shrine at Amyclae in Laconia and a three-day festival, the Hyacinthia, was held in his honour at Sparta.

Hyades. Nymphs who cared for Dionysus (q.v.) as a child on Mt. Nysa. Zeus (q.v.) placed their images in the sky as the "rain stars", part of the constellation of Taurus which rises at midnight in the rainy season.

Hydra of Lerna. The "water snake", offspring of Echidne (q.v.) and Typhon (q.v.) and raised by

Hera (q.v.). It was a monster with the body of a dog and 9 serpent heads. Heracles (q.v.) was sent to kill it by Eurystheus (q.v.). It lived at the source of the River Amymone in the swamp of Lerna. As Heracles lopped off a head two more grew. He also had to crush a giant crab which Hera placed among the signs of the zodiac. Finally he crushed the Hydra's heads with his club and Iolaus (q.v.) burned them to stop them regrowing. He dipped his arrows in the beast's blood thereby making them poisonous.

Hygeia. The wife or daughter of Asclepius (q.v.), a goddess of health.

Hylas. See Heracles.

Hyllus. The son of Heracles (q.v.) and Deianeira (q.v.). He conducted Heracles to his funeral pyre. Either he or Iolaus (q.v.) defeated Eurystheus (q.v.). Eventually he was slain by Echemus, king of Tegea.

Hymen. God of weddings.

Hyperboreans. A mythical race living far to the north, behind Boreas (q.v.) i.e. at the place where the north wind originates. Apollo (q.v.) spent time with them before going to Delphi and spent the winter months with them. A Hyperborean soothsayer, Olen, installed Apollo's oracle at Delphi. Their land was supposed to have perpetual sunshine and was a land of plenty, an earthly paradise where men lived in peace and ease on the fruits of the earth. Herodotus (**B31**) tells us that one of their priests, Aburis, travelled the world on a golden arrow and never needed to eat. He places their land in Southern Russia.

Hypenor. One of the Spartii (q.v.).

Hyperion. A Titan (q.v.) and sun-god, father of Helios (q.v.), Selene (q.v.) and Eos (q.v.), the sun, moon and dawn. In Keats' poem he is the last of the old gods to be deposed, the young Apollo (q.v.) taking his place.

Hypermestra. See Danaus.

Hypnus. The god of sleep.

I

Iacchus. Alternative name for Dionysus (q.v.) used in the Eleusian mysteries where he was regarded as the son of Zeus (q.v.) and Demeter (q.v.), not Semele (q.v.).

Iapetus. A Titan (q.v.), father of Prometheus (q.v.), Atlas (q.v.) and Epimetheus.

Iasion. Or Iasius or Iasus, the son of Zeus (q.v.) and Electra (q.v.), lover of Demeter (q.v.) who bore him a son Pluton. Zeus in his jealousy slew him with a thunderbolt.

Icarius. Father of Erigone. An Athenian to whom Dionysus (q.v.) taught cultivation of the vine and who gave wine to a band of shepherds. Mistaking drunkenness for witchcraft they slew him.

Icarus. See Daedalus.

Idaea. A nymph, mother of Teucer (q.v.) by Scamander (q.v.) of Crete.

Idas. The twin of Lynceus and a son of Poseidon (q.v.). He abducted Marpessa in a chariot given to him by Poseidon and fought Apollo (q.v.) for possession of her. Given the choice by Zeus (q.v.) she chose Idas. He and Lynceus took part in the voyage of the Argonauts (q.v.) and the hunt of the Calydonian boar (q.v.) and were killed in battle with their cousins the Dioscuri (q.v.).

Idomeneus. King of Crete who contributed 100 ships to the expedition against Troy (q.v.). Virgil adds that on his return from Troy he was caught in a storm and vowed to sacrifice the first person he met to Poseidon (q.v.) in return for safe passage. This proved to be his son and the sacrifice brought a pestilence on Crete. Idomeneus was banished to Calabria in Italy.

Ilia. A priestess of Vesta (q.v.) also called Rhea Silvia. The mother of Romulus (q.v.) and Remus.

Iliad. Homer's epic poem on the siege of Troy (q.v.). Although it hints at earlier and later events it covers only a period of weeks in the tenth year of the war, recounting Achilles' (q.v.) quarrel with Agamemnon (q.v.), the death of Patroclus (q.v.) and the death of Hector (q.v.). It ends with Achilles returning Hector's (q.v.) body to Priam (q.v.). Although many gods and heroes appear, Achilles and Hector are the main protagonists.

Ilioneus. An old and venerated Trojan who accompanied Aeneas (q.v.).

Ilithyiae. Daughters of Hera (q.v.) who helped women

in childbirth. Later only one goddess, Ilithyia, is mentioned in this connection.

Ilus. (1) The son of Tros (q.v.) and father of Laomedon (q.v.). An ancestor of the Trojans.
(2) Original name of Ascanius (q.v.) son of Aeneas (q.v.) and Creusa.

Inachus. The first king of Argos, son of Oceanus (q.v.) and Tethys. A river was named after him.

Ino. The daughter of Cadmus (q.v.) and Harmonia (q.v.), sister of Autonoe, Agave, Polydoras, Illyrus and Semele. She helped to rear Dionysus (q.v.) and her husband Athamas (q.v.) was punished for it by Hera (q.v.) who drove him into madness and the murder of his own children. Ino, Autonoe and Agave were Bacchae (q.v.) and they slew Pentheus, the son of Agave and heir to Cadmus, for opposing the worship of Dionysus. Ino committed suicide (see **Athamas**) and became a sea deity.

Io. The daughter of Inachus. Zeus (q.v.) loved her and turned her into a white heifer to deceive the jealous Hera (q.v.). He did not succeed in this and Hera set the hundred-eyed Argus to watch the heifer. But Hermes (q.v.) at Zeus' command cut off his head and placed his eyes in the tail of the peacock. He also sent a gadfly whose sting caused Io to wander the earth till she reached Egypt. On her wanderings she gave her name to the Ionian sea and to the Bosphorus ("ford of the cow"). In Egypt Zeus restored her to human form and she bore him a son, Epaphus, an ancestor of Danaus (q.v.).

Iobates. See Bellerophon.

Iolaus. Son of Iphicles (q.v.) and nephew of Heracles (q.v.) to whom he was charioteer and constant companion. He helped Heracles kill the Hydra (q.v.) and perform his other labours and in return Heracles gave him his wife Megara. He also sent Iolaus as the leader of his sons by the daughters of Thespius to settle in Sardinia.

Iolcus. The kingdom of Jason's (q.v.) father Aeson, usurped by his half brothers Pelias and Neleus.

Iole. See Deianeira.

Ion. The son of Xuthus and Creusa, brother of Achaeus. In Euripides' play *Ion* he is the son of Creusa and Apollo (q.v.) who is carried off to Delphi (q.v.), as a baby but is eventually restored to Creusa and adopted by Xuthus. The eponymous ancestor of the Ionian Greeks.

Iphicles. (1) One of the Argonauts (q.v.).
(2) The son of Amphitrion (q.v.) and Alcmene (q.v.) a night younger than Heracles (q.v.). The father of Iolaus (q.v.). He married the youngest daughter of Creon of Thebes when Heracles married Megara.

Iphigenia. The daughter of Agamemnon (q.v.) and Clytemnestra (q.v.), sacrificed by her father at Aulis to get a favourable wind for the Greek fleet sailing to Troy (q.v.). Euripides cites another tradition in which Artemis (q.v.) substituted a doe for Iphigenia at the last moment and carried her off to Tauris. Later Orestes (q.v.) found Iphigenia on the Tauric Chersonese and brought her home to Greece.

Iphitus. A son of Eurytus who argued that his father should deliver Iole (see **Deianeira**) to Heracles (q.v.). But in a rage Heracles slew him and though purified of the murder was told by an oracle to sell himself into slavery and give the proceeds to Iphitus' family.

Irene. The daughter of Zeus (q.v.) and Themis (q.v.), goddess of peace and one of the Horae (q.v.). The Romans identified her with Pax.

Iris. The personification of the rainbow and, in later myth, a messenger of the gods, particularly Hera (q.v.).

Isis. An Egyptian goddess, wife of Osiris and mother of Horus. In Hellenistic times she became one of the most important deities of the Mediterranean world, her cult arriving in Rome by the time of Augustus. Here the features of her worship, Egyptian priests, processions, initiation ceremonies etc. were described by Apuleius in his *Golden Ass*. One of her temples is preserved at Pompeii.

Ismene. The daughter of Oedipus (q.v.) and Jocasta (q.v.). She followed her father and her sister Antigone (q.v.) into exile.

Issa. The daughter of Macareus and his sister Canace, beloved by Apollo (q.v.).

Isthmian Games. Quadrennial games held at Corinth in honour of Poseidon (q.v.).

Ithaca. The island home of Odysseus (q.v.), one of the Ionian islands.

Itys, Itylus. *See* Procne.

Iulus. A name used for Ascanius (*q.v.*) by Virgil to indicate the descent of the Julian clan from Aeneas (*q.v.*).

J

Janus. A god of beginnings or new ventures, worshipped at Rome. He had a flamen (sacred priest) and was very important but the origin and nature of his worship is obscure. He had two faces and may represent the assimilation of an eastern god and an Etruscan (*see* **L41**) deity. Also associated with doorways and thresholds.

Jason. Son of Aeson, rightful king of Iolcus who was usurped by his half-brothers, Pelias and Neleus. The infant Jason was smuggled out of Iolcus and reared by Cheiron (*q.v.*) while Pelias expelled Neleus and ruled alone. When Jason returned to claim his birthright Pelias sent him to fetch the Golden Fleece from Colchis. This was the fleece of the ram on which Phrixus (*q.v.*) had escaped and which he had given to Aëtes, king of Colchis. Its presence was the cause of Colchis' prosperity and it hung from an oak tree in the grove of Ares (*q.v.*) where a dragon guarded it. After numerous adventures Jason and his Argonauts (*q.v.*) arrived at Colchis and Aëtes promised Jason the fleece if he could yoke two fire-breathing bulls with brazen feet made by Hephaestus (*q.v.*), and sow the grove of Ares with dragons' teeth left by Cadmus of Thebes (*q.v.*). Medea (*q.v.*) the sorceress gave him a fire-proof lotion which allowed him to complete the task and when her father Aëtes refused to give up the fleece, charmed the dragon to sleep while Jason stole it. Pursued by Aëtes the couple escaped when Medea murdered her half-brother Absyrtus and dropped pieces of his corpse into the sea, causing Aëtes to stop and collect them. They were purified of the murder by Circe (*q.v.*). At Iolchus Pelias had forced Aeson to commit suicide and in revenge Medea persuaded Pelias' daughters to boil their father alive pretending it would restore his youth. The couple were banished because of this and went to Corinth. Here Jason abandoned Medea for Glauce (*q.v.*) whom Medea killed. Jason took his own life though one tradition holds he was killed by the falling prow of the Argo (*q.v.*).

Jocasta. Daughter of Menoeceus, wife of Laius king of Thebes and mother of Oedipus (*q.v.*). When her unwitting incest with Oedipus brought a plague on Thebes Menoeceus sacrificed himself in answer to an oracle demanding the life of one of the Sparti (*q.v.*) i.e. a descendant of the "sown men". Jocasta hanged herself when she learned the truth of her marriage to Oedipus.

Jove. Alternative name for Jupiter (*q.v.*).

Juno. Italian goddess of womanhood and childbirth, associated by the Romans with the Greek Hera (*q.v.*) and regarded as the consort of Jupiter (*q.v.*).

Jupiter. Originally an Italian sky-god, later regarded by the Romans as *Dies Pater*—"Father Day", god of the day. Later still identified with Zeus (*q.v.*). His cult was introduced to Rome by the Etruscans and the temple to Jupiter Optimus Maximus (Best and Most High) stood on the Capitol. His *flamen*, the *flamen* Dialis was the most important of the college. He was guarantor of the *imperium* and city of Rome and triumphs were an act of Jupiter worship. Worshipped in various capacities as *Stator* (he who founds or maintains), *Teretrius* (he who strikes), *Ultor* ("Avenger") and *Tonans* ("Thunderer").

Juturna. (1) An Italian goddess of springs and streams.

(2) The sister of Turnus (*q.v.*).

Juventas. Italian goddess identified with Hebe (*q.v.*).

L

Labdacus. Mythical king of Thebes; a descendant of Cadmus (*q.v.*) and an ancestor of Oedipus (*q.v.*).

Lachesis. One of the Fates (*q.v.*).

Laelaps. A fleet-footed hound given to Procris by Cephalus (*q.v.*).

Laertes. The king of Ithaca, father of Odysseus (*q.v.*)

by Anticleia, daughter of the thief Autolycus. While Odysseus was at Troy (*q.v.*) Penelope's (*q.v.*) suitors forced him to retire to the country.

Laestrygones. A race of giant cannibals ruled by Lamus. At Telepylos, their capital city, Odysseus (*q.v.*) lost all but one of his twelve ships to them. Homer says their summer nights were so short that shepherds going out with their flocks in the morning met those returning at sunset. Traditionally located in eastern Sicily or at Formiae in central Italy.

Laius. *See* Oedipus.

Lamia. One of the Empusae (*q.v.*), daughter of Belus.

Lamus. *See* Laestrygones.

Laocoön. A Trojan prophet, son of Antenor and a priest of Apollo (*q.v.*) and Poseidon (*q.v.*). He warned the Trojans against the Wooden Horse (*q.v.*) and flung a spear at it. However he had angered Apollo by breaking his vows of celibacy and the god now sent two sea serpents which crushed him and his two sons. A famous group of statues depicting the scene, carved in Rhodes c. 25 B.C., now stands in the Vatican museum. The Trojans disastrously drew the wrong conclusion viz. that his death was punishment for striking the horse.

Laodamia. The daughter of Acastus and wife of Protesilaus of Thessaly, the first Greek ashore at Troy (*q.v.*) though he knew from an oracle the first Greek to land would die. Homer says he left his wife mourning and his house unfinished but Catullus, Virgil and Ovid follow another tradition in which she begged the gods that Protesilaus might return to life for three hours. When he died a second time she committed suicide. Wordsworth's poem *Laodamia* takes the tale as its subject.

Laodice. (1) A daughter of Priam (*q.v.*), sister of Cassandra (*q.v.*) and wife of Helicaon. When Troy (*q.v.*) fell the earth swallowed her.

(2) Alternative name for Electra (*q.v.*), Agamemnon's (*q.v.*) daughter.

Laomedon. The son of Ilus (*q.v.*), king of Troy (*q.v.*) and father of Hesione and Priam (*q.v.*). Apollo (*q.v.*) and Poseidon (*q.v.*) helped him build the walls of Troy and he refused to pay them. Poseidon then sent a sea monster to devour Hesione but Heracles (*q.v.*) saved her. Laomedon then refused to pay Heracles the agreed white horses left by Zeus (*q.v.*) in exchange for Ganymede (*q.v.*). Heracles and Telamon then sacked Troy and slew Laomedon and all his sons save Priam (*q.v.*).

Lapis Niger. Black marble paving in the Roman Forum said to cover the tomb of Romulus (*q.v.*).

Lapithae or **Lapiths.** Mythical tribe of Thessaly, governed by Pirithous, son of Ixion (*q.v.*) and thus half-brothers to the Centaurs (*q.v.*). At the wedding of Pirithous and Hippodamia, attended by Theseus (*q.v.*) a centaur tried to abduct the bride and a famous battle between the Lapithae and Centaurs ensued. It is described by Ovid and is depicted in the Parthenon and the frieze of Apollo's (*q.v.*) temple at Bassae. It is also the subject of a sculptured frieze by Michelangelo.

Lares. Originally fertility gods, worshipped by the Romans privately in the home and semi-publicly at crossroads. They were represented as youths with handfuls of fruit who wandered the farmstead incessantly whirling round and round. They kept away maleficent demons and ensured the prosperity of the family home. Each month they received offerings of oat cakes, milk, honey and flowers. Generally associated with the Penates, the spirits who guarded the household stores. Together the guardians of the hearth and home.

Larissa. A city in Thessaly near modern Volos. Reputed birthplace of Achilles (*q.v.*) hence his nickname "the Larissaen".

Lars Porsenna. Legendary Etruscan chief whom Livy tells us besieged Rome on behalf of the exiled Tarquinius Superbus. Lars means "overlord" and he is probably a symbol of Etruscan suzerainty over Rome. (*See* **Horatius Cocles**).

Latinus. Eponymous king of the Latini or Latins in Italy. Hesiod makes him the son of Odysseus (*q.v.*) and Circe (*q.v.*). Virgil makes him the son of Faunus (*q.v.*). Livy and Virgil portray him as opposing the settlement of Aeneas (*q.v.*) and the Trojans in Italy but then agreeing Aeneas should marry his daughter Lavinia. He next helps Aeneas fight Turnus king of the Rutuli, to whom Lavinia had been promised. Livy says he died in battle and Aeneas became king of the Latins; Virgil that he survived to celebrate the marriage and uniting of Latins and Trojans.

Leander. Mythical youth who drowned while swimming to meet Hero (*q.v.*).

Leda. Daughter of Thestius and wife of Tyndareus king of Sparta. Seduced by Zeus (*q.v.*) in the form of a swan she gave birth to two eggs, from one of which hatched Helen (*q.v.*) and Polydeuces (*q.v.*) from the other, Castor (*q.v.*) and Clytemnestra (*q.v.*). One tradition says that Helen was the daughter of Nemesis (*q.v.*) who left the egg for Leda to incubate.

Lemnos. A small island at the mouth of the Hellespont, home at one time of a primitive people known to the Greeks as the Pelasgi. Hephaestus (*q.v.*) was said to have landed on the island when Zeus (*q.v.*) hurled him out of heaven and supposedly had a forge here.

Lethe. "Forgetfulness", one of the rivers of the Underworld whose waters induced amnesia in those who drank of them. Virgil holds that here souls forgot their past prior to reincarnation and Ovid says that it flowed round the "cave of sleep".

Leto. Known to the Romans as Latona. The daughter of the Titans (*q.v.*) Coeus and Phoebe and the mother of Apollo (*q.v.*) and Artemis (*q.v.*) by Zeus (*q.v.*). While she carried the unborn gods the jealous Hera (*q.v.*) forced her to wander the earth until she finally gave birth to them at Ortygia, henceforth called Delos (*q.v.*). Hera sent the giant Tityus (*q.v.*) to rape her but her children slew him with their arrows. *See also* **Niobe.**

Leuce. A nymph loved by Hades (*q.v.*) who turned her into a white poplar tree.

Leucippus. (1) King of Messenia whose daughters Hilaera and Phoebe were abducted by the Dioscuri (*q.v.*) and whose brothers Idas (*q.v.*) and Lynceus (*q.v.*) fought to save them.

(2) The son of Oenomaus who loved Artemis (*q.v.*). To be near her he disguised himself as a nymph but when Apollo (*q.v.*) advised the nymphs to bathe naked he was discovered and torn to pieces by them.

Leucothea. Originally Ino, daughter of Cadmus (*q.v.*) and wife of Athamas who helped Zeus (*q.v.*) save Dionysus (*q.v.*) at the death of Semele (*q.v.*). In revenge Hera (*q.v.*) drove her mad and she leapt into the foaming sea to become the sea deity Leucothea—"the white goddess". In this role she helped Odysseus (*q.v.*) land on Scheria. Her son was Palaemon, a minor sea god.

Liber Pater. An ancient Italian god of the vine, early identified with Bacchus (*q.v.*) by the Romans.

Lichas. The herald of Heracles (*q.v.*) who took the shirt of Deineira (*q.v.*) to him. In his agony Heracles took him by the ankle, swung him round three times and threw him into the Euboean Sea where he became a rock of human shape which henceforth bore his name.

Linus. (1) The son of Psamathe of Argos and Apollo (*q.v.*). Fearful lest her father learn of her liaison with the god she exposed the baby who was reared by shepherds but later killed by her father's hounds. When her distress revealed her secret her father condemned her to death but Apollo sent a plague to the city which only abated when the Argives propitiated mother and son with dirges called *linoi*.

(2) The son of a Muse who was so gifted musically that the jealous Apollo killed him.

(3) Heracles' (*q.v.*) music tutor whom Heracles slew in a rage with his own lyre.

Lotophagi. ("The Lotus eaters"). A mythical people living on lotus fruit which induced trances and forgetfulness and made the eater lose any desire to return home. They gave the fruit to Odysseus' (*q.v.*) men. Herodotus placed them in western Libya, possibly the island of Jerba.

Luceres. One of the original three tribes into which Rome was divided and which were believed to date back to Romulus (*q.v.*). The other tribes were the Ramnes and Tities.

Lucifer. The "light bringer", the name given to the planet Venus which can be seen before dawn. In the evening sky the Greeks called it Hesperus.

Lucretia. Wife of Tarquinius Collatinus whose rape by Sextus, son of Tarquinius Superbus led her to stab herself in shame. Junius Brutus then swore by her spirit to expel the Tarquins which he did. The story is told by Livy and Ovid and inspired Shakespeare's poem *The Rape of Lucrece* and Brit-

ten's opera *The Rape of Lucretia*. A subject also for Titian, Botticelli, Tintoretto and Veronese.

Lucretius. *See* **B39.**

Lycaon. A mythical character who tricked Zeus (*q.v.*) by feeding him human flesh. Zeus killed him and all his sons save Nyctinus by lightning or turned them into wolves, hence Lycanthropy.

Lycomedes. The king of Scyros who murdered Theseus (*q.v.*). It was to his court that Thetis (*q.v.*) sent Achilles (*q.v.*), and Lycomedes' daughter Deidamia bore Achilles his son Neoptolemus (*q.v.*).

Lycurgus (1) Mythical king of Thrace who was made blind and mad for opposing the worship of Dionysus (*q.v.*).

(2) Mythical founder of the Spartan constitution and military regime, first mentioned by Herodotus and subject of a *Life* by Plutarch. Some traditions say the Pythia at Delphi gave him the constitution, others that he devised it while in Crete. In Sparta he was worshipped as a god.

Lynceus. (1) *See* **Danaus.**

(2) Twin of Idas (*q.v.*) noted for his keen eyesight.

Lyrnessus. City near Troy (*q.v.*) sacked by Achilles (*q.v.*).

M

Macareus. *See* **Issa.**

Macaria. *See* **Eurystheus.**

Machaon. The son of Asclepius the physician (*q.v.*).

Maenads. *See* **Bacchae.**

Maia. The daughter of Atlas (*q.v.*) and Pleione, eldest of the Pleiades (*q.v.*) and the most beautiful. By Zeus (*q.v.*) the mother of Hermes (*q.v.*). The Romans identified her with spring and as a nature goddess gave her name to the month of May.

Manes. "The good ones", the Roman name for the spirits of the dead, regarded as a collective divinity, *Di Manes*. On certain days they could leave the Underworld and were capable of great mischief. Thus they demanded propitiatory ceremonies at funerals and on set days when the head of the house, the *paterfamilias*, would go into the night and cast boiled beans to them. The Roman poets applied the term also to the gods of the Underworld and to the Underworld itself.

Marpessa. *See* **Idas.** The daughter of the river god Evenus.

Mars. Roman god of war, at one time also associated with agriculture. Later completely identified with Ares (*q.v.*).

Marsyas. A Phrygian, in some traditions a silenus (*q.v.*), who found the flute invented and discarded by Athene (*q.v.*). He challenged Apollo (*q.v.*) to a music contest, judged by the Muses (*q.v.*). Apollo won and had him flayed alive. The tears of the woodland spirits and animals which wept for him formed the river Meander.

Medea. The niece of Circe (*q.v.*) and daughter of Aëtes of Colchis some say by Hecate (*q.v.*). She loved Jason (*q.v.*) and helped him steal the Golden Fleece, murdering her half-brother in their escape. Having cut a goat in pieces, boiled them and pulled forth a lamb she persuaded the daughters of Pelias to boil him, causing his death. When Jason left her for Glauce (*q.v.*) she caused her death and slew her sons by Jason. She then escaped in a chariot drawn by winged serpents to Athens. Here she married Aegeus (*q.v.*). When Theseus (*q.v.*) returned she tried to poison him to secure the succession of her own son Medus (*q.v.*) but Aegeus recognised Theseus and saved him. She fled to wander the earth: some say she returned to Colchis and was reconciled to her father, others that she went to Asia Minor where her son gave his name to the Medes. She became an immortal.

Medus. Son of Medea (*q.v.*) and Aegeus (*q.v.*) eponymous ancestor of the Medes.

Medusa. *See* **Gorgons.** Slain and beheaded by Perseus (*q.v.*) as she slept. From her corpse sprang forth the fully grown Pegasus (*q.v.*) and the warrior Chrysaor.

Megaeia. One of the Erinnyes (*q.v.*).

Megara or **Megaera.** The eldest daughter of Creon of Thebes. Wife of Heracles (*q.v.*) and bore him several children. Later married Iolaus (*q.v.*) though one tradition says Eurystheus tried to kill her and Heracles instead killed Eurystheus. In revenge Hera (q.v.) drove Heracles mad and he killed Megara and his children.

Melampus. Son of Amythaon, a seer who introduced the worship of Dionysus (q.v.) to Greece. He and his brother Bias cured the women of Argos (including the daughter of the king, Proctus) of madness and received two thirds of his kingdom in reward.

Meleager. The son of Oeneus and Althaea. The Fates (q.v.) told his mother he would only die when a certain brand, which was on the fire, was burned. She extinguished and hid it. Meleager was one of the Argonauts (q.v.) and organised the hunt of the Calydonian Boar (q.v.). He fell in love with Atalanta who joined the hunt and having killed the boar himself gave her the hide on the pretext she had touched it first. This set the hunters quarrelling and in the dispute he killed his uncles, brothers of Althaea. She cursed their murderer, not realising the truth, and when she learned the Erinnyes (q.v.) were persecuting him because of the curse burned the brand and committed suicide. Her daughters (save Gorge and Deianeira) were turned into guinea-hens by Artemis. The son of Meleager and Atlanta was Parthenopaeus.

Melpomene. The Muse of Tragedy.

Memnon. The son of Eos (q.v.) and Tithonus, half-brother of Priam (q.v.). The king of Ethiopia who helped the Trojans and killed many Greeks. Achilles (q.v.) met him in single combat while Zeus (q.v.) weighed their fates in the balance. Achilles slew him but Zeus answered his mother's request that he be honoured by having the birds called *Memnonides* rise above his funeral pyre, then fall as a sacrifice. They annually visited his tomb on the Hellespont though one tradition says he survived the war and ruled five generations in Ethiopia before becoming an immortal. The Greeks assumed many monuments, which they called *Memnonia*, were dedicated to him including a huge statue in Egyptian Thebes.

Menelaus. Son of Atreus, younger brother of Agamemnon (q.v.) and husband of Helen (q.v.). When her father chose him from amongst many suitors he made the others swear to help him in any misfortune. He was thus able to summon the Greek forces for the war on Troy (q.v.). At one stage in the war he fought a duel with Paris (q.v.) to decide the war and was winning until Aphrodite (q.v.) carried Paris off. Because he failed to sacrifice to Athene (q.v.) he took eight years to return from Troy to Sparta.

Menoeceus. (1) See Jocasta.
(2) See **Seven against Thebes**.

Mentor. Friend and adviser of Odysseus (q.v.) who was too old to go to Troy (q.v.) and remained at Ithaca to watch over Odysseus' interests. Athene (q.v.) took his form to guide Telemachus' (q.v.) search for his father. The name is now synonymous with a trusted counsellor.

Mercury. The Roman equivalent of Hermes (q.v.).

Merope. A Pleiad. Wife of Sisyphus.

Metis. Counsellor of the young Zeus (q.v.) and his first wife. Mother of Athene (q.v.). Herself the daughter of Oceanus (q.v.) and Tethys.

Midas. Son of Gordius. See **Gordian Knot**. His hospitality to Silenus (q.v.) led Dionysus (q.v.) to grant him any wish: he wished that all he touched would turn to gold. When even his food became gold he begged to be relieved of his gift—and was—by bathing in the River Pactolus which was henceforth rich in gold. When he judged Pan (q.v.) a better musician than Apollo (q.v.) the latter gave him asses' ears which he hid under his hat. Only his barber knew, but when his barber told a hole in the ground, reeds grew from it which, via the wind, revealed his secret to the world.

Milanion. Husband of Atalanta (q.v.).

Miletus of Crete. The son of Aria and Apollo (q.v.), a beautiful youth over whom Minos (q.v.) and his brothers Rhadamanthus (q.v.) and Sarpedon quarrelled. Miletus chose Sarpedon and to escape Minos' jealousy they fled to Asia Minor where Miletus founded the city Miletus which bore his name.

Minerva. Etruscan goddess of wisdom, the arts and crafts. The Romans identified her with Athene (q.v.).

Minos. The son of Zeus (q.v.) and Europa (q.v.), brother of Rhadamanthus (q.v.) and Sarpedon (q.v.). Ruler of Crete and supported in this by Poseidon (q.v.) who gave him a magnificent white bull. See **Cretan Bull.** He gave Crete her laws and defended the island with the aid of Talos, a brazen

giant with a bull's head. He pursued the nymph Britomartis for nine months but she leapt into the sea. Artemis (q.v.) deified her and the two shared the epithet Dictynna. While besieging Nisa, the port of Megara, Scylla, the daughter of the king Nisus fell in love with Minos and cropped her hair on which Nisus' life depended. She let Minos into the city but he was repulsed by her parricide and deserted the girl who swam after his ship. According to one tradition her father's spirit in the form of an eagle seized her and she was transformed into the Ciris bird; according to another tradition Minos drowned her and she became a fish. Minos married Pasiphaë (q.v.) who bore him Ariadne (q.v.), Androgeos and Phaedra. When Androgeos won all the events at the Panathenaic games Aegeus (q.v.) had him murdered and in revenge Minos extracted a tribute of seven Athenian youths and maidens who were devoured by the Minotaur (q.v.). He was killed by the daughters of Cocalus of Sicily while pursuing Daedalus (q.v.) and became one of the three judges of the Underworld.

Minotaur. Offspring of Pasiphaë (q.v.) and the Cretan Bull (q.v.) which had the head of a bull and body of a man. It lived in a labyrinth devised by Daedalus (q.v.) where it devoured the maidens and youths of Athens delivered in tribute to Minos (q.v.). It was slain by Theseus (q.v.).

Minyans or **Minyae.** Prehistoric inhabitants of Boeotia (q.v.) and Thessaly whose reputed ancestor was Minyas.

Misenus. Trumpeter of Aeneas (q.v.) who was drowned by a Triton (q.v.) and buried in the Bay of Naples at the port which then bore the name Misenum (the modern Capo Miseno). From the time of Agrippa Misenum was a major Roman naval station.

Mithras. An Iranian deity whose worship was developed in Persia and spread throughout the Middle East. Known to the Greeks from the time of Herodotus his worship spread to Rome under the Republic and from the 2nd century A.D. spread throughout the empire. Mithras was linked with astrology and appears to have been linked with the sun following a fight with the sun-god. But the core of his cult was that man or the soul had fallen from grace and that Mithras could bring redemption and thus eternal life. Very popular with the Roman legions. Mithras was the one serious contender with Christianity for religious supremacy. His ritual involved seven stages of initiation and secret ceremonies conducted in underground caves or artificial subterranean chambers such as that found in London. These temples were called mithraea.

Mnemosyne. "Memory", the daughter of Uranus (q.v.) and by Zeus (q.v.) the mother of the Muses (q.v.).

Moirae or **Moerae.** See **Fates.**

Monoecus. "The lone dweller", Latin name for Heracles (q.v.) who was said to have dwelt alone for a time in the region of modern Monte Carlo.

Mopsus. The son of Apollo (q.v.) and Manto, daughter of Teiresias. When he beat Calchas (q.v.) in prophecy Calchas died of grief.

Morpheus. The Greek *Hypnos*. The son of the god of "Sleep". A god who sends dreams and visions of human form. In Ovid's *Metamorphoses*, Sleep sends him to Alcyone (q.v.) in the form of her dead husband.

Musaeus. A mythical poet who succeeded Orpheus (q.v.), the first poet.

Muses or **Musae.** The daughters of Zeus (q.v.) and Mnemosyne (q.v.) who presided over the arts and sciences. Originally three in number, Hesiod later names nine. Clio was muse of history, Euterpe of lyric poetry and music, Thalia of comedy, Melpomene of tragedy, Terpsichore of song and dance, Erato of mime, Polyhymnia or Polymnia of the hymn, Calliope of epic poetry and Urania of astronomy, though the attributions vary.

Myrmidons or **Myrmidones.** Tribe of southern Thessaly which provided Achilles' (q.v.) contingent at Troy.

Myrtilus. The son of Hermes (q.v.), the charioteer of Oenomaus whose death he caused by removing the lynch pin of his chariot and substituting a wax replica. He did this because Pelops (q.v.) had bribed him with the promise of half his kingdom, but instead Pelops flung him into the sea. He cursed the House of Pelops as he died and his father placed him amongst the stars.

N

Naiads or **Naiades.** Fresh-water nymphs in Greek mythology. They carried off Hylas (*q.v.*).

Narcissus. *See* Echo.

Nauplius. A king of Euboea who lured ships returning from Troy (*q.v.*) to their doom on the promontory of Caphareus by lighting misleading fires.

Nausicaa. Daughter of Alcinous, king of the Phaeacians who found Odysseus (*q.v.*) after a shipwreck while playing ball with her friends on the beach. She looked after him and her father gave him a ship.

Nectar. The drink of the Greek gods which conferred immortality.

Neleus. Twin of Pelias (*q.v.*), sons of Poseidon (*q.v.*) and the nymph Tyro. The twins were exposed by their mother but reared by a horse breeder. When Tyro married Cretheus, king of Iolcus, he adopted the boys who were thus half-brothers of Aeson. Pelias then later seized the kingdom, imprisoned Aeson and expelled Neleus who went to Pylus with Bias and Melampus and became its king. He and all twelve of his sons bar Nestor (*q.v.*) were killed by Heracles (*q.v.*) for aiding Augias (*q.v.*) in his war against Heracles.

Nemesis. Greek goddess, daughter of Oceanus. Originally she was envisaged as allotting to men their share of happiness and unhappiness, thereby chastening the over-fortunate. Later she was portrayed as the punisher of crime, the goddess of retribution. Some say she laid the egg from which Helen (*q.v.*), Clytemnestra (*q.v.*) and the Dioscuri (*q.v.*) were born. She had a sanctuary at Rhamnus from around 430 B.C.

Nemi. A lake in the Alban mountains, site of a sanctuary and sacred wood of Diana (*q.v.*).

Neoptolemus. Also called Pyrrhus, a son of Achilles (*q.v.*) and Deidamia. Odysseus (*q.v.*) and Diomedes (*q.v.*) persuaded his grandfather Lycomedes to let him go to Troy (*q.v.*) after his father's death. He was one of the Greeks inside the Wooden Horse. He slew Polites, the son of Priam (*q.v.*) and Hecuba (*q.v.*) before their eyes. He killed Priam at the altar of Zeus, smashed the skull of Astyanax (*q.v.*), Hector's (*q.v.*) child, and sacrificed Polyxena, Priam's daughter, on his father's tomb. He was given Andromache (*q.v.*) but back in Greece married Hermione (*q.v.*) with the blessing of Menelaus (*q.v.*) despite her prior betrothal to Orestes (*q.v.*). When their marriage proved barren he went to Delphi (*q.v.*) to consult the oracle and was slain either by Orestes or the priests of Apollo (*q.v.*).

Nephele. A phantom conjured up by Zeus (*q.v.*) to deceive Ixion. She later married Athamas.

Neptune. Italian sea-god whom the Romans identified with Poseidon (*q.v.*).

Nereids or **Nereides.** Fifty beautiful sea nymphs, the daughters of Nereus (*q.v.*) and Doris, of whom the most famous were Amphitrite (*q.v.*) and Thetis (*q.v.*).

Nereus. An ancient and benevolent sea god, the son of Pontus (the sea) and Ge (*q.v.*). Husband of Doris, the daughter of Oceanus (*q.v.*) by whom he was father of the Nereids (*q.v.*).

Nero. *See* **B44.**

Nessus. *See* Deianeira.

Nestor. King of Pylos, only one of Neleus' (*q.v.*) twelve sons spared by Heracles. He participated in the Calydonian Boar (*q.v.*) hunt and the battle of Lapithae (*q.v.*) and Centaurs (*q.v.*). The oldest of the Greeks at Troy (*q.v.*) he was famous for his eloquence and wisdom. The father of Antilochus, a friend of Achilles (*q.v.*) and one of the bravest Greeks at Troy. Nestor was the only Greek to return home without mishap.

Nike. Goddess of Victory, not only in war but in musical and athletic competitions in Hesiod's *Theogony*, the daughter of the Titan Pallas and Styx. A minor deity, later envisaged not as one goddess but as several spirits, represented as young girls with wings who flew across the heavens to carry the crown to the victor. Zeus honoured Nike for helping the Olympian gods in the Titanomachia (*q.v.*). She was sometimes identified with Athene (*q.v.*).

Niobe. Daughter of Tantalus, sister of Pelops (*q.v.*) and wife of Amphion (*q.v.*) by whom she had seven sons and seven daughters (according to Ovid, Homer makes it six of each). She boasted of being superior to Leto (*q.v.*) who only had two children and in revenge Apollo (*q.v.*) slew her sons and Artemis (*q.v.*) her daughters. She wept for nine days and nights and Zeus (*q.v.*) then turned her into a stone on Mt. Sipylus.

Nisus. *See* Minos.

Nomius. "The pasturer", a name given to Pan (*q.v.*), Apollo (*q.v.*) and Hermes (*q.v.*) in their roles as protectors of flocks and pastures.

Notus. The south-west wind, known to the Romans as Auster. The son of Astraeus (*q.v.*) and Eos (*q.v.*).

Numa. The name of two Italian warriors in the *Aeneid*.

Numa Pompilius. Legendary king of Rome. The second king, successor of Romulus (*q.v.*) he was said to have ruled between 717 and 673 B.C. Said to be of Sabine (*q.v.*) origin he reorganised Roman religion under the guidance of Egeria (*q.v.*). He was said to have been initiated into the mysteries of Pythagoras, an obvious anachronism as he predates Pythagoras' 6th century visit to Italy, but his reputed religious reforms signify a new strand in Roman religion, a disinterested search for knowledge as opposed to inspired action. He founded the cult of Janus (*q.v.*), organised the priests in *collegia* and established the flamens, and reorganised the Salii whose war dances in honour of Mars (*q.v.*) reflected a very ancient Italic rite. He also appointed the Pontifex Maximus, a high priest with responsibility for ensuring religious rites were properly performed and for preventing the growth of undesirable foreign cults. He also reformed the Roman calendar to achieve the maximum coincidence of lunar and solar cycles.

Numicius. A sacred river in Latium between Ardea and Lavinium.

Numitor. The grandfather of Romulus (*q.v.*) and Remus (*q.v.*).

Nymphae or **Nymphs.** Minor deities, the spirits of nature. These daughters of Zeus (*q.v.*) were semimortal and were generally benevolent, though they could be malevolent particularly to unresponsive lovers. Each was the tutelary deity of a rock, tree, cave or fountain and was better known to the local peasants than the great gods of Olympus (*q.v.*). Lavishly decorated monumental fountains (a "*nymphaeum*") were dedicated to the nymphs by both Greeks and Romans.

Nysa, Mt. Mountain in Libya where, according to tradition, Dionysus (*q.v.*) was raised.

O

Oceanides. Sea nymphs (*q.v.*) of the ocean, daughters of Oceanus (*q.v.*). Hesiod says they were 40 in number.

Oceanus. One of the Titans (*q.v.*), the son of Ge (*q.v.*) and Uranus (*q.v.*). The only Titan not to revolt against Uranus (*q.v.*). In Aeschylus' *Prometheus Bound* he preaches submission to the authority of Zeus (*q.v.*). He was seen originally as the river encircling the world from which all rivers and seas sprang. He is thus depicted as the rim on Achilles' (*q.v.*) shield. The husband of Tethys and by her father of, among others, Metis.

Odysseus. The hero of Homer's Odyssey, itself the model for James Joyce's *Ulysses*, Ulysses being the Roman name for him. The son of Laertes, king of Ithaca, and Anticleia, daughter of the wily thief Autolycus. However, one tradition makes him the son of Sisyphus (*q.v.*). He married Penelope (*q.v.*). Warned by an oracle not to go to Troy (*q.v.*) he feigned madness when the heralds arrived by sowing salt, but when Palamedes placed his son Telemachus (*q.v.*) before the plough he was forced to disclose his sanity and join the expedition. Later, at Troy, he avenged himself by having a letter signed in Priam's (*q.v.*) hand placed in Palamedes' tent. The letter was found and Palamedes was stoned to death. But Odysseus himself tricked Achilles (*q.v.*) into revealing his true identity and joining the expedition. At Troy Odysseus and Diomedes (*q.v.*) entered the city at night to kill Rhesus the Thracian and steal his white horses, because it was prophesied that if they drank of the Scamander (*q.v.*) Troy would not fall. He quarrelled with Ajax (*q.v.*) over the armour of Achilles and some say he killed him. He captured Helenus and from him learned the secret oracles which told how Troy would fall. In accordance with these he stole the Palladium of Athene (q.v.). It was also Odysseus who devised the stratagem of the Wooden Horse. When Troy fell he took Hecuba (q.v.) as a slave. His journey home lasted ten years and involved many adventures. He first went to Cicones to procure jars of sweet wine and then visited the Lotophagi (q.v.). After leaving them he landed in Sicily where he blinded Polyphemus the Cyclops (q.v.). Next he visited Aeolus (q.v.) and as a result was blown off course and lost all his ships save one at Telepylos. In this he reached Aeaea, land of Circe (q.v.) and on her advice sought the aid of Teiresias, a dead seer in the Underworld. In the land of the Cimmerians he summoned Teiresias' shade, and also those of his mother and former comrades, though Ajax (q.v.) held aloof. Then, with Circe's counsel he navigated the Scylla and Charybdis (q.v.) and neutralised the spell of the Sirens (q.v.) by blocking his crew's ears with wax but having himself tied to the mast that he might hear their song. At Thrinacia his men slaughtered the cattle of Helios (q.v.) and were punished by Zeus (q.v.), all but Odysseus dying in a subsequent shipwreck. He drifted to Ogygia on flotsam, where he spent eight years with the nymph Calypso (q.v.). On a raft he made land at Scheria, was found by Nausicaa (q.v.) and given a ship to Ithaca (q.v.). Here he was recognised by Eumaeus (q.v.) despite his disguise as a beggar. He found Laertes (q.v.) in the country and Penelope (q.v.) besieged by suitors. This drunken and unruly crew were headed by one Alcinous, their most persistent member. Penelope had kept them at bay by promising to marry one of them when she had finished weaving a robe for Laertes: a robe she unpicked each night. But betrayed by her servants she was now being forced to choose a husband. Meanwhile Telemachus (q.v.) who had sailed away to find Odysseus returned to find him with Laertes and they plotted revenge. Still dressed as a beggar Odysseus entered the palace and was recognised only by his nurse Eurycleia and his faithful hound Argus who died on seeing his long lost master. Penelope now announced she would marry the suitor who could fire Odysseus' bow. Only he was able to bend and string it. The suitors having failed Odysseus strung the bow and with Telemachus slew the suitors. The *Odyssey* ends when Athene (q.v.) reconciles the hero and the kinsmen of the suitors who were seeking revenge. Teiresias had prophesied that Odysseus had to set out on another journey to appease Poseidon (q.v.) for the blinding of his son Polyphemus and would then live to an old age until death came from the sea. One tradition tells how Telegonus, Odysseus' son by Circe came looking for his father, landed and began plundering for supplies. Odysseus and Telemachus gave battle and Telegonus killed Odysseus, not recognising his father. He also took Telemachus and Penelope to Aeaca where Circe married Telemachus and he himself married Penelope.

Odyssey. See under **Odysseus.**

Oedipus ("Swollen-foot"). The son of Laius, king of Thebes, and Jocasta (q.v.). The Delphic oracle said Laius would be killed by his son so he had the baby exposed on Mt. Cithaeron with a nail driven through its feet—hence "Oedipus". But he was found by a shepherd and raised by Polybus, king of Corinth, as his own son. As an adult Oedipus learned from the oracle that he would kill his own father and marry his own mother and believing himself the son of Polybus, left Corinth. He met Laius on the road and killed him in a quarrel. Laius had been on his way to Delphi to seek advice on ridding Thebes of the Sphinx (q.v.). This Oedipus did and was made king by the Thebans. He married Jocasta and they had four children, Eteocles (q.v.), Polynices (q.v.), Antigone (q.v.) and Ismene (q.v.). When Thebes suffered a plague because of their incest Oedipus contacted the seer Teiresias and learned whose son he was. When she heard the truth Jocasta hanged herself and Oedipus blinded himself with the pins from her dress. With Antigone and later Ismene he went into exile at the grove of the Eumenides (*see* **Erinnyes**) at Colonos in Attica. Here he was received by the gods, having first cursed the sons who had neglected him, saying they would divide their kingdom by the sword.

Oeneus. King of Pleuron and Calydon, husband of

Althaea and father of Tydeus (q.v.), Meleager (q.v.), Gorge and Deineira (q.v.). His realm was seized by his nephews but his grandson Diomedes (q.v.) avenged him and put Andraemon, husband of Gorge, on the throne. He accompanied Diomedes to the Peleponnesus where he was killed by two nephews who had escaped Diomedes. Deineira (q.v.) married Heracles (q.v.).

Oenomaus. A son of Ares (q.v.), king of Elis. An oracle said he would be killed by his son-in-law. Therefore he challenged all his daughter's suitors to a chariot race and if they won they would marry his daughter Hippodameia: if they lost they were put to death. His own chariot was drawn by wind-born horses, a gift from Ares. But he was murdered by Myrtilus at the instigation of Pelops (q.v.).

Oenone. A nymph who loved Paris (q.v.). He deserted her for Helen (q.v.) and when he was wounded by Philoctetes (q.v.) she refused to help him. Then, in-remorse at his death, she committed suicide.

Oileus. One of the Argonauts (q.v.), and father of Ajax (q.v.).

Olympia. A small province in the western Peloponnesus, isolated from the centre and east of the Peloponnesus by high mountains. The site of a major sanctuary of Zeus (q.v.) whose worship replaced that of an early female divinity in the 9th century B.C. However, it was not till about 470 B.C. that a magnificent temple was built to Zeus. From 776 B.C. though, the Olympic games had been celebrated at Olympia in honour of Zeus. These quadrennial contests were international in character and an international truce accompanied their celebration. The prestige of the games was great and from 776 Greek chronology was based on the games, an "Olympiad" being a four-year cycle. Hence Olympiad 12, 1 denoted the 1st year in a four-year period after 11 previous Olympiads. If the number of Olympiads is multiplied by 4 and deducted from 776 we have our date *e.g.* 11 × 4 = 44, subtracted from 776 is 732 B.C.

Olympius. A term for any deity or muse inhabiting Olympus and not the Underworld.

Olympus Mt. The highest peak in Greece on the borders of Thessaly and Macedonia. Its 2975 m are almost inaccessible and it was not climbed until 1913. It was believed to be the home of the twelve Olympian gods.

Omphale. Queen of Lydia and widow of Tmolus who purchased Heracles (q.v.) as a slave. He served her for three years and one tradition says he dressed as a woman and swapped clothes with Omphale during this period.

Ops. Roman goddess of plenty, a consort of Saturn (q.v.) and the personification of abundance.

Orcus. The Roman name for Hades (q.v.) and for his realm.

Orestes. The son of Clytemnestra (q.v.) and Agamemnon (q.v.). As a child he was smuggled out of Mycenae by his sister Electra (q.v.) when Clytemnestra and Aegisthus (q.v.) seized power. He took refuge at the court of king Strophius in Phocis, becoming a close friend of Pylades (q.v.), the king's son. When of age he, Pylades and Electra killed Aegisthus and Clytemnestra, and Orestes was punished for his matricide by the Erinnyes (q.v.). He fled to the Acropolis of Athens and embraced the image of the goddess. Athene (q.v.) then summoned the Areopagus to judge his case. Apollo (q.v.), whose oracle had encouraged his crime, defended him on the grounds that fatherhood was more important than motherhood. Athene's casting vote found him innocent. Another tradition says Apollo told him he could be free of the Erinnyes by fetching the statue of Artemis (q.v.) from the Tauric Chersonese. Orestes and Pylades went to Tauris and were seized by the natives for sacrifice to Artemis. But it transpired that his sister Iphigenia (q.v.) was the priestess and she helped them steal the statue and return to Greece. They met Electra and went on to Mycenae where Orestes killed Aegisthus' son and became king. Later he slew his rival Neoptolemus (q.v.) and married his cousin Hermione.

Oreithyia. See **Boreas.** He turned her into a wind.

Orion. A giant, son of Poseidon (q.v.) who was a renowned hunter and very handsome. He loved Merope, daughter of Oenopion of Chios and was promised her hand in return for ridding Chios of wild animals. This he did but Oenopion would not give up Merope which led Orion to seduce her. Oenopion, with the help of his father Dionysus, blinded Orion who was told by the oracle he could only recover his sight by going to the east and gazing on the sun as it rose. This he did with the help of Hephaestus (q.v.) and once there Eos (q.v.) fell in love with him and Helios (q.v.) restored his sight. Later he joined Artemis (q.v.) in a hunt. Apollo (q.v.) angry at his boasting that he would kill all the wild beasts and afraid he would seduce Artemis contrived his death at the unwitting hands of Artemis. She placed his image in the stars, his constellation rising with the sun at the autumnal equinox.

Orpheus. The son of king Oeagrus of Thrace and Calliope (q.v.). The Greeks regarded him as the first great poet. He could enchant the beasts and trees with his lyre, a gift from Apollo (q.v.). After returning from the voyage of the Argonauts (q.v.) he married Eurydice (q.v.). His grief at losing her after redeeming her from Hades (q.v.) led to a failure to honour Dionysus (q.v.) at a Bacchanalia and he was torn to pieces by Bacchae (q.v.). The muses buried the pieces at the foot of Mt. Olympus (q.v.) save his head which was thrown into the River Hebrus still singing. The head and his lyre eventually floated to Lesbos (q.v.) and were finally placed amongst the stars at the request of Apollo and the Muses. *See also* **Orphism, Section J.**

Orthrus. A giant two-headed dog, the offspring of Typhon (q.v.) and Echidne (q.v.) and, some say, the father of the Sphinx (q.v.) and Chimaera (q.v.). It was set to watch the oxen of Geryon (q.v.) and was slain by Heracles (q.v.).

Ortygia (1) Port of Syracuse in Sicily.
(2) Port of Delos (q.v.), birthplace of Artemis (q.v.).

Otus and Ephialtes. Twin sons of Iphimedeia and Poseidon (q.v.), named Aloeidae after their mother's later husband Aloeus. At an early age they imprisoned Ares (q.v.) and later swore to rape Hera (q.v.) and Artemis (q.v.). In a vain effort to achieve this they placed Mt. Pelion on top of Mt. Ossa and attacked Heaven. But Artemis induced them to seek her at Naxos. Here she leapt between them in the form of a doe and they accidentally slew each other. In Tartarus (q.v.) their shades were tied back to back by bonds of vipers.

Ovid. *See* **B46.**

P

Palaemon. A sea god, the son of Athamas and Ino who was originally named Melicertes.

Palamedes. *See* **Odysseus.**

Pales. Italic deity of flocks and herds, worshipped on the Palatine.

Palicus. An obscure god or hero worshipped in Sicily and mentioned in the *Aeneid* (q.v.).

Palinurus. "Wind Astern", the helmsman of Aeneas. He managed the ship between the Scylla and Charybdis (q.v.) and in the storm off the coast of Carthage but later fell asleep and into the sea. He was cast ashore but murdered by local tribesmen. His shade begged Aeneas for carriage across the Styx (q.v.) so it could be at rest, but the Sybil refused as he had not been properly buried. However she promised him a shrine, Capo Pulinuro in Lucania near modern Salerno.

Palladium. A mythical statue of Athene given to Dardanus (q.v.) by Zeus (q.v.) to ensure the protection of Troy. By one tradition it was stolen by Odysseus (q.v.) and Diomedes (q.v.). By another Aeneas (q.v.) saved it and brought it to Rome where it saved the city several times in its early years.

Pallas. (1) A title of Athene (q.v.) given to her by the Achaens. Pallas, Kore and Parthenos signify a virgin, maiden or girl.
(2) One of the 24 Giants (q.v.) who rebelled against Zeus (q.v.).
(3) A brother of Aegeus (q.v.). *See also* **Theseus.**
(4) An ancestor of Evander (q.v.).
(5) Evander's son who went to follow Aeneas (q.v.).

Pan. A god, half-man, half-goat, said by some to be a son of Zeus (q.v.) by others to be the son of Hermes (q.v.) and Penelope with whom he inhabited Arcadia. He was a patron of shepherds and herdsmen and a lover of mischief. When not frolicking with the nymphs he liked to startle peasants and flocks inspiring "panic". He loved and

pursued Syrinx whose flight from him resulted in her being transformed into a reed from which he made a seven-piped flute, the syrinx. He also seduced Selene (q.v.). Sometimes identified with the Roman Faunus (q.v.).

Pandarus. A Trojan archer who broke a truce by shooting at the Greeks. In Chaucer's *Troilus and Criseyde* and Shakespeare's *Troilus and Cressida* he is Cressida's uncle and the lovers' go-between. The word "pandar" is derived from his name for this reason.

Pandora. "All gifts", the first woman fashioned and given life by Hephaestus (q.v.) and Athene (q.v.). Zeus (q.v.) sent her to punish man after Prometheus (q.v.) had given him fire. She married the brother of Prometheus, Epimetheus. Her curiosity led her to open a box which it was forbidden to touch, and from it sprang all the evils and diseases which beset mankind. Only hope was left at the bottom of the box.

Parcae. The Roman equivalent of the "Fates" or Horae.

Paris. Son of Priam (q.v.) and Hecuba (q.v.) who dreamed during her pregnancy that she would bring forth a blazing firebrand. As a child he was exposed on Mt. Ida. Raised by shepherds he was named Paris or sometimes Alexander ("defender of men") because of his courage. He loved and deserted Oenone (q.v.) which eventually caused his death. Promised the fairest of women by Aphrodite (q.v.) if he gave her the apple of discord, he did as she bade. Reunited with his parents he then left for Sparta whence he seduced Helen (q.v.) thus starting the Trojan War. At one point in the war Aphrodite saved him from death in a duel with Menelaus. He shot the arrow which slew Achilles (q.v.) at the Scaean Gate but was himself mortally wounded by Philoctetes (q.v.).

Parnassus, Mt. 2461 m peak in the Pindus range, north-east of Delphi (q.v.). Home of Apollo (q.v.) and the Muses (q.v.) hence the name "Montparnasse" for the hill in Paris on which centred the university and cultural life of that city. On the original's slopes was also the Corycian Cave, a centre of the Bacchae (q.v.).

Parthenon. *See* **L94.**

Parthenope. A nymph whose body was said to have washed up at Neapolis (Naples) around 600 B.C. She gave her name to the short-lived Parthenopean Republic of Naples established by Napoleon in 1799.

Parthenopeus. *See* **Seven Against Thebes.**

Parthenos. *See* **Pallas.**

Pasiphaë. Daughter of Helios (q.v.) and Persë, and wife of Minos (q.v.). Mother of the Minotaur (q.v.) by the Cretan Bull (q.v.) and of many children, including Ariadne (q.v.), Glaucus and Phaedra, by Minos.

Patroclus. Cousin and bosom companion of Achilles (q.v.) whom he met at the court of Peleus (q.v.) while in exile for an accidental murder. Slain by Hector (q.v.) while wearing Achilles' armour, his death persuaded Achilles to re-enter the Trojan War.

Pausanias. Spartan king who intervened to moderate Lysander's arrogant attitude towards Athens and other Greek cities after the Peloponnesian War.

Pegasus. Winged horse, offspring of Poseidon (q.v.) and Medusa (q.v.). It was captured by Bellerophon (q.v.) at the fountain of Pirene and helped him slay the Chimaera (q.v.). It struck Mt. Helicon with its hoof and brought forth the spring of Hippocrene, sacred to the Muses.

Peleus. The son of Aeacus, king of Aegina. With his brother Telamon he killed their half-brother Phocus and the two were expelled to Phthia in Thessaly by Aeacus. Here Eurytion purified them of murder. They took part in the Calydonian Hunt when they accidentally killed Eurytion. They then fled to the court of Acastus (q.v.) of Iolcis. Zeus (q.v.) married him to Thetis (q.v.) though he himself loved Thetis. This was because the oracle foretold that her son would be greater than his father. Their son was Achilles (q.v.). All the gods save Eris (q.v.) were invited to the wedding and in revenge she cast the Apple of Discord. Peleus later ruled the Myrmidones at Phthia.

Pelias. *See* **Jason.**

Pelicles. Son of Peleus *i.e.* Achilles (q.v.).

Peloponnesus. The "island of Pelops" (q.v.), the large southern peninsula of mainland Greece, attached to northern Greece by the Corinthian isthmus.

Pelops. Son of Tantalus (q.v.) king of Lydia. Tantalus cut him in pieces and served him to the gods at a meal. Only Demeter (q.v.) grieving for Persephone (*q.v.*) did not realise and she ate Pelops' shoulder. Zeus (*q.v.*) restored him to life by having Hermes (*q.v.*) boil him in a pot. Demeter gave him an ivory shoulder, said to be the birthmark of his descendants. His shoulder blade was later taken to Troy (*q.v.*) by the Greeks as the oracle said this was necessary if the city were to fall. He married Hippodamia.

Pelorus. One of the Sparti (*q.v.*).

Penates. Roman deities of the home, confused from early times with the *genius* and the Lares. Eventually a wide variety of deities, *e.g.* Mars, Mercury, Venus, were regarded as *"di Penates"* that is, "guardians of the hearth".

Penelope. The wife of Odysseus (*q.v.*), usually seen as a symbol of fidelity. One tradition in the Peloponnesus made her adulterous and the mother of Pan (*q.v.*) by Hermes (*q.v.*) or by all of her many suitors.

Peneus. The son of Oceanus (*q.v.*) and Tethys. A river god and father of Daphne (*q.v.*) and Cyrene (*q.v.*). Identified with the River Peneus in Thessaly.

Penthesilea. Daughter of Otrere and Ares (*q.v.*), queen of the Amazons (*q.v.*) who helped the Trojans. Slain by Achilles (*q.v.*) they fell in love as she died and he later mourned her. When the wretched Thersites mocked his grief Achilles slew him which caused his kinsman Diomedes (*q.v.*) to throw her corpse into the Scamander. It was retrieved and honourably buried.

Pentheus. Grandson of Cadmus (*q.v.*) and king of Thebes. The subject of Euripedes' *Bacchae*. He refused to allow Dionysus (*q.v.*) into the city but the god, in disguise, persuaded him to dress as one of the Bacchae (*q.v.*) and watch their orgies. He was then torn to pieces by the Bacchae, led by his own mother who was in a trance.

Perdix (or **Talos**). *See* **Daedalus.**

Periclymenus. The son of Neleus (*q.v.*) and brother of Nestor (*q.v.*). An Argonaut (*q.v.*) he could assume any form he chose. Slain by Heracles (*q.v.*).

Periphetes. A giant residing at Epidaurus who murdered travellers with an iron club. Slain by Theseus (*q.v.*) who henceforth carried his club.

Perse. The daughter of Oceanus (*q.v.*). Wife of Helios (*q.v.*) to whom she bore Circe (*q.v.*), Pasiphaë (*q.v.*), Aeetes and Perses (*q.v.*).

Persephone. Daughter of Zeus (*q.v.*) and Demeter (*q.v.*). She spent the winter months with Hades (*q.v.*) when nothing grew and with Demeter she spent the fertile months. Thus she was a goddess of vegetation. She was also queen of the Underworld and was a symbol of death. Known to the Romans as Proserpina. Her companion in the Underworld was Hecate (*q.v.*).

Perses. The son of Helios (*q.v.*) and Perse (*q.v.*) father of Hecate (*q.v.*).

Perseus. Grandson of Acrisius (*q.v.*) king of Argos and the son of Zeus (*q.v.*) and Danae (*q.v.*). Raised at the court of Polydectes who sent him to fetch the head of Medusa (*q.v.*). Hermes (*q.v.*) gave him a sickle with which to do this and told him how, via the Graeae (*q.v.*) he could procure Hades' (*q.v.*) helmet of invisibility, winged sandals and a magic wallet to help him in the task. Once he had the head he petrified the Titan Atlas (*q.v.*) with it. He then flew to Aethiopia where he found Andromeda (*see* **Cassiopeia**). Returning to Seriphos he slew Polydectes, made Dictys (*q.v.*) king and returned to Argos. He went on later to exchange the kingdom of Argos for that of his cousin Megaperthes of Tiryns.

Phaebus ("Shining"). A name used for Apollo (*q.v.*) at Delos (*q.v.*) where he was associated with Artemis (*q.v.*).

Phaedra. The daughter of Minos (*q.v.*) and wife of Theseus (*q.v.*) to whom she bore Acamas and Demephon. *See also* **Hippolytus.**

Phaeton. The son of Helios (*q.v.*) and Clymene. Helios let him drive the chariot of the sun across the sky but he lost control of it and was killed by a thunderbolt from Zeus (*q.v.*) for almost setting the world on fire. He fell into the River Po and his sisters who mourned him were turned into poplar or alder trees and their tears into amber.

Phalanthus. Mythical founder of Tarentum in Italy.

Philemon. The husband of Baucis. This old Phrygian couple once received Zeus (*q.v.*) and Hermes (*q.v.*) with great hospitality.

Philoctetes. The son of Poecas, nephew of Protesilaus, and companion of Heracles (*q.v.*). He lit Heracles funeral pyre and received his bow and arrows. On the way to Troy (*q.v.*) one of the poisoned arrows wounded him, or he was bitten

by a snake on the island of Tenedos. The smell of the wound became so offensive that on the advice of Odysseus (*q.v.*) he was left on Lemnos. Later an oracle revealed that Troy would not fall till the bow and arrows of Heracles were brought to the Greeks and Odysseus and Diomedes (*q.v.*) fetched him to Troy. Here either Machaon or Podalirius, the sons of Asclepius (*q.v.*) cured him of his wound. He slew Paris (*q.v.*) and later settled in Italy.

Philomela. *See* **Procne.**

Phineus. King of Salmydessus in Thrace and the son of Agenor. He first married Cleopatra, then Idaca who falsely accused her stepsons of improper advances. Phineus imprisoned them and was made blind and pursued by the Harpies (*q.v.*). Eventually the Argonauts (*q.v.*) whose ranks included Zetes and Calais, Cleopatra's brothers, slew the Harpies. Phineus freed the stepsons and told Jason (*q.v.*) what course to set.

Phlegethon ("Blazing"). A river of the Underworld called the "river of flames" by Plato. The shades of those who had committed crimes of violence against their kin were roasted in it until they received forgiveness.

Phlegyas. A king of the Lapithae (*q.v.*) who burnt Apollo's (*q.v.*) shrine at Delphi and was punished for it in the Underworld by having to sit beneath a huge rock which was liable to fall at any time.

Phocis. Small mountainous province of northern Greece which held the oracle of Delphi.

Phocus. *See* **Peleus.**

Phoebe ("Bright"). In early myth the daughter of Heaven and Earth and mother of Leto (*q.v.*). Later identified with Artemis (*q.v.*) the moon-goddess.

Phoenix ("Red"). (1) Companion and tutor of Achilles (*q.v.*) who tried to reconcile him with Agamemnon (*q.v.*).

(2) The brother of Cadmus (*q.v.*) and Europa (*q.v.*), eponymous ancestor of the Phoenicians.

(3) A mythological Egyptian bird which died on a funeral pyre every 500 years before rising again from the ashes.

Phorcys. A sea-god, the father of Echidne (*q.v.*), Ladon, the Gorgons (*q.v.*) and the Graeae (*q.v.*).

Phrixus and **Helle.** Brother and sister, the children of Athamas king of Aeolia. Their stepmother, Ino (*q.v.*), had engineered their sacrifice by Athamas out of jealousy but they escaped on a flying ram with a golden fleece sent by Zeus (*q.v.*). Helle fell off into what was henceforth the Hellespont, but Phrixus reached Colchis and sacrificed the ram to Zeus (*see* **Jason**). The ram's image was placed amongst the stars as Aries.

Phyllis. *See* **Demophon.**

Picus. An ancient Italian god represented as a woodpecker *i.e.* "*picus*".

Pierides. A name applied to the Muses (*q.v.*). It was derived from the inhabitants of Pieria, on the south coast of Macedonia, who were noted for their worship of the Muses.

Also a name for nine daughters of Pierus king of Macedonia who were defeated in a contest by the Muses and turned into birds.

Pillars of Hercules. Two pillars, Calpe and Abyla, erected on either side of the straits of Gibraltar by Heracles (*q.v.*).

Pilumnus. An ancient minor Italian god, "the spearman".

Pindar. *See* **B48.**

Pirithous. Son of Ixion (*q.v.*) and Dia, companion of Theseus (*q.v.*) and king of the Lapithae (*q.v.*). He led the fight on the Centaurs (*q.v.*). On the death of his wife Hippodamia he and Theseus abducted the young Helen (*q.v.*) of Troy. She fell by lot to Theseus who, in return and despite misgivings, promised to help Pirithous abduct a daughter of Zeus (*q.v.*) for himself. They attempted to abduct Persephone (*q.v.*) from the Underworld but Hades (*q.v.*) chained them to a rock. Heracles (*q.v.*) later freed Theseus but Pirithous was left to suffer torment for his sins.

Pleiades. The seven daughters of Atlas (*q.v.*) and Pleione and companions of Artemis (*q.v.*). Zeus (*q.v.*) turned them into doves and placed their image in the stars to save them from the attentions of Orion (*q.v.*) who pursued them for five years. A group of seven poets in 3rd century B.C. Alexandria also called themselves the Pleiad.

Plutarch. *See* **B48.**

Pluto. (1) A Roman name for Hades (*q.v.*), "the rich one" who owns the riches of the earth itself.

(2) A nymph who was mother of Tantalus (q.v.) by Zeus (q.v.).

Podarces. (1) See **Priam**.

(2) Son of Iphiclus, leader of the Thessalians who fought at Troy (q.v.).

Polites. A son of Priam (q.v.) and Hecabe (q.v.), slain before their eyes by Neoptolemus (q.v.).

Pollux. The Roman name for Polydeuces. See **Castor**.

Polydeuces. See **Castor**.

Polydorus. (1) The son of Cadmus (q.v.) and Harmonia and ancestor of Oedipus (q.v.) and other great Theban kings.

(2) The youngest son of Priam (q.v.) and Hecabe (q.v.).

Polymnia. See **Muses**.

Polynices. The son of Jocasta and Oedipus (q.v.), brother of Eteocles (q.v.), Antigone (q.v.) and Ismene (q.v.). See also **Seven Against Thebes**. When Creon refused to allow his burial Antigone (q.v.) disregarded the order and buried the corpse.

Polypemon. Also known as Procrustes, "the stretcher". A robber who tied travellers to a bed and if they were too tall he cut off their legs; if too short he put them on a rack. Theseus (q.v.) did the same to him.

Polyphemus. See **Cyclopes and Galatea**.

Polyxena. The daughter of Priam (q.v.) and Hecuba (q.v.) beloved by Achilles (q.v.) whose shade requested her sacrifice by Neoptolemus (q.v.) after Troy's (q.v.) fall. This is the theme of Euripedes' *Hecabe*.

Pomona. An Italian goddess of tree-fruits (*poma*) e.g. apples. She was a minor deity but had her own priest and sanctuary near Rome. Ovid links her with Vertumnus, an Etruscan god with the power to change his shape. He was god of the changing seasons and the ripening fruits of autumn, and also of money changing. *Vertere* means "change" in Latin. He loved Pomona and pursued her disguised as a harvester, vine-dresser, herdsman and old woman, but only won her when he appeared as himself. His statue stood in the Vicus Tuscus, a busy street of brothels and shops named after him as an Etruscan.

Pontus. The sea, offspring of Ge (q.v.) the earth.

Pontus Euxinus. The "Hospitable Sea", the Greek name for the Black Sea. The name was an attempt to flatter and placate a hostile sea which was much feared by sailors.

Porphyrion. See **Giants**.

Porsenna. See **Lars Porsenna**.

Portunus. A Roman sea-deity associated with harbours.

Poseidon. The Roman N ntune, a god of earthquakes, and later of the sea. The eldest son of Cronus (q.v.) and Rhea. When he and Zeus (q.v.) and Hades (q.v.) cast lots for their realms he won the sea and had an underwater palace near Aegae in Euboea. Here he kept horses with brazen hoofs and gold manes who drew his chariot across the sea. Its passage calmed the sea. Poseidon created the horse and invented the bridle. As a horse he raped Demeter (q.v.) who was disguised as a mare. Their offspring was the horse Arion and the nymph Despoena and, some say, Persephone (q.v.). He resented Zeus (q.v.) and helped Hera (q.v.) and Apollo (q.v.) enchain him. In punishment Zeus made him a servant of Laomedon (q.v.) and he built the Neptunilia Pergama, the walls of Troy. He helped the Greeks at Troy but hated Odysseus (q.v.) who blinded Polyphemus (q.v.). He disputed the possession of Athens with Athene (q.v.) and lost, but Zeus gave him the Isthmus of Corinth instead. Here the Isthmian games were held in his honour. He married Amphitrite (q.v.). By mortal women he had many children including Pegasus (q.v.) and the Aloeidae (q.v.). He is usually portrayed with a trident which he used to shake the earth.

Priam. The son of Laomedon (q.v.) and husband of Hecuba (q.v.). Originally called Podarces his name was changed to Priam *i.e.* "ransomed" because Heracles (q.v.) spared him and sold him to Hesione (q.v.) his sister. He had fifty sons and fifty daughters, nineteen of whom were by Hecuba and included Hector (q.v.), Paris (q.v.), Helenus (q.v.) and Cassandra (q.v.). He begged Achilles (q.v.) to return Hector's body. Eventually slain at the altar of Zeus (q.v.) by Neoptolemus (q.v.).

Priapus. The son of Dionysus (q.v.) and Aphrodite (q.v.). A fertility god whose worship spread from the Hellespont to Greece and later Rome, though he was never taken seriously. He was often portrayed in the form of a red-faced scarecrow with a large detachable phallus and in this role was used to scare birds. The phallus became a truncheon to ward off other intruders. He was also a protector of cultivated gardens and a god of sailors. In Petronius' *Satyricon* he pursues the hero Encolpius and makes him impotent. Horace and Martial write of him lightheartedly and 85 obscene poems about him – *"priapeia"* - exist of unknown authorship. His sacrificial animal was the donkey, a symbol of lust.

Procne. The daughter of Pandion, king of Athens. Pandion gave her to Tereus in return for his assistance and they had a son Itys. But Tereus wanted her sister Philomela. He made Procne a slave and tore out her tongue, then seduced Philomela saying Procne was dead. Procne could only alert her sister and be free by stitching a message to her robe. Once free she slew Itys, cooked pieces of the corpse and fed it to Tereus. When Tereus learnt what had happened he chased the sisters with an axe but the gods turned him into a hawk, Procne into a swallow and Philomela a nightingale though some traditions say it was Philomela who lost her tongue and became a swallow.

Procris. Daughter of Erectheus of Athens and the wife of Cephalus. Eos (q.v.) who also loved Cephalus showed him that Procris was easily seduced in return for gold. Procris then fled to Crete and lived for a time with Minos (q.v.). On returning to Athens disguised as a youth she brought with her a hound and spear, gifts from Artemis (q.v.), which never missed their quarry. Cephalus so wanted the gifts that the couple were reconciled. But Procris suspected Cephalus of having an affair with Eos and followed him on a hunt where he accidentally killed her with the spear.

Procrustes. See **Polypemon**.

Proetus. The son of Abas (q.v.) king of Argolis. His twin brother Acrisius (q.v.) expelled him and he fled to Lydia where he married Anteia (also called Sthenebosa) daughter of king Iobates (see **Bellerophon**). He later returned to Argolis and forced Acrisius to give him half the kingdom. He ruled from Tiryns whose huge walls he built with the aid of the Cyclopes (q.v.). Eventually gave two thirds of his kingdom to Melampus (q.v.) and Bias.

Prometheus. A Titan (q.v.) and the brother of Epimetheus (q.v.) or "afterthought" and Atlas (q.v.). Sometimes said to be the maker of mankind. He supported Zeus (q.v.) against his brother Titans but stole fire from Olympus and gave it to men. This angered Zeus who took revenge on man through Pandora (q.v.) and punished Prometheus by chaining him to a rock in the Caucasus. Here an eagle tore at his liver each day. The liver was renewed daily and Prometheus suffered this torment until Heracles (q.v.) rescued him.

Proserpina. Roman counterpart of Persephone (q.v.).

Proteus. A sea god and a subject of Poseidon (q.v.). He had the power of prophecy and could change his form. He would avoid prophecy by changing form until tightly gripped; then he appeared in his true shape and spoke the truth. Said to live on the isle of Pharos in the Nile Delta. Menelaus (q.v.) mastered him while returning from Troy (q.v.) and forced him to reveal the way to Sparta.

Psyche. In Greek literature, the "soul" personified, often portrayed as a butterfly. As the centre of emotion she was tormented by *"eros"*. Her beauty made Aphrodite (q.v.) jealous and she sent Eros (q.v.) to torment her. Instead he fell in love with her though he would not let her see him or disclose his identity. But at the bidding of her two sisters she sought to discover who he was. For the first time she saw him, holding a candle above him as he slept, but hot wax fell on him. He woke and left her to seek him. After many trials she found him, became immortal and was united with Eros for ever.

Pygmalion. (1) The king of Tyre and brother of Dido (q.v.).

(2) The king of Cyprus who made and fell in love with a maiden's statue. Aphrodite (q.v.) answered his prayers and gave the statue life as the girl Galatea. They married and had two sons, Paphus and Metharme. In some versions the tale he is a sculptor. The basis of Shaw's *Pygmalion* and the musical *My Fair Lady*.

Pylades. Husband of Electra (q.v.). See also **Orestes**.

Pyramus and **Thisbe**. The lovers in a tale by Ovid which he heard in the East. Living in Babylon they are forbidden to meet but converse through a chink in a wall. They arrange a meeting at the tomb of Ninus but Thisbe, arriving first, was chased away by a lion and dropped her veil. Finding this, Pyramus thought her dead and committed suicide. She returned and slew herself on his sword. Since that time the nearby mulberry has borne fruit the colour of blood. This is the basis of Bottom's tale in Shakespeare's *A Midsummer Night's Dream*.

Pyrrhus. Another name for Neoptolemus.

Pythia. The priestess of Apollo (*q.v.*) at Delphi (*q.v.*).

Python. A she-dragon of Mt. Parnassus who controlled the oracle at Delphi (*q.v.*). The boy Apollo (*q.v.*) slew her and the Pythia (*q.v.*) took over her task of giving voice to oracles.

Q

Quirinus. A very ancient Roman deity whose cult was centred on the Quirinal. The Romans eventually forgot his original character and he was identified with Mars (*q.v.*) in classical times, though Romulus (*q.v.*) was also supposed to have adopted the name after his deification.

R

Rape of the Sabine Women. An episode recounted by Livy and Ovid to explain the intermarriage of the Roman settlers and natives. Romulus (*q.v.*) and his followers invited the surrounding tribes to celebrate a festival in the Circus Maximus then carried off the native girls. War broke out but the Sabine women, who had been well treated, intervened to restore peace. The event has been the subject of paintings by Poussin and Rubens and of a group of statues by Giovanni da Bologna.

Remus. *See* Romulus.

Rhadamanthus. The son of Zeus (*q.v.*) and Europa (*q.v.*), brother of Minos (*q.v.*) and Sarpedon (*q.v.*). Once the ruler of part of Crete but Minos forced him to flee to Boeotia (*q.v.*). Famed for his wisdom and justice he was made one of the judges of the Underworld after his death. He married Alcmene (*q.v.*) on the death of Amphitrion (*q.v.*).

Rhea. (1) A Titaness, daughter of Ge (*q.v.*) and Uranus (*q.v.*). *See* Cronus.
(2) *See* Romulus.

Rhesus. A Thracian king who helped the Trojans. An oracle said that if his magnificent snow-white horses ate the grass of the Trojan plain and drank of the River Scamander Troy would not fall. Diomedes (*q.v.*) and Odysseus (*q.v.*) raided his camp, slew him, and stole the horses.

Rhodos/Rhode. The daughter of Poseidon (*q.v.*), wife of Helios (*q.v.*).

Rome. The "eternal city" sited on the banks of the Tiber. Traditionally founded in 753 B.C. (year 1 of the Roman calendar) by Romulus (*q.v.*). It only really became a city in the 6th century under the Tarquins. Under the Republic it had a population of two or three hundred thousand, of 450,000 by the time of Augustus and 1,000,000 under the Antonines, though the population was occasionally reduced by wars, fires and plagues.

Romulus. The legendary founder of Rome (*q.v.*), twin brother of Remus and together the sons of Rhea or Rhea Silvia. She was the daughter of Numitor, king of Alba Longa (*q.v.*) who was deposed by his brother. Her uncle compelled her to become a Vestal Virgin (*q.v.*) but she bore Romulus and Remus, according to her, by Mars (*q.v.*). Her uncle then imprisoned her and threw the babies into the Tiber. The shepherd Faustulus (*q.v.*) found a wolf suckling them and reared them. When they reached manhood they returned to Alba Longa, restored Numitor to the throne and set off to found a city of their own. They went to the site of Rome and decided to consult the gods. Romulus chose the Palatine Hill, his childhood home, as the centre of the city, Remus the Aventine (*q.v.*). The gods favoured Romulus, sending him an extraordinary omen of twelve vultures, Remus only six. Thus Romulus was given the honour of founding Rome which he did by ploughing a furrow around the Palatine. As he commenced building the city wall Remus derisively jumped over it, a quarrel ensued and Romulus slew him. Romulus took in fugitives in order to populate the city, found them wives by the "Rape of the Sabine women" (*q.v.*) and reigned for forty years before disappearing in a whirlwind on the Campus Martius. He was deified and identified with the Sabine god Quirinus (*q.v.*).

Rubicon. *See* L107.

S

Sabines. A branch of the Samnite race and one of the Sabellian peoples who occupied the Etruscanised area on the middle valley of the Tiber around Falerii. To the south of Rome they held the mountainous land between Rome and Campania. They were a constant threat to early Rome and the tradition that one Titus Tatius, a Sabine prince, was offered joint rule by Romulus (*q.v.*) may indicate a period of Sabine occupation or domination of Rome.

Sabinus. A mythical Sabine king.

Salmoneus. The son of Aeolus (*q.v.*) and brother of Sisyphus (*q.v.*). The founder of Salmone. His pride led him to emulate the thunder and lightning of Zeus (*q.v.*) who slew him and crushed his city with a thunderbolt.

Sarpedon. The son of Zeus (*q.v.*) and Europa (*q.v.*), brother of Minos (*q.v.*) and Rhadamanthus (*q.v.*). The three brothers quarrelled over the love of the youth Miletus (*q.v.*). Sarpedon went to Asia Minor and became king of the Lycians after helping king Cilix of Cilicia defeat them. Zeus allowed him to live three generations and he helped Troy (*q.v.*) in the Trojan war. Patroclus (*q.v.*) slew him.

Saturn. From *Satus i.e.* "sown". Ancient Mediterranean god of agriculture, possibly of Ligurian origin and particularly revered in Sardinia (*q.v.*) and Africa (*q.v.*). Later identified with Cronus (*q.v.*) who supposedly emigrated to Italy after being deposed by Zeus (*q.v.*). Here he presided over a mythical "Golden Age". His temple in Rome was consecrated in 497 B.C. and housed the state treasury. His festival, the Saturnalia, was celebrated near the winter solstice, originally on 17 December but from the 4th century A.D. on New Year's Day. During the celebrations complete licence was given, slaves took the place of their masters, presents were given, a "Lord of Misrule" appointed and merrymaking and disorder of every kind was rife. It may be that in primitive times his worship involved the sacrifice of humans because in classical times rush dummies in human shape (*argei*) were flung into the Tiber each year on 15 May in his honour.

Satyrs. Young spirits of wildlife, the woods and hillsides. Sons of Hermes (*q.v.*) closely associated with Dionysus (*q.v.*). They were possessed by lechery and a love of wine and embodied the fertile force of nature. Usually they were personified with pointed ears, horns and a tail like Pan's (*q.v.*).

Scaean Gate. The "left hand", the gate in the walls of Troy (*q.v.*) where Achilles (*q.v.*) fell.

Scamander, River. River in Asia Minor near Troy (*q.v.*), originally called the Xanthus. Its name was changed when the mythical Scamander (*q.v.*) of Crete founded a colony in Phrygia and jumped into the river.

Scamander. One-time king of Crete, father of Teucer (*q.v.*) by the nymph Idaea and therefore an ancestor of the Trojans.

Sciron. A robber who dwelt on the border of Attica and Megara. He preyed on travellers and forced them to wash his feet on the Scironian rock. He then kicked them off the rock into the sea to be eaten by a giant turtle. Theseus (*q.v.*) slew him.

Scylla. (1) *See* Minos.
(2) *See* Charybdis.

Scyrus. Aegean isle, half-way between Lesbos and Euboea and off the major trade routes. It was of no importance save in legend: here Achilles (*q.v.*) was hidden by Lycomedes. It was also here that Lycomedes threw Theseus (*q.v.*) from a rock while the hero was in voluntary exile from Athens after giving the city its first constitution. In 470 B.C. Cimon expelled the local populace in order to install Athenian colonists. At the same time he found the reputed body of Theseus and took it back to Athens amidst great pomp.

Selene. Eastern goddess whom the Greeks identified with Artemis (q.v.) and the Romans with Diana (q.v.) or the older moon goddess Luna. Both also identified her with Hecate (q.v.) and thus the moon became associated with sorcery.

Semele. See **Dionysus.**

Semiramis. The wife of Ninus. These two were the mythical founders of Ninus or Nineveh.

Seven Against Thebes. Oedipus (q.v.) cursed his sons for neglecting him, saying they would divide their kingdom by the sword. To avoid this Eteocles and Polynices agreed to rule in turn but Eteocles then refused to give up the throne when his term expired. Polynices sought the help of Adrastus (q.v.) king of Argos and married his daughter Argia while her sister married Tydeus son of Oeneus of Calydon who was in exile because of a murder he had committed. Amphiaraus the seer (brother-in-law of Adrastus) prophesied death for all who marched on Thebes save Adrastus. But on the advice of Tydeus, Polynices bribed Eriphyle into persuading Amphiaraus to join them. These four were joined by Capaneus, Hippomedon and Parthenopaeus. The seven were initially successful but Teiresias (q.v.) prophesied that a Theban royal prince must sacrifice himself to save the city and Menoeceus did so. The fortunes of the seven now waned. Zeus (q.v.) killed Capaneus with a thunderbolt as he stormed the city walls. Tydeus was wounded by Melanippus but Athene (q.v.) intended to save him with an elixir from Zeus. But Amphiaraus, who had a grudge against him, persuaded him to drink the brains of Melanippus which so disgusted Athene she let him die. Hippomedon and Parthenopaeus were also slain. Polynices now fought a duel with Eteocles to settle the matter and both were mortally wounded. Amphiaraus was swallowed up by the earth and only Adrastus survived. See also **Antigone** and **Epigoni.**

Seven Hills of Rome. The Quirinal, Viminal, Esquiline, Caelian, Capitoline, Palatine and Aventine.

Seven Kings of Rome. Traditionally said to be Romulus, Numa Pompilius, Tullus Hostilius, Ancus Martius, Tarquinius Priscus, Servius Tullius and Tarquinius Superbus.

Seven Sages of Greece. Usually held to be Thales of Miletus, Bias of Priene, Solon, Chilo of Sparta who brought the bones of Orestes (q.v.) to Sparta, Periander of Corinth, Pittacus of Mytilene, a democrat, contemporary of Solon and opponent of Alcaeus, and Cleobulus of Rhodes.

Sibyl (Sibylla). A priestess and prophetess who uttered oracles. Localised in several places the term came to be used generically of many sibyls and Varro lists ten. The most famous was at Cumae in Campania and she told Aeneas (q.v.) how to enter the Underworld. Ovid says she was seven generations old when Aeneas met her and that Apollo (q.v.) had granted her request to live as many years as there were grains in a handful of sand. But she had forgotten to seek eternal youth and was now withered with age. In Petronius' *Satyricon* she hangs in a bottle and when asked what she wants replies "I want to die".

Sibylline Books. A Roman tradition tells how a sibyl (q.v.) offered Tarquinius Priscus nine prophetic books which he refused to buy at the price. She destroyed three and he still refused them; she burnt three more and he took the remaining three at the price demanded for the nine. Special priests kept them and they were consulted only when the Senate authorised it in time of need. In 83 B.C. the originals were destroyed by fire but replaced by new ones. Many later additions were made including Jewish and Christian forgeries and fourteen still exist. They were last consulted in the 4th century A.D. and shortly afterwards Stilicho had them burnt. The original books instructed the Romans to convey the sacred stone of Cybele to Rome.

Sigeum. Part of Troy (q.v.). Hence the Dardanelles were known as the "straits of Sigeum".

Sileni, Silenus. Scholars distinguish between *sileni* and satyrs (q.v.) but the two are very similar and the Greeks themselves seem to have made no distinction. They are regarded as companions of Dionysus (q.v.) and have pointed ears, flat noses and the tail of a horse or goat. By the 6th century B.C. one of their number, Silenus, stands out from his fellows for his wisdom and is sometimes said to have been the tutor of Dionysus. His special

knowledge comes from wine drinking and like his fellows he is usually drunk. An old man with horse-ears and tail he proves a good raconteur when captured, though something of a comic drunkard.

Silvanus. Ancient Italian god, a protector of uncultivated land.

Sinis or **Sinnis.** A robber of the Corinthian Isthmus who killed travellers by tying them to the tops of fir trees tied to the ground and then releasing the trees. Theseus (q.v.) slew him in the same fashion.

Sinon. A cousin of Odysseus (q.v.) and grandson of Autolycus the thief. When the Greeks pretended to leave Troy (q.v.) he remained in camp and persuaded the Trojans that the wooden horse was a gift in atonement for the theft of Athene's Palladium (q.v.). Once the horse was inside Troy he signalled the Greek fleet to return.

Sirens. In Homer two sisters who lure sailors to their death by their singing. Odysseus (q.v.) and the Argonauts (q.v.) withstood their fatal charms, the latter because Orpheus (q.v.) outsang them. They have been associated with the modern Galli islands. In non-Homeric tradition their number varies and they are portrayed as having the bodies of birds and heads of either sex. Some say they were daughters of Ge (q.v.) and companions of Persephone (q.v.) who escorted the dead to the Underworld. They were said to feed on the dead. Later they are given the heads of beautiful women and sing to console the dead they escort. Finally they lose their funerary and evil nature and develop fishes' tails like mermaids.

Sisyphus. The son of Aeolus and husband of the Pleiad Merope who bore him Glaucus. He was an ancestor of Bellerophon (q.v.) and also seduced Anticleia, mother of Odysseus (q.v.) and may have been his father. The founder of Ephyra (later Corinth) and an infamous rogue and knave he was condemned in the Underworld perpetually to push a large stone, uphill, only to see it always roll down, hence the term "labour of Sisyphus' to denote a futile task.

Sophocles. See **B56.**

Spartii. "The sown men" who sprang up when Cadmus (q.v.) sewed the dragon's teeth. They were fully armed and fought amongst themselves until only five remained, Echion, Udaeus, Chthonius, Hyperenor and Pelorus. These helped Cadmus build the Cadmea, citadel of Thebes, and were ancestors of the Thebans. The title was also given to their descendants. Cadmus saved some of the teeth and Jason (q.v.) had to sow these to get the Golden Fleece.

Sphinx. A fabulous monster with a human head and the body of a lion. In Egyptian mythology where it originates it could be of either sex but in Greek myth is a female and lives north of Thebes. It was the offspring of Echidne (q.v.) and Typhon (q.v.) or possibly Orthrus (q.v.) and the Chimaera (q.v.) and plagued Thebes by strangling and devouring all who could not answer her riddle: what walks on four legs at dawn, two at noon and three in the evening? Oedipus (q.v.) answered correctly that it was man who first crawls, then walks upright and finally uses a stick in old age. The sphinx then leapt from her rock and was dashed to pieces.

Stentor. Greek herald in the Trojan war who supposedly had a voice equal to that of fifty men. He died after Hermes (q.v.) beat him in a shouting match. His name gives us the word "stentorian' meaning extremely loud.

Steropes. One of the Cyclopes (q.v.).

Stheneboea. Another name for Anteia. See **Bellerophon.**

Sthenelus. (1) A king of Mycenae, the son of Perseus (q.v.) and Andromeda (q.v.). The husband of Nicippe by whom he was the father of Alcinoe, Medusa (q.v.) and Eurystheus (q.v.).

(2) The son of Capaneus and Evadne, a companion of Diomedes (q.v.) and one of the Epigoni (q.v.). One of the Greeks in the Wooden Horse (q.v.).

(3) A Trojan and companion of Aeneas (q.v.).

Stheno. One of the Gorgones (q.v.).

Strymon. River in Thrace, believed by the Greeks to be the home of the crane.

Stymphalian Birds. Monsters inhabiting Lake Stymphalus, a marshy area in northern Arcadia. They were huge birds with bronze beaks and claws that ate human flesh. They used their feathers as arrows. The birds were sacred to Ares (q.v.) but Heracles (q.v.) startled them with bronze castanets provided by Athene (q.v.) and shot them. Some say they flew to the Black Sea and were found there by the Argonauts (q.v.).

Styx. The river of "hate" in the Underworld and flowing several times around its perimeter. When dipped in it Achilles (q.v.) was made invulnerable. Ghosts could only cross it if they paid Charon (q.v.) to ferry them across and for this purpose a coin was placed beneath the tongue of corpses. On its far bank was Cerberus (q.v.). Aristophanes (q.v.) and others describe it as a marsh rather than a river though Herodotus (q.v.) identifies it with a trickle from the rock near Pheneus. It was associated with the cascade on Mt. Chelmos further west whose cold waters stain the rock black. Plutarch and Arrian say Alexander the Great was poisoned by water from here brought to him in a mule's hoof.

Sul or **Sulis.** A Celtic deity identified with Minerva (q.v.) by the Romans. The patron of Aquae Sulis.

Symplegades. Floating islands, like icebergs, at the entrance to the Bosphorus. They clashed together and crushed ships. Jason (q.v.), on the advice of Phineus, let loose a dove which made them recoil and as they did so the Argo (q.v.) slipped between them. Henceforth they remained stationary.

Syrinx. An Arcadian nymph. See **Pan.**

T

Talaus. The father of Adrastus (q.v.).

Talos. (1) A mythical brazen giant with a bull's head said to protect Crete.

(2) See **Daedalus.** Another name for Perdix.

Tantalus. A wealthy king, the son of Zeus (q.v.) and the nymph Pluto. The father of Pelops, Broteas and Niobe. He was favoured by Zeus and was invited to Olympian banquets but stole nectar (q.v.) and ambrosia (q.v.) and revealed Zeus' secrets. He received the golden dog made by Hephaestus (q.v.) for Rhea (q.v.) (which had watched Zeus' cradle) from Pandareus. This incensed the gods but Tantalus denied having seen it. Pandareus then put to a miserable death and his daughters were abducted by the Harpies (q.v.). His numerous other crimes included serving Pelops (q.v.) as a meal to the gods. For this he was punished in the Underworld, either by being placed beneath a huge rock which constantly threatened to fall and crush him or by being placed in a lake the waters of which receded whenever he tried to drink, while above his head were boughs of fruit "tantalisingly" behind his reach.

Tarchon. Legendary ancestor of the Etruscan "Tarquins" who lead a group of emigrants from Lydia to Italy and there founded Tarquinii and other Etruscan cities. He became an ally of Aeneas (q.v.).

Tarpeia. The daughter of Tarpeius, commander of the Roman garrison on the Capitol during the Sabine (q.v.) wars shortly after Rome's foundation. Her story is told by Livy. She treacherously offered to show the way into the citadel if the Sabine chief Tatius would give her that which his men "wore on their shield arms". By this she meant gold torques but instead the Sabines crushed her to death with their shields. The tale is an attempt to account for the name of the Tarpeian Rock (q.v.).

Tarpeian Rock. A precipice on the south-west corner of the Capitol from which traitors and other condemned criminals were thrown to their death. The last victim was an equestrian implicated in a conspiracy against Claudius in 43 A.D.

Tartarus. (1) Another name for Hades (q.v.) though in Homer it refers to the deepest reaches of the Underworld, a place of punishment to which the Titans (q.v.) and Centimani (q.v.) were consigned by Cronus (q.v.).

(2) Also the name of a son of Ge (q.v.) who was father, by his mother, of the monster Typhon (q.v.).

Teiresias or **Tiresias.** A blind Theban prophet, who, while young, had come upon Athene (q.v.) bathing in the nude. She had therefore blinded him but in compensation gave him the gift of prophecy. He revealed to Oedipus (q.v.) the truth of his incest. He helped Thebes against the Seven (q.v.) then died after drinking from the well of Tilphussa.

Odysseus (q.v.) consulted his shade in the land of the Cimmerians.

Telamon. The son of Aeacus and brother of Peleus (q.v.). After the two murdered their half-brother Phocus, his father expelled him to Salamis where he married Glauce and later succeeded her father as king. Next he married Periboea of Athens and she bore him Ajax (q.v.). A friend of Heracles (q.v.) and with him sacked Troy (q.v.). He carried off Hesione who bore him Teucer and his refusal to return her to her brother Priam (q.v.) was one cause of the Trojan war.

Telchines. Mythical beings, artists in metal work who made a sickle for Cronus (q.v.) and the trident for Poseidon (q.v.). They raised the infant Poseidon. At times they were destructive and interfered with the weather. They annoyed Zeus (q.v.) who drowned a number of them in a flood, and Apollo (q.v.) who took the form of a wolf to savage them.

Telemachus. See **Odysseus.**

Telephassa. The mother of Europa (q.v.) and Cadmus (q.v.) by Agenor.

Telephus. The son of Heracles (q.v.) and Auge (a priestess and daughter of Aleus, king of Tegea). Abandoned as a child, the Delphic oracle later directed him to the court of king Teuthras in Mysia where he found his mother married to Teuthras. He later succeeded Teuthras and married Laodice, daughter of Priam (q.v.). When the Greeks on their way to Troy (q.v.) landed in Mysia he repulsed them, but Dionysus (q.v.) caused him to trip on a vine and Achilles (q.v.) wounded him. An oracle told him he could only be cured by the one who wounded him while the Greeks were told they could not take Troy without his help. He therefore went to Achilles who cured the wound with rust from his spear and in return Telephus showed the Greeks the route to Troy.

Tempe. A vale in Thessaly where Apollo (q.v.) pursued Daphne (q.v.) and was purified of the killing of Python.

Tenedos. Small island off the coast of Asia Minor, south west of Troy (q.v.). Here Achilles (q.v.) slew king Tenes (q.v.) and his father Cyncus and here Philoctetes (q.v.) was wounded.

Tenes. The son of Apollo (q.v.) though reputed to be son of Cycnus, king of Colonae in Troas. His stepmother attempted to seduce him and, when he refused her, made false accusations against him. Cycnus then put Tenes and his sister Hemithea into a chest and cast it adrift at sea. It washed up on the isle of Leucophrys where Tenes became king and gave his name to the island, Tenedos (q.v.).

Tereus. See **Procne.**

Terpsichore. The muse of song and choral dance, portrayed with a lyre and plectrum.

Teucer. (1) The son of Scamander (q.v.) and the nymph Idaca. He gave the land to Dardanus (q.v.) on which Dardanus built Dardania. An ancestor of the Trojans.

(2) The son of Hesione and Telamon, half brother of Ajax (q.v.) behind whose shield he fought at Troy (q.v.).

Teucri. Name for the Trojans derived from that of their ancestor Teucer (q.v.).

Teuthras. See **Telephus.** The father of the girl Tecmessa. Ajax (q.v.) raided the Thracian Chersonese, slew him and abducted Tecmessa.

Tethys. A Titaness, mother of Oceanus (q.v.) of Metis.

Thalia. (1) Muse of comedy.

(2) One of the Charities (q.v.).

Thebe. The wife of Zethus, who gave her name to Thebes.

Themis. A Titaness, the daughter of Ge (q.v.) and Uranus (q.v.) and sister of Cronus (q.v.). The wife of Zeus (q.v.) before Hera (q.v.), she bore him the Horae (q.v.) and Moerae (q.v.). She determined religious rites, instituted laws and was the first to distinguish between that which was permitted and that which offended the divine order. Hence she became the personification of justice and represented the incarnation of divine law.

Therseander. See **Epigoni.**

Theocritus. See **B59.**

Thersites. A low-minded, ugly and mean spirited wretch amongst the Greek forces at Troy (q.v.). He accused Agamemnon (q.v.) of prolonging the war to serve his own interest until Odysseus (q.v.) beat him into silence.

Theseus. The son of Aethra, a princess of Troezen, by Aegeus (q.v.) though one tradition says Poseidon (q.v.) fathered him in the form of a bull.

Aegeus left her after seducing her but showed her a rock under which he had hidden his sword and sandals. Theseus was raised secretly by his mother at her father's court, and when he reached adolescence lifted the rock to claim Aegeus' sword and sandals. With these he set off for Athens and on the way had many adventures, slaying the wild sow of Crommyum, Sciron (q.v.), Periphetes (q.v.), Cercyon and Procrustes (q.v.). Arriving at Athens Aegeus recognised the sword and sandals and accepted him as his son despite the plots of Medea (q.v.). Theseus then scattered the Pallantides, fifty nephews of Aegeus and the sons of Pallas who hoped to claim the throne themselves. Next he captured the Cretan Bull (q.v.). But his greatest task was to go voluntarily to Crete to slay the Minotaur (q.v.). As one of the tribute demanded by Minos (q.v.) he was to be sacrificed to the monster but Minos' daughter Ariadne fell in love with him and gave him a sword with which to slay the beast and a thread by which he could retrace his steps through the massive labyrinth in which it lived. The couple then fled to Naxos where he left Ariadne and where she was loved by Dionysus (q.v.) whose sacred island it was. Aegeus tragically killed himself on Theseus' return and the hero then became king of Athens. Either alone or with Heracles (q.v.) he invaded the land of the Amazons and carried off either Antiope or Hippolyte. The Amazons attacked Athens but Theseus defeated them in the middle of Athens. By the Amazon queen he became father of Hippolytus (q.v.). Later he married Phaedra and was father by her of Acamas and Demophon (q.v.). A close friend of Pirithous (q.v.), the two shared many adventures. Eventually he returned again to Athens but was ousted by Menestheus and retired to Scyros where, for some reason he was murdered by Lycomedes. Unlike Heracles, Theseus was not worshipped throughout the Hellenistic world but was very much an Athenian hero and his reputed bones were brought to the city from Scyros in historical times. He is said to have gathered the villages of Attica into one state by the process of *synoecismus*.

Thetis. A Nereid (q.v.) who was raised by Hera (q.v.) and remained attached to her. Zeus (q.v.) and Poseidon (q.v.) desired her but it was foretold that her son would be greater than his father. She was thus forced to marry a mortal, Peleus (q.v.), but only after she had tried to avoid him by changing her shape, becoming various animals including a lion. Their wedding on Mt. Pelion was attended by all the gods save Eris (q.v.). They had a number of children who were killed when Thetis tried to make them immortal by throwing them into the fire. Peleus snatched their seventh child, Achilles (q.v.), from her as she tried yet again. Instead she dipped him in the Styx (q.v.). Angry at not giving birth to an immortal she left Peleus to live with her sister Neireids. She cared for Hephaestus (q.v.) when Zeus threw him into the sea, and for Dionysus (q.v.) though she and Briareus (q.v.) freed Zeus when the other gods enchained him.

Thoas. The son of Andraemon king of Calydon who took forty ships to Troy (q.v.) and was one of the Greeks in the Wooden Horse (q.v.).

Thyades. *See* **Thyia.**

Thyestes. The son of Pelops (q.v.) and Hippodamia and brother of Atreus, ancestor of the illustrious Atridae family. He and Atreus murdered their half-brother Chrysippus and fled to Mycenae. Here Atreus seized the kingdom and banished Thyestes. Thyestes had seduced Atreus' second wife Aerope and he now tricked Atreus into killing Pleisthenes, his son by his first wife. In revenge Atreus lured Thyestes to Mycenae, slew his three sons and served them to him. Thyestes unknowingly ate them. Not surprisingly he cursed the house of Atreus on learning the truth. The Delphic oracle told Thyestes he could get revenge by fathering a son on his own daughter Pelopia, a priestess at the court of Thres);; protus of Sicyon. He raped her and Atreus later married her, believing her to be the daughter of Thresprotus. He raised Thyestes' son Aegisthus (q.v.) as his own.

Thyia. The first woman to worship and sacrifice to Dionysus (q.v.). She gave her name to the Attic women who participated in the orgies of Dionysus at Parnassus, the Thyiades. These women were also called Thyades, "raging women", a similar name but of different origin.

Thyone. *See* **Semele.**

Thyrsus. A wand carried by the Maenads, covered with ivy wreaths and surmounted by a fir cone.

Tiryns. City reputedly founded by Proetus (q.v.) and built with the help of the Cyclopes (q.v.). The actual site is a mound 300 yd long on the Gulf of Argolis. It was first inhabited in the 3rd millennium B.C. and held a chief's residence and town. Around 1600 B.C. a larger palace was built and ramparts constructed. In the 14th and 13th centuries the rampart was rebuilt and enlarged. Its impressive ruins remain.

Tisiphone. One of the Eumenides (q.v.).

Titanesses. Sisters of the Titans (q.v.), daughters of Ge (q.v.) and Uranus (q.v.). Their numbers included Rhea (q.v.), Themis (q.v.), Tethys and Mnemosyne.

Titanomachia. The ten-year war, waged in Thessaly by Zeus (q.v.) and the Olympian gods against Cronos (q.v.) and the Titans (q.v.) led by Atlas (q.v.). Ge (q.v.) promised Zeus (who had usurped his Titan father Cronos) victory if he would free the Cyclopes (q.v.) and Hecatoncheires (q.v.) from Tartarus (q.v.). He did and the Cyclopes gave him the thunderbolt, Hades (q.v.) a helmet which conferred invisibility and Poseidon a trident. The three overcame Cronos and the Hecatoncheires stoned the other Titans who were defeated and consigned either to Tartarus or an island far to the west. Here the Hecatoncheires guarded them. Atlas was made to carry the sky as punishment but the Titanesses (q.v.) were spared. The war is the basis of Keats' *Hyperion*.

Titans. The sons of Ge (q.v.) and Uranus (q.v.). There were twelve of them though the lists given of their names are inconsistent. The most often named are Cronus (q.v.), Oceanus (q.v.), Hyperion, Iapetus and Atlas (q.v.). Brothers of the Titanesses (q.v.). When Uranus consigned the Cyclopes (q.v.) to Tartarus (q.v.) Ge persuaded Cronos and his brother Titans to depose Uranus. The Titans were in turn deposed in the Titanomachia (q.v.).

Tithonus. The son of Laomedon and Strymor and a half-brother of Priam (q.v.). By Eos (q.v.) the father of Memnon (q.v.). Eos begged Zeus (q.v.) to make him immortal, which he did, but forgot to ask for perpetual youth. Tithonus grew older and older until Eos tired of looking on him, turned him into a cicada and locked him in a cage.

Tities. One of the three primitive tribes of Rome.

Tityus. A giant son of Ge (q.v.) sent by Hera (q.v.) to violate Leto (q.v.) but Artemis (q.v.) and Apollo (q.v.) slew him with their arrows. In Hades (q.v.) he was pegged to the ground (he covered nine acres) while two vultures picked at his liver.

Tleopolemus. A son of Heracles (q.v.) who settled in Argos and later Rhodes.

Triptolemus. *See* **Demeter.**

Triton. The son of Poseidon (q.v.) and Amphitrite (q.v.) though sometimes several tritons are spoken of. He was a merman, his upper body being human, the lower fish. He blew a shell-trumpet, the concha, to calm the waves and Ovid tells us that he blew the concha to order the waters to recede after the Flood. (*See* Deucalion).

Troilus. A young son of Priam (q.v.) slain by Achilles (q.v.). His romance with Cressida is a medieval invention.

Trojan War. The ten-year siege of Troy (q.v.) and its eventual sack by Greek forces under Agamemnon (q.v.). The combined forces sought to restore Helen (q.v.) to Menelaus (q.v.). The story of the war is told in Homer's *Iliad* where Achilles (q.v.) is the major hero of the Greeks and Hector (q.v.) of the Trojans. According to Homer the war was ended by the Wooden Horse (q.v.) concocted by Odysseus (q.v.). The war is usually placed by tradition as occurring in the 12th century B.C. The war is not a purely mythical episode. Archaeological evidence from the site of Troy shows that the city occupying the seventh stratigraphical layer was destroyed by fire, though probably in the 14th century B.C. Archaeology also confirms the *Iliad's* description of the main towns in Trojan civilisation together with its picture of the Greek people and army.

Trophonius and **Agamedes.** Sons of Erginus who built a temple for Apollo (q.v.) at Delphi. They were rewarded by living merrily for six days and dying in their sleep on the seventh. Trophonius later had an oracle of his own at Lebadeia in Boeotia. Here, according to Pausanias, the questioner underwent a complex initiation, was dressed as a sacrificial victim and (carrying a honey-cake to placate the Underworld divinities) descended into a pot-hole. An underground stream swept him along some distance before he was returned to the light having heard invisible speakers in the cavern. Not surprisingly the questioner would look dazed and dejected and it became common to speak of a gloomy person as one who had been consulting Trophonius.

Tros. (1) The grandson of Dardanus (*q.v.*) and father of Ilus (*q.v.*) and Ganymede (*q.v.*). An ancestor of the Trojans, he gave his name to Troy (*q.v.*).

(2) A small town absorbed by the city of Troy (*q.v.*).

Troy. Also called Ilium, a city of Asia Minor near the sea not far from the straits of the Dardanelles. From its position the inhabitants could watch the sea traffic between the Aegean and Sea of Marmara. Many traders off-loaded cargo and used the land route to bypass the dangerous straits. Hence in the late 3rd millennium B.C. Troy became very prosperous from trade, a prosperity which returned at various periods in the 2nd millennium. In 1870 the German Heinrich Schliemann, an amateur archaeologist, sought the site near modern Hissarlik in Turkey. He found it and later excavations have distinguished nine strata of occupations, the richest dating from 2200 B.C. and the 7th showing signs of destruction by fire (*See* **Trojan War**). From the 14th century B.C. the site was of little importance until the Roman occupation when, as Ilium Nevum, it played a large part in provincial life. Homer's Troy had probably absorbed three neighbouring towns, Tros (*q.v.*), Dardania and Ilium and the names of three tribes, Ilians, Trojans and Dardanians are represented in the myths of its foundation.

Tyche or **Tuche.** The Roman "Fortuna", and always more popular in Rome. A daughter of Zeus (*q.v.*) and the goddess of luck who bestowed or denied gifts to men according to her whims. She often accompanied Pluto (*q.v.*). She is portrayed juggling a ball, symbolising the instability of fate, or with a rudder to guide men's affairs.

Tydeus. Son of Oeneus and Calydon, husband of Deipyle. After committing a murder in his youth he fled to the court of Adrastus (*q.v.*). *See* **Seven Against Thebes**.

Tyndareus. The brother of Hippocoon who deposed him as king of Sparta, but Heracles (*q.v.*) reinstated him. Helen (*q.v.*) was brought up at his court (she was his wife Leda's (*q.v.*) child by Zeus (*q.v.*)). Helen married Menelaus (*q.v.*) who succeeded Tyndareus. Tyndareus had had all the Greek nobles who sought Helen's hand swear an oath to defend her chosen husband. This was the reason why the Greeks allied in support of Menelaus in the Trojan War (*q.v.*). Tyndareus also helped Agamemnon (*q.v.*) expel Thyestes (*q.v.*) and regain his throne.

Typhon. The monstrous offspring of Ge (*q.v.*) and Tartarus (*q.v.*), whose eyes could expel fire and whose limbs ended in snakes' heads. He attacked Olympus and the gods fled to Egypt disguised as animals, Zeus (*q.v.*) as a ram, Apollo (*q.v.*) as a cow, Dionysus (*q.v.*) as a goat, Hera (*q.v.*) as a white cow, Artemis (*q.v.*) as a cat, Aphrodite (*q.v.*) as a fish, Ares (*q.v.*) as a boar and Hermes (*q.v.*) as an ibis. Athene (*q.v.*) did not flee and persuaded Zeus to fight. In a great struggle Zeus was saved by Hermes and Pan (*q.v.*) and then defeated Typhon with his thunderbolts. He was then buried under Mt. Etna. By Echidne (*q.v.*) Typhon was father of a variety of monsters.

Tyro. A nymph, the mother of Pelias (*q.v.*) and Neleus (*q.v.*) by Zeus (*q.v.*) and of Aeson by Cretheus. The grandmother of Jason (*q.v.*).

U

Udaeus. One of the Spartii (*q.v.*).

Ulysses. The Roman name for Odysseus (*q.v.*).

Urania. The Muse of Astronomy.

Uranus. The Sky, offspring of Ge (*q.v.*) the earth and brother of Pontus, the sea. The father by Ge of the Hecatoncheires (*q.v.*), the Cyclopes (*q.v.*) and the Titans (*q.v.*). He threw the rebellious Cyclopes into Tartarus (*q.v.*). Ge then persuaded the Titans to rise against their father and avenge their brothers. She gave Cronos (*q.v.*) a flint sickle with

which he castrated Uranus. The blood of Uranus which fell to earth produced the Erinyes and the blood which fell into the sea produced Aphrodite (*q.v.*). Uranus was deposed but cursed Cronos that his own children depose him.

V

Venus. Originally an Italian deity whose name meant "beauty" or "charm", she was a goddess of vegetable rather than animal fertility. She became identified with Aphrodite (*q.v.*) by way of Aphrodite's cult at Mt. Eryx in Sicily, said to have been founded by Aeneas (*q.v.*) on the death of Anchises (*q.v.*). In 217 B.C. Venus Erycina was given a temple at Rome and became completely associated with Aphrodite taking on her functions and attributes. She was patron goddess of Sulla and Pompey. In the imperial cult she played a very important role as the Julian family claimed descent from Aeneas and therefore Aphrodite. In this context she was Venus Genetrix, creator of all things, the universal mother and life giver.

Vesta. A primitive Roman goddess of the hearth, the counterpart of Hestia (*q.v.*). She was worshipped in each Roman house and officially in a circular temple in the Forum. The temple held a fire, said to have come from Troy (*q.v.*) which could never be allowed to go out. It was tended by the Vestal Virgins (*q.v.*). Her cult was purely Italian and never spread to the provinces.

Vestal Virgins. A college of priestesses of the cult of Vesta (*q.v.*). There were originally four of them, later six and finally seven. Candidates for the college were chosen at between six and ten years of age; both their parents had to be alive and they underwent a prolonged special training. They served for thirty years under the control of the Pontifex Maximus and during all this period had to remain virgins. The punishment for unchastity was burial alive. However they were highly honoured and had great privileges. For instance they could save from execution any criminal they met on the way to his death. They lived in a large residence near the temple of Vesta. The sacred fire of Vesta was tended by Vestal Virgins up to the 4th century A.D.

Virgil. *See* **B62**.

Victoria. The Roman goddess of victory, corresponding to the Greek *Nike* (*q.v.*).

Vulcan. The Roman god of fire, identified with Hephaestus (*q.v.*) and sometimes called Mulciber, "the smelter". His name gives us the word "volcano".

W

Wooden Horse of Troy. The "Trojan Horse", a stratagem devised by Odysseus (*q.v.*) which ended the Trojan War (*q.v.*). The Greeks had Epeius, son of Panopeus, build a large wooden horse. Athene (*q.v.*) helped him and it bore an inscription dedicated to her. Then twenty-three or more Greeks including Odysseus, Neoptolemus (*q.v.*), Sthenelus and Thoas hid inside it. The rest of the Greek force then burnt their camp and put to sea leaving only the wily Sinon (*q.v.*) to trick the Trojans into dragging the horse into Troy. (*See also* **Laocöon**). Inside the city Helen (*q.v.*) patted the horse and called out the names of those she suspected were inside it, but she was accompanied by the Trojan prince Deiphobus and Odysseus stopped the Greeks answering. At night the Greek fleet returned, Sinon let the men out of the horse, the gates of Troy were opened and the city was sacked.

X

Xenophon. *See* **B66**.

Xuthus. The son of Hellen and husband of Creusa, the daughter of Erectheus, king of Athens. By her the father of Achaeus and Ion. On the death of

Erectheus Xuthus was asked to determine which of the king's sons should succeed him. He chose Cecrops and was expelled to Achaia by the other heirs. Euripedes (q.v.) makes Ion the son of Apollo (q.v.) and Creusa.

Z

Zagreus. A son of Zeus (q.v.). He was torn apart and eaten by Titans (q.v.) except for his heart which Athene (q.v.) saved. He is sometimes identified with Dionysus (q.v.).

Zephyrus. The son of Astraeus and Eus. He was the west wind, originally imagined, like all winds, in the form of a horse. The father of Xanthus and Balius, the talking horses of Achilles (q.v.) which Poseidon (q.v.) had given to Peleus (q.v.) as a wedding gift. The husband of Iris (q.v.). He deflected the discus which killed Hyacinthus (q.v.). His Roman counterpart was Favonius.

Zetes. See **Calais.**

Zethus. See **Amphion.**

Zeus. The son of Cronos (q.v.) and Rhea (q.v.). He deposed his father and defeated the Titans (q.v.). Then he and his brothers Hades (q.v.) and Poseidon (q.v.) cast lots for their kingdoms and Zeus won the sky. The earth was common to all. Zeus was the king of the gods and was identified with Jupiter by the Romans. He was the father of men. In early legend his consort is Dione, but his consort on Mt. Olympus (q.v.) is the jealous Hera (q.v.). He first married Hetis who bore him Athene (q.v.) and his second wife was Themis (q.v.) who bore him the Horae and Maerae. Hera bore him Ares (q.v.), Hebe (q.v.) and Hephaestus (q.v.). His sister Demeter (q.v.) bore him Persephone (q.v.) and Eurynome bore him the Charities (q.v.) while by Mnemosyne he was father of the Muses (q.v.). By mortal women he was father of Hermes (q.v.), Apollo (q.v.) and Artemis (q.v.) and Dionysus (q.v.). Given the thunderbolt by the Cyclopes (q.v.) he was known as the thunderer.

IDEAS &
BELIEFS

This section explains many of the ideas and beliefs that have dominated our history during the centuries. The arrangement is alphabetical and the subjects range from a world-wide spectrum of religious and philosophical terms to the major political ideologies which have shaped modern history. A Special Topic in this edition looks at the development of human rights over the last half century.

IDEAS AND BELIEFS

THIS section explains many of the ideas and beliefs which people have held at different periods in history. Beliefs may be true or false, meaningful or totally meaningless, regardless of the degree of conviction with which they are held. Since man has been moved to action so often by his beliefs they are worth serious study. The section throws a vivid light on human history.

Man has always felt a deep need for emotional security, a sense of "belonging". This need has found expression in the framing of innumerable religious systems, nearly all of which have been concerned with man's relation to a divine ruling power. In the past, people have been accustomed to think of their own religion as true and of all others as false. Lately we have come to realise that in man's religious strivings there is common ground, for our need in the world today is a morality whereby human beings may live together in harmony.

There is also to be found in man an irresistible curiosity which demands an explanation of the world in which he finds himself. This urge to make the world intelligible takes him into the realm of science where the unknown is the constant challenge. Science is a creative process, always in the making, since the scientist's conjectures are constantly being submitted to severe critical tests. Basic scientific ideas are discussed in Section F, while major economic theories are to be found in Section G.

A

Abortion. See J57.

Activists, those in a political movement who insist on taking active steps towards their objectives rather than merely putting forward a programme. Lately activism has become an increasingly common facet of political life. This is probably because the undeniably rapid social changes which are taking place across the world at the moment are not generally being followed by appropriate shifts in political structures and ideals.

Acupuncture, a unique medical system originating in China and based on the established therapeutic effects of implanting fine gold needles in specific parts of the body. The site of needle implantation is decided according to traditional texts. The apparent lack of any logical relationship between the implantation sites and any known physiological or anatomical systems within the body has caused acupuncture to be held in low regard by Western medicine. Indeed it was certainly true that acupuncture and other similar practices tended to flourish in parts of the world where orthodox medicine has made little progress or where doctors and trained staff are scarce. Recent years however have seen a curious and unexpected revival of interest in acupuncture in Europe and America.

Adlerian Psychology. In 1911 the Viennese psychoanalyst Alfred Adler (1870–1937) together with his colleague Carl Gustav Jung broke with their friend Sigmund Freud over disputes concerning the latter's theoretic approach to psychoanalysis. Jung and Adler were themselves shortly also to part company, each to set up and develop his own "school" of psychoanalysis. Adler's system of psychotherapy is based on the idea, not of sex as a driving force as in the case of Freud, but on the concept of "compensation" or a drive for power in an attempt to overcome the "inferiority complex" which he held to be universal in human beings. The child naturally feels inferior to adults, but bullying, making him feel insignificant or guilty or contemptible, even spoiling, which makes him feel important within the family but relatively unimportant outside, increases this feeling. Or the child may have physical defects: he may be small or underweight, have to wear glasses, become lame, be constantly ill, or stupid at school. In these ways he develops a sense of inferiority which for the rest of his life he develops a technique to overcome.

This may be done in several ways: he may try to become capable in the very respects in which he feels incompetent—hence many great orators have originally had speech defects; many painters poor eyesight; many musicians have been partially deaf; like Nietzsche, the weakling, he may write about the superman, or like Sandow, the strong man, be born with poor health.

On the other hand he may overdo his attempt and overcompensate. Hence we have the bully who is really a coward, the small man who is self-assertive to an objectionable degree (Hitler, Napoleon, Stalin, and Mussolini were all small men) or the foreigner who like three of these men wanted to be the hero of his adopted country—Hitler the Austrian, Napoleon the Italian, Stalin the Georgian.

But what about the man who can do none of these things, who continues to fail to compensate? He, says Adler, becomes a neurotic because neurosis is an excuse which means "I could have done so-and-so but . . ." It is the unconscious flight into illness—the desire to be ill. Adler's treatment involves disclosing these subterfuges we play on ourselves so that we can deal with the real situation in a more realistic way. Adlerian psychoanalysis still attracts supporters, but its golden days were when the founder was at the head of the movement in the USA, when his views were considered to provide a more "acceptable" theory of the mind than the enormously controversial theories of Freud with their strong sexual orientation.

Adventists, a group of American religious sects, the most familiar being the Seventh-Day Adventist Church, which observes Saturday as the true Sabbath. With (1999) more than 5 million members throughout the world, it shares with other Adventists a belief in the imminent second coming of Christ (a doctrine fairly widespread in the USA during the early decades of the 19th cent. when the end of the world was predicted by William Miller for 1843, then for 1844). Modern Adventists content themselves with the conviction that the "signs" of the Advent are multiplying, the "blessed event" which will solve the world's ills. Believers will be saved, but the sects differ as to whether the unjust will be tortured in hell, annihilated, or merely remain asleep eternally.

Aestheticism. See Section M, Part II.

Agnosticism. See God and Man.

Albigenses, also known as Cathari. French heretical sect (named after the town of Albi in Provence) which appeared in the 11th cent. to challenge the Catholic Church on the way true Christians should lead their lives. They followed a life of extreme asceticism in contrast to the local clergy and their faith was adopted by the mass of the population, especially in Toulouse. Condemned as heretics by Pope Innocent III, the sect was exterminated in the savage Albigensian Crusade (1208–29), initially led by Simon de Montfort. (In his thoroughness, de Montfort also succeeded in destroying the high culture of the Troubadours.)

Alchemy, ancient art associated with magic and astrology in which modern chemistry has its roots. The earliest mention of alchemy comes from ancient Egypt but its later practitioners attributed its origins to such varied sources as the fallen angels of the Bible, to Moses and Aaron, but most commonly to Hermes Trismegistus, often identified with the Egyptian god Thoth, whose knowledge of the divine art was handed down only to the sons of kings (cf. the phrase "hermetically sealed"). Its main object was the transmutation of metals. Egyptian speculation concerning this reached its height during the 6th cent. in the Alexandrian period. Brought to Western Europe by the Moslems, one of its most famous Arab exponents was Jabir (c. 760–c. 815), known to the Latins as Geber, who had a laboratory at Kufa on the Tigris. One school of early Greek philosophy held that there was ultimately only one elemental matter of which everything was composed. Such men as Albertus Magnus (1206–80) and Roger Bacon (1214–94) assumed that, by removing impurities, this *materia prima* could be obtained. Although Bacon's ideas were in many ways ahead of his time, he firmly believed in the philosopher's stone, which could turn base metals into gold, and in an elixir of life which would give eternal youth. Modern science has, of course, shown in its researches into radioactivity, the possibility of transmutation of certain elements, but this phenomenon has little bearing on either the methods of the alchemist or the mysteries with which he surrounded them.

Anabaptists. *See* **Baptists.**

Analytical Psychology, the name given by Carl Gustav Jung (1875–1961) of Zürich to his system of psychology, which, like Adler's (*see* **Adlerian Psychology**), took its origin from Freud's psychoanalysis from which both diverged in 1911. Briefly, Jung differed from Freud: (1) in believing that the latter had laid too much emphasis on the sexual drive as the basic one in man and replacing it with the concept of *libido* or life energy of which sex forms a part; (2) in his theory of types: men are either extrovert or introvert (*i.e.* their interest is turned primarily outwards to the world or inwards to the self), and they apprehend experience in four main ways, one or other of which is predominant in any given individual—sensing, feeling, thinking, or intuiting; (3) in his belief that the individual's unconscious mind contains not only repressed materials which, as Freud maintained, were too unpleasant to be allowed into awareness, but also faculties which had not been allowed to develop—*e.g.*, the emotional side of the too rational man, the feminine side of the too masculine one; (4) in the importance he attaches to the existence of a collective unconscious at a still deeper level which contains traces of ancient ways of thought which mankind has inherited over the centuries. These are the *archetypes* and include primitive notions of magic, spirits and witches, birth and death, gods, virgin mothers, resurrection, etc. In the treatment of the neuroses Jung believed in the importance of (a) the present situation which the patient refuses to face; (b) the bringing together of conscious and unconscious and integrating them.

In the 1940s and 50s interest in Jung's ideas waned, at least in academic circles, as the emphasis among experimental psychologists shifted closer and closer to the "hard" scientific line. This was also true in the field of psychoanalysis where the Jungian as opposed to the Freudian point of view became progressively less popular. At the present time this trend is beginning to reverse, and while Jung's offbeat views on astrology, telepathy, etc., are still unfashionable, a reappraisal of the significance of his views on the nature of the unconscious is taking place and many psychologists feel that his contribution to our understanding of the nature of human mental processes has been greatly underrated. *See also* **Psychoanalysis**.

Anarchism, a political philosophy which holds, in the words of the American anarchist Josiah Warren (1798–1874), an early follower of Robert Owen, that "every man should be his own government, his own law, his own church." The idea that governmental interference or even the mere existence of authority is inherently bad is as old as Zeno, the Greek Stoic philosopher, who believed that compulsion perverts the normal nature of man. William Godwin's *Enquiry Concerning Political Justice* (1793) was the first systematic exposition of the doctrine. Godwin (father-in-law of Shelley) claimed that man is by nature sociable, co-operative, rational, and good when given the choice to act freely; that under such conditions men will form voluntary groups to work in complete social harmony. Such groups or communities would be based on equality of income, no state control, and no property: this state of affairs would be brought about by rational discussion and persuasion rather than by revolution.

The French economist Proudhon (1809–65) was the first to bring anarchism to the status of a mass movement. In his book *What is Property?* he stated bluntly that "property is theft" and "governments are the scourge of God". He urged the formation of co-operative credit banks where money could be had without interest and goods would be exchanged at cost value at a rate representing the hours of work needed to produce each commodity. Like Godwin, he disapproved of violence but, unlike Marx, disapproved of trade unions as representing organised groups.

In communistic anarchism these ideas were combined with a revolutionary philosophy, primarily by the Russians Michael Bakunin (1814–76) and Peter Kropotkin (1842–1921) who favoured training workers in the technique of "direct action" to overthrow the state by all possible means, including political assassination. In 1868 anarchists joined the First International which broke up a few years later after a bitter struggle between Bakuninists and Marxists. Subsequently small anarchist groups murdered such political figures as Tsar Alexander II of Russia, King Humbert of Italy, Presidents Carnot of France and MacKinley of America, and the Empress Elizabeth of Austria.

Anarchism and communism differ in three main ways: (1) anarchism forms no political party, rejects all relationship with established authority, and regards democratic reform as a setback; (2) communism is against capitalism, anarchism against the state as such; (3) both have the final goal of a classless society, but anarchism rejects the idea of an intermediate period of socialist state control accepted by communism. Philosophical anarchists, such as the American writer Henry David Thoreau (1817–62), were primarily individualists who believed in a return to nature, the non-payment of taxes, and passive resistance to state control; in these respects Thoreau strongly influenced Gandhi as did the Christian anarchist Tolstoy.

Anarchism has traditionally been criticised as being impractical—*e.g.*, in a non-authoritarian society, who is going to look after the sewers or clean the streets?—and there is a good deal of force to this argument. In fact anarchistic ideas became progressively less fashionable in the first half of this century. A curious and probably significant revival of interest has taken place in recent years, however, probably because of a growing sense of disillusion, particularly on the part of young people, with the progress of orthodox political systems. *See also* **Syndicalism**.

Anglicanism, adherence to the doctrine and discipline of the Anglican Church, as the genuine representative of the Catholic Church. *See* **Church of England**.

Anglo-Catholicism. To Queen Elizabeth I the Church of England was that of the "middle way" in which human reason and commonsense took their place beside Scripture and Church authority. The extent to which these various factors are stressed creates the distinctions between "high" and "low" church. Anglo-Catholics tend to reject the term "Protestant" and stress the term "Catholic" and, although few accept the infallibility of the Pope some Anglo-Catholic churches have introduced much or all of the Roman ritual and teach Roman dogmas. The ordination in March 1994 of the first women priests to the Anglican ministry caused over 200 former Anglican clergy (many of them married) to be received into the Catholic Church. See **Catholicism, Tractarianism**.

Animal Rights. See J57.

Animism. To early man and in primitive societies the distinction between animate and inanimate objects was not always obvious—it is not enough to say that living things move and non-living things do not, for leaves blow about in the wind and streams flow down a hillside. In the religions of early societies, therefore, we find a tendency to believe that life exists in all objects from rocks and pools to seas and mountains. This belief is technically known as *animatism*, which differs from *animism*, a somewhat more sophisticated view which holds that natural objects have no life in themselves but may be the abode of dead people, spirits, or gods who occasionally give them the appearance of life. The classic example of this, of course, is the assumption that an erupting volcano is an expression of anger on the part of the god who resides in it.

Anthropomorphism, the attribution of human form, thoughts or motives to non-human entities or life forms from gods to animals. At one end this can be summed up in the once widespread image of God as a "white-bearded old gentleman sitting on a cloud." At the other end is the very common tendency to invest domestic animals and pets with man-like wishes and personalities. At both extremes the belief could be seriously misleading. Firstly, it could be very unwise to assume that God, if he exists, necessarily thinks as humans do and has human interests at heart. Secondly, we shall learn very little about animal behaviour if we look upon them as mere extensions of our own personality, and we do them less than justice if we see them simply as human beings of diminutive intelligence.

Anthroposophy, a school of religious and philosophical thought based on the work of the German educationist and mystic Rudolf Steiner (1861–1925). Steiner was originally an adherent of Madame Blavatsky's theosophical movement (*cf* Theosophy) but in 1913 broke away to form his own splinter group, the Anthroposophical Society. Steiner was much influenced by the German poet and scientist, Goethe, and believed that an appreciation and love for art was one of the keys to spiritual development. One of the first tasks of his new movement was the construction of a vast temple of arts and sciences, known as the Goetheanum, to act as the headquarters of the society. This structure, which was of striking and revolutionary architectural style, was unfortunately burnt down in 1922 to be replaced by an even more imaginative one which today is one of the most interesting buildings of its kind in the world. Anthroposophy, which continued to expand greatly following its founder's death, is nowadays well-established in various parts of the world with specialised, and often very well equipped, schools and clinics which propagate the educational and therapeutic theories of the movement. These, which include the allegedly beneficial powers of music, coloured lights, *etc.*, have made an increasing impact on modern educational ideas, but the schools have acquired a reputation for success in the training of mentally handicapped children. Today (1999) there are over 750 Steiner schools worldwide, many clinics and homes for the handicapped, adult education centres, an international management consultancy, and several hundred thousand acres under biodynamic cultivation without the use of chemical pesticides, herbicides, or fertilizers. Interesting work continues to be done, in pharmacology, botany, mathematics and physics, and architecture. New banking systems, operating rather like credit unions, have arisen (Mercury in Britain, Prometheus in New Zealand).

Anticlericalism, resentment of priestly powers and privileges, traceable in England to Wyclif's insistence in the 14th cent. on the right of all men to have access to the Scriptures. The translation of the Bible into the common tongue was a great landmark in the history of the Bible and the English language. Wyclif's principles were condemned by the Roman Church of his time but were readily accepted during the Reformation. Tudor anticlericalism arose from motives ranging from a greedy desire to plunder the riches of the Church to a genuine dislike of the powers of the priesthood whose spiritual courts still had the right to decide on points of doctrine or morals in an age when the layman felt he was well able to decide for himself. In innumerable ways the Church was permitted to extort money from the laity. It is generally agreed, says Trevelyan, that the final submission of church to state in England was motivated quite as much by anticlericalism as by Protestantism. The rise of the Reformed churches in England satisfied the people generally and anticlericalism never became the fixed principle of permanent parties as happened in France and Italy from the time of Voltaire onwards.

Antisemitism, a term first applied about the middle of the last century to those who were anti-Jewish in their outlook. Although this attitude was prevalent for religious reasons throughout the Middle Ages, modern antisemitism differed (*a*) in being largely motivated by economic or political conditions, and (*b*) in being doctrinaire with a pseudo-scientific rationale presented by such men as Gobineau (1816–82) and Houston Stewart Chamberlain (1855–1927), and later by the Nazi and Fascist "philosophers". Beginning in Russia and Hungary with the pogroms of 1882 it gradually spread south and westwards where, in France, the Dreyfus case provided an unsavoury example in 1894. Thousands of Jews from Eastern Europe fled to Britain and America during this period; for in these countries antisemitism has rarely been more than a personal eccentricity. During the last war the murder of six million Jews by the Nazis and their accomplices led to a further exodus to various parts of the world and finally to the creation of the state of Israel.

The individual Jew-hater makes unconscious use of the psychological processes of projection and displacement: his greed or sexual guilt is projected on to the Jew (or Black or Catholic) because he cannot bear to accept them as his own emotions, and his sense of failure in life is blamed on his chosen scapegoat rather than on his own inadequacy.

But there are social causes too and politicians in some lands are well versed in the technique of blaming unsatisfactory conditions (which they themselves may have in part produced) upon minority groups and persuading others to do the same. Historically, the Jew is ideally suited for this role of scapegoat; (1) in the Middle Ages when usury was forbidden to Christians but not to Jews, the latter often became moneylenders incurring the opprobrium generally associated with this trade (*e.g.*, to the simple-minded Russian peasant the Jew often represented, not only the "Christ-killer", but also the moneylender or small shopkeeper to whom he owed money); (2) many trades being closed to Jews, it was natural that they concentrated in others, thus arousing suspicions of "influence" (*i.e.* Jews are felt to occupy a place in certain trades and professions which far exceeds their numerical proportion to the population as a whole); (3) even with the ending of ghetto life, Jews often occupy *en masse* some parts of cities rather than others and this may lead to resentment on the part of the original inhabitants who begin to feel themselves dispossessed; (4) Jews tend to form a closed society and incur the suspicions attached to all closed societies within which social contacts are largely limited to members; marriage outside the group is forbidden or strongly disapproved of, and the preservation, among the orthodox, of cultural and religious barriers tends to isolate them from their fellow citizens. Since 1990, with the political changes in Russia and Eastern Europe, neo-fascist extremists have begun a resurgence of antisemitism. See **Racism, Zionism, Judaism**.

Anti-vivisection, opposition to scientific experimentation upon live animals based, according to its supporters, both on the moral grounds of the suffering imposed, and also on the grounds that many doctors and scientists of repute have rejected the value of information gained in this way. It is true that the protagonists of the movement during its early days in the mid-19th cent. included a number of eminent physicians and surgeons. Many people today remain deeply concerned about the moral problems of vivisection, even though without animal experiments we would be unable to test out new drugs for safety before using them on human beings. There are in Britain many active anti-vivisection societies. Much of their work is co-ordinated through the British Council of Anti-Vivisection Societies. In Britain, experiments on live animals are covered by the 1986 Animals (Scientific Procedures) Act. It is estimated that worldwide 200 million animals are killed in experiments each year. Many people would like the number of experiments on animals reduced and the law changed to prohibit any experiments in which there is any risk of inflicting suffering. Recent years have seen an upsurge in support for organisations whose objective is to lessen the suffering of animals. The most militant group is the Animal Liberation Front. A recent account of activities in this field can be found in Barbara James, *The Young Persons Action Guide to Animal Rights* (Virago Press, 1992). *See also* **J57**.

Apartheid. An Afrikaans word meaning "apartness", which refers to the policy of total racial discrimination between black and white South Africans as enforced by successive governments of that country from 1948 until the early 1990s when the system was dismantled. At its height, apartheid was the most inhuman aspect of a system which denied even the most basic human rights to the African population. *See also* **Section C** for recent events in South Africa.

Arianism, formed the subject of the first great controversy within the Christian Church over the doctrine of Arius of Alexandria (d. 336) who denied the divinity of Christ. The doctrine, although at first influential, was condemned at the Council of Nicaea (325), called by the Emperor Constantine, at which Arius was opposed by Athanasius, also of Alexandria, who maintained the now orthodox view that the Son is of one substance with the Father. Arius was banished but the heresy persisted until the 7th cent., especially among the barbarians, the Goths, Vandals and Lombards. Disbelief in the divinity of Christ has formed part of the doctrine of many sects since (*e.g.* **Unitarianism** (*q.v.*).

Arminianism. A theological movement in Christianity, based on the teachings of the Dutch theologian Jacob Harmensen (or Hermansz) (1560–1609), whose name was Latinised as Jacobus Arminius. He reacted against the Calvinist doctrine of predestination. His followers formulated his three main beliefs as: divine sovereignty was compatible with real freewill in man; Christ died for all men (and not only the elect); and all who believe in him can be saved. Arminianism had an important influence on John Wesley and through him on Methodism.

Asceticism. The practice of self-discipline of both mind and body in order to achieve a spiritual ideal or goal. From the Greek *askein*, to practise or exercise. The term originally referred to the training carried out by athletes. The concept was then transformed into the idea of training for wisdom. This view is clearly articulated in Plato, who argued that one must free oneself from the desires of the body in order to achieve full spiritual insight. Since all religions exalt the soul over the body, the spiritual over the material, and eternal life over this world, they all have traces of asceticism. In many of them, there are adherents who have gone beyond self-denial to self-punishment. Important features of ascetic movements are celibacy, abdication of worldly possessions, abstinence and fasting. Some ascetics have dispensed with washing, or have isolated themselves in deserts or mountains. Extreme ascetics have resorted to self-laceration, wearing iron devices under their clothes, flagellation, even castration.

Ascetism has been very important in Christianity, most notably in the monastic movement (*see* **Monasticism**), though practices varied widely among monks, from the extravagant austerity of Egyptian hermits to the work-oriented community life of the Benedictines. Since the rise of Protestantism, however, extreme austerity has been less favoured. Hinduism also has a strong tradition of asceticism, and there are elements in Buddhism and Islam.

Assassins, a sect of Moslem Shi'ites, founded by the Persian Hasan i Sabbah (*c.* 1090), which for more than two centuries established a rule of terror all over Persia and Syria. The coming of the Mongols in 1256 destroyed them in Persia and the Syrian branch suffered a similar fate at the hands of the then Mamluk sultan of Egypt, *c.* 1270. It was a secret order, ruled over by a grand master, under whom the members were strictly organised into classes, according to the degree of initiation into the secrets of the order. The devotees, belonging to one of the lower groups, carried out the actual assassinations under strict laws of obedience, and total ignorance of the objects and ritual of the society. It is believed that the latter were given ecstatic visions under the influence of hashish, whence the term *hashshashin*, which became corrupted to "assassin".

Associationism. In psychology, the Associationist school of the 19th cent. accepted the association of ideas as the fundamental principle in mental life. It was represented in Britain by the two Mills and Herbert Spencer, in Germany by J. F. Herbart (1776–1841). To these, mental activity was nothing but the association of "ideas" conceived of as units of both thought and feeling—the emotion of anger or the perception of a chair were both "ideas"—and apart from them the self did not exist. Personality was simply a series of these units coming and going, adding to or cancelling each other out, in accordance with rigid scientific laws.

Astrology was once the best available theory for explaining the course of human life and bears much the same historical relationship to astronomy as alchemy does to chemistry. Originally it was divided into the two branches of Natural Astrology which dealt with the movements of the heavenly bodies and their calculations, and Judicial Astrology which studied the alleged influence of the stars and the planets on human life and fate. It was the former that developed into modern astronomy; the latter was, and remains, a primitive myth.

Astrology owes most to the early Babylonians (or Chaldeans) who, being largely nomadic in an environment which permitted an unobstructed view of the sky, readily accepted the idea that divine energy is manifested in the movements of the sun and planets. Gradually this concept became enlarged and the relative positions of the planets both in relation to each other and to the fixed stars became important together with the idea of omens—that, if a particular event occurred whilst the planets were in a particular position, the recurrence of that position heralded a recurrence of the same sort of event. Soon the planets became associated with almost every aspect of human life. They were bound up with the emotions, with parts of the body, so that astrology played quite a large part in medicine up to late mediaeval times. Not only was the position of the planet to be considered but also the particular sign of the zodiac (or house of heaven) it was occupying, and it was believed possible to foretell the destiny of an individual by calculating which star was in the ascendant (*i.e.* the sign of the zodiac nearest the eastern horizon and the star which arose at that precise moment) at the time of his birth. Astrology was popular among the Egyptians, the Romans (whose authorities found the Chaldean astrologers a nuisance and expelled them from time to time), and during the Middle Ages when astrologers were often highly respected.

Despite the apparent absurdity of astrological beliefs—for example, how could the pattern of light from stars billions of miles away possibly influence the temperament of single individuals on earth—a substantial number of intelligent and well-educated people take its study in all seriousness. The most interesting "convert" was the psychologist and philosopher, Carl Jung, who conducted a complex experiment in which he compared the "birth signs" of happily married and divorced couples and claimed to find that those most favourably matched in astrological terms were also those more likely to have permanent wedded bliss. Jung's findings were subsequently shown to have been based on a simple statistical fallacy, which did not prevent the brilliant but eccentric psychologist from offering them up as evidence in support of his own theory of "synchronicity" (**J50**), an involved and vaguely metaphysical notion which suggests that events in the universe may be significantly related in a "non-causal" fashion. To add fuel to the controversy however, the French mathematician, Michel Gauquelin, has recently offered up fresh data which apparently supports the general astrological view. In a carefully controlled study he noticed statistically significant correspondences between certain astrological signs and the professions of a large number of Frenchmen whose birth time and date were accurately recorded. Gauquelin claims to have repeated his study on a second large sample of his fellow countrymen, though he has been unable to use English people as the exact times of birth are not recorded on their birth certificates! This apparent shot in the arm for astrology is still a matter of great scientific controversy, though Gauquelin's work has been given support from the distinguished British psychologist. H. J. Eysenck, who has pronounced his statistical data to to be incontrovertible. Both scientists, however, carefully refrain from discussing the implications of these curious findings, and the controversy will no doubt increase rather than decrease in the near future.

Atheism. *See* **God and Man.**

Atlantis, a mythical continent supposed to have lain somewhere between Europe and America and a centre of advanced civilisation before it was inundated by some great natural catastrophe in pre-Christian times.

Atomism. In philosophy, the atomists were a group of early Greek thinkers, the most important of whom were Leucippus (fl. *c*. 440 B.C.) and his younger contemporary Democritus (*c*. 460–370 B.C.). Prior to these men, although it had been agreed that matter must be composed of tiny ultimate particles and that change must be due to the manner in which these mingled or separated from each other, it was supposed that there existed different types of particle for each material—*e.g.* for flesh, wood, hair, bone. The atomists taught that atoms were all made of a single substance and differed only in the connections (pictured as hooks, grooves, points, etc.) which enabled them to join each other in characteristic ways. Theirs was the first move towards modern atomic theory and a predecessor of the modern concept of chemical linkages.

Authoritarianism, a dictatorial form of government as contrasted with a democratic one based on popular sovereignty. Its alleged advantages are the avoidance of the delays and inefficiency said to be characteristic of the latter.

Automatism, the production of material, written or spoken in "automatic" fashion—*i.e.*, apparently not under the conscious or volitional control of the individual. This psychologically perplexing phenomenon has occurred from time to time throughout the history of literature and art, and while it has occasionally produced work of great merit (much of William Blake's poetry, Coleridge's "Kubla Khan", etc.) the bulk of it is indifferent and often simply rubbish. Spiritualists claim that the work is produced under the direct guidances of the spirit world, and their argument has attracted considerable attention through the compositions of the pianist Rosemary Brown who, with little or no academic background in musical theory, has produced a number of "original" piano pieces allegedly composed by Beethoven, Mozart, *etc.*, from the astral plane. While few music critics doubt Mrs. Brown's honesty and integrity, most consider her work to be clever pastiche and barely comparable in quality to the masterworks of the dead composers. Nevertheless automatism wants some explaining, and most psychologists today defer judgement, taking the view that it serves to remind us of the fund of material which lies in the unconscious mind, and which is prone to pop up from time to time without warning. Rather similar is the case of Matthew Manning, a young English student who produced clever and artistically intriguing drawings and sketches, allegedly guided by the hands of famous dead artists.

B

Baconian Method, the use of the inductive (as opposed to the deductive or Aristotelian) method of reasoning as proposed by Francis Bacon in the 17th cent. and J. S. Mill in the 19th cent. Deduction argues from supposedly certain first principles (such as the existence of God or Descartes's "I think, therefore I am") what the nature of the universe and its laws *must* be, whereas the only means of obtaining true knowledge of the universe, in Bacon's view, was by the amassing of facts and observations so that when enough were obtained the certain truth would be known in the same way that a child's numbered dots in a playbook joined together by a pencilled line create a picture. However, this is not the way science progresses in practice. Bacon had underrated the importance of hypothesis and theory and overrated the reliability of the senses. In discussing the scientific tradition, Sir Karl Popper in his book, *Conjecture and Refutations*, says: "The most important function of observation and reasoning, and even of intuition and imagination, is to help us in the critical examination of those bold conjectures which are the means by which we probe into the unknown." Two of the greatest men who clearly saw that there was no such thing as an inductive procedure were Galileo and Einstein.

Bahá'í Faith, a faith which teaches the unity of all religions and the unity of mankind. It arose in Iran from the teachings of the Bab (Mirza Ali Mohammed, 1820–50) and the Bahá'u'lláh (Mirza Husain Ali, 1817–92), thought to be manifestations of God, who in his essence is unknowable. Emphasis is laid on service to others. It has communities in many states and is surprisingly strong in England with a substantial following among university students. Its aims—universal peace, love, fellowship, sexual equality, etc.—are so laudable that it is hard to disagree with anything in the movement. Since the ruling fundamentalist Islamic regime of the Ayatollahs came to power in Iran in 1979 members of the faith have been persecuted. The movement is now guided and administered by an elected order, "The Universal House of Justice". Today (1999) the movement has over 5,750,000 followers, with some 6,000 in Britain.

Baptists, a Christian denomination whose distinctive doctrines are that members can only be received by baptism "upon the confession of their faith and sins" and that "baptism is no wise appertaineth to infants." Baptism is therefore by total immersion of adults. Modern Baptists base their doctrines upon the teaching of the Apostles and some hold that the Albigenses (*q.v.*) maintained the true belief through what they regarded as the corruption of the Roman Church in mediaeval times. On the other hand any connection with the Anabaptist movement during the Reformation is rejected and the beginning of the modern Church is traced to John Smyth, a minister of the Church of England who in Amsterdam came under the influence of the Arminians (*q.v.*) and Mennonites. Smyth died in 1612 when the first Baptist church in England was built at Newgate. This, the "General" Baptist Church, rejected Calvinistic beliefs and held the Arminian doctrine of redemption open to all, but some years later a split occurred with the formation of the "Particular" Baptist Church which was Calvinist in doctrine. In 1891 the two bodies were united in the Baptist Union and today the sect is spread throughout the world, notably in the United States. There are (1999) *c*. 147,000 Baptists in Great Britain.

The Anabaptists movement began in Zurich, Switzerland, in 1525, when Conrad Grebel, Felix Manz and Jörg Blaurock, their hearts moved by their failure to live according to the Gospel, decided to give their lives to following Christ's teaching, whatever the cost. The movement spread widely in Switzerland, Germany and Holland in the 16th century, and its followers suffered martyrdom by fire, water and the sword for the sake of their faith. They met with further condemnation and persecution because of the excesses of a violent and radical group, known as the Münster Anabaptists, whom they disowned.

The wider movement was non-violent and stood for baptism on confession of faith, love to one's enemies and obedience to the Spirit of Christ's Sermon on the Mount. This movement is the spiritual precursor of several of the Peace Churches of today: the Hutterians (named after their founder, Jakob Hutter), the Mennonites (after Menno Simons), and, later, the Amish.

The most radical of these groups is that of the Hutterian Brethren, who live, work, and hold their goods in common like the first Christians.

Beat Generation, a term first used by the American writer Jack Kerouac (d. 1969), author of *The Town and the City* and *On the Road,* to define various groups spread across the face of the country, but notably in New York and San Francisco, who, belonging to the post-war generation, represented a complex of attitudes, mainly rebellious.

Behaviourism, a school of psychology founded in 1914 by J. B. Watson (1878–1958), an animal psychologist at Johns Hopkins University, Baltimore. Its main tenet was that the method of introspection and the study of mental states were unscientific and should be replaced by the study of behaviour. When animals or human beings were exposed to specific stimuli and their responses objectively recorded, or when the development of a child, as seen in its changing behaviour, was noted, these alone were methods which were truly scientific. Watson contributed an important idea to psychology and did a great deal towards ridding it of the largely philosophical speculations of the past. But he also went to absurd extremes, as in his view that thought is nothing but subvocal speech, consisting of almost imperceptible movements of the tongue, throat, and larynx (*i.e.*, when we think, we are really talking to ourselves), and his further opinion that heredity is, except in grossly abnormal cases, of no importance. He claimed that by "conditioning", the ordinary individual could be made into any desired type, regardless of his or her inheritance.

The work of Ivan Pavlov had begun about 1901, but was unknown in America until about ten years later, and it was through another Russian, Vladimir Bekhterev, that the concept of "conditioning" was introduced into the country. Bekhterev's book *Objective Psychology,* describing his new science of "reflexology". was translated in 1913 and played a great part in the development of Behaviourist ideas. The conditioned reflex became central to Watson's theory of learning and habit, formation (*e.g.,* he showed that a year-old child, at first unafraid of white rats, became afraid of them when they came to be associated with a loud noise behind the head). Finally all behaviour, including abnormal behaviour, came to be explained in terms of conditioned responses; these were built up by association on the infant's three innate emotions of fear, rage, and love, of which the original stimuli were, for the first, loud noises and the fear of falling; for the second, interference with freedom of movement; and for the third, patting and stroking.

Because of its considerable theoretical simplicity and its implicit suggestion that human behaviour could be easily described (and even modified or controlled), Pavlovian psychology appeared very attractive to the Communist regime in Russia, and before long it became the "official" dogma in universities and research laboratories. Whereas in America and Western Europe its severe limitations became gradually apparent, in the former USSR these were ignored or disguised for ideological reasons with the inevitable outcome that Soviet psychology failed to evolve and, at one stage, seemed to be no more than a pallid offshoot of physiology. In non-Communist countries simple Watsonian behaviourism evolved into more sophisticated studies of animal learning, largely pioneered by the Harvard psychologist, Skinner. These techniques, which have shown that animals, from monkeys to rats, may be taught to solve a remarkable range of physical problems (such as pressing complex sequences of buttons or levers to escape from a cage) have themselves turned out to be rather disappointing in terms of advancing our general understanding of the workings of the human and animal brain. There is a growing feeling among psychologists that the real keys to the understanding of mankind will only be found through the study of man himself, and not his simpler animal cousins. *See also* **Gestalt Psychology.**

Benthamism. *See* **Utilitarianism.**

Bermuda Triangle, an area of sea, bounded by Bermuda, Florida and Puerto Rico where unexplained disappearances of aircraft and ships have led to many fanciful theories. Natural phenomenon are the most likely explanation.

Bio-terrorism. *See* **Terrorism, J52.**

Bolshevism, an alternative name for **Communism** (*q.v.*), usually used in the West in a derogatory sense. When the Russian Social Democratic Party at a conference held in London in 1903 split over the issue of radicalism or moderation, it was the radical faction headed by Lenin (who subsequently led the 1917 Revolution and became first Head of State of the Soviet Union) which polled the majority of votes. The Russian for majority is *bolshinstvo* and for minority *menshinstvo;* hence the radicals became known as Bolsheviki and the moderates as Mensheviki. *See* **Communism, Marxism.**

Brahmanism. A religion of ancient India which evolved out of the Vedas about 1000–800 B.C. and is still powerful today. It provides the orthodox core of traditional Hinduism. Characteristics of the faith were elaborate ceremonies, material offerings, animal sacrifice, a dominant priestly caste (the Brahmins), and a development of the idea of Brahman as the eternal, impersonal Absolute Principle. *See also* **Hinduism.**

Buchmanism. *See* **Moral Re-Armament.**

Buddhism, one of the great Oriental religions. It arose against the background of Brahminism in north India in the 6th cent. B.C., its founder being the Sākyan prince Siddhattha Gotama, known as the Buddha or "Enlightened One". Distressed by the problem of human suffering from which even death allowed no escape—since Buddha accepted a doctrine of a cycle of lives—he left his palace and his beloved family to become a religious mendicant and ascetic, studying for six years the beliefs of Brahmin hermits and self-torturing recluses. After this long search he sat down under a tree (the Banyan tree, which became known as the Bo-tree or tree of enlightenment because of his enlightenment) and finally came to understand the cause and release from suffering. The result of his meditations are enshrined in the "four noble truths" which are: (1) that all living is itself suffering; (2) suffering is caused by desire; (3) suffering ceases when desire is eradicated; (4) that it can be destroyed by following the "noble eightfold path" whose steps are: right views; right thought; right speech, plain and truthful; right conduct, including abstinence not only from immorality and the taking of life, whether human or animal; right livelihood, harming no one; right effort, always pressing on; right awareness of the present; and lastly, right meditation. The more man acquires merit by following these rules in his chain of lives, the sooner is *Nirvana* attained; he loses his individuality, not by annihilation, but "as the dewdrop slips into the shining sea," by merging with the universal life.

Buddhism teaches a way of liberation through ethics and meditation. In many Buddhist nations no word exists for the concept of an Almighty God, which was neither affirmed nor denied by Buddha himself but simply ignored. Nor did Buddha claim to be other than a man, although prayers were made to Buddha, ritual developed, sacred relics preserved under stupas, and the belief in a succession of Buddhas introduced; the sacred writings (*Tripitaka*) are divided into three parts; *Suttanta, Abhidhamma* and *Vinaya. Suttanta* are mostly teachings in everyday language, *Abhidhamma* are teachings using the analytical method and the *Vinaya* is the monastic rule for monks. They were gathered by devotees at various councils—the first held after the death of Buddha at the age of 80, a third at the order of King Asoka in 244 B.C. The founder himself wrote nothing.

Buddhism spread to Sri Lanka, Nepal, Tibet, Mongolia, Indo-China, Myanmar (Burma), Thailand, China, and Japan, although on the whole losing influence in India. In Tibet, Buddhism developed into Lamaism (q.v.). In Sri Lanka, Burma, Thailand etc., it persisted in its pure form (the Theravada), while in China and Japan it developed into the Mahayana. Today (1999) there are over 330 million Buddhists world-wide. Fragments of the oldest known Buddhist manuscript (the religion's equivalent to the Dead Sea Scrolls) were discovered by the British Library in 1996.

Bushido, the traditional code of honour of the Samurai or Japanese military caste corresponding to the European concept of knighthood and chivalry from which it took its separate origin in the 12th cent. Even today it is a potent influence among the upper classes, being based on the principles of simplicity, honesty, courage, and justice which together form a man's idea of personal honour.

C

Cabala, originally a collection of Jewish doctrines about the nature of the Universe, supposedly handed down by Moses to the Rabbis, which evolved into a kind of mystical interpretation of the Old Testament. Students of the history of religious belief have found its origins to be in fact extremely obscure, and some aspects appear to have been lifted from ancient Egyptian sources. Skilled Cabalists hold that the system contains a key to biblical interpretation based on the numerical values of the words and letters of the Scriptures which reveal hidden depths of meaning behind the allegorical Old Testament stories.

Calvinism, the branch of Protestantism founded basically (although preceded by Zwingli and others) by Jean Chauvin (1509–64), who was born in Noyon in Picardy. John Calvin, as he is usually called, from the Latin form of his name, Calvinius, provided in his Institutions of the Christian Religion the first logical definition and justification of Protestantism, thus becoming the intellectual leader of the Reformation as the older Martin Luther was its emotional instigator. The distinctive doctrine of Calvinism is its dogma of predestination which states that God has unalterably destined some souls to salvation to whom "efficacious grace and the gift of perseverance" is granted and others to eternal damnation. Calvinism, as defined in the Westminster Confession, is established in the Reformed or Presbyterian churches of France, Holland, Scotland, etc., as contrasted with the Lutheran churches, and its harsh but logical beliefs inspired the French Huguenots, the Dutch in their fight against Spanish Catholic domination, and the English Puritans. The rule set up under Calvin's influence in Geneva was marred by the burning at the stake of the anatomist Servetus for the heresy of "pantheism", or, as we should say, Unitarianism.

Perhaps its greatest single influence outside the Church was the result of Calvinist belief that to labour industriously was one of God's commands. This changed the mediaeval notions of the blessedness of poverty and the wickedness of usury, proclaimed that men should shun luxury and be thrifty, yet implied that financial success was a mark of God's favour. In this way it was related to the rise of capitalism either as cause or effect. Max Weber, the German sociologist, believed that Calvinism was a powerful incentive to, or even cause of, the rise of **capitalism** (q.v.): Marx, Sombart, and in England, Tawney, asserted the reverse view—that Calvinism was a result of developing capitalism, being its ideological justification.

Capitalism is an economic system under which the means of production and distribution are owned by a relatively small section of society which runs them at its own discretion for private profit. There exists, on the other hand, a propertyless class of those who exist by the sale of their labour power. Capitalism arose towards the end of the 18th cent. in England where the early factory owners working with small-scale units naturally approved of free enterprise and free trade. But free enterprise has no necessary connection with capitalism; by the beginning of this century monopolies were developing and state protection against foreign competition was demanded. Capitalism is opposed by those who believe in socialism (q.v.), first, for the moral reasons that it leads to economic inequality and the exploitation of labour and the consuming public, and that public welfare rather than private profit should motivate the economic system; secondly, for the practical reason that capitalism leads to recurrent economic crises. Any major world economic crisis led to great hopes on the part of Marxists and Communists that capitalism was involved in its final death throes.

Cartomancy, the art of fortunes or predicting the future by playing cards or by the Tarot pack.

Catholicism. For those who are not Roman Catholics the term "Catholic" has two separate meanings. The more general refers to the whole body of Christians throughout the world, the more specific refers to a particular view of Christianity. In this latter sense the Church of England, the Orthodox Eastern Churches, and others consider themselves "Catholic" meaning that (a) they belong to Christ's Church as organised on an accepted basis of faith and order; (b) they insist on the necessity of "liturgical" worship through established forms (e.g., baptism, holy communion); (c) they emphasise the continuity of Christian tradition by the use of ancient creeds (e.g., the Apostles' Creed, the Nicene Creed) and regard the ministry as a succession (Apostolic succession) deriving from early practice. In this sense there is thought to be no necessary contradiction between Catholicism and Protestantism regarded as a renewal of the Church in the 16th cent. by an appeal to the Scriptures as interpreted by the early Fathers of the Church. This definition obviously excludes Quakers, Christian Scientists, and many Nonconformist sects. See also **Roman Catholic Church, J46.**

Censorship. See J57.

Characterology, the attempt made over many centuries to classify people into personality types on the basis of physical or psychological characteristics. The first attempt was made by Hippocrates in the 5th cent. B.C. who classified temperaments into the sanguine (or optimistic), the melancholic, the choleric (or aggressive), and the phlegmatic (or placid); these were supposed to result from the predominance of the following "humours" in the body: red blood, black bile, yellow bile, or phlegm respectively. Theophrastus, a pupil of Aristotle, described, with examples, thirty extreme types of personality (e.g. the talkative, the boorish, the miserly, etc.); these were basically literary and imaginative but about the same time "physiognomy" arose which attempted to interpret character from the face. Physiognomy became of importance again during the Renaissance and there are still those today who believe in it in spite of the fact that, broadly speaking, there is no connection whatever between facial features and personality (i.e. although it may be possible to tell from the features that a man is an idiot or some extreme abnormal type and some idea of character may be obtained from an individual's characteristic facial expressions, it is not possible to tell (as Johann Lavater, the best-known physiognomist of the late 18th cent. believed) from the shape of the nose, height of the brow, or dominance of the lower jaw, whether anyone is weak, intellectual or determined). The contention of the 19th cent. Italian criminologist Cesare Lombroso that criminals show typical facial characteristics—prominent cheekbones and jaw, slanting eyes, receding brow, large ears of a particular shape—was convincingly disproved by Karl Pearson when he found that 3,000 criminals showed no major differences of features, carefully measured from a similar number of students at Oxford and Cambridge.

It has, however, been noted that people in general tend to be intellectual or emotional, inward- or outward-looking, and this observation is reflected in the classification of the Scottish psychologist, Alexander Bain (d. 1903), into intellectual, artistic, and practical; Nietzsche's Apollonian and Dionysian types; William James's "tender" and "toughminded"; and C. G. Jung's introvert and extrovert.

Some connection has been found between temperament and body-build. The German psychiatrist Ernst Kretschmer (1888–1964) showed that manic-depressive patients and normal people who are extroverted and tend to alternate in mood (as do manic-depressives to an exaggerated degree) were usually short and stout or thick-set in build; schizophrenics and normal people, who both show shyness, serious or introverted reactions, were usually tall and slender. The former of "pyknic" body-build are "cyclothyme" in temperament, the latter with "schizothyme" temperament are of two bodily types—the tall and thin or "asthenic" and the muscularly well-proportioned or "athletic". The American Sheldon has confirmed these observations on the whole and gone into further details. According to him the basic body types are: (1) *endomorphic* (rounded build), corresponding to Kretschmer's pyknic, normally associated with the *viscerotonic* temperament (relaxed, sociable); (2) *mesomorphic* (squarish, athletic build), normally associated with the *somatotonic* temperament (energetic, assertive); and (3) *ectomorphic* (linear build) normally associated with the *cerebrotonic* temperament (anxious, submissive, restless). Glandular and metabolic factors have considerable effect on human personality and also, to some extent, on physique. It is not too surprising, therefore, to find an association between body build (or "somatotype" as Sheldon termed it) and general mood. However, Sheldon's original clear-cut categories of body-type are no longer looked upon as reliable indicators of personality.

Charismatic, the evangelical, 'New Church' Christian movement that has broken away from the traditional Church. The 'house church' movement (with *c* 110,000 members) is part of this rapidly-growing movement, which started in Britain with the 1987 'March for Jesus'.

Chartism, a socialistic movement in England (1837–55) which attempted to better the conditions of the working classes. Named after "The People's Charter" of Francis Place (1838), its programme demanded: (1) universal manhood suffrage; (2) vote by ballot; (3) equal electoral districts; (4) annual parliament; (5) payment of members; (6) abolition of their property qualifications. Chartism was supported by the Christian socialists (*q.v.*), J. F. D. Maurice (1805–72), and Charles Kingsley (1819–75) with certain qualifications. The movement, the first mass organisation of the industrial working class, had considerable influence on the evolution of socialist ideas in England. It is worth noting that its demands—with the exception of the unworkable "annual parliament"—have largely been met today, though at the time they were thought by many to be both outrageous and impossible. The movement failed at the time from internal divisions.

Chauvinism, a term applied to any excessive devotion to cause, particularly a patriotic or military one. The word is derived from Nicholas Chauvin whose excessive devotion to Napoleon made him a laughing-stock.

Chirognomy, the study of the shape of the hands and fingernails.

Chirology, the subject concerned with the hand as an indicator of psychological and medical significance. Chirology derives from an Oriental tradition concerning mental and physical healing and spirituality and as such encompasses many associated arts and studies of direct relevance to modern day living. Palmistry in the main is a crude folk art and does not attempt to understand or clarify its own teachings. The Cheirological Society was founded in 1889 by Katherine St. Hill to promote the systematic study of the hand as a serious subject worthy of scientific attention bereft of superstition and fakery. It still exists today and has members throughout the world.

Chiromancy, the study of lineal formations of the hand.

Chiropractic, the art of manipulation of the joints, in particular the spine, as a means of curing disease. Some qualified doctors employ its principles and, as with its near-neighbour osteopathy, it seems on occasions to be a useful complement to medical treatment.

Christadelphians, a religious denomination formed in the USA in the late 1840s by John Thomas, an Englishman. They strive to represent the simple apostolic faith of the 1st century and hold that the Scriptures are the wholly inspired, infallible Word of God. They believe in the mortality of mankind—the teaching of the immortality of the soul is not of Bible origin and that salvation is dependent of belief followed by a baptism of total immersion in water. They believe in the imminent, personal return of Jesus Christ to the earth to judge the living and dead and reward the righteous with Eternal life.

Christianity, the religion founded by Jesus Christ whose teaching is found in the New Testament's four Gospels. Simple as His creed may seem it soon became complicated by the various ways in which Christians interpreted it, and the differences within the early Church are reflected in the numerous Councils held to define truth from heresy. The Eastern Church of the Byzantine Empire from the 5th cent. onwards had differed in various ways from the See of Rome and by 1054 the breach became permanent. The 16th cent. Reformation was the other great break in the unity of the Church and once Protestantism had given in effect the right to each man to interpret the Scriptures in his own way, the tendency to fragmentation increased so that, by 1650, there were no fewer than 180 sects, mostly dogmatic and intolerant towards each other. Today there are many more, some of which are mentioned in this section under the appropriate headings. Nevertheless there are signs today that the trend of disunity is being reversed. The modern ecumenical movement, which has its roots in the great missionary movement of the 19th cent., aims to bring about a reunion of Christendom by uniting Christians throughout the world on the simple basis of the acceptance of Jesus Christ as God and Saviour, *i.e.*, on the basis of Christian fellowship. The movement finds expression in the World Council of Churches (*q.v.*). The Christian life is expressed in the words of Christ: "Thou shalt love the Lord thy God with all thy heart and thy neighbour as thyself." For many it is the humanitarian side of Christianity that has meaning today; to accept responsibility for others, as well as for oneself. There are now (1999) over 1,760,000,000 Christians world-wide.

Christian Science claims that it is a religion based on the words and works of Christ Jesus. It draws its authority from the Bible, and its teachings are set forth in *Science and Health with Key to the Scriptures* by Mary Baker Eddy (1821–1910) the discoverer and founder of Christian Science. A distinctive part of Christian Science is its healing of physical disease as well as sin by spiritual means.

The Church of Christ, Scientist, was founded in 1879 when 15 students of Mrs Eddy met with their teacher and voted to organize a church designed to commemorate the words and works of the Master, which should reinstate primitive Christianity and its lost element of healing.

A few years later the church took its present and permanent form as The Mother Church, The First Church of Christ, Scientist, in Boston, Massachusetts, which together with its branch churches and societies throughout the world, constitutes the Christian Science denomination. Now (1999) more than 100 years after its founding there are over 2,700 branches in 60 countries.

Christian Socialism, a movement launched in 1848, a year of revolutions throughout the continent, by a group in England designed to commit the church to a programme of social reform. The leaders, notably J. F. D. Maurice, Charles Kingsley (both Anglican clergymen), and John Ludlow were deeply moved by the wretched conditions of the British working class and the two priests had, indeed, given active support to the

Chartist movement (*q.v.*). However, all insisted that socialism in its existing forms ignored the spiritual needs of mankind and must be tempered with Christianity. Tracts were written to expose the sweated industries, the consequences of unrestrained competition and the evils following the enclosure system; but, more concretely, Christian socialism fostered co-operative workshops and distributive societies based on those of the Rochdale pioneers, organised a working-man's college, and set up elementary classes for education. It also supported the emerging trade-union movement.

The traditions of Christian socialism have been carried on by the Fabian Society, by adherents of Guild Socialism, and by individuals who reject Marx's teaching of revolutionary change, and seek to bring it about by the methods of political action.

Church of England. There is some evidence of possible continuity with the Christianity of Roman Britain, but in the main the Church derives from the fusion of the ancient Celtic church with the missionary church of St. Augustine, who founded the See of Canterbury in A.D. 597. To archbishop Theodore in 673 is ascribed its organisation in dioceses with settled boundaries, and in parishes. St. Augustine's church was in communion with Rome from the first, but the Church of England was not brought within papal jurisdiction until after the Norman conquest, and was at no time under the complete domination of Rome. It remains the Catholic Church of England without break of continuity, but during the Reformation the royal supremacy was accepted and that of the pope repudiated. It is the Established Church (*i.e.*, the official church of the realm), crowns the sovereign, and its archbishops and bishops in the House of Lords can act as a kind of "conscience of the state" at every stage of legislation. The Church is organised in two ecclesiastical provinces (Canterbury and York) and 43 dioceses. Its traditional forms of worship are embodied in the Book of Common Prayer, but the Alternative Service Book of 1980 is now widely used.

In 1992, the General Synod finally accepted the ordination of women priests. The first 32 women priests were ordained on 12 March 1994 in Bristol Cathedral. The first 42 Anglican women priests in Scotland were ordained in the Scottish Episcopal Church in December 1994. Meanwhile the Anglican Church faced a financial crisis, with its assets having been severely eroded in the 1980s. Far-reaching changes in the organisation of the Anglican Church were proposed by the Turnbull Commission in 1995. The plans strengthen the role of the Archbishop of Canterbury and propose an autonomous National Council.

Recent developments include continued divisions over women bishops and gay priests, the signing of the 1996 Porvoo Agreement (ending the rift with Lutheranism) and a steadying of church attendance figures (although Sunday attendance was only 22 per thousand in 1994 compared to 35 in 1968). The first women priests in Wales were ordained in 1997, whilst in 1996 the Movement for the Ordination of Women was reformed to campaign for Anglican women bishops. By 1997, 10 % of Anglican clergy were women. In 1997 the General Synod formally agreed to hold unity talks with the Methodists. More recently, controversy has surrounded moves by the Church of England to relax its ban on divorcees remarrying in Church.

The Anglican Communion comprises the churches in all parts of the world which are in communion with the Church of England. All the bishops of the Anglican Communion meet every ten years in the Lambeth Conference (first held in 1867), over which the Archbishop of Canterbury by custom presides as *primus inter pares*. At the 1968 Conference observers and laymen were admitted for the first time. The last Conference met against a background of continued division over women, gay issues *etc.* The 1998 Lambeth Conference (attended by 798 bishops) strongly supported the traditionalists over homosexuality issues.

Church of Scotland, the established national church of Scotland, presbyterian in constitution, and governed by a hierarchy of courts—the kirk-sessions, the presbyteries, the synods, and the General Assembly. *See* **Presbyterianism.**

Clairvoyance. *See* **Telepathy.**

Collectivism. The theory of the collective ownership or control of all the means of production, and especially of the land, by the whole community or state, *i.e.* the people collectively, for the benefit of the people as a whole. The term has also acquired a broader sense, to denote the view that the individual is subordinate to the social collectivity. An influential expression of collectivist ideas can be found in Rousseau's *Du contrat social* (1762). It is an important theme in Hegel and Marx, and has been expressed in such movements as socialism, communism and fascism. Collectivism is to be contrasted with individualism (*q.v.*).

Colonialism. Colonialism refers to the kind of imperialism practised by European countries in for example Africa and S.E. Asia, where the colonised country was allowed to have partially autonomous legal and social institutions, while the mother country retained supreme power, and the colonial community had social and political rights denied to the natives. "Neo-colonialism" means the cultural and economic infiltration of developing countries by manipulation of market forces. *See also* **Imperialism.**

Communism, ideally refers to the type of society in which all property belongs to the community and social life is based on the principle "from each according to his ability, to each according to his needs." There would be public ownership of all enterprises and all goods would be free. Since no such society as yet exists, the word in practice refers to the attempt to achieve such a society by initially overthrowing the capitalist system and establishing a dictatorship of the proletariat (Marx identified the dictatorship with a democratic constitution). Communists believe that their first task is the establishment of socialism under which there remain class distinctions, private property to some extent, and differences between manual and brain workers. The state is regulated on the basis "from each according to his ability, to each according to his work". Lenin applied Marx's analysis to the new conditions which had arisen in 20th-cent. capitalist society. Marxism–Leninism develops continuously with practice since failure to apply its basic principles to changed circumstances and times would result in errors of dogmatism. Mao Tse-tung worked out the techniques of revolutionary action appropriate to China; Che Guevara the guerrilla tactics appropriate to the peasants of Latin America. His counsel "It is not necessary to wait until conditions for making revolution exist; the insurrection can create them", was the opposite of Mao Tse-tung's "Engage in no battle you are not sure of winning", and Lenin's "Never play with insurrection". Two fundamental principles of communism are (1) peaceful co-existence between countries of different social systems, and (2) the class struggle between oppressed and oppressing classes and between oppressed and oppressor nations. Maoism, for example, held that it was a mistake to lay one sided stress on peaceful transition towards socialism otherwise the revolutionary will of the proletariat becomes passive and unprepared for the tasks ahead.

In Russia the civil war developed *after* the revolution; in China the communists fought their civil war *before* they seized power: the Yugoslav partisans won their own guerrilla war *during* their stand against the fascist powers—differences which had important political consequences. Russia suffered three decades of isolationism and totalitarian suppression ("an isolated and besieged fortress") before the advent of Gorbachev heralded a new openness (*glasnost*) in Soviet politics. The dramatic collapse of Communism in Eastern Europe during 1989 and the collapse of the Soviet Union itself in 1991 left only China, Cuba, Vietnam and North Korea as communist states (at least in theory) in the 1990s. *See* **Maoism, Marxism** and **Trotskyism.**

Confucianism. Confucius (Latinised form of K'ung-Fo-tzu) was born in 551 B.C. in the feudal state of Lu in modern Shantung province. He was thus a contemporary of Buddha, although nobody could have been more dissimilar. Where Buddha was metaphysical in his thought, Confucius was practical; Buddha was original, Confucius had hardly an original idea in his head; Buddha wanted to convert individuals to an other-worldly philosophy. Confucius wanted to reform the feudal governments of his time, believing that in this way their subjects would be made happier. Other religions have in their time, been revolutionary; Confucius was a conservative who wanted to bring back a golden age from the past. The only respect in which Confucius agreed with the Buddha was that neither was particularly interested in the supernatural.

Much of his time was spent in going from the court of one feudal lord to another trying to impress them by his example. For he suffered from the curious belief that the example set by the ruler influences his subjects. He made much of etiquette, trembling and speaking in low tones and behaving with "lofty courtesy" to his inferiors. Promoting the idea of "the golden mean", he was not impressed by heroic deeds or unusual people, and was greatly displeased when he heard that a truthful son had reported that his father had stolen a sheep: "Those who are upright", he said, "are different from this; the father conceals the misconduct of the son, and the son conceals the misconduct of the father." One feels that Confucius would have felt not at all out of place in an English public school. Virtue brings its own reward in this world, ceremonial is important, politeness when universal would reduce jealousy and quarrels; "reverence the

spirits but keep them far off." Destiny decides to what class a man shall belong, and as destiny is but another name for Nature prayer is unnecessary, for once having received his destiny, a man can demand and obtain from Nature what he chooses, his own will decides.

Congregationalists, the oldest sect of Nonconformists who hold that each church should be independent of external ecclesiastical authority. They took their origin from the Brownists of Elizabeth's days. Robert Browne (c. 1550–c. 1633), an Anglican clergyman, who had come to reject bishops, was forced with his followers to seek refuge, first in Holland and then in Scotland where he was imprisoned by the Kirk. In later life he changed his views and is disowned by Congregationalists because of his reversion to Anglicanism. His former views were spread by Henry Barrow and John Greenwood who, under an Act passed in 1592 "for the punishment of persons obstinately refusing to come to church" (and largely designed for the suppression of this sect), were hanged at Tyburn. They had preached (a) that the only head of the church is Jesus Christ; (b) that, contrary to Elizabethan doctrine, the church had no relationship to the state; (c) that the only statute-book was the Bible whereas the Articles of Religion and Book of Common Prayer were mere Acts of Parliament; (d) that each congregation of believers was independent

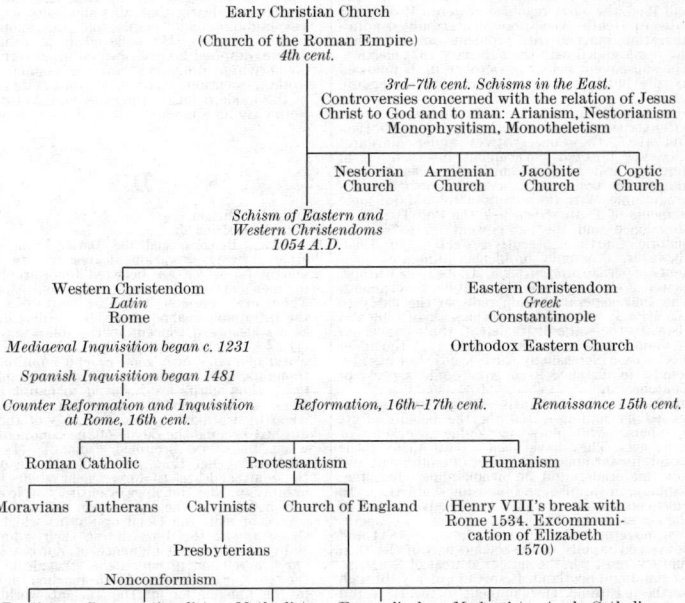

Early Christian Church

(Church of the Roman Empire)
4th cent.

3rd–7th cent. Schisms in the East.
Controversies concerned with the relation of Jesus
Christ to God and to man: Arianism, Nestorianism
Monophysitism, Monotheletism

Nestorian Church   Armenian Church   Jacobite Church   Coptic Church

Schism of Eastern and Western Christendoms 1054 A.D.

Western Christendom
Latin
Rome

Eastern Christendom
Greek
Constantinople

Mediaeval Inquisition began c. 1231

Orthodox Eastern Church

Spanish Inquisition began 1481

Counter Reformation and Inquisition at Rome, 16th cent.   *Reformation, 16th–17th cent.*   *Renaissance 15th cent.*

Roman Catholic   Protestantism   Humanism

Moravians   Lutherans   Calvinists   Church of England   (Henry VIII's break with Rome 1534. Excommunication of Elizabeth 1570)

Presbyterians

Nonconformism

Baptists   Congregationalists   Methodist   Evangelicals   Modernists   Anglo-Catholics and had the power of choosing its own ministers. The body fled once more to Holland and were among the Pilgrims who set sail in the *Mayflower* for America in 1620 whilst those who remained were joined by Puritans fleeing from Charles I. They became free once more to live in England under the Commonwealth only to be repressed again under Charles II. Finally full liberty of worship was granted under William III. In 1833 the Congregational Union of England and Wales was formed which had no legislative power. It had issued a Declaration of Faith by which no minister was bound; he was responsible to his own church and to nobody else. The sect is widespread both in Britain and the USA where it is held in special honour because of its connection with the Pilgrim Fathers. In 1972 the Congregational Church in England and Wales and the Presbyterian Church of England united to form the United Reformed Church. Those who did not join comprise the Congregational Federation.

Conservatism. The term "Conservative" came into general use after 1834 in place of the older name of "Tory". The modern Conservative Party has its origins in the period of "Tory Democracy" introduced by Disraeli between 1874 and 1880. Originally the party of church, aristocracy and landed gentry, Conservatism has been increasingly supported since the turn of the century by large business interests. Under Baldwin, Conservative-dominated administration held office for much of the inter-war period. The 1945 Labour victory caused the Conservative Party to undertake a basic review of its philosophy. From 1951 to 1964, Conservatives held office continuously, reaching a peak in Harold Macmillan's 1959 election victory. Though defeated by Labour in 1964 and 1966, the party regained power in 1970 under Edward Heath. The subsequent troubled administration, plagued with problems on the industrial front, ended with the February 1974 election. The subsequent defeat in October 1974, followed by the battle for the Conservative leadership, again caused the party to seek to review its philosophy as it had developed in recent years. After the three victories of the party in 1979, 1983 and 1987, the Conservatives under Margaret Thatcher rejected government intervention in industry and relied on market forces, a rigid monetarist policy and a major privatisation programme. With the advent of John Major some elements of Thatcherism (*e.g.* the Poll Tax) were abandoned and the party went on to win an historic fourth consecutive election in 1992. However, economic problems, numerous incidents of 'sleaze' and bitter divisions over Europe, as well as electoral reverses, beset his government. The 1997 general election reduced the party to 165 MPs. It was a defeat on the scale of 1906 and 1945. In the wake of its defeat, the party chose William Hague as its leader. Since 1997 the party has become increasingly Euro-sceptic but has also sought to distance itself from some aspects of Thatcherism.

Cooperativism. A cooperative is an organization owned by and operated for the benefit of its members, who may be either workers or customers. They have been set up all over the world, for farming, purchasing of equipment and raw materials, and in wholesaling, retailing, banking, insurance and housing industries. In most cooperatives the members receive a share of the net earnings. The modern consumer cooperative movement started in Rochdale in 1844 and developed rapidly in the second half of the 19th century, mostly in the industrial areas of Northern England and Scotland. It spread quickly through northern Europe. Development in the USA and Latin America came later in the 20th century.

Coptic Church, the sect of Egyptian Christians who, holding "Monophysite" opinions (*i.e.*, refusing to grant the two natures, God and Man, of Christ), were declared heretical by the Council of Chalcedon in 451. They practise circumcision and have dietary laws. Their language is a direct descendant of ancient Egyptian. Like the Armenians, they are regarded as an heretical branch of Eastern Christianity. Their religious head is the patriarch of Alexandria. The rise of Islamic fundamentalism threatens Egypt's 6 million Copts.

Counter-Reformation. A movement in the 16th and 17th centuries in Europe, by which the Roman Catholic church reformed itself, defined its doctrines, strengthened its discipline and halted the advance of Protestantism. The Council of Trent (1545–1563) aimed at removing abuses within the church and defining Catholic thought in the debate with Protestantism. New, more active religious orders were founded, in particular the Jesuits (1534). The greater control exercised over church doctrine was seen in the setting up of the Inquisition and an Index of Prohibited Books. Some historians now prefer the term Catholic Reformation to Counter-Reformation.

Creationism. The theory which attributes the origin of matter, the different species of plants and animals, *etc.*, to "special creation" out of nothing by a divinity. Creationists thus accept that the Book of Genesis is a literal description of the beginning of the world. It is this doctrine which fundamentalist Christians have opposed to the evolutionary theories of Darwin, which have come to be accepted by most scientists since the publication of *The Origin of Species* in 1859. An attempt was made in the 1980s in the United States to have creationism taught alongside evolution, but failed in the U.S. Supreme Court.

A second slightly older meaning of the term is in reference to the theory that God creates a soul for every being born.

Cynics, a school of philosophy founded in the time of Alexander the Great by Diogenes. Choosing to live like a dog by rejecting all conventions of religion, manners, or decency, and allegedly living in a tub, Diogenes unwittingly brought on his school the title "Cynic", meaning not "cynical", as the word is understood today, but "canine". His teacher, Antisthenes, who had been a disciple of Socrates, decided, after the latter's death, that all philosophy was useless quibbling and man's sole aim should be simple goodness. He believed in a return to nature, despised luxury, wanted no government, no private property, and associated with working men and slaves. Far from being cynics in the modern sense, Diogenes and Antisthenes were virtuous anarchists rather like old Tolstoy.

D

Daoism. *See* Taoism.

Deism. *See* God and Man.

Demonism, Demons, and the Devil. Demons are ethereal beings of various degrees of significance and power which are believed to be implicated in men's good, but especially evil, fortune. They are common to most cultures. From the anthropological point of view the demon arose as a widespread concept in the following ways: (1) as a psychological projection into the outer world of man's own good or evil emotions and thoughts; (2) as a survival of primitive animism (*q.v.*), thus spirits are believed to haunt places, trees, stones, and other natural objects; (3) when by warlike invasion the gods of the vanquished become the devils of the conquerors (as when the Jews occupied Canaan); (4) as a primitive belief that spirits of the dead continue after death to hover near their former habitation, and not always entirely welcome to the living; (5) the conception of a supreme source of evil (the Devil or Satan) which took shape among the Jews during their sojourn in Babylon under the influence of Zoroastrianism (*q.v.*), a religion in which the struggle between the two spirits, Good and Evil, reached its height in the imagination of the ancient world. The Satan of the Old Testament was first regarded as one of God's servants (in the Book of Job he goes up and down the earth to see whether God's commands are obeyed), but when the Jews returned from their captivity he had become identified with Ahriman, the spirit of evil, who was in continual conflict with Ahursa Mazda, the spirit of good. The primitive mind ascribed both good and evil to one power alone; the division into God and the Devil, priest and witch, belongs to a higher stage of civilisation. The worship of evil itself, or of its personification in Satan, is a curious practice which seems to have developed hand-in-hand with Christianity and to have received steady support from a small but measurable minority. Many of the ceremonies involved in Satanism or in the so-called Black Mass appear to have been no more than opportunities for sexual excesses of one kind or another—such indulgences being traditionally barred to devout Christians. The alleged power of sex as a form of magic was propagated by the talented but rather mad poet, Aleister Crowley (1875–1947).

Determinism and Free-will. The question of whether man is, or is not, free to mould his own destiny is one which has exercised the minds of philosophers since Greek mythology conceived of the Fates as weaving a web of destiny from which no man can free himself. Socrates emphasised that man could through knowledge influence his destiny whilst ignorance made him the plaything of fate; Plato went further in pointing out that man can, and does, defeat the purposes of the universe and its divine Creator. It is our duty to live a good life, but we can live a foolish and wicked one if we chose. Aristotle wrote "Virtue is a disposition or habit involving deliberate purpose or choice". If this were not so morality would be a sham.

The Problem for Theology. The last of the great philosophers of Antiquity and one of the great influences in moulding Catholic theology was Plotinus (c. 204–70). Soul, he taught, is free, but once enmeshed in the body loses its freedom in the life of sense. Nevertheless, man is free to turn away from sensuality and towards God who is perfect freedom; for even when incarnated in matter the soul does not entirely lose the ability to rescue itself. This conception was carried over into the beliefs of the early Christian Apologists because it appeared to be in line with the teaching of Jesus that He had come to save man from sin. Sin implies guilt, and guilt implies the freedom to act otherwise; furthermore an all-good God cannot be responsible for the sin in the world which must be man's responsiblity and this again implies freedom. Pelagius (c. 355–c. 425), a Welsh priest, not only believed in free-will but questioning the doctrine of original sin, said that when men act righteously it is through their own moral effort, and God rewards them for their virtues in heaven. This belief became fairly widespread and was declared a heresy by the Church, being attacked notably by St. Augustine (354–430), a contemporary of Pelagius, who believed in predestination—that, since the sin of Adam, God had chosen who in all future history would be saved and who damned. This represents one tradition in Christianity: the determinism which leads to Calvinism (q.v.). St. Thomas Aquinas (1227–74), the greatest figure of scholasticism and one of the principal saints in the Roman Catholic Church, compromised between the two positions in the sense that, believing man to be free, he yet held that Adam's sin was transmitted to all mankind and only divine grace can bring salvation. But even when God wishes to bestow this salvation, the human will must co-operate. God foresees that some will not accept the offer of grace and predestines them to eternal punishment.

The Problem for Philosophy. With the Renaissance, thinkers began to free themselves from the domination of the Church and so study the world objectively and freely without preconceptions. But the more man turned to science, the more he discovered that the world was ruled by apparently inexorable laws and, since the scientist must believe that every event has a cause, he was led back to determinism. Man as part of the universe was subject to law too and all that existed was a vast machine. Francis Bacon (1561–1626) separated the fields of religion and science but left man subject completely to the will of God. Thomas Hobbes (1588–1679) was a rigid determinist and materialist although, having had trouble with the church in France whence, as a royalist, he had fled, he took care to announce that the Christian God is the Prime Mover.

Modern philosophy begins with René Descartes (1596–1650), a Frenchman who tried to reconcile the mechanical scientific universe of his time with the spiritual need for freedom. He did this by separating completely mind and body; the former, he said, is free, the latter completely determined. But, by admitting that the will can produce states of body, he was left with the problem of how this could happen—a problem which the so-called Occasionists solved to their own satisfaction by stating that the will is free and God so arranges the universe that what a person wills happens. Baruch Spinoza (1632–77), a Dutch Jew whose independence of thought had led to his excommunication from the Amsterdam Synagogue in 1656, was a complete determinist. He asserted that God and Nature are one, everything that happens is a manifestation of God's inscrutable nature, and it is logically impossible that things could be other than they are. Thus both Hobbes and Spinoza were determinists for entirely opposed reasons. The former as a materialist, the latter because he believed in the absolute perfection and universality of God. Yet the great religious mystic and mathematician Blaise Pascal (1623–62) held that, no matter what reason and cold logic may indicate we *know* from direct religious experience that we are free. John Calvin (1509–64) and Martin Luther (1483–1546) were both determinists. *See* **Calvinism, Lutheranism**.

To the more practical British philosophers, John Locke (1632–1704) and David Hume (1711–76), free-will was related to personality. Locke believed that God had implanted in each individual certain desires and these determine the will; the desires are already there, but we use our will to satisfy them. Hume argued that a man's behaviour is the necessary result of his character and if he had a different character he would act otherwise. Accordingly, when a man's actions arise from his own nature and desires he is free. He is not free when external events compel him to act otherwise (e.g., if he strikes another because his own nature is such he is free as he is not if he is compelled to do so against his desire). Leibnitz (1646–1716), although as a German metaphysical philosopher holding very different general views, said much the same thing—that choice is simply selecting the desire that is strongest. But most of the 18th cent. thinkers after Voltaire, with the great exceptions of Rousseau and the later German philosophers Kant, Fichte, Schopenhauer, and Hegel, who were initially influenced by him, accepted determinism. Rousseau (1712–78) began to stem the tide by his declaration that man is a free soul striving to remain free and only prevented from being so by society and the cold science which stifles his feeling heart. Once again the will became important as Kant (1724–1804) asserted that belief in freedom is a moral necessity although it cannot be proved by reason; the moral nature of man shows that there is a "transcendental" world beyond the senses where freedom applies. Fichte and Schelling found freedom in the Absolute ego or God, of whom each individual was part and thus also free. Hegel (1770–1831) saw the whole universe as evolving towards self-awareness and freedom in man although this could only be fully realised in a society that makes for freedom. Even God himself only attains full consciousness and self-realisation through the minds of such individuals as are free. This is the goal of the dialectical process. (*See* **Dialectical Materialism**.)

The Scientist's View. For the scientist the law of cause and effect is a useful hypothesis since, by and large, it is necessary for him to assume that all events are caused. Nevertheless the modern tendency is to think in terms of statistical probability rather than relentless mechanistic causality, and, although the free-will problem does not concern the scientist as such, it is clear that freedom and determinism (assuming the terms to have any meaning at all) are not necessarily opposed. In sociology, for example, we *know* that certain actions will produce certain results upon the behaviour of people in general, e.g., that raising interest rates will discourage business expansion. But this does not mean that Mr. Brown who decides in the circumstances not to add a new wing to his factory is not using his free-will. Even in the case of atoms, as Dr. Bronowski has pointed out, the observed results of allowing gas under pressure in a cylinder to rush out occur because most of the atoms are "obeying" the scientific "law" relating to such situations. But this does not mean that some atoms are not busy rushing across the stream or even against it—they are, but the general tendency is outwards and that is what we note. Lastly, the modern philosophical school of Logical Analysis would probably ask, not whether Free-will or Determinism is the true belief, but whether the question has any meaning. For what scientific experiment could we set up to prove one or the other true? The reader will note that some of the philosophers mentioned above are using the words to mean quite different concepts.

Dialectical Materialism, the combination of Hegel's dialectic method with a materialist philosophy produced by Karl Marx (1818–83) and his friend Friedrich Engels (1820–95). It is the philosophical basis of **Marxism** (q.v.) and **Communism** (q.v.) "Dialectic" to the ancient Greek philosophers meant a kind of dialogue or conversation, as used particularly by Socrates, in which philosophical disputes were resolved by a series of successive contradictions: a thesis is put forward and the opposing side holds its contradiction or antithesis until in the course of argument a synthesis is reached in which the conflicting ideas are resolved.

From Thesis through Antithesis to Synthesis. Hegel in the 19th cent. put forward the view that this process applies to the course of nature and history as they strive towards the perfect state. But to him, as to the Greeks, the conflict was in the field of ideas. The "universal reason" behind events works through the ideas held by a particular society until they are challenged by those of another which supersedes them and in turn, usually by war, becomes the agent of universal reason until the arrival of a new challenger. Hegel therefore regarded war as an instrument of progress and his Prussian compatriots found no difficulty in identifying their own state as the new agent of progress by universal conquest. Feuerbach, Lassalle, and other early socialists were impressed by some of Hegel's ideas: e.g., that societies evolved (with the assumption that finally their own ideal society would be achieved) and that truth, morals, and concepts were relative so that a type of society that was "good" at one time was not necessarily so at another. But Marx and Engels in effect turned Hegel upside-down, accepted his dialectic but rejected his belief that ideas were the motive force. On the contrary, they said, ideas are determined by social and economic change as a result of materialistic forces. (*See* **Calvinism,** where it is pointed out that the Marxist view is not that Calvin changed men's economic ideas but rather that a developing capitalism unconsciously changed his.) The historical materialism of Marxism purports to show that the inexorable dialectic determines that feudalism is displaced by capitalism and capitalism by creating a proletariat (its antithesis) inevitably leads to socialism and a classless society. The state, as a tool of the dominant class, withers away. Dialectical materialism is applied in all spheres. As a philosophy there is little to be said for it save that it has shown us the close dependence of man's thoughts upon current material and social conditions. But as a battle-cry or a rationalisation of Marxism it wielded immense power over the minds of men. *See* **Marxism.**

Dianetics. *See* **Scientology.**

Diggers, one of the many sects which flourished under the Commonwealth (others were the Muggletonians, the Levellers, the Millennarians, and the Fifth Monarchy Men), so-called because they attempted to dig (*i.e.* cultivate) untilled land. Gerrard Winstanley, a profoundly religious man, and leader of the Diggers, believed in the economic and social equality of man and castigated the clergy for upholding the class structure of society. In his book *The True Leveller's Standard Advanced* (1649) he wrote: "Every day poor people are forced to work for fourpence a day, though corn is dear. And yet the tithing priest stops their mouth and tells them that "inward satisfaction of mind' was meant by the declaration "the poor shall inherit the earth'. I tell you, the Scripture is to be really and materially fulfilled. You jeer at the name "Leveller'; I tell you Jesus Christ is the Head Leveller".

Doukhobors, a religious sect of Russian origin, founded by a Prussian sergeant at Kharkov in the middle of the 18th cent., and now mainly settled in Canada. Like many other sects they belong to that type of Christianity which seeks direct communication with God and such bodies tend to have certain traits in common, such as belief in the "inner light", opposition to war and authority in general, and often ecstasies which show themselves in physical ways such as shaking, speaking in strange tongues (glossolalia), and other forms of what to the unbeliever seem mass hysteria. Liturgy, ritual, or ceremony is non-existent. The Doukhobors were persecuted in Tsarist Russia, but in 1898 Tolstoy used his influence to have them removed to Canada where the government granted them uninhabited land in what is now Saskatchewan.

Dowsing. *See* **Radiesthesia.**

Druidism, the religion of Celtic Britain and Gaul of which Druids were the priesthood. They were finally wiped out by the Roman general Suetonius Paulinus about A.D. 58 in their last stronghold, the island of Anglesey. There are two sources of our present beliefs in Druidism: (1) the brief and factual records of the Romans, notably Pliny and Julius Caesar, which tell us that they worshipped in sacred oak groves and presumably practised a religion doing reverence to the powers of nature which must have had its roots in early stone age times and had many cruel rites, *e.g.*, human sacrifice; (2) the beliefs put forward by William Stukeley, an amateur antiquarian who from 1718 did valuable work by his studies of the stone circles at Stonehenge and Avebury. However, influenced by the Romantic movement, he later put forward the most extravagant theories which unfortunately are those popularly accepted by those without archaeological knowledge today. Stonehenge and Avebury were depicted as the temples of the "white-haired Druid bard sublime" and an attempt was made to tie up Druidism with early Christianity, above all with the concept of the Trinity. In fact, these circles have no connection with the Druids. They may have made ceremonial use of them but recent evidence suggests that the megalithic stones at Stonehenge belong to a Bronze Age culture (2100–1600 B.C.). Nor have Druidism and Christianity any relationship. There are 35 Druid groups in Britain and c. 300 more world-wide.

Dualism, any philosophical or theological theory which implies that the universe has a double nature, notably Plato's distinction between appearance and reality, soul and body, ideas and material objects, reason and the evidence of the senses, which infers that behind the world as we perceive it there lies an "ideal" world which is more "real" than that of mere appearance. In religions such as Zoroastrianism or the Gnostic and Manichaeism heresies, it was believed that the universe was ruled by good and evil "principles"—in effect that there was a good God and a bad one. In psychology, dualism refers to the philosophical theories which believe mind and body to be separate entities. The opposite of dualism is monism which asserts the essential unity of the substance of the universe.

An essential problem in the dualistic view lies in the question as to how and where the two separate and distinct properties of the universe interact. Where, for example, does the "mind" actually mesh with the physical mechanics of the brain and body—where does the ghost sit in his machine? Descartes decided that mind and body must interact somewhere and he selected the pineal gland (an apparently functionless part of the brain) as the spot. But this did nothing to explain how two *totally different* aspects of nature can possibly influence each other, and today most philosophers and psychologists reject dualistic views of life and personality as posing more problems than they solve. *See also* **Psychology, Occam's Razor.**

E

Ecomovement. In the early 1970s widespread publicity was for the first time given to the urgent warnings of ecologists that the current exponential increase in (a) world population, (b) depletion of natural resources, and (c) pollution of the environment could not continue without global catastrophe. The most significant single event in the evolution of what is now being known as the "ecomovement" was probably the publication of the Club of Rome's paper on *The Limits to Growth*. From this sprang a movement, unfortunately initially drawn only from the middle class and better educated, which aimed to reduce environmental pollution, the extravagances of advertising and needless waste of natural resources. Its first campaigns were directed against such obvious targets as disposable glass bottles and unnecessary packaging and wrapping in shops and supermarkets. The ecomovement also protests against industrial firms which pollute rivers and seas and against aircraft noise and waste in general. Its early campaigns were greeted with some derision but have achieved dramatic point with the world pollution and economic crises which developed during the 1980s and 1990s.

Ecumenism, a world movement which springs from the Christian belief that all men are brothers and that the Christian Church should be re-structured to give reality to the belief. Christ's church exists not to serve its own members, but for the service of the whole world. Some see the answer in a united church of a federal type (unity in diversity), others in an organic structure with one set of rules. The period since the convening of the Second Vatican Council by Pope John has been one of prolonged discussion among Christian theologians with the aim of promoting Christian unity. *See* **World Council of Churches.**

Education. Education was no great problem to primitive man, but as societies became more complex people began to ask themselves such questions as: *What* should young people be taught? *How* should they be taught? Should the aim of their education be to bring out their individual qualities or rather to make them good servants of the state?

The first teachers were priests who knew most about the traditions, customs, and lore of their societies and thus the first schools were in religious meeting places. This was notably true of the Jews who learned from the rabbis in the synagogue.

The Greeks. We begin, as always, with the Greeks whose city-states, based on slavery, educated men (not women) for the sort of life described in Plato's *Dialogues*—the leisured life of gentlemen arguing the problems of the universe at their banquets or in the market-place. This made it necessary to learn debate and oratory (or rhetoric) especially for those who proposed to take up politics. The Sophist philosophy taught the need to build up convincing arguments in a persuasive manner, to learn the rules of logic and master the laws and customs of the Athenians, and to know the literature of the past so that illustrations might be drawn from it. These strolling philosophers who taught for a fee were individualists showing the student how to advance himself at all costs within his community.

Socrates had a more ethical approach, believing that education was good in itself, made a man happier and a better citizen, and emphasised his position as a member of a group. His method of teaching, the dialectic or "Socratic" method, involved argument and discussion rather than overwhelming others by rhetoric and is briefly mentioned under **Dialectical Materialism** (*q.v.*). Today this method is increasingly used in adult education where a lecture is followed by a period of discussion in which both lecturer and audience participate; for psychologists have shown that people accept ideas more readily when conviction arises through their own arguments than when they are passively thrust down their throats.

Socrates' pupil Plato produced in his book *The Republic* one of the first comprehensive systems of education and vocational selection. Believing that essentially men have very different and unequal abilities he considered that in an idealistic or utopian society they should be put into social classes corresponding to these differences, and suggested the following method: (1) For the first 18 years of a boy's life he should be taught gymnastics and sports, playing and singing music, reading and writing, a knowledge of literature, and if he passed this course sent on to the next stage; those who failed were to become tradesmen and merchants. (2) From 18–20 those successful in the first course were to be given two years of cadet training, the ones thought incapable of further education being placed in the military class as soldiers. (3) The remainder, who were to become the leaders of society, proceeded with advanced studies in philosophy, mathematics, science, and art. Such education was to be a state concern, state supported and controlled, selecting men and training them for service in the state according to their abilities.

Plato's pupil Aristotle even suggested that the state should determine shortly after birth which children should be allowed to live and destroy the physically or mentally handicapped; that marriage should be state-controlled to ensure desirable offspring. However, in their time the leisured and individualistic Sophists held the field and few accepted the educational views of Plato or his pupil.

Rome. The Romans were not philosophers and most of their culture came from Greece. Administration was their chief aptitude and Quintilian (A.D. *c.* 35–*c.* 95) based his higher education on the earlier classical tuition in public speaking, but he is important for emphasising the training of character and for his humanistic approach to the method of teaching that caused his *Institutio oratoria* to be influential for centuries later—indeed one might almost say up to the time of the great Dr. Arnold of Rugby. Education, he believed, should begin early but one must "take care that the child not old enough to love his studies does not come to hate them" by premature forcing; studies must be made pleasant and interesting and students encouraged by praise rather than discouraged when they sometimes fail; play is to be approved of as a sign of a lively disposition and because gloomy, depressed children are not likely to be good students; corporal punishment should never be used because "it is an insult as you will realise if you imagine it yourself". The world became interested not in *what* he taught but *how* he taught it; he was the pioneer of humanistic education and character-training from Vittorino d. Feltre (1378–1446) of Mantua, through Milton and Pope who commended his works to the modern educationists who have studied their pupils as well as their books.

The Middle Ages: The Religious View. With the development of Christianity education once more became a religious problem. The earliest converts had to be taught Christian doctrine and were given instruction in "catechumenal" schools before admission to the group, but as the religion came increasingly into contact with other religions or heresies a more serious training was necessary, and from these newer "catechetical" schools, where the method used was the catechism (*i.e.*, question and answer as known to all Presbyterian children today), the Apologists arose among whom were Clement of Alexandria and the great Origen. From this time education became an instrument of the church and in 529 the Emperor Justinian ordered all pagan schools to be closed.

As typical of the best in mediaeval education whilst the lamp of civilisation burned low during the Dark Ages, after the fall of Roman power, and survived only in the monasteries, we may mention St. Benedict (*c.* 480–*c.* 547) of Monte Cassino. There, in southern Italy, a rule was established which became a part of monastic life in general. Monastic schools were originally intended for the training of would-be monks, but later others were admitted who simply wanted some education; thus two types of school developed one for the *interni* and the other for *externi* or external pupils. Originally studies were merely reading in order to study the Bible, writing to copy the sacred books, and sufficient calculation to be able to work out the advent of holy days or festivals. But by the end of the 6th cent. the "seven liberal arts" (grammar, rhetoric, dialectic, arithmetic, geometry, music, and astronomy) were added.

The Renaissance. The close of the Middle Ages saw the development of two types of secular school. One came with the rise of the new merchant class and the skilled trader whose "guilds" or early trade unions established schools to train young men for their trades but ultimately gave rise to burgher or town schools; the other was the court school founded and supported by the wealthy rulers of the Italian cities—Vittorio da Feltre (mentioned above) presided over the most famous at Mantua.

These Renaissance developments are paralelled in northern Europe by the Protestant reformers who, having with Martin Luther held that everyone should know how to read his Bible in order to interpret it in his own way, were logically committed to popular education, compulsory and universal. In theory this was intended for biblical study, but writing, arithmetic, and other elementary subjects were taught and Luther said that, even if heaven and hell did not exist, education was important. Universal education is a Protestant conception.

Views of Philosophers. From this period onwards people were free to put forward any ideas about education, foolish or otherwise, and to create their own types of school. Of English philosophers who theorised about, but did not practise, education we may mention the rationalist Francis Bacon (1561–1626) who saw learning as the dissipation of all prejudices and the collection of concrete facts; the materialist and totalitarian Hobbes (1588–1679) who, as a royalist, believed that the right to determine the kind of education fit for his subjects is one of the absolute rights of the sovereign power or ruler; the gentlemanly Locke (1632–1704) whose ideal was a sound mind in a sound body to be attained by hard physical exercise, wide experience of the world, and enough knowledge to meet the requirements of the pupil's environment. The end result would be one able to get on with his fellows, pious but wise in the ways of the world, independent and able to look after himself, informed but reticent about his knowledge. Classics and religious study were not to be carried to excess, since Locke held that these subjects had been overrated in the past. Locke's pupil was the well-to-do, civilised young man of the 17th cent. who knew how to behave in society.

Jean-Jacques Rousseau (1712–78), a forerunner of the Romantic movement (*q.v.*), which despised society and its institutions, put emotion at a higher level than reason. His book *Emile* describes the education of a boy which is natural and spontaneous. Society, he holds, warps the growing mind and therefore the child should be protected from its influences until his development in accordance with his own nature is so complete that he cannot be harmed by it. During the first 4 years the body should be developed by physical training; from 5 to 12 the child would live in a state of nature such that he could develop his powers of observation and his senses; from 13 books would be used and intellectual training introduced, although only in line with the child's own interests, and he would be given instruction only as he came to ask for it. Moral training and contact with his fellows to learn the principles of sympathy, kindness, and helpfulness to mankind would be given between 15 and 20. Girls, however, should be educated to serve men in a spirit of modesty and restraint. His own five children he deposited in a foundling hospital.

Summary. Broadly speaking, then, there have been four main attitudes to education: (1) religious, with a view to a life beyond death; (2) state-controlled education, with a view to uniform subservience to authority; (3) "gentlemanly" education, with a view to social graces and easy congress in company; (4) the "child-centred" education, which attempts to follow the pupil's inner nature. It is unnecessary to mention the ordinary method of attempting to instil facts without any considerable degree of co-operation between pupil and teacher in order that the former may, with or without interest, follow some occupation in adult life; for this the philosophers did not consider. Today there remain the two fundamental principles: education for the advantage of the state and its ideology or education for individual development and freedom.

Four educationists of the modern period who have influenced us in the direction of freedom were Johann Pestalozzi of Switzerland (1746–1827) who, by trying to understand children, taught the "natural, progressive, and harmonious development of all the powers and capacities of the human being"; Friedrich Froebel (1782–1852) of Germany, the founder of the Kindergarten who, like Pestalozzi, was influenced by Rousseau but realised the need to combine complete personal development with social adjustment; Maria Montessori (1869–1952) whose free methods have revolutionised infant teaching; John Dewey (1859–1952) who held that the best interests of the group are served when the individual develops his own particular talents and nature.

Egalitarianism. The doctrine that human beings are, in an important sense, equal and that it is desirable to remove inequalities by social and political means. It was part of the famous slogan of the French Revolution: "Liberty, Equality, Fraternity." There has been much debate, however, as to what extent human beings are, in fact, equal. Critics of equality as a political ideal argue that it conflicts with other more valuable ideals or social values, and that the different kinds of equality are not compatible.

Eleatics, the philosophers of Elea in ancient Greece who, at the time when Heraclitus (*c.* 535–475 B.C.) was teaching that change is all that exists and nothing is permanent, were asserting that change is an illusion. Of the three leaders of this school, Xenophanes asserted that the universe was a solid immovable mass forever the same; Parmenides explained away change as an inconceivable process, its appearance being due to the fact that what we see is unreal; and Zeno (the best-known today) illustrated the same thesis with his famous argument of the arrow which, at any given moment of its flight, must be where it is since it cannot be where it is not. But if it is where it is, it cannot move, this is based, of course, on the delusion that motion is discontinuous. The Eleatics were contemporaries of Socrates.

Elitism. A political theory, largely drawn from the writings of V. Pareto (1848–1923). Power in a society will always be exercised by a minority (the elite) which takes the major decisions. An elite gains its dominant position through possessing certain resources or qualities valued in that particular society, *e.g.* priests or soldiers or senior state officials. Elites normally aim to continue their domination, but are not always capable of doing so and become displaced by another elite. If elite rule is inevitable then there can be no hope of an egalitarian, socialist society. This analysis of the importance of elites has been very influential. Some sociologists have extended the theory in recent years to argue that in all developed countries there is a plurality of competing elites within different systems of control. Such systems are politics, trade union organisations, cultural and educational institutions.

Empiricism. While not a single school of philosophy, empiricism is an approach to knowledge which holds that if a man wants to know what the universe is like the only correct way to do so is to go and look for himself, to collect facts which come to him through his senses. It is, in essence, the method of science as contrasted with rationalism (*q.v.*) which in philosophy implies that thinking or reasoning without necessarily referring to external observations can arrive at truth. Empiricism is typically an English attitude, for among the greatest empirical philosophers were John Locke, George Berkeley, and David Hume. *See* **Rationalism**.

Encyclopedists. The writers (all men) who contributed to the *Encyclopedie* published in France from 1751 to 1772. The work's full title was *Encyclopedie, ou dictionnaire raisonne des sciences, des arts et* *des metiers.* It was designed as a synoptic description of all branches of human knowledge, and is perhaps the most characteristic work of the Enlightenment (*q.v.*). The *Encyclopedie* was inspired by Chambers' *Cyclopedia, or a universal dictionary of arts and sciences* published in London in 1728. The project began in 1745, with Denis Diderot and Jean d'Alembert as editors. The latter resigned in 1758, leaving Diderot to shoulder most of the work. In 1772 the project reached 28 volumes; between 1776 and 1780 7 supplementary volumes were published.

Besides Diderot and d'Alembert and many obscure writers, Voltaire, Rousseau and d'Holbach contributed. The work was a showcase for representatives of new schools of thought in all branches of intellectual activity. The work was tolerant, liberal, and also innovative in giving attention to trades and mechanical arts. In its scepticism, its emphasis on being scientific, and its criticism of superstition and contemporary social institutions, the *Encyclopedie* had immense influence.

Enlightenment. A European intellectual movement of the 18th century. Enlightenment thinkers aimed to bring clarity, order and reason, in a word, *light* to regions where formerly there had been mystery, superstition and blind authority, that is, darkness. Man would become enlightened by knowledge and progress to greater happiness and freedom. The movement affected the arts, the sciences, political and social life.

The Enlightenment was prepared by the rise of science from the 16th century on. In particular, the success of Newton (1642–1727) in encapsulating the laws that govern the motion of the planets gave great hopes in man's capacity to attain extensive understanding. According to the German philosopher Kant (1724–1804) the motto of the Enlightenment was "Have courage to use your own understanding". Scientific knowledge was the ideal. If something was held to be true, it had to be based on dispassionate rational investigation. This overrode any claim to knowledge based on authority. One great source of authority was the Christian church, which was widely criticised by Enlightenment thinkers (*e.g.* in Voltaire's *Candide*); another was the despotism and arbitrary power of many states at the time. Although there is now a tendency to be sceptical about the Enlightenment and the power of reason, the belief in human progress through increased knowledge has been one of the most powerful ideas of the last 250 years.

Epicureanism. The two great schools of the Hellenistic period (*i.e.* the late Greek period beginning with the empire of Alexander the Great) were the Stoics and Epicureans, the former founded by Zeno of Citium (not to be confused with Zeno the Eleatic) (*q.v.*), the latter by Epicurus, born in Samos in 342 B.C. Both schools settled in Athens, where Epicurus taught that "pleasure is the beginning and end of a happy life." However, he was no sensualist and emphasised the importance of moderation in all things because excesses would lead to pain instead of pleasure and the best of all pleasures were mental ones. Pleasures could be active or passive but the former contain an element of pain since they are the process of satisfying desire not yet satiated. The latter involving the absence of desire are the more pleasant. In fact, Epicurus in his personal life was more stoical than many Stoics and wrote "when I live on bread and water I spit on luxurious pleasures." He disapproved of sexual enjoyment and thought friendship one of the highest of all joys. A materialist who accepted the atomic theory of Democritus, he was not a determinist, and if he did not disbelieve in the gods he regarded religion and the fear of death as the two primary sources of unhappiness.

Epiphenomenalism. *See* **Mind and Body.**

Erastianism, the theory that the state has the right to decide the religion of its members, wrongly attributed to Erastus of Switzerland (1524–83) who was believed to have held this doctrine. The term has usually been made use of in a derogatory sense–*e.g.,* by the Scottish churches which held that the "call" of the congregation was the only way to elect ministers at a time when, about the turn of the 17th and 18th

cent., they felt that Episcopalianism was being foisted on them. "Episcopalianism" (*i.e.* Anglicanism) with its state church, ecclesiastical hierarchy, and system of livings presented by patrons was to them "Erastian" in addition to its other "unscriptural practices."

Essenes, a Jewish sect which, during the oppressive rule of Herod (d. 4 B.C.), set up monastic communities in the region of the Dead Sea. They refused to be bound by the scriptural interpretations of the Pharisees and adhered rigorously to the letter of Holy Writ, although with additions of their own which cause them by orthodox Jews today to be regarded as a break-away from Judaism. Among their practices and beliefs were purification through baptism, renunciation of sexual pleasures, scrupulous cleanliness, strict observance of the Mosaic law, communal possession, asceticism. Akin in spirit, although not necessarily identical with them, were the writers of Apocalyptic literature preaching that the evils of the present would shortly be terminated by a new supernatural order heralded by a Messiah who would reign over a restored Israel. The casting out of demons and spiritual healing formed part of these general beliefs which were in the air at that time. The sect has an importance far beyond its size or what has been known about it in the past since the discovery from 1947 onwards of the Dead Sea Scrolls (*see* **Section L**) of the Qumran community occupying a monastery in the same area as the Essenes and holding the same type of belief. These scrolls with their references to a "Teacher of Righteousness" preceding the Messiah have obvious relevance to the sources of early Christianity and have given rise to speculations as to whether Jesus might have been influenced by views which, like His own, were unacceptable to orthodox Jews but in line with those of the Dead Sea communities. Scholars now think that early Christianity was not a sudden development but a gradual one which had its predecessors.

Ethical Church, a movement typical of 19th cent. rationalism which attempted to combine atheism (or at any rate the absence of any belief in a God which was inconsistent with reason or based on revelation) with the inculcation of moral principles. Prayers were not used and ordinarily the service consisted in the singing of edifying compositions interspersed with readings from poems or prose of a similar nature by great writers holding appropriate views. It terminated in a talk on an ethical or scientific theme. Conway Hall (built 1929) in Red Lion Square, London, belongs to the South Place Ethical Society, founded by Moncure Conway who preached at their Unitarian chapel in South Place, Finsbury, 1864–97.

Ethnocentrism, the exaggerated tendency to think the characteristics of one's own group or race superior to those of any others.

Eugenics, a 19th-cent. movement largely instigated by the British scientist and mathematician, Sir Francis Galton. Galton argued that many of the most satisfactory attributes of mankind—intelligence, physical strength, resistance to disease, *etc.*—were genetically determined and thus handed down in the normal process of inheritance. From this he reasoned that selective mating of physical "superior" individuals, and its converse, the controlled limitation on the breeding of criminals or the insane, would lead inevitably to a progressive improvement in the overall standards of the human race. In their simplest form these proposals are incontestable, though they do of course introduce marked restrictions on the choice of the individual for marriage and procreation. Worse yet is the way in which the argument can be misapplied or elaborated—as it was in Nazi Germany—to include the sterilisation of alcoholics, confirmed criminals and even epileptics. Nevertheless there remains the feeling that there are some aspects of eugenics which intuitively at any rate make good sense and of course the widespread application of birth control is itself an enactment of eugenic principles.

In 1997 it was revealed that extensive sterilisation of mentally-handicapped people had been carried out until the 1970s in Norway and Switzerland.

Euthanasia (mercy killing), the term applied to the painless killing of those (especially the old) suffering from unbearable pain and an illness for which there is no cure. In Britain, attempts in Parliament to introduce its legalisation have failed but in 1993 Holland voted to adopt routine legal procedures for euthanasia on the patient's request. Under these procedures, euthanasia is tolerated when the patient is conscious, suffers an incurable disease paired with intolerable pain and clearly requests a "soft death". The World Right to Die Organisation now has 36 branches across 20 countries. Legislation permitting voluntary euthanasia was passed in the Northern Territory of Australia in 1995 and the world's first legal euthanasia took place in 1996. In 1997 the Liberal Democrats became the first major party in Britain to debate legalisation. *See also* **J57**.

Evangelicalism, the belief of those Protestant sects which hold that the essence of the Gospel consists in the doctrine of salvation by faith in the atoning death of Christ and not by good works or the sacraments; that worship should be "free" rather than liturgical through established forms; that ritual is unacceptable and superstitious. Evangelicals are Low Churchmen.

Evangelism, the preaching of the Gospel, emphasising the necessity for a new birth or conversion. The evangelistic fervour of John Wesley and George Whitefield (*see* Methodism) aroused the great missionary spirit of the late 18th and 19th cent. George Fox, founder of the Society of Friends (*q.v.*), was also an evangelist. Evangelists can be Low, High, or Middle Churchmen.

Existentialism, a highly subjective philosophy which many people connect with such names as Jean-Paul Sartre (1905–80) or Albert Camus (1913–60) and assume to be a post-war movement. However, existentialism stems from Sören Kierkegaard (1813–55), the Danish "religious writer"—his own description of himself—in such works as *Either/Or, Fear and Trembling,* and *Concluding Unscientific Postscript.* Between the two wars translations of Kierkegaard into German influenced Martin Heidegger's great work *Being and Time* and the other great existentialist Karl Jaspers; it has strongly influenced modern Protestant theology notably in Karl Barth, Reinhold Niebuhr, and Paul Tillich and beyond that field the French philosopher Gabriel Marcel, the Spanish writer Unamuno in his well-known *The Tragic Sense of Life,* and Martin Buber of Israel in his *I and Thou.* We have it on Heidegger's authority that "Sartre is no philosopher" even if it is to his works that modern existentialists often turn.

Existentialism is extremely difficult for the non-metaphysically-minded to understand, it deals, not with the nature of the universe or what are ordinarily thought of as philosophical problems but describes an attitude to life or God held by the individual. Briefly, its main essentials are: (1) it distinguishes between *essence, i.e.,* that aspect of an entity which can be observed and known—and its *existence*—the fact of its having a place in a changing and dangerous world which is what really matters; (2) existence being basic, each self-aware individual can grasp his own existence on reflection in his own immediate experience of himself and his situation as a free being in the world; what he finds is not merely a knowing self but a self that fears, hopes, believes, wills, and is aware of its need to find a purpose, plan, and destiny in life; (3) but we cannot grasp our existence by thought alone; thus the fact "all men must die" relates to the essence of man but it is necessary to be involved, to draw the conclusion as a person that "I too must die" and experience its impact on our own individual existence; (4) because of the preceding, it is necessary to abandon our attitude of objectivity and theoretical detachment when faced by the problems relating to the ultimate purpose of our own life and the basis of our own conduct; life remains closed to those who take no part in it because it can have no significance; (5) it follows that the existentialist cannot be rationalist in his outlook for this is merely an escape into thought from the serious problems of existence; none of the important aspects of life—failure, evil, sin, folly—nor (in the view of Kierkegaard) even the existence of God or the truth of Christianity—can be proved by reason.

"God does not exist; He is eternal," was how he expressed it; (6) life is short and limited in space and time, therefore it is foolish to discuss in a leisurely fashion matters of life and death as if there were all eternity to argue them in. It is necessary to make a leap into the unknown, *e.g.,* accepting Christ (in the case of the Christian existentialist) by faith in the sense of giving and risking the self utterly. This means complete commitment, not a dependence on arguments as to whether certain historical events did, or did not, happen.

To summarise: existentialism of whatever type seems to the outsider to be an attitude to life concerning itself with the individual's ultimate problems (mine, not yours); to be anti-rationalist and anti-idealist (in the sense of being, as it seems to the believer, practical)—in effect it seems to say "life is too short to fool about with argument, you must dive in and become committed" to something. Sartre who called himself an "atheist existentialist" was apparently committed to the belief that "hell is other people," but for most critics the main argument against existentialist philosophy is that it often rests on a highly specialised personal experience and, as such, is incommunicable.

Existential Psychology, a new if rather diffuse movement in modern psychology with no specific founder but with a number of figures who have, perhaps against their will, acquired leader status. One of the key figures is the British psychiatrist, R. D. Laing, whose radical views on psychotherapy are counted as being heretical by the vast majority of his medical colleagues. Laing holds that many so-called neurotic and psychotic conditions are essentially not "abnormal" and merely represent extreme strategies by which an individual may adjust to environmental and personal stress. Instead of attempting to suppress or eliminate the psychosis in the traditional manner, one should lead the patient through it thus allowing the individual's "unconscious plan" for his own adjustment to be fulfilled.

Exorcism, the removal or ejection of an evil spirit by a ritual or prayer. It is easy to forget that the concept of insanity as representing a disorder of the brain, analogous to physical sickness of the body, is fairly recent in origin. Barely two centuries ago it was considered to be appropriate treatment to put lunatics into chains and beat them daily in the hope that the malevolent beings inhabiting them might be persuaded to depart. Tragically, many of the symptoms of severe forms of mental disorder induce such an apparent change in the personality of the individual as to suggest that an alien individual has indeed taken over their body, and this belief is still common in many parts of the world. Most religious systems have developed some ritual or set of rituals for expelling these demons.

F

Fabian Society. In 1848 (the year of *The Communist Manifesto* by Marx and Engels) Europe was in revolt. In most countries the workers and intellectuals started bloody revolutions against the feudal ruling classes which were no less violently suppressed; hence on the continent socialism took on a Marxist tinge which to some extent it still retains. But at the same time England was undergoing a slow but non-violent transition in her political and industrial life which led the workers in general to look forward to progress through evolution. Marxism never became an important movement in England even though it took its origin here. There were many reasons for this: the agitation of the Chartists (*q.v.*); the writings of Mill, Ruskin, and Carlyle; the reforms of Robert Owen; the religious movement led by the Wesleys; the Co-operative societies; the Christian socialists. Furthermore legislation stimulated by these bodies had led to an extension of the franchise to include a considerable number of wage-earners, remedial measures to correct some of the worst abuses of the factory system, recognition of the trade unions, etc.

This was the background against which the Fabian Society was founded in 1884 with the conviction that social change could be brought about by gradual parliamentary means. (The name is derived from Quintus Fabius Maximus, the Roman general nicknamed "Cunctator," the delayer, who achieved his successes in defending Rome against Hannibal by refusing to give direct battle.) It was a movement of brilliant intellectuals, chief among whom were Sidney and Beatrice Webb, H. G. Wells, G. B. Shaw, Graham Wallas, Sidney Olivier, and Edward Pease. The Society itself was basically a research institution which furnished the intellectual information for social reform and supported all contributing to the gradual attainment by parliamentary means of socialism.

The Webbs's analysis of society emphasised that individualist enterprise in capitalism was a hang-over from early days and was bound to defeat itself since socialism is the inevitable accompaniment of modern industrialism; the necessary result of popular government is control of their economic system by the people themselves. Utopian schemes had been doomed to failure because they were based on the fallacy that society is static and that islands of utopias could be formed in the midst of an unchanging and antagonistic environment. On the contrary, it was pointed out, society develops: "The new becomes old, often before it is consciously regarded as new." Social reorganisation cannot usefully be hastened by violent means but only through methods consonant with this natural historical progression—gradual, peaceful, and democratic. The Fabians were convinced that men are rational enough to accept in their common interest developments which can be demonstrated as necessary; thus public opinion will come to see that socialisation of the land and industries is essential in the same way that they came to accept the already-existing acts in respect of housing, insurance, medical care, and conditions of work.

The Society collaborated first in the formation of the Independent Labour Party and then with the more moderate Labour Party and the trade unions and Co-operative movement. But in general it disapproved of independent trade union action since change should come from the government and take political form. The class-war of Marx was rejected and so too was the idea of the exclusive role of the working class —reform must come from the enlightened co-operation of all classes.

Faith Healing, the belief and practice of curing physical and mental ills by faith in some supernatural power, either allegedly latent in the individual (as with Christian Science) or drawn in some way from God. It is a characteristic of faith healing that it is supposed to be publicly demonstrable—i.e., a "healer" will hold public meetings and invite sick people to come up to be cured on the platform. In the emotionally charged atmosphere which the healer generates, it is not unusual for people to show immediate and striking improvement in their illness, but the almost invariable rule is for relapses to occur within days or hours after the event. When remission is more permanent, the illness is generally hysterical in origin and will often return to the individual in some other form. Spiritualists claim that the healing in such cases is done not by "faith" but by direct intervention of the spirits of doctors, etc., who have died and passed on to another world. Perhaps the world's most famous faith healer in the post-war period was Harry Edwards (d. 1976), who had millions of letters from all parts of the world asking for the healing attention of his spirit guides. Many doctors, while remaining immensely sceptical about the origins and extent of this kind of therapy, are inclined to admit that it might have benefits when the sickness is mildly hysterical in origin. The real danger, of course, comes when patients seek unorthodox therapy before consulting their doctor.

Falangists. The Fascist Party of Spain founded in 1933 by José Antonio Primo de Rivera, son of the man who was dictator of the country from 1923 to 1930. The Falange was the only political party allowed in Spain during the Franco era. *See* **Fascism.**

Fascism. From the end of mediaeval times with the opening up of the world, the liberation of the mind and the release of business enterprise, a new spirit arose in Europe exemplified in such movements as the Renaissance, the Reformation, the struggle for democracy, the rise of capitalism, and the Industrial Revolution. With these movements there developed a certain tradition, which, in spite of hindrances and disagreement or failures, was universally held by both right- and left-wing parties however strongly they might fail to agree on the best means of attaining what was felt to be a universal ideal. The hard core of this tradition involved: belief in reason and the possibility of human progress; the essential sanctity and dignity of human life; tolerance of widely different religious and political views; reliance on popular government and the responsibility of the rulers to the ruled; freedom of thought and criticism; the necessity of universal education; impartial justice and the rule of law; the desirability of universal peace. Fascism was the negation of every aspect of this tradition and took pride in being so. Emotion took the place of reason, the "immutable, beneficial, and fruitful inequality of classes" and the right of a self-constituted élite to rule them replaced universal suffrage because absolute authority "quick, sure, unanimous" led to action rather than talk. Contrary opinions are not allowed and justice is in the service of the state; war is desirable to advance the power of the state; and racial inequality made a dogma. Those who belong to the "wrong" religion, political party, or race are outside the law.

The attacks on liberalism and exaltation of the state derive largely from Hegel and his German followers; the mystical irrationalism from such 19th cent. philosophers as Schopenhauer Nietzsche, and Bergson; from Sorel (*see* **Syndicalism**) came the idea of the "myth", and an image which would have the power to arouse the emotions of the masses and from Sorel also the rationale of violence and justification of force. But these philosophical justifications of fascism do not explain why it arose at all and why it arose where it did—in Italy, Germany, and Spain. These countries had one thing in common—disillusionment. Germany had lost the 1914–18 war, Italy had been on the winning side but was resentful about her small gains. Spain had sunk to the level of a third-rate power, and people were becoming increasingly restive under the reactionary powers of the Catholic Church, the landed aristocracy, and the army. In Marxist theory, fascism is the last fling of the ruling class and the bourgeoisie in their attempt to hold down the workers.

Italian Fascism. The corporate state set up by Benito Mussolini in Italy claimed to be neither capitalist nor socialist, and after its inception in 1922 the Fascist Party became the only recognised one. Its members wore black shirts, were organised in military formations, used the Roman greeting of the outstretched arm, and adopted as their slogan "Mussolini is always right". Membership of the Party was not allowed to exceed a number thought to be suited to the optimum size of a governing class and new candidates were drawn, after strict examinations, from the youth organisations. The Blackshirts, a fascist militia, existed separately from the army and were ruled by Fascist Headquarters.

At the head of government was Mussolini, "Il Duce" himself, a cabinet of fourteen ministers selected by him and approved by the King to supervise the various functions of government, and the Grand Council or directorate of the Fascist Party, all the members of which were chosen by the Duce. Parliament, which was not allowed to initiate legislation but only to approve decrees from above, consisted of a Senate with life-membership and a Chamber of Fasci and Corporations composed of nominated members of the Party, the National

Council of Corporations, and selected representatives of the employers' and employees' confederations. Private enterprise was encouraged and protected but rigidly controlled; strikes were forbidden, but a Charter of Labour enforced the collaboration of workers and employers whose disputes were settled in labour courts presided over by the Party. All decisions relating to industry were government-controlled (*e.g.*, wages, prices, conditions of employment and dismissal, the expansion or limitation of production), and some industries such as mining, shipping, and armaments were state-owned.

Italian fascism served as a model in other countries, notably for the German National Socialist Party, in Spain and Japan, and most European nations between the wars had their small Fascist parties, the British version led by Sir Oswald Mosley being known as the British Union which relied on "strong-arm tactics", marches and violence. The Public Order Act of 1936 was passed to deal with it. Although fascism in all countries has certain recognisable characteristics, it would be wrong to think of it as an international movement taking fixed forms and with a clearly thought-out rationale as in the case of communism. There were minor revivals of interest in Fascism in Italy after 1945 and more recently in France with the emergence of the National Front led by M. Le Pen. In the 1990s, elections in a variety of countries have showed increasing support for extreme right-wing or antiimmigrant parties. There is increasing support for neo-Fascism again in Italy and parts of Germany. For an excellent recent introduction to the subject, *see* Roger Eatwell, *Fascism* (1995). *See* **Falangists, Nazism**.

Fatalism. *See* **Determinism**.

Feminism. Feminism is an expression which emerged in the mid-19th century. It is an international movement (there was, for example, a feminist congress in Paris in 1890), which aimed at ending female inequality in male-dominated societies. In early 20th century Britain feminism sought political advance through a militant campaign for women's suffrage, This, and the part played by women in World War One, made it impossible for a male elite to deny women the right to vote. But in each country it became increasingly clear to women that the political process alone left many of their needs unsatisfied, if not unrecognised. However, in post-World War Two Britain, legislation made a gesture towards outlawing discrimination against women at work with the 1970 Equal Pay Act and the 1975 Sex Discrimination Act.

Activist feminism, the "Women's Liberation Movement" of the 1960s and 1970s (primarily in America and Europe as well as Britain), centred on questions of sexuality and the right of women to make choices, for example, over when (and whether) to become pregnant. The contraceptive pill appeared to open up sexual choice for women and to liberate them from traditional responsibilities for home, family and the welfare of children. In practice, it appeared to many women that the pill (as well as having physical side-effects) merely relieved men from a recognition of their own responsibility. The 1967 Abortion Act in Britain implied an acceptance of a woman's right to control her own reproduction, a right which has been systematically but unsuccessfully challenged since.

As western economies faltered in the late 1970s a recurring problem for the movement was consolidating the small gains that had been made. But the women's movement achievements cannot be measured by tangible results alone. A central aspect of the movement was "consciousness-raising", helping women recognise the social roots of their individual oppression. In their analysis of sexual stereotyping, late 20th century feminist writings—for example, Betty Friedan's *The Feminine Mystique* (1963) and Germaine Greer's *The Female Eunuch* (1970)—encouraged a change in some women's expectations. These writers, and many like them, enabled a new generation of women to challenge the dominant decision-making role of men and to demand acceptance of the principle of equality between the sexes. Dale Spender's *Man Made Language* (1980) pointed to the ways in which the "sexist" structure of language internalised the perpetuation of male dominance. A simple, but not superficial, result of this is the acceptance of the abbreviation "Ms" rather than "Mrs" or "Miss" on the grounds that the latter presupposed that a woman's identity depended on her marital status.

Although feminism as a movement was loosely structured—there were, for example, early on, differing emphases between socialists, black women, working class women, and lesbians, based on their own experiences—the movement became increasingly fragmented during the 1980s. Some women, who were now building individual careers, distanced themselves from agitation and thought little more could be achieved by collective action. Single-issue pressure groups evolved, focusing on campaigns for change in particular areas.

The Greenham Common Women's Peace Camp which began in the mid-1980s as a protest against the deployment of Cruise missiles in Britain, was able to develop from this into an exemplary feminist action which reverberated internationally. Self-organisation among miners' wives in the 1984–85 strike proved similarly effective.

The irony of "classical" feminism is that it became a concern of the generation that came to maturity in the late 1960s. Their children—and their younger sisters—had absorbed the earlier failures and successes and moved on. By the 1990s, for what became the older generation, there was a view that the earlier movement had implanted unrealistic expectations in women (particularly those with domestic responsibilities), the "double burden" of maintaining a career and home. This led at a time of growing recession and unemployment to an anti-feminist campaign or "backlash", not only among men (which was to be expected) but also among some women who described themselves as post-feminists. Susan Faludi, speaking for a younger generation in *Backlash: The Undeclared War Against Women* (1991) documents a process which has as a common thread the attempt to force women back into the home and a return to "traditional" family life. However, a significant recognition of the altered balance between the sexes came with the October 1991 House of Lords decision that rape within marriage was an offence.

The mid 1990s saw a new emphasis placed by political parties on the role of the family and its reputed breakdown as the root of many of the problems confronting Western society. This was interpreted by some as an attempt to reverse the social and economic advances achieved by some women in the past half century. Working mothers, for example, were accused of neglecting their prime duty as home-makers, although the research evidence presented was often contradictory.

The year 1997 marked the two hundredth anniversary of the death of the Anglo-Irish feminist and writer Mary Wollstonecraft at the age of 38. Wollstonecraft's *Vindication of Women*, published in 1792, is often seen as a pioneering work in its advocacy of equality between the sexes.

Fetichism, originally a practice of the natives of West Africa and elsewhere of attributing magical properties to an object which was used as an amulet, for putting spells on others, or regarded as possessing dangerous powers. In psychology the term refers to a sexual perversion in which objects such as shoes, brassières, hair, *etc.*, arouse sexual excitement.

Feudalism. The feudal system took its origins from Saxon times and broadly speaking lasted until the end of the 13th cent. It was a military and political organisation based on land tenure, for, of course, society throughout this period was based almost entirely on agriculture. The activities of men divided them into three classes or estates. The First Estate was the clergy, responsible for man's spiritual needs; the Second was the nobility, including kings and emperor as well as the lesser nobles; the Third was composed of all those who had to do with the economic and mainly agricultural life of Europe. The praying men, the fighting men and administrators, and the toilers were all held to be dependent on each other in a web of mutual responsibilities.

The theory of feudalism, although it by no means always worked out in practice, was as follows: the earth was God's and therefore no man owned land in the modern sense of the word. God had given the pope spiritual charge of men, and secular power over them to the emperor from whom kings held their kingdoms, and in turn the dukes and counts received the land over which they held sway from the king. Members of the Second Estate held their lands on the condition of fulfilling certain obligations to their overlord and to the people living under them, so when a noble received a fief or piece of land he became the vassal of the man who bestowed it. To him he owed military service for a specified period of the year, attendance at court, and giving his lord counsel. He undertook to ransom his lord when he fell into enemy hands and to contribute to his daughter's dowry and at the knighting of his son. In return the lord offered his vassal protection and justice, received the vassal's sons into his household and educated them for knighthood.

The system was complicated by the fact that large fiefs might be subdivided and abbots often governed church lands held in fief from nobles. The serf or toiling man dwelt on the land of a feudal noble or churchman where he rendered service by tilling the soil or carrying out his craft for his manorial lord in return for protection, justice, and the security of his life and land. He was given a share in the common lands or pastures from which he provided for his own needs. In the modern sense he was not free (although at a later stage he could buy his freedom) since he was attached to the soil and could not leave without the lord's permission. On the other hand he could neither be deprived of his land nor lose his livelihood. Feudal tenures were abolished in England by statute in 1660, although they had for long been inoperative. In Japan a feudal system existed up to 1871, in Russia until 1917.

Fideism. A term applied to religious doctrines which hold that the intellect or reason of man is incapable of attaining knowledge of divine matters and that religious faith is the way to truth. The word came into use in the late 19th century, although it is a doctrine that has a long history. The most notable modern thinker in this tradition is Soren Kierkegaard (1813–55).

Flying Saucers. In June 1947 an American private pilot, Kenneth Arnold, saw a series of wingless objects flying through the air at a speed which he estimated at thousands of miles an hour. What Kenneth Arnold actually saw has never been satisfactorily explained—it was probably a flight of jet fighters reflecting the sun's rays in a way that made them appear as discs—but since that date literally hundreds of thousands of people all over the world have reported the sighting of strange objects in the sky, coming in a bewildering range of shapes and sizes. Initially the American Air Force launched an official enquiry—Project Bluebook—to attempt to solve the mystery of these "unidentified flying objects" or "UFOs," which folded in 1969 after hesitantly concluding that the sightings were probably misinterpretations of natural phenomena. A CIA report in 1997 confirmed that over half of all the UFO sightings from the late 1950s to the 1960s were actually American spy planes on secret missions. However, despite all this, belief in the existence of flying saucers and their origin as alien space vehicles is widespread and is held very strongly by people in all walks of life.

Fourierism *See* Utopianism.

Freemasonry, a widespread, influential secret organisation of English origin. Although it can be traced back to the Middle Ages when itinerant working masons in England and Scotland were organised in lodges with secret signs for the recognition of fellow-members, modern freemasonry first arose in England in the early decades of the 18th cent. The first Grand Lodge was founded in London in 1716 and Freemasons' Hall was opened in 1776. With its clubs for discussion and social enjoyment (women were excluded) it met a need and became a well-known feature of English life. The movement quickly spread abroad to places which had direct trade links with England. The graded lodge structure, the social prestige conferred by membership, the symbolism, ritual and ceremony, and the emphasis on mutual help have had a lasting appeal. Interest in the occult had more appeal on the Continent than in England. Until two decades

or so ago, membership conferred definite business and social advantages, particularly in small communities where the leading middle-class figures were generally members. Recently this advantage has markedly declined and freemason lodges nowadays tend to be little more than worthy charitable organisations. Fear of secret societies has given freemasonry many opponents; it was condemned by the Roman Catholic Church, banned by Fascist dictators, and denounced by the Comintern. A statement from the Congregation for the Doctrine of the Faith in 1981 reminded Catholics that under Article 2335 of the Code of Canon Law they are forbidden under pain of excommunication from joining masonic or similar associations. Recently, there have been calls for Freemasons who are members of, for example, the judiciary to declare their membership openly.

Freudian theory. *See* Psychoanalysis.

Friends, The Society of. *See* Quakers.

Fundamentalism is a term covering a number of religious movements which adhere with the utmost rigidity to orthodox tenets; for example the Old Testament statement that the earth was created by God in six days and six nights would be held to be factual rather than allegorical or symbolic. Although the holding of rigid beliefs in the literal truth of the Bible might seem to be frequently contrary to modern scientific findings, the fundamentalists at least do not have the problems of compromise and interpretation to face, and to some people this is no doubt a great attraction. Since the coming to power of Khomeini in Iran, Islamic fundamentalism has become a potent force in much of the Middle East, North Africa (especially Egypt and Algeria) and Central Asia. In Afghanistan, the radical Taleban movement is attempting to impose a strict Islamic regime.

Futurism. *See* **Section L.**

G

Game Theory, an approach to understanding human and animal behaviour which takes the view that psychological insight is best gained by studying the decisions which all living things make constantly and which govern the course of their lives. It proposes that life is basically a strategic game following complex rules which can probably only be understood by a study of the "decision units" as and when they occur. Because one is dealing with highly variable animals controlled by highly complex brains, and not with simple clockwork or electro-mechanical systems, the study of the rules which operate in the game of life is enormously complicated and thus game theory has quickly taken off into advanced mathematics. Game theory, incidentally, can be used to apply to individual action or to the behaviour of groups.

Gay Movement, term for the campaign to remove legal and other discrimination from homosexual men and lesbian women and to allow them to lead their lives to the full in our society. Its first large-scale manifestation was in America in the 1970s, paralleled in Britain with organisations such as the Gay Liberation Front and, more recently, OutRage. Although much discrimination remains, many people now accept that the sexual orientation of a person should not be a ground for any form of discrimination. Issues such as gay rights, and the onset of AIDS, have continued to ensure that "gay rights" remains a controversial area. In a vote in the Commons in March 1999 on the question of equalising the age of consent (there is currently a higher minimum age of consent for male homosexual acts than for heterosexual) a majority of 281 to 82 was in favour, but the House of Lords again rejected the reform in April 1999.

Gestalt Psychology. In the latter half of the 19th cent. it became evident to psychologists that in principle there was no good reason why "mental" events should not be just as measurable and manageable as "physical" ones. Intensive studies of learning, memory, perception, and so on were therefore undertaken and the beginnings of an empirical science of psychology were underway. In the early part of the 20th cent. the experiments of Pavlov (*see* **Behaviourism**) and his co-workers suggested that the behaviour of an animal, or even men, might ultimately be reduced to a descriptive account of the activities of nervous reflex loops—the so-called conditioned reflexes. With the publication of Watson's important book on Behaviourism in 1914 it looked as though the transfer of psychological studies from the field of philosophy to that of science could now take place. Actually the over-simplified picture of cerebral and mental pictures which Behaviourism offered was rather comparable to the billiard ball view of the universe so fashionable in Victorian science. Just as Behaviourism implied that there was a fundamental building block (the conditioned reflex) from which all mental events could be constructed, so Victorian physics assumed that the entire universe could be described in terms of a vast collection of atoms pushing each other around like billiard balls. The development of nuclear physics was to shatter the latter dream and at the same time a challenge to the naïve "reflex psychology" came from the Gestalt experimental school.

The founders of this school were Max Wertheimer, Kurt Koffka and Wolfgang Köhler, three young psychologists who in 1912 were conducting experiments—notably in vision—which seemed to expose the inadequacies of the behaviourist position. The Pavlov–Watson view, as we have said, implied that complex sensory events were no more than a numerical sum of individual nervous impulses. Wertheimer's group proposed that certain facts of perceptual experiences (ruled out of court as subjective and therefore unreliable by Watson) implied that the whole (*Gestalt*) was something more than simply the sum of its parts. For example, the presentation of a number of photographs, each slightly different, in rapid series gives rise to cinematographic motion. In basic terms, the eye has received a number of discrete, "still" photographs, and yet "motion" is perceived. What, they asked, was the sensory input corresponding to this motion? Some processes within the brain clearly *added* something to the total input as defined in behaviourist terms. An obvious alternative—in a different sense modality—is that of the arrangement of musical notes. A cluster of notes played one way might be called a tune; played backwards they may form another tune, or may be meaningless. Yet in all cases the constituent parts are the same, and yet their relationship to one another is evidently vital. Once again the whole is something more than the sum of the parts.

The implications of all this appeared to be that the brain was equipped with the capacity to organise sensory input in certain well-defined ways, and that far from being misleading and scientifically unjustifiable, human subjective studies of visual experience might reveal the very principles of organisation which the brain employs. Take a field of dots, more or less randomly distributed; inspection of the field will soon reveal certain patterns or clusters standing out—the constellations in the night sky are a good illustration. There are many other examples, and Wertheimer and his colleagues in a famous series of experiments made some effort to catalogue them and reduce them to a finite number of "Laws of Perceptual Organisation" which are still quoted today.

Ghosts, belief in ghosts is one of the most common features of supernatural and mystical philosophy. At its roots it is based on the assumption that Man is essentially an individual created of two separate and distinct substances, mind and body. Most religious systems hold to this dualistic view (*see* **Dualism**), arguing that whereas the body is transient and destructible, the mind or spirit is permanent and survives the death of its physical host. The discarnate spirit is normally assumed to progress to some other realm ("Heaven," "Nirvana," "The Spirit World," *etc.*) whereupon it loses contact with the mortal world. Occasionally, however, for one reason or another, the spirits may not progress and may become trapped and unable to escape the material world. Traditionally this is supposed to occur when the death of the individual is precipitated by some great tragedy —murder, suicide, *etc.*—when the site of the tragedy is supposed to be haunted by the earthbound spirit. Although the library of the Society for Psychical Research is crammed with supposedly authentic accounts of hauntings of this kind, scientific interest in ghosts has been waning rapidly in recent years. At one time, in particular in the latter part of the 19th cent., with the upsurge of scientific interest in Spiritualism (*q.v.*), there were even attempts to call up ghosts in the laboratory. These led to spectacular opportunities for fraud on the part of Spiritualist mediums and the like, but in the long run added little to the cause of science. As we have said, belief in ghosts is largely dependent upon a parallel belief that the mind or soul of man is something essentially separate from the body. With the decline in belief of this notion has come an inevitable decline in belief in ghosts. For a recent, different view, *see* Percy Seymour, *The Paranormal: Beyond Sensory Science* (Penguin, 1992).

Gnosticism. Among the many heresies of early Christianity, especially during its first two centuries, was a group which came under the heading of Gnosticism. This was a system or set of systems which attempted to combine Christian beliefs with others derived from Oriental and Greek sources, especially those which were of a mystical and metaphysical nature, such as the doctrines of Plato and Pythagoras. There were many Gnostic sects, the most celebrated being the Alexandrian school of Valentius (fl. *c.* 136–*c.* 160). "Gnosis" was understood not as meaning "knowledge" or "understanding" as we understand these words, but "revelation." As in other mystical religions, the ultimate object was individual salvation; sacraments took the most varied forms. Many who professed themselves Christians accepted Gnostic doctrines and even orthodox Christianity contains some elements of Gnostic mysticism. It was left to the bishops and theologians to decide at what point Gnosticism ceased to be orthodox and a difficult task this proved to be. Two of the greatest, Clement of Alexandria and his pupil Origen, unwittingly slipped into heresy when they tried to show that such men as Socrates and Plato, who were in quest of truth, were Christian in intention, and by their lives and works had prepared the way for Christ. Thus they contradicted Church doctrine which specifically said *Extra ecclesiam nulla salus*—outside the Church there is no salvation.

God and Man. The idea of gods came before the idea of God and even earlier in the evolution of religious thought there existed belief in spirits (*see* **Animism**). It was only as a result of a long period of development that the notion of a universal "God" arose, a development particularly well documented in the Old Testament. Here we are concerned only with the views of philosophers, the views of specific religious bodies being given under the appropriate headings. First, however, some definitions.

Atheism is the positive disbelief in the existence of a God. **Agnosticism** (a term coined by T. H. Huxley, the 19th cent. biologist and contemporary of Darwin) signifies that one cannot know whether God exists or not. **Secularism** (prominent from the 1850s) pursued "a philosophy of life which ignores theology". **Deism** is the acceptance of the existence of God, not through revelation, but as a hypothesis required by reason. **Theism** also accepts the existence of God, but, unlike Deism, does not reject the evidence of revelation (*e.g.*, in the Bible or in the lives of the saints). **Pantheism** is the identification of God with all that exists (*i.e.*, with the whole universe). **Monotheism** is the belief in one God, **Polytheism** the belief in many (*see also* **Dualism**).

Early Greek Views. Among the early Greek philosophers, Thales (*c.* 624–565 B.C.) of Miletus, in Asia Minor, Anaximander (611–547 B.C.), his pupil, and Anaximenes (b. *c.* 570 B.C.), another Miletan, were men of scientific curiosity and their speculations about the origin of the universe were untouched by religious thought. They founded the scientific tradition of critical discussion. Heraclitus of Ephesus (c. 540–475 B.C.), was concerned with the problem of change. How does a thing change and yet remain itself? For him all things are flames—processes. "Everything is in flux, and nothing is at rest." Empedocles of Agrigentum in Sicily (c. 500–c. 430 B.C.) introduced the idea of opposition and affinity. All matter is composed of the so-called four elements—*earth, water, air,* and *fire*—which are in opposition or alliance with each other. All these were materialist philosophers who sought to explain the working of the universe without recourse to the gods.

Socrates, Plato, and Aristotle. Socrates (470–399 B.C.) was primarily concerned with ethical matters and conduct rather than the nature of the universe. For him goodness and virtue come from knowledge. He obeyed an "inner voice" and suffered death rather than give up his philosophy. He believed in the persistence of life after death and was essentially a monotheist. Plato (427–347 B.C.) was chiefly concerned with the nature of reality and thought in terms of absolute truths which were unchanging, logical, and mathematical. (*See* **Mind and Matter.**) Aristotle (384–322 B.C.) took his views of matter not from Democritus (atomic view) but from Empedocles (doctrine of four elements), a view which came to fit in well with orthodox mediaeval theology. Matter is conceived of as potentially alive and striving to attain its particular form, being moved by divine spirit or mind (*nous*). (An acorn, for example, is matter which contains the form "oak-tree" towards which it strives.) Thus there is a whole series from the simplest level of matter to the perfect living individual. But there must be a supreme source of all movement upon which the whole of Nature depends, a Being that Aristotle describes as the "Unmoved Mover", the ultimate cause of all becoming in the universe. This Being is pure intelligence, a philosopher's God, not a personal one. Unlike Plato, Aristotle did not believe in survival after death, holding that the divine, that is the immortal element in man, is mind.

Among the later Greek thinkers the Epicureans were polytheists whose gods, however, were denied supernatural powers. The Stoics built up a materialist theory of the universe, based on the Aristotelian model. To them God was an all-pervading force, related to the world as the soul is related to the body, but they conceived of it as material. They developed the mystical side of Plato's idealism and were much attracted by the astrology coming from Babylonia. They were pantheists. The Sceptics were agnostics.

From *Pagan to Christian Thought.* Philo, "the Jew of Alexandria," who was about 20 years older than Jesus, tried to show that the Jewish scriptures were in line with the best in Greek thought. He introduced the *Logos* as a bridge between the two systems. Philo's God is remote from the world, above and beyond all thought and being, and, as His perfection does not permit direct contact with matter the divine *Logos* acts as intermediary between God and man. Plotinus (204–70), a Roman, and the founder of Neoplatonism, was the last of the great pagan philosophers. Like Philo, he believed that God had created the world indirectly through emanations—beings coming from Him but not of Him. The world needs God but God does not need the world. Creation is a fall from God, especially the human soul when enmeshed in the body and the world of the senses, yet (*see* **Determinism**) man has the ability to free himself from sense domination and turn towards God. Neoplatonism was the final stage of Greek thought drawing inspiration from the mystical side of Plato's idealism and its ethics from Stoicism.

Christianity: The Fathers and the Schoolmen. It was mainly through St. Augustine (354–430), Bishop of Hippo in North Africa, that certain of the doctrines of Neoplatonism found their way into Christianity. Augustine also emphasised the concept of God as all good, all wise, all knowing, transcendent, the Creator of

the universe out of nothing. But, he added, since God knows everything, everything is determined by Him forever. This is the doctrine of predestination and its subsequent history is discussed under **Determinism**.

In the early centuries of Christianity, as we have seen, some found it difficult to reconcile God's perfection with His creation of the universe and introduced the concept of the *Logos* which many identified with Christ. Further, it came to be held that a power of divine origin permeated the universe, namely the Holy Spirit or Holy Ghost. Some theory had to be worked out to explain the relationships of these three entities whence arose the conception of the Trinity. God is One; but He is also Three: Father, Son (the *Logos* or Christ), and Holy Ghost.

This doctrine was argued by the Apologists and the Modalists. The former maintained that the *Logos* and the Holy Spirit were emanations from God and that Jesus was the *Logos* in the form of a man. The Modalists held that all three Persons of the Trinity were God in three forms or modes: the *Logos* is God creating, the Holy Spirit God reasoning, and God is God being. This led to a long discussion as to whether the *Logos* was an emanation from God or God in another form; was the *Logos* of like *nature* with God or of the same *substance*? This was resolved at the Council of Nicaea (325) when Athanasius formulated the orthodox doctrine against Arius (*q.v.*): that the one God is a Trinity of the same substance, three Persons of the same nature—Father, Son, and Holy Ghost.

St. Thomas Aquinas (1227–74), influenced greatly by Aristotle's doctrines, set the pattern for all subsequent Catholic belief even to the present time. He produced rational arguments for God's existence: *e.g.,* Aristotle's argument that, since movement exists, there must be a prime mover, the Unmoved Mover or God; further, we can see that things in the universe are related in a scale from the less to the more complex, from the less to the more perfect, and this leads us to suppose that at the peak there must be a Being with absolute perfection. God is the first and final cause of the universe, absolutely perfect, the Creator of everything out of nothing. He reveals Himself in his Creation and rules the universe through His perfect will. How Aquinas dealt with the problem of predestination is told under **Determinism**.

Break with Mediaeval Thought. Renaissance thinkers, free to think for themselves, doubted the validity of the arguments of the Schoolmen but most were unwilling to give up the idea of God (nor would it have been safe to do so). Mystics (*see* **Mysticism**) or near-mystics such as Nicholas of Cusa (c. 1401–64) and Jacob Boehme (1575–1624) taught that God was not to be found by reason but was a fact of the immediate intuition of the mystical experience, Giordano Bruno held that God was immanent in the infinite universe. He is the unity of all opposites, a unity without opposites, which the human mind cannot grasp. Bruno was burned at the stake in 1600 at the instigation of the Inquisition (a body which, so we are told, never caused pain to anyone since it was the civil power, not the Inquisition, that carried out the unpleasant sentences) for his heresy.

Francis Bacon, who died in 1626, separated, as was the tendency of that time, science from religion. The latter he divided into the two categories of natural and revealed theology. The former, through the study of nature, may give convincing proof of the existence of a God but nothing more. Of revealed theology he said: "we must quit the small vessel of human reason . . . as we are obliged to obey the divine law, though our will murmurs against it, so we are obliged to believe in the word of God, though our reason is shocked at it." Hobbes (d. 1679) was a complete materialist and one feels that his obeisance to the notion was politic rather than from conviction. However, he does mention God as starting the universe in motion; infers that God is corporeal but denies that His nature can be known.

From Descartes Onwards. Descartes (1596–1650) separated mind and body as different entities but believed that the existence of God could be deduced by the fact that the idea of him existed in the mind. Whatever God puts into man, including his ideas, must be real. God is self-caused, omniscient, omnipotent, eternal, all goodness and truth. But Descartes neglected to explain how mind separate from body can influence body, or God separate from the world can influence matter.

Spinoza (1632–77) declared that all existence is embraced in one substance—God, the all-in-all. He was a pantheist and as such was rejected by his Jewish brethren. But Spinoza's God has neither personality nor consciousness, intelligence nor purpose, although all things follow in strict law from His nature. All the thoughts of everyone in the world, make up God's thoughts.

Bishop Berkeley (1685–1753) took the view that things exist only when they are perceived, and this naturally implies that a tree, for example, ceases to exist when nobody is looking at it. This problem was solved to his own satisfaction by assuming that God, seeing everything, prevented objects from disappearing when we were not present. The world is a creation of God but it is a spiritual or mental world, not a material one.

Hume (1711–76), who was a sceptic, held that human reason cannot demonstrate the existence of God and all past arguments to show that it could were fallacious. Yet we must believe in God since the basis of all hope, morality, and society is based upon the belief. Kant (1724–1804) held a theory similar to that of Hume. We cannot know by reason that God exists, nor can we prove on the basis of argument anything about God. But we can form an idea of the whole of the universe, the one Absolute Whole, and personify it. We need the idea of God on which to base our moral life, although this idea of God is transcendent, *i.e.*, goes beyond experience.

William James (1842–1910), the American philosopher (*see* **Pragmatism**), held much the same view: God cannot be proved to exist, but we have a will to believe which must be satisfied, and the idea works in practice. Hegel (1770–1831) thought of God as a developing process, beginning with "the Absolute" or First Cause and finding its highest expression in man's mind, or reason. It is in man that God most clearly becomes aware of Himself. Finally Comte (1798–1857), the positivist, held that religion belongs to a more primitive state of society and, like many modern philosophers, turned the problem over to believers as being none of the business of science.

Good and Evil

Early Philosophers' Views. The early Greek philosophers were chiefly concerned with the laws of the universe, consequently it was common belief that knowledge of these laws, and living according to them, constituted the supreme good. Heraclitus, for example, who taught that all things carried with them their opposites, held that good and evil were like two notes in a harmony, necessary to each other. "It is the opposite which is good for us". Democritus, like Epicurus (*q.v.*), held that the main goal of life is happiness, but happiness in moderation. The good man is not merely the one who *does* good but who always *wants* to do so: "You can tell the good man not by his deeds alone but by his desires." Such goodness brings happiness, the ultimate goal. On the other hand, many of the wandering Sophist teachers taught that good was merely social convention, that there are no absolute principles of right and wrong, that each man should live according to his desires and make his own moral code. To Socrates knowledge was the highest good because doing wrong is the result of ignorance: "no man is voluntarily bad." Plato and Aristotle, differing in many other respects, drew attention to the fact that man is composed of three parts: his desires and appetites, his will, and his reason. A man whose reason rules his will and appetites is not only a good but a happy man; for happiness is not an aim in itself but a by-product of the good life. Aristotle, however, emphasised the goal

of self-realisation, and thought that if the goal of life is (as Plato had said) a rational attitude towards the feelings and desires, it needs to be further defined. Aristotle defined it as the "Golden Mean"—the good man is one who does not go to extremes but balances one extreme against another. Thus courage is a mean between cowardice and foolhardiness. The later philosophers Philo and Plotinus held that evil was in the very nature of the body and its senses. Goodness could only be achieved by giving up the life of the senses and, freed from the domination of the body, turning to God, the source of goodness.

Christian Views. St. Augustine taught that everything in the universe is good. Even those things which appear evil are good in that they fit with the harmony of the universe like shadows in a painting. Man should turn his back on the pleasures of the world and turn to the love of God. Peter Abelard (1079–1142) made the more sophisticated distinction when he suggested that the wrongness of an act lies not in the act itself, but in the intention of the doer: "God considers not what is done but in what spirit it is done; and the merit or praise of the agent lies not in the deed but in the intention." If we do what we believe to be right, we may err, but we do not sin. The only sinful man is he who deliberately sets out to do what he knows to be wrong. St. Thomas Aquinas agreed with Aristotle in that he believed the highest good to be realisation of self as God has ordained, and he also agreed with Abelard that intention is important. Even a good act is not good unless the doer intended it to have good consequences. Intention will not make a bad act good, but it is the only thing that will make a good act genuinely good.

In general, Christianity has had difficulties in solving the problem of the existence of evil; for even when one accepts that the evil men do is somehow tied up with the body, it is still difficult to answer the question: how could an all-good God create evil? This is answered in one of two ways: (*a*) that Adam was given free-will and chose to sin (an answer which still does not explain how sin could exist anywhere in the universe of a God who created everything); (*b*) by denying the reality of evil as some Christians have chosen to do (*e.g.*, Christian Science *q.v.*). The Eastern religions, (*see* **Zoroastrianism**), solved the problem in a more realistic way by a dualism which denied that their gods were the creators of the whole universe and allowed the existence of at least two gods, one good and one evil. In Christianity there is, of course, a Devil, but it is not explained whence his evil nature came.

Later Philosophic Views. Hobbes equated good with pleasure, evil with pain. They are relative to the individual man in the sense that "one man's meat is another man's poison." Descartes believed that the power to distinguish between good and evil given by God to man is not complete, so that man does evil through ignorance. We act with insufficient knowledge and on inadequate evidence. Locke, believing that at birth the mind is a blank slate, held that men get their opinions of right and wrong from their parents. By and large, happiness is good and pain is evil. But men do not always agree over what is pleasurable and what not. Hence laws exist and these fall into three categories: (1) the divine law; (2) civil laws; (3) matters of opinion or reputation which are enforced by the fact that men do not like to incur the disapproval of their friends. We learn by experience that evil brings pain and good acts bring pleasure and, basically, one is good because not to be so would bring discomfort.

Kant (*see* **God and Evil**) found moral beliefs to be inherent in man whether or not they can be proved by reason. There is a categorical imperative which makes us realise the validity of two universal laws: (1) "always act in such a way that the maxim determining your conduct might well become a universal law; act so that you can will that everybody shall follow the principle of your action; (2) "always act so as to treat humanity, whether in thine own person or in that of another, in every case as an end and never as a means."

Schopenhauer (1788–1860) was influenced by Buddhism and saw the will as a blind impelling striving, and desire as the cause of all suffering. The remedy is to regard sympathy and pity as the basis of all morality and to deny one's individual will. This is made easier if we realise that everyone is part of the Universal Will and therefore the one against whom we are struggling is part of the same whole as ourselves.

John Stuart Mill and Jeremy Bentham were both representatives of the Utilitarian school, believing that good is the greatest good (happiness) of the greatest number (see **Utilitarianism**). Lastly, there is the view held mostly by political thinkers that good is what is good for the state or society in general (see **State and Man**).

Guild Socialism, a British form of syndicalism (q.v.) created in 1906 by an architect, A. J. Penty, who was soon joined by A. R. Orage, S. G. Hobson, and G. D. H. Cole. The guild socialists advocated a restoration of the mediaeval guild system as was being recommended by the French syndicalists whose programme involved a return to direct economic action, a functional industrial structure, return of craftsmanship, and distrust of the state. Guild socialists believed that value was created by society as a whole rather than by individuals singly, and that capitalist economists had recommended the acquisition of wealth without emphasising the social responsibilities which wealth should bring. The trade unions were to be organised to take over and run their own industries after nationalisation. Thus guild socialists were not only against capitalism but also against state socialism in which the state took over the control of industry. Political authority was held to be uncongenial to human freedom and therefore nothing was to be gained by the substitution of state bureaucracy for capitalist control. The National Guilds League, formed in 1915, advocated abolition of the wages system, self-government in industry and control by a system of national guilds acting in conjunction with other functional democratic organisations in the community. This body was dissolved in 1925, but the theories of guild socialism have undoubtedly influenced British socialism.

Gurdjieff, Russian–Greek mystic who set up an occult commune at La Prieure in France, to which were attracted a host of the intellectual and literary avant-garde of the 1920s. His teachings, which are immensely obscure, are presented in allegorical form in a lengthy philosophical novel, *All and Everything*.

H

Hasidism (Chasidism). From the Hebrew *hasid*, pious or faithful one. A Jewish mystical movement which began in Poland in the 18th century, and which spread widely, first through Eastern Europe and then into Western Europe and America. The movement was founded by Israel ben Eliezer (1700–60), who came to be known as the Ba'al Shem Tov ("Master of the Good Name"). It was originally opposed to the authority of the rabbis and traditional Jewish practices. According to Hasidism, true religion comes not from study of the sacred texts but from purity of heart, prayer and observance of the commandments. The movement was also characterized by ecstatic forms of worship. Its present day followers are ultra-conservative orthodox Jews.

Hedonism. From Greek *hedone*, pleasure. The theory of ethics in which pleasure is regarded as the chief good, or proper end, of action. This is sometimes called ethical hedonism and is then distinguished from psychological hedonism, which is the theory that behaviour is primarily motivated by the pursuit of pleasure and the avoidance of pain. Psychological hedonism can of course be employed to support ethical hedonism.

This view, that only pleasure is ultimately good, has been held by many distinguished philosophers, including Epicurus, Locke, Hobbes, Hume, Bentham and Mill. In the case of the last two, it is closely associated with utilitarianism (q.v.). Although the term "pleasure" suggests physical enjoyments, hedonists have taken it to include intellectual pleasures also. They also argue that many things beside pleasure, such as virtue and knowledge, are desirable in that they produce pleasure.

Heresy, originally meant a sect or school of thought holding views different from others (e.g., Pharisees and Sadducees within Judaism). Later it came to mean beliefs contrary to orthodox teaching (e.g., Arianism, Jansenism, Pelagianism).

Hermeneutics. Originally, the study of the general principles of biblical interpretation. The term was imported into philosophy in the late 19th century to refer to a more general study of interpretation, namely the interpretation of the significance of human actions, utterances, products and institutions.

Hermeticism (or Hermetism). Philosophies based on the Hermetic writings, also called the Hermetica, works on occult, theological and philosophical subjects ascribed to the Egyptian God Thoth (referred to in Greek as Hermes Trismegistos, Hermes the thrice-greatest). This collection, written in Latin and Greek, dates from 2nd–3rd centuries A.D. It reached Europe, from the Arabs, in the late 15th century, and had some influence during the Renaissance. It continues to fascinate modern devotees of magic and astrology.

The term also has a literary sense. It refers to an Italian poetic movement of the 20th century, characterized by brevity and obscurity.

Hinduism, the religion and social institutions of the great majority of the people of India. Hinduism has no fixed scriptural canon but its doctrines are to be found in certain ancient works, notably the *Veda*, the *Brahmanas*, the *Upanishads*, and the *Bhagavad-gita*. The dark-skinned Dravidians invaded India between about 3250 and 2750 B.C. and established a civilisation in the Indus valley. They were polytheists who worshipped a number of nature-gods; some elements of their beliefs persisted into Hinduism. They were subdued by a light-skinned Nordic people who invaded from Asia Minor and Iran about 1500 B.C. The language of these Aryan people was Vedic, parent of Sanskrit in which their religious literature (the Vedas) came to be written after many centuries of oral transmission.

The *Veda* or Sacred Lore has come down to us in the form of mantras or hymns of which there are four great collections, the best-known being the *Rig-Veda*. These Vedic Aryans worshipped nature-deities, their favourites being Indra (rain), Agni (fire), and Surya (the sun). Their religion contained no idolatry but became influenced by the beliefs of the Dravidians, Sacrifice and ritual became predominant in a ceremonial religion.

As a reaction a more philosophic mind arose (c. 500 B.C.) with its scriptures in the *Upanishads*. At its highest level known as Brahmanism belief is in a subtle and sophisticated form of monotheism (Brahman is an impersonal, all-embracing spirit), but there is a tolerant acceptance of more primitive beliefs. Thus Vishnu (a conservative principle) and Siva (a destructive principle) grew out of Vedic conceptions. The two great doctrines of Hinduism are *karma* and transmigration. The universal desire to be reunited with the absolute (*atman* or Brahman) can be satisfied by following the path of knowledge. Life is a cycle of lives (*samsara*) in which man's destiny is determined by his deeds (*karma*) from which he may seek release (*moksa*) through ascetic practices or the discipline of Yoga (q.v.). Failure to achieve release means reincarnation—migration to a higher or lower form of life after death—until the ultimate goal of absorption in the absolute is reached.

In the great Sanskrit epic poems *Ramayana* and *Mahabharata* the deity takes three forms, represented by the divine personalities of Brahma, Vishnu, and Siva. There are also lower gods, demi-gods, supernatural beings, and members of the trinity may even become incarnate, as Vishnu became identified with Krishna, one of the heroes of the *Mahabharata* and the well-known *Bhagavad-gita*.

The ritual and legalistic side of Brahmanism is the caste system based on the elaborate codes of the *Law of Manu*, according to which God created distinct orders of men as He created distinct species of animals and plants. Men are born to be Brahmans, soldiers, agriculturists, or servants, but since a Brahman may marry a woman from any of these castes, an endless number of sub-castes arise.

Hinduism has historically shown great tolerance for varieties of belief and practice. Ideas pleasant and unpleasant have been assimilated: fetichism, demon-cults, animal-worship, sexual cults (such as the rites of *Kali* in Calcutta). Today, as would be expected in a country which is in the throes of vast social change, Hinduism itself is changing. Under the impact of modern conditions new ideas are destroying old beliefs and customs. A militant political Hinduism is now threatening the cohesion of India, fanned by the Bharatiya Janata Group (BJP) which extols Hindu fundamentalism. There are (1999) over 750,000,000 Hindus worldwide. The newly-completed Hindu temple in Neasden, north London, is the largest place of Hindu worship outside India. *See also* **Jainism, Sikhism.**

Homoeopathy, an alternative branch of medicine whose motto *Similia Similibus Curantur* (like cures like) sums up its particular approach to therapy. In essence the homoeopathists claim that a disease can be treated by administering quite minute doses of a substance which produce symptoms (in the healthy person) similar to those induced by the disease itself. The founder and populariser of this unusual approach to medicine was the German Samuel Hahnemann who was born in 1775, a friend of the physician Mesmer who propagated hypnotherapy. Hahnemann lived to see his ideas spread across the civilised world (despite the grave theoretical difficulties implicit in the question of how the very minute dosages actually achieve any result at all). Recent years have seen a major growth in public demand for homoeopathy. This has been testified to by general practitioners and hospital staff. The increased interest in homoeopathy, furthermore, is world-wide.

The amount of research being carried out in homoeopathy by medical doctors, physicists, molecular biologists, *etc.*, is phenomenal; furthermore, two real breakthroughs occurred in the UK when papers on homoeopathy were published in *The Lancet* in 1988 and in the *British Medical Journal* in 1989.

Human Rights. *See* **Special Topic, J58–60.**

Humanism, the term applied to (1) a system of education based on the Greek and Latin classics; and (2) the vigorous attitudes that accompanied the end of the Middle Ages and were represented at different periods by the Renaissance, the Reformation, the Industrial Revolution, and the struggle for democracy. These include: release from ecclesiastical authority, the liberation of the intellect, faith in progress, the belief that man himself can improve his own conditions without supernatural help and, indeed has a duty to do so. "Man is the measure of all things" is the keynote of humanism. The humanist has faith in man's intellectual and spiritual resources not only to bring knowledge and understanding of the world but to solve the moral problems of how to use that knowledge. That man should show respect to man irrespective of class, race or creed is fundamental to the humanist attitude to life. Among the fundamental moral principles he would count those of freedom, justice and tolerance.

Today the idea that people can live an honest, meaningful life without following a formal religious creed of some kind does not seem particularly shocking. Persons seeking to find out more about humanism can apply for information to the British Humanist Association, 47, Theobald's Road, London WC1X 8SP.

Hussites, the followers of John Hus, the most famous pupil of John Wyclif. He was the rector of Prague University and, although it is now by no means certain that his beliefs were heretical, he was condemned to death for heresy and burnt at the stake in 1415 at Constance whence he had come with a safe conduct issued by the Emperor Sigismund of Hungary. The latter based his action on the doctrine that no faith need be kept with heretics, but it is obvious that the main objection to Hus was his contempt for authority of any kind. After their leader's death, the Hussites became a formidable body in Bohemia and Moravia. They took up arms on behalf of their faith, their religion being strongly imbued with political feeling (hostility to Germanism and to the supremacy of the Roman Church). Their religious struggles for reform led to the Hussite Wars during which the movement splintered into several groups.

Hutterites. *See* **Mennonites, J31.**

I

I Ching, the Chinese "Book of Changes" which is supposed to provide a practical demonstration of the truths of ancient Chinese philosophy. The method consists of casting forty-nine sticks into two random heaps, or more simply, of tossing three coins to see if there is a preponderance of heads or tails. The coins are cast six times whereupon the head-tail sequence achieved is referred to a coded series of phrases in the book, which are supposed to relate in some way to the question held in the mind when the sticks or coins are being cast. The phrases are without exception vague, and platitudinous remarks such as "Evil people do not further the perseverance of the superior man," etc., abound. Consequently it is not difficult to read into such amorphous stuff a suitable "interpretation" or answer to one's unspoken question. The I Ching might well be looked upon as an entertaining parlour game, but it is currently a great fad in Europe and America and is taken with great seriousness by an astonishing number of people.

Idealism, in a philosophical sense, the belief that there is no matter in the universe, that all that exists is mind or spirit. *See* **Mind and Matter** and **Realism.**

Illuminati, a secret society founded in 1776 by Adam Weishaupt, a Bavarian professor of canon law at Ingolstadt, in an attempt to combat superstition and ignorance by founding an association for rational enlightenment and the regeneration of the world. "He tried to give the social ideals of the Enlightenment realisation by conspiratorial means" (J. M. Roberts, *The Mythology of the Secret Societies,* 1972). Under conditions of secrecy it sought to penetrate and control the masonic lodges for subversive purposes. Among its members were Goethe and Schiller. The Order spread to Austria, Italy and Hungary but was condemned by the Catholic Church and dissolved in 1785 by the Bavarian government.

Immortality. The belief in a life after death has been widely held since the earliest times. It has certainly not been universal, nor has it always taken a form which everyone would find satisfying. In the early stages of human history or prehistory everything contained a spirit (*see* **Animism**) and it is obvious from the objects left in early graves that the dead were expected to exist in some form after death. The experience of dreams, too, seemed to suggest to the unsophisticated that there was a part of man which could leave his body and wander elsewhere during sleep. In order to save space, it will be helpful to classify the various types of belief which have existed in philosophical thought regarding this problem: (1) There is the idea that, although *something* survives bodily death, it is not necessarily eternal. Thus most primitive peoples were prepared to believe that man's spirit haunted the place around his grave and that food and drink should be set out for it, but that this spirit did not go on forever and gradually faded away. (2) The ancient Greeks and Hebrews believed for the most part that the souls of the dead went to a place of shades there to pine for the world of men. Their whining ghosts spent eternity in a dark, uninviting region in misery and remorse. (3) Other people, and there were many more of these, believed in the transmigration of souls with the former life of the individual determining whether his next life would be at a higher or lower level. Sometimes this process seems to have been thought of as simply going on and on, by others (*e.g.*, in Hinduism and Buddhism) as terminating in either non-sentience or union with God but in any case in annihilation of the self as self. Believers in this theory were the Greek philosophers Pythagoras, Empedocles, Plato (who believed that soul comes from God and strives to return to God, according to his own rather confused notions of the deity. If it fails to free itself completely from the body it will sink lower and lower from one body to another.) Plotinus held similar views to Plato, and many other religious sects in addition to those mentioned have believed in transmigration. (4) The belief of Plato and Aristotle that if souls continue to exist after death there is no reason why they should not have existed before birth (this in part is covered by (3)), but some have pointed out that eternity does not mean "from now on," but the whole of the time before and after "now"—nobody, however, so far as one knows, held that *individual* souls so exist. (5) The theory that the soul does not exist at all and therefore immortality is meaningless: this was held by Anaximenes in early Greek times; by Leucippus, Democritus, and the other Greek atomists; by the Epicureans from the Greek Epicurus to the Roman Lucretius; by the British Hobbes and Hume; by Comte of France; and William James and John Dewey of America. (6) The thesis, held notably by Locke and Kant, that although we cannot prove the reality of soul and immortality by pure reason, belief in them should be held for moral ends. (For the orthodox Christian view *see* **God and Man, Determinism and Free-will.**) From this summary we can see that many philosophies and religions (with the important exceptions of Islam and Christianity) without denying a future life do deny the permanence of the individual soul in anything resembling its earthly form (*see* **Spiritualism, Psychic Research**).

Imperialism, the practice by a country, which has become a nation and embarked upon commercial and industrial expansion, of acquiring and administering territories, inhabited by peoples usually at a lower stage of development, as colonies or dependencies. Thus the "typical" imperialist powers of the mid-19th cent. and earlier were Britain, France, Belgium, Holland, Spain and Portugal, whilst Germany, Italy, and Japan, which either did not have unity during this period or adequate industrial expansion, tried to make good their weakness in this direction by war in the late 19th cent. The term "imperialism" is not easy to define today (although often enough used as a term of abuse). There is economic imperialism exerted, not through armies, but through economic penetration. There is what may be described as ideological imperialism, *e.g.,* the anti-communist crusade that led America (in the name of freedom) into a disastrous and widely-condemned war in Vietnam; the dogmatism that led the former Soviet Union into the invasion of Czechoslovakia and Israel into occupying neighbouring lands.

Individualism. The doctrine that the single person is the basic unit of political analysis. The term covers all political and social philosophies that place a high value on the freedom of the individual. It is believed that the interests of the individual are best served by allowing him maximum freedom and responsibility. Society is seen as a collection of individuals. So individualism opposes controls over the individual, especially when they are exercised by the state. The most extreme form is anarchism, but all individualists believe that government interference should be kept to a minimum, and is hence associated with right–wing policies. It is opposed to collectivism (*q.v.*). The term was originally used critically, to refer to self-centred conduct or egoism as a matter of principle.

Irrationalism. An attitude that puts emotion and passion before reason, and which can be exploited for dubious ends.

Islam, the religion of the Arabic and Iranian world of which Mohammed (570–632) was the prophet, the word signifying submission to the will of God. It is one of the most widespread of religions. Its adherents are called Moslems or Muslims. Islam came later than the other great monotheistic religions (Judaism and Christianity) and drew its inspiration mainly from Judaism and Nestorianism. Mohammed accepted the inspiration of the Old Testament and claimed to be a successor to Moses, but recognised Jesus only as a prophet.

The sacred book of Islam is the Koran. Its revelations are contained in 114 *suras* or chapters; all but one begin with the words: "In the name of Allah, the Merciful, the Compassionate." It is written in classical Arabic, and Moslems memorise much or all of it. Its ethical teachings are high. Like orthodox Judaism Islam is a literal-minded religion lived in everyday life. No Moslem is in any doubt as to exactly how he should carry on in the events of his day. He has five duties: (1) Once in his life he must say with absolute conviction: "There is no God but Allah, and Mohammed is His Prophet". (2) Prayer preceded by ablution must be five times daily—on rising, at noon, in mid-afternoon, after sunset, and before retiring. The face of the worshipper is turned in the direction of Mecca. (3) The giving of alms generously, including provisions for the poor. (4) The keeping of the fast of Ramadan, the holy month, during which believers in good health may neither eat nor drink nor indulge in wordly pleasures between sunrise and sunset. (5) Once in his life a Moslem, if he can, must make the pilgrimage to Mecca. In addition, drinking, gambling, and the eating of pork are forbidden and circumcision is practised. Polygamy is permitted, although decreasing; sexual relations outside marriage are disapproved of; marriage is only with the wife's consent; and divorce may be initiated by either husband or wife. A great advantage in the spread of Islam has been its lack of race prejudice.

Mohammed's main achievements were the destruction of idolatry, the welding of warring tribes into one community, the progress of a conquest which led after his death to the great and cultured empire which spread throughout the Middle East into north Africa, north India, and ultimately all over Europe was due to the Moslem defeat by Charles Martel at Poitiers in 732.

During the 1980s, militant Islam became a major political force in Iran (under Ayatollah Khomeini). Islamic fundamentalism is now, in the 1990s, a growing political force in, for example, Algeria, Egypt, Afghanistan and Pakistan. There are (1999) over 1,000 m. Moslems in the world.

Britain's Moslem population (1999) numbers over 1·5 million, with 70% under the age of 25. There are over 600 mosques and numerous prayer centres throughout Britain. The first was established at Woking in Surrey in 1890. The Central Mosque in Regent's Park, London has the largest congregation in Britain while other important centres include Liverpool, Manchester, Leicester and Glasgow.

J

Jainism. The Jains are an Indian sect, largely in commerce and finance. Their movement founded by Vardhamana, called Mahavira (the great hero), in the 6th cent. B.C. arose rather earlier than Buddhism in revolt against the ritualism and impersonality of **Hinduism** (*q.v.*). It rejects the authority of the early Hindu Vedas and does away with many of the Hindu deities whose place is largely taken by Jainism's twenty-four immortal saints; it despises caste distinctions and modifies the two great Hindu doctrines of *karma* and transmigration. Jain philosophy is based on *ahimsa*, the sacredness of all life, regarding even plants as the brethren of mankind, and refusing to kill even the smallest insect. The first Jain temple in the Western world opened in 1988 in Leicester. Of an estimated 3,900,000 Jains world-wide, there are *c* 3,700,000 in India. Jainism claims 30,000 devotees in Britain (1999).

Jansenism, the name given by the Roman Catholic Church to the heresy of Cornelius Jansen (1585–1638), a Dutch-born professor of theology at Louvain, derived from his work *Augustinus*, published after his death. He proposed that without special grace from God, the performance of his commandments is impossible, that man has no free will, and that most human beings are condemned to damnation. The movement based on these ideas was very influential in France in the 17th century.

Jehovah's Witnesses, a religious body who consider themselves to be the present-day representatives of a religious movement which has existed since Abel "offered unto God a more excellent sacrifice than Cain, by which he obtained witness that he was righteous." Abel was the first "witness," and amongst others were Enoch, Noah, Abraham, Moses, Jeremiah, and John the Baptist. Pre-eminent among witnesses, of course, was Jesus Christ who is described in the Book of Revelation as "the faithful and true witness."

Most people are aware that the original movement was founded by Charles Taze Russell (Pastor Russell) of Allegany, Pittsburgh, Pennsylvania, USA in 1881 under the name, adopted in 1896, of the Watch Tower Bible and Tract Society. Following Pastor Russell's death in 1916 J. F. Rutherford seized control of the Watch Tower Bible & Tract Society, dismissed the majority of the Board of Directors, began a revisionist change in doctrine and established dictatorial authority. In 1931 the present name (Jehovah's Witnesses) was adopted.

Their teaching centres upon the early establishment of God's new world on earth, preceded by the second coming of Christ. Witnesses believe this has already happened and that Armageddon "will come as soon as the Witness is completed." The millennial period will give sinners a second chance of salvation and "millions now living will never die" (the title of one of their pamphlets). The dead will be raised to the new earth until all the vacant places left after Armageddon are filled.

Every belief held by the movement, it is asserted, can be upheld, chapter and verse, by reference to the Scriptures. Witnesses regard the doctrine of the Trinity as devised by Satan. In both wars Witnesses have been in trouble for their refusal to take part in war and six thousand suffered in the same reason in German concentration camps. There are perhaps 5 million Witnesses world-wide (1999) and 125,000 in Britain.

Jesus People, one of the early revivals of interest in the teaching and personality of Jesus Christ which featured from the 1960s as part of the American "Hippy" scene. The Jesus People or Jesus Freaks, as they were sometimes called, were generally white but not necessarily of an orthodox Christian background. The cult developed in California and its adherents adopted the attire of the modern American Hippy.

Judaism, the religion of the Jews, the oldest of the great monotheist religions, parent of Christianity and Islam, the development of which is presented in the Old Testament. The creed of Judaism is based on the concept of a transcendent and omnipotent One True God, the revelation of His will in the *Torah*, and the special relation between God and His "Chosen People." The idea of Incarnation is rejected, Jesus is not recognised as the Messiah. The *Torah* is the Hebrew name for the Law of Moses (the Pentateuch) which, Judaism holds, was divinely revealed to Moses on Mount Sinai soon after the exodus of the Israelites from Egypt (1230 B.C.). Many critics deny the Mosaic authorship of the first five books of the Bible and believe them to be a compilation from four main sources known as J(Jahvist), E (Elohist), D (Deuteronomist) and P (Priestly Code), distinguished from each other by the name used for God, language, style, and internal evidence. From the historical point of view an important influence on Judaism may have been the monotheism of Akhenaten, the "heretic" Pharaoh (note, for example, the striking resemblance between Psalm 104 and Akhenaten's "Hymn to the Sun").

The Talmud is a book containing the civil and canonical laws of the Jews and includes the Mishna, a compilation from oral tradition written in Hebrew, and the Gemara, a collection of comments and criticisms by the Jewish rabbis, written in Aramaic. There are in fact two Talmuds: the one made in Palestine (the Jerusalem Talmud), finished at the beginning of the 5th cent., and the other made in Babylon, completed at the end of the 6th cent.

Judaism at the beginning of the Christian era had a number of sects: (1) the Pharisees (whose views include the first clear statement of the resurrection of the just to eternal life and the future punishment of the wicked) who held to the *Torah* and the universality of God; (2) the Sadducees, the upper class of priests and wealthy landowners, to whom God was essentially a national God and who placed the interests of the state before the *Torah*; they rejected ideas of resurrection and eternal life; (3) the Essenes (*q.v.*) who were regarded as a puritanical break-away movement by both parties. The views of the Pharisees prevailed.

Jewish writing continued through the years and some books were added to the *Torah*, among them the Three Major Prophets and certain books of the Twelve Minor Prophets. There were also the Apocalyptic writers who were unorthodox in their preaching of a divinely planned catastrophic end to the world with a "new Heaven and a new earth," preceded by a divine Messiah, and a future life—all of which beliefs influenced early Christianity. Judah Halevi of Toledo (*c.* 1085–*c.* 1140) and Moses Maimonides of Cordova (1135–1204) were the great Jewish philosophers.

Modern movements in Judaism stem from the Enlightenment, notably with Moses Mendelssohn in the 18th cent. who accepted, as was the tendency of the period, only that which could be proved by reason. He translated the Pentateuch into German thus encouraging German Jews to give up Yiddish and Hebrew for the language of the land and thereby preparing them for their vast contribution to Western civilisation. One of his disciples, David Friedländer (d. 1834) instituted "reform" Judaism. He wanted to eliminate anything that would hamper the relationships of Jews with their neighbours or tend to call in doubt their loyalty to their adopted state. A similar movement in America (1885) called for the rejection of dietary laws, the inauguration of Sunday services, and the repudiation of Jewish nationalism. Between "reform" and orthodoxy there arose the conservative movement which, in England, includes prayers in English in the service, does not segregate men and woman in the synagogue, and translates the Law in a more liberal way. Judaism is essentially a social and family religion which, more than almost any other concerns itself with the observances of every aspect of daily life. As in Islam (*q.v.*) details are laid down in the most minute way for the behaviour of the orthodox.

The home is the main Jewish institution and Jews, like Catholics, cannot surrender their religion. Circumcision takes place eight days after birth, and a boy becomes a man for religious purposes at his Bar Mitzvah at the age of thirteen. Women are spared most of this because their place in the home is considered sufficiently sacred. Among festivals are Passover, recalling the Exodus; Rosh Hashanah (the Jewish New Year), the anniversary of the Creation and the beginning of ten days of penitence ending with Yom Kippur (the Day of Atonement), a day of fasting spent in the synagogue; Purim, celebrating the deliverance of the Jews from Haman; and Chanukah, celebrating their victory against the Syrians under their leader Judas Maccabeus. A new and semi-religious festival is the Yom Haatzmaut, the anniversary of the birth of the new Jewish state of Israel. The total numbers of world Jewry are estimated to be over 18 million (1999).

K

Kabbala. *See* Cabala.

Ku Klux Klan. After the American Civil War (1861–65) southern conservatives and ex-Confederate leaders began to fear (as they had every reason to do) both Black and poor White rule. Taxes were rising owing to radical legislation and the tax-burdened and disenfranchised planters finally took to illegal means to achieve their ends by trying to effect an alliance with the poor White and small farmer through appealing to his anti-Black prejudice.

Hence the Ku Klux Klan was formed in 1866 as a secret society by a small group of Confederate veterans in Tennessee with the intention of frightening Blacks by dressing in ghostly white robes in the guise of the spirits of dead soldiers. But the movement spread like wild-fire throughout the South encouraged by small farmers and planters alike. General Nathan Bedford Forrest was appointed "Grand Wizard" of the Klan "empire" and in every community armed Klansmen riding at night horsewhipped "uppity" Blacks, beat Union soldiers, and threatened carpet-bag politicians (*i.e.*, fortunehunters from the North). Soon several similar organisations arose, many of which did not stop at torture, burning property, and murder. The Klan was a vicious and contemptible organisation in which former Southern leaders trying to regain control deliberately set poor and middle-class Whites against the Negroes by appeal to race prejudice. Congress struck back with laws and intervention of Federal troops, and after a large number of convictions in South Carolina much of the violence stopped.

After the 1914–18 war the movement, dormant since 1900, revived as a sadistic anti-Black, anti-Jewish, anti-Catholic society, spreading to the north as well as the south. By 1926, the Klan began to subside once more. While it revived again in the mid-60s, the Klan has recently suffered a loss of support. However, fuelled by events such as the 1992 Los Angeles race riots, another 20,000 Americans belong to a number of extremist groups, such as the Militia Movement.

L

Lamaism, the religion of Tibet. Its beliefs and worship derive from the Mahayana form of Buddhism which was introduced into Tibet in 749. The emphasis laid by its founder on the necessity for self-discipline and conversion through meditation and the study of philosophy deteriorated into formal monasticism and ritualism. The Dalai Lama, as the reincarnated Buddha, was both king and high priest, a sort of pope and emperor rolled into one. Under him was a hierarchy of officials in which the lowest order was that of the monks who became as numerous as one man in every six or seven of the population. The main work carried out by this vast church-state was the collection of taxes to maintain the monasteries and other religious offices. Second in power to the Dalai Lama was the Panchen or Tashi Lama believed to be a reincarnation of Amitabha, another Buddha. The last Dalai Lama fled to India in 1959 when the Chinese entered his country. For a brief period following his departure, the Panchen Lama surprised the Western world by publicly welcoming the Communist invasion, but he later renounced the regime and the suppression of Lamaism in Tibet continued unchecked.

Latter-day Saints. *See* **Mormons (J35).**

Levellers, an English military-politico-religious party prominent in the Parliamentary Army about 1647 which stood for the rights of the people. *See* **Diggers.**

Liberalism. The Liberal Party is the successor to the Whigs (a nickname derived from *Whiggamore*, used in the 17th cent. for Scottish dissenters) of the 18th and 19th cents. Under Gladstone's two great ministries (1868–74; and 1880–85), and again under Campbell-Bannerman and Asquith (1906–14) much reforming legislation was enacted. The Asquith–Lloyd George split of 1916, and the advent of Labour as a major party after 1918, caused the Liberals to be relegated as a much smaller, third party. In the decade after 1945, there were times when the Liberal Party barely survived. But revivals have since occurred under the leadership of Jo Grimond (1962), Jeremy Thorpe (1974), David Steel (1979) and Paddy Ashdown (from 1988 to 1999).

Liberal philosophy is moderately radical and progressive in terms of social reform. But the party strongly disapproves of state control or any form of monopoly, private or public. The main proposals favoured by the party are co-ownership in industry, proportional representation, greater protection of individual liberties, and separate Parliaments for Wales and Scotland. Many younger members of the party hold views to the left of official party policy. The phenomenon of "community politics" owed much to these younger and more radical Liberals. The 1987 election setback heralded a merger ("democratic fusion") between the Liberals and their SDP Alliance partners. The new Social and Liberal Democratic Party (SLD) was formed in 1988. The first leader of the new party is Paddy Ashdown, MP for Yeovil. The new party (known as the Liberal Democrats) has been faced with the twin problems of putting forward a clear political ideology and also dealing with the revived Labour Party. In the 1992 election, it failed to make significant inroads, returning 20 MPs, having gained 4 seats but lost 6. From 1992 to 1997, it won spectacular by-election victories and sweeping local council successes. It also elected its first 2 MEPs in the June 1994 European elections. In the 1997 election the party exceeded its wildest expectations, capturing 46 seats (its best result since 1929). Since 1997 it has pursued a policy of 'constructive opposition' to the Labour Government.

Libertarianism, a political belief in free trade, individual liberty and respect for the lives and property of others. Essentially it is the modern day form of classical liberalism. Today the tradition is carried on by, among others: Frederick Hayek, Murray Rothbard, Ayn Rand *etc.*

Literary Theory. Modern literary theory is concerned with ways in which meaning is constructed and with ideological influences. It challenges received notions of imagination and inspiration, moral significance, and the personality of the author. Its origins lie partly in semiology and formalism, which concentrate on the actual words and structure of a literary text. Marxism (*see* **J31**) is also important in the works of such critics as Georg Lukács and Louis Althusser. Later approaches include structuralism and post-structuralism. Feminism has become an increasingly significant form of criticism. Other theories are New Historicism, which examines social and cultural contexts, and Reader-Response Criticism, which analyses readers' constructions of meaning.

Logical Positivism, a school of philosophy founded in Vienna in the 1920s by a group known as "the Vienna circle": their work was based on that of Ernst Mach, but dates in essentials as far back as Hume. Of the leaders of the group, Schlick was murdered by a student, Wittgenstein came to Britain, and Carnap went to America following the entry of the Nazis. Briefly the philosophy differs from all others in that, while most people have believed that a statement might be (*a*) true, or (*b*) false, logical positivists consider there to be a third category; a statement may be meaningless. There are only two types of statement which can be said to have meaning: (1) those which are tautological, *i.e.*, those in which the statement is merely a definition of the subject, such as "a triangle is a three-sided plane figure" ("triangle" and "three-sided plane figure" are the same thing); and (2) those which can be tested by sense experience. This definition of meaningfulness excludes a great deal of what has previously been thought to be the field of philosophy; in particular it excludes the possibility of metaphysics. Thus the question as to whether there is a God or whether free-will exists is strictly meaningless for it is neither a tautological statement nor can it be tested by sense experience.

Lollards, a body of religious reformers and followers of Wyclif who were reviled and persecuted in the reign of Richard II. The name "Lollard" comes from a Flemish word meaning "mutterer"—a term of contempt used to describe the sect. Under Henry V, determined efforts were made to crush the Lollards. Their leader, Sir John Oldcastle, was burnt at the stake (December 1417).

Luddites, a group of peasants and working men who deliberately destroyed spinning and farm machinery in England in the early part of the 19th cent., fearing that such devices would destroy their livelihood. Their name was taken from the eccentric Ned Lud who had done the same in a less organised way two or three decades earlier. The Luddites' worst fears were of course not realised, for far from putting human beings out of work the industrial revolution created jobs for a vastly increased population. Luddism, dormant for over a century, is beginning to appear again, if in muted form.

Lutheranism. The Reformation had a long history before it became, under Luther and Calvin, an accepted fact. The mediaeval Church had held (as the Catholic Church holds today) that the sacraments were the indispensable means of salvation. Since these were exclusively administered by the clergy, any movement which attacked clerical abuses was forced by sheer necessity to deny the Church's exclusive control of the means of salvation, before it could become free from dependence on a corrupt priesthood. Hence the Albigenses and the Waldenses (*qq.v.*), the followers of John Hus and Wycliff (*see* **Anticlericalism**), were bound to deny the authority of the Church and emphasise that of the Bible. Luther began his movement primarily in order to reform the Church from its gross abuses and the famous ninety-five theses nailed to the door of the Church at Wittenberg in 1517 were not primarily theological but moral complaints dealing with the actual behaviour of the clergy rather than Church beliefs. But, unlike the earlier reformers, Luther had arrived at the right moment in history when economic individualism and the force of nationalism were bound, sooner or later, to cause the authorities in Germany to line up on his side. Thus he began with the support of the peasants who were genuinely shocked at the abuse of indulgences and other matters, but ended up by being supported by the noblemen who wanted to destroy the power of the pope over the German states and looked forward to confiscating the lands and property of the Church. When the peasants wanted the reform of actual economic abuses relating to the feudal system, Luther took the side of the nobles against them. The contemporary movement in Switzerland led by Ulrich Zwingli had no such secular support, and Zwingli was killed in 1531.

Martin Luther (1483–1546) was the son of a miner in Eisleben in Saxony, entered the order of Austin Friars in 1505, and later taught at the newly founded university of Wittenberg. After the publication of the theses the real issue so far as the Church was concerned was whether he was willing or not to submit to the authority of his superiors; Luther refused to compromise with his conscience in the famous words: "Here I stand; I can do no other." In a further statement Luther recommended the formation of a German national church, the abolition of indulgences and other means whereby Rome obtained money from Germany, and an end to the celibacy of the clergy. For this he was naturally excommunicated. His teaching was based on the German translation of the Bible, but he was by no means a fundamentalist: *e.g.*, he denied that the Book of Hebrews was written by Paul, would have nothing to do with the Apocrypha, and regarded the letter of James as "an epistle of straw." The Scriptures were open to all and could be interpreted by private judgment enlightened by the Spirit of God. Like Calvin, Luther was a predestinarian and determinist, but he was also a conservative and soon became alarmed about the position taken by many extremists once the Reformation was under way. He had really wanted the Church to reform itself, but when he alienated Rome he had perforce to rely more and more on the secular powers which finally resulted in the state-church form which became pronounced in Prussia and later elsewhere. Whereas Calvin wished the Church to be at least the equal of the State and in some respects its superior, Luther's rebellion resulted in the reverse, a state-controlled episcopalianism. *See* **Calvinism, Presbyterianism**.

Lycanthropy, the belief that men may, by the exercise of magical powers or because of some inherited affliction, occasionally transform into wolves. The so-called werewolf is an important feature of mid-European folklore and

much the same can be said of the were-tigers and were-bears of Africa and the Far East.

M

McLuhanism. According to Marshall McLuhan (1911–80), a Canadian, and former professor of English at Toronto, the *way* people communicate is more important than *what* they communicate: hence his famous slogan, "the medium is the message." There have been two great landmarks in human understanding since we learnt to speak and write: the invention of the printed book and the present electronic revolution. The printed word took us step by step along the linear, logical path to understanding; television comes at us from all directions at once. "Electronic circuitry has overthrown the regime of "time' and 'space' . . . Its message is Total Change."

McLuhan's importance lies in alerting us to the present clash between two great technologies, the literate and the electromagnetic, and in his vision, beyond the present chaos, of a world drawn tighter together in a "global village" where identity will merge in collectivity and we shall all be able to co-operate for the common good instead of being split up into warring nations.

Magic, a form of belief originating in very early days and based on the primitive's inability to distinguish between similarity and identity. The simplest example would perhaps be the fertility rites in which it is believed that a ceremony involving sexual relations between men and women will bring about fertility in the harvest. Or the idea that sticking pins in an image of an individual will bring about harm or even death to the real person. Magic is regarded by some as a form of early science in that man in his efforts to control Nature had recourse to magical practices when the only methods he knew had failed to bring the desired results. It filled a gap. By others magic is regarded as an elementary stage in the evolution of religion. It can be said to have served a purpose there too. Yet magic differs from religion, however closely at times it may come to be related with it in this important respect: religion depends upon a power *outside and beyond* human beings, whereas magic depends upon nothing but the casting of a spell or the performance of a ceremony—the result follows automatically.

The idea that "like produces like" is at the roots of imitative magic. It follows that an event can be compelled by imitating it. One engages in swinging, not for pleasure, but to produce a wind as the swing does; ball games are played to get rainy weather because the black ball represents dark rainclouds; other ball games, in which one attempts to catch the ball in a cup or hit it with a stick, represent the sexual act (as some gentlemen at Lords may be distressed to hear) and bring about fertility; in medicine until a few centuries ago herbs were chosen to cure a disease because in some respects their leaves or other parts looked like the part of the body affected (*e.g.*, the common wildflower still known as "eyebright" was used in bathing the eyes because the flower looks like a tiny eye). *See* **Witchcraft, Demonism.**

Malthusianism, the theory about population growth put forward by the Rev. Thomas Malthus (1766–1834) in *An Essay on Population* (1798). His three main propositions were (1) "Population is necessarily limited by means of subsistence." (2) "Population invariably increases where means of subsistence increase unless prevented by some very powerful and obvious checks." (3) "These checks, and the checks which repress the superior power of population, and keep its effects on a level with the means of subsistence, are all resolvable into moral restraint, vice and misery." In other words, no matter how great the food supply may become, human reproductive power will always adjust itself so that food will always be scarce in relation to population; the only means to deal with this is by "moral restraint" (*i.e.*, chastity or not marrying), "vice" (*i.e.*, birth-control methods), or misery (*i.e.*, starvation). More specifically, Malthus claimed that while food increases by arithmetical progression, population increases by geometrical progression. It is true that these gloomy predictions did not take place in Malthus's time largely owing to the opening up of new areas of land outside Europe, the development of new techniques in agriculture, the growth of international trade to poorer areas, the increased knowledge of birth-control, and developments in medical science which reduced the misery he had predicted. Furthermore, we now know that as a society becomes industrialised its birth-rate tends to fall. Growth in the world's population has increased from about 465 million in 1650 to reach 6,000 million in 1999.

Manichaeism, an Asiatic religion which developed from Zoroastrianism (*q.v.*) and shows the influence of Buddhism (*q.v.*) and Gnosticism (*q.v.*), being founded by Mani, a Persian who was born in Babylonia, *c.* 216 A.D. Mani presented himself to Shapur I as the founder of a new religion which was to be to Babylonia what Buddhism was to India or Christianity to the West. His aspiration was to convert the East and he himself made no attempt to interfere directly with Christianity although he represented himself as the Paraclete (the Holy Ghost or "Comforter") and, like Jesus, had twelve disciples. His success in Persia aroused the fury of the Zoroastrian priests who objected to his reforming zeal towards their religion and in 276 Mani was taken prisoner and crucified.

Of Mani's complicated system little can be said here, save that it is based on the struggle of two eternal conflicting principles, God and matter, or light and darkness. Although its founder had no intention of interfering with the West, after his death his followers soon spread the religion from Persia and Mesopotamia to India and China. It reached as far as Spain and Gaul and influenced many of the bishops in Alexandria and in Carthage where for a time St. Augustine accepted Manichaeism. Soon the toleration accorded it under Constantine ended and it was treated as a heresy and violently suppressed. Yet it later influenced many heresies, and even had some influence on orthodox Catholicism which had a genius for picking up elements in other religions which had been shown to appeal to worshippers provided they did not conflict unduly with fundamental beliefs.

Maoism is the branch of communism in China that was shaped by one of the most remarkable statesmen of modern times, Mao Tse-tung (1893–1976). He set the pattern of revolution for poor peasant societies and restored pride and confidence to his fellow countrymen after years of turmoil and brutality. Although Marxist theory guided the Chinese communists in their struggle for liberation from the old, bourgeois and feudal China, it was interpreted in a manner peculiar to China and developed to fit into the Chinese way of life and the "thoughts" of Chairman Mao. As early as 1926 Mao had pointed out that the Chinese proletariat had in the peasantry its staunchest and most numerous ally. "A rural revolution," he said, "is a revolution by which the peasantry overthrows the authority of the feudal landlord class." The struggles of 1925–49 (the Long March of the Red Army, the Anti-Japanese War, the Civil War against Chiang Kai-shek) were the foundations on which present-day China has been built. Maoism is against authoritarianism and for self-reliance; against bureaucracy and for revolutionary momentum; against rivalry between individuals and for common effort. Great efforts have been made to remove poverty, ignorance, corruption and disease from China. Mao taught that struggle is necessary for the revolution to endure. "Running water does not go stale and door-hinges do not become worm-eaten," Mao reminded his comrades. "We must," he said, "make every comrade understand that the highest criterion for judging the words and deeds of the communists is whether they conform with the best interests and win the support of the broadest masses of the people." The effect of the death of Mao Tse-tung on

Chinese communism has been a huge shift towards the modernisation of China.

Marxism. The sociological theories founded by Karl Marx and Friedrich Engels on which modern communist thought is based. Marx and Engels lived in a period of unrestrained capitalism when exploitation and misery were the lot of the industrial working classes, and it was their humanitarianism and concern for social justice which inspired their work. Marx wrote his *Communist Manifesto* in Brussels in 1848 and in his great work, *Das Kapital* (1867), he worked out a new theory of society. Marx showed that all social systems are economically motivated and change as a result of technical and economic changes in methods of production. The driving force of social change Marx found to be in the struggle which the oppressed classes wage to secure a better future. Thus in his celebrated theory of historical materialism he interpreted history in terms of economics and explained the evolution of society in terms of class struggle. (*See* **Dialectical Materialism.**) "In the social production of their means of existence," he wrote, "men enter into definite and unavoidable relations which are independent of their will. These productive relationships correspond to the particular stage in the development of their material productive forces." Marx's theory of historical materialism implies that history is propelled by class struggle with communism and the classless society as the final stage when man will have emancipated himself from the productive process. Marx was the first to put socialism on a rational and scientific basis, and he foretold that socialism would inevitably replace capitalism. His prophecy, however, came to realisation not in the advanced countries as he had envisaged but in backward Russia and China. *See* **Communism.**

Materialism. Any theory that tends to the view that only matter or material objects exist and that everything else, notably minds and mental experiences, can be described in material terms. Materialism is thus opposed to dualism or idealism and, in general, to any belief in God, in disembodied spirits *etc.* There is much contemporary philosophical debate as to whether "consciousness" is not a name for something mysterious, but simply a way of talking about the brain. *See also* **Mind and Matter.**

There is, of course, the popular and quite different sense of the term, which emphasizes the value of material possessions.

Mechanism. As a theory, the view that everything happens mechanically, that natural phenomena are to be explained by reference to certain laws of nature applied to the behaviour of matter in motion. Through the influence of science, there is a strong tendency in Western thought to compare the universe or parts of it, even human beings, to machines. It is a view closely connected with materialism.

Mennonites, a Christian sect rejecting infant baptism. Named after Menno Simons (1496–1559). Its members reject military service and refuse to hold public office. Hutterites share their beliefs.

Mesmerism, a rapidly vanishing name to denote the practice of hypnosis, which owes its popularity, though not its discovery, to the Austrian physician, Anton Mesmer (1733–1815). Mesmer's contribution was the realisation that a large number of what we would today call psychosomatic or hysterical conditions could be cured (or at least temporarily alleviated) by one or another form of suggestion. Mesmer himself relied on the idea of what he called "animal magnetism," a supposedly potent therapeutic force emanating from the living body which could be controlled by the trained individual. Mesmer used wands and impressive gadgetry to dispense the marvellous force and he effected a remarkable number of cures of complaints, hitherto looked upon as incurable or totally mysterious in origin—the most typical of these being hysterical blindness, paralysis or deafness, nervous skin conditions, and so on. Hypnosis, which is a valid if very poorly understood psychological phenomenon even today, would probably have been developed much further had not efficient general anaesthetics such as ether, nitrous oxide, *etc.*, been discovered, thus greatly diminishing its role as a pain reliever in surgery. Mesmer, who was three parts charlatan, never really troubled to think deeply about the cause of his undoubted success. The first man to treat hysteria as a formal class of illness and who made a scientific attempt to treat it with hypnosis was Ambrose Liébeault (1823–1904). He and his colleagues Hippolyte Bernheim (1840–1919) believed: (a) that hysteria was produced by suggestion, and particularly by autosuggestion on the part of the patient, and (b) that suggestion was a normal trait found in varying degrees in everyone. These conclusions are true, but as Freud showed later are far from being the whole truth.

Messianism. Most varieties of religious belief rely on the assumption that the deity is a supernatural being either permeating the universe or dwelling in some other sphere, and normally inaccessible to man. Where divine intervention is necessary, the deity is traditionally believed to nominate a human being—in the case of Christianity, for example, Jesus is believed to be the actual son of God. Messianic cults introduce a novel variant on the traditional theme. In these a human being is held to be God himself. He may either nominate himself for this role, relying on his own personality or native talent to acquire the necessary following, or for one reason or another large numbers of people may alight on one individual and declare him the Messiah. While it might seem that beliefs of this kind would be confined to earlier epochs in man's recorded history, this is in fact not the case. In the past century, and even within recent decades, a number of individuals have been held by groups to be actually divine.

To simple people the idea that God is to be found on earth and that one may even be personally introduced to him, is an obviously attractive one. The trouble is that all self-styled gods to this present date have eventually disappointed their supporters by performing that most human of acts—dying.

Metapsychology. Not to be confused with parapsychology (q.v.). The branch or off-shoot of psychology which goes beyond empirical and experimental studies to consider such philosophical matters as the nature of mind, the reality of free-will and the mind/body problem. It was originally used by Freud as a blanket descriptive term denoting all mental processes, but this usage is now obsolete.

Methodism, the religious movement founded by John Wesley in 1738, at a time when the Anglican Church was in one of its periodic phases of spiritual torpor, with the simple aim of spreading "scriptural holiness" throughout the land. Up to that time Wesley had been a High Churchman but on a visit to Georgia in the United States he was much impressed by the group known as Moravians (q.v.), and on his return to this country was introduced by his brother Charles, who had already become an adherent, to Peter Böhler, a Moravian minister in England. Passing through a period of spiritual commotion following the meeting, he first saw the light at a small service in Aldersgate in May 1738 "where one was reading Luther's preface to the Epistle to the Romans" and from this time forth all Wesley's energies were devoted to the single object of saving souls. He did this for fifty years and at the end of his life confessed that he had wasted fifteen minutes in that time by reading a worthless book. Even when he was over eighty he still rose at 4 a.m. and toiled all day long.

Soon Whitefield, a follower with Calvinist views, was preaching throughout the country and Charles Wesley was composing his well-known hymns; John's abilities at this time were taken up in organising the movement described as "People called Methodists." They were to be arranged in "societies" which were united into "circuits" under a minister, the circuits into "districts" and all knit together into a single body under a conference of ministers which has met annually since 1744. Local lay preachers were also employed and to maintain interest the ministers were moved from circuit to circuit each year. These chapel services were not originally meant to conflict with the Church of England of which Wesley still consid-

ered himself a member. They were purely supplementary, and it used to be the custom (before the Methodists began to count themselves as Nonconformists) for Methodists to attend Church in the morning and Chapel in the evening.

The class-meeting was the unit of the organisation where members met regularly under a chosen leader to tell their "experiences" upon which they were often subjected to severe cross-examination. At the end of every quarter, provided their attendances were regular, they received a ticket of membership which entitled them to come to monthly sacramental services. If attendance was inadequate the name was removed from the list, without appearance on which nobody was deemed a member. The price of the ticket was "a penny a week and a shilling a quarter" but Wesley was not interested in receiving money from anyone who was not utterly devoted to the cause.

The Work of Wesley

John Wesley introduced four other innovations, some of which were regarded by Churchmen who had previously been willing to commend his efforts in bringing religion to the poorer classes as dangerous: (1) He started the Sunday-school scheme and afterwards enthusiastically supported that of John Raikes, often regarded as the founder of the idea; this was of immense importance in the days before the Education Acts. (2) He reintroduced the Agapae or "love feasts" of the early Church which were fellowship meetings deepening the sense of brotherhood of the society. (3) He began to copy the open-air meetings of the eloquent Whitefield and soon unwittingly produced the most extraordinary results, finding that his sermons led to groans, tears, fainting fits, and all sorts of emotional expression. Even his open-air lay speakers produced like results and these came to be associated with Methodism and gave significance to the proud Anglican claim that *their* services would be "without enthusiasm." (4) After some hesitation he ventured to consecrate Dr. Thomas Coke, who was being sent as a missionary to America, as a bishop of his church. In addition to Wesley's religious work he was a great educator of the common man. Thus he introduced the cheap book and the church magazine, publishing books of any sort even when the views expressed were different from his own—e.g., Thomas à Kempis's *Imitation of Christ* and works of history, biography, science, and medicine in some cases written by himself. In this way the movement with its cheap books and reading rooms had an influence far beyond its actual membership. Both the Anglican Church and the Evangelical movement of Wilberforce and others profited from Wesley's work.

Later Schisms.

Methodism, especially after Wesley's death in 1791, began, like other movements, to develop schisms. These were the long-standing differences which the Baptist movement (q.v.) had shown too between Arminian and Calvinist sections—i.e., between those who did and those who did not accept the doctrine of predestination. In the case of the Methodists, this led to a complete break in 1811. Then there were differences associated with the status of the laity, or the relationship of the movement with the Anglican Church. The "Methodist New Connection" of 1797 differed only in giving the laity equal representation with the ministers but the more important break of the Primitive Methodists in 1810 gave still more power to the laity and reintroduced the "camp-meeting" type of service. In 1815 the Bryanites or "Bible Christians" were formed, and a further schism which was even brought before the law courts was ostensibly over the foundation of a theological college. The real reason, of course, was that the ministers were becoming more Tory, whilst the laity were becoming more Radical. Finally in 1932, at a conference in the Albert Hall in London, the Wesleyan Methodists, the Primitive Methodists, and the United

Methodists became one Church, the Methodist Church.

Adult Methodist membership has fallen recently, from 841,000 in 1930, to 729,000 in 1960 and now to c. 380,000 (1999). During 1998, Methodists began the first formal steps towards talks with Anglicans about reunion.

Millenarianism. The belief in a future "millenium", that is, the thousand year reign of Christ on earth. The idea however has pre-Christian roots and is reflected in Jewish and Islamic thought. It is not part of orthodox Christianity, but many sects in the 19th century, like the Plymouth Brethren and Adventists, espoused millenarianism. The idea has since broadened to mean any theory with an expectation of some transforming change: not only the Kingdom of God, but also, the just society, or harmony amongst peoples.

Mind and Matter.

Early Greek Views: Idealism and Dualism. Primitive peoples could see that there is a distinction between those things which move and do things by themselves and others, such as stones, which do not. Following the early state of **Animism** (q.v.), in which spirits were believed to have their abode in everything, they began to differentiate between matter or substance and a force which seems to move it and shape it into objects and things. Thus to the Greek Parmenides (fl. c. 475 B.C.), who was a philosopher of pure reason, thought or mind was the creator of what we observe and in some way not quite clear to himself it seemed that mind was the cause of everything. This is perhaps the first expression of the movement known as Idealism which says, in effect, that the whole universe is mental—a creation either of our own minds or the mind of God. But from Anaxagorus (488-428 B.C.) we have the clearer statement that mind or *nous* causes all movement but is distinct from the substance it moves. He does not, however, think in terms of individual minds but rather of a kind of generalised mind throughout the universe which can be used as an explanation of anything which cannot be explained otherwise. This is the position known as Dualism (q.v.) which holds that both mind and matter exist and interact but are separate entities.

Most people in practice are dualists since, rightly or wrongly, mind and body are thought of as two different things: it is the "commonsense" (although not necessarily the true) point of view. Plato in a much more complex way was also a dualist although he held that the world of matter we observe is in some sense not the genuine world. The real world is the world of ideas and the tree we see is not real but simply matter upon which mind or soul has imprinted the idea of a tree. Everything that exists has its corresponding form in the world of ideas and imprints its pattern upon matter. Mind has always existed and, having become entangled with matter, is constantly seeking to free itself and return to God.

Plato's pupil Aristotle had a much more scientific outlook and held that, although it was mind which gave matter its form, mind is not *outside* matter, as Plato had thought, but *inside* it as its formative principle. Therefore there could be no mind without matter and no matter without mind; for even the lowest forms of matter have some degree of mind which increases in quantity and quality as we move up the scale to more complex things.

So far, nobody had explained how two such different substances as matter and mind could influence each other in any way, and this remains, in spite of attempts to be mentioned later, a basic problem in philosophy.

Two later ideas, one of them rather foolish and the other simply refusing to answer the question, are typified by the Stoics and some members of the Sceptic school. The first is that only matter exists and what we call mind is merely matter of a finer texture, a view which as an explanation is unlikely to satisfy anyone; the other, that of some Sceptics, is that we can know nothing except the fleeting images or thoughts that flicker through our consciousness. Of either mind or matter we know nothing.

Renaissance Attitude. Christian doctrines have already been dealt with (*see* **God and Man, Determinism and Free-will**), and the past and future of the soul is dealt with under **Immortality**. Nor need we mention the Renaissance philosophers who were really much more concerned about how to use mind than about its nature. When they did consider the subject they usually dealt with it, as did Francis Bacon, by separating the sphere of science from that of religion and giving the orthodox view of the latter because there were still good reasons for not wishing to annoy the Church.

17th-cent. Views: Hobbes, Descartes, Guelincx, Spinoza, Locke, Berkeley. Thomas Hobbes in the 17th cent. was really one of the first to attempt a modern explanation of mind and matter even if his attempt was crude. As a materialist he held that all that exists is matter and hence our thoughts, ideas, images, and actions are really a form of motion taking place within the brain and nerves. This is the materialist theory which states that mind does not exist.

Thus there are three basic theories of the nature of mind and body: idealism, dualism, and materialism, and we may accept any one of the three. But, if we accept dualism, we shall have to explain precisely the relationship between body and mind. In some of his later writings Hobbes seems to suggest that mental processes are the effects of motion rather than motion itself; *i.e.,* they exist, but only as a result of physical processes just as a flame does on a candle. This theory of the relationship is known as *epiphenomenalism.*

Descartes, the great French contemporary of Hobbes, was a dualist who believed that mind and matter both exist and are entirely different entities; therefore he had to ask himself how, for example, the desire to walk leads to the physical motion of walking. His unsatisfactory answer was that, although animals are pure automatons, man is different in that he has a soul which resides in the pineal gland (a tiny structure in the brain which today we know to be a relic of evolution with no present function whatever). In this gland the mind comes in contact with the "vital spirits" of the body and thus there is interaction between the two. This theory is known as *interactionism,* and since we do not accept its basis in the function of the pineal gland, we are simply left with the notion of interaction but without the explanation of how it takes place.

One of Descartes's successors, Arnold Guelincx, produced the even more improbable theory of *psychophysical parallelism* sometimes known as the theory of the "two clocks". Imagine you have two clocks, each keeping perfect time, then supposing you saw one and heard the other, every time one points to the hour the other will strike, giving the impression that the first event causes the second, although in fact they are quite unrelated. So it is with the body and mind in Guelincx's view, each is "wound up" by God in the beginning in such a way as to keep time with the other so that when I have the desire to walk, purely unrelated physical events in my legs cause them to move at the same time. A variety of this theory is *occasionism,* which says that whenever something happens in the physical world, God affects us so that we *think* we are being affected by the happening.

The trouble about all these theories is (a) that they really explain nothing, and (b) that they give us a very peculiar view of God as a celestial showman treating us as puppets when it would surely have been easier to create a world in which mind and matter simply interacted by their very nature. Spinoza, too, believed in a sort of psychophysical parallelism in that he did not think that mind and body interacted. But since in his theory everything is God, mind and matter are simply two sides of the same penny.

John Locke, another contemporary, thought of the mind as a blank slate upon which the world writes in the form of sensations, for we have no innate or inborn ideas and mind and matter do interact although he does not tell us how. All we know are sensations—*i.e.,* sense impressions. Bishop Berkeley carried this idea to its logical conclusion: if we know nothing but sensations, we have no reason to suppose that matter exists at all. He was, therefore, an idealist.

18th cent. Views: Hume, Kant. David Hume went further still and pointed out that, if all we know are sensations, we cannot prove the existence of matter but we cannot prove the existence of mind either. All we can ever know is that ideas, impressions, thoughts, follow each other. We do not even experience a self or personality because every time we look into our "minds" all we really experience are thoughts and impressions. Hume was quick to point out that this was not the same as saying that the self did not exist; it only proved that we cannot know that it does.

Kant made it clear that, although there is a world outside ourselves, we can never know what it is really like. The mind receives impressions and forms them into patterns which conform not to the thing-in-itself but to the nature of mind. Space and time, for example, are not realities but only the form into which our mind fits its sensations. In other words our mind shapes impressions which are no more like the thing in itself than the map of a battlefield with pins showing the position of various army groups at any given moment is like the battlefield. This, of course, is true. From physics and physiology we know that the sounds we hear are "really" waves in the air, the sights we see "really" electromagnetic waves. What guarantee do we have that the source is "really" like the impression received in our brain? Kant was the leader of the great German Idealist movement of the 18th cent. which in effect said: "why bother about matter when all we can ever know is mental?"

19th and 20th cent. Views. The Englishman Bradley, and the Frenchman Henri Bergson in the 19th and early 20th cent. both held in one form or another the belief that mind in some way creates matter and were, therefore, idealists, whereas Comte, the positivist (*q.v.*), and the Americans William James and John Dewey, held that mind is a form of behaviour. Certain acts (*e.g.*, reflexes) are "mindless" because they are deliberate; others which are intended may be described for the sake of convenience as "minded" (*i.e.*, purposeful). But like the majority of modern psychologists—insofar as they take any interest in the subject—they regarded mind as a process going on in the living body. Is there any reason, many now ask, why we should think of mind as being any different in nature from digestion? Both are processes going on in the body, the one in the brain the other in the stomach and intestines. Why should we therefore regard them as "things"?

Mithraism, a sun-religion which originated in Persia with the worship of the mythical Mithra, the god of light and of truth. It was for two centuries one of early Christianity's most formidable rivals, particularly in the West since the more philosophical Hellenic Christianity of the East had little to fear from it. (Arnold Toynbee has described Mithraism as "a pre-Zoroastrian Iranian paganism—in a Hellenic dress"; Manichaeism as "Zoroastrianism—in a Christian dress".) Mithraism was a mystery faith with secret rites known only to devotees. It appealed to the soldiers of the Roman Army which explains its spread to the farthest limits of the Roman empire and its decline as the Romans retreated. The religion resembled Zoroastrianism (*q.v.*) in that it laid stress on the constant struggle between good and evil and there are a number of parallels with Christianity. *e.g.*, a miraculous birth, death, and a glorious resurrection, a belief in heaven and hell and the immortality of the soul, a last judgment. Both religions held Sunday as the holy day of the week, celebrated 25 December (date of the pagan winter solstice festival) as the birthday of the founder; both celebrated Easter, and in their ceremonies made use of bell, holy water, and the candle. Mithraism reached its height about 275 A.D. and afterwards declined both for the reason given above and, perhaps, because it excluded women, was emotional rather than philo-

sophical, and had no general organisation to direct its course. Yet even today, from the Euphrates to the Tyne, traces of the religion remain and antiquarians are familiar with the image of the sun-god and the inscription *Deo Soli Mithrae, Invicto, Seculari* (dedicated to the sun-god of Mithra, the unconquered). Mithraism enjoyed a brief revival of popular interest in the mid-1950s when workers excavating the foundations of the skyscraper, Bucklersbury House in the City of London, found the well-preserved remains of a Roman Mithraic temple. A campaign to save the temple as a national monument resulted in its now being on open display on a site in front of the skyscraper.

Modernism. The term has two main connotations:

1. A movement in the Roman Catholic church, *c.* 1890–1910. The 19th century stress on science and the application of scientific methods in fields like history, psychology and philosophy, raised serious problems for traditional Catholic doctrine. The Modernists sought to reinterpret orthodox church teaching in the light of this modern knowledge. The movement was condemned as heresy in 1907.

2. The term is more frequently used to refer to the "modern" movement in all the arts in the period *c.* 1900–30, though defining the period it covers is only one of the problems in describing the movement. It is generally seen as an artistic response to the changes which undermined the securities on which 19th century art and literature were founded. Modernism is marked by a greater ambition for works of art themselves. As well as being novels, or paintings, or music, *etc.*, they were increasingly considered, by artists and critics alike, as representing a theoretical programme, attempts to make the audience see or understand the world in a different way. So modernist characteristics include an increased self-consciousness of the artist, and formal experiment employing a wide variety of technical innovations. In literature the prime works of modernism are T. S. Eliot's *The Waste Land* and James Joyce's *Ulysses*, the most important painters include Picasso and Matisse; and among composers Schoenberg and Stravinsky stand out (*see* **Section E**).

Mohammedanism. *See* **Islam.**

Monasticism. When in the 4th cent. A.D. Constantine in effect united state and church there were naturally many who hastened to become Christians for the worldly benefits they expected it to bring in view of the new situation. But there were others who, in their efforts to escape from wordly involvement, went into the deserts of North Africa and Syria to live as hermits and so in these regions there grew up large communities of monks whose lives of renunciation made a considerable impression on the Christian world. They were men of all types but the two main groups were those who preferred to live alone and those who preferred a community life. Among the first must be included St. Anthony, the earliest of the hermits, who was born in Egypt *c.* 250 and who lived alone in a hut near his home for fifteen years and then in the desert for a further twenty. As his fame spread Anthony came forth to teach and advocate a life of extreme austerity, until by the end of his life the Thebaid (the desert around Thebes) was full of hermits following his example. (Not unnaturally, he was constantly assailed by lustful visions which he thoughtfully attributed to Satan.) In the Syrian desert St. Simeon Stylites and others were stimulated to even greater austerities and Simeon himself spent many years on the top of a pillar in a space so small that it was only possible to sit or stand.

The first monastery was founded by Pachomius of Egypt *c.* 315 and here the monks had a common life with communal meals, worship, and work mainly of agricultural type. In the Eastern part of the Empire St. Basil (*c.* 360) tried to check the growth of the extreme and spectacular practices of the hermits by organising monasteries in which the ascetic disciplines of fasting, meditation, and prayer, would be balanced by useful and healthy activities. His monasteries had orphanages and schools for boys—not only those who were intended for a monkish life. But the Eastern Church in general continued to favour the hermit life and ascetic extremes. Originally a spontaneous movement, the monastic life was introduced to the West by St. Athanasius in 339 who obtained its recognition from the Church of Rome and St. Augustine introduced it into North Africa beyond Egypt. The movement was promoted also by St. Jerome, St. Martin of Tours, who introduced it into France, and St. Patrick into Ireland. The monastery of Iona was founded by St. Colomba in 566. But it must be remembered that the Celtic Church had a life of its own which owed more to the Egyptian tradition than to Rome. Unlike the more elaborate monasteries of the Continent those of the early Celtic Church were often little more than a cluster of stone bee-hive huts, an oratory, and a stone cross. It had its own religious ceremonies and its own art (notably its beautifully carved crosses and the illuminated manuscripts such as the Lindisfarne Gospel (c. 700) and the Irish Book of Kells dating from about the same time). The Scottish St. Ninian played a major part in introducing Egyptian texts and art to Britain where, mixed with Byzantine influences and the art of the Vikings, it produced a typical culture of its own. Strangely enough, it was the relatively primitive Celts who played almost as large a part in preserving civilisation in Europe during the Dark Ages as the Italians have since. It was St. Columbanus (c. 540–615) who founded the great monasteries of Annegray, Luxeuil, and Fontaine in the Vosges country, St. Gall in Switzerland, and Bobbio in the Apennines. So, too, it was the Anglo-Saxon Alcuin (c. 735–804) who was called from York by Charlemagne to set up a system of education throughout his empire; the most famous of the monastic schools he founded was at Tours. Among those influenced by him was the philosopher John Scotus Erigena.

Meanwhile from the south, as the disintegrating Roman empire became increasingly corrupt, St. Benedict of Nursia (c. 480–c. 543) fled the pleasures of Rome to lead a hermit's life near Subiaco. Here he founded some small monasteries, but c. 520 made a new settlement, the great monastery of Monte Cassino in southern Italy, where he established a "Rule" for the government of monks. This included both study and work and emphasised that education was necessary for the continuance of Christianity. As his influence spread his Rule was adopted by other monasteries, and schools became part of monastic life. It is not possible to describe the many different orders of monks and nuns formed since, nor the mendicant orders of friars (e.g., Franciscans, Dominicans, Carmelites, Augustinians). Outside the Roman Catholic Church, both Eastern Orthodox and Anglican Christians owe much to the monastic movement. Monasticism, of course, is not peculiar to Christianity and forms a major aspect of Buddhism, especially in the form of Lamaism (q.v.) in Tibet.

Monetarism. See **Section G.**

Monophysitism, a heresy of the 5th cent. which grew out of a reaction against Nestorianism (q.v.). The majority of Egyptian Christians were Monophysites (Mono-physite = one nature)—i.e. they declared Christ's human and divine nature to be one and the same. This view was condemned at the Council of Chalcedon (A.D. 451) which pronounced that Jesus Christ, true God and true man, has two natures, at once perfectly distinct and inseparably joined in one person and partaking of the one divine substance. However, many continued to hold Monophysite opinions, including the Coptic Church (q.v.), declaring the Council to be unoecumenical (i.e. not holding the views of the true and universal Christian Church).

Montanism, a Phrygian form of primitive Puritanism with many peculiar tenets into which the early Christian theologian Tertullian (c. 150–c. 230) was driven by his extremist views that the Christian should keep himself aloof from the world and hold no social intercourse whatever with pagans. The sect had immediate expectation of Christ's second coming and indulged in prophetic utterance which they held to be inspired by the Holy Ghost but which their enemies put down to the work of the Devil.

Moonies. See **Unification Church, J52.**

Moral Re-Armament, a campaign launched in 1938 by an American evangelist of Lutheran background, Frank N. D. Buchman (1878–1961),

founder of the Oxford Group Movement, and at first associated with the First Century Church Fellowship, a fundamentalist Protestant revivalist movement. On a visit to England in 1920 Buchman preached "world-changing through life-changing" to undergraduates at Oxford, hence the name Oxford Group. This revivalist movement was based on Buchman's conviction that world civilisation was breaking down and a change had to be effected in the minds of men.

Two of the Group's most typical practices were group confession of sins openly and the "quiet time" set aside during the day to receive messages from the Almighty as to behaviour and current problems. In the eyes of non-Groupers the confession (often of trivial sins) appeared to be exhibitionist and there was felt to be a certain snobbery about the movement which made it strongly conscious of the social status of its converts.

The Oxford Group gave way to Moral Rearmament, the third phase of Buchmanism. MRA is open to all. Its starting point is the readiness of each person to make real in their own life the changes they wish to see in society. A commitment to search for God's will in daily life forms the basis for creative initiative and common action. Absolute moral standards of honesty, purity, unselfishness and love help to focus the challenge of personal and global change.

The peak of public interest in MRA was probably reached in the 1950s. Like so many movements of its kind it relied heavily for its motive force on the dynamism of its founder and leader. With the death of Dr. Buchman and the unexpected demise at an early age of his most promising protégé and successor-designate, the journalist Peter Howard, the movement began to lose some public impact. However, this work of reconciliation continues today, notably through the conferences held in Caux, Switzerland, each year. Much of the planning and preparation for these sessions is done by British MRA full-time workers. The phrase "moral rearmament" was coined by the English scientist W. H. Bragg and appropriated by Buchman.

Moravian Church, a revival of the Church of the "Bohemian Brethren" which originated (1457) among some of the followers of John Hus. It developed a kind of Quakerism that rejected the use of force, refused to take oaths, and had no hierarchy. It appears to have been sympathetic towards Calvinism but made unsuccessful approaches to Luther. As a Protestant sect it was ruthlessly persecuted by Ferdinand II and barely managed to survive. However, in the 18th cent. the body was re-established by Count Zinzendorf who offered it a place of safety in Saxony where a town called Herrnhut (God's protection) was built and this became the centre from which Moravian doctrine was spread by missionaries all over the world. Their chief belief (which had a fundamental influence on John Wesley—see **Methodism**) was that faith is a direct illumination from God which assures us beyond all possibility of doubt that we are saved, and that no goodness of behaviour, piety, or orthodoxy is of any use without this "sufficient sovereign, saving grace".

Mormons, or Latter-day Saints, one of the very numerous American religious churches; founded in 1830 by Joseph Smith, the son of a Vermont farmer, who, as a youth, had been influenced by a local religious revival though confused by the conflicting beliefs of the various denominations. He said that while praying for guidance he had been confronted by two heavenly messengers who forbade him to join any existing church but prepare to become the prophet of a new one. Soon, in a series of visions, he was told of a revelation written on golden plates concealed in a nearby hillside. These he unearthed in 1827 and with the help of "Urim and Thummin" translated the "reformed Egyptian" characters into English. Described as the *Book of Mormon*, this was published in 1830 and at the same time a little church of those few who accepted his testimony was founded in Fayette, N.Y. In addition the first of Joseph Smith's "miracles"—the casting out of a devil—was performed. The *Book of Mor-*

mon purports to be a record of early American history and religion, the American Indians being identified as part of the ten Lost Tribes of Israel. Jesus Christ is believed to have appeared in America after His resurrection and prior to His ascension. Smith's eloquence was able to influence quite educated people, including Sidney Rigdon with whom he went into business for a time. *Doctrine and Covenants* is the title of another book dealing with the revelations Smith claimed to have received. Soon the sect was in trouble with the community both because its members insisted on describing themselves as the Chosen People and others as Gentiles and because they took part in politics, voting as Smith ordered them to. Smith was constantly in trouble with the police. Therefore they were turned out from one city after another until they found a dwelling-place at Nauvoo, Illinois, on the Mississippi.

In 1844 Smith was murdered by a mob, and confusion reigned for a while. Brigham Young, Smith's successor, was quite an extraordinary leader, however, and soon stamped out the warring factions and drove out the recalcitrants, though persecutions from the outside continued. There followed the famous trek of more than a thousand miles across desert country in which he led the way, reaching his journey's end in the forbidding valley of the Great Salt Lake (then outside the area of the United States) on 24 July 1847. By 1851 30,000 Mormons had reached the Promised Land. Here they held their own in a hostile environment and under the practical genius of their leader carried through a vast irrigation scheme and built Salt Lake City which still serves as the headquarters of their sect. In 1850 their pioneer settlement was made Utah Territory, and in 1896 incorporated in the Union. The church was strictly ruled by its leader who also looked after affairs of state for thirty years until his death in 1877.

"Plural marriage" (or polygamy) is one of the things for which the church is best known. Though practised in the early years—as a restoration of the Old Testament practice, as Mormons believe—it was discontinued in 1890, by a formal statement issued by Wilford Woodruff, then the President of the Church.

Membership of The Church of Jesus Christ of Latter-day Saints has reached over 10 million, with members in 156 nations. There are *c.* 180,000 members in Britain (1999) having grown from 6,000 in 1958. Europe's newest and largest Mormon temple (the Preston Temple in Lancashire) opened in 1998.

The Reorganised Church of Jesus Christ of Latter-day Saints with its headquarters at Independence, Missouri, has been separate and distinct since 1852.

Muggletonians, one of the many sects which arose during the Commonwealth but, unlike most of the others (**Levellers** (*q.v.*), **Diggers** (*q.v.*), Fifth Monarchy Men, and the Millenarians) which tended to have a strongly political aspect, this was purely religious. Founded by two journeymen tailors, Lodowick Muggleton and John Reeve, who interpreted the Book of Revelation in their own peculiar way, it was decided that Reeve represented Moses, and Muggleton, Aaron. They also believed that the Father, not the Son, had died on the cross (an ancient heresy) but added the strange statement that He left Elijah in control during His period on earth. Rejecting the doctrine of the Trinity, they also asserted that God has a human body. Nevertheless, for a time, they had many followers.

Mystery Religions. *See* Orphism.

Mysticism, a religious attitude which concerns itself with direct relationship with God, "reality" as contrasted with appearance or the "ultimate" in one form or another. All the higher religions have had their mystics who have not always been regarded without suspicion by their more orthodox members, and, as Bertrand Russell points out, there has been a remarkable unity of opinion among mystics which almost transcends their religious differences. Thus, characteristic of the mystical experience in general, have been the following features; (1) a belief in insight as opposed to analytical knowledge which is accompanied in the actual experience by the sense of a mystery unveiled, a hidden wisdom become certain beyond the

possibility of doubt; this is often preceded by a period of utter hopelessness and isolation described as "the dark night of the soul"; (2) a belief in unity and a refusal to admit opposition or division anywhere; this sometimes appears in the form of what seem to be contradictory statements: "the way up and the way down is one and the same" (Heraclitus). There is no distinction between subject and object, the act of perception and the thing perceived; (3) a denial of the reality of time, since if all is one the distinction of past and future must be illusory; (4) a denial of the reality of evil (which does not maintain, *e.g.*, that cruelty is good but that it does not exist in the world of reality as opposed to the world of phantoms from which we are liberated by the insight of the vision). Among the great mystics have been Meister Eckhart and Jakob Boehme, the German religious mystics of the 13th and 16th cent. respectively, Acharya Sankara of India, and St. Theresa and St. John of the Cross of Spain. Mystical movements within the great religions have been: the Zen (*q.v.*) movement within Buddhism; Taoism in China; the Cabalists and Hasidim in Judaism; and the Sufis within Islam.

N

Nation of Islam, most influential of the US Black Muslim groups. Founded in 1930 it is now led by Louis Farrakhan. Its strident anti-white stance has sometimes been linked with anti-semitism.

Nationalism. Devotion to one's nation and its interests. Politically, this is translated into the theory that each nationality should be organised in a sovereign state. Nationalism first developed in Western Europe with the consolidation of nation states, and brought about the reorganization of Europe in the 19th and 20th centuries, *e.g.* the unification of Italy, the rise of Germany. At first, nationalism was liberal and democratic in tone, but it has also been associated with national expansion at the expense of other nations, and was an essential element of Fascism. In the 20th century it was important in the political awakening of Asia and Africa against colonialism. In Europe, the collapse of Communist regimes has led to a resurgence of nationalism (*e.g.* Serbia).

Natural Law, the philosophical doctrine which states that there is a natural moral law, irrespective of time and place, which man can know through his own reason. Originally a product of early rational philosophy, the Christian form of the doctrine is basically due to St. Thomas Aquinas who defined natural law in relation to eternal law, holding that the eternal law is God's reason which governs the relations of all things in the universe to each other. The natural law is that part of the eternal law which relates to man's behaviour. Catholic natural law assumes that the human reason is capable of deriving ultimate rules for right behaviour, since there are in man and his institutions certain stable structures produced by God's reason which man's reason can know to be correct and true. Thus, the basis of marriage, property, the state, and the contents of justice are held to be available to man's natural reason. The rules of positive morality and civil law are held to be valid only insofar as they conform to the natural law, which man is not only capable of knowing but also of obeying.

Protestant theologians criticise this notion. Thus Karl Barth and many others hold that sinful and fallen man cannot have any direct knowledge of God or His reason or will without the aid of revelation. Another theologian Niebuhr points out that the principles of the doctrines are too inflexible and that although they are the product of a particular time and circumstance, they are regarded as if they were absolute and eternal. In fact, as most social scientists would also agree, there is no law which can be regarded as "natural" for all men at all times. Nor does it seem sensible to suppose that all or even many men possess either the reason to discern natural law or the ability to obey it; whether or not we accept man's free-will (and all Protestant sects do not), we know as a fact of science that people are not always fully responsible for their actions and some not at all.

Such basic human rights as freedom of speech and religion, and freedom from fear and want, derive from natural law as later developed by John Locke.

Naturalism. 1. In general, the view that what is studied by the human sciences is all that there is, and that there is no need to go beyond or outside the universe for any explanation.

2. In ethics, the view that value terms can be defined in terms of neutral statements of fact, or derived from such statements.

Nazism, the term commonly used for the political and social ideology of the German National Socialist Party inspired and led by Hitler. The term *Nazi* was an abbreviation for *Nazional-socialistische Deutsche Arbeiterpartei*.

Neocolonialism. *See* **Colonialism.**

Neo-Fascism, term used for the post-war revival of Nazism (*see above*) and Fascism (*q.v.*) in France, Germany, Eastern Europe and now Russia.

Neoplatonism. Movement begun by Plotinus' interpretation of Plato and carried forward by various philosophers of the next three centuries and which had some influence in the Renaissance. Plotinus (205–270) saw reality as hierarchically ordered in a graded series from the divine to the material; man, who contains some part of the divine, longs for union with the highest level. Subsequent Neoplatonists include Porphyry, Iamblichus and Philoponus. (*See also* **Determinism and Free-will** and **God and Man**).

Nestorian heresy. The 5th cent. of the Christian Church saw a battle of personalities and opinions waged with fanatical fury between St. Cyril, the patriarch of Alexandria, and Nestorius, patriarch of Constantinople. Nestorius maintained that Mary should not be called the mother of God, as she was only the mother of the human and not of the divine nature of Jesus. This view was contradicted by Cyril (one of the most unpleasant saints who ever lived) who held the orthodox view. In addition to his utter destruction of Nestorius by stealthy and unremitting animosity Cyril was also responsible for the lynching of Hypatia, a distinguished mathematician and saintly woman, head of the Neoplatonist school at Alexandria. She was dragged from her chariot, stripped naked, butchered and torn to pieces in the church, and her remains burned. As if this were not enough Cyril took pains to stir up pogroms against the very large Jewish colony of Alexandria. At the Council of Ephesus (A.D. 431) the Western Bishops quickly decided for Cyril. This Council (reinforced by the Council of Chalcedon in 451) clarified orthodox Catholic doctrine (*see* **Monophysitism**). Nestorius became a heretic, was banished to Antioch where he had a short respite of peace, but later, and in spite of his age, was dragged about from one place to another on the borders of Egypt. Later the Nestorian church flourished in Syria and Persia and missions were sent to India and China.

New Age, a quasi-religious movement, based on a millenarian mysticism, astrology and ecology. Condemned by many Christians as pagan and heretical. It gained support in the 1980s.

Nihilism, the name commonly given to the earliest Russian form of revolutionary anarchism. It originated in the early years of Tsar Alexander II (1818–81), the liberator of the serfs, who, during his attempts to bring about a constitutional monarchy, was killed by a bomb. The term "nihilist", however, was first used in 1862 by Turgenev in his novel *Fathers and Children*. *See* **Anarchism.**

Nominalism. Early mediaeval thinkers were divided into two schools, those who regarded "universals" or abstract concepts as mere names without any corresponding realities (Nominalists), and those who held the opposite doctrine (**Realism**) that general concepts have an existence independent of individual things. The relation between universals and particulars was a subject of philosophical dispute all through the Middle Ages.

The first person to hold the nominalist doctrine was probably Roscelin or Roscellinus in the late 11th cent., but very little is known of him and none of his works remains except for a single letter to Peter Abelard who was his pupil. Roscelin was born in France, accused twice of heresy but recanted and fled to England where he attacked the views of Anselm, according to whom Roscelin used the phrase that universals

were a *flatus voci* or breath of the voice. The most important nominalist was the Englishman William of Occam in the 13th cent. who, once and for all, separated the two schools by saying in effect that science is about things (the nominalist view) whereas logic, philosophy, and religion are about terms or concepts (the Platonic tradition). Both are justified, but we must distinguish between them. The proposition "man is a species" is not a proposition of logic or philosophy but a scientific statement since we cannot say whether it is true or false without knowing about man. If we fail to realise that words are conventional signs and that it is important to decide whether or not they have a meaning and refer to something, then we shall fall into logical fallacies of the type: "Man is a species, Socrates is a man, therefore Socrates is a species." This, in effect, is the beginning of the modern philosophy of logical analysis which, to oversimplify, tells us that a statement is not just true or untrue, it may also be meaningless. Therefore, in all the philosophical problems we have discussed elsewhere there is the third possibility that the problem we are discussing has no meaning because the words refer to nothing and we must ask ourselves before going any further "what do we mean by God", and has the word "freewill" any definite meaning?

Nonconformity, the attitude of all those Christian bodies, which do not conform to the doctrines of the Church of England. Up to the passing of the Act of Uniformity in 1662 they were called "puritans" or "dissenters" and were often persecuted. The oldest bodies of nonconformists are the Baptists, Independents, and (in England) the Presbyterians; the Methodists, although dating from 1738, did not consider themselves nonconformists until some time later. The Presbyterians are, of course, the official Church of Scotland where it is the Anglicans (known as "Episcopalians") who are technically the nonconformists.

O

Occam's Razor, the philosophical maxim by which William of Occam, the 14th cent. Franciscan has become best-known. This states in the form which is most familiar: "Entities are not to be multiplied without necessity" and as such does not appear in his works. He did, however, say something much to the same effect: "It is vain to do with more what can be done with fewer." In other words, if everything in some science can be interpreted without assuming this or that hypothetical entity, there is no ground for assuming it. This is Bertrand Russell's version and he adds: "I have myself found this a most fruitful principle in logical analysis."

Occultism. *See* **Magic, Alchemy, Astrology,** and **Theosophy.**

Optimism. Originally the doctrine propounded by Leibnitz (1646–1716) that the actual world is the "best of all possible worlds", being chosen by the Creator out of all the possible worlds which were present in his thoughts as that in which the most good could be obtained at the cost of the least evil. This view was memorably mocked by Voltaire in *Candide*. The term is now more generally applied to any view which expects or hopes that there is or will be more good than evil in the world, or more pleasure than pain.

Opus Dei, a Roman Catholic organisation founded in 1928 by the Spanish priest Josemaría Escrivá de Balaguer (1902–75). Its aim is to spread, in all spheres of society, a deep awareness of the universal call to holiness, in the fulfilment—with freedom and responsibility—of one's professional work. In 1994, the Pope named Mgr Javier Echevarria to head Opus Dei. In 1996, the first church dedicated to the founder of Opus Dei was inaugurated in Rome.

Orangemen, members of a society formed in Ulster back in 1795 to uphold Protestantism. Their name is taken from King William III, Prince of Orange, who defeated James II at the Battle of the Boyne (1690), hence the enormous banners depicting "King Billy on the Boyne" carried in procession on 12 July each year. The Unionist Party of Northern Ireland (the ruling political party from 1921 to 1972) is largely maintained by the Orange Order. The Order also has branches in many English-speaking countries.

Orphism. The Greeks in general thought very little of their gods, regarding them as similar human beings with human failings and virtues although on a larger scale. But there was another aspect of Greek religion which was passsionate, ecstatic, and secret, dealing with the worship of various figures among whom were Bacchus or Dionysus, Orpheus, and Demeter and Persephone of the Eleusinian Mysteries. Dionysus (or Bacchus) was originally a god from Thrace where the people were primitive farmers naturally interested in fertility cults. Dionysus was the god of fertility who only later came to be associated with wine and the divine madness it produces. He assumed the form of a man or a bull and his worship by the time it arrived in Greece became associated with women (as was the case in most of the Mystery Religions) who spent nights on the hills dancing and possibly drinking wine in order to stimulate ecstasy; an unpleasant aspect of the cult was the tearing to pieces of wild animals whose flesh was eaten raw. Although the cult was disapproved of by the orthodox, it existed for a long time.

This primitive and savage religion in time was modified by that attributed to Orpheus whose cult was more spiritualised, ascetic, and substituted mental for physical intoxication. Orpheus may have been a real person or a legendary hero and he, too, is supposed to have come from Thrace, but his name indicates that he, or the movement associated with him, came from Crete and originally from Egypt, which seems to have been the source of many of its doctrines. Crete, it must be remembered, was the island through which Egypt influenced Greece in other respects. Orpheus is said to have been a reformer who was torn to pieces by the Maenad worshippers of Dionysus. The Orphics believed in the transmigration of souls and that the soul after death might obtain either eternal bliss or temporary or permanent torment according to its way of life upon earth. They held ceremonies of purification and the more orthodox abstained from animal food except on special occasions when it was eaten ritually. Man is partly earthly, partly heavenly, and a good life increases the heavenly part so that he may become one with Bacchus and be called a "Bacchus".

The religion had an elaborate theology. As the Bacchic rites were reformed by Orpheus, so the Orphic rites were reformed by Pythagoras (c. 582-c. 507 B.C.) who introduced the mystical element into Greek philosophy, which reached its heights in Plato. Other elements entered Greek life from Orphism. One of these was feminism which was notably lacking in Greek civilisation outside the Mystery Religions. The other was the drama which arose from the rites of Dionysus. The mysteries of Eleusis formed the most sacred part of the Athenian state religion, and it is clear that they had to do with fertility rites also, for they were in honour of Demeter and Persephone and all the myths speak of them as being associated with the supply of corn to the country. Without being provocative, it is accepted by most anthropologists and many theologians that Christianity, just as it accepted elements of Gnosticism and Mithraism, accepted elements from the Mystery Religions as they in turn must have done from earlier cults. The miraculous birth, the death and resurrection the sacramental feast of bread and wine, symbolising the eating of the flesh and drinking of the blood of the god, all these are common elements in early religions and not just in one. None of this means that what we are told about Jesus is not true, but it surely does mean: (a) that Christianity was not a sudden development; (b) that the early Church absorbed many of the elements of other religions; (c) that perhaps Jesus Himself made use of certain symbols which He knew had a timeless significance for man and invested them with new meaning.

Orthodox Eastern Church. There are two groups of Eastern churches: (1) those forming the Orthodox Church dealt with here which include the ancient Byzantine patriarchates of Constantinople, Alexandria, Antioch, and Jerusalem, and the national churches of Russia, Greece, Serbia, Bulgaria, Romania, etc. (although Orthodox communities exist all over the world and are no longer confined to geographical areas); (2) the churches which rejected Byzantine orthodoxy during various controversies from the 5th to the 7th cent., notably the Coptic church (q.v.) and the Armenian church. Although all Orthodox churches share the same doctrine and traditions they are arranged as national independent bodies each with its own hierarchy. They do not recognise the pope, and the primacy of the patriarch of Constantinople is largely an honorary one. Although claiming to be the One Holy, Catholic, and Apostolic Church its alleged infallibility rests on universal agreement rather than on any one individual, and agreement over the faith comes from the Scriptures interpreted in the light of the Tradition. The latter includes dogmas relating to the Trinity, Christology, Mariology, and Holy Icons; the testimony of the Fathers (St. Athanasius, St. Basil, St. John Chrysostom, St. Cyril of Alexandria, etc.); the canons or rules as formulated by the Councils and the Fathers. The Orthodox Church did not take part in the great Western controversies about the Bible, nor, of course, in the Reformation. Attempts have recently been made to improve relations bebetween Rome and Constantinople: the two Churches agreed in 1935 to retract the excommunications cast on each other in A.D. 1054, which formalised the Great Schism. Since the fall of communism in Russia, the Orthodox Church has flourished in the 1990s. In England, the first purpose-built Orthodox Cathedral is now under construction in west London.

Ouspensky, a contemporary of Gurdjieff (q.v.), Peter Ouspensky was another obscure mystic of Eastern European origin who believed he had an occult philosophical message to bring to the West.

Oxford Group. See **Moral Re-Armament.**

Oxford Movement. See **Tractarianism.**

P

Pacifism. The belief that, because violence and the taking of life is morally wrong, war and the employment of organized armed forces cannot be justified. The word first came into use to describe movements advocating the settlement of disputes by peaceful means. Since the First World War the word has been used to describe the refusal of individuals to undertake military service. The first pacificists were minority Christian groups like the Quakers and Plymouth Brethren. In the present century the movement has broadened and many democratic nations allow their citizens to abstain from fighting on grounds of principle, often described as "conscientious objection".

Paganism, a form of worship which has its roots in the ancient nature religions of Europe. Pagans reverence the sanctity of the Earth, its people and other life forms. Paganism is still a living religion, the main forms of which include Wicca (witchcraft), Druidry, Asatru and Shamanism. The Pagan Federation was founded in 1971 to provide information and to counter misconceptions about Paganism. There are an estimated 100,000 practising pagans in Britain (mainly Druids).

Pantheism. See **God and Man.**

Panpsychism. Literally, "all-soul-ism", the view that everything that really exists in the world is a mind or consciousness. To be distinguished from "hylozoism", which claims that everything is alive. Panpsychic views can be found in Leibniz and Schopenhauer, and in the 20th century philosopher A. N. Whitehead (1861–1947).

Papal Infallibility. The basis of papal infallibility is (a) that every question of morals and faith is not dealt with in the Bible so it is necessary that there should be a sure court of appeal in case of doubt, and this was provided by

Christ when he established the Church as His Teaching Authority upon earth; (b) ultimately this idea of the teaching function of the Church shapes the idea of papal infallibility which asserts that the Pope, when speaking officially on matters of faith or morals, is protected by God against the possibility of error. The doctrine was proclaimed in July 1870.

Infallibility is a strictly limited gift which does not mean that the Pope has extraordinary intelligence, that God helps him to find the answer to every conceivable question, or that Catholics have to accept the Pope's views on politics. He can make mistakes or fall into sin, his scientific or historical opinions may be quite wrong, he may write books that are full of errors. Only in two limited spheres is he infallible and in these only when he speaks officially as the supreme teacher and lawgiver of the Church, defining a doctrine that must be accepted by all its members. When, after studying a problem of faith as carefully as possible, he emerges with the Church's answer—on these occasions it is not strictly an answer, it is *the* answer.

Historically speaking, the Roman Catholic Church of the early 19th cent. was at its lowest ebb of power. Pope Pius IX, in fear of Italian nationalism, revealed his reactionary attitude by the feverish declaration of new dogmas, the canonisation of new saints, the denunciation of all modern ideals in the Syllabus of Errors, and the unqualified defence of his temporal power against the threat of Garibaldi. It is not too much to say that everything regarded as important by freedom-loving and democratic people was opposed by the papacy at that time. In 1870, after a long and protracted struggle, the Vatican Council, convened by Pius IX, pronounced the definition of his infallibility. Döllinger, a German priest and famous historian of the Church, was excommunicated because, like many others, he refused to accept the new dogma. There was clearly a connection between the pronouncement of the Pope's infallibility and his simultaneous loss of temporal power.

After the humanism of the Second Vatican Council (1962–5) Pope Paul's encyclical *Humanae Vitae* (1968), condemning birth control, came as a great disappointment to the many people (including theologians, priests, and laymen) who had expected there would be a change in the Church's teaching. The Church's moral guidance on this controversial issue, however, does not involve the doctrine of infallibility. (The Roman Catholic Church teaches that papal pronouncements are infallible only when they are specifically defined as such.) That there is unlikely to be any immediate softening of the Church's line on infallibility was made clear in July 1973 when the Vatican's Sacred Congregation for the Doctrine of the Faith published a document strongly reaffirming papal infallibility. The document also reminded Catholics of their obligation to accept the Catholic Church's unique claims to authenticity.

Parapsychology, the name given to the study of psychical research (q.v.) as an academic discipline, and chosen to denote the topic's supposed status as a branch of psychology. The impetus behind parapsychology came from the psychologist William MacDougall who persuaded Duke University in North Carolina, USA, to found a department of parapsychology under J. B. Rhine. Throughout the 1930s and 40s the work of Rhine and his colleagues, who claimed to have produced scientific evidence for the existence of ESP, attracted world-wide attention. Increasing reservations about the interpretation of Rhine's results and an apparent lack of any readily repeatable experiments, however, gradually eroded scientific confidence in the topic. The academic status of parapsychology is at the present time exceedingly uncertain. Rhine retired from university life in 1965 and the world-famous parapsychology laboratory at Duke University was closed. On the other hand the American Association for the Advancement of Science recently admitted the Parapsychology Association (the leading organisation for professional parapsychologists) as an affiliated member society. An American government body, the National Institute of Mental Health, has also officially supported some medical research into alleged telepathic dreams, the first "official" grant support of this kind.

Parsees. See **Zoroastrianism.**

Pavlovian theory. See **Behaviourism.**

Pelagianism. The Christian doctrine that each person has responsibility for ensuring his own salvation, apart from the assistance of divine grace. Its name is derived from Pelagius, a British lay monk who came to Rome about 400 A.D. and attacked Augustine's view that moral goodness is only possible through divine grace. Pelagius argued that if men and women were not held to be responsible for their actions, there would be nothing to restrain them from sin. His emphasis on free will and the essential goodness of human nature suggested an optimism that was at odds with doctrines of original sin. Augustine attacked Pelagius' views as heretical, a judgement that was confirmed by the church in 417, when Pelagius was excommunicated.

Pentecostalism, a religious movement within the Protestant churches, holding the belief that an essential feature of true Christianity is a vigorous and profound spiritual or mystical experience which occurs after, and seemingly reinforces the initial conversion. The origins of modern Pentecostalism appear to lie in the occasion on 1 January 1901 when a member of a Bible College in Topeka, Kansas, one Agnes N. Ozman, spontaneously began to speak in an apparently unknown language at one of the College's religious meetings. This "speaking in tongues" was assumed to be evidence of her conversion and "spirit baptism", and became a feature of most Pentecostal meetings in due course. The movement spread rapidly across America, particularly in rural communities, and also was a strong feature of Welsh religious life in the early part of the century. Pentecostal services are enthusiastic and rousing with a strong emphasis on music and participation on the part of the congregation. Pentecostalism is evangelistic in nature and is gaining in strength at the present time. Two of the leading Pentecostal groups in Britain are the Assemblies of God (with c. 55,000 members) and the Elim Pentecostal Church. There are also a growing number of Black Pentecostal churches.

Pessimism. Philosophically this refers to the doctrine associated with Arthur Schopenhauer (1788–1860), that in this world everything tends to evil, that the amount of pain is greater than the amount of pleasure. Of course, pessimistic ideas have a long history. As the Greeks said: "Call no man happy until he is dead." They are also present in the teachings of eastern and western religions, which emphasize the corruptness of this world and the possibility of happiness only in a hereafter. Schopenhauer's pessimism had a strong influence on Nietzsche, and through him on existentialism (q.v.).

Peyotism. A religious movement among North American Indians centred around the *peyote*, a part of the cactus which produces hallucinogenic effects.

Phrenology, a psychological "school" founded in 1800 by two Germans, Franz Josef Gall and Johann Gaspar Spurzheim. Gall was an anatomist who believed there to be some correspondence between mental faculties and the shape of the head. He tested these ideas in prisons and mental hospitals and began to lecture on his findings, arousing a great deal of interest throughout both Europe and America, where his doctrines were widely accepted. Phrenology became fashionable, and people would go to "have their bumps read" as later men and women of fashion have gone to be psychoanalysed. Roughly speaking, Gall divided the mind into thirty-seven faculties such as destructiveness, suavity, self-esteem, conscientiousness, and so on, and claimed that each of these was located in a definite area of the brain. He further claimed that the areas in the brain corresponded to "bumps" on the skull which could be read by the expert, thus giving a complete account of the character of the subject. In fact, (a) no such faculties are located in the brain anywhere, for this is simply not the way the brain works; (b) the faculties described by Gall are not pure traits which cannot be further analysed and are based on a long outdated psychology; (c) the shape of the brain bears no specific relationship to the shape of the skull. Phrenology is a pseudo-science; there is no truth in it whatever. But, even so, like astrology, it still has its practitioners.

Physiocrats. A French school of economic thought during the 18th cent., known at the time as *Les Economistes* but in later years named physiocrats by Du Pont de Nemours, a member of the School. Other members were Quesnay, Mirabeau, and the great financier Turgot. The physiocrats held the view, common to the 18th cent., and deriving ultimately from Rousseau, of the goodness and bounty of nature and the goodness of man "as he came from the bosom of nature". The aim of governments, therefore, should be to conform to nature; and so long as men do not interfere with each other's liberty and do not combine among themselves, governments should leave them free to find their own salvation. Criminals, madmen, and monopolists should be eliminated. Otherwise the duty of government is *laissez-faire, laissez passer.* From this follows the doctrine of free trade between nations on grounds of both justice and economy; for the greater the competition the more will each one strive to economise the cost of his labour to the general advantage. Adam Smith, although not sharing their confidence in human nature, learned much from the physiocrats, eliminated their errors, and greatly developed their teaching.

Physiognomy. *See* **Characterology.**

Pietism, a movement in the Lutheran Church at the end of the 17th cent.—the reaction, after the sufferings of the thirty years' war, of a pious and humiliated people against learning, pomp and ceremony, and stressing the importance of man's personal relationship with God. The writings of Johann Georg Hamann (1730–88) who came from a Pietist family of Königsberg influenced Kierkegaard. The Pietist movement was the root of the great Romantic movement of the 18th cent.

Platonism. Philosophical ideas that are inspired by the writings of Plato, usually embracing his belief in a realm of unchanging and eternal realities (specifically, abstract entities or universals) independent of the world perceived by the senses. Most working mathematicians are Platonists, in the sense that they believe that mathematical objects like numbers exist independently of our thought and hence that mathematical statements are true or false independently of our knowledge of them.

Pluralism. 1. In philosophy, any metaphysical view that the world must consist of more than one or two basic kinds of entity; these latter views would be called Monism or Dualism. Pluralists, such as William James, think of themselves as empiricists, reaffirming plain facts of experience against metaphysical extremists and pointing to the irreducible variety of things.

2. In political thought, it refers to the autonomy enjoyed by disparate groups or institutions within a society and also to the belief that such an arrangement for the distribution of political power should exist. As such it provides an alternative to collectivist doctrines, which may coerce the individual, and individualistic doctrines, which fail to provide an understanding of the individual's role in society. Pluralism is widely regarded as an ideal, but there is much argument as to how pluralism is to be interpreted in detail and how it is to be applied effectively within a modern society.

Plymouth Brethren, a religious sect founded by John Nelson Darby, a minister of the Protestant Church of Ireland, and Edward Cronin a former Roman Catholic, in 1827. Both were dissatisfied with the lack of spirituality in their own and other churches and joined together in small meetings in Dublin every Sunday for "the breaking of bread". Soon the movement began to spread through Darby's travels and writings and he finally settled in Plymouth, giving the popular name to the "Brethren". Beginning as a movement open to all who felt the need to "keep the unity of the Spirit", it soon exercised the right to exclude all who had unorthodox views and split up into smaller groups. Among these the main ones were the "Exclusives", the Kellyites, the Newtonites,

and "Bethesda" whose main differences were over problems of church government or prophetical powers. Some of these are further split among themselves. Readers of *Father and Son* by Sir Edmund Gosse, which describes life with his father, the eminent naturalist Philip Gosse, who belonged to the Brethren, will recall how this basically kind, honest, and learned man was led through their teachings to acts of unkindness (*e.g.,* in refusing to allow his son and other members of his household to celebrate Christmas and throwing out the small tokens they had secretly bought), and lack of scientific rigour (*e.g.,* in refusing for religious reasons alone to accept Darwinism when all his evidence pointed towards it).

Today, the majority of Brethren belong to the "Open Brethren" assemblies and, unlike the "Exclusives" hold that the Lord's Supper (a commemorative act of "breaking the bread" observed once a week) is for all Christians who care to join them. Baptism is required and Brethren believe in the personal premillennial second coming of Christ.

Poltergeist, allegedly a noisy type of spirit which specialises in throwing things about, making loud thumpings and bangings, and occasionally bringing in "apports", *i.e.,* objects from elsewhere. Most so-called poltergeist activities are plain frauds, but the others are almost invariably associated with the presence in the house of someone (often, but not always a child) who is suffering from an adolescent malaise or an epileptic condition. The inference is that those activities which are not simply fraudulent are either due to some unknown influence exuded by such mentally disturbed people, or that they are actually carried out by ordinary physical means by such people when in an hysterical state—*i.e.,* unconsciously. The second hypothesis is much the more probable. *See* **Psychic Research.**

Polytheism. *See* **God and Man.**

Populism. A form of politics which emphasizes the virtues of the common people against politicians and intellectuals, who are distrusted as devious and selfish. "The will of the people" can provide sufficient guidance to the statesman. It is not restricted to any one political view and can manifest itself in left, right or centrist forms.

Positivism, also known as the **Religion of Humanity,** was founded by Auguste Comte (1798–1857), a famous mathematician and philosopher born in Montpellier, France. His views up to the end of the century attracted many and it would have been impossible throughout that time to read a book on philosophy or sociology that did not mention them, but today his significance is purely of historical interest. In his *Cours de Philosophie Positive* (1830) he put forward the thesis that mankind had seen three great stages in human thought: (1) the theological, during which man seeks for supernatural causes to explain nature and invents gods and devils; (2) the metaphysical, through which he thinks in terms of philosophical and metaphysical abstractions; (3) the last positive or scientific stage when he will proceed by experimental and objective observation to reach in time "positive truth".

Broadly speaking, there is little to complain of in this analysis; for there does seem to have been some sort of general direction along these lines. However, Comte was not satisfied with having reached this point and felt that his system demanded a religion and, of course, one that was "scientific". This religion was to be the worship of Humanity in place of the personal Deity of earlier times, and for it he supplied not only a Positive Catechism but a treatise on Sociology in which he declared himself the High Priest of the cult. Since, as it stood, the religion was likely to appear somewhat abstract to many, Comte drew up a list of historical characters whom he regarded as worthy of the same sort of adoration as Catholics accord to their saints. The new Church attracted few members, even among those who had a high regard for Comte's scientific work, and its only significant adherents were a small group of Oxford scholars and some in his own country. Frederic Harrison was the best-known English adherent and throughout his life continued to preach Comtist doctrines in London to diminishing audiences.

Postmodernism. Given that "modernism" (J34) is a term difficult to define, "postmodernism" is an even more elusive concept, though a very fashionable one for describing contemporary art. The modernist tradition of formal and stylistic experiment, added to our increased knowledge of the history of Western and non-Western arts, has provided a vast range of styles, techniques and technologies for the artist to choose from. This extension of choice has simultaneously created uncertainty about their use. If no one or few styles have any authority, then the artist picks and chooses with little commitment, and so tends towards pastiche, parody, quotation, self-reference and eclecticism. The post-modern style is to have no settled style. But it is always dangerous to try and pin down an artistic movement that is still taking place.

Pragmatism, a typically American school of philosophy which comes under the heading of what Bertrand Russell described as a "practical" as opposed to a "theoretical" philosophy. Whereas the latter, to which most of the great philosophical systems belong, seeks disinterested knowledge for its own sake, the former (a) regards action as the supreme good, (b) considers happiness an effect and knowledge a mere instrument of successful activity.

The originator of pragmatism is usually considered to have been the psychologist William James (1842–1910) although he himself attributed its basic principles to his life-long friend, the American philosopher, Charles Sanders Peirce (1839–1914). The other famous pragmatist is John Dewey, best-known in Europe for his works on education (for although American text-books on philosophy express opinions to the contrary, few educated people in Europe have taken the slightest interest in pragmatism and generally regard it as an eccentricity peculiar to Americans). James in his book *The Will to Believe* (1896) points out that we are often compelled to take a decision where no adequate theoretical grounds for a decision exist; for even to do nothing is to decide. Thus in religion we have a right to adopt a believing attitude although not intellectually fully convinced. We should believe truth and shun error, but the failing of the sceptical philosopher is that he adheres only to the latter rule and thus fails to believe various truths which a less cautious man will accept. If believing truth and avoiding error are equally important, then it is a good idea when we are presented with an alternative to believe one of the possibilities at will, since we then have an even chance of being right, whereas we have none if we suspend judgment. The function of philosophy, according to James, is to find out what difference it makes to the individual if a particular philosophy or world-system is true: "An idea is 'true' so long as to believe it is profitable to our lives" and, he adds, the truth is only the expedient in our way of thinking . . . in the long run and on the whole of course". Thus "if the hypothesis of God works satisfactorily in the widest sense of the word, it is true". Bertrand Russell's reply to this assertion is: "I have always found that the hypothesis of Santa Claus "works satisfactorily in the widest sense of the word'; therefore 'Santa Claus exists' is true, although Santa Claus does not exist." Russell adds that James's concept of truth simply omits as unimportant the question whether God really *is* in His heaven; if He is a useful hypothesis that is enough. "God the Architect of the Cosmos is forgotten; all that is remembered is belief in God, and its effects upon the creatures inhabiting our petty planet. No wonder the Pope condemned the pragmatic defence of religion."

Predestination. *See* **Calvinism.**

Presbyterianism, a system of ecclesiastical government of the Protestant churches which look back to John Calvin as their Reformation leader. The ministry consists of presbyters who are all of equal rank. Its doctrinal standards are contained in the *Westminster Confession of Faith* (1647) which is, in general, accepted by English, Scottish, and American Presbyterians as the most thorough and logical statement in existence of the Calvinist creed. The Church of Scotland is the leading Presbyterian church in the British Isles.

The Reformation in Scotland was preceded by the same sort of awareness of the moral corruption of the Roman Church as had happened elsewhere, but for various political and emotional reasons, which need not be discussed here, the majority of the Scottish people (unlike the English who had been satisfied with the mere exchange of Crown for Pope) were determined on a fundamental change of doctrine, discipline, and worship, rather than a reform of manners. The church preachers had learned their Protestantism not from Luther but from Calvin and their leader John Knox had worked in Geneva with Calvin himself and was resolved to introduce the system into Scotland. In 1557 the "Lords of the Congregation" signed the Common Band (*i.e.,* a bond or covenant) to maintain "the blessed Word of God and his congregation" against their enemies, and demanded the right to worship as they had chosen. However, the real date of the Scottish Reformation is August 1500 when Mary of Guise (the regent for Mary Queen of Scots who was not yet of age) died and the Estates met to settle their affairs without foreign pressure; the *Scots Confession* was drawn up and signed by Knox and adopted by the Estates.

The ideas on which the Reformed Kirk was based are found in the *Scots Confession*, the *Book of Discipline*, and the *Book of Common Order*, the so-called Knox's liturgy. Knox's liturgy, the same as that used in Geneva but translated into English, was used until Laud's attempt to force an Anglican liturgy on the Kirk led to an abandonment of both in favour of "free prayers."

The Presbyterian tradition includes uncompromising stress upon the Word of God contained in the Scriptures of the Old and New Testaments as the supreme rule of faith and life, and upon the value of a highly trained ministry, which has given the Church of Scotland a high reputation for scholarship and has in turn influenced the standard of education in Scotland. The unity of the Church is guaranteed by providing for democratic representation in a hierarchy of courts (unlike the Anglican Church, which is a hierarchy of persons). The local kirk-session consists of the minister and popularly elected elders (laymen). Ministers, elected by their flocks, are ordained by presbyters (ministers already ordained). Above the kirk-session is the court of the presbytery which has jurisdiction over a specified area; above that the court of synod which rules over many presbyteries; and finally the General Assembly which is the Supreme Court of the Church with both judicial and legislative powers, and over which the Moderator of the General Assembly presides. The function of the elders is to help the minister in the work and government of the kirk. The episcopacy set up by James VI and I, and maintained by Charles I was brought to an end by the Glasgow Assembly (1638), but General Assemblies were abolished by Oliver Cromwell and at the Restoration Charles II re-established episcopacy. The Covenanters who resisted were hunted down, imprisoned, transported, or executed over a period of nearly thirty years before William of Orange came to the throne and Presbyterianism was re-established (1690).

In 1972 the Presbyterian and Congregationalist Churches in England were merged to form the United Reformed Church. *See* **Church of Scotland, Calvinism.**

Protestant, the name first applied to those who favoured the cause of Martin Luther and who protested against the intolerant decisions of the Catholic majority at the second Diet of Speyer (1529), revoking earlier decisions of the first Diet of Speyer tolerating the Reformers in certain cases (1526). In general the name "Protestant" is applied to those Churches which severed connection with Rome at the time of the Reformation. The essence of Protestantism is the acceptance by the individual Christian of his direct responsibility to God rather than to the Church. *See* **Lutheranism, Presbyterianism, Calvinism.**

Psychiatry, a branch of medicine concerned with the treatment of psychological problems and mental illness. It uses drugs and psychotherapeutic techniques.

Psychic Research is a general term for the various approaches to the scientific investigation of the paranormal, in particular supposed extra-sensory powers of the mind, but also manifestations such as ghosts, poltergeists, spiritualistic phenomena, etc. In recent years the word parapsychology has also come into use, particularly for the investigation of ESP in a laboratory setting, but it is really part of psychic research as the subject's fascinating history reveals.

For all recorded history, and no doubt very much earlier, man has been puzzled at his apparent ability to perceive features of the universe without the use of the normal senses—mind-to-mind contact, dreams about the future which come true, etc. He has also been intrigued by the notion that in addition to the natural world of people and things, there exists in parallel, a *supernatural* world of ghosts, spirits and other similar strange manifestations. Belief in such oddities has been tremendously widespread and still forms one of the major casual conversational topics raised when people see each other socially today. Of course, until the 19th cent. or thereabouts such phenomena, while bizarre, unpredictable and possibly frightening, were not at odds with man's view of himself and his world as revealed through basic religious beliefs. Man was supposed to be in essence a supernatural being with eternal life, and the world was seen as the happy hunting ground of dynamic evil forces which could intervene directly in the lives of humans. The rise of material science in the 19th cent. however began to shake the orthodox religious framework, and as a result in due course scientists began to question the basis of all supernatural powers and manifestations, putting forward the reasonable argument: "if such things *are* real then they should be demonstrable in scientific terms—like all other aspects of the universe are."

Once having advanced this argument, the next step was to carry it to its conclusion and set about the systematic investigation of the phenomena to see whether they *did* conform in any way to the immensely successful framework of 19th cent. science, and from this step psychic research was born. In fact one can date its origins rather precisely—to 1882 when a group of scholars formed the Society for Psychical Research in London—an organisation which still exists today. The first experiments in this slightly eccentric field of science were haphazard and tended to be confined to spiritualistic phenomena such as table tapping, mediumistic messages, ectoplasmic manifestations, *etc.*, which were having a great wave of popularity among the general public at the time. In fact what one might term as the first phase of psychic research—it has gone through three phases in its history—was really heavily tied up with Spiritualism. Before ridiculing it for this, it is only fair to point out that many of the most eminent figures of the time—the great physicists Sir Oliver Lodge and Sir William Crookes, Alfred Russell Wallace, 'co-discoverer with Darwin of the theory of evolution by natural selection, the brilliant author and creator of Sherlock Holmes, Sir Arthur Conan Doyle, and many others—became convinced Spiritualists as the result of their early experiments. Nevertheless, despite the ardent support of such intellectual giants, medium after medium was in due course detected in fraud—sometimes of the most blatant kind—and the majority of scientists gradually became more critical and less likely to be taken in by even the subtlest of trickery. As a result, interest slowly shifted from the séance room to a different realm, and as it did so the first phase of psychic research drew to a close.

The second phase was, broadly speaking, the era of the ghost hunter. With the idea of spirits materialising in laboratories seeming intrinsically less and less credible, scientists began to study what struck them at the time to be basically more "plausible" matters—haunted houses, poltergeist phenomena and so on. For some reason the idea of a house dominated by a psychic presence as the result of some tragic history seemed (at the turn of the century) *somehow* scientifically and philosophically more acceptable than did the old spiritualist notions about direct communication with the spirit world. The key figure in the "ghost hunting" era was Mr. Harry Price, an amateur magician who became the scourge of fraudulent mediums, but who staked his name and credibility on the authenticity of the alleged poltergeist phenomena at Borley Rectory in Suffolk, which became world famous through his book, *The Most Haunted House in England.* The ancient rectory's catalogue of ghosts and marvels allegedly witnessed by numerous "reliable witnesses" seemed irrefutable. Unfortunately investigations by the Society for Psychical Research after Price's death made it seem certain that Price was responsible for faking some of the Borley phenomena himself, and with these disclosures scientifically "respectable" ghost hunting took a nasty tumble. Thus, with an increasingly critical attitude developing among scientists, haunted houses and poltergeists gradually began to shift out of favour to usher in the third phase of psychic research.

The date of the commencement of this phase can be identified as 1927 when the Parapsychology Laboratory at Duke University in North Carolina was formed by Dr. J. B. Rhine. Here the emphasis was on laboratory studies along the traditional lines of experimental psychology; spirit forms and poltergeists were ignored in favour of the routine testing of literally thousands of people for telepathy, precognition (the ability to see into the future), etc., almost always involving card tests which could be rigidly controlled and the results statistically analysed. By the 1940s Rhine was claiming irrefutable evidence of telepathy achieved by these means, but once again critical forces began to gather and it was pointed out that results obtained in Rhine's laboratory rarely seemed to be replicable in other scientists' laboratories in different parts of the world. In fact the failure of ESP experiments of this kind to be easily repeatable has turned out to be crucial and has led to a growing scepticism on the part of uncommitted scientists who now question whether psychic research and parapsychology have really advanced our understanding of the world of the paranormal in any way.

To sum up the topic one could say that in a curious way, while the third phase of psychic research is now drawing to a close, the evidence suggests that a fourth phase is appearing, and that this may well feature a return to the study of the more sensational and dramatic phenomena reminiscent of the Victorian séance room. If this is so, a century after its foundation the wheel will have turned full circle and psychic research will be back where it started, without in the opinion of most scientists, having solved any of the basic questions which it had set out to answer. *See* **Parapsychology, Poltergeist, Telepathy, Spiritualism.**

Psychoanalysis, an approach to the study of human personality involving the rigorous probing, with the assistance of a specially trained practitioner, of an individual's personal problems, motives, goals and attitudes to life in general. Often, and quite understandably, confused with psychology (of which it is merely a part), psychoanalysis has an interesting historical background and has attracted the interest of philosophers, scientists and medical experts since it emerged as a radical and controversial form of mental therapy at the turn of the century. The traditionally accepted founder is the great Austrian Sigmund Freud, but he never failed to acknowledge the impetus that had been given to his own ideas by his talented friend, the physiologist Joseph Breuer, who for most of his working life had been interested in the curious phenomena associated with hypnosis. Breuer had successfully cured the hysterical paralysis of a young woman patient and had noticed that under hypnosis the girl seemed to be recalling emotional experiences, hitherto forgotten, which bore some relationship to the symptoms of her illness. Developing this with other patients Breuer then found that the mere recalling and discussing of the emotional events under hypnosis seemed to produce a dramatic alleviation of the symptoms—a phenomenon which came to be known as *catharsis*. Breuer also noticed another curious side-effect, that his women patients fell embarrassingly and violently in love with him, and he gradually dropped the practice of "mental catharsis", possibly feeling that it was a bit too dangerous to handle. This left the field clear for Freud, whose brilliant mind began to search beyond the therapeutic aspects of the topic to see what light might be thrown on the nature of human personality and psychological mechanisms in general. The most important question concerned the "forgotten" emotional material which turned up, apparently out of the blue, during the hypnotic session. Freud rightly saw that this posed problems for the current theories of memory, for how could something once forgotten (*a*) continue to have an effect on the individual without his being aware of it, and (*b*) ultimately be brought back to conscious memory again. It must be remembered that at this time memory was considered to be a fairly simple process—information was stored in the brain and was gradually eroded or destroyed with the passage of time and the decay of brain cells. Once lost, it was believed, memories were gone for ever, or at best only partially and inaccurately reproducible. Furthermore, human beings were supposed to be rational (if frequently wilful) creatures who never did anything without thinking about it (if only briefly) beforehand and without being well aware of their reasons for so doing. It was within this framework that Freud had his great insight, one which many people believe to be one of the most important ideas given to mankind. This was simply the realisation that the human mind was not a simple entity controlling the brain and body more or less at will, but a complex system made up of a number of integrated parts with at least two major subdivisions—the conscious and the unconscious. The former concerned itself with the normal round of human behaviour, including the larger part of rational thought, conversation, *etc.*, and large areas of memory. The latter was principally devoted to the automatic control of bodily functions, such as respiration, cardiac activity, various types of emotional behaviour not subject to much conscious modification and a large storehouse of relevant "memories" again not normally accessible to the conscious mind. Occasionally, Freud proposed, an exceedingly unpleasant emotional or otherwise painful event might be so troublesome if held in the conscious mind's store, that it would get shoved down into the unconscious or "repressed" where it would cease to trouble the individual in his normal life. The advantages of this mechanism are obvious, but they also brought with them hazards. With certain kinds of memory, particularly those involving psychological rather than physical pain—as for example a severe sexual conflict or marital problem—repression might be used as a device to save the individual from facing his problem in the "real" world, where he might be able ultimately to solve it, by merely hiding it away in the unconscious and thus pretending it did not exist. Unfortunately, Freud believed, conflicts of this kind were not snuffed out when consigned to the basements of the mind, but rather tended to smoulder on, affecting the individual in various ways which he could not understand. Repressed marital conflicts might give rise to impotence, for example, or perhaps to homosexual behaviour. Guilt at improper social actions similarly repressed might provoke nervous tics, local paralysis, *etc, etc*. Following this line of reasoning, Freud argued that if the unwisely repressed material could be dredged up and the individual forced to face the crisis instead of denying it, then dramatic alleviations of symptoms and full recovery should follow.

To the great psychologist and his growing band of followers the stage seemed to be set for a dramatic breakthrough not only in mental therapy but also in a general understanding of the nature of human personality. To his pleasure—for various reasons he was never too happy about hypnosis—Freud discovered that with due patience, skill and guidance an individual could be led to resurrect the material repressed in his unconscious mind in the normal, as opposed to the hypnotic, state. This technique, involving long sessions consisting of intimate discussions between patient and therapist became known as psychoanalysis, and it has steadily evolved from its experimental beginnings in the medical schools and universities of Vienna to being a major system of psychotherapy with a world-wide following and important theoretical connotations. Psychoanalysis, as practised today, consists of a number of meetings between doctor and patient in which the latter is slowly taught to approach and enter the *territory* of his subconscious mind, and examine the strange and "forgotten" material within. A successful analysis, it is claimed, gives the individual greater insight into his own personality and a fuller understanding of the potent unconscious forces which are at work within him.

Freud's initial ideas were of course tentative, and meant to be so. He was however a didactic and forceful personality himself, unwilling to compromise on many points which became controversial as the technique and practice of psychoanalysis developed. The outcome was that some of his early followers, notably the equally brilliant Carl Jung and Alfred Adler, broke away to found their own "schools" or versions of psychoanalysis. Jungian analysis, practised by the followers of C. G. Jung (*see* **B35**) is an important aspect of psycho-analysis. All psychoanalysts, Freudian and Jungian, must have a lengthy training analysis by a training analyst from a recognised institute. This is not restricted to individuals qualified in medicine or psychology. Today, psychoanalysis is coming under increasingly critical scrutiny, and its claims are being treated with a good deal of reservation. Notable antagonists include the English psychologist Professor H. J. Eysenck. Analysists respond by saying that their system is closer to an art than a craft and not amenable to routine scientific experiment. The controversy will no doubt continue for some time to come, but whatever its validity as therapy, the basic ideas behind psycho-analysis—notably the reality and power of the unconscious mind—are beyond question and have given human beings definite and major insights into the greatest enigma of all—the workings of the human mind.

Psychology is the study of people: how they think, how they act, react and interact. Psychology is concerned with all aspects of behaviour and the thoughts, feelings and motivation underlying such behaviour. Modern psychology is thus the science of human behaviour and experience. To study psychology, the student needs to learn a range of scientific methods (use of statistics, hypothesis testing *etc*.) *See* **Adlerian Psychology, Gestalt Psychology** *etc*.

Psychotherapy, a method aimed at alleviating mental and emotional suffering through a specialised relationship between therapist and patient. The whole range of psychotherapies is represented on the National Register, which is compiled by the UK Council for Psychotherapy. This incorporates eight different models, each one of which holds in common a theory about the human mind, a concept of the development of the individual, and a theory of change.

Puritans were a separate sect before the accession of Edward VI, but did not become prominent till the reign of Elizabeth. Afterwards they split up into Independents and Presbyterians, and the influence of Oliver Cromwell made the former supreme. Since the Revolution the word has been replaced by "Nonconformist' or "Dissenter', but, of course, Roman Catholics in England and Protestant Episcopalians in Scotland are just as much Nonconformists or Dissenters as Baptists or Methodists.

Pyramidology, a curious belief that the dimensions of the Great Pyramid at Giza, if studied carefully, reveal principles of fundamental historical and religious significance. The perpetrator of this was a Victorian publisher, John Taylor, who discovered that if you divide the height of the pyramid into twice the side of its base you get a number very similar to pi—a number of considerable mathematical importance. Later discoveries in the same vein include the finding that the base of the pyramid (when divided by the width of a single casing stone) equals exactly 365—number of days in the year.

Many books have been written on the interpretation of the dimensions of the pyramid, none of which has any scientific or archaeological validity. Pyramidology is simply a classic example of the well-known fact that hunting through even a random array of numbers will turn up sequences which appear to be "significant"—always provided that one carefully selects the numbers one wants and turns a blind eye to those one doesn't! **Pyrrhonism,** a sceptical philosophy which doubts everything. (*See* **Scepticism**)

Pythagoreanism. The school of thought initiated by the followers of Pythagoras (**B49**). To be distinguished from Pythagoras himself, whose own doctrines are difficult to determine. The Pythagoreans believed that at its deepest level, reality is mathematical in nature, that is, all things can be ultimately reduced to numerical relationships. Their theory of number was applied to music theory, acoustics, geometry and astronomy. The doctrine of the "harmony of the spheres" seems to have started with them: certain parameters characterizing the planets are related to one another "harmoniously" by a mathematical rule. The revolution of each planet produces a distinct tone, and the whole set corresponds to the notes of a scale. They also held a doctrine of metempsychosis: the soul transmigrates through successive reincarnations to union with the divine.

Q

Quakers, (**Religious Society of Friends**), a religious body founded in England in the 17th cent. by George Fox (1624–91). The essence of their faith is that every individual person has the power of direct communication with God who will guide him into the ways of truth. This power comes from the "inner light" of his own heart, the light of Christ, Quakers meet for worship avoiding all ritual, without ordained ministers or prepared sermons; often there is silence until someone is moved by the Holy Spirit to utter his message.

In the early days Quakers gave vent to violent outbursts and disturbed church services. Friends had the habit of preaching at anyone who happened to be nearby, their denunciation of "steeple-houses" and references to the "inner light," their addressing everyone as "thee" and "thou," their refusal to go beyond "yea" and "nay" in making an assertion and refusing to go further in taking an oath, must have played some part in bringing about the savage persecutions they were forced to endure. Many emigrated to Pennsylvania, founded by William Penn in 1682, and missionaries were sent to many parts of the world. The former violence gave way to gentleness. Friends not only refused to take part in war but even refused to resist personal violence. They took the lead in abolishing slavery, worked for prison reform and better education. As we know them today Quakers are quiet, sincere, undemonstrative people, given to a somewhat serious turn of mind. The former peculiarities of custom and dress have been dropped and interpretation of the Scriptures is more liberal. Although Quakers refuse to take part in warfare, they are always ready to help the victims of war. In Britain the Quakers have (1999) over 17,500 adult members. There are *c* 214,000 worldwide.

Quietism, a doctrine of extreme asceticism and contemplative devotion, embodied in the works of Michael Molinos, a 17th cent. Spanish priest, and condemned by Rome. It taught that the chief duty of man is to be occupied in the continual contemplation of God, so as to become totally independent of outward circumstances and the influence of the senses. Quietists taught that when this stage of perfection is reached the soul has no further need for prayer and other external devotional practices. Similar doctrines have been taught in the Moslem and Hindu religions. *See* **Yoga.**

R

Racism, the doctrine that one race is inherently superior or inferior to others, one of the bases of racial prejudice. It has no connection whatever with the study of race as a concept, nor with the investigation of racial differences, which is a science practised by the physical anthropologist (who studies physical differences), or the social anthropologist (who studies cultural differences). *See also* **Race, Section L.**

Radiesthesia, the detection, either by some "psychic" faculty or with special equipment, of radiations alleged to be given off by all living things and natural substances such as water, oil, metal, *etc.* The word radiesthesia is in fact a fancy modern name for the ancient practice of "dowsing," whereby an individual is supposed to be able to detect the presence of hidden underground water by following the movements of a hazel twig held in his hands. Dowsers, or water diviners, as they are sometimes called, claim also to be able to detect the presence of minerals and, hard though it may seem to believe, have actually been hired by major oil companies to prospect for desert wells—though without any notable success. The theory of dowsing is that all things give off a unique radiation signal which the trained individual (via his twig, pendulum, or whatever) can "tune in" to, a theory which, while not backed up by any data known to orthodox sciences, is at least not too fantastically far-fetched. It is when radiesthesists claim to be able to detect the presence of oil, water, or precious metals by holding their pendulum *over a map* of the territory and declare that it is not necessary for them to visit the area in person to find the required spot that the topic moves from the remotely possible to the absurdly improbable. Some practitioners of this art state that they are able to perform even more marvellous feats such as determining the sex of chickens while still in the egg, or diagnosing illness by studying the movements of a pendulum held over a blood sample from the sick individual. Such claims when put to simple scientific test have almost invariably turned out as fiascos.

There is an important link between radiesthesia and the pseudo-science of *radionics,* which holds that the twig or pendulum can be superseded by complicated equipment built vaguely according to electronic principles. A typical radionic device consists of a box covered with knobs, dials, *etc.*, by which the practitioner "tunes in" to the "vibration" given off by an object, such as a blood spot, a piece of hair, or even a signature. By the proper interpretation of the readings from the equipment the illness, or even the mental state, of the individual whose blood, hair, or signature is being tested, may be ascertained. The originator of radionics seems to have been a Dr. Albert Abrams who engaged in medical practice using radionic devices in America in the 1920s and 30s.

Ranters, a fanatical antinomian (the doctrine that Christians are not bound to keep the law of God) and pantheistic sect in Commonwealth England. The name was also applied to the Primitive Methodists because of their noisy preaching.

Rastafarianism, a Caribbean religious movement which took root in the 1930s following the teachings of Marcus Garvey who set up the "Black Star Liner" for the repatriation of Africans abroad. Rastafarians look to Ethiopia as their spiritual home since that country was the one part of Africa not to be colonised permanently (it was invaded by Mussolini in the 1930s). Reggae is their music.

Rationalism is defined as "the treating of reason as the ultimate authority in religion and the rejection of doctrines not consonant with reason." In practice, rationalism had a double significance: (1) the doctrine as defined above, and (2) a 19th cent. movement which was given to what was then known as "free-thought," "secularism," or agnosticism—*i.e.*, it was in the positive sense anti-religious and was represented by various bodies such as the Secular Society, the National Secular Society, and the Rationalist Press Association (founded in 1899).

In the first sense, which implies a particular

philosophical attitude to the universe and life, rationalism is not easy to pin down although, at first sight, it would appear that nothing could be simpler. Does it mean the use of pure reason and logic or does it mean, on the other hand, the use of what is generally called the "scientific method" based on a critical attitude to existing beliefs? If we are thinking in terms of the use of pure reason and logic then the Roman Catholic Church throughout most of its history has maintained, not that the whole truth about religion can be discovered by reason, but as St. Thomas Aquinas held, the basis of religion—e.g. the existence of God—can be rationally demonstrated. Nobody could have made more use of logic than the schoolmen of the Middle Ages, yet not many people today would accept their conclusions, nor would many non-Catholics accept St. Thomas's proofs of the existence of God even when they themselves are religious. The arguments of a First Cause or Prime Mover or the argument from Design on the whole leave us unmoved, partly because they do not lead up to the idea of a *personal God*, partly because we rightly distrust logic and pure reason divorced from facts and know that, if we begin from the wrong assumptions or premises, we can arrive at some very strange answers. If the existence of a Deity can be proved by reason, then one can also by the use of reason come to the conclusions, or rather paradoxes, such as the following: God is by definition all good, all knowing, all powerful—yet evil exists (because it if does not exist then it cannot be wrong to say "there is no God"). But if evil exists, then it must do so either because of God (in which case He is not all good) or in spite of God (in which case He is not all powerful).

Arguments of this sort do not appeal to the modern mind for two historical reasons: (1) many of us have been brought up in the Protestant tradition which—at least in one of its aspects—insists that we must believe in God by faith rather than by logic and in its reformed form insists on God as revealed by the "inner light"; (2) our increasing trust in the scientific method of observation, experiment and argument. Thus, no matter what Aristotle or St. Thomas may say about a Prime Mover or a First Cause, we remain unconvinced since at least one scientific theory suggests that the universe did not have a beginning and if scientific investigation proved this to be so, then we should be entirely indifferent to what formal logic had to say.

The secularist and rationalist movements of the 19th cent. were anti-religious—and quite rightly so—because at that time there were serious disabilities imposed even in Britain by the Established Church on atheism or agnosticism and freedom of thought. These are of little significance now because very little is left, largely thanks to their efforts, of these disabilities.

Finally, although most people are likely to accept the scientific method as the main means of discovering truth, there are other factors which equally make us doubt the value of "pure" logic and reason unaided by observation. The first of these is the influence of Freud which shows that much of our reasoning is mere rationalising—e.g., we are more likely to become atheists because we hated our father than because we can prove that there is no God. The second is the influence of a movement in philosophy which, in the form of logical positivism or logical analysis, makes us doubt whether metaphysical systems have any meaning at all. Today, instead of asking ourselves whether Plato was right or wrong, we are much more likely to ask whether he did anything but make for the most part meaningless noises. Religion is in a sense much safer today than it ever was in the 19th cent. when it made foolish statements over matters of science that could be *proved* wrong; now we tend to see it as an emotional attitude to the universe or God (a "feeling of being at home in the universe," as William James put it) which can no more be proved or disproved than being in love.

Realism is a word which has so many meanings, and such contradictory ones, in various spheres, that it is difficult to define. We shall limit ourselves to its significance in philosophy. In philosophy, "realism" has two different meanings, diametrically opposed. (1) The most usual meaning is the one we should least expect from the everyday sense of the word—*i.e.*, it refers to all those philosophies from Plato onwards which maintained that the world of appearance is illusory and that ideas, forms, or universals are the only true realities, belonging to the world beyond matter and appearance—the world of God or mind. In early mediaeval times St. Thomas Aquinas was the chief exponent of this doctrine which was held by the scholastics as opposed to the Nominalists (*q.v.*). (2) In its modern everyday meaning "realism" is the belief that the universe is real and not a creation of mind, that there is a reality that causes the appearance, the "thing-in-itself" as Kant described it. Material things may not really be what they appear to be (*e.g.* a noise is not the "bang" we experience but a series of shock-waves passing through the atmosphere), yet, for all that, we can be sure that matter exists and it is very possible (some might add) that mind does not.

Reformation, the great religious movement of the 16th cent., which resulted in the establishment of Protestantism. John Wyclif (d. 1384), John Hus (d. 1415) and others had sounded the warning note, and when later on Luther took up the cause in Germany, and Zwingli in Switzerland, adherents soon became numerous. The wholesale vending of indulgences by the papal agents had incensed the people, and when Luther denounced these things he spoke to willing ears. After much controversy, the reformers boldly propounded the principles of the new doctrine, and the struggle for religious supremacy grew bitter. They claimed justification (salvation) by faith, and the use as well as the authority of the Scriptures, rejecting the doctrine of transubstantiation, the adoration of the Virgin and Saints, and the headship of the Pope. Luther was excommunicated. But the Reformation principles spread and ultimately a great part of Germany, as well as Switzerland, the Low Countries, Scandinavia, England, and Scotland were won over to the new faith. In England Henry VIII readily espoused the cause of the Reformation, his own personal quarrel with the Pope acting as an incentive. Under Mary there was a brief and sanguinary reaction, but Elizabeth gave completeness to the work which her father had initiated. *See* **Lutheranism, Calvinism, Presbyterianism, Baptists, etc.**

Relativism. Theories or doctrines that truth, morality *etc.* are relative to situations and are not absolute. The view that all truth is relative is associated with Scepticism (*q.v.*). In the area of morality, it is the view that there are no absolute or universal criteria for ethical judgements. This view is often a reaction to the differences in moral belief between different societies. It is objected against relativism that there must be standards by which to measure the correctness of judgements or beliefs.

Religious Society of Friends. *See* **Quakers.**

Renaissance, the revival of art and letters, under the influence of classical models, which began in Italy in the 14th century. It is a term which must be used with care for the following reasons: (1) Although it was first used in the form *rinascita* (re-birth) by Vasari in 1550 and people living at that time certainly were aware that something new was happening, the word had no wide currency until used by the Swiss historian Jacob Burckhardt in his classic *The Civilization of the Renaissance in Italy* (1860). (2) The term as used today refers not only to art in its widest sense but to a total change in man's outlook on life which extended into philosophical, scientific, economic, and technical fields. (3) Spreading from Italy there were renaissance movements in France, Spain, Germany, and northern Europe, all widely different with varying delays in time. As the historian Edith Sichel says: "Out of the Italian Renaissance there issued a new-born art; out of the Northern Renaissance there came forth a new-born religion. There came forth also a great school of poetry, and a drama the greatest that the world had seen since the days of Greece. The religion was the offspring of Germany and the poetry that of England."

The real cause of the Renaissance was not the fall of Constantinople, the invention of printing, or the discovery of America, though these were phases in the process; it was, quite simply, money. The birth of a new merchant class gave rise to individualist attitudes in economic affairs which prepared the way for individualism and humanism. The new wealthy class in time became patrons of the arts whereas previously the Church had been the sole patron and controller. Thus the artist became more free to express himself, more respected, and being more well-to-do could afford to ignore the Church and even, in time, the views of his patrons.

It is true that art continued to serve to a considerable extent the purposes of faith, but it was judged from the standpoint of art. Mediaeval art was meant to elevate and teach man: Renaissance art to delight his senses and enrich his life. From this free and questing spirit acquired from economic individualism came the rise of modern science and technology; here Italy learned much from the Arab scholars who had translated and commented upon the philosophical, medical, and mathematical texts of antiquity, while denying themselves any interest in Greek art and literature. Arabic Latin versions of Aristotle were in use well into the 16th cent. The Byzantine culture, though it had preserved the Greek tradition and gave supremacy to Plato, had made no move forward. But the Greek scholars who fled to Italy after the fall of Constantinople brought with them an immense cargo of classical manuscripts. The recovery of these Greek masterpieces, their translation into the vernaculars, and the invention of printing, made possible a completer understanding of the Greek spirit. It was the bringing together of the two heritages, Greek science, and Greek literature, that gave birth to a new vision. But it was not only Aristotle and Plato who were being studied but Ovid, Catullus, Horace, Pliny and Lucretius. What interested Renaissance man was the humanism of the Latin writers, their attitude to science, their scepticism.

The period *c.* 1400-1500 is known as the **Early Renaissance**. During this time such painters as Masaccio, Uccello, Piero della Francesca, Botticelli, and Giovanni Bellini were laying the foundations of drawing and painting for all subsequent periods including our own. They concerned themselves with such problems as anatomy, composition, perspective, and representation of space, creating in effect a grammar or textbook of visual expression. The term **High Renaissance** is reserved for a very brief period when a pure, balanced, classical harmony was achieved and artists were in complete control of the techniques learned earlier. The High Renaissance lasted only from *c.* 1500 to 1527 (the date of the sack of Rome), yet that interval included the earlier works of Michelangelo, most of Leonardo's, and all the Roman works of Raphael.

Ritualism, a tendency which, during the 19th cent., developed in the High Church section of the Church of England to make use of those vestments, candles, incense, etc. which are usually regarded as features of the Church of Rome. Since some opposition was aroused, a Ritual Commission was appointed in 1904 to take evidence and try to find some common basis on which High and Low Church could agree with respect to ceremonial. The report of 1906 in effect recommended the giving of greater powers to bishops to suppress objectionable practices. Although they are often associated together, it is worth while pointing out that there was no special connection between the Oxford Movement or Tractarians (*q.v.*) and Ritualism because Pusey disliked ritual and even Newman, who eventually went over to Rome, held simple services at his church of St. Mary's.

Roman Catholic Church, the Christian organisation which acknowledges the Pope as the lawful successor of St. Peter, the apostle appointed by Christ to be the head of His Church. The reforming impulse at the Second Vatican Council (1962-5), summoned by Pope John, set in train movements towards religious unity and the reform and modernisation of the Church. Pope Paul made changes in the government and liturgy of the Church but refused to allow birth control, the marriage of priests or a greater role for women.

A historic meeting took place in 1982 between Rome and Canterbury when Pope John Paul II made the first papal visit to Britain. The 1993 papal encyclical, *Veritatis Splendor*, forcefully restating the Catholic opposition to artificial birth control, has reopened Catholic divisions on this issue. The English text of the Catechism of the Catholic Church, the first complete survey of Roman Catholic teaching since the 16th century, was published in 1994. Pope John Paul's book, *Crossing the Threshold of Hope* was published the same year. In 1995 the Pope's encyclical *Evangelium Vitae* (Gospel of Life) repeated his attacks on abortion, euthanasia, suicide and *in vitro* fertilisation. (*See also* Papal Infallibility J38–9.) Increasingly, many liberal Roman Catholics are unhappy with the more conservative pronouncements of the Pope (such as the document *Ad Tuendam Fidem*, On the Defence of Faith) published in 1998. Some may leave the Church.

Some Anglicans (opposed to women priests) have moved to join the Catholic Church. The resignation in September 1996 of the Bishop of Argyll reinforced the growing debate on celibacy in the priesthood (the celibacy rule dates from 1139). There are currently (1999) over 1,050 million Catholics worldwide. In 1998 the Pope paid a historic visit to Cuba. Over the last decade, attendance at Sunday Mass in England has declined from 1·4 million to 1·1 million. Similarly, since the 1960s, Catholic baptisms in England have fallen by around 25 %.

Romantic Movement or **Romanticism** is the name given not so much to an individual way of thinking but to the gradual but radical transformation of basic human values that occurred in the Western world round about the latter part of the 18th cent. It was a great breakthrough in European consciousness and arose through the writings of certain men living during the half-century or more following, say, 1760. It arose then because both time and place were propitious for the birth of these new ideas. There was a revolution in basic values— in art, morals, politics, religion, *etc.* The new view was of a world transcending the old one, infinitely larger and more varied.

To understand the Romantic movement it is necessary first to take note of the climate of thought preceding the great change; then to account for its beginning in Germany where it did (*see* Pietism) during the latter part of the 18th cent., and finally to appraise the writings of those men whose ideas fermented the new awakening. Briefly, the shift was away from French classicism and from belief in the all-pervasive power of human reason (the Enlightenment) towards the unfettered freedom that the new consciousness was able to engender. What mattered was to live a passionate and vigorous life, to dedicate oneself to an ideal, no matter what the cost (*e.g.*, Byron).

The ideas of the Enlightenment (*e.g.*, Fontenelle, Voltaire, Montesquieu) had been attacked by the Germans Hamann and Herder and by the ideas of the English philosopher Hume, but Kant, Schiller, and Fichte, Goethe's novel *Wilhelm Meister*, and the French Revolution all had profound effects on the aesthetic, moral, social, and political thought of the time. Friedrich Schlegel (1772–1829) said: "There is in man a terrible unsatisfied desire to soar into infinity; a feverish longing to break through the narrow bonds of individuality." Romanticism undermined the notion that in matters of value there are objective criteria which operate between men. Henceforth there was to be a resurgence of the human spirit, deep and profound, that is still going on.

Rosicrucians, an ancient mystical society founded in the 16th cent. by Christian Rosenkreuz which attempted to forge a theoretical link between the great Egyptian religions and the Church of Rome, drawing rituals and philosophy from both camps. The Society did not long survive the death of its founder (he managed to reach the age of 106 incidentally) but has been revived in succeeding centuries by a series of rivalling factions. Perhaps the most famous of these is the Rosicrucian Order (A.M.O.R.C) which has become well-known in the Western world as a result of its heavy advertising in the popular press. Founded by the American H. Spencer Lewis, this offers a simple and good-natured doctrine preaching the Brotherhood of Man, the reincarnation of the soul and the immense latent potential of the human mind. As with many American-based organisations of this kind, the boundary between business and religion is hard to define. It is probably best summed up as a modern secret society which serves an important function in the lives of many people of mystical inclinations.

S

Sabbatarianism, the belief held by those Christians who regard the first day of the week as the Sabbath and wish to respect it as a holy day according to the 4th Commandment. Sabbatarianism became a principal characteristic of Presbyterianism (q.v.). Observance of the Sabbath has declined in recent years along with the general fall in church attendance and the advent of sporting, leisure and now shopping activities on the Sabbath.

Salvation Army. The religious movement which in 1878 became known by this name arose from the Christian Mission meetings which the Rev. William Booth and his devoted wife had held in the East End of London for the previous thirteen years. Its primary aim was, and still is, to preach the gospel of Jesus Christ to men and women untouched by ordinary religious efforts. The founder devoted his life to the salvation of the submerged classes whose conditions at that time were unspeakably dreadful. Originally his aim had been to convert people and then send them on to the churches, but he soon found that few religious bodies would accept these "low-class" men and women. So it was that social work became part of their effort. Practical help like the provision of soup-kitchens, accompanied spiritual ministration. Soon, in the interests of more effective "warfare" against social evils, a military form of organisation, with uniforms, brass bands, and religious songs, was introduced. Its magazine *The War Cry* gave as its aim "to carry the Blood of Christ and the Fire of the Holy Ghost into every part of the world.'

General Booth saw with blinding clarity that conversion must be accompanied by an improvement of external conditions. Various books had earlier described the terrible conditions of the slums, but he produced a monumental survey entitled *In Darkest England and the Way Out.* From that time forward the Army was accepted and its facilities made use of by the authorities. Today (1999) the Army's spiritual and social activities have spread to over 94 countries across the world; every one, no matter what class, colour, or creed he belongs to, is a "brother for whom Christ died." Within Britain there are now (1999) over 1,700 officers (*i.e.* ordained ministers). The Salvation Army is now considering far-reaching changes to its image and organisation as the new century arrives.

Scepticism. From the Greek, *skepsis,* enquiry or questioning. The philosophical attitude of doubting claims to knowledge. It springs from observations that the senses are unreliable, that the best methods often fall short of reaching the truth, and that experts often disagree. Sceptical attitudes emerge early in ancient Greek philosophy, but were only systemized into a school of thought by Pyrrhon Elis (*c.* 360–*c.* 272 B.C.). The Greek Sceptics proposed *epoche,* or suspension of belief, and aimed at *ataraxia,* tranquility of mind.

Scepticism is a recurring theme in Western philosophy, for example in Montaigne (1533–92) and Bayle (1647–1706). The most powerful sceptical thinker of the modern age is David Hume (1711–76). His arguments throw doubt upon induction, the notion of causality, the identity of the self and the existence of the external world.

The term is also associated with Descartes (1596–1650), though Descartes himself is not a sceptic. It refers to his "method of doubt", which attempted to put knowledge upon a sure foundation by suspending Judgement on any proposition whose truth could be doubted, until one can be found that is absolutely certain. This secure point is the famous "I think therefore I am".

Schoolmen. From the time of Augustine to the middle of the 9th cent. philosophy, like science, was dead or merely a repetition of what had gone before. But about that time there arose a new interest in the subject, although (since by then Western Europe was entirely under the authority of the Catholic Church) the main form it took was an attempt to justify Church teaching in the light of Greek philosophy. Those who made this attempt to reconcile Christian beliefs with the best in Plato and Aristotle were known as "schoolmen" and the philosophies which they developed were known as "scholasticism." Among the most famous schoolmen must be counted John Scotus Erigena (*c.* 800–*c.* 877), born in Ireland and probably the earliest; St. Anselm, archbishop of Canterbury (1033–1109); the great Peter Abelard whose school was in Paris (1079–1142); Bernard of Chartres, his contemporary; and the best-known of all, St. Thomas Aquinas of Naples (1225–74), who was given the name of the "Angelic Doctor."

The philosophies of these men are discussed under various headings (**God and Man, Determinism and Free-will**), but being severely limited by the Church their doctrines differed from each other much less than those of later philosophical schools. However, one of the great arguments was between the orthodox Realists (*q.v.*) and the Nominalists (*q.v.*) and a second was between the Thomists (or followers of St. Thomas Aquinas) and the Scotists (followers of John Duns Scotus—not to be confused with John Scotus Erigena). The two latter schools were known as the Ancients, whilst the followers of William of Occam, the Nominalist, were known as the Terminalists. All became reconciled in 1482 in face of the threat from humanism of which the great exponent was Erasmus of Rotterdam (1466–1536).

Scientology, an applied religious philosophy dealing with the study of knowledge, which through the application of its technology, claims to bring about desirable changes in the conditions of life. The word Scientology comes from the Latin word *Scio* (knowing in the fullest meaning of the word) and the Greek word *Logos* (study of). Developed and founded by author, philosopher and humanitarian L. Ron Hubbard (1911–86). Scientology purports to explain all of life's difficulties and contradictions in terms of occurrences in past lives. These mental blocks are removed so the individual can return to the deified state from which he came many incarnations ago. Until the late 1960s the worldwide headquarters was in East Grinstead, Sussex and this is now the UK headquarters. Scientology ® is a registered trademark.

Scientology has come in for criticism in recent years, particularly for its recruitment techniques. It has been attacked by one government minister as a "socially harmful pseudo-philosophical cult". Certainly Hubbard's eldest son, Ronald E. DeWolf changed his last name to remove any associations with his father.

Secularism. *See* **God and Man, J22** and **Rationalism, J44.**

Semiology, semiotics. These two words are now used almost interchangeably. The original sense of semiotics was the study of signs and sign-using behaviour, and was propounded by the American philosopher Peirce (1839–1914). Semiotics was divided into three branches: syntactics, the study of grammar; semantics, the study of meaning; and pragmatics, the study of the purposes and effects of meaningful utterances. Under the influence of the French linguist de Saussure (1857–1913) the term has broadened to the study of any means by which human beings communicate, not only through language, but also through gestures, clothes, objects, advertisements *etc.* Societies have a multiplicity of language-like "codes" by which objects like cars and buildings have cultural meanings over and above their functions.

Shakers, members of a revivalist group, styled by themselves "The United Society of Believers in Christ's Second Appearing," who seceded from Quakerism in 1747 though adhering to many of the Quaker tenets. The community was joined in 1758 by Ann Lee, a young convert from Manchester, who had "revelations" that she was the female Christ; "Mother Ann" was accepted as their leader. Under the influence of her prophetic visions she set out with nine followers for "Immanuel's land" in America and the community settled near Albany, capital of New York state. They were known as the "Shakers" in ridicule because they were given to involuntary movements in moments of religious ecstasy. Central to their faith was the belief in the dual role of God through the male and female Christ: the male principle came to earth in Jesus; the female principle, in "Mother Ann." The sexes were equal and women preached as often as men at their meetings which sometimes included sacred dances—nevertheless the two sexes, even in dancing, kept apart. Their communistic way of living brought them economic prosperity, the Shakers becoming known as good agriculturists and craftsmen, noted for their furniture and textiles. After 1860, however, the movement began to decline and few are active today. There is now (1999) only one U.S. Shaker colony (in Maine).

Shamans, the medicine men found in all primitive societies who used their magical arts to work cures, and protect the group from evil influences. The *shaman* was a man apart and wore special garments to show his authority.

Shiites or Shia, a heretical Moslem sect in Persia, opposed by the orthodox Sunnites. The dispute, which came almost immediately after the death of the Prophet and led to bitter feuding, had little to do with matters of doctrine as such but with the succession. After Mohammed's death, there were three possible claimants: Ali, the husband of his daughter Fatima, and two others, one of whom gave up his claim in favour of the other, Abu Bakr. The orthodox selected Abu Bakr, who was shortly assassinated, and the same happened to his successor as Ali was passed over again. The Shiites maintain that Ali was the true vicar of the Prophet, and that the three orthodox predecessors were usurpers.

Shintoism, literally means "teaching of the Gods". It is a native Japanese religion, with a strong bias towards ancestor worship and the divine powers of natural forces. Unusual in that it had no recognised founder nor written dogma, Shintoism permeated Japanese life in a most vigorous way until the defeat of the country at the hands of the Allied Powers in 1945. In the 1500 years of its existence the Shinto religion produced tens of thousands of unique and beautiful shrines throughout Japan. Vast numbers of these were destroyed by bombing in the war. Shintoism was disestablished by the American occupying forces in 1945 and the Emperor Hirohito "abdicated" his divine powers. Dissatisfaction among many Japanese has led to a recent revival of interest in Shintoism.

Sikhism. The Sikh community of the Punjab, which has played a significant part in the history of modern India, came into being during a period of religious revival in India in the 15th and 16th cent. It was originally founded as a religious sect by Guru (teacher) Nanak (1469–1538) who emphasised the fundamental truth of all religions, and whose mission was to put an end to religious conflict. He condemned the formalism both of Hinduism and Islam, preaching the gospel of universal toleration, and the unity of the Godhead, whether He be called Allah, Vishnu, or God. His ideas were welcomed by the great Mogul Emperor Akbar (1542–1605). Thus a succession of Gurus were able to live in peace after Nanak's death; they established the great Sikh centre at Amritsar, compiled the sacred writings known as the *Adi Granth,* and improved their organisation as a sect. But the peace did not last long, for an emperor arose who was a fanatical Moslem, in face of whom the last Guru, Govind Singh (1666–1708), whose father was put to death for refusal to embrace Islam, had to make himself a warrior and instil into the Sikhs a more aggressive spirit. A number of ceremonies were instituted by Govind Singh; admission to the fraternity was by special rite; caste distinctions were abolished; hair was worn long; the word singh, meaning lion, was added to the original name. They were able to organise themselves into 12 *misls* or confederacies but divisions appeared with the disappearance of a common enemy and it was not until the rise of Ranjit Singh (1780–1839) that a single powerful Sikh kingdom was established, its influence only being checked by the English, with whom a treaty of friendship was made. After the death of Ranjit Singh two Anglo-Sikh wars followed, in 1845–46, and 1848–49, which resulted in British annexation of the Punjab and the end of Sikh independence. In the two world wars the Sikhs proved among the most loyal of Britain's Indian subjects. The partitioning of the continent of India in 1947 into two states, one predominantly Hindu and the other predominantly Moslem, presented a considerable problem in the Punjab, which was divided in such a way as to leave 2 million Sikhs in Pakistan, and a considerable number of Moslems in the Indian Punjab. Although numbering less than 3 per cent. of the population the Sikhs are a continuing factor in Indian political life. Demands for Sikh independence led to the storming by Indian troops of the Golden Temple at Amritsar on 6 June 1984. In October 1984, Mrs. Gandhi was assassinated by Sikh extremists. There are over 600,000 Sikhs in Britain (1999). There are *c.* 20m. Sikhs worldwide.

Socialism, is a form of society in which men and women are not divided into opposing economic classes but live together under conditions of approximate social and economic equality, using in common the means that lie to their hands of promoting social welfare. The brotherhood of man inspires the aims of socialism in foreign, colonial, social, and economic policies alike. The word "socialism" first came into general use in England about 1834 in connection with Robert Owen's "village of cooperation" at New Lanark. About the middle of the 19th cent., Charles Kingsley and others established a form of Christian socialism, and William Morris, John Burns, and others founded a Socialist League in 1886. With the development of trade unions the socialist movement took a more practical trend. Fabianism (*q.v.*) associated in its early days with the names of Beatrice and Sidney Webb and George Bernard Shaw, aimed at the gradual reorganisation of society by creating intelligent public opinion by education and legislation. The British Labour Party believed in peaceful and constitutional change to socialism by democratic methods based upon popular consent. The Labour Government of 1945–51 initiated a major period of social reform and public ownership.

Though beset by economic difficulties, the 1964–70 Labour Government continued a policy of radical reform. The minority Labour Government (of February–October 1974) and the subsequent administration continued this process, particularly in the area of state intervention in industry. The election defeats of 1979, 1983 and 1987 inevitably led to a questioning of the future direction the party should take and, under the leadership of Neil Kinnock, the party became (in effect) a modernised social democratic party. It fought the 1992 election on this platform but went down to its fourth consecutive defeat. Under John Smith (until his untimely death in 1994) and subsequently under Tony Blair, the party has continued its modernisation policy. The Labour Party's 1997 election manifesto effectively buried its commitment to socialism. Some socialists, unhappy with these changes, formed the Socialist Labour Party in May 1996. Its leading figure was Arthur Scargill. The outcome of the May 1997 election vindicated the Blairite approach as the party captured 418 seats, a greater tally than ever before.

Soka Gakkai, Japan's largest religious organisation with 10 million followers world-wide. Founded in 1930 as the lay arm of a venerable Buddhist sect, its enormous wealth and political influence have aroused much opposition.

Solipsism. The theory that nothing really exists but oneself and one's mental states. No philosopher has deliberately held this view, but it is often seen to follow from certain views, for example, the belief that all one can know is oneself and one's immediate knowledge. It is philosophically interesting in that though the theory is intrinsically absurd, it is difficult to refute. Ludwig Wittgenstein (1889–1951) argued that the fact that we have a language (in which to express this solipsism) depends on the existence of a mind-independent external world.

Spiritualism is a religion which requires to be distinguished from psychical research (q.v.) which is a scientific attempt carried on by both believers and non-believers to investigate psychic phenomena including those not necessarily connected with "spirits"—e.g., telepathy or clairvoyance and precognition. As a religion (although for that matter the whole of history is filled with attempts to get in touch with the "spirit world") Spiritualism begins with the American Andrew Jackson Davis who in 1847 published *Nature's Divine Revelations*, a book which is still widely read. In this Davis states that on the death of the physical body, the human spirit remains alive and moves on to one or another of a considerable range of worlds or "spheres" where it commences yet another stage of existence. Since the spirit has not died, but exists with full (and possibly even expanded) consciousness, there should be no reason, Davis argues, why it should not make its presence known to the beings it has temporarily left behind on earth. In 1847, the year of the publication of Davis's book, two young girls, Margaret and Kate Fox, living in a farmhouse at Hydesville, New York, began apparently to act as unwitting mediums for attempts at such between-worlds communication. The girls were the focus for strange rappings and bangs which it was alleged defied normal explanation and which spelt out, in the form of a simple alphabetical code, messages from the spirits of "the dead." The Fox sisters were later to confess that they had produced the raps by trickery, but by that time the fashion had spread across the world and before long "mediums" in all lands were issuing spirit communications (often in much more spectacular form).

In the late 19th cent. Spiritualism went into a phase of great expansion and for various reasons attracted the attention of many scientists. Among these were Sir William Crookes, Sir Oliver Lodge, Professor Charles Richet, Alfred Russell Wallace, to say nothing of the brilliant and shrewd creator of Sherlock Holmes, Sir Arthur Conan Doyle. Today many people find it astonishing that people of such brilliance should find the phenomena of the seance room of more than passing interest, but the commitment of the Victorian scientists is understandable if we realise that Spiritualists, after all, claim to do no more than demonstrate as fact what all Christians are called on to believe—that the human personality survives bodily death. Furthermore, at the time of the late 19th cent. peak of Spiritualism, much less was known about human psychology and about the great limitations of sensory perception in typical seance conditions, when lights are dimmed or extinguished and an emotionally charged atmosphere generated. Today the most striking phenomena of the seance room—the alleged materialisation of spirit people and the production of such half-spiritual, halfphysical substances as ectoplasm—are rarely if ever produced at Spiritualist meetings. Some say that the most probable explanation for this is that too many fraudulent mediums have been caught out and publicly exposed for the profession to be worth the risks. The movement today, which still has a large and often articulate following, now concentrates on the less controversial areas of "mental mediumship," clairvoyance and the like, or on the very widespread practice of "spirit healing." Where people are not deliberately deluded by bogus mediums acting for monetary reward (a practice which largely died out with the "death" of ectoplasm) Spiritualism probably has an important role to play in the life of many people whose happiness has been removed by the death of a much loved relative or spouse. It does not deserve the violent attacks that are often made on it by orthodox clergy who allege that Spiritualists are communicating not with the souls of the departed but with the devil or his emissaries. *See also* **Greater World Spiritualists.**

Stalinism. The methods and policies associated with Joseph Stalin (1879–1953), leader of the USSR from 1929 until his death. This form of despotism consisted of the concentration of power in his own hands, and the ruthless suppression of dissent in any form, plus a "cult of personality", which used every means of propaganda to present Stalin as a wise and benevolent ruler.

State and Man. Most of the early civilisations such as those of Egypt and Babylonia were theocratic, that is to say, they were arranged in a hierarchy with, at the peak, a king who was also an incarnation of the god. Needless to say, in such circumstances there was no room for philosophising about the nature of the state and the relationship which ought to exist between state and citizens. As usual, we have to turn to ancient Greece for the beginnings of thought about this problem. We do so as briefly as possible since in general it is only the later philosophers whose work has much contemporary interest and, in any case, most people today realise that the political philosophy of a particular time is bound to reflect the actual conditions prevailing then and as such is of mainly theoretical interest today.

The Greek Approach. The early pre-Socratic philosophers Democritus and the Pythagorean school for example, held that the individual should subordinate himself to the whole; they had no doubt that the citizen's first duty was to the state. The Greeks until the time of Plato were not really thinking in terms of individual rights, nor had they given much thought to what form the state should take—they simply accepted it. The first great attempt to describe the ideal state is to be found in Plato's *The Republic* which is referred to elsewhere (*see* **Education**). His pupil Aristotle did not try to form a utopia but made many comments on the nature of government. Thus, while agreeing that the state was more important than any individual person, he distinguished between good and bad states, and pointed out that to the extent that the state does not enable its citizens to lead virtuous and useful lives it is evil. A good constitution must recognise the inequalities between human beings and confer on them rights according to their abilities: among these inequalities are those of personal ability, property, birth, and status, as freeman or slave. The best forms of rule were monarchy, aristocracy, and democracy; the worst forms—tyranny, oligarchy (or rule of a powerful few), and ochlocracy (or mob-rule). The later Greek thinkers of Hellenistic times held two opposed points of view. The Epicureans (q.v.) taught that all social life is based upon self-interest and we become members of a group for our own convenience; therefore there are no absolute rights and laws—what is good is what members decide at that time to be good, and when they change their minds the law must change too. Injustice is not an evil in any god-given sense; we behave justly simply because if injustice became the general rule, we ourselves should suffer. The Stoics (q.v.), on the other hand, held that the state must dominate the individual completely and everyone must carry out, first and foremost, his social duties and be willing to sacrifice everything for it; but the state of the Stoics was no narrowly national one, but one that strove to become a universal brotherhood.

The Christian Approach. The orthodox Christian view is expressed in St. Augustine's book *The City of God.* Here it is held that the church, as the worldly incarnation of the City of God, is to be supreme over the state, and the head of the church is to be supreme over secular rulers. In addition it must be recognised that, whilst the secular ruler can make mistakes, the church does not, since it is the representative of God's kingdom on earth.

The Secular State. During the Renaissance (q.v.) people began to think for themselves and the results of their cogitations were not always pleasant; for it was during this time that many rulers, petty and otherwise, were seeking absolute authority. Two notable thinkers at this stage were Niccolo Machiavelli (1469–1527) in Italy and Thomas Hobbes (1588–1679) in England, where, of course, the Renaissance arrived later in history. Both supported absolute monarchy against the former domination of the church. The name of Machiavelli has become a by-word for any behaviour that is cunning and unscrupulous, but he was not really as bad as he is usually painted. It is, indeed, true that in his book *The Prince* he showed in the greatest detail the methods by which a ruler could gain absolute control and destroy civic freedom, but this despotism was intended as merely a necessary intermediate stage towards his real idea which was a free, united Italian nation wholly independent of the church. Hobbes was a materialist whose thesis was that man is naturally a ferocious animal whose basic impulse is war and pillage and the destruction of whatever stands in his way to gain his desires. But if he allowed himself to behave in this way his life would be "nasty, brutish, and short" so he creates a society in which he voluntarily gives up many of his rights and hands them over to a powerful ruler in his own interest. But having done this he must obey; even when the ruler is unjust, as he has no right to complain because anything is better than a return to his natural state. The religion of the king must be the religion of the people and the only things no ruler has the right to do is to cause a man to commit suicide or murder or to make him confess to a crime.

Views of Locke: Live and Let Live. John Locke (1632–1704) disagreed with these views. Man is naturally peaceful and co-operative and therefore social life comes readily to him. He sets up an authority in order to preserve the group and that is why laws are made; but the function of the state is strictly limited to maintaining the public good and beyond this men are to be left free. Therefore absolute power and the doctrine of the Divine Right of Kings were wrong because power ultimately rests with the people who have the right to make and break governments. It is also wrong that those who make the laws should be able to execute them. This is the important British doctrine of the separation of powers between the legislature and the executive which is regarded as one of the bases of democracy.

Rousseau's Social Doctrine. The only other views we need consider here are those of Jean-Jacques Rousseau (1712–78) and Herbert Spencer (1820–1903), since the views of the two important intervening figures, Hegel and Karl Marx, are dealt with elsewhere (*see* Dialectical **Materialism**) and after Spencer we come to a stage where political philosophy begins to merge with sociology and the social sciences. Rousseau is a puzzling figure. On the one hand he has been hailed as the prophet of freedom and on the other as the father of modern totalitarianism. His book *Social Contract* (1762) begins with the words: "Man is born free, and everywhere he is in chains." He says that he is in favour, not merely of democracy, but of direct democracy in which everyone has to give his assent to all measures as in the Greek city-states and in Geneva, of which city he was a citizen. (This method is still in force in respect of some measures in the Swiss cantons.) Natural society is based on a "social contract" or mutual agreement and Rousseau speaks of a "return to nature" which would ensure the sovereignty of the people at all times. Thus far, he seems to agree with Locke but soon we find that he is more akin to Hobbes, since (as we are learning in our own day) nothing is more tyrannical than the absolute rule of all the people. (Public opinion is more Hitlerian than Hitler.) As it turns out, then, the "social contract" consists in "the total alienation of each associate, together with all his rights, to the whole community" and "each of us puts his person and all his power in common under the supreme direction of the general will." Rousseau admired direct democracy in the small city-state, but if his doctrine is applied to large states, then the "general will" becomes absolute. It is in this sense that he is regarded as the forerunner of totalitarianism. Herbert Spencer is quoted only as an example of how the inappropriate application of a biological theory to social issues. Influenced by Darwin's thesis of natural selection, he saw in society a struggle

in which the fittest survived and the less fit perished. Each individual had the right to preserve himself, but in the case of human beings this depended upon group life in which, to some extent, each individual is limited by the rights of others. But this should not go too far, and he condemned the socialism of J. S. Mill which (a) would give over-much protection to the unfit, and (b) would give the state powers which it has no right to since the best government is the least government. In accordance with Darwinism free competition was essential.

Stoics, the followers of Zeno, a Greek philosopher in the 4th cent. B.C., who received their name from the fact that they were taught in the Stoa Poikile or Painted Porch of Athens. They believed that since the world is the creation of divine wisdom and is governed by divine law, it is man's duty to accept his fate. Zeno conceived virtue to be the highest good and condemned the passions. (*See* **God and Man, State and Ma⸱⸱, Determinism and Free-will** for a more detailed account of their beliefs.)

Structuralism. 1. *Psychology.* The name of a school of thought whose influence has not lasted. It sought to investigate the structure of consciousness through the analysis, by introspection, of simple forms of sensation, thought, images, *etc.* and then find out how these components fitted together in complex forms. The school, which is mainly identified with Edward Titchener (1867–1927), discounted the value of analysing the significance of mental experience, and of examining the functions of the mind.

2. *Linguistics.* The theory that language is best described in terms of its irreducible structural units in morphology (the study of word structure) and phonology (the study of sound systems).

3. *Social sciences.* Theories or methods of analysis characterised by a preoccupation, not simply with structures, but with such structures as can be held to underlie and generate the phenomena under observation. To use a distinction of the linguist Noam Chomsky (b. 1928), the concern is with deep structures rather than surface structures. The main influences on the movement have been the theories of the French anthropologist Claude Levi-Strauss (b. 1908). According to him, universal patterns of cultural and social systems are products of the invariant "deep" structure of the human mind. He believed that structural similarities underlie all cultures and that an analysis of the relationships between cultures could provide insight into innate and universal principles of human thought.

Structural analysis has also been applied to literary theory, notably by the French critic Roland Barthes (1915–80). *See* **Literary Theory, J29.**

Subjectivism. In moral philosophy, the belief that all moral attitudes are merely a matter of personal taste. According to this an assertion like "Abortion is wrong" does not express an objective truth but means that the speaker or, more broadly, his society, or people in general, disapprove of abortion.

Sufism. A mystical movement within Islam. It started as a reaction against the legalistic approach of early Islam, seeking to establish a more personal relationship with Allah, or God. The objective of Sufism is perfection of the individual and union with God. Sufi orders were first established in the 12th century and some are still thriving today. Sufism has been very important in the history of Islamic faith and had a great influence on Muslim literature, and created a genre of mystical love poetry.

Sunnites, the orthodox sect of Islam as contrasted with the Shiites or Shia (*q.v.*).

Surrealism. *See* **Section L.**

Swedenborgianism. The Church of the New Jerusalem, based on the writings of Emanuel Swedenborg (1688–1772), was founded by his followers eleven years after his death. The New Church is essentially a movement bearing the same relationship to Christianity as Christianity does to Judaism. Swedenborg's many works include the 12-volume *Arcana Caelestia* (*Heavenly Secrets*) (1749–56).

Symbolism. *See* **Section M.**

Synchronicity, an attempt by the psychologist, Carl Gustav Jung, to explain the apparently significant relationship between certain events in the physical universe which seem to have no obvious "causal" link. This rather involved concept is easily understood if one realises that almost all scientific and philosophical beliefs are based on the notion that the continuous process of change which is taking place in ourselves and in the universe around us is dependent upon a principle known as causality. We can express this another way by saying that an object moves because it has been pushed or pulled by another. We see because light strikes the retina and signals pass up the nervous system to the brain. A stone falls to the ground because the earth's gravity is pulling it towards its centre, etc., etc. For all practical purposes every event can be looked upon as being " caused" by some other prior event and this is obviously one of the most important principles of the operation of the universe. Jung, however, felt that there is a sufficiently large body of evidence to suggest that events may be linked in a significant (i.e., non-chance) way without there being any true causal relationship between them. The classic example he held to be the supposed predictive power of astrology by which there appears to be a relationship between the stellar configurations and the personality and life-pattern of individuals on earth. Jung was scientist enough to realise that there could be no causal connection between the aspect of the stars and the lives of people billions of miles from them, yet felt the evidence for astrology was strong enough to demand an alternative non-causal explanation. The trouble with synchronicity, which has not made much impact on the world of physics or of psychology, is that it is not really an explanation at all but merely a convenient word to describe some puzzling correspondences. The real question, of course, is whether there really are events occurring which are significantly but not causally linked, and most scientists today would hold that there were probably not. Still it was typical of the bold and imaginative mind of Jung to tackle head-on one of the principal mysteries of existence and come up with a hypothesis to attempt to meet it.

Syndicalism, a form of socialist doctrine which aims at the ownership and control of all industries by the workers, contrasted with the more conventional type of socialism which advocates ownership and control by the state. Since syndicalists have preferred to improve the conditions of the workers by direct action, e.g., strikes and working to rule, rather than through the usual parliamentary procedures, they have been closely related to anarchists (q.v.) and are sometimes described as anarcho-syndicalists. Under syndicalism there would be no state; for the state would be replaced by a federation of units based on functional economic organisation rather than on geographical representation. The movement had bodies in the United Kingdom, where guild socialism (q.v.) was strongly influenced by its doctrines, in France, Germany, Italy, Spain, Argentina, and Mexico, but these gradually declined after the first world war. Fascism (q.v.) was also strongly influenced by the revolutionary syndicalism of Georges Sorel.

T

Tantra. 1. *Tantric Buddhism.* Tantra refers to a series of ritual texts said to have been originally transmitted by the Buddha himself. The tantras speak of the evocation of various gods, the pursuit of magical powers, the use of chants, and the attainment of enlightenment through meditation and yoga. Tantric theory and practice is a development within the Mahayana Buddhist tradition. It died out in India but was taken to Tibet. The most famous tantra is the *Tibetan Book of the Dead.*

2. *Tantric Hinduism.* Within Hinduism tantra refers to a group of Sanskrit texts not part of the orthodox Veda (see **Hinduism**). These are concerned with acquiring spiritual power and liberation in life, through practices aiming at purifying the body and controlling one's mental processes. Tantric cults have fallen into disrepute, due to the use of erotic metaphors and, it is alleged, erotic practices.

Taoism, a religion which, although in a degenerate state, is still one of the great Eastern creeds. Its alleged founder, Lao-tze, is said to have been born in Honan about 604 B.C.; he is also said to be the author of the bible of Taoism, the *Tao-te-ching,* or in English *The Way of Life,* and to have disapproved of Confucius. This, if true, would hardly be surprising; for Taoism is eminently a mystical religion recommending doing nothing and resisting nothing, whereas **Confucianism** (q.v.) is eminently a practical code of living and its founder insisted on intervening in everything to do with social life. But the truth as revealed by modern scholarship is rather different. We are told that the poems of the *Tao-te-ching* are anonymous and probably originated among recluses in lonely valleys long before the time of Confucius; they were collected and given form at some time late in the 3rd cent. B.C. and their authorship attributed to Lao-tze. It is entirely possible that no such peson ever existed (unlike Confucius, who certainly did), but if there were such a man he appears to have used a pseudonym since "Lao" is not a surname but an adjective meaning "old" and it was customary to attribute important works to old men on account of their supposed wisdom. Lao-tze simply means "the old philosopher", and although the *Tao-te-ching* is one of the most remarkable and instructive books ever written it is as anonymous as the Border Ballads.

It is apparent that the religion learned both from the ancient Chinese mystics and from Brahmanism: *Tao,* the Way, is impalpable, invisible, and incapable of being expressed in words. But it can be attained by virtue, by compassion, humility, and non-violence. Out of weakness comes true strength whereas violence is not only wrong but defeats its own ends. There is no personal God and such gods as men imagine are mere emanations of *Tao* which gives life to all things. *Tao* is Being. Works are worthless and internal renunciation is far better than anything that follows from the use of force because passive resistance convinces the other from within that he is in error, whereas violence only compels the external appearance of conviction whilst inwardly the individual is as before. "It is wealth to be content; it is wilful to force one's way on others."

Later Lao-tze became a divinity and indeed one of a Trinity each worshipped in the form of idols (which the founder had hated). Soon there was worship of the forces of nature: the stars, the tides, the sun and moon, and a thousand other deities among whom Confucius was one. The purest mysticism and wisdom had been utterly corrupted by contact with the world.

Telepathy and Clairvoyance. Telepathy is the alleged communication between one mind and another other than through the ordinary sense channels. Clairvoyance is the supposed faculty of "seeing" objects or events which, by reason of space and time or other causes, are not discernible through the ordinary sense of vision. Such claims have been made from time immemorial but it was not until this century that the phenomena were investigated scientifically. The first studies were undertaken by the Society for Psychical Research, which was founded in 1882 with Professor Henry Sidgwick as its first president. Since then it has carried out a scholarly programme of research without —in accordance with its constitution—coming to any corporate conclusions. In America the centre of this research was the Parapsychology Laboratory at Duke University (see **Parapsychology**) where at one time it was claimed clear scientific evidence for extra-sensory perception (ESP) had been obtained. These claims have been treated with great reservation by the majority of scientists but despite the belief that the study of ESP was going into eclipse, there remains a small but measurable residue of interest in scientific research in this area. It would be odd if some scientists were not interested in ESP because of the enormous weight of anecdotal evidence which has built up over centuries to support it. The weakness of the scientific as opposed to the casual evidence is however exemplified by the failure of ESP researchers to produce a reliable "repeatable" experiment.

Terrorism. A form of political violence used against governments, groups or individuals with the purpose of creating a climate of fear in which the aims of the terrorists may be fulfilled. The term derives from the "Reign of Terror" in the French Revolution. In the 20th century it is most closely associated with the violence of small political movements of both the extreme left and right, attempting to overthrow existing political institutions. It has been used as part of nationalist movements seeking to remove colonial governments, as in the expulsion of Britain from Palestine and France from Algeria. There is also what is known as "*state terrorism*", as practised by totalitarian regimes such as Hitler's Germany and Stalin's Soviet Union. Today fears are growing of *bio-terrorism (e.g.* the possible use of deadly germ and bacterial warfare by a country such as Iraq).

Theism. *See* **God and Man.**

Theosophy (Sanskrit *Brahma Vidya* = divine wisdom), a system of thought that draws on the mystical teachings of those who assert the spiritual nature of the universe, and the divine nature of man. It insists that man is capable of intuitive insight into the nature of God. The way to wisdom, or self-knowledge, is through the practice of **Yoga** (*q.v.*). Theosophy has close connections with Indian thought through Vedic, Buddhist, and Brahmanist literature. The modern Theosophical Society was founded by Mme H. P. Blavatsky and others in 1875, and popularised by Mrs. Annie Besant.

Totalitarianism. Totalitarian government is one which tolerates only one political party, to which all other institutions are subordinated, and which usually demands the complete subservience of the individual to the government. The Italian dictator Mussolini coined the term in the 1920s to describe the new fascist state of Italy, and the word has become synonymous with absolute and oppressive single-party government, as in Nazi Germany or Soviet Russia. *See also* **Stalinism.**

Totemism. A totem is an animal, plant or object with which a social or religious group feels a special affinity and which is often considered to be the mythical ancestor of the group. The totem is worshipped or esteemed by members of the group or clan bearing its name. Totemism is the form of social organization consisting of such clans. Membership of the clan is inherited and lifelong; but marriage is usually with a partner outside the totemic clan. Totem poles (as erected by North American Indians) are a way of representing the clan's guardian spirit. Totemism has been important in the religion and society of many primitive peoples.

Tractarianism, a Catholic revival movement, also known as the **Oxford Movement** (not to be confused with the so-called Oxford Group), which had its beginnings at Oxford in 1833. The leaders included the Oxford high churchmen E. B. Pusey, J. Keble and J. H. Newman. Through the *Tracts for the Times* (1833–41), a series of pamphlets which were sent to every parsonage in England, they sought to expose the dangers which they considered to be threatening the church from secular authority. The immediate cause of the movement was the Reform Act (1832) which meant that the state was no longer in the safe keeping of Tories and Churchmen but that power was falling into the hands of Liberals and Dissenters. They advocated a higher degree of ceremonial in worship nearer the Roman communion. In *Tract 90* (the last) Newman showed how the Thirty-nine Articles themselves, which were regarded as the bulwark of Protestantism, could be made to square with Roman doctrine. It was obvious which direction the movement was taking and the romanizing tendency was widely resented. In 1845 Newman went over to Rome. Pusey and Keble persisted in their efforts to secure recognition of Catholic liturgy and doctrine in the Anglican Church. Catholicism of the Anglican type (*i.e.,* Catholic in ritual, ceremony, and everything save submission to the Pope) is termed Anglo-Catholicism (*q.v.*).

Transcendental Meditation, popularised in the West by the Maharishi Mahesh Yogi, who achieved sensational worldwide publicity by his "conversion" of the Beatles. This is a simple meditational system which it is claimed is an aid to relaxation and the reduction of psychological and physical stress. It is a technique which can be taught in a relatively short, concentrated period of time, provided that someone trained by the Maharishi is the teacher. The pupil or would-be meditator is given a *mantra*—letting his thoughts flow freely while sitting in a comfortable position. Very many claims are made on behalf of the system. As with most cults, religious and occult systems, there is an initial psychological benefit to anyone who becomes deeply involved. Nevertheless, apart from this simple "participation-effect", there is some evidence that the body's autonomic functions (heart rate, respiratory cycle, brain waves, *etc.*) can be modified by certain individuals including yogis. The TM movement in Britain is based at Mentmore Towers in Buckinghamshire. The movement recruits heavily on campuses in America, but has been the subject of many complaints by parents.

Transcendentalism. 1. A term used to refer to the transcendental idealism of Immanuel Kant (1724–1804). *See* **Mind and Matter.**

2. A movement established in the United States in the 1830s, much influenced by German idealism and Platonism, which included Ralph Waldo Emerson (1803–82) and Henry Thoreau (1817–62) among its members. Transcendentalism's characteristic belief was in the supremacy of insight over logic and experience for the revelation of the deepest truths. It tended towards mysticism, pantheism and optimism about the progress of the spirit. Although the movement's followers believed that true reform must come from within the individual, they took part in contemporary reform movements.

Transcendentalism itself faded with the coming of the American Civil War, but it had a strong influence on the writings of Whitman, Emily Dickinson and Hawthorne.

Transmigration of Souls. *See* **Immortality, Buddhism, Hinduism.**

Transubstantiation, the conversion in the Eucharist of the bread and wine into the body and blood of Christ—a doctrine of the Roman Catholic Church.

Trotskyism, a form of communism supporting the views of Leon Trotsky, the assumed name of Lev Bronstein (1879–1940) who, in 1924, was ousted from power by Stalin and later exiled and assassinated in Mexico. Trotsky held that excessive Russian nationalism was incompatible with genuine international communism and that Stalin was concentrating on the economic development of the Soviet Union to an extent which could only lead to a bureaucratic state with a purely nationalist outlook. After the Hungarian uprising in 1956, which was ruthlessly suppressed by the Soviet Armed Forces, a wave of resignations from Western Communist parties took place, many of the dissidents joining the Trotskyist movement.

U

Ufology, cultish interest in the study of strange and unexplained aerial phenomena (unidentified flying objects, hence UFOs). *See* **Flying Saucers.**

Uniates, the Eastern Orthodox Churches which are in full communion with the Roman Catholic Church, recognise the authority of the Pope and in faith and doctrine are totally Catholic. However, they retain their traditional liturgies and separate canon law and permit their priests to marry.

Unification Church, controversial religious group founded by Sun Myung Moon in Korea in 1954. Better known as the 'Moonies'. Its founder believes he is the Messiah completing the mission of Jesus Christ cut short by the crucifixion. Teachings are represented in the Divine Principle, Moon's own interpretation of the Bible. Worldwide the Moonies may have *c.* 500,000 members.

Unitarianism has no special doctrines, although clearly, as the name indicates, belief is in the single personality of God, *i.e.,* anti-trinitarian. This general statement, however, can be interpreted with varying degrees of subtlety. Thus unitarian belief may range from a sort of Arianism which accepts that, although Christ was not of divine nature, divine powers had been delegated to him by the Father, to the simple belief that Christ was a man like anyone else, and his goodness was of the same nature as that of many other great and good men. Indeed, today many Unitarians deny belief in a personal God and interpret their religion in purely moral terms, putting their faith in the value of love and the brotherhood of man. The Toleration Act (1689) excluded Unitarians but from 1813 they were legally tolerated in England. Nevertheless attempts were made to turn them out of their chapels on the ground that the preachers did not hold the views of the original founders of the endowments. But this ended with the Dissenting Chapels Act of 1845. In America no such difficulties existed, and in the Boston of the 19th cent. many of the great literary figures were openly unitarian in both belief and name: e.g., Emerson, Longfellow, Lowell, and Oliver Wendell Holmes.

United Reform Church. See **Presbyterianism (J41).**

Utilitarianism, a school of moral philosophy of which the main proponents were J. S. Mill (1806–73) and Jeremy Bentham (1748–1832). Bentham based his ethical theory upon the utilitarian principle that the greatest happiness of the greatest number is the criterion of morality. What is good is pleasure or happiness; what is bad is pain. If we act on this basis of self-interest (pursuing what we believe to be our own happiness), then what we do will automatically be for the general good. The serious failing of this thesis is (1) that it makes no distinction between the quality of one pleasure and another, and (2) that Bentham failed to see that the law might not be framed and administered by men as benevolent as himself. J. S. Mill accepted Bentham's position in general but seeing its failings emphasised (1) that self-interest was an inadequate basis for utilitarianism and suggested that we should take as the real criterion of good the social consequences of the act; (2) that some pleasures rank higher than others and held that those of the intellect are superior to those of the senses. Not only is the social factor emphasised, but emphasis is also placed on the nature of the act.

Utopias. The name "utopia" is taken from a Greek word meaning "nowhere" and was first used in 1516 by Sir Thomas More (1478–1535) as the title of his book referring to a mythical island in the south Pacific where he sited his ideal society. Since then it has been used of any ideal or fanciful society, and here a few will be mentioned. (The reader may recall that Samuel Butler's 19th cent. novel, describing an imaginary society in New Zealand where criminals were treated and the sick punished, was entitled *Erewhon* which is the word "nowhere" in reverse.) Not all utopias were entirely fanciful—e.g., Robert Owen's and François Fourier's beliefs, although found to be impractical, were, in fact, tried out.

Sir Thomas More. More wrote at a time when the rise of the wool-growing trade had resulted in farming land being turned over to pasture and there was a great wave of unemployment and a rise in crime among the dispossessed. More began to think in terms of the mediaeval ideal of small co-operative communities in which class interests and personal gain played a decreasing part, a society which would have the welfare of the people at heart both from the physical and intellectual points of view. His utopia was one in which there was no private property, because the desire for acquisition and private possessions lay at the root of human misery. There was, therefore, only common ownership of land and resources. Each class of worker was equipped to carry out its proper function in the economic scheme and each was fairly rewarded for its share in production so that there was neither wealth nor poverty to inspire conflict. Nobody was allowed to idle, until the time came for him to retire when he became free to enjoy whatever cultural pleasures he wished, but since the system was devoid of the waste associated with competition, the working day would be only six hours. There was to be compulsory schooling and free medical care for everybody, full religious toleration, complete equality of the sexes, and a modern system of dealing with crime which was free from vindictiveness and cruelty. Government was to be simple and direct by democratically-elected officials whose powers would be strictly limited and the public expenditure kept under close scrutiny. It will be seen that More was far in advance of his age, and to most democratically-minded people in advance of an earlier utopia, Plato's *Republic*, which is described under the heading of Education.

James Harrington. James Harrington published his book *The Commonwealth of Oceana* in 1656 and offered it to Oliver Cromwell for his consideration but without tangible results. Better than any other man of his time Harrington understood the nature of the economic revolution which was then taking place, and, like More, saw the private ownership of land as the main cause of conflict. He put forward the theory that the control of property, particularly in the shape of land, determines the character of the political structure of the state; if property were universally distributed among the people the sentiment for its protection would naturally result in a republican form of government. The Commonwealth of Oceana was a society "of laws and not of men"—i.e., it was to be legally based and structured so as to be independent of the good or ill-will of any individuals controlling it. Thus there must be a written constitution, a two-house legislature, frequent elections with a secret ballot, and separation of powers between legislature and executive—all today familiar features of parliamentary democracy, but unique in his time.

Saint-Simon. The utopias of the late 18th and 19th cent. come, of course, into the period of the industrial revolution and of laissez-faire capitalism. Individual enterprise and complete freedom of competition formed the outlook of the ruling class. Naturally the utopias of this period tended to have a strongly socialist tinge since such theories are obviously produced by those who are not satisfied with existing conditions. Saint-Simon's *New Christianity* (1825) is one such, and by many, Claude Henri, Comte de Saint-Simon (1760–1825) is regarded as the founder of French socialism. His book urged a dedication of society to the principle of human brotherhood and a community which would be led by men of science motivated by wholly spiritual aims. Production property was to be nationalised (or "socialised" as he describes the process) and employed to serve the public good rather than private gain; the worker was to produce according to his capacity and to be rewarded on the basis of individual merit; the principle of inheritance was to be abolished since it denied the principle of reward for accomplishment on which the society was to be founded. Saint-Simon's proposals were not directed towards the poorer classes alone, but to the conscience and intellect of all. He was deeply impressed with the productive power of the new machines and his scheme was, first and foremost, intended as a method of directing that power to the betterment of humanity as a whole.

Fourier. François Marie Charles Fourier (1772–1837), although by conviction a philosophical anarchist who held that human beings are naturally good if allowed to follow their natural desires, was the originator of what, on the face of it, one would suppose to be the most regimented of the utopias. It consisted of a system of "phalanxes" or co-operative communities each composed of a group of workers and technicians assured of a minimum income and sharing the surplus on an equitable basis. Agriculture was to be the chief occupation of each phalanx and industrial employment planned and so carefully assigned that work would become pleasant and creative rather than burdensome. One of his ideas was that necessary work should receive the highest pay, useful work the next, and pleasant work the least pay. The land was to be scientifically cultivated and natural resources carefully conserved. Most of the members' property was to be privately owned, but the ownership of each phalanx was to be widely diffused among members by the sale of shares. Such "parasitic and unproductive" occupations as stockbroker, soldier, economist, middle-man and philosopher would be eliminated and the education of children carried out along vocational lines to train them for their future employment.

The strange thing was that Fourier's suggestions appealed to many in both Europe and the USA and such men (admittedly no economic or technical experts) as Emerson, Thoreau, James Russell Lowell, and Nathaniel Hawthorne strongly supported them. An American Fourier colony known as Brook Farm was established and carried on for eight years when it was dissolved after a serious fire had destroyed most of its property.

Robert Owen. Robert Owen (1771–1858), a wealthy textile manufacturer and philanthropist, established communities founded on a kind of utopian socialism in Lanarkshire, Hampshire, and in America. Of his New Lanark community an American observer wrote: "There is not, I apprehend, to be found in any part of the world, a manufacturing community in which so much order, good government, tranquillity, and rational happiness prevail." The workers in Lanark were given better housing and education for their children, and it was administered as a co-operative self-supporting community in Scotland. Later in life Owen returned to sponsoring legislation that would remove some of the worst evils of industrial life in those days: reduction of the working day to twelve hours, prohibition of labour for children under the age of ten, public schools for elementary education, and so on. But he lived to see few of his reforms adopted.

V

Vedanta. An old-established system of Indian thought. It is expressed in commentaries on the *Brahma Sutras.* A key figure is Shankara (788–820 A.D.) who founded what is known as Advaita Vedanta.

Vegans, *see under* **Vegetarianism.**

Vegetarianism, a way of life practised by those who abstain from meat. Strict vegetarians (Vegans) also exclude all animal products (*e.g.* butter, eggs milk) from their diet.

Vitalism, the philosophical doctrine that the behaviour of the living organism is, at least in part, due to a vital principle which cannot possibly be explained wholly in terms of physics and chemistry. This belief was held by the rationalist thinker C. E. M. Joad (1891–1953) and is implicit in Henri Bergson's (1859–1941) theory of creative evolution. It was maintained by Bergson that evolution, like the work of an artist, is creative and therefore unpredictable; that a vague need exists beforehand within the animal or plant before the means of satisfying the need develops. Thus we might assume that sightless animals developed the need to become aware of objects before they were in physical contact with them and that this ultimately led to the origins of organs of sight. Earlier this century a form of vitalism described as "emergent evolution" was put forward. This theory maintains that when two or more simple entities come together there may arise a new property which none of them previously possessed. Today biologists would say that it is the *arrangement* of atoms that counts, different arrangements exhibiting different properties, and that biological organisation is an essentially dynamic affair.

W

Wahabis, members of an Arabian sect of Islam which originated in the teaching of Muhammad Ibn "Abd-al-Wahab, born at the end of the 17th cent. He was deeply resentful of the Turkish rule which, in addition to its tyranny, had brought about innovations in the religion which Muhammad regarded as a perversion of its original form. He proceeded to reform Islam to its primitive conditions and impressed his beliefs on Mohammed Ibn Saud, a sheikh who spread them with the aid of his sword. Under the successors of Ibn Saud the power of the Wahabis spread over much of Arabia where it is dominant today in Saudi Arabia. Its particular characteristic is that it refuses to accept symbolic or mystical interpretations of the words of the Prophet and accepts quite literally the teaching of Islam. It is, in fact, a sort of Moslem fundamentalism. Although crushed by the Turks in 1811–15, the movement remains an important element in Mohammedanism.

Waldenses, a movement also known as "The Poor Men of Lyons," founded by Peter Waldo of that city about the same time, and in the same part of southern France, as the Albigenses (*q.v.*) with whom, however, they had nothing in common. Their main belief was a return to Apostolic simplicity, based on reading the Bible in their own language; their doctrines were somewhat similar to those of the Mennonites and the Quakers. However, they did not wish to separate themselves from the Church and were originally protected by several Popes until the Lateran Council of 1215 excluded them mainly for the crime of preaching without ecclesiastical permission. From this time they were subjected to persecution, yet maintained some contact with the Church until the Reformation when they chose to take the side of the Protestants. Situated mainly on the sides of the Alps, half in Piedmont and half in France, they were persecuted or not according to the contemporary political convenience of the Dukes of Savoy, and the major attempt to destroy them called forth Oliver Cromwell's intervention and the famous sonnet of Milton. In spite of torture, murder, deportation, and even the kidnapping of their children, to have them brought up in the Roman Catholic faith, the sect survived, and still exists, having been granted full equality of rights with his Catholic subjects by Charles Edward of Piedmont in 1848.

Weathermen. Far left group whose aim was to overthrow the American political system. The group's name was borrowed from the lyrics of songwriter Bob Dylan. Its membership was drawn from a well-educated social strata, and it has committed specific and well-planned acts of violence.

Witchcraft. There are various interpretations and definitions of witchcraft from that of Pennethorne Hughes who states that "witchcraft, as it emerges into European history and literature, represents the old paleolithic fertility cult, plus the magical idea, plus various parodies of contemporary religions" to that of the fanatical Father Montague Summers who says that Spiritualism and witchcraft are the same thing. A leading authority on witchcraft, however, the late Dr. Margaret Murray, distinguishes between Operative Witchcraft (which is really Magic (*q.v.*)) and Ritual Witchcraft which, she says, "embraces the religious beliefs and ritual of the people known in late mediaeval times as "witches." That there were such people we know from history and we know, too, that many of them—the great majority of them women—were tortured or executed or both. Many innocent people perished, especially after the promulgation of the bull *Summis desiderantes* by Pope Innocent VIII in 1484. In 1494 they codified in the *Malleus Maleficarum* (Hammer of Witches) the ecclesiastical rules for detecting acts of witchcraft. Dr. Murray points out that there have ordinarily been two theories about witchcraft: (1) that there were such things as witches, that they possessed supernatural powers and that the evidence given at their trials was substantially correct; (2) that the witches were simply poor silly creatures who either deluded themselves into believing that they had certain powers or, more frequently, were tortured into admitting things that they did not do. She herself accepts a third theory: that there were such beings as witches, that they really did what they admitted to doing, but that they did not possess supernatural powers. They were in fact believers in the old religion of pre-Christian times and the Church took centuries to root them out. That there existed "covens" of witches who carried out peculiar rites Dr.

Murray has no doubt whatever. The first to show that witchcraft was a superstition and that the majority of so-called witches were people suffering from mental illness was the physician Johann Weyer of Cleves (1515–88). His views were denounced by the Catholic Church. In the 1990s, the Catholic Church established a commission in the Czech Republic to review the notorious Sumperk witch trials of 1679 (when 100 people were burnt alive in Moravia). It is a sign of changing attitudes. Few people realise how deeply the notion of witchcraft is implanted in our minds. For example, the Witchcraft Act was not repealed in this country until the 1950s.

Women's Liberation Movement. *See* **Feminism (J20).**

World Congress of Faiths, an inter-religious movement which aims to break down barriers between faiths. The first step was taken by the world's parliament of religions held in Chicago in 1893; similar gatherings were held subsequently at intervals in Europe; but the actual organisation was formed in 1936 by Sir Francis Younghusband; and now an annual conference is held and educational activity carried on.

World Council of Churches, a union of Christian Churches from over 100 countries (including the Churches of the Protestant, Anglican, and Orthodox traditions, but excluding the Roman Catholic Church), engaged in extending Christian mission and unity throughout the world. This modern ecumenical movement stems from the great World Missionary Conference held at Edinburgh in 1910. The World Council was founded in 1948 and meets for consultation from time to time. The 8th Assembly met in Harare, Zimbabwe, in 1998 but was overshadowed by doubts over the future for the council. Back in 1981, the Salvation Army resigned in protest at the movement's involvement in African liberation.

World Federalism, the extension of the principle of federalism (already an established political system in such countries as Canada, Germany, Switzerland and the USA) to a world, international order, to prevent wars and to tackle *global* issues on a *global* basis. The Association of World Federalists campaigns for this objective.

Y

Yin and **Yang,** the two basic forces in ancient Chinese thought. Yang is associated with masculinity, heat, light, creation *etc.*, yin with femininity, coldness, dark, passivity *etc. See also* **Confucianism, Taoism.**

Yoga, a Hindu discipline which teaches a technique for freeing the mind from attachment to the senses, so that once freed the soul may become fused with the universal spirit (*atman* or Brahman), which is its natural goal. This is the sole function of the psychological and physical exercises which the Yogi undertakes, although few ever reach the final stage of *Samadhi* or union with Brahman which is said to take place in eight levels of attainment. These are: (1) *Yama*, which involves the extinction of desire and egotism and their replacement by charity and unselfishness; (2) *Niyama*, during which certain rules of conduct must be adopted, such as cleanliness, the pursuit of devotional studies, and the carrying out of rituals of purification; (3) *Asana*, or the attainment of correct posture and the reduction to a minimum of all bodily movement (the usual posture of the concentrating Yogi is the "lotus position" familiar from pictures); (4) *Pranayama*, the right control of the life-force or breath in which there are two stages at which the practitioner hopes to arrive, the first being complete absorption in the act of breathing which empties the mind of any other thought, the second being the ability almost to cease to breathe which allegedly enables him to achieve marvellous feats of endurance; (5) *Pratyahara* or abstraction which means the mind's complete withdrawal from the world of sense; (6) *Dharana* in which an attempt is made to think of one thing only which finally becomes a repetition of the sacred syllable OM; (7)

dhyana, meditation, which finally leads to (8) *Samadhi* the trance state which is a sign of the complete unity of soul with reality.

Yoga is very old, and when the sage Patanjali (*c.* 300 B.C.) composed the book containing these instructions, the *Yoga Sutras*, he was probably collecting from many ancient traditions. Some of the claims made by Yogis seem, to the Western mind, frankly incredible; but in the West Yoga methods have been used at the lower levels in order to gain improved self-control, better posture, and improved health.

Z

Zen Buddhism, a Buddhist sect which is believed to have arisen in 6th cent. China but has flourished chiefly in Japan; for some reason it has of recent years begun to attract attention in the West thanks to the voluminous writings of Dr. D. T. Suzuki and the less numerous but doubtless much-read books of Mr. Christmas Humphreys. But the fact that these writings exist does not explain their being read, nor why of all possible Eastern sects this particular one should be chosen in our times. What is Zen's attraction and why should anyone take the trouble to read about something (the word "something" is used for reasons that will become evident) that is not a religion, has no doctrine, knows no God and no after-life, no good and no evil, and possesses no scriptures but has to be taught by parables which seem to be purposely meaningless? One of the heroes of Zen is the fierce-looking Indian monk Boddhidharma (fl. *c.* 516–34) who brought Buddhism to China, of whom it is recounted that when the Emperor asked him how much merit he had acquired by supporting the new creed, the monk shouted at him: "None whatever!" The emperor then wished to know what was the sacred doctrine of the creed and again the monk shouted: "It is empty—there is nothing sacred!" Dr. Suzuki, having affirmed that there is no God in Zen, goes on to state that this does not mean that Zen denies the existence of God because "neither denial nor affirmation concerns Zen." The most concrete statement that he is prepared to make is that the basic idea of Zen is to come in touch with the inner workings of our being, and to do this in the most direct way possible without resorting to anything external or superadded. Therefore anything that has the semblance of an external authority is rejected by Zen. Absolute faith is placed in a man's own inner being. Apparently the intention is that, so far from indulging in inward meditations or such practices as the Yogi uses, the student must learn to act spontaneously, without thinking, and without self-consciousness or hesitation. This is the main purpose of the *koan*, the logically insoluble riddle which the pupil must try to solve. One such is the question put by master to pupil: "A girl is walking down the street, is she the younger or the older sister?" The correct answer, it seems, is to say nothing but put on a mincing gait, to *become* the girl, thus showing that what matters is the experience of being and not its verbal description. Another *koan*: "What is the Buddha?" "Three pounds of flax" is attributed to T'ungshan in the 9th cent. and a later authority's comment is that "none can excel it as regards its irrationality which cuts off all passages to speculation." Zen, in effect, teaches the uselessness of trying to use words to discuss the Absolute.

Zen came to Japan in the 13th cent., more than five centuries after Confucianism or the orthodox forms of Buddhism, and immediately gained acceptance whilst becoming typically Japanese in the process. One of the reasons why it appealed must have been that its spontaneity and insistence on action without thought, its emphasis on the uselessness of mere words, and such categories as logical opposites, had an inevitable attraction for a people given to seriousness, formality, and logic to a degree which was almost stifling. Zen must have been to the Japanese what nonsense rhymes and nonsense books, like those of Edward Lear and Lewis Carroll, were to the English intellectuals. Lear's limericks, like some of the *koans*, end up with a line which, just at the time when one expects a point to be made, has no particular point at all, and *Alice in Wonderland* is the perfect example of a world, not without logic, but with a crazy logic of its own which has no relationship with that of everyday life. Therefore Zen began to impregnate every aspect of life in Japan, and one of the results of its emphasis on spontaneous action rather than reason was its acceptance by the Samurai, the ferocious warrior class, in such activities as swordsmanship, archery, Japanese wrestling, and later Judo and the Kamikaze dive-bombers. But much of Japanese art, especially landscape gardening and flower-arrangement, was influenced similarly, and Zen is even used in Japanese psychiatry. The very strict life of the Zen monks is based largely on doing things, learning through experience: the periods of meditation in the Zendo hall are punctuated by sharp slaps on the face administered by the abbot to those who are unsatisfactory pupils. Dr. Suzuki denies that Zen is nihilistic, but it is probably its appearance of nihilism and its appeal to the irrational and spontaneous which attracts the Western world at a time when to many the world seems without meaning and life over-regimented. However, it has influenced such various aspects of Western life as philosophy (Heidegger), psychiatry (Erich Fromm and Hubert Benoit), writing (Aldous Huxley), and painting (Die Zen Gruppe in Germany).

Zionism, a belief in the need to establish an autonomous Jewish home in Palestine which, in its modern form, began with Theodor Herzl (1860–1904), a Hungarian journalist working in Vienna. Although Herzl was a more or less assimilated Jew, he was forced by the Dreyfus case and the pogroms in Eastern Europe to conclude that there was no real safety for the Jewish people until they had a state of their own. The Jews, of course, had always in a religious sense thought of Palestine as a spiritual homeland and prayed "next year in Jerusalem," but the religious had thought of this in a philosophical way as affirming old loyalties, not as recommending the formation of an actual state. Therefore Herzl was opposed both by many of the religious Jews and, at the other extreme, by those who felt themselves to be assimilated and in many cases without religious faith. Even after the Balfour Declaration of 1917, there was not a considerable flow of Jews to Palestine, which at that time was populated mainly by Arabs. But the persecutions of Hitler changed all this and, after bitter struggles, the Jewish state was proclaimed in 1948. Today Zionism is supported by the vast majority of the Jewish communities everywhere. After 1990, a major exodus of Jews from Russia to Israel (made possible by the demise of the Soviet Union) introduced a new phase in the history of Zionism.

Zoroastrianism, at one time one of the great world religions, competing in the 2nd cent. A.D. on almost equal terms from its Persian home with Hellenism and the Roman Imperial Government. Under the Achaemenidae (*c.* 550–330 B.C.) Zoroastrianism was the state religion of Persia. Alexander's conquest in 331 B.C. brought disruption but the religion flourished again under the Sassanian dynasty (A.D. *c.* 226–640). With the advance of the Mohammedan Arabs in the 7th cent. Zoroastrianism finally gave way to Islam. A number of devotees fled to India there to become the Parsees. In Iran itself a few scattered societies remain.

The name Zoroaster is the Greek rendering of Zarathustra, the prophet who came to purify the ancient religion of Persia. It is thought that he lived at the beginning of the 6th cent. B.C. He never claimed for himself divine powers but was given them by his followers. The basis of Zoroastrianism is the age-long war between good and evil, Ahura Mazda heading the good spirits and Ahriman the evil ones. Morality is very important since by doing right the worshipper is supporting Ahura Mazda against Ahriman, and the evil-doers will be punished in the last days when Ahura Mazda wins his inevitable victory.

The sacred book of this religion is the *Avesta.* If Zoroastrianism has little authority today, it had a very considerable influence in the past. Its doctrines penetrated into Judaism (*q.v.*) and, through Gnosticism, Christianity. The worship of Mithra by the Romans was an impure version of Zoroastrianism. Manichaeism (*q.v.*) was a Zoroastrian heresy and the Albigensianism of mediaeval times was the last relic of a belief which had impressed itself deeply in the minds of men.

SPECIAL TOPICS

CURRENT ETHICAL DEBATES

ABORTION

Introduction

Abortion is the ending of the life of a foetus after conception and before birth. Is this ever morally right? After 1967 there was a liberalization of abortion laws throughout Europe, but opponents have not given up the argument, making abortion a bitter ethical issue. The Roman Catholic church in particular is strongly opposed to it. Defenders of abortion argue that an embryo is very different from us and that there is little difference between an early abortion and contraception. Opponents focus on the later stages of pregnancy. They talk of 'the unborn child' and claim that abortion is the deliberate killing of an innocent human being and in the same category as murder. So the debate is often about drawing the line as to where one becomes a human being or person. Is it at conception, birth, or somewhere in between, e.g. when a foetus becomes viable? The trouble with this is, first, that viability is being gradually reduced; it is becoming possible to bring fertilized eggs to maturity outside of the womb; secondly, viability varies according to medical expertise, so a foetus would have a right to live in London but not in the Amazonian forests. It may, therefore, be better to stop thinking in terms of sharp boundaries and acknowledge that becoming a person is complex and gradual, for a foetus is neither rational nor self-conscious and the capacity to have experiences only comes towards the end of pregnancy. In this case one can argue that there is not much wrong with an early abortion.

The Right to Chose?

Opponents of abortion concentrate on the state of the foetus. Defenders tend to concentrate on the mother and link their views to women's rights: a woman has a right to choose what happens to her own body. Argument centres around whether a woman's rights over her body are more important than the life of the person or part-person in her womb. Though one may not want to allow abortion simply because the pregnancy is inconvenient, there are many cases where unwanted pregnancy endangers the health of the woman. Should abortion in these cases be also prohibited? And what of pregnancies caused by rape or incest? (Some critics of abortion oppose it in all cases). There is another debate over the suggestion that principles about the sanctity of life might be abandoned and replaced by a set of principles concerning people's autonomy and the quality of their lives. This would justify the abortion of infants who will be severely handicapped. Another argument for abortion is a more pragmatic one; that the prohibition of abortion leads to highly undesirable consequences. Involuntary childbearing aggravates poverty, increases infant and child death rates, and places severe strain upon the resources of families and governments.

ANIMAL RIGHTS

The Background

In the first chaper of Genesis, God gave human beings dominion over the animals, and the Christian tradition continued to give low status to animals. Philosophers have been as harsh. Descartes, for example, thought of animals as machines without feelings. In modern societies most animals raised for food never see the light of day. They are so intensively confined that they may not be able to turn round or raise a wing. Then there are the vast numbers of animals used for scientific research. Finally, in the UK there has been an angry debate about the hunting of animals for sport.

The Modern Debate

A debate about the moral status of animals only really began in the 1970s. Peter Singer, for example, argued that there was no good reason for refusing to extend the basic principle of equality (the principle of equal consideration of interests) to non-human animals. On the question of food, he argued that where there are adequate alternatives to eating meat, we cannot justify the suffering inflicted on animals by the practices of commercial farming; therefore, vegetarianism is the only morally acceptable diet. On animal experiments, he suggested that we should ask whether we would perform the experiment on an orphaned human being with a mental level similar to that of the animal. Only if the answer were yes, could we say that we were not giving the interests of humans greater weight than that of animals. For to show a bias in favour of one's own species is unjustifiable. Other philosophers have gone on to claim that animals have basic rights. On the other hand, those who support animal research argue that animals are not morally equal to humans. On the hunting of animals (as in the case of fox-hunting) defenders of the practice tend to treat it as a tradition, a long-standing part of country life, and also as an important source of employment. But they rarely address the main point: that it is morally wrong to take pleasure in hunting animals to their deaths.

One strand runs throughout all discussions to do with animals. We should not continue to treat animals the way we, as a society, are treating them now. The burden of proof has shifted: it is now for those in favour of the gratuitous use of animals to justify themselves.

CENSORSHIP

Introduction

Freedom of speech is a crucial and precious civil liberty, one of the most important ingredients of a just, liberal and free society. In Britain and other Western democracies the merits of free speech (and freedom of the press, which is thought to follow from it) are widely accepted; what is in question is its scope and meaning. For this freedom is limited in certain respects; there are a number of legal restrictions, for example, the Official Secrets Act, Prevention of Terrorism Act, laws relating to libel and contempt of court. Any further attempt to restrict this freedom is branded as censorship. Justifications of censorship are made on the grounds of public welfare and morals.

Political Censorship

There is political censorship, where governments seek to silence criticism and dissent. An example of this was the ban on broadcasting interviews with terrorist organisations in Northern Ireland, which ran from 1988 to 1994. A second debate has run in recent months, especially since the death of Princess Diana. Should the UK introduce a law on privacy, to safeguard individuals from press intrusion? The press, in its own defence, argues that this is a threat to freedom of speech and, specifically, a threat to the investigation of and reporting on matters of public concern.

Moral Censorship

The issue of censorship also occurs frequently in what might be called areas of morality, taste and decency, with the depiction of sex and violence in the cinema and on television, and now on the Internet and via satellite and cable television channels. Should not adults be free to see what they wish to see? The argument then becomes one about harms: what are the bad effects of reading pornography or watching blue movies? Opponents of pornography argue that harm is done not to the consumer of it, but those affected by the consumer. For example, the exposure to pornography leads to sexual crime. But there is a lack of evidence for this connection. Similarly with violence: very many research studies have been carried out in recent years and nothing conclusive has been brought forward either to prove or disprove the existence of a causal link between violence on screen and violent behaviour. And perhaps such a link needs to be shown before we give up our bias towards free speech.

However, though it may not be right to deny access to such material to those who want access, this does not mean it should be made freely available. So it is possible to uphold free speech and at the same time place restrictions upon material that is 'offensive' to reasonable people.

EUTHANASIA

The word's etymology means 'good death', but in its present sense it refers to the killing of those who are incurably ill and in great pain or distress, for the sake of those killed, and to spare them further suffering or distress. In most countries of the world, except for Holland, it is illegal to assist a patient to die in this way. Most of the groups campaigning for changes in the law to allow euthanasia are campaigning for voluntary euthanasia—that is, euthanasia carried out at the request of the person killed.

Passive and Active Euthanasia

But we must draw a distinction between passive euthanasia, when death results from ceasing to use life-sustaining measures; active euthanasia on the other hand requires someone taking positive steps to bring about the death of the patient. The centre of discussion is over voluntary active euthanasia. The argument for it is that there are cases where finding relief from suffering supersedes all other consequences and that respect for the individual's dignity and autonomy obliges society to respect those who seek euthanasia. Those who oppose it (the courts now incline to allow passive euthanasia) refer first to the professional obligation to keeping patients alive: killing patients is inconsistent with the role of nursing, care-giving, and healing (though it is consistent with the medical aim of alleviating pain). The second reason is that the social consequences of allowing voluntary active euthanasia are too dangerous. Although particular acts of active killing may sometimes be justified, to allow it in general would run serious risks of misuse and abuse. We would be on a 'slippery slope'. The response to this is that if voluntary active euthanasia were to be permitted, it would be made the responsibility of the medical profession, who already hold a good deal of power over life and death, without being morally corrupted by it. Nor is there any real empirical evidence that justified killings will lead, as a matter of fact, to unjustified ones. It is sometimes argued that the Nazi mass murders had their beginnings in the Nazi euthanasia programme. But their examinations policy did not grow out of voluntary euthanasia, and it is not easy to see how a similar policy could grow out of the desire to relieve suffering and to respect an individual's wish, even if it is for death.

SOFT DRUGS

There is a substantial body of opinion which believes that the use of 'soft' drugs should no longer be treated as a serious criminal offence (as it is by the 1971 Misuse of Drugs Act) and could perhaps even be legalised. The drugs most often mentioned are cannabis and those such as Ecstasy, which are much used by young people. One argument for what is often called 'decriminalization' is that soft drugs are simply not harmful enough to justify prohibition. Whatever health risks there are, they are less than with tobacco and alcohol, which are perfectly legal. With cannabis, it is claimed that it is non-addictive and also has medicinal properties in the relief of discomfort and pain. On the other hand a percentage of cannabis users consider themselves addicted and complain of poor concentration and loss of long-term memory.

Comparisons with Prohibition

A second argument is that decriminalising soft drugs would have the advantage of decoupling soft drugs from hard drugs, in that they would no longer have the same atmosphere of illegality about them. For, the argument runs, it is the prohibition of the drugs, for which there is a continuing demand, which creates the 'drug problem', not the drug itself. Comparisons are frequently made with the Prohibition era in the United States during the 1920s, when the attempt to ban alcohol encouraged criminal activity and ultimately failed.

Opponents of Decriminalization

Opponents of decriminalization say that if the laws were relaxed, there would be a rapid increase in the use of soft drugs, which in turn would lead to harmful social consequences. They also believe that there would be an increase in the use of hard drugs, in that the use of soft drugs leads to hard drugs; they function as a 'gateway'. It is certainly true that cannabis use precedes the use of other illegal drugs, such as heroin and cocaine, but not that it necessarily or even usually leads to them. The Netherlands has experimented with decriminalization, in that the use of soft drugs is permitted in certain places, but the consequences of this are so far inconclusive.

THE HUMAN RIGHTS DEBATE

Introduction

The concept of human rights is based on the belief that individuals are entitled to certain basic political and social conditions by virtue of their existence as human beings. The most systematic expression of this concept in the 20th century was the Universal Declaration of Human Rights adopted by the United Nations General Assembly in 1948. The concept's roots have often been traced to the 1776 American Declaration of Independence (in which all individuals are said to be created with the rights to 'life, liberty and the pursuit of happiness') and the 1789 French Declaration of the Rights of Man and the Citizen. The UN Declaration's importance lay in its acknowledgement that the promotion and protection of human rights was a legitimate concern of the international community. It was followed by similar declarations including the 1951 European Convention for the Protection of Human Rights and Fundamental Freedoms, the 1969 American Convention on Human Rights, the 1981 African Charter on Human and People's Rights, together with UN conventions on racial discrimination, slavery, the status of women, religious intolerance and self determination. A recurring issue has been that while governments formally sign the conventions, governments are also responsible for infringing the rights those conventions seek to promote. The documentation and reporting of these infringements by such non-governmental bodies as the British-based Amnesty International (*see* **L6**) and the American-based Human Rights Watch act as a source of pressure in preserving human rights.

Fifty Years of Human Rights

The year 1998 marked the 50th anniversary of the adoption by the United Nations General Assembly of the Universal Declaration of Human Rights. As with the establishment of the United Nations itself, the Declaration represented the hope that the international community could put behind it a century of war and suffering, the inevitable result, the document's framers believed, of undemocratic political systems with a total disregard for fundamental human rights. In 1941 US President Roosevelt declared that the world which emerged from the war should be one that guaranteed the 'Four Freedoms' of speech, religion, freedom from want and freedom from fear.

The UN Declaration

The UN Declaration's Preamble asserted that 'recognition of the inherent dignity and of the equal and inalienable rights of all members of the human family is the foundation of freedom, justice and peace in the world', going on to say that 'disregard and contempt for human rights have resulted in barbarous acts which have outraged the conscience of mankind...' This could only be remedied by recognising that human rights were the international community's legitimate concern. The omens were, however, mixed. While the Declaration was in itself a laudable achievement, on the day of its adoption—10 December 1948—Saudi Arabia abstained while South Africa and the Soviet Union rejected the whole concept.

The Declaration's first article echoes the roots of human (or natural) rights in 18th century rationalism, the source, for example, of the 1776 American Declaration of Independence and the 1789 French Declaration of the Rights of Man and the Citizen. All human beings, it says, 'are born free and equal in dignity and status', are 'endowed with reason and conscience and should act towards one another in a spirit of brotherhood.' Each individual is entitled to the freedoms set out in the Declaration regardless of 'race, colour, sex, language, religion, political or other opinion, nationality or social origin, property, birth or status.'

The Declaration's potential strength rests in its comprehensiveness, with a recognition of the interlinked nature of economic, political, social and judicial rights. While calling for the 'right to life, liberty and security of the person', for freedom from slavery, torture and cruel or inhuman punishment, for equality before the law, and for the presumption of innocence, the Declaration also asserts the right to own property, to work and form trade unions, to social security and protection against unemployment. The right to freedom of thought, conscience and religion is accompanied by the right to express these opinions. The individual also has a right to meet those duties to the community 'in which alone the free and full development of his personality is possible.'

Recent Conventions

Although the Declaration has no formal legal standing, it has been built upon by, for example, an International Covenant on Civil and Political Rights and an International Covenant on Economic, Social and Cultural Rights, both adopted by the UN General Assembly in 1966. Further covenants and declarations have been adopted on racial discrimination, religious intolerance, slavery, torture, the rights of children, women's rights and self determination. There have also been regional agreements on human rights, including the 1951 European Convention for the Protection of Human Rights and Fundamental Freedoms (from which the European Court of Human Rights has developed), the 1969 American Convention on Human Rights and the 1981 African Charter on Human and People's Rights. The incorporation of the European Convention into British law under the Human Rights Act in 1998 marked a significant step forward.

Human Rights Organisations

There are two main non-governmental organisations which campaign for the protection and extension of human rights—the British-based Amnesty International and the American-based Human Rights Watch. Amnesty International was founded in 1961 to work for the release of non-violent prisoners of conscience. Amnesty also campaigns against torture, the death penalty, for the wider rights of prisoners, against extra-judicial executions and 'disappearances' (the kidnapping and murder of political opponents). The organisation was awarded the Nobel Peace Prize in 1977 and in 1999 claims over a million members in 150 countries. Human Rights Watch was founded in 1977 in response to appeals by Soviet bloc-based groups for the monitoring of compliance with the human rights provisions of the East-West Helsinki agreements. The organisation broadened its cover in the 1980s following concerns that the US government saw human rights abuses carried out by anti-Communist governments as less reprehensible.

Current Human Rights Abuses

Both Amnesty and Human Rights Watch act as pressure groups by investigating and publicising human rights violations. It is here that the effectiveness of the many declarations and covenants can be questioned. Amnesty International reported that in 1997 there were incidents of torture in 117 countries (with British companies involved in selling equipment to inflict electro-shock torture), 'disappearances' in 32 countries and extra-judicial executions in 55. China's human rights violations receive little more than perfunctory criticism from Western leaders concerned not to alienate a valuable source of trade and a target for investment. The French government refused to allow Chinese dissidents at celebrations of the UN Declaration in 1998 for fear of offending Beijing. Despite the Declaration's assertion of a right to asylum from political persecution, Britain detains asylum seekers in prison while their claims are assessed. In Algeria, a government-sponsored human rights commission condemns the violations of Islamic fundamentalists while ignoring abuses committed by government forces. In Egypt, the head of the British-funded Organisation for Human Rights was arrested for his activities in 1998.

The Rwandan Massacres

A very glaring failure came with the 1994 Rwandan massacres where, despite the provisions of the Convention on the Prevention and Punishment of the Crime of Genocide, the UN Security Council, aware that a systematic campaign of terror and murder was being waged, voted to reduce its peace mission in the country to an ineffective token force. More optimistically, however, the UN agreed in 1998 to establish a permanent international criminal court to try political leaders responsible for offences against human rights. The attempt to extradite the former Chilean military dictator Augusto Pinochet in 1998 for trial in Spain showed the potential effectiveness of such a court and served as a warning to future offenders. Similarly, the linkage by the World Bank and the International Monetary Fund between financial aid to Burma's military junta and the restoration of political rights to the opposition demonstrates another possible source of pressure.

The Kosovo Crisis

During the early months of 1999 the world witnessed the brutal and systematic 'ethnic cleansing' of the Kosovo Albanian population. Countless numbers were turned into refugees, and an unknown number murdered by Serb forces. All this was in Europe, not a remote part of Africa. For more on Kosovo, *see* **C68**.

Hopes for the Future

If the international human rights record in the 50 years since the UN Declaration is mixed, both the symbolic and the practical importance of such declarations and covenants cannot be over-emphasised. By creating a moral climate they provide a benchmark for what constitutes a civilised society and a base from which to argue and campaign. The most important aspect of the developments of the late 20th century is that human rights can no longer be viewed as the domestic concern of an individual state but are now a matter for international public opinion. In 1948 Nelson Mandela, struggling against the earliest manifestations of apartheid in South Africa, saw the UN Declaration as a 'sudden ray of hope at one of our darkest hours.' Half a century later he was president of a state in which apartheid had collapsed in the face of internal and external abhorrence at the system's violation of human rights.

GAZETTEER
OF THE
WORLD

An index and guide to the maps
with up-to-date descriptive matter.
Each year the Gazetteer is amended
to reflect recent place name changes,
new boundaries and frontiers, as
well as revised population figures as
they become available.

GAZETTEER OF THE WORLD

Measurement of Geographical Phenomena.

(1) Physical Features.

In using the gazetteer the reader should note that it is impossible to make absolutely correct measurements of geographical phenomena. For example, measurement of height of land above sea-level depends, in the first instance, upon the definition of the elusive concept of sea-level itself. This is constantly changing and so an arbitrary value of *mean sea-level* is normally used, but the value adopted varies from country to country. As a result, height above sea-level has inbuilt inconsistencies and inaccuracies. Similarly, the length of a river will depend upon the scale of the survey from which measurements are made. Large-scale maps and aerial photographs can show in great detail the sinuous course of rivers, whereas a map on a smaller scale must reduce the amount of information shown and thereby the apparent length.

The gazetteer now records the heights of mountains, lengths of rivers, and land and sea areas in metric units. English equivalents will be found on p. 1 of the **Atlas**.

(2) Definition of Urban Area.

An even more difficult problem of measurement relates to the definition of the urban area of a town or city. It is possible to define the extent of urban areas in three major ways, by using (1) the administrative area, (2) the physically built-up area, and (3) the socio-geographic, metropolitan area. This latter concept is in many ways the most meaningful for it relates to the notion that a city exerts a strong influence over the population resident beyond its administrative or built-up boundary. For example, the city may provide employment opportunities or shopping and entertainment facilities for a population resident some distance away from it. In order to define "city" in these terms some means of measuring the degree of connection between it and its surrounding hinterland (the city-region) must be found and, needless to say, there is considerable disagreement among workers in this field as to what are the most suitable criteria to use. Different criteria produce different definitions and even the most recent measurements are obsolete within a short space of time. However, the real significance of this less tangible concept of "city" may be illustrated by the fact that the reform of local government in England rests in part upon the concept of the city-region.

The population figures given in the gazetteer normally relate to the city's administrative area. In the case of some large cities two figures are given—(1) for the administrative city, and (2) for the more extensive metropolitan area which surrounds and includes the administrative city.

Place Names.

Where there have been recent changes in place names, the new name is used with the old name in brackets and a cross reference from old to new. The adoption of new names has increased in the 1990s with the fall of communism. New nations have emerged in central and eastern Europe. Towns and cities have abandoned their Soviet names (*e.g.* Leningrad is now St. Petersburg). Elsewhere change continues. Zaire has reverted to Congo. Bombay has become Mumbai. It is a constantly changing world.

Industries.

In many countries (not least Britain) old industries are gradually fading away. Because the gazetteer aims to be in part a historical guide, mention of these industries has been retained (even though the factories may have closed).

Population Figures.

Total population figures from a census count are no longer regarded as necessarily more accurate than estimates arrived at by other methods. The usefulness of censuses lies rather in the additional information which they provide. Even so, some countries like the Netherlands have given up censuses altogether. The gazetteer therefore no longer distinguishes between census figures and estimates but aims to include the latest reliable figures from whatever source.

Census 2001.

The next official census in the United Kingdom will take place on 29 April 2001 (the census is normally held at 10-year intervals, the last being in 1991). It is planned that there will be new questions on income, ethnic origin and religion to enable a fuller statistical picture of the population to emerge.

Local Government Reorganisation.

The eight counties of Wales were replaced on 1 April 1996 by 22 unitary authorities and the 12 regions of Scotland by 32 unitary authorities. Thirteen English unitary authorities were also created on that date, with a further 13 being created on 1 April 1997. The process was completed on 1 April 1998.

It is very difficult within the confines of short entries to make clear the complexity of these changes. In Scotland, for example, the name Angus has now been used for a historic county (until 1974), for a local government district within the Tayside Region (until 31 March 1996), and for a new unitary authority from 1 April 1996. On each occasion the area denoted by the name has changed. The new unitary authority called City of Dundee is not the same as the burgh of Dundee nor the same as the local government district of Dundee which it replaces.

ABBREVIATIONS USED IN THE GAZETTEER

Geographical Names

Ala. = Alabama
Ark. = Arkansas
Atl. Oc. = Atlantic Ocean
B.C. = British Columbia
BEF = British Expeditionary Forces
Brit. = British
Cal. = California
CERN = European Centre for Nuclear Research
Col. = Colorado
Conn. = Connecticut
Del. = Delaware
Eng. = England
E.U. = European Union
Fla. = Florida
Fr. = French
Ga. = Georgia
ICI = Imperial Chemical Industries
Ill. = Illinois
Ind. = Indiana
Kan. = Kansas
Ky. = Kentucky

La. = Louisiana
Land = prov. (Germany)
Mass. = Massachusetts
Md. = Maryland
Me. = Maine
Mich. = Michigan
Minn. = Minnesota
Miss. = Mississippi
Mo. = Missouri
Mont. = Montana
NATO = North Atlantic Treaty Organisation
N.C. = North Carolina
N.D. = North Dakota
Neth. = Netherlands
N.H. = New Hampshire
N.J. = New Jersey
N.M. = New Mexico
N.S.W. = New South Wales
N.T. = Northern Territory (Australia)
N.Y. = New York
N.Z. = New Zealand
O.F.S. = Orange Free State

Okla. = Oklahoma
OPEC = Organization of Petroleum Exporting Countries
Ore. = Oregon
Pac. Oc. = Pacific Ocean
Penns. = Pennsylvania
R.I. = Rhode Island
R.o.I. = Republic of Ireland
S.C. = South Carolina
Scot. = Scotland
S.D. = South Dakota
SHAPE = Supreme Headquarters, Allied Powers, Europe
Tenn. = Tennessee
U.K. = United Kingdom
U.N. = United Nations
USA = United States of America
Va. = Virginia
Vt. = Vermont
Wash. = Washington
W.I. = West Indies
Wis. = Wisconsin
Wyo. = Wyoming

Other Abbreviations

a. = area
admin. = administrative
agr. = agriculture
alt. = altitude
anc. = ancient
arch. = archaeological
a.s.l. = above sea-level
ass. = associated
auth. = authority
aut. rep. = autonomous republic
bdr. = border
bdy. = boundary
bldg. = building
bor. = borough
C. = cape
c. = city; circa, *c.* = about
can. = canton
cap. = capital
cas. = castle
cath. = cathedral
C.B. = county borough
ch. = chief
cm = centimetres
co. = county
col. = colony
colly. = colliery
comm. = commercial
conurb. = conurbation
cst. = coast
ctr. = centre
cty. = country
dep. = department
dist. = district
div. = division
E. = east or easterly
elec. = electrical
engin. = engineering
esp. = especially
exp. = exports

F. = firth
Fed. = Federation
fed. = federal
fish. pt. = fishing port
fortfd. = fortified
G. = Gulf
gen. = general
G.N.P. = gross national product
gr. = great, group
gtr. = greater
ha = hectares
hgst. = highest
I. = island
impt. = important
inc. = including
indep. = independent
inds. = industries
industl. = industrial
Is. = Islands
km = kilometres
km² = square kilometres
L. = lake
l. = length
lge. = large
l. gov. = local government
lgst. = largest
lt. = light
m = metres
machin. = machinery
M.B. = metropolitan borough
met. a. = metropolitan area
met. co. = metropolitan county
mftg. = manufacturing
mkg. = making
mkt. = market
mm = millimetres
mnfs. = manufactures
mng. = mining

mtn. = mountain
mun. = municipality
N. = north or northerly
nat. = national
non-met. co = non-metropolitan county
nr. = near
p. = population
par. = parish
penin. = peninsula
pref. = prefecture
prin. = principal
prod. = product
prot. = protectorate
prov. = province
pt. = port
R. = river
rep. = republic
residtl. = residential
rly. = railway
S. = south or southerly
shipbldg. = shipbuilding
sm. = small
spt. = seaport
st. = state
sta. = station
sub. = suburb
t. = town
terr. = territory
tr. = trade
trib. = tributary
U.D. = urban district
unit. = unitary
univ. = university
v. = village
W. = west or westerly
wat. pl. = watering place
wkg. = working
wks. = works
wkshps. = workshops

A

Aachen (**Aix-la-Chapelle**), t., N. Rhine-Westphalia, **Germany**; anc. spa t. in coal-field dist.; industl., route ctr.; contains tomb of Charlemagne; p. (1990) 243,200.

Aalen, t., Baden-Württemberg, **Germany**; on R. Kocher; iron, textiles, lens mkg.; p. (1986) 62,800.

Aalst (**Alost**), t., E. Flanders, **Belgium**, 24 km N.W. Brussels; industl., comm. ctr. at rly. junc.; agr. tr.; p. (1993) 76,514.

Aarau, t., cap. of Aargau can., **Switzerland**; precision tools and instruments, shoes, textiles; hydroelectric power; p. (1980) 15,788.

Aare, R., **Switzerland**; flows through Brienz and Thun Ls., thence into Rhine; Aare gorges above Meiringen; lgst R. wholly in Switzerland, 290 km long.

Aargau, can., N. **Switzerland**; occupies lower Aare R. valley; agr. in valleys, wooded uplands; cap. Aarau; a. 1,404 km²; p. (1990) 496,300.

Aba, t., **Nigeria**; N.E. of Pt. Harcourt; mkt., palm oil processing; p. (1992) 270,500.

Abaco, Gt., I., **Bahamas**, **W.I.**; sheltered harbours, yachting; exp. crayfish; p. (1990) 10,061.

Ābādān, c., **Iran**; spt., major oil terminal and refining ctr. on A.I. in Persian G.; permanently damaged by Iraqi air attack; now closed (1980); p. (1985) 294,000.

Abakan, t., **Russia**, on R. A.; recent rly.; sawmilling, food inds.; p. (1989) 154,000.

Abashiri, t., N. cst. Hokkaido, **Japan**; impt. fishing base; p. (1990) 44,416.

Abbeville, t., N. **France**; on R. Somme; connected with Paris and Belgium by canals; sugar-milling, carpets, biscuits, beer; p. (1982) 25,988.

Abbots-Langley, v., Herts., **Eng.**; birthplace of Nicholas Breakspeare (Pope Adrian IV).

Åbenrå, spt., S.E. Jutland, **Denmark**; at head of A. fjord and admin. ctr. of S. Jutland prov.; vehicles, clothing, food processing; p. (1990) 21,463.

Abeokuta, t., **Nigeria**; cap. Ogun st.; N. of Lagos; palm oil, textiles; p. (1992) 386,800.

Abercarn, t., Caerphilly, **Wales**; tinplate, knitting pins; former colliery t.; p. (1991) 14,069.

Aberdare, t., Rhondda, Cynon, Taff, **Wales**; on R. Cynon: wire cables; former coal-mng.; p. (1991) 29,040.

Aberdare Range, mtns., Nat. Park, **Kenya**; rise to 4,000 m; form a section of E. rim of Gr. Rift Valley; equable climate attractive to white settlers; camphor forests, fruit and pastoral agr. at higher alts.

Aberdeen, royal burgh, unit. auth. created in 1996, formerly part of Grampian, E. **Scot.**; between mouths of Rs. Dee and Don; impt. fishing pt.; established itself as centre of rapidly growing N. Sea oil ind.; "granite-city"— much granite used in central bldgs.; univs., cath.; p. (1991) 189,707 (c.), (1995) 219,120 (unit. auth.).

Aberdeen, t., S.D., **USA**; ctr. for wheat and livestock region; p. (1990) 24,927.

Aberdeenshire, E. **Scot.**, unit. auth. created in 1996, incorporating historic co. which became part of Grampian in 1974; bordered N. and E. by N. Sea; inc. cstl. ts. of Fraserburgh, Peterhead and Stonehaven; p. (1995) 226,530.

Aberfeldy, burgh, Perth and Kinross, **Scot.**; in Strath Tay, 6 km below Loch Tay; mkt.; salmon and trout fishing resort; p. (1991) 1,748.

Abergavenny, t., Monmouthshire, **Wales**; on R. Usk; scene of massacre of Welsh chiefs; light engin., concrete prods.; cattle mkt.; cas.; p. (1991) 14,092.

Aberlour, Charlestown of, burgh, Moray, **Scot.**; on R. Spey, 19 km S. of Elgin; p. (1991) 821.

Abernethy, burgh, Perth and Kinross, **Scot.**; on R. Tay, once cap. of Pictish Kings; p. (1991) 895.

Abertillery, t., Blaenau Gwent, **Wales**; collieries, tinplate; p. (1991) 11,680.

Aberystwyth, t., Ceredigion, **Wales**; on Cardigan Bay at mouth of R. Ystwyth, resort; cas., univ.; Nat. Library of Wales; p. (1991) 11,154.

Abidjan, c., replaced as cap. of **Côte d'Ivoire** by Yamoussoukro but remains seat of government; pt.; exp. palm oil, cocoa, copra, hardwood, rubber; oil refining at Vridi nearby; p. (1990) 2,500,000 (met. a.).

Abilene, t., Texas, **USA**; univ.; agr. processing, oil refining; p. (1990) 106,654.

Abilene, t., on Smoky Hill R., Kansas. **USA**; child-

hood home of Eisenhower; p. (1980) 6,572.

Abingdon, Vale of White Horse, Oxon., **Eng.**; mkt. t. on R. Thames; leather gds.; mediaeval and Georgian bldgs.; p. (1991) 35,234.

Abingdon, t., Va., **USA**; timber inds., agr. processing and tr., tobacco; tourist ctr.

Abinger Hammer, v., Surrey, **Eng.**; former centre of Weald iron industry.

Abkhazskaya, aut. rep., **Georgia**; borders Black Sea; sub-tropical crops, tourism; cap. Sukhumi; a. 8,599 km²; p. (1989) 537,500.

Abo. See **Turku**.

Abomey, t. anc. cap., former Kingdom of Dahomey, now **Benin**; former slave mkt.; cotton; p. (1982) 54,418.

Abovyan, t., **Armenia**; 16 km from Yerevan; new model t. founded 1963; p. (1990) 58,700.

Aboyne and Glentanner, par., Aberdeenshire, **Scot.**; on R. Dee nr. Ballater; Highland games; resort; p. (1991) 2,067.

Abraham, Plains of, nr. Quebec, **Canada**; Wolfe's victory over French under Montcalm, 1759.

Abram, t., Gtr. Manchester, **Eng.**; engin.; p. (1991) 11,482.

Abrantes, t., **Portugal**, on Tagus R.; French won battle here in Napoleonic Wars, 1807, dist. of Santarém; p. (1981) 48,653.

Abruzzo, region, central **Italy**; high limestone plateaus, narrow cstl. plain bordering Adriatic; poor agr., livestock; methane; forms part of Mezzogiorno; a. 8,513 km²; p. (1992) 1,255,549.

Abu Dhabi, I., emirate, lgst. of **United Arab Emirates**; S.E. Arabian pen.; rich oil reserves; a. 207,200 km²; p. (1985) 670,125.

Abuja, new t., **Nigeria**; became cap. of Nigeria in 1991; built from oil revenue; building slowing down with fall in oil prices; p. (1992) 305,900 (Federal Capital Territory).

Abu Qir, v. on A. Bay, **Egypt**; site of anc. Canopus; Battle of the Nile fought in the Bay 1798; offshore gasfield linked by pipeline to fertiliser plants near Alexandria.

Abu Simbel, Nile Valley, **Egypt**; anc. temples carved out of solid sandstone, one to Rameses II and the other to his Queen; saved from waters of Lake Nasser.

Abydos, anc. t. of Phrygia, Asia Minor, in present **Turkey**; resisted Philip of Macedon; famed for story of Leander and Hero.

Abydos, ruined c., Upper **Egypt**; celebrated for its temple of Osiris.

Abyssinia. See **Ethiopia**.

Acapulco de Juárez, spt., Pac. cst., **Mexico**; major modern resort in bay surrounded by steep mtns.; exp. agr. prods.; struck by Hurricane Pauline (1997); p. (1990) 592,187.

Accra, c., cap. of **Ghana**; spt.; univ.; airpt.; consumer gds.; p. (1984) 867,459 (c.), 1,431,099 (met. a. inc. Tema).

Accrington, t., Hyndburn, Lancs., **Eng.**; 32 km N. of Manchester; former cotton ctr.; textile machin., more diversified new inds.; p. (1991) 36,466.

Achill I., Mayo, **R.o.I.**; mtnous.; agr., fishing, tourism at Dugort and Keal; a. 148 km²; p. (1986) 3,161.

Acireale, spt., Sicily, **Italy**; cath.; sulphur springs, p. (1981) 47,888.

Aconcagua, mtn., Andes, **Argentina**; highest peak of Western Hemisphere, alt. 6,956 m.

Aconquija, Nevada de, mtn. range, in E. Andes, N. **Argentina**; rises steeply from Chaco lowland to 5,500 m.

A Coruña. See **La Coruña**.

Acre. See **Akko**.

Acre, st. W. **Brazil**; isolated within Amazon basin; rubber estates; producer of coagulated rubber; cap. Rio Branco; a. 153,170 km²; p. (1991) 417,317.

Acton. See **Ealing**.

Adamawa Highlands, Nigeria; rise to over 5,490 m; stock rearing.

Adam's Bridge, chain of sandbanks, 35 km long, in Palk Strait, between **India** and **Sri Lanka**; construction of rail causeway mooted.

Adana, t., **Turkey**; on Seijhan R.; ctr. for fruit and cotton, impt. exp, from Turkey; cas.; cap. of A. prov.; 4th. t. of Turkey; Yumurtalik Free Trade Zone (1987); p. (1990) 972,318, 1,934,907, (prov.).

Adapazari, t., **Turkey**; rly. junction; silk, linen; highgrade concentrate from low-grade iron ore deposits in Camdagi a.; p. (1985) 152,291.

Adda, R., N. **Italy**; flows through L. Como to R. Po.; agr. in wide valley above L. Como; 240 km long.

Addis Ababa, c., cap. of **Ethiopia**; at 2,440 m in central highlands; terminus of Djibouti rly., ctr. of coffee tr., main concentration of inds. in Ethiopa; consumer gds., food processing; new cotton mill (1981); admin. ctr.; univ., palaces; p. (1991) 1,700,000.

Adelaide, c., spt., cap. of S. **Australia**; on alluvial plain of R. Torrens with Mount Lofty Range to E. and Gulf St. Vincent to W.; growth based on wheat, wool and fruit but heavy inds. since war (nearby coal and iron); cars, electrical goods, textiles, chems., oil refining; p. (1993) 1,071,100.

Adélie Land (Terre Adélie), Antarctica; French terr. and dependency of Réunion.

Adelsberg, t., Yugoslavia. See Postojna.

Aden, spt., economic and commercial cap. of **Yemen;** former Brit. col.; bay behind headlands of Aden t. and Little Aden, excellent anchorage; p. (1987) 417,366.

Aden, G. of W. Arabian Sea; one of most impt. shipping lanes in world; pts. of Aden, Berbera, Djibouti; length 880 km, width 480 km at mouth.

Adige, R., N. **Italy;** upper course forms impt. routeway through Alps between Italy and N.; flows via Verona to Adriatic; 360 km long.

Adirondack, mtns., **USA;** hgst. peak Mt. Marcy (1,630 m), average height 1,200 m; scenically attractive, ski resorts, sanatoria, iron-ore deposits.

Adlington, t., Lancs., **Eng.**; nr. Chorley; former cotton spinning t.; p. (1991) 8,556.

Admiralty Is., 27 km of sm. coral Is., one lge. I., S.W. **Pac. Oc.**; part of Papua New Guinea; forms part of Bismarck Archipelago; anc. civilisation; pearl fishing, coconuts; ch. t. Lorengau.; a. 2,072 km².

Adour, R., S.W. **France;** rises in Pyrenees, enters Bay of Biscay below Bayonne; 331 km long.

Adria, mkt. t., Rovigo, **Italy;** formerly on cst., now 22 km inland, old Etruscan c.; p. (1981) 21,785.

Adrianople. See Edirne.

Adriatic Sea, branch of the Mediterranean, between Italy and Balkan Peninsula; forms G. of Venice on the N.; chief trading pts., Venice, Trieste, and Ancona on the N., Brindisi and Dürres on the S.; a. 134,680 km², 720 km long.

Adullam or Aidelma, Judean c. of Canaanite origin, S.W. Jerusalem, **Israel**, where David hid in cave from Saul.

Adur, l. gov. dist., West Sussex, **Eng.**; lower A. valley and ts. of Shoreham-by-Sea and South-wick; p. (1995) 58,500.

Adwick le Street, t., South Yorks, **Eng.**; coal; home of George Washington's family; p. (1991) 10,288.

Adygeyskaya (Adygei), aut. region, **Russia;** in foothills of Caucasus; mainly agr. and lumbering; cap. Maykop; a. 7,599 km²; p. (1989) 432,000.

Adzharskaya, aut. rep., **Georgia;** borders Turkey; mtnous.; sub-tropical crops; cap. Batumi; a. 2,849 km²; p. (1990) 382,000.

Aegades, gr. of rocky Is. off W. cst. of Sicily, **Italy;** ch. t. Favignana on I. of that name.

Aegean Is., between **Greece** and **Turkey;** called the Grecian Archipelago, inc. Crete, Cyclades, Sporades, and Dodecanese; a. 3,901 km²; p. (1981) 428,533.

Aegean Sea, branch of the Mediterranean; studded with Is., between **Greece** and **Turkey;** connected through the Dardanelles with Sea of Marmara and thence through the Bosporus Strait with the Black Sea; rich cultural history; coral sponge fishing; recent oil finds contested between Greece and Turkey; length 640 km, width 320 km.

Afan. See Por Talbot.

Afars and Issas. See Djibouti.

Afghanistan, rep. (1973), former kingdom, Asia; land locked, lies N. and W. of Pakistan; cap. Kabul; comm. ctrs. Kabul, Kandahar; mtnous.; ch. Rs., Kabul and Helm; intense summer heat, severe winter cold, scanty rainfall; ethnic variety, Pashtuns, Ghilzays, Uzbeks and Tadzhiks; many hill tribes; languages Pashtu and Farsi; religion Islam; geography causes fragmented settlement and slow economic progress; severe drought 1968–72; 75 percent depend on agric.; heavily dependent on irrigation; wheat staple crop, also cotton, rice, maize; sheep, goats, horses; handicraft inds. (carpets and weaving) more impt. than modern

inds.; mineral resources but poor transport hinders development; no rly.; refugees totalled 5,000,000 by 1985; hydroelectr. at Asadabad; invaded by Russian troops, Dec. 1979 but withdrew Feb.1989; continuing civil war; a. 647,500 km²; p. (1994) 20,500,000. Officially renamed Islamic Emirate of Afghanistan, 1997. Major earthquake, May 1998.

Africa, third lgst. continent contains 22 per cent of world's land a. but only 11 per cent of p.; diverse physical and cultural conditions; plateaux interrupted in N. and S. by steeply folded, sharply eroded mtn. ranges and by mtn. massifs of Sahara and E. Africa; climate and vegetation vary from hot desert to equatorial rain forest and from Mediterranean woodland to tropical savannah; sparse but ethnically varied p., concentrated mainly along N.W. Mediterranean cst., Nile valley, cst. of W. Africa and N.E. of L. Victoria; little urbanisation; economic development hindered by colonial legacy and neo-colonial international companies, poorly developed transport network, poor soils, inadequate rainfall and fluctuating prices of primary prods. on world mkt.; petroleum deposits providing revenue for devel. in few ctys.; those ctys. without oil severely handicapped by high cost of imports; schemes like Volta R. multipurpose development and the Cabora Bassa dam designed to alleviate this poverty; continent contains 40 per cent of world hydroelectric potential and is storehouse of non-energy producing minerals, but many exported in unprocessed form; agr. predominant economic activity, except in industl. enclaves of Egypt, Zimbabwe and S. Africa; a c. 30,259,000 km²; p. (1995) 721,000,000.

Agadir, spt., S. cst. **Morocco;** wrecked by earthquake, 1960; new t. built S. of former c. in a. of greater geological stability; p. (1982) 110,479.

Agana, cap. of **Guam**; reconstructed after second world war; p. (est. 1980) 3,000 (exc. armed forces).

Agen, t., cap. of Lot-et-Garonne, **France;** mkt. t.; aqueduct and bridge over Garonne R.; fruit tr. and processing; p. (1990) 32,223.

Agincourt (Azincourt), v., Pas-de-Calais, **France;** famed for battle in 1415 between English, led by Henry V and French under d'Albert.

Agra, c., Uttar Pradesh, **India;** on Jumna R., 184 km S.S.E. of Delhi; formerly cap. of Mogul Empire; famous Taj Mahal mausoleum; univ.; p. (1991) 892,000.

Agrigento, t., S. Sicily, **Italy;** spt., exp. sulphur, salt. Formerly Girgenti, founded Akragas, c. 580 B.C., famous for its temples; birthplace of Empedocles; p. (1981) 51,325.

Aguadilla, spt., **Puerto Rico**; exp. coffee and sugar.

Aguascalientes, st., **Mexico**; on central plateau at 1,800 m; agr.; mineral springs; cap. A.; a. 6,472 km²; p. (1990) 719,650.

Aguascalientes, t., cap. of A. st. **Mexico**; alt. over 1,800 m; 416 km N.W. of Mexico City; wide range of local inds.; hot springs; p. (1990) 506,384.

Agulhas, C., rocky projection, 160 km E. of C. of Good Hope, most southerly point of **Africa**.

Ahlen, t., N. Rhine–Westphalia, **Germany;** on R. Werse; coal mng., metal and engin. wks.; p. (1986) 51,900.

Ahmadabad, temporary cap. of Gujarat, **India;** Jain temple, mosques; univ.; impt. textile ctr.; oilfield at Nawagam nearby; p. (1991) 2,877,000.

Ahmadnagar, c., Maharashtra, **India;** admin. ctr.; old Bahmani cap.; lge. tr. in cotton and silk gds.; p. (1981) 143,937 (c.), 181,210 (met. a.).

Ahrewady. See Irrawaddy.

Ahvāz (Ahwāz), c., cap. of Khuzestan prov., **Iran;** airpt.; oil, aluminium, steel pipes; new steel plant; p. (1986) 589,529.

Aigues-Mortes, t., Gard dep., **France;** on Rhône delta; canal ctr., once spt., now 5 km from Mediterranean; salt works; much of mediaeval t. preserved; tourism; p. (1982) 4,475.

Aiguille d'Arves, mtn., Dauphiné Alps, S.E. **France;** 3 rock needles; hgst. alt. 3,511 m.

Aiguille du Midi, mtn., Mt. Blanc massif, S.E. **France;** rock needle, funicular rly.; alt. 3,845 m.

Aiguille Verte, mtn., Mt. Blanc massif, S.E. **France,** rock needle overlooking Chamonix; alt. 4,130 m.

Ailefroid, mtn., Dauphiné Alps, S.E. **France;** double summit; alt. 3,962 m.

Ailsa Craig, rocky I., S. Ayrshire, **Scot.**; alt. 340 m; gannetry.

Ain, dep., **France**; in Jura; mainly agr., famous for pigs and poultry; a. 5,822 km²; p. (1990) 471,000.

Ain, R., **France**; trib. of R. Rhône, flows S.S.W. from Jura; hydroelectric power; 194 km long.

Airdrie, burgh, N. Lanarkshire, **Scot.**; 19 km E. of Glasgow; iron inds., brick and concrete wks., steel tubes, pharmaceutics; p. (1991) 36,998.

Aire, R., West Yorks., **Eng.**; trib. of Ouse; major valley for power production; produces 20 per cent of U.K. power; length 112 km.

Aisne, dep., **France**; borders Ardennes; forested; mainly agr., sugar-beet; sm. textile ts.; cap. Laon; a. 7.423 km²; p. (1990) 537,500.

Aisne, R., N.E. **France**; navigation improved by regularisation; 240 km long.

Aitolia and Akarnania, Greece; mtnous. prov. on N. side of Patras; arable cultivation on cstl. plain; cap. Missolonghi; a. 5,390 km²; p. (1991) 228,180.

Aix-en-Provence, t., Bouches-du-Rhône, **France**; 29 km N. of Marseilles; old cap. of Provence; thermal springs; cultural and comm. ctr., agr., inds.; p. (1990) 126,854 (t) 130,888 (met. a.).

Aix-la-Chapelle. See Aachen.

Aix-les-Bains, health resort, Savoy, **France**; p. (1982) 23,534.

Aizuwakamatsu, t. N. Honshu, **Japan**; lacquer ware, candles; p. (1990) 119,084.

Ajaccio, spt., cap. Corse-du-Sud, Corsica, **France**; timber, flour, olive oil, tobacco; tourism; birthplace of Napoleon; p. (1990) 59,318.

Ajman, emirate, one of **United Arab Emirates**; p. (1985) 64,318.

Ajmer, t., Rajasthan, **India**; salt extraction, vegetable oils; p. (1991) 403,000.

Akhaia, prov., **Greece**; impt. currant producing a.; livestock; inc. pt. of Patras; a. 3,134 km²; p. (1991) 300,078.

Akhisar, t., **Turkey**; anc. Thyatira; in fertile agr. basin, p. (1985) 68,553

Akita, pref., **Japan**; a. 11,663 km²; contains Japan's lgst. oilfield and copper mine; mtns. and fertile lowlands; p. (1990) 1,227,000.

Akita, c., **Japan**; cap. Akita pref.; old cas. t., pt; oil refining ctr.; p. (1990) 302,359.

'Akko (Acre), c., spt., **Israel**; famous for sieges during Crusades; withstood Napoleon for 61 days in 1799; pt. functions now assumed by Haifa; p. (1982) 39,100.

Akmola, c. and prov. in **Kazakhstan**. Akmola became capital of Kazakhstan in 1995.

Akmolinsk. See Tselinograd.

Akola, t., Maharashtra, **India**; cotton; p. (1991) 328,000.

Akosombo, pt. **Ghana**; pt. and new t. S. of L. Volta; textile factory being built; planned p. 50,000.

Akranes, t., **Iceland**; N. of Reykjavik; lge. cement wks.; p. (1993) 5,233.

Akron, c., Ohio, **USA**; lge. rubber mftg. ctr.; maize, mills, woollens, machin., chemicals; univ.; p. (1990) 223,019 (c.), 657,575 (met. a.).

Aktyubinsk, t., N.W. **Kazakhstan**; at S. end of Ural mtns.; ferro-alloys, engin., lignite, elec. power, chemicals, copper; p. (1990) 261,100.

Akureyri, t., N. **Iceland**; herring fishery, food processing; 2nd. t. of Iceland; p. (1993) 14,799.

Akyab, See Sittwe.

Alabama, st., **USA**; cap. Montgomery, ch. pt. Mobile; "cotton st.", cattle-rearing; fertilisers, chemicals, mng.; lgst. c. Birmingham; settled 1702; admitted to union 1819; st. flower camelia, st. bird yellow-hammer; a. 133,667 km²; p. (1990) 4,040,587.

Alagôas, st., N.E. **Brazil**; hot, dry cattle rearing a., poor st. with low literacy rate; cap. Maceio; a. 28,648 km²; p. (1991) 2,512,515.

Alameda, spt. Cal., **USA**; on I. in San Francisco Bay; impt. naval and air base; pt. inds.; p. (1980) 63,852.

Aland Is. (Ahvenanmaa), group belonging to **Finland** at entrance of G. of Bothnia; a. 1,481 km²; p. (1993) 25,102.

Alaska, Arctic st., **USA**; separated from other sts.; bought from Russia (1868); mtnous.; furs, timber, salmon; major oil and natural gas discoveries on N. slope present difficult ecological problems for exploitation; pipeline from Prudhoe Bay to Valdez; lgst. c. Anchorage; admitted to union 1959; st. flower forget-me-not, st. bird Willow Ptarmigan; cap. Juneau (planned cap. at Willow South never built); a. 1,518,776 km²; p. (1990) 550,043.

Alaska G. of, S. cst. A., **USA.**; semi-circular G. with precipitous csts.; oil in Cook Inlet and

Controller B.; a. 5,000 km².

Alaska Highway, from Dawson Creek, B.C., **Canada,** to Fairbanks, Alaska, **USA**; 2,443 km long; built for second world war programme; main supply base and H.Q., Edmonton, Alberta.

Alaska Range, mtn. massif, S.A., **USA**; extends in arc of 640 km; separates S. cst. and N. tundra; S.E. flowing glaciers; many peaks over 3,000 m; Mt. McKinley, 6,182 m.

Alatau, mtns., bdy. of **Kazakhstan**; and Sinkiang, **China**; group of 5 ranges, outliers of Tien-Shan; alt. up to 4,600 m; highest peak Khan Tengri, 6,954 m.

Alava, Basque prov., N. **Spain**; ch. t. Vitoria; viticulture; a. 3,043 km²; p. (1991) 274,720.

Albacete, prov., S.E. **Spain**; stock-raising; a. 14,864 km²; p. (1991) 339,268.

Albacete, t., cap. of A. prov., **Spain**; agr, mkt.; fruit, saffron; p. (1991) 134,584.

Alba-Iulia, t., **Romania**; on R. Mures, formerly Carisburgh; union of Transylvania with Romania proclaimed here 1918; p. (1992) 71,254.

Albania, rep., S.E. Europe; lying along Adriatic, adjacent to Yugoslavia and Greece; food ch. ind.; petroleum reserves and refining, hydroelectric power, coal, chrome ore, copper, iron ore; first external rail link opened (1986); fastest growing p. in Europe; virtual anarchy, 1997; huge influx of Kosovo refugees, 1999; cap. Tirana; a. 27,529 km²; p. (1991) 3,412,000.

Albano, crater L., **Italy**; tourist attraction 24 km S.E. of Rome; steep sides; a. 8 km².

Albany, mkt. t., Ga., **USA**; on Flint R.; agr. ctr.; cotton, food; p. (1980) 74,471.

Albany, c., cap. of N.Y. st., **USA**; R. pt. on Hudson R.; admin. and industl. ctr.; p. (1990) 101,082 (c.), 874,000 (met. a. with Schenectady-Troy).

Albany, t., **W. Australia**; on King George Sound; founded (1826) as penal col.; first white settlement in W. Australia, established to counter Fr. settlement of W.; p. (1991) 11,186.

Albert, L. See Mobutu Seso, L.

Alberta, prov., W. **Canada**; part of prairies; Rockies in W.; wheat, livestock, feed crops; coal less impt. with development of rich oil and gas resources; chemicals, timber; cap. Edmonton; a. 661,188 km²; p. (1991) 2,545,553.

Albertville. See Kalemie.

Albi, t., cap. of Tarn dep., **France**; cath., industl. and comm. ctr.; p. (1990) 48,707.

Ålborg, c., cap. of N. Jutland prov., **Denmark**; spt. on S. side of Lim fjord; shipping., cement, textiles; airpt.; p. (1990) 155,019.

Albula Alps, mtn. range, Rhaetian Alps, E. **Switzerland**; summits intersected by low passes; inc. several impt. Dolomitic peaks.

Albuquerque, t., N.M., **USA**; on Rio Grande; alt. 1,525 m.; univ.; food prod., engin.; resort; p. (1990) 384,736 (c.), 481,000 (met. a.).

Albury-Wodonga, t., N.S.W., Vic., **Australia**; regional urban growth ctr. (1974) on Murray R.; p. (1983) 77,970.

Alcalá de Henares, t., **Spain**; nr. Madrid; univ.; birthplace of Cervantes; p. (1991) 162,780.

Alcamo, t., Sicily, **Italy**; nr. ruins of anc. Segesra; p. (1981) 42,059.

Alcatraz, I., Cal., **USA**; San Francisco Bay; former prison.

Alcoy, t., **Spain**; textiles, paper; p. (1981) 65,908.

Aldabra Is., Seychelles Rep.; 400 km N.W. of Madagascar; leased (1971–1985) to Royal Society for wildlife research (unique animal and plant species).

Aldan, R., E. Siberia, **Russia**; flows from Stanovoy Range to Lena R. via Tommot gold-mng. dist.; coal in lower course; 2,682 km long.

Aldeburgh, spt., Suffolk Coastal, Suffolk, **Eng.**; famous for annual music festival; p. (1991) 2,654.

Aldermaston, Berkshire, **Eng.**; atomic weapons research ctr.

Alderney, I., dependency of **Guernsey**; horticulture, tourism; a. 794 ha; p. (1994) 2,375.

Aldershot, t., Rushmoor, Hants., **Eng.**; bricks; lge. military camp; p. (1991) 51,356.

Aldridge, t., West Midlands, **Eng.**; plastics, packing cases; expanded t.; p. (1991) 16,862.

Alençon, t. cap. of Orne dep., **France**; textiles; p. (1990) 31,139.

Aleppo, c., **Syria**; 2nd. c. of Syria; in limestone hills; univ.; mkt and textile ctr.; p. (1993) 1,494,000.

Alès, t., Gard dep., **France**; sm. coalfield; chemicals; p. (1982) 70,180 (met. a.).

Alessandria, t., N. **Italy**; rly. ctr. on Tanaro R.; engin.; p. (1981) 100,523.

Alesund, spt. on Giske I., W. **Norway**, fishing, fish processing; airpt. on I. to N.; p. (1990) 23,741.

Aletsch, glacier, **Switzerland**; in Bernese Alps; lgst. in Europe; length 24 km.

Aletschhorn, mtn., Bernese Alps, **Switzerland**; alt. 4,198 m.

Aleutian Is.; Bering Sea, Alaska, **USA**; chain of over 150 Is. formed from partially submerged peaks of volcanic A. mtn. range; on earthquake belt; U.S. air base.

Alexander Archipelago, S.E. Alaska, **USA**; dense I. system; fjord scenery; well populated; furs, lumbering, fishing; a. 33,670 km².

Alexandria, (El Iskandariyah) ch. pt. and prov., **Egypt**; founded by Alexander the Great, 332 B.C.; floating dock; exp. cotton, wheat, rice, gum; second lgst. c. in Africa; new steel plant at El Dikhelia; pt. being expanded and new pt. at Dikhelia; linked to offshore gas field; rapid growth, second lgst. c. in Africa; p. (1990) 3,170,000 (c.), (1991) 3,295,000 (prov.).

Alexandria, c., spt., Va., **USA**; on Chesapeake Bay; indust. t.; p. (1990) 111,183.

Alford, t., East Lindsey, Lincs., **Eng.**; mkt.; engineering, knitwear, flexographic printing; p. (1991) 2,989.

Alfreton, t., Amber Valley, Derbys., **Eng.**; mkt. t.; formerly coal mng.; hosiery, knitwear; p. (1991) 22,822.

Algarve, prov., anc. kingdom, **Portugal**; in extreme S. of cty; tourism, fishing, fruit.

Algeciras, spt., **Spain**; W. of Gibraltar on A. Bay; nearby Campo de Gibraltar scheme for social and economic development; p. (1991) 101,365.

Algeria, indep. st. (1962), N. Africa; former French colony; fertile cstl. plain borders Mediterranean Sea where cereal, wine, fruit and olive production and incr. mkt. garden prods. for exp.; Land reform (1980) encouraging livestock; afforestation to prevent N. spread of Sahara; exp. of high grade iron ore, phosphates, petroleum and natural gas are financing ambitious industrialisation plans; incr. tourism; new roads link Saharan oilfields to cst.; cap. El Djezair; 60 per cent of p. under 19; a. 2,373,994 km²; p. (1995) 28,575,000. Civil war since 1992 against Muslim fundamentalists.

Algiers. See **El Djezair**

Alicante, spt., cap of A. prov., **Spain**; wine, fruits; oil refinery; p. (1991) 270,951, 1,315,712 (prov.).

Alice Springs, t., N.T., **Australia**; ch. t., of desert a.; major cattle raising ctr.; natural gas nearby; growth of winter tourism; p. (1991) 24,678.

Aligarh, t., Uttar Pradesh, **India**; 128 km S.E. of Delhi; univ.; p. (1991) 481,000.

Alkmaar, t., **Netherlands**; impt. cheese mkt. on N. Holland canal; p. (1994) 92,962.

Allahabad, t., Uttar Pradesh, **India**; at confluence of Jumna and Ganges Rs.; univ.; Hindu pilgrimage ctr.; p. (1991) 806,000 (c.).

Allegheny Mtns., **USA**; part of Appalachian system, inc. several parallel ranges; water-shed between Atlantic and Mississippi R. drainage; forested, tourism; average alt. 1,500 m.

Allegheny R., Penns., N.Y., **USA**; rises in A. mtns., flows to Ohio R.; Pittsburg met. a. on lower reaches where R. entrenched 120 m below plateau making urban development difficult; used for coal and ind. transport; 520 km long.

Allen, Bog of, R.o.I.; peat bogs, peat cutting, cultivation; a. 958 km².

Allentown, t., Penns., **USA**; coal, textiles, cement; p. (1990) 105,090 (c.), 687,000 (met. a.).

Alleppey, spt., Kerala, S. **India**; on sand spit coconut prods, p. (1981) 169,940.

Allerdale, l. gov. dist., Cumbria, **Eng.**; cstl. dist. inc. Workington, Maryport, Cockermouth and Keswick; p. (1995) 95,900.

Alliance, t., Ohio, **USA**; iron, steel, engin.; p. (1980) 24,315.

Allier, dep., **France**; N. of Massif Central; coal and iron mng.; mineral springs, wine, wheat; a. 4,786 km²; p. (1990) 357,700.

Alloa, sm. burgh, Clackmannan, **Scot.**; on N. bank of R. Forth; bricks, tiles, glass, distilling; p. (1991) 18,842.

Alma-Ata, See **Almaty**.

Almada, t., **Portugal**; on R. Tagus estuary opposite Lisbon; Salazar bridge (opened 1966) links it with Lisbon; p. (1987) 42,607.

Almaty, t., **Kazakhstan**; in foothills of Tien-Shan mtns.; univ.; comm. agr., and ind. ctr.; food processing, machin., printing; p. (1990) 1,147,100. Capital city (until 1995).

Almelo, t., Overijssel, **Neth.**; 40 km S.E. of Zwolle; cotton textile mnfs.; p. (1994) 64,589.

Almeria, spt. on G. of A., S.E. **Spain**; cap. A prov.; cath.; exp. grapes, oranges; p. (1991) 157,763, 461,938 (prov.).

Alnwick, t., l. gov. dist., Northumberland, **Eng.**; cas.; mkt. t.; p. (1995) 30,900 (dist.), (1991) 7,419 (t.).

Alor Setar, t., cap. of Kedah, **W. Malaysia**; on main W. cst. road and rly.; p. (1980) 71,682.

Alost. See **Aalst.**

Alpes-de-Haute-Provence (**Basses-Alpes**), dep., S.E. **France**; mtnous., infertile a. bordering Italy; olives, wines; cap. Digne; a. 6,988 km²; p. (1990) 130,900.

Alpes-Maritimes, dep., S.E. **France**; ceded by Italy in 1860; ch. t. Nice; olives, wines, fruit; a. 3,737 km²; p. (1990) 971,800.

Alphen, t., S. Holland, **Neth.**; on Old Rhine, 16 km S.E. of Leiden; p. (1994) 66,143.

Alps, hgst. mtns. in **Europe**; 960 km long, inc. 1,200 glaciers; separates S. and central Europe, forming a climatic divide; major tourist a., winter sports; hydroelec. power; main peaks Mont Blanc (4,814 m), Mont Rosa (4,641 m), Matterhorn (4,509 m).

Als, I., S. Denmark; in the Little Belt, a. 337 km²; linked to Jutland by bridge; p. (1990) 50,744.

Alsace-Lorraine, region, E. **France**; bordered to E. by W. Germany and Rhine R; incorporated into Germany at time of unification (1871), returned to France by Treaty of Versailles (1919); impt. iron-ore and iron and steel inds. in Lorraine; regional aid for economic development; well wooded; p. (1990) 1,624,400 (Alsace) See **Lorraine**.

Alsdorf, t., N. Rhine-Westphalia, **Germany**; 16 km N. of Aachen; p. (1986) 45,900.

Alston, t., Eden, Cumbria, **Eng.**; in upper reaches of south Tyne in N. Pennines; limestone quarrying.

Altai Mtns., Mongolia, **Russia**; border China; steppes and glaciers; silver and mercury; multipurpose R. project at Kamenna-Obi; ctr. of Russian atomic ind. at Ust Kamenogorsk; stock-rearing; average alt. 3,000 m, highst. alt. 4,656 m at Tabun Bogdo.

Alta, R., N. **Norway**; scene of major new h.e.p. sta. fiercely opposed by Lapp residents.

Altamura, caves, N. **Spain**; prehistoric shelters, paintings of animals (Magdalenian).

Altamura, t., Apulia, **Italy**; at foot of Apennines; wines, wool; cath.; p. (1981) 51,328.

Altdorf, t., cap. of Uri can., **Switzerland**; rubber gds., wood workings; statue of William Tell and Tell Theatre; p. (1980) 8,200.

Altenahr, t., N. Rhine-Westphalia, **Germany**; site of anc. cas. of Counts von der Marck; metals, wine; p. (1983) 23,400.

Altenburg, t., Saxony, **Germany**; lignite mng., engin., metallurgy, mnfs. playing cards, textiles; p. (1981) 55,827.

Althorp, (Northants), seat of Earl Spencer; burial place of Princess Diana (1997).

Alton, t., East Hants., **Eng.**; breweries, lt. engin.; p. (1991) 16,005.

Alton t., Ill., **USA**; on Mississippi R.; oil refining; p. (1980) 34,171.

Altoona, c., Penns., **USA**; rly. t.; p. (1984) 54,600 (c.), 134,400 (met. a.).

Altrincham, mkt. t., Trafford, Gtr. Manchester, **Eng.**; engin.; residtl.; p. (1991) 40,042.

Alva, burgh, Clackmannan, **Scot.**; at S. foot of Ochil Hills, 5 km N. of Alloa; woollens, printing, fruit and fish canning; p. (1991) 5,201.

Alvsborg, co., S.W. **Sweden**; cap. Vänersborg; a. 11,394 km²; p. (1992) 445,921.

Alwar, c., Rajasthan, **India**; in hilly agr. region; former cap. of A. princely st.; fort, palace; p. (1991) 205,086.

Amagasaki, c., **Japan**; nr. Osaka; chemicals polyethylene; iron and steel; oil refining; p. (1990) 498,998.

Amalfi, spt., **Italy**; on G. of Salerno; tourist resort; fisheries; p. (1981) 6,052.

Amapá, fed. terr., N. **Brazil**; on equator; tropical rain forest, sparse p.; a. 137,423 km²; p. (1991) 289,050.

Amārah, Al, pt., **Iraq**; on left bank of R. Tigris 400 km below Baghdad; Arab t. and agr. mkt. at R. crossing; p. (1985) 131,758.

Amārapura, t., **Myanmar**; on R. Irrawaddy 10 km. S.W. of Mandalay; former cap.; craft inds.

Amarillo, t., Texas, **USA**; oil refining, creameries, meat packing; p. (1990) 157,615.

Amasya, t. and prov., **Turkey**; on Yesil-Cekerek R.;

tr. ctr.; p. (1985) 53,431, (1990) 357,191 (prov.).

Amazon, gr. R., **S. America**; drains lgst. a. and carries more water than any other R. in world; main Andean headstreams Huarco Ucayali and Marañón from Peru unite to flow across Brazil to Atl. Oc., receiving waters of many Rs. inc. the Madeira; lgst. rain forest in world; ocean steamers penetrate to Iquitos, Peru, c. 3,680 km from mouth; a. drained c. 6 million km² of sparsely populated cty., mostly in Brazil; length 6,448 km; basin inc. 40% of S. America; ocean pt. Belém.

Amazonas, lgst. st. of **Brazil**; isolated; tropical rain forest; tree prods.; vast mineral reserves: cap. Manáus; a. 1,595,823 km²; p. (1991) 2,088,682.

Amazonas, fed. terr., **Venezuela**; cap. Puerto Ayacucho on Orinoco R., isolated, tropical rain forest; a. 181,300 km²; p. (1981) 45,667 (mainly Indian).

Amazonia, Peru, Colombia, Brazil; a. covered by Amazon R. and its tribs. and the surrounding lowland; thickly forested; underdeveloped.

Ambala, c., Haryana, **India**; cotton, flour; p. (1991) 139,889.

Ambato, c., **Ecuador**; S. of Quito, on slope of Mt. Chimborazo; alt. 2,702 m; textiles, canned fruits, leather gds.; p. (1990) 124,166.

Amberg, t., Bavaria, **Germany**; mediaeval walled t. on R. Vils; specialist steels, textiles; p. (1986) 43,300.

Amber Valley, l. gov. dist., Derbys., **Eng.**; S. of co., nr. Notts.; inc. Alfreton, Ripley, Heanor and Belper; p. (1995) 114,900.

Ambès, t., Gironde, **France**; nr. Bordeaux; oil refining; p. (1982) 2,715.

Ambleside, tourist ctr., Cumbria, **Eng.**; N. of L. Windermere; p. (1991) 2,905.

Amboise, t., Indre-et-Loire dep., **France**; 24 km E. of Tours; famous cas, and prison; p. (1982) 11,415.

Ambon, I., Moluccas, **Indonesia**; spices, coconuts; religious riots (1999); a. 818 km²; p. 73,000.

America, the lands of the Western hemisphere, comprising the continents of North and South America, separated by narrow Isthmus of Panama; most N. point over 14,400 km from C. Horn, the extreme S. point. See also **North, South, and Central America.**

American Samoa, Is, E.N.E. Fiji under US rule; a. 197 km²; p. (1993) 52,860.

Amersfoort, c., Utrecht, **Neth.**; walled c. on R. Eem; rapid growth of light inds.; p. (1994) 110,117.

Amersham, t., Bucks., **Eng.**; radio isotopes; lt. inds., 17th cent. mkt. hall; p. (1991) 21,711.

Ames, t., Iowa, **USA**; Iowa State Univ. of. Science and Technology and many fed. and st. institutes; p. (1990) 47,196.

Amiens, c., cap. of Somme dep; major textile ctr. of **France**, on R. Somme; cath.; p. (1990) 136,234 (c.), 156,120 (met. a.).

Amindiui, Is, Arabian Sea; joined with Lacadive & Minicoy Is. to form Lakshadweep, Union territory, **India**.

Amirante Isles, gr. of islands in the Indian Oc. belonging to **Seychelles**.

Amlwch, t., Isle of Anglesey, **Wales**; N. cst. resort; pt.; oil terminal; p. (1991) 3,519.

Amman, c., cap. of **Jordan**; N.E. of Dead Sea; site of biblical Raboth Ammon; textiles, cement, tobacco; airpt.; univ.; p. (1992) 1,272,000.

Ammanford, t., Carmarthenshire, **Wales**; brick mkg.; p. (1991) 12,106.

Amoy. See Xiamen.

Ampthill, Mid Beds., **Eng.**; mkt. t.; p. (1991) 6,230.

Amravati, c., Maharashtra, **India**; cotton ctr., univ.; p. (1991) 422,000.

Amritsar, c., Punjab, N.W. **India**; Golden Temple sacred to Sikhs; trade ctr. for shawls and carpets; soaps, paints, engin.; Massacre of Indian nationalists by troops under British control, 1919; p. (1991) 709,000.

Amroha, t., Uttar Pradesh, **India**; pilgrimage ctr.; p. (1991) 137.061.

Amsterdam, spt., cap. of **Netherlands**; at junction of R. Amstel and the IJ; built on 96 Is. joined by 300 bridges, harbour at terminus of N. Sea canal can hold 1,000 ships; two univs., Royal Palace, Bourse; extensive tr.; exp. dairy prod., sugar, tobacco; shipbldg., diamond polishing, aeronautical, marine, elec. machin., oil refining; p. (1994) 724,096 (c.), 1,100,120 (met. a.).

Amudarya (Oxus), R., marks boundary between **Turkmenistan**, **Uzbekistan** and **Afghanistan**; flows from Pamir mtns. to Aral Sea; Kara- and Ksyl-Kum deserts on either bank; rich in fish; 1,395 km long.

Amur (Heilong Jiang), major R. of E. **Asia**; flows from Mongolia between N.E. China and E. Siberia into Pac. Oc. opposite Sakhalin I.; with tribs. Argun and Ussuri forms lgst. R. frontier in world; crossed by Trans-Siberian rly. at Khabarovsk; 2,827 km long.

Anaconda, t., Mont., **USA**; one of lgst. copper mines in world; p. (1990) 10,278.

Anaheim, t., Cal., **USA**; tourism; Disneyland; p. (1990) 266,406 (c.), 2,411,000 (met. a.).

Anahuac, plateau, **Mexico**; average alt. 2,000 m; surrounded by higher cty. inc. volcano Popocatapetl (5,456 m); contains Mexico City heartland of Aztec Mexico; a. c. 3,900 km².

Anambas Is., Indonesia; 240 km W. of W. Malaysia; little development; p. c. 12,000.

Anatolia (Asia Minor), penin. approx. coextensive with Turkey bounded by Black Sea (N.), Mediterranean (S.), Aegean (W.).

Anching. See Anqing.

Anchorage, t., Alaska, **USA**; timber, salmon fishing and canning; earthquake 28 Mar. 1964; spt.; airpt.; p. (1990) 226,338.

Ancona, spt., central **Italy**; on the Adriatic Sea; founded by Dorians, 1500 B.C.; sugar refineries, shipbldg., petrochemicals; p. (1992) 100,701.

Andalucia, region, covering southern **Spain**; Córdoba, Seville, Jaén and Granada, celebrated ctrs. in Moorish times; irrigation for wines, olives, fruits.

Andaman and Nicobar Is., Bay of Bengal; constituted a union terr., **India**, 1956; hilly remnants of drowned mtn. chain; primitive pygmy tribes; a. 8,327 km²; p. (1991) 280,661.

Anderlecht, t., residtl. and industl. sub. of Brussels, **Belgium**; p. (1983) 94,715.

Andermatt, v., Uri, **Switzerland**; at foot of Mt. St. Gotthard; tourist ctr., winter health resort.

Anderson, t., Ind., **USA**; car components; p. (1990) 59,459.

Andes, gr. volcanic mtn. system, **S. America**; extends over 6,400 km from N.-S.; physical and climatic divide rising to over 6,000 m; densely populated; high tropical plateaus; rich in minerals; hgst. peak, Aconcagua (6,965 m).

Andhra Pradesh, st. S.E. **India**; cap. Hyderabad; inc. valleys of lower Godavari and Krishna Rs.; sugar, rice; a. 275,278 km²; p. (1991) 66,508,008.

Andizhan, c. **Uzbekistan**; once residence of Khans of Khokan; industl. ctr.; in irrigation a.; cotton, silk; oilfields; p. (1990) 296,800.

Andorra, sm. mtn. st., E. Pyrenees; under joint suzerainty of French President and Bishop of Urgel (Spain until 1993; now virtually indep.); livestock, wines, tobacco; tourism; alt. 900–3,000 m; a. 495 km²; p. (1994) 62,500.

Andover, mkt. t., Test Valley, Hants., **Eng.**; prehistoric earthwks.; expanded t.; p. (1991) 34,647.

Andria, t., S. **Italy**; Roman remains, cath., palaces; p. (1981) 83,319.

Andropov. See Rybinsk.

Andros, lgst. I., **Bahamas**; sponges, sisal, hemp; a. 5957 km²; p. (1990) 8,155.

Andújar, t., **Spain**; on Guadalquivir R.; mineral springs, pottery, soap, textiles, uranium plant; p. (1981) 30,875.

Angara, R., Siberia, **Russia**; trib. of Yenisey; navigable almost its entire length., rises nr. and flows through L. Baykal; length 2,080 km; hydro-electric power.

Angarsk, t., E. Siberia, **Russia**; on R. Angaar 32 km N.W. Irkutsk; engin., saw milling; p. (1989) 266,000.

Angel Falls (Salto del Angel), waterfall, **Venezuela**; nr. Ciudad Bolívar; 980 m drop.

Angerman, R., N. **Sweden** rises nr. Norwegian border, falls to G. of Bothnia; timber transport; 448 km long.

Angers, t., cap. of Maine-et-Loire dep., **France**; on R. Maine; mkt. t. for local produce, fruit, vegetables, Anjou wines, Cointreau; textiles; cath., cas.; p. (1990) 146,163 (t.), 206,276 (met. a.).

Angkor, c., **Cambodia**; jungle-covered ruins of c. from Khmer civilisation; discovered 1860.

Anglesey. See Isle of Anglesey.

Angola, People's Rep. of (Portuguese W. Africa), interior forms part of central African plateaus, bounded by transitional escarpments in W. which face on to narrow coastal plain; rainfall diminishes from N.-S. with consequent crop zoning; coffee, cotton, oil palm in N., corn, peanuts, sisal in drier interior, cattle in S., semidesert in S.E.; economy dependent upon primary inds., especially agr.; coffee major exp., produced on plantations; newly discovered oilfields; diamonds in remote N.E. Luanda dis.; iron-ore mng. impt. at Cassinga; little mftg.; hydroelectric scheme on Cuarza R.; pts. on natural harbours impt. transhipment points for land-locked central African ctys.; indep. 1975, followed by civil war between rival guerrilla groups; cap. Luanda; a. 1,246,375 km²; p. (1995) 11,500,000 (inc. Cabinda).

Angoulême, mftg. t., cap. of Charente dep., **France**; on R. Charente; cognac, paper; cath.; suffered during Huguenot wars; p. (1990) 46,194 (t.), 101,108 (met. a.).

Angra do Heroismo, t., cap. admin. dist. **Azores**; pt. on Terceira I.; p. (1981) 75,010.

Angren, t., **Uzbekistan**; E. of Tashkent; lgst. ctr. of lignite mng. in central Asia; p. (1990) 133,200.

Anguilla, I., Leeward Is., W.I.; dry climate, thin limestone soil; exp. cotton, salt; a. 91 km²; reverted to Brit. Crown after secession from St. Kitts–Nevis ass. st. 1967; status of separate Brit. dependency and withdrawal from St. Kitts–Nevis ass. statehood 1980; p. (1998) 10,000.

Angus, E.**Scot.**, unit. auth. created in 1996, reinstating most of historic co. which became part of Tayside in 1974; bordered E. by N. Sea; inc. ts. of Arbroath, Forfar and Montrose; p. (1995) 111,770.

Anhui (Anhwei), prov., E. central **China**; in delta region of Chang Jiang; a. 140,686 km²; cap. Hefei; soya-beans, rice, tea, coal and iron; p. (1992) 52,290,000.

Aniakchak, volcano, S.W. Alaska, **USA**; rich variety of flora and fauna on crater floor; alt. 1,384 m.

Anjou, former prov. of **France**; mainly S. of lower R. Loire; ch. t. Angers.

Ankara, c., cap. of **Turkey** since 1923; alt. 1,037 m; univ., cultural and admin. ctr.; p. (1990) 2,541,000, 3,236,626 (prov.).

Anklesvar, t., Gujarat, **India**; natural gas, oil; gas pipelines to Ultaran and Barodi; p. (1981) 36,123.

'Annaba, spt., dep., N. **Algeria**; on fertile plain; fertiliser factory supplied by phosphates from Djebel-Onk; iron and steel complex; p. (1987) 222,518 (t.), 453,151 (dep.).

Annaberg–Bucholz, t., Saxony, **Germany**; in Erz Mtns.; cobalt, tin, uranium mng.; p. (1989) 25,404.

Annam, region, **Vietnam**; formerly within French Union; divided by 17th parallel bdy. (1957); a. 147,560 km²; ch. t. Hué.

Annamese Cordillera, cstl. mtn. range, **Laos**, **Vietnam**; N.–S. watershed between Mekong and S. China Sea; rising to 2,000 m in Ngoc Linh; forested; inhabited by hill tribes.

Annan, royal burgh, Dumfries and Galloway, **Scot.**; on R. Annan, 3 km from its mouth in Solway F.; Chapelcross reactor sta.; p. (1991) 8,930.

Annapolis, c., cap. of Maryland, **USA**; naval academy; p. (1990) 33,187.

Annapolis Valley, Nova Scotia, **Canada**; famous fruit growing a., especially for apples.

Annapurna, massif, **Nepal**; part of Himalayas; many glaciers in W. and N.W.; alt. 8,080 m.

Ann Arbor, c., Mich., **USA**; on the Huron; univ. of Michigan.; motor lorries, farm implements, scientific instruments; p. (1990) 109,592 (c.), 283,000 (met. a.).

Annecy, t., **France**; dep. of Haute-Savoie; at lower end of beautiful L. Annecy; textiles, paper, watches; resort; p. (1990) 51,143 (t.), 122,622 (met. a.).

Anqing (Anching), c., Anhui prov., **China**; R. pt. on Chang Jiang; tr. in agr. prods.

Ansbach, t., Bavaria, **Germany**; machin., metallurgy, furniture indus.; rly. ctr.; p. (1986) 37,500.

An-shan, c., Liaoning, N. **China**; at foot of Qian Shan, 96 km S.W. of Shenyang; lgst. iron and steel complex in China (fully automated steel plant), elec., chemical and locomotive ind.; p. (1992) 1,390,000.

Antakya (Antioch), anc. c., S. **Turkey**; on R. Orontes; cap. of Hatay prov., major Roman cap. and early ctr. of Christian culture; p. (1985) 107,821.

Antalya, c., S.W. **Turkey**; freeport (1986) with shallow harbour from which Paul and Barnabas sailed to Antakya; tourism; p. (1990) 353,149, 1,132,211 (prov.).

Antananarivo (Tananarive), cap. of **Madagascar**; ctr. of commerce and communications; airpt.; lge meat preserving factories, plastics, radios, car assembly, shoes, knitted gds.; rice mills; univ.; p. (1990) 803,390.

Antarctica, plateau continent within A. circle; snow-covered, extensive ice sheets and glaciers;

volcanoes and Is.; alt. 2,000–3,000 m; dependencies of U.K., Australia, N.Z., France, Norway but a. S. of 60° S reserved for peaceful international scientific research; a. 16 million km². *See also* **L7**.

Antarctic Ocean, parts of Pac., Atl. and Indian Oceans, S. of 60° S.; cold and dangerous; no mammalian life other than whales.

Antibes, t., Alpes-Maritimes, N. of Cap d. A., S.E. **France**; spt. on Fr. Riviera; exp. oranges; flowers for perfume mnfs.; resort; Roman remains; p. (1990) 70,688.

Anticosti, barren I. in G. of St. Lawrence, Quebec, **Canada**; well wooded game reserve, lumbering; 224 km by 45 km.

Antigua, anc. c., **Guatemala**; 32 km W. of Guatemala c.; former cap., destroyed by earthquake 1773; comm. ctr. in coffee dist.; notable colonial ruins; tourism; p. (1989) 26,231.

Antigua and Barbuda, Leeward gr., W.I.; aut. st. in ass. with Gt. Britain; indep. 1981; semi-arid limestone; 75 per cent p. in N.E.; sugar, cotton, tourism; cap. St. Johns; a. (inc. Barbuda and Redonda) 440 km²; p. (1991) 65,962.

Antilles, Greater and Lesser, archipelago enclosing Caribbean Sea and G. of Mexico, **W.I.**; complex political structure, tropical climate and crops; a. c. 259,000 km².

Antioquia, mtnous. dep. **Colombia**; colonial mng.; agr. now more impt.; one of major p. clusters in Colombia inc. dep. cap. Medellin; a 65,791 km²; p. (1992) 4,467,914.

Antisana, volcano, central **Ecuador**; alt. 5,708 m.

Antofagasta, spt., **Chile**; cap., comm. and industl. ctr. of A. region; exps. copper from Chuquicamata; situated in desert, water supply 240 km by aqueduct from Andes; p. (1992) 226,749, 407,409 (prov.).

Antony, t., Hauts-de-Seine, **France**; brick wks., toys; sub. of Paris; p. (1990) 57,916.

Antrim, former co.; l. gov. dist., **N. Ireland**; fertile lowland a., arable agr.; borders L. Neagh in S.W. and A. mtns. in N.E.; p. (1991) 44,516.

Antrim, mkt. t., **N. Ireland**; on Lough Neagh; linen, nylon; p. (1991) 20,878.

Antsiranana, (Diego Suarez), t., extreme N. of **Madagascar**; oxygen plant; Fr. naval base; p. (1990) 54,418.

An-tung. *See* Dandong.

Antwerp, (Anvers), low-lying prov., N. **Belgium**: grain, flax; a. 2,859 km²; p. (1993) 1,619,613.

Antwerp, (Anvers), spt., **Belgium**; on Scheldt R., 88 km from sea; major transit pt. for EC, competes with Rotterdam; oil pt., refineries; diamonds; Gothic cath.; of artistic and historic interest; p. (1993) 465,102.

Anuradhapura, anc. cap., **Sri Lanka**; ctr. of Buddhism; comm. ctr of irrigated rice-growing a. in dry zone; p. (1981) 36,248.

An-yang, c., Henan prov., **China**; coal, cotton ind.; former cap. of Shang dynasty; p. (1984) 534,400.

Anzhero-Sudzhensk, t., S.W. Siberia, **Russia**; nr. Tomsk; coal mng., mng. equipment pharmaceutics; p. (1989) 108,000.

Aoraki, mtn. *See* Cook, mtn.

Aomori, spt., N. Honshu, **Japan**; on A. Bay; cstl. tr. of timber, fish with Hokkaido; S. outlet of Seiken Tunnel between Honshu and Hokkaido; cap. of apple-growing A. prov.; p. (1990) 287,813.

Aosta, t., cap. of Val d'Aosta, N. **Italy**; in valley of Dora Baltea at node of trans-Alpine routes; iron inds.; Mont Blanc road tunnel links to Chamonix, Switzerland, opened 1964; cath., p. (1981) 37,682.

Aotearoa, Maori name for New Zealand.

Apapa, spt., sub. of Lagos, **Nigeria**; on mainland opposite I. on which Lagos is situated; modern pt. terminus of W. Nigerian rly. system; exp. agr. prods.; imports industl. prods.

Apeldoorn, c., Gelderland, **Netherlands**; holiday resort; royal summer palace of Het Loo; p. (1994) 149,449.

Apennines, mtn. "backbone" of **Italy**; rich in minerals inc. Carrara marble; cultivation on lower slopes; earthquakes, in S.; barrier to E.–W. communications; hgst. alt. 2,916 m, (Grand Sasso d'Italia); length N.–S. 1,280 km; width 120 km.

Apia, spt., N. Upolu, cap. of **Samoa**; exp. agr. prods.; p. (1986) 32,196.

Apolda, t., Erfurt, **Germany**; ball-casting and museum; p. (est. 1989) 27,633.

Appalachian Mtns., parallel ranges between Atl. Oc. and Mississippi basin, stretching for 2,560 km from Me. to Ala., **USA**; afforestation, hydro-elec. power, coal in N., iron ore in S.; region of human poverty; average alt. 900 m; Mt. Mitchell 2,039 m.

Appenzell, can., N.E. **Switzerland**; divided into the half-cans. Appenzell Inner-Rhoden, a. 174 km², cap. Appenzell; and Appenzell Ausser-Rhoden; textiles, agr.; a. 243 km², cap. Herisau; p. (1990) 65,100.

Appenzell, picturesque t., cap. of A. can., **Switzerland**; on R. Sitter; lace, embroidery.

Appian Way, anc. highway; runs from Rome to Campania and S. **Italy**.

Appleby, t., Eden, Cumbria, **Eng.**; mkt. t. on R. Eden; cas.; p. (1991) 2,570.

Appleton, c., Wis., **USA**; industl. c. in rich dairy dist.; p. (1990) 65,695 (c.), 315,121 (met. a. with Oshkosh-Neenah).

Apsheron, peninsula, E. **Azerbaijan**; on W. side of the Caspian; petroleum wells (nr. Baku) and mud volcanoes.

Apulia, region, S.E. **Italy**; hilly, cstl., pastoral plain; grain, fruits, livestock; wine, olive oil; a, 19,347 km²; p. (1992) 4,049,972.

Aqaba, t., **Jordan**'s only spt. at head of G. of A., 88 km from Israeli Elat.; exp. phosphates, imports petroleum; p. (1983) 40,000.

Aqaba G., Red Sea, between **Sinai Peninsula** and **Saudi Arabia**; impt. Biblical waterway; few natural harbours, Dahab, Elat, Aqaba main pts; Elat ctr. of mng. a., and airpt.; length 160 km, width 24 km.

Aquila (L'Aquila), t., cap. of Abruzzi prov., **Italy**; on R. terrace of R. Aterno; mkt. and sm. inds. ass. with local farming; holiday resort; cath.; p. (1981) 63,678.

Aquitaine, region, S.W. **France**; inc. deps. Dordogne, Gironde, Landes, Lot-et-Garonne, Pyrénées-Atlantique; to W. and S.W. of Central Massif, to N. of Pyrenees, bordered on W. by Atl. Oc.; warm, wet, oceanic climate; rich agr. lowland; inc. Landes, reclaimed sandy area; ch. ts. Bordeaux, Toulouse; p. (1990) 2,795,800.

Arabia, peninsula, **S.W. Asia**; mainly desert plateau, lying between Red Sea and Persian Gulf; inc. Saudi Arabia, South Yemen, North Yemen, Oman, United Arab Emirates, Kuwait, Bahrain, Qatar; coffee, dates, gums, horses, camels; E. Arabia rich in oil reserves; a. 2,590,000 km²; p. 8,000,000.

Arabian Desert, E. **Egypt**; between R. Nile and Red Sea; alt. approx. 350–2,000 m; a. 207,200 km².

Arabian Mtns., ridge along W. and S.W. csts. of **Arabia**; volcanic, hgst. peaks in Yemen Arab Rep.; average alt. 1,500 m, rising to over 3,500 km.

Arabian Sea, N.W. part of Indian Oc., tr. in Arab dhows; width 2,880 km.

Aracaju, spt., cap. of Sergipe st., **Brazil**; sugar, soap, textiles, tanneries; p. (1991) 401,244.

Arad, new t. (1962) **Israel**; in Negev desert, nr. Beersheba; inds. to be based on gasfields at Zohar and Kanaim; chemicals.

Arad, t., **Romania**; industl., route ctr. on R. Mures; p. (1992) 190,088.

Arafura Sea, N. of Australia, S.W. of Papua-New Guinea, and E. of Timor.

Aragua, sm. upland cstl. st., **Venezuela**; lies in densely populated industl., agr., urban and political region of cty.; tropical climate; good road network; cap. Maracay in fertile Aragua valley; a. 7,014 km²; p. (1981) 891,623.

Araguaia, R., **Brazil**; trib. of Tocatins R.; splits into 2 parts in middle course to form Banaral I.; rapids; length 1,800 km.

Arak, t., **Iran**; mkt. and agr. processing ctr. for surrounding region on Trans-Iranian rly.; carpets; p. (1986) 268,405.

Aral Sea (Aral'skoye More), inland sea with no outlet, **Uzbekistan/Kazakhstan**; fed by Amu-Dar'ya and Syr Dar'ya Rs.; sparse p. on shore but attempts to develop agr.; a. 63,805 km².

Aran Is.; Galway, **R.o.I.**; inc. anc. religious ctr. and I. of Inishmore; fishing; agr.; a. 47 km²; p. (1986) 735.

Arandelovac, t., Serbia, **Yugoslavia**; industl. a. based on local sources of refractory clays; tourist resort.

Aranjuez, t., **Spain**; 18th cent. planned t. on R. Tagus; mkt. gardens; strawberries, asparagus; p. (1981) 35,484.

Ararat, volcanic mtn., **Turkey**; supposed resting-place of Noah's Ark.; 5.168 m.

Ararat, t., Victoria, **Australia**; former gold rush t.

on W. Highway and ctr. for Grampians; p. (1986) 8,015.

Aras (Araxes) R., flows from Bingöl Dağlari mtns. **(Turkey)** to Caspian Sea forming long sections of **USSR**–Iran frontier; valley in rich fruit growing a.; home of anc. civilisation; length 880 km.

Araucania, region., **Chile**; cap. Temuco; concentration of A. Indians, especially in Rio Tolten valley; a. 31,761 km²; p. (1992) 774,959.

Arbroath, royal burgh, Angus, **Scot.**; engin., textiles, fishing pt.; holiday resort; p. (1991) 23,474.

Arcachon, t., Gironde, S.W. **France**; on S. side of Bassin d'Arcachon, Bay of Biscay; fish. pt., oysters; resort; p. (1982) 13,664.

Arcadia, region of anc. **Greece** in Peloponnesus; tradition of pastoral agr. in dry a.; ch. c. was Megalopolis; p. (1991) 105,309.

Arctic Ocean, almost landlocked sea extending from N. Pole to Atl. Oc.; flora and fauna of scientific interest; a. 14,089,600 km².

Ardabil, anc. c. in fertile agr. a., Azerbaijan, **Iran**; tr. and route ctr.; carpets; p. (1986) 283,710.

Ardal, t., **Norway**; on Sogne fiord; site of aluminium wks.

Ardèche, dep., S. **France**; Cevennes Mtns.; olives, wine, silk, minerals; cap. Privas; a. 55,530 km²; p. (1990) 277,600.

Ardennes, hilly wooded region, **Belgium**, N. **France**, **Luxembourg**, rising to over 600 m; infertile; heavy fighting in both world wars.

Ardennes, dep., N.E. **France**; farming, woollens, iron; cap. Mézières; a. 5,250 km²; p. (1990) 296,400.

Ardglass, sm. t., Down, **N. Ireland**; one of N.I.'s impt. fishing pts; p. (1991) 1,651.

Ardnacrusha, Clare, **R.o.I.**; power sta. on R. Shannon, 5 km N. of Limerick; p. (1986) 481.

Ardrishaig, sm. spt., Argyll and Bute, **Scot.**; on Loch Gilp, at entrance to Crinan Canal; p. (1991) 1,315.

Ardrossan, burgh, N. Ayrshire, S.W. **Scot.**; resort and spt. on Firth of Clyde; oil storage, ship-bldg., road bitumen, engin.; p. (1991) 10,750.

Ards, l. gov. dist., **N. Ireland**; formerly part of Down; N. of Strangford L.; main t. New-townards; p. (1991) 64,764.

Arecibo, spt., N. cst. **Puerto Rico**; sited in rich agr. a.; local hydroelec. power; p. (1990) 93,385.

Arendal, spt. **Norway**; on Skagerrak; wood pulp, aluminium, shipping; p. (1990) 24,985.

Arequipa, c., **Peru**; cap. of A. prov. and former Inca c.; impt. wool mkt.; alpaca wool inds.; growth point for prov. industl. development; copper mng. nearby; earthquakes frequent; p. (1993) 916,806 (prov.), 619,156 (c.).

Arezzo, c., cap. of Arezzo prov., Tuscany, **Italy**; hill site in basin within Apennines at junc. of valley routes; in mediaeval times ctr. of learning and the arts; birthplace of Petrarch and Vasari; Gothic cath.; mkt. for silk, wine, olives; p. (1981) 92,105.

Argenteuil, t., Val-d'Oise, **France**; N.W. sub. of Paris; industl., mkt. gardens; p. (1990) 94,162.

Argentina, fed. rep., S. America; 2nd. in a., 3rd. in p. of S. American sts.; p. predominantly of European origin and highly urbanised; varied relief and climate, inc. Andes, tropical N., Chaco, Pampas, Patagonia in S.; agr. less impt. internally than other S. American sts., yet provides most of exp., inc. meat, wool, wheat, maize, cotton; petroleum, natural gas; cap. Buenos Aires; new cap. to be built on fringe of Patagonia to decentralize power from Buenos Aires by 1989; a. 2,797,109 km²; p. (1995) 34,586,635.

Argos, c. of anc. **Greece**; N.E. Peloponnesus; leading c. in 7th cent. B.C. under King Pheidon; p. (1991) 78,884.

Argostólion, cap. of Cephalonia I., **Greece**; ship-bldg.; earthquake 1953; p. (1981) 6,788.

Argyll and Bute, W. **Scot.**; unit. auth. created in 1996, incorporating most of historic co. of **Argyllshire** which became part of Strathclyde in 1974; rural a. N.W. of Glasgow conurb.; p. (1995) 91,310.

Arhus, c., **Denmark**; prin. spt. on E. cst. Jutland; admin. ctr. of A. prov.; Gothic cath.; univ.; comm. and industl. ctr.; pt. processing inds., oil refining; p. (1987) 256,000.

Arica, spt., N. **Chile**, free zone; exp. tin, copper, sulphur mainly from Bolivia; rly. to La Paz and oil pipeline connects to Sica-Sica in Bolivia; p. (1992) 169,217.

Ariège, dep., S. **France**; Pyrenees in S., fertile lowland in N.; livestock, fruit, iron, copper; cap. Foix; a. 4,900 km²; p. (1990) 136,500.

Arizona, st., **USA**; home of Apache Indians; much desert, rainfall increasing to E.; many lge. irrigation schemes for cotton, grain, fruit, vegetables; inc. Col. Plateau and Grand Canyon to N.; copper, lead mng. and refining; prin. ts. Phoenix (cap.), Tucson; huge meteorite crater nr. Winslow; admitted to union 1912; st. flower Saguaro Cactus blossom; st. bird cactus wren; a. 295,024 km²; p. (1990) 3,665,228.

Arkansas, st., **USA**; highland in N.W., inc. Ozark, Ouachita mtns., lowland in S.E. where Arkansas R. and Mississippi alluvium; humid climate; cotton cultivation; bauxite, coal, petroleum; admitted to union 1836; st. flower Apple Blossom, st. bird Mockingbird; cap. Little Rock; a. 137,534 km²; p. (1990) 2,350,725.

Arkansas, R., **USA**; rises in Rockies, trib. of Mississippi; completion (1971) of 704 km waterway (17 dams and locks), opening Okla. and Ark. to sea; flows through impt. agr. as.; several major cs. on banks; length 2,334 km.

Arkhangel'sk, c., major spt., **Russia**; on E. side Dvina estuary, White Sea; lge. harbour kept open in winter by ice breakers; fishery headquarters; inds. from local softwood resources; engin.; hydroelec. power; p. (1989) 416,000.

Arklow, t., spt., Wicklow, **R.o.I.**; fisheries, pottery; fertiliser plant under construction; resort; p. (1981) 8,646.

Arlberg, Alpine pass, 1,803 m; main western entry to Austria; rly. tunnel 10 km long; road tunnel (1979) 14 km long.

Arles, t., Provence, S. **France**; on Rhône delta; anc. Roman t.; historic bldgs and monuments; van Gogh and Gauguin painted here; p. (1990) 52,593.

Arlington, t., Texas, **USA**; aircraft, missiles; rapid expansion; p. (1990) 261,721.

Arlington, t., Va., **USA**; Arlington National Cemetery contains tombs of the Unknown Soldier and President Kennedy.

Arlon, t., cap. of Luxembourg prov., **Belgium**; p. (1982) 22,364.

Armadale, burgh, W. Lothian, **Scot.**; 16 km S.W. Linlithgow; p. (1991) 8,958.

Armagh, former co.; l. gov. dist., **N. Ireland**; lowland in N. rising to over 450 m adjoins **R.o.I.** border; mainly rural; p. (1991) 51,817.

Armagh, c., **N. Ireland**; caths.; linen, whiskey; p. (1991) 14,265.

Armavir, c., Krasnodar Terr., **Russia** on Kuban R.; rly. junc.; engin.; food processing; p. (1989) 161,000.

Armenia, CIS, former rep. USSR; former a. divided between Turkey, Russia, Iran; mineral inds.; subtropical agr.; hydroelec. stas. under constr.; earthquake 1988; disturbances 1989; cap. Yerevan; a. 30,821 km²; p. (1995) 3,742,000.

Armenia, t., **Colombia**; coffee; earthquake devastation (1999); p. (1992) 212,310.

Armentières, mftg. t., Nord, **France**; base of British operations against Lille in first world war; textiles; p. (1982) 55,913 (French met. a.).

Armidale, t., N.S.W., **Australia**; univ.; ctr. of New England wool producing dist.; p. (1981) 18,922.

Arnhem, c., cap. of Gelderland prov., **Neth.**; on R. Neder-Rhine; lge. tin smelter; lt. inds. using rubber and rayon; p. (1994) 133,670 (c.), 311,755 (met. a.).

Arnhem Land, N. part of N.T., **Australia**; an aboriginal reserve; bauxite worked, uranium finds.

Arno, R., central **Italy**; flows past Florence and Pisa into Mediterranean; Val d'Arno is the fruitful valley of the R.; length 120 km.

Arnold, t., Gedling, Notts., **Eng.**; almost continuous with Nottingham; hosiery, brick mkg.; p. (1991) 37,646.

Arnsberg, c. N. Rhine Westphalia, **Germany**; mftg. on R. Ruhr; p. (1989) 74,962.

Arnstadt, t., Erfurt, **Germany**; on R. Gera, 16 km S. of Erfurt; artificial silk, leather gds., engin.; p. (1989) 29,665.

Aroostook, dist., New England, **USA**; produces 12 per cent of USA potatoes.

Arran, I., N. Ayrshire, **Scot.**; in Firth of Clyde; contains many summer resorts; p. (1991) 4,474.

Arras, t., cap. of Pas-de-Calais dep., **France**; historic cap. of Artois; renowned for tapestry; agr. mkt.; brewing, textiles, metal inds.; almost destroyed in first world war; p. (1990) 42,715(t.), 79,607 (met. a.).

Árta, prov., Epirus, **Greece**; agr. area; Pindhos range; p. (1991) 78,884.

Artemovsk, t., **Ukraine**; industl. ctr. in Donets Basin; salt, coal, iron; p. (1990) 90,600.

Arthur's Seat, famous hill, Edinburgh, **Scot.**; 251 m.

Artois, former prov. of N. **France**; now mainly with dep. of Pas-de-Calais.

Aru Is., gr., **Indonesia**; S.W. of W. Irian; fertile; sago, rice, sugar, coconuts, tobacco; a. 8,402 km²; p. 18,139.

Aruba, I., Leeward Is., W.I.; closure of oil refinery (1985) which provided employment and one-third gov. receipts; shipping; guano; voted for indep. from spr. (1977) internal self-government granted 1986, (status aparte); a. 176 km²; p. (1991) 68,897.

Arun, l. gov. dist., West Sussex, **Eng.**; W. section of S. Downs and ts. of Arundel, Littlehampton and Bognor Regis; p. (1995) 136,200.

Arunachal Pradesh, new union terr. (1972), N.E. Assam, **India**; formerly N.E. Frontier Agency; in Himalayas bordering Tibet and Burma; tribal p.; cap. Itanagar; a. 81,424 km²; p. (1991) 864,558.

Arundel, t., Arun, West Sussex, **Eng.**; mkt. t. on Arun R.; Arundel Castle, seat of Duke of Norfolk; p. (1991) 3,033.

Arusha, t., **Tanzania**; S.W. of Mt. Meru; mkt. for coffee; H.Q. of E. African Common Market; airpt. at 1,388 m (W. of t.).

Aruwimi, R., **Congo**; trib. of R. Congo; route of Stanley's famous forest march in 1887; 992 km long.

Arvida, t., S. Quebec, **Canada**; aluminium plant; nearby Saguenay power development.

Arvika, t., N. of L. Vänern, **Sweden**; agr. machin. and implements, pianos, organs.

Asahikawa, c., Hokkaido, **Japan**; on Ishikari R.; industl., comm. and rly. ctr. for gr. agr. region; p. (1990) 359,069.

Asansol, t., W. Bengal, **India**; in Damodar valley; rly. junc.; coal mng., iron, steel; p. (1991) 262,000.

Ascension I., part of Brit. col. St. Helena, 1,216 km to S.E.; volcanic; ch. settlement Georgetown; nesting place of sooty tern; Brit. earth satellite sta. (1966); airstrip known as Miracle Mile; some arable and pastoral agr.; a. 88 km²; p. (1993) 1,117.

Aschaffenburg, t., Bavaria, **Germany**; pt. on R. Main and Trans-European waterway; cas.; synthetic fibres, scientific-based inds.; p. (1986) 59,600.

Aschersleben, t., Saxony-Anhalt, **Germany**; potash and lignite mng., chemicals, textiles, engin., horticulture; p. (1989) 33,891.

Ascoli Piceno, cath. c., central **Italy**; cap. of A.P. prov.; lies in wooded hills; agr. inds.; (1981) 54,298.

Ascot, v., Berks., **Eng.**; famous racecourse at Ascot Heath.

Asfordby, Leics., **Eng.**; site of deep mine colliery, closure announced (1997).

Ashanti, admin. region, central **Ghana**; formerly powerful native st.; timber, cocoa; growing importance of gold mines (15% Ghana's exp.); new mines opened 1984; cap. Kumasi; a. 24,390 km²; p. (1984) 2,089,683.

Ashbourne, t., Derbys. Dales, **Eng.**; nr. Dovedale; mkt. t.; quarrying, milk processing; p. (1991) 6,300.

Ashburton, t., Teignbridge, Devon, **Eng.**; old mkt. t., S. gateway to Dartmoor; anc. stannary t.; p. (1991) 3,564.

Ashburton, t., S. Island, **N.Z.**; ctr. of gr. wheat growing dist.; p. (1991) 24,435.

Ashby-de-la-Zouch, t., North West Leics., **Eng.**; hosiery; p. (1991) 10,595.

Ashdod, pt., **Israel**; new modern deepwater pt. on Med. cst., 32 km S. of Jaffa.

Ashdown Forest, East Sussex, **Eng.**; heath and woodland; site of former iron industry.

Asheville, c., N.C., **USA**; economic and cultural ctr. of mtnous. region; winter resort; glass; p. (1984) 58,600 (c.), 165,600 (met. a.).

Ashfield, l. gov. dist., Notts., **Eng.**; comprises Sutton-in-Ashfield, Hucknall and Kirkby-in-Ashfield; p. (1995) 109,200.

Ashford, t., l. gov. dist., Kent, **Eng.**; mkt. t., rly. works, site of international station at northern end of channel tunnel; p. (1995) 96,300 (dist.), (1991) 52,002 (t.).

Ashikaga, c., Honshu, **Japan**; cultural ctr.; old silk-weaving ctr.; anc. school with library of Chinese classics; p. (1990) 167,687.

Ashington, t., Wansbeck, Northumberland, **Eng.**; coal mng., p. (1991) 27,962.

Ashkhabad, c., cap. of **Turkmenistan**; in foothills of Kopet-Dag mtns.; textiles, clothing, food processing; univ.; p. (1990) 407,200.

Ashland, t., Ky., **USA**; on R. Ohio; iron, steel, lumber, leather; p. (1980) 27,064.

Ashmore and Cartier Is., uninhabited external territory of **Australia** lying 320 km off the N.W. Australian coast; a. 5 km².

Ashtabula, t., Ohio, **USA;** pt. on L. Erie handling iron ore, coal; many diversified inds.; p. (1980) 23,449.

Ashton-in-Makerfield, t. Gtr. Manchester, **Eng.;** nr. Wigan; former coal mng.; p. (1991) 28,105.

Ashton-under-Lyne, t., Tameside, Gtr. Manchester, **Eng.;** textiles, lt. engin., rubber, tobacco; p. (1991) 43,906.

Asia, largest continent, extends over nearly one-third of the land surface of the earth; chief mtn. ranges, Himalayas, Kunlun, Tien Shan, Altai, Tibetan plateau; ch. Rs., Ob, Yangtze, Yenisey, Lena, Amur, Hwang-ho, Mekong; deserts, Arabia, Thar, Takla Makan, Gobi; some very fertile valleys and plains; climate very varied, extreme in N., monsoonal in S. and E.; gold, coal, oil, iron, manganese, antimony, tin; principal countries in Asia: Turkey in Asia, Israel, Jordan, Iran, Iraq, Afghanistan, India, Pakistan, Sri Lanka, Myanmar (Burma), China, Vietnam, Indonesia, Thailand, Malaysia, South Korea, North Korea, Japan, Bangladesh, Cambodia, Laos, Philippines, Syria, Lebanon, Taiwan, and Russian Asia; industrialisation greatest in Japan, China, Korea, India, and Russian Asia; a. c. 43,250,000 km²; p. (1995) 3,400,000,000.

Asia Minor. See **Anatolia.**

Asir, dist., S.W. **Saudi Arabia;** desert cstl. plain with parallel A. mtns.

Askja, volcanic crater, L. and lava plain, E. **Iceland;** surrounded by Dyngju-fjöll Hills; alt. 1,450 m.

Asmara, c., cap. of **Eritrea;** alt. 2,226 m; on rly.; textiles, matches, soap, brewing; p. (1991) 367,300.

Asnières, t., sub. N.W. Paris, Hauts-de-Seine, **France;** regattas; p. (1990) 72,250.

Aspra Spitia, t. central **Greece;** new industl. t. close to Andikira Bay; aluminium wks.

Aspull, t., Gtr. Manchester, **Eng.;** nr. Wigan; former coal mng.; p. (1991) 4,765.

Assab, c., **Eritrea;** port giving access to the sea by Ethiopia following secession of Eritrea in 1993; p. (1989) 36,569.

Assam, st., **India;** on Brahmaputra R.; valley enclosed by mtns.; forested; extensive tea plantations; rice, cotton, coal; oil development at Rudrasagar; former cap. Shillong; since 1956 4 new sts. carved out – Nagaland (1963), Meghalaya, Manipur, Tripura (1972), and union terrs. of Arunachal Pradesh and Mizoram (1972); a. (1972) 121,973 km²; p. (1991) 22,414,322.

Assen, t., prov. cap. Drenthe, **Neth.;** route ctr.; food processing; p. (1994) 52,268.

Assiniboine, R., Manitoba, **Canada;** joins Red R. at Winnipeg; 720 km long.

Assisi, t., Umbria, central **Italy;** 24 km S.E. of Perugia; birthplace of St. Francis; cath. and old cas.; damaged by earthquake (1997); p. (1981) 24,440.

Assyria, gr. anc. empire, northern plain Mesopotamia **(Iraq),** cap. Nineveh; drained by R. Tigris; now mainly pastoral farming a.

Astara, pt., **Azerbaijan;** on Caspian Sea, at frontier with Iran; natural gas pipeline; p. (1990) 13,000.

Asti, t., **Italy;** route, industl., comm. ctr.; cath.; sparkling wines; p. (1981) 77,681.

Astin Tagh, (Aerchin Shan), mtn. range, S., Sinkiang, **China;** N. branch of Kunlun mtn. system which separates Tibet from Turkestan; rises to 5,000 m.

Astrakhan', c., **Russia;** major air and sea pt. on delta of R. Volga, 80 km from Caspian Sea; handles petroleum, timber; lge. fishing fleet; caviar; food and pt. processing inds.; astrakhan fur; cap. A. oblast; univ.; p. (1989) 509,000.

Asturias, region and former kingdom, N.W. **Spain;** S. of Bay of Biscay; now Oviedo prov.; isolated from rest of Spain by Cantabrian mtns.; coal mng; p. (1987) 1,115,016.

Asunción, c., cap. of **Paraguay;** at confluence of Rs. Paraguay and Pilcomayo; 25 per cent of p. of Paraguay in and around A.; admin., industl., comm. ctr.; cath.; p. (1992) 637,737 (met. a.).

Aswan, t. and prov., Upper **Egypt;** on Nile at first cataract; anc. name Syene. Aswan dam built 1902, 5 km S. of t., to control Nile flood; lge. cement plant; univ. proposed; p. (1986) 191,461 (t.), (1991) 925,000 (prov.).

Aswan High Dam (107 m high) opened 1971,

on R. Nile, **Egypt,** 6 km S. of old Aswan dam, has harnessed R. to bring electricity and irrigation to hundreds of vs. and prevent Nile's flood from being lost into Mediterranean. See also **Nile.**

Asyût, major c. and prov. of Upper **Egypt;** nr. A. dam on Nile R.; anc. Lycopolis; noted pottery, wood, ivory carving; caravan tr. ctr.; cap, of A. prov.; p. (1986) 273,191 (c.), (1991) 2,532,000 (prov.).

Atacama, region **Chile;** cap. Copiapo; a. 75,705km²; p. (1992) 230,786.

Atacama Desert, N. **Chile;** arid coastal tract rich in nitrates; one of world's driest deserts.

Atami, t., Honshu, **Japan;** on Sagami Bay; seaside hot-spring resort; p. (1990) 47,291.

Atbara, t., **Sudan;** at confluence of Atbara R. with Nile; heavy inds.; international airpt.; p. (1983) 73,000.

Atbara R., or **Black Nile, Ethiopia** and **Sudan;** trib. of Nile; provides irrigation water for Sudan; length 1,264 km.

Athelney, hill, formerly encircled by marsh nr. Taunton, Somerset, **Eng.;** between the Rs. Tone and Parret; King Alfred's hiding-place.

Athens (Athínai), c., cap of **Greece;** on plain of Attica; admin., economic and cultural ctr.; varied mnfs., notably textiles; anc. c. of Greek art and learning; Acropolis and many splendid temples; univ.; airpt; p. (1981) 772,072 (c.), (1991) 3,072,922 (met. a.).

Athens, t., Ga., **USA;** univ.; cotton gds.; lumber; p. (1984) 42,500 (c.), 136,600 (met. a.).

Athens, t., Ohio, **USA;** univ.; coal, lt. inds.; p. (1980) 19,743.

Atherstone, t., North Warwicks., **Eng.;** N. of Coventry; mkt. t., footwear, granite quarrying; p. (1991) 10,677.

Athlone, t., Westmeath, **R.o.I.;** on R. Shannon; radio sta.; textiles; p. (1986) 8,815.

Atholl, dist., N. Perth and Kinross, **Scot.;** extensive deer forests and grouse moors.

Athos, peninsula, Khalkidhiki, N.E. **Greece;** Mt. Athos (2,034 m) at S. tip, known as Holy Mountain, home of monastic community; ch. t. Karyes.

Athy, t., Kildare, **R.o.I.;** on Grand Canal; agr. machin.; p. (1986) 4,734.

Atitlán L., S.W. **Guatemala;** volcanic; famed for beauty; dense p. on shore; maize, fishing; a. 137 km².

Atlanta, c., st. cap. Ga., **USA;** univ.; cotton, paper, farm implements, printing, clothing; p. (1990) 394,017 (c.), 2,833,511 (met. a.).

Atlantic City, c., N.J., **USA;** summer resort, convention c.; p. (1990) 37,986 (c.), 319,000 (met. a.).

Atlantic Ocean, 2nd lgst ocean; a. est. 82,440,000 km²; connected to Pac. Oc. by Panama Canal; central ridge of volcanic activity runs S. from Iceland to Antarctic, some peaks emerging as Is. mainly in N. (e.g. Azores, Ascension, Tristan da Cunha); S, mainly a barren waste of water; chief deeps: Milwaukee Deep (9,225 m) nr. Bahamas and Nares Deep (8,531 m) nr. Puerto Rico.

Atlas, mtn. range, N.W. **Africa;** extends 2,400 km through Morocco, Algeria, to Tunisia; formed of several chains; mineralised, roads across passes; long been home of Berber tribes; average height 2,500–3,000 m; hgst. peak Jebel Toubkal, 4,141 m.

Atlixco Valley, t., **Mexico;** 16 km S.W. of Puebla; fertile volcanic soils; wheat, fruit, vegetables; p. (1990) 104,186.

Attica, (Attikí), dep., **Greece;** agr.; serving cap. Athens; a. 3,761 km²; p. (1991) 3,523,407.

Attleboro, c., Mass., **USA;** founded (1669) by immigrants from English Attleborough (Norfolk); jewellery, silverware; p. (1980) 34,196.

Attock, t., **Pakistan;** on Indus R. between Peshawar and Islamabad; oil wells, oil refining; impt. crossing of R. Indus.

Atyrau, (Guryev) c., **Kazakhstan;** pt. on R. Ural at entrance to Caspian Sea; oil refining; pipe-line to Orsk; p. (1990) 151,400.

Aubagne, t., Bouches-du-Rhône, **France;** bricks, tiles, corks, meat processing; p. (1981) 38,571.

Aube, dep., N.E. **France;** arid, infertile chalk in ctr. and N.W.; wooded and fertile S.E.; drained by Seine and A. Rs.; cap. Troyes; a. 6,024 km²; p. (1990) 289,200.

Aubervilliers, t., Seine-St. Denis, **France;** sub. of Paris; industl.; p. (1990) 67,836.

Auburn, t., N.Y., **USA;** shoes, woollens, farm implements; st. prison; p. (1980) 32,548.

Aubusson, t., Creuse dep., **France;** sited on Creuse R.; fine tapestries and carpets; p. (1982) 6,153.

Auch, t., cap. of Gers dep., **France;** agr., mkt., tr. in Armagnac brandy; agr. processing; p. (1990) 24,728.

Auchterarder, burgh, Perth and Kinross, **Scot.;** 24 km S.W. of Perth; health resort on S. slopes of Vale of Strathearn; woollen inds.; p. (1991) 3,549.

Auchtermuchty, burgh, Fife, **Scot.;** at S. foot of Lomond Hills, 40 km N.E. of Alloa; distilling (now closed down); p. (1991) 1,932.

Auckland, spt., c., N.I., **N.Z.;** lgst. c. in N.Z.; seat of government 1845–64; univ.; extensive tr. and shipping; sawmills, sugar refinery, shipbldg.; glass; steelwks. projected 40 km S. of A., in Waikato iron sand a.; p. (1991) 315,668 (c.), 855,571 (urban a.).

Aude, dep., S. **France;** mtnous.; fertile N., salt from S. cstl. lagoons; drained by A. R. to Mediterranean; cap. Carcassonne; a. 6,340 km² p. (1990) 298,700.

Audenshaw, t., Gtr. Manchester, **Eng.;** metals, leather, pharmaceuticals; p. (1991) 13,173.

Aue, t., Saxony, **Germany;** 32 km S.E. of Zwickau; uranium mng., metallurgy, textiles; p. (1989) 25,435.

Aughrim, v., Galway, **R.o.I.;** battle (1691) between William III and James II.

Augsburg, c., Bavaria, **Germany;** at confluence of Rs. Lech and Wertach; cath.; theological institute; major industl. ctr., textiles, engin.; route ctr.; p. (1990) 258,300.

Augusta, t., Sicily, **Italy;** on E. cst. peninsula; gd. harbour used as naval base; fishing; lubricants; p. (1981) 38,900.

Augusta, c., Maine, **USA;** state capital and commercial centre on Kennebec River; p. (1980) 21,820.

Augusta, c., Georgia, **USA;** pt.; on Savannah R. and boundary with S.C.; cotton, cotton-seed oil, chemicals, foundries; p. (1984) 46,000 (c.), (1990) 397,000 (met. a.).

Aulnay-sous-Bois, t., Seine-St. Denis, **France;** residtl. sub. of Paris; p. (1990) 82,537.

Aurangabad, t., admin. ctr., Maharashtra, **India;** textiles, grain tr.; p. (1991) 573,000.

Aurès, mtn. massif, **Algeria;** Berber stronghold.

Aurignac, v., Haute-Garonne, S. **France;** at foot of Pyrenees; caves, paleolithic remains.

Aurillac, t., cap., mkt. t. for dep. of Cantal, **France;** cheeses, umbrellas, leather goods; p. (1990) 32,654.

Aurora, t., Ill., **USA;** rly. wks., foundries, office equipment; p. (1990) 357,000 (met. a. with Elgin).

Auschwitz. *See* Oswiecim.

Aussig. *See* Usti Nad Labem.

Austin, st. cap., Texas, **USA;** educational and artistic ctr., st. univ.; food processing; international airpt.; p. (1990) 465,622 (c.), 782,000 (met. a.).

Australasia, div. of **Oceania;** inc. Australia, Tasmania, N.Z., New Guinea and neighbouring archipelagos.

Australia, Commonwealth of, lgst. I., smallest continent in world; forms part of Australasia; Cook took possession for Britain 1770; Commonwealth proclaimed 1901; fed. of N.S.W., Victoria, Queensland, S.A., W. Australia, Tasmania; inc. also Cap. Terr. (Canberra) and N.T.; p. and inds. concentrated around cst. and in st. caps.; 41 per cent live in Gtr. Sydney and Melbourne; agr. economy (sheep, wheat, dairying) giving way to mineral inds. esp. in W.A. where lge. and diverse deposits abound; offshore petroleum deposits; N. cst. tropical, interior dry, S.E. cst. more moderate, Mediterranean climate in S.W.; mtns. in E. form Gr. Dividing Range separating E. cst. from interior, where plains drained by Murray-Darling and L. Eyre R. systems (used for hydroelec. power and irrigation); referendum (1999) on issue of a republic; cap. Canberra; a. 7,682,300 km²; p. (1994) 17,935,800.

Australian Alps, form S. part of Gr. Dividing Range, between E. cst. and interior, **Australia;** extend for 320 km; contain hgst. mtns. in Australia; Mount Kosciusko (2,228 m.); snow melt vital for irrigation of S.E.; popular tourist and naturalist a.

Australian Antarctic Territory, part of Antarctica; between 145° E. and 160° E. and S. of 60° S.

excluding Adélie Land; research stas. of Mawson, Davis and Casey.

Australian Capital Territory, fed. terr. surrounding Canberra, seat of Fed. Govt. of **Australia;** also inc. a. around Jervis Bay, originally planned to serve as pt. p. (1993) 299,400.

Austria, rep., Europe; after long and glamorous history under the Habsburg, instability between Austria and Hungary a cause of first world war; forcibly incorporated in German Reich, 1938, liberated 1945, recovered indep. 1955; almost entirely within Alps; drained mainly by Danube; continental climate; magnificent scenery generates a major tourist ind. but much food must be imported; forests and timber inds.; mineralised, iron-ore of Styria; hydro-elec.; inds. located in ts.; cap. Vienna; joined EU 1995; a. 83,898 km²; p. (1994) 8,029,717.

Austria, Lower, st., **Austria;** impt. agr. a.; cap. Vienna; a. (excluding Vienna) 18,384 km²; p. (excluding Vienna) (1993) 1,505,266.

Austria, Upper, st., **Austria;** oil, gas, iron & steel, aluminium mftg.; cap. Linz; a. 11,980 km²; p. (1993) 1,373,317.

Auvergne, old prov. and present region of **France;** inc. deps. **Allier, Cantal, Haute-Loire, Puy-de-Dôme;** part of Massif Central; volcanic scenery; ch. t. Clermont-Ferrand; p. (1990) 1,321,200.

Auvergne Mtns., mtns., central **France;** in N.W. of Central Massif; highest peak Puy de Sancy in Mt. Dore, 1,887 m; volcanic landscape.

Auxerre, t., cap. of Yonne dep., **France;** comm. and industl. ctr.; wine; tr.; Gothic cath.; p. (1990) 40,597.

Ava, c., **Myanmar;** on the Irrawaddy R.; former cap.; many pagodas, now ruins; bridge over R.

Avebury, v., Wilts., **Eng.;** mediaeval v. outside Neolithic circle and avenues, nr. Silbury Hill; lgst. prehistoric structure in England.

Aveiro, t., **Portugal;** on Vouga estuary, connected to sea by canal; fish. pt. salt from lagoons; p. (1981) 28,625.

Avellaneda, industl. sub. of Buenos Aires, **Argentina;** hides, wood; p. (1980) 330,654.

Avellino, t., cap. of A. prov., **Italy;** on motorway from Naples to W.; monastery; sulphur mng. and refining; hats; p. (1981) 56,892.

Aversa, t. **Italy;** in fertile plain of Campania; agr. and route ctr.; p. (1981) 50,525.

Avesta, t., Kopparberg, **Sweden;** on Dal R.; iron, aluminium and charcoal wks.

Aveyron, dep., **France;** on S.W. rim of Central Massif, inc. Causses limestones; extensive forests; grain, dairying, sheep; coal; cap. Rodez; a. 8,767 km²; p. (1990) 270,100.

Aviemore, t., Highland, **Scot.;** on R. Spey, 19 km S.W. of Grantown; winter sports; p. (1993) 2,214.

Avignon, t., cap. of Vaucluse, dep., **France;** anc. Roman t. at crossing of R. Rhône; Provençal tourist ctr.; diversified inds. inc. wine tr.; p. (1990) 89,440 (t.), 181,136 (met. a.).

Avila, t., cap. of A. prov., **Spain;** in Old Castile; univ., cath.; mediaeval architecture; birth-place of St. Teresa; p. (1991) 45,000, 172,656 (prov.).

Avon, R., Wiltshire/Bath and N.E. Somerset/Bristol, **Eng.;** flows from Cotswolds to enter Bristol Channel at Avonmouth; spectacular limestone gorge between Bristol and the sea; length 128 km.

Avon, R., Warwicks, **Eng.;** flows past Stratford-on-A., to reach Severn R. at Tewkesbury; fertile agr. valley; string of ts. along course; length 152 km.

Avon, R., Wilts./Hants./Dorset, **Eng.;** flows past Salisbury into English Channel at Christchurch; length 112 km.

Avonmouth, outport of Bristol, at mouth of R. Avon, **Eng.;** docks; seed crushing, petrol refinery, non-ferrous metal and chemical plants.

Avranches, t., Manche, **France;** Normandy mkt. t.; cider and dairy produce; p. (1982) 10,419.

Awe, Loch, Argyll and Bute, **Scot.;** 13 km W. of Inveraray, bordered by Ben Cruachan; length 40 km; salmon and trout fishing; hydroelec. sta. at Cruachan.

Axholme, Isle of, flat lowland a., N. Lincs., **Eng.;** W. of Trent R.; drained by Vermuyden in 17th cent.

Axminster, t., East Devon, **Eng.**; brushes; flour and sawmills; carpet and press tool mftg; p. (1991) 3,472.

Ayacucho (Huamanga.) c., and prov., **Peru**; founded by Pizarro in 1539; lies in equable fertile valley; p. (1993) 492,507 (prov.), 105,918 (c.).

Aydin, t., **Turkey**; anc. Tralles; rly. and agr. tr. ctr. for surrounding a.; p. (1985) 90,449, (1990) 824,816 (prov.).

Ayers Rock, N.T., **Australia**; giant terra-cotta monolith rising abruptly to 335 m; sacred to Aborigines; major tourist attraction.

Aylesbury, co. t., Aylesbury Vale, Bucks., **Eng.**; mkt. t.; expanded t.; p. (1991) 58,085.

Aylesbury Vale, l. gov. dist., Bucks., **Eng.**; a. in N.W. of co. inc. Aylesbury and Buckingham; p. (1995) 153,600.

Aylesford, mkt. t., Kent, **Eng.**; N.W. Maidstone; p. (1991) 24,085.

Ayr, royal burgh, S. Ayrshire, **Scot.**; pt on F. of Clyde, 48 km S.W. of Glasgow; Burns born nearby; p. (1991) 47,962.

Ayrshire, historic co., W. **Scot.**; now divided into E., N., and S. Ayrshire.

Aysen, reg. **Chile**; cap. Coihaique; a. 108,997 km²; p. (1992) 82,017.

Aysgarth, v. Richmondshire, North Yorks., **Eng.**; on R. Ure in Wensleydale; famous waterfalls.

Ayutthaya, t., **Thailand**; former cap., on Menam Chao Phraya R. delta; p. (1980) 47,189.

Azarbaijan, E. and **W.**, provs., N. **Iran**; border Azabaijan and Turkey; cap. (E.A.) Tabriz; cap. (W.A.) Rezayeh; p. (1986) 4,180,376 (E) and 1,989,935 (W).

Azerbaijan, CIS, former rep. USSR; Transcaucasia, rep.; Caucasus and Lesser Caucasus separated by hot dry irrigated steppe; oil boom, 1990s; disturbances 1989; 86,661 km²; p. (1995) 7,431,000.

Azores, gr. of physically and climatically attractive Is. in mid-Atlantic about 1,440 km W. of Lisbon, **Portugal**; partial indep. by regional gov. (1977); volcanic; fruit, wine; ch. spts: Ponta Delgada, Horta, Angra do Heroismo; U.S. air bases on Terceira I.; a. 2,569 km²; p. (1986) 253,500.

Azov Sea (Azouskoye More), Ukraine/Russia; joins Black Sea by Kerch strait; receives Don R.; fisheries; a. 36,000 km².

Azpeitia, t., N. **Spain**; mineral springs; local quarrying; timber inds.; agr. processing; p. (1981) 12,509.

Azraq Desert Nat. Park, Jordan; first Jordanian nat. park around oasis of Azraq, 96 km E. of Amman; a. 3,900 km².

B

Baalbek, c., **Lebanon**, S.W. Asia; old Heliopolis; ruins; tourism.

Bab-el-Mandeb, strait connecting Red Sea and Indian Oc.; dangerous but impt. shipping lane; length 32 km, width 27 km.

Babergh, l. gov. dist., S. Suffolk, **Eng.**; inc. Sudbury and Hadleigh; p. (1995) 78,900.

Babylon, anc. cap. of Babylonian Empire, in Euphrates valley about 90 km S. of Baghdad, **Iraq**.

Bacau, t., E. **Romania**; on R. Bistrita; oil, sawmilling, textiles; p. (1992) 204,495.

Bacolod City, t., Negros, **Philippines**; sm. pt.; exp. sugar; p. (1995) 402,000.

Bacton, v., Norfolk, **Eng.**; terminal for S. gasfields in N. Sea; p. (1991) 1,435 (with Walcott).

Bacup, t., Rossendale, S.E. Lancs., **Eng.**; 32 km N. of Manchester; textiles, felts, footwear; p. (1991) 13,682.

Badagri, t., W. of Lagos, **Nigeria**; on the Bight of Benin; formerly a gr. slave pt.; coir sacks.

Badajoz, lgst. prov., **Spain**; gr. reclamation scheme in progress; a. 21,624 km²; p. (1991) 643,245.

Badajoz, c., cap. of B. prov., W. **Spain**, in Estremadura; anc. fortress c.; transit tr.; p. (1991) 129,737.

Badalona, c. nr. Barcelona, **Spain**; shipbldg.; p. (1991) 206,120.

Baden, t., **Switzerland**; health resort, mineral springs; p. (1986) 14,054.

Baden-Baden, t., Baden-Württemberg, **Germany**; fashionable spa; p. (1986) 49,300.

Baden-bei-Wien, wat. pl., **Austria**; 22 km S.W. of Vienna; p. (1991) 23,998.

Baden-Württemberg, Land, **Germany**; created 1952; bounded by Rhine in W., drained by Neckar and Donau R. systems; mtnous., inc. Black Forest and Swabian Jura; received much immigrant ind. from E. Europe, so encouraging prosperous and diversified industl. structure; several impt. industl. regions centred on Mannheim, Karlsruhe, and cap. Stuttgart; a. 35,750 km²; p. (1992) 10,002,000.

Bad Lands, S.D., **USA**; stretches of infertile badly eroded soil.

Badrinath, mtn. and t., Uttar Pradesh, **India**; pilgrim shrine of Vishnu.

Badulla, t., **Sri Lanka**; tea; anc. t.; rly. terminus; ctr. of tea estates; p. (1981) 32,954.

Badwater, salt pool, Cal., **USA**; 85 m below sea-level, lowest point in N. America.

Baeza, t., S. **Spain**; anc. Moorish c.; olives, wine; p. (1981) 12,841.

Baffin B., between **Greenland** and **Canada**; joined to Atl. Oc. by Davis Strait, to Arctic Oc. by Nares Strait; open 4 months per year; B.I., in W., ctr. of Arctic research and communications; length 1,120 km, width 100–650 km.

Bagé, t., S. **Brazil**; ctr. of cattle tr.; p. (1985) 106,300.

Baghdad, c., cap. of **Iraq**; anc. c. on R. Tigris; terminus Baghdad rly.; airport; univ.; textiles, gum, bricks, tiles, metal inds.; p. (1987) 3,841,268.

Baghdad, prov. or liwa, **Iraq**; between Iran and Syrian Desert; inc. some of the most fertile lands in the Tigris and Euphrates valleys; p. (1987) 4,648,609.

Baghlan, t., **Afghanistan**; new industl. t. in ctr. of sugar producing a.; alt. 518 m; p. (1982) 41,240.

Bagnolet, t., Seine-St. Denis, **France**; sub. of Paris; famous for "plaster of Paris" from local gypsum; textiles; p. (1982) 32,557.

Bagshot, t., Surrey Heath, Surrey, **Eng.**; heath of same name; historically old postal town, 42 km S.W. of London; residtl.; p. (1991) 5,190.

Baguio, Luzon, N.W. of Manila, summer cap. of **Philippines**, alt. 1,500 m; gold mines; p. (1990) 183,102.

Bahamas, indep. st. (1973) within Brit. Commonwealth, W.I.; more than 700 coral atolls; subtropical climate; infertile but valuable tourist tr.; exp. crayfish; cap. Nassau; a. 11,406 km²; p. (1995) 275,700.

Bahawalpur, t., **Pakistan**; former cap. of B. princely st.; impt. bridging point over Sutlej R.; p. (1981) 133,956.

Bahia, st., **Brazil**; cap. Salvador; cattle, cacao, sugar, coffee, tobacco; oil, extensive mineral deposits; a. 560,139 km²; p. (1991) 11,801,810.

Bahia Blanca, spt., **Argentina**; industl. ctr., oil refining; prin. shipping point of S.; exp. oil, grain, wool, hides; p. (1991) 271,467.

Bahrain, indep. st. (1971) in Persian G.; low sandy Is. linked by road causeway to Saudi Arabia (1985); springs allow cultivation of dates; oil wells, oil and aluminium refining; trading ctr., declining importance of agr. as incr. salinity of traditional water supplies; cap. Manamah; airpt. at Muharraq; a. 678 km²; p. (1995) 568,000.

Baia, historic v., Campania, **Italy**; beautifully situated on Bay of Naples; celebrated Roman pleasure resort; p. (1981) 2,087.

Baia-Mare, t., N.W. **Romania**; on Somesul R., in region mining copper, lead, zinc, gold, silver; mtn. resort; p. (1992) 148,815.

Baikal L. See **Baykal L.**

Baildon, t., West Yorks., **Eng.**; nr. Bradford; moorland resort; p. (1991) 15,385.

Baja, t., **Hungary**; impt. bridging point of R. Danube in Gr. Plain; p. (1997) 38,000.

Baja California. See **Lower California.**

Bakar, pt., **Croatia** (formerly Yugoslavia); S. of Rijeka; new pt. and oil harbour.

Bakersfield, c., Cal., **USA**; ctr. of oil prod. and refining; aircraft assembly; p. (1990) 174,820 (c.), 543,000 (met. a.).

Bakewell, t., Derbys Dales. **Eng.**; tourist ctr. Peak District; agr., mng.; p. (1991) 3,818.

Bakhchisaray, t., Crimea, **Ukraine**; old cap. of Tartar Khans; copper, leather; p. (1990) 25,700.

Bakhuis Gebergte mtns., W. **Suriname**; major aluminium complex based on local power and bauxite.

Bakony Wald, mtns., **Hungary**; forested; vineyards; bauxite, manganese.

Baku, cap. of **Azerbaijan**; pt. on Caspian Sea; univ.;

new oil boom in 1990s; oil pipeline connects with Batumi; shipbldg.; p. (1990) 1,148,700.

Bala, t., Gwynedd, N. **Wales**; mkt. town; tourism; p. (1991) 1,922.

Bala, L., Gwynedd, N. **Wales**; drained by the Dee.

Balaklava, pt., S. Crimea, **Ukraine**; scene of the charge of the Light Brigade (1854).

Balaton, L., lgst. in **Hungary**; a. 596 km²; long history of settlement in a.; shores forested; vineyards; tourism.

Balbriggan, spt., Dublin, **R.o.I.**; hosiery; p. (1986) 5,680.

Baldock, t., North Herts., **Eng.**; on N. edge of Chiltern Hills and Gr. N. Road; hosiery, malting, lt. engin.; p. (1991) 9,232.

Baldwin, t., N.Y., **USA**; on S. Long I.; fisheries; p. (1980) 31,630.

Balearic Is., in Mediterranean Sea, **Spain**; inc. Majorca, Minorca, Ibiza, Formentera; limestone scenery and mild climate encourage tourism which has swamped Moorish influence; agr.; ch. t. Palma; a. 5,014 km²; p. (1991) 739,501.

Bali, I. off Java, **Indonesia**, in Lesser Sundas; equable climate, fertile soil, luxurious vegetation; p. mainly engaged in agr.; noted native dancers; a. (inc. Lombok) 10,196 km²; p. (1983) 2,593,900.

Balikesir, t. and prov., **Turkey**; rly. junc.; ctr. of fertile agr. region; p. (1990) 973,314. (prov), 172,570 (t.).

Balikpapan, t., Kalimantan, **Indonesia**; new oil refinery; p. (1980) 280,875.

Baliuag, t., Luzon, **Philippines**; rice, bamboo hats, mkt.; p. (1990) 89,719.

Balkan Mtns., Bulgaria; fine alpine meadows, forested; tourism based on Sofia; average alt. 900–1,200 m, hgst. point Botev Peak, 2,377 m.

Balkan Peninsula, the easternmost of the three gr. southern peninsulas of Europe, between the Adriatic and Ionian seas on the W., and the Black Sea, Sea of Marmara and the Aegean Sea on the E., with an area of, roughly, 500,000 km²; includes Turkey, Yugoslavia, Croatia, Slovenia, Bosnia, Bulgaria, Albania, Macedonia and Greece; ch. mtns.: Rodopi, Pindhus, Balkan; ch. Rs.; Danube, Maritsa, Vardar; ch. Ls.; Scutari, Okhrida.

Balkh. *See* **Wazirabad.**

Balkhash, t., **Kazakhstan**; on N. shore of L.B.; smelting, esp. local copper; vermiculite deposits nearby, salt; p. (1990) 87,400.

Balkhash, L., **Kazakhstan**; receives Ili R., but has no outlet; salt water; fishing, salt-panning; a. 17,301 km².

Ballachulish, v., Highland, **Scot.**; on S. shore of Loch Leven, N.E. of Oban; tourism; ferry across Loch Linnhe, new road bridge; p. (1991) 557.

Ballarat, t., Victoria, **Australia**; 117 km N.W. of Melbourne, former gold-field dist.; mkt. ctr.; fine examples of 19th century architecture; 2 caths.; p. (1991) 64,980.

Ballater, burgh, Aberdeenshire, **Scot.**; on R. Dee, 59 km S.W. of Aberdeen; tourist resort, mineral wells; nr. the royal Highland residence of Balmoral; p. (1991) 1,362.

Ballina, t., spt., Mayo, **R.o.I.**; agr. machin. salmon fishing; p. (1991) 6,714.

Ballina, t., N.S.W., **Australia**; at mouth of Richmond R.; resort, fishing; p. (1981) 9,738.

Ballinasloe, t., Galway and Roscommon, **R.o.I.**; agr. ctr.; cattle mkt.; terminus of Grand Canal; p. (1986) 6,125.

Ballinrobe, t., Mayo, **R.o.I.**; E. of Lough Mask; trout fishing; p. (1986) 1,270.

Ballybunion, resort, Kerry, **R.o.I.**; at mouth of R. Shannon; p. (1986) 1,452.

Ballycastle, spt., mkt. t., Moyle, N. **Ireland**; abbey and cas. ruins; seaside resort; p. (1991) 4,005.

Ballyclare, t., Newtownabbey, N. **Ireland**; paper, linen, dyeing, asbestos-cement prod.; p. (1991) 7,108.

Ballymena, mkt. t., l. gov. dist., N. **Ireland**; on R. Braid; linen and dyeing; p. (1991) 28,112 (t.), 56,541, (dist.).

Ballymoney, mkt. t., l. gov. dist., N. **Ireland**; 64 km N.W. of Belfast; linen; p. (1991) 24,198 (dist), 7,818 (t.).

Ballynahinch, t., Down, N. **Ireland**; 19 km from Downpatrick; p. (1991) 4,591.

Ballyshannon, spt., Donegal, **R.o.I.**; at mouth of R. Erne; salmon fishery; resort; hydroelectric power plant; p. (1986) 2,573.

Balmoral Cas., Aberdeenshire, **Scot.**; royal residence, on R. Dee, 13 km W. of Ballater.

Balsas, R., and lowland, **Mexico**; R. flows E.

to Pacific through rich agr. valley of Morelos; length 800 km.

Baltic Sea, an arm of Atl. Oc., opens into N. Sea by narrow channels between Denmark and Sweden; joined to Arctic by White Sea Canal; low, dune-backed cst.; shallowness, tendency to freeze reduce its importance for shipping; a. 414,000 km².

Baltic White Canal. *See* **Volga Baltic Waterway.**

Baltimore, industl. c., spt., Md., **USA**; fine harbour nr. head of Chesapeake B.; pt. processing and diversified inds.; steel wks. at Sparrow's Point; educational, cultural ctr., seat of Johns Hopkins univ.; many fine bldgs. despite disastrous fire of 1904; p. (1990) 736,014 (c.), 2,382,172 (met. a.).

Baltoro Glacier, Karakoram Mtns., **Pakistan**; drains into tribs. of Indus; alt. 3,532 m.

Baluchistan, prov. (revived 1970), **Pakistan**; S. of Afghanistan; largely desert and rugged barren mtns.; cap. Quetta; cereals, potatoes, fruits, dates; new oil and natural gas discoveries; a. 137,011 km²; p. (1981) 4,332,349.

Bamako, cap. c. of **Mali**; impressive site at foot of escarpment on R. Niger; admin. and agr. tr. ctr.; R. pt.; univ.; main industl. ctr. of Mali; p. (1984) 740,000.

Bamberg, c., Bavaria, **Germany**; cath.; textiles, elec., leather and engin. inds.; impt. R. pt. on Trans-European waterway; p. (1986) 69,600.

Bamburgh, t., Northumberland, **Eng.**; former cap. of Bernicia and Northumbria; cas.; birthplace of Grace Darling.

Banaba I. *See* **Ocean I.**

Banagher, v., Offaly, **R.o.I.**; impt. crossing of R. Shannon; p. (1986) 1,465.

Banam, t., **Cambodia**; on Mekong R.; boat-bldg., rice milling.

Banant, terr., Vojvodina, N. Serbia, **Yugoslavia**; major source of petroleum, natural gas, vineyards, but economically backward.

Banbridge, t., l. gov. dist., **N. Ireland**; on Bann R.; linen; p. (1991) 11,448 (t.), 33,482 (dist.).

Banbury, mkt. t., Cherwell, Oxford, **Eng.**; 128 km from London; aluminium ind., furniture, printing, ladies' wear; expanded t.; old livestock market closed (1998); p. (1991) 39,906.

Banchory, burgh, Aberdeenshire, **Scot.**; on R. Dee, 27 km S.W. of Aberdeen; p. (1991) 6,230.

Banda Is., volcanic gr. in Moluccas, in Banda Sea **Indonesia**; nutmegs and mace; a. 103 km².

Bandama, R., **Ivory Coast**; major power and irrigation scheme at Kossou Dam; length c. 320 km.

Bandar. *See* **Masulipatnam.**

Bandar "Abbās, spt., S. **Iran**; airport; oil exploration; deepwater harbour; p. (1982) 175,000.

Bandar-e-Būshehūr (Bushire), spt., S.W. **Iran**; on Persian G., Iran's major pt.; petrochem. complex project; p. (1982) 120,000.

Bandar-e-Torkeman, spt., N. **Iran**; on Caspian Sea, on rly. from Tehran.

Bandar Khomeynī, spt., **Iran**, on Persian G., terminus of rly. from Tehran; petrochemical plant.

Bandar Seri Begawan, t., cap. of **Brunei**; 20 km from mouth of Brunei R.; airport; p. (1991) 45,867.

Bandjarmasin, c., cap. of Kalimantan, **Indonesia**; pt. on Martapura R., nr. confluence with Barito R.; tr. ctr.; oil, timber, rubber, printing plant; p. (1980) 381,286.

Bandon, t., Cork, **R.o.I.**; on B.R.; agr. processing; p. (1986) 1,943.

Bandung, c., W. Java, **Indonesia**; industl. and tourist ctr.; tech. institute; radio sta. at nearby Malabar; p. (1983) 1,602,000.

Banff Nat. Park, Canada; first Canadian Nat. Park; in Rocky Mtns.; variegated scenery, many tourist facilities; a. 6,695 km².

Banff, royal burgh, Aberdeenshire, **Scot.**; on Moray F. at mouth of R. Deveron; fisheries; tourism; p. (1991) 4,110.

Banffshire, historic co., E. **Scot.** now divided between Aberdeenshire and Moray.

Bangalore, c., Karnataka, **India**; well-planned c., former Brit. military sta. and admin. H.Q.; route ctr.; textiles, engin.; p. (1991) 2,661,000.

Bangka (Banka), I., between Sumatra and Kalimantan, **Indonesia**; tin; a. 11,942 km²; p. 280,000.

Bangkok (Krung Thep), cap. c., **Thailand**; pt. on Menam Chao Phraya R., 32 km from sea; built originally round canals; major industl. ctr.; royal palace, univ.; p. (1993) 5,572,712.

Bangladesh (East Pakistan), indep. sov. st., S. Asia; within Commonwealth (1972); occupies former

Indian prov. of E. Bengal and E. part of Ganges delta; dense rural p. engaged in intensive farming of rice and jute; illiteracy 80 per cent; poor internal communications hinder devel.; exp. textiles; susceptible to flooding and cyclones; major floods 1998; cstl. embankment project; open warfare between India and Pakistan (Dec. 1971) resulted in creation of indep. st.; cap. Dacca; a. 142,776 km²; p. (1994) 119,000,000.

Bangor, t., North Down, **N. Ireland;** spt. on S. shore of Belfast Lough, 16 km N.E. of Belfast; lt. inds.; carpets, hosiery; seaside resort; p. (1991) 52,437.

Bangor, t., S. Me., **USA;** pt. of entry on Penobscot R.; timber inds., shoes; p. (1980) 31,643.

Bangor, t., Gwynedd, **Wales;** pt. on S. shore of Menai Strait; cath., univ. college; lt. engin.; tourist ctr.; p. (1991) 12,330.

Bangui, c., cap. of **Central African Rep.;** pt. on R. Ubangi; airpt.; p. (1988) 451,690.

Bangweulu, L., **Zambia;** 240 km long, 128 km wide, contains 3 islands. Dr. Livingstone died at Illala, on S. shore of this L., in 1873.

Baniyas, spt., **Syria;** terminus of oil pipeline from Kirkuk, opened 1952.

Banja Luka, t., **Bosnia-Herzegovina,** formerly Yugoslavia; caths., mosques; recent industl. development; cellulose; rly. junc.; p. (1981) 183,618.

Banjul (Bathurst), t., cap. of **Gambia;** pt. at mouth of Gambia R., exp. groundnuts; airport; p. (1983) 44,188.

Banks I., Canada, Arctic Oc.; separated by McClure Strait from Melville I.

Banks Peninsula, dist. on E. cst. of S.I., **N.Z.;** feature of Canterbury cst.; p. (1991) 7,639.

Banks Strait, separating Furneaux Is. from Tasmania, **Australia.**

Bankura, t., W. Bengal, **India;** on Hooghly R.; shellac, silk; p. (1991) 114,876.

Bann, Upper and Lower R., **N. Ireland;** rises in Mtns. of Mourne, and flows through Lough Neagh to Atlantic nr. Coleraine; length 144 km.

Bannockburn, moor, t. nr. Stirling, **Scot.;** Bruce's victory over Edward II on 23–24 June, 1314 established Scotland's independence; p. (1991) 5,799.

Banovici, basin, **Bosnia-Herzegovina,** formerly Yugoslavia; brown coal.

Banská Bystrica, region, **Slovakia;** copper and silver mng., metal wks.; a. 9,230 km²; p. (1990) 87,000.

Banstead, Surrey, **Eng.;** dormitory t.; l. gov. dist. with Reigate; p. (1994) 118,300 (dist.), (1991) 37,245 (t.) (with Tadworth).

Bantam, t. and dist., W. Java, **Indonesia;** suffered severely from fever and volcanic eruption; former pt. and sultanate; cattle rearing.

Bantry, t., Cork, **R.o.I.;** tweed; p. (1986) 2,811.

Bantry Bay, Cork, **R.o.I.;** Atlantic inlet; natural harbour utilised mainly by oil-storage depot.

Baoding (Paoting), c., Hebei prov., **China;** on main rly. to Beijing; p. (1984) 522,800.

Baoji (Paoki), c., Shaanxi prov., **China;** ctr. of arable agr. a.; cotton weaving; nearby gorge on Huang-He used for multi-purpose dams; p. (1984) 352, 100.

Baotou (Paotow), c., Mongol Zizhiqu (Inner Mongolia), **China;** on left bank of Huang-He, on road and rly. routes to E. China; terminus of caravan routes through Gobi Desert and Tarim basin to Turkestan; tr. in non-perishable livestock prods., cereals; modern steel ind.; p. (1992) 1,200,000.

Bar, spt., Dalmatian cst., Montenegro, **Yugoslavia;** terminal of Belgrade-Bar rly.; p. (1981) 32,535.

Baracaldo, pt., N.E. **Spain;** rapidly growing industl. t. on Bilbao estuary; p. (1981) 117,422.

Baranovichi, c., **Belarus;** admin. ctr. of agr. dist.; impt. rly. ctr.; p. (1990) 162,800.

Barataria Bay, S.E. Louisiana, **USA;** 56 km S. of New Orleans; ctr. of shrimp ind., petroleum extraction; picturesque stilt vs.; a. 466 km².

Barauni, t., N. Central Bihar, **India;** oil refining; oil pipelines to Gauhati, and Kanpur and from Haldia; p. (1981) 56,366.

Barbados, I., indep. sovereign st., within Brit. Commonwealth, W.I.; fertile soils; economy based on intensive agr. supporting dense p.; sugar, molasses, rum; fishing; tourism; cap. and spt. Bridgetown; moves towards becoming a republic; a. 429 km²; p. (1994) 264,300.

Barbary Coast, gen. name applied to Mediterranean cst. of N. Africa between Strait of Gibraltar and C. Bon.

Barberton, t., Ohio, **USA;** S.W. of Akron; tyre mftg.; p. (1980) 29,751.

Barberton, t., Transvaal, **S. Africa;** developed from 19th cent. gold rush; ctr. of rich agr. dist.; p. (1980) 70,880 (dist.).

Barbican, dist., City of London, **Eng.;** inc. major housing scheme to attract p. back into c.; cultural amenities.

Barbizon, v., nr. forest of Fontainebleau, **France;** haunt of painters, especially those ass. with the Barbizon school.

Barbuda, I., Leeward gr., **Antigua and Barbuda;** sea-island cotton; a. 161 km²; p. (1991) 1,400.

Barcellona, t., N.E. cst., Sicily, **Italy;** mkt. t.; p. (1981) 36,869.

Barcelona, c., cap. of B. prov., major spt. of **Spain;** industl. and comm. ctr., textiles and varied inds.; exp. agr. prod. inc. cork; cath., univ.; p. (1991) 1,653,175, 4,605,710 (prov.).

Barcelona, t., N. **Venezuela;** cap. of Anzoátegui st.; agr. tr.; brewing; adjoins Puerto la Cruz on Caribbean cst.; joint p. (1990) 106,061.

Barcoo Creak. See **Cooper's Creek.**

Bardsey, I., Irish Sea; off cst. of **Wales,** nr. N. point of Cardigan Bay; lighthouse.

Bareilly, c., Uttar Pradesh, **India;** mkt., sugar refining, cotton mills, bamboo furniture; p. (1991) 591,000.

Barents Sea, part of Arctic Oc., E. of Spitzbergen to N. Cape; impt. cod fisheries; oil potential; short Rs. to be diverted from Sea to Volga to carry water to Karakum Desert.

Bargoed, t., Caerphilly, S. **Wales;** p. (1991) 14,979.

Bari, c., cap. of B. prov., Apulia, **Italy;** spt. on Adriatic handling agr. prods.; agr. processing inds., oil refinery; p. (1992) 342,129.

Barinas, t., cap. of B. st., **Venezuela;** cattle, oil in surrounding Llanos; p. (1990) 152,853 (t.), 456,246 (prov.).

Barisal, t., **Bangladesh;** nr. Tetulia at mouth of Ganges; river pt.; gr. damage and loss of life from cyclone 1965; p. (1991) 163,481.

Barito R, Borneo, **Indonesia;** a. of swampland in lower valley; proposals to develop valley for rice cultivation; length c. 440 km.

Barking and Dagenham, outer bor., E. London, **Eng.;** on Rs. Roding and Thames; diversified inds. inc. huge Ford motor wks.; p. (1995) 154,800.

Bar-le-Duc, t, cap. of Meuse dep., **France;** in picturesque Ornain valley; many fine old houses; varied inds.; p. (1990) 18,577.

Barletta, t., spt., **Italy;** diversified int. processing inds.; wine tr.; p. (1981) 83,719.

Barmouth, t., Gwynedd, **Wales;** pt. on Cardigan Bay; chemicals; resort; p. (1991) 2,306.

Barnard Castle, Teesdale, Durham, **Eng.;** mkt. t., resort; woollens, penicillin; cas.; p. (1991) 6,084.

Barnaul, t., W. Siberia, **Russia;** route ctr. in cotton-growing dist. nr. industl. Kuznetsk Basin; varied inds.; p. (1989) 602,000.

Barnet, former U.D., Herts., **Eng.;** now outer bor., Greater London; comprising Finchley, Hendon, Barnet, East Barnet and Friern Barnet; p. (1995) 312,400.

Barnsley, t., met. dist., South Yorks., **Eng.;** machin., plastics; carpets; p. (1995) 226,700 (dist.), (1991) 75,120 (t.).

Barnstaple, North Devon, **Eng.;** mkt. t., pt. on R. Taw; seaside resort; p. (1991) 27,691.

Baroda, t., Gujarat, **India;** univ.; palaces, Hindu temples; natural gas pipeline from Ankleshwar; oil refining nearby at Jawaharnagar; heavy water plant; p. (1987) 734,473.

Barquisimeto, t., **Venezuela;** well built c.; comm. ctr. for fertile agr. a.; p. (1990) 602,622.

Barra Is., Outer Hebrides, Western Isles, **Scot.;** lighthouse on Barra Head; p. (1991) 1,244.

Barrancabermeja, R. pt., **Colombia;** oilfield, oil refining, paper mkg., petrochemicals; p. (1983) 123,000.

Barranquilla, t., **Colombia;** major spt. nr. mouth of Magdalena R.; impt. industl. ctr.; international airpt.; p. (1992) 1,018,763.

Barreiro, t., Setúbal, **Portugal;** on S. bank of Tagus estuary; agr. processing; p. (1987) 50,863.

Barrow-in-Furness, spt., l. gov. dist., Cumbria, **Eng.;** iron and steel ind.; shipbldg., submarines; p. (1995) 71,800 (dist.), (1991) 48,947 (t.).

Barrow I., W. **Australia;** since 1967 one of Australia's richest oilfields.

Barrow Point, most N. headland in Alaska, **USA.**

Barry, pt., Vale of Glamorgan, Wales; rapid growth in 19th cent. as outport of Cardiff; modern light inds., replacing coal and tinplate inds.; p. (1991) 49,887.

Barth, spt., Mecklenburg - West Pomerania, Germany; shipyard engin., furniture, sugar; p. (1989) 11,721.

Bartlesville, t., Okla., USA; oil refining, metal inds.; p. (1980) 34,568.

Barton-on-Humber, mkt. t., N. Lincs., Eng.; anc. Eng. pt.; S. site of new Humber Bridge; p. (1991) 9,422.

Basel, c., cap. of B. can., 2nd. t. of Switzerland; cath., univ.; burial place of Erasmus; comm., industl, rly. ctr. at head of barge navigation on R. Rhine; p. (1990) 171,000 (c.) 358,500 (met. a.).

Basel, can., Switzerland; divided into 2 half cantons; (1) B.—Stadt; in immediate vicinity of B.c.; cap. B.; a. 36 km²; p. (est. 1990) 191,800; (2) B.—Land; on N. Jura slopes; watchmaking; cap. Liestal; a. 427 km²; p. (1990) 230,000.

Basford, t., Gedling, Notts., Eng.; outskirts of Nottingham; hosiery.

Bashkir (Bashirskaya) aut. rep. occupying Belaya R. basin in S.W. Urals, Russia; impt. mng. and metal inds., inc. major oilfield; arable agr.; cap. Ufa; a. 143,486 km²; p. (1989) 3,943,100.

Basildon, t., l. gov. dist., Essex, Eng.; in lower Thames valley; new t. 1949; light inds.; p. (1995) 162,800 (dist.), (1991) 100,924 (t.).

Basilicata, region, S. Italy; comprising provs. of Potenza and Matera, mtnous. in W., drains to G. of Taranto; arable agr.; a. 9,984 km²; p. (1992) 610,821.

Basingstoke, t., part of l. gov. dist. of Basingstoke and Deane, N. Hants., Eng.; 80 km W. of London; expanded t.; engin., light inds.; p. (1995) 147,400 (dist.), (1991) 77,837 (t.).

Basle. See Basel.

Basotho ba Borwa (S. Sotho), Bantu Terr. Authority, O.F.S., S. Africa; cap. Witziesnoek; a. 52,000 hectares; p. (1969) 144,000.

Basque Provs., N. Spain; comprise 3 provs.: Alava, Guipuzcoa and Vizcaya where Basque language spoken; recent claims that French dep. of Pyrénées-Atlantiques should be inc. within an indep. Basque prov.; regional parliaments for provs. in Spain to help offset separatist moves (1980); lgst. c. Bilbao; p. (1981) 2,141,809.

Basra, t., Iraq; cap. of B. prov.; R. pt., 64 km from mouth of Tigris R., on main rly. from Baghdad; exp. agr. prods.; p. (1985) 616,700.

Bas-Rhin, dep., E. France; N. part of Alsace; extends to Rhine rift valley, inc. Vosges Mtns.; impt. agr. dist.; many industl. ts.; cap. Strasbourg; a. 4,791 km²; p. (1990) 953,100.

Bass Rock, lighthouse in Firth of Forth, opposite Tantallon Cas., E. Lothian, Scot.; gannetry.

Bass Strait, Australia; between Victoria and Tasmania; length 320 km; width 224 km.

Bassano del Grappa; cap. of Vicenza prov., on R. Brenta, Italy; light and craft inds.; cath.; p. (1981) 64,676.

Bassein, t., Myanmar; on mouth of Irrawaddy R., univ.; airfield; rice tr. and milling; p. (1983) 144,000.

Basse-Normandie, region, N. France; inc. deps. Calvados, Manche, Orne; ch.t. Caen; p. (1990) 1,391,300. See Normandy.

Bassenthwaite, L., L. Dist., Cumbria, Eng.; most N. of lge. Ls.; drained to Solway Firth by R. Derwent; length 6 km, width 1·6 km.

Basses-Alpes. See Alpes-de-Haute-Provence.

Basses-Pyrénées. See Pyrénées-Atlantique.

Basse-Terre, l., cap. of Guadeloupe, Fr. W.I.; pt.; p. (1990) 14,107.

Basseterre, t., St. Kitts I., W.I.; cap. St. Kitts-Nevis-Anguilla ass. st.; pt.; sugar refining; p. (1980) 14,283 (latest figure).

Bassetlaw, l. gov. dist., N. Notts., Eng.; lge. a. based on Worksop and East Retford; p. (1995) 106,600.

Bastia, c. spt., cap. Haute Corse, N.E. Corsica, France; lgst. t. of Corsica; agr. exp. and inds.; tourism; p. (1990) 38,728

Basutoland. See Lesotho.

Bata, t., ch. spt., Equatorial Guinea; cap. of Rio Muni prov.; airpt.; p. (1986) 17,000.

Bataan, peninsula and prov., W. Luzon, Philippines; mtnous.; inc. t. of Balanga; timber inds., oil refining; p. (1990) 425,803.

Batangas, prov. and spt., S.W. Luzon, Philippines; oil refining; agr. tr.; p. (1990) 184,970.

Batavia. See Djakarta.

Bath, c., Bath and N.E. Somerset, Eng.; Roman baths, hot springs, medicinal waters; fine Regency architecture; univ.; elec. engin., metal inds.; p. (1991) 85,20.

Bath and North East Somerset, unit. auth. created in 1996, formerly part of Avon, Eng.; bordered by Mendips in S.; p. (1995) 164,600.

Bathgate, burgh, W. Lothian, Scot.; coal mng.; automobile ind.; p. (1991) 13,819.

Bathurst, t., N.S.W., Australia; former gold t., reliant on wool and wheat; diversifying with secondary inds.; with Orange to form site of major inland c. of 200,000; p. (1981) 19,640.

Bathurst, I., off cst. of N.T., Australia; separated from Melville I. by Apsley Str.; aboriginal reserve; cypress pine milling; (1981) 1,586.

Bathurst, t., N.B., Canada; pt. on Nipisiguit Bay; paper mill; salmon fishing; local mng.; p. (1991) 15,890.

Bathurst. See Banjul.

Bātinah, Al, fertile coastal plain, Oman, Arabia; produces early-ripening dates famous for flavour.

Batley, t. West Yorks., Eng.; heavy woollens, shoddy; p. (1991) 48,030.

Batna, t., dep., N. Algeria; p. (1987) 181,601 (t.), 757,059 (dep.).

Baton Rouge, st. cap., La., USA; on Mississippi; major tr. ctr.; univ.; oil refining, chemical plants; p. (1990) 219,531 (c.), 528,000 (met. a.).

Battambang, prov., Cambodia; N.W. of Phnom-Penh; rice growing, cotton mill; p. (1981) 551,860.

Battersea, dist., London, Eng.; S. of R. Thames; famous park; lge. power sta. now disused; part of Wandsworth.

Batticaloa, t., cap. of E. Prov., Sri Lanka; on E. cst.; comm. ctr.; p. (1981) 42,963.

Battle, t., Rother, East Sussex, Eng.; battle of Hastings 1066; abbey; p. (1991) 5,253.

Battle Creek, t., Mich., USA; on Kalamazoo R.; engin., local cereal prod.; p. (1984) 54,300, (t.), 137,800 (met. a.).

Batu Arang, t., Malaysia; ctr. of only worked coalfield in Malaya; 45 km from Kuala Lumpur.

Batumi, t., spt. on E. shore of Black Sea; Georgia; oil, engin., citrus fruits, tea; oil pipeline connects with Baku; resort; airpt; p. (1990) 137,300.

Bauchi, state, Nigeria; cap. Bauchi; ctr. of Jos plateau; tin-mng. ctr.; p. (1991) 4,294,413.

Bauld, C., northernmost part of Newfoundland, Canada.

Bauru, t., São Paulo st., Brazil; comm. ctr.; food inds.; p. (1985) 220,900.

Bautzen, t., Saxony, Germany; on R. Spree; textiles, engin., iron inds.; cath.; p. (1989) 50,627.

Bavaria (Bayern), Land, Germany; mtnous., bounded in S. by Alps, inc. Böhmerwald, Fichtelgebirge, Franconian Forest; main Rs. Danube and Main; fertile agr. valleys; forestry and agr.; economic life concentrated in ts., esp. cap. Munich, now a focus of p. immigration; rural beauty attracts tourist tr.; celebrated beer; a. 70,220 km²; p. (1992) 11,596,000.

Bavarian Alps, mtn. range, Germany, along Austrian border; Zugspitze (2,969 m) highest mtn.

Bavarian Forest. See Böhmerwald.

Bawdwin, t., Myanmar; in Shan plateau; impt. mng. ctr.; wolfram, lead, zinc, silver, rubies.

Bayamo, t. Cuba; early settlement; agr. & rly. ctr.; p. (1990) 125,021.

Bayamón, t., Puerto Rico; in fertile valley; oil refining; p. (1990) 220,262.

Baybay, t., Leyte, Philippines; impt. comm. pt.; p. (1990) 82,281.

Bay City, t., Mich., USA; comm. pt. nr. head of Saginaw B.; fishing; pt. processing inds.; p. (1980) 41,593 (c.), 119,881 (met. a.).

Bayeux, t., Calvados, France; mkt. t.; cath., museum, Bayeux tapestry; p. (1982) 15,237.

Baykal, L. (Ozero Baykal), Siberia, Russia; sixth largest fresh-water L. in world; basin forms deepest depression in world (1,616 m); many pts. around shores but frozen Nov.–May; skirted by Trans-Siberian rly.; sturgeon, salmon; tourism; a. 35,483 km².

Bayonne, c. spt., Pyrénées-Atlantique, S.W. France; cath.; noted for invention of bayonet; Basque Museum; p. (1990) 41,846 (t.), 136,334 (met.a).

Bayonne, t., N.J., USA; 10 km from New York; chemicals, oil refining; dry docks; p. (1990) 61,444.

Bayreuth, t., Bavaria, Germany; home of Wagner; famous for musical festivals in national theatre; p. (1986) 72,300.

Baytown, pt., S.E. Texas, USA; industl. t., oil

refining and exp.; p. (1980) 56,923.

Beachy Head, chalk headland, S.W. of Eastbourne, East Sussex, **Eng.**; 175 m high. Major cliff fall into sea, January 1999.

Beaconsfield, t., South Bucks., **Eng.**; residtl; home of Edmund Burke; p. (1991) 12,282.

Beardmore Glacier, Antarctica; one of world's lgst. valley glaciers; over 176 km in length.

Bear I. (Björnöya I.), Norway; in Arctic Oc., 208 km S. of Spitzbergen; cod fisheries.

Bearsden, burgh, E. Dunbartonshire, **Scot.**; residtl.; p. (1991), 27,806.

Beas (Bias), t., Punjab, **India;** trib. of Sutlej R.; part of irrigation scheme.; marked limit of Alexander's advance into India, 327 B.C.

Beattock, pass, S. Uplands, **Scot.**; gives access from valley of R. Clyde to R. Annan; used by main W. cst. rly. route from Carlisle to Glasgow and Edinburgh; alt. 309 m.

Beauce, region, central **France;** flat limestone plateau; arid, few surface streams; thin layer of loam (limon) permits agr.; impt. wheat growing a. ("the granary of France"); p. mainly grouped in vs.

Beaufort Sea, off N. Alaska, **USA;** part of Arctic Oc.

Beaujolais, France; in upper Rhône valley, N.E. Massif Central; wine-growing dist.

Beaulieu, v., Hants, **Eng.**; on Beaulieu R.; Cistercian abbey; car museum.

Beauly, t., Highland, **Scot.**; on Beauly R.; ruined priory; p. (1991) 1,354.

Beaumaris, t., Isle of Anglesey, N. **Wales;** pt. on Menai Strait; lt. engin.; resort; p. (1991) 1,561.

Beaumont, t.; 2nd. pt. of Texas, **USA;** ctr. of petrochemical inds.; p. (1990) 114,323 (t.), 361,000 (met. a. with Port Arthur).

Beaune, t., Cote d'Or, **France;** mediaeval walled t.; ctr. of wine tr.; p. (1982) 21,127.

Beauvais, agr. mkt. t., cap. of Oise dep., N. **France;** cath.; Gobelin tapestry removed to Paris; p. (1990) 56,278.

Bebington, Wirral, Merseyside, **Eng.**; part of pt. of Liverpool; soap, chemicals, engin.; p. (1991) 60,148.

Becancourt, t., Quebec, **Canada;** on S. bank of St. Lawrence; integrated steel mill projected.

Beccles, Waveney, Suffolk, **Eng.**; mkt. t. on R. Waveney S. of Broads; resort, agr. inds.; p. (1991) 10,337.

Béchar, t., dep., N.W. **Algeria;** a. 306,000 km²; p. (1987) 107,311 (t.), 183,896 (dep.).

Bechuanaland. *See* Botswana.

Beckum, t., N. Rhine–Westphalia, **Germany;** cement, chalk, engin. wks.; p. (1986) 36,500.

Beddington and Wallington. *See* Sutton.

Bedford, co. t. and l. gov. dist., **Eng.**; on R. Ouse, 80 km N. of London; gen. engin., inc. marine and elec., bricks, aero research; Bunyan imprisoned; p. (1995) 137,000 (dist.), (1991) 73,917 (t.).

Bedfordshire, non-met. co., **Eng.**; crossed by Chilterns; agr., mkt. gardening, brickmkg., cement, vehicles, engin.; p. (1995) 545,700.

Bedford Level, once over 162,000 ha. of peat marsh in S. Fenland, **Eng.**; first successful draining initiated by Earl of Bedford 1634.

Bedlington, t., Wansbeck, Northumberland, **Eng.**; nr. Blyth; former coal mng.; electronics; p. (1991) 15,431.

Bedloe's I., or Liberty I., N.Y. harbour, **USA;** on which the statue of Liberty stands.

Bedwas, t., Caerphilly, **Wales;** gas, coal and coke by-prods.; p. (1991) 8,488.

Bedworth, t., Warwicks., **Eng.**; l. gov. dist. with Nuneaton; nr. Coventry; coal mng., limestone quarrying, engin., textiles; p. (1991) 31,932.

Bedzin, t., S. **Poland;** coalmng. t. in Upper Silesia; p. (1989) 76,883.

Beerenberg, mtn., Jan Mayen I., **Norway,** Arctic Oc.; one of lgst. volcanic cones in world; glaciated; alt. 2,546 m.

Beersheba, t., **Israel;** ctr. for development of the Negev; p. (1992) 128,400.

Beeston and Stapleford, Broxtowe, Notts., **Eng.**; sub. of Nottingham; engin., drugs, telephones; p. (1991) 66,626.

Bègles, t., Gironde, **France;** mftg.; p. (1982) 23,426.

Begovat, t., E. **Uzbekistan;** on Syr Dar'ya R.; iron and steel wks.; hydroelectric power.

Behera, prov. **Egypt;** Nile delta; cap. Damandur; a. 10,129 km²; p. (1991) 3,730,000.

Beihai, spt., Guangxi prov., **China;** seafood cultivation, fishing; food processing and machin. inds.; offshore oil development; port being rebuilt to attract foreign investment as part of new open door policy; growth centre; p. (1984) 172,000.

Beijing (Peking), c. and mun., cap. of **China;** cultural ctr. and c. of gr. architectural beauty; for hundreds of years seat of Chinese emperors (Mongol, Ming, Manchu); formerly surrounded by walls; Imperial and Summer palaces; seat of govt.; univ.; Catholic cath. reopened (1985); many sm. factories producing a very wide range of goods, esp. chemicals, computers, textiles, synthetic fibres, machin., precision instruments, printing, publishing; route ctr., rly. junc., airpt.; a. 8,770 km²; p. (1992) 7,050,000, (1990) 10,870,000 (prov.).

Beira, spt., **Moçambique;** airpt; rly. runs inland to Harare (Zimbabwe) and Blantyre (Malawi); exp. sugar, maize, cotton; oil pipeline to Umtali; p. (1990) 299,300.

Beirut, c., cap. of **Lebanon;** pt. on Mediterranean; anc. Phoenician c., now busy shipping and mercantile ctr.; silk, wool, fruits; 4 univs.; p. (1988) 1·5m.

Beisan (Bet She'an), t., **Israel;** in Jordan valley, c. 90 m below sea-level; archaeological finds date from 1500 B.C.; rebuilt since 1948 by Israelis.

Bejaia (Bougie), spt., dep., N. **Algeria;** impt. tr. ctr.; exp. wood, hides; oil pipeline connection to Hassi-Messoud; p. (1987) 114,534 (t.), 697,669 (dep.).

Békéscsaba, t., **Hungary;** milling; rly. junc.; poultry processing plant; p. (1997) 65,000.

Belarus, CIS, former rep. USSR; low-lying; timber; agr. on drained marshes; peat; 209,790 km²; p. (1994) 10,367,000.

Belau, *See* Palau, Rep. of

Belaya Tserkov, t., N. **Ukraine;** agr. and comm. ctr.; p. (1990) 200,500.

Belém, spt., cap. of Pará st., **Brazil;** comm. ctr., ch. pt. of Amazon basin, entrepôt for riverside settlements, exp. forest prod. inc. jute, cocoa and cotton; inds. dominated by food processing and textiles; steel works; univ.; p. (1991) 1,246, 435.

Belfast, l. gov. dist., cap. of **N. Ireland;** pt. on Belfast Lough; Britain's lgst. single shipyard; freeport (1984) for air freight; linen mnf., rope, tobacco, distilling, aircraft, fertilisers, computers; oil refinery on E. side of harbour; univ.; Stormont Castle; p. (1991) 279,237.

Belfort, t., cap. of Belfort dep., E. **France,** in Alsace; fortress t. between Jura and Vosges; heavy inds., rly. wks., cotton ind.; elec. engin.; p. (1990) 51,913.

Belfort (Territoire de), dep., **France;** ch. t. Belfort; a. 608 km²; p. (1990) 134,100.

Belgaum, t., Karnataka, **India;** cotton; alt. 760 m; Jain temples; p. (1991) 326,000.

Belgium, kingdom, W. Europe, comprises 9 admin. provs.; low-lying except in Ardennes in S.E.; very high density of p., intensive agr. and highly industl.; severe social and economic problems have resulted from decline of Sambre- Meuse coalfield and associated heavy engin. inds., similar difficulties in textile inds. in N.W.; industl. expansion on Kempenland coalfield in N.E. and around Brussels, Antwerp, and Ghent; heavily dependent upon foreign tr. for economic survival; member of EU; major spt. of Antwerp competing with Rotterdam for hinterland; 2 language groups: Flemish (Dutch dialect) in N., French dialect in S. (Walloon a.); univs. at Brussels, Ghent, Liège, Louvain; cap. Brussels; a. 30,445 km²; p. (1996) 10,140,000.

Belgorod, t., **Russia;** N.W. of Kharkov, on N. Donets R.; rly. junc. in agr. region; p. (1989) 300,000.

Belgrade (Beograd), c., cap of Serbia and **Yugoslavia;** inland pt. on Danube at mouth of Sava R.; industl., admin. and cultural ctr.; univ.; airport; bombed by NATO, 1999; p. (1991) 1,136,786.

Belitung or Billiton, I., between Sumatra and Kalimantan, **Indonesia;** tin; a. 4.832 km²; p. 102,375.

Belize, indep. rep. (1981), Central America; formerly Brit. Honduras; almost totally underdeveloped; heavy rainfall, hurricanes; tropical forest; only 15 percent of land is cultivated; economy hit by fall in world sugar prices; recent sale of 13 percent of land a. to clear tropical forest for citrus production; 20 per cent unemployed; lowest p. density in Central America; new cap. Belmopan; a. 22,962 km²; p. (1994) 209,500.

Belize City, c., former cap. of **Belize;** almost devastated by hurricane 31 Oct. 1961; cap. moved to Belmopan 80 km further inland; spt.; p. (1991) 44,087.

Bellery, c., Karnataka, **India;** fort; cotton processing and tr.; p. (1991) 245,391.

Bell Bay, pt., Tasmania, **Australia;** on bank of Tamar R.; modern pt. and aluminium refinery

(1950s) for processing Queensland bauxite; ferry terminal; now part of Launceston.

Bell I., Newfoundland, E. **Canada**; in Conception Bay, 32 km N.W. of St. Johns; impt. Wabana iron-ore deposits outcrop on N.W. cst., smelted on Pictou coalfield, Nova Scotia; a. 31 km².

Belle Isle Strait, Canada; between Newfoundland and Labrador, on N. shipping route to Canada from Europe.

Belleville, pt., L. Ontario, **Canada**; agr. processing; white marble nearby, cement; light inds.; p. (1986) 36,041.

Belleville, t., Ill., **USA**; industl. ctr., domestic prod., coal; air force training school; p. (1980) 41,580.

Belleville, t., N.J., **USA**; machin., chemicals; p. (1980) 35,367.

Bellingham, t., spt., Wash., **USA**; agr. distribution ctr.; timber inds.; salmon canning; p. (1984) 45,100 (c.), 111,800 (met. a.).

Bellinzona, t., **Switzerland**; on R. Ticino; 22 km N. of Lugano; three castles built on hills dominating t.; rly. engin.; tourism; p. (1980) 16,743.

Bell Rock (Inchcape I.), rock and lighthouse 17 km S.E. of Arbroath, **Scot.**

Belluno, t., cap. of B. prov., Venezia, N. **Italy**; route ctr. at S. foot of Dolomites; cath.; engin.; p. (1981) 36,634.

Belmopan, new inland cap., **Belize**; (1991) 3,558.

Belo Horizonte, c., cap. of Minas Gerais st. **Brazil**; impt. inland c.; ctr. rich agr. and mng. region; steel mills, food inds., textiles, diamond cutting; oil pipeline from Guanabara; univ.; one of the fastest growing c. in Brazil, especially since building of Fiat factory; p. (1991) 2,048,861.

Beloretsk, t., Bashkir, aut. rep., **Russia**; in Ural Mtns. on Belaya R.; iron, metal inds.

Belovo, t., W. Siberia, **Russia**; in Kuznetsk basin; coal mng., zinc, engin.; p. (1985) 117,000.

Belper, mkt. t., Amber Valley, Derbys., **Eng.**; hosiery, textiles, oil wks., iron foundries; p. (1991) 18,213.

Belsen, v., 24 km N.W. of Celle, **Germany**; notorious second world war concentration camp.

Belterra, t., dist., Pará st., N.E. **Brazil**; nr. confluence of Tapajós and Amazon Rs; site of Fordlandia scheme.

Beltsy, t., **Moldova**; on trib. of Dniester R.; agr. ctr., food processing; p. (1990) 164,800.

Belvoir (pronounced Beaver), **Vale of**, Melton Leics., **Eng.**; clay vale, cattle, sheep; Stilton cheese; recent development of coalfield.

Bembridge, v., E. cst., I. of Wight, **Eng.**; resort; p. (1991) 3,397.

Benalla, t., dist., Victoria, **Australia**, pastoral and agr.; p. (1986) 8,490 (t.).

Benares. *See* Varanasi.

Benbecula I., Outer Hebrides, Western Isles, **Scot.**; between Is. of N. and S. Uist; airpt. in N.; fishing; p. (1991) 1,803.

Bendigo, c., Victoria, **Australia**; former goldmng. dist., gold rush 1851; mng. ceased 1955; primary prods.; impt. egg producing ctr.; p. (1991) 57,427.

Benevento, c., Campania, **Italy**; cap. of B. prov. which contains many Roman remains; cath.; agr. processing; p. (1981) 62,636.

Benfleet, t., Castle Point, Essex. **Eng.**; residtl.; p. (1991) 49,701.

Bengal, Bay of, part of **Indian Oc.** washing E. shores of India and W. shores of Burma, receives waters of Rs. Krishna, Ganges; Brahmaputra, Irrawaddy.

Bengbu (Pengpu), c., Anhui, **China**; on Kwo-Ho 168 km. NW of Nanjing; on Tianjin–Nanjing rly; p. (1984) 597,100.

Benghazi, joint cap. (with Tripoli) of **Libya**; spt. and airpt. on G. of Sirte; univ.; former Greek Hesperides; p. (1984) 485,386.

Benguela, t., **Angola**, S.W. Africa; rly. runs inland to Zaïre and Zambia; seaport now lost much tr. to Lobito.

Benha, t., **Egypt**; impt. mkt. t., rail and road ctr. in heart of cultivated a. of Nile delta 48 km N. of Cairo; airpt.; p. (1986) 115,571.

Beni, dep. **Bolivia**; drained by R. Mamoré; rubber, cattle; a. 213,564 km²; p. (1988) 215,400.

Benin City, t., **Nigeria**; cap. of Benin st.; former notorious slave ctr.; p. (1992) 207,200.

Benin, People's Republic of, (Dahomey), indep. st. (1960), West Africa; former French Colony; high standard of education reflected in heavy government sector and low level of productive activity in the economy; staple foods of groundnuts, palms, coffee, cocoa; intensive farming in fertile

Terre de Barre; land held collectively; full potential of drier N. not yet exploited; concern about desert encroachment; oil found offshore from main pt. Cotonou; inds. process primary prods.; joint Benin-Nigerian rly; much tropical rain forest in S.; dependence on Nigeria; many joint industl. projects; cap. Porto Novo; a. 112,622 km²; p. (1994) 5,234,000.

Beni Suef, t. and prov., **Egypt**; on Nile, 96 km S. of Cairo; ctr. of fertile agr. a.; carpets, cotton; p. (1986) 151,813 (t.), (1991) 1,656,000 (prov.).

Ben Lawers, mtn., Perth and Kinross, **Scot.**; by Loch Tay; arctic and alpine flora; alt. 1,215 m.

Ben Macdhui, mtn., Aberdeenshire, **Scot.**; Cairngorm gr.; second highest peak in Brit. Is.; alt. 1,310 m.

Ben Nevis, mtn., Highland, **Scot.**; volcanic; hgst. peak in Brit. Isles; alt. 1,344 m.

Benoni, t., Transvaal, **S. Africa**; gold mng. ctr.; engin.; p. (1980) 205,420 (dist.).

Bensheim, t., Hesse, **Germany**; ctr. of fruit and wine dist. on E. edge Rhine valley; textiles, paper, metallurgy; p. (1986) 33,500.

Bentley with Arksey, t., South Yorks., **Eng.**; p. (1991) 32,675.

Benton Harbor, t., Mich., **USA**; midway along E. cst. L. Michigan; p. (1984) 14,200 (t), 163,000 (met. a.).

Benue R., **Nigeria-Cameroon**; rises in Adamawa mtns.; forms ch. trib. of Niger R.; R. pts. and agr. tr.; length 1,392 km.

Ben Vorlich. mtn., Perth and Kinross, **Scot.**; alt. 983 m.

Ben Wyvis, mtn., Highland, **Scot.**; nr. Dingwall; alt. 1,046 m.

Benxi (Penki), c., Liaoning prov., **China**; metallurgical ctr.; p. (1984) 810,500.

Ben-y-Gloe, mtn., Glen Tilt, Perth and Kinross, **Scot.**; alt. 1,120 m.

Beograd. *See* Belgrade.

Beppu, c., Kyushu, **Japan**; hot spring resort: p. (1990) 130,323.

Berbera, pt., **Somalia**, on G. of Aden; exp. livestock from pastoral hinterland; new deepsea pt. completed 1969; airport; p. (1987) 65,000.

Berchtesgaden, v., **Germany**; mtn. resort 24 km S. of Salzburg; Hitler's mtn. retreat; tourism; potash.

Berck-Plage, resort, Pas-de-Calais, **France**, on Eng. Channel; p. (1982) 15,671.

Berdichev, t., **Ukraine**; ctr. of sugar a.; engin., lt. inds.; p. (1990) 92,600.

Berdyansk, c., **Ukraine**; pt. on Sea of Azov; agr. ctr.; machin.; health resort; p. (1990) 133,500.

Bere Regis, mkt. t., Dorset, **Eng.**; Saxon royal residence; p. (1991) 1,767.

Berezina, R., **Belarus**; trib. of Dnieper; forms part of Baltic-Black Sea waterway; 608 km long.

Berezniki, t., E. European Russia; pt. on Kolva R., W. Urals; salt, chemicals, paper; p. (1989) 201,000.

Bergama, t., **Turkey**; anc. Pergamos, ruins; morocco leather inds.; agr. tr.; p. (1985) 38,849.

Bergamo, c., Lombardy, **Italy**; 54 km N.E. Milan; cath. and academy; silk industry; p. (1992) 114,930.

Bergen, spt., W. cst. **Norway**; univ.; most impt. comm. pt. in kingdom; shipping, fishing; mftg. inds.; birthplace of Grieg; p. (1990) 187,382.

Bergen op Zoom, t. N. Brabant, **Neth.**; sugar refining. engin.; p. (1993) 47,546.

Bergerac, t., Dordogne, S.W. **France**; impt. bridge over Dordogne R.; mkt. for wines and luxury foods; anc. Huguenot stronghold; p. (1982) 27,704.

Bergisches Land, terr., N. Rhine-Westphalia, **Germany**; specialised iron and steel prod.; chemicals machin.; inc. ts. of Solingen, Remscheid, Velbert, Wuppertal.

Bergisch-Gladbach, t., N. Rhine-Westphalia, **Germany**; 11 km E. of Cologne, paper, metallurgy, textiles; p. (1990) 104,100.

Berhampur, t., Orissa, **India**; admin. and educational ctr.

Bering Current (Okhotsk Current, or Oyashio), ocean current, N. Pac. Oc.; flows through Bering Strait from Arctic, along E. cst. of Kamchatka and Japanese Is. Hokkaido, Honshu; relatively cold; moderate summer temperatures along csts. causes fogs.

Bering Sea, part of N. **Pac. Oc.** between Aleutian Is. and B. Strait; fishing; a. 2,274,020 km².

Bering Strait, narrow sea which separates Asia from N. America, and connects Bering Sea with Arctic Oc.; 58 km wide at narrowest part.

Berkeley, v., Gloucs., **Eng.**; nr. R. Severn, 24 km N. of Bristol; scene of murder of Edward II; nuclear power-sta. decommissioning.

Berkeley, c., Cal., USA; univ.; chemicals; now inc. in San Francisco; p. (1990) 102,724.

Berkhamsted, Dacorum, Herts., Eng.; mkt. t.; chemicals; cas. ruins, 17th cent. school; birthplace of William Cowper the poet; p. (1991) 18,044.

Berkshire, former co., Eng.; chalk downland inc. Inkpen Beacon, White Horse Hills; drained by Thames and tribs.; residtl.; electronics, biscuits; dairying; Windsor Gr. Park; Ascot racecourse.

Berlin, c., cap. of re-unified Germany; on Spree R.; formerly divided into 4 occupied zones 1945; Soviet (E. Berlin), British, American, French (W. Berlin); W. Berlin formed isolated enclave within E. Germany; focal point of escape attempts from E. to W. led to construction of "Berlin Wall", destroyed 1989; W. Berlin major industl. ctr. aided by American and W. German capital; educational, cultural and tourist ctr.; E. Berlin, former cap. of E. Germany, rebuilt as showpiece with high-rise housing, elect. manfs, machin., p. (1990) 3,437,000.

Bermuda, Brit. gr. coral Is. (360 in no. of which 20 are inhabited) N. Atlantic; about 1,120 km E. of S.C.; Hamilton, on Long I. is the ch. t.; Brit. and US air and naval stas.; favourite winter resort for Americans; inds. attracted by tax incentives; no surface water; total a. 54 km²; p. (1997) 60,500.

Bern, c., cap. of B. can. and fed. cap. Switzerland; on Aare R.; cath., univ.; textiles, musical instruments, chocolate; H.Q. of Postal Union; bear pit; p. (1990) 134,600 (c.) 298,700 (met. a.).

Bern, can., Switzerland; fertile valleys, dairying; watches; hydroelectric power; plans for separate can. in Jura reg.; a. 6,881 km²; p. (1990) 945,600.

Bernard, Great St., one of the Alps in the S. of the Valais, Switzerland; highest point 3,390 m; height of mtn. pass between Italy (Aosta) and Switzerland (Martigny), 2,477 m; famous hospice for travellers in monastery on mtn.; road tunnel completed 1964.

Bernard, Little St., one of Graian Alps, Savoy, S. of Mt. Blanc, France; pass traversed by Hannibal 218 B.C.

Bernburg, t., Saxony-Anhalt, Germany; cas.; chemicals, salt mng.; p. (1980) 46,000.

Bernese Oberland (Berner Alpen), alpine region, Switzerland; 35 peaks over 3,000 m inc. Finsteraarhorn and Jungfrau; tourist a. inc. resorts of Interlaken and Grindelwald.

Bernina Alps, Switzerland; alt. 4,050 m.

Berri, t., S. Australia; ctr. of irrigated fruit growing a. on R. Murray; wines; p. (1981) 3,419.

Berri, oilfield, Saudi Arabia; 72 km N.W. of Ras Tannura; the field extends offshore.

Berwick, t., Vic., Australia; satellite of Melbourne; to be expanded to planned p. of 100,000 by 1985; p. (1983) 41,400.

Berwickshire, historic co., S. Scot., now part of Borders.

Berwick-upon-Tweed, l. gov. dist., Northumberland, Eng.; spt. on mouth of Tweed; border t., changed between Eng. and Scot. 15 times in history; fishing, lt. engin., tweeds, knitwear; cas. ruins; p. (1995) 26,400 (dist.), (1991) 13,544 (t.).

Besançon, t., cap. of Doubs dep., France; cath., observatory, univ.; farm implements, textiles; watch- and clock-making; birthplace of Victor Hugo; p. (1990) 119,194 (t.), 122,623 (met.a.).

Beskids, W. and E., (Beskidy Zachodnie), mtn. range, Poland, Slovakia, E. Europe; northern range of Carpathian mtn. system, seldom exceeds alt. 1,200 m, many passes; forested; tourism; length 352 km.

Bessarabia, terr., ceded to former USSR by Romania 1940, and now part of Moldova; agr. region.

Bessemer, t., Ala., USA; iron and steel; p. (1980) 31,729.

Bethany (El Azarieh), v., on Mt. of Olives 6 km W. of Jerusalem.

Bethel, anc. c., the modern Beitin, Jordan; 16 km N. Jerusalem.

Bethesda, t., Gwynedd, Wales; slate, lt. engin; p. (1991) 3,558.

Bethlehem, t. 9 km S.W. Jerusalem; according to Matthew and Luke birthplace of Christ; p. (1980) 14,000.

Bethlehem, t., Penns., USA; 80 km N. of Philadelphia; iron-wks.; univ.; p. (1980) 70,419.

Bethnal Green, dist., London, Eng.; in E. End of London; now in Tower Hamlets.

Béthune, t., Pas-de-Calais, France; rail and canal ctr. for coalfield; mkt. t.; p. (1990) 25,261 (t.), 259,679 (met. a.).

Betteshanger, v., Kent, Eng.; on N. flank of N. Downs, 6 km W. of Deal; coal mng.

Betws-y-coed, t., Conwy, Wales; waterfalls; tourism.

Beuthan. See Bytom.

Beverley, mkt. t., E. Riding of Yorks., Eng.; famous minster (13th cent.); agr. processing; p. (1991) 23,632 (t.).

Beverly, c., Mass., USA; footwear, machin.; p. (1980) 37,655.

Beverly Hills, t., Cal., USA; sub. of Los Angeles; home of many film celebrities; p. (1980) 32,367.

Beverwijk, t., nr. Haarlem, N. Holland, Neth.; agr. prods.; p. (1993) 35,523.

Bewdley, Wyre Forest, Worcs., Eng.; mkt. t. on R. Severn; birthplace of Stanley Baldwin; residtl.; p. (1991) 9,009.

Bexhill-on-Sea, t., Rother, East Sussex, Eng.; resort; p. (1991) 38,905.

Bexley, former bor., W. Kent; now outer bor., Greater London, Eng.; inc. Sidcup, Crayford and Erith; p. (1995) 220,300.

Béziers, t., Hérault, France; ctr. of wine, brandy tr. and inds.; chemicals; p. (1990) 72,362 (t.), 76,304 (met. a.).

Bezwada. See Vijayawada.

Bhadravati, t., Karnataka, India; steel; p. (1981) 77,055 (t.), 130,606 (met. a.).

Bhagalpur, t., Bihar, India; agr. tr. ctr. on R. Ganges; p. (1981) 253,000.

Bhamo, t., Upper Myanmar; on Irrawaddy; inland limit of steam boats; mkt. ctr.; ruby mines.

Bhandara, cap. of Bhandara dist., Maharashtra, India; 48 km E. of Nagpur; cotton cloth, brass mftg.; p. (1981) 56,025.

Bharuch, t., Gujerat, India; world's lgst. stream urea fertiliser plant; nearby oilfield.; p. (1991) 133,102

Bhatpara, t., W. Bengal, India; on R. Hooghly; industl. t.; jute, engin.; p. (1991) 316,000.

Bhaunager, t., Gujarat, India; spt. on G. of Cambay; exp. cotton, oilseeds; p. (1991) 402,000.

Bhilai, t., Madhya Pradesh, India; steel plant; rails and rly. sleepers; p. (1981) 319,450.

Bhim-Gora, sacred pool, place of Hindu pilgrimage, Uttar Pradesh, India.

Bhopal, c., cap. of Madhya Pradesh, India; impt. tr. ctr.; varied inds.; prehistoric cave paintings nearby; 2,000 killed in world's worst chem. accident (1984); p. (1991) 1,063,000.

Bhubaneswar, t., cap. of Orissa, India; 29 km from Cuttack; admin. ctr.; Hindu temples, pilgrimage ctr.; p. (1991) 412,000.

Bhutan, kingdom, indep. mtn. st., E. Himalayas; heavy monsoon rain, rich tropical vegetation. valuable forests; N.–S. ridges and valleys result in semi-closed communities; first motor link with India opened 1962; cap. Thimphu; a. c. 46,620 km²; alt. 7,558 m (Kula Kangri); p. scattered and nomadic (1990) 600,000.

Biafra, Bight of. See Bonny, Bight of.

Biala Podlaska, t. and prov., E. Poland; wool, furniture; p. (1989) 52,119 (t.), 304,000 (prov.).

Białystok, t. and prov., Poland; nr. Grodno; major industl. ctr.; rly. ctr.; p. (1989) 267,670 (t.), 687,800 (prov.).

Biarritz, t., Pyrénées-Atlantique dep., France; on Bay of Biscay; seaside resort; p. (1982) 26,647.

Biberach, t., Baden-Württemberg, Germany; on R. Kinzig; spa; wood, metal and engin. inds.; p. (1986) 28,000.

Bicester, Cherwell, Oxford, Eng.; anc. mkt. t., N.E. of Oxford; p. (1991) 22,128.

Biddulph, t., Staffs. Moorlands, Staffs., Eng.; coal mng., machin., textiles, furniture; residtl.; p. (1991) 16,725.

Bideford, Torridge, N. Devon, Eng.; pt. on estuary R. Torridge; mkt., boat-bldg.; resort; p. (1991) 14,328.

Biel (Bienne), t., Berne, Switzerland; nr. Lake B.; watches; impt. industl. ctr.; p. (1990) 52,736.

Bielefeld, t., Rhine-Westphalia, Germany; ch. ctr. of linen industry; machin., bicycles; p. (1990) 320,000.

Biella, t., Vercelli, Italy; textiles; p. (1981) 53,572.

Bielsko-Biala, t., and prov., S. Poland; textiles, engin.; p. (1989) 181,072 (t), 895,400 (prov.).

Bien-hoa, t., nr. Ho Chi-minh City, S. Vietnam; sugar refining; cotton mills.

Bies-Bosch, reclaimed fenland area between N. Brabant and S.W. **Neth.**; sugar refining, dairying; a. 142 km².

Biggar, sm. burgh, S. Lanarkshire, **Scot.**; 213 m alt. in Southern Uplands; p. (1991) 1,994.

Biggin Hill, London Borough, Bromley, **Eng.**; nr. Orpington; famous airfield of Battle of Britain; p. (1991) 14,107.

Biggleswade, t., Mid Beds., **Eng.**; in valley of R. Ivel, 14 km S.E. of Bedford; ctr. of fruit-growing and mkt. gardening dist.; hydraulic machin. tools, hosiery, caravans; p. (1991) 12,350.

Big Horn Mtns., Wyo. and Mont., **USA**; Rockies; favourite film location; attractive agr. valleys; highest alt., 3,600 m.

Bihac, t., **Bosnia-Herzegovina,** formerly Yugoslavia; on R. Una; industl; timber processing.

Bihar, st., N.W. **India**; in Ganges basin; hilly; bulk of p. in agr. N.; irrigation; minerals in S.E.; coal, iron, mica; steelwks. at Jamshedpur, oil refining at Barauni; cap. Patna, admin. ctr. Ranchi; a. 173,882 km²; p. (1991) 86,374,465.

Bihar, t., Bihar, **India**; within middle Ganges valley nr. Patna; p. (1991) 201,323.

Biisk, c., Siberia, **Russia**; ctr. of rich agr. a.; meat packing, textiles; p. (1989) 233,000.

Bijagós, Achipelago dos (Bissagos Is.), off W. cst. **Guinea-Bissau**; c. 14 Is.; coconuts, rice; ch. t. Bolama on Bolama I.; a. 1,554 km².

Bijapur, t., Karnataka, **India**; cotton tr. and inds.; ruins; former cap. of B. kingdom; p. (1991) 186,939.

Bikaner, t., Rajasthan, **India**; in Thar desert; on former caravan route; wool tr., bldg. stone, handicrafts; p. (1991) 416,000.

Bikini, atoll, **Pac. Oc.**; atomic-bomb tests (1946).

Bilaspur, t., Madhya Pradesh, **India**; silks, cottons; p. (1991) 192,396.

Bilbao, spt., N. **Spain**; cap. Basque prov. of Viscaya; formerly famous for rapier making; iron ore, smelting; pipeline from Ayoluengo oilfield; new Guggenheim Museum opened, 1997; p. (1991) 372,191.

Billinge and **Winstanley,** t., Lancs., **Eng.**; former coal-mng. a.; p. (1991) 6,943.

Billingham, t., Stockton-on-Tees, **Eng.**; on N. of Tees estuary; major petrochemical plant; p. (1991) 36,867.

Billings, t., Mont., **USA**; agr. tr. ctr. in irrigated a.; sulphur plant; p. (1990) 81,151.

Billingsgate, London, **Eng.**; old river-gate and wharf, formerly ch. fish mkt. of England; now moved to Isle of Dogs.

Bilma (Kawar), oasis t., **Niger**; on caravan route from Tripoli to Agadès and L. Chad.

Billiton I. See Belitung.

Biloxi, t., Miss., **USA**; fishing, tourist ctr.; US Coast Guard air base; p. (1984) 48,700 (t.) 197,400 (met. a.).

Bilston, t., West Midlands, **Eng.**; part of Wolverhampton; iron and steel.

Bingen, t., Rhineland Palatinate, **Germany**; at S. entrance to Rhine gorge; wine; beautiful scenery; tourism; p. (1986) 22,100.

Bingerville, spt., Cote d'Ivoire, W. Africa; rubber processing.

Bingham Canyon, t., N. Utah, **USA**; silver, gold, lead; major open pit copper mine.

Binghamton, N.Y., **USA**; on Susquehanna R.; boot factories, aircraft components, cameras; p. (1990) 53,008 (t.), 264,100 (met. a.).

Bingley, West Yorks., **Eng.**; mkt. t. on R. Aire 26 km N.W. of Leeds; textiles, engin., agr.; p. (1991) 19,585.

Bintan I., lgst. island of Riouw archipelago, Indonesia; bauxite, tin.

Bintenne, dist., **Sri Lanka**; remote a., sparse p.; lge. Gal Oya reservoir; tea and rubber estates.

Biobio, reg. **Chile**; cap. Conception; a. 36,939 km²; p. (1992) 1,729,920.

Bioko, formerly Marcias Nguema (Fernando Po), I., **Equatorial Guinea**; in Bight of Bonny; mtnous.; coffee, cocoa, bananas, timber; p. (1983) 57,190.

Biratnagar, t., S.E. **Nepal**, in the Tarai; jute, sugar, cotton milling, stainless steel; p. (1991) 130,129.

Birbhum, dist., W. Bengal, **India**; cap. Suri; healthy climate; rice, sugar; mnfs. silk, cotton; a. 4,550 km²; p. (1981) 2,095,829.

Birkenhead, Wirral, Merseyside, **Eng.**; spt. on R. Mersey, opposite Liverpool; handles industl. goods; heavy and pt. processing inds.; shipbldg.; p. (1991) 93,087.

Birmingham, c., met. dist., West Midlands, **Eng.**; industl. cap. Midlands, second lgst. c. Gt. Britain;

metal inds.; motor vehicles, components and accessories; univ., cath.; freeport (1984) for air freight; p. (1995) 1,017,500 (dist.), (1991) 965,928 (c.).

Birmingham, t., Ala., **USA**; coal, iron, limestone, steel, aircraft, chemicals, textiles; p. (1990) 265,968 (t.), 907,810 (met. a.).

Birnam, v., Perth and Kinross, **Scot.**; location of Birnam Wood in *Macbeth*; former royal forest; p. (1991) 1,227 (with Dunkeld).

Birobidzhan, or Jewish aut. oblast, **Russia**; in Khabarovsk terr.; agr., timber and mng. inds.; a. 35,988 km²; cap. Birobidzhan City; p. (1980) 67,000 (inc. 15,000 Jews).

Birr, t. Offaly, **R.o.I.**; mkt. t. on Brosna R.; observatory; p. (1986) 3,417.

Bisbee, t., Arizona, **USA**; very rich copper deposits, gold, silver, lead; p. (1980) 7,154.

Biscarosse, Landes dep.; **France**; 72 km S.W. Bordeaux; rocket and missile testing range projected; p. (1982) 8,979.

Biscay, Bay of, stormy a. of Atl. Oc., W. of France and N. of Spain, from Ushant to C. Ortegal; the Roman Sinus Aquitanicus; heavy seas.

Bisceglie, t., Apulia, **Italy**; spt. on E. cst. 35 km N.W. of Bari; tr. in wine and olives; light inds.; cath.; p. (1981) 45,899.

Bischofswerda, t., Saxony, **Germany**; quarrying, glass and iron inds.; rly. ctr.; p. (1989) 13,174.

Bishkek, (Frunze), c., cap. of **Kyrgyzstan**; univ.; engin., textiles, meat-packing; p. (1990) 624,900.

Bishop Auckland, t., Wear Valley, Durham, **Eng.**; palace of Bishop of Durham; iron, lt. engin.; former coal mng.; p. (1991) 23,154.

Bishopbriggs, sm. burgh, E. Dunbartonshire, **Scot.**; p. (1991) 23,825.

Bishop Rock, isolated rock, lighthouse, Scilly Is., **Eng.**; 58 km S.W. of Land's End, Cornwall; recognised internationally as E. end of trans-Atlantic ocean crossing.

Bishop's Stortford, East Herts., **Eng.**; mkt. t. on Stort R.; light inds.; Norman cas.; p. (1991) 28,403.

Biskra, t., dep., Algeria; a. 109,729 km², p. (1987) 128,280 (t.), (1987) 429,217 (dep.).

Bisley, v., Surrey, **Eng.**; ranges of Nat. Rifle Ass. on B. common.

Bismarck, t., st. cap. N.D., **USA**; on Missouri R.; agr. mkt. ctr.; p. (1980) 44,485.

Bismarck Archipelago, volcanic gr., S.W. Pac. Oc., off New Guinea, admin. by **Australia**.

Bisotūn, t., **Iran**; in ruins; monuments to Darius I (the Great).

Bissagos Is. See **Bijagós, Achipelago dos.**

Bissau, t., cap of **Guinea-Bissau**; former ctr. of slave tr.; airpt.; plans to expand harbour; p. (1988) 125,000.

Bitola, t., **Macedonia,** formerly Yugoslavia; varied mnfs., recent industl. development; mosques; p. (1981) 137,835.

Bitonto, t., Apulia, on E. cst. 11 km N.W. of Bari; **Italy**; cath.

Bitterfeld, t. Saxony, **Germany**; lignite mng., engin. chemicals; p. (1989) 20,017.

Bitter Lakes, Isthmus of Suez, **Egypt**, utilised by Suez Canal.

Biwa-ko, lgst. lake in **Japan**, S. Honshu; 101 m a.s.l.; canal to Kyto provides hydroelectric power; superb scenery, historical associations; tourism; a. 675 km².

Biysk or **Bisk,** c., Altai terr., **Russia**; pt. on Biya R.; terminus of branch of Turk-Sib. rly.; p. (1989) 233,000.

Bizerte, c., **N. Tunisia**; pt. and naval sta. on Med.; the anc. Hippo Zaritus; fishing, oil refining, steel wks., tyres; p. (1984) 94,509.

Björnborg. See **Pori.**

Blaby, t. and l. gov. dist., Leics., **Eng.**; sm. a. S.W. of Leicester; p. (1995) 85,200 (dist.), (1991) 6,538 (t.).

Black Belt, coastlands of Miss. and Ala., **USA**, where black soil prairie land is good for cotton.

Blackburn, t., l. gov. dist., Lancs., **Eng.**; once major cotton weaving ctr.; engin., lt. inds.; p. (1995) 140,300 (dist.), (1991) 105,994 (t.).

Black Country, Midlands, **Eng.**; formerly impt. ironworking and coal-mng. dist. mainly in S. West Midlands; now area of light engineering; c. 130 km².

Blackdown Hills, Devon and Somerset, **Eng.**; sandstone hills rising over 305 m.

Black Forest. See **Schwarzwald.**

Blackheath, open common, S.E. London, **Eng.**;

mustering place of Wat Tyler's (1381) and Jack Cade's (1450) revolutionary peasants; now main attraction of expensive residtl. a.; a. 108 ha.

Black Hills, mtns. between S.D. and Wyo., **USA**; highest., Horney Peak, 2.208 m; form part of Nat. Park.

Black Isle, peninsula, between Cromarty and Beauly Firths, Highland, **Scot.**; agr., fisheries, quarrying.

Black Mtn., Powys and Carmarthenshire, S. **Wales**; rises to 802 m; sandstone plateau; moorland; valleys used for reservoirs.

Black Mtns., Powys, S. **Wales**; rise to 811 m at Waun Fâch.

Blackpool, t., l. gov. dist., Lancs., **Eng.**; on cst. of Fylde dist.; one of major Brit. resorts; p. (1995) 153,600 (dist.), (1991) 146,282 (t.).

Black Prairie, region Texas, **USA**; extends 560 km S.W. from Ouachita Mtns. to Austin; contains very fertile Black Waxy and Grande Prairie sub-regions devoted almost entirely to cotton growing; ch. ts., Dallas, Fort Worth, Austin; a. 77,700 km².

Blackrod, t., Gtr. Manchester, **Eng.**; nr. Chorley; former cotton weaving; p. (1991) 5,681.

Black Sea, bordered by 6 sts., **Ukraine, Russia, Georgia** (N. and E.), **Turkey** (S.), **Bulgaria, Romania** (W.); receives waters of Danube, Dniester, Dnieper, Don. Bug; stagnant and lifeless below 150 m; fisheries in N. and W.; oil exploration by Turkey; a. 424,760 km² (exc. Sea of Azov).

Blacksod Bay, cst. of Mayo, **R.o.I.**

Black Volta, R., rises in **Burkina Faso**, flows E. and S. into L. Volta, **Ghana**; length c. 1,200 km.

Blackwater, R., N. Ireland; rising in Dungannon, it forms border with **R.o.I.**; enters L. Neagh; 80 km long.

Blackwater, R., R.o.I.; flows from Knockanefune to enter Atl. Oc. at pt. and resort of Youghal; chain of sm. ts. along course; 144 km long.

Blackwood, t., Caerphilly, S.E. **Wales**; N. of Abercarn; p. (1991) 14,466.

Blaenau Ffestiniog, t., Gwynedd, N. **Wales**; at head of Vale of Ffestiniog, 14 km E. of Porthmadog; consists of Ffestiniog and Blaenau Ffestiniog; slate quarries; pumped-storage hydroelec. sta. (1963); cement; narrow gauge rly.; p. (1991) 4,546.

Blaenau Gwent, S. **Wales**, unit. auth. created in 1996 from former l. gov. dist.; inland valley a. inc. Ebbw Vale and Abertillery; p. (1995) 73,200.

Blaenavon, t., Torfaen, **Wales**; former coal mng. a.; p. (1991) 6,066.

Blagoveshchensk, t., E. Siberia, **Russia**, on Chinese bdr. and R. Amur; wat. pl.; engin., sawmilling, flour milling; on Trans-Siberian rly.; p. (1989) 206,000.

Blair Atholl, v., Perth and Kinross, **Scot.**; tourist resort; cas.; seat of Duke of Atholl.

Blairgowrie and **Rattray,** burgh, Perth and Kinross, Scot.; at foot of Scot. Highlands; mkt. t. in Strathmore fruit growing dist.; p. (1991) 8,001.

Blakeney, v., N. Norfolk, **Eng.**; nr. sand spit; yachting; wild fowl.

Blandford or **Blandford Forum,** North Dorset, **Eng.**; on R. Stour; pastoral mkt. t. since 13th cent.; p. (1991) 8,880.

Blantyre, c., **Malawi**; in Shire Highlands; linked by rail to Beira (Moçambique); comm. ctr.; timber processing; p. (1987) 331,588.

Blantyre, v., S. Lanarkshire, **Scot.**; Lower B. birthplace of David Livingstone; p. (1991) 18,484.

Blarney, v., 6 km N.W. Cork, **R.o.I.**; cas. and Blarney stone; p. (1986) 1,952.

Blasket Is., Kerry. **R.o.I.**; rocky Is.; p. (1986) 4.

Blaydon, t. Tyne and Wear. **Eng.**; former coal mng.; p. (1991) 15,510.

Bled, glacial L., **Slovenia** (formerly Yugoslavia); tourism.

Blekinge, co. **S. Sweden**; cap. Karlskrona; a. 2,909 km²; p. (1992) 151,266.

Blenheim, t., S.I., **N.Z.**; fruit; p. (1991) 23,637 (urban a.).

Blenheim, v., **Germany**; scene of battle (1704) when English and Austrians under Marlborough defeated the French and Bavarians; **Blenheim Palace,** Woodstock, Oxon. **Eng.**; named in honour of this victory.

Blessington, L., Wicklow, **R.o.I.**; glacial L., now serves as reservoir for Dublin.

Bletchley, Milton Keynes, **Eng.**; expanded t.; p. (1991) 41,435.

Blida. See El Boulaïda.

Bloemfontein, t. cap. O.F.S., **S. Africa**; on plateau, alt. 1,393 m; route and tr. ctr.; univ.; p. (1985) 205,420 (met. a.).

Blois, t., cap. of Loir-et-Cher dep., **France**; historic t. on Loire R.; Renaissance château; wines; p. (1990) 51,549.

Bloomfield, t., N.J., **USA**; pharmaceuticals, metal and elec. gds.; sub. N.J. c.; p. (1990) 45,006.

Bloomington, t., Ill., **USA**; comm. ctr. and industl. t. in rich agr. and coal-mng. a.; univ.; p. (1984) 46,600 (t.). 122,800 (met. a.).

Bloomington, t., Ind., **USA**; electronic equipment, furniture, structural glass; univ.; p. (1990) 60,633.

Bloomsbury, dist., London, **Eng.**; fashionable dist. with many squares; famous for B. gr. of authors in first quarter of 20th cent.; inc. Brit. Museum, Univ. of London.

Blue Grass, dist., Ky., **USA**; area where blue grass abundant; horse breeding.

Blue Mountains, t., N.S.W., **Australia**; tourist ctr.; new t. (1947); p. (1981) 55,877.

Blue Mtns., Jamaica; famous for coffee; dense forest; tourism; average alt. 900–1,200 m, rising to 2,294 m in Blue Mtn. peak.

Blue Nile (Bahr-el-Azraq), R., rises in tablelands of Ethiopia, joins the White Nile at Khartoum; its seasonal flooding provides the bulk of water for irrigation in Sudan and Egypt.

Blue Ridge Mtns., S. Penn., Ga., **USA**; inc. Shenandoah valley; superb scenery, resorts; average alt. 600–1,200 m, rising to 1,737 m in Grandfather Mtn.

Bluff, S.I., **N.Z.**; 29 km from Invercargill; spt. for Southland prov., major aluminium ctr.

Blumenau, mkt. t., Santa Catarina st., **Brazil**; butter, sugar; p. (1985) 192,900.

Blyth, spt., Northumberland, **Eng.**; on former coalfield; part of l. gov. dist. of **Blyth Valley**; p. (1995) 80,300 (dist.), (1991) 35,327 (t.).

Bo, t., **Sierra Leone**; gold; admin. H.Q.; p. (1988) 26,000.

Boa Vista, t., R. pt., cap. Roraima st., **Brazil**; p. (1977) 25,000.

Bobbio, t., Emilia-Romagna, **Italy**, in northern Apennines; ctr. European cultural life, 9th-12th cent.; St Columban founded monastery, 612; p. (1981) 4,215.

Bobo Dioulassa, t., **Burkina Faso**; agr. tr., gold mng.; p. (1985) 231,162.

Bobigny, N.E. sub of Paris, cap. of Seine-St. Denis dep., **France**; varied inds.; p. (1990) 44,841.

Bobruysk, t., **Belarus**; pt. on R. Berezina; engin., sawmilling, paper, grain; p. (1990) 222,900.

Bocholt, t., N. Rhine-Westphalia, **Germany**; machin., textiles, elec. gds.; p. (1986) 66,400.

Bochum, t., N. Rhine-Westphalia, **Germany**; heart of Ruhr iron and steel ind.; known since 9th cent.; Univ. of Ruhr; p. (1990) 397,400.

Bodensee (L. Constance), S.W. **Germany** and **Switzerland**; 72 km long, 14 km wide.; R. Rhine flows through; fruit and horticulture on warmer slopes of L.

Bodmin, co. t., North Cornwall, **Eng.**; on S.W. flank of Bodmin moor; china clay, lt. engin.; p. (1991) 12,553.

Bodmin Moor, upland, N.E. Cornwall, **Eng.**; lower slopes cultivated, higher slopes used for sheep pastures; average alt. 300 m, highest point, Brown Willy, alt, 419 m; major ctr. of china clay quarrying.

Bodø, t., **Norway**; nr. Lofoten Is.; spt., fish processing; N. rly, terminus; p. (1990) 30,252.

Bodrum, t., on Aegean cst., **Turkey**; anc. Halicarnassus; 15th cent. Crusader castle; fishing.

Boeotia, region of anc. **Greece**; scene of many battles; Thebes was the ch. c.; home of Hesiod and Pindar; p. (1991) 134,034.

Bogda Ula, massif, Sinkiang, **China**; forms N. perimeter of Turfan depression; 240 km wide, average alt. 4,000 m, rising to 5,479 m in Turpanat Targh.

Bognor Regis, t., Arun, West Sussex. **Eng.**; residtl.; seaside resort; p. (1991) 56,744.

Bogor, t., Java, **Indonesia**; rubber factory, textiles, footwear; p. (1983) 274,000.

Bogota, cap. and lgst. c. of **Colombia**; in E. Cordilleras, 2,745 m a.s.l.; univ., nat. observatory, colonial architecture; political, social and financial ctr. of rep.; p. (1992) 4,819,676.

Bo Hai (Pohai), G. of, N. **China**; together with G. of Liaotung forms shallow expanse of water almost cut off from Yellow Sea by Liaotung and Shandong peninsulas; receives water and silt from Huang He; a. approx. 38,900 km².

Bohemia, historic region, former kingdom, **Czech Rep.**; plateau drained by R. Elbe; borders W.

Germany; agr. dist.; minerals inc. lignite, graphite; textiles, sugar, pottery.

Böhmerwald (**Bohemian Forest**), forested range of mtns. between **Czech Rep.** and Bavaria, **Germany**; 240 km long; alt. 1,479 m at Aber; region of poor soils; sm. farms; some mng. and quarrying.

Bohol I., prov. **Philippines**; maize, coconuts, rice; a. 3,864 km²; p. (1990) 948,315.

Boise, t., cap. of Idaho, **USA**; financial ctr.; timber mills; hot springs; p. (1990) 125,738.

Boksburg, t., Transvaal, **S. Africa**; industl., former coal-mng.; t. p. (1980) 156,780.

Bolan Pass, Baluchistan, **Pakistan**; pass from Pakistan to Afghanistan; summit 1,800 m.

Bolbec, t., Seine-Maritime, **France**; 19 km E. of Le Havre; textiles; elec. engin.; p. (1982) 12,578.

Boldon, t., Tyne and Wear, **Eng.**; coal mng.; p. (1991) 12,420.

Boliden, t., N. **Sweden**; impt. deposits of copper and arsenic.

Bolivia, inland rep., S. America; land-locked, 9 deps.; cap. nominally Sucre, actual admin. H.Q. La Paz; much US investment but discouraged by nationalism from late 1960s; relief makes transport difficult; moves towards gaining access to cst. via internat. corridor; forests; savannahs; agr. in backward conditions; embryonic industl. devel. suffered from political instability; much social protest against military rule, return to democracy 1982; rubber, quinine, cattle, hides; ch. exp. gas and tin; petroleum; mafia cocaine tr.; exp. illegal narcotics; language Spanish; a. 1,331,661 km²; p. (1995) 8,070,000.

Bollington, t., Cheshire, **Eng.**; nr. Macclesfield; textile finishing; p. (1991) 6,767.

Bologna, c., N. **Italy**; cap. of B. prov. on N. flank of Apennines; impt. route ctr. commanding road and rly. across Apennines to Florence; preserved and restored in Arcadian style by Communist admin.; univ., service t.; p. (1992) 401,308.

Bolsena, L., Latium region, **Italy**; occupies lge. extinct volcanic crater in S. of Tuscan Hills 96 km N.W. of Rome; a. (approx.) 129 km²; p. (1981) 3,960.

Bolshoya Volga, t., **Russia**; 128 km N. of Moscow, at junct. of Volga and Moscow Volga Canal; Soviet Institute of Nuclear Studies.

Bolsover, t., l. gov. dist., Derbys., **Eng.**; limestone, textiles; cas.; Hardwick Hall 6 km to S.; p. (1995) 70,800, (1991) 11,743 (t.).

Bolton, t., met. dist., Gtr. Manchester, **Eng.**; cotton, textiles, engin.; p. (1995) 265,400 (dist.), (1991) 139,020 (t.).

Bolton Abbey, North Yorks. **Eng.**; ruined Augustinian Priory.

Bolzano, t., Trentino-Alto Adige **Italy**; on R. Isarco at S. approach to Brenner Pass; resort; p. (1984) 103,009.

Boma, t., **Congo**; pt. on estuary of R. Congo; exp. timber, cocoa, palm prods., bananas; p. (1991) 246,207.

Bombay, spt., cap. of Maharashtra st., **India**; harbour, docks, rly. ctr.; univ.; greatest cotton ctr. in republic; pt. handles nearly half of India's foreign tr.; oil refinery; film industry; univ., fine public bldgs.; new name Mumbai (1995); p. (1991) 12,596,000.

Bonaire I., **Neth. Antilles**; a. 287 km²; p. (1993) 11,378.

Bône. See Annaba.

Bo'ness, burgh, Falkirk, **Scot.**; spt. on Firth of Forth, 6 km E. of Grangemouth; foundries, timber yards; p. (1991) 14,595.

Bonifacio, spt., Corse du Sud, Corsica, **France**; opposite Sardinia, on Strait of Bonifacio; p. (1982) 2,736.

Bonin Is., Pac. Oc., **Japan**; 15 Is., volcanic; 960 km S. of Tokyo; a. 103 km².

Bonn, c., **Germany**; at confluence of Rs. Sieg and Rhine; univ.; former seat of W. German parliament; birthplace of Beethoven; founded in Roman times; varied inds. inc. printing, publishing; p. (1990) 294,300.

Bonnet a l'Eveque, mtn., **Haiti**; sheer sides, flat top; site of La Ferrière fortress, alt. 900 m.

Bonneville Dam, Ore., Wash., **USA**; across R. Columbia 64 km above Portland (Ore.), provides irrigation to valleys on Columbia-Snake Plateau; locks permit navigation and provide hydroelectric power.

Bonneville Salt Flats, Utah, **USA**; remains of anc. lake; world automobile speed test, 1937–47.

Bonny, t., S. **Nigeria**; at mouth of R. Bonny.

Niger delta; oil terminal.

Bonny, Bight of (Bight of Biafra until 1975), W. Africa; bay lying E. of the G. of Guinea between the Niger and C. Lopez.

Bonnyrigg and **Lasswade**, burgh, Midlothian, **Scot.**, 11 km S.E. of Edinburgh, p. (1991) 13,696.

Boothia, peninsula on Arctic cst., Franklin dist. **Canada**; separated from Baffin I., by G. of B.

Bootle, t., Sefton, Merseyside, **Eng.**; on E. side of entrance to Mersey estuary; dockside inds. inc. tanning, ship-repairing; tin plant; p. (1991) 65,454.

Bophuthatswana, indep. Bantu Terr. (1977) not recognised by UN, re-incorporated in S. Africa 1994; some mineral wealth (asbestos, platinum) but land produces only 10 per cent of agricultural requirements; home of Sun City, tourist centre; cap. Mmabatho; a. 40,330 km²; p. (1985) 1,660,000.

Bor, t., Serbia, **Yugoslavia**; copper mng. and processing; p. (1981) 56,486.

Borås, t., S. **Sweden**; on R. Viske, nr. Göteborg; ctr. of textile and clothing inds.; p. (1992) 102,840.

Bordeaux, spt., cap. of Gironde, **France**; nr. mouth of R. Garonne; cath., univ.; exp. wines, liqueurs, sugar, potatoes, pit props; oil refining nearby; p. (1990) 213,274.

Borders, unit. auth., created in 1996 from former Region, **Scot.**; occupies E. half of Southern Uplands; hilly cty. drained by R. Tweed and tribs.; rural a. interspersed by mkt. and mill ts.; p. (1995) 106,200.

Bordighera, t., **Italy**; Riviera winter resort.

Borehamwood, t., Herts., **Eng.**; lt. engin., computers, film studios; p. (1991) 29,873.

Borinage, dist. around Mons, **Belgium**; impt. but declining coalfield.

Borislav, t., **Ukraine**; formerly Polish (1919–39); oilfield, natural gas; richest ozocerite deposits in Europe; oil pipeline links to Drogobych and Dashava; p. (1990) 40,700.

Borisov, t., **Belarus**; defeat of Napoleon, 1812; chemicals, sawmills, hardware; p. (1990) 146,800.

Borkum, I. and t., **Germany**; off Ems R. estuary; a. 36 km²; p. (1989) 5,646 (t.).

Borlänge, t., **Sweden**; iron, paper, engin. and chemical wks.; p. (1992) 47,300.

Borneo, lgst. I. in Malay archipelago and 3rd lgst. in world; high mtn. range extends from ctr. to N. rising to 4,180 m; low-lying swamp in S.; politically divided into Kalimantan (Indonesian B.), Sabah and Sarawak (E. Malaysia) and Brunei; jungle-covered and underdeveloped; scattered tribes inc. Dyaks; few nodes of development around oilfields (Sarawak and Brunei); much recent clearance of virgin rain forest; new settlement in Barito valley (Kalimantan); a. 738,150 km²; p. (1983) 7,350,000.

Bornholm, I. in Baltic Sea, **Denmark**; mostly granite with poor soils; cattle rearing; kaolin; tourism and fishing impt.; cap. Rønne; a. 543 km²; p. (1990) 45,784.

Borno, state, **Nigeria**; S.W. of L. Chad; former Moslem st.; a. 132,090 km²; p. (1991) 2,596,589.

Borobudur, Java, **Indonesia**; gr. Buddhist temple; ruins now restored.

Borrowdale, valley, Cumbria, **Eng.**; tourist resort; former graphite mines.

Boscastle, spt., Cornwall, **Eng.**; resort; pilchard fishing; sm. harbour built for slate exp.

Bosnia-Herzegovina, rep., formerly part of Yugoslavia; mtnous., forested, watered by R. Sava and tribs.; one-fourth cultivated; tobacco, cereals, fruit; cattle, sheep, pigs; mineral deposits; civil war in early 1990s; cap. Sarajevo; a. 51,199 km²; p. (1991) 4,366,000.

Bosporus or **Strait of Constantinople** (**Karadeniz Boğazi**), between Black Sea and Sea of Marmara; suspension bridge, first to link Europe and S.W. Asia, opened 1973; badly polluted by sewage from Istanbul and oil spillage from shipping.

Bossier City, t., La., **USA**; oil refineries, rly. wks., chemical and processing plants; p. (1980) 50,817.

Boston, t., l. gov. dist., Lincs., **Eng.**; sm. pt. on Witham R., agr. mkt., fruit and vegetable canning; p. (1995) 54,100 (dist.), (1991) 34,606 (t.).

Boston, c., st. cap. Mass., **USA**; fine harbour and leading pt. at head of Boston Bay; cultural, comm. and financial ctr., impt. mkt. for fish and wool; 3 univs.; leading c. in 19th cent.; varied inds. inc. leather, rubber, textiles, shoes and elec. gds.; p. (1990) 574,283 (c.), 2,871,000 (met. a.).

Bosworth or **Market Bosworth**, t., Leics., **Eng.**; battle between Richard III and Henry VII, 1485; *see* **Hinckley.**

Botany Bay, N.S.W., **Australia**; inlet of Tasman Sea on E. cst., site of landing of James Cook, 1770; 8 km S. of Sydney; resort; first settled by Brit. in 1787; old penal colony; deep-water pt. (1961) for oil tankers supplementary to Pt. Jackson.

Botasani, t., N. Moldavia, **Romania**; in rich pastoral a.; p. (1992) 126,204.

Bothnia, G. of, N. of Baltic; between Finland and Sweden; shallow sea, many Is.

Botswana, Rep. of, indep. sov. st. within Brit. Commonwealth (1966), Southern Africa; stretches from Orange R. to Zambesi R., and merges in W. with Kalahari desert; land locked; depends on rly. link to Zimbabwe and S. Africa; coal produced since 1980 to reduce dependence on S. Africa; minerals located but few mined; diamonds since 1971 (50 percent of exp.); copper, nickel; limited livestock agr.; potential arable land of Okavango chobe swamp; few inds. cap. Gaborone; a. 582,000 km²; p. (1994) 1,400,000.

Bottrop, t., N. Rhine-Westphalia, **Germany**; once a sm. t., now ctr. of Ruhr coal basin; p. (1990) 118,700.

Bouches-du-Rhône, dep., S. **France**; covers Rhône delta and inc. the Camargue and Crau; lagoon cst.; mainly agr. but inc. industl. complex ass. with cap. of Marseilles; a. 5,270 km²; p. (1990) 1,759,400.

Bougainville, I. seceded from **Papua New Guinea** to form Rep. of N. Solomons; secessionist conflict continues; major reserve of copper in Panguna valley; new mng. ts. of Anewa Bay and Panguna; forested; a. 10,619 km².

Bougie. *See* **Bejaia.**

Boulder, t., Col., **USA**; gold- and silver-mng. dist.; univ.; resort; p. (1990) 83,312 (t.), 225,339 (met. a. with Longmont).

Boulder City, t., Nevada, **USA**; nr. Hoover Dam. gr. engin. project; model t., ctr. for Nat. Park services; p. (1980) 9,590.

Boulogne-Billancourt, S.W. sub. of Paris, **France**; car, aircraft inds.; p. (1990) 101,971.

Boulogne-sur-Mer, t., Pas-de-Calais dep., **France**; on English Channel; comm. and fish. pt.; Channel port; pt. inds.; p. (1990) 44,244 (t.), 95,930 (met. a.).

Bounty I., N.Z., S. Pac. Oc.; uninhabited guano covered I.

Bourg-en-Bresse, t., cap. of Ain dep., **France**; route ctr., varied inds.; p. (1990) 42,955

Bourges, t., cap. of Cher dep., **France**; cath., univ., industl. and transit ctr.; p. (1990) 78,773 (t.), 92,720 (met. a.).

Bourget, L., Savoie, **France**; tourist a.

Bourgogne, region, E. **France**; inc. deps Côte-d'Or, Nièvre, Saône-et-Loire, Yonne; upland region draining to the north-west into the Paris basin and to the south-east via the Saône into the Rhône; ch. t. Dijon; p. (1990) 1,609,700.

Bourkina Fasso. *See* Burkina Faso

Bourne, t., South Kesteven, Lincs., **Eng.**; home of Hereward the Wake; also of Raymond Mays, racing driver; agr. machin, printing; p. (1991) 8,777.

Bournemouth, t., unit. auth. created in 1997, formerly part of Dorset, **Eng.**; on S. cst., E. of Poole Harbour; seaside resort; conference ctr.; p. (1995) 160,900 (former dist.), (1991) 155,488 (t.).

Bournville, garden sub. founded by George Cadbury (1897), 6 km S.W. of Birmingham **Eng.**; chocolate and cocoa wks.

Bourton-on-the-Water, v., Gloucs. **Eng.**; tourist ctr.; p. (1991) 2,239.

Bouvet I., uninhabited island in S. Atlantic belonging to **Norway**; a. about 56 km².

Bovey Tracey, v., Devon, **Eng.**; ball clay excavating; p. (1991) 3,492.

Bow or **Stratford-de-Bow**, Tower Hamlets, E. London, **Eng.**; 5 km from St. Paul's.

Bow, R., Alberta, N.W. **Canada**; head of Saskatchewan R., flows through Banff Nat. Park; irrigation; 504 km long.

Bowdon, t., Gtr. Manchester, **Eng.**; p. (1991) 5,141.

Bow Fell, mtn., Cumbria, **Eng.**; at head of Borrowdale, 6 km N.W. of West Water alt. 903 m.

Bowland, Forest of, W. offshoot of Pennines, Lancs., **Eng.**; between Rs. Lune and Ribble; designated a. of outstanding natural beauty; reservoirs.

Bowling Green, t., Ky., **USA**; tr. ctr. for agr. a. producing tobacco, livestock, limestone and dairy prods.; univ.; p. (1990) 40,641.

Bowness, v., Cumbria, **Eng.**; W. end of Hadrian's Wall.

Bowness, t., Cumbria, **Eng.**; on L. Windermere; tourist ctr.

Box Hill, nr. Dorking, Surrey, **Eng.**; E. of R. Mole gap through N. Downs; chalk; wooded, fine views; alt. 233 m.

Boyle, mkt. t., Roscommon, **R.o.I.**; on R. Boyle; dairying; p. (1986) 1,859.

Boyne, R., **R.o.I.**; flows to Irish Sea; Battle of the Boyne (1690) fought at Oldbridge, 5 km W. of Drogheda; salmon fishing; 128 km long.

Boyoma Falls (Stanley Falls), on Upper Congo R., **Congo**; nr. equator; originally named after the explorer.

Bozrah, t., of anc. Edom, 'probably modern Buseira **(Jordan)**, S.E. of Dead Sea.

Brabant, prov., **Belgium**; S. section of former Duchy; fertile and wooded; many breweries; mnfs, linen, cloth, paper, lace; cap. Brussels; a. 3,281 km²; p. (1993) 2,262,896.

Brabant, North. *See* **Noord Brabant.**

Brač, I., Adriatic Sea, off coast of **Croatia**; lgst. of Dalmatian Is.; tourism, fishing; a. 393 km².

Brackley, t., South Northants., **Eng.**; flour milling, brewing; former prosperous wool tr.; p. (1991) 9,113.

Bracknell, t., part of l. gov. dist. of **Bracknell Forest**, Berks., **Eng.**; on Thames Valley terrace, 16 km S. of Windsor; new t. designated 1949 to meet overspill needs from London; Meteorological Office H.Q.; engin., sealing compounds, plastics; p. (1995) 107,700 (dist.), (1991) 60,894 (t.).

Bradford, c., met. dist., West Yorks., **Eng.**; 14 km W. of Leeds; comm. ctr. of wool-textile inds.; impt. for worsted; engin. and chem. inds.; univ.; birthplace of Delius and J. B. Priestley; p. (1995) 482,700, (1991) 289,376 (c.).

Bradford-on-Avon, t., West Wilts., **Eng.**; on E. flank of Cotswolds from which bldg. stone derived; former ctr. of wool ind.; p. (1991) 8,815.

Bradwell, v., Essex, **Eng.**; at mouth of R. Blackwater; Magnox nuclear power sta.

Braemar, dist. in Grampians, Aberdeenshire, **Scot.**; containing Balmoral estate.

Braeriach, mtn., Aberdeenshire, **Scot.**; alt. 1,296 m.

Braga, t., cap. of B. dist., N.W. **Portugal**; agr. tr. ctr.; religious ctr.; cath.; p. (1987) 63,033.

Bragança, t., cap. of B. dist., N.E. **Portugal**; agr. tr.; p. (1981) 13,900.

Brahmaputra, one of longer Rs. in **Asia**; flows for much of its length through Himalayas and Assam; called **Tsangpo** in Tibet; fertile agr. valley subject to flooding and silting; 2,880 km long.

Brăila, t., **Romania**; R. pt. on Danube, nr. Galati; grain tr., boatbldg., reed processing; p. (1992) 234,706.

Braintree, t., Mass., **USA**; elec. machin., rubber gds., glassware; p. (1980) 36,337.

Braintree, t., l. gov. dist., Essex, **Eng.**; on Blackwater; rayon mftg., metal windows, engin.; p. (1995) 125,100 (dist.), (1991) 32, 229 (t.).

Brakpan, t., Transvaal, **S. Africa**; gold mng.; p. (1980) 79,800 (dist.).

Brampton, t., Ontario, **Canada**; noted for its greenhouses; p. (1991) 234,445.

Brandenburg, *Land*, cap. Potsdam; **Germany**, pop. (1992) 2,543,000.

Brandenburg, t., **Germany**; on R. Havel; cath.; tractors, textiles, machin.; p. (1981) 94,680.

Brandon, t., Manitoba, **Canada**; on Assiniboine R., W. of Winnipeg; comm. ctr. wheat a.; agr. equipment oil refining; p. (1991) 38,567.

Brandon, t., Suffolk, **Eng.**; ctr. of Breckland; expanded t.; p. (1991) 7,804.

Brandon and Byshottles, ts., former U.D., Durham, **Eng.**; former coal-mng. a.; p. (1991) 9,162.

Brandywine Creek, R., Penns., **USA**; Americans defeated by British 1777; length 32 km.

Brantford, t., Ontario, **Canada**; on Grand R., S.W. of Hamilton; leading mnf. t.; farm implements, cycles, bus and truck parts; p. (1991) 81,997.

Brasilia, cap. of **Brazil**, Goiás st., 960 km N.W. of Rio de Janeiro; ch. of many cities designed to open up interior of rep.; modern architecture; inaugurated 1960; p. (1991) 1,596,274.

Brasov, t., **Romania**; at foot of Transylvanian Alps; aircraft, engin., lge. German and Hungarian p.; p. (1992) 323,835.

Bratislava, c., cap. of **Slovakia**; pt. on Danube 48 km below Vienna; univ.; industl. and comm. ctr.; textiles, chemicals; engin., oil refining; linked to Mozyr', **Belorussia**, by oil pipeline; p. (1990) 440,000.

Bratsk, c., central Irkutsk oblast, **Russia**; on

Angara R., ship-repair yards, lumber, iron-ore, wood processing, chemicals; lge. hydroelectric sta.; p. (1989) 256,000.

Braunschweig. *See* Brunswick.

Bray, t., Wicklow, **R.o.I.**; on Irish Sea cst.; popular resort; p. (1986) 24,686.

Brazil, Federative Republic of, S. America; a. 8,512,035 km²; 5th lgst. cty. in world, exceeded in size only by Russia, China, Canada and USA; covers variety of land and climate; in S., gr. Brazilian plateau, in N., Amazon R. basin (thickly forested); leading industl. nation of **Latin America**; agr.; coffee, cotton, sugar, cocoa, rubber, fruits, hardwoods; rapid exploitation of rainforests worries conservationists; cattle-raising; vast mineral reserves inc. manganese, iron, gold, diamonds; admin. through 22 sts., 4 terrs., and Fed. Dist.; cap. Brasilia; lgst. industl. ctr. São Paulo and Belo Horizonte; many multinational companies, inc. car mftg., chems., construction materials; p. mainly White, Negro, Indian, Mestizo; Portuguese official language; p. concentrated in coastal belt, leaving vast a. of interior relatively underdeveloped; oil shortages led to use of sugar alcohol for cars; incr. finds of oil offshore will lead to oil self-sufficiency by 1999; p. (1994) 159,100,000.

Brazos, R., Texas, **USA**; flows through agr. and industl. Young Co. via Waco to industl. Brazosport; length 1,520 km.

Brazzaville, c., cap. of **Congo Rep.**; connected by rly. with the Atlantic at Pointe-Noire; R. pt. under construction; airport; p. (1992) 937,579.

Brechin, royal burgh, Angus, **Scot.**; on S. Esk; cath.; linen, paper, whisky; p. (1991) 7,655.

Breckland, dist., S.W. Norfolk, N.W. Suffolk, **Eng.**; chalk overlain by glacial sands; heathland and coniferous plantations; l. gov. dist., inc. Thetford, Swaffham and East Dereham; p. (1995) 112,000.

Brecknockshire, historic co., S. **Wales**, now part of Powys.

Brecon (Brecknock), t., Powys, **Wales**; on R. Usk; agr. ctr.; p. (1991) 7,523.

Brecon Beacons, mtns., S. **Wales**; 8 km S. of Brecon; highest peak 888 m; sandstone moorland; Nat. Park.

Breda, c., N. Brabant prov., **Neth.**; mnf. ctr.; machin., foundries, canneries, refineries; historic t., 13th cent. cath.; p. (1994) 129,125 (c.), 165,729 (met. a.).

Bredbury and **Romiley,** ts., Gtr. Manchester, **Eng.**; paper, engin., dyeing, textiles; p. (1991) 28,205.

Bregenz, t., cap. of Vorarlberg, **Austria**; on Bodensee; hydroelec. power; textiles; resort nr. Bregenz Forest; p. (1991) 27,236.

Breidha Fjord, lge. inlet, W. cst. Iceland.

Bremen, *Land*, **Germany**; a. 404 km²; cap. Bremen; p. (1992) 684,000.

Bremen, c., cap. of *Land* B., **Germany**; old t. on right bank of Weser R., 64 km from N. Sea; new t., founded 17th cent., on left bank; leading pt., industl. and comm. ctr.; former member of Hanseatic League; p. (1990) 522,300.

Bremerhaven, c., Bremen, **Germany**; outport of Bremen at mouth of R. Weser; docks; impt. passenger and fish. pt.; shipbldg.; united with Wesermünde 1941; p. (1990) 130,800.

Bremerton, t., Wash., **USA**; on Puget Sound; naval dockyard; elec. equipment, machin.; p. (1984) 35,200 (t.), 164,800 (met. a.).

Brendon Hills, Somerset, **Eng.**; extension of Exmoor, rising to over 400 m.

Brenner Pass, lowest Alpine pass from Bolzano **(Italy)** to Innsbruck **(Austria)**; used by road and rail; frequent meeting place of Mussolini and Hitler (1940-2).

Brent, outer bor., Greater London, **Eng.**; inc. Wembley and Willesden; p. (1995) 245,300.

Brenta, R., N. **Italy**; rises in picturesque Alpine valley; forestry, silk, tourism; flows to Adriatic Sea; navigable in lower course; length 180 km.

Brentford and Chiswick. *See* Hounslow.

Brentwood, t., l. gov. dist., Essex, **Eng.**; residentl.; new R.C. cath. (1991); p. (1995) 71,700 (dist.), (1991) 49,463 (t.).

Brescia, c., cap. B. prov., Lombardy, N. **Italy**; industl. ctr.; iron, steel, engin., textiles; many historic bldgs.; p. (1992) 192,883.

Breslau. *See* Wroclaw.

Bressay I., Shetland Is., **Scot**; p. (1991) 352.

Brest, naval pt., Finistère dep., N.W. **France**; base of French Atlantic fleet; used by Germans as fortfd. submarine base 1940-4; exp. agr. prods.; impt. industl. ctr.; p. (1990) 153,099 (c.), 201,480 (met. a.).

Brest (Brest-Litovsk), c., **Belarus**; nr. Polish border; route ctr. and agr. mkt.; timber, foodprocessing, textiles. Captured by Germans in 1915. Treaty of Brest-Litovsk signed with Soviet Russia 1918; p. (1990) 268,800.

Bretagne. *See* Brittany.

Bretton Woods, resort, N.H., **USA**; site of US monetary and financial conference, 1944, leading to establishment of the International Monetary Fund and the World Bank.

Brezhnev. *See* Naberezhnyye Chelny.

Briançon, t., Hautes-Alpes, **France**; in upper Durance R. valley; winter sports; p. (1982) 11,851.

Bridgend, t., unit. auth. created in 1996 from former l. gov. dist. of Ogwr, S. **Wales**; industl. trading estate; iron, stone, paper; former coal mng. a.; p. (1991) 35,841 (t.), (1995) 130,700 (unit. auth.).

Bridge of Allen, burgh, Stirling, **Scot.**; 3 km N. of Stirling; p. (1991) 4,864.

Bridgeport, c., Conn., **USA**; on Long Island Sound; impt. industl. c., firearms, hardware, elec. equipment, metal products, plastics; p. (1990) 141,686.

Bridgetown, t., spt., cap. **Barbados**; deepwater harbour, comm. ctr.; exp. sugar, molasses, rum; tourism; p. (1990) 6,720.

Bridgewater Canal, Worsley-Manchester-Runcorn, Gtr. Manchester and Cheshire, **Eng.**; crosses ship canal by means of Barton swing bridge; 61 km long.

Bridgnorth, t., l. gov. dist., Shrops., **Eng.**; cas.;carpets, radio equipment; p. (1995) 50,500, (1991) 11,229 (t.).

Bridgwater, t., Sedgemoor, Somerset, **Eng.**; on R. Parrett, 16 km from Bristol Channel; engin., wire rope, fibre fabrics, cellophane; p. (1991) 34,610.

Bridlington, t., E. Riding of Yorks., **Eng.**; on Bridlington Bay, S. of Flamborough Head; fishing; seaside resort; p. (1991) 31,334.

Bridport, West Dorset, **Eng.**; mkt. t.; seaside resort; p. (1991) 11,667.

Brie, region, Marne and Seine-et-Marne deps., **France**; low, level plateau of limestones and clays, S.E. of Paris; loam (limon) cover and plentiful water supply encourage agr.; grains, sugar-beet, fruit, dairy cattle; famous cheese; densely populated.

Brienz, t., **Switzerland**; resort on L. Brienz; wood carving.

Brierley Hill, t., West Midlands, **Eng.**; on W. edge of Black Cty.; cut glass, castable metal gds., firebricks, roofing and tiling, iron and steel.

Brigg, mkt. t., N. Lincs., **Eng.**; ctr. of agr. dist. between Lincoln Heights and Wolds; sugar-beet, jam, seed crushing, canning; p. (1991) 5,768.

Brighouse, t., Calderdale, West Yorks., **Eng.**; on R. Calder, 5 km S.E. of Halifax; textiles and engin.; p. (1991) 32,198.

Brightlingsea, t., Tendring, Essex, **Eng.**; on R. Colne; oysters, boatbldg., yachting; p. (1991) 7,441.

Brighton, t., unit. auth. created in 1997, formerly part of East Sussex, **Eng.**; 80 km S. of London on S. cst.; seaside resort and residtl. t.; Royal Pavilion (1817), univ.; lt. inds.; p. (1995) 156,200 (former dist.), (1991) 124,851 (t.).

Brindisi, c., Apulia, S. **Italy**; spt. on Adriatic cst., sea and air connections to Middle E.; cath.; cas.; wine, olive oil, silk, petrochemicals; oil refining; p. (1981) 89,786.

Brisbane, t., cap. of Queensland, **Australia**; third c. of A., set on winding B. river, 20 km from attractive sandy cst.; caths., univ.; consumer goods, processing of primary prods.; severe flooding 1974; rapid growth in past 30 years; p. (1993) 1,421,600 (met. a.).

Brisbane Water, t., N.S.W., **Australia**; N. of Broken Bay; rapid growth with electrification of commuting rly. to Sydney; p. (1981) 71,984.

Bristol, c., unit. auth. created in 1996, formerly part of Avon, **Eng.**; pt. on R. Avon 14 km from Bristol Channel; outport at Avonmouth; cath., univ.; docks; aircraft engin., tobacco, paint, printing and lt. inds.; p. (1995) 400,700 (unit. auth.), (1991) 407,992 (c.).

Bristol, t., Conn., **USA**; foundries, ball bearings, clocks, bells; p. (1990) 79,000 (met. a.).

Bristol Channel, arm of Atl. Oc. between S. cst. of Wales and Somerset and Devon, **Eng.**; noted tidal bores.

British Antarctic Territory, Brit. col., created 1962; consists of all land and Is. S. of lat. 60° S. and between 20° and 80° W. longitude;

comprising Graham Land peninsula, S. Shetlands, S. Orkneys and smaller Is., excluding S. Georgia and S. Sandwich Is.; a. 1,222,500 km².

British Columbia, W. prov. separated from rest of **Canada** by Rockies, borders Pac. Oc.; little lowland; parallel N.W.–S.E. ranges of Rockies crossed by Rs. Fraser, Columbia, Kootenay and Peace; vast coniferous forest and hydroelec. resources; salmon fishing on cst.; mng.; p. concentrated in S.W. around Vancouver; a. 948,600 km²; p. (1991) 3,282,061.

British Honduras. *See* Belize.

British Indian Ocean Terr., Brit. col., created 1965; consists of the Chagos Archipelago (of which Diego Garcia is lgst. I.) 1,920 km N.E. of Mauritius, and formerly Is. of Aldabra, Farquhar, and Desroches in the W. Indian Oc. now part of Seychelles Rep.; no permanent p.

British Is., archipelago, N.W. Europe; comprising 2 lge. Is. of Great Britain and Ireland and 5,000 sm. Is.; a. 315,029 km².

British Solomon Is. *See* Solomon Is.

British West Africa, formerly comprised Gambia, Sierra Leone, Gold Coast (Ghana), Nigeria, and parts of Togoland and Cameroons. *See* under their separate headings.

Briton Ferry, t., Neath, Pt. Talbot, S. **Wales**; pt. at mouth of R. Neath; former ctr. for steel wks., engin., ship-breaking.

Brittany (Bretagne), region, N.W. **France**; inc. deps. Côtes-du-Nord, Finistère, Ille-et-Vilaine, Morbihan; penin. between Eng. Channel and Bay of Biscay; contrast between productive cst. lands (fishing, early vegetables, tourism) and barren moorland interior; economically depressed; p. (1990) 2,795,600.

Brive-la-Gaillarde, t., Corrèze dep., **France**; regional mkt. in fertile basin on edge of Central Massif; p. (1990) 52,677.

Brixham, S. Devon, **Eng.**; incorporated in Torbay; fishing; resort; p. (1991) 15,865.

Brno (Brünn), c., **Czech Rep.**; cap. of Moravia; finely situated at confluence of Svratka and Svitava Rs., 109 km N. of Vienna; industl. and communications ctr. with mnfs. of machin., precision tools, textiles; annual tr. fair; p. (1990) 391,000.

Broadstairs, Thanet, Kent, **Eng.**; seaside resort; 5 km N.E. of Ramsgate; p. (1991) 22,118.

Broads, The, Norfolk, **Eng.**; series of Ls. formed by mediaeval turf cutting in lower alluvial reaches of Rs. Bure, Waveney, and Yare; yachting, fishing, tourism; lge. part forms **Broadland,** l. gov. dist., p. (1995) 112,500.

Brockton, c., Mass., **USA**; S. of Boston; lge. shoe and leather ind., machin.; annual tr. fair; p. (1990) 189,000 (met. a.).

Brockville, t., Ontario, **Canada**; R. pt. on St. Lawrence R. below Thousand Is.; telephone equipment, wire cables, elec. tools; p. (1986) 20,880.

Broken Hill, t., N.S.W., **Australia**; major mng. (silver, lead, zinc) ctr. in arid W. of st.; p. (1981) 26,913.

Bromberg. *See* Bydgoszcz.

Bromley, outer bor. of London, **Eng.**; inc. Beckenham, Orpington, Penge, and Chislehurst; p. (1995) 293,400.

Bromsgrove, t. and l. gov. dist., Worcs., **Eng.**; mkt. t., 21 km S.W. Birmingham; wrought ironwk., lt. engin.; p. (1995) 85,100 (dist.), (1991) 26,365 (t.).

Bromyard, Worcs., **Eng.**; sm. mkt. t.; p. (1991) 3,117.

Bronx, The, one of the five bors. of New York City, **USA**; connected by bridges to bor. of Manhattan; residtl. with parks, zoological and botanical gardens, colleges and professional schools; p. (1990) 1,203,789.

Brooklyn, bor., N.Y. City, **USA**; linked with Manhattan bor. by Brooklyn, Manhattan, and Williamsburgh suspension bridges across East R.; and with Staten I. by Verrazano-Narrows bridge (longest in world); mainly residtl. with numerous mftg. and comm. interests; p. (1990) 2,291,604.

Brooks Range, mtns., N. Alaska, **USA**; forms N. section of Rocky Mtns.; Inuit p.; Arctic climate, flora and fauna; alt. 2,000 m rising to 2,818 m (Mt. Michelson).

Broom, Loch, N.W. cst. of Scot.

Brora, t., Highland, **Scot.**; on E. cst., 19 km N.E. of Dornoch Firth; Harris Tweed ind.; tourism; p. (1991) 1,687.

Brownhills, t., West Midlands, **Eng.**; former mng. t.; expanded t.; p. (1991) 18,159.

Brownsville, t., Texas, **USA**; pt. on Rio Grande nr. Mexican border; livestock, sugar-cane, fruit processing, chemicals; p. (1984) 94,700 (t.), (1990) 260,000 (met. a. with Harlingen).

Broxbourne, t., l. gov. dist., Herts., **Eng.**; on gravel terrace to W. of R. Lea; ctr. of very intensively cultivated dist.; lt. inds.; p. (1995) 82,200 (dist.).

Broxtowe, l. gov. dist., Notts., **Eng.**; made up of Beeston and Stapleford and Eastwood; p. (1995) 112,100.

Bruay-en-Artois, t., Pas-de-Calais, **France**; coal mng.; p. (1982) 23,200.

Bruchsal, t., Baden-Württemberg, **Germany**; tobacco, paper, machin.; p. (1986) 36,500.

Bruges. *See* Brugge.

Brugge (Bruges), c., cap. of W. Flanders prov., N. **Belgium**; mediaeval t. connected by canal to its outer pt. Zeebrugge; univ.; impt. mkt. for grain, cattle, horses; engin., ship-repairing, elec. gds., glass mkg., textiles, lace; p. (1993) 116,871.

Brühl, t., N. Rhine–Westphalia, **Germany**; 13 km S. of Cologne; cas.; lignite; p. (1986) 40,700.

Brunei, indep. st. (1984), N. Borneo; enclave of Sarawak; Brit. protectorate after 1888; thriving economy based on Seria and offshore oil and gas fields; oil and gas provide 95 per cent of exp.; need to diversify as reserves dwindle and prices fall; 80 percent of food is imported; agr. therefore being encouraged since only 15 per cent of land is cultivated; cap. Bandar Seri Begawan; a. 5,765 km²; p. (1993) 267,300.

Brünn. *See* Brno.

Brunswick (Braunschweig), c., Lower Saxony, **Germany**; on R. Oker; formerly cap. of st. of Brunswick, now a comm. and industl. ctr.; mnfs. inc. canning, tinplate, optics, pianos, lorries; p. (1990) 258,500.

Brussels (Bruxelles), cap. of **Belgium** and of prov. of Brabant; impt. comm., industl. and cultural ctr.; varied mnfs., inc. pharmaceuticals, electronic equipment, machine tools; lge. oil refinery at Feluy; noted for carpets and lace; occupied by the Germans 1914–18, 1940–4; univ.; mediaeval and Renaissance monuments; H.Q. of EU; p. (1993) 950,399.

Bryan, t., Texas, **USA**; mkt. ctr., agr. college; p. (1984) 59,000 (t.), 117,400 (met. a.).

Bryansk, c., cap. of B. oblast, **Russia**, on Desna R.; rly. junc.; a fortress until 19th cent.; sawmilling, engin., textiles, chemicals, steel; oil pipeline from Kuybyshev; p. inc. Bezhitsa (1989) 452,000.

Brynmawr, t., Blaenau Gwent, **Wales**; former coal mng. a.; industl. estate; p. (1991) 14,581.

Brzeg (Brieg), t. Opole, **Poland**; on R. Oder; German until 1945; textiles, leather, chemicals; p. (1989) 38,554.

Bucaramanga, c., N. central **Colombia**, 900 m a.s.l. in E. highlands of Andes; ctr. of coffee-growing dist.; cigar and cigarette mkg.; p. (1992) 349,403.

Buchan Ness, C., nr. Peterhead, E. Scot.

Bucharest (Bucresti), cap. and lgst. c. of **Romania**; "Little Paris," on the Dambovita, trib. of Danube; cath., univ.; textiles, chemicals, pharmaceuticals, oil refining, engin.; 20 per cent industl. output of rep.; badly damaged by earthquake (1977); p. (1992) 2,350,984.

Buckfastleigh, t., S. Devon, **Eng.**; wool, quarrying; nearby Benedictine abbey on site of mediaeval Cistercian abbey; p. (1991) 2,786.

Buckhaven and Methil, burgh, Fife, **Scot.**; on N. Side of Firth of Forth, 13 km N.E. of Kirkcaldy; coal; p. (1991) 17,069.

Buckie, burgh, Moray, **Scot.**; boat- and yacht-bldg.; fisheries; p. (1991) 8,425.

Buckingham, Aylesbury Vale, Bucks., **Eng.**; mkt. t. on R. Ouse, 24 km N.W. of Aylesbury; p. (1991) 10,168.

Buckinghamshire, non-met. co., **Eng.**; crossed by Chilterns and Vale of Aylesbury; rural and wooded, dairy farming; co. t. Aylesbury; mnfs. chiefly in High Wycombe; lace mkg. and furniture; p. (1995) 665,900.

Buckley, t., Flintshire, **Wales**; sm. castings; p. (1991) 17,753.

Budapest, cap. and lgst. c. of **Hungary**; stands on both banks of Danube (Buda on right, Pest on left); attractive townscape; univ.; varied mnfs., inc. steel, textiles, chemicals, engin., motorbuses, oil refining; employs 40 per cent industl. workers of Hungary; p. (1997) 1,885,000.

Budaun, t., Uttar Pradesh, **India**; agr. processing; ruins; p. (1991) 116,695.

Bude. *See* Stratton and Bude.

Budel, t., N. Brabant, S. **Neth.**; 19 km S. of Eindhoven; major zinc smelter project; p. (1991) 11,926.

Budge-Budge, t., W. Bengal, **India**; on lower Hooghly R.; hemp, rice; p. (1981) 66,424.

Budleigh Salterton, East Devon, **Eng.**; resort; birthplace of Raleigh; p. (1991) 3,759.

Buena Park, t., Cal., **USA**; agr. processing mkt.; oilfields; p. (1980) 64,165.

Buenaventura, spt., **Colombia**; lumber yards, tanning, fish canning; p. (1983) 156,000.

Buenos Aires, c., cap. of **Argentina**; B.A. now contains one third of A.'s p.; ch. spt. at head of Rio de la Plata, on E. edge of Pampa; connected to Uruguay, Paraguay, and Brazil by gr. R. system; industl. and tr. ctr. for outlying regions; p. (1991) 2,965,403.

Buenos Aires, prov., **Argentina**; cap. La Plata, agric.; p. (1991) 12, 594,974.

Buffalo, c., N.Y., **USA**; pt. on L. Erie; focus of communications on Gr. Ls. has encouraged many heavy inds.; diversified lt. inds.; univ.; p. (1990) 328,123 (c.), 969,000 (met. a.).

Bug, R., **Ukraine**; known as S. or Ukrainian B.; flows from Volyno–Podolsh upland to Black Sea; navigable in lower course; 853 km long.

Bug, R., the western Bug rises in **Ukraine**, not far from the southern Bug and flows N. to join the Vistula below Warsaw; forms bdy. between **Poland** and **Ukraine**; 774 km long.

Buganda, prov., **Uganda**, E. Africa; located W. of L. Victoria largely at alt. between 1,300 and 1,800 m; intensive cultivation, cotton (ch. comm. crop), plantains, millets; cap. Kampala.

Builth Wells, t., Powys, **Wales**; on upper course of R. Wye; medicinal springs; p. (1991) 2,474.

Buitenzorg. *See* Bogor.

Bujumbura, t., cap. of **Burundi**; pt. on L. Tanganyika; varied inds.; airpt.; p. (1994) 300,000.

Bukavu, t., **Congo**; cement, quinine processing; p. (1991) 209,566.

Bukhara (Bokhara), t., **Uzbekistan**; in Amu-Dar'ya valley at W. foot of Tien Shan; agr. mkt. at W. terminus of anc. caravan route from China; modern route ctr.; local natural gas, textiles; p. (1990) 227,900.

Bukittinggi, t., Sumatra, **Indonesia**; in Padang Highlands at 1,068 m; p. 53,700.

Bukoba, t., **Tanzania**; pt. midway along W. shore of L. Victoria; exp. coffee, rice and other foodstuffs to L. pts. in Kenya and Uganda.

Bukovina, Northern; terr., formerly belonging to Romania, ceded to **USSR** in 1940; now part of **Ukraine**; a. 5,542 km²; ch. t. Chernovitsy; Carpathian Mtns., forested; farming, cereals; cattle.

Bulawayo, t., **Zimbabwe**; impt. rly. ctr.; major ctr. of commerce and heavy engin., airpt.; p. (1992) 620,936.

Bulgaria, Rep. of, S.E. Europe; in E. Balkans, bounded by Black Sea in E., and by Danube R. in N. which separates it from Romania; Rodopi range in S.W.; Maritsa R. basin forms central lowland a.; sharp climatic contrasts between winter and summer; fertile lowland areas organised into lge.-scale cooperative farms producing grain; impt. exp. tr. in agr. prods., inc. fruit, vegetables, tobacco; rapidly increasing industl. output; mineral and oil resources; popular tourist a. on Black Sea cst.; cap. Sofia; a. 110,911 km²; p. (1994) 8,459,723.

Bunbury, t., spt., W. **Australia**; 3rd. t. of st., exp. hardwoods, coal, mineral sands; growth since 1970 with establishment of alumina refinery and expansion of pt.; p. (1991) 25,657.

Buncrana, mkt. t., Donegal, **R.o.I.**; salmon fishing; seaside resort; p. (1986) 3,106.

Bundaberg, t., Queensland, **Australia**; on Burnett R.; ctr. of sugar refining; p. (1991) 49,513 (met. a.).

Bundoran, v., Donegal, **R.o.I.**; fish, pt. and resort; p. (1986) 3,106.

Bungay, Waveney, Suffolk, **Eng.**; mkt. t. on R. Waveney; printing, leather gds.; p. (1991), 3,393.

Bungosuido Channel, **Japan**; E. entrance into Inland Sea.

Bunzlau. *See* Boleslawiec.

Buraimi, oases lying between **Oman** and United **Arab Emirates**; rich in oil.

Buraydah (Buraida), t. Nejd., **Saudi Arabia**; oasis; tr. ctr.; p. (1988) 184,000.

Burbank, c., Cal., **USA**; airpt.; aeroplanes, film studios; p. (1980) 84,625.

Burdwan, t., W. Bengal, **India**; agr. processing

and tr. ctr. in Damodar valley close to Raniganj coalfield.

Bure, R., Norfolk, **Eng.**; lower course forms part of Norfolk Broads; joins Yare at Yarmouth; 93 km.

Burg, t., Saxony-Anhalt, **Germany**; on Ihle Canal; p. (1989) 27,464.

Burgas, c., **Bulgaria**; spt. and comm. ctr. on Black Sea; ch. exp. pt. for rep.; pt. for oil tankers under construction; p. (1990) 204,915.

Burgenland, prov., **Austria**; bordered on E. by Hungary; low-lying in N., agr.; hilly in S.; cap. Eisenstadt; a. 3,962 km²; p. (1991) 273,541.

Burgess Hill, t., Mid Sussex, West Sussex, **Eng.**; bricks, tiles; p. (1991) 26,077.

Burghead, burgh, Moray, **Scot.**; fish pt., resort; p. (1991) 1,495.

Burgos, c., N. **Spain**; cap. of B. prov.; anc. cap. of Castile and cap. of Franco's regime 1936–9; cath; home of the Cid; tourism, varied inds.; p. (1991) 169,279.

Burgos, prov., Old Castile, **Spain**; cap. B.; a. 14,050 km²; p. (1991) 355,138.

Burgstädt, t., Saxony, **Germany**; textiles, machin.; p. (est. 1989) 12,968.

Burgundy, former kingdom and prov., N.E. **France**; composed largely of upper valley of R. Saône; famous vineyards; strategic position on route leading between plateau of Vosges and Jura Mtns., from Rhône valley to Rhine valley.

Burhanpur, t., Madhya Pradesh, **India**; anc. walled Mogul c.; textiles, brocades; p. (1991) 172,710.

Burkina Faso, (Upper Volta), W. Africa; landlocked st. under Fr. rule until 1960; savana and low hills, hot and dry desert in N.; p. concentrated in S. and dependent on nomadism and subsistence agr.; many migrate to Ivory Coast and Ghana for work; soil erosion and desert encroachment reduce potential; poorest cty. in Africa; low life expectancies; dependent on aid; much emigration; cap. Ouagadougou; a. 274,123 km²; p. (1994) 10,000,000.

Burlington, t., S. Ontario, **Canada**; on L. Ontario, sub., N.E. of Hamilton; in fruit-growing a.; industl.; tourism; p. (1991) 129,572.

Burlington, t., Iowa, **USA**; on bluffs of Mississippi R.; machin., furniture; p. (1990) 27,208.

Burlington, t., Vt., **USA**; on L. Champlain; pt. of entry and ch. industl. and comm. t. in st.; mnfs.; p. (1990) 39,127.

Burma. *See* Myanmar, Union of

Burnham Beeches, Berks./Bucks., **Eng.**; part of anc. forest acquired 1879 for public use; a. 243 ha.

Burnham-on-Crouch, t., Essex, **Eng.**; pt., yachting, boat-bldg.; p. (1991) 7,067.

Burnham-on-Sea, t., Sedgemoor, Somerset, **Eng.**; on Bridgwater Bay; resort; p. (1991) 19,588.

Burnie, spt., Tasmania, **Australia**; pulp and paper mills; impt. mineral pt. (tin); p. (1991) 20,483.

Burnley, t., l. gov. dist., Lancs., **Eng.**; textiles, engin., car accessories; p. (1995) 89,800 (dist.), (1991) 47,661 (t.).

Burntisland, royal burgh, Fife, **Scot.**; on F. of Forth; p. (1991) 5,951.

Burray, one of the Orkney Is., **Scot.**; p. (1991) 363.

Burrinjuck, t., N.S.W., **Australia**; on Murrumbidgee R., N. of Canberra; site of impt. dam providing irrigation in Riverina (dist.)

Burry Port, t., Carmarthenshire, **Wales**; p. (1991) 8,508.

Bursa, c. and prov., N.W. **Turkey**; noted for its textiles; cap. of anc. Bithynia (3rd cent. B.C.) and later of Ottoman empire; mosques; p. (1990) 1,603,137 (prov.), 775,388 (t.).

Burslem. *See* Stoke-on-Trent.

Burton-on-Trent, t., East Staffs., **Eng.**; brewing, malting, rubber gds.; p. (1991) 60,525.

Burundi, rep., E. central Africa; high plateau on N.E. shore of L. Tanganyika; tropical climate. irregular rainfall; economy based on agr., inc. subsistence crops of manioc. sweet potatoes, and cash crops of cotton, coffee; coffee major exp.; one of poorest states in world; sm. mftg. inds. developing, but no rlys.; home of ruling Tutsi and rebel Hutu; cap. Bujumbura; a. 27,834 km²; p. (1994) 5,800,000.

Bury, t., met. dist., Gtr. Manchester, **Eng.**; on R. Irwell to S. of Rossendale Fells; cotton, textiles; birthplace of Robert Peel; p. (1995) 181,900 (dist.), (1991) 62,633 (t.).

Buryat (Buryatskaya), aut. rep. **Russia**; borders L. Baykal; mtnous., forested; lge. mineral deposits; cap. Ulan Ude; a. 350,945 km²; p. (1989)

1,038,300.

Bury St. Edmunds, St. Edmundsbury, Suffolk, **Eng.;** old mkt. t., on R. Lark, abbey ruins; farm implements, sugar-beet processing; expanded t.; p. (1991) 31,237.

Bushey, t., Hertsmere, Herts., **Eng.;** residtl.; p. (1991) 16,488.

Bushir. See Bandar-e-Būshehr.

Busto Arsizio, t., Varese prov., N. **Italy;** 30 km. N.W. of Milan; cotton milling ctr., iron, steel, rayon, textile machin.; p. (1981) 79,769.

Bute, I, Argyll and Bute, **Scot;** p. (1991) 7,375.

Buteshire, historic co., W. **Scot.,** now divided between Argyll and Bute and N. Ayrshire.

Butte, t., Mont., **USA;** mng. t. (copper, zinc. silver, manganese, gold, lead, arsenic); also a farming ctr.; p. (1980) 37,205.

Buttermere, L., Cumbria, **Eng.**

Butt of Lewis, promontory with lighthouse; Lewis, Hebrides, **Scot.**

Buxton, t., High Peak, Derbys., **Eng.;** spa; lime-quarrying; p. (1991) 19,854.

Buzau, t., **Romania;** rly. ctr.; cath.; wheat, timber, petroleum; p. (1992) 148,247.

Bydgoszez, prov., **Poland;** cap. B.; drained by Rs. Vistula, Brda, and Notec; formerly called Pomorze; salt and lime deposits aid chemical inds.; a. 20,800 km²; p. (1989) 1·1 m.

Bydgoszcz (Bromberg), c., N. central **Poland;** on R. Brda; R. pt., rly. ctr.; elec. equipment, machine tools, timber mnfs.; p. (1989) 380,425.

Byron C., most E. point of **Australia,** Pacific cst. of N.S.W.

Bytom, c., S.W. **Poland;** formerly in Prussian prov. of Upper Silesia; ctr. of Katowice mng. a.; p. (1989) 229,991.

C

Cabinda, enclave, **Angola;** separated by Zaïre R. estuary from Angola; tropical climate encourages thick forest cover; tropical crops; offshore oil production; uranium; a. 7,236 km²; p. (1992) 152,100.

Cabot Strait, entrance of G. of St. Lawrence between C. Breton I. and Newfoundland, **Canada.**

Cáceres, c., and cap. of C. prov., W. **Spain;** in Estremadura, above Tagus valley; mkt. t. lies below the old t. topping the hill; p. (1987) 69,770; (1991) 401,956 (prov.).

Cachar, dist., Assam, **India;** tea-growing ctr.; a. 6,961 km².

Cachoeira, t., Bahia, **Brazil;** historic c.; p. (1985) 138,500.

Cachoeira do Sul, t., Rio Grande do Sul, **Brazil;** p. (1980) 112,500.

Cader Idris, mtn., Gwynedd, **Wales;** alt. 893 m.

Cádiz, maritime prov., S.W. **Spain;** cap. Cádiz; a. 7,321 km²; p. (1981) 988,378.

Cádiz, c., cap. of C. prov., S.W. **Spain;** in Andalusia; pt. on Bay of C.; fortress t., naval base; exp. sherry, cork, fruit, olive oil, tunny fish; univ., cath.; one of the most anc. ts. in Europe, built by Phoenicians, *c.* 1100 B.C.; p. (1991) 156,558, 1,090,773 (prov.).

Caen, c., cap. of Calvados dep., **France;** church and abbey, tomb of William the Conqueror; univ.; iron-ore mng. and processing; severely damaged in second world war; p. (1990) 115,624 (c.), 188,799 (met. a.).

Caerleon, t., Newport, **Wales;** on R. Usk, 5 km N.E. of Newport; Roman Isca Silurum remains; agr. machin., tools, bricks; p. (1991) 8,931.

Caernarfon, t., Gwynedd, N. **Wales;** pt. on S. shore of Menai strait; cas., birthplace of Edward II; bricks, plastics; p. (1991) 9,695.

Caernarvonshire, historic co., N.W. **Wales;** now part of Gwynedd.

Caerphilly, t., unit. auth. created in 1996 from former l. gov. dists. of Islwyn and Rhymney Valley, S. **Wales;** cas.; lt. inds.; former coal mng. a.; p. (1991) 28,481 (t.), (1995) 169,900 (unit. auth.).

Caesar Mazaca, anc. c., Asia Minor; residence of the Cappadocian Kings; the modern Kayeri, **Turkey.**

Caesarea Palestinae, old c., **Israel,** 32 km S. Mt. Carmel; cap. of Herod the Great.

Caeté, t., Minas Gerais st., **Brazil;** lge. iron and

steel wks.; p. (1985) 35,200.

Cagliari, cap. and ch. pt. of Sardinia, **Italy;** univ., cath.; p. (1992) 180,309.

Cahir, t., Tipperary, **R.o.I.;** on R. Suir; anc. cas. and abbey; salmon fishing; p. (1986) 2,118.

Cahors, t., cap. of Lot dep., **France;** comm. ctr.; many historic bldgs., inc. cath., palace; distilleries, shoe factory; p. (1990) 20,787.

Cairngorm, mtns., Moray, Aberdeenshire and Highland, **Scot.;** rise to 1,310 m (Ben Macdhui); form part of Highlands; nat. nature reserve of arctic flora and fauna; winter sports.

Cairns, spt., Queensland, **Australia;** on Trinity Bay; bulk sugar terminal; resort for Barrier Reef; p. (1991) 86,227 (met. a.).

Cairntoul, mtn., Aberdeenshire, **Scot.;** alt. 1,294 m.

Cairo (El Qâhira), c., cap. of **Egypt** and prov.; on E. bank of Nile, at head of delta; lgst. c. in rep.; univ.; mosques, palace; fortress of Babylon in old c.; rapid growth with rural depopulation p. (1990) 6,452,000 (c.). (1991) 6,663,000 (prov.); Greater Cairo (1987) 13·3m.

Caistor, t., West Lindsey, Lincs., **Eng.;** site of Roman camp in Lincs. Wolds; p. (1991) 2,502.

Caithness, historic co., N. **Scot.,** now part of Highland.

Cajamarca, t., cap. of C. dep., **Peru;** in mtn. valley, 2,745 m; impt. in Inca times; p. (1993) 1,259,808 (prov.), 92,447 (t.).

Calabar, spt., S.E. **Nigeria;** cap. Cross River st.; exp. palm oil, kernels, rubber, ivory, cement; p. (1992) 157,800.

Calabria, region, extreme S.W. **Italy;** mtnous. pen.; highest point Mt. Pollino 2,234 m; ch. R. Crati; socially and economically underdeveloped; cap. Catanzaro; p. (1992) 2,074,763.

Calais, spt., Pas-de-Calais, N.E. **France;** cross-channel ferry pt. opposite to and 33·6 km distant from Dover; nearby Sangatte exit of Channel Tunnel; p. (1990) 75,836 (t.), 101,768 (met. a.).

Calama, oasis, Antofagasta prov., N. **Chile;** in Atacama desert at foot of Andean Cordillera; water from R. Loa supplies Antofagasta and used for irrigation locally; p. (1992) 120,602.

Calatafimi, t., Sicily, **Italy;** Garibaldi defeated Neapolitans, May 1860; p. (1981) 8,159.

Calbayog, c. Samar, **Philippines;** hemp tr., fisheries; p. (1990) 115,390.

Calbe, t., Saxony-Anhalt, **Germany;** on R. Saale; p. (1989) 14,253.

Calcutta, c., cap. of W. Bengal st., **India;** pt. on Hooghly R., lgst. c. in rep. and one of most densely populated areas of world; vast tr. from Ganges plain; univ.; jute-mills, textiles, chems., engin.; exp. jute, cotton, sugar-cane, rice, tea, coal; p. (1991) 11,022,000.

Calder, R., West Yorks., **Eng.,** trib. of Aire R.

Calderdale, met. dist., West Yorks., **Eng.;** chief t. Halifax; also inc. Todmorden, Brighouse, Hebden Royd, Ripponden and Sowerby Bridge; p. (1995) 193,200.

Calder Hall, Cumbria, **Eng.;** first full-scale nuclear power sta. in world (1956); now closed.

Caldey, I., off Pembrokeshire cst., **Wales;** lighthouse; Trappist monastery.

Caledonian Canal, from Inverness to Fort William, **Scot.,** connecting North Sea with Atl. Oc.; 100 km long; opened 1822.

Calf of Man, sm. I., S.W. **Isle of Man,** a. 250 ha,

Calgary, ch. t., Alberta, **Canada;** ctr. of ranching cty.; lumber mills, tanneries, oil refining, flour milling; p. (1991) 710,677.

Cali, c., cap. of Valle del Cauca dep., W. **Colombia;** 1,068 m on Cauca R.; comm. and transport ctr. for rich agr. a.; p. (1992) 1,624,401.

Calicut (Kozhikade), t., Kerala, **India;** first pt. reached by Vasco da Gama (1498); gave its name to calico cloth; p. (1981) 394,447 (t.), 546,058 (met. a.).

California, st., W. **USA;** admitted to Union 1850; st. flower golden poppy, st. bird California Valley quail; mtnous., forested, fertile valleys; subject to earthquakes from San Andreas fault; rich in minerals, oil, natural gas, gold, silver, copper; fruits; film ind.; attractive climate and scenery; cap. Sacramento; ch. pt. San Francisco, lgst. c. Los Angeles; most populous st. in USA; a. 411,014 km²; p. (1990) 29,760,021.

California Current, E. Pac. Oc.; flows N. to S. along cst. of Ore. and Cal., **USA;** relatively cold water; reduces summer temp. and causes fog in cst. a. especially nr. San Francisco.

California, G. of, arm of Pac. Oc., N.W. **Mexico;**

1,120 km long; same rift as Imperial and Coachella valleys in S.E. Cal.

Callander, burgh, Stirling, **Scot.;** mkt. t. on R. Teith, 24 km N.W. of Stirling; "the gate of the Highlands", tourism; p. (1991) 2,622.

Callao, c. and prov., W. **Peru;** pt. of Lima; sheltered harbour; sacked by Drake in 16th cent.; p. (1993) 639,729 (prov.), 359,768 (c.).

Calne, North Wilts., **Eng.;** mkt. t. on Marden R.; p. (1991) 11,518.

Caltagirone, t., Catania, Sicily, **Italy;** cath.; majolica ware; p. (1981) 35,682.

Caltanissetta, t., cap. of C. prov., Sicily, **Italy;** cath.; agr., sulphur ctr.; p. (1981) 61,146.

Calvados, dep., N.E. **France;** low-lying cty. and damp climate aid dairying; butter and cheese prods.; apple orchards produce Calvados brandy; cap. Caen; a. 5,690 km²; p. (1990) 618,500.

Cam (Granta), R., Cambridge, **Eng.;** trib. of R. Ouse; flows through the "backs" at Cambridge; 64 km long.

Camagüey, c., **Cuba;** comm. ctr. in rich agr. region; cattle, sugar-cane; p. (1990) 125,021.

Camargue, delta dist., Bouches-du Rhône, **France;** at mouth of R. Rhône; famous ccol. of flamingoes; gypsies; bull-rearing; a. 777 km².

Camberley, t., Surrey, **Eng.;** Royal Military Staff College, Royal Military Academy; p. (1991) 46,120 (with Frimley).

Cambodia, State of (Kampuchea), S.E. Asia; between Thailand and Vietnam; former ass. st. of Fr. Union; cap. Phnom-Penh on Mekong R.; mainly agr., rice, rubber, maize, pepper, kapok, livestock; Tonle Sap impt. for fishing; car assembly, cigarette mkg., textiles, plywood, paper, tyres,cement; oil refinery nr. Kompong Som; ravaged by civil war; a. 181,300 km²; p. (1993) 9,287,000.

Camborne, t., Cornwall, **Eng.;** 18 km S.W. Truro; old tin and copper mines; engin., radio-television assembly; textiles, chemicals; p. (1991) 35,915 (inc. Redruth).

Cambourne, planned £450m. new town near Cambridge.

Cambrai, t., Nord dep., **France;** on R. Scheldt; textiles (gave its name to cambric), agr. processing; suffered in both world wars; p. (1982) 36,618.

Cambrian Mtns., Wales; collective name for mtns. of N. and Central Wales inc. Snowdonia and Cader Idris.

Cambridge, univ. c., co. t., l. gov. dist., Cambridgeshire, **Eng.;** on Cam R.; famous univ. with residtl. colleges; leading ctr. of research-based inds.; p. (1995) 114,800 (dist.), (1991) 95,682 (c.).

Cambridgeshire, non-met. co., **Eng.;** low-lying, sloping from E. Anglian Heights in S.E. to Fens in N.; crossed by Rs. flowing to Wash; rich soils aid intensive agr. and mkt. gardening; inc. former cos. of Huntingdon, Peterborough and Isle of Ely; ch. t. Cambridge; p. (1995) 693,900.

Cambridge, c., Mass., **USA;** 5 km from Boston; seat of Harvard Univ. and MIT; mftg.; impt. research ctr.; now inc. in Boston met. a.; p. (1980) 95,322.

Camden, inner bor., N. London, **Eng.;** inc. Hampstead, Holborn, and St. Pancras; p. (1995) 184,900.

Camden, c., N.J., **USA;** pt. of entry on Delaware R., opposite Philadelphia; comm., mftg. and residtl.; iron foundries, chemicals, shipbldg.; p. (1990) 87,992; inc. in Philadelphia met. a.

Camerino, t., central **Italy;** in Apennines; univ. cath.; the anc. Camerium; p. (1981) 7,920.

Cameroon, United Rep. of, unitary st. (1972) W. Africa; on G. of Guinea; fed. cap. Yaoundé; dependence on primary exports of coffee and cocoa now reduced by rapid incr. in petroleum production since 1977; growing industrial sector; now graduated to middle income developing country; a. 475,500 km²; p. (1992) 12,198,000

Cameroon Mtn., volcano, massif, **Cameroon;** cstl-mtn., hgst. in W. Africa; last eruption 1959; alt. 4,072 m.

Campagna di Roma, Latium, **Italy;** malarial coastal plain around Rome; now reclaimed and used for pasture.

Campania, region, S. **Italy;** comprising provs. Avellino, Benevento, Caserta, Naples, Salerno; admin. and comm. ctr. Naples; high p. density; fertile; intensive agr.; p. (1992) 5,668,895.

Campbelltown, t., N.S.W., **Australia;** dairy and poultry ctr. for Sydney; proposed growth ctr.

for 340,000; p. (1981) 91,525.

Campbeltown, royal burgh, spt., Argyll and Bute, **Scot.;** distilling, fishing; planned ctr. for construction of off-shore oil platforms; p. (1991) 5,722.

Campeche, spt., S.E. **Mexico;** on G. of Campeche; gives its name to prov. (a. 56,099 km²; p. (1990) 528,824); clothing; exp. timber, sisal hemp; p. (1990) 172,208.

Campina Grande, t., Paraiba, **Brazil;** inland mkt. t. industl. ctr; p. (1985) 280,700.

Campinas, t., **Brazil;** 88 km N. of São Paulo; coffee; machin.; rubber gds.; p. (1991) 846,084.

Campine or **Kempenland,** region in Limburg and Antwerp provs., **Belgium;** concealed coalfield in heathland a.

Campobasso, t., cap. of C. prov., S. **Italy;** agr. ctr.; cutlery; 15th cent. cas.; p. (1981) 48,291.

Campo Belo, t., Minas Gerais st., **Brazil;** impt. cattle ctr. nr. L. formed by Furnas Dam on Rio Grande; p. (1985) 42,900.

Campo Duran, terr., **Argentina;** oilfield and refining.

Campo Grande, c., cap. Mato Grosso de Sul st. **Brazil;** p. (1990) 459,554.

Campos, c., Rio de Janeiro st., **Brazil;** ctr. for rich agr. region; sugar refining; p. (1991) 388,640.

Campos do Jordão, t., **Brazil;** alt. 1,699 m; health resort, known as the Switzerland of Brazil; p. (1985) 32,600.

Campsie Fells, range of hills, Stirling/E. Dunbartonshire, **Scot.;** highest point, 578 m.

Canada, indep. st., within Commonwealth; occupies N. part of N. America; enclave of Alaska (USA) in N.W.; second lgst. cty. in world, consisting of 10 provs., 3 terrs.; coastal mtns. and Rockies in W., interior plains in ctr., Hudson Bay lowlands in N., plateau a. of Quebec and Newfoundland in E.; many Is. off Arctic cst.; continental climate, severe in interior but moderated on csts.; less than 8 per cent of total land a. classified as cultivated land but agr. prods. (especially wheat) very valuable exp.; enormous forest resources but many economically inaccessible; fur trapping in N., impt. fishing inds. on both Pac. and Atl. csts.; considerable mineral resources; lgst. world producer of asbestos, silver, nickel, zinc.; major oil and gas resources in Alberta; one of most urbanised ctys. in world; p. concentrated along E.–W. axis in S. parts of W. provs. and along Gr. Ls. and St. Lawrence lowland; economy highly integrated with USA; 80 per cent of mftg. inds. based on US investment and 78 per cent of external tr. with USA; major cultural differences between English and French communities; strong separatist movements in Quebec; both nat. languages official (30 per cent p. speak French); cap. Ottawa; a. 9,976,185 km²; p. (1996) 30,300,000.

Canada Dam, Bihar, **India;** on R. Mayurakshi, 256 km from Calcutta.

Canadian Coast Range, mtns., B.C., W. **Canada;** penetrated by deep inlets (fjords) with very little cst. plain; crossed only by R. Skeena in N., R. Fraser in S.

Canadian R., S.W. **USA;** trib. of Arkansas R., not navigable but impt. for irrigation; 1,440 km long.

Canadian Shield (Laurentian Shield), Canada; vast region of hard anc. rock surrounding Hudson Bay, deeply eroded by ice, and lake covered; mng. and forestry.

Canal du Centre, canal, **France;** links Rhône-Saône valley at Chalon-sur-Saône with R. Loire at Digoin; serves Le Creusot coalfield; length 96 km.

Canaries Current, ocean current, flows S. along N.W. coast of Africa from El Dar-el-Beida to C. Verde; relatively cold and has very marked cooling effect on Saharan coastlands.

Canary Is., or **Canaries,** N. Atl. Oc.; gr. of 7 volcanic Is. belong to Spain, 96 km off cst. Africa; desires independence; inc. Tenerife (the lgst. I.), Gran Canaria, La Palma, Gomera, Hierro, Fuerteventura, Lanzarote; dry sunny climate and impressive volcanic landscape encourage tourism; intensive, irrigated agr. for bananas, tomatoes, oranges and vegetables; cap. Las Palmas, the "Fortunate Isles" of myths; a. 7,272 km²; p. (1981) 1,444,626.

Canberra, cap. **Australia;** midway between Melbourne and Sydney, lgst. inland c.; rapid growth since cap. established (1912); half work-force employed in government; spacious planned c. centred around L. Burley Griffin, reliant on high car ownership; p. (1993) 324,600.

Candia. *See* Iráklion.

Canea. *See* Khaniá.

Canna, sm. I., Hebrides, Highland, **Scot.**; basaltic pillars.

Cannanore, t., Kerala, **India**; exp. timber, coconuts; p. (1981) 60,904 (t.), 157,797 (met. a.).

Cannes, spt., dep. Alpes-Maritimes, **France**; 32 km S.W. Nice; famous resort; perfumes; airpt.; annual spring international film festival; p. (1990) 69,363 (t.), 335,647 (met. a.).

Cannock Chase, upland a., Staffs., **Eng.**; close to Midlands conurb.; forms l. gov. dist. based on **Cannock** t.; p. (1995) 90,700 (dist.), (1991) 60,106 (t.).

Canopus, c. of anc. **Egypt**; 19 km E. of Alexandria; here bdy. between Asia and Africa was drawn; Aboukir nr. ruins of temple of Serapis.

Cantabrians (Sierra de Cantabria), mtns., N. **Spain**; stretch from Pyrenees to C. Finisterre; form barrier between sea and central plateau; thick vegetation on lower slopes; coal, iron, hydroelec. power; hgst. peak Peña Vieja (2,673 m).

Cantal, dep., S.E. **France**; volcanic a., part of Massif Central; hgst. peak Plomb du Cantal (1,859 m); difficult agr., sparse p.; cap. Aurillac; a. 5,778 km²; p. (1990) 158,700.

Canterbury, c., l. gov. dist., Kent, **Eng.**; at foot of N. Downs on R. Stour; univ.; cath. founded A.D. 597 by St. Augustine; shrine of Thomas Becket; p. (1995) 135,000 (dist.), (1991) 36,464 (t.).

Canterbury, region, rich grazing and wheat-growing dist., on merged alluvial fans; S.I., **N.Z.**; ch. t. Christchurch; ch. pt. Lyttelton; p. (1991) 442,392.

Can-tho, t., **Vietnam**; on Mekong R. delta, tr. ctr.; rice, fish; p. (1989) 208,326.

Canton. *See* Guangzhou.

Canton R. *See* Zhujiang.

Canton, c., Ohio, **USA**; iron and steel, pulleys, hydraulic presses; p. (1990) 84,161 (c.), 394,106 (met. a.).

Canvey I., Castle Point, Essex, **Eng.**; fronting the Thames; expanded t.; resort; radio components, bookbinding, iron and wire wks., oil storage; oil refinery; liquid gas terminal; p. (1991) 36,406.

Cap-de-la-Madeleine, t., S. Quebec, **Canada**; varied mnfs.; p. (1986) 32,800.

Cape Breton I., Nova Scotia, **Canada**; coalmng., steelwks; farming, timber, fishing; ch. t. Sydney; discovered in 1497 by John Cabot; a. 9,324 km².

Cape Canaveral, E. Fla., **USA**; formerly Cape Kennedy; barrier I. separating Banana R. lagoon from Atl. Oc.; military base for testing missiles.

Cape Coast, t., **Ghana**; pt. of G. of Guinea, 96 km S.W. of Accra; cap. of Gold Coast until 1876; exp. cacao; cas.; p. (1984) 51,653.

Cape Cod, low sandy penin., Mass. Bay, **USA**; resort; fishing, boat bldg.; encloses C. C. Bay where Pilgrim Fathers first arrived in America 1620.

Cape Giradeau, t., Mo., **USA**; on Mississippi R.; footwear, clothing; p. (1980) 34,361.

Cape Horn, Chile, most southerly point of S. America.

Cape Kennedy. *See* Cape Canaveral.

Cape of Good Hope, S. Africa; famous headland, S. of Cape Town; 305 m high.

Cape Province, prov., **Rep. of S. Africa**; formerly Cape of Good Hope Colony; southernmost tip of Africa; cap. Cape Town; mostly plateau; inc. Transkeian terrs. in E.; sheep raising; wheat, citrus fruits, grapes, tobacco; fisheries; diamond and copper mng. in Namaqualand; automobile assembly, textiles, food canning; a. 721,224 km²; p. (1985) 5 m.

Capernaüm, in time of Christ impt. place in Palestine, on N. shore of L. Galilee; the modern Tell Hum (Israel).

Cape Town, c., cap. of Province, and legislative cap. of **Rep. of S. Africa**; spt. on Table Bay, 48 km N. of C. of Good Hope; communication by rail direct with Zimbabwe, Transvaal, O.F.S., and Natal; docks; cath.; univ.; exp. wool, gold, diamonds; oil refinery under construction at Milnerton 10 km N.E., p. (1980) 858,940 (met. a.).

Cape Verde, most W. part of **Africa**; site of Dakar, cap. of Senegal.

Cape Verde, Is., archipelago off W. cst. Africa; former Portuguese col.; 15 volcanic Is. and islets, divided into two grs.; windward and

leeward; a. 4,040 km²; cap. Praia; agr. sugar, fruit-growing; São Vicente fuelling sta. for navigation to S. America; indep. achieved 1975; plans to develop infrastructure; irrigation and reafforestation projects; p. (1995) 359,500.

Cap-Haitien, t., N. **Haiti**; spt., on N. cst.. exp. coffee, cacao, sugar; p. (1992) 92,122.

Capraia, I., 26 km E. of Corsica, belonging to **Italy**; volcanic; part of Genoa prov.

Caprera, I., off N.E. cst. Sardinia, **Italy**; Garibaldi buried here.

Capri, I. and tourist resort in Bay of Naples, **Italy**; famous Blue Grotto; celebrated in times of Augustus and Tiberius; wines; a. 10 km²; p. (1981) 7,489.

Capua, t., Campania, S. **Italy**; on Volturno R.; founded by Etruscans, impt. ctr. under Roman rule, sacked by Gaiseric; modern t. 5 km N. of site of anc. Capua; cath., Roman bridge; p. (1981) 18,053.

Caracas, c., cap. of **Venezuela**; in mtn. valley 921 m a.s.l.; 13 km inland from its pt. La Guaira; modern c.; contains 20 per cent of p. of rep.; cath., univs.; oil, textile mills, sugar refining; p. (1990) 1,824,892.

Caradon, l. gov. dist., Cornwall, **Eng.**; a. between Tamar and S. cst.; inc. Looe, Saltash and Liskeard; p. (1995) 79,400.

Carbon County, N. Utah, **USA**; contains immense reserves of gd. coking coal suitable for blast furnaces; not yet developed.

Carbonia, t., Sardinia, **Italy**; built 1937-8 nr. lignite and barytes a.; p. (1981) 32,130.

Carcassonne, c., cap. of Aude dep., S. **France**; historic citadel guarding impt. routeway from Aquitaine to Rhône valley; old c. divided from new by Aude R.; tourism; p. (1990) 44,991.

Cardamom Hills, Kerala, S. **India**; highland formed where W. and E. Ghats meet; rise to over 2,400 m; hgst. land of Indian penin.; rainfall less seasonal than most of India; "China" tea plantations on middle slopes.

Cárdenas, t., W. **Cuba**; pt. on Cárdenas Bay; processes and exp. sugar.

Cardiff, c., cap. of **Wales**, unit. auth. created in 1996 from former l. gov. dist.; at mouth of R. Taff on Bristol Channel, one of world's gr. coal-shipping pts.; univ. colleges., cath., cas.; docks at Barry; iron and steel wks., flour mills; freeport (1984) to help redevelopment of docks; chosen (1998) as location of new Welsh Assembly; p. (1991) 272,129 (c.), (1995) 309,400 (unit. auth.).

Cardigan, t., Ceredigion, S. **Wales**; at mouth of Teifi R.; former pt., now mkt. ctr.; p. (1991) 3,758.

Cardiganshire. *See* Ceredigion.

Caribbean Sea, part of Atl. Oc., between W.I. and Central and S. America; warm sea, entirely within tropics; a. 19,425 km².

Cariboo Range, mtns., B.C., W. **Canada**; mass of anc. crystalline rocks inside the gr. bend of R. Fraser; widespread occurrence of lode and alluvial gold; mainly above 1,500 m; hgst. point Mt. Sir Wilfred Laurier (3,584 m).

Carinthia (Karnten), prov., **Austria**; cap. Klagenfurt; contains hgst. mtn. in Austria, Grossglockner, alt. 3,801 m; many Ls.; p. (1991) 552,421.

Carlisle, c., l. gov. dist., Cumbria, **Eng.**; on Eden R.; pt. and route ctr.; Norman cas.; cath.; textiles, plasterboard, flour, bacon, biscuits, metal boxes; p. (1995) 103,500 (dist.), (1991) 72,439 (c.).

Carlow, co., S.E. Leinster, **R.o.I.**; arable agr. and livestock; co. t. Carlow; a. 896 km²; p. (1986) 40,988.

Carlow, co. t., Carlow co., **R.o.I.**; cath.; mkt., agr. processing; p. (1986) 11,509.

Carlsbad, t., N.M., **USA**; tourist resort; impt. potash deposits; p. (1980) 25,496.

Carlsbad Caverns National Park, N.M., **USA**; in foothills of Guadalupe mtns.; limestone caves; a. 18,600 ha.

Carlton, t., Gedling, Notts., **Eng.**; 3 km N.E. Nottingham; hosiery; p. (1991) 47,302.

Carmarthen, t., Carmarthenshire, **Wales**; on Towy R.; impt. agr. ctr.; cas. ruins; p. (1991) 13,524.

Carmarthenshire, S.W. **Wales**, unit. auth. created in 1996 from former l. gov. dists. of Carmarthen, Dinefwr and Llanelli, reinstating historic co. split up in 1974; stock rearing and fattening; industl. in S.E.; p. (1995) 169,500.

Carmiel, t., N. **Israel**; new t. built built between Acre and Safad, in the Galilean hills.

Carmona, t., **Spain**; Roman walls and necropolis.

Carnac, sm. t., Brittany, N.W. France; famous for its megalithic monuments; p. (1982) 3,964.

Carnarvon, t., W. Australia; on R. Gascoyne; NASA tracking sta.

Carnoustie, burgh, Angus, Scot.; on N. Sea; 10 km S.W. of Arbroath; resort; p. (1991) 10,673.

Caroni, R., Venezuela, hydroelec. complex at confluence Orinoco R.; steelwks.

Carpathian Mtns., range, E. Europe; arc of mtns. extending from Slovakia into Ukraine and Romania; major European range; 1,288 km long; contains oilfields.

Carpentaria, G. of, N. Australia; between Arnhem Land and C. York.

Carpentras, t., Vaucluse, France; on R. Auzon; antiquities; sweetmeats; p. (1982) 25,886.

Carpi, t., central Italy; 16 km N. of Modena; cath.; food processing; p. (1981) 60,507.

Carrantuohill, mtn., Kerry, R.o.I.; 1,041 m, loftiest in all Ireland.

Carrara, t., Massa Carrara, central Italy; famed for white marble used by Michelangelo; p. (1981) 65,687.

Carrick, l. gov. dist., Cornwall, Eng.; stretches across penin. and surrounds Fal estuary; inc. Truro, Penryn and Falmouth; p. (1995) 84,600.

Carrickfergus, t., l. gov. dist., N. Ireland; pt. on N. shore of Belfast Lough; textiles, nylon fibres, tobacco inds.; p. (1991) 32,750 (dist.), 22,786 (t.).

Carrickmacross, mkt. t., Monaghan, R.o.I.; p. (1986) 1,815.

Carrick-on-Shannon, co. t., R. D., Leitrim, R.o.I.; on flat land in Upper Shannon valley; p. of t. (1986) 1,984.

Carrick-on-Suir, mkt. t., Tipperary, R.o.I.; leather prods.; N.W. of Waterford; p. (1986) 5,353.

Carron, v., Falkirk, Scot.; nr. Falkirk; site of first ironwks. in E. Lowlands of Scot; p. (1991) 3,605.

Carron, Loch, inlet, W. cst., Highland, Scot.; followed by rly. from Dingwall to Kyle of Lochalsh.

Carse of Gowrie, Perth and Kinross, Scot.; fertile coastal dist. between Perth and Dundee, S. of Sidlaw Hills; soft fruits, especially raspberries.

Carsington, reservoir opend May 1992, S. Derbyshire.

Carson City, cap. Nevada, USA; smallest st. cap. at 1,427 m; tourist ctr.; p. (1990) 40,443.

Carstenz Mtns., Irian Jaya, Indonesia; major copper and base metal deposits and mng.; slurry pipeline to pts. on Tipoeka R.

Cartagena, spt., cap. dep. Bolivar, Colombia; shares with Barranquilla tr. from Magdalena R. valley; platinum, coffee, chemicals, textiles, fertilisers, oil refinery; drugs summit 1990; p. (1985) 559,581.

Cartagena, t., Murcia prov., S.E. Spain; on Mediterranean; spt. and naval base; cath.; shipbldg., metalwkg.: p. (1991) 172,152.

Cartagena, t., port; cap. Bolivar dep., Colombia; founded 1533; p. (1992) 688,306.

Cartago, c., Costa Rica; former cap.; 1,504 m at foot of volcanic Mt. Irazu; coffee, fruits; subject to earthquakes; p. (1984) 29,564.

Cartago Basin, Meseta Central, Costa Rica; alt. 5,000 ft.; a. of early Spanish settlement.

Carter Fell, mtn., a summit of the Cheviot hills, on the Eng./Scot. border, 554 m.

Carthage, anc. c., N. Africa; on Bay of Tunis; destroyed by Romans 146 B.C.; site is sub. of Tunis.

Casablanca. See El Dar-el-Beida.

Casale Monferrato, t., Piedmont, Italy; on R. Po; cath.; cement.

Cascade Range, USA and Canada; extends N. and S. through B.C., Wash., and Ore. between Rocky Mtns. and Pac. cst.; timber resources, hydroelec. power; hgst. peak Mt. Rainier, 4,395 m.

Cascade Tunnel, longest rly. tunnel in N. America, Wash., USA; carries trunk rly. from Spokane to Seattle through Cascade Mtns.; length 12·5 km.

Caserta, t., Italy; on N.E. edge of plain of Campania; impt. route ctr. and agr. mkt.; cath.; palace; p. (1981) 66,318.

Cashel, mkt. t., Tipperary, R.o.I.; anc. seat of kings of Munster; ruins of cath. on Rock of Cashel; p. (1986) 2,458.

Casiquiare, R., and canal, Venezuela; joins Orinoco to the Rio Negro, a trib. of the Amazon.

Casper, t., Wyo., USA; petroleum; airpt.; p. (1990) 46,742.

Caspian Sea, salt lake, Kazakhstan, Turkmenistan, Russia, Azerbaijan and Iran, between Europe and Asia; lgst. inland sea in world; a. 422,170 km²

but shrinking; 28 m below sea level; maximum depth 975 m; fed by R. Volga; agr. and dense p. on S. shore; pts.; Astrakhan, at mouth of Volga, Baku (oil ctr.).

Casquets, dangerous rocks, 11 km W. of Alderney, Channel Is., Eng.; lighthouse.

Cassino, t., Frosinone, Italy; in Apennines, on Rapido R.; t. and nearby monastery (Montecassino) destroyed 1944, now rebuilt; p. (1981) 31,139.

Castel Gandolfo, t., central Italy; in Alban Hills; papal summer residence; tourist centre; p. (1981) 13,348.

Castellammare del Golfo, spt., N.W. Sicily, Italy; wat. pl., tuna fishing.

Castellammare di Stabia, t., Campania, Italy; on Bay of Naples, at foot of Vesuvius; historic arsenal and dockyards; mineral springs; cath.; resort; p. (1981) 70,317.

Castellón de la Plana, prov., Spain; on Mediterranean, part of anc. Valencia, mainly mtns. a. 6,679 km²; cap. Castellón; p. (1991) 446,683.

Castellón de la Plana, t., Spain; on plain inland from Mediterranean cst.; varied agr. inds.; oil refining; p. (1991) 137,456.

Castelnaudary, t., Aude dep., France; in strategic gap between Central Massif and Pyrenees; captured by Black Prince 1355; mkt. for cereals; pottery; p. (1982) 11,381.

Castelo Branco, t., Portugal, prov. cap. Beira Baixa; agr. mkt. t.; p. (1981) 21,300.

Castelvetrano, agr. t., W. Sicily, Italy; wine mkg.; p. (1981) 30,577.

Castile, region in the high plateaux of central Spain; former kingdom; divided into Old Castile in N. (Avila, Burgos, Logroño, Santander, Segovia, Soria) and New Castile in S. (Ciudad Real, Cuenca, Guadalajara, Madrid, Toledo). Its dialect became the standard language of Spain.

Castlebar, cap. Mayo, R.o.I.; mkt. t.; p. (1986) 6,349.

Castleblayney, Monaghan, R.o.I.; nr. Dundalk; mkt. t.; shoes; p. (1986) 2,157.

Castlecary, v., N. Lanarkshire, Scot.; sta. on Roman wall; silica, fire clay deposits.

Castle Donington, t., Derbyshire, Eng.; airpt; power sta.; p. (1991) 6,007.

Castle Douglas, burgh, Dumfries and Galloway, Scot.; nr. R. Dee; nearby cas.; stock mkt.; p. (1991) 3,697.

Castleford, t., West Yorks., Eng.; 16 km S.E. of Leeds at confluence of Rs. Aire and Calder; coal mng., chemical, glass, and clothing mnfs, flour milling, brick mkg.; p. (1981) 36,032.

Castle Morpeth, l. gov. dist., Northumberland, Eng.; based on Morpeth; p. (1995) 49,700.

Castle Point, l. gov. dist., Essex, Eng.; comprises Canvey I. and Benfleet; p. (1995) 85,400.

Castlereagh, l. gov. dist., N. Ireland; inc. S.E. outskirts of Belfast; p. (1991) 60,799.

Castleton, v., Derbys., Eng.; on Hope R.; tourist ctr. for the Peak District; nearby fluorspar mines.

Castletown, t., Isle of Man; former cap.; pt., cas. tower; p. (1991) 3,152.

Castres, t., Tarn, France; on R. Agout; former Huguenot stronghold; cath.; textiles, soap, earthenware; p. (1982) 46,877.

Castries, t., cap. St. Lucia, Windward Is., W.I.; fine harbour; p. (1992) 53,883.

Castrop-Rauxel or Kastrop Rauxel, t., N. Rhine-Westphalia, Germany; part of Ruhr conurb.; industl.; coal, cement, tar prod., tiles, brandy; p. (1986) 96,100.

Catalonia, region, N.E. Spain; ch. industl. a.; comprises 4 provs.; Barcelona, Gerona, Lérida, Tarragona; cap. Barcelona; hilly, drained by Ebro R.; cereals, olive oil, wines; textiles, cars; hydroelec. power stas.; nuclear power sta. projected; a. 32,185 km²; p. (1981) 5,956,598.

Catamarca, t., cap. of Catamarca prov., N.W. Argentina; in Andean foothills 128 km S. of San Miguel de Tucumán; ctr. of irrigated oasis producing vines, apricots, cherries, cotton; thermal springs; p. (1991) 132,626 (t.), 264,234 (prov.).

Catanduanes, I., prov. off S. Luzon, Philippines; hilly, fertile; rice, corn, cotton, hemp, coconuts; a. 1,429 km²; p. (1990) 187,000.

Catania, c., Sicily, Italy; cap. of C. prov.; pt. on E. cst. at foot of Mt. Etna; rebuilt several times after earthquakes and volcanic eruption; cath., univ., cas.; p. (1992) 329,898.

Catanzaro, t., S. **Italy**; univ.; service ctr., regional cap. of Calabria; p. (1984) 101,622.

Catastrophe, C., S. extremity of Eyre Peninsula, S. **Australia**.

Catawba, R., S. and N.C., **USA**; rises in Blue Ridge Range, flows to Santee R.; extensively dammed; 480 km long.

Caterham and **Warlingham**, ts., former U.D. Tandridge, Surrey, **Eng.**; on N. Downs; residtl.; p. (1991) 30,177.

Cathay, anc. name for China and E. Tartary.

Catoche, C., N.E. point of Yucatan, **Mexico**.

Catskill Mtns., N.Y., **USA**; gr. in Appalachians, W. of Hudson R., well wooded; resort for p. of N.Y. c.; alt. c. 900 m.

Cauca, dep., **Colombia**; cap. Popayán; a. 30,191 km²; p. (1985) 674,824.

Cauca, R., **Colombia**; trib. of Magdalena; 960 km long.

Caucasia, region between Black Sea and Caspian, occupied by parts of **Russia, Georgia, Azerbaijan** and **Armenia** divided by Caucasus Mtns. into N. or Cis-Caucasia and S. or Trans-Caucasia.

Caucasus (Bol'shoy **Kavkaz**), mtns., separate **Russia** from **Georgia** and **Azerbaijan**; run from Black Sea to Caspian Sea; divided into 3 ranges; hgst. summits Mt. Elbruz (5,631 m) and Kasbek (5,047 m); many lofty passes and glaciers; total l. c. 1,520 km.

Caucun, 1., off Yucatan penin., **Mexico**; developing tourist ctr.; airpt.

Causses, Les, limestone plateau, Aveyron, Tarn deps., S. **France**; on S.W. flank of Central Massif; caverns, gorges of Rs. Lot and Tarn; sheep provide milk for Roquefort cheese; alt. 900–1,800 m.

Cauvery, R., S. **India**; rises in W. Ghats, flows into Bay of Bengal through Karnataka and and Tamil Nadu; length 640 km; lge. irrigation and hydroelec. power project.

Caux, region of Normandy, **France**; fertile loess-covered chalk plateau adjacent to English Channel; arable agr.

Cava de' **Tirreni**, t., Salerno, **Italy**; summer resort; textiles; p. (1981) 50,558.

Cavaillon, t., Vaucluse, **France**; cath.; ctr. of mkt. gardening dist.; p. (1982) 20,830.

Cavan, inland co., **R.O.I.**; agr. a. with many Ls.; depopulation; borders Ulster; a. 1,932 km²; p. (1986) 53,965.

Cavan, , co. t., Cavan, **R.O.I.**; 115 km S.W. Belfast; mkt.; cath.; p. (1986) 3,381.

Cavite, spt., Luzon, **Philippines**; walled t.; oil refining nearby; p. (1990) 91,641.

Cavour Canal, irrigation canal. Piedmont and Lombardy regions, N. **Italy**; links R. Po nr. Chivassa with R. Ticino 16 km N.E. of Novara; provides water for 101,000 ha of rice-fields and meadow-land; length 128 km.

Cawnpore. See Kanpur.

Caxias do Sul, t., Rio Grande do Sul, **Brazil**; wines; p. (1980) 198,683.

Cayambe, volcanic mtn., Andes, **Ecuador**; alt. 5,958 m.

Cayenne, c., cap of French **Guiana**, at mouth of Cayenne R.; exp. gold; gave its name to Cayenne pepper; p. (1990) 41,659.

Cayman Is., W.I.; consists of Grand Cayman, cap. George Town; Little Cayman; and Cayman Brac.; turtle and shark fishing; a. 259 km²; p. (1998) 33,600.

Ceará, st., N. **Brazil**; stretches from Brazilian Plateau to Atl. cst.; poor cattle rearing a. with many droughts; cap. Fortaleza; a. 148,078 km²; p. (1991) 6,353,346.

Cebu, one of Visayan Is., prov. **Philippines**; mtnous.; forested; coal, oil, gold; coconuts, maize; 4,408 km²; p. (1990) 2,645,735.

Cebu, c., Cebu I., **Philippines**; tr. ctr. of Visayan Is.; pt. for abaca and copra; p. (1995) 662,000.

Cedar Falls, t., N. Iowa, **USA**; on Cedar R.; p. (1990) 34,298.

Cedar Mountain, hill, Va., **USA**; here Stonewall Jackson defeated Banks in Civil War (second battle of Bull Run, 1862).

Cedar Rapids, c., Iowa, **USA**; distribution and rly. ctr. for agr. a.; p. (1990) 108,751.

Cegléd, t., **Hungary**; on edge of Central Plain in fruit growing a.; vehicle repair shops; p. (1997) 36,000.

Celaya, mkt. t., Guanajuato, **Mexico**; rly. junc.; ctr. of rich farming a.; many inds.; sweet-meats; p. (1990) 315,577.

Celebes. See **Sulawesi**.

Celje, t., **Slovenia** (formerly Yugoslavia); industl., agr. ctr., zinc refining, fertilisers; close to Austrian border; p. (1981) 63,877.

Celle, t., Lower Saxony, **Germany**; on R. Aller; cas. was residence of dukes of Brunswick-Lüneburg until 1705; oil refining, machin., textiles; p. (1986) 70,200.

Celtic Sea, a. bounded by S. Ireland, Wales, Cornwall and Brittany; rich natural gas deposits 48 km S.W. of Kinsale.

Central African Republic, indep. st., former empire until 1979; within Fr. Community, Equatorial Africa; formerly Fr. colony of Ubangi-Shari; land-locked upland plateau covered by savannah grassland; S.W. forest zone likely to develop with proposed rail link with Transcameroon rly.; cotton, diamonds; cap. Bangui; a. 622,984 km²; p. (1994) 3,068,000.

Central America, stretch of land between Mexico and S. America, from the Isthmus of Tehuantepec to that of Panama; includes Guatemala, Honduras, Mexico, Nicaragua, Salvador, Costa Rica, Panama, Belize; tropical climate; forests, savannahs.

Central Asia, usually applied to regions between 30° and 40° N. lat. and 55° and 85° E. long.; the land between China and Afghanistan and the Caspian, consisting of Kazakhstan, Tajikistan, Turkmenistan, Uzbekistan and Kyrgyzstan.

Central Clydeside Conurbation, conurb., Scot., based on Glasgow and includes other urban areas (Bearsden, Milngavie, Clydebank, Cumbernauld, Kilsyth, East Kilbride, Eastwood, Hamilton, Monklands, Motherwell, Renfrew and Strathkelvin); p. (1993) 1,619,960.

Central Lancashire, new t., Lancs., **Eng.**; site of 14,186 ha.; t. created from expansion of Chorley and Leyland; biggest new t. in Eng.; p. (1981) 247,224.

Central Valley, Cal., **USA**; valleys of Rs. San Joaquin and Sacramento; main agr. a. of Cal.; vast scheme for irrigation, hydroelec. power, flood control and protection of wildlife.

Centre, region, **France**; inc. deps. Cher, Eure-et-Loir, Indre, Indre-et-Loire, Loir-et-Cher, Loiret; region based on the upper Loire and its tributaries; agr; vineyards; ch. ts. Orleans, Tours; p. (1990) 2,371,000.

Cephalonia (**Kefalliniá**), lgst. of Ionian Is., **Greece**; mtnous. with fertile valleys; impt. harbours of Argostólion and Lexourion; currant production; a. 751 km²; p. (1991) 32,474.

Ceram. See **Seram**.

Ceredigion, W. **Wales**, unit. auth. created in 1996 from former l. gov. dist., reinstating historic co. of **Cardiganshire** disbanded in 1974; upland a. drained by the Teifi and Ystwyth Rs.; ch. t. Aberystwyth; p. (1995) 70,200.

Cérignola, t., Apulia, **Italy**; agr. ctr.; Spanish victory over French in Italian wars 1503; p. (1981) 50,682.

Cerigo (**Kithira**) I., **Greece**; sm. I. between Crete and Peloponnesus.

Cernauti. See **Chernovtsy**.

Cerro de **Pasco**, t., Pasco dep., **Peru**; mng. ctr. at 4,403 m; univ.; copper, gold, lead, zinc; p. (1991) 62,749.

Cerro Rico, mtn., **Bolivia**; in Andes, W. of Potosi; alt. 4,782 m; rich silver, tin, tungsten ores.

Cesena, t., Emilia-Romagna, **Italy**; flourished in Renaissance times; cath., Malatesta library; agr. mkt. t.; p. (1981) 89,640.

České Budějovice (**Budweis**), t., **Czech Rep.**; on R. Vitava, 128 km S. of Prague, major industl. ctr.; pencils, porcelain, brewing, anthracite; p. (1990) 99,000.

Cesky Těšin, t., **Czech Rep.**; on Olše R., trib. of Oder; part of former t. of Teschen on Czech side of frontier with Poland; coal mng.

Cessnock-Bellbird, t., N.S.W., **Australia**; coal mng. declining since 1968; ctr. for Hunter Valley vineyards; p. (1981) 16,916.

Ceuta, spt., Spanish N. **Africa**; naval base; opposite to and 26 km from Gibraltar; cath.; the anc. Abyia, one of the Pillars of Hercules; p. (1981) 65,263.

Cevennes, mtns., S. **France**; separating basins of Rhône, Loire, and Tarn; highest point Mt. Mézenc, alt. 1,767 m.

Ceylon. See **Sri Lanka**.

Chaco, prov., N. **Argentina**; farming and prairie

land; cap. Resistencia; a. 99,632 km²; p. (1991) 839,677.

Chad, indep. st. within Fr. Community, Equatorial Africa; landlocked, focus of trans Sahara and Equatorial tr. routes; N. frontier (Aouzou Strip) rich in minerals and occupied by Libya; valuable uranium and oil reserves but no exploitation; severe droughts (1982–3) reduced cattle and restricted arable crops; cash crops of cotton and ground nuts; cap. Ndjamena; a. 1,282,050 km²; p. (1993) 6,279,931.

Chad, L., lge. sheet of water bordering Nigeria, Niger, Chad and Cameroon; a. 129,500 km² when in flood; varies in extent with season, and is drying up; shallow, many Is., lies between the wooded region of the Sudan and the steppes leading to the Sahara desert; joint project for devel. by neighbouring ctys.

Chadderton, t., Gtr. Manchester, Eng.; engin., chemicals, textiles; p. (1991) 34,026.

Chagos Is., 5 coral Is., Indian Oc.; since 1965 the British Indian Ocean Territory; fine harbour in Diego Garcia.

Chainat, t., Thailand; on Menam Chao Phraya; major barrage for hydroelec. power and flood control.

Chalcis, t., Greece; resort for Athens; joined to mainland by swing bridge; p. (1981) 44,867.

Chalfont St. Giles, v., Bucks., Eng.; in London commuter belt; home of Milton; p. (1991) 4,987.

Châlons-sur-Marne, t., cap. of Marne dep., N.E. France; comm. and industl.; cath., churches; p. (1990) 51,533.

Châlon-sur-Saône, t., Saône-et-Loire dep., E. France; R. pt., comm. ctr. for Burgundy; historic t.; p. (1990) 56,259.

Chambal, R., trib. of R. Jumna, rising in Vindhya hills, Madhya Pradesh, India; major power, irrigation and industl. scheme; agr. in lower valley causing soil erosion, major soil conservation projection; 880 km long.

Chambéry, t., cap. of Savoie dep., S.E. France; leather gds.; tourism; p. (1990) 55,603 (t.), 102,548 (met. a.)

Chambord, v., Loir-et-Cher dep., France; on R. Cosson, trib. of Loire; Renaissance château; p. (1981) 206.

Chamonix, t., Haute-Savoie, France; at foot of Mont Blanc, in valley of R. Arve; winter sports ctr., road tunnel links to Aosta; p. (1982) 9,255.

Champagne, former prov. now incorporated in Champagne-Ardenne region, France; inc. deps. Ardennes, Aube, Marne, Haute-Marne; famous for its champagne wine; wheat, sheep; Ardennes hilly and heavily wooded: ch. t. Reims; p. (1990) 1,347,800.

Champaign, t., Ill., USA; close to Urbana; univ.; foundries; food processing; p. (1984) 60,400 (t.), 170,300 (met. a.).

Champigny-sur-Marne, t., Val-de-Marne dep., France; E. sub. of Paris; varied inds.; p. (1990) 79,778.

Champlain Canal, N.Y., USA; follows gap between Adirondack Mtns. and Green Mtns. occupied by Hudson R.; links Albany with L. Champlain and allows through barge traffic between New York and St. Lawrence valley.

Champlain, L., USA; N. frontier of N.Y. st.; discharges by Richelieu R. into St. Lawrence; flanked by trunk route from New York to Montreal; forms link between Hudson R. and St. Lawrence waterway; a. 1,126 km².

Chanda, t., Nagpur, Maharashtra, India; anc. temples.

Chandausi, t., Uttar Pradesh, India; cotton, hemp; rly. ctr.; p. (1981) 66,970.

Chandernagore, t., W. Bengal, India; on Hooghly R., N. of Calcutta; founded by French 1686; p. (1981) 101,925.

Chandigarh, union terr. (1966) and former cap. of both Punjab and Haryana sts., India; new c. designed by Le Corbusier to replace former cap. Lahore, now in Pakistan; to be sole capital of Punjab on plateau at foot of Himalayas, S.W. of Simla, (now postponed because of Sikh unrest); univ.; a. of terr. 114 km²; p. (1991) 511,000 (c.), 642,015 (terr.).

Changchun, c., Jilin, China; rly. ctr.; univ.; China's biggest motor vehicle plant, machine tools; film production centre; p. (1992) 2,130,000.

Changnacheri, t., Kerala, S. India; tea, cotton-spinning, silk; p. (1981) 51,955.

Changbai Shan, mtns.; form bdy. between China and N. Korea; drained by Rs. Yalu and Tumen; hgst. point Pai-t'ou-shan, 2,442 m.

Chang Jiang (Yangtse Kiang), R., China; rises in plateau in Xizang Zizhiou (Tibet) and flows E. to E. China Sea nr. Shanghai; one of China's major Rs.; crosses "Red Basin' of Sichuan, a deep gorge above Yichang and finally a broad level plain; many lge. cs. on its banks inc. Yichang, Nanjing, Wuhan, Zhenjiang, Chongqing; major water control project; navigable by ocean-going vessels for 2,880 km. to Yichang; total length 5,600 km.; longest river in Asia.

Changsha, c., cap. of Hunan prov., China; pt. on Xiang Jiang; univ.; tea, rice, antimony; p. (1992) 1,330,000.

Changzhou (Changchow), c., Jiangsu, China; in valley of Chang Jiang, on Grand Canal 112 km S.E. of Nanjing; mkt. for intensively cultivated dist.; silk; p. (1984) 512,600.

Channel Is., gr. of self-governing Is. belonging to the Brit. Crown off N.W. cst. France, of which the lgst. are Jersey, Guernsey, Alderney, and Sark; part of the old duchy of Normandy; vegetables, flowers, fruit, granite; two famous breeds of dairy cattle; tourist resort; impt. banking and insurance ctr. encouraged by low taxes; retirement ctr.; a. 194 km²; p. (1985) 130,000.

Chantilly, t., Oise, France; famous racecourse; formerly famous for lace and porcelain; p. (1982) 10,208.

Chao Phraya. See Menam Chao Phraya.

Chaozhou (Chaochow), c., Guandong, S. China; on Han R., 32 km N. of Shantou; ctr. of cultivated plain; rice, sugar, tea; linked to Shantou by rly.; p. (1984) 191,400.

Chapala, t. and L., Mexico; chiefly in Jalisco st.; attractive site and climate encourage tourism; pastoral agr. on shores; a. 1,080 km²; p. (1990) 35,414.

Chapelcross, nr. Annan, Dumfries and Galloway, Scot.; AEA nuclear power sta., producing electricity for natl. grid.

Chapel-en-le-Frith, mkt. t., High Peak, Derbys., Eng.; brake-linings; p. (1991) 8,715.

Chapra, t., Bihar, India; on Ganges R.; ctr. of former saltpetre and indigo tr.; p. (1991) 136,877.

Chard, mkt. t., Somerset Eng.; lace, engin., shirt and cotton mftg.; p. (1991) 10,770.

Chardzhou, t., Turkmenistan; inland pt. on Amu-Dar'ya R.; shipyards, textiles, chemicals; major oil refinery project; p. (1990) 163,700.

Charente, dep., S.W. France; cap. Angoulême; ctr. of distilling tr., cognac; a. 5,970 km²; p. (1990) 342,000.

Charente, R., S.W. France; rises W. of Limoges and flows into Bay of Biscay below Rochefort; valley slopes beyond Angoulême produce celebrated grapes from which brandy is made at Cognac and Jarnac.

Charente-Maritime, dep., S.W. France; cap. La Rochelle; borders Bay of Biscay; wine, wheat; oysters, pilchards; a. 7,229 km²; p. (1990) 527,000.

Charleroi, t., Hainaut, Belgium; on R. Sambre; coal mng.; glass; p. (1993) 207,045.

Charleston, c., spt., S.C., USA; industl. and comm. ctr. on Atl. cst. founded 1670; scene of onset of Civil War; p. (1990) 80,414 (c.), 506,875 (met. a.).

Charleston, t., cap. W. Va., USA; on Kanawha R.; in bituminous coal dist.; chemicals, glass, tools, oil, natural gas, lumber, coal processing; p. (1984) 59,400 (t.), (1990) 250,000 (met. a.).

Charleville-Mézières, twin t., Ardennes dep., N.E. France; on Meuse R.; iron, bricks, nails, hardware; p. (1990) 59,439.

Charlotte, c., N.C., USA; key rly. junc.; machin., chemicals, textiles; p. (1990) 395,934 (c.), 1,162,093 (met. a. with Gastonia-Rock Hill).

Charlotte Amalie, t., cap. of Virgin Is. of USA; on St. Thomas I.; excellent natural harbour; former coaling sta.; p. (1985) 12,660.

Charlottesville, t., Va., USA; on Rivanna R.; in apple-growing region; univ.; Monticello nearby, home of Jefferson; textiles; p. (1984) 40,600 (t.), 118,300 (met. a.).

Charlottetown, t., ch. pt. Prince Edward I., Canada; originally named after Queen Charlotte, consort of George III; univ.; p. (1991) 15,396.

Charlton Kings, t., Cheltenham, Gloucs., Eng.; at foot of Cotswolds; p. (1991) 11,332.

Charnwood Forest, upland dist., Leics., Eng.; to W. of Soar valley, 19 km N.W. of Leicester;

composed of anc. rocks; stone-crushing; largely forests; alt. 180–275 m; forms l. gov. dist. of **Charnwood** inc. Loughborough and Shepshed; p. (1995) 154,400.

Charters Towers, t., N. Queensland, **Australia**; fine bldgs. remain from 1872 gold rush; ctr. of agr. dist.; p. (1984) 7,620.

Chartres, t., cap. of Eure-et-Loir dep., **France**; mkt. for cereals from Beauce region; famous Gothic cath.; p. (1990) 41,850.

Châteauroux, t., cap. of Indre dep., **France**; 96 km S.E. of Tours, on R. Indre; agr. ctr., woollens, pottery; p. (1990) 52,949.

Chateau Thierry, t., Aisne, **France**; on R. Marne; mkt. t.; cas.; precision instruments; p. (1982) 14,920.

Châtellerault, t., Vienne, **France**; 64 km S. of Tours on R. Vienne; cutlery, metallurgical and aeronautical engin. Descartes lived here; p. (1982) 36,870.

Chatham, t., Rochester upon Medway, Kent, **Eng.**; on estuary of R. Medway; lt. inds.; famous naval dockyard established by Henry VIII; now planned to become heritage site; p. (1991) 71,691.

Chatham, t., spt., N.B., **Canada**; lumbering, fish exporting; p. (1986) 6,219.

Chatham, c., Ont., **Canada**; on extinct L. plain on R. Thames; agr. prods.; p. (1986) 42,211.

Chatham Is., N.Z. dependency, S. **Pac. Oc.**; volcanic Is.; sheep rearing and fishing; a. 963 km²; p. (1991) 760.

Chatsworth, Derbys., **Eng.**; on R. Derwent; seat of the dukes of Devonshire.

Chattanooga, c. Tenn., **USA**; on Tennessee R.; univ.; rly. ctr.; cottons; iron, steel, chemicals, paper, metals; p. (1990) 152,466 (c.), 433,204 (met. a.).

Chatteris, Fenland, Cambridge, **Eng.**; mkt. t.; p. (1991) 7,261.

Chaudière Falls, on Ottawa R., above Ottawa, **Canada**; hydroelec. sta.

Chauk, t., **Myanmar**; on R. Irrawaddy; ctr. of oilfield; oil refining; fertilisers.

Chaumont, t., cap. of Haute-Marne dep., **France**; on R. Marne; gloves, leather; p. (1990) 28,900.

Chautauqua, L., N.Y. st., **USA**; summer resort; vineyards.

Chaux-de-Fonds, La, t., can. Neuchâtel, **Switzerland**; ctr. of watchmkg. ind.; p. (1990) 36,272.

Cheadle, t., Staffs. Moorland, Staffs., **Eng.**; metal mnfs.; former coal-mng. a.; p. (1991) 10,833.

Cheadle and Gatley, ts., Gtr. Manchester, **Eng.**; textile finishing and bleaching, engin.; residtl.; p. (1991) 58,457.

Cheb, t., **Czech Rep.**; nr. Bavarian frontier; comm. ctr.; machin.; p. (1984) 31,333.

Cheboksary, c., cap. of Chuvash aut. rep., **Russia**; R. pt. on Volga; agr. ctr.; hydroelec. plant; p. (1989) 420,000.

Chechen Republic, rep. **Russia**, formerly known as Checheno - Inguish rep; declared independence 1991; unrest 1995; a 19,300 km²; cap. Grozny; p. (1992) 1,308,000.

Cheddar, v., Somerset, **Eng.**; famous limestone caves and gorge in Mendips; cheese, strawberries; p. (1991) 4,484..

Chefoo. See Yantai.

Cheju (Quelpart), I. and prov., off **S. Korea**, E. China Sea; extinct volcano Mt. Halla, 1,968 m; p. (1990) 515,000.

Chekiang. See Zhijiang.

Che-ling Pass, on bdy. between Guandong and Hunan, S. **China**; historic route across Nanling mtns., now followed by Wuhan to Guangzhou trunk rly.; alt. 300 m.

Chelm, t. and prov., E. **Poland**; nr. Lublin; cath.; flour-milling; p. (1989) 64,683 (t.) 245,500 (prov.).

Chelmsford, co. t., l. gov. dist., Essex, **Eng.**; 48 km N.E. London; cath.; agr. mkt.; p. (1995) 156,500 (dist.), (1991) 97,451 (t.).

Chelsea, dist., London, **Eng.**; fashionable residtl. dist. See Kensington.

Chelsea, t., Mass., **USA**; industl. sub. on Boston harbour; p. (1980) 25,431.

Cheltenham, t., l. gov. dist., Gloucs., **Eng.**; spa; educational ctr.; precision instruments; birthplace of Gustav Holst; p. (1995) 106,600 (dist.), (1991) 91,301 (t.).

Chelyabinsk, t., **Russia**; major industl. ctr. on Miass R., Siberian lowlands; steel wks.; metallurgy, machin.; on natural gas pipeline from Gazli gasfield; p. (1989) 1,142,000.

Chelyuskin, Cape, most N. point in Asia, in Krasnoyarsk Terr., **Russia**; named after Russian navigator who discovered it in 1742.

Chemnitz, c., Saxony, **Germany**; leading industl. ctr.; cotton, woollens, machin., cars, furniture, chemicals, engin.; nr. lignite mines; p. (1990) 291,400.

Chemulpo. See Inchon.

Chenab, R., W. Punjab, **Pakistan**; one of "five rivers" of Punjab; rises in Himalayas, flows S.W. into R. Sutlej; dams at Marala and Khanki; c. 1,440 km long.

Chengchow. See Zhengzhou.

Chengdu (Chengtu), c., cap. of Sichuan prov., **China**; telecommunications centre, oil refinery; chemicals, electronics, textiles, machin.; p. (1992) 2,840,000.

Chennai. See Madras.

Chepstow, mkt. t., Monmouthshire, **Wales**; on R. Wye, 3 km above confluence with R. Severn; ruined cas.; p. (1991), 9,461.

Chequers, official residence of Brit. prime ministers, 3 km S. of Wendover, Bucks., **Eng.**; gift of Lord Lee of Fareham.

Cher, dep., **France**; cap. Bourges; crossed by Cher R.; a. 7,301 km²; p. (1990) 321,600.

Cher, R., central **France**; rises in Central Massif, joins Loire below Tours; length 320 km.

Cherbourg, spt., Manche, **France**; N. cst. of Contentin peninsula; opposite to and 128 km dist. from Portsmouth; naval arsenal, shipbldg.; metals, ropes, fishing; p. (1990) 28,773 (t.), 92,045 (met. a.).

Cherepovets, c., **Russia**; on Rybinskoye reservoir of R. Volga; steel, engin., sawmills, shipbldg.; p. (1989) 310,000.

Cheribon. See Tjirebon.

Cheriton, dist. near Folkestone, Kent, **Eng.**; Channel Tunnel, linked to Sangatte, Calais, France opened 1994.

Cherkassy, t., **Ukraine**; nr. Kiev, on reservoir formed by Dnieper R.; sugar, engin., sawmilling; p. (1990) 297,200.

Cherkessk, t., **Russia**; rly. terminus, industl. ctr.; p. (1989) 113,000.

Chernigov, t., **Ukraine**; on Desna R.; p. (1990) 301,100.

Chernobyl, Ukraine; site of world's worst nuclear accident (1986).

Chernovtsy, t., **Ukraine**; univ.; Greek cath.; wheat, dairy produce, textiles, engin., chemicals; p. (1990) 257,300.

Cherrapunji, t., Assam, **India**; in Khasi Hills; reputed wettest place in world, average annual rainfall 12,700 mm.

Chertsey, t., Runnymede, Surrey, **Eng.**; on S. bank of R. Thames, 6 km below Staines; residtl.; p. (1991) 10,016.

Cherwell, l. gov. dist., Oxon., **Eng.**; stretches from Banbury to Bicester; p. (1995) 131,300.

Cherwell, R., trib. of Thames, nr. Oxford, **Eng.**; length 48 km.

Chesapeake Bay, inlet on Atl. cst., **USA**; extending 320 km from mouth of Susquehanna R. to C. Charles; shellfish ind.; bridge-tunnel (opened 1964) spans entrance to Bay; p. of c. (1990) 151,976.

Chesham, t., Bucks., **Eng.**; in heart of Chiltern Hills; printing, textiles, lt. engin.; residtl. p. (1991) 20,290.

Cheshire, non-met. co., N.W. **Eng.**; lowland a. drained by Rs. Dee and Mersey, bounded by Pennines in E.; dairying and mkt. gardening; chemical ind. based on salt deposits around Northwich; heavy inds. in and around Warrington; attracting many high technology inds.; much of co. residtl. for Liverpool and Manchester; cap. Chester; p. (1995) 978,100.

Cheshunt, t., Herts., **Eng.**; in Lea valley, 11 km S. of Hertford; bricks, mkt. gardening, horticulture; p. (1991) 51,998.

Chesil Bank, Dorset, **Eng.**; shingle ridge enclosing the Fleet lagoon running from I. of Portland to Bridport.

Chester, c., l. gov. dist., Cheshire, **Eng.**; at head of estuary of R. Dee; cath., anc. walls and old timbered houses; Roman c. of Deva site of legionary barracks; engin., metal goods; p. (1995) 120,100 (dist.), (1991) 80,110 (c.).

Chester, t., Penns., **USA**; on Delaware R. S.W. Philadelphia; called Uppland by Swedish settlers 1643, renamed by William Penn; pt. of entry; shipbldg.; p. (1980) 45,794.

Chesterfield, mkt. t., colly. dist., l. gov. dist., Derbys., **Eng.**; on Rother R.; 13 km S. of Sheffield; variety of heavy inds.; 14th cent. church with crooked spire; p. (1995) 100,900 (dist.), (1991) 71,945 (t.).

Chesterfield Inlet, arm of Hudson Bay, **Canada**; 400 km by 40 km.

Chester-le-Street, t., l. gov. dist., Durham, **Eng.**; clothing, confectionery, sand wkg.; p. (1995) 55,300 (dist.), (1991) 35,123 (t.).

Cheviot Hills, range between **Scot.** and **Eng.**; hgst. summit, the Cheviot, 816 m.

Cheyenne, t., cap. of Wyo., **USA**; cattle-ranching dist.; rly. ctr.; p. (1990) 50,008.

Chiana, Val di, valley, central **Italy**; separates Tuscan hills from central Apennines; occupied by upper course of R. Arno, middle course of R. Tiber; followed by main route from Florence to Rome.

Chiang Mai, c., cap of C. prov., and 3rd c. of **Thailand**; rly. terminus on Ping R.; tr. ctr.; teak; p. (1991) 161,541.

Chiapa, R., flows N. from **Guatemala** through **Mexico** to G. of Campeche; impt. routeway in lower course; length 320 km.

Chiapas, Pac. st., **Mexico**; mtnous., forested; bananas, tobacco, sugar and cocoa; cattle; oil reserves; close associations with Guatemala; cap. Tuxtla-Gutierrez; a. 74,408 km²; p. (1990) 3,203,915.

Chiasso, frontier t., S. **Switzerland**; rly. sta. on Italian border.

Chiayi, c., co., W. central **Taiwan**; p. (1995) 261,749 (c.), 565,172 (co.).

Chiba, c., cap. of C. pref. **Japan**; part of Keihin conurb. on Tokyo B.; tr. ctr., giant shipyard, oil refining, aluminium, chemicals, iron and steel; airpt.; p. (1990) 829,467.

Chicago, c., Ill., **USA**; on S. shore of L. Michigan; economic heart of Mid-West; comm. ctr. called "The Loop"; immense tr. by rail and Gr. Ls.; univs.; grain mills, meat packing plants, iron and steel wks., major iron-ore mkt., electronic equipment, furniture; lgst. airport in world; p. (1990) 2,783,726 (c.), 6,070,000 (met.a.).

Chichester, t., l. gov. dist., West Sussex, **Eng.**; on S. cst. plain, 18 km W. of Arundel; cath.; yachting basin; p. (1995) 104,100 (dist.), (1991) 26,572 (t.).

Chickamauga Creek, **USA**; branch of Tennessee R. above Chattanooga, forming part of Tenn. Valley Authority scheme; Civil War battles; site of Nat. Park.

Chickerell, E. Dorset, **Eng.**; 5 km N.W. of Weymouth; East Fleet, a sea-fed tidal estuary, lies to the west of the village.

Chiclayo, c., Lambayeque dep., **Peru**; mkt. ctr. for irrigated desert a. between Andes and Pac. Oc. producing mainly rice and sugar; p. (1993) 411,536.

Chicopee, t., Mass., **USA**; on Connecticut R. nr. Springfield; p. (1980) 55,112.

Chicoutimi, t., Quebec, **Canada**; pt. on Chicoutimi R.; lumber, pulp, paper; hydroelectric power; p. (1991) 62,670 (t.), (1986) 158,468 (met. a. with Jonquière).

Chiemsee, L., lge. lake nr. Munich, **Germany**; c. 460 m a.s.l.

Chieti, t., cap. of C. prov., S. **Italy**; cath.; anc. Teate Marrucinorum; Europe's lgst. glass plant, using methane from Abruzzi field; p. (1981) 54,927.

Chigrik, t., **Uzbekistan**; new t. (1963) 34 km S. of Tashkent.

Chigwell, t., Epping Forest, Essex, **Eng.**; on borders of Epping Forest; Hainault Estate now incorporated in Redbridge, Greater London; resdtl.; p. (1991) 10,332.

Chihli, Gulf of. See Pohai.

Chihuahua, lgst. st. in **Mexico**; dry climate impedes agr.; mng., cotton, cattle, Chihuahua dogs; a. 247,024 km²; p. (1990) 2,439,954.

Chihuahua, c., cap. Chihuahua st., **Mexico**; univ., cath.; ctr. silver-mng. ind.; p. (1990) 530,487.

Chikchi, peninsula, **Russia**; world's first Arctic nuclear power sta. being built.

Chikugo, t., N. Kyushu, **Japan**; lgst. coal mines in country; p. (1990) 43,835.

Chilaw, t., **Sri Lanka**; ctr. of coconut plantations.

Chile, rep., S. America; extends between Andes and Pac. for 4,160 km to C. Horn, E. to W. 400 km; Atacama desert; Spanish language; Roman Catholic; similar climate to that of Argentina but lacks space for extensive agr.; dairying, sheep, wool; ch. exp. nitrates, copper, iron-ore, coal, iodine, petroleum, paper; cap. San-

tiago; ch. pt. Valparaíso; earthquake 1960, hgst. recorded magnitude; domestic and foreign protests against human rights abuses of government; a. 738,494 km²; world's lgst. producer of copper; p. (1995) 13,292,200.

Chillán, t., **Chile**; destroyed 1939 by one of world's worst recorded earthquakes; since rebuilt; agr. and comm. ctr.; p. (1992) 158,731.

Chilpancingo de los Bravos, t., cap. of Guerrero st., **Mexico**; ctr. of pre-Aztec culture; univ.; p. (1990) 136,243.

Chiltern, l. gov. dist., Bucks., **Eng.**; inc. part of C. Hills and Chesham and Amersham; p. (1995) 92,400.

Chiltern Hills, chalk escarpment, Oxon., Bucks., Beds., and Herts., **Eng.**; cut by no. of impt. gaps used by main communications; sheep and barley; hgst. point 276 m nr. Wendover.

Chimborazo, mtn., **Ecuador**; 6,286 m; Andes; extinct volcano, first explored by von Humboldt (1802), first scaled by Whymper (1880).

Chimbote, spt., **Peru**; steel, iron-ore, coal; tinned fish, fish-meal; p. (1985) 255,000.

Chimkent (Shymkent), t., **Kazakhstan**; in W. foothills of Tien Shan; nearby oasis fed by Arys R.; major industl. ctr.; lead smelting; p. (1990) 400,900.

China, People's Republic of, Asia; Third lgst. cty. of world; 22 provs., 3 municipalities and 6 autonomous regions; anc. conservative civilisation overthrown by long civil war and establishment of communist régime (1949); lge. p. crowded on cultivable valleys of Hwang-ho (Yellow R.), Yangtze and Si-kiang in E.; rest of cty. either mtnous. (plateau of Tibet) or desert (Sinkiang); rapid economic growth following onset of communist régime; agr. organised on commune basis, becomes increasingly intensive in S. where climate is less extreme; vast mineral resources; esp. iron ore and coal, many underdeveloped; mineral fuels major export; recent industl. growth; heavy inds. at Wuhan, Baotou and in N.E. (Manchuria); special economic zones to attract foreign investment; poor communications except in E.; increasingly self-sufficient in petroleum; 1984 economic reform liberalised state planning system to allow mkt. forces to restructure all but key sectors; consumer goods and services to be expanded; cap. Beijing; 35 m. only children resulting from one-child family birth control policy; Hong Kong returned (1997); a. 9,597,129 km²; p. (1997) 1,220,000,000.

China Sea, part of W. Pacific between Korea and Philippines; divided by the narrow Formosa Strait into two areas; E. China Sea, inc. Yellow Sea, and S. China Sea.

Chinandega, mkt. t., cap. of C. dep., **Nicaragua**; sugar refining; p. (1985) 68,000.

Chincho. See Jinzhou.

Chindwin, R., **Myanmar**; ch. trib. of Irrawaddy; rises in Patkai Hills, navigable in rainy season; dense p. on lower reaches; 800 km long.

Chinghai. See Qinghai.

Chinkiang. See Zhenjiang.

Chingola, t., **Zambia**; copper mng.; metal prod., printing; p. (1989) 201,000.

Chinon, t., Indre-et-Loire, central **France**; on R. Vienne, industl.; ruined cas., once a royal residency; nuclear power sta.; p. (1982) 8,873 (t.), 78,131 (met. a.).

Chinqui, volcano, **Panama**; 3,480 m.

Chinwangtao. See Qinhuangdao.

Chioggia, spt., cath. t., N. **Italy**; on I. in G. of Venice; fishing; p. (1981) 53,566.

Chios (Khios) I., in Aegean Sea, **Greece**; mainly agr.; wines, fruits and figs; supposed birthplace of Homer; p. (1991) 52,184.

Chippenham, North Wilts., **Eng.**; mkt. t. on R. Avon; rly. signal and brake equipment, bacon curing, tanning; p. (1991) 25,961.

Chipping Campden, v., Gloucs., **Eng.**; in Cotswold Hills; formerly impt. for woollens; tourism; p. (1991) 1,741.

Chipping Norton, mkt. t., Oxford, **Eng.**; nr. Banbury; formerly impt. for woollens; p. (1991) 5,386.

Chipping Sodbury, mkt. t., S. Gloucs., **Eng.**; 13 km N.E. of Bristol; p. (1991) 31,973.

Chirchik, c., **Uzbekistan**; 32 km N.E. Tashkent; engin., chemicals; hydroelec. power stas.; p. (1990) 158,600.

Chiricahua Mtns., Arizona, **USA**; form part of Coronado Nat. Forest; long inhabited by Apache Indians; spectacular volcanic scenery; alt. 2,987 m.

Chirk, t., Wrexham, **Wales**; on R. Cleriog, S. of

Wrexham; slate, former coal mng. a.; cas.; p. (1991) 4,264.

Chislehurst. *See* **Bromley.**

Chistyakovo. *See* **Torez.**

Chita, c., rly. ctr., Siberia, **Russia;** on upper R. Ingoda, 640 km E. of L. Baykal; coal, engin., chemicals, sawmilling; p. (1989) 366,000.

Chittagong, c., **Bangladesh;** main pt. on Karna-fuli R., nr. Bay of Bengal; exp. jute, tea; oil refining; steel mill; hydroelec. power; p. (1991) 1,363,998.

Chittaranjan, t., West Bengal, **India;** new t. on Barakhar R., in steel ctr. of Damodar valley; rly. locomotive wks.; p. (1981) 50,748.

Chkalov. *See* **Orenburg.**

Choisy-le-Roi, t., Val-de-Marne dep., **France,** industl. sub. of Paris on R. Seine; p. (1982) 35,531.

Cholet, t., Maine-et-Loire, **France;** textile ctr. on R. Seine; p. (1990) 56,540.

Cholon (Cho Lon), t., S. **Vietnam;** 16 km S.W. of Ho Chi-minh City; ctr. of rice tr.

Cholula, anc. c. of Puebla prov., **Mexico;** Aztec temple, pyramid of Cholula, and other remains.

Chomo Lhari, mtn., Tibet, **China** and **Bhutan;** sacred to Buddhists; part of Himalayas; alt. 7,319 m.

Chomutov, t., N. Czech Rep.; industl. ctr. of lignite mng. a.; coal, steel, glass; p. (1984) 57,398.

Chongqing (Chungking), c., S.E. Sichuan prov., **China;** on Chang Jiang; comm. ctr. of W. China chosen 1983 as centre for experimental economic reforms; ctr. of rich agr. dist. of Red Basin of Sichuan; coal, iron and steel, heavy machin.; lorries, vans, chemical fertilisers; textiles; former treaty pt.; p. (1992) 3,010,000.

Cho Oyu, mtn., between **Nepal** and Tibet, **China;** sixth hgst. in world; alt. 8,225 m.

Chorley, t., l. gov. dist., N. Lancs., **Eng.;** on W. flank of Rossendale Fells, 11 km S.E. of Preston; cotton, engin.; expansion as new t. with Leyland; p. (1995) 97,000 (dist.), (1991) 33,536 (t.). *See* **Central Lancashire.**

Chorleywood, t., Three Rivers, Herts., **Eng.;** nr. Watford; p. (1991) 9,025.

Chorrilos Pass, Argentina; in E. cordillera of Andes at alt. 4,470 m; used by rly. from San Miguel de Tucumán to Antofagasta.

Chorzów(Królewska Huta), t., Katowice, **Poland;** coal, iron and steel, chemicals, engin.; p. (1989) 131,850.

Chota Nagpur, plateau, Madhya Pradesh, **India;** produces lac; impt. mng. ctr.; bauxite, mica.

Chou Kou Tien, site nr. Beijing, **China;** discovery of fossil bones of Beijing (Peking) man (*Sinanthropus pekinensis*).

Christchurch, t., l. gov. dist., Dorset, **Eng.;** on S. cst. 8 km E. of Bournemouth; holiday resort, aircraft, lt. inds.; p. (1995) 43,100 (dist.), (1991) 36,379 (t.).

Christchurch, c., Canterbury region, S.I., **N.Z.;** lgst. c. of S.I.; comm. ctr. for lamb, wool, and grain; cath., univ.; airpt; p. (1991) 292,858 (c), 307,179 (met. a.).

Christianshåb, Danish settlement on Disko Bay, **W. Greenland;** meteorological sta.; p. (1990) 1,712.

Christmas I., in Indian Oc., external terr. of **Australia** since 1958; a. 140 km², healthy climate, phosphate deposits; p. (1990) 2,500.

Christmas I., lge. coral atoll in Pac. Oc., one of Line Is.; discovered by Cook 1777; a. 135 km²; nuclear test site, 1957–64.

Chu, R. **Kazakhstan;** rises in Tien Shan flows N.W. for 800 km into inland drainage basin; Chumysh Dam provides hydroelectricity and water for cultivation of cotton, sugar-beet, citrus fruits.

Chuanchow. *See* **Quauzhu.**

Chubut, R., **Argentina;** drains from Andes into Atl. Oc.; continual irrigation reducing soil fertility of valley; 640 km long.

Chubut, prov., **Argentina;** cap. Rawson; p. (1991) 357,189.

Chuchow. *See* **Zhuzhou.**

Chudleigh, mkt. t., Devon, **Eng.;** on R. Teign; stone quarrying; p. (1991) 3,046.

Chu-kiang. *See* **Zhujiang.**

Chukotskiy, peninsula, **Russia;** extreme N.E.; rich gold deposit; hunting.

Chukyo, industl. area, Honshu, **Japan;** centred on Nagoya; textiles, ceramics, chemicals.

Chula Vista, t., Cal., **USA;** agr., aircraft; p. (1990) 135,163.

Chungking *See* **Chongqing.**

Chuquibamba Mtns. (alt. c. 6,400 m), Peru.

Chuquicamata, t., N. Chile; 3,050 m in Andes; lgst copper mine in world.

Chuquisaca, dep. **Bolivia;** oil, agr.; cap. Sucre; a.

51,524 km²; p. (1988) 442,600.

Chur (Coire), t., cap. Graubünden, **Switzerland;** in valley of upper Rhine; historic bldgs.; fruit, wine, tourist ctr.; p. (1990) 30,975.

Church, Hyndburn, sub. of Accrington, Lancs., **Eng.;** engin.; p. (1991) 4,277.

Churchill, R., formerly Hamilton R., flows into Hamilton inlet, cst. of Labrador, **Canada;** magnificent waterfall, Churchill Falls with lge. hydroelec. scheme.

Church Stretton, mkt. t., Shrops., **Eng.;** tourism; p. (1991) 3,435.

Chusan I. *See* **Zhousan.**

Chuvash, aut. rep., **Russia;** in middle Volga valley; arable agr., lumbering, food processing; a. 18,407 km²; p. (1989) 1,338,000.

Cibao, lowland a., **Dominican Rep.,** Central America; extends along N. side of Cordillera de Cibao for 180 km; 16–56 km wide; early a. of Spanish settlement; E. part called Vega Real; richest agr. a. of Hispaniola; cacao, tobacco, maize; dense p.; ch. t. Santiago.

Cicero, t., Ill., **USA;** adjoins Chicago; electrical appliances, hardware; p. (1980) 61,232.

Ciechanów, t. and prov., **Poland;** 78 km N.W. of Warsaw; agr. inds.; p. (1989) 43,068 (t.), 425,600 (prov.).

Cienfuegos, t., **Cuba;** sugar, tobacco; picturesque; nuclear power sta.; p. (1990) 123,600.

Cieszyn, t., Bielsko-Biala prov., **Poland;** part of former Teschen on Polish side of frontier with Czech Republic; p. (1989) 36,682.

Cimpina, t., **Romania,** in Walachia; petroleum ctr.; oil pipeline links to Ploiesti and Constanta on Black Sea.

Cincinnati, c. Ohio, **USA;** route and comm. ctr. on terraces of Ohio R.; food processing and many varied inds.; univs.; p. (1990) 364,040 (c.), 1,452,645 (met. a.).

Cinderford, t., Gloucs., **Eng.;** former ctr. of coalmng. a. of Forest of Dean; new lt. industl. estate; p. (1991) 9,566.

Cinque Ports, confederation of anc. Eng. pts. on cst. of Kent and Sussex; original 5: Sandwich, Dover, Hythe, Romney, Hastings; Winchelsea, and Rye added later.

Cirencester, t., Cotswold, Gloucs., **Eng.;** Roman Corineum; former woollen t.; p. (1991) 15,221.

Ciskei, S. Africa; new cap. Bisho; former cap. Zwelitsha; p. (1985) 750,000.

Citta di Castello, walled t., **Italy;** in upper Tiber valley; impt. in Roman times; Renaissance cath., palaces; p. (1981) 37,242.

Citta Vecchia (Mdina), c., central **Malta;** former cap.; Roman remains; cath.

Ciudad Bolivar, c., Bolivar st., **Venezuela;** pt. on Orinoco R.; formerly called Angostura; coffee, cattle; ctr. of new industl. development on lower Orinoco; p. (1990) 225,846.

Ciudad del Este, t., **Paraguay;** rapidly growing t. close to Itaipú Dam on Parana R.; p. (1992) 133,893.

Ciudad Guayana, c., Bolivar st., **Venezuela;** spt. on R. Orinoco; heavy inds. ctr.; p. (1981) 314,000.

Ciudad Juarez, c., **Mexico;** comm. ctr. on USA border; agr. processing; tourism; p. (1990) 797,679.

Ciudad Madero, t., **Mexico;** styrene and detergent plants, oil refining; p. (1990) 159,644.

Ciudad Obregón, t., Sonora, **Mexico;** on Yaqui R.; ctr. of irrigated agr. a.; p. (1979) 181,733.

Ciudad Real, c., cap. of Ciudad Real prov., **Spain;** mkt. t. founded 1255; textiles; p. (1987) 55,072.

Ciudad Real, prov., central **Spain;** mostly at 600 m; covering la Mancha dist.; agr.; cap. C.R.; a. 19,741 km²; p. (1991) 467,242.

Ciudad Rodrigo, old fortress t., Salamanca prov., **Spain;** strategic position nr. Portuguese bdy.; in Peninsular War fell to Fr. (1810) and captured by Wellington (1812).

Civitavecchia, t. Latium, **Italy;** pt. for Rome on Tyrrhenian cst., 48 km N. of mouth of R. Tiber; p. (1981) 45,836.

Clackmannan, t., central Scot., unit. auth. created in 1996, reinstating historic co. of Clackmannanshire which became part of Central Region in 1974; bordered S.W. by R. Forth; ch. t. Alloa; p. (1991) 3,420 (t.), (1995) 48,820 (unit. auth.).

Clacton-on-Sea, t., Tendring, Essex, **Eng.;** on E. cst. 19 km S.E. of Colchester; seaside resort; lt. inds.; residtl.; p. (1991) 45,085.

Clairvaux, v., Aube, **France;** Cistercian abbey.

Clamart, t., Hauts-de-Seine, **France;** sub. of S.W. Paris; p. (1982) 48,678.

Clapham, S. London rly. junction; accident 1988.

Atlas of the World

Contents

Symbols

——— Principal Railways   ━ ━ ━ Internal Boundaries

═══ Motorways

——— Principal Roads   4125 Heights in Metres

▬▬▬ International Boundaries   ☼ Principal Airports

Height of Land

Cartography by Philip's, Copyright 1999 George Philip Ltd.

2

WORLD : Political

3

ARCTIC OCEAN
New Siberian Is.
Novaya Zemlya
SWEDEN FINLAND
Helsinki
St. Petersburg
Arkhangelsk
RUSSIA
Bering Sea
Stockholm
Moscow
Yekaterinburg
Novosibirsk
Copenhagen
POLAND Warsaw
Berlin
Vienna
Kiev
UKRAINE
KAZAKHSTAN
Irkutsk
Ulan Bator
Vladivostok
Sapporo
ROMANIA
Bucharest
BULGARIA
GREECE
Istanbul
UZBEKISTAN
Tashkent
MONGOLIA
Peking
KOREA JAPAN
Dalian
Tokyo
Athens
CYPRUS
SYRIA
TURKEY
Baku
TURKMENISTAN
CHINA
ASIA
Pusan
Osaka
Mediterranean Sea
LEB. Baghdad
ISRAEL IRAQ
Tehran
Islamabad
Kabul
Chungking
Shanghai
Tripoli
LIBYA
Alexandria
EGYPT
Cairo
KUWAIT
IRAN
PAKISTAN
Karachi
NEPAL
Delhi
BHUT.
BANGLA-
DESH
Dacca
BURMA
TAIWAN
Hong Kong
PACIFIC
Tropic of Cancer
Wake I.
(U.S.)
OCEAN
Red Sea
BAHRAIN
QATAR
U.A.E.
Mecca
SAUDI
ARABIA
OMAN
INDIA
Ahmadabad
Calcutta
Hanoi
Hue
VIETNAM
Manila
Northern
Marianas
(U.S.)
Guam
(U.S.)
MARSHALL IS.
NIGER
CHAD
Khartoum
SUDAN
YEMEN
Bombay
Arabian
Sea
Madras
Bay of
Bengal
Rangoon
THAILAND
Bangkok
CAM-
BODIA
Ho Chi Minh
City
PHILIPPINES
Kano
N'Djamena
ERITREA
DJIB.
Addis Ababa
ETHIOPIA
SOMALI
REP.
Colombo
SRI LANKA
Phnom
Penh
FEDERATED STATES
OF MICRONESIA
KIRIBATI
NIGERIA
Abuja
CAMEROON
Douala
CENTRAL
AFRICAN
REPUBLIC
Mogadishu
KENYA
MALDIVES
INDIAN
Padang
Sumatra
MALAYSIA
Kuala
Lumpur
SINGAPORE
BRUNEI
Borneo
Equator
GABON
DEM. REP. OF
THE CONGO
Kinshasa
Nairobi
RWANDA
BURUNDI
Mombasa
TANZANIA
Dar-es-Salaam
SEYCHELLES
OCEAN
Jakarta
Surabaya
INDONESIA
New
Guinea
PAPUA
NEW GUINEA
SOLOMON IS.
TUVALU
Luanda
CABINDA
ANGOLA
ZAMBIA
COMOROS
Port Moresby
VANUATU
FIJI
Harare
ZIMBABWE
Antananarivo
MADAGASCAR
MAURITIUS
Darwin
Coral
Sea
New
Caledonia
(Fr.)
NAMIBIA
BOTSWANA
MOZAMBIQUE
Reunion
(Fr.)
Alice Springs
AUSTRALIA
Tropic of Capricorn
Johannesburg
SOUTH
AFRICA
SWAZ.
Durban
Perth
Brisbane
Cape Town
Adelaide
Sydney
Canberra
Melbourne
Auckland
NEW
ZEALAND
Crozet Is.
(Fr.)
Kerguelen Is.
(Fr.)
Tasmania
Hobart
Christchurch
Dunedin

DEPENDENCY
Greenwich
AUSTRALIAN DEPENDENCY
ADELIE LAND

30 25 20 15 10 5 0 5 10 15

ICELAND
Reykjavík Akureyri Húsavík

Arctic Circle

Tro

Narvi

60

ATLANTIC OCEAN

Faroe Is.
(Dan.)

Shetland
Is.

Kristiansund
Trondheim
Östersund
Su

NORWAY

Inda

55

UNITED
KINGDOM

Hebrides

Inverness
Aberdeen
Dundee
SCOTLAND
Glasgow
Edinburgh

Orkney
Is.

Sogne Fd.
Bergen
Lillehammer
Hardanger Fd.
Stavanger
Skagerrak

Kattegat

Z. Oslo
Drammen
Vänern
Örebro
Göteborg
Jönköping

Uppsala
Eskil

SWEDEN

Vättern
Kalmar

Londonderry
N.I.
Belfast
REP.
OF IRELAND
Galway
Limerick
Dublin
Cork
C. Clear

I. of Man
Carlisle
Newcastle
York
Leeds
Hull
Sheffield
Liverpool
Manchester
ENGLAND

NORTH
SEA

DENMARK
Aalborg
Aarhus
COPENHAGEN
Esbjerg
Flensburg
Kiel

Karlskrona
Malmö

BALT

50

Swansea
WALES
Cardiff
Bristol
Birmingham
Norwich
Cambridge
LONDON
Southampton
Portsmouth
Plymouth
Scilly Is.
Ushant.

Amsterdam
Groningen
NETHER-
The Hague
Rotterdam
LANDS

Bremen
Hanover
Hamburg
Elbe
Magdeburg

Rostock
Szczecin
BERLIN
Poz

Gdynia
Gdań
Byd

POL

English Channel
Dover
Calais
Ostend
Le Havre
Cherbourg
Rouen
Brest
Rennes
Caen
Lille
BELGIUM
BRUSSELS
Antwerp
LUX
Reims
Le Mans
PARIS
Loire
Orléans
Metz
Strasbourg

GERMANY
Essen
Dortmund
Cologne
Frankfurt
Wiesbaden
Bonn
Würzburg
Nuremberg
Stuttgart

Halle
Leipzig
Chemnitz
Dresden

PRAGUE
Plzen
Brno
CZECH REP.
Katow
Wro

45

Nantes
FRANCE
Tours
Limoges
Clermont
Ferrand
St. Etienne
Lyons
Grenoble
Bordeaux
Dordogne
Garonne
Toulouse
Perigueux

Dijon
Mulhouse
Basel
Bern
SWITZERLAND
Geneva
Zürich
Freiburg
Munich
Salzburg
Innsbruck
Linz

VIENNA
Brat
SLO
AUSTRIA
Graz
BUDAPEST
HUN

BAY OF BISCAY

A Coruña
Finisterre
Vigo
Oviedo
Oporto
Santander
Bilbao
San Sebastian
Pamplona

Montpellier
Sète
Avignon
Manosque
Nîmes
Marseilles
Toulon
Nice
Cannes

Milan
Brescia
Turin
Genoa
La Spezia
Trento
Bologna
Venice
Trieste
SLOV
Ljubljana
Zagreb

ADRIATIC SE
CROATIA

40

Coimbra
PORTUGAL
Douro
Duero
Valladolid
Ebro
Zaragoza
SPAIN
MADRID
Toledo
Tagus
Guadiana
Badajoz

Andorra
Perpignan

Barcelona
Valencia
Balearic Is.
Minorca

Corsica
Ajaccio

Sardinia
Sassari

Florence
Livorno
San
Marino
Ravenna
Ancona
ITALY
Tiber
ROME
Naples

Split
Sarajev
BOSNIA
Dubrov
Bari
Taranto
Bru

LISBON
Lagos
Sevilla
Córdoba
Guadalquivir
Cádiz
Málaga
Granada
Almería
Murcia
Alicante
Cartagena
Str. of
Gibraltar
Gibraltar(Br.)
Tangier
Ceuta(Sp.)

Ibiza
Palma
Majorca

MEDITERRANEAN

Cagliari

Tyrrhenian Sea

Palermo
Messina
Réggio di Calc
Sicily
Catania

Ionia

35

Rabat
Fès
Meknes
MOROCCO
Melilla(Sp.)
Oran
Tlemcen
ALGERIA
Blida
Algiers
Skikda
Annaba
Constantine
Bizerte
Tunis
TUNISIA
Sousse

Pantelleria
(Ital.)
MALTA

Pe

5 West from Greenwich 0 East from Greenwich 5 10 15

5

EUROPE

0   100   200   300   400 miles
0   200   400   600 km

E.U. Members & Populations

Austria	8,200,000	Italy	57,750,000
Belgium	10,225,000	Luxembourg	425,000
Denmark	5,350,000	Netherlands	15,900,000
Finland	5,180,000	Portugal	10,100,000
France	58,800,000	Spain	39,300,000
Germany	82,300,000	Sweden	8,850,000
Greece	10,600,000	U.K.	58,600,000
Ireland	3,625,000		

ENGLAND AND WALES

| 0 | 20 | 40 | 60 miles |
| 0 | 20 40 | 60 | 80 | 100 km |

Unitary Authorities

19. Poole
20. Bournemouth
21. Southampton
22. Portsmouth
23. Brighton & Hove
24. Medway Towns
25. Thurrock
26. Southend-on-Sea
27. Wokingham
28. Bracknell Forest
29. Reading
30. Windsor & Maidenhead
31. Slough
32. Swindon
33. Luton
34. Milton Keynes
35. Leicester City
36. Rutland
37. Peterborough
38. Telford & Wrekin
39. Derby City
40. City of Nottingham
41. Stoke-on-Trent
42. Halton
43. Warrington
44. North East Lincolnshire
45. Kingston upon Hull
46. City of York
47. Blackburn with Darwen
48. Blackpool
49. Darlington
50. Stockton-on-Tees
51. Middlesbrough
52. Redcar & Cleveland
53. Hartlepool

Unitary Authorities

1. Swansea
2. Neath Port Talbot
3. Rhondda Cynon Taff
4. Bridgend
5. Merthyr Tydfil
6. Caerphilly
7. Vale of Glamorgan
8. Cardiff
9. Blaenau Gwent
10. Torfaen
11. Newport
12. Monmouthshire
13. South Gloucestershire
14. City of Bristol
15. North Somerset
16. Bath and N.E. Somerset
17. Plymouth
18. Torbay

West from Greenwich

East from Greenwich

COPYRIGHT GEORGE PHILIP & SON LTD.

FRANCE

ENGLISH CHANNEL

St. George's Channel

Cardigan Bay

8

SCOTLAND

0   20   40   60 miles
0 20 40 60 80 100 km

ATLANTIC OCEAN

Unitary Authorities

1. City of Aberdeen
2. Dundee City
3. West Dunbartonshire
4. East Dunbartonshire
5. City of Glasgow
6. Inverclyde
7. Renfrewshire
8. East Renfrewshire
9. North Lanarkshire
10. Falkirk
11. Clackmannan
12. West Lothian
13. City of Edinburgh
14. Midlothian

SHETLAND

Shetland Is.

Unst
Yell   Fetlar
Whalsay
Mainland
Bressay
Lerwick
Foula

Rona

On same scale   Sumburgh Hd.

Mainland

Sumburgh Hd.

Fair Isle

N. Ronaldsay
Westray
Rousay   Sanday
Eday
Shapinsay
ORKNEY   Stronsay
Mainland   Orkney Is.
Kirkwall
Hoy   South
Ronaldsay

Pentland Firth

C. Wrath   Strathy Pt.   Dunnet Hd.   John
o'Groats
Ben Hope   Thurso   Noss Hd.
927   Dounreay
Wick

NORTH

SEA

Butt of Lewis

L. Laxford

Eddrachillis Bay

B. More
Assynt 998

WESTERN
Lewis
Stornoway   Broad Bay
Harris
Tarbert

North Minch

Little Minch

ISLES
North Uist
Monach
Is.
Benbecula

South Uist

Barra

Barra Hd.

The Aird

Enard Bay
L. Assynt
Loch Shin
Lairg
L. Broom   Ullapool
B. Dearg
1081
L. Ewe   Fannich   Ben Wyvis
1045
Strome-
ferry

Golspie
Dornoch   Helmsdale
Dornoch Firth
Tarbat Ness
Tain
Invergordon
Cromarty
Dingwall
Conon   Nairn   Forres   Elgin   Buckie
Beauly   Inverness   Keith   Buchan
MORAY

Ord of Caithness

Moray Firth

Banff   Fraserburgh
Turriff
Peterhead
Huntly

Kinnairds Hd.

S. Sutor
Portree
Raasay
Kyle
Lochalsh
Cuillin
Hills
Cuillin Sound
Canna
Rhum
Eigg
Muck
Ardnamurchan
Point
Tobermory
Coll
Tiree
Staffa
Iona

Monach
Is.
Ben More
619

HIGHLAND
Glen Affric
Glen Moriston
L. Arkaig
Mallaig
L. Morar
Ben Nevis
1343
Fort
William
Ardgour
L. Shiel

Grantown-
on-Spey
Cairn Gorm
Cairngorm Mts.
1245
Ben Macdhui
Badenoch
Kingussie
Braemar
Balmoral Castle

Ballater
Banchory

ABERDEENSHIRE   Aberdeen
Don
Girdle Ness
Stonehaven

Loch
Hourn
Sound of Sleat
Kyle
of Skye

North West Highlands

Grampian Mountains

Brae   Mar
Braes of Angus
Cairn a' Craig
Lochnagar   ANGUS   Brechin
Pass of
Killiecrankie
Montrose
Pitlochry   Forfar

Drumochter

SCOTLAND

L. Rannoch
Ben Lawers
1214
L. Tay
Aberfeldy
Blairgowrie

Morvern
Sound of Mull
Mull
B. More
966
Loch Linnhe
Ben Cruachan
1124
Oban
L. Awe
Inveraray
B. Vorlich
Colonsay

Breadalbane
Crieff
Killin
Earn
L. Earn
Ben More
983
Ben Vorlich
L. Katrine
Trossachs
Loch
Lomond
Ben Lomond
974

KINROSS
Scone   Carse of Gowrie
Perth   FIFE
St. Andrews
Cupar
Leven   Fife Ness
Kinross   Anstruther
Buckhaven
Glenrothes
Kirkcaldy
Dunfermline   Bass Rock

PERTH &

Dundee
Firth of Tay
Newport
Carnoustie
Arbroath

ARGYLL &

Lochgilphead
Crinan

BUTE
Rothesay

Rudh a' Mhail
Islay
Bowmore
Gigha

Helensburgh
Dumbarton   Stirling
Dunoon
Greenock
Port Glasgow
Paisley
Clydebank
Glasgow
Largs
Ardrossan
Saltcoats
Irvine
Kilmarnock
Prestwick
Ayr

STIRLING
Alloa
Falkirk   LOTHIAN   Dunbar
Grangemouth
Knockburn
Coatbridge   Edinburgh
Motherwell   Leith
Wishaw   Musselburgh   Haddington
Carstairs   Dalkeith
Moorfoot
Hills
Lanark   Peebles
Hamilton

EAST
SOUTH
LANARK-
SHIRE
Broad
Law 840

SCOTTISH

BORDERS
Galashiels
Coldstream
Selkirk
Hawick
Jedburgh   Kelso

St. Abb's Hd.

Berwick-upon-
Tweed

Holy I.
Farne Is.

The Cheviot
816

AYRSHIRE
Goat Fell
874
Arran
Brodick
EAST
SOUTH
AYRSHIRE
Sanquhar
Girvan

Firth of Clyde

Rathlin I.
Fair Hd.
Mull of
Kintyre
Campbeltown

North Channel

Giants Causeway
Portrush
Moville
Coleraine
Ballymoney
NORTHERN
Ballymena
IRELAND
Antrim
Lough Neagh
Belfast
Bangor

Ballycastle
Larne
Carrickfergus

Merrick
843   Cross
Nith
New
Galloway

DUMFRIES
AND
GALLOWAY
Dumfries
Castle
Douglas
Kirkcudbright   Kirkcudbright Firth

Southern Uplands

Cheviot Hills

Alnwick
Coquet
Morpeth
Newcastle
Blaydon
Gateshead

Pennines

Cross Fell
893
Skiddaw
931
Keswick
Penrith

ENGLAND

Bishop
Auckland
Durham

Stranraer
Portpatrick
Wigtown
Mull of Galloway
Luce
Bay
Wigtown Bay

Solway Firth

Gretna Green   Tyne
Carlisle
Maryport   Derwent
Workington

Spelga Mts.
Slieve
Sawel
683

West from Greenwich

COPYRIGHT. GEORGE PHILIP & SON, LT

IRELAND

0	20	40		60	miles
0	20	40	60	80	100 km

ATLANTIC

OCEAN

SCOTLAND

Tiree
Staffa
B. More
Mull
996
Iona
Oban

Lochgilphead
Colonsay
Rudh a' Mhail

Bowmore
Islay
Gigha
Arran

Campbeltown

Giant's Causeway
Malin Hd.
Rathlin I.
Portrush
Fair Hd.
Mull of
Kintyre

Tory I.
Sheep Haven
Horn Hd.
Lough Swilly
Inishowen Pen.
Moville
Bloody Foreland
Bunbeg
Ballycastle
Ballymoney
Trostan
554
North Channel

Aran I.
Errigal
752
Derryveagh Mts.
Letterkenny
Coleraine
Ballymena
Larne

Gweebarra B.
DONEGAL
Glenties
Finn
Lifford
Londonderry
Strabane
Sperrin Mts.
Sawel
683
Carrickfergus

Loughros More B.
676
Bluestack
Bangor
Rossan Pt.
Rathlin O'Birne I.
Killybegs
Donegal
ULSTER
Omagh
NORTHERN
IRELAND
Lough
Neagh
Belfast
Newtownards

Donegal Bay
Ballyshannon
Lower
L. Erne
Dungannon
Portadown
(Craigavon)
Lurgan
Lisburn

Broad Haven
Erris Hd.
Killala Bay
Sligo B.
Sligo
LEITRIM
Enniskillen
Upper
L. Erne
Erne
Black
ARMAGH
Armagh
Banbridge
Downpatrick
Ards
Ardglass

Mullet
Peninsula
Ballina
Moy
SLIGO
L. Allen
Leitrim
Monaghan
MONAGHAN
Newry
Slieve
Gullion
852
Mourne Mts.
Dundrum
Bay

Blacksod Bay
Nephin
806
L. Conn
CAVAN
Cootehill
Castleblayney
Carlingford L.
Newcastle
Warrenpoint

Achill
Head
Achill I.
Castlebar
MAYO
Boyle
Carrick-on-Shannon
Cavan
L. Gowna
Louth
LOUTH
Dundalk
Dundalk
Bay

Clare I.
Clew Bay
765
Croagh Patrick
819
Westport
Mweelrea
ROSCOMMON
L. Mask
Claremorris
Longford
Sheelin
Ceananus Mor
(Kells)
Ardee
Drogheda

Inishbofin
Killary Harbour
Twelve Pins
Connemara
L. Corrib
Tuam
Roscommon
LONGFORD
L. Ree
Inny
WESTMEATH
An Uaimh
(Navan)
MEATH
Balbriggan

Slyne Hd.
GALWAY
Athenry
REPUBLIC
Athlone
Mullingar
Boyne
Maynooth
Howth Hd.
DUBLIN
Dublin (Baile Atha
Cliath)

Galway
Ballinasloe
Clare
Tullamore
L. Allen
Celbridge
Naas
Kippure
754
Dun
Laoghaire

Kilkieran B.
Inishmore
Galway Bay
Gort
Loughrea
OFFALY
Brosna
Birr
St. Bloom
Mountmellick
Portlaoise
KILDARE
Kildare
Poulaphouca
Res.
Bray

Aran Is.
Slieve Aughty
L. Derg
LEINSTER
LAOIS
Rosecrea
Athy
WICKLOW
Lugnaquilla
923
Wicklow

Liscannor Bay
Mal Bay
CLARE
Ennis
IRELAND
Nenagh
Nore
CARLOW
Carlow
Muine Bheag
Mizen Hd.
Arklow

Kilkee
Kilrush
Rathkeale
Foynes
Keeper
694
Thurles
TIPPERARY
Kilkenny
KILKENNY
Mt. Leinster
796
Gorey

Loop Hd.
Shannon
Listowel
LIMERICK
Limerick
Golden Vale
Tipperary
Sl. Naman
722
Enniscorthy
WEXFORD

Brandon Hd.
Tralee Bay
Fenit
Rath Luirc
(Charleville)
MUNSTER
Galtymore
920
Caher
Carrick-on-Suir
Clonmel
New Ross
Wexford Harbour
Rosslare

Brandon Hill
953
Dingle
Sl. Mish
Tralee
Mitchelstown
Knockmealdown
Mts.
Comeragh Mts.
Waterford
Greenore Pt.
Tuscar Rock
Carnsore Pt.

Great
Blasket
KERRY
Killarney
Mallow
Blackwater
Fermoy
Dungarvan
Dungarvan Bay
Tramore
Saltee Is.

Dingle Bay
Macgillycuddy's
Reeks
Lakes of
Killarney
Boggeragh Mts.
CORK
Cork
Youghal
Midleton
Youghal Harbour

Valentia
Harbour
Carrantuohill
1040
Kenmare
Macroom
Lee
Cobh

Valentia I.
Cahirciveen
Caha Mts.
Bandon
Clonakilty
Cork Harbour

Ball inskelligs
Kenmare River
Castletown Berehaven
Bantry
Old Head of Kinsale

Crow Head
Dunmanus Bay
Bantry Bay
Baltimore
Clonakilty Bay
Galley Hd.

Mizen Hd.
Clear I.
Fastnet Rock
Clear

St. George's Channel

FRANCE

0 20 40 60 80 100 miles
0 40 80 120 160 km

Swansea Newport
Cardiff   Bristol Bath   Swindon LONDON   Southend
Taunton   Marg
E N G L A N D
Southampton   Folkestone Dove
Exeter Exmouth   Chichester Brighton Hastings C. Gris
Torquay Weymouth Bournemouth Ryde Portsmouth Newhaven Nez Boulogne
St. Ives Truro Plymouth Dartmouth Portland   Montre
Land's Falmouth Eddystone
End Penzance   Somme
50   Le Tréport
E N G L I S H   C H A N N E L   Dieppe St. Valery Fécamp
C. de la Hague   Caux Yvetot S.Me.
Alderney Cherbourg Pte. de Barfleur Valognes Le Havre Bolbec Roue
Guernsey St. Peter   Trouville Honfleur Elbeuf Be
Channel Is. Sark Port   Bessin Bayeux Lisieux Ve
(Br.) Jersey St. Lo Caen Falaise Evreux Mantes
St. Helier Mt.St. Vire o Or. Perche Ver
Granville Michel Avranches Or. Dreux E.L.
Ushant   Morlaix Guingamp St. Malo Dinard Alençon Mayenne Chartres
Brest Mts. St. Brieuc Dinan Fougères   Béa
Pte. de Bd'Arree Rennes M A I N E
St. Mathieu F. R I.V. Laval May. Le Mans Orlé
48 Pte. du Raz Mts. Noire Vilaine Sarthe O LC
Quimper Mo. Châteaubriant Loir SA
Pte. de Penmarch Quimperlé Lorient Vannes A M. R Tours TOURAINE
Carnac Angers Loire Amboise
Quiberon N Saumur I.L. Loches
Belle I. St. Nazaire Nantes Cholet Chinon
Loire e Châtellerault Châteauroux
Ile de Noirmoutier D.S. Creuse
Ile d'Yeu La Roche P O I T O U Poitiers
Les Sables d'Olonne Fontenay Catinou Vi.
46 Ile de Ré Niort MA
B A Y La Rochelle H.V.
O F Ile d' Oléron A U N I S Limoges
Rochefort ANGOUMOIS
B I S C A Y Saintes Uzerche
Royan Cognac Angoulême L I M
Le Verdon Ch. Périgueux
Médoc D Perigord
Libourne Sarlat
Bordeaux Gi. Bergerac G U Y Lo
Arcachon Garonne Dordogne Cahors
44 L.G.
L. Agen T.G.
Mont-de-Marsan G A S C O N Y
Gulf of Armagnac Auch M
Gascony Adour Ge. Toulouse
Gijón Biarritz Orthez G.H.
Llanes Bayonne P.A. Pau
Oviedo Getxo Gernika-Lumo Hendaya B E A R N Tarbes
Picos de Sestao Bilbao Donostia- Lourdes H.P. Pyréné Ari.
Europa 2648 Durango San Sebastián Roncesvalles Pic du Midi Bigorre
Sa. de Alba Reinosa Tolosa Ronces Vielha 2887 Mt. Perdu Andorra
Vitoria- Pamplona Canfranc P. 3355 N La Cer
Léon Gasteiz Miranda Jaca 160
Saldaña Pancorbo S P A I N
Astorga S Logroño Tafalla
Sahagún Burgos A R
West from Greenwich   East from Greenwich

11

12

NETHERLANDS

0   10   20   30   40   50 miles
0   20   40   60   80 km

NORTH SEA

WEST FRISIAN ISLANDS

Norderney
Juist
Borkum
Rottumeroog
Schiermonnikoog
Ameland
Terschelling
West Terschelling
Vlieland
Texel
Den Burg

Norddeich
Norden
Uithuizen
R Ems
R Delfzijl
Zoutkamp
Holwerd
Dokkum
Bergum
Zuidhorn
Groningen
Slochteren
Winsc
Hoogezand
Veendam
Onstwedde
Stadskanaal

Leeuwarden
Franeker
Harlingen
Bolsward
Sneek FRIESLAND
Heerenveen
Drachten
Wolvega
Den Oever
Hippolytushoef
Schagen
Medemblik
Workum
Stavoren
Lemmer
Steenwijk
Assen
Borge
Beilen
Ter
Apelo
DRENTHE
Hoogeveen
Emmen
Emlichheim

Den Helder

IJsselmeer
HOLLAND
Enkhuizen
Noordoost-Polder
Urk
Vollenhove
Meppel
Coevorden
Hardenberg
Ommen
Vechte
Hardenberg
Bellingwolde
Nordhorn

Bergen
Alkmaar
Hoorn
Edam
Marken
Monnikendam
Volendam
FLEVOLAND
Lelystad
Kampen
Zwolle
Elburg
Heerde
Hellendoorn
Wierden
Almelo
Oldenzaal
OVERIJSSEL

Beverwijk
IJmuiden
Haarlem
Zandvoort
Heemstede
Velsen
AMSTERDAM
Bussum
Harderwijk
Ermelo
Epe
Deventer
Rijssen
Hengelo
Gronau

Noordwijk
Katwijk-aan-Zee
Wassenaar
Scheveningen
THE HAGUE
Hoek van Holland
Leiden
Hilversum
Soest
Amersfoort
Baarn
Nijkerk
Putten 107
Apeldoorn
Zutphen
Goor
Enschede

Voorburg
Delft
Rijswijk
Utrecht
Gouda
Zeist
Veenendaal
Barneveld
Ede
Rheden
Dieren
GELDERLAND
Ruurlo
Locnem
Winterswijk
Ahaus
Stadtlohn

Rijn
Oude
Rijn
Lek
EUROPOORT
Vlaardingen
Hellevoetsluis
Maassluis
Schiedam
ROTTERDAM
Wageningen
Tiel
Waal
Renkum
Arnhem
Doetinchem
Aalten
Bocholt
Borker

Ouddorp
Brouwershaven
Goeree
Over
Flakkee
ZUID
Dordrecht
Gorinchem
Geldermalsen
Oss
Nijmegen
Emmerich
Kleve
Rhein
Goch
Xanten
Wesel
Dorsten

Schouwen
Noord Beveland
Domburg
Zierikzee
R HOLLAND B R A
's-Hertogenbosch
Jennep
Niers
Geldern
Gelsenkirchen
Bottrop

Walcheren
Middelburg
Flushing
Goes
Bergen-op-Zoom
Oosterhout
Vught
Boxtel
Veghel
Venray
Maas
Oberhausen
DUISBURG
ESS
Mülhe

Breskens
Sluis
Westerschelde
Terneuzen
Oosterschelde
Roosendaal
Baarle
Nassau
Essen
Tilburg
Eindhoven
Helmond
Deurne
Geldrop
Venlo
Tegelen
Krefeld
DÜSSELDORF

Maldegem
Eekloo
Hulst
Brasschaat
Merksem
Turnhout
Mol
Overpelt
Weert
Valkenswaard
Viersen
Mönchen-gladbach
Neuss
Solingen
Rheydt

Zelzate
Zomergem
St. Niklaas
ANTWERP
Deurne
Lier
Herentals
Nethe
Maaseik
Roermond
Leopoldsburg
Gladbach
GERMANY
Leverkusen

Ghent
Boom
Hoboken
Mechelen
Diest
Beringen 95
Sittard
Brunssum
Geilenkirchen
Bergheim

Lys
Wetteren
Dendermonde
Aalst
Asse
Vilvoorde
Aarschot
Hasselt
Genk
Geleen
Jülich
COLOGNE
Heerlen

Denze
Ninove
Leuven
Tienen
Maastricht
Sittard
Kerkrade
Eschweiler
Brühl

Oudenaarde
Ronse
Geeraards-bergen
Holle
BRABANT
Landen
Tongeren
Aachen
Zülpich
Düren
Bonn

Lessines
Enghien
Waterloo
Wavre
St. Trond
Visé
Herstal
Raeren
Euskirchen
Rheinbach

Tournai
Ath
Soignies
Nivelles
Gembloux
Namur
Liège
Verviers
Eupen
Mechernich
Münstereifel
Schleiden
Ahrweiler

BELGIUM
Leuze
157
HAINAUT
Mons
Jumet
Charleroi
Huy
Andenne
Ohey
Seraing
Spa 694
Malmedy
Stavelot
Münstereifel
746

Condé
La Louvière
Binche
Thuin
Florennes
Ciney
Havelange
StE
697 Gerolstein 700

Valenciennes
Maubeuge
Hautmont
313
Dinant
Marche
652
Bavigny
St Vith
Prüm
Ernstberg

le
Quesnoy
Solesmes
Aulnoye
Philippeville

East from Greenwich

COPYRIGHT. GEORGE PHILIP & SON. LTD.

13

ICELAND
On same scale
as general map

Horn
Ísafjörður
Húnaflói
Akureyri
Jökulsá
Breiðafjörður
Neskaupstaður
Faxaflói
Hvítá
Vatnajökull
Reykjavík
Akranes
Öræfajökull
2119
Keflavík
Þjórsá
Vestmannaeyjar

Arctic Circle

ATLANTIC

OCEAN

Arctic Circle

Hammerfest
Söröya
North Cape
Nordkinn
Vardö
Vadsö

Senja
Tromsö
Tana
Indri
L. Inari

Vesterålen
Narvik
Torne
Lapland
Porttipahta Res.
Lokka Res.

Lofoten
West Fjord
2123
Kebnekaise
Kiruna
Storlulea
Kalixälv
Kelloselkä

Bodö
Sulitjelma
1913
Gällivare
Kemi
Rovaniemi

Vega
Mosjöen
Hornavan
Boden
Tornio
Kemi
Haparanda

Vikna
Folda Fjord
Storavan
Storuman
Skellefte
Luleå
Piteå
Oulu
L. Oulu

Trondheim Fjord
Norrland
Vilhelmina
Raahe
Kajaani

Kristiansund
Steinkjer
Levanger
Vännäs
Umeå
Örnsköldsvik
Vaasa
FINLAND
Iisalmi

Molde
Trondheim
Storsjön
Östersund
Ångerman
Härnösand
Kuopio
Jyväskylä

Ålesund
Snöhetta
2286
Dovre Fjell
Bräcke
Ange
Indal
Sundsvall

Stadlandet
Galdhöpiggen
2469
Jotun Fjell
Ljusnan
Hudiksvall
Tampere
Pori
Lahti

Florö
Lillehammer
Glåma
Öster Dal
Mora
Söderhamn
Uusikaupunki
Hämeenlinna
Kotka

Höyanger
Sogne Fjord
Hamar
Mjösa L.
Klar
Väster Dal
Falun
Gävle
Ahvenanmaa
Is.
Turku
Helsinki

Bergen
Hardanger
Fjord
Oslo
Svealand
Sala
Dannemora
Uppsala
Hankoo
Porkkala
Gulf of Finland
Tallinn

Haugesund
Drammen
Karlstad
Västerås
Hjälmaren
Malar
Hiiumaa
ESTONIA

Stavanger
Skien
Oslo Fjord
Fredrikstad
Halden
Örebro
Eskilstuna
Stockholm
Saaremaa
Pärnu

Egersund
Arendal
L.
Vänern
Norrköping
Gulf of
Riga
Volga

Kristiansand
Larvik
Trollhättan
L.
Vätter
Linköping
Västervik
Visby
Gotland
Ventspils
LATVIA
Riga

Lindesnes
Mandal
Skagen
Jönköping
Oskarshamn
Jelgava
Dvina

Skagerrak
Göteborg
Borås
Götaland
Varberg
Öland
Liepaja
Klaipeda
LITHUANIA

Aalborg
Kattegat
Randers
Halmstad
Kalmar
Karlskrona
BALTIC SEA

Lim Fjord
Jutland
Aarhus
DENMARK
Hälsingborg
The Sound

Esbjerg
Copenhagen
Lund
Klaipeda

Odense
Fyn
Sjælland
Malmö
Sovetsk
Neman
Kaunas

Flensburg
Gedser
Store Bælt
Bornholm
Gdynia
Gdańsk
Kaliningrad
Vilnius

Heligoland
Kiel
Canal
Stralsund
Sassnitz
Rügen

Groningen
NETH.
Altona
Lübeck
Hamburg
Rostock
POLAND
Szczecin

GERMANY
Bremen

SCANDINAVIA

0		100		200 miles
0	100	200	300	

COPYRIGHT. GEORGE PHILIP & SON. LTD.

14

CENTRAL EUROPE

15

East from Greenwich

ITALY AND
S.E. EUROPE

0   50   100   150   200 miles
0   100   200   300 km

East from Greenwich

Przemyśl
Lviv
Vinnitsa
eszyn
30
Tatha
2655
Kirovograd
UKRAINE
SLOVAK REP.
Kolomyia
Kamenets-Podolskiy
Uman
Pervomaysk
Krivoy Rog
Košice
Prut
Mogilev-Podolski
Balta
Banská
Btiavnica
Tisza
Chernovtsy
MOLDOVA
Voznesensk
Miskolc
Tokaj
Botoşanio
Beltsy
Nikolayev
Budapest
Debrecen
Pietrosu
2305
Iaşi
Kishinev
Bug
Tiraspol
Kherson
G A R Y
Oradea
Cluj-
Napoca
Pietrosu
2102
Belgorod
Dnestrovski
emét
Körös
Tighina
Odessa
Hódmezővásárhely
R O M A N I A
G. of Karkinitsk
Szeged
Arad
Mureşul
Sibiu
Negoiu
Braşov
Galaţi
Izmail
C. Tarkhankut
45
Subotica
Timişoara
2535
Brăila
Sulina
Sombor
Petrovaradin
Transylvanian Alps
Ploieşti
Drogea
Sad
Belgrade
Drobeta
Pitesti
B L A C K
Smederevo
Turnu-Severin
Bucharest
Constanţa
Kragujevac
Vidin
Craiova
Danube
Silistra
S E A
S
Y
Novi Pazar
Niš
Iskŭr
Pleven
Ruse
Dobrich
Durmitor
U
Morava
B
Velika Tŭrnovo
Varna
2522
G
a
Shipka
Stiven
ONTE
l
Mts.
EGRO
O
KOSOVO
Sofia
B U L G A R I A
Burgas
Podgorica
S
k
Musala
Zonguldak
Shkodër
L
2925
a
Plovdiv
Edirne
Ereğli
Skopje
Istanbul
2764
Vardar
n
Bosporus
Tirane
Strumica
Marifsa
Üsküdar
Bolu
rrës
MACEDONIA
Rhodope
Kocaeli
A
Bitola
Serrai
Xanthi
Tekirdağ
İznik Gölü
Sakarya
40
Elbasan
Kavalla
Komotini
Eñez
Sea of
Bursa
vlorë
GREECE
Alexandroúpolis
Gelibolu
Marmara
Bilecik
L
Thessaloniki
Bandirmo
Eskişehir
B
Áthos
İmroz
Çanakkale
Kütahya
A
Pindus
2033
Dardanelles
Balikesir
Sivrihisar
N
Olympus
Lemnos
I
2917
Ayvalik
T U R K E Y
r. of
Trikkala
Larissa
N. Sporades
Lésvos
Afyon
ranto
Ioannina
Vólos
Manisa
Bolvadin
Eğridir
Corfu
G
Euboea
Chios
Turgutly
Gölü
Levkás
R
Aegean
İzmir
Alaşehir
Eğridir
Navpaktos
E
Thebes
Athens
Andros
Sámos
Aydin
Menderes
Cephalonia
E
G.ofCorinth
Piraeus
Ikaría
Denizli
Burdur
Sparta
Patras
Corinth
Hermoúpolis
Muğla
Taurus Mts.
Antalya
Zákinthos
C
Syros
Cyclades
Dodecanese
Olympia
Peloponnesus
Náxos
Elmali
Kalamáto
Sparta
Ios
3086
Pílos
Milo
Rhodes
Kastellórizon
5121
Thira
Rhodes
4486
C. Matapán
Cerigo
Scarpanto
35
Andikithira
Khaniá
Iráklion
Mt. ídhi
2456
C r e t e

N E A N S E A

18

SPAIN
AND PORTUGAL

| 0 | 50 | 100 | 150 miles |
| 0 | 50 | 100 | 150 | 200 | 250 km |

COPYRIGHT GEORGE PHILIP & SON LTD.

West from Greenwich   0   East from Greenwich

MIDDLE EAST

0   100   200 miles
0   100   200   300 km

Division between Greeks and Turks
in Cyprus; Turks to the north.

East from Greenwich

MEDITERRANEAN SEA

CYPRUS
C. Andreas
C. Arnauti
Morphou
Xerinia
Nicosia
Famagusta
Larnaca
Limassol
1951

TURKEY
Adana
Tarsus
Mersin
İskenderun
Antakya
Gaziantep
Kilis
Nizip
Birecik
Urfa
Viranşehir
Mardin
Midyat
Cizre
Şanlıurfa
Osmaniye
1547

SYRIA
Aleppo
Hama
Homs
Latakia
Tartūs
Bāniyās
Jablah
Idlib
Ma'arrat an Nu'man
Palmyra (Tadmor)
Ar Raqqah
Dayr az Zawr
Al Ḥasakah
Abu Kamāl
Ar Rutbah

LEBANON
Tripoli
Beirut
Saida
Tyre
Zahlé
3083

ISRAEL
Tel Aviv Jaffa
Haifa
Acre
Hadera
Netanya
Rehovot
Ashqelon
Jerusalem
Beersheba
WEST BANK
GAZA STRIP
Nablus

JORDAN
Amman
Al Khalil
At Tafilah
Ma'an
Al 'Aqabah
Ḥaql
As Salt
Irbid
Az Zarqā'
653
493

EGYPT
CAIRO
Alexandria
Damietta
Port Said
Rosetta
Tanta
El Mahalla el Kubra
Mansura
Zagazig
Benha
Suez
Ismâ'îlîya
Helwan
Suez Canal
Bitter Lakes
El Faiyûm
Beni Suef
El Minya
Mallawi
El Gîza
Pyramids
Shibîn el Kôm
Sinnûris
El Kubra
Damanhûr
Moghagha
Beni Mazâr
El Wâsta
Dairût
Manfalût

SINAI
Gebel el Tîh
Abu Zenima
El Tûr
Ras Muhammad
Nakhl
2637
G. Mûsa
G. Katherîna 2285
Dahab
Ra's Farah

IRAQ
Baghdad
Mosul
Kirkūk
Sulaymānīyah
Irbīl
Kuwait
Basra
Al 'Amārah
An Nāṣirīyah
As Samāwah
An Najaf
Karbalā'
Al Hindīyah
Al Kūfah
Ad Dīwānīyah
Ar Ramādī
Al Fallūjah
Ba'qūbah
Khānaqīn
Mandalī
Sāmarrā'
Tikrīt
Nineveh
Al Ḥadr
Tall 'Afar
Sinjar
Ana
Haditha
Tuz Khurmātū
Kifrī
Kala't Sālih
Babylon
Nippur
Ash Shatrah
As Salmān
Ash Shabakah
W. al Khirr
Thartar Depression

IRAN
Hamadān
Zanjān
Qazvin
Saqqez
Sanandaj
Kermānshāh
Khorramābād
Borūjerd
Malāyer
Nahāvand
Ahvāz
Dezfūl
Ābādān
Khorramshahr
Qom
Arāk
Hamīd
Bākhtarān
Maragheh
Mahābād
Saqqez
Bījār
Kāshān

SAUDI ARABIA
KUWAIT
Al Jahrah
Mina Saud
Al Ahmadi
Ḥafar al Bāṭin
Al Qaysūmah
Al Lisāfah
Al Buşayyah
Ar'ar
Rafḥā'
Al Jalāmīd
Sakākah
Qārah
Al Jawf
Al Qaşab
Najaf
Turaif
Ash Shu'bah
Ad Duwayd
Badanah
Qal'at al Muazzam
Dabā
1128
940

SYRIAN DESERT
AL ḤAMĀD
Sahrā' al Ḥijārah

AN NAFUD

Tigris
Euphrates
W. al Ubayyiḍ
W. ar Ratqa
W. al Khar
W. at Tubayq
W. Fajr
W. Ghadaf

Gulf of Aqaba
Gulf of Suez
Nile
Dead Sea
L. Tiberias

32   36   40   44   48   36   32   28   44   40   28

ICELAND

ATLANTIC
OCEAN

Jan Mayen

A R C T I C

Spitsbergen

Franz Josef Land

BRITISH
ISLES

North Cape
Hammerfest
Narvik

Sev
Ze

Bergen
Trondheim

N O R W A Y

Barents
Sea

Novaya Zemlya

North
Sea

Oslo

S W E D E N

Murmansk
Kolguyev I.

Kola Pen.

Pechora
Gulf

Kara
Sea

Putih I.
Dickson

DENMARK
Hamburg
Esbjerg
Copenhagen
Malmö
Berlin
Szczecin
Kaliningrad

Göteborg

Uppsala
Stockholm

Gulf of Bothnia

Gävle
Tampere

Helsinki
G. of Finland

FINLAND
Oulu
Kemi

Tornio

Kandalaksha

White
Sea

Arkhangelsk

N. Dvina

Naryan Mar

Novy Port
Vorkuta

Khabarovo
Vaigach I.

Gulf of Ob

Urengoy

Taz

POLAND
Łódź
Wrocław
Warsaw

Gdańsk
LITHUANIA
Vilnius
Minsk

Baltic Sea
Riga
LATVIA
ESTONIA
Tallinn

St. Petersburg

Petrozavodsk
L. Onega

L. Ladoga

Vologda
Kostroma

Kotlas

Pechora

U
r
a
l
s

Teipos Iz
1894
1617

S

West

S i
b e r i a n

Urengoy

L'viv
UKRAINE

Kraków
Kishinev

Zhitomir
Gomel
BELARUS
Smolensk

Tver
Rybinsk
Yaroslavl
Moscow
Ivanovo
Nizhniy
Novgorod

Izhevsk

Kirov

Berezniki

Perm

Serov

Nizhniy Tagil

R
u
s
s
i
a
n

Kama

S i

Tyumen
Tobolsk

Isurgut

Plain

Dnepropetrovsk
Krivoy Rog
Nikolayev
Odessa

Kiev
Cherkasy
Kremenchug
Kharkov
Poltava

Kursk
Orel
Tula
Voronezh

Penza
Tambov
Ryazan

Simbirsk

Kazan
Ufa

Zlatoust

Yekaterinburg
Kurgan

Petropavlovsk

Irtysh

Omsk
Tatarsk

Tomsk

An

Sevastopol
Simferopol
Crimea

Novorossiysk

Zaporozhye
Donetsk
Makeyevka
Sea
of Azov
Rostov

Don

Saratov

Samara

Chapayevsk

Volsk

Ural

Chelyabinsk

Magnitogorsk

Kokshetau
Pavlodar

Slavgorod

Novosibirsk

Barnaul

Biysk

Black   Sea

Sochi
Trabzon

Krasnodar
Kropotkin
Stavropol
Elbrus 5633

Kerch

Volgograd
Engels

Uralsk

Orenburg
Orsk

Astana

Leninogor

Semey

Beluk

Batumi
Rize
GEORGIA
TURKEY
Erzurum
ARMENIA
Yerevan
Diyarbakir
AZERBAIJAN

Kurgan
Tbilisi

Grozny

Astrakhan

Caspian
Sea

Atyrau

Aktyubinsk

K

K i r g i z

S   t   e   p   p   e

Karaganda

Karsakpai

Karaganda

Aralsk

Balkhash

Ayaguz

Tachena

Mosul
IRAQ

Kirkuk

Baku

Ust Urt Plateau

Aral
Sea

Kzyl Orda

L. Balkhash

K A Z A K H S T A N

Almaty

Kuldja

Baghdad

Basra
Abadan
Kuwait

Rasht
Hamadan
Tehran
Demavend

Turkmenbashi

Ashkhabad
Bandar-e Torkeman
Mary

Khiva

Kara Kum
Chardzhou

Kyzyl Kum

UZBEKISTAN
Bukhara

Shymkent

Zhambyl

Bishkek

Tashkent

Namangan
Andizhan

KYRGYZSTAN

Przhevalsk
Pk. Pobedy
7439

XINJ
UY

Mashhad

TURKMENISTAN

Khujand

Samarkand

Kashi

Kand

Tarim Pend

The
Gulf
Bushire
Shiraz

Esfahan

P E R S I A (I R A N)
Yazd

Kerman

Herat

Termez

Dushanbe

TAJIKISTAN

Communism Pk
7495

Pamirs

Shache

Hotan

Tarim

XIZANG
(TIBET)

Zabol

AFGHANISTAN

Mazar-i-Sharif

Kabul

PAKISTAN

Kashmir

ALASKA

Bering Strait

St. Lawrence I. (U.S.A.)

Wrangel I.

Chukot Sea

Chukot Range

Gulf of Anadyr

Bering Sea

OCEAN

Komsomolets I.

October Revolution I.

Bolshevik I.

De Long Is.

New Siberian Is.

East Siberian Sea

Beruang I.

Anadyr

Amabarchik

Lyakhov Is.

Nizhne Kolymsk

Sredne Kolymsk

Kolyma

Komandorskiye Is.

Kamchatka

Fang Mts.

Taimyr Pen.

Laptev Sea

L. Taimyr

Nordvik

Tiksi

Buluno

Yana

Verkhoyansk

K o l y m a   R a.

Shelikhov Gulf

Gizhigo

Magadan

Ust Kamchatsk

4750 Klyuchevsk. Vol.

Petropavlovsk-Kamchatskiy

Khatanga

Katuy R.

Verkhoyansk Range

Zhigansk

Lena

Okhotsk

Sea of Okhotsk

Central

L. Taimyr

Circle

Siberian

Vilyuisk

Yakutsk

Aldan

Dzhugdzhur Ra.

Shantar Is.

Okha

Sakhalin

ower Tunguska

oginsk

b

e

Plateau

Olekminsk

Aldan

Nikolayevsk

Aleksandrovsk

Stony Tunguska

S   I   A

Lena

Kirensk

Bodaibo

Stanovoy   Ra.

Skovorodino

Belogorsk

Komsomolsk

Sovetskaya Gavan

Yuzhno-Sakhalinsk

Korsakov

Kuril Is.

Angara

Bratsk

Krasnoyarsk

Taishet

Nizhneudinsk

L. Baikal

Y a b l o n o v y y

Amur

Sretensk

Nerchinsk

Blagoveshchensk

Amur

Birobidzhan

Songhua

Khabarovsk

Sikhote Alin Range

Gulf of Tartary

Otaru

Sapporo

JAPAN

Hakodate

ISK

Achinsk

vo

Kuznetskiy

znetsk

Kansk

Tulun

Cheremkhovo

Angarsk

Ulan-Ude

Chita

Khilok

Oloyannaya

Hailar

Harbin

Ussuriysk

Vladivostok

Sea of Japan

Minusinsk

vsk

Munku-Sardyk 3491

Irkutsk

Petrovsk

Kyakhta

Selenga

Yenisei

Ulan Bator

MONGOLIA

Uliastay

Uliastay

Changchun

Shenyang

Yinggou N. Dandong

Wonsan

Seoul

KOREA

ind-Us

Gobi Desert

Beijing (Peking)

Pyongyang

Inchon

Pusan

Hiroshima

mqi

Turpan

Baotou

Datong

Tianjin

Dalian

Qingdao

Kunsan

Mokpo

Masan

Nagasaki

JAPAN

G

p Nur

C H I N A

GREAT   WALL

Hwang

Jinan

Lianyungang

Lanzhou

Xi'an

Zhengzhou

RUSSIA AND CENTRAL ASIA

| 0 | 200 | 400 | 600 | 800 miles |

| 0 | 200 | 400 | 600 | 800 | 1000 | 1200 | km |

COPYRIGHT. GEORGE PHILIP & SON. LTD.

22

S.W. ASIA

0	100	200	300	400	500 miles
0	200	400	600	800 km	

23

INDIA, PAKISTAN, SRI LANKA & BURMA

0   200   400   600 miles
0   200 400 600 800 km

COPYRIGHT GEORGE PHILIP & SON LTD.

East from Greenwich

24

HAINAN
(Same scale as main map)

Haiphong, Zhanjiang
Beihai
Leizhou Bandao
Haikou
Tongxing Chengmai Wuzhi Shan
Yaxian 1879

CHINA

| 0 | 100 | 200 | 300 | 400 | 500 miles |
| 0 | 200 | 400 | 600 | 800 | km |

CHINA

RUSSIA

Sikhote-Alin Range

Svetlaya

SAKHALIN

La Pérouse Strait

Sea of Okhotsk

Rebun
Wakkanai
Rishiri
Cape Soya

Cape Shiretoko
Abashiri
Bay

Mudanjiang

Iman

Lesozavodsk

Jixi

Spassk-Dalni

Tetyukhe
Pristan

HOKKAIDO

1 Mt. Asahi
2290
Abashiri

Rumoi
Meshike

I. Kutcharo

Asahikawa
HOKKAIDO
Nemuro

Ussuriysk

Artem

Suchan

Cape Kamu

Otaru
Ishikari Bay

Obihiro
Kushiro

Vladivostok

Yanji

Nakhodka

Sapporo
L. Shikotsu

Okushiri
L. Toya
▲Mt. Horoshiri
2052

Uriggi

SOUTH
KOREA

Kilchu

NORTH
KOREA

Muroran
Uchiura Bay

Hakodate

Cape Esan

Cape Shiragami
Tsugaru Strait
Cape Shiriya

SEA   OF

JAPAN

Cape Henashi
Hirosaki
Noshiro

Aomori

L. Towada
Mt. Iwate
2041

2

Hachinohe

Morioka
Miyako

Akita
3

4
Kamaishi

Ou Range

Kitakami

Pohang

Sado
Cape Suzu
Wajima

Sakata
Mogami

Ishinomaki

TOHOKU

Cape Nyudo

PUSAN

Oki Is.

Yamagata
5
Sendai

Niigata
Mt. Azuma
2024
Agano
Fukushima
6
7

Koriyama
Lake
Inawashiro

Noto

8
Nagaoka

Toyama
Toyama Bay

Maebashi

Iwaki

Kanazawa
10
CHUBU
9
Tone

18
Utsunomiya

Mito

Matsue
Tottori

Cape Kyo
Wakasa Bay

11
Hida Ra.
▲Mt. Hotaka
3190
12

17
19

20
KANTO
L. Kasumiga

Tsushima

Chugoku Mts.
L. Biwa

25
13
TOKYO

21

22
Choshi
Cape Inubo

CHUGOKU
Cape Hino

24

YOKOHAMA

Hiroshima
33
32

KYOTO
26
15
NAGOYA
Akaishi Ra.
Yokosuka
Boso

Okayama
28
OSAKA

Uji
377623

Kure
35
34
Sakai 29

Shizuoka
Cape Nojima

Shimonoseki
ITAKYUSHU

Matsuyama
38
SHIKOKU
36
Takamatsu
Tokushima
Wakayama
37

Hamamatsu
Toyohashi

Nii Is.

Miyake Is.

Fukuoka
40
41
44

39
Kochi
30
KINKI

Omuta

Kumamoto
43

Nagasaki
42

45
Miyazaki

KYUSHU
46

Kagoshima

KYUSHU

Kagoshima Bay
Osumi
Group
Tanega I.

Osumi Strait

1935 Yaku I.

Tokara Group

Amami
I.

Kosebo

pe Nomo

Arake Bay

Cape Ashizuri

SHIKOKU
Cape Shiono

Hachijo I.

O   C   E   A   N

P   A   C   I   F   I   C

Cape Muroto

Bungo Channel

Tosa Bay

Kuma R.

Cape Iro
O.I.

Cape Daio
Cape Iraki

Ise Bay

Kii Channel

Kii Range

REFERENCE TO PREFECTURES

HOKKAIDO DISTRICT	KANTO DISTRICT	CHUGOKU DISTRICT
1 Hokkaido	17 Gumma	31 Tottori
TOHOKU DISTRICT	18 Tochigi	32 Okayama
2 Aomori	19 Saitama	33 Shimane
3 Akita	20 Ibaraki	34 Hiroshima
4 Iwate	21 Tokyo	35 Yamaguchi
5 Yamagata	22 Chiba	
6 Miyagi	23 Kanagawa	SHIKOKU DISTRICT
7 Fukushima		36 Kagawa
	KINKI DISTRICT	37 Tokushima
CHUBU DISTRICT	24 Hyogo	38 Ehime
8 Niigata	25 Kyoto	39 Kochi
9 Ishikawa	26 Shiga	
10 Toyama	27 Osaka	KYUSHU DISTRICT
11 Fukui	28 Nara	40 Fukuoka
12 Gifu	29 Mie	41 Saga
13 Nagano	30 Wakayama	42 Nagasaki
14 Yamanashi		43 Kumamoto
15 Aichi		44 Oita
16 Shizuoka		45 Miyazaki
		46 Kagoshima

JAPAN

0   50   100   150   200 miles

0   50 100 150 200 250 300 km

East from Greenwich

130   135   140   145

SOUTH-EAST ASIA

km
0 200 400 600 800
0 200 400 600 miles

NORTHERN MARIANAS

Guam (U.S.A.)

FEDERATED STATES OF MICRONESIA

PACIFIC OCEAN

Yap Is.

Caroline Islands

PALAU

Bismarck Sea

New Britain

Admiralty Is.

New Ireland

Wewak

PAPUA NEW GUINEA

Owen Stanley Ra.

Madang

Port Moresby

Coral Sea

Torres Strait

IRIAN JAYA

Maoke Mts.

Jayapura

Schouten Is.
Biak

Equator

Vogelkop

C. Palau

Waigeo

Misool

Halmahera

North C.
Morotai

Ceram

Obira

Buru

Amboina

Ceram Sea

Banda Sea

Gt. Kei

Tanimbar Is.

Aru Is.

Yos Sudarso I.

Kaimana B.

McCluer Gulf

Arafura Sea

Babar

Leti Is.

Wetar

Timor

Roti

Savu

Sawu Sea

Sumba

Flores

Flores Sea

Flores Is.

SULAWESI (CELEBES)

G. of Tomini

G. of Bone

Menado

Celebes Sea

Sangihe

Talaud Is.

MINDANAO

Davao Gulf

C.S. Augustino

Mindanao Trench

PHILIPPINES

Luzon

Manila

Quezon City

Mindoro

Mindoro Strait

Calamian Group

Palawan

SOUTH CHINA SEA

Paracel Is.

Samar

Leyte

Cebu

Panay

Negros

Bohol

Iloilo

Bacolod

Masbate

Sulu Sea

Zamboanga

Jolo

Sulu Arch.

Sandakan

SABAH

Kota Kinabalu

Mt. Kinabalu

BRUNEI

Bandar Seri Begawan

SARAWAK

Kuching

BORNEO

KALIMANTAN

Pontianak

Banjarmasin

Balikpapan

Samarinda

Makassar Strait

Ujung Pandang

Bali

Lombok

Sumbawa

Java Sea

JAVA

Jakarta

Bandung

Semarang

Surabaya

Yogyakarta

I N D O N E S I A

INDIAN OCEAN

Sumatra

Palembang

Bangka

Belitung

Medan

Padang

Barisan Mts.

Mentawai Is.

Nias

Banda Aceh

Strait of Malacca

MALAYSIA

Kuala Lumpur

Melaka

Penang

George Town

Ipoh

SINGAPORE

Johor Baharu

Kota Baharu

THAILAND

Bangkok

Gulf of Thailand

Isthmus of Kra

Phuket

Chiang Mai

CAMBODIA

Phnom Penh

L A O S

Vientiane

VIETNAM

Hanoi

Haiphong

Gulf of Tongking

Ho Chi Minh City

Mekong

Hainan

COPYRIGHT GEORGE PHILIP & SON, LTD.

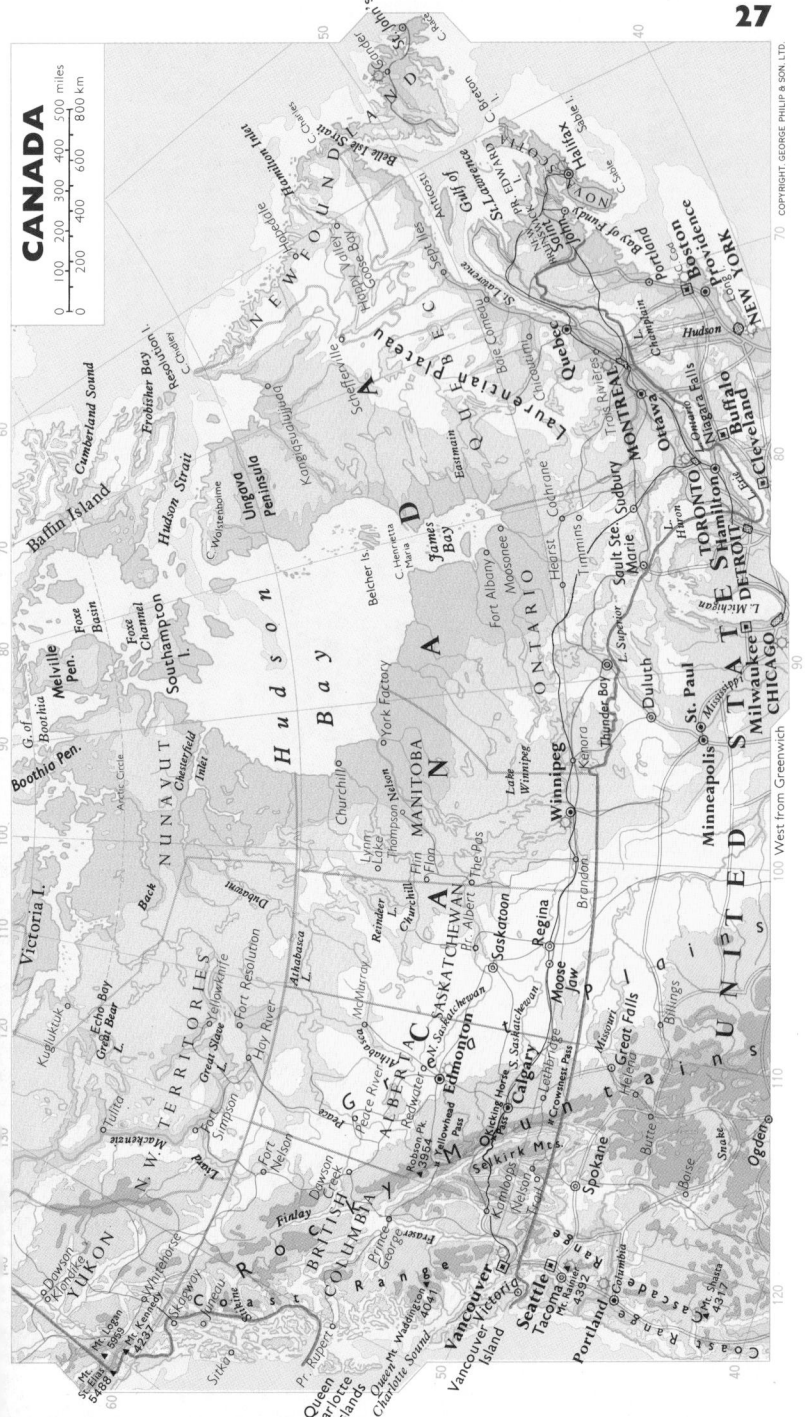

CANADA

0	100 200 300 400 500 miles	
0	200 400 600 800 km	

West from Greenwich

PACIFIC

OCEAN

Projection: *Bonne*

U.S.A.

0   100   200   300   400 miles
0   200   400   600 km

ADA

A

Cochrane

Laurentian Plateau

Arvida

Thunder Bay

Sudbury

Sault Ste. Marie

Quebec

Fredericton

MINNE-

Duluth

Lake Superior

Trois Rivières

Montreal

MAINE

Saint John

Sherbrooke

SOTA

St. Paul

WISCONSIN

Green Bay

MICHIGAN

Lake Huron

Georgian B.

Ottawa

Kingston

L. Ontario

VERMONT

N.H.

Portland

Manchester

neapolis

Austin

Madison

Milwaukee

L. Michigan

Saginaw

Toronto

Hamilton

Rochester

Troy

Albany

MASS.

Boston

R.I. C. Cod

Providence

City

IOWA

Des
Moines

CHICAGO

Grand
Rapids

London

Detroit

Windsor

Lake Erie

Buffalo

Scranton

Newark

New Haven

N.J.

NEW YORK

Cedar
Rapids

Council Bluffs

St. Joseph

Peoria

Illinois

Fort
Wayne

Toledo

Cleveland

Akron

PENNSYLVANIA

Pittsburgh

Philadelphia

St. Louis

ILLINOIS

INDIANA

Indianapolis

Dayton

OHIO

Columbus

Baltimore

M.D.

Delaware B.

Washington

Kansas City

Jefferson City

Cincinnati

Ohio

WEST
VIRGINIA

Huntington

Richmond

Chesapeake B.

MISSOURI

Evansville

Louisville

Lexington

Roanoke

VIRGINIA

Norfolk

Springfield

KENTUCKY

Oak Ridge

APPALACHIAN

Greensboro

Raleigh

C. Hatteras

ARKANSAS

Fort Smith
Arkansas

Little Rock

STATES

Nash-
ville

Knoxville

TENNESSEE

Chattanooga

Greenville

NORTH
CAROLINA

Charlotte

SOUTH
CAROLINA

Wilmington

Shreveport

Memphis

Tennessee

Gadsden

Savannah

Birmingham

MISSISSIPPI

Atlanta

GEORGIA

Charleston

Monroe

Jackson

Alabama

ALABAMA

Columbus

Montgomery

Albany

Savannah

ATLANTIC

LOUISIANA

Baton Rouge

Mobile

Dothan

Jacksonville

OCEAN

eaumont

Houston

Galveston

New Orleans

Mississippi
Delta

FLORIDA

hristi

os

Tampa

St. Petersburg

West Palm Beach

Freeport

BAHAMAS

Everglades

Miami

Nassau

Gulf of Mexico

C. Sable

Key West

Florida Strait

Matanzas

Havana

CUBA

Camagüey

Connecticut
Delaware
Maryland
Massachusetts
New Hampshire
New Jersey
Rhode Island

Yucatan
Strait

West from Greenwich   90

COPYRIGHT. GEORGE PHILIP & SON. LTD.

90   80   70   40   30   70

MEXICO AND THE CARIBBEAN

ATLANTIC OCEAN

Tropic of Cancer

Charleston
Savannah
Atlanta
Columbus
Montgomery
Jacksonville
Birmingham
UNITED STATES
Mobile
Jackson
Baton Rouge
New Orleans
Florida
Tampa
Miami
C. Sable
Florida Strait

BAHAMAS
NASSAU
Turks & Caicos Is. (Br.)

Havana
Sta. Clara
Holguin
Camaguey
Santiago de Cuba
Greater
Hispaniola
HAITI
DOMINICAN REP.
Santiago
Santo Domingo
Port au Prince
PUERTO RICO (U.S.)
San Juan
Virgin Is. (Br.)
Anguilla (Br.)
ANTIGUA & BARBUDA
ST. KITTS-NEVIS
GUADELOUPE (Fr.)
DOMINICA
MARTINIQUE (Fr.)
ST. LUCIA
ST. VINCENT & THE GRENADINES
BARBADOS
GRENADA
Port of Spain
TRINIDAD & TOBAGO
Tobago

Antilles
Yucatan Strait
Cayman Is. (Br.)
JAMAICA
Kingston
Caribbean Sea
Curaçao
NETH. ANTILLES
G. of Venezuela
Maracaibo
L. Maracaibo
Mérida
Barquisimeto
CARACAS
Ciudad Bolívar
VENEZUELA
Orinoco
Caroni
Caura
Apure

Yucatan
Mérida
C. Catoche
Gulf of Campeche
BELIZE
Belmopan
Villahermosa
GUATEMALA
Tuxtla Gutierrez
Coatzacoalcos
Gulf of Honduras
HONDURAS
Tegucigalpa
Chinandega
NICARAGUA
Managua
L. Nicaragua
COSTA RICA
San José
C. Gracias a Dios

C. Corrientes
Popocatepetl 5452
Puebla
MEXICO CITY
León
Aguascalientes
Guadalajara
Oaxaca
Acapulco
Salina Cruz
G. of Tehuantepec
San Salvador
EL SALVADOR

Corpus Christi
Matamoros
Tampico
Veracruz
Orizaba 5700
Gulf of Mexico
M e x i c o

El Paso
Ciudad Juarez
Chihuahua
Nogales
Hermosillo
Guaymas
Piedras Negras
Nuevo Laredo
Monterrey
Saltillo
Torreón
Durango
Mazatlan
Eastern Sierra Madre
San Luis Potosi
Western Sierra Madre
Mexicali
Lower California
Gulf of California
C. San Lucas
Revilla Gigedo Is. (Mexico)

Dallas
Fort Worth
Austin
San Antonio
Rio Grande

Colón
Panama
PANAMA
G. of Panama
G. of Darién
Barranquilla
Cartagena
Magdalena
Sa. Nevada de Sta. Marta 5800
Bucaramanga
Cúcuta
Medellín
COLOMBIA
Cordillera Mérida
Meta

PACIFIC OCEAN

	miles
0 100 200 300 400 500	miles
0 200 400 600 800 km	

SOUTH AMERICA

0   200   400   600   800 miles
0   200 400   800   1200 km

**Map labels:**

CARIBBEAN SEA

Santiago de Cuba   Sierra Maestra   Hispaniola
JAMAICA   HAITI   Port au   DOM.   S. Juan
Kingston   Prince   REP.   PUERTO RICO (U.S.)
Leeward Is.
Windward Is.
NICARAGUA   BARBADOS
Curaçao (Neth.)   TRINIDAD AND TOBAGO
Barranquilla   G. of Venezuela   Port of Spain
Maracaibo   Cabimas   Puerto Cruz
COSTA   G. of   La Guaira   Santo Tomé
RICA   PANAMA   Darién   Cartagena   Barquisimeto   Caracas   Ciudad Bolívar
Panamá   Gulf   Bucaraga   Maturin
Pereira   Medellín   Mérida   VENEZUELA   Kaieteur Falls   GUYANA   Georgetown
Manizales   Bogotá   Roraima   SURINAM   Paramaribo
Cali   COLOMBIA   2810   Sa. Pacaraima   Demerara
Pasto   Orinoco   Cayenne   FR. GUIANA
Papayán   Casiquiare   Sa. de Tumucumaque
ECUADOR   Quito   Cotopaxi   Putumayo   Japurá   Negro   Amazon   Macapá   Equator
Chimborazo   5897   Solimões   Marajó I.   Pará
6267   Guayaquil   Benjamin Constant   Belém
C. Pariña   Cuenca   Marañon   Iquitos   Amazon   Santarém   São Luís
Piura   Selvas   São Francisco   Fortaleza
Chiclayo   Purus   Madeira   Tapajós   Xingu   Imperatriz   Teresina   C. de São Roque
Trujillo   Pucallpa   Roosevelt   Parnaíba   Natal
S. Antonio   Branco   Paulistana   João Pessoa
Falls   B R A Z I L   Recife   C. Branco
PERU   Rio   São Francisco   Maceió
Callao   Lima   Huancayo   Branco   Barreiras   Aracaju
Pisco   Cuzco   Guaporé   Plateau of   Salvador   Alagoinhas
Lomas   Juliaca   Urubamba 6580   Mato Grosso   Ilhéus
Arequipa   Cuyabá   Goiânia   Brasília   Montes   Vitória de
BOLIVIA   Claros   Conquista
Mollendo   La Paz   Pindorà   Campos
Arica   Oruro   Cochabamba   Santa Cruz   Caravelas
Iquique   Sucre   Corumbá   Uberaba   Belo
Potosí   Uberlândia   Horizonte
Uyuni   Tarija   Ribeirão   Mantiqueira Mts.   Itabira
Tropic of Capricorn   PARAGUAY   Prêto   Campinas   Niteroi
Antofagasta   Salta   Asunción   São Paulo   Rio de Janeiro
Taltal   Ojos del Salado   Tucumán   Iguaçu   Curitiba   Santos   C. Frio
6863   Corrientes   Falls   Blumenau
Santiago   Paraná   Santo   Pôrto Alegre
del Estero   Maria   ATLANTIC
La Serena   ARGENTINA   Uruguaiana   Bagé   Lagoa dos Patos   Rio Grande do Sul   OCEAN
Aconcagua   Córdoba   Santa Fé   Uruguay   Pelotas
Viña del Mar   Mendoza   Paraná   URUGUAY
Valparaiso   Rosario   Rocha
Santiago   Mercedes   Montevideo
Juan   Buenos   Rio de la Plata
Fernández   Talca   Aires   La Plata
(Chile)   Santa   Mar del Plata
PACIFIC   Concepción   Rosa   Pta. Mogotes
Colorado   Azul   Mar del Plata
OCEAN   Neuquén   Bahía Blanca
Valdivia   Temuco   Negro   Viedma
Osorno   Chubut   G. of San Matías
Puerto Montt   Rawson
Chiloé   Comodoro   OCEAN
Chonos   Rivadavia
Arch.   G. of San Jorge
Patagonia
Rio Gallegos   Falkland Is.
Punta Arenas   (Br.)
Magellan's Str.   Stanley
Tierra del Fuego   South Georgia
C. Froward   Staten I.   (Br.)
C. Horn
Drake Passage   West from   Greenwich

33

AFRICA

| 0 | 200 | 400 | 600 | 800 miles |
0   200 400 600 800 1000 1200 km

West from Greenwich 0 East from Greenwich 10

SÃO TOMÉ & PRÍNCIPE

KENYA
Brava
Kismayu
Lak Dera
Lamu
Malindi
Mombasa
Nairobi
Kenya 5199
Athi
Kilimanjaro 5895
Arusha
Moshi
Tanga
Zanzibar
Dar-es-Salaam
Morogoro
Entebbe
Kampala
Bukoba
Mwanza
L. Victoria
L. Eyasi
Tabora
Iringa
RWANDA
BURUNDI
Bujumbura
L. Tanganyika
L. Edward
L. Kivu
Kongolo
Kolem
Rufiji
Mtwara
COMOROS
C. Amber
Antsiranana
Antalaha
Mananara
Toamasina
Antananarivo
Fianarantsoa
Manakara
MADAGASCAR
Ambllobe
Morondava
Ambato
Mahajanga
C. Ste. Marie
Aldabra
INDIAN OCEAN
Pemba
Mozambique
Quelimane
Nampula
Mozambique
Beira
Inhambane
Maputo
Durban
Pietermaritzburg
SWAZILAND
Pietersburg
LESOTHO
Ladysmith
East London
Grahamstown
Port Elizabeth

DEM. REP. OF THE CONGO
Kisangani
Kindu
Ubundu
Bandundu
Mbandaka
Busira
Irebu
Mai-Ndombe
Lomela
Lulonga
Kananga
Kasai
Kamina
Mbujimayi
Kabalo
Kalemie
Likasi
Lubumbashi
Kolwezi
Kafakumba
Sandoa
Lobito
Benguela
Luanda
Ambriz
N'Zeto
Kinshasa
Brazzaville
Pointe Noire
Cabinda
Soyo
Boma
GABON
Ogooue
CONGO

ANGOLA
Malanje
Huambo
Lubango
Namibe
C. Sta. Maria
Cunene
C. Fria
Ondjiva
Cuando
Cuanza

ZAMBIA
Mongu
Lusaka
Livingstone
L. Bangweulu
Chingola
Kitwe
Ndola
Kabwe
Kafue
L. Mweru
L. Kabamba
Zambezi
Kariba
Chipata
L. Malawi
MALAWI
L. Nyasa
Blantyre
Lilongwe

ZIMBABWE
Harare
Mutare
Bulawayo
Chegutu
Gweru
Masvingo
Save

BOTSWANA
Gaborone
Francistown
Mafikeng
Maun
Kalahari

NAMIBIA
Windhoek
Swakopmund
Walvis Bay
Lüderitz
Grootfontein
Etosha Pan
Tsumeb
Okavango
Tropic of Capricorn

SOUTH AFRICA
Johannesburg
Pretoria
Germiston
Kimberley
Bloemfontein
De Aar
Keetmanshoop
Orange
Cape Town
Simonstown
C. of Good Hope
Mossel Bay

SOUTH ATLANTIC OCEAN
St. Helena
Ascension I.

Ecuador
Equator

34

AUSTRALIA

| 0 | 100 | 200 | 300 | 400 | 500 miles |
| 0 | 200 | 400 | 600 | 800 km |

East from 130 Greenwich

PAPUA NEW GUINEA

Lae
Wau
Mt. Victoria
4073
G. of Papua
Port
Moresby
Rigo

Torres Strait
nce of Wales
I.
Cape York
D'Entrecasteaux Is.
Louisiade
Arch.

Bougainville
Choiseul
SOLOMON
Santa
Isabel
Indispensable Str.
ISLANDS
Malaita
S. Cristóbal

Weipa
Cape
York
Coleman
Peninsula
Cooktown
ellesley
Is.

Coral
Sea

PACIFIC

OCEAN

Chillagoe
Mt. Bartle Frere
Cairns
Innisfail
Normanton
rketown
Croydon

Chesterfield Is.

Norman
Townsville
Charters
Towers
Hughenden
Bowen
Mackay

Bird I.
Cato I.

QUEENSLAND
Longreach
Winton
Emerald
Mt. Morgan
Rockhampton
Gladstone
Bundaberg

Diamantina
Great
Grey
Range
Great
Windorah
Maryborough
Fraser I.
Gympie

A
u
s
t
r
a
l
i
a
n
Charleville
Darling
Toowoomba
Ipswich
Brisbane

Cunnamulla
Dirranbandi
Great
Divide

rdsville
Tibooburra
L. Callabonna
Bourke
Walgett
Moree
Grafton
Coffs
Harbour

NEW
SOUTH
Cobar
Wilcannia
Menindee
Dubbo
Roto
Whangarei
North C.
Doubtless B.

Broken
Hill
Darling
Murray River
Mildura
WALES
Bathurst
SYDNEY
Wollongong
Newcastle

North Island
Kaipara Harb.
Auckland
Manukau
North Shore City
Great Barrier I.
Thames
Hamilton
Tauranga
B. of Plenty

laide
Basin
Murray
Canberra
CAP.
TERR.
Goulburn
Queanbeyan
Jervis B.
Bateman's
B.

North Taranaki
Bight
New Plymouth
Palmerston North
Rotorua
Gisborne
Hawke Bay
Napier
Hastings

Hars'ham
Stawell
VICTORIA
Wangaratta
Mt. Kosciusko 2230
Bombala

NEW
ZEALAND
East C.

Ararat
Ballarat
MELBOURNE
Karamea B.
Nelson
Blenheim
Cook
Strait
Wellington

Colac
Geelong
Westport
Ross
Campbell

King I.
Bass Strait
Furneaux
Group

South Island
Mt. Cook 3753
Mt. Aspiring
303
Milford
Sd.
Canterbury
Plains
Christchurch
Lyttelton
Timaru
Oamaru

Chatham Is.
(N.Z.)

Burnie
Scottsdale
Devonport
Strahan
Launceston
Queenstown

Southern Alps
Queenstown
Port Chalmers
Otago Harb.
Dunedin

TASMANIA
Hobart
P. Davey
Tasman Penin.
P. Arthur
Storm B.
S.E. Cape

Stewart I.
Bluff
Invercargill
Bluff Harb.
Southwest C.

NEW ZEALAND
on same scale

COPYRIGHT. GEORGE PHILIP & SON. LTD

P A C I F I C

Aleutian Islands

O C E A N

C. Lopatka

Kuril Islands

Extreme limits of drift-ice

Petropavlovsk-
Kamchatskiy

Bering Sea

Sakhalin

Seas covered by pack-ice in Spring

Sea of
Okhotsk

Kodiak I.

Gulf of
Alaska

Nunivak

St. Lawrence
(U.S.A.)

Anadyr

Magadan

Okhotsk

Anchorage

Mt. McKinley
6194

Nome

C. Prince of
Wales

East C.

Arctic Circle

Chukot Ra.

Kolyma Ra.

Kamchatka

Verkhoyansk Ra.

Aldan

Juneau

Mt. Logan
5959

Whitehorse

ALASKA
(U.S.A.)

Fairbanks

Yukon

Chukot
Sea

Kolyma

Ust' Nera

Cherskiy Ra.

Yakutsk

Dawson

Brooks Ra.

Indigirka

Verkhoyansk

Lena

Mackenzie Mts.

Pt. Barrow

Wrangel I.

East Siberian
Sea

New Siberian
Is.

Tiksi

Lena

Mackenzie

Inuvik

Seas permanently covered
by pack-ice

Beaufort Sea

R U S S I A

Great Bear
Lake

Echo Bay

Banks I.

Laptev
Sea

Nordvik

Kotuy

Khatanga

Victoria
I.

Melville
I.

Pr. Patrick
I.

A R C T I C

Severnaya
Zemlya

Taimyr Pen.

Putorana
Mts.

Pr. of
Wales I.

Magnetic Pole 1988

Sverdrup
Is.

O C E A N

Norilsk

Yenisei

Igarka

Boothia
Pen.

Somerset
I.

Axel
Heiberg I.

Devon
I.

North
Pole

Dikson

Melville
Pen.

Ellesmere I.

Franz Josef
Land

Novy Port

Baffin Island

Qaanaaq
(Thule)

Baffin
Bay

Novaya
Zemlya

Kara
Sea

Yamal Pen.

Salekhard

Ob

Vorkuta

Ural Mts.

Davis Str.

Disko

Qegertarsuaq
(Godhavn)

GREENLAND
(Kalaallit Nunaat)

Spitsbergen
(Norway)

Barents
Sea

Naryan Mar

Pechora

Nuuk
(Godthåb)

Ittoqqortoormiit
(Scoresbysund)

Greenland Sea

North C.

Murmansk

Kola
Pen.

Syktyvkar

Arkhangelsk

Qaqortoq
(Julianehåb)

Mt. Forel
3360

Ammassalik

Jan Mayen
(Norway)

Hammerfest

White Sea

N. Dvina

C. Farewell

Denmark Strait

Akureyri

Norwegian

Narvik

FINLAND

L.
Onega

Nizhniy
Novgorod

Reykjavik

ICELAND

Sea

Trondheim

NORWAY

SWEDEN

G. of Bothnia

L.
Ladoga

St. Petersburg

Moscow

ATLANTIC

Faroe Is.
(Den.)

Bergen

Oslo

Helsinki

W. Dvina

OCEAN

Shetland Is.

Stockholm

Baltic Sea

North
Sea

DENMARK

Copenhagen

Warsaw

Kiev

UNITED
KINGDOM

Elbe

Berlin

POLAND

Dniester

NETH.

GERMANY

Rhine

Dnieper

London

Black Sea

NORTHERN
LANDS
AND SEAS

0   200   400   600   800 miles

0   400   800   1200 km

West from 10 Greenwich   0   East from 10 Greenwich

Clare, co., Munster, **R.o.I.**; cstl. co. bounded in S. and E. by R. Shannon; mainly agr. and tourism; inc. cliffs of Moher; Shannon airpt. and tax-free industl. development scheme; co. t. Ennis; a. 3,351 km²; p. (1986) 91,344.

Clare I., Clew Bay, Mayo, **R.o.I.**; p. (1986) 140.

Clarence Strait, between Melville I. and Darwin, N.T., **Australia**.

Clarksburg, t., W. Va., **USA**; industl. ctr. for coal mng. a., oil and natural gas fields; machin. glass, pottery; p. (1980) 22,371.

Clarksdale, t., Miss., **USA**; processing ctr. for rich farming a.; p. (1980) 21,137.

Clarksville, t., Tenn., **USA**; on Cumberland R.; tobacco mkt.; p. (1990) 75,494 (t.), 169,439 (met. a.).

Clay Cross, t., Derbys., **Eng.**; former ctr. coal mng. (first developed by George Stephenson 1838) iron, engin.; p. (1991) 24,271 (with North Wingfield).

Clayton-le-Moors, t., Hyndburn, Lancs., **Eng.**; nr. Blackburn; textile machin., cotton and blanket weaving, bristles, soap; p. (1991) 6,961.

Clear C., southernmost point of Ireland, Clear I., **R.o.I.**; off S.W. cst. of Cork.

Cleare, c., Alaska, **USA**; site of ballistic missile early warning sta.

Clearwater, t., Fla., **USA**; citrus fruit, flowers, fish; resort; p. (1990) 98,784.

Cleator Moor, t. Cumbria, **Eng.**; former colly. t.; p. (1991) 6,410

Cleckheaton t., West Yorks., **Eng.**; nr. Bradford; woollens, blankets, asbestos; p. (1991) 27,151.

Clee Hills, Shrops., **Eng.**; between Rs. Severn and Teme; alt. 550 m.

Cleethorpes, t., N.E. Lincs., **Eng.**; 5 km S. of Grimsby; resort; p. (1991) 32,179.

Clent Hills, Hereford and Worcs., **Eng.**; about 16 km S.W. of Birmingham, overlooking valley of R. Stour; recreation; maximum alt. 316 m.

Clerkenwell, industl. dist., London, **Eng.**; immediately N. of the City; noted for jewellry.

Clermont-Ferrand, c., cap. Puy-de-Dôme dep. central **France**; in Auvergne; rubber tyres, chemicals, food inds.; Gothic cath., Romanesque church; p. (1990) 140,167 (c.), 254,416 (met. a.).

Clevedon, t., N. Somerset, **Eng.**; at mouth of R. Severn; seaside resort; quarrying, bricks, footwear; p. (1991) 21,670.

Cleveland, c., Ohio, **USA**; impt. Gr. Ls. pt. handling iron ore and coal which support a major iron and steel ind.; oil refining, food processing, many varied inds.; univ.; p. (1990) 505,616 (c.), 1,831,122 (met. a.).

Cleveland Hills, North Yorks., Redcar and Cleveland, **Eng.**; part of N. York Moors; once mined for iron ore, impt. potash deposit.

Clichy, t., Hauts-de-Seine, **France**; N.W. sub. of Paris; oil refining, aircraft, automobile components; p. (1982) 47,000.

Clifton, sub., Bristol, **Eng.**; on R. Avon; mineral springs; famous suspension bridge.

Clifton, t., N.J., **USA**; industl. t., nr. Passaic; p. (1990) 71,742.

Clinton, t., Iowa, **USA**; on Mississippi R.; iron and steel, machin.; p. (1990) 29,201.

Clitheroe, t., Ribble Valley, Lancs., **Eng.**; in Ribble valley; mkt. t. for rural a.; limestone quarrying nearby; p. (1991) 13,548.

Clonakilty, t., Cork, **R.o.I.**; nr. Bandon; sm. harbour; agr. prods.; p. (1986) 2,567.

Cloncurry, t., Queensland, **Australia**; rly junction and air terminal in ctr. of copper field; uranium nearby; p. (1984) 3,040.

Clones, mkt. t. on Ulster border, Monaghan, **R.o.I.**; rly. ctr.; p. (1986) 2,280.

Clonmacnoise, v., Offaly, **R.o.I.**; ecclesiastical ruins.

Clonmel, t., Tipperary, **R.o.I.**; on R. Suir; agr. ctr.; fairs; cider, footwear; p. (1986) 11,759.

Clovelly, v., Devon, **Eng.**; seaside resort.

Clowne, t., Derbys., **Eng.**; coal mng.; p. (1991) 7,234.

Cluj, c., **Romania**; in Transylvania on Somesul R.; univs., historic bldgs.; industl. ctr.; p. (1992) 328,008.

Clutha R., R. of S.I., **N.Z.**, hydroelec. power; 320 km long; gives name to district.; p. (1991) 18,303.

Clwyd, R., Denbighshire, N. **Wales**; flows into Irish Sea at Rhyl; length 48 km.

Clydach, t., Swansea, **Wales**; on R. Tawe, 8 km N.E. Swansea; steel wks., nickel refineries.

Clyde, R., central **Scot.**; flows through industl. belt into Firth of C.; Glasgow, Greenock, Clydebank main pts.; hydroelec. stas.; twin-road tunnel under R. in Glasgow (Whiteinch-Linthouse) com-

pleted 1963; 170 km long.

Clydebank, t., W. Dunbartonshire, **Scot.**; on Clyde adjoining Glasgow; tyres, biscuits; p. (1991) 29,171.

Clyde, Firth of, stretches from Dumbarton to Ailsa Craig, **Scot.**; Bute, Arran, Gr. and Little Cumbrae ch. Is.; 102 km long.

Coachella Valley, arid region, S.E. Cal., **USA**; part of G. of Cal.; dates and citrus fruits grown from Imperial Valley irrigation system.

Coahuila, st., **Mexico**; 3rd st. of Mexico; lies S. of Texas, bordering Rio Grande valley; main coal deposits; mnfs. impt.; irrigated agr.; cap. Saltillo; a. 142,611 km²; p. (1990) 1,971,344.

Coalbrookdale, v., Shrops, **Eng.**; old coal and iron mines; home of iron master Abraham Darby. *See* Bridges, Section L.

Coalville, t., North West Leics., **Eng.**; nr. Ashby-de-la-Zouch; coal mng., engin., elastic webbing; p. (1991) 30,408.

Coast Range, mtns., **USA**; along Pac. cst.; wooded ranges causing rain shadow to E. valleys; alt. up to 600 m.

Coatbridge, burgh, N. Lanarkshire, **Scot.**, 16 km E. of Glasgow; coal, iron and steel, prefabricated houses, tubes engin.; p. (1991) 43,617.

Coats I., S. of Southampton I. Hudson Bay, **Canada**.

Coatzacoalcos (Puerto Mexico), spt., **Mexico**; on G. of Campeche; oil refinery; chemicals, fertilisers; p. (1990) 232,314.

Cobalt, t., Ont., **Canada**; silver, cobalt, arsenic, nickel; p. (1986) 1,640.

Cobán, t., **Guatemala**; mkt. t.; coffee and Peruvian bark tr.; p. (1989) 120,000.

Cóbh (Queenstown), c., Cork, **R.o.I.**; spt. on Great I. in Cork Harbour; lge. docks; H.Q. of Royal Cork Yacht Club; seaside resort; p. (1986) 6,369.

Coburg, t., Bavaria, **Germany**; old cas.; wickerwork, furniture, metal, machines, toy inds.; p. (est. 1986) 44,400.

Cochabamba, dep., **Bolivia**; E. of Andes; lgst. p. concentration of Bolivia in C. basin; a. 65,496 km²; p. (1988) 982,000.

Cochabamba, c., cap. of C. dep., **Bolivia**; second lgst. c. in rep.; alt. 2,559 m; univ., cath.; oil refining, shoes, rubber tyres, fruit-canning, modern milk plant; hydroelectric power; p. (1992) 404,102.

Cochin, spt., Kerala, **India**; on Malabar cst.; exp. coconut oil, tea; oil refining, silting pt.; p. (1981) 513,249.

Cockenzie and Port Seton, small burgh, E. Lothian, **Scot.**; two fishing pts. on F. of Forth; p. (1991) 4,235.

Cockermouth, t., Allerdale, Cumbria, **Eng.**; slate, shoe mftg., plywood, concrete prods.; birthplace of Wordsworth; p. (1991) 7,702.

Cockpit Country, upland a., W. **Jamaica**; classic karst landscape forming rugged upland; some cultivation in hollows; a. 500 km²; alt. 300–800 m.

Coco, R., **Honduras** and **Nicaragua**; flows to Caribbean Sea through economically impt. valley; agr., forestry, mng.; potential as routeway; 480 km long.

Cocos (Keeling) **Is.**, 27 coral atolls, Indian Oc.; since 1955 terr. of **Australia** purchased by Australia (1978) to ensure democracy; strategic position S.E. of Sri Lanka, radio and cable sta. German cruiser *Emden* destroyed by Australian cruiser *Sydney* on N. Keeling I. in 1914; uninhabited until 1826; developed by Clunies Ross family for coconut prod.; controlled emigration since 1948 to solve problem of overpopulation; voted to integrate with Northern Territory, Australia (1984); a. 13 km²; p. (1994) 670.

Coesfeld, t., N. Rhine–Westphalia, **Germany**; textiles, machin.; p. (1986) 31,600.

Cognac, t., Charente, **France**; cognac, bottles; p. (1982) 20,995.

Coihaique, t., Chile; cap. Aysen region; p. (1982) 31,167.

Coimbatore, t., Tamil Nadu, **India**; commands Palghat Gap; varied inds. benefit from local hydroelec. power; p. (1991) 816,000.

Coimbra, t., **Portugal**; cath., oldest univ. in Portugal; wine-growing; earthenware mfns.; p. (1981) 74,616 (t.), 138,930 (met. a.).

Colchester, t., l. gov. dist., Essex, **Eng.**; pre-Roman t. of Camulodunum on R. Colne; univ.; lt. inds., engin., oyster fisheries; pt.; p. (1995) 151,200 (dist.), (1991) 96,083 (t.).

Cold Fell, mtn., Northumberland, **Eng.**; 622 m.

Cold Harbour, v., Va., **USA**; battles between Grant and Lee 1864.

Coldstream, t., Borders, **Scot.**; on Eng. border; agr. machin., knitwear; p. (1991) 1,746.

Coleraine, t., l. gov. dist., **N. Ireland**; pt. on R. Bann, 6 km from sea; univ.inen, acrilan mftg., distilling; p. (1991) 50,721 (dist.), 50,438 (t.).

Coleshill, t., North Warwickshire, **Eng.**; lurgi gasification plant; p. (1991) 6,324.

Colima, mkt. t., **Mexico**; on Colima R. in fertile valley; univ.; agr. processing; p. (1990) 116,155.

Colima, st., **Mexico**; on Pac. cst.; cap. Colima; pt. Manzanillo; cotton, sugar, rice, coffee; a. 5,203 km². (1990) 424,656.

Colima, volcano (48 km N.E. of c.), **Mexico**, alt. 3,869 m.

Coll, I. off cst. of Mull, Argyll and Bute, **Scot.**; agr., lobster fishing; p. (1991) 172.

Collie, t., W. **Australia**; impt. coal deposits supply power for much of W. Australia; p. (1981) 7,667.

Collingwood, t., Ont., **Canada**; on Georgian Bay, L. Huron; shipbldg., steel; p. (1986) 12,127.

Colmar, t., cap. Haut-Rhin dep., **France**; ctr. of Alsace textile ind.; attractive mediaeval t.; mkt. for vineyards; p. (1990) 64,889 (t.), 83,816 (met. a.).

Colne, t., Pendle, E. Lancs., **Eng.**; cotton mnfs., felts; p. (1991) 18,776.

Colne, R., **Eng.**; trib. of Thames rising in Chilterns.

Cologne (Köln), c., N. Rhine–Westphalia, **Germany**; on Rhine at N. end of Rhine gorge; cath. univ.; impt. R. pt., route and comm. ctr., eau-de-Cologne, electro-technical ind., machin., metallurgy, paper, chemicals, cars, oil refining, textiles; p. (1990) 955,500.

Colombes, t., Hauts-de-Seine dep., **France**; sub. of Paris on R. Seine; p. (1990) 79,058.

Colombia, rep., N.W. S. America; cap. Bogotá; Andes contain most of p.; the savannahs (llanos) to S.E. are almost uninhabited; industl. employment growing; increasingly indep. of USA sphere of influence; agr. impt.; coffee, (50 percent of exports), bananas; major oil reserves discovered (1985), some exp.; rapidly expanding coal production in 1990s; eruption of Nevado del Ruiz (1985) Mount Galeras (1993); centre of drugs trade, a. 1,139,592 km²; p. (1994) 34,479,000.

Colombo, c., cap. of **Sri Lanka**; on W. cst.; univ.; impt. pt. (artificial) built by British; exp. tea, rubber, coconuts; p. (1983) 623,000.

Colón, t., **Panama**; at Atl. end of Panama Canal; free tr. zone; comm. and industl. ctr.; oil refining nearby; p. (1990) 140,908.

Colonsay, I., Inner Hebrides, Argyll and Bute, **Scot.**; 13 km long; ecclesiastical antiquities; p. (1991) 349.

Colorado, st., **USA**; admitted to Union 1876; st. flower Rocky Mtn. Columbine, st. bird Lark Bunting; hgst. st. in USA; in the Rockies extending up to 4,401 m (Mt. Elbert), no land below 1,000 m; drained by headwaters of Rs. Arkansas and Colorado; major stockrearing a.; many minerals esp. uranium, radium and molybdenum; cap. Denver; a. 270,000 km²; p. (1990) 3,294,394.

Colorado, plateau, Arizona, Utah, Col., N.M., **USA**; arid upland with spectacular scenery, inc. Grand Canyon; alt. 1,500–3,300 m.

Colorado, R., **Argentina**; flows from Andes to Atl. Oc.; limited irrigation in pastoral valley; length 848 km.

Colorado, major R. of W. **USA**; drains 8% of USA; formed by confluence of Green and Grand Rs.; spectacular canyons inc. Grand Canyon; hydroelec. power from many dams inc. Hoover Dam; irrigation supplies intensive horticultural a. in S. section and consequent rapid decrease in volume to a sm. stream in lower course; length 2,320 km.

Colorado, R., rises N.W. Texas, **USA**; flows to G. of Mexico; irrigation and power; 1,552 km long.

Colorado Desert, Cal., **USA**; inc. Imperial Valley, a fertile irrigated a.

Colorado Springs, t., Col., **USA**; 102 km S. Denver; resort; p. (1990) 281,140 (t.), 397,014 (met. a.).

Columbia, t., Mo., **USA**; W. of St. Louis; st. univ.; flour, lumber; p. (1990) 69,101.

Columbia, t., st. cap. S.C., **USA**; in ctr. of rich farming a.; textiles, clothing; burned down in Civil War 1865; p. (1990) 98,052 (t.), 453,331 (met. a.).

Columbia, District of (D.C.); area on east bank of Potomac R., coterminus with c. of Washington;

cap. of **USA**; a. 179 km²; p. (1990) 606,900.

Columbia, R., major R. of western N. **America**; rises in Rocky Mtns., B.C., flows though Washington, **USA**; power sources, inc. Grand Coulee Dam, Bonneville Dam; deepwater harbour at mouth; length 2,240 km.

Columbus, c., Ga., **USA**; at head of navigation on Chattahoochee R.; industl. and shipping ctr.; textile mills, food-processing; cotton-ginning machin.; p. (1990) 179,278.

Columbus, t., Ind., **USA**; engin.; leather gds.; p. (1980) 30,614.

Columbus, c., st. cap. Ohio, **USA**; rly. ctr.; st. univ.; machin., paper, aircraft machin., chemicals; p. (1990) 632,910 (c.), 1,377,419 (met. a.).

Colwyn Bay, t., Conwy, N. **Wales**; on cst. 10 km E. of Llandudno; seaside resort; p. (1991) 29,883.

Comayagüela, c., former cap. of **Honduras**; twin c. of Tegucigalpa from which it is separated by Choluteca R.; both cs. administered together as Central Dist.

Combe Martin, v., Devon, **Eng.**; 8 km E. of Ilfracombe; seaside resort; p. (1991) 2,453.

Comber, t., Ards, **N. Ireland**; linen; p. (1991) 8,333.

Commonwealth of Independent States, a community of independent states which is successor to USSR; members **Russia, Ukraine, Belarus, Armenia, Azerbaijan, Moldova, Kazakhstan, Kirghizia, Tajikistan, Turkmenistan, Uzbekistan.**; cap. Minsk; p. (1991) 276·65 m.

Como, c., N. **Italy**; at foot of Alps, on L. Como; oranges, olives; textiles; cath.; tourism; p. (1981) 95,571.

Como, L., N. **Italy**; beautiful mtn. scenery, tourism, villas; a. 145 km².

Comodoro Rivadavia, spt., Chubut prov., **Argentina**; on San Jorge G., 880 km S.W. of Bahía Blanca; military zone; univ.; ch. source of oil in Argentine; oil refining; p. (1980) 98,985.

Comorin, C., most S. point of **India**.

Comoros, Indian Oc.; in Moçambique channel, midway between African and Madagascar; cap. Moroni; total a. 2,170 km²; turtle fishing; vanilla, copra, sisal, timber, perfume plants; indep. from France declared 1975 but rejected by Mayotte Is.; p. (1995) 544,000.

Compiègne, t., Oise, **France**; sugar mills, rope; Armistice signed between Allies and Germany 1918; Fr. surrendered to Hitler 1940; resort; p. (1982) 62,778 (met. a.).

Compton, t., Cal., **USA**; residtl. for Los Angeles; heavy engin., glass, oil refining; p. (1980) 81,286.

Conakry, c., cap. of **Rep. of Guinea**; impt. pt. on offshore islet; exp. iron-ore and alumina; experimental fruit gardens; p. (1983) 705,280.

Concarneau, pt., Finistère, **France**; 19 km S.E. Quimper; fisheries; p. (1982) 18,225.

Concepción, c., cap. Biobio region, **Chile**; shipping ctr. through its pt. Talcahuano; univ.; comm. and cultural t.; severe earthquakes 1939 and 1960; nr. to coalfield; p. (1992) 330,448.

Concepción, t., cap. of C. prov., **Paraguay**; main comm. ctr. for Chaco, pt. on R. Paraguay; p. (1984) 25,607.

Conchos, R., Chihuahua prov., **Mexico**; flows N.E. from Madre Occidental to Rio Grande; cotton under irrigation in upper valley; hydroelec. power; length 560 km.

Concord, t., Cal., **USA**; residtl. and comm. ctr. in San Francisco met. a.; p. (1990) 111,348.

Concord, t., Mass., **USA**; literary ctr.; textiles; p. (1980) 16,293.

Concord, t., st. cap., N.H., **USA**; on Merrimack R.; granite, machin., textiles; p. (1980) 30,400.

Concordia, t., **Argentina**; pt. on Uruguay R.; exp. agr. prod.; p. (1991) 138,905.

Condamine, R., Queensland, **Australia**; trib. of R. Darling; used for irrigation.

Coney I., t., N.Y., **USA**; on Long I., 8 km long, comprises Manhattan Beach, Brighton Beach, W. Brighton, and W. End.

Congleton, t., l. gov. dist., E. Cheshire, **Eng.**; on S.W. margin of Pennines; once impt. for silk; p. (1995) 85,700 (dist.), (1991) 24,879 (t.).

Congo, Dem. Rep. of (formerly Zaïre), Central Africa; comprises eight provs. (caps. in brackets): Bas-Congo (Matadi), Bandundu (Bandundu), Equateur (Mbandaka), Haut-Congo (Kisangani), Kivu (Bukavu), Shaba (Lubumbashi), Kasai Oriental (Mbuji-Mayi), Kasai Occidental (Kananga); lies in vast basin of Congo R., mtns. on E. and S. borders; climate equatorial in N., tropical in S.; agr. exp. inc. palm oil, cotton, coffee, but economy based on mng., diamonds (Kasai), cobalt, non-ferrous metals (Shaba), major world producer of copper; radium deposits nr. Lubumbashi; extensive navigation on Congo R.; main pt. Matadi on estuary linked by rail to cap. Kinshasa; rebellion in E. in 1997; a. 2,345,457 km²; p. (1995) 43,814,000.

Congo, People's Rep. of the, indep. st. within Fr. Community. Equatorial Africa; cap. Brazzaville; a. 342,000 km²; p. (1995) 2,936,000.

Congo, gr. R. of **Equatorial Africa**; numerous tribs., drains 3,885,000 km²; navigable from sea to Matadi for ocean steamers, from Matadi to Pool Malebo interrupted by rapids and falls, again navigable to Boyoma Falls; proposed power project to be lgst. in Africa; estuary 11–16 km wide; c. 4,800 km long.

Conisborough, t., South Yorks., **Eng.**; limestone, bricks, tiles; p. (1991) 16,031.

Coniston, t., Ont., **Canada**; on rly. 13 km E. of Sudbury; nickel smelting; t. built by and for nickel-mng. company.

Coniston Water, L., Cumbria, **Eng.**; focus of tourism in L. Dist.; 8-8 km long.

Conjeeveram. *See* **Kanchipuram.**

Connacht, prov., **R.o.I.**; inc. Galway, Mayo, Sligo, Leitrim, Roscommon; mtnous in W.; farming, fishing; a. 17,775 km²; p. (1986) 431,409.

Connah's Quay, t., Flintshire, **Wales**; lt. engin.; p. (1991) 14,443.

Connaught Tunnel (Can. Pac. Rly.), B.C., **Canada**; longest in N. America (8 km) 1,500 m under mt. Sir Donald (Selkirk Mtns.).

Connecticut, R., New Eng.; **USA**; middle course forms fine agr. land; investment in navigation, irrigation and flood control; 566 km long.

Connecticut, st., New England, **USA**; one of original 13 sts.; admitted to Union 1788; st. flower mountain Laurel, st. bird robin; humid climate; arable agr.; diversified inds.; many natural harbours on cst.; cap. Hartford; lgst. c. Bridgeport; a. 12,973 km²; p. (1990) 3,287,116.

Connemara, mtns., dist., **R.o.I.**; Co. Galway; many lakes and bogs; tourist resort.

Consett, t., Derwentside, Durham, **Eng.**; on edge of Pennines, 16 km S.W. Newcastle; iron, steel closed (1980), coal mng.; p. (1991) 20,148.

Constance (**Konstanz**), c., Baden–Württemberg, **Germany**; on Bodensee; cath.; textiles, machin., chemicals, elec. inds.; route ctr.; p. (1983) 69,100.

Constance, L. *See* **Bodensee.**

Constanta, ch. spt. S.E. **Romania**; on Black Sea; oil pipeline to Ploiesti and Cimpina; Danube-Black Sea canal (1984) shortens route of Trans-European waterway to Black Sea; exp. petroleum, wheat; cement, chemicals; p. (1992) 350,476.

Constantine. *See* **Qacentina.**

Constantinople. *See* **Istanbul.**

Conwy, spt., N. **Wales**; mediaeval walled t. at mouth of R. Conwy; sm. seaside resort; cas.; quarrying, lt. engin.; unit. auth. created in 1996 from former l. gov. dists. of Aberconwy and Colwyn; inc. Conwy Valley and coastal resorts of Conwy, Llandudno and Colwyn Bay; p. (1991) 3,627 (t.), (1995) 111,200 (unit. auth.).

Cook, mtn., alt. 3,753 m; hgst. point in S. Alps. and **N.Z.**; 3 peaks. To be renamed Mt. Aoraki.

Cook Inlet, S. cst. Alaska, **USA**; oil pipeline connects oilfields of Granite Point with marine terminal at Dritt R.

Cook Is., Brit. gr. (Rarotonga lgst.) in S. Pac., annexed to **N.Z.** 1901; internal self-govt. 1965; bananas, oranges, copra; a. 241 km²; p. (1994) 18,500.

Cookstown, mkt. t., l. gov. dist., **N. Ireland**; cement wks.; p. (1991) 31,082 (dist.), 9,842 (t.).

Cook Strait, channel between N. and S. Is. of **N.Z.**; 24–29 km wide; undersea cable completed 1965.

Cooma, t., N.S.W., **Australia**; mkt. t.; tourist ctr. for Kosciusko Nat. Park; H.Q. of Snowy Mts. Authority; p. (1981) 7,978.

Coonoor, t., Tamil Nadu, **India**; in Nilgiri Hills; sanatorium c. 1,800 m a.s.l.; p. (1981) 44,750.

Cooper Creek (**Barcoo**), intermittent R., central **Australia**; rises in Warrego Range, Gr. Dividing Range, flows S.W. into marshes of L. Eyre; provides water for livestock in semi-arid region; 1,408 km long.

Copeland, l. gov. dist., Cumbria, **Eng.**; cstl. a. N. of Barrow and inc. Whitehaven and Millom; p. (1995) 70,700.

Copenhagen (**København**), ch. spt., cap. of **Denmark**; on E. cst. of Sjaelland I.; royal palace,

univ., library; naval sta.; freeport; steel, metal, textiles, clothing, breweries; p. (1990) 617,637.

Copiapó, t., cap. of Atacama region, **Chile**; copper- and iron-mng. ctr.; p. (1992) 100,946.

Coquet, R., Northumberland, **Eng.**; rises in the Cheviots and flows into North Sea.

Coquimbo, region Chile; cap. La Serena; a. 40,656 km²; p. (1992) 502,460.

Coquimbo, spt., **Chile**; exp. iron. copper, and manganese ores; p. (1992) 122,872.

Coral Sea, Pac Oc., extends from the New Hebrides to Australia.

Coral Sea Islands Territory, Fed. terr., **Australia**; scattered Is., E. of Gr. Barrier Reef, off Queensland cst.; possibility of oil exploration.

Corbeil-Essonnes, t., Essonne, **France**; on R. Seine, 19 km S.E. of Paris; flour mills, printing, paper; p. (1982) 38,081.

Corbridge, t., Northumberland, **Eng.**; on R. Tyne, nr. Hexham; 17th cent. bridge; Roman t. nearby; p. (1991) 2,719.

Corby, t., l. gov. dist., Northants., **Eng.**; 11 km N. of Kettering; new t.; former steel wks., clothing, lamps; p. (1995) 52,300 (dist.), (1991) 49,053 (t.).

Córdoba, c. and prov., central **Argentina**; univ.; cultural and comm. ctr.; exp. wheat, cattle, lumber; health resort; local hydroelec. power from La Vina; p. (1991) 1,208,713 (c.), 2,766,683 (prov.).

Córdoba, t., Veracruz, **Mexico**; mkt. t. in coffee growing a.; p. (1990) 150,428.

Córdoba, prov., Andalusia, **Spain**; cap. Córdova; olives, vines, livestock; a. 13,724 km²; p. (1991) 753,760.

Córdoba, c., Andalusia, **Spain**; cap. of C. prov., on Guadalquivir R.; cath. first built as a mosque in 8th cent.; tourist ctr.; p. (1991) 309,212.

Corfu (**Kérkira**), most N. of Ionian Is., **Greece**; traversed by mtns. but largely lowland producing olive oil, figs, wine, oranges; a. 637 km²; p. (1991) 107,592 (prov.).

Corinth (**Kórinthos**), t., cap. Corinthia prov., **Greece**; at end of Isthmus of C.; occupies site 5 km from anc. classic c. destroyed by earthquake 1858; raisins, wine; p. (1981) 22,658 (t.),(1991) 141,823 (prov.).

Corinth Canal, ship canal, S. **Greece**; traverses Isthmus of Corinth, links G. of Corinth and Ionian Sea with Saronic G. and Aegean Sea; opened 1893; length 5-6 km, depth 8 m.

Corinth, Isthmus of, connects the Peloponnesus with the mainland of **Greece**; cut across by canal.

Corinto, ch. spt., N.W. **Nicaragua**; handles 50 per cent of cty's tr.; exp. hides, sugar, coffee; p. (1985) 24,000.

Cork, co., **R.o.I.**; lgst. and most S.; mtns.; dairying, brewing, agr., fisheries; cap. Cork; a. 7,485 km²; p. (1986) 412,735.

Cork, spt., Cork, **R.o.I.**; at mouth of R. Lee; cath., univ.; woollens, butter, cattle, brewing, cars, rubber; p. (1986) 133,271.

Corner Brook, c., W. Newfoundland, **Canada**; gd. harbour; iron foundries, cement, gypsum; one of world's lgst. newsprint mills; p. (1991) 22,410.

Cornwall, t., Ont., **Canada**; on St. Lawrence R.; H.Q. of Seaway Authority; textiles, pulp, paper, flour; p. (1986) 46,425.

Cornwall and Isles of Scilly, non-met. co., S.W. **Eng.**; penin. bordering Atl. Oc. and Eng. Channel; granite moorlands supply kaolin; formerly tin mining; mild maritime climate encourages tourism, dairying, and mkt. gardening; many small fishing vs.; co. t. Bodmin; p. (1995) 482,700.

Coro, c., Falcón, **Venezuela**; on Paraguaná penin.; agr. processing; nearby oil refineries; p. (1990) 124,616.

Corocoro, t., La Paz dep., **Bolivia**; at alt. c. 4,000 m in central Andes, 80 km S. of La Paz; impt. copper-mng. ctr.

Coromandel Coast (**Carnatic region**), cst. of Tamil Nadu, **India**; where earliest European settlements established; extensive a. of flat land built up by R. Cauvery.

Coronation Gulf, arm of Beaufort Sea; extreme point N. Canadian mainland; discovered by Franklin.

Coronel Oviedo, t., **Paraguay**; comm. ctr.; p. (1982) 21,782.

Corpus Christi, c., Texas, **USA**; cotton, oil refining, chemicals; resort; p. (1990) 257,453 (c.), 350,000 (met. a.).

Corréze, dep., S. central **France**; part of Massif Central, mostly over 600 m; cap. Tulle; a. 5,884 km²; p. (1990) 237,900.

Corrib, Lough, Galway and Mayo, **R.o.I.**; drained

by Corrib R. into Galway Bay; impt. brown trout fishery; a. 176 km².

Corrientes, t. and prov., **Argentina**; agr. tr. ctr. on Paraná R.; univ.; cattle, sugar, rice, cotton; river navigation reduces isolation; p. (1991) 258,103 (t.), 795,594 (prov.).

Corryvreckan, strait and whirlpool between Jura and Scarba Is., Inner Hebrides, **Scot.**; whirlpool caused by tidal movement over variable sea bed.

Corse du Sud. *See* Corsica.

Corsica (**Corse**), I., **France**; in Mediterranean Sea; violent history in 16th and 17th cent.; high granite peaks (Monte Cinto), mtn. torrents, fertile plains; inland and sea fishing; rapid growth of tourism with little benefit to indigenous Corsicans; split into 2 deps. to help overcome autonomist agitation (1975); Haute Corse, cap. Bastia (1990) 131,600, Corse-du-Sud, cap. Ajaccio (1990) 118,800; a. 8,721 km²; p. (1990) 250,400.

Corsicana, t., Texas, **USA**; site of first oil drilling in USA; p. (1980) 21,712.

Cortona, t., Tuscany, **Italy**; nr. Perugia; Roman remains, cath.; p. (1981) 22,281.

Corunna. *See* La Coruña.

Corvallis, t., Ore., **USA**; in fertile farming valley; lumbering; univ.; p. (1990) 44,757.

Coryton, t., Essex, **Eng.**; on Thames, oil refining; oil pipeline to Stanlow refinery.

Cos (**KOS**), I., Dodecanese, **Greece**; in Aegean Sea, second lgst. of gr.; gave name to Cos lettuce; birthplace of Hippocrates; p. (1981) 20,350.

Cosenza, c., S. **Italy**; ctr. for figs, oranges, olive oil, wine; cath., univ., cas.; p. (1984) 106,376.

Costa Brava, region, Catalonia, **Spain**; tourism.

Costa del Sol, region, Málaga cst., **Spain**; tourism.

Costa Rica, rep., Central America; over half p. in equable Meseta Central; cap. San José; forests, volcanic mtns.; agr. 40 per cent G.N.P.; coffee, bananas, cacao; high literacy and living standards; a. 50,909 km²; p. (1995) 3,385,000.

Côte d'Azur, **France**; Mediterranean littoral E. of Rhône R.; inc. resorts of Nice, Cannes, Monte Carlo, and St. Tropez.

Côte d'Ivoire (**Ivory Coast**), rep., on G. of Guinea, formerly a Fr. overseas terr.; hot, humid climate; coastal lagoons, interior plateau (300– 1,200 m); economy based on subsistence agr. although an impt. coffee and timber producer; world's third lgst. coffee producer; half p. relies on coffee as principal source of income; underdeveloped mineral resources; poorly developed rail network but extensive road system; new tt. at San Pedro; Pt. Bouet outport of former cap. Abidjan; new cap. Yamoussoukro (1983); a. 322,481 km²; p. (1994) 13,720,000.

Côte d'Or, dep., E. **France**; heart of anc. Burgundy, traversed by R. Saône; cap. Dijon; wines, livestock, iron and steel; a. 8,783 km²; p. (1990) 493,900.

Cotentin, peninsula, N. **France**; 80 km long; Cherbourg, at its extremity, 128 km from Portsmouth.

Côtes-d'Armor, dep., N. Brittany, **France**; rugged cst. and Is. and mild climate encourage tourism; mkt. gardens along cst.; many fishing ts.; cap. St. Brieuc; a. 7,218 km²; p. (1990) 538,400.

Cotonou, pt., **Benin Rep.**; new artificial pt.; fishing; lt. inds.; offshore oilfields (drilling from 1982); p. (1982) 487,020.

Cotopaxi, volcano, (alt. 5,982 m) in the Andes of **Ecuador**, nr. Quito; loftiest active volcano in the world; recent eruptions have caused great damage to Ecuador.

Cotswold, l. gov. dist., Gloucs., **Eng.**; lge a. covering C. Hills and inc. Cirencester and Northleach; p. (1995) 81,400.

Cotswold Hills, W. **Eng.**; limestone escarpment; Gloucs., Oxon.; once famous for woollens; source of Thames and tribs.; highest point Cleeve Cloud, 309 m; tourism.

Cottbus or **Kottbus**, t, Brandenburg, **Germany**; on R. Spree; rly. ctr.; textile and metal mnfs.; p. (1990) 124,900.

Cottian Alps, mtn. range on border of France and Italy crossed by Hannibal; craggy; max. alt. 2,844 m (Monte Viso).

Coulsdon and Purley. *See* Croydon.

Council Bluffs, t., Iowa, **USA**; on Missouri R. nr. Omaha; rly. ctr.; farm implements, paper, machin.; p. (1990) 54,315.

Courantyne, R., **Guyana**; rises in Serra Acari; passes through bauxite mng. region to Atl. Oc.; navigation in lower course; 720 km long.

Courtrai. *See* Kortrijk.

Cove and **Kilcreggan**, burgh, Argyll and Bute, **Scot.**; at junction of Loch Long and R. Clyde; p. (1991) 1,586.

Coventry, c., met. dist., West Midlands, **Eng.**; 29 km E.S.E. of Birmingham; former ctr. of cycle, motor cycle, motor car and aircraft engines, tractors, engin.; tools; chemicals; projectiles, textiles; cath.; univ.; p. (1995) 303,600 (dist.), (1991) 299,316 (c.).

Covilhã, t., **Portugal**; cloth factories; p. (1981) 21,807 (c.), 60,945 (met. a.).

Covington, t., Ky., **USA**; on R. Ohio, opp. Cincinnati; machin., leather, furniture; p. (1990) 43,264.

Cowbridge, t., Vale of Glamorgan, S. **Wales**; nr. Cardiff; p. (1991) 3,682.

Cowdenbeath, burgh, Fife, **Scot.**; 8 km N.E. of Dunfermline; coal; p. (1991) 12,126.

Cowes, resort and pt., I. of Wight, **Eng.**; on estuary of R. Medina; regattas and yacht bldg.; hovercraft; p. (1991) 16,335.

Cowra, t., N.S.W., **Australia**; famous wheat dist. and site of state experimental farm; p. (1981) 7,900.

Cozumel I., E. of Yucatan peninsula, **Mexico**.

Craców. *See* Kraków.

Cradle, Mt., mtn., Tasmania, **Australia**; alt. 1,546 m; Nat. Park.

Cradock, t., Cape Prov., **S. Africa**; wool tr.; p. (1980) 39,160 (dist.).

Craigavon, c., l. gov. dist., **N. Ireland**; new "city in a garden" under construction, 16 km long, merging Portadown and Lurgan, linked by motorway, to provide major base for ind.; p. (1991) 74,986 (dist.), 9,201 (c.).

Crail, royal burgh, Fife, **Scot.**; cstl. resort; p. (1991) 1,449.

Craiova, c., S. **Romania**, in Wallachia; tr. ctr.; agr. processing, textiles, engin., chemicals; p. (1992) 303,520.

Cramlington, t., Northumberland, **Eng.**; 13 km N. of Newcastle; new t.; p. (1991) 26,238.

Cranborne Chase, Wilts., **Eng.**; chalk upland of over 275 m; extension of Salisbury Plain.

Cranbrook, mkt. t., Kent, **Eng.**; hops and grain; former weaving t.; p. (1991) 3,522.

Cranston, t., R.I., **USA**; machin., chemicals, textiles; p. (1980) 71,992.

Crater L., Ore., **USA**; in Nat. Park, is a body of water 600 m deep and 9·5 km across, set in a crater of an extinct volcano, *c.* 2,400 m high; varied flora and fauna on shore.

Craters of the Moon, dist., Idaho, **USA**; Nat. Monument of volcanic craters and cones; a. 192 km².

Crau, La, region, Bouches-du-Rhône dep., S.E. **France**; dry, pebbly area E. of Rhône delta; winter pasture for sheep.

Craven, dist., central Pennines, **Eng.**; relatively low limestone plateau, alt. mainly below 240 m; drained by R. Ribble to S.W., R. Aire to S.E.; sheep rearing in valleys, cattle for fattening, root and fodder crops; forms l. gov. dist. based on Skipton and Settle; p. (1995) 51,000.

Crawley, t., l. gov. dist., West Sussex, **Eng.**; on N.W. flank of Weald, 14 km S. of Reigate; new t. (1947); engin., pharmaceuticals, metal, leather, wooden goods; p. (1995) 91,900 (dist.), (1991) 88,203 (t.).

Crayford. *See* Bexley.

Creag Meagaidh, mtn., Highland, **Scot.**; alt. 1,128 m.

Crediton, mkt. t., Devon, **Eng.**; p. (1991) 8,142.

Cree, R., Dumfries and Galloway, **Scot.**; flows into Wigtown Bay.

Crema, industl. and agr. t., N. **Italy**; S.E. of Milan; cath.; p. (1981) 34,610.

Cremona, t., cap. of C. prov., Lombardy, N. **Italy**; famed as a ctr. of learning and later for mnf. of violins and violas; revived in last 20 years; birthplace of Stradivari; cath.; pt. on new Milan-Adriatic Waterway; p. (1981) 80,929.

Crete (**Kriti**), I., E. Mediterranean, lgst. I. of **Greece**; cradle of Minoan civilisation between 1600 and 1400 B.C.; mild climate; sm. a. of cultivable land; few minerals; part of Greece since Balkan Wars (1913); cap. Iraklion; birthplace of El Greco; a. 8,379 km²; p. (1991) 540,054 (admin. reg.).

Créteil, t., cap. Val-de-Marne dep., **France**; light inds.; p (1990) 82,390.

Creus, c., juts out into Mediterranean Sea, **Spain**; nr. Fr. border.

Creuse, dep., in Massif Central, **France**; soil infertile, harsh climate, limited agr.; a. 5,605 km² p. (1990) 131,300.

Crewe, t., Cheshire, **Eng.**; 32 km S.E. of Chester; lge. rly. wks.; impt. rly. junc.; aircraft and refrigerator wks., clothing, engin., motor vehicles; expanded t.; part of l. gov. dist. of **Crewe and Nantwich**; p. (1995) 113,600 (dist.), (1991) 63,351 (t.).

Crewkerne, mkt. t., Somerset, **Eng.**; 13 km S.W. of Yeovil; leather gds.; grammar school (1499); p. (1991) 7,142.

Criccieth, t., Gwynedd, N. **Wales**; on N. shore of Cardigan Bay; seaside resort; p. (1991) 1,720.

Cricklade, t., N. Wilts., **Eng.**; on R. Thames, 13 km N.W. of Swindon; fortified Saxon township; p. (1991) 3,808.

Crieff, t., Perth and Kinross, **Scot.**; on R. Earn; summer resort; p. (1991) 6,023.

Crimea (Krym) Peninsula, juts into Black Sea, **Ukraine**; wheat, tobacco, fruit; campaign 1854–55 between Russia and Allied Forces of Turkey, Britain, France, and Sardinia was chiefly fought out here (Alma, Balaclava, and Sevastopol); tourism, demands for independence (1992).

Crimmitschau, t., Saxony, **Germany**; nr. Zwickau; impt. textile ctr.; p. (1989) 23,455.

Crinan Canal, across peninsula of Argyll and Bute, S.W. **Scot.**; connects Loch Gilp with Atl. Oc.; 14 km long.

Croaghpatrick, mtns., May, **R.o.I.**; 766 m.

Croatia, formerly part of Yugoslavia, recognised as independent by EC, 1991; stretches from Istria on Adriatic cst. to Dinaric Alps; crossed by Drava and Sava Rs.; traditional agr. being replaced by new inds.; impt. aluminium wks. based on local bauxite; chemicals, shipbldg.; impt. oilfields; cap. Zagreb; a. 56,524 km² p. (1994) 4,837,000.

Crocodile R. *See* Limpopo.

Cromarty, burgh, Highland, **Scot.**; N.E. cst. of Black Isle; offshore oil platforms at Nigg, C. Firth; p. (1991) 721.

Cromer, t., North Norfolk, **Eng.**; on N. cst. of E. Anglia; seaside resort; p. (1991) 7,267.

Cromford, v., Derbys., **Eng.**; Richard Arkwright's first waterpowered mill (1777); cotton; p. (1991) 2,426 (with Matlock Bath).

Crook and Willington, ts., former U.D., Wear; p. (1991) 8,246.

Valley, Durham, **Eng.**; varied inds. to replace coal mng.; p. (1981) 21,619.

Crosby, t., Sefton, Merseyside, **Eng.**; on Liverpool Bay 5 km N. of Bootle, Seaforth container pt.; residtl.; seaside resort; p. (1991) 52,869.

Cross, R., S.E. **Nigeria**; rises in Cameroon Highlands, flows W. and S. into G. of Guinea at Calabar; useful inland waterway; 640 km long.

Cross River, state **Nigeria**; cap. Calabar; agric., cement, oil; a. 27,237 km²; p. (1991) 1,865,604.

Cross Fell, mtn., Cumbria, **Eng.**; on E. border of co.; alt. 894 m; highest point of the Pennines.

Crotone, t., S. **Italy**; pt. on E. cst. Calabria; electro-chemicals and metallurgical inds.; on site of anc. Crotona founded as Greek col.; home of Pythagoras; p. (1981) 58,281.

Crowland, t., Lincs., **Eng.**; mkt. t. in the Fens, on R. Welland; 8th-cent. abbey ruins; p. (1991) 3,172.

Crows Nest Pass, B.C., Alberta, **Canada**; southernmost pass across Canadian Rocky Mtns.; used by rly. from Medicine Hat to Syokane (USA); summit 1,360 m.

Croydon, residtl. t., **Eng.**; now outer bor., Greater London; inc. Coulsdon and Purley; lt. inds.; major office ctr.; p. (1995) 330,900.

Crummock Water, L. Dist., Cumbria, **Eng.**; ribbon L.

Csongrad, mkt. t., agr. dist., **Hungary**; at junc. of Rs. Tisza and Körös; p. (1984) 22,000.

Cuba, I., indep. rep., W.I.; cap. Havana; lies within tropics; highly fertile although half land a. is mtnous.; exp. sugar, nickel, tobacco, rum, citrus fruits; revolution (1959) reoriented economic and political connections away from USA towards USSR; excellent health care and education; 88 per cent of cultivated land in state farms or cooperatives; recent attempts to diversify economy but sugar still 75 per cent of exp; a. 114,494 km²; p. (1994) 10,977,000.

Cubatão, t., **Brazil**; N.E. of Santos; rapidly growing t. from industl. expansion; hydro-electric, oil refinery, petro-chems., new integrated steel wks. to aid vehicle ind. of São Paulo; p. (1980) 66,000.

Cuckfield, mkt. t., Mid Sussex, West Sussex, **Eng.**; p. (1991) 2,879.

Cuckmere, R., Sussex, **Eng.**; passes through S. Downs in beautiful gap; length 37 km.

Cúcuta, t., cap. of Norte de Santander, **Colombia**; close to Venezuelan border; nr. oilfield; destroyed by earthquake, 1875; new planned t.; p. (1992) 450,318.

Cuddalore, spt., Tamil Nadu, **India**; nr. Pondicherry; exp. oilseeds, cottons; p. (1991) 144,561.

Cuddapah, t., Andhra Pradesh, **India**; cotton, cloth factories, millet, rice; p. (1991) 121,422.

Cudworth, South Yorks., **Eng.**; p. (1991) 11,715.

Cuenca, t., cap. of Azuay prov., 3rd. c. of **Ecuador**; in fertile agr. basin of Andes; sugar, tyres, flour mills, Panama hats; p. (1990) 194,981.

Cuenca, agr. and mng. prov., central **Spain**; furniture, leather, paper; a. 17,063 km²; p. (1991) 200,383.

Cuenca, t., cap of C. prov., **Spain**; on gorge above R. Júcar; mkt. t.; famed in mediaeval times for silver and cloth mnfs.; p. (1987) 41,407.

Cuernavaca, t., cap. of Morelos st., central **Mexico**; anc. Indian t. captured by Cortes; tourist resort; univ.; p. (1990) 281,752.

Cuiabá, t., cap. of Mato Grosso st., **Brazil**; ctr. pastoral a.; gold and diamonds produced; galena deposit nearby; p. (1985) 283,100.

Cuillin Hills, mtns., I. of Skye, **Scot.**; attaining 992 m in Sgurr Alasdair.

Culiacán, c., of Sinaloa, N.W. **Mexico**; anc. c.; Pacific pt. Altata; p. (1990) 602,114.

Culloden Moor, 10 km E. of Inverness, **Scot.**; defeat of Prince Charles Edward Stuart's highlanders by Duke of Cumberland's forces (1746).

Culross, royal burgh, Fife, **Scot.**; belongs to Nat. Trust; abbey.

Culver City, t., Cal., **USA**; sub. of Los Angeles; lge. motion-picture plant; electronic equipment, machin., chemicals, tools; p. (1980) 38,139.

Cumaná, c., N.E. **Venezuela**; pt. on Caribbean; European settlement since 1510; exp. coffee, cacao; sardine canning; airpt.; p. (1990) 212,492.

Cumberland, historic co., N. **Eng.**; now part of Cumbria non-met. co.

Cumberland, industl. t., Md., **USA**; on Potomac R.; iron and steel, tyres, glassware; p. (1990) 23,706.

Cumberland Gap, Ky., **USA**; ch. break in high E. wall of Cumberland plateau; gives access from upper Tennessee valley to Cumberland and Ohio valleys; impt. routeway in colonisation of Ky.

Cumberland Is., off cst. of Queensland, **Australia**.

Cumberland Plateau, mtn. region, Ky., Tenn., Ala., **USA**; forms S.W. zone of Appalachian mtn. system terminating abruptly towards Tennessee valley to E., Cumberland valley to W.; drained W. by tribs. of Cumberland and Ohio Rs; composed of horizontal sandstones overlying coal; thinly populated by farming communities except where mng. ts. occur in valleys cut down to coal; mainly between 360–900 m.

Cumberland R., Tenn. and Ky., **USA**; trib. of Ohio R., rises in C. plateau; upper course forested; crosses coal-mng. a. and fertile agr. valley; part of Tenn. Valley Authority scheme; hydroelec. power; 1,104 km long.

Cumbernauld, new t. (1955), N. Lanarkshire, **Scot.**; to house 50,000 overspill from Glasgow; mnfs. of adding machines rapidly declining with use of computers; p. (1991) 48,762.

Cumbrae, Gt. and Little, Is. in F. of Clyde, off cst. of N. Ayrshire, **Scot.**; p. (1991) 1,393.

Cumbria, non-met. co., N.W. **Eng.**; centred on L. Dist. where rugged glaciated scenery encourages tourism, sheep farming, forestry and water storage; Cumberland coalfield on W. cst. and declining heavy inds. being replaced by new lt. inds.; ch. ts. Carlisle and Barrow; p. (1995) 490,300.

Cumbrian Mtns., L. Dist., Cumbria, **Eng.**

Cumnock, t., E. Ayrshire, **Scot.**, hilly dist. S. of Glasgow; p. (1991) 9,607.

Cundinamarca, dep., **Colombia**; contains many Andean Is. and the fed. cap. Bogotá; a. 23,585 km²; p. (1992) 1,658,751 (excluding Bogota).

Cunene. *See* Kunene R.

Cuneo, prov., **Italy**; a. 7,433 km²; p. (1981) 548,452.

Cuneo, t., cap. of C. prov., Piedmont, **Italy**; mkt. for prod. of surrounding a.; withstood many sieges under the rule of house of Savoy; p. (1981) 55,875.

Cupar, royal burgh, Fife, **Scot.**; on R. Eden, W. of St. Andrews; p. (1991) 7,545.

Curaçao, I., Neth. Antilles, off N. cst. Venezuela; major ctr. for refining and trans-shipping Venezuelan oil; threatened closure (1985) offset for 5 years to avoid economic collapse (provides 25 percent of C. income); picturesque Dutch architectur in cap. Willemstad; a. 544 km²; p. (1994) 149,376.

Curepipe, t., central **Mauritius**; health resort; p. (1993) 76,133.

Curicó, t., **Chile**; agr. and comm. ctr.; earthquake 1928; p. (1992) 103,919.

Curitiba, c., cap. of Paraná st., **Brazil**; univ.; industl. and comm. ctr. at *c.* 900 m; coffee, maté, chemicals, pharmaceutical and forest prods., foodstuffs; p. (1991) 1,290,142.

Curragh, plain, Kildare, **R.o.I.**; turf; racecourse.

Curtis I., Queensland, **Australia**; low volcanic I.; wooded; cattle.

Curzola. *See* **Korčula.**

Cuttack, t., Orissa st., **India**; on Mahanadi R.; long famous for gold and silver filigree work; p. (1991) 403,000.

Cuxhaven, spt., Lower Saxony, **Germany**; outport of Hamburg at the mouth of R. Elbe; fine harbour; p. (1986) 56,100.

Cuyahoga Falls, t., Ohio, **USA**; industl. and residtl.; p. (1990) 48,950.

Cuzco, dep., **Peru**; inc. Central Cordilleras, reaching *c.* 5,800 m; tropical climate; agr. varies with alt.; minerals; cap. C.; a. 144,304 km²; p. (1990) 1,041,800.

Cuzco, t., cap. of C. dep., S. **Peru**; in Andes at alt. 3,418 m in valley of Urubamba R.; once cap of Incas; sacked by Francisco Pizarro 1533; cath., ruins of Inca fortress; tr. ctr. for agr. prod.; p. (1993) 1,028,763 (prov.), 255,568 (t.).

Cwmbran, t., Torfaen, **Wales**; in valley of Afon Lwyd, 8 km N. of Newport; new t. (1949); motor accessories, wire, elec. prods., bricks, tiles, pipes; p. (1991) 46,021.

Cyclades (Kirkádhes), gr. of about 220 Is., **Greece**; rugged and barren csts, conceal sheltered agr. valleys; ch. t. and pt. Hermoupolis; a. 2,650 km²; p. (1991) 94,005.

Cyprus, Rep. of, I., indep. state, E. Mediterranean, 64 km S. of Turkey; Is., inc. main pt. of Famagusta, occupied by Turkey from 1974; indep. st. of Turkish Rep. of Cyprus declared (1983) but only recognised by Turkey; varied cst., limestone hills in N., forested mtns. in S., central plains of Messarois in which cap. Nicosia is situated; agr. employs 30 per cent of p.; many irrigation schemes also aid soil and water conservation; land reform programmes to reduce fragmentation of holdings; copper in Troodos mtns. but asbestos of increasing importance; lt. inds. and tourism helping to restructure economy but agr. provides over 50 per cent of exp., inc. wine, citrus fruit, vegetables; split of cty. by Attila line into 2 separate parts N. dependent on aid from Turkey but S. developing rapidly since 1974; applying for EU membership; a. 9,251 km²; p. (1994) 725,000.

Cyrenaica, prov., **Libya**; impt. region in anc. times; Greek col. 7th cent. B.C., Roman prov. 1st cent. B.C., captured by Arabs A.D. 642, part of Ottoman Empire 16th cent.; animal grazing, dates, oilwells; a. 854,700 km².

Czechoslovakia, former federal republic consisting of two nations of equal rights; landlocked country linked to sea by Elbe, Oder and Danube; socialist planned economy with coal, iron and steel; following elections in June 1992 division into **Czech Republic** and **Slovakia** took place on 1 January 1993; a. 127,897 km²; p. (1990) 15·7 m.

Czech Republic, western part of former Czechoslovakia, cap. Prague; 8 administrative regions; privatisation programme; applying for EU membership; a. 78,864 km²; p. (1995) 10,362,400.

Czernowitz. *See* **Chernovtsy.**

Czestochowa, c. and prov., S. **Poland**; on Warta R.; rly. and industl. ctr.; iron and steel, textiles; celebrated religious ctr.; monastery; p. (1989) 256,578 (c.), 773,400 (prov).

D

Dabrowa Gornicza, t., Katowice, **Poland**; coal, zinc, iron ore; p. (1989) 134,934.

Dacca (Dhaka), c., cap. of **Bangladesh**; on Buriganga R., old channel of Ganges; jute, muslin, paper mnfs.; medical radioisotope ctr.; univ.; p. (1991) 3,397,187.

Dachau, t., Bavaria, **Germany**; paper, elec. gds., brewing; concentration camp during last war; p. (1986) 32,900.

Dachstein, mtn., Salzkammergut, **Austria**; alt. 2,998 m.

Dacorum, l. gov. dist., Herts., **Eng.**; a. of Chilterns inc. Tring, Berkhamsted and Hemel Hempstead; p. (1995) 134,500.

Dadra and Nagar Haveli, union terr., **India**; admin. ctr. Silvassa; a. 490 km²; p. (1991) 138,477.

Dagenham, dist. former M.B., **Eng.**; now forms part of Greater London bor. of Bark-ing; on N. bank of R. Thames with river-side Ford motor works.

Dagestan, Caucasian aut rep., **Russia**; mtnous.; cap. Makhachkala; cotton, orchards and vineyards; machin., engin. oil; a. 50,246 km²; p. (1989) 1,802,200.

Dagupan, c., Pangasinan, Luzon, **Philippines**; on Lingayen Bay; comm. ctr.; p. (1990) 122,247.

Daharki Mari, t., **Pakistan**; 560 km N.E. of Karachi; fertiliser plant.

Dahlak Archipelago, Eritrea; in Red Sea; only 2 Is. inhabited; noted for pearl fishing.

Dahomey. *See* **Benin, People's Rep. of.**

Daimiel, mkt. t., Ciudad Real, **Spain**; cheeses, oil, wine; p. (1981) 16,260.

Dakar, spt., cap. of **Senegal**, W. Africa; S.E. of C. Verde behind Gorée I. on Atl. cst.; exp. groundnuts; some industl. development; free tr. zone, international airport; univ. and medical ctr.; p. (1992) 1,729,823.

Dakhla, oasis, Libyan Desert, **Egypt**; 272 km S.W. of Asyût; dates, olives; stage on caravan route from Cyrenaica to Upper Egypt; site of New Valley Project for irrigation.

Dalälven, R., S. central **Sweden**; length 520 km, used for timber transport.

Da Lat (Dalat), t., **Vietnam**; 224 km N.E. Ho Chiminh City; in Annamite hills; nuclear reactor (1963); airport.

Dalbeattie, burgh, Dumfries and Galloway, **Scot.**; granite, dairy prod., gloves; p. (1991) 4,421.

Dalby, t., Queensland, **Australia**; 1961 oil strike of Moonie oilfield; rich volcanic soils aid grain and beef production; p. (1984) 9,590.

Dalgety, t., on Fife cst., **Scot.**; new t. proposed; p. (1991) 7,860.

Dalian, spt., Liaoning prov., **China**; seafood cultivation; shipbldg., heavy engin., elec., chemical inds.; fully mechanised pt. and another being built; designated development zone in cty.'s new open door policy; p. (1992) 2,420,000.

Dalkeith, burgh, Midlothian, **Scot.**; 10 km S.E. of Edinburgh; mkt. t.; p. (1991) 11,567.

Dallas, c., Texas, **USA**; in cotton- and graingrowing a.; machin., aircraft, petroleum prod.; univ.; scene of assassination of President Kennedy (1963); p. (1990) 1,006,877 (c.), 2,553,362 (met. a.).

Dalmatia, region of **Croatia**, N.E. Adriatic cst.; high Karst plateaux; olive oil, wine; tourism; contains many resorts; a. 12,732 km².

Daltonganj, t., Bihar, **India**; on R. Koël; coal, cement; p. (1981) 51,952.

Dalton-in Furness, t., Cumbria, **Eng.**; limestone quarrying, textiles; abbey ruins; p. (1991) 7,550.

Daman (Damão), spt., Union Territory **India**; 160 km N. Bombay; fishing, ship-bldg., cotton; former Portuguese settlement; p. (1991), 62,101 (t.), 101,586 (terr.).

Damanhûr, t., **Egypt**; on W. margin of Nile delta, 40 km S.E. of Alexandria; mkt. for local agr. produce; p. (1986) 190,840.

Damaraland, region, **Namibia**; high plateau; pt., Walvis Bay; cattle rearing.

Damascus (Arabic **Esh-Sham**), cap. c., **Syria**; 91 km S.E. of its pt. Beirut; claims to be oldest continuously inhabited c. in world; metal-wk., glass, cement; univ.; p. (1993) 1,497,000.

Dambovitta (Dimbovita), R., **Romania**; rises in Mt. Omul (Transylvanian Alps), flows S. through Bucharest to R. Danube, via impt. oilfields; 320 km long.

Dammam, spt. on Persian G., **Saudi Arabia**; oil pt.; industry, univ.

Damodar, R., Bihar, **India**; flows through India's major coalfields; valley forms ch. industl. a. of India; multipurpose scheme for hydroelectric power, irrigation and flood control.

Dampier, spt., W. **Australia**; on Indian Oc.; ships iron ore from Mt. Tom Price and Mt. Wittenoom; pelletising plant.

Dampier Archipelago, gr. of sm. Is., off N.W. **Australia**, in Indian Oc.

Dampier Strait, Bismarck Archipelago, channel between W. New Britain and Umboi I.

Dampir Strait, channel between Irian Jaya and Waigeo I.

Danakil Land (Dankalia), coastal desert a., mainly in **Ethiopia**, but partly in **Djibouti**; includes D. depression; potash; sm. pt. and road projected.

Da-nang (Tourane), c., S. **Vietnam**; ch. pt. of Annam on S. China Sea; exp. agr. prod.; p. (1989) 370,670.

Danao, c., Cebu, **Philippines**; rice and sugar dist.; p. (1990) 73,358.

Dandenong, t., Victoria, **Australia**; 30 km E. of Melbourne; growing industl. ctr.; p. (1983) 58,200.

Dandong (Antung), c., Liaoning, **China**; pt. on Yalu R., 24 km from mouth; Chinese frontier sta. on main rly. from China into N. Korea; mkt. for agr. prod.; lumbering; p. (1984) 560,500.

Dannemora, t., **Sweden**; 40 km N.E. of Uppsala; iron ore worked since 1579.

Danube (Donau), R., second longest R. in Europe; rises in Black Forest, Germany, and flows E. into Black Sea; forms comm. highway; Iron Gate hydro-electric and navigation project inaugurated by 1978; increased no. of dams causing concern with conservationists; linked by canals with Main, Rhine and Oder; completion of Rhine-Main-Danube canal and Danube-Black Sea canal (1984) created Trans-Europe Waterway of 3,500 km.; Vienna, Budapest, Belgrade, and other lge. cs. on its banks; 2,706 km long.

Danube-Tisa Canal, Croatia; irrigation, flood control, navigable; 261 km long.

Danville, t., Ill., **USA**; coal; mftg. tr.; p. (1980) 38,985.

Danville, t., Va., **USA**; cotton, tobacco; p. (1984) 44,700.

Danzig. See Gdansk.

Dap Cau, t., **Vietnam**; bamboo pulp and paper factories.

Darbhanga, t., Bihar, **India**; rice, oil-seeds, grain, sugar tr.; univ.; p. (1991) 218,391.

Dardanelles, strait between European and Asian **Turkey**, connecting Aegean Sea with Sea of Marmara; (the anc. Hellespont), 64 km long.

Daresbury, v., Cheshire, **Eng.**; birthplace of C. L. Dodgson (Lewis Carroll).

Dar-es-Salaam, spt., former cap. of **Tanzania**; univ.; textile mill projected; oil refining; pipeline to Ndola, Zambia; naval base and Tanzam rly. built with Chinese aid; p. (1988) 1,360,850.

Darhan, new t., **Mongolia**, on R. Hara; industl.; p. (1990) 88,600.

Darien, region, **Panama**; tortoiseshell, pearls, gold, but agr. is basis of economy; cap. La Palma; a. 15,540 km²; p. (1990) 43,382.

Darien, Gulf of, inlet of Caribbean Sea; separates Colombia and Panama.

Darjeeling, hill t., W. Bengal, **India**; tea, quinine; Himalayan resort; p. (1984) 63,600.

Darlaston, t., West Midlands, **Eng.**; nuts, bolts, fabricated steel mnfs., drop forgings, car components; pig iron plant closed after 100 years of production.

Darling Downs, plateau, S.E. Queensland, **Australia**; rich agr. region, fertile black soils aid wheat growing; ch. t. Toowoomba.

Darling R., N.S.W., **Australia**; longest trib. of the Murray, forming part of the Murray-Darling Rs. scheme for irrigation and flood control; 2,723 km long.

Darlington, t., unit. auth. created in 1997, formerly part of Durham, **Eng.**; bridge bldg., woollen yarn mnf., engin., rly. wagons, steel wks.; p. (1995) 100,600 (former dist.), (1991) 86,757 (t.).

Darmstadt, c., Hesse, **Germany**; cas.; comm. ctr.; metallurgical prods., paper, machin., radio, chemicals, plastics; technical univ.; p. (1990) 139,500.

Dart, R., Devon, **Eng.**; rises in Dartmoor, flows S. into English Channel at Dartmouth; picturesque estuary; 74 km long.

Dartford, t., l. gov. dist., Kent, **Eng.**; S. side of Thames estuary; Dartford-Purfleet road tunnel (1963); road bridge (1991); engin., chemicals, quarrying, paper; mkt.; p. (1994) 83,600 (dist.), (1991) 59,411 (t.).

Dartmoor, high granite plateau, S.W. Devon, **Eng.**; rough moorland; sheep, cattle, and wild ponies; granite tors; Nat. Park; tourism; granite quarries, reservoirs; prison at Princetown; china clay (Lee Moor) now extends into Nat. Park; recent discovery of tungsten, lgst. deposit in W. Europe but conflicts with conservation; a. 583 km²; hgst. point High Willays, 622 m.

Dartmouth, spt., S. Devon, **Eng.**; on W. of estuary of R. Dart; Royal Naval College; pottery; yachting, holiday resort; p. (1991) 5,676.

Dartmouth, industl. spt., sub. of Halifax, Nova Scotia, **Canada**; oil refining, shipbldg.; p. (1991) 67,798.

Darvel, burgh, E. Ayrshire, **Scot.**; on R. Irvine, 13 km E. Kilmarnock; birthplace of Sir Alexander Fleming, discoverer of penicillin; p. (1991) 3,759.

Darwen, t., N.E. Lancs., **Eng.**; on flank of Rossendale Fells, 5 km S. of Blackburn; tile and glaze bricks, paint, wallpaper, plastics; p. (1991) 29,864.

Darwin, c., cap. N.T., **Australia**; pt. and regional ctr., invigorated in the 1950s by nearby uranium mng. (Rum Jungle); devastated by cyclone 1974, rebuilding complete by 1979; international airpt.; p. (1993) 77,900.

Daryal Gorge, Caucasus, **Georgia**; deep gorge (1,800 m) cut by Terek R.; identified as the classical Caspian or Iberian Gates from which distances were reckoned; forms part of Georgian military road.

Dashava, settlement on Lvov oblast, W. **Ukraine**; ctr. of rich natural gas field and starting point of gas pipeline to Kiev and Moscow, built after second world war.

Datia, t. Madhya-Pradesh, **India**; stone-walled, palaces; p. (1981) 60,991.

Datong (Tatung), c., Shanxi prov., **China**; impt. coalfield; steam and diesel locomotives; p. (1992) 1,110,000.

Datteln, t., N. Rhine-Westphalia, **Germany**; coal, leather, iron; p. (1983) 37,300.

Daugavpils, t., Latvia; on Dvina R.; textiles, engin., rly. repair wks., food prods.; p. (1991) 129,000.

Dauphiné Alps, mtn. range, S.E. **France**; 24 peaks over 3,050 m.

Davangere, t., Karnataka, S. **India**; on 600 m plateau in Indian Penin.; p. (1991) 266,000.

Davao, c., Mindanao, **Philippines**; pt. for sugar; p. (1995) 1,006,000.

Davenport, t., Iowa, **USA**; on Mississippi R. where it is spanned by bridges to Rock Island, Molise and East Molise; rly., comm. and industl. ctr.; p. (1990) 95,300 (t.), 351,000 (met. a. with Rock Is-Moline).

Daventry, t., l. gov. dist., Northampton, **Eng.**; 14 km S.E. of Rugby; boot-mkg., lt. engin.; radio-transmission sta.; expanded t.; p. (1995) 64,800 (dist.), (1991) 18,099 (t.).

David, t., cap. of Chiriquí prov., **Panama**; timber coffee, cacao, sugar; p. (1990) 102,678.

Davis Strait, channel between Greenland and Baffin I., N.W. Terr., **Canada**; connects Atl. Oc. with Baffin Bay; navigable.

Davos-Platz and **Dörfli**, ts., Grisons, **Switzerland**; Alpine winter resorts; alt. 1,478 m; p. (1980) 10,468.

Dawley, t., The Wrekin, Shrops., **Eng.**; on S.E. flank of the Wrekin; ironwks., pipe, cement, roadstone, asphalt and brick wks., engin.; part of Telford new t. (1963).

Dawlish, t., Teignbridge, S. Devon, **Eng.**; on S. cst. between estuaries of Rs. Exe and Teign; seaside resort; flower tr.; p. (1991) 9,648.

Dawson, t., Yukon Terr., **Canada**; on Yukon R., nr. Klondike goldfields; asbestos mng. projected 1968; p. (1991) 1,926.

Dayton, c., Ohio, **USA**; on Great Miami R.; univ.; aircraft, elec. machin., rubber gds.; p. (1990) 182,044 (c.), 951,270 (met. a. with Springfield).

Daytona Beach, t., Fla., **USA**; resort; shipping, ctr.; motor speed trials; p. (1984) 56,400 (t.), (1990) 371,000 (met. a.).

De Aar, t., rly. junc., Cape Prov., **S. Africa**; 500 m. from Cape Town; rlys. from N.W. (Luderitz, Walvis Bay) and S.E. (Pt. Elizabeth, E. London) join Cape Town to Johannesburg trunk rly.; p. (1980) 24,100 (dist.).

Dead Sea, salt-water L. between **Israel** and **Jordan**; surface 392 m below level of Mediterranean; a. 881 km², length 76 km, greatest width 15 km, greatest depth 399 m; receives waters of Jordan; high mineral content, very saline; Israeli plans to link to Mediterranean Sea by underground canal to generate hydro-electric power. Dead Sea now (1999) shrinking at an alarming rate.

Deal, anc. pt., E. Kent, **Eng.**; on S.E. cst., 11 km N.E. Dover; opposite Goodwin Sands; seaside resort; p. (1991) 28,504.

Dean, Forest of. See **Forest of Dean**.

Dearborn, t., Mich., **USA**; birthplace of Henry Ford; p. (1980) 90,660.

Death Valley, depression, Cal., **USA**; N. of Mojave Desert, 240 km N.E. of Los Angeles; completely arid; floor covered with saline deposits; tourist attraction; depth of valley floor 84 m below sealevel.

Deauville, seaside resort, Calvados dep., N. **France**; on Eng. Channel; racecourse, casino.

Debra Markos, t., cap. of Gojam prov., **Ethiopia**; vegetable oil extraction; p. (1984) 39,808.

Debrecen, t., **Hungary**; 183 km E. of Budapest; univ.; ctr. of pastoral dist.; fairs; pharmaceutics, medical instruments, furniture; ctr. of Calvinism; p. (1997) 210,000.

Decatur, t., Ala., **USA**; steel textiles; industl. development after establishment of Tenn. Valley Authority; p. (1980) 42,002.

Decatur, t., Ill., **USA**; on Sangamon R.; industl.; rly. engin., food processing; univ.; p. (1990) 83,885 (t.), 117,206 (met. a.).

Decazeville, t., Aveyron, S. **France**; ctr. of sm. coalfield (no longer worked), metallurgy; p. (1982) 9,204.

Deccan, The, upland of S. **India**, bounded by the Narbada and Kistna Rs.; coincides with Maharashtra st.; area of very fertile lava soils; impt. cotton-growing region.

Dee, R., N. **Wales** and Cheshire, **Eng.**; 144 km long; lge. silted estuary, use for water storage planned.

Dee, R., Aberdeenshire, **Scot.**; picturesque, tourism; 139 km long.

Dehiwala-Mt Lavina, t., **Sri Lanka**; on cst. S. of Colombo; p. (1983) 181,000.

Dehra Dun, t., Uttar Pradesh, **India**; important scientific research ctr.; sawmills; p. (1991) 368,000.

Deir-ez-Zor, t., **Syria**; on Euphrates R.; on motor route between Damascus and Baghdad.

Delabole, v., Cornwall, **Eng.**; on N.W. flank of Bodmin Moor; slate quarries.

Delagoa Bay, natural harbour, **Moçambique**; ch. pt. Maputo.

Delaware, st., **USA**; admitted to Union 1787, popular name First State; st. flower Peach Blossom, st. bird Blue Hen Chicken; low-lying a. of Atl. cst. plain; agr., lumber; fertilisers, minerals, leather, chemicals, machin.; cap. Dover; ch. pt. Wilmington; a. 6,138 km²; p. (1990) 666,168.

Delaware Bay, inlet, Atl. cst., **USA**; drowned estuary of R. Delaware, extends 128 km inland from C. May into heart of highly industl. a. of Philadelphia.

Delaware, R., flows between N.Y. st., **USA** along the Penns. border, through N.J. to Delaware Bay; 504 km long.

Delft, c., pt., S. Holland, **Neth.**; on Schie R. (canalised), nr. Rotterdam; technical univ.; ceramics (delft-ware), tool mftg., precision instruments; 13th cent. Old church and 15th cent. New church; p. (1994) 91,941.

Delhi, c., cap. of **India**; on watershed between Rs. Indus and Ganges; made up of Old Delhi with walls, palace, and fort, and New Delhi with admin. ctr.; univ.; p. (1991) 301,000 (New Delhi), 7,207,000.

Delhi, union terr., **India**; hot and arid region between Indus valley and alluvial plain of Ganges; irrigation to support agr.; New Delhi and Old Delhi ch. ctrs.; a. 1,497 km²; p. (1991) 9,420,644.

Delitzsch, t., Saxony, **Germany**; 26 km E. of Halle; sugar, chemicals; p. (1989) 27,894.

Delmarva, peninsula, Del., **USA**; between Chesapeake Bay and Del. Bay; horticulture, poultry, forestry, fishing.

Delmenhorst, t., Lower Saxony, **Germany**; nr. Bremen; jute, woollens, linoleum, foodstuffs; p. (1986) 70,500.

Delphi, anc. Phocis, central **Greece**; N. of G. of Corinth; famous for Delphic oracle on Mt. Parnassus.

Del Rio, t., Texas, **USA**; pt. of entry on Rio Grande; mkt. for agr. a.; grapes; exp. wool; border t., bridge to Mexico; p. (1980) 30,034.

Demavend, dormant volcano, **Iran**; hgst. peak in Elburz range, c. 5,673 m.

Demerara, co., **Guyana**; between Essequibo and Demerara Rs.; exp. sugar, molasses, rum.

Demerara, R., **Guyana**; drains N. to Atl. Oc.; bauxite transport.

Denain, t., Nord dep., N. **France**; industl. ctr.; p. (1982) 21,872.

Denbighshire, N. **Wales**, unit. auth. created in 1996 from former l. gov. dists. of Glyndŵr and Rhuddlan, reinstating part of historic co. split up in 1974; inc. cst. t. of Prestatyn and Rhyl and inland rural a.; p. (1995) 91,600.

Denbigh, t., Denbighshire, **Wales**; in Vale of Clwyd, 16 km S. of Rhyl; cas.; tourism; dairy prods.; birthplace of Stanley the explorer; p. (1991) 8,529.

Denby Dale, t., West Yorks., **Eng.**; 13 km W. of Barnsley; woollen textiles; earthenware pipes; p. (1991) 2,282.

Den Helder. See Helder.

Denholme, t., West Yorks., **Eng.**; nr. Bradford; dairying, textiles; p. (1991) 2,295.

Denizli, t., **Turkey**; 75 km S.E. of Izmir; gardens — "the Damascus of Anatolia"; nr. site of Laodica; p. (1990) 190,360, 750,882 (prov.).

Denmark, kingdom, N.W. Europe; part of Scandinavia; member of EU; consists of Jutland peninsula, Is. of Sjaelland, Fyn, Falster, Lolland, and Bornholm, and 400 smaller Is., between N. Sea and Baltic; emphasis on dairy agr., producing butter, eggs, and bacon; increasing industrialisation; industl. prods. now account for 62 per cent of exp.; cap. Copenhagen; a. 42,932 km²; p. (1995) 5,200,000.

Denny and Dunipace, burgh, Falkirk, **Scot.**; 10 km W. of Falkirk; steel castings, precast concrete, p. (1991) 13,481.

Dent du Midi, mtn. gr., Vaud can., S.W. **Switzerland**; rises to 10,694 ft. in Haut Cime.

Denton, t., Gtr. Manchester, **Eng.**; nr. Manchester; felt-hat mkg.; p. (1991) 37,785.

Denton, mkt. t., Texas, **USA**; univs.; food processing; p. (1980) 48,063.

Denver, c., cap. of Col., **USA**; on E. slope of Rockies, on South Platte R.; univs.; oil, electronic equipment, mng. machin., livestock, canning; tourism; p. (1990) 467,610 (c.), 1,622,980 (met. a.).

Deoghar, t., Bihar, **India**; temples, place of pilgrimage; p. (1981) 52,904.

Deptford. See Lewisham.

Dera Ghazi Khan, t., **Pakistan**; on W. bank of Indus R.; silk, brass; p. (1981) 103,000.

Dera Ismail Khan, t., **Pakistan**; on Indus R.; admin. ctr., caravan ctr.; p. (1981) 68,000.

Derby, c., unit. auth. creaed in 1997, formerly part of Derbys., **Eng.**; on R. Derwent; general engin., aero-engines, man-made fibres; p. (1995) 231,900 (former dist.), (1991) 223,836 (c.).

Derbyshire, non-met. co., **Eng.**; much of a. occupied by Pennines and Peak Dist. Nat. Park.; coalfield and industl. a. in E.; forms part of Manchester met. a. in N.W.; p. (1995) 957,900.

Derbyshire Dales, l. gov. dist., Derbys., **Eng.**; Pennine a. inc. Matlock, Bakewell and Ashbourne; p. (1995) 69,300.

Derg, Lough, in basin of R. Shannon, **R.o.I.**; separating Galway and Clare from Tipperary.

Derg, L., Donegal, **R.o.I.**, with cave on I. visited by R.C. pilgrims and known as "St Patrick's Purgatory".

Derry; l. gov. dist., **N. Ireland**; borders R.o.I. and L. Foyle; Sperrin Mtns. in S.; p. (1991) 95,371.

Derwent, lgst R. of Tasmania, **Australia**; flows to Storm Bay via Hobart; hydroelec. power; 190 km long.

Derwent, R., Derbys., **Eng.**; trib. of R. Trent; length 96 km.

Derwent, R., North Yorks, **Eng.**; trib. of R. Ouse; length 91 km.

Derwentside, l. gov. dist., Durham, **Eng.**; inc. Consett, Stanley and surrounding a.; p. (1995) 87,500.

Derwentwater, L., Cumbria, **Eng.**; 5 km long.

Desaguadero, R., **Bolivia**; outlet of L. Titicaca; used for irrigation; 320 km long.

Desborough, t., Northants., **Eng.**; boot and shoe mnfs., iron mng.; p. (1991) 7,351.

Des Moines, c., cap. of Iowa st., **USA**; in heart of corn belt; transport and industl. ctr.; univ.; p. (1990) 193,187 (c.), 393,000 (met. a.).

Des Moines, R., Iowa, **USA**; trib. of Mississippi rising in Minn.; 880 km long.

Desna, R., main trib. of Dnieper R., **Russia/Ukraine**; navigable below Bryansk; 1,184 km long.

Des Plaines, t., Ill., **USA**; sub. of Chicago on Des Plaines R.; p. (1980) 53,568.

Dessau, t., Saxony - Anhalt, **Germany**; at confluence of Mulde and Elbe Rs.; cas.; machin., rly. carriages, paper, sugar, chemicals; route ctr.; p. (1986) 103,000.

Detmold, t., N. Rhine–Westphalia, **Germany**; cas.; paints, wood inds.; p. (1986) 66,700.

Detroit, ch. c., pt., Mich., **USA**; busy comm. and industl. ctr.; univ.; gr. grain mart; and ctr. of the Ford motor-car wks., aeroplanes, military tanks, synthetic diamonds, pharmaceutics, tools, chemicals, steel; lgst exporting t. on Great Lakes; p. (1990) 1,027,974 (c.), 4,382,000 (met. a.).

Detroit, R., channel between L. St. Clair and L. Erie (40 km) separates st. of Mich., **USA**, from Ontario, **Canada**; carries more shipping than any other inland waterway in the world.

Deurne, t., **Belgium**; nr. Antwerp, airport; p. (1982) 76,744.

Deux-Sèvres, dep., Poitou-Charentes, **France**; cap. Niort; a. 6,053 km²; p. (1990) 346,000.

Deva, t. cap. Hunedoara prov. W. central **Romania**; agr., tourism; castle; p. (1990) 82,313.

Deventer, t., Overijssel, **Neth.**; on IJssel R.; indstl. ctr., Hanse t. in Middle Ages; p. (1994) 69,079.

Devil's Island (**I. du Diable**), I., Atl. Oc. off **Fr. Guiana**; former penal settlement where Dreyfus was confined in 1894.

Devizes, Kennet, Wilts., **Eng.**; mkt. t., on Kennet and Avon canal at foot of Marlborough Downs; bricks, tiles, bacon-curing; p. (1991) 13,205.

Devon, non-met. co., S.W. **Eng.**; between English and Bristol Channels; attractive cstl. scenery, Nat. Parks of Dartmoor and Exmoor encourage tourism; mixed farming; modern lt. inds.; major ctrs. of p. at Plymouth, Torbay, Exeter; p. (1995) 1,058,800.

Devonport, spt., N. Tasmania, **Australia**; pt. for fruit dist. of R. Mersey; mnfs. primary prods.; Mersey-Forth power project p. (1991) 24,622.

Devonport, Auckland, **N.Z.**; naval base and dockyard; p. (1987) 10,550.

Dewsbury, t., West Yorks., **Eng.**; on R. Calder, 13 km from Leeds; heavy woollens, shoddy, coalmng.; dyewks.; p. (1991) 50,168.

Dez Dam, over Dez R., Khurzistan prov., **Iran**; opened 1963.

Dezful, t., **Iran**; mkt. ctr.; oil fields nearby; p. (1986) 151,420.

Dhahran, spt., **Saudi Arabia**; main oil pt. of S.A.; College of Petroleum and Minerals.

Dhanbad, t., Bihar, **India**; lead, zinc, tools, radio assembly, fertilisers; p. (1991) 151,789, (t.), 815,000 (met. a.).

Dhanushkodi, t., Tamil Nadu, **India**; on I. in Palk Strait; ferry pt. for passenger traffic from India to Sri Lanka.

Dhar, t., Madhya Pradesh, **India**; cultural and tr. ctr.; p. (1981) 48,870.

Dharmsala, hill sta., Himachal Pradesh, **India**; 160 km N.E. of Amritsar; sanatorium; c. 1,800 m; imposing mtn. scenery; p. (1981) 14,522.

Dharwad, t., Karnataka, **India**; 112 km E. of Goa; univ.; cotton mnf.; p. (1981) 13,026.

Dhaulagiri, mtn. peak, 8,172 m, **Nepal**, 4 summits in Himalayas.

Dhekélia, Cyprus; Brit. sovereign base within Rep.

Dhufar, fertile prov., Oman, **Arabia**; sugar-cane, cattle; ch. t. Salālah; ch. pt. Mirbat.

Dhulia, t., Khandesh dist., Maharashtra, **India**; cotton ind.; rly. ctr.; p. (1991) 278,000.

Diamante, R., Mendoza prov., **Argentina**; rises in Andes, flows E. to R. Salado; irrigates oasis of San Rafael; 320 km long.

Diamantina, t., Minas Gerais, **Brazil**; former diamond mng. ctr.; p. (1985) 37,200.

Dibrugarh, t., Assam, **India**; former terminus of rail communications from Calcutta; p. (1991) 125,667.

Didcot, sm. t., Oxon, **Eng.**; 16 km S. of Oxford; Grand Prix engin.; rly. ctr.; p. (1991) 17,691.

Diego Garcia, I., **Brit. Indian Oc. Terr.**; Anglo-American naval communications ctr.; c. 1,000 islanders evacuated to Mauritius, 1966-71, now demanding return home. Major US military base.

Diego Suarez. See **Antsiranana**.

Dien Bien Phu, site of battle in **Vietnam** (Nov. 1953) which resulted in disastrous French defeat.

Dieppe, pt., Seine-Maritime, **France**; 56 km N. of Rouen; fisheries, shipbldg., machin.; cross-Channel ferry; p. (1982) 26,000.

Differdange, t., S.W. **Luxembourg**; iron ore; cattle; p. (1991) 15,740.

Digboi, N.E. Assam, **India**; oil fields and refinery.

Digne, t., cap. of Alpes-de-Haute-Provence, **France**; nr. Aix; cath.; p. (1990) 17,425.

Dijôn, c., cap. Côte-d'Or, E. **France**; the Roman Divonense castrum; route ctr.; Saône-Saône watershed; wine tr.; industl. ctr.; univ., cath.; p. (1990) 151,636, (c.), 226,025 (met. a.).

Dili, t., cap. of E. Timor, **Indonesia**; major spt.; exp. cotton, copra, coffee; p. (1980) 65,451.

Dimitrovgrad, t., **Bulgaria**; founded 1947; fer-

tilisers, chemicals, superphosphate plant, iron, thermo-electric sta.

Dimitrovo. See **Pernik**.

Dinajpur, t., **Bangladesh**; comm. ctr.; univ.; p. (1991) 126,189.

Dinan, t., Brittany, **France**; mediaeval t. above Rance R.; hosiery, brewing; holiday resort; p. (1982) 14,157.

Dinant, t., Namur, **Belgium**; on R. Meuse: mkt. t., tourist resort; exported copperware (dinanderie) in Middle Ages; cath., citadel (1040); p. (1982) 12,008.

Dinapur, t., Bihar, **India**; on Ganges R., nr. Patna; p. (1991) 126,189.

Dinard, t., Brittany, **France**; resort, especially for English; p. (1982) 10,016.

Dinaric Alps, mtn. range, extending 640 km along Adriatic; from **Albania** to **Italy**; hgst. peak Durmitor, 2,515 m.

Dindigul, t., Tamil Nadu, **India**; 40 km S. of Tiruchirapalli; cigars; p. (1991) 182,477.

Dingle B., Kerry, **R.o.I.**; long inlet of sea on Atl. cst.

Dingwall, royal burgh, Highland, **Scot.**; at head of Cromarty F.; rly. junction; cattle mkt., admin. ctr.; distilling, handloom weaving; p. (1991) 5,224.

Dinslaken, t. N. Rhine-Westphalia, **Germany**, N. of Duisburg; coal, steel, iron, footwear, timber; oil pipeline from Wesseling under construction; p. (1986) 61,300.

Diomede Is., two barren granitic islets in Bering Strait between Alaska and Siberia; accepted bdy. between Soviet and US terr.

Diredawa, t., **Ethiopia**; 40 km N. of Harar; rly. wks.; mkt and comm. ctr.; new cement wks.; p. (1984) 98,104.

Dirk Hartog I., off Shark Bay, W. **Australia**.

Disko U., off W. cst. of **Greenland** in Baffin Bay; contains harbour of Godhavn, cap. N. Greenland; rendezvous for whalers; shrimp beds; a. 8,288 km².

Dismal Swamp, morass, S. Va. and N.C., **USA**; contains L. Drummond and extends 50-65 km S. from nr. Norfolk.

Diss, South Norfolk, **Eng.**; mkt. t. on R. Waveney, 45 km S.W. of Norwich; agr. implements; p. (1991) 6,538.

Distaghil, major peak, Gr. Karakoram, N. Kashmir, **Pakistan**; two summits connected by a ridge, max. alt. 7,890 m.

Distrito Federal, federal dist., **Brazil**; inc. cap. c. of Brasilia; a. 5,815 km²; p. (1991) 1,596,274.

Ditchling Beacon, 10 km N. of Brighton, East Sussex, **Eng.**; hgst point of South Downs, 248 m.

Diu, spt., I., off S. cst. of Bombay Union Territory, **India**; oil nearby at Kayakov; p. (1991) 39,485.

Dīwānīyah, t., Iraq; cap. D. prov.; on Baghdad-Basra rly.; p. (1965) 60,553, (latest fig.)

Diyarbakir, c., cap. of D. prov., central **Turkey**; on Tigris R.; comm. and mnf. ctr.; flour and rice mills; the anc. Amida, old walls, gates, citadel; p. (1990) 371,038 (t.). 1,094,996 (prov.).

Djajapura (**Sukarnapura**), t., cap. of Irian Jaya, **Indonesia**; on Humboldt B., an inlet of Pac. Oc.

Djakarta. See **Jakarta**.

Djambi, dist., and t., Sumatra, **Indonesia**; on E. cst. plain 160 km N.W. of Palembang; univ.; field; a. (dist.) 44,924 km².

Djerba, t. and I., **Tunisia**, at S. entrance to G. of Gabès, joined to mainland by causeway; olives, textiles, pottery; a. 510 km²; p. (1984) 92,269.

Djibouti, c. cap. of **Djibouti**; rly. terminus; main pt. free pt. (1981), container terminal (1985); p. (1995) 383,000.

Djibouti, Rep. of, indep. st. (1977) N.E. Africa; former French Somaliland, renamed Fr. Terr. of Afars and Issas 1967; extends inland from straits of Bab-el-Mandeb; economy based on trade through international pt. of D.; plain, mainly below 180 m; hot, dry climate; shark and mother-of-pearl fisheries; little cultivable land; a. 23,051 km²; p. (1995) 586,000.

Dneprodzerzhinsk, t., **Ukraine**; W. of Dnepropetrovsk on Dnieper R.; iron and steel, engin., chemicals; hydroelec. sta. nearby; p. (1990) 283,600.

Dneproges (abbrev. Dnieper hydroelectric sta.), **Ukraine**; nr. Zaporoz'ye, on Dnieper: lgst dam and power sta. in Europe; destroyed by Germans, rebuilt 1944-9.

Dnepropetrovsk, c., **Ukraine**; on R. Dnieper; univ.; impt. rly. and industl. ctr., using iron ore (from Krivoy Rog), coal (Dombas), manganese (Nikopol) and electric power from Dnieper dam; heavy machin., chemicals; p. (1990) 1,186,700.

Dneprorudnyy, t., Ukraine; new t. on S. shore of Kakhvota reservoir; p. (1990) 23,300.

Dneprostroy. *See* **Zaporoz'ye.**

Dnieper (Dnepr), gr. R. of **Russia, Belarus, Ukraine;** 3rd longest R. of Europe; rises in Valdai hills, flows into Black Sea, 2,240 km long; connected by canals to Baltic; tribs. inc. Berezina, Pripet, Desna, Orel, Samara; since erection of Dneproges dam navigable almost entire length.

Dniester (Dnestr), R., Ukraine, Moldavia; rises in Carpathians and flows into the Black Sea; 1,403 km long.

Döbeln, t., Saxony, Germany; machin., metallurgy, wood, cigar and sugar inds.; p. (1989) 27,777.

Dobrich, t., N.E. Bulgaria; comm. and agr. ctr. of Dobruja; food-processing, textiles, furniture, agr. machin.; named **Tolbukhin** in honour of Russian soldier who took it from Germans during World War II, 1944; renamed Dobrich, 1991; p. (1990) 115,786.

Dobruja, historic region, S.E. **Europe;** along Black Sea cst., S.E. Romania, and N.E. Bulgaria; mainly agr.; ch. pt. Constanta.

Dobšiná, t., Slovakia; cave containing ice-field of 0·8 ha; asbestos, iron ore; p. 5,300.

Docklands, expanding area of former docks, E. London; commercial and office devt; expensive housing; light railway; Canary Wharf tallest blg. in London.

Dodecanese (S. Sporades), gr. of some 20 Greek Is. (originally 12) in S. Aegean Sea; most impt. are Rhodes, Cos, and Leros; Italian 1912–46; p. (1991) 163,476.

Dodoma, cap. of **Tanzania** since 1974; at geographical ctr. of T. in rural a.; p. (1988) 203,833.

Dodworth, t., South Yorks., Eng.; nr. Barnsley; coal; p. (1991) 4,964.

Dogger Bank, sandbank in N. Sea, between England and Denmark; depth varies from 6 to 37 m; valuable fishing ground.

Dogs, I. of, riverside dist., formed by bend in the R. Thames off Greenwich, London, **Eng.;** Millwall and India docks.

Doha, t., cap. of **Qatar;** spt. on E. of Qatar peninsula, Persian Gulf; internat. airpt., deep sea pt.; contains 80 per cent of p.; p. (1992) 313,639.

Dokai Bay, inlet, N. Kyushu, **Japan;** landlocked bay on S. side of Shimonoseki Straits; flanked by highly industl. zone inc. Yawata, Wakamatsu, Tobata cs.; requires constant dredging; length 6 km, width 0·8–2·4 km.

Dôle, t., Jura, E. **France;** on R. Doubs, nr. Dijon; industl. ctr.; anc. cap. of Franche-Comté, ceded to France in 1678; birthplace of Pasteur; p. (1982) 27,959.

Dolgarrog, Gwynedd, **Wales;** site of hydroelectric sta.

Dolgellau, t., Gwynedd, N. **Wales;** agr., quarrying, timber; p. (1991) 2,396.

Dollar, burgh, Clackmannan, **Scot.;** at foot of Ochil Hills; p. (1991) 2,670.

Dollar Law, mtn., nr. Peebles, **Scot.;** alt. 817 m.

Dolomites, gr. of limestone mtns., S. Tyrolese Alps, N.E. **Italy;** tourist dist.; peaks assume fantastic forms; principal peak Marmolada 3,355 m.

Dominica, Commonwealth of, W.I.; indep. st. (1978); most N. of Windward Is.; 25 per cent under cultivation; volcanic soils highly suitable for bananas; N.–S. mtn. range has spectacular volcanic scenery; cap. Roseau; a. 751 km²; p. (1994) 74,200.

Dominican Rep., rep., W.I.; shares I. of Hispaniola with Haiti; comprises Nat. Dist. (inc. cap. Santo Domingo) and 25 admin. provs.; mtnous. with sub-tropical climate; in path of tropical cyclones; badly devastated by hurricane (1979); comm. economy mainly agr.; transport system geared to exp. of sugar (now declining with U.S. quotas on imports); decline in tobacco sales causing farmers to abandon production; govt. investment in agr. and mng.; oil refining at Nigua; exp. bauxite; 48,430 km²; p. (1994) 7,770,000.

Domodossola, frontier t., Piedmont, N. **Italy;** nr. Alpine tourist resort in Toce valley, nr. Simplon; p. (1981) 20,069.

Don, R., South Yorks., **Eng.;** trib. of R. Ouse, 112 km long.

Don, R., Aberdeen/Aberdeenshire, **Scot.;** flows into N. Sea nr. Aberdeen; salmon; 131 km long.

Don, major R. of southern **Russia;** falls into Sea of Azov below Rostov, its ch. pt.; navigable

to Voronezh; ch. trib., Donets; access to Volga by Don–Volga canal; fisheries; 1,955 km long.

Donaghadee, t., Ards, **N. Ireland;** nearest point to Scot.; spt. and seaside resort; p. (1991) 4,455.

Donauwörth, t., W. Bavaria, **Germany;** bridge t. on N. bank of Danube at Wörnitz confluence; p. (1989) 17,546.

Donbas, industl. region, **Ukraine;** in valleys of Rs. Donets and lower Dnieper; about 23,300 km²; important coalfield; adjoins Krivoy Rog ironfields; many lge. industl. ts.

Doncaster, t., met. dist., South Yorks., **Eng.;** on Don R., 27 km N.E. of Sheffield; only Harworth colliery remains; tractors, nylon mftg.; racecourse; p. (1995) 292,900 (dist.), (1991) 71,595 (t.).

Donegal, spt., Co. Donegal, **R.o.I.;** on W. cst. on Donegal Bay; tweeds, carpets; p. (1986) 2,242.

Donegal (Tirconnail), co., N.W. **R.o.I.;** fishing poor agr.; cloth, hydroelectric power; co. t. Lifford; a. 4,830 km²; p. (1986) 129,664.

Donets, R., rises in uplands of central **Russia;** N.E. of Belgorod, flows S.E. to join R. Don; crosses Donets coalfield; length 1,040 km long. *See* **Donbas.**

Donetsk (Stalino), t., Ukraine; industl. ctr. of Donets coal basin; iron, steel, engin., chemicals; p. (1990) 1,116,900.

Donges, t., Loire Atlantique, **France;** nr. St. Nazaire; oil refinery; synthetic textiles, plastics.

Dongola (Dunqulah), t., Sudan; on left bank of Nile above Third Cataract; Old D. was 120 km to S.

Dong Ting (Tung Ting), lge. L., Hunan, **China;** receives water from Xi Jiang and Yuan Rs., drains N. to Chang Jiang; surrounded by flat intensively cultivated land; rice, sugar; size varies with season; max. (in late summer) 6,500 km².

Donner Pass, E. Cal., **USA;** highway pass through Sierra Nevada at 2,176 m.

Donzère-Mondragon, Vaucluse, **France;** site of Rhône barrage supplying hydroelectric power.

Dora Baltea, R., N. **Italy;** rises in Mt. Blanc, flows E. and S. through Val d'Aosta to R. Po at Chivasso; impt. routeway from N. Italy to Switzerland (through Gr. St. Bernard Pass) and France (through Little St. Bernard Pass); 152 km long.

Dorchester, co. t., West Dorset, **Eng.;** mkt. t. on R. Frome; lime, agr., engin.; Roman remains; nearby prehistoric Maiden Castle; linked with the name of Thomas Hardy; p. (1991) 15,037.

Dordogne, dep., S.W. **France;** cap. Périgueux; crossed by Dordogne R.; fertile valleys; p. (1990) 386,400.

Dordogne, R., S.W. **France;** rises in Central Massif, joins Garonne to form Gironde; vineyards; upper reaches used for hydroelectric power.

Dordrecht, c., nr. Rotterdam, **Neth.;** on R. Merwede; met. a. with Zwijndrecht; timber, shipbldg., seaplanes; p. (1994) 113,394 (c.) 213,074 (met. a.).

Dorking, t., Mole Valley, Surrey, **Eng.;** on R. Mole to S. of gap through N. Downs; mkt., residtl.; lt. inds.; p. (1991) 15,658.

Dornbirn, t., Vorarlberg, **Austria;** textiles; p. (1991) 40,881.

Dornoch, burgh, Highland, **Scot.;** N. of Dornoch F.; resort; p. (1991) 1,196.

Dorset, non-met. co., S. **Eng.;** borders English Channel along attractive cliffed cst. formed by E.–W. limestone ridges; Portland stone quarried; many tourist resorts; mkt. ts. serve agr. interior; p. (1995) 678,700.

Dorset Heights, hills, extend E. to W. across central Dorset, **Eng.;** chalk; pastoral farming, sheep; some cultivation where soil is deep enough; rise to 250–275 m.

Dorsten, t., N. Rhine–Westphalia, **Germany;** on R. Lippe; coal, iron, elec., chemical inds.; p. (1986) 74,100.

Dortmund, c., N. Rhine–Westphalia, **Germany;** on Dortmund–Ems Canal; industl. ctr. and pt. of Ruhr; coal, iron, steel; p. (1990) 599,900.

Dortmund–Ems Canal, N. Rhine–Westphalia, **Germany;** links Dortmund on Ruhr coalfield with R. Ems 8 km above Lingen; 144 km long.

Douai, t., Nord, **France;** nr. Lille on Scarpe R.; coal, iron and engin. wks.; bell founding, arsenal; p. (1990) 44,195 (t.), 199,562 (met. a.).

Douala, spt., Cameroon; rly. to Yaoundé; exp. hardwoods; p. (1991) 810,000.

Douarnenez, spt., Finistère, N.W. **France;** on D. Bay; sardine fisheries; p. (1982) 17,813.

Doubs, dep., E. **France;** traversed by Jura range and R. Doubs; mainly agr.; watchmkg., motor vehicles; cap. Besançon; a. 5,315 km²; p. (1990) 484,800.

Douglas, t., cap. of **Isle of Man**; 120 km W. of Liverpool, **Eng.**; spt; resort; nearby freeport (1983) gaining from low tax rate; p. (1991) 22,214.

Douglas Point, on shore of L. Huron, Ont., **Canada**; nuclear power sta.

Dounreay, Highland, **Scot.**; fast-breeder nuclear reactors; closure of reprocessing plant announced (1998).

Douro, R., **Portugal** and **Spain**; enters Atl. Oc. below Oporto; known as Duero R. in Spain; l. 776 km; famous port wine a.

Dove, R., Derbys. and Staffs., **Eng.**; trib. of Trent; flows through beautiful dales; 77 km long.

Dovedale, valley, Derbys., **Eng.**; steeply sloping limestone ravine of R. Dove; tourism.

Dover, packet pt., l. gov. dist., Kent, **Eng.**; Cinque pt.; nearest spt. to France, the Strait of D. being only 34 km wide; ch. pt. for Continent; cas.; p. (1995) 107,300 (dist.), (1991) 34,179 (t.).

Dovey, R., **Wales**; flows from Cambrian Mtns. and enters Cardigan Bay by a wide estuary.

Down, former co.; l. gov. dist., **N. Ireland**; borders Strangford Lough and Dundrum Bay; agr. and fisheries; p. (1991) 58,008.

Downham Market, t., West Norfolk, **Eng.**; on R. Ouse; flour-milling, malting, sheet-metal wks.; p. (1991) 5,841.

Downpatrick, t., Down, **N. Ireland**; on R. Quoile; linen; p. (1991) 10,113.

Downs, natural harbour of refuge for shipping between Kent cst. and Goodwin Sands in the English Channel.

Drachenfels, mtn. peak of the Rhine, **Germany**; the steepest of the Siebengebirge range, nr. Königswinter; alt. 325 m; ascended by lt. rly.; famous cave of legendary dragon.

Draguignan, t., S.E. **France**; cap. of Var. dep. until 1974; mkt. t., service ctr.; p. (1982) 28,194.

Drakensberg, mtn. chain between Natal and Orange Free State, **S. Africa**, and **Lesotho**; extending 800 km from Gt. Fish R. to Olifants R.; hgst. peak Mont-aux-Sources 3,283 m; rly. crosses range from Van Reenen Pass.

Drammen, spt., **Norway**; nr. Oslo, on the Drammen R.; shipyard; exp. timber, wood-pulp, paper; p. (1990) 58,717.

Drancy, t., Seine-St. Denis, **France**; N.E. sub. of Paris; p. (1990) 60,928.

Drava (Drau), R., trib. of Danube, **Austria** and **Yugoslavia**; flows from the Tyrol across Carinthia and Styria, joining Danube nr. Osijek; length 720 km; used for hydroelec. power.

Drax, West Yorks., **Eng.**; thermal elec. power sta. linked to Selby coalfield.

Drenthe, prov., **Neth.**; on German frontier; cap. Assen; a. 2,663 km²; p. (1994) 451,409.

Dresden, c., **Germany**; R. pt. on Elbe, 80 km E. of Leipzig; cap. Saxony *Land*; impt. route ctr.; engin., chemicals, optical and photographic apparatus, porcelain, glass, brewing; fine art collections; scientific research; oil pipeline from Schwedt under construction; p. (1990) 488,000.

Drin, R., N. **Albania**; rises in Yugoslavia and flows through deep gorges into Adriatic; hydroelec. power; 288 km long.

Drina, R., trib. of Sava R., **Yugoslavia**; forming boundary between Montenegro and Bosnia-Hercegovina; source of hydroelec. power; 480 km long.

Dröbak, spt., S.E. **Norway**; winter pt. for Oslo; summer resort.

Drobeta-Turnu Severin, c., S.W. **Romania**; R. pt. on Danube below Iron Gate cataracts; grain, salt, petroleum tr., shipbldg.; p. (1992) 115,526.

Drogheda, spt., Louth, **R.o.I.**; considerable pt. in agr. produce, salmon, etc.; stormed by Cromwell in 1649; p. (1986) 24,086.

Drogobych, t., **Ukraine**; 64 km S.W. of Lvov; ctr. of lge. oilfields, refineries; mftg.; p. (1990) 78,500.

Droitwich, t., Wychavon, Worcs., **Eng.**; brine baths; lt. inds.; expanded t.; p. (1991) 20,966.

Drôme, dep., S.E. **France**; traversed by Alps and watered by Rs. Rhône, Drôme, and Isère; cap. Valence; agr., forestry, sericulture, textile ind.; a. 6,560 km²; p. (1990) 414,100.

Dromore, mkt. t., Banbridge, **N. Ireland**; on Lagan R.; linen; p. (1991) 3,434.

Dronfield, t., North East Derbys., **Eng.**; between Chesterfield and Sheffield; edged tools, engin. and agr. implements; p. (1991) 22,985.

Droylsden, t., Gtr. Manchester, **Eng.**; sub. of Manchester; chemicals; textiles; p. (1991) 22,666.

Drumochter Pass, Grampian Mtns., **Scot.**; carries

main Perth to Inverness rly. and main road from Glen Garry into valley of R. Spey; highest alt. reached by any main rly. in Gt. Britain, 453 m.

Dschang, t., **Cameroon**; quinine processing; bauxite mng.; p. (1981) 21,705.

Dubai (Dubayy), emirate, one of **United Arab Emirates**, Arabian Gulf; recently developed as free pt. (modelled on Singapore); p. (1985) 419,104.

Dubbo, t., N.S.W., **Australia**; busy road, rail, air junction in rich agr. dist.; p. (1981) 23,986.

Dublin, co., **R.o.I.**; co. t. Dublin; a. (inc. c. of Dublin) 922 km²; p. (1981) 977,700.

Dublin (Irish *Baile Atha Cliath*), C.B., cap. of **R.o.I.**; co. t. Co. Dublin; at mouth of R. Liffey; ctr. of govt., commerce, ind., and culture; cath., univ., Abbey Theatre; brewing, distilling, food processing; Swift was buried here; p. (1986) 502,749 (c.), 1,021,449 (co.).

Dubrovnik (Ital. Ragusa), t., **Croatia** (formerly Yugoslavia); impt. pt. on Adriatic; retains much of its mediaeval architecture but damaged in civil war, 1991; tourism; airport; p. (1981) 66,131.

Dubuque, t., Iowa, **USA**; pt. on Mississippi R.; varied inds. inc. meat-packing; p. (1990) 57,546.

Dudley, t., met. dist., West Midlands, **Eng.**; cas.; engin.; cables, chains; p. (1995) 312,500 (dist.), (1991) 192,171 (t.).

Duisburg, c., N. Rhine–Westphalia, **Germany**; R. pt. on E. bank of Rhine at confluence with R. Ruhr, 16 km N. of Düsseldorf; iron and steel inds., machin., textiles, chemicals, pt. inds., route and R. tr. ctr.; p. (1990) 536,700.

Dukeries, dist., Sherwood Forest, Notts., **Eng.**; so called from ducal mansions in dist.; tourism.

Dukinfield, t., Tameside, Gtr. Manchester, **Eng.**; 10 km E. of Manchester; textiles, engin., rope and twine; p. (1991) 17,917.

Dukla Pass, 497 m. pass; anc. route across Carpathians, linking Poland, Hungary and Slovakia.

Duluth, pt., Minn., **USA**; at W. end of L. Superior; gr. tr. in grain, timber and iron ore; natural gas pipeline into the Mesabi Iron Range; p. (1984) 86,600 (c.), (1990) 239,971 (met. a. with Superior).

Dulwich, residtl. sub. in bor. of Southwark, Greater London, **Eng.**; village character with lge. park and public school.

Dumbarton, royal burgh, W. Dunbartonshire, **Scot.**; on N. bank of R. Clyde, 19 km below Glasgow; shipbldg., valve and tube-mkg., iron and brassware; p. (1991) 21,962.

Dum-Dum, t., W. Bengal, **India**; ammunition; impt. airpt.; p. (1991) 149,965 (N.), 232,811 (S.).

Dumfries, royal burgh, Dumfries and Galloway, **Scot.**; on R. Nith, 16 km from Solway F.; p. (1991) 32,136.

Dumfries and Galloway, unit. auth. created in 1996 from former Region, S. **Scot.**; occupies W. half of Southern Uplands; drained by S. flowing rivers to Solway F.; sparse rural p.; p. (1995) 147,900.

Dumfriesshire, historic co., S. **Scot.**; now part of Dumfries and Galloway.

Dumyât, t., Lower **Egypt**; on main distributary of R. Nile delta; cotton; p. (1986) 113,000.

Dunaujváros, t., **Hungary**; new t. built from v. of Dunapentele; iron and steel wks.; paper inds., engin. p. (1997) 57,000.

Dunbar, royal burgh, E. Lothian, **Scot.**; sm. fishing pt.; Cromwell's victory 1650; p. (1991) 6,518.

Dunbartonshire, historic co., central **Scot.**; now divided between Argyll and Bute, W. Dunbartonshire, E. Dunbartonshire and N. Lanarkshire.

Dunblane, mkt. burgh, Stirling, **Scot.**; on Allan Water, 8 km from Stirling; Gothic cath. now used as par. church; scene of horrific school massacre, 1996; p. (1991) 7,368.

Dundalk, t., cap. of Co. Louth, **R.o.I.**; harbour, rly. ctr.; engin., footwear, tobacco, brewing; p. (1986) 26,669.

Dundee, c., spt., royal burgh, unit. auth. created in 1996, formerly part of Tayside, E. **Scot.**; on F. of Tay, 80 km N. Edinburgh; jute mnf. (ended 1999); engin., computers, refrigerators, clocks, watches, preserves, linoleum; publishing., univ.; p. (1991) 158,981 (c.), (1995) 151,010 (unit. auth.).

Dundonald, t. E. of Belfast, **N. Ireland**; p. (1991) 12,943.

Dunedin, c., Otago, S.I., **N.Z.**; univ.; wool and dairy produce; named after the old name of Edinburgh; p. (1991) 116,577.

Dunfermline, royal burgh, Fife, **Scot.**; 22 km E. of Alloa; linen, rubber prods., synthetic fibre; birthplace of Charles I and Andrew Carnegie; cap. of Scot. 1057–93; p. (1991) 55,083.

Dungannon, mkt. t., l. gov. dist., **N. Ireland;** linen, bricks; p. (1991) 9,190 (t.), 45,428 (dist.).

Dungarvan, t. Co. Waterford, **R.o.I.;** spt., mkt. t.; leather processing; p. (1986) 6,849.

Dungeness, headland of shingle, Kent, **Eng.;** 16 km S.E. of Rye; two Magnox nuclear power stas.; linked by power cable to France 1961.

Dunkeld, t., Perth and Kinross, **Scot.;** on R. Tay at entrance to Strathmore; cath., ecclesiastical ctr. in 9th century; tourist resort; p. (1991) 1,227 (with Birnam).

Dunkirk (Dunkerque), spt., Nord dep., **France;** strong fort; gd. harbour and tr.; fisheries, shipbld., oil refining; steel mill; scene of evacuation of B.E.F. 1940; p. (1990) 71,071 (c.), 192,852 (met. a.).

Dun Laoghaire (Kingstown), t., Dublin, **R.o.I.;** spt., mail packet sta., fishing; ferry to Eng.; p. (1986) 54,715.

Dunmanway, t., Cork, **R.o.I.;** on R. Brandon; tweeds, blankets; p. (1986) 1,382.

Dunmurry, t. Lisburn, **N. Ireland;** engin.; p. (1991) 12,771.

Dunoon, burgh, Argyll and Bute, **Scot.;** on N. side of F. of Clyde, anc. cas.; holiday resort; p. (1991) 9,038.

Duns, burgh, Borders, **Scot.;** agr. and allied inds.; mkt. t.; cas.; p. (1991) 2,444.

Dunsinane, hill, Perth and Kinross, **Scot.;** nr. Perth; alt. 309 m; referred to by Shakespeare in *Macbeth.*

Dunstable, t., South Beds., **Eng.;** on N. edge of Chiltern Hills, 6 km W. of Luton; motor vehicles, engin., cement, rubber, and plastic gds.; p. (1991) 49,666.

Duque de Caxias, t., Brazil; Brazil's largest oil refinery, petro-chemicals; Alfa-Romeo car plant; p. (1991) 664,643.

Durance, R., S.E. France; trib. of Rhône; rapid current, 347 km long; provides irrigation and hydroelec. power.

Durango, c., cap. of D. st., Mexico; cath.; silver, gold, copper, iron-ore; p. (1990) 414,015.

Durango, st., N.W. **Mexico;** mng., agr., cotton, wheat; a. 109,484 km²; p. (1990) 1,352,156.

Durant, t., S. Okla, **USA;** cotton gins and compresses, cottonseed oil; p. (1980) 11,972.

Durban, c., **S. Africa;** on Durban Bay; ch. comm. c. of Natal; exp. coal, manganese, wool, hides; oil and sugar refining, chemicals, textiles, engin.; oil pipeline to Johannesburg; univ.; main pt. and seaside resort; p. (1985) 982,075.

Düren, t., N. Rhine–Westphalia, **Germany;** on R. Ruhr 37 km S.W. of Cologne; rly. ctr.; iron and steel wks., vehicles; p. (1986) 84,100.

Durgapur, t., W. Bengal, **India;** site of barrage on Damodar R.; p. (1991) 426,000.

Durham, c., co. t., l. gov. dist., Durham, N.E. **Eng.;** sited within a meander of R. Wear; cath., cas., univ.; carpets, organ mftg., confectionery; p. (1995) 89,700 (dist.), (1991) 36,937 (t.).

Durham, non-met. co., N.E. **Eng.;** between Rs. Tyne and Tees; stretches from attractive Pennine moorland in W. to coalfield and industl. a. with many sm. ts. in E.; borders the N. Sea; p. (1995) 607,700.

Durham, t., N.C., **USA;** tobacco ind., textiles; univ.; p. (1990) 136,611.

Durrës (Durazzo), ch. spt., **Albania;** on Adriatic; pt. for Tirana; tobacco ind., plastics; tourism; p. (1991) 86,900.

Dursley, t., Gloucs., **Eng.;** 21 km S.W. of Gloucester; engin., agr. machin.; 18th cent. mkt. house; p. (1991) 13,331.

Dushanbe, c., cap. of **Tajikistan;** univ.; industl. and agr. ctr.; rly. junc.; earlier called Stalinabad; 1989 ethnic unrest; p. (1986) 565,000.

Düsseldorf, c., cap. of N. Rhine-Westphalia, **Germany;** on R. Rhine, 32 km N. of Cologne; admin. and cultural ctr., art and medical academies; iron, steel, machin., soap, cars, paper, chemical inds.; impt. trans-shipment pt.; p. (1990) 576,700.

Dust Bowl, region, **USA;** name applied to great plains on E. flank of Rocky Mtns.; subject to severe soil erosion by wind, particularly in drought years (1933, 1936) due to destruction of natural vegetation by over-grazing or by excessive ploughing.

Dutch Guiana. *See* Suriname.

Dutch Harbour, t., Unalaska I., Aleutian gr., N. Pac. Oc.; strategic American naval base.

Dvina or **Northern Dvina,** R., **Russia;** flows to White Sea at Arkhangelsk, formed by the junction of Rs. Sukhona and Vychegda at Kotlas; con-

nected by canal with Neva and Volga; used for timber transport; 744 km long.

Dvina or **Western Dvina,** R., Russia, Latvia; rises in Valdai Hills nr. sources of Volga and Dnieper, flows through Latvia to G. of Riga; connected by canal to Berezina and Dnieper; c. 1,016 km long.

Dzaudzhikau. *See* Ordzhonikidze.

Dzerzhinsk, c., **Russia;** R. pt. of Oka; chemicals (fertilisers, explosives); p. (1989) 602,000.

Dzhalil, t., **Russia;** new t. 48 km N.E. of Almetyevsk to serve new oilfield there.

Dzhambul, c., **Kazakhstan;** on Talas R. and on Turk-Sib rly.; chemicals, food-processing; p. (1990) 310,900.

Dzhezkazgan, t., **Kazakhstan;** 560 km W. of L. Balkhash; copper-mines; manganese ore nearby; p. (1989) 109,000.

Dzierzoniow (Reichenbach), t., Walbrzych, S.W. **Poland;** mnf. ctr.; textiles, machin., formerly in Germany; p. (1989) 37,908.

Dzungaria, inland basin, Xinjiang prov., N.W. **China;** lies between Tien-Shan highlands and Altai mtns.; former historic kingdom of Zungaria.

E

Ealing, outer bor., Greater London, **Eng.;** comprising former bors. of Acton, Ealing, and Southall; p. (1995) 292,100.

Earl's Court, residtl. a., London, **Eng.;** Bor. of Kensington and Chelsea, contains E.C. exhibition hall.

Earn, R., Perth and Kinross, **Scot.;** issues from Loch Earn (10 km long) and flows into Tay R.; 74 km long.

Easington, l. gov. dist., Durham, **Eng.;** colly. closed 1993; now part of Peterlee new t.; p. (1995) 96,600.

Easington, v., E. Riding of Yorks., **Eng.;** nr. Hull; natural gas terminal; p. (1991) 7,593.

East Anglia, comprises Norfolk and Suffolk, **Eng.;** former Anglo-Saxon kingdom; one of Britain's most productive agr. regions.

East Anglian Heights, hills, extend S.W. to N.E. across N.E. Hertfordshire, N. Essex, and S.W. Suffolk, **Eng.;** chalk overlain by glacial clays and sands; smooth, rolling surface; region of lge. farms and lge. fields, mixed farms mainly grain; rarely exceed 180 m.

East Ayrshire, unit. auth. created in 1996, formerly part of Strathclyde, W. **Scot.;** ch. t. Kilmarnock; p. (1995) 123,110.

East Bergholt, v., Suffolk, **Eng.;** birthplace of Constable.

Eastbourne, t., l. gov. dist., East Sussex, **Eng.;** on S. cst. to E. of Beachy Head; seaside resort; p. (1995) 88,600 (dist.), (1991) 94,793 (t.).

East Cambridgeshire, l. gov. dist., Cambs., **Eng.;** a. N.E. of Cambridge inc. Ely; p. (1995) 64,900.

East Cape, extreme N.E. point of Asia; on Chukchi peninsula, **Russia;** Russian name Cape Dezhnova.

East Cape, extreme E. point of **N.Z.;** named by Cook on his first voyage in 1769.

East Chicago, t., Ind., **USA;** L. Michigan; iron and steel wks., oil refining; p. (1980) 39,786.

East Cleveland, t., Ohio, **USA;** residtl.; p. (1990) 33,096.

East Coast Bays, bor., N.I., **N.Z.;** series of settlements on bays N. of Auckland; amalgamated 1954; p. (1987) 31,600.

East Dereham, t., Breckland, Norfolk, **Eng.;** 22 km W. of Norwich; agr. implements; p. (1991) 12,974.

East Devon, l. gov. dist., Devon, **Eng.;** Exmouth, Sidmouth and Seaton on cst. and inland ts. Honiton and Ottery St. Mary; p. (1995) 123,600.

East Dorset, l. gov. dist., Dorset, **Eng.;** rural a. based on Wimborne Minster; p. (1995) 81,600.

East Dunbartonshire, unit. auth. created in 1996, formerly part of Strathclyde, central **Scot.;** lies immediately N. of Glasgow; p. (1995) 111,130.

Easter Island, S. Pac. Oc., 3,760 km W. of Chile; various theories to explain origin of gigantic statues; p. (1985) 2,000.

East Grinstead, t., West Sussex, **Eng.;** in ctr. of Weald, 14 km W. of Tunbridge Wells; famous hospital for plastic surgery; p. (1991) 27,058.

East Ham. *See* Newham.

East Hampshire, l. gov. dist., Hants., **Eng.;** stretches from Alton to Petersfield; p. (1995) 109,800.

East Hartford, t., Conn., **USA;** industl.; p. (1980) 52,563.

East Hertfordshire, l. gov. dist., Herts., **Eng.**; lge a. inc. Ware, Bishop's Stortford, Hertford and Sawbridgeworth; p. (1995) 122,600.

East Indies, name commonly applied to Is. between S.E. Asia and N. Australia, variously known as Malay archipelago, Malaysia, Indonesia.

East Kilbride, t., S. Lanarkshire, **Scot.**; 11 km S.S.E. of Glasgow; new t. 1947; lge. agr. machin., aero engines, engin., elec. prods., seawater distillation plant; knitwear, clothing; p. (1991) 70,422.

East Lansing, t., Mich., **USA**; residtl.; univ.; p. (1980) 51,392.

Eastleigh, t., l. gov. dist., Hants., **Eng.**; rly. engin., many new inds.; p. (1995) 111,300 (dist.), (1991) 49,934 (t.).

East Lindsey, l. gov. dist., Lincs., **Eng.**; lge. a. on E. cst. inc. Louth, Mablethorpe, Horncastle, Skegness and Alford; p. (1995) 122,400.

East London, spt., C. Prov., **S. Africa**; at mouth of Buffalo R.; holiday resort; trading ctr.; inds. inc. car assembly, textiles, engin.; titanium deposits nearby; p. (1985) 193,819 (met. a.).

East Lothian, E. **Scot.**, unit. auth. created in 1996, incorporating most of historic co. which became part of Lothian in 1974; lies E. of Edinburgh, bordered N.E. by N. Sea, S.W. by Lammermuir Hills; p. (1995) 87,630.

East Main, R., Quebec, **Canada**; flows into James Bay; 432 km long.

East Northamptonshire, l. gov. dist., Northants., **Eng.**; stretches from Oundle to Irthlingborough, Rushden, Raunds and Higham Ferrers; p. (1995) 70,500.

Easton, t., Penns., **USA**; on Delaware R.; rly. ctr., coal, steel, machin., p. (1980) 26,027.

East Orange, t., N.J., **USA**; residtl. sub. of New York; p. (1990) 73,552.

East Pakistan. *See* Bangladesh.

East Point, t., Ga., **USA**; textiles, fertilisers; p. (1980) 37,486.

East Providence, t., Rhode I., **USA**; textiles, machin.; p. (1980) 50,980.

East Renfrewshire, unit. auth. created in 1996, formerly part of Strathclyde, W. **Scot.**; lies immediately S.W. of Glasgow; p. (1995) 88,150.

East Retford, t., Bassetlaw, Notts., **Eng.**; on R. Idle, 10 km E. of Worksop; p. (1991) 20,679.

East Riding of Yorkshire, unit. auth. created in 1996, formerly part of Humberside, **Eng.**; lge. a. N. of the R. Humber inc. Holderness Peninsula and ts. of Beverley and Bridlington; p. (1995) 308,400.

East River, tidal strait about 26 km long and 180–1,200 m wide; separates the bors. of Manhattan and Bronx from the bors. of Queens and Brooklyn, N.Y., **USA.**

East St. Louis, t., R. pt., Ill., **USA**; on Mississippi R.; lge stockyards, meat-packing, aluminium, chemicals; p. (1980) 55,200.

East Staffordshire, l. gov. dist., Staffs., **Eng.**; stretches from Uttoxeter to Burton-on-Trent; p. (1995) 100,400.

East Sussex, non-met. co., S.E. **Eng.**; mainly rural, urban growth on cst., where resorts, retirement and dormitory ts. for London, inc. Hastings and Eastbourne; crossed by S. Downs in S. terminating at Beachy Head, Ashdown Forest in N.; p. (1995) 730,900.

East Timor, prov., Indonesia; Port. terr. until 1975; sovereignty claimed by Indonesia and territory seized by force; atrocities against local population; autonomy now (1999) promised; mtnous; underdeveloped; cap. Dili; a. 14,693 km²; p. (1985) 2,294,000.

Eastwood, t., Broxtowe, Notts., **Eng.**; birthplace of D. H. Lawrence; coal; p. (1991) 19,363.

Eau Claire, t., Wis., **USA**; on Chippewa R.; agr. mkt.; univ. food processing, varied mnfs.; p. (1990) 56,856.

Ebbw Vale, t., Blaenau Gwent, **Wales**; 27 km N.W. of Newport; coal, iron, tinplate, bricks, pipes, precast concrete; some steel wks. to close; p. (1991) 19,484.

Eberswalde, t., Brandenburg, **Germany**; N.E. of Berlin; iron, wood, and cardboard wks., chemicals; p. (1981) 53,183.

Ebro, ch. R. of N.E. **Spain**; flows to Mediterranean from Cantabrian Mtns.; feeds hydroelectric plants, irrigation, esp. around Zaragoza; 928 km long.

Eccles, Gtr. Manchester, **Eng.**; 6 km W. of Manchester; chemicals, oil refining, engin.; p. (1991) 36,000.

Echo L., Tasmania, **Australia**; used to store water for hydroelectric power.

Echuca, t., Victoria, **Australia**; major inland pt. on Murray R. in mid 19th century; in 1970s original pt. and bldgs. restored.

Ecija, t., Seville, **Spain**; olive oil, wine, pottery; the Roman Astigi; p. (1981) 34,619.

Eckernförde, spt., Schleswig-Holstein, **Germany**; on Baltic, N.W. of Kiel; p. (1986) 24,500.

Ecrins, mtn. peak, S.E. **France**; hgst. point of massif du Pelvoux and Dauphiné Alps; alt. 4,106 m.

Ecuador, rep., S. America; on equatorial Pac. cst., bounded by Colombia to N. and Peru to W. and S.; inc. Galapagos Is. in Pac. Oc.; lowland to E. and W. of central Andes; climate temperate in Andes and hot and humid in lowlands; comm. economy mainly agr. with impt. exp. of bananas, coffee, cocoa; petroleum impt. (68 per cent of exports); pipeline across Andes to cst. of Esmeraldas; communications difficult but vital for economic development; attempts to control illegal narcotics exp.; major pts. Guayaquil and Manta; official language Spanish; cap. Quito; a. inc. Galapagos Is. 454,752 km²; p. (1996) 11,698,496.

Edam, t., N. Holland, **Neth.**; on cst. IJsselmeer; cheese, tool mftg.; p. (1993) 25,242.

Eday, I., Orkney Is., **Scot.**; the Ocelli of Ptolemy; p. (1991) 166.

Eddystone, rock with lighthouse, Eng. Channel; S.W. of Plymouth.

Ede, t., Gelderland, **Neth.**; livestock; pianos; p. (1994) 98,220.

Edea, t., pt., **Cameroon**; aluminium smelting based on nearby hydroelectric power plant; p. (1981) 31,016.

Eden, Vale of, fertile belt in Cumbria, **Eng.**; between barren hills of Pennines and L. Dist.; occupied by R. Eden; mkt. ts. Appleby and Penrith; forms l. gov. dist. **Eden**, inc. Penrith, Alston and Appleby; p. (1995) 47,900.

Eder, R., **Germany**; joins Fulda R. S. of Kassel; Eder dam lgst. in Germany.

Edessa (Edhessa), t., N.E. **Greece**; agr. tr. ctr.; the anc. Ægae, burial place of Macedonian kings; p. (1981) 16,642.

Edgehill, ridge, 24 km S. of Warwick, **Eng.**; scene of first battle of civil war, 1642.

Edinburgh, c., cap. of **Scot.**, unit. auth. created in 1996, formerly part of Lothian; royal burgh on F. of Forth; univ., cas.; palace (Holyrood); printing, publishing, brewing, electronics equipment, rubber prods.; Edinburgh Festival in August; Leith, with docks is joined to E.; p. (1991) 401,910 (c.), (1995) 447,550 (unit. auth.).

Edirne, t. and prov., **Turkey**; in Thrace, on R. Maritsa; comm. ctr. with tr. in wine, tobacco, silk, perfume; the anc. Adrianople, named after the emperor Hadrian, later cap. of Ottoman sultans 1366–1453; p. (1985) 86,909, (1990) 404,599 (prov.).

Edmonton, c., cap. of Alberta, **Canada**; fast growing c. (119 km²) on both sides of N. Saskatchewan R.; high-level bridge links Strathcona; major military ctr.; univ.; international air ctr.; oilfields and farming; oil and chemical inds.; p. (1991) 616,741.

Edremit, t., Balikesir, N.W. **Turkey**; cereals, opium; silverwk.; p. (1985) 30,159.

Edward, L., on frontier of Uganda and Zaïre, one of the sources of R. Nile; occupies Gt. Rift Valley; alt. c. 900 m, 70km long, breadth 51km; salt, fishing, wildlife.

Eger, t., N.E. **Hungary**; mkt. t. in wine producing region; mediaeval fortress t.; p. (1997) 59,000.

Egersund, pt., S. cst. **Norway**; fishing; mentioned in Norwegian sagas.

Egham, t., Runnymede, Surrey, **Eng.**; on R. Thames, nr. Staines; contains field of Runnymede; residtl.; p. (1991) 23,816.

Egmont, mtn., N.I., **N.Z.**; extinct volcano; alt. 2,501 m. Maori name is Mt. Taranaki.

Egremont, mkt. t., Cumbria, **Eng.**; 10 km S. of Whitehaven; limestone; former iron ore mng.; p. (1991) 6,581.

Egypt, Arab Republic of, indep. st., N.E. corner Africa; member of Federation of Arab Reps.; 96 per cent a. is desert except Nile valley and delta where 95 per cent of p. live; agr. depends on annual rise of Nile waters and irrigation; cereals, sugarcane, vegetables, fruit; cotton main cash crop; phosphates; oilfield in Sinai and recent finds offshore in G. of Suez and in Western Desert; nat. gas since 1974; 6 oil refineries; major port development on Red Sea to handle mineral exp.;

textiles account for ⅓ of manuf. output; cap. Cairo; Aswan High Dam has produced problems; (1) silting up of reservoir (L. Nasser) behind dam; (2) reduction in fertilising silt deposits in lower Nile valley; (3) erosion of Nile delta itself; (4) reduction of fish p. in E. Med.; a. 999,740 km²; p. (1995) 58,819,000.

Eider, R., **Germany**; separates Holstein from Schleswig; flows into N. Sea; 125 m. long.

Eifel, plateau of volcanic rocks, **Germany**; lies N. of R. Moselle, forming W. edge of Rhine gorge between Koblenz and Bonn; formerly cultivated, now largely woodland and moorland; farming in valleys; rises to just over 600 m.

Eiger, mtn., one of the hgst. peaks of the Bernese Oberland, **Switzerland**; famous for steep N. wall; alt. 3,978 m.

Eigg, I., Inner Hebrides, Highland, **Scot.**; 24 km S.W. of Mallaig; basaltic rocks on cst.; rises to 393 m; p. (1991) 141.

Eilat, new spt., Negev, **Israel**; on G. of Aqaba; growing tourist tr.; copper at Timna; oil pipeline from Ashdod (1970).

Eildon Hills, Borders, **Scot.**; S. of Melrose; hgst. point 422 m.

Eindhoven, c., N. Brabant, **Neth.**; electronic equipment, motor vehicles, tobacco and textile inds.; technical univ.; p. (1994) 196,130 (c.), 393,326 (met. a.).

Eire. *See* **Ireland, Republic of.**

Eisenach, t., Erfurt, **Germany**; on R. Hörsel, at foot of Thuringian forest; ctr. of Werra potash field; cars, machin., textiles; birthplace of J. S. Bach; p. (1981) 50,674.

Eisenerz Alps, mtn. range, **Austria**; most N. range of Alps, overlooking Danube valley between Linz and Vienna; impt. iron-ore deposits; alt. from 1,800–2,700 m.

Eisenhüttenstadt, t., Brandenburg, **Germany**; iron smelting; terminus of Oder–Spree canal; p. (1989) 52,393.

Eisleben, t., Saxony - Anhalt, **Germany**; machin., copper and silver-mng. ctr.; birthplace of Luther; p. (1989) 26,530.

Ekibastuz, t., **Kazakhstan**; 120 km S.W. of Pavlodar; ctr. of rapidly developing mng. a. coal, gold, metals; p. (1990) 137,000.

El Aaiun, pt., **Western Sahara**; main pt. for exp. of phosphates; p. (1982) 96,784.

El Alamein, v., **Egypt**; in Libyan Desert 96 km S.W. of Alexandria, scene of Allied victory, second world war; oilfield nearby; terminal nr. Sidi Abd el-Rahman.

Elan, R. Powys, **Wales**; rises on S.E. sides of Plynlimon, flows into R. Wye; lower valley contains series of 4 lge. reservoirs, capacity 45,460 million litres; ch. source of water for Birmingham.

Elâzig, t. and prov., E. **Turkey**; dam and hydroelec. project at Keban, 48 km to N.W. at confluence of E. and W. branches of Euphrates; p. (1990) 498,225 (prov.), 218,121 (t.).

Elba, I., off Tuscan est., **Italy**; iron ore, wine, marble, salt; ch. t. Portoferraio; Napoleon's first exile here; a. 363 km²; p. (1981) 10,755.

Elbe (**Labe**), R., in **Czech Rep.** and **Germany**; rises in Riesengebirge and flows into N. Sea at Cuxhaven; navigable for 840 km of total l. of 1,160 km; connected with Rhine and Weser Rs. by Mittelland canal.

Elbasan, town in cent. **Albania.**

Elbert, mtn., Col., **USA**; hgst. peak of Rocky Mtns. in USA, 4,401 m.

Elblag or **Elbing**, spt. and prov., N. **Poland**; shipbldg., machin., vehicles; p. (1989) 125,778 (t.), 475,900 (prov.).

El Boulaïda (**Blida**), t., dep., **Algeria**; agr. ctr.; citrus fruits; p. (1987) 127,284 (t.), 704,462 (dep.).

Elbruz Mt., Caucasus, **Russia**; hgst. in Europe (5,636 m), over-topping Mont Blanc by 822 m; twin volcanic peaks.

Elburz, mtn. range, N. **Iran**; bordering on Caspian Sea; hgst. peak, Demavend, 5,642 m.

Elche, t., Alicante, **Spain**; palm groves; oil, soap, footwear; p. (1991) 181,192.

El Dar-el-Beida (**Casablanca**), c., **Morocco**; pt. on Atl. Oc.; artificial harbour; fish canning, textiles; exp. phosphate; p. (1982) 2,139,204.

Eldorado, radium mine, N.W. Terr., **Canada**; on E. shore of Gr. Bear Lake nr. Arctic Circle; produces 40 per cent of world's radium, sent to Pt. Hope, Ontario, for refining.

El Djezair (**Algiers**), dep., pt., cap. c. of **Algeria**; old

t. surmounted by 16th cent. Casbâh (fortress); univ.; exp. wine, citrus fruit, iron ore; oil refining at Maison Carrée; airpt. at Maison Blanche, 16 km E. of c.; p. (1995), 2,168,000 (c.), (1987) 1,687,579 (dep.).

Elektrenai, t., **Lithuania**; new township nr. Vievis, at site of thermal power sta. (1990) 15,800

Elektrostal, t., **Russia**; 56 km E. of Moscow; steel, engin.; p. (1989) 152,000.

Elephanta I., Bombay Harbour, **India**; Brahmanic caves with monolithic carvings.

Elephant Butte Dam, N.M., **USA**; on Rio Grande; built to control flood water; lake, a. 115 km² supplies irrigation water to 2,020 km² in N.M. and Texas, water also supplied to Mexico.

El Ferrol del Caudillo, spt., **Spain**; on N.W. cst.; fortfd., fishing; p. (1981) 91,764.

Elgin, royal burgh, Moray, **Scot.**; pt. Lossiemouth; whisky; ruins anc. cath.; p. (1991) 19,027.

Elgin, t., Ill., **USA**; watches, electrical equipment; p. (1990) 77,010.

El Giza, t. and prov., **Egypt**; on Nile, sub. of Cairo; nr. pyramids of Khufu (Cheops), Khafra (Chephren), and the Sphinx; film ind.; p. (1990) 2,156,000 (t.) (1991) 4,182,000 (prov.).

Elgon Mt., extinct volcano, bdy. of **Kenya** and **Uganda**; 4,300 m; cave dwellings on slopes.

Elie and **Earlsferry**, burgh, Fife, **Scot.**; summer resort; p. (1991) 903.

Elisabethville. *See* **Lubumbashi.**

Elizabeth, c., N.J., **USA**; univ.; sewing machines, oil refining, cars, aircraft components; now inc. in Newark; p. (1990) 110,002.

Elk I., Nat. Park, **Canada**; animal reserve, tourism.

El Khârga, oasis, Libyan desert, **Egypt**, 136 km S.W. of Asyût; site of New Valley Project for irrigation.

Elkhart, t., Ind., **USA**; E. of Chicago; paper, machin.; elec. equipment, musical instruments; p. (1984) 43,100.

Elk Mtns., W. Col., **USA**; highest point Castle Peak, 4,305 m.

Elland, t., West Yorks., **Eng.**; on R. Calder, 5 km S.E. of Halifax; textiles; p. (1991) 14,232.

Ellesmere, agr. dist., S.I., **N.Z.**; on Canterbury Plain nr. Christchurch.

Ellesmere, mkt. t., Shrops., **Eng.**; nearby lake; tourism; p. (1991) 2,967.

Ellesmere I., extreme N. of Arctic **Canada**; barren uninhabited; a. 106,200 km².

Ellesmere Port, t., N.W. Cheshire, **Eng.**; on Manchester Ship Canal and 14 km S.S.E. of Liverpool; metal mftg., paper, engin., oil refineries; cars; expanded t.; forms part of l. gov. dist. of **Ellesmere Port and Neston**; p. (1995) 81,000 (dist.), (1991) 64,504 (t.).

Elliot Lake, t., N. Ont., **Canada**; ctr. of uranium mines; p. (1981) 16,723.

Ellice Is. *See* **Tuvalu I.**

Ellis I., N.Y. harbour, **USA**; served as ch. immigration ctr., 1892–1943.

Ellon, burgh, Aberdeenshire, **Scot.**; on R. Ythan; p. (1991) 8,627.

El Mahalla el Kubra, t., **Egypt**; N. of Cairo on Nile delta; textile ctr.; p. (1986) 358,844.

Elmbridge, l. gov. dist., Surrey, **Eng.**; close to Gtr. London; inc. Esher, Walton and Weybridge; p. (1995) 122,200.

Elmira, t., N.Y., **USA**; rly. gds., farm implements; famous as burial place of Mark Twain; p. (1990) 33,724.

El Misti, mtn., S. **Peru**; dormant volcano with snow cap; alt. 5,846 m.

Elmshorn, t., **Germany**; N.W. of Hamburg; shipbldg.; p. (1986) 41,500.

El Paso, c., Texas, **USA**; on E. bank Rio Grande opposite Ciudad Juárez (Mexico); natural gas distribution, oil refining, metallurgy; tourism; p. (1990) 515,342 (c.), 592,000 (met. a.).

El Salvador, rep., on Pac. cst. of Central America; bounded by Guatemala to W. and Honduras to N. and E.; comprises 14 administrative departments; temperate volcanic uplands, hot humid coastal lowlands; comm. economy mainly agr., especially coffee, also developing comm. fisheries and iron and steel ind.; electric power from dam across Lempa R.; well-developed transport system, inc. Pan-American Highway; pt. at Acajutla and airport at Ilopango; member of Central American Common Market; protracted guerrilla warfare during much of the 1980s; cap. San Salvador; a. 21,331 km²; p. (1992) 5,047,925.

El Segundo, t., Cal., **USA**; lge. oil refinery; assembly of aircraft components; p. (1980) 13,752.

Elsinore. *See* Helsingør.

Elstow, v., Beds., **Eng.**; the birthplace of John Bunyan.

Elstree, t., Hertsmere, Herts., **Eng.**; 6 km W. of Barnet; residtl.; films, lt. engin., silk hosiery; p. (1991) 2,196.

Eluru, t., Andhra Pradesh, **India**; cotton, carpets, hosiery, oil; p. (1991) 212,918.

Elvas, mkt. t., **Portugal**; on Guadiana R.; plums, olives, jams; cath.; once strongly fortfd.; p. (1981) 12,880.

Ely, t., Cambridge, **Eng.**; on S. fringe of Fens; mkt., cath.; agr. ctr.; p. (1991) 10,329.

Ely, I. of. *See* Cambridgeshire.

Elyria, t., Ohio, **USA**; mftg.; p. (1990) 56,746.

Emba, R., **Kazakhstan**; rises in Urals, flows S.W. to Caspian Sea; crosses productive Ural–Emba oilfield; 608 km long.

Emden, t., Lower Saxony, **Germany**; impt. N. Sea pt. nr. mouth of R. Ems and on Dortmund–Ems and Ems–Jade canals; exp. coal and iron from Ruhr; shipyards, fisheries; p. (1986) 49,600.

Emene, t., **Nigeria**; nr. Enugu; steel plant; cement.

Emilia-Romagna, region, N. **Italy**; S. of Po R.; divided into 8 provs.; fertile agr. a.; a. 22,124 km²; p. (1992) 3,920,223.

Emmen, t., Drenthe, **Neth.**; 48 km S.E. of Groningen; elec. machin., ball bearings, tinplate, iron wks.; p. (1994) 93,476.

Emmental, dist., **Switzerland**; dairy produce, especially cheese.

Empoli, t., Tuscany, **Italy**; on R. Arno; textile mnfs., glass; p. (1981) 44,961.

Ems, R., N. **Germany**; rises in Teutoburger Wald, flows N. to N. Sea at Emden; 333 km long.

Emscher, R., **Germany**; rises in Sauerland, flows W. through heart of Ruhr coalfield to enter R. Rhine at Hamborn; canalised for most of its course; very highly polluted; 88 km long.

Encarnación, pt., cap. of Itapuá dep. S.E. **Paraguay**; on Paraná R.; exp. timber, maté, tobacco, cotton, hides; p. (1984) 31,445.

Enderby Land, Australian terr., S. of C. of Good Hope, **Antarctica**.

Enfield, outer bor., Greater London, **Eng.**; comprising Edmonton, Enfield, and Southgate; p. (1995) 261,300.

Enfield, t., Conn., **USA**; mftg.; p. (1980) 42,695.

Engadine, **Switzerland**; upper valley of Inn R., health resort; ch. t. St. Moritz; Swiss Nat. Park.

Enggano, I., Sumatra, **Indonesia**; sparse p.; hunting, fishing, shifting cultivation.

Engels. *See* Pokrovsk

England, southern and lgst. political div. of U.K.; bounded by Wales on W., by Scot. on N. and separated from continent of Europe by English Channel and North Sea; highly industl., circa 80 per cent of p. live in urban areas; major trading nation through main pts. London, Liverpool, Southampton; increasing contrast between prosperous S. and depressed N. and W.; very varied geology and topography produce contrasts in landscape, matched by climatic variability; increasingly attractive as tourist area although urban and agr. pressures on rural countryside cause concern in such a densely populated cty.; excellent road and rail network; rich and varied cultural heritage and numerous historic bldgs.; cap. London; p. (1995) 48,903,400.

Englewood, t., Col., **USA**; sub. of Denver; glasshouses; p. (1980) 30,021.

Englewood, t., N.J., **USA**; elevators, leather gds.; p. (1980) 23,701.

English Channel (La Manche), narrow sea separating England from France; extends from Strait of Dover to Land's End in Cornwall; length 480 km, greatest width 248 km.; now crossed by Channel Tunnel *See* Cheriton.

Enham-Alamein, Hants., **Eng.**; rehabilitation ctr. for disabled ex-service men; 4 km N. of Andover; lt. inds.

Enid, t., Okla., **USA**; univ.; ironwks., farm implements; wheat mkt.; p. (1980) 50,363.

Enna (Castrogiovanni), t., Sicily, **Italy**; sulphurmines; famous for its connection with the Proserpine legend; p. (1981) 27,838.

Ennepetal, t., N. Rhine–Westphalia, **Germany**; t. created 1949 with merging of Milspe and Voerde; iron, machin.; p. (1986) 33,700.

Ennerdale Water, L., Cumbria, **Eng.**

Enniscorthy, mkt. t., Wexford, **R.o.I.**; cath.; p. (1986) 4,483.

Enniskillen, t., Fermanagh, **N. Ireland**; brewing, nylon mftg., meat processing; p. (1991) 11,436.

Enschede, c., Overijssel, **Neth.**; textile ctr.; technical univ.; with Hengelo forms met. a.; p. (1994) 147,624 (c.), 254,063 (met. a.).

Ensenada, t., **Mexico**; spt., exp. cotton; fishing and fish processing; p. (1990) 260,905.

Entebbe, t., **Uganda**; on L. Victoria; univ.; cotton ginning; airport; p. (1991) 41,638.

Entre Rios, prov., **Argentina**; between Paraná and Uruguay Rs.; wheat, linseed, livestock; cap. Paraná; a. 76,216 km²; p. (1991) 1,020,257.

Enugu, cap. of E. prov., **Nigeria**; coal; cloth mill; p. (1992) 286,100, (1991) 3,161,295 (state).

Epernay, t., on S. bank of Marne, **France**; champagne ctr.; p. (1982) 28,876.

Ephesus, anc. Ionian c., in what is now **Turkey**, S. of Izmir; sacked by Goths A.D. 262; excavations.

Epinal, t., cap. of Vosges dep., **France**; on Moselle R.; textiles, printing, liqueur; p. (1990) 39,480.

Epirus, dist., N.W. **Greece**; a. 9,552 km²; p. (1991) 339,210.

Epping Forest, Essex, **Eng.**; forest a. N.E. of London free to public (opened by Queen Victoria 1882); formerly part of royal hunting forest; also l. gov. dist., inc. Chigwell, Waltham Abbey and Ongar; p. (1995) 118,800.

Epsom and Ewell, ts., l. gov. dist., Surrey, **Eng.**; 29 km S.W. of London; residtl., racecourse; p. (1995) 69,200 (dist.), (1991) 64,405 (ts.).

Epworth, v., N. Lincs., **Eng.**; birthplace of John Wesley; p. (1991) 3,359.

Equatorial Guinea, unitary state, W. **Africa**; former Spanish col.; indep. 1968; comprises 2 provs.; Rio Muni (mainland and Is. of Corisco, Elobey Grande, Elobey Chico) and Biako (Is. of Biako and Pagalu); narrow coastal plain and dissected upland plateau (600 m); economy almost entirely based on agr. and timber; exploration for oil; cap. Malabo on Biako I.; a. 28,051 km²; p. (1992) 420,000.

Erbil, t., **Iraq**; comm. ctr.; rly. terminus; p. (1985) 333,903.

Erebus, mtn., active volcano, Victoria Land, **Antarctica**; alt. 4,027 m.

Erewash, l. gov. dist., Derbys., **Eng.**; a. close to Nottingham nic. Ilkeston and Long Eaton; p. (1995) 106,700.

Erfurt, admin. dist., **Germany**; a. 7,322 km²; p. (1983) 1,238,200.

Erfurt, c., **Germany**; on Gera R.; cap. Thuringia *Land*; cath., ctr. of mkt. gardening and seedgrowing dist., textiles, machin., foodstuffs, footwear, radios, heavy engin.; p. (1990) 207,200.

Ericht, Loch, Scot.; in central Grampians; 25 km long; hydroelec. scheme.

Erie, c., N.W. Penns., **USA**; pt. on L. Erie; coal, iron, grain, petroleum; machin., domestic appliances; p. (1990) 108,718 (c.), 276,000 (met. a.).

Erie Canal. *See* New York State Barge Canal.

Erie, one of Great Lakes (the shallowest), N. America, separating Canada from USA; 386 km long, 48–91 km wide; polluted waters; petroleum resources.

Erith, former M.B., Kent, **Eng.**; on Thames estuary; plastics, paints, varnishes, timber, concrete; now inc. in London bor. of Bexley.

Eritrea, indep. st. N.E. Africa (1993); formerly prov., Ethiopia; tobacco, cereals, pearl fishing; demands for autonomy; secessionist rebellion crushed (1978); severe drought 1982–3; cap. Asmara, a. 124,320 km²; p. (1994) 3,525,000.

Erivan. *See* Yerevan.

Erlangen, t., Bavaria, **Germany**; univ.; textiles, elec. and precision engin., gloves; p. (1990) 102,600.

Ermelo, t., **Neth.**; ctr. of agr. dist.; p. (1993) 26,603.

Ernakulam, dist., Kerala, **India**; cotton, coffee, hides; p. (1991) 1,141,000.

Erne, R., N. Ireland/R.o.I.; links Ls. in Cavan and Fermanagh; 115 km long.

Erode, t., S. Tamil Nadu, **India**; on R. Cauvery; p. (1991) 159,232.

Erzgebirge (Ore Mtns.), mtn. range along border of Czech Rep. and **Germany**; reaching highest peak in Mt. Klinovec (1,240 m); uranium; tourism.

Erzurum, t., **Turkey**; agr. ctr. on fertile plateau c. 1,890 m a.s.l.; formerly of gr. strategic importance; univ.; earthquake (1983); p. (1990) 297,544. (t.), 848,201 (prov.).

Esbjerg, spt., **Denmark**; W. cst. of Jutland; export harbour on N. Sea cst.; exp. agr. prod.; fishing; airport; p. (1990) 81,504.

Esch-sur-Alzette, t., **Luxembourg**; mng. ctr.; steel; p. (1991) 24,012.

Eschwege, t., Hesse, **Germany**; cas.; machin., textiles, leather, cigars, chemicals; p. (1986) 22,900.

Eschweiler, t., N. Rhine-Westphalia, **Germany**; N.W. of Aachen; lignite mng., steel, iron metallurgy; p. (1986) 53,100.

Esdraelon, plain, **Israel**; between Carmel and Gilboa Mtns.

Esfahān (Isfahan, anc. Aspadana), c., central **Iran**; prov. cap.; historic, picturesque c. noted for carpets and metal ware; tourism, airpt.; new steel mill; impt. oil refining ctr.; p. (1986) 1,001,248.

Esher, t., Elmbridge, Surrey, **Eng.**; on R. Mole, residtl.; Sandown Park racecourse; p. (1991) 46,599.

Eshowe, health resort, Natal, **S. Africa**; 64 km from Tugela R.; p. (1980) 28,680 (dist.).

Esk, R., Borders, **Scot.**; Cumbria, **Eng.**; attractive agr. valley; flows into Solway F. from confluence of Black and White Esk Rs.; 37 km long.

Eskilstuna, t., **Sweden**; on R. of same name; iron, steel, machin.. machin. tools; p. (1992) 89,584.

Eskişehir, t. and prov., **Turkey**; W. of Ankara, anc. Dorylaeum; rly. ctr.; p. (1990) 415,831 (t.), (1990) 641,087 (prov.).

Esmeraldas, prov., **Ecuador**; cap. E. on R. of same name; cacao, tobacco; a. 14,152 km²; p. (1990) 306,628.

Esmeraldas, pt., **Ecuador**; bananas, timber, tobacco, cacao, rubber; gold mines nearby; terminal of petroleum pipeline from Oriente; p. (1990) 98,558.

Esneh. See Isna.

Espirito Santo, st., **Brazil**; sugar, cotton, coffee, fruits, lumber, thorium; cap. Vitória; a. 40,883 km²; p. (1991) 2,598,231.

Espiritu Santo, I., **Vanuatu**; volcanic I., lgst. of gr.; depopulation.

Essaouira (Mogador), spt., **Morocco**; cereals, almonds, gum-arabic, crude oil; p. (1982) 42,035.

Essen, c., N. Rhine-Westphalia, **Germany**; gr. industl. c., ctr. of Ruhr conurbation; coal, steel (Krupp), electric power, engin.; canal links with Dortmund-Ems and Mittelland canals and with Rhine; minster severely damaged in second world war; p. (1990) 626,100.

Essequibo, R.; flows N. from Brazilian border draining half **Guyana**; lower course navigable, rapids; timber in upper valley; 960 km long.

Essex, non-met. co., **Eng.**; bounded on S. by Thames, on E. by N. Sea; co. t. Chelmsford; on London clay and chalk; agr.; wheat, barley, sugar-beet; mkt. gardens; S.W. of co. forms part of Greater London with mftg. subs.; oil refineries at Shell Haven; civil nuclear power sta. at Bradwell; univ. at Colchester; p. (1995) 1,577,500.

Esslingen, t., Baden-Württemberg, **Germany**; on R. Neckar; mach. and rly. shops; textiles, chemicals, leather gds.; Liebfrauen church (1440); p. (1986) 86,900.

Essonne, dep., **France**; S. of Paris; cap. Evry; a. 1,810 km²; p. (1990) 1,084,800.

Esteli, cap., Esteli, **Nicaragua**; on Inter-American Highway; p. (1985) 30,635.

Eston, t., Redcar and Cleveland, **Eng.**; 5 km E. of Middlesbrough; shipbldg. and repairing; p. (1991) 37,343 (with South Bank).

Estonia (Estoniya), former USSR constituent rep.; borders on Baltic, G. of Finland, G. of Riga; lowland with many Ls.; farming and dairying, fishing; oil deposits; hydroelec. power; mainly Lutheran; univ.; cap. Tallinn; a. 45,610 km²; p. (1992) 1,595,000.

Estoril, wat. pl. and thermal spa, **Portugal**; N. side of Tagus estuary; holiday resort; p. (1981) 24,312.

Estremadura, maritime prov., **Portugal**; agr., tourism; cap. Lisbon; a. 5,348 km²; p. (1981) 1,064,976.

Estremadura, region, S.W. **Spain**; on the border of Portugal; largely plateau, alt. 450–900 m.; heathy moorland; sheep; less arid conditions than in remainder of central Spain allow olives, vines, cereals; irrigation in valleys of Tagus, Guadiana; govt. project to develop a. in progress.

Esztergom, t., **Hungary**; R. pt. on Danube; iron foundries, machine tools; mineral springs; cath.; p. (1997) 28,000.

Etang de Berre, lagoon, Bouches-du-Rhône, S.E. **France**; E. of Rhône delta; traversed by Rhône-Marseille canal; salt pans; oil refineries in a.; approx. a. 260 km².

Étaples, t., Pas-de-Calais, **France**; seaside resort; p. (1982) 11,310.

Etawah, t., Uttar Pradesh, **India**; textiles; p. (1991) 124,027.

Ethiopia (Abyssinia), indep. st. N.E. Africa; temperate climate as a result of high plateau terrain; coffee most impt. comm. crop, but poor communications inhibit economic development; low per capita income and rapid growth of p.; potential for hydro-electric power is lge., one sta. open on Awash R.; mftg. dominated by textiles; severe drought began in 1970s and continued in 1980s; cap. Addis Ababa; monarchy abolished 1975; a. 1,221,900 km²; p. (1994) 55,000,000.

Ethiopian Highlands, mtns., **Ethiopia**; rise over 4,500 m; source of headwaters of tribs. of R. Nile.

Etna, volcano, N.E. Sicily, **Italy**; most recent eruptions 1971, 1979, and 1992; alt. 3,276 m. It is Europe's largest active volcano.

Eton, t., Berks., **Eng.**; on N. bank of R. Thames opposite Windsor; public school, founded by Henry VI; p. (1991) 1,974.

Etruria, anc. dist., **Italy**; now forms Tuscany; home of the Etruscans and part of the Roman empire by 400 B.C.

Etruria, t., Stoke, **Eng.**; part of Stoke-on-Trent; seat of Josiah Wedgwood's potteries (1769).

Euboea (Evvoia), lgst. of Greek Is., Aegean Sea; mtnous. (Mt. Delphi 1,746 m); vines and olives in lowlands, sheep and goats in highlands; a. 3,864 km²; p. (1991) 209,132.

Euclid, t., Ohio, **USA**; electrical and agr. machin.; p. (1990) 54,875.

Eucumbene Dam and **L.,** N.S.W., **Australia**; major storage of Snowy Mtns. hydroelectric scheme; holds eight times as much water as Sydney harbour.

Eugene, c., Ore., **USA**; univ.; mkt. ctr. for rich agr. and lumbering region; fruit-canning, sawmilling; headquarters of Willamette National Forest; p. (1990) 112,669 (c.), 283,000 (met. a. with Springfield).

Euphrates, lgst. R. in S.W. **Asia**; rises in Armenian uplands and joined by the Tigris enters Persian G. as the Shatt-al Arab; anc. ctr. of civilisation; modern irrigation, navigation, high dam opened 1973 and Ataturk Dam (1981) part of multi-purpose project; 2,848 km long.

Eure, dep., Normandy, **France**; agr., fruit, livestock, textiles; cap. Evreux; a. 6,037 km²; p. (1990) 513,800.

Eure-et-Loir, dep., N. **France**; mainly agr.; cap. Chartres; a. 5,934 km²; p. (1990) 396,100.

Europe, continent; W. peninsula of Eurasian land mass; no well-defined bdy. with Asia but line normally accepted runs along Ural Mtns. to Caspian Sea and Caucasus to Black Sea, Sea of Marmara and Dardanelles; after Australia, Europe is smallest continent in a., but contains 11 per cent of world's p. and even more of world's economic activity; climate varies from Arctic to Mediterranean and from temperate maritime to severe continental; major physical features inc. Alps, Pyrenees in S., Baltic Shield in N.; many European countries now included within European Union (EU) which has expanded rapidly; old division of East and West has disappeared. Major concentration of p. and economic activity within Golden Triangle (q.v.); total a. c. 10,360,000 km²; p. (1995) 509,000,000 (excl. frmr. USSR).

Euro-port, name of the post-war expansion of the port of Rotterdam, **Neth.**; capable of handling 100,000 tonne oil-tankers; oil refining centre.

Evanston, t., Ill., **USA**; on L. Michigan, sub. of Chicago; univ.; p. (1980) 73,706.

Evansville, c., Ind., **USA**; on Ohio R.; shipping and comm. ctr. for agr. region; coal mng.; p. (1990) 116,646 (c.), 279,000 (met. a.).

Eveneki National Area, Siberia, **Russia**; forest and tundra covered; home of Eveneki people; cap. Tura; a. 740,740 km²; p. (1989) 24,800.

Everest, Mt. (Chomolungma = Goddess Mother of the Earth), Himalaya, on frontier of Nepal and Tibet, **China**; alt. 8,846 m; hgst. mtn. in the world; Hillary and Tenzing first to reach summit in 1953; within Nepal Nat. Park.

Everett, mftg. t., Mass., **USA**; nr. Boston; iron and steel; p. (1980) 37,195.

Everett, t., Wash., **USA**; on Puget Sound; harbour; comm. ctr.; timber; tourism; p. (1980) 54,413.

Everglades, Fla., **USA**; subtropical a.; extensive marshes; home of Seminole Indians; lge. scale drainage since 1905; emergency plan launched (1998) to save its endangered ecosystem.

Evesham, mkt. t., Wychavon, Worcs., **Eng.**; on R. Avon, in Vale of Evesham, 24 km S.E. of Worcester; fruit ctr.; tourism; p. (1991) 17,823.

Évora, t., cap. of Upper Alentejo prov., S. **Portugal**; mkt. for agr. prod.; cath.; p. (1987) 34,851.

Évreux, t., cap. of Eure dep., **France**; mkt. ctr.; p. (1990) 51,459.

Evros, prov., **Greece**; borders Bulgaria and Turkey; a. 4,191 km²; p. (1991) 143,791.

Evry, t. cap. of Essone dep., **France**; new cathedral inaugurated, April 1996.; p. (1990) 45,854.

Exe, R., Somerset and Devon, **Eng.**; rises on Exmoor, flows S. via Exeter to English Channel at Exmouth; 86 km long.

Exeter, l. gov. dist., cath. c., co. t., Devon, **Eng.**; former Roman Isca; E. of Dartmoor on R. Exe; mkt. t.; univ.; aircraft components; airport; p. (1995) 106,600 (dist.), (1991) 94,717 (c.).

Exmoor, Somerset and Devon, **Eng.**; sandstone moorland, deep wooded valleys; Nat. Park.

Exmouth, t., East Devon, **Eng.**; on estuary of R. Exe; holiday resort; p. (1991) 28,414.

Exploits, R., Newfoundland, **Canada**; length 240 km; used for hydroelectric power.

Eye, mkt. t., Mid Suffolk, **Eng.**; 29 km N. of Ipswich; anc. church; p. (1991) 1,741.

Eyemouth, burgh, Borders, **Scot.**; on E. cst. 14 km N. of Berwick; fishing; p. (1991) 3,473.

Eyre Lake, 2 shallow salt lakes in northern S. **Australia**; 12 m below sea level; receives water from flash flooding, sometimes dry; a. 7,800 km².

Eyre Peninsula, S. **Australia**; between Gr. Australian Bight and Spencer G.; iron-ore deposits; a. 51,800 km².

F

Fabriano, t., Marches, **Italy**; in Apennines; cath.; paper mills; p. (1981) 28,708.

Faenza, t., Ravenna, **Italy**; at foot of Apennines; majolica, textiles; p. (1981) 55,003.

Fagersta, t., Västmanland, **Sweden**; iron, steel smelting.

Failsworth, t. Gtr. Manchester, **Eng.**; N.E. of Manchester; textiles, elec. gds.; p. (1991) 20,160.

Fairbanks North Star, t., Alaska, **USA**; univ.; sawmilling; mng.; p. (1990) 77,720.

Fairfield, t., Conn., **USA**; chemicals, automobile parts; univ.; p. (1980) 54,849.

Fair I., midway between Shetland and Orkney, **Scot.**; bird sanctuary; famous for brightly patterned, hand-knitted articles; p. (1991) 67.

Fairmont, t., W. Va., **USA**; glass, machin., coal by-products; p. (1980) 23,863.

Faisalabad c. W. Punjab, **Pakistan**; univ. cotton chemicals, fertilizers; p. (1981) 1,092,000.

Faiyum (El Faiyûm), t. and prov. **Egypt**; oasis nr. L. Karun (anc. L. Moeris), fertilised by Nile water and silt; cereals, sugar-cane, fruits, cotton; archaeological finds; p. (1986) 212,523 (t.), (1991) 1,800,000 (prov.).

Faisalabad, t., Uttar Pradesh, **India**; rly. junc.; sugar refining; p. (1981) 101,873 (t.), 143,167 (met. a.).

Faizabad, t., Uttar Pradesh, **India**; mkt. t.; sugar refineries; p. (1991) 124,437.

Falaise, t., Calvados, **France**; birthplace of William the Conqueror; p. (1982) 8,820.

Falaise de l'Ile de France, low S.E.-facing escarpment, 80 km S.E. and E. of Paris, **France**; overlooks Champagne Pouilleuse; ch. vine-growing dist. for champagne-wine ind. of Reims, Epernay.

Falcón, st., **Venezuela**; bordering Caribbean Sea; cap. Coro; p. (1990) 632,513.

Falconara Marittima, t., **Italy**; nr. Ancona; spt.; oil refining, shipbldg.; p. (1981) 29,071.

Falkirk, burgh, unit. auth. created in 1996, formerly part of Central Region, **Scot.**; 16 km S.E. of Stirling, bordered N.E. by F. of Forth; foundries, bricks, chemical, aluminium wks., concrete, timber yards; battles 1298 and 1746; p. (1991) 35,610 (t.), (1995) 142,800, (unit. auth.).

Falkland, burgh, Fife, **Scot.**; 5 km S. of Auchtermuchty; mkt.; p. (1991) 1,197.

Falkland Is., Brit. Crown col., S. Atl., comprises E. and W. Falkland and adjacent Is.; known as Malvinas by Argentina; sheep rearing (for wool);

cap. Stanley on E. Falkland I.; invasion by Argentina led to Falklands War (1982); airpt. opened (1985) capable of taking long range wide bodied aircraft; a. 12,173 km²; p. (1997) 2,100.

Falkland Is. Dependencies, S. Atl.; inc. Is. of S. Orkney and S. Shetland; now form part of **Brit. Antarctic Terr.**

Fall River, c., Mass., **USA**; on Mt. Hope Bay; pt. of entry; clothing, rubber gds., food prods., paper; p. (1980) 92,574.

Falmouth, t., Carrick, Cornwall, **Eng.**; on W. side of estuary of R. Fal. 16 km S. of Truro; sheltered harbourage; offshore oil supply base; seaside resort; fisheries, ship repairing, mng., quarrying, lt. engin.; cas.; pt.; p. (1991) 20,297.

False Bay, inlet on E. side of C. of Good Hope peninsula, **S. Africa**.

Falster, I., Baltic, **Denmark**; cap. Nyköbing; p. (1990) 42,846.

Falun, t., Kopparberg, **Sweden**; paper; copper mines now exhausted; p. (1992) 54,653.

Famagusta, t., spt., **Cyprus**; on E. cst.; resort; anc. crusade pt.; p. (1985) 19,400.

Famatina, t., La Rioja prov., **Argentina**; in foothills of Andes, 576 km N.W. of Córdoba; copper-mines.

Fareham, t., l. gov. dist., Hants., **Eng.**; at N.W. corner of Portsmouth Harbour; p. (1995) 102,500 (dist.), (1991) 54,866 (t.).

Farewell (Kap Farvel), C., southernmost tip of **Greenland**.

Farewell, C., most N. point S.I., **N.Z.**

Fargo, t., N.D., **USA**; rly. ctr. and R. pt.; grain, farm machin.; p. (1984) 65,700 (t.), (1990) 157,000 (met. a.).

Faringdon, mkt. t., Vale of White Horse, Oxon., **Eng.**; Faringdon Folly; p. (1991) 5,235.

Farnborough, t., Rushmoor, Hants., **Eng.**; Aldershot military camp; Royal Aircraft Establishment; p. (1991) 52,535.

Farne Is., gr. of islets off Northumberland cst., **Eng.**; bird sanctuary; National Trust.

Farnham, t., Waverley, Surrey, **Eng.**; at N. foot of N. Downs, 16 km W. of Guildford; mkt.; p. (1991) 36,178.

Farnworth, t., Gtr. Manchester, **Eng.**; nr. Bolton, textiles, engin., paper; p. (1991) 25,053.

Faro, spt., cap. of Algarve prov., **Portugal**; cork, figs, oranges; p. (1981) 27,974.

Faroe Is., 320 km N.W. of the Shetlands; cap. Thórshavn (Strömö I.); Danish possession but not member of EU; impt. fisheries; now seeking independence; a. 1,399 km²; p. (1990) 47,946.

Farrukhabad, t., Uttar Pradesh, **India**; on Ganges R.; gold, lace, brass wk.; p. (1991) 194,567.

Fars, prov., S. **Iran**; agr.; cap. Shîrâz; p. (1982) 2 m.

Fastnet, lighthouse in Atl. Oc., 7·2 km S.W. C. Clear, Irish cst.

Fatima, v., W. **Portugal**, nr. Leiria; R.C. pilgrimage.

Fatshan *See* **Foshan**.

Faversham, pt., Swale, N.E. Kent, **Eng.**; at head of F. creek; mkt.; fruit, hops, bricks, brushes, engin.; p. (1991) 17,070.

Fawley, t., Hants., **Eng.**; on W. shore Southampton Water; lge. oil refinery with pipeline to Staines and Heathrow Airpt.; synthetic rubber; p. (1991) 13,034.

Fayetteville, t., N.C., **USA**; agr. processing; p. (1984) 66,100 (t.), (1990) 275,000 (met. a.).

Feather, R., N. Cal., **USA**; R. project for water supply irrigation, and hydroelectric power.

Featherstone, t., West Yorks., **Eng.**; p. (1991) 10,496.

Fécamp, sm. spt. on cst. of Normandy, **France**; fishing, tourism, 12th cent. abbey; p. (1982) 21,696.

Fedchenko, glacier, **Tajikistan**; in Pamir mtns; 80 km long; one of longest in world.

Federal German Republic. *See under* **Germany**.

Feira de Santana, t., Bahia, **Brazil**; inland mkt. t.; p. (1991) 405,691.

Feldberg, highest peak in Black Forest, **Germany**; alt. 1,495 m.

Feldkirch, t., Vorarlberg, **Austria**; on Swiss frontier; p. (1991) 26,743.

Felixstowe, pt., Suffolk Coastal, Suffolk, **Eng.**; container pt.; seaside resort; p. (1991) 28,606.

Felling, Tyne and Wear, **Eng.**; Tyneside mftg. dist.; p. (1991) 35,053.

Feltham. *See* **Hounslow**.

Fenland, l. gov. dist., Cambs., **Eng.**; agr. a. in N. of co. inc. Wisbech, Chatteris, March, Whittlesey and North Witchford; p. (1995) 78,900.

Fens, The, low-lying dist. around the Wash, **Eng.**;

artificial drainage begun in 17th cent.; impt. agr. dist.; root crops, wheat, fruit, bulbs; a. 3,367 km².

Feodosiya, t., **Ukraine;** in Crimea; major Black Sea pt., tobacco, hosiery; exp. wheat; resort and sanatoria; p. (1990) 85,000.

Ferghana, region, **Uzbekistan;** deep basin at W. end of Tien Shan Mtns.; drained W. by R. Syr Dar'ya; semi-arid but extensive irrigation system allows intensive cultivation of cotton, citrus fruits, silk, rice; ch. ts. Kokand, Namangan.

Ferghana, c., **Uzbekistan;** hydroelectric power, petroleum refining, textiles; deposits of ozocerite nearby; p. (1990) 197,800.

Fermanagh, former co.; l. gov. dist., **N. Ireland;** bisected by R. Erne and lakes; stock raising, dairying; p. (1991) 54,033.

Fermoy, t., Cork, **R.o.I.;** on R. Blackwater; cath.; woollens; p. (1986) 2,872.

Fernando de Noronha, I., fed. terr., N.E. cst. Brazil; penal settlement and met. sta.; cap. Vila dos Remédios; a. 26 km²; p. (1980) 1,279.

Fernando Po. See **Bioko.**

Ferrara, c., N. **Italy;** nr. head of Po delta; cath., univ., palaces; mkt. for fertile plain; silk, hemp, wine; oil refinery nearby; petrochemicals; birthplace of Savonarola; p. (1992) 137,099.

Ferro (Hierro), most S. of the **Canary Is.;** a. 275 km²; cap. Valverde; chosen by Ptolemy (A.D. 56) for his prime meridian and used by French scientists in 17th cent.; reckoned as exactly W. 20 ° of Paris.

Ferryhill, v., Durham, **Eng.;** 8 km S. of Durham, in gap through limestone ridge which separates Wear valley from Tees valley; commands main N. to S. route along lowland E. of Pennines; p. (1991) 11,610.

Fertile Crescent, an arc of fertile land from the Mediterranean Sea, N. of the Arabian Desert, to Persian G.; home of some very early civilisations and migrations.

Fez (Fès), c., **Morocco;** lies inland 160 km E. of Rabat; one of the sacred cities of Islam; univ. attached to mosque (one of lgst. in Africa); comm. ctr.; p. (1982) 448,823.

Fezzan, prov., S.W. **Libya;** desert plateau with numerous wells and inhabited oases.

Ffestiniog. See **Blaenau Ffestiniog.**

Fianarantsoa, t., **Madagascar;** rice mills, meat preserves; p. (1990) 124,489.

Fichtelgebirge, mtn. range, N.E. Bavaria, **Germany;** extending into CSSR, rising to 1,051 m in Schneeberg; forested slopes.

Fiesole, t., Tuscany, **Italy;** on summit of wooded hill overlooking Florence and the Arno; residtl.; 11th cent. cath.; p. (1981) 14,486.

Fife, E. **Scot.,** unit. auth. created in 1996, reinstating historic co. which became Region in 1974; occupies a. between Tay and Forth estuaries; industl. dist. based originally on coalfields; Longannet colliery remains; p. (1995) 351,600.

Fiji, S.W. Pac. Oc., former Brit. col., gained independence in 1970; comprises over 800 Is.; tropical climate; agr. basis of economy, especially sugar and coconut prods.; gold an impt. exp.; forestry and tourism developing; forms centre of communications in S.W. Pac. Oc.; fast-growing Indian population; international airport at Nadi, ch. pt. and cap. Suva; a. 18,272 km²; cosmopolitan p. (1995) 783,800. Rejoined Commonwealth, 1997.

Filey, t., North Yorks., **Eng.;** 8 km S.E. of Scarborough; seaside resort; p. (1991) 6,044.

Filton, Bristol, **Eng.;** aircraft wks.

Finchley. See **Barnet.**

Findhorn, v., Moray, **Scot.;** resort; 12th cent. abbey; fishing; p. (1991) 683.

Findlay, t., Ohio, **USA;** on Blanchard R.; agr. machin., tyres, beet sugar refining; p. (1980) 35,594.

Fingal's Cave, Staffa I., Inner Hebrides, W. **Scot.;** basaltic columns.

Finger Lakes, gr. of narrow glacial Ls., N.Y., **USA;** picturesque resorts and state parks.

Finistère, dep. N.W. **France,** in Brittany; cap. Quimper; fishing, tourism; a. 7,071 km²; p. (1990) 838,700.

Finland, rep., N. Europe; part of Scandinavia; low-lying plateau severely eroded by ice to form 60,000 Ls.; economy based on timber (forests cover 72 per cent of a.); world's leading exporter of pulp and paper; increasing importance of metal and engin. inds.; cap. Helsinki; joined EU 1995; a. 360,318 km²; p.

concentrated in S.; p. (1994) 5,098,754.

Finland, G. of, E. arm of Baltic Sea, between Finland and Russia.

Finnart, Argyll and Bute, **Scot.;** crude oil terminal situated in Loch Long. N.W. Glasgow; pipeline to Grangemouth.

Finnmark, most N. co., **Norway;** inhabited by Lapps; whale fisheries; lge. copper deposits discovered nr. Reppan fjord; a. 48,125 km²; p. (1990) 74,590.

Finsbury. See **Islington.**

Finsteraarhorn, highest peak in Bernese Oberland, **Switzerland;** 4,277 m.

Finucane I., pt., W. **Australia;** deepwater pt. to ship ion ore and new t. projected.

Firenze. See **Florence.**

Firozabad, t., Uttar Pradesh, **India;** glassware; agr. tr; p. (1991) 215,128.

Firozpur, t., Punjab st., N.W. **India;** rly. t.; admin. ctr.; p. (1991) 61,142.

Fishguard, spt., Pembrokeshire, **Wales;** on S. of Cardigan Bay; steamer connection to Rosslare (Ireland); p. (1991) 2,679.

Fitchburg, t., Mass., **USA;** paper, machin., textiles; p. (1980), 39,580 (t.), 99,957 (met. a.).

Fitzroy, R., W. **Australia;** flows into King Sound; dry in winter; irrigation; 560 km long.

Fiume. See **Rijeka.**

Flamborough Head, promontory of Yorks. cst., **Eng.;** steep chalk cliffs; lighthouse; anc., Brit. earthwork (Danes' dyke).

Flanders, region between R. Scheldt and cst., crossed by Franco-Belgian frontier; Dunkirk, Lille ctrs. of French F.; Belgian F. divided into 2 provs., E. and W., p. (1993) 1,116,244 and 1,344,263 respectively; caps. Bruges and Ghent.

Fleet, t., Hart, Hants., **Eng.;** 6 km N.W. of Aldershot; p. (1991) 30,391.

Fleetwood, spt., Wyre, Lancs., **Eng.;** at mouth of Wyre, Morecambe Bay; deep-sea fish. pt.; fish processing; lge. chemical plant nearby; p. (1991) 27,227.

Flensburg, spt., Schleswig-Holstein, **Germany;** on Baltic, close to Danish border; shipbld., machin., rum distilleries, fishing; p. (1986) 85,700.

Flevoland, prov., **Neth.;** estab. 1986; p. (1994) 253,699.

Flinders I., Australia; lgst I. in the Furneaux gr., Bass Strait; famous for mutton birds.

Flinders Range, chain of mtns., S. **Australia;** extending 400 km N.E. from head of Spencer G., reaching 1,190 m in St. Mary's Peak; named after Matthew Flinders; uranium ore at Mt. Painter.

Flint, t., Flintshire, **Wales;** viscose textile yarn, cas. ruins; p. (1991) 11,737.

Flint, t., Mich., **USA;** motorcars, aircraft engines; p. (1990) 140,761 (t.), 430,000 (met. a.).

Flintshire, N.E. **Wales,** unit. auth. created in 1996 from former l. gov. dists. of Alyn and Deeside and Delyn, reinstating part of historic co. split up in 1974; inc. ts. of Buckley, Connah's Quay, Flint and Mold; p. (1995) 145,700.

Flodden, v. Northumberland, **Eng.;** on R. Till; battle between James IV of Scot. and the English under the Earl of Surrey 1513.

Florø, t., **Norway;** new t. 136 km N. of Bergen.

Florence (Firenze), c., Tuscany, **Italy;** on R. Arno; univ.; leather-work; famous for art treasures, cath. and churches; ruled by Medici 1421–1737; birthplace of Dante and Machiavelli; severely affected by heavy floods Nov. 1966; p. (1992) 397,434.

Florence, t., N.W. Ala., **USA;** on Tennessee R., nr. Wilson dam; textile, steel plants; p. (1984) 36,000 (t.), 135,700 (met. a.).

Flores, I., most northwesterly of Azores gr.; Portuguese; cap. Santa Cruz; French ballistic missiles tracking sta.; a. 142 km².

Flores, I., Indonesia; mtnous.; volcanic, densely forested; a. 22,973 km².

Flores Sea, between Sulawesi and Flores, **Indonesia.**

Florianópolis, spt., cap. of Santa Catarina st., **Brazil;** comm. ctr., fishing; p. (1985) 218,900.

Florida, st., **USA;** Sunshine St.; admitted to Union 1845; st. flower Orange Blossom, st. bird Mockingbird; between Atl. Oc. and G. of Mexico; low-lying, swampy, inc. Ever-glades; sea resorts on Atl. cst.; citrus fruit and subtropical agr.; agr. processing; cap Tallahassee; a. 151,670 km²; p. (1990) 12,937,926; hgst. percentage of p. over 65 in USA (18.3).

Florida Keys, archipelago, **USA**; extends in an arc from S.E. cst. Florida W.S.W. to Key West in G. of Mexico; fishing resorts.

Florida Strait, between Florida and Bahama Is.; course of Gulf Stream from G. of Mexico.

Florina. *See* **Phlorina.**

Florissant (**St. Ferdinand**), t., Mo., **USA**; sub. of St. Louis on Missouri R.; p. (1990) 51,206.

Flushing. *See* **Vlissingen.**

Fly, lgst. R. of **Papua New Guinea**; flows S.E. from Victor Emmanuel Range to G. of Papua; 1,280 km long.

Fochabers, v., Moray, **Scot.**; nr. mouth of Spey; tourist resort; food canning; p. (1991) 1,534.

Focsani, t., **Romania**; at foot of Transylvanian Alps; wine and grain ctr.; p. (1992) 101,296.

Foggia, cath. c., S. **Italy**; rly. ctr. and mkt. ctr. for plain of Apulia; site of cas. of Frederick II; p. (1992) 155,674.

Foix, t., cap. of Ariège dep., S. **France**; historic t.; p. (1990) 10,446.

Foligno, t., central **Italy**; in Apennines, on Topino R.; cath., textiles, paper; p. (1981) 52,484.

Folkestone, t., Shepway, Kent, **Eng.**; seaside resort; p. (1991) 45,587.

Fond du Lac, t., Winnebago L., Wis., **USA**; cath.; machine tools, domestic appliances; resort; p. (1990) 37,757.

Fonseca, Gulf of, Honduras; lgst. indentation along Pac. cst. of Central America; sm. pt. of Amapala, US naval base, and new deepwater pt.

Fontainebleau, t., Seine-et-Marne, **France**; on R. Seine, 56 km S.E. Paris; in former royal forest (a. 17,200 ha); magnificent palace; p. (1982) 18,753.

Fontenoy, v., **Belgium**; nr. Tournai; scene of battle (1745) when the French under Marshal Saxe defeated the English and their allies.

Foochow. *See* **Fuzhou.**

Fordlandia. *See* **Belterra.**

Foreland, N. and **S.,** two headlands on E. cst. Kent, **Eng.**; between which are the Goodwin Sands and Pegwell Bay; lighthouses; sea battle between de Ruyter and Monk (1666).

Forest Heath, l. gov. dist., Suffolk, **Eng.**; part of Breckland inc. Mildenhall and Newmarket; p. (1995) 67,400.

Forest Hills, residtl. a., central Queen's bor., N.Y., **USA**; national and international matches played at West Side Tennis Club.

Forest of Dean, Gloucs., **Eng.**; between Wye and Severn Rs.; former Royal Forest; Forestry Commission plantations; former coal mng. a.; tourism; new lt. industl. estates; forms l. gov. dist.; p. (1995) 75,400.

Forfar, royal burgh, Angus, **Scot.**; jute, linen; p. (1991) 12,961.

Forli, c., Emilia-Romagna, central **Italy**; route ctr. in Apennine foothills; felt, textiles, footwear; p. (1992) 109,080.

Formby, t., Merseyside, **Eng.**; on W. cst., 10 km S.W. of Southport; residtl.; p. (1991) 25,356.

Formosa, t. and prov., N. **Argentina**; bordering on Paraguay; timber; cap. Formosa; a. 72,067 km²; p. (1991) 148,074 (t.), 398,413 (prov.).

Formosa. *See* **Taiwan.**

Forres, royal burgh, Moray, **Scot.**; on Findhorn R. nr. Moray F.; agr., forestry, engin., distilleries; cas.; p. (1991) 8,531.

Forst, t., Brandenburg, **Germany**; on R. Neisse; E. section of t. Polish since 1945; textiles; p. (1989) 26,313.

Fortaleza, c., cap. of Ceará st., **Brazil**; in the dry Sertão reg. of the N.E.; terminus of cattle droving route; growth resulting from planned industl. development to revitalise region: p. (1991) 1,758,334.

Fort Collins, t., Col., **USA**; ctr. of rich farming a.; grain, sugarbeet, livestock; univ.; p. (1990) 87,758 (t.), 186,136 (met. a.).

Fort de France, cap. of **Martinique,** Fr. W.I.; landlocked harbour; exp. sugar, rum; comm. ctr.; Fr. naval base; p. (1990) 101,544.

Fort George, t., W. Quebec, **Canada**; rises in Labrador and flows into Hudson Bay; 880 km long.

Fort Gouraud, t., **Mauritania**; modern iron-ore mines.

Forth, R., **Scot.**; formed by two headstreams rising to N. of Ben Lomond which meet nr. Aberfoyle; takes meandering course to Alloa, whence it expands into Firth of Forth; 165 km long.

Forth, Firth of, lge. inlet, E. cst. of **Scot.**; submerged estuary of R. Forth; navigable by lge. vessels for 64 km inland to Grangemouth; other pts., Leith, Rosyth (naval), Bo'ness; l. (to Alloa) 80 km; the Forth rly. bridge (1890) spans the F. at Queensferry; road bridge (1964).

Forth and Clyde Canal, Scot.; links F. of Forth at Grangemouth and F. of Clyde at Glasgow; not completely navigable; 61 km long.

Fort Johnston, t., S. **Malawi**, on L. Malombe; new t., 1966; tobacco; airpt.

Fort Knox, Ky., **USA**; nation's gold bullion depository; military air-base.

Fort Lamy. *See* **Ndjamene.**

Fort Lauderdale, c., Fla., **USA**; on Atl. cst. N. of Miami; lge. marina; citrus fruits, mkt. garden prod.; holiday resort; p. (1990) 149,377 (c.), 1,255,000 (met. a. with Hollywood-Pompano Beach).

Fort Myers, t., Fla., **USA**; on G. of Mexico; resort; Edison experimented here; p. (1984) 38,200 (t.), (1990) 335,000 (met. a. inc. Cape Coral).

Fortrose, t., royal burgh, Ross and Cromarty, **Scot.**; on S. cst. of Black Isle, on Moray F.; p. (1981) 1,319.

Fort Smith, c., Ark., **USA**; on Arkansas R.; mkt. ctr. for agr. a.; varied mnfs., inc. furniture, glass; coal and zinc mined nearby; p. (1990) 72,798 (c.), 142,083 (met. a.).

Fort Victoria, (**Masvingo**), t., **Zimbabwe**, agr. and mng. ctr., cattle, historic ruins in Zimbabwe Nat. Park; p. (1982) 30,600.

Fort Wayne, c., Ind., **USA**; at confluence of 2 headstreams of Maumee R.; rly. repair shops; elec. machin. and domestic appliances, originally a Fr. fort; p. (1990) 173,072 (c.), 364,000 (met. a.).

Fort William. *See* **Thunder Bay.**

Fort William, burgh, Highland, **Scot.**; nr. head of Loch Linnhe, at base of Ben Nevis; aluminium factory; pulp- and paper-mill at Corpach; p. (1991) 10,391.

Fort Worth, c., Texas, **USA**; rly. and comm. ctr. on Trinity R.; livestock and grain mkt.; oil refining, meat packing, oilfield equipment; p. (1990) 447,619 (c.), 1,332,053 (met. a. with Arlington).

Fort Yukon, trading sta. on Yukon R., N.E. Alaska, **USA**.

Foshan (**Fatshan**), c., Guandong, **China**; S.W. of Guangzhou; iron and steel, textiles; p. (1984) 299,800.

Fos-sur-Mer, t., Bouches-du-Rhône, S. **France**; nr. Marseilles; new deepwater pt. and oil refinery; bauxite terminal; iron and steel plant; p. (1982) 9,446.

Fotheringhay, v., Northampton, **Eng.**; on R. Nene; Mary Queen of Scots beheaded (1587) in F. Castle.

Fougères, t., Ille-et-Vilaine, **France**; cas.; footwear, clothing; p. (1982) 25,131.

Foulness I., S. Essex, **Eng.**; at mouth of R. Crouch; owned by Min. of Defence; site of projected third London airport at Maplin, now abandoned; projected container and oil pt.

Fountains Abbey, ruined 12th cent. Cistercian abbey, North Yorks., **Eng.**; nr. Ripon.

Fowey, sm. spt., Cornwall, **Eng.**; nr. mouth of R. Fowey; exp. kaolin; resort; fishing; p. (1991) 1,939.

Foxe Basin and Channel, to N. of Hudson Bay, between Baffin I. and Southampton I., **Canada**.

Foyers, Falls of, Highland, **Scot.**; E. of Loch Ness, nr. Fort Augustus; aluminium wks., the first hydroelectric plant erected in Britain (1896).

Foyle, Lough, inlet, N. **Ireland**; between Donegal (R.o.I.) and Londonderry; outlet of R. F.; Londonderry t. at head of inlet.

Foynes Is., R.o.I.; oil terminal on N. side, E. of Battery Point.

Foz do Iguaçú, t., Paraná, **Brazil**; highway (coffee road) from Paranaguá; rapid growth with opening of Itaipú Dam; p. (1985) 183,400.

Framingham, t., Mass., **USA**; 32 km W. of Boston; lt. inds.; p. (1980) 65,113.

Framlingham, mkt. t., Suffolk, **Eng.**; N.E. of Ipswich; cas.; p. (1991) 2,697.

Francavilla Fontana, t., Apulia, **Italy**; rly. junc.; agr. tr.; p. (1981) 32,588.

France, rep., W. Europe; bounded by 3 seas; Eng. Channel, Atl. Oc., Mediterranean; variety of climate and relief; leading agr. cty. of Europe; 75 per cent under cultivation; exps. grain, fruit, vegetables, wine; industl. expansion since second world war; lgst. inds. inc. iron and steel, motor vehicles, aircraft, engin., textiles, chemicals; tourism impt.; EU member; cap. Paris; 96 deps.; excessive social, economic, and political concentration around Paris promotes description of France as "Paris and the French Desert"; recent attempts to break this down using framework of 21 economic planning regions; a. 550,634 km²; p. (1996) 58,300,000.

Franceville, t., Gabon, Equatorial Africa; on R. Ogooué; lined to Libreville as part of the Trans-Gabon rly. project; manganese mines opened 1962; founded by De Brazza.

Franche-Comté, region E. **France** bordering Switzerland; inc. deps. Doubs, Jura, Haute-Saône, Territoire de Belfort; mainly mountainous and wooded but industrial round ch. ts. Belfort, Besançon; p. (1990) 1,097,300.

Francistown, t., Botswana; airpt.; butter, coppermng.; p. (1989) 52,725.

Frankenthal, t., Rhineland-Palatinate, **Germany;** in industl. dist. of Mannheim-Ludwigshafen, engin., machin.; p. (est. 1986) 44,300.

Frankfurt-on-Main, c., Hesse, **Germany;** local point in Rhine-Main urban region; rly. ctr., transit pt.; machin., cars, chemicals, elec. engin., publishing; airport; cath., univ.; birthplace of Goethe; p. (1990) 647,200.

Frankfurt-on-Oder, c., Brandenburg, **Germany;** agr. ctr., R. pt., rail junc.; machin., chemicals; E. part of t. (Słubice) Polish since 1945; p. (1981) 81,009.

Frankischer (Franconian) Jura, plateau with steep N.-facing edge, S.E. of **Germany;** runs 128 km S.W. from Fichtelgebirge; drained by Reg-nitz and Altmühl Rs.

Franklin, dist., N.W. Terr., **Canada;** comprising the Is. of Arctic Canada from Banks I. to Baffin I., including Boothia Peninsula and Melville Peninsula; sparsely populated; furs; a. 1,434,943 km².

Františkovy Lázne (Franzensbad), famous spa, W. Bohemia, **Czech Rep.;** 445 m a.s.l., between the Erzgebirge and the Fichtelgebirge.

Franz Josef Land (Zemlya Frantsalosifa), Russia; archipelago in Arctic Oc. N. of Novaya Zemlya; a. 20,720 km²; mainly ice-covered.

Frascati, t., Italy; 19 km S.E. of Rome; summer resort; famous villas and arch. remains; nuclear research ctr.; p. (1981) 18,728.

Fraser I. (Great Sandy I.), Queensland, **Australia;** low sandy I., timber reserve and Nat. Park; concern over ecology caused discontinuation of mineral sand exp. (1977).

Fraser, R., B.C., **Canada;** rises at c. 1,800 m on W. slopes Rocky Mtns.; famous salmon fisheries; routeway; Vancouver nr. delta; 1,360 km long.

Fraserburgh, spt., burgh, Aberdeenshire, **Scot.;** one of the main E. cst. herring pts.; p. (1991) 12,843.

Frauenfeld, t., cap. of Thurgau can., **Switzerland;** 11th cent. cas.; textiles; p. (1980) 18,607.

Fray Bentos, t., cap. of Rio Negro dep., **Uruguay;** pt. on R. Uruguay 80 km from mouth; meat-processing; p. (1985) 20,091.

Fredericia, t., pt., E. Jutland, **Denmark;** major rly. junc.; textiles, silver and electroplated gds., fertilisers; oil refinery; p. (1990) 46,072.

Fredericton, c., cap. of N.B., **Canada;** on St. John R.; univ., cath.; timber, shoes, plastics; p. (1991) 45,364.

Frederiksberg, sub. of Copenhagen, **Denmark,** with indep. municipal status; p. (1981) 88,167.

Frederikshåb, sm. spt. on W. cst. of **Greenland;** fish processing; p. (1990) 2,556.

Frederikshavn, fish. pt., N. Jutland, **Denmark,** on Kattegat; p. (1990) 35,500.

Frederikstad, t., **Norway;** at mouth of Glomma R.; ctr. of pulp and paper-producing ind.; electrotechnical inds., shipbldg., fish canning; p. (1990) 50,170.

Frederiksvaerk, t., Sjaelland, **Denmark;** impt. iron and steel wks.; p. (1990) 17,941.

Freetown, c., cap. of **Sierra Leone;** pt. on Atl. Oc.; one of lgst. natural harbours in world; humid, oppressive climate; exp. diamonds, palm oil; food processing, oil refining; fishing; much fighting (1999) in civil war; p. (1988) 469,776.

Freiberg, t. Saxony, **Germany;** S.W. of Dresden, at foot of Erzgebirge; mng. academy (silver discovered 12th cent.); metallurgy, textiles, glass, porcelain; p. (1981) 51,377.

Freiburg im Breisgau, c., Baden-Württenıberg, **Germany;** in Black Forest; cath., univ.; cultural ctr.; tourism; p. (1990) 191,600.

Freising, t., Bavaria, **Germany;** N.E. of Munich; cath.; agr. machin., textiles, chemicals; p. (1986) 36,200.

Freital, t. Saxony, **Germany;** S.W. Dresden; glass, uranium ore processing; coalmines nearby; p. (1989) 413,588.

Fréjus, t., Var dep., S.W. **France;** cath., Roman ruins; resort on Fr. Riviera; p. (1982) 32,698.

Fréjus, Col de, Alpine pass, **France** and **Italy,** 2,083 m, under which runs the Mont Cenis tunnel (13·6 km).

Fremantle, spt., W. **Australia;** at mouth of Swan R., 19 km S.W. from Perth, principal pt. in W. Australia and first Australian pt. of call for mail steamers; part of Perth met. a.; giant industl. complex at Kwinana; p. (1991) 23,834.

French Equatorial Africa, formerly included Gabon, Congo (Brazzaville), Ubangi-Shari and Chad, sts. which are now independent.

French Guiana (Guyane), Fr. Overseas dep., on N. cst. of **S.** America, between Surinam to W. and Brazil to S. and E.; tropical climate; little developed and thinly populated; ch. ctr. of p. and spt. at cap. of Cayenne; economy based on agr., especially sugar and forestry; some gold and bauxite mng.; a. 90,650 km²; p. (1990) 114,700.

French Polynesia, Fr. overseas terr., in S. Pac. Oc., comprising several archipelagos; Society Is., Marquesas Is., Tubuai Is., Tuamotu Is., and Gambier Is.; increased autonomy since 1977; cap. Papeete; a. 4,002 km²; p. (1994) 216,600.

French Somaliland. See Djibouti.

French Southern and Antarctic Terrs., Fr. overseas terr., comprising several grs. of Is. and Antarctic terr. of Adélie Land; a. 409,220 km²; no permanent p.

French West Africa, comprised former Fr. cols. of Dahomey (Benin), Ivory Coast, Mauritania, Niger, Fr. Guinea, Upper Volta, Senegal, Fr. Soudan (Mali).

Freshwater, sm. t., I. of Wight, **Eng.;** at W. end of I., 13 km W. of Newport; resort; p. (1991) 7,317 (with Totland).

Fresnillo de Gonzalez Echeverria, t., Zacatecas, **Mexico;** alt. 2,227 m; mkt. t., silver mng.; p. (1990) 160,208.

Fresno, c., Cal., **USA;** ctr. of vast irrigated fruit-growing dist.; p. (1990) 354,202 (c.), 667,000 (met. a.).

Fribourg (Freiburg), c., cap. of F. can., **Switzerland;** between Berne and Lausanne; viaduct and bridges; cath., univ.; p. (1990) 34,722.

Fribourg (Freiburg), can., **Switzerland;** mainly dairy farming; cereals, sugarbeet, cheese; a. 1,671 km²; p. (1990) 207,800.

Friedrichshafen, t., **Germany;** on Bodensee; machin., boat bldg., motors; resort; p. (1986) 52,100.

Friendly Is. See Tonga.

Friern Barnet. See Barnet.

Friesland, prov., N. **Neth.;** cap. Leeuwarden; dairying, horses, cattle; natural gas on Ameland I.; a. 3,432 km²; p. (1994) 607,016.

Frimley and Camberley, ts., Surrey Heath, former U.D., Surrey, **Eng.;** 5 km N. of Farnborough; lt. engin., plastics; military training ctr.; p. (1991) 46,120.

Frinton and Walton, Tendring, Essex, **Eng.;** on E. cst., 8 km N.E. of Clacton; seaside resort; p. (1991) 15,043.

Frisches Haff, shallow freshwater lagoon, Baltic cst. of **Poland;** 85 km long, 6–18 km broad.

Frisian Is., chain of Is. stretching from Den Helder to Jutland, along csts. of Neth., Germany, and Denmark; ch. Is. are Texel, Vlieland, Terschelling, Ameland (West F. Is.), Nordeney, Borkum (East F. Is.), Sylt, Föhr, Rømø (North F. Is.); severe erosion; Sylt now half size it was 500 years ago.

Friuli-Venezia Giulia, aut. reg. (created 1963), N.E. **Italy;** comprising 3 provs. Udine, Gorozia, Trieste; p. (1992) 1,195,055.

Frobisher Bay, inlet in S. Baffin I., N. **Canada,** extending 320 km between Cumberland Sound and Hudson Strait.

Frodingham, N. Lincs., **Eng.;** on W. flank of limestone ridge, Lincoln Edge; impt. iron-ore open-cast mines; mnfs. iron and steel.

Frome, mkt. t., Mendip, Somerset, **Eng.;** on R. Frome, 18 km S. of Bath; p. (1991) 23,159.

Frome, R., Dorset, **Eng.;** flows from N. Dorset Downs into Poole Harbour.

Frontignan, t., Hérault, S. **France;** oil refining; pipeline under sea from Sète; produces muscat; p. (1982) 14,961.

Frunze. See Bishkek.

Frýdek-Mistek, t., Czech Republic; on R. Ostravice on opposite banks; timber, textiles; p. (1990) 66,000.

Fuenlabrada, t. Madrid prov. C. Spain; rlwy, textiles; p. (1991) 144,720.

Fuerteventura, I., Canary gr.; a. 1,717 km².

Fujayrah, emirate, one of United Arab Emirates, Persian G.; p. (1985) 54,425.

Fujian (Fukien), prov., China; cap. Fuzhou; intensive agr., rice and sugar-cane; shellfish raised along cst.; a. 123,103 km²; p. (1990) 30,610,000.

Fujisawa, t., Honshu, Japan; bearings, machin.; p. (1990) 350,330.

Fujiyama, extinct volcano, Japan; 96 km S.W. of Tokyo; pilgrim resort; hgst. peak of Japan; alt. 3,780 m.

Fukui, c., cap. of F. pref., central Honshu, Japan; synthetic fibres, paper; old silk-weaving ctr.; p. (1990) 252,743.

Fukuoka, c., N. Kyushu, Japan; pt. on Hakata Bay; univ. ctr., old cas. t.; textiles, dolls, shipbldg.; p. (1990) 1,237,107.

Fukushima, c., N. Honshu, Japan; ceramics, foods, steel; publishing; p. (1990) 277,528.

Fukuyama, c., S. Hokkaido, Japan; p. (1990) 365,612.

Fulda, t., Hesse, Germany; nr. Kassel; on R. Fulda; palace, abbey; textiles, metallurgy, rubber; route ctr.; p. (1986) 54,100.

Fulham. See Hammersmith.

Fulwood, t., Lancs., Eng.; 3 km N.E. of Preston; part of Central Lancashire New Town.

Funchal, cap. of Madeira Is.; pt., winter resort; cath.; p. (1987) 44,111.

Fundy, Bay of, inlet between Nova Scotia and New Brunswick, Canada; lge. tidal range of 21 m.

Furka Pass, Switzerland; between Valais and Uri cans.; 2,433 m.

Furneaux Is., S.E. Australia; in Bass Strait, belonging to Tasmania; lgst. is Flinders I.

Furness, dist., Cumbria, Eng.; between More-cambe Bay and the Irish Sea.

Fürstenwalde, t., Brandenburg, Germany; on R. Spree; metallurgy, leather, tyres; p. (1989) 35,658.

Fürth, t., Bavaria, Germany; nr. Nürnberg; toy and glass inds.; p. (1990) 104,400.

Fusan. See Pusan.

Fuse, t., Honshu, Japan; machin., textiles, chemicals; now part of Higashiosaka.

Fushimi, c., Honshu, Japan; sub. of Kyoto; p. (1990) 280,276.

Fushun, c., Liaoning, N. China; at foot of Changbai Shan, 35 km N.E. of Shenyang; major industl. ctr.; possesses world's thickest bituminous coal seam (127 m) worked by deep and opencast mines; oil refinery based on local oil shales; steelwks., chemicals; electronics; timber inds.; diversifica-tion planned; p. (1992) 1,350,000.

Fuskiki, spt., Honshu, Japan; serves Toyama c. with metals, coal.

Futa, La, pass, Tusco-Emilian Apennines, N. Italy; used by main road from Bologna to Florence; alt. 903 m.

Futa Jalon (Fouta Djalon), upland dist., mostly in Guinea, W. Africa with parts in Liberia and Sierra Leone.

Fuxin (Fuzin), c., Liaoning, N. China; ctr. of lge. coalfield; p. (1984) 653,200.

Fuzhou (Foochow), c., cap. of Fujian prov., China; at mouth of Min R., major comm. and industl. ctr.; diverse light inds.; became impt. with tea exp.; former treaty pt.; p. (1992) 1,290,000.

Fylde, W. Lancs., Eng.; low plain behind coastal sand dunes; pig- and poultry-rearing dist.; ch. t. Blackpool; l. gov. dist. excluding Blackpool; p. (1995) 74,500.

Fylingdales, ballistic missile early warning sta. on N. Yorks. moors, Eng.

Fyn, I., Denmark; in Baltic Sea; a. 3,419 km²; cap. Odense; dairying, sugarbeet; p. (1990) 426,106.

Fyne, Loch, on Argyll and Bute cst., W. Scot.; an arm of F. of Clyde; offshore oil platform con-struction: 64 km long.

G

Gabès, spt., Tunisia; on G. of Gabès, 320 km S. of Tunis; dates, henna, wool; p. (1984) 92,259.

Gabon, rep., W. Africa; Cameroon to N., Zaire to S. and E.; tropical climate, hot, humid; much equato-rial rain forest; forestry main ind. but mng. in-creasingly impt.; petroleum exp. creating increas-ing prosperity; manganese at Moanda (S.), iron-

ore at Mekambo (N.E.); communications geared mainly to mng. areas; major pts. Libreville (cap.), Port Gentil; Trans-Gabon rly. project to promote exploitation of timber; first part opened 1979; intense forest cover makes internal air services very impt.; airport at Libreville; a. 266,770 km²; p. (1993) 1,011,710.

Gaborone (Gaberones), cap. Botswana; formerly sm. v.; chosen as cap. for new rep., bldg. began 1964; p. (1991) 138,471.

Gadag-Betgeri, t., Karnataka, India; cotton and silk weaving; p. (1991) 134,051.

Gaeta, t., naval pt., Italy; on promontory on shore of G. of Gaeta; the anc. Caietae Portus; cath.; p. (1981) 22,605.

Gafsa, t., Tunisia; phosphate mng. ctr.; p. (1984) 60,870.

Gaillard Cut, excavated channel, Panama; carries Panama Canal through Culebra Mtn. from L. Gatun to Pac. Oc.; 11 km long.

Gainesville, t., Fla., USA; univ.; mkt. gardening; electronics, wood prod.; p. (1990) 84,770.

Gainsborough, t., West Lindsey, Lincs., Eng.; on R. Trent; agr. implements, milling, packing and wrapping machin.; mkt.; George Eliot's St. Ogg's in Mill on the Floss; p. (1991) 19,704.

Gairdner, salt L., S. Australia; a. 4,766 km².

Gairloch, sea loch and v., Highland, Scot.; resort, fishing.

Galapagos, volcanic Is., Pac. Oc.; 960 km W. of Ecuador (to whom they belong) on equator; flora and fauna peculiar to each I.; visited by Darwin 1835; wildlife under increased threat; a. 7,428 km²; p. (1994) 12,000.

Galashiels, burgh, Borders, Scot.; on Gala Water, 3 km above confluence with R. Tweed; tweeds, woollens; p. (1991) 13,753.

Galati or Galatz, c., E. Romania; major inland pt. on lower Danube; cath.; p. (1992) 325,788.

Galesburg, t., Ill., USA; engin., coal mng.; p. (1980) 35,305.

Galicia, historic region, S.E. Poland and W. Ukraine.

Galicia, region, N.W. Spain; comprising provs. La Coruña, Lugo, Orense, and Pontevedra; p. (1981) 2,811,942.

Galilee, northern div. of Palestine in Roman times, containing the ts. Cana, Capernaum, Tiberias, Nazareth; the ch. scene of Christ's ministry; now Israel.

Galilee, Sea of (Lake Tiberias), also known as L. Gennesaret; Biblical associations; 207 m below level of Med.; Israel plans to draw water from L. to irrigate Negev; a. 166 km².

Gallarate, t., Italy; nr. Milan; textiles; p. (1981) 46,915.

Galle, c., pt. on S.W. cst. of Sri Lanka; exp. tea, rubber, coconut oil; suffered from competition with Colombo after construction of modern harbour there; p. (1983) 88,000.

Gallego, R., N.E. Spain; rises in Pyrenees, flows S. to R. Ebro at Zaragoza; provides irrigation around Zaragoza; valley used by main rly. across Pyrenees from Pau to Zaragoza; 176 km long.

Gallipoli. See Gelibolu.

Galloway, anc. dist. S.W. Scot.; now part of Dumfries and Galloway.

Galloway, Mull of, the extremity of the Rinns of G., the most southern pt. of Scot.

Galston, burgh, E. Ayrshire, Scot.; on R. Irvine, nr. Kilmarnock; p. (1991) 5,154.

Galveston, c., spt., Texas, USA; on I. in Bay at entrance to G. of Mexico; gr. cotton and sulphur pt. with lge. exp. of agr. prod.; mills, foundries, food-processing, chemicals; univ., resort; scene of worst hurricane disaster in U.S. history, 1900; p. (1990) 59,070 (c.), 217,000 (met. a. with Texas City).

Galway, co., Galway Bay, Connacht, R.o.I.; fishery, cattle, marble quarrying; a. 6,351 km²; p. (1986) 178,552.

Galway, co. t. and cultural ctr. Galway, R.o.I.; univ.; spt., fishing; sawmills, textiles, printing; p. (1986) 47,104.

Gambia, The, W. Africa, on Atl. Oc.; comprises St. Mary's I. (on which is Banjul, the cap.) and narrow mainland enclave (average width 32 km) extending 320 km inland astride R. Gambia, hot all year, summer rain, but savannah inland; agr. is basis of economy, esp. groundnuts; economic aid from Taiwan; communications developed around Banjul (spt. and airpt.); union with

Senegal (1982), dissolved 1989; one of Africa's smallest sts.; a. 11,295 km²; p. (1993) 1,025,867.

Gambia, R., **Gambia**, rises in Futa Jalon Plateau, flows N. and W. into Atl. Oc. at Banjul; forms main means of communication through Gambia, 1,120 km long.

Gambier Is., Fr. Polynesia, **S. Pac. Oc.**, 4 coral Is.; a. 31 km².

Gand. *See* Ghent.

Gandhinagar, new cap. of Gujarat, **India**; on Sabarmati R., 21 km N. of Ahmadabad; under construction; p. (1991) 123,359.

Ganges (**Ganga**), sacred R. of **India**; rises in Himalayas and flows to Bay of Bengal via alluvial cones at foot of Himalayas by several delta mouths, on one of which stands Calcutta; navigable for lge. ships from Allahabad; delta alone larger than Eng. and Wales; flood plain and delta very fertile and densely populated; removal of irrig. water by India causes friction with Bangladesh; agreement over division of water at Farraka barrage reached (1978); 2,400 km long.

Gangtok, t., cap. of, Sikkim st; **India**; E. Himalayas; agr. tr. ctr.; carpets; p. (1991) 25,024.

Gan Jiang (**Kan R.**), S. **China**; flows N. to L. Poyang; valley provides road route from Guandong to Jianxi prov.; *c*. 880 km long.

Gansu (**Kansu**), prov., N.W. **China**; borders Inner Mongolia; cap. Lanzhou; pastoral agr., wheat, cotton, tobacco; coal reserves; rich iron ore deposits; attemps to break down isolation by attracting foreign investment; a. 391,507 km²; p. (1990) 22,930,000.

Gap, t., Hautes Alpes, S.E. **France**; textiles; p. (1990) 35,647.

Gard, dep., S. **France**; in Languedoc, on Mediterranean; cap. Nîmes; vines, olives, sericulture; a. 5,879 km²; p. (1990) 585,000.

Garda, L., between Lombardy and Venezia, **Italy**; variety of scenery, winter resort; a. 370 km²; greatest depth, 346 m.

Gardéz, t., **Afghanistan**; alt. 2,287 m; ctr. of comm. and transport; p. (1984) 10,469.

Garforth, t., West Yorks., **Eng.**; coalmng., lt. inds.; p. (1991) 15,250.

Garigliano, R. and dist., S. central **Italy**; where Liri R. joins Gari R. below Cassino; nuclear power plant.

Garmisch-Partenkirchen, t., Bavaria, **Germany**; winter sports; p. (1986) 27,700.

Garonne, R., S.W. **France**; rises at foot of Mt. Maladetta (Pyrenees), flows via Toulouse and agr. valley, and enters Gironde estuary 32 km below Bordeaux; 720 km long.

Garrigue, region, Languedoc, S. **France**; low limestone hills, run N.E. to S.W., W. of Rhône delta; semi-arid; Mediterranean vegetation to which region gives name; winter pasture for sheep; olives; Montpellier, Nîmes located on S. flank.

Garut, t., W. Java, **Indonesia**, mtn. resort, lge. spinning mill; p. 24,219.

Gary, c., Ind., **USA**; on S. shore of L. Michigan; producer of steel, tinplate, cement; p. (1990) 116,646 (c.), 605,000 (met. a. with Hammond).

Gascony, anc. prov., S.W. **France**; now comprises deps. along Atl. cst. and Pyrenees; Landes, Gers, Hautes-Pyrenees, and parts of Lot-et-Garonne, Tarn-et-Garonne, Haute Garonne, Gironde, and Ariège. Battleground in Hundred Years War.

Gastonia, t., N.C., **USA**; impt. textile ctr.; p. (1980) 47,333.

Gateshead, t., met. dist., Tyne and Wear, Eng.; on R. Tyne opposite Newcastle; engin., food processing, pumps, paper; pt.; p. (1995) 201,800 (dist.), (1991) 83,159 (t.).

Gatineau, R., **Canada**; trib. of Ottawa R., which it joins nr. Ottawa; length 480 km; hydroelec. power; forested valley.

Gatwick, West Sussex, **Eng.**; ad S 38 London; first airport in world where trunk road, main rly. line and air facilities combined in one unit.

Gaul (Lat. *Gallia*), embraced the lands inhabited by Celtic peoples in Roman times, covering what is now modern France (Gaul proper), Belgium, N. Italy, and parts of Germany, Neth., and Switzerland. South of the Alps was known as Cisalpine Gaul, north of the Alps as Transalpine Gaul.

Gauri-Sankar, mtn. in Himalayas, Nepal and Tibet, **China**; 56 km W. of Mt. Everest; alt. 7,149 m.

Gävle, spt., **Sweden**; timber, textiles, steel, porcelain; p. (1992) 89,194.

Gävleborg, co., **Sweden**; ch. t., Gävle; a. 18,544 km²; p. (1992) 289,190.

Gaya, t., Bihar, **India**; Buddhist pilgrim ctr.; cottons, silks; p. (1991) 292,000.

Gaza, ch. t. of Gaza Strip (q.v.); in ancient times the t. where Samson brought down the temple; p. (1985) 1·608 m.

Gazankulu (**Machangana**), Bantu Terr. Authority (1969), **S. Africa**; home of Shangana and Tsonga p.; cap. Giyana; p. (1985) 497,000.

Gaza Strip, coastal a. under Egyptian admin. since 1949; occupied by Israeli troops, Nov. 1956–March 1957, and after June 1967; now granted limited Palestinian self-rule; first international Palestinian airport opened (1998); p. (1993) 748,400.

Gaziantep, t. and prov., **Turkey**; S.W. of Malatya; mkt. t.; p. (1990) 573,968 (t.), 1,140,594 (prov.).

Gazli, **Uzbekistan**; 96 km N.W. of Gukhara; natural gas field; pipeline to Chelyabinsk opened 1963; destroyed by earthquake (1976); p. (1990) 8,900.

Gdansk (**Danzig**), c., and prov., N. **Poland**; Baltic pt.; on branch of Vistula; annexed to Germany 1939, restored to Poland 1945; shipbldg., machin., chemicals, metals; Gdansk, Gdynia and Sopot admin. as single c. (Trójmiasto = tricity). Birthplace of Solidarity trade union movement; p. (1989) 462,076 (c.), 1,417,800 (prov.). Shipyards closed (1997).

Gdynia, spt., Gdansk, N. **Poland**; competes with spt. of Gdansk for Polish hinterland; impt. comm., rly. and industl. ctr.; part of the Trójmiasto; p. (1989) 251,303.

Gedling, l. gov. dist., Notts., **Eng.**; Basford, Carlton and Arnold and N.E. outskirts of Nottingham; p. (1995) 111,300.

Geelong, c., Victoria, **Australia**; spt. on Corio Bay (part of Pt. Phillip Bay); expanding comm. and industl. ctr.; improved pt. facilities in 1960s, bulk grain terminal; p. (1993) 151,900 (met. a.).

Gejiu (**Kokiu**), t., Yunnan prov., **China**; leading tin-mng. ctr. of China; p. (1984) 337,700.

Gela, t., S. Sicily, **Italy**; in cotton-growing a.; petrochemicals; p. (1981) 74,789.

Gelderland, prov., **Neth.**; E. and S. of Utrecht prov., a. 5,022 km²; cap. Arnhem; cereals, tobacco; cattle rearing; p. (1994) 1,851,402.

Geleen, with Sittard, met. a. Limburg, prov., N.E. of Maastricht **Neth.**; p. (1993) 34,123 (c.), (1994) 185,278 (met. a.).

Gelibolu (**Gallipoli**), pt. and penin. on the Dardanelles, **Turkey**; scene of unsuccessful landing by British and Anzac troops 1915; 176 km long.

Gelligaer, t., Caerphilly, **Wales**; 6 km N.E. of Pontypridd; former coal mng.; p. (1991) 15,906.

Gelsenkirchen, t., N. Rhine-Westphalia, **Germany**; in Ruhr conurb. on Rhine–Herne canal; coal, ironwks., glass, chemicals, oil refining; p. (1990) 293,400.

Geneva, c., cap of G. can., **Switzerland**; at exit of Rhône from L. Geneva; cath., univ.; former H.Q. of League of Nations; H.Q. of ILO, WHO, and Red Cross; watchmkg., jewellery, elec. gds., optical instruments; tourist resort; birthplace of Rousseau; p. (1990) 167,200 (c), 376,000 (canton).

Geneva (**L. Léman**), L., S.W. corner of **Switzerland**; forms a gr. crescent of water, source of poetic inspiration; 371 m a.s.l.; a. 578 km².

Génissiat, **France**; site of gr. barrage and hydroelec. power sta. on Rhône below Geneva.

Genk, t., Limburg, **Belgium**; stainless steel wks., petrochemicals; p. (1993) 61,765.

Gennevilliers, t., Hauts-de-Seine, **France**; N.W. sub. of Paris; R. pt.; p. (1982) 45,445.

Genoa (**Genova**), c., ch. pt. **Italy**; cath., univ., palaces; handles one-third of Italy's foreign tr.; pt. and airpt. expansion, shipyards, steelwks., engin., textiles, tanning; p. (1992) 667,563.

George L., N.Y., **USA**; Adirondack mtns.; picturesque resort.

George Town, cap., **Cayman Is.**; pt.; p. (1989) 12,921.

Georgetown (**Demerara**), c., cap. of **Guyana**; on Demerara R.; exp. sugar, cocoa, coffee, timber, gold, diamonds, bauxite; airpt. nearby; botanical gardens; p. (1983) 188,000, 187,056 (met. a.).

Georgetown. *See* Penang.

Georgia, st., S.E. **USA**; one of 13 original sts., admitted to Union 1788; st. flower Cherokee Rose, st. bird Brown Thrasher; on Atl. cst.; rising to Appalachians; impt. arable agr.; cotton and lumber inds.; major source of kaolin; ch. ts., Atlanta (cap.), Savannah; a. 152,489 km²; p. (1990) 6,478,216.

Georgia (Gruziya), former USSR constituent rep.; rich agr., fruit, tobacco, grain; mng. inc. manganese, gold, oil; several hydroelectric power plants; coastal and mtn. resorts; active Jewish community; ethnic unrest 1989; cap. Tbilisi; a. 69,671 km²; p. (1994) 5,429,000.

Georgian Bay, arm of L. Huron, S. Ont., **Canada;** separated from L. by Manitoulin I. and Saugeen peninsula; *c.* 160 km long, *c.* 80 km wide; L. pts., Owen Sound, Midland, Parry Sound; Georgian Bay Is., Nat. Park.

Gera, c., cap. of G. admin. dist., **Germany;** on White Elster R.; woollens, printing; lignite mined nearby; p. (1990) 128,000.

Geraldton, spt., W. **Australia;** N. outlet for wheat belt; also exps. wool and manganese; early tomatoes; super phosphate; p. (1991) 20,587.

Germany, reunified 3 October 1990 after partition into Democratic Rep. (E. Germany) and Federal Republic (W. Germany) since 1948; N. half part of N. European Plain; rises in S. to Bavarian Alps; 2nd lgst. trading nation of world; mainly industl. with core in Ruhr conurb.; motor vehicles, chemicals, precision engin.; member of EU; tourism; 16 admin. dists. (*Länder*); cap. Berlin (seat. of parliament, govt. to be decided); faced economic problems after reunification; a. 357,041 km²; p. (1994) 81,338,093

Germiston, t., Transvaal, **S. Africa;** nr. Johannesburg; gold-mng.; rly. wkshps., engin., machin., chemicals; gas pipeline from Sasolburg, p. (1980) 166,440 (dist.).

Gerona, *See* Girona.

Gerrards Cross, t., S.E. Bucks., **Eng.;** 14 km E. of High Wycombe; residtl.

Gers, dep. S.W. **France;** cap. Auch; grain, vines, brandy; a. 6,291 km²; p. (1990) 174,600.

Gersoppa Falls, Sharavati R., Karnataka, **India;** hgst. cascade 253 m; hydroelec. power.

Getalfe, t. Madrid prov. C. **Spain;** agric. ind., geog. centre of Spain; p. (1991) 140,104.

Gezira, dist., Sudan, N.E. Africa; between Blue and White Niles; *c.* 12,173 km² capable of irrigation provided by Blue Nile at Sennar Dam; lge-scale growing of high-quality cotton; total a. *c.* 20,200 km².

Ghadames (**Ghudamis**), oasis, Sahara Desert, **Libya;** at point where Tunis, Algeria, Libya converge 480 km S.W. of Tripoli.

Ghaghara (**Gogra**), sacred R., **India;** trib. of Ganges, rises in Tibet, flows through Uttar Pradesh; lge. catchment a. but poorly developed floodplain; 960 km long.

Ghana, rep., W. Africa; indep. st., member of Brit. Commonwealth; tropical monsoon climate, but rainfall decreases inland; badly affected by Sahelian drought; S. Ghana more developed than N.; agr. basis of comm. economy and cocoa (of which Ghana is world's lgst producer) 60 per cent of all exp. by value; Volta R. scheme produces power from main dam at Akosombo and an aluminium smelter plant began production in 1967; reservoir decreasing with drought in Sahel and reducing power production; oil refining and production; communications network based on Accra and Takoradi on cst., and inland ctr. of Kumasi; development of road network vital for expansion of comm. agr.; 3 univs.; tourism now third largest component of economy, pts. at Takoradi and Tema; cap. Accra; a. 238,539 km²; p. (1995) 16,470,000.

Ghardaia, dep., **Algeria;** N. of Sahara; includes Mzab valley; p. (1987) 215,955.

Ghats, mtn. ranges which border the Deccan plateau in S. **India.** The **Eastern Ghats** are broken by many Rs. and rise only to 1,362 m in Northern Circars. The **Western Ghats** form an almost unbroken range, reaching 2,672 m in Dodabetta in Nilgiri hills; rainfall extremely heavy; forests; hydroelectric power.

Ghaziabad, t., Uttar Pradesh, **India;** on R. Jumna opposite Delhi; p. (1991) 454,000.

Ghazipur, t., Uttar Pradesh, N. **India;** on Ganges, E. of Varanasi; p. (1981) 60,725.

Ghazni, mtn. t., E. **Afghanistan;** once cap. of empire of Mahmud, *c.* A.D. 1000; now mkt. t.; p. (1982) 31,985.

Ghent, c., cap. of E. Flanders prov., **Belgium;** pt. at confluence of Rs. Scheldt and Lys;

cath., univ.; textiles, steel, plastics, chemicals; oil refinery; p. (1993) 229,828.

Ghor, El, depression, **Jordan** and **Israel,** between Sea of Galilee and Dead Sea 3–24 km wide; agr. resettlement scheme.

Giant's Causeway, basaltic columns on promontory of N. cst. of Moyle, **N. Ireland.**

Gibraltar, City of, Brit. terr. at W. entrance to Mediterranean; rocky I., 426 m, joined to Spain by sandy isthmus; few natural resources; economy depends on tourism, Admiralty dockyard, services to shipping, and entrepôt tr., to close 1983; Spanish govt. lays claim to terr.; frontier with Spain in renewed dispute (1999); a. 6·5 km²; p. (1998) 31,000.

Gibraltar, Strait of, connects Mediterranean with Atl., 13·6 km wide; of strategic importance. Plans for tunnel to link with N. Africa.

Gidgelpha-Moomba, dist., S. **Australia;** lge. natural gas field; pipeline to Adelaide.

Giessen, t., Hesse, **Germany;** on R. Lahn; univ.; various mnfs.; p. (1986) 71,100.

Gifu, t., Central Honshu, **Japan;** cas.; fans, lanterns, textiles; tourism for cormorant fishing; p. (1990) 410,318.

Gigha, I, Argyll and Bute, **Scot.;** off W. cst. of Kintyre; 10 km by 3 km.; p. (1991) 143.

Gijón, spt., Oviedo, **Spain;** on Bay of Biscay; gd. harbour; tobacco, petroleum, coal, earthenware; steel wks. nearby; p. (1991) 260,254.

Gila, R., N.M. and Arizona, **USA;** trib. of R. Colorado; used for irrigation in Imperial valley; 1,040 km long.

Gilan, prov., N.W. **Iran;** on Caspian Sea, bounded by frmr. USSR; sub-tropical climate; agr., inc. cotton and rice; cap. Rasht; p. (1982) 1,581,872.

Gilbert Is. *See* **Kiribati.**

Gilgit, dist., Kashmir, **India;** mtnous., exceeding 6,000 m on N. and W.; with Ladakh links India with Tibet.

Gillingham, t., l. gov. dist., Kent, **Eng.;** 3 km E. of Chatham; on R. Medway; naval and military establishments; cement, lt. inds.; p. (1995) 95,800, (1991) 94,923 (t.).

Gippsland, dist., S.E. Victoria, **Australia;** between Dividing Range and cst.; main brown coal field supplying local power plants; intensive dairying and mkt. gardens for Melbourne; p. (1992) 169,760.

Girgenti. *See* **Agrigento.**

Girona, c., cap. of G. prov., **Spain;** cath.; textiles, p. (1987) 67,447 (c.), (1991) 504,046 (prov.).

Gironde, dep., S.W. **France;** vineyards, grain, fruit, wines; cap. Bordeaux; a. 10,723 km²; p. (1990) 1,213,500.

Gironde, estuary, S.W. **France;** formed by junc. of Rs. Garonne and Dordogne; navigable to Pauillac and Bordeaux.

Girvan, burgh, S. Ayrshire, **Scot.;** on F. of Clyde, 29 km S.W. of Ayr; summer resort; p. (1991) 7,449.

Gisborne, c. and dist., spt., N.I., **N.Z.;** on Poverty Bay, 96 km N.E. of Napier; freezing-wks.; fishing; p. (1991) 44,361 (dist.).

Giuba, R. *See* **Juba R.**

Giurgiu, t., **Romania;** pt. on Danube; opposite Ruse, Bulgaria; linked by oil pipelines with Ploiesti; p. (1992) 74,236.

Givors, t., Rhône dep., **France;** on Rhône R. 16 km S. of Lyons; mnfs. inc. glass; oil refining near by at Feyzin; p. (1982) 20,554.

Gjøvik, t., S. **Norway;** on L. Mjösa; furniture, footwear, lt. inds.; p. (1990) 15,514.

Glace Bay, t., Cape Breton I., Nova Scotia, **Canada;** coal; harbour; p. (1991) 19,501.

Glacier National Park, B.C., **Canada;** mtn. scenery, resorts; a. 1,349 km².

Glacier National Park, Mon., **USA;** Rocky mtns., picturesque; a. 4,040 km².

Gladbeck, t., N. Rhine–Westphalia, **Germany;** N. of Essen; coalmng; p. (1986) 76,600.

Gladstone, t., Queensland, **Australia;** pt. exports coal to Japan; alumina plant (1973), oil storage; p. (1991) 33,447.

Glamis, v., Angus, **Scot.;** G. cas. childhood home of Queen Elizabeth the Queen Mother, and featured in Shakespeare's *Macbeth.*

Glamorgan, historic co., S. **Wales,** now divided into 8 unit. auths. inc. Cardiff and Swansea.

Glamorgan, Vale of. *See* **Gwent, Plain of.**

Glarus, can., **Switzerland;** E. of Schwyz; a. 684 km²; sheep, cheese, cottons; p. (1990) 167,200.

Glarus, t., cap. of can. G., **Switzerland;** on R. Linth, nr. Wessen; p. (1980), 5,800.

Glasgow, c., burgh, unit. auth. created in 1996, formerly part of Strathclyde, W. **Scot.**; on R. Clyde; leading spt. and 3rd lgst. c. in Gt. Britain; major problems of urban renewal; ctr. of industl. belt; shipbldg., iron and steel, heavy and lt. engin., electronics equipment, printing; univ., cath.; p. (1991) 662,954 (c.), (1995) 618,430 (unit. auth.).

Glas Maol, mtn., Angus, **Scot.**; part of the Braes of Angus; alt. 1,068 m.

Glastonbury, t., Somerset, **Eng.**; on R. Brue, ruins of 10th century abbey; nearby prehistoric lake villages; p. (1991) 7,747.

Glatz. *See* **Kłodzko.**

Glauchau, t., Saxony, **Germany**; on R. Mulde; woollens, calicoes, dyes, machin.; p. (1989) 26,566.

Gleiwitz. *See* **Gliwice.**

Glen Affric, Highland, **Scot.**; 48 km S.W. of Inverness; drained E. to Moray F.; hydroelectric scheme.

Glencoe, Highland, **Scot.**; S.E. of Ballachulish; scene of massacre of MacDonalds 1692.

Glendalough, Wicklow, **R.o.I.**; scenic valley with Ls. and monastic ruins; tourism.

Glenelg, t., S. **Australia**; on St. Vincent G.; sub. of Adelaide; first free settlement in Australia; p. (1984) 13,720.

Glen Garry, Perth and Kinross, **Scot.**; used by Perth to Inverness rly. on S. approach to Drumochter Pass.

Glen More, Scottish valley traversed by Caledonian Canal from Fort William to Inverness.

Glenrothes, t., Fife, **Scot.**; new t. (1948); electronics; p. (1991) 38,650.

Glen Roy, Highland, **Scot.**; 24 km N.E. of Fort William; remarkable terraces, remains of series of glacial lakes.

Glen Spean, Highland, **Scot.**; used by Glasgow to Fort William rly.

Glittertind, mtn., Opland co., S. **Norway**; highest peak in Scandinavia; alt. 2,483 m.

Gliwice (Gleiwitz), c., S.W. **Poland** (since 1945); coal mng. and steel ctr. of Katowice region; machin., chemicals; p. (1989) 212,481.

Glomma (Glommen), R., S. **Norway**; lgst. R. in Scandinavia; flows to Skaggerak; timber inds.; hydroelec. power; 400 km long.

Glossop, t., High Peak, Derbys., **Eng.**; at foot of Pennines; paper, food-canning, textile finishing; mkt.; p. (1991) 30,771.

Gloucester, cath. c., l. gov. dist., **Eng.**; on R. Severn; the Roman Glevum; cath., on site of Benedictine abbey; aircraft mftg. and repair; engin., nylon; p. (1995) 105,800 (dist.), (1991) 114,003 (c.).

Gloucester, t., Mass., **USA**; pt. at head of G. Harbour; resort, fish-processing; p. (1980) 27,768.

Gloucestershire, non-met. co., W. **Eng.**; situated around lower Severn basin, Cotswolds, Forest of Dean; sheep, dairy and fruit farming; major ctrs. of p. at Gloucester and Cheltenham; p. (1995) 552,700.

Glyncorrwg, t., Neath Pt. Talbot, **Wales**; 6 km N. of Maesteg; coal mng. dist.

Glynde, v., Sussex, **Eng.**; nearby Tudor manor and opera house of Glyndebourne.

Gmünd. *See* **Schwäbisch-Gmünd.**

Gniezno (Gnesen), c., W. **Poland**; E. of Poznan; first cap. of Poland (11th cent.); cath.; p. (1989) 69,646.

Goa, India; former Portuguese enclave; statehood conferred 1987; cap. Panaji; iron pyrites, manganese, coconuts, fish, spices, cashew nuts, salt, copra; a. 3,693 km²; p. (1991) 1,169,793.

Goat Fell, mtn., I. of Arran, N. Ayrshire, **Scot.**; alt. 874 m.

Gobi, steppes and stony or sandy desert, China and **Mongolia**; divided into two principal divs.; Shamo in Central Mongolia, and the basins of the Tarim, E. Turkestan; l. about 2,400 km (E. to W.), breadth 800–1,120 km; average elevation 1,200 m; crossed by impt. Kalgan–Ulan Bator highway.

Godalming, t., Waverley, Surrey, **Eng.**; 6 km S.W. of Guildford; first public supply of elec. 1881; Charterhouse School; p. (1991) 20,630.

Godavari, sacred R., **India**; rises in W. Ghats, flows E. across Deccan through gap in E. Ghats to Bay of Bengal; forms lge. delta; used for irrigation and hydroelec. powers; c. 1,440 km long.

Godesberg, Bad, t., N. Rhine-Westphalia, **Germany**; part of Bonn; spa; meeting place of Chamberlain and Hitler 1938.

Godhavn, Danish settlement, Disco I., W. of **Greenland**; arctic research sta.; fish processing; p. (1990) 1,164.

Godoy Cruz, c., Mendoza prov., N.W. **Argentina**; p. (1980) 141,553.

Godthåb, t., admin. ctr., **Greenland**; first Danish col. 1721; sm. pt.; fish processing; p. (1990) 12,687.

Godwin-Austen Mt. or **K2**, peak (8,611 m) in Karakoram between Tibet and Sinkiang, **China**, after Everest highest in world; summit reached by Prof. Desio 1954; also named Chobrum.

Gogmagog Hills, Cambs., **Eng.**; low chalk upland, S. of Breckland; traces of Roman entrenchment.

Gora. *See* **Ghaghara R.**

Goiânia, t., cap of Goiás st., Brazil; comm. and industl. ctr.; p. (1991) 920,838.

Goiás, st., central Brazil; mtnous., forested; stock-raising, tobacco; gold, diamonds; cap. Goiânia, on Vermelho R.; a. 642,061 km²; p. (1991) 4,024,547.

Gökçeada I. (Imbroz I.), off W. **Turkey**, in Aegean Sea at entrance to Dardanelles; a. 280 km².

Golconda, fort and ruined c., nr. Hyderabad, S. **India**; famous for its legendary diamond troves.

Gold Coast, City of, Queensland, **Australia**; 40 km cstl. a. inc. 18 townships, named 1959; rapid tourist devel. inc. Surfer's Paradise; p. (1993) 300,200.

Golden Gate, strait between San Francisco Bay and Pac. Oc., Cal., **USA**; spanned by Golden Gate Bridge, opened 1937.

Golden Horn, peninsular on the Bosporus, forming the harbour of Istanbul, **Turkey**.

Golden Triangle, a. of Britain and Europe roughly bounded by Birmingham, Frankfurt, and Paris; economic core a. of **W. Europe**.

Golden Vale, dist., Limerick, Tipperary, **R.o.I.**; drained W. to Shannon and E. to Suir; rich farming a., beef and dairy cattle, pigs.

Gold River, t., B.C., **Canada**; on W. cst. of Vancouver I. at junc. of Heber and Gold Rs.; new t. 1967; p. (1986) 1,879.

Golspie, t., Highland, **Scot.**; p. (1991) 1,434.

Gomal Pass, a pass in Sulaiman ranges, **Pakistan**, leading from Indus valley to Afghanistan.

Gomel', c., S.E. **Belarus**; on R. Sozh, trib. of Dnieper; R. pt., agr. ctr.; engin., chemicals, clothing inds.; p. (1990) 506,100.

Gomera, I, **Canaries**; 21 km S.W. Tenerife; cap. San Sebastian.

Gondar, t. N.W. **Ethiopia**; N. of L. Tana; airport; p. (1984) 68,958.

Goodwin Sands, dangerous sandbanks off E. cst. of Kent, **Eng.**; shielding the Down roadstead.

Goodwood, v., West Sussex, **Eng.**; racecourse and motor racing; home of Dukes of Richmond.

Goole, t., **Eng.**; second pt. of Hull on Humber; shipbldg., flour milling, fertilisers, alum and dextrine mftg.; p. (1991) 19,410.

Goonhilly Downs, Cornwall, **Eng.**; satellite communications sta. of Post Office.

Göppingen, t., Baden-Württemberg, **Germany**; between Ulm and Stuttgart; machin., iron, wood, chemicals; p. (1986) 51,400.

Gorakhpur, t., Uttar Pradesh, **India**; on Rapti R., N. of Varanasi; grain, timber; fertilisers; univ.; p. (1991) 506,000.

Gorgàn, c. **Iran**, Mazandaran prov.; nr. Caspian Sea; p. (1982) 114,000.

Gori, t., central **Georgia**; at con-fluence of Bolshoy, Liakhvi, and Kura Rs.; birthplace of Stalin; p. (1990) 69,600.

Gorinchem, t., S. Holland, **Neth.**; on R. Merwede; p. (1993) 30,106.

Goring Gap, Berks./Oxon., **Eng.**; where R. Thames cuts through Chilterns and Berkshire Downs.

Gorizia (Görz), c., cap. of Gorizia prov., N.E. **Italy**; on Yugoslav border; cas.; agr. mkt., fruit, wine; textile machin.; p. (1981) 41,557.

Gorki or **Gorky** *See* **Nizhniy Novgorod.**

Görlitz, t. Brandenburg, **Germany**; on W. Neisse on Polish border; lignite mines; textile mills; mystic Jacob Boehme lived here; p. (1981) 80,831.

Gorlovka, t., **Ukraine**; in Donets Basin; coal, chemicals, engin.; oil pipeline connects with Grozny oilfields; p. (1990) 337,900.

Gorno-Altai, aut. region, S.E. Altai terr., **Russia**; in Altai mtns. on Mongolian border; cap. Gorno-Altaisk; forested, pastoral agr., mng. (gold, manganese, mercury); a. 92,567 km; p. (1989) 190,800.

Gorno-Altaisk, t., **Russia**; cap. of Gorno-Altai aut. region; nr. Chuya highway to Mongolia; food-processing of agr. prod. from region; p. (1986) 39,000.

Gorno Badakhshan, aut. region, S.E. **Tajikistan**; in Pamirs, bordered by China and Afghanistan; mng. (gold, mica, salt, limestone); livestock; cap. Khorog; a. 63,688 km²; p. (1990) 164,300.

Gornyy Snezhnogorsk, t., **Russia**; new t. in Siberia Arctic on R. Hantaiki, 56 km W.N.W. Komsomolsk; tin-mng.

Gorseinon, t., Swansea, S. **Wales**; nr. Loughour estuary, 6 km N.W. of Swansea; former steelwks., zinc refineries; p. (1991) 18,917.

Gorzów Wielkopolski (Landesberg an der Warthe), c., Gorzow prov. W. **Poland** (since 1945); industl. ctr.; lignite mines; p. (1989) 123,222 (c.), 497,400 (prov.).

Gosainthan (Xixabangma Feng), mtn. massif, **Nepal–Tibet** (China) border; part of Himalayas; rises to 8,091 m.

Gosford-Woy Woy, t., N.S.W., **Australia**; electric rly. connecting Sydney (80 km to S.) led to growth of commuting, dairying, mkt. gardening and tourism; p. (1981) 94,369.

Gosforth, t., sub. to Newcastle upon Tyne, Tyne and Wear, **Eng.**; p. (1991) 23,315.

Goslar, t., Lower Saxony, **Germany**; mng. ctr. at foot of Harz mtns.; tourism; p. (1986) 49,000.

Gosport, t., l. gov. dist., Hants., **Eng.**; naval depot W. of Portsmouth to which it is linked by ferry; marine engin.; p. (1995) 74,800 (dist.), (1991) 67,802 (t.).

Göta, R., **Sweden**; flows from L. Vänern to the Kattegat; also canal connecting L. Vänern with the Baltic; the G. Canal provides a popular tourist trip from Stockholm to Göteborg.

Göteborg or **Gothenburg**, c., cap. of Göteborg and Bohus, S.W. **Sweden**; at mouth of R. Göta on Kattegat; second c. in Sweden for commerce and ind.; univ.; shipbldg., oil refining; deepwater tanker terminal; p. (1992) 433,811 (t.), 747,849 (co.).

Gotha, t., Erfurt, **Germany**; iron, machin., engin., musical instruments, textiles, porcelain, printing, cartography; p. (1981) 57,573.

Gotham, v., Notts., **Eng.**; gypsum mng. and plaster wks; p. (1991) 1,638.

Gothenburg. See Göteborg.

Gotland, I. in the Baltic, **Sweden**; many historic bldgs.; cap. Visby; tourism; a. 3,173 km²; p. (1992) 57,578.

Göttingen, t., Lower Saxony, **Germany**; univ.; scientific instruments, pharmaceutics, film studios; p. (1990) 122,700.

Gottwaldov. See Zlin.

Gouda, t., S. Holland, **Neth.**; on R. IJssel, 18 km from Rotterdam; cheese, candles, ceramics, pipes; p. (1994) 69,917.

Gough I., Atl. Oc. dependency of **St. Helena**; breeding ground of the great shearwater; guano.

Goulburn, t., N.S.W., **Australia**; commands route across Gr. Dividing Range; in agr. dist. W. of Sydney; cath.; wool, shoes; p. (1992) 155,100 (met. a.).

Goulburn Is., N.T., **Australia**; 2 sm. Is. off N. cst. of Arnhem Land; Methodist Mission sta.

Goulburn, R., Victoria, **Australia**; irrigation.

Gourock, burgh, Inverclyde, **Scot.**; on F. of Clyde, 3 km W. of Greenock; ferry to Dunoon; resort; p. (1991) 11,743.

Gove Peninsula, N.T., **Australia**; N.E. extremiy of Arnhem Land; giant bauxite and alumina production complex (1968); model t. of Nhulunbuy.

Gower, peninsula, Swansea, **Wales**; tourism.

Gozo, I. in Mediterranean, belonging to **Malta**; the anc. Gaulos; surrounded by perpendicular cliffs; a. 67 km²; p. (1990) 26,064.

Grado-Aquileia, t., Friuli-Venezia Giulia, N.E. **Italy**; pleasure resort and former Roman spt.; early Christian mosaics and antiquities; Grado joined to mainland by bridge.

Graengesberg, dist., Kopparberg co., **Sweden**; on S. fringe of Scandinavian mtns.; iron ore.

Grafham Water, reservoir, Cambs., **Eng.**

Grafton, t., N.S.W., **Australia**; on Clarence R.; dairy prod., timber; annual jacaranda festival; p. (1981) 17,005.

Graham Land, part of British Antarctic Territory; mtnous., icebound; discovered 1832.

Grahamstown, t., C. Prov., S. **Africa**; univ. cath.; p. (1980) 25,120.

Graian Alps, mtns. between Savoie, **France**, and Piedmount, **Italy**; hgst. point Gran Paradiso, 4,063 m.

Grain Coast, name formerly applied to cst. of **Liberia**, W. Africa; "grain" refers to spices.

Grammichele, t., E. Sicily, **Italy**; 37 km S.W. of Catania; planned settlement after 1968 earthquake; p. (1981) 13,607.

Grampians, mtns. of **Scot.**; forming natural bdy. between Highlands and Lowlands; inc. Ben Nevis, the hgst. peak (1,344 m), the Cairngorms and Schiehallion.

Granada, t., W. **Nicaragua**; on L. Nicaragua; in rich agr. region; distilling, soap, furniture; p. (1985) 89,000.

Granada, c., cap. of G. prov., S. **Spain**; in Andalusia, at foot of Sierra Nevada; formerly cap. of Moorish kingdom of G.; univ., cath., famous 14th cent. Alhambra; tourism; p. (1991) 286,688.

Granada, prov., S. **Spain**; traversed by Sierra Nevada; wheat, olives, textiles, liqueurs, paper; a. 12,530 km²; p. (1991) 806,499.

Granby, t., Quebec, **Canada**; on Yamaska R.; sawmills, leather, textiles, rubber, plastics; p. (1986) 38,508.

Gran Chaco, extensive lowland plain, **Argentina**, **Paraguay**, and **Bolivia**, between Andes and Paraguay–Paraná Rs.; hot, wet, swampy region with forests containing quebracho trees, a source of tannin; potential for petroleum.

Grand Banks, submarine plateau, extending S.E. from Newfoundland, **Canada**; a. 1,295,000 km²; impt. cod fisheries.

Grand Bassam, t., spt., **Ivory Coast**; exp. bananas, palm-kernels.

Grand Canal, canal, N. **China**; c. 1,600 km long from Tianjing to Hangzhou; built between A.D. 605–18 and 1282–92; rebuilt for navigation and flood control.

Grand Canary, I., **Canaries**; cap. Las Palmas; tomatoes, bananas, potatoes; tourism; extinct volcanoes.

Grand Cayman I., **Cayman Is.**, W.I.; a. 220 km²; coconuts; cap. Georgetown; p. (1989) 23,881.

Grand Combin, mtn., **Switzerland**; part of Pennine Alps nr. Italian border; alt. 4,320 m.

Grand Coulee Dam, Wash., **USA**; on Columbia R., 176 km below Spokane; one of lgst. concrete dams in world, producing 1,924 mW hydroelec. power; reservoir (Franklin D. Roosevelt Lake) recreational a.; supplies irrigation water to 4,900 km² between Rs. Columbia and Snake.

Grand Falls, t., Newfoundland, **Canada**; newsprint; falls provide hydroelectric power; p. (1991) 14,693 (with Windsor).

Grand Island, t., Nebraska, **USA**; cattle and grain t.; p. (1980) 33,180.

Grand' Mère, t., Quebec, **Canada**; pulp and paper mills; p. (1986) 15,442.

Grand Prairie. See Black Prairie.

Grand Rapids, c., Mich., **USA**; on Grand R.; furniture mkg., car and aircraft parts, chemicals, paper; p. (1990) 189,126 (c.), 688,000 (met. a.).

Grand R., Mich., **USA**; enters L. Mich. at Grand Haven, navigable to Grand Rapids; hydroelec. power; 400 km long.

Grand Turk, I., cap. of **Turks and Caicos** Is.; p. (1990) 3,761.

Grange, t., South Lakeland, Cumbria, **Eng.**; on N. cst. of Morecambe Bay; summer resort; p. (1991) 4,473.

Grangemouth, burgh, Falkirk, **Scot.**; on F. of Forth; shipbldg. and repair, marine engin., oil refining, projected oil tanker terminal; petroleum prods., chemicals, pharmaceutics; electronics and elec. ind.; oil pipeline to Finnart; p. (1991) 18,739.

Granite City, Ill., **USA**; iron and steel, tinplate, rly. engin., chemicals; p. (1980) 36,185.

Gran Sasso d'Italia, rugged limestone highlands, Abruzzi e Molise, central **Italy**, in highest part of Apennines, rising to 2,923 m in Monte Corno; Mussolini was rescued from here by German paratroopers 1943; Aquila at foot of Gran Sasso winter sports ctr.

Grantham, t., S. Kesteven, Lincs., **Eng.**; on Witham R.; tanning, agr. machin., engin., brewing, malting, expanded t.; birthplace of Margaret Thatcher; p. (1991) 33,243.

Grantown-on-Spey, burgh, Highland, **Scot.**; on R. Spey; resort; p. (1991) 2,391.

Granville, spt., Manche dep., **France**; on Golfe de St. Malo; fisheries, food-processing; p. (1982) 15,015.

Grasmere, v., Cumbria, **Eng.**; at head of Grasmere L.; home of Wordsworth.

Grasse, t., Alpes-Maritimes dep., S.E. **France,** in Provence in hills above Cannes; perfumers; birthplace of Fragonard.

Graubünden. *See* **Grisons.**

Graudenz. *See* **Grudziadz.**

's-Gravenhage. *See* **Hague.**

Graves, Pointe de, N. point of Médoc peninsula, **France;** in famous wine dist.

Gravesend, spt., Gravesham, Kent, **Eng.;** S. bank R. Thames facing Tilbury; pilot sta. for Port of London; paper, cement; oil refinery projected; p. (1991) 51,435.

Gravesham, l. gov. dist., Kent, **Eng.;** based on Gravesend and surrounding dist.; p. (1995) 92,400.

Graz, c., cap. of Styria, **Austria;** on R. Mur at foothills of Alps; second lgst. c.; univ., cath.; machin., iron and steel, rly. wks.; p. (1991) 232,155.

Great Altai, range of mtns., lying mainly in **Outer Mongolia** but also in Western Siberia, **Russia;** rising to 4,200 m.

Great Artesian Basin, Central **Australia;** underlies plains of Queensland, N.S.W., S. **Australia;** supplies water for cattle and sheep stations; too saline for use in some a. and too hot in others (cooling towers necessary); a. 2 million km.[2]

Great Atlas (Haut Atlas), mtn., N.W. **Africa;** alt. *c.* 2,000 m; part of the Atlas mtns.

Great Australian Bight, gr. cstl. indentation s. of Nullarbor Plain, **Australia.**

Great Barrier Reef, coral reef barrier off N.E. cst. of **Australia;** 1,600 km long, 120–160 km from cst.; currently being eaten away by the star fish, *Acanthaster planci;* much marine pollution; many reef Is. form Nat. parks.

Great Basin, high plateau region between the Wasatch and Sierra Nevada mtns., **USA;** inc. most of Nevada, parts of Utah, Cal., Idaho, Ore., Wyo.; drainage ctr. Great Salt Lake; a. 543,900 km[2]; much desert; sparse p.

Great Bear Lake, lge. L., N.W. Terr., **Canada;** *c.* 280 km long; a. 36,260 km[2]; outlet through Great Bear R. to Mackenzie R.

Great Belt (Store Bælt), strait **Denmark;** separates Fyn I. from Sjaelland I.; sinuous shape makes navigation difficult; rly. ferry at narrowest point (18 km) between Nyborg and Korsor; 64 km long; proposed bridge.

Great Britain. *See* **England, Scotland, Wales, British Isles.**

Great Dividing Range, mtn. system, E. **Australia;** extends, under different local names, from Queensland to Victoria and separates E. cst. plains from interior; reaches max. alt. in Mt. Koskiusko (2,228 m), in Australian Alps, on bdy. between Victoria and N.S.W.

Great Driffield, t., E. Riding of Yorks, **Eng.;** on Yorks. Wolds 21 km N. of Beverley; p. (1991) 9,463.

Great Dunmow, mkt. t., Uttlesford, Essex, **Eng.;** on R. Chelmer; 16 km N.W. of Chelmsford; p. (1991) 4,907.

Greater Manchester, former met. co., gt., N.W. **Eng.;** lge. urban a. centred on major comm. ctr. of M., with former cotton spinning ts. to N., inc. Bolton, Bury and Rochdale; dormitory ts. to S.; former concentration on textile mftg. now reduced and inds. diversified; major industl. estate at Trafford Park; p. (1995) 2,578,300.

Great Falls, c., Mont., **USA;** on Missouri R.; lgst. c. in st.; mkt. for irrigated farming a.; ctr. of hydroelectric power, called the "electric city"; copper- and oil-refining, flour mills; p. (1990) 56,725.

Great Fisher Bank, submarine sandbank in N. Sea; 320 km E. of Aberdeen, 160 km S.W. of Stavanger; valuable fishing-ground; depth of water, from 45–75 m.

Great Gable, mtn., Cumbria, **Eng.;** alt. 899 m.

Great Grimsby, spt., N.E. Lincs., **Eng.;** on S. bank of R. Humber; major distant waters fish. pt.; food-processing; (1991) 90,703.

Great Harwood, t., Hyndburn, Lancs., **Eng.;** 8 km N.E. of Blackburn; textiles, aero-engin.; p. (1991) 10,562.

Great Lake, Tasmania, **Australia;** lgst. freshwater L. in Australia.

Great Lakes, N. **America;** 5 freshwater Ls.; Superior, Michigan, Huron, Erie, Ontario; glacial genesis; frozen 4 to 5 months in winter; traffic in cereals, iron, coal, etc.; major ctr. of heavy inds.; resorts; serious pollution; a. 248,640 km[2].

Great Plains, lowland a. of central **N. America;** extending E. from Rocky mtns., and S. from Mackenzie to S. Texas.

Great Rift Valley, geological fault system extending from S.W. Asia to E. Africa, 4,800 km in l.; inc. L. Tiberias (Sea of Galilee), Jordan valley, Dead Sea, G. of Aqaba, Red Sea, and chain of Ls., notably L. Rudolf and L. Malawi; a branch runs through Ls. Tanganyika, Mobutu and Edward; used for geothermal power.

Great Salt Lake, shallow salty L., N. Utah, **USA;** in Great Basin plateau of N. America; remnant of L. Bonneville; alt. 1,286 m; varies in size and depth; receives Bear, Jordan and Beaver Rs.; many Is., no outlet.

Great Sandy Desert, W. **Australia;** mostly sandhills, stony in ctr.; one of A. 3 great deserts.

Great Slave Lake, N.W. Terr., **Canada;** a. 28,490 km[2]; 496 km long; drained by Mackenzie R.; navigable.

Great Smoky Mtns., Tenn., **USA;** with Blue Ridge mtns. form E. zone of Appalachian mtn. system; hgst peak Clingmans Dome 2,026 m; largely preserved as Nat Park.

Great Torrington, t., Torridge, Devon, **Eng.;** on R. Torridge; mkt., processing of agr. prod.; p. (1991) 4,073.

Great Wall of China, wall built in N. **China** along S. edge of Mongolian plateau to keep out invading Mongols; length 2,400 km; begun in Ch'in dynasty by Shih Huang Ti, *c.* 220 B.C.; present form dates from Ming dynasty (1368–1644).

Great Whale R. (R. de la Baleine), Quebec, **Canada;** rises in L. Bienville, flows to Hudson Bay; difficult transport; 400 km long.

Great Yarmouth, pt., l. gov. dist., Norfolk, **Eng.;** at mouth of R. Yare; holiday resort; fish and food processing plants; base for N. Sea gas; p. (1994) 88,700 (dist.), (1991) 56,190 (t.).

Greece, rep., S.E. Europe; mtnous. peninsula, between Mediterranean and Aegean Sea, inc. many sm. Is. to S., lgst. Crete; inds. increasingly impt. but agr. prods. still ch. exp. (tobacco, olive oil, cotton, citrus fruit, wine); only 25 per cent a. cultivable; economy also helped by lge. merchant fleet and tourism; deposed king in exile; executive power held by military junta 1967–74; 10th member of EU (1981); territorial disputes with Turkey over Aegean islands and tension over Cyprus; cap. Athens; a. 132,561 km[2]; p. (1993) 10,400,000.

Green Bay, c. E. Wisconsin, **USA;** oldest settlement in Wisconsin at mouth of R. Fox; p. (1990) 96,466.

Greenland, I., between Arctic Oc. and Baffin Bay; lofty ice-capped plateau; peopled by coastal settlements of Inuits; fisheries; whale oil, seal skins; lge. uranium deposits, potential for petroleum; first onshore drilling (1984) in Scoresby Land; some coal, lead, zinc; US base at Thule; part of Danish kingdom; internal self-government 1981; cap. Godthåb; a. 2,175,600 km[2] of which 1,833,720 km[2] are under a permanent ice-cap; ice-cap now receding; p. (1993) 55,117.

Greenland Sea, Arctic Oc., between Greenland and Spitzbergen; ice-covered.

Green Mtns., Vt., **USA;** part of Appalachians reaching 1,340 m (Mt. Mansfield); Nat. Forest, tourism.

Greenock, spt., burgh, Inverclyde, **Scot.;** on S. shore of F. of Clyde, 40 km W. of Glasgow; container facilities; shipbldg., sugar refining, woollens, chemicals, aluminium casting, tin-plate inds.; birthplace of James Watt; p. (1991) 50,013.

Green River, Wyo., Utah, **USA;** rises in Wind R. Range (major watershed in Rockies); flows via spectacular scenery to Colorado R.; impt. routeway; 1,168 km long.

Greensboro', c., N.C., **USA;** cotton, tobacco, chemicals; regional financial ctr.; educational institutes; p. (1990) 183,521 (c.), 942,000 (met. a. inc. Winston-Salem-High Point).

Greenville, t., Miss., **USA;** on Mississippi R.; deep-water harbour; tr. ctr. for cotton, agr. prod.; chemicals, metal gds.; p. (1980) 40,613.

Greenville, t., S.C., **USA;** univ.; industl. and comm. ctr.; textile mills, farm prod. processing; p. (1990) 58,282 (t.), 641,000 (met. a. with Spartanburg).

Greenwich, inner bor., London, **Eng.;** inc. most of former bor. of Woolwich on S. bank of R. Thames; famous for its hospital, observatory (now moved to Cambridge) and R.N. College (now closed); longitudes conventionally calculated from Greenwich meridian; site of Millennium Exhibition and Village; p. (1995) 211,400.

Greenwich Village, lower Manhattan, N.Y. city, USA; bohemian quarter.

Greifswald, spt., Mecklenburg - West Pomerania, Germany; on Baltic inlet; shipbldg., textiles, wood inds.; p. (1981) 61,388.

Greiz, t., Gera, Germany; paper, textiles, chemicals; p. (1989) 33,441.

Grenada, W.I., most S. of Windward Is.; inc. Southern Grenadine Is.; known as the "spice islands" as major exp. is nutmeg; cloves and vanilla also grown; sugar and sugar prods.; cotton-ginning; cap. St. George's; former Brit. col., achieved indep. 1974; Pt. Salinas airport opened (1984); a. 344 km²; p. (1995) 96,000.

Grenadines, gr. of over 100 sm. Windward Is., W.I., attached to Grenada and St. Vincent and the Grenadines.

Grenoble, c., cap of Isère dep., S.E. France; on Isère R. at foot of Alps; univ.; thriving cultural and scientific ctr.; impt. hydroelectric ctr.; science-based inds., joint Franco-German nuclear research reactor; gloves, paper, cement, liqueurs; tourism based on skiing; p. (1990) 153,973 (c.), 400,141 (met. a.).

Gretna (Green), v., Dumfries and Galloway, Scot.; on Eng. border; famous as place of runaway marriages until 1940; p. (1991) 3,149.

Greymouth, spt., S.I., N.Z.; on W. cst. at mouth of Grey R.; ch. t. prov. of Westland; grew with gold mng., now replaced by coal and timber; p. (1987) 7,530.

Grimaldi, caves, N.W. Italy; remains of prehistoric man, late Paleolithic, found there.

Grimsby. See Great Grimsby.

Grindelwald, v., Bernese Oberland, Switzerland; tourist ctr.

Gris-Nez, C., N.E. France; nearest point on Fr. cst. to Dover.

Grisons (Graubünden), can., E. Switzerland; region of glaciers and magnificent peaks; ch. resorts Davos, Arosa, St. Moritz; Swiss Nat. Park; lgst. can.; sparse p.; ctr. Romansch language; a. 7,112 km²; p. (1986) 166,000.

Grodno, c., W. Belarus; pt. on Neman R.; a Polish t. until 1939; machine parts, cloth; historic bldgs.; p. (1990) 277,000.

Groningen, c., cap. of G. prov., Neth.; univ.; impt. trading ctr.; p. (1994) 170,535 (c.), 210,269 (met. a.).

Groningen, prov., N.E. Neth.; agr. and dairying; major natural gas deposits at Slochteren; a. 2,157 km²; p. (1994) 556,607.

Groote Eylandt, I., G. of Carpentaria; off cst. of N.T., Australia; aboriginal reserve; manganese ore-mng.

Grosseto, t., cap. of G. prov., Tuscany, Italy; cath.; agr. mkt.; severely affected by floods 1966; p. (1981) 69,523.

Gross Glockner, mtn. (3,801 m) and pass (2,370 m), Austria, part of Hohe Tauern range; hgst. peak in Austria. cap. Chechersop.

Grozny, t., cap. Chechen rep. Russia; on R. Terek; naphtha wells, refinery, engin.; starting point of oil pipelines to Makhachkala, Tuapse and Gorlovka; fell to Russian attack 1995; p. (1989) 400,000.

Grudziadz (Graudenz), t., on R. Vistula, Torun prov., Poland; mftg.; p. (1989) 101,571.

Grünberg. See Zielona Góra.

Gruyères, dist., can. Fribourg, Switzerland; cattle; cheese.

Gruziya. See Georgia.

Guadalajara, c., cap. of Jalisco st., W. Mexico; c. 1,500 m high; impt. industl. and comm. ctr.; textiles, agr. processing, traditional pottery and glassware; cath.; gas pipeline from Salamanca; health resort; p. (1990) 2,846,720.

Guadalajara, c., cap. of G. prov., Spain; on Henares R., N. of Madrid; palace of Mendoza family; battle of Spanish Civil War, March 1937, fought nearby; p. (1987) 59,492 (c.), (1991) 147,868 (prov.).

Guadalaviar, R., E. Spain; flows into Mediterranean, below Valencia; 208 km long.

Guadalcanal, volcanic I., Pac. Oc.; lgst. of Solomon Is.; jungle and mtns.; exp. copra; ch. t. Honiara.

Guadalquivir, R., S. Spain; flows through Andalusia via Seville to Atl.; c. 560 km long; hydroelec. plants; agr.

Guadalupe Hidalgo, place of pilgrimage, N.W. Mexico City, Mexico; basilica and shrine; treaty

ending Mexican–U.S. war signed here 1848.

Guadarrama, Sierra de, mtn. range, central Spain; rugged, forest covered; affects Madrid's climate; reaches 2,431 m.

Guadeloupe, overseas dep. France, W.I.; comprises most S. of Leeward gr., Basse-Terre, Grande-Terre, Marie-Galante and other Is.; economy based on sugar exports to France; rapidly rising p. aggravates process of econ. development; attempts to develop tourism and food-processing inds.; ch. comm. ctr. and pt. Pointe à Pitre (Grande Terre); cap. Basse-Terre; a. 1,748 km²; p. (1990) 387,000.

Guadiana, R., forms part of Spanish and Portuguese frontier; flows into G. of Cádiz; Estremadura valley reclamation scheme; 816 km long.

Guam, I., U.S. air and naval base in W. Pac.; developing tourist ind.; free-port and tax incentives aid investment; ch. t. Agaña; a. 541 km²; p. (1992) 140,200.

Guanajuato, st., central Mexico; average elevation 1,800 m; mng. (silver, gold, tin, copper, iron, lead, opals); a. 30,572 km²; p. (1990) 3,980,204.

Guanajuato, cap. of G. st., Mexico; 1,990 m high in gorge; resort; p. (1990) 113,580.

Guangdong (Kwantung), prov., S. China; on S. China Sea; cap. Guangzhou; occupied by delta of Xijiang and its confluents; Hong Kong in estuary; tropical monsoon climate; densely p. on R. plains and valley slopes; intensive farming of rice, sugar, fruits; 2 Special Economic Zones to encourage foreign investment; a. 221, 308 km²; p. (1990) 63,210,000.

Guangzhou (Canton), c., cap. Guangdong prov., S. China; industl. and educational ctr.; mnfs. inc. steel, ships, paper, cement; univ.; former treaty pt. and major spt. of S. China but site on Zhujiang R. delta results in silting and expensive harbour wks., hence Chinese interest in Hong Kong; ctr. of revolutionary movement from days of Sun Yat-Sen; p. (1992) 3,620,000.

Guang Zhuang (Kwangsi Chuang), aut. region, S. China; borders on Vietnam; cap. Nanning; drained by Xijiang and tribs.; rice most impt. crop; timber from sub-tropical forests; home of the Zhuang people (over 7 million); a. 221,321 km²; p. (1990) 42,530,000.

Guantánamo, c., S.E. Cuba; sugar, coffee, bananas, cacao; pt. at Caimanera on G. Bay; p. (1990) 200,381.

Guaporé, R., Brazil; rises in Mato Grosso st., forms Brazil–Bolivia bdy. before joining the Mamore; length 1,440 km.

Guarulhos, c., Brazil; N.E. of São Paulo; mechanical and electrical engin.; metals; benefits from rapid industl. growth of São Paulo; p. (1991) 781,499.

Guatemala, rep., Central America; straddles Central American isthmus; interior mtnous. with temperate climate; coastal lowlands hot and humid; economy based on agr., coffee accounting for half exp.; timber exploitation, food processing; two oil refineries; trades mainly with USA, ch. pts. Puerto Barrios, San José, Santos Tomas de Castilla; 4 univs.; cap. Guatemala City; a. 108,889 km²; p. (1992) 9,742,000.

Guatemala City, c., cap. of G. rep.; cath., univ.; fruit and vegetable mkts.; coffee tr.; remains Mayan civilisation; partially destroyed by earthquake (1976); p. (1989) 2 m.

Guayama, t., Puerto Rico; ctr. of agr. region; sugar-milling and food-processing.

Guayaquil, ch. pt., Ecuador; cap. of Guayas prov. on Guayas R., nr. Bay of G.; univ., cath.; sawmills, foundries, machin., brewing, oil refinery; p. (1990) 1,508,444.

Guayas, prov., Ecuador; cst. lowlands; plantations for coffee, cocoa, bananas, rice; cap. Guayaquil; p. (1990) 2,515,146.

Guaymallén, c., Mendoza prov. N.W. Argentina; agr. centre; p. (1980) 157,334.

Gudbrandsdal, valley, S. Norway; leads S.E. from Dovrefjell towards Oslo; drained by R. Logan; used by main road Oslo to Trondheim; provides relatively lge. a. of cultivable land; hay, oats, barley, dairy cattle; 368 km long.

Guelph, t., Ont., Canada; on Speed R.; univ.; mkt. ctr. in rich farming a.; cloth, elec. equipment; p. (1991) 87,976.

Guernsey, I., Channel Is., between cst. of France and Eng.; tomatoes, grapes (under glass), flowers, cattle, tourist resort, t. and ch. spt. St. Peter Port; banking; a. 6,335 ha; p. (1991) 58,867.

Guerrero, st., S. **Mexico**; on Pac. cst.; mtnous.; cereals, cotton, coffee, tobacco; cap. Chilpancingo; ch. pt. Acapulco; a. 64,452 km; p. (1990) 2,622,067.

Guiana Highlands, plateau, S. **America**; extend c. 1,440 km from E. to W. across S. parts of Venezuela, Guyana, Surinam, Fr. Guiana; steep sides, rounded tops c. 900 m but rise to 2,852 m in Mt. Roraima; chiefly composed of crystalline rocks rich in minerals.

Guienne, former prov., **France**, partly coincides with the Aquitaine basin (q.v.); controlled by England 1154–1451.

Guildford, co. t., l. gov. dist., Surrey, **Eng.**; 48 km S.W. London; on gap cut by R. Wey through N. Downs, cath., univ.; vehicles, agr. implements, lt. inds.; residtl., cas.; p. (1995) 125,100 (dist.), (1991) 65,998 (t.).

Guilin (**Kweilin**), c., Guangxi, **China**; on R. Li; univ.; textiles, sugar refining, timber; noted for its beautiful setting; p. (1984) 446,900.

Guinea, rep., W. Africa; climate hot and humid on cst. but temperate in higher interior; 95 per cent p. engaged in agr., but bauxite dominates exp. from deposits at Boké, (world's second largest producer); hydroelectric dam and aluminium smelter at Konkouré; pt. at Kamsar for mineral exp.; major spt. at cap. Conakry; a. 245,861 km²; p. (1994) 6,500,000.

Guinea, gen. name for W. African coastlands from Senegal to Angola.

Guinea-Bissau, formerly Portuguese Guinea, W. Africa; indep. 1974; cap. Bissau; poor econ. infrastructure; no manf. inds.; depends on agr. of rice, ground-nuts and stock raising; cst. edged by mangroves; offshore oil potential; a. 36,125 km²; p. (1994) 1,058,000.

Guinea, Spanish. See **Equatorial Guinea.**

Guinea Current, ocean current, flows W. to E. along Guinea cst., diverted away from cst. in Bight of Benin by C. Three Points.

Guinea, Gulf of, arm of Atl. Oc. formed by gr. bend of cst. of W. **Africa** between Ivory Coast and Gabon; Bight of Benin and Bight of Bonny are inner bays.

Guipúzcoa, smallest prov. **Spain**; cap. San Sebastian; on B of Biscay and French border; a. 1,997 km²; p. (1991) 671,743.

Guisborough, t., Redcar and Cleveland, **Eng.**; at foot of Cleveland Hills; former ctr. of iron mng.; 12th cent. abbey ruins; p. (1991) 18,156.

Guiyang (**Kweiyang**), c. and cap., Guizhou prov., **China**; univ.; comm. and industl.; coal; iron and steel, textiles, chemicals; p. (1992) 1,560,000.

Guizhou (**Kweichow**), inland prov., S.W. **China**; upland a. with p. concentrated in valley urban areas; cap. Guiyang; cereals, tung oil; forestry; coal, mercury; a. 176,480 km²; p. (1990) 32,730,000.

Gujarat, st., **India**; formerly part of Bombay st.; cap. temporarily Ahmedabad; new cap. Gandhinager, 21 km N. of A. under construction; oil development in Cambay area; fertiliser plant projected; a. 187,115 km²; p. (1991) 41,309,582.

Gujranwala, c. **Pakistan**; N. of Lahore; power plant, engin.; p. (1981) 597,000.

Gujrat, t., Rawalpindi, **Pakistan**; agr. ctr., handicraft inds.; p. (1981) 154,000.

Gulbarga, t., Karnataka, **India**; cotton, flour, paint; (1991) 304,000.

Gulfport, t., Miss., **USA**; pt. of entry; exp. wood, cottonseed; mnfs., textiles, fertilisers; resort; p. (1980) 39,676.

Gulf Stream, warm current of the Atl. Oc., issuing from G. of Mexico by Fla. Strait.

Guntur, c., Andhra Pradesh, **India**; on E. cst. N. of Madras; cotton mkt.; p. (1991) 273,000.

Guryev. See **Atyrau**.

Güstrow, t., Mecklenburg - West Pomerania, **Germany**; S. of Rostock; cas., cath.; mkt. t.; p. (1989) 38,527.

Gütersloh, t., N. Rhine–Westphalia, **Germany**; nr. Bielefeld; silk and cotton inds.; famous for its Pumpernickel (Westphalian rye bread); machin., furniture, publishing, metallurgy; p. (1986) 79,400.

Guwahati, t., **India**; temporary cap. of Assam being developed in E. suburb of Dispur; univ.; silk, cotton, lace, oil refinery; pipeline from Barauni; p. (1991) 577,591.

Guyana, rep., N. cst. S. America; former Brit. col.; largely covered by dense jungle, p. concentrated on narrow coastal belt; economy

based on agr., especially sugar and rice; forestry inds. limited by lack of transport; impt. bauxite deposits; high birth-rate creates social and economic problems, especially on overpopulated coastal belt; ethnic tension (1998); airport at Timehri; univ. at Turkeyen; cap. Georgetown; a. 214,970 km²; p. (1994) 730,000.

Gwalior, t., Madhya Pradesh, **India**; adjoins Lashkar (q.v.); dominated by rock of Gwalior with Jain sculptures; p. (1991) 691,000.

Gwent, Plain of (**Vale of Glamorgan**), lowland dist., S. **Wales**; lies S. of moorland of S. Wales coalfield, extends E. into Monmouthshire; fertile soils; mixed farming except in industl. areas of Cardiff, Barry.

Gweru, t. **Zimbabwe**; ctr. of farming dist.; shoes, glass, containers; p. (1992) 124,735.

Gwynedd, N.W. **Wales**, unit. auth. created in 1996 from former l. gov. dists. of Arfon, Dwyfor and Meirionnydd; mtnous. a. except cst.; sparse p. inland where hill farming; inc. Snowdonia Nat. Park, Lleyn Penin., and ts. of Bangor and Caernarfon; p. (1995) 118,000.

Gyandzha, (**Kirovabad**) c., W. **Azerbaijan**; on Gyandzha R.; industl. ctr.; textiles, agr. implements, wine; copper and manganese mines; aluminium plant; p. (1990) 281,000.

Gympie, t., Queensland, **Australia**; on Mary R., 106 m. from Brisbane; former goldfield; now dairying and pastoral dist., tropical fruits, especially pineapples; p. (1984) 11,380.

Györ, t., **Hungary**; at confluence of Rs. Raba and Danube; cath.; textile ctr., rolling stock, chemicals, machine tools; p. (1997) 127,000.

H

Haarlem, c., cap. of N. Holland prov., **Neth.**; nr. N. Sea cst.; tulip-growing, textiles, printing; 15th cent. church; p. (1994) 150,213 (c.), 214,152 (met. a.).

Hackney, inner bor., N.E. London, **Eng.**; incorporates former bors. of Shoreditch and Stoke Newington; furniture, clothing, p. (1995) 194,200.

Haddington, burgh, E. Lothian, **Scot.**; on R. Tyne, 26 km E. of Edinburgh; woollen mnf.; grain mkt., corn mills, lt. engin., hosiery; p. (1991) 8,844.

Haderslev, t. **Denmark**; tobacco, clothing, knitted goods; p. (1990) 30,330.

Hadhramaut, governorate, **Yemen**; ch. pt. and c. Al Mukallā; fertile coastal valley; frankincense, aloes, tobacco, shawls, carpets; p. (1986) 537,095.

Hadleigh, t., Babergh, Suffolk, **Eng.**; mkt.; flour-milling; p. (1991) 6,595.

Hadrian's Wall, part of frontier barrier, N. **Eng.**; stretching across Tyne–Solway isthmus, 118 km long. See **Roman Walls, Section L.**

Hafnarijördur, t., S. of Reykjavik, **Iceland**; p. (1993) 16,787.

Hagen, t., N. Rhine–Westphalia, **Germany**; N.E. of Wuppertal; iron, steel, chemicals, textiles, paper; p. (1990) 214,100.

Hagerstown, t., Md., **USA**; machin., furniture, chemicals, aircraft; p. (1990) 35,445.

Hagersville, t., Ont., **Canada**; gypsum producer.

Hagfors, t., Värmland, **Sweden**; site of lge. iron and steel wks. since 1878.

Hague, The, or **'s-Gravenhage** or **Den Haag**, c., S. Holland, **Neth.**; seat of government; permanent court of international justice; admin. ctr.; urban inds., machin. and metal wares; engin., printing; p. (1994) 445,279 (c.), 695,217 (met. a.).

Haifa, c., ch. spt., **Israel**; on Bay of Acre at foot of Mt. Carmel; terminus of Iraq oil pipeline; oil refining and heavy inds.; p. (1992) 251,000.

Haikou (**Hoihow**), c., ch. pt. of Hainan I., Guangdong prov., **China**.

Hail, t., and oasis, Neid, **Saudi Arabia**; p. (1986) 92,000.

Hailsham, mkt. t., Wealden, East Sussex, **Eng.**; 8 km N. of Eastbourne; mats, rope, and twine; p. (1991) 18,426.

Hainan, I., S. cst. of China; densely wooded; monsoon climate; seafood cultivation; sugarcane, rubber, peanuts, sesame main crops; recent industrial development; food processing, cement, electronics; a. 36,193 km²; p. (1990) 6,420,000.

Hainaut, prov., **Belgium**, adjoining N.E. border of **France**; industl. and agr.; coal- and iron-mines; a. 3,719 km²; p. (1993) 1,285,934.

Haiphong, c., ch. pt., **Vietnam**; on Red R. delta; comm. and trading ctr.; cotton, thread, soap, glass, enamel ware, fish-canning; former naval base of Fr. Indo-China; p. (1989) 456,049.

Haiti, rep., W.I., W. third of I. of Hispaniola; tropical climate modified by alt.; agr. basis of economy; coffee accounts for 45 per cent exp.; irrigation scheme in Artibonite valley; unexploited mineral resources, some bauxite mng. and exp.; sm.-scale inds.; well-developed road network and international shipping services; cap. Port-au-Prince; corrupt Duvalier dictatorship ousted in 1986. a. 27,713 km²; p. (1992) 6,763,746.

Hakodate, c., S. Hokkaido, **Japan**; Seikan rail tunnel to Honshu (Aomori) opened 1988; fishing pt.; fish food processing; p. (1990) 307,251.

Halberstadt, t., Saxony - Anhalt, **Germany**; cath.; metallurgy, rubber inds., engin., sugar refining; rly. junc.; p. (1989) 46,851.

Halden, t., S.E. **Norway**; wood-pulp, paper, footwear, cotton spinning; nuclear research reactor; p. (1990) 20,134.

Haldia, pt., W. Bengal, **India**; nr. mouth of R. Hooghly; satellite pt. for Calcutta to handle coal, ore, grain; oil pipeline to Barauni; refinery; p. (1991) 100,347.

Hale, t., Trafford, Gtr. Manchester, **Eng.**; residtl.; p. (1991) 15,868.

Halesowen, t., S.W. of Birmingham, West Midlands, **Eng.**; weldless tubes, elec. gds., stainless steel forgings, engin.; p. (1991) 57,918.

Halesworth, t., Suffolk, **Eng.**; on R. Blyth, 14 km S.W. of Beccles; p. (1991) 4,575.

Halifax, spt., cap. of Nova Scotia, **Canada**; univ.; naval sta. and dockyard, open in winter; machin., iron foundries, footwear, oil refining, food-processing; scene of explosion of munitions ship (1917); p. (1991) 114,455 (c.), (1986) 295,990 (met. a.).

Halifax, t., Calderdale, West Yorks., **Eng.**; on E. flanks of Pennines; carpets, textiles, machine tools; cast iron wks.; p. (1991) 91,069.

Halland, co. S.W. **Sweden.**; cap Halmstad; a. 5,448 km²; p. (1992) 261,172.

Halle, c. Saxony - Anhalt **Germany**; on R. Saale; univ.; lignite and potash mined nearby; engin., chemicals, p. (1990) 307,200.

Hallstatt, v., Upper **Austria**; in the Salzkammergut; early Iron Age culture type site.

Halmahera, I., **Indonesia**; mtnous., active volcanoes, tropical forests; spices, pearl fisheries, sago, rice; a. 17,218 km².

Halmstad, spt., Kattegat, **Sweden**; iron and steel wks., machin. engin., cycles, textiles, leather, jute, wood-pulp; p. (1992) 81,084.

Hälsingborg. See Helsingborg.

Halstead, t., Essex, **Eng.**; on R. Colne, N.W. of Colchester; rayon weaving; p. (1991) 9,775.

Halton, t. and l. gov. dist., Cheshire, **Eng.**; surrounds Mersey R. and inc. Runcorn and Widnes; p. (1995) 123,200, (1991) 2,332 (t.).

Haltwhistle, mkt. t., Tynedale, Northumberland, **Eng.**; on R. South Tyne; former coal-mng. dist.; p. (1991) 3,773.

Hama, c., N. **Syria**, on R. Orontes; the anc. Hamath, ctr. of Hittite culture; food tr., rural inds.; p. (1993) 229,000.

Hamadān, t., W. **Iran**; alt. c. 1,800 m; the anc. Ecbatana, cap. of Media; carpets, pottery; airport.; tomb of Avicenna; p. (1986) 274,274.

Hamamatsu, c., S. Honshu, **Japan**; on cst. plain 96 km S.E. of Nagoya; ctr. of impt. cotton-mftg. region; textiles, dyeing, musical instruments, motor cycles; p. (1990) 534,624.

Hamar, t., **Norway**; on L. Mjösa; ctr. of rich agr. dist.; tr. and mftg. inds.; p. (1990) 27,550.

Hamble, Hants, **Eng.**; popular yachting ctr.; p. (1991) 3,229.

Hambleton, t. and l. gov. dist., North Yorks., **Eng.**; inc. Northallerton, Bedale and Thirsk; p. (1995) 83,900 (dist.), (1991) 1,566 (t.).

Hamburg, c., Land H., **Germany**; astride R. Elbe, nr. N. Sea; 2nd. lgst. German c. and ch. pt.; freeport since 1189; pt. to be extended by reclaiming Is. of Neuwerk and Scharhörn; diversified tr. inc. liner traffic, barge traffic down Elbe, entrepôt goods; major pt. processing inds., airpt., univ.; cultural and musical ctr.; heavily bombed in second world war; p. (1990) 1,660,700 (c.), 1,669,000 (Land).

Hämeenlinna (Tavastehus), c., cap. of Häme co., S.W. **Finland**; L. pt.; tourist ctr.; birthplace of Sibelius; p. (1993) 44,176.

Hameln (Hamelin), t., Lower Saxony, **Germany**; pt. on R. Weser; iron, textiles; scene of legend of the Pied Piper; p. (1986) 55,400.

Hamhung, c., **N. Korea**; industl. and comm. ctr., oil refinery, petrochemicals; coal nearby; p. (1981) 775,000.

Hamilton, spt., cap. of **Bermuda**; tourism. comm. and service ctr.; p. (1994) 1,100.

Hamilton, c., and L. pt., S.E. Ont., **Canada**; at W. end of L. Ont.; univ.; varied metallurgical mnfs.; p. (1991) 318,499 (c.), (1986) 557,029 (met. a.).

Hamilton, c. ctr. of major pastoral region; N.I., **N.Z.**; on Waikato R.; univ.; p. (1991) 101,448 (c.), 148,625 (urban. a.). Moves to rename city Waikato.

Hamilton, burgh, S. Lanarkshire, **Scot.**; in Clyde valley, 16 km S.E. of Glasgow; admin. ctr.; elec. prods., carpet mftg., cottons, woollens, knitwear; Rudolf Hess landed near Duke of Hamilton's estate 1941; p. (1991) 49,991.

Hamilton, t., Ohio, **USA**; on Great Miami R.; industl. ctr.; mnfs. metal prods., paper, machin.; p. (1990) 61,368 (t.), 291,000 (met. a. with Middletown).

Hamm, t., N. Rhine–Westphalia, **Germany**; on R. Lippe, in Ruhr conurb.; rly. marshalling yards, iron and steel foundries; p. (1990) 180,100.

Hammerfest, spt., **Norway**; world's most N. t., on Kvalöya I.; fishing.

Hammersmith and Fulham, Thames-side inner bor., London, **Eng.**; inc. former bor. of Fulham; industl., residtl.; p. (1995) 156,100.

Hammond, c., N.W. Ind., **USA**; on Grand Calumet R., nr. Chicago; originally slaughtering and meat-pkg. ctr., now ch. mnfs., petroleum and steel prods., soap; p. (1990) 84,236.

Hampshire, non-met. co., S. **Eng.**; inc. Hampshire basin of chalk covered in clay and sand; inc. infertile heath and New Forest; lt. inds.; tourism, seaside resorts; co. t. Winchester; p. (1995) 1,616,700.

Hampstead, inc. in Greater London, **Eng.**; hilltop v. with nearby heathland. See Camden.

Hampton, Thames-side t., Richmond upon Thames, London, **Eng.**; Hampton Court Palace; Hampton Wick E. of H. Court.

Hampton, t., S.E. Va., **USA**; oldest English community in US; fishing, oyster and crab packing; p. (1990) 133,793.

Han, R., Hubei, **China**; rises in S.W. Shaanxi prov., flows E. to join Chang Jiang at Wuhan; ch. trib. of Chang Jiang; 1,280 km long.

Han, R., S. **China**; forms rich agr. delta nr. Shantou; c. 400 km long.

Hanau, t., Hesse, **Germany**; on Rs. Mein and Kinzig; jewellery ctr., rubber and non ferrous metals inds.; birthplace of Jakob and Wilhelm Grimm, Paul Hindemith; p. (1986) 85,200.

Hanchung. See Hanzhong.

Hangzhou (Hangchow), c., cap. of Zhejiang prov., E. **China**; picturesque setting at head of H. Bay; former treaty pt., now silted up; silk weaving, chemicals, jute cloth; tourism; p. (1984) 430,000 (c.).

Hankou, c., Hubei, **China**; at junc. of Han and Chang Jiang, 960 km from mouth of Yangtze but accessible to ocean-going ships; ch. comm. and mnf. ctr. of central China; former treaty pt., now part of Wuhan conurb.; machin., chemicals, cigarettes, silk. See Wuhan.

Hannibal, t., Mo., **USA**; on Mississippi R.; shoes, cement, metal gds.; boyhood home of Mark Twain; p. (1980) 18,811.

Hanoi, c., cap. of **Vietnam**; on Red R.; old Annamese fort, now modern comm. ctr.; univ.; cotton, silks, tobacco, pottery; superphosphate and magnesium phosphate nearby; bricks, concrete, rubber; p. (1989) 1,088,862.

Hanover (Hannover), c., cap. of Lower Saxony, **Germany**; route ctr.; iron, textiles, machin., paper, biscuits, cigarettes, cars, rubber-processing, chemicals; p. (1990) 514,400.

Hanyang. See Wuhan.

Hanzhong (Hanchung), c., S.W. Shaanxi, **China**; on Han R.; nr. Sichuan border; agr. and tr. ctr.; former Nancheng; p. (1984) 412,100.

Haparanda, spt., N. **Sweden**; salmon fishing; exp. timber, and prod. of the Lapps.

Happy Valley-Goose Bay, t., Labrador, **Canada**; on Churchill R., international airpt.; p. (1986) 7,248.

Hapur, t., W. Uttar Pradesh, **India**; tr. in sugar, timber, cotton, brassware; p. (1991) 146,262.

Harar, (Harer), t., cap. H. prov., **Ethiopia**; unique African hilltop t. with medieval walls, towers and gates; anc. c. of Islamic learning; overlooks Rift Valley; brewery; p. (1984) 62,160.

Harare (Salisbury), c., cap. of **Zimbabwe**; admin. and industl. ctr. in agr. region with gold and chrome mines nearby; tr. in agr. prods., inc. tobacco; clothing, furniture, fertilisers; univ.; airpt.; p. (1992) 1,184,169.

Harbin (Haerhpin), c., cap. of Heilongjiang prov., **China**; pt. on Sunghua Jiang; tr. and comm. ctr. of N.E. China; exp. soyabeans; food-processing, machin., paper-mills, oil refining, hydro-turbines, textiles; former treaty pt.; p. (1992) 2,840,000.

Harborough, l. gov. dist., S. Leics., **Eng.**; based on Market Harborough and Lutterworth; p. (1995) 72,100.

Hardanger Fjord, W. cst. **Norway**; 120 km long; magnificent scenery; tourism.

Hardt Mtns., **Germany**; northward continuation of Vosges on W. of Rhine rift valley; formerly forested, now largely cleared for pasture; hgst. points reach just over 600 m.

Hardwar, t., Uttar Pradesh, **India**; on R. Ganges; gr. annual fair and pilgrimage; nearby dam; p. (1991) 147,305.

Hargeisa, t., **Somalia**; comm. ctr. of livestock-raising region; airport; p. (1987) 400,000.

Har Homa, controversial Israeli settlement bordering Arab East Jerusalem.

Haringey, outer bor., Greater London, **Eng.**; comprising former bors. of Hornsey, Tottenham, and Wood Green; p. (1995) 213,300.

Hari-Rud, R., N. **Afghanistan** and **Iran**; the anc. "Arius"; length 1,040 km; (*Rud* = river).

Harlech, t., Gwynedd, **Wales**; on Cardigan Bay 16 km N. of Barmouth; farming; cas.; seaside resort; p. (1991) 1,233.

Harlem, upper Manhattan, N.Y. city, **USA**; residtl. and business section of c. with lge. black p.; depressed economic a. with much poverty.

Harlem, R., N.Y., **USA**; separates Manhattan I. from bor. of Bronx; with Spuyten Duyvi Creek forms waterway 13 km long from East R. to Hudson R.

Harlingen, spt., S. Texas, **USA**; ctr. of productive agr. a.; p. (1980) 43,543.

Harlow, t., l. gov. dist., Essex, **Eng.**; in valley of R. Stort, 35 km N.E. of London; new t. (1947); spreads S.W. from nucleus of old mkt. t. of H.; engin., glass, furniture mkg., metallurgy; p. (1995) 73,000 (dist.), (1991) 74,629 (t.).

Harpenden, t., Herts., **Eng.**; in Chiltern Hills, 8 km N. of St. Albans; Rothamsted agr. experimental sta.; residtl.; p. (1991) 28,097.

Harris, S. part of Lewis I., Outer Hebrides, Western Isles, **Scot.**; and several sm. Is.

Harrisburg, c., cap. of Penns., **USA**; on Susquehanna R.; iron and steel ind.; machin., cigarettes, cotton gds.; p. (1990) 588,000 (met. a. with Lebanon-Carlisle).

Harrogate, t., l. gov. dist., North Yorks., **Eng.**; in valley of R. Nidd, 22 km N. of Leeds; spa; favoured a. for retirement; p. (1995) 145,600 (dist.), (1991) 66,178 (t.).

Harrow, outer bor., Greater London, **Eng.**; public school; camera mftg.; p. (1995) 210,100.

Harspränget, t., Norrbotten, **Sweden**; lge. hydroelectric plant.

Harstad, ch. t., Lofoten Is., N.W. **Norway**; herring ind., woollen gds.; p. (1990) 32,327.

Hart, l. gov. dist., N.E. Hants., **Eng.**; comprises Fleet and Hartley Wintney; p. (1995) 84,100.

Hartbeespoort, Dam, Transvaal, **S. Africa**; on R. Crocodile (Limpopo), 40 km W. of Pretoria; supplies water for cultivation, under irrigation, of cotton, maize, tobacco.

Hartford, c., cap. of Conn., **USA**; comm. and insurance ctr.; univ.; sm. arms, typewriters, elec. machin., aircraft engin., ceramics; Mark Twain lived here; p. (1990) 139,739 (c.), 768,000 (met. a.).

Hartland Point, Barnstaple Bay, N. Devon, **Eng.**

Hartlepool, spt., unit. auth. created in 1996, formerly part of Cleveland, **Eng.**; on E. cst., 5 km N. of Tees estuary; shipbldg., lt. inds., timber, iron and steel inds., pipe making; advanced gas-cooled reactor nuclear power sta; p. (1995) 92,200 (unit. auth.), (1991) 87,310 (t.).

Harvey, t., N.E. Ill., **USA**; nr. Chicago; rolling stock, diesel engines, heavy machin.; p. (1980) 35,810.

Harwell, v. Oxon., **Eng.**; 19 km S. of Oxford; Atomic Energy Authority nuclear power research establishment; p. (1991) 2,236.

Harwich, spt., Tendring, Essex, **Eng.**; on S. cst. of estuary of R. Stour; ferry port for Belgium, Neth., Denmark; docks, container facilities,

naval base; p. (1991) 18,436.

Haryana, st. **India**; formed 1966 from Hindi-speaking areas of Punjab; former cap. Chandigarh; Hindu speaking a. transferred from Chandigarh (1986); a. 45,584 km²; p. (1991) 16,463,648.

Harz Mtns., range, **Germany**; between the Weser and the Elbe; highest peak the Brocken; ch. t. Goslar; forested slopes; rich in minerals; tourism.

Haslemere, t., Waverley, Surrey, **Eng.**; nr. Hindhead; mkt., residtl., lt. inds.; p. (1991) 12,218.

Haslingden, t., Rossendale, Lancs., **Eng.**; on Rossendale Fells, 5 km S. of Accrington; heavy industl. textiles, waste-spinning; p. (1991) 15,024.

Hasselt, t., prov., Limburg, **Belgium**; mkt. t.; gin distilleries; p. (1993) 67,080.

Hassi Massaoud, t., **Algeria**; lge. oilfield; pipeline to Bejaia; oil refinery.

Hassi R'Mel, t., **Algeria**; lge. natural gasfield.

Hastings, t., l. gov. dist., East Sussex, **Eng.**; on S. cst., midway between Beachy Head and Dungeness; seaside resort; Cinque Port; cas.; p. (1995) 82,600 (dist.), (1991) 81,139 (t.).

Hastings, c. and dist., N.I., **N.Z.**; on Hawke's Bay, nr. Napier; ctr. for fruit growing dist.; fruit-canning; p. (1991) 64,693 (dist.).

Hatay (Sanjak of Alexandretta), prov. and t., S. **Turkey**; comprising Antioch (now Antakya) and its pt. Alexandretta (now Iskenderun), ceded to Turkey by France 1939; p. (1990) 1,109,754 (prov.), 118,443 (t.).

Hatfield, t., Welwyn and Hatfield, Herts., **Eng.**; 30 km N. of London; new t. (1948) which grew around old t. of Bishops Hatfield; aircraft inds. (closed 1994); computers; p. (1991) 31,104.

Hathras, t., Aligarh dist., Uttar Pradesh, **India**; sugar, cotton, carved work; p. (1991) 113,285.

Hatteras, Cape, promontory on I. and cays off N.C., **USA**; stormy region, marked by lighthouse.

Hattiesburg, t., Miss., **USA**; sawmilling, clothing, fertilisers; p. (1980) 40,829.

Haugesund, spt., S. **Norway**; on S.W. cst., 35 m. N. of Stavanger; ch. ctr. of herring fishery; canning inds.; p. (1987) 27,000.

Hauraki Gulf, arm of Pac. Oc.; E. cst. N.I., **N.Z.**; forming entrance to harbour of Auckland; Nat. Park; gives name to dist.; p. (1991) 16,921.

Haute Corse. *See* Corsica.

Haute Garonne, dep., S. **France**; in Languedoc; cap. Toulouse; a. 6,366 km²; p. (1990) 926,000.

Haute-Loire, dep., **France**; mainly in Massif Central; cap. Le Puy; cattle, fruit, vineyards; a. 4,999 km²; p. (1990) 206,600.

Haute-Marne, dep., **France**; mainly in Champagne; metallurgical inds.; a. 6,268 km²; p. (1990) 204,100.

Haute-Normandie, region **N France**; inc. deps. Eure, Seine-Maritime; ch. t. Rouen; p. (1990) 1,737,200. *See* Normandy.

Hautes-Alpes, dep., **France**; mtnous.; on Italian border; sheep; cap. Gap; a. 5,641 km²; p. (1990) 113,300.

Haute-Saône, dep., **France**; inc. part of Vosges mtns.; mainly agr.; cap. Vesoul; a. 5,372 km²; p. (1990) 229,700.

Haute-Savoie, dep., **France**; borders on Italy and Switzerland; reaches highest alt. in Mont Blanc; cap. Annecy; winter sports; a. 4,595 km.; p. (1990) 568,300.

Hautes-Pyrénées, dep., S. **France**; rises in S. to steep peaks of Pyrenees, forming bdy. with Spain; Basques live on both sides of border; cap. Tarbes; Lourdes place of pilgrimage; a. 4,533 km²; p. (1990) 224,800.

Haute-Vienne, dep., **France**; entirely in Massif Central; cap. Limoges; cattle-raising; a. 5,488 km²; p. (1990) 353,600.

Haut-Rhin, dep., E. **France**; in lower Alsace; cap. Colmar; ch. industl. t. Mulhouse; a. 3,507 km²; p. (1990) 671,300.

Hauts-de-Seine, dep., **France**; W. of Paris; cap. Nanterre; a. 176 km²; p. (1990) 1,391,700.

Havana (La Habana), c., cap. of **Cuba**; ch. pt. of W.I., with lge. harbour; cigars, tobacco, sugar, rum, coffee, woollens, straw hats, iron-ore; oil refining on outskirts of c.; p. (1990) 2,096,054.

Havant, t., l. gov. dist., **Eng.**; at foot Portsdowns Hill, 10 km N.E. of Portsmouth; p. (1995) 118,100 (dist.), (1991) 46,510 (t.).

Havel, R., **Germany**; rises in Neubrandenburg L. region; flows to Elbe R.; partially canalised nr. Berlin; 354 km long.

Haverfordwest, t., Pembrokeshire, **Wales**; 10 km N.E. of Milford Haven; agr. mkt.; Norman cas.; p. (1991) 13,454.

Haverhill, t., St. Edmundsbury, Suffolk, Eng.; expanded t.; textiles; p. (1991) 19,086.

Haverhill, t., Mass., USA; industl.; shipping containers; p. (1990) 394,000 (met. a. with Lawrence).

Havering, outer bor., E. London, Eng.; inc. Hornchurch and Romford; p. (1995) 231,000.

Havirov, t. Czech Republic, S.E. of Ostrava; mnfs., mng.; p. (1990) 92,000.

Hawaii, I., N. central Pac. Oc.; lgst. of Hawaiian gr.; three gr. volcanic mtns., Mauna Kea (4,208 m), Mauna Loa (4,172 m), Hualalai (last erupted, 1801); ch. pt. Hilo (devastated by tidal wave, 1946); lava deserts, bamboo forests; sugar-cane, cattle, coffee; tourism; deep-sea fishing; p. (1980) 92,053.

Hawaii, st., Pac. Oc., admitted 1959 as 50th st. of USA; st. flower Hibiscus, st. bird Nene; chain of coral and 1959 as 50th st. of USA; chain of coral and volcanic Is.; cap. Honolulu on S.E. cst. of Oahu I.; tourism; ctr. of international shipping routes; sugar, pineapples; a. 16,638 km²; p. (1990) 1,108,229.

Hawarden, t., Flintshire, N. Wales; steel plant; home of Gladstone.

Hawes Water, L., Cumbria, Eng.; 4 km long.

Hawick, burgh, Borders, Scot.; on R. Teviot, 28 km S.W. of Kelso; hosiery, tweed, and woollens; p. (1991) 15,812.

Hawke's Bay, region, N.I., N.Z.; on E. cst.; cap. Napier; a. 11,033 km²; p. (1991) 139,479.

Hawkesbury, R., N.S.W., Australia; impt. waterway flowing into Broken Bay; spectacular gorges.

Haworth, t., West Yorks., Eng.; nr. Keighley; home of the Brontës; p. (1991) 4,956.

Hawthorne, t., S.W. Cal., USA; residtl.; in gas- and oil-producing a.; aircraft and electronics; p. (1980) 56,447.

Hay-on-Wye, t., Powys, Wales; on R. Wye; cas.; mkt.; large number of book shops; p. (1991) 1,407.

Hay, R., Alberta, Canada; flows into G. Slave Lake; 560 km long.

Haydock, t., Merseyside, Eng.; coal mng.; inc. H. Park racecourse; p. (1991) 16,705.

Hayes and Harlington. See Hillingdon.

Hayling Island, resort, Hants., Eng.; E. of Portsmouth; p. (1991) 14,054.

Hayward, t., Cal., USA; fruit-canning, poultry; p. (1990) 111,498.

Haywards Heath, residtl. t. West Sussex, Eng.; p. (1991) 28,923.

Hazel Grove and Bramhall, subs. of Stockport, Gtr. Manchester, Eng.; p. (1991) 39,730.

Hazleton, t., Penns., USA; anthracite region; textiles, iron and steel mnfs.; p. (1980) 27,318.

Headingley, sub., Leeds, West Yorks., Eng. mainly residtl.; county cricket ground. Vote (1997) to move to new ground near Wakefield.

Heanor, t., Amber Valley, Derbys., Eng.; 11 km N.E. of Derby; hosiery, pottery, prefabricated timber bldgs. mftg.; p. (1991) 22,180.

Heard, I., Australian terr. 4,000 km SW of Fremantle, Australia; volcanic, weather station.

Heathrow, London airport, Eng.; 24 km W. of central London, S. of M4 motorway; on Piccadilly tube line. See L57.

Hebburn, t., Tyne and Wear, Eng.; on R. Tyne 6 km below Gateshead; shipbldg., engin.; p. (1991) 18,183.

Hebei (Hopeh), prov., N.E. China; part of N. China plain; bounded on N. by Great Wall; cap. Shijiazhuang; wheat, kaolin, cotton, coal mng., a. 194,250 km²; p. (1990) 60,280,000.

Hebrides or Western Isles, Scot.; grouped as Outer and Inner Hebrides; ch. t. Stornoway, Lewis.

Hebron, t., 26 km. S.W. of Jerusalem.

Heckmondwike, t., West Yorks., Eng.; wool textiles; p. (1991) 9,855.

Hedon, t., E. Riding of Yorks., Eng.; former spt.; p. (1991) 6,646.

Heerenveen, t., Friesland prov., N. Neth.; bicycles; p. (1993) 38,728.

Heerlen, t., Limburg, Neth.; 22 km E. of Maastricht; coal mng.; with Kerkrade, met. a.; p. (1994) 95,794 (c.), 270,118 (met. a.).

Heide, t., Schleswig-Holstein, Germany; ctr. of Ditmarschen oilfields; p. (1986) 20,700.

Heidelberg, c., Baden-Württemberg, Germany; on R. Neckar, nr. Mannheim; celebrated univ., cas.; tobacco, wood, leather, rly. carriages; ; p. (1990) 138,000.

Heidenheim, t., Baden-Württemberg, Germany; N.E. of Ulm; textiles, machin., metallurgy, furniture; p. (1986) 47,600.

Heilbronn, t., R. pt., Baden-Württemberg, Germany; engin., vehicles, foodstuffs; p. (1990) 116,200.

Heilongjiang (Heilungkiang), prov., N.E. China; separated from USSR by Amur and Ussuri Rs.; mtnous.; crossed by Songhua R. in central plain; maize, soyabeans, millets; opencast coalmines; gold; cap. Harbin; a. 466,200 km²; p. (1990) 34,770,000.

Hejaz, W prov., Saudi Arabia; mainly desert; very poor communications; ch. t. Mecca; a. 388,500 km².

Hekla, volcano, Iceland; erupted in 1970; alt. 1,554 m.

Helder (Den Helder), t., N. Holland, Neth.; on strait between peninsula and I. of Texel; naval base; p. (1994) 61,024.

Helena, st. cap., Mont., USA; grew up as gold- and silver-mng. t.; bricks, pottery; resort; p. (1990) 24,569.

Helensburgh, t., Argyll and Bute, W. Scot.; on the Clyde; resort; p. (1991) 15,852.

Helford, R., Cornwall, Eng.; oysters, tourism.

Helicon, mtn. gr., Greece; abode of classical muses.

Heligoland (Helgoländ), sm. I., N. Sea; off mouth of Elbe; ceded by Britain to Germany 1890 in return for Zanzibar.

Hellespont. See Dardanelles.

Helmand or Helmund, R., Afghanistan; flows c. 1,360 km from mtns. of Kabul to Hamun-i-Helmand swamp on Iranian border; cultivation in valley; major irrigation project.

Helmond, t., N. Brabant, Neth.; on Zuid-Willemsvaart (canal); textiles; p. (1994) 72,293.

Helmsley, mkt. t., Ryedale, North Yorks., Eng.; cas.

Helmstedt, t., Lower Saxony, Germany; E. of Brunswick; on E. German border; textiles, machin.; p. (1986) 25,500.

Helsingborg (Hälsingborg), spt., Malmöhus, Sweden industl. ctr.; train ferry to Elsinore, Denmark; p. (1992) 110,614.

Helsingør, t., spt., Denmark; shipbldg.; setting of Shakespeare's Hamlet; p. (1990) 56,701.

Helsinki or Helsingfors, c., cap. of Finland; spt. on G. of Finland; harbour ice-bound Jan. to Apr., channel opened by ice-breakers; cultural ctr., univ.; timber, textiles, carpets; exp. mainly timber prods.; p. (1993) 508,588.

Helston, mkt. t., Kerrier, Cornwall, Eng.; on R. Cober, 13 km W. of Falmouth; tourist ctr.; famous for festival of floral dance (8 May); fishing, soup-canning; p. (1991) 8,505.

Helvellyn, mtn., L. Dist., Cumbria, Eng.; severely eroded by ice; alt. 951 m; sharp ridge of Striding Edge.

Helwan, t., Egypt; 24 km S. of Cairo; sulphur springs; iron and steel complex, recently expanded (1982); fertilisers, cement; car assembly; p. (1986) 328,000.

Hemel Hempstead, t., Dacorum, Herts., Eng.; new t. (1947), on S. slopes of Chilterns; scientific glass, elec. engin., cars; p. (1991) 79,235.

Henan (Honan), prov., Central China; traversed by Huang He; cap. Zhengzhou; densely p. in fertile E.; mainly agr.; wheat, cotton, kaolin, anthracite; a. 167,172 km²; p. (1990) 86,140,000.

Hengelo, t., Overijssel, Neth.; industl. ctr.; cattle mkt.; metals, textiles; p. (1994) 77,514.

Hengyang, c., Hunan, China; on Xiang Jiang in foothills to S. Chang Jiang plain; on main Guangzhau-Beijing rly.; lead and zinc mines nearby; p. (1984) 551,300.

Hénin-Beaumont, t., Pas-de-Calais, France; on coalfield; p. (1982) 26,212.

Henley-on-Thames, t., South Oxfordshire, Oxon., Eng.; 8 km N.E. of Reading; mkt. gardening, brewing; annual regatta; p. (1991) 10,558.

Hensbarrow, upland a., Cornwall, Eng.; granite; kaolin-mng. dist., kaolin exp. by sea from Fowey; rises to over 300 m; a. 70 km².

Henzada, t., Myanmar; on Irrawaddy delta; in tobacco and rice-growing dist.; p. (1983) 283,658.

Herakleion. See Iráklion.

Herât, c., cap. of H. prov., N.W. Afghanistan; on Hari Rud R.; of historic and strategic importance, has been called "the key of India"; crude petroleum and chrome-ore nearby; tr. ctr.; textiles; p. (1988) 177,300.

Hérault, dep. S.W. France; in Languedoc; agr.; cap. Montpellier; govt.-sponsored tourist developments along shores of Mediterranean; a. 6,221 km²; p. (1990) 794,600.

Herculaneum, anc. c., S. Italy; 6 km E. of Naples; buried along with Pompeii by eruption from Vesuvius A.D. 79; rediscovered 1709; site of modern Resina and Portici.

Hereford and Worcester, non-met. co. (until 1998), **Eng.;** crossed by Wye and Severn valleys, separated by Malvern Hills; mainly agr.; beef, dairy and fruit farming; major ts. Hereford and Worcester; p. (1995) 694,300. Worcs. and Hereford separated in 1998.

Hereford, c., l. gov. unit. auth., **Eng.;** on R. Wye; cath.; mkt.; tiles, engin., timber, cider and preserves; furniture, brass-ware; p. (1995) 49,500 (dist.), (1991) 54,326 (c.).

Herford, t., N. Rhine–Westphalia, **Germany;** on R. Werra; cotton, flax, furniture, cigars, confectionery, metallurgy; p. (1986) 59,500.

Herisau, t., cap. of Appenzell Ausser-Rhoden half-can., N.E. **Switzerland;** muslin, embroideries; p. (1980) 14,160.

Herm, sm. I., dependency of **Guernsey,** English Channel; 6 km N.W. Sark and N.E. of Guernsey; remarkable shell-beach; a. 130 ha.

Hermon, Mount (Jebel esh Sheikh), mtn., in Anti-Lebanon range, on **Syria–Lebanon** bdy., nr. Israel; alt. 2,862 m.

Hermosillo, c., cap. of Sonora st., N.W. **Mexico;** on San Miguel R.; oranges; agr. and mng. ctr.; p. (1990) 449,472.

Hermoupolis or **Hermopolis,** t., Syros I., **Greece;** cap. of Cyclades; Aegean pt. and comm. ctr.; p. (1981) 13,876.

Herne, t., N. Rhine–Westphalia, **Germany;** pt. on Rhine–Herne canal; industl. t. of Ruhr conurb.; p. (1990) 178,400.

Herne Bay, t., Kent, **Eng.;** on cst., 19 km W. of Margate; p. (1991) 31,861.

Herning, t., Jutland, **Denmark;** knitting ind.; p. (1990) 56,687.

Heröya, S. **Norway;** nuclear power plant; chemicals, fertilisers.

Herstal, t., **Belgium;** nr. Liège; armaments, aero-engines; p. (1993) 36,611.

Herstmonceux, v. nr. Hastings, Sussex, **Eng.;** cas.; frmr. site of Royal Greenwich Observatory.

Hertford, co. t., East Herts., **Eng.;** on R. Lea, 32 km N of London; pharmaceutics, flour milling, rolling stock, diesels, brewing; p. (1991) 21,665.

Hertfordshire, non-met. co., **Eng.;** borders Greater London on S.; ch. ctr. St. Albans; drained by Rs. Thames and Lea; intensive agr., lt. inds.; new ts. Welwyn, Stevenage, Hatfield, Hemel Hempstead; p. (1995) 1,011,200.

's-Hertogenbosch, t., **Neth.;** on Rs. Dommel and Aa; cap. of N. Brabant prov.; cath.; cattle mkt.; industl. development; p. (1994) 95,448 (t.), 197,888 (met. a.).

Hertsmere, l. gov. dist., Herts., **Eng.;** a. close to London, inc. Bushey, Elstree and Potters Bar; p. (1995) 94,800.

Hesse, *Land*, **Germany;** part of former Prussian prov. Hesse-Nassau; mainly upland; inds. at Frankfurt, Kassel, Darmstadt; wine produced along Rhine valley; cap. Wiesbaden; tourism; a. 21,103 km²; p. (1992) 5,837,000.

Hetch Hetchy Dam, Cal., **USA;** on R. Toulumne upstream from San Joaquin R.; ch. source of irrigation for middle San Joaquin valley; supplies water and generating power to San Francisco.

Hetton, t., Tyne and Wear, **Eng.;** 8 km N.E. of Durham; coal-mng. dist.; p. (1991) 13,538.

Hexham, mkt. t., Tynedale, Northumberland, **Eng.;** on R. Tyne, 32 km W. of Newcastle; priory; p. (1991) 11,008.

Heysham. *See* Morecambe and Heysham.

Heywood, t., Gtr. Manchester, **Eng.;** 5 km E. of Bury; chemicals, engin.; p. (1991) 29,286.

Hialeah, t., Fla., **USA;** sub. of Miami; racecourse; p. (1990) 145,254.

Hidalgo, st., central **Mexico;** mtnous. with fertile valleys in S. and W.; cap. Pachuca; mng. (silver, gold, copper, lead, iron, sulphur); maguey (type of lily), tobacco, cotton, coffee; a. 20,868 km²; p. (1990) 1,880,632.

Higashiosaka, c., **Japan;** E. of Osaka; formed from amalgamation of Fuse, Kawachi, Hiraoka and many sm. ts.; p. (1990) 518,251.

Higham Ferrers, mkt. t., East Northants, **Eng.;** 5 km E. of Wellingborough; footwear and leather dressing; p. (1991) 5,345.

Highgate, residtl. dist., N. London, **Eng.;** hilltop v. in bor. of Haringey.

Highland Park, t., Mich., **USA;** sub. of Detroit; grew up with expansion of motor-car ind.; p. (1980) 27,909.

Highland, N. Scot., unit. auth. created in 1996 from former Region and part of Strathclyde; inc. I. of Skye and Inner Hebrides; rugged mtns. inland; p.

concentrated around cst.; off-shore oil development; stock raising, forestry, tourism; p. (1995) 208,300.

High Peak, l. gov. dist., Derbys., **Eng.;** a. of Pennines inc. New Mills, Glossop, Whaley Bridge and Buxton; p. (1995) 87,900.

High Point, t., N.C., **USA;** furniture ctr., hosiery; p. (1980) 63,808.

High Willhays, hgst. summit, Dartmoor, Devon, **Eng.;** 621 m.

High Wycombe, t., Bucks., **Eng.;** 13 km N. of Maidenhead; furniture, paper-mkg., egg processing; in London commuter belt; p. (1991) 71,718.

Hildesheim, t., Lower Saxony, **Germany;** at foot of Harz mtns.; cath.; machin., farm implements, textiles, ceramics; p. (1990) 105,400.

Hillah, Al, mkt. t., Iraq; on R. Euphrates; nr. anc. Babylon; food tr. rugs, leather; p. (1985) 215,249.

Hillerød, t., **Denmark;** admin. ctr. of Frederiksborg prov.; p. (1990) 33,388.

Hillingdon, outer bor. Greater London, **Eng.;** comprising Hayes and Harlington, Ruislip and Northwood Yiewsley, W. Drayton, and Uxbridge; p. (1995) 245,300.

Hilo, t., **Hawaii;** pt. of entry and main tr. and shipping ctr. of I.; tourism; Mauna Loa volcano nearby; p. (1980) 35,269.

Hilversum, t., **Neth.;** nr. Utrecht; radio broadcasting ctr.; noteworthy modern architecture; p. (1994) 84,213 (t.), 102,369 (met. a.).

Himachal Pradesh, st., N.W. **India;** bounded by Tibet on E.; forested mtns., cultivated valleys; cap. Simla; a. 56,019 km²; p. (1991) 5,170,877.

Himalayas, vast chain of mtns. along N. border of India, between the Indus and Brahamaputra Rs., and lying in Pakistan, India, Nepal, Sikkim, Bhutan, and China; made up of several parallel-ranges inc. the Siwaliks, the Hindu Kush, and the Karakorams; crossed by passes, mainly in W.; 2,560 km long; hgst. peak Mt. Everest, 8,854 m.

Himeji, c., S. Honshu, **Japan;** mkt. ctr. on shore of Inland Sea, 48 km W. of Kobe; iron and steel ind., heavy engin.; oil refining; p. (1990) 454,360.

Hinckley, mkt. t., Leics., **Eng.;** hosiery, cardboard boxes, dye-wks., engin.; with Market Bosworth forms l. gov. dist. of **Hinckley and Bosworth;** p. (1995) 97,500 (dist.), (1991) 40,608 (t.).

Hindenburg. *See* Zabrze.

Hindhead, t. and hill common, Surrey, nr. Haslemere, **Eng.;** p. (1991) 7,473 (t.).

Hindiya Barrage, dam, Iraq; across R. Euphrates, 48 km above Al Hillah; provides flood control and irrigation in a. between Shatt al Hillah and R. Euphrates.

Hindley, t., Gtr. Manchester, **Eng.;** 3 km S.E. of Wigan; paint, knitwear, rubber, asbestos; p. (1991) 22,581.

Hindu Kush, mtn. range, mainly in N.E. **Afghanistan;** hgst. peak Tirich Mir (7,755 m) in Chitral dist., **Pakistan;** Salang tunnel (opened 1964) with 2-lane motor highway cuts H.K. at height of 3,300 m, runs 240 m below mtn. top, 3·2 km.

Hindustan, former name of part of N. **India** between Himalayas and Vindhya ranges.

Hinkley Point, Somerset, **Eng.;** two nuclear power-sta., one Magnox, one advanced gas-cooled reactor.

Hirfanli Dam, project on R. Kizilirmak, 144 km S.E. Ankara, **Turkey.**

Hirosaki, c., Honshu, **Japan;** mkt., lacquer-ware; cas.; p. (1990) 174,710.

Hiroshima, c., S.W. Honshu, **Japan;** on delta of Ota R.; first c. to be destroyed by atomic bomb (6 Aug. 1945); since rebuilt; motor vehicles, shipbldg.; p. (1990) 1,085,705.

Hirschberg. *See* Jelenia Góra.

Hispaniola, second lgst. I. of **W.I.;** lies between Cuba and Puerto Rico; divided between Haiti (Fr.-speaking) and Dominican Rep. (Spanish-speaking); complex relief, climate, and vegetation, but strong cultural differences make international bdy. a sharp divide; a. 76,498 km².

Hitchin, t., North Herts., **Eng.;** in gap through Chiltern Hills, 56 km N. of London; lt. engin., tanning, chemicals, distilling; mkt.; p. (1991) 32,221.

Hjälmaren Lake, central **Sweden;** drained into L. Malaren by Esk R.; linked by canal to Arboga; a. 474 km².

Hjörring, c., Jutland, N. **Denmark;** biscuit and clothing wks.; p. (1990) 34,558.

Hobart, cap. and ch. pt. of Tasmania, **Australia;** on R. Derwent; univ.; fruit exp.; mostly light inds.; zinc; cadmium, superphosphates, textiles; p. (1993) 193,200.

Hoboken, t., Antwerp, **Belgium**; shipbldg.; refractory metals; p. (1981) 34,563.

Hoboken, t., N.J., **USA**; on Hudson R. above Jersey City, opp. N.Y. to which it is linked by subway and ferry; pt. for ocean commerce; industl. ctr.; p. (1990) 33,397.

Ho Chi-minh City (Saigon), c., spt., **Vietnam**; former cap. of S. Vietnam; on Saigon R. to E. of Mekong Delta; tree-lined boulevards; cath., univ., modern airport; comm. ctr.; exp. rice, rubber; food processing; p. declining rapidly since reunification of Vietnam; p. (1992) 4 m (inc. Cholon).

Höchst, t., Hesse, **Germany**; industl. sub. of Frankfurt-on-Main; site of German chemical ind.

Hochstetter, mtn., S.I., **N.Z.**; in Southern Alps; alt. 3,416 m.

Hoddesdon, t., Herts., **Eng.**; in Lea valley, 6 km S. of Ware; food processing; p. (1991) 36,883.

Hodeida (Al Hudaydah), t., **Yemen**, on Red Sea; pt. and naval base; exp. dates, hides, coffee; p. (1987) 155,110.

Hódmezővásárhely, t., S.E. **Hungary**; wheat, fruit, tobacco, cattle; natural gas pipeline from Szeged; p. (1997) 50,000.

Hof, t., Bavaria, **Germany**; on R. Saale; textiles, iron, machin., porcelain, glass, brewing; p. (1986) 50,600.

Hofei or **Hefei**, c., cap. of Anhui prov., **China**; rice-growing a.; cotton and silk, iron and steel; p. (1983) 830,000.

Hoffman, mtn. peak of the Sierra Nevada, Cal., **USA**; alt. 2,473 m.

Hofuf (Al Hufuf), t., El Hasa, **Saudi Arabia**; dates, wheat, fruit; textiles, brass- and copper-ware; oil-fields nearby; p. (1986) 101,271.

Hog's Back, Surrey, **Eng.**; steep chalk ridge; alt. 154 m.

Hohenstein-Ernstal, t., Saxony, **Germany**; textiles, metal gds.; p. (1989) 16,707.

Hohe Tauern, Alpine range, Tyrol, **Austria**; rugged crystalline rocks; highest point Gross Glockner, 3,801 m; traversed by rly. tunnel 8 km long.

Hohhot (Huhehot), c., Nei Mongol (Inner Mongolia), **China**; diesel engines; new woollen mill; p. (1984) 778,000.

Hoihow. See **Haikou.**

Hokkaido, lge. I., **Japan**, N. of Honshu; colder than other Is.; less dense p.; temperate agr.; skiing; tunnel link with Honshu to aid economic development; a. 88,775 km²; p. of pref. (1990) 5,643,647.

Holbaek, t., Sjaelland, **Denmark**; W. of Copenhagen; engin. and motor wks.; p. (1990) 31,151.

Holbeach, mkt. t., S. Lincs., **Eng.**; in Fens, 11 km E. of Spalding; brewing; ctr. of bulb-growing dist.; p. (1991) 6,088.

Holborn. See **Camden.**

Holderness, peninsula, E. Riding of Yorks., **Eng.**; between R. Humber and N. Sea; agr.

Holguin, t., N.E. **Cuba**; comm. ctr.; sugar, tobacco, coffee, cattle; exps. handled by pt. Gibara; p. (1990) 228,052, 927,700 (dep).

Holland. See **Netherlands.**

Holland, N. See **Noord Holland.**

Holland, Parts of. See **Lincolnshire.**

Holland, S. See **Zuid Holland.**

Hollandia, former name of cap. W. Irian, **Indonesia**; renamed Kota Baru by Indonesia, then Sukarnapura, now Djajapura.

Holloman, t., N.M., **USA**; atomic and space research ctr.; site of 1st. man-made atomic explosion.

Hollywood, t., Fla., **USA**; seaside resort on Atl. cst.; cement, furniture; p. (1990) 121,697; part of Fort Lauderdale met. a.

Hollywood, sub. of Los Angeles, Cal., **USA**; ctr. of film industry.

Holmesdale, Vale of, Kent, E. Surrey, **Eng.**; extends along foot of N. Downs escarpment; drained by Rs. Mole, Darent, Medway, Len, Stour; heavy clay soils; ch. ts. Dorking, Reigate, Sevenoaks, Maidstone, Ashford, which have grown up in gaps through hills to N. and S. of Vale; length 96 km, average width 2 km.

Holmfirth, t., West Yorks., **Eng.**; 8 km S. of Huddersfield, textiles, engin.; p. (1991) 21,979.

Holt, mkt. t., N. Norfolk, **Eng.**; 8 km S.W. of Sheringham; 16th-cent. school; p. (1991) 2,972.

Holt, t., Wrexham, **Wales**; on R. Dee, 11 km S. of Chester; cas. ruins.

Holyhead, spt., Isle of Anglesey, **Wales**; on Holyhead I.; mail packet sta. for Ireland; lt. engin., woodwkg., clocks; site for aluminium smelter; p. (1991) 11,796.

Holy I. (**Lindisfarne**), off cst. of Northumberland, **Eng.**

Holy I., Scot., in F. of Clyde, nr. I. of Arran.

Holy I., off cst. of Isle of Anglesey, **Wales.**

Holyoke, t., Mass., **USA**; on Connecticut R., above Springfield; paper, machin.; p. (1980) 44,678.

Holywell, mkt. t., Flintshire, N. **Wales**; woollen, rayon and paper inds.; p. (1991) 7,531.

Holywood, spt., North Down, **N. Ireland**; on S. shore of Belfast Lough; seaside resort; p. (1991) 9,252.

Homburg (Bad Homburg), c., Hesse, **Germany**; famous spa; p. (1986) 51,100.

Home Counties, term applied to the geographical counties adjoining London, *i.e.*, Middlesex, Surrey, Essex, and Kent; sometimes Hertfordshire, Buckinghamshire, and Berkshire are included, and occasionally Sussex.

Homs, t., **W. Syria**; on R. Orontes in fertile plain; anc. Emesa; steel plants, fertilisers, lt. inds.; pipeline from Kirkūk oil fields; p. (1993) 537,000.

Honan. See **Henan.**

Honda, old Spanish t., **Colombia**; on Magdalena R., at rapids; former comm. ctr.

Honduras, rep., straddles Central American isthmus with longest cst. on Caribbean; comprises 18 deps. inc. offshore Bay Is.; coastal lowlands hot and humid, more temperate in interior highlands which rise to over 2,000 m; agr. basis of economy, especially American-owned banana plantations; bananas almost half exp.; some mng.; rlys. oriented to banana-producing areas to facilitate exp.; nationalised forests; land reform; devastated in 1998 hurricane; cap. Tegucigalpa; 5 airports.; a. 111,958 km², p. (1994) 5,294,000.

Honduras, British. See **Belize.**

Hong Kong, former Brit. Crown Col., S.E. cst. **China**, comprises Hong Kong I., Kowloon peninsula and New Territories; road and rail tunnels link H.K. with Kowloon; deepwater harbour of Victoria; industl. development rapid since second world war yet few natural resources; exp. clothing, toys, electronics, watches; dense p. increased by immigration from China and Vietnam; returned to Chinese sovereignty 1 July 1997 with status of special admin. reg.; capitalist system to remain for 50 years; new airport (Chep Lap Kok) opened, July 1998; a. 1,068 km², p. (1995) 6,189,800.

Honiara, t., cap. of **Solomon Is.**; on Guadalcanal I.; p. (1989) 33,749.

Honiton, t., East Devon, **Eng.**; on R. Otter, 26 km E. of Exeter; mkt.; trout-fishing; formerly lace making; p. (1991) 7,859.

Honolulu, c., cap. of **Hawaii**; on Oahu I.; social and comm. ctr. and ch. pt. of archipelago; gd harbour; univ.; airport; fruit-canning, sugar-processing; tourism; p. (1990) 365,272 (c.), 836,000 (met. a.).

Honshu, lgst. I. of **Japan**; contains most of p. along E. cst. in 320 km industl. belt; Seikan tunnel links I. to Hokkaido; a. 230,300 km²; p. (1990) 99,254,000.

Hoogeveen, t., Drenthe, **Neth.**; fruit- and vegetable-canning; p. (1993) 46,524.

Hooghly, R., arm of Ganges R., **India**; flows into Bay of Bengal; used in jute-milling and navigable as far as Calcutta; 256 km long.

Hooghly Chinsura, t., W. Bengal, **India**; on Hooghly R.; rice-milling; p. (1991) 151,806 (part of Calcutta met. a.).

Hook of Holland (Hoek van Holland), spt., **Neth.**; port with ferry connections to Harwich, Eng.

Hoorn, old fishing t., N. Holland, **Neth.**; on IJsselmeer, 39 km N. of Amsterdam; cattle mkts.; birthplace of Jan P. Coen, founder of Batavia; p. (1994) 60,979.

Hoover Dam, USA; on Colorado R.; used for irrigation (parts of Cal., Arizona, and Mexico), flood control and hydroelectric power; Lake Mead, 184 km long, 2–13 km wide, one of world's lgst. man-made Ls.

Hopeh. See **Hebei.**

Horbury, t., West Yorks., **Eng.**; nr. Wakefield; p. (1991) 9,186.

Horeb. See **Sinai.**

Hormuz, Strait of, between Persian G. and G. of Oman.

Horncastle, mkt. t., E. Lindsey, Lincs., **Eng.**; at confluence of Rs. Bain and Waring at foot of Lincoln Wolds; mkt.; vegetable-processing; p. (1991) 4,994.

Hornsea, t., E. Riding of Yorks., **Eng.**; on E. cst., N.E. of Hull; seaside resort; p. (1991) 7,573.

Hornsey. *See* Haringey.

Horsens, t., Denmark, E. Jutland; on inlet of Kattegat; industl. and comm. ctr.; p. (1990) 55,210.

Horsforth, t., West Yorks., Eng.; in Aire valley N.W. of Leeds; cloth, tanning, lt. engin.; p. (1991) 18,593.

Horsham, t., Victoria, Australia; on R. Wimmera; pastoral, dairying and agr. dist.; p. (1991) 12,552.

Horsham, t., l. gov. dist., West Sussex, Eng.; on R. Arun at W. end of forested dist. of the High Weald; agr., timber, engin., chemicals; Shelley's birthplace; impt. commuting centre; p. (1995) 116,200 (dist.), (1991) 42,552 (t.).

Horta, t., cap. of H. dist., Azores; on Fayal I.; excellent harbour and base for transatlantic flights; p. (1981) 6,910.

Horten, spt., Norway; nr. Oslo; naval base; shipbldg., mftg. inds.; p. (1990) 16,043.

Horton, R., N.W. Terr., Canada; flows into Beaufort Sea, Arctic Oc.; reindeer reserve along cst.

Horwich, t., Gtr. Manchester, Eng.; on W. edge of Rossendale Fells, N.W. of Bolton; rly. t.; engin.; rly. workshops closed (1983); p. (1991) 18,017.

Hospitalet de Llobregat, t., Spain; sub. of Barcelona, in Llobregat valley; p. (1981) 294,033.

Hotan (Khotan), c., S.W. Xinjiang, China; in fertile H. oasis at base of Kunlun Shan; silk, carpets, jade-ware; on anc. Silk Road; early ctr. of Buddhism; visited by Marco Polo 1274.

Hot Springs, c., Ark., USA; in Ouachita mtns. S.W. of Little Rock; Nat. Park since 1832; health resort; p. (1990) 32,462.

Houghton-le-Spring, t., Tyne and Wear, Eng.; S.W. of Sunderland; former coal mng.; p. (1991) 35,100.

Hounslow, outer bor., Greater London, Eng.; inc. former bors. of Brentford and Chiswick, Heston and Isleworth, Feltham and Hounslow; rubber goods; p. (1995) 204,000.

Housatonic, R., W. Mass., Conn., USA; falls attracted early Puritan settlement and industrialisation; dairy farming; 240 km long.

Houston, c., spt., S. Texas, USA; on Galveston Bay; gr. pt., lgst. c. of S.; univ.; oil refineries, oilfield machin., steel, chemicals, paper, processing, milling and assembling plants; NASA's manned space flight ctr. and lunar science institute; p. (1990) 1,630,553 (c.), 3,301,937 (met. a.).

Houston Ship Canal, Texas, USA; links Houston to head of shallow Galveston Bay and continues through bay to deep water; provides site for heavy inds.; opened 1915; total length 72 km.

Hove, t., Brighton and Hove, Eng.; on S. cst., contiguous with Brighton; residtl.; holiday resort; p. (1991) 67,602.

Howrah, c., W. Bengal, India; on W. bank of Hooghly R., in met. a. of Calcutta; p. (1981) 744,429.

Hoy, I., Orkney Is., Scot.; lofty cliffs along W. cst.; separated from Mainland I. by Sound of Hoy; Old Man of Hoy rock 137 m high; p. (1991) 447.

Hoylake, t., Wirral, Merseyside, Eng.; on N. cst. of Wirral peninsula; residtl.; golf course; p. (1991) 25,554.

Hradec Králové, t., Czech Rep.; at confluence of Elbe (Labe) and Orlice Rs.; industl. ctr.; mnfs. machin., precision instruments; 14th-cent. cath. and town hall; p. (1990) 101,000.

Hsinchu, c., co., N.W. Taiwan; p. (1995) 340,149 (c.), 340,149.

Huainan (Hwainan), c., Anhui prov., central China; ctr. of China's ch. coal mng. region; p. (1992) 1,200,000.

Huai He (Hwai-ho), R., China; flows E. between N. China plain and lower Chang Jiang; subject to disastrous floods and changes of course; since 1950 flood control and irrigation canal to sea; 1,224 km long.

Huamanga. *See* Ayacucho.

Huambo. *See* Nova Lisboa.

Huancayo, t., cap. of Junin dep., Peru; in high valley of Andes, *c.* 3,300 m; textiles; p. (1993) 258,209.

Huang Hai (Hwang-hai or Yellow Sea), arm of Pac. Oc. between Korea and China; branches into Gs. of Bo Hai and Liaotung; shallow sea rapidly infilling; named after yellow silt from Huang He; length 960 km, greatest width 640 km.

Huang He (Hwang Ho), R., China; the Yellow R., rises in Kunlun Shan; flows *c.* 4,800 km. into G. of Bo Hai; cuts through Shaanxi in a deep gorge;

filled with yellow silt (loess) from this a.; floods frequently and changes course (once entered sea S. of Shandong); in lower part forms fertile plain; now part of multipurpose scheme for hydro-electric power, irrigation and flood control; lgst. dam in China opened at Liuchia in 1975; flow now (1999) reduced to a trickle in parts; threat of major catastrophe; 4,640 km long.

Huangshi (Hwangshih), c., Hubei prov., China; main iron and steel ctr. of central China, built since 1950; p. (1984) 435,200.

Huarás or Huaráz, cap. of Ancash dep., Peru; on Santa R., *c.* 3,000 m; mainly agr., some mng.; avalanche 1941 killed 6,000 inhabitants; p. (1993) 66,888 (predominantly Indian).

Huascarán, extinct volcano, Peruvian Andes, nr. Huarás, 6,773 m high; avalanche 1970 killed 20,000 people.

Hua Shan (Tsinling Shan), mtn. range, central China; rises to over 1,830 m; watershed between Huang He and Chang Jiang basins; impt. climatic divide between temperate N. China and tropical S. China.

Hubei (Hupeh), prov., central China; N. of the Chang Jiang; many Ls. and Rs.; rice, wheat, cotton; iron ores; Wuhan is major industl. ctr. of prov. and central China; cap. Wuhan; a. 186,363 km²; p. (1990) 54,760,000.

Hubli, c., Karnataka, India; E. of Goa; textiles, rly. engin.; p. (1991) 648,000.

Hucknall, t., Ashfield, Nottingham, Eng.; hosiery, coal; p. (1991) 29,160.

Huddersfield, t., West Yorks., Eng.; on edge of Pennines, 16 km S. of Bradford; wool, textiles, chemicals, engin.; p. (1991) 143,726.

Hudson, R., N.Y., USA; flows from Adirondacks to N.Y. harbour; with valley of Mohawk R. makes gr. highway of tr. between Great Ls. and N.Y.; scenic; hydroelec. power; 560 km long.

Hudson Bay, gr. inland sea, Canada; communicates by Hudson Strait with Davis Strait (Atl. Oc.); ice-free mid-July to Oct.; salmon, cod; a. 1,398,600 km².

Hué, c., Vietnam; on Hué R., 16 km from S. China Sea; pt. and tr. ctr.; former cap. of Annam; royal palace; p. (1989) 211,085.

Huelva, coastal prov., S.W. Spain; copper mng., vine- and olive-growing, stock-raising, fisheries, brandy distilling; a. 10,117 km²; p. (1991) 441,778.

Huelva, c., cap. of Huelva prov., Spain; pt. on G. of Cadiz; oil refining, chemicals, food processing; exp. of minerals from nearby Rio Tinto; p. (1991) 143,576.

Huesca, c., cap. of H. prov., N.E. Spain; at foot of Pyrenees on R. Isuela; cath.; agr. ctr.; wine and timber tr. with France; p. (1987) 40,949, (1991) 218, 253 (prov.).

Hugh Town, cap. of the Scilly Isles, Eng.; on St. Mary's I.

Huhehot. *See* Hohhot.

Hula L. *See* Waters of Merom.

Hull, t., S.W. Quebec, Canada; within met. a. of Ottawa; sawmills, paper; p. (1991) 60,707.

Hull or Kingston upon Hull, c., unit. auth. of Kingston upon Hull created in 1996, formerly part of Humberside, Eng.; major spt. of UK; at influx of R. Hull in estuary of Humber; originally laid out by Edward I; lge. docks; premier distant water fishing pt.; inds. inc. oil-extracting, flour milling, sawmilling, chemicals, engin.; univ.; p. (1995) 268,600 (unit. auth.), (1991) 310,636 (c.).

Humber, estuary of Rs. Ouse and Trent, Eng.; fine waterway; 2–13 km wide, 61 km long; Humber bridge opened (1981), longest single span suspension bridge in Britain.

Humboldt, R., N. Nevada, USA; rises in Ruby Mtns., flows for 480 km before disappearing by evaporation and percolation; impt. 19th cent. routeway.

Humboldt Bay, inlet, Cal., USA; nuclear experimental breeder reactor.

Humboldt Current. *See* Peru Current.

Hume Lake, reservoir, N.S.W., Australia; formed by dam where R. Murray leaves Gr. Dividing Range; supplies water for irrigation in upper Riverina dist.; capacity *c.* 113 million m³.

Hunan, prov., central China; S. of the Chang Jiang; hilly in S. and W.; rice, wheat, beans; rich mineral resources, inc. mercury, tin, tungsten; cap. Changsha; Mao Tse-tung came from Hunan peasant stock; a. 205,589 km²; p. (1990) 54,760,000.

Hunedoara, dist., Romania; iron mining, cap. Deva; a. 7,016 km²; p. (1992) 547,993.

Hungary, rep., E. Europe; bounded by Ukraine, Slovakia, Romania, Yugoslavia, and Austria; lies in basin of middle Danube (Duna), with plain in E. and Carpathian mtns. in W.; mainly agr.; exp. meat, fruit, vegetables to EU; inds. increasingly impt. and now account for over 50 per cent of income; applying for EU and NATO membership; cap. Budapest; a. 93,012 km², p. (1997) 10,174,000.

Hunsrück (dog's back), forested highlands, Rhineland–Palatinate, **Germany**; between Mosel and Nahe Rs.; vineyards on S. slopes; hgst. point 816 m.

Hunstanton, t., West Norfolk, **Eng.**; S.E. shore of Wash; seaside resort; p. (1991) 4,634.

Hunter, R., N.S.W., **Australia**; rises in Liverpool range of Gr. Dividing Range, flows S. and E. into Tasman Sea at Newcastle; world famous grape growing and wine producing reg.; coal exp.; c. 400 km long; p. (1992) 539,100 (dist.).

Hunterston, N. Ayrshire, **Scot.**; civil nuclear power sta.; integrated iron and steel wks., engin. of oil platforms and oil terminal planned.

Huntingdon, t. located in the historic co. of **Huntingdonshire,** E. **Eng.**, now l. gov. dist. within Cambs. on R. Ouse; expanded t.; canning, engin., processed rubber, confectionery; birthplace of Cromwell and home of the poet Cowper; p. (1995) 149,600 (dist.), (1991) 15,575 (t.).

Huntington, c., W. Va., **USA**; on Ohio R.; R. pt. comm. ctr.; rly. wks., steel; p. (1990) 313,000 (met. a. with Ashland).

Huntly, burgh, Aberdeenshire, **Scot.**; at confluence of Rs. Bogie and Deveron; agr. mkt.; angling resort; p. (1991) 4,230.

Huntsville, c., Ala., **USA**; textiles; rocket research ctr.; p. (1990) 159,789 (c.), 238,912 (met. a.).

Hupeh. See Hubei.

Huron, L., between **Canada** and **USA**; one of the Gr. Ls. of the St. Lawrence basin; a. 59,596 km²; 330 km long.

Husum, spt., Schleswig-Holstein, **Germany**; on N. Sea cst.; cattle mkt.; p. (1986) 23,800.

Hutchinson, t., Kan., **USA**; salt-mng., meat-packing, flour milling, oil refining; p. (1980) 40,284.

Huyton with Roby, Knowsley, Merseyside, **Eng.**; sub. of Liverpool; p. (1991) 56,500.

Hwai-ho. See Huai He.

Hwainan. See Huainan.

Hwang-hai. See Huang Hai.

Hwang-ho. See Huang He.

Hwangshih. See Huangshi.

Hyde, t., Tameside, Gtr. Manchester, **Eng.**; on R. Tame, 11 km S.E. of Manchester; paints, chemicals, food-processing, tobacco, rubber; p. (1991) 30,666.

Hyderabad, ch. c., Andhra Pradesh, **India**; on R. Musi; walled t. and impt. comm. ctr.; univ., nuclear fuel fabrication plant; p. (1991) 3,146,000.

Hyderabad, c., **Pakistan**; 5 km W. of Indus; 144 km N.E. of Karachi; old cap. of Sind; univ.; noted for silk, gold and silver embroidery; now varied mnfs.; dam at nearby Kotri; p. (1981) 795,000.

Hyndburn, l. gov. dist., Lancs., **Eng.**; inc. Colne Valley ts. of Accrington, Great Harwood, Rishton, Clayton-le-Moors, Church and Oswaldtwistle; p. (1995) 80,200.

Hythe, t., Shepway, Kent, **Eng.**; on S. cst., 5 km W. of Folkestone; Cinque pt.; military canal passing through t., used for boating; p. (1991) 18,538.

I

Iasi (Jassy), c., **Romania**; former cap. of Moldavia; in fertile agr. region; univ., cath.; cultural ctr.; textiles, plastics, chems.; p. (1992) 342,994.

Ibadan, c., cap. Oyo st.; S.W. **Nigeria**; univ.; ctr. of rich agr. a., between the savannah and forest regions; p. mainly Yoruba; crafts, small inds.; p. (1992) 1,295,000.

Ibagué, c., cap. of Tolima dep., **Colombia**; transport ctr.; cotton, tobacco, sugar, leather gds.; p. (1992) 334,078.

Ibarra, t., **Ecuador**; alt. 2,226 m at foot of Imbabura volcano; on Pan-American highway; p. (1990) 80,991.

Iberian Peninsula, S.W. peninsula of Europe; containing sts. of **Spain** and **Portugal**; lge. a. of high tableland; interior isolation and regionalism; historical and contemporary importance for minerals; a. 593,250 km².

Ibiza. I., Balearic gr. in W. **Mediterranean**; Spanish, cath., tourism.

Iceland, rep., N. Atl. Oc.; volcanic I. with ice-covered plateaux; glacier fields cover 13,000 km²; only 1 per cent of a. cultivated; cold climate; hot house cultivation using thermal springs; economy dependent on fishing and fish-processing inds.; high standard of living; tourism increasingly impt.; 7 admin. dists.; cap. Reykjavik; a. 102,846 km²; p. (1994) 266,783.

Ichang. See Yichang.

Ichinomiya, c., S.E. Honshu, **Japan**; anc. Shinto shrine; textiles, pottery; p. (1990) 262,434.

Ichow. See Lin-i.

Icknield Way, prehistoric route running from near Avebury, Wilts., **Eng.**; along the Berkshire Downs, Chilterns and East Anglian Heights into Norfolk, crossing the Thames at Streatley.

Idaho, st., **USA**; Gem State; admitted to Union 1890; St. flower Syringa, St. bird Mountain Bluebird; one of the Rocky Mtn. sts.; rich in minerals; agr. mainly in irrigated Snake R. valley; cap. Boise; a. 216,413 km²; p. (1990) 1,006,749.

Idaho Falls, c., Idaho, **USA**; on Snake R.; food-processing, lumbering; silver, lead, and gold mines nearby; nuclear experimental breeder reactor; p. (1980) 39,590.

Ida Mountains, range, N.W. **Turkey**; volcanic, hot springs; max. alt. Mount Gargarus, 1,768 m.

Idle, t., West Yorks., **Eng.**; in Aire valley, 5 km N. of Bradford; woollens.

Ife, t., **Nigeria**; ctr. of the cacao tr.; univ.; p. (1992) 268,600.

Ifni, enclave, S. **Morocco**; ceded by Spain to Morocco (1969); cap. Sidi Ifni; a. 1,500 km².

Igarka, sm. t., Siberia, **Russia**; on R. Yenisey, 640 km from its mouth; graphite plant, nickel-mines, lumber mills.

Iglesias, t., Sardinia, **Italy**; N.W. of Cagliari; mng. for lead, pyrites, zinc; p. (1981) 30,117.

Iguaçu, R., trib. of Paraná; mostly in Brazil; famous falls where Argentina, Brazil, and Paraguay meet, height 20 m higher than Niagara; hydroelec. power potential.

Ijmuiden, c., N. Holland, **Neth.**; on cst. at mouth of N. Sea canal; fishing; gasification plant, major iron and steel plant.

Ijsselmeer (Lake Ijssel), freshwater reservoir, **Neth.**; formerly Zuider Zee; separated from N. Sea by Wieringen–Friesland Barrage; active land reclamation in progress; Wieringermeer drained 1930, N.E. Polder 1942, E. Flevoland 1957, S. Flevoland 1968, Markerwaard to remain undrained; when reclamation complete a. of Neth. will have increased by some 6 per cent.; ch. c. on inlet (IJ) Amsterdam.

Ilchester, t., Somerset, **Eng.**; on R. Yeo; N.W. of Yeovil; birthplace of Roger Bacon; p. (1991) 1,733.

Ilebo, t. **Congo**; rlwy. terminus on Kasai R.

Ile-de-France, region, **France**; inc. deps. Paris, Seine-et-Marne, Yvelines, Essonne, Hauts-de-Seine, Seine-Saint-Denis, Val-de-Marne, Val-d'Oise; the most populous region of France, centred on Paris; p. (1990) 10,660,600

Îles d'Hyères, I. gr., **France**; in Mediterranean off Toulon; tourism.

Ilesha, t., **Nigeria**; tr. ctr., cotton weaving; p. (1992) 342,400.

Ilford. See Redbridge.

Ilfracombe, t., North Devon, **Eng.**; sm. pt. on cst. of Bristol Channel; seaside resort; p. (1991) 10,429.

Ilhéus, spt., Bahia, **Brazil**; exp. cacao, timber; losing tr. to lge. pts.; p. (1985) 146,100.

Ili, R., **Central Asia**; rises in Tienshan, China, and flows into L. Balkhash in Russia.; new t. of I. at site of hydroelec. sta.; c. 1,200 km long.

Iligan, c., Mindanao, **Philippines**; integrated steel mill; cement; p. (1995) 273,000.

Ilkeston, t., Erewash, Derbys., **Eng.**; W. of Nottingham, iron, engin., locknit fabrics, needles, plastics; p. (1991) 35,134.

Ilkley, t., spa, West Yorks., **Eng.**; on R. Wharfe, N.W. of Leeds; local mkt.; p. (1991) 13,530.

Illawara, dist., N.S.W., **Australia**; forming belt of land between S. tableland and cst.; very fertile; dairy farming; coal seams; ch. ts., Kiama, Wollongong, Bulli, Gerringong; p. (1992) 355,100.

Ille-et-Vilaine, dep., N.W. **France**; on English Channel; a. 6,990 km²; agr.; cap. Rennes;

p. (1990) 798,700.

Illimani, one of the high peaks of the Cordillera Real, Andes, **Bolivia**, 6,461 m, E. of La Paz.

Illinois, st., **USA**; Prairie State; admitted to Union 1818; St. flower Native Violet; St. bird Cardinal; in Middle West; named after its principal R., a lge. trib. of Mississippi; many Rs.; cap. Springfield, metropolis Chicago; rich agr.; fuel and mineral resources; major coal-mng. st.; inds. inc. meat-processing, farm implements; a. 146,076 km²; p. (1990) 11,430,602.

Illinois, R., Ill., **USA**; glacial valley; long history of settlement; impt. routeway; 437 km long.

Illyria, region stretching along Adriatic Sea from Trieste in N. to **Albania** in S. and inland as far as Rs. Danube and Morava.

Ilmen, L., **Russia**; nr. Novgorod; drained by Volkhov R. into L. Ladoga; a. 932 km²; fisheries.

Ilminster, t., Somerset, **Eng.**; 16 km S.E. of Taunton; cutstone, concrete, collars, radio valves; p. (1991) 4,162.

Iloilo, c., cap. of I. prov., Panay, **Philippines**; ctr. of rly. network; impt. pt. exp. sugar, rice, copra, hemp; p. (1995) 334,000.

Ilorin, t., N. **Nigeria**; on Lagos–Kano rly.; agr. and caravan ctr.; govt. sugar-growing scheme at Bacita; p. (1992) 430,600.

Imabari, t., spt., N.W. Shikoku, **Japan**; on shore of Indian Sea; mnfs. cotton textiles, paper, canned fruits; p. (1990) 123,114.

Imatra, t., Kymi, **Finland**; hydroelec. power sta. supplies S. Finland; electro-metallurgy; p. (1993) 32,558.

Imbroz. *See* **Gökçeada I.**

Immingham, pt., N.E. Lincs., **Eng.**; on the Humber, N.W. of Grimsby; lge. docks; new deep-sea oil and coal terminals; chemical engin., refinery nearby at Killingholme; p. (1991) 12,278.

Imola, t., **Italy**; S.E. of Bologna; cath.; glass, pottery; p. (1981) 60,010.

Imperia, t., **Italy**; on G. of Genoa; sm. pt. olive-growing ctr.; resort; p. (1981) 41,609.

Imperial Valley, S. Cal., **USA**; extends 48 km S.E. from Salton Sea to Mexican bdy.; mainly below sea-level; hot, arid climate; irrigation from Colorado R. chiefly by All-American Canal nr. Yuma; total irrigated a. 405,000 ha; principal crops, fruit, dates, tomatoes, cotton, and dairy prod.

Imphal, cap. of Manipur, **India**; in rice-growing basin in hills of Assam nr. Burma bdy.; p. (1981) 156,622.

Inari L., extensive L., Lappi, **Finland**; outlet into Barents Sea; hydroelec. power; a. 1,774 km².

Ince-in-Makerfield, t., Gtr. Manchester, **Eng.**; nr. Wigan; engin.; p. (1991) 10,554.

Inchon, c., **S. Korea**; on Yellow Sea; pt. for Seoul; exp. soyabeans, rice; textile ctr., steel mill, glass, diesel engines; p. (1990) 1,818,293.

Independence, c., Mo., **USA**; E. of Kansas; oil refining; agr. machin.; p. (1990) 112,301.

India, rep., indep. st. (since 1947), S. Asia; second cty. of world by p.; 22 sts. and 9 union terrs.; peninsula bounded by Himalayas in N. extends in wide plateau to Indian Oc. in S.; most of p. concentrated in Indo-Gangetic Plain; unpredictable monsoon climate; heavy dependence on agr.; 70 per cent of p. farmers; few cash crops except cotton (the Deccan), tea (Himalayas), and jute (W. Bengal); 854 languages and dialects impede economic development; strong caste system; new inds. expanding rapidly; chems., engin. electronics; cap. New Delhi; main pts. Bombay (Mumbai), Calcutta; a. 3,268,580 km²; p. (1996) 913,200,000.

Indiana, st., **USA**; Hoosier State; admitted to Union 1816; St. flower peony; St. bird Cardinal; in Middle West, bounded by Mich., Ohio, Ill. and sep. from Ky. by Ohio R.; agr.; coal, limestone, petroleum; steel, metal prods., machin., food prod.; cap. Indianapolis; a. 93,994 km²; p. (1990) 5,544,159.

Indianapolis, c., cap. of Ind., **USA**; on White R.; univ.; rly. ctr.; meat-packing, jet engines, aircraft parts, chemicals, pharmaceutics; p. (1990) 741,952 (c.), 1,249,822 (met. a.).

Indian Ocean extends from S. of Asia and E. of Africa to the C. of Good Hope and C. Leeuwin in Australia, separated from the Pacific by the Malay Archipelago and Australia; a. 75,990,600 km².

Indigirka, R., Yakut ASSR, **Russia**; flows into Arctic Oc.; hydroelec. power; 1,760 km long.

Indo-China, S.E. Asia; federation in Fr. Union until end of hostilities July 1954; consisted of the three sts. of Vietnam, Cambodia, and Laos.

Indo-Gangetic Plain, India, **Bangladesh** and **Pakistan**; name applied to flat land created by the Indus and Ganges basins; densely populated a.

Indonesia, rep., S.E. Asia; former Neth. E. Indies; made up of many sm. Is. straddling equator for over 4,800 km; many Is. in W. volcanic and E. coral; geothermal energy supply being developed; lgst. Is. inc. Java, Sumatra, Kalimantan (S. Borneo), Sulawesi, and Irian (W. New Guinea); mostly underdeveloped except Java; intensive agr. employs 55 per cent of p.; rapidly developing oil and gas industry but falling oil revenues (70 per cent of exports); near to econ. and financial collapse, 1997; self-sufficient in rice, stored surpluses; 63 per cent p. on Java, Madura and Bali Is.; planned decentralisation to other Is.; cap. Djakarta; a. 1,907,566 km²; p. (1998) 202,000,000.

Indore, c., Madhya Pradesh, **India**; nr. valley of Narbada R.; comm. ctr.; cotton-mills; p. (1991) 1,092,000.

Indre, dep., central **France**; agr. and industl.; cap. Châteauroux; a. 6,905 km²; p. (1990) 237,500.

Indre-et-Loire, dep., central **France**; drained by Indre and Loire Rs.; vineyards, orchards; cap. Tours; a. 6,156 km²; p. (1990) 529,300.

Indus, R., **Pakistan**, rises in Tibet, flows through Kashmir, Punjab, Sind, to Arabian Sea; 5 tribs. Jhelum, Chenab, Ravi, Beas, Sutlej, form one of world's major R. systems, now used extensively to irrigate the Punjab and the Sind; impt. cotton, wheat, and sugar dist.; hydroelec. power; supported Indus valley civilisation 3000–1500 B.C.; 2,880 km long.

Ingleborough, mtn., near Settle, North Yorks., **Eng.**; underground caves, stalactites; made of limestone and millstone grit; alt. 724 m.

Inglewood, t., S. Cal., **USA**; sub. of Los Angeles; chinchilla farms; furniture, lt. engin., aircraft parts; p. (1990) 109,602.

Ingolstadt, t., Bavaria, **Germany**; on Danube, nr. Munich; cas.; machin., cars, tobacco, oil refining; pipeline from Genoa; transalpine oil pipeline from Trieste, through N.E. Italy and Austria to I.; p. (1990) 106,400.

Inhambane, spt., **Moçambique**; sugar, copra, oil-seeds, bricks, soap, tiles; p. (1980) 56,439.

Inishboffin, I., Galway, **R.o.I.**, sm. I. off Connemara; farming, fishing.

Inishmore, lgst. of Aran gr., Galway, **R.o.I.**; fishing.

Inkpen Beacon, hill, Berks., **Eng.**; highest point reached by chalk hills in Eng.; alt. 297 m.

Inland Sea, **Japan**; between Honshu on N. and Shikoku and Kyushu on S.; sheltered sea with many Is.; ch. spts. Osaka, Amagaski, Kōbe, Okayama, Hiroshima, Kure; Nat. Park; a. c. 9,500 km².

Inn, R., traversing **Switzerland**, the Tyrol, **Austria** and Bavaria; enters R. Danube at Passau; hydroelec. plants; 512 km long.

Innerleithen, burgh, Borders, **Scot.**; on R. Tweed, 8 km S.E. of Peebles; woollen cloth and knitwear; mineral springs; p. (1991) 2,515.

Inner Mongolia (Nei Mongol), Chinese aut. region, N.E. **China**; stretches along S. border of Mongolian People's Rep.; vast steppelands, sparse p.; st. farms for animal husbandry; peat beds; milk-processing; cap Hohhot; a. 1,177,518 km²; p. (1990) 21,110,000.

Innisfail, t., Queensland, **Australia**; ch. sugar-producing ctr. of Australia; p. (1981) 7,933.

Innsbruck, c., cap. of the Tyrol, W. **Austria**; on R. Inn; commands N. approach to Brenner Pass; univ.; tourism; fortfd. 12th cent.; p. (1991) 114,996.

Inowrocław, t., N. **Poland**; prov. Bydgoszcz; rock-salt. iron pyrites; agr. prod.; p. (1989) 76,497.

Insterburg. *See* **Chernyakhovsk.**

Inter-American Highway, section of Pan-American Highway system, from Mexico to Panama.

Interlaken, t., Bernese Oberland, Berne, **Switzerland**; on R. Aare between Ls. Thun and Brienz; tourist resort.

Intracoastal Waterway, **USA**; toll-free waterway along Atl. and Gulf of Mexico csts.; completed 1949 using bays, rivers and canals; 4,960 km long.

Inuvik, t., Arctic, **Canada**; above the permafrost; p. (1991) 3,206.

Inveraray, burgh, Argyll and Bute, **Scot.**; nr. head of Loch Fyne; herring fishing; p. (1991) 512.

Inverbervie, burgh, Aberdeenshire, **Scot.**; on E. cst.,

13 km S. of Stonehaven; linen; p. (1991) 1,879.

Invercargill, c., S.I., **N.Z.**; on S.E. cst.; sawmills, freezing wks.; aluminium smelter; served by Bluff Harbour; p. (1991) 56,148.

Inverclyde, unit. auth. created in 1996, formerly part of Strathclyde, W. **Scot.**; on F. of Clyde, inc. Gourock and Greenock; p. (1995) 88,690.

Inverell, t., N.S.W., **Australia**; 655 km N. of Sydney; wheat and lamb cty.; tin; p. (1981) 9,734.

Invergordon, burgh, spt., Highland, **Scot.**; on N. side of Cromarty F., 19 km N.E. of Dingwall; former naval pt.; whisky distillery; p. (1991) 3,929.

Inverkeithing, royal burgh, Fife, **Scot.**; on F. of Forth, nr. Dunfermline; shipbreaking, papermkg., quarrying; p. (1991) 6,001.

Inverkip, par., v., Inverclyde, **Scot.**; 10 km S.W. of Greenock; par. contains Gourock; expt; p. (1991) 1,258.

Inverness, royal burgh, Highland, N.E. **Scot.**; on Moray F.; distilling, lt. engin., tweeds; sm. pt. for general cargo; tourism; p. (1991) 41,234.

Inverness-shire, historic co., N.W. **Scot.**, now part of Highland.

Inverurie, royal burgh, Aberdeenshire, **Scot.**; on R. Don, 22 km N.W. of Aberdeen; rly. ctr., mkt. t.; tourism; p. (1991) 9,567.

Inyokern, t., E. Cal., **USA**; naval ordnance research sta.

Ioánnina (**Janina**), t., Epirus, **Greece**; nr. Albanian frontier; agr. tr.; embroidery; univ.; p. (1981) 44,829, (1991) 157,214 (reg.).

Iona, I., off cst. of Mull, Argyll and Bute, **Scot.**; early Scottish Christian ctr.; restored abbey; St. Columba's burial place; anc. burial place of Scottish kings; p. (1991) 130.

Ionian Is., gr. in Mediterranean, belonging to **Greece**; comprising Corfu, Paxos, Levkas, Cephalonia, Zakinthos, Ithake; severe earthquake 1953; total a. 1,948 km²; p. (1991) 193,734.

Ionian Sea. Mediterranean; between Greece on E.; Italy and Sicily on W.

Iowa, st., **USA**; Hawkeye St.; admitted to Union 1846; St. flower Wild Rose, St. bird Eastern Goldfinch; in Middle West; prairie cty.; watered by Mississippi and Missouri; rich farm land; maize, oats, and other grains; hogs, pigs; processing of farm prod.; flood control, reforestation; diverse inds.; cap. Des Moines; a. 145,791 km²; p. (1990) 2,776,755.

Iowa City, c., S.E. Iowa, **USA**; former st. cap. (1839–56); univ.; p. (1990) 59,738.

Ipoh, c., cap. of Perak st., N.W. **Malaya**; tin-mng. ctr.; Chinese rock temples; p. (1980) 300,727.

Ipswich, t., S.E. Queensland, **Australia**; nr. Brisbane; coalmng. ctr.; woollens; p. (est. 1984) 73,680.

Ipswich, co. t., l. gov. dist., Suffolk, **Eng.**; pt. on estuary of R. Orwell; increasingly impt. container pt.; exp. timber, grain and malt; birthplace of Cardinal Wolsey; diesel engines, gen. engin.; p. (1995) 114,100 (dist.), (1991) 130,157 (t.).

Iqaluit, cap, Nunavut region, **Canada**. Tiny population (5,000 in 1999).

Iquique, t., N. **Chile**; pt. on Pac. Oc.; exp. nitrates and iodine from Atacama desert; fish-canning; p. (1994) 63·2 m.

Iquitos, t., N.E. **Peru**; on Amazon, 3,680 km from mouth; comm. ctr.; exp. timber, cotton; sawmills, oil refining; p. (1993) 274,759.

Iráklion (**Candia** or **Herakleion**), t., cap. of Crete, **Greece**; impt. spt. on G. of I., arm of Aegean Sea; at foot of terraced hill slopes; wine, olive oil, fruit, fishing; tourism; p. (1991) 115,124.

Iran, former kingdom, Islamic st. (1979), S.W. Asia; known as Persia until 1935; interior plateau at c. 900 km, ringed by mtn. ranges of up to c. 5,500 m; much of a. desert; settled agr. limited to Caspian plain; heavy dependence on oil; oilfields centred on Abādān; hit by fall in world oil prices and sale losses due to Iraqi air attacks; pipeline to Iskenderun (Turkey) on Mediterranean cst. started (1986) as alternative exp. route; high quality carpets exported, esp. to USA; cap. Tehran; a. 1,626,520 km²; p. (1994) 63,200,000.

Irapuato, c., central **Mexico**; agr. tr. and processing; iron-founding; p. (1990) 362,471.

Iraq, rep., S.W. Asia; the anc. Mesopotamia; dominated by 2 Rs., Tigris and Euphrates; much of a. desert and semi-desert but irrigation in S. and centre enables settled agr. for barley, wheat, dates, and tobacco; only outlet to sea at N.W. end of Persian G.; oil principal source of wealth; main oilfield at Kirkūk; main oil pt. at Basra; pipelines to Lebanon and Syria; new inds. based on

oil; 14 provs.; cap. Baghdad; a. 435,120 km²; p. (1993) 19,410,000.

Irazu, active volcano, 3,437 m high, **Costa Rica**.

Irbid, t., **Jordan**; comm. and agr. tr. ctr.; p. (1992) 385,000.

Ireland, I., W. of Gt. Britain, separated by Irish Sea; divided politically into R.o.I. (Eire) and N. Ireland (Ulster, part of U.K.); ch. physical features, L. Neagh in N.E., Ls. of Killarney in S.W.; Rs. Shannon, Boyne, Blackwater; mtns. of Mourne, Wicklow, and Kerry; mild moist climate; called "emerald isle"; pastoral agr., especially dairying; tourism; a. 83,937 km².

Ireland, Republic of, indep. st., W. Europe; comprises 26 of 32 cos. making up I. of Ireland; member of EU; ring of highlands surround central lowland basin, much of which is peat-covered; economy based on agr., especially dairying; exps. butter, cheese, bacon; new govt.-encouraged inds.; mineral resources; tourism; cap. Dublin; a. 68,894 km²; p. (1993) 3,560,000.

Irian Jaya (formerly Dutch New Guinea, later W. Irian), prov., **Indonesia**; formerly W. New Guinea and Dutch col.; part of Indonesia, 1963; inaugurated as prov., 1969; primitive agr. of rice, poultry, cocoa; few oil deposits; cap. Djajapura; a. (inc. Ternate) 412,784 km²; p. (1983) 1,268,600.

Irish Sea, Brit. Is.; between Gt. Britain and Ireland, connecting N. and S. with Atl. Oc.; 320 km long; 80–224 km wide; greatest depth 840 m; a. 18,130 km².

Irkutsk, c., cap. of I. oblast, **Russia**; on Angara R. in E. Siberia; on Trans-Siberian rly., 64 km W. of L. Baykal; univ.; engin., sawmilling, petroleum refining, chemicals, hydroelec. power sta.; p. (1989) 626,000.

Irlam, t., Gtr. Manchester, **Eng.**; engin., tar, soap, glycerine, margarine; over-spill p.; p. (1991) 18,504.

Ironbridge, t., Shrops., **Eng.**; scene of Darby's iron ind.; derives name from first cast-iron bridge (1779) which here crosses Severn; now inc. in Telford new t.; p. (1991) 2,184.

Iron Country, Utah, **USA**; vast reserves of iron ore; undeveloped due to inaccessibility.

Iron Gate (**Portile de Fier**), **Romania**; famous rapids in R. Danube; Romanian-Yugoslavian hydroelectric and navigation project, 1964–71.

Irrawaddy, R., **Myanmar**; flows S. to Bay of Bengal; navigable for lge. steamers 1,440 km; irrigation wks.; major Asian rice bowl; 2,000 km long.

Irtysh, R., W. Siberia, **Russia**; ch. trib. of R. Ob'; crossed by Turk–Sib rly. at Semipalatinsk and by Trans-Siberian rly. at Omsk; hydroelectric power stas.; ambitious plans to divert R. South now postponed; 2,960 km long.

Irvine, royal burgh, N. Ayrshire, **Scot.**; nr. mouth of R. Irvine; new t. (1966); cas.; hosiery, lt. engin., bottle wks., chemicals; lorry plant closure announced (1999); p. (1991) 32,988.

Irvington, t., N.J., **USA**; industl. sub. of Newark; machin.; p. (1990) 61,018.

Irwell, R., Gtr. Manchester, **Eng.**; flows through Manchester to the Mersey via Manchester Ship Canal; 48 km long.

Isar, R., **Austria** and W. **Germany**; rises in Austrian Tyrol, flows N.E. to Danube; hydroelectric power stas. below Munich; 261 km long.

Isarco, R., N. **Italy**; rises nr. Brenner Pass, flows S. into R. Adige at Bolzano; 80 km long.

Isdud, anc. ct. of the Philistines. See Ashdod.

Ise (**Ujiyamada**), t., Honshu, **Japan**; sacred c. of Shintoism; p. (1990) 104,162.

Ise Bay, inlet, S. Honshu, **Japan**; flanked by ch. textile mftg. a. of cty, with 5 million people centred on Nagoya; 64 km long, 24–32 km wide.

Iseo, L., N. **Italy**; E. of Bergamo; 124 km².

Isère, dep., S.E. **France**; drained by Rs. Isère and Rhône; cap. Grenoble; mtnous.; cereals; wine, butter, cheese; iron, coal, lead, silver, copper; gloves, silks; a. 8,231 km²; p. (1990) 1,016,200.

Isère, R., S.E. **France**; rises in Graian Alps, flows W. into R. Rhône nr. Valence; used to generate hydroelec. power; used, with trib. R. Arc, by main rly. from France to N. Italy through Mt. Cenis (Fréjus) tunnel.

Iserlohn, t., N. Rhine–Westphalia, **Germany**; S.E. of Dortmund; metal gds.; p. (1986) 89,500.

Isfahan. See Esfahán.

Ishikari, t., Hokkaido, **Japan**; on cst. of Otaru Bay, 16 km N. of Sapporo; ctr. of second lgst. coalfield in Japan; sm. petroleum production.

Ishimbay, c., Bashkir aut. rep. **Russia**; on R.

Belaya; ctr. of Ishimbay oilfields; pipelines to Ufa, Orsk, and Shkaparo.

Isiro (Paulis), t., N.E. **Congo**; admin. offices; cotton ginneries; rly. repair shops.

Isis, R., headstream of R. Thames, **Eng.**; so named around and above Oxford.

Iskenderun (Alexandretta), spt., S. **Turkey**; recent modernisation for new Iran/Turkey rly.; new steel wks.; p. (1990) 175,998.

Islamabad, new cap. of **Pakistan**, to N. of Rawalpindi below Himalayas; nuclear power sta.; p. (1981) 201,000.

Islay, I. Inner Hebrides, Argyll and Bute, **Scot.**; farming, dairying, distilleries; p. (1991) 3,538.

Isle of Anglesey, N.W. **Wales**, separated from mainland by Menai Straits; former stronghold of Druids, attacked by Romans A.D. 61; mainly agr. and tourism; unit. auth. created in 1996 from former l. gov. dist., reinstating historic co. disbanded in 1974; p. (1995) 67,200.

Isle of Grain, Kent, **Eng.**; flat promontory at confluence of Thames and Medway, once separated from mainland by a tidal estuary; lge oil refinery; pipelines to Walton-on-Thames and Heathrow Airport.

Isle of Man, Brit. dependency, Irish Sea; high plateau N.E. to S.W.; ch. t. Douglas; old cap. Castle-town; admin. according to own laws; tourism; freeport (1983) to take advantage of low tax rate; a. 572 km²; p. (1994) 64,282.

Isles of Scilly, archipelago, l. gov. dist., 45 km. S.W. of Land's End, Cornwall, **Eng.**; early flowers and vegetables benefit from mild winter climate; tourism; p. (1995) 2,000.

Isle of Wight, unit. auth. created in 1995, **Eng.**; English Channel, separated from Hampshire by Spithead and the Solent; crossed by chalk hills, terminating in the Needles; popular holiday resort; ch. ts. Newport, Ryde, Cowes; p. (1995) 125,100.

Islington, inner bor., London, **Eng.**; N. of City; incorporates Finsbury; univ.; residtl.; clocks, precision engin.; p. (1995) 174,500.

Ismailia (Ismâ'îliya), t. and prov., **Egypt**; at mid-point of Suez Canal on L. Timsah; rail connections with Cairo, Suez, Port Said; declined during canal closure; p. (1986) 212,567, (1991) 632,000(02sp)(prov.).

Ispra, t., Varese, **Italy**; nr. L. Maggiore; nuclear research ctr.; p. (1981) 4,629.

Israel, rep., S.W. Asia; occupies narrow corridor between Jordan valley and Mediterranean Sea; extends S. into the Negev desert (half a. of rep.); Mediterranean climate enables cultivation of early fruits and vegetables, especially citrus fruits; special feature of agr. is cooperative settlements (Kibbutz); main factor limiting agr. development is availability of water; diamonds hgst. exp. earner; most highly industrialised cty. of S.W. Asia, especially for textiles and clothing; petroleum of increasing impt.; tourism; Jewish rep. since 1948; until then part of the mandate Palestine; surrounded by hostile Arab sts.; difficulties of increasing Jewish immigration; cap. Jerusalem; a. 20,850 km²; nat. a. in dispute, particularly since Arab-Israeli wars of 1967 and 1973 (*see* **Section C**); p. (1994) 5,470,000.

Issyk Kul, mtn. L., **Kyrgyzstan**; in Tien-Shan mtns., alt. 1,568 m; a. 6,216 km²; ice-free in winter.

Istanbul (Constantinople), ch. spt., former cap., **Turkey**; on Golden Horn peninsula on European cst. at entry of Bosporus into Sea of Marmara; divided into old "Stamboul" on S. side, and dists. of Galata and Beyoglu (Pera) on N.; the anc. Byzantium; magnificent mosque of Sta. Sophia; univ.; industl. and comm. ctr.; tourism; p. (1990) 6,293,000 (t.), 7,309,190 (prov.).

Istria, peninsula, N. Adriatic, **Croatia** (formerly Yugoslavia); ch. c. Pula; agr., olives, vines, oranges, maize; p. Yugoslav and Italian; a. c. 5,200 km².

Itabira, t., Minas Gerais st., **Brazil**; on Brazilian Plateau, 96 km N.E. of Belo Horizonte; lgst. deposits of iron ore in Brazil; p. (1985) 81,800.

Itabuna, t., Bahia, E. **Brazil**; cocoa, livestock; p. (1985) 178,700.

Itajaí, spt., Santa Catarina, S. **Brazil**; exp. lumber, cement, agr. prods.; (1985) 104,500.

Italy, rep., S. Europe; peninsula extending into Mediterranean; inc. 2 main Is. of Sicily and Sardinia; bounded by Alps to N.; central spine of Apennines; Mediterranean climate; contrast between industrialised N. and less developed agr. S. (Mezzogiorno); member of EU; agr. impt.,

especially in Po basin; tourism attracted by Roman and Renaissance architecture and by climate; inds. based on hydroelectric power in N., inc. elec. engin., motor vehicles and textiles, centred at Milan and Turin; 19 admin. regions; cap. Rome; a. 301,049 km²; p. (1992) 59,960,300.

Ithaca, t., N.Y., **USA**; on Cayuga L.; seat of Cornell Univ.; elec. clocks; machin.; p. (1980) 28,732.

Ithake, one of the Ionian Is., **Greece**; a. 96 km²; ch. t. Ithake; severe earthquake, 1953.

Itzehoe, t., Schleswig-Holstein, **Germany**; founded by Charlemagne; wood, cement, machin.; p. (1986) 31,700.

Ivano-Frankovsk (Stanislav), c., **Ukraine**; in Carpathian foothills; industl. ctr.; oilfields nearby; oil refineries, engin.; p. (1990) 219,900.

Ivanovo, t., **Russia**; N.E. of Moscow; textiles, iron and chemical wks.; peat-fed power stas.; p. (1989) 481,000.

Iviza. *See* Ibiza.

Ivory Coast. *See* Côte d'Ivoire.

Iwaki, t., Honshu, **Japan**; ctr. of apple producing dist., p. (1990) 355,817.

Iwakuni, t., Honshu, **Japan**; on Inland Sea; p. (1990) 109,530.

Iwo, t., **Nigeria**; nr. Ibadan; tr. ctr.; p. (1983) 262,000.

Izhevsk (Ustinov), c., cap. of Udmurt aut. rep. **Russia**; steel ctr., engin.; p. (1989) 635,000.

Izmail, c., **Ukraine**; in Bessarabia, on Danube delta, nr. Romanian border; naval base of Soviet Danube flotilla; former Turkish fortress; p. (1990) 94,100.

Izmir (Smyrna), c., **Turkey**; at head of G. of I., Anatolia; exp. figs, raisins, tobacco, carpets, rugs; anc. and historic c.; ch. comm. ctr. of the Levant; Nemrut Free Trade Zone (1987); ambitous industl. project, refinery and chem. complex (1972–86); univ.; p. (1990) 2,319,188 (t.), 2,694,770 (prov.).

Izmit, c., **Turkey**; E. end of Sea of Marmara; cereals, tobacco, oil refinery and polythene plant under construction; p. (1985) 233,338.

J

Jabalpur (Jubbulpore), c., Madhya Pradesh, **India**; rly. ctr.; ordnance wks.; p. (1991) 742,000.

Jablonec nad Nisou, t., **Czech Rep.**; on R. Neisse; glassware ctr., inc. glass jewellery and imitation stones; p. (1984) 44,742.

Jáchymov, t., **Czech Rep.**; spa; uranium mines, pitchblende, lead, silver, nickel, cobalt.

Jackson, t., Mich., **USA**; on Grand R.; locomotives, motorcar accessories, electronic equipment, metal gds.; p. (1984) 37,700 (t.), 145,300 (met. a.).

Jackson, t., cap. of Miss., **USA**; comm. and industl. ctr.; p. (1990) 196,637 (c.), 395,000 (met. a.).

Jacksonville, c., Fla., **USA**; pt. on St. John's R.; impt. ctr. on Atl. cst.; chemicals, shipbldg. and repair, printing, lumber, cigar mftg.; tourism; p. (1990) 672,971 (c.), 907,000 (met. a.).

Jacobabad, t., Sind, **Pakistan**; driest and hottest place in Indian sub-continent; p. (1981) 80,000.

Jacui, R., S. **Brazil**; rises in S. edge of Brazilian Plateau, enters Atl. Oc., through lagoon, Lagoa dos Patos; 560 km long.

Jadotville. *See* Likasi

Jaduguda, Bihar, **India**; uranium mine and mill to supply India's growing nuclear power production.

Jaén, t., cap. of prov. of Jaén, S. **Spain**; in foothills of Andalusian mtns.; cath.; olive oil, wine, chemicals; p. (1991) 105,545, 624,752 (prov.).

Jaffna, spt., N. **Sri Lanka**; on J. peninsula; second t. of rep.; p. (1983) 128,000.

Jaipur, c., cap. of Rajasthan, **India**; univ.; fine fabrics, jewellery; tourism; old cap. Amber is 8 km away; p. (1991) 1,458,000.

Jajce, t., **Bosnia-Herzegovina**, formerly Yugoslavia; at junc. of Rs. Vrbas and Pliva (hydroelectric power); Fed. People's Rep. of Yugoslavia declared here by Tito (1943).

Jakarta, **(Batavia)**, c., cap. of **Indonesia**, N.W. Java; comm. ctr.; textiles; exps. rubber, tea; printing; airport; p. (1996) 9,161,000.

Jalalabad, c., E. **Afghanistan**; on Kåbul R., nr. Khyber Pass; univ.; agr. tr. ctr.; p. (1988) 55,000.

Jalgaon, t., Maharashtra, **India**; in Tapti R. valley nr. Bhusawal; p. (1991) 242,193.

Jalisco, st., **Mexico**; on Pac. Oc.; traversed by Sierra Madre; well timbered, agr.; minerals; tourism; a. 80,876 km²; p. (1990) 5,287,987.

Jalón, R., **Spain;** rises in Iberian Mtns., flows N.E. into R. Ebro nr. Zaragoza; valley forms main rly., road route from Madrid to Ebro valley.

Jalpaiguri, t., W. Bengal, **India;** frontier t.; rly. ctr.; p. (1981) 61,743.

Jamaica, rep., W.I.; member of Brit. Commonwealth; mtnous.; Blue Mtn. range runs E. to W. and rises to 2,258 m; tropical climate modified by alt.; economy based on agr. and mng.; major exp. crops sugar and bananas; major world producer of bauxite (recent contraction) and alumina; tourist ind. expanding; member of Caribbean Free Trade Association; 25 per cent unemployment; major pts. Kingston, Montego Bay, Pt. Antonio; international airpt.; univ. at cap. Kingston; a. 11,424 km²; p. (1993) 2,471,600, of which 22 per cent are in Kingston.

James, R. Va., **USA;** hydroelec. power in upper reaches, wide estuary in lower course; outlet to Chesapeake Bay; 544 km long.

James Bay, S. arm of Hudson Bay, **Canada;** c. 480 km long, 224 km wide.

Jamestown, spt., cap. of **St. Helena** I.; flax; p. (1992) 1,500.

Jamestown, t., dist., Va., **USA;** nr. mouth of James R., where first English permanent settlement was founded 1607.

Jammu, t., J. and Kashmir, **India;** winter cap. of st.; univ., fort, palace; p. (1981) 206,135.

Jammu and Kashmir, st., N.W. **India;** traversed by ranges of Himalayas; wheat and rice; 1972 agreement divided state between India and Pakistan; disturbances 1989; cap. Indian sector Srinagar, cap. Pakistani sector Muzaffarabad; total a. 222,823 km²; p. (1981) 5,987,389.

Jamnagar, t., Gujarat, **India;** on G. of Kutch; p. (1991) 342,000.

Jamshedpur, c., Bihar, **India;** W. of Calcutta; major industl. ctr. of rep.; Tata iron and steel wks.; engin.; p. (1991) 461,000.

Jämtland, co. W. **Sweden;** cap. Ostersand; a. 49,857 km²; p. (1992) 135,910.

Janina. See **Ioánnina.**

Jan Mayen I., volcanic I. between Spitzbergen and Iceland, Arctic Oc.; annexed by **Norway** 1929; meteorological sta.; a. 373 km².

Japan, E. Asia; 4 main Is., Honshu (lgst.), Hokkaido, Shikoku, Kyushu; mtnous.; 18 active volcanoes; subject to earthquakes; only 17 per cent of land cultivable; intensive and mechanised agr.; rice, fruits, vegetables; few animals; inds. highly developed and based on imports of raw material and export of finished prods.; rapid industrialisation since second world war; economic growth has been rapid, but major financial crisis (1997); rapid technological innovation; stable labour management relationships; inds. inc. shipbldg., motor vehicles, textiles, steel, electronics, chemicals, cheap consumer gds.; cap. Tokyo, world financial ctr.; a. 370,370 km²; p. (1993) 125,568,504 (inc. Okinawa and Ryuku Is.).

Japan Current. See **Kuroshio.**

Japan, Sea of, portion of **Pac. Oc.** between Korea, USSR, and Japan.

Japurá, R., **Colombia, Brazil;** rises as Caquetá in Colombian Andes, flows S.E. through Brazil to Amazon; 2,080 km long.

Jari, new t., Amazonia, **Brazil;** ambitious project of timber and pulp plant in the rain forest; not as successful as hoped.

Jaroslaw, t., Przemysl., prov., S.E. **Poland;** on R. San; food-processing; founded 11th cent.; impt. tr. ctr. 16th cent.; p. (1989) 41,267.

Jarrow, t., South Tyneside, Tyne and Wear, **Eng.;** on S. bank of Tyne, 11 km below Gateshead; grew up as shipbldg. ctr.; in depression; hunger march to London 1936; new inds; steel and tube wks., oil storage; die-castings; home of the Venerable Bede; p. (1991) 29,325.

Jasper National Park, Alberta, **Canada;** Rocky mtns., tourism.

Jaunpur, t., Uttar Pradesh, **India;** mkt. t.; ctr. of Moslem learning and architecture in 15th cent.; p. (1991) 136,062.

Java, I., **Indonesia;** most developed of Indonesian Is.; traversed E. to W. by forested volcanic mtns.; fertile volcanic soils aid intensive rice cultivation; over-populated; contains 70 per cent of cty.'s p. yet only 8 per cent of land a.; exps. inc. coffee, rubber, sugar, copra, teak; noted for silver craft and batik work (anc. craft of fabric decoration); a. 130,510 km²; p. (1983) 96,892,900.

Javari, R., forms bdy. between **Peru** and **Brazil;**

trib. of R. Amazon.

Java Sea, part of the **Pac. Oc.** between N. cst. Java, Borneo, and Sumatra.

Jebel Aulia, v., **Sudan;** S. of Khartoum; dam across White Nile R.

Jebel-Hauran, high tableland of **Syria,** alt. c. 1,800 m.

Jedburgh, royal burgh, Borders, **Scot.;** on Jed Water, S.W. of Kelso; tweeds, woollens, rayon; abbey ruins; ctr. of Border warfare in Middle Ages; p. (1991) 4,118.

Jeddah. See **Jiddah.**

Jefferson City, st. cap. Mo., **USA;** on Missouri R.; univ.; comm. and processing ctr. of agr. a.; shoes, tiles, farm implements; p. (1980) 36,619.

Jelenia Góra (Hirschberg), t. and prov., S.W. **Poland** (since 1945), formerly in Lower Silesia; mftg.; spa; p. (1989) 93,205 (t.), 515,000 (prov.).

Jelgava (Mitau), t., **Latvia;** on Lielupe R.; textiles, foodstuffs, refractory materials; p. (1991) 74,500.

Jemappes, t., **Belgium;** 5 km W. of Mons; industl.; Fr. victory over Austria 1792; battle of Mons 1914.

Jena, c., **Germany;** on R. Saale, 72 km S.W. of Leipzig; univ., observatory; optical glass-ware, precision instruments; leading cultural ctr. late 18th and early 19th cent., defeat of Prussians by Fr. 1806; p. (1990) 101,900.

Jerez de la Frontera, t., **Spain;** in Andalusia, 22 km N.E. of Cádiz; in fertile agr. a.; sherry; p. (1991) 184,018.

Jericho, v., Jordan Valley, **Jordan;** est. through recent excavations as one of oldest towns in the world (6000 B.C.).

Jersey, lgst. of Channel Is., 21 km W. of Fr. cst.; potatoes, tomatoes, cauliflowers, flowers, fruit. cattle; tourist resort; banking; ch. t. St. Helier; a. 117 km²; p. (1991) 84,082.

Jersey City, c., N.J., **USA;** E. of Newark, on Hudson R.; comm. and industl. ctr.; diverse inds.; p. (1990) 228,537 (c.), 553,000 (met. a.).

Jerusalem, c., **Israel** and **Jordan;** 811 m a.s.l.; between Dead Sea and Mediterranean; the "Holy City" of the Jews and the sacred c. of the Christians and Moslems; Israeli western sector and Arab eastern sector declared by Israeli parliament (1980) united c. and cap.; modern mftg.; p. (1992) 544,200 inc. E. Jerusalem.

Jervis Bay, inlet of Pac. Oc., Australian Capital Territory, **Australia;** acquired by Fed Govt. as site for establishment of pt. for Canberra 1909; plans to develop pt. and steelworks. a. 73 km².

Jesselton. See **Kota Kinabalu.**

Jhang Maghiana, t., **Pakistan;** textiles; mkt.; on R. Chenab; p. (1981) 195,000.

Jhansi, c., Uttar Pradesh, **India;** ctr. rly. ctr., mkt.; formerly of strategic importance; p. (1991) 313,000.

Jharia, t., Bihar, **India;** ctr. of most impt. coalfield in India; p. (1981) 57,496.

Jhelum, R., W. Punjab, **Pakistan;** most W. of the five Rs. of the Punjab; forms Vale of Kashmir in upper course; Mangla Dam under Indus Waters Treaty, completed 1967.

Jhelum, c., **Pakistan;** on Jhelum R.; p. (1981) 106,000.

Jiamusi (Kiamusze), c., Heilongjiang, **China;** ch. pt. on Songhua R; p. (1984) 546,500.

Jiangsu (Kiangsu), coastal prov., **China;** on Yellow Sea; low lying a. N. of Chang Jiang delta; rich agr., dense p.; cotton, sericulture, tea, sugar, fish (many Ls.); cap. Nanjing; a. 109,000 km²; p. (1990) 68,170,000.

Jiangxi (Kiangsi), prov., S.E. **China;** in basin of navigable Gan R. which drains through L. Poyang to Chang Jiang; ch. cs. Shanghai, Zhenjiang, Wuxi, Nanchang (cap.); rice, wheat, tea, cotton; tungsten, coking coal, kaolin; a. 172,494 km²; p. (1990) 38,280,000.

Jiddah or **Jeddah,** c., admin. cap., Hejaz, **Saudi Arabia;** on Red Sea, pt. of Mecca; pilgrims; steel mill and oil refinery; new King Faisal Port nearby; univ. (with Mecca); p. (1986) 1·4 m.

Jihlava, t., Moravia, **Czech Rep.;** on Jihlava R.; 519 m a.s.l.; timber, grain, textiles; Prague Compactata signed here 1436; p. (1984) 52,828.

Jilin (Kirin), prov., N.E. **China;** N. of Korea and Liaotung peninsula; crossed by Songhua R.; in fertile Manchurian plain; impt. industl. a.; soya beans, grain, lumber, coal, gold, lead; cap. Changchun; a. 186,998 km²; p. (1990) 25,150,000.

Jilin (Kirin), c., Jilin, N.E. **China;** former prov. cap.; on Songhua R., at outlet of Songhua reservoir; impt. position on rly. from Changchun to coastal pts.; chemical fertilisers, steel, oil refinery; p. (1992) 1,270,000.

Jimma, t., **Ethiopia**; ch. prod. Jimma coffee; connected by road with Addis Ababa; Agricultural Technical School; p. (1984) 60,992.

Jinan (Tsinan), c., cap of Shandong prov., **China**; on S. bank of Huang He, 160 km. from G. of Bo Hai; agr. ctr.; textiles, foodstuffs, chemicals, trucks; univ.; p. (1992) 2,350,000.

Jinja, t., **Uganda**; on N. shore of L. Victoria where Nile drains from L. over Ripon Falls; (now submerged by the construction of Owen Falls dam 2·4 km downstream); cotton mnfs., copper smelting, flour and maize milling; rly. to Kampala; p. (1991) 60,979.

Jinzhou (Chincho), c., Liaoning prov., **China**; cement, glass, bricks, tiles, paper, wood and pulp, oil; p. (1984) 748,700.

Jiujiang (Kiukiang), c., Jianxi prov., **China**; pt. of Chang Jiang at foot of forested mtn.; entrepôt tr.; former treaty pt.; p. (1984) 378,100.

João Pessoa, t., cap. of Paraíba st., **Brazil**; through its pt. Cabedelo expts. cotton, sugar, minerals; industl. expansion; p. (1991) 497,214.

Joban, dist., N.E. Honshu, **Japan**; third lgst. coalfield in Japan; ch. t. Fukushima.

Jodhpur, t., Rajasthan, **India**; ctr. of Thar desert; old fortress t.; p. (1991) 668,000.

Jogjakarta, c., Java, **Indonesia**; univ., cultural ctr.; handicrafts; citadel with palace; p. (1980) 342,267.

Johannesburg, c., Transvaal, S. **Africa**; univ.; gold-mng. ctr. of Witwatersrand; diamond cutting, engin., textiles, chemicals; oil pipeline from Durban; p. (1985) 1,609,408 (met. a.).

John o' Groat's House, place nr. Duncansby Head, Highland, **Scot.**

Johnston Atoll, two sm. Is. 1,150 km S.W. of Hawaii, belonging to **USA**; p. (1990) 173.

Johnstone, burgh, Renfrewshire, **Scot.**; on R. Black Cart, nr. Paisley; machine tools, textiles, iron and brass foundry; p. (1991) 18,635.

Johnstown, industl. t., Penns., **USA**; on Conemaugh R.; coal-mng. and steel ctr.; machin.; p. (1984) 33,100 (t.), 259,000 (met. a.).

Johore, st., **Malaysia**; at S. end of Malaya; forested; cap. Johor Baharo; rubber, rice, copra, pineapples; tin, iron, bauxite; a. 18,985 km²; p. (1980) 1,638,229.

Joina Falls, **Mali**; dam projected for hydroelectric power and irrigation under auspices of Organisation of Riparian States of R. Senegal (Guinea, Mali, Mauritania, Senegal).

Joinville, t., Santa Catarina, **Brazil**; exp. timber, maté tea; textiles, machin., car parts, plastics; p. (1991) 346,095.

Joliet, c., Ill., **USA**; on Des Plaines R., S.W. of Chicago; R. pt.; coal and limestone nearby; rly. engin., oil refining; p. (1990) 76,836 (c.), 390,000 (met. a.).

Joliette, t., Quebec, **Canada**; textile mills, paper, tobacco-processing; p. (1986) 16,845.

Jönköping, t., cap. of J. co., **Sweden**; safetymatches, textiles, footwear; p. (1992) 112,802 (t.) 309,867 (co.).

Jonquière, t., S. Quebec, **Canada**; paper and pulp mills; p. (1991) 57,933. See **Chicoutimi.**

Joplin, t., Mo., **USA**; in dairy and livestock region; lead and zinc mng.; mnfs. metal and leather gds.; p. (1990) 40,961.

Jordan, kingdom, S.W. Asia; bounded by Israel, Syria, Saudi Arabia, and Iraq; consists of high plateau (600 m), Jordan valley, and hill cty. to W. of R. Jordan; only 25 per cent of a. sufficiently humid for agr., much is migratory herding of animals and subsistence agr.; sm. mineral wealth; only outlet to sea Aqaba, pt. on G. of Aqaba; only one single-track rly.; new rail link built to Al-Hara phosphate mines, now major exp.; dependant on oil imports; cap. Amman; W. Bank of R. Jordan occupied by Israeli forces since June 1967; for recent developments in peace process, *see* **Section C**; a. 101,140 km²; p. (1994) 4,950,000.

Jordan, R., **Israel** and **Jordan**; flows S. from Anti-Lebanon along sinuous course, mostly below sea-level to Dead Sea; its rapidly and variant depth render it unnavigable, and no t. of any importance has ever been built on its banks; Jesus was baptised in its waters; contemporary strife over use for irrigation; 368 km long.

Jos, t., central **Nigeria**; on Bauchi Plateau, 96 km S.W. of Bauchi; impt. tin mines; steel rolling mill; p. (1992) 185,600.

Jostedalsbre, icefield, W. **Norway**, lgst. icefield of

European mainland; a. 881 km²; rises to 2,043 m.

Jotunheimen, mtn. region, central **Norway** hgst. in Scandinavia; Galdhopiggen 2,470 m, Glittertind 2,482 m.

Juan Fernández, two rocky volcanic Is., S. **Pac. Oc.**, belonging to **Chile**; a. 98 km²; the buccaneer Alexander Selkirk marooned here 1704–9 gave idea for Defoe's *Robinson Crusoe.*

Juan les Pins, resort, Alpes-Maritimes dep., S.E. **France**.

Juba (Giuba), R., **Somalia**; narrow fertile valley, imp. agr. a.; 872 km long.

Jubbulpore. See **Jabalpur.**

Jucar, R., E. **Spain**; rises in Montes Universales, and flows to Mediterranean; irrigation and hydroelec. power; 400 km long.

Judaea, div. of Palestine in the Roman period.

Juggernaut. See **Puri.**

Juiz de Fora, t., Minas Gerais, **Brazil**; textile ctr.; p. (1991) 385,756.

Julfa (Jolfa), c., N. **Iran**; on frontier with USSR, customs and transit ctr. on overland route from Europe.

Julian Alps, mtn. range, **Slovenia** (formerly Yugoslavia) and **Italy**; hgst. peak 2,865 m.

Julianehåb, t., S.W. **Greenland**; N.W. of C. Farewell; tr. ctr., fish. pt.; p. (1990) 3,543.

Jülich, t., N. Rhine-Westphalia, **Germany**; nuclear reactor; p. (1986) 30,200.

Jullundur, c., Punjab, **India**; rly. ctr.; st. cap. until Chandigarh was built; p. (1981) 408,196.

Jumna, R., N. **India**; ch. trib. of R. Ganges; rises in the Himalayas and flows past Delhi and Agra to Allahabad; 1,376 km long.

Junagadh, t., Gujarat, **India**; agr. tr. and foodprocessing; industl. ctr.; formerly cap. of principality of J.; p. (1991) 130,484.

Jundiai, t., São Paulo st., **Brazil**; industl. ctr.; nr. São Paulo; p. (1991) 312,517.

Juneau, c., cap. of Alaska, **USA**; at foot of Chilkoot mtns., lumbering; fisheries; gold settlement (1881); p. (1990) 26,751. See **Willow South.**

Jungfrau, peak, Bernese Oberland, **Switzerland**; height 4,161 m; electric rly. from Kleine Scheidegg to Jungfraujoch.

Junin, t., **Argentina**; agr. tr., rly. engin., pottery, furniture; p. (1980) 62,080.

Jura, dep., E. **France**; named from mtn. range on Franco-Swiss border; agr. and pastoral; cap. Lons-le-Saunier; a. 5,053 km²; p. (1990) 248,800.

Jura, I., Argyll and Bute, **Scot.**; off W. cst.; p. (1991) 196.

Jura, mtn. range, **Switzerland** and **France**; folded parallel ranges separated by deep R. valleys; hgst. peak Crêt de la Neige, 1,724 m; 240 km long, breadth 48–64 km.

Jura, canton, **Switzerland**; between Berne and Basle in a strong French speaking dist. in Jura Mtns; p. (1990) 65,700.

Juruá R., lge. trib. of Amazon; rises in E. **Peru** and flows through Acre and Amazonas sts., **Brazil**; over 3,200 km long.

Jujuy, prov., N.W. **Argentina**; p. (1991) 512,329.

Jylland (Jutland), peninsula region, **Denmark**; intensive agr. and poultry farming; sandy heath in W.; more fertile clay in E. used for dairying; a. 29,554 km²; p. (1990) 2,378,348.

Jyväskylä, t., central **Finland**; pt. on L. Päijänne; pulp. paper, plywood; univ.; p. (1993) 71,842.

K

K2. See **Godwin-Austen, Mt.**

Kabardin-Balkar, aut. rep., Transcaucasia, **Russia**; cap. Nalchik; livestock, lumber, wheat, fruit; nonferrous metals; hydro-metallurgy plant; a. 12,432 km²; p. (1989) 753,500.

Kabelega Falls (Murchison Falls), on Victoria Nile, **Uganda**; falls between L. Kioga and L. Mobutu Seso.

Kabinda. See **Cabinda.**

Kābul, c., cap. of **Afghanistan**; on Kābul R. S. of Hindu Kush; 2,104 m a.s.l.; excellent climate; univ.; comm. and cultural ctr.; textiles, leather, timber inds.; p. (1993) 700,000.

Kābul, R., flows from Hindu Kush through gorges in Khyber Pass to Indus; site of dam for hydroelec. power and irrigation; length c. 480 km.

Kabwe (Broken Hill), **Zambia**; comm. and mng. ctr.; lead, zinc, cadmium, silver; p. (1989) 210,000.

Kachchh, peninsula, Gujarat st., N.W. **India**; bounded on N. by Pakistan; largely barren except for fertile strip along Arabian Sea; p. (1981) 1,050,161.

Kachin State, semi-aut. st., **Myanmar**; comprising former Myitkyina and Bhamo dists.; home of Kachins; a. 89,042 km²; p. (1983) 903,982.

Kadiyevka, t., **Ukraine**; coal, iron and steel, synthetic rubber; p. (1990) 112,300.

Kaduna, t., N. **Nigeria**; cap of Kaduna st.; rly. junc.; aluminium wks.; spinning and weaving; new oil refinery; p. (1992) 309,600 (t.), (1991) 3,969,252 (state).

Kaffa, region, **Ethiopia**; mtnous., forested; natural habitat of coffee plant; p. (1984) 2,450,369.

Kagoshima, c., at S. end of Kyushu I., **Japan**; pt. on K. Bay; univs., cas.; porcelain, silk and cotton clothing, food-processing, publishing; rocket launching site at Uchinoura; p. (1990) 536,685.

Kahoolawe, I., **Hawaii**; a. 117 km²; uninhabited.

Kaieteur Falls, waterfall, **Guyana**; where R. Potaro leaves Guiana Highlands; among world's hgst. falls (226 m).

K'ai-feng, c., Henan, **China**; nr. S. bank of Huang He; one of the most anc. cities in China; cottons, chemicals; p. (1984) 619,200.

Kai Islands, Is., **Indonesia**; between New Guinea and Timor; timber; a. 1,761 km²; p. 51,000.

Kaikoura, dist., S.I., **N.Z.**; on E. cst., 128 km N.E. of Christchurch; in this region are the Kaikoura ranges, in which the hgst. peaks are Tapuaenuku (2,887 m) and Alarm (2,867 m); p. (1991) 3,711.

Kailas (**Kang-ti-ssu Shan**), range and peak, S.W. Tibet, **China**; unclimbed sacred mtn.; source of Indus, Ganges, Sutlej and Zangbo (headstream of Brahmaputra).

Kainji Dam, **Nigeria**; power sta. transmission system and river transportation on R. Niger.

K'ai-ping, t., Hebei, N. **China**; second lgst. coalmng. a. (Kailan mines) in China; coal exported through Qinhuangdao.

Kairouan, holy c. of Moslems, **Tunisia**; 128 km S.S.E. of Tunis; founded A.D. 670; mosque; p. (1984) 72,254.

Kaiserslautern, c., Rhineland–Palatinate, **Germany**; nr. Mannheim; iron, textiles, machin., tobacco, wood; p. (1986) 96,800.

Kaiser Wilhelm's Land, Australian dependency, **Antarctica**.

Kakamega, t., **Kenya**; E. Africa; 48 km N. of Kisumu; ctr. of gold-mng. dist.

Kakinada, t., spt., Adhra Pradesh, **India**; cotton, oilseeds; p. (1991) 280,000.

Kalahari Desert, region of semi-desert, southern **Africa**; between Orange and Zambesi Rs.; mainly in **Botswana**; alt. 1,128 m; a. 51,800 km²; inhabited chiefly by Bushmen; new Trans-Kalahari highway completed (1998).

Kalamata, t., Peloponnesus, **Greece**; nr. Sparta; figs, currants, flour-milling, cigarette mftg.; p. (1981) 43,235.

Kalamazoo, c., Mich., **USA**; industl. and comm. ctr. in farming a.; paper, pharmaceuticals; fish hatchery nearby; p. (1984) 77,200 (c.), 215,200 (met. a.).

Kalemie (**Albertville**), t., **Congo**; on L. Tanganyika; rail-steamer transfer point.

Kalewa, t., **Myanmar**; at confluence of Irrawaddy and Chindwin Rs.; coal deposits.

Kalgan See **Zhangjiakou**.

Kalgoorlie, t., W. **Australia**; gold mng. ctr. in arid region adjacent to "Golden Mile" auriferous reef; nickel mng.; p. (1991) 26,079 (inc. Boulder).

Kalimantan (**Indonesian Borneo**); straddles equator; sparse p.; poor soils; lge. areas of swamp; plans for reclamation; coal, oil, diamonds, gold in sm. quantities; rice, pepper, copra; a. 539,461 km²; p. (1980) 6.7 m.

Kalinin. See **Tver**.

Kaliningrad (**Königsberg**), c., **Russia**, former cap. of E. Prussia; on R. Pregel, linked by canal to outer pt. Pillau; univ., cath.; shipbldg., machin., wood-pulp, chemicals, exp. agr. prods.; Kant lived here all his life; p. (1989) 401,000.

Kalisz, t. and prov., **Poland**; on R. Prosna; industl. ctr., textiles; oldest Polish t. mentioned in 2nd cent. A.D. by Ptolemy; p. (1989) 106,031 (t.), 706,500 (prov.).

Kalmar, co. and t., spt., S. **Sweden**; on I. in Kalmar Sound; cath., cas.; matches, food inds., shipbldg.; p. (1992) 56,863 (t.), 241,912 (co.).

Kalmuk (**Kalmytskaya**), aut. rep., **Russia**; on Caspian Sea; harsh and infertile steppe; pastoral agr.; cap. Elista; a. 75,887 km²; p. (1989) 322,600.

Kalna, v., on Mt. Stara Planina, Serbia, **Yugoslavia**; uranium mine and plant; nuclear power sta.

Kaluga, c., **Russia**; pt. on Oka R.; chemicals, engin., hydroelec. power plant; p. (1989) 311,000.

Kalyan, spt., Maharashtra, **India**; nr. Bombay; bricks, tiles; p. (1991) 1,015,000.

Kalymnos, I., Dodecanese, **Greece**; mtnous.; a. 106 km²; p. 13,600.

Kama, R., **Russia**; ch. trib. of Volga which it joins below Kazan; rises in foothills of Urals; lge. hydroelectric sta. at Perm; navigable; 2,016 km long.

Kamaishi, t., spt., N.E. Honshu, **Japan**; serves Kamaishi-Sennin iron-ore field, lgst. worked deposits and reserves in Japan; impt. iron and steel ind; p. (1990) 52,484.

Kamakura, t., Honshu, **Japan**; on shore of Sagami Bay; tourism; p. (1990) 174,307.

Kamaran I., Red Sea, **Yemen**; formerly under Brit. occupation, 1915–67; a. 57 km².

Kamchatka, peninsula, E. Siberia, **Russia**; volcanic ranges; geothermal power sta.; mineral wealth, fisheries on cst.; climate cold, wet and foggy; contains part of Koryak nat. okrug; cap. Petropavlovsk.

Kamenets-Podolskiy, t., **Ukraine**, on Smotrich R.; lt. inds.; mediaeval fortress t.; p. (1990) 103,300.

Kamensk-Uralsk, c., **Russia**; aluminium, iron, steel, engin.; p. (1989) 208,000.

Kamet, Himalayan peak, on border of **India** and Tibet, **China**; 7,761 m; highest mtn. climbed (Smythe, 1931) until 1953 (Everest).

Kamloops, t., B.C., **Canada**; on Thompson R.; formerly Fort Thompson; on transcontinental rlys.; suppl ctr. for mng. and grazing dist.; fruit and livestock mkts.; p. (1991) 67,057.

Kampala, c., cap. of **Uganda**; univ., ch. comm. ctr.; lt. inds., coffee-processing; p. (1991) 773,463.

Kampen, t., Overijssel, **Neth.**; on R. IJssel; cigar-mkg.; p. (1993) 32,571.

Kampot, prov., **Cambodia**; on G. of Siam; ctr. of pepper ind.; p. (1981) 337,879.

Kampuchea, Democratic. See **Cambodia**.

Kamyshin, t., **Russia**; pt. on Volga; textiles, mkt. gardening, grain; p. (1989) 122,000.

Kan, R. See **Gan Jiang**.

Kananga (**Luluabourg**), c., cap. of Kasai Occidental prov., **Congo**; on Lulua R.; comm. and communications ctr. in cotton-growing a.; p. (1991) 371,862.

Kanawha, R., W. Va., **USA**; rises in Allegheny mtns., flows into R. Ohio; runs through ch. mng. a. of W. Va. coalfield nr. Charleston.

Kanazawa, c., Honshu, **Japan**; in Kana plain, on Sea of Japan; machin., silk and cotton textiles; landscape gardens; No theatre; p. (1990) 442,868.

Kanchenjunga, mtn., on Nepal–Sikkim bdy., N.E. **India**; third hgst. mtn. in world, 8,585 m.

Kanchipuram (**Conjeeveram**), t., Tamil Nadu, S. **India**; on plain S.W. of Madras; pilgrimage ctr.; textiles; p. (1991) 144,955.

Kandahar. See **Qandahar**.

Kandy, c., **Sri Lanka**; in mtns. in ctr. of I.; 120 km from Colombo; univ. at sub. of Peradeniya; resort in hot season; tea, cocoa; p. (1981) 97,872.

Kangaroo I., lgst. I. off S. **Australia** cst.; tourists attracted by spectacular granite scenery and varied flora and fauna.

KaNgwane, homeland, Natal, **S. Africa**; chief town Eerstehoek; pop. (1985) 392,782.

Kano, c., N. **Nigeria**; trading centre for whole of Sudan region; impt. airport and rly. terminus; groundnut ctr.; p. (1992) 699,900 (c.), (1991) 5,632,040.

Kanpur (**Cawnpore**), c., Uttar Pradesh, N. **India**; on R. Ganges; impt. mftg. ctr.; textiles, chemicals, leather goods, foodstuffs; p. (1991) 1,879,000.

Kansas, st., **USA**; called the "sunflower state"; prairie; farming, maize, wheat; cattle, dairying, pigs; coal, petroleum, natural gas, lead, meat packing, flour milling, aircraft, chemicals, machin.; admitted to Union 1861; st. flower sunflower, st. bird Western Meadowlark; cap. Topeka; a. 213,095 km²; p. (1990) 2,477,574.

Kansas, R., Kan., **USA**; trib. of Missouri R., confluence at Kansas City; vegetable growing in valley; periodic flooding; 272 km long.

Kansas City, Kansas and Mo., **USA**; at confluence of Kansas and Missouri Rs.; univ.; gr. livestock mart, car and aircraft assembly, steel prods., meat-packing, food processing; p. (1990) 149,767 (Kansas) 435,146 (Mo.); 1,566,280 (joint met. a.).

Kansu. See Gansu.

Kant, t., **Kyrgyzstan;** 19 km E. of Frunze; to be expanded to industl. c.; proposed p. 100,000.

Kaohsiung, spt., co., **Taiwan;** on S.W. cst.; industl. ctr., road and rly. terminus; oil refining, aluminium wks.; p. (1995) 1,423,821 (c.) 1,191,258 (co.).

Kaolack, inland pt., **Senegal;** 112 km up Saloum R.; groundnut ctr., integrated textile complex; p. (1992) 179,894.

Kaposvár, t., S.W. **Hungary;** on Kapos R.; comm. ctr.; textiles, foodstuffs; p. (1997) 68,000.

Kara-Bogaz-Gol, lge. shallow bay, **Turkmenistan;** an arm of Caspian Sea; rapid evaporation allows huge quantities of salt from Caspian to be deposited along its shores (world's lgst. source of Glauber's salt); a. 18,130 km².

Karabuk, t., **Turkey;** N. of Ankara; steel wks.; p. (1985) 94,818.

Karacheyevo-Cherkesskaya, aut. region, **Russia;** in Greater Caucasus; cap. Cherkessk; livestock, grain; coal, lead, zinc; a. 14,095 km²; p. (1989) 415,000.

Karachi, c., **Pakistan;** on Arabian Sea, nr. Indus delta; former cap. of Pakistan; univ.; spt., air ctr.; oil refining, industl. gases, steel mill, natural gas from Sui; nuclear power sta.; p. (1981) 5,103,000.

Karaganda, c., **Kazakhstan;** on impt. coalfield developed since 1926; supplies industl. ctrs. of Urals; iron and steel wks., power sta.; p. (1990) 613,200.

Kara-Kalpak, aut. rep., N.W. **Uzbekistan;** inc. Ust-Urt plateau, Kyzyl-Kum desert; irrigated agr.; cap. Nukus; a. 165,553 km²; p. (1990) 1,244,700.

Karakoram Range, part of Himalayas between **Kashmir** and **China;** many lofty peaks, inc. Mt. Godwin-Austen; Karakoram highway linking Pakistan with Xinjiang prov. of China, opened 1971.

Kara-Kum, sand desert, **Turkmenistan;** E. of S.E. shore of Caspian Sea; to be irrigated with water diverted from Rs. which flow to Barents Sea. a. 349,650 km²; canal 1,440 km long across desert.

Karamay (K'o-la-ma-i), t. Xianjiang, **China;** ctr. of lge. oilfield; pipeline to Fushantzu refinery; p. (1984) 180,100.

Kara Sea, Arctic Oc.; E. of Novaya Zemlya; navigation to and from Siberian pts. July–Sept.

Karbala, c., **Iraq;** N.W. of Al Hillah; ctr. of pilgrimage; sacred c. of Moslem Shiite sect; p. (1985) 184,574.

Karelian, aut. rep., **Russia;** between Kola peninsula and Finland; lake-covered, coniferous forests; cap. Petrozavodsk; rich in timber, minerals, precious metals; granite and mica quarried; paper and pulp milling; a. 179,408 km²; p. (1989) 790,200.

Karelian Isthmus, Russia; strategic route between Finland and Russia impt. for defence of St. Petersburg (Leningrad).

Kariba Dam, in Kariba gorge of Zambesi R., on **Zimbabwe–Zambia** border; operated jointly by the two govts.; one of lgst. dams in world with vast artificial lake supplying hydroelectric power to Zimbabwe and the copperbelt of Zambia; badly polluted with use of D.D.T. in tsetse and malaria control; involved resettlement of Batonka peoples; completed 1960.

Karikal, former Fr. settlement on E. cst. of **India;** part of Union Territory of Pondicherry; p. (1991) 145,723.

Karkonosze. See Riesengebirge.

Karl-Marx-Stadt. See Chemnitz.

Karlovac, t., **Croatia,** (formerly Yugoslavia); S.W. of Zagreb; chemicals, textiles, food processing; p. (1981) 78,363.

Karlový Vary (Carlsbad), t., Bohemia, **Czech Rep.;** on R. Ohre; hot mineral springs; health resort; porcelain; p. (1984) 59,183.

Karlskoga, t., **Sweden;** E. of L. Vänern; seat of Bofors armament wks.; iron and steel, explosives, chemicals; p. (1983) 35,539.

Karlskrona, spt., S. **Sweden;** on Baltic Sea; main naval sta.; lighting fixtures, china; p. (1992) 59,390.

Karlsruhe, c., Baden-Württemberg, **Germany;** road and rly. ctr.; outport on Rhine; chemicals, engin., elec., tobacco inds., oil refining; nuclear reactor; oil pipeline to Lavera, nr. Marseilles; p. (1990) 276,500.

Karlstad, t., **Sweden;** on N. shore L. Väner; ironwks., engin., machin.; p. (1992) 77,290.

Karnak, t., **Egypt;** on Nile, E. of Luxor; site of the anc. Thebes; ruined temples.

Karnal, t., Haryana, **India;** clothing inds.; p. (1991) 173,751.

Karnataka (Mysore), st., S.W. **India;** borders Arabian Oc.; inc. W. Ghats where high rainfall and hydroelec. power; rainfall decreases to E.; cap. Bangalore; a. 192,203 km²; p. (1991) 44,977,201.

Karpathos, I., Dodecanese, **Greece;** Aegean Sea; between Rhodes and Crete; p. (1981) 4,645.

Karroo, W. Cape Prov., **S. Africa;** high plateau, scrub-covered; irrigated by Verwoerd dam on Orange R.

Kars, t. and prov., N.E. **Turkey;** in Armenia, alt. c. 1,800 m, in strategic position nr. Soviet border; p. (1985) 69,293, (1990) 662,155 (prov.).

Karst, dist., **Slovenia** (formerly Yugoslavia); in Dinaric Alps; gives name to limestone landforms which are well developed here.

Karun, R., S.W. **Iran;** mainly mtn. torrent; difficult access, sparse p.; 752 km long.

Karvina, t., **Czech Rep.;** on Polish border; ctr. of Ostrava-Karvina coalfield; p. (1990) 70,000.

Kasai, R., **Angola** and **Congo,** Central Africa; rises in Bihé Plateau (Angola) and flows over 1,920 km into R. Congo 192 km above Kinshasa; alluvial diamond mng. at Chicopa.

Kasai, former prov., **Congo;** agr.; impt. source of industl. diamonds; attempted secession 1960; now divided into E. Kasai (cap. Mbuji-Mayi), and W. Kasai (cap. Luluabourg).

Kāshān, c., central **Iran;** in agr. oasis; carpets, velvet; p. (1982) 110,000.

Kashi (Kashgar) c., Xinjiang, prov., **China;** on anc. imperial silk route through central Asia; growth rapid with irrigation; visited by Marco Polo 1275; p. (1984) 187,100.

Kashmir. See Jammu and Kashmir.

Kassala, t., N.E. **Sudan;** ctr. of cotton-growing dist.

Kassel, c., Hesse, **Germany;** on R. Fulda; cas.; machin., vehicles, science-based inds.; route ctr.; p. (1990) 194,800.

Kastamonu, t., N. **Turkey;** cap. of K. prov.; ctr. of dist. rich in minerals; textiles, copper gds.; p. (1985) 46,986.

Katanga. See Shaba.

Kathiawar, peninsula, Gujarat, **India;** between G. of Kutch and G. of Cambay; ch. pt. Bhaunagar; very dry a.

Katmai, Mount, S. Alaska, **USA;** active volcano with crater L.; alt. 2,135 m.

Katmandu (Kathmandu), cap. of **Nepal;** on Vishnumati R., 120 km from Indian frontier; highway to Kodari; hydroelec. sta.; brick and tile wks.; many palaces and temples; p. (1991) 419,073.

Katoomba, t., N.S.W., **Australia;** holiday resort at 1,017 m in the Blue Mountains; since 1947 part of City of Blue Mtns.; p. (1981) 13,942 (inc. Wentworth Falls).

Katowice, prov., S. **Poland;** in Upper Silesia; cap. K.; mng. and industl. a. drained by Warta R.; a. 9,516 km²; p. (1989) 3,953,800.

Katowice, c., S. **Poland;** cap. of K. prov.; impt. iron-mng. and industl. ctr.; heavy machin. chemicals; p. (1989) 366,077.

Katrine, Loch, Stirling, **Scot.;** beautiful woodland and moorland scenery; source of Glasgow water supply; scene of Scott's *Lady of the Lake*; 13 km long, *c*. 1·6 km wide.

Katsina, t., **Nigeria;** nr. Niger border; agr. tr. ctr., groundnuts, cotton; rural craft inds.; steel rolling mill; Hausa cultural ctr.; p. (1992) 186,900, (1991) 3,878,344 (state).

Kattegat, arm of N. Sea linked with Baltic; separates **Denmark** (Jutland) from **Sweden;** 64–112 km wide.

Katwijk, t., S. Holland, **Neth.;** on N. Sea 24 km from the Hague; resort; synthetic resins; p. (1993) 40,682.

Kaufbeuren, t., Bavaria, **Germany;** on R. Wertach; textile mnfs.; p. (1986) 41,500.

Kaunas (Kovno), c., **Lithuania;** on R. Nemen; R. pt. and comm. ctr.; univ.; 11th cent. c.; metal gds., chemicals, textiles, hydroelec. power; Jewish p. (circa 30 per cent) exterminated during German occupation 1941–4; p. (1990) 429,700.

Kavalla, c., E. Macedonia, **Greece;** on Bay of Kavalla; processes and exp. tobacco; the anc. Neapolis; p. (1981) 56,705.

Kawagoe, c., Honshu, **Japan;** in Kanto plain; silk textiles; p. (1990) 304,860.

Kawasaki, S. sub. Tokyo, Honshu, **Japan;** pt. for import of industl. raw materials; heavy inds.; p. (1990) 1,173,606.

Kawthoolei State, st., **Myanmar;** former Karen st.,

extended to inc. areas in Tenasserim and Irrawaddy; a. 30,383 km²; p. (1983) 1,057,505.

Kayah State, semi-aut. st., **Myanmar;** on Thai border; forested plateau; tungsten mines; teak; a. 11,730 km²; p. (1983) 168,355.

Kayseri, c. and prov., **Turkey;** S.E. of Ankara; textiles, carpets, food tr.; anc. Hittite c.; p. (1990) 943,484 (prov.), 461,415 (c.).

Kazakhstan, CIS, former USSR constituent rep., located in central Asia; cap. Akmola; steppe with stock-raising; lge. desert areas being made fertile by irrigation; plans to divert Ob R.; grain in N.; coal in Karaganda; asbestos at Dzhetygara; minerals inc. metaborite (richest boron mineral); oil; atomic power sta. to W. of Caspian Sea; cosmodrome at Leninsk, E. of Aral Sea; a. 2,778,544 km²; p. (1994) 16,942,000.

Kazan, c., **Russia;** cap. of Tatar aut. rep.; pt. on Volga; impt. tr. ctr. for E. Russia, Turkestan Bokhara and Iran; cath., univ. (where Tolstoy and Lenin were educated); engin., chemicals, synthetic rubber, textiles, paper, oil refining; natural gas pipeline to Minnibayevo; p. (1989) 1,094,000.

Kazanluk, t., central **Bulgaria;** in region famous for attar of roses.

Kazan-retto or **Volcanic Is.;** gr. of Is., W. Pac. Oc. S. of Tokyo; sugar plantations, sulphur; returned to **Japan** by USA 1968.

Kazbek, extinct volcano, N. **Georgia;** second hgst. peak of Caucasus; alt. 5,045 m.

Kāzerūn, t., S.W. **Iran;** ctr. of agr. dist. where fruit, tobacco, opium, cotton grown.

Kazvin or **Qazvin,** c., N.W. **Iran;** transit tr.; carpets, textiles; p. (1983) 244,265.

Kearsley, t., Gtr. Manchester, **Eng.;** chemicals, paper; p. (1991) 9,287.

Keban Dam, S.E. **Turkey;** at confluence of the E. and W. branches of Euphrates.

Kecskemet, c., central **Hungary;** fruit-canning and wine-distilling from locally grown prods.; 4th cent. c.; p. (1997) 105,000.

Kedah, st., **Malaysia;** on Strait of Malacca, N.W. Malaya; rice, rubber, coconuts, tungsten; cap. Alor Star; a. 9,479 km²; p. (1980) 1,116,140.

Kediri, t., E. Java, **Indonesia;** food processing; p. (1980) 221,830.

Keeling Is. See **Cocos Is.**

Keelung, c., N. **Taiwan;** on E. China Sea; naval base and ch. pt.; exp. agr. prods.; chemicals; gold, sulphur, copper mined nearby; p. (1995) 368,173.

Keewatin, dist., N.W. Terr., **Canada;** barren grounds; fur a. 590,934 km².

Kegworth, v. Leics., **Eng;** scene of M1 air crash; p. (1991) 3,405.

Keighley, t., West Yorks., **Eng.;** in Aire valley, 24 km N.W. of Leeds; engin., woollen and worsteds; p. (1991) 49,567.

Keihin, vast conurb. of Tokyo, Yokohama and Kawasaki, **Japan.**

Keith, burgh, Moray, **Scot.;** mkt. t. in agr. dist.; p. (1991) 4,793.

Kelantan, st., **Malaysia;** one of most fertile areas on E. cst. Malaya; cap. Kota Bharu; rice, coconuts, rubber; a. 14,815 km²; p. (1980) 893,753.

Kells or **Ceannanus Mor,** mkt. t., Co. Meath, **R.o.I.;** notable for monastic remains and illuminated Book of Kells, now in library of Trinity College, Dublin; p. (1986) 2,413.

Kelso, burgh, Borders, **Scot.;** at confluence of Rs. Teviot and Tweed; p. (1991) 5,989.

Kemerovo, c., **Russia;** S.E. of Tomsk; coalmng. ctr.; chemicals, textiles, plastics; p. (1989) 520,000.

Kemi, t., N.E. **Finland;** spt. on G. of Bothnia; sawmills; p. (1993) 25,095.

Kemi, R., N.E. **Finland;** used for hydroelectric power and timber transport; 480 km long.

Kempten, t., Bavaria, **Germany;** nr. Bodensee; Benedictine abbey; p. (1986) 57,000.

Kendal, l. gov. dist., Cumbria, **Eng.;** mkt. ctr.; tourism; p. (1991) 25,461.

Kenilworth, t., Warwicks., **Eng.;** 6 km S.W. of Coventry; mkt.; ruined cas.; p. (1991) 21,623.

Kenitra. See **Mina Hassan Tani.**

Kennet, l. gov. dist., Wiltshire, **Eng.;** stretches from Marlborough to Devizes; p. (1995) 74,700.

Kennet, R., Wilts. and Berks., **Eng.;** trib. of R. Thames; followed by main rly. London to W. of Eng.; 70 km long.

Kennington, dist., in London bor. of Lambeth, **Eng.;** inc. the Oval cricket ground, home of Surrey C.C.; p. (1991) 4,290.

Kenosha, t., Wis., **USA;** on W. shore of L. Mich.; p. (1990) 80,352 (t.), 128,000 (met. a.).

Kensington and Chelsea, Royal Borough of, inner bor., W. London, **Eng.;** mainly residtl.; contains Kensington Palace and Gardens; p. (1995) 153,900.

Kent, non-met. co., **Eng.;** intensive agr., mkt. gardening, orchards, hops; "Garden of England"; crossed by N. Downs and Weald; industl. zone bordering Thames and Medway estuaries; tourist resorts and cross-channel ferry pts. on cst.; London commuter hinterland; co. t. Maidstone; p. (1995) 1,551,300.

Kentucky, E. central st., **USA;** in W. foothills of Appalachians and crossed by tribs. of Mississippi; "Bluegrass" st.; mainly agr.; some coal; cap. Frankfort; lgst. c. Louisville, at falls of Ohio R.; hydroelec. power; tourism; admitted to Union 1792; st. flower Goldenrod, st. bird Cardinal; a. 104,623 km²; p. (1990) 3,685,296.

Kentucky, R., Ky., **USA;** flows from Cumberland plateau to Ohio R.; length 400 km.

Kenya, rep., E. Africa; member of Brit. Commonwealth; comprises 7 provs.; straddles equator but climate modified by alt.; marked contrast between sparsely populated and arid N. and well-developed S. where upland climate has attracted the European p.; economy based on prod. and processing of arable and pastoral prods., inc. dairy prod.; relatively well developed cooperative African farming; 80 per cent of p. earn living on the land; most industl. of E. African cty., mostly exp. orientated; growth in exp. of cement and fluorspar; tourism incr. impt; ch. spt. Mombasa, airports at Nairobi and Mombasa; famous for big game; univ.; cap. Nairobi; a. 582,646 km²; p. (1995) 26,440,000.

Kenya, Mt., volcano, **Kenya;** just S. of equator; snow-covered; alt. 5,197 m; 2nd hgst. peak in Africa; Nat. Park.

Kephallenia. See **Cephalonia.**

Kerala, st., **India;** cap. Trivandrum; plantations producing rubber, tea, pepper; higher proportion of literacy than in any other st.; a. 38,855 km²; p. (1991) 20,098,518.

Kerch, c., **Ukraine;** in Crimea, commanding K. strait connecting Black Sea and Azov Sea; spt. and industl. ctr.; metallurgical plant, iron and steel mills, shipbldg., fisheries; iron-ore, vanadium, natural gas nearby; p. (1990) 176,300.

Kerguelen, archipelago, S. **Indian Oc.;** part of Fr. Antarctic terr.; whaling, fishing; famous for K. cabbage (*Pringlea antiscorbutica*).

Kerkrade, t., Limburg prov., **Neth.;** coal mng.; anc. abbey; p. (1994) 52,848.

Kérkira. See **Corfu.**

Kermadec Is., volcanic gr. Pac. Oc.; 960 km N.E. of N.Z.; a. 34 km²; met. sta. on Sunday I. (Raoul I.) (lgst. of gr.); annexed to **N.Z.** 1887; p. (1986) 5.

Kerman, region, S.E. **Iran;** mtnous., much desert land; agr.; carpet-weaving; coal and iron-ore mng. being developed; recent copper find; irrigation scheme projected; p. (1982) 1,078,875.

Kermān, c., S.E. **Iran;** prov. cap.; carpet-weaving ctr.; textile mftg.; airpt.; mediaeval mosques; multi-million dollar complex for mining and refining copper; p. (1986) 254,786.

Kermānshāh, (Qahremānshahr) t., N.W. **Iran;** cap. of Kermānshāhān prov.; agr., comm. and route ctr.; airpt.; oil refinery; p. (1986) 565,544. **Kern,** R., E. Cal., **USA;** one of most impt. power-generating Rs. in st.

Kerrier, l. gov. dist., Cornwall, **Eng.;** a. inc. Lizard penin. and Helston; p. (1995) 88,800.

Kerry, coastal co., Munster, **R.o.I.;** deeply indented cst.; cap. Tralee; tourism; a. 4,703 km²; p. (1986) 124,159.

Kerulen, R., N.E. **Mongolia** and **China;** flows parallel to edge of Gobi Desert; a. designated for economic development; 1,256 km long.

Keswick, Allerdale, Cumbria, **Eng.;** on Greta R.; at N. end of L. Derwentwater; tourist ctr.; mkt.; pencils; p. (1991) 4,836.

Kettering, l. gov. dist., mkt. t., Northants., **Eng.;** nr. Wellingborough; footwear; iron mng.; p. (1995) 79,900 (dist.), (1991) 47,186 (t.).

Kew, dist., London bor. of Richmond upon Thames, **Eng.;** contains Kew botanical gardens.

Keweenaw, peninsula, L. Superior, **USA;** former impt. copper deposits.

Keynsham, t., Bath and N .E. Somerset, **Eng.;** expanded t.; p. (1991) 15,193.

Key West, c., Fla., **USA;** on I. *c.* 240 km from mainland; naval sta., coastguard base; cigarmftg.; tourism; p. (1980) 24,382.

Khabarovsk, c., **Russia;** cap. of K. terr., E. Siberia, on Amur R.; cath.; oil refining, aircraft engin., wood and paper inds.; pipeline links with oilfields in N. Sakhalin; transport ctr. of Far East; p. (1989) 601,000.

Khakass Autonomous Oblast, admin. div. of Krasnoyarsk region, **Russia;** pastoral agr., timber and mng. inds.; a. 61,784 km²; p. (1989) 566,900.

Khandwa, t., Madhya Pradesh, **India;** S. of Indore; cotton, oil-pressing; p. (1991) 145,133.

Khaniá, or **Canea,** c., Crete, **Greece;** in sheltered bay on W. cst.; historic sites; p. (1981) 47,451.

Khanka, L., **China-USSR** border; dairy farming, fishing; branch of Trans-Siberian rly. to W. shore; a. 4,403 km².

Khanty-Mansi, admin. div., **Russia;** in W. Siberian lowland; sparse p.; cap. KhantyMansiisk (at confluence of Ob' and Irtysh Rs.); natural gas; a. 556,850 km²; p. (1989) 1,282,400.

Kharagpur, c., W. Bengal, **India;** industl., scientific research ctr.; rly. junc.; p. (1991) 265,000.

Khārg, I., Persian Gulf, **Iran;** oil terminal for supertankers, 48 km from mainland; repeated Iraqi air attacks resulted in floating terminal at Sirri island and plans for replacement terminal.

Khar'kov, c., **Ukraine;** impt. industl. ctr. in Donets coal region; cap. of K. region; univ., cath.; rly. ctr.; extensively rebuilt after second world war; p. (1990) 1,618,400.

Khartoum, c., cap. of the **Sudan;** at confluence of Blue and White Niles; univ.; famous siege under Gordon 1884–5; p. (1983) 476,218.

Khashm el Girba, t., **Sudan;** new t. on Atbara R., between Khartoum and Ethiopian border; for p. of Wadi Halfa inundated by Aswan L.; sugar refinery.

Khasi Hills, Meghalaya, N.E. **India;** form abrupt S. edge to middle Brahmaputra valley; very heavy monsoon rains on S.-facing slopes; lower slopes forested; middle slopes impt. tea-growing region; rise to over 1,800 m.

Khaskovo, t., **Bulgaria;** woollens, carpets, tobacco; p. (1990) 95,807.

Kherson, c., **Ukraine;** 24 km up R. Dnieper from Black Sea; sea and R. pt., rly. junc.; grain, oil refining, engin., textiles, shipbldg; founded by Catherine the Great as fortress t.; p. (1990) 361,200.

Khingan, Gr. and Little, mtn. ranges, Inner Mongolia and Heilongjiang prov., N.E. **China;** rich timber resources; rise to over 1,800 m.

Khios or **Chios,** I., **Greece;** in Aegean Sea; wines, figs, fruits; marble; cap. Khios; supposed birthplace of Homer; p. (1981) 48,700.

Khiva, former vassal st. of Russia; now part of **Uzbekistan and Turkmenistan.**

Khiva, c., N.W. **Uzbekistan;** in oasis nr. Kara-Kum desert; cottons, carpets; anc. c.; p. (1990) 40,600.

Khmel'nitskiy (Proskurov), c., **Ukraine;** on R. Bug; machin. tools, textiles, food inds.; p. (1990) 241,000.

Khmer Republic. See **Cambodia.**

Khor Abdulla, Iraq; in Persian G. nr. Basra; deepwater oil-loading island terminal.

Khorāsan or **Khurasan,** prov., N.E. **Iran;** sparsely p.; agr.; wool; turquoises; cap. Mashhad; p. (1982) 3,264,398.

Khorramshahr, spt., S.W. **Iran,** leading pt. on Persian G.; increased in importance in second world war when harbour facilities expanded; handles major part of foreign trade; main exp. dates; linked by pipeline to oilfields and by road and rail to Ahvāz and Tehran.

Khotan. See **Hotan.**

Khovu-Aksy, t., Tuva aut. rep., **Russia;** on R. Elegest, 80 km S.W. of Kyzyl; new t. 1956; cobalt deposit being developed.

Khudzhand, (Leninabad), c., **Tajikistan;** on Syr Dar'ya R., S. of Tashkent; silks, cottons, fruit-preserving; hydroelectric power sta.; p. (1990) 163,100.

Khulna, c., **Bangladesh;** in low-lying a. in W. Ganges delta; p. (1991) 545,849.

Khunjerab Pass, Kashmir, **India;** 5,000 m. pass in Karakoram Range; links Sinkiang (China) with Pakistan and Middle East; new metal route opened (1982) making shorter route to W. for China and took 20 years to build.

Khuzestan, prov., W. **Iran;** frontier Iraq; leading petroleum ctr.; lge. dams; cap. Ahvāz; p. (1982) 2,196,920.

Khyber Pass, pass in Hindu Kush mtns., between Pakistan and **Afghanistan;** followed by route from Peshawar to Kabul; historically most famous route into India, used by many invaders, inc. Alexander the Great.

Kiamusze. See **Jiamusi.**

Kianga-Moura, dist., Queensland, **Australia;** lge. coalfield; coking coal exp. to Japan via Gladstone.

Kiangsi. See **Jiangxi.**

Kiangsu. See **Jiangsu.**

Kicking Horse Pass, mtn. pass (1,628 m), over Rocky Mtns., B.C., **Canada;** used by Canadian Pac. rly.

Kidderminster, t., Wyre Forest, Worcs., **Eng.;** on R. Stour 6 km above its confluence with R. Severn; carpets, engin., sugar-beet refining, textile machin., elec. vehicles, drop forgings; p. (1991) 54,644.

Kidsgrove, t., "Potteries," Stoke, **Eng.;** 5 km N.W. of Stoke-on-Trent; chemicals, metal wks., rayon, silk and nylon spinning, precast concrete, ceramics; p. (1991) 27,702.

Kidwelly, Carmarthenshire, **Wales;** mkt. t.; sm. harbour; cas.; p. (1991) 2,664.

Kiel, spt., cap. of Schleswig-Holstein, **Germany;** univ.; Baltic naval pt.; shipbldg. and allied inds., elec. gds., textiles, fishing; p. (1990) 246,600.

Kiel Canal (North Sea-Baltic Canal or Kaiser-Wilhelm-Kanal) Germany; connects Elbe estuary on North Sea with Baltic; 98 km long; opened 1895, reconstructed 1914; internationalised 1919 by Treaty of Versailles, but repudiated by Hitler 1936.

Kielce, c. and prov., central **Poland;** in Swietokrzyskie mtns.; cath., route ctr.; agr. machin., chemicals; minerals quarried in prov.; founded 12th cent.; p. (1989) 213,012 (c.), 1,123,700 (prov.).

Kielder, reservoir, Northumberland, **Eng.;** one of lgst. man-made lakes in Europe.

Kiev (Kiyev), c., cap. of **Ukraine;** on R. Dnieper; leading cultural, industl. and comm. ctr.; cath., univ.; machin., textiles; in a. of rich mineral deposits; natural gas pipeline runs from Dashava; historic c., once cap. of Muscovite empire; p. (1990) 2,616,000.

Kigali, cap. of **Rwanda;** comm. ctr.; airport; new tungsten and iron foundries; p. (1993) 234,500.

Kigoma, t., W. **Tanzania;** pt. on E. shore of L. Tanganyika; W. terminus of Central rly. to Dar-es-Salaam.

Kii, peninsula, **Japan;** highland area and inlet of same name, S. Honshu.

Kikinda, t., Vojvodina, **Serbia, Yugoslavia;** agr. tr.; rly. junc.; p. (1981) 69,854.

Kilauea, crater, 1,112 m high, on S.E. slope of Mauna Loa, **Hawaii,** one of lgst. active craters in world; over 3 km in diameter.

Kildare, inland co., Leinster, **R.o.I.;** dairying, cereals; co. t. Naas; a. 1,694 km²; p. (1986) 116,247.

Kildare, mkt. t., cap. of Kildare, **R.o.I.;** cath.; close by is the famous racecourse, the Curragh of Kildare; p. (1986) 4,268.

Kilimanjaro, volcanic mtn., N. **Tanzania;** hgst. peak in Africa, 5,895 m; international airpt. at 894 m on Sanya Plain; Nat. Park.

Kilindini, spt., **Kenya;** adjoins Mombasa; the finest harbour on E. cst. of Africa.

Kilkenny, inland co., Leinster, **R.o.I.;** cap. Kilkenny; pastoral farming, black marble; a. 2,062 km²; p. (1986) 73,186.

Kilkenny, t., cap. of Kilkenny, **R.o.I.;** on R. Nore; local mkt., caths., cas.; p. (1986) 8,969.

Killala Bay, Mayo and Sligo, **R.o.I.,** wide bay fed by R. Hoy.

Killaloe, v., Co. Clare, **R.o.I.;** crossing point for R. Shannon; cath.; p. (1986) 1,033

Killarney, t., Kerry, **R.o.I.;** local mkt.; tourist ctr. for the Ls. of K.; p. (1986) 7,837.

Killarney, Lakes of, Kerry, **R.o.I.;** Lower, Middle, and Upper, celebrated for their beauty; tourist resorts; Muckross on Middle L. site of anc. abbey.

Killiecrankie, Pass of, Scot.; on R. Garry; at S. approach to Drumochter Pass; used by main rly. Perth to Inverness; scene of battle 1691.

Killingworth, t., Tyne and Wear, **Eng.;** 6 km N.E. of Newcastle; new t.; proposed p. 20,000.

Kilmarnock, burgh, E. Ayrshire, Scot.; on R. Irvine, 17 km N.E. of Ayr.; p. (1991) 44,307.

Kilo-Moto, goldfield, **Congo;** in N.E. of st., 80 km W. of L. Kasenyi; linked by motor road to R. Congo (Kisangani) and L. Kasenyi.

Kilrenny and Anstruther, t., Fife, Scot., at entrance to F. of Forth; fishing, hosiery, oilskin mnfs; p. (1991) 3,154.

Kilrush, sm. spt., U.D., Co. Clare, **R.o.I.;** on R. Shannon; p. (1986) 2,961.

Kilsyth, burgh, N. Lanarkshire, **Scot.;** at S. foot of Campsie Fells, 16 km W. of Falkirk; p. (1991) 9,918.

Kilwinning, burgh, N. Ayrshire, **Scot.;** 8 km E. of Ardrossan; p. (1991) 15,479.

Kimberley, former goldfield dist., W. **Australia;** sparsely populated beef producing a., bauxite and iron mng.

Kimberley, t., B.C., **Canada;** on R. Kootenay; site of Sullivan mine, silver, lead, zinc; ores smelted at Trail; p. (1986) 6,732.

Kimberley, t., C. Prov., **S. Africa;** diamond-mng. dist.; asbestos, manganese, iron, cement, engin.; founded 1871; p. (1985) 149,667 (met. a.).

Kinabalu, Mount, Sabah, **Malaysia;** in Crocker mtns.; hgst. peak in Borneo, alt. 4,104 m.

Kincardineshire, historic co., E. **Scot.,** now part of Aberdeenshire.

Kinder Scout, mtn., N. Derbys., **Eng.;** hgst. point of the Peak dist.; alt. 637 m.

Kindia, t., **Guinea;** rich bauxite deposits worked since 1974 but output restricted by poor rail links.

Kineshma, c., **Russia;** on Volga, N.W. of Gorki; pt. for Ivanovo industl. a.; textiles; dates from early 15th cent.; p. (1989) 105,000.

King George's Sound, W. **Australia;** nr. Albany; fine harbour and bay.

Kinghorn, t., Fife, **Scot.;** on F. of Forth, 5 km S. of Kirkcaldy; p. (1991) 2,931.

Kingsbridge, t., South Hams, S. Devon, **Eng.;** at head of Kingsbridge estuary, 16 km S.W. of Dartmouth; mkt.; p. (1991) 5,258.

King's Lynn, spt., West Norfolk, **Eng.;** at mouth of Gr. Ouse; docks; fishing base; agr. machin., canning, chemical fertilisers, shoes; expanded t.; part of l. gov. dist. of **King's Lynn and West Norfolk;** p. (1991) 41,281 (t.), (1995) 131,100 (dist.).

Kingston, t., Ont., **Canada;** E. end of L. Ontario; univ., military college; p. (1986) 55,050.

Kingston, spt., cap. of **Jamaica;** ch. comm. ctr. for J.; landlocked harbour; agr.-processing; univ.; p. (1991) 587,798.

Kingston upon Hull. *See* **Hull.**

Kingston upon Thames, former M.B., Surrey, **Eng.;** now **The Royal Borough of Kingston-upon-Thames,** outer bor. of Greater London; inc. bors. of Malden and Coombe and Surbiton; residtl. with Richmond Park, Hampton Court, Bushey Park nearby; aircraft parts; p. (1995) 140,100.

Kingstown, spt., cap. of **St. Vincent,** W.I.; cath., botanic gardens; p. (1991) 26,223.

Kingswood, t., S. Gloucs., **Eng.;** nr. Bristol; elec. vehicles, motor cycles, boots, brushes, tools; school founded by John Wesley; p. (1991) 60,192 .

Kington, mkt. t., Hereford, **Eng.;** 19 km W. of Leominster; p. (1991) 2,197.

Kinki, dist., S.W. Honshu, **Japan;** agr., industl. and comm. complex centred on Osaka, Kyoto, and Kōbe; p. (1990) 22,207,000.

Kinlochleven, v., Highland, **Scot.;** at head of Loch Leven; hydroelec. power sta.; aluminium smelting; p. (1991) 1,076.

Kinnairds Head, promontory, nr. Fraserburgh, on N.E. cst. of **Scot.**

Kinross, burgh, Perth and Kinross, **Scot.;** on Loch Leven, 26 km N.E. of Alloa; textiles; resort; p. (1991) 4,552.

Kinross-shire, historic co., E. **Scot.,** now part of Perth and Kinross.

Kinsale, t., Cork, **R.o.I.;** sm. fish pt. on K. harbour; tourism; natural gas field; p. (1986) 1,811.

Kinshasa (**Leopoldville**), c., cap. of **Congo;** above the cataracts on R. Congo; univ.; textiles, shoes; founded by Stanley 1887; p. (1991) 3,804,000.

Kinta Valley, S.E. Perak, **W. Malaysia;** tin mng., rubber plantations.

Kintyre, peninsula, Argyll and Bute, **Scot.;** terminates in Mull of Kintyre; 67 km long, 16 km wide.

Kioga (**Kyoga**), L., **Uganda;** on R. Nile midway between L. Victoria and L. Mobuto Seso.

Kiölen or **Kjölen,** mtn. range, **Norway** and **Sweden;** hgst. point Mt. Sulitjelma, 1,876 m.

Kirghizia, CIS, former USSR constituent rep.; S.W. of Siberia; mtnous. cty., in Tienshan and Pamir systems; livestock breeding; mineral resources, food processing; cap. Frunze; a 196,581 km²; p. (1994) 4,463,000.

Kiribati (**Gilbert Is**), indep. st. (1979), former Brit. col., central Pac. Oc.; chain of coral Is. across equator; economy based on phosphate mng. and copra; cap. Tarawa; Ellice Is. separated 1976 and renamed Tuvalu; a. 956 km²; p. (1995) 80,000.

Kirin. *See* **Jilin.**

Kirkburton, t., West Yorks., **Eng.;** S.E. of Huddersfield; woollens; p. (1991) 4,121.

Kirkby, t., Knowsley, Merseyside, **Eng.;** p. (1981) 50,898.

Kirkby in Ashfield, t., Ashfield, Notts., **Eng.;** 16 km N.W. of Nottingham; p. (1991) 27,014.

Kirkbymoorside, t., Ryedale, North Yorks., **Eng.;** nr. Vale of Pickering; mkt.-place; sailplanes, gliders; p. (1991) 2,650.

Kirkcaldy, royal burgh, Fife, **Scot.;** spt. on N. side of F. of Forth; linoleum, engin.; birthplace of Adam Smith; p. (1991) 47,155.

Kirkcudbright, royal burgh, Dumfries and Galloway, **Scot.;** on R. Dee at influx into K. Bay, S.W. of Dumfries; agr. ctr., hosiery; cas., abbey; p. (1991) 3,588.

Kirkcudbrightshire, historic co., S. **Scot.,** now part of Dumfries and Galloway.

Kirkenes, t., Finnmark prov., N.E. **Norway;** on S. arm of Varanger fjord, nr. Soviet border; pt. for iron-mng. dist.

Kirkham, t., Kirklees, Lancs., **Eng.;** textiles; p. (1991) 9,038.

Kirkintilloch, burgh, E. Dunbartonshire, **Scot.;** on Forth and Clyde Canal; engin.; p. (1991) 20,780.

Kirklees, met. dist., West Yorks., **Eng.;** comprises Huddersfield, Dewsbury, Batley, Spenborough, Colne Valley, Meltham, Holmfirth, Denby Dale, Kirkburton, Heckmondwike and Mirfield; p. (1995) 387,700.

Kirkstone Pass, mtn. pass, Cumbria, **Eng.;** used by main road between Ullswater and Windermere Lakes.

Kirkūk, t., **Iraq;** most imp. centre of Iraqi oil industry; p. (1970) 207,852 (no recent figs.).

Kirkwall, royal burgh, Mainland I., Orkney Is., **Scot.;** cath.; p. (1991) 6,469.

Kirov. *See* **Vyatka.**

Kirovabad. *See* **Gyandzha.**

Kirovograd. c., **Ukraine;** on Ingul R.; cap. of K. oblast; agr. ctr.; engin.; p. (1990) 274,200.

Kirovsk, c., **Russia;** on Kola peninsula; apatite and nephelite mng.; chemicals.

Kirriemuir, burgh, Angus, **Scot.;** on N. margin of Strathmore, 8 km W. of Forfar; jute-weaving; birthplace of J. M. Barrie; p. (1991) 5,571.

Kirtland, t., N.M., **USA;** atomic and space research sta.

Kiruna, t., N. **Sweden;** inside Arctic Circle, N.W. of Luleå; linked by rly. to Narvik (Norway); impt. deposits of iron ore; p. (1983) 28,638.

Kiryu, c., Honshu, **Japan;** major textile ctr.; p. (1990) 126,443.

Kisangani (**Stanleyville**), t., **Congo;** on R. Congo nr. Boyoma Falls; airpt.; univ.; p. (1991) 373,397.

Kiselevsk, c., S.W. Siberia, **Russia;** coal-mng. ctr. in Kuznetsk basin; p. (1989) 128,000.

Kishinev, c., cap. of **Moldova;** on Byk R., trib. of Dniester; cath., univ.; industl., comm. ctr. in rich farming a.; tourism; p. (1990) 675,500.

Kislovodsk, c., **Russia;** in N. Caucasus; famous spa; p. (1989) 114,000.

Kismayo, pt., **Somalia;** new deep-water harbour; airpt.; p. (1987) 200,000

Kisumu, spt., cap. of Nyanza prov., **Kenya;** at head of Kavirondo G. on L. Victoria; handles bulk of cotton from Buganda and coffee from N. Tanzania for transhipment E. by rail; lge. brewery; p. (1984) 167,100.

Kitakyūshū, c., N. Kyushu, **Japan;** one of Japan's lgst. muns. on merging (1963) of ts. Moji, Kokura, Tobata, Yawata, and Wakamatsu; sixth c. to enjoy special aut. rights; p. (1990) 1,026,467.

Kitami, c., Hokkaido, **Japan;** mkt.; food-processing; p. (1990) 107,247.

Kitchener, c., Ont., **Canada;** agr. machin., tyres, hardware, agr. processing; p. (1991) 168,281 (c.), (1986) 311,194 (met. a.).

Kithira. *See* **Cerigo.**

Kitimat, t., B.C., **Canada;** lge. aluminium smelter powered by hydroelectricity from diversion of R. Fraser trib. through the Rockies; p. (1986) 11,196.

Kitwe, t., **Zambia;** contiguous to mng. township of Nkana, ctr. of copperbelt; p. (1989) 495,000.

Kiukiang. *See* Jiujiang.

Kivu, L., on border of **Congo** and **Rwanda;** in highlands of Gr. Rift Valley; natural gas discoveries; 1,473 m high, 96 km long.

Kizil, lgst. R. of **Turkey;** rises in Kisil Dagh, flows to Black Sea via Sivas; 1,120 km long.

Kladno, t., **Czech Rep.;** 16 km N.W. of Prague; coalmng. ctr.; iron and steel wks., machin.; p. (1990) 73,000.

Klagenfurt, t., cap. of Carinthia, **Austria;** winter sports ctr.; varied mnfs.; p. (1991) 89,502.

Klaipeda (Memel), c. **Lithuania;** ice-free spt. on Baltic Sea; exp. timber, textiles, chemicals, paper; p. (1990) 206,200.

Klamath, mtns., N. Cal., S.W. Ore., **USA;** beautiful ranges containing Nat. Park and Indian reserve; hgst. alt. Mt. Eddy, 2,757 m.

Klamono, t., W. Irian, **Indonesia;** ctr. of oilfield; pipeline to Sorong harbour.

Klerksdorp, t., S. Transvaal, **S. Africa;** gold, diamonds; p. (1980) 238,680.

Klodzko (Glatz), t., Walbrzych prov. S.W. **Poland;** formerly in Prussian Silesia; rly. junc.; on R. Neisse; comm. and mftg.; p. (1989) 30,261.

Klondike, R., Yukon, **Canada;** sm. trib. of Yukon in gold-mng. region; gold rush 1896; 160 km long.

Klyuchevskaya Sopka, one of 18 active volcanoes, **Russia;** in N.E. Siberia, on Kamchatka peninsula; alt. 4,748 m.

Knaresborough, t., North Yorks., **Eng.;** 5 km N.E. of Harrogate; mkt.; cas. ruins; p. (1991) 13,380.

Knighton, t., Powys, **Wales;** on R. Teme; mkt.; p. (1991) 2,972.

Knockmealdown Mtns., Waterford and Tipperary, **R.o.I.;** highest point 796 m; tourism.

Knob Lake. *See* Schefferville.

Knossos, ruined c., cap. of anc. Crete, **Greece;** S.E. of Iráklion; ctr. of Cretan bronze age culture, 1800 B.C.; archaeological source of knowledge about the Minoans.

Knottingley, t., West Yorks., **Eng.;** on R. Aire, 19 km S.E. of Leeds; engin., glass, tar distilling, chemicals; coal mng; p. (1991) 14,690.

Knowsley, met. dist., Merseyside, **Eng.;** comprises Kirkby, Prescot and Huyton with Roby; p. (1995) 154,000.

Knoxville, c., Tenn., **USA;** univ.; livestock and tobacco mkt.; textiles, marble, plastics, chemicals, aluminium; p. (1990) 165,121 (c.), 605,000 (met. a.).

Knutsford, t., N.E. Cheshire, **Eng.;** mkt.; home of Mrs. Gaskell, author of *Cranford;* p. (1991) 13,352.

Kōbe, c., spt., Honshu, **Japan;** at E. end of Inland Sea; 5th c. of Japan; developed as pt. for Osaka and Kinki plain; iron and steel, shipbldg., rubber; major earthquake January 1995; p. (1990) 1,477,423.

Koblenz (Coblenz), t. Rhineland-Palatinate, **Germany;** at confluence of Rs. Rhine and Moselle; fine buildings; wine, paper, machin., leather, ceramics; p. (1990) 108,800.

Kōchi, plain and c., Shikoku, **Japan;** early vegetables, double rice cropping; p. (1990) 317,090.

Kodiak I., lgst. of Is. of Alaska, **USA;** 144 km long; forested mtns.; fur-trading, salmon-fishing, canning; earthquake 1964; p. (1990) 13,309.

Kōfu, basin and c., Honshu, **Japan;** rice, vineyards, orchards, silk, wine; p. (1990) 200,630.

Kohat, t., **Pakistan;** on trib. of Indus; military t.; cement wks.; p. (1981) 78,000.

Koh-I-Baba Mtns., Afghanistan, spur of the Hindu Kush; highest point 5,380 m.

Kokand, c., **Uzbekistan;** in the Ferghana Valley; mftg. ctr., textiles, chemicals, engin.; p. (1990) 175,700.

Kokiu. *See* Gejiu.

Kokkoka (Gamla Karleby), t. **Finland;** on cst. of G. of Bothnia; sulphur plant; p. (1993) 35,269.

Kokomo, c., Ind., **USA;** on Wild Cat R.; ctr. of agr. region; car components; p. (1984) 45,400, (c.), 101,000 (met. a.).

Koko-Nor. *See* Qinghai Hu.

Kokura. *See* Kitakyūshū.

Kola Peninsula, peninsula, **Russia;** extension of Lapland; rich mineral deposits; hydroelectric plants and missile base.

Kolar, c., Karnataka, **India;** p. (1981) 144,385 (met. a.).

Kolarovgrad. *See* Shumen.

Kolding, c., at head of Kolding fjord, Jutland,

Denmark; spt. and fishing base; lt. inds.; p. (1990) 57,285.

Kolhapur, c., Maharashtra, S.W. **India;** cap. of former princely st. of K.; bauxite; anc. Buddhist ctr.; p. (1991) 406,000.

Köln. *See* Cologne.

Kolobrzeg (Kolberg), t., Koszalin prov., N.W. **Poland;** spt. on Baltic cst.; comm. and fishing harbour; resort and spa; p. (1989) 44,426.

Kolomna, c., **Russia;** on Moskva R., nr. confluence with Oka R.; industl. ctr.; engin., locomotives, machin., synthetic rubber; p. (1989) 162,000.

Kolomyya, c., **Ukraine;** on Pruth R.; in Carpathian foothills; agr. tr., metal gds., oil refining, textiles.

Kolwezi, c., S. Shaba, **Congo;** comm. ctr. for mng. dist. (cobalt and copper); p. (1991) 544,497.

Kolyma, R., N.E. Siberia, **Russia;** flows into Arctic Oc., via Kolyma goldfields; navigable in summer; basin largely covered with tundra, sparsely p.; 2,560 km long.

Komárno, c., **Slovakia;** on left bank, of Danube, opposite Hungarian Komárom, on right bank; R. pt., shipbldg., oil refining; p. (1984) 35,396.

Komi, aut. rep., **Russia;** wooded lowland, pastoral agr.; coal from Pechora basin, oil at Ukhta and Troitsko-Pechorsk; mng. now ch. economic activity; cap. Syktyvkar, lumber ctr.; a. 415,799 km²; p. (1989) 1,250,800.

Komi-Permyak, admin. div., **Russia;** forestry, cellulose, paper; cap. Kudymbar; a. 31,080 km²; p. (1989) 158,500.

Komló, t., **Hungary;** new mng. t.; coking coal; p. (1997) 28,000.

Kompong Som (Sihanoukville) c., **Cambodia;** deepwater pt. on G. of Thailand; linked to Phnom Penh by modern highway; textile mills, tractors, oil refining.

Kommunarsk (Voroshilovsk), t., **Ukraine;** 40 km S.W. of Lugansk; ctr. of iron, steel and coking inds.; p. (1990) 125,700.

Komsomolsk, c., **Russia;** built by volunteer youth labour, after 1932; heavy industl. development; oil refining; pipeline connects with oilfield in N. Sakhalin; p. (1989) 315,000.

Konin, t. and prov., C. **Poland;** brown coal, rlwy, aluminium; p. (1989) 79,315 (t.) 465,900 (prov.).

Köniz, t. Bern canton, **Switzerland;** printing, rlwy, castle; p. (1990) 35,925.

Konstantinovka, industl. t., **Ukraine;** in heart of Donbas industl. region, 61 km N. of Donetsk; heavy engin., iron and steel, zinc smelting; p. (1990) 107,700.

Konya, c., **Turkey;** cap. of K. prov.; agr. tr. ctr.; mnfs. textiles, carpets, leather gds.; the anc. Iconium, fortress of the Hittite empire; p. (1990) 543,460 (c.), 1,750,303 (prov.).

Kooland I., W. **Australia;** rugged I. with iron-ore deposits worked since 1960 and exp. to **Japan.**

Koolyanobbing, mng. t., W. **Australia;** high-grade haematite and limonite ores mined since 1961 and t. constructed as residential and service ctr.

Kootenay or **Kootenai,** R., flows from B.C., **Canada;** through Montana and Idaho, **USA,** into K. L., draining it by narrow channel into Colombia R.; beautiful scenery; 720 km long.

Kopparberg , co. C. **Sweden;** cap. Falun; a. 28,350 km²; p. (1992) 290,245.

Korat Plateau, t. Thailand; headwaters of Mekong tribs.; cattle-rearing; tr. ctr. Korat.

Korçë (Koritsa), t., S.E. **Albania;** in infertile basin at 854 m nr. Greek border; mkt.; cultural ctr.; p. (1991) 67,100.

Korcula (Curzola), I., off **Croatia;** sm. I. in Adriatic Sea; ch. pt. K.; a. 277 km² .

Korea, Democratic People's Republic of (N. Korea), occupies N. part of Korean peninsula (N. of 38th parallel), E. Asia; bounded on N. by China and Russia; continental climate; cold dry winters, hot humid summers; predominantly mtnous. with many uninhabited offshire Is.; all inds. nationalised and collective agr.; rapid mechanisation, agr. employs 43 per cent working p.; development emphasis on mng. resources of coal, iron-ore and on growth of heavy inds.; most industl. resources located in N. Korea; rapid incr. in industrialisation; international airport at cap. of Pyongyang; longest surviving hard-line Communist ruling dynasty in Asia; widespread famine in mid-1990s; a. 121,248 km²; p. (1998)

22,000,000 (est.).

Korea, Rep. of (S. Korea), occupies S. part of Korean peninsula (S. of 38th parallel); climate resembles N. Korea's, topography less rugged; massive US aid revitalised economy after Korean war and Korea acquired one of world's largest foreign debts; 20 per cent work-force engaged in agr.; undergoing rapid industrialisation; textiles, electronics, shipbldg., vehicles; iron and steel ind. at Pusan; major debt and financial crisis, 1997; irrigation and power project (1971–81) for 4 Rs.— Hangang, Naktangang, Kum-Gang, and Yongsan-Gang; cap. Seoul; a. 98,992 km²; p. (1995) 44,851,000.

Korea Bay, Yellow Sea; between N. Korea and North-East China (Manchuria).

Koriyama, Honshu, **Japan**; textiles, chemicals; p. (1990) 314,642.

Korsör, spt., Sjaelland I., **Denmark**; fine harbour; glass wks.; p. (1990) 20,443.

Kortrijk (Courtrai), t., W. Flanders prov., N.W. **Belgium**; textiles; 13th cent. Notre Dame church; battle of the Spurs 1302; p. (1993) 76,264.

Koryak, admin. div., N.E. Siberia, **Russia**; sparse p.; a. 393,680 km²; p. (1989) 39,900.

Kos, I. *See* Cos, I.

Kosciusko, Mount, N.S.W., in Australian Alps; highest peak in **Australia**; 2,228 m; Nat. Park popular for skiing.

Kosi, R., **India**; flows from Himalayas to Ganges; site of barrage for hydroelectric power and irrigation.

Košiče, c., S.E. **Slovakia**; lies in fertile basin; major industl. ctr.; heavy inds., iron and steel plant; agr.-processing; univ., Gothic cath.; mediaeval fortress t.; p. (1990) 236,000.

Kosovo-Metohija, aut. region, S.W. Serbia, **Yugoslavia**; mtnous., fertile valleys; stock raising, forestry; overwhelmingly Albanian p. causing agitation for independence; Serb repression led to war and ethnic cleansing (1999); ch. t. Priština; a. 10,352 km²; p. (1981) 1,584,441. *See* **Section C**.

Kostroma, c., cap. of K. oblast, **Russia**; at confluence of Volga and Kostroma; in flax growing a.; textiles, engin.; cath.; p. (1989) 278,000.

Koszalin (Köslin), c. and prov., N.W. **Poland**; nr. Baltic cst.; paper mills, textiles, building materials; p. (1989) 107,592 (c.), 502,700 (prov.).

Kota, t., Rajasthan, **India**; on R. Chambal; textiles; two nuclear reactors and heavy water plant; p. (1991) 537,000.

Kota Kinabalu (Jesselton), t., cap of Sabah, **Malaysia**; on W. cst.; main rubber pt.; rly. terminal; p. (1991) 208,484.

Köthen, t., Saxony - Anhalt, **Germany**; in former st. of Saxony-Anhalt; lignite mines, sugar-refining, machin., chemicals; p. (1989) 33,970.

Kotka, spt., S.E. **Finland**; on G. of Finland, at mouth of Kymi R.; major exp. pt. for timber, paper, pulp; p. (1993) 56,267.

Kotor, spt., S. Montenegro, **Yugoslavia**; on Bay of K., inlet of Adriatic; cath.; tourism.

Kotri, t., **Pakistan**; on R. Indus, opposite Hyderabad; barrage N. of the t., to help irrigate Sind.

Kottbus. *See* Cottbus.

Koulikoro, t., **Mali**, W. Africa; on upper course of R. Niger; mkt. for groundnuts, gumarabic, sisal; linked by R. to Timbuktu and Gao; 1,216 km from Dakar.

Kovrov, c., **Russia**; on Gorki rly. line and R. Klyazma; impt. agr. exp. ctr.; engin., textiles; p. (1989) 160,000.

Kowloon, peninsula, S.E. **China**; on mainland opposite Hong Kong I.; pt. installations; major industl. and tr. ctr.; held by Britain on lease expiring 1997; p. (1986) 424,000.

Kozáni, dep., Macedonia, **Greece**; cap. K.; mainly agr.; a. 6,143 km²; p. (1991) 150,386.

Kozhikode. *See* Calicut.

Kra Isthmus, neck of land between B. of Bengal and G. of Thailand, linking Malay peninsula with continent of Asia.

Kragujevac, t., central Serbia, **Yugoslavia**; on both banks of Lepenica R.; cath.; arsenal and garrison; route ctr., developing agr. and industl. ctr.; p. (1991) 146,607.

Krakatoa (Rakata), volcanic I., Sunda strait, **Indonesia**; between Java and Sumatra; greater part disappeared in violent eruption 1883.

Kraków (Cracow), c. and prov., S. **Poland**; pt. on Vistula; cultural ctr., univ. (Copernicus matricu-

lated here); many historic monuments; inc. c. of Nowa Huta lgst. iron and steel ctr. of rep.; machin., chemicals, farm implements; p. (1989) 745,568, (c.), 1,223,100 (prov.).

Kramatorsk, c., **Ukraine**; in Donets basin; heavy engin., metallurgy; p. (1990) 199,300.

Kramfors, t., **Sweden**; on G. of Bothnia; papermill and sulphite pulp wks.

Krasnodar Territory, region, **Russia**; extends from Sea of Azov and Black Sea to N.W. end of Caucasus; contains Kuban steppe and Maikop oilfields; fertile black soil; main pt. Tuapse; many health resorts; p. (1989) 5,052,900.

Krasnodar, c., cap. of K. region, **Russia**; R. pt. Kuban R.; ctr. of industl. and agr. region; p. (1989) 621,000.

Krasnovodsk, c., **Turkmenistan**; pt. on Caspian Sea; oil-refining ctr.; handles agr. and oil prods.; p. (1990) 59,200. Renamed Türkmenbashi.

Krasnoyarsk Territory, extensive region, **Russia**; extends across Siberia to Arctic Oc.; traversed by Yenisey and tribs.; minerals, grain from Minusinska basin and timber from coniferous forests; cap. K.; a. of labour camps in Stalin era; p. (1989) 3,605,500.

Krasnoyarsk, c., cap. of K. terr., E. Siberia, **Russia**; on Trans-Siberian rly. at crossing of Yenisey R.; hydroelectric sta.; industl. ctr.; local copper and iron-ore deposits; ctr. for grain and timber; p. (1989) 913,000.

Krefeld, t., N. Rhine-Westphalia, **Germany**; chemicals, steel, machin., textiles, soap; former ctr. of silk inds.; p. (1990) 245,000.

Kremenchug, c., **Ukraine**; on R. Dnieper; timber, engin., textiles; hydroelectric sta.; oil refining; p. (1990) 238,000.

Krems, mkt. t., **Austria**; on R. Danube; fruit processing; founded in 10th cent. as imperial fortress; p. (1991) 22,829.

Kreuznach, Bad, t., Rhineland Palatinate, **Germany**; on R. Nahe; metallurgy, leather, optical and chemical inds.; viticulture, mineral baths; p. (1986) 39,700.

Krishna (Kistna), R., S. **India**; rises in W. Ghats, flows E. across Deccan plateau into Bay of Bengal; lower valley and delta under intensive rice cultivation; densely populated; 1,360 km long.

Kristiansand, spt., S. **Norway**; on Skagerrak; shipbldg., ships, timber, paper, pulp, fish; electro-metallurgy; p. (1990) 54,267.

Kristianstad, c., cap. of K. prov., **Sweden**; on Helge R.; its pt. Ahus is on Baltic; foodprocessing, clothing, machin.; founded 1614 as fortress; p. (1992) 72,789 (t.), 292,993 (co.).

Kristiansund, spt., W. cst. **Norway**; built on 3 Is.; trawler fleet base; exp. dried fish; heavily damaged in second world war; since rebuilt; p. (1990) 17,093.

Kristinehamn, L. pt. on L. Vänern, central **Sweden**; p. (1983) 26,623.

Krivoy Rog., c., **Ukraine**; on R. Ingulets; ctr. of ch. iron-mng. a. of USSR; p. (1990) 717,400.

Krk, I., N. Adriatic Sea, off **Croatia**; S. of Rijeke; agr.; tourism; ch. t., K.; p. 14,500.

Krkonose. *See* Riesengebirge.

Kronoberg, co. S. **Sweden**; cap. Växjö; a. 8,459 km²; p. (1992) 178,961.

Kronshlot (Kronstadt), spt., on I. of Kotlin, **Russia**; at head of G. of Finland, nr. St. Petersburg; Baltic pt. and naval base; scene of naval mutiny which precipitated the Russian revolution; founded by Peter the Great 1710.

Kroonstad, t., O.F.S., **S. Africa**; on R. Vals; rly. junc.; agr. mkt.; engin., milling; p. (1980) 104,160 (dist.).

Krosno, t. and prov., S.E. **Poland**; R. Wislok; oil centre; p. (1989) 49,094 (t.), 491,500 (prov.).

Kruger Nat. Park, N.E. Transvaal, **S. Africa**; game reserve; a. 20,720 km².

Krugersdorp, t. Transvaal, **S. Africa**; gold mng., uranium, manganese; p. (1980) 153,880 (dist.).

Kuala Lumpur, c., fed. terr., **W. Malaysia**; cap. of Fed. of Malaysia and of Selangor st.; univ.; ctr. of rubber and tin dist.; outport Port Kelang; new Sepang airport, 1998; p. (1986) 1,000,000.

Kuangchow. *See* Guangzhou.

Kuantan, main t. on E. cst. **W. Malaysia**; linked to Kuala Lumpur; tin mng; p. (1980) 136,625.

Kuching, c., cap. of Sarawak, **Malaysia**; pt. on Sarawak R.; gold discovered nearby at Bau; p. (1989) 157,000.

Kucově (Qyteti Stalin), **Albania**; nr. Berat; oil prod. and refining; pipeline connects to Vlorë.

Kufra, oasis, **Libya**; dates, barley; on caravan route.

Kuldja. *See* **Yining.**

Kumamoto, c., W. Kyushu, **Japan**; 3rd c. of K.; cas., univs.; food inds.; business ctr.; p. (1990) 579,305.

Kumasi, c., cap. of Ashanti region, **Ghana**; univ.; aerodrome; road and rly. junc.; ctr. of cocoa-producing a.; bauxite nearby; jute bags; p. (1984) 260,286 (c.), 345,117 (met. a.).

Kumayri (Leninakan), c., **Armenia**; nr. Turkish border; textiles, engin., rug-mkg.; earthquake 1988; p. (1990) 122,600.

Kumba Konam, t., Tamil Nadu, **India**; on Cauvery delta; silks, cotton; sacred Hindu c.; p. (1981) 132,832.

Kunene (Cunene), R., **Angola**; scheme to channel water from Angola to S.W. Africa; 1,200 km long.

Kun Lun (Kwen Lun), mtn. ranges, Xizang Zizhiou (Tibet), **China**; extend 2,900 km E. from Pamirs along N. edge of high plateau of Xizang Zizhiou; drained N. into inland drainage basin of Lop Nor; alt. frequently exceeds 5,400 m; rising to 7,729 m.

Kunming, c., cap. of Yunnan prov., S.W. **China**; univ.; comm. and cultural ctr., noted for its scenic beauty; iron and steel, milling and boring machin., textiles, chemicals; p. (1992) 1,580,000.

Kununurra Dam, Ord R., **W. Australia**; opened 1963; to irrigate 81,000 ha of semi-arid land for cotton, rice, and cattle.

Kuopio, t., **Finland**; on L. Kalki; timber inds.; tourism; p. (1993) 83,097.

Kura, R., rises in **Turkey**, chief R. of Transcaucasia, **Russia**; flows into Caspian Sea; agr., fishing, hydroelec. power; 1,504 km long.

Kurdistan (Country of the Kurds), includes parts of E. Turkey, Armenia, N.E. Iraq, and N.W. Iran; attempts at autonomy.

Kure, c., S.W. Honshu, **Japan**; spt. and naval base; engin.; shipbldg.; p. (1990) 216,723.

Kurgan, c., **Russia**; on Tobol R.; impt. junc. on Trans-Siberian rly.; tr. in cattle and foodstuffs; agr. engin.; p. (1989) 356,000.

Kuria Muria Is., 5 barren Is. in Arabian Sea off cst. of Oman; admin. by U.K. until 1967 now ceded to **Oman**.

Kurile Is., chain of volcanic Is., N. Pac., **Russia**; extend from Kamchatka to Hokkaido; mainly mtnous.; sulphur, hunting, fishing; Japan claims sovereignty over 4 Is. (Kunashiri, Etorofu, Shikotan, Habomai); a. 15,592 km².

Kurisches Haff (Kurštu Martos), shallow lagoon, Baltic cst. of **Lithuania**; receives water of R. Niemen; narrow entrance to Baltic Sea at N. end of lagoon commanded by pt. of Klaipeda (Memel); length 92 km, maximum width 32 km.

Kurische Nehrung, sandspit, Baltic Sea; almost cuts off Kurisches Haff from Baltic Sea; 88 km long.

Kurnool, t., Andhra Pradesh, **India**; agr. comm. ctr.; p. (1981) 206,700.

Kuroshio (Japan Current), ocean current, flows N.E. along Pac. cst. of Kyushu, Shikoku and S. Honshu, relatively warm water, exerts slight warming influence on this cst. in winter.

Kursk, c., cap. of K. oblast, **Russia**; on Tuskor R.; rly. junc.; in fertile fruit-growing a.; engin., textiles, synthetic rubber; p. (1989) 424,000.

Kurume, t., W. Kyushu, **Japan**; on Chikugo plain; comm. ctr.; p. (1990) 228,300.

Kushiro, spt., S.E. Hokkaido, **Japan**; exp. lumber; local coal; fishing; p. (1990) 205,640.

Kustanay, c., **Kazakhstan**; on Tobol R.; agr.-processing, lt. inds.; p. (1990) 228,400.

Kütahya, t., cap. of K. prov., central **Turkey**; agr. mkt. ctr.; ceramics; chemical complex; p. (1990) 135,432 (t.), 578,020 (prov.).

Kutaisi, c., **Georgia**; on R. Rion (hydroelectric plant; chemicals, textiles, mng. equipment; big coal deposits being mined; mkt. gardening a.; p. (1990) 236,400.

Kut-al-Amara, t., cap. of K. prov., Iraq; on R. Tigris; agr. tr. ctr.; p. (1970) 58,647 (latest fig.).

Kutch, Rann of, desert region covered with salt, but flooded during monsoons; nine-tenths belongs to India; one-tenth to Pakistan.

Kutchan, t., S.W. Hokkaido, **Japan**; ctr. of lge. iron-ore field; ore smelted at Muroran.

Kutno, t. Plock, **Poland**; route ctr.; sm. textile ind.; p. (1989) 49,753.

Kuwait, indep. Arab st., S.W. Asia; under Brit. protection until 1961; invaded by Iraq, August 1990; lies at head of Persian G.; inc. mainland and 9 sm Is.; mainly desert with a few oases; imports most of food requirements; possesses 13 per cent of the proved world reserves of oil; heavily dependent on oil and natural gas exports; freshwater scarce; one of hgst. incomes per capita in world, but most of p. remains poor; a. 24,235 km²; p. (1995) 1,590,013.

Kuwait, c., cap. of **Kuwait**; pt. with natural harbour on Persian G.; univ.; p. (1993) 31,241.

Kuybyshev. *See* **Samara.**

Kuzbas (Kuznetsk Basin), industl. region, Siberia, **Russia**; lies S. of Trans-Siberian rly. in upper valleys of Rs. Ob and Tom; coal, iron and steel mftg., heavy metallurgical ind.; ch. ts., Novosibirsk, Novokuznetsk, Kemerovo, Leninsk-Kuznetsky.

Kwa Ndebele, homeland Transvaal, **S. Africa**; chief town Moutjana; pop. (1985) 235,855.

Kwangsi Chuang. *See* **Guang Zhuang.**

Kwantung. *See* **Guangdong.**

Kwanto Plain, S.E. Honshu, **Japan**; lgst. a. of continuous lowland in Japan, extends 128 km inland from Tokyo; plain devoted to intensive rice cultivation; higher, drier terraces under mulberry, vegetables, tea, tobacco; very dense rural p.; lge. number of urban ctrs., inc. Tokyo, Yokohama; a. 13,000 km².

Kwazulu, former Bantu Terr. Authority (1970), E. **S. Africa**; runs 480 km from Moçambique to Cape Prov; cap. Nongoma in N. highland; p. (1985) 3·7 m.

Kweichow. *See* **Guizhou.**

Kweilin. *See* **Guilin.**

Kweiyang. *See* **Guiyang.**

Kwidzyn (Marienwerder), c., Elblag prov., N. **Poland** (since 1945); cath., cas.; industl. ctr. nr. Vistula R.; p. (1989) 36,409.

Kwinana, new t. (1952), pt., W. **Australia**; oil refinery and steel plant, alumina reduction, integrated steelwks.; p. (1981) 12,355.

Kyle of Lochalsh, v., Highland, **Scot.**; at entrance to Loch Alsh, facing S. end of I. of Skye; terminus of rly. across Highlands from Dingwall; ch. pt. for ferries to N.W. cst., I. of Skye, Outer Hebrides; p. (1991) 862.

Kymi, R., **Finland**; rises in L. Päijänne, flows to G. of Finland; many Ls., timber transport, hydroelec. power; 144 km long.

Kyoto, c., Honshu, **Japan**; cultural and religious ctr., without lge.-scale inds.; former cap. 794–1868; univ.; shrines, old Imperial palace; p. (1990) 1,461,140.

Kyushu, most S. of 4 major Is. of **Japan**; mtnous.; coal mng. in Chikugo basin; heavy inds.; agr. on coastal lowlands; joined to Honshu by bridge and rly.; a. 42,007 km²; p. (1990) 13,296,000.

Kyustendil, t., **Bulgaria**; in foothills of Osogovo mtns.; lge. lead and zinc deposits; combined plant for mng. and ore dressing projected.

Kzyl Orda, R. and t., **Kazakhstan**; lge. dam to irrigate rice plantations; p. of t. (1990) 155,500.

L

Laaland I. *See* **Lolland I.**

Labrador, mainland a. of prov. Newfoundland, **Canada**; separated from I. by Strait of Belle I.; barren, severe climate; impt. cod fisheries; rich iron ore reserves nr. Quebec bdy.; Churchill R. power project; cap. Battle Harbour; a. 292,219 km².

Labrador City, t., Newfoundland, **Canada**; new t. built 1965, nr. Wabush L. to house workers of iron-ore mines; p. (1991) 9,061.

Labuan, I., Sabah, **Malaysia**; rubber, rice, coconuts; cap. Victoria; a. 81 km²; p. (1991) 54,307.

Laccadive, coral Is., Arabian Sea; about 320 km off Malabar cst. joined with Minicoy and Amindivi Is. to form union terr. Lakshadweep, **India**.

Lachine, c., Quebec, **Canada** now part of gter. Montreal; on Montreal I. where St. Lawrence R. leaves St. Louis L.; iron and steel, wire, rope; Lachine canal by-passes rapids; p. (1986) 34,906.

Lachlan, R., N.S.W., **Australia**; main trib. of R. Murrumbidgee; irrigation; 1,472 km long.

La Coruña (A Coruña), spt., cap. of La Coruña prov., N.W. **Spain**; fishing; p. (1991) 251,342 (c.), 1,089,810 (prov.).

Ladakh, dist., of the Upper Indus, **India**, bordering Tibet; ch. t. Leh; isolated and remote; alt. 3,600 m; p. (1981) 68,380.

Ladoga (Ladozhskoye), L., St. Petersburg, **Russia**; a. 18,389 km²; (lgst. in Europe); drained to G. of Finland by R. Neva; fishing; link in new deepwater canal between White and Baltic Seas.

Ladybank, burgh, Fife, **Scot.**; 8 km S.W. of Cupar; p. (1991) 1,373.

Ladysmith, t. Natal, **S. Africa**; cotton mills; besieged by Boers 1899–1900; p. (1980) 105,020 (dist.).

Lae, t., **Papua New Guinea**; pt. on Huon Gulf serving goldmng. dist.; outlet for Morobe; plywood; air ctr.; p. (1990) 80,655.

Lagan (Laggan), R., **N. Ireland**; flows into Belfast Lough; canal link to Lough Neagh; 56 km long.

Lagôa dos Patos, L., **Brazil**; drained by Rio Grande do Sul; 224 km long.

Lagôa Mirim, L., on bdy. between **Brazil** and **Uruguay**; drains N.; 176 km long.

Lagos, spt., former cap. of **Nigeria**; unhealthy and congested; cap. recently moved to Abuja; gd. natural harbour; exp. cocoa, groundnuts, palm oil and kernels, timber, hides and skins, cotton, rubber, crude oil; mnfs. textiles, confectionery, chemicals, car assembly; univ.; p. (1992) 1,347,000, (1991) 5,685,781 (state).

La Grande Chartreuse, limestone region between Chambéry and Grenoble, **France**; famous monastery and liqueur.

La Grande Rivière, N. Quebec, **Canada**; major hydroelec. scheme; mineral and timber inds.

Laguna, dist., Durango st., **Mexico**; former L. bed irrigated by Rs. Nazas and Aguanaval; ch. cotton-growing region in Mexico; ch. t., Torréon; a. 259,000 km².

Lahore, ch. c., **Pakistan**; univ., cath., temples, mosques; textiles, pottery, carpets, industl. gases; atomic research ctr.; second c. of Pakistan; p. (1981) 2,922,000.

Lahti, t., S. **Finland**; wood, plywood, brewing, textiles; p. (1993) 94,160.

Lake Champlain, N.Y., **USA**; forms lowland a. for main routes between Montreal and N.Y.

Lake Charles, c., La., **USA**; spt. at mouth of Calcasieu R.; connected to G. of Mexico by channel; exp. oil, chemicals, rice, cotton; p. (1984) 75,100 (c.), 175,000 (met. a.).

Lake District, almost circular mtnous. a., Cumbria, **Eng.**; 17 major and many smaller Ls. formed by glacial erosion and deposition; increasing tourist pressure on Nat. Park as motorways improve accessibility.

Lakeland, c., Fla., **USA**; citrus fruit ctr.; holiday resort; p. (1990) 70,576 (c.), 405,000 (met. a. with Winter Haven).

Lake of the Woods, L., Ont., S.E. of Winnipeg, on bdy. between **Canada** and **USA**; in pine forest; tourism.

Lakeview, t., Ont., **Canada**; thermal elec. power plant projected; to be lgst. in world.

Lakshadweep, union terr., **India**; made up of Laccadive, Minicoy and Aminidivi Is; coir, coconuts; a. 32 km²; p. (1991) 51,707.

La Laguna, second lgst. t., former cap. Tenerife, Canary Is; p. (1991) 116,539.

La Linea, t., **Spain**; on isthmus connecting Gibraltar with mainland; p. (1981) 55,590.

La Mancha, plain, Cuidad-Real prov., S. **Spain**; in shallow depression on central plateau, alt. between 450–900 m, drained by headstreams of R. Guadiana; semi-arid climate with hot summers, cold winters; widespread salt deposits; Merino sheep, esparto grass; Spain's lgst. grape-growing region.

Lambaréné, t., **Gabon**; site of Schweitzer's hospital on Ogooué R.

Lambayeque, prov., N.W. **Peru**; ctr. of irrigated dists.; sugar, cotton, tobacco; cap. Chiclayo, ch. pt. Pimental; a. 11,948 km²; p. (1993) 920,795.

Lambeth, inner bor., London, **Eng.**; L. palace, residence of Archbishop of Canterbury; p. (1995) 261,700.

Lammermuir Hills, E. Lothian, **Scot.**; highest peak Lammer Law, 529 m.

Lampang, t., **Thailand**; modern sugar plant; p. (1980) 42,301.

Lampedusa, lgst. of Pelagi Is., between Malta and Tunisian cst., belonging to **Italy**; barren limestone; a. 21 km²; p. (1981) 4,792.

Lampeter, t., Ceredigion, S. **Wales**; on R. Teifi; mkt.; univ. college; p. (1991) 1,989.

Lamu, t., **Kenya**; impt. historical and tourist ctr. on Indian Ocean.

Lanark, royal burgh, S. Lanarkshire, **Scot.**; in Clyde valley 35 km S.E. of Glasgow; hosiery; ctr. of mkt. gardening a.; nr. New Lanark model t. built by Robert Owen; p. (1991) 8,877.

Lanarkshire, historic co., central **Scot.**; now divided between Glasgow, N. and S. Lanarkshire.

Lancashire, non-met. co., N.W. **Eng.**; major growth of p. in 19th cent. based on prod. of cotton and coal; main industl. ctrs. now outside co. in Merseyside and Gtr. Manchester met. cos.; Pennines in E.; extensive lowland in W.; admin. ctr. Preston; p. (1995) 1,426,000.

Lancaster, c., co. t., l. gov. dist., Lancs., **Eng.**; 10 km up R. Lune; mediaeval cas., univ.; linoleum, vinyl, clothing; p. (1995) 136,200 (dist.), (1991) 44,497 (t.).

Lancaster, c., Penns., **USA**; agr. ctr., tobacco mkt.; stockyards; mnfs. linoleum, watches; birthplace of Robert Fulton; p. (1984) 56,300 (c.), (1990) 423,000 (met. a.).

Lanchow. See Lanzhou.

Lancing, v., West Sussex, **Eng.**; on S. cst., 3 km E. of Worthing; seaside resort; lt. inds.; public school.

Landau, t., Rhineland-Palatinate, **Germany**; on R. Queich; cigar mftg., wine, iron ind.; here the carriages called landaus were first made; p. (1986) 35,300.

Landes, dep., S.W. **France**; on Atl. cst.; agr., vineyards, resin; cap. Mont-de-Marsan; a. 9,334 km²; p. (1990) 306,000.

Landes, Les, region, Aquitaine, S.W. **France**; fringes Bay of Biscay from Pointe de Grave to Biarritz; coastal sand dunes and lagoons backed by low, flat plain of alternate sandy tracts and marsh; reclaimed by drainage and afforestation, now over half a. covered by pine forests; turpentine; timber; oilfield.

Land's End, extreme S.W. point of **Eng.** on Cornish cst.

Landshut, t., Bavaria, **Germany**; on R. Isar; cas.; elec. inds., glass, metallurgy, textiles, coal; rly. junc.; p. (1986) 57,100.

Landskrona, spt., **Sweden**; on the Sound; shipping and tr. ctr.; agr.-processing; on nearby I. of Ven; Tycho Brahe built his observatory; p. (1983) 35,656.

Langdale Pikes, L. Dist., **Eng.**; 2 peaks Harrison Stickle (733 m), Pike o'-Stickel (709 m); popular rambling and climbing a.; 5 km W. of Grasmere.

Langebergen, mtns., Cape Prov., **S. Africa**; 240 km E. to W. parallel to S. cst. of Africa; form barrier to access from cst. plain to Little Karroo, broken across by valley of R. Gouritz; max. alt. exceeds 1,370 m.

Langreo, t., N. **Spain**; in Asturias, 19 km S.E. of Oviedo; coal and iron mines; p. (1981) 55,758.

Langres, t., Haute-Marne, **France**; cath., mediaeval fortifications; famous for its cutlery; birthplace of Diderot; p. (1982) 11,359.

Languedoc, former prov. now incorporated in **Languedoc-Roussillon** region, S. **France**; inc. deps. Aude, Gard, Hérault, Lozère, Pyrénées-Orientales; major govt. sponsored investment in tourist inds., along Mediterranean cst.; mono-cultural vine prod., irrigation scheme to aid agr. diversification; p. (1990) 2,115,000.

Lannemezan, region, Aquitaine, S.W. **France**; belt 80 km wide stretches over 160 km along foot of Pyrenees W. of Toulouse; consists of immense deltas of glacial gravel deeply cut by tribs. of Rs. Garonne and Adour; valleys liable to severe floods in summer, intervening plateau dry, bare; scantily populated.

Lansing, c., cap of Mich., **USA**; on Grand R. at confluence with Cedar R.; automobiles, chemicals; p. (1990) 127,321 (c.), 433,000 (met. a. with E. Lansing).

Lanzarote, I., **Canary Is.**; volcanic mtns.; developing tourist ind.; cochineal; cap. Arrecife.

Lanzhou (Lanchou), c., cap. of Gansu prov., **China**; on Huang He; tr. ctr.; oil refining, gaseous diffusion plant, woollen mills, coal mng. nearby; p. (1991) 1,530,000.

Laoag, c., N. Luzon I., **Philippines**; agr.-processing; p. (1990) 83,756.

Laoighis or **Leix Co.**, Leinster, **R.o.I.**; mtns. and bog; inland pasture and tillage; cap. Port Laoighise (Maryborough); a. 1,720 km²; p. (1986) 53,284.

Laon, t., cap. of Aisne dep., **France**; on rocky height above plain; historic fortress t.; cath.; p. (1990) 28,670.

Laois. *See* **Laoighis.**

Laos, People's Democratic Rep. of, S.E. Asia; kingdom until 1975; bordered by China, Vietnam, Kampuchea, Thailand and Burma; formerly part of Fr. Indo- China; under-developed and isolated cty.; considerable mineral resources but only tin exploited; disrupted by civil war, drought, crop pests; economic ctr. is Mekong valley, scene of recent Mekong R. Development Project; elsewhere thickly forested mtns.; 70 per cent of p. engaged in subsistence agr. for dry rice; now produces rice surplus; main exp., hardwoods; no rlys.; royal cap. Luang Prabang, admin. cap. Vientiane; a. 231,399 km²; p. (1994) 4,600,000.

La Pampa, prov., central **Argentina**; p. (1991) 259,996.

La Paz, dep., **Bolivia**; traversed by Andes; de facto cap. La Paz, legal cap. Sucre; cocoa, coffee, rubber, tin-mng. at Catari; a. 105,377 km²; p. (1988) 1,926,200.

La Paz, c., **Bolivia**; seat of govt.; comm. ctr.; copper, alpaca wool, cinchona, textiles; highest cap. c. in world; p. (1992) 711,036.

Lapland, terr., N. **Europe**, in Norway, Sweden, Finland and Russia, extending from Norwegian cst. to White Sea; mainly mtn. and moorland, with many lakes; Lapps are nomadic pastoralists with reindeer herds; iron-ore at Kiruna and Gällivare; a. 336,700 km²; p. of Swedish Co. of L. (1983) 118,819.

La Plata, c., spt., **Argentina**; cap. of Buenos Aires prov., univ.; mftg. ctr.; iron and steel, oil refining, refrigerated meat prods.; p. (1991) 542,567.

La Plata, Rio de. *See* **Plata, Rio de la.**

Laptev Sea (Nordenskjöld Sea), inlet of Arctic Oc.; between Severnaya Zemlya and New Siberian Is., **Russia.**

Larache, spt., **Morocco**; on Atl. cst. 64 km S. of Tangier; exp. cork, wool; p. (1982) 63,893.

Laramie, t., Wyo., **USA**; univ.; industl. ctr. for cattle and timber region; rly. engin.; p. (1990) 26,687.

Laredo, t., Texas, **USA**; frontier t. on Rio Grande; smuggling; ctr. of Chicanos; p. (1990) 122,899.

Largo, v., Fife, **Scot.**; fishing, holiday resort; birth-place of Alexander Selkirk.

Largs, burgh, N. Ayrshire, **Scot.**; on F. of Clyde opposite Is. of Bute and Cumbrae; seaside resort, fishing; battle 1263 defeating last attempt by Norsemen to conquer Scot.; p. (1991) 10,925.

La Rioja, t. and prov., N.W. **Argentina**; a. 92,331 km²; p. (1991) 103,727 (t.), 220,729 (prov.).

Larissa, dep., Thessaly, **Greece**; inc. infertile basin of R. Piniós; cap. Larissa; ch. pt. Volos; p. (1991) 112,777 (c.), 270,612 (dep.).

Larnaca, spt., **Cyprus**; the anc. Citium; grain, cotton, fruit; oil refinery; growing tourist ctr.; p. (1997) 106,000.

Larne, spt., l. gov. dist., **N. Ireland**; at entrance to Larne Lough; cross channel service to Stranraer; tourism; p. (1991) 26,419 (dist.), 17,525 (t.).

La Rochelle, spt., cap. of Charente-Maritime dep., **France**; on Atl. cst.; its deepwater pt. is La Pallice; cath.; fishing pt.; chemicals, food-processing; tourism; p. (1990) 73,744.

La Roche-sur-Yon, t., cap of Vendée dep., **France**; on R. Yon; built by Napoleon I; p. (1990) 48,518.

Larut Hills, W. Malaysia; rise to over 1,500 m; lge. tin-field.

Larvik, spt., **Norway**; S.W. of Oslo; seaside resort; engin., pulp, stone; former whaling pt; p. (1990) 20,594.

Las Cruces, t., N.M., **USA**; on Rio Grande R.; irrigated agr.; univ.; p. (1990) 62,126.

La Serena, c., cap. of Coquimbo prov., **Chile**; 14 km inland from its pt. Coquimbo; cath.; resort; p. (1992) 120,336.

Lashio, t., **Myanmar**; on R. Salween; rly. terminus; Burma road links with China; ctr. of silver-lead mines.

Lashkar, c., Madhya Pradesh, central **India**; modern industl. t., adjoining Gwalior.

La Skhirra, pt. on G. of Gabès, **Tunisia**; oil; pipeline to Edjelé.

Las Palmas, prov., Canary Is., **Spain**; inc. Gran Canaria, Lanzarote, Fuerteventura and smaller Is.; intensive irrigated agr. of bananas, tomatoes, potatoes; tourism encouraged by climate and volcanic landscape; a. 4,053 km²; p. (1991) 836,556.

Las Palmas, c., N.E. Gran Canaria, ch. pt. of **Canary Is.**; exp. agr. prods.; cath.; p. (1991) 347,668.

La Spezia, spt., Liguria, N.W. **Italy**; on Bay of Spezia; ch. Italian naval sta., arsenal and docks; maritime inds., elec. machin., olive oil, oil refining; p. (1992) 100,458.

Lassen Peak, Nat. Park, Cascade Range, Cal.; only active volcano in **USA.**

Lasswade. *See* **Bonnyrigg and Lasswade.**

Las Vegas, c., Nevada, **USA**; noted for its gambling casinos; ranching and mng. a.; p. (1990) 258,295 (c.), 741,000 (met. a.).

Latacunga, t., **Ecuador**; at about 2,740 m in Andean basin, not far from Cotopaxi volcano; anc. Inca t.; ctr.; p. (1990) 39,882.

Latakia, spt., **Syria**; exp. tobacco, olive oil, sponges; p. (1993) 293,000.

Latina (Littoria), c., cap. of Latina prov., in Latium central **Italy**; in ctr. of reclaimed a. of Pontine marshes; mkt. ctr., on which planned road system converges; built since 1932; nuclear power sta. nearby; p. (1981) 93,738.

Latin America, the Spanish-, Portuguese- and Fr.-speaking countries of N. America, S. America, Central America, and the W.I., inc. the reps. of Argentina, Bolivia, Brazil, Chile, Colombia, Costa Rica, Cuba, Dominican Republic, Ecuador, Salvador, Guatemala, Haiti, Honduras, Mexico, Nicaragua, Panama, Paraguay, Peru, Uruguay, and Venezuela; sometimes Puerto Rico, Fr. W.I., and other Is. of the W.I. are included, and occasionally Belize, Guyana, Fr. Guiana, and Surinam; p. (1995) 480,000,000.

Latium (Lazio), region, central **Italy**; between Apennines and Tyrrhenian Sea, comprising provs. of Rome, Frosinone, Latina, Rieti, Viterbo; a. 17,182 km²; p. (1992) 5,162,073.

Latrobe Valley, one of most impt. economic a. in Victoria, **Australia**; major brown coal and electric power production; secondary inds. attracted by cheap power.

Latvia, former constituent rep., USSR; dairying, stock-raising, forestry; cap. Riga; spts. Ventspils, Liepaya; a. 66,278 km²; p. (1995) 2,505,900.

Launceston, t., Tasmania, **Australia**; at head of Tamar estuary, inc. Bell Bay where many heavy inds.; p. (1991) 93,347.

Launceston, t., North Cornwall, **Eng.**; agr. mkt.; quarrying, lt. engin.; p. (1991) 6,466.

Laurencekirk, burgh, Aberdeenshire, **Scot.**; agr. ctr. in the Howe of Mearns; p. (1991) 1,611.

Laurion or **Laurium,** pt. on Attic peninsula, **Greece**; lead, manganese, zinc, and silver mines; silver mined 5th cent. B.C.

Lausanne, c., cap. of Vaud can., **Switzerland**; nr. L. Geneva; cath.; univ.; impt. rly. junc.; seat of Swiss high courts of justice; tourism; p. (1990) 123,200 (c.), 262,900 (met. a.).

Lauterbrunnen, Alpine valley, Bern can., **Switzerland**; famous for its waterfalls, the highest of which is Staubbach 299 m; tourist and winter sports ctr.

Laval, t., cap. of Mayenne dep., **France**; Mayenne R. divides old and modern parts; cotton, paper, machin., marble; cas., church; p. (1990) 53,479.

Lavenham, t., Suffolk, **Eng.**; a ctr. of the wool tr. in 15th cent., still preserves its mediaeval character; p. (1991) 1,231.

Lavera, pt., nr. Marseilles, S.E. **France** commencement of 752 km oil pipeline to Karlsruhe, W. Germany; oil refining.

Lawrence, t., Mass., **USA**; on Merrimac R., N.W. of Boston; textiles, paper, footwear, engin.; p. (1990) 394,000 (met. a. with Haverhill).

Lawton, t., Okla., **USA**; mnfs. cottonseed oil; p. (1984) 85,600 (t.), 119,400 (met. a.).

Laxey, v., Isle of **Man**; flour milling, woollen mills, meerschaum pipes.

Lazio. *See* **Latium.**

Lea or **Lee,** R., **Eng.**; rises in Chiltern Hills nr. Luton, flows S. and E. into R. Thames through industl. zone of N.E. London; valley to become a regional park; mkt. gardening a.; 74 km long.

Leamington (Royal Leamington Spa), t., Warwicks., **Eng.**; on R. Leam, trib. of Avon, 3 km N.E. of Warwick; fashionable spa; engin. inds.; p. (1991) 55,396.

Leatherhead, t., Mole Valley, Surrey, **Eng.**; on R. Mole to N. of gap through N. Downs; residtl.; p. (1991) 42,903.

Lebanon, mtn. range, **Lebanon**, extending to cst. of Syria; snow-capped most of year;

highest peak Timarum, 3,214 m; famous in anc. times for cedar forests.

Lebanon, rep., S.W. Asia; at E. end of Mediterranean Sea; bordered by Syria to N. and Israel to S.; narrow coastal strip backed by mtnous. interior; free mkt. a., with economy based on transit tr.; most of p. involved in tourism, finance and commerce; oil refining based on imports; cap. Beirut; strife-torn by civil war, now being rebuilt; a. 8,806 km²; p. (1995) 2,925,000.

Le Bourget, t., N.E. of Paris, **France**; airpt.; p. (1982) 11,021.

Lebórk (Lauenburg), t. Slupsk prov., **Poland** (since 1945); in agr. dist.; timber and food inds.; p. (1980) 33,981.

Lebowa Territory, Bantu Terr., **S. Africa**; home of N. Sotho and Ndebele peoples; self-gov. Oct. 1972; cap. Seshego; p. (1985) 1·8 m.

Lecce, c., Apulia, S. **Italy**; agr. and route ctr. with ceramic and glass inds.; anc. Greek col.; baroque churches and palaces; p. (1992) 100,508.

Lecco, t., **Italy**; in Lombardy, on L. Como; iron and copper wks., agr.-processing, cheese.

Lech, R., rises in Austria and flows past Augsburg in Bavaria, **Germany**, to join Danube; 283 km long.

Le Creusot, t., Saône-et-Loire, **France**; ctr. of one of sm. coalfields bordering the Massif Central; steel, engin.; p. (1982) 32,309.

Ledbury, t., Hereford, **Eng.**; at W. foot of Malvern hills; fruit preserving, tanning; 17th cent. mkt. hall; birthplace of John Masefield; p. (1991) 6,216.

Leeds, c., met. dist., West Yorks., **Eng.**; on R. Aire; at E. margin of Pennines; univ.; lge. clothing ind., varied engin. mnfs., paper and printing; with Bradford forms conurb. of W. Yorks., p. (1995) 725,000 (dist.), (1991) 424,194 (c.).

Leek, mkt. t., Moorlands, Staffs., **Eng.**; 18 km N.E. of Stoke-on-Trent; silk mnfs., butter; expanded t.; p. (1991) 18,167.

Lee-on-Solent, t., Hants., **Eng.**; on Southampton Water; p. (1991) 7,259.

Leeuwarden, c., cap. of Friesland prov., **Neth.**; noted cattle mkt.; rly. junc.; p. (1994) 87,464.

Leeuwin, C., S.W. point of **Australia**; notorious storms; Nat. Park (1971).

Leeward Is., **W.I.**, northern gr. of Lesser Antilles archipelago; so-called because winds in this a. generally blow from E.; inc. Virgin Is. of US; Fr. I. of Guadaloupe, Dutch Is. of St. Eustatius and Saba, and Brit. Leeward Is. (Montserrat, Virgin Is., and former cols. of Antigua, St. Kitt-Nevis, Anguilla).

Lefkosia. *See* Nicosia.

Leganes, t. Madrid prov., C. **Spain**; mineral springs, electronics; p. (1991) 173,043.

Legazpi, c., cap. of Albay prov., **Philippines**; spt. in S.E. Luzon; linked by rly. with Manila; p. (1990) 121,116.

Leghorn. *See* Livorno.

Legionowo, t., **Poland**; on outskirts of Warsaw; nr. artificial L. in R. Bug valley; p. (1989) 50,577.

Legnano, t., Lombardy, **Italy**; N.W. of Milan; textiles, machin.; p. (1981) 49,308.

Legnica (Liegnitz), c. and prov., S.W. **Poland** (since 1945); on Katzbach R., in rich agr. region; p. (1989) 103,949 (c.), 510,200 (prov.).

Leh, cap. of Ladakh, Kashmir, **India**; isolated t. in Himalayas on caravan route to Tibet; p. (1981) 8,000.

Le Havre, spt., Seine-Maritime dep., N. **France**; at mouth of Seine on English Channel; shipbldg., engin., chemicals, ropes, cottons, oil refining; pipeline to Grandpuits; p. (1990) 197, 219 (c.), 253,627 (met.a.).

Leicester, c., unit. auth. created in 1997, formerly part of Leics., **Eng.**; on R. Soar; univs. (Leicester and De Montfort); footwear, hosiery, knitwear, textile machin.; major shopping complex at Fosse Park; Roman remains; p. (1995) 295,700 (former dist.), (1991) 318,518 (c.).

Leicestershire, non-met. co., **Eng.**; mainly rural, low-lying Midland co., but inc. Charnwood Forest; mixed agr., sm. coalfield; hosiery and footwear inds.; p. (1995) 923,000.

Leiden or **Leyden**, c., S. Holland prov., **Neth.**; on Oude Rijn; famous univ.; printing, textiles, medical equipment; gr. weaving ctr. in Middle Ages; revolt against Spanish rule 1573–4; birthplace of Rembrandt; p. (1994) 114,892 (c.), 194,051 (met. a.).

Leigh, t., Gtr. Manchester, **Eng.**; 8 km S.E. of

Wigan; textiles; p. (1991) 43,150.

Leighton Buzzard, t., South Beds., **Eng.**; at N.E. end of Vale of Aylesbury; tiles, engin., sand quarrying; p. (1991) 32,610 (inc. Linslade).

Leinster, S.E. prov., **R.o.I.**; bulk of recent Irish p. increase; a. 19,637 km²; p. (1986) 1,852,649.

Leipzig, c. Saxony, **Germany**; comm., industl., and cultural ctr. at junc. of Rs. Pleisse, Elster, and Parthe; famous univ.; inds. inc. publishing, steel, textiles, chemicals, machin., cars; tr. fairs; Bach was organist at Thomaskirche; birthplace of Leibnitz and Wagner; p. (1990) 507,800.

Leiston-cum-Sizewell, t., Suffolk Coastal, Suffolk, **Eng.**; on cst. 6 km E. of Saxmundham; agr. implements; important nuclear power sta.; p. (1991) 5,950.

Leith, t., Edinburgh, **Scot.**; shipbldg., timber, whisky; outport for Edinburgh.

Leith Hill, Surrey, **Eng.**; nr. Dorking; alt. 294 m; Lower Greensand crest.

Leitmeritz. *See* Litomèřice.

Leitrim, co., Connacht, **R.o.I.**; agr.; cap. Carrick-on-Shannon; a. 1,588 km²; p. (1986) 27,035.

Leix. *See* Laoighis.

Leixões, the modern harbour of Oporto, **Portugal**; oil refinery.

Lek, R., **Neth.**; one of the branches of the Neder Rijn; from Wijk-bij-Duurstede to Krimpen nr. Rotterdam; 64 km long.

Le Locle, t., Neuchâtel, **Switzerland**; ctr. of watch-mkg. ind.; p. (1986) 10,900.

Léman L. *See* Geneva, L.

Le Mans, t., cap. of Sarthe dep., N.W. **France**; cath.; linen, ironmongery, chemicals, motor cars, aeroplanes; motor-racing; p. (1990) 148,465 (t.), 189,107 (met.a.).

Lemnos, Greek I., Aegean Sea, **Greece**; 64 km S.W. of Dardanelles; ch. t. Kastro (the anc. Myrina); tobacco, wine; a. 466 km²; part of Lesvos dep.

Lena, one of gr. Siberian Rs., **Russia**; rises in Oc.; navigable; 4,480 km long.

Leninabad. *See* Khudzhand.

Leninakan. *See* Kumayri.

Lenin Dam (Dnieper Dam). *See* Zaporozh'ye.

Leningrad. *See* St. Petersburg.

Leninogorsk. *See* Ridder.

Lenin Peak (Mt. Kaufmann); Trans-Altai Range, **Tajikistan-Khirghizia**; adjoining glacier; 7,132 m.

Leninsk-Kuznetski, t., **Russia**; in W. Siberia on Inya R.; coalfield in Kuznetsk basin; heavy engin., power sta.; p. (1989) 134,000.

Lenkoran, c., pt. **Azerbaijan**; on Caspian Sea, nr. Iranian border; rice, citrus fruits, tea, fisheries, food-processing; p. (1990) 45,500.

Lennoxtown, t., E. Dunbartonshire, **Scot.**; aluminium wks.; p. (1991) 4,524.

Lens, t., Pas-de-Calais dep., N. **France**; industl. ctr. in coal a.; p. (1990) 35,278 (t.), 323,174 (met.a.).

Leoben, t., Styria, **Austria**; lignite mng. ctr.; p. (1991) 28,504.

Leominster, mkt. t., Hereford, **Eng.**; 19 km N. of Hereford; once famed for woollen ind.; p. (1995) 41,200 (dist.), (1991) 9,453 (t.).

León, c., central **Mexico**; at c. 1,700 m; comm., agr. and mng. ctr. (gold, copper, silver, lead, tin); textiles, leather; p. (1990) 872,453.

León, c., cap. of León dep., N.W. **Nicaragua**; cath., univ.; ctr. for agr. and industl. prods.; footwear, textiles; p. (1985) 101,000.

León, cap. of L. prov., N.W. **Spain**; gothic cath.; craft inds.; p. (1991) 146,720, 517,176 (prov.).

Léopoldville. *See* Kinshasa.

Lepontine Alps, major gr., **Switzerland–Italy**; alt. over 3,300 m.

Le Puy, t., cap. of Haute Loire dep., **France**; lace, liqueurs; cath. sited on old volcanic plug; tourism; p. (1990) 23,434.

Lérida, t., cap. of L. prov., **Spain**; on R. Segre; 2 caths.; textiles, leather, glass; p. (1991) 119,167 (t.), 358,123 (prov.).

Lerwick, t., Shetland Is., **Scot.**; on Mainland; fishing; p. (1991) 7,336.

Lesbos. *See* Lesvos.

Les Causses. *See* Causses, Les.

Leskovac, t., Serbia, **Yugoslavia**; on Morava R.; in economically backward a.; textiles, soap, furniture, tobacco-processing; p. (1991) 61,693.

Les Landes. *See* Landes, Les.

Leslie, burgh, Aberdeenshire, **Scot.**; 11 km N. of Kirkcaldy; paper, bleaching; p. (1991) 3,062.

Lesotho (Basutoland), kingdom, southern Africa; surrounded by Rep. of S. Africa; at head of Orange R. and enclosed by Drakensberg mtns.;

economy mainly agr., especially pastoral farming; exp. livestock, wool, mohair, diamonds; 50 per cent revenue from U.K. grants; poor communications; many workers migrate to S. Africa; inds. encouraged by tax concessions becoming increasingly impt.; Highlands Water Project started (1986) to export water from Orange R. to S. Africa and generate hydro-electr. from 6 dams; cap. Maseru; a. 30,344 km²; p. (1992) 1,889,000.

Lesser Antilles. *See* **Antilles.**

Lesvos (Lesbos, Mytilene), I., off Turkey, Aegean Sea, belonging to **Greece**; highest point 939 m; agr., antimony, marbles; cap. Mytilene; a. 1,601 km²; p. (1991) 103,700 (dep.).

Leszno, t. and prov., W. **Poland**; engin., distilling, tobacco; p. (1989) 57,673 (t.) 383,300 (prov.).

Letchworth (Garden City), t., North Herts., **Eng.**; at foot of Chiltern Hills, 3 km N.E. of Hitchin; first garden c., founded by Sir Ebenezer Howard 1903; engin., office equipment; expanded t.; p. (1991) 31,418.

Lethbridge, c., Alberta, **Canada**; in foothills of Rockies; ctr. of lge. coal-mng. dist. and of irrigated wheat-growing a.; p. (1991) 60,974.

Le Touquet-Paris Plage, fashionable resort, W. cst. **France**; S. of Canche estuary.

Letterkenny, t., Co. Donegal, **R.o.I.**; on Lough Swilly; tourist ctr.; p. (1986) 6,691.

Leuna, t., Saxony - Anhalt, **Germany**; 5 km S. of Merseburg; synthetic chemical ind.; oil pipeline from Schwedt; p. (1989) 8,647.

Levant, French and Italian name for E. cst. of Mediterranean.

Leven, burgh, Fife, **Scot.**; on N. side of F. of Forth; resort; p. (1991) 8,317.

Leven, Loch, Perth and Kinross, **Scot.**; ass. with escape of Mary Queen of Scots from Castle I. 1568.

Leverkusen, t., N. Rhine-Westphalia, **Germany**; on R. Rhine, N. of Cologne; iron, machin., textiles, chemicals; p. (1990) 161,000.

Levkás or **Santa Maura**, one of Ionian Is., off W. **Greece**; wine, olive oil, currants; p. (1991) 20,900.

Lewes, t., l. gov. dist., East Sussex, **Eng.**; on R. Ouse at N. entrance to gap through S. Downs; mkt., cas., printing, light inds.; p. (1995) 88,000 (dist.), (1991) 15,376 (t.).

Lewis, I., Outer Hebrides, Western Isles, **Scot.**; fishing, tweeds; ch. t. Stornoway; p. (1991) 21,731 (with Harris).

Lewisham, inner bor., London, **Eng.**; inc. Deptford; residtl.; industl.; p. (1995) 239,700.

Lewiston, t., Maine, **USA**; power for textile mill supplied by waterfall since early 19th cent.; p. (1980) 40,481.

Lexington-Fayette, c., Ky., **USA**; in heart of Blue Grass region; univ.; ch. tobacco mkt. and horsebreeding ctr. of USA; p. (1990) 225,366 (c.), 348,000 (met. a.).

Lexington, t., Mass., **USA**; nr. Boston; residtl.; first battle in war of independence 19 Apr. 1775; p. (1980) 29,479.

Leyburn, t., Richmondshire, North Yorks., **Eng.**; in lower Wensleydale; mkt; p. (1991) 1,716.

Leyden. *See* **Leiden.**

Leyland, t., Lancs., **Eng.**; 8 km S. of Preston; motor vehicles, rubber; p. (1991) 37,331. *See* **Central Lancashire.**

Leyte, one of Visayan Is., prov. central **Philippines**; maize, abaca, rice; Japanese fleet defeated by US in battle of Leyte Gulf 1944; a. 7,213 km²; p. (1990) 1,368,510.

Leyton. *See* **Waltham Forest.**

Lhasa (Lasa), c., cap. of Tibet, **China**; "forbidden" c.; Buddhist ctr., temple, monasteries, shrines; caravan tr. in carpets, silk, lace, gold, tea; pharmaceutical factory, turbine pumps, fertilisers; much hotel bldg. and restoration of Buddhist sites to encourage tourism and break down isolation; p. (1982) 343,200.

Lhotse, mtn., Tibet, **China-Nepal**; 4th hgst. mtn. in world; alt. 8,506 m.

Lianyungang, spt., Jiangsu, **China**; impt. fishing and tea centre; rapid industrial development, esp. mineral processing, chemicals and motors; univ.; attracting foreign investment as "open" c. under China's new economic policy; p. (1984) 450,000.

Liao-ho, R., Liaoning, N.E. **China**; flows into G. of Liaotung, Yellow Sea; navigable for last 640 km of course; c. 1,600 km long.

Liaoning, prov., N.E. **China**; inc. lower course and delta of Liao-ho; part of N.E. China (formerly called Manchuria); maize, millets, soyabeans; lge.

mineral reserves of coal and iron ore; cap. Shenyang; a. 150,220 km²; p. (1990) 39,980,000.

Liaotung, peninsula, N.E. **China**; nr. G. of same name.

Liaoyang, c., E. Liaoning prov., N.E. **China**; in fertile valley of Liao-ho; cotton-growing; textile mills; p. (1984) 565,300.

Liao-yuang, c., S.W. Jilin, **China**; lge. coal-mng. ctr.; p. (1984) 375,600.

Liberec, t., Czech **Rep.**; on R. Neisse; univ.; textiles, chemicals, tr. ctr.; p. (1990) 104,000.

Liberia, rep., W. **Africa**; founded (1847) by free slaves from USA; tropical climate; few cash crops, inc. rubber and cocoa; rich iron deposits provide main exp.; world's lgst. merchant fleet as result of "flag of convenience"; civil war in 1990s; cap. and ch. pt. Monrovia; a. 99,068 km²; p. (1993) 2,825,000.

Libertador, reg. **Chile**; cap. Rancagua; a. 16,456 km²; p. (1992) 688,385.

Libourne, t., Gironde, **France**; on R. Dordogne, 35 km N.E. of Bordeaux; wine tr.; p. (1982) 23,312.

Libreville, c., cap. of **Gabon**; pt. on G. of Guinea; exp. tropical hardwoods, rubber, cacao; Trans-Gabon rly. project to link L. to Booué to promote timber exploitation; p. (1992) 352,000.

Libya, (Great Socialist People's Libyan Arab Republic) (since 1977), rep., N. Africa; on Mediterranean cst.; desert conditions prevail; radical attitude towards oil companies as oil accounts for 99 per cent of exp. earnings and forms basis of newfound wealth; petro-chemical inds.; over half working p. are foreigners; most of p. engaged in subsistence agr. (nomadic pastoralism); most food and mnfs. imported; joint caps. Tripoli (site of government deps.), Benghazi; a. 1,759,537 km²; p. (1990) 4,000,000.

Libyan Desert, part of the Sahara, **Africa.**

Licata, t., Sicily, **Italy**; spt.; sulphur-processing; p. (1981) 40,050.

Lichfield, c., l. gov. dist., Staffs., **Eng.**; cath.; agr. and lt. inds.; expanded t.; birthplace of Dr. Samuel Johnson; p. (1995) 93,300 (dist.), (1991) 28,666 (c.).

Lickey Hills, gr. of hills, Hereford and Worcs., **Eng.**; 6 km S.W. of Birmingham; reveal anc. rocks underlying younger sediments; rise to 292 m, largely wooded.

Liechtenstein, principality, between Austria and Switzerland; official language German; economy based on sm.-scale inds. and tourism in picturesque Alpine scenery aided by mild climate; wine; cap. Vaduz; a. 161 km²; p. (1994) 30,629, one-third foreign born.

Liège (Luik), industl. c. and prov., E. **Belgium**; on R. Meuse nr. confluence of Ourthe; cath., univ.; conurb. inc. Herstal, Bressoux, Ougrée, Angleur, Grivegnée; metallurgy, armaments, vehicles, chemicals, textiles, glassware, tyres; p. (1993) 196,632 (c.), 1,011,368 (prov.).

Liepaja (Libau), c., **Latvia**; ice-free pt. on Baltic Sea, second to Riga; shipyards, steel-wks.; paper mills, chemicals; exp. timber, grain; p. (1991) 114,900.

Liestal, t., cap. of the half-can. Baselland, **Switzerland**; p. (1980) 12,158.

Liffey, R., **R.o.I.**; rises in Wicklow Mtns. and enters Irish Sea at Dublin; water supply for Dublin; inds. along estuary.

Liguria, region, N.W. **Italy**; inc. provs. of Genoa and Porto Maurizio; a. 5,411 km²; p. (1992) 1,667,896.

Ligurian Sea, Mediterranean; N. of Corsica.

Likasi (Jadotville), t., **Congo**; ctr. for copper mng. and refining; p. (1991) 279,839.

Lille, c., cap. of Nord dep., N. **France**; on R. Deûle; mftg., comm. and cultural ctr.; former cap. of Fr. Flanders (1668); textiles (the term lisle derived from earlier spelling of city's name), metallurgy, engin.; univ., art museums; p. (1990) 178,301 (c.), 950,256 (met.a.).

Lilongwe, c., main ctr. of Central Region, **Malawi**; replaced Zomba as cap. 1975; p. (1987) 233,973.

Lima, c., cap. of **Peru**; 13 km from its pt. Callao; dominates comm., industl. and social life of cty.; cath., univ.; imposing architecture; seaside subs. Miraflores, Barranco, Chorillos; shanty ts. on outskirts; p. (1993) 5,706,127.

Lima, t., Ohio, **USA**; on Ottawa R.; rly. wks., oil, car bodies, refrigerators; p. (1990) 45,549.

Limassol, t., S. **Cyprus**; spt. on Akrotiri Bay; new artificial harbour; ctr. of admin. dist.; wine, agr.-processing; exp. foodstuffs; tourism; p. (1997) 183,000.

Limavady, t., l. gov. dist., **N. Ireland**; mkt.; linen; p. (1991) 29,567 (dist.), 10,350 (t.).

Limbach, t., Saxony, **Germany**; hosiery, textiles, machines; p. (1989) 22,526.

Limbe. *See* Blantyre-Limbe.

Limbourg, prov., N.E. **Belgium**; bordering Neth.; mainly agr.; coal-mng. in Campine region; cap. Hasselt; a. 2,409 km²; p. (1993) 763,565.

Limburg, prov., S.E. **Neth.**; bordering on Belgium and W. Germany; drained by R. Maas; former coalmng.; new inds. to relieve unemployment; a. 2,191 km²; p. (1994) 1,125,187.

Limeira, t., São Paulo, **Brazil**; ctr. of orange cultivation; hats, matches; p. (1985) 187,800.

Limerick, co., Munster, **R.o.I.**; agr., livestock, fishing: a. 3,385 km²; p. (1986) 164,569.

Limerick, cap. of Limerick, **R.o.I.**; spt. at head of Shannon estuary; bacon, tanning, shipbldg.; p. (1986) 56,279.

Limmat, R., **Switzerland**; trib. of R. Aare; flows through c. of Zürich; 128 km long.

Lim Fjord, shallow strait, Jutland, **Denmark**; connects N. Sea with Kattegat; contains I. of Mors.

Limoges, c., cap. of Haute-Vienne dep., **France**; to N.W. of Central Massif; anc. t., celebrated in middle ages for goldsmith's work, later for enamel ware and porcelain; cath.; p. (1990) 136,407 (c.), 170,065 (met.a.).

Limón, spt., **Costa Rica**; on Caribbean; oil refining nearby; p. (1984) 67,784 (dist.).

Limousin, region and former prov., central **France**; to W. of Auvergne; inc. deps. Corrèze, Haute-Vienne, Creuse, plateau, average alt. 300 m, composed of old crystalline rocks; exposed damp climate; infertile, some pastoral agr.; kaolin; ch. t.; Limoges; p. (1990) 722,900.

Limpopo or **Crocodile R., S. Africa, Moçambique**, and **Zimbabwe**; lower R. forms a fertile valley 1,600 km long.

Linares, t., Jaén prov., **Spain**; silver-lead mines; metallurgical inds.; p. (1981) 51,278.

Lincoln, c., co. t., l. gov. dist., Lincs., **Eng.**; on R. Witham in gap through Lincoln Edge; impt. Roman t.; cath., cas.; heavy engin., iron foundries, bricks, lime, seed milling, malting; p. (1995) 84,300 (dist.), (1991) 80,281 (c.).

Lincoln, c., cap. of Nebraska, **USA**; univ.; educational ctr.; grain and cattle mkt.; flour mills, agr. machin., cars, chemicals, rubber gds.; p. (1990) 191,972.

Lincoln Edge, limestone ridge, Lincs. and N. Lincs., **Eng.**; runs N. from Ancaster through Lincoln to Humber; narrow ridge with steep scarp slope to W., broken by R. Witham at Lincoln; iron-ore deposits worked in N. nr. Scunthorpe; sheep, barley; rarely exceeds 90 m alt.

Lincolnshire, non-met. co., **Eng.**; between the Humber R. and the Wash; fertile soil on low-lying fenland; intensive agr., arable crops, bulbs, market gardening; food processing; formerly divided into 3 admin. parts: Holland, Kesteven, and Lindsey; p. (1995) 611,800.

Lincoln Wolds, low plateau, Lincs. and N. Lincs., **Eng.**; runs N. 72 km from Wash to Humber; chalk covered with glacial deposits; mixed farming, grains, roots, sheep; lge. farm units; scantily populated; rise to approx. 135 m.

Lindau, t. Baden-Württemberg, **Germany**; on I. in Bodensee; tourist resort; p. (1986) 23,100.

Lindisfarne or **Holy I.**, off cst. of Northumberland, **Eng.**; connected to mainland by stretch of sand and causeway at low tide; abbey founded 635 A.D. as first establishment of Celtic Christianity in Eng.

Lindsey. *See* Lincolnshire.

Line Is., Pac. Oc., coral gr. admin. by U.K., except Palmyra, Kingman and Jarvis, which belong to USA; coconuts; airfields, meteorological stas.

Lin-i (formerly **Ichow**), t., Shandong, **China**; at foot of Shandong Highlands.

Linköping, t., S.E. **Sweden**; aero-engin., pianos, furniture; cath.; p. (1992) 126,377.

Linlithgow, burgh, W. Lothian, **Scot.**; distilling, brewing, paper, shoes; birthplace of Mary Queen of Scots; p. (1991) 11,866.

Linnhe, Loch, Highland, Argyll and Bute, **Scot.**; 21 miles long; entrance to Caledonian Canal.

Linslade. *See* Leighton Buzzard.

Linz, c., cap. of Upper Austria; pt. on Danube; comm. and industl. ctr. with iron and steel wks.; cath.; p. (1991) 202,855.

Lipa, c., Luzon, **Philippines**; sugar, tobacco, cocoa, maize; processing; p. (1990) 160,117.

Lipari Is. or **Aeolian Is.**, volcanic gr. between Sicily and toe of **Italy**; inc. Stromboli (927 m), Lipari, Vulcano, Salina; olives, grapes, currants, pumice; p. (1981) 10,208.

Lipetsk, c., **Russia**; on Voronezh R.; ctr. of iron-ore mng. a.; engin., steel, ferro-alloys; health resort; p. (1989) 450,000.

Lippe, R., **Germany**; trib. of Rhine; paralleled by L. canal; forms N. bdy. of Ruhr industl. dist.; 176 km long.

Lippstadt, t., N. Rhine-Westphalia, **Germany**; on R. Lippe; metallurgy, textiles rly. ctr.; p. (1986) 60,100.

Liri, R., central **Italy**; rises in Alban Hills, flows S.E. to Cassino and then S.W. to G. of Gaeta; valley followed by main road from Rome to Naples; length 168 km.

Lisbon (Lisboa), c., cap of **Portugal**; on R. Tagus, 14 km from mouth; spt. with fine natural harbour; cas., cath., univ.; admin., comm., and industl. ctr.; expanding inds., airpt.; attracts p. from rural areas; p. (1987) 830,500.

Lisburn, t., l. gov. dist., **N. Ireland**; on R. Lagan, 10 km S.W. of Belfast; p. (1991) 99,458 (dist.), 42,110 (t.).

Lisieux, t., Calvados dep., N. **France**; historic t., severely damaged in second world war; cath.; Camembert cheese; p. (1982) 25,823.

Liskeard, mkt. t., Caradon, Cornwall, **Eng.**; on R. Looe at S. edge of Bodmin Moor; p. (1991) 7,044.

Lismore, t., N.S.W., **Australia**; pt. on Richmond R.; dairying, sugar refining, maize, potatoes, textiles, engin., bacon; p. (1981) 24,033.

Lismore, mkt. t., Waterford, **R.o.I.**; on Blackwater R.; cas.; p. (1986) 703.

Listowel, t., Kerry, **R.o.I.**; on R. Feale; cas. ruins; p. (1986) 3,494.

Litherland, t., Sefton, Merseyside, **Eng.**; N. sub. of Liverpool; p. (1991) 20,905.

Lithuania, former constituent rep., USSR; borders Baltic Sea; agr. development on reclaimed marshland; dairy farming, stockraising, fishing, timber inds., food-processing, ship bldg., textiles, machin.; cap. Vilnius; a. 65,201 km²; p. (1994) 3,724,000.

Litoměřice, t., **Czech Rep.**; in Bohemia on R. Elbe (Labe); cath.; brewing, agr. ctr.; p. (1984) 28,844.

Little Belt (Lille Bælt), strait, **Denmark**; separates Fyn I. from Jutland; too shallow for lge. ships; road/rly., motorway bridges cross narrow N. section nr. Frederidicia; 48 km long.

Little Bighorn, R., Wyo., Mont., **USA**; Custer's last battle on ridge overlooking R. (1876); 144 km long.

Littleborough, t., Gtr. Manchester, **Eng.**; textiles and textile finishing; p. (1991) 13,638.

Little Dunmow, v., 3 km E. of Great Dunmow; Uttlesford, Essex, **Eng.**; historic Dunmow Flitch (side of bacon); bacon factory closed (1983).

Littlehampton, t., Arun, West Sussex, **Eng.**; on S. cst. at mouth of R. Arun; holiday resort, sm. spt.; p. (1991) 50,408.

Little Lever, t., Gtr. Manchester, **Eng.**; 5 km S.E. of Bolton; residtl. and industl.; p. (1991) 11,589.

Little Rock, c., cap. of Ark., **USA**; N.E. of Hot Springs, on Ark. R. opposite N. Little Rock; comm. and mnf. ctr. in rich cotton and dairy farming a.; bauxite nearby; p. (1990) 175,795 (c.), 513,117 (met. a. with N. Little Rock).

Littoria. *See* Latina.

Liuchow. *See* Liuzhou.

Liuzhou (Liuchow), c., Guangxi, S. **China**; on trib. of Xijiang; route ctr. and R. pt.; p. (1984) 446,900.

Liverpool, c., spt., met. dist., Merseyside, **Eng.**; on N. bank at entrance to Mersey estuary; deep-sea container berths at Seaforth; shipping and ship-repairing; elec. mnfs. and engin., flour milling, sugar refining, seed and rubber processing, cars; cath., univ.; second Mersey tunnel opened 1971; freeport (1984) to help revive docks; p. (1995) 470,800 (dist), (1991) 481,786 (c.).

Liverpool, t., N.S.W., **Australia**; within met. a. of Sydney; major source of poultry, vegetables and dairy prods. for Sydney.

Livingston, new t. (1962), W. Lothian, **Scot.**; p. (1991) 41,647.

Livingstone, t., **Zambia**; on Zambesi R. where rly. bridges R.; stands at *c.* 900 m; former cap.; sawmilling ctr.; p. (1989) 102,000

Livorno (Leghorn), spt., cap. of L. prov., **Italy**; on Ligurian Sea; shipbldg., machin., chemicals, iron and steel wks., oil refining; exp. wine, olive oil, textiles, marble; p. (1992) 166,394.

Lizard, The, C., Cornwall, **Eng.**; S. point of Eng.

Ljubljana, c., cap. of **Slovenia** (formerly Yugoslavia); on trib. of Sava R.; industl. ctr., local coal, hydroelectric power; route ctr.; airport; univ., mediaeval fortress; ctr. of Slovene nat. movement in 19th cent.; p. (1981) 305,211.

Llanberis, pass, Gwynedd, N. **Wales**; between Snowdon and Glyder Fawr; road carries heavy tourist traffic; summit 356 m; nearby tourist resort of Llanberis; p. (1991) 1,859.

Llandarcy, v., S. **Wales**; on cst. Swansea Bay, Bristol Channel; lge. oil refinery; pipeline to Angle Bay, Pembrokeshire.

Llandeilo, mkt. t., Carmarthenshire, **Wales**; in Vale of Towy, E. of Carmarthen; cas.; p. (1991) 1,666.

Llandovery, t., Carmarthenshire, **Wales**; on R. Bran, nr. confluence with Towy; mkt. ctr. for rural a.; p. (1991) 2,037.

Llandrindod Wells, t., Powys, **Wales**; medicinal waters; p. (1991) 4,362.

Llandudno, t., Conwy, **Wales**; between Gr. Ormes and Little Ormes headlands; resort; p. (1991) 14,576.

Llanelli, t., Carmarthenshire, **Wales**; pt. on Burry inlet, 18 km N.W. of Swansea; industl. and comm. ctr.; coal mng., steel and tinplate wks., mng. machin.; cas.; p. (1991) 44,953.

Llanfairfechan, t., Conwy, **Wales**; at foot of Penmaenmawr mtn.; seaside resort; granite quarrying; p. (1991) 3,338.

Llangefni, t., Isle of Anglesey, **Wales**; in ctr. of the I.; mkt. and agr. t.; p. (1991) 4,643.

Llangollen, t., Denbighshire, **Wales**; on R. Dee; Vale of L., tourist ctr.; annual International Eisteddfod; p. (1991) 3,267.

Llanidloes, t., Powys, **Wales**; on R. Severn; surrounded by hills; anc. mkt. house; p. (1991) 2,616.

Llanos, lowland region, **Venezuela** and **Colombia**, S. America; drained by R. Orinoco and tribs.; high temperatures throughout year, but rain chiefly in summer; ch. vegetation, coarse grass which withers during dry season (Dec. to May).

Llanos de Urgel, upland region, Lérida, N.E. **Spain**; semi-arid; formerly steppe-land, now irrigated by R. Segre; vine, olive, maize, tobacco.

Llanrwst, mkt. t., Conwy, **Wales**; on R. Conwy; tourist ctr.; p. (1991) 3,012.

Llanstephan, v., Carmarthenshire, **Wales**; at mouth of R. Towy; ruins of Norman cas.

Llantrisant, new t., Rhondda, Cynon, Taff, S. **Wales**; iron-ore quarrying; Royal Mint; p. (1991) 9,136 (with Pontyclun).

Llantwit Major, t. Vale of Glamorgan, **Wales**; famous centre of learning in Celtic times.

Lleyn, peninsula, Gwynedd, N. **Wales**; from Snowdonia to Bardsey I.; crystalline rocks form hills in E., otherwise low, undulating; pastoral farming, sheep, cattle; sm. seaside resorts; ch. t. Pwllheli.

Llwchwr or **Loughor**, R., S. **Wales**; in lower course forms bdy. between Carmarthenshire and Swansea, empties into Burry inlet.

Loanhead, burgh, Midlothian, **Scot.**; 8 km S.E. of Edinburgh; coal, engin.; p. (1991) 5,659.

Lobito, spt., **Angola**; on Atl. Oc.; 29 km N. of Benguela; fine natural deepwater harbour; rly. terminus; varied exps.; oil-refinery.

Locarno, t., **Switzerland**; on L. Maggiore; tourist ctr.; L. treaty 1925; p. (1986) 14,341.

Lochalsh. See Kyle of Lochalsh.

Lochgelly, burgh, Fife, **Scot.**; nr. Dunfermline; p. (1991), 7,044.

Lochgilphead, Argyll and Bute, **Scot.**; at head of Loch Gilp, 3 km N. of Ardrishaig; tourist ctr.; p. (1991) 2,421.

Lochmaben, burgh, Dumfries and Galloway, **Scot.**; in Annandale, 11 km N.E. of Dumfries; p. (1991) 2,024.

Lockerbie, burgh, Dumfries and Galloway, **Scot.**; in Annandale, 16 km E. of Dumfries; sheep mkt.; air disaster 1988, caused by terrorist bomb; p. (1991) 3,982.

Lockport, t., N.Y., **USA**; on N.Y. st. barge canal, 38 km N.E. of Buffalo; power from Niagara falls supplies paper, metal, and other inds.; p. (1980) 24,844.

Lodi, t., **Italy**; on R. Adda, S.E. of Milan; cath.; scene of Napoleon's victory over Austrians 1796; p. (1981) 42,873.

Lodore Falls, waterfalls, Cumbria, **Eng.**; in Watendlath beck at foot of Derwentwater.

Lódz, c. and prov., central **Poland**; second c. of rep. and ctr. of textile ind.; machin., elec. equipment,

chemicals, metals; univ.; cultural ctr.; problems of water-supply; p. (1989) 849,204 (c.), 1,139,400 (prov.).

Lofoten Is., storm-swept chain of Is. off N.W. cst. **Norway** within Arctic Oc., stretching 240 km; cod and herring fisheries among richest in world.

Loftus, t. Redcar and Cleveland, **Eng.**; on N.E.flank of Cleveland Hills; p. (1991) 5,931.

Logan, Mount, S.E. Yukon, **Canada**, E. of Alaska; alt. 5,959 m.

Logroño, t., N. **Spain**; on Ebro R.; in wine growing a.; industl. and agr. ctr.; p. (1991) 126,760.

Loire, R., **France**; longest in cty., flows from Cevennes mtns. to Atl. Oc. at St. Nazaire; vineyards and many castles in attractive valley; 1,000 km long.

Loire, dep., E. central **France**; in part of the former provs. of Beaujolais and Lyonnais; agr.; coal mng., cattle raising; cap. St. Etienne; a. 4,799 km²; p. (1990) 746,300.

Loire-Atlantique, dep., W. **France**; mainly agr., salt-marsh on cst.; inds. at cap. Nantes; a. 6,980 km²; p. (1990) 1,052,200.

Loiret, dep., N. central **France**; agr., vineyards, distilling, mftg.; cap. Orléans; a. 6,812 km²; p. (1990) 580,600.

Loir-et-Cher, dep., central **France**; contains fertile a. of Beauce; cap. Blois; a. 6,421 km²; p. (1990) 305,900.

Lokeren, industl. t., **Belgium**; between Ghent and Antwerp; textiles, chemicals, tobacco; p. (1993) 35,435.

Lokoja, t. **Nigeria**; at confluence of Rs. Niger and Benue; R. pt.; iron-ore nearby.

Lolland or **Laaland**, Danish I. part of **Denmark** in Baltic Sea; a. 1,241 km²; agr. forests; ch. ts. Maribo, Nakshov; p. (1990) 73,191.

Lomami, R., central **Congo**; trib. of Congo R., rich coal-bearing strata at confluence; 1,812 km long.

Lombardy, Plain of, N. **Italy**; extensive lowland flanked by Alps, Apennines, Adriatic Sea; built up by alluvium from R. Po, its tribs. and R. Adige; intensively cultivated; rice, maize, flax, clover, lucerne, wheat, apples, dairy cattle; densely populated; many industl. ts., Milan, Novara, Pavia, etc.; p. of region (1992) 8,882,408

Lombok, one of the lesser Sunda Is., **Indonesia**; mtnous. volcanic terrain; Wallace's Line passes between Lombok and Bali; ch. t. Mataram; p. 1,300,000.

Lomé, spt., cap. of **Togo**, W. Africa; on G. of Guinea; deepwater pt.; exp. cacao, cotton, palm prods.; phosphates; p. (1990) 450,000.

Lomond, Loch, Stirling, lgst. loch in **Scot.**; studded with Is., surrounded by hills with Ben Lomond on E. side.

Lomza, t. and prov., **Poland**; on Narew R., metal inds., foodstuffs; p. (1989) 57,976 (t.), 344,500 (prov.).

London, cap. of U.K., **Eng.**; at head of Thames estuary; seat of govt., world ctr. of finance and communication; cultural and artistic ctr.; comprises the City, 12 inner and 20 outer bors.; Port of London; upstream docks now closed; main pt. downstream at Tilbury; currently losing p. and inds. to outer met. a.; univs. (London, Brunel, City etc.), caths., historic bldgs., theatres, museums, galleries, libraries, and parks; p. (1995) 5,200 (City of London), 3,647,000 (Inner London), 7,007,100 (Greater London).

London, t., Ont., **Canada**; on R. Thames, 104 km W. of Hamilton; industl. ctr.; univ.; p. (1991) 303,165 (c.), (1986) 342,302 (met a.).

Londonderry c., Derry, **N. Ireland**; on left bank of R. Foyle, 6 km upstream from Lough Foyle; shirt mftg.; textiles; acetylene from naphtha; training ctr. for ind.; p. (1991) 21,485.

Londrina, c., Paraná, **Brazil**; industl. and agr. ctr., coffee, maize, cotton, livestock; p. (1991) 540,982.

Long Beach, c., Cal., **USA**; Pac. cst. resort and industl. suburb of Los Angeles met. a.; p. (1990) 429,433 (c.). See Los Angeles.

Long Eaton, t. Erewash, Derbys., **Eng.**; on R. Trent, 8 km S.W. of Nottingham; former ctr. for lace mftg., elec. cables, flexible tubing, hosiery; p. (1991) 44,826.

Longford, co., Leinster, **R.o.I.**; peat bogs; dairy farming; co. t. Longford; a. 1,090 km²; p. (1986) 31,496.

Longford, co. t., Longford, **R.o.I.**; cas., cath.; mkt. t.; p. (1986) 6,457.

Long Forties Bank, submarine sandbank, N. Sea; 128 km E. of Aberdeen; valuable fishing-grounds; depth of water, from 45-75 m.

Long I., part of N.Y., **USA**; separated from mainland by East R.; contains Queens and Brooklyn bors. of N.Y. City; mkt. gardening, fisheries, oysters, holiday resorts; a. 4,356 km².

Longreach, t. Queensland, **Australia**; in ctr. of Gr. Australian (artesian) basin; collecting ctr. for cattle and wool.

Longridge, t., Ribble Valley, Lancs., **Eng.**; 10 km N.E. of Preston; p. (1991) 7,351.

Longview, t. Texas, **USA**; oil, chemicals, plastics; p. (1984) 73,300 (t.), 168,400 (met. a.).

Longwy, t., Meurthe-et-Moselle dep., N.E. **France**; on Belgian–Luxembourg frontier; upper part fortfd.; lower part industl. with iron and steel ind.

Lons-le-Saunier, cap. of Jura dep., E. **France**; saline springs; agr. ctr.; p. (1990) 20,140.

Looe, t. Caradon, Cornwall, **Eng.**; on Looe estuary; holiday resort; p. (1991) 5,022.

Lopburi, t., **Thailand**; ctr. of haematite iron deposits; former cap.

Lop Nor, marsh, Xinjiang, W. **China**; in Tarim Basin at foot of Altun Shan; ctr. of inland drainage, receives water from R. Tarim; atomic testing grounds.

Lorain, t., Ohio, **USA**; on L. Erie; shipbldg., steelwks., fisheries; p. (1990) 71,245 (c.), 271,000 (met. a. with Elyria).

Lorca, t., Murcia, **Spain**; agr. prod., woollens, chemicals; bishop's palace; p. (1981) 60,627.

Lord Howe I., forested volcanic I., S. Pac. Oc., 698 km N.E. of Sydney; palm seed ind.; ad-min. by N.S.W. **Australia**; p. (1991) 320.

Lorient, spt., Morbihan dep., N.W. **France**; on Atl.; naval shipyard, fishing harbour; p. (1982) 64,675.

Lorraine, region and former prov., N.E. **France**; inc. deps. Moselle, Meurthe-et-Moselle, Meuse, and Vosges; ch. t. Nancy; rich iron-ore deposits; impt. but declining industl. a.; mkt. gardening, vineyards; with Alsace long disputed between Germany and France; p. (1990) 2,305,700.

Los Alamos, t., N.M., **USA**; site of research for first atomic bomb; p. (1980) 11,039.

Los Angeles, c., S. Cal., **USA**; booming modern c. ("the city of angels"), busiest pt. in Cal.; fine harbour; riots 1992; many prosperous inds., inc. aircraft, missiles, chemicals, machin., electronic equipment, food-processing, oil refining; film ctr.; earthquake 1994; p. (1990) 3,485,398 (c.), 8,863,000 (met. a. with Long Beach).

Los Lagos, reg. Chile; cap. Puerto Montt; a. 67,247 km²; p. (1992) 953,330.

Lossiemouth, burgh, Moray, **Scot.**; on Moray F., 8 km N. of Elgin; birthplace of Ramsay MacDonald; fishing; p. (1991) 7,184.

Lostwithiel, mkt. t. Cornwall, **Eng.**; on R. Fowey S.E. of Bodmin; anc. Stannary t.; p. (1991) 2,452.

Lot, dep., S.W. **France**; livestock, wine, cereals, coals, iron; a. 5,227 km²; cap. Cahors; p. (1990) 155,800.

Lot, R., S. France; trib. of Garonne R., 435 km long.

Lot-et-Garonne, dep., S.W. **France**; agr. (cereals, vines, fruit); cap. Agen; a. 5,385 km²; p. (1990) 306,000.

Lötschental, picturesque valley, Valais, **Switzer-land**; ch. v. Kippel.

Loughborough, t., Charnwood, Leics., **Eng.**; on R. Soar 16 km N. of Leicester; engin., elec. gds., chemicals, textiles; univ.; former hosiery t.; bell foundry; p. (1991) 46,867.

Loughor. See **Llwchwr.**

Loughrea, mkt. t., Galway, **R.o.I.**; cotton mill; p. (1986) 3,360.

Louisiana, southern st., **USA**; Pelican St.; admitted to Union 1812; st. flower Magnolia, st. bird East-ern Brown Pelican; leading producer of rice, sugarcane, sweet potatoes, also cotton, maize, tobacco, oil, natural gas, lumber; cap. Baton Rouge; New Orleans major pt.; a. 125,675 km²; p. (1990) 4,219,973.

Louisville, c., Ky., **USA**; on Ohio R.; univ.; lgst. tobacco mkt. in world; chemicals, paints, cars, machin., elec. gds., synthetic rubber; p. (1990) 269,063 (c.), 953,000 (met. a.).

Lourdes, t., **France**; on R. Pau; Catholic pilgrim centre.; slate, marble; p. (1982) 17,619.

Lourenço Marques. See **Maputo.**

Louth, t., East Lindsey, Lincs., **Eng.**; on E. edge of Lincoln Wolds; abbey ruins; cattle mkt., farm implements, plastic bags, corrugated board; p. (1991) 14,248.

Louth, maritime co., Leinster, **R.o.I.**; mtns., bog and barren land; salmon fishing; cap. Dundalk; a. 818 km²; p. (1986) 91,810.

Louvain (Leuven), c., Brabant prov., **Belgium**; on R. Dyle; univ. (Erasmus taught here); brewing ctr., bell foundries; p. (1993) 85,592.

Low Archipelago. See **Tuamotu Is.**

Low Countries, name for Belgium and the Neth.

Lowell, c., Mass., **USA**; at junc. of Merrimac and Concord Rs.; 48 km N. of Boston; textiles, machin., chemicals, carpets; birthplace of Whis-tler; p. (1990) 103,439 (c.), 273,000 (met. a.).

Lower California (Baja California), peninsula, N.W. **Mexico**; separating G. of Cal. and Pac. Oc.; isolated, arid; divided into 2 sts., Baja California (cap. Tijuana) p. (1990) 1,657,927, and Baja California, Territorio Sur (cap. La Paz) p. (1990) 317,326; a. 143,963 km².

Lower Hutt, c., N.I., **N.Z.**; rapid industl. devel. in last 45 years; engin., plastics, textiles, vehicle assembly; p. (1991) 94,540.

Lower Saxony (Nieder Sachsen), Land, **Germany**; inc. Lüneburg heath and Harz mtns.; cap. Hanover; a. 47,205 km²; p. (1992) 7,476,000.

Lowestoft, fish pt., Waveney, Suffolk, **Eng.**; on E. Anglian cst. 14 km S. of Gr. Yarmouth; holiday resort, nr. Broads; food processing plants; base for N. Sea gas; p. (1991) 62,907.

Lowther Hills, mtns., between S. Lanarkshire and Dumfries and Galloway **Scot.**; hgst. point 733 m.

Loyalty Is., S. **Pac. Oc.**; included in Fr. ad-ministration of New Caledonia; copra; lgst. Is. Maré, Lifou, Uvéa; a. c. 2,100 km².

Lozère, dep., S.E. **France**; traversed by Cevennes mtns.; cap. Mende; a. 5,170 km²; p. (1990) 72,800.

Lualaba, R., **Congo**, central **Africa**; rises nr. Lubumbashi in Shaba prov., flows N. circa 800 km to Kikondja, where joined by R. Lufira to form R. Congo; name also applied to main stream of R. Congo as far downstream as Ponthierville.

Luanda, c. cap. of **Angola**; pt. on Atl. Oc.; exp. coffee, cotton, palm prod.; industl. ctr.; foodstuffs, tobacco, plastics; oil refining; hydro-electric power; p. (1995) 2,250,000.

Luang Prabang, c., N.W. **Laos**; at confluence of Mekong and Kahn Rs.; rubber, rice, teak; former royal cap.; p. (1985) 68,399.

Lubbock, c., N.W. Texas, **USA**; on Double Mountain fork of Brazos R.; ctr. of cotton-growing a.; p. (1990) 186,206.

Lübeck, c., pt. of Schleswig-Holstein, **Germany**; on Baltic Sea at mouth of Trave R.; cath.; shipbldg., machin., chemicals, textiles, iron, foodstuffs; birthplace of Thomas Mann; p. (1990) 215,200.

Lublin, c. and prov., E. **Poland**; motor vehicle and elec. engin.; agr. tr. and processing; cultural ctr., univ.; cas.; p. (1989) 348,881 (c.), 1,010,600 (prov.).

Lubumbashi (Elizabethville), t., Shaba, **Congo**; copper-mng. ctr.; p. (1991) 739,082.

Lucca, c., cap. of L. prov., Tuscany, **Italy**; cath., churches, palaces; noted for olive oil, pasta, wine; silk, cotton, jute, tobacco inds.; p. (1981) 91,246.

Lucena, t., Córdoba, **Spain**; olive oil, ceramics, gilt metals, wine; p. (1981) 29,717.

Lucenec, t., Czech **Rep.**; on Hungarian border; magnesite, textiles, sawmilling; p. (1984) 27,477.

Lucerne (Luzern), can., **Switzerland**; agr., pastoral, vineyards; oil refinery projected at Schötz/Ettiswil; cap. Lucerne; a. 1,492 km²; p. (1990) 319,500.

Lucerne (Luzern), c., cap. of L. can., **Switzerland**; at N.W. end of L. Lucerne; aluminium gds., sewing machin.; tourist ctr.; p. (1990), 60,035 (c.), 161,000 (met. a.).

Lucerne, L., Switzerland; also known as L. of the Four Cantons; length 37 km; a. 70 km².

Luchon or **Bagnères-de-Luchon**, resort in Fr. Pyrenees, Haute-Garonne dep., S. **France**; warm sulphur springs; winter sports ctr.

Luchow. See **Zuzhou.**

Luckenwalde, t., **Germany**; on R. Nuthe; textiles, footwear, machin., wood and metals, chemicals;

p. (1989) 26,552.

Lucknow, c., cap. of Uttar Pradesh st., N. India; on R. Gumti (trib. of Ganges); educational and cultural ctr. with textile inds.; rly. ctr.; scene of 1857 mutiny; p. (1991) 1,619,000.

Lüda, special mun., S. Liaoning prov., China; comprising Port Arthur Naval Base District and the pts. of Port Arthur and Talien (Dairen); chemicals, machin., shipbldg., textiles; p. (1984) 1·59 m.

Lüdenscheid, t., N. Rhine-Westphalia, Germany; metal mngs., domestic hardware; supplied structures for first Zeppelins; p. (1986) 73,400.

Lüderitz, t., Namibia; rly. pt. on desert cst.; diamonds, fishing; p. (1990) 6,000.

Ludhiana, t., Punjab st., N.W. India; S. of Sutlej R.; industl. ctr.; hosiery, knitwear; p. (1991) 1,043,000.

Ludlow, t., South Shrops., Eng.; agr. mkt.; agr. engin.; cas.; p. (1991) 9,040.

Ludwigsburg, t. Baden-Württemberg, Germany; N. of Stuttgart; cas.; textiles, foodstuffs, machin., toys; p. (1986) 76,900.

Ludwigshafen, t., Rhine-Palatinate, Germany; on R. Rhine, opposite Mannheim; chemicals, marine diesel engines, metallurgy, glass; R. pt. and rly. junc.; oil pipeline from Rotterdam under construction; p. (1990) 163,700.

Lugano, t., Ticino can., Switzerland; on L. Lugano; tourist resort; p. (1980) 27,815.

Lugano, L., lies at S. foot of Alps between Switzerland and Italy; attractive scenery, tourism; a. 49 km².

Lugansk (Voroshilovgrad), industl. t., Ukraine; S. of R. Donets in Donbas Region; impt. rly. engin. factories; textiles; p. (1990) 501,100.

Lugnaquilla, mtn., loftiest summit in Wicklow, R.o.I.; 927 m.

Lugo, c., cap. of L. prov., N.W. Spain; in Galicia, on Miño R.; in fertile agr. a.; cath.; p. (1987) 77,043, (est. 1991) 379,077 (prov.).

Lukuga, intermittent outlet of L. Tanganyika, Congo, linking with R. Congo.

Luleå, spt., N. Sweden, cap. of Norrbotten co.; on Lule R. at head of G. of Bothnia; iron ore; smelting plant, engin.; p. (1992) 68,924.

Luluabourg. See Kananga.

Lulworth Cove, sm. inlet, Dorset, Eng.; formed by sea breaching limestone cliffs and eroding clay behind; tourism.

Lund, t., S. Sweden; 16 km N.E. of Malmö; 11th cent. Romanesque cath.; univ.; publishing ctr.; p. (1992) 92,027.

Lundy I., Bristol Channel, N. Devon, Eng.; 19 km N.W. of Hartland Point; wildlife sanctuary; about 5 km long and 1 km wide.

Lune, R., Cumbria, Eng.; flows 72 km to Irish Sea; attractive valley.

Lüneburg, t., Lower Saxony, Germany; on Ilmenau R., S.E. of Hamburg; rly. junc., R. pt.; iron wks., chemicals; dates from 8th cent.; p. (1986) 59,500.

Lüneburg Heath, Lower Saxony, Germany; lies to S. of Lüneburg; glacial outwash plain of sands and gravels; heather, scrub; some agr. but infertile acid soils.

Lünen, t., N. Rhine-Westphalia, Germany; in Ruhr conurb.; coal, metallurgy, glass, wood; R. pt. and rly. ctr.; p. (1986) 84,400.

Lunéville, t., Meurthe-et-Moselle dep., N.E. France; in Lorraine, on R. Meurthe; 18th cent. château.

Lungi, t., Sierra Leone, W. Africa; nr. Freetown; only civil airport in st.

Luoyang (Loyang) c., Henan prov., China; industl.; ball bearing and mng. machin.; lge. car and tractor plant, oil refinery, textiles; p. (1992) 1,190,000.

Lupata Gorge, Moçambique, E. Africa; narrow pass occupied by R. Zambezi.

Lurgan, t., Craigavon, N. Ireland; textiles, tobacco mftg.; merging with Portadown to form new c. of Craigavon; p. (1991) 21,905.

Lusaka, c., cap. of Zambia; comm. and admin. ctr.; at junc. of routes to Tanzania and Malawi; motor assembly, footwear, metal prods., clothing; p. (1989) 921,000.

Lushun. See Lüda.

Lutherstadt-Wittenberg. See Wittenburg.

Luton, t., unit. auth. created in 1997, formerly part of Beds., Eng.; in Chiltern Hills nr. source of R. Lea; motor vehicles, engin., hat mkg., aircraft, instruments; expanded t.; univ.; airport (recently renamed London Luton Airport); p. (1995)

181,400 (former dist.), (1991) 171,671 (t.).

Lutong, main oil pt. of Sarawak, E. Malaysia; oil refining.

Lutsk, c., Ukraine; pt. on Styr R.; one of oldest ts. in Volhynia; coal mng., machin.; architectural monuments; p. (1990) 204,100.

Lutterworth, t., Leics., Eng.; church with relics of John Wyclif, religious reformer; p. (1991) 7,380.

Luxembourg, prov., S.E. Belgium; on Fr. border; wooded and hilly; a. 2,784 km²; cap. Arlon; p. (1993) 236,850.

Luxembourg, grand duchy, W. Europe; lies between Belgium, Germany, and France; divided into 12 admin. cans.; official language French though German frequently used; well wooded, most of a. over 300 m; economic prosperity based upon iron and steel inds. and lge. deposits of iron-ore; agr. and cattle raising impt.; sm. size of home market makes L. keen member of EU and cap. of L. contains many European organisations; tourist ind. based upon scenery and cas. ts.; a. 2,587 km²; p. (1995) 406,600.

Luxembourg, c., cap. of grand duchy of Luxembourg; historic t., perched above valleys of Alzette and Petrusse Rs.; cath.; seat of European Court of Justice; p. (1991) 75,833.

Luxor, t., Upper Egypt; on E. bank of Nile; site of Thebes; tomb of Tutankhamun; p. (1986) 138,000.

Luzon, I., lgst. and most N. of Philippines; mtn. ranges; fertile Cagayan valley; rice, sugar cane, cotton, coffee, hemp, tobacco; mineral deposits; cap. Manila; a. 104,688 km²; p. (1990) 28,289,866.

Lviv (Lvov), c., Ukraine; founded 13th cent.; univ., caths.; major industl. ctr.; petroleum refining, natural gas nearby; p. (1990) 797,800.

Lvov. See Lviv.

Lyalpur. See Faisalabad.

Lydd, Shepway, Kent, Eng.; anc. t. on Romney marsh, at edge of Dungeness shingle; explosive lyddite mnf.; airport; p. (1991) 3,173.

Lydda, c., Israel, S.E. of Tel Aviv; major airport.

Lydney, t., Gloucs., Eng.; in Forest of Dean; spt. on Severn estuary; timber imports; new lt. inds.; p. (1991) 7,413.

Lyme Regis, spt., West Dorset, Eng.; on bdy. between Devon and Dorset; holiday resort; p. (1991) 3,851.

Lymington, t., Hants., Eng.; on the Solent; ferry to I. of Wight; abbey; p. (1991) 13,508.

Lymm, t., Cheshire, Eng.; 8 km W. of Altrincham; mainly residtl.; p. (1991) 9,721.

Lynchburg, c., Va., USA; on James R. in foothills of Appalachians; tobacco ctr.; p. (1984) 67,300 (c.), 142,600 (met. a.).

Lyndhurst, v., Hants, Eng.; recognised as cap. of New Forest; tourisml; p. (1991) 2,381.

Lynemouth, nr. Blyth, Northumberland, Eng.; aluminium smelter; p. (1991) 2,024.

Lynn, industl. c., Mass., USA; on Mass. Bay; footwear, elec. appliances; Mary Baker Eddy lived here; p. (1980) 78,471.

Lynton, t., North Devon, Eng.; 27 km W. of Minehead on Bristol Channel; tourist ctr. for Exmoor; sm. harbour of Lynmouth 130 m below; devastating flood of R. Lyn 1952; p. (1981) 2,037.

Lyons, c., cap. of Rhône dep., France; at confluence of Rs. Saône and Rhône; silk, rayon, chemicals, engin., heavy lorries; oil refinery nearby; univ.; world ctr. for cancer research; p. (1990) 422,444 (c.), 1,262,223 (met.a.).

Lytham St. Annes, t., N. Lancs., Eng.; on N. cst. of Ribble estuary, 6 km S. of Blackpool holiday ctr.; p. (1991) 40,866.

Lyttelton, spt., S.I., N.Z., on N. cst. of Banks peninsula; imp. pt.

M

Ma'an, t., S. Jordan, terminus of rly. through Amman to Beirut; Hijaz rail line to Medina; p. (1989) 108,300.

Maas, R., Dutch name for the R. Meuse after it has entered the Neth.

Maastricht, t., cap. of Limburg prov., Neth.; on R. Maas; pottery, glass, textiles, brewing; p. (1994) 118,102 (c.) 164,153 (met. a.).

Mablethorpe, t., East Lindsey, Lincs., Eng.; holiday resort; p. (1991) 9,719.

Macao, Portuguese col., S.E. China; increased indep. since 1975; to be returned to China in 1999; gambling, tourism, recreation for Hong Kong; new deep water port; rapid recent industl. growth (toys, textiles and transistors) with influx of capital; oldest European col. in Far East (1557); a. 17 km²; p. (1994) 395,304.

Macapá, c., cap. of Amapá st., **Brazil**; at mouth of R. Amazon; rubber, cattle tr.; p. (1985) 169,600.

Macclesfield, t., l. gov. dist., Cheshire, **Eng.**; at foot of Pennines, 16 km S. of Stockport; on R. Bollin; mkt., textiles, clothing, paper prods., engin.; expanded t.; p. (1995) 151,800 (dist.), (1991) 50,270 (t.).

Macdonald Is., terr. of **Australia**, Antarctica.

Macdonnell Range, mtns., N.T., **Australia**; highest part of desert tableland, centrally situated within the continent; some gold and mica mines, but development hampered by aridity and isolation; highest alt. 1,500 m.

Macduff, spt., burgh, Aberdeenshire, **Scot.**; 3 km E. of Banff; fishing; p. (1991) 3,894.

Macedonia, region of Balkan peninsula, covering parts of Greece, Yugoslavia, and Bulgaria.

Macedonia, dist., **Greece**; mtnous.; cereals, tobacco; chromium; cap. and pt. Salonika; a. 33,945 km²; p. (1991) 2,236,019.

Macedonia, rep., formerly Yugoslavia; agr., chromium; cap. Skopje; a. 27,436 km²; p. (1994) 1,936,877. Huge refugee influx, 1999.

Maceio, spt. cap. of Alagôas st., **Brazil**; cotton, sugar, tobacco, soap, sawmills, distilleries; p. (1991) 628,209.

Macerata, t., cap. of M. prov., **Italy**; cath., univ.; terracotta, glass, chemicals; p. (1981) 43,782.

Macgillicuddy's Reeks, mtns., Kerry, **R.o.I.**; highest peak, Carantuohil, 1,041 m.

Machala, t., Tibet, **China**; hgst. coalmine in world.

Machilipatnam (Bandar, Masulipatnam), spt., Andhra Pradesh, **India**; on Coromandel cst.; cotton mftg., rice; p. (1991) 159,007.

Machynlleth, t., Powys, **Wales**; on R. Dovey; clothing; tourism; p. (1991) 2,033.

Macintyre, R., N.S.W., **Australia**; forms border between Queensland and N.S.W.; trib. of R. Darling; 645 km. long.

Mackay, spt., Queensland, **Australia**; sugar; artificial deep-water pt. for sugar exp.; p. (1991) 53,225 (met.a.)

Mackenzie, R., N.W. Terr., **Canada**; lgst. in N. America; rises in Rocky mtns. as Athabaska, flows into Athabaska L., leaves as Slave R., thence into Gr. Slave L., below which it is known as Mackenzie R., across arctic plains to Beaufort Sea; 4,000 km. long.

Mackenzie Mtns., N.W. Terr., **Canada**; range of Rockies, still much unexplored; game preserve; max. alt. 2,760 m.

Mâcon, t., cap. of Saône-et-Loire dep., **France**; on R. Saône; Burgundy wines; p. (1990) 38,508.

Macon, c., Ga., **USA**; on Ocmulgee R.; industl. and shipping ctr. for agr. a., cotton, livestock; cotton mftg.; p. (1990) 106,612 (c.), 281,000 (met. a. with Warner Robins).

Macquarie, I., Australian I., **S. Pac.**; 1,440 km S.E. of Tasmania; rich in wildlife, Tasmanian st. reserve (1972).

Macquarie, R., N.S.W., **Australia**; trib. of R. Darling; 960 km long.

Macroom, t., Cork, **R.o.I.**; on R. Sullane; agr., fishing; p. (1986) 2,449.

Madagascar (formerly **Malagasy Rep.**), I. off Moçambique; former Fr. col.; distinctive evolution of flora and fauna; p. engaged in agr.; rice staple food, coffee and cloves main exp.; inds. based on processing; offshore petroleum deposits; new refinery at ch. pt. of Toamasina; cap. Antananarivo; a. 587,041 km²; p. (1994) 13,469,000.

Madang, t., **Papua New Guinea**; entrepôt pt. on N. cst.; international airpt.; p. (1990) 27,057.

Madeira, R., **Brazil**; trib. of Amazon; with Mamoré R., c. 3,200 km long.

Madeira Is., volcanic archipelago, Atl. Oc., part of met. **Portugal**; partial autonomy by regional gov. (1977); wine, sugar, fruits; tourism; cap. Funchal on Madeira I., lgst. of gr.; a. 790 km²; p. (1986) 269,500.

Madhya Pradesh, st., **India**; absorbed sts. Bhopal, Vindhya Pradesh, Madhya Bharat, 1956; rice, jute, pulses, oilseeds, cotton; forests; manganese, coal, marble, limestone; cotton textile mftg.;

cap. Bhopai; a. 443,452 km²; p. (1991) 66,181,170.

Madinat ash Sha'b (Al Ittihad), t. **Yemen**; cap. of Democratic Rep. of Yemen; N.W. of Aden.

Madison, c., cap. of Wis., **USA**; educational and admin. ctr.; univ.; mnfs. agr. tools, footwear; p. (1990) 191,262 (c.), 367,085 (met. a.).

Madiun, t., Java, **Indonesia**; agr. and comm. ctr.; engin.; p. (1980) 150,502.

Madras, c., cap. of Tamil Nadu st., **India**; spt. on Bay of Bengal, on Coromandel cst.; cath., univ.; comm. and mftg. ctr.; textile mills, tanneries, potteries, chemical plants; oil refinery projected; p. (1991) 3,841,000. Now renamed Chennai.

Madras. See Tamil Nadu.

Madre de Dios, R., **Bolivia**; trib. of R. Madeira; rises in Peru; 960 km long.

Madrid, c., cap. of **Spain**; and of M. prov. on Manzanares R.; stands at 665 m (highest cap. in Europe) in vast open plains; although remote with relatively few inds. is ctr. of Spanish admin. and communications; univ., cath., Prado gallery; printing, publishing; p. (1991) 2,984,576 (c.), 4,935,642 (prov.).

Madura, I., **Indonesia**; off N.E. Java; dry climate, limestone soils; arable and pastoral agr.; salt; a. 4,584 km²; p. c. 2,000,000.

Madurai, t., Tamil Nadu, **India**; univ., impt. textile ctr.; p. (1991) 941,000.

Maebashi, c., central Honshu, **Japan**; N.W. Kanto plain; silk textile ctr.; p. (1990) 286,261.

Maelstrom, tidewater whirlpool, in Lofoten Is., **Norway**.

Maentwrog, v., Gwynedd, N. **Wales**; in Vale of Ffestiniog, 3 km E. of Ffestiniog; hydroelectric power sta. run by Nuclear Electric.

Maesteg, t., Bridgend, **Wales**; dormitory t. for steel wks. at Pt. Talbot; cosmetics; p. (1991) 20,576.

Mafeking (Mafikeng) t., N.E. Cape Prov., **S. Africa**; famous siege at outbreak of Boer War 1899–1900; p. (1980) 6,500.

Magadan, spt., **Russia**; on N. side of Sea of Okhotsk; marine engin.; fishing; p. (1989) 152,000.

Magadi, L., Kenya; in Gr. Rift valley; carbonate of soda extracted.

Magallaces, reg. **Chile**; cap. Punta Arenas; a. 132,034 km²; p. (1992) 143,058.

Magdalena, R., **Colombia**; forms basis of inland navigation system, opening up interior; 1,600 km long.

Magdeburg, cap., Saxony - Anhalt *Land*, **Germany**; on R. Elbe; cath.; beet-sugar ctr., sugar-refineries; chemicals, steel, mng. machin., heavy engin.; route ctr. and lge. inland pt.; p. (1990) 277,200.

Magelang, t., Java, **Indonesia**; tr. ctr.; tannery; p. (1980) 123,484.

Magellan, strait, between Tierra del Fuego and Chile, separates Atl. and Pac. Ocs.

Maggiore, L., N. **Italy**-**Switzerland**; a. 212 km²; contains Borromean Is.; tourist resort.

Magherafelt, l. gov. dist., centred on t. of M., **N. Ireland**; agr. a. bordering L. Neagh; (1991) 36,293 (dist.), 6,682 (t.).

Maghreb, collective name given to Arabic-speaking countries bordering Mediterranean in N. Africa, inc. Algeria, Morocco and Tunisia.

Magnet Mtn., S. Urals, **Russia**; very rich deposit of magnetite iron ore; smelted at Magnitogorsk, and in Kuzbas region.

Magnitogorsk, c., **Russia**; in S. Urals, on R. Ural; sited on magnetite deposits; metallurgical ctr.; oil pipeline from Shkapovo in Bashkira; p. (1989) 440,000.

Mahajanga (Majunga), t., **Madagascar**; second t. and pt.; meat conserves, sacks, cement; p. (1990) 121,967.

Mahalapye, c., C. **Botswana**; rly; p. (1989) 104,450.

Mahalla El Kubra. See El Mahalla el Kubra.

Mahanadi, R., **India**; flows from Orissa to Bay of Bengal; forms extensive delta; sugar and rice growing; 832 km long.

Maharashtra, st., W. **India**; on Arabian Sea; ch. ts. Bombay (cap.), Poona, Nagpur; fertile lava soils; impt. cotton-growing dist. of Deccan; a. 307,477 km²; p. (1991) 78,937,187.

Mahé, former Fr. prov., S. **India**; united with India 1954; cap. Mahé part of Union Territory of Pondicherry; p. (1991) 33,425.

Mahon, spt., cap. of Minorca, Balearic Is., **Spain**; p. (1981) 21,624.

Maidenhead, t., Windsor and Maidenhead,

Berks., **Eng.;** on R. Thames, 14 km above Windsor; residtl.; p. (1991) 59,605; *See* **Windsor.**

Maidens, The, gr. of dangerous rocks off Larne cst., **N. Ireland.**

Maidstone, co. t., l. gov. dist., Kent, **Eng.;** on R. Medway; regional ctr.; brewing, paper, agr. tools, confectionery, timber inds.; p. (1995) 139,300 (dist.), (1991) 90,878 (t.).

Maiduguri, t., **Nigeria;** cap. Bornu st.; on rly. from Bornu; mkt.; p. (1992) 289,100.

Maikop, c. cap. of Adygei aut. oblast, Krasnodar terr., **Russia;** oilfields nearby; oil-refineries, woodwkg., food-processing; p. (1989) 149,000.

Main, R., **Germany;** joins Rhine opposite Mainz; linked with Danube via Ludwig canal; and newer Rhine-Main-Danube canal creating waterway from N. Sea to Black Sea of 3,500 km; 448 km long.

Main Range, central mtns. of **W. Malaysia;** rise to over 2,100 m.

Maine, st., New England, **USA;** Pine tree St.; admitted to Union 1820; st. flower White Pine Tassel, st. bird Chickadee; mtnous., with much forest; potatoes, paper, pulp, metals, woollens, shoes, processed foods; cap. Augusta; ch. spt. Portland; a. 86,027 km²; p. (1990) 1,227,928.

Maine-et-Loire, dep., **France;** agr. vineyards; cap. Angers; a. 7,280 km²; p. (1990) 705,900.

Mainland, I., lgst. of Shetland Is., **Scot.;** p. (1991) 17,596.

Mainland, I., Orkney Is. *See* **Pomona.**

Mainz, c., cap of Rhineland-Palatinate, **Germany;** at confluence of Rs. Rhine and Main; R. pt.; cath., univ., cas.; cement, engin., optical glass, food-processing; p. (1990) 180,800.

Maisons-Alfort, t., **France;** S.E. sub. of Paris; p. (1990) 54,065.

Maitland, t., N.S.W., **Australia;** on R. Hunter, nr. Newcastle; ctr. for fertile Hunter Valley; coal mng. decreasing; p. (1981) 38,865.

Majes, R., S. **Peru;** valley a. site of projected irrigation scheme; 240 km. long.

Majorca (Mallorca), lgst of Balearic Is., **Spain;** major tourist ctr.; ch. t. and pt. Palma; a. 3,639 km²; p. (1981) 561,215.

Majunga. *See* **Mahajanga.**

Makalu, mtn., Nepal and Tibet, **China;** fifth hgst. mtn. in world; part of Himalayas; alt. 8,486 m.

Makasar. *See* **Ujung Pandang.**

Makassar, strait, **Indonesia;** separates Kalimantan from Sulawesi; 384 km wide.

Makeyevka, c., **Ukraine;** in Donets basin; metallurgical and coal-mng. ctr.; p. (1990) 426,700.

Makhachkala, c., cap. of Dagestan aut. rep., **Russia;** pt. on Caspian Sea; comm. and industl. ctr.; oil refineries linked by pipeline to Grozny fields; p. (1989) 317,000.

Makó, t., **Hungary;** on Maros R., nr. Romanian bdy.; comm. and agr. ctr.; p. (1997) 26,000.

Makran, dist., **Pakistan** and **Iran;** coastal dist.; lowland route between India and Middle E.

Makurdi, t. **Nigeria,** W. Africa; on R. Benue; mkt. for palm prod., groundnuts; rly. bridge across R. Benue; p. (1992) 111,410.

Makwar, v., **Sudan,** N.E. Africa; on Blue Nile; site of Sennar Dam.

Malabar Coast, India; name applied to W. cst. of India from Goa to southern tip of peninsula at C. Comorin; sand dunes backed by lagoons; coastlands intensively cultivated, rice, spices, rubber, coconuts; ch. pt. Cochin.

Malabo (Santa Isabel), cap of **Equatorial Guinea;** on Marcias Nguema I.; ch. pt. for I., exp. cacao; comm. and financial ctr.; p. (1986) 10,000.

Malacca, st., S.W. **W. Malaysia;** originally part of Brit. Straits Settlements (*q.v.*); cap. M.; a. 1,658 km²; p. (1980) 464,754.

Malacca, strait, separates Sumatra, **Indonesia,** from **W. Malaysia;** 38 km wide at narrowest point; international routeway but attempts by Malaysia and Indonesia to claim it as territorial water.

Maladetta, with **Pic d'Anéto,** hgst. point in Pyrenees, **Spain;** alt. 3,408 m.

Malaga, c. cap. of Malaga prov., **Spain;** in Andalusia on Bay of M.; impt. spt.; olive oil, wine, fruit; oil pipeline from Puertollano; winter resort; cath.; citadel; birthplace of Picasso; p. (1991) 524,748 (c.), 1,177,259 (prov.).

Malagasy Rep. *See* **Madagascar.**

Malang, t., Java, **Indonesia;** ctr. of fertile agr. basin; p. (1983) 560,000.

Mälar, L., S.E. Sweden; connected with Baltic by Södertelge canal; 1,260 Is.; length 128 km; a. 1,235 km².

Malatya, c., cap. of M. prov., central **Turkey;** at foot of Taurus mtns.; ctr. of rich agr. a.; fruit, opium; p. (1990) 304,760 (c.), 702,055 (prov.).

Malawi, land locked rep., Central Africa; L. Malawi to S. and E.; tropical climate modified by alt.; few natural resources; economy based on agr.; one of most fertile soils in Africa but only 50 per cent cultivated; exp. tobacco and tea; new cap at Lilongwe (old cap. Zomba); a. 117,614 km²; p. (1994) 9,700,000.

Malawi, L., central **Africa;** southward extension of the Gr. Rift valley; c. 450 m a.s.l.; 560 km by 64 km; drains by R. Shire into R. Zambezi; petroleum under L. bed.

Malaya. *See* **Malaysia, West.**

Malay Archipelago, lge. gr. of Is. extending 7,680 km from Nicobar Is. in Bay of Bengal to Solomon Is. in Pac.; inc. Sumatra, Java, Kalimantan, Sulawesi, Philippines, New Guinea, Bismarck archipelago.

Malaysia, East, part of **Fed. of Malaysia;** inc. Sarawak and Sabah (formerly Brit. N. Borneo); less developed than W. Malaysia; p. concentrated on cst; hill tribes engaged in hunting in interior; diversification of Malaysian agr. has introduced cocoa as a major crop; oil major exp., exploration off cst.; separated from W. Malaysia by S. China Sea; a. 200,971 km²; p. (1980) 2,318,628.

Malaysia, Federation of, indep. federation (1963), S.E.Asia; member of Brit. Commonwealth; inc. W. Malaysia (Malaya) and E. Malaysia (Borneo sts. of Sarawak and Sabah); cap. Kuala Lumpur; a. 329,293 km²; p. (1994) 19,500,000.

Malaysia, West (Malaya), part of **Federation of Malaysia;** consists of wide peninsula S. of Thailand; most developed in W.; world's leading producer of natural rubber; worlds leading exporter of tin; but decline in world prices of both these prod. has encouraged economic diversification; timber exports also declining due to efforts to conserve rainforest; palm oil, petrol, electrical and electronic machin. now impt. export; new gas discoveries, attempts to convert palm oil into diesel fuel; free port at Pasir Gudang to divert exports from Singapore; 35 per cent of p. Chinese; a. 131,588 km²; p. (1985) 15,557,000.

Malbork (Marienburg), t., Elblag prov., **Poland;** R. pt. on Nogat R.; p. (1989) 39,016.

Malden, t., Mass., **USA;** mftg. sub. of Boston; rubber gds., hosiery, furniture; p. (1980) 53,386.

Maldive Is., indep. rep. (1968), former Brit. prot., Indian Oc.; chain of coral atolls c. 640 km S.W. of Sri Lanka; 1,067 Is., 193 inhabited; economy based on fishing (bonito and tuna); dried fish main exp.; modernisation of fishing with Japanese aid; coconuts, copra, coconut oil, coir, cowrie shells; cap. Male; former Brit. air base on Gan. I. (until 1976); a. 298 km²; p. (1996) 253,300.

Maldon, t., l. gov. dist., Essex, **Eng.;** sm. pt. at head of Blackwater estuary; agr. machin., steel window-frames, flour-milling; p. (1995) 54,300 (dist.), (1991) 15,841 (t.).

Malegaon, t., Maharashtra, **India;** in Satmala Hills N.E. of Bombay; p. (1991) 342,000.

Malham Cove, North Yorks., **Eng.;** in Craven dist. of N. Pennines, 16 km N.W. of Skipton; semicircular amphitheatre limestone cliffs from base of which emerges R. Aire.

Mali, Rep. of, W. Africa; landlocked st.; former Fr. col. of Soudan; dry semi-desert climate in S.; extends into Sahara desert in N.; badly affected by Sahelian drought after 1971; few natural resources; nomadic pastoralist p. in N.; only 20 per cent of a. cultivable; livestock basis of inds. (hides, wool, etc.) and exps.; many minerals but not exploited; cap. Bamako; a. 1,204,350 km²; p. (1995) 10,500,000.

Malinda, t., **Kenya;** growing tourist resort on Indian Ocean cst.

Malin Head, Donegal, **R.o.I.;** most N. point.

Malines (Mechelen), t., **Belgium;** on R. Dyle; cath.; rly. ctr., textiles, furniture; once famous for lace; p. (1993) 75,740.

Malling, t., Kent, **Eng.;** 5 km W. of Maidstone; fruit, chemicals. *See* **Tonbridge.**

Mallow, mkt. t., Cork, **R.o.I.;** on R. Blackwater; agr. fishing, flour mills, tanneries, condensed milk, dehydrated foods; p. (1986) 6,488.

Malmesbury, t., North Wilts., **Eng.;** anc. hilltop t. in Cotswolds; mkt.; abbey; elec. engin.; birthplace of Thomas Hobbes; p. (1991) 4,439.

Malmö, c., spt., S. **Sweden;** on the Sound opposite

Copenhagen; third lgst. c. in cty.; naval and comm. pt.; former ctr. for shipbldg., textiles, machin.; founded in 12th cent.; car and aerospace engin. plant to relieve unemployment; p. (1992) 236,684.

Malta, indep. st. within Brit. Commonwealth (1964), rep. (1974); I. in Mediterranean, 93 km S. of Sicily; strategic location; former British naval and military base; agr. ch. occupation with ship-repairing at dry- docks of Valletta; sm.-scale inds. growing; tourism exploits Mediterranean climate; major airport at Luqa; awarded George Cross for bravery in second world war; applying for EU membership; cap. Valletta; a. 316 km²; p. (1995) 370,402 (inc. Gozo and Comino).

Maltby, t., Rotherham, South Yorks., Eng.; mine still open 1994; p. (1991) 18,158.

Malton, mkt. t., North Yorks., Eng.; on R. Derwent, in S.W. of Vale of Pickering; brewing; p. (1991) 4,294.

Malvern, t., Worcs., Eng.; at E. foot of Malvern hills; spa; annual dramatic festival; Elgar lived here; p. (1991) 31,537.

Malvern Hills, narrow ridge forming bdy. between Worcs. and Hereford, Eng.; rises very abruptly from Severn valley to over 300 m between Malvern and Bromsberrow; moorland, wood-land on lower slopes; forms l. gov. dist.; p. (1995) 91,700.

Mammoth Cave, Ky., USA; to S. of Green R. in hilly forested parkland; spectacular limestone formations (stalactites, stalagmites), lakes and rivers (e.g. Echo R., 110 m below surface) in avenues aggregating 240 km long; included in Nat. Park.

Mamoré, R., N. Bolivia and Brazil; rises in Andes; 1,920 km long.

Mam Soul, mtn., Highland, Scot.; alt. 1,178 m.

Manacle Rocks, dangerous reef off cst. of Cornwall, Eng.; 12 km S. of Falmouth.

Manacor, t., Majorca, Spain; artificial pearls, wine, stalactite caves of Drach and Hams; p. (1981) 24,153.

Managua, c., cap. of Nicaragua; on S. shore of L. Managua; industl. and comm. ctr.; oil refining, agr. processing, textiles, steel; univ.; 48 km from pt. Puerto Somoza; violent earthquake Dec. 1972; p. (1985) 682,111.

Managua, L., Nicaragua; second lgst. L. in Central America.

Manāmah, Al, cap. and ch. pt. Bahrain, Persian G.; free pt., comm. ctr.; declining pearl-fishing ind.; linked by causeway to internat. airpt.; p. (1988) 151,500.

Manáus (Manaos), c., cap. of Amazonas st., N.W. Brazil; on Rio Negro nr. confluence with Amazon; impt. R. pt., airport.; oil refinery; former rubber ctr.; in free zone (10,360 km²) recently set up to encourage development in Amazonas; new inds. include steel wks., oil refinery; boom now far ex-ceeds 19th century rubber boom; tourism; inter-nat. airpt.; p. (1991) 1,010,558.

Manche, dep., N.W. France; on English Channel; agr. and dairying; cap. Saint Lô; ch. pt. Cherbourg; a. 6,410 km²; p. (1990) 479,600.

Manchester, c., Gtr. Manchester, Eng.; on R. Irwell; terminus of Manchester Ship Canal; ctr. of cotton and man- made fibre textile inds.; heavy, lt., and elec. engin., machine tools, petro-chemicals, dyestuffs, pharmaceutical prods.; univ.; comm., cultural and recreational cap. of N.W. Eng.; p. (1995) 432,600 (met. dist.), (1991) 402,889 (c.).

Manchester, t., Conn., USA; textiles (silk); p. (1980) 49,761.

Manchester, c., N.H., USA; at Amoskeag falls, on the Merrimac R.; textiles, footwear, machin.; p. (1984) 94,900 (c.), 136,400 (met. a.).

Manchester Ship Canal, ship canal, Cheshire/Merseyside/Gtr. Manchester, Eng.; joins Man-chester to Mersey estuary at Eastham; 57 km long.

Manchuria. *See* North-East China.

Mandalay, c., Myanmar; on R. Irrawaddy, 640 km N. of Rangoon; former cap.; lost importance with rise of Irrawaddy delta; many temples, palaces; p. (1983) 532,895.

Manfredonia, mkt. t., Foggia, Italy; fish. pt.; cath.; p. (1981) 52,674.

Mangalore, spt., Karnataka, India; exp. coffee, coconuts, rice, spices, fertiliser; p. (1991) 273,000.

Mangere, N.I., N.Z.; 21 km S. of Auckland; in-ternational airport (opened 1965).

Mangla Dam, Pakistan; world's lgst. earth-filled dam, on Jhelum R., part of Indus Basin irriga-tion scheme.

Manhattan, I., N.Y., U.S.A.; at mouth of Hudson R.; a. 57 km²; forms major part of bor. of Manhattan of N.Y. City; p. (1990) 1,487,536 (bor.).

Manila, c., S.W. Luzon, Philippines; cap. and ch. pt. of Is.; entrepôt tr.; modern skyscrapers; univ., cath.: airpt.; p. (1995) 9,450,000.

Manipur, new st. (1972), E. India; borders Myanmar (Burma); former princely st.; cap. Imphal; a. 22,274 km²; p. (1991) 1,837,149.

Manisa, c., cap. of M. prov., W. Turkey; agr. ctr.; mineral deposits nearby; p. (1990) 158,426, 1,154,418 (prov.).

Manitoba, prov., Canada; wheat, rich mineral deposits, fisheries; diverse inds.; cap. Winni-peg; a. 650,090 km²; p. (1991) 1,091,942.

Manitowac, c., Wis., USA; on L. Mich.; shipbldg., aluminium wks., flour mills; p. (1980) 32,547.

Manizales, c., cap. of Caldas, Colombia; at 2,155 m in the Central Cordillera; in rich coffee a.; route ctr.; p. (1992) 327,115.

Mannar, G., with Palk Strait separates India from Sri Lanka.

Mannheim, c., Baden-Württemberg, Germany; major R. pt. at confluence of Rs. Neckar and Rhine, opposite Ludwigshafen; heavy and lt. inds., notably precision instruments, machin., vehicles; p. (1990) 312,000.

Manono, t. Congo; ctr. for tin-mng.; now in ruins.

Manresa, industl. t., N.E. Spain; in Catalonia; textiles; associated with Ignatius of Loyola; place of pilgrimage; p. (1981) 64,745.

Mansfield, t., l. gov. dist., Notts., Eng.; on E. flank of Pennines, 19 km N. of Nottingham; 2 remaining coal mines; sand-quarrying, textiles, footwear, metal boxes, machin.; p. (1995) 101,600 (dist.), (1991) 71,853.

Mansfield, c., Ohio, USA; machin. farm tools, paper, rubber gds.; p. (1990) 50,627.

Mansfield Woodhouse, t., Notts., Eng.; 3 km N. of Mansfield; stone quarries; Roman remains; p. (1991)18,204.

Mansûra, c., Lower Egypt; pt. on Nile; cotton mftg.; univ. p. (1986) 316,870.

Mantua, c., cap. of M. prov., N. Italy; on R. Mincio; comm. and agr. ctr.; old fortfd. c.; p. (1981) 60,866.

Manukau, c., N.I., N.Z.; new c. (1965) formed from amalgamation of suburban communities around Auckland; p. (1991) 226,147, now lgst. c. of N.Z.

Manukau Harbour, N.I., N.Z.; lge. shallow inlet on W. cst. of Auckland peninsula; provides additional harbour facilities for spt. of Auck-land; recreational sailing; fishing.

Manych, R., Russia; trib. of R. Don; 480 km long; canal being built through R. to Caspian to provide through connection with Black Sea.

Manzala (Menzala), lagoon, Mediterranean cst., Egypt; extends E. from Damietta mouth of Nile to Pt. Said; fringed by salt marsh; a. 2,072 km².

Manzanillo, spt., S.E. Cuba; exp. sugar, rice, tobacco; p. (1990) 107,650.

Manzanillo, c. Colima, W. Mexico; ch. pt. on Pac. Oc.; exp. coffee, timber, minerals; p. (1990) 92,168.

Maputo (Lourenço Marques), spt., cap. of Moçambique; at head of Delagoa Bay; rly. terminus; oil refining, deposits of bentonite worked nearby; ore terminal, much transit tr.; second lgst. pt. in Africa; p. (1991) 1,098,000.

Maracaibo, spt. cap. of Zulia st., Venezuela; deepwater harbour; on W. of narrow entrance on L. Maracaibo; univ.; oilfields and re-fineries; exp. coffee, cocoa; p. (1990) 1,207,513.

Maracaibo, G., and L., Zulia st., Venezuela; brack-ish lake, 192 km long, 96 km wide; oilwells on fringes and drilled into lake floor.

Maracay, c., N. Venezuela; on L. Valencia, 112 km from Carácas; p. (1990) 354,428.

Maragheh, t., Iran; on N. end of L. Urmia; comm. and fruit ctr.

Marajó, I., at mouth of the Rs. Amazon and Pará, Brazil; a. 38,850 km².

Maralinga, S. Australia; 320 km N.E. Eucla; joint U.K.-Australian atomic testing ground, first weapon exploded here 27 Sept. 1956.

Maranhão, st., N.E. Brazil; rice, cotton, sugar, tobacco, coffee, cattle, gold, copper; oil in the Barrierinhas a.; cap. São Luiz; a. 334,812 km²; p. (1991) 4,922,339.

Marañon, R. *See* Amazon, R.

Maras, t. and prov., S. central **Turkey;** tr. in Kurdish carpets; p. (1985) 210,371, (1990) 892,952 (prov.).

Marathon, v. and plain, **Greece;** 32 km N.E. of Athens; here the Athenians defeated the Persians 490 B.C.

Marazion, mkt. t., Cornwall, **Eng.;** on Mount's Bay, nr. St. Michael's Mount; pilchard fisheries; p. (1991) 1,381.

Marble Bar, t., W. **Australia;** 136 km inland by rail from Pt. Hedland; ctr. of Pilbara goldfields.

Marburg on Lahn, t., Hesse, **Germany;** univ., cas.; noted for optical instruments; p. (1986) 77,100.

March, mkt. t., Fenland, Cambs., **Eng.;** on R. Nene in Fens; rly. junc.; farm tools; p. (1981) 14,475.

Marches, The, region, central **Italy;** extending from eastern slopes of Apennines to Adriatic cst.; embracing provs. of Macerata, Ascoli-Piceno, Ancona, and Pesaro e Urbino; a. 9,697 km²; p. (1992) 1,433,994.

Marchfeld, plain, Lower **Austria;** between Rs. Danube and Morava which here forms bdy. between Austria and Czech Republic.

Marcias Nguema. *See* Biako.

Mar del Plata, c., **Argentina;** on C. Corrientes; Atl. cst. resort; p. (1980) 407,024.

Maree, Loch, Highland, **Scot.;** 21 km long, c. 3 km wide; rocky shores; studded with wooded islets.

Maremma, coastal region along Tyrrhenean Sea, S. Tuscany, **Italy;** once malarial, now drained with wide fertile areas.

Mareotis or **Birket-et-Mariut,** L., Lower **Egypt;** separated from Mediterranean by ridge of sand on which stands Alexandria; 80 km long, 32 km wide.

Margam, part of Pt. Talbot, Neath Pt. Talbot, S. **Wales;** on cst. of Swansea Bay; lge. new steel-wks., lgst. steel-rolling mill in Europe.

Margarita, I., in Caribbean off N. **Venezuela;** tourism; formerly pearl-fishing ctr.; cap. Asunción; a. 1,166 km².

Margate, t., Kent, **Eng.;** W. of N. Foreland, in the Isle of Thanet; seaside resort; p. (1991) 56,734.

Margolan, t., E. **Uzbekistan;** in Ferghana Valley; noted for silk ind.; p. (1990) 124,900.

Mari, aut. rep., **Russia;** timber, paper inds.; p. (1986) 729,000.

Maribor, t., **Slovenia** (formerly Yugoslavia); on Drava R., nr. Austrian border; metallurgical inds.; ctr. of agr. a.; p. (1981) 185,699.

Marilia, t., São Paulo st., **Brazil;** coffee, cotton, oil peanuts; p. (1985) 136,500.

Mariinsk Canal. *See* Volga Baltic Waterway.

Marion, c., Ind., **USA;** mkt. ctr. within corn belt; varied inds.; p. (1980) 35,874.

Marion, t., Ohio, **USA;** agr. ctr., with varied agr. mnfs.; p. (1990) 34,075.

Maritime Provinces, group of provs. in **Canada**— Nova Scotia, New Brunswick, Prince Edward I.

Maritsa, R., **Bulgaria** and **Greece;** used for irrigation and hydroelectric power; 416 km long.

Mariupol, (Zhdanov), spt., S.E. **Ukraine;** on Sea of Azov; metallurgical ctr., chemicals; fishing and fish-processing; p. (1990) 519,900.

Market Drayton, t., North Shrops., **Eng.;** on R. Tern, 21 km S.W. of Newcastle-under-Lyme; agr. implements, nylon mftg.; p. (1991) 9,482.

Market Harborough, t., Harborough, Leics., **Eng.;** on R. Welland, 13 km N.W. of Kettering; elec. engin., foodstuffs, corsetry; p. (1991) 16,563.

Market Rasen, t., West Lindsey, Lincs., **Eng.;** agr. ctr.; racecourse; p. (1991) 2,948.

Markinch, burgh, Fife, **Scot.;** 13 km N. of Kirkcaldy; paper mftg., whisky blending and bottling factory closed 1983; p. (1991) 2,176.

Marl, t., N. Rhine–Westphalia, **Germany;** in Ruhr; coal mng.; chemicals; p. (1986) 87,800.

Marlborough, t., Wycombe, Wilts., **Eng.;** on R. Kennet in heart of Marlborough Downs; public school; p. (1991) 6,429.

Marlborough, dist., S.I., **N.Z.;** pastoral; a. 10,930 km²; cap. Blenheim; p. (1991) 36,765.

Marlborough Downs, hills, Wilts., **Eng.;** chalk; highest point, Milk Hill, 298 m.

Marlow, t., Bucks., **Eng.;** on R. Thames; mkt., tourist ctr.; home of Shelley; p. (1991) 17,771.

Marmara, Sea of, separates Europe from Asia; connected with Black Sea through the Bosporus, with Aegean Sea through Dardanelles; shores belong to Turkey.

Marne, dep., N.E. **France;** in Champagne; ctr. of champagne ind.; cap. Châlons-sur-Marne; a. 8,205 km²; p. (1990) 558,200.

Marne, R., central **France;** rises in Plateau de Langres, flows across Champagne Humide,

Champagne Pouilleuse, and Beauce, joins R. Seine just above Paris; with Marne–Rhine and Marne–Saône canals forms impt. inland waterway linking Seine with Rhine and Rhône valleys; c. 520 km. long.

Marple, t., Gtr. Manchester, **Eng.;** 5 km. E. of Stockport; engin., residtl.; p. (1991) 19,829.

Marquesas Is., volcanic gr. in central **Pac. Oc.,** part of Fr. Polynesia; lgst. Nukuhiva and Hivaoa; mtnous., fertile; exp. copra, vanilla, tobacco, cotton; a. 1,274 km²; p. (1983) 6,548.

Marrakesh, c., **Morocco;** tourist ctr.; leather gds., carpets; p. (1982) 439,728.

Marsa el-Brega, new pt., G. of Sirte, **Libya;** oil pipeline from Zelten; gas liquefaction plant opened 1970; airport.

Marsala, pt., Sicily, **Italy;** on site of anc. Carthaginian settlement; wine ctr.; p. (1981) 79,093.

Marseille, c., spt., cap. of Bouche-du-Rhône dep., S. **France;** on Provence cst.; passenger and gds. traffic; pt. inds., marine engin., oil refining; oil pipeline to Karlsruhe; industl. expansion at G. of Fos; cath., univ., palace; founded as Massilia by Phocaean Greeks of Asia Minor 600 B.C.; p. (1990) 807,726 (c.), 1,087,376 (met.a.).

Marshall Is., Rep. of, gr. of coral Is., central Pac. Oc.; internal self-government (1978), comprising 34 atolls; exp. copra, sugar, coffee; admin. ctr. Jaluit I.; joined UN 1991; nuclear bomb tests; a. 181 km²; survival threatened by long-term global warming; p. (1994) 54,000.

Marske-by-the-Sea, t., Langbaurgh, Cleveland, **Eng.;** seaside resort; p. (1991) 8,936.

Martha's Vineyard, I., S.E. Mass., **USA;** state forest; summer resort; ch. ts., Vineyard Haven, Oak Bluffs, Edgartown.

Martigny, t., Valais, **Switzerland;** linked by road tunnel to Aosta, Italy; p. 6,572.

Martin, t. **Slovakia,** S. E. of Zilina; rly.; p. (1990) 66,000.

Martina Franca, t., S. **Italy;** in Apulia; wine, olive oil; summer resort.

Martinique, I., Fr. overseas dep., Windward Is., **W.I.;** dominated by volcanic peak Mt. Pelée which erupted 1902 destroying t. of St. Pierre; hurricanes, earthquakes; economy based on sugar-cane and fruit prod.; much emigration to France; cap. Fort de France; a. 1,088 km²; p. (1990) 359,600

Martos, t., Jaen prov., Andalusia, **Spain;** castled hilltop t.; wines, sulphur springs; mftg.; p. (1981) 21,672.

Mary (Merv), c., **Turkmenistan;** in oasis in Kara-Kum desert; anc. c. founded 3rd cent. B.C.; textile ctr.; p. (1990) 93,800.

Maryborough, t., Queensland, **Australia;** pt. on Mary R.; exp. fruit, sugar, timber, coal; p. (1991) 23,286.

Maryborough. *See* Port Laoighise, Ireland.

Mary Kathleen, t., Queensland, **Australia;** new t., nr. uranium field in Cloncurry a.

Maryland, one of original 13 sts. of **USA;** Old Line St.; admitted to Union 1788; st. flower Black eyed Susan, st. bird Baltimore Oriel; on shores of Chesapeake Bay; humid continental climate; arable agr. and mkt. gardening; sea-fishing; cap. Annapolis; lgst. c. Baltimore; a. 27,394 km²; p. (1990) 4,781,468.

Maryport, t., Allerdale, Cumbria, **Eng.;** former pt.; modern lt. inds. in industl. estate to S. of t.; p. (1991) 9,797.

Masaya, t., W. **Nicaragua;** comm. ctr. in rich agr. a.; p. (1985) 75,000.

Masbate, I., prov. **Philippines;** gold mng.; a. 3,269 km²; p. (1990) 599,915.

Mascarene Is., collective name of **Mauritius, Rodriguez and Réunion, in Indian Oc.**

Maseru, t., cap. **Lesotho;** nr. border with S. Africa on Caledon R.; two new industl. estates to encourage light inds.; tourists from S. Africa; p. (1992) 367,000.

Masham, t., North Yorks., **Eng.;** on R. Ure; 14 km N.W. of Ripon; mkt.

Mashhad, c., N.E. **Iran;** cap. of Khorassan prov.; linked by oil pipeline to Esfahan and rly. to Turkmenistan; p. (1986) 1,466,018.

Mashonaland, dist., **Zimbabwe;** a. inhabited by the Mashona tribe; ch. t. Salisbury; p. (1992) 857,318 (C.) 1,033,336 (E.).

Masjid-i-Sulamain, t., **Iran;** impt. oilfield and refinery; p. (1982) 117,000.

Mask, L., Mayo and Galway, **R.o.I.**; 19 km long 3–6 km wide.

Mason City, t., Iowa, **USA**; on Sheel Rock R.; tr. ctr. of lge. agr. a.; p. (1990) 29,040.

Mason–Dixon Line. *See* Section L.

Massachusetts, st., New England, **USA**; Bay St.; admitted to Union 1788; st. flower Mayflower, st. bird Chickadee; on Atl. cst.; humid continental climate; hilly interior severed by N.–S. Connecticut valley; major fishing ind.; replacement of traditional textile inds. by modern science-based inds., especially around M. Institute of Technology; impt. arable gr. a.; cap. Boston; a. 21,386 km²; p. (1990) 6,016,425.

Massa di Carrara. *See* Carrara.

Massawa. *See* Mits'iwa.

Massif Central, upland a., **France**; variable geology and scenery inc. volcanic Auvergne and limestone Causses; much rural depopulation, pastoral agr.; industl. ts. inc. St. Etienne based on sm. coalfields in N.E.; others ts. inc. Limoges and Clermont-Ferrand.

Masterton, dist., N.I., **N.Z.**; meat-packing; dairy prods., woollen mills; p. (1991) 22,947.

Masulipatnam. *See* Machilipatnam.

Masvingo. *See* Fort Victoria.

Matabeleland, dist., **Zimbabwe**; a. inhabited by Matabele tribe; ch. t. Bulawayo; p. (1992) 640,957 (N.), 591,747 (S.).

Matadi, spt., **Congo**; on R. Congo; main pt.; exp. forest prod.; proposed Inga power project nearby; p. (1990) 172,926.

Matagalpa, t., **Nicaragua**; ctr. of agr. a., food processing; second lgst. t. of Nicaragua; p. (1985) 37,000.

Matamoros, irrigated region, **Mexico**; around t. of M. on Rio Grande delta; Mexico's leading producer of cotton.

Matamoros, t., **Mexico**; on Rio Grande; livestock tr. ctr.; p. (1990) 303,392.

Matanzas, spt., cap. of M. prov., **Cuba**; exp. sugar, cigars; rayon plant; p. (1990) 113,724, 599,500 (prov.).

Matarani, new spt., S. **Peru**; oil refinery.

Mataró, spt., **Spain**; nr. Barcelona; fisheries, textiles, chemicals, paper; p. (1991) 101,172.

Matera, t., cap. of M. prov., S. **Italy**; stands on limestone ridge cleft by canyon; agr. ctr.; 13th cent. cath. and cas.; p. (1981) 50,712.

Mathura (Muttra), t., Uttar Pradesh, **India**; sacred t. on R. Jumna; Hindu pilgrimage ctr.; textiles; p. (1991) 226,691.

Matlock, t., Derbys. Dales, **Eng.**; on R. Derwent; 24 km N. of Derby; admin. ctr.; tourist ctr., limestone quarrying, lt. inds.; p. (1991) 14,680.

Mato Grosso, st., **Brazil**; cap. Cuiabá; a. 1,232,081 km²; p. (1991) 2,020,581.

Mato Grosso, plateau, Mato Grosso st., **Brazil**; average alt. 900 m, acts as divide between Amazon and Paraná–Paraguay R. systems; reserves of gold, diamonds, manganese but largely undeveloped; lge. areas of tropical rain forest.

Mato Grosso de Sul, st. Brazil; cap. Campo Grande; separated from Mato Grosso state in 1979; a. 350,548 km²; p. (1991) 1,778,494.

Matosinhos, t., **Portugal**; fish. pt. at mouth of Leca R.; seaside resort; p. (1981) 43,488.

Matsue, c., S.W. Honshu, **Japan**; on L. Shinji; old cas.; p. (1990) 142,956.

Matsumoto, c., central Honshu, **Japan**; machin., food-processing, paper; once impt. for silk; remains of 16th cent. cas.; p. (1990) 200,723.

Matsuyama, c., **Japan**; pt. based inds. of oil refining and petrochemicals; univ., feudal cas.; p. (1990) 443,317.

Matterhorn (Fr. Mt. Cervin. It. **Monte Cervino**); alt. 4,477 m; Pennine Alps, **Switzerland**.

Mauchline, mkt. t., E. Ayrshire, **Scot.**; associated with Robert Burns; p. (1991) 3,931.

Maule, reg. Chile; cap. Talca; a. 30,518 km²; p. (1992) 834,053.

Mauna Kea, volcano, **Hawaii**; alt. 4,208 m; now dormant.

Mauna Loa, volcano, **Hawaii**; alt. 4,172 m; one of the world's lgst. volcanoes.

Mauritania, Islamic Rep. of, W. Africa; desert in N., S. more fertile; Senegal R. forms main artery of transport; mainly pastoral agr. (nomadic); severe effects of Sahelian drought since 1971 caused p. to become settled and move to ts.; urban p. 35% (1984); deposits of iron ore (Fort Gouraud) and copper (Bakel Akjoujt); fishing; new pt. develop-

ment at Nouadhibou; cap. Nouakchott; a. 1,085,210 km²; p. (1994) 2,400,000.

Mauritius, I., rep. within Brit. Commonwealth; Indian Oc.; volcanic I., surrounded by coral reefs, 800 km E. of Madagascar; subtropical climate, prone to cyclone; racially mixed; dependent on sugar for 95 per cent of exps.; attempts to decr. this dependence by Export Processing Zone (tax-free industrial zone), and incr. tea output; dense p. and unemployment cause social tension; former residents of Chagos Arch. resettled on 2 of Agalega Is.; tourism incr. impt.; cap. Port Louis; a. (inc. Rodriguez and Agalega) 2,038 km²; p. (1995) 1,140,000.

Mawson, national research base for Australia, Antarctica.

Mayagüez, c., spt., **Puerto Rico**; ctr. of fertile region producing sugar, coffee, tobacco; cultural and educational ctr.; p. (1990) 100,371.

Maybole, burgh, S. Ayrshire, **Scot.**; 13 km S. of Ayr; commuter centre for Ayr etc; cas.; p. (1991) 4,737.

Mayenne, dep., N.W. **France**; pastoral and agr.; cap. Laval; a. 5,146 km²; p. (1990) 278,000.

Mayfair, dist., City of Westminster, London, **Eng.**; fashionable residtl. and comm. a., to E. of Hyde Park; clubs and hotels.

Mayo, maritime co., Connacht, **R.o.I.**; broken cst., much barren mtn. land, many lge. lakes; agr., fishery; co. t. Castlebar, a. 5,506 km²; p. (1986) 115,184.

Mayotte, I., Comoro Archipelago, Moçambique Channel; rejected indep. to remain Fr. terr. (1975); sugar-cane, vanilla, cacao; a. 363 km²; p. (1994) 109,600.

Mazandaran, prov., N.E. **Iran**; Caspian Sea; subtropical climate; agr.; cap. Sari; p. (1982) 2,375,994.

Mazar-i-Sharif, c., **Afghanistan**; chemical fertilisers from natural gas; textiles, bricks, flour-milling; noted mosque; p. (1988) 130,600.

Mazatlán, c., N.W. **Mexico**; major spt. on Pac. cst.; comm. and industl. ctr.; exp. metals, hides, fish prods., woods; oil refinery; fishing, tourism; p. (1990) 314,249.

Mbabane, cap. of **Swaziland**; stands at c. 1,160 m; admin. ctr.; tin mng.; p. (1986) 38,290.

M'Bao, Senegal, W. Africa; oil refinery.

McMurdo Sound, ice-locked channel, Antarctica; base for many expeditions.

Mead, L., Arizona/Nevada., **USA**; on R. Colorado behind Hoover Dam; one of world's lgst. reservoirs; stores water for irrigation in Imperial Valley and Yuma dist.; tourist attraction; 184 km long, 2–13 km wide.

Meath, maritime co., Leinster, **R.o.I.**; pastoral; co. t., Trim; a. 2,347 km²; p. (1986) 103,881.

Meaux, t., Seine-et-Marne dep., **France**; on R. Marne; cath.; comm. and industl. ctr.; p. (1982) 55,797 (met. a.).

Mecca, holy c. of Islam, cap. of **Saudi Arabia**; birthplace of Mohammed; pilgrimage ctr.; Gr. Mosque enclosing the Kaaba; univ. (with Jidda); p. (1986) 618,000.

Mechelen. *See* Malines.

Mecklenburg-West Pomerania, Land, **Germany**; part of N. European plain, bordering Baltic Sea; cap. Schwerin; a. 22,947 km²; pop. (1992) 1,892,000.

Medan, c., cap. of N. Sumatra prov., **Indonesia**; ctr. for rubber, tobacco, tea; printing; univ.; pt. is Belawan; p. (1983) 1,966,000.

Médéa, dep., t. 80 km S. of El Djezair, **Algeria**; projected industl. complex; p. (1983) 84,292 (t.), (1987) 650,623 (dep.).

Medellin, c., cap. of Antiquia prov., **Colombia**; at 1,533 m in Central Cordillera; second c. of rep.; univ.; ctr. of drug trade; coffee; textiles, steel, sugar refining, glass; coal, gold, silver mined nearby; hydroelec. power; p. (1992) 1,581,364.

Medicine Hat, t., Alberta, **Canada**; on S. Saskatchewan R.; rly. junc.; coal, natural gas, flour mills; p. (1991) 43,265.

Medina, c., Hejaz, **Saudi Arabia**; 352 km N. of Mecca; tomb of Mohammed; place of Moslem pilgrimage; univ.; harbour at Yanbu' on Red Sea; p. (1986) 500,000.

Medinipur, t., W. Bengal, **India**; mkt. for agr. prods.; (1981) 86,118.

Mediterranean, gr. inland sea, almost tideless, dividing Europe from Africa; communicating with Atl. by Strait of Gibraltar and Black Sea by Dardanelles, Sea of Marmara and Bosporus, E. part touches Asia in the Levant; total length W. to E. 3,520 km; greatest width of sea proper c. 1,120 km; water a. 2,331,000 km²; greatest depth 4,482 m; ch. Is.; Corsica, Sardinia, Sicily, Crete, Cyprus, and the Balearic, Lipari, Maltese, Ionian grs., also Greek arch.

Médoc, region, Gironde, **France**; extending for about 77 km along Garonne R.; noted for wines.

Medway, R., Kent, **Eng.**; flows N.E. past Tonbridge, Maidstone and Rochester (where it becomes estuarial) to mouth of Thames; 112 km long; Medway Bridge completed 1962.

Meekatharra, t., W. **Australia**; Flying Doctor and School of the Air ctr.

Meerut, c., Uttar Pradesh, **India**; scene of outbreak of Indian mutiny 1857; p. (1991) 850,000

Meghalaya ("Home of the Clouds"), new st. (1970), **India**; former Khasi-Jaintia Hills and Garo Hills dists. of Assam; cap. Shillong; a. 22,549 km²; p. (1991) 1,774,778.

Meiling Pass, on bdy. between Guandong, Jianxi, S. **China**; provides historic routeway across Nanling mtns., followed by old imperial highway from Nanjing to Guangzhou; alt. c. 300 m.

Meiningen, t., **Germany**; on R. Werra; cas.; machin., chemicals, timber inds.; drama ctr. in second half 19th cent.; p. (1989) 25,474.

Meissen, t., Saxony, **Germany**; on R. Elbe; cath.; famous porcelain popularly known as Dresden china; p. (1981) 39,276.

Meknès, t., **Morocco**; one of the caps. of M.; agr. ctr., olives; p. (1982) 319,783.

Mekong, R., S.E. **Asia**; rises in Tibet, flows through China, Laos, Cambodia and Vietnam, entering China Sea in extensive swampy delta; used for sm. boats but many rapids; 4,000 km long; new R. project for flood control, irrigation and hydroelectric power.

Melanesia, archipelago, S.W. **Pac. Oc.**; inc. Admiralty, Solomon, Santa Cruz, Vanuatu, Loyalty, New Caledonian, and Fiji Is.; New Guinea is sometimes included; ethnic region.

Melbourne, c., cap. of Victoria, **Australia**; at mouth of Yarra R. and N. head of Port Phillip Bay; focal point of trade, transport and inds.; produces 30 per cent of total factory output in Australia; varied inds. inc. car and aircraft assembly, petrochemicals, foodstuffs; internat. airport; 2 univs., 2 caths.; p. (1993) 3,189,200 (met. a.), 71 per cent of st. p.

Melilla, spt. and enclave in **Morocco**, on Mediterranean cst., belonging to Spain; exp. iron ore; p. (1981) 53,593.

Melitopol, c., **Ukraine**; on Molochnoy R.; ctr. of rich fruit-growing a.; heavy machin., food-processing; p. (1990) 175,800.

Melksham, t., West Wilts., **Eng.**; on R. Avon, 8 km N.E. of Bradford-on-Avon; rubber wks., engin., flour mills, creameries, rope and matting; p. (1991)13,074.

Melrose, burgh, Borders, **Scot.**; on R. Tweed; 6 km E. of Galashiels; ruined abbey; p. (1991) 2,270.

Melton Mowbray, t., Leics., **Eng.**; on Lincoln Heights, 24 km N.E. of Leicester; mkt., hunting dist.; famous pork pies; footwear, pet foods, Stilton cheese; with surrounding a. forms l. gov. dist. of **Melton**; p. (1995) 46,500 (dist.), (1991) 24,348 (t.).

Melun, t., cap. of Seine-et-Marne dep., N. **France**; on R. Seine; agr. tools and prod.; Romanesque church; p. (1990) 36,489 (t.), 92,459 (met.a.).

Melville I., off N. cst., Arnhem Land, **Australia**; Aboriginal settlement; a. 4,350 km².

Melville I., N.W. Terr., Arctic **Canada**; natural gas; a. 41,958 km².

Memaliaj, t., **Albania**; new mng. t. on banks of R. Vjosa.

Memel. *See* Klaipeda.

Memmingen, t., Bavaria, **Germany**; rly. junc.; machin., textiles; p. (1986) 37,300.

Memphis, anc. c., **Egypt**; on R. Nile; 19 km S. of Cairo; nearby are Saqqara ruins.

Memphis, c., Tenn., **USA**; on R. Mississippi; rly. ctr., pt. of entry, lgst. c. in st., mkt. ctr. for cotton and hardwoods; cottonseed oil, textiles, farm machin.; natural gas and hydroelectric power; univ.; Martin Luther King assassinated (1968); p. (1990) 610,337 (c.), 981,747 (met. a.).

Menado, t., Sulawesi, **Indonesia**; second t. of I.; pt. for transit tr.; p. (1980) 217,159.

Menai Strait, separates Isle of Anglesey from mainland, **Wales**; crossed by Telford's suspension bridge (1825) and Britannia rly. bridge (1850).

Menam Chao Phraya, R., **Thailand**; main R. of

cty.; dense p. in valley; lge. multi-purpose scheme for hydroelectric power and irrigation; 1,120 km long.

Mendip Hills, Somerset, **Eng.**; limestone range containing many karst features inc. Cheddar gorge and Wookey Hole; a. of outstanding natural beauty; quarrying; motor-way; hgst. point 325 m; forms l. gov. dist. **Mendip**, inc. Frome, Wells, Shepton Mallet, Glastonbury and Street; p. (1995) 98,600.

Mendoza, prov., W. **Argentina**, on Chilean border; Andean peaks Aconcagua and Tupungato; oilfields; alfalfa, vines, olives, fruit, peppermint; cap. M.; a. 148,783 km²; p. (1991) 1,412,481.

Mendoza, c., cap. of M. prov., W. **Argentina**; stands at c. 730 m in oasis known as "garden of the Andes"; starting point of Transandine rly.; univ.; wine, fruit; petroleum, agr. processing; p. (1991) 121,696.

Mendoza, R., **Argentina**; enters L. Guanacache; used for hydroelectric power; 320 km long.

Menin (Meenen), t., **Belgium**; on R. Lys on Fr. border; mediaeval cloth ctr.; tobacco tr., textiles, rubber gds., soap; scene of fierce fighting in first world war; p. (1981) 33,542.

Mentawei Is., S.W. Sumatra, **Indonesia**; hilly and forested; fishing, shifting cultivation.

Menteith, Lake of, Stirling, **Scot.**; contains 3 Is.; 2·4 km by 1·6 km.

Menton, t., Alpes-Maritimes dep. S. **France**; Riviera resort; p. (1982) 25,449.

Meppel, t., Drenthe, **Neth.**, 21 km N. of Zwolle; shipbldg.; p. (1993) 24,217.

Merauke, t. W. Irian, **Indonesia**; pt. on S. cst.; ctr. of livestock raising region.

Mercedes, t., S.W. **Uruguay**; livestock ctr., E. of its pt. Fray Bentos; p. (1985) 37,110.

Mergui, archipelago, Tenasserim cst., S. **Myanmar**; teak, rice, pearl fishing.

Mérida, c., cap. of Yucatan st., S.E. **Mexico**; sisal-hemp; Spanish colonial architecture; tourism; Mayan ruins; p. (1990) 557,340.

Mérida, c. Badajoz prov., S.W. **Spain**; on Guadiana R.; comm. ctr. of Estremadura; impt. Roman remains; p. (1981) 41,783.

Mérida, t. cap. of M. st., **Venezuela**; in Andes; univ., cath.; tourist ctr.; world's highest cable rly. to Espejo peak (4,690 m); p. (1990) 167,922 (t.), 615,503 (st.).

Meriden, t., Conn., **USA**; hardware mftg.; p. (1980) 57,118.

Meridian, t., Miss., **USA**; mkt. ctr. in cotton, livestock, lumber a.; rly. and route ctr.; textiles, clothing; p. (1980) 46,577.

Merionethshire, historic co., N.W. **Wales**, now part of Gwynedd.

Merksem, industl. t., Antwerp, **Belgium**; p. (1982) 41,782.

Merrick, mtn., Dumfries and Galloway, **Scot.**; hgst. peak in S. Uplands of Scot.; alt. 843 m.

Mersea, I., at mouth of R. Colne, Essex, **Eng.**; oysters; holiday resort; 8 km long, 3 km wide.

Merseburg, c., Saxony - Anhalt, **Germany**; on R. Saale; ctr. of gr. lignite field; paper mills, chemical wks.; historic c.; p. (1981) 50,932.

Merse of Berwick, region, S.E. **Scot.**; lower valleys of Rs. Tweed and Teviot; glacial clays; arable agr. for barley, wheat; dairy cattle; ch. t. Berwick-on-Tweed.

Mersey, R., Cheshire/Gtr. Manchester/Merseyside, **Eng.**; enters Irish Sea by fine estuary at Liverpool; 109 km long.

Merseyside, former met. co., N.W. **Eng.**; a. around lower Mersey estuary inc. N. Wirral penin., pts. of Liverpool, Birkenhead and Bootle; manychem. and pt. processing inds.; p. (1995) 1,427,200.

Mersin, c., S. **Turkey**; freeport (1986), on Mediterranean cst.; oil refinery; dates from c. 3,600 B.C.; p. (1980) 216,308.

Merthyr Tydfil, t., unit. auth. created in 1996 from former l. gov. dist., S. **Wales**; in narrow valley of R. Taff, 35 km N.W. of Cardiff; former coal mng. ctr.; hosiery, aircraft, bricks, elec. domestic prods.; p. (1991) 39,482 (t.), (1995) 58,700 (unit. auth.).

Merton, outer bor., Greater London, **Eng.**; inc. former bors. of Mitcham, Wimbledon, and Merton and Morden; p. (1995) 179,200.

Meru, mtn., **Tanzania**, E. Africa; extinct volcano overlooking E. arm of Gt. Rift valley; coffee plantations at alt. 1,500–1,800 m, some rubber below 1,200 m; alt. summit 4,560 m.

Merv. *See* Mary.

Mesa, t., Arizona, **USA**; in Salt River Valley, founded by Mormons 1878; agr. ctr., helicopter mftg.; p. (1990) 288,091.

Mesa Central, plateau, **Mexico**; part of Mexican plateau, major a. of comm. agr. (maize, wheat, agave); contains cap. Mexico City; dense p. and industl. comm. ctrs.

Mesa del Norte, plateau, **Mexico**; northern part of Mexican plateau.

Mesabi Range, hills, N.E. Minn., **USA**; vast iron ore deposits, now running out.

Mesa Verde National Park, S.W. Col., **USA**; Indian cliff dwellings.

Mesopotamia, anc. region, S.W. **Asia**; between Tigris and Euphrates Rs.; a. of early civilisation.

Messenia, anc. region, Peloponnesus, **Greece**; corresponding to present Messinia, densely p. agr. dep., cap. Kalamata; a. 3,406 km²; p. (1991) 166,964.

Messina, c., spt., Sicily, **Italy**; opposite Reggio; univ.; exp. fruit, wine, oil; p. (1992) 232,911.

Messina, strait, between Sicily and Italian mainland; length 35 km, minimum width 5 km.

Mesta, R., **Bulgaria**, **Greece**; rises in Rodopi mtns., flows S.E. into Aegean Sea 24 km E of Kavalla; valley famous for tobacco; known in Greece as Nestos; c. 280 km long.

Mestre, t., **Italy**; on lagoon at landward end of causeway linking Venice to mainland.

Meta, R., **Colombia** and **Venezuela**; navigable for 640 km; trib. of R. Orinoco; 1,200 km long.

Metz, c., cap of Moselle dep., N.E. **France**; on R. Moselle 40 km N. of Nancy; cultural and comm. ctr. of Lorraine; impt. iron mines; wines, preserved fruits; mediaeval bldgs.; birthplace of Verlaine; p. (1990) 123,920(c.), 193,117 (met. a.).

Meudon, t., Hauts-de-Seine, **France**; S.W. sub. of Paris; observatory; glass, linen, ammunition; p. (1982) 49,004.

Meurthe, R., N.E. **France**; rises in Vosges and joins Moselle N. of Nancy.

Meurthe-et-Moselle, dep., N.E. **France**; borders on Belgium and Luxembourg; cap. Nancy; a. 5,276 km²; p. (1990) 711,800.

Meuse, dep., N.E. **France**; borders on Belgium; cap. Bar-le-Duc; a. 6,237 km²; p. (1990) 196,300.

Meuse (Maas), R., **France**; rises in Haute-Marne, flows past Verdun into Belgium past Namur, and Liège into the Neth. and joins the Waal, left arm of the Rhine; impt. routeway; 912 km long.

Mexborough, t., South Yorks., **Eng.**; on R. Don, 16 km above Doncaster; potteries; p. (1991) 15,282.

Mexicali, c., Baja Cal., **Mexico**; border resort; p. (1990) 602,390.

Mexican Plateau, central plateau, **Mexico**; between the branches of the Sierra Madre; highest point over 2,400 m; impt. landform and a. of human settlement.

Mexico, fed. rep., Central America; inc. 31 sts., and fed. dist. of Mexico City; mtnous.; Sierra Madre covers most of rep.; variety of climate according to alt.; W. mostly desert; one of world's fastest-growing p.; agr. requires irrigation; major world exporter of cotton, fruit, sulphur, silver, oil; 14 oil refineries, new petrochemical complex at Cosoleacaque; rapid industl. expansion for consumer gds.; attempts to decentralise inds. from Mexico City not very successful; tourism for Americans; cap. Mexico City; a. 1,972,360 km²; p. (1994) 93,000,000 (est.).

Mexico, st., **Mexico**; encircles fed. dist. of Mexico City; cap. Toluca; a. 21,412 km²; p. (1990) 9,815,901.

Mexico City, c., cap. of **Mexico**; lgst. c. in Latin America; on plain at 2,275 m; altitude and basin site trap pollutants; many note-worthy bldgs., cath., univ.; admin., comm. and industl. ctr.; nuclear reactor nearby; lge. earthquake (1985) destroyed many parts of c.; surrounded by shanty ts.; p. (1990) 8,236,960 (fed. dist.).

Mexico, Gulf of, lge. inlet of Atl. Oc. (1,600 km E. to W.) by 1,280 km N. to S.) lying S. of USA and E. of Mexico; communicates by Florida strait with Atl. and by Yucatan strait with Caribbean Sea; submarine oil drilling.

Mexico, Valley of, Meseta Central, **Mexico**; major industl. zone; over 60 per cent by value of Mexican mngs. produced; wide range of inds.; major ctr. Mexico City; attempts to decentralise p. and economic activity throughout Mexico; once ctr. of Aztec p.

Meyrin, t., **Switzerland**; H.Q. of CERN Organisation Européené pour la Recherche Nucléaire; nr. Geneva.

Mezhdurechensk, t., **Russia**; W. Siberia, on R. Rom'; new coal-mng. ctr.; p. (1989) 107,000.

Mezzogiorno, lge. underdeveloped region, southern **Italy**; comprising Abruzzo and Molise, Campania, Basilicata, Apulia, Calabria and the Is. of Sicily and Sardinia; major govt. attempts to develop a.; agr. reforms and industl. growth, oil refining, iron and steel, petrochemicals; contains 35 per cent of p. of Italy, much emigration; much devastated by earthquake (1980); p. (1981) 20,053,334.

Miami, c., Fla., **USA**; on Biscayne Bay, at mouth of Miami R.; famous resort and recreational ctr.; varied inds.; international airport; world's 5th lgst. cargo airpt.; 3rd container pt. on U.S. East cst.; lge. freeport; M. beach across Biscayne Bay; ctr. of Cuban exiles; p. (1990) 358,548 (c.), 1,937,000 (met. a. with Hialeah).

Miass, c., **Russia**; in Urals, 90 km S.W. of Chelyabinsk; gold-mng. ctr.; cars; p. (1989) 168,000.

Michigan, st., **USA**; Wolverine St.; admitted to Union 1837; st. flower Apple Blossom, st. bird Robin; in valley of Gr. Ls.; industl.; cars, iron and steel gds., petroleum, minerals; some agr.; cap. Lansing; a. 150,779 km²; p. (1990) 9,295,297.

Michigan Lake, 3rd lgst of Gr. Ls. and the only one wholly in **USA**; in basin of St. Lawrence R., enclosed by two peninsulas of the st. of Mich. and by Wis., Ill., and Ind.; a. 61,901 km²; discharges by Straits of Mackinac to L. Huron.

Michipicoten, R., Ont., **Canada**; flows 200 km to L. Superior; iron ore deposits in valley.

Michoacan, st., **Mexico**; on Pac. Oc.; mtnous., rich in minerals; cap. Morelia; a. 60,088 km²; p. (1990) 3,534,042.

Michurinsk, t., **Russia**; N.W. of Tambov; engin., textiles, food inds.; agr. exp. ctr.; p. (1989) 109,000.

Micronesia, Federated States of, ind. state, includes W. Pac. Is. of Yap, Truk, Ponape and Kosrae; p. (1994), 104,000.

Mid Bedfordshire, l. gov. dist., Beds., **Eng.**; a. N. of Luton and inc. Biggleswade, Sandy and Ampthill; p. (1995) 116,400.

Mid Devon, l. gov. dist., Devon, **Eng.**; based on Tiverton; p. (1995) 66,000.

Middleburg, t. cap. of Zeeland prov., **Neth.**; on Walcheren I. nr. Flushing; margarine, timber, optical instruments; cloth ctr. in mediaeval times; p. (1994) 40,118.

Middlesbrough, t., unit. auth. created in 1996, formerly part of Cleveland, **Eng.**; expanded t.; pt. on S. side of Tees estuary; impt. iron and steel ind., heavy engin., chemicals; p. (1995) 147,500 (unit. auth.), (1991) 147,430 (t.).

Middlesex, historic co., S.E. **Eng.**; N. of R. Thames; largely absorbed in Greater London 1964.

Middleton, t., Gtr. Manchester, **Eng.**; in valley of R. Irk; textiles, engin., chemicals, foam rubber; p. (1991) 45,621.

Middletown, t., Ohio, **USA**; on Miami R. and canal; steel, paper; p. (1990) 46,022.

Middlewich, t., Cheshire, **Eng.**; on Rs. Dane, Wheelock and Croco, 8 km N. of Crewe; salt, chemicals, clothing; p. (1991) 10,100.

Midhurst, t., West Sussex, **Eng.**; on R. Rother; famous polo grounds; birthplace of Richard Cobden; p. (1991) 6,451.

Midi-Pyrénées, region, S.W. **France**; inc. deps. Ariège, Aveyron. Haute-Garonne, Gers, Lot, Hautes-Pyrénées, Tarn, Tarn-et-Garonne; mountainous region on Spanish border descending to agricultural lowlands north-eastwards; p. (1990) 2,430,700

Midland, t., Texas, **USA**; oilfield ctr., cotton ginning, natural gas; p. (1990) 89,443.

Midlands, region, **Eng.**; comprises non-met. cos. of Staffs, Derbys., Notts., Leics., Warwicks., Northants., and met. co. of West Midlands; impt. a. for lt. engin.

Midlothian, E. Scot., unit. auth. created in 1996, incorporating part of historic co. which was divided between the Borders and Lothian in 1974 and is now divided between Borders, E. Lothian, Edinburgh, Midlothian and W. Lothian; p. (1995) 79,880.

Mid Suffolk, l. gov. dist., Suffolk, **Eng.**; rural a. inc. Eye and Stowmarket; p. (1995) 79,600.

Mid Sussex, l. gov. dist., West Sussex, **Eng.**; a. inc. Cuckfield and Burgess Hill; p. (1995) 126,100.

Midway Islands, I., **Pac. Oc.**; calling-place on air-routes betweeen San Francisco and Asia, midway between Asia and **USA** (to which it belongs); p. (1981) 453 (excl. military personnel).

Mieres, t., Oviedo prov., N. **Spain**; in Asturias; coal-mng. ctr., iron and steel inds.; p. (1981) 58,098.

Mikkeli, c., cap. of M. prov., **Finland**; L. pt. in Saimaa L. region; p. (1993) 32,394.

Milan, c., cap. of M. prov., N. **Italy**; route ctr. in Lombard plain; second lgst. c. in rep.; ctr. of commerce and ind.; textiles, chemicals, printing, publishing, machin., cars, aircraft, porcelain; cath., univ.; p. (1992) 1,358,627.

Mildenhall, t., Forest Heath, Suffolk, **Eng.**; on R. Lark; 13th cent. church; R.A.F. sta. nearby; expanded t.; p. (1991) 10,468.

Mildura, t., Victoria, **Australia**; on R. Murray; irrigation ctr.; wine, citrus fruits, tomatoes; ctr. for dried fruit; p. (1986) 18,382.

Milford Haven, spt., Pembrokeshire, **Wales**; magnificent deepwater harbour; major tanker terminal (250,000 tonnes); 2 refineries; pipeline from Angle Bay to Llandarcy (nr. Swansea); major white fish pt.; trawlers built and repaired; net mkg.; p. (1991) 13,194.

Milford Sound, inlet, at S. of S.I., **N.Z.**; tourist resort; noted for scenery and rare birds.

Millau, t., Aveyron, **France**; on R. Tarn; glove mnfs.; p. (1982) 22,256.

Millom, t., Copeland, Cumbria, **Eng.**; on N.W. cst. of Duddon estuary; ironwks. (closed 1968 after 100 years); hosiery; declining p.; p. (1991) 6,455.

Millport, burgh, N. Ayrshire, **Scot.**; on Gr. Cumbrae I., in F. of Clyde; resort; cath.; quarries; p. (1991) 1,340.

Milngavie, burgh, E. Dunbartonshire, **Scot.**; 8 km N.W. of Glasgow; textiles; p. (1991) 12,592.

Milnrow, t., Gtr. Manchester, **Eng.**; sub. of Rochdale; cotton and waste spinning engin., brick mkg., paper and tub mftg.; p. (1991) 12,541.

Milo or **Melos,** I., Cyclades, **Greece**; cap. Plaka, nr. site of anc. c.; famous statue of Venus of Milo (now in Louvre) found here in 1820.

Milton Keynes, t., unit. auth. created in 1997, formerly part of Bucks., **Eng.**; new c. for London overspill comprising Bletchley, Wolverton and Stony Stratford; Open University; p. (1995) 192,900 (former dist.).

Milwaukee, c., Wis., USA; lgst. c. and ch. pt. of st.; on L. Mich.; 112 km N. of Chicago; univ.; major mftg. ctr. with numerous inds., notably machin. and transport equipment, meat-canning, beer; p. (1990) 628,088 (c.), 1,432,149 (met. a.).

Min, R., Fujian, S. **China**; descends steeply on S.E. course to enter S. China Sea nr. Fuzhou, length 480 km, navigable.

Min, R., Sichuan, W. **China**; flows S., diverted into irrigation channels; joins Chang Jiang at Yibin; length 800 km, navigable.

Mina Hassan Tani (Kenitra), spt., **Morocco**; exp. grain; p. (1981) 450,000.

Minas Gerais, st., **Brazil**; vast iron ore reserves; gold, diamonds, manganese, uranium, aluminium; cotton, coffee; hydroelec. power sta.; cap. Belo Horizonte; heavy inds.; a. 585,472 km²; p. (1991) 15,746,200.

Minas Novas, t., Minas Gerais, **Brazil**; p. (1985) 28,400.

Mina Sulman, free transit pt., **Bahrain**; deepwater pt., dry dock for OPEC super-tankers, entrepôt.

Minatitlán, t., E. **Mexico**; petroleum refineries; petrochemicals; p. (1990) 199,840.

Minch, The, channel between the mainland of **Scot.** and the N. portion of Outer Hebrides, 38–64 km wide; very rapid current.

Minch, The Little, channel between I. of Skye, **Scot.** and the middle portion of Outer Hebrides, 22–32 km wide.

Minchinhampton, t., Gloucs., **Eng.**; in Cotswolds, 6 km S.E. of Stroud; p. (1991) 3,201.

Mindanao, second lgst. I. of **Philippines**; forested mtns., volcano Mt. Apo; exp. pineapples, hemp, coconuts, coffee; iron, gold, copper mined; plywoods and veneer, paper, pulp; ch. ts. Zamboanga, Davao; a. of govnt. sponsored immigration; lge. Moslem p.; greatest ocean depth Mindanao Deep, off Philippines, 11,524 m; a. 94,628 km²; p. (1990) 14,297,462.

Minden, t., N. Rhine–Westphalia, **Germany**; on R. Weser at crossing of Mittelland canal; pt., rly. junc.; cath. (12th–14th cent.) destroyed in second world war; p. (1986) 75,400.

Mindoro, I., **Philippines**, S. of Luzon; mtnous., thickly forested; rice, coconuts grown on cst., a. 9,376 km²; p. (1990) 832,642.

Minehead, t., West Somerset, **Eng.**; at N. foot of Exmoor, on Bristol Channel cst.; mkt., holiday resort; p. (1991) 9,158.

Minho, R., separates Portugal from Spain in N.W.; length 272 km.

Minicoy Is., Arabian Sea; joined with Laccadive and Amindivi Is. to form union terr. of Lakshadweep, **India**.

Minneapolis, c., Minn., USA; on Mississippi R., at falls of St. Anthony; lgst. c. of st., pt. of entry, rly. terminus; wheat mkt., comm. and industl. ctr.; wide range of inds.; univ.; p. (1990) 368,383 (c.), 2,464,124 (met. a. inc. St. Paul which it faces).

Minnesota, st., USA; North Star St.; admitted to Union 1858; st. flower Lady's Slipper, st. bird Common Loon; W. of L. Superior; studded with Ls., many Rs.; iron ore; maize, wheat, livestock, dairying; cap. St. Paul; a. 217,736 km²; p. (1990) 4,375,099.

Minorca (Menorca), I. off **Spain**; 2nd lgst. of Balearic Is.; Mediterranean agr.; developing tourism; cap. Mahón; a. 733 km²; p. (1981) 58,727.

Minsk, c., cap. of **Belarus**; lge. rly. junc.; cultural and industl. ctr.; univ.; engin., computers; rebuilt since second world war; p. (1990) 1,612,800.

Minya, c. and prov., central **Egypt**; on Nile; cotton tr. ctr.; p. (1986) 179,136 (c.), (1991) 3,003,000 (prov.).

Minya Konka, mtn., S.W. Sichuan prov., **China**; in Himalayas; highest peak in China; 7,570 m.

Mirfield, t., West Yorks., **Eng.**; on R. Calder, 5 km S.W. of Dewsbury; woollens; p. (1991) 18,459.

Miri, t., Sarawak, E. **Malaysia**; impt. oil ctr.; p. (1980) 91,000.

Mirzapur, t. Uttar Pradesh, **India**; on R. Ganges; carpets, brassware; p. (1991) 169,336.

Misiones, prov., N.E. **Argentina**; densely forested subtropical region; sugar cane, tea, timber, sandstone and basalt mining; cap. Posadas; a. 29,801 km²; p. (1991) 788,915.

Miskolc, c., N.E. **Hungary**; impt. industl. ctr.; iron ore, lignite nearby; varied inds., inc. textiles, porcelain, engin., bricks, refrigeration plants; p. (1997) 178,000.

Mississauga, c., Ontario, **Canada**; lies to W. of Toronto; part of T. met. a.; p. (1991) 463,388.

Mississippi, st., S. USA; Magnolia St.; admitted to Union 1817; st. flower Magnolia, st. bird Mockingbird; in lower M. valley; bounded on S. by G. of Mexico; cotton, sweet potatoes, pecan nuts, rice, sugar-cane, sorghum-cane, fruit, livestock raising; petroleum, natural gas; cotton textiles, chemicals, fish-processing; cap. Jackson; a. 123,584 km²; p. (1990) 2,573,216.

Mississippi, principal R. of USA; rises in N. Minn. nr. L. Itasca; drains c. 3,170,000 km²; enters G. of Mexico in lge. delta nr. New Orleans; navigable, flood control problems; length 3,760 km (Mississippi–Missouri–Red Rock 6,176 km).

Missolonghi, t., **Greece**; pt. on inlet of G. of Patras; fish, tobacco; Byron died here 1824; p. (1981) 11,375.

Missoula, t., Mont., USA; on Klark R.; univ.; rly. wks., agr., fruit, oil refinery; tourism; p. (1990) 42,918.

Missouri, st., central USA; Show-me St.; admitted to Union 1821; st. flower Hawthorn, st. bird Bluebird; dominated by Mississippi and Missouri Rs.; predominantly agr.; livestock, maize; coal, iron; transport equipment; cap. Jefferson City; ch. t. St. Louis; a. 180,456 km²; p. (1990) 5,117,073.

Missouri, longest R. of USA; 3,942 km; trib. of Mississippi R.; main headstream Jackson R.; flood, power and irrigation schemes.

Missouri Coteau, hill ridge, N. **America**; runs N.W. to S.E. across prairies of Saskatchewan (Canada), N. and S. Dakota (USA); rises abruptly from 480–600 m.

Mistassini, L., Quebec, **Canada**; 160 km long.

Misurata, t., Tripolitania, **Libya**; on cst. of Mediterranean, 176 km E. of Tripoli; mkt. for local agr. produce; p. (1984) 178,295.

Mitau. See Jelgava.

Mitchelstown, t., Cork, **R.o.I.**; nr. Fermoy; dairy prods.; p. (1986) 3,210.

Mitidja, plain, **Algeria**, N. Africa; borders Mediterranean; intensive cultivation of vine; ch. ts. Algiers, Blida.

Mito, c. Honshu, **Japan**; cas., comm. ctr.; famous for lime trees; site of two nuclear power plants nearby; p. (1990) 234,970.

Mits'iwa (Massawa), spt., **Eritrea** on Red Sea; fine harbour; fishing; fish meal; p. (1989) 19,404.

Mittelland Canal, inland waterway system, Germany; system of canals and canalised Rs.; links Dortmund-Ems canal nr. Rheine through Minden, Hanover, Magdeburg, Berlin to R. Oder at Frankfurt-on-Oder; makes use of natural E.-W. troughs across the N. German plain.

Mittweida, t., Saxony, **Germany**; metallurgy, textiles; p. (1989) 17,633.

Miyazaki, c., Kyushu, **Japan**; famous shrine; ctr. of sandy plain with lagoons; p. (1990) 287,367.

Mizoram ("Land of Highlanders"), union terr. (1972); new st. (1986); Assam, N.E. **India**; former Mizo Hills dist. of Assam; 80 per cent p. Christian; 44 per cent literate, higher proportion than any other a. except Kerala; new cap. Aizawl; a. 21,238 km²; p. (1991) 689,756.

Mjosa, lgst. L., **Norway**; 88 km long.

Mladá Boleslav (Jungbunziau), t., Bohemia, **Czech Rep.**; vehicles, agr. machin., textiles; once ctr. of Bohemian Brethren (followers of John Hus); p. (1984) 47,686.

Moanda, spt. at mouth of Congo R., **Congo**; oil refinery, aluminium smelter.

Mobutu Sese Seko, L., (L. Albert), Congo, Uganda; on floor of Gt. Rift Valley; crocodile farming; tourism; main pt. Kasenyi; 160 km long, 32 km wide; alt. 640 m; a. 5,346 km².

Mobile, c., spt., Ala., **USA**; on R. M.; shipbldg. pt. inds.; exp. cotton; p. (1990) 196,278 (c.), 476,923 (met. a.).

Moçambique, former Portuguese prov., indep. st. (1975), E. Africa; wide cstl. plain rising inland to 2,100 m; crossed by Zambesi R.; few exp. inc. cashew nuts, cotton, sugar, tea; deposits of coal and bauxite; Beira and Maputo (cap.) serve as import pts. for transit tr.; 40 % GNP from tourism and transport; Cabora Bassa Dam in Tete dist.; severely hit by drought since 1984; civil war against Renamo rebels ended 1992; joined Brit. Commonwealth, 1995; a. 771,820 km²; p. (1995) 16,500,000.

Moçambique Channel, strait, **Indian Oc.**; separates Madagascar from mainland of Africa; 1,600 km long, 400–960 km wide.

Moçambique Current, ocean current, flows N. to S. along E. cst. of Moçambique and Natal, E. Africa; relatively warm water.

Moçâmedes. *See* Namibe.

Modane, t., S.E. Savoie, **France**; commands routes via Mont Cenis Pass and tunnel; electrometallurgy; p. (1982) 4,877.

Modena, t., cap. of M. prov. **Italy**; cath.; univ.; textiles, leather, engin.; p. (1992) 176,972.

Modesto, t., Cal., **USA**; fruit (especially peaches), vegetable-processing; p. (1990) 164,730 (t.), 371,000 (met. a.).

Modica, t., S.E. Sicily, **Italy**; agr. ctr.; limestone grottoes, cave dwellings; Cava d'Ispica; p. (1981) 45,769.

Moe. *See* Yallourn.

Moers, t. North Rhine-Westphalia, **Germany**; W of Duisburg in the Ruhr; ind. coal; p. (1990) 105,000.

Moffat, burgh, Dumfries and Galloway, **Scot.**; 24 km N.W. of Lockerbie; resort; p. (1991) 2,342.

Moffat Tunnel, Col., **USA**; carries trunk rly. from Chicago to San Francisco under Rocky mtns. between Denver and Salt Lake City; 10 km long; alt. 2,774 m.

Mogadishu, c., cap. of Rep. of Somalia; on Indian Oc.; modernised deep-sea pt., airpt.; p. (1987) 1,000,000.

Mogador. *See* Essaouira.

Mogi das Cruzes, t., São Paulo, **Brazil**; agr.; bauxite mng.; p. (1985) 234,900.

Mogilev, c., Belarus; on R. Dnieper; industl.; rly. and route junc.; p. (1990) 362,600.

Mohács, t., S. **Hungary**; on Danube; impt. R. pt.; strategic site; battle 1526; p. (1997) 20,000.

Mohammedia, t., Morocco, N. Africa; oil refining; p. (1982) 105,120.

Mohawk, R., N.Y., **USA**; trib. of Hudson R.; followed by impt. road, rly. and canal routes across Appalachian mtns.; 280 km long.

Mojave or **Mohave**, S. Cal., **USA**; desert region of mtns. and valleys; a. 38,850 km².

Moji, spt., Kyushu, **Japan**; exp. coal, cement, timber; linked by bridge to Honshu. *See* Kitakyushu.

Mokpo, spt., W. cst. **S. Korea**; ctr. of food-processing and cotton-ginning; p. (1983) 228,000.

Mol, t., N.E. **Belgium**; nuclear energy research ctr.; p. (1983) 29,970.

Mold, t., Flintshire, N. **Wales**; on R. Alyn;

chemicals, roadstone; p. (1991) 8,745.

Moldau. *See* Vltava.

Moldova, CIS former constituent rep., USSR; fertile fruit growing a. especially for vines; inds. based on fruit; cap. Kishinev; a. 34,188 km²; p. (1994) 4,353,000.

Mole Valley, l. gov. dist., Surrey, **Eng.**; based on Mole R. ts. of Leatherhead and Dorking; p. (1995) 79,400.

Mole R., Surrey, **Eng.**; rises in central Weald, flows N. into R. Thames nr. Molesey; cuts impt. gap through N. Downs between Dorking and Leatherhead; 80 km long.

Molenbeek-Saint-Joan, t., **Belgium**; nr. Brussels; lge mftg. ctr.; p. (1983) 71,181.

Molfetta, spt., Apulia, **Italy**; olive oil, macaroni, wine, caths.; p. (1981) 65,951.

Moline, t., Ill., **USA**; on Mississippi R.; agr. implements, ironwks., flour; p. (1980) 46,278.

Molise, region, central **Italy**; subsistence arable and pastoral farming; a. 4,437 km²; p. (1992) 331,494.

Mölndal, t., S.W. **Sweden**; paper, textiles; margarine; p. (1992) 52,423.

Moluccas or **Spice Is.**, prov. **Indonesia**; gr. of Is. between Sulawesi and W. Irian; mtnous., fertile; spices, sago, timber, pearls, rice, copra, ch. t. Ternate; attempts at secession by S. Moluccans; a. 496,454 km²; p. (1983) 1,534,300.

Mombasa, spt., **Kenya**; ch. harbour, Kilindini; rly. terminus; oil refinery; exp. tropical produce (ivory, hides, rubber, etc.); fertiliser plant, sheet glass, steel rolling mill; p. (1984) 425,634.

Møn, I., off cst. of Sjaelland, **Denmark**; a. 233 km²; cap. Stege; p. (1990) 10,132.

Monaco, principality on Mediterranean cst. between France and Italy, W. Europe; economy based on tourism; benefits from climate and amenities, inc. famous casino; tax laws attract p. and shortage of land causes M. to build out into sea; much revenue derived from transactional laws, sales of tobacco and postage stamps; cap. Monte Carlo; a. 146 ha; p. (1995) 31,000.

Monadhliath Mtns., Highland, **Scot.**; between Spey R. and Loch Ness; hgst. peak Carn Mairg, 1,216 m.

Monadnock Mt., peak, 965 m high, N.H., **USA**; name used as a term for the geomorphological feature of an isolated hill which has successfully resisted erosion.

Monaghan, co., **R.o.I.**; mainly pastoral and agr.; a. 1,295 km²; p. (1986) 52,379.

Monaghan, co. t., Monaghan, **R.o.I.**; on the Ulster canal; cath.; p. (1986) 6,075.

Mona Passage, strait, Caribbean Sea; separates Hispaniola from Puerto Rico.

Monastir. *See* Bitola.

Mönch, peak, Bernese Alps, **Switzerland**; 4,101 m.

Mönchengladbach, t., N. Rhine-Westphalia, **Germany**; 26 km W. of Düsseldorf; rly. ctr. textiles; p. (1990) 260,700.

Monchique, t., Algarve, **Portugal**; spa; wine, oil, chestnuts; p. (1981) 9,609.

Moncton, t., N.B., **Canada**; rly. ctr., textiles; oil nearby; p. (1991) 80,744.

Monfalcone, t., N.E. **Italy**; on Adriatic; modern industl. t.; shipbldg., oil refining; p. (1981) 30,277.

Monferrato, low hills, Piedmont, N. **Italy**; S. and S.E. of Turin between valleys of Po and Tanaro; celebrated vineyards, produce Asti Spumante wines; alt. never exceeds 460 m.

Mongla, pt., **Bangladesh**; on Pussur R.; shipping pt. under construction.

Mongolia, Inner. *See* Inner Mongolia.

Mongolia, People's Rep. of (Outer Mongolia), central Asia; land-locked, extensive plateau at 1,200 m bordering Gobi desert in S.; dry continental climate with extremely cold winters; pastoral agr. collectively organised for horses, sheep, camels, oxen, and goats; cap. Ulan Bator; incr. mechanisation; food processing, livestock prods.; a. 1,564,360 km²; p. (1995) 2,200,000.

Monmouth, t., Monmouthshire, **Wales**; at confluence of Rs. Wye and Monnow; mkt. ctr.; timber, crushed limestone, wrought ironwk.; p. (1991) 7,246.

Monmouthshire, S.E. **Wales**, unit. auth. created in 1996 from former l. gov. dist., reinstating part of historic co. split up in 1974; drained by the Usk and Wye Rs.; inc. ts. of Abergavenny, Chepstow and Monmouth; p. (1995) 85,600.

Monongahela, R., W. Va., **USA**; joins Allegheny R. at Pittsburgh to form Ohio R.; impt. waterway.

Monopoli, spt., Apulia, **Italy**; oil, wine, fruit, flour tr.; p. (1981) 43,424.

Monroe, t., La., **USA**; cotton ctr., natural gas,

paper, printing ink; p. (1984) 56,000 (t.), 142,700 (met. a.).

Monrovia, c., cap. of **Liberia,** W. Africa; free port and industl. free zone on Atl. at mouth of St. Paul R.; exp. rubber, palm oil; ship registration; p. (1984) 425,000.

Mons, c., cap. of Hainaut prov., W. **Belgium,** nr. Fr. border; cath.; inds. linked with Borinage coal-mng. dist.; varied mnfs.; scene of many battles; NATO (SHAPE) H.Q. nearby at Casteau; p. (1993) 92,533.

Montana, st., N.W. **USA;** Treasure St.; admitted to Union 1889; st. flower Bitterroot, st. bird Western Meadowlark; in Rocky mtns. region; cap. Helena; lgst. c. Great Falls; copper, silver, gold, zinc, lead, manganese; coal, petroleum, natural gas; pastoral agr.; Glacier Nat. Park, tourism; a. 377,456 km²; p. (1990) 799,065.

Montauban, t., Tarn-et-Garonne dep., **France;** on R. Tarn; cath.; agr. prod., wines; p. (1990) 53,278.

Montbéliard, t., Doubs dep., **France;** S. of Belfort; textiles, watches, typewriters, vehicles; p. (1990) 30,639(t.), 117,510 (met. a.).

Mont Blanc, mtn., Alps; on confines of **Italy** and **France;** alt. 4,814 m; longest road tunnel in world (opened to traffic 1965) linking Courmayeur (Italy) and Chamonix (France), length 12 km.

Montceau-les-Mines, t., Saône-et-Loire dep., **France;** coal, textiles, metal-working; p. (1982) 51,290 (met. a.).

Mont Cenis Pass and Tunnel, W. Alps; on bdy. between **France** and **Italy;** approached from W. by Isère Arc valleys, from E. by Dora Riparia; alt. 2,097 m; tunnel carries main rly. from Lyons to Turin under Col de Fréjus; opened 1871; 12 km long.

Montclair, t., N.J., **USA;** residtl. sub. of N.Y.; paper gds. manfs.; p. (1990) 37,792.

Mont-de-Marsan, t., Landes dep., **France;** mkt. ctr.; p. (1990) 31,864.

Mont-Dore, spa, Puy-de-Dôme dep., **France;** 48 km S.W. of Clermont-Ferrand; Puy de Sancy (1,887 m) hgst. peak of Mont-Dore mtn. gr.; p. (1982) 2,394.

Monte Bello Is., gr. off N.W. cst., **Australia;** about 136 km N. of pt. of Onslow; first Brit. atomic weapon exploded here 3 Oct. 1952.

Monte Carlo, t., **Monaco;** tourist resort, casino; p. (1985) 12,000.

Monte Corno, mtn., **Italy;** in Central Apennines; alt. 2,923 m.

Monte Cristo, Italian I., 42 km S. of Elba, in Tyrrhenian Sea; famed by novel by Dumas.

Monte Gargano, peninsula, S. **Italy;** projects into Adriatic Sea nr. plain of Foggia; formed by limestone plateau, alt. over 900 m; pasture on upper slopes, woodland on lower; a. 1,030 km².

Montego Bay, spt., **Jamaica;** main ctr. for tourism; p. (1991) 83,446.

Montélimar, t., Drôme dep., **France;** bricks, tiles, nougat; hydroelectric barrage on R. Rhône; p. (1982) 30,213.

Montenegro, constituent rep., S.W. **Yugoslavia;** agr., pastoral; cap. Podgorica; a. 13,812 km²; p. (1981) 584,310.

Monterey, t., Cal., **USA;** S. of San Francisco, resort of artists and writers; sardine ind., fruit and vegetable canneries; p. (1980) 27,558.

Monteria, c., cap. of Cordoba prov., **Colombia;** tobacco, cacao, cotton, sugar; p. (1992) 265,754.

Monte Rosa, hgst. peak, 4,637 m, Pennine Alps, on border of **Italy** and **Switzerland.**

Monte Rotondo, hgst. mtn., Corsica, **France;** 2,767 m.

Monterrey, t., cap. of Nuevo León prov., **Mexico;** third lgst. c.; cath.; textiles, brewing, ironwks., minerals; thermoelec. plant; sheet metal; p. (1990) 1,064,197.

Monte Sant'Angelo, hilltop t., **Italy;** on Gargano promontory; notable ctr. of pilgrimage; p. (1981) 16,500.

Montevideo, c., cap. **Uruguay;** major pt. on Rio de la Plata; dominates life of rep. as financial, comm. and industl. ctr.; fisheries, oil-refining, food-processing, tourism; cath., univ.; p. (1992) 1,383,660.

Montgomery, t., Powys, central **Wales;** in upper Severn valley, 13 km N.E. of Newtown; agr. mkt.; cas.

Montgomery, c., cap. of Ala., **USA;** at head of Alabama R.; cotton, livestock, timber, dairying, fertilisers; hydroelec. power; p. (1990) 187,106 (c.), 292,517 (met. a.).

Montgomeryshire, historic co., central Wales, now

part of Powys.

Montluçon, t., Allier dep., **France;** on R. Cher; terminus of Berry canal, linking Commentry coalfields with Loire; iron foundries, glassmaking; cas.; p. (1982) 51,765.

Montmartre, dist., N. Paris, **France;** on Butte de M. (101 m), commands superb view S. over Paris; picturesque square, frequented by artists; basilica of Sacré Coeur.

Montparnasse, dist., Paris, **France;** on left bank of Seine R.; haunt of artists and writers.

Montpelier, st. cap., Vermont, **USA;** sm. t. in Green Mtns. and on Winooski R.

Montpellier, t., cap. of Hérault dep., **France;** 8 km N. of Mediterranean cst. on coastal lowland route to S.W. France; comm. and cultural ctr.; univ.; wines, fruit tr.; silk, chemicals; many anc. bldgs. inc. cath.; p. (1990) 210,866(t.), 236,788 (met. a.).

Montreal, c., spt., Quebec, **Canada;** at confluence of Ottawa and St. Lawrence Rs.; caths., univs.; major industl., comm. and financial ctr.; extensive harbour installations, lge. grain exp.; diverse mnfs.; lgst. c. and spt. in Canada; p. mainly French-speaking; p. (1991) 1,017,666 (c.), (1986) 2,921,357 (met. a.).

Montreuil-sous-Bois, E. sub. Paris, **France;** hothouse flowers and fruit for Paris mkt.; peach growing; mnfs.; p. (1990) 95,038.

Montreux, t., **Switzerland;** on L. Geneva; tourist ctr.; Chillon cas.; p. (1980) 19,685.

Montrose, spt., burgh, Angus, **Scot.;** on E. cst. at mouth of S. Esk R.; chemicals, rope wks., vegetable-canning, boat-bldg., fishing; supply base for N. Sea oil; p. (1991) 11,440.

Mont-Saint-Michel, rocky granite I., in English Channel, off Normandy cst., **France;** tourist ctr. with Benedictine abbey; connected to mainland by causeway; alt. 79 m.; p. (1982) 80.

Montserrat, volcanic I., Brit. crown col., Leeward Is., W.I.; chiefly agr.; exp. sea-island cotton, limes, sugar-cane and tomatoes; cap. Plymouth; a. 101 km²; p. (1997) 12,000. Devastated by major volcanic eruption, 1997.

Montserrat, mtn., Catalonia, **Spain;** Benedictine monastery, alt. 1,236 m.

Monument Valley, Utah and Arizona, **USA;** home of Navajo Indians.

Monza, c., Lombardy, N. **Italy;** 14 km from Milan; cath.; textiles, leather, hats; former royal residence; motor-racing circuit; p. (1992) 120,054.

Moonie, t., Queensland, **Australia;** 320 km W. of Brisbane; oilfields; pipeline to Lytton, at mouth of Brisbane R.

Moose Jaw, c., Saskatchewan, **Canada;** rly. junc.; agr. ctr.; agr. implements, oil refining, p. (1991) 33,593.

Moradabad, c., Uttar Pradesh, N. **India;** rly. junc.; cotton mills, brassware; mosque; p. (1991) 444,000.

Morava, R., Slovakia and Austria; trib. of R. Danube; navigable in lower course; 339 km long.

Morava, R., Serbia, **Yugoslavia;** formed from W. Morava and S. Morava, flows N. into Danube 80 km below Belgrade to Istanbul; 560 km long.

Moravia, region, **Czech Rep.;** part of Bohemian plateau, drained by Morava R.; inc. fertile agr. a.; mineral resources and industl. ts.

Moray, E. **Scot.,** unit. auth. created in 1996, incorporating historic co. of Morayshire which became part of Grampian in 1974; borders M. Firth; arable agr. benefiting from glacial soils; p. (1995) 87,150.

Moray Firth, arm of N. Sea; on Scottish E. cst., between Highland and; plans for lge.-scale industl. expansion; offshore oil platforms at Arderseir; valuable inshore oilfield.

Morbihan, dep., N.W. **France;** on Bay of Biscay; agr., fishing; cap. Vannes; a. 7,094 km²; p. (1990) 619,800.

Mordovia, aut. rep., **Russia;** forested steppe between Rs. Oka and Volga; pastoral agr.; lumbering; food processing; a. 25,493 km²; p. (1989) 963,500.

Morea. See Peloponnesus.

Morecambe and Heysham, t., N. Lancs., **Eng.;** on S. shore of M. Bay; M. holiday resort; H., pt. for N. Ireland and oil refinery; two advanced gas-cooled reactor nuclear power stas.; p. (1991) 46,657.

Morecambe Bay, between Lancs. and Cumbria, **Eng.;** isolates Furness dist. of Lancs.; many proposed barrages across Bay, now project increasingly probable as water shortage in N.W. Eng. grows; discoveries of nat. gas.

Morelia, c., cap. of Michoacán st., W. **Mexico**; on rocky hill, 1,891 m in fertile valley; cath.; textiles, pottery; p. (1990) 489,758.

Morelos, inland st., **Mexico**; mtns., forested; arable agr.; cap. Cuernavaca; a. 4,962 km²; p. (1990) 1,195,381.

Morez, t., Jura dep., **France**; precision instruments, optical equipment; winter sports.

Morgan, t., R. pt., S. **Australia**; transhipment ctr.; from here water pumped from R. Murray and sent by pipeline to Whyalla.

Morgantown, c., W. Va., **USA**; univ.; coal, oil, gas fields; chemicals, heavy ind.; p. (1980) 27,605.

Morioka, c., N. Honshu, **Japan**; textiles, ironwks.; p. (1990) 235,440.

Morlaix, spt., Finistère, **France**; tobacco, paper, brewing, agr.; p. (1982) 19,541.

Morley, t., West Yorks., **Eng.**; 5 km S.W. of Leeds; woollens, stone quarrying; p. (1991) 47,579.

Morocco, kingdom, N.W. Africa; csts. on Atl. Oc. and Mediterranean Sea; rises to Atlas mtns. inland; leading world producer of phosphates; other minerals inc. iron-ore, lead and manganese; agr. main occupation, provides 30 per cent of exp.; fishing and tourism well developed; cap. Rabat; a. 466,200 km²; p. (1994) 26,500,000.

Morogoro, t., **Tanzania**, E. Africa; on E. edge of Central African plateau, alt. *c.* 900 m, 176 km by rail W. of Dar-es-Salaam; ctr. of sisal and cotton-growing a.

Moron, t., **Venezuela**; on cst. nr. Puerto Cabello; industl.; natural gas, oil refining.

Morón de la Frontera, t., S.W. **Spain**; agr. tr. ctr.; ruined Moorish cas.; p. (1981) 27,311.

Morpeth, t., Northumberland, **Eng.**; finely situated in valley of Wansbeck; coal mng., iron-founding; mkt.; Norman cas. remains; p. (1991) 14,393.

Morro Velho, gold mng. dist., Minas Gerais, **Brazil**; in Serra do Espinhaco; ch. t. Nova Lima.

Mors, I., N. Jutland, **Denmark**; in Lim fjord; a. 357 km²; p. (1990) 23,774.

Morwell, t., Victoria, **Australia**; ctr., for brown coal extraction and briquettes; inds. attracted by cheap power; p. (1991) 15,423.

Moscow, c., cap. of **Russia**; leading cultural, political, comm., industl. and route ctr.; on Moskva R.; served by several airpts., R. and canal pts.; contains Kremlin in c. ctr. with Red Square; caths., univs., palaces, many famous theatres and art galleries; p. (1989) 8,771,000 (c.), 8,970,000 (met. a.).

Moscow Sea (**Ucha Reservoir**), artificial L., **Russia**; created behind dam on R. Volga at Ivankovo; supplies water to Moscow, maintains level on Moscow–Volga canal, and supplies water to 8 hydroelec. power-stas.; a. 329 km².

Moscow–Volga Canal, **Russia**; links R. Volga at Ivankovo with Khimki sub. of Moscow; forms part of St. Petersburg–Moscow inland waterway; opened 1937; 128 km long.

Moselle, dep., N.E. **France**; iron-ore, coal mng.; metal inds.; cap. Metz; a. 6,224 km²; p. (1990) 1,011,300.

Moselle, R., **France** and **Germany**; trib. of R. Rhine; canalised between Thionville and Koblenz (269 km); lower valley forms famous wine dist.; 525 km long.

Moshi, t., N. **Tanzania**; on southern slope of Mt. Kilimanjaro; ctr. of coffee-growing dist., airpt. at 854 m (S.W. of t.).

Mosi-oa-Toenja. *See* **Victoria Falls.** The local name means "Smoke of the Thunders."

Mosjoen, t., N. **Norway**; recent aluminium wks; p. (1990) 9,391.

Moskva, R., central **Russia**; trib. of R. Oka; Moscow stands on its banks; linked with upper Volga by Moscow–Volga canal (128 km long); 400 km long.

Mosonmagyaróvár, t., **Hungary**; aluminium wks.; agr. machin.; p. (1997) 30,000.

Mosquito Cst., lowland, E. cst. **Nicaragua**; 400 km N.-S., 192 km E.-W.; lumbering, bananas; ch. t. Bluefields; sparse p.

Moss, spt., **Norway**; pulp, paper, machin., textile inds.; p. (1990) 29,363.

Mossamedes. *See* **Moçâmedes.**

Mossel Bay, pt. and seaside resort, Cape Prov., **S. Africa**; between Cape Town and Port Elizabeth; p. (1980) 33,240 (dist.).

Mossley, t., Tameside, Gtr. Manchester, **Eng.** 5 km E. of Oldham; mkt. t., textiles; p. (1991) 10,569.

Most, t., Czech **Rep.**; lignite, chemicals; Druzhba crude oil pipeline extended to chemical wks.; p. (1990) 71,000.

Mostaganem, t., dep., N.W. **Algeria**; spt. on Mediterranean cst., E. of Oran; exp. wine and fruits; gas pipeline from Hassi Massaoud; p. (1987) 114,037 (t.), 504,124 (dep.).

Mostar, t., **Bosnia-Herzegovina**, formerly Yugoslavia; on R. Naretva; bauxite, lignite; inds., wine, food processing, aluminium plant; devastated in civil war 1993; p. (1981) 110,377.

Móstoles, t. Madrid prov. C. **Spain**; agr. ctr.; p. (1991) 193,056.

Mosul, t., N. **Iraq**; on R. Tigris; in region producing cereals, citrus fruit, cattle; impt. oilfields nearby; metal works; impt. during crusades; p. (1985) 570,926.

Motala, t., on L. Vättern, **Sweden**; radio sta.; engin., woollen gds.; p. (1992) 42,264.

Motherwell, burgh, N. Lanarkshire, **Scot.**; in Clyde valley, 24 km S.E. of Glasgow; iron, steel, machin., engin., textiles; p. (1991) 30,717.

Moulins, c., cap. of Allier dep., **France**; on Allier R.; leather gds., clothing; cath., ruined château, art treasures; p. (1990) 23,353.

Moulmein, spt., **Myanmar**, on R. Salween; exp. teak, rice; p. (1983) 219,991.

Mountain Ash, t., Rhondda, Cynon, Taff, **Wales**; in narrow valley 5 km S.E. of Aberdare; former coal mng. a.; p. (1991) 21,301.

Mount Adams, mtn., S. Wash. **USA**; beautiful volcanic scenery in Cascade Range; pine forests; alt. 3,803 m.

Mount Alberta, mtn., W. Alberta, **Canada**; in Canadian Rockies and Jasper Nat. Park; alt. 3,622 m.

Mount Assiniboine, mtn., Alberta, B.C., **Canada**; "Matterhorn" of Canadian Rockies; alt. 3,620 m.

Mount Carmel, mtn., N.W. **Israel**; rises to 554 m and extends 10 km as penin. into Mediterranean Sea, forming S. limit to Bay of Acre; ass. with prophets Elijah and Elisha.

Mount Gambier, t., S. **Australia**; at foot of extinct volcano; forestry, sawmilling of radiata pine; p. (1991) 21,156.

Mount Goldsworthy, t., W. **Australia**; new t. being developed in iron ore mng. a.

Mount Isa, t., W. Queensland, **Australia**; in Selwyn Range 128 km W. of Cloncurry; copper, silver, lead mng.; p. (1991) 23,935.

Mount Lofty Range, mtn. range, S. **Australia**; forms barrier to routes leaving Adelaide; lower slopes support vineyards and outer suburbs of Adelaide; rises to over 700 m.

Mount Lyell, Tasmania, **Australia**; impt. copper mines, and refinery.

Mount McKinley, Alaska, **USA**; in Alaska Range and Nat. Park; highest point in N. America, c. 6,191 m.

Mountmellick, t., Laoighis, **R.o.I.**; p. (1986) 2,789.

Mount Newman, W. **Australia**; t. built 1967 to exploit nearby iron ore.

Mount of Olives, **Jordan**; ridge (817 m), E. of Jerusalem; Garden of Gethsemane on lower slopes.

Mount's Bay, inlet, S. cst., Cornwall, **Eng.**; 32 km wide; fishery grounds.

Mount Tom Price, t., W. **Australia**; new t., being developed in iron ore mng. a.

Mount Vernon, c., N.Y., **USA**; on Bronx R.; sub. of N.Y.; residtl.; takes name from George Washington's house on Potomac, Va., 24 km S. of Washington D.C.; varied inds., notably electronic equipment; p. (1990) 67,153.

Mourenx, t., Pyrénées-Atlantique, **France**; nr. Lacq; new t., in oil dist.; p. (1982) 9,036.

Mourne Mtns., Newry and Mourne, N. **Ireland**; hgst. peak, 853 m.

Mouscron, t., **Belgium**; textile ctr. nr. Fr. border; p. (1993) 53,606.

Moyle, l. gov. dist., N. **Ireland**; borders N.E. cst.; inc. Rathlin I., Giants Causeway; main t. Ballycastle; p. (1991) 14,789.

Mozambique. *See* **Moçambique.**

Mudanjiang (**Mutankiang**), c., Heilongjiang prov., **China**; pulp, paper, machin., flour milling; site of dam on Mudan R.; oil shale found locally; p. (1984) 603,300.

Mühlhausen, t., Erfurt, **Germany**; on R. Unstrut; textiles, machin., tobacco; p. (1981) 43,348.

Mukden. *See* Shenyang.

Mulhacen, mtn., Sierra Nevada range, Spain; 3,483 m (hgst. peak Europe, outside Alps).

Mülheim-an-der-Ruhr, t., N. Rhine–Westphalia, Germany; on R. Ruhr; cas.; coal mng., iron, steel., tobacco, engin., elec., oil refining; airpt.; p. (1990) 177,200.

Mulhouse, t., Haut-Rhin dep., France; impt. textile ctr.; potash deposits to N. supply chemical inds.; p. (1990) 109,905(t.), 223,856 (met.a.)

Mull, I., Argyll and Bute, Scot.; included in Hebrides; pastoral farming, fishing, tourism; ch. t. Tobermory; p. (1991) 2,708.

Mullet, The, peninsula, W. cst. Mayo, R.o.I.

Mullingar, c. t., Westmeath, R.o.I.; on Brosna R.; mkt. agr. ctr.; cath.; p. (1986) 8,077.

Multan, t., W. Punjab, Pakistan; on R. Chenab; carpets, silks, pottery, steel, thermal sta.; import gas pipeline to Lyallpur; nuclear fuel enrichment plant based on Pakistan's main uranium deposits nearby; p. (1981) 730,000.

Mumbai. *See* Bombay.

Muncie, t., Ind. USA; on White R.; iron, steel, glass and paper; p. (1990) 71,035.

Munger, t., Bihar, India; on R. Ganges; mkt. ctr.; p. (1981) 129,260.

Munich or München, c., cap. Bavaria, Germany; on R. Isar; cultural ctr. with univ., cath., many old bldgs.; inds. varied, notably scientific instruments, brewing, elec. engin., chemicals; famous film studios; annual beer festival; p. (1990) 1,236,500.

Münster, c., N. Rhine–Westphalia, Germany; pt. on Dortmund–Ems canal; heavy machin., with varied mnfs.; cath., univ. and mediæval bldgs. damaged or destroyed in second world war; p. (1990) 261,400.

Munster, prov., S.W. R.o.I.; includes cos. Waterford, Kerry, Cork, Limerick, Clare, Tipperary; a. 24,540 km²; p. (1986) 1,020,577.

Muonio, R., part of bdy. between Finland and Sweden; flows into G. of Bothnia.

Murano, t., Venice, Italy; famous since Middle Ages for glass ind.

Murchison Falls. *See* Kabelega Falls.

Murchison, R., W. Australia; flows to Indian Oc., spectacular gorge, Nat. Park; length 1,280 km.

Murcia, prov. and former Moorish kingdom, S.E. Spain, on Mediterranean, irrigated agr., cereals and fruit; cap. Murcia; a. 8.467 km²; p. (1991) 1,046,561.

Murcia, c., cap. of Murcia prov., S.E. Spain; on R. Segura; cath., univ.; textiles and food inds.; p. (1991) 328,847.

Murgab or Murghab, R., Afghanistan; flows 400 km to desert swamps.

Murmansk, spt., Russia; on Kola peninsula; ice-free throughout year; engin., elec. power; fishing, shipbldg.; submarine base; marine power sta. utilising tidal energy projected; p. (1989) 468,000.

Murom, t., Russia; pt. on Oka R.; anc. t.; textiles, engin.; p. (1989) 124,000.

Muroran, spt., Hokkaido, Japan; on W. cst.; impt. iron and steel ctr.; p. (1990) 136,209.

Murray, R., separates N.S.W. and Victoria, Australia; major irrigation schemes support intensive agr.; hydro-electric power; 2,560 km long; length Murray-Darling system 3,696 km.; p. (1992) 109,600 (dist.).

Murrumbidgee, R., N.S.W., Australia; trib. of R. Murray; used extensively for irrigation; 2,160 km long; p. (1992) 148,300 (dist.).

Mururoa, coral Is., S. Pac.; used by France as nuclear testing site; p. (1985) 3,000.

Musa Jebel, mtn., Egypt; 2,249 m; identified with the biblical Sinai.

Muscat, t., cap. of Oman, Arabia; on S. cst. of G. of Oman; gd. harbour; dates, mother-of-pearl; terminal of oil pipeline; p. (1990) 380,000 (met. a.).

Muscat and Oman. *See* Oman.

Musgrave Range, mtns., on bdy. between S. Australia and N.T., Australia; isolated highland in ctr. of continent; arid; rise to 1,520 m.

Muskingum, R., Ohio, USA; trib. of Ohio R.; canalised for navigation; 384 km long.

Musselburgh, burgh, East Lothian, Scot.; on F. of Forth at mouth of R. Esk; wire, cables, nets, twine; paper mkg.; golf course; p. (1991) 20,630.

Mutankiang. *See* Mudanjiang.

Mutari. *See* Umtali.

Mutrah, t., Oman; ch. comm. ctr.; agr. tr.; site of Port Qaboos, deep water pt.; p. (1980) 15,000.

Muttra. *See* Mathura.

Muzaffarnagar, t., Uttar Pradesh, India; N.E. of Delhi; p. (1991) 240,609.

Muzaffarpur, t., Bihar, India; in middle Ganges valley N. of Patna; p. (1991) 241,107.

Mwanza, t., N. Tanzania; pt. on L. Victoria; rly. term.; gold and diamonds mined; p. (1988) 233,013.

Mweelrea, mtn., Mayo, R.o.I.; 820 m.

Mweru, L., between Congo and Zambia; a. 6,993 km² at c. 900 m.

Myanmar, Union of, until 1989 Burma; rep., S.E. Asia; Irrawaddy R. basin, developed by British in 19th cent., forms major cluster of p., routeways and source of rice of which M. is one of few exporters; surrounding mtns. relatively underdeveloped, although they are a source of teak and hardwood exps.; almost self-sufficient in petroleum from deposits in N.; natural gas prod. increasingly impt.; monsoon climate; p. mainly Buddhist; secessionist moves in Moslem Arakan st., ch. ts., Mandalay, cap. Rangoon; a. 676,580 km²; p. (1995) 43,920,000.

Mycenae, anc. c., N.E. Peloponnesus, Greece; excavations by Schliemann.

Myingyan, t., Myanmar; on R. Irrawaddy, S.W. of Mandalay; cotton spinning mill, zinc smelting, chemicals, fertilisers.

Myitkyina, t., Myanmar; on R. Irrawaddy; terminus of caravan route to China.

Mymensingh, t., Bangladesh; rice, jute; p. (1991) 185,517.

Myslowice, t., Katowice, Poland; ctr. of coal-mng. dist.; technical porcelain; p. (1989) 92,009.

Mysore. *See* Karnataka.

Mysore, t., Karnataka, India; univ.; new inds. based on hydroelec. power; p. (1991) 481,000.

Mytilene, pt. Aegean Sea, Greece; ch. c. of I. of Lesvos (sometimes called Mytilene); p. (1981) 24,991.

N

Naantali, t., S.W. Finland; pt. for Turku, on Baltic Sea; oil-refining, chemicals; founded 15th cent.

Naas, co. t., Co. Kildare, R.o.I.; former cap. of Leinster prov.; p. (1986) 10,017.

Naberezhnyye Chelny, t. S. Urals, Russia; S. shore of Nizhnekamsk reservoir; named Brezhnev for a time after Soviet leader; p. (1989) 500,000.

Nabeul, governorate, Tunisia, N. Africa; p. (1984) 461,405.

Nablus, t., Jordan, N. of Jerusalem; nr. site of anc. Schechem and Jacob's Well.

Nadiad, t., Gujarat, India; S. of Ahmadabad; p. (1991) 167,051.

Nagaland, st., India formerly part of Assam; separate st. since 1963; many border disputes; incorporates Naga Hills and Tuengsang; tribal a., cap. Kohima; a. 16,488 km²; p. (1991) 1,209,546.

Nagano, c., central Honshu, Japan; on R. Sinanogawa, 160 km S.W. of Nigata; cultural ctr.; publishing, machin., food-processing; textiles; site of 1998 Winter Olympics. p. (1990) 347,036.

Nagaoka, t., N.W. Honshu, Japan; lge. oil production ctr; p. (1990) 185,938.

Nagapattinam, t., Tamil Nadu, India; spt. at mouth of R. Vettar; exp. cotton, tobacco, groundnuts; rly. terminus; p. (1981) 82,828.

Nagasaki, c., spt., Kyushu, Japan; on narrow peninsula; second c. destroyed by atomic bomb in second world war; impt. shipbldg. ctr. and associated engin.; p. (1990) 444,616.

Nagercoil, t., Tamil Nadu, India; extreme S. of Indian peninsula; coconut-processing; p. (1991) 190,084.

Nagh Hamadi (Nag' Hammâdi), t., Upper Egypt; on R. Nile 256 km above Asyût; site of barrage (opened 1930) to regulate Nile flood and ensure irrigation of Girga prov.; barrage carries Cairo-Shellal rly. across Nile.

Nagorno-Karabakh, aut. oblast, S.W. Azerbaijan; on E. of Lesser Caucasus; forested mtns.; unrest 1990; cap. Stepanakert; a. 4,403 km²; p. (1990) 192,400.

Nagoya, third c. of Japan; on Ise Bay, central Honshu; major pt. and industl. ctr.; univ.; textile mills, ceramic ctr., oil-refining; 16th cent. fortress t.; p. (1990) 2,154,664.

Nagpur, c., Maharashtra st., **India**; univ.; admin. ctr.; textiles; Hindu temples; p. (1991) 1,625,000.

Nagy Banya. *See* **Baia-Mare.**

Nagykanizsa, t., S.W. **Hungary**; industl. ctr.; heavy equipment, glasswks., beer; p. (1997) 52,000.

Nagykörös, mkt. t., N. **Hungary**; in fruit-growing region; wine, food-processing; p. (1997) 27,000.

Nagymáros, t., **Hungary**; on Danube R. between Budapest and Austrian border; site of hydro-electr. dam built jointly with Austria.

Naha, spt., cap. of Okinawa I., Ryuku Is. **Japan**; p. (1990) 304,896.

Nailsworth, t., Gloucs., **Eng.**; in Cotswold Hills 6 km S. of Stroud; p. (1991) 5,242.

Nairn, royal burgh, Highland, N.E. **Scot.**; fishing ctr.; cas.; p. (1991) 7,892.

Nairnshire, historic co., E. **Scot.**, now part of Highland.

Nairobi, c., cap. of **Kenya**; stands at *c*. 1,500 m on edge of Kenya highlands; modern c., 528 km from Mombasa; univ.; tourist ctr.; lt. inds.; steel rolling mill; inland ctr. for containers; wildlife game reserve; p. (1984) 1,103,554.

Naivasha, L., **Kenya**; on floor of Gt. African Rift Valley; alt. 1,800 m.

Najaf or **Nejef**, c., **Iraq**; in Euphrates valley; Shiite Moslem pilgrimage ctr.; p. (1985) 242,603.

Nakhichevan, c. **Azerbaijan**; food and wine inds.; ctr. of Nakhichevan aut. region; p. (1990) 60,100.

Nakhicheva, aut. rep. **Azerbaijan**; borders Iran and Turkey; cotton, tobacco, rice, wheat in irrigated lowlands; salt and mineral deposits; a. 5,439 km²; p. (1990) 300,400.

Nakhodka, t., **Russia**; outpt. for Vladivostok on Sea of Japan; p. (1989) 160,000.

Nakhon Pathom, t., **Thailand**; in central plain, S.W. of Bangkok; mkt. t.; p. (1980) 45,242.

Nakhon Ratchasima, t., **Thailand**; on Mun R., in Korat plateau; rly. junc.; copper deposits nearby; p. (1991) 202,503.

Nakhon si Thammarat, t., **Thailand**; in S. of Isthmus of Kra, on G. of Siam; anc. t.; mkt.; p. (1980) 102,123.

Nakskov, spt., Lolland I., **Denmark**; sugar-refining; p. (1990) 16,037.

Nakuru, t., **Kenya** rift valley (1,837 m), E. Africa; protected bird sanctuary (flamingoes) on L. Nakuru; wool-processing, fertilisers; p. (1984) 101,700.

Nalchik, c., cap. of Kabardino-Balkar aut. rep., **Russia**; in foothills of N. Caucasus; food-processing; tourist resort; p. (1989) 235,000.

Namangan, c., **Uzbekistan**; on Syr Dar'ya R., in Ferghana Valley; textiles, leather; p. (1990) 312,000.

Namaqualand, region, S.W. cst. of **Africa**; divided by Orange R. into Gr. N. in Namibia, and Little N. in Cape Prov., Rep. of S. Africa; semi-arid; a. 259,000 km²; copper, diamonds.

Nam Co (Nam Tso), L., Tibet, **China.**

Namhol. *See* **Foshan.**

Namib Desert, desert a. along S.W. coastal strip of Africa for 1,200 km; very dry a., and almost unused.

Namibe (Moçâmedes) pt. **Angola**, S.W. Africa; rail link to Cassinga mines; p. (1981) 100,000.

Namibia, indep. st. (1990); formerly mandated territory under S.Af. rule; became (1990) 50th member of Commonwealth; scanty rainfall; stock rearing; alluvial diamonds from Lüderitz on Orange R.; copper, lead, zinc mng. in Grootfontein dist.; coal and offshore natural gas discovered; minerals provide 60 per cent exp. earnings; ch. pt. Walvis Bay; cap. Windhoek; summer cap. Swakopmund; a. 824,296 km²; p. (1995) 1,511,000.

Namsos, spt., central **Norway**; on Folda fjord; lumber, fish canning; textiles; copper; p. (1990) 8,437.

Namur, c., cap. of N. prov., **Belgium**; at confluence of Meuse and Sambre Rs.; agr. process-sing, cutlery, glass; p. (1993) 104,372 (c.), 429,536 (prov.).

Nanaimo, t., B.C., **Canada**; pt. on Vancouver I.; timber and allied inds.; fisheries; boating and yachting; tourism; p. (1991) 60,129.

Nanchong, c., Sichuan, **China**; on Kan R.; major transportation and industl. ctr.; textiles, machin., chemicals, paper; tractor wks.; dates from Sung dynasty (12th cent.); p. (1984) 231,700.

Nancheng. *See* **Hanzhong.**

Nancy, c., Meurthe-et-Moselle dep., **France**; industl. and admin. ctr.; univ., cath.; chemical ind. (based on local salt); anc. cap. of duchy of Lorraine; p. (1990) 102,410 (c.), 310,628 (met. a.).

Nanda Devi, mtn., Uttar Pradesh, **India**; in Himalayas, 7,822 m; first scaled, 1936.

Nanded, t., Maharashtra, **India**; p. (1991) 275,000.

Nanga Parbat, mtn., N.W. Kashmir, **India**, in W. Himalayas; alt. 8,131 m.

Nanjing (Nanking), c., Jiangsu, **China**; on Chang Jiang; cap. of China during Kuomintang régime 1928–49; famous seat of learning; tombs of founders of Ming dynasty; lge. motor vehicle plant, electronics, precision instruments, insecticides, cotton cloth, oil-refining; road-rail bridge over lowest reaches of Chang Jiang opened 1969; p. (1992) 2,520,000.

Nanling, mtns., S. **China**; form divide between Rs. flowing N. to Chang Jiang and S. to Xi R.; crossed by historic Cheling and Meiling Passes; alt. mainly below 1,800 m.

Nanning, c., cap. of Guangxi prov., **China**; on Yu R.; ch. mkt. on S. frontier; rice transplanter factory; p. (1992) 1,070,000.

Nan Shan, mtns., central **China**; branch range of Kunlun; rise to over 3,600 m.

Nanterre, N.W. sub. of Paris, **France**; cap. of Hauts-de-Seine dep.; aluminium mftg.; p. (1990) 86,627.

Nantes, spt., cap. of Loire-Atlantique dep., W. **France**; on R. Loire; ocean pt. St. Nazaire; impt. industl. and shipping ctr.; univ., cath., cas.; p. (1990) 252,029 (c.), 492,255 (met. a.).

Nantong (Nantung) c., Jiangsu, **China**; on N. bank of Chang Jiang estuary; cotton; p. (1984) 402,700.

Nantucket, I., Mass., **USA**; official W. end of trans-Atlantic sea-crossing; summer resort; fishing; p. (1980) 3,229.

Nantung. *See* **Nantong.**

Nantwich, mkt. t., Crewe and N. Cheshire, **Eng.**; on R. Weaver, 5 km S.W. of Crewe; brine baths; clothing, food prods.; p. (1991) 11,695; *see* **Crewe.**

Nantyglo and Blaina, t., Blaenau Gwent, **Wales**; in narrow valley 3 km N. of Abertillery; footwear, rubber prods.; p. (1981) 9,862.

Napier, c., N.I., **N.Z.**; pt. and ch. c. of Hawke's Bay prov. dist.; exp. frozen meat; timber processing, fishing; p. (1991) 51,645.

Naples (Napoli), c., Campania, S. **Italy**; spt. on Bay of N., at foot of Vesuvius, opposite anc. Pompeii; exp. food prods.; impt. industl. ctr.; shipbldg., oil refining, food-processing; cultural and artistic ctr.; univ., cath.; tourism; earthquake, 1980; p. (1992) 1,071,744.

Nara, c., S. Honshu, **Japan**; anc. religious ctr. and place of pilgrimage; colossal image of Buddha (16·3 m high); cap. of Japan A.D. 710–84; tourism; p. (1990) 349,356.

Nara Basin, Honshu, **Japan**; agr. dist. serving the Kinki plain; intensive rice and vegetable cultivation.

Narayanganj, c., **Bangladesh**; S. of Dacca in middle Ganges delta; p. (1991) 268,952.

Narberth, mkt. t., Pembrokeshire, **Wales**; nr. head of Milford Haven; p. (1991) 1,801.

Narbonne, t., Aude dep., S. **France**; in Languedoc; nr. Mediterranean cst.; in wine-growing a.; impt. in Roman times; cath., palace (now town hall); p. (1982) 42,657.

Narew, R., **Poland** and **Russia**; flows to R. Vistula nr. Warsaw, *c*. 432 km long; ch. trib. W. Bug.

Narmada, R., central **India**; flows W. through Madhya Pradesh and Gujarat to G. of Cambay; 1,280 km long.

Narrabri, t., N.S.W., **Australia**; 570 km N.W. Sydney; observatory with stellar interferometer.

Narrandera, t., N.S.W., **Australia**; on R. Murrum-bidgee; collecting ctr. for wool, mutton, wheat, fruits produced in irrigated a.

Narrogin, t., W. **Australia**; major ctr. of wheat belt; p. (1981) 4,969.

Narva, t., N.E. **Estonia**; textiles, machin., sawmills; hydroelectric power; founded by Danes 1223; p. (1991) 87,000.

Narvik, spt., N.W. **Norway**; sheltered by Lofoten Is.; ice-free; linked by rly. to iron-ore fields in N. Sweden; scene of fierce sea-battles between British and Germans 1940; p. (1990) 13,873.

Naseby, v., Northants., **Eng.**; battle where parliamentarians under Fairfax and Cromwell beat royalists under Charles I and Prince Rupert 1645.

Nashville, c., st. cap. Tenn., **USA**; pt. on Cumberland R.; rly. ctr.; impt. shipping, industl. and educational ctr.; food and tobacco prods., cellophane, rayon; univs. and colleges; p. (1990) 487,973 (c.), 985,026 (met. a. with Davidson).

Nasik, t., Maharashtra, **India**; on R. Godavari; Hindu pilgrimage ctr.; metal work; p. (1991) 657,000.

Nassau, spt., cap. Bahamas, **W.I.**; exp. forest, sea and agr. prods.; resort; p. (1980) 3,233 (t.), 135,437 (met. a.).

Nassau, l., Cook Is., S. **Pac. Oc.; N.Z.** terr.; uninhabited; radio telegraph sta.

Nasser City, t., **Egypt**; rural development at Kom Ombo, N. of Aswan, for resettlement of 50,000 Nubians before formation of Lake Nasser behind the High Dam.

Natal, spt., cap. of Rio Grande do Norte st., **Brazil**; above mouth of Potengi R.; exp. sugar, cotton, salt, carnauba wax, hides; industl. expansion(02sp); textile mills; airport on main routes from Africa to S. America; p. (1991) 606,541.

Natal, prov., **S. Africa**; subtropical coastal climate; sugar-cane, tea, cereals; coal; cap. Pietermaritzburg; a. 91,385 km²; p. (1985) 2,145,018.

Natanya or **Nathania**, t., **Israel**; resort on Mediterranean cst.; food-processing; p. (1992) 139,700.

Natauna Is., **Indonesia**; I. gr. in S. China Sea, N.W. of Borneo; little developed; a. 2,113 km²; p. 27,000.

Naucratis, anc. c., **Egypt**; between Cairo and Alexandria; excavated by Flinders Petrie and Gardiner.

Naumburg, t., Saxony - Anhalt, **Germany**; on R. Saale; cath.; textiles, leather, toys; p. (1989) 30,706.

Nauplia (Gr. **Nauplion**), pt. and comm. ctr., on E. cst. Peloponnesus, **Greece**; the anc. Argos; first cap. of indep. Greece 1830-4, when it was superseded by Athens; p. (1981) 10,611.

Nauru, I., indep. rep. (1967), central Pac. Oc.; formerly admin. by Australia; coral I., heavily dependent on phosphate-mng.; 80% uninhabitable because of this; island threatened by rising sea levels; a. 21 km²; p. (1990) 8,100.

Navan (**An Uamh**), t., Meath, **R.o.I.**; carpets; lead and zinc ores; p. (1986) 3,660.

Navarre, prov., N. **Spain**; bounded by Pyrenees; thickly wooded; cap. Pamplona; sugar-beet, cereals, cattle, hardwoods, vineyards; former kingdom; p. Basque; p. (1991) 521,940.

Naver, R., Highland, **Scot.**; flows N. to Pentland Firth; valley once densely p., cleared early 19th cent. to make room for sheep.

Naxos, I., **Greece**; in Aegean Sea, lgst. of the Cyclades; famous for wine and fruit; a. 425 km²; p. 19,000.

Nayarit, st. W. **Mexico**; agr.; cap. Tepic; a. 26,979 km²; p. (1990) 816,112.

Nazareth, t., **Israel**; 34 km S.E. Acre; home of Jesus Christ.

Naze, The, headland in Essex, 5 m. s. of Harwich.

Nazilli, t., S.W. **Turkey**; on R. Menderes; agr.; especially olives; p. (1985) 77,627.

Ndjamena (**Fort Lamy**), c., cap. of **Chad Rep.**; at confluence of Shari and Logone Rs.; isolated but ctr. of caravan tr.; airpt.; p. (1993) 529,555.

Ndola, t., **Zambia**; nr. bdy. with Congo, 176 km by rail N. of Kabwe; ctr. of rich copper-mng. a., less impt. lead- and zinc-mng.; minerals despatched by rail E. to Beira and W. to Lobito Bay; oil refining nearby; international airpt. being built; p. (1989) 467,000.

Neagh, Lough, L., **N. Ireland**; lgst. freshwater L. in Brit. Is.; a. 396 km²; drained by R. Bann.

Neath, t., Neath Pt. Talbot, **Wales**; 10 km up R. Neath from Swansea Bay; coal, aluminium inds., oil refining; cas., abbey; p. (1991) 45,965.

Neath Port Talbot, S. **Wales**, unit. auth. created in 1996 from former l. gov. dists. of Neath and Pt. Talbot; p. (1995) 139,600.

Nebraska, st., **USA**; Cornhusker St.; admitted to Union 1867; st. flower Golden rod, st. bird Western Meadowlark; mainly prairie; cap. Lincoln; farming, meat-packing, wheat, maize, hay, potatoes, sugar-beet, apples, wool, livestock, petroleum, cement; a. 200,147 km²; p. (1990) 1,578,385.

Neckar, R., **Germany**; rises between Swabian Jura and Black Forest; flows through Baden-Württemberg to Rhine at Mannheim; 384 km long.

Needles, chalk stacks in English Channel, off W. cst. of I. of Wight, **Eng.**

Neftyne Kamni, t., **Russia**; built on piles over Caspian Sea for Russian oil workers.

Negev, desert, region, S. **Israel**; new a. of irrigated agr.; oil and natural gas.

Negombo, t., S.W. **Sri Lanka**; at mouth of Negombo lagoon; ctr. of coconut belt; metalware, ceramics; p. (1981) 61,376.

Negril Beach, Jamaica; 40 km W. of Montego Bay; new resort to further Jamaica's tourist tr.

Negri Sembilan, st., W. **Malaysia**; on Strait of Malacca; tin and rubber; cap. Seremban; a. 6,682 km²; p. (1980) 573,578.

Negro Rio, R., **Argentina**; flows into G. of St. Mathias, Atl. Oc.; used for irrigation, partly navigable.

Negro Rio, R., **Brazil**; one of ch. tribs. of R. Amazon; rises in Colombia, joins Amazon nr. Manaus; c. 1,520 km long.

Negro Rio, R., **Uruguay**; flows from Brazil border to Uruguay R.; major multi-purpose project at Rincon del Bonete; 800 km long.

Negros, I., **Philippines**; S. of Mindanao; impt. sugar producing I.; copper deposits; a. 12,704 km²; p. (1990) 3,182,219.

Neheim-Hüsten, t., N. Rhine–Westphalia, **Germany**; at confluence of Rs. Möhne and Ruhr; chemicals; part of Arnsberg.

Neijiang (**Neikiang**), c., Sichuan prov., **China**; on To R.; agr. ctr.; p. (1984) 289,100.

Neisse or Nisa, two tribs. of R. Oder, (1) Western or Glatzer Neisse, frontier between Poland and E. Germany, 224 km long; (2) Eastern or Lausitzer Neisse, E. Silesia, Poland, 192 km long.

Neiva, t., **Colombia**; at head of navigation of R. Magdalena; tr. in cattle and coffee; panama hats; p. (1992) 232,610.

Nejd, C. prov.; with Hejaz, forms kingdom of **Saudi Arabia**; mainly desert; impt. oil wells, horses, camels, dates, various fruits; cap. Riyadh; a. 1,087,800 km²;

Nellore, t., Andhra Pradesh, **India**; admin. ctr.; p. (1991) 316,000.

Nelson, R., **Canada**; drains L. Winnipeg to Hudson Bay; length (with its gr. trib. the Saskatchewan) 2,320 km.

Nelson, t., Pendle, Lancs., **Eng.**; on N. flank of Rossendale 5 km N.E. of Burnley; cotton, iron and brick wks., lt. engin., paper; p. (1991) 29,120.

Nelson, c., S.I., **N.Z.**; pt. nr. head of Tasman Bay; fishing, fruit-packing, timber; coalfield; cath.; p. (1991) 37,943.

Neman (Pol. **Nieman**, Ger. **Memel**), R., **Lithuania** and **Belarus**; rises S.W. of Minsk and flows c. 920 km into Kurisches Haff (Courland Lagoon), Baltic Sea, forming sm. delta.

Nene, R., Northants., **Eng.**; rises nr. Naseby and flows 144 km to the Wash.

Nepal, indep. kingdom, S.E. Asia; on S. slopes of Himalayas and inc. Mt. Everest; isolated from India by malarial forested zone of Terai; N. mostly tropical forest and jungle; home of Gurkhas; poor infrastructure hinders development; only 5,000 km of road; agr. in fertile valleys, rice, wheat, maize; forestry impt. but deforestation a problem; growing guerrilla revolt; cap. Katmandu; a. 141,414 km²; p. (1992) 19,360,000.

Nerbudda. *See* Narmada.

Ness, Loch, Highland, **Scot.**; occupies N.E. end of Glen More; forms link in Caledonian Canal; very deep; 36·4 km long.

Neston, t., Cheshire, **Eng.**; on N. side of Dee estuary; residtl.; sea bed engin.; p. (1991) 15,585; *See* Ellesmere Port.

Nestos, R. *See* Mesta.

Netherlands, kingdom, N.W. Europe; bounded by N. Sea, Belgium and W. Germany; comprises 11 provs.; since second world war has taken advantage of location at mouth of Rhine, opposite Thames estuary, to develop lge.-scale coastal inds., inc. iron and steel at IJmuiden, oil refining, petrochemicals at major European pt. complex of Rotterdam–Europort; similarly major industl. growth in conurbation of Randstad Holland in steering economy far away from formerly predominant agr. basis; agr. still impt. and major sea-flood control schemes around IJsselmeer and Rhine estuary have created valuable land for intensive agr. in a densely populated cty.; important discoveries of natural gas in Groningen have turned cty. into major supplier of energy for European mkts.; practises advanced policy of social welfare; EU member; cap. Amsterdam; seat of govt. at The Hague; a. 36,175 km²; p. (1995) 15,424,122.

Netherlands Antilles, 2 gr. of Is. in Caribbean Sea, part of Lesser Antilles; main gr. off Venezuela inc. Curaçao, Bonaire and formerly Aruba; 2nd gr. inc. volcanic Is. of St. Eustatius, Saba, and St. Maarten (S. part only); agr. of sm. importance as a result of low rainfall; benefits from Venezuelan oil ind.; oil refineries in Curaçao; petrochemical inds.; indep. planned; Aruba separated (1986) with full internal self- government; cap. Willemstad; a. 1,020 km²; p. (1994) 202,244.

Netze. *See* **Notec.**

Neubrandenburg, c., Brandenburg, N. **Germany;** fibreglass, machin., chemicals; p. (1982) 620,600 (dist.).

Neuchâtel, can., **Switzerland;** in Jura mtns.; forested with some pastures; cattle, cheese, wine; watches, cutlery, cottons, hosiery; asphalt from Val de Travers; a. 800 km²; p. (1990) 160,600.

Neuchâtel, cap. of Neuchâtel can., **Switzerland;** on N. slope of Lake Neuchâtel; cas.; univ.; watches, jewellery, condensed milk; p. (1990) 33,060.

Neuchâtel, L., **Switzerland;** at S.E. foot of Jura mtns.; drains N.E. to R. Aare; vineyards on S. facing slopes; remains of lake dwellings, anc. Celtic site of La Tène culture.

Neuilly-sur-Seine, sub., W. of Paris, Hauts-de-Seine, **France;** fine bridge and cas.; engin.; p. (1990) 62,033.

Neumünster, t., Schleswig-Holstein, **Germany;** rly. ctr.; leather, paper and textile inds.; p. (1986) 77,900.

Neunkirchen, t., Saarland, **Germany;** iron and steel mngs.; coal mng.; p. (1986) 49,500.

Neuquén, prov., S. **Argentina;** natural gas reserves; pipeline planned to feed urban ctrs. of Pampas; p. (1991) 388,833.

Neuquén, t., cap. of N. prov., **Argentina;** at confluence of Rs. Limay and Neuquén, in ctr. of fruit-farming dist.; p. (1991) 243,803.

Neusalz. *See* **Nowa Sól.**

Neusandetz. *See* **Nowy Sacz.**

Neuss, c., N. Rhine-Westphalia, **Germany;** rly. junc., canal pt.; nr. Rhine, opposite Düsseldorf; metal gds., food-processing; p. (1990) 147,200.

Neustadt, t., Rhineland-Palatinate, **Germany;** on R. Haardt; agr. machinery; impt. wine tr.; p. (1990) 147,200.

Neustadt. *See* **Wiener-Neustadt.**

Neutitschein. *See* **Nov_Ji_in.**

Neva, R., **Russia,** on which St. Petersburg stands; drains L. Ladoga to G. of Finland; navigable but liable to flooding; 74 km long.

Nevada, st., **USA;** Silver St.; admitted to Union 1864; st. flower Sagebrush, st. bird Mountain Bluebird; in Rocky mtns., continental climate; mng. basis of economy gold, silver, copper, tungsten, gypsum, iron, lead; livestock agr.; timber; tourism; ts. inc. Las Vegas and cap. Carson City; a. 286,299 km²; p. (1990) 1,201,833.

Nevers, c., cap. of Nièvre dep., **France;** on R. Loire; anc. iron and steel ind.; porcelain and faience; cath., historic bldgs.; p. (1990) 43,889.

Nevis, I., Lesser Antilles, W.I.; cotton, sugar; ch. t. Charlestown; part of ind. country of St. Kitts-Nevis; separatist demands (1997); a. 130 km²; p. (1991) 8,794.

New Albany, c., Ind., **USA;** on R. Ohio; domestic glassware, furniture, leather, iron and steel, car bodies; p. (1980) 37,103.

New Amsterdam, spt., **Guyana;** on Berbice R.; processes agr. prods. from surrounding lowland.

New Amsterdam, Dutch settlement, Manhattan I., **USA;** taken by English 1664, and renamed New York.

Newark, mkt. t., part of l. gov. dist. of Newark and Sherwood, Notts., **Eng.;** on R. Trent 27 km N.E. of Nottingham; ball bearings, brewing and malting; cas.; coal mining at Bilsthorpe; p. (1995) 104,100 (dist.), (1991) 35,129 (t.).

Newark, c., N.J., **USA;** meat-packing, printing, elec. gds., paints, chemicals, cars, aircraft, leather; p. (1990) 275,221 (c.), 1,824,000 (met. a.).

New Bedford, c., spt., Mass., **USA;** on estuary of R. Acushnet; whale-fishery ctr.; mnfs. cottons, cordage, glass, shoes; resort; p. (1984) 97,700 (c.), 167,700 (met. a.).

Newbiggin-by-the-Sea, t., Wansbeck, Northumberland, **Eng.;** sm. seaside resort; p. (1991) 7,100.

New Brighton, t., Merseyside, **Eng.;** at entrance to Mersey estuary; residtl. dist. of Wallasey; resort.

New Britain, t., Conn., **USA;** iron and brass mnfs.; p. (1990) 148,000 (met. a.).

New Brunswick, maritime prov., **Canada;** forest-clad mtns.; impt. timber inds.; fishing and fish-processing; many minerals; road and rail

link with Prince Edward I.; cap. Fredericton; a. 72,481 km²; p. (1991) 723,900.

New Brunswick, t., N.J., **USA;** on Raritan R.; chemicals, motor lorries, leather, hosiery and hardware; univ.; p. (1980) 596,000 (met. a.).

Newburgh, burgh, Fife, **Scot.;** on S. side of F. of Tay, 13 km E. of Perth; fish. pt.; former linoleum industry; p. (1991) 1,401.

Newburn, t., Tyne and Wear, **Eng.;** on R. Tyne. 5 km W. of Newcastle; pure graphite for nuclear reactors; p. (1991) 42,897.

Newbury, t., l. gov. dist., Berks., **Eng.;** on R. Kennet, 27 km S.W. of Reading; engin., furniture, paper, cardboard box making; mkt.; race-course; controversial by-pass opened, 1998; p. (1995) 142,600 (dist.), (1991) 33,273 (t.).

New Caledonia, overseas terr. of **France;** volcanic I. in S. Pac. Oc.; nickel and chrome deposits; nickel processing; cap. Nouméa; independence movements to establish separate Melanesian reg. in S. Pacific and much unrest since 1984; referendum on full independence planned; a. 22,139 km² p. (1994) 183,200.

Newcastle, c., N.S.W., **Australia;** spt. at mouth of R. Hunter; second c. of st.; lgst. exporter of coal in Australia; iron and steel based on coal resources; new inds. on reclaimed land; mineral sand mng. (rutile, zircon); p. (1993) 454,800 (met. a.).

Newcastle, spt., on Dundrum Bay; Down, N. **Ireland;** resort; p. (1991) 7,214.

New Castle, t., Penns., **USA;** tinplate, glass, steel wire, iron, coal, limestone; p. (1980) 33,621.

Newcastle Emlyn, t., Carmarthenshire, **Wales;** on R. Teifi; p. (1991) 1,506.

Newcastle-under-Lyme, t., l. gov. dist., Staffs., **Eng.;** 3 km W. of Stoke-on-Trent, on Lyme Brook; coal mng.; brick and tile mnfs.; p. (1995) 123,100 (dist.), (1991) 73,731 (t.).

Newcastle upon Tyne, c., met. dist., Tyne and Wear, **Eng.;** spt. on N. bank of Tyne R., 16 km from N. Sea; shipbldg., heavy engin., chemicals; connected by bridges across Tyne to Gateshead; univ., cath., many fine public bldgs., partially preserved in redevelopment of c. ctr.; airport; metro system; p. (1995) 283,100 (dist.), (1991) 189,500 (c.).

New Delhi. *See* **Delhi.**

New England, N.S.W., **Australia;** dist. of N. Tablelands; pastoral cty. for sheep and beef; ch. ts. Armidale, Glen Innes, and Tenterfield.

New England, the six N.E. Atl. sts. of **USA;** Me., N.H., Vt., Mass., R.I., Conn.; humid-continental climate, infertile soils, poor agr. conditions; fishing; recent industl. meta-morphosis as traditional inds. are replaced by modern science-based, high-value inds.; tourism; ch. t. Boston; p. (1990) 13,206,943.

Newent, mkt. t., Gloucs., **Eng.;** 13 km S. of Ledbury; p. (1991) 4,111.

New Forest, forest and heathland, Hants., **Eng.;** relic of Royal Forest; now partly owned by Forestry Commission; pasture, ponies, tourism, residtl.; oil reserves but no drilling yet as conflicts with conservation; ch. t. Lyndhurst; forms l. gov. dist.; p. (1995) 168,800.

Newfoundland, I., with Labrador, prov., of **Canada;** E. of the G. of St. Lawrence; in E. low; in W. rugged mtns., many Ls.; coniferous forest; fishing, cod, salmon, halibut, lobster, seal; lumber, wood-pulp, paper; iron ore, lead, zinc, copper, asbestos; hydroelec. power; climate is severe; cap. St. John's; a. prov. 404,519 km² (I. 112,300 km², Labrador 292,219 km²); p. (1991) 568,474.

New Galloway, burgh, Dumfries and Galloway, **Scot.;** on R. Dee; nearby Clatteringshaws hydroelec. sta..

New Guinea, I., S.W. Pac. Oc.; N. of Australia; equatorial climate; dense forest; central mtn. chain; lge. a. of lowland in S.; divided politic-ally between Irian Jaya in W. (Indonesia) and Papua New Guinea in E.; economically under-developed; a. 831,390 km². *See* **Papua New Guinea, Irian Jaya.**

Newham, inner bor., Greater London, **Eng.;** W. of R. Lea; contained Royal group of London docks (now all closed); p. and industl. decentralisation from a.; p. (1995) 228,400.

New Hampshire, st., New England, **USA;** borders on **Canada;** Granite St.; admitted to Union 1788; st. flower Purple Lilac, st. bird Purple Finch; forested mtns.; agr., fruit-growing; paper and forest prods.; textiles, shoes; granite; cap.

Concord; ch. spt. Portsmouth; ch. mftg. ctr. Manchester; a. 24,097 km²; p. (1990) 1,109,252.

Newhaven, t., East Sussex, **Eng.**; on S. cst. at mouth of R. Ouse, 14 km E. of Brighton; passenger pt. for Dieppe; boat-bldg. and lt. indus.; p. (1991) 11,208.

New Haven, c., pt., Conn., **USA**; on inlet of Long I. Sound; Yale Univ.; firearms, clocks, hardware, radiators, rubber gds.; p. (1990) 130,374 (c.), 530,000. (met. a. with Meriden).

New Hebrides. See **Vanuatu.**

New Holland, v., N. Lincs., **Eng.**; rly. terminus, ferry pt. for crossing to Hull.

New Ireland, volcanic I., **Papua New Guinea**, in Bismarck archipelago; mtnous.; ch. pt. Kavieng; exp. copra; a. (with adjacent Is.) 9,842 km²; p. (1990) 87,194.

New Jersey, st., **USA**; Garden St.; admitted to Union 1787; st. flower Purple Violet. st. bird Eastern Gold Finch; on Atl. cst. plain, adjacent to N.Y. c.; intensive agr., mkt. gardening; heavily industrialised; oil refining, glass sand, zinc, iron ore, clay, chemicals, motor vehicles; cap. Trenton; ch. cs. Newark, Jersey City; a. 20,295 km²; p. (1990) 7,730,188.

Newmarket, t., Forest Heath, Suffolk, **Eng.**; at foot of E. Anglian Heights; horse racing centre; p. (1991) 16,498.

New Mexico, st., **USA**; popular name "Land of Enchantment"; admitted to Union 1912; st. flower Yucca, st. bird Road Runner; N. of Mexico, S. of Col. st.; traversed by Rocky mtns.; dry climate; agr. dependent upon irrigation; dry farming, arable crops, livestock; uranium, potash salts, pumice, beryllium, copper, petroleum; ch. ts., Albuquerque and cap. Santa Fé; a. 315,115 km²; p. (1990) 1,515,069.

New Mills, industl. t., High Peak, Derbys., **Eng.**; at W. foot of Pennines; textile printing, bleaching and dyeing; rayon, paper; confectionery; p. (1991) 9,092.

Newmilns and Greenholm, burgh, E. Ayrshire, **Scot.**; on R. Irvine, 19 km E. of Kilmarnock; muslin and lace curtain mnf.; p. (1991) 3,436.

New Mirpir, t., **Pakistan**; new t. 3 km. from old Mirpur submerged by Mangla L. 1967.

New Orleans, c., spt., La., **USA**; on delta of Mississippi R.; the gr. cotton mart of America, busy comm., mftg. and cultural ctr., home of jazz; sugar refining, oil refining; p. (1990) 496,938 (c.), 1,238,816 (met. a.).

New Plymouth,|02sp|dist., N.I., **N.Z.**; on W. cst. at N. foot of Mt. Egmont; oil and natural gas deposits; dairy-farming; p. (1991) 67,951.

Newport-on-Tay, burgh, Fife, **Scot.**; on S. side of F. of Tay, opposite Dundee; p. (1991) 4,343.

Newport, cap. I. of Wight, **Eng.**; on R. Medina, in gap through central chalk ridge; mkt.; brewing, joinery, bait mnfs.; prison; p. (1991) 20,574.

Newport, mkt. t., The Wrekin, Shrops., **Eng.**; 13 km N.E. of Wellington; p. (1991) 10,964.

Newport, spt., **Vietnam**; on N. outskirts of Ho Chi-minh City; lge. pt. inaugurated 1967.

Newport, t., R.I., **USA**; on Narragansett Bay; fashionable seaside resort; precision instruments; p. (1980) 29,259.

Newport, t., unit. auth. created in 1996 from former l. gov. dist., S.E. **Wales**; on R. Usk, 8 km from its mouth; timber terminal and deep-water berth; engin., iron and steel, aluminium, paperboard, confectionery, chemicals, plastics; p. (1991) 115,522 (t.), (1995) 137,200 (unit. auth.).

Newport News, c., spt., Va., **USA**; on N. shore of estuary of James R. on Hampton Roads; lge. harbour; shipbldg.; outlet for Virginian tobacco and Appalachian coal; p. (1990) 170,045 (c.), 1,396,000 (met. a. with Norfolk-Virginia Beach).

Newport Pagnell, mkt. t., Milton Keynes, **Eng.**; on R. Ouse; mnfs. Aston Martin cars; p. (1991) 12,285.

New Quay, t., Ceredigion, **Wales**; on cst. of Cardigan Bay; fishing; resort; p. (1981) 766.

Newquay, t., Restormel, Cornwall, **Eng.**; on N. Cornish cst.; seaside resort; p. (1991) 17,390.

New Radnor, t., Powys, **Wales**; on slope of Radnor Forest, 10 km S.W. of Presteign.

New Rochelle, t., N.Y., **USA**; on Long I. Sound; residtl.; p. (1990) 67,265.

New Romney, t., Shepway, Kent, **Eng.**; nr. S. cst. to E. of Dungeness; in rich agr. dist. of Romney Marsh; Cinque pt.; old harbour silted up by shingle, now a mile from sea; p. (1991) 8,340.

New Ross, mkt. t. Wexford, **R.o.I.**; brewing and malting; p. (1986) 5,343.

Newry, t., Newry and Mourne, **N. Ireland**; pt. at head of Carlingford Lough; machin., rope, brewing, granite; p. (1991) 21,633.

Newry and Mourne, l. gov. dist., **N. Ireland**; surrounds t. of N., borders R.o.I., Irish Sea; inc. Mtns. of Mourne; p. (1991) 82,943.

New South Wales, st., S.E. **Australia**; first col. established by Brit. in A.; much mineral wealth in tablelands and mtns.; climate equable and well suited to both arable and pastoral agr.; leading agr. st. in Australia; major irrigation schemes in drier E. plains of Murray, Murrumbidgee, and Lachlan Rs.; coal mng. and heavy inds. at Newcastle, Port Kembla, Wollongong; hydroelectric power from Snowy mtns. scheme; lge. concentration of p. in cap. c. of Sydney; a. 801,431 km² (excluding Cap. Terr. of Canberra); p. (1993) 6,023,500.

Newton, t., Mass., **USA**; on R. Charles; in met. a. of Boston; lt. inds.; p. (1980) 83,622.

Newtownabbey, t., l. gov. dist., **N. Ireland**; sub. of Belfast, textiles, lt. inds.; p. (1991) 74,035 (dist.), 56,811 (t.).

Newton Abbot, mk. t., Teignbridge, Devon, **Eng.**; at head of Teign estuary; rly. junc.; pottery, lt. engin.; agr. processing; p. (1991) 23,801.

Newton Aycliffe, t., Durham, **Eng.**; 10 km N.W. of Darlington; new t. (1947); engin., textiles, plastics, paint; p. (1991) 25,085.

Newton-le-Willows, t., Merseyside, **Eng.**; engin., printing, sugar-refining; p. (1991) 19,416.

Newton-Stewart, burgh, Dumfries and Galloway, **Scot.**; on R. Cree, 8 km N. of Wigtown; mkt.; wool, creameries and agr. inds.; p. (1991) 3,673.

Newtown and **Llanllwchaiarn**, mkt. t., Powys, **Wales**; on R. Severn 13 km S.W. of Montgomery; precision instruments, machine tools; p. (1991) 10,548.

Newtownards, spt., mkt., Ards, **N. Ireland**; 11 km E. of Belfast; textile and engin. inds.; p. (1991) 23,869.

Newton St Boswells, burgh, Borders, **Scot.**; p. (1991) 1,108.

New Waterway. See **Nieuwe Waterweg.**

New Westminster, t., B.C., **Canada**; spt. on estuary of R. Fraser; exp. timber; agr. ctr., food-processing and canning; fishing; oil refining; forms part of Vancouver met. a.; p. (1986) 39,972.

New York, st., N.E. **USA**; popular name "Empire St."; admitted to Union 1788; st. flower Rose, st. bird Bluebird; one of 13 original sts., borders Canada on N., faces Atl. Oc. in S.; Adirondack mtns. in N., with lowland in E. alongside L. Ontario; Hudson valley impt. routeway; humid-continental climate; second lgst. st. in p. size and despite p. movement to W., remains major a. of urbanisation (megalopolis) with comm. and industl. activity; ch. ts. inc. Buffalo, Rochester, Syracuse; st. cap. Albany, metropolis New York city; decline of N. ts. offset by inds. from Quebec, leaving Canada because of separatist moves; dairy farming and intensive agr. serve urban mkts.; a. 128,402 km²; p. (1990) 17,990,455.

New York, c., spt., N.Y., **USA**; on N.Y. Bay at mouth of Hudson R.; lgst. c. in USA and one of lgst. in world; comprises 5 bors., Manhattan, Bronx, Queens, Brooklyn, Richmond; originally founded by Dutch settlers as New Amsterdam on Manhattan I.; gr. comm. ctr. and cultural cap.; univ.; fine parks, bridges, skyscrapers, and deepwater harbour; varied inds., inc. clothing, food-processing, printing and publishing, shipbldg.; despite p. and industl. decentralisation concentration of socially needy in c. causing financial difficulties to c. govt.; 2 intern. airports; p. (1990) 7,322,564 (c.), 8,546.846 (met. a.).

New York State Barge Canal (Erie Canal), N.Y. st., **USA**; links Tonawanda on Niagara R. with Hudson R. via the Mohawk gap through Appalachian mtns.; provides through water route from N.Y. to Gr. Ls.; opened as Erie Canal 1825, improved 1918; length 542 km (with branches 840 km), depth 4 m.

New Zealand, indep. sov. st. within Brit. Commonwealth, S. Pac. Oc.; 1,920 km E. of Sydney. Australia; consists of two major Is., N.I. and S.I., separated by Cook Strait, and several smaller Is., inc. Stewart I. to S.; mtnous., glaciated, volcanic; landscapes with superb scenery; dependent upon pastoral prods., taking advantage of equable climate and excellent grass growing conditions, but mainly reliant on Brit. mkts.; economic diversification;

expansion of lt. indus., inc. car assembly, pulp and paper, textiles; oil and natural gas discovered; advanced social services; cap. Wellington; ch. pt. Auckland; a. 268,676 km²; p. (1995) 3,592,400. The Maori name for New Zealand is Aotearoa.

Neyland, t., Pembrokeshire, **Wales**; on Milford Haven; rly. terminus and sm. pt.; p. (1991) 3,006.

Ngami, L., **Botswana**, S.W. Africa; swamp, the remnant of a much larger L.

Ngauruhoe, mtn., N.I., **N.Z.**; an active volcano; 2,292 m.

Niagara, R., forms part of boundary between **Canada** and **USA**; flows from L. Erie to L. Ontario; rapids and famous falls utilised by gr. hydroelec. power sta. heavily polluted with toxic waste; 56 km long.

Niagara Falls, waterfall, Niagara R., on bdy. of **USA** and **Canada**; in two sections, American (51 m high) and Canadian (48 m high), separated by Goat I.; major tourist attraction and hydroelec. power sta.

Niagara Falls, t., Ontario, **Canada**; opposite the falls; hydroelectric power sta.; timber and agr., inds., tourism; p. (1986) 72,107.

Niagara Falls, c., N.Y., **USA**; extends along summit of cliff for 5 km; paper, flour, aluminium, chemicals, hydroelectric power stas.; univ.; p. (1990) 61,840 (c.), 221,000 (met. a.).

Niamey, t., cap of **Rep. of Niger**, W. Africa; one of the termini (the other is Zinder) of the trans-Sahara motor routes; agr. tr. ctr.; p. (1988) 398,265.

Nicaragua, rep., Central America; civil war (1970), lies across isthmus with Pac. Oc. to W., Caribbean Sea to E.; sparsely populated; central mtn. range, marshy E. cst.; tropical rain forest and climate; limited a. of fertile soils but 70 per cent. p. farmers; main exps. coffee, cotton; industl. growth was based on US investment, gold and silver mng.; food shortages caused by war and US trade embargo; declining coffee exports; devastated by 1998 hurricane; cap. Managua; a. 148,006 km²; p. (1994) 4,395,000.

Nicaragua, Lake, S.W. **Nicaragua**; lgst. L. in Central America; 24 km from Pac. Oc., but discharges into Caribbean via San Juan R.; fisheries; 160 km N.W. to S.E., 67 km S.W. to N.E.

Nicaraguan Depression, lowland, **Nicaragua**; contains Ls. Maragua and Nicaragua.

Nice, c., spt., cap. of Alpes Maritimes dep., **France**; on Mediterranean cst., at foot of Alps; pleasant climate and surroundings; adjoins anc. t. of Cimiez; ceded to France 1860 by Sardinia; resort; fruit and flower exp., perfume mftg.; attracting science-based inds.; major airport; p. (1990) 345,647 (c.), 475,507 (met.a.).

Nicobar Is. See **Andaman and Nicobar Is.**

Nicosia, c., cap. of **Cyprus**; agr. tr. ctr.; textiles, cigarettes, leather, pottery mnfs.; remains of Venetian fortifications; mosques; airport; cap. of admin. dist. of Nicosia; tourism; new name Lefkosia (1995); p. (1997) 250,000.

Nidd, R., trib. of R. Ouse, North Yorks., **Eng.**; 80 km long.

Nidwalden. See **Unterwalden**.

Nieder Sachsen. See **Lower Saxony**.

Nieuwe Waterweg, ship canal, S. Holland, **Neth.**; connects R. Lek 11 km below Rotterdam with N. Sea cst. at Hook of Holland.

Nieuwveld Range, mtns., Cape Prov., **S. Africa**; part of S. terminal escarpment of African tableland; overlooks Gr. Karroo to its S.; forms impenetrable barrier to routes; mainly over 1,500 m. max. alt. 1,914 m.

Nièvre, dep., central **France**; traversed by Morvan mtns., forests, arable agr.; cap. Nevers; a. 6,887 km²; p. (1990) 233,300.

Nigel, t., Transvaal, **S. Africa**; gold mng.; industl.; p. (1980) 76,700 (dist.).

Niger, landlocked rep., W. Africa; 90 per cent p. dependent upon agr. but only 3 per cent of land cultivated; livestock (cattle, sheep, goats), cotton; exp. of groundnuts main source of wealth; rainfall diminishes to N. giving way to Sahara Desert; discovery and exploitation of uranium (1967), 75 per cent of exp. earnings in 1980 but now declining; fishing in L. Chad; game hunting; close economic ties with France; cap. Niamey; a. 1,253,560 km²; p. (1994) 8,807,000.

Niger, R., W. Africa; rises nr. sea in outer mtn. zone of W. Africa as R. Tembi, sweeps round by

Timbuktu to delta in G. of Guinea, on circuitous course of 4,160 km, receiving its gr. trib., the R. Benue, about 400 km from the mouth; navigable for 1,600 km; Kainji (Nigeria) hydroelec. plant and dam opened 1969; now organised by international Niger Basin Authority.

Nigeria, fed rep., W. Africa; within Brit. Commonwealth, susp. 1996-9; federation of 19 sts.; climate, wet, tropical in S., increasingly dry to N.; main economic development in S.; exp. agr. prods., especially cocoa; exp. hardwoods; economic growth based on cstal. oil deposits (sulphur free); fall in oil prices causing decline in production and exp.; 2nd oil producer in Africa; former cap. Lagos, lgst. c. Ibadan; cap. Abuja; a. 923,773 km²; p. (1993) 93,300,000.

Niigata, c., Honshu., **Japan**; pt. on W. cst. exp. locally produced petroleum; chemical inds.; p. (1990) 486,097.

Niihama, c., N. Shikoku, **Japan**; on cst. of Inland Sea, 32 km S.E. of Imabari; refines copper obtained from Besshi mines 19 km to the S.; petrochemicals; p. (1990) 129,151.

Nijmegen, c., E. **Neth.**; on R. Waal, nr. German bdr., 18 km S. of Arnhem; Hanse t. in Middle Ages; historic bldgs., univ.; p. (1994) 147,018 (c.), 247,822 (met. a.).

Nijni-Novgorod. See **Gorki**.

Nikko, t., Honshu, **Japan**; famous temples and shrines; tourist resort; p. (1990) 20,128.

Nikolayev, c., cap. of N. oblast, **Ukraine**; major spt. at head of Dnieper-Bug estuary on Black Sea; shipbldg., ctr.; exp. minerals, grains; founded 1784 as fortress; p. (1990) 507,900.

Nikolayevsk, R. pt., Khabarovsk terr., **Russia**; on R. Amur; shipyards; fishing, canning, lumbering, oil refining.

Nikopol, c., **Ukraine**; on Dnieper; manganese mng. ctr.; steel, machin.; p. (1990) 158,000.

Nikšić, t., Montenegro, **Yugoslavia**; N. of Cetinje; bauxite mng., growing industl. ctr.; p. (1981) 72,299.

Nile, longest R. in Africa (see **White Nile** (Bahr-el-Abiad) and **Blue Nile** (Bahr-el-Azrek);); flows through a longer stretch of basin (over 3,920 km in a direct line) than any other R., and along all its windings measures 6,670 km; on Upper Nile navigation is hindered by sudd (floating vegetation); R. rises April, overflows Sept.; formerly cultivation entirely dependent on annual floods, but now assisted by dams, at Asyût, Aswan, Sennar, for regulating flow and navigation; Aswan High Dam completed 1970, but complex problems of delta erosion and dam-lake silting. See also **Egypt**.

Nilgiri Hills, Tamil Nadu, S. **India**; tea-growing dist.; resort a.

Nîmes, c., cap. of Gard dep., S. **France**; in Cevennes; Roman antiquities, notably Maison Carrée; silk, cotton, carpets, wines; tourism; p. (1990) 133,607.

Nineveh, celebrated anc. c., **Iraq**, stood on E. bank of upper R. Tigris, opposite modern Mosul.

Ningbo (Ningpo), c., spt., Zhejiang, **China**; 160 km from Shanghai; leading fish. pt., comm. and mnf. ctr.; exp. agr. and fish prods.; c. opened to foreign investment under new economic reforms; p. (1992) 1,090,000.

Ningxia Hui, aut. region, N.W. **China**; bounded on N. by Inner Mongolia; dry a. but modern irrigation projects allow growth of spring wheat and rice; coal reserves, salt; cap. Yingchuan; a. 66,408 km²; p. (1990) 4,660,000.

Niobrara, R., **USA**; trib. of Missouri R.; flows from Wyoming to Nebraska; 960 km long.

Niort, c., cap. of Deux-Sèvres dep., W. **France**; noted for mkt. gardens and leather gds. (gloves); birthplace of Mme de Maintenon; p. (1990) 58,660.

Nipigon, Lake, in Thunder Bay dist., Ont., **Canada**; 106 km long, 74 km wide; studded with Is.; discharges by Nipigon R. to L. Superior.

Nipissing, Lake, S. Ont., **Canada**; 855 km²; drained by French R. to Georgian Bay.

Niš, t., Serbia, **Yugoslavia**; on R. Nishava; route ctr.; rly. engin., developing mftg.; univ.; p. (1991) 175,555.

Nišava, R., Serbia, **Yugoslavia**; flows N.W. into R. Morava nr. Niš; valley used by trunk rly. from Belgrade to Istanbul; length over 160 km.

Nishapur, mkt. t., N.E. **Iran**; S.W. of Mashhad; in fertile a.; cotton, fruits; famous turquoise mines nearby; birthplace of Omar Khayyám; impt. archaeological finds dating 9th and 10th cent.

Nishinomiya, c., S. Honshu, **Japan**; produces famous liquor called saké; machin., chemicals; p. (1990) 426,919.

Niterói, t., cap. of Rio de Janeiro st., **Brazil**; shipbldg.; residtl. sub. of Rio de Janeiro c. to which it is linked by bridge; p. (1991) 416,123.

Nith, R., S.W. **Scot.**; flows to Solway F., S. of Dumfries; followed by main rly. from Carlisle to Kilmarnock and Glasgow; 114 km long.

Nitra, t. **Slovakia**, on R. Nitra N.E. of Bratislava; first Christian church in region there; agric. industries; p. (1990) 91,000.

Niue (Savage) I., Pac. Oc.; one of Cook Is., overseas terr. of **N.Z.**, self government 1974; ch. pt. Alofi; copra, plaited basketware, sweet potatoes; a. 259 km²; p. (1993) 1,977.

Nivernais, former prov. of **France**, now forming Nièvre prov. and part of Cher.

Nizamabad, t., Andhra Pradesh, **India**; road and rly. ctr. N. of Hyderabad; p. (1991) 240,924.

Nizhneudinsk, t., W. Irkutsk, **Russia**; new mftg. t.

Nizhniy Novgorod, (Gorki), c., **Russia**; cap. of forested region, on Rs. Oka and Volga; univ., churches, 13th cent. kremlin; gr. industl. ctr. with heavy engin., steel, textiles, chemicals, oil refining, cars, glass, timber inds.; birthplace of Maxim Gorky; p. (1989) 1,438,000.

Nizhniy Tagil, t., **Russia**; in Ural mtns.; metallurgical ctr. using ore from Mt. Visokaya; rly. cars, iron, and steel plants, chemicals; p. (1989) 440,000.

No, Lake, Bahr-el-Ghazal prov., **Sudan**; N.E. Africa; vast swamp a., 906 km S.W. of Khartoum; flow of water blocked by papyrus reed and floating weed (sudd).

Nobeoka, t., Kyushu, **Japan**; on E. cst.; p. (1990) 130,615.

Nobi Plain, S. Honshu, **Japan**; at head of Ise Bay; consists of low, badly drained alluvial plain on W. under intensive rice cultivation, with higher, drier, terraces on E. under mulberry, vegetables, pine-woods; very dense urban and rural p.; ch. textile and pottery mftg. a. in Japan; inc. cs. Nagoya, Gifu, Yokkaichi; a. 1,865 km².

Nocera Inferiore, t., Italy; nr. Naples; vegetablecanning, textile mnfs.; p. (1981) 47,698.

Nogales, Sonora, **Mexico**; mng. and agr. ctr.; p. (1990) 107,119.

Noginsk, t., **Russia**; nr. Moscow; textiles, metals; natural gas pipeline from Central Asia projected; p. (1989) 123,000.

Nola, c., **Italy**; at foot of Vesuvius, 19 km N.E. of Naples; ctr. of fertile arable agr. a. in Campania plain; anc. c., home of Giordano Bruno; p. (1981) 30,979.

Nome, c., W. Alaska, **USA**; on Seward peninsula; gold rush (1900); now admin. and route ctr.; airport; tourism; p. (1990) 8,288.

Noord Brabant, prov., **Neth.**; s. of Gelderland; N. half former Duchy; cattle, grain, hops; cap. 's-Hertogenbosch; a. 4,973 km²; p. (1994) 2,259,779.

Noord Holland, prov., **Neth.**; a. 2,722 km²; cap. Haarlem; natural gas in Schermer Polder nr. Alkmaar; p. (1994) 2,457,329.

Noordoostpolder, Overijssel, **Neth.**; land reclaimed from Zuider Zee, 1942; now used for intensive agr.; a. 479 km²; p. (1993) 39,053.

Nord, dep., N. **France**; borders on Belgium and N. Sea; flourishing agr., mng. iron and coal, textile and chemical mnfs.; cap. Lille; a. 5,773 km²; p. (1990) 2,531,900.

Nordenham, pt. on Lower Weser R., Lower Saxony, **Germany**; lead and zinc smelting; fishing; p. (1986) 28,800.

Norderney, one of the E. Frisian Is., **Germany**; low-lying sand-dunes; resort at Nordseebad.

Nordhorn, t., Lower Saxony, **Germany**; nr. Neth. frontier; textiles; p. (1986) 48,000.

Nordkyn, Cape, northernmost pt. of European mainland, Finnmark prov., N. **Norway**.

Nordland, co., N. **Norway**; fjord cst.; p. on cst. lowlands; fishing, livestock; iron-ore, electrochemical and metallurgical inds. based on local hydroelec. power; spt. Narvik; a. 38,146 km²; p. (1990) 238,345.

Nord-Pas-de-Calais, region, N.E. **France**; inc. deps. Nord, Pas-de-Calais; north-eastern corner of France, bordering Belgium; inc. ports of Boulogne, Calais, Dunkirk and southern end of Channel Tunnel; p. (1990) 3,965,100.

Norfolk, non-met. co., E. **Eng.**; low-lying fens in W.; low sandy cst. suffers from erosion; intensive arable agr. on lge. farms; wheat, barley, root crops; inds. based on agr. processing and pro-

vision of agr. requisites; tourism intensively developed on Norfolk Broads; co. t.. Norwich; p. (1995) 772,400.

Norfolk, c., Va., **USA**; naval base on Hampton Roads; fine deepwater harbour; exp. coal, industl. prods.; shipbldg., car assembly, food-processing, timber inds., fertilisers; p. (1990) 261,229 (c.), 1,396,107 (met. a. with Virginia Beach-Newport News).

Norfolk I., remote dependency of **Australia**; Pac. Oc.; volcanic I., 1,676 km N.E. of Sydney; unique ecology; fertile agr.; discovered by Cook 1774; penal settlement 1788–1853; tourism; a. 34 km²; p. (1993) 2,665.

Norilsk, t., Krasnoyarsk terr., **Russia**; in N. Siberia; northernmost t. in Russia; mng. of coal, uranium, nickel, copper; natural gas pipeline from W. Siberia; p. (1989) 175,000.

Normandy, historic prov. of **France**; on English Channel; now divided into deps. Manche, Calvados, Eure, Seine-Maritime and part of Orne; Rouen was cap.; Channel Is. were part of the old duchy; conquered England 1066; allied invasion of Europe 1944.

Normanton, t., West Yorks., **Eng.**; 5 km N.E. of Wakefield; coal mng.; p. (1991) 18,775.

Norman Wells, t., N.W. Terr., **Canada**; at confluence of R. Mackenzie and Gr. Bear R., 112 km W. of Gr. Bear L.; ctr. of rich oil-field; p. (1986) 627.

Norrbotten, prov., N. **Sweden**; rich iron deposits at Kiruna; ore exp. via ice-free Narvik on Norwegian cst.; many Ls. and Rs., highest peak in Sweden, Kebnekaise; cap. Pitea; a. 105,553 km²; p. (1992) 266,089.

Norris Dam, Tenn., **USA**; across R. Clinch at confluence with R. Tennessee, N.W. of Knoxville; lgst. dam Tenn. Valley Authority (TVA); built for flood control and hydroelectric power.

Norrköping, c., S.E. **Sweden**; nr. inlet of Baltic Sea; industl. and shipping ctr.; ocean-going shipping through Lindö canal; p. (1992) 120,798.

Northallerton, mkt. t., Hambleton, North Yorks.; admin. ctr., **Eng.**; in broad gap between Cleveland hills and Pennines; in dairy farming and agr. dist.; p. (1991) 13,774.

North America, northern continent of W. hemisphere; comprises Greenland (on N. American continental shelf), Canada, USA, Mexico; high W. Cordilleras, inc. Rocky mtns., run N. to S. from Alaska to Mexico; lower range of Appalachian mtns. in E. with vast interior basin, inc. Gr. Ls., Saskatchewan, St. Lawrence, and Miss.-Mo. R. systems; gr. variation in climate and vegetation from subtropical in S. and Mediterranean in W. to Arctic in N. and continental in interior; enormous endowment of natural resources provide basis for vast economies of USA and Canada, but contemporary public concern for natural environment of continent; formerly inhabited by Indians, now mainly occupied by a white p. with lge. European minorities, and an African-based, black p.; p. (1994) 373 m. (inc. Hawaii).

Northampton, co. t., l. gov. dist., Northants., **Eng.**; on R. Nene; footwear, engin., leather prods.; new t. designation; p. (1995) 189,700 (dist.), (1991) 179,596 (t.).

Northamptonshire, non-met. co., **Eng.**; E. Midlands; chiefly agr.; iron mng. and mftg.; footwear, engin., leather; p. (1995) 599,300.

North Atlantic Drift, drift of surface waters of Atl. Oc. N.E. from Gulf Stream towards Europe; relatively warm; supplies prevailing S.W. winds with warmth and moisture to modify climate of Brit. Is. and N.W. Europe.

North Ayrshire, unit. auth. created in 1996, formerly part of Strathclyde, W. **Scot.**, borders F. of Clyde and inc. I. of Arran; p. (1995) 139,520.

North Bay, t., Ont., **Canada**; on L. Nipissing; air base; tourism, route ctr.; p. (1986) 50,623.

North Berwick, royal burgh, E. Lothian, **Scot.**; on S. of F. of Forth, 32 km E. of Edinburgh; seaside resort; golf course; fishing pt.; p. (1991) 5,687.

North Beveland, I., **Neth.**; in Scheldt estuary; arable agr.; a. 91 km².

North Carolina, st., S.E. **USA**; Tarheel St.; admitted to Union 1789; st. flower Flowering Dogwood., st. bird Cardinal; bounded on E. by Atl. Oc.; one of 13 original sts.; sandy, indented cst., rising in W. to Appalachian mtns.; humid subtropical climate, modified by alt.; agr. impt., maize, cotton, tobacco; mica; textiles; ch. pt.

Wilmington; cap. Raleigh; a. 136,524 km²; p. (1990) 6,628,637.

North Channel, gives access from Atl. Oc. to Irish Sea between S.W. Scotland (Dumfries and Galloway) and N.E. Ireland (Larne); length 96 km; narrowest width 24 km.

North China Plain, China; alluvial lowland of Huang-He basin; notorious floods but R. now controlled; wheat and millets; very dense p.

North Cornwall, l. gov. dist., **Eng.;** lge. a. on cst. stretching from Bodmin to Bude; p. (1995) 77,800.

North Crimean Canal, Ukraine; links R. Dnieper with Black Sea and Sea of Azov, crossing steppes of S. Ukraine and Crimea, terminating at Kerch; first section (123 km long) opened 1963; when completed will be 352 km long, 200 km of which will be navigable.

North Dakota, st., N.W. **USA;** Flickerhill St.; admitted to Union 1889; st. flower Wild Prairie Rose, st. bird Western Meadowlark; rolling prairie, rising from E.-W.; drained by Missouri R., controlled by multi-purpose Garrison Reservoir; arable agr., mainly grains, but eroded "Badlands" in S.; coal mng., petroleum; cap. Bismarck; a. 183,022 km²; p. (1990) 638,800.

North Devon, l. gov. dist., **Eng.;** inc. Exmoor and ts. of Barnstaple, Ilfracombe and Lynton; p. (1995) 85,600.

North Dorset, l. gov. dist., Dorset, **Eng.;** mainly rural but inc. ts. of Shaftesbury, Sturminster Newton and Blandford Forum; p. (1995) 56,900.

North Down, l. gov. dist., **N. Ireland;** borders Belfast Lough; main ts. Bangor, Holywood; p. (1991) 71,823.

North Downs, Surrey/Kent, **Eng.;** chalk escarpment running E. to W. across S.E. Eng.; form "white cliffs of Dover"; followed in part by Pilgrim's Way; Box Hill 233 m.

North-East China, formerly known as Manchuria, comprising provs.—Liaoning, Jilin, Heilongjiang; mtnous., N.W. and E.; drained to N. by Songhua Jiang and S. by Liao Rs.; forested; soya-beans, wheat, coal, iron; impt. a. for iron and steel; occupied by Japanese in 1931 and returned to China in 1947.

North East Derbyshire, l. gov. dist., Derbys., **Eng.;** industl. a. of Clay Cross and Dronfield; p. (1995) 99,300.

North-East Frontier Agency. *See* **Arunachal Pradesh.**

North East Lincolnshire, unit. auth. created in 1996, formerly part of Humberside, **Eng.;** inc. t. of Great Grimsby and Humberside resort of Cleethorpes; p. (1995) 160,100.

North East Passage, along N. cst. Europe and Asia between Atl. and Pac. *See* **Section L.**

Northern Ireland, part of **U.K.;** occupies N.E. a. of Ireland, consisting of 26 l. gov. dists.; mild, temperate climate, exploited by dairy farming using excellent grass; arable agr. inc. barley, potatoes; traditional inds. inc. linen, shipbldg., food-processing, tobacco; modern inds. encouraged by extensive government aid inc. artificial fibres, carpets, elec. and aero-engin.; heavily dependent upon Brit. mkt.; serious social disturbance after 1969, based upon longstanding religious differences between Roman Catholic and Protestant as a result of discrimination against minority; Stormont Parliament replaced by Assembly (suspended 29 May 1974 and direct rule resumed); new Assembly created (*see* **Section D**); returns 18 members to Westminster (17 prior to May 1997 general election); a. 14,121 km²; p. (1991) 1,577,836.

Northern Marianas, chain of Is., W. Pac.; former US Trust Terr. now a commonwealth in union with USA; a. 479 km²; p. (1995) 47,200.

Northern Territory, self governing st. (1978) N. **Australia;** variable rainfall decreasing inland from N. to S.; land rises generally N. to S. and reaches over 1,800 m in Macdonnell ranges; lge. semi-nomadic Aboriginal p.; livestock agr. dependent upon rail, road access to mkt.; mng.; newly opened uranium mines abuse aborigine terr.; ch. ts. Darwin on N. cst., Alice Springs; a. 1,356,176 km²; p. (1993) 170,500.

Northfleet, t., Kent, **Eng.;** on S. bank of R. Thames, adjoining Gravesend; cement, paper, rubber, tyres, cables; p. (1991) 21,397.

North Foreland, E. Kent, **Eng.;** chalk headland.

North Hertfordshire, l. gov. dist., Herts., **Eng.;** stretches from Baldock, Letchworth and Hitchin to Royston; p. (1995) 114,900.

North Island, I., N.Z.; one of the two major Is. of N.Z., separated from S.I. by Cook Strait, volcanic mtns., Waikato R. drains L. Taupo, cap. Wellington, spt. Auckland, oil deposits on E. and W. csts.; a. 114,688 km²; p. (1991) 2,553,413.

North Kesteven, l. gov. dist., Lincs., **Eng.;** rural a. based on Sleaford; p. (1995) 84,900.

North Lanarkshire, unit. auth. created in 1996, formerly part of Strathclyde, central **Scot.;** lies immediately E. of Glasgow; p. (1995) 326,740.

Northleach, t., Cotswold, Gloucs., **Eng.;** once impt. woollen tr.

North Lincolnshire, unit. auth. created in 1996, formerly part of Humberside, **Eng.;** a. S. of the R. Humber inc. lowland a. of I. of Axholme and ts. of Barton-on-Humber, Brigg, Goole and Scunthorpe; p. (1995) 152,100.

North Little Rock, t., Ark., **USA;** agr. processing, engin.; p. (1990) 61,741.

North Norfolk, l. gov. dist., Norfolk, **Eng.;** cstl. a. inc. Wells-next-the-Sea, Cromer, Sheringham, Walsingham and North Walsham; p. (1995) 95,700.

North Ossetia, aut. rep., **Russia** on N. slope of Gr. Caucasus; cap. Vladikavkaz; agr. in valleys; lead, silver, zinc, and oil deposits with metallurgical and food-processing inds.; a. 8,029 km²; p. (1989) 632,400.

North Platte, t., Nebraska, **USA;** on N. Platte R.; p. (1980) 24,509.

North Platte, R., USA; rises N. Col., flows 1,088 km through Wyo., across W. Nebraska to join S. Platte at c. of North Platte; extensive power and irrigation developments.

North Rhine–Westphalia, *Land,* **Germany;** highly industrialised, coal mng., iron and steel, textiles; cap. Dusseldorf; a. 34,066 km²; p. (1992) 17,510,000.

North River (Beijiang), Guandong, **S. China;** rises in Nanling mtns., flows S. into Xi Jiang delta; 480 km long.

North Sea, arm of the Atl., E. of Gr. Brit., W. of Norway, Sweden, and N. Germany, and N. of Holland, Belgium, and France; length 960 km, width 640 km; gd. fisheries; major natural gas, coal and oil deposits.

North Sea Canal, ship canal, N. Holland, Neth.; connects Amsterdam to N. Sea at Ijmuiden; depth 14 m, length 26 k.

North Shields, t., frm. Tyne and Wear, **Eng.;** Tyne pt.; fishing pt.; marine engines, chain cables, anchors, rope; mkt.; p. (1991) 38,119.

North Shropshire, l. gov. dist., Shrops., **Eng.;** a. N. of Shrewsbury and inc. Market Drayton; p. (1995) 54,400.

North Solomons, Rep. of, formed 1975 when Bougainville I. seceded from Papua New Guinea; p. (1981) 128,794.

North Somerset, unit. auth. created in 1996, formerly part of Avon, **Eng.;** inc. Severnside ts. of Clevedon and Weston-super-Mare; p. (1995) 183,800.

North Tonawanda, t., N.Y., **USA;** on Niagara R.; timber tr., paper mnfs.; p. (1990) 34,989.

North Tyneside, met. bor., frm. Tyne and Wear, **Eng.;** comprises Tynemouth, Whitley Bay and Wallsend; p. (1995) 193,900.

Northumberland, non-met. co., N. **Eng.;** on border of Scot. along Cheviots and R. Tweed; drained by Tyne, Blyth, Coquet Rs.; pastoral agr., especially sheep; coal mng., with former impt. exp. to London and S.E. Eng.; isolation and wild landscape attractive to tourists; p. (1994) 307,700.

Northumberland Straits, separate Prince Edward I. from Nova Scotia and New Brunswick, **Canada;** 14 km combined road and rail tunnel, bridge and causeway to link provs. projected.

Northumbria, Anglo-Saxon kingdom stretching from the Humber to the Forth; conquered by the Danes 9th cent.

North Walsham, mkt. t., North Norfolk, **Eng.;** 22 km N. of Norwich; former wool-weaving ctr.; p. (1991) 9,534.

North Warwickshire, l. gov. dist., Warwicks., **Eng.;** close to Midlands conurb., based on Atherstone; p. (1995) 61,500.

North West Leicestershire, l. gov. dist., Leics., **Eng.;** inc. Ashby de la Zouch, Ashby Woulds, Coalville and Castle Donington; p. (1995) 83,800.

North-West Passage, between Atl. and Pac. along Arctic cst. of **Canada;** potentially of gr. importance as a W. outlet for Alaskan oil; sovereignty claimed by Canada but disputed by U.S.A. who claims it is an internat. strait. *See* **Section L.**

Northwest Territories, N.W. region and terr. of **Canada**; N. of 60° Lat. N., between Yukon (W.) and Hudson Bay (E.); comprises 3 dists., Franklin, Mackenzie, Keewatin; varied physical geography, inc. vast areas of lowland with some of highest peaks in E.N. America; tree-line marks physical bdy. between N. and S.; drained in W. by Mackenzie R.; major inds. gold and silver mng. around cap. Yellowknife, zinc and lead in the High Arctic; petroleum, fur-trapping, fisheries; incr. indep. since 1983; first diamond mine opened (1998); new Inuit self-governing territory of Nunavut came into being 1 April 1999.

Northwich, t., Cheshire, **Eng.**; on R. Weaver; impt. chemical inds. based originally upon local salt deposits, now much subsidence in a. due to salt extraction; p. (1991) 34,520.

North Wiltshire, l. gov. dist., Wilts., **Eng.**; rural a. inc. ts. of Calne, Chippenham and Malmesbury; p. (1995) 121,600.

North York Moors, limestone plateau, North Yorks., **Eng.**; lies S. of estuary of R. Tees, heather moorland; some pastoral farming on lower slopes; alt. varies from 300–450 m; formerly impt. iron-ore quarrying along N. edge.

North Yorkshire, non-met. co., N. **Eng.**; inc. much of former N. Riding; stretches from Pennines (W.) to Vale of York (central), N. York Moors and Yorks. Wolds (E.); crossed by R. Ouse and tribs.; mainly rural, mixed agr.; ch. ts. cstl. resort of Scarborough and spa of Harrogate; p. (1995) 556,200.

Norton-Radstock, t., Bath and N.E. Somerset, **Eng.**; footwear, sm. coalfield; p. (1991) 19,032.

Norwalk, t., Cal., **USA**; oil refining; p. (1980) 85,286.

Norwalk, t., Conn., **USA**; gd. harbour on Long I. Sound; lt. inds., clothing; formerly impt. oyster ind. diminished by industl. pollution; p. (1990) 127,000 (met. a.).

Norway, kingdom, W. Scandinavia, N. Europe; long fjord cst. stretches from Arctic to N. Sea; mtnous.; cool damp climate, influenced by prevailing W. winds; excellent conditions for hydroelectric power and electro-inds.; sm. p. makes N. heavily dependent upon foreign tr., especially exp. of aluminium, wood-pulp, paper, fish; now possesses lge. deposits of petroleum in N. Sea; arable agr. limited to fjord lowlands and a. around cap. Oslo; a. 322,600 km², p. (1994) 4,347,695.

Norwich, c., co. t., l. gov. dist., Norfolk, **Eng.**; on R. Wensum just above confluence with R. Yare; univ.; cath., cas.; cultural and agr. ctr.; food mnfs., footwear, printing; decentralization of office employment from London; p. (1995) 126,700 (dist.), (1991) 171,304 (c.).

Norwich, t., Conn., **USA**; sm. pt. on Thames R.; machin., textiles; p. (1980) 38,074.

Notec (**Netze**), R., **Poland**; trib. R. Warta; partially navigable; 224 km long.

Notodden, t., S. **Norway**; nr. Tinnfoss falls which provide hydroelectric power; iron smelting, nitrates; p. (1990) 8,275.

Nottingham, c., co. t., l. gov. dist., Notts., **Eng.**; a bridging point over Trent R.; lace, hosiery, tobacco, pharmaceutical and cycle inds.; univ., cas.; p. (1995) 283,800 (dist.), (1991) 270,222 (c.).

Nottinghamshire, non-met. co., Midlands, **Eng.**; contains part of productive E. Midlands coalfield serving many power stas. along Trent R.; urban growth concentrated mainly on coalfield; engin., hosiery; wheat, barley, cattle, roses; brilliantly characterised in writings of D. H. Lawrence; p. (1995) 1,031,900.

Nouadhibou, pt., **Mauritania**; new pt. for bulk carriers to exp. iron ore; fish processing plants; pelletizing plant; p. (1988) 59,198.

Nouakchott, t., cap. of **Mauritania**, W. Africa; comm. ctr. on caravan route; tr. in agr. prods.; planned industl. zone; rapid growth with mass migration of nomadic p. to shanty ts. as response to Sahelian drought; p. (1988) 393,325.

Nouméa (**Port de France**), t., cap. of Fr. **New Caledonia**; ch. pt. of Is.; exp. nickel, chrome; p. (1983) 60,112.

Nouvelle Amsterdam, I., **Indian Oc.**; part of Fr. Southern and Antarctic Terrs.; volcanic; ctr. of meteorological research; a. 65 km².

Nova Friburgo, t., Rio de Janeiro, **Brazil**; health resort; p. (1985) 144,000.

Nova Iguaçú, t., Rio de Janeiro, **Brazil**; steel, tyres, chemicals; p. (1991) 1,286,337.

Nova Lima, t., Minas Gerais st., **Brazil**; in Serra do Espinhaço, 16 km S. of Belo Horizonte; adjacent to impt. gold-mines of Morro Velho; p. (1985) 47,400.

Nova Lisboa (**Huambo**), central **Angola**, Africa; E. of Benguela; rly. repair shops; agr. comm. ctr.; p. (1995) 400,000.

Novara, c., cap. of N. prov., N. **Italy**; agr. and mnf. ctr., textiles, chemicals, cheese; Romanesque church; p. (1992) 102,029.

Nova Scotia, maritime prov., **Canada**; mainly fertile upland and rich valleys with agr. aided by temperate maritime climate; fruit, livestock, dairying; forested uplands along cst. nr Bay of Fundy give rise to impt. timber inds. with many pts. along indented cst.; fishing and fish-processing; local coal supplies, iron and steel ind.; cap. Halifax; a. 54,556 km²; p. (1991) 899,942.

Novaya Kakhovka, c., **Ukraine**; built (1951) on K. Sea nr. hydroelec. power sta. on Dnieper R.; tourism; p. (1990) 57,700.

Novaya Zemlya, archipelago, Arctic Oc. **Russia**; 2 main Is.; lofty and rugged, severe climate; nuclear testing a.; a. 90,750 km².

Novgorod, c., **Russia**; on Volkhov R. nr. exit from L. Ilmen; food and timber inds., engin.; in mediaeval times gr. comm. and cultural ctr., cap. of an indep. rep.; architectural monuments; damaged by Germans in second world war; p. (1989) 229,000.

Novi Sad, c., Serbia, **Yugoslavia**; R. pt. on Danube R., formerly royal free c.; almost destroyed by Austrians 1849; tr. in fruit, wine, vegetables, corn; Danube bridges attacked by NATO, 1999; p. (1991) 178,896.

Novokuybyshevsk, t., **Russia**; S.W. of Kuybyshev; lge. oil processing plant; p. (1989) 113,000.

Novo Kuznetsk, c. **Russia**; grew up as iron and steel ctr. of Kuznetsk Basin; engin., chemicals, aluminium, ferro-alloys; p. (1989) 600,000.

Novomoskovsk, c., **Russia**; on R. Don; lignite, fertilisers, p. (1989) 146,000.

Novorossiisk, spt., **Russia**; on N.E. cst. of Black Sea; engin., textiles; lgst. cement producer in Russia; exp. industl. prods.; p. (1989) 186,000.

Novoshakhtinsk, c., **Russia**; on Rostov–Kharkov highway; coal mng., chemicals; p. (1989) 108,000.

Novosibirsk, c., **Russia**; on Ob R. and Trans-Siberian rly.; lgst. industl. ctr. of Siberia, nr. Kuznetz Basin; hydroelec. power; varied inds., uranium nearby; univ.; p. (1989) 1,437,000.

Novo Troitsk, t., **Russia**; in Urals, 18 km S.W. of Orsk; cement, special steels; p. (1989) 106,000.

Novovoronezh, Russia; on R. Don, S. of Voronezh; nuclear power sta.

Nowa Huta, t., **Poland**; 10 km S.E. Kracόw on Vistula R.; heavily polluted Lenin metallurgical combine and modern residtl. a. within c. of Kracόw; p. (1989) 224,386.

Nowa Sól (**Neusalz**), t., Zielona Góra, **Poland**; pt. on R. Oder; metal-working, food and timber inds.; p. (1989) 43,053.

Nowgong, t., Assam, **India**; agr. and comm. ctr.; rice, tea.

Nowra-Bomaderry, t., N.S.W., **Australia**; on E. cst. at mouth of Shoalhaven R.; expanded (1979) into c. of Shoalhaven; collecting ctr. for coastal agr. prod.; powdered milk, paper mill; p. (1981) 17,887.

Nowy Sacz, t. and prov., S. **Poland**; on Dunajec R.; lignite nearby; rly. engin., mftg.; ctr. of a. renowned for beauty and tourist attractions; p. (1989) 76,658.

Noý Jičín (**Neutitschein**), t., Moravia, **Czech Rep.**; farm machin., and eng.

Nubia, anc. region, N.E. **Africa**, extending on both sides of Nile from first cataract at Aswan to Khartoum, Sudan; largely desert, some irrigation alongside Nile.

Nueva Esparta, st., **Venezuela**; consists of over 70 Is.; impt. fisheries; cap. La Asunción; a. 1,150 km²; p. (1990) 280,777.

Nueva San Salvador, t., **El Salvador**; agr. comm. ctr. in coffee-growing and livestock region; p. (1992) 116,575.

Nuevo Laredo, c., N.E. **Mexico**; entry point for American tourists driving to Mexico; tr. ctr. in pastoral and arable agr. a.; p. (1990) 217,912.

Nuevo Léon, st., N.E. **Mexico**; arable agr. needs irrigation in arid climate; impt. iron and steel inds.; cap. Monterrey; a. 65,097 km²; p. (1990) 3,086,466.

Nuku'alofa, cap. of Polynesian kingdom of **Tonga**; p. (1986) 28,899.

Nukus, c., cap. of Karakalpak aut. rep., **Uzbekistan**;

on Amu Dar'ya R. in Khorezm oasis; clothing inds.; p. (1985) 139,000.

Nullarbor Plain, S. **Australia;** low, level, limestone plateau fringing Gr. Australian Bight; arid; treeless, salt-bush scrub; crossed by Trans-continental rly. between Naretha (W. Australia) and Ooldea; rly. is dead straight, dead level for 477 km.

Numazu, t., Honshu, **Japan;** nr. Tokyo; ctr. of industl. dist. with varied mnfs. inc. machin.; p. (1990) 211,731.

Nunavut, self-gov. region, **Canada;** capital Iqaluit; estab. 1999 from N.W. Territories; area larger than Alaska.

Nuneaton, t., part of l. gov. dist. of **Nuneaton and Bedworth,** Warwicks., **Eng.;** on Anker R.; coal mng., textiles, lt. inds.; mkt.; birthplace of George Eliot; p. (1995) 119,000 (dist.), (1991) 66,715 (t.).

Nunivak, I., Alaska, **USA;** lge. reindeer herds.

Nunjiang, former prov., N.E. **China;** crossed by Nen Jiang, trib. of Songhua Jiang; now part of Heilung-kiang prov.

Nürnberg (Nuremberg), c., Bavaria, **Germany;** historic c. of architectural beauty; indust.. ctr. with elec. mnfs., machin., heavy vehicles, precision instruments, chemicals, toys, pencils and crayons; rly. junc.; inland pt. on Rhine–Danube waterway; p. (1990) 494,900.

Nusa Tenggara, Is., **Indonesia;** part of Lesser Sunda Is.; p. (1980) 5,461,830.

Nuwara Eliya, hill t., (c. 1,800 m), **Sri Lanka;** health resort; p. (1981) 20,471.

Nyasa, L. See Malawi L.

Nyasaland. See Malawi.

Nyíregyháza, t., N.E. Hungary; ctr. of reclaimed agr. a.; mkt. for tobacco, wine, fruits; domestic ware; p. (1997) 113,000.

Nyborg, pt., Denmark; on Fyn I.; terminal of train-ferry across Gr. Belt; shipyards; textile ind.; p. (1990) 18,207.

Nykøbing, spt., Falster I., **Denmark;** admin. ctr. of Storstrøms prov.; p. (1990) 25,214.

Nyköping, spt., **Sweden;** at head of inlet on Baltic cst.; comm. and industl. ctr.; p. (1992) 68,093.

Nystad. See Uusikaupunki.

O

Oadby, t., Leics., **Eng.;** 5 km S.E. of Leicester; footwear; part of l. gov. dist. of **Oadby and Wigston,** S. of Leicester; p. (1995) 53,200 (dist.), (1991) 18,538 (t.).

Oahu, I., **Hawaii,** Pac. Oc.; sugar, pineapples; tourist tr.; cap. Honolulu; a. 1,564 km²; p. (1988) 838,500.

Oakengates, t., The Wrekin, Shrops., **Eng.;** 24 km N.W. of Wolverhampton; iron and steel, pre-cast concrete, engin.; now part of new t. of Telford; p. (1991) 27,366.

Oakham, t., Rutland, **Eng.;** mkt.; hosiery, footwear; p. (1991) 8,691.

Oakland, c., Cal., **USA;** on San Francisco Bay; residtl. sub.; cars, shipbldg., fruit canning, elec. machin., clothing, tanneries, chemicals; p. (1990) 372,242 (c.), 2,083,000 (met. a.).

Oak Park Village, t., Ill., **USA;** now included in Chicago; birthplace of Ernest Hemingway; p. (1980) 54,887.

Oak Ridge, t., Tenn., **USA;** Atomic Energy Commission's major research ctr.; p. (1990) 27,310.

Oamaru, bor., spt., S.I., **N.Z.;** wool, frozen meat; exp. agr. prods.; p. (1987) 12,550.

Oaxaca, st., Pac. cst., S. **Mexico;** mtnous.. subsistence agr. in fertile valleys; comm. prod. of coffee, cotton, tobacco; stock-raising; mng. in mtns.; cap. Oaxaca; a. 94,201 km²; p. (1990) 3,021,513.

Oaxaca, c., cap. of O. st., S. **Mexico;** stands at c. 1,500 m; coffee; gold and silver mines; handi-craft mkt.; table linen weaving, wool zarapes; tourist ctr.; p. (1990) 212,943.

Ob', R., W. Siberia, **Russia;** one of the world's lgst. Rs., flows from Altai mtns. to G. of Ob'; crossed by Turk-Sib. rly. at Barnaul and by Trans-Siberian rly. at Novosibirsk; ch. trib. Irtysh; hydroelec. power; navigable; oilfields in middle section; outlet of Ob basin Novy-Port (Gdansk); plans to divert waters to irrigate Kazakhstan by 2,500 km canal; 4,160 km long.

Oban, spt., burgh, Argyll and Bute, **Scot.;** on F. of Lorne; resort; ctr. for local shipping; woollens, tartans; p. (1991) 8,203.

Obed, Alberta, **Canada;** 240 km W. of Edmonton;

major natural gas a.

Obeid, El, t., Kordofan, **Sudan;** economically dependent upon rly. link to Khartoum; agr. tr. ctr.; p. (1983) 140,024.

Oberammergau, v., Upper Bavaria, **Germany;** scene of decennial Passion Play; winter sports; p. (1989) 4,980.

Oberhausen, t., N. Rhine–Westphalia, **Germany;** industl. ctr. of Ruhr conurb.; rly. junc., canal pt.; p. (1990) 224,000.

Obihiro, t., Hokkaido, **Japan;** mkt; sugar-beet refining, flax, dairy prods.; p. (1990) 167,389.

Obuasi, t. **Ghana,** W. Africa; ctr. of gold mng.; lge. deep-level mine, modernised 1984.

Obwalden, demi-canton, **Switzerland;** a. 492 km²; p. (1990) 28,800.

Ocean City, t., N.J., **USA;** seaside resort founded by the Methodists; p. (1980) 13,949.

Ocean I. (Banaba), Kiribati, Pac. Oc.; high grade phosphate (guano) worked by Brit.; p. (1990) 284.

Oceania, name given to the Is. of the Pacific; comprising Australasia, Polynesia, Melanesia, Micronesia; p. (1995) 28,000,000.

Ochil Hills, volcanic hill-range, **Scot.;** stretching 40 km N.E. to S.W. from F. of Tay to nr. Stirling; loftiest Ben Cleugh, 721 m; beautiful glens and valleys.

Odawara, t., **Japan;** pt. with rail connections to Tokyo, 48 km to N.E.; p. (1990) 193,417.

Odemis, t., Asiatic Turkey; N.E. of Aydin; to-bacco, cereals, silk, cotton, flax, olives, raisins, figs; minerals; p. (1985) 47,475.

Odense, spt., **Denmark;** admin. ctr. of Fyn prov.; varied inds.; exp. dairy prod.; birthplace of Hans Andersen; p. (1990) 176,133.

Odenwald, forested hills, Hesse and Baden-Württemberg, **Germany;** highest point Katzen-buckel 626 m.

Oder (Pol. **Odra**), R., central **Europe;** flows from Moravia to Baltic through Silesia and Pomer-ania, forming from junc. with Neisse R. fron-tier between Poland and Germany, ch. trib. Warta R.; impt. comm. waterway below Wroclaw; 896 km long.

Odessa, t., Texas, **USA;** impt. oil ctr., chemicals, foundry prod., livestock tr.; p. (1990) 89,699.

Odessa, spt., **Ukraine;** on Black Sea; cultural, industl. ctr.; cath., univ.; gr. grain exp.; engin., oil refining, chemicals; ice-bound for a few weeks in winter; p. (1990) 1,106,400.

Offaly, co., Leinster, **R.o.I.;** much marshy land (inc. Bog of Allen), barren uplands (inc. Slieve Bloom); pastoral agr., wheat; p. mainly rural; agr. processing inds. in ts.; co. t. Tullamore; a. 1,999 km²; p. (1986) 59,835.

Offa's Dyke, earthwork constructed by Offa, king of Mercia (757–96) as bdy. between the English and the Welsh; still forms part of border between the two countries; long-distance footpath along the Welsh marches, 269 km.

Offenbach, t., Hesse, **Germany;** on R. Main; cas., leather museum; machin., chemicals, leather gds., metals; p. (1990) 115,200.

Offenburg, t., Baden-Württemberg, **Germany;** on R. Kinzig; textiles, glass, rly. junc.; cas.; p. (1986) 50,500.

Ogaden, arid region, S.W. **Ethiopia;** on border of Rep. of Somalia. Territory still disputed by Somalia.

Ogaki, t., Honshu, **Japan;** route ctr. in lowland em-bayment, 40 km N.W. of Nagoya; p. (1990) 148,281.

Ogbomosho, t., S.W. **Nigeria;** ctr. of agr. dist.; cotton weaving; p. (1992) 660,600.

Ogden, c., Utah, **USA;** stands at 1,324 m., nr. Gr. Salt L.; rly. ctr.; beet-sugar, meat-packing, flour-milling, clothing, cement; p. (1980) 64,407.

Ogdensburg, c., pt., N.Y., **USA;** on St. Lawrence R., opposite Prescott; impt. R. pt.; p. (1980) 12,375.

Ogmore Vale, t., Bridgend, **Wales;** in narrow valley, 10 km N. of Bridgend; industl.; cas.; p. (1991) 6,693.

Ogooué, R., Gabon, **Congo;** site of Schweitzer's hospital at Lambaréné; 800 km long.

Ohau, Lake, S.I., **N.Z.;** in Mt. Cook dist.; fed by glaciers; 19 km by 35 km; hydroelectric power potential.

Ohio, R., trib. of Mississippi R., **USA;** formed in Penns., by junc. of Monongahela and Alleg-heny Rs. at Pittsburgh, thence navigable for 1,560 km to Cairo in Ky.; an impt. comm. waterway for industl. raw materials; flood pro-tection schemes.

Ohio, st., N. **USA**; Buckeye St.; admitted to Union 1803; st. flower Scarlet Carnation, st. bird Cardinal; gr. agr. and industl. region; maize, wheat, cattle; major deposits of coal form basis of heavy inds., especially in major ts. of Cleveland, Cincinnati, Toledo, Akron, Dayton, Youngstown; petroleum; timber inds.; cap. Columbus; a. 106,508 km²; p. (1990) 10,847,115.

Ohre (**Eger**), R., Bohemia, **Czech Rep.**; rises in Fichtelgebirge, flows N.E. into Labe (Elbe) and through Karlovy Vary; 224 km long.

Ohrid or **Ochrida**, L., forms part of bdy. between **Albania** and **Macedonia**; alt. c. 850 m; deepest L. in Balkans; scenic tourist a.; monasteries on shores.

Ohrid or **Ochrida**, t., Macedonia, **Yugoslavia**; on N.E. shore of L.; airport and tourist ctr.; p. (1981) 64,245.

Oich, Loch, Gr. Glen, Highland, **Scot.**; forms part of Caledonian Canal.

Oise, dep., N. **France**; traversed by R. Oise; fertile, forested; cap. Beauvais; a. 5,884 km²; p. (1990) 725,600.

Oise, R., trib. of R. Seine, **France**; canalised navigable to Chauny; 298 km long.

Oita, c., spt., N.E. Kyushu, **Japan**; on Beppu Bay; wire, carbon, iron, and steel; oil refinery; p. (1990) 408,502.

Ojos del Salado, mtn., N.W. **Argentina**; alt. 6,884 m.

Oka, R., Kursk, **Russia**; rises S. of Orel, flows past Kaluga, Serpukhov, Kolomna, Ryazan, Murom, to become trib. of Volga at Gorki; navigable, carrying grain and timber; 1,520 km long.

Oka, R., Irkutsk, Siberia, **Russia**; joins Angara R. below Bratsk; 800 km long.

Okavango, R.; rises in **Angola**, flows to Ngami depression, **Botswana**, where it forms swampy delta; 1,600 km long.

Okayama, c., Honshu, **Japan**; textiles; lt. inds.; p. (1990) 593,730.

Okazaki, t., Honshu, **Japan**; nr. G. of Ovari; industl. ctr.; textiles, chemicals, machin.; p. (1990) 306,821.

Okeechobee, L., S. Fla., **USA**; drains to Atl. Oc. via Everglades; tourist attraction especially for fishing; also comm. fisheries.

Okefenokee, swamp, Ga./Fla., **USA**; forms O. Nat. Wildlife Refuge.

Okehampton, mt. t., West Devon, **Eng.**; on N. flank of Dartmoor; granite quarries; p. (1991) 4,841.

Okha, spt., E. cst. Sakhalin I., **Russia**; exp. petroleum; lge. refinery.

Okhotsk, Sea of, N.E. **Asia**; 1,600 km by 800 km; enclosed by the Siberian mainland, Kamchatka, the Kurils and Sakhalin I.

Oki Is., off cst. of Honshu, **Japan**; a. 350 km².

Okinawa, I., **Japan**, under U.S. control until 1972; lgst. and most impt. of Ryuku Is. US air bases at Kadena and cap. Naha; a. 1,500 km²; p. (1990) 1,222,398.

Oklahoma, st., **USA**; Sooner St.; admitted to Union 1907; st. flower Mistletoe, st. bird Scissor-tailed Fly-catcher; prairie, plains and mtns.; continental climate; cereals, cotton, stock-raising; petroleum, gas, zinc, coal, gypsum, lead; ch. ind. petroleum refining; cap. Oklahoma City; a. 181,090 km²; p. (1990) 3,145,585.

Oklahoma City, c., cap. of Okla. st., **USA**; univ.; livestock mkt.; tr. and processing ctr.; oil and by-prods., field machin., flour mills, meat-packing; scene of horrific extremist bombing, April 1995; p. (1990) 444,719 (c.), 959,000 (met. a.).

Oktyabrsky, t., Bashkir aut. rep., **Russia**; on R. Ik; in new oil-mng. dist., the "New Baku"; p. (1989) 105,000.

Öland, I., Baltic Sea; off E. cst. **Sweden**; connected by Europe's longest bridge to mainland; agr., limestone quarries; ch. t. Borgholm; seaside resorts; a. 1,341 km²; p. (1983) 23,874.

Oldbury. *See* **Warley**.

Oldbury-on-Severn, S. Gloucs., **Eng.**; nuclear power sta.

Old Castile, historical div., **Spain**; now divided into Santander, Soria, Segovia, Logrono, Avila, Valladolid, Palencia, and Burgos provs.

Oldenburg, c., Lower Saxony, **Germany**; on R. Hunte nr. Hunte–Ems canal; rly. junc.; mkt. for horses and cattle; lt. inds.; natural gas nr. to cst.; p. (1990) 143,800.

Oldham, c., met. dist., Gtr. Manchester, **Eng.**; on R. Medlock, 11 km N.E. of Manchester; manmade fibre and cotton textiles, machin.; industl. diversification inc. electro- and aero-engin., leather, paints; p. (1995) 220,000 (dist.), (1991) 103,931 (c.).

Oldmeldrum, burgh, Aberdeenshire, **Scot.**; 6 km N.E. of Inverurie; p. (1991) 1,976.

Olenek, R., **Russia**; N. Siberia; flows W. of Lena R. into Laptev Sea, Arctic Oc.; abounds in fish; 2,160 km long, 960 km navigable.

Oléron, Ile d', I., Charente-Maritime dep., **France**; lies off estuary of Charente, Bay of Biscay; oysters, early vegetables; a. 176 km².

Olifant, R., Transvaal, **S. Africa**; trib. of Limpopo; irrigation scheme for intensive agr. in valley.

Olinda, c., Pernambuco st., **Brazil**; seaside resort; phosphates; p. (1991) 340,673.

Oliva, t., Valencia, **Spain**; nr. Alicante; wine dist., ducal palace; p. (1981) 19,232.

Olivos, sub., Buenos Aires, **Argentina**.

Olmütz. *See* Olomouc.

Olney, t., Milton Keynes, **Eng.**; mkt., dairy produce; annual Shrove Tuesday pancake race; p. (1991) 4,484.

Oloibiri, S. **Nigeria**; oilfields; pipeline to Pt. Harcourt, 128 km W.

Olomouc (**Olmutz**), Czech Rep.; industl. ctr., steel wks., elec. equipment, textiles, food prod.; cath., univ.; formerly one of ch. fortresses of Austria; p. (1990) 107,000.

Oloron-Sainte-Marie, t., Pyrénées-Atlantique, **France**; in Pyrenean foothills; caths.; p. (1982) 12,237.

Olsztyn (**Allenstein**), t., and prov. N.W. **Poland**; on R. Alle, 160 km N. of Warsaw; cas.; machin., wood inds.; p. (1989) 160,956 (t.) 746,200 (prov.).

Olten, t., N. **Switzerland**; rly. junc., on R. Aare; p. (1986) 18,025.

Olympia, anc. c., Peloponnesus, S. **Greece**; at confluence of Alphaeus and Cladeus Rs.; site of gr. temple of Zeus and scene of Olympic games; modern v. of O. nearby; museum.

Olympia, cap. of Washington st., **USA**; spt. on Puget Sound; exp. timber; machin., agr.-processing inds.; p. (1984) 29,200 (c.), 138,300 (met. a.).

Olympus, Mt., highest mtn. in **Greece**; on border of Thessaly and Macedonia, nr. Aegean cst.; alt. 2,975 m; regarded by anc. Greeks as home of the Olympian gods.

Omagh, t., l. gov. dist., **N. Ireland**; on R.; Stule agr. mkt.; tourist ctr.; p. (1991) 45,809 (dist.), 17,280 (t.).

Omaha, c., Nebraska, **USA**; on Missouri R.; one of lgst. livestock and meat-packing ctrs. in US, gold and silver smelting and refining, steel fabrication, industl. alcohol prod.; univ.; p. (1990) 335,795 (c.), 618,000 (met. a.).

Oman (**Muscat and Oman** until 1970), sultanate, S.W. Asia; fertile coastal plain, interior desert plateau; irrigated agr., especially impt. for dates; fishing; oil discovered 1964, now main exp.; a. 212,380 km²; p. (1994) 2,097,000.

Oman, G. of, Arabian Sea; connected through strait of Kormuz to Persian G.; length 480 km, width 208 km.

Omaruru, t. and dist. **Namibia**; creamery; aerodrome; p. (1991) 7,446 (dist).

Omdurman, c., central **Sudan**; on Nile, opposite Khartoum; site of Mahdi's tomb; here Kitchener defeated the dervishes 1898; native mkts.; p. (1983) 526,287.

Ometepe, I., L. Nicaragua, **Nicaragua**; volcanic; alt. 1,753 m.

Omsk, c., W. Siberia, **Russia**; at confluence of Irtysh and Om Rs.; major R. pt. on Trans-Siberian rly.; in agr. region; engin., chemicals, textiles, oil refining, food processing; cath.; founded as fortress 1716; p. (1989) 1,148,000.

Omuta, t., W. Kyushu, **Japan**; on Amakusa Sea; local coal at Miike giving rise to chemical inds.; pt. exp. coal; p. (1990) 150,461.

Onega, Lake, **Russia**; between L. Ladoga and White Sea; second lgst. L. in Europe (L. Ladoga is lgst.); a. 9,751 km²; ch. c. Petrozavodsk; Onega canal forms part of Volga-Baltic waterway.

Onega, R., **Russia**; flows to G. of Onega; 640 km long.

Onitsha, t., **Nigeria**; on R. Niger; agr. tr. ctr.; p. (1992) 336,600.

Ontario, prov., **Canada**; bounded on N. by Hudson Bay, on S. by Gr. Ls.; extreme continental climate in N., milder in S. peninsula; extensive coniferous forest in N.; temperate agr. in S.; leading mineral producer, nickel, uranium, copper, gold; well-developed inds. using plentiful hydroelectric power; agr.-processing, machin., engin.; cap. Toronto;

contains fed. cap. of Ottawa; a. 1,068,587 km²; p. (1991) 10,084,885, concentrated in S.E.

Ontario, L., N. America; smallest of the Gr. Ls. of the St. Lawrence basin, separating the Canadian prov. of Ont. from N.Y., USA; navigable, carries industl. raw materials; polluted waters; a. 19,425 km²; depth 226 m.

Ontario, t., Cal., USA; aircraft components; fruit comm. ctr.; p. (1990) 133,179.

Onteniente, t., Valencia, **Spain;** on R. Clariano; woollen gds., paper mills; p. (1981) 28,123.

Oosterhout, t., N. Brabant, **Neth.;** nr. Breda; footwear, tobacco; p. (1994) 50,038.

Ootacamund, t., Tamil Nadu, **India;** in Nilgiri hills, c. 2,100 m; summer H.Q. of st. govt.; sanatorium.

Opatija (It. Abbazia), t., Croatia (formerly Yugoslavia); tourist resort, known as the Nice of the Adriatic; p. (1981) 29,274.

Opava (Troppau), t., N. Moravia, **Czech Rep.;** nr. Polish border; industl. ctr. in agr. a.; p. (1984) 60,961.

Opland or **Oppland,** co., central **Norway;** mtnous. N. inc. alpine region of Jotunheimen; forestry prods.; a. 24,885 km²; p. (1990) 182,593.

Opole (Oppeln), c. and prov., S. **Poland;** on R. Oder; R. pt., rly. junc.; cement, metals, furniture; 3 univ. schools; cap. Prussian prov. of Upper Silesia 1919–45; p. (1989) 126,962 (c.), 1,010,400 (prov.).

Oporto (Porto), c., spt., **Portugal;** second c. of rep., built high above Douro R.; ctr. of port wine tr.; cath., univ., historic bldgs.; sardine fisheries, cotton and wool textiles, sugar refining, distilling, oil refining; outer harbour at Leixöes; p. (1981) 327,368 (c.), 1,562,287 (met. a.).

Oradea t., W. Romania, on Crisul Repede R., nr. Hungarian border; cap. Bihor prov.; baroque architecture; p. (1992) 220,848.

Öraefa Jokull, hgst mtn., **Iceland;** alt. 1,955 m.

Oran. See **Ouahran.**

Orange, t., N.S.W., **Australia;** in fertile fruit growing a., agr. processing; tourism; with Bathurst is planned growth ctr.; p. (1981) 27,626.

Orange, historic t., Vaucluse, **France;** title founded by Charlemagne passed to William the Silent of the house of Nassau; Roman amphitheatre; tourism; p. (1982) 27,502.

Orange, R., Cape Prov., S. **Africa;** flows from Lesotho to Atl.; part forms S. bdy. between Cape Prov. and Orange Free State; Verwoerd dam (1972) for power, irrigation, flood control; Highlands Water Project (1986) to export water from Lesotho to S. Africa; 2,080 km long.

Orange Free State, prov., **Rep. of S. Africa;** plateau land, Drakensberg to N.E., Rs. Orange, Vaal and Caledon; sheep, cattle, horses, wheat, maize, fruit, tobacco, coal, diamonds; cap. Bloemfontein; a. 128,586 km²; p. (1985) 1·8 m.

Oranienburg, t., Potsdam, **Germany;** on R. Havel; industl.; chemicals, metals; p. (1989) 28,978.

Ord of Caithness, hill, headland, nr. Helmsdale, **Scot.;** alt. 366 m.

Ordos, desert region, Inner Mongolia, **China;** lies S. of Huang He; mean alt. 1,000 m; dry cropping, especially millets; pastoral farming.

Ord, R., W. Australia; in Kimberley dist.; since 1972 Ord Irrigation Project; hydroelectric power.

Ordu, spt. and prov., **Turkey;** on Black Sea; exp. manganese; p. (1985) 80,828 (t.), (1990) 850,105 (prov.).

Qrdzhonikidze. See **Vladikavkaz.**

Orebro, c., cap. of Örebro prov., **Sweden;** on R. Svartå at entrance to Hjälmar L.; anc. t., cas.; footwear, biscuits; p. (1992) 123,188 (t.), 274,325 (prov.).

Oregon, st., N.W. **USA;** Beaver St.; admitted to Union 1859; st. flower Oregon Grape, st. bird Western Meadowlark; borders Pac. Oc.; ch. physical features, Coast ranges, Cascade mtn. region, Blue mtns., Columbia R. and tribs., Willamette valley; rainy cst., drier interior (agr. with irrigation); cereals, sugar-beet, fruit, cattle; gold, silver, copper, coal, uranium; fisheries, canning, meat-packing, timber, milling; cap. Salem; a. 250,948 km²; p. (1990) 2,842,321.

Orekhovo-Zuyevo, t., Russia; E. of Moscow, on R. Klyazma; textile inds.; p. (1989) 137,000. Now called Oryakhovo.

Orel, c., **Russia;** on R. Oka; univ.; rly. junc.; engin., textile mills, food prods.; birthplace of Turgenev; p. (1989) 337,000.

Orenburg (Chkalov), c., cap. of Orenburg oblast,

Russia; on Ural R.; rly. junc.; food processing, agr. machin.; oil and natural gas in region; p. (1989) 547,000.

Orense, c., cap. of Orense prov., **Spain;** on R. Minho; flour, leather, iron; p. (1991) 107,247, 351,529 (prov.).

Ore Sound, strait, between Sjaelland, Denmark, and S. Sweden; protected by agreement of adjacent countries; freezes occasionally.

Orford Ness, coastal sandspit, Suffolk, **Eng.;** cas. keep at Orford.

Oriente, terr., **Peru/Ecuador;** for long in dispute between the two ctys., partially settled by treaty (1942); lies E. of Andes, between Putumayo and Marañon Rs.; mainly dense forest, reputedly rich in minerals.

Orihuela, t., Alicante, **Spain;** on R. Segura; leather, textiles, wine; univ., cath.; p. (1981) 49,851.

Orinoco, R., Venezuela; rises in Parima mtns., flows to Atl., connected to Rio Negro and Amazon; impt. industl. development on lower O., based on hydroelec. power and iron ore; experimental scheme to reclaim delta for agr.; 2,368 km long.

Orissa, st., **India;** agr. with few ts.; Hirakud dam across Mahanadi R.; Paradeep being developed as pt.; rice; cap. Bhuvaneshwar; a. 155,825 km²; p. (1991) 31,659,736.

Orizaba, t., Veracruz, **Mexico;** textiles, paper mills, breweries; resort; p. (1990) 113,516.

Orizaba, mtn., Veracruz, **Mexico;** volcanic; called Citlatepetl in Aztec times; alt. 5,704 m.

Orkney Islands, l. gov. auth., **Scot.;** gr. of 68 Is. in N. Sea, inc. Pomona, Sanday, Westray; 29 inhabited; antiquarian remains, stone circles; farming, fishing; North Sea oil; cap. Kirkwall; total a. c. 932 km²; p. (1995) 19,870.

Orlando, c., Fla., **USA;** winter resort; inds. based on citrus fruit and mkt. garden prods.; p. (1990) 164,693 (c.), 1,073,000 (met. a.).

Orléannais, region and former prov., **France;** inc. deps. of Loire-et-Cher, Loiret, and parts of Eure-et-Loire and Yonne.

Orléans, c., cap. of Loiret dep., **France;** on R. Loire; cath., univ.; regional tr. ctr.; wine, textiles, chemicals, farm implements; statue of Joan of Arc; p. (1990) 107,965 (c.), 243,153 (met. a.).

Ormoc, c., W. Leyte, **Philippines;** pt. and agr. ctr., exp. hemp, rice; disastrous floods Nov. 1991; p. (1990) 129,456.

Ormskirk, t., West Lancs., **Eng.;** 22 km N.E. of Liverpool; in mkt. gardening a.; lt. engin., clothing; p. (1991) 23,425.

Orne, dep., N. **France;** agr., dairying, stockkeeping, fruit-growing. Camembert cheese; cap. Alençon; a. 6,143 km²; p. (1990) 293,200.

Orontes, R., rises in Lebanon, flows through **Syria** past Hama into **Turkey** past Antioch to Mediterranean; unnavigable but used for irrigation; part of valley followed by rly.; irrigated areas intensively cultivated; c. 400 km long.

Orpington. See **Bromley.**

Orsha, c., **Belarus;** impt. industl. and transport ctr. on R. Dnieper; textiles, food-processing; once a frontier fortress; p. (1990) 124,000.

Orsk, c., **Russia;** in Ural mtns. on Ural R.; inds. based on surrounding mng. a.; oil pipeline terminus; oil refining; hydroelectric power sta. nearby; p. (1989) 271,000.

Orta, L., Italy; W. of Lago Maggiore; a. 18 km².

Orthez, t., Pyrénées-Atlantique, **France;** scene of Wellington's victory over Soult (1814); Bayonne hams; p. (1982) 11,542.

Orumiyeh. See **Rezaiyeh.**

Oruro, t., Bolivia; cap. of O. prov. at alt. 3,709 m; once impt. ctr. for silver mng.; now other minerals impt.; tin smelter; p. (1992) 183,194 (t.), (1988) 388,300 (dep.).

Oruwala, t., Sri Lanka; steel rolling mill.

Orvieto, t., Umbria, **Italy;** on R. Paglia; cath., Etruscan antiquities; wines, olive oil, cereals; pottery.

Oryakhovo. See **Orekhovo.**

Osaka, c., Honshu, **Japan;** ctr. of Kinki plain; built on delta in shallow O. Bay; comm. ctr.; banking, heavy industry, metals, machin., clothing; p. (1990) 2,623,831.

Osasco, t., São Paulo st., **Brazil;** industl. satellite of São Paulo with traditional and new inds.; p. (1991) 563,419.

Osh, t., Kirghizia; textiles, food-processing; one of oldest ts. in central Asia; p. (1990) 217,500.

Oshawa, t., Ont. **Canada;** pt. on L. Ont.; motor

vehicles; p. (1991) 129,344 (c.), (1986) 203,543 (met. a.).

Oshima, I., Tokyo Bay, **Japan**; lgst. and most N. of Izu-shichito gr.; site of volcanic Mt. Mihara (755 m).

Oshkosh, t., Wis., **USA**; on Fox R.; meat packing, flour, motors; p. (1990) 55,006 (c.), 315,000 (met. a. Appleton-Oshkosh-Neenah).

Oshogbo, t., **Nigeria**; comm. and educational ctr.; serves agr. dist.; cotton-ginning; new steel rolling mill; p. (1992) 441,600.

Osijek, t., **Croatia** (formerly Yugoslavia); on Drava R.; growing industl. ctr. for textiles and leather; p. (1991) 104,761.

Osinniki, t., **Russia**; W. Siberia; new ctr. of coal mng.; thermal power sta.

Osipenko. *See* Berdyansk.

Oslo (Christiania), c., cap. of **Norway**; at head of Oslo Fjord; ch. spt., comm., industl., and cultural ctr.; ice-free harbour, cath., univ.; exp. timber, fish, matches; wood pulp, paper; new airport (Gardermoen) opened, 1998; p. (1990) 461,644.

Osnabrück, c., Lower Saxony, **Germany**; on R. Hase; stands on a branch of the Mittelland canal; inland pt. and industl. ctr.; iron and steel; mach., textile and paper mnfs.; p. (1990) 164,000.

Osorno, t., **Chile**; agr. ctr.; in beautiful forested cty.; Germanic influence; food-processing; tourism; p. (1992) 128,709.

Ossett, t., West Yorks., **Eng.**; 5 km W. of Wakefield; woollens, shoddy-processing, engin.; p. (1991) 20,405.

Ostend, spt., **Belgium**; passenger route between Britain and continent of Europe; popular resort; casino, fisheries, shipbldg., textiles, tobacco; p. (1993) 69,148.

Östergötland, co., **Sweden**; on Baltic cst.; rises to uplands of Småland in S. where p. declining; lowland, a. crossed by Gota canal; cap. Linköping; a. 11,050 km²; p. (1992) 408,268.

Östersund, t., Jämtland, **Sweden**; on Storsjön L.; p. (1992) 59,019.

Östfold, co., S.E. **Norway**; hilly a. crossed by R. Glomma; dairy prods. for Oslo; a. 4,178 km²; p. (1990) 238,345.

Ostia, anc. c., **Italy**; once pt. of Rome, at mouth of R. Tiber, founded 4th cent. B.C.; layout revealed by excavations; modern v. of O. nearby on plain reclaimed from salt marsh.

Ostrava, c., **Czech Rep.**; at junc. of Oder and Ostravice Rs.; industl. ctr. of Ostrava-Karvinna coalmng. region; iron and steel, machin., chemicals, oil refining; p. (1990) 331,000.

Ostroleka, t. and prov., N.E. central **Poland**; on R. Narew; cellulose, paper; p. (1989) 49,032 (t.), 393,400 (prov.).

Ostrow Wielkopolski, t., Kalisz prov., **Poland**; agr. machin., clothing; p. (1989) 72,085.

Ostrowiec Swietokrzyski (Ostrovets), t., Kielce, **Poland**; on R. Kamienna; ceramic and metallurgical inds.; p. (1989) 77,466.

Oswaldtwistle, t., Hyndburn, Lancs., **Eng.**; at N. foot of Rossendale Fells; chemicals, textiles; p. (1991) 12,176.

Oswego, t., N.Y., **USA**; pt. on L. Ontario; mnfs. hosiery, matches, textiles, boiler engines, paper; p. (1980) 19,793.

Oswestry, t., l. gov. dist., Shrops., **Eng.**; at foot of Welsh mtns., cas.; engin.; p. (1995) 34,800 (dist.), (1991) 15,612 (t.).

Oswiecim (Ger. **Auschwitz**), t., Bielsko prov., **Poland**; at confluence of Rs. Iola and Vistula; lge. chemical wks.; German concentration camp (1940–44); p. (1989) 45,402.

Otago, reg., S.I., **N.Z.**; forested mtns.; gold; farming, sheep, fruit; lge. deposit of jade found at head of L. Wakatipu; coalfields; cap. Dunedin; a. 65,320 km²; p. (1991) 186,067.

Otago Harbour, Otago dist., S.I., **N.Z.**; Dunedin and Port Chalmers are ports on this harbour.

Otanmäki, **Finland**; rich deposit of magnetite-ilmenite ore.

Otaru, reg., Hokkaido, **Japan**; herring fisheries; coal mng., lumbering; p. (1990) 163,215.

Otley, t., West Yorks., **Eng.**; on R. Wharfe; printing, machin., wool, paper mkg., leather, furnishings; birthplace of Thomas Chippendale; p. (1991) 13,596.

Otranto, t. S. **Italy**; on Strait O.; once a flourishing c., fine mosaic pavement, cath., cas.; submarine cable sta.; bauxite exp., fishing; p. (1981) 4,811.

Otsu, t., Honshu, **Japan**; on L. Biwa; p. (1990) 260,004.

Ottawa, c. Ont. cap. of **Canada**; on R. Ottawa; univ., caths., parliament bldgs.; hydroelec, power, lumbering, sawmills, paper, flour, leather, matches, machin., ironware; p. (1986) 300,763 (c.), 819,263 (met. a. with Hull).

Ottawa, R., **Canada**; trib. of St. Lawrence, forming bdy. between Ont. and Quebec; timber transport, hydroelec. power; 1,000 km long.

Ottery St. Mary, mkt. t., East Devon, **Eng.**; 16 km E. of Exeter; birthplace of Coleridge; p. (1991) 3,253.

Ottumwa, t., Iowa, **USA**; on Des Moines R.; in coalfield and agr. dist.; iron and steel, meat-packing; p. (1990) 24,488.

Ötzal, valley, **Austria**; longest side valley of R. Inn; tourist dist.

Ouachita or **Washita**, R., Ark., **USA**; trib. of Red R.; 880 km long.

Ouachita National Forest, Ark., Okla., **USA**; part of forested O. highlands.

Ouagadougou, cap. of **Burkina Faso**; tex., soap, comm.; p. (1985) 442,223.

Ouahran (Oran), spt., dep., N. **Algeria**; founded by Moors 10th cent.; occupied by French 1831–1962; handles wines, wool, cereals, meat, skins; fine roadstead at Mers-el-Kebir; former French naval and military sta.; p. (1987) 609,823 (t.), 916,578 (dep.).

Oudenaarde (Audenarde), t., **Belgium**, on R. Scheldt; textile ctr.; scene of Marlborough's victory over French 1708; p. (1981) 27,318.

Ouenza, dist., **Algeria**; 75 per cent of Algerian iron-ore produced in dist.

Oujda, t., N.E. **Morocco**; comm. ctr.; phosphate, lead and zinc-mng. dist.; p. (1982) 260,082.

Oulton Broad, L., Suffolk, **Eng.**; nr. Lowestoft. *See* Broads.

Oulu, spt., cap. of Oulu prov., N.W. **Finland**; on G. of Bothnia at mouth of R. Oulu; univ.; p. (1993) 104,346.

Oundle, mkt. t., East Northants., **Eng.**; on R. Nene; public school; p. (1991) 3,996.

Ouro Prêto, old colonial t., **Brazil**; former cap. of Minas Gerais st.; as gold mng. ctr.; founded 1711; school of mines.

Ouse or Great Ouse, R., **Eng.**; rises in S. Northamptonshire and flows N.E. via the Fens to the Wash; 250 km long.

Ouse, R., East Sussex, **Eng.**; flows to English Channel at Newhaven; 48 km long.

Ouse, R., York/North Yorks., **Eng.**; formed by Rs. Swale and Ure, flows to Humber estuary; 208 km long.

Overijssel, prov., **Neth.**; dairying, fishing; ch. ind. textiles; a. 3,364 km²; p. (1994) 1,044,648.

Oviedo, coastal. prov., N. **Spain**; agr., fruit, sardine, and other fisheries; cap. O.; a. 10,888 km²; p. (1991) 1,096,155.

Oviedo, c., cap. of O. prov., **Spain**; on R. Nalón; cath., univ.; industl. and comm. ctr. for agr. and mng. dists. of Asturia; p. (1991) 203,189.

Owenus, pt., **Liberia**, deepwater pt. built to serve iron ore mines at Belinga.

Owen Falls, **Uganda**; dam inaugurated 1954 to supply Uganda with hydroelectric power; also converts L. Victoria into reservoir for irrigation of Egypt.

Owensboro', t., Ky., **USA**; petroleum; ctr. for stock raising and tobacco growing a.; p. (1990) 53,549.

Owens, L., S. Cal., **USA**; on E. flank of Sierra Nevada, 32 km S.E. of Mt. Whitney; water taken by 360 km-long aqueduct to Los Angeles; a. 311 km².

Owen Sound, t., L. pt., Ont., **Canada**; on S.W. cst. of Georgian Bay, L. Huron; E. terminus of lgst. wheat-carrying L. steamers; linked by rly. to Toronto (200 km) and Montreal; p. (1981) 19,883.

Oxelösund, spt., E. **Sweden**; on Baltic cst., S. of Stockholm; steelwks., glass.

Oxford, c., l. gov. dist., Oxon., **Eng.**; between R. Thames and R. Cherwell; 13th cent. univ. and residtl. colleges; printing, cars, elec. engin.; p. (1995) 134,800 (dist.), (1991) 118,795 (c.).

Oxfordshire, non-met. co., **Eng.**; formed by Chilterns and Cotswolds, drained by R. Thames and tribs.; mainly agr. with lge. arable farms; p. (1995) 598,400.

Oxnard, t., Cal., **USA**; citrus fruits, sugar beet, oil refining; p. (1990) 142,216 (t.), 669,000 (met. a. with Ventura).

Oxus, R. *See* Amu Dar'ya.

Oyashio. *See* Bering Current.

Oyo, t., Nigeria; cotton weaving; mkt.; p. (1992) 237,400 (t.), (1991) 3,488,789 (state).

Ozark Mtns., Okla. and Ark., USA; lead, zinc; ch. t, Joplin; forested.

P

Paarl, t., Cape Prov., S. Africa; summer resort extending along Gt. Berg R.; wines, fruit, tobacco; flour, saw and textile mills; p. (1980) 108,860 (dist.).

Pabianice, t., Poland; nr. Lodz; textiles, farming implements, paper; p. (1989) 74,755.

Pabna, t., and dist., Bengal, Bangladesh; dist. is a fertile alluvial plain; t. serves as trading, industl. and admin. ctr. for a.; hosiery, carpets; p. (1991) 104,479 (t.), 4,305,000 (dist.).

Pachitea, R., Peru; rises in Andes, flows N. to R. Ucayali; sm. German immigrant colonies in upper valley; 512 km long.

Pachmarhi, Madhya Pradesh, India; summer cap., tourist ctr.

Pachuca, cap., Hidalgo st., Mexico; silver mnfs. and mng.; woollen and leather gds.; p. (1990) 179,440.

Pacific Islands, Trust Terr. of, external terr. of USA held under U.N. trusteeship; consists of Mariana Is. (except Guam), Caroline and Marshall Is., W. Pac. Oc.; inc. 2,141 Is., grouped into 6 admin. dists.; cap. (provisional) Saipan, Mariana Is.; total land a. *c.* 1,800 km²; p. (1985) 154,000.

Pacific Ocean, a. 176,120,000 km²; lgst. ocean in the world; extends from W. cst of America to E. cst. of Asia and Australia and the S. Ocean in the S.; enters Arctic Oc. via Bering Strait; greatest length N. to S. 1,280 km; breadth, 16,000 km; mean depth 3,830 m, 11,524 m in the Mindanao trench; many coral and volcanic Is. in S.W.

Padang, t., prov., W. cst. Sumatra, Indonesia; exp. agr. prods., coffee, copra, rubber and coal; cement mnfs.; univ.; p. (1983) 726,000.

Paddington. *See* Westminster, City of.

Paderborn, c., N. Rhine–Westphalia, Germany; cath. and other historic bldgs. severely damaged in second world war; foodstuffs, textiles, metals; p. (1990) 122,700.

Padiham, t., Lancs., Eng.; at N. foot of Rossen-dale Fells, textiles, engin., gas appliances; p. (1991) 12,570.

Padstow, mkt. t. Camel estuary, Cornwall, Eng.; silting has caused pt. decline; lt. inds.; seaside resort; p. (1991) 2,460.

Padua (Padova), c., cap. of P. prov., N.E. Italy; cath., arcades, anc. bridges; univ. founded 1222 (Galileo taught here); flourished as artistic ctr.; birthplace of Livy; machin., chemicals, cloth, distilling; agr. ctr.; p. (1992) 213,656.

Paducah, c., Ky., USA; pt. on Ohio R.; saw-mills, tobacco, railway wks.; atomic energy plant; p. (1990) 27,256.

Paestum, anc. c., S. Italy; S.E. of Salerno; founded by the Greeks 600 B.C.; ruins of temples, Roman forum and amphitheatre.

Pagan, ruined c., central Myanmar; on Irrawaddy R.; founded circa 849, sacked 1299; in ctr. of a. covered with pagodas, place of Burmese pilgrim-age; lacquer work.

Pago Pago, spt., cap. of American Samoa, S. Pac.; on Tutuila I., magnificent harbour; US naval and radio sta.; airport; p. (1990) 46,773.

Pahang, st., Malaysia, central Malaya; isolated from rest of Malaya, less economically de-veloped; largely covered with forest; some rubber production, gold, tin mng.; cap. Kuala Lipis; a. 34,395 km²; p. (1980) 798,782.

Pahlevi. *See* Bandar-e-Pahlevi.

Paignton, t., S. Devon, Eng.; incorporated in Torbay; resort; p. (1991) 42,989.

Painted Desert, Arizona, USA; a. of bare multi-coloured shale and sandstones; arid; a. c. 19,400 km².

Paisley, burgh, Renfrewshire, Scot.; 8 km W. of Glasgow; anc. abbey; former inds. included ship-bldg., chemicals, engin., preserves, car bodies, cotton thread; p. (1991) 75,526.

Paita, pt., Peru; exp. cotton, wool, flax, panama hats; lge. whaling sta. to S.

Pakistan, Islamic Rep. of, forms part of Indian subcontinent, S. Asia; formerly split into two separate units, E. Pakistan (cap. Dacca) and W. Pakistan, (cap. Lahore), 1,600 km apart; politi-cally separate since 1972; W. part now forms Pakistan; rejoined Commonwealth 1989; E. part indep. st. of Bangladesh; dry semi-desert, irrigated by Indus R. and tribs.; cash crops, sugar, wheat, cotton; natural gas fields; new cap. Islamabad; main spt. Karachi; a. 803,944 km²; p. (1996) 134,000,000.

Paknampoh, t., Thailand; on R. Menam, at upper limit of navigation; terminus of private rly.; fish breeding in L. created from swamp.

Pakokku, t., Upper Myanmar; pt. on Irrawaddy R.; shipping ctr. for a. producing sugar, tobacco, peanuts, teak, petroleum; Yenangyaung oilfields nearby.

Paktia, prov., Afghanistan; mtnous., forested; difficult to govern, inhabited by sm. and indep. tribes, but sparse p.; livestock basis of agr.; timber exp; a. c. 12,950 km²; p. (1984) 525,000.

Palau, Rep. of, formerly Western Carolines; group of Is. 300 km. E. of Philippines; renamed 1981; part of U.S. Trust Terr. of Pacific Is.; p. (1994) 18,000.

Palawan I., prov. Philippines; elongated I., rising to 1,731 m; coffee, resin, timber; prov. a. 11,784 km²; p. (1990) 528,287.

Palembang, cap. of S. Sumatra prov., Indonesia; R. pt. of Musi R., 80 km from sea; terminus of S. Sumatran rly. systems; exp. coffee and petroleum prods. from nearby oilfields; inds. based on agr. processing and oil refining; p. (1981) 903,000.

Palencia, t., cap. of P. prov., N.W. Spain; industl. ctr.; rly. engin.; cath.; p. (1987) 75,951; (1991) 183,908 (prov.).

Palermo, spt., Sicily, Italy; cath., univ.; ship-repairing; processes agr. prod. from surround-ing fertile Conca d'Oro; p. (1992) 696,735.

Palestine or The Holy Land, historic region, bounded by Syria and Lebanon on the N., Jordan on the E., the Egyptian prov. of Sinai on the S., and the Mediterranean on the W.; a. when under Brit. mandate 2,701 km². *See* Israel.

Palghat, t., Kerala, India; commands Palghat gap through W. Ghats; p. (1981) 117,986.

Palitana, t., Gujarat, India; t. of Jain temples inhabited by priests and their servants; p. (1981) 34,449.

Palk Strait, separates India from Sri Lanka.

Palma de Mallorca, spt., Mallorca I., Spain; cath., palaces, varied inds.; agr. exp.; well-known tourist resort; p. (1991) 308,616.

Palm Beach, t., Fla., USA; Atl. coastal resort; permanent p. (1980) 9,729.

Palmerston North, c., N.I., N.Z.; rly. junc. at ctr. of Manawatu R. lowlands; sheep and dairy prod.; univ.; p. (1991) 70,318. Moves to rename city Manawatu.

Palmira, t., W. Colombia; agr. ctr. in Cauca valley; p. (1983) 179,000.

Palm Springs, Cal., USA; resort; p. (1980) 32,366.

Palmyra, anc. c. in Syrian desert, 192 km. N.E. of Damascus; extensive ruins.

Palmyra Is. *See* Line Is.

Palo Alto, t., sub. development 48 km S.E. San Francisco, Cal., USA; attractive wooded site of variable relief; on shore of San Francisco Bay peninsula; Stanford Univ.; science-based inds.; p. (1980) 55,225.

Palomar, Mount, peak, 1,868 m high, S. Cal., USA; observatory with 5,080 mm reflecting telescope.

Palos de la Frontera, t., Huelva, S.W. Spain; on Rio Tinto; starting point for Columbus in 1492; pt. now silted up; p. (1981) 4,014.

Palua, pt., Venezuela; pt. of shipment for iron mines at El Pao; nearby Caroni hydroelec. plant serves steel wks. and aluminium plant.

Pamir Mtns., high mtn. plateau ("roof of the world"), Tajikistan, Central Asia; Mt. Commu-nism (7,400 m) climbed by Russo-British team 1962; name derives from high mtn. valleys known as pamirs.

Pampas, Argentina; vast plains stretching from the Rio Negro on the S. to the Gran Chaco in the N., and E. from the Andes to the Atl.; woodless, level country; rich pastures in E., supporting countless numbers of sheep and cattle, a major influence upon the Argentinian economy, source of livestock exps.; W. mostly barren.

Pamplona, c., cap. of Navarre, N. **Spain**; at foot of Pyrenees, anc. Baxque c.; cath., fortress, univ.; industl. ctr. with varied mnfs.; p. (1991) 191,112.

Panaji, cap. of Goa state, **India**; p. (1981) 77,226.

Panama, rep., **Central America**; narrow strip of terr. at S. end of isthmus separating N. and S. America; mtnous. and tropical, thickly forested; 9 prov. and 1 autonomous Indian reservation; split by Canal Area from which rep. earns 25 per cent of revenue; shipping registration and other services impt.; subsistence agr.; exp. bananas, shrimps, sugar, coffee; rich copper deposits found 1975; poor communications; Cap. Panama City; a. 74,009 km²; p. (1990) 2,329,329.

Panama Canal Area, Panama; strip of land 82 km long 16 km wide on either side of Canal; 1979 former Canal Zone transferred by US to Panamanian sovereignty; a. 1,675 km².

Panama City, c. spt., cap. of **Panama**; free pt. at S. entrance to Canal; cath.; oil refining, steel rolling mill, cement plant, lt. inds.; contains 25 per cent p. Panama rep.; p. (1990) 584,803.

Panama City, t., Fla., **USA**; pulp and paper mill; resort; p. (1984) 34,100 (t.), 108,500 (met. a.).

Pan American Highway, international road project, not yet fully complete, from Alaska to Chile, down W. csts. of continents; section between USA and Mexico is called Central American Inter-American Highway.

Panay, I., **Philippines**; between Negros I. and Mindoro I.; coconuts, maize grown in E., fertile lowland; ch. t. Iloilo; a. 11,515 km²; p. (1990) 8,031,271.

Pančevo, t., N.E. Serbia, **Yugoslavia**; agr. ctr. for grain growing a., flour-milling; developing industl. ctr., fertilizers, oil refining; p. (1991) 72,717.

Pangalanes Canal (Canal Des Pangalanes), Madagascar; follows E. cst from Farafangana to Tamatave, through series of lagoons; 480 km long.

Panipat, t., Haryana, N.W. **India**; on Jumna R.; on route from Afghanistan to central India; scene of battles; p. (1991) 191,212.

Panjim, cap. of Goa, **India**; pt.; old cap. (Velha Goa) in ruins; p. (1981) 43,165.

Panjsher Valley, Afghanistan; silver and mica mines.

Pantelleria, volcanic I., Mediterranean, **Italy**; midway between W. Sicily and Tunisia; figs, raisins, vines, capers, cereals; fishing; a. 150 km²; ch. t. P.; p. (1981) 7,917.

Pantin, N.E. sub., Paris, Seine-St. Denis, **France**; glasswks., sugar refining, tobacco factories, chemicals, leather, tallow; p. (1982) 43,553.

Paoki. *See* Baoji.

Paoting. *See* Baoding.

Paotow. *See* Baotou.

Papakura, dist., N.I., **N.Z.**; residtl. a. for Auckland; p. (1991) 36,553.

Papaloa, R., **Mexico**; agr. and industl. development; Papaloan project for flood control and electricity generation.

Papal States, Italy, areas ruled by the Pope until 1870; comprised Latium, Umbria, the Marches, and Emilia-Romagna.

Papatoetoe, c., N.I., **N.Z.**; residtl. ctr. close to Auckland; p. (1987) 21,900.

Papeete, t., pt., **Tahiti I.**, Pac. Oc.; cap. Tahiti and of Fr. Settlements in Oceania; exp. copra, vanilla, phosphates and mother-of-pearl; p. (1983) 78,814.

Paphos (Pafos), admin. dist., W. cst. **Cyprus**; anc. c.; Old P. dates from 3000 B.C., New P. impt. spt.; rich deposits of copper and iron pyrites, sulphur in Vretsia a.; scene of ambitious project (completed 1983) to grow tropical fruits (mango, avocado, papaya) with irrigation; p. (1992) 32,575 (c.).

Papua New Guinea, E. New Guinea, S.E. Asia; indep. st. (1975); mtnous., thickly forested;underdeveloped; copra, rubber and timber prods.; many valuable reserves of gold and copper; cap. Pt. Moresby; a. 461,693 km²; p. (1992) 3,850,000.

Pará, st., **Brazil**; densely forested; rubber, fruits, cacao, Brazil nuts; massive iron ore deposits in Serra do Carajás with new road and rail access; cap. Belem; a. 1,228,061 km²; p. (1991) 5,084,726.

Paracel Is., S. China Sea; claimed by China, Taiwan and Vietnam.

Paraguay, landlocked rep., S. America; undulating cty.; swamps, forest; hot summers, warm winters, high but seasonal rainfall; sm. densely populated areas, lge. areas with no p.; most economically developed in E.; in and around cap. Asunción 25 per cent p.; economy based on agr., decline of meat and timber but agr. expansion in other prods.; cereals, livestock, fruit, cotton, oil-seeds, but food imported; aid from USA for rural development; few fuel resources (a few oilfields in the Chaco Borea) and low energy consumption; hydroelectric plant on Paraná (Itaipu dam), Paraguay Rs. and at Guaira Falls; electricity exp. to Brazil; new inds. with cheap power; first steel mill (1982); some agr. based inds.; a. 406,630 km²; p. (1993) 4,500,000.

Paraguay, R., S. America; rises in plateau of Mato Grosso, flows S. and joins R. Paraná nr. Corrientes; forms bdy. between Brazil and Bolivia, Brazil and Paraguay; impt. navigable waterway to Cáceres (Brazil); 1,920 km long.

Paraíba, st., N.E. **Brazil**; livestock, cotton, sugar cane; tin, scheelite; cap. João Pessoa; a. 56,462 km²; p. (1991) 3,200,620.

Paraíba do Sul, R., S. **Brazil**; rises in São Paulo st., and flows between Rio de Janeiro and Minas Gerais to Atl. N.E. of Rio de Janeiro; forms routeway between São Paulo and Rio de Janeiro; 1,040 km long.

Paramaribo, spt., cap. of **Suriname**; on Suriname R.; exp. bauxite, timber, rubber, rice, fruit; t. built on grid pattern with canals and tree-lined streets; p. (1993) 200,970.

Paraná, c., cap. of Entre Rios prov., N.E. **Argentina**; pt. of P. R. for grain, cattle, sheep; road tunnel to Santa Fé; p. (1991) 277,338.

Paraná, R., S.W. **Brazil**; formed by junc. of Rs. Rio Grande and Paranaíba; flows W. between Paraguay and Argentina; flows into Rio de la Plata; navigable to Brazil frontier nr. Iguaçu Falls; forms part of international inland waterway system; hydroelec. power, Itaipú lgst. sta. in world; joint hydroelec. scheme between Paraguay, Brazil and Argentina; 3,280 km long; rapid rise in p. with indust. expansion from electricity.

Paraná, st., S. **Brazil**; between Paraná R. and Atl. Oc.; extensively forested; maté, timber, coffee; cap. Curitiba; a. 201,287 km²; p. (1991) 8,415,659.

Paranaguá, spt., Paraná st., **Brazil**; ch. pt. for Paraná; in lagoon harbour; modern highway links with Asunción (Paraguay); p. (1986) 94,800.

Pardubice, t., **Czech Rep.**; univ., cath.; rly. junc., industl. ctr.; distilling, oil refining; p. (1990) 96,000.

Paricutin, Mt. Michoacán, **Mexico**; volcano formed between 1943 and 1952, 2,501 m high; of great interest to scientists.

Paris, c., cap. of **France**; dominates rep. politically, economically, and socially, partly as result of extreme centralisation of political power in cap.; on R. Seine, 176 km from mouth, in ctr. of Paris Basin; forms major ctr. of communications; planning of Haussmann gives spacious appearance, 12 boulevards radiate from Arc de Triomphe; many historic bldgs., especially on and around Ile de la Cité, an I. on R. Seine, site of cath. of Notre Dame; major cultural and tourist ctr.; univs.; comprises 20 admin. arrondissements; major ctr. of inds. with concentration of modern science-based inds. hindering planned attempts at decentralisation; p. (1990) 2,152,400 (c.), (1982) 9,060,257 (met. a.).

Paris Basin, concentric limestone escarpments form saucer-shaped depression with Paris at ctr.; impt. agr. dist., wheat, dairy prod. and wines.

Parkersburg, t., W. Va., **USA**; on Ohio R.; iron- and steel-wks., oil and natural gas, coal, glassware, rayon, porcelain; p. (1984) 39,400 (t.), 157,900 (met. a.).

Parkes, t., N.S.W., **Australia**; mkt.; rly. junc.; radio telescope; p. (1981) 9,047.

Parma, c., cap. of P. prov., **Italy**; between Apennines and Po R.; tr. ctr. rly. junc.; food-processing, wine, Parmesan cheese, precision instruments, agr. machin.; Roman remains, many historic bldgs., univ., cath.; p. (1992) 170,555.

Parma, t., Ohio, **USA**; motor vehicle parts; residtl.; p. (1990) 87,876.

Parnaíba, spt., Piauí, **Brazil**; agr. comm. ctr., cotton, cattle; exp. agr. prods.; p. (1986) 116,206.

Parnaíba, R., rises in Brazil; flows into N. Atl. Oc., forms bdy. between Maranhão and Piauí; 1,200 km long.

Parnassus, mtn. ridge, **Greece**; 133 km N.W. of Athens, nr. the anc. Delphi, the modern Liakhura; hgst. peak Licoreia 2,461 m.

Parnu or **Pyarnu**, spt., S.W. **Estonia**; of G. of Riga; exp. timber flax; health resort; p. (1991) 58,600.

Páros, I., Grecian Archipelago; W. of Naxos; source of Parian marble; cap. of P.; a. 163 km².

Parramatta, c., N.S.W., **Australia**; pt. nr. head of Parramatta R. in met. a. of Sydney; 2nd Brit. settlement in Australia.

Parrett, R., Somerset, **Eng.**; flows to Bristol Channel, nr. Bridgwater; 56 km long.

Pasadena, c., Cal., **USA**; N. of Los Angeles; in fruit-growing region, base of San Gabriel mtns.; 5,080 mm telescope on Mt. Palomar; famous for its carnival; p. (1990) 131,591.

Pasco, t., Wash., **USA**; on Snake R.; atomic energy plant; p. (1980) 18,425.

Pasco. See Cerro de Pasco.

Pas-de-Calais, dep., N. **France**; impt. heavy industl. a. based upon local extensive coal deposits; heavy inds. inc. iron and steel, but many ts. in decline as importance of coal diminishes; prosperous agr. based on arable farming; N. cst. faces English Channel and inc. pts. of Calais and Boulogne; severe devastation in both world wars; cap. Arras; a. 6,750 km²; p. (1990) 1,433,200.

Pasir Gudang, free port , **Malaysia**; across Jahore Str. from Singapore; opened (1984) to divert M.'s exports from Singapore.

Passage West, t. Cork, **R.o.I.**; declining pt., fishing; p. (1986) 3,511.

Passaic, c., N.J., **USA**; rubber gds., springs, steel cabinets, tin cans; p. (1990) 58,041.

Passau, c., **Germany**, at confluence of Rs. Danube, Inn and Ilz, nr. Austrian frontier; trans-shipment base, inds. inc. leather, porcelain, tobacco and brewing; cath., picturesque tourist ctr.; p. (1986) 52,700.

Passchendaele, t., **Belgium**; strategic point in first world war; battle 31 July–6 Nov. 1917.

Passero I., Mediterranean Sea; off S.E. cst. of Sicily, **Italy**.

Passy, residtl. part of W. Paris, **France**; between Bois de Boulogne and right bank of Seine; residence of Balzac.

Pasto, t., cap. of Narino dep., **Colombia**; on flank of Pasto volcano; univ.; agr. comm. ctr.; gold nearby; p. (1992) 303,401.

Patagonia, extensive region, E. of Andes, **Argentina/Chile**; elevated plateau, arid, sterile; prin. Rs. Colorado, Rio Negro, and Chubut; impt. source of oil at Commodoro Rivadavia; lge. tracts of grazing for livestock; much of p. Welsh descendants; plans to decentralise cap. of A. to small Ts. of Viedma and Carmen de Patagones.

Patan, c. **Nepal**; impt. ctr. of Buddhism; gold and silver gds.; p. (1991) 117,203.

Patani or **Pattani**, pt., S. **Thailand**; on E. cst. of Malay peninsula; spices, rubber, coconuts; tin mng.; former Malay sultanate.

Paterno, t., Sicily, **Italy**; N.W. of Catania; cath., cas.; mineral springs, wines; p. (1981) 45,144.

Paterson, c., N.J., **USA**; on Passaic R. whose falls provide hydroelectric power for gr. silk mnf. ind.; now inds. diversified; in addition to textiles and textile machin., aeroplane engines, metallurgical inds., electronic equipment; p. (1990) 140,891.

Patiala, t., Punjab, **India**; metal gds., flour; cement; p. (1981) 206,254.

Patino Mines. See Unicia.

Pátmos, I., one of the Dodecanese, **Greece**; in Aegean Sea; St. John wrote the Revelation here; a. 34 km²; p. 3,000.

Patna, c., cap. of Bihar, **India**; univ.; rly. junc.; agr. tr., rice, oilseeds, cotton; handicraft inds.; p. (1991) 917,000.

Patras (Pátrai), spt., cap. of Akhaia, **Greece**; citadel and cas., exp. currants, raisins, figs, olive oil; inds. based on agr. processing; p. (1991) 152,570.

Pau, c., cap. of Pyrénées-Atlantique dep., **France**; on Gave-de-Pau; impt. mkt. and regional ctr.; summer and winter resort; linen, chocolate, hams, wine; natural gas nearby; p. (1990) 83,923 (c.), 134,625 (met. a.).

Pauillac, t., Gironde dep., **France**; pt. on Gironde estuary; ships, wines, timber; oil refinery, natural gas; p. (1982) 6,359.

Paulo Affonso, falls, São Francisco R., **Brazil**; 79 m; Tres Marias dam and power sta. opened 1960; in Nat. Park.

Pavia, c., prov. cap., N. **Italy**; on R. Ticino; route ctr. and agr. mkt. in Po valley; olives, wine, Parmesan cheese; oil refining at Spineto; walled c.; battle 1525; birthplace of Lanfranc; p. (1981) 85,029.

Pavlodar, pt., **Kazakhstan**; on R. Irtysh; chemicals, sulphates, agr. machin., locomotives, aluminium, oil processing; food prod.; p. (1990) 336,800.

Pawtucket, c., R.I., **USA**; on Pawtucket R. at head of navigation; first water-power cotton spinning factory in USA 1790; textiles remain most impt. ind.; p. (1990) 329,000 (met. a. with Woonsocket–Attleboro).

Paysandú, dep., W. **Uruguay**; rich pastoral a.; ranching, cattle, sheep; arable agr., cereals, mkt. gardening around c. of P.; a. 13,406 km²; p. (1985) 103,487.

Paysandú, cap. of P. dep., W. **Uruguay**; pt. on Uruguay R. with meat-packing, soap and footwear inds.; p. (1985) 74,014.

Pays de la Loire, region, W. **France**; inc. deps. Loire Atlantique, Maine-et-Loire, Mayenne, Sarthe, Vendée; region based upon lower reaches of R. Loire; ch. ts. Le Mans, Nantes; p. (1990) 3,059,100.

Pazardzhik, t., **Bulgaria**; on main rly. line to Istanbul; industl., hemp spinning and weaving; p. (1990) 87,277.

Paz de Rio, t., Boyacá, **Colombia**; iron and steel wks.; iron ore, coal, limestone nearby.

Peace, R., **Canada**; one of ch. headstreams of Mackenzie R.; rises in Rocky mtns., and flows generally N. to Gr. Slave R. nr. L. Athabaska; a. of very mild climate in lower course, fertile agr. valley; 1,680 km long.

Peak Dist., Pennine hill dist., mid-**Eng.**; extends from Chesterfield to Buxton, and Ashbourne to Glossop; composed of limestone with typical karst features; within P.D. Nat. Park, tourist and recreation a. for cities to E. (Sheffield) and W. (Manchester); limestone quarrying for cement; Kinder Scout 634 m.

Pearl Harbor, landlocked harbour, Oahu I., **Hawaii**, one of finest natural harbours in E. Pac.; US naval base; attacked by Japanese without warning 7 Dec. 1941 (7.55 a.m., local time), precipitating U.S. entry into Second World War.

Pearl Is., archipelago, G. of Panama; sea fishing, pearls.

Pearl R. See Chu-kiang.

Pechenga (Petsamo), spt., **Russia**; on inlet of Barents Sea; formerly Finnish, ceded to USSR Sept. 1944; ice-free throughout year; exp. nickel, timber, cobalt.

Pechora, dist., **Russia**; E. of Urals; coalfields; coking coal; ch. ts., Vorkuta and Inta.

Pechora, R., **Russia**; rises in Urals and flows N. into Arctic Oc.; 1,120 km navigable between June and Sept. for transport of timber from its basin; fishing; 1,792 km long.

Pecos, R., N.M. and Texas, **USA**; trib. of Rio Grande; water control schemes provide irrigation for lge. a.; 1,482 km long.

Pécs, c., S.W. **Hungary**; on Yugoslav border; one of oldest and most pleasantly situated ts. of Hungary; cath., univ., airport; in coal-mng. a.; coke, chemicals, majolica, leather gds., engin., brewing; p. (1997) 161,000.

Peebles, royal burgh, Borders, **Scot.**; on upper course of R. Tweed; woollen cloth, knitwear; mkt., tourist ctr.; p. (1991) 7,065.

Peeblesshire, historic co., S. **Scot.**; now part of Borders.

Peel, t., Isle of Man; resort, fishing pt. midway along W. cst.; cas., cath.; p. (1991) 3,829.

Peel Fell, mtn. Northumberland, Eng.; 1,964 ft.

Pegu, c., Pegu prov., S. **Myanmar**; R. pt., rly. junc.; many temples, notably Shwe May Daw Pagoda; once cap. of Burmese kingdom; came under Brit. rule 1852; p. (1983) 150,447.

Pegu Yoma, mtns., **Myanmar**; between valleys of Rs. Irrawaddy and Sittang; thickly forested with teak which is comm. exploited and forms impt. exp.

Peine, t., Lower Saxony, **Germany**; N.W. of Brunswick; iron, furniture, textiles; p. (1986) 45,600.

Peipus, Lake, Estonia; drained by Narva R. into G. of Finland; Pskov lies to S.; scene of Alexander Nevsky's victory over the Germans 1242; a. 3,626 km².

Pekalongan, t., N. cst. Java, **Indonesia**; exp. sugar, rubber; p. (1980) 132,558.

Peking. See Beijing.

Pelagi, gr. of Italian Is., inc. Lampedusa and Linosa, between Malta and Tunisian cst.

Pelée, mtn., **Martinique;** active volcano, devastated town of St. Pierre 1902; alt. 1,342 m.

Pella, dep. of Macedonia, **Greece;** mtnous.; cotton, wheat, tobacco; cap. Edessa; a. 2,802 km²; p. (1991) 138,761.

Peloponnesus (Peloponnisos), peninsula and reg., S. **Greece;** separated from mainland by G. of Corinth, but joined in N.E. by Isthmus of Corinth; mtnous.; livestock agr., drought-resistant sheep and goats; ch. ts., Kalamata, Tripolis; a. 21,642 km²; p. (1991) 1,086,935 (inc. region of Peloponnesus and district of Akhaia and Elia).

Pelotas, t., Rio Grande do Sul, **Brazil;** pt. on lagoon S.S.W. Pôrto Alegre; meat-packing and industl. ctr.; p. (1985) 278,400.

Pemba, I., part of **Tanzania;** cloves, copra, coconuts; exp. mangrove bark for tannin; a. 984 km²; p. (1988) 265,039.

Pemba (Port Amelia), spt., **Moçambique;** sisal, coconuts, cotton, maize, groundnuts; p. (1980) 41,166.

Pembroke, mkt. t., Pembrokeshire, **Wales;** on S. side of Milford Haven; sm. pt.; dock facilities; cas., ruins of Monkton priory; birth-place of Henry VII; p. (1991) 6,773.

Pembroke Dock, Pembrokeshire, **Wales;** site of government dockyard (1814) with consequent growth of a new t.; p. (1991) 8,651.

Pembrokeshire, S.W. **Wales,** unit. auth. created in 1996 from former l. gov. dists. of Preseli, Pembrokeshire and South Pembrokeshire, reinstating historic co. split up in 1974; p. (1995) 113,500.

Penang, I., st. W. **Malaysia;** cap. Georgetown, pt. for N. Malaya handling rubber and tin; paper mill; the first Brit. Straits Settlement (q.v.); linked by bridge (1985) to mainland; longest bridge (13 km.) in Asia; a. 1,036 km²; p. (1980) 954,638.

Penarth, t., Vale of Glamorgan, **Wales;** former sm. pt. on Severn estuary, 3 km S. of Cardiff; seaside resort; p. (1991) 20,319.

Pendle, l. gov. dist., Lancs., **Eng.;** ts. of Barrowford, Colne and Nelson; p. (1995) 85,300.

Pengpu. See Bengbu.

Penicuik, burgh, Midlothian, **Scot.;** on R. Esk; paper; p. (1991) 17,173.

Penistone, t., South Yorks., **Eng.;** on R. Don; steel; mkt.; p. (1991) 8,627.

Penki. See Benxi.

Penmaenmawr, t., Conwy, **Wales;** 6 km. S.W. of Conwy; resort; p. (1991) 2,681.

Pennine Alps, Switzerland; div. of Alpine system; ch. peaks; Mont Blanc (4,814 m) Monte Rosa (4,637 m), Matterhorn (4,477 m); winter sports.

Pennine Range, mtn. range, "backbone of England," extends 224 km southwards from Cheviot hills to Derbyshire; limestone, millstone grit; moorland sheep, dairying in valleys, quarrying, tourism; inc. Peak Dist. Nat. Park and Pennine Way long distance route; water supply, forestry; Cross Fell, 895 m.

Pennsylvania, st., **USA;** "Keystone St."; admitted to Union 1787; st. flower Mountain Laurel, st. bird Ruffed Grouse; originally proprietary colony of Penn family, later one of the 13 original sts. in the Union; traversed N.E. to S.W. by Appalachians; ch. Rs.: Delaware, Susquehanna, Allegheny, and Monogahela; major industl. st.; iron and steel, coal (bituminous and anthracite), natural gas, petroleum; maize, wheat, oats, rye; textiles, machin., motor cars, tobacco; cap. Harrisburg; ch. ts.; Pittsburgh, Philadelphia; a. 117,412 km²; p. (1990) 11,881,643.

Penrith, t., N.S.W., **Australia;** in Sydney met. a.; ctr. for mkt. gardening.

Penrith, mkt. t., Eden, Cumbria, **Eng.;** at N. foot of Shap Fell, 29 km S.E. of Carlisle; agr. mkt.; tourist ctr.; p. (1991) 12,049.

Penryn, t., Carrick, Cornwall, **Eng.;** on R. Fal estuary; sm. pt., boat repairs; once ctr. of granite quarrying; p. (1991) 7,027.

Pensacola, t., Fla., **USA;** on N. shore of P. Bay; originally a Spanish settlement, retaining much Spanish influence in squares, bldgs., street names; fishing, sea food inds.; univ.; naval air training school; p. (1984) 62,000 (t.), 318,700 (met. a.).

Penticton, B.C., **Canada;** comm. fruit ctr.; p.

(1991) 27,258.

Pentonville, dist., London, **Eng.;** prison; birthplace of John Stuart Mill.

Pentland Firth, strait, between Orkney Is. and Highland, **Scot.,** connecting N. Sea and Atl. Oc.; dangerous tidal currents.

Pentland Hills, range, **Scot.;** extend from Lanark to Edinburgh; hgst. Scald Law, 878 m.

Penwith, l. gov. dist., Cornwall, **Eng.;** S.W. tip of Cornwall inc. Penzance, St. Just and St. Ives; p. (1995) 60,000.

Pen-y-Ghent, peak, Pennines, North Yorks., **Eng.;** alt. 680 m.

Penza, c., cap. of P. oblast, **Russia;** on Sura R.; rly. junc.; agr. ctr., especially for grain tr. to Moscow; food-processing and wide range of mnfs.; oil pipeline from Mozyr'; p. (1989) 543,000.

Penzance, t., Penwith, Cornwall, **Eng.;** on Mount's Bay; tourist ctr.; ferry to Scilly Isles; engin.; birthplace of Sir Humphrey Davy; p. (1991) 19,709.

Peoria, t., Ill., **USA;** machin., domestic gds.; grain tr.; univ.; p. (1990) 113,504 (t.), 339,172 (met. a.).

Perak, st., **W. Malaysia;** ch. tin-dredging a., in basin of Perak R.; rubber; cap. Taiping; a. 20,668 km²; p. (1980) 1,805,198.

Pereira, t., Caldas, **Colombia;** cath.; comm. ctr. for coffee; severe earthquake devastation (1999); p. (1992) 335,960.

Perekop, Isthmus of, connects Crimea with Ukraine.

Pergamino, t., Buenos Aires, **Argentina;** road and rail focus in maize-growing dist.

Périgord, dist., S.W. **France;** limestone plateau crossed by Dordogne R.; famous for truffles.

Périgueux, t., cap. Dordogne, **France;** on R. Isle; cath.; famous for pâté de foie gras; engin., china; p. (1990) 32,848.

Perim, I. in strait of Bab-el-Mandeb at S. entrance to Red Sea; part of **Yemen;** former coaling sta.; a. 13 km²; p. 1,700.

Perlis, st., **W. Malaysia;** agr. dist. for rice and coconuts; tin; a. 803 km²; p. (1980) 148,276.

Perm, oblast, Russia; major mng., timber, and paper dist.; produces oil (Krasnokamsk), coal (Kizel), hydroelectricity, and potash (Solikamsh); cap. Perm.

Perm (Molotov), c., cap. of P. oblast, **Russia;** on Kama R.; machin., chemicals, oil refineries; univ.; p. (1989) 1,091,000.

Pernambuco, st., N.E. **Brazil;** mtnous. interior, cst. fertile; cap. Recife; sugar, cotton, manioc, tobacco, fruits; a. 98,322 km²; p. (1991) 7,109,626.

Pernik (Dimitrovo), c., **Bulgaria;** iron and steel inds.; p. (1990) 99,643.

Pernis, t., opposite Rotterdam, **Neth.;** lge. oil refinery; pipeline to Wesserling (nr. Cologne).

Perovo, t., **Russia;** nr. Moscow; engin., chemicals; agr. research institute; p. inc. in Moscow.

Perpignan, c., cap. of Pyrénées-Orientales dep., **France;** nr. Spanish border and Mediterranean; on Paris–Barcelona rly.; mkt. and comm. ctr. for wines and fruits; cath.; tourism; p. (1990) 108,049 (c.), 138,735 (met. a.).

Persepolis, anc. c., **Iran;** former cap. of Persian empire, now in ruins; tourism.

Pershore, t., Wychavon, Worcs., **Eng.;** on R. Avon; ctr. of fruit-growing a.; p. (1991) 7,087.

Persia. See Iran.

Persian Gulf, inlet from Indian Oc. through G. of Oman and Strait of Hormuz, between Iran and Arabia; oilfields in surrounding land and now in G. itself; ch. pts. Bandar-e-Bushehr, Abadan, Kuwait, Dubai; Bahrain, lgst. I.

Perth, c., cap. of W. **Australia;** on R. Swan; well planned garden c.; univ., cath., airport; many employed in services; inds. moving to Fremantle (pt.) or to Kwinana; p. (1993) 1,221,200 (met. a., 73 per cent of st. p.).

Perth, c., royal burgh, Perth and Kinross, **Scot.;** on R. Tay; rly. junction; cap. of Scot. until assassination of James I, 1437; dyeing, textiles, whisky distilling; cath; p. (1991) 41,453.

Perth and Kinross, unit. auth. created in 1996, formerly part of Tayside, E. **Scot.;** p. (1995) 132,820.

Perthshire, historic co., E. **Scot.,** now divided between Perth and Kinross and Stirling.

Peru, Andean rep., S. America; consists of 3 N.W.-S.E. regions; Costa (cst.) Sierra (Andes, rising to over 6,100 m) and Selva (interior *montaña* and R. basins); 40 per cent p. in Costa, 60 per cent in Sierra, yet Selva covers 70 per cent total a.; ch. Rs. Ucayali, Marañon; L. Titicaca shared with Bolivia; El Misti volcano in S.; cap. Lima on Pac. cst. with 20 per cent p.; agr. diversified and being extended by irrigation schemes; fishing main single ind.; mng. impt. in Andes; major world producer of silver, phosphates, potash, copper, petroleum; social, economic and political problems provoking long-lasting guerrilla revolt; seizure of foreign diplomats (1997); a. 1,249,048 km²; p. (1994) 23,130,300.

Peru Current (Humboldt), ocean current, S. Pac. Oc.; flows N. along cst. of N. Chile and Peru; causes clouds and fog.

Perugia, t., Umbria, **Italy**; on R. Tiber; univ., observatory; woollens, silks, lace; foodstuffs, furniture, pottery, chemicals, agr. machin.; p. (1992) 146,160.

Pervouralsk, t., **Russia**; in Urals; metallurgical ctr.; p. (1989) 142,000.

Pesaro, c., central **Italy**; on Adriatic cst.; agr. ctr., seaside resort; birthplace of Rossini; p. (1981) 90,412 (inc. Urbino).

Pescadores Is. (**P'eng-hu Lieh-tao**), archipelago, between Taiwan and mainland **China**; fishing, fish-processing; a. 132 km²

Pescara, c., cap. of P. prov., S. **Italy**; on estuary of R. Aterno; fish. pt., olive oil, soap, pasta, pottery; resort; birthplace of D'Annunzio; p. (1992) 121,424.

Peshawar, c., cap. of North-West Frontier Prov., **Pakistan**; 18 km E. of Khyber pass, commanding route to Afghanistan; military sta.; univ.; handicrafts, textiles, furniture; p. (1981) 555,000.

Petah Tikva, oldest modern Jewish settlement in **Israel** (1878); ctr. for oranges; mnfs. inc. textiles; p. (1992) 148,900.

Petaling Jaya, t., **W. Malaysia**; industl. estate nr. Kuala Lumpur; tyres, aluminium rolling mill.

Peter I., uninhabited I., **Antarctic Oc.**, belonging to Norway, a. *c.* 243 km².

Peterborough, t., Ont., **Canada**; flour-milling, elec. machin., trailers, agr. equipment, plastics, textiles, paper; p. (1986) 61,049.

Peterborough, c., l. gov. dist., Cambs., **Eng.**; on R. Nene on margin of Fens; cath.; rly ctr.; ctr. of brick ind. (Oxford clay around Fletton); diesel engines, agr. machin., gen. engin.; expanding t.; p. (1995) 159,300 (dist.), (1991) 134,788 (c.).

Peterborough, Soke of. *See* **Cambridgeshire**.

Peterhead, spt., burgh, Aberdeenshire, **Scot.**; on E. cst., 43 km N.E. of Aberdeen; herring fisheries, leading U.K. fish. pt. by value of fish landed (1982); fish-processing, granite quarrying; supply base for N. Sea oil; p. (1991) 18,674.

Peterlee, new t. (1948), Durham, **Eng.**; coal-mng. dist.; textiles, science-based inds.; p. (1991) 31,139.

Petersfield, t., East Hants., **Eng.**; on R. Rother, N.W. of Chichester; mkt.; p. (1991) 12,177.

Petra, anc. c., **Jordan**; temples, rock tombs and Roman ruins; called Sela in Bible (2 Kings 14. 7); rediscovered by Burckhardt 1812. Now threatened by erosion.

Petropavlovsk, t., **Kazakhstan**; on Ishim R.; rly. junc.; flour, leather, meat canneries, furs, engin.; p. (1990) 245,200.

Petropavlovsk-Kamchatsky, t., **Russia**; spt. on Pac. cst.; shipyard, timber mills, engin.; fishing and whaling fleet; p. (1989) 269,000.

Petrópolis, t., Rio de Janeiro, **Brazil**; health resort, *c.* 700 m a.s.l.; cath.; p. (1985) 275,100.

Petsamo. *See* **Pechenga**.

Petten, t., **Neth.**; 48 km N.W. of Amsterdam, on cst.; atomic research ctr.

Petworth, mkt. t., West Sussex, **Eng.**; in Rother valley, 19 km N.E. of Chichester; associated with Turner; p. (1991) 2,156.

Pevensey Levels, marshy a., East Sussex, **Eng.**; lie behind coastal sand-bars between Eastbourne and Bexhill, extend 8 km inland to Hailsham; now largely drained, cattle pastures; a. 62 km².

Pforzheim, t., Baden-Württemberg, **Germany**; S.E. of Karlsruhe; gold, silver, metal wks., jewellery; p. (1990) 113,600.

Phetburi, t. and prov., **Thailand**; on Isthmus of Kra crossed by Phetburi R.; p. (1980) 366,612 (prov.).

Philadelphia, c., pt., Penns., **USA**; on Delaware R.; comm., industl. and cultural ctr.; univ., R.C. cath., masonic temple, mint, academy of fine arts; shipbldg., locomotives, machin., surgical instruments, carpets, woollens, cottons, worsteds; sugar, and petroleum refining; ctr. of War of Independence 1775–1783; founded as Quaker col. by William Penn 1682; p. (1990) 1,585,577 (c.), 4,857,000 (met. a.).

Philippeville. *See* **Skikda**.

Philippines, Rep. of, S.E. Asia; chain of 7,100 Is. in Pac. Oc., stretching over 1,760 km; ch. Is. Luzon, Mindanao, Negros, Cebu, Mindoro, and Palawar; lie in track of cyclones; tropical climate; mtnous., agr. aided by intricate terracing system; most Is. underdeveloped except Luzon where p. concentrated; subsistence agr. rice and maize; 60 per cent of households live below the poverty line; coconuts major export crop; sugar impt. once but falling world prices have curtailed production; electronics and garments also exported; income generated by Filipinos working abroad sending wages home; geothermal energy used; coconut shells burnt for fuel; cap. Manila; a. 299,681 km²; p. (1994) 68,624,247.

Phlorina (Florina), t., Macedonia, **Greece**; in basin at 900 m, 16 km from Yugoslav border; agr. ctr.; p. (1981) 12,573.

Phnom-Penh, c., cap. of **Cambodia**, S.E. Asia; pt. on Mekong R.; handles ships up to 2,500 tonnes; linked to Kompong Som by modern highway; multi-purpose dam to W.; univ., royal palace; airport; p. (1994) 920,000.

Phoenix, c., Arizona, **USA**; on Salt R., ctr. of Salt River Valley irrigated region; electronics research, steel, aircraft, clothing; p. (1990) 983,403 (c.), 2,122,101 (met. a.).

Phoenix Group, Is., **Pac. Oc.**; part of Kiribati; a. 41 km²; US have some rights over Canton and Enderbury; Canton used as international airport; p. (1985) 24.

Phuket I., **Thailand**; off Kra Isthmus; main alluvial tin-working region of Thailand; ch. t. Phuket; a. 534 km².

Piacenza, c., cap. of P. prov., **Italy**; in Emilia-Romagna, on R. Po; agr. and comm. ctr.; cath., palaces, arsenal; cars, chemicals, cement; p. (1992) 102,161.

Piatra-Neamt, t., Moldavia, **Romania**; timber, pharmaceuticals, soap; oil refineries; p. (1992) 123,173.

Piaui, st., **Brazil**; semi-arid, underdeveloped dist.; thorn scrub; livestock rearing; cap. Teresina; a. 249,319 km²; p. (1991) 2,581,054.

Piave, R., N.E. **Italy**; flows to Adriatic, 200 km long.

Picardy (Picardie), former prov. and region inc. deps. Aisne, Oise, Somme, **France**; old battle sites, Agincourt and Crécy; rich agr. a.; textiles; p. (1990) 1,810,700.

Pichincha, prov., **Ecuador**; p. concentrated in Andes; many natural resources inc. lime, gypsum, silver; tropical hardwoods; cattle raising; cap. Quito; a. 16,105 km²; p. (1990) 1,756,228.

Pickering, mkt. t., Ryedale, North Yorks., **Eng.**; on N. margin of Vale of P.; church with murals; cas.; gas terminal; p. (1991) 5,914.

Pickering, Vale of, North Yorks., **Eng.**, wide, flat-floored vale, once occupied by glacial lake; bounded to N. by N. York Moors, to S. by York Wolds; drained W. by R. Derwent, alluvial soils, marshy in ctr.; crop farming along margins, cattle grazing in damper meadows in ctr., ch. ts. Pickering, Malton, Helmsley.

Picos de Europa, mtn. massif, N. **Spain**; hgst. massif in Cantabrian mtns., rising to 2,650 m; partially inc. in Nat. Park.

Picton, t., S.I., **N.Z.**; freezing wks.; tourist and fishing ctr.; pt.

Pictou, t., Nova Scotia, **Canada**; on Northumberland Strait; founded by Scottish settlers; p. (1986) 4,413.

Pidurutalagala, mtn., **Sri Lanka**; alt. 2,530 m; hgst. peak in rep.

Piedmont, region, N. **Italy**; rice, wheat, vines, fruits; cottons, woollens; a. 25,416 km²; p. (1992) 4,303,830.

Pietermaritzburg, c., cap. of Natal, **S. Africa**; named after Piet Retief and Gerhardus Maritz, two Boer leaders; lt. inds.; tanning; iron-ore mng. in a.; part of univ. of Natal; 2 caths.; p. (1985) 192,417 (met. a.).

Pietersburg, t., Transvaal, **S. Africa**; gold, asbestos, tin; comm. ctr. for cereals, tobacco, cotton, citrus fruits; p. (1980) 115,480 (dist.).

Pila (Schneidemühl), t. and prov., N.W. **Poland** (since 1945); formerly in Prussian prov. of Pomerania; tr. ctr., lignite mines nearby; p. (1989) 71,109 (t.), 476,000 (prov.).

Pilar, t., **Paraguay**; impt. R. pt.; sawmills; textiles; p. (1984) 26,352.

Pilbara, dist., W. **Australia**; extensive iron mng.; other minerals inc. salt, oil, nat. gas; rapid growth of p.

Pilcomayo, R., northernmost R. of **Argentina**; rises in Bolivian Andes, flows across the Gran Chaco, to enter Paraguay, joining the Paraguay R. nr. Asunción; hydroelec. power; 1,120 km long.

Pilibhit, t., Uttar Pradesh, N. **India**; admin. ctr.; sugar-refining; p. (1991) 106,605.

Pilsen. See Plzeň.

Pinar del Rio, c., prov. cap., **Cuba**; tobacco; p. (1990) 121,774 (1989) 681,500 (prov.).

Pinatubo, volcano **Philippines**; erupted June 1991.

Pinawa, t., Manitoba, **Canada**; 88 km N.E. of Winnipeg; nuclear research; p. (1986) 2,078.

Pindus, mtn. chain, between Thessaly and Albania, **Greece**; hgst. peak 2,455 m.

Pingxiang, c., Jianxi, **China**; supplies coking coal to Wuhan. p. (1984) 1,270,400.

Pinneberg, t., Schleswig-Holstein, **Germany**; N.W. of Hamburg; rose cultivation, metals, leather; p. (1986) 35,600.

Pinsk, c., **Belarus**; in Pripet Marshes, pt. on Pina R.; paper, wood-working inds., matches; Jewish residents exterminated during German occupation second world war; p. (1990) 121,600.

Piombino, t., **Italy**; mainland pt. for island of Elba; steel wks.; p. (1981) 39,389.

Piotrkow Trybunalski, t. and prov., **Poland**; cas.; timber and glass inds.; new textile combine; p. (1989) 80,598 (t.), 638,900 (prov.).

Piqua, t., Ohio, **USA**; N. of Dayton: ironwks., woollens; nuclear reactor; p. (1980) 20,480.

Piracicaba, t., São Paulo, **Brazil**; ctr. of agr. dist.; sugar-refining, brandy, flour; p. (1985) 252,900.

Piraeus, c., **Greece**; pt. of Athens and prin. pt. of Greece; major industl. and comm. ctr.; p. (1991) 182,671.

Pirmasens, t., Rhineland-Palatinate, **Germany**; S.W. of Mannheim; footwear, leather gds.; p. (1986) 46,100.

Pirna, t., Saxony, **Germany**; on R. Elbe; textiles, paper, glass; p. (1989) 43,486.

Pirot, t., Serbia, **Yugoslavia**; nr. Bulgarian border; in economic development a.; p. (1981) 69,653.

Pisa, c., **Italy**; at head of Arno delta, 19 km N.E. of Livorno; famous leaning tower, cath., univ.; textiles, chemicals, engin.; airport; tourism; p. (1984) 103,894.

Pistoia, t., Tuscany, **Italy**; on Arno plain, N.W. of Florence; iron and steel gds., macaroni; p. (1981) 92,274.

Pit, R., Cal., **USA**; rises in Goose L.; cuts spectacular gorges in the Cascades; used for hydroelectric power.

Pitcairn I., E. Pac. Oc., Brit. col.; inc. atolls of Ducie and Oeno and I. of Henderson; sweet potatoes, bananas, oranges, coconuts; a. 5 km²; mostly descendants of mutineers of the *Bounty*; p. (1997) 57.

Pitch Lake, Trinidad, W.I.; S. of I., 16 km S.W. of San Fernando; natural deposit of asphalt; tourism; a. 86 ha.

Pitea, spt., N. **Sweden**; on G. of Bothnia; saw-mills; p. (1992) 40,766.

Pitesti, t., **Romania**; on Arges R.; petroleum, fruit, grain; lge. automobile plant; oil refinery; p. (1992) 179,479.

Pitlochry, burgh, Perth and Kinross, **Scot.**; on R. Tummel, 8 km S. of Pass of Killiecrankie; summer resort; distilleries, hydros; p. (1991) 2,541.

Pittenweem, burgh, Fife, **Scot.**; at entrance to F. of Forth; fisheries; p. (1991) 1,561.

Pittsburgh, c., Penns., **USA**; univ.; R.C. cath.; pt. on Ohio R.; ctr. of richest American coal-field; natural gas, petroleum, iron and steel, machin., metal gds., meat-packing, glass, alu-minium, chemicals, p. (1990) 369,379 (c.), 2,057,000 (met. a.).

Pittsfield, c., Mass., **USA**; textiles, paper, plastics, elec. machin.; resort; p. (1980) 51,974.

Piura, prov. and t., N. **Peru**; on Piura R.; oldest Spanish t. in Peru; cotton mkt. and processing, p. (1993) 1,388,264 (prov.), 277,964 (t.).

Pladju, t., S. Sumatra, **Indonesia**; oil refining; linked by pipeline with Tempino and Bejubang.

Plata, Rio de la (Plate R.), estuary between **Argentina** and **Uruguay**; receives waters of Rs. Paraná and Uruguay; cst. provides sites for lge. spts., Buenos Aires, La Plata, Montevideo.

Platte, R., Nebraska, **USA**; formed by union of N. Platte and S. Platte Rs.; total length 2,240 km; irrigation, hydroelec. power.

Plauen, t., Saxony, **Germany**; textiles, machin., cable, leather, paper, radios; rly. junc; p. (1981) 78,800.

Plenty, Bay of, reg. and bay, N.I., **N.Z.**; on E. cst.; 208 km wide; p. (1991) 208,163.

Plettenberg, t., N. Rhine–Westphalia, **Germany**; on R. Lenne; iron wks.; p. (1986) 27,600.

Pleven, mkt. t., **Bulgaria**; many mosques; famous siege 1877; textiles, wines; p. (1990) 138,323.

Plitvička Jezera, lakes, W. Croatia{02sp}(formerly Yugoslavia); beautiful scenery; tourism; fishing.

Ploče, new spt., **Croatia** (formerly Yugoslavia); on Dalmatian cst.; industl. and rly. ctr.

Plock, t. and prov., **Poland**; on R. Vistula, nr. Warsaw; agr.; oil refinery and petrochemical plant; food processing; agr. machin.; p. (1989) 120,933 (t.), 512,600 (prov.).

Ploiesti, t., Prahova dist., **Romania**; petroleum, engin.; p. (1992) 252,073.

Plovdiv (Philippopolis), c., **Bulgaria**; on R. Maritsa; univ., Greek cath.; second c. of rep.; agr. processing, clothing, metals, engin.; p. (1990) 379,083.

Plymouth, c., spt., l. gov. dist., S. Devon, **Eng.**; on Plymouth Sound; comprises the "three towns" of Plymouth, Devonport, and Stonehouse; Brit. fleet faced Armada 1588; R.C. cath., guildhall, museum; Naval dockyard; seaside resort; fishing and fish-canning, lt. inds.; deposit of tungsten thought to be lgst. in W. Europe but lies within Dartmoor Nat. Park; p. (1995) 257,500 (dist.), (1991) 245,295 (c.).

Plymouth, ch. t., **Montserrat I.**, W.I.; p. (1985) 3,500. Volcanic destruction, 1997. Depopulated.

Plymouth, spt., Mass., **USA**; on Plymouth Bay, S.E. of Boston; here Pilgrim Fathers landed 1620 from *Mayflower* to form first English col.; Pilgrim Hall, Pilgrim Rock; textiles, cordage, machin.; tourism; p. (1980) 7,232.

Plynlimmon, mtn., Powys and Ceredigion, **Wales**; alt. 753 m; source of R. Severn.

Plzeň (Pilsen), c., W. Bohemia, **Czech Rep.**; ctr. of coal-mng. region; famous for beer and Lenin (former Skoda) armament wks.; p. (1990) 175,000.

Po, R., **Italy**; flows from Monte Viso, through Piedmont and Lombardy to the Adriatic; valley forms a major component of N. Italian lowland; natural gas deposits in valley; liable to flooding; 648 km long.

Pocklington, mkt. t., East Riding of Yorks., **Eng.**; foot of York Wolds, 19 km E. of York; ctr. of agr. dist.; 16th cent. grammar school; p. (1991) 5,908.

Podgorica, **(Titograd)** t., cap. of Montenegro, **S. Yugoslavia**; nr. Albanian frontier; anc. t. but now mainly modern with growing industl. activity; agr. processing, aluminium smelting; airport; p. (1991) 118,059.

Podolsk, t., **Russia**; on main rly. from Moscow to S.; engin., tin-smelting, food-processing; p. (1989) 209,000.

Pohai. See Bo Hai.

Point-à-Pierre, Trinidad; oil refinery; natural gas pipeline from Forest Reserve field.

Point-à-Pitre, ch. t. and pt. **Guadeloupe**, Fr. W.I.; on Grande Terre I.; exp. agr. prods., bananas, sugar; p. (1982) 25,310.

Pointe-des-Galets or **Le Port**, ch. pt., **La Réunion** (Fr.), Indian Oc.

Pointe-Noire, spt., **Congo Rep.**; airport, rly. to Brazzaville; agr. exp.; potash deposits nearby; linked to deepwater terminal for bulk carriers but mine closed due to flooding; petroleum refinery (1982); gas reserves; p. (1992) 576,206.

Point Fortin, t., **Trinidad**; oilfield and refinery.

Poitiers, c., cap. of Vienne dep., **France**; many attractive bldgs., cath.; agr. tr.; mnfs. chemicals, hosiery; Black Prince defeated Fr. 1356; p. (1990) 82,507 (c.), 105,268 (met. a.).

Poitou-Charentes, region, **France**; on western seaboard inc. deps. Charente, Charente-Maritime, Deux-Sèvres, Vienne; agr., vineyards; p. (1990) 1,595,100.

Pokrovsk (**Engels**), c., **Russia**; on Volga; R. pt., mftg. and food-processing ctr.; engin., petroleum refining, textiles; p. (1989) 181,000.

Poland, rep., E. Europe; history of country dominated by constantly changing sovereignty between E. and W. powers; strong national identity, based esp. on Catholic church; mainly lowland; continental climate; economy retarded by history of political fluctuation; growth of export-based inds. almost halted in 1980s depression; major ctr. of mng. and heavy inds. in conurb. of Upper Silesia, agr. land remains largely in private ownership, but govt. attempts to rationalise farm structure, major pts. at Gdynia, Gdansk, and Szczecin, international airport at cap. Warsaw, 17 historic provs. replaced by 49 large dists.; border with Germany fixed along Oder-Neisse line; applying for EU membership; a. 311,700 km²; p. (1995) 38,581,000.

Polotsk, c., **Belarus**; cath.; gasoline prod., oil refining; pipeline to Latvian pt. of Ventspils; food processing; p. (1990) 77,800.

Polotskiy, t. **Belarus**; 13 km W. of Polotsk; oil.

Poltava, c., **Ukraine**; industl. and food-processing ctr. in rich agr. dist.; countryside described in Gogol's work; textiles, synthetic diamond plant; battle 1709 between Swedish and Russian armies; p. (1990) 317,000.

Polynesia, ethnic region, **Oceania**; I. grs. in Pac. Oc. within 30° N. and S. of equator; between longitude 135° E. and W.; p. (1984) 498,000.

Pomerania, former prov., N. **Germany**; in post-war redivision part E. of R. Oder to **Poland**; part W. of R. Oder incorporated in Mecklenburg, E. **Germany**; farming, shipbldg., fishing.

Pomona (**Mainland**), lgst of the Orkney Is., **Scot.**; Kirkwall (cap.) and Stromness on I.; p. (1991) 15,128.

Pomorze. See Bydgoszcz.

Pompeii, ruined c., **Italy**; stood 21 km S.E. of Naples, at foot of Vesuvius; destroyed A.D. 79 by volcanic eruption, site re-discovered 1748; many interesting excavations; also modern c. nearby; fine church with famous collection of silver and gold plate; p. (1981) 22,896.

Ponape, volcanic I., **Micronesia**, W. Pac. Oc.; copra, ivory, nuts, starch, bauxite; a. 334 km²; p. (1990) 30,000.

Ponce, c., **Puerto Rico**; recently improved harbour on S. cst.; well connected with other ts. in rep.; ctr. of fertile, irrigated sugar-cane a.; industl. ctr.; p. (1990) 187,749.

Pondicherry, spt., Tamil Nadu st., **India**; on Coromandel cst.; cap. of P. Union Territory.; tr. ctr. for local prod.; p. (1991) 203,065 (c.), 807,785 (terr.).

Ponta Grossa, t., Paraná, **Brazil**; rly. junc.; comm. ctr.; maté, rice, timber, tobacco, bananas, cattle, jerked beef; p. (1985) 224,000.

Pontardawe, t., Neath Pt. Talbot, S. **Wales**; on R. Tawe, N.E. of Swansea; zinc smelting and refining; p. (1991) 18,479.

Pontchartrain, Lake, shallow L., lower Mississippi flood plain, **USA**; connected by canal to New Orleans 10 km to S., and by deltaic channels to G. of Mexico.

Pontefract, mkt. t., West Yorks., **Eng.**; 11 km E. of Wakefield; coal, furniture, confectionery, mkt. gardening; cas. ruins; p. (1991) 28,358.

Pontevedra, prov., **Spain**; on deeply indented Atl. cst.; transatlantic pt. Vigo; scenery and fiesta attractions for tourists; agr., livestock, timber, fisheries; cap. P.; a. 4,390 km²; p. (1991) 879,872.

Pontevedra, c., cap. of P. prov., N.W. **Spain**; fish. pt., handicrafts, agr. tr.; p. (1987) 67,314.

Pontiac, t., Mich., **USA**; on Clinton R.; fishing and shooting, motor cars, rubber gds., machin., varnish; p. (1980) 76,715.

Pontianak, t., cap. of Kalimantan, **Indonesia**; exp. rubber, copra; rubber processing; p. (1983) 355,000.

Pontine Is., off W. cst. of **Italy**; in Tyrrhenian Sea; a. 11·6 km²; p. 6,000.

Pontine Marshes, region, Latium, S. **Italy**; coastal zone S.E. of Rome extending from Velletri to

Terracina; formerly highly malarial fens, largely drained and colonised 1930–35; 3,200 new farms, 4 new ts.; ch. t. Littoria; a. 647 km².

Pontresina, t., Grisons, **Switzerland**; E. of St. Moritz; tourist resort.

Pontypool, t., Torfaen, **Wales**; coal, steel, glass, bricks, tin galvanising, nylon at Manhilad; p. (1991) 35,564.

Pontypridd, t., Rhondda, Cynon, Taff, **Wales**; on R. Taff, 19 km N.W. of Cardiff; formerly coal, iron-founding; p. (1991) 28,487.

Pool Malebo (**Stanley Pool**), **Congo** and **Congo Rep.**; lake formed by expansion of R. Congo; length 40 km.; width 26 km.

Poole, t., unit. auth. created in 1997, formerly part of Dorset, **Eng.**; spt. on Poole Harbour, 6 km W. of Bournemouth; imports clay for local pottery inds; petroleum production began 1979; tourism, yachting, marine engin., chemicals; p. (1995) 138,900 (former dist.), (1991) 138,479 (t.).

Poona. See Pune.

Poopó, salt L., Oruro dep., **Bolivia**; fed from L. Titicaca by R. Desaguadero, which flows over saline beds; no outlet; c. 3,600 m a.s.l.; a. 2,600 km².

Popayan, c., S.W. **Columbia**; 1,677 m above Cauca R.; cath., univ.; food processing, coffee, flour; mng. nearby; p. (1992) 203,722.

Poplar. See Tower Hamlets.

Popocatepetl, volcano, nr. Puebla, **Mexico**; alt. 5,456 m; dormant since 1702.

Porbander, spt., Gujarat, **India**; exp. silk, cotton; imports coal, dates, timber, machin., petroleum; birthplace of Mahatma Gandhi; p. (1991) 116,671.

Pori (**Björneborg**), spt., S. **Finland**; at mouth of R. Kokemäen; copper refinery, rolling mills, match, paper and pulp wks.; p. (1993) 76,422.

Porirua, c., Wellington, N.I., **N.Z.**; dormitory for Wellington; p. (1991) 46,601.

Porjus, t., Norrbotten, N. **Sweden**; on R. Lulea, hydroelectric plant supplies power to iron-ore mng. dists. of Gallivare and Kiruna, also to Narvik rly.

Porsgrunn, spt., **Norway**; timber, shipping, engin., porcelain, explosives; p. (1990) 35,172.

Port Adelaide, main pt., S. **Australia**; serves Adelaide; exp. agr. prods. from hinterland; imports bulk cargoes (petroleum, phosphate, limestone).

Portadown, t., Craigavon, N. **Ireland**; on R. Bann, 40 km S.W. of Belfast; linen, food processing; merged with Lurgan to form new c. of Craigavon; p. (1991) 21,299.

Portaferry, spt., Ards, N. **Ireland**; shipping fisheries; p. (1991) 2,324.

Portage la Prairie, t., Manitoba, **Canada**; sm. pt. on Assiniboine R.; grain and potato tr.; p. (1991) 13,186.

Port Alberni, spt., Vancouver I., B.C., **Canada**; exp. timber; fisheries; timber inds.; p. (1991) 18,403.

Port Alfred, pt., **Canada**; upper St. Lawrence R.; imports bauxite for smelting at Arvida.

Port Amelia. See Pemba.

Portarlington, mkt. t., Offaly, **R.o.I.**; farming; first place to have elec. power-sta. using local peat fuel; p. (1986) 3,295.

Port Arthur. (Canada) See Thunder Bay.

Port Arthur (China). See Lushun.

Port Arthur, t., Texas, **USA**; pt. on L. Sabine; exp. petroleum, chemicals, grain; p. (1980) 61,251.

Port Arzew, pt., **Algeria**; world's first plant to liquefy natural gas (1964); oil pipeline from Haoud el Hamra; oil refinery.

Port Augusta, t., spt., S. **Australia**; at head of Spencer G.; fine harbour; salt field; exp. wheat, fruit; impt. rly. junction; p. (1991) 14,966.

Port-au-Prince, c., cap. of **Haiti**; spt. on bay in G. of La Gonave; cultural and political ctr.; univ., cath.; food processing and exp.; oil refinery; p. (1992) 1,255,078.

Port Blair, spt., cap. of Andaman and Nicobar Is., **India**; p. (1991) 74,955.

Port Chalmers, t., bor., S.I. **N.Z.**; container pt., timber exp.

Port Colborne, t., Ont., **Canada**; pt. on L. Erie; iron smelting; nickel and copper refining; power from Niagara falls; p. (1986) 18,281.

Port Elizabeth, spt., Cape Prov., S. **Africa**; on Algoa Bay; bilingual univ.; exp. skins, wool, ostrich feathers, mohair; foundries, soap, chemicals, car assembly, food preservation, sawmills; p. (1985) 651,993 (met. a.).

Port Erin, v., **Isle of Man**; on S.E. cst.; seaside resort, fisheries.

Port Essington, N. point, of Coburg peninsula, N.T., **Australia**; pearl culture experiments.

Port Etienne, *See* Nouadhibou.

Port Franequi, *See* Ilebo.

Port Gentil, spt., **Gabon**, Eq. Africa; exp. palmoil, mahogany, ebony; sawmills, fishing, centre of Gabon's main oil reserves, oil refining; p. (1983) 123,300.

Port Glasgow, burgh, spt., Inverclyde, **Scot.**; on S. bank of R. Clyde, 27 km below Glasgow; shipbldg. and repairing, textiles, rope, canvas mftg.; p. (1991) 19,693.

Port Harcourt, spt., **Nigeria**; 48 km from sea on E. branch of Niger delta; terminus of E. Nigerian rly. system; tin, palm oil, groundnuts; bitumen plant, tyres; oil refining; p. (1992) 371,000.

Porthcawl, t., Bridgend, **Wales**; on cst. 16 km S.E. of Pt. Talbot; resort; p. (1991) 15,922.

Port Hedland, sm. spt., **W. Australia**; new t. being built 8 km inland to absorb impact of Mt. Newman ore project; twin ts. linked by industl. belt; exp. iron ore to Japan; p. (1991) 12,599.

Porthmadog (**Portmadoc**), t., Gwynedd, **Wales**; pt. on Tremadog Bay; terminus of Festiniog lt. rly.; p. (1991) 3,048.

Port Hope, t., Ont., **Canada**; midway along N. shore of L. Ont.; fruit, dairying, radium refining; p. (1986) 10,281.

Port Huron, t., Mich., **USA**; on L. Huron; summer resort, dry docks, grain elevators; motor-car parts; p. (1980) 33,981.

Portici, spt., Campania, **S. Italy**; on Bay of Naples; dockland sub. of Naples; p. (1981) 79,259.

Portile de Fier. *See* Iron Gate.

Portishead, pt., N. Somerset, **Eng.**; on Severn estuary 5 km S.W. of Avonmouth; shipping; p. (1991) 14,721.

Port Jackson, N.S.W., **Australia**; deep natural harbour used by Sydney and crossed by Sydney bridge.

Port Kelang (**Port Swettenham**), major spt. of **Malaysia**; 48 km W. of Kuala Lumpur; exp. primary prods. inc. tin, rubber, fruit; imports mnfs.; p. 11,300.

Port Kembla, spt., N.S.W., **Australia**; part of Wollongong; artificial pt. built to exp. coal; many expansion programmes; integrated steelworks; p. (1981) 208,651 (inc. Wollongong).

Portknockie, burgh, Moray, **Scot.**; on N. Buchan cst., 8 km E. of Buckie; sm. fish. pt.; p. (1991) 1,296.

Portland, t., Weymouth and P., Dorset, **Eng.**; 6 km S. of Weymouth on sheltered N.E. side of I. of Portland; lge artificial harbour; naval base closing, prison; p. (1981) 10,915.

Portland, t., spt., Me., **USA**; comm. cap. of Me.; lge fisheries; paper, pulp, lumber, processed food, clothing; p. (1984) 61,800 (t.), 201,200 (met. a.).

Portland, c., Ore., **USA**; gr. wheat and wool tr.; flour milling, shipbldg., fishing and canning, aluminium, lumber; p. (1990) 437,319 (c.), (1990) 1,240,000 (met. a.).

Portland Canal, fjord, N.W. cst of America, forming bdy. between Alaska and B.C.

Portland, I. of, Dorset, **Eng.**; limestone mass, linked to mainland by shingle spit, Chesil Bank, terminates S. in Portland Bill; naval base, Borstal institution; limestone quarrying; masonry wks.

Portlaoighise, mkt., t., Laoighis, **R.o.I.**; flour, malting; p. (1986) 3,773.

Port Louis, c., cap., of **Mauritius**; pt. on Indian Oc.; exp. sugar; contains 42% of Mauritius p. in met.a.; port extension and bulk sugar terminal; p. (1993) 144,250.

Port Macquarie, t., N.S.W., **Australia**; former penal settlement on Hastings R.; resort; p. (1981) 19,581.

Port Moresby, t., cap. of **Papua New Guinea**, 2,880 km from Sydney; spt., airpt.; univ.; p. (1990) 193,242.

Port Nelson, spt., Manitoba, **Canada**; on cst. of Hudson Bay at mouth of R. Nelson; linked by rly. to trans-continental systems; exp. wheat, minerals; closed by ice for 7 months each year.

Port Nolloth, spt., Cape Prov., **S. Africa**; serves

copper- and diamond-mng. dists.; declining crayfish pt.

Pôrto Alegre, c., cap. of Rio Grande do Sul st., **Brazil**; exp. lard, preserved meats, rice, timber, tobacco; textiles, chemicals, furniture, brewing, metallurgy; oil refinery under construction; pipeline connects with Rio Grande; 2 univs.; p. (1991) 1,262,631.

Portobello, resort, **Scot.**; on F. of Forth, 5 km E. of Edinburgh.

Port of Spain, c., cap. of **Trinidad**; attractive c. with squares; 2 caths.; mosque; spt. exp. cocoa, sugar, asphalt, oil; natural gas pipeline from Penal; food processing; p. (1990) 58,400.

Porto Marghera, spt., Venezia, **N. Italy**; the modern pt. of Venice, reached by ship canal dredged through shallow lagoon; oil refineries; chemicals, metal refining.

Porto Novo, t., cap. of **Benin Rep.**; on coastal lagoon; spt.; fishing; many old colonial bldgs.; p. (1982) 208,258.

Pôrto Velho, c., cap of Rondônia st., **Brazil**; in a. producing maize, rice, rubber, tin; p. (1985) 202,000.

Portoviejo, t., **Ecuador**; mkt. and comm. ctr. for agr. dist.; p. (1990) 132,937.

Port Phillip, lge. inlet., Victoria, **Australia**, landlocked bay, Melbourne on N., Geelong on W.

Port Pirie, t., spt., **S. Australia**; major pt. on Spencer Gulf; refines zinc and lead from Broken Hill; exp. wheat; p. (1991) 14,398.

Port Radium, t., N.W. Terr., **Canada**; on Gr. Bear L.; pitchblende deposits.

Portree, spt., v., I. of Skye, Highland, **Scot.**; landlocked harbour on P. Bay, Sound of Raasay; fishing; tweed mill; p. (1991) 2,126.

Portrush, spt., Coleraine, **N. Ireland**; 8 km N. of Coleraine; tourism; p. (1991) 5,598.

Port Said, (**Bur Sa'id**), spt. and prov., **Egypt**; at N. end of Suez Canal; free tr. a.; impt. fuelling sta.; entrepôt tr.; p. (1991) 449,000, (1990) 461,000 (prov.).

Port St. Mary, v., **Isle of Man**; on S.E. cst.; resort; fisheries, boat-bldg.

Portsdown Hill, chalk ridge, Hants., **Eng.**; extends E. to W. behind Portsmouth from Havant to Fareham.

Portsea I., fortfd. I., between Portsmouth and Langston harbours, Portsmouth, **Eng**.

Portslade-by-Sea, t., Brighton and Hove, **Eng.**; W. of Hove; p. (1991) 17,762.

Portsmouth, c., naval pt., unit. auth. created in 1997, formerly part of Hants., **Eng.**; opposite I. of Wight; naval establishment; Portsmouth is the garrison t.; Portsea has the naval dockyards, Landport is residtl., and Southsea is a popular resort; naval dockyard for fleet maintenance and repair closed 1984; across the harbour is Gosport; shipbldg.; gen. mnfs.; birthplace of Dickens and I. K. Brunel; p. (1995) 189,900 (former dist.), (1991) 174,669 (c.).

Portsmouth, t., N.H., **USA**; summer resort, naval dockyard, cotton; the 1905 Peace Treaty between Japan and Russia was negotiated here; p. (1984) 27,800 (t.), 206,500 (met. a.).

Portsmouth, t., Ohio, **USA**; iron and steel gds., aircraft, boots, shoes, bricks; p. (1980) 25,943.

Portsmouth, spt., Va., **USA**; naval dockyard; farm produce, cotton, rly. wks.; p. (1990) 103,907.

Portsoy, burgh, Aberdeenshire, **Scot.**; spt. 8 km W. of Banff; fisheries and meal milling; p. (1991) 1,822.

Port Stanvac, **S. Australia**; 24 km S. of Adelaide; oil refining.

Port Sudan, spt., **Sudan**; 48 km N. of Suakin; linked by rail to Atbara and Khartoum; oil refining; p. (1983) 206,727.

Port Sunlight, Merseyside, **Eng.**; garden v. founded 1888 by Lord Leverhulme for the employees of the Port Sunlight factories.

Port Swettenham. *See* **Port Kelang**.

Port Talbot, t., Neath Port Talbot, S. **Wales**; on E. side of Swansea Bay; impt. iron and steel ind., copper, coal; new deep-water harbour serves as ore terminal; p. (1991) 37,647.

Portugal, rep., Iberia, W. Europe; member of EU (1986); mild temperate climate on cst., drier and hotter in interior; economy based on an inefficient agr. sector, located in wide fertile valleys, and associated processing inds.; major exp. of cork, but few industl. raw materials; textiles; post-war growth of tourist inds.; cap. and airport Lisbon; a. 91,945 km²; p. (1994) 9,902,200.

Portuguesa, st., **Venezuela**; inc. llanos plains; livestock raising; cap. Guanare; a. 15,200 km²; p. (1990) 625,576.

Portuguese Guinea. *See* Guinea-Bissau.

Portuguese Timor. *See* East Timor.

Portuguese West Africa. *See* Angola, People's Rep. of.

Porvoo, spt., S. **Finland**; on G. of Finland; exp. ctr. for forest prods.

Porz, t., N. Rhine–Westphalia, **Germany**; on R. Rhine, part of Cologne; glass, metals, paper.

Posadas, c., cap. of Misiones prov., N.E. **Argentina**; on upper Paraná R.; on border of Paraguay; yerba-maté, tobacco, cereals; connection for Iguaça falls; p. (1991) 210,755.

Posen. *See* Poznan.

Pössneck, t., Gera, **Germany**; S.E. of Weimar; porcelain, textiles, leather; p. (1989) 17,410.

Postillon Is., Lesser Sunda Is., **Indonesia**; coconuts.

Postojna (**Adelsberg**), t., **Slovenia** (formerly Yugoslavia); 32 km N.E. of Trieste; extensive grotto and stalactite cavern.

Potchefstroom, t., Transvaal, **S. Africa**; on Mooi R.; univ.; agr.; malt, timber, engin.; p. (1980) 141,000 (dist.).

Potenza, t., cap. of P. prov., **Italy**; on hill 220 m above Basento R.; agr. and industl. ctr.; univ.; p. (1981) 64,358.

Poti, spt., **Georgia**; exp. manganese; fish processing, timber-milling, engin.; p. (1990) 137,300.

Potomac, R., **USA**; divides Va. from Md.; flows past Wash., to Chesapeake Bay; 464 km long.

Potosi, dep., **Bolivia**; famous for silver- and tin-mines; zinc ore; cap. Potosi; a. 116,630 km²; p. (1988) 667,800.

Potosi, c., **Bolivia**; on slope of Cerro Gordo de Potosi, 4,072 m a.s.l.; tin, silver, copper, lead mng.; p. (1992) 112,291.

Potsdam, c., cap. of Brandenburg *Land*, **Germany**; on R. Havel, 29 km S.E. of Berlin; beautiful parks and gardens, many palaces; scene of conference between Allies on bdy. questions, 1945; motor and locomotive wks., engin.; precision instruments; p. (1990) 139,500.

Potteries, The, dist., Stoke, **Eng.**; ctr. of earthenware ind., comprising ts. Burslem, Hanley, Fenton, Tunstall, Stoke and Longton.

Potters Bar, t., Hertsmere, Herts., **Eng.**; residtl.; in London commuter belt; p. (1991) 22,414.

Poulton-le-Fylde, t., Lancs., **Eng.**; ctr. of mkt. gardening, poultry rearing dist.; p. (1991) 18,939.

Powys, central **Wales**, unit. auth. created in 1996 from former l. gov. dists. of Brecknock, Montgomeryshire and Radnorshire; mtnous a. bordering Eng.; forestry, stockraising and water catchment for Eng.; crossed by Rs. Wye and Severn; sparse p.; p. (1995) 122,300.

Powys, Vale of, Powys, **Wales**; drained by R. Severn; cattle-rearing; ch. t. Welshpool.

Poyang Hu, lge. L., Jiangxi, **China**; on S. margin of Chang Jiang plain; surrounded by flat, intensively cultivated land, rice, sugar, mulberry; size varies greatly with season, max. a. (in late summer) 4,662 km².

Poznan, prov., W. **Poland**; drained by Warta and Notec Rs.; mainly agr.; stock-raising; mnfs. inc. locomotives; a. 26,705 km²; p. (1989) 1,323,400.

Poznan, c., cap. of P. prov., **Poland**; on Warta R.; route ctr., industl. and educational ctr.; cath. univ.; cap. of Poland; iron-founding, chemicals; anc. c., once cap. of Poland; p. (1989) 586,908.

Pozzuoli, t., **Italy**; 3 km W. of Naples; anc. Puteoli; mineral baths, ordnance wks.; Roman ruins; p. (1981) 70,350.

Prague (**Praha**), c., cap. of Czech Rep.; picturesque, anc. c. on R. Vltava; comm. and cultural ctr.; univ. (founded 1348); outstanding architecture; extensive mnfs.; machin., sugar, leather, milling, chemicals; p. (1990) 1,215,000.

Prahova, R., Walachia, **Romania**; rises in Transylvanian Alps, flows S. into R. Ialomita; c. 176 km long.

Prato, t., **Italy**; 13 km N.W. of Florence; cath.; mediaeval cas. and fortifications; cottons, woollens, machin.; p. (1992) 166,108.

Predeal Pass, **Romania**; carries main road and rly. across Transylvanian Alps from Bucharest to Brasov; alt. over 1,200 m.

Preesall, t., Lancs., **Eng.**; N. of Blackpool; p. (1991) 5,168.

Pregel, R., **Poland**; flows to Frisches Haff, nr. Kaliningrad; 200 km long.

Prek Ihnot, **Cambodia**; power and irrigation development project on lower Mekong R.

Prerov, t., **Czech Rep.**; S.E. of Olomouc; hardware, textiles; p. (1984) 50,241.

Prescot, mftg. t., Knowsley, Merseyside, **Eng.**; 6 km. S.W. of St. Helens; mkt., elec. cable ind.; p. (1991) 37,486.

Prešov, mkt. t., **Slovakia**; linen mnfs.; p. (1990) 89,000.

Prestatyn, t., Denbighshire, **Wales**; on N. cst., 5 km E. of Rhyl; seaside resort; p. (1991) 15,020.

Presteigne, mkt. t., Powys, **Wales**; on R. Lugg, 16 km N.W. of Leominster; p. (1991) 1,815.

Preston, t., l. gov. dist., Lancs., **Eng.**; pt. on R. Ribble; textiles, engin., aircraft wks.; p. (1995) 134,300 (dist.), (1991) 177,660 (t.).

Prestonpans, burgh, E. Lothian, S.E. **Scot.**; on F. of Forth, 14 km E. of Edinburgh; scene of Jacobite victory 1745; p. (1991) 7,014.

Prestwich, t., Gtr. Manchester, **Eng.**; in valley of R. Irwell, 6 km N.W. of Manchester; cotton bleaching and dyeing, soap, furnishings; p. (1991) 31,801.

Prestwick, burgh, S. Ayrshire, **Scot.**; on F. of Clyde, 5 km N. of Ayr; golfing ctr. and trans- atlantic airpt. and freeport (1984); resort; p. (1991) 13,705.

Pretoria, c., Transvaal, admin. cap. of **Rep. of S. Africa**; univ., tr. ctr.; inds. inc. engin., chemicals, iron, and steel; p. (1985) 822,925 (met. a.).

Preveza, ch. pt. and t. of P. dep. of Epirus, N.W. **Greece**; guards G. of Arta; p. (1981) 13,624 (c.), (1991) 58,910 (dep.).

Pribilof Is., off S.W. Alaska, **USA**; seal fur; a. 168 km².

Pribram, t., Bohemia, **Czech Rep.**; impt. lead and silver mines, zinc, barium and antimony; p. (1984) 38,787.

Prijedor, t., **Bosnia-Herzegovina**, formerly Yugoslavia; on E. flank of Dinaric Alps, 104 km S.E. of Zagreb; rly. junc.; iron-ore mines.

Prilep, t., **Macedonia**, formerly Yugoslavia; mkt., refractory materials, tobacco processing; p. (1981) 99,770.

Primorskiy Kray, terr., **Russia**; S.E. Siberia, on Sea of Japan; coal, iron ore, and various metals in vicinity; fisheries; millet and rice; slow economic development results from isolation; wants economic links with China; ch. cs., Vladivostok (cap.), Ussuriysk; a. 168,350 km²; p. (1989) 2,256,100.

Prince Albert, t., Saskatchewan, **Canada**; lumbering, furs; p. (1991) 34,181.

Prince Edward I., prov., **Canada**; sm. I. in G. of St. Lawrence; physically poorly endowed; rocky, with thin soils; pastoral agr., furfarming, fishing; cap. Charlottetown; a. 5,657 km²; p. (1991) 129,765.

Prince George, t., B.C., **Canada**; oil refining; lumbering, mng., fur tr.; p. (1991) 69,653.

Prince Rupert, t., B.C., **Canada**; Pac. pt. of Canadian National rly.; service ctr., fishing and fish-processing; p. (1986) 15,755.

Princeton, bor., N.J., **USA**; seat of Princeton Univ.; p. (1980) 12,035.

Principe. *See* São Tomé.

Pripet Marshes, **Belarus**; forested swampy region crossed by Pripet R. and its streams; greater part reclaimed; coal and petroleum; a. 46,620 km².

Pripet (**Pripyat**), R., **Belarus**; trib. of R. Dnieper; 560 km long.

Privas, t., cap. of **Ardèche** dep., **France**; p. (1990) 10,490.

Pristina, c., cap. of Kossovo aut. region, S.W. Serbia, **Yugoslavia**; on Sitnic R.; admin. ctr.; many mosques; devastated in 1999 war.

Prokopyevsk, t., S.W. Siberia, **Russia**; in Novosibirsk dist.; one of the main coalfields of Kuznetsk Basin; mng. machin., metallurgy; p. (1989) 274,000.

Prome, c. **Myanmar**; pt. on R. Irrawaddy; connected by rail and road to Rangoon; tr. in rice, cotton, tobacco; one of oldest cs. in Burma, founded 8th cent.

Proskurov. *See* Khmel'nitskiy.

Prostejov, t., N. Moravia, **Czech Rep.**; rly. junc.; agr. machin., textiles; historic bldgs.; p. (1984) 51,100.

Provence, former prov. now incorporated in Provence-Alpes-Côte d'Azur, **France**; inc. deps. Alpes-de-Haute-Provence, Hautes-Alpes, Alpes-Maritimes, Bouches-du-Rhône, Var, Vaucluse; mkt. gardening, tourism esp. along coast; ch. city Marseille; p. (1990) 4,257,900.

Providence, c., R.I. **USA**; at head of Narragansett Bay; univ.; jewellery, textiles, silverware, rubber gds., machin., oil, coal; p. (1990) 160,728 (c.), 655,000 (met. a.).

Provo, t., Utah, **USA**; at base of Wasatch mtns., nr. shore of Utah L.; univ.; flour, bricks, blast furnaces; p. (1990) 264,000 (met. a. with Orem).

Prudhoe, Tynedale, Northumberland, **Eng.**; former coal mng. t.; chemicals, paper; p. (1991) 11,204.

Prudhoe Bay, N.E. Alaska, **USA**; the jewel in Alaska's oil crown; arctic conditions make extraction and transport of oil difficult and ecologically dangerous but despite opposition from environmentalist groups 1,262 km pipeline to ice-free pt. of Valdez.

Prussia, former kingdom (1701–1806); former st. (1806–1945), **Germany**; consisted of 13 provs., cap. Berlin; formally abolished 1947; E. Prussia partitioned between USSR and Poland.

Pruszkow, t., **Poland**; nr. Warsaw; elec. plant; engin.; p. (1989) 53,889.

Prut, R., rises in Ukraine and then forms the boundary between **Romania** and **Moldova** as it flows from the Carpathian mtns. to the Danube R.; 576 km long.

Przemyśl, c. and prov., S.E. **Poland**; on San R. (trib. of Vistula) nr. bdy. between Poland and Ukraine; anc. fortress t.; sewing machin.; p. (1989) 68,121 (c.), 404,200 (prov.).

Pskov, c., **Russia**; on R. Velikaya, nr. entry to L. Peipus; rly. junc.; flax tr.; historic bldgs.; scene of abdication of Nicholas II, March 1917; p. (1989) 204,000.

Pudsey, t., West Yorks., **Eng.**; between Leeds and Bradford; woollens; p. (1991) 31,636.

Puebla, c., cap. of P. st., **Mexico**; one of oldest and most impt. cs. of rep.; fine cath., theatre, univ.; cotton mills, onyx quarries, glazed tiles; p. (1990) 1,054,921.

Puebla, st., **Mexico**; on interior plateau at 2,400 m; fertile valleys for coffee and sugar; mng. impt.; dense p.; a. 33,991 km^2; p. (1989) 4,118,059.

Pueblo, c., Col., **USA**; on R. Arkansas, in foothills of Rockies; iron and steel ctr.; coal and various metals nearby; p. (1990) 98,640 (t.), 123,051 (met. a.).

Puente-Genil, t., Córdoba, **Spain**; olive oil, quince pulp; p. (1981) 25,615.

Puerto Barrios, pt., **Guatemala**; rly. terminus; oil refining; p. (1989) 338,000.

Puerto Cabello, spt., N. **Venezuela**; on Caribbean nr. Valencia; excellent harbour; linked by rail and highway to Carácas; asbestos, vegetable oils, soap, candles, meat-packing; p. (1980) 94,000.

Puerto Cortés, spt., N.W. **Honduras**; on Caribbean; exp. bananas, hardwoods; p. (1988) 43,300.

Puerto de Santa Maria, El, spt., S.W. **Spain**; on Bay of Cadiz; exp. mainly sherry; p. (1981) 45,933.

Puerto la Cruz, t., **Venezuela**; 16 km from Barcelona; oil refining; p. with Barcelona (1981) 81,800.

Puerto Limón. See Limón.

Puerto Montt, spt., **Chile**; cap. Los Lagos region; in sheep-farming dist.; S. terminus of rlys.; devastated by earthquake 1960; p. (1992) 130,737.

Puerto Ordaz. See Santo Tomé de la Guayana.

Puerto Rico, I., terr. of **USA**, W.I.; since 1952 free commonwealth ass. with USA; democratic economic growth aided recently by falling birth-rate; mtnous., eroded soils, alt. modifies tropical climate; exp. mnfs., but agr. impt. internally; 80 per cent land under cultivation, sugar, tobacco, coffee; tourism; cap. San Juan; a. 8,866 km^2; p. (1993) 3,522,037.

Puerto Saurez, R. pt., **Bolivia**; on R. Paraguay; collecting ctr. for rubber, coffee, Brazil nuts.

Puget Sound, Wash., **USA**; inlet of Pac. Oc.

Puket. See Phuket.

Pula, spt., **Croatia**, (formerly Yugoslavia); on Adriatic; industl. ctr. with shipyards, docks, and various inds.; ch. naval base of Habsburg empire; tourism; Roman remains; p. (1981) 77,278.

Pulia. See Apulia.

Puna, cold, bleak, and barren plateau of Andes in Peru and Bolivia, 3,600–5,500 m.

Pune (Poona), c., Maharashtra, **India**; in W. Ghats; temperate pleasant climate; cultural, educational (univ.) and political ctr.; military base; agr. tr. ctr.; cotton gds., paper; p. (1991) 1,567,000.

Punjab, region N.W. Indus plains, Indian sub-continent; extensive irrigation from the "five rivers"—Jhelum, Chenab, Ravi, Bias, Sutlej; now divided politically between India and Pakistan; impt. cotton, wheat, and sugar dist.; coal deposits.

Punjab (East), former st., **India**; partitioned on linguistic basis 1966; Punjab-speaking Punjab st. (a. 50,375 km^2; p. (1981) 16,788,915 inc. 55 per

cent Sikh); and Hindi-speaking Haryana st. (a. 44,056 km^2; p. (1991) 20,281,969; joint cap. Chandigarh.

Punjab (West), prov., **Pakistan**; old prov. revived 1970; p. (1981) 47,292,441.

Punta Arenas, c., cap. of Magallanes prov., S. **Chile**; most S. c. in world; mutton, wool; coal nearby; natural gas pipeline from Kimiri-Aike; p. (1992) 113,661.

Puntarenas, spt., **Costa Rica**, on G. of Nicoya; fishing; fish-processing; resort; p. (1984) 37,390 (dist.).

Purbeck, I. of, sm. penin., Dorset cst., **Eng.**; anc. v. of Corfe Castle in ctr.; limestone ("Purbeck marble") quarries; site of Britain's lgst. onshore oilfield; once a royal deer forest; forms 1. gov. dist. of Purbeck, inc. Wareham and Swanage; p. (1995) 44,900.

Puri, t., Orissa, **India**; long famous for its temple and festival of the god Vishnu and his monster car, Juggernaut; p. (1991) 125,199.

Purus, R., Peru and Brazil; rises in Andes, flows to Amazon R. through underdeveloped a.; 3,360 km long.

Pusan, main pt. of **S. Korea**; on Korean Strait at head of Naktong R. basin; textiles; steel mill at Pohang nearby; Korea's first nuclear power sta.; p. (1990) 3,797,566.

Pushkin, c., **Russia**; nr. St. Petersburg; summer palaces of Tsars; Pushkin museum; Pulkovo observatory nearby.

Puteaux, sub. Paris, **France**; woollens, dyes, engin., printing; p. (1982) 36,143.

Putney, sub. of London, **Eng.**; residtl.; Thames-side dist.

Putrid Sea. See Sivash.

Putumayo, R., trib. of R. Amazon; rises in Colombia, forming bdy. with Ecuador and Peru; here in wild-rubber region, Roger Casement exposed cruel exploitation of native labour; 1,600 km long.

Puy-de-Dôme, extinct volcano, Massif Central, **France**; hgst peak of Auvergne mtns., 1,466 m.

Puy-de-Dôme, dep., **France**; in Auvergne; cap. Clermont-Ferrand, industl. ctr. Thiers; a. 8,003 km^2; p. (1990) 598,200.

Puymorens Tunnel, Pyrenees, on bdy. between France and Spain; carries main rly. between Toulouse and Barcelona.

Pwllheli, t., Gwynedd, N. **Wales**; sm. pt. on S. cst. Lleyn Peninsula; seaside resort; in-shore fishing, boat-bldg.; p. (1991) 3,974.

Pyatigorsk, c., N. Caucasus, **Russia**; ctr. of Caucasian mineral water springs; Lermontov shot here in duel 1841; p. (1989) 129,000.

Pylos, pt., S.W. Peloponnesus, **Greece**; shipbldg. and repair yard, heavy metal wks. projected; sea-battles 1827 (Navarino), 425 B.C.

Pyongyang, c., cap. of **N. Korea**; stands high above Taedong R.; major industl. ctr. with coal and iron ore deposits nearby; univ.; many historic relics; p. (1984) 2·6 m.

Pyrenees, range of mtns., S.W. **Europe**; dividing France from Iberian Peninsula; 432 km long; hgst peak Pic d'Anéto (Maladetta) 3,408 m.

Pyrénées-Atlantiques, dep., S.W. **France**; mainly agr., sheep and cattle raising; ch. ts. Pau (cap.), Bayonne, Biarritz; a. 7,713 km^2; p. (1990) 578,500.

Pyrénées-Orientales, dep., S. **France**; on Mediterranean; wine, fruit, olives; cap. Perpignan; a. 4,141 km^2; p. (1990) 363,800.

Pyrgos, t., Elis, S.W. **Greece**; has suffered from earthquakes; p. (1981) 21,958.

Q

Qaanaaq. See Thule.

Qaidam (Tsaidam), depression, Qinghai prov., **China**; a. of salt marsh and Ls.; rich deposits of oil; state farms for intensive animals husbandry.

Qacentina (Constantine), c., dep., N. E. **Algeria**; 650 m. alt. on gorge of R. Rhumel; textile and engin. wks.; lge tractor and diesel engine complex; p. (1987) 440,842 (c.), 662,330 (dep.).

Qandahar, c., former cap of **Afghanistan**; alt. 1,037 m.; fruit preserving and canning; airpt. built with U.S. aid; textiles; p. (1982) 225,500.

Qarun (Birker el Qarum), See Karun.

Qatar, emirate, indep. st. (1971), Arabia; crown prince appointed (1979); peninsula on Persian G.; economy based on oil; inland production declining, but increasing offshore drilling; political stability less certain after withdrawal of Brit. military protection (1971); cap. Doha; a. 10,360 km²; p. (1994) 539,000, of whom 75 per cent are foreign nationals.

Qattara Depression, N. **Egypt;** 134 m below sea level, salt marsh produced by seepage and evaporation of artesian water; marshes; few inhabitants; scheme to flood depression with sea water to generate electricity now under construction.

Qenâ, t. and prov., central **Egypt;** on R. Nile; water jars and bottles; agr. tr., cereals, dates; p. (1986) 119,794 (t.). (1991) 2,598,000 (prov.).

Qingdao (Tsingtao), c., Shandong prov., **China;** spt. with excellent harbour at head of bay; tourism impt.; mnfs. locomotives, cement, textiles, machin., chemicals; special development zone to attract high technology inds.; oil jetty for Shengli oil field; p. (1992) 2,060,000.

Qinghai (Tsinghai), prov., W. **China;** between Xinjiang and Xizang Zizhou (Tibet), inc. c. plateau; local coal and iron ore but exploitation hindered by isolation; two new iron and steel plants; new rly.; massive hydro-electricity plant; international airpt. link with Hong Kong; attempts to increase economic development; oil exploration; a. 721,004 km²; p. (1990) 4,430,000.

Qinghai Hu (Koko Nor), salt L., Qinghai prov., **China;** at over 3,000 m. in Tibetan highlands; a. 5,957 km²; no outlet.

Qinhuangdao (Chinwangtao), c., spt., former treaty pt., Hebei, N. **China;** on Yellow Sea cst. 240 km N.E. of Tianjin; only good natural harbour on N. China cst.; exp. coal from Gailan mines; machin., textiles, chemical inds.; designated a development zone to attract foreign investment; p. (1984) 425,300.

Qiqihar (Tsitsihar), c., Heilongjiang prov., N. **China;** on Vladivostok portion of Trans-Siberian rly.; food processing and tr., chemicals; potential oilfield; p. (1992) 1,380,000.

Qisil-Qum, desert region, **Central Asia;** covering dried-up a. of extended Pleistocene Aral Sea.

Qizan, spt., **Saudi Arabia;** cereals, pearl-fishing, salt.

Qom (Qum), c., **Iran;** pilgrimage ctr., shrine of Fatima; rly. junction; p. (1986) 550,630.

Qornet es Sauda, mtn., Lebanon range, Levant, **Lebanon;** max. alt. 3,050 m.

Quantock Hills, Somerset, **Eng.;** S. of Bridgwater Bay; hgst. pt. 385 m.

Quauzhu. See Zhengzhou.

Queanbeyan, t., N.S.W., **Australia;** rapid growth as commuter ctr. as only 13 km from Canberra; pastoral, dairying dist.; mkt. and service ctr.; p. (1981) 19,056.

Quebec, c., cap. of Q. prov., **Canada;** spt. with fine harbour on St. Lawrence R. at mouth of St. Charles; cultural cap. of French Canada; inds. based on local raw materials of timber, agr. prods.; oil refining at St. Romauld; historic c. with many fine bldgs., univ., tourism; p. (1991) 167,517 (c.), (1986) 603,267 (met. a.).

Quebec, prov., **Canada;** mainly within Canadian Shield; continental climate; forests and timber inds.; agr. in S.; hydroelectric power and abundant minerals; p. mainly French-speaking; ch. cs., Quebec (cap.), Montreal; strong separatist movements causing decline in investment and movement of some inds. to USA; a. 1,540,687 km²; p. (1997) 7,400,000.

Quebec-Labrador Trough, Canada; geological formation extending through central Quebec prov. to Ungava Bay, Hudson Strait; immense reserves of iron-ore (locally "red-gold").

Quedlinburg, t., Saxony-Anhalt, **Germany;** at foot of Harz mtns.; cas., cath.; aniline dyes, metals, engin., horticultural mkt. t.; p. (1989) 29,096.

Queen Charlotte's Is., archipelago, N. of Vancouver I., off cst. B.C., **Canada;** halibut fishing, lumbering.

Queen Charlotte Sound, strait, separating Vancouver I. from B.C. mainland **Canada;** a continuation of Johnstone Strait.

Queen Elizabeth Is., Canada; I. gr. in Canadian Arctic; most N. land of N. America; a. 349,443 km².

Queen Maud Land, Norwegian sector of **Antarctica;** ice crystal mtns., 3,050 m high for 160 km along cst.

Queens, bor., N.Y. City, USA; residtl. dist.; lgst. bor. of N.Y. c.; p. 1,951,598.

Queensbury and Shelf, t., West Yorks., **Eng.;** textiles; p. (1991) 11,661.

Queensferry, royal burgh, Edinburgh, **Scot.;** at S. end of Forth road and rail bridges; p. (1991) 8,887.

Queensland, st., N.E. **Australia;** sub-tropical a. rising from cst. to Gt. Dividing Range and Western Plains (inc. Gt. Artesian Basin); Barrier Reef off cst.; p. concentrated on cst. where sugar cane and tropical fruits grown, popular all year tourist resorts and retirement ctrs.; all year mkt. gardening replaced by extensive cattle and sheep ranching in W.; coal, copper, uranium, bauxite; oil at Moonie; mftg.; cap. Brisbane; a. 1,727,200 km²; p. (1993) 3,155,400.

Queenstown. See Cobh.

Queenstown, t., Tasmania, **Australia;** copper mng. t.; prosperity depends on continuation of mng. at Mount Lyell.

Queenstown, S.I., N.Z., tourist ctr. on L. Wakatipu in S. Alps; p. (1991) 15,123.

Queenstown, t., Cape Prov., **S. Africa;** in agr. region producing wool and wheat; p. (1980) 48,860 (dist.).

Quelimane, pt., **Moçambique;** at head of estuary; rly. terminus; exp. copra, sisal, tea; notorious in 18th and 19th cent. as slave mkt.; p. (1980) 60,151.

Quelpart. See Cheju.

Quemoy, gr. of Is. off Chinese mainland nr. Amoy.

QueQue, t., **Zimbabwe;** major new steel works has attracted many ancillary inds.; p. (1982) 47,600.

Querétaro, t., cap. of Q. st., **Mexico;** site of pre-Aztec settlement at 1,881 m; cath., many colonial bldgs.; old cotton ind.; p. (1990) 454,049.

Querétaro, st., **Mexico;** in Central Plateau; arid with fertile valleys; variety of crops; mng. impt.; famous for opals; cap. Q.; a. 11,479 km²; p. (1990) 1,044,227.

Quetta, t., cap. of Baluchistan, **Pakistan;** at 5,000 ft., commands routes to Bolan Pass; ctr. of irrigated agr. a.; military ctr.; coal mng. nearby; damaged by severe earthquake (1935); p. (1981) 285,000.

Quezaltenango, t., S.W. **Guatemala;** second c. of rep.; at 2,333 m at foot of Santa Maria volcano; univ.; comm. ctr. for rich agr. region; textiles, handicrafts; p. (1989) 246,000.

Quezon City, c., **Philippines;** new city within metropolitan Manila; univ.; p. (1995) 1,989,000.

Quibdó, t., **Colombia;** in forested a. on R. Atrato; platinum, gold mng.; p. (1992) 119,027.

Quillon, t., Kerala, **India;** on Malabar cst., ctr. of coconut tr. and processing; p. (1981) 137,943 (t.), 167,598 (met. a.).

Quilmes, t., Buenos Aires, **Argentina;** on Rio de la Plata estuary; English public school; resort; oil refining, textiles, glass; p. (1980) 441,780.

Quimper, t., cap. Finistère dep., **France;** tourist ctr. for S. Brittany; Breton pottery; Gothic cath.; p. (1990) 62,541.

Quincy, t., Ill., **USA;** at bridging point of R. Mississippi; agr. machin., clothing, footwear, food inds.; p. (1980) 42,554.

Quincy, t., Mass., **USA;** in Mass. B., 13 km S.E. of Boston; shipbldg. ctr.; p. (1980) 84,743.

Quindio, pass, **Colombia;** provides impt. routeway through Cordillera Central; 11,099 ft.

Qui Nhon, t., S. **Vietnam;** on E. cst.; tr. in coconut prods.; fishing.

Quintana Roo, st., S.E. **Mexico;** on Caribbean; low-lying swamp, underdeveloped; cap. Chetumal; a. 50,344 km²; p. (1990) 493,605.

Quito, c., cap. of **Ecuador;** in Andes at 2,852 m, 24 km S. of equator; anc. Inca c., cath., univ., slower growth than coastal ts.; impt. textile ctr.; p. (1990) 1,100,847.

Quorndon or **Quorn,** sm. t., Leics., **Eng.;** on R. Soar, 5 km S. of Loughborough; ctr. of fox-hunting dist.; p. (1991) 4,614.

Qwaqwa, frmr. homeland, **S. Africa;** p. (1985) 181,559.

R

Raake, t., N. **Finland;** spt.; iron wks.

Raasay, I., E. of Skye, Highland, **Scot.;** 21 km long, 5-6 km wide; p. (1991) 163.

Rab I., at head of Adriatic, off **Croatia;** tourism; a. 192 km².

Rabat, c., cap. of **Morocco;** spt. at mouth of Bu Regreg R. on Atl. cst.; cath., univ.; textiles, carpets, rugs; p. (1982) 518,616.

Rabaul, spt., New Britain, **Papua New Guinea;** ch. pt., exp. copra; damaged by volcanic eruption (1937) former cap. of New Guinea; p. (1990) 17,022.

Raciborz (Ratibor), t., Upper Silesia, Poland (since 1945); on R. Oder; textiles, metals, wood engin.; p. (1989) 62,733.

Racine, c., Wis., USA; sm. pt. on L. Mich., 16 km S. of Milwaukee; agr. machin., tractors, car parts; p. (1990) 84,298 (c.), 175,034 (met. a.).

Radcliffe, t., Gtr. Manchester, Eng.; N.W. of Manchester; paper, rubber, paint, engin.; p. (1991) 32,587.

Radebeul, t., Saxony, Germany; on R. Elbe; satellite of Dresden; p. (1989) 32,011.

Radium Hill, v., S. Australia; ctr. for radium mng. 1920–30 and uranium later; mines now closed (since 1961).

Radnorshire, historic co., central Wales, now part of Powys.

Radom, t. and prov., Poland; in Radomska Plain; route ctr.; metal and chemical inds.; lge. tobacco factory; p. (1989) 226,025 (t.), 745,400 (prov.).

Radomosko, t., Piotrków, Poland; on edge of Lodz Upland; metallurgical wks., food inds.; bentwood chairs for exp.; p. (1989) 50,059.

Ragaz, Bad, spa, St. Gall can., Switzerland; at mouth of Tamina R.; hot springs from nearby v. of Pfäfers.

Ragusa. See Dubrovnik.

Ragusa, t., Sicily, Italy; oil and asphalt production; p. (1981) 64,492.

Rahway, t., N.J., USA; on R. Rahway; residtl. suburb for N.Y.; p. (1980) 26,723.

Raichur, t., Karnataka, India; comm. ctr.; agr. processing; p. (1991) 157,551.

Rainford, t., Merseyside, Eng.; nr. St. Helens; former coal-mng. a.; p. (1991) 6,382.

Rainier, mtn., Wash., USA; 4,432 m; forms Nat. Park.

Rainy, L., on border of Canada and Minn., USA; drained by Rainy R. to L. of the Woods.

Raipur, t., Madhya Pradesh, India; ctr. of fertile rice growing a.; p. (1991) 439,000.

Rajahmundry, t., Andhra Pradesh, India; on delta of Godivari R.; agr. tr.; p. (1991) 325,000 .

Rajasthan, st., India; dry a. inc. Thar desert; sparse p. where primitive irrigation; agr., millets, pulses, cotton; impt. gypsum deposits; cap. Jaipur; a. 342,274 km²; p. (1991) 44,005,990.

Rajkot, t., Gujarat, India; p. (1991) 559,000.

Rajshahi, t., Rajshahi dist., Bangladesh; on R. Ganges; univ.; silk inds.; p. (1991) 299,671.

Raki-Ura I. See Stewart I.

Raleigh, c., cap. of N.C., USA; educational ctr. univ.; printing, cotton tr. and processing; p. (1990) 207,951 (c.), 735,000 (met. a. with Durham).

Ralik, W. chain of Is., Marshall gr., Pac. Oc.; lgst. atoll Kwajalein; parallel with Ratak chain.

Ramat Gan, t., Israel; in plain of Sharon; univ.; lt. inds.; p. (1992) 122,700.

Rambouillet, t., Yvelines, France; nr. Versailles; anc. château; p. (1982) 22,487.

Rameswaram, t., Tamil Nadu. India; on Rameswaram I., Palk Strait; contains Dravidian temple, Hindu holy place of pilgrimage; p. (1981) 27,928.

Ramla, t., Israel; S. of Lydda; former cap. of Palestine; ass. with crusaders.

Rampur, t., Uttar Pradesh, India; N.W. of Bareilly; agr. tr.; sugar refining; chemicals; cap. of former princely st. of R.; p. (1991) 243,742.

Ramree I., Myanmar; in Bay of Bengal, off Arakan cst.; 80 km long.

Ramsbottom, t., Lancs., Eng.; on R. Irwell, 6 km N. of Bury; engin., paper, textiles; p. (1991) 17,318.

Ramsey, mkt. t., Cambs., Eng.; on edge of Fens, 11 km N. of St. Ives; engin.; abbey ruins; p. (1991) 7,577.

Ramsey, t., spt., I. of Man, Eng.; on N.E. cst.; holiday resort; p. (1991) 6,496.

Ramsgate, t., Kent, Eng.; on S. cst. of I. of Thanet; seaside resort; p. (1991) 37,895.

Rancagua, t., cap. Libertador region, Chile; ctr. of fertile valley in Andean foothills; tractors, agr. processing; p. (1992) 184,134.

Rance, R., Brittany, France; world's first major tidal hydroelectric power sta. (opened 1966).

Ranchi, t., Bihar, India; hot season seat of govt. in Chota Nagpur plateau; univ.; heavy engin.; p. (1991) 599,000.

Rand. See Witwatersrand.

Randers, pt., Denmark; on Randers Fjord, inlet of Kattegat; machin., foundries; exp. dairy prod.; mediaeval monastery; p. (1990) 61,020.

Randfontein, t., Transvaal, S. Africa; gold-mng. ctr.; uranium plant; p. (1980) 91,460 (dist.).

Randstad, conurb., Neth.; Dutch "urban ring." inc. Rotterdam, The Hague, Leiden, Amsterdam and Utrecht, contained within radius of 16 km; a. of rapid industrialisation.

Rangitaiki, R., N.I., N.Z.; flows into Bay of Plenty; 192 km long.

Rangoon, c., cap. of Myanmar; on E. arm of Irrawaddy delta; 2 caths., many mosques, temples and pagodas; replaced Mandalay as cap.; ctr. of rice tr. and exp.; oil refining; teak collecting ctr.; p. (1983) 2,458,712.

Rangpur, t., Bangladesh; on R. Ghaghat; jute; p. (1991) 203,931.

Raniganj, t., W. Bengal, India; coalfield in Damodar basin; engin.; p. (1981) 48,702 (t.), 119,101 (met. a.).

Rannoch, Loch, Perth and Kinross, Scot.; 14 km long, 1·6 km wide; drained to R. Tay.

Raoul I. See Sunday I.

Rapallo, t., Liguria, N.W. Italy; on G. of Genoa, 35 km E. of Genoa; most celebrated resort on Italian Riviera di Levante; p. (1981) 28,318.

Rapanui. See Easter I.

Rapid City, t., S.D., USA; second t. of st.; comm. ctr. for agr. and mng. a.; p. (1990) 54,523.

Rarotonga, volcanic I., Pac. Oc.; lgst. of Cook Is.; fruit canning; ch. t. and pt. Avarua; p. (1981) 9,530.

Ra's al Khaimah, emirate, member of the United Arab Emirates; p. (1985) 116,470.

Rasht (Resht), c., Iran; cap. of Gilan prov., in a. producing rice, cotton, silk; carpets; nearby Pahlevi serves as pt.; p. (1986) 293,881.

Ras Lanug, oil terminal, on G. of Sidra, Libya; pipeline from Hofra oilfield.

Ras Tannura, spt., Nejd, Saudi Arabia; lge. oil refinery; oil exp.

Ratak, E., chain of Is., Marshall Group, Pac. Oc.; ch. I. Majuro; parallel with Ralik chain.

Rathenow, t., Brandenburg, Germany; on R. Havel; optical and precision instruments; p. (1989) 30,935.

Rathlin, I., off Fair Head, Moyle, N. Ireland; 8 km by 1·6 km.

Ratibor. See Raciborz.

Ratingen, t., N. Rhine–Westphalia, Germany; N.E. of Düsseldorf; textiles, machin., glass; famous for Blue L.; p. (1986) 89,200.

Ratisbon. See Regensburg.

Ratlam, t., Madhya Pradesh, India; rly. junc. in Malwa Plateau; p. (1991) 195,776.

Ratnapura, t., Sri Lanka; former ctr. of gem mng.; p. (1981) 37,354.

Rauma, spt., S.W. Finland; on Baltic Sea; p. (1993) 38,133.

Raunds, t., East Northants., Eng.; 8 km N.E. of Wellingborough; p. (1991) 7,493.

Raurkela, t., Orissa, India; steel, tinplate, iron, fertilisers; p. (1991) 398,864.

Ravenglass, t., Cumbria, Eng.; nr. mouth of R. Esk; old pt.; Roman remains.

Ravenna, c., cap. of Ravenna prov., Emilia-Romagna, Italy; on reclaimed plain nr. Po delta; connected to Adriatic by canal; ctr. of fertile agr. dist., agr. processing; new inds. aided by discovery of methane N. of c.; oil refineries, chemicals, fertilisers; cath., mausoleum, famous mosaics; p. (1992) 136,009.

Ravenna, prov., Emilia-Romagna, Italy; N. Italian plain rising to Apennines; fertile agr. a.; cap. R.; a. 1,852 km²; p. (1981) 358,654.

Ravensburg, t., Baden-Württemberg, Germany; nr. Konstanz; engin., textiles; p. (1986) 43,200.

Ravi, R., Punjab, India; trib. of Chenab; used for irrigation; 720 km long.

Rawalpindi, c., Pakistan; seat of govt. until completion of Islamabad; admin., comm. and rly. ctr.; foundries, oil refining, industl. gases; p. (1981) 928,000.

Rawmarsh, t., South Yorks., Eng.; 3 km N.E. of Rotherham; engin.; p. (1991) 18,085.

Rawson, cap. of Chubut prov., S. central Argentina; spt.; p. (1991) 19,161.

Rawtenstall, t., Rossendale, Lancs., Eng.; on R. Irwell in ctr. of Rossendale Fells; felts; footwear, textiles; p. (1991) 21,933.

Rayleigh, t., Rochford, Essex, Eng.; 8 km N.W. of Southend; lt. inds.; dormitory for London; p. (1991) 28,912.

Ré, Ile de, I., W. cst. of Charente-Maritime dep. France; off La Rochelle; citadel (built 1681) at St. Martin de Ré is now a prison.

Reading, t., l. gov. dist., Berks., Eng.; at confluence of Rs. Thames and Kennet; univ.; biscuits, engin., electronics, mkt. gardening, tinbox mftg., printing; p. (1995) 141,500 (dist.), (1991) 213,474 (t.).

Reading, c., Penns., **USA**; on Schuylkill R.; steelwks. using local coal, optical gds.; p. (1990) 337,000 (met. a.).

Recife, spt., cap. of Pernambuco st., N.E. **Brazil**; fine natural harbour; univ.; processing and exp. of sugar from surrounding a.; "Venice of Brazil" because of I. and peninsula site; lge. petrochemical wks. nearby; recent industl. expansion and diversification; engin., chem., electrical and telecommunications equipment; integrated steel wks.; p. (1991) 1,290,149 .

Recklinghausen, t., N. Rhine–Westphalia, **Germany**; nr. Dortmund; collieries, iron, machin., textiles, chemicals; p. (1990) 125,500.

Recôncavo, dist., Bahia st., N.E. **Brazil**; surrounds bay at mouth of R. Paraguassu; intensive cultivation of sugar-cane, cotton, tobacco, rice, by Negro farmers; oil production; ch. ts. São Salvador, Cachoeira.

Redbridge, outer bor., E. London, **Eng.**; incorporates Ilford, Wanstead and Woodford, Chigwell (Hainault Estate), Dagenham (N. Chadwell Heath ward); mainly residtl.; p. (1995) 227,300.

Redcar, t., Redcar and Cleveland, **Eng.**; lge. iron and steel wks.; p. (1991) 35,877.

Redcar and Cleveland, unit. auth. created in 1996, formerly part of Cleveland, **Eng.**; inc. Cleveland Hills and ts. of Guisborough, Redcar and Skelton; p. (1995) 141,400.

Redcliff, t., **Zimbabwe**; iron-mng.; iron and steel wks.; fertilisers.

Red Deer, t., Alberta, **Canada**; on Red Deer R.; mkt. t. in farming a.; lge. natural gas processing plant nearby; p. (1991) 58,134.

Redditch, t., l. gov. dist., Worcs., **Eng.**; 19 km S. of Birmingham; needles, fishing tackle, cycles, springs, aluminium alloys; new t. (1964); p. (1995) 77,900 (dist.), (1991) 73,372 (t.).

Redhill. See **Reigate**.

Redlands, t., Cal., **USA**; univ.; citrus fruit packing and canning; p. (1980) 43,619.

Redonda, I., Leeward gr., **Antigua and Barbuda**; between Montserrat and Nevis; uninhabited.

Redondo Beach, t., Cal., **USA**; residtl.; tourism; p. (1980) 57,102.

Red R. (China and Vietnam). See **Song-koi**.

Red R., **USA**; southernmost of lge. tribs. of Mississippi R.; derives name and colour from red clay in upper course; dammed for flood control and hydroelec. power; 2,560 km long.

Red R. of the North, **USA**; rises in Minn., flows N. into Canada to empty into L. Winnipeg; 1,040 km long.

Redruth, t., Cornwall, **Eng.**; once major ctr. of tin mng.; most mines now closed, although recent revival of some; p. (1991) 35,915 (inc. Camborne).

Red Sea, arm of sea separating Arabia from Africa; connects with Indian Oc. by Straits of Bab-el-Mandeb; extension of Great African Rift Valley which further N. encloses the Dead Sea; 2,240 km long.

Redwood City, t., W. Cal., **USA**; timber tr.; electronics; p. (1980) 54,951.

Ree, Lough, L., R.o.I.; between Roscommon, Longford and Westmeath, an extension of R. Shannon; 27 km long.

Regensburg (Ratisbon), c., R. pt., Bavaria, **Germany**; N.E. of Munich on R. Danube; timber processing, chemicals; p. (1990) 122,300.

Reggio di Calabria, spt., Calabria, **Italy**; on Strait of Messina; cath.; fishing, ferry to Sicily; mkt. for citrus fruit; tourism; agr. processing; rebuilt after 1908 earthquake; p. (1992) 178,312.

Reggio nell' Emilia, c., cap. of prov. of same name, in Emilia-Romagna, N. **Italy**; at foot of Apennines; Renaissance church of the Madonna della Ghiara; locomotives, aircraft, agr. engin.; birthplace of Ariosto; p. (1992) 133,191.

Regina, t., cap. of Saskatchewan, **Canada**; ctr. of wheat growing dist. of Prairies; connected by pipeline to Alberta oilfields; oil refining, chemicals, agr. machin.; p. (1991) 179,178 (c.), (1986) 186,521.

Rehovoth, Israel; t., in citrus fruit dist.; Weizmann Institute of Science.

Reichenbach, t., Saxony, **Germany**; at foot of Erzgebirge; p. (1989) 25,663.

Reichenberg. See **Liberec**.

Reigate, t., Surrey, **Eng.**; at foot of N. Downs, 8 km

E. of Dorking; dormitory for London; part of l. gov. dist., **Reigate and Banstead**; p. (1995) 118,700 (dist.), (1991) 47,602 (t.) (with Redhill).

Reims, c., Marne dep., N.E. **France**; on R. Vesle; famous Gothic cath.; univ.; champagne ctr., textiles; p. (1990) 185,164 (c.), 206,362 (met. a.).

Reindeer L., Saskatchewan, Manitoba, **Canada**; Indian settlement on shore; a. 6,475 km[2].

Rejang R., Sarawak; **Malaysia**; navigable for 72 km by ocean boats; main R. of Sarawak.

Rembang, pt., N. cst. Java, **Indonesia**; in dry limestone R. plateau; proposed nuclear power plant.

Remscheid, t., N. Rhine–Westphalia, **Germany**; nr. Düsseldorf; iron and steel ctr.; machin. tools; p. (1990) 123,400.

Renaix. See **Ronse**.

Rendsburg, t., Schleswig-Holstein, **Germany**; on Kiel Canal; shipbldg., elec. gds.; p. (1986) 30,600.

Renfrew, royal burgh, Renfrewshire, **Scot.**; nr. R. Clyde, 8 km W. of Glasgow; p. (1991) 20,764.

Renfrewshire, W. **Scot.**, unit. auth. created in 1996, incorporating part of historic co. which became part of Strathclyde in 1974 and is now divided between Inverclyde, E. Renfrewshire and Renfrewshire; lies immediately W. of Glasgow; p. (1995) 178,340.

Renkum, t., Gelderland. **Neth.**; 13 km W. of Arnhem; paper mnfs.; p. (1993) 32,867.

Rennes, c., cap. of Ille-et-Vilaine dep., **France**; only major inland t. of Brittany, in fertile agr. basin; univ., comm. ctr.; cars, engin.; p. (1990) 203, 533 (c.), 245, 065 (met. a.).

Reno, lgst. t. of Nevada, **USA**; univ.; st. agr. college; famous for easy divorce procedure and gambling; p. (1990) 133,850 (t.), 255,000 (met. a.).

Repton, t., South Derbyshire, **Eng.**; famous public school in priory; former Saxon cap. of Mercia; p. (1991) 2,012.

Resende, t., Rio de Janeiro st., **Brazil**; chemicals, rly. junc.; univ.; p. (1985) 102,900.

Resht. See **Rasht**.

Resina, t., S. **Italy**; on Bay of Naples at W. foot of Vesuvius; nr. site of anc. Herculaneum; resort.

Resistencia, t., cap. of Chaco prov., **Argentina**; served by R. pt. of Barranqueras on R. Paraná; tr. in cattle, timber, cotton; agr. processing; p. (1991) 292,350.

Resita, t., Banat region, **Romania**; steel inds. based on local iron ore; heavy engin.; p. (1992) 96,798.

Restormel, l. gov. dist., Cornwall, **Eng.**; inc. N. and S. cst. and ts. of Newquay and St. Austell; p. (1995) 90,200.

Retalhuleu, dep., **Guatemala**; ctr. for coffee; sugar; a. 1858 km[2]; p. (1991) 238,857.

Réunion (Ile de Bourbon), I., overseas terr. of **France**; in Indian Oc., between Mauritius and Madagascar; volcanic I.; impt. sugar producer; cap. St. Denis; a. 2,512 km[2]; p. (1990) 597,800.

Reus, t., Tarragona, prov., **Spain**; textiles; agr. tr.; p. (1981) 75,987.

Reuss, R., **Switzerland**; flows N. from the St. Gotthard Pass through L. Lucerne, joining Aare R. nr. Brugg; 157 km long.

Reutlingen, t., Baden-Württemberg, **Germany**; S. of Stuttgart; textiles, metals, machin., leather; p. (1990) 104,300.

Reval. See **Tallin**.

Revelstoke, t., B.C., **Canada**; rly. junc.; in timber producing a.; ctr. for R. Nat. Park; p. (1986) 8,279.

Revillagigedo Islands, archipelago, Pac. Oc., off S.W. **Mexico**; ch. Is., Socorro, San Benedicto (volcano suddenly arose on I. 1952).

Reykjavik, c., cap. of **Iceland**; on S.W. cst.; impt. fish. pt.; fish exp. and processing; water piped from geysers; airport; univ.; 2 caths.; p. (1993) 101,824.

Rezayeh, (**Orūmiyeh**) c., **Iran**; cap. of W. Azerbaijan prov.; comm. ctr. of agr. region; p. (1986) 304,823.

Rheidol, R., Ceredigion, **Wales**; flows from Plynlimmon in deeply incised valley (Devil's Bridge) to Aberystwyth; hydroelec. power; 38 km long.

Rheine, t., N. Rhine–Westphalia, **Germany**; on R. Ems; textiles, machin.; p. (1983) 71,200.

Rheingau, dist., **Germany**; famous wine a. on right bank of Rhine from Biebrich to Assmanshausen.

Rheinhausen, t., Rhine–Westphalia, **Germany**; on

left bank of Rhine opposite Duisburg; coal mng., iron, textiles.

Rhin (**Bas**). *See* **Bas Rhin**.

Rhine, R., rises in Switzerland, can. Grisons, passes through L. Constance, skirts Baden, traverses Hesse, Rhineland, and the Neth., flowing to N. Sea by two arms, Oude Rijn and the Waal (the latter discharging finally by the Maas); famous for its beauty, especially between Bonn and Bingen; ch. falls at Schaff hausen; once a natural barrier between E. and W. Europe spanned by 30 rly. bridges; linked to Rhône by 1985 and Rhine-Main-Danube canal allows navigation from N. Sea to Black Sea for 3,500 km. (Trans European waterway); very polluted; 1,280 km long.

Rhine-Hern, canal, **Germany**; impt. Ruhr waterway, part of Mitelland Canal; 38 km long.

Rhineland Palatinate (**Rheinland-Pfalz**), *Land*, Germany; borders France, Luxembourg and Belgium; drained by Rhine and Moselle, inc. Hunsrück and Eifel mtns.; arable agr. in Rhine valley; vineyards; cap. Mainz; a. 19,852 km; p. (1992) 3,821,000.

Rhode Island, st., New England, **USA**; "Little Rhody'; admitted to Union 1790; st. flower violet, st. bird R.I. Red; washed by Atl. Oc., surrounded by Mass. and Conn.; divided by Narragansett Bay, with many Is. lgst. being that from which the st. takes its name; smallest and most densely populated st.; famous for poultry; major ind. textiles; cap. Providence; a. 3,144 km²; p. (1990) 1,003,464.

Rhodes (**Rhodos**), I., Dodecanese Is.; off S.W. cst., Anatolia, belonging to **Greece**; cap. R.; p. (1981) 87,831.

Rhodes, cap. of I. of Rhodes, **Greece**; on N.E. cst.; picturesque; p. (1981) 41,425.

Rhodesia. *See* **Zimbabwe**.

Rhodope Mtns. *See* **Rodopi Mtns.**

Rhondda, t., Rhondda, Cynon, Taff, **Wales**; in narrow R. valley; former coal mng. ctr.; lt. inds. introduced since 1930s depression; picturesque a. in upper R. valley; p. (1991) 59,947.

Rhondda, Cynon, Taff, S. **Wales**, unit. auth. created in 1996 from former l. gov. dists. of Cynon Valley, Rhondda and Taff-Ely; upland in N. dissected by deep R. valleys containing former coal mng. settlements; inc. ts. of Aberdare and Pontypridd; p. (1995) 239,900.

Rhône, dep., S.E. **France**; drained by R. Rhône, and its trib. R. Saône, which unite at Lyons; agr. grain, potatoes, wine; vine-growing, many mnfs., silks, textiles; cap. Lyons; a. 2,859 km²; p. (1990) 1,509,000.

Rhône, R., **Switzerland** and **France**; rises in Rhône glacier of St. Gotthard mtn. gr., and flows through L. of Geneva and E. France to G. of Lyons in Mediterranean; power stas. at Sion and Geneva; canals, dams, locks and power stas. form part of Fr. Rhône Valley project (1937–72); linked to Rhine by 1985; 811 km long.

Rhône-Alpes, region, S.E. **France**; inc.deps. Ain, Ardèche, Drôme, Isère, Loire, Rhône, Savoie, Haute-Savoie; based on the upper Rhône valley, inc. important industrial ctrs. of Lyon and Grenoble; p. (1990) 5,350,700.

Rhône-Saône Corridor, routeway, **France**; impt. transport artery using Rhône, Saône R. valleys as a means for linking Paris, Lorraine and Rhine rift valley with Mediterranean cst.; rlys., roads, with major pt. of Marseille serving the S. terminus.

Rhuddlan, t., Denbighshire, **Wales**; p. (1991) 3,182.

Rhyl, t., Denbighshire, N. **Wales**; at entrance Vale of Clwyd; resort developed from sm. fishing v.; p. (1991) 24,909.

Rhymney, t., Caerphilly, **Wales**; on R. Rhymney, E. of Merthyr Tydfil; former colly. and iron founding ctr.; engin.; p. (1991) 7,991.

Ribble, R., North Yorks., Lancs., **Eng.**; rises in Pennines, flows W. to Irish Sea nr. pt. of Preston; 120 km long.

Ribble Valley, l. gov. dist., N. Lancs., **Eng.**; inc. Forest of Bowland and ts. of Clitheroe and Longridge; p. (1995) 52,000.

Ribe, mkt. t., Jutland, S. **Denmark**; admin. ctr. of R. prov.; impt, mediaeval c.; Romanesque cath.; many fine bldgs.; p. (1990) 17,872.

Ribeirão Prêto, t., São Paulo st., **Brazil**; mkt. in rich agr. a., coffee, cotton, sugar; p. (1991) 430,805.

Richard's Bay, Natal, S. **Africa**; new pt. to supplement congested Durban; on natural harbour; silting problem but designed for bulk carriers;

plans to attract ass. industl. development.

Richborough, pt., Kent, **Eng.**; at mouth of R. Stour; Caesar's ch. pt., Roman remains; pt. has been privately redeveloped; chemicals.

Richmond, t., North Yorks., **Eng.**; at E. foot of Pennines on R. Swale; mkt. t., agr. tr.; 14th cent. grammar school; Norman cas.; forms l. gov. dist. of Richmondshire with surrounding a. of Aysgarth and Leyburn; p. (1995) 46,300 (dist.), (1991) 7,862 (t.).

Richmond, c., Cal., **USA**; deepwater pt.; oil refining; car assembly, chemicals, electronics; p. (1980) 74,676.

Richmond, c., cap. of Va., **USA**; on falls on R. James; pt. at head of navigation; financial, and tr. ctr.; tobacco inds., and mkt.; chemicals, iron and steel; p. (1990) 203,056 (c.), 866,000 (met. a. with Petersburg).

Richmond upon Thames, outer bor., Greater London, **Eng.**; inc. Barnes, Richmond and Twickenham; industl. and residtl.; park and Kew Gardens ; p. (1995) 175,600.

Rickmansworth, t., Three Rivers, Herts., **Eng.**; residtl. sub of London; p. (1991) 10,767.

Ridder, (**Leninogorsk**), c. **Kazakhstan**; in Altai mtns.; lead, zinc, and silver mines; metallurgical plants; p. (1990) 69,200.

Rideau Canal, Ont., **Canada**; from Ottawa R. at Ottawa to Kingston on L. Ontario; 211 km long.

Riesa, t., Saxony, **Germany**; R. pt. on Elbe R. nr. Meissen; p. (1981) 51,857.

Riesengebirge, mtn. range, between Silesia (**Poland**) and Bohemia (**Czech Rep.**); highest peak Schneekoppe (Czech Snežka, Polish Sniezka), 1,604 m.

Rieti, Latium, **Italy**; an anc. Sabine c. with mediaeval townscape, in fertile Apennine basin; route ctr. and cap. of R. prov.; chemicals, sugar refinery, textiles; p. (1981) 43,079.

Riff or **Rif**, mtns. **Morocco**, N.W. Africa; extend along N. African cst. for 320 km from Straits of Gibraltar; inaccessible and economically unattractive, terr. of semi-nomadic tribes; rise to over 2,100 m in many places.

Riga, cap. of **Latvia**; Baltic pt.; exp. wheat, flax, hemp, dairy produce; industl. ctr., diesel rly. engin., furniture; univ.; local bathing beaches; p. (1991) 910,200.

Rigi, mtn., nr. L. Lucerne, **Switzerland**; viewpoint reached by rack and pinion rly.; 1,801 m.

Rijeka-Susak, c., **Croatia** (formerly Yugoslavia); formerly Fiume, ceded to Yugoslavia by Italy after second world war; rival pt. to Trieste on Adriatic Sea; oil refining, shipbldg., tobacco, chemicals; hydroelectric power; p. (1991) 167,364.

Rimac, R., Lima dep., **Peru**; rises in W. cordillera of Andes and flows W. to Pac. Oc.; provides water for irrigation and for c. of Lima; 120 km long.

Rimini, c., Emilia-Romagna, **Italy**; on Adriatic cst. at junc. of Via Emilia and Via Flaminia; mkt. for fertile agr. a.; sm. inds.; bathing resort; p. (1992) 129,876.

Ringerike, t., Buskerud, **Norway**; new t. 40 km N.W. of Oslo and inc. former t. of Hönefoss; p. (1990) 27,433.

Riobamba, t., Chimborazo, **Ecuador**; on R. St. Juan; woollens, cotton gds., cement, ceramics; Inca palace ruins; p. (1990) 94,505.

Rio Branco, R., flows c. 560 km from Guiana Highlands through Brazil to join Rio Negro.

Rio Branco, t., cap. of Acre st., **Brazil**; p. (1985) 145,900.

Rio Cuarto, t., Cordoba prov., **Argentina**; agr. ctr.; p. (1991) 217,717.

Rio de Janeiro, c., spt., S.E. **Brazil**; cap. of Guanabara st., on G. Bay, Alt. Oc.; former fed. cap.; beautiful natural harbour, many fine bldgs.; Sugar Loaf mtn., Copacabana beach; flourishing tr. and inds.; mnfs. inc. textiles, foodstuffs, pharmaceutics, china, sheet glass; oil refining; p. (1991) 5,336,178 .

Rio de Janeiro, st., S.E. **Brazil**; on Atl. Oc.; consolidated with Guanabara (1975); consists of cst. plain, central Sero do Mar escarpment, fertile Paraiba R. basin in W.; coffee, sugar, fruit; ctr. of heavy ind.; cement, textiles, sugar refineries at Campos, steel wks. at Volta Redonda; offshore oil finds in Campos basin; cap. Niterói; a. 42,735 km²; p. (1991) 12,584,108.

Rio Gallegos, cap. of Santa Cruz prov., S. **Argentina**; agr. ctr.; p. (1991) 64,640.

Rio Grande, headstream of R. Paraná., **Brazil**;

Furnas dam, Estreito dam for hydroelec. power; 1,040 km long.

Rio Grande, R., flows from st. of Col. through N.M. to G. of Mexico; forms bdy. between Texas, **USA** and **Mexico**; Elephant Butte, Caballo, and Falcon multi-purpose dams; known also as Rio Grande do Norte and Rio Bravo; c. 3,016 km long.

Rio Grande do Norte, st., N.E. **Brazil**; cst. plain rising to S. plateau; climate semi-arid; cotton, sugar, salt, scheelite; cap. Natal; a. 53,038 km²; p. (1991) 2,413,618.

Rio Grande do Sul, st., S. **Brazil**; grassy plains, rolling plateaux; cool climate; stock-raising, meat-processing, wheat, wine, wool; lge. coal deposits at São Jeronimo; cap. Pôrto Alegre; a. 267,684 km²; p. (1991) 9,127,611.

Rioja, region and prov., N. **Spain**; upper Ebro valley; famous for wines and orange groves; ch. ctr. Logroño; p. (1991) 265,823.

Riom, t., Puy-de-Dôme dep., **France**; former cap. of Auvergne; old bldgs. built of lava; p. (1982) 18,901.

Rio Muni, terr., **Equatorial Guinea**; former Spanish terr., on cst. between Cameroon and Gabon, inc. offshore Is. of Corisco, Elobey Grande, Elobey Chico; with Biako forms Equatorial Guinea; equatorial forest; exp. tree prods. of cacao, coffee, hardwood; ch. t. Bata; a. 26,003 km²; p. (1983) 240,804.

Rion, R., **Georgia**; flows from Caucasus to Black Sea; lower half navigable; hydroelec. sta. at Kutaisi. (In Greek mythology the R. Phasis of the Argonauts.)

Rio Negro, prov., **Argentina**; in N. Patagonia; irrigated agr. in R. valley, fruits, grain crops; elsewhere stock-raising; cap. Viedma; a. 201,010 km²; p. (1991) 506,772.

Rio Negro, dep., **Uruguay**; livestock fattening from N. Uruguay; grain crops; ch. t. and cap. Fray Bentos; a. 8,466 km²; p. (1985) 48,241.

Rio Tinto, t., **Spain**; W. end of Sierra Morena 64 km N.E. of Huelva; major world ctr. of copper production.

Riouw-Lingga Archipelago, I. gr., **Indonesia**; S. of Malaya; Bintan lgst. I. where bauxite mng.; pepper and rubber cultivation; a. 5,905 km².

Ripley, mkt. t., Amber Valley, Derbys., **Eng.**; 11 km N.E. of Derby; coal, iron, heavy engin., bricks, agr. implements; p. (1991) 18,310.

Ripon, c., North Yorks., **Eng.**; on R. Ure; cath.; old mkt. square; old custom of wakeman; tourism; p. (1991) 13,806.

Risca, t., Caerphilly, **Wales**; on R. Ebbw; former coal mng. dist.; limestone quarrying; bricks, plastics; p. (1991) 15,124.

Risdon, t., Tasmania, **Australia**; first white settlement in Tasmania, opposite Hobart; electrometallurgy.

Rishton, t., Hyndburn, Lancs., **Eng.**; at N. foot of Rossendale Fells, 6 km N.E. of Blackburn; p. (1991) 6,773.

Rive-de-Gier, t., Loire dep., **France**; on R. Gier, nr. Lyons; coal mng., iron and steel, glass; p. (1982) 15,850.

Rivera, dep., **Uruguay**; on Brazilian border; noted for cattle and sheep ranches; cap. R.; a. 9,824 km²; p. (1985) 88,800.

Rivera, t., cap. of R. dep., **Uruguay**; on Brazilian frontier opposite Santa Ana; agr. mkt.; p. (1985) 56,335.

Riverina, pastoral cty., N.S.W., **Australia**; between Lachlan-Murrumbidgee and Murray Rs.; merino sheep in W., good wheat yields in E.; gtr. crop variety with irrigation; a. 68,894 km²;

River Rouge, t., Mich., **USA**; ctr. of Ford car mnf.; many heavy inds.; rapidly growing t. p. (1980) 12,912.

Riverside, t., Cal., **USA**; ctr. for citrus fruit packing and tr.; resort; p. (1990) 226,605 (t.), 2,589,000 (met. a. with San Bernardino).

Riviera, the belt of cst. between the Alps and the Mediterranean from Spezia to Hyères, **France** and **Italy**; picturesque scenery, sheltered, mild climate; fashionable health resorts.

Riyadh, t., royal cap. of **Saudi Arabia**; 368 km inland from Persian G.; palace; univ.; route and tr. ctr., linked by rail with pt. of Zahran; p. (1988) 2 m.

Rizaiyeh (Urmia), c., cap. of Azerbaijan prov., **Iran**; nr. L. Urmia; comm. ctr.; birthplace of Zoroaster; p. (1983) 262,588.

Rizal, prov., central Luzon, **Philippines**; rapidly growing prov. in fertile Central Plain; new inds. developing; cap. Pasig; a. 2,049 km²; p. (1990) 980,194.

Rize, t. and prov., **Turkey**; nr. Trabzon, on Black Sea; ctr. of Turkish tea inds.; p. (1985) 50,221 (t.), (1990) 348,776 (prov.).

Road Town, spt., Tortola; cap. of the Brit. **Virgin Is.**; tr. in fish, poultry; p. (1991) 6,330.

Roanne, t., Loire dep., **France**; on R. Loire; château ruins; textiles; p. (1990) 42,848 (t.), 77,160 (met.a.).

Roanoke, R., Va., and N.C., **USA**; flows into Albemarle Sound; hydroelec. power; 656 km long.

Roanoke, c., S.W. Va., **USA**; between Blue Ridge and Allegheny mtns.; rly. junc.; engin. p. (1984) 100,700 (c.), 222,700 (met. a.).

Roanoke I., off cst. N.C., **USA**; attempted settlement of colony by Raleigh.

Roaring Creek, Belize, Central America; site of new cap. 80 km inland, at junc. of W. highway with Hummingbird highway.

Robben I., at entrance of Table Bay, Cape Prov., **S. Africa**; penal settlement which housed Nelson Mandela; now called Siqithini (Xhosa for 'place of healing').

Robin Hood's Bay, v., North Yorks., **Eng.**; picturesque site in inlet; tourism, fishing.

Robson, Mt., **Canada**; on B.C. and Alberta border; alt. 3,956 m; in Nat. Park.

Rocha, dep., **Uruguay**; borders Atl. Oc.; a. of cattle and sheep rearing; cap. R.; a. 11,850 km²; p. (1985) 66,440.

Rochdale, t., met. dist., Gtr. Manchester, **Eng.**; at S. foot of Rossendale Fells, on R. Roch; textiles, engin., asbestos; co-operative movement started (1844); p. (1995) 207,600 (dist.), (1991) 94,313 (t.).

Rochefort, c., Charente-Maritime dep., **France**; fishing pt.; former impt. naval base; p. (1982) 27,716.

Rochester, t., part of l. gov. dist. of **Rochester-upon-Medway**, Kent, **Eng.**; on R. Medway, adjoining Chatham; cath., cas.; many associations with Dickens; aeronautical, elec. and mechanical engin., paint, varnish, cement; p. (1995) 144,200 (dist.), (1991) 23,971 (t.).

Rochester, t., Minn., **USA**; famous for Mayo clinic, and Mayo medical research ctr.; p. (1980) 57,890.

Rochester, c., N.Y., **USA**; on Genesee R.; univ.; cameras, films, optical instruments, thermometers, electronic equipment; hydroelectric power; p. (1990) 231,636 (c.), 1,002,000 (met. a.).

Rochford, t. and l. gov. dist., Essex, **Eng.**; cstl. a. inc. Rochford and Rayleigh; p. (1995) 76,100 (dist.), (1991) 15,081 (t.).

Rock, R., Wis., Ill., **USA**; formerly home of native Indians; focus of white settlement since 1830; 456 km long.

Rockall, sm. I., **Atl. Oc.**; lies 320 km W. of Outer Hebrides; forms hgst. part of submarine bank which forms good fishing-ground; uninhabited; annexed by Britain 1955; formally incorporated into Inverness-shire (1972) to ensure control of oil and natural gas deposits; claimed also by Ireland and Iceland; rock samples aged 1,000 million years place it with some Canadian rocks.

Rockall Deep, submarine trench, N. **Atl. Oc.**; between N.W. Ireland and Rockall I.; suspected oil and natural gas reserves.

Rockford, c., Ill., **USA**; serves agr. dist.; agr. machin., machin. tools; p. (1990) 139,426 (c.), 283,719 (met. a.).

Rockhampton, t., pt., Queensland, **Australia**; on Tropic of Capricorn; outlet for vast pastoral and mng. a.; comm. cap. of central Queensland; meat-preserving; p. (1991) 63,598.

Rockingham, t., W. **Australia**; satellite of Perth; major pt. planned to serve Kwinana; p. (1981) 24,932.

Rock Island, c., Ill., **USA**; on R. Mississippi; former site of US arsenal; agr. machin., timber and agr. processing; p. (1980) 46,928.

Rocky Mtns., vast mtn. chain, N. **America**; extend from Alaska, through Canada, USA to Mexico; made up of several parallel ranges separated by intermontane basins and plateaux; barrier to spread of settlers to W. cst. in 19th cent.; climatic barrier; extensive snow and glacier fields in N.; dry desert landscapes in S.; many Nat. Parks; sparse p.; hydroelectric power; hgst. peak Mt. Logan (6,054 m); length 5,120 km.

Rodez, t., cap. of Aveyron dep., **France**; on R. Aveyron; cath.; woollens; p. (1990) 26,794.

Rodopi (Rhodope) Mtns., range S. **Bulgaria**; rise to 3,100 m.

Rodosto. *See* **Tekirdag.**

Rodriguez, I., Brit. dependency of **Mauritius**, Indian Oc.; 560 km N.E. of Mauritius; mainly agr. and fishing; cap. Port Mathurin; a. 109 km²; p. (1993) 34,536.

Roermond, t., Limburg prov., **Neth.**; on R. Maas; minster; textiles; p. (1993) 42,744.

Roeselare, (Roulers) t., W. Flanders, **Belgium**; on R. Lys, nr. Kortrijk, textile ctr.; p. (1993) 53,455.

Rohtak, t., Haryana, **India**; N.W. of Delhi; p. (1991) 216,096.

Roissy-en-France; 26 km N.E. of Paris, **France**; site of Charles de Gaulle airport; p. (1982) 1,411.

Roman, t., **Romania**; on R. Moldava; cath.; agr. processing; p. (1983) 67,962.

Romania, Rep. of, S.E. Europe; country bounded by Ukraine, Moldova, Hungary, Yugoslavia, Bulgaria, and Black Sea; Carpathian mtns., Transylvanian Alps, wide Walachian plain, Moldavian plateau; drained by Danube and its tribs.; cold winters and hot summers; since second world war transformation of economy from agr. to industl. basis, although agr. still impt., contributing many exps., especially timber, wine, fruit; major pt. Constanta on Black Sea; oilfields at Ploiesti; cap. Bucharest; ch. tr. partners former USSR and E. Europe; Danube used for navigation; Iron Gates power and navigation system being constructed in co-operation with Yugoslavia; tourism from W. Europe and N. America encouraged; measures to stimulate birth rate; revolution 1989, popular uprising against Ceausescu dictatorship; a. 237,428 km²; p. (1993) 22,755,260.

Rome (Roma), cap. of **Italy**, and of Latium and Rome prov.; on R. Tiber, 24 km from sea; in Roman legend founded by Romulus 753 B.C.; once cap. of anc. Roman empire; inc. Vatican c., ctr. of Roman Catholic Church; situated on original "seven hills," and along the R.; leading cultural ctr.; St. Peter's church, Colosseum, Pantheon; univ.; admin. ctr.; tourism; created cap. of United Italy 1871; p. (1992) 2,723,327.

Romford. *See* **Havering.**

Romney Marsh, coastal marsh, Shepway, Kent, **Eng.**; formed by blocking of R. Rother by shingle spit of Dungeness which extends from Rye to Hythe; largely drained; pastures for special Romney Marsh breed of sheep; a. 129 km².

Romsey, t., Test Valley, Hants., **Eng.**; on R. Test, 14 km N.W. of Southampton; mkt. ctr.; Norman abbey; p. (1991) 17,032.

Ronaldshay, North, most N. of Orkney Is., **Scot.**; p. (1991) 92.

Ronaldshay, South, most S. of Orkney Is. **Scot.**; p. (1991) 943.

Roncesvalles, mtn. pass in Pyrenees, Navarre, **Spain**; 32 km N.E. of Pamplona; defeat and death of Roland 778.

Ronda, t., Málaga, **Spain**; in Andalusia; anc. Moorish t., divided by deep gorge crossed by bridge; p. (1981) 31,383.

Rondônia, st., **Brazil**; on Bolivian border; forest covered; forest prods.; nomadic Indian tribes; cap. Pôrto Velho; a. 243,071 km²; p. (1991) 1,130,400.

Rønne, t., **Denmark**; cap. of Bornholm I.; fish. pt.; shipyards, ceramics; p. (1990) 15,187.

Ronse (Renaix), t., **Belgium**; nr. Ghent; textile ctr.; p. (1982) 24,287.

Roodepoort-Maraisburg, t., Transvaal, **S. Africa**; ctr. Witwatersrand goldfields; p. (1980) 165,315.

Roosendaal, t., S.W. of N. Brabant, **Neth.**, sugar-refining; p. (1994) 62,784.

Roosevelt Dam (1903–11), Arizona, **USA**; on R. Salt in canyon E. of Phoenix on edge of Col. plateau; used for irrigation and hydroelectric power; part of Salt river project.

Roquefort-sur-Soulzon, t., S.E. Aveyron, **France**; caves in limestone cliffs used for ripening cheese; p. (1982) 880.

Roraima, mtn., at junc. of boundaries of Brazil, Guyana, and Venezuela; 2,852 m, hgst. point of Guiana Highlands.

Roraima (Rio Branco), fed. terr., **Brazil**; under-developed rain forest; devastation caused by forest fires (1998); cap. Boa Vista; a. 214,320 km²; p. (1991) 215,790.

Rosa Monte, Pennine Alps, Swiss-Italian border; alt. 4,637 m.

Rosario, t., Santa Fé prov., **Argentina**; second t. of rep.; R. pt. on Paraná R.; agr.-processing, iron and steel, lt. inds.; univ., cath.; p. (1991) 1,078,374.

Roscommon, co. t., Roscommon, **R.o.I.**; mkt.; cas., priory; p. (1986) 1,673.

Roscommon, inland co., Connaught, **R.o.I.**; extensive peat bog and Ls.; pastoral agr., cap. R.; a. 2,458 km²; p. (1986) 54,592.

Roseau, t., cap. **Dominica**, W.I.; p. (1991) 15,853.

Rosetta (Rashid), t., Lower **Egypt**; nr. Rosetta mouth of Nile; Rosetta stone found nearby gave key to Egyptian hieroglyphics.

Roskilde, t., spt., Sjaelland, **Denmark**; former cap.; cath. contains tombs of kings; admin. ctr. of R. prov.; p. (1990) 49,081.

Ross and Cromarty, historic co., N.W. **Scot.**, now part of Highland.

Rossendale Fells (or Forest), upland, S.E. Lancs./ Gtr. Manchester, **Eng.**; extension of Pennines between Rs. Mersey and Ribble; millstone grit moorland used for reservoirs; alt. mainly above 360 m; forms l. gov. dist. **Rossendale** in Lancs., inc. ts. of Haslingden, Rawtenstall, Bacup and Whitworth; p. (1995) 65,400.

Ross Dependency, Antarctica; N.Z. sector; inlet of Ross Sea; a. 414,400 km²; no permanent p.

Rosslare, spt., Wexford, **R.o.I.**; on extreme S.E. of Ireland; connections to Fishguard; p. (1986) 704.

Ross-on-Wye, t., South Herefordshire, Hereford, **Eng.**; mkt., tourism; p. (1991) 9,606.

Ross Sea, sea extending to 85° S. in **Antarctic**.

Rostock, c. Mecklenburg - West Pomerania, **Germany**; pt. nr. Baltic cst., outport of Warnemünde; shipbldg., fish-processing, chemicals; univ.; medi-aeval t.; p. (1990) 246,600.

Rostov, c., **Russia**; pt. on R. Don, nr. Azov Sea (Black Sea); one of Russia's finest and oldest cs.; ctr. of agr. dist.; grain mkt.; agr.-processing; univ.; p. (1989) 1,019,000.

Rosyth, t., Fife, **Scot.**; naval dockyard (closed 1995).

Rothamsted, v., Herts., **Eng.**; in Chiltern Hills, S. of Harpenden; famous agr. research sta.

Rother, l. gov. dist., East Sussex, **Eng.**; rural a. inc. Rye, Bexhill and Battle; p. (1995) 87,200.

Rother, R., Derbys. and South Yorks., **Eng.**; flows to R. Don at Rotherham; 34 km long.

Rother, R., East Sussex and Kent, **Eng.**; rises in the Weald, flows S.E. into English Channel at Rye; 50 km long.

Rotherham, t., met. dist., South Yorks., **Eng.**; on R. Don, 6 km N.E. of Sheffield; coal mining, iron, steel, wire, springs, glass; p. (1995) 255,800 (dist.), (1991) 121,380 (t.).

Rothes, burgh, Moray, **Scot.**; on R. Spey 19 km S.E. of Elgin; p. (1991) 1,345.

Rothesay, royal burgh, Argyll and Bute., **Scot.**; on E. cst. of I. of Bute in F. of Clyde; tourism; p. (1991) 5,264.

Rothwell, West Yorks., **Eng.**; on R. Aire, suburb of Leeds; coal-ming. ctr., engin.; p. (1991) 7,070.

Rotorua, c., leading spa of **N.Z.**; on volcanic plateau, Auckland, N.I.; hot springs; p. (1991) 65,096.

Rotterdam, c., spt. **Neth.**; Europe's lgst. spt., on Nieuwe Maas, part of Rhine-Maas-Scheldt delta; linked to outport Europoort (q.v) by New Waterway; serves hinterland of Rhine valley and central Europe; freeport; processing of imports, especially oil refining and petrochemical inds.; badly damaged in second world war; p. (1994) 598,521 (c.), 1,074,387 (met. a.).

Roubaix, t., Nord dep., **France**; nr. Lille; on Roubaix canal close to Belgian frontier; major textile ctr., especially for woollens; p. (1990) 98,179.

Rouen, c., Seine-Maritime dep., **France**; gr. R. pt., 125 km up R. Seine; oil refining, textiles, chemicals; cath.; Joan of Arc burned here; birthplace of Corneille and Flaubert; badly damaged in second world war; p. (1990) 105,470 (c.), 380,161 (met. a.).

Rousay, I., Orkney Is., **Scot.**; p. (1991) 291.

Roussillon, former prov., S. **France**; now part of Pyrénées-Orientales; irrigated by many sm. streams; olives, wine, fruit; historical cap. Perpignan.

Rovaniemi, t., **Finland**; on Kemi R.; timber and saw mills; p. (1993) 34,438.

Rovigo, prov., Venetia, **Italy**; part of N. Italian plain extending to Adriatic; impt. agr. dist.; cap. R.; a. 218 km²; p. (1981) 253,508.

Rovigo, t., cap. of R. prov., **Italy**; on R. Adige, cath., cas. ruins, palace; p. (1981) 52,218.

Rovno, c., cap. of R., oblast, **Ukraine**; rly. junct.; industl. ctr.; ruins of mediaeval palace; p. (1990) 232,900.

Roxburghshire, historic co., S. **Scot.**; now part of Borders.

Royal Oak, t., Mich., **USA**; residtl.; Detroit zoological park here; p. (1980) 70,893.

Royston, mkt. t., North Herts., **Eng.**; at N. foot of E. Anglian Heights, 11 km N.E. of Baldock; p. (1991) 14,087.

Royton, t., Gtr. Manchester, **Eng.**; 13 km N.E. of Manchester; textiles; p. (1991) 21,475.

Ruanda-Urundi. *See* Rwanda and Burundi.

Ruapehu, highest mtn., N.I., **N.Z.**; volcanic peak at S. extremity of central volcanic dist.; crater L. at summit; alt. 2,798 m; gives name to dist.; p. (1991) 18,104.

Rubicon, R., central **Italy**; flows to Adriatic; crossed by Julius Caesar and his armies 49 B.C.; has been identified with the Fiumicino or the Uso.

Rubtsovsk, t., W. Siberia, **Russia**; agr. engin.; p. (1989) 172,000.

Ruby Mines, dist., Mandalay, Upper **Myanmar**; hilly region of Shan plateau, once famous for rubies.

Ruda Slaska, t., Katowice, **Poland**; coal-mng. ctr.; iron and steel wks.; p. (1989) 169,017.

Rudnyy, t., **Kazakhstan**; t. 48 km S.W. of Kustanay; iron-ore mng. and dressing plant supplying Magnitogorsk; p. (1990) 126,200.

Rudolf, L., N.W. **Kenya**; in Great Rift Valley; a. 9,065 km²; ctr. of semi-arid region; renamed **Turkana.**

Rudolph I., N. of Franz Josef Land Arctic Oc.; **Russia** naval base; met. sta.

Rudolstadt, t., **Germany**; on R. Saale, in former st. of Thuringia; seat of counts of Schwarzburg-Rudolstadt (1584–1918); tourism; porcelain; p. (1989) 31,776.

Rueil-Malmaison, sub. of Paris, **France**; château; tomb of the empress Josephine; p. (1990) 67,323.

Rufiji, R., **Tanzania**; E. Africa; flows to Indian Oc.; 720 km long.

Rufisque, t., **Senegal** sm. spt. nr. Dakar; growing industl. ctr. for consumer gds.

Rugby, mkt. t., l. gov. dist., Warwicks, **Eng.**; on R. Avon, 18 km E. of Coventry; famous public school; elec. and gen. engin., motor and aircraft patterns; p. (1995) 87,000 (dist.), (1991) 61,106 (t.).

Rugeley, mkt. t., Staffs, **Eng.**; on R. Trent, 14 km S.E. of Stafford; coal, iron, tanning; expanded t.; p. (1991) 22,975.

Rügen, I., **Germany**; in Baltic Sea, off Stralsund; ch. t. Bergen; pt. Sassnitz, terminus of train ferry; steamer services to Trelleborg, Sweden.

Ruhr, industl. dist., **Germany**; lies to E. of R. Rhine, on either side of R. Ruhr; rich coalfield; impt. iron and steel, heavy engin. inds. based on local coal and iron ore from Luxembourg, Spain, Sweden; water communications to N. Sea along R. Rhine and Dortmund–Ems Canal; ch. ts. Essen, Duisburg, Düsseldorf, Dortmund, Bochum.

Ruhr, R., **Germany**; trib. of Rhine; flows S. of Ruhr conurb.; 232 km long.

Rukwa, L., E. **Africa**; between L. Tanganyika and L. Malawi in the rift valley; 48 km by 19 im, a. increasing.

Rum, I., Inner Hebrides, Highland, **Scot.**; nature reserve, highland ecology.

Rumaila, **Iraq**; oilfield; pipeline links to the Zubair–Fao system.

Rum Jungle, N.T., **Australia**; 64 km S.E. of Darwin; site of Australia's first major uranium project; ceased operation in 1970.

Runcorn, t., Halton, Cheshire, **Eng.**; on S. side of Mersey estuary; new t. (1964); chemicals; pipeline carrying petrochemical feedstock from Teeside; p. (1991) 64,154.

Rungis, Paris, **France**; site of major new mkt. to replace Les Halles; nr. Orly airpt., Val de Marne dep.; p. (1982) 2,650.

Runnymede, site of signing of Magna Carta; l. gov. dist., Surrey, **Eng.**; comprises Egham and Chertsey; p. (1995) 75,600.

Ruse, t., **Bulgaria**; on R. Danube, opposite Giurgiu in Romania; univ.; Roman t.; agr. processing; p. (1990) 192,365.

Rushcliffe, l. gov. dist., Notts., **Eng.**; a. S.E. of Nottingham inc. West Bridgeford; p. (1995) 103,200.

Rushden, t., East Northants., **Eng.**; 5 km E. of Wellingborough; shoes; p. (1991) 23,854.

Rushmoor, l. gov. dist., Hants., **Eng.**; small a. of Farnborough and Aldershot; p. (1995) 86,300.

Rüsselsheim, t., **Germany**; impt. car factory; p. (1986) 57,300.

Russia, CIS former constituent rep., USSR; lgst. rep. by a. and p.; economic development; inds. centred on St Petersburg and Moscow with new inds. being developed in Urals and Kuznetz basin; extends from Baltic to Pac. Oc. (8,000 km), from Arctic to Caspian Sea (4,000 km); part of N. European plain in W. and Siberian plain in E., separated by Ural mtns.; major Rs. Volga, Don, Ob, Yenisey, Lena, Amur; gr. variety in climate and p. density; major agr. region for wheat, sugarbeet, livestock; vast mineral deposits have aided economic growth; oil around Volga valley; metallic ores from Ural and Black Sea; hydroelectric power from Volga, Yenesey and Ob Rs.; cap. Moscow; a. 16,838,885 km²; p. (1996) 148,100,000.

Rustavi, t., **Georgia**; t., 32 km S.E. Tbilisi; iron and steel; lge. metallurgical plant; p. (1990) 160,400.

Rustenburg, t., Transvaal, **S. Africa**; on N.W. edge of High Veld, 96 km W. of Pretoria; local mkt. for agr. produce; agr.-processing.

Rutbah, t., **Iraq**; on oil pipeline from Iraq to Haifa; impt. ctr. on trans-desert routes.

Rutherglen, royal burgh, Glasgow, **Scot.**; on R. Clyde, S.E. of Glasgow; chemicals, tubes, paper, wire ropes, bolts.

Ruthin, t., Denbighshire, **Wales**; Vale of Clwyd, 13 km S.E. of Denbigh; p. (1991) 5,029.

Rutland, **Eng.**, unit. auth. created in 1997, reinstating historic Midland co. based on Oakham which became part of Leics. in 1974; p. (1995) 34,600.

Rutland Water, reservoir, Rutland, **Eng**.

Ruwenzori mtn. range, on **Uganda-Zaïre** border; overlooking W. arm of Gt. Rift Valley, midway between L. Mobutu Seso and L. Edward; hgst. peaks, Mt. Margherita (5,123 m), Mt. Alexandra (5,109 m); lower slopes covered in equatorial rain forest, coffee plantations on middle slopes above 1,500 m.

Rwanda, indep. rep., Central Africa; former kingdom of Ruanda, part of UN trust terr. of Ruanda-Urundi under Belgian admin. (until 1962); sm., landlocked st., S. of equator, consisting of upland plateau at 1,200 m; mainly subsistence agr. under gt. strain with rapid p. growth; coffee (ch. exp.), cotton, pyrethrum; cattle; tin, tungsten and natural gas discoveries; little ind.; bitter tribal warfare 1994–; cap. Kigali; a. 26,338 km²; p. (1993) 7,459,000.

Ryazan, c., cap. of R. oblast, **Russia**; on Oka R.; food inds., agr. machin., footwear, chemicals; mediaeval architecture; p. (1989) 515,000.

Rybinsk, c., cap. of R. oblast, **Russia**; on Upper Volga; tr. and shipping ctr. since 16th cent.; site of hydroelectric power sta.; shipbldg., engin.; renamed Andropov 1984 to honour dead General Secretary; p. (1989) 251,000.

Rybinsk Sea (**Rybinsk Reservoir**), **Russia**; artificial L.; created behind dams on R. Volga and R. Sheksna at Rybinsk; part of scheme to regulate flow of R. Volga and to incorporate it in a vast inland waterway system; opened 1945; a. 3,885 km.

Rybnik, t., Katowice prov., S.W. **Poland**; ctr. of coal-mng. dist.; p. (1989) 142,059.

Rydal Water, L., nr. Ambleside, Cumbria, **Eng.**; adjacent v. contains Rydal Mount, home of Wordsworth.

Ryde, t., I. of Wight, **Eng.**; on N.E. cst.; yachting ctr. and seaside resort; boat and yacht bldg.; steamer connection across Spithead to Portsmouth; p. (1991) 20,502.

Rye, t., Rother, East Sussex, **Eng.**; at mouth of R. Rother to W. of Dungeness; Cinque pts.; Ypres cas.; tourist ctr.; p. (1991) 3,708.

Ryedale, l. gov. dist., North Yorks., **Eng.**; lge. a. inc. Malton, Pickering, Norton, Kirby Moorside and Helmsley; p. (1994) 48,000.

Ryton, t., Tyne and Wear, **Eng.**; on R. Tyne, W. of Newcastle; p. (1991) 15,952.

Ryukyu Is., archipelago, between Kyushu I., **Japan**, and Taiwan; ch. t. Naha on Okinawa I.; following second world war Is. S. of Lat. 30° N. occupied by USA; Amami and Tokara grs. returned to Japan 1953; American military installations on Okinawa withdrawn 1972; lge. Is. mtnous., volcanic; sweet potatoes, sugarcane, pineapples; 3 lge. oil refineries; a. 2,196 km²; p. (1990) 1,222,398.

Rzeszów, c. and prov., S.E. **Poland**; at foot of Carpathian highlands; route ctr.; growing industl. t.; p. (1989) 150,702, (c.), 716,300 (prov.).

S

Saale, R., Germany; rises in Fichtelgebirge flows N. through Thuringia to Elbe; attractive, well wooded valley; irrigation; hydroelec. power; 360 km long.

Saalfeld, t., Gera, Germany; on R. Saale; famous cas., iron-mng.; machin., chocolate; p. (1989) 34,037.

Saarbrücken, c., cap. of Saarland, **Germany**; on R. Saar, nr. Fr. border; cas.; rich coalfield; iron and steel wks., textiles, leather, paper, oil refining at Klarenthal nearby; p. (1990) 191,500.

Saaremaa (Osel), I., Baltic Sea; at entrance to G. of Riga, **Estonia**; low plateau, bleak and barren; ch. t. Kingisepp (Kuressaare); a. 2,720 km².

Saarland, *Land*, **Germany**; heavy inds. based on lge. coalfields; drained by R. Saar; cap. Saarbrücken; admin. by League of Nations 1919–35, returned to Germany after plebiscite; economic attachment to France after second world war; reunited politically with W. Germany 1957; a. 2,567 km²; p. (1992) 1,077,000.

Saarlouis (Saarlautern), Saarland, **Germany**; on R. Saar; coal mng.; wood and metal inds.; founded by Louis XIV; birthplace of Marshal Ney; p. (1986) 37,400.

Sabadell, t., **Spain**; N.W. of Barcelona; textiles, fertilisers, paper; p. (1991) 184,190.

Sabah, E. Malaysia; attempted secession 1975; formerly N. Borneo; underdeveloped; tropical forest; forest prods., inc. rubber, the major exp.; main pt. Sandakan; cap. Kota Kinabalu; a. 76,112 km²; p. (1991) 1,736,902

Sabahiyah, t., Kuwait; new t. being built between Ahmadi and Fahahil.

Sabara, t., Minas Gerais, **Brazil**; historic c.; museum of gold.

Sabine, R., Texas and La., **USA**; flows through S. Lake (an expansion of the R. 29 km long) to G. of Mexico; 936 km long.

Sable I., off S.E. cst. Nova Scotia, **Canada**; sandy I., scene of many shipwrecks.

Sacramento, c., st. cap. Cal., **USA**; on R. Sacramento; shipping and industl. ctr.; rly. wk.-shps., smelting, meat and fruit packing, flour, lumber, metal prods., rocket and missiles ind.; p. (1990) 369,365 (c.), 1,481,102 (met. a.).

Sacramento, R., Cal., **USA**; forms N. section of Central Valley projected for irrigation, hydro-electric power and flood control; 624 km long.

Saddleback (Blencathra), mtn., Cumbria, **Eng.**; nr. Keswick; alt. 868 m.

Saddleworth, t., Gtr. Manchester, **Eng.**; in Pennines, 8 km N.E. of Oldham; woollens, paper mkg., engin.; p. (1981) 21,851.

Saffron Walden, mkt. t., Uttlesford, Essex, **Eng.**; on E. Anglian heights; cas., abbey ruins; saffron crocus once cultivated here; p. (1991) 13,201.

Safi, spt., **Morocco**; on Atl. Oc.; linked by rail to phosphate deposits at Youssoufia; pottery, fish-processing; resort; p. (1982) 197,616.

Saga, c., cap. of S. pref., Kyushu, **Japan**; coal-mng. ctr., textiles, ceramics; p. (1990) 169,964.

Saganoseki, t., N.E. Kyushu, **Japan**; on Bungo strait; impt. gold, copper, and silver mines; smelting.

Sagar, t., Karnataka, **India**; nr. Krishna R. valley; p. (1991) 195,346.

Saginaw, c., Mich., **USA**; on R. Saginaw; former fur and lumbering region; coal; beans, sugarbeet; various mnfs.; p. (1990) 399,000 (met. a. with Bay City–Midland).

Saguenay, R., Quebec, **Canada**; trib. of St. Lawrence R.; outlet of L. St. John; used for hydroelec. power; tourism; length c. 176 km.

Sagunto, t., Spain; nr. Valencia; integrated steelwks. projected; anc. t., sieged by Hannibal; p. (1981) 54,759 (met. a.).

Sahara, the gr. N. African desert between the Sudan and the Barbary sts., extending from the Atl. to the Nile, inc. Tripoli and Fezzan; a. 16,835,000 km²; numerous oases with ts. and tr. ctrs.; oil pipelines to Algerian and Tunisian csts.; nomadic Arab and Berber tribes. The Sahara abounded with lakes and grassland until c. 6,000 years ago.

Saharan Arab Democratic Rep. *See* **Western Sahara**.

Saharan Atlas, S. range of Atlas mtns. in **Algeria**; ch. peaks., Jebel Aurès, 2,331 m. J. Aissa, 2,242 m, J. Ksel, 2,011 m.

Saharanpur, c., Uttar Pradesh, N.W. **India**; wood-carving, furniture, agr.-processing inds.; p. (1991) 375,000.

Sahel, region of **W. Africa**, inc. Chad, Mali, Mauritania, Niger, Senegal and Bourkina Faso; suffered severe famine and drought 1972–4 and 1984–5 caused by desertification.

Saïda (Sidon), t., **Lebanon**; on Mediterranean, S. of Beirut; terminus of oil pipeline from Saudi Arabia; refinery; p. (1988) 38,000.

Saigon. *See* **Ho Chi-minh City**.

Saimaa, L. system, **Finland**; a. of water which forms basin of R. Vuoksi; canal connects with C. of Finland and runs partly through Russian terr.; a. 1,699 km².

Saingdin Falls, Myanmar; on Kaladan R.; site of new hydroelec. power sta.

St. Abb's Head, rocky promontory, lighthouse, Borders, Scot.

St. Albans, c., l. gov. dist., Herts., **Eng.**; on N. margin of Vale of St. Albans, 32 km N.W. of London; faces remains of Roman Verulamium across R. Ver; lt. inds., electronics, instrument mkg.; cath.; residtl.; p. (1995) 129,600 (dist.), (1991) 80,376 (c.).

St. Amand, t., Cher dep., **France**; on R. Cher; Roman remains; new recreational park; p. (1982) 12,801.

St. Andrews, royal burgh, Fife, **Scot.**; seaside resort; univ.; famous golf course; p. (1991) 11,136.

St. Anthony, waterfalls, on R. Mississippi, **USA**; predominant factor in site of Minneapolis.

St. Asaph, t., Denbighshire, N. **Wales**; on R. Clwyd; p. (1991) 3,399.

St. Austell, mkt. t., Restormel, Cornwall, **Eng.**; on S. flank of Hensbarrow; ctr. of Cornwall's china clay ind.; p. (1991) 21,622.

St. Barthélemy, Fr. I., **W.I.**; dependency of Guadeloupe; cash crops of sugar, bananas, cacao; cap. Gustavia; p. (1982) 3,059.

St. Bees Head, promontory, 4 km N.W. of St. Bees, Cumbria, **Eng.**; freestone quarries, anhydrite.

St. Bernard Pass, Great, on Italian–Swiss bdy., W. Alps; carries main road from W. Switzerland to Plain of Lombardy; 2,477 m a.s.l.; road tunnel (5·6 km) constr. 1958–62 links Cantine de Proz (Valais can., Switzerland) and St. Rhémy (Italy); under tunnel will run projected 416 km pipeline from Genoa to Aigle.

St. Bernard Pass, Little, on French–Italian bdy. W. Alps; links Isère valley with Val d'Aosta; alt. 2,190 m.

St. Boniface, t., Manitoba, **Canada**; sub. of Winnipeg; meat-packing, petroleum prods.

St. Brides Bay, Pembrokeshire, **Wales**.

St. Brieuc, t., cap. of Côtes-du-Nord dep., N.W. **France**; sm. fish. pt.; iron and steel wks.; cath.; p. (1990) 47,340 (t.), 83,661 (met.a.).

St. Catharines, c., Ont., **Canada**; on Welland Ship Canal; mkt. for Niagara fruit-growing region; agr. implements, textile, paper and flour mills, vehicle components; resort; p. (1991) 129,300 (c.), (1986) 343,258 (met. a. with Niagara).

St. Chamond, t., Loire, **France**; nr. St. Etienne; ribbons, rayon; rly. wks.; coal mng.; p. (1990) 39,262 (t.), 81,795 (met. a.).

St. Clair, L., Canada–USA; part of link between L. Huron and L. Erie; a. 1,191 km².

St. Clair, R., N. America; flows from L. Huron through L. of St. Clair into L. Erie; forms bdy. between Mich. (USA) and Ont. (Canada); impt. link in Gr. Ls. waterway; length 136 km, depth dredged to 6 m.

St. Clair Shores, t., Mich., **USA**; residtl. sub. of Detroit; p. (1980) 76,210.

St. Cloud, W. sub. of Paris, **France**; fine park; porcelain; p. (1982) 28,760.

St. Cloud, t., Minn., **USA**; on R. Mississippi; granite quarries; st. college; p. (1984) 42,100 (t.), 171,300 (met. a.).

St.-Cyr-l'Ecole, t., Yvelines, **France**; once famous for military school founded by Napoleon; bldgs. destroyed second world war; p. (1982) 16,380.

St. Davids, c., Pembrokeshire, **Wales**; 24 km S.W. of Fishguard; on site of anc. Minevia; cath., ruins of Bishop Gower's palace (1342); p. (1991) 1,627.

St. David's Head, promontory, Pembrokeshire, **Wales**.

St. Denis, t., N. sub., Paris, **France**; on R. Seine; abbey, burial place of Fr. kings; chemicals., machin.; p. (1990) 90,086.

St. Denis, spt., cap. of Ile de la Réunion (Fr.), Indian Oc.; p. (1990) 122,875.

St. Dié, t., Vosges, **France**; on R. Meurthe; cath.; textile ctr., hosiery; p. (1982) 24,816.

St. Dizier, t., Haute-Marne, dep. **France**; on R. Marne; metallurgy; p. (1982) 37,445.

St. Edmundsbury, l. gov. dist., Suffolk, **Eng.**; based on Bury St. Edmunds and inc. Haverhill; p. (1995) 93,100.

St. Elias, mtns., Alaska, **USA**; and Yukon, **Canada**; inc. Mt. McKinley (5,780 m); source of world's lgst. icefield outside polar regions.

Saintes, t., Charente-Maritime dep., **France**; cath.; Roman antiquities; suffered in Huguenot wars; agr. implements; earthenware; p. (1982) 27,486.

St. Etienne, t., cap. of Loire dep., **France**; nr. Lyons; in sm. coal basin on edge of Central Massif; famous for firearms; modern inds. inc. engin., dyes, chemicals, textiles, glass; p. (1990) 201,569 (t.), 313,388 (met.a.).

St. Gall (**St. Gallen**), t., cap. of can. St. G., **Switzerland**; founded around Benedictine monastery (7th-8th cent.); embroidered cottons; p. (1990) 74,136.

St. Gall (**St. Gallen**), can., **Switzerland**; borders L. Constance, rising to S.; mainly industl.; ch. ind. textiles; cap. St. G.; a. 2,012 km²; p. (1990) 420,300.

St. George's Channel, part of Irish Sea, separating Wales from Ireland.

St. George's, t., cap. of **Grenada**, W.I.; ch. spt.; built around submerged volcanic crater forming St. G. Bay; p. (1989) 35,742.

St. Germain-en-Laye, t., Yvelines, **France**; on R. Seine; outer sub. of Paris; residtl.; popular resort; birthplace of Debussy; p. (1982) 40,829.

Saint Gotthard, mtn. gr., Alps, S. central **Switzerland**; crossed by St. G. pass (2,115 m); rly. passes through St. G. tunnel (14·8 km, max. alt. 1,155 m); road tunnel (16·3 km) opened 1980, longest in world; motorways link pass with Zürich, Basle, and Lugano.

St. Govan's Head, promontory, Pembrokeshire, **Wales**.

St. Helena, I., Brit., col., Atl. Oc.; 1,920 km from W. cst. Africa; spt. and only t. Jamestown; Napoleon imprisoned 1815-21, and Boer captives 1900; famous for its wirebird, species of plover peculiar to I.; a. 122 km²; p. (1997) 6,000.

St. Helens, t., met. dist., Merseyside, **Eng.**; 19 km E. of Liverpool; connected by canal with R. Mersey; coal, iron, alkali; copper smelting, glass, fibreglass, plastics; p. (1995) 179,900 (dist.), (1991) 106,293 (t.).

St. Helier, spt., **Jersey**, Channel Is.; resort; cas.; tr. in early vegetables.

Saint-Hyacinthe, t., spt., Quebec, **Canada**; on Yamaska R.; cath.; famous for organs; lt. inds.; p. (1986) 38,603.

St. Ives, t., Penwith, Cornwall, **Eng.**; at entrance to St. Ives Bay; fishing, holiday resort; p. (1991) 10,092.

St. Ives, t., Camb., **Eng.**; on R. Ouse, 6 km E. of Huntingdon; borders the Fens; R. Ouse crossed by 16th cent. bridge containing a chapel; p. (1991) 16,510.

Saint-Jean, t., Quebec, **Canada**; on Richelieu R.; timber, grain exps.; textiles, sewing machines, p. (1986) 34,745.

Saint John, c., spt., N.B., **Canada**; lgst. c. of N.B.; ice-free pt.; lge. dry docks; rly. terminus; impt. inds. inc. sugar- and oil-refining, paper, textiles; p. (1991) 90,457 (c.), (1986) 121,265 (met. a.).

St. John, L., Quebec, **Canada**; on Saguenay R.; tourism; a. 971 km².

St. John, R., Maine, N.B., **Canada**, **USA**; flows to B. of Fundy forming section of international boundary; 720 km long.

St. John's, t., cap. of **Antigua**, W.I.; pt., airpt.; cath.; ch. comm. ctr. of I.; p. (1982) 30,000.

St. John's, c. spt., cap. of Newfoundland, **Canada**; on E. cst.; first English settlement in America early 16th cent.; gr. tr. in fish with allied inds.; univ., 2 caths.; p. (1986) 96,216 (c.), (1991) 171,859 (met. a.).

St. Johns, R., **USA**; drains swamps of central Fla., 21 km from Atl. Oc.; 560 km long.

St. John's Wood, residtl. dist., Westminster London, **Eng.**; contains Lord's Cricket Ground, home of English cricket.

St. Joseph, t., Mich., **USA**; pt. on L. Mich.; ctr. of fruit-growing a.; resort; p. (1980) 9,622.

St. Joseph, t., Mo., **USA**; declining pt. on R. Mississippi; agr. tr. and processing; p. (1990) 71,852.

St. Just, t., Penwith, Cornwall, **Eng.**; nr. Lands End, 10 km W. of Penzance; former tin-mng. ctr.; p. (1991) 2,092.

St. Kilda, rocky I., most W. of the Hebrides, **Scot.**; 5 km long; bird sanctuary, famous for its wren, a sub-species.

St. Kitts-Nevis, Leeward gr. of Is., W.I.; aut. st. in association with Gt. Britain; indep. (1983); sugar, sea island cotton, molasses; a. 262 km²; cap. Basseterre; p. (1993) 43,520.

Saint-Laurent, t., Quebec, **Canada**; industl. t. on Montreal I., W. of Montreal; p. (1991) 72,402.

St. Lawrence, G. of, Canada; arm of Atl. Oc., partly enclosed by Newfoundland and Nova Scotia; impt. fisheries.

St. Lawrence I., Alaska, **USA**; in Bering Sea; 160 km long.

St. Lawrence, R., Canada; major outlet from Gr. Lakes; forms bdy. between USA and Canada; ch. tribs. Ottawa, Richelieu, St. Maurice, Saguenay Rs.; with St. L. Seaway forms a major waterway facing Europe; grain, timber, oil, iron-ore traffic; used for hydro-electric power; total length from source (St. Louis) 3,360 km.

St. Lawrence Seaway, N. America; joint Canada-USA project links head of the Gr. Lakes with Atl. Oc., providing channel for lge. ocean-going vessels to reach American continent; provides major source of hydroelectric power to industl. a.; opened 1959.

St. Lô, t. cap. of Manche dep., N.W. **France**; built on rocky hill overlooking R. Vire; cath.; p. (1990) 22,819.

St. Louis, t., Réunion, overseas territory of France, Indian Ocean.

Saint-Louis, t., Senegal, W. Africa; at mouth of R. Senegal; cath.; former cap.; comm. ctr.; impt. fish. pt.; p. (1992) 125,717.

St. Louis, c., Mo., **USA**; on R. Mississippi 16 km below confluence of Rs. Mississippi and Missouri; two univs.; impt. rly. and river junc.; mkt. for furs, livestock, grain, farm prod.; banking and fin. ctr.; varied mnfs.; machin., cars, aircraft, leather gds., beer, chemicals; p. (1990) 396,685 (c.), 2,444,099 (met. a.).

St. Lucia I., indep. st. (1979) within Commonwealth; Windward Is., W.I.; volcanic, forested, fertile valleys; exp. bananas and other tropical agr. prod.; airpt.; cap. Castries; a. 616 km²; hurricane disaster 1980; p. (1993) 136,000.

St. Malo, spt., Ile-et-Vilaine dep., N.W. **France**; on Normandy cst.; cath.; once fortfd.; shipping, fishing, and tourist inds.; p. (1982) 47,324.

St. Martin, I., Leeward Is., W.I.; N. part Fr. dependency of Guadeloupe, S. part belongs to Neth. Antilles; divided since 1648; ch. exp. salt; total p. (1981) 13,156.

St. Marylebone. See **Westminster, City of.**

St. Maur-des-Fossés, residtl. garden sub. of Paris, Val-de-Marne dep., **France**; p. (1990) 77,492.

St. Maurice, v., Valais, **Switzerland**; nr. Martigny; 6th-cent. abbey; once a leading Burgundian t.; p. c. 10,000.

St. Maurice, R., Quebec, **Canada**; trib. of St. Lawrence R.; used for timber transport and hydroelec. power; 520 km long.

St. Mawes, v., Cornwall, **Eng.**; on E. cst. of estuary of R. Fal; cas.; holiday resort, fishing.

St. Michael's Mt., castled rock, Cornwall, **Eng.**; the anc. Ictis; alt. 70 m.

St. Monance, burgh, Fife, **Scot.**; resort; p. (1991) 1,373.

St. Moritz, resort and winter sports ctr., **Switzerland**; in the Upper Engadine; alt. 1,857 m.

St. Nazaire, t., Loire-Atlantique dep., W. **France**; spt. at mouth of R. Loire, outport for Nantes; growing pt. and industl. ctr.; shipyds., iron and steel, fertilisers, aircraft, oil refining; p. (1990) 66,087 (t.), 131,511 (met.a.).

St. Neots, mkt. t., Cambs. **Eng.**; on R. Ouse, 16 km N.E. of Bedford; brewing, milling, paper-mkg.; expanded t.; p. (1991) 13,471.

St. Niklaas, mftg. t., E. Flanders, **Belgium**; nr. Antwerp; textile ctr., carpets; p. (1993) 68,472.

St. Omer, t., Pas-de-Calais dep., N. **France**; ctr. of mkt.-gardening a.; textiles, food inds.; cath., abbey ruins; p. (1982) 53,748 (met. a.).

St. Ouen, N. sub. of Paris, Seine-St. Denis dep., **France**; on R. Seine at base of Butte de Monmartre; metals, chemicals, glues, tanning; p. (1982) 43,743.

St. Pancras. See **Camden.**

St. Paul, spt., **Réunion**, French territory, Indian Ocean; p. (1990) 71,952.

St. Paul, c., cap. of Minn., **USA**; faces Minneapolis across Mississippi; cath.; univ.; ctr. of agr. dist.; agr. mkt. and processing; car assembly, oil refining, electronics; p. (1990) 272,235 (c.), 2,464,000 (met. a. with Minneapolis.)

St. Paul, I., **Indian Oc.**; bare volcanic islet rising to 493 m; part of Fr. Southern and Antarctic Terr.; uninhabited.

St. Peter Port, spt., cap. of **Guernsey**, exp. fruit, flowers, vegetables; resort.

St. Petersburg, c., formerly Leningrad, **Russia**; at mouth of Neva R.; cultural ctr. with many fine bldgs., inc. winter palace, Hermitage museum, cath., admiralty bldg.; former cap. of Russia; major pt. and industl. ctr.; exp. timber, furs, and raw materials; ice-bound December–March; founded (1703) by Peter the Great as St. Petersburg; p. (1989) 4,460,000 (c.), 5,024,000 (met. a.).

St. Petersburg, c., Fla., **USA**; resort on Tampa Bay; p. (1990) 238,629.

St. Pierre, t., Martinique I., Fr. **W.I.**; utterly destroyed and all inhabitants save one by eruption of Mt. Pelée 1902; tourism.

St. Pierre, t., **Réunion**, French Territory, Indian Ocean; sm. artificial harbour.

St. Pierre and Miquelon, Fr. terr. consisting of 8 sm. Is. off S. cst. of Newfoundland; a. of St. Pierre gr. 26 km²; a. of Miquelon gr., 215 km²; ch. t. St. Pierre, fisheries; p. of St. P. and M. (1990) 6,392.

St. Pölten, cap. of Lower **Austria**; nr. Vienna; founded round an abbey; textiles, machin.; p. (1991) 49,805.

St. Quentin, t., Aisne dep., **France**; on R. Somme; impt. textile ctr.; p. (1990) 62,085.

St. Raphaël, t., Var dep., S.E. **France**; resort on Fr. Riviera, S.W. of Cannes; marina; p. (1982) 24,310.

St. Rémy, t., Bouches-du-Rhône dep., **France**; Roman antiquities; p. (1982) 8,439.

St. Thomas, t., Ont., **Canada**; ctr. of agr. dist., rly. ctr.; lt. inds.; p. (1986) 28,851.

St. Thomas, I., Atl. Oc.; main economic ctr. of **USA Virgin Is.**; tourism; p. (1990) 48,166.

St. Thomas I. See **São Tomé.**

St. Trond, t., Limburg, **Belgium**; impt. fruit mkt.; p. (1982) 36,591.

St. Tropez, t., Var dep., S.E. **France**; on Fr. Riviera; popular, expanding tourist resort; marina; p. (1982) 6,248.

St. Vincent, C., S.W. **Portugal**; Spanish fleet defeated by British 1797.

St. Vincent, Gulf of, lge. inlet, S. **Australia**; penetrates 160 km inland, max. width 65 km; Pt. Adelaide is on E. side.

St. Vincent, I., part of **St. Vincent and the Grenadines**, ind. st. (1979) within Commonwealth; one of Windward gr., **W.I.**; volcanic; exp. bananas, arrowroot from alluvial soils in S.W. which has majority of p.; subsistence agr. on hill slopes; cap. Kingstown; a. 389 km² (inc. attached Grenadine Is.); p. (1994) 109,000.

Sakai, sub. of Osaka, Honshu, **Japan**; industl. ctr., engin., chemicals, textiles, electricity generation; p. (1990) 807,859.

Sakhalin, I., off cst. of Siberia; with Kuriles forms Sakhalin oblast of **Russia**; herring fisheries, coal, naphtha, alluvial gold, oil, timber, natural gas; oil pipelines connected to Komsomolsk and Khabarovsk refineries; a. c. 63,610 km².

Sakashima Is. See **Ryuku.**

Sakura-jima, peninsula, S. Kyushu, **Japan**; former I. joined to mainland by lava flows; famed for fruit and vegetables.

Sala, t., Västmanland, **Sweden**; silver mine worked

for over 400 years, now to limited extent; lime, bricks.

Salado, R., N.W. **Argentina**; impt. Andean trib. of Paraná R.; 800 km long.

Salamanca, t., Guanajuato st., **Mexico**; oil refining; ammonia plant; natural gas pipeline to Guadalajara; p. (1990) 206,275.

Salamanca, t., cap. of S. prov., **Spain**; on R. Tormes; old univ., 2 caths., many convents; p. (1991) 185,992, 370,624 (prov.).

Salamis, I., **Greece**; opposite harbour of Athens; spt. and ch. t. S.; famous naval battle 480 B.C.; p. (1981) 20,807.

Salar de Uyumi, windswept, dry, salt flat, S.W. **Bolivia.**

Salavat, t., **Russia**; in Bashkiria, 144 km S. of Ufa; ctr. of oilfield; glass factory; became t. in 1954; p. (1989) 150,000.

Sala-y-Gomez, barren, uninhabited volcanic I., **Pac. Oc.**; belonging to **Chile**, 328 km E.N.E. of Easter I.

Salazar, **Mexico**; nr. Mexico City; alt. 2,897 m; nuclear reactor for radioisotopes for medical, industl. and agr. purposes.

Salcombe, t., South Hams, S. Devon, **Eng.**; mkt.; fishing; resort; p. (1991) 1,921.

Saldanha Bay, inlet on W. cst. C. of Good Hope, **S. Africa**; whaling, fishing; fish-canning at t. of S.B.

Sale, t., Victoria, **Australia**; tr. of lge. irrigated agr. a.; gas processing and crude oil stabilisation plant (1969); p. (1991) 13,858.

Sale, t., Trafford, Gtr. Manchester, **Eng.**; residtl. sub. of Manchester; p. (1991) 56,052.

Sale or Salch, spt., Fez, **Morocco**; former pirate headquarters; fishing, fish-processing, carpets; p. (1982) 289,391.

Salekhard, t., R. pt., N.W. Siberia, **Russia**; on R. Ob; fisheries, collecting ctr. for furs; exp. timber.

Salem, t., Tamil Nadu, **India**; industl. ctr., rly. junc. in picturesque valley; local iron ore, manganese mng.; mineral processing, textiles; p. (1991) 367,000.

Salem, t., Mass., **USA**; 24 km from Boston; one of oldest New England ts.; many fine bldgs.; textiles, leather prods., machin., electronics; p. (1990) 264,000 (met. a. with Gloucester).

Salem, t., st. cap. Ore., **USA**; on Willamette R.; univ.; fruit packing, flour milling and canning; p. (1990) 107,786 (t.), 278,000 (met. a.).

Salerni, t., Sicily, **Italy**; the anc. Halicyæ; famous Norman cas., terracotta vases; p. (1981) 12,289.

Salerno, c., cap. of Salerno prov., in Campania, S. **Italy**; on G. of S.; fishing pt. and comm. ctr.; machin., textiles, food processing; univ.; famous for Allied landing 1943; p. (1992) 147,564.

Salford, t., met. dist., Gtr. Manchester, **Eng.**; on R. Irwell, adjoining Manchester; inc. terminal docks of Manchester Ship Canal; univ.; varied inds.; p. and industl. decentralization; p. (1995) 230,500 (dist.), (1991) 79,755 (c.).

Salgótarján, t., N. **Hungary**; coal mng., agr. machin., tools, glass; p. (1997) 45,000.

Salina, t., Kan., **USA**; on Smoky Hill R.; univ.; flour milling, cattle mkt., farm implements; p. (1980) 41,843.

Salinas, t., Cal., **USA**; comm., tr. and processing ctr. for fertile Salinas valley; birthplace of John Steinbeck; p. (1990) 108,777 (t.), 356,000 (met. a. with Seaside-Monterey).

Salinas, R., Cal., **USA**; rises in US Coast Range, flows N.W. into Bay of Monterey, Pac. Oc.; fertile valley floor irrigated to produce hard and stone fruits, mkt. garden produce (especially lettuce), alfalfa; 166 km long.

Salinas-Grandes, Las, gr. salt marsh region, **Argentina**; provs. Santiago del Estero and Cordoba; dry, no Rs.

Salisbury, t., South **Australia**; part of Adelaide; research ctr. for long-range weapons.

Salisbury (New Sarum), cath. c., historic county town and l. gov. dist., Wilts., **Eng.**; on S. edge of Salisbury Plain at confluence of Rs. Avon, Ebble, Nadder, Wylye and Bourne; Old Sarum to N. was the Roman Sorbiodunum and present site represents a move (1220) to a more sheltered and better watered in. valley; cath. pure Early English with tallest spire in Eng. (123 m); ctr. mediaeval woollen ind.; engin. ind.; p. (1995) 110,800 (dist.), (1991) 39,268 (c.).

Salisbury. See **Harare.**

Salisbury Plain, Wilts., **Eng.**; chalk upland, N. of Salisbury; Stonehenge; army training a.; a. 777 km².

Salonika. See Thessaloniki.

Salmon, R., Idaho, **USA**; canyon c. 1·6 km deep and 16 km wide in places; rapids navigable downstream only, thus its name of River of No Return; l. c. 680 km.

Salop. See Shropshire.

Salsette, I., **India**; connected by bridge and causeway with Bombay; popular seaside resort at Juhu; a. 624 km².

Salt, R., Arizona, **USA**; rises in Colorado plateau, flows into Gila R. below Phoenix; rich, irrigated fruit growing valley in lower course; many multipurpose schemes in Salt River Valley project; length 384 km. See also **Roosevelt Dam**.

Salta, c., cap. of Salta prov., **Argentina**; on R. Salta; picturesque c. with colonial atmosphere; cath.; comm. ctr. for rich agr. a.; p. (1991) 370,904 (c.), 866,153 (prov.).

Saltash, mkt. t., Caradon, Cornwall, **Eng.**; on W. side of Tamar estuary; lowest bridging point of Tamar by Brunel's rly. bridge (1859) and toll road bridge; p. (1991) 14,139.

Saltburn-by-the-Sea, t., Redcar and Cleveland, **Eng.**; seaside resort; 16 km E. of Middlesbrough; p. (1991) 6,145.

Saltcoats, burgh, N. Ayrshire, **Scot.**; on Firth of Clyde 3 km S. of Ardrossan; sm. harbour; hosiery; mainly residtl.; p. (1991) 11,865.

Saltillo, c., cap. of Coahuila st., **Mexico**; comm., industl., and mng. ctr.; p. (1990) 440,845.

Salt Lake City, c., cap. of Utah, **USA**; nr. Gr. Salt L., H.Q. of Mormonism; temple and univ.; agr. comm. ctr. for irrigated a.; meat packing; p. (1990) 159,936 (c.), 1,072,227 (met. a. with Ogden).

Salto, c., cap. of S. dep., **Uruguay**; on Uruguay R., nr. Concordia (Argentina); rly. and tr. ctr. for agr. a.; citrus fruit, grapes, wine; p. (1985) 80,787.

Salton Sea, L., S. Cal., **USA**; 80 m below sea-level in depression which extends N.W. from head of G. of Cal.; ctr. of inland drainage; a. 699 km². See also **Imperial Valley**.

Salvador, spt., cap. of Bahia, **Brazil**; Brazil's first cap.; many years of economic stagnation now replaced by rapid growth; Brazil's first oil strike here in 1939; refining less impt. than petrochemicals at Camaçari complex (started 1972); new pt., naval base; hydro-elect. from Paulo Afonso encouraging many new light inds.; cement, aluminium, laminated timber, special alloys; p. (1991) 2,056,013 .

Salween, R., S.E. **Asia**; rises in E. Tibet, crosses Yunnan, descending into Burma to empty in G. of Martaban; many rapids; navigable to Moulmein; hydroelec. scheme; 2,880 km long.

Salzburg, c., cap. of Salzburg prov., **Austria**; on R. Salzach; cath., cas.; birthplace of Mozart; tourist resort; annual music festival; p. (1991) 143,971.

Salzburg, prov., **Austria**; adjoins Bavaria and the Tyrol, on N. slope of E. Alps; pastoral agr.; timber and some mineral wealth; hydro-electric power; cap. Salzburg; a. 7,154 km²; p. (1991) 483,880.

Salzgitter, t., Lower Saxony, **Germany**; S.W. of Brunswick; steel, engin., wagon bldg., fertilisers; p. (1990) 144,800.

Salzkammergut, lake dist., Upper **Austria**; saline baths at Aussee and Ischl; tourist region; stock-raising forestry.

Samar, I., **Philippines**; separated from Leyte by narrow strait; mainly forested mtns.; hemp, rice in lowlands; cap. Catbalogan; typhoons; a. 13,080 km²; p. (1990) 1,246,722.

Samara, **(Kuybyshev)**, c., cap. of S. oblast, **Russia**; on R. Volga; major R. pt., rly. junc. on Moscow–Siberian line, airport; hydroelectric power sta.; comm. ctr. with varied mnfs., inc. cars, aircraft, textiles, synthetic rubber; oil refining; grain and livestock exp.; p. (1989) 1,254,000.

Samarkand, c., **Uzbekistan**; one of oldest cs. in world, sited in productive oasis on Zeravshan R.; many historical associations and anc. bldgs; agr. tr. ctr.; food processing; cotton, silk; univ.; p. (1990) 369,900.

Samarra, t., **Iraq**; on Tigris R., N. of Baghdad; holy c. of Shiite sect; p. (1970) 62,008 (latest fig.).

Sambalpur, t., Orissa, **India**; on Hirakud reservoir of Mahandi R.; p. (1991) 131,138.

Sambhar, salt lake, Rajasthan, **India**; exploited on lge. scale; a. 233 km².

Sambre, R., trib. of R. Meuse at Namur; crosses Franco-Belgian coal basin; part of N. Fr.–S. Belgian waterway system; 176 km long.

Samnan, t., N. **Iran**; in foothills of Elburz mtns.; iron, sulphur ores, petroleum.

Samoa, archipelago, S. **Pac. Oc.**; volcanic mtns., tropical climate; agr., fishing; divided into two parts. See **Western Samoa, American Samoa**.

Sámos, I., Aegean Sea, off W. cst. Anatolia. belonging to **Greece**; mtnous., fine climate, fertile soils; wine, tobacco, Med. crops; ch. t. Vathy; a. 466 km²; p. (1991) 41,965.

Samothrace, I., Aegean Sea, **Greece**; barren, mtnous.; sparse p.; goats, grain, olives, sponge fishing; a. 184 km²; p. c. 4,000.

Samsö, I., Kattegat, **Denmark**; a. 109 km².

Samsun, spt., Trabzon, **Turkey**; on Black Sea cst.; exp. tobacco, grain, timber, wax, wool, skins, copper gds., antimony, chemical complex; p. (1990) 277,222 (t.), 1,158,400 (prov.).

San, R., S.E. **Poland**; trib. of R. Vistula; bdy. between Poland and Ukraine; navigable in lower course; 442 km long.

Sana'a, c., cap. of **Yemen**; walled c. at 2,217 m; tr. in silk, cottons, hides, grapes; handicraft inds.; Islamic cultural and educational ctr.; p. (1990) 500,000.

San Andreas Fault, Cal., **USA**; shearing plate bdy. which extends from G. of Cal. to San Francisco; stress liable to cause sudden sharp earthquakes.

San Angelo, t., Texas, **USA**; on R. Concho; cattle, wool, mohair mkt.; dairy produce, petroleum, machine-shop prod.; p. (1990) 84,474.

San Antonio, sm. coastal t., **Angola**, Africa; at mouth of R. Zaïre; serves as occasional pt. of embarkation for travellers from lower regions of Zaïre.

San Antonio, C., most W. point of Cuba.

San Antonio, c., cap. of Bexar co., Texas, **USA**; in fertile San Antonio valley; serves farming and livestock a.; oil refining, food processing, meat packing; military installations in a.; warm climate attracts winter tourist tr.; Mexican atmosphere; siege of Alamo (1836); p. (1990) 935,933 (c.), 1,302,099 (met. a.).

San Bernardino, c., Cal., **USA**; founded and planned by Mormons (1852) rly. ctr.; citrus fruit packing and tr.; p. (1990) 164,164.

San Bruno, t., Cal., **USA**; 16 km S. of San Francisco; site of international airpt.; printing, mainly residtl.; p. (1980) 35,417.

San Carlos, t., Luzon, **Philippines**; p. (1990) 124,529.

San Cristóbal, c., cap. of Táchira st., **Venezuela**; at 830 m nr. Colombian bdy.; mng. and comm. ctr.; coffee, cacao, sugar; food-processing, cement; cath.; p. (1990) 220,697.

Sancti Spiritus, t., Las Villas, **Cuba**; comm. ctr. in grazing dist.; tr. in sugar tobacco; agr. processing; p. (1986) 75,600.

Sandakan, t., Sabah, **Malaysia**; fine natural harbour on N.E. cst.; exp. agr. prods., timber, rubber; sawmilling, fishing; p. (1990) 223,432.

Sanday, I., Barra Is., Orkney Is., **Scot.**; flat, many shipwrecks; agr., fishing; p. (1991) 533 .

Sandbach, mkt. t., Cheshire, **Eng.**; 8 km N.E. of Crewe; salt, chemicals, comm. vehicles; p. (1991) 15,839.

Sandefjord, t., Vestfold prov., S.E. **Norway**; whaling pt. nr. mouth of Oslo Fjord; shipyds., whale-processing; chemicals; p. (1990) 32,718.

Sandhurst, v., Berkshire, **Eng.**; 16 km S.E. of Reading; Royal Military Academy, National Army Museum; p. (1991) 19,153.

Sandia, t., N.M., **USA**; atomic research ctr.

San Diego, c., Cal., **USA**; first Spanish settlement in Cal. 1542; on Pac. cst., 16 km N. of Mexican border; fine natural harbour, naval base; fish-canning, aircraft; comm. ctr. for fruit-and vegetable-growing dist.; p. (1990) 1,110,549 (c.), 2,498,016 (met. a.).

Sandlings, The, S.E. Suffolk, **Eng.**; a. of glacial sands, forming heathland; difficult agr. conditions.

Sandown-Shanklin, t., I. of Wight, **Eng.**; on Sandown Bay; resort; p. (1991) 17,305.

Sandringham, v., Norfolk, **Eng.**; Royal residence since 1861.

Sandusky, c., Ohio, **USA**; on S. cst. L. Erie; tr. in coal, fruit, foodstuffs; paper, farm implements, chemicals; summer resort of Cedar Point nearby; p. (1980) 31,360.

Sandviken, t., Gävleborg, **Sweden**; impt. steel inds.; p. (1986) 40,000.

Sandwell, met. dist., West Midlands, **Eng.**; comprises Warley and West Bromwich; p. (1995) 293,700.

Sandwich, t., Kent, **Eng.**; Cinque pt. at mouth of Stour R.; harbour silted up 16th cent.; mkt. lt. inds.; p. (1991) 4,164.

Sandy, t., Mid Beds., **Eng.**; 5 km N.W. of Biggleswade; mkt. gardening; p. (1991) 8,554.

Sandy Hook, peninsula, N.J., **USA**; projects into lower bay of N.Y.; government reservation.

San Felipe, cap. of Yaracuy st., **Venezuela**; ctr. of agr. dist. producing coffee, sugar and other tropical prods.; p. (1980) 57,526.

San Fernando, N.W. sub. of Buenos Aires, **Argentina**; spt. on Rio de la Plata; industl. ctr., footwear, furniture, fish canning.

San Fernando, t., Bay of Cadiz, S. **Spain**; pt. has naval arsenal; salt mftg.; much of surrounding marshland now reclaimed; p. (1981) 78,048.

San Fernando, spt., Trinidad, W.I.; on W. cst. 40 km S. of Port of Spain; exp. sugar, asphalt, petrol; p. (1990) 30,100.

San Fernando, t., Venezuela; ctr. cattle ranching region of upper Llanos; oil; p. (1980) 57,308.

San Francisco, c., Cal., **USA**; spt. on S. F. Bay; entrance spanned by Golden Gate Bridge; attractive hilly site; cosmopolitan c. with several immigrant quarters; comm. and financial ctr. with many varied inds.; univ.; sudden earthquake (1906) destroyed much of c. (*see* **F9**); p. (1990) 723,959 (c.), 1,604,000 (met. a.).

Sangihe Is., Indonesia; volcanic archipelago between Kalimantan and Philippines; sago, nutmeg, copra; ch. t. and spt. Tahuna; a. 813 km², p. c. 90,000.

San Gimignano, hill t., Tuscany, **Italy**; overlooks Val d'Elsa; 13th cent. mediaeval t., preserved as national monument; tourist ctr.; p. (1981) 7,377.

San Giovanni in Fiore, t., Calabria, **Italy**; agr. ctr. at 1,006 m nr. confluence of Neto and Arvo Rs.; p. (1981) 20,154.

Sangli, t., Maharastra, **India**; nr. Miraj on Karnataka border; p. (1991) 193,197.

Sangre de Cristo Mtns., part of Rocky mtns. **USA**; name (Span.—Blood of Christ) derives from reddish hue seen at sunset; highest summit Blanca Peak 4,367 m.

San Joaquin, R., Cal., **USA**; forms part of Central Valley project for irrigation of farmlands of R. valley; 512 km long.

San José, prov., **Costa Rica**; bauxite mng. nr. San Isidro del General projected with road to Punta Uvita where sm. pt. will be built; cap. San José; a. 4960 km²; p. (1984) 1,105,844.

San José, c., cap. of **Costa Rica**; sited at c. 1,160 m in S. J. basin; cath., univ., observatory, theatre, park; ch. industl. and comm. ctr. of rep.; oil refining, agr. processing; major route ctr., international airport; p. (1984) 296,625.

San José, t., cap. of San José prov., Uruguay; impt. mkt.; flour-milling; p. (1985) 31,732.

San José, c., Cal, **USA**; in fertile Santa Clara valley; fruit and vegetable canning and processing, chemicals, paper, electronics; p. (1990) 782,248 (c.), 1,498,000 (met. a.).

San Juan, prov., **Argentina**; at foot of Andes; gold, copper mng.; cap. S. J.; a. 89,179 km²; p. (1991) 528,715.

San Juan, c., cap. of San Juan prov., **Argentina**; comm. ctr. of agr. a., tr. in wine, fruit, cattle; p. (1991) 352,691.

San Juan, c., cap of Puerto Rico; built in part on I.; major spt. on N.E. cst.; exp. agr. prod. to USA; agr. processing; modern inds. inc. oil refining, cement, metallurgy, pharmaceuticals; cath., univ.; p. (1990) 437,745.

San Juan, R., Central America; divides Nicaragua and Costa Rica; plans made for its canalisation, which would give both countries a clear waterway from Caribbean to Pac.; 144 km long.

San Juan, R., Col., N.M., and Utah., **USA**; flows in goose-neck incised meanders; Navajo Dam part of Colorado River storage project, bringing irrigation to Navajo Indian reservation; 640 km long.

San Juan del Norte (Greytown), pt. on Caribbean cst. of Nicaragua; silting; sm. exp. of bananas, hardwoods.

San Juan del Sur, spt., on Pac. cst., **Nicaragua**; exp. ctr. for coffee, sugar, cocoa, balsam.

Sankt Ingbert, t., Saarland, **Germany**; N.E. of Saarbrücken; coal mng.; iron, glass, machin., textiles, leather; p. (1986) 40,500.

San Leandro, t., Cal., **USA**; food processing; Portuguese residents have annual religious festival; p. (1980) 63,952.

Sanliurfa, (Urfa), t., **Turkey**; nr. Syrian bdr.; handicrafts, local agr. tr.; p. (1990) 239,604.

San Lorenzo, t., Argentina; 22 km N. Rosario; lge. chemical wks., oil refining.

Sanlúcar de Barrameda, pt., Cadiz prov., **Spain**; nr. mouth of R. Guadalquivir; wines and agr. prod.; mediaeval cas.; bathing resort; p. (1981) 48,496.

San Luis, c., cap. of S. L. prov., **Argentina**; ctr. of cattle, grain, wine producing dist.; rich mineral deposits in surrounding a.; hydro-electric power sta. and irrigation dam nearby; p. (1991) 110,136 (c.), 286,458 (prov.).

San Luis Potosí, st., **Mexico**; leading mng. st.; metals melting, food-processing; cap. San Luis Potosí; a. 63,235 km²; p. (1990) 2,001,966.

San Luis Potosí, t., cap. of San Luis Potosí st., **Mexico**; industl. and comm. ctr.; metallurgy textiles; cath.; palace; p. (1990) 525,819.

San Marino, sm. indep. rep., Italy; in Apennines nr. Rimini; has kept its independence since 4th cent. A.D.; exp. wine, textiles, building stone; cap. San Marino; a. 62 km²; p. (1993) 24,003.

San Marino, t., cap. of **San Marino**; on slope of Mt. Titano, 19 km. S.W. of Rimini; tourism; p. (1993) 4,335.

San Miguel, c., **El Salvador**, at foot of San Miguel volcano; sisal-fibre, coffee, cattle, cotton, indigo; cath.; p. (1992) 182,817.

San Miguel Allende, t., Guanajuato st., **Mexico**; picturesque hilly site; famous art institute; p. (1990) 110,057.

San Miguel de Tucumán, c., cap. Tucumán prov., **Argentina**; on R. Sali; univ.; breweries, sawmills, flour, sugar; p. (1991) 622,324 (c.), 1,142,105 prov.).

San Millán de la Cogolla, Spain; oldest (6th cent.) monastic foundation in Spain; in Cárdenas valley (Logrono prov.); p. (1981) 298.

San Nicolas, R. pt., Argentina; on Paraná R.; cattle, flour, agr. prod., distillery, steel plant; p. (1980) 96,313.

Sanniya Hor, shallow L., Iraq; linked to R. Tigris; acts as flood control reservoir.

Sanok, t., Krosno prov., S.E. Poland; site on steep banks of San R.; industl. ctr., comm. vehicles, rubber gds.; p. (1989) 15,481.

San-Pedro, spt., Côte d'Ivoire; pt. linked with development of timber production in hinterland and to Bangolo iron ore deposits; iron pelletizing plant; p. (1980) 50,000.

San Pedro, spt., a. of Los Angeles, Cal., **USA**; shipyds., oil refining, fruit canning.

San Pedro de Macoris, spt., **Dominican Rep.**; on Caribbean; exp. sugar, sugar prods.; clothing, soap; p. (1991) 137,000.

San Pedro Sula, t., Honduras; ctr. for banana and sugar inds.; food processing; p. (1991) 325,900.

Sanquhar, burgh, Dumfries and Galloway, **Scot.**; coal mng., brick mkg.; p. (1991) 2,095.

San Rafael, t., W. Argentina; comm. ctr. for agr. a.; food processing, meat, wine, fruit; p. (1980) 70,477.

San Remo, sm. pt., **Italy**; winter resort on Italian Riviera; flower mkt., olive oil, lemons, wine; 12th cent. church; p. (1981) 60,787.

San Salvador (Watling's I.), Bahama Is., **W.I.**; discovered by Columbus 1492, his first sight of the New World; a. 155 km²; p. (1990) 539.

San Salvador, c., cap. of El Salvador; stands c. 600 m a.s.l.; ch. comm. and industl. ctr.; food processing, textile and tobacco inds.; univ., observatory; oil refining; liable to earthquakes; p. (1992) 422,570.

San Salvador de Juyjuy, cap. of Juyjuy prov., N. Argentina; tourist resort, cath., agr. and tr. centre; p. (1991) 180,102.

Sansanding, t., **Mali**, W. Africa; lge. barrage across R. Niger.

San Sebastian, c., cap. of Guipúzcoa prov., N. **Spain**; spt. on Bay of Biscay, at foot of Mt. Urgull; seaside resort; fishing, textiles, paper, glass; captured by Wellington 1813; p. (1991) 174,219.

San Severo, mkt. t., S. **Italy**; hilltop site, 24 km N.W. of Foggia, Apulia; cath.; wine ctr., cream of tartar, bricks; p. (1981) 54,273.

Santa Ana, c., W. **El Salvador**; second lgst. c. of rep.; coffee, sugar, cattle; Santa Ana volcano nearby; p. (1992) 202,337.

Santa Ana, c., Cal., **USA**; S.E. of Los Angeles; in fruit farming a.; fruit pkg., walnuts, oranges; p. (1990) 293,740.

Santa Barbara, c., Cal., **USA**; resort on Pac. cst., picturesque setting, mild climate; p. (1990) 370,000 (met. a. with Santa Maria-Lompoc).

Santa Barbara Is., **USA**; along S. cst. of Cal.; inc. Santa Catalina I., a favourite resort.

Santa Catarina, st., **Brazil**; between Atl. and Argentina; tobacco, manioc, fruit, hogs; impt. coal producer; cap. Florianópolis; a. 95,830 km²; p. (1991) 4,536,433.

Santa Clara, c., **Cuba**; attractive site at over 360 m; agr. and comm. ctr. for sugar and tobacco; decisive victory for guerrilla army of Fidel Castro 1959; remains of Che Guevara interred here (1997); p. (1990) 194,354.

Santa Clara, c., W. Cal., **USA**; citrus fruit pkg.; electronics, plastics, chemicals; univ.; p. (1980) 87,700.

Santa Clara Valley, Cal., **USA**; extends S. from San Francisco Bay; intensive fruit-growing under irrigation, prunes; ch. t. San José.

Santa Cruz, prov., S. **Argentina**, cap. Rio Gallegos; a. 243,943 km²; p. (1991) 159,839.

Santa Cruz, c., cap. of S.C. dep., **Bolivia**; alt. 457 m; agr. mkt. for sugar, coffee, rice, cattle; oil refining; gas pipeline planned; international airport; impt. reserves iron ore; univ.; p. (1992), 694,616 (c.), (1988); 1,110,100 (dep.).

Santa Cruz de Tenerife, pt. on Tenerife I., **Canary Is.**; cap. of S.C. de T. prov., Spain; gd. harbour, oil refinery; exp. agr. prods.; developing resort in attractive a. with mild climate; p. (1991) 191,974, 765,260 (prov.).

Santa Cruz Is., volcanic gr., S. Pac. Oc.; part of **Solomon Is.**; exp. copra.

Santa Fé, c., cap. of S.F. prov., **Argentina**; impt. R. pt. on I. in Salado R.; comm. ctr. for surrounding grain and livestock a.; food processing; univ., cath.; p. (1991) 406,388 (c.), 2,798,422 (prov.).

Santa Fé, t., N.M., **USA**; at base of Sangre de Cristo range; oldest capital in US founded by Spaniards 1610; tourist and comm. ctr.; p. (1990) 55,859.

Santa Isabel. *See* Malabo.

Santa Maria, t., Rio Grande do Sul, **Brazil**; rly. junc., rly. engin., agr. tr. and processing; p. (1985) 197,200.

Santa Maria de Garoña, **Spain**; nr. Burgos; nuclear power plant being built.

Santa Marta, spt., cap of Magdalena dep., **Colombia**; banana pt. on deep bay at mouth of Manzanares R., serving local plantations; p. (1992) 286,471.

Santa Monica, c., Cal., **USA**; W. of Los Angeles; attractive site on Santa Monica Bay; aircraft, plastics, cosmetics; p. (1980) 88,314.

Santander, c., cap. of Santander prov., N. **Spain**; spt. and seaside resort on Bay of Biscay; exp. iron and zinc ore, agr. prods.; heavy inds., shipbldg., oil refining, chemicals; former summer resort of Spanish court; cath.; p. (1991) 194,214, 526,866 (prov.).

Santarém, t., Pará, **Brazil**; rubber, cacao, Brazil nuts, sugar; p. (1985) 227,400

Santarém, t., cap. of Ribatejo prov., **Portugal**; on slope of hill overlooking Tagus R.; Moorish cas.; mkt. for agr. prod.; p. (1981) 52,138.

Santa Rosa, t., cap. of La Pampa prov., **Argentina**; p. (1991) 80,592.

Santa Rosa, t., Cal., **USA**; tr. and industl. ctr. for Somona Valley fruit-growing a.; p. (1990) 113,000 (t.), 388,000 (met. a. with Petaluma).

Santiago, c., cap of **Chile** and Metropolitan reg.; planned t. ctr. in broad valley of Mapoche R., one of lgst. and most attractive cs. in S. America; cultural, comm., political and financial ctr., focus of routes; univ.; textiles, chemicals, paper, iron and steel; rapidly growing p.; p. (1992) 4,385,481 (c.), 5,180,757 (met. a.).

Santiago de Compostela, c., La Coruña, **Spain**; on R. Sar, surrounded by hills; univ., palace, cath. (with tomb of St. James); famous place of pilgrimage; agr. tr., food processing, tourism; p. (1991) 105,527.

Santiago de Cuba, c., **Cuba**; spt. on S. cst., exp. minerals, agr. prods., sugar, tobacco; oil refining, cigars, soap; cath., univ.; p. (1990) 405,354.

Santiago del Estero, c., cap. of S. del E. prov., **Argentina**; transportation ctr. of Argentine Chaco; agr. tr. ctr., cattle, food processing; p. (1991) 263,471 (c.), 671,988 (prov.).

Santiago de los Caballeros, t., **Dominican Rep.**; comm. agr. ctr. in fertile a.; food processing, coffee, rice, tobacco; cigars, cigarettes; p. (1991) 375,000.

Santis, mtn., on border cans. St. Gallen and Appenzell, **Switzerland**; alt. 2,506 m. Europe's hgst. television transmitter on summit.

Santo Andre, c., **Brazil**; part of industl. complex built to S.E. of São Paulo to relieve congestion; specialises in metalware and chems., p. (1991) 613,672.

Santo Dominigo, cap. **Dominican Rep.**; pt. on S. cst. exp. agr. prods.; reputed burial place of Columbus; univ.; p. (1991) 2,055,000.

Santorine. *See* Thira.

Santos, c., spt., São Paulo, **Brazil**; world's ch. coffee pt.; also exp. oranges, bananas, cotton, and industl. prod. from modern harbour; p. (1991) 428,526.

Santo Tomé de la Guayana (Puerto Ordaz) c., S.E. **Venezuela**; new industl. c. nr. confluence of Orinoco and Caroni Rs.; iron mines, steel, hydroelec. power and aluminium plants in a.; industl. complex.

San Vicente, t., cap. of S.V. dep., **El Salvador**; ctr. for coffee, sugar, tobacco; mnfs. leather gds., shawls, hats; p. (1992) 45,842.

São Bernardo, c., **Brazil**; part of industl. complex built to relieve congestion in São Paulo which lies to N.W.; p. (1991) 565,171.

São Caetano, c., **Brazil**; ctr. for metalwk. built to S.E. of São Paulo to relieve congestion; p. (1985) 171,200.

São Carlos, t., São Paulo st., **Brazil**; 192 km N.W. of São Paulo; ctr. of coffee-growing a.; textiles, refrigerators, furniture; p. (1985) 140,400.

São Francisco, R., **Brazil**; flows from Minas Gerais prov. to Alt.; navigable for 1,440 km of middle course; used for hydroelectric power at Paulo Afonso falls and Três Marias dam; 2,560 km long.

São Goncalo, c., Rio de Janeiro, **Brazil**; fast-growing c.; p. (1991) 747,891.

São Jeronimo, t., Rio Grande do Sul, **Brazil**; low-grade coal; p. (1985) 30,600.

São João do Meriti, c., Rio de Janeiro, **Brazil**; industl. and comm. ctr.; p. (1991) 425,038.

São José dos Campos, c., São Paulo, **Brazil**; ctr. of Brazil's aircraft ind.; synthetic fibres, telecommunication equipment, chems., motor vehicle components; p. (1991) 442,728.

São Leopoldo, t., Rio Grande do Sul, S. **Brazil**; 32 km N. of Porto Alegre; mkt. t.; p. (1985) 114,100.

São Luis, pt., cap. of Maranhão st., **Brazil**; on São Luis I.; noted cultural ctr. in 19th cent.; aluminium plant; p. (1991) 695,780.

São Miguel, I., **Azores**; lgst. and most productive I. of archipelago; ch. t. and spt. Ponta Delgada, exp. agr. prods., pineapples; volcanic landscape a tourist attraction; p. (1981) 131,908.

Saône, R., **France**; rises in Vosges and flows to R. Rhône at Lyons; navigable, canalised; 451 km long.

Saone-et-Loire, dep., **France**; mtnous.; noted vineyards; cap. Mâcon; a. 8,627 km²; p. (1990) 559,400.

São Paulo, st., **Brazil**; on Atl. cst.; major industl. a. of S. America; coffee, cotton, sugar, rice, maize; vehicles, elec. gds., chemicals, textiles, telecomm. equipment, metal-wkg. plants; cap. São Paulo; Santos lgst pt. in Brazil; a. 247,226 km²; p. (1991) 31,192,818.

São Paulo, c., cap. of São Paulo st., **Brazil**; fast-growing c., comm. and industl. ctr. of rep. and leading c. of S. America; vehicles, machin., elec. gds., textiles, pharmaceuticals; aluminium refinery; nearby pt. Santos ships rich agr. prod. from hinterland; univs., cath.; p. (1991) 9,480,427.

São Roque, Cape of, Rio Grande do Norte, N.E. **Brazil**; most N.E. point of S. America.

São Tomé, cap. **São Tomé and Principe**; p. (1991) 43,420.

São Tomé and Principe, former Portuguese col., W. Africa ; volcanic Is. in G. of Guinea; cocoa, coffee; cap. São Tomé; a. 963 km²; airpt. extended to encourage tourism; indep. achieved as democratic rep. 1975; p. (1995) 131,100.

São Vicente, c., S.E. São Paulo, **Brazil**; first Portuguese settlement in Brazil (1532), on I. off mainland; sub. of Santos; fashionable beach resort; p. (1985) 240,800.

Sapele, t., Benin st., **Nigeria**; S. of Benin; lge. lumber mill and plywood plant; p. (1992) 126,000.

Sapporo, c., Hokkaido, **Japan**; main t. of Hokkaido; planned t.; univ.; brewing, dairy processing, sawmills; p. (1990) 1,671,765.

Saqqara, v., **Egypt**; necropolis of anc. Memphis; step pyramids.

Sarajevo, c., cap. of **Bosnia-Herzegovina**, formerly Yugoslavia; major route ctr., airport; ctr. of Yugoslav Moslems; mosques, caths.; diversified mnfs., metallurgy, elec. prods., textiles, tobacco, pottery; assassination 28 June 1914 of Archduke Francis Ferdinand precipitated First World War; under siege in civil war, 1992; p. (1981) 448,500.

Saransk, c., Mordovian aut. rep., **Russia**; 232 km S.E. of Gorki; univ.; elec. equipment, engin., agr. processing; p. (1989) 312,000.

Sarapul, c., **Russia**; pt. on R. Kama; radio equipment, machin., footwear, gloves; p. (1989) 110,000.

Sarasota, Fla., **USA**; exp. fruit, veg.; resort; p. (1990) 278,000 (met. a.).

Saratoga Springs, N.Y., **USA**; summer resort at foot of Adirondack mtns., mineral springs; horse-racing; casino; p. (1980) 23,906.

Saratov, c., **Russia**; pt. on R. Volga; regional ctr. for agr. prod. of lower Volga valley and oil from Baku; univ.; engin., ball-bearings, textiles, oil refining, sawmilling; p. (1989) 905,000.

Sarawak, st., **E. Malaysia**; mtnous. inland with sparse p.; rubber, sago, pepper grown along coast.; oil; cap. Kuching; a. 121,914 km²; p. (1992) 1,583,000.

Sardinia, I., aut. region, **Italy**; mtnous., dry climate; fertile Campidano plain with fruit, wines, sheep; zinc and lead mng.; tourism; fishing; major petrochemical complex at Ottana; part of former kingdom of Sardinia belonging to house of Savoy; a. 24,002 km²; p. (1992) 1,651,902.

Sargasso Sea, zone S.W. of N. Atl. Oc.; relatively still sea within swirl of warm ocean currents; noted for abundance of gulf-weed on its surface, rich in marine life; named by Columbus.

Sari, c., cap. of Mazandaran prov., **Iran**; p. (1983) 124,663.

Sark, I., dependency of **Guernsey**, Channel Is.; 10 km E. of Guernsey; picturesque scenery; tourist ctr.; farming; a. 516 ha; p. (1986) 550.

Sark, R., forms extreme W. bdy. between **Scot.** and **Eng.**

Sarnia, c., and pt., Ont., **Canada**; on St. Clair R.; connected to Port Huron by rly. tunnel; oil refineries, petrochemical inds., agr. tr.; p. (1986) 49,033.

Sarno, t., Campania, **Italy**; spa at foot of mtns. on E. edge of fertile Sarno plain; agr. mkt., textile ctr.; cas.; p. (1981) 30,583.

Šar-Planina, mt. range on border of Macedonia and Serbia, **Yugoslavia**; impt. chrome deposits; ctr. of mtn. tourism.

Sarpsborg, t., **Norway**; on R. Glommen; lgst. pulp and paper concern in kingdom; hydro-electric power sta.; p. (1990) 39,772.

Sarreguemines, t., Moselle dep., **France**; in Lorraine; potteries based on local clay; coal mng.; p. (1982) 25,178.

Sarthe, dep., N.W. **France**; undulating surface; farming, apples, livestock; coal, linen, potteries; cap. Le Mans; a. 6,247 km²; p. (1990) 513,700.

Sarthe, R., **France**; trib. of R. Loire; 265 km long.

Sasebo, spt., Kyushu, **Japan**; ctr. of coalfield; engin., shipbldg.; p. (1990) 244,693.

Saskatchewan, prov., **Canada**; coniferous forests and plains; Rs. Saskatchewan and Churchill; many lge. Ls.; extreme climate; hydroelec. power; gr. wheat prov.; livestock, dairying; oil, copper, uranium, helium plants, furs, fisheries; cap. Regina; a. 651,903 km²; p. (1991) 994,900.

Saskatchewan, R., **Canada**; flows from Rocky mtns. through L. Winnipeg and thence by R. Nelson to Hudson Bay; 2,320 km long.

Saskatoon, c., Saskatchewan, **Canada**; grew rapidly after arrival of rly. (1890); comm. ctr. for grain producing a.; meat packing and tr.; varied inds., cement, oil refining; univ.; p. (1991) 186,058 (c.), (1986) 200,665 (met. a.).

Sasolburg, t., O.F.S., **S. Africa**; oil from coal production; gas pipeline to Germiston a. p. (1980) 77,680 (dist.).

Sassari, t., Sardinia, **Italy**; nr. G. of Asinara; cath., univ., palaces; tobacco and macaroni wks., cheese; p. (1992) 121,961.

Sattahip, pt., **Thailand**; new pt. inaugurated 1967.

Satu Mare, t., N.W. **Romania**; agr. machin., handicraft inds. based on local prods., food-processing; cath.; p. (1992) 131,859.

Saudi Arabia, kingdom, Arabian peninsula, S.W. Asia; mainly desert, agr. in oases and S.W. upland region of Asir; lgst. producer of oil in Middle East; oil sales account for 85 per cent govt. revenue; steel inds. and oil refinery at Jiddah, petrochemicals at Dammam; Moslem holy cs. Mecca and Medina; cap. Riyadh (royal), Mecca (religious), Jiddah (admin.); main pt. King Faisal Port.; a. 2,400,930 km²; p. (1992) 16,900,000. (1,500,000 foreign workers).

Sauerland, dist., N. Rhine–Westphalia, **Germany**; plateau, alt. from 150–450 m E. of Rhine; agriculturally poor, largely forested; crossed by R. Wupper, with which are associated industl. ts. Wuppertal (textiles), Solingen and Remsched (cutlery and special steel); supplies hydroelectric power to Ruhr.

Sault Ste. Marie, t., Ont., **Canada**; pt. on St. Mary's R., opposite Sault Ste. Marie, Mich., to which it is connected by bridge; pulp, paper, iron and steel; tourist ctr. for L. and forest region; p. (1986) 80,905.

Sault Ste. Marie, t., Mich., **USA**; pt. on St. Mary's R.; opposite Sault Ste. Marie, Ont.; calcium carbide; tourist ctr. for fishing, hunting a.; p. (1980) 14,448.

Sault Ste. Marie Canals (Soo), **Canada** and **USA**; twin canals on Canadian and American side of shallow channel linking L. Superior and L. Huron; traversed by all wheat and iron-ore traffic from L. Superior pts.; length (Canadian) 2 km; depth 5 m.

Saumur, t., Maine-et-Loire dep., **France**; on R. Loire, 48 km S.W. of Tours; sparkling wines, brandy; flower, vegetable mkt.; cas.; p. (1982) 33,953.

Sauternes, v., Gironde, **France**; name applied to white wines of dist.

Sava, R., **Slovenia**, joins Danube at Belgrade; used for hydroelectric power; agr. in valleys; transport axis; 928 km long.

Savage I. *See* Niue.

Savai'i I., lgst. is. of **Western Samoa**, Pac. Oc.; volcanic, mtnous., fertile; exp. bananas, copra, cocoa; a. 1,821 km²; p. (1986) 44,930.

Savannah, c., Ga., **USA**; spt. nr. mouth of Savannah R.; rly., fishing and comm. ctr. for Sea Is., Savannah valley and surrounding plantations; mkt. for naval stores; sugar refining, paper, oil refining, diverse mnfs.; tourist ind. stimulated by mild climate; p. (1990) 137,560.

Savannah, R., **USA**; flows between Ga. and S.C., to Atl. Oc.; used for hydroelectric power; 720 km long.

Saverne, Col de, low pass, N.E. **France**; carries trunk rly. from Paris to Strasbourg and the East between Vosges and Hardt mtns.; gradual approach from W., steep descent to E. into Rhine valley.

Savoie (**Savoy**), dep., **France**; borders Italy in Savoy Alps; part of former duchy; dairying and vineyards; hydroelectricity forms basis of metallurgical inds.; first Fr. National Park (Vanoise Park); cap. Chambéry; a. 6,188 km²; p. (1990) 348,300.

Savona, spt., Genoa, **Italy**; cath.; iron, shipbldg., glass and tinplate wks.; exp. preserved fruits and tomatoes; imports coal, oil, iron-ore; p. (1981) 75,353.

Savonlinna, t., Mikkeli, E. **Finland**; in Saimaa L. region; route ctr.; timber inds.; p. (1993) 28,640.

Sawankalok, t., **Thailand**; impt. teak collecting ctr.

Sawbridgeworth, t., East Herts., **Eng.**; on R. Stort, 6 km S. of Bishops Stortford; malting, fruit preserving; p. (1991) 9,432.

Saxham, t., Suffolk, **Eng.**; agr. machin.

Saxmundham, mkt. t., Suffolk Coastal, Suffolk, **Eng.**; 29 km N.E. of Ipswich; p. (1991) 2,529.

Saxony, *Land*, **Germany**; turbulent political and territorial history, now comprises admin. dists. of Leipzig, Dresden, Chemnitz inc. Erzgebirge; kaolin deposits basis for porcelain ind. at Meissen; industrialised in 19th and 20th cent. with notable textile ind.; coal mng. nr. Zwickau; inds. concentrated around Chemnitz; cap. Dresden; comm. ctr. at Leipzig; a. 16,996 km²; pop. (1992) 4,679,000.

Saxony-Anhalt, *Land*, **Germany**; inc. Halle and Magdeburg; cap. Magdeburg; pop. (1992) 2,823,000.

Sayan Mtns., range of mtns.; between Rs. Yenisey and Angra, **Russia**; form part of Sino-Russian border; mineral resources.

Scafell Pike, mtn., Cumbria, **Eng.**; in Cumbrian Mtns, Lake Dist.; highest in Eng.; alt. 979 m.

Scalby, t., North Yorks., **Eng.**; 5 km N.W. of Scarborough; p. (1991) 9,019.

Scalloway, Shetland Is., **Scot.**; on W. cst. of Mainland; the anc. cap.; ruined cas.; fish. pt.; p. (1991) 1,056.

Scalpay, I., off E. cst. of Skye, Highland, **Scot.**

Scalpay, I., Harris, Outer Hebrides, Western Isles, **Scot.**; p. (1991) 382.

Scandinavia, name given to lge. peninsula in N.W. Europe; comprises kingdoms of Sweden and Norway; sometimes inc. Denmark, Finland and Iceland; rugged a. of anc. peneplained rocks; climate varies from arctic (N.) to humid maritime (S.W.); rich in timber and mineral ores, esp. iron and copper; W. cst. waters valuable fishing grounds.

Scapa Flow, strait, N. **Scot.**; between Pomona and Hoy, Orkney Is.; surrendered German fleet scuttled 1919; Brit. battleship *Royal Oak* sunk at anchor 1939.

Scarba, I., Argyll and Bute, **Scot.**; off N. end of Jura, red deer in woods and moorlands; p. (1991) 547.

Scarborough, c., Ontario, **Canada**; part of Toronto met. a.; p. (1991) 524,568.

Scarborough, t., l. gov. dist., North Yorks., **Eng.**; on E. cst.; seaside resort; cas.; former spa; p. (1995) 108,900 (dist.), (1991) 38,809 (t.).

Scarpanto. *See* **Karpathos.**

Schaffhausen, most. N. can., **Switzerland**; on R. Rhine; pastoral, forested; cereals, fruit, vegetables, wine; hydroelectric power from S. falls on Rhine; cap. S.; a. 298 km²; p. (1990) 71,700.

Schaffhausen, c., cap. of S. can., **Switzerland**; on Rhine below L. Constance; falls to S.W. of c.; hydroelectricity supplies power for electro-chemical ind. and aluminium wks.; p. (1990) 34,324.

Schefferville, t., **Canada**; 576 km N. of St. Lawrence estuary and connected to it (at Seven Islands) by rly.; ctr. of iron-ore mines in Quebec-Labrador trough; p. (1986) 322.

Scheldt (Dutch **Schelde**, French **Escaut**), R., **France**, **Belgium**, **Neth.**; rises in Aisne, France, flows to N. Sea forming extensive delta with Rhine (Rijn) and Meuss (Maas) in Netherlands; navigable; 432 km long; network of canals.

Schenectady, c., N.Y., **USA**; on Mohawk R., N.W. of Albany; electrical plants, locomotive wks.; p. (1990) 65,566.

Scheveningen, seaside resort, **Neth.**; 3 km N.W. of The Hague; fish. pt.

Schiedam, t., **Neth.**, on Nieuwe Maas, 4 km downstream from Rotterdam; forms part of Rotterdam–Europoort; diverse pt.-based inds.; gin; p. (1994) 72,515.

Schiehallion, mtn., Perth and Kinross, **Scot.**; alt. 1,082 m.

Schio, t., Veneto, **Italy**; at foot of Alps on Leogra R.; woollens, textiles, machin.; p. (1981) 35,596.

Schleswig, t., Schleswig-Holstein, **Germany**; fish. pt. on Schlei inlet; lt. inds.; p. (1986) 23,300.

Schleswig-Holstein, *Land*, **Germany**; occupies S. part of Jutland peninsula; a. disputed between Denmark and Prussia in 19th cent.; mainly agr.; many sm. pts.; crossed by Kiel Canal; cap. Kiel; a. 15,664 km²; p. (1992) 2,649,000.

Schneidemühtl. *See* **Pila.**

Schönebeck, t., Saxony - Anhalt, **Germany**; pt. on R. Elbe; metals, chemicals, machin.; p. (1989) 44,660.

Schoonebeek, v., Drenthe, **Neth.**; S. of Emmen; lge. oilfield.

Schouten I., W. Irian, **Indonesia**; in Geelvink Bay; p. 25,487.

Schouwen-Duiveland, I., Zeeland prov., **Neth.**; cap. Zierikee; formerly 2 separate Is.

Schuylkill, R., Penns., **USA**; flows into Delaware R.; navigable; length 208 km.

Schwäbish-Gmünd, t., Baden–Württemberg, **Germany**; at foot of Swabian Jura, E. of Stuttgart; clocks, glass, optical, precious metal and jewellery inds.; mediaeval and baroque bldgs.; p. (1986) 56,100.

Schwarzwald (Black Forest), forested mtn. range, Baden–Württemberg, **Germany**; highest peak Feldberg 1,496 m; tourism; famous for clock and toy inds.

Schwedt, t., Brandenburg, **Germany**; on R. Oder; lge. oil refinery; pipeline from Mozyr' (USSR); paper, fertilisers; p. (1981) 52,291.

Schweinfurt, t., Bavaria, **Germany**; on R. Main, N.E. of Würzburg; metals machin., ball bearings, dyes, brewing; p. (1986) 50,600.

Schwelm, t., N. Rhine–Westphalia, **Germany**; E. of Wuppertal; metals machin., textiles; p. (1986) 29,800.

Schwenningen, t., Baden–Württemberg, **Germany**; clocks, precision instruments, optical apparatus; p. with Villingen (1986) 76,200.

Schwerin, c., cap. of Mecklenburg-West Pomerania, *Land*, **Germany**; on Schwerin L., surrounded by smaller Ls.; comm. and industl. ctr. of agr. dist.; food processing, engin., furniture; cath., cas.; p. (1990) 126,800.

Schwyz, can., **Switzerland**; mtnous. in S.; forested; dairying impt.; original member of confederation; cap. S.; a. 907 km²; p. (1990) 110,500.

Schwyz, c., of Schwyz can., **Switzerland**; tourist ctr. nr. Lucerne; p. (1980) 12,100.

Sciacca, sm. pt., Sicily, **Italy**; nr. Agrigento; mineral springs; p. (1981) 34,294.

Scilly Is., *See* **Isles of Scilly.**

Scioto, R., Ohio, **USA**; joins Ohio at Portsmouth; 400 km long.

Scone, par., Perth and Kinross, **Scot.**; place of residence and coronation of early Scottish kings; from here Edward I removed Stone of Destiny to Westminster Abbey 1297; tourist ctr.; civil aerodrome.

Scoresbysund, E. **Greenland**; lgst. fjord system in the world; length 304 m; fishing and hunting; onshore oil drilling (1984); p. (est. 1990) 554.

Scotland, Brit. Is., N. part of **Gt. Britain**; 32 unit, auths. created in 1996; home affairs admin. by Dep. of Secretary of State for Scot.; referendum in 1997 opened way for Scottish Parliament; physically divided into 3 parts; (1) the Highlands and Is., an upland a. suffering from depopulation, economically reliant on stock-rearing, tourism, hydroelec. power, whisky and fishing; intrusive impact of N. Sea oil on N.E. cst.; (2) the Central Lowlands, containing most p., based in industl. ts. on sm. coalfields, inc. lgst. c. Glasgow and cap. Edinburgh; (3) the S. Uplands, a stock-rearing a. bordering Eng.; p. (1995) 5,136,600.

Scott Base, main base Ross Dependency, **Antarctica**.

Scrabster, pt. nr. Thurso, Highland, **Scot.**; main ferry terminal for Orkneys.

Scranton, c., Penns., **USA**; on Lackawanna R.; anthracite ctr.; chemicals, shoes, textiles; univ.; p. (1990) 734,000 (met. a. with Wilkes-Barre).

Scunthorpe, t., N. Lincs., **Eng.**; on Lincoln Edge, 10 km S. of Humber; iron, limestone mng. and major iron and steel ind.; p. (1991) 75,982 (t.).

Scutari (Albania). *See* **Shkodër.**

Scutari (Turkey). *See* **Usküdar.**

Seaford, t., East Sussex, **Eng.**; 5 km E. of Newhaven; seaside resort; declined as a pt. with shift of Ouse R. channel to Newhaven; p. (1991) 19,622.

Seaforth, Loch, Lewis, Outer Hebrides, **Scot.**; 22 km long.

Seaham, spt., Durham, **Eng.**; Seaham Harbour on E. cst. 6 km S. of Sunderland; colly. workings extend under sea, closed 1993; p. (1991) 22,130.

Sea Islands, **USA**; chain of Is. off Atl. cst. of S.C., Ga. and Fla.; formerly impt. for sea-island cotton but since 1919 infested with boll weevil.

Seathwaite, v., Cumbria, **Eng.**; 11 km from Keswick, close to Styhead (436 m); exceptionally heavy annual rainfall (above 3,800 mm).

Seaton, t., East Devon, **Eng.**; on Lyme Bay at mouth of R. Axe, seaside resort; freestone quarries; p. (1991) 7,579.

Seaton Delaval, t., Blyth Valley, Northumberland, **Eng.**; former coal mng.; p. (1991) 7,333.

Seattle, c., Wash., **USA**; spt. between Puget Sound and L. Wash.; S.E. is Mt. Rainier, N.E. Mt. Baker; tr. with Far East and Alaska from wooded, agr. hinterland; fishing and fish exp.; lgst. c. of Wash., a major industl. and comm. ctr.; aircraft (home of Boeing), shipbld., food processing; univs., cath.; p. (1990) 516,259 (c.), 1,973,000 (met. a.).

Secunderabad, t., Andhra Pradesh, **India**; now incorporated within Hyderabad; comm. ctr., rly. junc.; p. (1981) 135,994.

Sedan, t., Ardennes dep., **France**; on R. Meuse; machin., metal ware, woollens, flour; Napoleon III surrendered to Prussians 1870; p. (1982) 24,535.

Sedbergh, mkt. t., South Lakeland, Cumbria, **Eng.**; woollen ind., public school; p. (1991) 1,670.

Sedgefield, t., l. gov. dist., S.E. Durham, **Eng.**; in fertile agr. a.; cattle mkt.; racecourse; p. (1995) 90,800 (dist.), (1991) 4,424.

Sedgemoor, l. gov. dist., Somerset, **Eng.**; based on Bridgwater, Burnham and surrounding a.; p. (1995) 101,100.

Sefton, met. dist., Merseyside, **Eng.**; comprises Crosby, Bootle and Litherland; p. (1995) 291,000.

Ségou, t., R. pt., **Mali**; W. Africa; on R. Niger; ctr. of irrigation scheme; cotton, hides, cattle; cap. of former kingdom; p. (1984) 99,000.

Ségou Canal, **Mali**, W. Africa; leaves R. Niger 6 km below Bamako, extends 208 km N.E. to Segou; irrigates 7,770 km² on right bank of Niger and assists navigation.

Segovia, c., cap. of S. prov., Old Castile, **Spain**; on rocky hill above Eresma R.; Roman aqueduct, cath.; p. (1991) 55,000, 1,606,357 (prov.).

Segovia, R., rises in N.W. Nicaragua, flows N.E. to Caribbean; forms part of S. limit of Mosquito cst., and bdy. between **Honduras** and **Nicaragua**; 480 km long.

Segre, R., Lérida, N.E. **Spain**; rises in E. Pyrenees flows S.W. into R. Ebro; water irrigates the a. around Lérida, the lgst. block of irrigated land in Spain; c. 272 km long.

Segura, R., **Spain**; flows to Mediterranean at Guardamar; 288 km long.

Seïkan Tunnel, **Japan**; links Honshu with Hokkaido under Tsugaru strait; 37 km long.

Seine, R., **France**; rises in Côte d'Or dep. and flows past Paris and Rouen to English Channel at Havre; navigable, part of French waterway network; 757 km long.

Seine-et-Marne, dep., N. **France**; agr., stock-raising, dairying; impt. source of food for Paris mkts.; Brie cheese; cap. Melun; a. 5,892 km²; p. (1990) 1,078,200.

Seine-Maritime, dep., N. **France**; undulating and fertile; grain, dairying; heavy inds. at cap. Rouen; oil refineries; beach resorts; p. (1990) 1,223,400.

Seine-Saint Denis, dep., N.E. Paris, **France**; mkt. gardens; cap. Bobigny; p. (1990) 1,381,200.

Seistan and Baluchistan, twin prov., **Iran**; co. ts. Zabol, Zahedan; rly. terminus Pakistan rly. from Quetta through Mirjaveh.

Sekondi-Takoradi, t., S.W. **Ghana**; spt. on G. of Guinea; developed after construction of rly. (1903) to tap mineral, agr. and forest wealth of hinterland; deepwater harbour at Takoradi constructed 1928; fisheries, saw milling; p. (1984) 91,874 (c.), 160,868 (met. a.).

Selangor, st., central Malaya, **W. Malaysia**; former sultanate; economically well developed; chemicals, rubber, tin, coal, pineapples; ch. pt., Pt. Swettenham; fisheries; new st. cap. designated at Klang to relieve congestion of Kuala Lumpur; p. (1980) 1,515,536.

Selby, mkt. t., l. gov. dist., North Yorks., **Eng.**; on R. Ouse, 20 km. S. of York; anc. abbey church; flour milling, flax, oil-cake; development of major coalfield since 1983 linked to bldg. of power sta. in Aire Valley; p. (1995) 72,500 (dist.), (1991) 15,292 (t.).

Sele, R., S. Italy; rises in S. Apennines, flows W. into G. of Salerno; headwater carried E. through gr. Apennine tunnel (11 km) to irrigate plateau of Apulia in S.E. Italy.

Selenga, Asiatic R., rises in Mongolia, enters **Russia** nr. Kiachta from where it is navigable to its delta in L. Baykal; c. 1,100 km long.

Selkirk, royal burgh, Borders, **Scot.**; on Etterick Water; 6 km S. of Galashiels; mkt. t.; tartans, tweeds; p. (1991) 5,922.

Selkirk Mtns., B.C. **Canada**; run N.W. to S.E. parallel with Rocky mtns.; anc. rocks, highly mineralised; rise to over 2,700 m.

Selkirkshire, historic co., S. **Scot.**; now part of Borders.

Sellafield, nuclear power plant, Cumbria, **Eng.**; formerly Windscale; reprocesses nuclear waste.

Selma, t., Ala., **USA**; on Alabama R., in cotton, dairying, lumbering region; food processing, fertilisers; p. (1980) 26,684.

Selsey Bill, peninsula between Bognor Regis and Portsmouth, West Sussex, **Eng.**

Selukwe, t., **Zimbabwe**; alt. 1,444 m; gold mng., chrome ore, molybdenum; ranching.

Selwyn Range, mtns., Queensland, **Australia**; extend 560 km W. from Gr. Dividing Range.

Semarang, spt., Java, **Indonesia**; exp. sugar, tobacco, tapioca, kapok; shipbldg., rly. repairs, cement, sawmills, tyres, elec. equipment; univ.; p. (1983) 1,269,000.

Semipalatinsk (**Semey**), t., **Kazakhstan**; on R. Irtysh; lge. meat-packing plant; textiles, engin.; rich gold deposit found in a. 1965; p. (1990) 338,800.

Semmering Pass, low pass, **Austria**; provides route across E. Alps for rly. from Vienna to Venice; scenic resort; alt. below 915 m.

Semnan, t., Central Prov., **Iran**; comm. ctr. for tobacco growing region; p. (1986) 418,152.

Sena, t., **Moçambique**; on R. Zambesi; iron-ore mng.

Sendai, t., Honshu, **Japan**; cas.; univ.; metallurgy, food processing, lacquer ware; p. (1990) 918,378.

Senegal, rep., W. cst. Africa; union with Gambia (1982), dissolved 1989; flat savannah; tropical climate with long dry season; agr. main occupation, groundnuts accounting for 72 per cent exp.; production hit by severe drought (1982–3); ground-nut and agr. processing provide industl. basis; bauxite, phosphate, titanium, zirconium mng.; oil refinery at cap. Dakar; a. 197,109 km²; p. (1993) 7,970,000.

Senegal, R., **W. Africa**; flows from Kong mtns. W. and N.W. to Atl. at St. Louis, above Cape Verde; lower valley forms fertile agr. land; partially navigable; plans for economic development of valley; joint water scheme with 3 dams to relieve water shortages, improve navigation and provide hydro-electric power for Mali, Senegambia and Mauritania; 1,600 km long.

Senegambia, former rep., W. cst Africa; formed (1982) from unification of Senegal and Gambia following attempted coup (1981); union dissolved, 1989. *See* **Senegal** and **Gambia**.

Senftenberg, t., Brandenburg, **Germany**; inds. based on local lignite deposits; glassware, tiles; p. (1989) 31,580.

Senigallia, t., **Italy**; resort and spt. on Adriatic; fishing and agr. ctr.; food processing, agr. machin.; p. (1981) 40,108.

Senlis, t., Oise dep., **France**; Gallo-Roman wall; tourist ctr. in forested region, 43 km N.E. of Paris; mkt. t., furniture, rubber gds.; p. (1982) 15,280.

Sennar, t., **Sudan**; on Blue Nile, on rly. route to Khartoum, Suakin, Pt. Sudan; dam for irrigation, flood control and hydroelectric power; p. c. 8,000.

Sens, t., Yonne dep., **France**; on r. Yonne; known to Romans as Agedincum; Gothic cath.; agr. tr., food processing, farm implements, boots, chemicals, cutlery; p. (1982) 27,501.

Sensuntepeque, t., **El Salvador**; pottery, distilling; p. (1992) 38,073.

Senta, t., Serbia, **Yugoslavia**; pt. on Tisa R.; agr. ctr.; food processing, agr. machin., chemicals.

Seoul, c., cap. of **S. Korea**; in Han R. valley; food processing, textiles, rly. engin.; univs., anc. walls; international airport, connected by rly. to out-port of Inchon; host of 1988 Olympic games; p. (1990) 10,627,790.

Sepik, R., N. **Papua New Guinea**; flows E. to Bismarck Sea; drains vast mtn. a.; very fast flow; navigable by shallow craft; 800 km long.

Sept-Iles (**Seven Islands**), t., on St. Lawrence, Quebec, **Canada**; iron brought by rail from Schefferville; airline service but no highway; p. (1986) 25,637.

Sequoia National Park, Cal., **USA**; sequoia trees.

Seraing, t., Liège, **Belgium**; on R. Meuse; coal mng.; iron and steel heavy inds.; seat of famous Cockerill iron wks. (1817) and glass wks. (1825); p. (1993) 61,225.

Seram (Ceram), I., Moluccas, **Indonesia**; W.-E. mtn. range rising to 3,357 m; tobacco; sago; a. 17,143 km².

Serampore, t., W. Bengal, **India**; former Danish settlement; cotton and silk weaving, pottery, jute and paper mills; p. (1991) 137,028.

Serbia, constituent rep., N.E. **Yugoslavia**; lgst. and most impt. rep., "bread basket" of Yugoslavia; grain, fruit; mng. copper and antimony; cap. Belgrade; a. 87,879 km²; p. (1981) 9,313,676.

Seremban, t., cap. of Negri Sembilan st., **W. Malaysia**; on Linggi R.; linked by rly. to Pt. Dickson; comm. ctr. for rubber and tin a.; p. (1980) 136,625.

Sereth, R., rises in Carpathians, W. **Ukraine** and enters **Romania** to join Danube above Galati; 720 km long.

Sergipe, cst. st., **Brazil**; sandy cst. rising to undulating plateau in interior; well wooded and cropped for sugar, cotton; drier interior devoted mainly to stock-raising; oil deposits; a. 21,054 km²; p. (1991) 1,492,400.

Sergiyev Posad, **(Zagorsk)** c., **Russia**; 70 km N.E. of Moscow; woodcarving, toy mkg.; site of famous Troitse-Sergiyeva Lavra monastery, converted into museum 1920; p. (1989) 115,000.

Sergo. See Kadiyevka.

Seria, t., **Brunei**; coastal t., protected from sea by 8 km dyke; oil ctr., linked by pipeline with Lutong; p. (1988) 23,415.

Serov, t., **Russia**; in Urals; iron and steel; natural gas pipeline from Ingrim; p. (1989) 104,000.

Serowe, t., **Botswana**, Southern Africa; seat of Bamanguato tribe; mkt. ctr.; lge coal reserves widening economic base of Botswana and reducing dependence on S. Africa; p. (1989) 95,041.

Serpukhov, t., R. pt., **Russia**; on R. Oka, planned canal link to Moscow; p. (1989) 144,000.

Serra da Mantiqueira, mtn. range, hgst. in Brazil.

Serra do Espinhaco, mtns., **Brazil**; highest peak, Itambe, 2,045 m; iron-ore deposits.

Serra do Mar, mtns., **Brazil**; form steep E. edge of Brazilian Plateau S. from Rio de Janeiro.

Serrai (Seres), dep., Macedonia, N. **Greece**; N. mtns. form frontier with Bulgaria in gorge of Struma R. valley; lower Struma R. basin fertile agr. a., producing cotton, tobacco; mkt. ctr. at cap. Serrai; a. 4,053 km²; p. (1981) 46,317 (t.).

Sertão, semi-arid hinterland, N.E. **Brazil**; stockraising, but drought causes migration to Amazon basin; hydroelectric power and irrigation schemes.

Sesto San Giovanni, sub., Milan, **Italy**; machin., glass, chemicals, plastics; p. (1981) 94,738.

Sète, spt., Hérault dep., **France**; on Med. cst.; chemicals, fisheries; exp. oysters, brandy, wine; oil pipeline under sea to Frontignan; importance originally based upon canal network, now supplanted by rlys.; tourism of growing importance; p. (1982) 58,865 (met. a.).

Setesdal (Saetersdal), Aust-Agder, S. **Norway**; remote valley retaining traditional social customs; arable pastoral agr.

Sétif. See Stif.

Seto, t., central Honshu, **Japan**; porcelain ctr. (since 13th cent.); based on local deposits of kaolin; p. (1990) 126,343.

Setouchi, dist., S.W. Honshu, **Japan**; rice, mandarin oranges, reeds, salt, textiles; part of Japan's industl. belt.

Setté Cama, spt., **Gabon**, Equatorial Africa; open roadstead, landing difficult owing to swell; exp. timber; oil nearby.

Settle, mkt. t., Craven, North Yorks., **Eng.**; on R. Ribble in heart of Craven dist.; tourist ctr. for limestone cty. of N. Pennines; textiles; p. (1991) 3,082.

Settsu Plain, S. Honshu, **Japan**; at head of Osaka Bay at E. end of Inland Sea; intensively cultivated alluvial lowlands, ch. crops, rice, vegetables, oranges; gr. industl. belt extends along cst. through Kobe, Osaka, Kishiwada; engin., chemicals, textiles; a. 1,295 km².

Setubal, t., Estremadura, S. **Portugal**; impt. pt. on Sado R., estuary; exp. cork, wine, oranges; fishing, fish processing, shipyds.; p. (1987) 77,885.

Sevan (Gokcha), lge. l., **Armenia**; alt. 1,934 m; never freezes; surrounded by high barren mtns.; drained by Razdan R.; several hydroelectric power stas.

Sevastopol, spt., **Ukraine**; built on ruins left after famous siege 1855; Black Sea resort; rebuilt after

second world war; one of most beautiful Crimean cs.; p. (1990) 361,400.

Sevenoaks, mkt. t., l. gov. dist., Kent, **Eng.**; in Vale of Holmesdale; residtl.; agr., lt. inds.; Knole Park; public school founded in 1432; p. (1995) 109,700 (dist.), (1991) 24,489 (t.).

Severn, R., Ont., **Canada**; flows to Hudson Bay; tr. post at mouth; 560 km long.

Severn, R., W. of **Eng.** and N. **Wales**; rises in Powys and flows to Bristol Channel; suspension bridge at estuary opened 1966; several proposals for major economic development around shores of estuary; 344 km long.

Severn Tunnel, **Eng.**; under estuary of R. Severn between Pilning (S. Gloucs.) and Severn Tunnel Junction (Monmouthshire); carries main rly. from London to S. **Wales**; longest main-line rly. tunnel in Brit. Is.; 7 km long.

Severodvinsk, t., **Russia**; on Dvina Bay, White Sea; metals, bldg. materials; p. (1989) 249,000.

Seville, c., cap. of Seville prov. and of Andalusia, **Spain**; spt. on Guadalquivir R., canal link with Atl. Oc.; exp. agr. prod., imports industl. raw materials; major industl., comm. and cultural ctr.; diverse mnfs.; beautiful c. with Moorish influence, prominent in narrow streets of ctr. a.; Alcázar palace; Gothic cath.; bullfighting, tourist ctr.; p. (1987) 655,435.

Sèvres, t., Hauts-de-Seine, dep., N. **France**; S.W. sub. of Paris on Seine R.; celebrated porcelain mnfs.; headquarters of International Bureau of Weights and Measures; p. (1982) 20,225.

Seward, t., S. Alaska, **USA**; rly. terminal, airfield and ice-free harbour make it an impt. supply ctr. for interior Alaska; p. (1980) 1,843.

Seychelles Is., indep. rep. (1976) within Commonwealth, Indian Oc.; consists of 86 Is. (37 granitic, 49 coralline), among most beautiful in world; lgst. I. Mahé; cap. Victoria; fishing, heavy dependence on tourism pays for dependence on imported food; petroleum exploration; exp. copra, cinnamon bark; famous for species of nut; total a. 404 km²; p. (1993) 72,253.

Seyne, or **La Seyne-sur-Mer**, t., Var dep., **France**; nr. Toulon; shipbld.; p. (1982) 58,146.

Sfax, spt., **Tunisia**; admin. ctr.; exp. phosphate, olive oil, salt, esparto grass, cereals, dates, hides; imports food, coal, textiles, soap; sponges; fishing; natural gas found in a.; surrounded by irrigated gardens and olive groves; p. (1984) 231,911.

Sgurr Mor, mtn., Highland, **Scot.**; alt. 1,109 m.

Shaanxi (Shensi), prov., N. **China**; Great Wall runs nr. N. border with Inner Mongolia; from N.-S. four main regions: (1) dry, fertile loess plateau, notorious famine region, but increasingly irrigated; (2) fertile Wei R. valley, ctr. of p. and agr.; (3) Hua Shan (4) agr. a. of upper Han R.; grain, livestock; coal, petroleum; developing transportation network aiding economic development; cap. Xi'an; a. 188,860 km²; p. (1990) 32,470,000.

Shaba (Katanga), prov., **Congo**; many varied mineral deposits inc. copper, tin, iron-ore, cobalt, radium; cap. Lubumbashi; a. 466,200 km²; (1991) 5,207,000.

Shache (Yarkand), c., Xinjiang prov., **China**; tr. ctr. in S. oasis; tr. in wheat, rice, beans, fruit, carpets, textiles; p. (1985) 60,000

Shache (Yarkand), R., Xinjiang prov., **China**; trib. of Gan R.; 800 km long.

Shaftesbury, mkt. t, North Dorset, **Eng.**; Saxon hilltop t., abbey ruins; ctr. for agr. a.; p. (1991) 6,203.

Shahjahanpur, t., Uttar Pradesh, **India**; on Deoha R.; agr. mkt. t. and rly junc.; grain, sugar tr. and processing; p. (1991) 237,717 .

Shakhty (Alexandrovsk Grushevski), t., **Russia**; anthracite mng. in Donets Basin; leather, textiles, metal wkg., food inds.; p. (1989) 226,000.

Shamaldy-Say, t., **Kyrgyzstan**; new t. on site of Uch-Kurgan hydroelectric power sta.

Shandaken Tunnel, N.Y. st., **USA**; carries water under Catskill mtns. to augment water supply of c. of N.Y.; 29 km long.

Shandong (Shantung), coastal prov., N. **China**; S. of fertile plain of Huang He; dense p. but agr. potential limited by dry climate; wheat, millet, maize, soyabeans, cotton, hemp, fruits; E. mtns. contain coal, iron, bauxite, kaolin; iron and steel inds. and cotton mills at main industl. ts. of Jinan and Qingdao; special economic zones to encourage foreign investment; birthplace of Confucius at foot of sacred peak Tai; cap. Jinan; a. 146,198 km²; p. (1990) 83,430,000.

Shanghai, c. and mun., **China**; major spt. on left bank of Huangbu; its strategic location developed, largely by Brit. businessmen, as ctr. for imperialist trading; rich agr. region; handles major share of Chinese shipping but dredging required; machin., chemicals, electronics, cars, steel, shipbldg., are main inds.; major educational and research ctr.; open to foreign investment, esp. for high technology inds.; new business district (Pudong); a. 6,186 km²; 3rd most populous c. in world; p. (1990) 13,510,000 (prov.), (1992) 7,860,000 (c.).

Shannon Airport, Clare, **R.o.I.**; N.W. of Limerick; on main transatlantic air route; ctr. of customs-free industl. estate built (1958) to compensate for decline in air traffic with larger planes; p. (1981) 7,998 (t.).

Shannon, R., **Ireland**; separates Connaught from provs. of Leinster and Munster, flows to Atl. at Loop Head; hydroelectric power sta. at Ardnacrusha; 358 km long.

Shan State, div., **Myanmar**; elevated plateau through which flows Salween R.; impt. mng. dist., lead, zinc, silver at Bawdwin, smelters at Namtu; also tungsten, tin, antimony, manganese; home of Shan people; former Shan and Wa sts.; cap. Taunggyi; a. 155,801 km²; p. (1983) 3,718,706.

Shantou (Swatow), c., spt., S.E. Guandong, **China**; at mouth of Han R.; mftg. and exp. tr.; univ.; special economic zone to attract foreign inds. and new dock being built; p. (1984) 899,900.

Shanxi (Shansi), prov., N. **China**; bounded W. and S. by Huang He; mainly high plateaux; fertile loess deposits, but drought conditions limit agr. potential; dry crops and livestock; coal, iron-ore, petroleum; cap. Taiyuan; a. 156,420 km²; p. (1990) 28,180,000.

Shaohing. See Shaoxing.

Shaoxing (Shaohing), c., N. Zhejiang prov., S.E. **China**; agr. ctr. on Hangzhou Bay; rice, wheat, cotton; p. (1984) 244,100.

Shaoyang, c., Hunan prov., **China**; coal and iron mng.; timber; p. (1984) 416,500.

Shap, mkt. t., Cumbria, **Eng.**; nearby in Shap Fell 279 m, an impt. pass traversed by rly. and by a main road; granite quarries.

Shapinsay, I., Orkney Is., **Scot.**; p. (1991) 322.

Shari, R., central **Africa**; formed by several head-streams in Central African Rep., flows across Chad Rep. into L. Chad in wide delta; navigable.

Shārjah, emirate, member of the **United Arab Emirates** (1971), Persian Gulf; international airport at cap. Shārjah (p. 25,000); natural harbour at Khawr Fakhan; oil exploration, fishing; p. (1985) 268,722.

Sharon, plain, **Israel**; citrus fruits, vines, poultry.

Shashi, t., S. Hubei prov., **China**; agr. mkt. ctr. and canalised R. pt.; tr. in cotton, grain; flour milling, textiles; p. (1984) 246,800.

Shasta Dam, Cal., **USA**; dams water of Rs. Pit, McCloud, Sacramento for hydroelectric power; irrigation, flood control and reclamation of lower Sacramento valley.

Shatt-al-Arab, R., **Iraq**; formed by union of Tigris and Euphrates, flows thence to head of Persian G.; swampy delta in rich agr. a.; deepest-water line of R.'s estuary defined (1975) as new Iraq/Iran bdy.; 192 km long.

Shawinigan Falls, c., Quebec, **Canada**; pulp and paper, chemicals, aluminium inds., powered by hydroelectric power from falls on St. Maurice R.; p. (1986) 24,470.

Shawnee, c., Okla., **USA**; rly. and tr. ctr. for rich agr. a.; electronics, aircraft components; p. (1980) 26,506.

Sheaf, R., South Yorks., **Eng.**; rises in S.E. Pennines, flows N.E. to join R. Don at Sheffield; 18 km long.

Shebelinka, natural gas fields nr. Kharkov, **Ukraine**; pipelines to Kharkov-Bryansk and Dnepropetrovsk-Odessa.

Sheboygan, t., Wis., **USA**; on L. Michigan; ctr. for dairy farming and resort a.; cheese, leather gds., hardware; p. (1990) 49,676.

Sheerness, Kent, **Eng.**; on I. of Sheppey at entrance to estuary of R. Medway; former royal dockyard and garrison; deepwater comm. pt.; electronics, furniture, coach bldg.; p. (1991) 11,653

Sheffield, c., met. dist., South Yorks., **Eng.**; on cramped site at confluence of Rs. Sheaf and Don; univs.; heavy engin. ctr., famous for high quality steels, cutlery, tools; major post-war redevelopment of c. ctr.; National Centre for Popular Music (opened 1999); p. (1995) 528,500 (dist.), (1991) 431,607 (c.).

Sheksna, R., **Russia**; rises in L. Beloye and flows S. to Rybinsk Reservoir; forms part of Volga–Baltic waterway; 160 km long.

Shellhaven, oil refineries, Essex, **Eng.**; on N. side of Thames estuary, nr. Standord-le-Hope.

Shenandoah National Park, Va., **USA**; extends along forested Blue Ridge mtns.; views of Shenandoah valley and Allegheny mtns.

Shenandoah, R., Va., **USA**; trib. of Potomac R.; picturesque valley noted for rich apple orchards and pastures; scene of several campaigns in Civil War; 272 km long.

Shensi. See Shaanxi.

Shen-yang (Mukden), c., cap. of Liaoning prov., N.E. **China**; on Hun R. in narrowest part of lowland with hilly country on both sides; impt. rly. junc. with main routes N. to Harbin and Trans-Siberian rly., S. to Beijing, Luta and into Korea; comm. and educational ctr.; impt. textile ctr., heavy inds., univ.; p. (1992) 4,580,000.

Shenzhen, special economic zone, Guandong, **China**; a. selected (1980) to encourage foreign investment; close to Hong Kong; soft drinks, cement, electronic equipment, petrochems. relocated from Hong Kong; spt.; univ.; planned nuclear power plant to supply Hong Kong; p. (1984) 337,000 (146,000 temporary workers).

Shepparton-Mooroopna, t., Victoria, **Australia**; ctr. of vegetable and orchard a. of Goulburn valley irrigation; p. (1991) 30,511.

Sheppey, I. of, Kent, Swale, **Eng.**; in Thames estuary E. of mouth of R. Medway; sheep-raising; steel wks.; ch. t., Sheerness; a. 117 km².

Shepshed, t., Charnwood, Leics., **Eng.**; 5 km W. of Loughborough; hosiery; p. (1991) 12,961.

Shepton Mallet, mkt. t., Mendip, Somerset, **Eng.**; at foot of Mendip Hills, 8 km S.E of Wells; old woollen ctr.; bacon curing, brewing; p. (1991) 7,581.

Shepway, l. gov. dist., S.E. Kent, **Eng.**; cstl. a. of Folkestone, Hythe, New Romney and Lydd; p. (1995) 97,000.

Sherborne, mkt. t., West Dorset, **Eng.**; 6 km E. of Yeovil; famous abbey and school; Norman cas. ruins; glass fibre; p. (1991) 7,606.

Sherbrook, t., S.E. Quebec, **Canada**; comm. and mkt. ctr. for surrounding agr. region; inds. based on local sources of hydroelectric power from Magog R.; textiles, paper mills, machin., flour milling; deposits of asbestos nearby; p. (1991) 76,429 (c.), (1986) 129,960 (met. a.).

Sheringham, t., North Norfolk, **Eng.**; on cst. 6 km W. of Cromer; resort; fishing; p. (1991) 7,620.

Sherwood Forest, anc. royal woodland, Notts., **Eng.**; now restricted to infertile Bunter Sandstone cty.; inc. several estates and parks, notably the Dukeries.

Shetland Is., l. gov. auth., **Scot.**; 80 km N.E. of the Orkneys; about 100 in gr., ch. 1., Mainland; lge. number of rainy days, but climate mild and tourists attracted by isolation, scenery and wildlife; Fair Isle famous for knitted clothes; fishing, livestock, agr., potatoes; rapid growth with oil drilling in N. Sea; lge. oil terminal of Sullum Voe; wreck of oil tanker Braer, Jan 1992; ch. t. Lerwick; p. (1995) 23,090.

Shibin el Kôm, Menûfiya, **Egypt**; rly. and mkt. ctr. in agr. a. of Nile delta; tobacco, textiles; p. (1986) 132,751.

Shigatze. See Zigaze.

Shijiazhuang (Shihkiachwang) c., Hebei prov., **China**; cotton milling, glass mftg.; grew rapidly with coming of rly.; p. (1992) 1,320,000.

Shikarpur, t., N. Sind, **Pakistan**; tr. ctr. for grain, precious stones; engin., food processing; p. (1981) 88,000.

Shikoku, I., **Japan**; S. of Honshu; smallest of Japan's 4 main Is.; sparsely populated, mtnous. interior, heavily forested; arable agr. in lowlands; ch. cs., Matsuyama, Kochi, Tokushima; a. 18,772 km²; p. (1990) 4,195,000.

Shilka, R., E. Siberia, **Russia**; trib. of R. Amur; 552 km long.

Shillelagh, v., Wicklow, **R.o.I.**; oak forest, gave its name to oak or blackthorn cudgel; p. (1986) 334.

Shillong, c., cap. Meghalaya, former cap. of Assam,

India; at alt. 1,372 m in Khasi hills; ctr. of impt. tea-growing dist.; admin. technical education; pleasant climate attracts summer tourists; p. (1981) 109,244 (c), 174,703 (met. a).

Shimizu, spt., **Japan**; exp. tea, oranges; fishing; p. (1990) 241,524.

Shimoda, spt., Honshu, **Japan**; between Nagoya and Yokohama; fishing; p. (1990) 30,081.

Shimoga, t., Karnataka, **India**; on Tunga R.; cotton-ginning, rice-milling; p. (1991) 178,882.

Shimonoseki, spt., Honshu I., **Japan**; at extreme S.W. of I.; tunnel and bridge links island of Kyushu; rly. ctr.; engin., chemicals based on local coal; fishing; p. (1990) 262,635.

Shin, Loch, Highland, **Scot.**; 26 km long; drained by R. Shin to R. Oykell.

Shipka Pass, Bulgaria; over the Balkan mtns., 75 km N.E. of Plovdiv.

Shipley, t., West Yorks., **Eng.**; on R. Aire, 13 km N.W. of Leeds; worsted mnfs.; inc. model v. of Saltaire, built by Titus Salt (1851) to house his alpaca mill workers; p. (1991) 28,165.

Shiraz, c., cap. of Fars prov., **Iran**; beautifully sited in vine-growing dist.; textiles, rugs, metal wks., lt. elec ind., tourist ctr.; tombs of mediaeval poets Saadi and Hafez; known as "city of roses and nightingales"; pleasant winter climate; univ., airpt.; oil refinery; p. (1986) 848,011.

Shire, R., flows out of L. Malawi south through **Malawi** and **Moçambique** to Zambesi; lge. hydro-elect. potential; 592 km long.

Shirwa or **Chilwah**, shallow L., **Malawi**; 64 km long, 22 km wide; has 4 Is.

Shizuoka, c., cap. of S. pref., Honshu, **Japan**; pt. on Suruga Bay; impt. ctr. for tea and oranges; lacquer-ware, textiles; p. (1990) 472,199.

Shkodër (Scutari), c., N. **Albania**; stands at foot of L. Scutari, 26 km from Adriatic; mkt. ctr., tobacco, cement, textiles; enjoyed greatest comm. prosperity after Ottoman conquest; several mosques; rail link to Podgorica, Albania's first external rail link, used mainly for metal ore export; p. (1991) 83,700.

Shkodër (Scutari), L., on borders of Montenegro **(Yugoslavia)** and **Albania**; outlet via R. Boyana into Adriatic, 46 km long.

Sholapur, c., Maharashtra, **India**; between Hyder-abad and Poona; rly. junc.; impt. textile ctr.; p. (1991) 604,000.

Shoreham-by-Sea, t., Adur, West Sussex, **Eng.**; at mouth of R. Adur, 6 km E. of Worthing; spt. and mkt. t.; oil jetty; boat bldg., chemicals, soap, preserves; p. (1991) 17,332.

Shoshone Falls, on Snake R., Idaho, **USA**; height 61 m, used for irrigation projects.

Shott el Jerid, Algeria and **Tunisia**; deep depres-sion in the desert.

Shotts, plateau, N. **Africa**; upland region with salt Ls., within Atlas mtns.

Shreveport, c., La., **USA**; industl. ctr. in cotton-growing dist.; petroleum; p. (1990) 198,525 (c.), 334,000 (met. a.).

Shrewsbury, co. t., Shrops., **Eng.**; on R. Severn 19 km above Ironbridge gorge between the Wrekin and Wenlock Edge; agr. and dairy equipment, machin., elec. prods.; cattle and sheep mkt.; public school; part of l. gov. dist. of Shrewsbury and Atcham; p. (1995) 95,800 (dist.), (1991) 64,219 (t.).

Shropshire (Salop), non-met co., **Eng.**; on Welsh border, crossed by R. Severn; fine pastoral cty.; with hills and woodland, agr. and dairying; industl. activity at co. t. Shrewsbury; p. (1995) 419,900.

Shumen, c., cap. of S. prov., N. E. **Bulgaria**; agr. tr.; Moslem architecture; p. (1990) 111,754.

Shusha, t., Azerbaijan; health resort; silk spinning, rug making; Armenian p. massacred by Tartars 1926; p. *c.* 6,000.

Shustar, t., Iran; carpets, woollens, pottery; shallow-draught boats can reach Shallili, nr. S. by R. Karun.

Shymkent. *See* Chimkent.

Sialkot, t., Pakistan; N.E. of Lahore; sports gds., musical and surgical instruments, paper; agr. tr. and processing ctr.; p. (1981) 296,000.

Siam. *See* Thailand.

Sian. *See* Xi'an.

Siangtan. *See* Xiangtan.

Siauliai, t., Lithuania; 184 km N.W. of Vilna; rly. junc.; food and leather inds.; p. (1990) 147,600.

Sibenik, t., Croatia (formerly Yugoslavia); Adriatic spt.; exp. timber, bauxite; aluminium, chemical and textile inds.; p. (1981) 80,148.

Siberia, terr., **Russia**; extends from Urals to Sea of

Okhotsk and Bering Strait, bounded by Arctic on N. and by Mongolia and Turkestan on S.; climate mostly severe; ch. ts., Novosibirsk (cap. W. S.) and Irkutsk (cap. E. S.); rich in coal, iron, minerals; oil and gas in W. Siberian lowland; liquified coal pipeline under construction to Moscow; p. and economic activity clustered around rlys.. esp. Trans-Siberian rly.; affected by global warming, 1990s; a. *c.* 12,950,000 km²; p. (1983) 29,587,000.

Sibiu, t., central **Romania**; picturesque site at foot of Transylvanian Alps; retains mediaeval character despite being an impt. industl. ctr.; lge. German minority p.; caths.; p. (1992) 169,696.

Sibu, t., Sarawak, E. **Malaysia**; 128 km up R. Rejang; comm. ctr. at head of ocean naviga-tion; airport; p. (1989) 114,000.

Sichuan (Szechwan), prov., S.W. **China**; mostly occupied by Chang Jiang; known as Red Basin because of colour of its sandstone; fertile a. with mild climate; rice, tea, citrus fruits, tobacco, sugar-cane; lge coal reserves; exp. tung oil; silk producing a.; most populous prov.; cap. Chengdu; a. 568,977 km²; p. (1990) 106,370,000.

Sicily, lgst. I., Mediterranean Sea; former kingdom and now aut. region of **Italy**; pleasant climate, mtnous.; fertile lowlands, especially plain of Catania, but gr. hampered by primitive methods, absentee landlords and need for irrigation; lge. range of Mediterranean crops; fishing; sulphur; petroleum reserves, refining and petrochemical inds.; volcanic Mt. Etna erupted in 1971; a. 25,708 km²; p. (1992) 4,997,705.

Sidi-bel-Abbès, t., dep., W. **Algeria**; old fortress t., became H.Q. of Fr. Foreign Legion; agr. mkt. ctr. for region producing grain, grapes, olives, live-stock; p. (1987) 152,778 (t.), 444,047 (dep.).

Sidlaw Hills, low mtn. range, Angus, **Scot.**; max. alt. 455 m.

Sidmouth, mkt. t., East Devon, **Eng.**; on S. cst., 24 km S.E. of Exeter; seaside resort; retire-ment ctr.; p. (1991) 10,767.

Sidon. *See* Saïda.

Siebengebirge, sm. wooded range of seven hills, **Germany**; of volcanic origin rising to 457 m on right bank of Rhine; famous for Drachenfels association with the Siegfried saga.

Siedlce, t. and prov., **Poland**; E. of Warsaw; rly. junc.; agr. inds.; p. (1989) 70,529 (t.), 648,100 (prov.).

Siegburg, t., N. Rhine–Westphalia, **Germany**; on R. Sieg; Benedictine abbey; dyes, iron, ceramics; p. (1986) 34,100.

Siegen, t., N. Rhine–Westphalia, **Germany**; on R. Sieg; 2 cas.; iron mng. and smelting, machin., leather; p. (1990) 109,800.

Siemianowice Slaskie, t., **Poland**; nr. Katowice; ctr. of mng., industl. region; iron and steel, machin.; cas.; p. (1989) 80,412.

Siena, hill-town, Tuscany, **Italy**; 51 km S. of Florence; spreads over three hilltops with Piazza del Campo in between where celebrated Palio festival (horse-races) are held; 13th- and 14th-cent. arch., cath.; agr. mkt., tanning, glass, textiles, bricks; *panforte* confectionery; tourist ctr.; p. (1981) 61,989.

Sieradz, t. and prov., central **Poland**; R. Warta; old medieval t.; tourism; p. (1989) 42,041 (t.), 408,100 (prov.).

Sierra Leone, rep., W. cst. Africa; mangrove swamps on cst., high plateau, with peaks over 1,800 m in interior; climate hot, humid; economy based on subsistence agr. with rice, coffee and cocoa for exp.; iron ore mng. at Marampa; main exp. diamonds; fishing along cst.; civil war in 1990s; cap. Freetown; a. 72,326 km²; p. (1993) 4,460,000.

Sierra Madre Occidental, mtn. range, **Mexico**; volcanic, forms W. edge of Mexican plateau; average alt. 2,100 m.

Sierra Madre Oriental, mtn. range, **Mexico**; limestone, forms E. edge of Mexican plateau; average alt. 2,400 m.

Sierra Maestra, mtn. range, Oriente prov., S.E. **Cuba**; rises abruptly from cst.; rich in minerals.

Sierra Morena, mtn. range, **Spain**; between Guadalquivir and Guadiana basins, highest point 1,677 m; rich in minerals.

Sierra Nevada, mtn. range, Granada, **Spain**; highest summit Mulhacén 3,483 m.

Sierra Nevada, mtn. chain, Cal., **USA**; highest peak Mt. Whitney 4,544 m; nat. parks.

Sierra Nevada de Mérida, mtn. range, W. Vene-zuela; extends N.E. from San Cristóbal to

Barquisimeto; extension of E. range of Andes, alt. over 4,880 m; impt. coffee plantations from 900–1,800 m on slopes.

Sierra Pacaraima, mtn. range, **Brazil, Venezuela**; forms part of international bdy. and watershed between Amazon and Orinoco basins.

Sighet, frontier t., N. **Romania**; on R. Tisa, on border with USSR; extreme, continental climate; timber, agr. and livestock tr.; cotton textiles.

Siglufjörd, spt., N. **Iceland**; impt. herring fisheries; p. (1993) 1,781.

Sigtuna, t., Stockholm, **Sweden**; on Mälaren L.; first cap. of Sweden; educational ctr., tourist resort; p. (1983) 28,681.

Sihanoukville. *See* Kompong Som.

Sikhote-Alin, mtn. range, S.E. Asiatic **Russia**; rises to 1,800 m and extends for 1,200 km parallel to Pac. cst.; hinders access to W. basins; forestry, minerals.

Si-Kiang. *See* Xi Jiang.

Sikkim, st., **India**; on S. slopes of Himalayas; incorporated as 22nd st. 1975; forest covered; economically underdeveloped; scene of rivalry between India and China; cap. Gangtok; a. 7,110 km²; p. (1991) 406,457.

Sila, La, massif, Calabria, S. **Italy**; granite mass occupying full width of peninsula; alt. over 1,060 m, max. 1,930 m.

Silchester, par., Hants., **Eng.**; ruins of Roman t., Calleva Atrebatum; impt. ctr. of Roman communications network.

Silesia (Polish **Slask**, Czech **Slezsko**, German **Schlesien**), geographical region, **Central Europe**; since 1945 divided between Poland, Czech Republic and Germany; extends along both banks of Oder R.; bounded in S. by Sudeten mtns.; forested mtns., fertile arable agr. in lowlands; major concentration of economic activity based on coalfield of Upper Silesia (ceded to Poland 1922); complex territorial history; now forms highly urbanised industl. conurb. mainly in Poland, admin. by Katowice, Opole, Wroclaw, Wroclaw (c.), and part of Zielona Gora; Czech Republic portion forms part of N. Moravia; Germany retains sm. part of Lower Silesia W. of Neisse R.; total a. 46,600 km².

Silistra, t., **Bulgaria**; on Danube opposite Romanian t. of Calarasi; cereals and timber tr.; mnfs. foodstuffs, ceramics, furniture; mosques.

Silkeborg, t., Jutland, **Denmark**; tourist resort in beautiful forest and lake region; p. (1990) 48,280.

Silsden, t., West Yorks., **Eng.**; wool textiles; p. (1991) 6,284.

Silver Spring, t., Md., **USA**; sub. N. of Washington, D.C.; science-based inds. and research laboratories; p. (1990) 76,046.

Simbirsk, (**Ulyanovsk**), c., cap. of S. oblast, **Russia**; industl. ctr. of middle Volga region; birthplace of Lenin whose real name was Ulyanov; p. (1989) 625,000.

Simcoe, L., S. Ont., **Canada**; several resorts; boating, fishing; 48 km by 42 km.

Simeulue, I., S.W. of Sumatra, **Indonesia**; primitive islanders; fishing and shifting cultivation.

Simferopol, t., **Ukraine**; on R. Salghir nr. Sevastopol; industl. ctr. in rich agr. a., fruit-canning, tobacco, machin.; p. (1990) 348,900.

Simla, t., Himachal Pradesh, **India**; famous hill-station c. 2,158 m high on forested ridge of Himalayas, 280 km N. of Delhi.

Simonstown, W. Cape Prov., **S. Africa**; naval sta, docks; p. (1980) 48,520 (dist.).

Simplon, mtn., **Switzerland**; alt. 3,567 m; the pass over the Simplon (alt. 2,011 m) from Domodossola, Italy, to Brig in the Rhône valley, Switzerland, was originally made by Napoleon I. The Simplon rly. tunnel leads from Brig on the Swiss side to Iselle in the Val di Vedro on the Italian and is the longest in the world, 19.7 km.

Simpson Desert, Central **Australia**; uninhabited arid a. covered in ridge dunes and spinifex; a. 77,000 km².

Sinai, peninsula, easternmost part of **Egypt**; between Gs. of Aqaba and Suez, at head of Red Sea; mainly desert in N., granitic ridges in S. rising to 2,592 m at Jebel Katrun; Jebel Musa or Mt. Sinai (2,244 m) is one of numerous peaks; mineral resources; coal mine at Maghâra; occupied by Israeli troops, Nov. 1956–March 1957, and since June 1967; phased Israeli withdrawal began 1979, completed 1982; prov. N. Sinai and S. Sinai; a. 28,632 km²; p. (1991) 223,000 (N.), 41,000 (S.).

Sinaia, t., S. **Romania**; health and winter sports resort in Transylvanian Alps; until 1947 summer residence of Romanian kings; palaces.

Sinaloa, st., **Mexico**; on G. of Cal.; agr. and mng., rich in gold, silver, copper, iron and lead; cereals on uplands; sugar, cotton on lowlands; cap. Culiacán; a. 48,482 km²; p. (1990) 2,210,766.

Sind, prov. (revived 1970), **Pakistan**; lower Indus valley; dry climate; E. part reaches edge of Thar desert; agr. depends on irrigation; irrigated by Sukkur and Kotri systems; wheat, rice, cotton, oilseeds, sugar-cane, fruits; handicraft inds. in ts.; ch. ts., Karachi, Hyderabad, Sukkur, Shikarpur; a. 129,500 km² p. (1981) 19,028,666.

Singapore, rep., S.E. Asia; I. separated from Malaysian mainland by Johore Strait and linked by causeway; equatorial climate; cap. Singapore on S. cst. has fine natural harbour; p. (1991) 2·69 m; currently world's biggest port; world ctr. of rubber and tin mkts.; tr. in machinery, petrol prods., mnfs., with Japan, Malaysia and USA; increasingly impt. as regional financial centre; oil refining, shipbldg., but industl. development slowing down since 1985; only 20 per cent of land cultivated; fruit, mkt. gardening; second hst. standard of living in Asia; reduction in Brit. military presence from base on N. cst. of I.; a. 620 km²; p. (1994) 2,930,200.

Singhbhum, dist., Bihar, **India**; iron and steel wks. based on local iron mng.; a. 13,445 km²; p. (1981) 2,861,799.

Sinhailion. *See* Lianyungang.

Sining. *See* Xining.

Sinkiang-Uighur. *See* Xinjiang Uygur.

Sinop, cap. of S. prov., **Turkey**; sm. pt. with gd. harbour on Black Sea but poor communications with hinterland; p. (1985) 23,148 (t.), (1990) 265,153 (prov.).

Sintra (**Cintra**), t., **Portugal**; summer resort, 29 km from Lisbon; Moorish castle, royal palace; p. (1981) 126,010 (met. a.).

Sinuiju, c., **W. N. Korea**; spt. at mouth of Yalu R. on Yellow Sea; linked by bridge to Antung (China); industl. ctr.; chemicals, aluminium inds., using power from Supung Dam; p. (1984) 500,000.

Sinyang. *See* Xinyang.

Sion, t., cap. of Valais can., **Switzerland**; on R. Rhône; built on two castled hills; cath.; horticultural mkt. ctr.; hydroelectric power stas. and coal mines nearby; p. (1980) 22,877.

Sioux City, Iowa, **USA**; on R. Missouri; meat-packing, foundries, elec. gds., cement; p. (1990) 80,508.

Sioux Falls, t., S.D., **USA**; on Big Sioux R.; in rich wheat region; machin., cars, farming implements; nuclear reactor; p. (1990) 100,814.

Siping (**Szeping**), c., Jilin prov., **China**; agr. distributing ctr.; cement; p. (1984) 353,300.

Siret, R., Romania, Ukraine; flows S. from Carpathians to Danube; steep forested left bank, fertile terraced right bank; hydroelectric power and irrigation schemes; 448 km long.

Sisak, t., Croatia (formerly Yugoslavia); developing indust. ctr. and R. pt.; iron and steel, oil refining.

Sistan and Baluchistan, twin prov., **Iran**; bounded by Afghanistan and Pakistan; cap. Zahedan; much desert land; arid, very hot; p. (1982) 664,292.

Sitapur, t., Uttar Pradesh, **India**; rly. junc.; agr. tr. ctr.; eye hospital; p. (1991) 121,842.

Sitra, I., Persian G.; forms part of st. of **Bahrain**, 5 km long and 1·6 km wide; oil pipeline and causeway carrying road extends out to sea for 5 km to deep-water anchorage; oil refinery; power sta. and desalinisation plant.

Sittang, R., **Myanmar**; rises in Pegu Yoma, flows S. to. G. of Martaban through delta; valley intensively cultivated, delta forested; irrigation project; 976 km long.

Sittard, mkt. t., Limburg, **Neth.**; tanning; p. (1993) 46,578, 184,097 (met. a. with Geleen).

Sittingbourne and Milton, mkt. t., Swale, Kent, **Eng.**; on Milton Creek, 14 km E. of Chatham; paper mills, brick wks.; cement; insecticides; ctr. of fruit-growing dist.; p. (1991) 38,771.

Sittwe (**Akyab**), spt., **Myanmar**; at mouth of Kaladan R.; exp. rice; (1983) 107,907.

Sivas, c., cap. of S. prov., **Turkey**; impt. tr. and agr. ctr. in Kizil Irmak valley; cement, rugs; copper mng. nearby; foundations of modern Turkey laid here by Atatürk 1919; p. (1990) 219,949 (c.), 767,481 (prov.).

Sivash Sea or Putrid Sea, lagoon on N.E. cst. of Crimea, **Ukraine**; 20 per cent salt; a. 2,590 km².

Siwa, oasis, Egypt; in Libyan Desert, c. 480 km S.W.

of Alexandria; dates, olives; remains of temple of Zeus Ammon (visited by Alexander the Great); 32 km long, 1·6 km wide.

Sizewell, Suffolk, **Eng.**; Magnox nuclear power sta.; Britain's 1st pressurised water nuclear reactor sta. under construction.

Sjaelland, I., **Denmark**; lgst. I., separated from Fyn I. by the Gr. Belt; fertile glacial clays but rapidly spreading ts.; ch. c. Copenhagen; a. 7,356 km²; p. (1990) 1,972,711.

Skagerrak, arm of N. Sea, giving access to the Kattegat, between Norway and Denmark, 112–144 km wide.

Skagway, sm. spt., Alaska, **USA**; at head of Lynn Canal inlet, 640 km N.W. of Prince Rupert; linked by rly. to Whitehorse on upper R. Yukon; boomed in gold rush (1898), p. (1990) 4,385 (inc. Yakutat and Angoon).

Skåne (Scania), old prov. and peninsula, extreme S. of **Sweden**; corresponds approx. to cos. Malmöhus, Kristianstad; most favoured part of Sweden in relief, soil, climate; intensive farming, wheat, barley, sugar-beet, fodder crops, dairy cattle; ch. ts. Malmö, Lund, Hälsingborg; a. 10,939 km².

Skaraborg, co., **Sweden**; between Ls. Vänern and Vättern; dairy agr.; a. 8,467 km²; p. (1992) 278,860.

Skara Brae, prehistoric v., Mainland, Orkney Is. **Scot.**; v. excavated from under sand dunes.

Skarzysko-Kamienna, t., Kielce, **Poland**; ctr. of metallurgical ind.; p. (1989) 50,455.

Skaw The (Grenen), C., at extreme N. of **Denmark**.

Skeena, R., B.C., **Canada**; rises in N. Rocky mtns., flows S.W. to Pac. Oc. at Prince Rupert; lower valley used by Canadian National Rly.; 640 km long.

Skegness, t., East Lindsey, Lincs., **Eng.**; on E. cst.; resort; lt. engin.; p. (1991) 15,149.

Skelleftea, t., N. **Sweden**; on Bothnia G.; growing since discovery of Boliden ores nearby; iron and copper ore smelting; p. (1992) 73,734.

Skelmersdale, t., West Lancs., **Eng.**; coal, bricks, drainpipes; new t. (1961); p. (1991) 42,104.

Skelton, t., Redcar and Cleveland, **Eng.**; at N. foot of Cleveland Hills, 16 km E. of Middlesbrough; steel flooring; p. (1991) 10,088.

Skiddaw, mtn., Cumbria, **Eng.**; E. of Bassenthwaite L.; alt. 931 m.

Skien, spt., Bratsberg, **Norway**; on R. Skien; saw-mills, timber tr.; birthplace of Ibsen; p. (1990) 29,328.

Skierniewice, t. and prov. central **Poland**; fruit and vegetables, elec. engin; p. (1989) 43,963 (t.), 416,700 (prov.).

Skikda (Philippeville), t., spt., dep., N.E. **Algeria**; exp. prods. from Saharan oases; oil pipeline to Mesdar; vast petrochemical plant; p. (1987) 128,747 (t.), 619,094 (dep.).

Skipton, t., Craven, North Yorks., **Eng.**; on R. Aire; cotton and rayon inds.; cas.; p. (1991) 13,583.

Skopje, t., cap. of **Macedonia**, formerly Yugoslavia; anc. Scupi, one of oldest ts. in Balkans; oriental appearance; destroyed by massive earthquake (1963); food processing, iron and steel wks.; new oil refinery; airpt., route ctr.; p. (1981) 506,547.

Skövde, t., **Sweden**; between Ls. Vänern and Vättern; garrison t., chemicals, cement; p. (1992) 48,460.

Skye, I., lgst. of Inner Hebrides, Highland, **Scot.**; connected by bridge to mainland 1995; mtnous.; sheep-farming and fisheries; tourism; only t. Portree; a. 1,417 km²; p. (1991) 8,868.

Skyros, I., Sporades, **Greece**; in Aegean Sea; mainly agr.; a. 199 km².

Slagelse, t., Sjaelland, **Denmark**; food inds.; iron wks.; 11th cent. church; p. (1990) 34,279.

Slave Coast, name given to the Guinea cst. of W. Africa between the Volta and Niger deltas where slaves were shipped from 16th to 19th cent.

Slave, R., N.W. Terr., **Canada**; flows into Gr. Slave L.; length 416 km.

Slavonia, historic region, **Croatia** (formerly Yugoslavia); between Drava R. (N.) and Sava R. (S.); ch. t. Osijek.

Slavyansk, t., **Ukraine**; in Donets basin; chemicals, engin.; p. (1990) 136,000.

Sleaford, mkt. t., North Kesteven, Lincs., **Eng.**; 19 km N.E. of Grantham; agr. and agr. implements; p. (1991) 10,388.

Sleat, Sound of, Highland, **Scot.**; separates I. of Skye from the mainland; 11 km wide.

Slezsko. See Silesia.

Sliema, t., **Malta**; E. of Valletta; resort; p. (1983) 20,123.

Slieve Bloom, hill range, Offaly and Laoghis cos., **R.o.I.**; highest point 529 m.

Slieve Donard, mtn., **N. Ireland**; highest of the Mourne mtns.; alt. 835 m.

Sligo, co., Connacht, **R.o.I.**; borders Atl. Oc.; rises to Ox Mtns. over 600 m; pastoral agr., fishing; co. t. S.; a. 1,909 km²; p. (1986) 56,046.

Sligo, co. t., Sligo, **R.o.I.**; on S. Bay; pt., exp. agr. prods.; abbey ruins; cath.; p. (1986) 17,259.

Slioch, mtn., Highland, **Scot.**; alt. 981 m.

Sliven, t., **Bulgaria**; in Balkan mtns.; impt. woollen mnf. ctr.; carpets; p. (1990) 112,220.

Slough, t., l. gov. dist., Berks., **Eng.**; on river terrace N. of R. Thames, 37 km W. of London; many lt. inds.; p. (1995) 109,300 (dist.), (1991) 110,708 (t.).

Slovakia, formerly eastern part of Czechoslovakia, cap. Bratislava; extends from Carpathians to Danube valley; mainly agricultural, depressed industry; a. 49,035 km²; p. (1993) 5,324,632.

Slovenia, former constituent rep., Yugoslavia; independence recognised by EC, 1991; mtnous., but many minerals inc. coal; highly developed region; cap. Ljubljana; a. 16,229 km²; p. (1992) 1,996,800.

Slupsk (Stolp), t. and prov., N.W. **Poland** (since 1945); formerly in Pomerania; on R. Stupia, nr. Baltic Sea; cas.; wood, metal, food processing; p. (1989) 100,127 (t.), 410,000 (prov.).

Småland, historic prov., S. **Sweden**; barren upland a. S. of L. Vättern; moorland, deciduous forest; contrasts greatly with remainder of S. Sweden; a. 29,322 km².

Smederevo, t., Serbia, **Yugoslavia**; nr. Belgrade; pt. on R. Danube; walled t.; steel wks.; p. (1991) 64,257.

Smethwick. See Warley.

Smolensk, c., cap. of S. oblast, **Russia**; on upper Dnieper; anc. c. damaged in many wars; route ctr.; vehicles, machin., food processing; p. (1989) 344,000.

Smyrna. See Izmir.

Snaefell, highest mtn., **Isle of Man**; alt. 620 m.

Snake R., or **Lewis Fork**, trib. of Columbia R., flows from Wyo. to Wash., **USA**; gorges; hydroelectric power; 1,680 km long.

Sneek, t., Friesland, **Neth.**; butter, cheese mkt.; yachting ctr.; p. (1993) 29,234.

Sneeuwbergen, mtn. range, Cape Prov., **S. Africa**.

Snowdon, mtn., Gwynedd, **Wales**; highest in Eng. and Wales, alt. 1,086 m; forms part of Snowdonia Nat. Park.

Snowy Mtns., N.S.W., **Australia**; part of Australian Alps inc. Australia's hgst. peak (Mount Kosciusko); rise to over 2,000 m; S.M. scheme (1950) diverts water from headstreams in tunnels through mtns. to provide water for irrigation and hydroelectric power; completed 1972.

Snowy, R., N.S.W. and Victoria, **Australia**; rises in Mt. Kosciusko, flows S. into Bass strait 128 km W. of C. Howe; part of Snowy Mtn. scheme; 432 km long.

Soar, R., Leics., Notts., **Eng.**; rises S. of Leics., flows N.W. to join R. Trent; 69 km long.

Sobat, R., **Sudan** and **Ethiopia**; made up of several sm. Rs.; trib. of White Nile; 800 km long.

Soche. See Yarkand.

Sochi, t., **Russia**; on Black Sea at foot of main Caucasian range; health resort with subtropical climate and sulphur springs; developed since 1933; p. (1989) 337,000.

Society Is., Fr. Polynesia, S. **Pac. Oc.**; comprise Windward Is. (Tahiti, Moorea, Mehetia, etc.) and Leeward Is. (Huahine, Raiatea, etc.); visited by Captain Cook; main prods. phosphate and copper; cap. Papeete; a. 1,647 km²; p. (1983) 142,129.

Socotra, I., G. of Aden, Indian Oc.; since 1967 part of **Yemen**; under Brit. protection 1886–1967; lofty tableland; myrrh, frankincense, aloes; cap. Tamrida; a. 3,626 km².

Söderhamn, spt., **Sweden**; on G. of Bothnia, N. of Gavle; timber, wood-pulp; p. (1983) 30,736.

Södermanland, co., **Sweden**; between Baltic cst. and L. Mälar; cattle-rearing; mng.; a. 6,822 km²; p. (1992) 257,858.

Södertälje, t., **Sweden**; on S. canal linking L. Mälar with Baltic cst.; vehicles, chemicals, tobacco; p. (1992) 81,770.

Soest, c., N. Rhine–Westphalia, **Germany;** one of oldest ts., member of Hanseatic league; suffered heavily in second world war; soap, textile machin., engin.; p. (1993) 41,785.

Soest, t., Utrecht, **Neth.;** residtl., agr. ctr.; p. (1987) 41,000.

Sofia, c., cap. of **Bulgaria;** Roman Serdica, and Triaditsa of Byzantine Greeks; nr. Yugoslav border; impt. route ctr. and ch. industl. ctr. of rep.; machin., textiles, chemicals, elec. engin.; cath., univ., and many historic bldgs.; p. (1990) 1,141,142.

Sogne Fjord, Norway; longest fjord in Norway; length 176 km; tourism.

Sogn og Fjordane, co., W. **Norway;** borders Atl. Oc., indented by Sogne Fjord; lge. hydroelectric power resources; tourism; a. 18,480 km²; p. (1990) 106,614.

Sohag, t. and prov., Egypt; on R. Nile; cotton processing; p. (1986) 132,965 (t.), (1991) 2,763,000 (prov.).

Soho, dist., London, Eng.; settled by Fr. Huguenots 16th cent.; high proportion of foreign residents, sometimes known as London's "Latin quarter"; night-clubs, theatres, restaurants, film-company offices.

Soissons, t., Aisne dep., **France;** anc. Augusta Suessionum; commands N.E. approaches to Paris; cath.; agr. tr.; p. (1982) 32,236.

Sokoto, t., Nigeria, W. Africa; founded 1809 as cap. of native st. of S., p. mainly Hausa and Fulani; tr. ctr.; p. (est. 1983) 148,000, (1991) 4,392,391 (state).

Solent, The, strait separating I. of Wight from Hampshire mainland, Eng.;

Solihull, t., met. dist., West Midlands, **Eng.;** 8 km S.W. of Birmingham; residtl.; motor vehicles; p. (1995) 202,900 (dist.), (1991) 94,531 (t.).

Solikamsk, t., Russia; on R. Kama; chemicals from local potash; rapidly growing t.; p. (1989) 110,000.

Solingen, t., N. Rhine–Westphalia, **Germany;** 24 km E. of Düsseldorf; cutlery ctr.; p. (1990) 165,600.

Solnechnyy. See Gornyy Snezhnogorsk.

Solomon Is., S. Pac. Oc.; internal self-gov. (1976); full independence (July 1978); archipelago of volcanic Is.; N. Is. form part of Papua New Guinea; remainder were Brit.; dependent on exp. of copra, timber, fish; threatened by insect pests; a. 29,785 km²; p. (1993) 349,500 (mostly Melanesian).

Solothurn (Soleure), can., N.W. **Switzerland,** crossed by Jura mtns., and R. Aare; 97 per cent cultivated; dairying; many industl. ts.; cap. S.; a. 793 km²; p. (1990) 226,700.

Solothurn (Soleure), t., cap. of S. can., **Switzerland;** on R. Aare; anc. t.; cath.; watches, motor mnf.; p. (1980) 15,778.

Solway Firth, arm of Irish Sea, Dumfries and Galloway, Scot., and Cumbria, Eng.; 6 km long.

Somalia (Somali Democratic Rep.), E. cst. Africa; narrow cst. plain in N., widens in S., interior plateau reaching c. 2,400 m; dry, hot climate; 75 per cent. p. nomadic; livestock herding; permanent agr. in irrigated R. valleys; sugar, banana plantations in Webi Shebeli and Juba Rs. in S.; potential for mineral exploitation; continuing civil war, famine; UN intervention 1992; severe floods (1997); cap. Mogadishu; a. 637,658 km²; p. (1992) 9,200,000.

Somaliland, French. See Djibouti.

Sombor, t., Serbia, **Yugoslavia;** cattle, grain tr.; textiles; p. (1981) 99,168.

Somersby, v., Lincs., **Eng.;** the birthplace of Tennyson.

Somerset, non-met. co., S.W. Eng.; inc. part of Exmoor, Mendips, Quantocks and Blackdown Hills; to N. is drained marshland of Somerset levels; dairying; coastal resorts; co. t. Taunton; p. (1995) 481,000.

Somme, dep., N. **France;** borders Eng. Channel; crossed by R. Somme; low-lying agr. a.; textile inds.; cap. Amiens; a. 6,327 km²; p. (1990) 547,800.

Somme, R., France; flows in deps. Aisne and Somme to English Channel; scene of battles 1916; linked to Rs. Oise and Scheldt by canal 186 km long.

Somport Tunnel, on bdy. France–Spain; carries main rly. from Pau to Zaragoza under Pyrénées; 8 km long.

Sönderborg, spt., S. Jutland, Denmark; older part of c. on Als I.; palace; p. (1990) 28,291.

Sondrio, t., cap. of S. prov., Italy; commands the Adda valley, impt. routeway through Alps; agr. mkt.; textiles; p. (1981) 22,747.

Songhua R., (**Sungari R.**), N.E. **China;** trib. of R. Amur; length 1,840 km.; hydroelectric power.

Songkhla, t., **Thailand;** most S. t.; ctr. of rubber growing dist.; third t. of cty.; p. (1980) 172,604.

Song-koi (Red R.), R., rises in Yunnan plateau, S.W. **China,** flows S.E. through N. **Vietnam,** enters G. of Tongking; Hanoi is nr. head of delta; Haiphong nr. one of R. mouths; lower valley densely populated and intensively cultivated; c. 1,280 km long.

Sonora, st., **Mexico;** on G. of Cal.; crossed by Sierra Madre Occidental; irrigated agr.; ch. producer of wheat, cattle; fish exp.; cap. Hermosillo; a. 182,535 km²; p. (1990) 1,822,247.

Sonoran Desert, Arizona, **USA;** alt. 900 m; enclosed basins and salt marshes.

Sonsonate, t., El Salvador; old t. with cath.; comm. ctr. of richest agr. region of rep., famed for coffee and dairy prod.; nr. Isalco volcano; p. (1992) 76,200.

Soo Canals. See Sault Ste. Marie Canals.

Soochow. See Suzhou.

Sopot, spt., Gdansk, **Poland;** on Gdansk Bay; resort, spa; part of Trójmiasto; p. (1989) 46,874.

Sopron, t., N.W. **Hungary;** on R. Hunte; nr. Austrian border; textiles, chemicals; p. (1997) 54,000.

Sorau. See Zary.

Soria, t., cap. of prov. of Soria, **Spain;** on R. Duero at c. 900 m; agr.-processing; retains mediaeval appearance; p. (1987) 31,507; (1991) 93,950 (prov.).

Sorocaba, t., São Paulo st., **Brazil;** textiles, food processing; p. (1991) 377,270.

Sorrento, cst. t., S. **Italy;** nr. S. extremity G. of Naples; popular resort, celebrated for its wines in anc. times; p. (1981) 17,301.

Sosnowiec, t., Katowice prov., **Poland;** coal-mng. ctr., iron wks.; metal and textile inds.; cas.; p. (1989) 259,318.

Soufrière, volcano, St. Vincent, **W.I.;** alt. 1,235 m.

Sound, The, channel between Kattegat and Baltic, 5 km across at narrowest part; proposed tunnel between Denmark and Sweden.

Sousse (Susa), spt., **Tunisia;** exp. olive oil, phosphates; resort; p. (1984) 83,509.

South Africa, Republic of, lies in most S. part of Africa between Atl. and Indian Ocs.; comprises 4 provs., Cape Prov., Natal, O.F.S., Transvaal; narrow cst. plain, several interior plateaux (600–1,800 m) with upland grasslands (Veld) and fringed by escarpments; climate warm and sunny; most highly developed cty. in Africa, based on mineral resources of gold and diamonds, and more recent successful economic diversification; coal in Witbank and Vryheid dists. serves iron and steel ind. at Pretoria; growing textile, foodprocessing inds. at pts. Cape Town, Durban and rubber at Pt. Elizabeth; agr. dependent upon water supply; rich fruit growing a. around Cape Town, extensive grain growing and pastoral areas extended by irrigation; caps. Pretoria (admin.), Cape Town (legislative), Bloemfontein (judicial); a. 1,224,254 km²; p. (1995) 41,244,000. A census estimate in 1997 reduced this figure to 38 million.

South America, S. continent of Western Hemisphere; inc. all ctys. S. of Panama. See **Latin America.**

Southampton, c., spt., unit. auth. created in 1997, formerly part of Hants., **Eng.;** at head of Southampton Water on peninsula between estuaries of Rs. Test and Itchen; univ.; decline of passenger liners, now one of Britain's biggest container pts.; ship repairing, oil refining, cable mkg., electronics, synthetic rubber; free-port (1984); p. (1995) 213,400 (former dist.), (1991) 210,138 (c.).

Southampton Water, inlet, Hants., **Eng.;** comprises drowned estuaries of Rs. Itchen and Test; gives access from Solent and Spithead to spt. of Southampton; 14 km by 1·6–2·4 km.

South Australia, st. of the **Australian Commonwealth;** the "desert state"; barren undulating interior forms part of central plateau of continent but inc. mtns. in S. and S.E. and L. Eyre basin 12 m below sea level; Nullarbor Plain in S.W.; sheep in S.E., intensive agr. in Murray R. valley; some interior mng. inds. but st. cap. of Adelaide contains most inds. and 69 per cent of p.; a. 984,381 km²; p. (1993) 1,466,500.

South Ayrshire, unit. auth. created in 1996, formerly part of Strathclyde, S.W. Scot.; borders F. of Clyde; ch. t. Ayr; p. (1995) 114,570.

South Bedfordshire, l. gov. dist., Beds., **Eng.**; close to Luton and inc. Dunstable and Leighton-Linslade; p. (1995) 110,900.

South Bend, c., Ind., **USA**; on St. Joseph R.; ctr. of fruit and dairy region; motorcars, aircraft, agr. machin.; p. (1990) 105,511.

South Buckinghamshire, l. gov. dist., Bucks., **Eng.**; based on Beaconsfield; p. (1995) 62,900.

South Cambridgeshire, l. gov. dist., Cambs., **Eng.**; rural a. surrounding Cambridge; p. (1995) 126,300.

South Carolina, st., **USA**; "Palmetto St."; admitted to Union 1788; st. flower Carolina Jessamine, st. bird Carolina Wren; level in E., mtns. in W.; subtropical climate; part of cotton belt; pigs and maize also impt.; cotton textiles; cap. Columbia; a. 80,432 km²; p. (1990) 3,486,703.

South Dakota, st., **USA**; "Cayote St."; admitted to Union 1889; st. flower Pasque flower, st. bird Ring Necked Pheasant; lies in Gt. Plains; crossed by R. Missouri; irrigated agr.; part of spring wheat belt, but now more diversified crops; agr. processing; cap. Pierre; a. 199,552 km²; p. (1990) 699,004 (inc. 25,000 Indians).

South Derbyshire, l. gov. dist., Derbys., **Eng.**; a. S. of Derby and inc. Repton and Swadlingcote; p. (1995) 76,200.

South Downs, chalk escarpment, East and West Sussex and Hants., **Eng.**; stretch from Chichester to Eastbourne; rise to over 240 m.

Southend-on-Sea, t., l. gov. dist., Essex, **Eng.**; on N. side of Thames estuary; varied lt. inds.; air ferry terminal; resort; dormitory for London; p. (1995) 171,200 (dist.), (1991) 158,517 (t.).

Southern Alps, mtns., S.I., **N.Z.**; alt. 3,000 m.

Southern Ocean, surrounds **Antarctica**; pack ice.

Southern Uplands, region, S. **Scot.**; broad belt of hilly cty., N. part bleak moorland, S. part deeply cut by glens; sheep-rearing; dairying in valleys.

South Georgia, Brit. I., S. Atl. Oc.; former whaling ctr; no permanent population; a. 4,144 km².

South Gloucestershire, unit. auth. created in 1996, formerly part of Avon, **Eng.**; inc. ts. of Chipping Sodbury and Kingswood; p. (1995) 233,200.

South Hams, l. gov. dist., S. Devon, **Eng.**; a. between Torquay and Plymouth inc. Totnes, Kingsbridge and Salcombe; p. (1995) 79,100.

South Herefordshire, l. gov. dist., Hereford., **Eng.**; lge rural a. which inc. Ross-on-Wye; p. (1995) 54,700.

South Holland, l. gov. dist., Lincs., **Eng.**; fenland a. around Spalding; p. (1995) 71,100.

South I., lge. I., **N.Z.**; inc. S. Alps (highest Mt. Cook, 3,764 m), Canterbury Plains, impt. sheep-rearing dist.; cool climate; considerable hydroelectric power resources; tourism; a. 150,461 km²; p. (1991) 881,537.

South Kensington, dist., W. London, **Eng.**; contains Victoria and Albert Museum, Geological and Science Museums, British Museum of Natural History, Commonwealth Institute, Albert Hall.

South Kesteven, l. gov. dist., Lincs., **Eng.**; rural a. and ts. of Grantham and Bourne; p. (1995) 117,500.

South Lakeland, l. gov. dist., Cumbria, **Eng.**; lge. a. surrounding Morecambe Bay and inc. Ulverston, Grange, Kendal and Sedbergh; p. (1995) 100,400.

South Lanarkshire, unit. auth. created in 1996, formerly part of Strathclyde, S. **Scot.**; lies S. of central Clydeside conurb.; p. (1995) 307,420.

South Norfolk, l. gov. dist., Norfolk, **Eng.**; lge. a. inc. Diss and Wymondham; p. (1995) 105,400.

South Northamptonshire, l. gov. dist., Northants., **Eng.**; inc. Brackley and Towcester; p. (1995) 73,900.

South Orkney Is., Antarctica; S.W. of S. Georgia; part of Brit. Antarctic Terr. (1962); meteorological sta.

South Ossetian, aut. oblast, **Georgia**; in Caucasus mtns.; goat and sheep rearing dist.; a. 3,898 km²; p. (1990) 99,200.

South Oxfordshire, l. gov. dist., Oxon., **Eng.**; Wallingford, Thame and Henley-on-Thames; p. (1995) 123,300.

Southport, t., Sefton, Merseyside, **Eng.**; on S. side

of Ribble estuary; 29 km N. of Liverpool; leisure centre; residtl.; p. (1991) 90,959.

South Ribble, l. gov. dist., Lancs., **Eng.**; a. S. of Preston and inc. Walton-le-Dale; p. (1995) 103,100.

South Sandwich Is., Brit. dependency, Antarctica; sm. volcanic Is.; a. 337 km²; no permanent p.

South Shetland, archipelago, S. Atl. Oc.; 640 km S. of C. Horn; part of Brit. Antarctic Terr. (1962).

South Shields, t., frm. Tyne and Wear, **Eng.**; pt. on S. bank at mouth of R. Tyne; holiday resort; marine engin., new lt. inds.; p. (1991) 83,704.

South Shropshire, l. gov. dist., Shrops., **Eng.**; S. of Shrewsbury and inc. Ludlow; p. (1995) 39,800.

South Somerset, l. gov. dist. inc. Yeovil; p. (1995) 150,400.

South Staffordshire, l. gov. dist., Staffs., **Eng.**; a. bordering W. Midlands conurb.; p. (1995) 104,300.

South Tyneside, met. bor., frm. Tyne and Wear, **Eng.**; comprises Jarrow, Hebburn and South Shields; p. (1995) 156,300.

Southwark, inner bor., London, **Eng.**; S. of R. Thames, incorporating former bors. of Bermondsey and Camberwell; cath.; site of former Globe theatre; p. (1995) 232,000.

South West Africa. See **Namibia.**

Southwick, t., Adur, West Sussex, **Eng.**; on S. cst. 6 km W. of Brighton; p. (1991) 11,067.

Southwold, spt., Waveney, Suffolk, **Eng.**; on E. cst. 13 km S. of Lowestoft; fishing; resort; p. (1991) 3,905.

South Yorkshire, former met. co., **Eng.**; mainly industl. a. E. of Pennines; inc. productive coalfield nr. Barnsley and Doncaster and steel producing ts. of Sheffield and Rotherham; p. (1995) 1,303,900.

Sovetsk (Tilsit), t., **Russia** (since 1945); on R. Niemen, formerly in E. Prussia; timber and paper inds.; famous for Treaty of Tilsit between Napoleon and Russia 1807.

Sowerby Bridge, t., Calderdale, West Yorks., **Eng.**; on R. Calder, 5 km W. of Halifax; woollens; p. (1981) 15,546.

Spa, t., Liège, **Belgium**; mineral springs, resort; gave name to "spas"; p. (1981) 9,619.

Spain, indep. sov. st., Iberia, S.W. Europe; member of EU (1986); lge. land a. takes up 80 per cent of Iberian peninsula and helps to make climate continental; mtnous. interior and narrow coastal strip encourages regional isolation and development of regional culture; civil war 1936–9 hindered modern economic growth; economy based on agr., but much of land is arid and although industl. raw materials in N. Spain and an oil refinery recently constructed at Bilbao, economic development has depended largely upon the spectacular growth of tourism; 42 million visitors each year; Europe's biggest car exporter; inds. attracted by labour costs; monarchy revived 1975; cap. Madrid; a. 504,747 km²; p. (1994) 39,190,000.

Spalding, mkt. t., South Holland, Lincs., **Eng.**; in Fens, 16 km up R. Welland from Wash; agr.; bulb mkt.; agr. machin.; sugar-beet, fruit canning; p. (1991) 18,731.

Spandau, t., Potsdam, **Germany**; previously gr. military ctr.; at confluence of Rs. Havel and Spree; now part of Berlin.

Spanish Guinea. See **Equatorial Guinea.**

Spanish Sahara (Spanish West Africa). See **Western Sahara.**

Sparrows Point, t., Md., **USA**; situated on Chesapeake Bay; impt. iron and steel inds.

Sparta (Spárti), famous anc. c., **Greece**; on R. Eurotas, in Peloponnesus; passed under Roman rule 146 B.C.; modern c. dates from 1834; p. (1981) 14,388.

Spelthorne, l. gov. dist., Surrey, **Eng.**; close to Gtr. London; inc. Staines and Sunbury-on-Thames; p. (1995) 89,400.

Spencer Gulf, lge. inlet, S. **Australia**; penetrates 384 km inland, many impt. pts. along cst. (Whyalla, Pt. Pirie, Pt. Augusta).

Spennymoor, t., Durham, **Eng.**; growing industl. t. S. of Durham; p. (1991) 17,381.

Sperrin Mtns., Strabane, **N. Ireland**; peat-covered schists; Sawell, 683 m.

Spey, R., Moray, Highland, the most rapid in **Scot.**, flows N.E. to Moray Firth; used for hydroelec. power; 171·2 km long.

Speyer, t., Rhineland–Palatinate, **Germany**; Roman origin; Romanesque cath.; famous Diet 1529 condemning Reformation gave rise to term "Protestant"; cas; publishing, engin.; p. (1986) 42,900.

Spitalfields, par., E. London, **Eng.**; formerly noted for silk weaving, introduced by Huguenots 17th cent.; name derives from spital or hospital of St. Mary, founded 12th cent.

Spithead, roadstead, between Portsmouth and I. of Wight, **Eng.**; used by ships of Royal Navy.

Spitsbergen (Svalbard), I. gr. belonging to **Norway**; within Arctic; mtnous.; sealing and whaling; coal mng.; asbestos, copper, gypsum; a. 62,921 km²; p. (1990) 3,405.

Split (Spalato), t., **Croatia** (formerly Yugoslavia); spt. on Adriatic; airport; food processing; p. (1991) 189,388.

Spokane, c., Wash., **USA**; on R. Spokane at falls used for hydroelec. power; timber tr. impt.; flour and saw mills, elec. gds.; lge. aluminium wks.; p. (1990) 177,196 (c.), 361,000 (met. a.).

Spoleto, c., Umbria, central **Italy**; cath., many Roman remains; textiles; p. (1981) 36,839.

Sporades, scattered Is. belonging to **Greece** in Aegean Sea, inc. Skyros, Skiathos and Skopelos.

Spratley Is., **S. China Sea**; cluster of about 50 reefs and sand bars, thought to contain petroleum; ownership disputed by China, Taiwan, Philippines, and Vietnam.

Spree, R., **Germany**; flows W. past Berlin to the Havel at Spandau; 363 km long.

Spremberg, t., Brandenburg, **Germany**; on R. Spree; cas., older part of t. on I.; glass, textiles; p. (1989) 24,547.

Springfield, c., cap. of Ill., **USA**; in rich agr. and coal mng. a.; farming and elec. machin., food processing; home of Abraham Lincoln; p. (1990) 105,227 (c.), 189,550 (met. a.).

Springfield, c., Mass., **USA**; varied mnfs.; US armoury establ. 1794; p. (1990) 156,983 (c.), 530,000 (met. a.).

Springfield, c., Mo., **USA**; agr. ctr.; flour milling, engin.; p. (1990) 140,494.

Springfield, t., Ohio, **USA**; agr. mach., motor lorries; p. (1990) 70,487.

Springs, t., Transvaal, **S. Africa**; E. of Johannesburg; gold mng., engin.; cars, elec. gds.; uranium plant; p. (1980) 170,180 (dist.).

Spurn Head, E. Riding of Yorks., **Eng.**; sand spit at mouth of Humber estuary.

Sri Lanka (Ceylon), indep. rep. (1972) within Brit. Commonwealth (1948); in Indian Oc.; S.E. of India; fertile plains with cash crops of coconuts and rubber (S.W.) but dry in N.; mtnous. interior ameliorates climate where tea cultivation; varied p. composition inc. Sinhalese (70 per cent of p.), Tamils, Burghers (Portuguese and Dutch); agitation for Tamil independence; dependent on exp. of primary produce; inds. growing; cap. and ch. spt. Colombo; a. 65,610 km²; p. (1992) 17,405,000.

Srinagar, t., cap. of Kashmir, **India**; in vale at c. 1,600 m. on Jhelum R. in W. Himalayas; beautiful surrounding cty.; summer resorts; mnfs. silks, woollens, carpets; tourism; p. (1991) 595,000.

Srirangam, t., Tamil Nadu, **India**; on R. Cauvery; temple dedicated to Vishnu; pilgrimage ctr.; p. (1981) 64,241.

Stade, t., Lower Saxony, **Germany**; nr. Hamburg; pt. on R. Schwinge; leather, wood, textiles; p. (1986) 43,000.

Staffa, I. on Inner Hebrides, W. **Scot.**; 10 km N. of Iona, off W. cst. Mull; grand basaltic caverns, inc. Fingal's Cave, 69 m long, 13 m wide, 20 m high.

Stafford, co. t., l. gov. dist., Staffs., **Eng.**; on R. Sow, 24 km N. of Wolverhampton; heavy elec. and other engin.; expanded t.; p. (1995) 123,300 (dist.), (1991) 61,885 t.).

Staffordshire, non-met. co., W. Midlands, **Eng.**; plain drained by R. Trent and tribs.; N. Staffs. coalfield; S. Staffs. coal-field now inc. in W. Midlands met. co.; p. (1995) 1,056,400.

Staffordshire Moorlands, l. gov. dist., Staffs., **Eng.**; borders S. Pennines and inc. Leek, Biddulph and Cheadle; p. (1995) 94,800.

Staines, mkt. t., Spelthorne, Surrey, **Eng.**; on R. Thames, 6 km S.E. of Windsor; linoleum, machin.; nr. birthplace of Matthew Arnold; p. (1991) 51,167.

Stainmore, pass, North Yorks./Durham, **Eng.**; crosses N. Pennines from Greta valley into upper Eden valley; used by main road; alt. 418 m.

Staithes, v., North Yorks., **Eng.**; potash mng.

Stalino. *See* Donetsk.

Stalybridge, t., Gtr. Manchester, **Eng.**; on R. Tame, 13 km E. of Manchester; cotton and wool engin., plastics, rubber, gds., elec. cables; p. (1991) 22,921.

Stamboul. *See* Istanbul.

Stamford, mkt. t., Lincs., **Eng.**; old bldgs., one of 5 Danelaw ts.; agr. inds., elec. gds., plastics; p. (1991) 17,492.

Stamford, c., Conn., **USA**; on shore of Long I. Sound; chemicals, engin.; p. (1990) 108,056 (c.), 203,000 (met. a.).

Stanislav. *See* Ivano-Frankovsk.

Stanley, t., Derwentside, Durham, **Eng.**; former colly. dist.; p. (1991) 18,905.

Stanley, spt., cap of **Falkland Is.**; former whaling port., contains over half p. of Falklands; p. (1991) 1,557.

Stanley Falls. *See* Boyoma Falls.

Stanley Pool. *See* Pool Malebo.

Stanleyville. *See* Kisangani.

Stanlow, Cheshire, **Eng.**; petrol refinery, oil storage, docks, chemicals, linked to Anglesey by pipeline.

Stanovoy Mtns., range of mtns., **Russia**; extending from N. of R. Amur to nr. Sea of Okhotsk.

Stara Zagora, t., central **Bulgaria**; textiles, agr. processing; educational ctr.; p. (1990) 164,553.

Stargard Szczecinski, t., N.W. **Poland** (since 1945); formerly in Pomerania; rly. junc.; metal chemical, and food inds.; devastated in second world war; p. (1989) 69,852.

Start Point, C., nr. Dartmouth, Devon, **Eng.**

Stassfurt, t., Saxony - Anhalt, **Germany**; in gr. potash mng. region; chemicals, machin., metals; p. (1989) 26,466.

Staten I., the most S. point N.Y. st. **USA**; shipyds.; linked with Brooklyn by Verrazano-Narrows bridge (opened 1964); residtl; p. (1990) 378,977.

Staten I., off Tierra del Fuego, **S. America**.

Stavanger, spt., cap. of Rogaland prov., S.W. **Norway**; comm. and industl. ctr.; fish curing and canning; oil refinery at Sola; cath.,airport; p. (1990) 97,328.

Staveley, t., Derbys., **Eng.**; 5 km N.E. of Chesterfield; iron, chemicals, concrete and iron pipes; p. (1991) 27,665.

Stellenbosch, t., Cape Prov., **S. Africa**; 40 km. E. of Cape Town; univ.; wines, saw milling, brick and tile mkg.; p. (1980) 64,100 (dist.).

Stelvio Pass, between **Italy** and **Switzerland**; road pass, alt. 2,762 m.

Stendal, c., Saxony - Anhalt, **Germany**; impt. rly. junct.; sugar, metal and food inds.; cath.; Stendhal (Henri Beyle) took his name from the c.; p. (1989) 50,717.

Stepney. *See* Tower Hamlets.

Sterlitamak, t., Bashkir aut. rep., **Russia**; on S.W. flank of Ural mtns.; impt. oil refineries on "second Baku" oilfield; linked by pipeline to Togliatti; p. (1989) 247,000.

Stettin. *See* Szczecin.

Stettiner Haff, lagoon, **Germany** and **Poland**; separated from Baltic Sea by Is. Usedom and Wollin; receives R. Oder; 56 km long.

Stevenage, t., l. gov. dist., Herts., **Eng.**; 6 km S.E. of Hitchin; first new t. to be designated under the New Towns Act 1946; old t. known in Domesday as Stevenach; agr., lt. engin., elec. goods, chemicals, aircraft parts; p. (1995) 76,100 (dist.), (1991) 76,064 (t.).

Stevenson, burgh, N. Ayrshire, **Scot.**; explosives factory; p. (1991) 10,153.

Steventon, v., Hants., **Eng.**; birthplace of Jane Austen.

Stewart I., S. of S.I., **N.Z.**; a. 1,735 km²; rises to over 900 m; famous for oysters.

Stewarton, burgh, E. Ayrshire, **Scot.**; woollens, carpets; p. (1991) 6,481.

Steyning, v., West Sussex, **Eng.**; on R. Adur, 6 km N. of Shoreham at entrance to gap through S. Downs; residtl.; p. (1991), 8,962 (with Upper Beading)

Steyr, t., **Austria**; at confluence of Rs. Enns and Steyr; industl. ctr.; historic bldgs.; p. (1991) 39,542.

Stif (Sétif), t., dep., N.E. **Algeria**; agr. ctr. for surrounding plateaux; grain, livestock; phosphates in a.; p. (1987) 170,182 (t.), 997,482 (dep.).

Stilton, v., Cambs., **Eng.**; 10 km S.W. of Peterborough; famous for cheese; p. (1991) 2,219.

Stirling, royal burgh, unit. auth. created in 1996, formerly part of Central Region, **Scot.**; stretches from Grampian mtns. to Central Lowlands; t. lies on R. Forth in gap between Campsie Fells and Ochil Hills; cas., univ.; coal mng., engin., concrete, wool, rubber prods.; p. (1991) 30,515 (t.), (1995) 82,280 (unit. auth.).

Stirlingshire, historic co., central **Scot.**; now divided between E. Dunbartonshire, Falkirk, N. Lanarkshire and Stirling.

Stockholm, c., cap. of **Sweden**; freeport; on I. at outlet of L. Malar; called the "Queen of the Baltic" for the beauty of its surroundings; comm. ctr.; machin., textiles, leather, sugar, chemicals; univ. and many academic institutions; chosen Cultural Capital of Europe, 1998; p. (1992) 684,576.

Stockport, t., met. dist., Gtr. Manchester, **Eng.**; on R. Mersey, S.E. of Manchester; cotton manmade fibres, engin.; p. (1995) 290,600 (dist.), (1991) 132,813 (t.).

Stocksbridge, t., South Yorks., **Eng.**; iron and steel; p. (1991) 13,182.

Stockton, t., Cal., **USA**; R. pt. on San Joaquin R.; agr. processing, farm implements; p. (1990) 210,943 (t.), 481,000 (met. a.).

Stockton-on-Tees, mkt. t. 6 km W. of Middlesbrough, **Eng.**; unit. auth. created in 1996, formerly part of Cleveland; inc. t. of Billingham; impt. iron and steel inds., plywood; first rly. for passenger traffic opened 1825 between Stockton and Darlington; 18th cent. town hall; racecourse; p. (1995) 178,100 (unit. auth.), (1991) 83,576 (t.).

Stoke Newington. *See* **Hackney**.

Stoke-on-Trent, c., unit. auth. of **Stoke** created in 1997, formerly part of Staffs., **Eng.**; at S.W. foot of the Pennines; formed in 1910 by union of the five towns of Arnold Bennett's novels, Hanley, Burslem, Tunstall, Longton, and Fenton (with Stoke-on-Trent); ceramics, iron and steel, engin., brick and tile works, precast concrete, rubber prods.; p. (1995) 254,300 (former dist.), (1991) 266,243 (c.).

Stolberg, t., N. Rhine–Westphalia, **Germany**; E. of Aachen; metals, glass, wood, chemicals; p. (1986) 56,400.

Stolp. *See* **Slupsk**.

Stone, mkt. t., Staffs., **Eng.**; on R. Trent, 11 km S. of Stoke-on-Trent; footwear, tiles, porcelain, scientific glassware; p. (1991) 12,305.

Stonehaven, t., burgh, Aberdeenshire, **Scot.**; fish. pt. on E. cst., 22 km S. of Aberdeen, distilling, net mftg.; p. (1991) 9,445.

Stonehenge, prehistoric gr. of monumental stones, on Salisbury Plain, Wilts., **Eng.**; date of erection est. between 2100–1600 B.C.

Stornoway, spt., burgh, Western Isles, **Scot.**; on E. cst. of I. of Lewis, Outer Hebrides; ctr. Harris Tweed ind.; fishing ctr.; p. (1991) 5,975.

Stour, R., Kent, **Eng.**; flows past Canterbury to Pegwell Bay; 64 km long.

Stour, R., Somerset, Dorset, **Eng.**; trib. of R. Avon; 88 km long.

Stour, R., Suffolk and Essex, **Eng.**; flows E. to sea at Harwich; 67 km long.

Stour, R., Hereford and Worcs./West Midlands, **Eng.**; trib. of R. Severn; 32 km long.

Stourbridge, t., West Midlands, **Eng.**; on R. Stour; 14 km W. of Birmingham; brick and glass wks.; p. (1991) 55,624.

Stourport-on-Severn, mkt. t., Worcs., **Eng.**; at confluence of Rs. Stour and Severn; carpets, iron and steel gds., porcelain, ceramics; old canal and R. pt.; p. (1991) 18,283.

Stowmarket, t., Mid Suffolk, **Eng.**; on R. Gipping, 18 km N.W. of Ipswich; I.C.I. paint factory; p. (1991) 13,229.

Strabane, t., l. gov. dist., **N. Ireland**; agr. ctr., shirt mkg.; p. (1991) 36,141 (dist.), 11,670 (t.).

Straits Settlements, former Brit. crown col. of Penang, Malacca, and Singapore, established 1867, dissolved 1946. *See* **Malaysia, West.**

Stralsund, spt., Mecklenburg - West Pomerania, **Germany**; opposite Rügen I.; grain tr., machin., metals, fish smoking, shipbldg.; p. (1981) 74,421.

Strangford Lough, arm of sea, Down and Ards, **N. Ireland**; 29 km long, 10 km wide at entrance.

Stranraer, royal burgh, Dumfries and Galloway, **Scot.**; at head of Loch Ryan; steamer service to Larne, N. Ireland; creameries, brewing, knitwear; cas.; mkt.; p. (1991) 11,348.

Strasbourg, c., cap. of Bas-Rhin dep., E. **France**; impt. pt. in Rhine valley on Ill R., 16 km S. of confluence with Rhine; terminus of Marne–Rhine and Rhône–Rhine canals; industl., comm. and cultural ctr. of economically impt. Alsace region; food processing and varied mnfs.; historic c., with many fine bldgs., inc. cath., univ., imperial palace; surrendered to Germany

1871, recovered 1919; meeting-place of European Parliament; p. (1990) 255,937 (c), 388,483 (met.a.).

Stratford. *See* **Newham**.

Stratford-on-Avon, t., l. gov. dist., Warwicks., **Eng.**; on R. Avon; birthplace of Shakespeare; memorial theatre, library; many bldgs. ass. with Shakespeare; tourist ctr.; lt. inds.; p. (1995) 110,500 (dist.), (1991) 22,231 (t.).

Strathmore, lowland belt, central **Scot.**; flanked to N. by Grampians, to S. by Sidlaw and Ochil Hills; drained by Rs. Earn, Tay, Isla, S. Esk; famous for cereals and small fruits; length 96 km, width 11–16 km.

Strathspey, valley of the Spey, **Scot.**; 112 km long.

Stratton and Bude, North Cornwall, **Eng.**; 19 km S. of Hartland Point; resort; p. (1991) 5,979.

Straubing, t., Lower Bavaria, **Germany**; agr. mkt. ctr.; machin.; p. (1986) 41,600.

Strawberry, R., Utah, **USA**; on E. slopes of Wasatch mtns. 128 km S.E. of Salt Lake City; dammed to supply irrigation water led through tunnel under Wasatch mtns. to 259 km^2 cultivable land round L. Utah.

Street, t., Mendip, Somerset, **Eng.**; at foot of Polden Hills, 11 km S.W. of Wells; footwear, leather; p. (1991) 10,539.

Stretford, t., Gtr. Manchester, **Eng.**; borders Manchester Ship Canal; inc. Trafford Park industl. estate; residtl.; Lancashire co. cricket ground, Manchester United football ground at Old Trafford; p. (1991) 43,953.

Stromboli, I., Lipari Is., Tyrrhenian Sea, N. of Sicily, **Italy**; active volcano, alt. 927 m.

Stromness, burgh, Mainland, Orkney Is., **Scot.**; 21 km W. of Kirkwall; mkt., fish. pt.; p. (1991) 1,890.

Stronsay, I., Orkney Is., **Scot.**; p. (1991) 382

Stroud, mkt. t., l. gov. dist., Gloucs., **Eng.**; on R. Frome, in Cotswolds; former ctr. of impt. cloth ind. in W. Eng.; woollens, dyes, plastics, engin.; p. (1995) 107,300 (dist.), (1991) 38,835 (t.).

Sturminster Newton, t., North Dorset, **Eng.**; impt. cattle mkt. on Stour R.; creameries; p. (1991) 2,155.

Sturts Stony Desert, a. N.W. of S. **Australia**; named after Charles Sturt, explorer.

Stuttgart, c., cap. of Baden-Württemberg, **Germany**; on Neckar R.; cas., cath., rly. junc.; industl. and comm. ctr.; publishing, science-based inds.; oil refinery nearby; p. (1990) 583,700.

Styria, prov., **Austria**; borders Slovenia on S.; mtnous. with forests and pastures; lignite and iron mng., inds. around cap. Graz; grain, wine, fruit, stock-rearing; tourism; p. (1991) 1,184,593

Suakin, former pt., **Sudan**, N.E. Africa; on Red Sea; now used only for pilgrim traffic to Jeddah; replaced by Pt. Sudan.

Subotica, t., Serbia, **Yugoslavia**; univ.; agr. ctr. with Hungarian culture; agr. processing; expanding industl. ctr.; p. (1991) 100,219.

Suceava, t., S. Bukovina, N.E. **Romania**; mkt. t. on Suceava R.; once the residence of Moldavian princes; p. (1992) 114,355.

Suchow. *See* **Zuzhou.**

Sucre, c., cap. of Chuquisaca dep. and *de jura* cap. of **Bolivia** (La Paz is *de facto* cap.); in valley of Andes at 2,600 m; agr. ctr., oil refining; p. (1992) 130,952.

Sucre, st., **Venezuela**; on Caribbean cst.; coffee and cacao; fishing impt.; fish canning at cap. Cumaná; a. 11,800 km^2; p (1991) 722,707.

Sudan, The, rep., N.E. Africa; climatic transition from N. desert to rainy equatorial S.; mainly plateaux, dissected by Nile R. system; sporadic conflict between N. and S.; 3 southern provs. now form an autonomous reg.; long staple cotton, grown in irrigated areas, provides most valuable exp.; gum arabic from lge. forest areas; food processing; dams constructed on Atbara and Blue Nile Rs.; suffering from famine, 1998; protracted civil war; cap. Khartoum; a. 2,530,430 km^2; p. (1994) 28,200,000.

Sudbury, t., Ont., **Canada**; nickel, copper mng.; refining; univ.; p. (1991) 92,727 (c.), (1986) 148,877 (met. a.).

Sudbury, t., Babergh, Suffolk, **Eng.**; on R. Stour, 19 km N.W. of Colchester; p. (1991) 19,512.

Sudene, terr., N.E. **Brazil**; government sponsored economic development.

Sudetenland, region of **Czech Rep.** bordering Germany, until 1945 German-speaking; annexed by

Hitler 1938, recovered by Czechoslavakia 1945; named after Sudeten mtns.

Sudeten Mtns. or **Sudetes**, mtn. range along borders of **Czech Rep.** and **Poland**; separating Bohemia and Moravia from Silesia; minerals.

Suez (Es-Suweis), spt. and prov., **Egypt**; the anc. Arsinoë; at head of G. of Suez (arm of Red Sea) and S. entrance of Suez canal, which crosses the isthmus of Suez to the Mediterranean at Port Said; Port Tewfiq adjoining has quay and docks; declined during closure of canal 1967–75; oil refining, fertilisers; p. (1990) 392,000 (c.), (1991) 376,000 (prov.).

Suez Canal, ship canal, **Egypt**; connects Mediterranean Sea (Pt. Said) with Red Sea (Suez) through Ls. Manzala, Timsah, and Bitter; length 162 km; closed after Arab-Israeli war of June 1967; reopened 1975; tunnel links Egypt and Israel (1980); widening and deepening of canal to accommodate larger oil tankers, complete (1980).

Suez, G., Red Sea; N.W. arm of Red Sea between Arabian desert and Sinai peninsula, **Egypt**; southern approach to Suez canal; length 304 km., width varies from 19–40 km.

Suffolk, non-met. co., E. Anglia, **Eng.**; bounded on E. by N. Sea, drowned coastline; rises to 90 m in E. Anglian Heights in W.; impt. agr. a., lge. farms, mixed farming; inds. based on agr.; many expanded ts. in S.; co. t. Ipswich; p. (1995) 656,800.

Suffolk Coastal, l. gov. dist., E. Suffolk, **Eng.**; lge. rural a. inc. ts. of Leiston-cum-Sizewell, Saxmundham, Aldeburgh, Woodbridge and Felixstowe; p. (1995) 116,000.

Suhl, t., Suhl, **Germany**; once famous for armaments; motor-cycles; p. (1981) 49,849.

Sui, Baluchistan, **Pakistan**; natural gas; pipeline to Karachi.

Sukhumi, spt., **Georgia**; agr. processing; resort; p. (1990) 121,700.

Sukkur, t., **Pakistan**; major bridging point of R. Indus; 368 km N.E. of Karachi; dam for irrigation; thermal sta.; p. (1981) 193,000.

Sula Is., I. gr. in Molucca Sea, E. of Sulawesi, **Indonesia**; little developed.

Sulawesi (Celebes), I., **Indonesia**; mtnous., lge. forests; copra, coffee, gold, nickel, copper, asphalt; ch. pts. Menado, Makasar; a. 189,484 km²; p. (1983) 11,112,200.

Sulaymäniyah, t., **Iraq**; in hill dist. nr. Iran border; p. (1985) 279,424.

Sullum Voe, Shetland Is., **Scot.**; oil terminal and receiving ctr. for N. Sea oil.

Sultanabad. See Arak.

Sulu Is., prov. **Philippines**; archipelago between Borneo and the Philippines; inc. over 400 volcanic Is. and coral islets; a. 2,461 km²; under US control 1899–1940; p. (1990) 469,971.

Sumatra, I., **Indonesia**; relatively underdeveloped; growing p.; main development in Cultuurgebied, rubber, oil palm, sisal, tobacco; impt. oil deposits and new oil refineries; much resettlement in 1990s from other islands; a. 473,607 km²; p. (1981) 30,928,500.

Sumba or **Sandalwood I.**, S. of Flores, **Indonesia**; horse-breeding; rice, maize, tobacco, timber, cinnamon; cap. Waingapu; a. 11,150 km².

Sumbawa, I., **Indonesia**; between Flores and Lombok; wet climate, sparse p.; a. (inc. nearby Is.) 13,572 km²; p. (1980) 320,000.

Sumgait, t., **Azerbaijan**; on Caspian Sea; 40 km N.W. of Baku; metallurgical ind.; chemicals; p. (1990) 234,600.

Sumy, t., **Ukraine**; engin., chemicals, textiles, agr. processing; p. (1990) 296,000.

Sunbury-on-Thames, t., Spelthorne, Surrey, **Eng.**; W. of London; residtl., water wks., gravel pits; petrol research establishment; p. (1991) 27,392.

Sunda Is., **Indonesia**; between S. China Sea and Indian Oc.; form two grs., Greater Sunda Is., inc. Java, Sumatra, Borneo, Sulawesi, Banka, and the Lesser Sunda Is. (renamed Nusa Tenggara 1954) inc. Bali, Lombok, Sumbawa, Timor.

Sundarbans, The, tract of forest and swamps, fringing the delta of the Ganges, **India/Bangladesh**; 130 km wide; rice grown in N.; tigers and crocodiles found in S.

Sunda Strait, between Java and Sumatra, **Indonesia**; 21 km wide, contains the volcanic I. of Krakatao.

Sunday I. or **Raoul I.**, lgst. and only inhabited of

Kermadec Is., **N.Z.**; 32 km in circuit; meteorological and radio sta.

Sundbyberg, t., **Sweden**; adjoins Stockholm; chemicals, paper; p. (1983) 26,985.

Sunderland, C. (1992), spt., met. dist., Tyne and Wear, **Eng.**; at mouth of R. Wear; precision and aero-engin., clothing, shipbldg.; Nissan car plant; p. (1995) 295,800 (dist.), (1991) 183,310 (c.).

Sundsvall, spt., Västernorrland, **Sweden**; on a wide bay of the Baltic nr. Hernösand; timber and wood-pulp inds.; p. (1992) 94,329.

Sungari. See **Songhua R.**

Sunnyvale, t., Cal., **USA**; ctr. of fruit-growing a.; lt. inds.; p. (1990) 117,229.

Superior, t., Wis., **USA**; at head of L. Superior; tr. in grain, timber, coal; shipbldg. and flour mills; oil refining; p. (1980) 29,571.

Superior, L., N. America; lgst. sheet of fresh water in the world; lies between **Canada** and **USA**; one of chain of gr. Ls. in St. Lawrence system; outlet to L. Huron by St. Mary's R.; receives waters of St. Louis, Pigeon and Nipigon; impt. waterway; a. 82,880 km².

Surabaya, spt., Java, **Indonesia**; ch. naval base; handles nearly half Indonesia's tr.; shipbldg., oil refining, food processing; p. (1983) 2,289,000.

Surakarta (Solo), Java, **Indonesia**; on Solo R.; tr. ctr. for agr. region; former sultan's palace; p. (1980) 469,888.

Surat, c., Gujarat, **India**; on R. Tapti; gold and textile ctr.; notable as first English trading post 1612; plague (1994); p. (1991) 1,499,000.

Surbiton, Gtr. London, **Eng.**; on R. Thames, inc. in Royal Borough of Kingston-upon-Thames; residtl.; lt. engin., elec. components.

Suresnes, t., Hauts-de-Seine dep., **France**; sub. of Paris; cars, chemicals; p. (1982) 35,744.

Suriname (Dutch Guiana), former self-gov. terr. of Neth.; indep. 1975; S. America; sub-tropical climate; p. concentrated on cst. where rice, sugar, and citrus fruits grown; great agr. potential; main exp. bauxite (80 per cent of total exp. though recently declining); iron ore, timber, hydroelectr. oil; cap. Paramaribo; a. 163,265 sq. km; p. (1994) 402,900.

Surinumu Dam, 48 km from Port Moresby, **Papua New Guinea**; part of hydroelectric scheme; opened 1963.

Surrey, non-met. co., S. **Eng.**; S. of R. Thames inc. part of N. Downs; serves as dormitory a. and recreational dist. for London; mkt. gardening, dairying; co. t. Guildford; p. (1995) 1,044,400.

Surrey Heath, l. gov. dist., Surrey, **Eng.**; based on Bagshot, Frimley and Camberley; p. (1995) 82,100.

Susa. See **Sousse**.

Susquehanna, R., N.Y., Penns., and Md., **USA**; flows to Chesapeake Bay through highly industl. a.; routeway W. from Philadelphia and Baltimore across Appalachian mtns.; not navigable; hydroelectric power; 675 km long.

Sussex. See **East Sussex**, and **West Sussex**.

Susten Pass, alpine road, alt. 2,225 m between Hasli Tal and Reuss valley, links Bernese Oberland with Gotthard road, **Switzerland**.

Sutherland, historic co., N.W. **Scot.**, now part of Highland.

Sutlej, R., **Pakistan**; rises in the Himalayas and flows to the R. Indus; used for lge. scale irrigation; 1,600 km long.

Sutton, outer bor., Greater London, **Eng.**; inc. former bors. of Beddington and Wallington, Sutton and Cheam, and Carshalton; residtl.; p. (1995) 174,400.

Sutton Coldfield, t., West Midlands, **Eng.**; 10 km N.E. of Birmingham; residtl.; hardware, plastics; p. (1991) 106,001.

Sutton-in-Ashfield, t., Ashfield, Notts., **Eng.**; 5 km S.W. of Mansfield; lt. engin.; hosiery; former coalmng. dist.; p. (1991) 37,890.

Suva, c., cap. of Fiji Is.; on Viti Levu I.; fine harbour; exp. coconut prods., sugar; international airport; p. (1986) 71,608.

Suwalki, t. and prov., N.E. **Poland**; nr. Lithuanian bdy.; timber, grain, woollens; p. (1989) 59,684 (t.), 467,100 (prov.).

Suwannee, R., Fla., and Ga., **USA**; flows to G. of Mexico; known as Swanee River, 400 km long.

Suzhou (Soochow), c., Jiangsu, **China**; nr. Shanghai; former treaty pt.; textile ctr.; p. (1984) 695,500.

Svalbard. See **Spitsbergen**.

Svendborg, spt., Fyn, **Denmark**; exp. dairy prods.; textiles, machin.; p. (1990) 41,030.

Sverdlovsk *See* Yekaterinburg.

Svir, R., **Russia**; flows between L. Onega and L. Ladoga; hydroelectric power; navigable; 200 km long.

Svishtov (Sistova), t., N. **Bulgaria**; R. pt. on Danube in vine-growing dist., nr. Romanian bdr.; cath., univ.

Swabia, historic region, mediaeval duchy, **Germany**; now forms part of Baden–Württemberg and Bavaria; contains Black Forest.

Swabian Alps, mtns., Baden–Württemberg, **Germany**; inc. the Swabian Jura range between valleys of Neckar and Danube.

Swadlincote, t., South Derbys., **Eng.**; 5 km E. of Burton-on-Trent; potteries, engin., clothing; p. (1991) 36,859.

Swaffham, mkt. t., Breckland, Norfolk, **Eng.**; fruit canning; p. (1991) 5,332.

Swale, R., North Yorks., **Eng.**; joins R. Ure to form R. Ouse, 96 km long.

Swale, l. gov. dist., mid Kent, **Eng.**; nr. Thames estuary inc. Sittingbourne, Faversham and I. of Sheppey; p. (1995) 117,900.

Swanage, mkt. t., Dorset, **Eng.**; on bay, E. cst. I. of Purbeck; seaside resort; p. (1991) 9,947.

Swansea, c., spt., **Wales**; on Swansea Bay; univ.; grew with exp. of coal; now imports minerals; copper and zinc refining; steel, aluminium, wire, plastics; unit. auth. created in 1996 from former l. gov. dists. of Lliw Valley and Swansea; inc. Gower Penin.; p. (1991) 171,083 (c.), (1995) 230,600 (unit. auth.).

Swatow. *See* Shantou.

Swaziland, indep. kingdom, S. Africa; within Brit. Commonwealth (1968), govt. based on tribal communities; bordered by S. Africa on S., W., and N. and by Moçambique on E.; four north-south regions; high, middle, low veld and Lebombo escarpment; rainfall increases with alt.; agr. basis of economy and sugar impt. exp., but iron-ore major exp.; asbestos mng., food processing inds.; cattle raising main internal activity; cap. Mbabane; a. 17,363 km²; p. (1993) 818,000.

Sweden, kingdom, Scandinavia, N.W. Europe; divided for admin. purposes into 24 cos.; cap. c. Stockholm; mtnous. in N. and S. with central lowland belt containing major agr. a. and lge. proportion of p.; sm. home mkt. makes for dependency on exps., especially of mftg. products and minerals; inc. high-grade iron-ore from Kiruna and Malmberget, N. of Arctic circle; development of high-value science-based inds.; furniture, porcelain and glass mnfs. have international reputation; social democratic st. since 1932; remained neutral in second world war; highly advanced system of social security; joined EU 1995; a. 449,792 km²; p. (1995) 8,816,381.

Swidnica (Schweidnitz), t., Walbrzych, **Poland** (since 1945); formerly in Lower Silesia; metals, elec. machin., leather, textiles; p. (1989) 62,424.

Swilly, Lough, N.E. Donegal, **R.o.I.**; arm of Atl. Oc. between Fanad Point and Dunaff Head; extends 40 km inland.

Swindon, t., unit. auth. created in 1997, formerly part of Wilts., **Eng.**; in upper Thames Valley (Vale of White Horse), 43 km S.W. of Oxford; impt. rly. junc.; rly. workshops closed (1986); mkt. for local dist.; heavy engin., textiles, tobacco; expanded t.; one of largest housing projects in Europe; ctr. for micro-electronics inds.; p. (1991) 145,236.

Swinoujscie (Swinemünde), spt., N.W. **Poland** (since 1945); formerly in Pomerania; on I. of Usedom (Uznam), Baltic Sea; spt. for Szczecin; spa and summer resort; fishing; p. (1989) 42,932.

Swinton and Pendlebury, ts., Gtr. Manchester, **Eng.**; 8 km W. of Manchester; cotton spinning, engin.; p. (1991) 43,155.

Switzerland, confederation, central Europe; landlocked mtnous. st. with major physical features dominated by Alpine mtn. system; divided into 26 cantons and half-cantons for purposes of govt.; 3 official languages: German (72 per cent), French (20 per cent), Italian (6 per cent) in addition to Romansch; like Norway, major natural resource is water power; industl. specialisation on precision engin., especially watch and clock mnfs.; agr. in valleys with impt. output of dairy prod., transhumance between mtn. pastures and valley bottoms; tourism provides valuable source of income; neutral; voted to remain non- member of U.N. (1986); cap. Berne; a. 41,310 km²; p. (1995) 7,020,000.

Sydney, c., cap. of N.S.W., **Australia**; pt. and c. built around natural harbour of Pt. Jackson, crossed by S. Harbour Bridge and bordered bymany impt. bldgs. and parks (Opera House, Government bldgs.); one of best harbours on E. cst., pt. developed with improved transport; site of first European settlement; contains 61 per cent of state p., 22 per cent of Australia's p.; covers vast a. as suburbs grow rapidly; caths., 3 univs., airpt. on Botany Bay where heavy inds. developing; services most impt. employment, vast range of inds.; p. (1993) 3,713,500 (met. a.).

Sydney, spt., Cape Breton I., Nova Scotia, **Canada**; coal mng. and exp.; steel, chemicals; p. (1991) 26,063.

Syktyvkar, c., Komi, aut. rep., **Russia**; R. pt. on Vychegda R.; shipyds., sawmilling, engin.; cultural ctr. of Komi people; p. (1989) 232,000.

Sylhet, t., **Bangladesh**; on Surma R. in tea growing dist.; fertilisers; p. (1991) 169,000.

Syracuse, c., S.E. Sicily, **Italy**; old t. on Ortygia I., off E. cst., modern t. on mainland, connected by bridge; founded c. 734 B.C.; ctr. of anc. Greek culture; exp. olive oil, oranges, lemons, wine; chemicals at Priolo; many Greek and Roman remains; p. (1992) 126,800.

Syracuse, c., N.Y., **USA**; on Erie Barge canal; impt. industl. ctr. for chemicals, electronics, machin.; formerly salt-producing ctr.; univ.; p. (1990) 163,860 (c.), 660,000 (met. a.).

Syrdarya, one of main Rs. of central Asia; formed in Ferghana Valley in **Uzbekistan**; flows through **Tajikistan** and **Kazakhstan** to Aral Sea; not navigable but used for irrigation and hydroelectric power; 2,400 km long.

Syria (Syrian Arab Rep.), S.W. Asia; on E. cst. Mediterranean; much of a. mtnous. and semidesert; climate hot, but cold winters in highland interior; 32 per cent p. engaged in agr. which provides 20 per cent nat. income; mainly pastoral, but grains, fruit and cotton grown in well watered Euphrates R. valley and along cst.; oil exp. since 1968; phosphate mines in Palmyra a.; textiles, food processing in Aleppo and cap. Damascus; a. 187,086 km²; p. (1995) 14,186,074.

Syriam, t., **Myanmar**; nr. Rangoon; main oil refining ctr. of cty.

Syros or **Syra**, I., one of Cyclades, Aegean Sea, S. **Greece**; heath-covered; most populous of Cyclades; ch. t. Hermoupolis.

Syzran, c., **Russia**; impt. R. pt. on Volga nr. confluence with Syzran R.; rly. ctr.; engin., oil refining; p. (1989) 174,000.

Szazhalombatta, t., **Hungary**; on Danube, 24 km S. of Budapest; lgst. oil refinery in rep.; oil supplied through Druzhba pipeline.

Szczecin (Stettin), c., N.W. **Poland** (since 1945); formerly cap. of Prussian prov. of Pomerania; impt. spt. at mouth of R. Oder; deep-sea fishing base; shipbldg., metallurgy, engin., chemicals, technical univ.; p. (1989) 411,275.

Szczecin, prov., **Poland**; borders Baltic Sea; drained by R. Oder; mainly agr.; a. 31,339 km²; p. (1989) 964,300.

Szechwan. *See* Sichuan.

Szeged, t., **Hungary**; nr. confluence of Rs. Tisza and Maros; anc. R. pt. destroyed by floods 1879, since rebuilt; univ.; tr. in cereals, paprika; textiles; p. (1997) 166,000.

Szekesfehérvár, t., **Hungary**; nr. Budapest; mkt. t., with aluminium and metal inds., food processing; known since Roman times; once cap. of Hungarian kings; p. (1997) 106,000.

Szeping. *See* Siping.

Szolnok, t., **Hungary**; pt. on R. Tisa, E. of Budapest; route ctr.; machin., paper, cellulose, chemicals; p. (1997) 78,000.

Szombathely, t., W. **Hungary**; rly. ctr.; agr. machin., textiles, shoes; birthplace of St. Martin of Tours (c. A.D. 316); p. (1997) 84,000.

T

Tabasco, coastal st., **Mexico**; on Bay of Campeche; low-lying; rapid development with drainage of swamps; cash crops of cacao, coffee, sugar, tobacco; major petroleum deposits aiding industl. development; cap. Villa Hermosa; a. 25,335 km²; p. (1990) 1,501,183.

Table Bay, inlet of Atl., cst. of C. of Good Hope, S. **Africa**; site of Cape Town.

Table Mountain, Cape Prov., **S. Africa**; nr. Cape Town; alt. 1,082 m.

Tabor, t., **Czech Rep.**; S. of Prague, on R. Luznice; rly. junc.; textiles, tobacco; p. (1984) 33,757.

Tabora, t., central **Tanzania**, E. Africa; at junc. of rlys. from Dar es Salaam and L. Victoria; p. (1985) 134,000.

Tabriz, c., **Iran**; cap. of Azerbaijan; metal inds., carpets, leather, soap; famous blue mosque; univ.; impt. oil refining ctr.; p. (1986) 994,377.

Tachira, st., **Venezuela**; mtnous. inland st. bordering Colombia; coffee; cap. San Cristobal; a. 11,100 km²; p. (1990) 859,861.

Tacna, t., cap. of Tacna prov., **Peru**; in fertile valley of mtnous. region; agr. t.; p. (1990) 150,200.

Tacna, prov. and t., **Peru**; mtnous. and arid, some irrigated valleys; transferred from Chile by treaty 1929; subject to earthquakes; a. 12,769 km²; p. (1993), 218,353 (prov), 174,335 (t.).

Tacoma, spt., Wash., **USA**; on Puget Sound; shipping, fishing; grew with Alaskan and Pac. tr.; port inds. and agr. processing; p. (1990) 176,664 (c.), 586,000 (met. a.).

Tacuarembo, dep., **Uruguay**; N. of Rio Negro R., which provides hydroelectricity; mainly agr.; cap. T.; a. 15,812 km²; p. (1985) 82,809.

Tadoussac, v., Quebec, **Canada**; on R. Saguenay, where it enters St. Lawrence R.; tourist ctr.; settlement dates from 1599; p. (1986) 838.

Taegu, c., **S. Korea**; textiles, agr. processing; p. (1990) 2,228,834.

Taejon, t., **S. Korea**; S. of Seoul; fish, petroleum; p. (1990) 1,062,084

Taff, R., S.**Wales**; rises in Brecon Beacons, flows S.E. across coalfield to Bristol Channel at Cardiff; 64 km long.

Tafilalet, Morocco, N. Africa; oasis of the Sahara, E. of Atlas; dates.

Tagab, c., **Afghanistan**; in Panjshir R. valley N.W. of Kābul.

Taganrog, c., **Russia**; spt. on Sea of Azov; iron and steel, engin.; site of fortress founded by Peter the Great 1698; birthplace of Chekhov; p. (1989) 292,000.

Tagliamento, R., N.E. **Italy**; rises in Carnic Alps, flows W. into Adriatic; 160 km long.

Tagus, R., **Spain** and **Portugal**; rises in E. Spain and flows across the Meseta to Atl. Oc. at Lisbon where there is a magnificent bridge; its estuary forms one of the finest harbours in Europe.

Tahiti, ch. I., Society Is., **Fr. Polynesia**; contains Papeete, main admin. ctr. of Fr. Oceania; fertile alluvial belt; exp. copra, phosphates, vanilla; tourism; a. 1,041 km²; p. (1983) 115,820.

Taichow. See **Taizhou.**

Taichung, t., co., **Taiwan**; agr. mkt.; food processing; p. (1995) 655,196 (c.), 849,549 (co.).

Taif, t., Hejaz, **Saudi Arabia**; 80 km E. of Mecca; 1,800 m a.s.l.; summer resort.

Tai Hu, L., Jiangsu, **China**; focus of intensive system of small canals and waterways, 96 km N. of Shanghai; a. c. 260 km².

Taimyr Peninsula, N. cst., Siberia, **Russia**; terminates with C. Chelyuskin; occupies most of Taimyr National Area, inhabited by nomadic Samoyeds; p. (1986) 54,000.

Tainan, t., co., S.W. cst. of **Taiwan**; former cap.; univ.; p. (1995) 705,940 (c.), 705,940 (co.).

Taipei, c., co., cap. of **Taiwan**; on cst. plain in N. Taiwan, nucleus of major industl. a.; major transport ctr.; international airpt.; univ.; p. (1995) 2,639,283 (c.), 3,297,579 (co.).

Taiwan (Formosa), I., off cst. of S.E. China; beautiful I. with intensive agr. on W. cst.; most densely populated cty. in the world; part of Japan 1895–1945; returned to China 1945; occupied by Nationalist government since 1949; growing political isolation; USA aid has built growth economy, textiles, plastics, electronics exp. to USA esp.; cap. Taipei; a. 35,975 km²; p. (1998) 21,500,000.

Taiyüan, c., cap. of Shanxi prov., N. **China**; on Fen R.; walled c.; univ.; ctr. of rapid industl. development; integrated iron and steel plant; chemicals, machin., paper, textiles; p. (1992) 1,980,000.

Taiz, t., **Yemen**; in fertile valley; former cap.; p. (1987) 178,043.

Taizhou (Taichow), c., Jiangsu prov., **China**; rice ctr.; p. (1984) 161,300.

Tajikistan, CIS, former constituent rep., USSR;

borders China and Afghanistan; mainly mtnous., inc. Pamirs and Turkestan and part of highly cultivated Ferghana Valley; cattle breeding; cotton main cash crop; impt. oil and hydroelec. power resources; cap. Dushanbe; a. 144,263 km²; p. (1994) 5,704,000.

Takamatsu, t., **Japan**; N. cst. Shikoku; ferry terminal; univ.; tourism; p. (1990) 329,684.

Takaoka, t., Honshu, **Japan**; ctr. of rice tr.; lacquer wk.; cars; p. (1990) 175,466.

Takapuna, c., N.I., **N.Z.**; connected by motorway to Auckland; residtl. ctr.; p. (1987) 70,000.

Takasaki, t., Honshu, **Japan**; radiation chemistry research ctr.; textiles; p. (1990) 236,463.

Taklimakan Shamo, desert, W. **China**; basin of inland drainage; home of the Turko people; surrounded by a ring of oases.

Takoradi. See Sekondi-Takoradi.

Talaud I., Indonesia; N.E. of Sulawesi; copra; underdeveloped; a. 1,279 km².

Talavera de la Reina, t., Toledo prov., central **Spain**; on Tagus R.; ceramics; scene of battle 1809; p. (1981) 69,307.

Talca, t., cap. of Maule region., **Chile**; S. of Santiago; lge. mftg. ctr.; matches, footwear, paper, and flour mills, foundries; p. (1992) 171,467.

Talcahuano, spt., **Chile**, nr. Concepción; naval sta.; steel plant at Huachipato; fish processing, oil refining; p. (1992) 246,566.

Talien. See Lushun.

Tallahassee, t., Fla., **USA**; univ.; timber-based inds.; p. (1990) 124,773.

Tallinn, spt., cap. of **Estonia**; on G. of Finland; diverse inds. inc. radio equipment; mediaeval architecture; p. (1991) 502,400.

Tamale, t., cap. of Kaduna st., **Ghana**, W. Africa; admin. ctr.; cotton milling, peanut processing; p. (1984) 83,653.

Tamar, R., Tasmania, **Australia**; formed at confluence of N. Esk and S. Esk at Launceston, flows into Bass Strait nr. George Town.

Tamar, R., Devon and Cornwall, **Eng.**; flows S. to Plymouth Sound; 72 km long.

Tamatave. See **Toamasina.**

Tamaulipas, st., **Mexico**; on G. of Mexico, S. of Texas; petroleum is main resource; fishing along lagoon cst.; cotton, livestock; cap. Ciudad Victoria; a. 79,593 km²; p. (1990) 2,244,208.

Tambao, t., **Bourkina Fasso**; rich deposits of manganese could diversify economy and provide valuable exports; development depends on railway extension.

Tambov, c., cap. of Tambov oblast, **Russia**; on Tsna R.; regional ctr. serving agr. dist.; engin.; p. (1989) 305,000.

Tameside, met. dist., Gtr. Manchester, **Eng.**; comprises Dukinfield, Ashton-under-Lyne, Hyde and Mossley; p. (1995) 221,500.

Tamil Nadu (formerly Madras), st., **India**; on S.E. cst. of peninsula; home of Tamils; crossed by R. Cauvery; dry crops; acute water shortages relieved by water and sewerage development plan; cst. ts. Madras, Madura; a. 130,357 km²; p. (1991) 55,858,946.

Tampa, c., Fla., **USA**; popular winter resort, cigar factories, phosphates, electronics; fruit growing and canning; p. (1990) 280,015 (c.), 2,067,959 (met. a. with St. Petersburg-Clearwater).

Tampere (Tammerfors), t., S. **Finland**; on rly. between Helsinki and Vaasa; textiles, leather, paper, based on local hydroelec. power; cath.; p. (1993) 176,149.

Tampico, spt., **Mexico**; on R. Panuco, 14 km from G. of Mexico; exp. petroleum; oil refining, fish processing, chemicals; tourism; p. (1990) 271,636.

Tamworth, t., N.S.W., **Australia**; impt. service and shopping ctr. for N. Tablelands; p. (1981) 29,657.

Tamworth, t., l. gov. dist., Staffs., **Eng.**; on R. Tame, 8 km S.E. of Lichfield; anc. cas.; lt. engin.; expanded t.; p. (1995) 72,200 (dist.), (1991) 68,440 (t.).

Tana, lge. freshwater L., N.W. **Ethiopia**, nr. Gondar; source of Blue Nile, surrounded by marsh, papyrus swamp.

Tana, R., **Kenya**; rises nr. Mt. Kenya and flows to Indian Oc.; impt. elephant habitat in valley; 5 major hydro-elect. sta..; 800 km long.

Tananarive. See Antananarivo.

Tandridge, l. gov. dist., Surrey, **Eng.**; S. of Gtr. London, inc. Caterham and Godstone; p. (1995) 77,000.

Tanga, spt., **Tanzania,** E. Africa; on plateau overlooking Tanga Bay; rly. terminus; new plywood plant; p. (1988) 187,634.

Tanganyika, gr. L., E. **Central Africa;** lies in Gt. Rift Valley; c. 672 km long, 24–32 km wide; second lgst. L. in Africa and except for L. Baykal deepest L. in world; c. 823 m a.s.l.; discovered by Burton and Speke 1858, explored by Livingstone and Stanley 1871.

Tangier, free pt., **Morocco,** N. Africa; on Strait of Gibraltar; no longer internationalised zone but integral part of kingdom of Morocco; summer cap.; shipyard; cigarettes, fishing; p. (1982) 266,346.

Tangshan, c., Hebei prov., **China;** impt. industl. ctr.; steel, machin.; textiles, cement, oil refining; devastated by a series of earthquakes (1976); p. (1990) 1,500,000.

Tanimbar Is., Indonesia; gr. of Is. in Banda Sea, S. Moluccas; forests, swamps; maize, rice, coconuts, sago.

Tanta, t., Lower **Egypt;** 88 km N. of Cairo; impt. rly. junc.; religious fairs; cotton processing; univ. proposed; p. (1986) 334,505.

Tanzania, rep., E. cst. Africa; inc. Is. of Zanzibar and Pemba, united since 1964; narrow coastal plain rises to inland plateau (Mt. Kilimanjaro, 5,895 m, hgst. peak in Africa); climate varies with alt., tropical in Zanzibar, temperate inland; predominantly subsistence agr., maize, millet, groundnuts, livestock; comm. crops inc. sisal, sugar, cotton, coffee; cloves on Is., especially Pemba; food processing, textile inds.; 5-year planning system to assist economic development; 12 National Parks (inc. Serengeti); old cap. Dar es Salaam; new cap. Dodoma (since 1974); a. 939,706 km²; p. (1994) 29,700,000.

Taormino, resort, E. Sicily, **Italy;** 230 m above sea at foot of Mt. Etna; magnificent scenery and anc. ruins.

Tapachula, c., Chiapas st., S. **Mexico;** on Pac. cst. lowlands; comm. ctr. for agr. dist.; p. (1990) 222,282.

Tapti, R., W. **India;** flows W. to G. of Cambay from Betul dist., Madhya Pradesh; 702 km.

Tarai, marshy, jungle tract at foot of Himalayas, **India,** Nepal; barrier to economic development of Nepal, now much modified and reduced in area by human occupation.

Taranaki, reg., N.I., **N.Z.;** impt. stock rearing and dairying a.; offshore oil and gas fields; a. 9,713 km²; p. (1991) 107,222.

Taranto, t., Lecce, **Italy;** on G. of Taranto, inlet of Ionian Sea; maritime arsenal with gr. comm. and industl. interests; strong cas.; steel wks.; cement; oil refinery; famous for its oyster and mussel fisheries; p. (1992) 230,207.

Tarapacá, region, N. **Chile;** cap. Iquique; hot, arid desert; nitrate deposits; a. 55,270 km²; p. (1992) 341,112.

Tarascon, t., Bouches-du-Rhône dep., **France;** connected by bridges with Beaucaire on opposite bank of R. Rhône; old cas.; famous festival; p. (1982) 11,024.

Tarawera Mtn., volcanic peak, N.I., **N.Z.;** 305 m; in Hot Springs dist.; eruption 1886 destroyed L. Rotomahana (water later returned to form bigger and deeper L.).

Tarbes, t., cap. of Hautes-Pyrénées dep., **France;** on R. Adour; cath.; p. (1990) 50,228.

Tarifa, t., **Spain;** on Gibraltar Strait; most S. point of mainland of Europe; fish tr., cereals, oranges, wines; p. (1981) 15,220.

Tarija, dep. **Bolivia;** part of Gran Chaco rising to W.; extensive agr. and forests; cap. T.; a. 64,196 km²; p. (1988) 246,600.

Tarija, t., cap. of T. prov., **Bolivia;** alt. 1,906 m; cath., univ.; mkt. t.; p. (1992) 90,000.

Tarim Basin, depression, Xinjiang, **China;** desert with oases; crossed by Silk Road; anc. civilisation; state farms for wheat, millet, maize, cotton.

Tarn, dep., S. **France;** watered by Tarn and its tribs.; between Central Massif and basin of Aquitaine; mainly agr.; cap. Albi; a. 5,781 km²; p. (1990) 342,700.

Tarn, R., **France;** trib. of R. Garonne; rocky gorge 50 km long in its upper course; 376 km long.

Tarn-et-Garonne, dep., W. **France;** alluvial plain

formed by Rs. Tarn, Garonne and Aveyron; mainly agr.; cap. Montauban; a. 3,730 km²; p. (1990) 200,200.

Tarnobrzeg, t. and prov., S.E. **Poland;** sulphur mng. and processing; p. (1989) 45,702 (t.), 594,200 (prov.).

Tarnow, t. and prov., **Poland;** E. of Kraków; industl. ctr.; lge. nitrogen factory; synthetic fibres, metallurgy; cath.; p. (1989) 120,639 (t.), 664,900 (prov.).

Tarpon Springs, t., Fla., **USA;** pt.; main source of sponges in USA.

Tarragona, prov., **Spain;** on Mediterranean; vineyards and agr.; cap. Tarragona; a. 6,283 km²; p. (1991) 540,360.

Tarragona, spt., cap. of T. prov., **Spain;** at mouth of R. Francoli; exp. agr. prod. of Ebro valley; cath.; many Roman remains, inc. aqueduct; liqueur; p. (1991) 112,655.

Tarsus, anc. c., S. **Turkey;** nr. Adana; orange and citrus groves; ruined Roman temple; birthplace of St. Paul; p. (1990) 168,654.

Tartu c., **Estonia;** pt. on Emayygi R.; rly. junc.; famous univ. founded 1632; agr. machin., tobacco ind.; p (1991) 115,300.

Tashkent, c., cap. of **Uzbekistan;** cultural, industl. and scientific ctr. of central Asia; on Trans-Caspian rly. in fertile Ferghana valley; univ.; diverse inds.; terminus of gas pipeline; p. (1990) 2,093,900.

Tasman Bay, lge inlet, S.I., **N.Z.;** penetrates N. cst., between Separation Point and D'Urville I.; enclosed by mtns., sheltered, fertile, coastal fringe; ch. ts. Nelson, Motueka; gives name to dist.; p. (1991) 36,416.

Tasman Glacier, S.I., **N.Z.;** one of the lgst. in the world.

Tasmania (formerly **Van Diemen's Land**), I., st., **Australia;** smallest and least populous st. of Australia, second to be colonised (in 1803); mountainous with rugged cst.; temperate climate aids hydro-electric development and consequent rapid industl. ex-pansion; plans for hydro-electric sta. on Franklin R. to help relieve high unemployment but fiercely opposed because of region's rare and striking natural beauty; 9 Nat. Parks; mng.; pastoral agr.; for-estry; cap. Hobart; a. 67,897 km²; p. (1993) 472,100.

Tasman Sea, Australia; part of Pac. Oc. between Australia and New Zealand.

Tatabánya, t., N. **Hungary;** lignite mng. ctr.; aluminium refining, chemicals; p. (1997) 72,000.

Tatar, aut. rep., **Russia;** in middle Volga valley; wooded steppeland; extensive oil deposits and natural gas fields; cap. Kazan; a. 67,988 km²; p. (1989) 3,641,700.

Tatra Mtns., highest mtn. gr. of W. Carpathians, on border of **Slovakia** and **Poland;** highest peak Gerlach in Slovakia, 2,664 m; mountaineering and winter sports.

Tatung. See Datong.

Taubaté, t., São Paulo st., **Brazil;** industl. ctr.; p. (1985) 205,900.

Taunton, co. t., Somerset, **Eng.;** on R. Tone at W. end of Vale of Taunton; old cas.; with Wellington forms l. gov. dist. of **Taunton Deane;** p. (1995) 98,700 (dist.), (1991) 55,856 (t.).

Taunton, t., Mass., **USA;** cotton, iron foundries, machin., plastics; p. (1980) 45,001.

Taunus, mtn. range, Hesse, **Germany;** between Rs. Lahn and Rhine and Main; forests, vineyards and spas.

Taupo, L., N.I., **N.Z.;** lgst. L. in N.Z.; geysers, hot springs in vicinity; 40 km by 27 km; gives name to dist.; p. (1991) 30,721.

Tauranga, t. and dist., N.I., **N.Z.;** spt. on Bay of Plenty; tourism; fishing; p. (1991) 67,333 (dist.).

Taurus Mtns., range, S. **Turkey;** rise to over 3,660 m.

Tavastehus. See Hämeenlinna.

Tavistock, mkt. t., West Devon, **Eng.;** on R. Tavy; anc, stannary t.; Drake born nearby; p. (1991) 10,222.

Taw, R., Devon, **Eng.;** flows from Dartmoor to Barnstaple Bay; 80 km long.

Tawe, R., S. **Wales;** flows into Swansea Bay; 104 km long.

Taxco, t., **Mexico;** alt. 1,700 m; gold- and silver-mng.; tourist ctr.; anc. Aztec t.; p. (1990) 86,811.

Taxila, ruined c., **Pakistan;** nr. Rawalpindi; anc. seat of learning; ruins of Buddhist univ.

Tay, R., Scot.; flows S.E. from Loch Tay in Perth and Kinross, to Firth of Tay; longest R. in Scot., 188 km; salmon fisheries.

Tay, Firth of, lge. inlet, E. cst. **Scot.;** extends inland almost to Perth.

Tayeh, t., Hupeh, **China;** lies to S. of Yangtze R., 67 km S.E. of Wuhan; impt. iron-ore deposits; supplies Hwangshih; iron and steel inds., heavy engin.

Tayport, burgh, Fife, **Scot.;** at entrance to Firth of Tay; opposite Broughty Ferry; linen, jute; p. (1991) 3,346.

Tbilisi (Tiflis), c., Georgia; route ctr. on Kura R.; major admin., economic and cultural ctr. of Transcaucasia; machin., textiles, tanneries, furniture, food processing; power from hydroelectric power stas.; anc. tr. ctr.; some mediaeval fragments in c. ctr.; p. (1990) 1,267,500.

Tczew (Dirschau), t., Gdansk prov., N. **Poland;** pt. on Vistula; rly. junc.; agr. implements; p. (1989) 58,887.

Team Valley, Tyne and Wear, **Eng.;** impt. trading estate.

Tebessa, t., dep., N.E. **Algeria;** in Atlas mtns., at 851 m; mkt.; carpets; phosphate deposits nearby; p. (1987) 107,559 (t.), 409,317 (dep.).

Tees, R., N. **Eng.;** rises on Cross Fell, Cumbria, flows E. to N. Sea between Hartlepool and Redcar; heavy inds. in lower section; 112 km long.

Teesdale, l. gov. dist., Durham, **Eng.;** Pennine a. inc. Barnard Castle; p. (1995) 24,200.

Teesport, oil refinery, between Redcar and Middlesbrough, Redcar and Cleveland, **Eng.**

Teesside, former admin. dist., N.E. **Eng.;** inc. Middlesbrough, Redcar, Thornaby-on-Tees, Stockton-on-Tees, Billingham, and Eston.

Tegal, spt., Java, **Indonesia;** textiles, sugar refining; lge. dam nearby; p. (1980) 131,728.

Tegucigalpa, c., cap. of **Honduras;** on R. Choluteca at 976 m; inter-ocean highway connects with Caribbean and Pac. Oc.; former ctr. of silver mng.; inc. Comayaguela, the modern part of c., where the nat. univ. is situated; p. (1991) 670,100.

Tehran (Teheran), c., cap. of **Iran,** 112 km S. of Caspian Sea; mftg. and comm. ctr.; modern bldgs.; gas pipeline to north; international airpt.; univ.; car assembly, textiles, chemicals, glass; new oil refinery; ctr. for more than 90 per cent of all industl. firms in Iran; p. (1986) 6,022,078.

Tehuantepec, Isthmus of, separates G. of Mexico from Pac. Oc. at narrowest point of **Mexico;** width 200 km.

Teifi, R., S. **Wales;** rises in Cambrian mtns., flows S.W. to Cardigan Bay; 150 km long.

Teign, R., Devon, **Eng.;** flows to sea at pt. of Teignmouth from Dartmoor; picturesque estuary; 48 km long.

Teignbridge, l. gov. dist., S. Devon, **Eng.;** lower T. valley and ts. of Dawlish, Teignmouth, Newton Abbot and Ashburton; p. (1995) 114,700.

Teignmouth, t., Teignbridge, Devon, **Eng.;** at mouth of R. Teign, 21 km S. of Exeter; resort; revival of pt. with ball clay exp.; p. (1991) 13,528.

Tekirdag, t. and prov., **Turkey;** on Sea of Marmara, W. of Istanbul; former Greek settlement; p. (1985) 63,215 (t.), (1990) 468,842 (prov.).

Tel Aviv-Jaffa, c., Israel; on Mediterranean; lgst. c. of cty.; financial and cultural ctr.; univ.; founded by Zionists 1909; p. (1992) 353,200.

Telemark, co., **Norway;** borders Skagerrak; mtnous., lake-covered, much forested; hydroelectric power forms basis for electrochemical inds.; a. 15,118 km²; p. (1990) 162,869.

Telford, new t. (1963), Shropshire, **Eng.;** 32 km W. of Wolverhampton; p. (1981) 103,411.

Tellicherry, t., spt., Kerala, **India;** exp. pepper; lge. college; furniture; p. (1981) 75,561.

Telok Betong, spt., Sumatra, **Indonesia;** exp. pepper, agr. products.

Tema, pt. (opened 1962), nr. Accra, **Ghana;** deepwater harbour, oil refinery, aluminium smelter; impt. industl. development; p. (1984) 60,767.

Teme, R., on border of Wales and Hereford and Worcs., **Eng.;** trib. of R. Severn; 112 km long.

Temir-Tau, c., Kazakhstan; on Nura R.; industl. ctr.; iron, steel, synthetic rubber, soda; lge. thermal power sta.; p. (1990) 213,100.

Temuco, c., cap. of Araucania region., **Chile;** cath.;

tr. in cereals, apples, timber; Araucanian Indian mkt.; p. (1992) 240,880.

Tenali, t., Andhra Pradesh, **India;** nr. Guntur in Krishna delta; p. (1991) 143,836.

Tenasserim, div., lower **Myanmar;** on Thailand border; extends along Isthmus of Kra; tin and rubber; a. 92,945 km². p. (1983) 917,628.

Tenby, mkt. t., Pembrokeshire, **Wales;** on W. side of Carmarthen Bay, Bristol Channel; seaside resort; walled cas. t.; p. (1991) 5,619.

Tendring, l. gov. dist., E. Essex, **Eng.;** inc. cstl. ts. of Harwich, Frinton, Clacton and Brightlingsea; p. (1995) 131,600.

Tenerife, I., Canary Is.; volcanic landscapes and mild climate attracts tourists; cap. Santa Cruz; a. 2,025 km².

Tennessee, R., Tenn., U.S., **USA;** lgst. and most impt. branch of Ohio R.; valley once liable to flooding, now controlled by dams, and improved by the Tenn. Valley Authority; 1,251 km long.

Tennessee, st., **USA;** "Volunteer St."; admitted to Union 1796; st. flower Iris, st. bird Mockingbird; rises to Appalachians in E., crossed by Tennessee R. and tribs.; a. of heavy rainfall and severe soil erosion necessitated the public Tenn. Valley Authority scheme of conservation, dam bldg., and afforestation; cap. Nashville; a. 109,412 km²; p. (1990) 4,877,185.

Tenterden, mkt. t., Kent, **Eng.;** 13 km N. of Rye; grew with wool tr., church with famous tower; p. (1991) 6,803.

Teófilo Otoni, t., Minas Gerais, **Brazil;** semi-precious stone polishing; p. (1985) 126,200.

Tepic, c., cap. of Nayarit st., **Mexico,** comm. ctr. for agr. dist.; nr. Sanguaney volcano; p. (1990) 238,101.

Teplice, watering pl., **Czech Rep.;** N.W. of Prague; textile and hardware inds.; mineral springs; p. (1984) 53,508.

Teramo, c., cap. of T. prov., **Italy;** 24 km from Adriatic; route and agr. ctr.; cath.; textiles; the anc. Interamnium; p. (1981) 51,092.

Terek, R., N. Caucasia, **Russia;** flows to Caspian Sea; used for irrigation and hydroelectric power in lower course; 592 km long.

Teresina, t., cap. of Piauí st., **Brazil;** comm. ctr.; lt. inds.; p. (1991) 598,449.

Terezópolis, t., Rio de Janeiro, **Brazil;** health resort; textiles; p. (1985) 115,900.

Terneuzen, t., Neth.; on W. Schelde R.; pipeline from Pernis; p. (1993) 35,429.

Terni, t., Perugia, **Italy;** among the Apennines; iron and steel wks., arms factory; cath.; p. (1992) 108,150.

Ternopol (Tarnopol), t., Ukraine; E. of Lvov; rly. junc., mkt.; agr. machin., food inds.; p. (1990) 211,600.

Terrassa, t., Barcelona, **Spain;** textile ctr.; p. (1991) 153,519.

Terre Adélie, part of Fr. Antarctic terr., S. **Indian Oc.;** research stn.; est. a. 424,400 km².

Terre Haute, t., Ind., **USA;** coal, natural gas, flour, paper, glass, foundries; p. (1990) 57,483.

Teruel, t., cap. of Teruel prov., **Spain;** on R. Turia; walled t.; cath.; p. (1987) 27,475, (1991) 141,006 (prov.).

Test Valley, l. gov. dist., W. Hants., **Eng.;** stretches from Andover to Romsey; p. (1995) 105,900.

Tete, t., central **Moçambique;** on R. Zambesi; ctr. of coalfield; iron-ore, graphite, radioactive materials.

Tetovo, t., Macedonia, formerly Yugoslavia; chemicals, electro-metallurgy, textiles.

Tetuan, ch. spt., **Morocco,** N. Africa; walled t. p. (1982) 199,615.

Teviot, R., Borders, **Scot.;** trib. of R. Tweed; 59 km long.

Tewkesbury, mkt. t., l. gov. dist., Gloucs., **Eng.;** on R. Avon, close to confluence with R. Severn; Norman abbey; p. (1995) 76,200 (dist.), (1991) 9,488 (t.).

Texarkana, t., Texas and Ark., **USA;** bdy. passes down middle of main street; timber and cotton region; total p. (1984) 32,900 (t.), 118,500 (met. a.).

Texas, st., S.W. **USA;** "Lone Star St."; admitted to Union 1845; st. flower Bluebonnet, st. bird Mocking bird; second lgst. st. by a.; borders Mexico; dry plains in W., humid cst. in E.; problems of soil erosion yet leading agr. st.; leading producer of petroleum and natural gas; cap. Austin; a. 692,408 km²; p. (1990) 16,986,510.

Texel, one of the W. Frisian Is., **Neth.**; scene of several naval battles; p. (1991) 12,726.

Thailand (Siam), kingdom, S.E. Asia; 4 main regions; parallel N.–S. hill ranges (2,400 m) and valleys in N. producing teak; rice growing, fertile plain of Chao Phraya R. in ctr.; thinly populated E. plateau, drained by Mekong; S. coastal strip on G. of Siam; monsoon climate; predominantly agr., accounting for 60 per cent of p. and 60 per cent of exports; fifth lgst. exporter of foodstuffs in the world, mainly rice, tapioca, rubber and maize to U.S.A., Japan & Singapore esp.; desire to conserve rainforest now resulting in the intensification of agr.; recent offshore gas discoveries; mnfg. development centres on cap. Bangkok; tourism and fishery increasingly impt.; a. 519,083 km², p. (1993) 58,336,072.

Thailand, G. of, lge. inlet, S. China Sea; sheltered with shallow water; length 616 km N.W. to S.E.

Thal Desert, Pakistan; W. of Punjab; now irrigated for wheat and cotton.

Thame, mkt. t., South Oxford, **Eng.**; on R. Thame, 11 km S.W. of Aylesbury; p. (1991) 10,806.

Thames, R., **Eng.**; rises in Cotswold hills and flows past Oxford, Reading, Windsor, and London to the N. Sea; tribs. inc. Windrush, Cherwell, Thame, Kennet, Colne, Lea, and Roding; estuary impt. industl. a. with many oil refineries; flood barrier at Silvertown in Woolwich (1983), 336 km long.

Thameshaven, lge. oil refinery, Essex, **Eng.**; on N. cst. of Thames estuary 13 km below Tilbury.

Thana, t., Maharashtra, **India**; textiles, chemicals; p. (1991) 803,000.

Thanet, I. of, lge. promontory, N.E. extremity of Kent, **Eng.**; formed by bifurcation of R. Stour; also forms l. gov. dist. of **Thanet**, inc. Margate, Ramsgate, and Broadstairs; p. (1995) 125,300.

Thanjavur, t., Tamil Nadu, **India**; silks, carpets, jewellery, inlaid metals; impt. Brahman ctr.; p. (1991) 202,013.

Thar Desert, on bdy. of **India** and **Pakistan**; covers slopes between N.W. Deccan and R. Indus; barren, lack of Rs. or level land prevents irrigation; crossed by caravan routes.

Thebes, t., of Boeotia, in anc. **Greece**; Mycenaean site; destroyed by Alexander the Great 335 B.C.; modern c. of Thivai occupies site; p. (1981) 18,712.

Thebes, t. of anc. **Egypt**; on banks of Nile; site now partly occupied by vs. Karnak and Luxor; archeological discoveries in Valley of the Kings 1922, inc. tomb of Tutankhamun.

The Entrance, t., N.S.W., **Australia**; tourist resort on waterway from L. Tuggerah to Tasman Sea; fishing; p. (1981) 37,891.

Thermopylae, celebrated pass between Mt. Oeta and the sea, N.E. **Greece**; heroic battle between Spartans and Persians 480 B.C.

Thessaloniki, c., **Greece**; spt. at head of G. of T.; with fiscal free zone; second c. of Greece; impt. route and industl. ctr.; univ.; p. (1991) 383,967.

Thessaly, prov., central **Greece**; fertile plain drained by R. Piniós; mainly agr.; a. 13,489 km²; p. (1991) 734,846.

Thetford, t., Breckland, Norfolk, **Eng.**; on Little Ouse; industl. estate for London overspill; fruit and vegetable canning, pulp mftg., engin.; p. (1991) 20,058.

Thetford Mines, t., Quebec, **Canada**; asbestos mng. ctr.; p. (1986) 18,561.

Thienen (Tirlemont), t., Brabant prov., **Belgium**; ctr. of Belgian beet-sugar refining; captured by Marlborough 1705; p. (1981) 32,620.

Thiès, t., **Senegal**; rly. ctr. and wkshps.; aluminium, phosphate quarrying; p. (1992) 201,350.

Thimphu, t., cap. **Bhutan**; hydroelectric plant; 176 km road link to Phuntsholing (Sikkim) 1968; p. (1993) 30,340.

Thionville, t., Moselle dep., N. **France**; in Lorraine ironfield conurb.; metallurgical and chemical inds.; p. (1990) 40,835 (t.), 132,413 (met.).

Thira (Santorine), volcanic I., Cyclades, **Greece**; wine prods.; max. alt. 567 m; a. 75 km².

Thirlmere, L., Cumbria, **Eng.**; 5 km long; furnishes part of water supply of Manchester.

Thirsk, mkt. t., Hambleton, North Yorks., **Eng.**; in wide gap between Pennines and Cleveland Hills, 11 km S.E. of Northallerton; racecourse; p. (1991) 6,860.

Thompson, R., B.C., **Canada**; trib. of R. Fraser; forms impt. routeway through Rocky mtns.; 448 km long.

Thon Buri, c., **Thailand**; on R. Menam opposite Bangkok; second c. of T.; former cap., "Temple of Dawn"; p. (1991) 264,201.

Thorez (Chistyakovo), **Ukraine**; coal mng.; p. (1990) 88,200.

Thornaby-on-Tees. See Teesside.

Thornbury, mkt. t., S. Gloucs., **Eng.**; 16 km N. of Bristol; aircraft mftg.; expanded t.; Oldbury Magnox nuclear power sta.; p. (1991) 12,108.

Thornton Cleveleys, t., Wyre, Lancs., **Eng.**; 6 km N.E. of Blackpool; resort; p. (1991) 28,061.

Thórshavn, c., on Stromo I.; cap. of **Faroe Is.**; fish. pt.; anc. fortress; lighthouse; p. (1986) 15,287.

Thousand Isles, gr. of over 1,500 Is. in St. Lawrence R. which extend up-river for c. 48 km from Brockville to Gananoque, at junc. of L. Ont. and St. Lawrence R.; partly in N.Y. st. and partly in Canada.

Thrace, anc. name of terr. in S.E. Europe, part of which has been added to **Greece**; successively under Macedonian, Roman, Byzantine, and Turkish rule, before passing to Greece; consists of districts of Euros, Rhodope, Xanthi; tobacco; a. 8,586 km²; p. of dep. (1991) 338,005.

Three Gorges Dam (China). On Yangtze R., the largest planned dam in the world (1·3 miles long, 610 feet high). It will hold 39·3 billion cubic metres of water. Completion due, 2009.

Three Rivers, l. gov. dist., S.W. Herts., **Eng.**; close to London and inc. Rickmansworth and Chorleywood; p. (1995) 84,000.

Thule (Qaanaaq), N.W. **Greenland**; 1,600 km from N. Pole; American air base and site of ballistic missile early warning sta.; spt. open 2–3 months per annum; p. (1990) 846.

Thumba, Kerala, **India**; space science and technological ctr.

Thun, L., Berne can., **Switzerland**; occupies valleys of R. Aare where it leaves Alpine region; separated from L. Brienz by deltaic neck of land on which is Interlaken; a. 98 km².

Thun, t., Berne, **Switzerland**; on N.W. end of L. Thun; cas. on hill above t.; tourism; p. (1990) 38,124.

Thunder Bay, t., Ontario **Canada**; formed from Port Arthur and Port William; pt. on N.W. cst. of L. Superior; grain exp. ctr.; p. (1991) 113,746 (c.), (1986) 122,217 (met. a.).

Thurgau, can., N.E. **Switzerland**; on L. Constance, bordered by R. Rhine; prosperous agr. a.; inds. ass, with textiles; cap. Frauenfeld; a. 1,005 km²; p. (1990) 205,900.

Thuringia, Land, Germany; bordered by Bavaria, Saxony-Anhalt, Lower Saxony, and Hesse; drained by Rs. Saale and Werra; crossed by Thüringer Wald and extending to Harz mtns.; fertile arable agr. a.; cap. Erfurt; pop. (1992) 2,572,000.

Thuringian Forest or **Thüringer Wald**, forested range of hills **Germany**; rising to 982 m in Beerberg; famous for romantic scenery and legends; resorts.

Thurles, mkt. t., Tipperary, **R.o.I.**; on R. Suir; agr. processing; cath., cas.; p. (1986) 7,049.

Thurrock, t., l. gov. dist. Essex, **Eng.**; on Thames, nr. Tilbury; oil refining, metal refining, cement, paper board; p. (1995) 131,600 (dist.).

Thurso, burgh, Highland, **Scot.**; nr. Dounreay; anc. stronghold of Vikings; p. (1991) 8,488.

Tianjin (Tientsin) c. and mun., **China** 112 km S.E. of Beijing; impt. pt. using poor harbour on Hai R.; industl. ctr., oil refining, textiles, elec. instruments, steel rolling mills, machine tools, chemicals, tobacco, food processing; univ.; p. (1990) 8,830,000 (met. a.), (1992) 5,090,000 (c).

Tiaret, t., dep., W. **Algeria**; N. Africa; in strategic pass; walled; agr. mkt.; cereals, wool, cattle; p. (1987) 574,786 (dep.).

Tiber, R., **Italy**; flows from Apennines to Mediterranean, through Rome; 352 km long.

Tiberias, t., **Israel**; on Sea of Galilee (L. Tiberias); agr. ctr.; health resort with medicinal springs.

Tibesti, mtns., on bdy. between **Libya** and **Chad**, Equatorial Africa; barren in spite of slight rainfall; mainly above 1,800 m max. alt. 3,401 m.

Tibet (Xizang Zizhiqu), aut. region, **China**; lofty plateau called "the roof of the world" its lowest plains being 3,660 m a.s.l.; semi-desert; network of roads inc. one across Himalayas to Katmandu;

pastoral agr. sheep; arable agr. in R. valleys, especially Zangbo valley, wheat, barley, fruit, vegetables; tr. of wool, musk, gold, skins, drugs traditionally carried by yaks which can stand intense cold; salt, alluvial gold, radioactive ores; cap. Lhasa; a. 1,217,308 km²; p. (1990) 2,220,000.

Ticino, R. **Switzerland** and **Italy;** trib. of Po; forms S. approach to St. Gotthard Pass; irrigation in lower course; length 240 km.

Ticino, can., **Switzerland;** on S. slopes of central Alps, bordering Italy; contains parts of Ls. Maggiore and Lugano; mainly pastoral agr., but wine, corn, tobacco in valleys; industl. a., in S. based on hydroelectric power, chemicals, metallurgy; many tourist resorts inc. Locarno, Lugano; cap. Bellinzona; a. 2,813 km²; p. (1990) 286,700.

Ticonderoga, V., N.E., N.Y., **USA;** resort between Ls. George and Champlain; L. George falls provide hydroelectric power for paper mill; local graphite used in pencil ind.; p. (1980) 2,938.

Tideswell, t., Derbys., **Eng.;** tourist ctr.; limestone quarrying in a.; lge. 14th cent. church known as "cath. of the Peak." p. (1991) 1,717.

Tidore I., Moluccas, **Indonesia;** volcanic; densely populated; coffee, tobacco, spices, fruit; a. 78 km².

Tien Shan (Celestial Mtns.) mtn. chain, central Asia, along **China–Russia** border; highest peak 7,320 m; source of Syr-Dar'ya, Chu, Ili and many other Rs.

Tierra del Fuego, archipelago, southernmost part of S. America; separated from Patagonia by Strait of Magellan; W. **Chile** and E. prov. of **Argentina;** timber, pastoral agr., sheep; oilfield at Rio Grande; mng.; a. of Argentinian prov. 21,571 km²; p. (1991) 69,369.

Tigre, st., **Ethiopia;** formerly an independent kingdom; cap. Adua; severe drought 1982–3.

Tigris, R., S.W. **Asia;** rises in Taurus mtns. S. Turkey, flows through Iraq where it is joined by the Euphrates and proceeds to Persian G.; comm. routeway; dams for flood control and irrigation; many of the earliest cs. located in valley; 1,840 km long.

Tijuana, t., Baja Cal. st., **Mexico;** resort catering for Americans; casinos, race-tracks, bull-fights; p. (1990) 742,686.

Tiksi, t., **Russia;** Arctic spt., at mouth of Lena R.; local coal deposits; linked by air and R; to Yakutsk.

Tilburg, c., N. Brabant, **Neth.;** nr. Breda; woollens, textiles, tobacco, leather; p. (1994) 163,383 (c.), 236,838 (met. a.).

Tilbury, pt., Essex, **Eng.;** on N. Bank of R. Thames 32 km E. of London; within Port of London; major container terminal; p. (1991) 11,658.

Tilimsen (Tlemcen), t., dep., N. W. **Algeria;** picturesque medieval t.; agr. ctr. in fertile region; textiles, furniture, handicrafts; p. (1987) 107,632 (t.), 707,453 (dep.).

Tillicoultry, burgh, Clackmannan, **Scot.;** on Devon R.; woollen and worsted fabrics, paper; p. (1991) 5,269.

Tilsit. See **Sovetsk.**

Timaru, c. and dist., S.I., **N.Z.;** E. cst. spt., exp. frozen foods; fishing; regional ctr. for S. Canterbury; p. (1991) 34,208 (dist.).

Timbuktu. See **Tombouctou.**

Timisoara, c., W. **Romania;** comm., industl. and educational ctr.; univ., 2 caths., cas.; once a frontier fortress; p. (1992) 334,278.

Timmins, t., Ont., **Canada;** gold mng. declining; vast deposits of copper, zinc, silver, discovered 1964; timber inds., brewing; p. (1986) 46,657.

Timok Basin, Serbia, **Yugoslavia;** industl. region; coal mng., copper smelting, chemicals, glass, food processing; arable agr., vines.

Timor, lgst. of Lesser Sunda Is., **E. Indies;** divided politically until 1975 into W. Timor part of Indonesia and East Timor; now both part of Indonesia; a. 33,748 km²; p. (1990) 4,017,000.

Timor Sea, that part of the Indian Oc. N.W. of W. Australia, and S. of Timor I.

Tinogasta, t., Catamarca prov., **Argentina;** in E. foothills of Andes, 192 km N.W. of Catamarca; impt. copper mines.

Tintagel, v., Cornwall, **Eng.;** ruined Norman cas.; reputed birthplace of King Arthur; tourism.

Tintern, v., Monmouthshire, **Wales;** Cistercian abbey.

Tinto, R., Huelva prov., S.W. **Spain;** in Andalusia; flows W. to Alt. Oc.; gives its name to Rio Tinto copper mng. region which it crosses; 104 km long.

Tipperary, inland co., Munster, **R.o.I.;** drained by Rs. Suir and Shannon; mtnous., Knockmealdown and Galty mtns.; fertile Golden Vale in S.W.; dairying, sugar-beet; divided into N. and S. Ridings; co. t. Clonmel; p. (1986) 59,522 (N.R.), 77,097 (S.R.).

Tipperary, t., Tipperary, **R.o.I.;** 46 km S.E. Limerick; dairy processing; p. (1986) 5,033.

Tirana, t., cap. of **Albania;** agr. processing, engin., clothing, glass; univ.; airport; virtual anarchy (1997); p. (1991) 251,000.

Tiraspol, c., S.E. **Moldova;** on R. Dniester; agr. processing ctr.; heat and power sta. recently constructed; p. (1990) 183,700.

Tiree, I., Inner Hebrides, Argyll and Bute, **Scot.;** off cst. of Mull; 22 km long, up to 10 km wide; sm. freshwater lochs and prehistoric forts; p. (1991) 768.

Tirgu Mures, c., **Romania;** on R. Mures; ch. t. of Magyar aut. region in Transylvania; old fort, Gothic Calvinist cath.; agr. tr. and processing; p. (1992) 163,625

Tiruchirapalli (Trichinopoly), c., Tamil Nadu, S.E. **India;** on R. Cauvery; rly. ctr.; textiles, cigars, goldsmithery; p. (1991) 387,000.

Tirunelveli (Tinnevelly), c., Tamil Nadu, S.E. **India;** agr. tr. ctr. with sugar refinery; p. (1991) 135,825.

Tiruppur, t., Tamil Nadu, **India;** nr. Coimbatore; p. (1981) 165,223 (t.), 215,859 (met. a.).

Tisa (Tisza), R., **E. Europe;** rises in E. Carpathians, W. Ukraine, flows across Hungary into Yugoslavia where it joins the Danube 72 km below Novi Sad; ch. tribs. Koros and Mures; length c. 960 km; navigable in part.

Titicaca, L., **S. America;** between two ranges of Andes, on borders of Bolivia and Peru; 3,812 m a.s.l.; highest lge. L. in world; max. depth 300 m; crossed by steamers; fishing; a. c. 8,300 km².

Titograd. See **Podgorica.**

Titov Veles, t., central **Macedonia,** formerly Yugoslavia; on R. Vardar, and main rly. to Belgrade; recent industl. growth; textiles; p. (1981) 64,799.

Tiverton, mkt. t., Mid Devon, **Eng.;** 22 km N. Exeter; once famous for lace; textiles, engin.; p. (1991) 14,805.

Tivoli, the anc. Tibur, nr. Rome, **Italy;** on Aniene R., magnificent situations; hydroelec. power; resort; remains of Hadrian's villa; p. (1981) 50,969.

Tjirebon (Cheribon), spt., Java, **Indonesia;** on N. cst. 192 km E. of Djakarta; rice, tea, coffee tr.; ctr. of irrigation scheme; oil refining.

Tlaxcala, smallest st., **Mexico;** on Mesa Central; dense p.; mainly agr.; cap. T.; a. 4,027 km²; p. (1990) 763,683.

Tlemcen. See **Tilimsen.**

Toamasina (Tamatave), t., **Madagascar;** lge seapt. on Indian Oc., handles 70 per cent of M. tr.; industl. complex, car assembly, oil refinery; p. (1990) 145,431.

Tobago, southernmost I., Windward Is., **W.I.;** volcanic, forested, picturesque, irregular topography; resorts utilising pleasant climate; exp. coconuts, copra, cacao, limes; ch. t. Scarborough; seeks internal self-gov.; a. 300 km²; p. (1990) 46,400. See **Trinidad and Tobago.**

Tobata. See **Kitakyushu.**

Tobermory, burgh, Argyll and Bute, **Scot.;** on I. of Mull at N. entrance to Sound of Mull; fish. pt., resort; p. (1991) 825.

Tobol, R., W. Siberia, **Russia;** trib. of R. Irtysh; navigable in lower course; 800 km long.

Tobolsk, c., W. Siberia, **Russia;** R. pt. on Irtysh R.; shipbldg., sawmilling, fishing.

Tobruk, spt., **Libya,** N. Africa; on cst. 352 km E. of Benghazi; exp. oil, served by pipeline from Libyan oilfields; p. (1984) 94,006.

Tocantins, R., central **Brazil;** rises in Goias prov., flows N. across plateau of Brazil through Pará estuary to Atl. Oc.; navigation interrupted by rapids 320 km above Pará; ch. trib. Araguaya R.; 2,560 km long.

Toce, R., N. **Italy;** rises in Lepontine Alps, flows S. and S.E. into L. Maggiore; valley used by trunk rly. from Milan to Berne as S. approach to Simplon Tunnel; 86 km long.

Todmorden, mkt. t., Calderdale, West Yorks., **Eng.**; nr. source of R. Calder, 10 km N.E. of Rochdale; cottons, machin.; p. (1991) 11,969.

Togo, Rep. of, W. Africa; narrow strip between Ghana (W.) and Benin (E.); N. and S. lowlands separated by mtns. (1,000 m); climate hot and humid, but drier savannah conditions in N.; coffee on slopes of central mtns., cacao, copra in S., maize in N.; phosphate mng., major iron ore deposits in N. now form ch. exp.; developing food-processing inds.; cap. Lomé; a. 54,960 km²; p. (1991) 3,455,000.

Tokaido, Japan, one of gr. feudal highways, along S. cst. Honshu, now forms main line of modern communications network.

Tokaj, t., **Hungary;** at confluence of Bodrog and Tisa Rs.; nearby slopes of Hegyalia produce Tokay wine.

Tokat, t., cap. of T. prov., **Turkey;** copper refining, leather mnfs.; p. (1985) 73,008 (t.), (1990) 719,251 (prov.).

Tokelau (Union Isles), gr. of 3 coral atolls, S. Pac., N. of W. Samoa, belonging to **N.Z.;** Fakaofo, Nukunono and Atafu; natives are Polynesians; subsistence economy; copra; a. 10 km²; p. (1991) 1,577.

Tokoroa, co. t., N.I., **N.Z.;** kraft paper, pulp, and sawn timber; p. (1987) 17,400.

Tokushima, t., Shikoku, **Japan;** spt. on E. cst.; mkt. ctr., cotton mnfs.; p. (1990) 263,356.

Tokyo, c., cap. of **Japan;** spt. with deepened harbour handling mainly S. coastal tr.; major industl. ctr. with diverse mnfs. and major problems of pollution; built on marshy site with much expensive reclamation from sea; planned decentralisation of p. and economic activity in progress; with Osaka–Kobe–Kyoto conurbs. (480 km long ribbon development) spoken of as Tokaido (*q.v.*) megalopolis; major educational ctr. with many univs.; p. (1990) 8,163,127 (c.).

Tolbukhin, *See* Dobrich.

Toledo, prov., **Spain;** mtnous.; agr., vineyards, stock-raising; a. 15,346 km²; p. (1987) 487,867.

Toledo, anc. c., cap. of T. prov., **Spain;** in New Castile; on hill above Tagus R.; Gothic, Moorish, and Castillian architecture; picturesque narrow streets; Alcázar citadel; associated with El Greco; sword mkg. still flourishes; sm. arms; tourism; p. (1987) 58,297, (1991) 489,640 (prov.).

Toledo, c., Ohio, **USA;** rly. ctr. and L. pt. with natural harbour on Maumee R.; exp. mnfs., oil, coal, agr. prod.; imports iron-ore; glass mkg., shipbldg., car components and many varied mnfs.; p. (1990) 332,943 (c.), 614,128 (met. a.).

Tolentino, t., in the Marches, central **Italy;** on R. Chienti; mediaeval walls and houses; cath.; sm. handicraft inds.; spa and tourist ctr.; p. (1981) 17,984.

Toliary, spt. S.W. **Madagascar;** cap. T. prov.; p. (1990) 61,460.

Tolosa, t., Guipúzcoa prov., **Spain;** in the Basque cty.; mediaeval bldgs., and armour; paper mills; (p. (1981) 18,894.

Tolpuddle, v., Dorset, **Eng.;** 11 km N.E. of Dorchester; famous for Tolpuddle martyrs, agr. labourers condemned to transportation for trying to form a trade union (1834).

Toluca, c., cap. of Mexico st., central **Mexico;** stands at 2,672 m; brewing, flour, cottons, pottery; especially noted for basket weaving; p. (1990) 487,630.

Tol'yatti, c., **Russia;** on R. Volga 56 km W.N.W. of Kuybyshev; engin., motor wks., natural gas pipeline to Moscow; chemicals; p. (1989) 631,000.

Tom, R., Siberia, **Russia;** flows through Kuznetsk Basin and joins R. Ob; 704 km long.

Tomaszow Mazowieki, t., Piotrków prov., central **Poland;** industl. t. on Pilica R., surrounded by forests; textile ind., artificial silk; p. (1989) 69,579.

Tombigbee, R., Miss., **USA;** flows S. to join Alabama R. to form Mobile and Tensaw Rs.; navigable, partially canalised; length 654 km.

Tombouctou, formerly Timbuktu, **Mali,** W. **Africa;** nr. Niger R. on border of Sahara; salt tr., handicraft inds.; flourished as comm. mart and Moslem ctr. 14th–16th cent.; p. (1987) 453,032 (reg.).

Tomsk, c., cap. of marshy T. oblast, **Russia;** one of few lge. ts. in N. Siberia; major pt. on R. Tom; rly. junc. on Trans-Siberian rly.; educa-

tional ctr.; univ., cath.; engin., chemicals; p. (1989) 502,000.

Tonawanda, t., N.Y. st., **USA;** on Niagara R. at terminus of Erie Barge Canal; steel, plastics, chemicals; power from Niagara Falls, adjacent to N. Tonawanda; p. (1980) 18,693.

Tonbridge, t., Kent, **Eng.;** on R. Medway; food processing; lt. inds., inc. cricket balls; Norman cas. gatehouse; public school; part of l. gov. dist. of **Tonbridge and Malling;** p. (1995) 104,100 (dist.), (1991) 34,260 (t.).

Tone, R., Honshu, **Japan;** flows E. across Kanto Plain to Pac. Oc., N. of Tokyo; longest R. in Japan.

Tonga, I. gr., S. Pac. Oc.; Polynesian kingdom, gained independence 1970; 158 coral and volcanic Is.; 50 per cent. p. on Tongatabu I.; exp. copra, bananas; fishing; oil discovered 1969; airport; cap. Nuku'alofa; a. 699 km²; p. (1991) 103,000.

Tongariro, volcanic peak, N.I., **N.Z.;** nat. park in ctr. of volcanic dist.; alt. 1,970 m.

Tongeren (Tongres), t., Limburg prov., N.E. **Belgium;** mkt. ctr. for fertile Hesbaye region; historic bldgs.; p. (1982) 29,765.

Tonghua (Tunghwa), c., S.W. Jilin, **China;** rly junc.; soya bean processing; local iron and coal reserves; p. (1984) 363,400.

Tonkin, region, N. **Vietnam;** mtns. in N. and W., alluvial plain in E. around delta of Red R., containing most p. and lge. cs.; fertile agr.; ch. t. Hanoi; ch. pt. Haiphong; a. 104,973 km².

Tonle Sap, L., **Cambodia;** major comm. fishing a.; L. acts as natural reservoir to control floods of Mekong R.

Tönsberg, c., Vestfold prov., S.E. **Norway;** one of oldest Norwegian cs., on Skagerrak at entrance to Oslo fjord; ctr. of whaling fleet; oil mills; p. (1990) 38,333.

Toowoomba, t., S.E. Queensland, **Australia;** regional ctr. for Darling Downs, a rich wool and beef a; planned with parks and gardens: agr. based inds., engin.; p. (1991) 82,438.

Topeka, c., cap. of Kansas st., **USA;** on Kansas R.; impt. tr. ctr. in rich agr. region; food processing, rly. ctr. and engin.; p. (1990) 119,883.

Torbay, l. gov. dist., S. Devon, **Eng.;** formed by amalgamation of Torquay, Paignton and Brixham; located around Tor Bay; tourism; p. (1995) 123,900.

Torcello, I., with anc. Byzantine cath., on lagoon nr. Venice, **Italy.**

Torfaen, S.E. **Wales,** unit. auth. created in 1996 from former l. gov. dist.; inc. ts. of Cwmbran and Pontypool; p. (1995) 90,400.

Torgau, t., **Germany;** R. pt. on Elbe; industl. ctr.; American and Soviet armies met here 1945; p. (1990) 22,742.

Torne, R., N. Europe; rises in Sweden, drains L. Tornetrask and flows S.W. to G. of Bothnia, forming Finno-Swedish bdy.; rich in salmon; 512 km long.

Torness, East Lothian, **Scot.**; site of advanced gas cooled nuclear power sta.

Toronto, c., cap. of Ont. prov., **Canada;** major Gt. Ls. pt., on L. Ont.; spacious harbour; exp. lge. quantities of wheat; comm., financial, industl. and educational ctr.; many varied mnfs., univ.; notable bldgs., parks; a. 622 km²; p. (1991) 635,395 (c.), (1986) 3,427,168 (met. a.), lgst. c. of C.

Torpoint, t., Cornwall, **Eng.;** on Plymouth Sound; p. (1991) 8,238.

Torquay, t., S. Devon, **Eng.;** incorporated in Torbay; on N. side of Tor Bay; seaside resort with all-year season; p. (1991) 59,587.

Torre Annunziata, Campania, **Italy;** at foot of Vesuvius; spt., spa, bathing resort on Bay of Naples; arms factory, pasta mnf.; p. (1981) 57,097.

Torre del Greco, t., Campania, **Italy;** spt. and resort on Bay of Naples at foot of Vesuvius; coral fishing; pasta mnf.; p. (1992) 100,688.

Torremolinos, cst. resort, **Spain;** S. of Malaga; p. (1981) 22,535.

Torrens, L., S. **Australia;** 2nd lgst. salt L. in A.; varies from brackish lake to salt marsh.

Torreon, c., Coahuila, N. **Mexico;** cotton in surrounding Laguna dist.; cotton mills, rubber, smelting, food processing; rly. connection with ts. in S. Mexico; p. (1990) 459,809.

Torres Strait, between C. York, Queensland, **Australia,** and **New Guinea;** 144 km wide, strong tidal currents endanger navigation; contains volcanic and coral Torres Strait Is., 20 of which are inhabited by Australian Melanesians; p. (1986) 4,837.

Torridge, R., Devon, **Eng.;** flows from Hartland dist. to a confluence with the Taw at Bideford Bay; 85 km long.

Torridge, l. gov. dist., N.W. Devon, **Eng.;** inc. N. cst. ts. of Northam and Bideford and stretches inland to Great Torrington; p. (1995) 55,000.

Tortona, t., Piedmont, N. **Italy;** on Scrivia R.; textiles, metallurgy, engin., wines; cath.; the Roman Dertona; p. (1981) 28,806.

Tortosa, c., Tarragona prov., N.E. **Spain;** pt. on Ebro R., 35 km from mouth; food processing, soap, pottery; cath.; impt. Moorish t.; p. (1981) 31,445.

Tororo, t., **Uganda;** lge. chemical wks., cement, fertilisers.

Tortuga or **Ile de la Tortue,** I., Caribbean Sea; off N. cst. **Haiti;** provides shelter from N.E. tr. winds for Port-de-Paix; private development to convert I. into free pt. with tax incentives for inds.; scenic attractions being tapped to develop tourist tr.; airport under construction; subsistence agr. fishing; a. c. 65 km[2].

Torun (Ger. **Thorn**), c. and prov., **Poland;** rly. junc., pt. on Vistula; industl. ctr.; chemicals, elec. gds., clothing, metallurgy, engin., food processing; univ. bears name of Copernicus who was born here; p. (1989) 200,800 (c.), 656,400 (prov.).

Tory I., off N.W. cst., Donegal, **R.o.I.;** lighthouse; fishing; p. (1986) 136.

Totnes, t., South Hams, Devon, **Eng.;** on R. Dart 10 km N.W. of Dartmouth; mediaeval t.; agr. mkt., food processing; p. (1991) 6,929.

Tottenham. *See* **Haringey.**

Tottori, t., Honshu, **Japan;** spt. on Sea of Japan, exp. lumber, raw silk, fruit; industl. ctr.; p. (1990) 142,477.

Touggourt or **Tuggurt,** t., S. **Algeria;** on edge of Sahara; rly. terminus; dates.

Toulon, c., Var dep., S.W. **France;** reinstated as cap. of Var dep. (1974); on Mediterranean cst.; base of Fr. navy; fine natural harbour; comm. pt. and industl. ctr.; many fine bldgs.; Port-Cros Nat. Park nearby; p. (1990) 170,167 (c.), 437,553 (met.a.).

Toulouse, c., cap. of Haute-Garonne dep., S. **France;** in Languedoc on Garonne R. and Canal du Midi, commanding route through Gate of Carcassonne; industl. and agr. tr. ctr.; food processing, varied mnfs.; aircraft (home of Airbus Industries); many fine bldgs., notably mediaeval univ., basilica, Gothic cath.; p. (1990) 365,933 (c.), 608,430 (met.a.).

Touraine, former prov. of **France,** of which Tours was the cap.; now occupied by Indre-et-Loire dep. and part of Vienne dep.; known as the "garden of France."

Tourcoing, c., Nord dep., N. **France;** 16 km N.E. of Lille; with twin t. of Roubaix forms major wool textile ctr.; p. (1990) 94,425.

Tournai, c., Hainaut prov., W. **Belgium;** on R. Scheldt, nr. Mons; historic c.; famous cath.; textiles, carpet mftg., ctr. of cement ind.; p. (1993) 67,875.

Tours, c., cap. of Indre-et-Loire dep., **France;** in Touraine, on R. Loire; tourist ctr. for the châteaux of the Loire; route ctr.; agr. inds.; printing, engin.; Gothic cath.; p. (1990) 133,403 (c.), 271,927 (met.a.).

Towcester, mkt. t., South Northants., **Eng.;** 14 km S.W. of Northampton; "Eatanswill" of *Pickwick Papers*; p. (1991) 7,006.

Tower Hamlets, inner bor., E. London, **Eng.;** inc. former bors. of Bethnal Green, Stepney and Poplar; undergoing rapid economic and social change as p. and inds. are decentralised; site of lge. a. of London Docks now all closed but redeveloped; clothing, brewing; p. (1995) 172,800.

Townsville, spt., Queensland, **Australia;** coastal outlet for rich dairying, pastoral and mng. a. along Great Northern Rly; artificial harbour; univ.; copper refining; p. (1993) 121,700.

Towton, v., North Yorks., **Eng.;** nearby Towton field, scene of bloodiest battle of Wars of the Roses 1461; Lancastrians under Henry VI defeated by Yorkists under Edward IV.

Toyama, c., Honshu, **Japan;** on Etchu plain to E. of Noto peninsula; regional admin. and comm. ctr.; patent medicines, aluminium smelting, machin.; p. (1990) 321,254.

Toyohashi, t., Honshu, **Japan;** food processing, textiles; p. (1990) 337,988.

Trabzon or **Trebizond,** spt., **Turkey;** on Black Sea; exp. tobacco, food prods., carpets; once a gr. tr. ctr. on caravan route between Persia and Europe;

founded 8th cent. B.C. by Greek colonists; p. (1990) 173,354 (t.), 795,849 (prov.).

Trafalgar, C., S.W. cst., Cadiz, **Spain;** Nelson's famous victory 1805.

Trafford, met. dist., Gtr. Manchester **Eng.;** comprises Sale, Hale, Altrincham, Urmston and Stretford; p. (1995) 218,300.

Trail, t., B.C., **Canada;** lgst. metallurgical smelter in Commonwealth using local non-ferrous metals; chemicals; p. (1986) 7,948.

Tralee, mkt. t., spt., Kerry, **R.o.I.;** on R. Lee; exp. grain, butter; p. (1986) 17,109.

Trani, spt., N. Apulia, **Italy;** on Adriatic; mkt. t. for fertile coastal a.; fishing, food processing; cath., cas.; p. (1981) 44,235.

Transbaykal, region, Siberia, **Russia;** E. of L. Baykal; mineral wealth; ch. t., Chita.

Transcaucasia, region between the Black Sea and the Caspian Sea; comprising the constituent reps. of **Georgia, Armenia,** and **Azerbaijan;** ch. t. Tbilisi.

Transkei, former indep. Bantu Terr. (1976), **S. Africa;** agr., maize and livestock; heavily dependent on S. Africa; p. mainly employed in mines in Transvaal and Orange Free State; cap. Umtata; a. 42,849 km[2]; p. (1985) 2·9 m.

Transvaal, prov., **Rep. of S. Africa;** high veld plateau (900–1,200 m) with Kruger Nat. Park in N.E.; hot summers, temperate winters; livestock on grasslands, grains, citrus fruits and temperate crops on irrigated land; lge. mineral wealth, especially gold in Witwatersrand; diamonds, uranium, platinum; inds. in ch. cs., Johannesburg and cap. Pretoria; a. 286,066 km[2]; p. (1985) 7·5 m.

Transylvania, historic region and prov., central **Romania;** high plateau surrounded by Carpathians; forested; mineral wealth not yet fully realised; arable agr. in valleys; ch. ts. Cluj, Brasov.

Transylvanian Alps, range of mtns., **Romania.**

Trapani, t., cap. of T. prov. W. Sicily, **Italy;** spt. on promontory, sheltering natural harbour; exp. wine, pasta, tuna fish caught locally; p. (1981) 71,927.

Traralgon, t., Victoria, **Australia;** industl. growth based on Yallourn brown coal; tourism; p. (1991) 19,699.

Trasimeno, L., Umbria, central **Italy;** occupies lge. extinct volcanic crater; drained S. to R. Tiber; a. c. 155 km[2].

Tras-os-Montes e Alto-Douro, prov., N. **Portugal;** high, bleak plateau, cultivated valleys; climate cold except in S.; port wine cty. of Douro R.; remote, sparsely populated; a. 11,834 km[2].

Trawsfynydd, Gwynedd, N. **Wales;** within Snowdonia Nat. Park; nuclear power sta. decommissioning began in 1993.

Trebizond. *See* **Trabzon.**

Tredegar, t., Blaenau Gwent, **Wales;** in narrow valley 5 km W. of Ebbw Vale; engin.; home of Aneurin Bevan; p. (1991) 15,390.

Treforest, t., Rhondda, Cynon, Taff, **Wales;** on R. Taff; lge. trading estate established in 1930s to alleviate unemployment in primary inds. of S. Wales; aircraft accessories, electronics, chemical, pharmaceutical, rayon, metal wks.

Trelleborg, spt., S. **Sweden;** on Baltic Sea; most impt. rubber factory in cty.; p. (1983) 34,146.

Trengganu, st., **Malaysia;** N.E. Malaya; rice, rubber, coconuts; tin, iron; cap. Kuala Trengganu; a. 13,080 km[2]; p. (1980) 540,627.

Trent, R., **Eng.;** rises in N. Staffs, flows round S. Pennines and joins the Ouse to form estuary of the Humber; many power stas. along its banks; polluted waterway, especially between Humber and Nottingham; 240 km long.

Trentino-Alto Adige, aut. region, N.E. **Italy,** between Austrian and Swiss Frontiers and L. Garda; embraces provs. Trento and Bolzano; cap. Trento; formerly called Venetia Tridentina; a. 13,598 km[2]; p. (1992) 896,722.

Trento, t., cap. of Trento prov. and ch. t. of Trentino-Alto Adige, N. **Italy;** on R. Adige and route to Brenner Pass; chemicals, cement, elec. engin.; picturesque t.; cath.; p. (1981) 99,179.

Trenton, c., cap. N.J. st., **USA;** on Delaware R.; transport and industl. ctr.; noted for its wire-rope and pottery inds., established mid-19th cent.; crockery, machin., metal and rubber gds.; p. (1990) 88,675 (c.), 326,000 (met. a.).

Trèves. *See* **Trier.**

Treviso, c., cap. of T. prov., Venetia, N.E. **Italy;** on R. Sile; agr. ctr. on fertile Venetian plain; silk mills, paper, furniture, fertilisers, pottery; p. (1981) 87,696.

Trichinopoly. *See* Tiruchirapalli.

Trichur, t., Kerala, India; comm. and educational ctr.; p. (1981) 77,923 (t.), 170,122 (met. a.).

Trier (Trèves), c., Rhineland-Palatinate, Germany; on R. Moselle; Roman origin. (Augusta Trevorum, the Rome of the North), cath.. Porta Nigra; ctr. of Moselle wine reg.; textiles, leather goods; birthplace of Marx; p. (1986) 93,100.

Trieste, spt., cap. of T. prov., Friuli-Venezia Giulia, N.E. Italy; shipbldg., fishing, oil refining; pipeline to Schwechat, nr. Vienna; cath., cas., Roman antiquities; univ.; p. (1992) 228,398.

Trieste Free Territory, former free st. on the Adriatic; constituted by Peace Treaty with Italy, 1947, as compromise between conflicting Yugoslav and Italian claims; a. 743 km²; Zone A handed over to Italy, Zone B to Yugoslavia 1954. Yugoslav/Italian agreement 1975 settled border dispute and established free industl. zone on both sides of border in region of Sezana-Fernetti.

Trikkala, t., cap. of T. dep., W. Thessaly, N. Greece; mkt. t. for pastoral prods.; damaged by earthquake 1954; p. (1981) 45,160, (1991) 137,819 (dep.).

Trim, co. t., Meath, R.o.I.; mkt. t. on R. Boyne; anc. seat of Irish Parliament; p. (1986) 1,967.

Trincomalee, t., N.E. cst. Sri Lanka; excellent natural harbour; formerly a British naval base; p. (1981) 44,913.

Tring, mkt. t., Dacorum, Herts., Eng.; in gap through Chiltern hills, 14 km N.W. of Hemel Hempstead; p. (1991) 11,455.

Trinidad, I., W.I.; N. of Venezuela; climate warm and humid; oil, natural gas, asphalt, sugar, rum, coconut oil, molasses, citrus fruits; tourism; cap. Port of Spain; a. 4,828 km². *See* Trinidad and Tobago.

Trinidad, t., central Cuba; picturesque old t. of colonial period declared a national monument.

Trinidad and Tobago, indep. st. within Commonwealth (1962), rep. (1976), W.I.; main exps. crude oil and petroleum prods. which with natural asphalt represent over 20 per cent national income; lge. offshore gas deposits with rising production; oil refining; tropical crops and food processing; sugar, molasses, rum, fruits, textiles; cap. and major spt. Port of Spain; internal self-gov. sought by Tobago; a. 5,128 km²; p. (1991) 1,250,000.

Trinity, R., Texas, USA; flows S.E. to Galveston Bay; used for reservoirs; valley contains lge. p. and much economic activity; 800 km long.

Trino, Piedmont, N. Italy; 18 km S.S.W. of Vercelli; nuclear power sta.

Tripoli, c., Lebanon; spt. on Mediterranean; admin. ctr. for N. Lebanon; terminus of oil pipeline from Iraq; oil refining; exp. agr. prods.; p. (1988) 160,000.

Tripoli, c., joint cap. of Libya (with Benghazi), on Mediterranean; stands on edge of palmoasis, site of anc. Oea; tourist, comm. and mnf. ctr.; gd. harbour; p. (1984) 990,687.

Tripura, st. India; N.E. Ganges delta, bordering Assam and Bangladesh; cap. Agartala; rice, jute, cotton, sugar-cane; a. 10,360 km²; p. (1991) 2,757,205.

Tristan da Cunha, sm. gr. of Is., S. Atl. Oc.; dependency of Brit. col. St. Helena; ch. I. Tristan; evacuated 1961 (volcanic eruption) but resettled 1963; weather sta. (Gough I.); a. 117 km²; p. (1988) 313.

Trivandrum, c., cap. of Kerala st., S.W. India; pt. on Arabian Sea; textiles coconut processing; univ.; p. (1981) 483,086 (c.), 520,125 (met. a.).

Trnava, c., W. Slovakia; mkt. t. in fertile agr. region on Váh R.; food processing, steel wks.; cath., monasteries, called "little Rome"; p. (1990) 73,000.

Trnovo or Tirnovo, c., Bulgaria; on Jantra R.; food processing, textiles, leather; anc. cap. of Bulgaria.

Trogir, t., Croatia (formerly Yugoslavia); sm. pt. and seaside resort, partly sited on I. of Čiovo; mediaeval bldgs., inc. cath., palaces; p. c. 20,000.

Trois Rivières, t., Quebec, Canada; industl. ctr. on St. Lawrence R.; noted for newsprint; hydroelectric power from St. Maurice R.; p. (1986) 50,122 (c.), 128,888 (met. a.).

Trojmiasto (Tri-City), Poland; name given to the three municipalities of Gdansk, Gdynia, and Sopot, a loosely-knit conurb.

Trollhättan, t., S.W. Sweden; on Göta R., nr. T. falls which generate power for metallurgical

and chemical inds.; car and aircraft components; p. (1992) 51,673.

Trombay, I., off Bombay, India; oil refining; atomic reactor; uranium processing and nuclear waste reprocessing plant; zirconium metal produced; fertilisers.

Troms, co., N. Norway; deep fjords, offshore Is.; fishing, livestock, boat-bldg.; cap. Tromsö; a. 25,916 km²; p. (1990) 146,816.

Tromsö, t., cap. of Troms prov., N. Norway; spt. on sm. I. of T. in Norwegian Sea; arctic fishing, sealing; fish processing; p. (1990) 41,651.

Trondheim, c., spt., Norway; on W. cst. on S. side of T. fjord; shipbldg., engin.; exp. timber and wood-pulp, butter, fish, copper; anc. cath.; burial place of early Norwegian kings and place of coronation of recent sovereigns; p. (1990) 130,522.

Troon, burgh, S. Ayrshire, Scot.; on F. of Clyde, 10 km N. of Ayr; good harbour and graving docks; shipbldg., hosiery; seawater distillation research ctr. project; resort; p. (1991) 15,231.

Troppau. *See* Opava.

Trossachs, Stirling, Scot.; picturesque wooded glen; tourist resort.

Trouville, t., Calvados dep., N. France; popular seaside resort and fishing pt. on Normandy cst.; p. (1982) 6,012.

Trowbridge, mkt. t. and county admin. ctr., West Wilts., Eng.; cloth wks., bacon curing, dairying, engin.; p. (1991) 29,334.

Troy, c., N.Y., USA; at confluence of Rs. Hudson and Mohawk; gr. shirt-mftg. ctr.; p. (1990) 54,269.

Troyes, c., cap. of Aube dep., N.E. France; on R. Seine; once cap. of Champagne; hosiery, textile machin., food processing; cath.; site of mediaeval fairs which standardised Troy weight; p. (1990) 60,755 (c.), 122,763 (met.a.).

Trucial States. *See* United Arab Emirates.

Trujillo, c., N.W. Peru; comm. and mkt. ctr. for irrigated agr. region, on Moche R., in foothills of Andes; sugar, cocaine; univ., cath.; p. (1993) 509,312.

Trujillo, t., cap. of T. st., W. Venezuela; on Transandean highway at 805 m; agr. mkt. for region producing coffee, cacao, tobacco, maize; p. (1980) 31,774 (t.), (1990) 520,292 (st.).

Truro, t., Nova Scotia, Canada; on Salmon R.; hosiery, lumber mills, printing, metallurgy, machin.; p. (1991) 11,683.

Truro, c., Carrick, Cornwall, Eng.; at confluence of Rs. Kenwyn and Allen; mkt. t. and former sm. pt.; admin. ctr. of Cornwall; cath.; p. (1991) 18,966.

Tsavo, major National Park in Kenya.

Tselinograd (Aqmola), c., Kazakhstan; cap. Virgin Lands terr.; on Ishim R., nr. Karaganda coalfield; chemicals, agr. machin.; p. (1990) 281,400.

Tskhinvali, c., N. Georgia; elec. prods., lumber mills, fruit canning; p. (1990) 43,300.

Tsu, t., Honshu, Japan; textiles; p. (1990) 157,178.

Tsugaru Strait, Japan; separates Is. Hokkaido and Honshu; links Sea of Japan with Pac. Oc.; 72 km long, 24–32 km wide.

Tsuruga, spt., Japan; on W. cst. Honshu; rayon textiles, cotton, atomic power plant; p. (1990) 68,041.

Tuam, mkt. t., Galway, R.o.I.; sugar refining; p. (1986) 4,109.

Tuamotu, coral archipelago, Fr. Polynesia, S. Pac. Oc.; pearl fisheries; p. of gr. (1983) 11,793.

Tuapse, c., S. Krasnodar terr., Russia; at foot of Caucasus on Black Sea; major petroleum pt. at W. end of pipeline from Baku and Makhachkala; oil refineries.

Tübingen, t., Baden-Württemberg, Germany; on R. Neckar; 15th cent. univ., cas.; mediaeval c.ctr.; birthplace of Hölderlin; p. (1986) 76,200.

Tubuai, archipelago, Fr. Polynesia. S. Pac. Oc.; a. 163 km².

Tucson, c., S.E. Arizona, USA; mkt. and distribution ctr. on Santa Cruz R.; cultural ctr. and winter resort based on Spanish heritage and warm dry climate; food processing, missile components; p. (1990) 405,390 (c.), 667,000 (met. a.).

Tucumán. *See* San Miguel de Tucumán.

Tudela, t., Navarre, N. Spain; mkt. ctr. for fertile fruit-growing dist. and I. of La Majana in Ebro R.; fine cath., Roman bridge; p. (1981) 24,629.

Tuggurt. *See* Touggourt.

Tula, c., cap. of T. oblast, Russia; mnf. ctr. in Moscow industl. region; local iron and lignite mng.; Yasnaya Polyana, home of Tolstoy, nearby; p. (1989) 540,000.

Tulare, L., S. Cal., **USA**; ctr. of inland drainage 64 km S. of Fresno; streams feeding it used for irrigation; in drought years L. dries up completely; a. 233 km².

Tullamore, mkt. t., Offaly, **R.o.I.**; on Grand Canal; farming, distilling, brewing; p. (1986) 8,484.

Tulle-sur-Mer, t., cap. of Corrèze dep., **France**; firearms, textiles; p. (1982) 20,642.

Tulsa, c., Okla., **USA**; impt. oil ctr., based on lge. racial deposits; machin., aeroplanes; well laid out with many parks; p. (1990) 367,302 (c.), 709,000 (met. a.).

Tumaco, t., S.W. **Colombia**; spt. on Pac. Oc., on sm. I. off cst.; exp. agr. prods.; climate hot and humid.

Tummel, R., Perth and Kinross, **Scot.**; trib. of R. Tay; used by Perth to Inverness rly. as S. approach to Drumochter Pass; hydroelec. scheme nr. Pitlochry; 88 km long.

Tunbridge Wells (officially **Royal Tunbridge Wells**), t., l. gov. dist., Kent, **Eng.**; on border of East Sussex; chalybeate waters; attractive 17th cent. promenade known as "The Pantiles"; p. (1995) 103,300 (dist.), (1991) 60,272 (t.).

Tunghwa. See **Tonghua**.

Tung Ting Hu. See **Dong Ting**.

Tunguska, Upper, Stony and Lower, Rs., Siberia, **Russia**; all rise in Sayan mtns. nr. L. Baykal and flow N.W. into R. Yenisey.

Tunguska Basin, coalfield between Yenisey and Lena Rs., **Russia**; main ts., Norilsk, Igarka, Yeniseysk.

Tunis, c., cap. of **Tunisia**, N. Africa; spt. on inlet of Mediterranean; exp. raw materials; base for fishing fleets; univ.; notable mosques; tourist ctr.; ruins of anc. Carthage to N.E.; p. (1984) 596,654.

Tunisia, indep. st., N. Africa; bounded by Algeria on W., by Libya on E., indented Mediterranean cst.; Atlas mtns. penetrate into N.; temperate cst. climate, hot and dry in S. desert; agr. and mng. basis of economy; wheat, olive oil, wine, fruits, limited to wetter coastal areas and irrigated valleys; phosphates around Ghafsa; iron ore and lead in N.W.; steelwks. at Menzel Bourguiba; chemical and paper inds. based on local phosphates; economy hit by fall in world oil prices and lower remittances from Tunisians working abroad (immigration controls in France); cap. Tunis; a. 164,108 km²; p. (1994) 8,800,000.

Tunja, c., cap. of Boyacá dep., **Colombia**; route and agr. tr. ctr.; p. (1992) 112,360.

Turda, t., Transylvania, **Romania**; local salt mines and quarrying aid chemical and ceramic inds.; p. (1983) 59,695.

Turfan, depression, E. Xinjiang prov., **China**; on S. slopes of Tien Shan mtns.; desert a. irrigated by wells and canals for animal husbandry, fruit, cotton, grain; 275 m below sea level; ch. t. Turfan; archaeological finds.

Turgutlu (Kassaba), t., Manisa prov., **Turkey**; 48 km E.N.E. of Izmir; lignite, cotton, melons; p. (1985) 65,740.

Turin or **Torino,** c., cap. of T. prov., N. **Italy**; on R. Po at confluence with the Dora Riparia; former cap. of Piedmont and kingdom of Sardinia; univ., cath., many historic monuments; headquarters of Italian motor ind.; clothing, machin., furniture, chemicals; oil refinery nearby; p. (1992) 952,736.

Turkana, L. See **Rudolf, L.**

Turkestan E., terr. included in Xinjiang, **China**; separated from W. or former Russian Turkestan by Pamir plateau; mainly desert.

Turkestan W., terr. inc. **Turkmenistan, Uzbekistan, Tajikistan, Kirghizia,** and part of **Kazakhstan**.

Turkey, rep., S.W. Asia and E. Europe; occupies mtnous. Anatolian penin.; equable climate on coastal margins, continental severity in interior; economy predominantly agr. but hampered by poor land resources; grain grown on Anatolian plateau and a Mediterranean variety of crops around cst.; noted for tobacco; industl. development based on mng. resources and oil in S.E.; lge cities in W. act as magnet for the poorer areas of E.; 30 percent of p. in 5 cities; many migrate to Europe & Middle East as migrant workers; violence by Kurdish separatists; cap. Ankara; a. 814,578 km²; p. (1994) 61,183,000.

Türkmenbashi. See **Krasnovodsk**.

Turkmenistan, CIS former constituent rep., USSR;

borders on Afghanistan, Iran, and the Caspian Sea; much of a. in Kara-Kum desert; agr. based on irrigation; fruit, cotton, wool; sulphates, petroleum; p. concentrated in oases and industl. ctrs. of cap. Ashkhabad, Mary-Chadzhou, along Trans-Caspian rly.; a. 491,072 km²; p. (1994) 4,358,000.

Turks and Caicos, Is., Caribbean Sea, **W.I.**; about 30 sm. Is., geographically S.E. continuation of Bahamas; dry climate, poor limestone soil; exp. salt, crawfish; cap. Grand Turk; a. 430 km²; p. (1997) 13,500.

Turku (Abo), spt., S.W. **Finland**; on Baltic Sea; ctr. of fertile agr. a.; exp. agr. prods.; industl. ctr.; shipbldg., steel, machin., textiles; Finnish and Swedish univs.; p. (1993) 160,390.

Turnhout, t., N.E. **Belgium**, nr. Antwerp, on Campine canal; textiles, lace, printing; p. (1993) 38,419.

Tuscaloosa, c., Ala., **USA**; on Black Warrior R.; rly. and industl. ctr. based on local coal, iron, cotton, timber; univ.; p. (1990) 77,759 (c.), 150,522 (met. a.).

Tuscany, region, central **Italy**; inc. provs. Arezzo, Firenze, Livorno, Siena, Grosseto, Lucca, Pisa, Massa and Carrara, Pistoia; mainly mtnous., drained by Arno R. system; wines, olive oil, cereals; iron ore from Elba, marble from Apuan Alps around Carrara; pt. at Livorno (Leghorn); cap. Firenze (Florence); a. 22,989 km²; p. (1992) 3,528,735.

Tuticorin, t., Tamil Nadu, S.E. **India**; on G. of Manaar; fertiliser plant; declining cotton and tea pt.; heavy water plant; p. (1991) 199,854.

Tuttlingen, t., Baden-Württemberg, **Germany**; on R. Danube; surgical instruments; footwear; p. (1986) 30,800.

Tuva aut. rep., **Russia**; bounded by Siberia and Mongolia; mtn. basin, forested; timber inds., coal mng., asbestos, pastoral agr.; cap. Kyzyl; a. c. 165,800 km²; p. (1989) 308,600.

Tuvalu, formerly Ellice Is., until 1975 part of Gilbert and Ellice Is., W. Pac. Oc.; indep. (1978); p. mainly Polynesian; cap. Funafuti; coconut cultivation in high temps on poor coral soils; exp. copra; a. 25 km²; p. (1991) 10,090.

Tuxtla Gutiérrez, c., cap. of Chiapas st., **Mexico**; in fertile valley at 450 m; ctr. for sisal, tobacco, coffee, cattle; on Inter-American Highway; Mayan ruins nearby; p. (1990) 295,615.

Tuz, L., **Turkey**; salt L.; a. 1,619 km² in winter, much reduced in summer.

Tuzla, t., Bosnia-Herzegovina, formerly Yugoslavia; salt, lignite, coal; hydroelectric power in a.; agr. mkt. ctr.; textiles; civil war 1992 onwards; p. (1981) 121,717.

Tver (Kalinin), c., **Russia**; on upper Volga; diversified inds.; 17th cent. cath. and cas.; p. (1989) 451,000.

Tweed, R., S.E. **Scot.**; rises in Tweeddale, and reaches sea at Berwick; salmon fisheries; length 155 km.

Twelve Pins, star-shaped mtn. range, Galway, **R.o.I.**; Benbaum, 730 m.

Twickenham. See **Richmond-upon-Thames**.

Tychy, t., Katowice prov., **Poland**; on edge of Upper Silesian industl. a.; surrounded by forest; brewing; p. (1989) 189,816.

Tyler, c., Texas, **USA**; oil ctr. on E. Texan field; agr. ctr. for local mkt. gardening; famous for rose growing; p. (1990) 75,450.

Tyne, R., frmer Tyne and Wear, Durham and Northumberland, **Eng.**; formed by confluence of N. Tyne and S. Tyne at Hexham; flows E. to sea at Tyne-mouth and S. Shields; valley gives easy route across mtns. from Newcastle to Carlisle; lower course forms harbour (with shipbldg. and other wks.) from Newcastle to Tynemouth; road tunnel between Wallsend and Jarrow; 128 km long.

Tynedale, l. gov. dist., W. Northumberland, **Eng.**; lge. inland a. inc. Haltwhistle, Hexham and Prudoe; p. (1995) 57,700.

Tynemouth, t., North Tyneside, frmly Tyne and Wear, **Eng.**; pt. on N. bank of Tyne R.; ruined priory and cas.; residtl.; resort; p. (1991) 17,422.

Tyne and Wear, former met. co., N.E. **Eng.**; mainly industl. a. around lower T. and W. Rs.; inc. Newcastle-upon-Tyne, Tynemouth, Gateshead, South Shields and Sunderland; traditionally ass. with shipbldg. and coal mng., but inds. increasingly diversified; p. (1995) 1,131,000.

Tyre (Sur), Lebanon; anc. Phoenician c. and spt. founded c. 15th cent. B.C.; now sm. comm. t., tr. in cotton, tobacco; p. (1988) 14,000.

Tyrol, Alpine region, **Europe**; falls within Austria and Italy, linked by Brenner Pass; embraces highest peaks of Austrian Alps, culminating in Ortler Spitz; two-fifths forest, timber inds.; mtn. pasture; tourism; Austrian prov. of Tyrol; cap. Innsbruck; a. 12,650 km²; p. (1991) 630,358.

Tyrone, former co., **N. Ireland**; now replaced by Strabane, Omagh, Dungannon and Cookstown l. gov. dists.

Tyrrhenian Sea, part of Mediterranean between Italy and Corsica, Sardinia and Sicily.

Tyumen, c., **Russia**; one of oldest Siberian ts., rly. ctr. on Trans-Siberian rly., R. pt. on Tura R.; many heavy inds.; ctr. of oil and natural gas region; p. (1989) 477,000.

Tywyn, mkt. t., Gwynedd, **Wales**; on cst. of Cardigan Bay, 5 km N.W. of Aberdyfi; p. (1991) 2,864.

Tzekung. *See* Zigong.

Tzepo. *See* Zibo.

U

Ubangi, major R., **Central Africa**; trib. of R. Zaire, rises on bdr. of Central Africa Emp. and Zaire flows W. and S. to join Zaire R. at Irebu; partially navigable, 2,240 km long.

Ube, spt., S. Honshu, **Japan**; coal mng. and industl. ctr.; machin., synthetic petroleum; p. (1990) 175,053.

Ubeda, t., Jaén prov., **Spain**; on plateau between Guadalquivir and Guadalimar; food processing, olive oil, soap; p. (1981) 27,441.

Uberaba, t., Minas Gerais, **Brazil**; ctr. of cattle rearing and arable agr. region; sugar milling, mnfs. lime; p. (1985) 245,900.

Uberlandia, t., Minas Gerais st., **Brazil**; rail junc., agr. processing; p. (1991) 366,711.

Ucayali, R., **Peru**; headstream of R. Amazon; over 2,240 km long, navigable for 1,600 km; gives name to prov.; p. (1993) 314,810.

Uckfield, mkt. t., East Sussex, **Eng.**; 13 km N.E. of Lewes; a. ctr. of former Sussex iron ind.; p. (1991) 13,531.

Udaipur, c., Rajasthan, N.W. **India**; in picturesque valley at 760 m a.s.l.; cap. of former princely st. of U.; maharajah's palace; p. (1991) 309,000.

Uddevalla, spt., S. **Sweden**; N. Göteborg; former shipyds., prefab. houses, timber, granite quarrying, textiles; p. (1992) 48,178.

Udi, t., S. **Nigeria,** W. Africa; 160 km N. of Pt. Harcourt; impt. mng. ctr. on Enugu coalfield; linked by rail to Kaduna and Pt. Harcourt.

Udine, c., cap. of U. prov., Friuli-Venezia Giulia, N.E. **Italy**; between Alps and G. of Venice; route and industl. ctr. in agr. region; textiles, chemicals, engin., leather, woodwork; cath., many attractive bldgs., piazzas; severe earthquakes (1976); p. (1984) 101,179.

Udmurt aut. rep. Russia; part of Urals industl. a.; two-fifths forested, timber inds.; arable agr., flax; steel inds. at cap. Izhevsk, Votkinsk, Sarapul; p. (1989) 1,605,700.

Udokan Khrebet, mtns., **Russia**; world's lgst. reserve of copper.

Ufa, c., cap. of Bashkir aut. rep. **Russia**; in Urals industl. a., at confluence of Rs. Belaya and Ufa; p. (1989) 1,082,000.

Uganda, rep., E. Africa; dictatorship overthrown (1979); 4 regs. established for economic devel.; equatorial cty., climate modified by alt.; forms part of E. African plateau (1,200 m); well-developed economy; coffee, tea, tobacco, cotton for exp.; developing pastoral economy, fishing on L. Victoria; copper at Kilembe, tin; hydroelectric power from Owen Falls, second project at Kabelega Falls; electricity exp. to Kenya; savannah areas contain abundant wildlife in Nat. Parks and Game Reserves; cap. Kampala; a. 235,887 km²; p. (1991) 16,582,700.

Uist, N. and **S.,** Is., Outer Hebrides, Western Isles, **Scot.**; indented csts.; N. Uist boggy in E., hilly in W.; S. Uist smaller but mtnous.; crofting, fishing; p. (1991) 1,404 (N.), 2,106 (S.).

Uitenhage, t., Cape prov., S. **Africa**; fruit, wool, rly. wks., tyres, car assembly, textiles; summer resort; p. (1980) 134,640 (dist.).

Ujiji, t., in sm. terr. same name (a. 2,383 km²) on E. shore L. Tanganyika, **Tanzania**; where

Stanley found Livingstone 1871.

Ujiyamada. *See* Ise.

Ujjain, t., Madhya Pradesh, **India**; sacred c. and formerly cap. of Malwa; univ.; p. (1991) 362,000.

Ujpest, industl. sub., Budapest, **Hungary**; elec. engin., leather, shoes, textiles, furniture, pharmaceuticals.

Ujung Pandang (Makasar), c., Sulawesi, **Indonesia**; in dist. of rich volcanic soils; major spt. and airpt., entrepot tr.; p. (est. 1983) 888,000.

Ukhta t., **Russia**; ctr. of natural gas field in Pechora Basin; p. (1989) 111,000.

Ukraine, CIS former constituent rep., USSR; in Eastern Europe; of dominating importance in Soviet economy; drained by Rs. Dnieper Dniester, S. Bug, Donets; Pripet Marshes in N., wooded steppes in ctr., fertile black-earth a. in S.; major wheat-growing a. of Europe; highly mineralised, many industl. raw materials and ctrs. of metallurgical and heavy inds.; cap. Kiev; a. 582,750 km²; p. (1994) 52,114,000.

Ulan Bator, c., cap. of **Mongolian People's Rep.**; in stock-raising region; industl. ctr. of cty.; woollen gds., saddles, knitwear; new indust. ctr. at Darkhan nearby; rly. link to China and Russia; contains one-quarter of p. of rep.; p. (1996) 619,000.

Ulan-Ude (Verkhneudinsk), t., Siberia, **Russia**; major route and mnf. ctr.; pt. on R. Ude, junc. on Trans-Siberian rly., linked by rail to Beijing; engin., textiles, glass, leather; p. (1989) 353,000.

Ullapool, v., Highland, **Scot.**; fish. pt. (herring landings), on L. Broom, 72 km N.W. of Inverness; landed more fish in 1981 than any other British pt.; attractive mtn. and cst. scenery in a.; p. (1991) 1,231.

Ullswater, L., Cumbria, **Eng.**; 13 km long; supplies water to Manchester; attractive tourist a.

Ulm, c., Baden-Württemberg, **Germany**; route ctr. at limit of barge navigation on Danube, although navigable limits being extended by canalisation; food-processing, metal gds., textiles, cement; p. (1990) 111,000.

Ulsan, t., **South Korea**; oil refining, fertilisers; nuclear power sta. (1983) built to reduce oil imports; p. (1990) 682,978.

Ulster. anc. prov of **Ireland**. consisting of counties of Cavan, Donegal, Monaghan and the six counties now **N. Ireland.** Prov. Ulster, part of consists of Cavan, Donegal and Monaghan; p. (1986) 236,008.

Ulúa-Chamelhcón, R. basin, N. cst. **Honduras**; major banana region of Central American cst.

Ulva, I., Argyll and Bute, **Scot.**; off W. cst. of Mull; 8 km long.

Ulverston, mkt. t., South Lakeland, Cumbria, **Eng.**; nr. Morecambe Bay; antibiotics, elec. gds., tanning; p. (1991) 11,866.

Ulyanovsk. *See* Simbirsk.

Uman, c., **Ukraine**; at confluence of Kamenka and Umanka Rs.; rly. junc.; agr.-processing; p. (1990) 91,300.

Umanak, t., W. **Greenland**; hunting and fishing base on arm of Baffin Sea; marble mng.; p. (1990) 2,677.

Umbria, region, central **Italy**; comprising provs. of Perugia and Terni, crossed by Apennines and upper Tiber; agr. mainstay of economy; inds. based on hydroelectric power at Terni; chemicals; tourist ctr.; cap. Perugia; a. 8,472 km²; p. (1992) 814,796.

Ume, R., **Sweden**; flows S.E. to the G. of Bothnia; length 400 km.

Umeå, c., cap. of Västerbotten prov., N.E. **Sweden**; on G. of Bothnia at mouth of Ume R.; cultural ctr.; woodpulp; p. (1992) 94,912.

Umm-al-Quaywayn, emirate, member of **United Arab Emirates**; p. (1985) 29,229.

Umm Qasr, t., **Kuwait**; on Iraq border; new deepwater port planned.

Umtali (Mutare), t., **Zimbabwe**; comm. ctr. for rich agr. a.; oil refinery at Feruka; pipeline to Beira; paper milling, food processing, vehicle assembly; p. (1982) 69,600.

Umtata, t., Cape Prov., S. **Africa**; admin. ctr.; cath.; p. (1976) 24,805 (latest fig.).

Uncia, t., Oruro dep., **Bolivia**; alt. 3,900 m in E. Cordillera of Andes, 96 km S.E. of Oruro; site of impt. Patino tin mines.

Ungava Bay, arm of Hudson Strait, projecting into Labrador, N.E. **Canada**; minerals abundant, recent exploitation of impt. medium and low-grade iron deposits.

Union Isles. *See* Tokelau.

Union of South Africa. *See* South Africa, Rep. of.

Union of Soviet Socialist Republics (USSR), E. Europe, N. Asia; until 1991 major world economic and political power; ctr. of European communist bloc; extended over 9,600 km W.-E., 4,800 km N.-S.; continental climate with marked regional variations; centrally planned economy emphasised development of heavy inds. at major sources of natural resources, and development of new resources in E.; timber inds. and textiles impt. with lge.-scale, mechanised agr. with planned prod. reflecting regional variations in physical conditions; cap. Moscow; a. 22,272,290 km²; p. (1991) 290 m.

United Arab Emirates (Trucial Sts.), indep. sov. st. on Persian G., S.W. Asia; formed (1971) from Trucial Sts. (Abū Dhabi, Ajmān, Dubai, Al Fujayrah, Ra's al Khaimah, Shārjah, Umm-al-Quaywayn) after withdrawal of Brit. forces and termination of special defence treaty (1820–1971); p. immigration from Middle and Far East as oil-based economic growth proceeds, esp. in Abu Dhabi; a. 82,880 km²; p. (1993) 2,083,000.

United Kingdom, cty., N.W. Europe; separated from continent of Europe by English Channel; consists of Gr. Britain (Eng., Wales, Scot.) and N. Ireland; member of EU; a. 244,022 km²; p. (1997) 58,823,000.

United States of America, fed. rep., N. Amrica; world's major economic power; variety of climatic and physical conditions (*see* **N. America**); economically self-supporting, but imports petroleum, coffee, machin., textiles; extremely diversified mnfs.; exp. capital goods, industl. supplies, vehicles and food; consists of 50 sts. and Dist. of Columbia, co-extensive with cap. of Washington; outlying dependencies inc. Puerto Rico, U.S. Virgin Is., Panama Canal Zone, Guam, American Samoa, Trust Terr. of the Pac. Is.; assertive foreign policy; a. 9,363,169 km²; p. (1996) 265,300,000.

Unst, I., Shetland Is., **Scot.**; most N. of gr.; length 20 km; p. (1991) 1,055.

Unterwalden, can., **Switzerland**; divided into Obwalden and Nidwalden; dairying, fruit and livestock; cap. Stans; a. 767 km²; p. (1986) 58,000.

Upernavik, t., W. Greenland; on sm. I. in Baffin Bay; sealing and whaling base; meteorological sta.; p. (1990) 2,375.

Upper Austria, prov., **Austria**; borders on W. Germany and Slovakia; hilly and forested; drained by Danube R. system; inc. Salzkammergut resort a.; agr., forestry; inds. centred on Linz (cap.), Steyr and Wels; a. 11,979 km²; p. (1991) 1,340,076

Upper Hutt, c., N.I., **N.Z.**; shares rapid industl. growth of Hutt Valley; p. (1991) 37,092.

Upper Volta. *See* Burkina Faso.

Uppingham, mkt. t., Rutland, **Eng.**; 16th cent. school; p. (1991) 3,140.

Uppsala, c., cap. of U. prov., **Sweden**; on R. Sala, 72 km from Stockholm; historic ctr. of anc. Sweden; cultural ctr., famous univ. (Linnaeus taught there); cath.; lt. inds.; p. (1992) 174,554 (t.), 278,610 (prov.).

Ur, anc. Chaldean c., Iraq; 208 km W.N.W. of Basra; ruins; flourished about 3,000 B.C.

Ural, R., **Russia**; flows S.W. and S. to Caspian Sea; used for domestic and industl. water supply; navigable; 2,400 km long.

Ural Mts., Russia; mtn. system, forms bdy. between Europe and Asia and separates Russian plain from W. Siberian lowlands; extends N.-S. for 2,400 km; highest peaks Narodnaya and Telpos-Iz; rich mineral resources have given rise to huge ctrs. of heavy ind., inc. Sverdlovsk, Chelyabinsk, Magnitogorsk.

Uralsk, N.W., **Kazakhstan**; on R. Ural; grain-trading and cattle-mart ctr.; flour, leather, woollens, iron-ware; p. (1990) 206,700.

Uranium City, N. Saskatchewan, **Canada**; nr. N. shore of L. Athabasca, ctr. of Beaverlodge uranium-mng. a.; founded 1951; p. (1986) 2,748.

Urawa, t., Honshu, **Japan**; sub. of Tokyo; p. (1990) 418,267.

Urbino, t., in the Marches, central **Italy**; agr. mkt. and route ctr.; picturesque tourist ctr.; cath., univ., palace; b. with Pesaro (1981) 15,918.

Ure, R., North Yorks., **Eng.**; flows E. and S.E. to the Swale to form the Ouse; upper part of valley known as Wensleydale; 80 km long.

Urengoy, dist., Siberia, **Russia**; lge. natural gas field with 5,400 km. pipeline to W. Europe.

Urfa, prov. S.E. **Turkey**; a. 18,584 km²; p. (1990) 1,001,455.

Urgench, t., cap. of Khorezm oblast, **Uzbekistan**; pt. on Amu Dar'ya R. in Khiva oasis; cotton, food-processing; p. (1990) 128,900.

Uri, can., **Switzerland**; S. of L. of Lucerne; forest and mtns.; traversed by St. Gotthard rly. and R. Reuss; sparse p., German speaking; cap. Altdorf; a. 1,075 km²; p. (1990) 33,700.

Urmia, L., nr. Tabriz, N.W. **Iran**; 136 km by 48 km; salt and shallow; no outlet.

Urmston, Trafford, Gtr. Manchester, **Eng.**; residtl. sub. of Manchester; inc. part of Trafford Park industl. estate; p. (1991) 41,804.

Uruapan, t., Michoacán, W. **Mexico**; mkt. ctr. for semi-tropical mtnous. a.; famous handicrafts; parks, gardens; p. (1990) 217,142.

Urubamba, R., **Peru**; rises in E. Cordillera of Andes; forms one of headstreams of R. Amazon; length 560 km.

Urubupunga, t., **Brazil**; new. t. for 10,000, at site of hydroelectric power sta.

Uruguaiana, t., **Brazil**; on R. Uruguay; cattle ctr.; jerked beef, soap, candles; p. (1985) 105,900.

Uruguay, rep., S. America; smallest of S. American reps.; situated on N. bank of Rio de la Plata estuary; low hills in N.; temperate climate; 60 per cent land a. devoted to livestock rearing, especially cattle, sheep, based on extensive natural grasslands; arable land in S., grains; ch. t. Montevideo, cap. and main ctr. of inds.; food processing, leather, metallurgy, textiles, rubber; a. 186,925 km²; p. (1995) 3,170,000.

Uruguay, R., **S. America**; rises in S. Brazil, flows 1,360 km to Rio de la Plata; forms bdy. between Argentina and Uruguay and part of bdy. between Argentina and Brazil.

Ürümqi (Wulumuchi), c., cap. of Xinjiang Aut. Reg., N.W. **China**; admin., comm. and industl. ctr.; iron and steel, cement, textiles, nitrogenous fertilisers, agr. machin.; local coal, tin, silver mng.; p. (1992) 1,160,000.

Usak, t. and prov., **Turkey**; connected by rail with Izmir; noted for pile carpet-weaving; p. (1985) 88,267 (t.), (1990) 290,283 (prov).

Usambara, mtns., N.E. **Tanzania**; scene of early European settlement (1902); lumber, tea, coffee produced on slopes; max. alt. 2,560 m.

Usedom (Uznam), I., Baltic Sea; off mouth of R. Oder; since 1945 E. part belongs to **Poland**, W. (the larger part) to Germany; a. 445 km²; p. 45,000.

Ushant, I., off cst. of Finistère, **France**; at entrance to English Channel; it was off Ushant that Lord Howe gained his gr. naval victory on the "glorious first of June" 1794; lighthouse, fishing; p. 2,000.

Ushuaia, t., cap. Tierra del Fuego prov., **Argentina**; most S. t. in world; sheep farming, timber, furs; freezing plant; p. (1991) 29,166.

Usk, mkt. t., Monmouthshire, **Wales**; 13th cent. cas.; p. (1991) 2,187.

Usk, R., Gwent, S. **Wales**; flows S. through Monmouthshire and Newport to Bristol Channel; picturesque, good fishing; 91 km long.

Usküdar (Scutari), t., **Turkey**; on Bosporus, opposite Istanbul; mkt. ctr.; new bridge to European side of Bosporus; Crimean memorial cemetery for Brit. troops; Muslim cemeteries.

Uspallata Pass, 3,800 m high over Andes between Mendoza, **Argentina**, and Santiago, **Chile**; monument "Christ of the Andes" marks international bdy. settlement; used by Mendoza–Valparaiso rly.

Ussuri, R., rises in Maritime prov. of **Russia**, flows *c.* 800 km to R. Amur; final 480 km forms Sino-Russian bdy.

Ussuriysk (Voroshilov), t., **Russia**; 112 km N. of Vladivostok; rly. junc. of Trans-Siberian and Chinese Eastern rlys.; engin., agr. prod.; p. (1989) 158,000.

Ustica, I., Palermo, **Italy**; basalt; agr., fishing, handicrafts; a. 8 km²; p. (1981) 1,157.

Usti-nad-Labem (Aussig), c., Bohemia, **Czech Rep.**; R. pt. on Elbe; route and industl. ctr.; chemicals, textiles, machin.; p. (1990) 106,000.

Ustinov. *See* Izhevsk.

Ust Kamenogorsk, c., **Kazakhstan**; on Irtysh R.; mng. ctr.; food processing, clothing; hydroelectric power sta. nearby; p. (1990) 329,900.

Usumbura. *See* **Bujumbura.**

Utah, st., **USA;** "Beehive St.'; admitted to Union 1896; st. flower Sego Lily, st. bird Sea Gull; Rocky mtns. in E.; forms part of Gr. Basin in W.; Gr. Salt L. in N.W.; dry continental climate; poor agr. conditions, soil erosion; copper, gold; tourism; Nat. Parks; cap. Salt L. City; a. 219,932 km²; p. (1990) 1,722,850.

Utica, c., N.Y., **USA;** on Mohawk R. and Barge Canal; in rich dairying region; textiles, electronics, tools, firearms; p. (1990) 68,637 (c.), 317,000 (met. a. with Rome).

Utrecht, c., **Neth.;** on Old Rhine (Oude Rijn); univ., cath.; chemical and cigar factories; printing, machin., woollens, silks, velvets; major transport and financial ctr.; picturesque; p. (1994) 234,108 (c.), 545,796 (met. a.).

Utrecht, prov., **Neth.;** between Gelderland and N. and S. Holland; fertile agr., cattle rearing, horticulture; a. 1,362 km²; p. (1994) 1,851,402.

Utsunomiya, t., Honshu, **Japan;** ctr. for Nikko Nat. Park; p. (1990) 426,809.

Uttar Pradesh, st., **India;** Himalayas on N. bdy., drained by Ganges and Jumna; irrigation; wheat, rice, millet, barley, maize, cotton, sugar, oil-seeds; ch. ts. Allahabad, Lucknow (cap.), Varanasi, Kanpur, Agra, Meerut; a. 293,732 km²; p. (1991) 139,112,287.

Uttlesford, l. gov. dist., Essex, **Eng.;** inc. Saffron Walden and Dunmow; p. (1995) 68,300.

Uttoxeter, t., East Staffs., **Eng.;** on R. Dove; machin., biscuit mftg.; expanded t.; p. (1991) 10,329.

Uusikaupunki (Swed. **Nystad**), spt., Abo-Bjorneborg, S.W. **Finland;** on G. of Bothnia.

Uzbekistan, CIS former constituent rep., USSR; crossed by Rs. Amu Dar'ya and Syr Dar'ya; contains part of fertile Ferghana Valley; intensive farming based on irrigation; rice, cotton, fruits, silk, cattle, sheep; ch. cs. Tashkent (cap.), Samarkand; alluvial gold deposits and bauxite in Kizil-Kum desert; a. 412,250 km²; p. (1994) 22,199,000.

Uzhgorod, c., **Ukraine;** economic and cultural ctr.; friendship pipeline from Kuybyshev; univ.; p. (1990) 119,600.

V

Vaal, R., **S. Africa;** rises in Drakensberg mtns., flows between the Transvaal and Orange Free State to join the Orange R. nr. Kimberley. V. dam irrigates lge. a. of Witwatersrand; 896 km long.

Vaasa, c., cap. of Vaasa prov., W. **Finland;** pt. on G. of Bothnia; exp. timber and timber prods.; agr. ctr.; food processing, textiles, timber inds.; p. (1993) 54,713.

Vác, t., **Hungary;** on R. Danube; comm. ctr.; summer resort for Budapest; cath.; p. (1997) 34,000.

Vadso, cap. of Finnmark prov., N.E. **Norway;** ice-free Arctic pt. on N. side of Varangar fjord.

Vaduz, mkt. t., cap. of **Liechtenstein;** on Rhine; sm. tourist resort; p. (1991) 4,887.

Vaigach, sm. I., between Novaya Zemlya and mainland of Russia; geological extension of Urals; low-lying reindeer pasture; seal fishing.

Valais, can., **Switzerland;** in upper valley of R. Rhône; surrounded by mtns., forested on slopes; vines and cereals in valleys; ch. resort Zermatt, cap. Sion; a. 5,234 km²; p. (1990) 248,300.

Valdai Hills, morainic ridges between Leningrad and Moscow, **Russia;** rise to *c.* 348 m and form ch. watershed of rivers, Vlga, Dvina and Dniester.

Val d'Aosta, aut. region, N.W. **Italy;** high Alpine cty., borders France and Switzerland; cap. Aosta; agr., hydroelectric power; winter resorts; a. 3,263 km²; p. (1992) 117,204.

Val-de-Marne, dep., S.E. of Paris, **France;** cap.. Créteil; a. 243 km²; p. (1990) 1,215,500.

Valdez, t., Alaska, **USA;** ice-free pt., fishing; terminal of oil pipeline from North Slope; p. (1990) 9,952 (with Cordova).

Valdivia, c., S. **Chile;** on R. Callecalle nr. the sea (pt. Corral); damaged by earthquake and tidal wave 1960; univ.; metal, wood and leather gds.; paper, flour, brewing; p. (1992) 122,436.

Val d'Oise, dep., N.W. of Paris, **France;** cap.

Pontoise; a. 1,248 km²; p. (1990) 1,049,600.

Valdosta, t., Ga., **USA;** rly. and tr. ctr. for region producing tobacco, cotton, timber; p. (1980) 37,596.

Valence, t., cap. of Drôme dep., S.E. **France;** on R. Rhône; silks., hosiery, vineyards; agr. mkt.; p. (1990) 65,026 (t.), 107,965 (met. a.).

Valencia, region, E. **Spain;** on Mediterranean; comprises provs. of Alicante, Castellón de la Plana and Valencia; mtnous., with densely populated, fertile coastal plain; irrigation makes a. a major producer of Mediterranean fruit and crops; a. 23,305 km²; p. (1991) 2,135,846.

Valencia, c., cap. of V. prov., E. **Spain;** pt. on Mediterranean at mouth of R. Turia; one of most impt. agr. ts. of cty., and active industl. and comm. ctr.; univ., cath.; resort; p. (1991) 777,247.

Valencia, c., N. **Venezuela;** nr. L. Valencia; ctr. of agr. a., sugar-cane, cotton; leading industl. t.; cattle mart; cotton mills, meat packing; cath.; p. (1990) 903,076.

Valenciennes, c., Nord dep., N. **France;** in Hainaut cty. on R. Escaut (Scheldt); metallurgical and chemical inds.; once famous for hand-made lace; birthplace of Froissart and Watteau; chosen (1997) as site for new Toyota car factory; p. (1990) 39,276 (c.), 336,481 (met. a.).

Valentia, I., S.W. Kerry, **R.o.I.;** in Dingle Bay; agr., fishing; 10 km by 3 km.

Vale of Glamorgan, The, S. **Wales,** unit. auth. created in 1996 from former l. gov. dist; lowland bordering Bristol Channel; inc. cstl. ts. of Barry and Penarth; p. (1995) 118,800.

Vale of White Horse, l. gov. dist., Oxon., **Eng.;** based on Abingdon, Faringdon and Wantage; p. (1995) 113,100.

Vale Royal, l. gov. dist., Cheshire, **Eng.;** a. in ctr. of co. and inc. saltfield ts. of Northwich and Winsford; p. (1995) 114,700.

Valladolid, c., cap. of V. prov., **Spain;** on R. Pisuerga (trib. of Douro); grain tr.; route, industl. and comm. ctr.; food processing, textiles; cath., univ.; p. (1991) 345,259 (c.), 505,309 (prov.).

Valle del General, upland, S.W. **Costa Rica;** pioneer subsistence agr., maize, tropical fruit, cattle; improving transport.

Vallejo, t., Cal., **USA;** at mouth of Napa R. on San Pablo Bay; pt. and processing ctr. for farm prod.; naval shipyard; p. (1990) 109,199 (t.), 451,000 (met. a. with Fairfield-Napa).

Valletta, c., cap. of **Malta;** ch. spt. on rocky penin. of Mt. Scebarras, E. cst.; formerly naval base; cath., univ.; p. (1990) 9,199, 101,749 (urban harbour area.).

Valli di Comacchio, lagoon a., N.E. **Italy;** ctr. of an impt. eel industry; a. 259 km².

Valparaiso, c., central **Chile;** leading pt. on Pac. cst. of S. America; attractive c. with backdrop of steep hills; mftg., comm. and industl. ctr. of rep. with textile mills, sugar refineries, paint, shoe and chemical factories; univ.; p. (1992) 276,736, (1992) 1,373,967 (region).

Valtellina, fertile valley, **Italy;** in Lombard Alps above I. Como; impt. for vine cultivation; hydroelectric power resources; tourism.

Van, c., cap. of Van prov., S.E. **Turkey;** stands at 1,726 m on shore of salty L. Van; tr. ctr. of wheat-growing a.; new Turkish-Iranian rail link; p. (1990) 126,010 (t.), 637,433 (prov.).

Vancouver, c., B.C., **Canada;** Pac. cst. spt. with excellent natural harbour; international airport and terminus of transcontinental rly.; timber inds., shipbldg., fishing, oil and sugar refining; exp. prod. from these inds.; protection by mountains and mild climate make c. a major tourist ctr.; fastest-growing city in Canada; second lgst. Chinese community outside China; univ.; p. (1986) 431,147 (c.), (1991) 1,602,502 (met. a.).

Vancouver, I., B.C., **Canada;** off W. cst.; mtnous., forested; woodpulp, paper; indented cst. provides many natural harbours; fishing; cap. Victoria; a. 33,797 km².

Vancouver, t., Wash., **USA;** spt. on Columbia R. opposite Portland (Ore.); exp. grain, timber; food processing; p. (1990) 238,000 (met. a.).

Vandellos, Tarragona, **Spain;** nuclear power sta.; p. (1981) 3,838.

Vanderbijlpark, t., Transvaal, **S. Africa;** on Vaal R.; ctr. for steel wks.; p. (1980) 294,082 (dist.).

Vänern, lge. L., **Sweden;** W.N.W. of L. Vättern, with which it is connected by canal (and thence with the Baltic); a. 5,566 km².

Vänersborg, L. pt., **Sweden**; on tongue of land between R. Göta and the Vasobotten (southernmost bay of L. Väner); footwear, wood and sulphite pulp; p. (1983) 34,976.

Vannes, t., cap. of Morbihan dep., N.W. **France**; sm. pt. on S. cst. Brittany; cath.; dates from Roman times; p. (1982) 45,397.

Vanuatu, (New Hebrides), former Anglo-French condominion, S. Pac. Oc.; between New Caledonia and Fiji Is.; indep. st. 1980; strong separist moves in Santo I.; mostly subsistence agr.; few cash crops; ch. crop coconuts; no worked minerals; thickly forested; cap. Vila; a. 14,763 km²; p. (1996) 160,000.

Var, dep., S.E. **France**; in Provence, on Mediterranean; mainly agr. with some inds. at Draguignan and Toulon (cap. since 1974); bauxite at Brignoles; rapid growth of p.; inc. many coastal resorts; a. 6,042 km²; p. (1990) 815,400.

Varanasi (Benares), c., Uttar Pradesh, **India**; famous holy c. on Ganges, 640 km N.W. of Calcutta; place of annual pilgrimage; univ.; handicrafts, brasses, brocades, embroideries; p. (1991) 932,000.

Varanger Fjord, inlet of Arctic Oc. into Finnmark, **Norway**; iron mng. on S. shore.

Vardar, R., flows through Yugoslav and Greek Macedonia into Aegean Sea nr. Salonika; inc. V. agr. region; hydroelectric power; routeway; 448 km long.

Varde, t., W. Jutland, **Denmark**; agr. and route ctr.; food processing; steelwks; p. (1990) 19,134.

Vardö, t., Finnmark prov., N.E. **Norway**; sm. ice-free pt. on Vardoy I. with fish and oil interests; p. (1990) 3,008.

Vares, t., **Bosnia-Herzegovina**, formerly Yugoslavia; iron mng.; developing mnfs.

Varese, t., Lombardy, **Italy**; in Alpine foothills; resort and industl. ctr.; engin., furniture, paper, textiles, wines; p. (1981) 90,527.

Värmland, prov., **Sweden**; agr., iron mng. and processing, timber inds.; cap. Karlstad; a. 19,236 km²; p. (1992) 284,691.

Varna, t., **Bulgaria**; spt. on Black Sea; industl. ctr. of heavy inds.; summer resorts on cst. nearby; p. (1990) 314,913.

Varnsdorf, t., **Czech Rep.**; rly. junc. on German bdr.; impt. textile ctr.

Västerås, c., cap. of Västmanland prov., **Sweden**; on L. Mälar; impt. elec. and metallurgical inds.; power sta.; impt. mediaeval c., cath., cas.; p. (1992) 120,889.

Västerbotten, prov., **Sweden**; forested; timber inds.; cap. Umea; a. 59,153 km²; p. (1992) 255,987.

Västernorrland, prov., **Sweden**; forests and timber inds.; cap. Harnosand; a. 25,706 km²; p. (1992) 260,829.

Vastervik, t., Kalmar prov., **Sweden**; on Baltic cst. engin., chemicals, paper; p. (1992) 39,731.

Västmanland, prov., **Sweden**; N. of L. Mälar; mkt. gardening in S.; iron and silver mng. in N.; iron and steel inds.; cap. Västerås; a. 8,363 km²; p. (1992) 260,096.

Vasto, t., Abruzzi e Molise, **Italy**; agr. ctr. on steep-sided, vine-producing plateau; sm. Adriatic fishing pt.; p. (1981) 30,036.

Vatican City, indep. sov. Papal st., **Italy**; forms an enclave in Rome; inc. Papal residence, St. Peter's cath.; a. 44 ha; p. (1993) 1,000.

Vatna Jökull, mtn., **Iceland**; elevated snowfield; active volcano; alt. 2,120 m.

Vättern, L., **Sweden**; 40 km S.E. L. Vänern; a. 1,898 km².

Vaucluse, dep. S.E. **France**; in Provence; cap. Avignon; a. 3,577 km²; p. (1990) 467,100.

Vaud, can., W. **Switzerland**; N. of L. Geneva; forests and vineyards; cap. Lausanne; a. 3,209 km²; p. (1990) 583,600.

Växjö, t., S. **Sweden**; engin., timber wks., hosiery; p. (1992) 70,704.

Vejle, spt., Jutland, **Denmark**; admin. ctr. V. prov.; industl.; p. (1990) 51,263.

Velbert, t., N. Rhine–Westphalia, **Germany**; N.W. of Wuppertal; metal ind., locks and keys; p. (1986) 88,600.

Vélez-Málaga, t., Málaga prov., S. **Spain**; famous for wine, raisins, sugar, olive oil; Moorish cas.; p. (1981) 41,776.

Velletri, t., central **Italy**; at foot of Alban hills overlooking Pontine marshes; noted for its wine; Garibaldi routed Neapolitans here 1849; p. (1981) 41,114.

Vellore, t., Tamil Nadu, **India**; agr. mkt. t.; scene of Sepoy mutiny 1806; p. (1991) 175,061.

Velsen, t., N. Holland prov., **Neth.**; nr. entrance to N. Sea Canal, inc. IJmuiden iron and steel wks.; lge. paper mill; met. a. with Beverwijk; p. (1994) 63,617 (c), 133,704 (met. a.).

Veluwe, dist., Gelderland, **Neth.**; between Arnhem and IJselmeer; low hills of glacial sands and sand-dunes; heathland and pinewoods; relatively low p. density.

Venda, Bantu homeland, Transvaal, **S. Africa**; 3rd homeland granted "independence" (1979); nr. Zimbabwe border; p. (1985) 459,986.

Vendée, dep., W. **France**; on Bay of Biscay; fish. pts., beach resorts, agr. pasturage, vineyards; cap. La Roche-sur-Yon; a. 6,972 km²; p. (1990) 509,400.

Vendôme, t., Loir-et-Cher dep., **France**; on R. Loire; leather gds., cottons; mediaeval cas.; p. (1982) 18,218.

Venetia (Veneto), region, N.E. **Italy**; between the Alps and the Adriatic; embraces provs. Vicenza, Verona, Venice, Udine, Treviso, Padua, Belluno, and Rovigo; mtnous. in N., inc. Dolomite Alps; fertile plain of Po R. in S.; intensive arable agr.; ch. c. Venice; a. 18,384 km²; p. (1992) 4,395,263.

Venezia Giulia. See **Friuli-Venezia Giulia.**

Venezuela, fed. rep., N. cst. S. America; wealth derived from long-established oil ind. (90 per cent of exp. are oil); tropical climate, with temperate uplands, tropical forests and tall grass savannah lands (llanos); most economically advanced a. around cap. Carácas and oilfield a. of L. Maracaibo; counter pole of development based on hydroelectric power resources and iron ore in Caroní R. region; growing steel inds., government investment in lge. agr. areas, esp. maize and cereals; coffee from highlands main comm. agr. crop and exp.; large foreign debt; a. 912,050 km²; p. (1993) 20,407,000.

Venice (Venezia), c., cap. of V. prov. and ch. c. of Venetia, N.E. **Italy**; built on gr. of islets within lagoon in G. of V., at head of Adriatic; splendid architecture, rich in art treasures and historic associations; extensive canal network, inc. Grand Canal, intensive use leading to erosion of bldgs.; gradually sinking into Adriatic, lge.-scale projects to preserve c.; industl. zone on landward side in subs. of Porto Marghera and Mestre; craft and heavy inds.; p. (1992) 305,617.

Venlo, t., **Neth.**; on R. Maas; agr. mkt. and rly. junc.; chemicals, optical instruments, electric lamps; p. (1994) 65,367.

Ventimiglia, t., Liguria, N.W. **Italy**; on Mediterranean cst. on Fr. border; cath.; flower mkt.; tourism; p. (1981) 26,373.

Ventnor, t., I. of Wight, **Eng.**; on S. cst. 18 km S. of Ryde; mild climate, tourist and health resort; p. (1991) 5,710.

Veracruz, st., E. **Mexico**; narrow coastal plain rising to Sierra Madre Oriental; contains volcano Orizaba; recent agr. improvements; growth of petroleum inds.; cap. Jalapa; a. 71,836 km²; p. (1990) 6,215,142.

Veracruz, c., V. st., E. **Mexico**; spt. on G. of Mexico; comm. and industl. ctr. of oil region; nearby Laguna Grande, Mexico's first nuclear power sta. (1984); nr. site where Cortés landed 1519; p. (1990) 327,522.

Vercelli, c., cap. of V. prov., N. **Italy**; in Piedmont, on Sesia R.; rice mkt. for lge. irrigated plain textiles, machin., aircraft parts; p. (1981) 52,488.

Verdun, t., Quebec, **Canada**; sub. of Montreal; p. (1991) 61,307.

Verdun, t., Meuse dep., N.E. **France**; in Lorraine, on R. Meuse; strategic ctr. with varied mnfs.; 12th cent. cath.; scene of famous battle 1916; p. (1982) 24,120.

Vereeniging, c., Transvaal prov., **S. Africa**; on Vaal R.; coal, iron and steel, bricks; Treaty of Vereeniging 1902 ended Boer War; p. (1985) 177,220 (dist.).

Verkhneudinsk. See **Ulan-Ude.**

Verkhoyansk, t., Yakutsk, aut. rep., **Russia**; in N.E. Siberia; coldest permanently inhabited place in world; mean Jan. temp. of −59° F.; ctr. of fur trapping a.

Vermont, st., New England, **USA**; "Green Mtn. St.'; admitted to Union 1791; st. flower Red Clover, st. bird Hermitt Thrush; traversed by the Green mtns.; farming, dairying, stock-raising, lumbering, quarrying, machine tool and textile mftg.;

traditional inds. revitalised by new inds. coming from neighbouring Quebec; cap. Montpelier; famous for autumn colours; a. 24,887 km²; p. (1990) 562,758.

Verona, c., cap. of V. prov., N.E. **Italy**; on R. Adige; commands route from central Europe to Brenner pass and from Venice to Milan; cath. and notable monuments; active agr. tr. and inds., printing; p. (1992) 255,492.

Versailles, c., cap. of Yvelines dep., N. **France**; S.W. sub. of Paris; famous royal palace; mkt. gardening, distilleries; Treaty of Versailles 1919; p. (1990) 91,029.

Verviers, t., **Belgium**; nr. Liège; ctr. of textile ind. in Ardennes; p. (1993) 53,731.

Vesoul, t., cap. Haute-Saône dep., **France**; p. (1990) 19,404.

Vestmannaeyjar or **Westman Is.**, archipelago, S. W. **Iceland**; impt. cod fishing ind. based on Heimaey I; p. (1993) 4,886.

Vesuvius, famous active volcano, S. **Italy**; on shore of Bay of Naples; alt. c. 1,186 m; its eruption in A.D. 79 destroyed Pompeii and Herculaneum, and frequent eruptions have since been recorded; observatory founded 1844; funicular rly. from base of mtn. to rim of crater existed from 1880 to 1944 (destroyed by eruption).

Veszprem, c., **Hungary**; in fruit-growing dist., 96 km S. of Budapest; cath., univ. for chemical ind.; p. (1997) 64,000.

Vevey, t., Vaud can., **Switzerland**; on N. shore of L. Geneva; beautiful situation; chocolate, watches; resort; p. (1986) 15,149.

Viareggio, beach resort, Tuscany, **Italy**; on Tyrrhenian Sea, nr. Pisa; monument to Shelley; p. (1981) 58,136.

Viborg, t., Jutland, **Denmark**; admin. ctr. V. prov.; comm. and route ctr.; anc. cath.; textiles, machin., food processing; p. (1990) 39,395.

Vicenza, c. cap. of V. prov., N.E. **Italy**; in Venetia; mkt. ctr. for surrounding fertile agr. plain; textiles, iron and steel; many examples of Palladian architecture; p. (1992) 107,481.

Vichy, t., Allier dep., **France**; on Allier R.; famous spa; hot mineral springs; lge. exp. of V. water; seat of Pétain govt. during German occupation 1940–3; p. (1982) 63,501 (met. a.).

Vicksburg, t., Miss., **USA**; R. pt., on bluffs of Mississippi at junc. of Yazoo canal; shipping and mftg. ctr. in cotton and timber region; prominent in American Civil War; Confederate surrender 1863; p. (1980) 25,434.

Victoria, st., **Australia**; settled rapidly in 19th century with gold rush; now most densely populated yet smallest mainland st.; Latrobe brown coal, offshore natural gas, hydroelectric power encourage rapid industrialisation; dominated by cap. Melbourne; rural a. of Great Dividing Range produces wheat, sheep and dairy prods.; a. 227,516 km²; p. (1993) 4,468,300.

Victoria, c., cap. of B.C., **Canada**; spt. on Vancouver I.; fishing and fish-processing; sawmills, chemicals, cement; beautiful scenery; tourist ctr.; p. (1986) 66,303 (c.), (1991) 287,897 (met. a.).

Victoria, main pt. and harbour between Hong Kong I. and Kowloon, **China**; built on reclaimed land; admin. ctr. of Hong Kong.

Victoria, t., cap. of Labuan I., Sabah, **Malaysia**; fine harbour; p. 3,213.

Victoria, t., cap. of **Seychelles**, Ind. Oc.; harbour on lgst. and most impt. I. of Mahé p. (1987) 59,500 (island).

Victoria, t., S. Texas, **USA**; comm. ctr. in prosperous agr. a.; local oilfields; p. (1980) 50,695.

Victoria Falls (**Mosi-oa-Toenja**), on R. Zambesi, **Zambia**; discovered by Livingstone 1855; falls are 1,674 m wide and broken by islands and rocks.

Victoria, Lake, lgst. L. of **Africa**; bordered by Kenya, Uganda, Tanzania; in depression of Gt. Rift Valley, at alt. 999 m. a. c. 67,340 km²; discharges into Victoria Nile; impt. fisheries; discovered by Speke 1858.

Victoria Land, region, **Antarctica**; discovered by Ross in 1841.

Victoria Nile, R., **Uganda**; E. Africa; name of R. Nile from its source at L. Victoria until it enters L. Mobuto Seso.

Viedma, cap. of Rio Negro prov., S. central **Argentina**; agr. centre; p. (1991) 57,473.

Vienna (**Wien**), c., cap. of **Austria**; R. pt. on branch of Danube; surrounded by Wiener Wald (Vienna forest) and Carpathian foothills; major industl.,

comm. and transport ctr.; many fine bldgs., inc. univ., cath., parliament bldgs., magnificent Prater park; influential ctr. of music, cultural and scientific ctr.; home of Haydn, Mozart, Beethoven, Schubert, Mahler, Brahms, and Freud; p. (1991) 1,533,176.

Vienne, dep., W. **France**; drained by R. Vienne; mainly agr. dist.; cap. Poitiers; a. 7,021 km²; p. (1990) 380,000.

Vienne, t., Isère, **France**; nr. Grenoble, on R. Rhône; textiles, metallurgical inds.; Roman remains; overshadowed by Lyons 27 km to N.; p. (1982) 372,000.

Vienne, R., **France**; trib. of the Loire; rises in Massif Central; 354 km long.

Vientiane, admin. cap., **Laos**; pt. and comm. ctr. on Mekong R.; p. (1985) 377,409.

Viersen, t., N. Rhine–Westphalia, **Germany**; S.W. of Krefeld; textiles, machin., furniture, paper ind.; p. (1986) 78,100.

Vierzon, t., Cher dep., **France**; on R. Cher; bricks, tiles, porcelain from local sands, clay; agr. machin.; p. (1982) 34,886.

Vietnam, **Socialist Rep. of**, S.E. Asia; comprises regions of Cochinchina and Tonkin in former French Indo-China; from 1954–76 two separate countries, N. and S. Vietnam, based on two rivers, Song-koi and Mekong respectively, and separated by the high Annamite chain of mtns.; long period of civil war resulted in reunification; intensive agr. based on rice cultivation now largely collectivised; monsoon climate and river irrigation aid high yields; coffee, tea, rubber, sugar, main comm. crops but much devastation as result of war; minerals mainly concentrated in the N. with impt. anthracite deposit at Quang-Yen; industl. devel. also mainly in N. around Hanoi and ch. pt. Haiphong; hill tribes practising subsistence agr. inhabit the intervening Annamite mtns.; since reunification ts. declining rapidly; a. 335,724 km²; p. (1996) 75,300,000.

Viet-Tri, t., N. **Vietnam**; 128 km N.W. of Hanoi; chemicals, paper mill, sugar refining.

Vigevano, t., Lombardy, **Italy**; on R. Ticino; impt. agr. and industl. ctr.; footwear, plastics, textiles; cath.; p. (1981) 65,228.

Vigo, spt., **Spain**; transatlantic pt. on V. Bay; processing of imports; oil refining; p. (1981) 261,329.

Vijayanagar, ruined c., S.E. **India**; once cap. c. of Hindu empire in S. Deccan; 96 km in circumference; destroyed by Moslem forces at battle of Talikota 1565.

Vijayavada, t., Andhra Pradesh, **India**; rly. junc., comm. ctr.; irrigation dam, Kistna R.; p. (1991) 702,000.

Vila, t. cap. of **Vanuatu**, on S.W. coast of Efate I; p. (1989) 19,400.

Vila Real de Santo António, pt., Faro, **Portugal**; on W. bank of Guadiana R.; exp. copper ore, fish, fruit; p. (1981) 7,390.

Villach, t., Carinthia, S. **Austria**; at junc. of Gail and Drava Rs.; impt. route ctr.; tourism; p. (1991) 55,165.

Villahermosa, c., cap. of Tabasco, S.E. **Mexico**; agr. mkt., sugar processing; rich local petroleum deposits; p. (1990) 390,161.

Villa Maria, t., **Argentina**; rly. junc.; ctr. of grain, timber, dairying dist.; p. (1980) 67,490.

Villarrica, t., S.E. **Paraguay**; agr. tr. ctr. for cattle, tobacco, fruit; wines, yerba-maté grown in surrounding a.; p. (1982) 21,203.

Villavicencio, t., E. **Colombia**; in foothills of Andes; comm. ctr. for the llanos; cattle tr.; p. (1992) 233,026.

Villaviciosa, t., Oviedo prov., N.W. **Spain**; major fishing pt. on Bay of Biscay; p. (1981) 15,703.

Villeurbanne, t., Rhône dep., **France**; forming part of Lyons agglomeration; metallurgy, chemicals, leather, textiles; p. (1990) 119,848.

Vilnius, (Pol. **Wilno**), c., cap. of **Lithuania** on Vilija R. (trib. of Niemen); cultural ctr., cath., univ., historic bldgs.; held by Poland 1920–39; lt. inds., food processing; p. (1990) 592,500.

Vilvoorde, t. Brabant, **Belgium**; on Willebroek Canal NE of Brussels; p. (1993) 33,253.

Vilyui, R., Yakut aut. rep., **Russia**; flows E. from Siberian uplands into Lena R.; R. basin impt. agr. and mng. a.; fishing; 2,400 km long.

Vimy, t., Pas-de-Calais dep., N. **France**; nearby Vimy Ridge, site of Allied victory led by Canadians 1915; p. (1982) 3,621.

Viña del Mar, seaside t., central **Chile,** nr. Valparaiso: fashionable S. American resort; oil and sugar refining, textiles; p. (1992) 302,765.

Vincennes, t., Val-de-Marne dep., **France;** sub. of Paris; famous cas. and Bois; industl. and residtl.; p. (1982) 43,068.

Vindhya Hills, mtn. range, central **India;** separating the Deccan from the Ganges basin; *c.* 640 km long.

Vinnitsa, t., **Ukraine;** on R. Bug 192 km S.W. of Kiev; agr. mkt. t.; engin. chemicals, textiles; p. (1990) 378,800.

Virginia, st., **USA;** one of original 13 sts.; "Old Dominion" St.; admitted to Union 1788; st. flower Dogwood, st. bird Cardinal; wide Atl. coastal plain rising inland to Blue Ridge; famous for high quality "Virginia Leaf" tobacco; industl. ts. of Norfolk, Richmond, Portsmouth and Newport News; cap. Richmond; a. 105,711 km²; p. (1990) 6,187,358.

Virgin Is. (Brit.), W.I.; gr. of Is. E. of Greater Antilles; most impt. Tortola, Virgin Gorda, Anegada; water scarcity, semi-subsistence agr. economy; livestock, fish, fruit, vegetables; a. 153 km²; p. (1993) 17,000.

Virgin Is. (USA), W.I.; external terr. of USA E. of Greater Antilles, 64 km E. of Puerto Rico; 3 main Is., St. Thomas, St. John, St. Croix; bought from Denmark 1917; favourite tourist a. in Caribbean; cap. Charlotte Amalie on St. Thomas; livestock, sugar; rum distilling; a. 344 km²; p. (1990) 101,809.

Vis (Lissa), I., off **Croatia,** Adriatic; fish-canning ctr.; a. 91 km²; anc. remains; resort; sea battle 1866 between Italian and Austrian ironclads; p. 3,000.

Visby, old spt., **Sweden;** on Gotland I. in Baltic Sea; rich in historic interest; resort; p. (1984) 20,000.

Vishakhapatnam, spt., Andhra Pradesh, **India;** deepwater harbour on Bay of Bengal; exp. manganese and oilseeds from Madhya Pradesh; shipbldg.; p. (1991) 752,000.

Vistula, R., **Poland;** rises in Beskids range of Carpathians, flows through Poland past Krakow to Baltic Sea nr. Gdansk; forms major link in E. European waterway system; coal and timber transport; 1,056 km long.

Vitebsk, c., **Belarus;** R. pt. on W. Dvina and impt. rly. junc., in agr. region; textiles, machine tools, food processing; p. (1990) 356,400.

Viterbo, c., cap. of V. prov., **Italy;** N. of Rome; agr. ctr., food-processing; 12th cent. cath. and historic bldgs.; p. (1981) 57,632.

Vitim, R., E. Siberia, **Russia;** flows to R. Lena; navigable for 5 months of year; coal and grain tr.; 1,400 km long.

Vitória, spt., Espirito Santo, **Brazil;** new ocean terminal capturing tr. from Rio de Janeiro; exp. coffee, cocoa, fruit, iron ore; sugar refining, shoes, textiles, cement; p. (1985) 254,400.

Vitoria, c., cap. of Alava prov., **Spain;** in Basque cty.; stands on hill at 534 m; furniture mnf.; defeat of Fr. by Wellington 1813; p. (1991) 208,569.

Vitry-le-François, t., Marne dep., N.E. **France;** on Marne R.; industl., textiles, earthenware; agr. mkt. for Champagne Pouilleuse; p. (1982) 18,829.

Vitry-sur-Seine, S.E. sub., Paris, **France;** flower growing on sand and gravel terraces of Seine R., acreage being reduced by competition from housing and inds.; p. (1990) 82,820.

Vittoria, t., Sicily, **Italy;** mkt. for wine; p. (1981) 50,220.

Vittorio Veneto, t., **Italy;** N. of Venice; resort; textiles; p. (1981) 30,028.

Vizcaya, Basque prov., N. **Spain;** on Bay of Biscay; iron mng.; iron and steel inds.; dense p.; cap. Bilbao; a. 2,165 km²; p. (1991) 1,153,515.

Vlaardingen, t., S. Holland prov., **Neth.;** 8 km W. of Rotterdam, on Nieuwe Maas; leading fish. pt.; p. (1994) 73,820.

Vladikavkaz (Ordzhonikidze), c., cap. of N. Ossetian aut. rep., **Russia;** on R. Terek at foot of Caucasus, ind. ctr., metallurgical inds.; natural gas pipe-line to Tbilisi; hydroelec. power sta.; p. (1989) 300,000.

Vladimir, c., cap. of V. oblast, **Russia;** between Gorki and Moscow, on trib. of Oka R.; founded 12th cent.; caths., historic bldgs.; machine tools, agr. machin., textiles; p. (1989) 350,000.

Vladimir-Volynski, c., N.W. **Ukraine;** one of oldest Ukrainian settlements, founded 9th cent.; agr. mkt. ctr.; p. (1990) 38,400.

Vladivostok, c., spt., **Russia;** ch. pt. and naval base on Pac.; terminus of Trans-Siberian rly. and airline from Moscow; ch. cultural ctr. of Far East; shipyards, fisheries, oil refining, engin., chemicals; economic development in hinterland hindered by distance from major ctrs. of p. and ind.; p. (1989) 634,000.

Vlieland, Friesian I., at entrance to IJsselmeer, **Neth.;** resort, nature reserve.

Vlissingen or **Flushing,** spt., Zeeland prov., S.W. **Neth.;** on Walcheren I.; shipyards, oil refining, fishing; resort; birthplace of Admiral de Ruyter; p. (1993) 44,147.

Vlorë, spt., S.W. **Albania;** on Strait of Otranto, Adriatic Sea; salt; oil pipeline connects from Kucovë nr. Berat; p. (1991) 76,000.

Vltava or **Moldau,** R., Bohemia, **Czech Rep.;** rises in Sumava mtns. (Bohemian Forest) and flows to R. Elbe below Prague; used for hydro-electric power; *c.* 416 km long.

Voghera, t., Lombardy, **Italy;** rly. junc. and agr. mkt.; textiles, machin. engin.; cas., cath.; p. (1981) 42,639.

Voi, t., **Kenya,** E. Africa; 144 km N.W. of Mombasa on rly. to Nairobi; branch connection with Tanzania rly. system allows agr. prod. from Arusha and Moshi dists. to pass through Mombasa as alternative to Tanga; shoe factory.

Voiron, t., Isère dep., **France;** on Morge R., 24 km N.W. of Grenoble; textiles, paper; p. (1982) 19,658.

Vojvodina, aut. prov., N. Serbia, **Yugoslavia;** impt. and fertile agr. dist. crossed by Danube R.; intensive agr., prosperous and dense p.; fruit, vegetables, livestock, food processing; ch. c. Novi Sad; a. 22,489 km²; p. (1981) 2,034,772.

Volcano Is., Japan; 3 volcanic Is. in Pac. Oc., S. of Japan, admin. by USA until 1968, now Japanese.

Volga, R., **Russia;** rises in Valdai hills, flows in serpentine course to Caspian at Astrakhan in wide delta; ch. tribs., Oka, Sura, Vetluga, Kama, Samara; major waterway linked to Baltic Sea, Azov, and Black Seas, and to Moscow; hydroelectric developments reducing sturgeon in Caspian Sea and caviar prod. declining; longest R. in Europe, 3,720 km.

Volga Baltic Waterway (Mariinsk Waterway), Russia; inland deepwater navigation network linking Black Sea and Caspian Sea in S. with Baltic Sea and White Sea in N.

Volgograd (Stalingrad), c., **Russia;** R. pt. on Volga and major rly. ctr.; exp. raw materials, fish; industl. ctr. for steel, engin., chemicals, oil refining; hydroelectric power sta.; fierce siege and successful defence 1942 turning point of second world war; p. (1989) 999,000.

Volhynia, historic region, **Ukraine;** on Polish frontier; rich agr. lowland; coal mng. at Novovodinsk; cap. Lutsk.

Volkhov, R., **Russia;** flows from L. Ilmen to L. Ladoga; navigable; hydroelectric power sta. and aluminium smelting plant at Volkhov (St. Petersburg oblast); 208 km long.

Volkingen, t., Saarland, **Germany;** on Saar R., 13 km W. of Saarbrücken; coal mng., iron and steel; p. (1986) 43,100.

Vologda, c., **Russia;** R. and rly. junc. on upper Sukhona R.; in dairying a.; engin., textiles, sawmilling, paper, dairy inds.; cath., historic bldgs.; p. (1989) 283,000.

Volos, spt., **Greece;** at head of G. of V.; impt. transport, industl., comm. ctr.; exp. agr. prods.; car mnfs.; p. (1981) 71,378.

Volsk, c., **Russia;** R. pt. on Volga R.; cement, tanneries, metallurgy, food processing.

Volta (White Volta), major R., **W. Africa;** drains extensive terr. in Niger bend, flows S. through Ghana to delta on Guinea cst., 112 km E. of Accra; main means of communication but rapids make through navigation impossible; Volta R. project for industrialisation of Ghana; dam and power plant at Akosombo, aluminium smelter at Tema; power decr. with decline in reservoir size from drought in Sahel; 1,520 km long. *See also* Black Volta.

Volta Redonda, t., Rio de Janeiro, **Brazil;** state-owned steel plant; p. (1985) 220,100.

Volterra, hill t., Tuscany, **Italy;** Etruscan and mediaeval walls; alabaster, salt; p. (1981) 14,080.

Volzhsky, t., **Russia;** industl. t. on Volga R.; aluminium smelting, chemicals; p. (1989) 269,000.

Voorburg, t., **Neth.;** industl. ctr. E. of the Hague; p. (1993) 39,734.

Vorarlberg, prov., Austria; forestry, dairying, tourism; inds. based on hydroelectric power; textiles; cap. Bregenz; a. 2,600 km²; p. (1991) 333,128.

Vorkuta, ctr. of Pechora coal basin, Russia; beyond Arctic circle, which supplies entire European N. Russia; p. (1989) 116,000.

Voronezh, c., Russia; R. pt. on Voronezh R. nr. junc. with Don; impt. comm. ctr. in fertile agr. dist.; machin., rubber, oil refining, food processing; nuclear power sta.; univ., cath.; p. (1989) 887,000.

Voroshilovgrad, See Lugansk.

Voroshilovsk. See Kommunarsk.

Vosges, dep., E. France; on Franco-German frontier; dairying, vineyards, stone quarrying, textiles; cap. Epinal; a. 5,970 km²; p. (1990) 386,300.

Vosges, highlands, E. France; structurally similar to Black Forest, from which they are separated by Rhine rift valley; forested slopes, vineyards; source of Meurthe, Moselle, Sarve, Ill, and Saône Rs.; highest summit Ballon de Guebwiller, 1,425 m.

Votkinsk, t., Russia; 61 km N.E. of Izhevsk; lge. engin. plant; hydroelectric power sta.; birthplace of Tchaikovsky; p. (1989) 104,000.

Vranja, t., Croatia (formerly Yugoslavia); flax and hemp culture and mnf.; developing industl. ctr. based on handicrafts.

Vratsa, t., Bulgaria; on R. Vratcanska; jewellery, wine, silk, tanning; p. (1990) 85,272.

Vrsac, t., Yugoslavia; milling, wine, brandy; p. (1981) 61,005.

Vulcano, I., Lipari gr., Italy; off N.E. cst. Sicily; active volcano; gave its name as generic title for this type of mtn.

Vyatka, (Kirov), c., Russia; pt. on Vyatka R.; rly. junc.; engin., saw milling, chemicals, leather inds.; cath.; p. (1989) 478,000.

Vyatka, R., Russia; rises in foothills of Urals, flows past Vyotka into Kama R.; timber transport, fishing; c. 1,360 km long.

Vyborg (Viipuri), c., Russia; spt. on G. of Finland, occupies strategic site on Karelian Isthmus, N.W. of St. Petersburg; Finnish until 1945; exp. timber; shipyards, engin., food processing.

Vychegda, R., Russia; rises in Urals, flows W. to N. Dvina R.; timber transport; 1,120 km long.

Vyrnwy, L., reservoir, Powys, Wales; with dam 360 m long supplies water for Liverpool; a. 454 ha.

W

Waal, R., Neth.; S. arm of R. Rhine.

Waco, c., Texas, USA; in Brazos valley; route ctr., airport; regional cultural ctr.; univ.; textiles, leather; p. (1990) 103,590.

Waddenzee, stretch of shallow water between W. Frisian Is. and Neth. mainland.

Wadebridge, spt., Cornwall, Eng.; at head of Camel estuary, 10 km N.W. of Bodmin; agr. mkt.; p. (1991) 5,291.

Wadi Halfa, t., Sudan; on R. Nile at second cataract; rly. terminus of Sudan rlys.; inundated by Aswan L.; new t. Khashm el Girba for inhabitants.

Wadi Medani, t., cap. of Blue Nile prov., Sudan; ctr. of cotton growing dist.; p. (1983) 141,065.

Wagadugu. See Ouagadougou.

Wagga Wagga, t., N.S.W., Australia; on R. Murrumbidgee; ctr. of agr. and pastoral dist.; p. (1981) 36,837.

Wahiawa, t., Oahu I., Hawaii; pineapples.

Waikaremoana, L., N.I., N.Z.; hydroelectric power.

Waikato, R., N.I., N.Z.; rises in L. Taupo and flows N.W. into Tasman Sea; coalfields, hydroelec. power stas.; longest R. of N.Z.; 422 km long; gives name to dist. and region; p. (1991) 37,556 (dist.), 338,959 (region).

Wairakei, N.I., N.Z.; on L. Taupo; health resort; geothermal power sta.

Waitemata, c., N.I., N.Z.; part of Auckland on picturesque inlet; p. (1987) 98,500.

Wakamatsu. See Kitakyushu.

Wakatipu, L., Otago, S.I., N.Z.; 83 km long, 5 km wide, 360 m deep, 320 m a.s.l.

Wakayama, spt., Honshu, Japan; textiles; new iron and steel plant; p. (1990) 396,553.

Wakefield, c., met. dist., West Yorks., Eng.; on R. Calder; 13 km S. of Leeds; cath.; former ctr. of coal mng. a.; woollen and worsted prods., chemicals, engin.; p. (1995) 317,100 (dist.), (1991) 73,955 (c.).

Wakefield, t., Va., USA; on Potomac R., nr. Fredericksburg; birthplace of George Washington; p. (1980) 1,355.

Wake I., coral atoll, Pac. Oc.; between Marianas and Hawaii; comm. and naval base on route to Far East, belonging to USA; p. (1980) 302.

Walachia, region, S. Romania; wide plain bounded by Transylvanian Alps and separated from Yugoslavia by Danube; rich agr. a., "the bread-basket of Romania"; Ploiesti oilfields; inds. nr. ch. c. Bucharest; a. 76,563 km²;

Walbrzych (Waldenburg), c. and prov., S.W. Poland (since 1945); formerly in Lower Silesia; industl. and mng. ctr. at 427 m; porcelain, machin., engin.; p. (1989) 141,504 (c.), 738,100 (prov.).

Walchensee, Lake, Bavaria, Germany; a. 16 km²; hydroelectric power sta.

Walcheren, I., Zeeland prov., S.W. Neth.; in N. Sea at entrance to Scheldt estuary; mainly agr.; ch. ts., Vlissingen, Middelburg; flooded 1944 to stop German advance; tourism.

Waldenburg. See Walbrzych.

Wales, principality, Great Britain; mostly mtnous.; Cambrian mtns. rise to 1,085 m at Snowdon; contrast between N. and Central Wales (pastoral farming, forestry, water supply, tourism, rural depopulation) and S. Wales (former coalfield, metal-based inds., lge. ts.); referendum (1997) paved way for Welsh Assembly; cap. Cardiff; p. (1995) 2,916,800.

Wallasey, t., Wirral, adjoining Birkenhead, Merseyside, Eng.; residtl., seaside resort (New Brighton); p. (1991) 60,895.

Wallensee, L., Switzerland; 18 km long.

Wallingford, t., South Oxon., Eng.; on R. Thames, to N. of its gap between Chilterns and Lambourn Downs; p. (1991) 9,315.

Wallis and Futuna Is., gr. of coral Is., S. Pac. Oc.; overseas terr. of France; copra; a. 275 km²; p. (1993) 14,400 (mostly Polynesians).

Wallsend, t., frmly. Tyne and Wear, Eng.; on N. bank of Tyne, 6 km below Newcastle; Tyne tunnel links with Jarrow; shipbldg., engin., iron, plywood; at end of Hadrian's Wall; p. (1991) 45,280.

Walmer, t., Kent, Eng.; 3 km S. of Deal; holiday resort; cas., residence of Warden of Cinque Ports.

Walney, I., off cst. of Cumbria, Eng.; opposite Barrow.

Walsall, t., met. dist., West Midlands, Eng.; 8 km E. of Wolverhampton; leather and iron prods., engin., steel tubes; p. (1995) 262,800 (dist.), (1991) 174,739 (t.).

Walsingham, v., North Norfolk, Eng.; many old bldgs., priory ruins, abbey; pilgrimage ctr.

Walsum, t., N. Rhine-Westphalia, Germany; at confluence of Rhine and Emscher canal; R. pt. for Oberhausen steelwks.

Waltham, c., Mass., USA; nr. Boston; science-based inds.; univ.; p. (1980) 58,200.

Waltham Abbey, t., Epping Forest, Essex, Eng.; 21 km N.E. London, on edge of Epping Forest; tomatoes; Norman nave of abbey part of parish church; p. (1991) 15,629.

Waltham Forest, outer bor., E. London, Eng.; incorporating former bors. of Chingford, Leyton, Walthamstow; industl. and residtl.; p. (1995) 221,100.

Walthamstow. See Waltham Forest.

Walton and Weybridge, ts., Elmbridge, Surrey, Eng.; on R. Thames, 27 km S.W. of London; eng., aircraft; p. (1991) 52,802.

Walvis Bay, spt., South Africa, enclave in Namibia; on Walvis Bay, Atl. Oc.; fishing, fish processing; impt. base for S. Africa who wishes to keep it separate from Namibia; p. (1980) 20,740 (dist.).

Wandsworth, inner bor., S.W. London, Eng.; inc. Battersea; on R. Wandle at influx into Thames; oil mills, metal wks., paper, brewing; p. (1995) 265,100.

Wanganui, c. and dist., N.I., N.Z.; pt. on R. Wanganui; tr. ctr. for wool, grain, meat, dairy prod.; agr. processing, steel-pipes, fertilisers; iron ore deposits; p. (1991) 45,082.

Wanganui, R., N.I., N.Z.; famous for its beauty; 265 km long.

Wangaratta, t., Victoria, **Australia**; 232 km from Melbourne; ctr. of varied agr. dist. supplying prods. (milk, wool) for processing; p. (1991) 15,984.

Wankie, t., **Zimbabwe**; site of coal-mng. ind.; 344 km N.W. of Bulawayo; modern coal fired power sta.; p. (1982) 39,200.

Wanne-Eickel, t., N. Rhine–Westphalia, **Germany**; pt. on Rhine–Herne canal; coal-mng. ctr. of Ruhr.

Wansbeck, R., Northumberland, **Eng.**; flows E. from Pennines into N. Sea 5 km N. of Blyth.

Wansbeck, l. gov. dist., Northumberland, **Eng.**; inc. Newbiggin, Ashington and Bedlington; p. (1995) 62,200.

Wantage, mkt. t., Oxon., **Eng.**; in Vale of the White Horse; birthplace of King Alfred; p. (1991) 9,452.

Wapping, Thames-side dist., London, **Eng.**

Warangal, t., Andhra Pradesh, **India**; textiles, carpets; p. (1991) 448,000.

Ware, mkt. t., East Herts., **Eng.**; on R. Lea; 3 km N.E. of Hertford; p. (1991) 17,000.

Wareham, mkt. t., Purbeck, Dorset, **Eng.**; on R. Frome, on N. of I. of Purbeck, 13 km S.W. of Poole; p. (1991) 6,500 (est.).

Warminster, t., West Wilts., **Eng.**; on Wylye watershed at edge of Salisbury Plain; agr. mkt., gloves; p. (1991) 16,379.

Warnemünde, spt., **Germany**; ferry pt. for rail traffic between Berlin and Copenhagen; shipbldg.; outport for Rostock; resort.

Warrego, R., Queensland, N.S.W., **Australia**; trib. of R. Darling; 640 km long.

Warren, t., Ohio, **USA**; on Mahoning R.; iron and steel mftg.; p. (1990) 50,793.

Warrenpoint, spt., Newry and Mourne, **N. Ireland**; at head of Carlingford Lough; p. (1991) 5,408.

Warrington, t., l. gov. dist., Cheshire, **Eng.**; on R. Mersey and Manchester Ship Canal; metal inds. (wire-drawing), chemicals, brewing, paper; expanded as new c. (to take people from Manchester); attracting high technology inds.; p. (1995) 188,800 (dist.), (1991) 82,812 (t.).

Warrnambool, t., spt., Victoria, **Australia**; former pt. on Lady Bay; wool processing, rugs, blankets; p. (1991) 23,946.

Warsaw (Warszawa), c., cap. of Poland; on R. Vistula; devastated 1939–45; facsimile rebuilding based on Canaletto's paintings; cath., univ.; rly. ctr.; iron, steel, engin., textiles, chemicals; p. (1989) 1,651,255 (c.), 2,415,900 (prov.).

Warsop, t., Notts., **Eng.**; 6 km N.E. of Mansfield; limestone, gravel; p. (1991) 10,083.

Warta, R., Poland; trib. of R. Oder; connected to R. Vistula by canal; 720 km long.

Warwick, t., Queensland, **Australia**; sawmilling, agr. processing; p. (1992) 9,540.

Warwick, co. t., l. gov. dist., Warwicks., **Eng.**; on R. Avon, 13 km S.W. of Coventry; cas.; agr. implements, brewing, malting; p. (1995) 120,700 (dist.); (1991) 22,476 (t.).

Warwick, c., R.I., **USA**; on Narragansett Bay; textile ctr.; p. (1980) 87,123.

Warwickshire, non-met. co., W. Midlands, **Eng.**; undulating, drained by tribs. of Rs. Severn and Trent, crossed by Cotswolds to S.; sm. coalfield to N.; potential new coalfield in S.; p. (1995) 498,700.

Wash, The, bay, N. Sea between Lincs. and Norfolk, **Eng.**; 35 km long, 24 km wide; partly reclaimed to form the Fens; proposed barrage to aid further reclamation and water storage.

Washington, t., Tyne and Wear, **Eng.**; 8 km S.E. of Gateshead; coal, iron and steel, stone quarrying, chemicals; new t. 1964; p. (1991) 56,848.

Washington, c., cap. of **USA**; in Dist. of Columbia on Potomac R.; c. planned as national seat of Government; White House, Capitol, 5 univs.; over half p. Black; p. (1990) 606,900 (c.), 3,923,574 (met. a.).

Washington, st., **USA**; 'Evergreen St.' admitted to Union 1889; st. flower Western Rhododendron, st bird Willow Goldfinch; in extreme N.W., stretching from Pac. Oc. into Rocky mtns.; over half a. forested; Colombia R. and tribs. provide hydroelectric power; timber, fishing, tourism; cap. Olympia; a. 176,617 km²; p. (1990) 4,886,692.

Wassatch Mtns., range of Rocky mtns., Utah and Idaho, **USA**; alt. 3,600 m.

Wast Water, L. Dist., deepest L. in **Eng.**; 5 km long, 79 m deep.

Watchet, t., West Somerset, **Eng.**; sm. pt. on cst. of Bristol Channel; p. (1991) 3,147.

Watenstedt-Salzgitter. *See* Salzgitter.

Waterbury, c., Conn., **USA**; on Naugatuck R.; ctr. of brass ind. and metal gds.; p. (1990) 108,961.

Waterford, co., Munster, **R.o.I.**; mtnous. co. in S.E.; mainly agr., dairying, pigs; fishing; co. t. Waterford; a. 1,867 km²; p. (1986) 91,151.

Waterford, co. t., spt., Waterford, **R.o.I.**; on R. Suir; cath.; brewing, fishing, glass mnfs.; p. (1986) 39,529 (t.).

Waterloo, t., Brabant prov., **Belgium**, nr. Brussels; battle nearby 1815; p. (1982) 24,936.

Waterloo, c., Ont., **Canada**; known as "the insurance capital of Canada"; two major universities; a city since 1948; p. (1995) 89,663.

Waterloo, c., Iowa, **USA**; on Cedar R.; agr. prod. and tools; p. (1990) 66,467.

Waters of Merom (L. Hula), Upper Galilee, **Israel**; extensive drainage completed 1957; a. 14 km².

Waterton Glacier International Peace Park, Albert and Mont., **Canada** and **USA**; glacial and lake scenery; a. 596 km².

Watertown, t., Mass., **USA**; on Charles R.; textiles, clothing; p. (1980) 34,384.

Watertown, t., N.Y., **USA**; on Black R.; engin., paper; p. (1990) 29,429.

Watford, t., l. gov. dist., Herts., **Eng.**; on R. Colne, 26 km N.W. of London; mkt.; varied inds., inc. lt. and elec. engin., paper, printing; p. (1995) 77,200 (dist.), (1991) 113,800 (t.).

Wattenscheid, t., N. Rhine–Westphalia, **Germany**; E. of Essen; coal, metals, footwear; p. (1980) 67,653.

Waukegan, c., Ill., **USA**; on L. Michigan; summer resort; steel, brass, motors, sugar refining; p. (1980) 67,653.

Wauwatosa, t., Wis., **USA**; sub. of Milwaukee; metals, concrete, chemicals; p. (1990) 49,366.

Waveney, R., Norfolk and Suffolk, **Eng.**; 80 km long.

Waveney, l. gov. dist., Suffolk, **Eng.**; based on Lowestoft, Beccles and Bungay; p. (1995) 107,700.

Waverley, l. gov. dist., Surrey, **Eng.**; inc. Farnham, Godalming and Haslemere; p. (1995) 115,300.

Wayatinah, hydroelectric commission v., Tasmania, **Australia**; dam, lagoon and power sta. at confluence of Rs. Nive and Derwent.

Wazirabad (Balkh), t., **Afghanistan**; anc. Bactra, cap. of Bactria, called the "mother of cities", destroyed by Genghiz Khan 1221; textile plant projected; p. c. 13,000.

Weald, The, wooded and pastoral tracts S.E. **Eng.**; extending from Folkestone, Kent, through Surrey, Hants., and Sussex to the sea at Beachy Head; former a. of iron working; name derived from German *Wald* = forest.

Wealden, l. gov. dist., East Sussex, **Eng.**; stretches from Uckfield to S. cst.; p. (1995) 136,300.

Wear, R., Durham/Tyne and Wear, **Eng.**; rises in Pennines, flows through Durham to N. Sea at Sunderland; 96 km long.

Wear Valley, l. gov. dist., Durham, **Eng.**; Pennine a. inc. Bishop Auckland, Crook and Willington; p. (1995) 63,000.

Weaver, R., Cheshire, **Eng.**; industl. trib. of R. Mersey; 72 km long.

Weddell Sea, arm of S. Atl. Oc., **Antarctica**; whaling and sealing.

Wednesbury, t, West Midlands, **Eng.**; former metal wkg. t.

Wednesfield, t., West Midlands, **Eng.**; metal tubes, materials handling engin.; expanded t.

Wei, R., Shaanxi prov., W. China; rises in highlands of Kansu, flows E. between highlands of Shaanxi and Hua Shan to join Yellow R; valley contains very fertile loess soils; formed cradle of Chinese civilisation; c. 800 km long.

Weifang, c., Shandong prov., China; coal-mng. ctr.; tobacco processing; p. (1984) 1,033,200.

Weihai, c., Shandong prov., China; naval base; fishing; vegetable-oil processing, textiles; p. (1984) 216,400.

Weimar, t., Erfurt, **Germany**; on R. Ilm; ctr. of music and culture in 19th cent., associated with Goethe, Schiller, Nietzsche, Liszt, Herder; scene of establishment of German rep. 1919; elec. and metal inds., musical instruments, glass; European City of Culture (1999); p. (1981) 63,725.

Weipa, Queensland, **Australia**; Aboriginal community t., since 1965 taken over by Queensland to overcome opposition to bldg. of new t., pt., and alumina plant; bauxite nearby at Aurukin.

Weisshorn, mtn. peak, **Switzerland**; alt. 4,505 m.

Wejherowo, t., Gdansk, **Poland**; on R. Reda; mediaeval stronghold; palace; p. (1989) 46,465.

Welkom, t., O.F.S., **S. Africa**; ctr. of O.F.S. goldfields; p. (1980) 187,660 (dist.).

Welland, t., Ont., **Canada**; on Welland Canal; industl. t.; p. (1986) 45,054.

Welland, R., Northants. and Lincs., **Eng.**; rises in Northampton heights and flows N.E. into the Wash; 112 km long.

Welland Ship Canal, Ont., **Canada**; connects Ls. Erie and Ont.; 43 km long; 2-lane waterway.

Wellingborough, t., l. gov. dist., Northants., **Eng.**; on R. Nene, 14 km N.E. of Northampton; mkt.; footwear; expanded t.; p. (1995) 68,300 (dist.), (1991) 41,602 (t.).

Wellington, mkt. t., The Wrekin, Shrops., **Eng.**; brewing, sugar refining, timber, toys; name derived from "Watling Town" (stood on Watling Street); with Dawley and Oakengates forms new t. of Telford; p. (1991) 18,494.

Wellington, mkt. t., Somerset, **Eng.**; 10 km S.W. Taunton, anc. woollen ind. still survives; dairy prod.; p. (1991) 9,621.

Wellington, c., spt., N.I., cap. of **N.Z.**; univ.; impt. exp. ctr. for dairy prod., wool, meat; new inds. developing in Hutt valley with vehicle assembly, rubber, oil refineries; p. (1991) 150,301, 356,682 (urban a.).

Wellington, prov., N.I., **N.Z.**; mtnous., pastoral and dairy farming; a. 28,153 km²; p. (1985) 587,700.

Wells, cath. t., Mendip, Somerset, **Eng.**; on S. flank of Mendip hills; cath.; bishop's palace; paper mftg.; tourism; p. (1991) 9,763.

Wels, t., Upper **Austria**; on Traun R.; mkt. for agr. a.; cas.; p. (1991) 53,042.

Welshpool, mkt. t., Powys, **Wales**; on R. Severn; nearby is Powys cas.; p. (1991) 5,724.

Welwyn Garden City, t., Welwyn-Hatfield, Herts., **Eng.**; 34 km N. of London; founded by Sir Ebenezer Howard (1920) as first satellite t. of London; new t. 1948; pharmaceuticals, plastics, radio, and electronics, lt. inds.; p. (1991) 42,087.

Welwyn Hatfield, l. gov. dist., Herts., **Eng.**; comprises Welwyn Garden City and Hatfield; p. (1995) 95,200.

Wembley, former M.B., Middx., **Eng.**; now inc. in Brent outer bor. Greater London; lt. inds., sports ctr.; British Empire Exhibition 1924-5.

Wenlock Edge, narrow ridge, Shrops., **Eng.**; extends 29 km S.W. from Much Wenlock to Craven Arms; limestone; moorland, mainly above 290 m.

Wensleydale, North Yorks., **Eng.**; valley in N. Pennines drained E. by R. Ure; cattle reared for fattening on lowland farms; some dairying (cheese); length 56 km.

Wenzhou (Wenchow), c., spt., Zhejiang prov., **China**; pt. on estuary of Wu R., E. China Sea; fishing, coastal tr.; exp. wood, tea, agr. prod.; univ.; textile, leather and medicine inds.; designated an economic development zone, communications being improved; p. (1984) 519,100.

Wernigerode, t., Saxony - Anhalt, **Germany**; on N. slopes of Harz mtns.; mediaeval cas.; tourism; p. (1989) 36,778.

Wesel, t., N. Rhine–Westphalia, **Germany**; R. pt. at confluence of Rs. Lippe and Rhine, Ruhr conurb.; p. (1986) 54,600.

Weser, R., **Germany**; formed by confluence of Fulda and Werra Rs. at Münden; flows N. to N. Sea at Bremerhaven; linked by Mittelland canal to Rhine, Ems, and Elbe; navigable for entire length of 330 m.

Wesermünde. See Bremerhaven.

Wessex, anc. kingdom, S. **Eng.**; inc. Berks., Hants., Wilts., Dorset, Somerset and Devon.

West Bengal, st., N.E. **India**; W., mainly Hindu section of former presidency of B. (Muslim E.B. now Bangladesh); on Ganges delta and flood plain; humid sub-tropical climate; very dense p.; rice, jute; ch. c. Calcutta; a. 87,617 km²; p. (1991) 68,077,965.

West Bridgford, t., Rushcliffe, Notts., **Eng.**; at junc. of Grantham canal with R. Trent; residtl. sub. of Nottingham; p. (1991) 33,843.

West Bromwich, t., Sandwell, West Midlands, **Eng.**; on R. Thame, 8 km N.W. of Birmingham;

heavy engin. and allied inds., chemicals, springs, oil refining; p. (1991) 146,386.

West Derbyshire. See Derbyshire Dales.

West Devon, l. gov. dist., Devon, **Eng.**; rural W. of Dartmoor and ts. of Tavistock and Okehampton; p. (1995) 46,600.

West Dorset, l. gov. dist., Dorset, **Eng.**; inc. Lyme Regis, Bridport, Sherborne and Dorchester; p. (1995) 89,700.

West Dunbartonshire, unit. auth. created in 1996, formerly part of Strathclyde, W. **Scot.**; bordered S. by R. Clyde and N. by Loch Lomond; p. (1995) 96,290.

Western Australia, st. of the **Australian Commonwealth**; cut off from the rest of A. by desert; lgst. st., nearly a third of continent with only 9 per cent of p. concentrated in S.W. around st. cap. of Perth in fertile Mediterranean-like a.; diversity of relief, Hammersley range in N.W., Kimberley range in N.E., Gibson desert in interior; rich but irregularly distributed mineral deposits; intensive agr. in S.W., wheat and sheep in interior; a. 2,525,500 km²; p. (1993) 1,687,300.

Western Desert, Egypt; part of Libyan Desert; inc. Qattara depression; coastal road from Cairo to Tripoli; fighting in second world war.

Western Isles, l. gov. auth., **Scot.**; remote a. of Outer Hebrides where pastoral farming and fishing are the traditional livelihood; p. (1995) 29,040.

Western Pacific High Commission Territories, inc. Solomon Is. and Kiribati and Tuvalu Is.

Westernport, inlet, Vic., **Australia**; major heavy industl. a. close to Melbourne, rapidly growing.

Western Sahara (Spanish Sahara), N.W. African cst.; comprising Rio de Oro and Sagui el Hamra; desert; rich phosphate mines at Bou Craa connected to El Aaiun pt. by rly.; upon decolonisation terr. split between Morocco and Mauritania (1976) but declared Saharan Arab Democratic Rep. by Algerians (Polisario) and still disputed; UN peace resolution 1991; a. 265,993 km², p. largely nomadic (1993) 214,000.

Western Samoa, indep. sov. st., S. Pac. Oc.; member of Commonwealth (1970); gained independence from N.Z. 1962; consists of 2 lge Is. (Savai'i, Upolu) and 7 sm. Is.; 70 per cent p. in agr.; c. 30 per cent a. devoted to bananas; exp. bananas, copra, cacao beans; ch. spt. Apia on Upolu I.; a. 2,841 km²; p. (1994) 163,000. Recently changed name to Samoa.

Westerwald, plateau of old volcanic rocks, **Germany**; ending in steep slope E. of R. Rhine; fertile soil; pastureland or deciduous woodland; sm. quantities of iron ore in Siegerland.

West Ham, former C.B., Essex, **Eng.**; sub. to E. of London; bordered by Rs. Thames and Lea; now inc. in Newham bor., Greater London.

West Hartford, t., Conn., **USA**; residtl. sub. of Hartford; metal gds., ctr. for dairying, tobacco-growing dist.; p. (1980) 61,301.

West Indies or **Antilles**, I. grs., **Atl. Oc.**; extend between csts. of Fla. and Venezuela, separating Caribbean Sea and G. of Mexico from Atl.; inc. Cuba, Haiti, Dominican Rep., Bahamas, Barbados, Jamaica, Leeward Is., Trinidad and Tobago, Windward Is., Guadeloupe, Martinique, Curaçao, Puerto Rico, Virgin Is.; mostly volcanic and coral Is.; former colonial terrs. developed for plantation agr. worked by W. African slaves; most of indigenous Indians killed.

West Irian. See Irian Jaya.

West Lancashire, l. gov. dist., Lancs., **Eng.**; N. of Merseyside, inc. Skelmersdale and Ormskirk; p. (1995) 110,200.

West Lindsey, l. gov. dist., Lincs., **Eng.**; lge a. N. of Lincoln and inc. Market Rasen and Gainsborough; p. (1995) 77,600.

West Lothian, central **Scot.**; unit. auth. created in 1996, incorporating most of historic co. which became part of Lothian in 1974 and is now divided between Edinburgh, Falkirk, and W. Lothian; industl. dist. in Central Lowlands close to Edinburgh; p. (1995) 149,540.

Westmeath, co., Leinster, **R.o.I.**; low-lying, drained by R. Shannon, many Ls.; dairying; co. to Mullingar; ch. t. Athlone; a. 1,834 km²; p. (1986) 63,379.

West Mersea, t., Essex, **Eng.**; on Mersea I.; p. (1991) 6,602.

West Midlands, former met. co., **Eng.**; mainly industl. a. centred around Birmingham and the S. Staffs. coalfield (Black Country) and Coventry and the Warwicks. coalfield; many forms of engin. and light inds. inc. vehicle mftg.; p. (1995) 2,637,200.

Westminster, City of, inner bor., London, **Eng.**; on N. bank of R. Thames; W. of City of London; incorporates former bors. of Paddington and St. Marylebone; contains Houses of Parliament, Westminster Abbey, Government offices, Royal Palaces (Buckingham Palace and St. James's); p. (1995) 195,300.

Westmorland, historic co., **Eng.**; now part of Cumbria non-met. co.

Weston-super-Mare, t., N. Somerset, **Eng.**; on Bristol Channel, 32 km S.W. of Bristol; holiday resort; expanded t.; p. (1991) 69,372.

West Orange, t., N.J., **USA**; elec. equipment; home of T. A. Edison; p. (1980) 39,510.

West Oxfordshire, l. gov. dist., Oxon., **Eng.**; inc. Cotswolds and ts. of Chipping Norton, Witney and Woodstock; p. (1995) 95,800.

West Palm Beach, Fla., **USA**; domestic hardware; spt.; tourism; p. (1990) 864,000 (met. a. with Boca Raton-Delray Beach).

Westphalia. See North Rhine-Westphalia.

West Point, military sta., N.Y., **USA**; on Hudson R.; military academy.

Westport, spt., Mayo, **R.o.I.**; on Clew Bay; fishing; mkt.; p. (1986) 3,456.

Westray, I., Orkney Is., **Scot.**; 16 km long; p. (1991) 704.

West Somerset, l. gov. dist., Somerset, **Eng.**; inc. Exmoor and cstl. ts. of Watchet and Minehead; p. (1995) 32,400.

West Sussex, non-met. co., S.E. **Eng.**; crossed by E.–W. chalk ridge of S. Downs and forested Weald; diverse agr.; dormitory, retirement and tourist ts. on cst. inc. Bognor Regis and Worthing; Crawley new t. in N.; p. (1995) 731,500.

West Virginia, st., **USA**; "Mountain St.' admitted to Union 1863; st. flower Big Rhododendron, st. bird Cardinal; inc. Allegheny plateau; impt. mng. st. for coal; fruit farming; many industl. ts.; cap. Charleston; a. 62,629 km²; p. (1990) 1,793,477.

Westward Ho!, v., N. Devon, **Eng.**; named after Kingsley's novel.

West Wiltshire, l. gov. dist., Wilts., **Eng.**; stretches from Melksham, Bradford-on-Avon and Trowbridge to Warminster; p. (1995) 109,700.

West Yorkshire, former met. co., **Eng.**; industl. and mainly built-up a. E. of Pennines; traditionally ass. with woollen textile mftg.; inc. major ctrs. of Bradford and Leeds; p. (1995) 2,105,800.

Wetar I., Indonesia; N. of Timor I.; mtns.; underdeveloped; sparse p.; a. 31,080 km².

Wetherby, t., West Yorks., **Eng.**; on R. Wharfe; mkt., t.; racecourse; p. (1991) 8,154.

Wethersfield, t. Conn., **USA**; oldest settlement (1634) in st.; aircraft parts, agr. implements.

Wetterhorn, mtn., **Switzerland**; alt. 3,710 m.

Wetzlar, t., Hesse, **Germany**; on R. Lahn; metallurgical and optical inds.; p. (1986) 50,300.

Wexford, coastal co., Leinster, S.E. **R.o.I.**; mixed farming, fishing; cap. Wexford; a. 2,334 km²; p. (1986) 102,552.

Wexford, t., cap. of Wexford; Leinster, S.E. **R.o.I.**; on R. Slaney; agr. processing; outport at Rosslare; p. (1986) 10,336.

Wey, R., Hants., Surrey, **Eng.**; rises in W. Weald, flows N. into R. Thames nr. Weybridge; cuts impt. gap through N. Downs at Guildford; length 56 km.

Weybridge. See Walton and Weybridge.

Weymouth, t., part of l. gov. dist. of Weymouth and Portland, Dorset, **Eng.**; on Weymouth Bay, 13 km S. of Dorchester; torpedo and boatbldg., bricks, tiles, engin.; holiday resort; p. (1995) 62,900 (dist.), (1991) 46,065 (t.).

Whaley Bridge, t., High Peak, Derbys., **Eng.**; textile bleaching and finishing; p. (1991) 4,530.

Whangarei, c. and dist., N.I., **N.Z.**; deep harbour; oil refining; natural gas pipelines from Kapuni; fertilisers, sheet glass; p. (1991) 62,644.

Wharfe, R., West and North Yorks., **Eng.**; trib. of R. Ouse; 96 km long.

Wheeling, c., W. Va., **USA**; pt. on Ohio R.; comm. and mftg. ctr. in coal and natural gas a.; iron, steel, and metal plants; p. (1984) 42,100 (c.), 183,200 (met. a.).

Whickham, t., Tyne and Wear, **Eng.**; nr. Gateshead; chemicals, paper; p. (1991) 17,428.

Whitburn, burgh, W. Lothian, **Scot.**; 32 km S.W. of Edinburgh; coal, limestone; p. (1991) 11,511.

Whitby, t., North Yorks., **Eng.**; at mouth of R. Esk, 27 km N.W. of Scarborough; anc. spt. and fishing t.; residtl. and coastal resort; abbey; famous for jet ornaments; potash to be mined nearby; p. (1991) 13,640.

Whitchurch, t., Shrops., **Eng.**; 21 km S.W. of Crewe; dairy prods; p. (1991) 7,868.

White, R., Ark. and Mo., **USA**; trib. of Mississippi; hydroelectric power; 1,104 km long.

Whiteadder, R., Borders, **Scot.**; trib. of R. Tweed; 54 km long.

Whitehaven, spt., Copeland, Cumbria, **Eng.**; on Solway F. 5 km N. of St. Bees Head; coal, methane gas, cement, chemicals; p. (1991) 26,542.

Whitehead, t., Carrickfergus, **N. Ireland**; at entrance to Belfast Lough; seaside resort; p. (1991) 3,761.

Whitehorse, t., cap. of Yukon terr., **Canada**; ctr. coal and copper mng., hunting and fur trapping; once a gold "boom town"; H.Q. Royal Canadian Mounted Police; end of Alaska highway linking Edmonton, Alberta; p. (1991) 22,907.

White Mtns., part. of Appalachian system, N.H., **USA**; highest summit Mt. Washington, 1,918 m.

White Nile (Bahr-el-Abiad), R., **Sudan**; N.E. Africa; strictly, name applied to stretch of R. Nile between L. No and Khartoum; 800 km long.

White Plains, t., N.Y., **USA**; on Bronx R.; residtl.; battle 1776; p. (1990) 48,718.

White Russia. See Belorussia.

White Sea or **G. of Arkangelsk,** inlet of Barents Sea, **Russia**; frozen for 6 months of year; connected to Baltic Sea by deep-water canal; impt. fisheries.

Whitley Bay, t., North Tyneside, **Eng.**; 5 km N. of Tynemouth; seaside resort; plastics; p. (1991) 33,335.

Whitstable, spt., Kent, **Eng.**; on Thames estuary 10 km N. of Canterbury; holiday resort, oysters; p. (1991) 28,907.

Whittlesey, t., Fenland, Cambs., **Eng.**; in the Fens, 13 km W. of March; bricks, mkt. gardening; p. (1991) 10,275.

Whyalla, t., spt., S. **Australia**; t. on N.W. shore of Spencer Gulf developed by Broken Hill Co. in 1901 as terminal for Iron Knob iron exp.; major iron and steel wks.; shipbldg. now in difficulties; p. (1991) 25,740.

Wichita, c., Kans., **USA**; in Arkansas valley; rly. wks., oil refineries and equipment, meatpacking ctr. in agr. and stock-raising region; univ.; p. (1990) 304,011 (c.), 485,000 (met. a.).

Wichita Falls, c., Texas, **USA**; oil refining, ctr. in agr. and ranching a.; p. (1990) 92,259.

Wick, spt., sm. burgh, Highland, **Scot.**; on E. cst., 22 km S. of John O'Groats; airport to Orkneys and Shetlands; herring fishing ctr.; p. (1991) 7,681.

Wicklow, coastal co., Leinster, **R.o.I.**; crossed by Wicklow mtns.; pastoral agr. and tourism; cap. Wicklow; a. 2,033 km²; p. (1986) 94,542.

Wicklow, t., cap. of Wicklow, Leinster, **R.o.I.**; on S.E. cst., 56 km S. of Dublin; mkt.; sm. seaside resort; p. (1986) 5,304.

Wicklow, mtns., Wicklow, **R.o.I.**; highest summit Lugnaquillia, 927 m.

Widecombe, v., Devon, **Eng.**; Dartmoor tourist ctr.; famous through ballad "Widecombe Fair."

Widnes, t., Halton, Cheshire, **Eng.**; on R. Mersey 19 km E. of Liverpool; impt. chemical inds.; expanded t.; p. (1991) 57,162.

Wiener Neustadt, t., Lower **Austria**; rly. and industl. ctr.; heavy machin.; founded 1192; anc. bldgs., cas., cath.; education ctr.; p. (1991) 35,268.

Wieringermeer Polder, reclaimed a., N. Holland, **Neth.**; N.W. of IJsselmeer; a. 202 km².

Wiesbaden, c., cap. of Hesse, **Germany**; on Rhine, at S. foot of the Taunus; famous spa.; cas.; ctr. for Rhine wines; chemicals, metal gds.; p. (1990) 261,800.

Wigan, t., met. dist., Gtr. Manchester, **Eng.**; 26 km N.E. of Liverpool; engin., chemicals, cement, food processing, paper; former coal mng. ctr.; p. (1995) 309,800 (dist.), (1991) 85,819 (t.).

Wigston, t., Leics., **Eng.**; 6 km S. of Leicester; engin., hosiery; p. (1991) 32,864. See Oadby.

Wigtown, sm. burgh, Dumfries and Galloway, **Scot.**; on W. Bay, Solway F.; located in historic co. of Wigtownshire, now part of Dumfries and Galloway; p. (1991) 1,117.

Wilhelmshaven, c., Lower Saxony, **Germany**; on inlet of N. Sea, 64 km N.W. of Bremen; ch.

German naval base until 1945; industl. ctr. with heavy machin., elec. equipment, textiles, furniture; oil pipeline; p. (1986) 94,900.

Wilkes-Barre, c., Penns., **USA**; on Susquehanna R.; industl. ctr. in anthracite mng. a.; p. (1980) 51,551.

Wilkes Land, **Antarctica**; featureless plateau, alt. 2,900 m; immense glaciers; U.S. base taken over by Australia 1959.

Willamette, R., Ore., **USA**; rises in Cascade mtns., flows N. into Columbia R. below Portland; valley gives rich agr. land, wheat, rootcrops, dairy prod., hard and soft fruits; ch. ts. Eugene, Salem, Oregon City, Portland; used for hydroelectric power; 480 km long.

Willemstad, pt., cap. of **Neth. Antilles**; on Curaçao I.; oil refining; tourism; p. (1983) 50,000.

Willenhall, t., West Midlands, **Eng.**; locks and keys, drop forgings.

Willesden, former M.B., Middx., **Eng.**; now inc. in Brent outer bor., Greater London impt. rly. junc.; residtl. and industl.

Williamsburg, c., Va., **USA**; between James and York Rs.; historic t., settled 1632; rebuilt in 1920s to original plan; in Colonial Nat. Historical Park; p. (1980) 9,870.

Williamsport, t., Penns., **USA**; on Susquehanna R.; rly. ctr., timber, machin.; summer resort; p. (1984) 32,300 (t.), 117,100 (met. a.).

Willow South, was to be new cap. (1977), Alaska, **USA**; replacing Juneau; closer to ctr. of p.; lack of finance halted construction.

Wilmington, t., spt., Del., **USA**; on Delaware R.; shipbldg., machin., iron and steel wks.; chemicals; leather, cork, rubber gds.; p. (1990) 71,592 (t.), 579,000 (met. a.).

Wilmington, spt., N.C., **USA**; exp. cotton, tobacco, timber, fertilizers, shipbldg., textiles, chemicals; p. (1984) 44,800 (t.), 110,400 (met. a.).

Wilmslow, t., Cheshire, **Eng.**; on R. Bollen, 10 km S.W. of Stockport; residtl.; pharmaceuticals; p. (1991) 28,604.

Wilton, t., Wilts., **Eng.**; on R. Wylye, 5 km W. of Salisbury; agr. mkt., carpets, felt; anc. cap. of Wessex; many old bldgs.; p. (1991) 3,717.

Wilton, industl. estate, Redcar and Cleveland, **Eng.**; on S. side of Tees estuary; heavy organic- and petro-chemicals; nylon polymer plant.

Wiltshire, non-met. co., **Eng.**; crossed by chalk downland and Salisbury Plain; barley, wheat, dairying, pigs; co. t. Salisbury; p. (1995) 590,600.

Wimbledon, dist., London, **Eng.**; lge. open common; site of international tennis tournament; part of London Bor. of Merton.

Wimborne Minster, mkt. t., Dorset, **Eng.**; on R. Stour; Roman settlement and home of early Saxon kings; Badbury Rings earthworks nearby; p. (1991) 15,274.

Winchcombe, t., Gloucs., **Eng.**; nr. Cheltenham; old mills; pottery, paper; nearby cas.; p. (1991) 4,243.

Winchelsea, anc. t., East Sussex, **Eng.**; 3 km S.W. of Rye; once impt. walled spt. and Cinque port, now 3 km inland.

Winchester, cath. c., l. gov. dist., Hants., **Eng.**; on R. Itchen, 19 km N. of Southampton; anc. Anglo-Saxon cap.; meeting place of parliaments until time of Henry VII; magnificent cath., famous public school; p. (1995) 104,400 (dist.), (1991) 36,121 (t.).

Windermere, t. Cumbria, **Eng.** and lgst. English L.; outlet to Morecambe Bay; supplies water to Manchester; 16 km long, 1·6 km wide; p. (1991) 6,847.

Windhoek, t., cap. of **Namibia**; in hills at 1,700 m; comm. ctr., agr. processing; tr. in karakul (Persian lamb); p. (1990) 125,000.

Windrush, R., Oxford, Gloucs., **Eng.**; trib. of R. Thames.

Windscale. See **Sellafield**.

Windsor, c., pt., Ont., **Canada**; on Detroit R., linked to Detroit, USA, by tunnel, bridge and ferry; ctr. for car mftg., salt wks., chemicals, paints; univ.; p. (1991) 191,435 (c.), (1986) 253,988 (met. a.).

Windsor, t., part of l. gov. dist. of **Windsor and Maidenhead**, Berks., **Eng.**; on R. Thames, 32 km W. of London; Windsor has famous royal cas. (founded by William the Conqueror) and park, St. George's Chapel and the Royal Mausoleum; p. (1995) 140,200 (dist.) (1991) 30,135 (t.) (with Eton).

Windward Is., **W.I.**; extend S. from Leeward Is.; consist of Fr. Martinique and former Brit. cols. of Grenada, St. Vincent, St. Lucia and Dominica with their dependencies (the Grenadines divided between Grenada and St. Vincent) which attained associated statehood 1967; sm. limited resources, economically depressed; volcanic; p. (1984) 419,000.

Windward Passage, channel, 96 km wide, between Cuba and Haiti.

Winnebago, L., Wis., **USA**; 43 km long; lgst. L. in Wis.

Winnipeg, c., cap. of Manitoba, **Canada**; at junc. of Red and Assiniboine Rs.; cath., univ.; rly. ctr.; ch. world wheat mkt.; meat packing and food processing; lgst. garment mnf. ctr. in cty.; oil refining; p. (1986) 594,551 (c.), (1991) 652,355 (met. a.).

Winnipeg, L., Manitoba, **Canada**; 64 km N. of Winnipeg; 416 km long, 49–96 km wide; contains several lge. Is. (Reindeer, 181 km²; Big I., 155 km²); used for hydroelectric power.

Winnipegosis, L., Manitoba and Saskatchewan, **Canada**; a. (exclusive of Is.) 5,180 km²; 80 km W. of L. Winnipeg, into which it drains.

Winsford, t., Cheshire, **Eng.**; on R. Weaver; 6 km S. of Northwich; ctr. of salt inds., chemicals; expanded t.; computer peripherals; p. (1991) 26,839.

Winston-Salem, t., N.C., **USA**; formed 1913 from union of 2 adjacent ts.; tobacco ctr.; p. (1990) 143,485.

Winterthur, t., Zurich, **Switzerland**; on Eulach R.; rly. ctr., locomotives, machines, cottons; p. (1990) 86,143.

Wirksworth, t., West Derbys., **Eng.**; in Pennines, 8 km S. of Matlock; limestone, fluorspar wks., ctr. of Derbys. former lead mng.; p. (1991) 4,235.

Wirral, penin., met. dist., Merseyside, **Eng.**; between estuaries of Dee and Mersey; residtl.; comprises Wallasey, Birkenhead, Bebington and Hoylake; p. (1995) 331,500.

Wisbech, t., Fenland, Cambs., **Eng.**; on R. Nene, 18 km from its mouth in the Wash; mkt. gardening, fruit growing and canning, agr. implements; p. (1991) 24,981.

Wisconsin, st., **USA**; "Badger St."; admitted to Union 1848; st. flower Wood Violet. st. bird Robin; bounded by Gr. Ls.; low lying; leading dairying st.; industl. ts. around Gt. Ls.; cap. Madison; ch. t. Milwaukee; a. 145,439 km²; p. (1990) 4,891,769.

Wisconsin, R., Wis., **USA**; trib. of R. Mississippi; used for hydroelectric power; 960 km long.

Wismar, spt., Mecklenburg West Pomerania, **Germany**; on Baltic Sea, N. of Schwerin; oil pt. and industl. ctr. with shipyards and food processing inds.; p. (1981) 57,718.

Witbank, t., Transvaal, **S. Africa**; leading coalmng. dist. with power sta. and carbide and cyanide factories; p. (1980) 154,400 (dist.).

Witham, t., Essex, **Eng.**; 14 km N.E. of Chelmsford; ctr. of mkt. gardening a.; expanded t.; p. (1991) 22,684.

Witham, R., Leics. and Lincs., **Eng.**; flows into the Wash; cuts impressive gap through Lincoln.

Witney, t., Oxford, **Eng.**; on R. Windrush, 16 km W. of Oxford; woollens, blankets, gloves; p. (1991) 20,377.

Witten, t., N. Rhine–Westphalia, **Germany**; on R. Ruhr; glass, machin., metals, chemicals, optical inds.; p. (1990) 105,300.

Wittenberg, t., Saxony - Anhalt, **Germany**; on R. Elbe; ctr. of Reformation and burial place of Luther (Schlosskirche); cas.; machin., textiles; p. (1981) 53,874. Now called Lutherstadt-Wittenberg.

Wittenberge, t., Mecklenburg - West Pomerania, **Germany**; on R. Elbe; rly. junc., repair wkshps., machin.; p. (1989) 29,572.

Witwatersrand, dist., Transvaal, **S. Africa**; goldmng. dist. producing over 25 % of world's gold.

Wivenhoe, t., Essex, **Eng.**; on R. Colne; boat-bldg., oysters, lt. inds.; p. (1991) 7,073.

Wloclawek, t. and prov., river pt., N. **Poland**; on R. Vistula; impt. paper mnfs., ceramics; p. (1989) 120,680 (t.), 427,400 (prov.).

Woburn, t., Beds., **Eng.**; 8 km N.E. of Leighton Buzzard; Woburn Abbey (seat of Dukes of Bedford).

Woking, t., l. gov. dist., Surrey, **Eng.**; 6 km N. of Guildford; residtl.; p. (1995) 90,300 (dist.), (1991) 98,138 (t.) (with Byfleet).

Wokingham, mkt. t., l. gov. dist., Berks., **Eng.**; 8 km S.E. of Reading; agr. tr. and machin., bricks; p. (1995) 142,000 (dist.), (1991) 38,063 (t.).

Wolfenbüttel, t., Lower Saxony, **Germany**; on R.

Oker, 11 km S. of Brunswick; noted for ducal library, founded 17th cent., of which Leibnitz and Lessing were librarians; p. (1986) 48,600.

Wolf Rock, isolated rock with lighthouse, at approach to English Channel from Bay of Biscay; 14 km S.W. of Lands End, Cornwall.

Wolfsburg, t., Lower Saxony, **Germany**; on R. Aller, N.E. of Brunswick; Volkswagen wks.; p. (1990) 129,200.

Wolin, I., Baltic Sea; off mouth of R. Oder, Szczecin, **Poland**; Nat. Park; fishing, tourism; a. 344 km[2]; p. (1989) 4,495.

Wollongong Greater, t., N.S.W., **Australia**; 7th. c. of A.; heavy inds. attracted by local coal especially at Pt. Kembla; iron, steel, chems.; Australia's only tinplate plant; p. (1993) 249,500.

Wolsingham, t., Durham, **Eng.**; on R. Wear; impt. steel wks.; p. (1991) 1,286.

Wolverhampton, t., met. dist., West Midlands, **Eng.**; heavy and lt. engin., boilers, rayon, elec. engin. and apparatus, iron wks., aircraft and motor components, hollow-ware, tools, strongrooms and safes, paints; p. (1995) 244,300 (dist.), (1991) 257,943 (t.).

Wolverton, t., Milton Keynes, **Eng.**; on R. Ouse, 24 km S.W. of Bedford; rly.-carriage wks.; p. (1991) 55,733.

Wombwell, t., South Yorks., **Eng.**; at E. foot of Pennines, 11 km N. of Sheffield; coal mng., bricks; p. (1991) 15,462.

Wonsan, spt., **N. Korea**; on Sea of Japan; major pt. and rly. ctr.; Japanese naval base in second world war; oil refining; p. (1984) 350,000.

Woodbridge, t., Suffolk Coastal, Suffolk, **Eng.**; on R. Deben; engin., brush mkg.; p. (1991) 10,950.

Wood Green, former M.B., Middx., **Eng.**; now inc. in Haringey outer bor., Greater London.

Woodhall Spa, t., East Lindsey, Lincs., **Eng.**; 6 km S.W. of Horncastle; former spa, bromo-iodine springs; resort; p. (1991) 3,337.

Woodstock, t., Ont., **Canada**; on R. Thames; ctr. of agr. dist.; lt. mnfs. based on hydro-electric power; p. (1986) 26,603.

Woodstock, t., Oxford, **Eng.**; on Glyme R., 11 km N.W. of Oxford; glove mnfs.; Blenheim Palace; p. (1991) 2,898.

Wookey Hole, cave, Mendip Hills, Somerset, **Eng.**; at foot of limestone hills, 3 km N.W. of Wells; R. Axe emerges from the cave.

Woolwich, dist. former met. bor., London, **Eng.**; on either side of R. Thames; impt. Tudor dockyard, now closed; now part of Greenwich and Newham bors.

Woomera, S. **Australia**; c., 432 km N.W. of Adelaide; base for joint U.K.-Australian guided-weapon testing range extending N.W. across the continent; established 1947; p. (1981) 1,658.

Woonsocket, t., R.I., **USA**; on Blackstone R.; textiles, rubber gds.; p. (1980) 45,914.

Wootton Bassett, mkt. t., N. Wilts., **Eng.**; expanded since the 1960s to provide housing for people wkg. in Swindon; p. (1991) 10,524.

Worcester, c. and l. gov. dist., Worcs., **Eng.**; on R. Severn, 38 km N. of Gloucester; cath.; machin., porcelain, glove mkg.; birthplace of Elgar; p. (1995) 91,100 (dist.), (1991) 82,661 (c.).

Worcester, t., Cape Prov., **S. Africa**; viticultural and industl. ctr.; Goudini spa nearby; p. (1980) 95,100 (dist.).

Worcester, c., Mass., **USA**; univ.; cultural ctr.; machine tools, elec. engin.; p. (1990) 169,759 (c.), 437,000 (met. a.).

Worcestershire, historic Midland co., **Eng.**; part of Hereford and Worcs. until 1998; now recreated separate county.

Workington, t., Allerdale, Cumbria, **Eng.**; sm. spt. on Solway F. at mouth of Derwent R., first Bessemer steel plant, closed (1981), engin.; industl. diversification on nearby industl. estates, inc. bus wks.; p. (1991) 25,579.

Worksop, t., Bassetlaw, Notts., **Eng.**; 24 km S.E. of Sheffield; coal-mng. dist.; brewing, knitwear, glass, flour; p. (1991) 37,247.

Worms, t., Rhineland-Palatinate, **Germany**; on left bank of Rhine; historic ctr.; famous imperial diet 1521 when Luther refused to retract; scene of *Nibelungenlied*; ctr. for Liebfraumilch wines; chemical, textile, leather and metal inds.; p. (1986) 72,000.

Worms Head, promontory at W. end of Gower Peninsula, S. **Wales**.

Worthing, t., l. gov. dist., West Sussex, **Eng.**; on S. cst., 16 km W. of Brighton; holiday resort, popular as retirement ctr. in mkt. gardening dist.; p. (1995) 98,500 (dist.), (1991) 95,732 (t.).

Woy Woy, t., N.S.W., **Australia**; resort and commuter t. for Sydney; clothing; p. inc. in Gosford.

Wrangel I., Arctic Oc., off Khabarovsk terr., **Russia**; weather sta.

Wrath, C., N.W. **Scot.**

Wrekin, hill, Shrops., **Eng.**; alt. 403 m.

Wrekin, The, l. gov. dist., Shrops., **Eng.**; inc. Newport, Wellington, Oakengates and Dawley; p. (1995) 144,600.

Wrexham, t. 18 km S.W. of Chester, N.E. **Wales**, unit. auth. created in 1996 from former l. gov. dists. of Wrexham Maelor and Glyndwr; p. (1991) 40,614 (t.), (1995) 123,400 (unit. auth.).

Wrocław (Breslau), c., Silesia, **Poland**; on R. Oder; impt. route ctr. and R. pt.; univ., cath.; rapid industl. development; ctr. of electronics inds.; p. (1989) 640,557.

Wrocław (Breslau), prov., Lower Silesia, **Poland**; until 1945 part of Germany; heavy inds. based on local minerals; cap. Wrocław; a. 24,740 km[2]; p. (1989) 1,122,800

Wroxeter, v., Shrops., **Eng.**; on R. Severn, 8 km S.E. Shrewsbury; Roman sta. Uriconium.

Wuchow. See Wuzhou.

Wuhan, c., Hubei prov., **China**; formed by union of Hankan, Hanyang and Zhifang; major metropolis on Chang Jiang; integrated iron and steel wks., machine tools, walking tractors, textiles, shipbldg.; univ.; p. (1992) 3,790,000.

Wuhu, c., Anhui prov., **China**; former treaty pt. on Chang Jiang; textiles; p. (1984) 491,700.

Wupper, R., **Germany**; trib. of Rhine; industl. concentration along middle course; 64 km long.

Wuppertal, t., N. Rhine-Westphalia, **Germany**; formed by amalgamation of Barmen and Elberfeld; textiles, rubber gds., paper, metals, pharmaceuticals; p. (1990) 383,900.

Würzburg, c., Bavaria, **Germany**; on R. Main; univ., cath.; historic bldgs., engin., chemicals, printing; p. (1990) 128,000.

Wurzen, t., Saxony, **Germany**; on R. Mulde; cath., cas.; machin., furniture, leather, foodstuffs; p. (1989) 18,830.

Wuxi (Wusih), c., Jiangsu prov., **China**; on N. shore of Tai L., 120 km W. of Shanghai; univ.; industl. ctr. with cotton mills, chemical wks.; former treaty pt.; p. (1984) 825,100.

Wuzhou (Wuchow), c., R. pt., Guangxi, **China**; on Xijiang; tr. ctr.; exp. tung oil, hides; p. (1984) 256,500.

Wyandotte, t., Mich., **USA**; on Detroit R.; salt deposits; chemical ind.; p. (1980) 34,006.

Wychavon, l. gov. dist., Worcs., **Eng.**; inc. Vale of Evesham and Pershore in S. and Droitwich in N.; p. (1995) 106,000.

Wycombe, l. gov. dist., Bucks., **Eng.**; close to Oxon. and inc. High Wycombe and Marlow; p. (1995) 164,100.

Wye, R., Bucks., **Eng.**; rises in Chiltern hills, flows S.E. to R. Thames at Cookham.

Wye, R., **Eng.** and **Wales**; rises in Plynlimmon, flows S.E. into R. Severn at Chepstow; forms deeply incised valley at Symond's Yat; 208 km long.

Wye, t., Kent, **Eng.**; nr. Ashford; impt. agr. college (Univ. of London).

Wylfa Head, Anglesey, Isle of, N. **Wales**; Magnox nuclear power sta.

Wymondham, t., South Norfolk, **Eng.**; 14 km S.W. of Norwich; mkt.; Benedictine abbey founded 1107; p. (1991) 10,159.

Wyoming, st., **USA**; "Equality St."; admitted to Union 1890; st. flower Indian Paintbrush, st. bird Meadowlark; inc. areas of Rocky mtns. and great plains; Yellowstone Nat. Park; scant rainfall; irrigation; cattle and sheep ranching; petroleum; sparse p.; cap. Cheyenne; a. 253,597 km[2]; p. (1990) 453,588.

Wyre, R., Lancs., **Eng.**; rises in Pennines, flows W. into Lancaster Bay at Fleetwood; 45 km.

Wyre, l. gov. dist., Lancs., **Eng.**; inc. Preesall, Fleetwood and Thornton Cleveleys; p. (1995) 104,300.

Wyre Forest, l. gov. dist., Worcs., **Eng.**; inc. Bewdley, Kidderminster and Stourport; p. (1995) 97,000.

X

Xalapa, c., cap. of Veracruz st., **Mexico**; c. 1,370 m. a.s.l.; luxuriant vegetation; agr. ctr.; tourism; p. (1990) 288,331.

Xanthi, t. and dep. Thrace, **Greece**; on R. Mesta; ctr. of tobacco-growing a.; p. (1991) 91,063 (dep.).

Xanthus, ruined c., **Turkey**; on R. Xanthus; destroyed 43 B.C.; tourism.

Xauen, t., **Morocco**, N. Africa; holy t. founded 15th cent.

Xiamen (Amoy), c., Fujian, **China**; rail link to Jianxi; tea, fruit, machin., chemicals, textiles, electronics, tourism; univ.; formerly treaty pt.; in special Economic Zone to encourage foreign investment; p. (1984) 532,600.

Xi'an (Sian), cap. of Shaanxi prov., **China**; impt. route and industl. ctr.; machin.; tourism; research ctr.; iron and steel, textiles, chemicals; p. (1992) 2,790,000.

Xiangtan (Siangtan), c., Hunan prov., **China**; on navigable Xijiang; regional tr. ctr., tea, cotton, electrical goods, machin., textiles; Mao Tse Tung born nearby; p. (1984) 501,700.

Xi Jiang (Si Kiang), ch. R., S. **China**; headstreams rise in Yunnan plateau, R. then flows E. enters S. China Sea through lge delta nr. Hong Kong; lower valley intensively cultivated, rice, sugar cane, tea; tropical climate permits continuous cultivation of most crops through year; valley densely populated; c. 2,000 km. long.

Xingu, R., **Brazil**; trib. of Amazon; navigable in its lower course; Nat. Park and Indian reserve threatened by new cattle ranches; 1,920 km long.

Xinhailion. See Lianyungang.

Xining (Sining), cap. of Qinghai prov., **China**; ctr. of spring wheat a.; woollen mills, iron and steel; new rly. completed to help reduce isolation; p. (1984) 576,400.

Xinjiang Uygur (Sinkiang-Uighur), aut. region, N. W. **China**; very dry climate; remote until new roads and rlys. penetrated a.; ethnic minority p. of Turkish background and Islamic faith; many attempts to develop natural resources and industry by Chinese government; pastoral agr.; sheep, goats; new st. arable farms, wheat, maize, millet; lge. oil reserves; cap. Ürümqi; a. 1,646,800 km²; p. (1990) 15,370,000.

Xinyang (Sinyang), t., S. Henan, **China**; regional ctr. for S. Henan and Hubei; p. (1984) 226,600.

Xizang Zizhqu. See Tibet.

Y

Yablonovyy, mtn. range, Siberia, **Russia**; E. of L. Baykal; highest peak, Sokhondo, 2,510 m; crossed by Trans-Siberian rly.

Yaila Mtns., Ukraine; form S.E. margin of Crimea penin., extend from Sevastopol to Kerch; form marked climate barrier between Black Sea littoral and N. part.

Yakima, t., Wash., **USA**; agr. ctr. of irrigated valley, noted for fruit; p. (1984) 48,900 (t.), 179,500 (met. a.).

Yakima, R., Wash., **USA**; trib. of Columbia R.; used for irrigation; 333 km long.

Yakut, aut. rep., **Russia**; borders Arctic Oc.; home of Yakuts; tundra and forest region, isolated; fur trapping, diamond and gold mng., state farms; a. 3,963,355 km²; p. (1989) 1,094,100.

Yakutsk, t., cap. of Yakut, aut. rep., **Russia**; pt. on Lena R.; univ.; airport; p. (1989) 187,000.

Yallahs Valley, Jamaica; severe soil erosion; govt. improvement scheme of afforestation and new crops; a. 181 km².

Yallourn, t., Victoria, **Australia**; ctr. of lignite mng. a.; p. (1991) 17,990 (inc. Moe).

Yalta, spt., **Ukraine**; sub-tropical resort on Black Sea, sheltered by Yaila mtns.; conference between Churchill, Roosevelt, and Stalin 1945; p. (1990) 88,800.

Yalu, R., forms bdy. between N.E. China, and N. **Korea**; flows into Yellow Sea; used for hydroelectric power.

Yamagata, t., Honshu, **Japan**; ctr. of rice-growing a.; cas.; p. (1990) 249,487.

Yamaguchi, t., cap. of Y. prov., S.W. Honshu, **Japan**; cas.; comm. ctr., chemicals; p. (1990) 129,461.

Yamal-Nenets National Okrug, Russia; inc. Yamal penin.; permafrost; hunting, fishing; cap. Salekhard; lge. natural gas finds; a. 670,810 km²; p. (1989) 494,800.

Yambol, t., **Bulgaria**; on R. Tunja; ruined mosque; agr. tr.; recent inds. inc. canning, farm machin., textiles, ceramics; p. (1990) 99,225.

Yamethin, dist., Upper Myanmar; teak forests, rice; ch. t. Yamethin; site of irrigation project.

Yamoussoukro, t., Côte d'Ivoire; cap. replaced Abidjan (1983) to relieve congestion; p. (1990) 120,000.

Yana, R., Siberia, **Russia**; flows into Arctic Sea; navigable; 1,600 km long.

Yangchow. See Yangzhou.

Yangchuan. See Yanqan.

Yangi-yer, t., **Uzbekistan**; founded 1957 as ctr. for new irrigated cotton lands of E. Uzbekistan.

Yangon, See Rangoon.

Yangtze River. See Chang Jiang.

Yangzhou, c., Jiangsu, **China**; in valley of Chang Jiang, N.W. of Shanghai; mkt. for local agr. prods.; p. (1984) 382,200.

Yanqan (Yangchuan), c., Shaanxi prov., **China**; iron working ctr.; p. (1982) 477,600.

Yantai, spt., Shangdong prov., **China**; anc. c.; food processing, light ind., textiles, cement, steel; exp. foodstuffs esp. prawns & wines; pt. being enlarged as c. declared an economic development zone to attract foreign investment, esp. high technology; p. (1984) 699,400.

Yaoundé, t., cap. of Cameroon Rep., W. **Africa**; lt. inds. inc. beer, cigarettes, textiles; p. (1991) 649,000.

Yapura, R., Brazil and Colombia, S. America; trib. of R. Amazon; length 2,400 km.

Yaracuy, st., Venezuela; crossed by Y. valley impt. agr. a. for bananas, coffee, sugar, tobacco; crossed by Pan-American Highway; cap. San Felipe; a. 7,099 km²; p. (1990) 411,980.

Yare, R., Norfolk, **Eng.**; flows E. to N. Sea at Gorleston; forms part of Norfolk Broads navigable waterways; 80 km long.

Yarkand. See Shache.

Yarmouth, spt., Nova Scotia, **Canada**; fisheries; p. (1991) 7,781.

Yarmouth. See Great Yarmouth.

Yaroslavl, c., cap. of Y. oblast, **Russia**; on upper Volga in Moscow industl. region; founded 1010; comm. and industl. ctr.; mnfs. inc. textiles, motor vehicles, synthetic rubber, agr. machin.; Volkov theatre, 12th cent. monastery, churches; p. (1989) 633,000.

Yasan, N., **Bulgaria**; lge. refinery and petro-chemicals complex.

Yatsushiro, t., Kyushu, **Japan**; p. (1990) 108,135.

Yazd, c., Isfahan prov., **Iran**; in desert a. at 1,190 m; fine silks, carpets; p. (1986) 248,874.

Yazoo, dist., Miss., **USA**; flood plain of R. Mississippi and R. Yazoo; very fertile alluvial soil, but subject to disastrous floods; one of ch. cotton-growing dists. in USA.

Yegoryevsk, t., **Russia**; 115 km S.E. of Moscow; lge textile ind.; phosphorite deposits.

Yekaterinburg, (Sverdlovsk), c., cap. of Y. oblast, **Russia**; on R. Iset in E. foothills of Ural mtns.; on Trans-Siberian rly.; industl. expansion during second world war; heavy machin., metallurgical and chemical plants; univ.; p. (1989) 1,365,000.

Yeletz, t., **Russia**; on R. Sosna; grain and cattle tr.; cultural ctr.; rly. junc.

Yelizavetgrad. See Kirovograd.

Yell, I., Shetland Is., **Scot.**; 27 km long; covered in peat moorland; p. (1991) 1,075.

Yellowhead Pass, B.C., Alberta, **Canada**; most N. and lowest of main passes across Rocky mtns.; carries Canadian Nat. rly. on route from Edmonton to Vancouver and Prince Rupert; summit alt. 1,130 m.

Yellowknife, t., N.W. Terr., **Canada**; on N. shore of Gr. Slave L.; ctr. of impt. gold-mng. dist.; linked by air to Edmonton, Alberta; p. (1991) 15,179.

Yellow R. See Huang He.

Yellow Sea. See Huang Hai.

Yellowstone, L., Wyo., **USA**; 32 km long, 24 km wide; alt. 2,360 m; in Y. Nat. Park.

Yellowstone National Park, N.W. Wyo., **USA**; volcanic scenery, geysers; a. 8,956 km².

Yemen, Rep. of, S.W. Arabian peninsula; cap.

Sana'a, economic and commercial cap. Aden; divided since 1967 into Yemen Arab Republic (N. Yemen) and People's Democratic Rep. of Yemen (S. Yemen); reunification May 1990; climate hot and humid coastal strip, summer rainfall on high plateau and desert interior; agr. millet, maize, sorghum, oats (fruit, Mocha coffee; oil (1984); rich fishing grounds; British withdrawal and closure of Suez canal led to ec. decline in south; a. 540,000 km²; p. (1994) 15,800,000.

Yenangyaung, t., R. pt., **Myanmar**; on left bank of R. Irrawaddy, 448 km N. of Rangoon; ctr. of Burma oilfields.

Yenisey, R., Siberia, **Russia**; rises in Sayan mtns., flows N. into Arctic Oc.; ch. tribs., Angara, Stony Tunguska, Lower Tunguska; hydroelectric power sta. at Krasnoyarsk; linked to Ob R. by canal; middle course navigable; 5,280 km long.

Yeo or **Ivel**, R., Dorset, Somerset, **Eng.**; trib. of R. Parrett; 38 km long.

Yeovil, mkt. t., Somerset, **Eng.**; on R. Yeo; glove mnf., aero-engin., agr. machin., dairy processing; p. (1991) 38,805.

Yerevan or **Erivan**, c., cap. of **Armenia**; on Zanga R. in deep valley of Caucasus mtns.; earthquake 1988; major science-based, industl. ctr.; p. (1990) 1,201,500.

Yes Tor, second highest summit, Dartmoor, Devon, **Eng.**; 618 m.

Yevpatoriya or **Eupatoria**, spt., Crimea, on Black Sea, **Ukraine**; popular resort; children's sanatoria; chemicals, leather, locks, dried fish; new pt. being built; p. (1990) 108,900.

Yezd. See Yazd.

Yibin (Ipin), c., Sichuan prov., **China**, at junction of Chang Jiang and Min Jiang.

Yichang (Ichang), c., S.W. Hubei, **China**; on Chang Jiang; site of famous gorges; terminus of lge. vessels from Shanghai.

Yiewsley and West Drayton, former U.D., Middx., **Eng.**; now inc. in Hillingdon outer bor. Greater London; varied lt. inds.

Yingchuan, t., cap. of Ninxia, aut. region, **China**; on Huang He; ctr. of fertile agr. a.; new lt. inds.; p. (1982) 576,000.

Yingkou (Yingkow), c., Liaoning prov., N.E. **China**; 32 km upstream from mouth of Liao R.; soyabean prods.

Yining (Kuldja), c., Xinjiang prov., **China**; on highway to Turkestan; coalfield; recent industl. development inc. iron and steel.

Ynys Môn. See Isle of Anglesey.

Yokkaichi, c., spt., S. Honshu, **Japan**; on Ise Bay, 37 km S. of Nagoya; textiles, petrochemicals, synthetic rubber, porcelain; p. (1990) 274,184.

Yokohama, leading spt., Honshu, **Japan**; on W. shore of Tokyo Bay; steel, chemicals, cars, oil refining, shipyards; univs.; with Tokyo and Kawasaki forms conurb. of Keihin; p. (1990) 3,220,350.

Yokosuka, spt., Honshu, **Japan**; S. of Tokyo; holiday resort; thermal power sta.; p. (1990) 433,358.

Yonkers, c., N.Y., **USA**; on E. bank of Hudson R.; residtl.; lt. inds., textiles; p. (1990) 188,082.

Yonne, dep., **France**; in S.E. of Paris basin, inc. Champagne, Burgundy, Orléanais; drained by R. Yonne; cap. Auxerre; agr., Chablis wines; a. 7,495 km²; p. (1990) 323,100.

Yonne, R., **France**; major trib. of R. Seine; 288 km long.

York, c., unit. auth. created in 1996, formerly part of North Yorks. **Eng.**; on R. Ouse; in central position in Vale of York; anc. part of c. enclosed by walls; minster, cas., univ.; chocolate, confectionery, rly. wkshps.; p. (1995) 174,400 (unit. auth.), (1991) 124,609 (c.).

York, c., Penn., **USA**; ctr. of fertile agr. region; varied inds., inc. agr. tools, machin., textiles, metal gds.; p. (1990) 437,000 (met. a.).

York, C., Queensland, **Australia**; most N. point on mainland of Australia.

York, Vale of, broad lowland, North Yorks/York, **Eng.**; between Pennines and N. Yorks. Moors and Yorks. Wolds; drained to Humber by R. Ouse and tribs.; glacial and alluvial soils have required draining; crop farming, wheat, barley, root-crops, associated with fattening of beef cattle; settlement mainly marginal; ch. t. York; length 96 km, width from 16 km in N. to 48 km in S.

Yorke, penin., S. **Australia**; separates Spencer G. and G. of St. Vincent; 160 km long, 48 km wide.

Yorkshire, historic co., N. **Eng.**; formerly divided into 3 separate admin. parts (Ridings); N., E.,

and W.; now split into the non-met. co. of N. Yorks., the met. cos. of W. Yorks. and S. Yorks., and 8 unit. auths. inc. Kingston upon Hull, Middlesbrough and York.

Yorkshire Moors, hills, North Yorks. and Redcar and Cleveland, **Eng.**; inc. N. Yorks. Moors, Cleveland Hills and Hambleton Hills; bounded to N. by Tees valley, S. by Vale of Pickering, W. by Swale valley, E. by sea; composed of oolitic limestone; good sheep pastures; impt. iron-ore deposits worked in Cleveland Hills; max. alt. 454 m.

Yorkshire Wolds, hills, E. Riding of Yorks., **Eng.**; extend N.E. from Humber and terminate in Flamborough Head; chalk; good sheep pasture; average alt. 180 m.

Yorktown, v., Va., **USA**; scene of surrender by Lord Cornwallis to Washington 1781.

Yosemite National Park, Cal., **USA**; in Sierra Nevada; contains Yosemite creek and canyon with three famous cataracts.

Yoshkar-Ola, t., Mari, aut. rep., **Russia**; 128 km N.W. of Kazan; cultural ctr.; wood processing, food inds.; p. (1989) 242,000.

Youghal, spt., Cork, **R.o.I.**; on estuary of the Blackwater; resort; p. (1986) 5,706.

Youngstown, c., Ohio, **USA**; on Mahoning R.; 91 km N.W. of Pittsburgh; ctr. of one of most impt. iron and steel dists. in USA; heavy engin.; univ.; p. (1990) 95,732 (c.), 492,619 (met. a. with Warren).

Yoyang. See Yueyang.

Ypres (Ieper), t., W. Flanders prov., N.W. **Belgium**; textiles and textile machin.; ctr. of cloth ind. in middle ages; scene of battles 1914–17; p. (1981) 34,426.

Ypsilanti, t., Mich., **USA**; on Huron R.; residtl., agr. mkt., mnfs.; univ.; p. (1980) 24,031.

Ystwyth, R., Ceredigion, **Wales**; flows 40 km to join R. Rheidol at Aberystwyth.

Yuan, R., N.W. Hunan prov., **China**; flows into Dongting Hu and Chang Jiang R.; rapids; 640 km long.

Yucatán, st., S.E. **Mexico**; limestone lowlands poor soils; henequen (sisal hemp), chicle (resin from which chewing gum is made); cap. Mérida; a. 61,968 km²; p. (1990) 1,363,540.

Yueyang (Yoyang), t., Hunan, **China**; at outlet of Dongting Hu and Chang Jiang; p. 4,800.

Yugoslavia, Socialist Fed. Rep. of, S.E. Europe; comprises reps. of Serbia, Montenegro, and aut. regions of Kosovo and Vojvodina; former constituent reps. of Croatia and Slovenia recognised as independent by EU 1991; Bosnia-Herzegovina and Macedonia have declared independence; new conflict in Kosovo (1999); long W. cst. on Adriatic Sea with well-developed limestone karstic topography; hilly interior; climate Mediterranean on cst., continental in interior; distinctive political development after second world war; refused to accept Soviet hegemony; well-developed links with W.; with major attempts to industrialise, based on energy, heavy and consumer inds. less p. engaged in agr.; economic decision-making increasingly freed from central control; developing tourist tr., especially with countries of W. Europe, based on climate and attractive Adriatic littoral, with many sm. Is.; cap. Belgrade; a. 255,698 km²; p. (1994) 10,513,710. See Section C.

Yukon, R., **Canada** and **Alaska**, **USA**; flows N.W. and W. into Bering Strait; navigable for 1,920 km; 3,200 km long.

Yukon Territory, prov., N.W. **Canada**; mtnous. (Mt. Logan 6,050 m); gold, silver, lead, zinc; Alaska Highway links with B.C. and Alberta; ch. ts. Dawson, and Whitehorse (cap.); incr. indep. since 1983; a. 536,327 km²; p. (1991) 27,797.

Yuma, t., Arizona, **USA**; at confluence of Rs. Gila and Colorado, nr. Mexican bdr.; ctr. of irrigated agr. region; p. (1980) 42,481.

Yumen, c., N.W. Gansu prov., **China**; leading petroleum ctr.; drilling equipment, precision instruments; on Old Silk Road to Xinjiang; p. (1984) 158,100.

Yunnan, prov., S. **China**; adjoins Burma; mtnous. a. of minority groups; rice, tobacco, tea, cotton; copper, tin; cap. Kunming; a. 420,466 km²; p. (1990) 36,750,000.

Yuzhno-Sakhalinsk, t., **Russia**; at S. end of Sakhalin I.; paper, lt. inds.; p. (1989) 159,000.

Yvelines, dep., **France**; W. of Paris; cap. Versailles; a. 2,271 km²; p. (1990) 1,307,200.

Yverdon, t., Vaud, **Switzerland**; typewriters; p. (1980) 20,802.

Z

Zaanstadt, t., N. Holland **Neth.**; industl. dist.; food processing p. (1994) 132,508.

Zabrze, t., Upper Silesia, Katowice, **Poland**; impt. coal-mng. ctr. with associated heavy inds.; cultural ctr.; p. (1989) 202,824.

Zacapa, t., cap. of Z. prov., **Guatemala**; mkt. t. at rly. junc.; tobacco tr. and processing; sulphur springs; p. (1989) 35,769.

Zacatecas, st., **Mexico**; on central plateau at 2,100 m; dry, agr. dist.; sm. mng. ctrs.; a. 72,836 km²; p. (1990) 1,278,279.

Zacatecas, t., cap. of Z. st., **Mexico**; cath.; ctr. of silver mng., pottery, clothing; p. (1990) 108,528.

Zacatecoluca, t., **El Salvador**; cigar mkg., hand looms; coffee, cotton, sugar, vanilla in a.; p. (1992) 57,032.

Zadar (Zara), t., **Croatia** (formerly Yugoslavia); spt. on cst. of Adriatic Sea; formerly Italian (1920–47); Roman remains; cath.; car ferry to Pesaro (Italy); tourism; p. (1981) 116,174.

Zagan (Sagan), t., Zielona Gora, W. **Poland** (since 1945); on R. Bober; cas.; textiles, paper, lignite mines; p. (1989) 27,333.

Zagazig, t., **Egypt**; on Nile Delta; tr. ctr. of fertile agr. a. producing cotton, grains; cotton mills; p. (1986) 255,000.

Zagorsk. *See* Sergiyev Posad.

Zagreb, c., cap. of **Croatia** (formerly Yugoslavia); on Sava R.; cath., univ.; tr. fair; many inds., notably petrochemicals based on local petroleum reserves, elec. engin.; airport; second c. of rep.; p. (1991) 726,770.

Zagros, mtns., **Iran**; inc. Iran's major oilfield; highest peak Zardesh Kuh, 4,551 m.

Zahedan, c., **Iran**; cap. of Sistan and Baluchistan prov.; airport; terminus of rly. from Pakistan; p. (1982) 165,000.

Zahle, t., Lebanon, S.W. Asia; on slopes of L. mtn.; p. (1988) 45,000.

Zaïre. *See* Congo, Dem. Rep. of.

Zaïre, R. *See under* Congo.

Zakinthos (Zante), Ionian I., **Greece**; cap. Zakinthos (Zante); devastated by earthquake 1953; a. 717 km²; p. (1981) 30,014.

Zakinthos (Zante), t., Zakinthos I., **Greece**; spt. on E. cst.; agr. tr. and processing; p. (1981) 9,764.

Zakopane, t., Nowy Sacz prov., **Poland**; in High Tatra mtns.; base for mountaineering and winter sports; health resort; tourism; p. (1989) 28,417.

Zalaegerszeg, t., **Hungary**; in Göcsej dist.; oil refining; mkt. t. for grain and livestock; p. (1997) 62,000.

Zambesi, R., S.E. **Africa**; flows E. to Moçambique Channel, Indian Oc.; forms frontier between Zambia and Zimbabwe; inc. Victoria Falls and Kariba and Cabora Bassa dams; navigable but impeded by rapids; 3,520 km long.

Zambia, rep., Central Africa; member of Commonwealth; tropical climate, modified by alt.; plateau (1,200 m); subsistence agr.; livestock on uplands free from tsetse fly; mng. basis of economy, especially in copperbelt; world's 4th lgst copper producer; exp. disrupted by Rhodesian U.D.I. (1965); falling copper output as mines near exhaustion; need to develop alternative routes to cst.; pipeline from Ndola to Dar-es-Salaam; construction of Tan-Zam rly. financed by Chinese aid; cap. Lusaka; a. 752,618 km²; p. (1993) 8,940,000.

Zamboanga, c., Mindanao, **Philippines**; spt. on Basilian Strait, exp. prod. timber; p. (1995) 511,000.

Zamora, prov., **Spain**; borders Portugal; drained by R. Duero; cereals, wine, merino sheep; cap. Zamora; a. 10,559 km²; p. (1991) 210,822.

Zamora, t., cap. of Zamora prov., **Spain**; on R. Duero; cath.; agr. tr. and processing ctr.; developing mnfs.; p. (1987) 60,708.

Zamosc, t. and prov., Lublin, **Poland**; Renaissance planned t. in valley of Lubianka R.; industl., comm. and cultural ctr.; p. (1989) 60,565.

Zanesville, t., Ohio, **USA**; textiles, pottery, machin.; p. (1990) 26,778.

Zangbo (Tsangpo), R., Tibet, **China**; one of headstreams of R. Brahmaputra; 1,350 km. long.

Zanjan, c., **Iran**; cap. of Gilan prov.; cotton, woollen gds.; p. (1986) 215,458.

Zanzibar, terr., E. **Africa**; comprises Is. of Z. and Pemba; joined Tanganyika to form **Tan-**

zania (1964); major world source of cloves; coconut and coconut prod. major exp. and basis of processing inds.; cap. Zanzibar; a. 2,642 km²; p. (1988) 640,578.

Zanzibar, spt., Zanzibar I., **Tanzania**; on W. cst. 35 km from E. Africa; outlet for clove exp., entrepot tr.; former slave mkt.; p. (1988) 157,634.

Zaporozh'ye, t., **Ukraine**; on R. Dnieper, nr. dam and hydroelec. power sta.; metal inds. based on Donets coal and Krivoi Rog iron ore; p. (1990) 891,000.

Zaragoza, prov., **Spain**; largely barren plain suffering from climatic extremes; a. 17,122 km²; cap. Z.; p. (1991) 852,766.

Zaragoza, cap. Z. prov., **Spain**; on R. Ebro; 2 caths., univ.; former cap. of Aragon; rly. junc.; comm. ctr.; p. (1987) 575,317.

Zarate, t., Entre Rios prov., **Argentina**; paper wks., agr. ctr., meat packing; p. (1980) 65,504.

Zaria, c., N. **Nigeria**; founded 15th cent., old part surrounded by walls; univ., cotton ctr.; rly. ctr.; p. (1992) 345,200.

Zarga, t. **Jordan**; ind. ctr., phosphates; p. (1986) 404,500.

Zary (Sorau), t., Zielona Gora, **Poland** (since 1945); textiles; p. (1989) 39,172.

Zawiercie, t., **Poland**; industl. ctr.; coal, iron, textiles, glass; p. (1989) 56,017.

Zdunska Wola, t. Sieradz, **Poland**; nr. Lodz; textiles, engin.; p. (1989) 44,686.

Zealand. *See* Sjaelland.

Zeebrugge, spt., **Belgium**; 14 km N. of Bruges; exp. coal, chemicals; oil refining; linked by canal to Bruges.

Zeeland, prov., **Neth.**; a. covering part of Scheldt estuary and Is.; low-lying; dairying; cap. Middelburg; a. 1,787 km²; p. (1994) 363,867.

Zeist, t., Utrecht, **Neth.**; chemicals, toys; p. (1994) 59,258.

Zeitz, t., Saxony - Anhalt, **Germany**; textiles, chemicals; p. (1991) 59,357.

Zelten, Libya, N. Africa; oilfield; 320 km S. of Benghazi; pipeline to Mersa al-Brega.

Zenica, t., **Bosnia-Herzegovina**, formerly Yugoslavia; lge. iron and steel wks.; ctr. of Z. basin; rly. junc.; p. (1981) 132,733.

Zeravshan, R., **Tajikistan** and **Uzbekistan**; flows for 736 km before evaporating in desert region N. of Chardzhou.

Zetland. *See* Shetland.

Zgierz, t., Lodz. prov., central **Poland**; nr. source of R. Bzura; textiles, chemicals, textile machin.; p. (1989) 58,836.

Zhangjiakou (Kalgan), c., Hebei, **China**; nr. Great Wall, 160 km N.W. of Beijing; a main route to Mongolia; tea wool, hides; p. (1984) 607,900.

Zhangzhou (Chuangchow), c., Fujian prov., **China**; former pt. now silted up; p. (1984) 210,600.

Zhanjiang (Tsamkong), c., Guandong prov., **China**; spt. on Liuzhou peninsula; machin., chemicals, elec. inds.; designated economic development zone; cotton, milling, leather mnfs.; p. (1984) 899,500.

Zhdanov. *See* Mariupol.

Zhengzhou, (Quauzhu), c., cap. Henan prov., **China**; 24 km. S of Huang He where it emerges on to N. China Plain; impt. route ctr. and rly. junc.; p. (1992) 1,730,000.

Zhenjiang (Chinkiang), c., Jiangsu, **China**; former treaty pt. on Chang Jiang, 77 km. below Nanjing; tr. ctr.; p. (1984) 397,300.

Zhijiang (Chekiang), coastal prov., S.E. **China**; cap. Hangzhou; impt. rice growing a.; major natural gas field; a. 102,269 km²; p. (1990) 40,840,000.

Zhitomir, t., **Ukraine**; engin., clothing; route ctr.; p. (1990) 295,900.

Zhousan (Chusan), I., and archipelago off E. cst. of China and Chang Jiang delta; ch. ctr. Dinghai on Zhousan I.; valuable fishing grounds.

Zhuhai, special economic zone, **China**, N. of Macau; selected (1983) to attract foreign investment; new pt.; p. (1984) 144,400.

Zhujiang (Chukiang or Pearl R.), Guandong, S. **China**; one of most impt. waterways of China; 176 km. long from Guangzhou to Hong Kong; fertile delta known as "land of fish, rice and fruit"; around Guangzhou network of elec., drainage and irrigation stas; built since 1959; estuary now silting.

Zhuzhou (Chuchau), c., Hunan prov., **China**; on Xiang Jiang; rly.; p. (1984) 487,800.

Zibo (Tzepo), c., Shandong, **China**; formed by merging of several coal mng. ts. in the 1950s; p. (1991) 2,460,000.

Zielona Gora (Grünberg), c., W. **Poland** (since 1945);

K178

in valley surrounded by wooded hills; admin. and industl. ctr., cap. of Z.G. prov.; textiles, food processing, machin.; viticulture; p. (1989) 113,108.

Zielona Gora, prov., **Poland;** borders E. Germany; glacial sands, wooded; brown coal deposits; cap. Z.G.; a. 14,514 km²; p. (1989) 655,000.

Zigaze (Shigatze), t., Tibet, **China;** on R. Zangbo; tr. ctr. on main caravan routes.

Zigong (Tzekung), c., Sichuan, **China;** petroleum, natural gas, salt wks.; p. (1984) 899,700.

Ziguinchor, t., **Senegal;** pt. on R. Casamance; exp. groundnuts; p. (1992) 148,831.

Zilina, t., Slovakia; on R. Vah; paper, fertilisers; p. (1990) 97,000.

Zimbabwe, Central Africa; former Brit. col. (Rhodesia); indep rep. 1980; landlocked st.; much of land high veld above 900 m covered in savannah; impressive economic growth with removal of sanctions and end of warfare; manuf. limited by lack of skilled labour; still heavy dependence on agr., maize and tobacco; mng. also impt.; Wankie coal mine lgst. in world; also asbestos, chrome and copper; power from Kariba dam encourages lt. inds.; growing econ. and social unrest, 1998; cap. Harare; a. 389,329 km²; p. (1995) 11,536,000.

Zimbabwe National Park; site nr. Victoria, Mashonaland, of ruined t. built c. 15th cent. A.D. by a Bantu people; discovered 1868.

Zinder, t., **Niger,** W. Africa; terminus of trans-Saharan motor route; tr. ctr.; former cap.; second t. of Niger; p. (1988) 119,838.

Zion National Park, Utah, **USA;** contains Z. canyon; a. 596 km².

Zipaquirá, t., **Colombia;** 48 km N. of Bogotá; salt mng., chemicals; cattle-rearing a.

Zistersdorf, t., Lower **Austria;** recently developed oilfields.

Zittau, t., Saxony, **Germany;** on R. Mandau; woollens, linens, machin., cars, chemicals; p. (1989) 36,246.

Zlatoust, t., S.W. **Russia;** in Ural mtns.; metallurgical ctr.; steel, chemicals, sawmilling; p. (1989) 208,000.

Zletovo, terr., N.E. **Macedonia,** formerly Yugoslavia; oil shales, lead, zinc deposits.

Zlin (Gottwaldov), t., **Czech Rep.;** 64 km E. of Brno; footwear, leather and domestic woodware inds.; home of Bata footwear; p. (1990) 87,000.

Znojmo or **Znaim,** t., **Czech Rep.;** anc. t., cas.; ctr. of fertile agr. dist.; p. (1984) 38,321.

Zomba, t., former cap. of **Malawi,** 884 m a.s.l. on slopes of Zomba mtn., 67 km N.E. Blantyre; Malawi's univ. t.; p. (1983) 46,000.

Zonguldak, t. and prov., **Turkey;** spt. on Black Sea; coal-mng. a.; p. (1990) 124,862 (t.), 1,073,560 (prov.).

Zorita De Los Canes, Guadalajara, **Spain;** on R. Tagus; nuclear power plant.

Zrenjanin, t., Vojvodina, Serbia, **Yugoslavia;** pt. on R. Begej; ctr. of agr. dist.; agr. processing; p. (1991) 81,328.

Zuetina, oil pt. (1968), **Libya;** pipeline links shore storage sta. with offshore berths.

Zug, smallest can., **Switzerland;** drained by R. Reuss; contains part of L. Z.; dairying, fruit; cap. Z.; a. 241 km²; p. (1990) 84,900.

Zug, t., cap. of Zug can., **Switzerland;** on L. Z.; elec. engin., printing; p. (1980) 21,609.

Zugspitze, mtn., Bavarian Alps, on Bavarian-Austrian bdr.; highest peak in **Germany,** 2,965 m; connected by rack-and-pinion to Garmisch-Partenkirchen at foot.

Zuider Zee. See IJsselmeer.

Zuid Holland, prov. **Neth;** crossed by R. Rhine; mkt gardening; a. 2,927 km²; p. (1994) 3,313,193.

Zulia, st., **Venezuela;** centred on L. Maracaibo, producing 70 per cent of Venezuelan oil; timber reserves; cap. Maracaibo; a. 63,902 km²; p. (1990) 2,387,208.

Zürich, c., cap. of Z. can., **Switzerland;** on L. Z. and R. Limmat; cath., univ.; leading world banking ctr.; inds. inc. textiles, paper; p. (1990), 341,300 (c.), 840,000 (met. a.).

Zürich, can., **Switzerland;** forested and agr. a.stretching N. from L. Z.; inds. at cap. Z. and Winterthur; a. 1,728 km²; p. (1990) 1,150,500.

Zürich, L. Z., **Switzerland;** drained by R. Limmat; length 40 km.

Zutphen, t., Gelderland, **Neth.;** on R. Ijssel; textiles, paper; Sir Philip Sidney died here 1586; p. (1993) 31,117.

Zuzhou (Suchow), c., Jiangsu, **China;** at junct. of N. China plain and Chang Jiang basin; rly. junct.

Zuzhou (Luchow), c., Sichuan, **China;** coal, iron, kaolin; synthetic ammonia plant.

Zweibrücken, t., Rhineland-Palatinate, **Germany;** nr. Saarbrücken; cas.; machin., footwear, textiles; p. (1986) 32,700.

Zwickau, c., Saxony, **Germany;** on R. Mulde; cas.; coal, motors, machin., tex-tiles; birthplace of Schumann; p. (1990) 113,600.

Zwolle, t., Overijssel, **Neth.;** canal ctr.; cattle mkt.; p. (1994) 99,139.

Zyrardow, t., Skierniewice, **Poland;** nr. Warsaw; specialised textile ctr.; p. (1989) 42,068.

Zyryanovsk, t., **Kazakhstan;** lead, zinc; p. (1990) 53,400.

GENERAL
INFORMATION

This section contains some three thousand entries, arranged alphabetically, including a number of scientific terms and explanations. Entries range across a wide spectrum of human knowledge, from the animal kingdom and historical terms to such contemporary topics as biodiversity, population growth and world climate trends. Cross references direct the reader to fuller information elsewhere in the book.

MEASUREMENTS ARE GIVEN IN METRIC UNITS

Abbreviations

mm	= millimetre	m^2	= square metre
cm	= centimetre	km^2	= square kilometre
m	= metre	ha	= hectare
km	= kilometre	m^3	= cubic metre
km/h	= kilometres per hour	s	= second
g	= gram	min	= minute
kg	= kilogram	h	= hour
tonne	= metric ton		

Equivalents

Length   *Reciprocal*

1 cm	= 0·394 in	2·540
1 m	= 1·094 yd	0·914
1 km	= 0·621 mile	1·609

Area

$1 \, m^2$	= 1·196 yd^2	0·836
$1 \, km^2$	= 0·386 $mile^2$	2·590
1 hectare	= 2·471 acres	0·405

Volume

$1 \, m^3$	= 1·308 yd^3	0·765
1 litre	= 0·220 gallon	4·546

Mass

1 kg	= 2·205 lb	0·454
1 tonne	= 0·984 ton	1·016

Temperature

$$C = (F - 32) \div 1·8$$
$$F = (1·8 \times C) + 32$$

See also **Metric Equivalents, F66–70**

GENERAL INFORMATION

A

Aard-vark (Dutch *aarde* = earth + *vark* = pig), a large nocturnal mammal found only in Africa. It feeds on termites and ants.

Abacus, a device for making arithmetical calculations, consisting of parallel bars on which are strung movable coloured beads. The earliest form of this instrument was used in Mesopotamia about 3000 B.C., and its use spread westwards throughout the Graeco-Roman world and eastwards to China. An efficient form of the abacus is still used in parts of Asia.

Abdication. The term usually refers to the renunciation of the royal office by a reigning monarch. Both Edward II (1327) and Richard II (1399) were forced to abdicate, James II left the throne vacant without waiting for a formal deposition, and the abdication of Edward VIII was effected by the Declaration of Abdication Act, 1936. Since 1688 when Parliament declared James II to have abdicated, no British monarch can abdicate without the consent of Parliament.

Aberration, in astronomy, is the apparent displacement of a star due to the speed of the observer with the earth (*see* **Parallax**). In optics (i) spherical aberration is when there is blurring of the image and fringes of colour at its edges, due to failure of lens to bring light to a single focus; (ii) chromatic aberration is due to the refractive index of glass being different for light of different colours. For instance, violet light is bent more than red.

Abiogenesis, or spontaneous generation; the origination of living from non-living matter. The term is applied to such discredited ideas as that frogs could be generated spontaneously by the action of sunlight on mud, or maggots arise spontaneously in dead meat without any eggs from which the maggots hatch being present. Spallanzani (1729–99) upset the hypothesis of spontaneous generation; Pasteur dealt it a death-blow.

Abominable Snowman. *See* **Yeti.**

Aborigines, a term first applied to an ancient mythical people of central Italy, derives from the Latin *ab origine* = from the beginning. It now signifies the original inhabitants of any country, in particular the aboriginal tribes of Australia. In contrast to their highly complex social and religious customs, the material culture of Australian aboriginals is very low and ill adapted to stand up to contact with European civilisation. Originally estimated at 300,000, their number has dropped in the last 200 years to some 225,000. The 1988 Australian bicentenary focused attention on their lack of legal right to ancient tribal lands and their welfare problems. The passage of the Native Rights Act in 1993 has generated heated debate and led to the controversial Native Title Amendment Bill.

Absolute Temperature, Absolute Zero. This is a refined notion requiring some study of thermodynamics for its full understanding. For setting up an absolute temperature scale one must first assign a numerical value to one fixed temperature. For this, the triple point of water has been chosen, *i.e.*, the temperature at which solid, liquid, and gaseous water are all in equilibrium. The triple point is defined to be 273·16 K where K is read for kelvin (after Lord Kelvin). This temperature is 0·01°C on the Celsius scale (*q.v.*) and is thus very close to the melting point of ice. Suppose the pressure and volume of a mass of gas are measured (i) at the triple point of water, giving (pV)tr as the product of the pressure and volume; and (ii) at any unknown temperature T K, giving (pV) as the product. Then the absolute temperature, T K, is defined by

$$T \text{ K} = 273 \cdot 16 \; \frac{(pV)}{(pV)\text{tr}}$$

It is to be understood that the gas pressure is very low. The nature of the gas is immaterial. More subtly, it can be shown that the temperature so defined is identical with that derived in a rather abstract way in the science of thermodynamics. The absolute scale is therefore also called the thermodynamic scale. Absolute temperatures can be obtained from Celsius temperatures by adding 273·15; thus the absolute temperature of melting ice is 273·15 K. Conversely, absolute zero is a temperature 273·15 K below the temperature of melting ice, *i.e.*, −273·15°C. Theory shows that absolute zero is unattainable, but it has been approached to within about 1 millionth of a degree. Within ten or so degrees of absolute zero, matter develops some remarkable properties. *See* **Kelvin, Cryogenics, Superconductor, Helium.**

Abstract Art, a term applied to 20th cent. plastic arts in which form and colour possess aesthetic value apart from the subject. Usually represented as a modern movement beginning with Cézanne. The idea is ancient, abstract design being found in the Neolithic period, in folk-art, and particularly in Moslem art (which forbids naturalistic representations especially of the human figure). Among those in the tradition are Kandinsky, Braque, Mondrian, Calder.

Acadians. *See* **Cajuns (L21).**

Acetic Acid, an organic acid produced when ordinary (ethyl) alcohol is fermented by the organism called *Acetobacter aceti*. The same oxidation process yields vinegar: this is a weak and crude solution of acetic acid obtained by trickling dilute alcoholic liquor over beechwood shavings at 35°C. The souring of wine is due to the same process. Acetic acid is used as a food preservative and flavouring material, and in the manufacture of cellulose acetate and white lead.

Acetylene (also called ethyne), a compound of carbon and hydrogen prepared from calcium carbide and water. A very reactive gas, it is used industrially on a large scale to prepare acetaldehyde, chlorohydrocarbon solvents, and many intermediates for plastics manufacture. Burns in air with a highly luminous flame, formerly used for lighting purposes, but is now widely used, with oxygen, in welding. For safe storage and transportation it is dissolved in acetone.

Acid Rain is the name given to rain, snow or sleet contaminated with acid substances so that its acidity is greater than the limit expected by normal concentrations of carbon dioxide dissolving in the rain to give carbonic acid (pH 5·5–5·6). The pH (*see* **L95**) of acid rain therefore is less than about 5·5. The increased acidity is caused by larger concentrations of a number of contaminants, principally the strong acids, nitric and sulphuric, which arise from industrial effluents containing oxides of nitrogen and sulphur. The European emission of sulphur dioxide doubled between 1940 and 1980. In some European and North American areas such contamination can give a rain pH as low as 3 (which is 100 times more acid than pH 5). The acid rain can mark fruit and leaves, and adversely affect soil but its main effect is on the aquatic ecosystems especially in regions which cannot naturally buffer acidic inputs such as those with thin soils and granite rocks.

Acids, substances having a tendency to lose a positive ion (a proton). This general definition overcomes difficulties of earlier views which merely described their properties and asserted that they are chemically opposite to bases. As a whole acids contain ionisable hydrogen, replaceable by a metal, to form a salt. Inorganic acids are compounds of non-metals or metalloids, *e.g.*, sulphuric, phosphoric acid. Carboxylic acids contain the group –COOH.

Act of Settlement. *See* **L110.**

Act of Union. *See* **Union, Treaty of (L124).**

Actinides, the fourteen metallic elements from thorium (no. 90) to lawrencium (no. 103). All known isotopes of these elements are radioactive

L4

and those with atomic number greater than 92 (uranium) have been produced only in significant quantities artificially. Plutonium (no. 94) is obtained from uranium during the course of nuclear reactor operation and the higher transuranic elements can be made from it by the successive capture of neutrons or nuclei of light atoms. The availability of only minute quantities of short-lived isotopes makes the determination of the physical and chemical properties of the higher actinides very difficult. Claims for the discovery of new elements can therefore be controversial and since the discoverers can name the elements their naming is also controversial. There were three different reports for Nobelium (no. 102). Lawrencium (no. 103) is called Jolistium by Russian authors. Element no. 104 was reported in 1964 by a Russian group and called Kurchatovium but is called Rutherfordium (Rf) in the West. Element no. 105 is called Hahnium (Hn).

Advent, a period devoted to religious preparation for the coming celebration of the Nativity (Christmas). It includes the four Sundays immediately preceding the festival.

Advocatus Diaboli ("the devil's advocate"), a Roman Catholic functionary who presents opposing evidence in regard to the life of any deceased person it may be proposed to canonise.

Aerodynamics, the science of gases (especially air) in motion, particularly in relation to aircraft (aeronautics). The idea of imitating the birds by the use of wings is of ancient origin. Leonardo da Vinci first carried out experiments in a scientific manner. The invention of the balloon in 1783 and the researches of scientists and engineers in the 19th cent. ultimately led to the development of the aeroplane.

Aerolites, the name given to the class of meteorites composed chiefly of heavy silicates. The other two main classes are *siderolites* (nickel–iron and silicates) and *siderites* (nickel–iron).

Aerosol, a suspension of a liquid in a gas; for example, a fog is very small drops of water suspended in air. Formed by spraying the liquid in air, aerosols are used to disperse liquid over a wide area in crop spraying, air freshening and pest control. *See also* **Fluorocarbons.**

Afrikander, type of cattle bred in South Africa.

Afrikaner, an Afrikaans-speaking South African, usually of Dutch descent.

After-damp occurs in a mine after an explosion, causing suffocation. It is composed mainly of carbon dioxide and nitrogen and contains water vapour and carbon monoxide (produced by the burning, in a restricted supply of air, of fine coal dust).

Agaric, large fungi of the family *Agaricaceae,* which includes the mushroom and what are popularly called "toadstools", though the idea that these two lay terms sharply differentiate between edible and poisonous fungi is an incorrect one. Characteristic of the agarics is the presence of a cap or *pileus* (bearing underneath the spore-shedding gills) and a stalk or *stipe.*

Agave, the American aloe or Century Plant which sometimes does not attain to flowering maturity under sixty or seventy years, and then dies. The flower spray may reach a height of 6 m and in its development the rush of sap is so great that the Mexicans collect for brewing the strong spirit called mescal. 1,000 litres of sap can be obtained from a single plant. Some species of agave yield sisal used for making cord and rope.

Aggression. After many years of consideration a definition of aggression was agreed at the United Nations in 1974. It is the use of armed force by a state against the sovereignty, territorial integrity, or political independence of another state or in any other manner inconsistent with the Charter of the UN. Iraq's invasion of Kuwait in 1990 was one recent example.

Air, a mixture of gases in the earth's atmosphere, the main constituents being nitrogen, oxygen and argon. Dry air contains these gases in the following proportions by volume: nitrogen 78·06%, oxygen 21%, argon 0·94%. Other gases are also present in small amounts. Of particular importance are water vapour and carbon dioxide. Water vapour is not only critical for life forms on land but also a major factor in the behaviour of the atmosphere—weather and climate. Carbon dioxide is util-

ised by green plants in photosynthesis (**F32**). Air also contains traces of ammonia, nitrogen oxides, hydrogen, sulphur dioxide, ozone, and of the rare gases, helium, krypton, neon and xenon. Near cities and industrial areas there are also large quantities of dust and smoke particles (up to 100,000 particles per cc), and traces of other gases from industrial processes. A litre of air at 0°C and 760 mm pressure weighs 1·2932 g. *See also* **Atmosphere, Pollution.**

Air Glow is the general name given to a large number of relatively weak optical emissions from the earth's upper atmosphere in the height range 70 to 400 km (approx.). It is distinct from the aurora polaris (*q.v.*) which is usually much brighter and normally only observable at high latitudes. Air glow is produced by a combination of photochemical reactions in the upper atmosphere, excitation by photoelectrons, or by solar ultra-violet light. In the latter case it is more correctly called "dayglow". These emissions occur in the ultra-violet and infra-red spectral regions as well as in visible light.

Alabaster, a soft crystalline form of sulphate of lime, or granulated gypsum, easily worked for statuary and other ornamental articles, and capable of being highly polished. Volterra, in Tuscany, yields the finest; that in highest ancient repute came from Alabastron in Egypt, near to the modern Antinoë.

Alb, white vestment reaching to the feet, worn by priests in religious ceremonies.

Albatross, a large sea-bird of almost pure white, black and white, or brown plumage. It nests in colonies on remote islands, but at other times rarely approaches land. Of the thirteen species, nine are found in the southern oceans, one in the tropics, three others in the North Pacific. Modern fishing methods are threatening the albatross with extinction. Their number worldwide are estimated (1998) at only 40,000.

Albert Memorial, a large Gothic monument designed by Sir George Gilbert Scott, and embellished with sculptures by eminent artists. Erected in memory of Prince Albert in Kensington Gardens at a cost of £117,000.

Alcázar the palace at Seville, famed for the beauty of its halls and gardens, formerly the residence of the Moorish kings.

Alchemy. *See* Section J.

Alcohols. A class of organic compounds of general formula R–OH, where R is an aliphatic radical. "Alcohol" is the name used for ethyl alcohol (ethanol); this is produced by distilling fermented liquors, and synthetically from ethylene, a product of petroleum cracking. Industrially ethyl alcohol is used in the manufacture of chloroform, ether, perfumes, etc. Diluted with wood alcohol or other denaturants ethyl alcohol is called "methylated spirits"; the denaturants are varied according to the industrial purposes for which it is required, the methylated spirits then being largely exempt from duty. Wood alcohol (methyl alcohol or methanol) can be obtained by distilling wood or synthetically from water gas.

Alcoholic Strength. In 1980 Great Britain adopted the OIML (International Organisation of Legal Metrology) system of spirit strength measurement in metric units as required by EEC directive. The alcoholic strength of wine is expressed in percentage volume ("% vol") terms, *i.e.,* the number of volumes of pure alcohol in 100 volumes of the product at 20°C. For spirits the quantity for duty is the litre of alcohol at 20°C. For example, a case of 12 bottles of 75 cl each = 9 litres; at 40% volume 9 litres = 9 × 40% = 3.60 litres of alcohol. The alcoholic strength of spirits and liqueurs appearing on bottle labels is increasingly shown in % vol. terms (*e.g.,* "40.5% vol"). The USA continues to use the US proof gallon (1.37 US proof gallons = 1 British proof gallon).

Aldehyde, the generic term for a class of chemical compounds of general formula R–CHO, where R is an organic radical. Except for formaldehyde, which is a gas, aldehydes are volatile liquids. They are produced by oxidation of primary alcohols. Most important aldehyde is formaldehyde (methanal) used in making the plastics described as formaldehyde resins. Formalin (formaldehyde solution in water) is much used for preserving zoological specimens.

Alder, a river-side tree of the genus *Alnus*, including some 30 species and found in north temperate regions and the Andes. The only species native to Britain is *A. glutinosa*, which has been described as "guardian of river-banks" because of the way its roots bind together the sand and stones, and so slow down erosion. The wood is used for furniture and charcoal.

Aldine Editions are the beautiful books printed in Venice by the Renaissance printer Aldo Pio Manuzio and his family between 1490 and 1597. Italics were first introduced in these books.

Algae, flowerless plants living mostly in water. Seaweeds and the green pond scums are the best known algae. The green powder found on trees is a microscopic alga (*Protococcus*).

Algebra, a branch of mathematics in which symbols are used in place of numbers. Sir Isaac Newton styled it the "universal arithmetic". The Chinese were able to solve the quadratic equation before the Christian era but it was Al-Khowarizmi, an Arab mathematician of the early 9th cent., who introduced algebra to Europe.

Alhambra, the ancient palace of the Moorish kings at Granada in Spain, built in the 13th and 14th cent. Though part of the castle was turned into a modern palace under Charles V, the most beautiful parts of the interior are still preserved—the graceful halls and dwelling-rooms grouped round the Court of Alberca and the Court of Lions, with their fountains, arcades, and lovely gardens.

Aliphatic describes derivatives of hydrocarbons having chains of carbon atoms, as distinct from rings of carbon atoms as in benzene (*see* **Aromatic**). The gas butane is aliphatic.

Alkali, the general name given to a number of chemicals which are bases (*q.v.*). The term should be limited to the hydroxides of metals in the first and second group of the periodic table and of ammonia, *e.g.*, $NaOH$, KOH. They are used commercially in the manufacture of paper, glass, soap, and artificial silk. The word comes from the Arabic *al-kali* meaning calcined wood ashes. Alkalis are extremely soluble in water and neutralise acids to form salts and water.

Alkaloids, a large group of natural products which contain nitrogen; they are usually basic. Isolated from plants and animals, they include some hormones, vitamins, and drugs. Examples are nicotine, adrenalin, and cocaine. Many alkaloids are made synthetically for medicinal use, *e.g.*, morphine, quinine. Their function in plants is not well understood. *See* **Belladonna.**

Alligator, the crocodile of America, found in the lower Mississippi and adjacent lakes and marshes. There is also a Chinese species. Alligators have broader snouts than other crocodiles.

Allotropy. Depending on the temperature, pressure or method of preparation, an element may exist in one of several forms, each having different physical properties (crystal structure, electrical conductivity, melting point, etc.). This is known as allotropy and the different forms of the element are called allotropes. Many elements exhibit allotropy, *e.g.*, sulphur, phosphorus, oxygen, tin and carbon, the most well-known allotropes of carbon being diamond and graphite.

Alloys are combinations of metals made for their valuable special properties, *e.g.*, durability, strength, lightness, magnetism, rust-resistance, *etc.* Some well-known ones are brass (zinc + copper), coinage bronze (copper + zinc + tin), steels (iron + carbon + various other materials), soft solder (tin + lead), dental fillings (mercury + various ingredients).

All Saints' Day (Nov. 1) is common to both the Anglican and Roman Catholic Churches, and is in commemoration of the saints generally, or such as have no special day set apart for them. Instituted by Pope Boniface IV, early in the 7th cent., this ecclesiastical festival was formerly called "All Hallows".

All Souls' Day (Nov. 2) is a festival of the Roman Church, intended for the mitigation by prayer of the sufferings of souls in purgatory. The commemoration was enjoined by Abbot Odilo of Cluny during the 11th cent. upon the monastic order over which he presided, and was afterwards adopted generally throughout the Roman Communion.

Allspice, a flavouring obtained from a West Indian tree of the myrtle family, *Pimenta officinalis*, likened to the flavour of cinnamon, nutmeg and cloves combined. The berries resemble peppercorns and are used as a spice in mincemeat, etc.

Alluvium, river transported deposits of sand, mud and gravel which accumulate to form distinctive features such as levées, flood plains and deltas. The frequent renewal of alluvium by flooding causes riverine lands to be some of the most fertile. In Asia alluvial lands support high densities of population, *e.g.*, The Hwang-ho plains and the Ganges delta.

Almond, the fruit of the *Amygdalus communis*, originally indigenous to Persia, Asia Minor and N. Africa; now cultivated in Italy, Spain, France, the USA and Australia. It yields both bitter and sweet oil. Bitter almond oil is obtained by macerating and distilling the ripe seeds; it is used for flavouring and scenting purposes, its fragrant odour being due to the presence of benzaldehyde and hydrogen cyanide. When the seeds are pressed sweet almond oil results: this is used in perfumery, and also as a lubricant for very delicate machinery.

Almuce, a fur stole worn by certain canons.

Aloe, large plants of the lily family, with about 180 species found mainly in the S. African veldt and karroo. The bitter purgative drug (aloes) is prepared by evaporating the plant's sap. *See* **Agave.**

Alpaca, a South American ruminant related to the llama whose long, fine wool is woven into a soft dress fabric known by the same name. Sir Titus Salt first manufactured alpaca cloth (1836). Saltaire, near Bradford, remains to evidence the success which for many years attended the enterprise.

Alpha Particle, or alpha-ray, fast-moving helium nucleus ejected by some radioactive atoms, *e.g.*, polonium. It is a combination of 2 neutrons and 2 protons.

Alphabet (so called from the first two letters of the Greek alphabet—alpha, beta) is the term applied to the collection of letters from which the words of a language are made up. It grew out of the knowledge that all words can be expressed by a limited number of sounds arranged in various combinations. The Phoenicians were the first to make use of an alphabetic script derived from an earlier Semitic alphabet (earliest known inscriptions *c.* 1500–950 B.C.) from which all other alphabets have sprung. The stages in the development of the alphabet were mnemonic (memory aids), pictorial (actual pictures), ideographic (symbols), and lastly phonetic. All the ideographic systems died out, with the exception of that of the Chinese.

Altimeter, an instrument used in aircraft to estimate altitude; its usual essential feature is an aneroid barometer which registers the decrease of pressure with height. Roughly 1 millibar corresponds to 9 m. To read an aircraft altimeter correct for its destination, the zero setting must be adjusted for difference of ground height and difference of surface pressure, especially when pressure is falling or when flying towards low pressure.

Altitude, an astronomical term used to signify the angular elevation of a heavenly body; this is measured with a quadrant or sextant. In aeronautics it is the height above sea-level.

Alto-Relievo, a term applied to sculptured designs which are depicted in prominent relief on a flat surface, technically signifying that the projections exceeds one-half the true proportions of the objects represented. Basso-relievo is carving kept lower than one-half such projection.

Alum is a compound salt used in various industrial processes, especially dyeing, its constituents being the sulphate of one univalent metal or radical (*e.g.*, potassium, sodium, ammonium, rubidium, caesium, silver, thallium) and the sulphate of a tervalent metal (*e.g.*, aluminium, iron, chromium, manganese), and water of crystallisation.

Alumina is the oxide of aluminium. Very valuable as a refractory material. The ruby is almost 100 per cent. alumina; so also are the emerald, oriental amethyst, etc. An hydrated aluminium oxide is bauxite, chief ore of alu-

L6

minium from which the metal is extracted electrolytically.

Aluminium, element no. 13, symbol Al, is a light metal which conducts electricity well. Its specific gravity at 20°C is 2·705. Melting point of aluminium is 660·2°C. It is made commercially by electrolysing bauxite dissolved in cryolite (double fluoride of aluminium and sodium). Aluminium alloys are being increasingly used for construction purposes.

Amadavat, a popular cage bird of the weaver family, mainly crimson with spots, so named because the first specimens came from Ahmadabad in India about 1700.

Amalgam is the term applied to any alloy of which mercury forms a part.

Amber, a brittle resinous substance; in origin, fossilised resin. Obtained mostly from the Baltic coasts, and used for ornaments, pipe mouth-pieces, *etc.*

Ambergris is a waxy substance produced in the intestines of the sperm whale, and generally found floating on the sea. It is a valuable perfumery material.

Amblyopsis, a species of fish, practically sightless, and with inoperative organs of hearing and feeling, that inhabit the Mammoth Cave of Kentucky. A remarkable illustration of the failure of senses not brought into use.

America's Cup. In 1851 the Royal Yacht Squadron put up for competition a silver cup that has become the most famous trophy in yachting. In that year the New York Y.C. sent the schooner *America* across the Atlantic to compete in a 53-mile (85 km) race round the Isle of Wight; it captured the trophy which now bears its name. Until 1983 none of the many challenges by yachtsmen from Great Britain, Canada, and latterly, Australia, had been successful. In that year, however, in Rhode Island Sound *Australia II*, skippered by John Bertrand, won on the 25th challenge. The triumph was short-lived. The 1992 winner was Bill Koch's *America*[3] which claimed the 141-year-old trophy 4-1. In 1995 the New Zealand yacht *Black Magic* achieved a sensational 5-0 victory over the Americans. In February 2000 the holders, New Zealand, have to defend their title.

Amethyst, the violet variety of quartz, used as a precious stone, containing traces of manganese, titanium and iron. The finest coloured specimens come from Brazil and the Urals.

Amice, a white linen vestment worn by Roman Catholic and many Anglican priests when officiating at Mass or Holy Eucharist.

Amines, organic chemicals composed of carbon, hydrogen and nitrogen. They are derived from ammonia, which they resemble in smell and chemical characteristics. The smell of bad fish is due to the presence of amines. Important industrially as intermediates in a wide variety of products, for example, the synthesis of dyestuffs and man-made fibres such as nylon.

Amino acids, organic compounds containing an amine group and a carboxylic acid group. They are the "building bricks" of proteins (*q.v.*).

Ammeter, an instrument for measuring the current flowing in an electric circuit. A contraction of ampere-meter. *See* **Ampere.**

Ammonia, a colourless gaseous compound comprising three atoms of hydrogen to one of nitrogen. Formerly it was made by heating the horns and hoofs of deer, acquiring the name of spirits of hartshorn. The ammonia of commerce is now procured by coal decomposition in the course of gas-making and by direct synthesis. In the very important Haber process of ammonia production by fixation of atmospheric nitrogen, the nitrogen is made to combine with hydrogen and the ammonia so prepared is converted into nitric acid, ammonium nitrate or ammonium sulphate. The Haber process made Germany self-sufficient in nitrates in the first world war.

Ammonites, extinct animals related to the Nautilus. The chambered shell is coiled, usually in a plane spiral. They are confined to Mesozoic rocks.

Ammonium, the basic radical of ammonium salts. Composed of one atom of nitrogen and four of hydrogen, it behaves chemically like an ion of a monovalent alkali metal. Ammonium chloride is known as "sal ammoniac". "Sal volatile" is ammonium carbonate.

Amnesty, an act of grace by which a ruler or governing power pardons political offenders.

Amnesty International is the world's largest human rights (*see* **J58–60**) organisation. It seeks to secure the release of prisoners of conscience, works for fair and prompt trials for all political prisoners, and campaigns against torture and the death penalty. Since 1961, Amnesty has taken on over 43,500 cases. There are now (1999) over 1 million members in 92 countries.

Amorphous, a term used to indicate the absence of crystalline form in any body or substance.

Ampere, unit of electric current in the SI system of units; named after André Marie Ampère, who in the 1820s helped to lay the foundations of modern electromagnetism. Defined as that constant current which, if maintained in two parallel rectilinear conductors of infinite length, of negligible circular cross section, and placed at a distance of one metre apart in a vacuum, would produce between these conductors a force which is equal to 2×10^{-7} newton per metre.

Amphioxus *or* **Lancelet,** a primitive chordate (**F36(2)**), occurring in sand-banks around British shores and elsewhere.

Anabolism. *See* **Catabolism.**

Analysis is one of the major branches of modern pure mathematics and includes the theories of differentiation, integration, differential equations and analytic functions.

Anchor, an instrument used for keeping ships stationary. Great improvements have been introduced in recent years, stockless anchors being now chiefly used, consisting of a shank and a loose fluke. Lloyd's rules prescribe the number and weight of anchors which must be carried by merchant ships.

Anchorite is a religious person who retires into solitude to employ himself with holy thoughts. Among the early Christians, anchorites were numerous, but in the Western Church they have been few. Their reputation for wisdom and prescience was high, and kings and rulers in olden days would visit their cells for counsel. An anchorite or "ankret" was in mediaeval times a source of fame and profit to the monastic house within which he was voluntarily immured.

Anchovy, a fish of the herring family, distinguished by its large mouth and projecting snout, plentiful in the Mediterranean.

Ancient Lights are rights of light enjoyed by a property owner over adjoining land. Such a right is obtained either by uninterrupted enjoyment for twenty years, or by written authority, and once legally established cannot be upset, no building being permissible that would seriously interfere with the privilege.

Anemometer, an instrument for measuring the strength of the wind. In the most widely used pattern the rotation, about a vertical axis, of a group of hemispherical or conical cups gives a measure of the total flow of air past the cups, various registering devices being employed. The Dines anemograph provides a continuous record of the variation in both velocity and direction; changes of pressure produced in a horizontal tube, kept pointing into the wind by a vane, cause a float, to which a pen is attached, to rise and fall in sympathy with the gusts and lulls. The hot-wire anemometer, depending upon the change of electrical resistance experienced by a heated wire when cooled, enables very gentle air currents to be investigated.

Aneroid is the kind of barometer which does not depend upon atmospheric support of a mercury (or other liquid) column. It consists of a metallic box, partially exhausted of air, with a corrugated lid which moves with atmospheric changes. A lever system magnifies the lid movements about 200 times and atmospheric pressure is read from a dial. The construction of the vacuum chamber provides automatic compensation for temperature changes. An aneroid barometer is the basic component of an altimeter.

Angelica, an aromatic plant of the Umbelliferae order, *Angelica officinalis*, valuable as a flavouring and possessing medical properties. In olden times supposed to protect against poison.

Angelus, a church bell rung in Roman Catholic countries, at morn, noon, and sunset, to remind the faithful to say their Angelic Salutation.

Angevin Dynasty includes the Plantagenet kings from Henry II to Richard II. The name was derived from Henry II's father, Geoffrey, Count of Anjou.

Angles, a northern tribe originally settled in Schleswig, who with the Saxons and Jutes invaded Britain in the 5th cent.

Ångström, a unit of wavelength, named after the Swedish physicist A. J. Ångström (1814–74), equal to one hundred-millionth of a centimetre ($10^{.8}$ cm). It is used to measure wavelengths of light, X-rays, *etc.*

Aniline, a simple aromatic compound ($C_6H_5NH_2$) related to benzene and ammonia. It is obtained from coal-tar. The name recalls the fact that it was first prepared by distilling indigo (*anil* is Portuguese for indigo). In 1856 W. H. Perkin (1838–1907) discovered the first aniline or coal-tar dye, mauve, and thus founded the modern dyestuff industry.

Animal Kingdom. *See* **F36.**

Anise, an umbelliferous plant (*Pimpinella anisum*) found in Egypt and the Levant, and valued for its fruit, aniseed, possessing certain medicinal properties and yielding an aromatic, volatile oil. Also used in cooking. The anise of the Bible is *Anethum graveolens, i.e.,* dill.

Annates were acknowledgments formerly paid to the Popes by way of fee or tax in respect of ecclesiastical preferment and consisted usually of a proportion of the income ("first-fruits") of the office. Introduced into England in the 13th cent.; annexed to the Crown under Henry VIII; transferred to a perpetual fund for the benefit of the poorer clergy in 1704. *See* **Queen Anne's Bounty.**

"Annual Register", a yearly record of political and literary events, founded by Edmund Burke (as editor) in 1759 and Robert Dorsley, the bookseller.

Annunciation, Feast of the (25 March), is a Church festival commemorating the message of the incarnation of Christ brought by the angel Gabriel to the Virgin Mary, hence the title Lady Day.

Anointing is the pouring of consecrated oil upon the body as a mark of supreme honour. In England it is restricted chiefly to the ceremony of the monarch's coronation, and the spoon with which the oil is applied forms part of the English regalia. In the Roman Catholic Church anointing represents the sacrament of extreme unction.

Ant. There are about 6,000 species of ants, which belong to the same order (Hymenoptera) as the bees, wasps and ichneumon flies. They are social in habit, living in communities of varying size and development. There are three basic castes in ants—the females or *queens,* the *males,* and the *workers* (the last-named being neuter), although specialised forms of workers are sometimes found, *e.g.,* the *soldiers* of the harvesting ants. In the communities of those species of ants which evolved most recently there is a highly complex social life and well-developed division of labour. Some species of these ants make slaves of other species, stealing the cocoons before the adult forms emerge. Many ants "milk" green-flies, which they protect for their honey-like secretion, and most ants' nests contain many "guests", such as beetles and silver fish. Some ants harvest grains of corn, and others, from S. America, live on fungi which they cultivate in underground "mushroom beds".

Antarctic Exploration. In earlier centuries it was thought that a great continent must exist in the southern hemisphere, around the South Pole, to balance the known land masses in the north. Its supposed extent was greatly reduced in the 18th cent., particularly when Capt. Cook sailed for the first time south of the Antarctic Circle and reached the edge of the ice-pack. A portion of the ice-covered continent—the coast of Graham Land—was first sighted by Lieut. Edward Bransfield in 1820. The first extensive exploration was made by Capt. James Clarke Ross, who with the *Erebus* and *Terror* penetrated into the Ross Sea in 1841, and discovered the great Ross Ice Barrier in 78° South lat. Interest in the Antarctic did not revive until after 1890, when an international scheme of research was drawn up. A Norwegian, C. E. Borchgrevink, in 1898–1900, was the first to winter in the Antarctic and to travel on the ice barrier. The British share in this work was carried out by Capt. R. F. Scott's expedition in

the *Discovery*, 1901–4. Scott's party sledged across the barrier to 82° 17′ South, then a record "farthest south". A little later, Ernest Shackleton beat this by travelling to within 160 km of the South Pole. The Scottish polar explorer William Spiers Bruce led the Scottish national Antarctic Expedition of 1902 in the *Scotia* and discovered Coats Land and founded a meteorological observatory on the South Orkneys. In 1910 Scott organised his second expedition in *Terra Nova*, and became engaged against his will in a "race for the Pole" when, after his departure, the Norwegian Arctic explorer, Roald Amundsen, suddenly announced that he was sailing for the Antarctic. Amundsen set up his base at the eastern end of the Barrier, and, relying on dog teams for hauling his sledges, reached the Pole on 14 December 1911. Meanwhile Scott and his party, their start delayed by adverse weather, were marching southwards, man-hauling their sledges, for Scott was against the use of dogs. After an arduous journey they reached the Pole one month after Amundsen. The return was a struggle against the weather and increasing weakness, probably due to scurvy, until at last they perished within a few kilometres of their base. After the first world war the development of the whaling industry greatly stimulated further exploration. Outstanding expeditions included that of Admiral R. E. Byrd, 1929, when he flew over the South Pole; the British Graham Land expedition, 1934, which carried out the first extensive mapping of any part of the Antarctic continent; and the US Navy's Antarctic Expedition of 1940, when the whole continent was circumnavigated and great areas photographed from the air. The Antarctic was the scene of high adventure during the International Geophysical Year (1957–58), when scientists from many countries participated in the explorations. The Commonwealth Trans-Antarctic Expedition set out from opposite sides of the continent and met at the South Pole, the UK party, led by Sir Vivian Fuchs, from the Falklands, and Sir Edmund Hillary and his party from New Zealand. The UK party accomplished the first crossing of the White Continent in 99 days. In 1993, the explorers Sir Ranulph Fiennes and Dr Michael Stroud completed the first unsupported crossing of the Antarctic land mass and the longest unsupported polar journey—both world records. In December 1994, Liv Arnesen (Norway) became the first woman to reach the South Pole alone. In January 1996 David Hempleman-Adams became the first Briton to walk solo and unsupported to the South Pole. Scientists working in Antarctica have discovered that over 100,000,000 years ago the frozen waste was once a huge forest roamed by plant-eating dinosaurs. Meanwhile climate warming has led to the loss of 25 per cent of its sea ice this century. The ozone hole over Antarctica is now (1999) larger than ever. In 1998 scientists made plans to explore a huge lake, two miles below the Antarctic ice-cap, insulated by ice for millions of years. It could hold living creatures which inhabited the planet over 30 million years ago.

Anteaters, a small family (the Myrmecophagidae) of mammals from Central and South America. They feed on ants, termites and other insects which they gather with a long tongue covered with sticky saliva.

Antennae, paired feelers of insects and crustaceans. In radio, the term "antenna" is equivalent to "aerial".

Anthem, a choral composition, with or without instrumental accompaniment, usually sung after the third collect in the Church of England services. The words are from the Scriptures, and the composition may be for solo voices only, for full choir, or for both. Among the chief British composers of anthems are Tallis, Purcell, Croft, Boyce, Goss and Stainer.

Anthracite is a black coal with a brilliant lustre. It contains 92 per cent. and over of carbon and burns slowly, without smoke or flame. *See* **Coal.**

Anthropoid, meaning "resembling man", a sub-order of the primate mammals including man and also the gibbon, chimpanzee, orang-utan, and gorilla.

Antibiotics, a collective name for any substance

derived from micro-organisms or fungi which is capable of destroying infections, *e.g.*, penicillin.

Anticyclone, a region where barometric pressure is greater than that of its surroundings. Such a system is distinguished on weather charts by a pattern of isobars, usually circular or oval-shaped, enclosing the centre of high pressure where the air is calm. In the remaining areas light or moderately strong winds blow spirally outwards in a clockwise direction in the Northern Hemisphere (and in the reverse direction in the Southern Hemisphere), in accordance with Buys Ballot's law (an observer with back to wind in Northern Hemisphere has lower pressure to left; in Southern to right). Over the British Isles anticyclonic weather is generally quiet and settled, being fair, warm, and sunny in summer and either very cold and often foggy or overcast and gloomy in winter. These systems move slowly and sometimes remain practically stationary for days at a time, that over Siberia being particularly well defined. Extensive belts of almost permanent anti-cyclones occur in latitudes 30° N and 30° S. Persistent anticyclonic weather with easterly winds during the months December 1962 to March 1963, brought the coldest and hardest winter to Britain since 1740.

Antimony. Metal element, no. 51, symbol Sb. In group 5 of the periodic table. Exists in various forms, the stable form being a grey metal with a layer structure. The other forms are non-conductors. On being burned, it gives off dense fumes of oxide of antimony. By itself it is not of special utility; but as an alloy for hardening other metals, it is much used. As an alloy with lead for type-metal, and with tin and copper or zinc for Britannia-metal, it is of great value. Most important antimony ore is stibnite (antimony sulphide).

Anti-Pope, one elected in opposition to one held to be canonically chosen; applied to the popes Clement VII and Benedict XIII, who resided at Avignon during the Great Schism (1378–1417).

Anti-proton, the "negative proton", an atomic particle created in high energy collisions of nuclear particles. Its existence was confirmed in Oct. 1955. *See* **Section F.**

Antisemitism. *See* **Section J.**

Antlers are the branched horns of deer, the branches being called tines. Antlers originate as outgrowths of the frontal bone, and are usually shed once a year. Except in the reindeer and caribou they are restricted to the male.

Aotearoa, meaning "Long White Cloud', the Maori name for New Zealand.

Apartheid. *See* **Section J.**

Ape, a term applied to the gorilla, chimpanzee, orang-utan and gibbon—the anthropoid apes.

Aphelion, the point in the orbit of a planet farthest from the sun; the opposite of perihelion. At aphelion the earth is 1.52×10^8 km from the sun.

Aphids, green-flies or plant lice, a numerous species of destructive insects living on young shoots and foliage, some on roots. Reproduction is by parthenogenesis (virgin birth).

Apis, the sacred bull worshipped by the ancient Egyptians; also the scientific name for the bee.

Apocalyptic writings are those which deal with revelation and prophecy, more especially the Revelation of St. John.

Apocrypha (hidden writings), the books which were included in the Septuagint (Greek) and Vulgate (Latin) versions of the Old Testament but ex- cluded from the sacred canon at the Reformation by the Protestants on the grounds that they were not originally written in Hebrew nor re- garded as genuine by the Jews. The books include: 1 and 2 Esdras, Tobit, Judith, additions to Esther, Wisdom of Solomon, Ecclesiasticus, Baruch, Song of the Three Holy Children, History of Susannah, Bel and the Dragon, Prayer of Manasses, 1 and 2 Maccabees. The term is usually applied to the additions to the Old Testament, but there are also numerous Christian writings of the same character. *The New English Bible,* which contains the Apocrypha, was published in 1970.

Apogee, that point in the orbit of a heavenly body which is farthest from the earth; used in relation to the sun, moon and artificial satellites. The sun's apogee corresponds to the earth's aphelion. *See* **Perigee.**

Apostasy is a revolt, by an individual or party, from one form of opinions or doctrinate to another. Julian, the Roman Emperor (331–63), brought up as a Christian, became converted to paganism and on coming to the throne (361), proclaimed religious toleration. Hence his name, Julian the Apostate.

Apostles. The twelve apostles who were disciples of Jesus were: Simon Peter and Andrew (his brother), James and John (sons of Zebedee), Philip, Bartholomew, Thomas, Matthew, James, Thaddaeus, Simon, and Judas Iscariot. After the Ascension Matthias was chosen to take the place of Judas. St. Paul was the leading apostle in the mission to the Gentiles, though he was not one of the twelve. St. Barnabas has also been called an apostle.

Apostles' Creed, the name of the most ancient of the Church's statements of its belief: "I believe in God the Father Almighty; and in Jesus Christ his only Son our Lord, who was born of the Holy Ghost and the Virgin Mary. . . ." A later version is used in the Church of England at morning and evening prayer.

Apostolic Fathers were the immediate disciples or followers of the apostles, especially such as left writings behind. They included Barnabas, Clement of Rome, Ignatius of Antioch, Hermas, Papias of Hieropolis and Polycarp.

Appeasement Policy. The name of the policy during 1937 and 1938 of yielding to the demands of Hitler and Mussolini in the hope that a point would be reached when the dictators would co-operate in the maintenance of peace. The policy culminated in the Munich Agreement (which was the subject of much criticism) after a series of concessions including the recognition of the Italian conquest of Abyssinia and the German annexation of Austria. The policy was finally demonstrated as futile when Hitler seized Czechoslovakia in March 1939.

Appian Way, the oldest and finest of the Roman roads originally laid by Appius Claudius (312 B.C.) from Rome to Capua and thence to Brundisium (Brindisi).

Approved Schools were residential schools, subject to Home Office inspection, for the training of young persons under 17 who, because of disturbed behaviour as a result of unfavourable influences such as bad environment or parental neglect, were guilty of offences or in need of care and protection and had been sent to them by magistrates from juvenile or other courts. The approved school order was abolished by the Children and Young Persons Act 1969. Such young people may now be committed to the care of a local authority and accommodated in a system of community homes ranging from children's homes to borstal type institutions.

April, the fourth month of the year, from the Roman *Aprilis* derived from *aperire* "to open" —the period when the buds begin to open.

Apse is a semicircular recess, arched or dome-roofed, at the end of the choir, aisles, or nave of a church.

Aqueducts are conduits in which water flows or is conveyed from its source to the place where it is to be used. Most famous builders were the Romans and the oldest Roman aqueduct was the Aqua Appia, which dates from about 310 B.C. Among modern aqueducts may be mentioned that of Glasgow, which brings water to that city from Loch Katrine; that of Manchester, which taps Thirlmere; that of Liverpool, with Lake Vyrnwy in North Wales as its source, and the Fron Aqueduct, Powys, which carries water from the Elan Valley to Birmingham.

Arabian Nights Entertainment or **Book of a Thousand and One Nights,** a collection of fascinating tales of the Orient, of mixed Indian, Persian, Arabic, and Egyptian origination, and first made known in Europe by Antoine Galland's French translation (1704–17) from Arabian texts. The "master" tale tells how the princess Shahrazad so beguiles the king through the telling of the tales over one thousand and one nights that her life was spared. English translators include E. W. Lane (1840), Sir Richard Burton (1885–8), John Payne (1882–4).

Arabic Numerals. The modern system of numbering, 0, 1, 2, 3, 4, 5, 6, 7, 8, 9, in which the digits depend on their position for their value is called the Arabic numerical notation. The method is, in fact, of Indian origin. By the 9th cent. Hindu science was available in Arabic, and the Persian mathematician Al-Kwarizimi (c. 830) in his *Arithmetic* used the so-called "Arabic" system of numbering. Gradually the method spread to Europe, taking the place of the Roman system which was useless for calculation. The West is indebted to the Arabs for the zero symbol. It made the invention of decimal fractions possible.

Aragonite, the unstable form of calcium carbonate found as a mineral in some young deposits. It crystallises in the orthorhombic system but tends to revert to calcite.

Aramaic Languages, the Semitic dialects current in Mesopotamia and the regions extending southwest from the Euphrates to Palestine from about the 12th cent. B.C. until after the rise of Islam, when Aramaic was superseded by Arabic. Both Aramaic and Greek were spoken in Palestine during the time of Christ.

Archaeopteryx, a fossil bird providing a connecting link between reptiles and birds. It had feathers, jaws with teeth, no bill, reptilian bones and skull, a long tail, and it probably used its fore-limbs for gliding flight. The first specimen, found in 1861, in the Solenhofen limestone of Bavaria, is in London's Natural History Museum.

Archbishop, the chief of the bishops of an ecclesiastical province in the Greek, Roman, and Anglican churches. In the Church of England there are two archbishops, the Archbishop of Canterbury, called the Primate of *all* England, and the Archbishop of York, styled the Primate of England.

Archimedes' Principle. When a body is weighed in air and then in any fluid, the apparent loss in weight is equal to the weight of fluid displaced. This scientific fact was noted by the Syracusan philosopher Archimedes (287–212 B.C.) and is often used as a basis for density measurements.

Architecture, the art and science of building. The provision of shelter for mankind by the orderly arrangement of materials in a manner which expresses man's attitude to living. The forms which buildings take are the outcome of the function for which they are to be used, of the architect's aesthetic sensibility and the structural method adopted. Until the last hundred years structural methods were limited to timber frames, and columns, lintels, load-bearing walls, arches, vaults, and domes in brick or stone. From these few basic elements have evolved the great variety of historic styles of building to be found throughout the world. To give but one example, the Greeks created those systems of decorated columns and beams, known as the Orders, which were adapted by the Romans, revived decoratively rather than structurally during the Renaissance and are still used in debased form on the more presumptuous type of modern building. In recent years, however, architecture has taken on a new meaning. Once confined to the rich, in the form of Church, State or Commerce, it is now, with the coming of democracy, recognised as an essential social service for all. This, and the development of new structural techniques and materials (steel, aluminium, sheet glass, reinforced concrete, plastics and plywoods, to name a few), have made the interest in historic styles, the mainstay of the older architect, of secondary importance. Modern architecture is the creation of buildings with the highest possible standards of functional performance in terms of efficient planning and structure, good artificial and natural lighting, adequate heating or cooling, and proper acoustic conditions.

Arctic Exploration. Modern exploration of the Arctic begins in the 16th cent. when men sought to reach the East Indies by sailing through the Arctic to the Pacific Ocean. The North-east Passage, via the shores of northern Asia, was the first attempted. In 1553 and 1554 the English navigators Sir Richard Chancellor and Stephen Burrough sailed into the White Sea, but were prevented by storms and ice from advancing farther eastwards. The project was later revived by the Dutch; Barendts in 1594 discovered Spitsbergen, but also failed to get beyond Novaya Zemlya. It was not, in fact, until 1879 that the Swede, A. E.

Nordenskjöld, in the *Vega*, succeeded in reaching the Pacific. The attempts to find a North-west Passage were more numerous and determined. In 1585 John Davis penetrated Davis Strait and coasted along Baffin Island. Hopes ran high when Henry Hudson discovered Hudson Bay in 1610, but a practicable passage continued to elude explorers. The problem was to find a navigable route through the maze of channels in the short summer season, and to avoid being frozen in with supplies exhausted. After the Napoleonic Wars the Admiralty sent out many naval expeditions which culminated in Sir John Franklin's expedition with the *Erebus* and *Terror* in 1845. The ships were beset by ice in Victoria Channel and, after Franklin's death, were abandoned by their crews, who perished from scurvy and starvation on their march southwards. To ascertain their fate, several further expeditions were despatched, and the crew of the *Investigator*, commanded by R. J. M'Clure, sailing eastwards from Bering Strait, were the first to make the Passage, though in doing so they were obliged to abandon their ship. It was thirty years before the Norwegian, Roald Amundsen, succeeded in sailing the *Gjoa* from the east to west. In the meantime, the North Pole had become the goal of explorers. Nansen, in 1893, put the *Fram* into the ice-pack to drift across the Polar basin, and himself made an unsuccessful attempt on the Pole across the pack. This was eventually achieved by the American explorer Robert E. Peary, who after several expeditions in the North Greenland region, sledged to the Pole with Eskimo companions in 1909. The next phase was the employment of airships and aeroplanes in Arctic exploration. In 1926 Admiral Byrd made the first flight over the Pole, and in the same year Amundsen and Lincoln Ellsworth flew the airship *Norge* from Spitsbergern to Point Barrow Alaska. Two years later, the *Italia*, commanded by the Italian, Nobile, was wrecked on a return flight from the Pole, and Amundsen lost his life in an attempt to rescue the survivors. With modern developments in aircraft and navigation, flights over the Polar basin are almost a routine matter. The first voyage under the North Pole was made in 1958 by the American nuclear-powered submarine *Nautilus*. In 1995 scientists reported that a part of the Arctic ice-cap the size of Norway had melted in the previous 16 years. Scientists are now (1999) reporting that the ozone hole above the Arctic is growing.

Arenaceous Rocks, the rocks composed of grains of sand, chiefly sandstones; quartz is the most abundant mineral in these rocks.

Argillaceous Rocks are a sedimentary group, including the shales and clays.

Argon, chemical element no. 18, symbol A. This was the first of the inert gases (**F14**) to be isolated from air by Rayleigh and Ramsay in 1894. Argon is used for filling gas-filled metal filament electric lamps. In gas discharge tube it gives a blue glow. *See also* **Rare Gases.**

Arithmetic, the branch of mathematics that deals with numerical calculations as in counting, measuring, weighing. The early civilisations used simple arithmetic for commercial purposes, employing symbols and later letters of the alphabet as numerals. When Hindu-Arabic numerals replaced Roman numerals in the Middle Ages it meant a great step forward and led to rapid developments—the invention of logarithms, slide-rule, calculating machines.

Arithmetic Progression, a sequence of numbers in which the successor of each number is obtained by adding or subtracting a fixed number, for example 2, 5, 8, 11, . . . or 100, 95, 90, 85. . . .

Ark of the Covenant was the sacred chest of the Hebrews and symbolised God's presence. It was overlaid with gold inside and outside. It accompanied the Israelites into battle and was once captured by the Philistines. Eventually it found a resting-place in Solomon's Temple.

Armada, Spanish, the naval expedition fitted out by Philip II of Spain in 1588 against England, commanded by the Duke of Medina Sidonia. It comprised 127 ships, was manned by 8,000 sailors and carried 19,000 soldiers and more than 2,000 cannon. Against this formidable force

Elizabeth had only 80 ships, manned by 9,000 sailors, under Lord Howard of Effingham, under whom served Drake, Hawkins and Frobisher. The British Fleet awaited the Armada off Plymouth, and at Tilbury there was a considerable defensive land force under the command of the Earl of Leicester. On 19 July the ships of the Armada were sighted off the Lizard, disposed in a crescent 11 km long from horn to horn. The excellent manoeuvring of the English, their fire-ships and a gale from the N.W. combined so effectively to cripple the Spanish ships that the Armada was scattered, reaching home via the North of Scotland. It was impossible to embark the army of Parma waiting in the Netherlands. Elizabeth had a medal struck bearing in Latin the inscription, "God blew and they were scattered".

Armadillo, a genus of animals related to the sloths and anteaters, belonging to South America, and carrying a hard bony covering over the back, under which one species (*Tolypeutes*) can completely conceal itself when attacked, rolling itself up like a hedgehog.

Armageddon, according to the Revelation of St. John, the great battle in which the last conflict between good and evil is to be fought.

Armillary Sphere, an early form of astronomical apparatus with a number of circles representing equator, meridian, ecliptic, *etc.* Used by Hipparchus and Ptolemy and up to the time of Tycho Brahe for determining the position of the stars.

Aromatic. A term used by chemists, originally to describe compounds like benzene, having a characteristic smell. It is a term which implies a collection of chemical characteristics, the salient features being a flat ring structure and a general similarity to benzene.

Arsenic, a metalloid element, no. 33, symbol As in group 5 of the periodic table usually met with as a constituent of other minerals, sometimes by itself. Its compounds are very poisonous. Lead arsenate is a powerful insecticide used for spraying fruit trees. The more stable allotropic form (grey) has a layer structure, and conducts electricity.

Art Deco, the name given by modern collectors to the decorative style of the 1920s and 1930s; it is derived from the long official name of the Paris Exhibition of 1925, which was almost exclusively devoted to "les Arts Décoratifs". Art Deco runs parallel in time with Functionalism (*q.v.*) but unlike that austere and philosophical style, Art Deco is gay, elegant and even frivolous, being a creation of fashionable Paris. It is related superficially to Cubism, using squares, circles and triangles in interesting combinations for ornament. Another popular motif is the modern girl with her shingled head dancing the tango or drinking cocktails. The style is brash and worldly, but in its best expressions full of charm and vitality. Famous names within the style are the glassmaker Rene Lalique (1860–1945), the fashion designers Gabrielle Chanel and Elsa Schiaparelli, and the decorator and illustrator Erte (Roman de Tirtoff, b. 1829). There has been a nostalgic revival of Art Deco, *e.g.*, in films like "Bonny and Clyde" (1967) or "The Great Gatsby" (1974) based on F. Scott Fitzgerald's novel (1925).

Artesian Wells take their name from Artois in France, where the first wells of this kind were constructed in 1126. They are to be found only when a water-bearing bed is sandwiched between two impervious beds. When a boring is made to the lower part of the bed, the pressure of water is sufficient to cause the water to overflow at the surface. Artesian wells were known to ancient Egypt and China, and have existed in the Sahara since the earliest times. The fountains in Trafalgar Square were once fed by artesian wells sunk through the London clay into the chalk about 250 m.

Articles. The *Six Articles* are those contained in an Act of Henry VIII, and were of Roman Catholic origin. The *Thirty-nine Articles* were drawn up for the English church at the Reformation. They are printed at the back of the Prayer Book. Candidates for holy orders in the Church of England are required to subscribe to them.

Artificial Intelligence. *See* V2.

Art Nouveau (German *Jugend Stil*) was prevalent in architecture and decoration in Europe and the USA *c*, 1885–1910. It was rooted in the thoughts of Ruskin and William Morris. In reaction against the impersonal uniformity of industrial products which were flooding the market, artists turned to Nature for their inspiration, choosing organically growing forms, flowers or animals, as motifs for decoration or even for shaping whole objects. Another favourite motif was Romantic Woman with long robes and flowing hair, as interpreted so beautifully by Aubrey Beardsley. The sharply undulating line with a whiplash rhythm is a recurring theme. Famous names are the glassmakers Emile Gallé in France and Louis Comfort Tiffany in New York, the English goldsmith Charles Robert Ashbee (1863–1942), Henry Van de Velde (1867–1942) in Belgium and Charles Rennie Mackintosh (1868–1928) in Scotland, both architects and interior decorators, and in pure architecture Antonio Gaudí of Barcelona (1852–1926) and Victor Horta of Brussels (1861–1946).

Arts and Crafts Movement, the English revival of decorative art which began about 1875 as a revolt against the existing vulgarity of internal decoration and furnishings and the pettiness of academic art. Inspired by William Morris and Burne-Jones together with Rossetti, it was strongly influenced by the former's mediaevalism, his hatred of industrialism, and his own version of socialism which included the regeneration of man by handicrafts. His firm of Morris & Co. produced wallpapers, tapestries, furniture, stained-glass windows, carpets and fabrics in a style totally different from that of contemporary Victorian decoration. Morris's Kelmscott Press did much to raise the standards of book design and printing. *See* **Art Nouveau** (above).

Arum, a genus of plants of the *Araceae* family of which there is but one British species, the wake-robin or cuckoo-pint, sometimes also styled "Lords and Ladies".

Arundel Marbles, a collection of ancient Greek sculptures formed by Thomas Howard, Earl of Arundel in the 17th cent. and presented to Oxford University by his grandson, Henry Howard, who became Duke of Norfolk.

Aryans, nomadic peoples who made their way in successive waves from the Eurasian steppes to the Indus and the Nile during the first half of the 2nd millennium B.C. They crossed the Hindu Kush into N.W. India and settled in the valleys of the Indus and Ganges, where an earlier Indus civilisation had flourished, *c.* 3240–2750 B.C. Their religious ideas are reflected in the Veda (oldest Hindu scriptures, written down many centuries later in Vedic, parent language of Sanskrit). Those who made their way to Syria and Egypt founded the Hyksos empire (*c.* 1720–1550 B.C.). The Aryans introduced the horse-drawn chariot and spoke a language from which the great Indo-European family of languages is derived, with one group in India and Iran, and another in Europe. Because of the misuse of the term by the Nazis, Aryan is now referred to as proto-Indo-European.

Asafoetida, an acrid, strong-smelling gum resin exuded from the stem of umbelliferous plant, *Ferula foetida*, found in Iran and Afghanistan. Formerly used medicinally to treat hysteria; still used in cooking in India, Iran and France.

Ascension Day, or Holy Thursday, is the 40th day after Easter.

Ascot Races are an annual fashionable function dating from 1711 and taking place on Ascot Heath, only 10 km from Windsor, in June. These races have always had royal patronage. The course is *c*. 3 km long.

Ash, a familiar deciduous tree of the genus *Fraxinus*, of over 60 species, native to North temperate regions. The ash held an important place in Norse mythology, as it was supposed to support the heavens with its roots in Hell. The species native to Britain, and to Europe, is *F. excelsior*, a tall tree with compound leaves, greenish flowers, winged seeds, and black buds in winter. It is a valuable timber tree, tough and elastic, and largely used for wheels and handles. The rowan, or mountain ash, *Sorbus aucuparia*, with similar leaves and orange berries, belongs to a different family. F.

pendula or weeping ash is a strain which makes an ideal natural summer house.

Ashes, The, the symbol which distinguishes the winning cricket team in the Australian Test Matches. In 1882 the Australians won at the Oval by 7 runs. After the match the following epitaph appeared in the *Sporting Times*: "In affectionate remembrance of English Cricket which died at the Oval on 29 Aug. 1882, deeply lamented by a large circle of sorrowing friends and acquaintances. R.I.P. NB. The body will be cremated and the ashes taken to Australia." When the English Eleven went to Australia the same winter it was said that they had come to recover the "ashes". England won two out of three matches, and after the third match the ashes of what was believed to have been a bail were presented in an urn to Ivo Bligh, later Lord Darnley. He bequeathed the urn to the M.C.C. It is now in the Memorial Gallery at Lord's. Recently, several historians have doubted the truth of this story. The Ashes are now (1999) held by Australia.

Ash Wednesday, first day of Lent, the seventh Wednesday before Easter.

Assassination, treacherous murder for political ends, usually of a ruler or distinguished person. Among the most notable: Julius Caesar, 44 B.C.; Thomas Becket, 1170; David Rizzio, 1566; William the Silent, 1584; Henry IV of France, 1610; Jean Paul Marat, 1793; Abraham Lincoln, 1865; Alexander II of Russia, 1881; Archduke Francis Ferdinand of Austria, 1914; Mahatma Gandhi, 1948; Liaquat Ali Khan, 1951; King Feisal of Iraq, 1958; President Kennedy, 1963; Malcolm X, 1965; Dr. Verwoerd, 1966; Dr. Martin Luther King, 1968; Senator Robert Kennedy, 1968; Mr. Tom Mboya, 1969; King Faisal, 1975; Lord Mountbatten, 1979; John Lennon, 1980; Pres. Sadat, 1981; Indira Gandhi, 1984; Olof Palme, 1986; Rajiv Gandhi, 1991; President Premadasa of Sri Lanka, 1993; and Israeli Prime Minister Yitzhak Rabin, 1995.

Asteroids or the minor planets are relatively small objects which move in orbits mainly between those of Mars and Jupiter. The first to be discovered (by Piazzi in 1801) was Ceres. Many thousands more have since been discovered, of which nearly 2,000 now have well-determined orbits and have been named. The largest are Ceres (800 km), Pallas (500 km), Vesta (530 km) and Juno (240 km). Few others have diameters of more than 80 km, while those of the majority are less than 5 or 10 km. Of particular interest are the Trojan group, located at the two stable "Lagrangian" points in Jupiter's orbit round the sun, where their locations make isosceles triangles with the sun and Jupiter. Also, a number of asteroids have orbits like that of Icarus which at perigee (*q.v.*) comes close to the sun. The first space probe designed to study asteroids (NEAR, Near Asteroid Rendezvous) was launched in 1996 to reach the Eros 433 asteroid in January 2000.

Astrolabe, a mediaeval scientific instrument for taking altitudes, observing the sun by day and the stars by night, and used for telling the time and finding the latitude. Used by the ancient Greeks, later by the Arabs and Persians, and introduced into Europe by way of Spain in the 14th cent. Chaucer is said to have sent his son Lois, a ten-year-old student at Oxford, an astrolabe with a treatise on its use in 1391.

Astronaut, a person who travels in space.

Astronomical Unit, the mean distance between the centres of the sun and earth, or the semi-major axis of the earth's orbit, has a value of about 1.495979×10^8 km (149,597,900 km). This value has been constantly improved over the past 300 years, first using observations of the planets, later transits of Venus across the sun's disc, then observations of minor planets such as Eros as they came near the earth, and now by the transit time of a radar beam bounced off the planet Venus. The astronomical unit is fundamental for astronomers.

Astronomy. The Pythagoreans believed the stars and planets moved with uniform circular velocity in crystalline spheres, centred round the earth (the "harmony of the spheres"). Hipparchus (190–120 B.C.) made the first star catalogue, discovered the precession of the

equinoxes and introduced the idea of epicyclic motion. His planetary system, in the form it was presented by Ptolemy 200 years later, held until the Renaissance when Copernicus revived the heretical view first put forward by Aristarchus of Samos (310–230 B.C.) that the sun and not the earth was at the centre. Galileo, accurate observer and experimenter, went beyond Copernicus; helped by the contributions of Tycho Brahe, Giordano Bruno, Kepler and others, he was able to overthrow the Ptolemaic system of the heavenly spheres and Aristotelian philosophy and pave the way for Newton and modern astronomy. To Galileo we owe the conception of acceleration; to Newton the theory of universal gravitation; they showed that the same laws govern both celestial and terrestrial physics. Three landmarks in more recent times were the discovery of Uranus by Herschel in 1781 which extended the solar system as then recognised; the estimation by Hubble in 1924 of the distance of Andromeda, which showed that our Galaxy was just one of many; and Einstein's theory of relativity which improved on Newton's theory of the solar system by bringing gravitation into the domain of space-time. Today radio-telescopes and space probes are advancing astronomical knowledge and making it possible to explore regions beyond the scope of optical telescopes. The following have held the position of **Astronomer Royal** (period of office in brackets): John Flamsteed (1675–1719), Edmund Halley (1719–42), James Bradley (1742–62), Nathaniel Bliss (1762–65), Nevil Maskelyne (1765–1811), John Pond (1811–35), Sir George Airy (1835–81), Sir William Christie (1881–1910), Sir Frank Dyson (1910–33), Sir Harold Spencer Jones (1933–55), Sir Richard Woolley (1956–72), Sir Martin Ryle (1972–82), Sir Francis Graham Smith (1982–90), Sir Arnold Wolfendale (1991–95) and Sir Martin Rees (1995–). See **F5–7**, *also* **Radio Astronomy.**

Astrophysics, a branch of astronomy concerned with the physical nature and constitution of the various objects within the universe. Recent developments in radio astronomy and in space research technology, opening up gamma-ray, X-ray, ultra-violet and infra-red parts of the spectrum, have all advanced this science.

Athanasian Creed, one of the three ancient creeds of the Christian Church, often referred to as the *Quicunque Vult*, is a statement of the doctrine of the Trinity and the Incarnation, and though named after St. Athanasius, it is thought to be the work of St. Ambrose (339–97).

Atmosphere is the gaseous envelope of the earth, and consists of a mixture of gases (*see* **Air**) and water vapour, the variability of the latter being of great importance meteorologically. The ozone layer, which absorbs solar ultra-violet radiation which would be lethal to plant life if it reached the ground lies between 12 to 50 km above the earth. The lower level of the atmosphere up to a height of about 12 km (10 km at the Poles and 16 km at the Equator) is known as the *troposphere*, and it is in this region that nearly all weather phenomena occur. This is the region of most interest to the forecaster studying temperature, humidity, wind-speed, and the movement of air masses. Temperature falls with height by about 1°C per 152 m in this layer. The *tropopause* is the boundary between the troposphere and the *stratosphere*. Temperature varies little in the lower levels of this region: it is mainly cloudless, and has no vertical currents. Strangely enough, the lowest temperatures of the atmosphere are to be found not at the Poles, but at about 18 km above the Equator, where a temperature as low as −80°C has been recorded! Temperatures begin to rise about 32 km from the earth's surface at about the same rate as they fall in the troposphere owing to the absorption of solar radiation by the concentration of ozone. The stratospheric air is extremely dry. Near the 100 km level a number of important atmospheric phenomena occur. Above this level the oxygen becomes predominantly monatomic in contrast to the normal diatomic form at lower altitudes. This is the *ionosphere* (*q.v.*). This layer acts as an electrical radio mirror which makes long-distance radio transmission possible. The region of the Van Allen belts (q.v.) above the earth is called the magnetosphere (q.v.). The auroras are most frequently observed at altitudes between about 100 and 400 km but do extend at times far higher. Many aspects of the upper air can only be studied through space-research techniques. These include the composition and temperature of the charged particles in the ionosphere, the location of the electric currents in the ionosphere which produce the regular variations of the compass needle, as well as those which circulate during magnetic storms, the variation of the intensity of different radiation in the air-glow (q.v.) with height, the composition of the air at heights above 32 km, and so on. In addition, the pressures, density, temperatures, and wind distribution of the neutral atmosphere can be studied more directly, in much greater detail, and up to much greater altitudes than is possible if one is confined to the use of equipment on the ground. Instruments outside the atmosphere can make systematic observations on a world-wide basis of the atmospheric circulation, through observation of cloud cover and of the thermal radiation into space from the atmosphere. Such observations are of great importance for meteorology. The atmospheres of the other planets are vastly different to our own. For example, the Venusian atmosphere is considerably denser than the Earth's and is composed primarily of carbon dioxide. Carbon dioxide is also the main constituent of the Martian atmosphere, although this is much thinner than that of the Earth. Titan, the largest satellite of Saturn, has a nitrogen-rich atmosphere. *See also* **Ionosphere.**

Atmospherics are electrical impulses which are believed to originate in atmospheric electrical discharges such as lightning. They give rise to crashing background noises in the loudspeakers of radio sets, interfering with reception at distances of up to 6,400 km from the centre of the disturbance. The location of atmospherics with the aid of radio direction-finding methods gives warning of thunderstorms.

Atom. *See* **F10–17, F23.**

Atomic Pile, an apparatus containing a fissionable element and a moderator, such as heavy water or graphite, in which a self-sustaining fission process proceeds at a controllable rate. The first atomic pile, constructed on a squash court at Chicago, was operated for the first time on 2 December 1942, under the direction of Enrico Fermi. The pile contained 12,400 lb (5,580 kg) of uranium. *See* **Nuclear Reactors.**

Augsburg Confession, name given to the doctrine of faith of the Lutheran churches, drawn up by Melanchthon and endorsed by Luther for the Diet of Augsburg (1530).

August, named after the Emperor Augustus, because it was his "lucky" month.

Auks, duck-like sea-birds, black and white, with short, narrow wings, compact bodies and legs set well back. Breed in colonies on rocky coasts of N. Europe (incl. British Isles) and spend most time in coastal waters. Migrate south in winter. The Auk family includes the Razorbill, Little Auk, Guillemot and Puffin. The Great Auk became extinct in the 19th cent. after ruthless hunting for its feathers.

Aurora polaris. This wonderful phenomenon of the night sky is a common sight at high northern and southern latitudes, where it is called the aurora borealis and the aurora australis respectively. It is visible less often at temperate latitudes, and only rarely in the tropics. The auroral ovals, or zones of maximum frequency of aurora, surround both of the earth's geomagnetic poles, and the northern auroral oval includes the northern parts of Scandinavia, Canada and Alaska. The aurora is the visible manifestation of complex plasma processes occurring within the earth's magnetosphere (q.v.), whereby streams of high-energy electrons and protons (mainly) are accelerated and dumped via the earth's magnetic field lines into the upper atmosphere. This mechanism produces the light emission of the aurora. The brightest aurora, which may also extend to lower latitudes, occurs during geomagnetic storms, which are complex and large-scale plasma instabilities within the magnetosphere

triggered by fluctuations in the solar wind (q.v.) —usually ascribed to "M" regions on the sun associated with coronal holes, flares and active sunspot groups. Auroral displays may take several forms—a faint glow, a diffuse ribbon of light crossing the heavens, great folded waving curtains or draperies, or the entire sky may be flooded with a rapidly varying brilliant panoply of light. Specially instrumented spacecraft which can directly explore the magnetosphere and high-latitude ionosphere have provided a great deal of our knowledge about this fascinating and complex phenomenon. The aurora is a kind of light essentially different from that of the rainbow which is a partly subjective phenomenon. Each beholder sees his own rainbow, whose light is sunlight refracted and reflected by many raindrops. The raindrops that produce his rainbow depend on his position as well as on the direction of the sun. The aurora, on the contrary, is a light as objective as that of a candle, though produced differently. It is a self-luminescence of the air in regions of the atmosphere that lie far above the clouds.

Austerlitz, Battle of, was fought near Brünn, in Moravia, on 2 December 1805. Napoleon defeated the Russians and Austrians under Kutuzov.

Auto-da-Fé, or Act of Faith, was the ceremony connected with the sentencing of heretics under the Inquisition of Spain and Portugal, the persons found guilty being imprisoned or burned alive. The ceremony took place in some public square, often in the presence of the king and court.

Automation is a modern word used to designate the adoption of methods of automatic control either of manufacturing processes or of any business process involving a large mass of routine work. The word is used in broader and narrower senses. In its broadest sense it covers any form of mechanisation which largely replaces human labour by the work of automatic or semi-automatic machines, such as has been in progress continuously since the Industrial Revolution; but it it better kept to a narrower meaning, in which it is confined to the recent development of electronic or similar devices, involving feedback (automatic detection and correction of malfunction). Human labour is eliminated save for that needed for watching and maintaining the elaborate machines used.

Autumn, the third season of the year, begins with the autumnal equinox, and ends with the winter solstice, but the term is generally understood as covering the period from mid-August to mid-November.

Auxins, "plant hormones", organic substances produced by plants to regulate growth. Synthetic auxins are now widely used, *e.g.*, for promotion of root formation in cuttings, differential weed control, prevention of premature dropping of fruit, in storage of potatoes *etc.* and to overcome frost damage to fruit buds.

Avalanches occur when layers of snow become unstable. Each of these 'white deaths' can send more than 1 million tons of ice, rock and snow thundering down mountain-sides.

Average is a single number designed to give a typical example of a set of numbers, *e.g.*, a cricketer's batting average for a season gives an idea of his typical score. There are several kinds of average and their uses are studied in the science of statistics (q.v.). A statement that "so and so is the average value" can be misleading if one does not know which average is meant. Three common averages are: the arithmetic average (or mean), the mode, and the median. The arithmetic average of n numbers is found by adding them together and dividing by n; this is a very common method of averaging. The mode of n numbers is the most frequently occurring number. The median is the middle number, *i.e.*, the number which is smaller than just as many of the other numbers as it exceeds. Of the numbers 1, 2, 2, 2, 3, 3, 4, 5, 6, 8, 9, the arithmetic means is 4, the mode is 2, the median is 3.

Avocet, a graceful wading bird related to the stilts, of black-and-white plumage, bluish legs, and slender upturned bill. There are four species. Avocets nest in colonies. The return of the avocet as a breeding bird since the last war has been a success story for the Royal Society for the Protection of Birds.

Avogadro's Hypothesis. This is a fundamental concept of chemistry. Equal volumes of all gases under the same conditions of temperature and pressure contain the same number of molecules. This law was instrumental in assigning the formulae of molecules. The hypothesis was put forward in 1811, but was not generally accepted until 1860.

Avogadro's Number. *See* **F24.**

Ayers Rock. *See* Section K.

Aztecs, the name of a powerful race found in Mexico when the Spaniards first discovered that country, and with difficulty subdued.

B

Babiroussa, a ferocious, long-legged wild pig, native of Sulawesi, sometimes called the horned-hog, because of the long upper tusks in the teeth of the male, which are developments of the canine teeth which grow upwards, piercing the upper lip, and curving backwards.

Baboon, monkeys belonging to the African genus *Papio.* They are considered the lowest of the Old World (Catarrhine) monkeys, and walk on all fours. In the main terrestrial, but take to trees after food. The mandrill is closely related.

Babylonian Captivity, the period spent by the Jews in Babylon after Jerusalem was captured by Nebuchadnezzar, the Babylonian emperor, in 586 B.C. Traditionally the captivity lasted 70 years, but when Babylon was in turn taken by Cyrus in 538 B.C., the exiles were permitted to return to Jerusalem. The term is also applied in church history to the period 1309–78 when the papacy moved to Avignon.

Bacteria. *See* **F44.**

Bacteriophage (Phage), literally "bacteria eater", *i.e.,* a virus which specifically infects bacteria. In common with viruses which attack animal or plant cells, isolated phages are inert, and can only reproduce by making use of the chemical apparatus of a more sophisticated host cell (in this case a bacterium). However phages may be of two types, virulent or temperate. Virulent phages completely disrupt the normal functioning of the infected bacterium and adapt its reproductive mechanism to produce more phage. This eventually kills the bacterium and the newly assembled phages are released. Temperate phages on the other hand may enter into a remarkable symbiotic relationship with the bacterium, known as lysogeny. The phage genetic material is incorporated into that of the bacterium and is reproduced each time the still functioning bacterium subsequently divides. Furthermore the bacterium is immune from attack by potentially virulent phages of the same type. When such lysogenic bacteria die, phage particles may again be released. Phages carried in lysogenic bacteria are in a state known as prophage and it is often difficult to obtain pure, prophage-free strains of bacteria. Because of their relatively simple structure, phages have been extensively used in research on genetics and molecular biology.

Badger, a carnivorous mammal related to the weasel, of nocturnal and burrowing habits, inoffensive, subsisting chiefly on roots and insects, though sometimes mice, young rabbits and eggs form part of its diet. Badger-baiting was a favourite sport in Britain until it was prohibited in the middle of 19th cent. The badger does little harm and quite a lot of good; badger digging is to be condemned as a cruel sport. In Britain the badger is partly protected, but Ministry officials may destroy the animal in areas where bovine tuberculosis (a growing threat) exists.

Bagpipe. Once popular all over Europe, this instrument is still played in Scotland, Ireland, Brittany and elsewhere. The bag acts as a reservoir of air and, when squeezed by the player's arm, forces air through the pipes. One of these, the Chanter pipe, provides the tune and is played by the fingers as in a flageolet. The remainder, the Drone pipes, give a continuous, unvarying note.

Bailey Bridge, invented by Sir Donald Bailey and first used in the N. African campaign 1942–3. Built up of prefabricated girders, it can be easily transported and erected.

Bailiwick, a feudal term denoting the limits of a bailiff 's jurisdiction. The term has survived in the Channel Islands, where Jersey and Guernsey are Bailiwicks.

Balance of Power was the doctrine in British policy whereby European groups should be so balanced as to prevent the emergence of a dominating Power. Thus the balance was maintained between the Triple Alliance (Germany, Austria and Italy) and the Triple Entente (Great Britain, France and Russia) and preserved peace from 1871 to 1914. After the first world war there was tentative support of Germany's recovery to counterweigh the possible French hegemony; but when Germany's power grew under Hitler leading to the second world war, Britain, France and Russia again became allies.

Baldachin (It. *Baldachino*), a canopy usually supported by four pillars over throne, altar, or other sacred object. The name is also applied to the silken canopy used in processions by the priest who carries the Host.

Balearic Crane, the crowned crane of the Balearic Islands and the North African mainland, distinguished by its yellowish, black-tipped occipital tuft and by its trumpet note.

Baleen *or* "whalebone" the name given to a series of horny plates growing from the roof of the mouth in those whales classified as Whalebone or Baleen Whales (*Mystacoceti*). There are 300–400 or so plates on each side, and their inner edges are frayed, the whole system constituting a filter for collecting minute organisms used for food. The Baleen Whales include the Right-Whales, the Pacific Grey-Whale and the Rorquals. *See* **Whales.**

Ballet is a combination of four arts; dancing, music, painting, and drama, each of which is ideally of equal importance. The movement of the individual dancers and the "orchestration" of the whole group is in the hands of the choreographer. The dancer's training follows certain basic rules but save in classical ballet there is considerable freedom of movement. Ballet as we know it today developed professionally at the Court of King Louis XIV of France, though it owes its origins to Italy and in the earliest times to Greece and Rome. Its movements were made up from the dances of courtiers, country folk and tumblers. Technique grew more complex as costume became modified, the body gaining complete freedom with the invention of tights. A succession of great dancers—French, Italian and latterly Russian left their imprint on the art. Contemporary ballet reflects the aesthetics of the Russian, Sergei Diaghilev. In England Dame Ninette de Valois laid the foundation of a national ballet, at Sadler's Wells and Covent Garden. A Royal Charter was granted in 1957 setting up the Royal Ballet to co-ordinate the activities of the Sadler's Wells group.

Ballistics, the science dealing with the motion of projectiles, especially shells, bombs and rockets. Great advances have been made in this science.

Balloon, the modern balloon consists of a bag of plastic material inflated with a gas lighter than air. The first ascent by man in a hot-air balloon was made on 21 November 1783, and in a hydrogen balloon on 1 December 1783. The most famous of the early scientific flights by manned balloons were those of the Englishmen Coxwell and Glaisher, in 1862, when a height of 11 km was reached. The first aerial crossing of the English Channel by Blanchard and Jeffries was made on 7 January 1785. Piccard's ascent to 16 km, in 1931, marked the conquest of the stratosphere. Four years later the American balloon *Explorer II*, inflated with nearly 112,000 m³ of helium, carried a team of scientists with their floating laboratory to an altitude of 23 km. Captive kite-balloons were widely used in the war as defensive measures against air attack. Meteorologists send their instruments up in balloons to collect data about the upper atmosphere, and of recent years physicists have learned much about cosmic radiation from the study of photographic plates sent to the upper regions in balloons. In March 1999 Brian Jones (from Britain) and his co-pilot Bertrand Piccard completed the first non-stop flight around the world in their balloon *Breitling Orbiter 3.*

Balsam, a big genus (140 species) of flowering plants. Many species are cultivated for their showy flowers, *e.g.*, *Impatiens noli-me-tangere*, the yellow balsam or "touch-me-not", so called because the fruit explodes when touched, slinging out the seeds. Balsam fir is a conifer (*Abies balsamea*) from which Canada balsam gum is obtained.

Bamboo, a genus of strong grasses, some species growing to over 36 m in height; much used in Asia for all kinds of purposes. The young shoots of some species are tender and esculent.

Banana (family *Musaceae*), a large herbaceous plant cultivated in moist regions of the tropics, and one of the most productive plants known. The main areas of commercial cultivation are in tropical America, the Canary Islands and West Africa. Bananas are currently (1999) at the centre of a trade war with the USA.

Bandicoots, Australasian marsupial mammals, of the size of a large rat or rabbit. They are burrowing animals living largely on insects. The rabbit-eared bandicoot, restricted to Australia, has shrew-like snout, long ears like a rabbit, long crested tail, and a silky coat. The long-nosed bandicoot has a spiny coat and comes from E. Australia. The pig-footed bandicoot has two functional toes on the foot, like a pig.

Bank of England. Founded by Royal Charter on 27 July 1694. Known as "The Old Lady of Threadneedle Street". Prior to 1759 the lowest denomination note issued was £20. The Labour Government elected in 1997 restored independence to the Bank in determining interest rates.

Bank Holidays. *See* Section Z.

Bank Rate, the rate at which the Bank of England is prepared to lend to the clearing banks. If raised it has the immediate effect of raising the rate of discount on Treasury Bills. Known as the Minimum Lending Rate from 1972 to 1981.

Bantu (native word = people), term loosely used for large family of Negro races of Southern Africa.

Baobab, a tropical African tree. The species *Adansonia digitata* is one of the largest trees known, though not the tallest; the trunk can reach 9 m in thickness. The fruit is woody, but its juice provides a cooling beverage. The bark yields a fibre used for making rope and cloth.

Barbary Ape, a large monkey belonging to the genus *Macaca*. It is the only monkey living in relative freedom in Europe, a small colony existing on the Rock of Gibraltar. It has no tail.

Barberry, a genus of berry-producing shrubs containing a hundred species. Several species are cultivated for their flowers and bright berries. Has an interesting pollination mechanism; the base of each stamen is sensitive to touch, and insects probing for nectar cause top of stamen to spring inwards, so dusting visitor's head with pollen which can then be carried to the next flower visited. The common barberry (*Berberis communis*) harbours one stage of the fungus that causes rust of wheat.

Barbican, a fortified entrance to a castle or city, with projecting towers. In the London area called Barbican there was formerly a barbican in front of the city gates.

Barbiturates. A group of drugs derived from a parent compound called barbituric acid: phenobarbitone is the best-known example. They induce sleep and are used in the manufacture of sleeping pills, but they can be habit forming.

Barbizon School, a school of mid-19th-cent. landscape painters whose main tenet was a return to nature with an exact rendering of peasant life and country scenery painted on the spot. It was named after the village of that name in the Forest of Fontainebleau, where its chief members—Millet, Theodore Rousseau, Daubigny and Diaz—made their home. Their practice of painting direct from nature, made them the precursors of Impressionism (*q.v.*).

Barcarolle, a Venetian gondolier's song applied to instrumental as well as vocal compositions.

Bard, among the ancient Celts a poet or minstrel whose mission was to sing of heroic deeds. He was supposed to have the gift of prophecy, and was exempt from taxes and military service.

Barilla, soda carbonate or soda ash obtained by burning certain salt-marsh plants (*e.g.*, the saltwort, *Salsola kali*). It used to be in great demand, until the product of the Leblanc and then the Solvay ammonia-soda process was made available by the chemical industry.

Barium, metal element, no. 56, symbol Ba. In group

2 of the periodic table. The metal is soft and easily cut. It occurs as the sulphate and carbonate in nature. It was first prepared by Sir Humphry Davy in 1808, as an amalgam, by electrolysis of barium chloride. The pure metal was not isolated until 1901.

Barium meal. Barium sulphate is opaque to X-rays and before X-ray pictures of the alimentary canal radiologists give a "barium meal" to the patients so that the alimentary canal shows up more clearly.

Barnacles constitute a sub-class (*Cirripedia*) of the Crustacea. The barnacle fouling the bottom of ships is the Goose Barnacle, which has a long muscular stalk and a shell composed of five plates. The Acorn Barnacles, which cover rocks, breakwaters, etc., just below high-water mark are similarly constructed, but have no stalk. The manner of feeding of barnacles was vividly described by T. H. Huxley, who said the barnacle is "a crustacean fixed by its head kicking the food into its mouth with its legs". It was a naval surgeon, J. Vaughan Thompson, who discovered in 1830 that barnacles have a free-swimming larva (or nauplius). In the Middle Ages a curious myth grew up to the effect that the Barnacle changed into a sea-bird called, for that reason, the Barnacle Goose.

Barnard's Star. A star discovered by the American astronomer Edward Emerson Barnard in 1916 and which has the largest stellar proper motion known. Barnard's Star is one of the closest stars to us and also one of the intrinsically faintest stars known.

Barometer is an instrument for measuring atmospheric pressure, invented at Florence by Torricelli, pupil of Galileo, in 1644. The standard method consists of balancing the air column against a column of mercury, used on account of its high density. The mercury is contained in a long glass tube, closed at one end, and inverted in a cistern also containing mercury. The height of the mercury column, supporting the air column, is taken as the pressure at the time, and can be read off very accurately by means of a vernier scale. Present-day tendency is to express the readings in units of pressure instead of length, the millibar being adopted (1 mb = 1,000 dynes per sq. cm.; 1,000 mb ≡ 75 cm of mercury approx.). The standard instrument is correct for pressures at 0°C in Lat. 45°, so that corrections have to be applied for temperatures and latitudes other than these. Also a correction has to be made for reducing the pressure to mean sea level. *See* **Aneroid.**

Baron, title given in feudal England to a man who held his land directly from the king by military or other honourable service. The first baron created by letters patent was John Beauchamp de Holt, Baron of Kidderminster, in 1387. A baron is a member of the fifth and last grade of the peerage of the United Kingdom and is addressed as "Lord". Life peers and life peeresses rank with hereditary barons and baronesses according to the date of their creation. In Scotland the term baron is used of the possessor of a feudal fief, or the representative by descent of such a fief. The equivalent of the English baron, as a rank of the Scottish peerage, is Lord of Parliament.

Baronet, the lowest hereditary title, instituted by James I to provide funds for the colonisation of Ulster. The first baronet was Sir Nicholas Bacon. Between 1964 and 1983 no recommendations for hereditary honours were made. In 1990 the Queen bestowed the title on Denis Thatcher.

Baroque, a term used for the art style of the period *c.* 1600–1720 which was the artistic accompaniment of the Jesuit counter-Reformation. Its most obvious characteristics are: (*a*) its emotional appeal and dramatic intensity both related to its deliberate intention as propaganda ("a good picture makes better religious propaganda than a sermon" said one of its exponents); (*b*) in architecture, a style which is heavily and sometimes almost grotesquely ornate, plentifully covered with voluptuous sculpture on which draperies float rather than hang, with twisted and spiral instead of plain or fluted columns, and unnecessary windows or recesses added for ornament rather than use; (*c*) its emphasis on the whole at the expense of the parts such that a building's sculpture merges into its architecture and both into its painting (Baroque paintings are as closely knit as a jigsaw puzzle so that one cannot isolate individual figures as would be possible in a Renaissance one). Baroque architecure owing to its origin is found mainly in the Catholic countries; Italy, France, Austria, Bavaria, *e.g.*, the Barberini Palace, Rome, designed by its greatest exponent Bernini and others; the Church of the Invalides, Paris. Baroque artists include Caravaggio, Guido Reni, Murillo and Rubens the greatest Northern Baroque painter. The Baroque style merges gradually into Rococo (*q.v.*).

Barque, a small sailing vessel with three or four masts. A three-masted barque has fore- and mainmasts square-rigged, the mizzenmast fore-and aft-rigged.

Barrow is an ancient artificial mound of earth or stone raised over the site of a burial. In Britain barrows were built from 2500 B.C. until the late Saxon period, but the Egyptian are the earliest barrows known, the great pyramids being a spectacular development of the custom of ceremonial burial. Silbury Hill, south of Avebury, is the biggest artificial mound in Europe, 512 m in circuit at the base, 96 m at top, and 41 m high.

Bartholomew, Massacre of St., occurred in Paris on the night of 24 August 1572, when over two thousand Huguenots were massacred by order of the Catholic French Court.

Baryons, the group of heavier subatomic particles which includes the proton, neutron, lambda and omega-minus particles (and their corresponding anti-particles, called anti-baryons). Baryons interact by means of all the known forces of nature (strong, weak, electromagnetic and gravitational). However, in any closed system the total baryon number (*i.e.*, the number of baryons minus the number of anti-baryons) is constant. This means that the proton, being the lightest known baryon, must be stable against spontaneous decay. Unlike the lighter leptons (*q.v.*), baryons are now thought to have internal structure reflecting the fact that they are composed of quarks (*q.v.*) See **F15**.

Basalt Rocks are fine-grained, dark coloured, of igneous origin and occur either as lava flows as in Mull and Staffa, or as intrusive sheets, like the Edinburgh Castle Rock and Salisbury Crags. One of the best examples of columnar basalt is the Giant's Causeway in Ireland.

Basanite, a smooth black siliceous mineral, or flinty jasper; a crypto-crystalline quartz used as a touchstone for testing the purity of gold, *etc.*, by means of the mark left after rubbing the metal with it. Sometimes styled the Lydian stone.

Base, a substance having a tendency to accept a proton (H-). This is a wide definition and covers unconventional types of compounds. In aqueous solution bases dissolve with formation of hydroxyl ions, and will neutralise an acid to form a salt. In non-aqueous solvents, like liquid ammonia or hydrogen fluoride, compounds classically regarded as salts can be bases, *e.g.*, sodium fluoride is a base in hydrogen fluoride solution.

Basilisk, is a lizard of aquatic habits, with an elevated crest (which it can erect or depress at will) down the centre of its back.

Basques, people of N. Spain and S.W. France, oldest surviving racial group in Europe, who have preserved their ancient language which is unrelated to any other tongue.

Bas-Relief ("low relief "), a term used to denote a class of sculptures the figures of which are only slightly raised from the surface of the stone or clay upon which the design is wrought.

Bastille, a castle or fortress in Paris, built in the 14th cent., and used as a state prison, especially for political offenders. Its bad repute as an instrument of despotism excited the hatred of the populace, who stormed and demolished it on 14 July 1789, at the start of the Revolution.

Bastinado, an oriental punishment, by beating with a pliable cane on the soles of the feet.

Bats. These mammals fly by means of a membrane stretched between each of the long fingers of the hand and between the fifth finger and the body. Another membrane stretches between the legs and the tail. Most British bats, including the pipistrelle, long-eared bats, noctules,

belong to the family Vespertilionidae (with the exception of the horseshoe bats which belong to the family Rhinolophidae). These all feed on insects which they catch on the wing. The problem of how bats can detect their insect prey and avoid obstacles when flying in total darkness has interested zoologists for a very long time. The problem was solved with the advent of sensitive ultrasonic recording devices. Blindness does not affect this ability but deafness leaves bats comparatively helpless. One of the most interesting types of bat is the fishing bat (*Noctilio*) found in central America, which can detect fish by being able to receive echoes from the ripples they make on the water surface. New European legislation to protect bats came into force in 1994. There are 16 species of bat in Britain, but their numbers are declining. Research has shown that bats play a vital (if almost unrecognized) role in the regeneration of rain forests. See **Ultrasonics**.

Bath, Order of the, Britain's second oldest order of knighthood. Exclusive to men since its institution by Henry IV in 1399, women became eligible for admission to the order in 1971. The order has three grades: Knight Grand Cross (G.C.B.), Knight Commander (K.C.B.), and Companion (C.B.). Women members of the order are known as Dame Grand Cross, Dame Commander and Companion.

Battery, Electric, the common term for an electric cell but really meaning a combination of two or more cells. A cell is a device for converting stored chemical energy into electricity which can then be used for heat, light, traction, or any desired purpose. A *primary* cell will do this until the chemical action is completed and the cell is then useless. In a *secondary* cell, the chemical actions are reversible and the cell can be returned to its initial condition and used again. This is done by passing an electric current through—a process called recharging. A common primary cell is the Leclanché dry cell; used in torches. This works by the action of sal-ammoniac on electrodes made of zinc and carbon. About a century after it came into common use it is still the chief source of power for portable equipment in armed forces. A common secondary cell is the lead and sulphuric acid accumulator used in cars. Many other types of cell are known and some are under development because the demands of space travel, medicine, warfare, *etc.*, call for batteries of lighter weight, greater reliability, or special properties. See **Fuel Cell, Energy Conversion**.

Bauhaus, a German institution for the training of architects, artists and industrial designers founded in 1919 at Weimar by Walter Gropius, (d. 1969). It was closed by Hitler in 1933 and re-opened at Chicago. The Bauhaus doctrine held that there should be no separation between architecture and the fine and applied arts; that art, science and technology should co-operate to create "the compositely inseparable work of art, the great building". Thus it was an organisation with a social purpose. The original institution, at the instigation of Gropius, included on its teaching staff not only architects and technicians but also such noted artists as Paul Klee and Wassily Kandinsky.

Bauxite, the chief ore of aluminium. Chemically it is aluminium oxide. Aluminium metal is made industrially by electrolysing purified bauxite dissolved in fused cryolite. Chief producing areas; Jamaica, Australia, Surinam, Russia, Guyana, France, Greece, Guinea, USA, Hungary and ex-Yugoslavia.

Bayeux Tapestry, a famous tapestry representing the conquest of England by William the Conqueror. It is embroidered on a band of linen 70 m long and 51 cm wide in blue, green, red and yellow, divided into 72 scenes ranging over the whole story of the conquest. The accepted view is that the tapestry was commissioned for Bayeux Cathedral, but a new interpretation is that it is an Anglo-Norman secular work of art, much influenced by the contemporary *chansons de geste* (songs of deeds), executed by English embroiderers for a Norman patron. A representation can be seen in the Victoria and Albert Museum in London.

Beagle, a small hound that tracks by scent, and extensively used for hare hunting.

Bears belong to the Ursidae family of the Carnivora. They are plantigrade mammals, walking (like man) on the soles of their feet. Found in most parts of the world except Australia. The common Brown Bear was once spread over the whole of Europe; it became extinct in England about the 11th cent.; 2–2·5 m in length, and stands 1 m or more at the shoulder. The Grizzly Bear of N. America is larger, and the coat is shorter and greyer. The Polar Bear is remarkable in having a white coat all the year round; it spends much time in water, and unlike other bears is entirely carnivorous. Bear-baiting was made illegal in England in 1835.

Beaufort Scale of wind force is used to specify numerically the strength of the wind. Since the introduction of anemometers to measure the actual velocity, equivalent values of the ranges in miles per hour at a standard height in the open have been agreed. See **Section Z**.

Beaver, a genus of mammals of the Rodentia order, with short, scaly ears, webbed hind feet, and a long broad scaly tail. They grow up to 1·2 m long, and live in communities, constructing dams and lodges where they breed. A campaign is now being launched to bring back beavers to Britain where they have been extinct for 400 years after being mercilessly hunted for their valuable pelt. The beaver, Europe's largest rodent, weighs nearly 45lbs.

Bedlam (a corruption of Bethlehem) was a priory in Bishopsgate, afterwards converted into a hospital for lunatics. The asylum was transferred to St. George's Field, Lambeth, in 1815. The term "bedlamite" came to be applied to any person behaving like a madman.

Beech, a deciduous tree belonging to the genus *Fagus* of some eight or nine species found in north temperate regions. The common beech, *F. sylvatica*, is believed to be native to Britain and is one of our finest trees, with massive trunk, long, pointed winter buds, and smooth, grey bark. There is little undergrowth under its dense shade. It is shorter-lived than the oak taking about 200 years to reach full size and then declining. The timber of beech has a variety of uses, *e.g.*, spoons, handles, chairs, *etc*.

Bee-eater, name of a family of brilliantly coloured birds closely related to the rollers and king-fishers inhabiting the tropical and sub-tropical parts of Africa, Asia and Europe. The European species successfully nested in Britain for the first time in 1955 and a pair nested in Alderney in 1956. With their long curved beaks they catch insects on the wing, especially bees and butterflies, and lay their eggs in dark tunnels.

Beef crisis. See **Mad Cow Disease, L77.**

Beefeater, See **Yeomen of the Guard.**

Beeswax, the secretion of the bee, used for the formation of the cells or honey-comb of the hive; when melted it is what is commercially known as yellow wax, white wax being made by bleaching. Being impervious to water, it acts as a good resistant and is an article of much utility.

Beetles (Coleoptera) constitute one of the biggest orders of insects, numbering over 200,000 species. There are two pairs of wings; the hind pair are used for flight, while the front pair are hardened to form a pair of protective covers (elytra). Some beetles have lost the power of flight and then the elytra are joined together.

Bel and the Dragon is the title of certain supplementary chapters to the "Book of Daniel" of an apocryphal character. First appeared in the Septuagint, but the Jewish Church did not accept it as inspired. In 1546 the Council of Trent declared it to be canonical.

Bell, a hollow body of metal used for making sounds. Bells are usually made from bell-metal, an alloy of copper and tin. Small bells used for interior functions are often made of silver, gold or brass. Ordinary hand-bells are of brass. From the 7th cent. large bells have been used in England in cathedrals, churches and monasteries. The greatest bell in the world is the "King of Bells" in the Kremlin at Moscow which weighs about 198 tonnes, is 627 cm high and 691 cm in diameter. It was cast in 1733 but cracked in the furnace (the broken part weighed 11 tonnes) and is now preserved as a national treasure. Other large bells in Russia include the 171 tonne one at Krasnogvardersk, near St Petersburg, and the

one of 110 tonnes at Moscow. The Great Bell (Great Paul) at St. Paul's, cast in 1881, weighs nearly 17 tonnes and is the largest in the United Kingdom. Other gigantic bells are the Great Bell at Peking (53 tonnes); Nanking (22 tonnes); Cologne Cathedral (25 tonnes); Big Ben, Westminster (over 13 tonnes); Great Peter, York Minster (10 tonnes). The Curfew Bell is rung in some parts of England to this day, notably at Ripon. The number of changes that can be rung on a peal of bells is the *factorial* of the number of bells. Thus four bells allow 24 and eight bells 40,320.

Belladonna or **Deadly Nightshade** (*Atropa belladonna*), a well-known poisonous wild plant found in Southern Europe and Western Asia. The alkaloid atropine it contains is valuable in medicine, although a large dose is poisonous.

Bell, Book and Candle. To curse by "bell, book, and candle" was a form of excommunication in the Roman Church ending with the words: "Close the book, quench the candle, ring the bell".

Benedicite, the canticle in the Book of Common Prayer, known also as "The Song of the Three Holy Children".

Benedictines are monks and nuns of the Benedictine Order who live under the rule of St. Benedict—the monastic code whose influence on the religious and cultural life of the West has been so powerful. The rule is marked by an absence of extravagant asceticism. The greatest of the early Benedictines was Pope Gregory I (590–604) who sent St. Augustine of Canterbury to Anglo-Saxon England. Gregorian plainsong is named after him.

Benzene. An aromatic hydrocarbon obtained from coal tar and some petroleum fractions. It is a volatile inflammable liquid with a characteristic smell. The molecule consists of a flat ring of six carbon atoms, each bound to one hydrogen atom. Benzene is the parent member of many aromatic organic compounds and is widely used in industry to synthesise intermediates for fibres, dyestuffs, explosives and pharmaceutical chemicals.

Berlin Wall, construction formerly dividing Berlin. Symbol of the Cold War from 1961 to 1989.

Beryl, a mineral, of which the emerald is a grass-green variety. Composed of beryllium and aluminium silicates. The pure mineral is colourless; the colour of most beryl comes from traces of impurities, notably iron and chromium. Otherwise it is yellowish, greenish-yellow, or blue, and is found in veins which traverse granite or gneiss, or embedded in granite, and sometimes in alluvial soil formed from such rocks.

Beryllium. Metallic element, no. 4, symbol Be. Very similar to aluminium, it is stronger than steel and only one-quarter its weight. It is not very abundant, its main source is the mineral, beryl. Copper containing 2 per cent. beryllium is used for making springs. Because of its special properties the metal is used as a component in spacecraft, missiles and nuclear reactors. This accounts for its recent development on a technical scale. The metal powder is toxic.

Bessemer Process for making steel depends on the forcing of atmospheric air into molten pig iron to burn out the impurities. Ousted by the oxygen converter. See **Steel.**

Betel, the leaf of an Indian climbing plant, of pungent, narcotic properties. It is destructive to the teeth, and reddens the gums and lips.

Bhang, the Indian name for the hemp plant *Cannabis sativa*, the leaves and seed-capsules of which are chewed or smoked. The drug which comes from flowers of the female plant is called hashish in Arabia and marihuana in the USA.

Bible (Greek *biblion* = scroll of paper; pl. *biblia* = writings) includes the Hebrew sacred Scriptures (Old Testament) and those held sacred by the Christians (New Testament). The Old Testament—the prehistoric portion—consists of 39 books, and is divided into three parts: (1) the Law, (2) the Prophets, (3) Miscellaneous Writings. The Old Testament was written in Hebrew except for parts of Ezra and Daniel, which were in Aramaic. It was not until the 9th cent. A.D. that a complete Hebrew text was made, the so-called Massoretic text. Before that the main versions were the Alexandrian Greek translation (Septuagint) made in the 2nd cent. B.C. and St.

Jerome's Latin Vulgate of the 4th cent. A.D. (It was Jerome who used the Latin word "testament" (formed from *testis* = a witness).) Portions were translated into the Anglo-Saxon in the 8th cent. and the Venerable Bede put the greater part of St. John's gospel into English, but it was not until 1535 that a complete, printed English version appeared—the Coverdale Translation. The Authorised Version dates from 1611 in the reign of James I, and its beautiful phraseology has given it a lasting appeal. The Revised Version dates from 1885. *The New English Bible*, with the Apocrypha, was published in 1970. It is a new translation in plain English prose of the earliest Hebrew, Aramaic, and Greek manuscripts. The finding of the Dead Sea Scrolls (since 1947) has added to our knowledge of Scripture. By the mid-1990s the complete Bible had been translated into 322 languages, the New Testament alone into 695. It remains the world's best-selling book.

Biedermeier, style in interior decoration and the decorative arts developed from Empire (*q.v.*). It was created in Vienna *c.* 1815 and the name was derived from a fantasy figure in Viennese writing personifying all that which is sedate and bourgeois. Biedermeier furniture is less austere and grandiose than Empire's predecessors, more intimate and homely. A most important creation is the large circular table on a stem-like foot, which became the centre of family life, around which chairs could be grouped freely, not formally against walls as previously. In Vienna itself the style died out *c.* 1830, but in other Continental countries it survived well into the second half of the 19th cent. Its English equivalent is Early Victorian.

Billion, formerly in English usage a million million; now a thousand million or 10^9.

Bill of Rights, or Declaration of Rights, was the document setting forth the conditions upon which the British throne was offered to William and Mary in 1688. This was accepted and ultimately became an Act of Parliament. The pressure group Charter 88 currently campaigns for a Bill of Rights to enshrine civil liberties. *See* **Human Rights, J58–60.**

Binary Notation, for numbers, is a way of representing numbers using only two digits, 0 and 1. Electronic digital computers handle numbers in this form and many people these days are having to learn it. Many school children find it both easy and fascinating—as did the great philosopher and mathematician Leibniz. The ordinary, or decimal numbers, 0, 1, 2, 3, 4, 5, 6, 7, 8, 9, 10 are written in binary notation as follows: 0, 1, 10, 11, 100, 101, 110, 111, 1000, 1001, 1010. The reader might divine the rules from this. The point is you "carry 1", *i.e.*, move the digit 1 a place to the left, when you reach 2. In decimal notation you move 1 a place left when you reach 10. In other words, instead of columns for units, tens, hundreds, thousands, etc., the columns are for units, twos, fours, eights, etc. In binary notation: "1 + 1 = 0 with 1 to carry". Since every digit in binary notation is either 0 or 1 it requires one bit of information to specify a binary digit.

Bioarchaeology, the study of human remains from archaeological sites.

Biological Clock. All living organisms undergo cyclical changes in activity of some sort. These are linked to the changes in their environment which are produced by the alternation of night and day, the phases of the moon and the tides, and the cycle of the seasons. These cycles of activity frequently persist if the organism is put into a constant environment in which there appear to be no external clues as to what time or what season it is. A squirrel, for example, wakes up at about the same time each evening even when it is put into constant darkness. It is usual to refer to these activity patterns as being driven by a biological clock inside the organism. But very little is known about how these biological clocks work.

Biological Warfare, is the use for warlike purposes of bacteria, viruses, fungi, or other biological agents. This sort of research can be done in many countries; it is much cheaper and easier to hide than nuclear weapons research.

Biosensors, micro-electronic or optoelectronic devices used to sense the presence of chemicals.

This new technique for diagnosis and analysis could have a host of applications in medicine (*e.g.* blood analysis), industry *etc.*

Biosphere, that part of the earth in which life exists—a very thin layer near the surface bounded by regions too hostile for life processes to occur. The upper limit is at about 9,000 m above sea level and the lower limit at about 10,000 m in the deep oceans. Ample supplies of solar energy, liquid water and places where liquid, solid and gas all meet seem to be requirements for a biosphere to exist and for all the biological cycles of water, oxygen, mineral, nitrogen, *etc.*, to function.

Birch, a genus of deciduous trees including about 40 species and found only in northern regions. Birches native to Britain, and to Europe generally, are of two species—the silver birch, *Betula pendula*, with its graceful, drooping branches and triangular leaves, and the white birch, *Betula pubescens*, which has erect branches and soft oval leaves. Birch timber is an important plywood timber, the bark is used for tanning leather, and wintergreen oil comes from the bark of black birch, *Betula lenta*, a North American species. The birch is not a long-lived tree.

Birds, or Aves, are, next to mammals, the highest class of animal life. There are two kinds of modern birds—*Carinatae*, possessing keeled breast-bones and having power of flight; *Ratitae*, having raft-like breast-bones, and incapable of flight; and a sub-class of fossil birds, Archaeornithes, including *Archaeopteryx*. Estimates of the total number of birds breeding in the British Isles vary, but there are 229 breeding species. Of these the commonest are wrens, house sparrows, blackbirds, chaffinches, robins and starlings.

The wheatear is usually the first of the migratory birds to return, often reaching Britain at the end of February and always before the middle of March; the sand martin is the first of the "early swallows" to return, followed by the house martin. The first cuckoo arrives about the middle of April, and the whinchat, garden warbler, and sedge warbler during the last week in April. The nightjar, spotted flycatcher, and red-backed shrike are not seen until the first week in May. The swift is among the last to return from Africa and the earliest to depart. Bird-nesting is illegal in Britain. With the passing of the Wildlife and Countryside Act in 1980 the trapping and caging of robins, nightingales, larks, kingfishers, cuckoos, owls, martins, fieldfares, flycatchers, ravens and other birds was made illegal in Britain. *See also* **F36**(2).

Birds of Paradise, over 40 species of tropical birds inhabiting the dense forests of New Guinea and neighbouring islands. The male birds are remarkable for their brilliant plumage, long tail feathers, and ruffs on wings and neck, which are displayed to advantage during courtship. Related to the Bower Birds of Australia.

Biretta, a four-cornered head-covering worn by ecclesiastics of the Roman Church and varying in colour according to the rank of the wearer. A cardinal's biretta is red, a bishop's purple, a priest's black.

Bise, a keen dry north wind prevalent in Switzerland and South France.

Bishop is a Christian ecclesiastic, a person consecrated for the spiritual government of an area, a diocese or province, to the spiritual oversight of which he has been appointed (diocesan bishops), or to aid a bishop so appointed (suffragan bishops). In the Church of England there are forty-three diocesan bishops, all nominated by the Crown. Two, Canterbury and York, are archbishops having primacy in the respective provinces. The archbishops of Canterbury and York and the bishops of London, Durham and Winchester and twenty-one other diocesan bishops in order of seniority are spiritual peers, and sit in the House of Lords. The (Disestablished) Church of Ireland has two archbishops and twelve bishops; the (Disestablished) Church of Wales an archbishop and five bishops and the Episcopal Church in Scotland seven bishops. *See also* **Cardinal.**

Bismuth, metallic element, no. 83, symbol Bi, in group 5 of the periodic table. Like antimony, the stable form is a grey, brittle, layer structure;

electrical conductor. It is readily fusible, melting at 264°C and boiling at about 1420°C. Wood's metal, an alloy with one of the lowest melting points (under 65°C, so that a spoon made of it will melt when placed in a cup of hot tea), contains four parts bismuth, two parts lead, one part tin, one part cadmium.

Bison, a genus of wild cattle, distinguished from the ox by its shorter, wider skull, beard under the chin, high forequarters, and, in winter, a great mane of woolly hair covering head and forequarters. There are two species, the European and the American bison. The European bison, which tends to browse (or munch trees and leaves rather than graze) is now poised to return.

Bit, formerly the word often referred to the metal piece in the mouth of a bridled horse, now more likely to be a technical expression in the mouth of a computer expert. A bit is a unit of information; it is the information that can be conveyed by indicating which of two possibilities obtains. Any object that can be either of two states can therefore store one bit of information. In a technical device, the two states could be the presence or the absence of a magnetic field, or of an electric voltage. Since all numbers can be represented in the binary system (*see* **Binary Notation**) by a row of digits which are *either* 0 *or* 1, it takes one bit of information to specify a binary digit. Bit is short for binary digit.

Bittern, a bird of the heron genus, with long, loose plumage on the front and sides of the neck. It is a solitary bird inhabiting marshes, but rare in Britain where it is confined to about 15 breeding pairs in Norfolk, Suffolk and Lancashire. An ambitious scheme was launched in 1995 to save it from extinction and a recovery is now underway.

Bivalves, shell-fish whose shell consists of two hinged valves, lying one on each side of the body, such as mussels, oysters and cockles.

Blackbird, or **Merle,** a member of the Thrush family, a familiar song bird in Britain. Male is all-black with orange bill; female is mottled brown with brown bill; the young are spotted brown.

Blackcock and Greyhen (as the female is called) are closely related to the Capercaillies but smaller. They nest on the ground and prefer wooded country to open moors. Found in northern half of northern hemisphere. Polygamous, they perform excited courtship dances; the male is a handsome blue-black bird with white undertail, the female dark brown mottled.

Black Death, the plague which swept across Europe in the years 1348–50, beginning in the ports of Italy, brought in by merchant ships from Black Sea ports. It was the worst scourge man has ever known; at least a quarter of the European population was wiped out in the first epidemic of 1348. It reached England in the winter of that year. The disease was transmitted to man by fleas from black rats, though this was not known at the time, the specific organism being *Bacillus pestis.* The disease continued to ravage Europe in recurrent outbreaks up to the late 17th cent. The epidemic in England in 1665 wiped out whole villages and one-tenth of London's population, then estimated at 460,000. Samuel Pepys wrote a grim account of it in his *Diary. See also* **Labourers, English Statute of.**

Black Hole of Calcutta, the name given to the place where a captured British garrison was confined in 1756, during the struggle for India between the French and British. Into a confined space, about 6 m square, 146 persons were driven and only 23 were found alive the next morning. The authenticity of the story has been called into question.

Black Holes. *See* **Astronomy, Section F, Part I.**

Black-letter, the Old English or Gothic type first used in printing blocks.

Black Woodpecker (*Dryocopus martius*), a black bird about the size of a rook, with slightly crested scarlet crown, found in parts of Europe.

Blenny, a group of marine fishes with spiny rays part of the fin running along the back. Several species are found around the British coast.

Blood Groups. *See* **Index to Section P.**

Bloody Assizes, the assizes conducted in 1685 by George Jeffreys, Lord Chief Justice, at which participants in the Duke of Monmouth's rebellion against King James II were tried. They were marked by relentless cruelty.

Bluebird, a migratory bird of North America, de-

riving its name from its deep blue plumage, it has a pleasant warbling song and is a familiar sight in the woods from early spring to November. In India and Malaya there is the Fairy Blue-bird; the male is black with shiny blue upper parts. Used as the symbol of happiness by Maeterlinck in his play *The Blue Bird.*

Blue Peter, a blue flag with a white square in the centre, is hoisted 24 hours before a ship leaves harbour (the letter P in the alphabet of the International Code of Signals).

Blue Ribbon, a term in general use to denote the highest honour or prize attainable in any field or competition. Thus the Derby is the blue ribbon of the turf. The expression is derived from the highest Order of Knighthood in the gift of the British Crown, the insignia of which is a garter of blue velvet.

Blue Stocking, a term used to describe a learned or literary woman, particularly if pedantic and undomesticated. It is said that the term derives from the Bas-Bleu club of Paris, which was attended by the literary savantes of the 17th cent. In England a similar literary club was formed about 1780, whose members were distinguished by their blue stockings.

"Blue" Sun, Moon, etc., a phenomenon caused by the scattering of sunlight by transparent particles suspended in the atmosphere, the effect being that blue light is transmitted, and red light extinguished to direct vision. The dust from the Krakatoa eruption in 1883 and the drifting layer of smoke from the forest fires in Alberta, Canada, in September 1950 gave rise to "blue" moons and suns, phenomena sufficiently rare to be described as occurring "once in a blue moon".

Boa, a term applied to a family of snakes of large size, some attaining a length of 9 m. They are not poisonous, but kill their prey by crushing —constriction—hence the name "boa constrictor". They occur both in the Old World and the New, but are more abundant in the latter. Most Boas retain the eggs within the body until young are fully developed, whereas the Pythons almost all lay leather-shelled eggs.

Boar, or Wild Hog, an animal largely distributed over the forest regions of Europe, Asia, Africa and South America. It has a longer snout and shorter ears than its descendant the domestic hog, and is provided with tusks. Having to forage for itself, it is a more active and intelligent animal than the pig of the sty, and offered good sport to the hunter.

Boat, an open vessel, propelled by oars or sails, or both. The boats of a ship of war are the launch, barge, pinnace, yawl, cutters, jolly boat and gig; of a merchant vessel, the launch, skiff, jolly boat or yawl, stern boat, quarter-boat and captain's gig. Every ship is compelled to carry fully provisioned and equipped lifeboats.

Boat Race. *See* **Section R.**

Bode's Law, a numerical relationship formulated by Bode in 1772 (though pointed out earlier by J. D. Titius of Wittenberg), which states that the relative mean distances of the planets from the sun are found by adding 4 to each of the terms 0, 3, 6, 12, 24, 48, 96, and dividing each number by 10. The gap between Mars and Jupiter caused Bode to predict the existence of a planet there, which was later confirmed by the discovery of Ceres and other minor planets. The law breaks down for Neptune and Pluto.

Boer War lasted from 11 October 1899, when the Boers invaded Natal, to 31 May 1902, when the Treaty of Vereeniging ended hostilities. At first the operations of the British troops in Cape Colony were unsuccessful and disastrous reverses were sustained. Lord Roberts was then sent out as Commander-in-Chief, with Lord Kitchener as Chief-of-Staff, and from February 1900, when Kimberley was relieved and Cronje was compelled to surrender and Ladysmith and Mafeking were relieved, the struggle was practically over.

Boiling-point is the temperature at which a liquid boils. At that point the pressure of the vapour is equal to the pressure of the atmosphere. Under increased pressure the b.p. rises and under less pressure, as on the top of a mountain, it is lower. At standard atmospheric pressure (760 mm of mercury) the b.p. of water is 100°C; alcohol 78·4°C; ether 35·6°C.

Book of Hours, the most widespread devotional work of the Middle Ages. Most surviving copies are 15th century, but the earliest (the de Brailes Hours) dates from *c*.1240.

Books, Classification of. All libraries are classified to facilitate reference, but the favourite system is the Dewey Decimal System, which divides the whole field of knowledge into ten Main Classes. Each of these Main Classes is again subdivided into ten main divisions. As an example: the main class of Sociology receives the number 300. This range 300 to 400 (the next main class) is graduated into tens, and Economics is 330. The range 330 to 340 is again graduated, and the subject of Labour and Capital is 331. This process is carried on by decimals so that 331·2 deals with Remuneration for Work, 331·22 with Wage Scales, and 331·225 with Extra Pay.

Borax (Sodium Pyroborate) is a white, soluble, crystalline salt. It is widely and diversely used, *e.g.*, as a mild antiseptic, in glazing pottery, in soldering, in the making of pyrex glass, as a cleansing agent and sometimes as a food preservative. Borax occurs naturally in the salt lakes of Tibet, where it is called tincal.

Bore. In physical geography, an almost vertical wall of water which passes upstream along certain estuaries. Its formation requires special conditions of river flow, incoming high tide, and shape of river channel. It can be spectacular and dangerous on some rivers. In Britain the best known is the Severn bore which can be over a metre high and move at 16–19 km/h. In parts of Britain the bore is called an eagre.

Boron. A metalloid element, no. 5, symbol B. There are two forms, one crystalline, the other amorphous. It is not very abundant in nature but occurs in concentrated deposits. It is best known in boric acid, which is used as a mild antiseptic (called boracic acid) and borax (*q.v.*). Boron compounds are essential to some plants, *e.g.*, beans. Used in the preparation of various special-purpose alloys, such as impact resistant steel. Compounds of boron and hydrogen are used as rocket fuels.

Borstal, an institution where young offenders under 21 on conviction were sent for detention and reform. Emphasis was placed on vocational training in skilled trades. The first was opened in 1902 at Borstal, near Rochester in Kent. Borstals were abolished by the 1982 Criminal Justice Act. Young offenders' are now referred to the Young Offenders' Institution (*q.v.*).

Boston Tea Party, an incident which occurred on 16 December 1773, on board some tea-ships in Boston Harbour. High taxation imposed by the British Parliament under George III had caused bitter feelings, and instigated by popular meetings, a party of citizens, disguised as Indians, boarded the tea-ships and threw the tea overboard. This incident was a prelude to the American War of Independence (1775–83) which resulted in Britain's loss of her American colonies.

Bounds Beating, an old Anglo-Saxon custom. The parish clergyman and officials go round the parish boundaries accompanied by boys who beat the boundary stones with long sticks of willow. The ceremony takes place on the Rogation days preceding Ascension Day.

Bourgeoisie, a term used by Marxists to indicate those who do not, like the proletariat, live by the sale of their labour. They include, on the one hand, industrialists and financiers or members of the liberal professions and, on the other, small artisans and shop-keepers who, although their standard of living may not be appreciably higher (and today is often lower) than that of the proletariat, are described as the "petty bourgeoisie". According to the Marxist view of history, the bourgeoisie arose with modern industrialism after it had overthrown the old feudal aristocracy and thus replaced it as the ruling class.

Bovine Spongiform Encephalopathy (BSE), see **Mad Cow Disease**.

Bow, an instrument for propelling arrows, and, in the days when it was a weapon of war, was usually made of yew or ash, and was about 2 m long, with an arrow *c.* 1 m long. It was the weapon with which Crécy, Poitiers and Agincourt were won. The cross-bow was Italian and was adopted in France, but did not become popular in Britain.

Bow Bells is the peal of the London church of St. Mary-le-Bow, Cheapside, within sound of which one must be born to be entitled to be called a "cockney". Bow Bells had not been heard since 1939, but they once again rang out over the City of London on 20 December 1961.

Bowdlerise, to expurgate a book. Derived from Thomas Bowdler (1754–1825), the editor of the Family Shakespeare, in which "those words and expressions are omitted which cannot with propriety be read aloud in a family". He treated Gibbon's *History of the Decline and Fall of the Roman Empire* in the same way, omitting "all passages of an irreligious and immoral tendency". Such prudery met with ridicule and hence the words "bowdlerism" "bowdlerist", *etc.*

Bower Bird, native to Australia and New Guinea and related to the Bird of Paradise, though often less striking in appearance. In the mating season the male builds a "bower" of sticks and grasses for courtship displays and as a playground. The Gardener Bower Bird of Papua makes a lawn in front of his bower and adorns it with bright coloured pebbles and flowers which are replaced as they wither. The female builds her nest away from the bower.

Boxgrove. Site near Halnaker, West Sussex. In 1993 archaeologists discovered the 500,000 year old left shin bone of "Boxgrove Man", making it the site of the oldest human inhabitant in England.

Boycott, a term used in connection with a person that the general body of people, or a party or society, refuse to have dealings with. Originally used when Captain Boycott (1832–97) was made the victim of a conspiracy by the Irish Land League which prevented him making any purchases or holding any social intercourse in his district. He had incurred the League's hostility by a number of evictions.

Brass, an exceedingly useful alloy of copper and zinc. Much brass is about two-thirds copper but different proportions give different properties. It is harder than copper and easily worked. Brass in the Bible (Matt. x, 9) probably refers to bronze.

Breadfruit Tree (*Artocarpus altilis*), a native of the South Sea Islands; the fruits are a brownish green, about the size of a melon, and contain a white pulpy substance which is roasted before being eaten. The tree grows 12 m or more. Captain Bligh's ship *Bounty* was on a voyage to Jamaica carrying a cargo of 1,000 breadfruit trees when the mutiny occurred.

Breeder Reactor, a kind of nuclear reactor (*q.v.*) which besides producing energy by the fission process also produces ("breeds") more nuclear fuel at the same time. A typical reaction is: a neutron induces fission of a U-235 nucleus which breaks up into two medium-sized nuclei and some neutrons; one of the latter then enters a U-238 nucleus turning it into U-239 which then decays radioactively *via* neptunium into plutonium which is useful fuel. There are technical problems in breeder reactors which have delayed their practical use.

Breviary (Lat. *breviarium* = abridgment), the short prayer-book of the Roman Catholic Church which gives the Divine Office, *i.e.*, the services to be said daily. The directions for Mass are in the Missal. The current Roman breviary is a simplified version of the one decreed by the Council of Trent, 1568. *See also* **Matins**.

Bridges are structures for continuing a road, railway, or canal across a river, valley, ravine, or a road or railway at a lower level. From early times bridges were made of timber, stone, or brick, and it was not until the 19th cent. that wrought- and cast-iron were used. Today the materials mostly used are steel and reinforced concrete. Among the most famous of ancient bridges is that of S. Angelo at Rome, built by Hadrian as the Pons Aelius, A.D. 134. The Rialto bridge at Venice dates from 1588. The Ponte Santa Trinita at Florence, one of the finest Renaissance bridges and deemed the most beautiful in the world, was destroyed by German mines in 1944 but has now been reconstructed just as it was before. The first stone bridge across the Thames was begun in 1176. It had 19 arches and was lined with houses and stood until 1831 when it was replaced by the granite bridge designed by Sir John Rennie which stood until 1972. This has been replaced by a three-span concrete bridge with a six-lane carriageway and two footways. The first cast-iron bridge (recently repaired) was built by Abraham Darby at Coalbrookdale, Shropshire, in 1779. Telford's Menai suspension bridge (1825) has since been enlarged, the original design maintained. Robert Stephenson's tubular bridge across the Menai Straits (1850) was the prototype of all modern plate girder railway bridges. Other famous bridges are the Niagara (suspension), Forth railway bridge (cantilever), London Tower bridge (suspension), Tay railway bridge, Victoria Jubilee bridge across the St. Lawrence at Montreal (an open steel structure), Sydney Harbour bridge, Lower Zambesi bridge, Storstrom bridge in Denmark, Auckland Harbour bridge, and Verrazano- Narrows bridge spanning New York's harbour from Brooklyn to Staten I., exceeding by 18 m the centre span of San Francisco's Golden Gate bridge. Work on a suspension bridge 2-miles long, linking Italy and Sicily, is planned to begin in 1999. Europe's longest bridge (opened 1998) is the 11-mile Vasco da Gama Bridge across the Tagus river north of Lisbon. The longest suspension bridge in the world, linking Hong Kong to its new airport, is currently (1999) under construction.

British bridges include the road suspension bridge across the Firth of Forth, completed 1964, the Severn suspension bridge (from which the design principles for the new bridge across the Bosporus were taken) and the Tay road bridge, both completed 1966, the Tinsley viaduct, near Sheffield, opened 1968 and the Humber suspension bridge, linking Hull and Grimsby, opened in 1981. When completed, it was the longest single-span suspension bridge in the world (1,410 m). The M25 "Dartford" bridge (opened 1991) is the largest cable-stayed bridge in Europe. The second Severn bridge, which opened in June 1996 is the longest in Britain. Europe's longest suspension bridge (opened in 1998) links the Danish island of Sjaelland (on which Copenhagen stands) to Funen (both at the mouth of the Baltic).

Bridleway. In English law (sec. 27(6) of the National Parks and Access to the Countryside Act 1949) a highway over which the public have the following, but no other, rights of way: that is to say, a right of way on foot and a right of way on horseback or leading a horse, with or without a right to drive animals of any description along the highway.

Britannia Metal, an alloy of tin, antimony and copper, harder than pure tin, corrosion-resistant, used for teapots, jugs (often electro-plated).

British Association for the Advancement of Science, The, was founded in 1831 by a group of British scientists under the leadership of Charles Babbage (1792–1871) to stimulate scientific inquiry. Its meetings are held annually.

British Legion, see Royal British Legion.

British Museum, was created by an Act of Parliament in 1753, when the Sir Hans Sloane collection, which the British Government had acquired for £20,000, was added to the Cottonian Library and the Harleian Manuscripts. It was opened to the public in 1759 at Montague House Bloomsbury. The acquisition of the library of George III (known as the King's Library) in 1823 led to the construction of the present building with the new wing (1829), quadrangle (1852), domed reading room (1857), and later additions. The books and the reading room are now part of the British Library (see Libraries). The Natural History Department was transferred to South Kensington in the 1880s. As a museum it is perhaps the most famous in the world, since it has many priceless collections. It attracted over 6,500,000 visitors in 1998. Its treasures include the Elgin Marbles (q.v.), the Rosetta Stone (q.v.) and the Portland Vase (q.v.). The famous domed Reading Room closed in 1997.

British Rail (British Railways). The name under which the railways of Britain were unified on 1 January 1948. Instead of the former four main railway systems six regions were formed: London Midland region (former LMSR), Western (former GWR), Southern (formerly SR), Eastern (southern area of former LNER), NE region (NE of former LNER), Scottish region (Scottish system of the former LMSR and LNER). Under the Transport Act 1962 the British Railways Board was set up to manage railway affairs. The most far-reaching change since 1955 has been the replacement of steam traction by electric and diesel locomotives. Under the chairmanship of Lord (then Dr.) Richard Beeching the British Railways Board planned a viable railway system by closing uneconomic branch lines, by developing new services on the liner train principle, and by utilising a more limited trunk route system. Under the Transport Act 1968 some railway passenger services became eligible for grants on social grounds, including urban railways and unprofitable rural services. High-speed inter-city passenger services came into operation in 1976 and in 1985 it was announced that the Advanced Passenger Train (the Electra) would go into production. Following the 1993 Railways Act, the privatisation of British Rail began on 1 April 1994 when a new company, Railtrack, took over the management of the track, signalling and other infrastructure. In 1994, the government announced its intention to privatise Railtrack, which owned 2,500 stations and 11,000 miles of track. This took place in 1996. The first privatised rail services since 1948 began in February 1996.

A new world speed record was set in April 1999 when a Japanese maglev (magnetically-levitated) train reached 343 m.p.h.

British Standard Time, The British Standard Time Act of 1968 put Britain an hour ahead of Greenwich Mean Time (GMT) throughout the year for an experimental 3 years. This brought Britain into line with countries in Western Europe where Central European Time is observed. In 1970 Parliament called for the restoration of the previous position—BST in the summer months and GMT in the winter months—as from 31 October 1971. An attempt to change the law once again to give lighter evenings (but darker mornings) is currently (1999) underway.

Brocken-spectre or Glory. The series of coloured rings which an observer sees around the shadow of his own head (or an aeroplane in which he is travelling) as cast upon a bank of mist or thin cloud. This effect is produced by reflection and refraction of sunlight in minute water-droplets in the air just as in a rainbow.

Bromine. A non-metal element, no. 35, symbol Br, member of the halogen family (q.v.). It is a red, evil-smelling liquid (Greek bromos, a stink). It is an abundant element. In the USA bromine is extracted from sea-water on a large scale. It unites readily with many other elements, the products being termed bromides. Its derivatives with organic compounds are used in synthetic chemistry. Bromoform is a liquid resembling chloroform. Bromides are used in medicine to calm excitement.

Bronze is primarily an alloy of copper and tin, and was one of the earliest alloys known, the Bronze Age (began c. 4,000 B.C. in Middle East) in the evolution of tool-using man coming before the Iron Age (c. 2,000 B.C.) Some modern bronzes contain zinc or lead also, and a trace of· phosphorus is present in "Phosphor-bronze".

BSE, see Mad Cow Disease.

Bubble Chamber. An instrument used by physicists to reveal the tracks of fast fundamental particles (e.g., those produced in large accelerating machines) in a form suitable for photography; closely related to the Wilson cloud chamber (q.v.), but the particles leave trails of small bubbles in a superheated liquid (often liquid hydrogen) instead of droplets of liquid in a supersaturated gas.

Buckingham Palace, London residence of British sovereigns since 1837. Originally built for the Duke of Buckingham (1703); bought by George III in 1762 and remodelled by Nash 1825–36. Part of the palace was opened to visitors in 1993.

Buntings, name of a group of finches, seed-eating birds, usually found in open country. The Yellowhammer, Reed Bunting, Corn Bunting and Cirl Bunting are resident in Britain; the Snow Bunting (which breeds in small numbers in Scotland) and Lapland Bunting are regular winter visitors. The Ortolan is a rare visitor.

Bustard, type of bird, related to the crane.

Butane, a colourless inflammable gas made of carbon and hydrogen; formula C_4H_{10}. Found in natural gas and made as a by-product of oil refining. Butane, like propane (q.v.), can easily be liquefied and moved safely in cans and tanks. It is thus useful as a "portable gas supply"; also used in internal combustion fuels.

Buzzard, magnificent dark brown birds, three feet long, with an eye as large as a human eye. They need woods to nest in and land to forage over.

Byzantine Art developed in the eastern part of the Roman empire after Constantine founded the city of Constantinople (A.D. 330). It has many sources—Greek, Syrian, Egyptian and Islamic —and reached its zenith in the reign of Justinian (527–65). The major art form was ecclesiastical architecture, the basic plan of which was Roman—either basilican (symmetrical about an axis) or centralised (symmetrical about a point). Arched construction was developed, and the dome became the most typical feature, although, unlike the Roman dome which was placed on a round apartment, the Byzantine dome was placed on a square one on independent pendentives. Frequently small domes were clustered round a large one as in the case of the great church of Santa Sophia (537), the climax of Byzantine architecture. Usually the churches were small and include those of SS. Sergius and Bacchus, Sta. Irene (in Constantinople), S. Vitale in Ravenna, and the much later and larger St. Mark's in Venice. Byzantine art also took the form of miniatures, enamels, jewels, and textiles, but mosaics, frescos, and icons (*q.v.*) are its greatest treasures.

C

Cacao, Theobroma cacao, is an evergreen tree, from 4–6 m high, growing abundantly in tropical America, West Africa, the West Indies, Sri Lanka, *etc.*, yielding seeds, called cocoa beans from which cocoa and chocolate are manufactured. The fruit is 17–25 cm long, hard and ridged; inside are the beans, covered with a reddish-brown skin, which are first fermented, then dried. The trees mature at five to eight years and produce two crops a year.

Cactus, a family of flowering plants numbering about a thousand species adapted to living in very dry situations. The stem is usually fleshy, being composed of succulent tissue, remarkably retentive of water; commonly equipped with sharp thorns which deter animals from eating them. The roots are generally very long, tapping soil water over a large area; a "prickly pear" cactus may have roots covering a circular area 7 m or more in diameter. The leaves are commonly insignificant or absent, and the stem takes over the photosynthetic leaf function and becomes accordingly flattened to expose greater area to sunlight and air. In some kinds of cactus (*e.g., Echinocactus*) the stem is shaped almost like a sea-urchin.

Cadmium. A metallic element, no. 48, symbol Cd, chemically similar to zinc and mercury. Used in alloys to lower the melting point, as in Wood's metal with bismuth and tin. Alloyed with copper to make electric cables. Like zinc, it is a protective metal and is used in electroplating. The cadmium-vapour lamp gives a characteristic frequency used in measuring wavelength.

Caesium, also spelt **Cesium,** is an alkali metal element, no. 55, symbol Cs, in first group of the periodic table. It resembles rubidium and potassium and was discovered by Bunsen and Kirchoff in 1860. It was the first element whose existence was discovered spectroscopically. The caesium atom consists of a heavy nucleus surrounded by 55 electrons, 54 of which are arranged in stable orbits, and one of which, known as the valency electron, is in a less stable orbit surrounding them. Used in the construction of photo-electric cells and as an accurate time standard (atomic clock).

Cajuns, corruption of Acadians. French-speaking inhabitants of Louisiana, descended from French Canadians who emigrated from Nova Scotia.

Calcium, a silvery-white metallic element, no. 20, symbol Ca. It melts at 810°C and is very reactive. It was discovered by Sir Humphry Davy in 1808, but not until 1898 was it obtained pure,

by Moissan. Does not occur as metal in nature, but calcium compounds make up a large part of the earth's crust. Most important calcium sources are marble, limestone, chalk (all three are, chemically, calcium carbonate); dolomite, which is the double carbonate of calcium and magnesium; gypsum, a hydrated calcium sulphate; calcium phosphate and calcium fluoride. Igneous rocks contain much calcium silicate. Calcium compounds are essential to plants and are used in fertilisers. Animals require calcium and phosphorus for bone and teeth formation; deficiency is treated by administration of calcium phosphate. Strontium is chemically similar to calcium, and the radioactive strontium 90 from atomic "fall-out" is therefore easily assimilated by the body.

Calendar, a collection of tables showing the days and months of the year, astronomical recurrences, chronological references, etc. The Julian Calendar, with its leap year, introduced by Julius Caesar, fixed the average length of the year at 365¼ days, which was about 11 minutes too long (the earth completes its orbit in 365 days 5 hours 48 minutes 46 seconds of mean solar time). The cumulative error was rectified by the Gregorian Calendar, introduced in Italy in 1582, whereby century years do not count as leap years unless divisible by 400. This is the rule we now follow. England did not adopt the reformed calendar until 1752, when she found herself 11 days behind the Continent. Until then, New Year's Day in England was on 25 March. Hence, in 1752, after the 11 days had been rectified, the new financial year began on 6 April—as it still does! The Gregorian Calendar did not come into use in Russia until 1918. Old Style and New Style dates are classed as "O.S." "N.S.".

Calends, the first day of the month in the Roman calendar.

Calorie. Unit of quantity of heat. The "small" or fundamental calorie is the amount of heat required to raise the temperature of 1 gram of water from 14·5° to 15·5°C and is equal to 4·185 joules. This is the gram-calorie used in physics and chemistry. The large Calorie (written with a capital C), commonly used in nutritional connotations, is equal to 1000 small calories and is called the kilogram-calorie.

Calvinism. See **Section J.**

Calypso, West Indian song in the form of a doggerel lampoon composed spontaneously and sung to a guitar.

Cambridge University had a sufficiently good teaching reputation to attract Oxford students in 1209, when lectures at their own university were suspended. In 1226 it had a Chancellor who was recognised by King and Pope. The first college to be founded was Peterhouse in 1284. The university was reorganised and granted a Charter of Incorporation by an act of Elizabeth in 1571. The colleges with their dates of foundation are Christ's (1505), Churchill (1960), Clare (1326), Clare Hall (1966), Corpus Christi (1352), Darwin (1964), Downing (1800), Emmanuel (1584), Fitzwilliam (1966), Gonville and Caius (1348), Jesus (1496), King's (1441), Magdalene (1542), Pembroke (1347), Peterhouse (1284), Queens' (1448), Robinson (1977) St. Catharine's (1473), St. Edmund's House (1896), St. John's (1511), Selwyn (1882), Sidney Sussex (1596), Trinity (1546), Trinity Hall (1350), Wolfson (1965). The women's colleges were: Girton (1869), Newnham (1871), New Hall (1954) and Hughes Hall (formerly Cambridge T. C.) (1885). Lucy Cavendish College (1965) (for women research students and other graduates) received full college status in 1997. Homerton (f. 1824) takes B.Ed students. Women were admitted to degrees (though not allowed to sit for examination) in 1920, and to full membership of the University in 1948. Newnham and New Hall still remain as all-women colleges.

Camel, a large ruminant quadruped, inhabiting Asia and Africa, where it is largely used as a beast of burden. There are two species—the Arabian camel or dromedary, with only one hump; and the Bactrian, or double-humped camel. There are no wild dromedaries, and the only wild bactrians occur in the Gobi Desert. The camel is able to go for long periods without water, not, as was formerly believed, because it stored water in its hump, but because of the unique mechanism of its physiology which enables it to conserve water at the expense of not sweating until 40°C is reached. The last wild camels are found in Mongolia and China.

Campanile, or bell-tower, is separate from but usually adjoining its parent church. The most famous are in Italy. Giotto's tower at Florence, adjoining the cathedral of Santa Maria del Fiore, is architecturally the finest in the world. Others are at Cremona, the loftiest in Italy (110 m) and Pisa (the leaning tower). The magnificent pointed campanile of St. Mark's, Venice, which collapsed in 1902 (and since rebuilt in its original form), was begun in 902.

Canal, an artificial watercourse used for navigation which changes its level by means of locks. The completion of the Bridgewater Canal in 1761 to take coal from Worsley to Manchester marked the beginning of canal building in industrial Britain. There are over 4,000 km of navigable inland waterways in Great Britain today, c. 3,200 km of which are under the control of British Waterways The English network is based on the four great estuaries, Mersey, Humber, Severn and Thames. Many canals are now being developed for boating, fishing and other leisure pursuits. The first new stretch of canal in Britain since 1905 was opened in April 1995 near Leeds. Many canals are finding a new use in the 1990s. The largest optical fibre network in Britain is currently (1999) being laid along their banks.

Candela unit of luminous intensity, symbol cd. An idea of the value which this unit represents may be gained from the fact that light obtained from a 40 W filament-type electric lamp or bulb is approximately the same as would be given by a point source of luminous intensity 30 cd. See **S.I. units, F66.**

Candlemas, an English and Roman Church festival in celebration of the Purification of the Virgin Mary. The date is 2 February.

Cannabis, a bushy plant found wild in many parts of the world. A "soft drug", it is illegal in Britain.

Canon, a term applied to signify a recognised rule for the guide of conduct in matters legal, ecclesiastical and artistic, or an authoritative ordinance: thus we have Canonical Scriptures, Canon Law, etc. A Canon is also a dignitary of the Church, usually a member of a cathedral chapter in the Anglican communion, or in the Roman Church a member of an order standing between regular monks and secular clergy.

Canonical Hours were seven in number in the Western Church; Matins and Lauds, before dawn; Prime, early morning service; Terce, 9 a.m.; Sext, noon; Nones, 3 p.m.; Vespers, 4 p.m.; Compline, bed-time.

Canonisation, the entering of one of the faithful departed on the list of saints of the Roman Catholic Church. The rules governing canonisation were simplified by papal decree in 1969. The forty English martyrs, of whom Edmund Campion was one, executed between 1535 and 1679 and beatified long ago, were canonised in 1970. Beatification, by which a person is called blessed, is usually followed by canonisation, but not necessarily.

Canticles, the name given to the scriptural passages from the Bible sung by the congregation in the various Christian liturgies. They are the *Benedicite, Benedictus, Magnificat, Nunc Dimittis.*

Capercaillie, the largest of the grouse family, found in the Scottish highlands and the pine forests and mountainous regions of Northern and Central Europe and Asia. The bird was reintroduced to Scotland by Sir Thomas Buxton in 1830. Now (1999) its numbers are down to 2,000.

Capet, the family name of the royal house of France, founded by Hugh Capet in 987, with its collateral branches. The main line of the dynasty came to an end in 1328 with the death of Charles IV when the throne passed to the related house of Valois. The direct Valois line ended in 1498 with the death of Charles VIII. The first of the Bourbon line was Henry IV whose descendants ruled France (except during the Revolution and the Napoleonic era) until 1848.

Capitalism. See **Section J.**

Capuchins are members of a mendicant order of Franciscans, founded in the 16th cent. with the aim of restoring the primitive and stricter observance of the rule of St. Francis, so called from the capuce (pointed cowl) worn by them.

Caracals, the largest of the African small cats. They are very agile.

Carat, a term used in assessing the value of gold and precious stones. In connection with gold, it represents the proportion of pure gold contained in any gold alloy, and for this purpose the metal is divided into 24 parts. Thus 24-carat indicates pure gold, and any lesser number of carats shows the proportion of gold contained in the alloy. The carat as a measure of weight is now obsolete, having been replaced by the *metric carat* of 0·2 grams.

Caravan, a band of travellers or traders journeying together for safety across the Eastern deserts, sometimes numbering many hundreds. There are several allusions to caravans in the Old Testament. The great caravan routes of this period from Egypt to Babylon and from Palestine to Yemen linked up with the Syrian ports and so with Western sea commerce.

Carbohydrates. See **Diet, Section P.**

Carbon, a non-metallic chemical element no. 6, symbol C, which occurs in crystalline form as diamonds and graphite; amorphous forms of carbon include charcoal and soot, while coke consists mainly of elementary carbon. The biochemistry of plants and animals largely hinges upon carbon compounds. The study of carbon compounds is called Organic Chemistry.

Carbon 14. A radioactive isotope of carbon, with a half- life c. 6,000 years, used in following the path of compounds and their assimilation in the body. Also used in determination of the age of carbon-containing materials such as trees.

Carbonari, members of a secret political society originating in Naples, and at one time very numerous. Their chief aim was to free Italy from foreign rule, and they exerted considerable influence in the various revolutionary movements in the first half of the 19th cent. Their name was adopted from the charcoal-burners (*carbonari*), and their passwords, signs, etc., were all in the phraseology of the fraternity.

Carbon dioxide. Commonest of the oxides of carbon. It is formed when carbon and its compounds are burnt with abundant supply of air, and when carbon compounds are oxidised in the respiration process of animals. The atmosphere contains carbon dioxide to the extent of about 325 ppm and is increasing by about 1 ppm per year, principally because of the burning of fossil fuels and possibly because of deforestation which not only leaves more oxidisible material but lowers the amount of carbon dioxide removed by photosynthesis.

Carbon monoxide is a colourless gas with no taste or smell. It is formed when coal and coke are burnt with a restricted supply of air; the blue flame to be seen in a coke brazier, for instance, is the flame of carbon monoxide. This gas is very poisonous, forming with the haemoglobin of the blood a compound which is useless for respiration and cherry red in colour, which gives a visible sympton of poisoning by carbon monoxide. With nickel it forms a volatile compound, called nickel carbonyl, and this reaction is the basis of the Mond process for extracting nickel.

Cardinal, one of the chief dignitaries of the Roman Catholic Church who constitute the Pope's council, or Sacred College, and when the papal chair is vacant elect by secret ballot a Pope from among themselves. There are three orders: cardinal bishops, members of the Roman Curia (the central administration of the Church) and bishops of sees near Rome; cardinal deacons, also members of the Curia, holding titular bishoprics; and cardinal priests who exercise pastoral duties over sees removed from Rome, though some are members of the Curia. Pope John Paul I, who had been elected in Aug. 1978 to succeed Pope Paul VI, died suddenly after only 33 days. He was succeeded by Pope John Paul II (Cardinal Karol Wojtyla, Archbishop of Cracow). Pope John Paul II created 22 new cardinals in 1998. The College of Cardinals comprises 120 members eligible to elect a new pope. Papal insignia were trimmed of embellishment by papal decree in 1969 with the abolition, subsequently revoked, of the famous red hat (the galero) and the shoes with buckles. Cardinals aged 80 and over may not enter a conclave to elect a pope.

Cardinal Virtues, according to Plato these were

justice, prudence, temperance, fortitude—*natural* virtues as distinct from the *theological* virtues of the Roman Catholic Church, faith, hope, charity. The phrase "seven cardinal virtues", combining the two, figures in mediaeval literature. *See* **Sins, Seven Deadly.**

Caribou, the reindeer (*see* **L104**) of North America.

Carmelites, a body of mendicant friars taking their name from Mount Carmel, where the order was first established in the 12th cent. The original rule of the order required absolute poverty, abstinence from meat and a hermit life. The rigidity of the rule of the order was mitigated by Innocent IV. They wear a brown habit with white mantle, hence their name of White Friars. The order of Carmelite nuns was instituted in the 15th cent.

Carolingians, dynasty of Frankish rulers founded in the 7th cent. The family was at its height when represented by Charlemagne. It ruled, with interruptions, until 987 when the Capetian dynasty succeeded.

Carp, a well-known fresh-water fish, found in plenty in most European and Asiatic still waters; reaches a length of about 60 cm and under favourable conditions lives for about 40 years. Familiar British members of the family are the roach, rudd, dace, chub, gudgeon, tench, minnow, barbel, bream and bleak. The goldfish, popular in ornamental ponds, is the domesticated variety of a Far Eastern member of the carp family.

Carthusians, an order of monks founded in 1084 by St. Bruno at the Grande Chartreuse near Grenoble, and introduced into England about a century later. They built the Charterhouse (corruption of Chartreuse) in London in 1371. The chief characteristics of the order are a separate dwelling-house in the precincts of the charterhouse for each monk, and the general assembly in the Church twice in the day and once at night. They wear a white habit, with white scapular and hood. The liqueur *Chartreuse* was invented by the order and is still their valuable secret. The order of Carthusian nuns dates from the 12th cent.

Casein, the chief protein in milk and cheese. It is coagulated by the action of rennet or acid. An important class of plastics ("casein plastics") are produced from it, and these plastics are converted into buttons, kitting-needles, *etc.* 36,000 litres of milk yield about 1 tonne of casein.

Cassowary, a genus of ostrich-like birds which, together with the emu, forms a separate order found only in Australasia. All species are black, with brightly coloured necks, and with a horny crest on the head. Noted for fierceness.

Castor-oil Plant (*Ricinus communis*), an African shrub now cultivated in most tropical countries. It has broad palmate leaves and bears a spiny fruit containing seeds which when pressed yield the well-known oil.

Cat, the general name for all members of the class *Felidae* of the carnivorous order, from the lion down to the domestic cat. The latter is believed to be descended from the European and African wild cats. Egypt is credited with being the first country in which the cat was domesticated.

Catabolism, Anabolism, are the terms used to describe the two types of metabolic pathway. Catabolic pathways are routes by which large organic molecules are broken up by enzymes into their simpler constituents *e.g.*, starch into glucose. The anabolic pathways are the routes by which complex molecules are synthesised from simple sub-units, *e.g.*, proteins from amino acids.

Catalyst. A substance which alters the rate of reaction without itself being chemically changed. Various aluminium and titanium compounds are catalysts in the formation of polythene from ethylene. Palladium catalyses the reaction of hydrogen with oxygen (hence its use in gas lighters). Enzymes in the body hasten the breakdown of carbohydrates and proteins by catalytic action. *See* **F26.**

Cataracts are gigantic waterfalls. The most famous are those of Niagara in North America, the Orinoco in South America, the Victoria Falls on the Zambesi in Africa, and the Falls of the Rhine at Schaffhausen.

Catechism, an elementary book of principles in any science or art, but more particularly in religion, in the form of questions and answers. There is a great variety of these, including the Lutheran, prepared by Luther in 1529, Calvin's Geneva (in 1536), and the Anglican, in the Book of Common Prayer.

Caterpillar, the larva of a butterfly or moth, worm-like in its segmented body, with 3 pairs of jointed true legs, often curiously marked and coloured, and frequently more or less hairy.

Cathedral, the chief church of a diocese, so called from its containing a Bishop's seat, or episcopal chair. The town in which it is situated is a cathedral city. Some celebrated cathedrals are St. John Lateran of Rome, Notre Dame of Paris, the cathedrals of Cologne and Milan, St. Paul's in London, Canterbury Cathedral, York Minster, and the cathedrals of Durham, Bristol, Gloucester, Peterborough, Exeter, Liverpool, and Coventry (destroyed by bombs, now rebuilt).

Cat's eye, a kind of quartz, much valued as a gem, opalescent, and of various shades.

Cavalier, a name adopted during the troubles of the Civil War to designate the Royalist party; it is also used generally in reference to a knightly, gallant or imperious personage.

Caves, natural hollow places in the earth, frequently found in Carboniferous limestone areas. The underground caves are formed by the action of rainwater carrying carbon dioxide, a dilute acid which slowly attacks the limestone rocks. The main caves in the British Isles are in the Mendips, Derbyshire, Yorkshire, S. Wales and in County Clare. Many British inland caves are thought to have been formed at the end of the Ice Age when the water table rose. The scientific study of caves is known as spelaeology.

Caviar. *See under* **Sturgeon.**

Cedar, a dark-leaved, cone-bearing, horizontal-branched evergreen tree that grows to a considerable height and girth, the best known species in Britain being the Cedar of Lebanon, which was introduced in the 17th cent.

Celluloid, one of the first synthetic thermoplastic materials, discovered by Alexander Parkes in 1865 when he was attempting to produce synthetic horn. It is made by treating cellulose nitrate with camphor and alcohol. Photographic film is made of a similar, but less-inflammable material, formed by the use of cellulose acetate instead of the nitrate.

Cellulose, a carbohydrate, and a constituent of nearly all plants. Cellulose occurs in an almost pure state in the fibres of linen (flax), absorbent cotton, jute, and filter-paper (used in laboratories).

Celsius was an 18th cent. Swedish scientist (**B13**) after whom the modern Celsius temperature scale is named. Since 1954, °C stands for "degree Celsius" instead of "degree Centigrade" but this is only a change in name. Both symbols refer to the temperature scale which calls the melting point of ice 0°C and the boiling point of water at one atmosphere pressure 100°C. *See* **Absolute Temperature.**

Celts, an ancient race found late in the third millennium B.C. in S.W. Germany, united by a common language and culture, who spread westward into Spain, northward into Britain, eastward to the Black Sea, reaching Galatia in Asia Minor. The "La Tène" iron-age Celts invaded Britain *c.* 250 B.C. After Britain was conquered by the Romans and invaded by the Angles and Saxons there remained as areas of Celtic speech only Wales (Brythonic speakers), Ireland, Scotland, the Isle of Man (Gaelic speakers), and in Cornwall. The late Celtic period in Britain produced a distinctive Christian art (*e.g.*, the Lindisfarne Gospel *c,* 700, and the Irish Book of Kells, dating from about the same time). Surviving Celtic languages are Welsh, Irish, Breton, Scots Gaelic and a tiny Cornish tradition. Manx Gaelic is on the point of extinction. Modern research is shedding new light on the emergence of "Celtic" civilisations.

Census. *See* **K2.**

Centrifuge, a machine which produces large accelerations by utilising the radial force caused by rotating a body about a fixed centre. Centrifuges have found extensive application in modern science. They can be used for the separation of one size of particle from another in biochemistry or in the training of astronauts where the accelerations occurring during rocket lift off can be simulated in a centrifuge on the ground.

Ceramics, are substances in which a combination of one or more metals with oxygen confers special and valuable properties. These include hardness, and resistance to heat and chemicals. Ceramic comes from the Greeek word for pottery, and pottery materials of mud and clay were probably the first man-made ceramics. Nowadays the range is enormous and growing; apart from all the pottery materials, there are firebricks, gems, glasses, concretes, nuclear reactor fuel elements, special materials for electronic devices, coloured pigments, electrical insulators, abrasives, and many other things. The scientific study of ceramics is part of materials science (*see* **Materials Science**). The need to design ceramic objects has inspired great art, and the production of ceramics has become a major industry.

Cerium, a scarce metallic element, no. 58, symbol Ce, discovered by Berzelius in 1803. A mixture of cerium and thorium nitrates is used in the manufacture of gas mantles, which owe their incandescent property to the deposit of cerium and thorium oxide with which they are coated.

Cern, French acronym for the European Laboratory for Particle Physics in Geneva. In 1989, the Large Electron Positron collider (LEP) was opened there. It recreates the swirl of matter just after the "Big Bang" which scientists believe created the universe 15 billion years ago.

Chain reaction. *See* **F13(1).**

Chalcedony, a mixture of crystalline silica and amorphous hydrated silica, *i.e.*, of quartz and opal. It has a waxy lustre, and is much used by jewellers for necklaces, bracelets, etc. Commonly it is white or creamy. Its bright orange-red variety is called carnelian; its brown variety, sard. Chrysoprase, plasma, bloodstone are varieties which are respectively pale apple-green, dark leek-green, green with red spots.

Chalk, a white limestone, calcium carbonate, found in the Upper Cretaceous deposits (formed from the shells of minute marine organisms). As chalk is porous, few streams form on its surface and consequently it is eroded slowly, although generally speaking it is a soft rock. Its juxtaposition with soft impervious clay in some areas results in its forming steep ridges known as escarpments, *e.g.*, N. and S. Downs and Chilterns. In contrast to the dry upland surfaces of chalk, lower levels are frequently saturated with water which subsequently emerges as springs.

Chamberlain, Lord, the senior officer of The Royal Household who is responsible for all ceremonial within the palace (levées, courts, garden parties, entertainment of foreign royalties and heads of state) but not the coronation or state opening of parliament. He is also in charge of appointments to The Royal Household. His office as censor of plays was abolished in 1968.

Chamberlain, Lord Great, one of the great officers of state whose duties are now mainly ceremonial. He attends the monarch at the state opening of parliament and at the coronation and is custodian of the Palace of Westminster (Houses of Parliament). The office is hereditary, dating from Norman times, and is held for one reign in turn by the descendants of the De Veres, Earls of Oxford.

Chameleon, a family of lizards with numerous species. Their ability to change colour is well known, but exaggerated, and is due to the movement of pigment cells beneath the skin. They are slow in movement, arboreal, and mainly insectivorous. Found in Africa, India, Sri Lanka, Madagascar and Arabia.

Chamois, a species of antelope, native of Western Europe and Asia. About the size of a goat, it lives in mountainous regions, and possesses wonderful leaping power, so that it is very difficult to capture. Its flesh is much esteemed, and from its skin chamois leather is made, although today sheep and goat skins are usually substituted. The mating season is October–November and the fawns are born in May or June. Live to be 20–25 years old.

Channel Tunnel, a scheme to bore a tunnel through 32–48 km of chalk under the sea between Dover and Calais has been a subject for discussion ever since Albert Mathieu first conceived the idea as a practical possibility in 1802. In the 1830s proposals for a bridge were made. In

the 1980s plans for a cross channel fixed link began to surface again.

The announcement in January 1986 of the intention by Britain and France to construct a 31-mile tunnel under the Channel between Cheriton, Kent and Frethun in northern France brought the idea of a Channel Tunnel very close to realisation. According to the original plans, by May 1993 a direct "fixed link" would be ready for travellers. Delays were to put back this date. The tunnel (which is the longest underwater tunnel in the world) was officially opened on 6 May 1994, but fare paying passenger services did not start until 14 November 1994. The tunnel carried 20 million passengers in 1998.

Chapel Royal, the church dedicated to the use of the Sovereign and Court. There are, among others, chapels royal at St. James's Palace, Buckingham Palace, Windsor, Hampton Court, the Tower, and Holyrood. *See also* **E4(2).**

Charcoal, a term applied to wood that has been subjected to a process of slow smothered combustion. More generally it refers to the carbonaceous remains of vegetable, animal, or combustible mineral substances submitted to a similar process. Charcoal from special woods (in particular buckthorn) is used in making gunpowder. Bone charcoal finds use in sugar refining, as it removes dark colouring matter present in the crude syrup.

Charter 88, pressure group working for major constitutional reform, including a Bill of Rights, fair electoral system, democratic Upper House *etc.* Many of its proposals are the subject of proposed legislation by the current Labour Government.

Chasuble, a sleeveless vestment worn by ecclesiastics over the alb during the celebration of Mass (to symbolise the seamless coat of Christ).

Cheese, an article of food made from the curd of milk, which is separated from the whey and pressed in moulds and gradually dried. There are about 500 varieties differing with method of preparation and quality of milk. They used to be made in the regions after which they are named but nowadays many of them are massproduced, *e.g.*, Cheddar is made not only in all parts of Britain but in Canada, New Zealand, Australia, Holland and the USA. Cheeses may be divided into 3 main classes: (1) soft, *e.g.*, Camembert, Cambridge, l'Evêque; (2) blue-veined, *e.g.*, Stilton, Gorgonzola, Roquefort (made from ewe's milk), (3) hard-pressed, *e.g.*, Cheddar, Cheshire, Gruyère, Parmesan, Gouda.

Cheetah or "hunting leopard", the large spotted cat of Africa and Southern Asia, the swiftest four-footed animal alive. In the 1990s cheetah numbers have declined rapidly.

Chemical Warfare. This term is usually restricted to mean the use in war of anti-personnel gases, aerosols and smokes, although explosives, napalm, herbicides and defoliants are also chemical agents that are used in war. Poison gas was first used on a large scale in the first world war; over 100,000 fatalities resulted from the use of principally chlorine, phosgene and mustard gas. Worldwide revulsion at the hideous effects of chemical weapons and their potential as indiscriminate weapons of mass destruction resulted in the Geneva Protocol of 1925 which prohibited the use of both chemical and bacteriological weapons. It has now been ratified by over 90 nations including all the major powers (although Japan and America are only recent signatories). The Protocol has been generally well observed although notable violations have been by the Italians in Abyssinia (1935–6), the Japanese in China during the second world war (when over 100,000 were killed in Zhejiang Province), the Americans in S.E. Asia in the 1960s and Iraq (against the Kurds in the 1980s).

Under the 1993 Chemical Weapons Convention (in force since 1997) signatories are obliged to remove chemical weapons left in other countries.

Chemistry is the science of the elements and their compounds. It is concerned with the laws of their combination and behaviour under various conditions. It had its roots in alchemy and has gradually developed into a science of vast magnitude and importance. Organic chemistry deals with the chemistry of the compounds of carbon; inorganic chemistry is concerned with the chemistry of the elements; physical chemistry is concerned with the study of chemical reactions and with the theories and laws of chemistry. See **F23–8.**

Chernobyl Disaster Site in the Ukraine of 1986 Soviet nuclear disaster, which caused major radioactive fallout across many countries. The scale of the disaster was kept from the Russian people.

Chestnut, the fruit of trees of the genus *Castanea*, members of the family *Fagaceae*. *C. sativa* is the sweet or Spanish chestnut, *C. dentata* the American chestnut and *C. crenata* the Japanese chestnut. The nut is edible. The wood is used in carpentry and fencing. See also **Horse Chestnut.**

Chiaroscuro, a term used in painting to denote the disposition of light and shade. Rembrandt is unrivalled as a painter for his contrasts of light and shadows.

Children Act (1989) was the outcome of numerous child-abuse scandals (*e.g.* Cleveland). It has two main elements, namely parents' rights and responsibilities and children's rights and welfare. The child's welfare is of paramount concern.

Chiltern Hundreds, three hundreds—Stoke, Burnham and Desborough—the stewardship of which is now a nominal office under the Chancellor of the Exchequer. Since about 1750 the nomination to it has been used as a method of enabling a member of Parliament to resign his seat on the plea that he holds an office of honour and profit under the crown. An alternate symbolic post for an M.P. giving up his seat is the stewardship of the Manor of Northstead in Yorkshire.

Chimpanzee, a large anthropoid ape, a native of tropical Africa, of a dark brown colour, with arms reaching to the knee, and capable of walking upright. Its brain is about a third of the weight of the human brain, but is anatomically similar. The animal has considerable intelligence and powers of learning. The AIDS virus is believed to have come from chimpanzees.

Chinchilla, a South American burrowing rodent. Grey in colour, and white underneath.

Chippendale Furniture was introduced in the reign of George I by Thomas Chippendale, a cabinetmaker from Yorkshire who migrated to London and set up for himself in St. Martin's Lane, Charing Cross. He was fonder of inventing designs for furniture than of making it, and in 1752 published a book of patterns; the London furniture-makers of the day soon began to model their work upon it.

Chivalry an international brotherhood of knights formed primarily during the 13th cent. to fight against the infidels in the Crusades. For the French the major battle was against the Moslems in the Holy Land and North Africa, the Spaniards fought the same enemy in their own country, and the Germans were concerned with the heathen of Baltic lands, but Chaucer's "very perfect gentle knight" had fought in all these areas. One did not easily become a knight who had to be of noble birth and then pass through a period of probation, beginning as a boy page in the castle of some great lord, serving his elders and betters humbly while he was taught good manners, singing, playing musical instruments, and the composition of verse. Probably he learned Latin, but he certainly learned French, which was the international language of knights as Latin was of scholars. At fourteen he became a squire and learned to fight with sword, battle-axe and lance, and to endure conditions of hard living while carrying out his duties of waiting on his lord, looking after his horses, and in time accompanying him in battle. Only if he showed himself suitable was he finally knighted by a stroke of the hand or sword on the shoulder from the king or lord. Knighthood was an international order and had its special code of behaviour; to honour one's sworn word, to protect the weak, to respect women, and defend the Faith.

Chlorine, a gaseous element, no. 17, symbol Cl, of the halogen family, first isolated in 1774 by Scheele by the action of manganese dioxide in hydrochloric acid. It unites easily with many other elements, the compounds resulting being termed chlorides. The gaseous element is greenish-white, with a pungent odour. It is a suffocating gas, injuring the lungs at a concentration as low as 1 part in 50,000, and was used during the first world war as a poison gas. Has a powerful bleaching action, usually being used in form of bleaching powder, made by combining lime and chlorine.

Chloroform, a volatile colourless liquid, compounded of carbon, hydrogen, and chlorine. It is a powerful solvent, not naturally occurring but synthesised on a large scale. When the vapour is inhaled it produces unconsciousness and insensibility to pain. It owes its discovery to Liebig, and its first application for medical purposes to Sir James Young Simpson.

Chlorophyll, the green pigment contained in the leaves of plants, first discovered by P. J. Pelletier (1788–1829) and J. B. Caventou (1795–1877) in 1818. Enables the plant to absorb sunlight and so to build up sugar. The total synthesis of chlorophyll was reported in 1960 by Prof. R. B. Woodward. This was an outstanding achievement. See **Photosynthesis, F32(1).**

Chouans, the name given to the band of peasants, mainly smugglers and dealers in contraband salt, who rose in revolt in the west of France in 1793 and joined the royalists of La Vendée. Balzac gives a picture of the people and the country in which they operated in his novel *Les Chouans*. They used the hoot of an owl as a signal—hence the name.

Chough, a member of the crow family, of glossy blue-green-black plumage, whose long curved bill and legs are coral red. It used to be abundant on the cliffs of Cornwall, but its haunts are now restricted to the rocky outcrops of the western coasts and in the mountains near by. It nests in cleft rocks and caves. The Alpine chough with yellow bill inhabits the mountainous districts of Europe and Asia and is not found in Britain.

Christmas means "mass of Christ" from the old English *Cristes maesse*, which is celebrated by the Western church on 25 December. The actual day on which Christ was born is not known and there is some uncertainty about the year. 25 December as the day of Nativity was not generally observed until the 5th cent. A.D., though, as the winter solstice, it had long been observed as a pagan festival of *sol invictus* (unconquered sun). The first Christmas card dates from about 1843 and the Christmas tree, of pagan origin, was introduced into England from Germany where it had been a tradition since the Middle Ages. Santa Claus is a corruption of Santa Nikolaus (St. Nicholas) patron saint of children, whose feast day is on 6 December.

Chromium, a very hard, bluish-white metal element, no. 24, symbol Cr, melting at very high temperature (above 1,900°C). Its chief ore is chromite or chrome iron-ore (ferrous chromite). "Ferro-chrome" is produced by heating chromite and anthracite in an electric furnace, and chrome steels are prepared by adding the pre-calculated amount of ferro-chrome to melted steel. Best known chrome steel is stainless steel first made by Brearley in 1912 and since then developed greatly at Sheffield. A typical formula is 18 per cent. chromium, 8 per cent. nickel, 74 per cent. iron. Equally important are Stellite alloys, containing chromium, cobalt, tungsten (or molybdenum), which have made possible modern high-speed cutting tools. Dies used in manufacture of plastics are commonly of chrome steel. The elementary metal finds little use alone except in chromium-plating for motor cars, *etc.*

Chromosomes, the structures contained within the nucleus of every animal and plant cell by which genetic information is transmitted. The chromosome number in somatic (body) cells is constant for each species of plant and animal, *e.g.*, man (46), cat (38), mouse (40) honey bee (16), fruit fly *Drosophila* (8), potato (48). Chromosomes are long molecules composed of deoxyribonucleoproteins (*i.e.*, proteins and DNA). Human chromosomes have been the subject of much recent research since it has been found that certain disorders are associated with chromosomal aberration, *e.g.*, in Mongolism an extra chromosome is present. In 1997 American scientists created the first artificial human chromosomes See also **Genes, Chromosome Theory (F31), Cell Division (F33(2)).**

Church Commissioners. The Church Commissioners were established in 1948 by the amalgamation of Queen Anne's Bounty (established 1704) and the Ecclesiastical Commissioners (established 1836) to administer Church revenues and to manage Church property.

Cid, El, a famous Spanish hero of the 11th cent., Don Rodrigo Diaz de Vivar, also called Cid Campeador, whose exploits, against Christians and Moors alike, are celebrated in poem and play.

Cilia, minute hair-like projections on the surface of some cells, which beat together in wavelike movements like the wind over a corn-field. These movements can be used as a means of locomotion as in the aquatic organism paramecium. Cilia are also found on the outer layers of the human trachea where they waft particles upwards to the throat, thus protecting the lungs. See **F37, Index to Section P** *and also* **Flagella.**

Cinque Ports, a number of seaport towns on the coast of Kent and Sussex, originally five; Hastings, New Romney, Hythe, Dover and Sandwich. Winchelsea and Rye were added later. These ports were required to furnish a certain number of ships, ready for service, and in return they were granted many privileges. The official residence of the Lord Warden is Walmer Castle, near Dover. The holder of the office is the Queen Mother, the first-ever woman to be appointed.

Cistercians, an order of monks and nuns taking their names from Citeaux, near Dijon, where their first monastery was established in 1098. The order was noted for the severity of its rule. They were famous agriculturists. The habit is white, with a black cowl or hood.

City Technology Colleges (CTCs), new concept of educational institute introduced by the Conservative Government after 1987. The first three to be opened were at Solihull, Nottingham and Middlesbrough.

Civil List is the estimate of the expenses to be incurred by the Sovereign in conducting her official business and engagements and those of the members of her family during each year. The amount is granted by Parliament upon the recommendation of a Select Committee and has to be settled afresh in the first six months of a new reign. The Civil List of Queen Victoria was £385,000; Edward VII and George V, £470,000; Edward VIII and George VI, £410,000; Elizabeth II £475,000. In 1990, a fixed 10-year Civil List arrangement was agreed for all the Royal Family. This was changed in 1992 so that only the Queen (£7·9m), the Queen Mother (£643,000) and Prince Philip (£359,000) now receive Civil List payments.

The Prince of Wales does not receive a Civil List payment but derives his revenue from the Duchy of Cornwall. Other resources available to the Queen include (1) the sums which Parliament votes to government departments each year, *e.g.*, upkeep of palaces (Department of the Environment) and the royal flight (Ministry of Defence); (2) privy purse (revenues of the Duchy of Lancaster); (3) personal fortune, the size of which is not disclosed. In 1992 the Queen agreed to pay tax on her private income and meet the working expenses of most junior members of the Royal Family. The system under which annual payments are made by the Government to the Queen was changed by the Civil List Act 1975; payments are now included in the annual estimates in the same way as the expenditure of a government department, and subject to scrutiny in the House of Commons.

Cleopatra's Needle on the Thames Embankment is of the time of Tuthmosis III (1500–1450 B.C.). The monolith had nothing to do with Cleopatra, as it only came to Alexandria after her death. It was first erected at the Biblical On (Greek Heliopolis), sacred City of the Sun. It was presented to the British Government by Mehemet Ali in 1819, but not brought to this country until 1878. Weight *c.* 183 tonnes; height, 20·8 m. Pollution has now changed its former rose-red granite to a grubby grey.

Climate has been defined by Professor H. H. Lamb as the total experience of the weather at any place over some specific period of time. Not only averages but extremes of temperature, variation of humidity, duration of sunshine and cloud cover, amount of rainfall and frequency of snow, frost, gales, etc., are amongst the data normally investigated. The interiors of great land masses are characterised by large ranges of temperature and low rainfall (continental climate), while proximity to oceans has an ameliorating effect with increase in rainfall (oceanic climate). Presence of mountain ranges and lakes and configuration generally produce local modifications of climate, also apparent between the centre and the outlying suburbs of a city. Latitude introduces zones of climate, *e.g.*, tropical rain, subtropical steppe and desert, temperate rain and polar. The climate is always changing in greater or less degree. Every year, every decade, every century brings a somewhat different experience. The tendency between 1880 and 1940 was for most parts of the world to become warmer. See **L132–133** for the current debate.

Clock, a device for measuring the passage of time. The earliest timekeeper was the shadow-clock, a primitive form of sundial, used in Ancient Egypt about 1500 B.C. To find the time at night the water clock or clepsydra was used. The sand-glass dates from the 15th cent. No one knows when the first mechanical clocks were invented, but it is known that a complicated mechanical clock driven by water and controlled by a weighbridge escarpment was built in Peking in 1090. The Dover Clock in the Science Museum is not the earliest surviving clock in England, as was once believed, but early 17th cent. The Salisbury Cathedral clock dates from 1386 and that of Wells Cathedral from 1392. The pendulum clock was invented by the Dutch scientist Christiaan Huygens (1625–95). The first watches were made in Nuremberg shortly after 1500. The marine chronometer is a high-precision timepiece used at sea for giving Greenwich mean time. The quartz-crystal clocks are accurate to one thousandth of a second a day, and the improved atomic clock, developed at the British National Physical Laboratory, which makes use of the natural vibrations of the caesium atom, is an almost absolute measure of time. Its accuracy of 1 sec. in 300 years has been improved to 1 sec. in 1,000 years.

Cloud Chamber, an apparatus invented by C. T. R. Wilson in which the tracks of atomic particles can be made visible. Just as the vapour trails tell of the track of an invisible aircraft high up in the air, so the vapour trails of an unseeable particle can tell of its behaviour. The rays under investigation pass through a chamber containing a gas, *e.g.*, air thoroughly cleansed of dust, supersaturated with water, or alcohol-vapour. As the particle passes through it forms a track of tiny water droplets which can be photographed. After a long and honourable history this wonderful instrument is now virtually obsolete. A later ingenious device for tracking fast fundamental particles is the Bubble chamber *(q.v.).*

Clouds are formed by the cooling of moist air, the type depending on the way the air cools and the height at which condensation occurs. There are three main classes: (1) high cloud (about 6,100 m)—cirrus (delicate and fibrous), cirrostratus (thin white veil), and cirrocumulus (delicately rippled) consisting of ice crystals; (2) medium cloud (above 2,100 m)—altostratus (dense, greyish veil) and altocumulus (broken flattened cloudlets)—chiefly water particles, often supercooled; (3) low cloud (from near ground to 2,100 m)—cumulus (fair weather, broken, dome-topped), cumulominbus (heavy, towering to great heights), stratocumulus (layer of globular masses or rolls), stratus (like fog but off the ground), nimbostratus (low, rainy cloud). The highest clouds of all, and the rarest, are the noctilucent, seen only on summer nights in high latitudes. They form at about 80 km above the earth and consist of ice-coated dust from meteors.

Clover, plants of the *Trifolium* genus, family *Leguminosae,* with about 250 species. These are "nitrogen fixing" plants and include red clover, white clover, alsike clover and crimson clover. They are of great importance in agriculture because in a good pasture they supply directly or indirectly most of the protein available to the animals. Seed of "wild white" clover has been accepted since about 1939 as the indispensable plant of good United Kingdom grassland, largely through the efforts of pioneers like D. A. Gilchrist (1859–1927).

Coal. Until recently the most important single fuel has been coal. It is a mineral of organic origin, formed from the remains of vegetation which over millions of years has changed to coal by the effects of heat and pressure from overlying rock or water. All coal contains moisture, inflammable volatiles, mineral impurities (some of which remain as coal ash after the coal is burnt), and fixed carbon (the coke that is left after the volatiles have been driven off). The relative proportions vary—from Anthracite, a hard coal containing the highest proportion of fixed carbon, to Lignite or brown coal which is little more than a hard peat. World reserves of bituminous coal have been estimated at 7.5×10^{12} tonnes. If one adds the reserves of brown coal and lignite, this figure is increased by about 15 per cent. The proportion of the reserves that could be economically recovered varies from country to country and estimates vary from 50 to 100 per cent of the reserves. The reserves are highly localised—over half being located in the former Soviet Union. In the United Kingdom coal has formed the basis of past industrial prosperity. Peak output occurred in 1913 when 290 million tonnes were mined one third of which was exported. At the end of the second world war production had fallen to 186 million tonnes and was far below demand. In 1947 the British coal industry was brought under public ownership and all its assets were vested in the National Coal Board. During the next ten years great efforts were made to increase coal output but, quite suddenly in 1956, demand for coal fell as oil became a popular fuel. The fall in demand was accompanied by increasing productivity, both mines and miners having been cut in their numbers by over half. Then as a result of the high cost of oil in 1973 came expansion of the industry. From 1984 the coal industry faced a bitter strike over plans to make large-scale pit closures. The defeat of the miners weakened the NUM and its leader, Arthur Scargill. The Government decision (in 1992) to close many of the remaining collieries and to privatise the industry created a bitter political controversy. By the beginning of 1995 the last pits had been privatised and the workforce reduced to 10,000 by 1999. Reduced demand for coal has threatened further job losses.

Coat of Arms, in heraldry, a device containing a family's armorial bearings. In mediaeval times the coat upon which such device was embroidered; knights wore it over their armour.

Cobalt, element no. 27, symbol Co, a white metal melting at 1490°C. Two main ores are *cobalt glance* (in which the element is combined with arsenic and sulphur) and *smaltite* (cobalt arsenide). The principal sources are Ontario and Zaïre. Various cobalt alloys are important, *e.g.*, stellite, ferrocobalt and carboloy. Its monoxide is an important colouring medium, and is used for colouring glass and porcelain blue.

Cobra, hooded and very venomous snakes. The best known species are the Indian Cobra, the Egyptian Cobra, and the Black-necked Cobra. Their food consists chiefly of small rodents. The King Cobra is almost exclusively a snake-eater. "Spitting" Cobras (or Ringhals) of S. Africa are a related genus, capable of spitting their venom several yards. The King Cobra possesses enough venom to kill 100 people.

Coca, a S. American shrub, *Erythroxylon coca*, also cultivated in Java. The leaves yield cocaine, classified as a dangerous drug. When the local people chew the leaves they are enabled to withstand hunger and fatigue, as cocaine acts both as a mental stimulant and as an anaesthetic on the mucous lining of the stomach.

Cochineal *or* **Carmine,** a dyestuff consisting of the dried bodies of the female scale insect (*Dactylopius coccus*) which feeds on cacti. Of ancient origin, the dye was well known to the Aztecs, and was used widely in the Middle Ages. The scarlet tunics worn by the English during the Napoleonic wars owed their colour to carmine.

Cockatoo, a member of the parrot family, bearing a crest of feathers on the head, native to Australia and adjacent regions. Predominant colour is white tinged with yellow or scarlet while some species have dark plumage. The cockatoo of New Guniea is slaty black with pale red cheeks and can crack Kanary nuts which require a hammer to break them open.

Cockchafer (*Melolontha*), one of the most destructive of beetles, the larvae feeding on roots.

It is about 2·5 cm in length, of a brownish colour, and emits a loud whirring sound when flying.

Cockle, the popular name of the bi-valve shellfish of the genus *Cardium*, found in sandy bays.

Cockroach, inaccurately called the "black beetle"; a pest of bakeries and kitchens. In Britain two species are commonly found; the Common Cockroach (*Blatta orientalis*), resident since the time of Elizabeth I, dark brown, about 2·5 cm long, with the wing covers long in the male and short in the female; and the German Cockroach (*Blatta germanica*), now the most common, half the size, dark yellow, with both sexes fully winged. All species have long antennae and flattened, leathery, shiny bodies. They are nocturnal and omnivorous.

Coconut Palm (*Cocos nucifera*), a tropical tree, growing to a height of 30 m, with a slender trunk surmounted by giant feather-like leaves. One of the most important sources of food and raw material for people living in the tropics. The juice of the fruit, or coconut, is drunk; the kernel is eaten fresh or dried to form copra, which yields animal feeding stuffs and oil, used in the manufacture of soap, margarine, cosmetics, synthetic rubber, *etc.*; leaves are used for thatching; leaf stalks for canes, fence posts, needles, *etc.*, and the trunk for houses and bridges. Main producing areas: Indonesia, Philippines, Malaysia, Sri Lanka and S. India.

Codes, a term used to designate a system of laws properly classified. The Code of Hammurabi, king of Babylon, *c.* 1751 B.C., had extensive influence over a long period. The Romans formulated several codes of historic importance including the Theodosian Code which summarised the Roman laws from the time of Constantine to 438 A.D. The final codification was made under order of the Emperor Justinian by his chief minister Tribonian and published in 529 with a new edition in 534. The most important of modern codes is the *Code Napoléon*, compiled between 1803 and 1810, and still in force. It has been used as an example for the codification of the laws of a number of countries from America to Japan. Under Frederick the Great the law of Prussia was codified. English law has never been codified, although the law on certain subjects has been gathered up into a single statute. The Law Commission Act, 1965, sought to consolidate and codify the law.

Codex, a manuscript volume of the Scriptures comprising the Sinaiaticus of the 4th cent., the Vatican codex of the same period, the Alexandrine codex of the 5th cent., and others. The British Museum, in 1933, purchased the *Codex Sinaiticus* from the Soviet Government for £100,000. The Sinaiaticus was written on 347 vellum leaves some fifteen to sixteen hundred years ago and the binding into 2 volumes was completed by Douglas Cockerill and his son in 1936. It was sold in 1981 for $5·2 million.

Coelacanth, a deeply primitive fish living off the Comoros Islands (and also off Indonesia).

Coffee, a shrub found originally in Arabia and Ethiopia, but now extensively grown in Brazil, Colombia, Ivory Coast, Uganda, Angola and Central America. It yields a seed or berry which after undergoing the necessary preparation, is ground and used in most countries as a breakfast beverage. The best coffee is the Mocha, an Arabian variety. The stimulating effect of coffee is due to the caffeine, which is also present in tea. The beverage was introduced into Europe in the 17th cent., and the first London coffee shop was opened in 1652.

Coinage, *see* **Currency, L31.**

Coke is the solid residue remaining when coal is carbonised and nearly all the volatile constituents have been driven off. Used as fuel, and as an agent for reducing metallic oxides to metals, *e.g.*, iron ore to iron, in making steel.

Colorado Beetle, a serious pest of potato crops. Both adults and larvae feed on the foliage where the orange eggs are laid. The grub is reddish, with two rows of small black spots on each side. The adults are about 1·2 cm long with yellow and black striped wing cases. The beetle is avoided by birds because of its nasty taste, and is controlled by arsenical sprays.

Colosseum, the name of the Flavian amphitheatre at Rome, begun by Vespasian and finished by

Titus A.D. 80. In general outline it still remains one of the most magnificent ruins in the world. In the arena the famous gladiatorial displays and mimic naval battles used to be given, and about 50,000 spectators could be accommodated.

Colossus is the name which the ancients gave to any statue of gigantic size. The Colossus at Rhodes, which was a bronze statue of the sun god, Helios, was the most famous, and reckoned among the seven wonders of the world. It stood over 30 m high at the mouth of the harbour. There is no truth in the legend that ships could pass between its legs. It fell in an earthquake in 224 B.C.

Colugo, also known as "flying lemur," caguan or kubuk, a remarkable mammal which may be regarded as an aberrant insectivore or an aberrant form of the earliest ancestor of the bats. It has nothing to do with lemurs. There are two genera, one inhabiting the Philippines and one inhabiting Malaya. They have a parachute-like membrane which covers them from the neck to the tip of the tail, by means of which they can glide from treetop to ground.

Column, in architecture, is an upright solid body serving as a support or decoration to a building. Columns consist of a pedestal, a shaft, and a capital, over which the supported entablature rises. They are named according to the styles of architecture of which they form part, e.g. Doric, Tuscan, Ionic, Corinthian or Composite .

Comets are celestial bodies which generally move about the solar system in elongated elliptical or nearly parabolic orbits. Most comets are in the latter category, having extremely long orbital periods, up to millions of years, and have therefore only been seen once in recorded history. They spend most of their lifetimes at extremely large distances from the sun, far outside Pluto's orbit. Those in elliptical orbits appear periodically and a few have been observed regularly. Halley's comet, named after Edmund Halley, who first correctly predicted that this comet would reappear in 1758, was first observed in Roman times and is one of the brightest of the periodic comets. The nucleus of a comet, which appears as a faint star when the comet is very far from the sun, is believed to be a frozen mixture of dust and materials called "ices"—CO_2, H_2O, NH_3 and CH_4, frozen at the low temperatures in the outer solar system. Approaching the sun, the comet is heated by sunlight and the surface "ices" are first vaporised and later photo-dissociated and ionised by sunlight, also freeing the surface dust. The dust, gases and ions produce the fuzzy appearance of the coma of the comet. Under the influence of sunlight acting on dust, and the solar wind and interplanetary field acting on the ions, the cometary tail (often multiple) is produced. This may stretch up to 200 million km, pointing away from the sun. Donati's comet (1858) was possibly the most spectacular of all and was visible even in daylight. Kohoutek's comet (1975) was the first to be observed from space, by the American Skylab and Russian Soyuz. Images from the Hubble space telescope suggest there are at least 200 million comets orbiting the Sun in a belt that lies beyond the orbit of Neptune and engulfs that of Pluto. A very spectacular comet appearance in 1997 was comet Hale-Bopp (which was last visible from Earth c. 2600 B.C. The Rosetta space mission (scheduled for 2003) is planned to land on the comet Wirtanen in 2011. The Stardust space probe, launched in 1999, aims to collect dust from the comet Wild-2 in 2004. See also **F4**(1).

Commons are the remnants of the mediaeval open fields round villages in which the villagers had rights in common, e.g., (i) estover—the right of taking wood for house building or firewood; (ii) pasture—the right of grazing beasts; (iii) turbary—the right of digging turf; (iv) piscary—the right to fish. Many of these common lands were enclosed during the agrarian revolution which went on steadily in England from the 15th cent. onwards, and with their enclosure common rights vanished. A Royal Commission on Common Land described the commons in 1965 as the "last reservoir of uncommitted land" which provide, as far as the public is concerned, by far the largest part of the accessible open spaces of the country. Under the Commons Registration Act, 1965, it was the duty of County Councils and County Borough Councils to make a register of all common land and all town and village greens in their areas.

Commons, House of, see **Section D.**

Commune of Paris has twice played a dramatic part in the history of France. In 1792 it was able, through its control of the administrative organisation of Paris, to override the National Assembly. In 1871, after the withdrawal of the Prussian troops, it tried to assert its authority. Public buildings were destroyed by members of the Commune and civil war raged during April and half May, but Government troops savagely suppressed the rising.

Community Charge, see **Poll Tax (L98).**

Compass or **Mariner's Compass.** It has been known since very early times that an iron needle, suspended freely to hang horizontally when not magnetised, comes to rest roughly along the geographical north–south line when magnetised. Further, it generally does not hang horizontally. This is the essential behaviour of the *compass,* a navigational instrument whose invention is obscure but which seems to have been known to the Chinese 4,500 years ago. That the behaviour of the compass shows the existence of a *magnetic field* associated with the Earth was first fully recognised by William Gilbert in 1600. Aircraft and ships now largely employ gyrostatic compasses which are not affected by electrical and magnetic disturbances. Sperry, Brown and Anschutz are three important types of gyroscopic compass.

Composite Materials, or more simply composites, are materials which derive useful properties by combining the virtues of two or more components. Combining clay with straw to make tougher bricks is an ancient example in which fibres (straw) are embedded in a matrix or body (the clay). A modern example is fibreglass in which glass fibres are embedded in a plastic matrix. Nature also uses composites as in bamboo in which a lignin matrix binds together the fibres of cellulose to make a light strong structure. Composites may contain flakes or particles embedded in the matrix instead of fibres—it depends on the application. Although the idea is not new composite technology has made rapid strides in the last few decades guided by scientific insight into the nature of solids and the origin of their stengths and weaknesses. The motivation had been that scientifically designed composites offer materials with exceptional strength/weight ratio, desirable magnetic properties and other technological advantages which meet the extreme demands of a variety of industries. For example, composite aluminium containing boron fibres or resin containing graphite fibres can have strength/weight ratios over twice that of highstrength solid aluminium. Composites of many kinds are now widespread in industrial use.

Computer, a technical device for accepting an input of information, processing this information according to some prescribed programme of operations and supplying an output of processed information. Many types of operation can be performed on many types of information and computers are now indispensable in science, business, warfare, government and other activities. Early thinkers in this field were Pascal (17th cent.), Babbage (19th cent.) and Turing (1930s), but electronic computers as we know them appeared during the second world war and the first commercial machine was on sale in 1950. See **Section V.**

Conclave, an assembly of Roman Catholic cardinals met together to elect a pope. The last Conclave was held in the Vatican in Oct. 1978, when Cardinal Wojtyla, the Archbishop of Cracow, was elected Pope John Paul II.

Concordat, an agreement of convention between the Pope and a secular government regarding ecclesiastical matters. The Concordat of Worms in 1122 between Calixtus II and the Emperor Henry V was famous as deciding a long struggle in regard to investiture. In 1801, Napoleon concluded a concordat with Pius VII defining the restored relations between the head of the Church and the French Roman Catholics.

Condor, a large eagle of brilliant black plumage with a circlet of white feathers round its neck.

It is a native of the Andes. There are two types of New World condor, the Andean and the Californian. Both are black, but the Andean condor has a pink head, the Californian a yellow head and red neck. They are among the rarest birds in the world.

Confederation is a free association of sovereign states united for some common purpose. It s to be distinguished from a Federation, which is a union of states with one central government, each state relinquishing its sovereignty, though retaining some independence in internal affairs.

Confucianism. *See* **Section J.**

Coniferae are cone-bearing trees, including firs, pines, cedars, cypresses, junipers, yews, etc., and are widely distributed in temperate regions.

Constellation, a grouping of stars that forms a pattern when seen from Earth. There are a total of 88 constellations in use on modern star charts, some of which are much larger than others. The stars within a particular constellation are not necessarily close to each other in space. In most cases they only appear close together due to their lying in more or less the same line of sight as seen from Earth.

Constitution, the fundamental organic law or principles of government of a nation, state, society, or other organisation, embodied in written documents, or implied in the institutions and customs of the country or society. The government of the USA, unlike Great Britain, works upon a written Constitution. It was framed when the USA came into existence as a sovereign body, when the Constitution built a republic out of a federation of thirteen states, based on representative government. The constitution was adopted in 1789, and its strength has been tested by the fact that, substantially unchanged, it is the groundwork for a federation which now comprises fifty states. *See also* **Section D.**

Continent, a word used in physical geography to denote the larger continuous land masses in contrast to the great oceans of the earth. They are: Eurasia (conventionally regarded as 2 continents, Europe and Asia), Africa, North America, South America, Australia and Antarctica. (Australasia is Australia, New Zealand and adjacent islands. Oceania is Australasia and the many islands of the S.W. Pacific.)

Continental Drift. The hypothesis of drifting continents is due to F. B. Taylor, an American geologist who published his theory in 1908, and to the Austrian meteorologist Alfred Wegener in 1910. The latter was impressed by the matching coasts of South America and Africa, which seemed to him to fit together like the pieces of a jigsaw puzzle. Since then many other people have taken up and developed the idea. Acccording to Wegener, at one time there were two primary super-continents. Laurasia and Gondwanaland. The one in the northern hemisphere consisted of North America, Europe, and the northern part of Asia. Its southern counterpart included Antarctica, Australia, India, Africa and South America. These super-continents broke up, and their various bits moved apart. In particular, the southern hemisphere continents drifted radially northwards away from the south pole, and the two Americas shifted westwards from Europe and Africa. What would have been the leading edges of the land masses on this hypothesis, are now heavily buckled up into mountain belts, such as the Cordillera and the Alpine-Himalayan chain. The resistance afforded to drifting by the strong ocean floors may well have been the cause of such structures. Despite the wealth of geological facts which have a bearing on the problem of continental drift, none of these has been able to decide the issue in a conclusive manner. Further studies of rock magnetism (*q.v.*) and of fossil climates should ultimately establish the concept of continental drift on a firm basis. *See also* **Earth, F8.**

Conurbation, a term used in reference to an extensive and continuous area of urban land-use. Conurbations are frequently formed by the physical coalescence of several formerly free-standing towns. They may themselves coalesce to form a higher order of physical urbanisation, known as a megalopolis.

Convention is an assembly of delegates, representa-tives, members of a party met to accomplish some specific civil, social, political, ecclesiastical or other important object.

Convention Parliaments, terms used to describe the Parliaments of 1660 (after the dissolution of the Long Parliament) and 1689, (summoned by William of Orange).

Convocation, an assembly called together to deliberate ecclesiastical affairs. In the Church of England the provinces of Canterbury and York each have their convocation. The term is also applied to assemblies of the graduates of certain universities.

Coot. A very widely distributed bird of the rail family and a common resident of the British Isles. The adult is black with a conspicuous white bald shield on the forehead and a white bill. The juvenile is brownish grey with whitish breast and throat. The coot flies heavily, but swims well. It dives frequently and can remain submerged for a considerable time. It is pugnacious and in winter gregarious. The food is chiefly vegetable. The large nest is usually built among aquatic vegetation and the young are fed by both parents. Another species, the Crested Coot, occurs in S. Europe.

Copper, one of the most familiar of metals, element no. 29, symbol Cu, used in ancient times as an alloy with tin in producing bronze, and preceding iron as an industrial material. Copper ores are most abundant in the USA, Chile, Canada, Zambia and Congo. All copper compounds are poisonous.

Copyright. Under the Copyright Act, 1956, copyright subsists in every original literary, dramatic musical, and artistic work if the author is a British subject or a citizen of the Republic of Ireland or resident in the United Kingdom, or if the work is first published in the United Kingdom. The Act provided that, except in certain special cases, the author of the work shall be the first owner of the copyright, and there are no formalities, such as registration or payment of fees, to be accomplished. Copyright includes the right to reproduce the work in any material form, to perform the work in public, or, if the work is unpublished, to publish the work. The Act also protected sound recordings, films and television and sound broadcasts. Literary, dramatic, musical and artistic works which enjoy the protection of the Act are automatically protected in those countries which are parties to the Berne Copyright Convention or the Universal Copyright Convention. In general, copyright in literary, dramatic, musical and artistic works is vested in the author for the period of his lifetime and 50 years following after which it passes into the public domain and becomes freely available to any who wish to make use of it. The Copyright Libraries, entitled to receive copies of books published in the United Kingdom are given under **Libraries.** The Berne Copyright Convention and the Universal Copyright Convention were revised at a diplomatic conference held in Paris in 1971. The effect of the revisions allows any national of a developing country to obtain, under certain conditions, a compulsory licence to translate and publish a copyright work for the purpose of teaching, scholarship and research, upon payment of compensation to the copyright owner of the original work. The Copyright Designs and Patents Act, 1988, updated the old law on copyright (and has itself been amended in the light of EU rulings).

Coral, an order of small marine animals closely related to the sea-anemone, but differing from it in their ability to develop a limy skeleton. They multiply sexually and by budding. The structure of the coral secretions assumes a variety of forms, fan-like, tree-like, mushroom shape, and so forth. Red coral (the skeleton of *Corallium rubrum*) is mainly obtained from the Mediterranean. The coral reefs of the Pacific and Indian Oceans are often many miles in extent. Living corals occur only in warm seas at about 23°C. Rising sea temperatures are now threatening many coral reefs.

Cordite, a smokeless explosive adopted for small arms and heavy artillery by the British Government in the naval and military services in 1889, and composed of 58 parts of nitro-glycerine, 37 of gun-cotton, and 5 of vaseline. It is a jelly or plastic dough, and used in the form of sticks. Invented by Sir Frederick Abel and Sir James Dewar in 1889.

Cork, the bark of a species of oak, *Quercus suber*, grown largely in the South of Europe and North America. The cork tree is said to yield bark every six to ten years for 150 years, and grows to a height of from 6–12 m. Its lightness, impermeability, and elasticity enable it to be used for a variety of commercial purposes, especially for stoppers of bottles.

Cormorant, a large, long-billed water-bird which captures fish by diving. The common cormorant has bronze-black plumage with white cheeks and sides and is found round the sea coasts of most parts of the world, including the British Isles. It nests in colonies on sea cliffs and rocky ledges. The Shag or Green Cormorant is a smaller bird with green-black plumage and a crest.

Corncrake. See Landrail.

Corn Laws were statutes intended for the benefit of British agriculture, and restricted import and export of grain. From the 14th to the mid-19th cent. such laws were in force, and were often of a stringent nature. They became so oppressive and caused corn to reach so high a price that the poorer classes were plunged into distress. A powerful anti-corn law agitation was organised of which Cobden, Bright and Villiers were the leaders, and Sir Robert Peel, in 1846, at the time of the Irish potato famine, carried through free trade. The repeal of the Corn Laws marked an important phase in the transformation of an agricultural to an industrial Britain.

Corona or **Solar Corona,** the outer atmosphere of the sun. This glows by virtue of light emitted by the sun and scattered by electrons and dust particles at various heights in the sun's atmosphere and also by light emitted from ionised atoms in the corona itself. Corona light is much fainter than the bright disc of the sun and is invisible against the normal blue of the sky. During total solar eclipses, the corona can be seen by the human eye as a faint glow extending irregularly outwards a few solar diameters from the sun. The sun's atmosphere extends much further than this but is invisible to the eye at large distances from the sun. The corona gases are thought to be very hot (millions of degrees) and in complex violent motion; the gross structure of the corona is connected with the sunspot cycle.

Cortes, the Parliaments of Spain and Portugal.

Cosmic Rays are a form of radiation coming from outer space, of deep penetrating power and of great scientific interest. The rays consist of extremely energetic atomic particles—protons, electrons and some heavier nucleons—travelling at speeds very close to that of light. A complex series of events result from their collision with the atmosphere, giving rise to showers of secondary high-energy particles containing many of those listed on **F16.** Cosmic rays are now investigated with instruments buried in deep mines, as well as those in satellites, and the great interest is because we now believe their origin to be in, or associated with, some of the most interesting objects in the universe—supernovae, neutron stars, pulsars and perhaps some gigantic galactic nuclei. See **F3(2).**

Cosmology is the science which studies the whole universe, its origin, its nature, its size, age and evolution. It is presently a very active science because of many new discoveries of radio astronomy and space astronomy (X-ray, ultraviolet and infra-red) of extremely distant and luminous objects whose radiation has taken many thousands of millions of years to reach us, and whose explanation is taxing many of the world's best theoretical scientists. See **F3–8.**

Cosmonaut, the Russian term for a space traveller.

Cotton, the name of a plant of several species bearing large yellow flowers with purple centres. These centres expand into pods, which at maturity burst and yield the white fibrous substances known as cotton. The raw cotton contains a large proportion of seeds which are removed by "ginning". Long before the Christian era, cotton had been grown and used with great skill in India to make fabrics. The industry was not introduced into England until the middle of the 17th cent. when Protestant refugees from Flanders came to settle in the

wool textile districts of East Anglia and Lancashire. With improvements in machinery and expansion of overseas trade in the 18th and 19th cent., Lancashire became the centre of the world's cotton industry but now man-made fibres have taken the place of cotton. The largest cotton producers in the world are the United States, China and Uzbekistan.

Coulomb, a unit of electric charge, named after the French naval engineer, Charles Augustin de Coulomb (1736–1806), equal to the quantity of electricity transferred in one second by a current of one ampere.

Council Tax. See **Section H.**

County. After the 1972 reorganisation of local government in the United Kingdom the distinction between *administrative* counties and *geographical* counties no longer existed. Certain geographical counties have disappeared (*e.g.,* Rutland and Pembroke), new counties have appeared (*e.g.,* Avon and Gwynedd), while former counties have been modified (*e.g.* Glamorgan and Yorkshire). In 1991 a new Local Government Commission was established to make proposals for the reform of local government. These proposals included the abolition of the counties of Avon, Cleveland and Humberside. See **D10.**

Coup d'État, a violent change in the government of a state carried out by force or illegally. Examples are the overthrow of the French Republic in 1851 by Louis Napoleon, who then became Emperor, and, since 1945, the military *coups* in the Middle East (*e.g.* Egypt in 1952, Iraq in 1958). The 1991 attempted *coup* in the Soviet Union helped precipitate the collapse of the USSR.

Court Leet, a court of record held annually before the steward of any particular manor or lordship; originally there was only one court for a manor, but in the time of Edward I it branched into two, the court baton and the court leet.

Coypu or **Nutria rat,** a large beaver-like rodent found in S. America; it became wild in E. Anglia, where it caused damage to dykes and crops, having escaped from farms where it is bred for its fur. Eradicated in E. Anglia by 1989.

Crane, a large, graceful wading-bird with elegant long legs and neck, greyish plumage, superficially resembling the heron and related to the bustard. They migrate in **V** or **W** formation and have trumpet-like voices. There are fourteen species, found in all continents except S. America, including the Crowned Crane with golden coronet and the Demoiselle with tuftlike crest of white feathers. The Common Crane nested in East Anglia in mediaeval times.

Credit is an advance of money or of goods or services in consideration of a promise of payment later. Trade credit is such an advance from trader to customer; bank credit is an advance of money by a bank to a client, whether a business firm or a private person, in consideration of an interest payment by the borrower.

Creed (Latin *credo* = I believe), a formal statement of belief. The three orthodox Christian creeds are the Apostles' Creed (a summary of their teaching), the Nicene Creed (drawn up by the Church Council at Nicaea in A.D. 325 to define its theological doctrines), and the Athanasian Creed (on the nature and divinity of Christ).

Cremation, the ancient custom, revived in modern times, of burning the dead. Cremation was first legalised in Great Britain in 1885 and the first crematorium opened at Woking in that year. Application for cremation must be accompanied by two medical certificates.

Creutzfeldt-Jakob Disease, See Mad Cow Disease, **L77.**

Cricket, a genus of insects of the grasshopper order which move by leaps. The male produces a chirping noise by rubbing its wing-covers together. Just as the males inherit the nerve machinery for emitting the song of the species, so the females receive and respond to that song and to no other.

Crimean War (1853–56). This war between Russia and the allied powers of Turkey, Britain, France and Sardinia, was connected with the Eastern Question (*q.v.*) and the desire of Russia for a port on the Mediterranean. Chief engagements were the Alma, Balaclava and Inkerman. Fighting virtually ceased with fall of Sevastopol in September 1855. The Treaty of Paris was signed 30 March 1856.

Criminal Justice Act. A controversial measure

whose main proposals limit a defendant's right to silence, gives powers to the police to establish a DNA database, extends offences for which 10-13 year olds can be given custodial offences *etc*.

Crinoids. *See* **Sea Lily (L109).**

Crocodiles and their allies (alligators, caimans and gavials) are the largest of modern reptiles. They are well equipped for a predatory life in shallow waters, having powerful tails and strong jaws. Their eggs are laid on land, in sand or decomposing vegetation.

Crow, a family of birds including many well-known species such as the rook, raven, jackdaw, carrion crow, hooded crow, magpie, nutcracker, jaw and chough.

Crusades were military expeditions undertaken by some of the Christian nations of Europe with the object of ensuring the safety of pilgrims visiting the Holy Sepulchre and to retain in Christian hands the Holy Places. For two centuries nine crusades were undertaken: First, 1095–99, under Godfrey of Bouillon, which succeeded in capturing Jerusalem; Second, 1147–49, led by Louis VII of France, a dismal failure, which ended with the fall of Jerusalem; Third, 1180–92, in which Richard I of England took part, making a truce with Saladin; Fourth, 1202–4, led by French and Flemish nobles, a shameful expedition, resulting in the founding of a Latin empire in Constantinople; Fifth, 1217–21, led by John of Brienne; Sixth, 1228–29, under the Emperor Frederick II; Seventh, 1248–54, under St. Louis of France; Eighth, 1270, under the same leadership, but cut short by his death on an ill-judged expedition to Tunis; Ninth, 1271–72, led by Prince Edward of England, which accomplished nothing. Millions of lives and an enormous amount of treasure were sacrificed in these enterprises and Jerusalem remained in the possession of the "infidels". The chief material beneficiaries were the Italian maritime cities; the chief spiritual beneficiary was the Pope; and in literature Europe benefited enormously.

Crux. *See under* **Southern Cross, L113.**

Cryogenics (Greek roots: productive of cold) is the science dealing with the production of very low temperatures and the study of their physical and technological consequences. "Very low" is often taken to mean below about $-150°$C. The growth of cryogenics (essentially a 20th-cent. science) is connected with the discovery of how to liquefy all gases including even helium which resisted liquefaction until 1908. Scientifically, cryogenics is important partly because special phenomena (*e.g.*, superconductivity (*q.v.*)) appear at lower temperatures and partly because more can be learned about ordinary properties by studying them in the absence of heat. Technologically, cryogenics is becoming more and more significant, for example, liquefied gases are rocket propellants, superconductors make valuable magnets, tissue-freezing techniques (using very cold liquids) have been introduced into surgery. *See* **Absolute Temperature.**

Crystal, in everyday usage, a solid chemical substance bounded by plane surfaces which show a regular geometrical arrangement as, *e.g.*, quartz crystals, rock salt, snow flakes. In physics the term means any substances whose atoms are arranged in a regular three-dimensional array. This includes most solids, even those not particularly crystalline in appearance, *e.g.*, a lump of lead. *See* **Glass** and **Liquid Crystals.**

Cubism, the name of a revolutionary movement in art created in the years 1907–9 by the two painters Picasso and Braque. Rejecting purely visual effects, they approached nature from an intellectual point of view, reducing it to mathematical orderliness. Its respectable grandparent was Cézanne who had once written: "you must see in nature the cylinder, the sphere, and the cone"—a concept which, together with the contemporary interest in Negro sculpture, moved the two founders of the movement to experiment with the reduction of natural forms to their basic geometrical shapes. In practice, this meant combining several views of the object all more or less superimposed in order to express the idea of the object rather than any one view of it. The name Cubism was derisive and the movement aroused the same opposition as Impressionism, Fauvism and the

later Futurism. Picasso's *Les Demoiselles d'Avignon* (1907; Museum of Modern Art, New York) was his first Cubist painting. Three phases are recognised: (1) Cubism under the influence of Cézanne; (2) high or analytical Cubism (*c.* 1909–12) concentrating on the breaking-down of form to the exclusion of interest in colour; (3) synthetic Cubism (*c.* 1913) making use of *collage* in which pieces of pasted-on paper (illustrations, wallpaper, newspaper) and other materials were used in addition to paint. Amongst other early cubist painters were Metzinger, Gleizes, Gris and Léger.

Cuckoo, a well-known migratory bird which is found in Great Britain from April to July, hawk-like in shape, with a very characteristic note, uttered during the mating season only by the male. The hen has a soft bubbling call. It lays its eggs in the nests of other birds, *e.g.*, the meadow pipit and hedge sparrow, but only one egg in each nest. Feeds mainly on insects, particularly hairy caterpillars.

Cuneiform, (Latin = *wedge-shaped*), an ancient method of writing by impressing wedge-like strokes into tablets of damp clay which when dried and hardened formed a permanent script. Cuneiform writing developed from its original pictographic form into a phonetic writing and can be traced back to the non-Semitic Sumerians of ancient Mesopotamia, the earliest civilisation known to us. It passed to the Semitic Accadians of Babylonia in the 3rd millennium B.C. who adapted it to their own language. Decipherment by Sir Henry Rawlinson, 1835.

Curfew (Old F. *covre-feu* = cover fire), a regulation common throughout Europe in mediaeval times by which, at a fixed hour in the evening, the church bell was rung as a signal that fires were to be put out and the people were to go to bed. The custom originated in the fear of fire when buildings were built of timber. Nowadays a curfew is imposed by the military in areas where riots or disturbances are expected, compelling the civilian population to remain in doors after nightfall.

Curia, the central government of the Roman Catholic Church. By the reform which came into force in 1968, its twelve Sacred Congregations or "ministries" were reduced to nine.

Curie, a measure of the rate at which radioactive material emits radiation. One curie is a disintegration rate of $3 \cdot 7 \times 10^{10}$ disintegrations per second.

Curlew, a wading-bird of which there are several species. It frequents marshy places, feeds on worms, insects, molluscs and berries and possesses a very long, down-curved bill.

Currency is the name given to the types of cash money—metal or paper—in use in an area (*e.g.* pound, sterling, dollar, franc). It also designates the actual coins or notes issued. Its amount is usually subject to regulation by the Government, or by a Central Bank acting on the Government's behalf. Britain changed over to a £-based decimal currency in February 1971. On 1 January 1985, ½p coins ceased to be legal tender. The old "halfpenny" first appeared in 1280. The Royal Mint has now produced a smaller and lighter 50p coin. The old 50p ceased to be legal tender on 28 February 1998. The first two-colour coin (the £2 coin) entered circulation in June 1998. *See also* **National Currencies (Z9)** and **Euro (L41).**

Cybernetics, the science concerned with the automatic control and communication processes in both animals and machines. Thus it is concerned with brain function, information theory, electronic computers, and automation.

Cyclone, a term usually applied to a tropical revolving storm. Cyclones often occur towards the end of the hot seasons and are mainly confined to tracks in the western areas of the oceans, being known as hurricanes (Caribbean and Pacific), cyclones (Indian Ocean) and typhoons (China Seas). The circulation of air in a cyclone is similar to that in the *depression* of temperate latitudes, but the region of low pressure is much more localised and the pressure gradients steeper. Winds of hurricane strength and torrential rain occur generally, although at the centre of the storm there is a small area, known as the "eye", where fair, calm weather prevails. Hurricane Andrew, which hit Florida in August 1992, left 250,000 people homeless. The 1998 Atlantic hurricane season was the worst for 200 years.

Hurricane Mitch devastated Honduras and Nicaragua. Hurricanes are graded in five classes. Many scientists predict that the global warming of the 1990s will lead to more—and more powerful—hurricanes. It seems this is now beginning to happen.

Cyclotron, a machine for accelerating charged particles such as protons to very high energies. Devised by E. O. Lawrence in California in 1930, it uses a magnetic field to make the particles traverse nearly circular paths and an electric field to give them an additional pulse of energy each time round. The accelerated particles impinge on targets, and the resulting events are a basic source of information for nuclear physicists. The cyclotron is obsolescent and has led to the development of other machines, *e.g.*, betatrons, synchrotrons. Britain has two major national high-energy machines: a 7 GeV proton synchroton (to be closed and replaced by a "spallation neutron source"), and a 5 GeV electron synchrotron. The European Organisation for Nuclear Research (CERN), carries out research at higher energies. *See* **L24.**

D

Dactylopterus, a fish of the gurnard family, with wing-like pectoral fins; sometimes known as the flying fish, though that appellation is more generally given to *Exocetus exiliens.*

Dadaism (French *Dada* = hobby-horse) was a hysterical and nihilistic precursor of **Surrealism** *(q.v.)* resulting from the shock produced by the first world war. Beginning in Zurich about 1915, it spread to other continental cities, such as Berlin and Paris, dying out in 1922. The movement was deliberately anti-art, destructive, and without meaning; it intended to scandalise by such tricks as "compositions" made out of anything that came to hand—buttons, bus tickets, pieces of wire, bits of tin, *etc.* Other excesses included incoherent poetry, Dada night-clubs, plays, and short-lived newspapers. Many Dadaist painters became Surrealists at a later stage, but where Surrealism is a deliberate attempt to present dreamlike images, Dadaism was sheer anarchism. Leading Dadaists were Hans Arp, Marcel Duchamp, André Breton, Kurt Schwitters and Max Ernst.

Daddy Longlegs, or **Crane-fly,** a slender long-legged fly of the family Tipulidae. The larvae which do damage to lawns and plants are called leather-jackets. The Americans call Harvestmen *(q.v.)* daddy longlegs.

Daguerreotype, the first practical photographic process, invented in Paris by M. Daguerre during the years 1824–39. The light-sensitive plate was prepared by bringing iodine in contact with a plate of silver. After exposure a positive image came by development of the plate in mercury vapour. Even for openair scenes the first daguerreotypes involved exposure of 5–10 minutes. The picture came in one copy and the process was therefore of limited use. The wet collodion process (1851) rendered the technique obsolete.

Dail Eireann, the name of the national parliament of the Irish Republic.

Dalai Lama, the temporal and religious leader of Tibet. The present Dalai Lama, Tenzin Gyabo (b. 1935), the 14th reincarnation, fled to India in 1959. Awarded the 1989 Nobel Peace Prize.

Damaskeening, the art of inlaying one metal upon another, largely practised in the East in mediaeval times, in the decoration of sword blades.

Dandies, the name given to a group prominent in early Victorian days who attracted attention by excessive regard for dress.

Danegeld, tax imposed in England in Anglo-Saxon times to raise funds for resisting the Danes or to buy them off. Edward the Confessor abolished the tax, but it was revived by the Conqueror and subsequently retained, under another name, after the danger from the Danes was past. It is the basis of all taxation in this country. Domesday Book *(q.v.)* was originally drawn up for the purpose of teaching the State how to levy the tax.

Danelaw, the law enforced by the Danes in the

kingdoms of Northumbria, East Anglia, and in the districts of the five (Danish) boroughs—lands grouped round Leicester, Nottingham, Derby, Stamford and Lincoln—which they occupied during the Viking invasions of the 9th and 10th cent. The country occupied was also called the Danelaw or Danelagh.

Darter, 1. Snakebirds, a genus of the pelican family, with long, pointed bill and serpent-like neck and resembling cormorants in appearance. There are 5 species. 2. Numerous species of small freshwater fish belonging to the perch family, found in N. America.

Date Palm. *Phoenix dactylifera,* one of the oldest known food plants widely cultivated in N. Africa and W. Asia. It grows to 30 m and continues to bear for 2 or 3 centuries, its fruit being of great value as a food. From the leaves the Africans make roofs for their huts; ropes are made from the fibrous parts of the stalks; and the sap furnishes a stimulating beverage.

Dauphin, the title borne by the eldest sons of the Kings of France from 1349 to 1830.

Day is the most natural unit of time and may be defined as the period of rotation of the earth relative to any selected heavenly body. Relative to the sun it is called the *solar day.* Relative to a fixed star it is called the *sidereal day.* Owing to irregularities in the earth's movements, the time taken for the earth to rotate through 360° relative to the sun is variable, and so the *mean solar day* of 24 hours has been introduced, which is the average throughout the year. The *mean solar day* is our standard, used for purposes of the calendar, and astronomers use *sidereal* clocks to check mean solar time. In practice, for convenience, the sidereal day is determined by the earth's rotation relative to the vernal equinox or first point of Aries, and is equal to 23 hours 56 minutes and 4·091 seconds of mean solar time (*i.e.*, about 4 minutes shorter than a solar day). The lengths of day on other planets can differ greatly to that of the Earth. Jupiter spins once every 10 hours or so while the length of a day on Venus is equal to 243·01 Earth-days, longer than its year of 224·7 days. *See* **Time.**

D-Day, the allied invasion of Normandy on 6 June 1944 which began the liberation of France in World War II. Allied troops landed on the coast of Normandy between the river Orne and the Cotentin peninsula, in the largest ever seaborne invasion. Three divisions from the Canadian and British army landed on 'Gold', 'Juno', and 'Sword' beaches and two divisions of the American First Army at 'Omaha' and 'Utah' beaches. After a fierce battle on 'Omaha' a substantial beach-head—24 miles long and 4 miles deep—was established by nightfall.

DDT (dichloro-dephenyl-trichloroethane). A very powerful insecticide which has had wide success in the control of diseases, such as malaria and typhus which are carried by insects. Mosquito swamps are sprayed with DDT to kill the carriers. Because this toxic chemical breaks down very slowly it builds up in birds and animals and its use is now banned in Britain. Its detection in Antarctic wild life confirmed that DDT pollution was virtually worldwide.

Deacon, an ecclesiastical official, who assists in some of the smaller ministerial duties in church or chapel.

Dead Languages are such as the ancient Greek and Roman tongues, which are no longer spoken but are preserved in literature.

Dead Sea Scrolls, a group of ancient Jewish documents, consisting of scrolls and fragments which have been recovered since 1947 in the vicinity of Qumran near the Dead Sea and which represent one of the most important finds ever made in the field of biblical archaeology and Christian origins. The scrolls written in Hebrew or Aramaic, were found in caves, the first by chance by an Arab shepherd in 1947. These consisted of biblical texts older by a thousand years than the earliest Hebrew manuscript of the Old Testament (A.D. 895). Many fragments have since been discovered, comprising the whole of the Old Testament with the exception of Esther. In addition there are commentaries and other non-biblical writings, including one called "The War of the Sons of Light with the Sons of Darkness". The writing on the scrolls indicates that they were written over a period of two centuries, the greater proportion before the birth of Christ. A nearby ruin is believed to have been the home of a religious sect called the Essenes (J17), to whom the scrolls belonged. By the aid of the latest scientific techniques, including radiocarbon tests, the age of the scrolls has been confirmed as between the second cent. B.C. and first century A.D.

Dean, a Church of England dignitary, ranking below a bishop, and the head of the chapter of a cathedral. A Rural Dean supervises a *deanery* or group of parishes. There are also Deans of Faculties in some universities, and at Oxford and Cambridge the Dean is in charge of chapel services and disciplinary arrangements.

Death Watch Beetle (*Xestobium rufovillosum*), a wood-boring beetle, larger than the common furniture beetle, found chiefly in the old oak beams of churches and other historic buildings. The grub bores from 4–12 years. The name "death watch" comes from the superstition that the ticking sound, made by the beetle striking its head against the wood, is a sign of approaching death. The death watch beetle found in the roof of Westminster Hall was smoked out by means of an insecticide called gamma benzine hexachloride. *See also* **Furniture Beetle, Woodworm.**

Decalogue, the name given to the Ten Commandments of the Old Testament. There are two versions of them, differing in detail: Exodus xx. 2–17 and Deuteronomy v. 6–21. They are of Hebrew origin and are recognised by Jews and Christians as the divine law given by God to Moses on Mt. Sinai. Most of them are prohibitions in contrast to the beatitudes (pronounced by Christ in the Sermon on the Mount) which are positive, *e.g.,* Blessed are the merciful.

December, the last month of the year in our calendar, and the tenth in the old Roman.

Deciduous Trees are such as shed their leaves at certain seasons as distinguished from evergreens or permanent foliaged trees or shrubs.

Declaration of Independence was an Act by which the American Congress, on 4 July 1776, declared the American colonies to be independent of Great Britain. "Independence Day" is a holiday in the United States.

Defender of the Faith (*Defensor Fidei*), the title conferred upon Henry VIII by Pope Leo X in 1521 for entering the debate against Luther with his pamphlet in defence of the Seven Sacraments. After Henry assumed headship of the Church of England the Pope withdrew the title but it was confirmed to him by Parliament in 1544 and has been used ever since by English monarchs.

Deflation. *See* **Section G.**

Dehydrate, to eliminate the water from a substance. The process of dehydration is now used in the food industry, as a result of wartime research, in making such things as dried egg and packet soups. Most vegetables contain over 90 per cent of water, and much of this can be removed under vacuum at low temperatures without appreciably impairing the flavour.

Deliquescence, the process of dissolving by the absorption of moisture from the atmosphere. For instance, chromic acid crystals on exposure to the air quickly deliquesce.

Deluge, a flood, commonly applied to the story of the Deluge in the Bible, in which Noah and the Ark figure. A similar tradition lingers in the mythologies of all ancient peoples.

Democratic Party, one of the two great American political parties, originated about 1787, advocating restrictions on the federal governments and in opposition to the federalists. It was in 1825 that a group who were in favour of high tariffs seceded, later to become the Republican Party. The Democratic Party was split again over slavery before the Civil War (1861–65), and in the main the southern states have been supporters of the Democrats. The economic depression helped the Democrats to power in 1932 (*see* **New Deal**) and they held office until 1953 when Eisenhower became President. In 1960 Kennedy narrowly won the Presidency and in 1964 Lyndon Johnson swept in with a landslide victory over the Republican candidate. In 1968 and 1972 the Democratic candidates were beaten by Nixon. In 1976 Jimmy Carter won an easy victory, but after that the Democrats lost three successive presidential elections (1980, 1984, 1988) before winning a narrow

but convincing victory under Bill Clinton in the 1992 election. The party suffered reverses in the 1994 mid-term elections but went on to victory in 1996. The unsuccessful impeachment proceedings against Clinton dominated politics early in 1999 (*see* **Section C**). The symbol of the party is a donkey, invented, like the Republican's elephant, by the cartoonist Thomas Nast.

Dendrochronology. The science of establishing the age of trees. *See* **Tree Rings, L122.**

Dendrite, a stone or mineral on or in which treelike tracery appears, the result of the action of the hydrous oxide of manganese.

Density, a measure of the mass per unit volume of a material, usually expressed in grams per cubic centimetre. *Specific gravity* is the ratio of the density of a material at the termperature under consideration to that of water at the temperature of its maximum density (4°C). In grams per cubic centimetre the density of gold is 19·3, silver 10·5, lead 11·3, water 0·99997, air 0·00129.

Depreciation of a currency is a fall in its value in terms of gold or of other currencies. *See* **Section G.**

Depression, a region where barometric pressure is lower than that of its surroundings. These areas of low pressure are usually less extensive than anticyclones (*q.v.*) and may vary from hundreds to thousands of kilometres in diameter. The winds, often of gale force where the depression is deep, blow round the system in an anticlockwise direction in the Northern Hemisphere (in the reverse direction in the Southern Hemisphere). Well above the earth's surface the winds blow along rather than down the pressure gradient but near the surface, friction causes the winds to blow slightly (*c.* 15°) across the isobars. The depression exists only as long as more air diverges out of its upper parts than converges into its lower parts. The majority of depressions which cross the British Isles travel from the Atlantic, sometimes in series or families at rates from a few kilometres to a thousand kilometres a day, bringing their generally unsettled weather with them.

Derby, The, the most famous flat race for 3-year-old fillies. First run at Epsom in 1780. The most successful Derby jockey is Lester Piggott (9 wins). The largest Derby field was 34 in 1862. In June 1996 Alex Greaves, riding *Portuguese Lil,* became the first woman jockey to ride in the Derby. *See* **Section R.**

Desalinisation, the process of removing minerals, chiefly salt, from sea or brackish water to provide pure water for drinking or industry. Small-scale desalinisation by distillation has been practised for many years on ships and small islands. By the 1960s, many large-scale distillation plants were in operation, many of them in hot dry countries as in the Middle East. Kuwait, for example, used oil revenues to buy desalination plant and powers the plant with natural gas. As water for large population centres becomes more precious and desalinisation techniques more efficient, the process may be more and more used though it is expensive in capital outlay and in the cost of heating required to distil the water. Methods other than distillation are under investigation but not as yet much used.

Deserts, vast, barren, stone or sandy wastes where there is almost no rainfall and little or no vegetation. These regions are found in the interior of the continents Africa, Asia and America between 20° and 30° north and south of the equator. Europe is the only continent without deserts. The most famous are the Sahara, the largest in the world, the Gobi desert of central Asia, the Kalahari desert of southwest Africa and the great Australian desert. The growing extension of deserts (desertification) is a topic of considerable debate. The increasing size of deserts is thought to result from both climatic change and also man's interference.

Detention Centres in Britain were for young people (boys and girls) over 14 but under 21 who have been found guilty of an offence for which an adult could be sent to prison. They have now been replaced by Young Offenders' Institutions.

Determinism and Free-will. *See* **Section J.**

Deuterium or "heavy hydrogen". The second isotope of hydrogen; the third is called tritium. Deuterium atoms have in their nuclei a neutron as well as a proton; tritium nuclei have two neutrons and one proton. In ordinary hydrogen gas about one out of every 5,000 atoms is a deuterium atom. Deuterium was discovered in 1932 by Professor Harold Urey. The oxide of deuterium corresponding to water is called "heavy water". The nucleus of the deuterium atom is called a deuteron. An anti-deuteron consisting of anti-proton and anti-neutron was produced at Brookhaven in 1965, the first compound anti-nucleus ever to be produced.

Devaluation is a definite, official downward valuation of a country's currency in terms of its exchange value with other currencies. The £ was devalued in 1949, when an official exchange rate of £1 = $2.8 was established, and again in 1967, to a rate of £1 = $2.4. *See* **Section G.**

Devonian System in geology refers to the strata between the Silurian and the Carboniferous formations. It includes the Old Red Sandstone formation. The fauna of the Devonian include the group of fishes known as the Rhipidistra (on the evolutionary route towards the amphibians), Actinistia (coelacanth), and the Dipnoi or lung fishes.

Dew, moisture deposited by condensation of water vapour on exposed objects especially during calm, cloudless nights. The loss of heat from the ground after sunset, by radiation, causes the layer of atmosphere close to the surface to be chilled below the temperature, known as the dew-point, at which the air is saturated with vapour. Part of the vapour condensed may be transpired from blades of grass and foliage of plants.

Dew Pond is a shallow artificial pond which is on high ground and rarely dries up, even during prolonged droughts, despite being used by cattle and sheep as a drinking source. The name arose from the belief that dew deposits at night provided the moisture for replenishment. Drainage of rain-water and mist condensed on neighbouring trees and shrubs are probably more important factors.

Dialectical Materialism. *See* **Section J.**

Diamond, a mineral, one of the two crystalline forms of the element carbon (the other is graphite), the hardest known substance, used as a gem and in industry. India was the first country to mine diamonds (the Koh-i-noor, which means "mountain of light", known since 1304, came from Golconda near Hyderabad and came into British possession when the Punjab was annexed in 1849). The celebrated diamond mines of South Africa were discovered in the 1870s. Other important diamond producing countries today are Russia, Congo, Ghana, Sierra Leone, Namibia, Angola and Tanzania. The world's biggest diamond is the 3,106-carat Cullinan, discovered near Pretoria, South Africa, in 1905. Diamonds can be made artificially by subjecting carbon to very high temperatures and pressures; many industrial diamonds are made this way. Antwerp is the main diamond centre of the world, London the main marketing centre, Amsterdam the main diamond cutting centre.

Diatoms. One-celled algae, common in fresh and salt water. Distinctive feature is the siliceous wall which is in two halves, one fitting over the other like the lid of a box. These walls are often very finely and beautifully sculptured. The diatoms constitute a class of the plant kingdom known as the Bacillariophyta. *Diatom ooze* is a deep-sea deposit made up of diatom shells. *Diatomite* or *diatomaceous earth* is the mineral form that such diatom oozes assume (sometimes known as kieselguhr which mixed with nitroglycerine yields dynamite).

Diesel Engine, an engine in which the liquid fuel is introduced into a compressed or partially compressed charge of air, and which does not need an extraneous source of ignition. The modern oil engine has been evolved mainly from the principles enunciated by Herbert Akroyd-Stuart in his patent of 1890 and, like the steam and other inventions, represents the improvements achieved by many men, including those by Rudolf Diesel of Germany, in respect of high compression pressures and greater fuel economy.

Diet, in German history, an assembly of dignitaries or delegates called together to debate upon and decide important political or ecclesiastical questions. The most famous imperial

Diets were those held at Worms (1521), Speyer (1529), and Augsburg (1530), all of which dealt with matters arising from the Reformation.

Diffusion is the process of mixing which occurs when two liquids or gases are in contact. It is most rapid between gases, and, as laid down by Graham's law, "the rates of diffusion of different gases are in the inverse proportion to the square roots of their relative densities". Diffusion arises through the continual movement of molecules. Even in solids diffusion can occur. If a block of gold and a block of silver are welded together, after some time particles of gold are found in the silver, and *vice versa*.

Digital Television. *See* **Television, L118.**

Dimensions in common speech are the magnitudes of length, breadth and thickness giving, the size of an object, thus a line has only one dimension: length; a plane surface two: length and breadth; and a solid three: length breadth and thickness. In mathematics, hypothetical objects with any number of dimensions are considered. In physics and mechanics, dimensions are numbers which relate the units in which any quantity is measured to the so-called fundamental units. The latter are usually but not necessarily those of length, mass and time. "Dimensional analysis" is an important technique of scientific reasoning.

Dimorphism, the quality of assuming two distinct forms. For instance, carbon, which is graphite in one form, is the diamond in another.

Dinosaur, the name given to a group of extinct reptiles of the Mesozoic period, some of which were of immense size. A recent theory suggests a huge cosmic impact may have ended their 160 million year reign, but many scientists now (1998) discount this. *See* **Diplodocus.**

Dip Needle. Instrument for measuring the *dip* or inclination of the earth's magnetic field.

Diplodocus, one of the best known of the extinct mammoth dinosaurs. Fossil remains have been discovered in the Jurassic rocks of the United States. Some reached a length of over 24 m.

Dipnoi *or* **Lung Fishes.** These have the air bladder adapted to function as a lung, and they can remain alive when the stream or marsh in which they live dries up. Species of lung fish occur in Australia, Africa and S. America.

Diptera, an order of insects. Their main characteristic is that they are two-winged, and the common house-fly is the best-known example. There are at least 50,000 species of these insects, including gnats, blow-flies, mosquitoes and tsetses.

Diptych was a folding two-leaved tablet of wood, ivory, or metal, with polished inner surfaces, utilised for writing with the style by the ancient Greeks and Romans. The same term was applied to the tablets on which the names of the persons to be commemorated were inscribed in the early Church. In art any pair of pictures hinged together is styled a diptych, a set of three, a triptych.

Discus, a circular piece of metal or stone about 30 cm in diameter, used in athletic contests by the ancient Greeks and Romans. Throwing the discus was a very favourite game, which was deemed worthy of celebration in Myron's famous *Discobolus* (c. 460 B.C.–450 B.C.), the best copy of which is in Rome.

Disk, an astronomical term denoting the seemingly flat surface of celestial bodies as seen by the eye.

Distillation, a process used to separate liquids of different boiling points. This is effected by placing the mixture in a distillation apparatus and heating. The liquid with the lower boiling point distils over first, the vapour being condensed and collected, forming the first *fraction*. With continued heating the second liquid reaches its boiling point, distils over and the mixture is said to be *fractionated*. Mixtures of liquids with close very high boiling points require more elaborate apparatus. Fractional distillation is a common process in the chemical industry, particularly in the refining of petroleum.

Diwali, the festival of light, marking the triumph of good over evil, celebrated by Hindus, Sikhs and Jains. Sweets and gifts are exchanged.

DNA (Deoxyribonucleic acid), a polymer molecule

in the form of a double-strand helix containing many thousands of sub-units. Contains the genetic information coded in sequences of sub units called bases. The Nobel Prize for medicine was awarded in 1962 for the discovery of the structure of DNA. *See* **Human Genome Project, Nucleic Acids.** and **Special Topic.** and **Section F.**

DNA Database. The world's first police DNA database was established at the Forensic Science Laboratory, Birmingham in April 1995. The database, which will eventually hold up to 5 million samples, will allow police to compare genetic material from crime scenes with DNA profiles of convicted criminals. DNA profiling has been developed from genetic fingerprinting, an earlier technique created in the mid 1980s by Sir Alec Jeffreys of Leicester University.

Docks are enclosed water spaces where ships rest while being loaded or unloaded, repaired, or waiting for cargo. There are three main types: the wet dock in which water is maintained at the level of high tide so that vessels remain afloat while loading and unloading; the tidal dock, with open entrance to permit free ebb and flow of tide (*e.g.*, Glasgow, Southampton (which has double tides)); and the dry dock, or graving dock, for overhauling and repairing vessels, so constructed that, after a ship has been docked, the water can be drawn off (*e.g.*, Southampton, Tilbury). The floating dock is a type of dry dock. Technological advances in the handling of cargo, *e.g.*, containers (sealed boxes of cargo), have led to modernisation of the docks. Under the 1991 Ports Act, many ports have now been privatised.

Dodo, an extinct bird, giant and flightless, which lived on the island of Mauritius up until 250 years ago. Another species, the white dodo, lived on Réunion. Some reached exceptional sizes. By the end of the 17th cent. Mauritius, Rodriguez, and Réunion had all been colonised, and the dodo along with many other birds vanished forever because of their inability to stand up to man and the animals imported by him.

Dog-days, a period of 40 days (3 July–11 August) when Sirius rises and sets with the sun. The ancient superstition, which can be traced back in Greek literature to Hesiod (8th cent. B.C.), was that this star affected the canine race.

Doge, the chief magistrate in the old republics of Venice (697–1797) and Genoa (1339–1797, 1802–5).

Dogfish, a large family of small sharks, seldom more than 1 m in length. The flesh is sold as "rock salmon." The eggs are contained in horny cases called "mermaid's purses". The commonest of the British dogfishes are the spurdogs.

Doldrums, a nautical term applied to those areas of the Atlantic and Pacific within a few degrees of the Equator towards which the trade winds blow and where the weather is calm, hot and sultry. Pressure is low and the air often rises to produce heavy tropical rainfall and squalls, rendering navigation difficult.

Dolomite, a name applied to a limestone containing appreciable magnesium; also the mineral dolomite, a double carbonate of magnesium and calcium.

Dolphin, a mammal of the whale order, from 2–2·4 m long, with a long, sharp snout, and of an active disposition. They abound in most seas and swim in shoals. A few species live in large rivers (Ganges and Amazon). They can cruise for long periods at around 15 knots and produce bursts of speed in the region of 20 knots, the water apparently flowing smoothly past their bodies. Dolphins are some of the most intelligent of mammals and are currently the subject of scientific experiments in communication. Name also for the fish, dorado. In 1990, a virus (linked to the one which killed 18,000 North Sea seals) was held responsible for dolphin deaths in the Mediterranean.

Domesday Book is the famous register of the lands of England framed by order of William the Conqueror. According to Stowe, the name was derived from *Domus dei*, the name of the place where the book was deposited in Winchester Cathedral; though by others it is connected with doom in the sense of judgment. Its compilation was determined upon in 1085, in order that William might compute what he considered to be due to him in the way of tax from his subjects. William sent into each county commissioners to make survey. They were to inquire the name of each place, the possessor, how many hides of land were in the manor, how many ploughs were in demesne, how many homagers, villeins, cottars, serving men, free tenants, and tenants in soccage; how much wood, meadow, and pasture; the number of mills and fish ponds; what had been added to or taken away from the place; what was the gross value at the time of Edward the Confessor. So minute was the survey that the Saxon chronicler of the time reports "there was not a single hide, nor one virgate of land, nor even, it is shame to tell, though it seemed no shame to do, an ox, nor a cow, nor a swine was left that was not set down". The record, which did not take in Northumberland, Cumberland, Durham and parts of Lancashire and Westmorland, was completed in 1086, and was comprised in two volumes—one a large folio, sometimes called the Little Domesday, which deals with Essex, Norfolk and Suffolk, the other a quarto, sometimes called the Great Domesday. The first is written on 384 double pages of vellum in one and the same hand, and in a small but plain character, each page having a double column. The quarto is written on 450 pages of vellum, but in a single column and in a large, fair character. The original is preserved in the Public Record Office at Kew. *See also* **Danegeld.**

Dominicans, an order of mendicant preaching friars founded by St. Dominic in Languedoc in 1215 and confirmed by the Pope in 1216. The rule of the order was rigorous. The dress was a white habit and scapular with a long black mantle. This gave them the name of Black Friars. Their official name is Friars Preachers.

Donjon, the keep, or inner tower of a castle, and the strongest and most secure portion of the structure. This was the last refuge of the garrison, and there was usually a prison on the lower floor, hence the name *dungeon*.

Don Juan, the legendary hero of many famous works, supposedly based on the life and character of the unscrupulous gallant Don Juan Tenorio of 14th-cent. Seville. The first dramatisation of the legend and the most famous is Tirso de Molina's *El Burlador de Sevilla*. Don Juan was also the subject of Molière's *Le Festin de Pierre*, Mozart's *Don Giovanni*, Byron's *Don Juan*, and José Zorilla's *Don Juan Tenorio*. The latter is played on All Saints' Day throughout Spanish-speaking countries.

Don Quixote, the "knight of the doleful countenance", the hero and title of Cervantes' classic novel of 16th-cent. Spain. Don Quijote de la Mancha, a gentle country gentleman of lofty but unpractical ideals, having read many chivalric romances, believes he is called upon to redress the wrongs of the world. Mounted on his nag Rosinante and accompanied by his companion Sancho Panza, a hard-headed and practical peasant, he sets out on his journeys of knight-errantry.

Dormouse, a family of small, squirrel-like rodents widely distributed throughout Europe and Asia, and living mainly on fruit and nuts. It is of nocturnal habits and sleeps through the winter. One of nature's most secretive creatures, it is now making a comeback in Britain after nearly becoming extinct.

Dot, a French term indicating the property which a wife brings to her husband on marriage and is usually settled on the woman, being her separate property, though the income from it may go towards the general household expenses.

Dotterel, a handsome bird of the plover family found in northern Europe and Siberia.

Doukhobors. *See* **Section J.**

Drachm (or Drachma), an ancient Greek silver coin and weight. One drachma was equivalent to six obols. The word has survived as the name of a weight: Avoirdupois, one-sixteenth part of an ounce; Apothecaries' Weight, one-eighth part of an ounce.

Drag. Term used in mechanics for resistance offered by a fluid to the passage of a body moving through it. When speed of sound is reached drag increases abruptly. The lift/drag ratio gives the aeroplane designer his measure of aerodynamic efficiency.

Dragon, a fabulous monster common to folk-lore in most countries; generally represented as a winged reptile with fiery eyes and breath of flame. A dragon guarded the garden of the Hesperides; in the New Testament there is mention of the "dragon, that old serpent, which is the devil"; St. George, England's patron saint, is supposed to have overcome the dragon; in heraldry the dragon has also a conspicuous place; and in China it was the imperial emblem.

Dragonet, the name of the fish of the *Callionymus* genus, beautifully coloured, and about 30 cm in length. They are common on the British coast and in the Mediterranean.

Dragon Fly, the common name of a well-known order of insects having two pairs of membraneous wings, and often of very brilliant colours. They are swift of flight and may be seen hovering over sheets of water in the sunshine all through the summer. Their chief food is mosquitoes.

Dragon's Blood, a dark-red resinous substance obtained from the fruit of a Malay palm, and possessing medicinal virtues. In a special technique used for making line blocks in printing, dragon's blood is used.

Drawbridge, a bridge that can be lifted up so that no passage can be made across it. It was a usual feature of a fortified castle in the Middle Ages, and was raised or lowered by chains and levers. It spanned the fosse, and on the approach of an attacking party was raised and formed a special barricade to the gate. Modern drawbridges are such as are raised to allow of the passage of boats up and down a river or estuary. The Tower Bridge is a famous London bridge of this type.

Driving Standards Agency, the national body responsible for driving tests for cars, lorries, buses *etc.* It also supervises approved driving instructors and training bodies.

Driving Test. The cost of a driving test rose to £36.75 in May 1999 when a longer, more difficult, test was introduced. The new driving test now takes around 40 minutes.

Drongo. The King Crow or Indian Black Drongo is frequently seen in India perched on branches or telegraph wires, darting suddenly to catch insects and to attack crows and hawks. Other members of the family are found in Asia, Africa and Australia. Its plumage is black with steel-blue gloss.

Drosophila or **Fruit Fly.** More has been learnt by geneticists from breeding experiments with this insect than with any other.

Dross, the name applied to the refuse of molten metal, composed of slag, scales and cinders.

Drought occurs when there has been an absence of rain for a long period or a marked deficiency of precipitation over a much longer period in a climatic zone where precipitation is ordinarily adequate for vegetation or agriculture, river flow and water supplies. It is different from aridity which refers to the extreme dryness of desert or arid regions where rainless periods characterise the climate. Hitherto in the British Isles "an absolute drought" was defined as "a period of at least 15 consecutive days without measurable rainfall", but arbitrary definitions of this type are not now normally used. In the British Isles droughts occur from time to time but very long rainless spells at a place are rather rare. The longest recorded spell in the British Isles with no measurable daily rainfall lasted 61 days at Liss (Hants) from 16 March to 15 May 1893. Over the country as a whole the 12-month period beginning 1 May 1975 was the driest such period since records began. The South of England's longest drought this century was ended by rain at the end of November 1992. In many places the summer of 1995 was the driest since records began in 1727, whilst the lack of rainfall in 1996 and early 1997 led to predictions of severe water shortages. Disruption of weather patterns by the effects of El Niño is threatening areas of the world with drought (*see* **L132**).

Druidism. *See* **Section J.**

Drupe is the scientific term for stone fruit. The stone forms the inner part (endocarp) of the fruit, and encloses a seed or kernel which is liberated after the flesh part (pericarp) rots.

Dry-rot, the term was first used about 1775 to describe the fungal decay of timber in buildings. Creosote distilled from coal tar is the standard material for preservation of timber, and pentachlorophenol and copper naphthenate are two compounds now extensively used. Dry wood always escapes dry-rot. Chief fungi causing dry-rot are *Merulius* and *Poria*.

Duck, water bird smaller than the related goose and swan, which together form the family Antidae. Duck refers to the female, drake to the male. The duck family falls into two separate groups: the river or freshwater (surface feeding) ducks, such as the mallard, pintail, wigeon, shoveler, mandarin, teal, garganey; and the sea (diving) ducks, such as the goldeneye, pochard, scoter, eider, and the fish-eating mergansers or "sawbills". The ancestor of all domestic breeds, with the exception of the muscovy, is the mallard.

Duckbill, *Ornithorhynchus anatinus,* also duck-billed platypus, a fur-covered, egg-laying, nest-building mammal inhabiting Australia and Tasmania. It has webbed feet and a muzzle like a duck's bill and is about 50 cm long.

Ductility is a property possessed by most metals which renders them capable of being stretched without breaking. Gold is the most, and lead the least ductile of metals, the order being gold, silver, platinum, iron, copper, palladium, aluminium, zinc, tin, lead. In animated nature the spider and the silkworm produce secretions of notable ductility.

Dugong. A marine mammal, belonging to the order Sirenia (sea-cows). Inhabits Red Sea and Indian Ocean; also found as far East as the Philippines and Australia. Lives on seaweed. Related to the Manatee.

Duke, the highest rank in the British peerage. Edward, the Black Prince, eldest son of Edward III, who died before his father, was the first English duke, being created Duke of Cornwall in 1337. Since then all Princes of Wales have held that title.

Dukeries, a stretch of English woodland and park country, mainly in Nottinghamshire, comprising the adjacent demesnes of several English dukes and nobles. The Dukeries include Sherwood Forest and the estates of Welbeck Abbey, Clumber Park, Worksop Manor and Thoresby Hall.

Dunes. Sand dunes are elliptical or crescent-shaped mounds of loose sand produced by wind action. The dune has a gentle slope on windward side; a steep slope on the leeward side.

Dunlin, very common small wading-bird of the Sandpiper family nesting in Britain. Its range extends to other areas where it also breeds.

Dunmow Flitch, a custom which originated in the parish of Little Dunmow, Essex, in the reign of Henry III, which was that the husband who was prepared to swear before the prior, convent, and townsfolk of Dunmow that he had not repented of marriage or quarrelled with his wife for a year and a day, should be rewarded with the gift of a flitch of bacon. The custom has frequently been revived.

Dunnock (*Prunella modularis*), a small bird of rich brown and dark grey plumage common in gardens and hedgerows. Sings a cheerful song all the year round. Called hedge-sparrow in southern England. Another member of the same family, the larger Alpine Accentor (*Prunella collaris*), is found on rocky mountain slopes of Europe and Asia.

Duodecimo, a sheet of paper folded into twelve leaves, written "12mo".

Durbar, a term used in India from the Persian word *darbár* meaning "court" or "audience". The word was applied to great gatherings like Lord Lytton's durbar for the proclamation of the Queen-Empress in 1877 and the Delhi durbar of 1911.

Dust, solid particles of matter floating in the atmosphere, produced chiefly by volcanic eruptions, sand-storms in desert regions, and industrial and domestic smoke. When the island of Krakatoa erupted in 1883, more than 4 km^2 of dust was thrown into the air and carried three times round the earth by the explosive wave. The particles in dust-storms are much finer than those in sand-storms and are swept up to far greater heights. The local whirlwinds which form over loose dry soils are termed dust-devils.

Dutch Elm Disease. *See under* **Elm, L39.**

Dyke. A wall-like intrusion of igneous rock which cuts across the bedding or other layered structure of the country rock; the word also signifies in alternative usage, a sea-wall and an open drain.

Dynamite, a powerful explosive whose chief element is nitro-glycerine. It was discovered by Nobel in 1867, who absorbed nitro-glycerine in kieselguhr; has a disruptive force of about eight times that of gunpowder.

Dynamo. Machine for transforming mechanical energy into electrical energy. Depends on principle of electromagnetic induction whereby a current is produced in a conductor (*e.g.*, copper wire) traversing a magnetic field. The two essential parts of a dynamo are the conductors or *armature* and the *field magnets.*

Dynasty, a succession of monarchs of the same family *e.g.* Romanovs, Bourbons.

E

Eagle, large bird of prey with huge hooked bill, related to the buzzard, kite, hawk, harrier, falcon and vulture, together forming the family Falconidae. There are many species to be found throughout the world, the Golden, Imperial, Tawny, Spotted and Lesser Spotted being found in Europe. The Golden Eagle, a magnificent-looking bird, nests in the Scottish Highlands, and the White-tailed Sea Eagle, which used to breed in Britain, is now only an occasional visitor. The eagle has been the symbol of royal power since the earliest times, and the American or Bald Eagle is the emblem of the United States.

Earl, a British title of nobility of the third rank, duke and marquis coming first and second. The title dates from Saxon times, and until 1337 ranked highest in our peerage.

Earl-Marshal, in England ranks as the eighth of the great officers of state, is head of the College of Arms, attends the sovereign in opening and closing the session of Parliament, arranges state processions (especially coronations) and assists in introducing newly created peers in the House of Lords. The office is hereditary in the family of the Dukes of Norfolk.

Earth, our habitable globe, is the third of the planets of the solar system in order from the sun and on an average throughout the year takes 24 hours to turn completely round relative to the sun, the whole earth revolving round the sun in a slightly elliptical orbit once in a year of 365·2564 days. The mean distance of the earth from the sun is 149,597,900 km. Recent earth satellite studies have shown that small variations of the surface gravity field (or geoid) occur which are believed to be related more to the structures deep within the earth's mantle than to the location and dimension of crustal features, such as oceans, continents and mountain ranges. The crust consists of a skin, 30 km thick under the continents, but only about 6–8 km thick under the ocean bed, comprised of rocks and sediments or soil. At the base of the crust is a sharp discontinuity (the Mohorovičić Discontinuity) to denser rocks of the mantle. This region, nearly 3,000 km thick, is in a process of slow but inexorable change, one of convection responding to heat sources (due mainly to radioactivity of the materials within the earth). This slow convection is responsible for many changes in the surface of the earth—continental drift (*q.v.*), earthquakes and volcanic activity. The core is a region of very high density and temperature, comprised of heavy elements such as iron and nickel. The crustal rocks are mainly comprised of oxygen, silicon, aluminium, sodium, potassium, iron, calcium and magnesium, with traces of many other elements. The mass of the earth is about 6,000 million million million tonnes, and it was formed about 4,600 million years ago. The earth has one natural satellite, the moon. *See also* **F8–10.**

Earthquake, a sudden violent disturbance of the earth's crust; the region of the surface immediately above the "focus", or source where the earthquake originates, is termed the "epicentre". On account of their destructive power earthquakes have attracted attention from the earliest times, but accurate study dates only from the last century and the development of a world-wide network of recording stations from the present one. The majority of severe earthquakes result from fractures, usually along existing faults, in underlying rock strata subjected to great strains, the shearing movement sometimes extending to the surface. These dislocations set up vibrations which are propagated as waves throughout the bulk of the earth or round the crust. Frequently the main shock is followed by a series of smaller aftershocks. Minor local earthquakes may be attributed to the effects of volcanic activity, but most of the larger ones originate in non-volcanic regions along well-marked lines of weakness in the earth's crust. Generally the ground is felt to tremble, undergoing oscillations which may gradually or suddenly increase to a maximum and accompanied by sounds. When there is movement of the sea-bed a tsunami (*q.v.*) may result. One of the greatest of historic times was that which destroyed and flooded Lisbon in 1755. Among the notable shocks of the present century rank those of San Francisco (1906), Messina, Italy (1908), China (1920), Japan (1923), Napier, New Zealand (1931), Ionian Is. (1953), Chile (1960), Iran (1962), Yugoslavia (1963), E. Turkey (1966), W. Sicily (1968), Peru (1970), China (1976), Mexico (1985) Armenia (1988), N.W. Iran (1990), Los Angeles (1994), Kobe (Japan), 1995 and Afghanistan (1998). The most devastating earthquake in recorded history hit Shanxi (China) in 1556, killing 830,000 people. Recent research has suggested that the collapse of the walls of Jericho in biblical times was due to an earthquake. In 1997 earthquakes in central Italy seriously damaged Assisi. Over 2 million people have been killed in earthquakes since 1900. *See* **Richter Scale** and **F9(2).**

Earthworm, of which there are several species, has a cylindrical body, tapering at both ends and segmented into rings. It moves by contraction of its rings, aided by retractive bristles; is eyeless, but has a mouth, gullet and stomach. Earthworms exist in immense numbers, and perform an important part in the scheme of nature by loosening the soil and rendering it more amenable to tillage. They also form a valuable food for birds and many mammals, and are unequalled as bait for certain kinds of fish. The New Zealand flatworm (now spreading in Britain) is devouring native earthworms.

Earwig, a genus of insects possessing two pairs of wings and anal forceps. It is nocturnal, lives on vegetable matter, and hides by day under stones or in flowers, *e.g.*, dahlias. The old belief that it deliberately creeps into people's ears is altogether unfounded.

Easter, the annual Christian festival in commemoration of the resurrection of Christ, the English name being derived from Eostre, goddess of Spring. The date cannot fall earlier than 22 March nor later than 25 April. Many disputes arose among the early Christians as to the proper time to celebrate this day which governs all other movable feasts. It was eventually ruled at the Council of Nicaea in 325 that Easter Day should be the first Sunday after the full moon following the vernal equinox. If this happens to be a Sunday, then Easter Day is the Sunday after. *See also* **Section Z.**

Eastern Front, the battlefront between Russia and Germany in both World Wars.

Eastern Question, a term formerly applied to the problems arising from the instability of the Ottoman Empire and its relations with the other nations of Europe. Later connected with other problems of the Near East such as the possession of Constantinople and rivalries in the Balkans.

East India Company was incorporated by Elizabeth in 1600. In 1613 the Company set up a factory at Surat, India, and in 1662 Bombay came under the Company's influence and developed into an important trading port. Dupleix wanted to establish French power in India and a struggle for supremacy took place. Clive gained the victory for England and thenceforward British dominion in India remained undisputed except by native princes. In 1772 Warren Hastings was appointed the first Governor-General and in 1784 Pitt's India Act established a Board of Control for the India Company. A great increase of trade resulted, and this rule continued down to 1858, when, as a result of the mutiny, the Crown assumed the sovereignty. British dominion ended in 1947.

Eau-de-Cologne, a popular distilled perfume first manufactured at Cologne in the 18th cent. by Johann Maria Farina, an Italian, and since made in large quantities in Cologne and elsewhere.

Ebony, a name applied to various hard black woods, the best of which are grown in Mauritius and Sri Lanka. There are also Indian and American varieties. Only the inner portions, the heartwood, of the trees are of the necessary hardness and blackness. Ebony is largely used in ornamental cabinet work, for piano keys, *etc.*

Ecce Homo ("Behold the Man!"), used in reference to the pictures and sculptures representing Christ crowned with thorns.

Ecclesiastical Courts, courts for administering ecclesiastical law and maintaining the discipline of the Church of England. Introduced by the Normans. Originally they had jurisdiction over both clergy and laity.

echidna, the spiny anteater, a native of the Australian outback.

Eclipse, the partial or complete obscuring of one heavenly body by another. An eclipse of the sun occurs when the moon, which is 1/400th of the diameter of the sun and about 1/390th as far away, obscures some portion of the sun as seen by an observer on the earth. A total eclipse occurs when the whole of the sun's disc is covered by the moon. Astronomers travel many thousands of miles to observe the outer layers of the sun and its corona, which is only possible when the light from the sun is totally obscured by the moon during the few minutes of an eclipse. The solar eclipse of 11 August 1999 attracted great attention (being Britain's first total solar eclipse for 70 years). It could be seen only from Cornwall. Total solar eclipses have occurred over parts of the British Isles in the years 1424, 1433, 1598, 1652, 1715, 1724, 1927, 1954 (visible from the Shetland Is.). An eclipse of the Moon occurs when the Moon moves into the Earth's shadow. When this happens, the sunlight is cut off and the lunar surface becomes quite dark until it emerges from the shadow again. Lunar eclipses can be either partial or total, depending on whether all or part of the Moon moves into the Earth's shadow. They are more common than solar eclipses. *See also* **Z11.**

Ecliptic is the sun's apparent path in the sky: the great circle described by the sun from west to east in the course of a year. The sun is exactly on the equator on approx. 21 March, and 23 September, and the points where the celestial equator and ecliptic intersect on these days are called the *equinoctial points.* On approx. 21 June and 22 December the sun reaches its greatest and least midday elevation and its greatest distance north and south of the equator, and the points on the ecliptic on these days are called the *solstices* (*see* **Seasons, Section Z**). These four points are equidistant from each other by 90°. The angle of the ecliptic to the earth's equator is called the obliquity of the ecliptic. Due to the gravitational perturbations of the other planets, both the equinoctial point and the obliquity of the ecliptic change with time. The value of the obliquity is *c.* 23·5.

Ecology, a term first described by the German biologist Haeckel in the 19th cent., is the study of the inter-relationships between living organisms and their environment. **Autecology** is the study of the environmental relationships of *individual* plants and species. **Synecology** is the study of plant and animal *communities* living together as groups.

Ecotourism is the form of tourism based on the natural ecological attractions of a country.

Ecumenical Council, a general council of the Christian Church summoned when important questions of Church doctrine and policy are to be decided. The early councils were predominantly Greek and convoked by the emperor. Those summoned by the pope when they meet at the Lateran Palace in Rome are called Lateran Councils; others have met at Constance, Florence, Trent and the Vatican. Their decisions are not binding on the rest of Christendom. Only 21 Ecumenical Councils have been held in the history of Christendom. The first

was held at Nicaea in 325 when the mystery of the Trinity was defined. The 21st (known as the 2nd Vatican Council), convened by Pope John, opened in October 1962 in St. Peter's, Rome, and ended in December 1965. Two of the principal themes were the reunion of all Christians with the Church of Rome and the Church's place in the modern world. At the last session of the Council the Pope announced his decision to establish for the first time an international synod of bishops in Rome for consultation and collaboration in the government of the Roman Church. This Senate of Bishops provides the balancing factor alongside the Curia, which represents the Papacy and not the episcopacy.

Edda, the name given to two important collections of early Icelandic literature—*the Elder or Poetic Edda,* poems handed down from the 9th and 10th cent., probably Norwegian in origin, and the *Younger* or *Prose Edda* of Snorri Sturluson compiled about 1230. They treat of legends of an early Scandinavian civilisation.

Eddystone Lighthouse, 21 km south of Plymouth, is one of the most isolated in the world. The tower is 51 m high, and its light can be seen for 28 km. The present structure is the fourth that has occupied this dangerous position. The first was of wood, completed by Winstanley in 1698, but it was destroyed by storm in 1703. In 1708 a second and stronger lighthouse was built by Rudyerd. This lasted until 1755, when it was destroyed by fire. Smeaton built the third lighthouse of granite and this withstood storm and tempest for over a hundred years, 1759–1881. The present lighthouse, also of granite, was built 1879–81 on a nearby rock by Sir James Douglass.

Eels, edible fishes of the order Apodes, with snakelike body covered with minute scales embedded in the skin. The common or freshwater eel *Anguilla anguilla* is found in the Atlantic coastal areas of N. America and Europe and in the Mediterranean, and breeds S.E. of Bermuda. The electric eel of S. America is able to cause electric shocks. Commercial sand eel fishing in the North Sea is currently depriving many birds, fish and marine mammals of their food.

Egret, a slender, graceful bird of the heron family, of pure white plumage, famed for its beautiful silky plumes (aigrettes), which appear in the breeding season, and for which it was ruthlessly hunted and would have been exterminated had not international action been taken to protect it. The Little Egret with black bill, black legs, and yellow feet breeds in Mediterranean lands.

Eider, a large diving duck, found along the rocky coasts of northern latitudes, well known for the beautifully warm soft down, called "eider down", which the female bird plucks from her breast to line her nest. In Norway and Iceland the haunts of the eider are preserved and the birds protected by law on account of the much prized "eider down", which is collected from the nests just before the breeding season. "Eider down" is so elastic that a kilogram of it will fill an ordinary bed covering.

Eiffel Tower, built by the French engineer Alexandre Gustave Eiffel (1832–1923) for the Paris Exhibition of 1889. The tower which is made of iron is 300 m high and weighs about 7,000 tonnes. It is France's most popular tourist site, attracting 5·4 million visitors each year.

Eisteddfod (a sitting) was originally a congress of Welsh bards and minstrels, and dates from before the 12th cent. These assemblies, discontinued for a long period, were resumed in 1819, and have been held yearly since, each lasting three or four days. Their object is to foster the Welsh patriotic spirit; they are devoted to orations and competitions in poetry, singing and harp-playing. Prizes are awarded.

Eland, largest species of antelope, native of Africa; large pointed horns, stands 1·5 m high at the withers, and weighs several hundred kg.

Elder, small trees of the *Sambucus* genus, with pinnate leaves, and clusters of white flowers and, later, small purplish-black berries. The black elder, the best known, thrives in Britain. A wine is made from its berries.

El Dorado, a "golden land", was an idea much favoured in the days of the early Spanish explorers. It was believed that somewhere on the South American continent there was a country abounding in gold and precious stones. Many expeditions were fitted out to discover it. Sir Walter Raleigh also embarked on this quest.

Electret, a piece of solid matter which retains a permanent electric polarisation analogous to the magnetic polarisation of a permanent magnet. There are various recipes for making them; carnauba wax is a common constituent.

Electricity. *See* **F21,** *also* **Energy Conversion.**

Electric Telegraph may be said to date from 1836, when Sir Charles Wheatstone and his co-inventor Cooke introduced their Single-Needle instrument, which was soon followed by the Double-Needle apparatus, Morse, in 1837, invented his famous recording instrument. The first electric cable was between Dover and France, and was laid in 1850. The first Atlantic cable was laid in 1858, and the second in 1866. It was in 1899 that the first Marconi wireless telegraph messages were sent between England and France.

Electroencephalograph, an instrument which records the minute voltages produced by the electrical activity of the brain by means of electrodes taped to the scalp. The record of brain waves, known as EEG, shows that there is a general cycle of activity in the brain that underlies both sleep and wakefulness.

Electrolysis is the condition established when an electric current passes through a conducting substance, between electrodes, resulting in decomposition and separation into constituents. Water thus becomes decomposed into hydrogen and oxygen.

Electromagnetic radiation. Radiation consisting of oscillating electronic and magnetic fields travelling together through space. Including visible light, the speed of travel is around 300,000 kms per second. Together with visible light, many different types exist including gamma rays, X-rays, ultraviolet and infrared radiation, microwaves and radio waves.

Electromagnetic waves. *See* **F14.**

Electron. *See* **F11, 16.**

Electronic News Gathering (ENG), also known in the United States as Electronic Journalism (EJ) or Electronic Camera Coverage (ECC), is a system for obtaining television pictures by means of very lightweight, portable electronic cameras. It is usually operated by a crew of two—cameraman and engineer—who are also equipped with a van or field car serving as a mobile base. Pictures from the unit can be used in three ways: they can be transmitted "live", beamed back by radio link to the studio, or recorded on to a videotape cassette on site and taken back to headquarters for editing and transmission. The chief advantage of ENG lies in its speed, as the use of electronic equipment avoids the delay which occurs in the chemical processing of film before it can be transmitted.

Electronics. The science which deals with the behaviour and control of free electrons. It started with the discovery of the electron by Sir J. J. Thomson in 1897. The practical applications, constituting electronic engineering, have given us radio, radar, photo-electric cells, cathode-ray oscillographs, electronic microscopes, television. Nowadays electronics uses devices like transistors such that the electrons move inside solid matter instead of *in vacuo*. This is sometimes referred to as "solid state electronics". *See also* **Microelectronics.**

Electron Microscope. A microscope in which beams of electrons are focused by magnetic lenses in a manner analogous to the focusing of light beams in the ordinary optical microscope. Modern electron microscopes have very high resolving power and can magnify up to 1,500,000 times, making it possible to explore the cell and the virus. A development of the electron microscope is the scanning electron microscope (stereoscan), developed at Cambridge, which can examine an essentially thick object, giving a very large depth of focus.

Electronvolt, unit of energy used in nuclear physics. It is the amount of energy required to move one electronic charge through a potential difference of one volt. It is very small—1.6×10^{19} joules—and therefore suited to atomic physics. 1 MeV = a million electronvolts; 1 GeV = a thousand million electronvolts; these

larger units are used in high energy physics.

Elementary Particle, one of the basic constituents of the material universe. The idea that matter consists of tiny particles goes back to classical times but the modern concept of the atom grew out of the chemistry and physics of the 19th cent. With the discovery of the electron in 1897 and the rise of nuclear physics in the 20th cent., the chemical atom was understood to be a structure built of even more fundamental particles—the electron, the proton and the neutron. In the last few decades, many more particles have been discovered, especially in the study of cosmic rays and by the use of large accelerating machines like those at CERN (Geneva) and Brookhaven National Laboratory (Long Island, New York). Among the later discoveries are the neutrino, the positron, the antiproton, the muon, the pion. These differ in electric charge and mass and other intrinsic properties and many have only a very short lifetime before they change into something else. Whether there is a small number of really elementary particles out of which all the others can be constructed is an unanswered question of contemporary physics. *See* **F15–17.**

Elements. In chemistry, substances which cannot be separated into two or more simpler chemical substances. 91 elements are found naturally on the earth, some are observed spectroscopically in the stars and planets, and a further fourteen have been made artificially. Between them these elements can appear in some 1,200 different isotopes, of which 317 occur in Nature. (There are 274 stable isotopes among 81 stable elements.) *See* **F6, F23,** and **F64.**

Elephant, a proboscidian mammal of which only two species survive—the Asiatic, in India, and the African elephant. No other animals possess a trunk. Both males and females have large ivory tusks, of considerable commercial value. The Indian elephant is usually about 2·7 m high and weighs about 3 tonnes; African elephants are larger, weighing about 6 tonnes, and are usually much fiercer. Several fossil elephants of still larger bulk have been discovered, including the mammoth and the mastodon. The Indian elephant is domesticated and used as a beast of burden, and may live 70 years. The ivory trade (banned in 1989) was responsible for the mass slaughter of perhaps 700,000 elephants. This evil trade still continues clandestinely. Today (1999) less than 50,000 Asian elephants still survive, with perhaps *c* 600,000 African elephants.

Elephant Seal. *See* **Sea Elephant, L109.**

Eleusinian Mysteries, festivals common throughout ancient Greece, agricultural in their symbolism.

Elgin Marbles, a collection of ancient Greek sculptures and architectural fragments got together by the 7th Earl of Elgin and brought to England between 1802 and 1812. These celebrated treasures had originally formed part of the Parthenon at Athens, and were probably carved by pupils of the sculptor Phidias. Lord Elgin expended over £70,000 upon them, and they were purchased for £35,000 for the British Museum. In May 1997 the new Labour Government ruled out their return to Greece.

Elk, the largest animal of the deer family, possessing enormous antlers, and standing, when mature, about 2 m high. The American moose is of the same family.

Elm, a stately, wide-spreading tree having some 20 species spread over north-temperate regions, several of which are native and peculiar to Britain. The grandest of the field elms is the English elm, *Ulmus procera*, which may reach a height of *c.* 42 m and a girth of 8 m. The wych elm, *U. glabra*, or Scots elm, is a valuable hardwood and used in boat-building. The fungus that causes Dutch elm disease is carried from tree to tree by a bark beetle. The fungus came from infected veneer logs from central Europe. Ironically the disease was named after the Dutch workers who discovered its cause! Since re-entering Britain in 1963, Dutch elm disease has caused the death of 12 million trees.

El Niño. *See* **L132.**

Elzevir, the name of a celebrated family of Dutch printers, who produced editions of Latin, French and German classics, which were highly valued for their beauty of type and accuracy of printing. They flourished in the 17th cent.

Ember-days are set apart for fasting and prayer in the Western Church, at the periods appointed for ordination, viz., the Wednesday, Friday and Saturday after the first Sunday in Lent, Whit-Sunday, 14 September (Holy Cross Day), and 13 December (St. Lucia's Day); of very ancient origin.

Embossing, the art of stamping in relief, letters or designs upon pliant substances.

Emerald. The rich green variety of beryl (beryllium aluminium silicate). The colour is due to the presence of chromium oxide.

Empire, the style created in France during the reign of Napoleon in architecture and all the arts. It is austerely classical, making much use of columns, pediments and the like in buildings as well as furniture, with eagles and sphinxes, reminiscent of Napoleon's campaigns, as ornaments. The style is heavy, grandiose and with a strong element of the heroic. A typical monument is the *Arc de Triomphe* in Paris (begun 1806), almost a repetition of a Roman model. In painting Jacques Louis David interpreted the style with heroic subjects taken from classical mythology or from Napoleon's career. The style was transmitted to the rest of Europe, remaining magnificent and rich at all the Bonaparte courts. In bourgeois surroundings in Germany and Scandinavia it became simple and domesticated.

Encaenia, a festival commemorating a dedication; at Oxford University the annual commemoration of benefactors, accompanied by the conferring of honorary degrees, is held in June.

Encyclical Letters, a term used in reference to letters addressed by the Pope to his bishops upon matters of doctrine or discipline.

Encyclopaedists, a term first applied to the eminent writers who collaborated in the French *Encyclopédie* (1751–65). They included Diderot, D'Alembert, Voltaire, Helvetius; their writings had great influence in popularising the social ideas which resulted in the French Revolution.

Energy. One of the most fundamental concepts of science. A body in motion possesses *kinetic energy* as a result of the *work* done by the forces creating the motion. But a force which does work to stretch a spring does not create motion. Instead, the work is stored up in the spring and is one example of *potential energy.* A raised body also possesses potential energy which turns into kinetic when the body falls. The *heat energy* contained in a body is the sum of the kinetic and potential energy of the constituent atoms which are vibrating all the time. Heat and motion are obtainable from electrical, magnetic, chemical, atomic, and other sources, and physicists therefore define corresponding forms of energy. The vital point is that all forms of energy are transferable into one another *without loss or gain.* This is the Law of Conservation of Energy. It is one of the most fundamental laws of science, and its general validity is the reason why energy is an important idea. Since Einstein, it has been recognised that mass also is interchangeable with energy. See **F18,** *also* **Nuclear Energy.**

Energy Conversion. For practical purposes it is frequently necessary to change energy from one into another of its many forms; indeed almost every activity does this in one way or another. The primary sources of energy are the sun, uranium and other elements from which nuclear energy can be drawn, and the tides. The sun is not much used *directly* because its heat is intermittent and not very intense, but solar cookers and refrigerators have been invented and solar batteries (*q.v.*) are used in spacecraft. The sun can be used *indirectly* because it has produced, *via* living processes, fossil fuels like coal and oil and still continues to generate winds, rain and rivers and hence hydroelectric and wind power. Commonly both fossil fuels and the energy of river or tidal waters are converted into electricity. Windmill type electricity generators are also quite common. The bulk of electricity production is a two-stage process: first fossil or nuclear fuel is used to create heat (*see* **Nuclear Reactors**); then the heat is used to raise steam and drive generators. Efforts are being made to convert heat into electricity more directly, *e.g.,* by using thermoelectric or thermionic effects (*q.v.*), but these have not been used for large-scale produc-

tion. Once electrical energy is available, factories can make chemical batteries in great numbers and these can then be used as portable energy sources, as can petrol and other refined forms of fossil fuel. *See* **Battery, Fuel Cell, Solar Battery.**

Engraving is the art of cutting or otherwise forming designs of pictures on wood, stone, or metal surfaces for reproduction by some method of printing. Wood-engraving was the earliest in the field, dating from the 15th cent. Later, engraving on steel and copper plates was introduced, and mezzotint, lithography, stipple, aquatint, *etc.* Most modern methods of reproduction are based on photography.

Entablature, that portion of a building which surmounts the columns and extends to the roof of the tympana of the pediments; it comprises the architrave, the frieze and the cornice.

Enthalpy, another name for the heat content (H) of a system in thermodynamics. If a system generates heat it is presumed that the heat comes from the enthalpy of the system which by the 1st law of thermodynamics thus falls. It can be combined with the entropy (S) in an equation which defines the important thermodynamic quantity called the Gibbs Free Energy: $G = H - TS$ where T is the thermodynamic temperature. G is important in the prediction of chemical change.

Entropy, one of the most important quantities in thermodynamics, symbol S. According to Clausius' statement of the Second Law the entropy of an isolated system cannot decrease. Although introduced by Clausius it arose from a consideration of Carnot's studies of the limitation of the convertibility of heat into work. It is most easily viewed as disorder in the statistical approach introduced by Boltzmann. This may be illustrated by considering the separate sets of coloured balls in a box. This is an ordered arrangement (of low entropy). The natural tendency is for the balls to mix and for the colours to become disordered (of higher entropy). We do not expect the opposite process for the balls to spontaneously separate, *i.e.,* we do not expect the entropy to decrease. In the context of energy changes, say in heat engines, the entropy change is equal to the heat change divided by the (thermodynamic) temperature (*see* **L3**).

Environment Agency, the government body established in 1996 to police emissions to air, land, rivers and coastal waters. It has merged the powers of the National Rivers Authority, Her Majesty's Inspectorate of Pollution and local waste regulation authorities.

Enzymes. Organic catalysts which accelerate chemical processes occurring in living organisms. There are a large number present in the cell, and most have a high degree of specificity. Enzyme mechanisms are the key to basic biological processes. See **Section F.**

Ephemoptera or **May-flies,** an order of insects. In the larval condition they exist from two to three years aquatically, but no sooner do they arrive at maturity than their lives are hurried to a close. They rise up in pyramids on warm summer nights, take no food, propagate and perish. The Latin name expresses the fact that the adults have an ephemeral existence.

Epiphany, a Christian festival celebrated on 6 January, originally an old solstice festival, celebrating the birth of light.

Equator, the imaginary great circle of the earth, every point of which is 90 degrees from the earth's poles, and dividing the northern from the southern hemisphere. It is from this circle that the latitude of places north and south is reckoned. The celestial equator is the circle in which the plane of the earth's equator meets the celestial sphere (the imaginary sphere, in which the observer is at the centre, used for representing the apparent positions of the heavenly bodies).

Equinox, the time when the sun crosses the plane of the earth's equator, making day and night of equal length.

Eras are distinctive periods of time associated with some remarkable historical event or personage. *The Christian era* is computed according to a 6th-cent. reckoning to begin with Jesus's birth, AD. 1. The date is placed some years too late. Scholars now believe that Jesus was born *c.* 4 B.C. The *Jewish era* dates

from 3761 B.C.; the *Julian era* from the altera-
tion of the calendar by Julius Caesar 45 B.C.; the
Mohammedan era from the date of the *Hejira*,
or the flight of Mohammed from Mecca to
Medina, which is A.D. 622, 16 July, in the
Julian Calendar.

Erbium, belongs to the group of rare-earth metals
discovered by Mosander in 1842. Element no. 68,
symbol Er.

Erg, the unit of work and energy in the centimetre-
gram-second system; the energy involved
when a force of 1 dyne moves its point of
application through a distance of 1 cm.

Ernie, the name given to the "electronic random
number indicator equipment", the electronic
machine which selected the prizewinning numbers in the first Premium Bond draw, June 1957.

Eros. This asteroid is 24–32 km in diameter.
It comes closer to the earth than any other
member of the solar system with the exception
of the moon and several very small asteroids.
Determination of solar parallax based on
observations of Eros in 1930–31 yielded until
then the most accurate estimate of the distance of
the sun from the earth. *See* **Astronomical unit.**

Erse, a term used by Lowland Scottish, and
English writers for the Gaelic language spoken
in the Highlands of Scotland. Sometimes
erroneously applied to Irish, the Gaelic language
as spoken in Ireland and revived as an official
language in recent times. Dr. Johnson, Sir
Walter Scott, and other writers used "Erse"
to signify Scottish Gaelic. The language of the
Scottish Lowlands (that used by Robert Burns)
is related to the English language and not to
Gaelic and is variously termed Scots, Braid
Scots, the Doric, the Scottish vernacular, and
fashionably of late, Lallans.

Escurial or **Escorial,** Spanish monastery built in
the mountains near Madrid by Philip II to
commemorate the victory over the French at
Saint-Quentin (1557). A palace was added later
and it also includes a church, library and royal
mausoleum. Built in granite in sombre style, it is
one of the finest buildings in Europe.

Eskimo. Popular name for the Inuit peoples of the
Arctic, living in Canada, Greenland, Alaska and
the northern territories of Russia. Canada has
recently agreed to grant self-government to an
Arctic Eskimo territory (Nunavut) (effective
from 1999).

Esperanto, an artificial international language
created by Ludwig Zamenhof of Warsaw and first
published in 1887. It does not seek to replace
national languages but to serve as a second
language for international communication. It
is based on the internationality of many words
in the principal modern languages, and is entirely
phonetic in spelling and pronunciation. In 1998
there were *c.* 10,000 British speakers of the language. Other artificial languages are Volapuk, Ido
and Glosa, a grammar-free international language
based on Latin and Greek.

Estates of the Realm in Britain are the Lords
Spiritual, the Lords Temporal and the Commons.

Esters. Organic chemicals formed by combining
an alcohol with an acid. They have a pleasant
smell, and occur naturally in plants as the
scent of flowers. Manufactured for use in the
perfumery industry, and as flavourings in food.
Some esters are used as solvents, notably amyl-
acetate ("pear drops") in quick-drying
paints. The polymeric fibre "Terylene"
consists of chains of molecules containing many
ester groups, formed by reacting an alcohol
having two alcoholic (OH) groups with an acid
having two acid (COOH) groups.

Etching, a technical method for producing graphic
work and works of art. A plate, traditionally
of copper, is covered with wax; the design or
picture desired is drawn with a sharp implement
which penetrates the wax. When the plate is
exposed to the action of an acid this will etch
into the copper where the lines have been drawn.
The wax is then removed, ink is applied to the
plate with its engraving, and the design or
picture can be printed on to paper in many
copies. Rembrandt, Goya and others made
great and original works of art in the technique,
but it was also widely used for reproductive
purposes before the invention of photography.
Hogarth painted his famous pictures in oil and
reproduced them graphically.

Ether, in chemistry, is a volatile inflammable
liquid composed of carbon, hydrogen and
oxygen. It is a valuable anaesthetic obtained
by heating alcohol with sulphuric acid. In
physics, in the 19th cent., all space was supposed
to be filled with a substance called ether, the
chief property of which was to carry light waves,
i.e., light was supposed to be waves in this all-
pervading medium known as the ether. Speculation and experiment concerned with the ether
were very fruitful in advancing physics. Ultimately the attempts by Michelson and Morley
to detect the motion of the earth through the
ether were unsuccessful in this respect but profoundly successful in stimulating the theory of
relativity. The ether concept has now been
abandoned.

Ethylene (also called ethene). A gas compounded
of carbon and hydrogen, it is related to acetylene
and ethane. Industrially it is obtained as a by-
product in petroleum refining. It has wide uses as
a starting material in the industrial manufacture of intermediates, especially alcohol. Its
most important application is in the production of
polythene (poly-ethylene). *See* **Catalyst.**

Etruscans, people believed to have come from
Asia Minor who colonised Italy about 900 B.C.,
settled in what is now Tuscany and part of
Umbria, reached the height of their civilisation
about 500 B.C., and were ultimately absorbed by
the Romans. They were skilled technicians in
bronze, silver and goldwork. Evidence of their
advanced civilisation was unearthed in 1998
beneath the ruins of Pompeii.

Etymology, the study of the origin and history of
words.

Euro, the name for the single European currency
agreed at the 1995 Madrid summit. It was
launched on 1 January 1999. A 'National
Changeover Plan' has been proposed to prepare
for possible British entry. *See* **Section G.**

Euro-dollar Market. An international financial
market, located mainly in Britain and Europe,
for lending and borrowing dollars, *i.e.*, titles to
dollar deposits in United States banks.

Europa, one of the moons of the planet Jupiter, on
which scientists believe the preconditions for life
could exist. For Jupiter, *see* **L69.**

Europe Day, designated 9 May (the anniversary of
the launch of the Schuman Plan in 1950).

European Space Agency was created in 1975 with
headquarters in Paris. Examples of space research
which it has undertaken include the Giotto probe
to Halley's Comet, involvement with the Cassini
mission to Saturn and the space station Spacelab.

Europium, element no. 63, symbol Eu, discovered
by Demarcay in 1906. A member of the rare-earth
metal group.

Euthanasia. *See* **J18.**

Evaporation is the process by which a solid or liquid
is resolved into vapour by heat. The opposite
process is condensation. Wherever a liquid or solid
surface is exposed, evaporation takes place into
the space above. If the vapour is continually
removed the solid or liquid vanishes into vapour;
the higher the temperature the quicker the
process. If the vapour is confined, then it collects,
getting more concentrated until as many atoms of
vapour are condensing as are evaporating. The
vapour is then said to be saturated. Evaporation
of water from sea, soil, plants, skin, *etc.*, is
continuously in progress.

Everest Expeditions. For many years after Mt.
Everest had been shown to be the highest
mountain in the world, political conditions in
Nepal, lying south of the summit, and in
Tibet, to the north, prevented mountaineers
from attempting an ascent. At last in 1921
the Tibetan authorities gave permission, and
the first expedition, organised by a joint committee of the Royal Geographical Society and the
Alpine Club, was sent out. This was primarily a
reconnaissance; besides mapping the northern
flanks, it found a practicable route up the
mountain. By 1939, six further expeditions
had climbed on the northern face. Some were
baulked by bad weather, others by problems
previously little known, such as the effect of
high altitudes on the human body and spirit.
Nevertheless, notable climbs were accomplished. In 1924, for example, Col. E. F.
Norton reached 8,589 m, and it was on this
expedition that George Mallory and Andrew

Irvine were seen going well at about the same height. They never returned, however. (The body of Mallory was eventually found in 1999, re-opening speculation that he may have reached the summit).

When the 1953 Expedition led by Col. John Hunt (later Lord Hunt), was being organised, stress was laid on three main points; proper acclimatisation of the climbers; use of oxygen for the final stages; and the establishment of very high altitude camps, so that the final assault parties would set out fresh and unencumbered. Great attention was also paid to recent developments in diet, clothing and equipment. In all these matters the 1953 expedition was able to draw on the accumulated experience of its predecessors. By the end of April, a base camp had been established below the ice-fall, and with the aid of thirty-four Sherpa porters supplies had been carried up into the Western Cwm. The next critical stage was the ascent of the steep head of the cwm, the Lhotse face, with the threat of avalanches always present. By most strenuous efforts, a camp was established on the South Col (7,869 m) on 21 May. From this camp on 26 May, T. D. Bourdillon and R. C. Evans climbed the South Peak of Everest (8,760 m), then the highest altitude ever attained. On 28 May Edmund Hillary and the Sherpa leader, Tenzing Norgay, spent the night at the highest camp (8,510 m) and on the following day, 29 May, climbed to the South Summit, negotiated the difficult final ridge, and reached the summit of Everest. On 17 May 1993 (exactly 40 years later) Rebecca Stephens became the first British woman to conquer Everest. In May 1995 the English climber Alison Hargreaves became the first woman to climb Everest without oxygen (she died later the same year on K2).

Evolution, in the words of Sir Julian Huxley (d. 1975), "a natural process of irreversible change which generates novelty, variety and increase of organisation". The theory, as laid down by Darwin, is that all existing species, genera and classes of animals and plants have developed from a few simple forms by processes of change and selection. Up to the time of Darwin a large part of the western world believed that life had been created suddenly at the beginning of the world which God had created, according to Archbishop Usher, on 22 October 4004 B.C. The evidence of the rocks, however, has given a more convincing theory of creation, and by studying the fossils preserved in the various layers of the earth's crust the past history of the earth has been pieced together. Darwin has been called the Newton of biology. *See* **Section F.**

Exchequer, which derives its name from the checkered tablecloth on which accounts were calculated in early Norman times, is a term connected with the revenues of the Crown. In former times it had jurisdiction in all revenue matters. The term Exchequer is now applied to the Governmental department which deals with the public revenues.

Existentialism. *See* **Section J.**

Exploration. Modern exploration began in the second half of the 15th cent. with the voyages of the great Portuguese and Spanish discoverers. They were followed by sailors of other European nations, who profited from their developments in navigation and from their charts, and in less than one hundred years the coastlines of much of the Americas, Africa and South-west Asia had been revealed and the globe circumnavigated. The motives of these early explorers were mixed: they were seeking adventure, trade, plunder, national power and conversion of the local people. Few if any were directly interested in advancing scientific knowledge. But from the reports of their voyages and travels, scholars at home compiled descriptions of the strange new world which stimulated their successors to undertake more systematic enquiries. One of the earliest English expeditions to be despatched for scientific research was that of William Dampier on the *Roebuck*, which was sent out by the Admiralty in 1699 to examine the coasts of North-west Australia. In the 18th cent. British explorers were at work mainly in the Pacific Ocean, with the object of breaking the Spanish monopoly of trade. Capt. James Cook sailed thither in 1769 to observe

first the transit of Venus at Tahiti, and then to search for the alleged great southern continent. On this voyage he discovered and charted much of the coasts of New Zealand and the east coast of Australia. On his second voyage he was the first to sail across the Antarctic Circle, and he showed that the southern continent was much smaller than had been supposed. By 1800 the general outlines of the continents, except for Antarctica were known, and explorers in the 19th cent. were largely engaged in opening up the interiors. In Africa British explorers solved two problems which had puzzled men for centuries: Mungo Park and Richard Lander established the true course of the River Niger, and Sir Richard Burton, J. H. Speke, Sir Samuel Baker and others revealed the true sources of the Nile. The greatest African explorer of that age was undoubtedly David Livingstone, the missionary, who in three great journeys explored the Zambesi and the region of the Great Lakes, spreading the Gospel, fighting the slave trade, and opening up the interior to settlement and trade. In North America Alexander Mackenzie was the first to cross the main breadth of the continent from sea to sea. In Asia motives were also mixed; men like Charles Doughty, who explored in Arabia, and Sir Francis Younghusband, who journeyed from China to India across the Gobi and the Himalayas, were impelled by a love of adventure and the quest for knowledge, but political considerations were often involved.

Explosives, substances which burn violently to produce gases in such volume that an explosion is induced. Gunpowder was the first explosive to be used; Roger Bacon's powder, consisting of charcoal, sulphur and saltpetre, was the only effective explosive until the 19th cent., but it was difficult to control. Nitroglycerine (glyceryl trinitrate) was first compounded in 1847 by adding glycerine to a mixture of sulphuric acid and nitric acid. In 1866 Alfred Nobel discovered how to make dynamite by absorbing nitroglycerine in the fine sand kieselguhr. Cordite was the joint invention of Sir Frederick Abel and Sir James Dewar (1889). It came into general use as a propellant. High explosives, providing bursting charge for shells and bombs, include TNT (trinitrotoluene), picric acid, cyclonite (RDX) and many others. Slurry explosives can be pumped on to the site and therefore offer advantages in transportation and safety; they are also waterproof. Chemical explosives have now been eclipsed by nuclear explosives.

Expressionism, a modern art movement confined primarily to the non-Latin countries of Europe which sought to give expression to intimate and personal emotions by means of distortions of line and colour and simplified style which carried a greater impact in terms of feeling. Broadly speaking, this has been characteristic of northern art in general. (*See* **Gothic**) The term is usually used of the modern movement which influenced the Post-impressionists and subsequent movements in France. Tired of the naturalism of the Impressionists, such artists as van Gogh, Gauguin, Matisse and Rouault, together with the Fauvists (*q.v.*) made use of simple outlines and strong colours. Apart from Toulouse-Lautrec, the principal Expressionists were Norwegian, like Munch, or German, like the painters of *Die Brücke* and *Der Blaue Reiter* groups. Individual artists were Ensor, Kokoschka, Nolde, Rouault and Soutine.

F

Fabian Society. *See* **Section J.**

Fables are fictitious narratives intended to enforce some moral precept, and may be either in prose or verse, and deal with personified animals and objects or with human beings. Aesop in ancient times and Hans Christian Andersen and the Brothers Grimm (in many of their stories) in later days, have given fables. Mention must also be made of La Fontaine and Krylov.

Fairs were established in mediaeval times as a

means of bringing traders and customers together at stated periods, and formed the chief means of distribution. The great English fairs of early times were those of Winchester and Stourbridge near Cambridge. Traders from the Netherlands and the Baltic gathered there with the great merchants of London, and goods of every kind, wholesale and retail, were sold. One of the biggest trade fairs was at Nijni-Novgorod, founded in the 17th cent.; other big continental fairs were those of Leipzig (founded in the 12th cent.), Lyons and Prague. Expositions of advanced industrial products are still popular today.

Fairy Rings are the circles caused in grassland by certain fungi. The circles expand outwards as the fungus spreads, the fruiting bodies being at the periphery. Farther inward where the fungi are decaying the grass grows more strongly, fertilised by the nitrogen released from the rotting fungi. In olden times these rings were held to be the scene of fairy dances.

Falcon, name given to diurnal birds of prey which belong to the same family, *Falconidae*, as the hawk, eagle, buzzard, kite and harrier. They are swift of wing and feed on birds and small mammals. These birds have long, pointed wings, strong, hooked and notched bill, long, curved claws and an eye of great power. They are found all over the world. Those that breed in Britain are the Kestrel (the most common), Hobby (one of the swiftest of European birds), Merlin and Peregrine, a swift and magnificent bird with slate-grey back, blackish crown, black "moustache" and whitish breast. Other members of the family are the Gyr Falcon from northern latitudes, Iceland and Greenland, which is a winter visitor to Britain, the Lanner, Saker, Eleonora's falcon, Red-footed falcon and the Lesser Kestrel. The Gyr Falcon and the Peregrine were used in the sport of falconry in olden times. Because of its fearlessness and larger size, the female bird was used. When the quarry was sighted, the bird was unhooded, set free, and after mounting high into the air would dart swiftly down to strike the prey. The heron was the usual victim. Recent research has proved that diving peregrine falcons are the fastest birds in the world.

Fall-out. Radioactive material produced by nuclear explosions which may cause bodily and genetic damage. (1) *Local fall-out*, due to the return to earth of larger particles, occurs locally, and within a few hours after the explosion; (2) *Tropospheric fall-out*, due to particles which remain in the troposphere and come down within a month or so, possibly all over the world, but within the altitude in which the explosion occurred; (3) *Stratospheric fall-out*, which comes from fragments taken up into the stratosphere and then deposited, in the course of many years, uniformly all over the globe. The two radioactive materials which have given rise to the greatest concern for the health of the individual are strontium-90 and iodine-131. Both these materials are liable to become concentrated in certain parts of the human body, strontium-90 in bone and iodine-131 in the thyroid gland. Radiation exposure may produce genetic effects, that is effects which may show up in succeeding generations. An extensive survey was carried out by scientists of the US Atomic Energy Commission on the islands of Bikini atoll, site of some 23 nuclear tests, 1946–58. Their records, published in 1969, revealed that the intensity of radioactivity underneath the point of explosion was still exceedingly high. Most of the radiation remaining was due to the radioactive isotope caesium-137. The variation in intensity from one place to another seemed to be correlated with the variations of vegetation: where there was little vegetation weathering had been rapid.

Fantail, a variety of the domestic pigeon; also a genus of Australian birds of the *Muscicapidae* family. A small New Zealand bird is called a fantail.

Fan Tracery, a complicated style of roof-vaulting, elaborately moulded, in which the lines of the curves in the masonry or other material employed diverge equally in every direction. It is characteristic of the late Perpendicular period

of Gothic architecture, and may be seen in St. George's Chapel at Windsor and the Chapel of Henry VII at Westminster Abbey.

Farmer-General, the name given to the financiers who in the days of the old French monarchy farmed certain taxes, contracting to pay the Government a fixed sum yearly, on condition that the unspecified taxes were collected and appropriated by themselves. The revolution of 1789 swept the Farmer-General away.

Fascism. *See* **Section J.**

Fata Morgana, the name given to a curious mirage often observed over the Straits of Messina, attributed to the magic of the fairy Morgana, half-sister of King Arthur, who was fabled to live in Calabria.

Fathers of the Church were early writers who laid the foundations of Christian ritual and doctrine. The earliest were the Apostolic Fathers (*q.v.*). The Four Fathers of the Latin Church were St. Ambrose, St. Jerome, St. Augustine and St. Gregory the Great. The Four Fathers of the Greek Church were St. Basil, St. Gregory Nazianzen, St. John Chrysostom and St. Athanasius.

Fathom, a nautical measure, the six-foot stretch (1·8 m) of a man's arms. Replaced by the metre on British Admiralty charts, but continued on yachtsmen's coastal charts.

Fatigue, a condition leading to breakage when a solid component, *e.g.*, an axle, is subjected to a large number of fluctuating repetitive stresses. Fatigue is the cause of most failures in service of metal engineering components though fatigue is not confined to metallic materials alone. Fatigue failures result from the *repetition*, not simply from the *size* of the stresses; indeed, fatigue breakage can result from stresses much lower than the material could stand if the load were applied steadily. Fatigue causes minute cracks, usually at the surface, which grow and spread. Early detection is difficult and fatigue, discovered by the railway engineers of the 19th cent., remains a severe engineering problem.

Fats are important foodstuffs. In physiology they constitute a valuable form of reserve food. They contain carbon, hydrogen and oxygen; chemically they are described as esters of glycerol (glycerine). Commonest fats are stearin, palmitin and olein, esters formed by the combination of glycerol with stearic, palmitic and oleic acid respectively. Fats are converted into soap by alkali; this process (saponification) also releases glycerol.

Fatwa, an edict issued by a Moslem religious leader (*e.g.* the death threat to Salman Rushdie issued in 1989 by Ayatollah Khomeini).

Fault, a term designating a breakage coupled with displacement of geological strata. *See* **F9**(2).

Fauvism (French *Fauve* = wild beast), a term used, at first contemptuously, to describe the work of a group of French painters who first exhibited at the Salon d'Automne in Paris in 1905. The most prominent among them was Henri Matisse. Forms are freely distorted and colours are selected and applied for their emotive power with no necessary reference to the "real" colour of the object in question. Other famous *Fauves* were Derain, Vlaminck and Rouault. By 1908 the group had lost its cohesion and its members went their separate ways.

February, the second month of the year, contains in ordinary years 28 days, but in leap years 29 days. When first introduced into the Roman calendar by Numa, *c.* 700 B.C. it was made the last month of the year, preceding January, but in 452 B.C. the position of the two months was changed, February following January.

Federation. *See* **Confederation.**

Félibrige, a movement founded in 1854 to revive the ancient glories of Provence, initiated by the French poet Frédéric Mistral.

Felspar, the name given to a group of minerals, silicates of aluminium with some calcium and sodium, or potassium, which make up probably more than half of the earth's crust. It is formed in granite and other rocks, both igneous and metamorphic.

Fenestella, the niche set apart on the south side of the altar for the piscina in Roman Catholic churches.

Fermentation, the action of chemical ferments or *enzymes* in bringing about chemical changes in the materials of living animals and plants, *e.g.*, the breaking-down of sugar by yeast into alcohol.

Ferret, a domesticated polecat. It is about half the size of a cat and is bred in captivity to hunt rats and rabbits. It has a long sinuous body and short legs which enable it to enter rabbit and rat holes and chase the quarry out to guns or into nets. Such ferreting is a popular country sport.

Ferrites are compounds containing iron, oxygen, and one or two of a certain range of other possible metallic elements. Ferrites have recently become very important technically, because, unlike ordinary magnetic materials, they combine strong magnetism with electrical insulating properties. Ferrite-rod aerials are now common in portable radios, and ferrite devices are used in radar.

Feudalism. See **Section J.**

Fieldfare, the largest member of the thrush family, a regular winter visitor to Britain from Scandinavia. It is brown in colour with a lighter spotted breast and a grey head.

Field-Marshal, the highest ranking title in the British army, and only bestowed on royal personages and generals who have attained great distinction. The first British Field-Marshal was created in 1736, when John, Duke of Argyll, had the title conferred upon him by George II.

Fifth Column. When Franco, the Spanish dictator, revolted against the Spanish Republic in 1936 and attacked Madrid with four armies, his commander, General Mola declared that a group of fascists within the city was assisting the besiegers. The term is used to describe a body of spies behind a fighting front.

Fighting-Fish, small pugnacious Thai fish with long caudal and ventral fins. They are kept in glass globes in Thailand, and when brought into contact will fight to the death, these encounters being the occasion of much gambling.

Filibuster, a name first given to pirates and buccaneers in the 17th cent. who took possession of small islands or lonely coast lands, and there maintained themselves apart from any governing authority. In later times the term was used to specify men taking part in expeditions whose object was to appropriate tracts of country, and settle upon them in disregard of international law. The most notable expeditions of this kind in modern times were those of Narciso Lopez against Cuba in 1850-51, and of William Walker against Nicaragua, between 1855 and 1860. Both leaders were captured and executed. The term is also used to express the right of a minority in the United States Senate for unlimited debate, which is used on occasions to delay legislation.

Finches, a large family of small birds belonging to the Passerine or perching order of birds. There are about 200 species, including greenfinch, hawfinch, chaffinch, goldfinch, siskin, bullfinch, crossbill, linnet, twite and bunting.

Fir, a cone-bearing tree with small evergreen leaves and of considerable use as timber. There are two types: the Silver Firs and the Douglas Firs numbering about 25 species. All these firs attain to a considerable height, and all yield turpentine or other resinous material.

Fire-damp. See **Methane.**

Fire-Fly, a small winged insect of the *Eleteridae* family, is able to throw out a strong phosphorescent light in the dark. There are some remarkable specimens in tropical countries.

Fire of London, of 1666, extended from East to West, from the Tower to the Temple church, and northward to Holborn Bridge. It broke out in a baker's shop in Pudding Lane, and lasted four days, and destroyed 87 churches, including St. Paul's Cathedral, and many public buildings, among them the Royal Exchange, the Custom House and the Guildhall. In the ruins were 13,200 houses and 400 streets. About 100,000 people were made homeless yet in about 10 years all the houses had been rebuilt. The plague had not disappeared from London when the fire occurred.

Firkin, a former measure of capacity, the fourth part of a barrel, now only used in reference to a small cask or tub for butter, lard, *etc.*

Fischer-Tropsch Process. A process for making synthetic petrol from carbon monoxide and hydrogen. The synthesis is accelerated by cobalt-thoria and nickel-thoria catalysts.

Fish Louse. Parasitic crustacea found on marine and fresh-water fishes and whales.

Fission, Nuclear. A nuclear reaction in which the nucleus of an atom (*e.g.*, uranium 235, plutonium) captures a neutron, and the unstable nucleus so produced breaks into two nearly equal fragments and throws out several neutrons as well. In biology the term fission is applied to reproduction by fragmentation of a single-cell organism, as in amoeba.

Flagella, single hair-like projections found on many micro-organisms. Their sole function is, by complicated motion, to move the organism about. They are longer and less versatile than cilia (*q.v.*).

Flag Officer, a British naval officer who enjoys the right of carrying a flag at the mast-head of his ship, and is of the rank of Admiral of the Fleet, Admiral, Vice-Admiral or Rear-Admiral.

Flagship, the ship that flies the Admiral's flag, and from which orders proceed.

Flamingo, a strangely beautiful, extremely slender wading bird of white and rose-pink plumage with long, slender legs and neck and a long, down-curved bill with which it rakes the mud and obtains its food of worms and molluscs. The wings are bright crimson, bordered with black, and a flock in flight is a picture of singular beauty. There is a large and famous colony in the Camargue, S.E. France.

Flash-Point. This is found by heating an oil in a special cup and taking the temperature at which sufficient vapour is produced to ignite when a small flame is applied. It is an index of the inflammability of oils.

Fleas. Fleas are small parasitic insects belonging to the order *Aphaniptera* (so called because these creatures have no wings). They obtain their food by sucking blood from their host. They are laterally compressed, which immediately distinguishes them from lice. The human flea (*Pulex irritans*) is able to jump vertically a distance of over 18 cm.

Fleet Prison, a noted debtors' prison that stood on the east side of Farringdon Street, London. It was notorious for the cruelties inflicted on prisoners, particularly under the wardenship of Thomas Bainbridge who took charge in 1728. It was pulled down in 1846.

Fleet Street, a famous thoroughfare in London, until 1990 the centre of journalism and newspaperdom, though it was long celebrated for its taverns. It takes its name from the Fleet stream which used to run from Hampstead through Holborn to the Thames at Blackfriars.

Flemings, the Dutch-speaking people of Flanders, whose medieval ancestors excelled in the textile arts: England owes its early eminence as a manufacturing nation to the migration of numbers of Flemings to this country in the 16th and 17th cent. *See also* **Walloons.**

Fleur de Lis, the former national emblem of France, the flower of the lily. It was superseded by the Tricolour in 1789, but is still adhered to by the supporters of the old French monarchy.

Flint, consists of granular chalcedony with some opaline silica, and occurs as nodules and bands in the Chalk. It is hard and has a conchoidal fracture, so enabling it to be used in making cutting implements in prehistoric times. Before the invention of lucifer matches, it was used along with steel for striking lights.

Flint implements are objects found in the younger geological strata, and constituting evidence of the condition and life of the period. They include knives, clubs, arrow-heads, scrapers, *etc.*, used as weapons, tools and possibly as surgical instruments and in religious ceremonies. Similar to prehistoric specimens are the flint and obsidian implements of some of the primitive peoples of today. Ritual weapons and sacrificial knives continued to be made of stone long after the introduction of metals for practical purposes.

Flounder, one of the most familiar of the smaller flat fishes common round the British coasts, and seldom attaining a weight of over 1·3 kg.

Fluoridation, the process of adding the element fluorine, in the form of suitable compounds, to something deficient in it. Commonly met with as a proposal to add fluorides (fluorine compounds) to drinking water to combat dental decay, especially in children. Some toothpastes are fluoridated and fluoride can also be taken as tablets and in other ways. In 1976 a working party of the Royal College of Physicians recommended that water supplies should be fluoridated when the natural fluoride level is below 1 mg/litre. This recommendation drew on many investigations throughout the world giving evidence for the effectiveness of fluoride in the prevention of decay without harmful side-effects. There is, however, a body of opinion unconvinced by this and opposed to adding fluoride to drinking water, one argument being that to take or not to take fluoride should be a personal decision.

Fluorine, chemical element, no. 9, member of the halogen family, symbol F, it is found in combination with calcium in fluorspar, and occurs in minute quantities in certain other minerals. Discovered by Scheele in 1771, it was first obtained by Moissan in 1886. A pale yellow gas, it is very reactive and combines with most elements except oxygen. Its acid, hydrogen fluoride, etches glass, the fluorine combining with the silicon to form volatile silicon fluoride. Organic fluorine compounds have found use as very stable polymers which resist a wide variety of chemical actions.

Fluorescent Lamp. *See* **Electric Light and Ultra-Violet Rays.**

Fluorocarbons are hydrocarbons in which some or all of the hydrogen atoms have been replaced by atoms of chlorine or fluorine. They are non-toxic, non-flammable and chemically inert gases or low boiling point liquids. These properties make them very suitable for use as refrigerants, and propellants in fire-extinguishers and aerosols. The most widely used fluorocarbons are the chlorofluoromethanes (CCl_2F_2, CCl_3F and $CHClF_2$). In 1974 it was first suggested that the vast release of fluorocarbons into the atmosphere due to the greatly increased use of aerosols could cause a significant depletion of the protective ozone (*q.v.*) layer in the upper atmosphere. The mechanism for this involves the decomposition of fluorocarbons at high altitudes as a result of intense solar irradiation. The chlorine atoms so released can then catalyse the conversion of ozone into ordinary molecular oxygen. The degree of ozone depletion that will result is a matter of considerable current controversy. Similarly, opinions differ as to the detrimental effect ozone depletion might have on the incidence of skin cancer and on the climate.

Fluorspar, a mineral; chemically calcium fluoride. Can be colourless, green or yellow, but is most commonly purple. Blue fluorspar under the name of Derbyshire "blue John" has been used for ornamental purposes.

Fly, the popular name for a large number of insects with one pair of wings and a proboscis terminating in a sucker through which fluid substances can be drawn up. The best-known species are the common house-fly, the blue-bottle and the blow-fly. In the larval form flies are maggots, and feed upon decaying substances, animal flesh, *etc.* Flies are able to walk upon ceilings or upright surfaces by having suckers at the soles of their feet. *See* **Diptera.**

Flycatcher, name of a large family of small birds, the Muscicapidae. They are insect feeders, catch their food in the air, and are distributed over most countries of the world. The spotted and the pied nest in Britain, which they visit from April to September.

Flying Fish are frequently to be seen in southern waters, and are capable of gliding considerable distances without touching the water. To build up speed for its "take-off " the fish swims rapidly, to break the surface at 24–32 km/h. Maximum air speed is about 64 km/h.

Flying Fox, a member of the bat family, but of much larger size, and confined to the tropical and sub-tropical Old World. Like the bats, it is nocturnal, but it feeds entirely on fruits.

Flying Lemur. *See* **Colugo.**

Flying Lizard, or *Draco,* an Asiatic lizard, pos-

sessing wing-like projections from each side which enable it to make flying leaps through the air, though not sufficient for continuous flight.

Flying Saucers. *See* **Section J.**

Flying Squirrel, rodents of which there are several species in Europe, Asia and America. It possesses a parachute-like fold of skin by means of which it projects itself through the air. In appearance they are much like ordinary squirrels, to which they are related. The African flying squirrels belong to a different family.

Fog is caused by the presence of particles of condensed water vapour or smoke in the surface layers of the atmosphere, the term being applied meteorologically when the resulting obscurity is such as to render objects invisible at distances of up to 1 km. Fogs are frequently formed when the air near the ground is cooled below its dew-point temperature by radiation on a still, cloudless night; by flowing over a relatively cold land or water mass; or by mixing with a colder air stream. An accumulation of smoke over a large city may cause a high fog cutting off the daylight and producing gloom. *See* **Pollution, Aerosol.**

Foliation, a geological term applied to rocks whose component minerals are arranged in parallel layers as the result of strong metamorphic action.

Folio, a printing term for a sheet of paper folded once, a half sheet constituting a leaf.

Folklore concerns itself with the mental and spiritual life of the people—both civilised and primitive—as expressed in the traditional beliefs, customs, institutions and sayings that have been handed down from generation to generation by word of mouth and with the observation, recording and interpretation of such traditions. (The word *folklore* itself was first suggested and used—as two words *Folk Lore*—by W. J. Thoms in the *Athenaeum* of 22 August 1846, and was at once absorbed into the English language.) Traditional lore of the kind included in the term folklore takes many forms and ranges from omens of good and bad luck (spilling the salt, breaking a mirror, dropping an umbrella, *etc.*) and the wearing of amulets or the possession of talismans (such as the horseshoe) as protection against misfortune, to elaborate ceremonial dances such as the Abbots Bromley Horn Dance, the Hobby horses of Padstow and Minehead the Northern sword-dances and the Christmas mummers' plays. Especially important are the beliefs and customs associated with birth, babyhood, marriage and death such being occasions when the individuals concerned require special protection or when unusual happenings can be used for foretelling their future. The child born on a Sunday will be the luckiest; rocking on an empty cradle will ensure the speedy arrival of a new baby; throwing an old shoe after a newly-married couple brings them luck; the bride should be carried over the threshold of the new home; on the sea-coast, death is believed to take place at the ebb-tide; the bees must be told of the death of the master of the house, or they will leave the hive. Another very large section of the subject deals with the traditional sayings and practices associated with particular days and seasons of the year—calendar customs, as they are called. The eating of pancakes on Shrove Tuesday; Mother Sunday customs and the simnel cake; Good Friday as the right day for planting potatoes, but emphatically the wrong day for washing clothes or cutting one's finger-nails; the necessity of wearing something new on Easter Sunday; the children's maypole dances and May garlands; midsummer fires; All Hallowe'en as the most favourable occasion for divining the future—especially in respect of marriage—and for games and sports such as apple-bobbing; the numerous practices accompanying the harvest. All these are examples of calendar customs; their full story would occupy several volumes. Folklorists are interested in all such oral tradition because they think that to a large extent it represents what folk have mentally stored up from the past and transmitted to their descendants throughout the centuries, and because therefore it is able to assist other historic methods—ethnographical, linguistic, archaeological, etc.—in the elucidation of the early story of man. In those countries with a great diversity of peoples in all stages of culture, a knowledge of folklore and what it can teach is of great importance. The Folk-Lore Society was founded in 1878, and that part of the subject represented by song and dance has now its own English Folk Dance and Song Society.

Food Standards Agency, an independent watchdog proposed by the Government to restore consumer confidence in food safety.

Footpath. In English law a highway over which the public have a right of way on foot only, other than such a highway at the side of a public road. *See also* **Long-Distance Walks.**

Force, as a term in physics, signifies an influence or exertion which, when made to act upon a body, tends to move it if at rest, or to affect or stop its progress if it be already in motion. In the c.g.s. system, the unit of force is the dyne; in the foot-pound-second system, the poundal; in the SI system, the newton.

Formaldehyde. Chemically it lies between methyl alcohol and formic acid; oxidation of methyl alcohol yields formaldehyde, and oxidation of formaldehyde produces formic acid. It is used as a disinfectant, in silvering mirrors, and in the manufacture of phenolformaldehyde plastics (of which bakelite is the best-known example). Solutions of formaldehyde in water, formalin, are used to preserve biological specimens.

Forme, a body of letterpress type, composed and secured for printing from; or a stereotype or electrotype. The former is used more for newspaper formes and the latter in book work.

Formic Acid can be obtained from a colourless fluid secreted by ants and other insects and plants. It is a strong irritant. Commercially it is obtained from sodium formate, which is synthesised by the absorption of carbon monoxide in caustic soda. It is used in the electroplating, tanning and textile industries.

Fossils. Remains of animals and plants, or direct evidence of their presence, preserved in rocks. They include petrified skeletons and shells, leaf imprints, footprints, *etc.*

Four Freedoms, a phrase coined by President Roosevelt in January 1941, embodying what should be the goal of the Allies. They were (1) Freedom of speech and expression; (2) Freedom of every person to worship God in his own way; (3) Freedom from want; (4) Freedom from fear.

Fox, carnivorous animal of the canine family, found in considerable numbers in most parts of the world. The common fox *Vulpes vulpes* of Europe is a burrowing animal of nocturnal habits, living upon birds, rabbits and domestic poultry, in the capture of which it displays much cunning. The fox in Britain is preserved from extinction chiefly for hunting purposes. Among other notable species are the Arctic fox and the red fox of North America, of which the valuable silver fox, coveted for its fur, is a variety. An estimated 15% of foxes are now to be found in the suburbs, scavenging the streets at night for left-over food. In 1997 the House of Commons voted overwhelmingly to ban the hunting of foxes with dogs, but the Bill failed to become law.

Fox-Shark *or* **Thresher Shark,** a large species of shark common in the Atlantic and in the Mediterranean. It is very destructive to small fish, but although it attains a length of 4·5 m it is not dangerous to man.

Franciscans. *See* **Friars.**

Franco-German War (1870–71) was opened by a declaration of war by Napoleon III, but the Germans who were better prepared than the French, won victory after victory. On 12 September Napoleon with 104,000 men were made prisoners at Sedan, a republic was then proclaimed, and Paris sustained a four months' siege. In the end France ceded Alsace and part of Lorraine to Germany, who claimed a war indemnity of £200 million. Revenge for the loss of these territories played an important part in French politics.

Frankincense is of two kinds, one being used as incense in certain religious services and obtained

from olibanum, an Eastern shrub, the other is a resinous exudation derived from firs and pines, and largely used in pharmacy.

Franklin, the name given in feudal times to a country landowner who was independent of the territorial lord, and performed many of the minor functions of local government, such as serving as magistrate.

Freeport, a port exempt from customs duties and regulations. The north German towns of the Hanseatic League (**L56**) were among the earliest and most famous freeports.

Freira, small grey and white sea bird. Extremely rare, it nests on the island of Madeira. Likely to become the first European species to face extinction since the Great Auk in 1844.

Fresco, a painting executed upon plaster walls or ceilings, a technique which has remained unchanged since it was practised by the great Renaissance artists.

Friars, members of certain mendicant orders of the Roman Catholic Church. The four chief orders are the Franciscans or Grey Friars, the Dominicans or Black Friars, the Carmelites or White Friars and the Augustinians (Austin Friars).

Friday, the 6th day of the week, named after Frigga, the wife of Odin. It is the Mohammedan Sabbath, a general abstinence day of the Roman Catholic Church, and according to popular superstition, an unlucky day.

Friends, The Society of. *See* **Quakers, Section J.**

Frigate-Bird, a web-footed bird widely distributed over tropical latitudes, and deriving its name from its great expanse of wing and forked tail, resembling the shape of a swift vessel. It feeds on flying fish mostly, being unable to dive and also steals from other birds. A frigate-bird was found dying on the Hebridean island of Tiree in July 1953; only twice previously had one been recorded in Europe—the first on the German coast in 1792, and the second on the coast of France in 1902.

Frog, a familiar amphibian, breathing through gills in the earlier (tadpole) part of its existence and through lungs later. It remains three months in the tadpole stage. The frog hibernates underwater in the mud during the winter. Britain now (1999) has only one species of native frog, the common frog (*Rana temporaria*).

Frost occurs when the temperature falls to, or below, 0°C, which is freezing point. Hoar frost is applied to the needles or feather-like crystals of the ice deposited on the ground, in the same manner as dew. Glazed frost is the clear icy coating which may be formed as a result of rain falling on objects whose temperatures are below the freezing point. These layers of ice, often rendering roads impassable for traffic, damaging overhead power and communication systems and endangering aircraft, can also be caused by condensation from warm, damp winds coming into contact with very cold air and freezing surfaces.

Froth-Hopper *or* **Frog-Hopper.** A family of bugs (belonging to the insect order *Hemiptera*) which in the larval stage surround themselves with a protective mass of froth ("cuckoo spit"). These insects, which suck the sap of plants, bear a faint resemblance to frogs, and the adults possess great leaping powers.

Fuel Cells. A recent development is a type of battery into which the active chemicals are fed from external fuel tanks. This is the *fuel cell*, which is being developed in a number of versions in several countries. One was demonstrated in action when in 1959 Bacon of Cambridge University used his fuel cell to drive a fork-lift truck and a welding machine. The Bacon fuel cell consists of two electrodes of porous nickel dipping into a solution of caustic potash in water. One electrode is supplied with hydrogen gas from an outside cylinder and the other with oxygen. These gases, forming layers on the nickel, are the active chemicals. The oxygen combines with water to make two negatively charged ions, each consisting of an oxygen and a hydrogen atom joined together (a hydroxyl ion). The hydroxyl ions travel through the solution to the hydrogen electrode, where they combine with hydrogen to form neutral water. Their negative charge (one electron per ion involved) has now arrived at the hydrogen electrode and is ready to flow back to the other electrode through any outside circuit that is provided. This flow constitutes the useful electric current, and it has been provided at the expense of creating water out of the original hydrogen and oxygen. The water can be removed in the form of steam. What is the advantage of all this? In the first place the fuel gases are easy to make and to store in cylinders. Supplying a new gas cylinder is easier and quicker than recharging an ordinary accumulator. Furthermore, a fuel cell is lighter for a given power than an accumulator; satellite designers have found them useful. The fuel cell is not damaged by heavy overloading, and this is valuable for application to vehicle driving. Fuel-cell-driven buses could combine the advantage of diesel buses and trolleybuses. Fuel cells are still in the development stage. It is not certain how they will compete with combustion engines or, in an oil-less future, with improved ordinary batteries.

Fulani, a non-Negro people of Hamitic stock widely distributed in N.W. Africa, chiefly in Nigeria. There are two main branches: the dark-skinned Fulani, settled farmers and city dwellers, Moslem in religion; and the light-coloured Bororo'en who are semi-nomadic herdsmen. The Fulani are different from any tribe in W. Africa though they resemble in some ways the Masai of E. Africa. The Fulani conquered the Hausa states at the beginning of the 19th cent. which passed under British suzerainty after 1903. Sokoto, built in 1810, was capital of the Fulani empire.

Fuller's Earth, a special kind of clay or marl possessing highly absorbent qualities, originally used in the "fulling"—that is, cleansing and felting—of cloth. Now used in clarifying oils. Deposits in America and in south of England.

Function. In mathematics, one quantity y is said to be a function of another quantity x, written $y = f(x)$, if a change in x results in some corresponding change in y. Thus $\sin x$ or $\log x$ are functions of x. If y depends not only on x but on several other quantities as well, y is called a function of many variables.

Functionalism, in architecture, a movement originated by Le Corbusier, Swiss-born French architect and town-planner, who applied the austere principles of the Purist movement in painting to his own art. From about 1924 he designed in concrete, steel and glass, buildings in which every part had a significance in terms of function on the theory that objects created to carry out their particular function to perfection cannot help being beautiful. "A house is a machine for living in." The style was in vogue between the two wars and it is still the basis of most modern architecture.

Fungi, a class of simple plants, which reproduce from spores and lack the green colouring matter *chlorophyll.* It includes moulds, rusts, mildews, smuts, mushrooms, etc. Potato blight is a fungus disease which caused the failure of the potato crop in Ireland in 1846. 50,000 different fungi are known. *See also* **F44(2).**

Furniture Beetle (*Anobium punctatum*). The common furniture beetle is responsible for 80 per cent of all woodworm damage and is the great pest of the comparatively modern house, causing damage in the main to softwood roofing and flooring timbers. Adults are 3 mm long. The grub tunnels for about 33 months. *See also* **Woodworm, Death Watch Beetle.**

Futurism, an Italian school of art and literature initiated by Marinetti, an Italian writer and mountebank friend of Mussolini at a later period. Its origin took the form of a manifesto published in Paris in 1909 in which Marinetti glorified violence, war and the machine age. In its aggression it favoured the growth of fascism. One of the distinctive features of Futurist art was the use of the principle of "simultaneity" in which the same figure (*e.g.*, a woman descending a flight of stairs) is represented in successive positions like film "stills" superimposed on each other. In spite of two further manifestoes it was not until 1911 that the first examples of Futurist painting and sculpture appeared by the artists Severini, Balla and Boccioni. Apart from the principle of simultaneity, Futurism derived from Cubist and Post-impressionist techniques. The movement faded out early in the first world war.

G

Gabardine, or a long, loose, coarse, over-garment, worn by men of the common class in the Middle Ages, and prescribed by law as the distinctive garment of the Jews. The name is now given to a closely woven cloth of wool and cotton used to make raincoats.

Gabbro, a kind of igneous rock, often very coarse-grained, containing a good deal of plagioclase felspar, and monoclinic pyroxene; it may occasionally also include biotite, magnetite, ilmenite and hornblende. A gabbro containing nickel at Sudbury in Canada is one of the richest sources known of that metal.

Gadfly, a widely distributed family of flies with only one pair of wings, including the horse fly. The females are very voracious, being able to bite through the skin and suck the blood of animals. The males are harmless.

Gadolinium. An element, no. 64, symbol Gd, belonging to the rare-earths metals discovered in 1886 by Marignac. It is strongly magnetic.

Gaelic, relating to the Gaels and their language, a term now applied only to the Celtic people inhabiting the Highlands of Scotland, but formerly also to the Celts of Ireland and the Isle of Man.

Galago, "Bush Babies", related to the lemur, native to Africa, large-eyed, in keeping with its nocturnal characteristics.

Galaxy or **Milky Way Galaxy** is the huge disk-shaped cloud of gas and stars (some 100,000 million, one of which is the sun) that is turning in space like a great wheel, with a diameter of about 100,000 light years. The Milky Way (that part of the heavens in Milton's words "powdered with stars") is really only a small part of this disk, and every star in the galaxy is moving round the centre under the gravitational control of the whole. The sun and planets lie near the edge of the disk, and it takes them about 250 million years to travel once round. The number of stars that can be seen with the unaided eye is about 3,000, and they all belong to the Milky Way Galaxy, as do most of the stars that can be seen with anything but the greatest telescopes. With the large modern optical and radar telescopes many other systems, similar in size and weight to our galaxy, have been discovered, scattered more or less uniformly through space, and the universe is known to include at least 10,000 million such galaxies. In 1996, astronomers found the most distant galaxy ever detected at 14 billion light years from Earth in the constellation of Virgo. The oldest known star in the Milky Way Galaxy, known as ESO 439–26, is *c.* 12 billion years old. In 1997 the Hubble telescope discovered perhaps the brightest star in the Milky Way—glowing with the radiance of 10 million suns. *See also* **F4(2).**

Gale, a high wind now technically defined as one of at least Beaufort force 8. Between thirty and forty gales a year occur on the north and west coasts of the British Isles and only about half of this number in the south-east. At St. Ann's Head, Dyfed, the anemometer registered a gust of 113 mile/h (182 km/h) on 18 Jan. 1945, which is a record for these islands. Gusts exceeding 113 km/h are rarely experienced in London. Gale warnings are issued for specified areas by the Meteorological Office, the warnings taking the form of radio broadcasts and the hoisting of storm signals at certain points on the coast. *See* **Beaufort Wind Scale, Section Z.**

Gall, abnormal vegetable growths caused by insects, mites, bacteria, or fungi, found on all parts of the plant. Oak-apples, Robin's pin-cushion (on wild rose), "witches' brooms" (on trees) are examples. Some are useful commercially, *e.g.*, oak apples yield tannic acid and the black oak gall is used in America as animal food.

Galleon, the name given to the old three-decked Spanish treasure vessels employed in conveying the precious minerals from the American colonies to Spain. The term is often applied to any large, especially stately, sailing vessel.

Galley, an oar-propelled sea-boat used by the ancient Greeks and Romans for transport purposes, manned by slaves. They were also used as warships from classical to relatively modern times, *e.g.*, Lepanto 1571. When so used the sides were raised to protect the rowers.

Gallic Acid, obtained from gall nuts, sumach, tea, coffee, and the seeds of the mango, is used in the manufacture of inks and as an astringent in medicine. It was discovered by C. W. Scheele (1742–86), a Swedish chemist.

Gallium, metallic element, no. 31, symbol Ga, related to aluminium, but which can be cut with a knife. It was discovered spectroscopically by L. de Boisbaudran in 1875. Long before Mendeleyev had predicted that an element with its properties would be found to fill the then existing gap in the Periodic Table; this gap came immediately below aluminium, so he suggested the name "eka aluminium" for it.

Gallup Poll, a system, introduced by Dr. Gallup in the United States, for testing public opinion on topical subjects by taking a test poll on questions framed to elicit opinions.

Galvanised Iron is iron coated with zinc. The name comes from the fact that such a coat protective against rust could be deposited electrolytically. Electrodeposition is sometimes used, but the cheaper and more common process depends on dipping the iron in a bath of molten zinc.

Gamboge, a resinous gum obtained from the sap of *Garcinia morella*, a tree native to Thailand, Cambodia and Sri Lanka, and used as a yellow pigment in paints and also as a purgative.

Game is the term applied to wild animals which are protected from indiscriminate slaughter by Game Laws. In the United Kingdom game comprehends deer, hares, pheasants, partridges, grouse, black game, moor game, woodcocks, bustards and certain other birds and animals of the chase. Game can only be killed (with few exceptions) by persons holding game licences. Occupiers of land and one other person authorised by them in each case are allowed to kill hares and rabbits on their land without licence. Game cannot be sold except by a person holding a proper licence. There is a "close time" prescribed for the different classes of game; for instance, the selling or exposing for sale of any hare or leveret during March, April, May, June or July is prohibited by law. Grouse cannot be shot between 11 December and 11 August; partridges between 2 February and 31 August; pheasants between 2 February and 30 September; and black game between 11 December and 10 August. In regard to foxes and stags, custom prescribes a certain law which sportsmen observe. Game reserves are legally protected areas where natural vegetation and wild life are allowed to remain unmolested by sportsmen or those who might destroy for economic ends.

Gaming, *or* **Gambling**—i.e., staking money on the chances of a game—differs from betting in that it depends upon the result of a trial of skill or a turn of chance. The 1959 Betting and Gaming Act replaced all the old laws on gaming, which went back to an Act of 1541 entitled "An Acte for Mayntenance of Artyllarie and debarringe of unlauful games", under which some games were unlawful if played for money in any circumstances. Roulette and any game of dice were among such games. Under the 1959 Act any game was lawful, subject to certain conditions. Since then the Betting, Gaming and Lotteries Act, 1963, and the Gaming Act, 1968, have been passed, to deal with unlawful gaming and to prevent the exploitation of gaming by commercial interests. The playing of bingo is now restricted to clubs licensed for bingo only. Sunday betting on dogs and horses became legal in January 1995. The government put forward proposals in February 1996 to ease the tight restrictions on casinos. Playing of fruit machines in betting shops is now legal. *See also* **National Lottery.**

Gammexane, a powerful insecticide, used particularly to kill the tsetse fly and mosquito.

Gangue. Useless minerals associated with metallic ores.

Gannet, a fish-eating bird which dives on its prey from a great height, swallowing it under water, is found in large numbers off the coast of Scotland, and has breeding stations in the Hebrides, St. Kilda, Ailsa Craig, the Bass Rock, Grassholme Island and on Ortac and Les Etacs (rocks off Alderney). It is a bird of white plumage, black tips to long narrow wings and wedge-shaped tail, and weighs about 3 kg. The gannet breeds in colonies on ledges of steep, rocky, island cliffs. Related to the cormorants, pelicans and frigate-birds.

Garden Cities in England were founded by Ebenezer Howard (1850–1928), and his ideas were put forward in his book *Tomorrow—A Peaceful Path to Real Reform* (later re-issued as *Garden Cities of Tomorrow*). New towns should be so placed and planned as to get the best of town and country life, an adaptation of the model villages of certain industrial philanthropists such as Salt, Richardson, Cadbury, Leverhulme and others. The Garden City Association (later the Town and Country Planning Association) was formed in 1899, and the first garden city was begun at Letchworth in 1903 and successfully established. Welwyn Garden City (1919) was Howard's foundation.

Gardener-Bird, a bird possessing many of the characteristics of the bower bird, found only in Papua-New Guinea. *See also* **Bower Bird.**

Gargantua, the giant hero of Rabelais' satire, of immense eating and drinking capacity, symbolical of the greed of the Church.

Gargoyle, a projecting spout for carrying off water from the roof gutter of a building. Gargoyles are only found in old structures, modern waterpipe systems having rendered them unnecessary. In Gothic architecture they were turned to architectural account and made to take all kinds of grotesque forms—grinning goblins, hideous monsters, dragons and so forth.

Garlic, a bulbous plant of the same genus as the onion and the leek, and a favourite condiment among the people of Southern Europe. It possesses a very strong odour and pungent taste and its culinary use is agelong.

Garnet, a group of minerals; chemically they are orthosilicates of the metals calcium, magnesium, titanium, iron, aluminium. Garnets can be coloured yellow, brown, black, green or red; the blood-red garnet is an important gemstone.

Garrotte, a method of strangulation used as capital punishment in Spain, and consisting of a collar which is compressed by a screw that causes death by piercing the spinal marrow. Garrotting was also applied to a system of highway robbery common in England in 1862–63, the assailants seizing their victims from behind, and by a sudden compression of the windpipe disabling them until the robbery was completed.

Garter. The Most Noble Order of the Garter was founded (*c.* 1348) by King Edward III, and is the premier order of knighthood in Great Britain. The traditional story associating the garter and the motto with the Countess of Salisbury, who it was said dropped her garter while dancing with the King, who remarked "honi soit qui mal y pense" cannot be accepted. The order was originally limited to the Sovereign and 25 knights, but the number has been extended, and it may now be bestowed on royal personages and leading representatives of the British peerage. The insignia of the order are the garter of dark-blue velvet with the motto in letters of gold, the mantle of dark-blue velvet lined with white silk, the surcoat and hood, and the gold-and-enamel collar. The garter is worn on the left leg below the knee and by women as a sash over the left shoulder. Recent recipients have been James Callaghan (1987), Sir Edward Heath (1992), the Princess Royal (1994), Sir Edmund Hillary and Baroness Thatcher (1995). *See* **Knighthood.**

Gas is an elastic fluid substance, the molecules of which are in constant rapid motion, and exerting pressure. The technique whereby gases are liquefied depends on increasing pressure and diminishing temperature. Each gas has a critical point; unless the temperature is brought down to this point no amount of pressure will bring about

L49

liquefaction. Last gas to be liquefied was helium (1908) which boils at −209°C.

Gas from coal was first used as an illuminating agent by William Murdoch towards the end of the 18th cent. in Birmingham, and about 1807 was introduced in London, one side of Pall Mall being lighted with it. It became widely used as an illuminant, and for space heating and cooking. In the UK increasing attention has been paid to the use of a primary fuel—natural gas— instead of producing gas from coal or oil.

Gas, Natural, natural mixture of gases often present with deposits of petroleum, found issuing from the ground in many parts of the world—in the oilfields of Venezuela and the Caucasus, in China, Saudi Arabia, but chiefly in North America. Its chief component is methane. Large industrial centres have made use of this gas since the latter part of the 19th cent., but much of this valuable fuel still goes to waste. Pipelines have been constructed to deliver the gas to where it is wanted. Britain began to ship liquid methane from the Saharan oilfield in 1964. Some of the world's largest natural gas fields have been discovered in the North Sea and are being actively exploited.

Domestic gas appliances have to be modified if the natural product is substituted for ordinary town gas because the burning characteristics are different. Oil production from the North Sea fields began in 1975 and the main single source of gas in the UK is now natural gas.

Gas Turbine. In this kind of engine mechanical movement is produced by a jet of gas impinging on a turbine wheel; used in aeroplanes, locomotives and ships. These engines are mechanically simple compared with internal combustion engines, and require less maintenance.

Gauge, a standard dimension or measurement, applied in various branches of construction. Thus the standard railway gauge is 4 ft 8½ in (143·5 cm) in the UK, USA and most European countries. The former Soviet Union used the broader gauge of 5 ft (152 cm). Narrow railway gauges of different standards are in use on very steep inclines in various countries. Other standard gauges are fixed in building and gun-boring.

Gauls were inhabitants of ancient Gaul, the country which comprised what is now France, Belgium and parts of the Netherlands, Switzerland and Germany.

Gault, a stratum of blue clay between the Lower Greensand and the Chalk. A typical section of the Gault can be seen at Folkestone.

Gauss, a unit of magnetic induction in the c.g.s. system, named after the great German mathematician and astronomer, K. F. Gauss.

Gavelkind, an old English custom of land tenure in Kent and other places in England, whereby on the death, intestate, of a property owner his property is divided equally among his children and not according to the law of primogeniture.

Gay Rights. See **Section J**.

Gazelles, a group of small, graceful antelopes which live in the drier regions of Africa and Asia. They can run very fast: speeds of over 64 km/h have been recorded.

GCSE, (**General Certificate of Secondary Education**), the school-leaving examination, introduced in 1988, which replaced the existing GCE and CSE.

Gegenschein. A faint oval-shaped glow situated at the point in the sky directly opposite the Sun and caused by the reflection of sunlight from tiny interplanetary dust particles.

Geiger Counter, an electrical device, invented by Geiger, which can detect individual atomic particles, e.g., electrons, protons, etc. It often consists of a tube of gas at a few cm Hg pressure, fitted with two electrodes—a cylinder and an axial wire. A high voltage is kept across the electrodes, and the passage of a charged particle through the gas releases ions which permit a momentary discharge between the electrodes. Electronic circuits register this discharge as a "count". Geiger counters are used to detect and measure radioactivity and cosmic rays both for technical and research purposes.

Gelatine, a transparent, tasteless, organic substance obtained from animal membranes, bones, tendons, etc., by boiling in water. It is of various kinds, according to the substance used in making it. Isinglass, the purest form of it, is made from air-bladders and other membranes of fish, while the coarser kind—glue—is made from hoofs, skin, hides, etc. Its constituents are carbon, hydrogen, oxygen and nitrogen. Gelatine is applied to an immense variety of purposes, from the making of food jellies to photographic materials.

Gemsbok, a large South African antelope of the open dry plains, sandy coloured with black and white markings on its face, and with long straight horns.

General, a military title next in rank to that of Field-Marshal, the highest officer in the army.

Generation, a time-measure reckoned at about 30 years when children are ready to replace parents; also the body of persons existing at the same time or period. In the 1990s, the generation gap is now even fewer years apart.

Generation, Spontaneous. See **Abiogenesis**.

Genes, the elementary units of heredity. They exist as highly differentiated regions arranged along the length of the chromosomes which the nuclei of cells carry. A chromosome may carry hundreds or even thousands of genes, each with its own particular structure and specific properties. The position of a particular gene on a chromosome is called its locus. The material of the gene is DNA (q.v.). See **F33** and **end Section F**.

Genesis, the first book of the Pentateuch, compiled in the 5th cent. B.C. from earlier documents, which carries the scriptural narrative from the creation to the death of Joseph. Sometimes there is disagreement, as in the story of the creation, Gen. i and ii. Gen. i reflects the views of the ancient Greek scientist Thales (c. 640–546 B.C.) and may be said to be the first scientific account of the creation of the world. The conditions described around the figures of Abraham, Isaac, Jacob and Joseph have a genuine historical basis.

Genetic Code. The elucidation of the structure of DNA (q.v.) for which Crick, Wilkins and Watson were jointly awarded the 1962 Nobel Prize for medicine, revealed the code or chemical dictionary out of which messages serving as blueprints for living structures can be made. See **Protein synthesis, F32**(2) and **F70–76**.

Genetic Engineering is the name given to the introduction of human choice and design criteria into the construction and combination of genes. This refers not to breeding by selection, a traditional process, but to the biochemical alteration of the actual DNA in cells (see **Section F, Part IV**) so as to produce novel self-reproducing organisms. Such manipulations became possible when techniques were recently discovered for severing and rejoining DNA molecules and inserting sections into them. Many people regard this development as fraught with enormous significance. Like nuclear power, it can lead to good, to evil, and to accidental hazards, not all of which can be foreseen. Thus when biologists realised they could create new lifeforms, e.g., bacteria, with novel genes, they appreciated that, as well as medically beneficial strains, new virulent forms might by accident be produced and escape into the world. Ultimately, human beings may be able to design the genes of higher animals and even of humans themselves and thus consciously influence biological evolution. See **F70–76**.

Genetic Fingerprinting. See **DNA Database**.

Genetically-Modified Food. See **L134**.

Genetics. See **F30**(2) and **F70–76**.

Geneva Convention, an agreement made by the European Powers at Geneva in 1864, establishing humane regulations regarding the treatment of the sick and wounded in war and the status of those who minister to them. All persons, hospitals, hospital ships are required to display the Geneva cross—a red cross on a white ground. A second conference held at Geneva in 1868 drew up a supplementary agreement. A major result of this Convention was the establishment of the Red Cross Society in 1870.

Genocide is an international crime, defined by the General Assembly of the United Nations in 1948 as "acts committed with intent to destroy, in whole or in part a national, ethnic, racial or religious group as such". The UN Convention came into force in 1951. Some recent conflicts (as in Rwanda in Africa) have seen acts of genocide.

Genus, a term applied in biology to designate a group of similar species. A group of similar genera is called a family.

Geodesy, the science of calculating the configuration and extent of the earth's surface, and determining exact geographical positions and directions, with variations of gravity etc. Land-surveying is a branch of geodesy.

Geography, science concerned with the spatial organisation of natural features and life and man-made artifacts upon and immediately above the surface of the earth. It is increasingly concerned with the processes by which such patterns are generated and this concern is leading to both a greater degree of specialisation within the subject and the merging of its constituent parts with related disciplines of economics, sociology, political science, geology, biology and meteorology.

Geology, the science which deals with the condition and structure of the earth, and the evidence afforded of ancient forms of life. The geological strata are classified in the following categories: *Primary* or *Palaeozoic* (the oldest fossil-bearing rocks including the Cambrian, Ordovician, Silurian, Devonian, Carboniferous, Permian); *Secondary* or *Mesozoic* (Triassic, Jurassic, Cretaceous); *Tertiary* or *Cainozoic* (Eocene, Oligocene, Miocene, Pliocene, Pleistocene); *Post tertiary* (most recent rocks). *See* **F48.**

Geometrical Progression, term used to indicate a succession of numbers which increase or decrease at an equal ratio—as 3, 9, 27; or 64, 16, 4.

Geometry is the branch of mathematics which demonstrates the properties of figures, and the distances of points of space from each other by means of deductions. It is a science of reason from fundamental axioms, and was perfected by Euclid about 300 B.C. The books of Euclid contain a full elucidation of the science, though supplemented in modern times by Descartes, Newton and Carnot. Of recent years non-Euclidean geometry has been developed.

Geophysics, the branches of physics which are concerned with the earth and its atmosphere. Meteorology, geomagnetism, aurora and airglow, ionosphere, solar activity, cosmic rays, glaciology, oceanography, seismology, nuclear radiation in the atmosphere, rockets and satellites—all these are geophysical subjects. The object of the International Geophysical Year, 1957–58, was to investigate the physical phenomena occurring on and around the earth by means of carefully co-ordinated observations made simultaneously all over the globe.

Geothermal Energy. Some of the heavy elements within the earth's crust are radioactive and this gives rise to a temperature rise towards the centre of the earth. The practical exploitation of this geothermal energy comes about when there are hot springs or geysers. It is believed that these are caused by rainwater slowly percolating down to the hot rocks and blowing out as steam. The homes of people living in Reykjavik are heated by geothermal steam and there are a number of small power stations in various parts of the world. Although the costs in the few cases where geothermal power has actually been exploited are remarkably low, the expense of drilling, *etc.*, required when attempting to exploit the heat in the rocks where surface manifestations do not occur, is likely to limit the use of this source of power.

Geothermal Heating. The earth's interior is hot and in certain localities, often adjacent to volcanic or earthquake-prone regions, reservoirs of hot water or steam exist at accessible depths. Natural hot geysers occur in many such places and people, *e.g.*, the ancient Romans and present-day Japanese, use natural hot water for bathing, cooking and laundry. Occasionally the subterranean reserves permit large-scale power generation by drilling for hot steam and passing it into turbines to produce electricity. Pioneering work on this was done at Lardarello in Italy which can produce hundreds of megawatts. Other sites are in New Zealand, California, Japan and Iceland. There are possibilities in S.W. England.

Germanium. A grey, hard, brittle chemical element, no. 32, symbol Ge, chemically related to silicon and tin. Discovered by Winkler in 1886. Its richest ore is germanite containing 6% of the metal. Coal is also a relatively rich source. Since 1948 it has assumed great importance as a semi-conducting material for making transistors (*q.v.*). Because of this it has been so intensively studied that more is known about its physical properties than about those of any other element.

Gesta Romanorum (Latin = deeds of the Romans), a mediaeval collection of Latin stories of unknown authorship which circulated widely in Europe during the Middle Ages. First printed in the 15th cent. The stories were used by Chaucer, Shakespeare and other writers who found many romantic incidents and legends which they were able to turn to good account.

Gestation, the carrying of young in animals during pregnancy, varies considerably in its length. In the case of an elephant, the period is 21 months; a camel, 12 months; a cow, 9 months; a cat, 8 weeks; a horse, 48 weeks; a dog, 9 weeks; and a pig, 16 weeks. Hens "sit" for 21 days; geese, 30; swans, 42; turkeys, 28; pigeons, 18.

Geysers, hot springs of volcanic origination and action, are remarkable for the fact that they throw out huge streams of boiling water instead of lava as in the case of a volcano. The most famous geysers are those of Iceland, which number over a hundred, the principal one having an opening of 21 m in diameter and discharging a column of water to a height of 61 m. There are also geysers in the Yellowstone region of America, and some in New Zealand.

Ghost-Moth or **Ghost Swift,** an interesting nocturnal insect (*Hepialus humuli*) common in England, possessing in the male a white collar and known for its habit of hovering with a pendulum-like action in the twilight over a particular spot where the female is concealed.

Gibbon, the name of a long-armed ape mainly inhabiting S.E. Asia. It is without tail, and possesses the power of very rapid movement among the trees of the forests.

Gin, a well-known spirit distilled from malt or barley and flavoured with the juniper berry. The principal varieties are the English and American, known as "Gin" or "Dry Gin", and the Dutch, referred to as "jenever" or "Hollandse jenever". In Germany and Austria it is called "Schnapps". The word "Gin" is an abbreviation of "Geneva", both being primarily derived from the French *genièvre* (juniper).

Giraffe, the tallest of existing animals, reaching a height of from 5–6 m when full grown. Its sloping back and elongated neck seem to be the natural evolution of an animal that has to feed on the branches of trees. It is a native of Africa, is of a light fawn colour marked with darker spots and has a prehensile tongue.

Giralda, a beautiful and remarkable example of Arabian art, erected in 1195 at Seville, still in existence.

Glaciers form in the higher Alpine ranges, and are immense consolidated masses of snow, which are gradually impelled by their force down the mountain-sides until they reach a point where the temperature causes them to melt, and they run off in streams. From such glaciers the five great rivers, the Rhine, the Po, the Rhône, the Inn and the Adige, have their source. The longest of the Swiss glaciers is the Gross Aletsch, which sometimes extends over 16 km. Some of the glaciers of the Himalayas are four times as long. The Muir in Alaska is of enormous magnitude, and that of Justeldals Brae in Norway is the largest in Europe. Recent high levels of glacial activity no doubt reflect global warming.

Gladiators were professional athletes and combatants in ancient Rome, contesting with each other or with wild beasts. At first they were drawn from the slave and prisoner classes exclusively, but so much were the successful gladiators held in esteem that men came to make a profession of athletics, and gladiatorial training schools were established. When a gladiator was vanquished without being killed in combat, it was left with the spectators to decide his fate, death being voted by holding the hands out with the thumb turned inward, and life by putting forth the hands with the thumb extended.

Gladiatorial shows were the chief public displays in Rome from the 3rd to the 4th cent. A.D.

Glass is an amorphous, man-made substance, fluid when hot, solid, though fragile, when cooled. It is made of sand mixed with an alkaline flux, usually soda or potash. While hot, glass can be formed into almost any shape by moulding, blowing or, since the early 19th cent., by machine pressing. Unrefined glass normally has a greenish tinge, due to the iron content of most sands, but it is transparent or at least translucent. To make truly colourless glass is a difficult and expensive process, and such glass resembling the natural mineral, rock crystal, is given the name crystal. Glass can be tinted by the addition of various metallic oxides, cobalt producing blue, manganese mauve, *etc.* Because it is at once solid and transparent, glass is the perfect material for windows for which it has been used since Roman times. And since it can be made cheaply and is easy to clean, it has been used for containers in homes, shops and pharmacies, again since Roman days. Glass can also be made into things of beauty, by the use of coloured glass and by cutting, engraving, painting and gilding. The earliest vessels of glass so far found come from Egypt and date back to *c.* 1500 B.C. With the invention of glass-blowing in the 1st cent. A.D., the use of glass spread throughout the Roman empire. Many varieties were made, including superb art glass like the Portland vase (*q.v.*) The Arabs were great glassmakers from the 7th to 15th cent. During the Renaissance the Venetians created luxurious art glass, rich in colour and often manipulated into fantastic forms, Bohemia's 17th-cent. glass is wonderfully engraved with pictures and cut into glittering facets. During the 1670s in England George Ravenscroft invented a new, heavy, water-clear crystal, with an addition of lead as the magic ingredient, and English lead glass is still the basis for all modern crystals.

Glass-Snake, genus, *Ophisaurus,* of legless lizards with long fragile tails capable of re-generation when broken. Six species are known; in S.E. Europe, S.W. Asia, S.E. Asia and N. America. Attains a length of about 60 cm; main colouring, green, with black and yellow markings.

Glauconite. A green mineral, chemically a hydrated silicate of potassium and iron. Commonly found in marine sands (hence these rocks are known as "greensands") and sandstones.

Glaucus is a curious genus of sea slugs often called the Sea Lizard belonging to the molluscs. It is without shell and has a soft body, with horny mouth and four tentacles. It is a native of the Atlantic, and is not more than 30 cm in length.

Glee, an unaccompanied piece for three or more voices. Glee-singing was popular in England during the 18th and early 19th cent. and glee-clubs are still in existence.

Global Warming. *See* L132.

Globe Theatre. The original Globe Theatre was built on Bankside, London in 1599 and pulled down in 1644. Its foundations were excavated in 1989. Sam Wanamaker (1919–93), the actor, and Theo Crosby (1925–94), the architect had already conceived and designed a near-replica, which was built near the site of the Elizabethan theatre using traditional materials.

Globigerina, an oceanic unicellular animalcule with a perforated shell, and occurring in certain parts of the Atlantic in such vast numbers as to form a bed of chalk ooze with their empty shells.

Glockenspiel, an instrument composed of metal bars each of which is tuned to a note. The bars are struck by hand-hammers and give forth chiming sounds.

Glow-worm, a beetle, possessing the power (much stronger in the female than the male) of emitting phosphorescent light from the hind end of the body. The female is wingless.

Glucinium. *See* Beryllium.

Glucose, Dextrose *or* **Grape Sugar** is a carbohydrate (*q.v.*). It is produced by hydrolysis from cane sugar, dextrine, starch, cellulose, *etc.*, by the action of reagents. It also occurs in many plants, fruits and honey. For brewing purposes glucose is prepared by the conversion of starch by sulphuric acid. Malt also converts starch into glucose.

Glutton *or* **Wolverine,** the biggest animal of the weasel family, inhabits the northernmost parts of Europe and America. In build it resembles the bear, and is rather larger than a badger. Its fur is of a brown-black hue, but coarse.

Glycerine *or* **Glycerol,** occurs in natural fats combined with fatty acids, and is obtained by decomposing those substances with alkalis or by superheated steam. It is colourless and oily and sweet, and is put to a variety of commercial uses, being widely utilised for medicaments, for lubricating purposes, and in the manufacture of nitro-glycerine.

Glycols. Organic compounds containing two alcohol groups. Ethylene glycol is the most widely known example; it is used as an antifreeze in motor-car radiators on account of its property of greatly reducing the freezing point of water. Also used in the manufacture of "Terylene". *See* Esters.

Glyptodon, an extinct species of gigantic armadillo, fossil remains of which have been discovered in S. America. It was some 2·7 m long, carried a huge tortoise-like shell and had fluted teeth.

Gneiss, a metamorphic rock usually containing quartz, felspar and mica. It is banded, the light-coloured minerals being concentrated apart from the dark minerals.

Gnosticism. *See* Section J.

Gnu *or* **Wildebeest,** a large antelope from Africa south of the Sahara, distinguished by its excessively short thick neck and large head with a pronounced roman nose. There are two species; the white-tailed gnu is almost extinct, the brindled gnu is still common and migrates in large herds.

Goat-Moth (*Cossus cossus*), a large moth of the *Cossidae* family, common in Britain, evil-smelling and very destructive in the larval stage to trees of the poplar and willow genus, into the wood of which the caterpillar bores during its three years' period of development.

Goats are horned ruminant quadrupeds, indigenous to the Eastern Hemisphere, but now domesticated in all parts of the world. Though related to the sheep, they are a much hardier and more active animal. The male has a tuft of hair under the chin. Many species, including those of Cashmere and Angora, are valuable for their hair, which is used for fine textile fabrics. Goat milk is nutritive, and goat-skins are in demand for leather for gloves, shoes, *etc.*

God and Man. *See* Section J.

Gog and Magog, two legendary City of London giants who were brought captive to London and made to serve as prisoners at the Palace of Brute, which stood on the site of Guildhall. Effigies of the giants have stood in Guildhall since the time of Henry V. They were destroyed in the Great Fire of 1666, replaced in 1672 and used to be carried through the streets of London in the Lord Mayor's Show. The present figures replaced those carved in 1708 by Richard Saunders, which were destroyed in an air raid during the last war. In the Bible, Ezekiel also makes reference to Gog and Magog.

Gold. Metallic element, no. 79, symbol Au (Latin *Aurum*) related to silver and copper, the coinage metals. The greatest amount of gold is obtained by treating gold-bearing quartz by the cyanide process. The gold is dissolved out by cyanide solution, which is then run into long boxes filled with zinc shavings when the gold is precipitated as a black slime. This is melted with an oxidising agent to remove the zinc.

Gold-Beaters' Skin is the outside membrane of the large intestine of the ox, specially prepared and used by gold-beaters for placing between the leaves of gold while they beat them. Thin membrane is of great tenacity, and gets beaten to such extreme thinness that it is used to put on cuts and bruises.

Gold Standard. Under the gold-standard system which was widely prevalent up to 1941, each gold-standard country fixed the value of its currency in terms of a weight of gold of a certain fineness and was, broadly speaking, ready to exchange its currency freely for gold, which could then be exported without restriction. This involved keeping a gold reserve big enough to meet all likely demands and also to serve as a backing for the issue of notes. The gold standard had to be given up during the first world war; and though it was in substance restored in Great Britain in 1925 (when Churchill was Chancellor), the restoration was never complete, as the gold reserve remained too small for complete freedom to export to be practicable. Sterling had to be devalued in the financial crisis of 1931 (which caused the fall of the Labour Government) and Great Britain was forced off the gold standard. *See also* **Section G.**

Goldeneye, a species of wild duck, widely distributed over Arctic regions. It is a passage-migrant and winter-visitor to the British Isles. Has nested in Cheshire. Distinguished by a large white spot in front of each eye on a dark ground.

Golden Dawn. See **Section J.**

Golden Number, the number of any year in the metonic cycle of 19 years, deriving its name from the fact that in the old calendars it was always printed in gold. It is found by adding 1 to the number of the year A.D. and dividing by 19, the remainder being the Golden Number; or, if no remainder, the Golden Number is 19.

Goldsmiths Company, one of the richest London City Companies; the official assayers of gold and silver, invested with the power of "hall-marking" the quality of objects made from these metals. First charter granted in 1327.

Gondola, the old regulation black boats so common on the canals of Venice, propelled by a gondolier with one oar who stands at the stern. The covered part in the centre (*felze*) is rarely seen nowadays as most passengers are tourists who want to see the city.

Gondwana, the name of the ancient southern land mass that linked Antarctica, Australia, India *etc.*

Gonfalon, the pennon affixed to a lance, spear or standard, consisting usually of two or three streamers and made to turn like a weather-cock.

Gophers. Rodent mammals. The pocket gophers are stout-bodied burrowers common in the USA. The slender burrowing gophers, also called "ground squirrels", occur in central and western USA. The sisel or suslik is a related European species. They are a great pest.

Gordon Riots of 1780 were an anti-popery agitation fomented by Lord George Gordon. Called also "No-Popery Riots".

Gorilla, the largest of the anthropoid apes, found in the forests of Equatorial Africa, and at maturity standing from 1·2–1·5 m high. Mountain gorillas are one of the most endangered species in the world. Now (late-1990s) only 650 survive in the Congo, Rwanda and Uganda.

Goshawk (*Accipiter gentilis*), a diurnal bird of prey, fearless and extremely agile; loves wooded country and is very destructive of poultry and game-birds. It resembles the peregrine falcon in appearance, but has shorter, rounded wings. This bird was a great favourite of falconers in mediaeval times. A few have now been reintroduced from Scandinavia.

Gospels are those portions of the New Testament which deal with the life, death, resurrection and teachings of Christ. They are the gospels of Matthew, Mark, Luke and John, all probably compiled in the later part of the 1st cent. The first three are called the *synoptic gospels* because of their general unity of narrative. Mark was probably the first to be written and John the last, and it is to Mark that scholars have turned for the most reliable source of knowledge of the life of Jesus. The word *gospel* comes from two Anglo-Saxon words *gode* (good) and *spell* (tidings), a translation of the Greek *evangelion* = evangel, evangelist. Recent research suggests Matthew was written much earlier than thought.

Gothic, the predominant style of architecture in northern Europe from 12th–15th cent. Its most striking characteristic is the extensive use of the pointed arch, but this is really a mere external reflection of the important structural invention of the 12th cent., that of the rib vault, whereby the whole pressure of the stone vaulting is supported on slim ribs which cross each other at a rising centre. On the outside of the building, the pressure from the vaults is caught up and supported by flying buttresses. A complete Gothic construction gives a marvellous effect of airy lightness, also of something striving upwards, towards the heavens, and this is further accentuated when the churches are crowned by lofty towers and spires. The vital

structural elements of Gothic architecture were first put into use in the abbey church of St. Denis in Paris *c.* 1140. The style was further developed in a glorious sequence of cathedrals in northern France: Notre Dame in Paris, Rheims, Amiens, Beauvais and others. When, as in Chartres, the windows are filled with stained glass of glowing colours and the doorways flanked with magnificently carved life-size figures of saints and apostles, the whole effect is one of unsurpassed solemnity and grandeur. From France the style spread to other lands in each of which it developed its own characteristics; thus the English churches tended to have massive towers and delicate spires and, as at Salisbury, were often set in open grounds surrounded by lawns; Flemish and Dutch churches were sometimes built of brick as were those in north Germany and Scandinavia; in Spain the Flamboyant style was followed. The main Gothic cathedral in Italy, that of Milan, although begun in 1386 was not completed until the early 19th cent. Late English Gothic is seen, for example, at King's College Chapel, Cambridge, Henry's Chapel at Westminster and St. George's Chapel at Windsor (all *c.* 1500).

Gothic is also found in secular buildings, *e.g.*, Little Wenham Hall in Suffolk, the castle at Ghent, the town halls of Louvain and Middelburg and the streets of Gothic houses in Bruges still in use today. Virtually Gothic as a style (excluding the "Gothic revival" of 19th cent. England) ended at the close of the 15th cent. Gothic art is best seen in the illuminated manuscripts of the 13th and 14th cent. and in the church sculpture. Its characteristic is a complete departure from the cool, perfectionist realism of classical times with distortion to produce emotional effects. The human figures are not ideal forms but recognisable as people we might meet in the street: yet there was also the element of wild imagination, intricate design and a wealth of feeling which might be grotesque, humorous, macabre, or even obscene. Gothic style also found expression in the decorative arts, retaining its architectural character even in small-scale works like caskets, chalices and the like in metalwork and ivory.

Goths. A Teutonic people who originally came from southern Sweden (Gotland) and by the 3rd cent. were settled in the region north of the Black Sea. They began to encroach on the Roman Empire and early in the 4th cent. split into two divisions: the "wise" Goths or Visigoths between the Danube and the Dniester (referred to as the West Goths), and the "bright" Goths or Ostrogoths in southern Russia on the Dnieper (referred to as the East Goths). The Ostrogoths were conquered by the Huns *c.* 370, while the Visigoths under Alaric devastated Greece and sacked Rome in 410. Eventually the Visigoths spread to France and Spain and their last king Roderick fell in battle against the Moors in 711. The Ostrogoths regained their independence on the death of Attila in 453 and under king Theodoric the Great conquered Italy in 493. They lost their identity after Justinian regained Italy, 525–552.

Gourd Family *or* **Cucurbitaceae.** This family of about 650 species of flowering plants includes the gourds, pumpkins, cantaloupes, cucumber, gherkin, water-melon and squashes. Most abundant in the tropics, the cucurbits are mainly climbing annuals with very rapid growth. The bathroom loofah is the skeleton of one cucurbit fruit, *Luffa cylindrica*. The squirting cucumber is another member of the family.

Governor. A device attached to an engine, turbine, compressor, *etc.*, which automatically controls the engine's speed in accordance with power demand. Most governors depend upon the centrifugal action of two or more balls which are thrown outwards as their speed of rotation increases and actuate a throttle valve or cut-off. The centrifugal governor was invented by Thomas Mead, patented by him in 1787. Watt adapted it to the steam engine.

Grail, Legend of the Holy, a tale of Celtic origin which became part of Arthurian legend and the subject of many mediaeval quest-romances. According to the Christian version the grail was the cup which Christ used at the Last Supper, brought to England by St. Joseph of Arimathea.

Grand Prix, the "French Derby" was established by Napoleon III, in 1863. It is the chief French race and is for three-year-olds.

Granite is a coarsely crystalline igneous rock consisting of quartz and alkali felspars plus mica or hornblende. It is a much used ornamental and building stone; it forms the high ground of Dartmoor and Bodmin Moor.

Graphite or **Plumbago**, commonly called black-lead, is a form of carbon occurring in foliated masses in marble, schist, etc. It is soft, will make black marks on paper or other plain surfaces, and is mainly used for lead pencils. It is also a valuable lubricant. Pure graphite has found a new use with the construction of atomic piles. Important deposits occur in Siberia, Sri Lanka, Malagasy, Canada and USA.

Graphology, the science which interprets and analyses the way letters are formed and shaped.

Graptolites, fossil animals confined to Cambrian, Ordovician and Silurian strata. Once classified as hydrazoa but now considered more likely to be hemichordates.

Grasshopper. There are many species of these leaping insects which are related to the locusts and crickets. Most are vegetarians; some eat flies and caterpillars also. The chirping sound they make is made by scraping the hind legs against the wings; in some species a noise is produced by rubbing the wings together.

Gravitation. One of the four types of force known to physics. The others are electromagnetic, the weak nuclear and the strong nuclear forces. Gravitational forces are an attraction that one piece of matter has for another; they dominate astronomical phenomena, but inside the atom they are negligible compared with the other types of force. Einstein's General Theory of Relativity is the only theory at present extant which attempts to interpret gravitational forces in terms of more fundamental concepts.

Graylag, the ordinary wild grey goose of Europe, the species from which domestic geese are derived; frequents fens and marshes; breeds in Iceland, Scandinavia and Scotland; distinguished by pinkish legs and feet and lack of black markings on bill.

Great Barrier Reef. See Section K.

Great Wall of China, the enormous wall (1,500 miles in length) built to protect China's northern frontier. Completed 204 B.C.

Grebe, a diving bird of beautiful plumage found over a great part of the world on lakes and oceans. The two species familiar in Great Britain are the Dabchick or Little Grebe and the large and handsome Great Crested Grebe, which has a feathery tuft, lost in the autumn, on each side of the head. Grebes have remarkable courtship displays. The breast feathers are of a downy softness and silver lustre, for which they were formerly much hunted.

Greek Art. See Hellenic Art.

Greek Fire, a combustible supposed to have been composed of sulphur, nitre, naphtha and asphalt, used with destructive effect by the Greeks of the Eastern Empire in their wars.

Greek Kalends, equivalent to never, as only the Romans, not the Greeks, had kalends.

Green Revolution. See Section G, Part III.

Greenwich Mean Time. The first Nautical Almanac, for the use of navigators and astronomers, was published by the Astronomer Royal in 1767. It was based on the meridian at Greenwich, with longitude measured east and west of 0°. A master clock, which still exists, was built at Greenwich Observatory in 1852 to control the railway station clocks and Greenwich Mean Time, or Railway Time as it was sometimes called, prevailed. In 1884 Greenwich was chosen as the prime meridian of the world and GMT became known as Universal Time. The time-keeping role is now done by the International Bureau of Weights and Measures. GMT has become CUT (Coordinated Universal Time). Recently, the Daylight Extra Now group has campaigned to abolish GMT and have an extra hour of daylight in the evening. A Bill is currently (1999) before Parliament. See also British Standard Time and F68.

Gregorian Calendar. See Calendar.

Gresham's Law states that if money, i.e., money with the higher intrinsic value, and bad money are in circulation together, the bad money will tend to drive out the good money from circulation. For instance, the good money is more likely to be melted down or demanded in payment by foreign creditors.

Gretna Green, a celebrated village in Annandale and Eskdale, just over the border from England, where runaway marriages were performed from 1754 to 1856, though only completely stopped during present century.

Griffin, in ancient mythology, a winged creature with an eagle's head and the body of a lion, found in ancient sculptures of Persia and Assyria. Its origin is traced to the Hittites.

Grilse, a young salmon that has only been once to the sea.

Grimm's Law, formulated by Jacob Grimm, an eminent German philologist, lays down a principle of consonantal change in the Germanic languages. For instance, Lat. *pater*, Eng. *father*, Ger. *Vater*; Lat. *frater*, Eng. *brother*, Ger. *Bruder*; Lat. *decem*, Eng. *ten*, Ger. *zehn*.

Grogram (French = *gros grain*), a kind of rough fabric made of wool and some other fibre, such as silk, mohair or cotton, formerly much used for commoner kinds of wearing apparel.

Grotto, a natural or artificial cave. Among the most famous are the blue grotto of Capri and the grotto of Antiparos (Cyclades, Aegean).

Ground Wave, that part of the energy emitted by a radio transmitter which travels along the ground; as opposed to the sky wave which is reflected back to earth by the ionosphere. With the lower radio-frequencies, the ground wave can be picked up over several thousand miles; in the broadcasting band, over a hundred or so miles; it is virtually useless at high frequencies.

Grouse, game bird of the northern latitudes where some 20 species occur. They are stout, compact, ground-dwelling birds, protectively plumaged (the willow grouse turns white in winter), the male usually being larger and more brightly coloured than the female. The red grouse of the British moorlands has been introduced into Belgium and Germany. Of the same family are the blackcock, ptarmigan, capercaillie, American prairie-hen and the partridge. Grouse shooting begins in Britain on 12 Aug. The black grouse in Britain is in rapid decline.

Guanaco, a large species of llama, common to South America. Utilised as a beast of burden.

Guano, the excrement of sea-birds, found in large quantities on the rocky islands of the western coasts of South America and Nauru Is. It forms a useful fertilising agent, being rich in phosphate and ammonia, and first came into use in 1841, since which time Peruvian guano has been a recognised article of commerce. Beds of guano from 15–18 m in thickness are not uncommon. Fish guano and bat guano from caves in South America and the Bahamas are also used as fertilisers.

Gudgeon, a small fresh-water fish of the carp family with 2 small barbels on the upper lip.

Guelph and Ghibelline, italianised forms of the German words "Welf" and "Waiblingen", the names of two rival princely families whose conflicts made much of the history of Germany and Italy during the Middle Ages. The feuds between these two factions continued in Italy during the campaigns of Emperor Frederick I, and later developed into the fierce struggles of the 13th cent. between emperor and pope. In Italy the Ghibellines supported the side of the German emperors and the Guelphs the cause of the Pope. The present Royal Family of England and other Northern monarchies are descended by different routes from the Guelph George I, Duke of Brunswick-Lüneburg of the House of Hanover.

Guildhall, the place of assembly of the members of a guild, and at one time, when guilds were in full strength, was practically the Town Hall. The London Guildhall is today the hall of meeting for the City of London Corporation.

Guilds for the fostering and protection of various trades have existed in England since Anglo-Saxon times and from the 12th to the 16th cent. exercised great influence and enjoyed many privileges. There were trades' guilds and craftsmen's guilds, and in all large cities and towns there was a guild hall. Their successes in the Middle Ages led to many monopolistic abuses, and in the end it became necessary to free the country from their restrictive power. The City Guilds (Livery Companies of the City of London) derive their name from the distinctive dress assumed by their members in the 14th cent.

Guild Socialism. *See* **Section J**.

Guillemot, a genus of sea-birds of the auk family, common in Northern Europe, two species—the Common Guillemot and the Black Guillemot—being natives of our own sea coasts, nesting on the cliffs. Brünnich's Guillemot, an Arctic species, is a rare straggler in Britain.

Guinea, an English gold coin of the value of twenty-one shillings, current from 1663–1817, and deriving its name from the first guinea coinage having been struck from gold obtained on the coast of Guinea.

Guinea-Pig, a rodent of the cavy family about 25 cm in length and with a tail so short that it does not project outside the body. It makes an excellent pet, though easily frightened. Its ancestors were species of the wild cavy of S. America said to have been domesticated by the Incas of Peru.

Gules, a heraldic term, denoting a rose of red tincture, indicated by vertical lines drawn or engraved without colour.

Gulf Stream is confined entirely to the western side of the N. Atlantic and is the warm-water current flowing through the Straits of Florida from the Gulf of Mexico parallel to the American coast up as far as Cape Hatteras. From there it continues north-eastwards as a slower, broader, cooler (yet even so, relatively warm) drift of water, merging with the North Atlantic Drift and losing its identity about 40° N. Lat., 60° W. Long. It is a common error to attribute the warmth of the British Isles and Western Europe generally to the Gulf Stream but this has no influence whatever except in so far as it feeds the North Atlantic Drift. Both the Gulf Stream and the North Atlantic Drift owe their movement to the direction of the prevailing winds, and it is the south-westerly airstream coming from warmer regions and passing over the surface waters of the Atlantic Drift that brings the warmth inland to influence the climate of Western Europe.

Gull. An extremely well-known, long-winged sea-bird with rather short legs and webbed feet. In almost all adults the body and tail are white whilst the back and most of the wings are grey or black. In the majority of cases the plumage of juveniles is partly or entirely dusky. Gulls are omnivorous, and are very useful as scavengers. They follow ships and quickly seize upon any refuse which may be thrown overboard. There are 44 species, which vary in size from moderately small to large. With certain exceptions, such as the Kittiwake in the North Atlantic, they are not found very far from land. They are sociable and mostly breed in colonies on cliff-ledges, on islands, beaches and sandhills and among vegetation in swamps, sometimes a long way from the sea. The nest is usually substantial, and the eggs generally number from two to three. Of the 29 species breeding in the northern hemisphere, 14 occur in the British Isles. The pure white Ivory Gull is the most northerly of birds. Sabine's and the Swallow-tailed Gull have forked tails. Ross's Gull has a black ring round the neck and one species, Franklin's Gull, migrates from the North, where it breeds, to pass the winter in the Southern hemisphere.

Gums are glutinous compounds obtained from vegetable sources, soluble in cold or hot water, but not in alcohol. There are innumerable varieties. Gum Arabic is exuded from a species of acacia grown in Senegal, the Sudan, Arabia, India and other countries, and is a valuable commercial product, used in dyeing, ink-making, as a mucilage, and in medicine. India-rubber is an elastic gum. Gums are also made from starch, potatoes, wheat, *etc.*, from seeds, bark, roots and weeds. Many so-called gums are resins.

Gun-Cotton, a powerful explosive manufactured by subjecting a prepared cotton to the prolonged action of a mixture of three parts sulphuric acid and one part of nitric acid. It burns without explosion on ignition, but by percussion explodes with a force five times greater than gunpowder does.

Gunpowder, also called "black powder", the oldest of explosive mixtures, consists of salt-petre, sulphur and charcoal, intimately mixed, the proportions being varied for different intended uses.

Gunpowder Plot was a conspiracy by a desperate band of Roman Catholics in the reign of James I to avenge the harsh treatment to which Catholics were subjected. Barrels of gunpowder were secreted in the vaults underneath the Houses of Parliament, and it was proposed to fire these when the King and his Ministers assembled on 5 November 1605. The plot was betrayed and Guy Fawkes and his co-conspirators were arrested and executed. The date serves to perpetuate the ancient custom of burning the effigy of Fawkes.

Gurnard, a sea-fish, with large, bony head and diminutive body, of which there are some forty species. They are plentiful in British waters.

Gymnasium, originally the name given in ancient Greece to the public places where Greek youth used to exercise and receive instruction. Plato, Aristotle and other great teachers lectured there. The Greek institution was never very popular with the Romans, and it was not until the 18th and 19th cent. that the cult of combining physical with intellectual activity again found a place in educational systems. In Germany the name was applied to the classical grammar school; in this country and America to the halls where gymnastics were practised.

Gypsies, a nomadic race, believed to be of Indian origin; their language, Romany, is related to the languages of N.W. India. The Rom are spread over many parts of the world, but are most common in Europe where they appeared towards the end of the Middle Ages. The English name *gypsy* comes from the Spanish *gitano* = Egyptian; other European names are *Zigeuner* (Ger.), *zingaro* (It.), *fzigany* (Magyar), all resembling the Persian *singar* = a saddler. Their history has been one of persecution. Hitler treated them like the Jews. In Britain since the war they have been kept increasingly on the move, but in 1968 Parliament passed a Bill to make the provision of sites a duty of local authorities. However, the 1994 Criminal Justice and Public Order Act made it much easier to move on unwelcome gypsies. Economic pressure has largely removed their traditional crafts of tinkering, basket-making and peg-making. The majority now deal in scrap-iron. Today (1999) there are *c.* 12 million Gypsies and in parts of Europe (such as Bulgaria and the Czech Republic) they are again subject to systematic ill-treatment.

Gypsum, a whitish mineral consisting of hydrated sulphate of calcium. The finest gypsum is alabaster. When heated gypsum is converted into the powder called Plaster of Paris; the water it loses can be taken up when the plaster is wetted, and the reconversion of Plaster of Paris into gypsum accounts for the way in which the former sets hard. The name "Plaster of Paris" came from the location of important gypsum quarries in the Montmartre district of Paris. It was found after the flood disasters of January 1953 that gypsum could undo the effect of sea-water. By spreading it for the rain to wash into the soil, thousands of acres of farmland in Holland and Britain were made productive again.

Gyroscope is a symmetrical rapidly rotating object, typically wheel-like, which because of its mass and rotation possesses a lot of the dynamical property known as angular momentum. Basic dynamical laws tell us that angular momentum is conserved and a consequence of this is that the axis of rotation tends to stay pointing in the same direction. Disturbing influences make a gyroscope's motion complicated but the general effect of the presence of a gyroscope attached to any body is to help to stabilise the body's motion. This is made use of in reducing the rocking of ships and in compasses and control systems in aircraft, torpedoes and missiles.

H

Habeas Corpus, the name given to a writ ordering

the body of a person under restraint or imprisonment to be brought into court for full inquiry into the legality of the restraint to be made. The first Habeas Corpus Act was passed in 1679, though nominally such a right had existed from Magna Carta, but some of the more despotic kings had disregarded it. In times of public peril the privilege of *habeas corpus* is sometimes temporarily suspended.

Haber–Ostveldt Process, the important industrial process for synthesising ammonia from atmospheric nitrogen. Nitrogen and hydrogen are combined at high pressure (*c.* 350 atmospheres) and moderately high temperature (500°C) using a catalyst (made largely of iron). A yield of 30% is obtained. The majority of the world's ammonia is produced in this way or from methods derived from it.

Habsburg (Hapsburg), the ruling house of Austria, 1282–1918; held title of Roman Emperor, 1438–1806, except for 1740–5. The aggrandisement of the Habsburg family was mainly brought about by a series of fortunate marriages. In 1521 when the Habsburg power was at its zenith, Charles V divided his dominions into two branches—Austrian Habsburg and Spanish Habsburg. The Habsburg Danubian Monarchy dates from 1526 when the Hungarian and Bohemian crowns were united with the Austrian patrimony of the Habsburg. The triple union lasted 400 years. The murder of the heir to the Habsburg thrones, Francis Ferdinand, at Sarajevo in 1914, provoked the outbreak of the first world war. Francis Joseph's great-nephew, Charles, went into exile in 1918.

Haddock, one of the best-known fishes abounding in northern seas and averaging about 1·8 kg in weight. Related to the cod. Largely used for curing, and sold as "finnan haddies".

Hade of veins, a mining term indicating the particular inclination that any vein, seam or strata may have from the perpendicular; thus, in Weardale the veins mainly "hade" to the north.

Hadrian's Wall. *See* **Roman walls.**

Haematite, ferric oxide, one of the principal iron ores, containing about 70% of the metal. It is usually found in kidney-shaped masses, and is specular, red or brown, in thin fragments but greyish in bulk.

Haemocyanin, the respiratory pigment of crustaceans and molluscs. It functions like haemoglobin, from which it differs in containing copper instead of iron and being blue when oxidised instead of red.

Haemoglobin, the pigment containing iron which gives red blood corpuscles their colour. It is a respiratory pigment, having the property of picking up oxygen when the blood passes through the lungs to produce the compound known as oxyhaemoglobin. In other parts of the body the oxyhaemoglobin breaks down, liberating oxygen, which is used in the oxidation process (respiration) that the body tissues carry on.

Hafiz, besides being the pseudonym of a famous Persian poet, is a title conferred upon any Mohammedan who has committed the whole of the Koran to memory.

Hafnium, a metallic element, no. 72, symbol Hf, discovered by Coster and Hevesy in 1922 and important in the atomic-energy field. It occurs in most zirconium minerals to the extent of *c.* 5%.

Hagiology, a branch of literature that is wholly given up to the history of the saints, and the setting forth of their stories and legends.

Hail, hard, roughly spherical balls of ice, consisting of white cores covered by layers of both transparent and opaque ice, frequently falling during thunderstorms. They usually do not exceed 2·5 cm in size, but hailstones as large as tennis balls have been observed. The general theory of a hailstone is that near the top of a cumulonimbus cloud a raindrop becomes frozen, grows in size by condensation and through collisions with snow particles, and eventually becomes so weighty as to overcome the ascending air currents in the cloud. Falling, it first encounters supercooled water drops, immediately freezing on it, increasing the white core, and then at lower levels ordinary water drops, freezing more slowly, producing a layer of clear ice. Before the hailstone arrives at the ground

gusts and lulls may transport it several times up and down both regions, adding alternate coatings of soft white and hard clear ice.

Halcyon, a term associated in olden times with the kingfisher and days of soothing calm, "halcyon days" being a frequently used expression. The legend was that the kingfisher laid its eggs on the surface of the sea at the time of the winter solstice when the sea was unruffled. (Halcyon is the Greek for kingfisher.)

Halibut, one of the largest of the flat fishes, averaging when full grown from 1·2–1·8 m in length, and highly esteemed for the table. Specimens of still larger size occasionally occur. It is plentifully distributed. Its two eyes are on the right side of the head.

Hallmark. A mark or group of marks, impressed by an assay office on gold or silver articles (and on platinum since 1974) guaranteeing the standard of fineness of the precious metal used in them. These marks, which have been applied to silver made in London since the beginning of the 14th cent. and perhaps earlier, make it possible to establish the year and place of assay and also the name of the maker. English pieces of silver usually have not less than four marks, viz., (1) town mark; (2) maker's mark; (3) date letter; (4) sterling mark.

The town mark is rarely changed; in London a crowned leopard's head was used from the earliest days until 1820 with only minor modifications, except for the period 1697–1720 when a lion's head erased was substituted; since 1820 the crown has been omitted.

Until the late 17th cent. a symbol was often used as a maker's mark, from 1696–1720 the first two letters of the maker's surname, and subsequently the maker's initials. Owing to the destruction of the earlier mark plates at Goldsmiths' Hall no maker's name prior to the late 17th cent. can be identified with certainty.

The London date letter is changed at the end of May each year, so each letter covers seven months of one year and five months of the following. The London date cycle has usually consisted of twenty letters: the alphabet of each cycle is of different style, and the letters are enclosed in shields of different shape.

The sterling mark, the lion passant, was introduced in 1544 and continued in use until 1697, when the higher Britannia standard was introduced in order to discourage the practice current amongst goldsmiths of melting down coin of the realm to make plate. The leopard's head crowned and the lion passant were then replaced by a figure of Britannia and a lion's head erased. Though the regulation imposing a higher standard was withdrawn in 1720, a small amount of Britannia standard silver continued to be made and still is made.

From 1784 until 1890 a plate tax was levied on all silver assayed in Great Britain and an additional duty mark, the sovereign's head, was used during this period. A Jubilee mark bearing the head of George V and of Queen Mary was used between the years 1933 and 1935, and in 1953 a coronation mark with the head of Queen Elizabeth was introduced. A special Millennium hallmark will be available only in 1999 and 2000.

Under the Hallmarking Act 1973 the hallmarking of platinum is now compulsory; the hallmark symbol is an orb surmounted by a cross and encompassed by a pentagon. There are now assay offices in London, Birmingham, Sheffield and Edinburgh.

Halloween (31 October), the eve of All Saints' Day, a time associated, especially in Scotland, with certain traditions attractively set forth in Burns's famous poem "Hallowe'en". It is the night when young men and maidens are supposed, by observing certain rites, to have their future wives and husbands disclosed to them.

Hallucinogen, a drug which acts upon the brain to create sensory illusions or hallucinations with a variety of emotional effects. One of the most widely studied is LSD (*q.v.*) which will produce symptoms very similar to those found in some mental disorders.

Halo, a luminous circle usually of 22° radius, surrounding sun or moon, produced by the refraction and reflection of light by ice crystals of high cirrus cloud. It is a very common occurrence, in the British Isles almost one day in three. The inner side is red and the outer a whitish-yellow colour. "Mock suns", *i.e.*, patches of light at the same elevation as the sun are much rarer occurrences, sometimes being of great beauty and brilliance. Halo is the Greek for threshing-floor. *See* **Corona.**

Halogens, the group name for the five non-metallic elements fluorine, chlorine, bromine, iodine and astatine. The term "halogen" means "salt-producer".

Halteres, the modified hind-wings of the two-winged flies or *Diptera* (*e.g.*, the house-fly). The equilibrium in flight of these insects depends on the halteres, which are commonly called "balancers".

Hampton Court Conference, presided over at Hampton Court Palace by James I in 1604 and which brought about his authorised translation of the Bible, had an important bearing on the religious differences of the time. James refused to grant tolerations to the Puritans. This sowed the seeds of civil war. Following the conference three hundred English Puritan clergy were ejected from their livings.

Hanaper Office, a former Chancery office, deriving its name from the fact that its writs and papers were kept in a hanaper (hamper). The Chancellor's office thus came to be known as the Hanaper. The Comptrollers of the Hanaper were abolished in England in 1842.

Hand, a measure of 4 in (10 cm), the average size of the palm; used in reckoning height of horses.

Handfasting, an informal marriage custom once prevalent in Scotland, whereby a man and woman bound themselves to cohabit for a year and a day, and at the end of that period either confirmed their contract by a regular marriage or separated.

Hanoverians, Royal dynasty which ruled Great Britain and Ireland, from 1714 to 1901. From the Brünswick-Luneburg branch of the Guelph family, they took their name from the German state of Hanover where they were Electors of the Holy Roman Empire. Their succession to the English, and later British, crown was secured by the 1710 Act of Settlement. In 1837 the crown of Hanover went to the uncle of Queen Victoria, Ernest, Duke of Cumberland and the personal union of the Hanoverian and British crowns ceased.

The British Hanoverian monarchs were George I (ruled 1714–27); his son George II (1727–60); George III, grandson of George II (1760–1820); his eldest son George IV (1820–30 and Prince Regent from 1812); William IV, third son of George III (1830–37) and Queen Victoria, granddaughter of George III (1837–1901).

Hansard, the title given to the official reports of Parliamentary debates, so named after Luke Hansard who in 1774 became partner in a firm of printers to the House of Commons. His son T. C. Hansard was first the printer and then the publisher of an unofficial series of parliamentary debates inaugurated by William Cobbett in 1803. In 1909 production was taken over by H.M. Stationery Office and today's volumes contain full, substantially verbatim, reports of what is said in both Houses of Parliament.

Hanseatic League was a confederation of North German towns established about 1241 for purposes of mutual protection in carrying on international commerce. The League became so powerful that it was able to dominate the foreign trade of Norway, Sweden, Denmark, and even to some extent of London. A branch was established in London and had its guild hall in Cannon Street for hundreds of years. The League existed down to the middle of the 17th cent. Hamburg, Lübeck and Bremen are the only cities which, as free ports, still by commercial courtesy retain the name of Hanse towns. *Hansa* is Old High German for Association or Merchants' Guild. *See also* **Freeport.**

Hapsburg, *see* **Habsburg.**

Hara-kiri, the custom of suicide, as formerly practised in Japan, when in disgrace.

Hardware. *See* **Section V.**

Hare, a rabbit-like animal with longer ears and legs. There are many kinds of hare distributed over the northern hemisphere and in Africa south to the Cape. They do not burrow as do rabbits but rely on camouflage, speed and

mobility for safety. Sightings of hares across Britain have declined sharply since the 1960s. Today (1999) this decline is causing concern. *See* **Game.**

Harleian MSS. comprise some thousands of volumes of MSS. and documents, collected by the first Earl of Oxford (1661–1724) and his son Edward. After the death of the latter, his widow handed the MSS. over to the nation for £10,000, and they are deposited in the British Museum.

Harlequin, the buffoon of ancient Italian comedy. As adapted to the British stage, however, harlequin is a pantomime character only, in love with Columbine, appearing in parti-coloured garments and carrying a wand, by which he exercises a magic influence in thwarting the fantastic tricks of the clown and pantaloon.

Harmattan, a dry wind which may blow between January and May across the Sahara to the Gulf of Guinea. Although affording relief from the tropical heat, vegetation withers because of its extreme dryness and much irritation is caused by the clouds of fine dust which it carries.

Harmonic Motion, regular periodic motion of the kind exemplified by a ball bobbing up and down at the end of a spring, and by the piston in a steam engine. It may be simple (simple harmonic motion) or composed of two or more simple harmonic motions. In simple harmonic motion the acceleration is proportional to the distance of the moving body from its original rest position.

Harp-seal, the ordinary Greenland seal, with a dark harp-shaped marking on its back, hence its name. It abounds in Newfoundland waters and further northward towards the Arctic.

Harpy Eagle, a large bird of prey named from the winged monsters of Greek mythology, inhabiting the forest regions of Central and South America. There are eight species, one with handsome grey plumage and large crest which attacks and kills animals much larger than itself, and was called by the Aztecs "winged wolf".

Harrier, a bird of prey of the falcon family; of the various species distributed over the world, three breed in Britain: the moorland Hen harrier, the Marsh harrier and Montagu's harrier. They are large birds with long tails, long legs, long wings and gliding flight. They nest on the ground and eat small mammals, frogs, lizards and small birds.

Hartebeest, common African antelope of a grey-brown colour, with ringed and knotted horns bending backward and tapering to sharp points; gregarious, of large size. There are several species.

Harvest Bug, a very small insect, of a dark red colour, which appears in large numbers in the fields in autumn, and is peculiarly irritating to animals and man by the tenacity with which it attaches itself to the skin and burrows underneath. Probably the larvae of spinning mites (Trombidoids). In the USA they are called "chiggers".

Harvest Moon, the full moon that occurs nearest to the autumn equinox, in September. It rises for several nights running about the same time, and yields an unusually brilliant series of moonlight nights.

Harvestmen are, like spiders, members of the arachnid class but belong to the distinctly different order of Phalangida. They are common in the countryside in autumn and have small oval bodies and eight long slender legs which besides being mere organs of locomotion also act as sense organs. Known as "daddy longlegs" in America and Britain.

Hashish, an Arabic word for the narcotic substance prepared from the hemp plant (*Cannabis sativa*). It is known by a variety of names, *e.g.*, bhang in India and marijuana in America.

Hatchment, in heraldry, is a square board, in vertical diagonal position, placed outside a house or on the tomb at the death of a member of a family and so arranged that it indicates the sex and condition of the deceased.

Hawfinch, a well-known European bird of the finch family, having a variegated plumage, a sturdy bill and black-and-white tail. In England it is found in the Midland and Eastern counties, and locally in Scotland.

Hawk. This name is applied to almost any diurnal bird of prey other than eagle, falcon or vulture, but in its strict sense applies only to the *Accipiter* genus—the small Sparrow Hawk and the larger Goshawk, round-winged, long-tailed birds with barred under-parts. They prey upon small birds captured in flight and small mammals.

Hawk-moths, large species of moths, thick of body and strong of wing, which fly with rapid swooping motion, hence the name. There are numerous handsome species in Britain.

Hearth-Money was a tax laid on hearths (in all houses paying the church and poor rates). Charles II introduced it in 1662, and it was repealed in the reign of William and Mary.

Heat, after prolonged controversy over whether or not heat is a "substance" (formerly called "caloric"), it was established in the 19th cent. that heat is a form of energy; it is in fact the combined kinetic and potential energy of the atoms of which a body is composed. Heat can be turned into other forms of energy, *e.g.*, a red hot body loses heat by radiating it in the form of electromagnetic waves ("radiant heat"—chiefly infra-red rays). Heat may also be transferred from one place to another by conduction and, in fluids, by convection. All three processes occur when a glowing fire heats a room. A unit quantity of heat is the calorie, which is the amount of heat sufficient to raise the temperature of 1 g of water by 1°C. In general, adding heat to a body raises its temperature. The number of calories required per gram of material to raise the temperature 1°C is called the *specific heat* of the material. However, adding heat may not raise the temperature—but may instead cause a change of state, *e.g.*, from solid to liquid (melting) or liquid to gas (evaporation). The amount of heat required to melt 1 gram of a solid is called the latent heat of melting. Similarly, there is a latent heat of evaporation. Strictly speaking, the specific and latent heats of a substance depend on how much its pressure and volume are allowed to vary during the measurements. Water has a high specific heat, and this makes the oceans a vast heat reservoir, a factor of great meteorological significance. The science of heat is called thermodynamics.

Heat Pump, essentially a refrigerator working in reverse, *i.e.*, a device which warms up one place, say, a house by releasing into it heat transferred from another place, say, the air or earth outside the house. The idea is attributed to Lord Kelvin (1852) and later Haldane used a heat pump to heat his house in Scotland. In Summer, a house could be cooled by operating the device in reverse. As in a domestic refrigerator, the heat is transferred by a suitable fluid whose circulation has to be driven by an external supply of energy, *e.g.*, by running a mechanical compressor. With good design and favourable conditions, the energy required to run the heat pump is considerably less than would be required to produce the same warming effect directly. Since the 1930s heat pumps have been produced commercially for domestic and industrial use but, as always, careful consideration is needed to decide whether in a particular application they are cheaper to run than alternative methods of heating.

Heath, flowering plants of the *Ericaceae* family. Heaths are widely distributed over uncultivated spaces of Europe and Africa. In Britain they are represented by heather (of which there are several species) and ling (*Calluna vulgaris*), which cover thousands of acres of moorland. Some of the African or Cape heaths are very beautiful and much prized by florists. One species of heath (*Erica arborea*) which grows in S. Europe and N. Africa has close-grained woody rootstock used for making briar pipes. In N. Europe acid heathlands, dominated by heather and ling, form one of the most widespread vegetation areas created by man through the destruction of forests, grazing and burning.

Heathrow Airport, originally called London Airport (Heathrow) and named after a village where Terminal 3 now stands, opened on 1 January 1946. The airport handles more than 90 airlines from 85 countries and offers direct flights to more than 200 destinations. It employs 54,000 staff. In 1998 the airport handled 54 million passengers. This total may rise to 80 million by 2013. The proposed new Terminal 5 is currently awaiting the verdict of Britain's longest-ever planning inquiry. If built, Terminal 5 will cost £1·2 bn and will be three times the size of Terminal 4. The Heathrow Express Paddington link was opened in June 1998.

Hegira, an Arab term signifying departure or flight, used in reference to Mohammed's departure from Mecca, A.D. 622, from which date the Mohammedan era is reckoned.

Helicopter, heavier-than-air aircraft which obtains its lift from blades rotating above the fuselage in windmill-fashion. The first successful helicopters were the Focke-Wulf 61, a German machine (1936), and the VS-300, designed by Igor Sikorsky, flown in 1937. Helicopters can hover, and rise and descend vertically, in addition to being capable of horizontal flight.

Heliotrope, a favourite sweet-scented flowering plant, common in tropical and sub-tropical countries; the Peruvian heliotrope is the "cherry pie" of our summer garden borders.

Helium, a gaseous element, no. 2, symbol He, first discovered by means of the spectroscope in the sun's atmosphere. This discovery, made in 1868 by the astronomer Sir Norman Lockyer, was followed in 1895 by Sir William Ramsay's proof that the element existed on earth. He found it in the uranium ore, clevite. Later it was established that helium is formed by the radioactive decay of many elements which emit α-particles (nuclei of helium atoms) and is contained in all radioactive minerals. The largest source of helium is natural gas, the richest in helium being the gas from certain wells in Utah, USA. Next to hydrogen, helium is the lightest gas known, has a lifting power equal to 92% of hydrogen and the advantage that it is inert and non-inflammable. It is used for inflating airships. Ordinary air contains 1 part in 200,000 of helium. It was the last gaseous element to be liquefied, this being achieved by Onnes in 1908 in Leyden. Liquid helium has many remarkable properties only imperfectly understood. As well as being scientifically fascinating it is indispensable in cryogenics (*q.v.*) as a medium for cooling other substances to temperatures near absolute zero. Hydrogen fusion in the "H bomb" produces helium.

Hellebore, a plant of the *Ranunculaceae* (buttercup) family. The best-known British examples are the green and stinking varieties. There is also a garden kind which flowers in December called the Christmas Rose. Hellebore yields a bitter substance which was once much used as a purgative.

Hellenic Art. The art of ancient Greece may be roughly divided into three periods: the prehistoric period (*c.* 1500–1000 B.C.) of the bronze age Mycenaeans; the archaic period (*c.* 600–500 B.C.); and the classical period (*c.* 500–300 B.C.). Of the first period centred on Mycenae in Peloponnesus but extending to the coasts of Asia and the city of Troy we can mention only the massive stone gateways and the shaft graves of Mycenae, where the archaeologist Schliemann discovered painted vases, gold cups, bronze swords and ornaments of what had once been a great, if primitive, civilisation. During the archaic period sculpture was the principal form of art expression. The magnificent male and female figures are reminiscent of Egyptian art, but are distinctive in liveliness of facial expression. The vase-paintings of this period became more elaborate, depicting scenes from mythology or ceremonial events. Typical of classical Greek art is the representation of the beautiful and healthy human body deliberately posed and often carrying out heroic or athletic acts. The vast majority of these statues are known to us only through Roman copies. The *Hermes* of Praxiteles (born *c.* 385 B.C.) is possibly the only existing statue which can be assigned with any degree of certainty to an individual artist.

Almost the whole of the Greek genius in architecture was expended on temples which are all basically similar in design—a rectangle with a low-pitched gabled roof resting on side walls. The three orders Doric, Corinthian and Ionic mainly referred to the type of column used, but naturally the whole building was influenced thereby. Some of the main buildings are on the Acropolis, a hill outside Athens, on which stand the Parthenon (from the outer frieze of which the Elgin marbles (*q.v.*), now mostly in the British Museum, were taken), the Erechtheum, famous for its Porch of Maidens, and the gateway known as the Propylaea with its broad flight of marble steps. Apart from that on vases, no Greek painting has come down to us, although Greek painters existed and were noted in their time. All we have are copies in mosaic and fresco made by the Romans, at Naples and Pompeii. Of Greek literature in prose, verse and the drama little can be said here. To the early period (*i.e.*, the archaic age) belong Homer's *Iliad* and *Odyssey*. Hesiod's long poem *Work and Days* and Sappho's love poems, and Pindar's Odes. The period of Pericles in the 5th cent. B.C. produced more great literature than any comparable period in history: the philosophical writings of Plato and Aristotle, the tragedies of Aeschylus, Euripides and Sophocles, the comedies of Aristophanes—all these are still part of the European tradition, and together with Greek architecture played a major part in the Renaissance (*see* **Section J**).

Hellenistic Art, the age of the period of Greek civilisation which began with the conquests of Alexander the Great (356-323 B.C.) and lasted until his former empire (which encompassed most of the Middle East and part of North Africa) was conquered by the Romans in 146 B.C. Culturally it was an important period because it spread Greek culture far beyond its original boundaries—even as far as the north of India, and its centres spread from Athens to the cities of Alexandria in Egypt, Antioch in Syria and Pergamum in Asia Minor. But equally Eastern culture spread to the West: democracy was replaced by absolute monarchy, cosmopolitanism took the place of the Greek tendency to believe that all who were not Greeks were barbarians, and mystical philosophies took the place of Greek rationalism. This was a sensuous, secular, pleasure-loving, rootless society, and these tendencies were reflected in its art.

Hellenistic sculpture was sensual, effeminate and violently emotional, depicting individuals and not always noble or beautiful ones. (Classical Greek sculpture was idealistic, showed types rather than individuals and appealed to the intellect rather than the emotions.) Some of the best examples came from the school at Pergamum and later from the island of Rhodes, and the titles themselves speak of their nature: *The Dying Gaul, Gaul Slaying his Wife and Himself* and the famous *Laocoön* (representing Laocoön and his two sons being crushed by two enormous serpents). All these date from about 240 to 50 B.C.—for the culture did not immediately end with the Roman conquest. The enormous frieze of the altar of the temple in Pergamum depicts a battle between gods and giants with tremendous realism and brutal violence far removed from the serene art of classical times. Portrait sculpture is typical of Hellenistic art, where it may almost be said to have been invented, since such ventures in the past had been idealistic rather than realistic. The great Hellenistic cities were geometrically planned and fine public buildings made their appearance in which the slender and graceful Ionic of the ornate Corinthian columns took the place of the more austere and heavy classical ones. Alexandria was celebrated for its vast libraries and was the centre of a brilliant intellectual life (the Septuagint or Greek translation of the Bible was prepared here). Here too worked the mathematicians Euclid and Archimedes, the physicians Erasistratus and Herophilus, and the geographer Pytheas. But Hellenistic literature was a pale reflection of the glories of the past and we mention only the comedies of Menander and the pastoral verse of Theocritus of Syracuse.

Hemiptera, the order of insects to which belong the true bugs. Their wing structure is in most species incomplete, hence the term hemiptera (half-wing). This order includes the familiar water insects, the water boatman and water skater, also the aphids, cicadas, leaf hoppers, scale insects.

Hemlock, a plant of the *Umbelliferae* family, growing in all parts of Britain, and containing a strong alkaloid poison. Used medicinally, this alkaline substance is of considerable service, being a powerful sedative. According to Pliny, hemlock was the poison used by the Athenians in putting criminals to death.

Hemp (*Cannabis sativa*), name of a plant native to Asia, now cultivated widely for the valuable fibre contained in the stalk or in some species in the leaves. Hemp fibre has been replaced by cotton for textiles and by jute for sacks and is now chiefly used for cordage and twine. It contains a resinous substance from which the narcotic hashish is made. The seed yields a valuable oil. The term hemp is also used for other fibre plants, *e.g.* manila hemp from the Philippines, sunn hemp from India, sisal from W. and E. Africa and phormium from New Zealand.

Henbane, a plant found in Britain and other parts of Europe and Northern Asia. It belongs to the potato family *Solanaceae*, grows mostly on waste ground and bears yellow-brown flowers veined with purple. The leaves yield a poisonous alkaloid substance which is of great use in medicine. Tincture of henbane is often preferred to laudanum.

Heptarchy, a word derived from the Greek *hepta*, seven, and denoting the seven kingdoms (*archai*) into which Anglo-Saxon England was divided before 900. The seven were Kent, Essex, Sussex, Wessex, Mercia, East Anglia and Northumbria.

Heracleum, a plant of the *Umbelliferae* family, common in southern and central Europe, though only one species, the cow parsnip, grows in England. It has a bitter root, and from the juice of the stem an intoxicating liquor is occasionally prepared.

Herald, an officer of state empowered to make formal proclamations and deliver messages from the sovereign or other high personage whom he serves. In the developments which took place in armorial bearings, the herald was the functionary charged with the duty of their proper depiction.

Heraldry, the knowledge of armorial bearings, was mainly the outcome of the love of outward distinction which prevailed in mediaeval times, "Heraldry," says Stubbs, "became a handmaid of chivalry, and the marshalling of badges, crests, coat-armour, pennons, helmets and other devices of distinction grew into an important branch of knowledge." The *shield*, or *escutcheon*, is the ground upon which armorial signs are traced, the colour of the shield being called the *tincture*, the signs recorded the *charges*. There are seven *tinctures—or* (gold), *argent* (silver), *gules* (red), *azure* (blue), *vert* (green), *purpure* (purple) and *sable* (black). The *charges* are classed as "Honourable" and "Subordinate" ordinaries, comprising lines and geometrical forms; and "Common" ordinaries, which latter includes all representations of natural objects. There is also a system of external signs, such as crowns, coronets, mitres, helmets, mantlings, wreaths and crests, each having its distinctive significance. For other distinguishing marks *see* **Hatchment, Quartering, Rampant.**

Heralds' College or College of Arms, was incorporated by Richard III in 1483. Its head is the Earl Marshal (an office hereditary in the family of the Dukes of Norfolk), and there are three Kings of Arms, six Heralds and four Pursuivants. The business transacted is wholly connected with the tracing of genealogies and the granting of armorial bearings. In Scotland the Heraldic functions are performed by the Lord Lyon King of Arms.

Herbarium, a systematically classified collection of preserved plants. One of the largest in the world is at the Royal Botanic Gardens at Kew.

Heredity is the study of the transmission of physical and mental characteristics from one generation to another. Gregor Mendel (1822-84), a great experimenter in the field of inheritance, established the principle embodied in Mendel's law in his work published in 1866. The ideas which he then put forward were forgotten until the early years of this century, but today they form the basis of the modern study of genetics. Genes are the units of heredity; they are contained in the chromosomes of the cell nucleus. In human cells there are 46 chromosomes—22 pairs of characteristic shape, and a 23rd (the sex chromosomes) similar in women and dissimilar in men, which unite in the process of fertilisation. An individual can only develop, even under the most favourable surroundings, as far as his inherited characteristics, *i.e.*, his genes will allow him to do. It is in the development of personality that the interplay between heredity and environment becomes most apparent. *See* **Evolution, Section F, Part IV.**

Hermaphrodite, animals or plants possessing both male and female reproductive organs, *e.g.*, snail, earthworms, most flowering plants.

Hermit Crab, a decapod, with a soft asymmetrical body which it protects by thrusting it into an empty gastropod shell, *e.g.*, whelk, which it carries about, only abandoning it when necessary for a larger one. Found in all seas, many live in commensal relationship with sea anemones *etc.*

Heron, a large wading bird with long curved neck and pointed bill, is a member of the *Ardeidae* family, of which there are many species. Egrets and bitterns are included as herons. Herons are to be met with in marsh lands and near rivers and lakes, where they feed on fish and frogs. They nest in trees in large numbers, these colonies being called heronries. The common heron is native to England, and other species from the Continent are frequent visitors.

Herring (*Clupes harengus*), an important food-fish inhabiting the North Sea which has been subjected to much overfishing. In Britain the herring industry is based on the Shetlands and the coastal ports of E. Scotland and N.E. England. Marine biologists have recently reported on its unique structure for hearing which makes it receptive to sound frequencies over a very wide range and able to determine distance, direction and source of sound.

Hibernation, the dormant condition in which numerous mammals, reptiles, amphibians, insects, plants, *etc.*, pass the winter. The rate of metabolism slows down, and the body temperature drops to that of the surroundings. Work on these low temperatures and their physiological effect has led to improved surgical techniques. Animals of the torrid regions pass through an analogous period (aestivation) during the hot season, when the sources of food are dried up.

Hickory, several species of American tree of the walnut family, remarkable for its very hard, solid, heavy white wood, and bearing an edible, four-lobed nut.

Hieratic Art, a type of art (typified by the major part of the art of ancient Egypt) which is (*a*) exclusively religious and (*b*) conventionally based on earlier forms and traditions.

Hieroglyphics are the earliest form of pictured symbolic expressionn, and are supposed to have been introduced by the ancient Egyptians. They consist of rude depictions of animals, plants, signs and objects, and in their later examples express, in abridged form, ideas and records from which significant historical information has been gleaned. The deciphering of Egyptian hieroglyphics long formed an ardent study, but gradually the key to the riddle was discovered, and most of the ancient records can now be understood. Besides the Egyptian there are also Hittite, Minoan and Mayan hieroglyphic scripts. *See* **Rosetta Stone.**

Hi-Fi (High Fidelity). A term used since the late 1940s to describe domestic sound reproducing equipment and originally implying superlative performance and particularly stereo capability as opposed to mere mono. In this usage it is now somewhat dated. The criteria for hi-fidelity performance were originally difficult to achieve in practise and therefore the appellation was of some consequence, but recent advances in technology, design, component standards and quality assurance procedures have ensured that the criteria can be met by almost every product on the market. Recent usage does not necessarily imply a qualitative judgment but simply describes equipment for home use. A Hi Fi system will probably include a number of sources such as a turntable and a tonearm combination for replaying vinyl discs, a tuner for receiving radio broadcasts or a compact disc (CD) player, in combination with a

pre-amplifier/amplifier and loudspeakers or headphones. Quite frequently some sort of recording device such as a cassette deck will also be present. Since the early 1980s compact disc has become the primary distribution medium for prerecorded music, almost completely replacing vinyl discs. It was not until the late 1980s that digital recording systems such as RDAT (Rotary-head Digital Audio Tape) became available, but these have still not made a very substantial impact on the domestic market. With the more recent developments of DCC (Digital Compact Cassette) and MD (Mini Disc), consumers now have a choice of three digital recording systems and this has probably left many wondering which to choose.

Hindi, the official language of India.

Hinduism. *See* **Section J.**

Hindustani, the spoken form of Hindi (written in Devanagari script) and Urdu (written in Arabic characters).

Hippogriff, a fabulous animal like a horse in body, but with the head, wings and front legs and claws of an eagle. The monster frequently appears in the romances of the Middle Ages.

Hippopotamus or "river-horse" the largest living representative of the hippopotamidae family, widely distributed over Africa, where it lives in herds. It is of immense bulk, attaining a length of 3·6 m and a weight of 4 tonnes and stands about 1·5 m high. Its skin is hairless and about 5 cm thick, and it has a pair of tusks often weighing as much as 2·7 kg. It leads an amphibious way of life, and lives entirely on vegetation, both aquatic and terrestrial. The pigmy hippopotamus, which occurs in forests and swamps in W. Africa, is only half the size.

Histology is the study of the structure of plant and animal tissues. These mainly consist of groups of cells with similar functions, *e.g.*, muscle, brain tissue.

Hittites. *See* **S12.**

Hobby, a member of the falcon family, 30–35 cm long. Local breeding visitor to England and Wales, April–September; irregular visitor to Scotland and Ireland. They winter in Africa.

Hog, the common name of animals of the Suidae family, including the wild boar, pig and sow. The wild boar, *Sus scrofa*, is the common ancestor. The skin of the hog is covered with bristles, the snout truncated and each foot has four hoofed toes. Hogs are omnivorous feeders and eat almost anything that is given them.

Hogmanay, the Scottish New Year's Eve festival and a national holiday of the country. The custom of demanding Hogmanay bread is still upheld in many parts of Scotland.

Hogshead, a cask of varying capacity, also a specific measure. In the old English measure a hogshead was 63 old gallons of wine (=52¼ imperial gallons = 238·6 litres). Of beer 54 old gallons make a hogshead.

Holly, a hardy evergreen shrub, largely grown in England. Its bright dark green prickly curved leaves and clusters of red berries are familiar in all parts of the country, and used as house decoration between Christmas Eve and Twelfth Night, probably a relic from Roman and Teutonic customs. Its wood is white and hard, valued for carved work, while its bark yields a gummy substance which is converted into bird-lime.

Hologram, a photographic record, taken under special optical conditions, of light reflected from a scene or object. The hologram is typically a piece of film. However it is nothing like a photographic negative of the ordinary kind; for one thing it will show an unintelligible pattern of light and dark patches. Nevertheless if it is illuminated (again under special optical conditions) the light coming through it will form a *three dimensional* image of the original object. Another radical difference between a hologram and an ordinary film is that if the hologram is cut up, each fragment can be used to construct the entire image. Holography, as a method of recording and reproducing photographic information, was conceived by Gabor in 1947 but was only fully realised in practice after the invention of the laser (*q.v.*), which made available powerful sources of coherent light. The use of laser light is one of the "special conditions" referred to above. Technical applications are being explored in many laboratories. Gabor received the 1971 Nobel prize.

Holothurians. See **Sea Cucumbers**.

Holy Alliance, an alliance ostensibly for conserving religion, justice and peace in Europe, but used for repressing popular tendencies towards constitutional government. Formed by Alexander I of Russia, Francis I of Austria and Frederick William III of Prussia, at Paris on 26 September 1815. Subsequently joined by all the sovereigns of Europe, except the Pope and the King of England. It ended after the 1830 revolution in France.

Holy Coat of Trèves, a garment preserved in the Cathedral of Trèves, said to have been worn by Christ. It was brought from Jerusalem by the Empress Helena in the 4th century.

Holy Roman Empire, the title traditionally given (although the term "Holy" does not appear in a document until 1157) to the revived Empire when the German king Otto I was crowned in Rome by Pope John XII in 962. It endured until Napoleonic times (1806) two years after Francis II had assumed the title of Emperor of Austria.

Holy Rood, an annual Roman Catholic festival held on 14 September to celebrate the Elevation of the Cross in commemoration of its re-erection in Jerusalem by the Emperor Heraclius in 628 after retaking it from the Persians. Also included in the Church of England calendar.

Holyrood, the ancient royal palace at Edinburgh, dating from the 15th cent., and inhabited by many Scottish sovereigns, notably Mary Stuart, the rooms occupied by her (including the one in which Rizzio was murdered) being still shown. It is now known as Holyrood House and is still used as a royal residence.

Holy Water, water blessed by a priest and kept in small fonts at the entrance to Roman Catholic and some Anglican churches.

Holy Week is the week preceding Easter Sunday, and embraces the days of the Sufferings of Christ. It includes Good Friday and Holy Saturday.

Homoeopathy. See **Section J**.

Honey, the sweet syrup formed by bees from the nectar of flower , the sucrose in the nectar being converted into a mixture of the simple sugars, glucose and fructose. Hybla, an ancient town of Sicily, on the southern slope of Mt. Etna, was famous for its honey.

Honey-eater, an Australian bird (of which there are many species) provided with a long curved bill and tufted tongue. It lives by sucking the nectar from the flowers which abound in rural parts of Australia and New Zealand.

Hookah, an Oriental pipe for tobacco smoking, the smoke being drawn through the water of a goblet (commonly a coconut shell) by means of a long flexible tube.

Hoopoe, a remarkably handsome bird with vivid black and white-barred wings and tail and black-tipped crest which opens like a fan. Ranges over Europe, Asia and Africa. It has bred in England and Wales and occurs in the British Isles in small numbers at all seasons. Other species are confined to Africa, Madagascar and India.

Hops, the female "cones" of the hop plant used in brewing; their essential oils give beer an aromatic flavour, and their tannin and resin act as a preservative as well as accounting for the bitter taste desired. The hop is a perennial climber belonging to the mulberry family. The male and female organs are on separate plants; as only the female flower-heads are commercially useful, female plants predominate in a hop garden, only a very few male plants being grown so that the female flowers can be fertilised.

Horizon, the limit of vision, the apparent line where sea and sky, or land and sky meet. This is termed the visible horizon. An ordinary person at the height of 1·5 m can see for 4·8 km, at 6 m 9·6 km, at 15 m 14·8 km and at 305 m 67·5 km. The figures are approximate.

Hormone, a chemical substance which is released by one part of the body and produces a response in other parts after having been carried there by the bloodstream or some other transport system. Prolactin, for example, is a hormone produced by the pituitary gland of nursing mothers and serves to stimulate and maintain the milk supply.

Horn or **French Horn,** a brass instrument of the trumpet family (i.e., played by three valves) whose tube is very thin and long (Horn in F = 12 ft). In consequence the tube is curled in a complicated manner. Owing to the sweet tone it is capable of producing, the Horn sometimes plays as part of the wood-wind.

Hornbill, large bird found in Africa and oriental regions. Some species have a casque or a horny growth above the very powerful beak. It feeds on fruits. When the female has laid her eggs in the hollow of a tree, the male bird stops up the entrance, and keeps her imprisoned until the hatching is completed and the young ones are able to fly. There are about 45 species.

Hornblende, the commonest member of the amphibole group of minerals, a silicate of calcium, magnesium, iron and aluminium, of a dark green colour. It is a constituent of numerous rocks, including diorite, syenite and hornblende schist.

Horned Viper, any of a number of species of African viper which have scales over each eye resembling horns. Their bite is usually very poisonous. The significance of the horns is not known.

Hornet, a general name for many of the bigger wasps. It usually nests in hollow trees, and despite its rather fiercesome appearance does not sting unless unduly provoked.

Horology, the science of time-measurement, including the construction and management of clocks, watches, etc. Instruments of this kind are not known to have existed before the 12th cent. and until the introduction of the pendulum in the 17th cent., clocks were ill-regulated and inaccurate. The time-recording mechanisms of the present day include (a) the clock, which shows the hours and minutes by hands, and strikes the hours, and sometimes quarters; (b) the timepiece, which is not generally a fixture and shows the time, but does not strike; (c) the watch, which is a pocket time-keeper; (d) the chronometer, which indicates the minutest portions of times; (e) electric timepieces, mains electric clocks; (f) the highly accurate quartz-crystal and atomic clocks used for astronomical purposes. See **Clock**.

Horse Chestnut, one of the large forest trees, with ample branches, and full foliage, and much esteemed for parks and ornamental grounds. The flowers, which appear in May, are white tinged with red and yellow. The tree is native to the mountainous regions of northern Greece. See also **Chestnut**.

Horse Guards, the building in Whitehall which until 1872 was the headquarters of the Commander-in-Chief of the British Army. The archway is still sentinelled by mounted guards.

Horse Latitudes, the latitudes of the sub-tropical high pressure systems, between the trade winds and the prevailing westerlies, characterised by light variable winds and low humidity.

Hospitallers, Knights, were of the order of St. John of Jerusalem, at first devoted to the aid of the sick, but afterwards military monks, who became prominent figures in the Crusades of the 12th cent. They adopted the Benedictine black habit with the eight-pointed cross worn by the modern St. John Ambulance Brigade. In 1309 they took Rhodes, but were expelled by the Ottomans in 1522. In 1530 the emperor Charles V gave them the island of Malta, which as Knights of Malta, they held until 1798, when they were dislodged by Napoleon. The Knights still survive as a sovereign order, with headquarters in Rome. See **Templars** and **Teutonic Order**.

Hottentots, name given to certain African people by Dutch settlers in the 17th cent. They used to occupy the greater part of Cape Colony and though driven out a number still survive in Namibia. They appear to be related to the Bushmen, though their culture is more advanced. In addition to herding, they practise some farming and know how to smelt iron.

Hounds are dogs that were originally bred and trained for hunting, such as the greyhound, fox-hound, bloodhound, wolf hound, deerhound, beagle, harrier, etc., but now often kept also as domestic dogs. The greyhound, deerhound and wolf hound hunt by sight, the others, with the bloodhound first in order, track by scent.

House Flies are world-wide and prolific. Their eggs are hatched within 24 hours of being laid, and full maturity is attained in a month. They feed on decayed animals and vegetable matter.

Hovercraft, or air cushion vehicle, is a craft which is lifted on a pad of air underneath it. This pad or cushion must be at a pressure higher than that of the atmosphere and it is made by sucking in air above the craft and ejecting it in a downward stream all round the lower edge. Hovercraft were devised by Cockerell in the 1950s and a full-scale example appeared in June 1959. The air pad support means that hovercraft can move over land, water or marsh. Cross-Channel hovercraft were introduced in 1966.

Howler Monkey, a genus of South American monkey noted for a laryngeal conformation which enables it to emit a loud reverberant noise something between a yell and a howl.

Huanuco-bark, a medicinal bark, brought from the Peruvian town of that name, and derived from the *Cinchona micrantha* tree.

Hubble Telescope. *See* **Telescope, L118.**

Huguenots, a name applied to the French Protestant communities of the 16th and 17th cent. Henry of Navarre, by the Edict of Nantes in 1598, granted them religious freedom, but more than a quarter of a century before—24 August 1572—thousands had been put to death in the massacre of St. Bartholomew. The revocation of the Edict of Nantes by Louis XIV in 1685 drove thousands into exile in England, Holland, Germany and America.

Human Genome Project, a 15-year £2 billion global effort launched in the 1990s to unravel the human genetic blueprint. When scientists work out the order of the 3 billion letters that compose human DNA, medicine will be revolutionised. Part of the work should be completed by 2001. The tiny nematode worm has become the first creature to have its entire genetic blueprint decoded.

Humble-bee or **Bumble-bee,** the common name of the insects of the genus *bombus,* of the Hymenoptera order. They live in small communities comprising males, females and drones, their habitations being underground. They do not have one queen bee only like the hive bee, but several females occupy the same nest, and these alone live through the winter, breeding and forming new colonies in the spring. Their sting does not have a barb like the honey bee's.

Humidity, the state of the atmosphere with respect to the water-vapour it contains. "Absolute humidity" is defined as the density of the vapour present, while "relative humidity", more frequently employed indicates the degree of saturation, *i.e.,* the ratio of the actual vapour pressure to the saturation vapour pressure at the particular temperature, expressed as a percentage.

Humming Birds are so called because of the humming noise made by the vibration of their wings in flying. They are of radiant plumage, and are among the smallest birds. The smallest bird in the world is the Fairy or Princess Helen's humming bird of Cuba, whose body is only 5·7 cm long. There are from four to five hundred species, and they are confined wholly to North and South America, being most numerous in the tropical latitudes. They have long, slender bills and tubular tongues which reach down into flowers to suck up the nectar on which they feed.

Hummum, the original name for what is now called the Turkish Bath in this country. One of the first of these baths was the Hummum in Covent Garden, London.

Hundred, the ancient divisonal name given to a portion of a county for administration or military purposes. It is supposed to imply the territory occupied by a hundred families; or the space of a hundred hides of land, or the capacity of providing 100 soldiers. Each hundred had its hundred court, with powers similar to those of a manor court, but this was abolished in 1867 by County Court Act.

Hundred Days, the interval of time between Napoleon Bonaparte's entry into Paris after his escape from Elba and his departure after his abdication, extending from 20 March 1815 to 28 June. During this period occurred the battle of Waterloo, 18 June. *See* **L128.**

Hundred Years' War, a term applied to the almost incessant contest between England and France, lasting from 1338 to 1453, including such famous battles as Crécy, Poitiers and Agincourt, and engaging successively Edward III, Henry V and Henry VI, among English kings.

Huns, a fierce Asiatic race which swept over eastern Europe in the 4th cent. Under Attila about the middle of the 5th cent, they obtained control of a large portion of central and eastern Europe, forcing even Rome to pay tribute. Their defeat at Châlons-sur-Marne in 451 by an army of Romans, Goths and Teutonic tribes, and the death of Attila in 453 ended their empire.

Hurdy-Gurdy, a rustic musical stringed instrument of the lute order, the sounds of which are produced by the action of a rosined wheel turned by the right hand, the notes being made by the fingering of the left hand. It dates from at least the 12th century.

Hussites. *See* **Section J.**

Hurricane. *See* **Cyclone, Wind.**

Hydra, an aquatic animal of simple structure, whose body is in the form of a cylindrical tube, with a disc-shaped base by which it attaches itself to any shifting substance. Its mouth is surrounded by tentacles by which it catches its food. The Hydra has the power of reproducing lost parts.

Hydrates are compounds containing water of crystallisation.

Hydraulic Ram, a form of automatic pump, used to raise water to a height by the action of its own falling velocity.

Hydraulics, the science of applied hydrodynamics, or water-machine engineering, ranging from pumps to marine engines.

Hydrocarbons are compounds of carbon and hydrogen. They include the *paraffins,* which are saturated compounds (*e.g.,* methane); the ethylene, acetylene and other series which are unsaturated; compounds with ring structures, *e.g.,* benzene, naphthalene and anthracene. Petroleum is composed almost entirely of hydrocarbons.

Hydrochloric Acid, a solution of hydrogen chloride gas in water, and resulting in considerable quantities as a by-product of the soda-ash or salt-cake manufacture. Its solution forms the common hydrochloric or muriatic acid of commerce. It is present to the extent of nearly half a per cent, in the digestive juice secreted by the stomach.

Hydrocyanic Acid, cyanide of hydrogen or prussic acid; very poisonous, and of the odour of bitter almonds. It is formed by the action of acids on sodium or potassium cyanide. Used to kill wasps (and in the gas chamber in the USA). It is a very important chemical on account of the reactions of its derivatives in many synthetic fields. Discovered by Scheele in 1782.

Hydroelectric Schemes. The sun's energy has been indirectly exploited in the past by harnessing the energy of the winds and rain. The climate is due, essentially, to differential heating of the earth. The resulting convection currents in the air (the motion of which is complicated by the rotation of the earth) give rise to winds. Moisture is collected from the sea and deposited high up on mountains as rain. Some of the gravitational energy may be collected as hydropower. Simple windmills or waterwheels are so undependable that they have not been used to any extent since the beginning of the Industrial Revolution. However, the modern form of the waterwheel—the hydro-electric generation plant —is extensively used in mountainous countries and about a third of the world's electricity is produced by this means. The essential requirements for a modern hydroelectric scheme are a river with a sufficient flow of water to provide the required power, a large "head" of water so that a cheap, compact turbine can be used and a dam so that water can be stored until it is required. In some cases a hydroelectric scheme is made economic by being associated with an irrigation or drainage scheme. Such multi-purpose schemes are especially important in India and Pakistan, where most hydro projects are of this type. Other well-known examples include the Snowy Mountains scheme in Australia and the Aswan High Dam in Egypt.

Although over 90 per cent of the electricity in certain individual countries, notably Norway, Sweden, Portugal, Switzerland and Uganda is produced from hydroelectric schemes, only a relatively small fraction of the total potential has been exploited. This fraction varies from about a third in Western Europe to a quarter in the United States to a very small fraction in Alaska, Canada, Africa and the hinterland of Asia.

Hydrofluoric Acid is obtained by distillation of fluorspar with sulphuric acid, and is a compound of fluorine and hydrogen. Its action is highly corrosive; a valuable agent in etching on glass, and a rapid decomposer of animal matter.

Hydrogen, symbol H, the simplest element, with an atomic number of 1, colourless, and the lightest of all substances. Cavendish in 1766 was the first to recognise that it was an element. It is 14·4 times as light as air, and is found in a free state in volcanic regions. It can be obtained by the action of metals on acids, and forms an explosive mixture with air, burning with oxygen to form water. Commercially it is used to produce the very hot flame of the oxyhydrogen blowpipe for cutting metals; to fill balloons and airships; to harden certain oils and render them suitable for margarine- and soapproduction. The gas can be liquefied, and the presence of the isotope deuterium was detected by Urey in 1931 in the residue of the evaporated liquid. The third isotope, tritium, is very rare. *See also* **Deuterium, Tritium.**

Hydrography, the science of water measurement, as applied to seas, rivers, lakes, currents, rocks, reefs, *etc.,* and embracing the whole art of navigation.

Hydrometer, an instrument for measuring the specific gravity of liquids, especially for ascertaining the strength of spiritous liquors and solutions. It is usually in the form of a glass bulb, to the lower end of which a smaller bulb, containing mercury, is attached which forces the instrument to sink into the liquid which it is to test. The larger bulb has a scale fixed to it, and the indication on this scale of the sinking point shows the specific gravity. There are many varieties: Twaddell's—a pear-shaped bulb containing mercury: Beaumé's, of similar construction, but applicable to liquids both heavier and lighter than water: Sykes', largely employed for determinining the strength of alcohol: and Nicholson's, used for taking the specific gravities of solids.

Hydropathy, the method of treating disease with water, either by bathing or drinking. Natural springs of special chemical and therapeutic properties, such as sulphur springs, and other mineral sources, have been used since prehistoric times for this purpose. It is probably one of the most ancient methods of cure. Recently the beneficial effects of pure water treatment have been advocated. Hydropathic establishments have been set up in many health resorts.

Hydroponics, or soilless growth, is the craft and science of growing plants in liquid nutrients instead of soil. Originally a laboratory technique, hydroponics has become since the 1930s a practical method of vegetable, fruit and flower production on both small and large scale. Basically, the growing plants have their roots in troughs of nutrient solution, either in or out of doors. Advantages include: much higher crop yields; the close control of weeds and diseases; quicker growth; and, very important, the possibilities of growing food in places where ordinary agriculture would be impracticable, *e.g.,* deserts and stony land, city roofs, in houses and in remote situations like Antarctic stations. Hydroponics is widely practised and contributes usefully to agriculture and horticulture in many countries, including the USA, Britain, India and France. Its value in spaceships and planetary colonies has often been pointed out by technological prophets.

Hydrostatics, the science of the pressure and equilibrium of liquids that are non-elastic.

Hydrozoa are a class of water animals of the *Coelenterata* phylum to which hydra (*q.v.*) belongs. In one order of the hydrozoa, freeswimming colonies showing marked division of labour between the individual units occur; this order includes the Portuguese man-of-war.

Hyena, a nocturnal carnivore with powerful jaws. The striped hyenas inhabit N. Africa and S.W. India. The brown hyenas with long shaggy hair are natives of S. Africa. The spotted, or laughing hyena, noted for the peculiar cry from which its name is derived, is also confined to Africa.

Hygrometer, an instrument for measuring the amount of water vapour in the atmosphere. A simple form of hygrometer, known as the wet-and-dry bulb, consists of two vertical thermometers affixed to a frame. One bulb is exposed to the air, and the other is covered with muslin which dips into a water-bath to keep it moist. If the air is saturated, it takes up no moisture from the wet bulb and the two thermometers read the same. If the air is not saturated, evaporation takes place from the wet bulb, latent heat is absorbed from the air and the temperature of the wet bulb is lower than that of the dry bulb. Relative humidity and dew-point of the air can then be derived from suitable tables. Hygrometers depending upon the expansion of human hair and goldbeater's skin and the deposition of dew on a polished surface, when cooled sufficiently, are also in general use. *See* **Humidity.**

Hymenoptera, the order of insects to which bees, wasps, hornets, ants and sawflies belong. They have a well-defined waist, two pairs of membranous wings coupled together, mouth parts modified for biting or sucking; the females possess an ovipositor used for depositing eggs and is sometimes modified for stinging. There are about 70,000 species in this order and many live in highly organised communities. *See also* **Ichneumon Fly.**

Hyperbola. A curve described by certain comets that go round the sun and never return.

Hypsometer, an instrument formerly used by mountaineers to find the height above sea-level by indirectly measuring the atmospheric pressure by determining the boiling point of water at the particular height. Based on the fact that as pressure decreases with height so the boiling point is lowered. Superseded by the aneroid barometer.

I

Ibex, wild goats of several species found in the mountain regions of Europe, Asia and Africa. The male has exceedingly large curved ridged horns. The species that lives in the Alps is called the Steinbock or bouquetin.

Ibis, belongs to a family of birds related to the stork. The sacred ibis of ancient Egypt is now extinct in Egypt but is found in the lakes and swamps of the Sudan near the Upper Nile. It has white and black plumage and a long curved beak. Other species are found elsewhere, the Glossy Ibis (black plumage glossed with purple and green) occasionally visiting England. There are now less than 220 Bald Ibis in the world (all in Morocco).

Ibo (Igbo), a large tribe of S.E. Nigeria. After the end of British rule they were active in their struggle for national independence and under their leader, Ojukwu, embarked upon the secessionist state of Biafra and the unsuccessful civil war against Federal forces. Today (1999) there are over 17 million Ibo speakers. The Hausa and the Yoruba are the other main Nigerian groups.

Ice is frozen water. It is a colourless, crystalline and brittle solid. Being only 92% as dense as water, it floats on the latter; the expansion which occurs as water changes into ice causes the fracture of water-pipes, though the fracture only becomes obvious when the ice melts and leaks out through the crack. The temperature at which ice forms is $0°C$, $32°F$. Ice can be melted by pressure, and the ease and smoothness with which one is able to skate on ice depends on this phenomenon.

Ice Ages. Periods during which the continents were partly or largely covered by ice-sheets and glaciers. The present-day ice-sheets of Greenland and Antarctica are relics of the most recent ice age (one of the eight major ones during the past 700,000 years), which began in the Pleistocene and ended about 10,000 years ago. During this last great glaciation ice sheets covered the northern part of Europe, Asia and North America. There is strong evidence that periodic changes in the earth's orbit around the sun caused the ice ages. The earth is now in one of its warm periods.

Icebergs are detached masses of glacier which subside into the sea and float as wind or current may take them. About one-ninth of an iceberg is above sea-level. The North Atlantic is the chief home of icebergs, which reach the ocean from the ice-clad plateaux of Greenland. Some of these floating masses of ice are of enormous proportions, and constitute in the spring and early summer seasons a great menace to the safety of ships, as was disastrously shown in the *Titanic* catastrophe of 1912. The increasing numbers of icebergs provide evidence of global warming.

Ice-breaker, a special heavy bow-plated ship for forcing a way through ice and used especially at ports of the Baltic Sea and the Great Lakes region of Canada which freeze during the winter months.

Icelandic Literature, the old Norse literature, centred about Iceland, which includes numerous works of poetry, mythology and history of interest and importance. Much of this literature is in the saga form. *See also* **Edda.**

Iceland Moss, a kind of lichen (*Cetrario islandica*) which grows in great quantities in the mountain regions of Iceland and other Northern countries. It possesses certain nutritive qualities and is of some value in medicine.

Iceland Spar, a colourless form of calcite (calcium carbonate), frequently found in association with metallic ores; it has the power to produce strong double refraction of light so that two images are seen of an object viewed through a piece of Iceland spar. It was formerly used in optical apparatus for producing polarised light.

Iceni, an ancient British race who in early times lived in Norfolk and other parts of Eastern England. Their most famous ruler was Queen Boadicea, who led her people against the Romans in A.D. 61.

Ice Man, name given to the frozen corpse of a middle-aged man, 5,300 years old, found in 1991 on a glacier in the Ötztal Alps.

Ice Plant, also called "dew plant" and "diamond plant". A South African mesembryanthemum commonly grown in British gardens. Introduced in 1690.

Ice Saints, St. Mamertus, St. Pancras and St. Servatius, so called because of the legendary cold on these Saints' Days, namely, 11–13 May.

Ichneumon, the Egyptian mongoose, popularly known as "Pharaoh's Rat". It is of great use in checking the multiplication of reptiles. It is frequently domesticated.

Ichneumon Fly, a numerous group of parasitic hymenopterous insects abounding in many lands, and all having the peculiarity of depositing their eggs in the bodies of other insects. It destroys swarms of caterpillars, which become the unwilling hosts of its progeny.

Ichthyology, the natural history of fishes.

Ichthyosaurus was a gigantic marine reptile of the Mesozoic age. The fossils are mostly found in the lias formation. Some were over 9 m.

Icon, an image of a sacred personage used in the home or in churches for devotional purposes by Christians of the Eastern Orthodox churches. Icons can be painted on wood, perhaps with the figures picked out against a golden background, or they can be cast in bronze, in the form of a crucifix, diptych (*q.v.*) or triptych with details in coloured enamels. Subjects are taken from the life of Christ or of the Saints. In churches several icons are sometimes placed together on a screen (the iconostasis, which divides the altar and sanctuary from the main body of

the church). The earliest preserved icons date from the 12th cent. Icons were venerated in Russia until the Revolution and remain, still in their archaic stylised form of mediaeval origin, a characteristic feature of the Greek and Russian Orthodox Churches.

Ides, in the ancient Roman Calendar, the 15th of March, May, July, October, and the 13th of all other months; always the eighth day after the Nones.

Idiom, an expression characteristic of a country, district, dialect or language, which usually gives strength and force to a phrase or sentence. The idioms of a language are its distinctive marks, and the best writers are the most idiomatic.

Idris, a famous giant belonging to the myths of Wales, commemorated by a chair of rock on the top of the Cader Idris mountain in Gwynedd.

Igneous Rocks are such as have been molten under conditions of great heat at some stage in their history; *e.g.*, granite, basalt. *See* **F9(1).**

Ignis Fatuus *or* **"Will-o'-the-wisp",** a phosphorescent light which may often be seen on summer and autumn evenings hovering over marshy ground or graveyards. Its nature is hardly understood, though it is generally believed to be the result of the spontaneous combustion of the gases from decaying organic matter. In olden times when marshy grounds were more common than now, this "dancing light" was very frequently visible and was regarded with superstition.

Iguana, large South American lizard, with a long tail, a scaly back and head, a thick fleshy tongue and a prominent dew-lap in the throat. Specimens of the different species average 1·2–1·5 m in length, and they live mostly in trees, though they are equally at home on land or in the water. The flesh of some species is good eating, as are also the eggs.

Iguanodon, a genus of extinct dinosaurs, whose fossils are found in the Jurassic and Cretaceous rocks. Iguanodons were 4·5–7·6 m long, and walked on their hind legs, the front legs being small and adapted for grasping the branches of trees on the leaves of which they fed.

Ilex, mentioned by classical authors, the holm- or holly-oak, which flourishes round the Mediterranean. To botanists Ilex is the genus to which the holly and maté plant belong.

Iliad, the great epic poem of ancient Greece attributed to Homer (*c.* 700 B.C.). It consists of ancient folk tale and saga, welded into an artistic unity, having as plot the carrying off of Helen by Paris to Troy and the subsequent siege of Troy.

Illuminated MSS. of great value and beauty of decoration exist in most public museums and in many private collections, some of them being of great antiquity, especially those of ancient Egypt executed on papyri. Greek and Latin specimens are also numerous, and the British Museum contains fine examples of all these kinds and also an extensive collection of mediaeval English MSS.

Illuminati. *See* **Section J.**

Ilmenite, a mineral widespread in igneous rocks; chemically it is an oxide of iron and titanium. Rich deposits have recently been found in the Allard Lake area of Quebec; the Travancore sands are also a source of ilmenite.

Immortality. *See* **Section J.**

Immortelles are wreaths, crosses or other designs made from what are called everlasting flowers, which are obtained from certain plants of the Composite order, and retain their colours and compactness for a long time. Immortelles are largely used as mementoes for decorating graves, especially in France.

Impeachment, a special arraignment, usually before Parliament or other high tribunal, of a person charged with some offence against the State. The custom in England was for the impeachment to be made in the House of Commons, and the trial to be before the House of Lords. The first instance occurred in 1376 when Lord Latimer was impeached. With present parliamentary procedure, impeachment is no longer necessary, since the Cabinet is responsible for the individual actions of its ministers, who, acting as a team, must carry the Commons with them, or resign, when it fails to the Leader of the Opposition to form a new Cabinet. Other famous impeachments were those of the Lord High Chancellor Francis Bacon (1621), Earl of Strafford and Archbishop Laud (1640), Warren Hastings (1788), the last being that of Lord Melville (1805). Under the constitution of the United States the President may be impeached by the House of Representatives and tried by the Senate. The first case was that of President Andrew Johnson who was saved from impeachment in 1868 by one vote. President Clinton became only the second president in US history to be impeached in December 1998. The trial ended in February 1999 with his acquittal (*See* **Section C**).

Imperialism. *See* **Section J.**

Impressionism, the most important and influential movement in 19th cent. European painting. It gained its name, at first contemptuously, in 1874 from a picture painted by Claude Monet and named by the artist *Impression: soleil levant*, which showed the play of light on water with the observer looking straight into the rising sun. Although intended to be the ultimate form of naturalism the inspiration of the school had been the scientific study of light with an attempt to render the play of light on the surface of objects.

Feeling that putting a line around a form was bound to cause it to look unnatural, they used bright colours corresponding to the spectrum and unmixed on the palette, and noted that an object of any given colour casts a shadow tinged with the complementary one (*e.g.*, red-green, yellow-blue). Hence bright sunlight was represented in clear yellows and orange with violet shadows. The first Impressionist exhibition held in Paris in 1874 aroused derision with its paintings by Monet, Renoir, Sisley, Pissaro, Cézanne and Degas among others. Impressionism subsequently led to the entirely artistic and anti-naturalist movement of Post-impressionism. Cézanne, who felt that he wanted to produce "something solid and durable, like the art of the museums" was only dubiously impressionist, as were also Degas and Renoir. Of course, in the wider sense of the word (*i.e.*, the recording of an ephemeral impression of a scene), Whistler, Turner and even Rembrandt used the technique.

Impressment, the forced seizure of persons for military service resorted to by many countries before the establishment of conscription. Press gangs forcibly recruited men for British warships especially during the Napoleonic wars, but such measures were abandoned after *c* 1850.

Imprimatur, originally an official licence to print and an important formula in the early days of printing. The term is now used in the wider significance of authority, or endorsement.

Incas, an Indian people who inhabited ancient Peru, founded a great empire and reached a high level of civilisation; overthrown by the Spaniards in 1533.

Incense, an aromatic resinous substance which, under combustion, exhales a pungent odour, and is used, mixed with certain fragment perfumes, in the celebration of Mass in Roman Catholic churches. Olibanum or frankincense is ordinarily the leading ingredient.

Incisors, the sharp-edged cutting teeth at the front of mammalian jaws. Rodents have long, sharp incisor teeth. Elephant tusks are modified incisors.

Independence Day, commemorates the adoption of the Declaration of Independence on 4 July 1776. 4 July is celebrated as a holiday in the USA.

Independent Schools. *See* Public Schools, **L100.**

Index. The name given to a list of books, prepared by papal authority, which are declared to be dangerous to faith and morals, and therefore forbidden to Roman Catholics, called the *Index librorum prohibitorum*. One of the reforms of the Vatican Council was the closing in 1966 of the Curia office which judged writings for the Church's Index of forbidden books, though the Index itself still remains. The Pope ordered that nothing should be placed on the Index until the author had been given a chance of explaining his views. The first Index was issued by Pope Pius IV, in 1559.

Indian Mutiny. This turning-point in the history of modern India occurred in 1857-58. The ostensible cause was the serving out to the native troops of cartridges greased with animal fat, for contact with this was forbidden both by the Hindu and Mohammedan faiths. A rebellious feeling, however, had long been developing, and when the Sepoys at Meerut in May 1857 refused to obey the English officers, overpowered and put them to death, the mutiny spread like wildfire. The rebels took Delhi and Lucknow, and for many months terrible massacres and atrocities were committed; men, women and children were slain in thousands. Order was re-established in the autumn of 1858 when the governing power was transferred from the East India Company to the Crown.

Indicators, substances which by a marked change in colour are used to indicate the course of a chemical reaction. Litmus paper, for instance, is red with acids and blue with alkalis. In biological work some radioactive substances are used as tracer elements.

Indigo, the substance obtained from the plant *Indigofera tinctoria*, a native of S. Asia, India being the chief producing country. The colouring matter is the result of the decomposition and fermentation of a glucoside contained in the plant. This is afterwards dried and becomes the caked indigo of commerce. Natural indigo has been eclipsed by artificial indigo, a coal-tar dye which came into commercial production at the end of the last century, and which is cheaper and more uniform in quality.

Indium, a scarce lead-coloured metallic element, no. 49, symbol In, found in zinc blende in Saxony and certain other ores. Discovered in 1863 by Reich and Richter. It is an important material in the manufacture of transistors.

Indulgence. In the Roman Catholic Church the remission granted by ecclesiastical authority to a repentant sinner of the temporal punishment still due after the guilt of sin has been forgiven by God. The indiscriminate sale of Indulgences by Tetzel and other Papal agents in the 16th cent. was one of the grievances which led to the Reformation (*see* **Section J**); the Council of Trent made such traffic unlawful. They were associated with some of the worst examples of corruption and hypocrisy in the history of the Church.

Indulgence, Declaration of, was the proclamation by which James II suspended the penal laws against Roman Catholics and Dissenters. It was issued in 1688, but the clergy as a body refused to obey, and the trial of the Seven Bishops and their acquittal by a jury followed. An invitation was thereupon sent to William of Orange to become King.

Industrialisation is simply a name for industrial development. It is customarily used in particular to designate the course of events in a hitherto underdeveloped country which is seeking to increase its wealth and productivity by the introduction of more advanced techniques and by the establishment of industries previously not carried on within it. The word usually covers not only the development of modern industrial production but also the provision of electric power-stations, irrigation works and transport and other developments designed to improve production in any field by methods involving large capital investments. One often-quoted example in our time of rapid industrialisation has been the Soviet Union, which, unable to get the capital from abroad, had to carry it through by ruthless restriction of the people's consuming power so as to achieve an unprecedentedly high ratio of investment to total production. Industrialisation has in practice meant a high concentration on the expansion of the basic heavy industries and of power supply, coupled with much slower development of the industries supplying consumer goods and of agricultural production; but there is no reason why this should always be the case. It may well be that in most underdeveloped countries development can but be devoted largely to the industries making consumers' goods and to measures designed to increase agricultural production and productivity.

Industrial Revolution. The name, first given by Engels in 1844, to describe the radical changes that took place in Britain during *c.* 1730-1850 to transform a mainly agricultural country into one predominantly industrial. It began with the mechanisation of the textile industry (Hargreave's spinning jenny, 1764, Arkwright's water-frame, 1769, Crompton's mule, 1770, and Watt's steam-engine, 1785), with subsequent major developments in mining, transport and industrial organisation. It was based on Britain's rich mineral resources, particularly coal and iron ore. With the use of the steam-engine as power, industry became concentrated round the coalfields and the great new industrial towns developed—Birmingham, Manchester, Newcastle and Glasgow. Britain became supreme in constructional ironwork (Telford, George and Robert Stephenson). Canals, bridges, railways and ships were built, and great advances were made in the practical application of scientific principles. Aided by colonial exploitation Britain became the most prosperous country in the world. The new industrial capitalists began to replace the country squires as ruling class. But the great accumulation of wealth at one pole of society was matched at the other by poverty and misery, for child labour, long working hours, low wages and slums were features of the industrial revolution in its infancy. As with all great technological developments, the industrial revolution produced related changes in all fields of social life—in politics, art, religion, literature and morals.

Inertia, a term used in mechanics for the property of matter by which it offers resistance to a change in its state of rest or in its state or direction of motion.

Inertial Navigation, an automatic method of dead-reckoning which at present finds its chief application in guided missiles, submarines and aircraft. Navigation by this means is carried out with reference to inertial space (*i.e.,* space which is stationary with respect to the fixed stars) and not to the surface of the earth as in normal navigation (latitude and longitude). This is done by means of high-accuracy gyro-scopes combined with highly sensitive accelero-meters in an apparatus known as the Ship's Inertial Navigation System. The American nuclear-powered submarine *Nautilus* pioneered the new north-west passage under the polar ice pack by this method of dead-reckoning in August 1958.

Inflorescence, a flowering shoot. Many arrange-ments of the flowers are possible and there are many kinds of inflorescence; *e.g.,* the spike, catkin, umbel, capitulum (in composites).

Infra-red Rays *or* **Radiation.** This is the range of rays which come between the visible red rays and the ultra-short Hertzian radiation. The wavelengths involved range between 0·75 micron (0·75 × 10⁻⁶m) and 100 micron (1 millimetre). Infra-red rays penetrate haze; hence landscapes obscured by haze or cloud can be photographed using plates sensitive to infrared. Many substances strongly absorb these rays and thereby become hot; this happens in toasting bread. Many industries use infra-red lamps for drying paints and lacquers. Very important to chemists, as a tool in the investigation of the structure of compounds, since various groups of elements absorb infra-red radiation at a characteristic frequency. Infrared astronomy has developed in recent years.

Infra-red Space Observatory (ISO), an orbiting tele-scope launched in 1995. By peering into the clouds of gas and dust in deep space it astonished astronomers by discovering vast quantities of water in the deserts of space. It ceased function-ing in 1998.

Infula, a sacred fillet, of woollen material, worn on the forehead by priests, magistrats and rulers in Roman times, also by persons fleeing for protection to sanctuary. Later, each of the two lappets of a bishop's mitre.

Ingoldsby Legends, a series of whimsical metrical tales full of droll humour written by the Rev. R. H. Barham, and first published in *Bentley's Miscellany* in 1837. The best known is the *Jackdaw of Rheims.*

Ink, a liquid pigment ordinarily made from an infusion of nut-galls, copperas and gum arabic. Shumac is substituted for nut-galls for inferior inks. An acid is sometimes added to prevent oxidation, and for the blue-black inks a small quantity of solution of indigo serves for colouring. Copying ink contains glycerine or sugar, which keeps the ink moist. Lampblack used to be the leading ingredient in printer's ink but now new methods of manufacturing have been developed. Marking ink is composed of a solution of nitrate of silver, gum, ammonia and carbonate of soda. For red, blue and other coloured inks, colouring solutions are used, *e.g.* Prussian blue. The earliest examples of ink writing (on wooden tablets) ever found in Britain were recovered from the well of a Roman villa (3rd cent. A.D.) at Chew Stoke, Somerset in 1954.

Ink Sac, a glandular organ found in squids and other cephalopods which contains an inky solu-tion. When roused the animal discharges the contents of the ink sac into the water, to make a cloud through which its enemies cannot see. The pigment, sepia, comes from the ink sac of the cuttlefish.

Inns of Court, the four bodies in London which enjoy the privilege of calling candidates to the bar after they have studied for a certain number of terms and passed certain examinations. The Inns are: the Inner Temple, the Middle Temple, Lincoln's Inn and Gray's Inn.

Inquisition, a Roman Catholic ecclesiastical court which became a formidable weapon of the Church in the 13th cent. under Pope Innocent III in dealing with charges of heresy. It was effectively set up in the various Catholic countries of the Continent, obtaining its fullest and most sweeping organisation in Spain in the days of Ferdinand and Isabella, when Torquemada was made Grand Inquisitor, and used its powers with terrible severity. *See* **Auto-da-fé.** In the 18th century its influence began to wane, and the jurisdiction of the Congregation of the Holy Office at Rome was limited to the suppression of heretical literature (*see* Index). The attitude of the Catholic Church to the Inquisition is now being debated. For a recent scholarly study, *see* Henry Kamen, *The Spanish Inquisition* (1997).

Insectivorous Plants, plants which trap insects with special mechanisms. Plant enzymes or bacteria digest the prey, providing the plants with nitrogen usually scarce in the soil in which they grow. The most common British species are the Sun-dew and the Bladderwort.

Insects. This huge class of invertebrate animals (*see* **Arthropods** (**F36**)) includes about 100,000 species. Insects are ubiquitous except in the sea, only a very few species being adapted to marine existence. Characteristic features are: the body is divided into three parts, head, thorax and abdomen: the head carries a pair of antennae, the thorax three pairs of legs and usually two pairs of wings. The most primitive insects constituting the sub-class *Apterygota* are wingless. The other sub-class, *Pterygota*, is divided into the *Exopterygota* (*Hemimetabola*), which have a simple metamorphosis, *e.g.*, cockroach, and the *Endopterygota* (*Holome-tabola*), with a complex metamorphosis, *e.g.*, butterfly, bee. Although many are parasitic on man, animals and plants, innumerable animals and some plants use them as food, and many flowering plants are dependent on a variety of insects for pollination.

Insignia, marks or badges of office or honour, such as stars, ribbons, crosses, medallions or other designating objects, worn by members of special Orders or holders of prominent offices.

Instinct. *See* **F40(2).**

Institut de France was formed in 1795, and after various modifications was in 1832 organised on its present basis. Its five academies are—the Académie Française, Académie des Inscriptions et Belles-Lettres, Académie des Sciences, Acadé-mie des Beaux-Arts, and the Académie des Sciences morales et politiques. It is restricted to 40 members.

Instruments, Musical. Musical instruments may be classified in a number of ways, but in general they fall into one of the three main classes, String, Wind and Percussion, according to how the sound is produced. **Stringed Instruments** are those which produce the sound by the vibra-tion of a string: (*a*) by plucking, as in Harp, Lyre, Psaltery, Zither, Lute, Guitar, Balalaika, Ukelele, Harpsichord; (*b*) by friction (bowed), as in Crwth, Rebec, Viol, Violin, Marine

Trumpet, Hurdy-Gurdy; (c) by striking (hammered), as in Dulcimer, Pianoforte, Clavichord; (d) by wind (blown), as in the Aeolian Harp. **Wind Instruments** are those in which the air in the instruments is set in vibration: (a) by blowing into a tube (flue-voiced), as in Recorder, Pandean Pipe, Flute, Organ; (b) by means of reeds (reed-voiced), as in Oboe, Clarinet, Saxophone, Bagpipe, Cor Anglais, Bassoon, Organ reed-stops; (c) those in which the sound is produced by the vibration of the player's lips against the mouthpiece (lip-voiced), as in Bugle, Horn, Trumpet, Tuba, Trombone, Saxhorn, Flügelhorn, Cornet. In a modern orchestra these are known as the *Brass*: instruments of the flute, oboe and clarinet families as the *Woodwinds*. Then there are the **Percussion Instruments**, which include the Drums, Cymbals, Tambourines, Castenets.

Insulator, a substance that will not conduct electric current. Many solids, liquids and gases are important insulators—rubber, cotton, silk, plastics, porcelain, glass, air, oil. If the applied voltage is too high, all insulators will "break down", *i.e.*, conduct electricity perhaps with resulting breakage, puncture or charring. Thermal insulators will not conduct heat; they are usually the same kinds of substance as electrical insulators.

Insulin is a hormone which controls the supply of sugar from the blood to muscles. The breakdown of sugar provides energy. In diabetes there is a lack of insulin, causing a build-up of blood sugar which can be released by the injection of insulin. It is secreted by the islet tissue of the pancreas, from which it was isolated in 1922 by Banting and Best. Dr. F. Sanger of Cambridge won the 1958 Nobel Prize in Chemistry for isolating and identifying its amino acid components. Prof. Dorothy Hodgkin and her team at the Dept. of Molecular Biophysics at Oxford succeeded in determining the structure of insulin, a task which would not have been possible without the electronic computer. In 1980 insulin became the first product of genetic engineering techniques to reach clinical trials.

Intelligence. Intelligence has been variously defined as the innate potential of a person to learn and understand; to make appropriate judgments; to see the relationships between things; to profit from experience; or to meet adequately new problems and conditions in life. There are many lines of evidence to show that intellectual capacity is closely related to heredity and influenced by environmental factors. The idea of intelligence testing was first devised by the French psychologist Binet at the beginning of this century. He was asked by the French government to invent a test which would weed out backward children in state schools, and thus save public money and avoid holding back the work of the class by teaching children who were incapable of learning at a given standard. Briefly, a series of problems are given to a large number of children and it is thus found out which series can be solved by the average child of a given age-group; if a child of 7 can only pass the tests suitable to the average child of 6, then his mental age is 6. The intelligence quotient or IQ is discovered by dividing his mental age by his chronological age and multiplying by 100. A gifted child can usually be spotted at an early age. Although IQ tests are the standard method of estimating intelligence, they are not universally accepted as a criterion; a teacher's general judgment may be the best assessment. High intelligence may be inherited, but fail to develop to the full because facilities for education are not available. Recent research suggests that the growth of the brain may be permanently affected by undernutrition at the time of its fastest growth (the last weeks before birth, and, to a lesser extent, the first weeks after birth). At this vulnerable period even quite minor deprivation can affect the rate and ultimate extent of growth of the brain. This has significance not only for the severely under-nourished babies in the poor parts of the world, but for babies of low birth weight in our own communities in the Western world.

Interest is the payment made for the use of

borrowed money over time. The rate of interest is the rate per cent per annum charged for such loans. There are many such rates, varying with the plenty or scarcity of borrowable money, with the length of time for which the loans are made, and with the degree of risk, if any, that the loans will not be duly repaid. Short-term loans are usually cheaper than long-term: the lowest rates are usually for "call money" repayable immediately on demand. These are used principally in short-term financial transactions, such as bill discounting. Bank loans, though usually made for fairly short terms, command higher rates. Long-term loans are made chiefly to public authorities, or as bonds or debentures to business concerns. The rates obtained vary with the demand and the supply of such accommodation.

Interferon, identified in 1957 as a defence protein produced in animal cells, is also produced in human immune systems. Its use as a possible anti-cancer agent as well as for other complaints has been limited by extraction problems. Modern production is likely to be by genetic engineering. In 1980 the amino acid sequence was determined for the 150 residues in human interferon.

International Date Line, a line along the 180° meridian marking the difference in time between E. and W. For the westward-bound traveller crossing the line the date would be put forward one day, for the eastward-bound, back one day. To avoid difference of date in adjacent land areas, the line deviates from the 180° meridian where this crosses land.

Internet. *See* **V16–18.**

Introit, the psalm sung by the choir as the priest approaches the altar to celebrate the Eucharist.

Inuit. *See under* **Eskimo, L41.**

Invention of the Cross, a Roman Catholic festival held on 3 May, to celebrate the finding of the alleged True Cross at Calvary by the Empress St. Helena in 326. Also included in the Church of England calendar. *See* **Holy Rood.**

In vitro. *See* **F75.**

Iodine, a non-metal element, no. 53, symbol I, member of the halogen family (*q.v.*), a substance formerly exclusively obtained from the ribbon-wrack seaweeds. These were burnt and the ashes (kelp) extracted with water. After concentrating the iodides, these were distilled with manganese dioxide and sulphuric acid to yield iodine vapour which was condensed in stoneware bottles. Nearly all iodine now in use is derived from the iodine salt present in Chile saltpetre (natural sodium nitrate). Iodine is used in photography, as an antiseptic solution in alcohol or potassium iodide (tincture of iodine), and in medicine. Discovered by Courtois in 1812.

Ionosphere. Although a certain degree of ionisation occurs at all levels of the atmosphere due to cosmic rays and the radioactivity of rocks, *etc.*, the ionosphere is normally denoted as the region above about 70 km where the ultra-violet component of sunlight is able to ionise a significant fraction of the atoms and molecules present. This ionisation causes the reflection of radio waves by which the ionosphere was initially discovered and for many years, explored. The nomenclature of the ionospheric layers— "D" region up to about 95 km, "E" region 95 km to about 180 km, and "F" region above 180 km—is due to the historical observations of radio wave reflections from "layers". Satellite and rocket observations have shown that the structure is in fact more continuous. Solar flares and aurora cause enhancements of the electron density in the ionosphere, which may result in the disturbance of radio communications over large distances (radio blackouts). *See also* **Atmosphere, Aurora, Magnetosphere.**

Ions, electrically charged atoms, or groups of atoms. Atoms of the metals lose electrons to become positively charged ions, *e.g.*, the sodium ion (Na-) has one electron less than the atom. The non-metal ions are negatively charged, *e.g.*, the chloride ion (Cl-) has one electron more than the atom. Similarly, a group like the sulphate ion ($SO_4{}^{2-}$) has more electrons than the constituent atoms. Thus, the hydrogen atom without its electron is a hydrogen ion or *proton* and the helium atom without its two electrons is a helium ion or *alpha-particle.* When an electric force is applied to certain solutions, the ions into which molecules of the dissolved substance are broken up are attracted to the oppositely charged electrodes, their movements constituting an electric current through the solution. In the same way gases, including air, conduct electricity by virtue of free ions. Combustion, radio-activity and ultra-violet and cosmic radiations produce ionisation.

Iridium, a white and very hard metallic element, no. 77, symbol Ir, discovered by Tennant in 1804. It occurs naturally as an alloy with platinum or osmium; tips for fountain-pen nibs have been made from the former native alloy. The former standard metre was composed of platinum–iridium alloy (*see* **Metre**) as are parts of scientific apparatus and surgical tools that must be non-corrodible.

Iris, the typical genus of the botanical order *Iridaceae,* with tuberous rhizomes and sword-shaped leaves, many of the family having beautiful flowers. About 100 species of Iris are recorded from the northern temperate zone, the most common species wild in Britain being the yellow flag. Orris root, used in perfumery, comes from another iris species.

Iron is a metallic element, no. 26, symbol Fe (Latin *ferrum*), occurring widely in nature in such ores as haematite, loadstone (magnetic iron oxide), spathic ore and iron pyrites. It is extracted by a process known as smelting, with coke and limestone in a furnace. Its many uses are familiar, the most important being in the manufacture of cast- and wrought-iron products and of steels, which are alloys mainly of iron with added carbon and various metals. Iron rust is formed by the action of oxygen and water, and is a coating of iron oxide. *See* **Smelting.**

Ironclads, ships of war cased in iron or steel plates of sufficient thickness to resist projectiles. They were first introduced (1858) in the French Navy, and in 1860 the first British ironclad, the *Warrior,* was launched.

Iron Curtain. In a speech at Fulton, USA, on 5 March 1946, Sir Winston Churchill used this phrase to describe the dividing line behind which, he said, lie all the capitals of the ancient States of Central and Eastern Europe—Warsaw, Berlin, Prague, Vienna, Budapest, Belgrade, Bucharest and Sofia. The Iron Curtain was symbolised by the Berlin Wall (dividing that city in half) and the rival military groupings of NATO and the Warsaw Pact. The dramatic changes in Eastern Europe since 1989 and the collapse of the Soviet Union in 1991 have ended all this as some former Communist countries increasingly look to membership of the European Union and NATO.

Ironsides were Cromwell's special troopers, so called because of their solidity and firmness in battle.

Irrational Number, a number such as the square root of two, or pi, which cannot be expressed as the ratio of two whole numbers. *See* **Rational Number,** and *Pi.*

Irredentists, a political party organised in Italy about 1878 with the object of incorporating within Italy neighbouring regions. Also a person, group or party advocating policies for the restoration to their country of territory formerly belonging to it but later lost.

Irrigation, an artificial method of providing water for the growth of plants on lands where the natural supply of water is deficient. For many hundreds of years techniques of irrigation have been slow and primitive (*e.g.,* tanks, inundation canals and the Archimedes screw) and consequent inefficiencies include large water losses by evaporation and seepage, and the watering of only a small area. New developments in perennial irrigation, using barrages, large reservoirs and pumping stations, permit vast tracts of land to be irrigated. Yet these are not without their problems as witnessed after the construction of the Aswan High Dam on the Nile where complex problems of delta erosion and dam lake silting ensued. Irrigation also serves the purpose of supplying *warmth* in winter; *e.g.,* in the English water-meadows, and in the more highly developed Italian *marcite* and winter-meadows, where the water is mostly applied in winter when there is plenty of rain. There are several other functions of irrigation; *e.g.,* washing out of excess salts and the renewing of fertility by the addition of alluvium.

Islam. *See* **Section J**.

Isobars are the lines drawn on charts linking together points of equal barometric pressure.

Isochasms, lines connecting places at which there is an equal probability of seeing an aurora, taking the average over a number of years, based on the auroral catalogue of Fritz.

Isomers are chemical compounds having the same composition but different structural arrangements, and consequently different physical and chemical properties. For example, ethyl alcohol and methyl ether are isomers, since the molecules of both are built up of two atoms of carbon, six of hydrogen and one of oxygen, *viz.,* C_2H_6O; ethyl alcohol, C_2H_5OH; and methyl ether, CH_3OCH_3.

Isotherms are lines drawn on charts through points of equal temperature.

Isotopes. When one talks of an element, say, uranium or lead, the name of the element is a generic name for a collection of uranium species and lead species. The different species are called isotopes. For any particular element, the number and arrangement of electrons around the nucleus are the same in all the isotopes, so all the isotopes have the same chemical properties. Soddy has described isotopes as "elements, the atoms of which have similar outsides but different insides". For example, in the nucleus of the uranium isotopes, U 235, U 238 and U 239, there are respectively 143, 146 and 147 neutrons, but all have 92 protons. The isotopes have different atomic weights, in this instance respectively 235, 238 and 239. But all have the same chemical properties.

Ivory, the dentine substance of which the tusks of the elephant, hippopotamus, walrus, *etc.,* are composed. The tusks of the African elephant sometimes weigh as much as 45 kg, and reach a length of 2·4–2·7 m. A world-wide ban on trading in ivory was imposed in 1989, but pressure has grown for a partial lifting of this ban.

Ivory Gull, a small, beautifully shaped sea-bird with striking all-white plumage and black legs which breeds on the rocky shores of the Arctic, being found farther north than any other bird; it occasionally wanders south in the winter.

J

Jabiru, the Brazilian name for the giant stork of South America.

Jacamar, from *Jacameri,* the Brazilian name for a smallish bird with long, sharply pointed bill and brilliant plumage which inhabits the tropical regions of South America east of the Andes. These birds are seen sitting motionless on trees, darting off at intervals, like flycatchers, to catch insects on the wing.

Jacanas, small water birds with immensely long toes which enable them to walk on water lily leaves. They are sometimes called "lily-trotters" and are found in tropical Africa and America. They live in swamps and feed on seeds and insects. Sometimes brilliantly coloured.

Jack, a small schooner-rigged vessel, used in the Newfoundland fisheries; a pike; an oscillating lever; a device used in roasting meat.

Jackal, *Canis aureus,* a small wild dog related to the wolf and resembling a fox. The Common Jackal is found in S.E. Europe, India and Sri Lanka; other species inhabit Africa and Egypt. The jackal is a well-known scavenger. It hunts singly or in pairs, unlike the wolf, which usually hunts in packs.

Jackdaw, one of the smaller members of the Crow family. This European bird is typically black with grey collar. It is easily tamed, makes an amusing pet and delights in making off with and taking to its nest bright objects, such as silverware.

Jacobins, a French revolutionary club or party, formed in 1789, and accustomed to meet at a Jacobin convent, hence the name. It became a controlling force in the Revolution, especially in the movement which led to the Terror. Robespierre was its chief spokesman.

Jacobites, adherents of the Stuart cause after the abdication of James II. First James himself, then his son (the Old Pretender), and later his grandson (the Young Pretender) tried to fan the flame of rebellion in Scotland and Ireland, but after the defeat at Culloden on 16 April 1746 the cause was lost. Also the name of the monophysite heretics of Syria, so named after their leader Jacobus Baradaeus in the 6th cent. A.D.

Jade, an exquisite kind of hardstone, ranging in colour from a whitish green to a deep mauvish brown. It can be translucent or opaque and sometimes it is veined. Jade is the common name for two minerals—the rarer *jadeite* (found in Burma, Tibet and China), a sodium-aluminium-silicate, and *nephrite* (found in New Zealand, China, Turkestan and Siberia), a calcium-magnesium silicate. The presence of small quantities of other chemicals accounts for the wide range of shades. In China jade has for centuries been looked upon with great veneration, magical powers have been ascribed to it, and it has been fashioned into ritual objects, also into miniature sculptures of animals or even whole landscapes, charming to look at and incredibly skilfully made. The Chinese word for jade is *yü*, used as a symbol for all that is noble, beautiful and pure.

Jaguar, a South American carnivorous animal resembling the leopard, but larger and more powerful. It preys on other animals but rarely attacks man.

Jainism. *See* **Section J.**

Janeite, a devotee of Jane Austen and her writings.

Janissaries, an élite band of Ottoman foot soldiers who acted as the Sultan's bodyguard. They were conscripts, raised by the "tribute of children" from conquered Christian countries, mainly Serbia and Albania. First recruited under Murad I (14th cent.). They were not allowed to marry. They gained great power under the Ottoman Empire. In 1826 the Sultan Mahmud II had them massacred.

January, the first month of the year, named after Janus, the two-faced god of the Romans. It was the *Wolf monath* and *Aefter Yule* of the Saxons.

Jasmine, a graceful climber belonging to the olive family with odoriferous blossom, originally a Persian plant, but now acclimatised in many varieties in almost all parts of the world. Two species of jasmine (the common jasmine and the Spanish jasmine) yield oils used in perfumery.

Jasper, a precious stone of the chalcedony variety, opaque, and coloured red, brown, yellow and sometimes green. It was greatly esteemed by the ancients, the Bible having numerous allusions to it.

Jay, a gaily-coloured bird of the Crow family, of many species—the Blue Jay of N. America, the Canada jay, sometimes called "whisky jack", the Siberian jay and the British jay, fawn-coloured with black and whitish crest and bright blue feathers in the wings. It lives in woods and like the magpie, takes the eggs and young of small nesting birds.

Jazz, a rhythmical syncopated music characterised by a strong element of improvisation in the performance, probably originating among the black population of the Southern States of the USA. It became popular during the first world war and, in a commercialised form, has held the popular field ever since. *See* **Section E.**

Jean, a stout kind of twilled cotton cloth much worn in olden times, and resembling fustian. Blue jeans, adopted by American city youngsters from farmworkers, are now the fashion elsewhere and worn not only as overalls by workmen but by both sexes in leisure time.

Jelly-fish. The jelly-fishes, which have gelatinous, translucent bodies fringed at the margin with delicate tentacles, constitute the coelenterate order *Scyphozoa*. The mouth, with a squarish opening, is seen on the underside, and there are four horseshoe-shaped sex organs.

Jerboa, small jumping mammals of the Rodent order. These mice-like animals have long tufted tails and very long hind legs, the front legs not being used for locomotion.

Jeremiad, any utterance or writing in which sorrow or complaint is the chief characteristic, so named as recalling the style of the "Lamentations of Jeremiah", in the Old Testament.

Jerusalem Chamber, a room in Westminster Abbey, deriving its name from the circumstance of its having originally been decorated with a view of Jerusalem. Henry IV died in this chamber, and the Committee for the Revision of the Bible met there in 1870 and later.

Jesuits, members of the Roman Catholic religious order founded by Ignatius Loyola in 1540. A long and vigorous course of study is prescribed before they are admitted into the privileges of full membership. They are required to take the vows of voluntary poverty, perfect chastity, perfect obedience and complete submission to the Pope with regard to the Mission of the Order. Pope Paul VI gave them the particular mission of initiating a dialogue with atheists.

Jet, a deep black fossil substance admitting of a high polish and much used for jewellery, ornaments and trimming. It is a form of lignite, the most important British deposit being found near Whitby, where jet manufacture has been an established industry for a long period.

Jet Engine, an aeroplane engine which derives its thrust from the high velocity of the gases it ejects. The essential units in a jet engine are a rotary compressor and a gas turbine, the latter driving the compressor. The first reliable, high-performance jet propulsion engine for aircraft was invented by Sir Frank Whittle.

Jet Stream, a meteorological term coined in 1946 to describe the relatively narrow belt of strong winds (160–320 km/h) at levels in the atmosphere from 5–11 km. These winds are important in forecasting weather, and can be a valuable aid to aircraft. From the ground, where there may be little wind, the jet stream can sometimes be seen as high cirrus cloud moving across the sky at high speed.

Jew's Harp. The name is believed to be a corruption of "jaws harp". This instrument consists of a metal frame with a central tongue of spring steel. The frame is pressed against the teeth, and the tongue of the harp is twanged with the finger, the mouth acting as a resonating chamber. By altering the shape of the mouth the resonant frequency and therefore the note can be varied.

Jockey Club, the governing body that, although possessing no legal status, frames rules and laws by which horse-racing and turf matters are regulated. The club-house is at Newmarket.

John Bull, the typical figure of an Englishman, bluff, big and burly. Arbuthnot's *History of John Bull* is supposed to have originated the character.

John Dory, a fish found in most temperate seas and common in British waters. It is of a golden-yellow colour (*jaune doré*), has a high dorsal fin with long filaments projecting from the spines, very protractile jaws and is much valued as a table fish. According to legend the dark spot on each side of its body is the thumbprint of St. Peter who took a coin from the fish's mouth (Matt. XVII 24–7).

John o' Groat's House, W. of Duncansby Head, Caithness, popularly named as the northernmost point of Scotland. According to legend the house, which has now disappeared, was built in octagonal form by a Dutchman Jan de Groot who came to live there in the 16th cent. The site is marked and an inn erected near it in 1876.

Jongleurs were minstrels and jesters who wandered from town to town singing songs, playing musical instruments, dancing and giving entertainments in mediaeval France and Norman England. Jongleurs were low-born in contrast to the Troubadours, who were often of the nobility.

Joule, a unit of energy in the SI system of units, defined as the work done when the point of application of a force of one newton is displaced

L69

through a distance of one metre in the direction of the force. Named after J. P. Joule (1818–89). The relationship between mechanical energy and heat energy is called the mechanical equivalent of heat. One British Thermal Unit (Btu) is equivalent to 778 ft.lb or 252 calories or 1.054×10^{10} ergs or, in S.I. units, 1054·35 joules. *See* **F20(1).**

Julian Calendar, named after Julius Caesar, who in 45 B.C., finding the Roman year 90 days in advance of the real time, was the first to adopt the calculation of time by the solar year, the average length being fixed at 365¼ days. There was still an overplus of a few minutes every year, and this was rectified by the Gregorian Calendar, introduced in Italy in 1582 and adopted in England in 1752, from which date what is called the "New Style" begins.

July, the seventh month of the year, named after Julius Caesar. It was the *Maed monath* (Meadmonth) of the Saxons.

June, the sixth month of the year, containing 30 days and deriving its name from Juno. It was the *Sear (Dry) monath* of the Saxons.

Jupiter is the largest of the planets, 11 times the diameter of the earth, 318 times its mass but only one fourth its density. It is the fifth farthest from the sun and is the second brightest. Our knowledge of Jupiter, its sixteen moons, its ring and its magnetosphere was enormously increased in 1979 by data from the Voyager 1 and 2 space-probes which passed the planet at distances of 349,000 km and 722,000 km on March 5 and July 9 respectively. Jupiter is a gaseous planet composed mainly of hydrogen and helium like the sun, possibly with a small molten core of silicates. The centre is presumed to be at a very high temperature (30,000°C) and enormous pressures—a hundred million earth atmospheres—which make hydrogen not only liquid but metallic. This metallic flux leads to intense magnetic fields. Jupiter's large magnetosphere is distorted by the solar wind and contains trapped high energy particles in radiation belts which would be lethal to man. Its existence was first inferred from its radio emissions and was confirmed by Pioneer 11 in 1974.

Jupiter's outer gaseous surface is very cold (−120°C) and consists of three layers of crystal clouds (ice ammonium hydrogensulphide and ammonia) interspersed with gaseous hydrogen and helium. It shows massive persistent features like the swirling high pressure Red Spot (larger when first seen in 1664 but which could hold two earths) and the neighbouring white oval formations. All these features are in relative motion, some moving east and others west which account for Jupiter's banded appearance. The persistence of the features arises because Jupiter has no terrain to break them up and because the surface temperature is low. Lightning continuously flashes over the Jovian surface and at the poles there are large auroras caused by an electric current of five million amperes which flows from the poles out to Io, one of the four moons discovered in 1610 by Galileo. The others are Europa, Ganymede and Callisto. The fourteenth moon was discovered in 1979 by Voyager 2 at the outer edge of the thin ring of particles discovered by Voyager 1, which also discovered high plumes due to volcanic activity on Io, the first seen beyond earth (although a recent suggestion is that the plumes are caused by the electric current). Io's sulphurous surface shows no meteoric craters and Europa's smooth ice surface shows only a few impacts and is probably young, unlike the older Ganymede and Callisto whose ice-crust surfaces have many. Ganymede's crust has been reworked, however, by extensive tectonic movements. Ganymede is now known to be the largest moon in the solar system, larger than the planet Mercury. In 1994, Jupiter was struck by the Shoemaker-Levy-9 comet whose impact sent seismic waves across the planet.

In 1995, the Hubble telescope found oxygen on Europa, one of Jupiter's moons. More recently salt has been discovered. Late in 1995 the Galileo spacecraft successfully entered the atmosphere of Jupiter. First data from Galileo suggested Jupiter's atmosphere was hotter and drier than expected with hurricane winds of 330 m.p.h. Images from Galileo in 1997 appeared to show iceberg-like structures on Europa. The origin of

Jupiter's swirling rings was discovered in 1998 to be the detritus thrown up by meteoroids crashing into the moons Amalthea, Thebe *etc.* Colour images of 10 have shown great volcanic activity. *See* **F8.**

Jurassic Formation, a series of rocks (the evidences of which are most marked in the Jura Mountains) coming between the Cretaceous and Triassic groups and including the Oolite and the Lias. It is a formation rich in fauna, abounding in echinoids, lamellibranchs, ammonites and belemnites; large reptiles, marine and land, are common, as are the plants called cyads. In Britain the Jurassic outcrop extends from the Dorset coast to the Yorkshire moors.

Jury, a body of private citizens chosen and sworn to hear and pass verdict upon evidence brought forward at a trial, inquest or inquiry. The origin of the English jury is obscure but it is thought to have been introduced by the Normans. The jurors are the sole judges of the true facts upon the evidence laid before them. Under the Criminal Justice Act of 1967 their verdicts in criminal courts in England and Wales no longer have to be unanimous but may be by a majority of 10 to 2. The age limit has been reduced from 21 to 18 and raised from 60 to 65. In Scotland 45 jurors are summoned in criminal cases, of whom 15 are chosen by ballot, and majority verdicts are accepted: not guilty, not proven and guilty.

Jute, the name given to the fibre of a plant grown largely in Bangladesh in the Ganges delta and used for the manufacture of coarse cloths, cordage and sacks. Calcutta is the biggest jute-manufacturing centre of the world, as Dundee was in the 19th cent.

Jutes, a Low German race who in the 5th cent. invaded the south-eastern part of England, establishing themselves in Kent and making Canterbury their capital.

Juvenile Court, (now called Youth Court). This is a special kind of Magistrates' Court to deal with persons under 18 (as of 1999) accused of criminal offences. The Magistrates chosen are specially qualified for the work, and the court normally contains at least one man and at least one woman. The Court is held in private away from the ordinary court room. The object of the Youth Court is to introduce into the trial a plan to reform the offender by providing for the care and protection which he may need. New powers to detain 'bail bandits' aged 12 to 15 were introduced from June 1999. The court's former civil jurisdiction (care proceedings) no longer exists – such proceedings are now the concern of Family Proceedings Courts (at Magistrates' level), the High Court and County Courts.

K

Kangaroo, pouched (marsupial) mammals of Australia and adjacent islands. There are over 20 species, the smaller ones being known as "wallabies". Kangaroos leap in a succession of springy bounds 3–6 m long, the forefeet not touching the ground. They can reach a height of over 2 m and a weight of 90 kg. First seen by white men when Capt. Cook's expedition visited Australia in 1770. Related genera include the tree kangaroos, rat kangaroos and the Tasmanian Jerboa kangaroo. There are an estimated 20 million Kangaroos in Australia.

Kaolin or **China Clay** is an essential ingredient in hard-paste porcelain (*q.v.*). It results from the decomposition of felspar, and is widely found in China, Japan and the USA. The richest deposits in Europe are in Cornwall, near Limoges in France, and in the Czech and Slovak Republics.

Kea, the Alpine parrot of New Zealand.

Kelvin. Lord Kelvin, an important 19th-cent. physicist, gave his name to the kelvin, symbol K, a measure of temperature on the absolute scale. The Kelvin scale is a development of the scale invented by Celsius (*q.v.*) for everyday use, long known as the "centigrade" scale; the degree interval on both scales is the same. The conversion formula for the or Kelvin scale is $K = C + 273·15$. *See* **Absolute Temperature.**

Kernewek. The native language of Cornwall which died out *c.* 1770 but is now being revived.

Kestrel, the most common British falcon, well known for its habit of hovering for minutes at a time with vibrating wings and then swooping down to attack mice and insects. The male has spotted chestnut-brown back, greyish head and tail, with a broad black band near tip.

Ketones. A class of organic compounds, related to aldehydes, of general formula R_2CO (where R is an organic radical). The simpler ketones, especially acetone, are widely used as solvents for lacquers, synthetic rubber and polymers, such as cellulose acetate and perspex. More complex ketones occur in nature, and some are used in the perfumery industry, muscone (from the musk deer (*q.v.*)) is an example.

Kew Gardens, officially known as the Royal Botanic Gardens, are among the most celebrated gardens in the world. They were started in 1759 by Princess Augusta of Saxe-Gotha, widow of Frederick, Prince of Wales, and mother of George III. They remained private property until 1841, when control passed to the Commissioners of Woods and Forests. They now cover 121 hectares and are administered by an independent body under the 1983 National Heritage Act. Since 1841 the gardens have been open to the public, and form one of the most attractive resorts near London. They suffered severe damage in the 1987 hurricane.

Keys, House of, is the Manx representative assembly. *See* **Tynwald.**

Keystone, the stone which occupies the centre and highest point of an arch and is usually the last to be inserted.

Khaki, a clay-coloured cloth adopted for uniforms in the British Army in the time of the war with the Boers, and used in the first and second world wars. First used by Indian regiments.

Kilderkin, once a common liquid measure in England, representing 18 gallons or 82 litres.

Kilogram, unit of mass, defined as the mass of the international prototype kilogram of platinum-iridium kept at the International Bureau of Weights and Measures at Sèvres. A remeasurement of Avogadro's Number (**F24(1)**) may lead to an atomic standard of mass (the second and the metre are already defined in atomic terms), but this will depend on the precision with which atoms can be counted.

Kilowatt. Unit of power, equal to one thousand watts. *See* **Watt.**

Kinetic Art denotes works of art which actually move or give the illusion of so doing. An early exponent of kinetic art was the American sculptor Alexander Calder (1898–1976) when he launched his famous "mobiles" in the early 1950s. Since then, constructions which rotate, jump, blink with lights, *etc.* have been made by many artists and the genre is being further elaborated upon today. Kinetic painters give a visual illusion of movement to their pictures by the use of particular colour contrasts or by a skilful play with spirals, squares, *etc.* in black and white, sometimes with colours blended in.

Kinetic Energy, the energy (*q.v.*) possessed by a particle or body in virtue of its motion. If the motion is destroyed, *e.g.*, by the impact of the body with an obstacle, the kinetic energy vanishes, being turned into some other form of energy such as heat and sound. If the body has mass m and speed v its kinetic energy (leaving out corrections due to relativity) is $\frac{1}{2}mv^2$.

King Crab, remarkable arthropods now classified separately from both Arachnids and Crustacea which they resemble, inhabiting the sea coasts of America, Japan, India and Malay Peninsula, carrying a shield-shaped shell, and having a long pointed spine projecting from the posterior. The body comprises three separate sections articulated together. These crabs—in America known commonly as the horseshoe crab because of their shape—are from 45–60 cm in length. Fossil king crabs are found as far back as the Silurian. There are about six living species.

Kingfisher, a well-known family of brilliant-plumaged birds, found in all continents, comprising some 250 species and sub-species. The British kingfisher, *Aceldo atthis*, haunts the rivers and streams, and is one of the most beautiful of native birds, having iridescent blue-green, white and rich chestnut in its plumage and bright-red feet. All kingfishers have long, dagger-shaped bills. In the Malayan region, New Guinea, the Moluccas and Australia, the varieties are very numerous. The quaint *Laughing Jackass* of Australia is among the largest of the kingfisher family. The European kingfisher is the bird of the Greek legend of the Halcyon. Cleaner rivers and more sensible management of river banks are encouraging the kingfisher to return.

King-of-Arms, the name of the chief officials of the Heralds' College. There are several in England —the principal being those of the Garter, Norroy and Ulster, Clarenceux. *See* **Heralds' College.**

Kiosk, a word of Russian or Turkish origin meaning a small open pavilion of light construction much used in Eastern countries as a place of shade and rest. Similar structures are common in the streets of Paris as news and advertisement stands, and in London as telephone boxes.

Kirimon (*Kiri no go Mon*) and **Kikumon** (*Kiki no go Mon*), the two Japanese imperial crests, the first a design of leaves, stems and flowers of the Paulownia plant, and the other representing the sixteen-petalled chrysanthemum.

Kite, name of several birds of prey, widely distributed, related to the hawks and eagles, graceful in flight, and distinguished by their long wings and deeply forked tails. The red kite, light chestnut brown, once the most familiar bird of prey in Britain, seen scavenging the streets of London, is now the rarest, and found only in Wales. The Egyptian kite and the pariah kite of India, notorious for their daring thefts, are closely related to the black kite, a smaller European species, with less forked tail and blackish-brown plumage.

Kittiwake, a beautiful white and pearl-grey gull with black legs, dark eyes and greenish-yellow bill. Its range is wide, and includes the British Isles, where it is a local resident. The flight of this only truly oceanic gull, which except in the breeding-season is generally found offshore, is graceful, swift and buoyant. A triangular black patch, noticeable on the ends of the wings when open, is characteristic of the species, as is the call kitti-wake, from which the bird derives its name. It nests in colonies on the ledges of caves and steep cliffs.

Kiwi, flightless, stoutly-built birds of New Zealand now very rare and carefully protected by the Government. They are little larger than a domestic hen, and lay astonishingly large eggs for their size. Incubation and care of chicks fall to the male bird. They have rudimentary wings concealed by the plumage, and the feathers are hair-like. They are nocturnal.

Knighthood is a degree of honour or title common in Europe since the Middle Ages, and was at first exclusively a military order. In Great Britain the four main orders of knighthood are those of the Garter, the Bath, the Thistle and St. Patrick; in addition to which there are several other orders, such as the Order of St. Michael and St. George, the Star of India, *etc.* There are also Knights Bachelors not associated with any special order. The title is not hereditary, and ranks below that of a baronet, though both are entitled to the prefix "Sir".

Knot, a nautical measure of speed (1 sea mile per hour), and formerly measured by a log-line, divided by knots at equal distances $\frac{1}{120}$ of a geographical mile. The number of knots travelled by the ship in a half a minute corresponded to the numbers of sea miles it travelled per hour. A sea mile is equal to about $1\frac{1}{5}$ of a statute mile or 1·9 km. Also, a grey and white wading bird, usually a winter visitor to Britain found in flocks on the coast.

Knout, a whip of many thongs, often fatal in its effects, formerly used in Russia for flogging.

Koala, the Australian arboreal marsupial mammal that looks like a toy teddy-bear, with ashy-grey fur, bushy ears and rudimentary tail. It feeds on the leaves and shoots of certain eucalyptus trees, and is not more than 60 cm in length. Today fewer than 100,000 remain and their habitat is threatened by development and the motor car.

Kohl, a powder prepared from antimony or burnt almond shells, and in common use by the women of the East for darkening the eyelids.

Koto, a musical instrument in general use in Japan consisting of a series of 13 silken strings stretched across a curved wooden surface, and played with the fingers. Each string is 1·5 m long, and has a separate bridge so fixed as to give the vibration necessary for the note it has to produce. It is a sort of horizontal harp, and in the hands of an expert player is capable of giving forth excellent music.

Kremlin, the citadel or walled city within a Russian city which during the Middle Ages served as an administrative and religious centre and offered protection. That of Moscow, now the headquarters of the Russian government, contains the cathedral where the Tsars were crowned, an imperial palace and the "King of Bells" (*see* **Bells**). Its walls which are topped with towers were built in the 15th cent.

Krypton, one of the rare gas elements, No. 36, symbol Kr, occurring in the air to the extent of 1 part in 20 million. It was discovered in 1898 by Ramsay and Travers. It is used in gas-filled electric lamps.

Kumara. *See* **Sweet Potato, L117.**

Kurds, an Arab people with no homeland of their own. Persecuted by Saddam Hussein in Iraq. *See* **Section C** (under Iraq) and **Special Topic, C67.**

Kusti, the sacred cord or girdle of the Parsees, consisting of 72 threads—the number of the chapters of the *Yasna*—and two branches, each branch containing six knots, together standing for the 12 months of the year.

Kyrie Eleison ("Lord, have mercy"), the name of a common form of prayer in the Anglican, Roman Catholic and Greek Churches; also applied to the English Church responses after the recital of the commandments.

Kyrle Society, named after Pope's "Man of Ross", John Kyrle, founded by Miss Miranda and Miss Octavia Hill in 1875, and having for its object, the decoration of workmen's clubs, hospitals, *etc.* and the promotion among the poor of a taste for literature, music and outdoor recreation.

L

Labarum, the standard of Constantine the Great, adopted after his conversion to Christianity, marked with his seal and represented upon the coinage.

Labourers, English Statute of, was passed 1350–51, with the object of compelling labourers to accept a certain rate of wages and not leave their employers' service, the Plague having rendered labourers so scarce that they were in great demand and had been insisting on higher pay. These enactments were bitterly opposed and led to the "Peasants' Revolt", headed by Wat Tyler.

Labradorite, a felspar rich in calcium and of a pearly lustre on cleavage, found in masses in igneous rocks, the best samples of which come from Labrador.

Labyrinth, or Maze, a combination of roads and passages so constructed as to render it difficult for anyone ignorant of the clue to trace the way to the central part. The Egyptian labyrinth near Lake Moeris had 3,000 rooms, half of them subterranean and the remainder above ground. The labyrinth in Crete, according to Greek myth, was built by Daedalus to house the Minotaur. There was one at Lemnos, renowned for its stalactite columns; and another at Clusium constructed by Porsenna, King of Etruria, about 520 B.C. The labyrinth in which Fair Rosamond was concealed was at Woodstock. Hampton Court maze dates from the 16th cent.

Labyrinthodonts, gigantic fossil amphibians which get their name from the curious labyrinthine structure of their teeth, probably an evolutionary link between fishes and reptiles. They occur in the Carboniferous, Permian and Triassic formations, and remains have been found in Britain and other parts of Europe. Their heads were long, and their footprints, by which they were discovered, closely resemble the prints of the human hand.

Lac, a resinous matter deposited on the branches of a number of tropical trees by the females of the lac insect, the exudation including eggs and a viscous covering. At the gathering time the twigs are broken off and dried in the sun, when the insects die, and the lac that remains is termed *stick-lac*. From this, by the removal of extraneous accretions and dissolving, *seed-lac* is produced. *Shell-lac* is seed-lac after it has been melted and otherwise prepared, and this is the best known of the lacs, being used in printing and the manufacture of varnishes and sealing-wax, and for other commercial purposes.

Lace, a delicate fabric of linen, silk or cotton threads, made by hand or machinery, and worked in various ornamental designs. The kinds of lace are many, deriving their distinctive names either from the method employed in production or from the place where any special variety was originally made. The best-known makes are pillow or bobbin-lace, woven and plaited by hand; needle-point lace, worked by the needle over a traced design; and machine lace, which practically dates from Heathcote's invention of the early part of the 19th cent. Some of the most famed laces are the following: *Alençon*, a needle-point lace; *Brussels*, a very fine kind, with needle-point sprigs and flowers; *Chantilly*, a silk variety with flowers and open-work; *Cluny*, a netlace with darned stitch; *Honiton*, a delicate kind with dainty sprigs and figures; *Mechlin*, generally made in one piece and very varied in design; and *Valenciennes*, or bobbin lace, of great durability, the pattern and ground of which are made at the same time, being one of the best and most costly of laces, now manufactured mainly in Belgium. Nottingham was famous for its lace.

Lace-Wings, insects with frail, transparent and much-veined wings whose grubs eat large numbers of insect pests such as aphids. The eggs are borne at the ends of threads attached to plants.

Ladybird, the common name of a large family of beetles—the *Coccinellidae*. The insect is usually of a red or yellow colour with small black or coloured spots. Ladybirds are of good service to the gardener because their larvae feed on aphids. There are about 2,000 species.

Lady-Day, the day of the festival of the Annunciation of the Virgin Mary, 25 March. One of the four English quarter days.

Lake Dwelling, the name given to certain prehistoric habitations which were thought to have stood on platforms over lakes, like villages in certain Pacific islands. Major excavations at the Lake of Burgäschi in Switzerland show that the prehistoric Swiss pile dwellings probably stood on the shores of lakes, not on platforms over the water. Also found at Mere and Glastonbury, Somerset.

Lakes are bodies of water collected in depressions of the earth's surface. The most notable lakes are the Great Lake series of North America, including Superior, Michigan, Huron, Erie and Ontario, all discharging into the St. Lawrence River. Africa has an enormous area of lakes, including the Mobutu Seso and the Victoria, forming the sources of the White Nile. Smaller lakes are numerous in other countries—Switzerland, Finland, Italy, England, Ireland, Scotland, all having their lake regions, where the scenery is invariably beautiful and romantic. The Kariba Dam (Zimbabwe-Zambia border) and the Nasser (Egypt) are the largest man-made lakes in the world.

Lake School, the name given, at first in ridicule, to a distinguished trio of poets—Wordsworth, Coleridge and Southey—who made their homes in the English Lake District.

Lamellibranchs (Pelecypods), the class of aquatic, bi-valve molluscs to which the oysters, cockles, mussels, clams and scallops belong. In these animals the body, which is compressed laterally, is enclosed in two hinged shells held together by muscular action. The gills are thin plates hence the name "lamellibranchs".

Lamination, stratification on a very fine scale, as in shales.

Lammas Day is one of the oldest of the Church festivals, probably derived from the loaf-mass (*hlafmaesse*) of the Anglo-Saxons. It occurs on 1 August. In the olden times it was the day when loaves were given in place of first-fruit offerings.

Lammergeyer, the bearded vulture of alpine regions, resembling an eagle in appearance. It has a white head with black tufts at base of the bill, and its general plumage is dark brown, nearly black. It is found in the remote mountain ranges from southern Spain and parts of Africa to China, and is becoming scarce.

Lampblack, a carboniferous pigment obtained from flame-smoke, and now produced in specially constructed furnaces in which bodies rich in carbon, such as tar, resin, petroleum, *etc.*, are burned. The smoke or soot resulting is collected from the sides of the furnace, and forms lampblack. It finds use in making printer's ink, black paint, *etc.* Being a very pure form of carbon, it is also utilised in the manufacture of dynamo brushes and arc-lamp carbons.

Lamprey. Eel-like fish having no scales, bones, paired fins or jaws. They attach themselves by their mouths to fish whose blood they suck. Together with the hagfishes, the lampreys are placed in a special class—the Cyclostomes. There are three British lampreys.

"Lancet", the name of a noted English medical journal, established in 1823 by Dr. Wakley.

Land Crab, a family of crabs (*Gecarcinidae*) which live mainly on land, though migrating to the seas to deposit their eggs.

Land League, an association formed in 1879, with Parnell as president, for compelling a reduction in the rents of land, and a reconstruction of the land laws in Ireland, and in case of non-compliance refusing to pay rent. For a time this League exercised great political influence and was an important aid to the Home Rule agitation.

Landrail, popularly known as the Corncrake, was once a regular summer visitor to Britain. Its harsh and piercing note was a familiar sound in English cornfields. It is decreasing almost everywhere and international efforts were launched in 1994 to try and save it from extinction. These are now bearing fruit.

Landslip, a sudden downward sliding under gravity of large masses of rock, soil, *etc.*; often set off by earthquake shock or saturation of a particular stratum with water. Many serious landslides have occurred from time to time. In 1618, an earthfall happened at Plurs, on Lake Como, involving the destruction of many buildings and the loss of numerous lives. In 1806 a portion of Rossberg mountain in Switzerland slipped from its position, and falling into the valley below buried many villages and hamlets and over 800 people. A chalk cliff 30–45 m high and 1·2 km long fell at Lyme Regis, in Dorset, in 1839, doing great damage. Over 200 people were killed by a landslip in Naini Tal, in India, in 1880; and at Quebec, in 1889, a rocky eminence called Cape Diamond gave way, many buildings being destroyed and lives lost. Notable landslips in recent times have occurred at Amalfi (Italy) in 1924, at Murchiston (New Zealand) in 1929, at Aberfan (Wales) in 1966 and near St. Gervais (France) in 1970. Submarine landslips (*i.e.* landslips under the oceans) may give rise to tsunamis.

Langue d'oc and Langue d'oïl, the two principal mediaeval French dialects, *oc* and *oïl* being their respective words for the affirmative particle (modern French *oui*). *Langue d'oc,* spoken south of the Loire, was the language of the troubadors. Provençal, one of its dialects had a literary revival in the 19th cent. under the influence of the poet Frédéric Mistral. *Langue d'oïl* was spoken in northern France, and it was the dialect of the Paris region which developed into modern French.

Lantern Fly, bugs belonging to the family *Fulgoridae* in which the head is drawn out to form a lantern-like structure. In no instance is the "lantern" luminous, though naturalists used to think it was.

Lanthanides, the fourteen metallic elements following lanthanum in the Periodic Table, *i.e.*, the elements cerium (no. 58) to lutetium (no. 71). They are also known as the rare-earth metals, though they are in fact all more terrestrially abundant than, for instance, mercury or arsenic (with the exception of the unstable radioactive element promethium, no. 61). The lanthanide atoms are distinguished by having an incomplete inner electron sub-shell (the 4f level), this feature giving them interesting magnetic properties. For instance, gadolinium, holmium and dysprosium are ferromagnetic at low temperatures. Chemically, the lanthanides behave similarly, being highly reactive metals usually forming trivalent salts. *See* **Periodic Table, F65.**

Lapis Lazuli, an azure-blue mineral, being a silicate of aluminium and sodium. The pigment ultramarine is made by grinding it, though artificial ultramarine has largely superseded it. The mineral (also called *lazurite*) has been used as a gemstone from antiquity.

Lapwing *or* **Green Plover,** familiar British bird on moors and marshlands with iridescent greenishblack plumage, white underparts and black crest. Often called "peewit" from its cry. Protected under Protection of Birds Act, 1967. It is nevertheless in serious decline in Britain.

Larboard is the old nautical term indicating the left-hand side of a ship, and changed by Admiralty order to "port" in 1844. Starboard is the right-hand side.

Larch, a familiar coniferous tree in the mountain regions of northern Europe, and though not native to Britain, the Common Larch is successfully cultivated in various parts of the kingdom. It is one of the best of all turpentine-yielding trees, and the bark is valued for tanning. The larch is an unusual conifer in being deciduous.

Lark, a family of song birds (*Alaudidae*) of many species, some of which—notably the skylark—are famed for their habit of soaring into the air, singing all the while. They build their nests on the ground in the open country and, except for the black lark of Russia, have streaked brown plumage. The skylark and woodlark are the best known British species, while the crested lark and shore lark are among the occasional visitors. Africa has the greatest number of larks; America has only one species, the horned lark.

Larkspur, the common name of the genus *Delphinium,* a favourite flower introduced into British gardens from Switzerland in 1573. The common larkspur is *D. consolida.*

Larva, the undeveloped form of any animal which, before maturity undergoes metamorphosis, usually differ from the adult in structure and habits.

Laser. A remarkable kind of light source that was discovered in 1960. With the laser it is possible to probe the behaviour of matter under the influence of enormous energy densities, range and survey vast distances to microscopic accuracy and send millions of telephone and television messages between any two points that can see each other with telescopes. Laser light, in contrast to natural light, is coherent and can be expressed as a regular progression of waves carrying energy along a particular path. Thus the essential difference is that laser light is an orderly sort of wave motion in contrast to ordinary light which is inherently unsteady and therefore an inefficient carrier of information in time. The name *maser,* which is the microwave parent of the laser, derives from the expression "microwave amplification by the stimulated emission of radiation". Upon application to light wavelengths the microwave part of the name lost its meaning and the term maser became generally descriptive of any device in which stimulated emission dominates.

Laser Fusion is a method by which it has been proposed that thermonuclear reactions may be controlled and exploited as a source of energy (*see* **Nuclear Fusion**). The idea is to irradiate a millimetre-sized pellet of a mixture of frozen deuterium and tritium with a short ($\sim 10^{-9}$ s) but very intense pulse of energy in the form of laser light. This has the effect of both compressing the pellet by a factor of at least a thousand and heating it to about 10^8 °C. Under these conditions, thermonuclear reactions (principally $^2D + {}^3T \rightarrow {}^4He + {}^1n$) proceed sufficiently fast that a net output of energy is obtained before the pellet explosively separates. Formidable technical problems need to be solved before laser fusion can become a practical proposition. These include the development of efficient high-powered lasers and the design of a suitable reactor that can withstand up to 100 micro-hydrogen bomb explosions per second. It is still not clear whether this method of controlling nuclear fusion is more practical than the more conventional approach involving the magnetic confinement of plasmas.

Latent Heat is the quantity of heat required to convert 1 gram of a substance from one form into another. For example, when a solid changes into a liquid or a liquid into a gas, the addition of heat to bring about the change produces no rise in temperature, the energy being absorbed in the form of latent heat. An equal amount is released when the process is reversed. The latent heat of fusion of ice is about 79·6 calories per gram, that of the vaporisation of water about 539 calories per gram.

Lateran Councils were the religious conventions held in the Lateran basilica at Rome for deciding important questions of Church doctrine. The most brilliant was that of 1215 which pronounced in favour of a Crusade.

Lateran Treaty, 1929, between Italy and the Vatican established the Vatican City as an independent sovereign state.

Laterite refers to any tropical soil or soil horizon rich in hydrated ferric and aluminium oxides which harden when exposed to the atmosphere. It is difficult to cultivate and is commonly used for bricks and road metal. Laterite buildings have been known to withstand the weathering for many centuries and a number of fine examples are found in India and S.E. Asia.

Latin America. The Spanish-speaking, Portuguese-speaking and French-speaking countries of N. America, S. America, Central America and the W. Indies. *See* **Section K.**

Latitude of a point on the earth's surface is its angular distance from the equator, measured on the surface of the earth in degrees, minutes and seconds. Thus the equator is 0° Lat. and the poles 90° Lat. (N. or S.). First determined by Hipparchus of Nicaea about 160 B.C. Latitude introduces zones of climate, *e.g.*, tropical rain, subtropical steppe and desert, temperate rain and polar.

Laughing Gas. *See* **Nitrous oxide.**

Launce *or* **Sand Eel,** a family of eel-like sea fishes found in large numbers on the coasts of North America and Europe. There are two species common to British waters. These fishes are of a bright silvery hue, and live much in the sand underneath the water. They are prized as human food and as bait.

Laurentian Shield refers to the Pre-Cambrian rocks in the region of the Upper Lakes of Canada, nearly 5 million sq km in extent. Of enormous importance to Canada on account of the mineral wealth, forests yielding valuable timber and wood-pulp, and water-power.

Lava, the molten rock which is erupted from a volcanic vent or fissure. Also the same material which has cooled and solidified.

Lawn, very fine sun-bleached linen, in olden time called "cloth of Rheims".

Lead, a soft malleable metallic element, no. 82, symbol Pb (Latin *plumbum*), occurring in numerous ores, which are easily smelted. Its most important source is the mineral galena which consists chiefly of lead sulphide; rarely is it found free. Lead is largely used in plumbing on account of its pliability, and in nuclear reactors as a shield against radiation because of its very high density. As an alloy element it combines in the formation of type metal, stereo metal, shot metal, pewter and many other compounds. Oxides of lead are used in some types of glass and in the manufacture of paints (red lead). All lead compounds are poisonous. Leading producers of lead are the United States (Missouri), Australia (Broken Hill) and Russia.

Leaf Miners, insect larvae which tunnel between the upper and lower skins of leaves. Most leaf miners are caterpillars of tiny moths; some sawfly larvae have the same habit.

Leagues, or combinations of kings, countries, communities, have been frequent since the kings of Canaan united against the Israelites. Among the most famous leagues may be mentioned the Holy or Catholic League, which prevented the recognition of Henry IV as King of France until he became a Roman Catholic; and the League of Augsburg against Louis XIV of France in 1686.

League of Nations, was founded on 10 January 1920, with the object of promoting international peace and security. The original members were the signatories to the Peace Treaties at Versailles, and membership grew to fifty-three as new nations and ex-enemy States were admitted. Two notable absentees were the United States and Soviet Russia, the latter not being represented until 1934. Germany was a member from 1926 to 1933. The League had an Assembly which met at Geneva every year and a Council which met five or six times a year. The Permanent Court of International Justice (now under the UN) sits at The Hague. The League held its last Assembly at Geneva in April 1946. Its place was taken by the United Nations. The International Labour Organisation, set up by the League of Nations, met in April 1944 at Philadelphia and resumed its work at Geneva under the UN in 1946.

Leap Year *or* **Bissextile,** was fixed by Julius Caesar, 45 B.C., the addition of one day in every four years bringing the measure of the calendar year even with the astronomical year with three minutes per year over. The Gregorian Calendar corrected this by dropping leap year at the centuries not divisible by 400. For instance, 1700, 1800 and 1900 were not leap years.

Learning. *See* **F40(2).**

Leather was made in ancient Egypt, Greece and Rome, and has through succeeding centuries played an important part in the service of man. It consists of the dressed hides or skins of animals after the process of tanning has been gone through. Untanned skins are known as pelts. Leather is classed either according to the skins from which it is made or the system of preparation employed. The best-known kinds are morocco, kid, Russian, chamois, Cordovan, grained, patent, russet, tan, calf, Hungarian.

Leech, an aquatic blood-sucking worm, mostly found in fresh-water ponds. Each end of the body is provided with a sucker, but that at the head end has jaws and teeth. The medicinal leech has three jaws. The leech attaches itself with avidity to animal bodies and sucks until glutted. Its saliva contains an anti-coagulant.

Leeward, a nautical term, meaning the sheltered side of a vessel—that is, the opposite side to that from which the wind is blowing.

Legion, a body of Roman troops, varying in numbers at different periods. A legion was divided into 10 cohorts, and every cohort into three maniples. Three legions composed the Roman army of occupation in Britain.

Legion of Honour, the French order for distinguished services, military or civil, was instituted by Napoleon I in 1802, and confirmed and modified under later rules. There are five grades—Grands Croix, Grands Officiers, Commandeurs, Officiers and Chevaliers.

Legume, the fruit typical of the pea, bean family, or *Leguminosae.*

Lemming, small light-brown rodents with dark spots, abounding in Scandinavian countries and in Siberia, about 12 cm long, with a short stump of a tail. The migrations of the lemming are famous, probably caused by overbreeding when food is plentiful. So insistent is the urge to keep moving that these animals will march on into the sea in their thousands and be drowned.

Lemur, almost the most primitive member of the primate order of mammals (to which man, apes and monkeys also belong). They are noted for having strong pliant toes enabling them to use their feet as hands, and also well-developed thumbs on the hands. They have long squirrel-like tails, fox-shaped heads and large staring eyes. True lemurs are confined to the Malagasy Rep.; closely related are the "bush-babies" of S. Africa.

Lend-Lease. During the earlier phases of the second world war the bulk of British investments in the USA had to be either sold or pledged to Americans in payment for dollar supplies. After the United States entered the war this drain was stopped by the Lend-Lease arrangement, under which Great Britain met the costs of American consumption in Great Britain, while the United States paid for British supplies from America. This arrangement was abruptly terminated on the ending of hostilities; and Great Britain and other belligerent countries found themselves without means of paying in dollars for indispensable American supplies, including the foodstuffs, materials and capital goods needed for economic reconstruction. In these circumstances Great Britain negotiated with the United States and also with Canada a large loan, which was used for buying dollar supplies and played an inportant part in helping the West European economies to maintain themselves and feed their people while they were carrying through the earlier stages of post-war reconstruction. These loans involved large charges for interest and amortisation in future years, but proved far too small to meet the dollar deficit for more than a short period. In face of this situation the United States launched the Marshall Plan.

Lenses, pieces of transparent material designed to focus an image of an illuminated object. Usually of glass, but plastic lenses are common, and quartz, *etc.* are used for special purposes. The surfaces of the simplest lenses are parts of spheres. Lenses which are thickest, or thinnest, at the centre are called convex and concave respectively. Lenses of complex shape are often used in microscopes, *etc.* Electron lenses are arrangements of electric or magnetic fields which focus beams of electrons, *e.g.*, on to TV screens.

Lent, the forty days' period of fasting that precedes Easter.

Lepidoptera, the order of insects with scaly wings and bodies, to which the 90,000 butterflies and moths belong.

Leptons. A group of particles which include electrons, neutrinos and muons. All are much lighter than protons or any baryons (*q.v.*).

Lepus, the constellation of the Hare, situated under the Orion group, and one of the constellations with which the ancients were familiar.

Lettres de Cachet, sealed letters which the kings of France issued to their agents to secure the imprisonment of distrusted or disliked persons without trial. Abolished in 1789.

Levée, a State reception held by the Sovereign or his representative and attended by men only.

Lewis, a contrivance for stone-lifting, the principle of which was known to the ancient Romans; it consists of two dovetail tenons of iron or other metal, expanded by an intervening key in a dovetail-shaped mortice in the stone, and shackled by a ringed bolt to the hoisting chain.

Leyden Jar, the earliest form of electrical condenser. Its invention is usually credited to Muschenbroeck of Leyden (1745). It consisted of a jar coated inside and out with tinfoil for about two-thirds of its height and having its inner coating connected with the top by a brass knob and chain. The jar was charged by connecting it to an electrostatic machine.

Lias, a geological term referring to the lower section of the Jurassic group, and mainly comprising shales and limestones.

Liberalism. *See* **Section J.**

Libraries, before the invention of printing, were few, and treasured together at enormous cost. At Nineveh remains of libraries, consisting of tablets of baked clay, have been discovered. There were two libraries at Alexandria containing a vast collection of rolls or volumes, founded by Ptolemy I Soter (367–382 B.C.) and established by Ptolemy II Philadelphus (309–246 B.C.). Among the great libraries of later times may be mentioned the Vatican Library at Rome, moved to its present premises in 1588; the Royal Library in Paris which later became the Bibliothèque Nationale; The Astor Library, New York; and in England, the Bodleian Library, Oxford, and the British Library (*see below*). Since 1850 public libraries have been established in all the chief cities and towns of the kingdom. The first lending library was opened in Edinburgh in 1726. The British Library in London, the National Library of Scotland, in Edinburgh, that of Wales in Aberystwyth, the Bodleian Library of Oxford, Cambridge University Library and Trinity College Dublin comprise the "copyright" libraries, entitled to receive a copy of each new book and journal published in Britain. The British Library Act 1972 brought together into a single organisation (a) the former British Museum Library (the books remaining in the Museum) and the Science Reference Library in Holborn and Bayswater, the whole now being known as the British

Library, Reference Division; (b) the former National Lending Library for Science and Technology and its arts and humanities counterpart, the National Central Library, together now known as the British Library, Lending Division and located at Boston Spa, Yorkshire. The new Reference Division, near Euston Station, was officially opened on 25 June 1998. Lending Division remains in Yorkshire. In 1994 the government commissioned a full-scale review of public libraries. Great emphasis is now being placed on new developments in information technology to transform libraries into a 21st cent. electronic network.

Libretto (It. booklet), the literary text of an opera or oratorio. Usually the composer and the librettist collaborate in the writing of an opera, but several composers (*e.g.*, Wagner) write their own librettos. Boito, librettist to Verdi for *Otello* and *Falstaff*, himself composed two operas *Mefistofele* and *Nerone*. Most famous of Italian opera librettists was the poet and dramatist Metastasio (1698–1782). His librettos were set to music by many composers, including Gluck, Handel, Mozart, Rossini.

Licence is a permission given to do some act, which without such permission, it would be unlawful to do. Licences are required for operating a television receiving set, for driving a motor vehicle, for killing game, for setting up as a bookmaker, for selling beer, wines and spirits, tobacco, *etc.* and for importing certain items such as arms, ammunition, radioactive materials, animals, plants, drugs and explosives. The dog licence was abolished in 1988.

Lichens. In every lichen, two plants are associated, one being an alga and the other a fungus. The fungus derives its food from the alga; probably the alga gains too from the association, being protected against desiccation by the fungus (an example of symbiosis). Lichens are the first plants to colonise bare rocks.

Life-Boats were invented by three men, Lionel Lukin who converted a coble into a boat for saving life in 1785; William Wouldhave, who discovered how to make a boat right herself if she capsized; and Henry Greathead, who built a life-boat, partly from Wouldhave's model, in 1789. This boat was stationed at South Shields, although the earliest recorded reference to a lifeboat station was in 1770 at Formby, Lancs. It was not until 1851 that the first lifeboat able to self-right was built, and a motor was first installed in a life-boat in 1904. Mersey class lifeboats, introduced in 1988, have twin turbo-charged diesel engines with maximum speed of 17·5 knots. Most coastal life-boats in this country are maintained by the Royal National Lifeboat Institution founded by Sir William Hillary on 4 March 1824. It is supported entirely by voluntary contributions, and has saved over 125,000 people. Its headquarters are in Poole, Dorset. In 1999, it costs over £80m. to maintain the service. The last traditional double-ended lifeboat was phased out of service in 1993. There are 215 lifeboat stations around the UK and Ireland.

Light, a particular kind of electromagnetic disturbance capable of travelling through space, and some kinds of matter, and of affecting our eyes to cause vision. Its finite speed was first demonstrated by O. Römer, using observations of the eclipses of Jupiter's satellites in 1675. In 1860 Maxwell showed that light waves are electromagnetic. Since Einstein's theory of relativity (1905) it has been generally realised that the speed of light is a fundamental natural constant. Visible light with wavelengths between about 4 and 7×10^{-5} cm is only a small part of the electromagnetic spectrum. The speed of light in vacuum is c. $2·997925 \times 10^8$ m/s.

Light Year, a measure of astronomical distance, equal to the distance light travels in a period of one year. A light year is $9·463 \times 10^{12}$ km but the unit parsec is now preferred. (1 pc = 3·2616 l.y.).

Lighthouses, to warn ships of dangerous places and indicate coasts, points, harbours, *etc.*, have existed since the building of the Pharos, a tower of white marble 183 m high, built by Ptolemy II Philadelphus at Alexandria about 280 B.C. In early lighthouses the lights were simple fires. The most famous and one of the earliest British lighthouses is the Eddystone (*q.v.*). Dungeness lighthouse, opened in 1960, was very modern in design, capable of automatic operation and the first of its kind to incorporate the xenon electric arc lamp as a source of illumination. The electric fog signal consists of sixty loud-speaker units built into the tower just below the lantern, giving a honeycomb effect. The lighthouses of England and Wales, the Channel Islands and Gibraltar are under the control of Trinity House; Commissioners of Northern Lighthouses control those of Scotland; and the Commissioners of Irish Lights control the coasts of Ireland. Particulars of lights in all parts of the world are published for the guidance of navigation in the *Admiralty Lists of Lights*, compiled annually by the British Admiralty. Under the 1987 Pilotage Act, responsibility for pilotage now rests with harbour authorities. All lighthouses are now automatic, the last manned lighthouse in Britain went over to computer control in 1998. Trinity House built its first lighthouse at Lowestoft in 1609. *See also* Eddystone Lighthouse, L38.

Lightning, the flash of a discharge of electricity between two clouds, or between a cloud and the earth, when the strength of the electric fields becomes so great as to break down the resistance of the intervening air. With "forked" lightning the actual path, often branched, is visible, while with "sheet" lightning the flash is hidden by the clouds which themselves are illuminated. "Ball" lightning or fireballs is the name given to the luminous balls which have been seen floating in the air during a thunderstorm. The Boys camera has provided much information regarding the sequence of events in a lightning discharge. It is found that a flash consists of a number of separate strokes, usually four or five, and that the discharge of electricity to earth begins with a faintly luminous "leader" moving downwards and branching at intervals. As the ground is approached a much brighter luminosity travels back along the conducting channels, lighting up with several branches. The multiple strokes which follow in fractions of a second have the same "return" nature and are rarely branched. Lightning flashes to earth damage structures, cause loss of life and endanger overhead power systems, often interrupting electricity supply. Such storms generally affect radio transmissions and present hazards to aircraft. Thunderclouds may develop energy far exceeding that of our largest power generating stations.

Lightning Conductor, a metal rod, the upper part of which is of copper with a conical point, the lower portion being iron, which extends into the earth. Its effect is to gather to itself the surrounding electricity and discharge it into the earth, thus preventing its falling upon the protected building. In ships, lightning conductors are fixed to the masts and carried down through the ship's keel-sheathing. Benjamin Franklin was the first to realise the possibilities of lightning protection and, in 1752, carried out his famous experiment of drawing electricity from thunder-clouds, with the aid of a sharp-pointed conductor fixed to a kite.

Lillibulero, an old marching song arranged by Purcell. With words by Wharton, it is said to have "sung James II out of three kingdoms". Used by the wartime BBC as a station identification signal preceding news bulletins.

Lily Family (Liliaceae), one of the largest families of flowering plants, with 200 genera and 2,500 species. It includes the true lilies (*Lilium*), tulips and hyacinths. Vegetables belonging to the family are the onion and asparagus.

Limes, trees of the genus *Tilia*, including some 30 species spread over north temperate regions. The word is a corruption of "linden". Limes native to Britain are the small-leaved *T. cordata* and the broad-leaved *T. platyphyllos*. The hybrid *T. vulgaris* was introduced into Britain from the Continent during the 17th cent. and is frequently seen in streets and parks. Lime-wood was used by Grinling Gibbons for his fruit, flower and bird decorations.

Limestones, sedimentary rocks composed wholly or largely of calcium carbonate and formed by two main processes, (1) organic (skeletal remains of organisms), *e.g.*, chalk (*q.v.*) and (2) chemical (precipitation of calcium carbonate), *e.g.*, oolite (*q.v.*). Marble is limestone that will polish after cutting.

Linen, a textile fabric manufactured from flax fibre, known to the ancient Egyptians, and first manufactured in England under Henry III by Flemish weavers. The greatest linen-manufacturing region in the world is Northern Ireland (largely yarns and the lighter types of fabrics); Scotland produces coarse linens and canvas as well as household linens.

Ling, a sea-fish common on the coasts of Britain, and abounding in more northern waters. It averages about 1 m in length, and is a voracious feeder, living chiefly on small fish. Ling is also the name applied to *Calluna vulgaris*, the plant commonly called "heather".

Linseed, the seed of the flax plant, containing, apart from its fibrous substance, certain oily and nitrogenous matter of considerable commercial value. This yields linseed oil. Some of the residue is used to make cattle food.

Lion, the most impressive of the Cat family. It is chiefly found in open bush country in Africa, being comparatively rare in Asia. Its large square head, its flowing mane (in the males only) and its tufted tail distinguish it. Tip to tip it can reach a length of 3m; a weight of 225 kg.

Lion and Unicorn, the supporting figures of the royal arms of Great Britain, date from the union of Scotland with England (1603) at the accession of James I (James VI of Scotland), the lion representing England and the unicorn Scotland.

Liqueurs are essences combined with alcoholic liquid, and are of many kinds, named according to their flavouring or place of production, and include Cointreau, Chartreuse, Curaçao, Benedictine, Tia Maria, Drambuie *etc.*

Liquid, the name given to matter in such state that it takes its shape from the containing vessel. The volume it occupies is independent of the container, however.

Liquid Crystals form a special class of substance and are true liquids in that they flow easily and can be poured. However, unlike ordinary liquids, liquid crystals have their molecules arranged with geometrical regularity in one or two dimensions, so that they have a certain internal structure similar to that of solid crystals. They are fairly complicated chemicals with somewhat elongated molecules. Liquid crystals are of interest to biologists as well as to chemists and physicists, and not just because they account for the iridescence of beetles. Some body fluids are in fact liquid crystals. There are also technological applications because of their unique electrical and optical properties.

Litanies were first used in church processions in the 5th cent. The first English litany was commanded to be recited in the Reformed churches by Henry VIII in 1544.

Lithium, a soft metallic element, no. 3, symbol Li, similar to sodium. It is very reactive and is stored under paraffin oil. It is the lightest metal element.

Lithography, the art of drawing on stone and printing therefrom, was discovered by Alois Senefelder about 1796, and was introduced into England a few years later. Many improvements in the art have been made, especially in chrome-lithography and photo-lithography.

Litre, a metric measure, was abolished in 1964 as a scientific unit of volume, but remains as a special name for the cubic decimetre and as an everyday unit, *e.g.*, a litre of petrol.

Liturgy, the name given to the Church ritual, though strictly applying only to the portion used in the celebration of the Eucharist or Lord's Supper. The Anglican liturgy is laid down in the Book of Common Prayer (1662). Temporary powers granted by Parliament in 1965 to the Church to make changes in the form of worship were made permanent in 1974. The Alternative Service Book was introduced in 1980.

Liverworts (Hepatics), a class of simple green plants related to the mosses. Liverworts are most common in damp situations, such as the banks of ditches. The majority of British species are leafy, only some are thalloid.

Lizard, the name given to a diversified order of reptiles, of which there are about 1,600 species. They include the geckos, chameleons, glass snakes, skinks and blind worms.

Llama, mammals related to the camels, from which they differ in small size, absence of the humps, and more woolly coat. The domestic

llama of S. America is used as a beast of burden, also providing wool, meat and milk. *See also* **Alpaca, Guanaco.**

Loadstone *or* **Lodestone,** an oxide of iron, found chiefly in Sweden and Norway. Its scientific name is magnetite. It has the power of attracting pieces of iron and served as the first magnets used in compasses. One of the class of non-metallic magnetic materials nowadays known as "ferrites" (*q.v.*).

Lobby Correspondents are political correspondents of newspapers who interpret political news and events.

Lobsters are marine crustacean animals existing in large numbers in the northern seas of Europe and America and in fair proportion on some parts of the British coasts, especially in the neighbourhood of the Channel Islands.

Locarno, Treaty of, 1925, whereby Germany, France and Belgium undertook to maintain their present frontiers and to abstain from the use of force against each other. Hitler broke the pact by re-occupying the Rhineland.

Locust, insects of the grasshopper family, but much more powerful. They are inhabitants of hot countries, and often make their appearance in untold millions, like clouds, devastating all the vegetation that comes within their course. The locust-tree (*Ceratonia siliqua*) is supposed to have furnished food to St. John the Baptist in the wilderness, and its "beans" have accordingly been styled "St. John's Bread".

Loess, a deposit of silt or marl laid down by wind action. The biggest loess deposits are in Asia, the source of the dust of which they are composed probably being the deserts of Central Asia. Large deposits in Europe originated from the edge of ice sheets during the Ice Age.

Logarithms, a system of calculation invented by John Napier in 1614, and developed by Henry Briggs a few years later. Thus if a number is expressed as the power of another number, *i.e.*, if $a = b\ n$, then n is said to be the logarithm of a to base b, written logba. Common logs are to base 10 and Napierian to base $2 \cdot 7182818 \ldots$, expressed as e.

Lombards, a German people, originating on the Elber, who settled in Italy in the 6th cent., occupying northern and central regions, and establishing a kingdom with Pavia as capital. They were conquered by Charlemagne in 774, but left their name to the region of Lombardy. Lombard Street, London, takes its name from the Lombard merchants and bankers who came to settle there in the 12th cent.

London Clay, geological stratum which occupies much of the London Basin and part of the Hampshire Basin. It represents the lower stratum of the Eocene. Outside the metropolis, brickfields utilise the clay for brickmaking. Water held down in the Chalk by this impervious stratum is tapped by a number of artesian wells in London. The tunnels of the underground run through the London Clay.

London University is recognised as one of the great universities of the world. Originated in the foundation of a non-sectarian college in Gower Street in 1828. Among the chief colleges are: University College London, King's College, (inc. former Chelsea College and Queen Elizabeth), Imperial College of Science and Technology, London School of Economics, School of Oriental and African Studies, Queen Mary and Westfield, Birkbeck, together with Royal Holloway and Bedford New College. London University was the first to throw open all degrees to women (1878).

Long Distance Walks. The National Parks and Access to the Countryside Act 1949 provided for the establishment in England and Wales of Long Distance Footpaths and Bridleways. The following walks have been opened: Pennine Way (the first long-distance footpath, a magnificent hill walk of 270 miles from Edale in Derbyshire along the Pennines over the Cheviots and the Scottish border); Pembrokeshire Coast Path (from St. Dogmael's to Amroth, 170 miles); Offa's Dyke Path (176 miles along the marches of Wales, one of the most important remaining earthworks of its kind in northwestern Europe); South Downs Way (Beachy Head to Buriton in Hants, 80 miles); South-West Peninsula Coast path (Minehead to Poole Harbour, 520 miles); Coast to Coast Walk from Robin Hood's Bay to

St. Bee's (190 miles); Ridgeway (Avebury to Ivinghoe Beacon, 90 miles); Pilgrim's Way (Winchester to Canterbury, 116 miles); Cotswold Way (Bath to Chipping Campden, 95 miles); West Highland Way (Glasgow to Fort William, 95 miles). Recently opened paths include (1989) the 83-mile Centenary Way from York to the North Sea at Filey, the 278-mile Icknield Way, reputed to be the oldest road in Britain (1993), the 147-mile Grand Union Canal walk (1993), the 88-mile Jurassic Way from Banbury to Stamford (1994) and the 225-mile Midshires Way (which will link with the Pennine Bridleway). The 180-mile Thames Path, inaugurated in 1996, is the Countryside Commission's newest national trail (running from Kemble, Gloucs., to the Thames Barrier). Also in 1996 the first six-mile section of the planned 150-mile London Outer Orbital Path opened. Britain's longest riverside walk, the 220-mile Severn Way, was opened in 1998. It runs from the Plynlimon plateau in Powys to the Bristol Channel. A carriageway for horses along the Pennine Way is planned to open in December 2002. *See also* **National Parks.**

Longitude of a point on the earth's surface is the angle which the meridian through the poles and that point makes with some standard meridian. The meridian through Greenwich is usually accepted as the standard meridian and the longitude is measured east or west of that line. As the earth revolves through 360° in 24 h, 15° longitude represent 1 hour's difference in apparent time.

Long Parliament (1640–60), marked the end of Charles I's 11-year attempt to govern without Parliament. It carried through what has come to be called "the English Revolution" and was the parliament of the civil war (1642–49).

Lord Lieutenant is the Queen's representative in the county, and his office is now largely ceremonial. On his recommendation the magistrates or JPs are appointed by the Lord Chancellor. The office was created in 1549 to take over the military duties of the sheriff.

Lords, House of, *See* **Section D.**

Louse, parasitic insect found on the skin of birds and mammals. The two sub-species that parasitise man are the body louse and the head louse. Typhus can be transmitted by lice.

Louvre, one of the old royal palaces of Paris, was built in its present form partly by Francis I and added to by later monarchs, Louis XIV completing the edifice. Napoleon I turned it into a museum and enriched it with the plunder of many foreign art galleries. The great extension to the Louvre building begun by Napoleon I was completed under Napoleon III in 1857. Much injury was done to the building during the Commune of 1871. Amongst other famous treasures it houses the Venus de Milo and Leonardo da Vinci's masterpiece, *La Gioconda.*

LSD (d-lysergic acid diethylamide). This hallucinogenic drug has achieved wide notoriety because of its use by certain people to give themselves abnormal mental experiences. Doctors have frequently warned against the dangers of its use. It is active in extremely small quantities and a dose as small as a fifty-millionth part of a gram can cause marked disturbances of the mental function in man. LSD has been used in the study of mental disease because it produces symptoms very similar to mental disorders such as schizophrenia.

Luddites, a combination of workmen formed in 1811, in a period of great distress, with the object of destroying the new textile machinery then being largely adopted, which they regarded as the cause of their troubles. Their first outbreak was at Nottingham, and was stated to have been started by a young apprentice named Ned Ludd. Afterwards, serious Luddite riots occurred in various parts of the country, especially in West Yorkshire, where many people were killed, mills were destroyed and numbers of rioters were tried and executed. Charlotte Brontë used the period in her novel, *Shirley.*

Lutecium, element (no. 71) of the rare-earth metal group discovered in 1907 by Urbain. Symbol Lu.

Lutheranism. *See* **Section J.**

Lynx, cats of sturdy build, with tufted ears and spotted fur, inhabiting many parts of the world, including Northern and Central Europe. They commit serious ravages among sheep and goats.

Lyon King of Arms, the President of the Scottish Lyon Court, and head of the heraldic organisation for Scotland.

Lyre-Bird, a remarkable family of Australian birds, the males of which possess a beautiful lyre-shaped tail. The bird is not more than 38 cm long, but its tail, displayed during its remarkable courtship dance, is 58 cm in length. There are two species: the Superb and Albert's Lyrebird.

M

Macaque. A family of monkeys which includes the Barbary ape (specimens of which live on Gibraltar), the Rhesus macaque (the organ grinder's monkey and the one used for experimental work in the investigation of disease), the Bonnet monkey of southern India and Sri Lanka, the Crab-eating and the Pig-tailed monkeys of south-eastern Asia.

Macaw, a genus of large parrots with brilliant scarlet and sky-blue plumage, with interminglings of green. Native to South and Central America.

McCarthyism, the term given to the wave of anti-Communist hysteria, associated with the name of Senator McCarthy (1908–57). The campaign lasted from early 1947 to late 1954.

Mace, originally a weapon of offence, now an ensign of authority borne before officers of state and other dignitaries. In the House of Commons the mace is handed to an official of the Crown by the Sergeant-at-Arms at the close of a parliamentary session.

Mach Number. Unit of flight speed. The ratio of speed of flight to speed of sound under same conditions of pressure and density. Speed of sound at sea-level is 762 mile/h (1,226 km/h), so flight speed of 381 mile/h (613 km/h) is equivalent to a Mach Number of $\frac{1}{2}$. At supersonic speeds the Mach Number is greater than 1; subsonic speeds, less than 1.

Mackerel, a sea-fish existing in large numbers in the northern Atlantic off America and Europe. They are beautiful fish with a streamlined body and among the fastest fish in the sea.

Macromolecules are very large molecules about 10,000 times or more as heavy as ordinary small molecules like hydrogen. Most are built up from a large number of simple sub-units, i.e., are polymers (q.v.). The term macromolecule is often used in biology, e.g., starch and cellulose are biological macromolecules, both built from glucose sub-units. Other important ones are proteins and nucleic acids. The properties of macromolecules depend on the sub-units of which they are composed.

Mad Cow Disease, the common name for Bovine Spongiform Encephalopathy (BSE), a fatal brain disease in cattle. Concern resurfaced in 1996 over possible links with the incurable Creutzfeldt-Jakob disease which affects humans. The Government admitted that it was possible that mad cow disease might be passed to humans by eating beef. Beef sales temporarily collapsed and the EU banned the import of British beef (this ban has now been lifted). Selective culling of cattle born between 1988 and 1993 was begun. The number of cases of BSE in Britain has declined from a peak of 36,000 in 1992. However, renewed concerns about long-term health risks to humans led the government to impose a ban on the sale of all cuts of beef off the bone in 1997.

Madder, one of the most important of dye-stuffs, largely used in producing Turkey-red dye, but now superseded by synthetic alizarin. Natural madder is the root of the *Rubia tinctorum*.

Maelstrom, a great whirlpool. The most famous is that off the coast of Norway, between the islands of Moskenës and Mosken, of the Lofoten group the power of which has been much exaggerated.

Mafia. A term which is connected with Italo-American organised crime. Historically, remoteness from the central government of Italy encouraged the growth in Sicily in the 19th cent. of *mafiosi*, key-men who gained power through fear and violence. Contem-

porary police records give details of *mafia* behaviour in defending their authority. Emigration of vast numbers of southern Italians to the United States led to a new type of urban *mafioso* who became connected with gangsterism and vice. Sometimes called the *Cosa Nostra*, the organisation has infiltrated city governments and is reputed to be in control of drug smuggling and other illegal operations. Organisations of gangsters similar to the Mafia are thriving in post-communist Russia and eastern Europe.

Magellan, Clouds of, the name given to a pair of small galaxies, satellite systems of our own galaxy, visible only from the southern hemisphere. On account of their relative nearness to the earth (186,000 light-years), they are receiving much attention from astronomers.

Magenta, a blue-red aniline dye discovered in 1859 by Sir W. H. Perkin, and named after the battle of that year between the French and Austrians.

Magic. See Section J.

Magic Circle, the world's most famous magical society. Its motto is *Indocilis Privata Loqui* which means "not apt to disclose secrets". This prestigious institution was established in 1905. With 1400 members, its new headquarters is at 12 Stephenson Way (near Euston Station) London NW1 2HD.

Magistrates or **Justices of the Peace** preside over petty sessional and Youth Courts (as well as Family Proceedings Courts, liquor licensing committees etc.), and are appointed by the Lord Chancellor on the recommendation of the Lord Lieutenant of the County. Most JPs are laymen and are unpaid. In certain big towns a legally-qualified, paid, full-time magistrate is appointed, known as a stipendiary magistrate. In London stipendiaries are known as Metropolitan Stipendiary Magistrates. JPs are no longer appointed over the age of 60 and they must retire when they reach 70. The judicial office of Justice of the Peace derives from a statute of 1361. Magistrates, though mostly laymen and unpaid, are now subject to compulsory training.

Magma, molten rock material rich in volatile constituents prior to its eruption at the surface. With the loss of volatiles it becomes lava.

Magna Carta was sealed by King John at Runnymede on 15 June 1215, in obedience to the insistent demands of the barons and has been confirmed many times by later monarchs. It was not a revolutionary document. It laid down what the barons took to be the recognised and fundamental principles for the government of the realm and bound king and barons alike to maintain them. Its main provisions were that no man should be punished without fair trial, that ancient liberties generally should be preserved, and that no demands should be made by an overlord to his vassal (other than those recognised) without the sanction of the great council of the realm.

Magnesium, a metallic element, no. 12, symbol Mg, first isolated in 1808 by Sir Humphry Davy, who prepared it by electrolysing the chloride. Its chief ores are magnesite and dolomite. Industrially it is obtained by electrolysis. Many important light alloys contain magnesium. The metal burns with a very bright light, and for this reason it is used in photographers' flash bulbs and also in firework manufacture.

Magnetic Storms. These are the effects of magnetospheric storms observed world-wide at ground level as fluctuations of as much as 5 % in the earth's magnetic field. The largest effects are observed at high latitudes, in the auroral ovals, and are due to electric currents flowing in the ionosphere and between the ionosphere and the magnetosphere. There may be concurrent disruption of radio communications. See **Magnetosphere.**

Magnetism, originally the name given to the quality of attraction for iron possessed by lodestone (q.v.). Now known to be a phenomenon inseparably connected with electricity. Strong magnetic attraction is possessed by a comparatively small class of substances; iron, nickel and cobalt are the most common elements, but there are several less well known, e.g., gadolinium. Many alloys have valuable magnetic properties which make possible numberless technical devices. New magnetic substances are always being developed (see **Ferrites**). The earth acts like a huge magnet with its axis inclined at about 11° to the axis of rotation, the magnetic poles being on the Boothia Peninsula (North Canada) and South Victoria Land (Antarctica). The magnetic field at the surface consists of the regular field of a magnetised sphere with an irregular field superimposed upon it. Variation in the magnetic forces occurs from place to place and from time to time, and maps showing the distribution over the globe of points of the same declination (i.e., the angle which the magnetic meridian makes with the geographical one) are of the utmost importance in navigation. Little is known regarding the origin of the main (regular) field of the earth, but it is believed that the irregularities are due to the presence of intense electric currents in the upper atmosphere and local magnetisation of rock strata. In 1967 the discovery was claimed of isolated magnetic poles, i.e., north and south magnetic poles existing separately, just as positive and negative electrical charges exist separately. If this is confirmed it will probably rank as one of the most important experimental results of the 20th cent., because of its significance for the theory of electromagnetism and fundamental particles. Magnetic field strengths are measured in gauss (c.g.s.) or tesla (S.I.) units.

Magnetohydro-dynamics. A current-carrying wire always experiences a force if it is in a magnetic field. This is the well-known electrodynamic force, and electric motors work because of it. If the current is carried in a fluid, e.g., a liquid metal or a plasma, these forces cause bodily movements to the fluid, which are in general very difficult to calculate. The forces are then called *magnetohydro-dynamic forces*. Now magnetic fields are themselves produced by electric currents; so a current flowing in a fluid produces a magnetic field, which then reacts on the fluid itself by means of the magnetohydrodynamic forces. In the Harwell machine Zeta, which was used to study technical problems of thermonuclear reactions, this effect acted so as to constrict the electric discharge on to the axis of the tube and thus keeps it away from the walls. This action was assisted by an extra magnetic field produced by a separate current flowing in metallic conductors outside the tube. Thus the hot plasma was contained by magnetohydro-dynamic forces and not at all by the material tube wall. In practical devices of the future magnetic forces may have to sustain plasma pressure of 60 atmospheres—a pressure for which a thick steel wall would normally be used! See also **Plasma Physics.**

Magnetosphere. The magnetic field of the earth prevents the plasma of the solar wind from directly impinging on the earth's upper atmosphere and ionosphere. The cavity thus maintained within the solar wind is known as the magnetosphere. The tenuous plasma within this cavity is partly of solar and partly of terrestrial origin, from the solar wind and the ionosphere respectively. These plasmas are subject to large perturbations, known as magnetospheric storms, triggered by fluctuations within the solar wind. These storms generate intense auroral displays, magnetic field fluctuations at ground level, and often major disturbances of the upper atmosphere and ionosphere which may result in disruption of radio communications. The inner parts of the magnetosphere contain the Van Allen radiation belts (q.v.). On the sunward side the magnetosphere extends to between 12 and 20 earth radii. However, on the side of the earth away from the sun it extends, like a comet tail, for many millions of km. Jupiter's large magnetic field produces a large magnetosphere, one of the largest features in our planetary system being as large as the sun itself.

Magnificat, the hymn of the Virgin Mary, given in Luke 1, 46 beginning in the Vulgate with the words "Magnificat anima mea Dominum" ("My soul doth magnify the Lord").

Magnitude in astronomy is a measure of the apparent brightness of a star, which is inversely proportional to the square of its distance. A low number indicates a bright star, and a high one a faint star. The *absolute magnitude* is a measure of *real* brightness, i.e., the brightness a star would have at a standard distance away of 10 parsecs (32·6 light years). The distance can be calculated if the apparent and absolute magnitudes are known. Another magnitude system used by astronomers is bolometric magnitude, which is a measure of the total radiation emitted by a star at all wavelengths.

Magpie, a well-known bird of the crow family, of glossy black and white plumage, famed for its intelligence and mischievous propensities.

Magyars, the Hungarian race who came to eastern Europe from S.W. Asia and settled in Hungary in the 10th cent. Their language belongs to the Finno-Ugrian group.

Mahdi an Arab leader of great influence, invested with powers akin to those of a Messiah in the Mohammedan mind. The title was taken by Mohammed Ahmed, who overran the Egyptian Sudan, and in 1885 captured Khartoum.

Maidenhair Tree or **Ginkgo.** This tree takes its name from the shape of its leaves, which resemble those of the maidenhair fern. Widely cultivated in China and Japan. It is the only survivor of an order of gymnosperms which flourished in Mesozoic times. Botanically interesting because the male gametes are motile.

Malmaison, château at Rueil-Malmaison, a western suburb of Paris. It derives its name from having been inhabited in the 11th cent. by the Norman brigand Odon, and afterwards, according to the tradition, by evil spirits, exorcised by the monks of St. Denis. It was the residence of Napoleon and of the Empress Josephine after her divorce. She died there in 1814. In 1900 it was given to the nation.

Mamluks, commonly known as Mameluks, were originally—in the 13th cent.—a bodyguard of Turkish and Circassian slaves in the service of the Sultan of Egypt, and attained such influence that in 1250 they were strong enough to appoint one of their own body to the throne of Egypt. After that a succession of Mamluk Sultans reigned down to 1517. Then the Turks annexed Egypt, and the Mamluks were taken into the service of the Beys. They again came to the front after Napoleon's conquest of Egypt, but in 1811 they were massacred by order of Mehemet Ali.

Mammoth, extinct elephants of gigantic size. In 1799 the first perfectly preserved specimen was found in Siberia in a block of ice. It was in prehistoric times found in Britain and other parts of Europe, as well as in Asia and America.

Mammoth Cave of Kentucky, one of the largest known limestone caverns in the world, with subterranean passages at different levels, lakes and rivers (the Echo R. flows 110 m below the surface); stalactites and stalagmites abound.

Manatee, an aquatic mammal of the sea cow (Sirenia) order of mammals, averaging when full grown from 3–3·6 m in length, with shovel-shaped tail, and forelimbs and nails which almost give the appearance of arms and hands. Gentle and trusting they are under threat from man. Protected in Florida. In spite of their ungainly aspect, they are believed to have given rise to the legend of mermaids. They now number only an estimated 2,600.

Manchus, originally nomads inhabiting northern Manchuria who invaded China early in the 17th cent. A Manchu dynasty occupied the imperial throne of China from 1644 to 1911.

Mandarin, the name given to a powerful Chinese official, civil or military, under the old régime, whose rank was shown by the wearing of a button on the cap. Mandarin is the major language of N. China.

Manganese, a metallic element, no. 25, symbol Mn, discovered by Scheele, 1774. It is silver-white, not very hard (it forms a hard alloy with carbon), brittle, and tarnishes when exposed to air. Its chief ore is pyrolusite (manganese dioxide). Steels containing manganese are very tough, used for making machine parts.

Maniple, eucharistic vestment worn over left arm.

Manna, a tree of the ash genus, *Fraxinus ornus*, growing in the South of Europe and in the East and exuding a sweet substance which is gathered, boiled and eaten.

Manometer, instrument used to measure gas pressure. Usually a ᴨ-tube containing water or mercury, one end open to the atmosphere, the other to the gas whose pressure is to be measured. More sensitive for small pressures than the Bourdon gauge.

Mansion House, the official residence of the Lord Mayor of London, stands opposite to the Bank of England, and was erected in 1739–53 from the designs of George Dance.

Mantis. Large insects belonging to the same order as the locusts and grasshoppers. The manner in which the forelegs are held, as though in suppliance, has gained for these insects the common name of "praying mantis". They are distributed throughout the warmer countries.

Manx, the Celtic dialect (Manx Gaelic) of the Isle of Man, now on the point of extinction.

Maoism. *See* Section J.

Maoris, the race living in New Zealand at the time it was first visited by Captain Cook in 1769. They are believed to have migrated from Polynesia about 1350. Up to 1871 they were frequently in arms against the European settlers but their high intelligence and stamina enabled them to adapt themselves and the New Zealand laws have encouraged equal citizenship. They number *c.* 325,000 (1999). In 1994 Maoris in the upper North Island were offered land and money in compensation for land seized in the 19th century.

Maple, trees native to the northern hemisphere. There are over 100 species. The sycamore is the best-known species growing in Britain. The sugar maple abounds in Canada and the eastern parts of the United States. The sugar is tapped by boring holes in the tree in February and March, and the juice that escapes is collected and evaporated. The maple-leaf is the Canadian national emblem.

Mappa Mundi, the world-famous medieval map of the world, now housed in Hereford Cathedral.

Maquis, name of the dense scrub in Mediterranean France and Corsica, providing good cover for bandits and outlaws. The French resistance movement, 1940–45, adopted the name Maquis.

Marathon, first run by Pheidippides from Marathon to Athens to announce the Greek victory over the Persians. The modern marathon is 26 miles 385 yards.

Marble is limestone in its hardest and most crystalline form. There are many varieties—33 were used in the building of the Paris Opera House—but white is the purest and rarest. White marble was used by the ancient Greeks for their temples and statues. Among the famous marbles of Italy are the Carrara and Siena marbles. Devonshire and Derbyshire yield some beautiful marbles and Connemara furnishes a serpentine-marble.

March, the third month of the year, and the first of the old Roman Calendar. It was named after the god Mars, and was the *Hlyd* (storm) *monath* of the Anglo-Saxons.

Mardi Gras, the last day of the Carnival in France, Shrove Tuesday.

Marine Nature Reserve (MNR), sea areas within territorial waters, to conserve marine fauna, flora *etc.* Lundy Island (England) and Skomer Island (Wales) are examples.

Marionettes are puppets moved by strings. They originated in the *Fantoccini* of the 15th cent. which had such a vogue in Italy and elsewhere on the Continent. The English *Punch and Judy* is a version of Punchinello.

Marmoset, small monkeys confined to the New World. Very squirrel-like in appearance, with long bushy tails, and thick woolly fur, they are pretty little animals and the smallest of all monkeys. There are claws, not nails, on their digits, the big toe excepted.

Maronite, Christian sect living mainly in Lebanon and Syria. Now part of the Catholic Church.

Marprelate Tracts, seditious pamphlets written with great maliciousness by a group of Elizabethan puritans about 1586, and intended to discredit the episcopacy, caused a great sensation in their time, and led to the execution of their supposed author, John Penry.

Marquess *or* **Marquis,** the title next in precedent to that of duke. The first English marquess was Rovery de Vere, Earl of Oxford, who was honoured by Richard II, in 1385.

Mars, the fourth nearest planet to the sun (*see* **F8**). The enormous amount of new information from the pioneer visits to Mars, primarily by the US *Mariner* and *Viking* spacecraft, in 1971 and 1976 respectively, has revolutionised our understanding of the planet. These missions showed that the planet's surface displayed many contrasts—the ancient crated terrains glimpsed previously, enormous volcanos, far larger than any on earth, vast wastelands, particularly near the polar regions, scoured by wind-blown dust over many aeons, and most tantalising, in many regions water had set unmistakable marks. We see the plains which have been subject to torrential deluges of rain in, probably, a number of different episodes over hundreds of millions of years. Other regions, extending over hundreds of km, show great gorges and canyons cut by catastrophic floods, when some natural dam has burst, releasing the pent-up waters of a gigantic lake or sea. This pictorial evidence, and more detailed informa-tion of the atmosphere and surface obtained from the *Viking* spacecraft tell us that there must have been episodes in the planet's history when its climate was quite different from that observed today. The atmosphere, if only for brief interludes, must have been much denser, and warmer, and rain must have been able to fall. Mars is today too cold and dry for water but there are polar ice caps, and the nature of the meteoric craters suggests that the surface is rock over ice and solid carbon dioxide. The search for life carried out by *Viking* produced much new information, but no traces of organic compounds as evidence, or precursors, of life. Mars has two small moons, Phobos and Deimos. Early findings from the Mars *Pathfinder* mission (which landed on Mars in 1997) suggest there was abundant water in the past and also that Mars may be much more like Earth than previously thought. Further data may come from the Mars *Polar Lander* (launched in January 1999).

Marseillaise, the French national hymn, written and composed by Rouget de L'Isle, a French engineer officer, who was inspired to write it in 1792 to encourage the Strasburg conscripts. It immediately became popular, and received its name because it was sung by the Marseillaise troops while marching into Paris.

Marshalsea, a former prison in Southwark, London, closed 1849. It existed as early as Edward III's time and was used as a jail for royal servants convicted of offences. In its later days it became a debtors' prison. Dickens described it in *Little Dorrit.*

Marston Moor, near York, was the scene of the famous battle between Prince Rupert and Cromwell on 2 July 1644. Cromwell's victory was the turning-point in the Civil War.

Marsupials, members of the order of pouched mammals. Except for the opossums of America, all marsupials occur in Australasia, and include kangaroos, wallabies and wombats.

Martello Towers, circular forts erected on the coasts of England, Ireland and the Channel Isles early in the 19th cent. as defences against the threatened Napoleonic invasion. So called from the circular fort at Mortella (Corsica), which resisted an English sea attack in 1794.

Marten, carnivorous animals of the weasel family; one species (the Pine Marten) was once common in Britain. Now it is only found in remoter areas. Most famous for their fur are the Siberian Sable and the American Marten.

Martial Law, the suspension of normal civil law and its replacement by military authority.

Martin, a well-known bird-visitor to Britain. It belongs to the swallow family, and the two species that spend their summers here are the house-martin, which makes its nest of mud under the eaves of houses, and the sand martin, which builds in sandy banks.

Martinmas *or* **St. Martin's Day,** falls on 11 November, and is one of the Scottish quarter days. St. Martin was a popular Saint with our ancestors and Martinmas was a busy time for the mediaeval housewife. It was the date when "Martlemas Beef" was dried in the chimney, and enough bacon and mutton cured to last until the spring. This diet of dried meat without vegetables caused scurvy. St. Martin (c. 316–400) was regarded as the patron saint of drinking, as well as of reformed drunkards. The late spell of fine weather sometimes occurring at Martinmas is called St. Martin's Summer.

Martyrs. People who suffer death in testimony to their faith. Stephen (Acts 6; 7) was the first Christian martyr in 39. The first English martyr was St. Alban, 286, and in Tudor times many eminent churchmen went to the stake. The Smithfield martyrs' memorial church used to be St. Peter's, St. John Street, Clerkenwell. After its demolition the memorial moved to the Church of St. James, Clerkenwell Green.

Mary Rose, the flagship of Henry VIII's navy. A 700-ton carrack, she sank in July 1545. Raised from the silt of the Solent 437 years later.

Marxism. *See Section J.*

Mason and Dixon Line, boundary line between Pennsylvania and Maryland, for long a source of dispute, drawn up by two English surveyors, Charles Mason and Jeremiah Dixon, between 1763 and 1767. It came to designate the boundary dividing the slave states from the free states of America, and is still used in distinguishing the "North" from the "South".

Masques were light dramatic compositions set to music and performed on special occasions. One famous example is Milton's "Comus", which was given at Ludlow Castle in 1634.

Mass, the service in the Roman Catholic Church defined as the Propitiary Sacrifice of Calvary, reoffered by the Priest acting *in persona Christi.* It was first celebrated in Latin in the 4th cent., and was introduced into England in the 7th cent. The use of a vernacular language was sanctioned by the 2nd Vatican Council (1965).

Mass Spectrograph, an instrument for separating isotopes. It works by sorting electrified particles according to their masses; the particles stream through a magnetic and possibly an electric field, and the lightest particles undergo the greatest deflection.

Massorah, a collection of criticisms on the Hebrew text of the Scriptures, and rules for its correct interpretation.

Mast, a long round piece of timber or tubular steel or iron, standing upright in a vessel, and supporting the yards, sails and rigging in general. The earliest ships had only one mast, carrying a simple sail. The number increased until there were 4 or 5, or even more. Above the lower mast of a sailing-ship comes the topmast, and above that, the topgallantmast and royalmast. The position of each mast is indicated by a prefix, as foremast, foretopmast, foretopgallantmast, foreroyalmast, mainmast, maintopmast, *etc.* The foremast is in the fore of the ship, the mainmast in the centre and the mizzen nearest the stern. In large vessels nowadays the mast does not extend to the keel, as it formerly did, but is usually stopped at the second deck.

Master of the Revels was an important Court official upon whom devolved the arrangement of Court festivities. The office is at least as old as the time of Edward III. By 1737 it seems to have died.

Master of the Rolls, one of the English judges, formerly a judge of Chancery, but since 1881 a judge of the Court of Appeal only. He has charge of the rolls or records of Chancery and ranks next to the Lord Chancellor and Lord Chief Justice.

Mastodon, an extinct order of quadruped closely resembling the elephant, but larger.

Materials Science is a blend of science and technology; it is the use of scientific research methods to study and improve materials for practical use. The deeper understanding so obtained enables scientists to design new substances with hitherto unknown combinations of properties that are useful in engineering, aircraft, nuclear power, surgery, *etc.* Materials science institutes or university departments will usually contain an assortment of chemists, physicists, metallurgists, ceramicists, engineers *etc.* because materials science brings to bear on materials many specialised techniques.

Mathematics is a body of knowledge expressed in a language of symbols. *Pure* mathematics studies the propositions that can be deduced in this language by applying definite rules of reasoning to sets of axioms. In *Applied* mathematics, the mathematical language is used, often with great effect, to discuss problems of the real world, such as mechanics, statistics and science generally. In range, subtlety, complexity and depth mathematics is un-surpassed among the intellectual disciplines and its study has attracted some of the most brilliant men in history.

Matins, the first of the canonical hours or services of the day in the Roman Catholic Church and Morning Prayer in the Anglican Church. The daily service in the Roman breviary *(q.v.)* used to consist of eight offices or "hours", fixed by canon, for prayer and devotion but since the second Vatican Council the structure has been simplified. Formerly, Matins was recited or sung at midnight, Lauds at sunrise, Prime at 6 a.m., Terce at 9 a.m., Sext at midday, Nones at 3. p.m., Vespers at sunset and Compline before retiring for the night. Lauds are now commonly joined to Matins.

Matrix, a rectangular array of numbers considered as a single mathematical object. There are special rules for multiplying and adding matrices and they are often used in mathematics, physics and elsewhere to simplify calculations and as a notational device.

Mau-Mau, a secret, anti-European, terrorist movement which agitated the Kikuyu tribe of Kenya during the years 1953–57. Mau-Mau was a symptom of African insecurity and discontent; emergency powers were lifted in November 1959, and large-scale reforms were instituted. Kenya attained independence in 1963 with Jomo Kenyatta as the Prime Minister.

Maundy Thursday, the day before Good Friday, commemorates the Last Supper. "Maundy" derives from Christ's command (mandatum) to his disciples on that day to love one another. It was the custom in the monasteries for the monks to wash the feet of the poor on this day, and for many centuries the sovereigns of England, through their almoners, have distributed money, food and clothing to "as many old men and as many old women as the Sovereign is years of age". The Royal Maundy ceremony is still observed, maundy coins being struck from standard silver.

Mausoleum, a special place of sepulture, generally for the reception of the remains of members of a royal or other family of distinction. The name is derived from the tomb of King Mausolus at Halicarnassus, erected 352 B.C., and forming one of the seven wonders of the ancient world. Another mausoleum of antiquity is that of Hadrian in Rome.

Mauve, a colouring matter produced from lichens by Dr. Stenhouse in 1848, but in 1856 obtained from aniline by William Perkin (1838–1907), who gave it the name Mauveen. This was the first synthetic organic dyestuff ever to be produced, which led to the building up of the great synthetic dyestuffs industry (which Germany dominated before the first world war).

May, the fifth month of the year, but the third of the ancient Roman calendar. Supposed to be named after Maia, the mother of Mercury, to whom sacrifices were offered on the first day of this month. In England in former days May Day was made the occasion of many festivities, including the crowning of the May Queen, dancing round the Maypole, *etc.*

"Mayflower", the name of the ship which in 1620 conveyed the Pilgrim Fathers, 101 in number, from England to America. *See* **Pilgrim Fathers.**

May Fly. *See* **Ephemoptera.**

Mazarin Bible, an edition of the Latin Vulgate, acknowledged as the masterpiece of the Gutenberg press (1456). It was the first book completely printed from movable types. It is called the Mazarin Bible because the first copy to capture the attention of scholars was found in the library of Cardinal Mazarin, in Paris. Also called the Gutenberg or the 42-line Bible.

Mean. In statistics and mathematics generally understood to be the arithmetic mean. The geometric mean between two quantities is the square root of their product. *See* **Average.**

Mechanical Equivalent of Heat. *See* **Joule.**

Medals, as decorations for military service, were first issued in this country by Charles I, who ordered medals for gallantry to be distributed to certain soldiers in 1643. Medals were also issued to officers and men who were victorious against the Dutch fleet in 1653. After Lord Howe's victory in 1794 a naval medal was instituted. Medals were also struck for the victory of Waterloo, and since that time special medals have been issued in connection with all our wars. The Victoria Cross, a special reward for personal gallantry, was instituted in 1856. The George Cross for gallantry instituted in 1940 ranks next to the Victoria Cross. The Military Cross was instituted in 1914.

Megalith, a prehistoric monument, consisting of a large single stone or a group of such stones, in a circle as at Stonehenge or in burial chambers as at New Grange, Ireland. Megalithic monuments have been constructed by different peoples in different parts of the world since the third millennium B.C.

Meiosis, special type of cell division by which the gametes or sex cells are generated, resulting in the sperm or ovum receiving only half the number of chromosomes found in a somatic cell. *See* **Mitosis.**

Mendelian Law. *See* **F30(2).**

Mendicant Friars, certain religious orders which spread over Europe in the 13th cent., and comprised the Franciscans, Dominicans, Augustines and Carmelites. Originally they depended entirely on alms.

Mercator's Projection, a method of indicating meridians and parallels of latitudes on maps, introduced by Mercator in the 16th cent., and still universally used in navigators' charts.

Mercury, the second smallest of the planets (*c.* one-twentieth of the earth's mass) is the closest to the sun at little more than one-third of the earth's average distance. It appears to resemble the earth in its interior and has about the same density but its surface resembles the moon and is heavily cratered. Mercury was visited by Mariner 10 which passed within a few hundred kilometres in March 1974 and which relayed pictures on the two following passes in September 1974 and March 1975 before control of its altitude was lost. It nevertheless continues to revisit Mercury every 176 days (two mercurian years). Mariner 10 was guided to Mercury by the gravitational field of Venus before it became a satellite of the smallest planet. The relayed pictures showed that the planet has an approximately 59-day rotation period exactly two thirds of its orbital period of 88 days. This relationship means that unlike on earth the seasonal variations are with longitude not latitude. Surface temperatures vary from 400°C to −200°C and there is virtually no atmosphere except a thin envelope of helium gas. Mariner 10 measured a small magnetic field at the surface about 1% of the earth's but much stronger than for Venus or Mars.

Mercury *or* **Quicksilver,** element no. 80, symbol Hg (Latin *hydrargyrum*) is one of the oldest-known metals, whose chief ore is the sulphide, cinnabar, found in certain parts of Spain, China, Japan and South America. It is liquid at ordinary temperature and is used in the construction of barometers and thermometers. Alloys of mercury are called amalgams. It is also of great value in medicine. The metal is used in the mercury-vapour (or "sunlight") lamp, since the vapour gives a bright yellow-white glow in an electric discharge.

Mercy-killing. *See under* **Euthanasia, J18.**

Meridian, an imaginary circle extending through the North and South Poles and any given place. When the sun is at its midday height at any place it is "on the meridian"; hence the terms ante-meridian (a.m.) and post-meridian (p.m.). *See also* **Greenwich Mean Time.**

Merino Sheep were imported into England from Spain in 1788 and had great influence in improving native breeds, especially in regard to the quality of the wool.

Merit, Order of, founded by King Edward VII in 1902 as a special distinction for eminent men and women without conferring a knighthood upon them. The Order has twenty-four British companions in addition to foreign honorary members limited in number, as the choice of members is, by the Sovereign's pleasure. Lord Kelvin was the founder companion. Florence Nightingale (1907), Professor Dorothy Hodgkin (1965), Dame Veronica Wedgwood (1969), Mother Theresa of Calcutta (honorary member, 1983) and Margaret Thatcher (1990) are the only women to have received this coveted decoration. Nelson Mandela was appointed an honorary

member in 1995. Ted Hughes, the Poet Laureate, was awarded the honour in 1998.

Merovingians, the name given to the family that ruled over France from about 500 to 750. Clovis was first of the line and Childeric the last. The "long-haired kings" have become the centre of much recent speculative history.

Mesons (from Greek *meso* = middle). One of the four groups of sub-atomic particle given by the Standard Model: gauge bosons (the most famous of which is the photon), the leptons (very light particles, including the electron), the mesons and the baryons. The latter two groups (together termed hadrons) are not truly fundamental, being made up of different combinations of quarks (three quarks forming a baryon, two a meson). The mesons are characterised by their instability; their life expectancy does not exceed 5×10^{-8} seconds. Examples of the meson group are the pions, the kaons, the charmed D's, the upsilon particle and the bottom B's.

Mesozoic. The geological era, including the Triassic, Jurassic and Cretaceous rocks.

Metamorphic Rocks are such geological deposits as have undergone alterations of structure and mineral reorganisation. The most active agents in producing these metamorphic changes are heat, water and pressure.

Metamorphosis, period of development from egg to adult, during which the animals have different forms, as found, *e.g.*, in the life histories of frog and butterfly.

Meteorites are small bodies, asteroids, or fragments of asteroids, which survive their fiery passage through the earth's atmosphere and hit the ground. The present surfaces of the moon, Mars and Mercury tell us that all the planets have been subjected since their formation to bombardment by meteorites. Though some large craters are still to be found on the earth, most have disappeared due to extensive weathering over thousands of millions of years. In some meteorites iron and nickel are the chief metals (siderites), others are like rock (aerolites). The iron meteorites are more common amongst those which have been preserved, but falls of rock-like meteorites occur more frequently. At L'Aigle in France in 1803 from 2000 to 3000 meteorite stones fell; this fall is famous because it convinced scientists that meteorites really came from outside our atmosphere. The largest meteorite stone actually known to have fallen to earth is one which descended in Emmott County, Iowa, in 1870, weighing 197 kg. A meteorite weighing no less than 37 tonnes found in Greenland is now in New York. On 30 June 1908, an enormous object fell in Siberia in a sparsely-inhabited region. A hot blast destoyed all trees within a radius of about 8–16 km. There is still controversy about the Siberian meteorite, whether it was an asteroid or the nucleus of a small comet.

Meteoroid, a tiny solid object in space. When meteroids are drawn into the atmosphere at high speed by the Earth's gravity they burn up producing a meteor.

Meteorology, the science of the atmosphere considered as a heat engine. Deals with weather, climate, optical phenomena, atmospheric electricity, physical processes such as radiation and precipitation, the dynamics and structure of cyclones, anticyclones, *etc.* Wide application to problems of aviation, agriculture, commerce and shipping. Meteorological observing stations are in operation all over the world, and on the simultaneous or synoptic reports of their instrument readings and estimates of pressure, temperature, humidity, speed and direction of wind, rain, character and amount of cloud, visibility, etc., forecasts, gale, snow and frost warnings are based. Instruments carried by earth satellites (*e.g.*, *Tiros, Nimbus*) outside the atmosphere can make systematic observations on a worldwide basis of the atmospheric circulation, through observation of cloud cover and of the thermal radiation into space from the atmosphere. Such observations together with the use of computers are of great importance for weather analysis and forecasting. The main communications centre for the UK is at the headquarters of the Meteorological Office at Bracknell, Berkshire, where the collection, editing and re-transmission of weather messages continue according to strict schedules day and night throughout the year.

Meteors or more commonly, "shooting stars", are small objects which enter the upper atmosphere to burn up in a bright streak of light. Their origin is mainly in the dust particles ejected in large quantities from comets. Some, particularly the larger and more brilliant ones, called fireballs, are debris of asteroids. Those which reach the earth's surface are called meteorites (q.v.).

Methane. The simplest hydrocarbon, compounded of one carbon atom and four hydrogen atoms. This gas occurs over marshes and swamps, where it is liberated in the decay of vegetable matter. It is the main constituent of natural gas, and also occurs in coal-mines, where it is called "fire-damp" because of the explosive character of its mixture with air. Formerly this natural gas was removed from the coal seams and ran to waste; now in many countries (including Britain) it is being used for commercial purposes.

Methylated Spirit, a mixture of 90 parts by volume ethyl alcohol, 9½ parts wood naphtha (methyl alcohol), ⅛ part crude pyridine, together with small amounts of petroleum oil and methyl violet dye. Industrial methylated spirit consists of a mixture of 95 parts by volume ethyl alcohol and 5 parts wood naphtha. It is used as a solvent and a fuel.

Metre, the rhythmical pattern of Verse.

Metre, unit of length in the metric system; since 1983 has been redefined as "the length of the path travelled by light in vacuum during a time interval of 1/299 792 458 of a second". This definition replaces that adopted in 1960 which used the wavelength of the orange-red line of krypton-86. Before that the "international prototype metre" was the distance between marks on the platinum-iridium bar placed at Sèvres in 1889.

Metric System, the system of weights and measures based on the gram and the metre, smaller and larger units being decimals and multiples of the primary units respectively. A decimal currency was adopted in France in 1795 and the metric system of weights and measures in 1799. (In that year the quadrant of the earth was surveyed and the standard metre adopted.) Nevertheless the change was accepted slowly, and as late as 1837 the French Government had to pass a law forbidding the use of the old measures. Since then the metric system has been adopted in most of the continental countries and is used universally in scientific work. Although there have been many attempts to get the system adopted in Britain, it was not until 1965 that the Government encouraged the adoption of the metric system of weights and measures. The changeover to decimal coinage was made in 1971; the system of weights and measures in industry is now mainly metric and "Metrication Day" for the ordinary shopper came on 1 October 1995. The final changeover to the metric system comes on 31 December 2009. *See* **F66–69** for **SI** units.

Mezzotint, a technical method for producing graphic work and works of art. A copper plate is made rough by close cross-hatching, so that a print from it produces an even black. When parts of the cross-hatching are scraped away, these areas will come out white when printed. By skilful use of his tools, the artist or technician can produce pictures finely graded from black to white and with a velvety black as background. The principles of the method were known and practised, for instance, by Rembrandt, but mezzotint became most popular for the reproduction of famous paintings from the end of the 18th century.

Mica. The mica of commerce is a nearly transparent mineral, which has great heat-resisting power, and can be split into thin plates. The most important micas are muscovite (potassium mica), the commoner variety, phlogopite (magnesium mica) and biotite (the magnesium and iron mica).

Michael, St., and George, St., an order of knighthood originally founded for the Ionian Isles and Malta in 1818, and reorganised in 1869, so as to admit Crown servants connected with the Colonies. The Earl of Derby, Earl Russell and Earl Grey were the first of the new knights.

Michaelmas Day, the festival day of St. Michael and All Angels, 29 September, one of the English quarter days.

Microbe, a term proposed by Sédillot in 1878 to denote any microscopic organism, vegetable or animal, or found on the borderland between the two great natural kingdoms. The term is commonly used, but not by scientists.

Microelectronics, a rapidly developing technology of the 1960s which reduces entire electronic circuits to minute size and embeds them in tiny chips of solid material. These are then called integrated circuits. A circuit consisting of, say, a dozen transistors and fifty resistors can be built into a small piece of semiconductor (q.v.) measuring not more than a couple of millimetres in any direction. Hundreds of these circuits can be made simultaneously in penny-size wafers of silicon about one-hundredth of an inch thick. There are great advantages in cheapness, reliability, robustness and speed of electronic performance. The small size is in itself an advantage in space vehicles and medical instruments. Applications to computers and communications equipment are no doubt only the first fruits of this new achievement of the current technological revolution.

Micrometer, an instrument for measuring minute distances; usually attached to the eye-pieces of a microscope or telescope, and consisting of two very fine hairs or wires stretched across the field of view, one fixed, the other movable. It was invented by William Gascoigne in the 17th cent. and improved by later inventors. Sir Joseph Whitworth made one in 1858 designed to measure the millionth part of an inch.

Micro-organisms, the collective term applied to several types of organism, the most important of which are fungi, viruses, bacteria and protozoa. It is a classification of convenience in biological studies. These organisms are generally simple in their environmental requirements (e.g., have simple nutritional needs) and in cellular organisation. This makes them very suitable for modern biological research. Much of the information on the nature of the genetic code was obtained from experiments on these organisms.

Microphone, device for converting the acoustic energy of sound waves into waves of electrical energy, used in sound amplifying systems. Developed independently by Edison (1877) and Hughes (1878).

Microscope, invented about 1590 by Janssen, and improved by Galileo, Fontana and others, is an instrument which by a lens system magnifies minute objects. Microscopes are simple, compound and binocular. *See also* **Electron Microscope, L39** and **Nanotechnology (F76)**.

Middle Ages (c. A.D. 400–1500), usually considered to be the period between the decline and fall of the Western Roman Empire and the fall of Constantinople to the Turks in 1453. The period covers (a) an earlier part ending with the 12th cent. (sometimes called the Dark Ages) when science was dead, when theology was the main preoccupation, and when the language of the learned West was Latin; and (b) a later age of Arabian influence when alchemy and astrology (at that time indistinguishable from astronomy) were central interests, technology was advancing, and Greek learning was transmitted by Arab scholars. Characteristic features of the mediaeval scene were monasticism (**Section J**), the Crusades (q.v.), Gothic art (q.v.), feudalism (**Section J**), and the supremacy of Islam in the field of learning. The period came to an end with the general decline of Christendom and the ushering in of the Renaissance (**Section J**). The term "Middle Ages" was coined by the 17th-cent. German historian Christoph Keller.

Midrash, name given to the homiletical interpretation of some of the Hebrew Scriptures in which allegory and legendary illustration were freely used. Compiled by Jewish rabbis from c. A.D. 200.

Milky Way. *See* **Galaxy, L47.**

Millenary Petition was presented to James I in 1603, on behalf of nearly 1000 Puritan Ministers against certain of the rites and ceremonies of the Church of England. The Hampton Court Conference was the outcome of this petition.

Millennium, a period of a thousand years. The term is specifically used of the period of a thousand years during which, according to Rev. xx. 1-5, Christ will reign in person on earth. The Millenarians are a sect that interprets the "Millennium" as beginning with the commencement of the 6001st year from the Creation, which, according to Archbishop Ussher (1581-1650), was in 4004 B.C. A Millennium Commission was established in February 1994 to distribute 20% of money allocated to good causes by the National Lottery for projects associated with the millennium. In 1996 Greenwich was chosen as the site for the Millennium Exhibition. The term 'Millennium Time Bomb' reflects concerns that computer technology will find the transition from 31 December 1999 to 1 January 2000 very difficult.

Millipede. Arthropods (**F36**) allied to the centipedes, from which they differ in having two pairs of legs to each body segment (except the first three) instead of one pair. Worm-like in shape but with a pair of antennae on the head, they can do much harm to garden plants, unlike centipedes which are beneficial.

Millstone-Grit, a series of grits and sandstones of deltaic origin underlying the coal measures of the Carboniferous system and attaining in England a thickness in parts of 1,525 m. It is from this rock that millstones have been made from time immemorial.

Mimicry, protective similarity of an animal to another animal or to inanimate objects. Examples of the former are the hover flies, which mimic wasps and bees; of the latter, leaf insects, stick insects and caterpillars that look like dead twigs.

Mink. Semi-aquatic mammals closely related to polecats. There is one American species and one European. The fur, which varies light to dark brown, is soft and thick, and is among the most valuable of commercial furs. They are now well-established in the wild in the British Isles. An estimated 60,000 mink are housed on 15 fur farms. Mink usually produce a litter of up to 10 kits.

Minnesingers were minstrel poets of Germany who, during the 12th and 13th cent., composed and sang verses of heroism and love. They were of knightly rank, the counterpart of the French troubadours.

Minnow, a small fresh-water fish of the carp family, abounding in all the waters of Europe; it has a mottled back and silvery belly, and forms a popular bait for trout.

Minor Planets. *See* Asteroids, **L11**

Minstrels were originally specially appointed instrumentalists and singers—pipers, harpers and gleemen—engaged by barons and manorial lords to amuse their tenants. Later, minstrels assumed nomadic habits, made their way into the houses of the great and were generally welcome. By Elizabeth's time, however, they were too numerous, and were classed as "rogues and vagabonds", along with actors.

Miracle Plays, mediaeval verse plays, popular in England in the 15th cent., usually religious in character, representing Bible incidents.

Mirage, an optical illusion caused by unequal temperatures in different layers of the atmosphere near the earth's surface. These temperature variations alter the refracting power of the air and cause light rays to be curved, making the air act as a huge distorting lens. This can happen at sea, in deserts and elsewhere and various types of mirage are known. A common kind in deserts curves light from the sky so that it appears to come from the ground, deceiving the observer into thinking that the sky is reflected in a lake of water.

Mishna, the first part of the Talmud, setting forth the "Oral Law" of the Jews.

Missal, the name of the mass-book of the Roman Church compiled 492–96 by Pope Gelasius I. The missal used until modern times was sanctioned by the Council of Trent, 1546–63, but the current missal was authorised by Pope Paul VI in 1969 after the Second Vatican Council. In the Anglican Communion the Book of Common Prayer superseded the Missal in 1549.

Mistle Thrush receives its name from its partiality to the mistletoe-berry. Larger than the song-thrush, with spotted breast rather than speckled.

Mistletoe, a parasitic evergreen with white berries used as a decoration at Christmas-time. The familiar mistletoe of Europe is the *Viscum*

album, which grows on the boughs of lime, willow, apple, poplar, maple, ash, hawthorn but seldom on oak-trees. It was sacred to the Druids, and in Norse mythology it was a mistletoe dart that killed the god Baldur.

Mistral, a cold, dry, northerly wind peculiar to the French coast of the Mediterranean.

Mitosis, cell division whereby each daughter cell receives the same number of chromosomes as the parent cell. When the gametes (sex cells) are formed a special type of division occurs (meiosis) in which the number of chromosomes is halved.

Mitre, the twofold pointed head-dress of bishops and certain abbots of the Western Church and occasionally of other ecclesiastics.

Moa, the name for several species of ostrich-like extinct birds related to the New Zealand kiwi. The largest species, *Diornis maximus,* stood 2·6 m high, the smallest, *Anomalopteryx parca,* was nearer the size of a turkey. This wingless bird became extinct because of hunting by the Maoris from whom the name comes.

Moabite Stone, a stone of the 9th cent. B.C. containing the earliest known inscription in Phoenician characters, and discovered in the highlands of Moab in 1868. It is now in the Louvre, Paris. It records the campaign between Moab and Israel (c. 850 B.C.), an account of which is given in the Old Testament (2 Kings 3:27).

Moderator, a material used to slow down neutrons in an atomic pile. Examples of moderators are pure graphite and heavy water. *See* **Nuclear Reactors.**

Mohole Project, a scheme to bore through the earth's crust to take samples of the mantle rocks beneath. Drilling trials, led by an American team of geophysicists, began in 1961 near the island of Guadalupe off the Mexican coast in the Pacific. The project, however, was cancelled in 1966 on account of the escalating cost. Russian geophysicists started on a similar experiment, boring through land rocks. The name "Anti-Cosmos" was given to the project. The boundary between the earth's crustal and mantle rocks is known as the Mohorovičić Discontinuity, or, more simply, as the Moho. The technology of deep sea drilling came from this project.

Molasses, sugar-cane juice in its uncrystallised form after boiling. The crystallised part is the raw sugar. Used to make rum.

Mole, a small burrowing animal with long, sensitive nose, about the size of a small rat, with short legs and forefeet armed with strong claws for digging in the earth. Their subterranean dwellings are of curiously ingenious construction, and they do not often leave them except to make raids on mice, frogs, snails, *etc.* The earth-worm, however, is the mole's chief item of food. Not to be confused with the vole which has a blunt nose.

Mole, or gram molecular weight.

Molecular Biology, a rapidly expanding branch of science mainly concerned with cell structure and function at a molecular level, in particular with genes and enzymes and the interaction between the two. Research work in Britain led to the unravelling of the structure of DNA, the hereditary substance of the genes, and played a major part in uncovering the molecular mechanism of the transfer of hereditary information and the nature of the genetic code. Crystallisation of the first enzyme (urease) took place in 1929; the gene as a definite chemical entity was discovered in 1943. *See* **Section F.**

Molecule. A group of atoms held together by chemical forces. *See* **Section F,** *also* **Macro-molecule.**

Molybdenum, element no. 42, symbol Mo, a fairly hard white metal with properties resembling those of chromium. Its commonest ore is the sulphide, molybdenite. The chief use of the metals is in the manufacture of alloy steels.

Monazite, a cerium mineral containing some thorium. Occurs as grains, often as sand ("monazite sands"), derived from granites. Deposits occur in India (Travancore), Russia, Norway, Malagasy Rep., S. Africa, Brazil, USA.

Monday, the second day of the week, called by the Anglo-Saxons *Monandaeg* (moon-day).

Mongoose, species of mammals related to the civets, feeding on vermin and reptiles. These animals, which have long tails and short legs, occur in Africa and Asia (especially India).

The biggest mongoose is the Egyptian ichneumon, and this has been introduced into the W. Indies because of its ability to kill large poisonous snakes.

Monitor, a family of lizards most resembling dragons. There are about 30 species widely distributed over the tropics.

Monroe Doctrine, a principle of American policy declining any European intervention in political affairs of the American continent, outlined by President Monroe in 1823. At the same time interference was disclaimed with existing European colonies in the Western Hemisphere. The American Civil War hampered the application of the doctrine for some time, but afterwards the United States firmly insisted on it.

Monsoons, regular persistent winds which blow at certain seasons in middle latitudes, mainly in South and East Asia. Their occurrence is related to the great changes of pressure which take place between summer and winter over the land mass. In India the south-west monsoon (June–October) is moisture-laden from its long passage over the sea and in the higher regions, especially, there is heavy rainfall. Sudden reversal of the wind results in the cold north-east monsoon (October–March) which is dry on account of the shelter afforded by the mountain ranges to the north. Frequently the term "monsoon" is applied to denote the associated rainfall, not the actual winds.

Monstrance, an ornamental transparent receptacle in which the Sacred Host is carried in procession or exposed for adoration.

Month, the 12th part of the calendar year. A lunar month is the interval of new moon to new moon or full moon to full moon; mean length, 29 days, 12 hours, 44 minutes, 2·87 seconds. A sidereal month represents the time of the moon's revolution from a given star back to the same again, 27 days, 7 hours, 43 minutes, 11·5 seconds. In English law, since 1926, a month means a calendar month.

Monument of London, a 202 ft (61·6 m) column, overlooking Billingsgate, designed by Wren and erected (1671–77) to mark the starting-point of the Great Fire of London (1666). The original inscription upon it ascribed the fire to "the treachery and malice of the popish faction", which stood until 1831, when the words were erased as objectionable. The black marble staircase has 345 steps (311 to the balcony).

Moon, the earth's satellite, 3,475 km in diameter and 384,400 km distant from the earth. It rotates in the same time as it revolves round the earth (27 days 7 hours 43 minutes), so that the same face is always presented to the earth. The lunar surface is pockmarked by innumerable collisions with solid particles of all sizes. Unlike the earth, it is unprotected by any atmosphere and for aeons of time it has been exposed to every kind of cosmic influence, including the parching effect of solar radiation. All moonlight derives from the sun but on the whole it is a pretty poor reflector. The exploration of the moon by means of rockets began in 1959 when the Russian *Luna 2* crashlanded on the plains of the *Mare Imbrium.* 1969 will be remembered as the year of the U.S. *Apollo* triumphs when man first set foot on the moon. The samples of lunar rock and dust brought back to earth were closely studied by lunar scientists. Samples date back further than any found on Earth as yet. The most famous, known as the Genesis Rock, is 4,100 million years old. Scientists believe ice may exist in a deep crater near the lunar south pole. The existence of water was confirmed by the *Lunar Prospector* probe in 1998, the first moonshot for 25 years.

Moorhen, a widely distributed bird of the rail family, a common resident in the British Isles. The adult is blackish with white under tail coverts, a white line on the flanks and a yellow-tipped bill. The frontal shield and the base of the bill are vermilion. It bobs its head, flirts its tail and dives well. The nest is usually placed close to the water's edge or on an overhanging branch. In feeding the young the parents are sometimes helped by their offspring of a previous brood of the season. In N. America it is known as the Florida Gallinule.

Moors, the name given to the Moslems who live in N.W. Africa and to those who once lived in Spain. In 711 Moorish Arabs invaded Spain and spread beyond the Pyrenees into France, where they were driven back by the end of the century. Spain, however, remained virtually under Moorish domination until the 11th cent. and during that period was the most civilised and prosperous part of Western Europe. In the arts and sciences the impact of Moorish culture was profound and lasting. Examples of the brilliant splendour of Moorish architecture are still to be seen in Toledo, Córdoba, Seville and Granada. During the long struggle for the Christian reconquest thousands were killed and expelled, and in 1492 Granada, their last remaining kingdom, was forced to surrender. They were virtually exterminated by the Inquisition, and the last were expelled in 1609.

Moose, the largest members of the deer family. The N. American Moose stands up to 2·4 m high, and has huge palmate antlers. There is another New World species, occurring in Alaska. The European species is known as the elk.

Morse Alphabet, a system of dots and dashes intended to be used in combination with the indicator in telegraphy; but usually read by sound, the receiving operator writing down the words in the system as transmitted. This system of signals was invented by the American inventor and artist Samuel Finley Breese Morse (1791–1872) of Charlestown, Massachusetts. The Morse Code was replaced on 31 December 1997 by more advanced technology.

Mosaic, art of arranging small pieces of coloured glass, marble, or other materials in such a fashion as to produce a decorative pattern. Some of the best examples of Byzantine mosaics are to be seen at Ravenna, Rome, Venice and Sicily.

Mosque, a Mohammedan church, the greatest being that of Santa Sophia at Istanbul, now converted into a museum of Byzantine art.

Mosquito, small two-winged flies with long legs and slender body. Their larvae are aquatic. The females of some species are blood-suckers, and thus come to transmit the blood parasites which cause malaria and yellow fever, for example. *See* **DDT** *and* **Gammexane.**

Mosses. With liverworts, mosses comprise an important group of relatively simple non-vascular land plants, the bryophytes (**F42**). In the main they are small plants, the largest between 30–70 cm high, having been recorded in the Southern Hemisphere. Mosses rarely occur singly, but usually form cushions or small colonies on moist soil, bark, wood, rock or walls. The genus *sphagnum* known as "peat" or "bog moss" is of commercial value in horticulture. In Lancashire and Cheshire lowland moors in which sphagnum is common are known as "mosses". Reindeer moss is a lichen and Spanish moss a seed plant.

Moths, of the insect order, *Lepidoptera,* differing from butterflies which have clubbed antennae, in having feathery, sometimes thin, pointed antennae, rarely clubbed. Most are nocturnal, and the pupae are usually brown and enclosed in a cocoon unlike those of the butterfly, which are usually naked. *See also* **Lepidoptera.**

Motion, Laws of. According to Newton: (1) A body continues in its state of rest or uniform motion in a straight line except in so far as it is compelled by external forces to change that state. (2) Rate of change of momentum is proportional to the applied force, and takes place in the direction in which the force acts. (3) To every action there is an equal and opposite reaction. These laws are the basis of almost all engineering and everyday mechanics. Corrections to them have been made by relativity and the quantum theory. *See* **F17, 19.**

Mule, a cross between a male ass and a horse mare; a hinny is a cross between an ass mare and a horse stallion. Also the name of the spinning machine invented by Crompton in 1779 which combined the principle of Hargreaves' spinning jenny with the machine invented by Arkwright.

Mullions, the vertical bars dividing the lights in a window, forming a highly decorative feature in the Tudor period of English Gothic architecture. The cross-beam or horizontal bar of wood or stone in a mullioned window is styled a transom. *See* **Windows.**

Munich Agreement. In September 1938 Mr. Neville Chamberlain and M. Daladier, British and French Premiers, reached agreement with Hitler at Munich for the dismemberment of Czechoslovakia, primarily for the benefit of Germany. Czechoslovakia itself was not consulted, nor Russia. Chamberlain declared on his return that he had secured "Peace in our Time".

Muscles. *See* **F37**(1).

Musk Deer, a small deer of the Himalayas, standing about 51 cm high. It is grey in colour, slightly brindled, and carries a small pouch in the abdominal region, containing what is commercially known as musk, an article which is of great value in the manufacture of various perfumes. The active constituent of musk, muscone, is now made synthetically.

Mutton Bird, an Australian name of controversial origin for a shearwater or petrel, *e.g.*, the Short-tailed and Sooty Shearwaters and the Great-winged, Kermadec, and White-headed Petrels. The young are taken by hand from their burrows for human food.

Myrrh, a resinous substance obtained from a tree of the natural order *Amyridaceae*, growing plentifully in Ethiopia and Arabia. Its use for embalming, medical and aromatic purposes may be traced back to the most remote times.

Mysteries, Greek, secret mystic ceremonies of the ancient Greeks, religious drama accompanied by dancing, the most well known being the Eleusinian and Orphic ceremonies.

Mystery Plays were mediaeval religious dramas performed at great ecclesiastical festivals, particularly in France and Bavaria, staging the Nativity, Passion and Resurrection stories.

N

Nadir, one of the two poles of the horizon, the other being the zenith. The nadir is the pole vertically below the observer's feet.

Nahum, one of the books of the Minor Prophets of the Old Testament. It is a prophecy of doom on the approaching sack of Nineveh which fell in 612 B.C. to the Medes and Babylonians.

Nano-technology, *See* **Section F, Special Topic.**

Nantes, Edict of, was a decree promulgated by Henry IV of France in 1598, giving full freedom of worship to the Protestants of the country. It was the revocation of this edict in 1685 by Louis XIV that drove hundreds of thousands of French Huguenots abroad.

Naphtha, a liquid combustible believed to have been one of the ingredients of "Greek fire". Naphtha is a light, highly inflammable oil obtained by distilling petroleum, shale oil, or coal tar. The petroleum naphtha consists of a mixture of paraffins; that from shale contains olefines as well as paraffins. Coal-tar naphtha contains xylol.

Naphthalene is an aromatic hydrocarbon; it is obtained from coal tar, and its derivatives are much used in the manufactures of colours for dyers and printers. "Moth balls" are made of naphthalene.

Narcotic, a medical dictionary definition is that a narcotic is a drug that produces stupor; complete insanity or sleep. In terms of drug addiction, it has been defined as altering the user's perception of himself and of the external world, being taken primarily for that purpose.

Nardus, a genus of coarse grasses, growing on bleak upland heaths and hill slopes. *Nardus stricta*, known as "mat-weed", is a British species.

Narghile, an oriental tobacco pipe so constructed that smoke passes through water and up a long flexible tube before reaching lips of the smoker.

Narrative Art, a type of art popular during the late 19th cent. based on the principle: "every picture tells a story"—*e.g.*, such paintings as the little Royalist boy surrounded by his anxious family and confronted across a table by the Roundheads bearing the title: "When did you last see your father?" The term, although often applied derisively, suitably describes many works of considerable artistic merit: *e.g.*, Hogarth's *Marriage à la Mode*, the Bayeux Tapestry, *etc.*

NASA, the United States government agency which carries out research into spaceflight and aeronautics. NASA was founded in 1958.

Naseby, Battle of, was fought on 14 June 1645, between the Royalists under the command of Prince Rupert and the King, and the Parliamentarians under Fairfax and Cromwell. Charles I was decisively defeated.

National Aeronautics and Space Administration. *See under* **NASA.**

National Anthem, a musical composition with words, officially adopted for ceremonial use as an expression of patriotism and loyalty to a national cause. The national anthem of the United Kingdom, "God save the King (Queen)", probably dates from the late-17th cent, to mid-18th cent. It was sung in 1745, the year of the landing of the Young Pretender. It had no one composer and was probably a recasting of folk-tunes and plainsong. Resemblances can be traced in pieces by Purcell and John Bull.

National Assembly, the name taken by the body responsible for the opening stages of the French Revolution and subsequently by other sovereign bodies in France and elsewhere.

National Covenant, an oath and declaration subscribed to by the Scottish Presbyterians in 1638 to maintain their religion against Charles I.

National Curriculum. The Education Reform Act (1988) originally provided for a national curriculum in state schools in England and Wales with three *core subjects* – maths, English and science – and seven *foundation subjects* – history, geography, technology, music, art, physical education, and a modern language. In 1995 the compulsory curriculum was reduced (history and geography were no longer compulsory after 14) and attempts to reduce teachers' workloads were made. Now, each summer, although all children aged 7, 11 and 14 take national tests in English and maths, and 11- and 14-year-olds take tests in science as well, the compulsory national curriculum has effectively been abandoned.

National Forest, a new forest given approval by the government in 1994. The National Forest area covers 194 sq. miles in Derbyshire, Leicestershire and Staffordshire.

National Gallery, established in 1824 at Pall Mall, London, with the Angerstein Collection of 38 pictures, purchased for £60,000, as a nucleus. The existing building which was opened in 1838 has been enlarged several times. The National Gallery at Millbank, the Tate Gallery, was given to the nation by Sir Henry Tate in 1897.

Nationalisation is the taking over by the State of the ownership and operation of an industry or service—*e.g.*, coal-mining, railways, transport, gas and electricity. The administration of the nationalised service is usually by a publicly appointed Board or Corporation acting, with greater or lesser autonomy, under the direction of a Minister responsible to Parliament. Most nationalised industries have now been privatised.

National Lottery, proposed in 1992 Budget. The first National Lottery draw was on 19 November 1994. The last previous national lottery in Britain was in 1826. Most European countries, and 22 US states, have similar schemes. Oflot is the Office of the National Lottery. The mid-week lottery draw began in February 1997.

National Marine Reserves *See* **Marine Nature Reserves.**

National Minimum Wage. This became law on 1 April 1999. Workers aged 22 or more must be paid a minimum £3.60 per hour (18–21 year olds at least £3.00).

National Nature Reserves (NNRs), reserves to safeguard flora, fauna and physical features, managed by English Nature, the Countryside Council for Wales and Scottish Natural Heritage.

National Parks. Under the National Parks Act 1949 a National Parks Commission was set up to create National Parks in England and Wales. Ten have been established: Peak District, Lake District, Snowdonia, Yorkshire Dales, Exmoor, Brecon Beacons, Dartmoor, Pembrokeshire Coast (the only coastal national park), North York Moors and Northumberland. They cover an area of some 13,618 km^2, or 9 per cent of the total area of England and Wales. It is not intended to change the character of these territories but to control their development so as to harmonise with the two dominant principles:

(a) that the characteristic beauty of the landscape within the Park area shall be preserved and (b) that the visiting public shall have ample access and facilities for recreation and enjoyment. The establishment of a new national park has been proposed for mid-Wales. The Commission also has power to designate areas in England and Wales outside the national parks as "areas of outstanding natural beauty". Thirty- three areas had been designated by 1977. Under the Countryside Act, 1968, the National Parks Commission was reconstituted as the Countryside Commission. In 1988, a special authority was established to manage the 120 miles of waterways constituting the Norfolk Broads and in 1991 national park status was granted to the New Forest. After growing pressure, plans were announced in 1997 to create Scotland's first national park (covering Loch Lomond and the Trossachs). Under the 1995 Environment Act, new independent authorities have run the National Parks since April 1997. *See also* **Long Distance Walks** and **Marine Nature Reserves.**

National Physical Laboratory, situated at Teddington, is one of the world's largest and best-equipped laboratories. It conducts research in its three main groups: Measurement, Materials and Engineering Sciences, and maintains British primary standards and physical units. First established in 1900 and managed by the Royal Society. Under privatisation it became an Executive Agency in 1990.

National Portrait Gallery, established in 1856, and now located in a building in St. Martin's Lane adjoining the National Gallery. Contains portraits of eminent people in British history and a valuable collection of medals and autographs.

National Rivers Authority (NRA), established in July 1989, has overall responsibility for the management of rivers, water resources and water environment. It operates via 10 regional units. In April 1996 the NRA became part of the new Environment Agency.

National Trust, founded in 1895. "A non-profit-making organisation incorporated by Act of Parliament for the purposes of promoting the permanent preservation of lands and buildings of historic interest or natural beauty for the benefit and access of the people." As a consequence of gifts and public-spirited individuals the Trust, now Britain's largest conservation charity, protects 590,000 acres of countryside, 500 miles of coastline and more than 200 historic houses. Since 1946 lands and houses may be given to the National Trust in lieu of death duties.

Nativity. There are three nativity festivals of the Christian Church: Christmas, 25 December, festival of birth of Christ; birthday of the Virgin Mary (8 Sept.); and St. John the Baptist (24 June).

NATO, the North Atlantic Treaty Organisation, established 4 April 1949. A defence grouping of Western European states, America and Canada. Britain is a member. The Russian equivalent was the Warsaw Pact (signed 1955, disbanded, 1991). NATO's Secretary-General is Javier Solana. On 12 March 1999 NATO was extended to include Hungary, Poland and the Czech Republic. The military action against Yugoslavia over Kosovo is discussed at the end of **Section C.**

Natterjack, a curious warty, prominent-eyed, brown toad (*Bufo calamita*), having a bright yellow line down the middle of its back. It utters a muttering sort of croak, hence its name.

Naturalism in painting has been defined as "a direct and spontaneous approach to nature"—to landscape primarily. Constable, Turner and Boudin were among the great naturalist painters of the 19th cent.

Natural Numbers, the counting numbers 1, 2, 3, 4, 5, . . .

"Nautical Almanac", published under the authority of the Admiralty, is always issued four years in advance, and contains information specially prepared for the use of navigators and astronomers. It first appeared in 1767.

Nautilus, a term now applied only to the pearly-shelled nautilus, the sole surviving example of the four-gilled section of the *Cephalopoda.* Its fossil relatives are called Ammonites. The spiral shell is divided into a number of compartments, the animal living in the last and largest chamber. There are three or four species, all living in tropical seas. The Paper Nautilus is not related to the Pearly Nautilus, belonging to the same order as the octopus.

Nave is the body or main open portion of a cathedral or church, and extends from the chief entrance to the choir, or chancel, and is usually flanked by aisles.

Neanderthal, the name of the valley lying between Düsseldorf and Wuppertal, where in a limestone cave a skull of a very early species of prehistoric man was discovered in 1856.

Nebula, a cloud of gas and dust in space. There are three basic types; emission nebulae create their own light, shining through the effects of very hot stars embedded within them; dust particles within reflection nebulae simply reflect the light from accompanying stars; dark nebulae contain no stars and appear as dark patches against a brighter background.

Nekton, term used to differentiate actively swimming aquatic organisms (*e.g.,* fishes) from the "drifters" or plankton.

Nelson Column, in Trafalgar Square, London, designed by Mr. William Railton, was chosen from among a number of designs—temples, obelisks and various sculptural groups—sent in as a result of a competition held in 1839. The erection of the column was begun in 1840. Twenty-six years later the lions designed by Landseer were set up at the foot of the completed column. The statue of Nelson himself was made by E. H. Bailey and the bronze reliefs at the base executed by Carew, Woodington, Ternouth and Watson, representing the Battles of the Nile, St. Vincent, Copenhagen and Trafalgar. Height 52 m, executed in Dartmoor granite from Foggin Tor quarries, at a cost of £46,000.

Néné *or* **Hawaiian Goose.** At the Severn Wildfowl Trust at Slimbridge Sir Peter Scott saved this bird from extinction.

Neo-Classical Style, term applied to the revival of classical logic and order after the extravagances of Rococo (*q.v.*), beginning in France in the mid-18th cent. and finding expression in architecture and the decorative arts. The style retains some of the daintiness of Rococo, furniture is on a small scale, often gilt, and silks and porcelain favour pastel shades. Straight lines take the place of the wild curvatures of Rococo and classical details like festoons and urn forms are used in many contexts and materials. Its English version is closely associated with the name of the architect Robert Adam whose light and graceful adaptations of Greek and Roman forms were introduced into English country houses. In France the style is sometimes called *Style Louis XVI.* Eventually the Neo-Classical style merges into Empire (*q.v.*).

Neodymium, element no. 60, symbol Nd, belonging to the rare earth metals. Discovered 1885. Named after the Greek word for "new twin', from twin lines in its spectrum.

Neo-Impressionism, a development of Impressionism (*q.v.*) by Seurat and Signac during the 1880s who devised the method of painting known as *pointillism* (the application of pure colours in minute touches to form a composite whole, based on a knowledge of the laws of colour and optics). One of the best-known examples of this technique is Seurat's *Sunday Afternoon on the Grand Jatte.*

Neon, inert gas present in air to the extent of about 1 part in 65,000. The crimson glow produced when an electric discharge passes through the gas is familiar in advertising signs. Element no. 10, symbol Ne.

Nepotism, the bestowal of patronage by reason of relationship rather than of merit.

Neptune. Apart from Pluto this is the most distant of the planets, estimated to be about $4,497 \times 10^6$ km from the sun, and taking about 165 years to revolve around it. Discovered by the German astronomers Galle and D'Arrest in Sept. 1846, after its existence had been predicted by Leverrier and Adams. The planet was visited by Voyager 2 in 1989, its last planetary stop. This revealed Neptune had eight moons (not just Triton and Nereid as previously thought) and a ring system. Its diameter is 49,528 km. A huge Earth-sized storm has been observed, which has been named the "Great Dark Spot'. Winds blow at nearly 900 mph around Neptune's equator, making it the windiest corner of the solar system.

Neptunium, element no. 93, symbol Np, one of the four new elements discovered during the progress of the atomic bomb project in the second world war. Neptunium is formed when a neutron enters nucleus of Uranium 238, and it decays radioactively to yield plutonium.

Neutrino, a neutral particle which carries energy and spin and although possessing little or no mass plays an important part in the interaction of other fundamental particles. The discovery that there are in fact two distinct neutrinos, each with its counterpart, was discovered in 1962 as a result of an experiment made with the 30,000 million-electronvolt proton accelerator at Brookhaven. See **F16.**

Neutron, a neutral particle present in all atomic nuclei except the hydrogen nucleus which is a single proton. In the development of nuclear science and technology the neutron has played a most important role and neutrons produce the radioisotopes now widely used in medicine, agriculture and industry. Neutrons and protons are termed nucleons. See **F11(2), F16.**

Neutron Bomb, a thermonuclear fusion weapon which produces increased lethal radiation while the destructive blast and fallout are significantly less than for a fission weapon of equivalent yield; it kills organic life while sparing property, except within a small radius. In 1978 President Carter reserved his decision on production; in 1981 the new Reagan administration decided to go ahead and stockpile the weapon. See also **F13(2).**

New Deal. The measures taken by President Roosevelt in USA in 1933 to overcome the great economic crisis which broke out at the end of 1929 and to restore the social security threatened by it. The measures were drawn up by a group of experts called a Brains Trust and they provided for recovery by a programme of public works, including large-scale construction of houses and large-scale assistance to farmers. Loans were granted and authorities formed to stimulate activities which reduced the workless from 17 millions to between 7 and 10 millions.

Newgate Prison was situated at the western end of Newgate Street, opposite the Old Bailey at the site of one of the old London city gates. There is a record of a prison upon this spot in the 13th cent. Later a new one was built by the executors of Richard Whittington, but this was destroyed by the Great Fire in 1666. Still another new prison on this site was erected between 1778 and 1780. In the Gordon Riots of the latter year it was destroyed by fire and re-erected. It was not used as a prison after 1880 and was demolished in 1902–3.

Newspapers. The first news-books to be published at regular intervals in Britain appeared in 1662 with news of what was going on abroad translated from German and Italian news-sheets. Licence to print was obtained from the Star Chamber, which until its abolition in 1641 allowed only the printing of foreign news. With the lifting of the ban on domestic news the Press became free. In the reign of Queen Anne English newspapers employed writers of great intellectual power and versatility. Despite the newspaper tax introduced in 1712, the number of newspapers published in London in 1776 had increased to 53, though the standard of writing was below that of earlier times. The development of the Press was greatly assisted in the 19th cent. by the abolition of the "taxes on knowledge", by the introduction of the cheap postal system and by improvements in printing, distribution, collection of news and advertising. The *London Gazette,* founded in 1665 (and still appearing twice weekly as the official organ of the Government), is the oldest newspaper living. *The Times,* known throughout the world, began as the *Daily Universal Register* in 1785, and adopted its present title in 1788. The *Manchester Guardian* (renamed *Guardian* in 1959), began as a weekly in 1821, and became a daily in 1855. The *Scotsman,* founded as a weekly in 1817 and established as a daily in 1855, and the *Glasgow Herald,* which began as the *Glasgow Advertiser* in 1783, are the leading Scottish newspapers. The first evening newspaper, the *Star and Evening Advertiser* was published in London in 1788. During 1989, the last national newspapers left Fleet St. In 1993 *The Guardian* acquired *The Observer.*

Newt, amphibian of lizard shape and mottled markings. There are three British species, the largest being the Great-Crested Newt (*Triturus cristatus*), which attains a length of 15 cm.

Newton, the unit of force in the SI system of units. Under its influence a body with a mass of 1 kilogram will accelerate at a rate of 1 metre per second each second.

Newton's Rings. Concentric circular rings, due to the phenomenon of interference, which are seen around the point of contact of a slightly convex lens with a flat plate of glass.

New Towns. Under the New Town Act 1946 and subsequent Acts some 33 new towns were designated in Britain; 23 are in England and Wales, five in Scotland and four in Northern Ireland. They were: Basildon, Bracknell, Crawley, Harlow, Hatfield, Hemel Hempstead, Milton Keynes, Northampton, Peterborough, Stevenage and Welwyn (to relieve housing problems in Greater London); Newton Aycliffe, Corby, Cwmbran, Peterlee and Washington (to serve the special needs of their areas); Newtown (to help stem rural depopulation in mid-Wales); Runcorn and Skelmersdale (to meet the overspill needs of Liverpool and north Merseyside); Telford and Redditch (to take population from Birmingham); Warrington (expanded to take people from Liverpool and Manchester); Central Lancashire New Town (new regional city based on existing towns of Preston, Leyland and Chorley). The five Scottish new towns are Cumbernauld, East Kilbride, Glenrothes, Irvine and Livingston. In Northern Ireland Craigavon was developed as a new city; Antrim and Ballymena were to become centres of economic growth; Londonderry and the surrounding district were designated as an area of special development. Rising population led planners to suggest in 1996 that 27 new towns will be needed by the year 2016, involving a total of 4·4 million new houses.

New Year's Day, 1 January. The first New Year's festival of which we know is that constituted by Numa 713 B.C., and dedicated to Janus.

Nibelungenlied, the German epic of the early 13th cent. comprising numerous mythical poems or sagas. Wagner's *The Ring of the Nibelungs* was based on Norse legends and the Nibelungenlied.

Nicene Creed, a summary of the principles of Christian faith, first issued in 325 by the Council of Nicaea (summoned by the emperor Constantine the Great) for the purpose of thwarting the Arian heresy and asserting the godhead of Christ. Date of Easter fixed at Council of Nicaea.

Nickel, silver-coloured metallic element, no. 28, symbol Ni, fairly soft though harder than iron. Chief source of the metal is the nickel sulphide in iron-copper pyrites deposits in Ontario. Chief uses are: in electroplating, in coins, as an element in alloy steels. A novel method of making pure nickel (by treating the metal with carbon monoxide and heating the resulting liquid, nickel carbonyl) was developed in 1890 by Mond. This discovery led to many technical advances in industrial chemistry, one of which is the production of catalysts. Discovered by Crondstedt in 1751 as an impurity in copper ore. Substituted for silver in French coinage in about 1882.

Night Heron, a stocky, short-legged heron of black and white plumage, red eyes and yellowish legs, crepuscular except in breeding season, and an occasional visitor to Britain.

Nightingale, a familiar singing bird which visits the southern counties of England every summer, and is sometimes found as far north as Yorkshire. It is a shy, brown bird, not often seen, but the song of the male, usually heard in the late evening or at early morn, is of remarkable sweetness and variety. After its wooing period is over its song ceases. Their numbers have fallen by a third to 5,000 in the last two decades.

Nightjar, nocturnal, insectivorous bird, owl-like in appearance, with mottled brown plumage of "dead leaf" pattern, and a churring song. It is a common breeding visitor to the British Isles, April to September, laying its eggs on bare ground.

Niobium is a metal element, no. 41, symbol Nb,

related to vanadium. Technical development has been slow because of its rare occurrence, although niobium is now used in ferrous alloys to increase resistance to corrosion and produce steel which can be used at high temperatures.

Nitre or **Saltpetre,** is now mostly manufactured by the double decomposition of sodium nitrate and potassium chloride. Its chief use is the manufacture of gunpowder and fireworks. It has been manufactured in England since 1625.

Nitrogen, a non-combustible gaseous element, no. 7, symbol N, devoid of taste or smell, and constituting nearly four-fifths of the atmospheric air. Nitrogen compounds are essential to plants and animals, and are used in fertilisers.

Nitro-Glycerine, an explosive yellow fluid produced by mixing small quantities of glycerine with a combination of one part of nitric acid and two parts of sulphuric acid. By itself it is a dangerously explosive substance to handle. In 1867, Nobel produced dynamite, a safe explosive made by absorbing nitro-glycerine in kieselguhr.

Nitrous Oxide, a compound of nitrogen and oxygen possessing mild anaesthetic power. Termed "laughing gas" on account of its exhilarating effect. It is still used in dentistry, and for minor operations and has proved useful in a new technique for finding leaks in water mains.

Nobel Prizes. The Nobel Foundation was established at the beginning of the century to give effect to the wishes expressed by Alfred Nobel in his Will. By the terms of the Will the judges are the Swedish Academy of Science, the Caroline Medico-Surgical Institute, the Swedish Academy and five members of the Norwegian Storting. The award of a Nobel Prize is accepted as the highest form of international recognition in the field in which it is given: physics, chemistry, medicine, literature, peace and, since 1969, economics. *See* **Section Z** for winners.

Nones were dates of the Roman calendar which fell on the 5th of each month, excepting March, May, July and October, when they fell on the 7th.

Norman Architecture is English Romanesque (*q.v.*), which flourished from the time of the Norman Conquest and was gradually superseded through a transition period (*c.* 1175–1200) by the introduction of the pointed arch characteristic of the Early English (first Gothic style). Typical of Norman churches are the round arches, thick walls, massive cylindrical columns, with throughout the basic pattern of the square and the circle. Some churches (*e.g.*, the Temple church in London or the chapel at Ludlow Castle) are wholly circular. Roofs in the early days were flat and towers, usually placed at the "crossing", were square but occasionally round; the spire of all these towers have perished, but it seems likely that they were squat and pyramidal.

North-East Passage, from the North Atlantic to Bering Strait was rapidly developed by the former USSR as a northern sea route to render accessible vast areas of northern Siberia. Attempts to find a North-East passage were made by Englishmen and Dutchmen in the 16th cent. but they were always defeated by the ice, for the sea is completely frozen for some 4,800 km for 9 months of the year. A Swede succeeded in sailing from Europe to Japan via the Arctic in the late 19th cent. *See also* **Arctic Exploration.**

North-West Passage, from the Atlantic to the Pacific through the Arctic Seas, has been the dream of navigators for centuries. Attempts to find it were made in the 16th and early 17th cent. by John and Sebastian Cabot, Frobisher, Gilbert, Davis, Hudson and Baffin. Two centuries later Ross, Parry, Franklin and others made the attempt; but it was not until 1903–5 that Amundsen, discoverer of the South Pole, made the complete voyage in the *Gjöa.* The Canadian icebreaker *Labrador* was the first deep-draft vessel to traverse the North-West Passage (1954) and the US tanker *Manhattan* was the first commercial vessel to do so (1969).

Notre Dame, the famous Paris cathedral, was founded in 1163, and is one of the finest specimens of Gothic architecture in Europe.

November, the 9th month of the year originally, but from *c.* 700 B.C., when Numa added January and February, it became the 11th month.

Nuclear Energy. Atomic nuclei consist of protons and neutrons joined in various proportions (**F11**). The heaviest naturally occurring nucleus contains 238 particles (92 protons, 146 neutrons) and is uranium 238 (U^{238}); the lightest is hydrogen, which consists of 1 proton. Neutrons and protons attract one another by very strong forces which are not at all well understood; they are called *nuclear forces.* Consequently it requires energy to be supplied if a nucleus is to be pulled apart into its constituent particles. The energy is required to overcome the attractions of the nuclear forces. Conversely, when the particles rush together to form a nucleus energy is released in the form of heat or radiation. The energy released when protons and neutrons coalesce to form a nucleus is called *Binding Energy.* The binding energy of a nucleus divided by the number of particles involved is called the binding energy per particle, which we will call B. It is very difficult to overestimate the importance of B to the human race. B varies from nucleus to nucleus, and the exact form of its variation is only roughly understood at the present time. But the most significant thing is that B is greatest for elements of medium atomic weight and lowest at the heavy (uranium) and light (hydrogen) ends of the periodic table. This means that if middleweight nuclei can be formed either from heavy ones or from light ones, B increases and energy is released in either case.

Nuclear Fission. *See* **F13**(1).

Nuclear Fusion. If light nuclei are hurled at high speeds into intimate contact they sometimes coalesce and release binding energy (*see* **Nuclear Energy**). This has been studied in laboratories where powerful and energy-consuming machines accelerate small numbers of particles for purely experimental purposes. If useful amounts of energy are to be gained these fusion reactions will have to occur on a bigger scale in an apparatus from which the resulting heat can be extracted in a controlled way. The one "useful" fusion device so far made is the thermonuclear bomb ("H-bomb"). Thermonuclear is the important word. If a suitable gas can be raised to a very high temperature the nuclei are stripped of their electrons and all particles move with very high speeds. The gas is then called a plasma. High enough temperatures will make speeds great enough for fusion reactions to occur and nuclear energy to be released. This is a thermonuclear reaction. For example, in deuterium gas, at temperatures over a million degrees Centigrade, the deuterium nuclei (*i.e.*, heavy hydrogen nuclei consisting of 1 proton joined to 1 neutron) interact to produce helium nuclei. To obtain a net gain in energy from this process, the temperature must be raised to about 100 million degrees C and maintained long enough; otherwise the energy released is less than that required to heat the fuel and to make up for heat losses. Many attempts to study the staggering technical problems are being made, and fusion research is very active in Britain, the USA, Japan and the Russian Federation. The joint European Torus (JET) fusion research project sited at Culham near Oxford aims to develop a new source of energy for the generation of electricity for the 21st cent. In 1991, the JET project achieved a two minute successful nuclear fusion, bringing nearer the prospect of new energy sources.

Nuclear Power Stations. In 1997 Britain generated 28 per cent of her electricity in nuclear power stations. Among numerous older nuclear power stations are Bradwell, Essex (1962), Hunterston "A", Scotland (1964), Hinkley Point "A", Somerset (1965), Dungeness "A", Kent (1966), Sizewell, Suffolk (1966), Oldbury, Avon (1968) and Wylfa, Anglesey (1970). They were all developed from the classic Calder Hall type, burning natural uranium inserted in a graphite moderator and cooled by carbon dioxide gas. They are called Magnox stations because the fuel elements of natural uranium rods are encased in magnesium alloy cans. A second nuclear power programme is based on the advanced gas cooled reactor (AGR) at Windscale, and include the reactors at Dungeness "B", (1983) and those at Hinkley Point "B", Hunterston "B", Hartlepool (Cleveland) and Heysham (Lancashire). In 1987, after the Layfield Report, the Government gave approval for the Sizewell B project to become Britain's first pressurised water reactor. Closure of the Berkeley (Gloucs) nuclear power station began in 1989. In 1994 the Government gave the go-ahead for the controversial Thorp nuclear reprocessing plant at Sellafield. The Sizewell B PWR became Britain's latest (and possibly last) nuclear power station in February 1995. After the Government's 1995 Nuclear Review, the industry was substantially restructured in preparation for privatisation in July 1996. The future of nuclear power in Britain became more uncertain in December 1995 when plans to build two new nuclear reactors, Sizewell C in Suffolk and Hinkley C in Somerset, were abandoned. Under a 15-nation agreement in 1998, eight old Magnox stations will have to be closed and discharges from Sellafield massively reduced by 2020. The troubled Dounreay plant is also to be closed.

Nuclear Reactors are pieces of apparatus designed to permit nuclear chain reactions to occur under controlled conditions. (Uncontrolled chain reactions are dangerous, *e.g.* atomic bombs.) The success of a reactor depends on the neutrons reaching the U^{235} nuclei to produce more fissions and not being wasted in irrelevant processes or simply escaping through the wall of the apparatus (neutrons are quite difficult to contain). The neutrons leaving the scene of fission are rapidly moving, and they stand more chance of causing another fission if they are slowed down. Consequently a material other than the uranium has to be present to facilitate this, and it is called a moderator. A useful moderator is pure graphite. Thus a reactor may consist of alternate blocks of uranium and graphite. If the reactor is too small so many neutrons escape that there are not enough to keep the chain reaction going. The reactor must therefore be greater than a certain *critical size*. In order to intensify or damp down the chain reaction it is arranged for pieces of neutron-absorbing material, such as cadmium, to be inserted or withdrawn as required. While the chain re-action is proceeding countless numbers of fissions are occurring, each one liberating energy which turns into heat. The temperature therefore increases, and to prevent a catastrophic rise, cooling has to be provided. The reactor therefore has cooling pipes through which a fluid coolant is pumped. The coolant carries the heat away and, in a reactor designed to produce electrical power, the heat is taken to steam-raising boilers and the high-pressure steam is led to turbines which drive the electric generators.

What has been briefly described is the type of reactor first used for serious power production at Calder Hall (1956). This was a graphite-moderated, gas-cooled reactor using as fuel natural uranium (*i.e.*, fissile U^{235} greatly diluted with U^{238}). Other thermal types of nuclear reactor are the advanced gas-cooled reactor (AGR), the high temperature reactor (HTR), the steam-generating heavy-water (SGHWR) and the light-water reactor (LWR). It is also possible to make reactors work without slowing the neutrons with a moderator; these are called *fast reactors*. The design of the prototype fast reactor (PFR) at Dounreay was based on experience gained with the Dounreay experimental fast breeder reactor (closed 1977 after 17 years' safe operation) which was the first to produce electricity on a commercial scale (1962) and achieved the highest power output of any of its type in the world. These fast reactors can produce new nuclear fuel in the course of their operation and therefore offer great economies; but they are more difficult to develop than thermal reactors. The fuel is made from the mixed oxides of plutonium and uranium and the coolant is liquid sodium metal.

Environmental considerations have become of increasing concern. Most of the products of the fission process are of necessity radioactive isotopes: they could be gaseous, like krypton, xenon and tritium or solid like strontium, caesium, zirconium and ruthenium. There are also present the new radioactive elements plutonium, curium, actinium, etc. Further, in both the nuclear reactor and in the plant which is used to chemically treat and reprocess the nuclear fuel, radioactivity will be induced in associated structural materials, to varying degrees. In this latter case, unlike the former, the radioactive waste with which one is left can to a great extent be selected and is largely overshadowed in importance by the waste arising from the fission and breeding processes. Even if the whole of the UK electrical power was produced by nuclear means, the volumes of such wastes would be relatively small and need in principle tens of acres of storage area. Much of the activity would decay in a decade, a great deal more in a century, but that associated with the elements bred from uranium, would be present for thousands of years: Pu^{239} has a half-life of 25,000 years. Segregation of the various types of activity is feasible; their incorporation into physically and chemically stable form has received a great deal of study so that storage, readily monitored even for many generations, seems entirely possible. The radioactive properties of these wastes can only be changed by nuclear reactions. Bombardment with neutrons or other highly energetic particles can bring about such reactions so that forms of "nuclear incineration" are feasible but are not yet fully explored.

Nucleic Acids. Living matter is built up of cells each of which has a nucleus surrounded by cytoplasm. Cell nuclei are composed chiefly of substances called nucleoproteins, which consist of a protein attached to a nucleic acid (this original name is still used, although nucleic acids are found in the cytoplasm as well as the nucleus). Nucleic acids are complex organic structures made up of chains of compounds called nucleotides (**F32(2)**). Nucleotide molecules have a sugar group attached to a nitrogenous base and a phosphate group. Only two sugar groups are found in the nucleotides, ribose, giving rise to ribonucleic acids (RNAs, found mainly in the cytoplasm) and deoxyribose, which forms deoxyribonucleic acids (DNAs, found mainly in cell nuclei). Seven different nitrogenous bases have been isolated, so that a number of different nucleotides are possible. A repeating, regular pattern of nucleotides is linked by the phosphate groups, forming nucleic acids. The functions of nucleic acids are of fundamental importance. They are concerned in the process of transmission of inherited qualities in reproduction and in building up body proteins.

Nuremberg Trial. On 21 November 1945, an International Military Tribunal, consisting of one American, one British, one Russian and one French member, began the trial of twenty-four Nazi leaders. Twelve were condemned to hanging of whom ten were hanged on 16 October 1946. Goering committed suicide; Bormann is now dead; Papen, Schacht and Fritsche were acquitted. The rest received terms of imprisonment.

Nuthatch, name of a number of tree-creeping birds, plump, with a short tail, bluish-grey plumage and black stripe under eye. Nest in holes and wedge nuts in bark of trees, hammering them to get a kernel. There are three European species, one, *Sitta europaea*, resident in England and now one of our most thriving birds.

Nylon, a generic term for any long-chain synthetic polymeric amide which has recurring amide groups as an integral part of the main polymer chain, and which is capable of being formed into a filament in which the structural elements are orientated in the direction of the axis. The first nylon of commercial interest was made in 1935, and the world's first nylon factory—in the United States—began production in 1940.

O

Oak, a tree of the genus *Quercus*, including some 300 species distributed over the northern hemisphere and into the tropics. Two species are native to Britain, where the oak is the commonest tree (1 in 3)—*Q. petraea*, more common in the west and north on shallower, lighter soils, and *Q. robur*, more common in the south on deeper, heavier soils. Oak timber is much prized for its strength and durability, and from the time of the Spanish Armada to Nelson's day was in great demand for naval construction. It has always been used for building, flooring, furniture and cabinet work. The oak is attacked by many insects, the round nut-like oak galls, or oak-apples, being produced by the sting of certain minute gall wasps.

"Oaks", a famous race for three-year-old fillies run at Epsom three days after the "Derby".

Obelisk, a tapering monolithic column, square at the base and pyramidal at the top, regarded by the ancient Egyptians as a sacred stone and usually found at the entrance to the sun temples. Many were transported from Egypt and set up at various times: there is one in the Place de la Concorde in Paris, and one on the Embankment in London—Cleopatra's Needle—originally erected at Heliopolis, centre of the sun-cult, by Tuthmosis III *c.* 1500 B.C.

Observatories. *See* **Astronomy** *and* **Telescope**.

Occam's Razor. *See* **Section J.**

Occultation, the passage of one celestial object in front of another, where the closer object has a larger apparent diameter than the more distant one and which, therefore, temporarily hides it from view. An example is the passage of the Moon across the Sun during a total solar eclipse.

Ocean, comprises the great body of water which covers seven-tenths of the surface of the earth, and has an average depth of 3·2 km. The principal oceans are the Pacific, Atlantic, Indian and Arctic. The greatest ocean depth is in the Pacific, in the Mindanao Deep, 37,782 ft (11,524 m).

Ocean Currents are well-defined streams running over certain portions of the ocean and caused mainly by wind-friction, slope of the sea surface and differences in density of the water, all movements being influenced by the deflective forces due to the earth's rotation. The climatic importance of the great ocean currents is that they constitute one means whereby heat is transferred from lower to higher latitudes.

Oceanography is the scientific study of the world ocean, *i.e.*, the single connected body of water that covers 70·8 per cent of the earth's surface. Modern oceanography dates from the voyage of HMS *Challenger* (1872–6) during which wide-ranging observations of the ocean were made, for the first time going well beyond what was directly required to assist shipping. Since then oceanography has matured into a highly technical and interdisciplinary science which may be roughly divided into: biological oceanography (the study of marine organisms and marine ecology); chemical oceanography (concerned with the composition of sea-water); physical oceanography (the study of ocean currents, tides and waves and the role played by the oceans in climate and weather); and geological oceanography (concerned with the formation, composition and evolution of the ocean basins).

Ocelot, the most common wild cat of S. America. It is about 1·2 m in length, including tail, and of a grey or tawny colour and spotted. Closely related to the Leopard cats.

Octane Number, the index of the knock-rating of petrol. It is based on the arbitrary scale in which iso-octane (which does not cause "knocking") has a value of 100, and normal heptane (which is prone to "knocking") has a value of 0. A good fuel for modern cars must have an octane number greater than 80.

Octarch, the kings of the English heptarchy, Hengist (455) being the first, Egbert (800) the last.

October, the 10th month, but the 8th in the old Roman calendar. It was held sacred to Mars.

Octopus, a genus of marine molluscs with eight tentacles that bear suckers.

Odin, the chief god of Scandinavian mythology.

Odyssey, Homer's epic setting forth the incidents of the wanderings of Odysseus on his way back to Ithaca after the siege of Troy.

Oersted, a unit of magnetic-field intensity in the c.g.s. system.

Offa's Dyke, largest remaining earthwork in Britain, supposed to have been built by Offa (A.D. 757–96) as a defensive boundary line between the English settlers and the dispossessed Welsh of Gwynedd, Powys and Gwent.

Office for National Statistics, formed in April 1996 by a merger of the Central Statistical Office and the Office of Population, Censuses and Surveys.

Ohm's Law, propounded by G. S. Ohm in 1826, is expressed in the equation: electromotive force (in volts) = current (in amperes) × resistance (in ohms). The ohm is the unit of electrical resistance in the metre-kilogram-second system.

Oil. The great expansion in energy demand over recent years has been met to a large extent by petroleum oil. This contains a wide range of hydrocarbon molecules of varying complexity. The various components are separated from each other by making use of their different boiling points. Crude oil is heated in the base of a fractionating tower; the various components condense at different temperatures in trays at different levels of the tower. The fraction of a given composition can be increased by "cracking" or breaking down the heavier hydrocarbons into lighter ones. The total world reserves of petroleum oil are still uncertain since large parts of the world are still not fully prospected. The cutback and the rise in the price of Middle Eastern oil following the 1973 Arab-Israeli war has now been succeeded by a glut of oil and falling prices. In 1997, British offshore oil production was 115·1m tonnes, down from 116·5m the previous year. Development started in 1996 of oil production in the Atlantic (there are huge reserves in the Foinaven field west of the Shetland Islands). This area is known as the "new North Sea". The first British North Sea field (the Argyll) dried up in 1992 having produced 97m barrels. Britain's largest on-shore oilfield is at Wytch Farm (Dorset). Major new oilfields were discovered in the early 1990s in Azerbaijan, Colombia and Mexico.

Okapi, nocturnal ruminant mammal, smaller than the giraffe, chestnut brown in colour with zebra-striped legs, native to the African Congo.

Olbers' Comet was discovered in 1815 by Olbers the German astronomer. Olbers also discovered the asteroids Pallas and Vesta (1802–07).

Old Red Sandstone, the continental rocks formed during the Devonian period. *See* **F48.**

Olefines, a series of hydrocarbons, in which the hydrogen atoms are double the number of carbon. The first member of the series is ethylene.

Oléron Laws *or* **Judgments**, were a code of maritime laws, introduced into England in the reign of Richard I in the 12th cent. Oléron is an island off the west coast of France, opposite the mouth of the Charente.

Olive. This small tree, whose fruit yields olive oil, is a native of the eastern Mediterranean countries, but has been introduced into cultivation elsewhere. The green unripe fruit is pickled in brine for table olives.

Olympiads were periods of four years which elapsed between each celebration of the Olympic games, held at Olympia in honour of Zeus. These festivals included competitions in literature, art, drama, rhetoric, music and gymnastics, and they were continued, with intervals, from 776 B.C. to A.D. 394. Modern Olympics have taken place at Athens 1896, Paris 1900, St. Louis 1904, London 1908, Stockholm 1912, Antwerp 1920, Paris 1924, Amsterdam 1928, Los Angeles 1932, Berlin 1936, London 1948, Helsinki 1952, Melbourne 1956, Rome 1960, Tokyo 1964, Mexico City 1968, Munich 1972, Montreal 1976, Moscow 1980, Los Angeles 1984, Seoul 1988, Barcelona in 1992, and Atlanta, Georgia, 1996 (the Centennial Olympics). The first Winter Olympics were held at Chamonix in 1924. The last were in 1998 at Nagano in Japan. The next will be at Salt Lake City in 2002. Sydney is host to the 2000 (Millennium) Olympics. The 2004 Olympics are to be held in Athens. London is planning a bid to host the 2008 Olympics.

Ombudsman. *See* **Section D.**

Onomasticians are scientists who study the fascinating subject of names—names of places and names of people—to find out their origins. They tell us, for example, that Cambridge is an Anglo-Norman corruption of *Grantabrycg* =bridge over the Granta; that Harrow-on-the-Hill was an early Anglo-Saxon settlement—"heathen temple on the hill"; that we owe the ridings of Yorkshire to the Vikings (Old Norse *thrithungr* = third part); that in Scotland *-ton* and *-toun* indicate not a town but a hamlet or village. Onomasticians are also concerned with international standardisation of place names.

Onyx *or* **Sardonyx**, a variety of chalcedony built up of different-coloured layers, which are parallel and straight (not curved as in agate).

Oolite, a geological term for the Jurassic oolitic limestones existing through a long stretch of country extending from Yorkshire to Dorset. It abounds in fossils of molluscs and reptiles.

The term "oolite" derives from the fact that these rocks are made of egg-shaped particles of calcium carbonate.

Opal, a mineral consisting of hydrous silica, occurring in numerous varieties and colours. Opals have been prized as gems since at least 400 B.C. but the secret of their unique internal "fire" or opalescence has only recently been learned. It is a result of the diffraction of light by a regular array of tiny silica spheres, about 100 nm in diameter, of which gem opals are now known to be composed. Opal miners are called gougers. Chief source—the Andanooka and Coober Pedy fields of South Australia.

Opium was known to the ancients, and used by them as a medicine. It is obtained from the poppy (*Papaver somniferum*), the unripe "head" or seed capsule of that flower yielding a juice which when dried becomes the opium of commerce. The poppy is cultivated in India, Iran, Turkey, Afghanistan and China for the sake of this juice, which yields various alkaloids, such as morphine, narcotine, codeine, *etc.* These days the drug is rarely used medicinally.

Opossum, marsupial mammals found in the more southerly of the United States, South America and Australasia. They are arboreal except for the water-opossum, which eats fish.

Optics, the branch of physics which investigates the nature and properties of light and the phenomena of colour. Burning lenses were known to the ancient Greeks and Ptolemy wrote a treatise on optics A.D. 150. Lenses as visual aids were known in ancient China but eyeglasses were not in use until the 13th cent. Spectacles were in more general use after the invention of printing in the 15th cent. The camera obscura was invented in the 16th cent. and the telescope and microscope early in the 17th cent.

Oracles were in ancient times supposed to be words spoken by the gods, and it was the custom on important occasions to consult them about the future. The Greeks had the Oracles of Zeus at Dodona, and Apollo at Delphi, while the Romans consulted the Oracles of Mars, Fortune and others.

Orange, a fruit growing in most sub-tropical climates and in universal demand. It is grown on an evergreen tree that attains a height of about 6 m at maturity.

Orang-utan, one of the largest of the anthropoid apes, found only in the swampy forests of Borneo and Sumatra. When full-grown it stands over 1·2 m in height and weighs *c.* 67 kg. Fruit is the mainstay of their diet. The male may live up to 45 years. Many have perished in the forest fires which raged after 1997.

Orbit, is the path of one celestial object around another. For example, the path of the Earth around the Sun. Also applied to the path of an artificial satellite around the Earth.

Orchestra, a group of instruments and instrumentalists whose playing is under the direction of a conductor. The composition of a typical symphony orchestra is as follows: STRINGS: 1st Violin (16), 2nd Violin (16), Viola (12), Violoncello (12), Double Bass (8). WOODWIND: Flute (3–4), Piccolo (1), Oboe (3), Cor Anglais (1), Bass Oboe (1), Clarinet (3), Bass Clarinet (1), Bassoon (3), Contra-bassoon (1). BRASS: Horn (6), Trumpet (5), Trombone (3–4), Tuba (2). PERCUSSION: Timpani (3–6), Side Drum (1), Bass Drum (1), Cymbals (1), Harp (2).

Order of Merit. *See* Merit, Order of.

Orders in Council are issued by the sovereign on the advice of a few selected members of the Privy Council. They must not seriously alter the law of the land. Another class of Orders in Council are issued by authority of an Act of Parliament for the carrying out of its provisions.

Ordination, the ceremony of installing ministers or clergymen in clerical offices, has existed from the earliest times. In the Anglican and Roman Catholic Churches the rites of Ordination are performed by bishops; among Nonconformists it is done by the governing bodies. The first women were ordained Anglican priests in Bristol Cathedral in March 1994. The Church in Wales ordained its first woman in January 1997. The Catholic Church does not admit women priests.

Organ is a musical wind instrument of ancient origin whose tones are produced by the vibra-

tions of air in pipes of varying length. Basically, an organ consists of a number of pipes grouped in rows or ranks according to their special tone-character. The air is fed by bellows or, in modern organs, by a rotary fan electrically driven. Each rank is controlled by a slider, and the knob that controls the slider is called a stop. The organist pulls out the stops to give the tones he wants, the other pipes being kept out of action by the slider. When a particular note on the keyboard is depressed the player may hear, by pulling out the appropriate stop, not only the normal pitch but the note in several octaves. A stop of which the notes are of normal pitch is called an 8-foot stop, a 16-foot stop would give an octave lower, a 4-foot stop an octave higher and a 2-foot stop two octaves higher. The hand keyboard is called a manual, and the foot keyboard the pedal board. The basic tone of an organ is its diapason tone, and is normally of 8-foot length and pitch. Most large organs have four manual keyboards and one pedal board. The most important manual is the great organ which comprises the majority of basic stops. The next in importance is the swell organ, so called because the pipes are enclosed in a box fitted with movable shutters operated by a swell-pedal. The effect provides a controlled crescendo or diminuendo. The tone of a typical English swell has a reedy character. The third manual controls the choir organ—a collection of stops suitable for vocal accompaniment. The fourth manual controls the solo organ—a group of stops which, singly or in combination, may provide a solo melody which the remainder of the organ accompanies. The pedal keyboard controls most of the bass stops. In some very large organs there is a fifth manual controlling the echo organ. This is a small group of stops usually set high in the roof of the building to give the effect of distant music. Most church organs have two or three manuals. Digital organs were introduced in the 1970s.

Organic Chemistry. *See* F23.

Organic Farming, means the production of food or other farm produce without artificial fertilisers or chemical pesticides.

Oriel Window is a window projected from the front of a building, rectangular, triangular, or pentagonal. The ordinary bay window and bow window are varieties of Oriel. When an Oriel window does not reach to the ground it usually rests upon moulded sills supported by corbels.

Oriflamme, the name of the original banner of the abbey of St. Denis, and adopted by Louis VI as his standard. It remained the national emblem of France for three centuries. The flag was of red silk, the outer edge being cut in the form of flames.

Original Sin, according to Christian doctrine the corruption that is born with us, as a result of Adam's fall.

Orimulsion, an emulsified bitumen fuel which comes from Venezuela.

Orioles, brilliantly coloured birds, members of the passerine family *Oriolidae,* found in the tropical regions of Asia, Africa and Australia. The golden oriole, perhaps the most beautiful of them all, with brilliant yellow plumage, black wings and tail, winters in Africa, visits England and is known to have nested here.

Orion, a famous constellation of the heavens, comprising nearly a hundred stars, all visible to the naked eye. It contains three stars of the second magnitude in a line, and these are called "Orion's Belt".

Ormer, a shellfish (*Haliotis tuberculata*) which occurs in the Channel Islands and on parts of the French coast. It is a great delicacy.

Ornithology, the scientific study of birds.

Ornithorhynchus. *See* Duckbill.

Orogeny, large-scale earth movements, including faulting and folding and sometimes igneous activity, which produce a linear belt of mountains, *e.g.,* the Alpine orogeny in Europe which produced the Alps.

Orphism. *See* Section J.

Orphrey, the name of an ornamental strip richly embroidered on ecclesiastical vestments.

Orrery, an instrument used in the 18th and early 19th cent. which showed the motions of the planets round the sun and the satellites round their primaries. The first orrery made was named after Charles Boyle, Earl of Orrery.

Orthodox Eastern Church. *See* **Section J.**

Osborne House, near Cowes, in the Isle of Wight. Queen Victoria's favourite winter-residence, and where she died.

Osier, a species of willow growing in damp soils and yielding branches utilised in basket-making.

Osmium, a very hard, bluish-white metallic element, no. 76, symbol Os, of the platinum group and one of the heaviest of known metals. It is obtained from certain sands of S. America, California, Australia and Russia. The alloy of osmium and iridium (osmiridium) provides tips for gold fountain-pen nibs. Discovered by Tennant in 1803.

Osmosis, the process by which absorption of liquids through semi-permeable membranes takes place. A solution exerts osmotic pressure (O.P.) or suction in proportion to concentration but also depending on kind of dissolved substance. The roots of the higher plants are covered with fine root-hairs, within the cell-walls of which the sap is normally of a higher concentration than the dissolved matter in the surrounding soil. The root-hairs, therefore, draw into themselves these weaker salt-solutions. (The explanation of water and salt exchanges is complicated by the selective ability of some cells (*e.g.*, roots) to accept or reject particular dissolved substances along with the water. The absorption of salts by a plant is selective, each plant selecting through the semi-permeable membranes of its root-hairs those substances which are most suited to it.)

Osprey (*Pandion haliaëtus*), a large and magnificent bird of prey, dark brown above and nearly white below. The head is whitish with a dark band from eye to nape. To the British Isles it is a rare passage migrant. In 1955, thanks to the energy of the Royal Society for the Protection of Birds, a pair nested in a Scots pine in Inverness-shire and reared three young. Since then more young ospreys have been safely fledged. The food consists almost entirely of fish, which the bird seizes with its talons. The so-called osprey plumes in fact come from the egret.

Ostrich, the largest living bird, related to the rhea, emu and extinct moa, now found only on the sandy plains of Africa and parts of S.W. Asia. The male has beautiful white plumes on wings and tail. The wings are useless in flight, but the birds have a speed exceeding that of the swiftest horse. An ostrich's egg weighs 1·3 kg.

Otary, any seal which has external ears (as opposed to the *true seals* which lack them). The eared seals make up the family *Otariidae*, which includes the Sea-lion and the Fur-seal.

Otter, an aquatic carnivorous mammal widely distributed over Europe, and until the 1950s very common in England and Wales. The otter averages about 60 cm in length, exclusive of tail, has web-feet and is a very expert swimmer. Otters are harmless and their hunting is a cruel and senseless blood sport. Having almost disappeared by 1980, the otter is now protected by the 1981 Wildlife and Countryside Act. In 1995 the otter was officially declared "saved" in England and Wales. The Otter Trust is based at Earsham near Bungay, Suffolk. Otters have the densest fur in the animal world.

Ounce or **Snow Leopard,** a very beautiful pale spotted cat from the Himalayas the size of a labrador retriever but with a long furry tail.

Outcrop. Where a bed of rock appears at the surface of the ground, there is an outcrop of the particular rock. The mining of outcrop coal is called open-cast mining.

Oviparous, a term referring to animals which lay eggs to be hatched outside the body of the parent.

Ovipositor, the organ by means of which female insects lay their eggs.

Owls, nocturnal birds of prey, distributed over the greater part of the world. Their forward-looking eyes, embedded in rings of feathers, give them a characteristic "owl-like" appearance, and their plumage, usually a mottled blend of browns and greys, is so soft that their flight is almost noiseless. Owls live on small mammals, reptiles, birds, insects and fish, and are very valuable birds to the farmer. British owls include the barn owl (screech owl), short-eared owl, long-eared owl, tawny owl and little owl. The decline in barn owl numbers is now (1999) reported to have been halted.

Ox, the popular name of the mammals included in the genus *Bos*. They are hollow-horned ruminants and hoofed quadrupeds, and include the various classes of domestic cattle as well as the different wild species. The adult male is called a bull, the female a cow and the young a calf. The best-known breeds of domesticated cattle are the Durham or Shorthorn, the Angus, the Jersey, Ayrshire, Suffolk and Hereford.

Oxalic Acid, an organic acid obtained from numerous plants, such as sorrel and rhubarb, and produced artificially for commercial purposes from sawdust, treated with caustic potash or caustic soda. It combines with metals to form oxalates; used in the manufacture of ink.

Oxford Clay, a geological formation consisting of a bed of blue clay *c.* 200 m thick, and forming the lower portion of the Upper Jurassic. It makes good bricks.

Oxford Movement. *See* **Tractarianism, Section J.**

Oxford University. The early history of the university is obscure. There was a school at Oxford as early as 1115 and it is known that Robert Pullen, a theologian from Paris, lectured there in 1133. Allusions to Oxford as the most celebrated centre of learning in England occurred in a work of Gerald of Wales in 1184–5. The earliest colleges to be founded were University College (1249), Balliol (about 1263), Merton (1264). In 1571 the university was reorganised and granted a Charter of Incorporation by an Act of Elizabeth. Other colleges and halls with their dates of foundation incude: All Souls (1438), Brasenose (1509), Christ Church (1546), Corpus Christi (1517), Exeter (1314), Hertford (1874), Jesus (1571), Keble (1868), Linacre (1962), Lincoln (1427), Magdalen (1458), New College (1379), Nuffield (1937), Oriel (1326), Pembroke (1624), Queen's (1340), St. Anthony's (1950), St. Catherine's (1962), St. Cross (1965), St. Edmund Hall (1270), St. John's (1555), St. Peter's (1929), Trinity (1554), Wadham (1612), Wolfson (1965), Worcester (1714), Campion Hall (1962), St. Benet's Hall (1964), Mansfield (1886), Regent's Park (1958), Greyfriar's Hall (1953), Harris Manchester College (1990) and Kellogg College (1990, formerly Rewley House). The most recent foundation is the postgraduate Green College. The original women's colleges were:— Lady Margaret Hall (1878), Somerville (1879), St. Hugh's (1886), St. Hilda's (1893) and St. Anne's (1952). Women were not admitted to degrees (though allowed to sit for examination) till 1920. The last college only to admit women is St Hilda's. Construction of a new Oxford American Institute began in 1998.

Oxygen is the most abundant of all terrestrial elements, no. 8, symbol O. In combination, this gaseous element forms about 46% of the earth's crust; one-fifth of the atmosphere; eight-ninths by weight of all water. Discovered independently by Scheele (*c.* 1773) and Priestley (1774). It is colourless, tasteless and odourless, and forms the chief life-supporting element of our world.

Oyster, a bivalve mollusc, of the genus *Ostrea*, having very numerous species and abounding in nearly all seas. The shell is rough and irregular. Oysters are exceedingly prolific, spawning in May and June. In England and Scotland deep-sea oysters are not allowed to be sold between 15 June and 4 August, and other kinds between 14 May and 4 August. In Ireland, no oysters may be taken between 1 May and 1 September, except in certain waters. The Whitstable oyster beds have existed since pre-Roman times.

Oystercatcher, a wading bird with black and white plumage and long, orange bill, inhabiting estuaries and sea-shores. Feeds on mussels, shell fish, *etc.*, but not oysters.

Ozone, a modified form of oxygen, containing three atoms of oxygen per molecule instead of two. It is prepared by passing oxygen through a silent electric discharge. When present in air to the extent of 1 part in 4 million parts of air it kills bacteria, and has been used for this purpose in ventilating systems, *e.g.*, that of underground railways. It is present in extremely small quantities in the lower atmosphere (*q.v.*) but is comparatively plentiful at heights between 12 and 50 km. As ozone absorbs ultraviolet light of certain wavelengths spectroscopic methods, involving the analysis of sunlight, are chiefly used in ozone determination.

P

Paca, a genus of large rodents found in Central and South America, and resembling the guinea-pig. It is of nocturnal habits, has streaked and spotted fur and lives on fruits and plants.

Pacific Ocean. The first European to recognise the Pacific as distinct from the Atlantic was the Spanish explorer, Vasco Nunlt]ez de Balboa, who discovered its eastern shore from a peak in Panama in 1513. The first European to sail upon it was Magellan, who entered it by the strait that bears his name in 1520. Sir Francis Drake was the first Englishman to sail upon it in 1577. The world's greatest known ocean depth is in the Mindanao Trench, off the Philippines, 37,782 ft (11,524 m).

Pagan, a person who does not worship God; a heathen. The word is derived from the Latin *paganus* (a countryman or uncultivated person). In the Middle Ages the term was used largely to describe Muslims (Moors, Saracens, *etc.*). See **Paganism, Section J.**

Pagoda, the name given in China, India *etc.* to a high pyramidal tower, usually, but not necessarily, connected with a temple.

Pahlevi, family name of the last Shahs of Iran.

Palaeontology, the science which is devoted to the investigation of fossils: animal (palaeozoology) and plants (palaeobotany). By studying the markings and fossils of living things in the stratified rocks, palaeontologists have been able to establish with astonishing accuracy a record of the evolution of life through geological time. The geologist at the same time with the evidence of the fossils has been able to work out the order and the age of the rocks. *See also* **Section F.**

Palatinate, a term formerly applied to two German regions, historically related, the Upper and Lower Palatinates. Now provinces of Bavaria.

Pale, the name given to the part of Ireland colonised by the English and comprising portions of the counties of Louth, Dublin, Meath and Kildare. The Anglo-Norman rulers were styled "Lords of the Pale".

Palimpsests are ancient MSS. or parchments which have been partly effaced and used for fresh writings. Many valuable MSS. were thus lost, but sometimes the second writing has been washed out, enabling the original writings to be deciphered. Among such restorations are a dialogue of Cicero's, a part of a book of Livy.

Palladium, a scarce metallic element, no. 46, symbol Pd, similar to platinum, with which it is usually found. It is an expensive metal, with desirable properties as a catalyst in reactions involving hydrogen, since it has a remarkable capacity for absorbing this gas; for example, coal gas and air will inflame in the presence of palladium at room temperature. It forms a silver-white alloy with gold, and this is used in some kinds of jewellery. It is used in expensive watches to make non-magnetic springs.

Pallium, a vestmental ornamentation of white wool presented by the Pope to archbishops on their appointment.

Palm, a large straight-trunked plant or tree common to tropical countries, and usually fruit yielding, such as dates, coconuts, *etc.* Many commodities useful to man are obtained from plants of the Palm family (*Palmaceae*).

Palm Sunday, the Sunday before Easter, upon which occasion it is customary to carry palms to the churches in some countries, in commemoration of Christ's entry into Jerusalem for the Feast of the Passover, when the people went forth to greet Him with palm branches.

Panama Canal. In 1903 the United States signed a treaty with Panama (which had previously seceded from Columbia) which gave the United States rights in perpetuity over a 16 km-wide strip of land extending across the isthmus for the purposes of building and running the canal. The canal connects the Atlantic and Pacific Oceans, is just over 80 kilometres long (with sea approaches) and the depth varies from 12 to 26 m. It is constructed above sea-level, with locks, and has been available for commercial shipping since 3 August 1914. Agreement was reached in 1978 for the waterway to be turned over to Panama by the year 2000.

Panda, *or* **Cat-Bear,** is related to the Raccoon. There are two kinds, the Red or True Panda, resembling a large domestic cat, which lives in the eastern Himalayas and S.W. China, and the Giant Panda, which is more like a bear in appearance and inhabits the mountains of western China. Both frequent the dense bamboo forests of those regions. Now (1999) only about 1,000 giant pandas survive in the wild in China and their natural habitat (bamboo groves) is being whittled away by man.

Pangolin, the scientific name of the "scaly ant-eater", a toothless mammal, found in W. Africa and S.E. Asia. It has a long extensible tongue which it uses in catching ants and termites, its chief food. When attacked the pangolin rolls itself into a ball, and its scales assume the form of sharp spikes. Pangolins have an Order of their own—the Pholidota, the scale-bearers.

Pantagruel, the leading character in one of the satires of Rabelais.

Pantheon, the famous temple in Rome, originally consecrated to the gods, built by Agrippa in 27 B.C. and rebuilt in the 2nd cent. by Hadrian. Its splendid dome and portico make it one of the most interesting architectural monuments of ancient days. Since the 7th cent. it has been used as a Christian church.

Panther, another name for the leopard, *Panthera pardus*, related to the lion, carnivorous, active climber, found in India, and other parts of Asia, also in Africa.

Papal Infallibility. *See* **Section J.**

Paper has been known in one form or another from very early times. The papyrus reeds of the Nile swamps served the ancient Egyptians for sheets upon which to inscribe their records. The Chinese and Japanese, centuries later, were using something more akin to modern paper in substance, an Asiatic paper-mulberry, yielding a smooth fibrous material, being utilised. With the spread of learning in Western Europe the necessity of a readier medium made itself felt and paper began to be manufactured from pulped rags and other substances. The first known English paper-mill was Sele mill near Stevenage, built about 1490, which produced the paper for an edition of Chaucer in 1498. Other mills were set up under Elizabeth, using linen and cotton as raw material. Other papermaking staples were later introduced, such as surat, esparto grass and wood-pulp. The chief raw material in the world paper industry is wood-pulp, the main exporters being the timber-growing countries of Canada, Sweden and Finland. Canada is the world's chief producer of newsprint.

Papyrus, the earliest known paper made in Egypt at a very remote period from a large species of reed, *Cyperus papyrus*. This plant is to be found all over tropical Africa, especially in the "sudd" region of the White Nile.

Parachute, the umbrella-shaped safety device used in emergency by the crew and passengers of aircraft. The first parachute descent from a great height was made in 1797 by André Garnerin who dropped 915 m from a balloon. Rate of descent for a parachute jump is *c.* 5 m/s.

Paraclete (the Holy Ghost, or Comforter), the name used in the English translations of St. John's Gospel, and adopted by Abelard to designate the convent in Champagne founded by him, of which Héloïse became the abbess.

Paradise, a Persian word used by the translators of the Old Testament to designate the Garden of Eden, and since meaning any place of happiness.

Paraffin, a mixture of hydrocarbons of higher boiling point than petrol. Paraffin was first obtained by distillation of coal, the process being discovered about 1830. About 1848, James Young procured it from mineral oil, and Irish peat also yielded it. The main source of paraffin supply today is crude petroleum. Used in the manufacture of candles, for waterproofing and numerous other purposes.

Parakeets, various small parrots of vivid plumage native to Australia, Polynesia, Asia and Africa. One of the loveliest of the parakeets is the budgerigar of Australia.

Parallax, the change in direction of a body caused by a change in position of the observer. If the parallax is measured (in degrees of angle) and the distance between the two observation points is known the distance of the observed body can be calculated. The distance of heavenly bodies has been found this way. The first stellar distances were so obtained in 1838 by Henderson, Struve and Bessel. Stellar distances are so great that even when the two observations are made at opposite points of the earth's orbit round the sun, the parallax is always less than 1·0″ of arc. *See* **Aberration.**

Parameter, a number which is fixed for the application of a theory to one particular situation but may be different for other situations. For example, in a theory of motion near the surface of a planet the acceleration due to gravity may be regarded as a parameter constant for a particular planet but differing from planet to planet. The word is often used in a similar way in discussions of economic affairs.

Parapsychology. *See* **Section J.**

Parchment, made chiefly from the skins of animals, usually of goats and sheep, was employed in olden times before printing was invented and superseded papyrus as writing material. Vegetable parchment, invented by W. E. Gaine in 1853, though not equal in strength and durability to skin parchment, is about five times stronger than ordinary paper. Vellum is parchment made from the skins of young calves or lambs.

Parliament, is the name given to the supreme legislature of the United Kingdom. It consists of the Queen, the Lords spiritual and temporal and the Commons. It meets in two houses: the House of Lords (the Upper or Second Chamber) and the House of Commons. It derives from the Anglo-Saxon *Witans* (*see* **Witan**). The Statute of Westminster (1275) first uses "parlement" of the Great Council in England. *See* **Section D.**

Parliamentary Correspondents sit in the Press Gallery of the House of Commons and describe its proceedings for the news media.

Parquetry, the name of a style of flooring consisting of small rectangular wooden blocks laid down according to geometrical pattern.

Parrot, the popular name of a widely distributed family of tropical birds, including the African grey parrot, the green parrot of South America —both familiar cage pets in this country—and the various parakeets, cockatoos, macaws, lories, *etc.* Many of these birds possess a remarkable gift of imitating sound, especially human voices.

Parsec, modern unit of astronomical distance, the distance at which the diameter of the earth's orbit subtends an angle of 1 arc second. 1 parsec (pc) = $3·0857 \times 10^{13}$ km.

Parthenogenesis. The development of animals from unfertilised eggs. The drones of the honey bee are parthenogenetic, and the phenomenon is also common among aphids.

Parthenon, the famous Temple of Athena on the Acropolis at Athens, was built under the rule of Pericles between 447 B.C. and 432 B.C. It was made wholly of marble without mortar. The famous sculptured friezes, known as the Elgin Marbles, are now in the British Museum.

Particulates, microscopic specks of acids and chemicals in the atmosphere. When inhaled into the lungs they can cause serious health problems (*e.g.* asthma and lung cancer).

Partridge, a well-known British game-bird. Close time: 2 February to 31 August. Two species are common in Britain.

Passport is an official document issued to a person by his own government, certifying to his citizenship and permitting him to travel abroad. Passports to British subjects issued by the United Kingdom Passport Agency (an Executive Agency of the Home Office) authorise bearer to leave the country and guarantee him the state's protection. Passports now (1999) cost £21—and are issued for a period of 10 years. Children over 16 already require separate passports. Family passports are to be abolished from October 1998 and children will then need their own passports. For those making frequent visits abroad a 94-page passport was first issued in 1973, which costs £31 (1999). From July 1988, British citizens began using a common wine-coloured EU passport. Existing blue passports will remain valid until they expire. They will disappear entirely after 31 December 1999. The old one-year British visitor's passport and the British Excursion Document (used by short-stay visitors to France) were abolished from early 1996. To facilitate obtaining a 10-year passport, an application can now be handed in at any post office, for an additional charge of £3·20. Reform of the quarantine laws led in 1998 to proposals for 'pet passports' with animals fitted with electronic tagging devices.

Patricians, the aristocracy of ancient Rome.

Paul's Cathedral, St., is the third cathedral church to be built on the site. It was preceded by a Norman building which was practically destroyed by the Great Fire in 1666. This followed a Saxon church which was burnt in 1086. The present building was designed by Sir Christopher Wren. The foundation stone was laid in 1675 and the structure was completed in 1710. It cost a little under £748,000. Its central feature is the dome, crowned by its cupola and lantern with the golden ball and cross. It escaped serious damage during the air raids of the blitz.

*p***C Value,** introduced by Dr. C. L. Whittles in 1935 as a measure of salinity of aqueous solutions (soil extract, irrigation water, *etc.*); defined as the negative logarithm of specific electrical conductivity in reciprocal ohms. Alone or joined with *p***H** (*q.v.*) is useful as an index of osmotic pressure (*see* **Osmosis**) and related hindrance to plant growth resulting from excess of fertiliser or soil salts. If manuring is balanced, growth is best about *p***C** 3.3.

Peacock, a bird of large size and beautiful plumage, its characteristic feature being a tail of brilliant "eyed" feathers, which it can erect and spread out, the males possessing resplendent feathering to a much greater extent than the females. It is related to the pheasant; one species is found wild in the forests of India, and another inhabits Burma and the Malaysian regions. In Africa there is the Congo Peacock.

Peanut, Groundnut *or* **Monkey Nut.** A member of the pea family native to S. America, but now cultivated in many parts of the world. After pollination, the flower stalk bends down and buries the pod containing the peas ("nuts") in the ground. The oil from these "nuts" can be used for margarine manufacture.

Pearl is produced by certain shelled molluscs, chiefly the oyster. The inner surface of the shells of the pearl oyster yield "mother-ofpearl", and distinct pearls are believed to be morbid secretions, caused by some external irritation. Many fine pearls are found in the actual body of the oyster. The Persian Gulf, Sri Lanka, the north-west coast of Western Australia, many Pacific islands and the Gulf of Mexico are among the most productive pearlfishing grounds. In ancient times Britain was renowned for its pearl fisheries, the pearls being obtained from a species of freshwater mussel. Western Australia has produced a 40-grain pearl, the finest the world has seen. The largest pearl ever found was the "Beresford-Hope Pearl", which weighed 1,800 grains, over six times as much as the oyster that produced it.

Peat, decayed vegetable matter found mostly in marshy positions, and common in Ireland and Scotland. Peat is coal in its first stage of development; burnt for fuel in many cottages.

Peccary, a pig-like animal native to the Americas. There are two species: the collared peccary and the white-lipped peccary, the latter being a vicious and dangerous animal.

Pelican, a genus of bird with long depressed bill pouched underneath, thus able to hold fish in reserve. It has immense wings and webbed feet. There are eight species.

Pemmican, venison or other meat, sliced, dried, pounded and made into cakes, used by explorers and others when out of reach of fresh meat.

Penguin, a genus of flightless, fish-eating sea-birds of the southern hemisphere. They are stoutbodied, short-necked and of small, moderate or large size. The Emperor and King Penguins make no nest but protect and incubate the single egg by carrying it in the down feathers between the feet and the body. Other species brood in the usual way and may lay as many as three eggs. Penguins use their flippers for swimming under water. All 17 species are bluish-grey or blackish above and white below. They are very sociable and breed in colonies. They have more feathers than any other bird.

Penicillin. An antibiotic drug produced by the mould *Penicillium notatum*, and discovered by Sir Alexander Fleming in 1928. It is one of the most effective chemotherapeutic agents known. The mould produces a number of penicillins, all of which are effective antibiotics.

Peninsular War lasted from 1808 to 1814. Fought in Spain and Portugal (the Iberian peninsula) by the British, Spanish and Portuguese forces, chiefly under Wellington, against the French. The latter were defeated.

Pentagon, government office in Washington (the largest in the world), housing many thousands of military and civilian workers in the War Department of the United States.

Pentateuch. *See* S21.

Penumbra, the half shadow of the Earth or Moon during an eclipse. The term is also used to describe the lighter, outer part of a sunspot.

Pepys Diary, by Samuel Pepys, was first published in 1825. It gives a picture of the social life of the period 1 January 1660 to 31 May 1669. He bequeathed the manuscript, together with his library, to Magdalene College, Cambridge.

Perch, a well-known family of fresh-water fish, with dark striped sides. The common perch of British rivers and lakes falls an easy prey to the angler because of its voracity.

Peregrine. *See under* Falcon.

Perfumes are essences or odours obtained from floral and other substances. The chief flower perfumes are those obtained from rose, jasmine, orange flower, violet and acacia. Heliotrope perfume is largely obtained from vanilla and almonds. Among the aromatic herbs which yield attractive perfumes are the rosemary, thyme, geranium, lavender, *etc.*, while orange peel, citron peel, musk, sandalwood, patchouli and other vegetable products are largely drawn upon. Many of the popular perfumes of today are chemically prepared *See* **Musk Deer.**

Perigee, the closest point of the orbit of an object such as a satellite to the earth. The opposite of apogee (*q.v.*).

Perihelion. That point in a planet's orbit when it is nearest to the sun; opposite of aphelion. The earth is at perihelion (1.47×10^8 km) in mid-winter, about 3 January.

Peripatus, an animal which stands as a link between the annelid worms and the arthropods. Wormlike with short unjointed legs it breathes by a system of air tubes like those in insects. Certain other points of internal structure point to a relationship with annelid worms. There are some fifty species, the best known being the S. African *Peripatus capensis.*

Perjury, the offence of giving false evidence. The ancient Romans threw the perjurer from the Tarpeian Rock, and after the Empire was Christianised, those who swore falsely upon the Gospel had their tongues cut out. The usual punishment in England from the 16th to 19th cent. was the pillory, fine and imprisonment.

Permian Formation, a group of rocks lying between the Trias and the Carboniferous strata. It has three subdivisions, Upper, Middle and Lower Permian.

Per Procurationem signature means that the subject of the correspondence has been put into the writer's care by his principal for him to use his personal judgment in the matter, and that he is authorised to sign on behalf of his principal. Normally contracted to *per pro* or *p.p.*

Peruke, the name given to the wigs worn by men in the latter half of the 18th cent. The custom of wearing wigs was gradually superseded by powdering the natural hair. Wigs are still worn by the Speaker of the House of Commons, judges and barristers.

Petrel, the name given to a member of a large, widely-distributed family of sea-birds of great diversity of size and colouring and distinguished by tube-like external nostrils. They usually skim low over the waves, and some, for this reason, are known as shearwaters. The storm petrel or Mother Carey's chicken occasionally patters along the surface, and is often called Little Peter—a reference to St. Peter walking on the water. Except when breeding, petrels are always at sea. They mostly nest in holes and crevices on islands and lay one egg, which is invariably white. The storm petrel, Leach's

petrel, Manx shearwater and the fulmar petrel are resident in the British Isles. *See also* **Mutton Bird.**

Petroleum. *See* Oil.

Pewter, alloy of tin and lead formerly used for making household utensils and ornaments.

***pH* Value.** Introduced in 1909 by the Danish chemist Sørensen to indicate hydrogen-ion concentration on the basis of electrical conductivity and a view of ionisation since discarded; is now taken as a logarithmic scale of acidity or alkalinity of aqueous solutions: acidity 0–7, neutrality at 7·0, alkalinity 7–14. The *pH* of blood is about 7·6 (faintly alkaline).

Phalanger, pouched marsupial mammals. They are arboreal and superficially resemble squirrels. There are two genera of flying phalangers or flying squirrels, which have a remarkable membrane along each side of the body enabling the animals to glide through the air. The members of the phalanger family are confined to the Australasian and oriental regions.

Phalangid, a member of the arachnid family Phalangida: popularly known as "harvesters".

Phalanx, a name applied by the ancient Greeks to a body of pike-men drawn up in close array, with overlapping shields, and eight, ten or more rows deep. The Macedonians stood sixteen rows deep. As many as 500 men could be in the front row.

Pharisees and Sadducees, two ancient Jewish sects. *See* **Judaism, Section J.**

Pharmacopoeia, an official publication containing information on the recognised drugs used in medicine. Each country has its own pharmacopoeia. The British Pharmacopoeia (B.P.) is published under the direction of the General Medical Council. The Pharmaceutical Society issues the British Pharmaceutical Codex (B.P.C.); there is also an International Pharmacopoeia (2 vols.), issued by the World Health Organisation.

Pharos, the name of the first lighthouse, built by Ptolemy II about 280 B.C., on the Isle of Pharos, at the entrance to the harbour of Alexandria. It was said to be 180 m high but this is doubtful. One of the "seven wonders".

Pheasant, game birds related to the partridges, quails, peacocks, chickens and turkeys, males distinguished by their brilliant plumage and long tapering tail. First found by the Greeks in Georgia where the River Phasis flows through to the Black Sea. Close time: 2 February to 30 September.

Phillippics, the oration delivered by Demosthenes, 352–341 B.C., against Philip of Macedon—remarkable for their bitter invective. The word was also used for Cicero's speeches against Antony. In modern use, any impassioned invective.

Philosopher's Stone. *See* **Alchemy, Section J.**

Phosphorus is a non-metal element, no. 15, symbol P. Most familiar as a waxy, yellow solid which is spontaneously inflammable in air. It has chemical similarities to arsenic, like which it is very poisonous. It was discovered by Brandt in urine in 1669. It is found in most animal and vegetable tissues. It is an essential element of all plants and of the bones of animals. In combination with various metals it forms different phosphates, which are largely utilised as manures. The chief commercial use of phosphorus is in the preparation of matches.

Photoelectric Cell, a device which gives a useful electrical response to light falling on it. There are several kinds depending on the different effects which light may have on a suitably chosen solid (usually a semiconductor), viz., the emission of electrons from the surface ("photoemissive cell"); change in electrical resistance ("photoconducting cell"); generation of electric current from a specially designed sensitive structure ("barrier layer" or "photovoltaic cell", "solar battery"). Different cells respond differently to lights of various wavelength and must be chosen for each application. *See also* **Solar Battery.**

Photogrammetry, the science of measurement from photographs taken from an aircraft. Aerial photography has many uses and is of great value to military intelligence and for mapmaking.

Photon. When light behaves like a stream of discrete particles and not like waves, the particles are called photons. *See* **F14, 16.**

Photosynthesis. *See* **F32(1), 43(1).**

Phrenology. *See* **Section J.**

Phylloxera, a genus of plant-lice related to the aphids, which attacks the grape vine. Many vineyards of France, in common with the rest of Europe, were replanted with native vines grafted on immune stocks from California in 1879 after being ravaged by the insect (which came from America). Curiously enough, the remedy also came from America, the vine stocks there being immune to *phylloxera*.

Pi is the unique number denoted by the Greek letter π and obtained by dividing the length of the circumference of any circle by its diameter. Its value is approximately 3·14159.

Picts, inhabitants of Scotland in pre-Roman times, are held by some historians to be a branch of the old Celtic race, by others to have been of Scythian origin. They occupied the north-eastern portion of Scotland, and were subdued by the Scots in Argyll in the 9th cent., Kenneth MacAlpin becoming king of a united kingdom of the Picts and Scots—the kingdom of Alban.

Pike, a familiar fresh-water fish abundant in the temperate regions of both hemispheres. It forms good sport for the angler in rivers and lakes, and sometimes attains a weight of from 9–13 kg. It is extremely voracious, is covered with small scales and has a ferocious-looking head.

Pilchard, a fish of the herring family, but with smaller scales and more rounded body. It appears off the Cornish coasts in vast shoals.

Pilgrimage. The undertaking of a journey to a distant place or shrine to satisfy a religious vow or secure spiritual benefit, was resorted to in early Christian times. The first recorded pilgrimage is that of the Empress Helena to Jerusalem in 326. In thhe Middle Ages pilgrimages became common, and were undertaken by monarchs and people of rank in all Christian countries. Moslems have been making pilgrimages to Mecca since the death of the Prophet, such duty being enjoined by the Koran. Among the great centres of Christian pilgrimages are Jerusalem, Rome, the tomb of Becket at Canterbury and Lourdes in France.

Pilgrimage of Grace (1536), the rising in Lincolnshire and Yorkshire in the reign of Henry VIII against religious innovations and the dissolution of the smaller monasteries, which overlapped with discontents caused by taxation, rising prices, enclosures and land speculation. The insurrection was followed by many executions.

Pilgrim Fathers, the 101 English Puritans who, after living some years in exile in Holland, to escape persecution in their own country, set sail for America in the *Mayflower*, 6 September 1620, landing at Plymouth, Mass., 4 December. They founded the settlement of Plymouth, and are regarded as the pioneers of American colonisation although 13 years earlier a small Virginian colony had been established.

Pillory, a wooden instrument of punishment in use in England until 1837. It consisted of a pair of movable boards with holes through which the culprit's head and hands were put, and was usually erected on a scaffold. While a person was undergoing this punishment the mob generally pelted him with stones and rubbish, sometimes to his serious injury. People convicted of forgery, perjury or libel were often condemned to the pillory, but from 1816–1837 the only offence for which it could be inflicted was perjury.

Pine, a conifer of the genus *Pinus*, which flourishes all over the northern hemisphere and includes 80–90 species, which afford valuable timber and yield turpentine and tar. The Scots Pine, *Pinus silvestris*, with its blue-green, short needles, set in pairs, and its rosy-orange branches, is native to Britain, as it is to the whole of Europe. It provides the red and yellow deal in everyday use.

Pine marten. *See under* **Marten.**

Pitcairn Islanders were originally the mutineers of the *Bounty*. They took possession of the island in 1790, and it was not until 1814 that their whereabouts was ascertained, accidentally, by a passing ship. The mutineers, under their leader, Adams, had settled down to a communal existence, married Tahitian women and increased so in numbers that in the course of years they were too many for the island to support, and in 1856 they were removed by the

British Government to Norfolk Island. A small number returned to Pitcairn.

Pitchblende *or* **Uraninite,** a relatively scarce mineral. It is nearly all uranium oxide, but lead, thorium, *etc.*, are also present. Pitchblende was the material in which radium was discovered by the Curies. Sources include the Great Lakes region of Canada and the Congo.

Pitohui, a song-bird found in Papua New Guinea which produces a powerful nerve toxin.

Placebo, medical treatment that the therapist uses deliberately although he knows it is without any specific effect on the condition being treated. There may be various medical reasons for using placebos, *e.g.*, for the beneficial psychological effect on people who like to feel something is being done for them; for differentiating during clinical trials of a new treatment between those persons given the real thing and a control or comparison group of persons given a placebo or inactive imitation.

Plainsong, a style of musical composition sung in unison (all voices singing the same tune without harmony), familiar in the Western Church from very early times and still performed, principally in the Roman Catholic Church. Though restrained and contemplative in spirit, it is capable of expressing deep emotion. *See* **E3(2).**

Planetarium, a complex optical system which projects into the interior of a dome a replica of all the phenomena of the sky that can be seen by the naked eye, *e.g.*, sun, moon, planets, stars, comets, meteors, aurora, eclipses and clouds. There is a planetarium in the Marylebone Road, London.

Planets, the name given to such celestial bodies as revolve round the sun in elliptical orbits. The name was first used by the Greeks to indicate their difference from the fixed stars. There are nine major planets, Mercury, Venus, Earth, Mars, Jupiter, Saturn, Uranus, Neptune and Pluto. There are also a large number of minor planets or asteroids. Saturn, Uranus and Jupiter are ringed. Many important questions can be answered by means of probes sent to the neighbourhood of the planets. These include the measurement of the magnetic field, if any, of the planets, the study of their atmospheres, much of which can be done without actually penetrating to the surface. With instruments landed gently on the surface it is possible to investigate surface conditions and composition by many methods. Even without a soft-landing information on these questions can be obtained by photography and subsequent transmission of the picture back to earth by some form of television scanning. The US Mars probe *Mariner IV* transmitted pictures of the Martian surface in 1965, the Russian *Venus IV* in 1967 made a soft-landing on Venus, and the US *Pioneer 11* came within 43,000 km of Jupiter in December 1974. Two US *Voyager* spacecraft were launched in 1977 flying by Jupiter (1979), Saturn (1980, 1981) Uranus (1986) and Neptune (1989), sending back important new data. Exciting pictures were received in 1998 from the Hubble telescope of a planet outside our own solar system. *See also* **Section Topic, Section F.**

Plankton, a word which first came into biological use in 1886 to describe the usually microscopic plants and animals floating, swimming and drifting in the surface waters of the sea. To be distinguished from *nekton* (swimming animals like fishes and squids) and *benthos* (plants and animals living on the sea bottom, like fixed algae, sponges, oysters, crabs, *etc.*). Of great economic importance, providing food for fish and whales.

Plantagenets, the kings who reigned in England between 1154 and 1485 and included the Houses of Lancaster and York. More correctly they are styled Angevins, from Anjou, of which Geoffrey, father of Henry II, was Count. His badge was a sprig of broom (*Planta genista*).

Plasma Physics is the physics of wholly ionised gases, *i.e.*, gases in which the atoms initially present have lost practically the whole of the electrons that usually surround their nuclei, so that the gas consists of a mixture of two components, positively charged ions and negatively charged electrons. The physical properties of a *plasma* are very different from those of an un-ionised gas. In particular, a plasma has a high electrical conductivity and can carry large currents. *See also* **Nuclear Fusion.**

Plastics, a broad term covering those substances which become plastic when subjected to increased temperatures or pressures. The Plastics Industry is based on synthetic organic examples of this group. There are two classes of plastics: the *thermoplastic*, which become plastic every time they are heated (*e.g.* cellulosic plastics) and *thermosetting*, which undergo chemical change when heated, so that once set they cannot be rendered plastic again (*e.g.*, Bakelite). Plastics are composed of long-chained molecules, *e.g.*, polyethylene.

Plate Tectonics, the contemporary and by now well-developed theory of the movements of the earth's crust. The view is that the surface of the Earth consists of about a dozen rigid plates. Some larger than continents, some much smaller, all in ceaseless motion relative to one another. Their separation and approach and their friction and collision are closely related to the evolution of mountain ranges, oceans and rift valleys and to phenomena like earthquakes. *See* **F77.**

Platinum, a metallic element, no. 78, symbol Pt. It is a scarce white metal generally allied with iridium, osmium, ruthenium and palladium. It can only be melted in an oxyhydrogen or electric furnace, but can be rolled out into a film-like sheet, or drawn out to the finest wire; being resistant to acids it is termed a noble metal. Named after the Spanish for "silver-coloured" *–platina*. First found in the sands of the River Pinto in S. America.

Platonic Solids, five regular solid figures known to the ancient world. They are: the tetrahedron (4 triangular faces), cube (6 square faces), octahedron (8 triangular faces), dodecahedron (12 five-sided faces), icosahedron (20 triangular faces). All the faces and angles of each solid are identical.

Pleiades, famous cluster of stars in the constellation of Taurus. Of the seven principal stars in the group, one is rather faint, and many myths have sprung up about this "lost Pleiad". *See also* **I23.**

Pleistocene, the geological period that succeeded the Pliocene. During the Pleistocene, also known as the *Great Ice Age*, there were four cold periods, when the ice sheets covered northern Europe and N. America, separated by warm periods when the glaciers drew back into the mountains. From recent studies based on rock magnetic measurements the transition to Pleistocene took place *c.* 1,850,000 years ago.

Pliocene, the geological period preceding the Pleistocene, and the last major division of the Tertiary strata. It began about fifteen million years ago.

Plough Monday, the first Monday after the Epiphany, when in olden times the rural population returned to work after the Christmas festivities.

Plover, wading birds, widely distributed over marshy places of Europe. Several species occur in Britain, including the Golden-plover, which breeds on the moors of Devon, Somerset, Wales, N.E. Yorkshire and Scotland, and the Ringed plover, Kentish plover and Dotterel.

Pluto, the last planet to be discovered was searched for following the 1914 predictions of P. Lowell and discovered by C. W. Tombaugh at the Flagstaff Observatory in Arizona in January 1930. Generally the most distant of the planets its orbit is much more elliptical than the other planetary orbits and so it sometimes approaches the sun closer than Neptune. It was thought to be different from the other outer Jovian planets which are gaseous and to consist of rock covered in frozen methane gas. Recently the size of Pluto has been revised downwards by inter-ferometric measurement of its diameter. The diameter of Pluto is currently (1999) estimated to be 2250 km. It is the only planet in the solar system not yet visited by spacecraft, but NASA plans a probe in 2003. Pluto's own moon, Charon, was also detected by earth-based telescopes using special photometric measurements. It is composed almost entirely of ice. Images of the surface of Pluto reveal ragged icy polar caps and clusters of bright and dark features. Some astronomers do not think Pluto should be classed as a planet. *See* **F8.**

Plutonium, a chemical element, no. 94, symbol Pu, capable of nuclear fission in the same way as

Uranium 235. Not until after it had been synthesised in atomic piles during the second world war was it shown to occur in infinitesimally small traces in nature. Its synthesis in the atomic pile depends on the capture by Uranium 238 nuclei of neutrons; immediate product of this reaction is the element neptunium, but this undergoes rapid radioactive disintegration to plutonium.

Poet Laureate is the poet attached to the royal household, an office officially established in 1668, though its origins go back to the early Middle Ages, when minstrels were employed at the courts of English kings. Chaucer, Skelton and Spenser, though not court poets, were all unofficial poets laureate. Ben Jonson has been called the first "official laureate" (1616), but the office was not officially recognised until 1668, when Dryden was formally granted the office. It is customary for the poet laureate to write verse in celebration of events of national importance. Ted Hughes (*see* **B33**) was Poet Laureate from 1984 to 1998. Other holders of the title have been John Dryden 1668–1689, Thomas Shadwell 1689–1692. Nahum Tate 1692–1715, Nicholas Rowe 1715–1718, Laurence Eusden 1718–1730, Colley Cibber 1730–1757, William Whitehead 1757–1785, Thomas Warton 1785–1790, Henry Pye 1790–1813, Robert Southey 1813–1843, William Wordsworth 1843–1850, Alfred Tennyson 1850–1892, Alfred Austin 1896–1913, Robert Bridges 1913–1930, John Masefield 1930–1967, Cecil Day-Lewis 1968–1972, John Betjeman 1972–1984 and Ted Hughes 1984–98.

Pogrom. Russian word meaning "destruction". First used to describe the Czarist attacks on the Jews in 1881 in Russia. In 1938 Hitler ordered a general pogrom which led on to the holocaust.

Poitiers, Battle of, was fought on 19 September 1356, during the Hundred Years' War, when Edward the Black Prince gained a complete victory over John, King of France, who was taken prisoner and brought to London.

Polecat, an animal of a dark-brown colour, about 46 cm in length, exclusive of tail; the ears and face-markings are white or light brown. It is carnivorous and belongs to the weasel family.

Pole-Star is of the second magnitude, and the last in the tail of the Little Bear constellation. Being near the North pole of the heavens—never more than about one degree from due north—it always remains visible in the Northern hemisphere; hence its use as a guide to seamen.

Police, a regular force established for the preservation of law and order and the prevention and detection of crime. The powers they have vary from country to country and with the type of government; the more civilised and democratic the state, the less police intervention. England, compared with countries abroad, was slow to develop a police force, and it was not until 1829 that Sir Robert Peel's Metropolitan Police Act established a regular force for the metropolis, later legislation establishing county and borough forces maintained by local police authorities throughout England and Wales. Up to that time police duties were discharged by individual constables and watchmen appointed by local areas in England and Wales. The police service in Great Britain today has recently undergone the most radical review since 1966. Some forces are being amalgamated and radical changes implemented. At present, however, the structure is:

1. County forces (43 in 1999) under a police committee of local councillors and magistrates.
2. Combined forces, covering more than one county, also under a police committee consisting of local councillors and magistrates and representatives from constituent areas.
3. The Metropolitan Police Force, covering an area within a 15-mile (24-km) radius of Charing Cross, but excluding the City of London (under the Home Secretary).
4. The City of London force under the Court of Common Council.

In Scotland the police authorities, (since April 1996), are four joint police boards made up of local councillors. Police ranks are: chief constable, assistant chief constable, chief superintendent, superintendent, chief inspector, inspector, sergeant and constable. In the Metropolitan Police area the chief officer is the Commissioner of Police of the Metropolis. Central authority rests with the

Home Secretary in England and Wales and the Secretary of State for Scotland in Scotland. In the present troubles in Northern Ireland responsibility for law and order is retained at Westminster. Great opposition faced the Sheehy Report when it proposed fixed-term contracts and performance-related pay. The 1994 Police and Magistrates Court Act has changed the relationship between central government, police authorities and chief constables. The new National Crime Squad (NCS) to tackle organised crime was launched in April 1998. In 1997 Britain ratified the treaty creating Europol (the first EU country to do so). Chief constables were given increased powers in 1998 to dismiss corrupt or inefficient officers. The problem of racism in the police force is currently of particular concern.

Poll Tax, common name for the Community Charge, which replaced the rates. It was replaced by the Council Tax from 1993. See **Section H**.

Polonium, a radioactive element, no. 84, symbol Po, discovered by Madame Curie in 1898, and named after her native land of Poland.

Polymerisation is the linking together of small molecules to make a large long-chain molecule. The general name for polymers of ethylene is Polythene, a wax-like plastic solid.

Pomology, the science of fruit-growing.

Pontifex, the title assigned in ancient Rome to members of the college of pontifices. "Pontifex maximus" was the official head of Roman religion. It was as "pontifex maximus" that Julius Caesar revised the calendar in 46 B.C., and when after the rise of Christianity the Popes took over the title the revision fell to them.

Pope, The, the head of the Roman Catholic Church, recognised by that Church as the lawful successor of St. Peter. He is elected by the body of Cardinals. Since 1870, when the King of Italy deposed the holder from temporal power, no Pope had left the Vatican between appointment and death until 1929, when peace was made between the Church and State in Italy and compensation was paid to the Holy See for the loss of temporal power. See also **Z13**.

Population. See **World Population, L130**.

Porcelain. The word is thought to be derived from the Italian *porcellana*, indicating the texture of a piglet. The majority of porcelain made on the continent was of "hard-paste", or true porcelain, similar to that discovered by the Chinese as early as the T'ang Dynasty (A.D. 618–907). It was composed of *kaolin* (china-clay) and *petuntse* (china-stone) which when fired in a kiln at a temperature of *c.* 1300°C became an extremely hard and translucent material. The recipe of "hard-paste" porcelain remained a secret of the Chinese until 1709, when it was re-discovered in Europe by Johann Böttger of the Meissen factory (popularly known as Dresden). Aided by disloyal Meissen workmen, factories were later established at Vienna, Venice and in many parts of Germany. Plymouth and Bristol were the only English factories to produce this type of porcelain, from 1768 to 1781. Elsewhere, both in England and France, the material manufactured was known as "soft-paste" or artificial porcelain which was made by blending varying white-firing clays with the ingredients of glass. The French factory of Sèvres began to make some hard-paste porcelain by 1768 and by the 19th cent. such porcelain was the only type being made throughout the whole of the continent. In England Josiah Spode is credited with the introduction of "bone-china" about 1794. This hybrid-paste was quickly adopted by many other factories and remains very popular.

Porphyry, a form of crystalline rock of many varieties that in ancient Egypt was quarried and used for the decorative portions of buildings and vessels. The term is applied generally to the eruptive rocks in which large well-formed crystals of one mineral are set in a matrix of other minerals.

Porpoise, a highly intelligent marine mammal of the dolphin and whale family, and a common inhabitant of northern seas. Porpoises travel in shoals, their progression being marked by constant leapings and plungings. Their average length is from 1·2-1·5 m. There are several species, nearly all confined to northern oceans.

Port, a special kind of red Portuguese wine, taking

its name from Oporto. It was little known in England until the Methuen Treaty of 1703, when it could be imported at a low duty.

Portland Vase, one of the most renowned specimens of ancient art, long in the possession of the Portland family. In 1810 it was loaned to the British Museum. Here it was shattered in 1845 by a stone from a maniac's hand, but has been skilfully restored. It is said to have been found in the 17th cent. in an ancient tomb near Rome. It was purchased from the Barberini family in 1770 by Sir Wm. Hamilton, subsequently sold to the Duchess of Portland. The vase, which is actually a two-handled urn, stands about 25 cm high, is of transparent dark blue glass, ornamented with figures cut in relief in overlaid white opaque glass. It was purchased by the British Museum in 1945. See also **Glass**.

Portreeve in olden times was an official appointed to superintend a port or harbour, and before the name of mayor was used the chief magistrate of London was styled the Portreeve.

Positivism. See **Section J**.

Positron, the "positive electron", an atomic particle having the same mass but an electric charge equal but opposite to that of an electron. It was discovered in 1932. See also **F16**.

Post-Impressionism, a term introduced by Roger Fry to describe the exhibition of paintings sponsored by himself in London (1910–11) officially entitled "Manet and the Post-Impressionists". The exhibition included paintings by Manet, Cézanne, Gauguin, Van Gogh, Seurat, Signac, works by Matisse, Rouault and the *Fauves* (*q.v.*), and sculpture by Maillol. In a second exhibition, held in 1912, Picasso and the Cubists were also represented. The term therefore refers to the movement in modern art which reacted against the transient naturalism of the Impressionists by concerning itself primarily with colour, form and solidity. Most artists include Cézanne, Van Gogh and Gauguin as the main Post-Impressionists and maintain that it prepared the way for Fauvism, Cubism and Expressionism.

Post Office, The, is made up of three separate companies, Royal Mail, Parcelforce and Post Office Counters. The Post Office employs 194,000 people and has a turnover of £6·3 bn. Britain is the only country with two urban deliveries daily.

Potassium, a metal, no. 19, symbol K (German *Kalium*). It is similar to sodium, reacting violently with water. It was discovered by Sir Humphry Davy in 1807, and is now generally obtained by the electrolysis of fused potassium hydroxide or chloride/fluoride mixture. Its principal minerals are carnallite and kainite, and it is relatively common in rocks, accounting for about 2½% of the earth's crust. An essential element for healthy plant growth; the ashes of plants are relatively rich in potassium.

Potato Famine. Term for the disaster in Ireland in 1845 and 1846 when the failure of the potato crop led to a million deaths from starvation.

Potsdam Agreement was signed by Truman, Stalin and Attlee in August 1945. By this Agreement a Council of Foreign Ministers was established, representing the five principal Powers: China, France, Soviet Russia, the United Kingdom and United States of America, with the task of drawing up the peace treaties for submission to the United Nations. It laid down, *inter alia*, that German militarism and Hitlerism should be destroyed and that industrial power should be reduced. The Potsdam Agreement became a dead letter with the creation of a communist régime in the Russian zone of Germany, and marked the beginning of the "cold war".

Prado Gallery, the great public picture collection of Madrid, containing a superb collection of paintings by Velasquez, Murillo, Raphael, Titian, Dürer, Van Dyck, Rubens and Goya.

Pragmatism. See **Section J**.

Prefect, chief magistrates in ancient Rome. The title is now applied to the chiefs of administration of the departments of France.

Pre-Raphaelite Brotherhood was the name given to their school of thought by three British artists, Dante Gabriel Rossetti, J. E. Millais and W. Holman Hunt, who in 1848 revolted against the academic art of their time and advocated a return to the style of the Italian painters prior to Raphael—the simple naturalism of the Primitives, such as Botticelli, Fra Angelico and Filippo Lippi. Thus they avoided the use of heavy shadows and painted on a white ground in bright colours—a technique which aroused the ire of those used to the dark and murky canvases of the contemporary romantic artists. Although they held these principles in common the three members of the "P.R.B.", as it was popularly called, were really quite different in other respects. Thus Rossetti (who for some reason is always thought of as the typical Pre-Raphaelite) produced works of a highly romanticised mediaevalism which, apart from certain aspects of technique, bear not the slightest resemblance to the sentimental naturalism of Millais or the much more dramatic realism of Holman Hunt (e.g., in *The Scapegoat*). The Brotherhood was later joined by a number of lesser artists, but its works are not commonly accepted with enthusiasm today when the general feeling is that they are sentimental and religiose rather than the product of deeply-felt emotions. Ruskin in his writings had defended their work but the movement ended in 1853.

Presbyterianism. *See* **Section J.**

Prescription charges rose by 10p to £5.90 from 1 April 1999.

Press-Gang, a body of sailors employed to impress men into naval service, frequently resorted to in England, especially during the war with France in the early 19th cent. Press gangs were not used after about 1850.

Primitive Art. The word "primitive" has a number of different meanings: (1) the art of prehistoric communities (e.g., the famous animal cave-drawings of the Aurignacians, c. 25,000 B.C., at Altamira in Spain); (2) the art of modern primitive communities (e.g., Bushman rock-paintings); (3) child art; (4) peasant art which springs from a spontaneous desire to impart beauty to objects of daily use and shows a tendency towards abstraction. Peasant art has many features in common the world over, the woodcarving of the Norsemen being almost indistinguishable from that of the Maoris; (5) the modern school of primitive painting in which naïveté of presentation is either the aim of a highly sophisticated mind (e.g., the self-taught French painter Le Douanier Rousseau (d. 1910), or arises naturally from a simple one (the American "grandma" Moses (d. 1961) who began to paint in her seventies).

Printing by movable types was first used in Europe in 1454 by Johann Gutenberg, a citizen of Mainz. The invention is also claimed for Laurens Koster of Haarlem. It was introduced into England by Caxton, who set up a printing press in Westminster in 1476. Gothic characters were first used, being superseded by Roman letters in 1518. In 1798 Earl Stanhope replaced the wood printing press by one of iron. In 1814 Friedrich Koenig applied the principle of steam power to the press. Mr. John Walter, of *The Times* newspaper, was the first to use the steam press. Improvements were introduced by Applegarth and Cowper in 1828 and great strides were made in 1858 when the Hoe machine was put on the market. Then came the Walter press in 1866 which printed on continuous rolls of paper from curved stereotyped plates. The Monotype machine casts single letters and the Linotype whole lines. The term letterpress is used for all printing methods using plates where the characters stand in *relief*. The other main printing methods are *intaglio* and *planographic*. The development of computer technology using electronic methods has introduced a new era in printing.

prion, a tiny micro-organism, one hundred times smaller than a virus.

Privatisation, selling of state-owned industries to private businesses and individuals, encouraged by the government after 1979 as part of its free market policies. Among the industries partly or wholly sold off were British Aerospace and Britoil (1983), British Telecom (1984) and British Gas (1986). Others included British Airways, British Coal and later British Rail. A further aspect of privatisation was the requirement of local authorities to contract out activities to private companies and the introduction of "internal markets" in the National Health Service. Labour

in power has not reversed the privatisation process since 1997. *See* **Section G.**

The Privy Council is the Sovereign's own council, consisting of about 300 persons who have reached eminence in some branch of public affairs (Cabinet ministers must be Privy Counsellors), on whose advice and through which the Sovereign exercises his or her statutory and a number of prerogative powers. From it have sprung many organs of the constitution and many of our government departments have grown from committees of the Privy Council. For example the Judiciary or courts of justice have grown from the Sovereign's Council sitting as a Court of Justice, and today the Judicial Committee of the Privy Council is a body of distinguished lawyers acting as a Court of Appeal from courts of the Commonwealth.

Probation Officers are attached to particular Courts, sometimes a Magistrates' or a higher court. Sometimes an offender is not sentenced to punishment, but is released "on probation", that is on the condition that he behaves well and follows directions given by the Court or by a probation officer. Such an officer is a trained man (or woman) who advises, assists and befriends people who are placed under his supervision by a court of law. The probation officer, by his assessment of the social background of the offender, can advise the court upon the wisdom of putting the offender on probation. The probation officer by his understanding can so befriend an offender as to provide a basis for his rehabilitation. He undertakes the "after care" of those released from prison or Young Offenders' Institutions. A merger of the probation and prison services has been mooted.

Productivity. Physical productivity is the output of products during a time unit, e.g., so many products per man hour, or day, or year. Total productivity is the sum of all the units of product created during the given time. Labour productivity is the part of the total that is attributed to labour as a factor of production. Productivity of capital is the element attributed to capital as a factor. Productivity of land is the element attributed to the natural powers of the soil, as distinct from what is contributed by the application to it of capital or labour.

Propane, a colourless inflammable gas made of carbon and hydrogen; formula C_3H_8. It is easily liquefied and transported liquid in cylinders and tanks. In this form it is familiar as a "portable gas supply" for domestic and industrial uses. It is sometimes mixed with butane (q.v.) for this purpose. Propane occurs in natural gas and is a by-product of oil refining.

Proteins are the main chemical substances of living matter: they are a part of every living cell and are found in all animals and plants. All proteins are basically constructed of carbon hydrogen, oxygen and nitrogen, and some contain sulphur, phosphorus (nucleoproteins) and iron (haemoglobin). Proteins are built up of very long chains of amino-acids connected by amide linkages (the synthetic polymers such as "nylon" and casein plastics (from milk) are built up of the same linkages). The structure of protein molecules allows a variety of function. Enzymes, which bring about chemical reactions in living cells, are proteins having specific properties. *See* **F32–3,** *also* **Diet, Section P.**

Proton, a basic constituent of the atomic nucleus, positively charged, having a mass about 1836 times that of the electron. It is a positive hydrogen ion.

Prout's hypothesis. The English chemist William Prout (1785–1850) advanced the idea that all atoms are made of hydrogen, and their weights are exact multiples of the weight of a hydrogen atom. With the modification that neutrons as well as protons occur in the nucleus, Prout's belief has been substantially vindicated.

Provost, a Scottish official similar in rank to an English mayor. The Provosts of Edinburgh, Glasgow, Aberdeen, Perth and Dundee are styled Lords Provost. The title of provost is also given to the heads of certain colleges.

Prud'hommes (Prudent Men), **Councils of,** were French trade tribunals, of masters and workmen, formed to decide on disputes. Originally mediaeval, they were revived by Napoleon in 1806, and carried on by the Third Republic.

Psalms, Book of, for many years attributed to David, but present-day scholars are of the view that the psalms were written by a series of authors at different times and for different purposes, and that few, if any, were written by David. The Holy Scriptures contain 150.

Psychic Research. *See* **Section J**.

Psychoanalysis. *See* **Section J**.

Ptarmigan, birds of the grouse family, one species of which inhabits the Scottish Highlands. In the winter the bird assumes a white plumage.

Ptomaines, amino acids produced during the putrefaction of proteins of animal origin. Not a cause of food poisoning, as was once generally supposed, which is almost invariably due to certain specific bacteria.

Publicans, under the Roman Empire, were people who farmed the public taxes. It is this class of officials that is alluded to in the "publicans and sinners" phrase in the New Testament.

Public Corporations, statutory bodies which operated major industries and services in the public interest, *e.g.*, UK Atomic Energy Authority, Bank of England, BBC, Electricity Authorities, Gas Council, British Coal Corporation, British Steel Corporation, British Railways Board, the Post Office, British National Oil Corporation, British Nuclear Fuels, British Airports Authority. They were accountable to Parliament but their staffs were not civil servants. Conservative Governments from 1979 to 1997 pursued a policy of privatisation of most of these bodies, and many (*e.g.* British Gas) became public companies.

Public Record Office. *See* **Record Office**.

Public Schools. The Public Schools Act of 1864 named nine "public" schools: Eton, Harrow, Rugby, Winchester, Westminster, Shrewsbury, Charterhouse, St. Paul's and Merchant Taylors'. Today the term embraces many more, and can be applied to all those schools which are financed by bodies other than the State and whose headmasters belong to the Headmasters' Conference as distinct from the Headmasters' Association. There are very many such schools in Britain, including among others: Bedford School (founded 1552); Bradfield College, Berks. (1850); Charterhouse, Godalming (1611); Cheltenham College (1841); Christ's Hospital, Horsham (1553); City of London (1442); Clifton College, Bristol (1862); Dulwich College (1619); Eton College (1440); Felsted, Dunmow, Essex (1564); Haileybury College (1862); Harrow (1571); King Edward's, Birmingham (1552); King's School, Canterbury (600); Malvern College (1865); Manchester Grammar School (1515); Marlborough College (1843); Merchant Taylors' (1561); Mill Hill (1807); Oundle (1556); Radley College, Abingdon (1847); Repton, Derbyshire (1557); Rugby School (1567); St. Albans (948); St. Paul's (1509); Sevenoaks School (1418); Sherborne (1550); Shrewsbury School (1552); Stonyhurst College (1593); Stowe School, Bucks. (1923); Tonbridge (1553); Uppingham, Leics. (1584); Warwick (914); Wellington College (1859); Westminster (1560); Winchester College (1382). Public schools for girls include: Christ's Hospital, Hertford (1552), Cheltenham Ladies' College (founded by Miss Beale in 1853), North London Collegiate School (founded by Miss Buss in 1850), Roedean (1885), Wycombe Abbey (1806). Many public schools have become coeducational. Public Schools are now known as Independant Schools.

Puffin, bird of the auk family (*see* **L12**). It has a large deep bill and is found in the N.E. Atlantic. In Britain, the largest colony is found on the archipelago of St Kilda, off the west coast of Scotland.

Pulsars, cosmic objects discovered in 1967 by the Radio Astronomy group at Cambridge; of great scientific interest, since they are probably neutron stars, and extremely dense. Unlike quasars (*q.v.*) they are nearby objects within our own galaxy. *See* **F5**.

Puma, mountain-lion or cougar, a large wild cat found throughout the Americas. It looks like a lean greyish lioness. It is known as the "lion of the Andes".

Puritans. *See* **Section J**.

Pyramidology. *See* **Section J**.

Pyramids of Egypt, on the west bank of the Nile, are vast stone or brick-built structures with inner chambers and subterranean entrances, built by the Pharaohs as royal tombs and dating from about 2700 B.C. The most celebrated are at Gizeh built during the 4th dynasty. The largest, originally 147 m high, is called the Great Pyramid, one of the seven wonders of the world, built by the Pharaoh Khufu, better known as Cheops, and there he was buried. 100,000 men, according to Herodotus, being employed for 20 years upon it. Chephren, successor of Cheops, erected the second pyramid, and the third was built by Mycerinus, a son of Cheops. The pyramid at Meidum built by King Snefru, founder of the 4th dynasty, is the most imposing of all.

Pythons, large snakes, non-poisonous and destroying their prey by crushing it. Some species may reach 9 m in length, and prey upon deer and other small mammals. Found in Asia, Africa and Australia. They lay eggs.

Q

Quadrant, an astronomical instrument for measuring altitudes, superseded for navigational purposes in modern times by the sextant. It consists of a graduated arc of 90° with a movable radius for measuring angles on it.

Quagga, an extinct African animal, resembling a zebra from the front and a horse from the back.

Quai d'Orsay. An embankment in Paris where the French Foreign Office is situated.

Quail, an edible bird of the partridge family, of which only one species, the Common Quail, is found in England. It is not more than 20 cm long. It is found in most of the warmer regions of the world. In England and Wales the Quail is covered by the Wild Bird Protection Acts.

Quantum Theory. The rapid development of quantum theory has been almost entirely due to the experimental and theoretical study of the interactions between electromagnetic radiation and matter. One of the first steps was taken when it was discovered that the electrons emitted from metals due to the action of ultra-violet radiation have an energy which is not related to the intensity of the incident radiation, but is dependent on its wavelength. Einstein showed in 1905 that this could only be explained on the basis that energy is transferred between radiation and matter in finite amounts, or *quanta*, which are inversely proportional to wavelength. *See* **F17(2)**.

Quarks are hypothetical subnuclear particles which were postulated by theoretical physicists concerned with the so-called elementary particles. There are believed to be six kinds of quarks. Quarks carry electrical charges which are fractions of those carried by familiar particles like electrons and protons. This and other special properties of quarks make them suitable for explaining the existence of the large number of other particles referred to on **F16–17**. Now the existence of the sixth and final quark has been demonstrated by experiment. *See* **F15(2)**.

Quartering, in heraldry, is the disposition of various escutcheons or coats of arms in their proper "quarters" of the family shield, in such order as indicates the alliances with other families.

Quartermaster, a military officer charged with the provisioning and superintendence of soldiers in camp or barracks, and holding the equivalent rank to a lieutenant. The Quartermaster-General is an officer who presides over the provisioning department of the whole army. A Quartermaster in the Navy is a petty officer responsible to the Officer of the Watch; at sea for the correct steering of the ship and in harbour for the running of the ship's routine.

Quarto, a sheet of paper folded twice to make four leaves, or eight pages; abbreviated to "4to".

Quartz is a common and usually colourless mineral, occurring both crystallised and massive. In the first form it is in hexagonal prisms, terminating in pyramids. When pure its specific gravity is 2·66. It is one of the constituents of granite, gneiss, *etc.* Among the quartz varieties are *rock crystal* (colourless), *smoky quartz* (yellow or brown), *amethyst* (purple), *rose quartz* (pink) and *milky quartz* (white). Quartz veins in metamorphic rocks may yield rich deposits of gold. Mining for gold in the rock is termed quartzmining.

Quasars, or in preferred terminology, quasi-stellar radio-sources, form a new class of astronomical objects, first identified in the period 1960 to 1962. They have enormous energy output, and are at vast distances. Many are strong sources of radio waves and fluctuate in intensity. There is still controversy over the nature of these objects. We presently consider that the intense emission comes from a relatively small region at the centre of peculiar galaxies. While a plausible explanation would be the existence of a gigantic black hole formed by the gravitational collapse of the nucleus of the galaxy, dragging in surrounding material, including entire star systems, our information is not yet conclusive, and has been further questioned by the findings of the Hubble telescope. *See* **F5.**

Queen Anne's Bounty, established by Queen Anne in 1704 for the augmentation of the maintenance of the poor clergy. Since 1 April 1948 Queen Anne's Bounty and the Ecclesiastical Commissioners ceased to exist and became embodied in the Church Commissioners for England.

Queen's (or **King's**) **Speech** is the speech prepared by the Government in consultation with the Queen and delivered by Her Majesty in person or by her deputy, at the opening or closing of a Parliamentary session.

Quetzal, a green bird with iridescent plumage, once revered as a god by the Aztecs.

Quinine, a vegetable alkaloid obtained from the bark of several trees of the *Cinchona* genus. It is colourless and extremely bitter. The drug, sulphate of quinine, is one of the most valuable medicines, forming a powerful tonic. It is antiperiodic, antipyretic and antineuralgic. In cases of malaria it is the most efficacious remedy of natural origin known.

Quirinal, one of the seven hills of Rome.

Quisling, term which came into use during the second world war to denote traitor, collaborator or fifth-columnist. After Vidkun Quisling, who became head of the puppet government after the German invasion of Norway in 1940.

Quorum, the number of members of any body or company necessary to be present at any meeting or commission before business can be transacted. The House of Commons needs a quorum of 40, the Lords a quorum of 3.

R

Rabbi, a Jewish term applied to specially ordained officials who pronounce upon questions of legal form and ritual, and also generally accorded to any Jewish scholar of eminence.

Rabbits, rodent burrowing mammals. In their wild state they have brownish fur and erect ears. They breed rapidly, having several litters a year. Decimated by the disease myxomatosis, they are now (1996) threatened by a deadly new disease RVHD (Rabbit Viral Haemorrhagic Disease), first reported in China in 1984. Pets that live in hutches in the garden are vulnerable as it is believed the disease is carried by birds.

Rabies, a virus infection affecting animals (*e.g.* dogs, foxes). Since strict quarantine laws in 1901, Britain has been free of rabies. Proposals for reviewing Britain's anti-rabies laws have recently been put forward.

Raccoon, plantigrade carnivorous mammals common to the American continent. There are several species. The common Raccoon (*Procyon lotor*) is about 60 cm long, with a bush ringed tail and sharp snout. Its skin is valuable.

Race. In the old text-books anthropologists were much concerned with the differences between the various races of Man; they described the Black Man (Negro), the Yellow Man (Mongol), the Red Man (American Indian), the Brown Man (Indian), and the White Man (European). Those who study Man from this point of view further subdivide each group into others. Thus White Man may be divided into

Nordic, Alpine and Mediterranean; Black Man into Hamitic, Bushman and so on. Each of these groups tends to have physical traits which its members hold in common, although, of course, there are no *pure* racial types. All existing races have been fairly thoroughly mixed. What, in view of recent experience, is really important, is that races or even nations do not have psychological traits—at least not *innate* traits. Anthropology dismisses all theories of a superior race as unscientific: there is not the slightest evidence that one race differs in any way from another in its psychological potentialities; Jews, Irish, Scots, Italians do differ: but their differences are due to their situation and not to anything inborn. *See* **Racism, Section J.**

Raceme, an inflorescence in which the main stem bears stalked flowers, *e.g.*, lupin, foxglove. The youngest flowers at the tip of this axis.

Radar. The basic principle of radar is very similar to that of sight. We switch on a light in the dark, and we *see* an object because the light waves are reflected from it and return to our eye, which is able to detect them. Similarly, the radar station *sees* an object because the invisible radio waves sent out from the transmitter are reflected from it and return to the receiver, which is able to detect them. Thus radar is the use of radio signals that man broadcasts.

The utilisation of radio waves for the detection of reflecting surfaces began with the classical experiment of the late Sir Edward Appleton in 1925, which he conducted in order to demonstrate the existence of the Heaviside layer in the upper atmospheres. During the course of the last war developments took place which tremendously improved the methods and instruments used. As in the case of so many of the inventions primarily developed for the purpose of waging war, many useful applications have been found for radar in times of peace, and, in particular, it has proved of great service as an aid to aerial and marine navigation, and in meteorology and astronomy. Radar astronomy investigates the solar system with the echoes of signals sent out from the Earth.

Radiation, energy emitted in the form of a beam of rays or waves, *e.g.*, acoustic (sound) radiation from a loudspeaker, radiant heat from a fire, β-radiation from a radioactive substance. The radiation of electromagnetic waves from a body depends on its temperature, the amount of energy radiated per second being proportional to the fourth power of the absolute temperature. The hotter the body, the shorter the wavelengths of the radiation; thus the colour of a glowing body depends on its temperature. Of paramount importance to us is radiation from the sun. Amongst other radiations, the sun sends ultra-violet, visible and infra-red (heat) waves. The principal gases of the atmosphere are transparent to practically all of the solar and sky radiation and also that which the earth re-transmits to space. Carbon dioxide and water vapour, however, strongly absorb certain types, the latter, as clouds, playing an important rôle in regulating the temperature of the globe. The cooling of the ground on a clear night is a result of the outgoing long-wave radiation exceeding that coming down from the sky; at sunrise cooling ceases as the incoming radiation becomes sufficient to compensate for the loss of heat.

Radiation, Cosmic. *See* **F3(2).**

Radio. The theory of electromagnetic waves—of which the radio wave is one—was originated by the British physicist James Clerk Maxwell (**F14**). He showed that both electrical and optical phenomena in space are essentially similar in character, and that the waves if short in wavelength are those of light, and if of longer wavelength those of radio waves. Heinrich Hertz made many useful discoveries about the waves themselves, and about their behaviour under differing conditions, and also about the apparatus for producing them. Marconi developed the use of radio waves as a practical means of communication.

Radio methods are vital for the transmission of observed data from space vehicles back to earth, a process known as "telemetering". This is done by converting the observations into electrical pulses which actuate a suitable radio transmitter so that it radiates a signal, in coded form, which can be received at a ground station and decoded. The transmission of such a signal can also be remotely controlled by means of signals from the earth. Photographic and television techniques may also be employed for obtaining the desired information and sending it back to earth, as in the case of the Russian picture of the reverse side of the moon and the American pictures of the lunar surface. The information may be stored within the spacecraft for a time, and then, upon receipt of a particular radio signal from the earth transmitted by the spacecraft at a time convenient for its reception. Soviet scientists, by a special technique, were able in the case of their *Venus IV* probe (October 1967) to parachute an instrumented canister from the spacecraft so that it could descend slowly to the surface of the planet. Another breathtaking achievement was the transformation of the faintest of signals from a billion miles away into superb pictures of the planet Saturn and its rings (*see* **Voyagers 1 and 2**). *See also* **Radio Astronomy, Telemetry.**

Radioactivity is the spontaneous transformation of atomic nuclei, accompanied by the emission of ionising radiations. It was discovered in 1896 by Becquerel, who noticed that salts containing uranium sent off radiations which, like X-rays, can blacken a photographic plate. Two years later Marie and Pierre Curie discovered several new chemical elements which possessed the same property, but many times more intense than uranium; the most important of these was radium. Shortly afterwards it was established, mainly by Rutherford, that three types of radiations called α-, β- and γ- rays, are emitted from radioactive substances. It was also Rutherford who, jointly with Soddy, deduced that the emission of the radiations is associated with the spontaneous disintegration of atoms which result in the transformation of one radioactive substance into another. A series of such transformations ends when a stable element is produced. All of the heavy radioactive elements can be arranged in three radioactive series, called, the uranium, thorium and actinium series. Initially, radioactivity was thought to be a property confined only to a few elements occurring in nature. In 1934, however, Irene and Frederick Joliot-Curie discovered that ordinary elements can be transformed into radioactive forms by subjecting them to bombardment with α-particles. Following this, it was found that beams of other fast particles produced in accelerators can also render ordinary substances radioactive. Nowadays it is known that radioactivity is a general property of matter; any chemical element can be produced in one or more radioactive forms, or isotopes. *See* **F12**(1).

Radio Astronomy. The science of radio astronomy makes use of radio apparatus and techniques for the observation of events occurring in far distant parts of the universe, and, in so doing, is able to enlarge upon the observational field of optical astronomy in a remarkable way. By means of radio telescopes it is possible to observe parts of the universe so far distant that the radio waves received have taken thousands of millions of years to travel from their source to the earth, and thus to observe happenings which may have occurred near the beginning of the history of the universe. Thus radio astronomy works with signals broadcast by objects in space.

There are two main types of radio telescope. The first, known as the interferometer, uses aerials spaced at large distances to obtain very high angular resolution. Indeed, the so-called very long baseline interferometers (VLBI) use receivers with separations of many thousands of km to obtain higher resolution than any optical telescope. The second, and "steerable" type, is that of the radio telescope at Jodrell Bank, Cheshire, which consists of an enormous concave metal bowl, with the radio aerials at its centre. This, though it has a lower "resolution", can be directed or "steered" on to any part of the sky which is above the horizon. The interferometers, particularly the VLBI, have been used to examine the fine structure of many

objects, including the nuclei of large and unusual galaxies. The jet-like structures recently found in several galaxies are of particular interest. As well as exploring the structure of gas clouds and clusters in our own galaxy and in more distant ones, several of the large steerable telescopes have been used as radar antennae, for example to explore the surface of the cloud-covered Venus, and to locate suitable landing sites for the *Viking* spacecraft exploring Mars. Increasingly the radio telescope is used as one of an armoury of instruments available to explore objects of astronomical interest.

Radiocarbon Dating is a method of dating the origin of organic materials or objects by observing their radioactivity. It is of great importance to archaeology because it enables prehistoric dates back to about 50,000 B.C. to be established for animal and vegetable remains. It works because cosmic rays (*q.v.*) entering the atmosphere create neutrons which convert nitrogen in the air to radioactive carbon. This forms radioactive carbon dioxide and gets incorporated into animals and vegetables throughout the world along with ordinary carbon dioxide in a definite ratio, approximately 1 radio carbon atom to 0.8×10^{12} ordinary carbon atoms. When the tissue dies it stops interchanging its carbon with the atmosphere, *e.g.*, by breathing, and the radioactive carbon in it gradually turns into nitrogen emitting a β-particle (*see* **F12**(1)). The radiocarbon content decreases by about 1% in 88 years. By measuring the proportion of radioactive carbon left in, say, dead wood, and comparing it with living wood, the age of the dead sample can be calculated. This needs careful laboratory experiments. It is now believed that the proportion of radioactive carbon in the atmosphere varied from time to time in the past because changes in the earth's magnetic field affected the cosmic rays. This has to be allowed for in calculating the radiocarbon date. One use of radiocarbon dating has been to trace the spread of agriculture through the world from its origin in the Near East *c.* 7000 B.C. *See* **Tree rings.**

Radiosonde, a weather station in miniature carried aloft by a free balloon to heights normally in the neighbourhood of 16 km. Signals representative of values of atmospheric pressure, temperature and humidity are transmitted simultaneously by radio to ground receiving apparatus. The position of the balloon at any instant can be determined by radar, enabling the speed and direction of the upper winds to be deduced.

Radium, a radioactive metallic element, no. 88, symbol Ra, discovered by Marie and Pierre Curie in 1898. Atomic weight 226. Radiotherapy (use of X-rays from radium) is used in the treatment of cancer.

Radon, a radioactive gaseous element, no. 86, symbol Rn, formed by radioactive decay of radium. Its discovery completed the series of elements known as the inert (or rare) gases. Radon has increasingly been linked to lung cancer.

Railways. *See under* **British Rail.**

Rain. When moist air rises into lower temperatures and becomes saturated, condensation takes place on the numerous hygroscopic particles present in the atmosphere. If the temperature is above freezing a cloud of small droplets is formed. These droplets may then grow larger by coalescing with each other as they pass through the cloud until their weight is great enough to make them fall to the earth as rain. In clouds which extend above freezing level, snow and rain both form from the prefer-ential growth of ice crystals at the expense of liquid water droplets. If the resultant ice particle melts as it falls to earth, it gives rain: if not it gives snow. *See also* **Acid Rain.**

Rainbow, a beautiful colour effect visible to an observer with back to the sun and facing a rain shower, caused by the refraction and reflection of sunlight in minute water-droplets in the air. From high in the air it would be possible to see a rainbow as a complete circle, but from the ground the most that can be seen is a semicircle when the sun is just on the horizon; the higher the sun is, the smaller the arc of the rainbow. When conditions are suitable two bows are seen, the secondary with the colours of the spectrum reversed. The colours the rainbow are seven; red, orange, yellow, green, blue, indigo and violet—the colours of the spectrum. See *also* **Aurora**.

Raingauge, an instrument consisting of a deep metal funnel whose stem dips into a graduated glass jar from which the depth of the rain water collected can be read. Continuous records of rainfall are provided by self-registering instruments.

Rain Making is a facility long desired by mankind, especially in the drought-ridden regions, and attempted throughout history by numerous non-scientific means. Since the second world war it has been proved that clouds can sometimes be made to rain or snow by dropping into them from an aeroplane very cold particles of solid carbon dioxide or by burning a solution containing silver iodide. This makes the moisture of the cloud form tiny ice crystals which grow big and finally fall out of the cloud. Research in this area still continues.

Ramblers' Association, an organisation formed with 1,200 members in 1935 and which now numbers 93,000. It has played a decisive influence on the creation of new long-distance paths (*see* **L76**) and the improvement of the footpath network. It supports the "Right to Roam" across all uncultivated land and in 1996 launched the 'Free Your Paths' campaign. In 1999 walkers were promised a statutory "right to roam" across 4 million acres of mountain, moors and common land.

Rambouillet, a royal French château (14th cent., rebuilt 18th cent.), near Paris, and the official summer residence of the President of the French Republic. Also the name of the literary salon of the Marquise de Rambouillet (1588–1665).

Rampant, in heraldry, is a term applied to the figure of an animal with forelegs elevated, the dexter uppermost. When the animal is shown side-faced it is *rampant displayed*; when full-face, *rampant guardant*; when looking back *rampant reguardant*; and when in sitting position *rampant sejant*.

Rape, a cruciferous plant yielding coleseed or rapeseed, extensively grown in all parts of Europe and India. Rape oil is made from the seeds and as oilcake is a valuable animal feeding-stuff.

Rare Gases (also called **Inert Gases**). These are a group of elements which are chemically inert, comprising helium, neon, argon, krypton, xenon and radon. Cavendish in 1785 noticed that there was in air some gas which was not oxygen, nitrogen or carbon dioxide, but it was not until 1894 that the first of the rare gases was found by Rayleigh and Ramsay. This they called argon (inert). After the discovery of helium in 1895 Kayser, Rayleigh and Travers soon isolated the other gases except radon, which was later detected as a radioactive decay product of radium. Some of these inert gases are used to fill electric-light bulbs, and helium is used in balloons, since it is very light and non-imflammable.

Rat, a well-known group of rodent embracing many species. The *brown rat* appeared in Europe early in the 18th cent., coming from the East and entering by way of Russia; now it is widespread and met with in Britain and all parts of the Continent. The *black rat*, which was the common rat before the arrival of the brown species, is a smaller animal and now comparatively scarce. There are numerous other kinds, all of them gross feeders. The 1990s has seen an explosion in their numbers.

Rational Number, a number which can be expressed as a ratio of two whole numbers. Examples are 2, ⅓, 0·3, −8. *See* **Irrational Number**.

Rationalism. *See* **Section J**.

Rattlesnake, venomous snakes which obtain their name from the possession of a rattle in the end of their tail, consisting of horny pieces so arranged that when vibrated they make a rattling sound. They are only found in N. and S. America.

Raven, a black-plumaged bird of the crow family, with raucous voice and massive bill. Occurs in many parts of Europe, Asia and America. Ravens are easily domesticated and form interesting pets. Dickens had one, described in *Barnaby Rudge*.

Ray, fish with a very flat body and broad and fleshy pectoral fins, related to the sharks. There are about 140 species. In Britain they are generally called *skate*.

Razorbill, a sea-bird of the auk family, having a high, furrowed bill and black-and-white plum-

age. It inhabits rocky cliffs during the breeding season, and at other times is mostly out on the open sea.

Realism is a vague term. As a movement in art it can be said to have started with Gustave Courbet in the mid-19th cent. in his revolt against the classicism of Ingres and the romanticism of Delacroix. He was a man of strong radical views, and like Zola, Balzac and Flaubert in literature, turned to the actuality of everyday life, recording it with frankness and vigour. Some young English painters, notably Bratby, of the "kitchen sink" school, practise what some describe as social realism. In another sense, realism is an attitude concerned with interpreting the essential nature of the subject, revealing truths hidden by the accidentals of ordinary visual appearance. Thus form becomes more significant than content: Beginning with Cézanne and Van Gogh this trend passes on to Cubist and Abstract painting. *See also* **Section J** (philosophy).

Record Office, in Chancery Lane, London, the place where the Public Records of England were preserved, including Domesday Book. These records have now been moved to Kew and Chancery Lane was closed to readers of original documents from December 1996. Modern records are subject to at least a 30-year restriction on access. Some records may be closed for 100 years. Since 1992 the PRO has been an Executive Agency.

Rectifier, an electrical device which will allow electric current to flow in one direction only and can therefore be used for turning alternating current into direct current. Since electricity is usually supplied in alternating form and frequently needed in direct form, rectifiers are of very common use in both industry and the home, for example in radio and television and for battery chargers. Rectifying properties are possessed by a number of different devices, one of which is a thermionic diode (*see* **Valve**). Very large valves filled with mercury vapour are often used for rectifying heavy currents for industrial purposes. Many other rectifiers use semiconductors in close contact with metals or with other semiconductors because such junctions have the property of passing electric current easily only in one direction.

Recusants, people who refused to attend the Anglican Church or to acknowledge the ecclesiastical supremacy of the Crown in. the 16th and 17th cent.

Recycling, the process of sorting and re-using waste products. By no means a new idea, and already much used in industry and by the whole community in war-time, recycling assumes prominence when materials are scarce and prices high. There is much evidence from several countries that the public responds well to properly organised schemes for the collection, sorting and re-use of paper, plastic, *etc*.

Red Rum, the most famouse racehorse of modern times. Winner of three Grand Nationals (1973, 1974, 1977).

Redstart, a small bird of the Thrush family of handsome plumage and striking song. Two species visit Great Britain: the Common Redstart, with bright chestnut rump and tail, white forehead and black cheeks, favours wooded country, and the Black Redstart, with black breast and throat, chestnut tail and white wing bars, prefers rocky ground or ruins, and breeds in S. England.

Redwing, a bird of the Thrush family which finds its way to this country for the winter. Resembles the song thrush, but distinguished by smaller size, buffish-white eye-stripe, chestnut flanks and underwings. It has bred in Scotland and on Fair Isle.

Redwood *or* **Sequoia**. This genus of coniferous tree comprises two species of Redwoods occuring in N.W. America. Specimens of one species, the Giant Redwood, reach a height of over 90 m and a thickness of 11 m. The age of the largest, the General Sherman tree, is put at over 3,500 years.

Referendum and Initiative, two methods by which the wishes of electors may be expressed with regard to proposed legislation. It is developed to the highest extent in Switzerland. In a *Referendum* some specific matter is referred to the electors. The *Initiative* is the means by which electors can compel their representatives to consider a specific issue. Gen. de Gaulle made use of the referendum in seeking the consent of the French nation for his policies. The British Labour Government held a referendum in June 1975, asking voters whether they wanted to remain in or withdraw from the European Economic Community. An Act of Parliament was required to authorise the referendum (which was something new in British constitutional history). The result was for continued membership. More recently Norway rejected membership of the EU in 1994, whilst in 1995 Ireland voted narrowly to legalise divorce and Quebec voted equally narrowly to remain part of Canada. Following the Labour victory in the 1997 election, referenda have been held in Scotland and Wales over devolution of power to elected assemblies. In May 1998 Londoners voted in favour of an elected Assembly and Mayor. In November 1999 Australia votes on whether to become a republic.

Reformation. *See* **Section J.**

Reform Bills. The principal Bills have been passed for the reform of the Parliamentary franchise. The first was the great Reform Bill of 1832, introduced by Lord John Russell and enacted under the Whig administration of Lord Grey. In addition to a sweeping redistribution of seats, this Act greatly extended the franchise but still left many people without the right to vote. The second Bill, passed by Disraeli in 1867, by giving the vote to workers in towns, established household suffrage. A third Bill, passed in 1884 under a Gladstone ministry, removed the distinction between borough and county franchise, enfranchised agricultural workers, and thus gave the vote to all men over 21. Women had to wait until 1918 to get the vote at the age of 30. The Representation of the People (Equal Franchise) Act, 1928, gave them the right to be registered as Parliamentary electors at the age of 21, thus making England into a true democracy. The Representation of the People Act, 1948, abolished the representation of the universities and the separate representation of the City of London and the business-premises vote. The Representation of the People Act, 1969, reduced the voting age to 18.

Refraction. The change of direction which light rays undergo when passing from one medium to another. The phenomenon is due to the fact that in different media light (and other forms of radiation) has different speeds.

Refractory, a substance capable of standing high temperatures and therefore useful for making furnaces and allied apparatus. Some insulating refractories are fire-clay, alumina, porcelain, carborundum, graphite and silica. Some refractory metals are platinum, molybdenum, tungsten, tantalum and the alloys nichrome, chromel and alumel.

Regency Style is the English version of the French Empire (*q.v.*) and approximately covers the period of the regency of Prince George, later George IV, from 1810 to 1820. It is somewhat less austere than the French style, and contains elements of the fantastic and exotic absent from Empire. The most famous monument of Regency style is the Royal Pavilion at Brighton, built for the Prince Regent by John Nash. (Regency style should not be confused with the *Régence* style in France, fashionable during the regency period between the death of Louis XIV in 1715 and the ascent to the throne of Louis XV in 1723. Here the English equivalent is Queen Anne style.)

Reindeer, a genus of deer horned in both sexes, occurring only in northerly regions. It has an average height of 1·3 m, is very fleet of foot and the Laplanders utilise it for draught purposes and for food. All reindeer antlers are a unique shape.

Relativity. The laws of relativity have been substantially proved and have revolutionised our ideas as to the nature of space, time, matter and energy and forced us to think along new lines. In 1949 a new theory by Einstein was announced which sets forth in a series of equations the laws governing both gravitation and electromagnetism, which is said to bridge the gap that separates the universe of the stars and galaxies and the universe of the atom. At present the one is explained by relativity, the other rests on the quantum theory. *See* **F17–19.**

Relief in sculpture is of three kinds—high relief (*alto-relievo*), in which the figures stand out to the extent of one-half of their natural propor-

tions, low-relief (*basso-relievo*) when the figures project but slightly; and middle-relief (*mezzo-relievo*), when the projection is intermediate.

Renaissance. *See* **Section J.**

Republican Party of the United States was born by the fusion in 1854 of the group who called themselves National Republicans, having split from the Democrats over tariffs in 1825, and the northern Democrats, both of them being opposed to slavery. It came to power when Abraham Lincoln was elected President in 1860 and won 14 of the 18 presidential elections held between 1860 and 1932. It was defeated in 1932 largely as a result of the economic depression and reached its lowest ebb in the years of Roosevelt's New Deal (*q.v.*) The Party went on being defeated every four years until Eisenhower's victory in 1952. Nixon narrowly failed to defeat Kennedy in 1960 and Goldwater was decisively beaten by Lyndon Johnson in 1964. In 1968 and again in 1972 Nixon was successful in winning the Presidency. His fall from power in the aftermath of Watergate made 1974 a bad year for the Republican Party. In 1980 and in 1984, Ronald Reagan won landslide victories. George Bush completed a trio of Republican victories in 1988. However George Bush was defeated by Bill Clinton in 1992. In the 1994 mid-term elections, Republicans won landslide victories but were again defeated in the 1996 presidential election. The symbol of the Party is an elephant, the invention of Thomas Nast, a cartoonist, in 1874.

Requiem. Properly a mass for the dead, the term is extended to cover musical settings by Palestrina, Mozart, Verdi and others.

Reredos, the ornamental screen at the back of the altar or communion table. It is often of a highly decorative character and is an architectural feature in many churches in Spain. Other examples are to be found in the following cathedrals in England: Southwark, St. Albans, Winchester, Durham and Liverpool.

Resins, natural resins are vegetable compounds largely employed in the industrial arts. They comprise india-rubber, amber, mastic, copal, *etc.* "Synthetic resins" is a term sometimes used as a synonym for "plastics".

Reuter, an international news agency, founded by Baron J. de Reuter in 1849. It became a private trust in 1916 and a public company in 1984.

Rhea, a large flightless bird, the "ostrich" of S. America, distinguished from the ostrich proper by smaller size, longer beak, larger wings, no tail and 3 toes instead of 2. There are 2 species.

Rheology, science of flow. *See* **F21(1).**

Rhinoceros, a large almost hairless animal related to the horse. Two kinds in Africa and several others in Asia. They have a horn, sometimes two, over the snout composed of modified hair. Most are leaf eaters but the largest species, the white rhino of South Africa, is a grazer. They have been much hunted for their horns. The numbers of rhinos, which fell sharply in the last two decades, are now (1999) reviving.

Rhodium, a metallic element, no. 45, symbol Rh, discovered by Wollaston in 1804. It is found in platinum ores in small amounts, generally less than 2 per cent. With platinum it gives a very hard and durable alloy. It is also used, instead of silver, in putting the reflecting layer on a mirror.

Ribbon Fish *or* **Oarfish,** a deep-sea fish, deriving its name from its ribbon-like shape. Though fairly long, it is only a few centimetres thick. The ribbon fish is rarely met with because of its habitat, and most of what is known about it was first learnt from specimens cast ashore.

Rice, a grain-yielding grass, of which thousands of strains are known today, extensively cultivated in China, India, S.E. Asia and certain parts of America, and forming the main food of the peoples of China, Japan, India and S.E. Asia. Some 95 per cent. of the world's rice is produced and consumed in the Orient. The grain with the husk is known as "paddy". Arrack, an alcoholic liquor, is made from fermented rice seeds. There are over 70,000 varieties of rice, including long grain, Basmati, Italian risotto rice and Japanese sticky rice.

Richter Scale, a series of numbers used to record the relative magnitude of earthquakes. Devised by F. Richter of the California Institute of Technology. An earthquake is given a number on the scale by measuring the amplitude of earth movements, *i.e.*, the size of the to and fro motion in an earthquake wave, with a special instrument called a seismometer. The reading is corrected by calculation to allow for the distance of the instrument from the earthquake and the corrected results by observers at different places agree quite well. The scale is logarithmic, *i.e.*, earthquakes differing by one unit on the Richter scale are a factor 10 different in amplitude. An earthquake allotted zero on the scale would give a reading of 10^{-6} m on a standard seismometer 100 km from the centre of the earthquake. Smaller disturbances would have negative values on the scale. The largest known earthquakes had Richter values between +8 and +9, *i.e.*, they had 10^{+8} to 10^{+9} bigger amplitudes than earthquakes of magnitude zero. It is a widespread misconception that the scale has an upper limit of 10; there are no upper or lower limits to the scale.

Rime, a crystalline deposit of ice formed on objects exposed to wet fog at the same time as frost.

Rinderpest *or* **Cattle Plague,** is a highly contagious disease affecting cattle, sheep and other ruminants. In Europe the disease has been eradicated, but it was formerly very widespread and caused great loss of life among cattle. The disease is caused by a filtrable virus, and is attended by fever and congestion of the mucous membranes.

Ring Dove *or* **Wood Pigeon,** a blue-grey bird, distinguished from other pigeons by larger size (41 cm), white wing-bar, glossy green-and-purple neck and white half-collar. It is very common in Britain.

Rituale, the book of rites used in the Roman Catholic Church for the administration of certain sacraments and other church ceremonies.

RNA (Ribonucleic Acid). *See* **Nucleic Acids.**

Roaring Forties, name applied to the prevailing westerly winds over the oceans in the temperate latitudes of the Southern Hemisphere. Because unimpeded by large land areas the winds are more regular and stronger than the westerlies in the Northern Hemisphere.

Robin (or Redbreast). A small bird with olive-brown upper parts and orange-red forehead, throat and breast; both sexes look alike. The young are speckled, lacking the red breast. Its wide European distribution includes the British Isles, where it is the national bird. It also occurs in N. Africa and W. Asia. The nest is placed in a great variety of situations including holes in banks, trees and walls; in sheds, amongst ivy and sometimes in old tins. Nesting-boxes are readily adopted, but care should be taken to ensure that the entrance-hole is small enough to exclude starlings. Robins are pugnacious and defend their territories with vigour. Their attractive appearance, trustful disposition, engaging ways and sweet song make them extremely popular. Robin numbers which were declining because of cold and rain, habitat loss and pollution have revived in the late 1990s. The name robin is also applied to a number of very different birds, one of which, the American Robin, occasionally wanders to Europe.

Rock Dove, the grey pigeon *Columbia livia* of Europe and Asia, ancestor of the domestic pigeons as Darwin was the first to show.

Rockets were invented by the Chinese as long ago as the 11th cent. The Germans devised the huge V2 rocket, carrying a ton of explosive, which was used near the end of the war to bombard London. Rockets are propelled by the burning of fuel (*e.g.*, oxygen or nitric acid), the exhaust, being ejected at high velocity, thrusts the rocket forward. For the study of the properties of the atmosphere vertical sounding rockets are used. Rocket flight in outer space was first presented as practicable by the Russian rocket expert, K. E. Tsiolkovsky, in 1903. The provision of sufficient launching velocity involves the use of rocket motors with adequate thrust. To launch a satellite into an orbit circulating within a few hundred kilometres of the surface a velocity of 29,000 km/h must be imparted. This may be done by using a multi-stage launching system. When the first-stage motor has burned out it drops off, so that, when the second-stage motor ignites, it does not have to support the weight of the first-stage, and so

on. If the launching velocity is increased to 40,000 km/h the vehicle will not return to the neighbourhood of the earth but pass out of the range of the earth's gravitational pull completely. Unless the launching velocity reaches 161,000 km/h it will not escape from the sun and will become an artificial planet.

Rock Magnetism. The study of naturally occurring magnetism in rocks is a subject which has gained considerable importance in recent years. There are two principal reasons for this. One is that this so-called "fossilised magnetism" may be able to tell us more about the past history of the earth's magnetic field. The other is that after many years of heated dispute between geologists rock magnetism promises to settle once and for all the controversy as to whether or not the continents have changed their relative positions in past times (continental drift theory (*q.v.*)). This branch of geophysical research, in addition to its academic interest, may well have important economic consequences. It might, for instance, become possible to locate mineral deposits once accumulated under special conditions at certain latitudes but now drifted to other places. Salt and similar deposits formed by the continuous evaporation of solutions in hot countries are one example; oil may well be another. There has been a *steady* change in rock magnetisation direction with geological time. It is known with some accuracy that the most recent reversal took place 700,000 years ago. It has been found that the older the rock, the farther removed is its fossil magnetisation from the present field.

Rococo, an architectural style which was, in effect, the final stage of **Baroque** (*q.v.*). The name first came into use about 1830 to describe the period 1720–70 and means "shell- shaped" (French *Rocaille*), since the shell was a favourite motif in Rococo ornamentation. At about the beginning of the 18th cent. the heavy older type of Baroque began to show even less restraint than had characterised it in the past; it became still less utilitarian, and showed a kind of playful light-hearted vitality which manifested itself in a wealth of ornamental invention. Baroque was flamboyant and robust, Rococo dainty, graceful and smiling. Its ornaments are frequently asymmetrical, and in this Rococo is unique among the historical styles of Europe. In architecture Rococo is naturally found in those areas where the Baroque had flourished, *i.e.*, Munich, Prague, Vienna and Dresden. In painting, the best expressions of Rococo are to be seen in the works of the French painters Watteau (d. 1721), Boucher (d. 1770), a favourite of Mme de Pompadour, and famous as a decorator of boudoirs, and Fragonard (d. 1806).

Roe, popular name given to organs in fish which produce eggs and sperms. "Hard roe" is that of the female and consists of eggs; that of the male is the soft roe or milt.

Roe Deer (*Capreolus capreolus*) deer native to Europe and found in England and Scotland but not Ireland. "Roebuck" is the name of the male adult.

Roller, a tropical Old World bird of the *Coraciidae* family, related to the hoopoe, kingfisher and bee-eater, of strikingly brilliant blue, chestnut, greenish-blue plumage. There are fifteen species, one of which breeds in the far north and visits the British Isles on its migrations to and from its winter quarters in Africa.

Romanesque Architecture, prevailed throughout Europe from the mid-10th to the 13th cent., and implies an art which developed from that of the Romans. Notable in Romanesque style were the rounded arch and masonry vaulting. Romanesque led to the graceful and more complex Gothic (*q.v.*). The Italians never regarded Gothic highly and Romanesque churches, generally based on the basilican plan (oblong with double colonnades and a semi-circular apse at the end), continued to be built there until the beginning of the 15th cent. Some of the best examples can be seen at Pisa (11th cent.), Florence (San Miniato, 1013), Lucca (12th cent.) and Milan (the 12th cent. San Ambrogio, most famous of all). In Germany Romanesque architecture flourished longer than in France or England; the most famous churches are in the valley of the Rhine, at Cologne (completely destroyed during the second world war), Mainz and Speyer. In France Romanesque churches are found in Burgundy, Provence and Normandy. *See* Norman Architecture.

Roman Roads, highways constructed by the Romans. They were of great durability. The best known British roads were Ermine Street (London, Lincoln, York), Fosse Way (Lincoln through Leicester, Cirencester, Bath, Exeter), Watling Street (Channel Ports, London to Shropshire).

Romanticism, a term for a movement in the arts—whether in music, painting, sculpture or literature—which seeks to give expression to the artist's feelings about his subject rather than to be concerned with form or reality. The romantic view is that art is nature seen through a temperament; the realist view is that art is a slice of life. In painting Delacroix (1798–1863) is the romantic artist *par excellence* with his uncontrolled expression of the passions and love of the exotic. In literature the Romantic movement reached its finest form in the works of Goethe, Schiller and Heine; in the poetry of Byron, Keats, Wordsworth, Shelley and Blake; and in the writings of Victor Hugo. Since Romanticism is partly a matter of temperament in the artist just as Classicism is. Cubism, for example, with its attention to form is classical whereas Surrealism with its attention to content is romantic. *See* Romantic Movement, Section J.

Roman Towns, among Roman towns were Aquae Sulis (Bath), Durovernum (Canterbury), Eboracum (York), Londinium (London), Ratae Coritanorum (Leicester), Venta Belgarum (Winchester) and Verulamium (St. Albans).

Roman Walls were built as frontier barriers under the Emperors Hadrian (76–138) and Antoninus Pius (86–161). Hadrian's works, linking Wallsend-on-Tyne with Bowness-on-Solway, comprised a twenty-foot stone wall, ditches, turrets, "milecastles", fortresses and a double earthen mound, or "Vallum". Impressive ruins are still visible at Chesters and Housesteads. Antoninus Pius, Hadrian's successor, made a further advance, but the turf wall which he built between Forth and Clyde was soon abandoned. Septimius Severus (146–211) restored Hadrian's wall after the assassination of Commodus and the subsequent civil wars. It was finally abandoned between 380 and 390. Hadrian's Wall is now a UNESCO World Heritage Site.

Romany. *See* Gypsies, L54.

Rood Screen, an ornamental partition, separating the choir from the nave in a church, and supporting a crucifix or rood.

Rook, a member of the crow family, abounding in most parts of the British Isles and found in Europe, Asia and N. Africa. It has been introduced into New Zealand. Rooks usually nest in colonies in tall trees. They are highly intelligent birds, and their ways have long been the subject of much careful study.

Rosary, a circular chain of beads, used by Catholics when reciting a particular form of prayer. Each bead represents an entire prayer, and the combined prayers constitute the Rosary.

Roses, Wars of the (1455–85), between the rival houses of York and Lancaster, for the possession of the English crown, began in the reign of Henry VI and ended with the death of Richard III on Bosworth Field. The emblem or badge of the Lancastrians was the red rose and of the Yorkists the white rose. All rivalry between The Roses ended by the marriage of Henry VII, the Lancastrian, with the Princess Elizabeth, daughter of Edward IV, the Yorkist.

Rosetta Stone, discovered in 1799 by the French at Rosetta in Egypt, and deposited in the British Museum. It is a piece of black basalt about 91 cm long, and contains a decree of the Egyptian priests of Ptolemy V Epiphanes (205–181 B.C.) in (1) hieroglyphics, (2) demotic and (3) Greek characters. It was the three different inscriptions on the same stone that enabled hieroglyphic writing to be deciphered. In 1996 Egypt asked for the return of the Rosetta Stone.

Rotten Row, a corruption of *route de roi* (king's drive), the riding resort in Hyde Park.

Rouge et Noir, a well-known gambling card game played on a table divided into two sections and marked with two black and two red lozenges.

Any number of players can take part, and the money is staked on the red or black spaces. The cards are dealt out, first to Noir, until the pips aggregate more than 30; then in like manner to the Rouge, and the packet coming nearest to 31 wins the stakes.

Roulette, a gambling game played on a table carrying a revolving wheel divided into 37 compartments. Each compartment bears a number, 0 (zero) and 1 to 36. The numbers are mixed and do not follow any particular order. Of these 37 numbers 18 are black and 18 are red, whereas zero is green. The players stake their money on any compartment, colour or combination of numbers they please. The wheel is whirled round and a ball is set rolling in the opposite direction, dropping finally into one of the compartments, thus deciding the winning number and colour.

Roundhead. In the reign of Charles I and later, a Puritan or member of the Parliamentary party who wore his hair cut short. It was originally a term of derision applied by the Royalists, who usually wore ringlets.

Round Towers, high circular towers with conical roof and massive masonry walls, built during the early Middle Ages (*c*. 10th cent.). It is believed that they served as refuges and lookouts. These buildings are numerous in Ireland, and two remain in Scotland, at Brechin, which is attached to the church, and at Abernethy.

Royal Academy of Arts was founded in London in 1768, under the patronage of George III. The early exhibitions of the Academy were held first in Pall Mall, and later in Somerset House where the exhibitions continued to be held until 1836, when the National Gallery being built, the Academy moved its quarters to that building. In 1869 the present Royal Academy at Burlington House was opened. List of presidents: Sir Joshua Reynolds (1768), Benjamin West (1792), James Wyatt (1805), B. West (1806), Sir Thomas Lawrence (1820), Sir M. A. Shee (1830), Sir C. Eastlake (1850), Sir F. Grant (1866), Lord Leighton, (1878), Sir J. E. Millais (1896), Sir E. J. Poynter (1896), Sir Aston Webb (1919), Sir F. Dicksee (1924), Sir William Llewellyn (1928), Sir E. Lutyens (1938), Sir A. J. Munnings (1944), Sir Gerald F. Kelly (1949), Sir A. E. Richardson (1954), Sir Charles Wheeler (1956), Sir Thomas Monnington (1966), Sir Hugh Casson (1976), Sir Roger de Grey (1984) and Sir Philip Dowson (1993). The Royal Academy of Arts holds an exhibition of pictures, designs *etc.* every summer.

Royal British Legion, the ex-servicemen's welfare organization founded by Earl Haig in 1921. A non-political organization, it organizes the sale of poppies on Remembrance Day.

Royal Hospital, Chelsea, built by Wren, opened in 1694 as an institution for invalid soldiers.

Royal Institution, established 1799, and incorporated by Royal Charter in 1800 for "the promotion, extension and diffusion of Science and of Useful Knowledge". It was in the building of the Institution that Faraday conducted his experiments. Today it has extensive research laboratories. It is now also famous for its Christmas lectures for young people.

Royal Society was founded in 1660 and incorporated by Royal Charter in 1662. Viscount Brouncker being named the first president. Its *Philosophical Transactions* date from 1665. Among those who served as president of the Royal Society are Sir Christopher Wren, Pepys, Sir Isaac Newton, Sir Joseph Banks, Sir Humphry Davy, Prof. T. H. Huxley, Lord Rayleigh, Sir Archibald Geikie, Sir J. J. Thomson, O.M., Professor Sir C. Sherrington, O.M., Lord Rutherford, O.M., Sir William Henry Bragg, O.M., Sir Henry Dale, O.M., Sir Robert Robinson, O.M., Lord Adrian, O.M., Sir Cyril Hinshelwood, O.M., Lord Florey, O.M., Lord Blackett O.M., Sir Alan Hodgkin, O.M., Lord Todd O.M., Sir Andrew Huxley and Lord Porter. The current (1999) President is Sir Aaron Klug.

Royal Society for the Protection of Birds (RSPB), one of the foremost conservation societies. With over 1 million members it is the largest wildlife organisation in Western Europe.

Rubber, substance obtained from the milky juice (latex) exuded by certain tropical trees and shrubs after tapping. Demand spread so rapidly in the

19th cent. that plantations were established wherever the tree would grow. Seeds of the Para rubber tree (*Hevea brasiliensis*) native to the Amazon basin were obtained by Kew, the young plants shipped to Ceylon and it was from these cultivated trees that the vast plantations of Malaysia and Indonesia developed. Recent years have seen great advances in the production of synthetic rubber.

Rubicon, a small river falling into the Adriatic, and forming one of the Italian boundaries, the crossing of which anciently involved decisive action and constituted a declaration of war. Thus the phrase "crossing the Rubicon", denoting an act from which there is no withdrawal.

Rubidium, a metallic element, no. 37, symbol Rb, most closely resembling potassium. It is silverwhite and very soft, and was discovered in 1861 by Bunsen and Kirchhoff, using the spectroscope. It is rare, occurring in small amounts in the mica called lepidolite and in potash salts of the Stassfurt deposits in Germany.

Rubrics are instructions in regard to the ceremonies of the Church, appearing in red in the Prayer Book.

Ruby is a deep red variety of Corundum (aluminium oxide); one of the most valued of precious stones. Myanmar (Burma) yields some of the finest, and rubies of inferior colour are found in Thailand, Sri Lanka, South Africa and Brazil.

Rudd, a fresh-water fish of wide distribution, plentiful in the rivers of Britain. It is of a reddishgold colour, with a greenish-blue beard.

Ruff, a bird related to the common sandpiper, at one time common in the Fen districts. The males have a ruff of feathers round the neck in the breeding season. The female is the Reeve.

Ruffe or **Pope,** a small fresh-water fish common in most parts of central Europe, and similar in appearance to the ordinary perch. It is found in British rivers.

"Rule, Britannia!" the national sea-song of England, was written by James Thomson (1700–48), the author of the "Seasons", and set to music by Dr. Arne about 1740. The poet's words were "Britannia, rule the waves!" but it is usually rendered "Britannia rules the waves."

Rum, a ardent spirit distilled from molasses, and containing from 40 to 50 per cent. of alcohol. It is chiefly manufactured in the West Indies, and derives its special flavour from a volatile oil.

Ruminants, animals that chew the cud, being provided with a compartmented stomach, enabling them to swallow food, and later to bring it back to the mouth for mastication; *e.g.,* sheep, goats, oxen, *etc.* While in the rumen some digestion of food, especially cellulose, takes place by bacterial action.

Runcible spoon, a kind of fork used for pickles having three broad prongs. The word was used by Edward Lear about 1870 as a nonsense word and may be derived from *Rouncival* meaning large or huge from the bones said to have been dug up at *Roncesvalles* where Roland fell. Rouncival peas are the large peas called "marrowfats".

Runes, certain characters of an alphabet found in inscriptions in the Germanic languages, found cut into buildings and implements of stone or wood in many parts of northern Europe, including Britain. The runic alphabet originally had 24 letters. Scholars agree that some runes derive from Greek, others from Latin.

Ruskin College, the first residential college for working people, founded at Oxford in 1899 by the American Walter Vrooman. Ruskin celebrated its centenary in 1999.

Rust Belt, the old industrial states in the USA, now in decline.

Rusts, parasitic fungi, some common species of which have reddish spores which in a mass have a rusty appearance. A well-known species is the Wheat Rust (*Puccinia graminis*), which has an alternative host in the barberry.

Ruthenium, a greyish-white metallic element, no. 44, symbol Ru, discovered by Claus in 1845. It is harder and more brittle than platinum, in whose ores it occurs.

Rutile, mineral titanium dioxide. It is found in many igneous rocks, and in gneisses and schists, Its commonest colour is reddish-brown.

S

Sabaoth, a Hebrew word, meaning an army or host, and applied sometimes to the Supreme Being, *e.g.,* "the Lord of Hosts" (Rom. ix. 29).

Sabbath and Sunday. Sunday, or the Lord's Day, is the first day of the week in the Christian year. It was substituted for the Jewish Sabbath in the 1st cent. A.D. as the Christian day of worship in commemoration of the Resurrection. The Sabbath, in the Jewish system, was the last day of the week (Saturday in the Christian calendar), designated as the day of religious rest in the fourth commandment of the Decalogue. It was the Puritans at the time of the Reformation who applied the term Sabbath to the Christian Sunday and the two terms have been used indiscriminately ever since.

Sabbatical Year was instituted by the Jews in ancient times for the purpose of giving the soil a rest from cultivation. This was every seventh year. In universities a sabbatical year is a year of absence from duty for the purpose of study and travel, granted to professors at certain intervals.

Sable, a furred mammal of the weasel family mainly inhabiting Siberia. It is bright brown in colour, and has a long, bushy tail. American sable is a marten.

Saccharin, a white crystalline solid manufactured from toluene, 550 times as sweet as cane sugar. It is used as a sweetening agent; as a substitute for sugar when sugar is forbidden, as in certain diseases, or when there is a shortage. It has no value as a food.

Safety Lamp, as used in coal-mines, was invented by Sir Humphry Davy in 1816. The flame is enclosed in a cage of fine-meshed wire which allows air to enter and promote burning, but conducts away the heat generated in combustion so that no product of combustion escapes at a temperature high enough to ignite explosive gases in the mine.

Saffron, a plant similar to a purple crocus. It is used for orange flavouring and colouring.

Sainfoin, a widely cultivated forage plant, especially adapted for sheep. It is of strong, leafy growth and bears bright red flowers. It belongs to the same family of flowering plants as peas and beans.

St. Elmo's Fire, a glowing brush-like discharge of electricity which takes place from sharppointed objects on mountains or the masts of ships exposed to the intense electric fields of thunder-clouds.

Saints' Days. In the liturgy of the Roman Catholic church a saint is commemorated and his intercession sought on a special day (saint's day), usually the anniversary of his death. Pope Paul decreed that from 1 January 1970 the following saints were to be dropped from the calendar; Christopher, Catherine of Alexandria, Alexis, Pudenzia, Susan, Margaret, Viviana, Eustace, Martina, Venantius and Domitilla. Many others, including our own Saint George, and Nicholas (Santa Claus) were demoted, though they may be venerated locally. There are now only 153 saints' days in addition to those in honour of the Apostles, Saint Joseph and the Virgin Mary. The festival of All Saints is on 1 November.

Salamanders are amphibia superficially resembling lizards, from which they differ in having a moist skin and no scales.

Salic Law was probably instituted in France in the 5th cent. for the purpose of excluding females from inheriting the Crown. The Bourbons introduced the same law into Spain, but this was abolished by decree in 1830 to enable Isabella II to succeed.

Salmon, a fish notable for its habit of returning from the sea to spawn in the river where it was itself hatched. Their origin can be inferred from the chemical composition of certain blood proteins. Salmon from the two sides of the Atlantic migrate to communal feeding grounds off Greenland.

Saltpetre. *See* Nitre.

Salvarsan, the organic arsenical compound asphenamine, which Ehrlich discovered was able to kill inside the human body the spirochaete germ that causes syphilis. Also known as

"606". It has been superseded by neosalvarsan.

Salvation Army. *See* Section J.

Samarium, metallic element, no. 62, symbol Sm, one of the lanthanides (**L72**). Discovered in 1879 by Boisbaudran.

Sami (Laplanders). The bedouin of the far north, the last nomadic tribes of Europe. Their way of life is intimately bound up with the reindeer. The reindeer herds feed, clothe and shelter the Sami. The Sami are found in, for example, Finland, Norway and Sweden.

San Andreas Fault, is the dividing line between the North American plate and the North Pacific Ocean plate where "plate" means one of the rigid sections of the earth's crust as conceived in the theory of plate tectonics (*q.v.*). The fault runs roughly north-west-south-east in California passing near San Francisco. The Pacific Ocean bed and the North American continent are sliding past each other along this fault at about 5 cm per year. As at all plate-to-plate boundaries—another is the Western Pacific coast—the San Andreas fault is the scene of great earthquake activity. Between 1934 and 1970 there were over 7,000 earth-quakes severer than magnitude 4 on Richter scale (*q.v.*) in and near southern California. Because of large population centres, the activity of San Andreas region is studied with great care and some apprehension about a repeat of the San Francisco earthquake of 1906 which caused displacements of up to 6·4 m along the San Andreas Fault. *See also* **F9**.

Sanderling, small wading bird of sandpiper family; breeds in tundra regions of far north, and is seen on sandy beaches of Britain as a winter visitor. Conspicuous white wing stripe and, like Curlew, Sandpiper, Knot, Dunlin and other members of sandpiper family, has marked change of plumage between winter and summer.

Sandpiper, small- to medium-sized wading birds of several species whose migratory powers are so great that they are found in most parts of the world. They include the Common Sandpiper, a bird about 18 cm long, greenish-brown head and back, white under-parts, beak long and slender; Purple, Wood and Curlew-Sandpipers.

Sans-culottes (French = without knee breeches), a term applied by the aristocrats to the revolutionary leaders during the French Revolution who wore long trousers instead of knee breeches.

Sanskrit is the language of ancient India, spoken by the Brahmins, and existing in early Oriental literature. It was the language of literature and government and is now confined to temples and places of learning. Its relationship to the modern Indian languages is like that of Latin and Greek to modern European languages.

Saponin. The term is a generic one applied to a range of organic compounds which produce frothy, soapy solutions. Saponins are ex-tracted from the soapwort root, horse chestnut seeds, *etc.* Saponin is the basis of the "foam" used for fire fighting; it can be used like soap to make insecticides and fungicides adhere to the leaves of plants. Also used as detergents.

Sapphic Verse, a form of verse said to have been invented by Sappho, the lyric poetess of Lesbos, who flourished about 600 B.C.

Sapphire, a valuable deep blue variety of Corun-dum (aluminium oxide) found mostly in India, Sri Lanka and Northern Italy. Synthetic sapphire is often used for gramophone styli.

Saracen, the name given in classic times to the Arab tribes of Syria and adjacent territories. In the Middle Ages the current designation among Christians for their Muslim enemies.

Sarcophagus, the name given to a stone coffin, such as was used by the ancient Egyptians, Greeks, and Romans, for receiving the remains of their famous dead. These sarcophagi were often decorated with carvings and sculptures.

Sassanides were a dynasty of Persian rulers de-scended from Artaxerxes from 226 to 625.

Satellite Communication, the system for trans-mitting telephone and television signals over long distances. The global satellite system Intelsat (Inter-national Telecommunications Satellite Organisa-tion) was founded in 1964 to establish a world-wide system on a commercial basis. The first generation of Intelsat satellites to be launched from Florida was *Early Bird*, which went into service in June 1965. Further series have been introduced since then. For example, in 1981 Intelsat had five satellites covering the Atlantic, Indian and Pacific oceans. Today, satellite com-munication has expanded out of all recognition.

Satrap, the name given to the governor of a province (satrapy) in the ancient Persian monarchy.

Saturday, the seventh day of the week (the Jewish Sabbath), derived name from planet Saturn.

Saturn, the sixth planet in order from the sun, from which it is distant 1427×10^6 km and around which it makes a revolution in 29.46 years (**F8**). It is 120,200 km in diameter or 9.42 times as large as the Earth and rotates on its axis in 10h 14 min. Saturn is noted for its magnificent ring system which is composed of myriads of ice-covered particles. Among the planet's 18 moons are Mimas, Enceladus, Tethys, Dione, Titan, Rhea, Hyperion, Iapetus and Phoebe. Titan is the largest (radius 2,575 km), being the second largest satellite in the solar system, about the size of the planet Mercury. Galileo was the first to observe that Saturn was ringed; Christiaan Huygens the first to study the nature of the rings; and Jacques Cassini the first to suggest that they were composed of myriads of particles. Our knowledge of the planet and its moons and rings has been greatly increased by the camera observations of the spacecrafts Pioneer 11 (flyby Sept 1979), Voyager 1 (flyby autumn 1980) and Voyager 2 (flyby Aug 1981). The Cassini space probe, launched back in 1997, is planned to reach Titan (where water vapour is believed to exist) in 2004. *See also* **Voyager 1 and 2, L127.**

Saturnalia, festivals held in ancient Rome in honour of the god Saturnus.

Sawfly. These insects are considered to be the most primitive members of the order (*Hymeno-petra*) to which the bees and wasps belong. In appearance they resemble somewhat the latter, but there is no waist separating thorax and abdomen. The ovipositor is never used as a sting; usually it is saw-like so that the female can use it to make incisions into tissues of plants where the eggs are laid. The larvae look like caterpillars of butterflies and moths.

Saxons, a Teutonic race originally inhabiting what is now Holstein. By the 7th cent. they had, with the Angles and Jutes, conquered and colonised most of England. The three main Anglo-Saxon kingdoms were Northumbria, Mercia and Wessex. The Saxons first arrived *c.* 449 A.D.

Scallop, marine bivalve molluscs of the genus *Pecten*, which is widely distributed. The scalloped edge to the shell results from a pattern of radiating groves. Related to the oyster.

Scandium, a metallic element, no. 21, symbol Sc. It was discovered in 1879 by Nilson, and occurs in small quantities in certain rarer minerals such as wolframite.

Scarabaeidae, a family of beetles (Scarabs) widely distributed through Africa and Asia and the inner parts of Europe. It is to this genus that the "Sacred Beetle" of the Egyptians belongs, and numerous representations of it are found on ancient monuments.

Sceptre, the staff or rod used since ancient times to symbolise supreme authority. The sceptre used for the coronation of Queen Elizabeth II is the one made for Charles II. It is about 90 cm long and tipped with a jewelled cross.

Schism, an ecclesiastical term for division in a church. The East–West Schism was the separation of the Greek Church from the Latin, finally estab-lished in 1054. The Great Schism was the division in the Roman Catholic Church from 1378 to 1415, when there were two lines of popes, one at Rome and one at Avignon.

Schist, the geological name of certain metamorphic rocks composed for the most part of mineral with thin plate-like crystals (*e.g.*, mica) so that the layers of a schist are closely parallel. Quartz occurs in schists, and where it preponderates the term "quartz schist" is applied.

Schoolmen, the great scholastic philosophers of the Middle Ages who devoted themselves to the study and exposition of questions of religious inquiry, and attempted to reconcile the teaching of the Church with that of Aristotle. The chief Schoolmen were Archbishop Anselm, Albertus Magnus, Thomas Aquinas, Peter Lombard, Duns Scotus. *See also* **Section J.**

Scientific Units. The International Bureau of Weights and Measures at Sèvres near Paris, is the custodian of accurate scientific measurement in terms of internationally agreed units.

Methods of measurement are continually being improved and measurements of new kinds coming into use. In defining units certain principles have evolved which can be expressed as a statement of priorities:

(i) units should be so defined that measurements made in one laboratory should be reproducible in another with as much consistency as possible;

(ii) units of all kinds should, so far as practical, form an interrelated system based on as few fundamental units as possible;

(iii) the fundamental units adopted should have a natural basis, independent of particular man-made objects such as metal bars or weights. An invariable universal natural standard was achieved for the metre in 1958 when it was defined in terms of the wavelength of a line in the spectrum of krypton-86. This was changed in 1983. See **L82** and **S.I. Units**.

Scone, Stone of, the ancient symbol of Scottish sovereignty. Known as the 'Stone of Destiny' it was placed in Edinburgh Castle in November 1996 (having been taken from Scotland in 1296 by Edward I, the 'Hammer of the Scots').

Scorpion. The scorpions constitute an order of the arthropods. Distinctive features are the pair of powerful claws at the head and a "sting" at the tail, which curves over the back in attack or defence so that it points forwards. The poison injected by the sting is potent, causing instant death in spiders, centipedes, *etc.*, and acute discomfort to humans. The idea that a cornered scorpion can sting itself to death is a myth; scorpions are immune to their own poison.

Scorpion Fly, the scorpion fly, of which there are less than 500 species, constitute a separate order of insects, the *Mecoptera*. They have 2 pairs of membranous wings, and gain their popular name because in some species the end of the abdomen is turned up, though it does not function as a sting.

Scree or **Talus,** the mass of loose, angular rock fragments which accumulate towards the bottom of hill-sides and mountain-sides. These fragments have been detached by weathering processes, in particular frost action.

Scythians, nomadic conquerors and skilled horsemen (9th—3rd cent. B.C.) who inhabited much of Southern Europe and Asiatic Russia.

Sea Anemones or **Actinaria,** an order of marine animals of the coelenterate class *Antozia.* They form a large and varied group of about 1,100 species and occur in many beautiful colours, flower-like in form.

Seaborgium, 106th element in the periodic table, named in 1994 after Nobel laureate Glenn T. Seaborg (1912–99).

Sea Butterfly, marine molluscs which propel themselves by two "wings", or side expansions of the foot. They constitute the order *Pteropoda.*

Sea Cow. See **Manatee** and **Dugong.**

Sea Cucumbers or **Holothurians.** These animals constitute the class of echinoderms called *Holothuroidea.* They are elongated and worm-like, with a ring of about twenty tentacles round the mouth. There are about 500 species.

Sea Eagle, a genus of flesh-eating birds related to the true eagles, kites and other birds of prey. Examples are the Bald Eagle, emblem of the USA, White-tailed Eagle (Grey Sea Eagle), and Steller's Sea Eagle of the Pacific coast of Asia. Last known in Britain in 1911, but successfully reintroduced from Norway in 1976 to the coast of Scotland.

Sea Elephant or **Elephant Seal,** a curious genus of seal, the males of which possess a proboscis of *c.* 30 cm in length that suggests an elephant's trunk. They are found on the coast of California and in parts of the Southern Ocean. Antarctic elephant seals can dive to 6,000 ft. and stay submerged for up to two hours—a world record for lung power.

Sea Gravimeter, an instrument to determine the density of the earth's crust beneath the oceans. Designed by Dr. A. Graf of Munich and Dr. J. Lamar Worzel of Columbia University, it can detect changes of one-millionth of the value of gravity at the earth's surface.

Sea Hare, a genus of molluscs (*Aplysia*), so-called because of resemblance to a crouching hare. The shell is thin curved plate largely sunk in the animal's body. They have four tentacles, occur in Britain in the laminaria or ribbon wrack zone, and discharge a purple fluid when molested.

Sea Horse, sea-fish (*Hippocampus*), very numerous in the tropics and comprising some twenty species. Their bodies are ringed and they have prehensile tails. Their heads are horse-shaped, and they swim in a vertical position. The seahorse is unique in that males become pregnant. Seahorses are no longer thought to be monogamous.

Seal, a marine mammal of the *Phocidae* family. They are found in the cold seas of the world, including the waters around Britain. In 1988, over 17,000 perished in the outbreak of deadly seal distemper.

Sea Lily. A class of echinoderms, the sea lilies may be roughly described as "stalked star-fishes". There are about 400 living species and several thousand extinct species are known. Otherwise called Crinoids.

Sea Mouse, a genus of marine worms called *Aphrodite*, oval in shape, 20–23 cm long, iridescent, covered with fine bristles.

Seasons comprise the four natural divisions of the year, and are due to the inclinations of the earth's axis to the plane of the ecliptic (*q.v.*). See **Z10.**

Sea Squirts or **Tunicates.** These animals are placed in the sub-phylum called *Urochorda*; found growing in rounded, jelly-like masses on rocks near low-water level. They get their name through the water jets they discharge.

Sea Urchin, species forming the class *Echinoidae.* The body is globular and covered with spines which may be used for both defence and locomotion. The main organs of locomotion are, however, the tube feet, as in starfishes.

Secondary Sexual Characters, characters of animals which are distinctive of sex, but have no direct connection with the reproductive process. Examples are: the mane of the lion and the antlers of some deer.

Secretary Bird, so called because of the quill-like plumes about its ears, is a bird of prey related to the eagles and vultures; common in Africa, and of considerable service as an exterminator of snakes. It is a large bird about 1·2 m in height.

Sedimentary Rocks. See **F9(1).**

Seismology, the branch of geophysics devoted to the study of earthquakes and other earth movements. The instruments used for the registration of earth tremors are termed seismographs and consist in principle of a pendulum system, the supporting framework following the ground movement and the bob remaining at rest, thus setting up a relative movement between two parts. In order to record the displacements completely, at one station, three seismographs are necessary to show the two horizontal and the vertical components of the motion. See also **Richter Scale.**

Selenium, a non-metallic element, no. 34, symbol Se; related to sulphur it is a dark red colour, and solid, found associated with sulphur, iron, pyrites, etc., though only in small quantities. It is a semiconductor (*q.v.*) and its special electrical properties have led to its use in photo-electric cells and rectifiers. Selenium is widely used in the chemical industry as a catalyst (*q.v.*) in producing aromatic hydrocarbons from less useful hydrocarbons. Also used in making some types of glass.

Semiconductors, substances with numerous special and useful electrical properties. These include:

(i) they conduct electricity much better than do insulators, but much less well than metals (hence their name);

(ii) their power to conduct depends strongly on their temperatures—which makes them useful for temperature sensitive devices;

(iii) they are sensitive to light—hence their use in photoelectric cells and solar batteries;

(iv) when in contact with metals, or with other suitable semiconductors, they form a boundary layer which conducts electricity much better one way than the other—this is the basis of many rectifiers some of which, called crystal diodes, are an important component in radios and electronic devices;

(v) their electrical properties can be greatly influenced by putting in minute amounts of impurity, this enables semiconductor devices, especially transistors, to be made with carefully selected properties.

Semiconductors were known to Faraday, but the semiconductor age really arrived with the invention of the transistor (q.v.) in 1947. The ubiquitous transistor is only one of very many semiconductor devices which perform a variety of functions in technical apparatus of all kinds. Semiconductors used in technology are usually small crystals, frequently of germanium or silicon, and their robustness and small power consumption often make them superior to other devices, such as thermionic valves, which they often replace. Other semiconducting materials are cadmium sulphide, selenium lead telluride, indium antimonide.

Senate, the higher governing Assembly of a Legislature. The word, applied primarily to the Roman council, is also used to denote the upper chamber in the legislatures of France, the United States, etc. In certain universities the governing body is also called the Senate.

Sensitive Plant. A species of Mimosa (*Mimosa pudica*), whose leaves are extremely sensitive to touch, shaking and burning.

Sepia, the "ink" of the cuttlefish. *See* **Ink Sac.**

September, the ninth month of the year, and the seventh of the old Roman calendar; hence the name, from Septimus. The designation was several times changed by the Emperors, but none of the new names survived for long.

Septuagesima Sunday, the 3rd Sunday before Lent.

Septuagint, the Greek translation of the Old Testament made by Alexandrian Jews between 250 B.C. and 100 B.C. from Hebrew texts now lost. There are many differences between the Septuagint and the Massoretic version (A.D. 900), and therefore it is of great value for textual criticism. The symbol for the Septuagint is LXX.

Sequoia. *See under* **Redwood.**

Serfs, the name given to the peasants formerly existing in Russia, who answered to the condition of the feudal "villeins" of England. They were attached to the soil and were transferred with it in all sales or leases. Serfdom existed in Prussia until 1807 and in Russia until 1861.

Serpentine, a mineral: chemically a hydrous silicate of magnesium. Green serpentine is used as an ornament stone. Fibrous serpentine is called asbestos.

Serval, a collie-dog-sized cat, long-limbed and spotted, from Africa. Preys on a variety of animals, from lizards to small antelope. Black servals occur mainly in mountainous regions.

Set, both in everyday speech (as in tea set, chess set) and in mathematics, a set is a collection of things. The members of the set can be specified by listing them or by describing the properties necessary for membership of the set, *e.g.*, the set of ginger-haired boxers. Set theory is a very important branch of mathematics founded by a great mathematician, Georg Cantor (1845–1918). Its development has influenced many other branches of mathematics.

Settlement, Act of, passed in 1701, assigned the Crown to the House of Hanover in case of Anne's death without children. The decision represented the determination of the squires and the Anglican Church never again to trust themselves to a Roman Catholic king.

Seven Champions of Christendom, as set forth in mediaeval literature, were St. George of England, St. Andrew of Scotland, St. Patrick of Ireland, St. David of Wales, St. James of Spain, St. Denis of France, and St. Antony of Italy.

Seven Churches of Asia, referred to in the Revelation of St. John, were those of Ephesus, founded by St. Paul in 57, Smyrna, Pergamos, Thyatira, Sardis, Philadelphia (Lydia) and Laodicea (Phrygia), all in W. Asia Minor.

Seven Wonders of the World were: 1. The Pyramids of Egypt; 2. the tomb of Mausolus, King of Caria (hence the word mausoleum); 3. the Temple of Diana at Ephesus; 4. the Walls and Hanging Gardens of Babylon; 5. the Colossus at Rhodes; 6. the Ivory and Gold Statue of Jupiter Olympus; and 7. the Pharos, or Watch Tower, built at Alexandria by Ptolemy Philadelphus, King of Egypt.

Seven Years War was waged by Frederick the Great and England against Austria, France, and Russia, from 1756 to 1763. It resulted in the retention of Silesia by Prussia, the breaking of French power in India and the strengthening of the British Indian Empire.

Severn Barrage, a barrier across the River Severn estuary proposed with a view to extracting useful electrical energy from tidal power. Essentially the idea is to let the tidal water flow into a reservoir upstream from the barrage and then to flow seaward under gravity through specially designed hydroelectric generators situated on the barrage. *See also* **Tidal Power.**

Sexagesima Sunday is the 2nd Sunday before Lent.

Sextant, a reflecting instrument for measuring the angular distances of objects. It is of special importance in navigation and surveying, and contains 60 degrees described on a graduated arc. A small telescope is attached and there are also a couple of mirrors which reflect the distant objects so as to enable them to be accurately observed. The invention is attributed to John Hadley, and to Thomas Godfrey independently, about 1780. The principle had been foreseen, and its application described, at earlier dates by Newton, Halley and Hooke.

Shad, a marine fish belonging to the same genus as the herring. It is found along the Atlantic Coast of the USA, and ascends rivers to spawn.

Shagreen, shark's skin: also untanned leather of peculiar grain made from skins of wild asses, camels and horses.

Shalloon, a kind of cloth manufactured from wool and worsted, and used chiefly for women's dresses and coat linings. It gets its name from the fact that it was originally made at Châlons-sur-Marne. It was called "chalouns" by Chaucer and "shalloons" by Swift.

Shamrock, the three-leaved clover-like plant native to Ireland and its national emblem.

Shark, a large and powerful ocean fish, comprising many species, very widely distributed, but most numerous in tropical seas. They have formidable teeth and are the most carnivorous of all fishes. They usually attain a large size, the whale-shark being often of a length of 15 m. Commercially the shark yields shagreen from its skin, the fins are made into gelatine, and an oil is obtained from the liver. Recent research on white sharks in the Mediterranean has shown their diet to consist of tuna and dolphin.

Sheep, a well-known family of ruminants of great utility as wool-producers, and for food. From the earliest times sheep have been a source of wealth to England. So much were they valued in the 15th and 16th cent., that their exportation was frequently prohibited. Sheep are classified under (1) longwools; (2) shortwools; and (3) mountain breeds. Most of the longwools carry Leicester blood in their ancestry and the shortwooled Down breeds carry the blood of the Southdown. The Southdown produced the present Suffolk, one of the most popular breeds. Cheviot is an important mountain breed. Of the foreign breeds the most valued are the Merino sheep of Spain, which yield a fine long wool. Australia, China, New Zealand, India, Argentina, South Africa, Turkey, Iran and Great Britain are among the chief wool-producing countries in the world. The first successful cloning of an adult sheep (Dolly) was achieved in 1997.

Shelduck, a handsome genus of surface-feeding ducks, one of which, the common shelduck, is an inhabitant of Great Britain. It is a beautiful white-and-chestnut plumaged bird with dark-green head and neck and red bill. Another species, the ruddy shelduck, appears in Britain only occasionally.

Shellac. This resin is the secretion of the lac insect (*Coccus lacca*), which occurs in forests of Assam and Thailand. It is used for making varnish and in the manufacture of gramophone records. *See also* **Lac.**

Shelter, the charity for the homeless, founded in 1966.

Sherardizing. Process for coating steel or iron parts with zinc to prevent corrosion; this is done by heating the parts in a closed rotating drum containing zinc dust.

Shilling has been an English coin from Saxon times, but it was not of the value of 12 pence until after the Conquest. It is interchangeable with the 5 new pence decimal piece which came into circulation in 1968. A new, smaller 5p coin was introduced after 1991.

Ships have existed from prehistoric times. There is mention of one that sailed from Egypt to Greece in 1485 B.C., and in 786 B.C. the Tyrians built a double-decked vessel. No double-decked ship was known in England, however, before the *Royal Harry* was built by Henry VII, and it was not until the 17th cent. that ship-building was carried on in Great Britain as a prominent industry.

Shoddy, the name given to a kind of cloth mainly composed of woollen or worsted rags, torn up and re-fabricated by powerful machinery. It was first made at Batley in Yorkshire *c.* 1813, and became a very important local industry.

Shooting Star, the popular name for a meteor.

Shot, the name given to solid projectiles fired from guns. In the time of Henry V stone shot was used, later leaden shot, then iron shot, and finally steel shot, introduced by Sir Joseph Whitworth.

Shrike, a large and varied family of birds of hawk-like behaviour found in all continents except S. America. The Red-backed Shrike, which winters in Africa, is a breeding visitor to England and Wales. It is commonly called the "Butcher Bird" from the way it impales its prey (small birds and insects) on thorn-twigs. The other species on the British list are the Great Grey Shrike, the Lesser Grey Shrike, the Woodchat Shrike, and the Masked Shrike.

Shrove Tuesday, the day before the first day of Lent, receiving its name from the old custom of shriving, or making confession, on that day. In England the day has always been associated with the making of pancakes.

Sicilian Vespers, the term applied to the terrible massacre of French people in Sicily in 1282. The French under Charles of Anjou were then in occupation of the island and had been guilty of many cruelties. It began at Palermo on Easter Monday at the hour of vespers and resulted in the expulsion of the French king and the introduction of Spanish rule.

Silence, Tower of, or *dakhma,* a tower about 8 m high, built by the Parsees for their dead. The corpse is taken inside by professional corpse-bearers and left to be consumed by vultures. Parsees do not burn or bury their dead, and the *dakhma* is to protect the living and the elements from defilement.

Silicon, an important non-metallic element, no. 14, symbol Si, it is related to carbon. Next to oxygen, it is the most abundant constituent of the earth's crust (27% by weight). It occurs in many rocks, and its oxide occurs in many forms (*e.g.* quartz, sand, flint, agate, chalcedony, opal, *etc.*). Principally used as a semi-conducting material for making transistors and similar devices. The circuitry of the computer is etched on a chip of silicon.

Silicones are synthetic organic derivatives of silicon which because of their high resistance to heat and moisture have special uses, *e.g.*, lubricants, heat-resistant resins and lacquers, and water-repellent finishes. Silicones are compounds in which the molecules consist of chains of atoms of silicon and oxygen alternately. Silicones were developed in the United States from discoveries first made by Prof. F. S. Kipping at Nottingham University. Manufacture began in Britain in 1950, and in the form of fluids, resins, rubbers and greases they find wide use in industry.

Silk, the name given to a soft glossy fabric manufactured from the fine thread produced by the silkworm. It was known to, and highly prized by the ancients, being at one time paid for, weight for weight, with gold. The manufacture of silk was carried on in Sicily in the 12th cent., later spreading to Italy, Spain and France, where Lyons has been the great centre of production from 1450 to this day. It was not manufactured in England before 1604; but when certain French refugees established themselves at Spitalfields in 1688, the industry was developed and became of importance. In the 18th cent. the Lombes of Derby achieved great success in this industry. Japan, China, Italy, and Korea are the chief silk-producing countries. Silk was produced in ancient China in the Shang dynasty (1176–1122 B.C.).

Silkworm, the larva of a species of moth, *Bombyx mori.* It is native to China, and has been cultivated with success in India, Iran, Turkey and Italy. The silkworm of commerce feeds on mulberry leaves and produces a cocoon of silk varying in colour from white to orange. The cocoon is the silken habitation constructed by the worm for its entrance upon the pupal condition, and to obtain the silk the pupa is killed by immersing in hot water.

Sill, a sheet-like mass of igneous rock which has been intruded parallel with the stratification of the country rock, *cf.* a dyke.

Silurian. This geological period is one of the major subdivisions of the Palaeozoic era. Its beginning is estimated at 440 million years ago, and the period lasted about 40 million years. Maximum thickness of the Silurian strata in Britain measures 4,575 m.

Silver, a white precious metallic element, no. 47, symbol Ag (Latin *argentum*) found in a free state, also in certain combinations, and in a variety of ores. The chief silver-producing regions are the Andes and Cordilleras. Peru, Bolivia and Mexico have yielded vast supplies of the metal since the 16th century, and Colorado and Nevada in the United States have also been very prolific in silver yield. In England standard silver (that used for coinage) formerly contained 92½ per cent. fine silver and 7½ per cent. alloy, but when the price rose to 89½d. per oz and the coins became worth more than the face value, the Coinage Act of 1920 was passed, reducing the fineness to half. To provide silver bullion for industry and for a fund towards the redemption of our silver debt to America, it was decided in 1946 to replace the United Kingdom silver coinage by one made of cupro-nickel (75 per cent. copper, 25 per cent. nickel). Maundy money, however, is of the original silver standard. Silver chloride and bromide are light-sensitive compounds and are used in photography.

Simony, the offence of trading in church offices, has been contrary to English law since the time of Edward VI. Elizabeth also promulgated laws against simony. Strict laws against simony are now in existence.

Sinn Fein (*Irish* = ourselves alone), Irish nationalistic movement founded in 1905 which developed into a mass republican party and triumphed in the establishment of the Irish Free State. A continuing group has survived which represents politically the outlawed IRA. In Northern Ireland Sinn Fein was legalized in 1974.

Sins, The Seven Deadly or Capital sins are pride, avarice, lust, anger, gluttony, envy, sloth.

Sirius, the dog-star, so called because of its situation in the mouth of the Dog (Canis Major); it is the brightest star in the sky, and is also one of the nearest to us.

Sirocco, a warm, southerly, often dust-laden, wind blowing across Mediterranean lands from the Sahara, in advance of an eastward-moving depression over the Mediterranean.

Siskin, a small bird of the finch family, common in Northern regions, nesting in Britain. The common Siskin has a yellow-green colour and is a lively, swift-flying bird with a stout bill.

Sistine Chapel, the chapel of the Pope in the Vatican, renowned for its frescoes by Michelangelo.

S.I. Units (*Système International d'Unités*) form an internationally recognised system of metric units for scientific and technical quantities. The basic units of length, time, mass, electric current, temperature, amount of substance, and luminous intensity are, respectively the metre, second, kilogram, ampere, kelvin (*see* **Absolute Temperature**) mole (*see* **F24**) and candela. The S.I. was recommended for general adoption by a number of international organisations such as the General Conference on Weights and Measures (1960). Many countries have made or are making the S.I. the only legally recognised set of Units. Gt. Britain's decision to "go metric" has brought general use of S.I. units in its train. These units command the widespread though not absolutely unanimous support of industrialists, technologists, and scientists. Many have urged their adoption to end the confusing multiplicity of units on the world scene. *See also* **F66–69.**

Six Articles, The Statute of the, was passed in 1539 for compelling adhesion to the chief doctrines of Roman Catholic faith: transubstantiation, communion in one kind only for the laity, vows of chastity, celibacy of the clergy, private masses and auricular confession; those who refused to subscribe to the Articles were treated as heretics. The Act was repealed in 1547.

Skink. The skinks constitute a large family of lizards with large smooth scales, under each of which is a bony plate. The largest species, found in Australia, is about 61 cm long. Some skinks have adopted a burrowing habit and degeneration of the limbs is associated with this. The Common Skink is a small species *c.* 12 cm long, living in deserts of N. Africa.

Skua, falcon-like marine birds related to the gulls found throughout the world. Known as "Robber Birds" because they steal not only the young and eggs of other birds (including penguins) but also their food, which they force them to disgorge in mid-air. The Arctic Skua breeds as far south as Scotland. The Great Skua breeds in both Antarctica and Arctica. Other species are the Pomarine, the Long-tailed, and McCormick's Skua.

Skunk, a North American mammal of the weasel family, with short legs and long bushy tail. All fifteen species are black and white, some being striped and the rest spotted. It secretes and ejects at will a foul-smelling fluid.

Sky. The blue colour of the sky on a summer's day is the result of the scattering of light waves by particles of dust and vapour in the earth's atmosphere. Blue light having almost the smallest wavelength in the visible spectrum (0·00004 cm) is scattered laterally about 10 times as much as the red (0·00007 cm).

Skyscraper. Owing to lack of ground space, increasing cost of land, and growth of modern cities, buildings are being made higher than broader; hence the name. The structures are constructed of steel framework usually clothed in concrete or reinforced concrete. The first modern skyscraper of steel skeletal construction was the Home Insurance Building in Chicago, designed (1883) by William Le Baron. The New York skyscrapers include the World Trade Center building (110 stories), Empire State building (102 stories), Chrysler (77 stories), Rockefeller Center (70 stories), and 60 Wall Tower (67 stories). Even taller than any New York skyscraper is the Sears Tower, Chicago (447m). The Petronas Towers in Kuala Lumpur (opened in 1996) reach 450 m (1477ft). Even taller will be the Daewoo Centre in Shanghai, China. The Grollo Tower in Melbourne (Australia) is planned to be the world's tallest tower. The tallest building in Britain is the 50-storey Canary Wharf tower (243·7m), visible from 20 miles away in Kent. It has overtaken the International Financial Centre (formerly the NatWest Bank tower) (183m) and the BT radio tower (177m). The tallest *structure* in Britain is the IBA mast at Belmont, Lincs. (387·1m).

Slate, fine-grained clayey rocks which have undergone metamorphism. They cleave easily, and it is this property of cleavage which makes them a valuable source of roofing material. Important quarries producing mainly green slate are in the Coniston–Ambleside area of the Lake District.

Slavery. In its earlier forms, as in the times of ancient Greece and Rome, in the feudal ages, when vassalage and villeinage existed, and in the serfdom of Russia and other northern nations, slavery was attended by many inhumanities and evils; but perhaps in the slavery system which prevailed in the British colonies for upwards of 200 years and in certain parts of the United States up to 1865, it attained its highest point of cruelty. In 1833 the Act of Emancipation was passed, emancipating all slaves in British territories, though slavery continued to be tolerated in northern Nigeria, Sierra Leone and in the Anglo-Egyptian Sudan long after that date. For a recent study, *see* Hugh Thomas, *The Slave Trade* (1997).

Slide Rule, an instrument which consists of two logarithmic scales sliding alongside each other. By its use multiplication, division, extraction of roots, *etc.*, are speedily carried out.

Sloth, a curious family of mammals, only found in Central and South America. They dwell almost entirely in the trees, proceeding from branch to branch with their bodies hanging downwards, their weight being supported by their large hook-like claws. They eat foliage.

Slow-Worm, a species of lizard found in Britain which lacks legs. Silver with longitudinal brown stripes, it lives almost entirely on slugs.

Smelting. The process of heating an ore with a reducing agent to convert ore into metal, and with a flux to convert rocky impurities into a slag that will float on top of the molten metal. Slag and metal can then be tapped separately. An example is iron smelting; the reducing agent is coke, and limestone is added as the flux; the smelting is carried out in a blast furnace.

Snake. The snakes constitute the important reptilian order *Ophidia*. Snakes have a scaly, cylindrical, limbless body, lidless eyes, forked tongue, and the upper and lower jaws joined by an elastic ligament. All snakes have teeth used for seizing prey, and the poisonous varieties are furnished with poison fangs in the upper jaw. These fangs are hollow modified teeth and the venom passes into them from a special gland situated behind the angle of the mouth. Some 2,500 species of snakes are known, divided into 13 families. There are 3 British species—the grass-snake, smooth-snake, and adder.

Snipe, a wading bird, long-legged, with long, slender, straight bill, brown plumage, and zig-zag flight. The Common Snipe breeds locally throughout Britain; the Great Snipe and small Jack Snipe are occasional visitors. The close season is 1 February to 11 August.

Snow. When water vapour condenses at high levels at a temperature below freezing (sub-limation), a cloud of ice particles is formed. If these frozen droplets are small, they fall slowly and gradually assume a feathery crystalline structure, reaching the earth as snowflakes if the temperature remains below freezing.

Snow Leopard. *See* Ounce.

Soda, carbonate of sodium, is now mainly obtained by certain processes of manufacture from common salt. It was formerly obtained from the ashes of plants. Bicarbonate of sodium is the primary product in the Solvay or Ammoniasoda method for commercial manufacture of soda; it is also formed when carbon dioxide is passed into strong soda solution. The bicarbonate is used in medicine and in the preparation of baking powder.

Sodium, a metallic element, no. 11, symbol Na (Latin *Natrium*), first obtained by Sir Humphry Davy in 1807 from caustic soda by means of the electric battery. Its chloride is *common salt*; the deposits of salt (*e.g.*, in Cheshire and at Stassfurt) have come into existence through the drying up of inland seas. Salt occurs in sea-water to the extent of about 3 per cent.; the Dead Sea contains about 22 per cent. The blood of animals is maintained at a level of about 0·6% sodium chloride. That there is sodium in the sun's atmosphere was confirmed in 1859 by Kirchhoff from his spectroscopic observations. Liquid sodium metal has properties which make it suitable as a coolant in some nuclear reactors; a technique of handling this very reactive liquid has had to be developed.

Soil Erosion occurs when the soil is removed from an area at a faster rate than soil formation. This situation usually occurs as a result of man's interference with the natural balance of the environment by the removal of natural vegetation, overgrazing or by poor farming techniques. Soil thus exposed is then removed by the wind (as in the Dust Bowl in the 1930s) or by rain in the form of gully or sheet erosion (as in the Tennessee Valley, USA). Methods introduced to stop soil erosion include contour ploughing, afforestation and dry farming techniques.

Solar Battery, one of the innumerable devices made possible by the development of semi-conducting materials, notably germanium and silicon. This device creates an electric current from light falling on it. The current can be put to use or stored in storage batteries. The energy of the current is derived from the sunlight. The solar battery is thus an *energy converting* apparatus. Solar batteries have provided power for the instruments in satellites.

Solar Eclipse, *See* Eclipse, **L38.**

Solar System, the system dominated by the Sun, containing the nine major planets and their satellites, the asteroids, comets, meteoroids and interplanetary gas and dust. *See also* **Section F.**

Solar Wind, a continuous stream of electrically charged particles blowing outwards from the sun, supplemented from time to time by intense outbursts from particular regions of the sun's surface. These streams of protons and electrons on encountering the earth's magnetic field distort it and cause magnetic storms (*q.v.*) and aurorae (*q.v.*).

Soldering is a means of joining together two pieces of material, usually metals, by melting a third metal (the solder) into the joint. The solder solidifies in the pores of the other metals and holds them together. The materials to be joined are not themselves melted so the technique requires less heat than welding. Solders are alloys; there are many kinds depending on the materials to be joined and the strength of joint desired. *See* **Welding.**

Solstice, an astronomical term indicating the point at which the sun is most distant from the equator. *See* **Seasons, Section Z.**

Solvents. The abuse of solvents such as glue, paints, nail-varnish removers *etc.* has grown recently among teenagers. Solvent abuse causes feelings of well-being or drowsiness and can lead to brain damage and dependence.

Soundings at sea, to determine depth at any point, have been taken in all seas, and with considerable accuracy. A deep reading was that of the *Challenger* expedition in 1873, near St. Thomas's in the North Atlantic, when 3,875 fathoms (7,091 m) were sounded. In 1851 H.M.S. *Challenger* recorded the then maximum ocean depth in the Marianas Trench (W. Pacific) by echo-sounding as between 5,882 and 5,950 fathoms (10,764 and 10,800 m). Another deep was located in the S. Pacific in 1952–53 of 5,814 fathoms (10,640 m) in the Tonga Trench, 290 km S. of Tonga Tabu. Since then greater depths have been recorded, in the Marianas Trench and the Mindanao Deep. *See* **Pacific Ocean.**

Southern Cross, popular name of *Crux*, is the smallest constellation in the entire sky and can be observed from latitudes below +30°. Its four brightest stars form a conspicuous Latin cross. The constellation is a vital guide to seafarers.

South Sea Bubble, the name given to a series of financial projects which began with the formation of the South Sea Company in 1711 and ended nine years later in disaster after a mania of speculation. The idea behind the parent scheme was that the state should sell certain trading monopolies in the South seas in return for a sum of money to pay off the National Debt (which stood at £51,300,000 in 1719 when the scheme started). The idea fascinated the public, fabulous profits being dreamt of, and the price of the stock rose out of all proportion to the earnings of the Company. Many dishonest speculative ventures sprang up in imitation with the inevitable result that thousands were ruined. All classes had joined in the gamble and a Committee of Secrecy set up by the House of Commons in December 1720 to investigate the affairs of the Company proved that there had been fraud and corruption on a large scale in the affairs of the Company. Sir Robert Walpole dealt with the crisis.

Space Flight. The Soviet Union was the first country to launch a man into space and bring him safely back to earth. This epoch-making event took place on 12 April 1961, when Yuri Gagarin, tragically killed in an air crash in 1968, circled the earth in a spaceship weighing about 4,826 kg. It was launched by rocket in an elliptical orbit with greatest height 300 km and least 175 km. The inclination of the orbit to the equator was 65° 4', and the period of revolution was 89 min. 6s. Since then, the Russian *Vostok* cosmonauts Titov (17 orbits), Nikolaev (64 orbits), Popovich (48 orbits), Bykovsky (81 orbits), Tereshkova, the first woman space traveller (48 orbits), the *Voskhod* cosmonauts Komarov, Feoktistov and Yegorov (16 orbits), Belyaev and Leonov (17 orbits), the American *Mercury* astronauts Glenn (3 orbits), Carpenter (3 orbits), Schirra (6 orbits), Cooper (22 orbits), the *Gemini* astronauts Grissom and Young (3 orbits), McDivitt and White (62 orbits), Cooper and Conrad (120 orbits), Borman and Lovell (206 orbits), Schirra and Stafford (15 orbits), Armstrong and Scott (6·6 orbits), Stafford and Cernan (44 orbits), Young and Collins (43 orbits), Conrad and Gordon (44 orbits), Lovell and Aldrin (60 orbits) were among the first to complete successful missions in space. Leonov was the first to perform the extra-vehicular (EVA) experiment (1965), *i.e.*, to leave an orbiting spaceship and float in space. Russia was the first to achieve an automatic docking (link-up) between two unmanned spacecraft in orbital flight (October 1967), and of two unmanned spacecraft (January 1969). The American *Apollo* mission was accomplished when Armstrong and Aldrin became the first men to set foot on the moon (July 1969). A joint Soviet-American project culminated in a *Soyuz-Apollo* link-up 225 km up on 17 July 1975. On 11 January 1978 two Soviet spacecraft docked with an orbiting laboratory, the first triple link-up in space. The longest endurance record is held by Valentin Lebedev and Anatoly Berezevoy (211 days in space aboard *Salyut* 7 in 1982). The first free walk in space was made by two American astronauts on 7 February 1984 from the space shuttle *Challenger*. The *Challenger* disaster in January 1986 disrupted America's space programme. *Challenger* has been succeeded by *Endeavour*, the most technologically advanced shuttle yet developed. Details emerged in 1996 of the next generation of U.S. spacecraft. These re-usable delta-shaped craft (the X-33) will be the first new rocket design since 1972. They are planned to be in service by 2007.

In 1991, Helen Sharman became the first Briton in space, whilst in 1995, Michael Foale became the first Briton to walk in space. In 1995, the Russian cosmonaut Valeri Poliakov broke the record for the longest time spent in space when he completed 438 days aboard the Mir space station. The US astronaut Shannon Lucid spent 188 days and 5 hours in space in 1996, a record for a woman.

Space Research. By space research we mean scientific research work which can only be carried to otherwise inaccessible observing locations by rocket propulsion. Such propulsion does not rely on the presence of an atmosphere to provide oxygen so that it is capable in principle of conveying objects to unlimited distances. The subject of space research is, therefore, one which is concerned with scientific applications in various fields of a single highly specialised and powerful technique. It is not a single discipline, but can provide data of great importance for many, such as the physics of the earth, the sun, moon and other bodies of the solar system, astronomy, geodesy and the study of gravitation. The prospect of investigating the biological conditions on different planets such as Mars and Venus is also opened, as well as that of experimental biological studies under conditions of zero gravity.

During recent years both the American and Russian space programmes have developed the concept of space stations for providing facilities for continuous manned observatories and laboratories in the future. There have now been successful soft landings on Mars and Venus, and "fly by" visits to Jupiter and Saturn. Voyager 2 left Saturn in Aug. 1981 visiting the planets Uranus (1986) and Neptune (1989) and continuing beyond. *See also* **Voyagers 1 and 2.** More recently, the launching of the Galileo probe into the atmosphere around Jupiter late in 1995 has greatly increased our knowledge of that planet. The Cassini Mission to Saturn was launched in 1997. Work is now well-advanced on the projected 400-ton Russian-American International Space Station (named Alpha).

Space Shuttle. The first reusable manned space vehicle, *Columbia*, was launched on 12 April 1981 from Cape Canaveral, Florida. It orbited the earth 36 times and returned on 14 April landing in California after a flight of 34 h 22 min with its two crew members controlling its landing. The 1986 *Challenger* disaster was a severe blow.

Spanish Civil War, 1936 to 1939. The war began with a revolt by the Fascist General Franco against the Republic which had succeeded the Monarchy in 1931. Germany and Italy aided the rebels who besieged Madrid for over 2 years. An International Brigade was formed to help the Republic, but the Spanish Government was faced with the greater part of the Army, and very effective assistance from Italy and Germany. Those powers seized the opportunity to have a curtain-raiser to the world conflict which they intended to precipitate. After a total loss of a million men the Fascists overpowered the Republic.

Sparrow, name given to finch-like birds found in most parts of the world, of which the House Sparrow *Passer domesticus,* is the most familiar of British birds. Also native to Britain is the rural Tree Sparrow, distinguished from the male House Sparrow by its chestnut crown. Other European species are the Italian, Spanish and Rock Sparrows.

Special Areas of Conservation (SAC). These areas of environmental sites of importance have now replaced Sites of Special Scientific Interest. In Britain they include woods (such as Windsor Forest and Great Park), mountains and moorlands (Ben Nevis, the Cairngorm plateau, Rannoch Moor *etc.*), whole river systems (the Itchen, Wye, Usk, Tweed, Spey *etc.*) and marine nature reserves (Morecambe Bay, Moray Firth).

Specific Gravity, defined as the ratio of the mass of a particular volume of a substance to the mass of an equal volume of water at 4°C. *See* **Hydrometer.**

Spectroscopy. Newton's arrangement with the prism was the first spectroscope; its function was to separate out the colour components of a source of light. Two hundred years elapsed before this apparatus was developed into a precise scientific instrument, capable of measuring both the wavelength and intensity of each colour component. In this form it is called a spectrometer. All atoms and molecules have well defined characteristic spectra which can be used to recognise them. In order to produce emission spectra it is necessary to energise the material under investigation by some means, such as by heating in a flame. The resulting radiation then consists largely of sharp bright lines, characteristic of the material. Absorption spectra are produced by interposing the experimental material between a white light source and the spectrometer. Then dark lines are seen, corresponding to absorptions of energy, in exactly the same places as the bright lines are observed in the emission spectra. Spectroscopic techniques have now been developed to such an extent that accurate measurements of wavelength and intensity are possible not only in the visible region, but over almost the whole of the electromagnetic spectrum. Two of the most useful types for the chemist are infrared spectroscopy which reveals absorption characteristic of the type of chemical bonds because of their different bond vibration frequencies and nuclear magnetic resonance spectroscopy which operates in the radiofrequency region. It reveals the structure environments of atoms containing particular nuclei. Not only does spectroscopy play an important rôle in probing the structure of matter, but it can be applied in the field of astronomy. The use of radio wave spectroscopy has led to the discovery of several new types of stellar object, and this data has produced a major reappraisal of our understanding of the universe. *See* **F14**(2).

Sphinx, in Greek mythology, a winged creature with a woman's head and a lion's body. The sphinx of ancient Egypt represented the pharaoh in a divine form.

Spiders. *See* **F36**(1) under arthropods.

Spiritualism. *See* **Section J.**

Spirituals, negro melodies with religious inspiration and which are still spontaneously created, but have also passed into art-music.

Sponge. *See* **Porifera, F36**(1).

Spoonbill, a long-legged, marsh bird, closely related to the ibis and stork, remarkable for its snowwhite plumage and broad, flat, spoon-shaped bill. The European species has not bred in England since the beginning of the 17th cent., but is still a regular summer visitor from the Netherlands, where it nests in colonies in reed beds and islets (*e.g.* Texel).

Sputniks, the name of the Russian earth satellites first launched in 1957. *Sputnik I,* launched 4 October 1957, became the first man-made earth satellite. *Sputnik II,* launched a month later carried a dog as passenger. *Sputnik III,* launched in May 1958, and weighing well over 2 tonnes, became the first fully-equipped laboratory to operate in space.

Stalactites are deposits of calcium carbonate formed on the roofs and sides of limestone caves,

and in tunnels, under bridges, and other places where the carbonic acid of rain-water percolates through and partly dissolves the limestone, resulting in the growth of icicle-like forms that often assume groupings. The water that drops from these may deposit further calcium carbonate, which accumulates and hardens into sharp mounds or hillocks called stalagmites.

Standard Deviation. In statistics it is often desirable to compare the variability or "spread" of different sets of data. For example, two kinds of light bulb could have the same average life but one kind could be more uniform or consistent than the other. The standard deviation is one of the commonest measures of spread. It is found as follows. If x is one of the data and x̄ is the mean of all the x's, then x − x̄ is called the deviation. Every deviation is now squared and the average squared deviation calculated. The standard deviation is then the square root of the average squared deviation. The lifetimes of the more uniform kind of light bulb would have a smaller standard deviation than those of the more erratic one.

Star, a luminous ball of hot gas which produces its own light and energy. *See* **Section F.**

Star Chamber, an ancient tribunal of state in existence in 1487 and possibly earlier, charged with the duty of trying offences against the government, unfettered by the ordinary rules of law. It was in effect a Privy Council entrusted with judicial functions. Under Charles I the Star Chamber was used by the King and his party to persecute opponents; and in 1641 a Bill carried in both Houses abolished it.

Starling (*Sturnus vulgaris*), a well-known European bird now common in many parts of the world. It has handsome iridescent blackish plumage and nests in holes and crevices. Flocks of starlings are often seen wheeling in the air; thousands roost on buildings in the heart of London. Other European species are the Spotless and Rose-coloured starlings. The latter sometimes wanders to the British Isles.

States-General, national assembly in which the chief estates of the realm were represented as separate bodies. The name, though not the institution, has survived in the Netherlands, where the two houses of parliament are known as states-general. In France the states-general consisted of three orders, clergy, nobility and commons. Philip IV first summoned it in 1302 to support him in his quarrel with Pope Boniface VIII. While absolute monarchy was establishing itself it met rarely, and not at all from 1614 until 1789, when it was convoked as a last resort by Louis XVI. But when it met it declared itself the National Assembly which marked the beginning of the revolution.

Statistics is a science that deals with the collection of numerical facts and the evaluation of their significance. The word is also used to refer to the facts themselves as in "trade statistics". This science gives precise meanings to words like "average" and to statements like "this set of data is significantly different from that". *See* **Average.**

Statue of Liberty, presented to the USA by Frenchman Ferdinand de Lesseps in 1884.

Statute of Westminster 1931. An Act of parliament which gave a basis of equality to the British Dominions. The Dominions as well as the United Kingdom were defined by the Balfour Memorandum of 1926 as "autonomous communities within the British Empire, equal in status, in no way subordinate one to another in any aspect of their domestic or external affairs, though united by a common allegiance to the Crown, and freely associated as members of the British Commonwealth of Nations". The Statute was the sequel. The Dominions are sovereign States governed solely by their own Parliaments and Governments.

Steam Engine, a machine whereby steam becomes the active agent of the working of machinery, and of very wide application. The leading types of steam engine are: (*a*) condensing, or low-pressure engines, where the steam is generated by a boiler; (*b*) non-condensing, in which the cylinder exhausts its steam into the open air. Engines of the latter type are used where portable engines are required.

Steam-hammer, invented (1839) by the Scottish engineer James Nasmyth. Consists basically of a vertical steam cylinder atop two legs with piston-rod passing through cylinder base and attached to a tup (hammer) of from 100 kg to 15 tonnes which rests on an anvil. The tup slides in V grooves on inside of legs. Length of stroke and therefore weight of blow can be accurately controlled from a light tap to a massive punch. It made possible the forging in one piece of multi-throw crankshafts for marine engines, *etc.* and the mass production of high-class axles and wheels, con rods and buffers, *etc.* for locomotives and rolling stock.

Stearin is the portion of fatty matters and oils which remains solid at an ordinary temperature, and is a compound of stearic acid with glycerine. It is largely used in the manufacture of candles. With caustic soda stearin forms a soap (sodium stearate), which is present in most commercial soaps which contain sodium palmitate and oleate in addition.

Steel, an alloy of iron and carbon, with varying proportions of other minerals. The famous blades of Damascus and steels of Toledo were made by the cementation and crucible method. The metal produced by the "Bessemer process" (*q.v.*) is of the highest value for structural purposes, rails, *etc.* The technique known as continuous casting bypasses some major steps in the conventional process of steel-making.

Stereophonic Broadcasting. A person having normal hearing is able to determine the direction from which a sound reaches him by virtue of the fact that he has two ears, and, therefore, the sound will reach one of them a fraction of a second before it reaches the other. This difference in arrival time allows the brain to calculate direction. It will, therefore, be apparent that if the same person listens to, say, an orchestral concert in a large hall he will be able to determine—even with his eyes shut—the approximate position of a particular instrument with respect to the rest of the orchestra. If, however, he listens at home to a broadcast of the same concert, then, due to the fact that he hears the music after it has been picked up by a single microphone located at one point and radiated over a single-channel transmission system, he will be unable to allocate a definite position to any instrument. The aim of stereophonic broadcasting, or sound reproduction therefore, is to restore the listener's ability to locate the position in space of the various sources of sound and to follow movement. To do this it is necessary to use two microphones in the studio—to simulate the two human ears—and to transmit their outputs, through two similar, but separate, chains of equipment, to two radio receivers and their two loudspeakers, which must be placed some distance apart, in the listener's home. The fundamental work on two-channel stereophony was done by A. D. Blumlein (1903–42), his original patent being dated 1931.

Stereotype, a metal cast taken from movable type which has been set up in the ordinary way. The first to introduce the process in practical form in this country was William Ged, of Edinburgh, who made stereotype plates in 1730. An impression of the type matter is first taken by means of a mould of prepared plaster of Paris or moistened sheets of specially prepared paper and when molten stereo metal is poured upon the mould and allowed to cool and harden, the stereo plate is formed, and can be printed from as a solid block for some time.

Steroids. A class of structurally related compounds, based on a system of condensed rings of carbon and hydrogen, which are widely distributed in animals and plants. Included in the steroid family are sterols, found in all animal cells, vitamin D, sex hormones, bile acids and cortisone, a drug used in the treatment of rheumatic fever.

Stickleback, a family of small spiny-finned fish widely distributed in both fresh and salt water. Male constructs roofed nest held together by sticky secretion from glands near kidneys. Several females deposit eggs therein which he jealously guards until after young are hatched.

Stirrup, a loop of metal 7-shaped strap suspended from the sides of the saddle, used for mounting and to support the horseman's foot. Some authorities allege their use as far back as the early Iron Age, and it is generally believed that they were used in battle in A.D. 378, when the Gothic cavalry defeated the legionaries of the Emperor Valens at Adrianople. Stirrups relieved the tension of the rider's knees and so enabled him to be armed from top to toe.

Stoat, a slender, carnivorous mammal with short legs, related to the weasels. The stoat is distinguished from the latter by its longer tail, which has a black tip. The black tip is retained even in the winter when the animal turns white, the fur then being known as "ermine". It is found in northern latitudes, and is abundant in Arctic America.

Stoma (pl. **stomata**), microscopic pores on the surfaces of leaves through which gaseous exchanges take place and water is lost. It is estimated that a single maize plant bears 200 million stomata, usually closed at night.

Stone of Scone. *See under* **Scone.**

Stone-Flies, comprise the order of insects called *Plecoptera,* which includes some 700 species, of which about thirty occur in Britain. The wings are membranous, and two long, thread-like feelers protrude at the tail end. The larvae are aquatic.

Stonehenge, a remarkable collection of Bronze Age monuments on Salisbury Plain. The site which contains ditches, earthwork-banks and megaliths (large stones) has long been recognised for its architectural innovations (the trilithon or free-standing arch and the circle of dressed and lintelled stone blocks) and for its astronomical, numerical and geometrical properties. The building and rebuilding, according to modern archaeological research, lasted from about 2100 to 1600 B.C.

Stork, a family of heron-like birds with long bills, freely distributed over Europe, Asia, Africa and S. America. The White Stork is an occasional visitor to England, and, more rarely, the Black Stork; these are the only two European storks.

Stratosphere, a layer of the earth's atmosphere which lies between the tropopause (*c.* 12 km above the earth) and the stratopause (*c.* 50 km). The ozone layer lies within the stratosphere and is responsible for the relatively high temperature there. The region is less turbulent than the troposphere, and is usually clear of clouds *etc,* making it attractive for air transport.

Stratum (pl. **strata**), a bed or layer of rock.

Strontium. This silver-white metallic element, no. 38, was discovered by Hope and Klaproth in 1793, and isolated by Sir Humphry Davy in 1808. The chief strontium minerals are celestite (sulphate) and strontianite (carbonate). Compounds of strontium give a brilliant colour to fireworks and signal flares. Radioactive isotopes of strontium (strontium-90) are formed as fission products in nuclear explosions and tend to collect in bone on account of the chemical similarity of strontium and calcium (*q.v.*). This hazard is a cause of great alarm. *See* **Fall-out.**

Sturgeon, a large fish found in northern seas and rivers with five rows of bony plates along the back and sides and pointed mouth with four barbels. Caviar is prepared from sturgeon ova. The Caspian sturgeon is now a fast-disappearing species and urgent measures are needed to protect all sturgeon.

Sublimation, when a solid substance is heated and turns into vapour without passing through the liquid stage and then condenses as a solid on a cold surface, it is said to "sublime" and the process is called "sublimation". Iodine behaves in this way, and sublimation is used as a method of purifying it.

Submarine, the first submarine, the *Nautilus,* was designed by Robert Fulton and tried out in the river Seine and in the sea off Brest in 1801. The idea was too revolutionary to find acceptance and it was not until electricity for under-water propulsion became available that the submarine underwent extensive development. Britain became interested about 1900 and the Germans developed it and made it into an instrument of warfare. The first voyage under the North Pole was made in 1958 by the American nuclear-powered submarine *Nautilus* (*q.v.*). The Government in March 1982 decided to replace the Polaris force with a new fleet of Trident II submarines at a cost of £7,500m. The first Trident submarine, HMS *Vanguard*, was launched in 1992. The fourth (and final) Trident submarine was launched in September 1998. The last Polaris submarine was withdrawn in 1996.

Suez Canal, connecting the Mediterranean and the Red Sea, was built by the French engineer Ferdinand de Lesseps and opened in 1869. An Egyptian company, *Canal Maritime de Suez*, was formed in 1866 with a capital of 200 million francs. The British Government acquired 176,602 shares out of a total of 400,000 for £4 million. Under the Convention of 1888 all nations were granted freedom of navigation without discrimination in peace or war. The right was recognised by Egypt in the Anglo-Egyptian Agreement of 1954, under which Britain agreed to give up the Suez base. The Suez Canal Company was nationalised by the Egyptian Government without warning in 1956, since when it has been widened and deepened and the average time of transit reduced.

Suffragette, member of the Women's Suffrage Movement who in the early part of this century agitated to obtain the parliamentary vote. The movement ended in 1918, when women of 30 were given the vote. In 1928 a Bill was passed which granted equal suffrage to men and women. The leaders of the Women's Suffrage Movement were Mrs. Pankhurst and her two daughters, Sylvia and Dame Christabel, Mrs. Fawcett, Annie Kenney and others.

Sugar, to the chemist the term is a generic one covering a group of carbohydrates, including cane sugar (sucrose), glucose, fructose, and maltose. In ordinary parlance sugar means sucrose, which is obtained from the sugar cane, sugar beet or sugar maple.

Sulphur, element no. 16, is a brittle, crystalline solid, symbol S, abounding in the vicinity of volcanoes. It is yellow in colour. It occurs in combination with other elements, as sulphates and sulphides, and allied with oxygen, hydrogen, chlorine, *etc.*, is of great commercial utility. Used in its pure state it constitutes the inflammable element in gunpowder; it is also used for matches and for making sulphuric acid.

Sulphuric Acid, a compound of great commercial importance, used in many manufactures, and composed of sulphur, oxygen and hydrogen. Extremely corrosive, and is present in acid rain (*q.v.*).

Sun, the centre of our solar system, is only one of millions of stars in our galaxy. The earth orbits the sun, which has a diameter of 1·39 million km, at a distance of 149·6 million km. The sun thus has a volume a million times that of the earth. At the surface, the gravitational field is 28 times that at the earth's surface. It rotates on its axis from east to west, though not as a solid, the solar equator turning once in about 25½ days and the poles in about 34 days. Large spots are observed on the sun which form and disappear at irregular intervals. The area of the disc covered by the spots, however, reaches a maximum roughly every 11 years, when the sun's heat seems rather greater than usual and magnetic storms more frequent (sunspot cycle). Spectrum analysis shows that the sun is composed of many elements found in the earth. Its surface temperature is *c.* 6,000°C.

The earth is in the outer atmosphere of the sun and subject to its winds and storms. The apparently inexhaustible heat of the sun, which has maintained life on the earth for millions of years, is derived from the destruction of matter, involved in the transmutation of hydrogen nuclei into helium nuclei, in which process about four million tonnes of matter are destroyed every second. At this rate of conversion the sun will go on radiating for 30,000 million years. The Soviet space rocket *Lunik I*, fired on 2 January 1959, became the first artificial planet of the sun. Recent research has shown that the Sun blows out bubbles—known as coronal mass ejections (CMEs)—every few days at a speed of 90,000 miles an hour. These can wipe out satellite communications and bring down power systems on Earth. The interior of the Sun is also more strange than suspected. Astronomers have found that, while the Sun's surface is resonating, regions below the surface appear to be smooth and flat.

Eventually, in 6 billion years time, the Sun will expand into a red giant and burn the Earth to a cinder. *See also* **F8.**

Superconductor, a metal in a state in which its electrical resistance has entirely vanished so that electric currents can flow indefinitely without generating heat or decreasing in strength. The superconducting state of metals was first discovered in mercury by Onnes in 1911. There are many magnetic and thermal properties associated with superconductivity and the phenomenon as a whole has proved to be of great scientific interest: it resisted explanation till about 1957. In the meantime many metals and alloys were found to show the property but only at very low temperatures—below *c.* −260°C. There is a growing number of practical applications, *e.g.*, coils of superconducting wire (kept very cold by liquid helium) can be made to carry enough electric current to produce strong magnetic fields. Such fields are very constant and do not require the large supply of electrical power that ordinary electromagnets need. By 1990, scientists seemed on the point of developing a revolutionary material that would superconduct (*i.e.* lose all electrical resistance) at *room temperature*. Such a development would revolutionise computers, power transmission and medicine.

Supersonic Speed, a speed greater than the speed of sound (in air at sea-level sound waves travel at about 1223 km/h). When a body travels at a speed which is greater than the speed at which disturbances themselves can travel, a mechanism exists for the generation of waves of enhanced intensity. Thus aircraft travelling at supersonic speeds produce shock waves in the air somewhat analogous to the bow waves of fast-moving ships. These shock waves are regions of intensely disturbed air which produce the sonic boom effect so distressing to people living near supersonic routes. *Supersonic* is not to be confused with *ultrasonic* (*q.v.*).

Surface Tension. The surfaces of fluids behave in some respects as though they were covered by a stretched elastic membrane. This property is called "surface tension". The action of detergents may be attributed in part to a reduction in the surface tension of water, allowing it to wet the surface of dirty articles.

Surrealism. The aim of the Surrealist school of painting and sculpture is to overcome the barriers between conscious and unconscious mind, the real and unreal worlds of waking and dreaming. As such it has a long and respectable ancestry, although the term was not in use until 1922 when it was picked by André Breton from Guillaume Apollinaire who had used it in connection with certain works by Chagall. However, Bosch in the 15th cent., Fuseli and Goya in the 18th, and many other purveyors of the weird and fantastic were the forerunners of modern Surrealism. The modern movement has broadly speaking taken two different directions: the first was towards complete fantasy and absurdity which took the form of "found objects"—*e.g.* a bird-cage filled with sugarcubes and a thermometer, a bottle-dryer, a bicycle wheel, or abstract works with strange and apparently irrelevant titles such as Paul Klee's *Twittering Machine*; the second towards highly detailed and realistic paintings of objects placed in strange juxtapositions—*e.g.*, Salvador Dali's trees with limp watches drooping over their branches. On the whole Surrealism has spent its force and become almost respectable.

Swans, large, graceful birds which together with the ducks and geese form the family Anatidae. There are three European species with white plumage; the Mute Swan distinguished by its orange bill with black knob (less prominent in female), a familiar sight on the rivers and ornamental lakes of Great Britain. Two wild swans are winter visitors here, the Whooper and Bewick's Swan. The "pen" (female) and "cob" (male) mate for life and the young swans are called "cygnets".

Swan-upping. The annual marking of the Thames swans which takes place during the third week of July. This ancient ceremony dates back to the 15th cent. when all the Thames swans were declared to be Royal birds owned by the Crown. Two city guilds—the Vintners' and Dyers' Companies—own about a third of the 200 swans now on the Thames. This privilege was granted to them by King Edward IV in return for money grants. Vintners' birds are marked with a nick on each side of the bill, the Dyers' with a nick on the right side only. The Queen's birds are unmarked.

Sweet Potato. This plant (*Ipomoea batatas*), which is a climbing perennial belonging to the convolvulus family, has thick roots that are rich in starch, and are eaten like potatoes. A native of the W. Indies and Central America, new varieties of sweet potato have been bred which stand cooler climates and can be grown as far north as Cape Cod. The sweet potato of New Zealand is called the Kumara.

Swift, a bird so-called from the extreme speed of its flight, resembling a swallow but related to the humming-bird. It has long, scythe-like wings, sooty-black plumage and greyish-white chin. There are several species inhabiting most parts of the world, particularly the tropics. The British breeding bird is among the latest to return from Africa and the earliest to go. Swifts are the only birds to use saliva for their nests. One oriental species builds its nest entirely from saliva.

Sword, hand weapon of metal used in open combat, characterised by a longish blade. During the Middle Ages the most famous blades were those made by the Arabs at Damascus and those made at Toledo.

Symbiosis. When two organisms live together and both derive mutual benefit from the association, the partnership is known as symbiosis. An example is the symbiosis of an alga and a fungus in lichens; another is the ordinary pea plant and the bacteria which live in the nodules on the pea's roots.

Synapse is the point of association between one nerve cell and another. The nervous impulse travelling along one nerve has to be transmitted to the next across a minute gap. This is the synaptic gap. The mode of transmission is chemical though it was at first thought to be electrical. The impulse arriving at the synapse releases a chemical transmitter which diffuses across the gap and stimulates an impulse in the adjacent nerve cell.

Syndicalism. *See* Section J.

Synod, an assembly of the clergy of a particular church, state, province, or diocese. The Synod of Whitby (664) settled the dispute between the Celtic and the Roman churches in the matter of Easter in favour of the Roman system of reckoning.

Synoptic Charts. These are meteorological charts used in forecasting on which weather conditions at a network of stations, at a standard hour of observation, are recorded, using symbols of the international weather code. Surface weather maps have been drawn regularly for more than a hundred years and the modern advance is the drawing of other maps showing conditions in the upper air. The plotting is done quickly by computer.

Synoptists. The writers of the first three Gospels whose narratives in the main agree, though Matthew and Luke add material not found in Mark; all three differ from John's Gospel.

T

Tactical Voting. A voting decision based on support for the candidate who appears to have the best prospect of defeating a least preferred candidate, rather than party loyalty (*e.g.* Labour supporters voting Liberal Democrat to defeat a Conservative). There was much evidence of tactical voting in the May 1997 general election, with the Liberal Democrats securing victory in 46 seats.

Taiping Rebellion, 1850–64, most famous of China's many peasant uprisings. It took place in Hunan (the province where Mao Tse-tung was born) and was savagely suppressed with the help of foreign powers.

Taj Mahal, the white marble mausoleum built at Agra by Shah Jehan in memory of his favourite wife who died 1629. Over 20,000 men were occupied for over 20 years in its erection.

Takahe or Notornis, large New Zealand bird of the rail family which for many years was believed to be extinct. Small colony found in 1948 in remote valley of mountainous part of the S. Island. The bird is strictly protected.

Take-Over Bid describes an offer made to all the shareholders of a company to purchase their shares at a named price and conditional upon acceptance by the holders of a named proportion of the total share issue. If accepted the purchaser thus gains control of the company.

Tallage, in Norman times, were taxes levied by the Crown upon lands of the royal demesnes. The levying of tallage was taken away by a statute of 1340 which required the consent of Parliament for all direct taxes.

Tammany, an organisation founded in New York (c. 1786) and formed from a benevolent society named after an Indian chief. It came to exert a powerful influence over political movements in that city. The leaders of the organisation used their power when their party was successful at the polls to appoint their nominee to every prominent office, and exacted bribes for concessions and privileges, and generally Tammany rule has meant wholesale corruption.

Tantalum, a scarce bluish metallic element, no. 73, symbol Ta, discovered by Ekeburg in 1802. Chemically related to vanadium and niobium, it is usually associated with the latter in nature. For several purposes it can be used in place of platinum, and it finds application in the making of surgical instruments. Tantalum is very hard, and resistant to acids (other than hydrofluoric acid); it is used in alloys.

Taoism. *See* Section J.

Taoiseach, the name for the Prime Minister of the Republic of Ireland.

Tapestry, a fabric largely used in former times for wall decoration and hangings. It was known to the ancient Greeks, but in its modern form came into prominence in the 15th and 16th cent., when it was manufactured in a marked degree of excellence by the weavers of Flanders, especially those of Arras. The manufacture was introduced into England early in the 17th cent., and was attended by considerable success. At the present day the term is applied to worsted cloths for furniture coverings, and there are also various kinds of tapestry carpets now made. The most famous tapestries of olden times were the Aubusson Tapestry and the Savonnerie. The Gobelin Tapestry factory, originated in Paris in the reign of Francis I, is still a national establishment. *See also* **Bayeux Tapestry.**

Tapirs. The tapirs constitute a family close to the horse family and the rhinoceros in the Ungulate order. They have four toes on the front feet and three on the hind. The snout is drawn out into a short trunk. The largest tapir is the Malayan tapir, which stands 1 m at the shoulder. Four species occur in C. and S. America.

Tar is a dark viscid product obtained from the destructive distillation of wood, coal, peat, *etc.* Wood tar is acid owing to the presence of acetic acid ("pyroligneous acid"). The highest proportion of coal tar goes into road making. Distillation of coal tar yields many valuable compounds, including benzene, phenol (carbolic acid), naphthalene and creosote; the final residue after distillation is pitch. Based on the chemical manipulation of compounds from coal tar is the preparation of many perfumes, food essences, drugs, antiseptics and plastics.

Tarpeian Rock at Rome received its name from the tradition that Tarpeia, the daughter of the Governor of the Citadel who betrayed the fortress of the Sabines, was crushed to death by their shields and buried beneath the rock. From this height persons guilty of treason were hurled to death.

Tate Gallery, named after its founder, Sir Henry Tate, at Millbank, London, was opened in 1897; Sir Henry Tate bore the cost of the building (£80,000) and also gave the nucleus of the present collection. "The Turner Wing", the gift of Sir Joseph Duveen, was added in 1910. A new Tate Gallery of Modern Art on the site of the derelict Bankside power station is currently being planned.

Tayberry, a high-yielding fruit, which is a cross between a raspberry and a blackberry.

Tay Bridge spans the Tay at Dundee, opened for rail traffic on 20 June 1887. A previous bridge, completed in 1877, was blown down on 28 December 1879, as a train was passing over it. A new bridge was opened on 18 August 1966 for road traffic, 2,244 m in length, the longest road bridge in Britain when it was first opened.

Tea was introduced into England about the middle of the 17th cent., when it was a great luxury, and fetched from £6 to £10 a pound. It is an Asiatic plant, native properly to China, Japan and India. Up to *c.* 1885 most of the tea imported into this country came from China. The bulk now comes from India and Sri Lanka.

Teal, the smallest of the European ducks and next to the Mallard the commonest British species. It is a handsome swift flier, but not as swift as the Garganey or Summer Teal.

Telecommunications. The sending of messages over a distance. The term is generally applied to the sending of messages by telegraph, telephone, radio, television or radar. The first submarine telegraph cable between England and France was laid in 1850 and, following Hertz's investigations into electric waves, Marconi's invention led to Britain being linked with Europe by wireless telegraphy in 1899. The first permanently successful telegraph cable across the Atlantic was laid in 1866. The first telephone service between London and Paris was opened in 1891. The electromagnetic telephone was invented by Alexander Graham Bell, a Scottish-born American, in 1876. The first submarine telephone cable to span the Atlantic was laid in 1956 connecting Britain with Canada and the United States, and many submarine telephone cables have since been laid including the Commonwealth cable system completed in 1967. The spectacular advances in space research depended on the new tools of work provided by parallel developments in telecommunications, *e.g.*, long-range radio and television transmission, electronic computer control. *See* **Satellite Communication, Radar, Radio, Television.**

Telemetry, measurement at remote distances by means of a radio-link from the object (missile or satellite) to the ground. The third Russian sputnik, for instance, carried apparatus for measuring, among other things, the pressure and composition of the atmosphere, and the intensity of different kinds of radiation from the sun. Its radio transmitter, powered by solar-energy batteries, sent out the information in coded form by means of uninterrupted signals at 20·005 megacycles with a duration of 150–300 milli-seconds. Radio telemetry from inside the body is increasingly used in medical and biological research; miniature radio transmitters can be swallowed or implanted in man or animal to detect physiological conditions.

Teleprinter, a telegraph transmitter with a typewriter keyboard, by which characters of a message are transmitted electrically in combinations of 5 units, being recorded similarly by the receiving instrument, which then translates the matter mechanically into printed characters. The telex service provides direct person-to-person transmission of written messages.

Telescope, an optical instrument for viewing objects at a distance, "the astronomer's intelligencer". Lippershey is credited with construction of the first in 1608; Galileo constructed several from 1609 and Newton was the first to construct a reflecting telescope. The ordinary telescope consists of an object-glass and an eye-lens, with two intermediates to bring the object into an erect position. A lens brings it near to us, and the magnifier enlarges it for inspection. A refracting telescope gathers the rays together near the eyepiece and is necessarily limited as to size, but the reflecting telescope collects the rays on a larger mirror, and these are thrown back to the eyepiece. The world's largest reflectors are at Mount Kea, USA (10m), Mount Pastukov, Caucasus (6m), Mount Palomar, USA (5·08m), Mount Hopkins, USA (4·5m), Cerro Tololo, Chile (4m) and the Anglo-Australian Telescope in Australia (3·89m). The *Hale* 200 in telescope at Mount Palomar revealed objects never before photographed; it is able to probe space and photograph remote galaxies out to a limiting distance of 2,000 million light years. The *Schmidt* telescope at

Mount Palomar has been used to make a huge photographic map of the universe. The giant steerable radio telescope built by Manchester University at Jodrell Bank, Cheshire, has a 250 ft reflector. The largest single radio dish in the world is the non-steerable 300 m instrument at Arecibo in Puerto Rico. Another instrument of radio astronomy is the interferometer which consists of spaced aerials. The biggest of these is in New Mexico. In 1990, the project to put the Hubble Space Telescope into space became reality, but the telescope suffered initial malfunctions. The Hubble uses gravity to magnify distant galaxies and its findings are giving scientists new evidence of the age of the universe. A new type of telescope named COAST (Cambridge Optical Aperture Synthesis Telescope) has been perfected that can take even sharper pictures than the Hubble. The world's biggest radio telescope, the Very Long Baseline Interferometer, (VLBI), a series of linked instruments stretching from the Caribbean to Hawaii, is now operational. This huge array of detectors is capable of seeing detail equivalent to a postage stamp 7,500 miles away. Astronomers will gain unprecedented insights into such mysteries as the birth of galaxies. The new (1999) Japanese Subaru telescope, the biggest infra-red telescope yet built, could help solve the mystery of how life was created. *See also* **F3, Astronomy, Radio Astronomy** and **Infra-Red Space Observatory.**

Teletext, the system of displaying printed information and simple diagrams on domestic TV.

Television, or the transmission of images of moving objects by radio or via the cable and satellite systems. To understand the problems of television it is necessary to consider the action of the human eye. Basically the eye consists of a lens which projects an image of the scene before it upon the retina, a light-sensitive screen at the back of the eye. The retina is made up of several millions of tiny light sensitive elements, each quite separate and distinct from its neighbours, and each separately connected to the brain by an individual fibre in the optic nerve. Thus the eye is a very complex organ, and it is able to pick up numbers of tiny details from a scene and convey each detail separately and simultaneously to the brain. It does not send a blend of different points of light and shade in the same way that the ear sends a blend of different sounds; if it did the brain would receive a completely unintelligible blur. From this it is clear that a television system which transmitted a mixture of detail would be useless; it must transmit all the details in a scene separately, yet almost simultaneously, and re-assemble them at such a speed that the eye cannot observe the building-up process. A means of doing this was provided by Nipkow in 1884, when he invented his famous scanning disc, and later Weiller invented the mirror drum for the same purpose. Such mechanical devices as these held the field for many years and in 1923 Baird in this country and Jenkins in America were both using them for the experiments which, in 1925, led to the successful transmission of shadows and simple outlines. It was not until 1926, however, that the first practical demonstration of television, as we understand it, took place when Baird transmitted by radio moving pictures of living human faces over a short distance. The BBC began televised broadcasts in 1930; the ITA in 1955. The first television exchange across the Atlantic was made in 1962 by way of the *Telstar* satellite.

A major development underway in the 1990s was the advent of digital television. For the past 75 years, television broadcasting has used the same analogue technology. Over the next few years the change to digital systems will dramatically increase the number of channels available for broadcast. In 1996 the British government legislated to allow licensing for six groups of digital channels, or multiplexes. The BBC, for example, has been granted its own multiplex and a financing deal designed to help with the transition to digital formats. It is hoped that one day the new technology will allow not only vastly more audio and visual services, but also a degree of interaction; the use of a television will blur with that of a telephone or a computer. For the time being, both industry and consumers face a bewildering array of unstandardised technologies. In autumn 1998 the BBC began transmissions of BBC1 and BBC2 in digital widescreen format and BSkyB has a 200-channel digital service. BBC Choice was BBC's first new general television channel for 34 years.

Television Licence. The cost of a current colour TV licence rose from £97.50 to £101 from April 1999. The black and white licence costs £33.50.

Tellurium, a relatively scarce element, no. 52, symbol Te, discovered in 1782 by von Reichenstein. Chemically it behaves rather like sulphur; its salts are known as tellurides. It occurs chiefly combined with metals in ores of gold, silver, copper and lead. It is a semiconductor, and some of its compounds (also semiconductors) are coming into use in technical devices.

Temperature. See **F66.**

Templars were soldier knights organised in the 12th cent. for the purpose of protecting pilgrims in their journeyings to and from Jerusalem, and obtained their name from having had granted to them by Baldwin II a temple for their accommodation. At first they were nonmilitary, and wore neither crests nor helmets, but a long wide mantle and a red cross on the left shoulder. They were established in England about 1180. During the crusades they rendered valuable service, showing great bravery and devotion. In the 12th cent. they founded numerous religious houses in various parts of Europe and became possessed of considerable wealth. It was this that caused their downfall. Kings and Popes alike grew jealous of their influence, and they were subjected to much persecution, and Pope Clement V abolished the Order in 1312. Edward II in 1308 seized all the property of the English Templars. The English possessions of the Order were transferred to the Hospitallers of St. John, afterwards called the Knights of Malta. See also **Hospitallers, Knights, Teutonic Order.**

Temple, a building dedicated to the worship of a deity or deities. Those built by the ancient Greeks at Olympia, Athens and Delphi were the most famous. The Temple of Diana at Ephesus was another. The Temple of Solomon at Jerusalem was destroyed and rebuilt several times; Herod's Temple was destroyed by the Romans in A.D. 70.

Temple Bar, an historic gateway (designed by Sir Christopher Wren in 1672) that until 1877 stood at the junction of the Strand and Fleet Street, London, dividing the City from Westminster. It was re-erected at the entrance to Theobald's Park, near Cheshunt, Herts., in 1888.

Terbium, an element, no. 65, symbol Tb, discovered in 1842 by Mosander, belonging to the group of rare-earth metals.

Teredo, the scientific name of the ship-worm, a peculiar bivalve mollusc, which lodges itself when young on the bottoms of wooden ships and bores its way inwards, causing much injury.

Termites, also known as *White Ants,* though they are not related to the true ants and are placed in an entirely different insect order (*Isoptera*). They abound in the tropics and also occur in temperate countries, though only two species are common in Europe. There is no British species. They live in colonies and their nests take the form of mounds of earth and wood, cemented together with saliva, and up to 6 m in height. Five separate castes are recognised, three of them being capable of reproduction, and the other two are sterile.

Tern. This slender, gull-like bird has long pointed wings, a deeply-forked tail, pale grey and white plumage, black cap, and is a very graceful flier. There are several species, some of which are summer migrants to Britain. The Arctic tern winters in the Antarctic, returning to find a nesting place in the spring. In 1997 a common tern set a world record for the longest known flight by a bird—16,000 miles from Finland to Victoria (Australia).

Terracotta Army, the thousands of life-sized figures in fired clay of soldiers who were to guard China's Emperor Qiu Shihuangdi after his death in the 3rd century B.C. Discovered by peasants digging a well in 1974, at Xian, it is often referred to as the Eighth Wonder of the World.

Terrapin, a kind of fresh-water tortoise. There are several species in the Northern Hemisphere.

Tertiary Rocks, in geology the rocks formed during the Caenozoic era comprising the Eocene, Oligocene, Miocene and Pliocene periods.

Teutonic Order, of German military knights, was founded in the Holy Land at the end of the 12th cent. for succouring the wounded of the Christian army before Acre. They were dispersed in the 15th cent. but the Order continued to exist until 1809, when Napoleon I confiscated its properties. In 1840 the order was resuscitated in Austria as a semi-religious knighthood. See also **Hospitallers, Knights, Templars.**

Textured Vegetable Protein, often referred to as TVP, is an edible protein material given a fibrous texture in the course of its manufacture from agricultural products. Nutritionally the material resembles meat and the extent to which it also resembles meat in succulence, flavour, feel in the mouth, suitability for chewing, *etc.* depends on the sophistication of the manufacturing technique and on the skill of the cook. The common starting material is the soya bean which is rich in protein and oil. The latter is removed, also for use in the food industry, and the residue is further processed to concentrate the protein and to remove unwanted flavours. A paste of suitable consistency is then forced under pressure through small holes and solidified as fibres. Bound together with a suitable binder and appropriately flavoured, these fibres form a lump of protein substance like meat.

Thallium, a blue-grey metallic element, no. 81, symbol Tl, discovered by Crookes in 1861. It is obtained from the flue dust resulting from the burning of pyrites for sulphuric acid manufacture.

Thanksgiving Day, a national holiday in the United States, observed on the fourth Thursday in November; instituted by the Pilgrim Fathers in 1621 to celebrate their first successful harvest.

Theodolite. The instrument used by surveyors for measuring angles in the horizontal and vertical planes; also used in meteorology for following balloons to measure windspeed *etc.*

Therm. The charges for gas for lighting and heating (formerly reckoned at per cubic foot) are now based on the calorific, or heat, value of the gas, and the unit used is termed a therm. The therm is 100,000 British thermal units.

Thermionic Emission is the departure of charged particles from matter under the influence of heat. The higher the temperature the greater the flow of escaping particles. The most common example is the emission of electrons from red-hot electrodes—this is the basic phenomenon made use of in thermionic valves (*see* **Valve**). If the hot electrode (the cathode) is enclosed in an evacuated or gas-filled bulb, the emitted electrons can be collected at another electrode (the anode) and will flow through an external circuit back to the emitter. Thus an electric current has been generated by heat.

Thermodynamics, a term first applied by Joule to designate that branch of physical science which treats of the relations of heat to work. What is called the first law of thermodynamics is thus stated by Clerk Maxwell: "When work is transformed into heat, or heat into work, the quantity of work is mechanically equivalent to the quantity of heat." In one of its many formulations, the second law asserts that "the heat tends to flow from a body of hotter temperature to one that is colder, and will not naturally flow in any other way".

Thermo-electric Devices. If two wires of different materials are formed into a loop and if the two joins are kept at different temperatures a current flows in the loop. This was discovered by Seebeck in 1822, and the device is called a thermocouple. The electric current could in principle be made to drive some useful machine, and the energy comes from the heat that is absorbed by the thermocouple—if one part of the thermocouple is not hotter than the others it will not work. It has long been realised that this is a device that converts heat directly into electricity without raising steam and driving dynamos as in a power-station. However, until recently nobody has used thermocouples for much besides temperature measurement, for which they are exceedingly useful. The new development is the manufacture of semiconductors (*q.v.*); for the thermo-electric effects of these new materials are much greater than those of metals. A material much studied in this connection is a compound of bismuth and tellurium, bismuth telluride. It now seems practicable to generate useful electricity from suitably designed thermocouples. For example, Russia produces a thermo-electric device which uses the heat from the chimney of a domestic oil-lamp to produce enough electricity to work a radio. Presumably this is very useful in remote parts with no electricity supply. But the possibilities do not stop there. Indeed, an eminent Russian authority has stated that thermocouples could produce electricity direct from the warmth of sunlight on a scale and at a cost comparable with conventional fuel-burning power-stations. Even if solar energy cannot be so used, it might be possible to use the heat of nuclear reactors, but this means that the thermo-electric devices would have to stand up to very heavy radioactivity and still work.

Thermometer, an instrument by which the temperature of bodies is ascertained. The most familiar kind of thermometer consists of a glass tube with a very small bore, containing, in general, mercury or alcohol. This expands or contracts with variation in the temperature, and the length of the thread of mercury or alcohol gives the temperature reading on a scale graduated in degrees. *See also* **F66–69.**

Thermonuclear Reactions. *See* **Nuclear Fusion.**

Thirty-nine Articles. *See* **Articles.**

Thistle, Order of. *See* **Knighthood.**

Thorium, a scarce, dark grey, metal element, no. 90, symbol Th, discovered by Berzelius in 1828. All substances containing thorium are radioactive. Chief source of thorium is monazite sand, big deposits of which occur in Travancore (India), Brazil and the USA. Important as a potential source of atomic energy since the discovery that it can be transmuted into U^{233}, which is capable of fission like U^{235}.

Thrush, a large family of song-birds of the *Passeriform* order, distributed all over the world. The British species include the robin, redstart, nightingale, song-thrush (or mavis), blackbird, mistle-thrush, ring-ouzel of the mountains and large numbers of migrant fieldfares and redwings from northern Europe are winter visitors.

Thunder, the sound heard after the occurrence of a lightning flash. It is due to vibrations of the air along the path of the flash, which are set up by the sudden heating (and expansion) followed by the rapid cooling (and contraction) to which the air is subjected. It is unusual for thunder to be heard more than 16 km away, the distance being estimated roughly by allowing 1 km for every 3 seconds which elapse between seeing the flash and hearing the thunder. Continued rolling of thunder results from the zig-zag nature of the flash and the multiple strokes of which it is composed, variations in the energy developed along the path, and echo effects. Thunderstorms are caused by powerful rising currents of air within towering cumulonimbus clouds and are most frequent during the afternoons and evenings of sunny summer days.

Thursday, the 5th day of the week, named after Thor, the Scandinavian deity. To the Romans Thursday was *dies Jovis,* or Jupiter's day.

Tiananmen Square, central square in Beijing (Peking). Scene of 1989 massacre of protesters.

Tidal Power. The principle of exploiting the energy of the tides is similar to hydro-power since it involves the harnessing of falling water. A barrage across a bay or estuary is filled during flow tide and closed during ebb tide creating a difference in level. When the water is allowed to fall towards the lower side of the barrage it operates a turbine which drives a generator. More sophisticated schemes would incorporate pumped storage facilities. An essential requirement is a large tidal range in order to get a sufficient head of water. Britain's first commercial wave-power station is likely to open on the west coast of Scotland. *See also* **Hydroelectric Schemes.**

Tides, the periodical rise and fall of the waters of the ocean and its arms, are due to the gravitational effect of the moon and sun. Newton was the first to give a general explanation of the phenomenon of the tides. He supposed the ocean to cover the whole earth and to assume at each instant a figure of equilibrium, under the combined gravitational influence of earth, sun and moon, thus making and controlling the tides. At most places there are two tides a day, and the times of high-and low-water vary according to the positions of the sun and moon relative to the earth. When earth, moon and sun are in line (at full moon and new moon) the gravitational pull is greatest and we get "spring" tides. When sun and moon are at right angles (first and third quarters of the moon's phases) we get the smaller "neap" tides.

Tiers Etat, the lowest of the three estates of the realm as reckoned in France—nobility, clergy and commons (*tiers état*)—prior to the Revolution.

Tiger, a powerful carnivorous animal of the cat family, which occurs in India and certain other parts of Asia. Its skin is of a tawny yellow, relieved by black stripings of great beauty of formation. Some tigers attain a length of from 3 to 3·6 m. There are now (1999) only an estimated 5,000 to 7,500 tigers in the wild, whereas in 1900 there were 40,000 tigers in India alone. The Siberian tiger is the world's largest cat. Only an estimated 500 now remain in the wild.

Tilapia, alternative name for St Peter's fish.

Time. The measurement of time has become of increasing importance to man with the advance of civilisation. It was at first almost inevitably based on the succession of night and day, the waxing and the waning of the moon, and on the changing seasons of the year, and the astronomical observation of these three periodic effects has served as the basis of time measurement until recent years. The precision of the observations has continually increased, and clocks have been developed for dividing the day into smaller units. The clocks were adjusted so as to keep in step with the rotation of the earth on its axis, but during recent years an atomic standard of time has been developed, and clocks are now adjusted so as to keep in step with the natural period of an atomic vibration. *See* **Clock, Greenwich Mean Time, British Standard Time.**

Tin is a white, metal element, no. 50, symbol Sn (Latin *Stannum*), whose commonest ore is cassiterite (tin oxide), which occurs in Malaya, Indonesia, Bolivia, Zaïre, Nigeria and Cornwall. It protects iron from rusting, and the tin coating on tinplate is applied by dipping the thin steel sheet in molten tin or by electrolysis. Tin alloys of importance include solder, bronze, pewter and Britannia metal. South Crofty, the last tin mine in Europe, was closed in March 1998, thus ending a 2,500 year tradition in Cornwall (but there are reports it may re-open).

Tit *or* **Titmouse,** a small insectivorous bird of the woodlands and forests, bright of plumage and very active and agile, often seen hanging upside down searching for food. There are over fifty species, eight of which occur in Britain: the Great and Blue Tits, familiar in gardens and countryside, the Cole Tit, Marsh Tit, Willow Tit, Bearded Tit, Long-tailed or "Bottle" Tit and the Scottish Crested Tit.

Titan, the largest moon of Saturn (*q.v.*).

Titanium, a scarce metallic element, no. 22, symbol Ti, difficult to extract from ores, found in association with oxygen in rutile, anatase and brookite, as well as with certain magnetic iron ores. It combines with nitrogen at a high temperature. Discovered by the Rev. William Gregor in 1791. Titanium alloys, being very resistant to stress and corrosion, and combining strength with lightness, and finding wide application not only in marine and chemical engineering but in the building of aircraft, rockets, and the nuclear-energy field. Titanium dioxide is now widely used in making paints.

Tithes, an ecclesiastical tax consisting of a tenth part of the annual produce known to the ancient Jews, and first imposed by Christian authorities in the 4th cent., although not made compulsory in England before the 9th cent. Tithes derived from land were termed "praedial", those derived from cattle being styled "mixed", while others are personal. After the passing of the Tithes' Commutation Act of 1836, tithes were gradually converted into rent charges, and today the old form of tithes exists only to a small degree.

TNT (**Trinitrotoluene**). A high explosive formed by the action of a mixture of nitric and sulphuric acids on toluene. Not highly sensitive to shock, it can be used in shells without danger, and is exploded by a time, or detonator, fuse. Apart from wartime applications, it is used in blasting in quarries and mines.

Toad, an amphibian, differing from the frog in having a dry, warty skin, a heavier, squat build and shorter limbs. It has a similar metamorphosis, is largely nocturnal, and will wander far from water after the breeding season. Two toads occur in Britain, the Common Toad and the Natterjack. The latter have a narrow light stripe running down the middle of the back.

Tobacco is made from the leaves of various narcotic plants of the *Nicotiana* family, which contain a volatile oil and an alkaloid called nicotine. Tobacco is grown in countries with a warm climate. It undergoes various processes of preparation. The leaves are first dried, then cut into small pieces, moistened and compressed, and in this form it is known as cut or "shag" tobacco; when moistened with syrup or treacle and pressed into cakes, it is Cavendish; when twisted into string form, it is "twist" or "pig-tail". For cigars the midribs of the dry leaves are removed, and what is left is moistened and rolled into cylindrical shape. For snuff, the tobacco leaves are moistened and allowed to ferment, then dried, powdered and scented. The world's largest producers of tobacco are China, the USA and India. Recently, nicotine has been discovered in mummies from ancient Egypt. In 1997, the EU agreed to ban tobacco advertising, the ban to be phased in over an 8-year period. The NHS currently spends over £600 million a year treating smoking-related illnesses.

Tolls. Payments for privileges of passage were first exacted in respect of ships passing up rivers, tolls being demanded on the Elbe in 1109. Tolls for land passage are said to have originated in England in 1269, toll-bars being erected at certain distances on the high-roads in the 17th cent., where toll had to be paid for all vehicles passing to and fro. After about 1825 they began to disappear, but still linger on some country roads and bridges. Tolls on London river bridges ceased in 1878–79. Today, tolls are a feature of motorways and major bridges.

Tolpuddle Martyrs. Six agricultural workers from Tolpuddle in Dorset who formed a union branch in 1834, were found guilty of taking a seditious oath and were given the maximum sentence of transportation to Australia for seven years. A widespread public outcry led to a pardon in 1836.

Tonic Sol-Fa, a system of musical notation in which monosyllables are substituted for notes. Thus the major diatonic scale is represented by Doh, Ray, Me, Fah, Soh, La, Te, Doh. The system was invented by a Miss Glover of Norwich in about 1840 and has proved of great assistance in the teaching of music in schools.

Tonsure, the shaven part of the head of a Roman Catholic ecclesiastic, dates from the 5th or 6th cent. In the Roman Catholic Churches only a circle, or a crown, is shaved, while in the Greek Church shaving is forbidden.

Topaz, a transparent mineral gem, being a silicate and fluoride of aluminium and generally found in granite rocks. Its colour is yellow, but it also occurs in pink and blue shades. The best kinds come from Brazil.

Topiary, the art of clipping and trimming trees, shrubs, *etc.*, into ornamental shapes. In Britain this art goes back before Elizabethan times when gardens were formal and the shapes simple and symmetrical. By the end of Queen Anne's reign topiary had become much more elaborate, and all kinds of fanciful shapes were produced. Pliny in his *Letters* tells how box hedges were clipped into different shapes in Roman times.

Topology is a branch of mathematics which studies geometrical objects from the point of view of their general shape rather than their precise measurements. For example, from the point of view of topology a ring doughnut and a picture frame have the same shape because they both have one single hole through them. Topology is used, for example, to deduce geometrical facts about an irregularly shaped object such as the Earth from the geometry of a regular

object such as a perfect sphere of the same general shape. Topology is an important tool in other parts of mathematics.

Tornado, a violent whirlwind, characterised by a black, funnel-shaped cloud hanging from heavy cumulonimbus and travelling at speeds up to 60 km/h. Tornadoes vary in diameter from less than a metre to a kilometre and occur frequently in the Mid-West region of the USA (known as tornado alley), where it has been estimated that the circling winds of the vortex may reach a velocity of 600 km/h. In West Africa the term is applied to thundery squalls.

Tortoises and Turtles, are cold-blooded reptiles, four-footed and encased in a strong shell protection, the shells of some species being of beautifully horny substance and design, once in much demand for combs, spectacle frames and ornamental work. It is the custom to designate the land species as tortoises and the aquatic kinds as turtles. The green turtle, so called because its fat has a green tinge, is in great demand for soup. Together the tortoises and turtles make up the reptilian order called *Chelonia*, the biggest representatives of which are the giant land tortoises of the Galapagos Islands, reaching a weight of 225 kg and living a century. Some of these giant tortoises are even said to have lived 200 or 300 years.

Toucan, a South and Central American family of brilliantly coloured birds, noted for their huge bills. Toucans live on fruit, are of arboreal habits, and nest in holes. There are about 37 species.

Touchstone, a kind of jasper called by the ancients "Lydian stone", of economic value in testing the quality of metal alloys, especially gold alloys. The testing process is very simple. The alloy is drawn across the broken surface of the Touchstone, and from the nature of the mark or streak it makes the quality of the alloy can be ascertained.

Tourmaline, a mineral occurring in different colours in prismatic crystals. It is a well-known example of a pyro-electric crystal, *i.e.*, one that has a permanent electric polarisation. A double silicate of aluminium and boron, it occurs in S.W. England, S. America and Asia.

Tournaments were equestrian contests between military knights and others armed with lances, and frequent in the Middle Ages. The Normans introduced them to England.

Tower of London was built as a fortress by William the Conqueror. It was a royal palace in the Middle Ages and later used as a garrison and prison. Many distinguished prisoners were executed there, or on the neighbouring Tower Hill, including Anne Boleyn, Catherine Howard, Lady Jane Grey, the 2nd Earl of Essex, and the Duke of Monmouth. The Chapel Royal of St. Peter ad Vincula in the Tower was built in 1105 and took its present shape in the reign of Henry VII. The Crown Jewels are kept at the Tower, and in the Armoury a fine collection of armour is preserved. The staff (in Tudor dress) are called Yeomen Warders of the Tower.

Trademark, a mark used in relation to goods for the purpose of indicating a connection in the course of trade between the goods and some person having the right, either as a proprietor or registered user, to use the mark. Trade marks can be registered, the registration holding good for 7 years and being renewable thereafter indefinitely for periods of 14 years. Infringement of a registered trademark renders the infringer liable to damages. In 1994, a new law was brought in to harmonise British trademark law with the EU. Owners of registered trademarks will now also be able to have their sign protected in international law.

Trade Winds form part of the circulation of air round the great permanent anticyclones of the tropics and blow inwards from north-east (Northern Hemisphere) and south-east (Southern Hemisphere) towards the equatorial region of low pressure. Atlantic trades are more regular than those of the Pacific. The belts may extend over 2,400 km of latitude and, together with the Doldrums, move north and south in sympathy with the seasonal changes in the sun's declination, the average annual range being about 5 degrees of latitude.

Trafalgar, Battle of, was fought off Cape Trafalgar on 21 October 1805, between the British under Nelson and the French and Spanish under Villeneuve and

Gravina. It was a complete victory for the British, but Nelson was killed.

Trafalgar Square. The site has often been referred to as the finest in Europe. It was conceived originally as a square by John Nash (1752–1835) when the project was considered of linking Whitehall with Bloomsbury and the British Museum. It was to be named after the new monarch as King William the Fourth's Square but on the suggestion of George Ledwell Taylor (a property owner near the site) alteration to the more popular name Trafalgar Square was agreed to by the King. On the north side the National Gallery was planned by Nash and erected by William Wilkins on the place of the Royal Mews—a work of William Kent a century before. The lay-out was the idea of Charles Barry but he did not approve the erection of the Nelson column (which see). His idea was for the square to have a grand flight of steps from the north side with sculptural figures of Wellington and Nelson but the Commons decided otherwise and the column as designed by William Railton was begun in 1840. The two fountains by Barry were supplanted in 1948 by ones designed (1938) by Sir Edwin Lutyens. Executed in Portland stone they are flanked by some bronze sculptures. In the same year memorial busts of Lords Jellicoe and Beatty were placed by the north wall.

Transept. The cross aisles of a church, projecting at right angles from the nave or choir.

Transistor. An electronic device consisting of a small piece of semiconducting solid (usually germanium or silicon) to which contact is made at appropriate places by three wires. The three parts resemble in function (not construction or behaviour) the cathode, anode, and grid of a thermionic valve, and transistors can perform many of the operations that valves had originally been used for in radio, television, etc. They possess several advantages over valves since there is no need for evacuated glass bulbs nor for a heated emitter to give off electrons. This lead to much greater compactness and economy as well as to a much longer life. Just as the valve was superseded by the transistor, the transistor has now been replaced with the integrated circuit. The transistor was invented by the Americans Bardeen, Brattain and Shockley in 1948.

Transubstantiation. See Section J.

Treasure-Trove, a legal term applying to treasure (coin, bullion, gold or silver articles) found hidden in the earth or other place, for which no owner can be discovered. The treasure legally belongs to the Crown, but it is the practice to return to the finder all articles not required for national museums and to reward him with the full market value of such as may be retained. It is the duty of the finder to report to the Coroner for the district in which the find is made. The old treasure-trove inquest with a jury has now been abolished. The coroner alone makes decisions. In England concealment is a criminal offence. See also **Wreck.**

Tree Council, an organisation founded in 1974 whose aim is to promote the improvement of the environment by the planting and conservation of trees and woods throughout the United Kingdom.

Tree Frog, occurs most commonly in America and Australasia. The common European tree frog is a brilliant green animal, the adhesive discs at the tips of its fingers and toes enabling it to cling to trees, etc., with ease.

Tree Rings as Natural Calendar. The approximate relationship between radiocarbon dating (q.v.) and true calendar age for the past 7,000 years has been established from measurements on tree-rings. Because one tree-ring is formed annually and its thickness is characteristic of the climatic conditions during its growth, it is possible, by comparing distinctive groups of rings, to date a series of trees. By using the long-lived Bristle Cone pines, tree-rings dating back to 500 B.C. have been obtained. It has been found that the radiocarbon age around, say, 3000 B.C. is too young by c. 600 years and because of short-term fluctuations near, say, 2000 B.C., a particular radiocarbon age can correspond to more than one true calendar age. These corrections are far less than those proved necessary after the publication of the first radiocarbon dates. Tree-rings (based on the measurement of deuterium in wood) can also show the pattern of temperature fluctuations and thus make it possible to trace climatic changes before written records began. The term for tree-ring dating is dendrochronology.

Tree Shrew, an arboreal insectivorous mammal of Asia belonging to the family Tupaiidae. Tree shrews are related to the shrews, though in appearance they resemble squirrels except for their sharply pointed snout. They occur in Borneo, Thailand, China and Malaya.

Trees. See under Ash, Elm, Oak etc.

Trent, Council of, the longest and one of the most important in the history of the Roman Catholic Church, was convened to combat the doctrines of Martin Luther. It first sat in 1545, the last sitting being in 1563. At this Council the general policy, principles and dogmas of the Roman Catholic Church were settled.

Triassic or **Trias,** the earliest geological period in the Mesozoic era, which began some 225 million years ago. Triassic formations 7,600 m thick occur in the Alps. Modern insects were appearing, and also small reptile-like mammals. Other important Triassic animals were: dinosaurs, ichthyosaurs (marine reptiles), and pterosaurs (flying reptiles). See Section F.

Tribunes, name assigned to officers of different descriptions in ancient Rome. The original tribunes were the commanders of contingents of cavalry and infantry. The most important tribunes were the tribunes of the plebs, first elected in 494 B.C. as the outcome of the struggle between the patrician and the plebeian orders. They held the power of veto and their persons were sacred.

Trichoptera. This is the insect order comprising the Caddis-flies. These are moth-like insects having hairs on the wings. They are usually found fluttering weakly near water. The larvae are aquatic and are remarkable for the cases (caddis cases) which they build out of sticks, small stones, sand grains, and shells.

Tricolour, the flag of the French Republic since 1789, consisting of three nearly equal vertical bands of blue, white and red (ratio 90 : 99 : 111).

Trilobites, extinct marine arthropods, most abundant in the Cambrian and Ordovician systems. Their appearance may be roughly described as resembling that of a woodlouse, and like that animal the trilobites were capable of rolling their bodies up into a ball.

Trinity. The Christian doctrine that God exists in three persons, all co-equal, and indivisible, of the same substance—God the Father, God the Son (who became incarnate as Jesus), begotten of the Father, and God the Holy Ghost, proceeding from Father and Son. The system denying the Trinity is Unitarianism. See Section J.

Trinity House, on Tower Hill, London, was incorporated in 1514 as an association for piloting ships, and has ever since been entrusted with various matters connected with the regulation of British navigation. Since 1854 the lighthouses of the country have been under its supervision. The acting Elder Brethren act as Nautical Assessors in Marine cases which are tried by the High Court of Justice. Under the 1987 Pilotage Act, Trinity House lost its responsibility as the principal pilotage authority in Britain to local harbour authorities.

Trireme, an ancient vessel with three rows of oars of great effectuality in early naval warfare. Mentioned by Thucydides. It was a long, narrow vessel propelled by 170 rowers. The Romans copied it from the Greeks.

Tritium, a radioactive isotope of hydrogen which has three times the weight of the ordinary hydrogen atom. It is produced by bombarding an isotope of lithium with neutrons and has a half-life of $12\frac{1}{4}$ years, decaying with the emission of β-particles (electrons).

Triumvirate, a term used to denote a coalition of three persons in the exercise of supreme authority. The first Roman triumvirate was that of Pompey, Julius Caesar, and Crassus, 60 B.C.: the second was that of Mark Antony, Octavus and Lepidus, 43 B.C.

Tropic-Bird, a long-tailed sea bird, of which there are 3 species (the Red-billed, the White-tailed, and the Red-tailed), frequenting the tropical regions of the Atlantic, Pacific and Indian oceans. They are often called Bo'sun Birds.

Troposphere. The atmospheric layer which extends from the earth's surface to the stratosphere. As a general rule temperature falls as altitude increases. *See* **Atmosphere.**

Troubadours, lyric poets who flourished from the 12th to the end of the 13th cent., chiefly in Provence and the north of Italy. They were often knightly amateurs, and cultivated a lyrical poetry intricate in metre and rhyme and usually of a romantic amatory strain, written in the *langue d'oc.* They did much to cultivate the romantic sentiment in days when society was somewhat barbaric and helped considerably in the formation of those unwritten codes of honour which served to mitigate the rudeness of mediaeval days. *See also* **Jongleurs.**

Trouvère *or* **Trouveur,** mediaeval poet of northern France, whose compositions were of a more elaborate character—epics, romances, fables, and chansons de geste—than those of the troubadour of the south. The poetry was written in the *langue d'oïl.* Flourished between the 12th and 13th cent.

Truffles are subterranean edible fungi much esteemed for seasoning purposes. There are many species, and they are found in considerable quantities in France and Italy, less commonly in Britain. They are often met with under beech or oak trees, and prefer calcareous soils, but there are no positive indications on the surface to show where they are, and they are not to be cultivated. Hogs, and sometimes dogs, are used to scent them out, the former, by reason of their rooting propensities, being the most successful in the work.

Tsetse, an African dipterous fly belonging to the same family as the house-fly. It is a serious economic pest as it transmits the protozoon causing African sleeping sickness when it pierces human skin in order to suck blood.

Tsunami, a seismic sea wave originating from any one of several submarine geological phenomena such as volcanic explosions, landslides or earth movements. Tsunamis are extremely long waves which travel in the open ocean at speeds up to 640 km/h. In deep water their height is only barely perceptible, but on reaching shallow coastal water they may attain heights of up to 30 m and can cause devastation to low-lying areas. The Pacific Ocean, whose rim is a seismically active area, is particularly susceptible to tsunamis. Tsunamis are often incorrectly referred to as tidal waves. Scientists are planning to deploy instruments on the ocean floor to predict and track tsunamis.

Tuatara *or* **Sphenodon,** a reptile of great antiquity, the sole surviving species of the *Rhynchocephalia,* found in New Zealand. It has a rudimentary third eye on the top of the head; this is called the pineal eye and corresponds to tissue which in mammals forms the pineal gland.

Tube Foot, the characteristic organ of locomotion of starfishes and kindred animals. They are arranged in pairs along the underside of the arms, and their sucker-like ends can grip a surface very tightly. The action of the suckers depends on hydraulic pressure.

Tudor Period extends from 1485 to 1603. The first Tudor sovereign was Henry VII, descended from Owen Tudor; then followed Henry VIII, Edward VI, Mary and Elizabeth, last of the line.

Tuesday, the third day of the week, named from the Saxon deity Tuisto, Tiw or Tuesco. To the Romans it was the day of Mars.

Tuileries, a French royal and imperial palace dating from 1564. It was attacked by insurgents during the outbreaks of 1792, 1830 and 1848, and was burned down during the Commune of Paris in 1871.

Tumulus, a mound of earth raised over the bodies of the dead. The mound of Marathon, enclosing the bodies of the Athenians who were killed in the famous battle with the Persians, is a celebrated tumulus. Such mounds were commonly raised over the tombs of the distinguished dead in ancient times, and sometimes enclosed heavy structures of masonry. The Roman "barrows" were tumuli. Evidence of such mounds are frequent in prehistoric remains.

Tuna *or* **Tunny,** a large marine fish belonging to the mackerel family, frequenting the warm waters of the Atlantic, Pacific and Mediterranean. Tuna fisheries are an important industry. The Japanese appetite for raw tuna (served as sushi) is leading to the extinction of the southern bluefin tuna.

Tundra, the vast treeless plains lying in northern N. America and northern Russia where long severe winters and permanently frozen subsoils (permafrost) have resulted in specially adapted plant communities. The summer thaw and impervious permafrost cause waterlogging of lowland areas and marsh plants occur on these sites. In summer the ground cover of lichens and mosses with some flowering plants is distinctive. Stunted willows and birches occur in certain sites.

Tungsten, a hard, brittle metallic element, no. 74, symbol W (it was formerly called wolfram), silver to grey in colour. Its chief ores are wolframite (iron and manganese tungstate) and scheelite (calcium tungstate). Tungsten is alloyed in steel for the manufacture of cutting tools; also in the non-ferrous alloy stellite. Electric lamp filaments are made from tungsten. Tungsten carbide is one of the hardest substances known and is used for tipping tools.

Turbines propelled by steam provide power for the propulsion of many ships, and on land steam turbines are a principal source of power, being used in large central electricity stations, for instance, to convert heat energy into electrical energy. The first gas-turbine ship had its trials in 1947.

Turbot, a large flat fish, highly valued as food. It often attains from 13 to 18 kg in weight. Its flesh is white and firm. It is confined to European waters, and is caught by line or trawl.

Turkey, a fowl of American origin, brought to Europe from America soon after the discovery of that country. It was a domesticated bird in England in the first half of the 16th cent.

Turpentine, an oily substance obtained from coniferous trees, mostly pines and firs. It is widely used especially in making paints and varnishes, and also has medicinal properties.

Turquoise, formerly called Turkey-Stone, is a blue or greenish-blue precious stone, the earliest and best specimens of which came from Persia. It is composed of a phosphate of aluminium, with small proportions of copper and iron. India, Tibet, and Silesia yield turquoises, and a variety is found in New Mexico and Nevada. It derives its name from the fact that the first specimens were imported through Turkey.

Turtle Dove, a summer visitor from Africa to southern England. It is a small, slender bird with reddish-brown upper parts, pinkish throat, black tail with white edges, and a repeated purring note.

Tweed. A rough-surfaced fabric of the twilled type, usually all-wool, though cheaper kinds may include cotton. Of a soft, open, flexible texture, it may have a check, twill or herringbone pattern. Harris, Lewis, Bannockburn and Donegal tweeds are well known. "Tweeds" is said to have been written in error by a clerk for "twill".

Twelfth Night is the eve of the feast of the Epiphany. It was once the most popular festival next to Christmas.

Twilight. There are several different classifications of twilight, each of which is based on the angular distance of the Sun below the observer's horizon. Civil twilight begins or ends when the centre of the solar disc is 6° below the horizon, nautical twilight beginning and ending when the centre is 12° below. The brightest stars are visible during nautical twilight. The third is astronomical twilight, at which time stars of 6th magnitude are visible provided the sky is clear. Astronomical twilight starts and finishes when the centre of the Sun is 18° below the horizon.

Tyburn, a former small tributary of the Thames, which gave its name to the district where now stands the Marble Arch, Hyde Park. Here public executions formerly took place.

Tycoon, the title by which the commander-in-chief of the Japanese army (virtually the ruler of Japan) was formerly described by foreigners. (In Japanese *taikun* means great lord or prince.) The term is now applied, usually in a derogatory sense, to an influential business magnate.

Tympanum is, in architectural phraseology, the triangular space at the back of a pediment, or, indeed, any space in a similar position, as over window or between the lintel and the arch of a doorway. In ecclesiastical edifices the tympanum is often adorned with sculpture.

Tynwald, the title given to the Parliament of the Isle of Man, which includes the Governor and Council (the Upper House), and the House of Keys, the representative assembly. This practically constitutes Home Rule, the Acts passed by the Tynwald simply requiring the assent of the Sovereign.

U

Uhlan, a light cavalry soldier armed with lance, pistol, and sabre and employed chiefly as skirmisher or scout. Marshal Saxe had a corps of them in the French Army; and in the Franco-German war of 1870 the Prussian Uhlans won fame.

Ultramarine, a sky-blue pigment obtained from *Lapis lazuli*, a stone found in Tibet, Iran, Siberia and some other countries. A cheaper ultramarine is now produced by grinding and heating a mixture of clay, sulphur, carbonate of soda and resin.

Ultrasonics, sound waves of frequency so high as to be inaudible to humans, *i.e.,* above 15,000 Hz (Hz is SI unit for cycle per sec.). Ultrasonic waves are commonly produced by causing a solid object to vibrate with a suitable high frequency and to impart its vibrations to the air or other fluid. The object may be a quartz or other crystal in which vibrations are excited electrically, or a nickel component which is magnetically energised. There are numerous technical applications, *e.g.* submarine echo soundings, flaw detection in castings, drilling glass and ceramics, emulsification. Ultrasonic waves are an important tool of research in physics. Bats produce very loud sounds when they are flying, but at ultrasonic frequencies (20,000 to 150,000 Hz), so that we cannot ourselves hear them.

Ultra-Violet Rays. These are invisible electromagnetic rays whose wavelengths are less than 3900 Å. (Angstrom = one hundred-millionth of a centimetre.) The sun's radiation is rich in ultra-violet light, but much of it never reaches the earth, being absorbed by molecules of atmospheric gases (in particular, ozone) as well as by soot and smoke particles. One beneficial effect of ultra-violet light on human beings is that it brings about synthesis of vitamin-D from certain fatty substances (called sterols) in the skin. The wavelengths which effect this vitamin synthesis also cause sun tan and sun burn. Ultra-violet lamps (which are mercury-vapour discharge lamps) are also used for sterilising the air inside buildings, their rays being lethal to bacteria. Many substances fluoresce under ultra-violet light; for instance, zinc silicate glows green, while cadmium borate throws out red light. This phenomenon is applied practically in fluorescent lamps, the light of requisite hue being secured by judicious mixture of the fluorescent materials which coat the lamp.

Umbra, the full shadow of the earth or moon during an eclipse. The term is also used to describe the darker, cooler central region of a sunspot.

Unciae. The Romans took over the Egyptian cubit and divided it into 16 digits as well as into 12 parts called *unciae,* the *uncia* being the origin of the inch.

Underdeveloped Countries are those in which economic structure and development are held back, or, as some would have it, countries which are underdeveloped in the transitive sense of the word. *See* **Section G.**

Unicorn, a fabulous single-horned animal. In heraldry its form is horse-like, with the tail of a lion and pointed single horn growing out of the forehead. In the Middle Ages the unicorn was a symbol of virginity.

UNIDO (United Nations Industrial Development Organization). This is the central coordinating body for industrial activities within the United Nations system. It assists in the formulation of development, scientific and technological programmes and plans for industrialization in the public, cooperative and private sectors.

Union Jack, the flag of the United Kingdom since 1801 (the Union with Ireland). Jack derives from the nautical term for flag.

Union of Great Britain and Ireland was proposed in the Irish Parliament in January 1799 after the 1798 Rebellion and came into force on 1 January 1801. The troubled history of Ireland, associated with the question of self-government, nationalism, land and religion, culminated in the Easter revolution of 1916. A treaty giving the 26 southern counties independence in 1921, as the Irish Free State, was followed by a period of internal dissension. In 1937 a new constitution was enacted in Ireland in which no reference was made to the Crown. This, however, left in force the External Relations Act of 1936 and with its repeal in 1948, Ireland separated itself from the British Crown and thus severed the last constitutional link with the Commonwealth, and became an independent Republic.

Union of Soviet Socialist Republics (USSR). The Union of Soviet Socialist Republics was formally constituted on 6 July 1923, covering most of the old Russian Empire overthrown in the Communist revolution of 1917, minus the territories which formed Finland, Poland, the Baltic Republics and East Prussia. With the fall of communism, it collapsed in 1991.

Union, Treaty of, was the treaty by which Scotland became formally united to England, the two countries being incorporated as the United Kingdom of Great Britain, the same Parliament to represent both, Scotland electing sixteen peers and forty-five members of the House of Commons. Uniformity of coins, weights, and measures was provided for, Scottish trade laws and customs were assimilated to those of England, and as regards religion and the practices of the law, Scotland was to continue as before. This Act was ratified on 1 May 1707.

Universe in astronomy means not only the star system (of which the sun and planets are a small part) but all the countless star systems or nebulae which may be separated from each other by millions of light-years. *See* **F3-8.**

Universities are institutions of higher education whose principal objects are the increase of knowledge over a wide field through original thought and research and its extension by the teaching of students. Such societies existed in the ancient world, notably in Greece and India, but the origin of the University as we know it today lies in mediaeval Europe, the word *universitas* being a contraction of the Latin term for corporations of teachers and students organised for the promotion of higher learning.

The first bodies to become recognised under this description were at Bologna and Paris in the first half of the 12th cent.; Oxford was founded by an early migration of scholars from Paris, and Cambridge began with a further migration from Oxford. Other Universities sprang up all over Europe, including three in Scotland—St. Andrews (1411), Glasgow (1451) and Aberdeen (1494)—which were followed by Edinburgh in 1582. These six bodies remained the only Universities in Great Britain until the foundation in 1826-29 of University and King's Colleges in London (resulting in the establishment of the University of London in 1836) and of the University of Durham in 1832. The 34 old-established universities in England were: Aston, Bath, Birmingham, Bradford, Bristol, Brunel, Buckingham, Cambridge, The City, Durham, East Anglia, Essex, Exeter, Hull, Keele, Kent, Lancaster, Leeds, Leicester, Liverpool, London, Loughborough, Manchester, Newcastle, Nottingham, Open, Oxford, Reading, Salford, Sheffield, Southampton, Surrey, Sussex, Warwick and York. Other old institutions of university standard were the University of Manchester Institute of Science and Technology; the Manchester Business School; the London Graduate School of Business Studies; Cranfield Institute of Technology; and the Royal College of Art. Formed from colleges of technology, art and design, commerce and other institutions, over thirty polytechnics were established in England and Wales as centres of higher education (*see below*). Wales used to have one University (The University of Wales with colleges at Aberystwyth, Bangor, Cardiff and Swansea) in addition to the

Welsh National School of Medicine, the Institute of Science and Technology, and St. David's, Lampeter. Scotland had eight: Aberdeen, Dundee (1967), Edinburgh, Glasgow, Heriot-Watt (1966), St. Andrews, Stirling (1967), and Strathclyde (1964), Britain's first technological University. Northern Ireland has two: Queen's University, Belfast and the New University of Ulster at Coleraine. The Open University received its charter in 1969; it provides degrees and other courses together with radio and television programmes and began its broadcasts in January 1971. The Republic of Ireland has the University of Dublin (Trinity College, Dublin), the National University of Ireland, Dublin City University and the University of Limerick

In the United States, the development of higher education has left the Universities less sharply defined than in Europe and the Commonwealth, among the best known being Harvard (1636), Yale (1701), Princeton (1746), Columbia (1754), Cornell (1865), California (Berkeley), Massachusetts Institute of Technology. In 1972 the European University Institute was established with headquarters in Florence. In Britain, universities receive aid from the State mainly in the form of grants from the Higher Education Funding Council which oversees the distribution of state finance. But they are selfgoverning institutions free from State control. In 1992, the distinction between the former polytechnics and the older universities ended.

The former polytechnics have now adopted university names (*e.g.* Leicester Polytechnic is now the De Montfort University). A University of the Highlands and Islands, based on a high-technology federal campus, is currently (1999) being planned. The Labour Government elected in 1997 is pledged to establish a 'University for Industry'. The ending of free tuition for students (from September 1998) and the other implications of the 1997 Dearing Report, will signal a revolution in higher education. A different type of organisation is the University of the Third Age, which is essentially a collective of older people who meet to participate in an exchange of information and ideas. *See also* separate entries for **Cambridge University, Oxford University** and **London University**.

Uranium, a metallic element, no. 92, symbol U, discovered by Klaproth in 1789 in pitchblende. It is a white metal which tarnishes readily in air. Great developments have followed the discovery that the nucleus of the uranium isotope U^{235} undergoes fission, and uranium minerals have become very important since it was found that atomic energy could be released controllably by taking advantage of fission. Before atomic energy work began to take the major part of the world's output of uranium minerals, the chief users of uranium compounds were the ceramics and textile industries. *See also* **Nuclear Reactors, Nuclear Fission, F13**(1).

Uranus. This planet was discovered by Herschel in March 1781. Its diameter is 51,118 km and its mean distance from the Sun is $2,871 \times 10^6$ km. When Voyager 2 visited Uranus in January 1986, it raised the number of known moons orbiting the planet from five to 15 (two further moons, Caliban and Sycorax, were discovered in 1998). The number of known rings surrounding Uranus was also increased to 11. Uranus has a large axial tilt which means that it rotates on its side. Each pole faces the Sun every half-revolution around the Sun, *i.e.* every 42 years. *See* **F8 and Voyager.**

Urea, the final product in mammals of the breakdown of nitrogenous waste, *e.g.*, excess aminoacids. It is very soluble in water and is excreted in urine. In 1828 Wöhler synthesised urea from inorganic matter. This was the first laboratory synthesis of an organic substance and refuted the idea that living creatures or life force are needed to create such substances.

Ursa Major and **Ursa Minor** ("Greater Bear" and "Lesser Bear"), two celebrated constellations, each of seven stars, in the northern celestial hemisphere, familiar since ancient times. Ursa Major has also been called the "Plough", "Charles's (Charlemagne's) Wain" or "the Wagon". The "Pointers" in this group of bright stars point to the brightest star in Ursa Minor, the Pole Star. Called the Big Dipper and the Little Dipper in the USA.

V

Valency. A term used by chemists to describe the combining ability of an element with respect to hydrogen. Thus oxygen, which forms water, H_2O, with hydrogen is said to have a valency of two, nitrogen (forms ammonia, NH_3) three, and carbon (forms methane, CH_4) four. Chlorine forms hydrogen chloride, HCl, and is said to be monovalent. This empirical approach cannot account for valency in such compounds as carbon monoxide, CO, which appears to require both elements to have the same valency. With the discovery of the electron it was realised that the concept of valency and chemical bonds is intimately concerned with the electronic structure of atoms, and theories have been advanced to explain why the same element can have different valencies in different compounds. Iron, for example, can have a valency of two ($FeCl_2$, ferrous chloride) or three ($FeCl_3$, ferric chloride). *See* **F11**(1), **F24**(2) and **Table of Elements** (F64).

Valentine's Day (14 February), is a festival in celebration of St. Valentine, one of the Christian martyrs of the 3rd cent. A sweetheart or Valentine is chosen on that day and letters or tokens sent secretly to the object of affection.

Valhalla, in Scandinavian mythology, is the special Paradise to which the souls of warriors slain in battle were transported.

Valkyries, the chosen handmaidens of Odin, appointed to serve at the Valhalla banquets. Their most important office, however, according to the Norse mythology, was to ride through the air at a time of battle and point out the heroes who were to fall. One of these Valkyries is made the heroine of Wagner's opera "*Die Walküre*".

Valve, an electronic device consisting of two or more metal plates (electrodes) usually enclosed in an evacuated glass bulb. One of the electrodes is heated causing electrons to be emitted. If a positive voltage is applied to the other electrode, the electrons will move towards it and the valve must conduct electricity. The current will only flow in one direction as the electrons are emitted only from one direction. A valve with two electrodes is called a diode, but by putting in one or more intermediate electrodes the flow of current can be sensitively controlled and the valves are then called triodes, pentodes, *etc.*, according to the total number of electrodes in them. Valves originally found extensive applications in amplifiers, rectifiers, oscillators and many electronic devices, but have now been superseded by transistors, which in turn have been replaced by the integrated circuit and the micro-chip.

Vanadium, a scarce metallic element, no. 23, symbol V, whose chief ores are carnotite and patronite. Some iron ores contain it. Most of the vanadium commercially produced finds its way into vanadium steels, which are used for tools and parts of vehicles, being hard, tough and very resistant to shocks. The oxide is used as a catalyst in industry, especially in making sulphuric aicd.

Van Allen Belts. One of the most remarkable discoveries made during the IGY, 1957–58, was that the earth is surrounded by a great belt of radiation. Evidence came from *Sputnik II* (which carried the dog Laika) and from the American satellites, *Explorers I* and *III*. The American scientist, J. A. van Allen, was able to explain the puzzling data collected from these satellites. Subsequent observations with deep space-probes showed that there are in fact two zones of high intensity particle radiation surrounding the earth, one concentrated at a distance of about 1,600 km, the other at about 24,000 km. A close relation exists between the shapes of the zones and the earth's magnetic field. Recent evidence suggests that Jupiter also is surrounded by a dense belt of trapped high-energy particles.

Vatican, the Papal residence at Rome, a famous palace on the hill adjacent to St. Peter's. Its museum is a rich treasure-house of literary and artistic objects. Works of Michelangelo glorify the Sistine Chapel.

Vauxhall Gardens, a famous London pleasure

resort from the early part of the 18th to the middle of the 19th cent. It was here that many great singers appeared and where the earliest balloon ascents were made.

Ventriloquism, the art of projecting or throwing the voice so that it seems to come from a different source.

Venus, the brightest of all the planets, whose orbit lies between the orbits of Mercury and Earth, is second in order from the sun (*see* **F8**). It approaches the earth to within 40 million km. It moves around the sun in the same direction as Earth and the other planets but rotates in the opposite sense. It has been visited by a number of American and Russian probes, some flybys, some soft-landings, others atmospheric probes. Venus has 100 times the atmospheric pressure of the earth and temperatures of 500°C. It is covered in a very thick cloud mainly of carbon dioxide which some scientists believe acts like a green-house trapping the heat from the sun. Complex reactions occur in the atmosphere and the rain consists mainly of sulphuric and hydrochloric acid. The cloud rotates about six times faster than Venus rotates and swirls into the polar regions like giant whirlpools. The terrain has been studied by radar, much of it ground-based, but a vast amount of information has come from both the Pioneer Venus orbiter and the recent successful Magellan probe, which between them have mapped nearly the entire Venusian surface. There are two major continents, Aphrodite Terra, is about the size of Africa, and the smaller Ishtar Terra, about the size of Australia, which consists of a very high plateau (*c.* 3,300 m) and a mountain range dominated by Maxwell Montes (at 10,600 m higher than Everest). Aphrodite Terra has a deep trench 2,900 m below "sea level". Most of the planet (60 per cent) is relatively flat. The Magellan probe (1990) revealed a carbon dioxide atmosphere, 100 times thicker than Earth's, with sulphur escaped from volcanoes as well as the longest channel (4,200 miles) in the solar system. It also found that there are no asteroid impact craters bigger than 5 miles across.

Venus Fly-trap, a well-known insectivorous plant (*Dionaea muscipula*) occurring in Carolina in damp mossy places. It is related to the Sundew. The leaf is the organ that catches the insects. The leaf blade is in two halves, hinged along the centre line. Each half bears three sensitive hairs called "trigger hairs". When an insect touches a trigger, the two halves of the leaf clap together, trapping the insect between them, when it is digested by a secretion (digestive enzymes) from the leaf, which afterwards absorbs the soluble products.

Vernalization. Seeds which, after being exposed to a low temperature, produce plants that flower earlier than usual are said to have been "vernalized". This technique of seed treatment devised by Lysenko is called vernalization. It is claimed to have been widely used in Russia to obtain cereal crops in places where climatic conditions are favourable for only a short season.

Versailles, Treaty of. The Peace Treaty, 1919, ending the first world war. The first half was devoted to the organisation of the League of Nations. Among the territorial changes Germany ceded Alsace-Lorraine to France, Posen and the Corridor to Poland. Germany undertook to disarm, to abolish universal military service, to keep only a small army of 100,000 and a small navy. Her colonies were to be shared out among the Allies under League Mandates. Reparations were to be paid, but were gradually reduced and entirely ceased in 1932. Hitler took unilateral action against the Treaty especially in regard to rearmament and the annexation of Austria.

Victoria and Albert Museum, in Kensington, London, was begun in 1852 as the Museum of Ornamental Art at Marlborough House. The present building was completed in 1909. It is one of the great museums of the world for the fine arts. The V & A also administers the Wellington Museum (Apsley House, Piccadilly), Ham House (Richmond, Surrey), and Osterley Park House (Middx). The Museum of Childhood (Bethnal Green) is a branch of the V & A.

Victoria Cross, an order of merit for conspicuous valour, awarded to members of the Army, Navy and Air Force, was established in 1856.

Videotape recording (VTR), technique for recording television programmes on to magnetic tape. The original means of storing programmes for broadcast or library purposes was by filming productions from high-quality monitors, an expensive and slow process, since the film had to be chemically developed and edited in the conventional way. The difficulty in establishing an instant play-back system along the lines of the sound tape recording system lay in the high speed and large amount of tape needed to accommodate the picture signal. The BBC experimented with a machine called VERA (Vision Electronic Recording Apparatus), but it was an American machine, the Ampex VR100, which provided the break-through. This recorded the picture across a wider tape rather than along it, and moving at a slower speed. The modern domestic recorder is usually of the VHS standard, while broadcasters use the higher quality systems, such as Betacam. The on-going simplification of hand-held video cameras is a stimulus for further innovations and technical development.

Vienna Congress, sat at Vienna from September 1814 to June 1815, and settled the delineation of the territories of the various European nations after the defeat of Napoleon. The Treaty of Vienna which resulted gave Sri Lanka, Mauritius, Cape Colony, Heligoland, Malta and part of Guyana to England; Belgium, Holland and Luxemburg were united in the Kingdom of the Netherlands; Austria took Lombardy-Venetia; Russia took part of Poland; and Prussia, part of Saxony and the Rhenish province. Except for one or two changes the clauses of the treaty were maintained for over forty years.

Vikings. Scandinavian pirates who from the 8th to the 10th cent. were the terror of northern waters. Sometimes the Viking raids reached south to the Mediterranean and east to the White Sea. Their leader Rurik founded the first Russian kingdom of Novgorod in A.D. 862. The Icelandic Vikings under Eric the Red discovered Greenland in A.D. 982 and a warm period in world climate allowed many to settle there. Their expeditions took them to Labrador and Newfoundland. They excelled in shipbuilding, were fine sailors and craftsmen. The name may derive from *vik*, a sheltered deep-water bay now called a *fjord*.

Vinyl Plastics are polymers made from derivatives of ethylene, examples are polyvinyl chloride (PVC), which is used in making plastic pipes and kitchen utensils, among other things; polyvinyl acetate used in the paint industry and in bonding laminated articles like plywood; and polystyrene (polyvinyl benzene) used in making electrical fittings and for lenses.

Viper, a family of poisonous snakes in which the venom-conducting fangs hinge forward when the snake bites. One species is found in Britain, the common viper or adder.

Virus. *See* Index to P and **F31**(2).

Visibility is defined by the distance at which the farthest of a series of objects, specially selected to show against the skyline or in good contrast with their background, can be distinguished. Visibility depends chiefly upon the concentration of water or dust particles suspended in the air. Instruments are available to measure the obscurity of the atmosphere more directly, including that at night. A large lapse rate of temperature and a strong wind are favourable to good visibility; a small lapse rate, calm or light wind favourable to bad visibility. Fog is when the visibility is less than 1,000 m; mist or haze when it is between 1,000 and 2,000 m. *See* **Pollution**.

Viscount, a title of rank coming between that of Earl and Baron. The title originally stood for deputy-earl. The first English Viscount was Viscount Beaumont, created in 1440.

Vitamins, name of a group of organic substances found in relatively minute amounts in certain foodstuffs, essential for growth and the maintenance of normal bodily structure and function. The Hungarian biochemist Szent-Györgyi, who first isolated vitamin C or ascorbic acid, defined the vitamin as "a substance that makes you ill if you don't eat it!".

Volcanoes are vents through which magma reaches the surface as lava flows, or as the solid products, e.g., ashes and bombs, of explosive eruption. The vent may be cylindrical or it may be a long fissure. The former type usually builds up cones, e.g., Vesuvius. Notable active volcanoes are Etna, Vesuvius and Stromboli, in Italy; Soufrière on Montserrat; and Mont Pelée on Martinique. The last-named was in violent eruption in 1902, when the chief town of St. Pierre was completely destroyed. Volcanic eruptions are sometimes linked with brilliant sunset phenomena, e.g., the Indonesian island of Krakatoa (1883), whose atmospheric and tidal effects were recorded all over the world, and Agung on the island of Bali (1963), which had been dormant for 120 years. In 1991, the eruption of Mt Pinatubo in the Philippines killed 300 people, while in 1997 much of Montserrat was threatened by the Soufrière eruption. The huge eruption at Tambora (Indonesia) in 1815 killed an estimated 90,000 people. Many scientists now believe that the world is overdue a major volcanic eruption. There are volcanoes on Mars far higher than any on Earth.

Vole, a small rodent with blunt nose, round face and short tail. Three kinds occur in Britain: the field, the bank and the water vole.

Volt, the electromotive force unit, named after Alessandro Volta (1745–1827), and defined in terms of the coulomb, the second and the joule.

Voyagers 1 and 2. These spacecraft were launched from Earth on 5 Sept. 1977 and 20 Aug. 1977 respectively as a follow-on mission to the earlier and successful Pioneer 10 and 11 spacecraft. Both were targeted initially to swing by Jupiter (q.v.), with Voyager 1 on the faster trajectory, to make the next phase of investigation of Jupiter and its moons, before continuing to Saturn (q.v.) and beyond, using the enormous gravitational field of Jupiter to assist them in their journeys. (It was this planet's gravitational field that flung Pioneer 10 (launched 1972) into space in June 1983 to make it the first man-made object to leave the solar system.) Voyager 1, in flying through the Jovian system in 1979, discovered the unique features of Io, the most volcanically active object yet found in the solar system, photographed the ice-covered moons—Europa, Ganymede and Callisto—and made many new discoveries of Jupiter, the largest and most massive planet of the solar system. Voyager 1 began surveying Saturn in Aug. 1980, and continued sending back a vast amount of new data, including some 18,000 pictures of the planet, its moons and, perhaps most spectacularly, its fascinating and complex system of rings. The measurements included infra-red and ultra-violet measurements of the structure of the planet's atmosphere, as well as data on the magnetic field and charged particle environment of the planet.

The flyby of Saturn by Voyager 2 in Aug. 1981 was carefully planned to obtain the maximum of new information to complement that obtained from Voyager 1 to help understand some of the perplexing new phenomena, and revealed even more new features of this beautiful and still enigmatic planet. Even after its Saturn flyby, the work of Voyager 2 was far from complete: its swing by Saturn redirected it toward Uranus, on which it provided our first close-up data in Jan. 1986, and from there it continued to Neptune in 1989, taking maximum advantage of a unique arrangement of all four of the outer planets, Jupiter, Saturn, Uranus and Neptune, which only occurs once every 200 years. Voyager 1, which would not pass particularly close to any planet after Saturn, carries a multi-lingual goodwill message as well as musical selections to far outside our solar system. It will not reach its nearest star, Sirius, for 360,000 years. In March 1990, Voyager 1 beamed back its last colour photographs before leaving the solar system for outer space. By then it was 3,500 million miles from Earth, travelling at 37,000 mph.

Vraic, a name for seaweed in the Channel Islands, where it is extensively used as a manure.

Vulgate, a term used to designate the Latin version of the Scriptures sanctioned by the Council of Trent. The work of St. Jerome in the late 4th cent. A.D. and still the official Bible of the Roman Catholic Church.

Vulture, a famous bird of prey of two distinctive groups; that of the Old World, whose nostrils are separated by a bony partition, and the New World vulture, which has no such division. Vultures feed on carrion and are the great scavengers of tropical regions. The European species are the Egyptian vulture, Griffon vulture, Black vulture and Bearded vulture. Vultures have no feathers on the head and neck.

W

Wading Birds, *Charadriiformes,* an order of migratory, long-legged, long-billed birds, frequenting marshes and shallow waters. They include the plovers, avocets, stilts, oystercatchers, curlews, phalaropes, godwits, dunlins, sandpipers, redshanks, greenshanks, snipe, woodcocks, the pratincole of the Mediterranean and the sun bittern of tropical America. Many species breed in Britain.

Wagtails, familar long-tailed small birds, the most common British species being the Pied or Water (with sub-species White) Grey and the Yellow (sub-species Blue). Wagtails nest in holes and are active of habit.

Walloons, name given to the French-speaking population of the southern provinces of Belgium, in contrast to the Flemings or Dutch-speaking population of the northern provinces. The Walloon areas contain the mining and heavy industries of the country.

Walpurgis Night, the night before 1 May, when witches and creatures of evil are supposed to have liberty to roam. Named after St Walpurgis, an English nun, who went on a mission to Germany in the 8th cent.

Walrus, a very large marine mammal, related to the seals having in the upper jaw two large curved tusks, which average in length from 38 to 60 cm. It lives on bi-valve molluscs, and inhabits the Arctic seas. An adult walrus can exceed 4 m in length and weigh over a tonne.

Wankel Engine *or* **Rotary Engine,** is an internal combustion engine invented by Felix Wankel in the 1930s and greatly developed since by large automobile firms in several countries. The ordinary internal combustion engine has to convert reciprocating motion of the pistons into rotary motion. In the Wankel engine the explosion of the fuel and air mixture drives a moving part (the rotor) directly into rotatory motion, and the rotor itself opens and closes the fuel inlet and exhaust ports. The three spaces between the triangular rotor and its specially shaped housing act successively as intake, compression, explosion and exhaust chambers as the rotor revolves. There are no valves and far fewer moving parts than in an ordinary piston engine. The Wankel engine is claimed to have many advantages in that it is smaller and lighter for a given horse-power, relatively simple, quieter and freer from vibration, and could contribute to pollution control. There are cars now on sale with the Wankel engine and continuous research and development will no doubt test in practice the claim of some protagonists that this engine is the agent of a technological revolution in the automobile.

Wapentake, the ancient name given in the northern countries to territorial divisions corresponding to the Hundreds of southern counties.

Warblers, a family of small, lively song-birds closely related to the flycatchers and thrushes. Represented in Britain by about 36 species, including the chiffchaff, one of the earliest spring visitors, willow-wren, wood-warbler, blackcap, garden-warbler, whitethroat, sedge and grasshopper-warbler.

Warsaw Pact. *See under* **NATO, L86.**

Water is the simplest compound of hydrogen and oxygen. It is formed when an electric spark is passed through a mixture of the gases, and is a product of combustion of all hydrogen-containing compounds, e.g., petrol, coal, coal gas and wood. Water is essential to living matter, and is the medium which carries food to animals and plants. Salts in hard water may be removed by distillation of the water or by a process known as ion-exchange (water softening). Pure water freezes at 0°C and boils at 100°C and is used as a standard of temperature on this scale. It has a maximum density at 4°C. Heating water above 100°C converts it into steam, which is used under pressure to convert heat energy into useful work, as in electrical power stations and steam engines. Water gas is a mixture mainly of carbon monoxide and hydrogen formed by blowing steam and oxygen through red-hot coke: it is used as a fuel. Water is one of the very few compounds which freezes from the surface down rather than from the bulk of the liquid up. This property has important consequences on the preservation of life in rivers and lakes when they are frozen. The Drinking Water Inspectorate set up in January 1990 has responsibility for checking that water supplied by the water companies is wholesome and fit to drink when it reaches your home. The privatisation of the water industry, followed by the widespread water shortages during the 1995 drought, have caused much debate on the whole question of domestic water supplies.

Water Hyacinth (*Eichhornia crassipes*), a beautiful aquatic plant native to Brazil which has spread to other favourable equatorial regions of the world causing havoc on account of its abnormal rate of reproduction away from its natural environment. In recent years it has invaded the Nile and the Congo, forming vast floating carpets which block the channels, clog the paddles of river craft and deoxygenate the water, killing the fish. It is being held in check by spraying with herbicides.

Waterloo, Battle of, was fought on 18 June 1815. The Allies (British, German and Dutch) under Wellington and Blücher defeated the French under Napoleon, ending Napoleon's career.

Waterloo Bridge, crossing the Thames, was built by Rennie, and opened in 1817. It had nine arches, each 120 ft (36 m) span, was built of granite, and had a length (including approaches) of 2,456 ft (749 m). The present bridge, completed in 1942, and formally opened 10 December 1945, is a fine example of reinforced concrete construction. (Architect, Sir Giles Gilbert-Scott.)

Watling Street, the name of the old Roman road which ran from the Channel ports by way of London to Shropshire. *See also* **Roman Roads.**

Watt. A unit of electrical power equivalent to 1 joule of work per second, named after James Watt (1736–1819). *See* **F66–69.**

Waxbill, a small Oriental and African bird of the *Estrildidae* family, with wax-like bill and beautifully variegated plumage. The Java sparrow, and the Blue-breasted waxbill are attractive, and often find their way into cages.

Wayz-Goose, the name given to a festive gathering of people employed in printing and other works, so called from the fact that in earlier times a goose was the principal dish of the feast.

Weasel. A carnivore mammal found in Britain, smallest member of the group including the Stoat, Polecat, and Pine-marten, about 20 cm long. Its fur is reddish on the upper side of the animal, white on the under side; it may all turn white in winter with the exception of the tail.

Weather is generally accepted as being the current state of the atmosphere, particularly as regards its pressure and temperature, wind, cloud and precipitation. Many other features such as fog, sunshine duration, humidity, pressure tendency, may be added to the list, all items of which are routinely observed by specially instrumented stations usually sponsored by the national meteorological services. Day-to-day changes in the weather as experienced by the individual are due to the passage of circulation systems, many of which bring clearly recognisable areas of "good" (*i.e.*, calm and sunny) weather as frequently occurs in anticyclones and "bad" (*i.e.*, cold, windy, cloudy and rainy) weather. Clearly, the weather in any place at any time is primarily determined by the frequency and intensity of synoptic-scale weather circulation systems (*c.* 3,000 km across). Local weather (over areas of *c.* 100 km) may be heavily influenced by topography, *e.g.*, valley fogs, frost hollows.

Weather Lore. Before instruments were invented to measure atmospheric conditions, man relied on his own observation of wind and sky, behaviour of birds and animals, and came to associate certain phenomena with types of weather. Many popular weather rhymes have

survived the centuries, and as long as forecasting is confined to the next 24 hours there is perhaps something to be said for them, particularly those dealing with the winds. What is very unlikely is that next year's summer can be predicted from this year's winter, or that one month's weather is related to that of another. The study of past records reveals too many exceptions for firm future predictions.

Weaver Bird, the popular name for a large group of finch-like birds belonging to the family *Ploceidae*, found principally in Africa but also in Southern Asia, Australia, and Europe and remarkable for their habit of building nests formed of blades of grass dexterously interwoven and suspended from the boughs of trees.

Weaving. The interlacing of two or more threads at right angles to form a fabric is a craft that has been practised since ancient times. The main principle of the weaving loom is the same to-day as it was thousands of years ago; a warp extends lengthwise through the loom, the threads being held in separate regular order by being passed through a reed or "slay", while the weft is crossed through alternating threads of the warp by means of a shuttle which holds the weft. Thus the fabric is built up. Weaving was done by hand up to the early part of the 19th cent., when Cartwright's steam-power loom was invented. The Jacquard loom for weaving figured designs dates from 1801.

Wedding Anniversaries are: first, Paper; second, Cotton; third, Leather; fourth, Fruit and Flowers; fifth, Wooden; sixth, Sugar; seventh, Woollen; eighth, Bronze; ninth, Pottery; tenth, Tin; twelfth, Silk and Fine Linen; fifteenth, Crystal; twentieth, China; twenty-fifth, Silver; thirtieth, Pearl; thirty-fifth, Coral; fortieth, Ruby; forty-fifth, Sapphire; fiftieth, Golden; fifty-fifth, Emerald; sixtieth, Diamond; sixty-fifth, Platinum or Blue Sapphire; seventieth, Platinum; seventy-fifth, Diamond or Odin.

Wednesday, the 4th day of the week, derived its name from Woden or Odin, the Norse god of war.

Weights and Measures. *See* **F66–69.**

Welding is a means of joining together two pieces of material, often metals, by heating the joint until the substances melt locally, run together, and then solidify. The heating can be by burning gas (*e.g.*, oxy-acetylene welding) or electric current (electric arc welding). Techniques exist for welding anything from hair-like wires to massive steel plates. *See* **Soldering.**

Werewolf, a man or woman, who according to mediaeval belief, could be turned by witchcraft or magic into a wolf, eat human flesh or drink human blood and turn into himself again. This belief was widely held in Europe, and similar superstitions prevail among most primitive peoples, *e.g.*, the "leopard man" of certain African tribes. Lycanthropy (from Gr. = wolfman) is a form of madness in which the patient imagines himself a beast.

Westminster Abbey stands on the site of an old church and Benedictine foundation of the 7th cent. It was rebuilt under Edward the Confessor, and again under Henry III, and important additions were made by Edward II, Edward III, Richard II, Richard III and Henry VII, the latter erecting the beautiful eastern chapel in the perpendicular style which bears his name. The west towers and gable were designed by Hawksmoor (1661–1736). The Abbey contains tombs of many sovereigns, of the Unknown Warrior, and many other illustrious persons are commemorated by monuments. An admission charge of £5 was introduced in 1998.

Westminster Cathedral, seat of the Roman Catholic Archbishop of Westminster. It was designed by J. F. Bentley and built betwen 1895 and 1910. It is of red brick, in early Christian Byzantine style with a domed campanile, 283 ft (86 m) high, and a decorative interior.

Westminster Hall, adjoining the House of Parliament, was built as a Banqueting Hall by William Rufus, and many courtly festivals were held there in succeeding centuries. King John established the Law Courts there. It now forms a gigantic hallway, leading to the Houses of Parliament. Charles I, Sir Thomas More, and Warren Hastings were tried there.

Whale, a completely aquatic mammal; the forelimbs are modified to form fin-like paddles and there is virtually no external trace of the hind-limbs. There are two major groups of whales—the *Toothed Whales*, including the Sperm-whale (Cachalot), Dolphin, Killer-whales and Porpoises; and the *Whalebone Whales*. In the latter a series of whalebone plates grow down from the roof of the mouth, and, being frayed at their edges into a hairy fringe, together constitute a filtering mecha-nism. The animal takes in sea water containing minute organisms on which it feeds; the mouth is then closed and the tongue raised when the water is forced out through the filter, on which is left the food. As the tongue is lowered, the whalebone plates straighten up, flicking the food on to the tongue, which transfers it to the gut. Most whale oil is obtained from the thick layer of fat under the skin (blubber), but in the Sperm-whale there is a large reserve of oil in the head. One of the major users of sperm oil is the leather industry. Ambergris used in perfumery comes from the intestine of whales. The number of whales that may be killed in a season is limited by Inter-national Convention. Today the three main whaling nations are Japan, Norway and Russia. In 1994 a whale sanctuary around Antarctica was established by the International Whaling Commis-sion. The sactuary bans commercial whaling in the Southern Ocean for at least 10 years. Sadly, blue whales, the world's largest creatures, have seen their population fall from a high of 400,000 to 12,000 in 1999. Scientists have found that Beluga whales travel thousands of miles to feast on stocks of cod and halibut after navigating by the stars or Earth's magnetic field.

Whiskers in physics and materials science (*q.v.*) are tiny rods of crystal, thinner than human hair and perhaps 1 cm long. Their importance lies in the fact that such crystals are free from the defects described on **F21.** They are also free from surface cracks and steps. This means they are immensely strong because failures of strength in ordinary solids are due to imperfections and cracks of one kind or another. Large numbers of whiskers of strong solids like graphite, silicon, or silicon carbide embedded in a matrix of softer matter such as plastic or metal make a very strong new material.

White Ants. *See* **Termites, L119.**

White Elephant, a term in common use to desig-nate a gift that causes the recipient more trouble or cost than it is worth; derived from an old-time custom of the Kings of Thailand who presented a white elephant to a courtier whom it was desired to ruin.

Whitehall Palace, built within sight of Westminster by Hubert de Burgh, Earl of Kent, round about 1240, was the residence of the Archbishops of York until Wolsey presented it to Henry VIII in 1530. From then until 1697, when it was burned down, it continued to be the favourite town residence of royalty, and to the Stuarts especially it was a great centre of court festivities. In those days, with its grounds, it extended from the Strand to the river. The only portion of Whitehall Palace now standing is the Banqueting Hall built by Inigo Jones, on a scaffold projected from the front of which Charles I was beheaded. A block of government buildings has been built on part of the site of the old Palace.

White House, the official residence at Washington of the President of the United States. It was built in 1792, having been designed by an Irishman, James Hoban. In 1814 British troops captured Washington and set fire to the White House.

Whitsuntide, the festival celebrating the descent of the Holy Ghost and occurring seven weeks after Easter.

Widow Bird, certain species of African weaver birds with predominantly black plumage. In the breeding season the male birds are strikingly beautiful, with scarlet and buff markings and long tail feathers. They are social parasites and trick other birds into rearing their young.

Wigeon, a surface-feeding duck of northern Europe, known in Britain more as a winter visitor than a nesting bird. It feeds in flocks in the muddy estuaries and has a characteristic "whee-oo" call.

Wildebeest. *See* **Gnu (L51).**

Willow, a water-side-loving tree of the genus *Salix*, to which the osiers belong. The best cricket-bat blades are made from a white willow, *S. alba* var. *caerulea*, a fine tree with bluish-green leaves, mostly found in Essex. Willow is also used for polo balls. Weeping willow, *S. baby-lonica*, is native to China and is the willow seen on Old China willow-pattern plates.

Wind, air set in motion by special atmospheric conditions, is of various degrees, from a slight rustling breeze to a hurricane. Winds are *constant*, as in trade winds or anti-trade winds; *periodic*, as in monsoons and other windvisitations occurring according to influences of season; *cyclonic* and *anti-cyclonic*, when their motion is spiral: *whirl-winds*, *hurricanes*, and *tornados*, when high tem-perature and great density induce extreme agita-tion. Ordinarily, a wind is named from the point of the compass from which it blows, or it may be expressed in degrees from true north. The *sirocco*, the *mistral*, and the *simoom* are local forms of winds of great velocity. A *blizzard* is a biting blast of icy temperature. *See* **Beaufort Scale, Z10.**

Windmills were in use in the East in ancient times, but were not much seen in Europe before the 13th cent. Wind sawmills were invented by a Dutchman in the 17th cent., and one was erected near the Strand in London in 1633. Great im-provements have been made in these mills, especially in the United States, where, by the application of the windshaft principle, much space is saved and the mills can be used for pumping, grinding and other purposes.

Windows (Old Norse *vindauga* = wind-eye), an opening in a wall of a building to admit light and air, and to afford a view of what is outside. In northern Europe windows, as the derivation of the word implies, were first used for ventilation and glass was not used in private houses before the end of the 12th cent. In early Gothic (12th cent.) windows were still small and narrow, with rounded heads. In Early English (13th cent.) they became longer and the heads pointed. In the Decorated period (14th cent.) windows were mullioned (divided by slender bars into panes) and the pointed heads often traceried. In Tudor times when the Renaissance had found its way to England, windows were larger and the bay-window (projecting from the wall) and the oriel window (*q.v.*) were much in vogue; in the late 18th cent. curved bays (called bow-windows) became fashionable. Sash windows (invented by the English) with wooden frames and divided into equal rectangular panes were used in Queen Anne and Georgian houses. Their design was influenced by a passion for symmetry; they were very efficient ventilators. The French window reaches to the floor and has double casements opening as doors. A Dormer window is a vertical window set on the sloping side of a roof. One of the main features of modern architecture is the large area de-voted to windows, a development made possible by improved heating systems.

Windsor Castle, the famous British royal residence on the banks of the Thames, as it now stands, was mainly built by Henry III, though a royal residence had existed there from the time of the Conqueror. Additions were made by Henry VIII, Elizabeth and Charles II. Windsor Park and Forest comprise over 5,200 ha. A serious fire in 1992 caused very extensive damage, destroying St. George's Hall and gutting the Queen's Chapel. After completion of restoration work costing £40m, visitors were readmitted in 1997.

Witan *or* **Witenagemot,** the name given to the king's council of "wise men" in Anglo-Saxon times, composed of the archbishops, bishops, abbots of the greater abbeys, earldormen and influential thanes.

Witchcraft. *See* **Section J.**

Woad, a plant (*Isastis tinctoria*) that in olden days was largely used in England for the blue dye obtained from the leaves. It is a biennial plant belonging to the same family (*Cruciferae*) as the wallflower.

Wolves, well-known carnivorous animals still found in many parts of Europe, but not existing in Britain since the middle of the 17th cent. They usually hunt in packs. In parts of Europe, careful conservation has seen their numbers increase, as in north-west Spain.

Women's Institutes (WI) were originally founded in Canada in 1897. The movement spread to Britain, with the first branch opening in Wales in 1915. The organisation is particularly active in rural areas. In its centenary year (1997) there were nearly 9,000 WIs in this country.

Women's Liberation Movement. *See* **Feminism, J20.**

Woodcock, a wading bird, valued for its flesh. It is a member of the snipe family, and breeds in Britain. The parent bird is able to carry its young between its thigh and body when flying to and from the feeding spots. It is one of the birds protected by the Game Laws.

Woodhenge, popular name for the traces of an elaborate wooden temple, dating back 5,000 years, located at Stanton Drew in Somerset. Discovered in 1997, archaeologists think nine concentric rings of oak pillars once towered above the site.

Woodpecker, a familiar tree-climbing, insectivorous bird of conspicuous plumage, of which four species are found in Britain, the green woodpecker or yaffle (because of its harsh cry), the great spotted, the lesser spotted, and the wryneck. They build in the hollows of trees. Yaffle has a long sticky tongue for licking up ground insects, especially ants. The great and lesser woodpeckers obtain insects by digging into tree trunks with strong, chisel-like bills, spearing the insects with a sharp tongue. The metallic drumming sound made by the birds in spring is thought to be caused by their beaks hammering away at some hard resounding substance.

Wood's Metal, an alloy with a very low melting point (65°C, under 150°F) so that a spoon made of it will melt when used to stir a cup of tea. Contains bismuth 4 parts, lead 2 parts, tin 1 part, cadmium 1 part. Its use as a heat exchanger has now been largely superseded by silicone oils, which have a wider temperature range.

Woodworm. Four beetles are mainly responsible for woodworm damage: common furniture beetle (*Anobium punctatum*), powder post beetle (*Lyctus brunneus*), death watch beetle (*Xestobium rufovillosum*), and house longhorn beetle (*Hylotrupes bajulus*). Particular attention should be paid to wood in damp, dark and out-of-the-way places, and the backs and underneaths of furniture. The most frequent cause of woodworm damage is the common furniture beetle (*q.v.*).

Wool is a fibre, made up of very long protein molecules. It has been largely grown and used in the manufacture of cloth in England since before the Roman invasion. It is grown on the backs of sheep, and is of various kinds, according to the breed of sheep from which it is derived. Wool differs from hair in that it has a wavy, serrated fibre, its curl being a notable characteristic, whereas hair has a smooth surface comparatively free from serratures. Long wools are mostly used for the manufacture of worsted goods, and short wools for woollen cloths, though the improvements in machinery in recent years have enabled manufacturers to utilise short wools to a great extent for dress fabrics as well as for woollens. The finest wools are obtained from the fleece of the Spanish merino sheep. Australia, New Zealand, Argentina and South Africa are among the greatest wool-producing countries.

Woolsack, the name given to the seat occupied by the Lord Chancellor in the House of Lords. It is a large square bag of wool, without back or arms, covered with red cloth. At the time when it was first used, in the reign of Edward III, wool was the great staple commodity of the country and, it is said, chosen for the seat of judges as a constant reminder of the main source of the national wealth. The Lord Chancellor is "appointed to the woolsack".

World Heritage Sites, established under the World Heritage Convention to secure lasting protection for sites of outstanding universal value. In Britain they include Canterbury Cathedral, Ironbridge Gorge, Blenheim Palace, Hadrian's Wall *etc.*

World Population. According to United Nations sources world population has now (1999) exceeded 6,000,000,000 (it passed this landmark in June 1999). More than half the total live in Asia. Different countries are at different stages in a demographic transition from the stability provided by a combination of high birth rate and high death rate to that provided by a combination of low birth rate and low death rate. Their recent population history and current trend of growth, the age-structure of their population, and conse-

quently their population potential for the near future are all widely different. Most rapid growth is in Africa with rates of over 3 per cent in some countries. In most European countries the rate is less than 1 per cent. A baby girl born in Norway may expect to live the longest (77·6 years) and a baby boy in Sweden (72·1 years), but a baby born in some African countries may not live to reach 40 years. It is estimated that about one in 25 of all human beings who have ever lived are alive today. It took 115 years for the world's population to rise from one to two thousand million; in a further 35 years it rose from two thousand million to three; in only 15 more years from four to five thousand million. It is estimated to reach over 9 billion before 2050 and over ten billion by 2080.

Life expectancy in Britain today is 73·8 for men and 79·2 for women (compared to 48 and 51 in 1906). Life expectancy is increasing in Britain. Women are expected to live until the age of 80 and men to 74½ within a few years. Already Britain has the oldest population in the EU. One in 5 Britons are now over 60 and nearly 2 million are over 80. There are now (1999) over 8,000 centenarians in Britain. Highest life expectancies in the world for women are currently Japan (82·8), Sweden (81·4) and Hong Kong (81·2). For men, Japan leads with 76·4, Sweden comes second (76·1) and Hong Kong third (75·8). A report published in 1998 by the UN predicts that by 2030 the elderly will make up 40% of the population of Germany and Japan. Projections show the population of Britain will reach 61·6 million by 2016.

Wreck, the name given to trove found under water, usually from a maritime wreck.

Wren, a family of small passerine birds possessing upturned tails and most abundant in South America. The British species is an interesting singing bird with a surprising loud note for its size.

X

Xenon a rare gaseous element, no.54, symbol Xe, occurring in minute quantities in the atmosphere, discovered by Sir William Ramsay and M. W. Travers in 1898. *See* **Rare Gases.**

X-Rays were discovered in 1895 by Professor Röntgen, of Wurzburg. X-rays are produced when heavy metal atoms (*e.g.* tungsten) are struck by electrons of sufficient energy. X-rays are now commonly used to examine the internal structure of many opaque objects. In medicine, industry and for security, examination may be conducted without physical invasion. X-rays may also be used to probe the structure of matter, for example the atomic structure of crystals. The discovery in the 1960s that cosmic objects emitted intense X-rays has led to many important new astronomical phenomena being discovered. *See* **F12.**

Xylem, the woody tissue of higher plants whose function is to conduct water and mineral salts upwards, and to provide mechanical support.

Y

Yacht, a light vessel now much used for pleasure trips and racing. The first yachting club was the Cork Harbour Club, started about 1720; and in 1812 the Royal Yacht Squadron was founded at Cowes. The Royal Thames Yacht Club dates from 1823. The most famous international yachting trophy is *The America's Cup* (**L6**).

Yak, a curious, long-haired ox, found in Tibet. Used as a beast of burden, and also kept for milk and meat.

Yard, a standard measure of 36 in, the word being derived from the Saxon *gyrd*, or rod. The yard and pound are now defined by reference to the metre and the kilogram: yard = 0·9144 of a metre; pound = 0·45359237 of a kilogram. By international agreement the metre is defined by reference to the wavelength of krypton-86 light.

Yardies. Jamaican criminal gangs, in some ways similar to the Chinese Triads or Italian mafia.

Yellowhammer, a common British bird of the bunting family, of lemon-yellow and brown plumage. Nests on or near the ground.

Yeomen of the Guard are a body of Foot Guards established in the reign of Henry VII for the protection of the Royal Person. Yeomen are now about 100 in number, and their duties consist in being present on ceremonial State occasions, the yearly distribution of Maundy Money, and the searching of the vaults of the Houses of Parliament on Guy Fawkes' day. "Beefeater" is the nickname of both Yeomen of the Guard and Yeomen Warders of the Tower, and they both wear the style of dress of the Tudor period, but with one distinction, the Yeomen of the Guard wear a cross belt, the Warders do not.

Yeti, opinions differ as to whether this is a mythical inhabitant of the Himalayas, a primitive primate or bear. Evidence to date is inconclusive.

Yoga. See Section J.

York Minster, one of the oldest and finest of English cathedrals, is 160 m long, its nave is 73 m broad, and the central tower is 66 m high. The present edifice, in parts, dates back to the 12th cent., but a church stood on the site in the 7th cent. In 1829 it was set on fire by a lunatic named Jonathan Martin. In July 1984, a serious fire caused by lightning wrought severe damage to the south transept.

Young Offenders' Institutions. See **Detention Centres, L33.**

Youth Courts. See **Juvenile Courts (L69).**

Ytterbium, a chemical, no.70, symbol Yb, element discovered by Urbain in 1907; one of the group of rare earth metals.

Yttrium, a chemical element, no.39, symbol Y, discovered by Mosander in 1842. It is found in a few rare minerals such as gadolinite, xenotime, fergusonite and euxenite. One of the group of rare earth metals.

Z

Zamboni Pile, a dry galvanic battery, which can provide small amounts of high-voltage current over a very long time. At Oxford a couple of Zamboni piles have kept a bell ringing for over a hundred years. These piles in the second world war were perfected and produced in quantity, being the most convenient source of current for infra-red signalling devices.

Zebra, an African quadruped of whitish-grey colour, with regular black striping, perhaps the most beautiful member of the Equine family. Rather larger than an ass and smaller than the horse, it has a tufted tail, is of light build, wild and fleet of foot. The Zebra may be threatened with extinction—already the fate of the Quagga species—because of its slaughter by man for its beautiful skin.

Zen Buddhism. See Section J.

Zenith, the highest point in the heavens above an observer's head, the opposite pole to the nadir.

Zero, the cypher signifying nothing originally came from China. The West is indebted to the Arabs for it, who themselves obtained it from India and passed it to European mathematicians towards the end of the Middle Ages. The zero has also been found in Babylonian cuneiform. The Greeks had no such symbol, which hindered the development of their mathematics. The use of zero led to the invention of decimal fractions and to the later developments in astronomy, physics and

chemistry. For absolute zero on the temperature scale see **Absolute Temperature.**

Zinc, a familiar metallic element, no.30, symbol Zn, known to the ancients, and used by them in the making of brass. It occurs as the sulphide, carbonate, etc. The ores of zinc are crushed, roasted and reduced with coal. In combination with copper it constitutes the familiar alloy called brass, and zinc itself is much used for roofing and other protective purposes. Zinc ores are mined in Canada, the USA, Mexico, Poland, Australia, Russia, Italy, Spain and many other parts of the world. Zinc smelting is carried on in most industrial countries.

Zionism. See **Section J.**

Zirconium, metallic element, no.40, symbol Zr, was discovered by Klaproth in the sand of the rivers of Sri Lanka in 1789. The crystalline metal is white, soft and ductile; in its amorphous condition it is a blue-black powder. Zirconium is used in atomic reactors as containers for fuel elements, since it does not absorb neutrons.

Zodiac, an imaginary zone or belt of the sky enclosing the circuit over which the principal planets travel. It is divided into 12 equal spaces of 30 degrees each, comprising respectively the 12 signs of the zodiac—Aries, Taurus, Gemini, Cancer, Leo, Virgo, Libra, Scorpio, Sagittarius, Capricornus, Aquarius and Pisces. The idea of the zodiac originated with the Babylonians about 2000 B.C. and passed by way of the Greeks to the Western world. The traditional 12 signs of the zodiac were thrown into turmoil recently when a 13th sign – Ophiucus – was added by astronomers.

Zodiacal Band, a very faint band of light sometimes seen stretching along the ecliptic joining the Zodiacal Light to the Gegenschein and, like them, caused by the reflection of sunlight from interplanetary dust particles.

Zodiacal Light, a faint cone of light occasionally seen stretching along the zodiac from the western horizon after evening twilight or the eastern horizon before morning twilight. It is believed to be due to the scattering of the sun's light by dust particles in orbit round the sun and extending beyond the earth. Recent observations at the high altitudes station at Chacaltaya in the Andes suggest that the dust is travelling round the sun in regular planetary orbits.

Zonda, a warm moist wind in Argentina of great velocity blowing from the north or northwest, and, like the Sirocco in Southern Europe, causing much discomfort. It happens when a depression is moving across the pampas, bringing with it a mass of air from the humid tropics. It is followed by a refreshing wind from the south east.

Zoological Gardens of London were opened in 1828, and belong to the Zoological Society of London. They contain one of the largest and most varied collections of living animals in the world. The Society maintains an open-air zoo at Whipsnade, on the edge of Dunstable Downs; this was opened in 1931. The future of London Zoo was secured in 1992 by a £1·7 million cost-cutting programme and many generous donations.

Zoology, the branch of science concerned with animal life, embracing many aspects such as anatomy, behaviour, classification, distribution and ecology.

Zoroastrianism. See **Section J.**

Zulus, one of the peoples of South Africa. Prior to white rule, the Zulus were ruled by a succession of paramount chiefs, reaching the zenith of their powers under King Shaka in the 1820s. Their power was crushed by the British at Ulundi in 1879 (after the Zulus had earlier routed the British at Isandlwana).

SPECIAL TOPICS

CURRENT ENVIRONMENTAL DEBATES

CLIMATE CHANGE AND GLOBAL WARMING.

It may be thought incongruous to describe climate change as a current environmental controversy. It is after all nothing new. The last Ice Age finally retreated from Britain perhaps only some 12,000 years ago, and the North African coastal plains, much of which are now desert, were the granary of the Roman Empire. What, though, as new is the speed of change and the risk it poses that eco-systems will be unable to adapt at the same rate. The fears of some members of the UN Intergovernmental Panel on Climate Change that southern Africa could face a 100-year drought, and that it is the climate refugee rather than the political refugee who will characterise the 21st century, convey the scale of that risk. Even if there is overall adaptation, localised impacts could still be severe. Other members of the Panel have speculated, for example, that diversion of the Gulf Stream could give the United Kingdom a climate akin to that of Labrador.

The impact of climate change to date is, however, anything but speculative. Figures released by Munich Re, one of the world's largest reinsurance companies, at the end of December 1998, indicated that natural disasters across the globe were now three times as frequent as when the company started to monitor them 25 years ago. The human cost of some 50,000 deaths in 1998 alone is high, but the economic cost is even higher. Floods during the year were responsible for 85 % of economic losses of some £60 billion, nine times more in real terms than 25 years earlier. As one direct consequence, large tracts of low-lying land across the globe are rapidly becoming uninsurable with highly adverse consequences for countries, notably those in the Caribbean, parts of Asia and the Pacific, dependent on inward investment for tourism and other forms of economic development.

The Phenomenon of Global Warming.

Climate change is a comprehensive term for the changes arising from the phenomenon of global warming generated by the build up of what are known as "greenhouse gases" in the atmosphere. The best known of those "greenhouse gases" is carbon dioxide (CO_2), and the first area of controversy, which is essentially scientific, is the actual rate of change and the extent to which it is man-made. The Intergovernmental Panel on Climate Change currently estimates that warming is occurring at a speed of between 1°C and 3·5°C every century, rates which may sound modest but which at the higher end of the scale could raise sea levels by up to one metre in the same period. Scientific opinion increasingly supports estimates at the higher end of the range, but the argument is far from closed. Similarly, there is growing but not unanimous acceptance that global warming is being accelerated by greenhouse gas emissions from the burning of fossil fuels, particularly coal and oil, with natural gas as a lesser but still important contributor. Although most greenhouse gas emissions are produced by domestic households, industry, commerce and agriculture, road transport is responsible for 21 % and that proportion is increasing. Improvements in the domestic and industrial sectors are steadily being outweighed by the increasing levels of use of cars and lorries. Even the substantial gains of 50 % or more in fuel efficiency over the last 20 years have been outweighed by longer journeys and the preference for more powerful models. The net result has been that CO_2 emissions from road vehicles have increased by 70 %–80 % throughout the European Union alone in the last 20 years. These trends may seem slightly remote to the ordinary citizen but in practice they are not. The potential of the ordinary family car to contribute to global warming, for example, may be assessed from the statistic that on average each one emits about a ton of carbon dioxide every year.

Rising Sea Levels.

Rising sea levels are a daunting threat not only to countries like Bangladesh, where more than 100 million people live on land barely above sea level, but also to those extensive areas of north western Europe like East Anglia, the Netherlands and the German coastal plain where the land drainage of centuries past has caused the soil to dry out and shrink, putting much land significantly below the present sea level.

Such anxieties were aired at the United Nations Conference on Environment and Development held in Rio in 1992, and led to the drafting of the Convention on Climate Change. The European Union for its part had earlier agreed after much argument to stabilise CO_2 emissions at 1990 levels by the year 2000. The results of these initiatives, in themselves fairly undemanding, remain modest. It is widely feared that the EU target will be missed despite the substantial contribution made in some countries, notably the UK, by the substitution of natural gas for coal to generate electricity, although that change is controversial for other reasons. Some observers also fear that emissions will rise steeply in the coming years as public opinion, notably in Germany, refuses to countenance the building of another generation of nuclear power stations and much reliance again has to be placed on coal.

The first conference of the parties to the UN Convention on Climate Change, held in Berlin in April 1995, likewise had only modest results. The reason is not far to seek. Greenhouse gas emissions are unlikely to be stabilised let alone reduced unless fuel use becomes more expensive, which in practice means taxation of energy generated from fossil fuel sources. Although such taxation has the potential to be popular as one facet of a movement away from taxing incomes and employment towards taxing resource consumption, which would help to reduce unemployment, it will be seen as a regressive additional burden unless it forms part of a comprehensive redistributive package. Moreover, it is feared by many in industry, particularly in fields such as chemicals where energy use is high, by governments such as those of Japan and the US which are apprehensive of the impact on their competitiveness, by developing countries who fear their development might be stifled, and by the oil producing countries who do not wish to see a reduction in the sales of what may be their sole significant export.

Taxation in some form is, however, almost certain to come because the challenge of climate change will not go away. Recent years have been the warmest for well over a century, and both droughts and flooding have grown in frequency. Some, like the 1995 floods in Germany and the Netherlands, were extremely severe and could easily have become major disasters. February 1995 saw the breaking away of an Antarctic iceberg the size of Oxfordshire.

The Kyoto Conference.

It is not surprising against this overall background that the second conference of the 150 parties to the Convention on Climate Change, held in Kyoto, Japan, in December 1997, was politically charged. The European Union, strongly supported by the Association of Small Island States, urged a target of a 15 per cent reduction in emissions of three key greenhouse gases by the year 2010 with Britain being ready to reduce its emissions by 20 per cent in any event. America and Canada were initially unwilling to envisage any reduction at all, although America expected China and India to commit themselves to future reductions. China and the G7 group of developing nations, on the other hand, called for reductions of 35 per cent by the wealthier countries by the year 2020.

It is perhaps remarkable in these circumstances that any agreement was reached at all, even if it was dubbed second-rate. A Protocol was nevertheless adopted stipulating a binding target of a 5·2 per cent average reduction by the major industrialised countries on 1990 levels of emissions of a "basket" of six greenhouse gases by the years 2008–12. The different regions will, however, receive differential treatment. The EU will make a reduction of 8 per cent as will most of the countries of central and eastern Europe, the United States one of 7 per cent, and Japan and Canada 6 per cent. New Zealand, Russia and the Ukraine will stabilise emissions at 1990 levels but Australia will be allowed an increase of 8 per cent. No emission reductions are required of the developing countries, but America did, however, gain acceptance of the controversial concept of "carbon trading" between developed and developing countries, which is on the one hand a politically realistic approach but on the other a disincentive to real domestic change—a case of do as I say, rather than do as I do.

The third conference of the parties held in Buenos Aires, Argentina, in November 1998 was widely seen as a disappointment after Kyoto. Although a Plan of Action was approved, the measures are not generally binding and the Protocol is not now expected to enter into force until the year 2000, or even as late as 2003 if some environmental experts are to be believed.

Outlook.

The Kyoto Conference decisions represent a considerable advance on the non-binding undertakings entered into at Rio in 1992, but their adequacy is controversial. For those who still doubt the extent to which man is responsible for global warming, they are a gratuitous economic hurdle. For the much larger number who accept that humanity is accelerating a natural phenomenon, they are a very weak response. A reduction in emissions of greenhouse gases of 5·2 per cent on 1990 levels by the developed countries by 2008–12 has to be set against the estimate of the Intergovernmental Panel on Climate Change in 1990 that a global reduction of 60 per cent in carbon dioxide emissions was required then, if the atmosphere was to enjoy a stable equilibrium.

Temperatures in 1997 and 1998.

The year 1997 was the world's hottest since global records began in the 1860s with air temperatures rising to 0·43°C above the long-term annual average. Britain enjoyed its second warmest summer on record with temperatures 3°C above the monthly average. These trends were continued in 1998, and scientists have little doubt that the twentieth century will prove to be the hottest for at least a millenium. July 1998 was the hottest month on record for the planet since reliable statistics were first kept 120 years ago. Although the temperature variations involved may appear modest in themselves, they need to be set against the estimate that the last Ice Age was provoked by average temperatures only 4–5°C lower than those with which we are familiar. The sensitivity of the human body to very small fluctuations in blood temperature may be a useful parallel.

Although the average Briton might still instinctively react that such an increase for the traditional holiday month was a positive asset, the global reality is very different from the perspective of the Pacific and the Caribbean. Some twenty states including the Maldives, the Cook Islands, Nauru, Kiribati, the Seychelles, Antigua, Barbuda and the Federated States of Micronesia are at risk of becoming uninhabitable through the saline pollution of all water supplies or through simply being submerged. One of the leading members of the islands' lobbying body, the Association of Small Island States (Aosis), is the Marshall Islands with an average height above sea level of 6-feet and a maximum height of 20-feet but with a population of 56,000. It is projected that 80 per cent of the main island and its capital will be under water within a century, which has led to the preparation of a strategy of total evacuation and abandonment.

Precedent is not encouraging for the ready welcome of such refugees, and even if they do receive a welcome their national culture will almost certainly be lost. The possible host nations may also have problems of their own. Vulnerable coastal cities range from New Orleans in the United States to Hamburg and Venice in Europe, and Bangkok, Hong Kong, Shanghai and Tokyo in Asia.

El Niño.

The most dramatic recent expression of the destructive potential of global warming, however, has been provided by El Niño, although its precise relationship with the wider global phenomenon is the subject of scientific argument. El Niño is a complex of storms and hurricanes routinely generated at five to six year intervals by the warming of the Pacific. An area of warm water comparable in size to the continent of Europe is displaced from off Indonesia towards the South American coast 3,000 miles away, and instead of provoking the familiar south-east Asian monsoon it brings torrential rain and floods the length of the western littoral of the Americas. Moreover its scale is such that it disrupts weather patterns as far away as Africa.

Although the phenomenon is ancient, it appears to be growing in frequency and intensity, fuelling speculation that it is being aggravated by global warming. The rise of 5°C in the surface water temperature of the Pacific in 1997 was expected to provoke rainfall 200 per cent of normal before Christmas and 300 per cent afterwards along the Pacific seaboard of the United States. In an apparently perverse contradiction, it can provoke compensating snowstorms and blizzards further inland.

The Impact of El Niño.

The impact can be devastating. The 1983 visitation saw damage of £9 billion worldwide and the death of at least 1,200 people, with the Californian coast being amongst the areas worst affected. The Peruvian GDP was reduced by some 5 per cent. The consequences in 1997 promise to have been even more severe when the full impact can be assessed, as the extent of ocean warming was already the century's second largest by September.

In Indonesia, the 1997 coffee crop fell by perhaps 40 per cent through drought and the same lack of rain led to thousands of deaths from starvation and malaria in Irian Jaya, the Indonesian half of New Guinea, in the first three months of 1998. More than 1,000 forest fires devastated hundreds of thousands of hectares in Borneo, and the copper industry in Papua New Guinea had to be suspended when the rivers became too low for commercial use. Crops in both Australia and the Phillippines also suffered severely, with February 1998 being one of the driest February months on record across south-east Asia.

The prediction of heavy rainfall on the Pacific seaboard of the United States proved fully justified and California suffered severely. 1998 had become San Francisco's wettest year since 1867 before even the end of February and states of emergency declared in 35 of the state's 59 counties.

Devastation in America.

Despite earlier predictions by meteorologists that El Niño would continue to disrupt global weather conditions until May 1998, there is good reason to believe that it contributed to two later phenomena. In accordance with the expectation that the eastern seaboard of the United States would experience the reverse of the western, July 1998 saw one of the worst droughts in Texan history, with temperatures in Dallas remaining at 37°C (100°F) for the whole month. The drought was then followed by torrential rains resulting in floods which affected a quarter of the state's territory. This faded into insignificance, however, against the impact of Hurricane Mitch on Honduras and neighbouring Nicaragua at the beginning of November 1998. Central America's worst storm on record, during which the equivalent of perhaps three years' rainfall fell in just four days, killed up to 10,000 people in Honduras, central America's poorest state, and rendered some 800,000 people, more than 10 per cent of the population, homeless. It also destroyed some 70 per cent of agricultural output, with preliminary estimates suggesting that that loss alone would amount to some £1·2 billion, equivalent to more than 60 per cent of annual national income.

The Debate on the Proper Response.

Disaster on this scale poses in acute form the key question of who is ultimately going to pay the enormous and escalating costs associated with climate change. Wealth transfers are comparatively straightforward within a single prosperous country such as the United States but are much less so between and within developing countries. A rise of, say, 15 per cent in global food commodity prices, for example, could spell starvation and social unrest in less fortunate regions. Moreover, richer countries invariably seek to retain their favourable position. Saudi Arabia and Kuwait are already claiming the right to compensation if the global fight against global warming leads to a reduction in the demand for oil.

Although in the case of central America foreign emergency aid was rapidly forthcoming, not least from Europe, there has been heated argument over the appropriate longer-term response to natural disasters in countries which are already desperately poor. Nicaragua pays more than 38 % of its national income on servicing its national debt, and pressure groups, such as the Jubilee 2000 campaign, strongly backed by the churches, have called for the general cancellation of Third World debt for the millenium. On 1 December, the Pope issued a Papal Bull and apostolic letter urging debt relief for those poorer nations in particular who were oppressed by a debt so huge that repayment was practically impossible, so as to remove from them "the shadow of death". In direct response to the specific challenge of the hurricane, France agreed to cancel part or all of the debt owed to it by the four central American states of Honduras, Nicaragua, Guatemala and El Salvador. Indebtedness to France, however, only represents about 2 per cent of the £4·1 billion and £6·1 billion owed by Honduras and Nicaragua respectively, and the French initiative remains unique. Even Britain, which is owed just £300,000 and £900,000 by the two countries, is unwilling to countenance outright debt cancellation although it is certainly willing both to support a repayments moratorium and to contribute to a special trust fund.

There are some legitimate anxieties behind this reluctance. Clare Short, the International Development Secretary, speaks for many when she fears that a general approach of unconditional debt relief would penalise those countries which did pay their debts, and fuel tyranny and corruption elsewhere. Others though maintain that both Britain and the immensely influential International Monetary Fund (IMF) are primarily concerned with retaining the leverage enjoyed by creditors to insist on economic approaches to which they are sympathetic. The rigidity with which those approaches are interpreted by the IMF does, however, have many critics and the Fund's insistence on reducing public expenditure is not self-evidently apppropriate in a disaster situation. Peru, despite the national emergency again created by El Niño, is so conscious of these pressures, that it has refused to try to negotiate any rescheduliinng of its debt payments. The intention of the multinational fruit companies to dismiss their entire workforce in Honduras, announced almost immediately, only serves to underline the total vulnerability of the countries concerned.

The whole question of who will pay, and how, the costs arising from climate change was also reflected in two political initiatives much closer to home during the year—the emergence of the Greens as important, albeit junior, partners in the new German government and in the UK's White Paper on transport.

GENETICALLY-MODIFIED FOODS.

Genetically-modified foods attracted particular public concern at the beginning of 1999. The potential advantages of genetically-modified food crops are substantial, as they can be more nutritious, more pleasing to the eye and longer lasting than their unmodified equivalents. They can also help the farmer by being more resistant to weather and disease. Moreover, their supporters argue that genetic modification is no different in essence from the plant breeding which has been practised virtually since agriculture began.

Many others, however, are far from reassured. They are not satisfied that the risk of modified organisms having unrecognised properties which could damage the whole food chain has been properly addressed and are mindful of earlier food safety assurances which were later found to have been inadequate.

The problem is compounded by the different interests involved. The pioneering producer of GM

soya, Monsanto, is a US concern and stands to benefit greatly from American governmental pressures for the elimination of barriers to global trade. The individual consumer has no comparable defender. Moreover, those EU member states which have banned GM products may have infringed both EU and international law.

BIOGEOGRAPHY

Biogeography is the study of the diversity, abundance and distribution of living things in space and time. It aims to answer questions about why organisms live in some places and not in others, and how these patterns of distribution developed. Biogeography in its modern form began in the age of exploration. The early explorers were the first to have the opportunity to compare fauna and flora from different parts of the world. They collected and catalogued many new species. In the nineteenth century, Alfred Russell Wallace, Charles Darwin, and Joseph Hooker revolutionised our understanding of the history of the earth's organisms.

Following in the footsteps of these pioneers, biogeographers today study the patterns of distribution of species and try to understand the processes that caused these patterns to develop. Why and how organisms live where they do are the fundamental questions of ecological biogeography. How they came to be there is the main question of historical biogeography.

ECOLOGICAL BIOGEOGRAPHY.

Geographical Range.

The geographical range of a species is influenced by *abiotic* and *biotic* factors. *Abiotic* factors are the characteristics of the environment, such as temperature, rainfall and salinity. *Biotic* factors are the interactions with other living organisms, and include competition, predation and herbivory.

a) Abiotic factors.

Each species has a set of fundamental physical requirements that must be met if it is to survive in a particular area. For terrestrial species, temperature and water availability are key factors. Disturbance, for example by fire, flood, or volcanic activity, is also important. For aquatic species, temperature, oxygen concentration, and salinity are the main abiotic factors. Water, light and the availability of nutrients have a major effect on plant distribution. Each species has an optimal set of conditions, but can tolerate some variation either side of this optimum. Beyond the minimum and maximum of this tolerance range, the species can not survive.

b) Biotic factors.

The range of most organisms is smaller than would be predicted from an analysis of the physical conditions that they can tolerate. This is usually because of interactions with other organisms. One such interaction is competition, which is where two organisms both need the same resource to survive. Lotka and Volterra developed mathematical models, which predicted that competing organisms cannot coexist indefinitely; any slight difference in competitive ability would ultimately lead to the exclusion of the least competitive species. Their predictions were confirmed in laboratory experiments by Gause and field observations by J.H. Connell. Connell studied the distribution of two species of barnacles, *Cthalamus* and *Balanus*, in the intertidal zone. *Cthalamus* is capable of surviving over the entire range between low and high tide marks, but, in the presence of *Balanus*, is confined to a narrow area near the high tide mark. *Balanus* is more vulnerable to desiccation than *Cthalamus*, and therefore cannot survive near the high tide mark.

Ecological Niches.

The fundamental "ecological niche" is the theoretical space in a habitat occupied by an organism. Its boundaries are the upper and lower limits of all of the biotic and abiotic factors that can be tolerated by an organism. A more tangible concept is the organism's realised niche, which is the actual set of conditions in which it exists.

When conditions are near the limits of tolerance for a species, abundance tends to be lower and reproduction is less effective. Near the limits of an organism's geographical range, recruitment tends to be low; the birth rate may be lower than the death rate. The population would die out without the immigration of individuals from areas of more favourable conditions. Therefore, some populations act as sources, some as sinks.

Life-history Strategies.

The life history of an organism is the story of its life, from how it came into being, how it lives, feeds and reproduces to how it dies. Many organisms have developed complicated adaptations to their environment. Some enable them to withstand extreme environmental conditions, while others provide defences against predators or herbivores. Others help them to avoid competition, for example by highly specialised diets, which allow many species to co-exist on the same food plant.

Two basic types of life-history strategy have been recognised, though these categories are really the opposite ends of a continuous spectrum. Thus r-selected species are adapted to exploit a changing environment. They tend to have good dispersal abilities, a short life span and they often produce many offspring. Examples of r-selected species are the field poppy and the locust. K-selected species tend to live in more stable, or at least predictable, environments. They tend to be long lived and to produce relatively few offspring. In animals, K-selected species are characterised by a high degree of parental care and a dependence on learned behaviour for survival. Examples of K-selected species are the oak and the elephant.

HISTORICAL BIOGEOGRAPHY.

It is impossible to understand the distribution of organisms today without an appreciation of their origins and the changes in the environment that shaped them. As long ago as 355 B.C. Aristotle realised that the surface of the earth was constantly changing; "... the same parts of the earth as a whole are not always sea, nor always mainland, but in process of time all change." Three factors are important in reconstructing the history of fauna and floras; the distribution of related taxa (as described in ecological biogeography), the relative age of the taxa and the dispersal ability of the taxa.

Historical biogeographers aim to reconstruct the origin, evolution and dispersal of organisms and the environmental changes on the earth's surface. Plate tectonics (**F77**) and the fossil record are important elements of this discipline. The fossil record provides evidence of the past distribution of organisms and the existence of long-extinct animals, such as the dinosaurs. Fossil pollen can be used to reconstruct past vegetation types. Changes in vegetation type can also help us to understand how the climate changed in the past, since some plant assemblages are indicators of particular climatic conditions.

The Origin of Species.

Charles Darwin's theory of evolution revolutionised human understanding of the origin of species. Darwin, and his contemporary Alfred Wallace, proposed that evolution is an adaptive process, driven by the process of natural selection. Natural selection causes gradual changes in organisms over long periods of time, by favouring the persistence of characteristics that confer a survival advantage. Darwin realised that these advantageous characteristics could be passed on between generations. There was no knowledge of the genetic mechanisms of inheritance in Darwin's time. Eventually, natural selection can cause organisms to be so different from their ancestors that they become an entirely new species; this process is known as *speciation*.

Darwin believed that species originate in a particular location, the centre of origin, and gradually disperse from there. Provided that dispersal is slow enough for natural selection to operate, then survival of those individuals best adapted to the new

territories will be favoured. Ernst Mayr, amongst others, developed this idea further in the twentieth century.

Leon Croizat tested Darwin's idea by mapping the distributions of hundreds of plant and animal species. He argued that some species had similar distribution patterns, despite having completely different dispersal abilities. This led him to conclude that current distributions are the remaining fragments of wider distributions in the past. The fragmentation process is known as *vicariance*. Tectonic movements, climatic change, and alterations in sea level all play a role in facilitating dispersal and subsequent fragmentation.

CURRENT ISSUES IN BIOGEOGRAPHY.

Biodiversity and Conservation.

Biodiversity is a measure of the number of species and their relative abundance. Biodiversity is highest in the tropics and lowest at the poles. The reason for this is still a matter of debate and probably results from the complex interaction of many factors, both biotic and abiotic. At the poles, climate excludes all but the most specialised organisms. In contrast, the tropics tend to be warm and wet, with little fluctuation in temperature. These conditions encourage specialisation, and thus eventually speciation (the origin of new species). It is also suggested that organisms in the tropics have smaller ecological niches and thus can be packed more tightly than those at higher latitudes. Areas that are particularly rich in endemic species are known as "biodiversity hotspots". Tropical rainforests contain many animals and plants that have never been identified and catalogued; many will become extinct before they have ever been recognised by science.

Biodiversity increases when the rate of speciation is higher than that of extinction. Humans are increasing the rate of extinction through habitat destruction and degradation, over-harvesting, pollution and wildlife trade. Tropical rainforests, wetlands and coral reefs are especially sensitive to human disturbance. Species are particularly vulnerable to extinction if they are peripheral (*i.e.* at the edge of their range), geographically localised (exist in isolated habitat patches), highly specialised (and therefore less adaptable), poor dispersers, or are climatically sensitive.

There are three main reasons for conserving biodiversity;

1) Biodiversity represents a genetic resource, which is of potential use in agriculture and medicine.

2) Destruction of biodiversity could disrupt the biogeochemical cycles, which are our life support systems. Such cycles include the water cycle and the carbon cycle.

3) Humans have drastically increased the rate of extinction of other organisms. Many people believe that this is ethically unacceptable and that humans have a responsibility to safeguard the survival of other species.

Conservation of species and biodiversity may be *in situ* or *ex situ*. *In situ* conservation aims to protect entire ecosystems. It is generally accepted that only *in situ* conservation ensures the long-term survival of species and their habitats. *Ex situ* conservation keeps or breeds endangered species in controlled conditions. *Ex-situ* conservation includes the establishment of gene banks, where seeds, sperm and other genetic materials are stored, and botanic gardens, arboreta and zoological gardens. There are particular problems with the ex-situ conservation of some animals, which fail to breed in captivity or are difficult to return to the wild.

Island Biogeography.

Islands are of special interest to biogeographers. Their geographic isolation prevents intermixing with other populations, so that the origins of island species are often easier to understand than those of continental organisms. Distribution, speciation and adaptation can often be more clearly understood on islands. For these reasons, islands have been

L136

described as "evolutionary laboratories". Darwin's visits to the Galapagos Islands fuelled his ground-breaking ideas on evolution and speciation.

Nineteenth century biogeographers had noted that bigger islands tend to have more species. They also noticed that more isolated islands tended to have fewer species. Smaller islands tend to have a higher rate of extinction, because the probability of extinction increases the smaller the population. More isolated islands have a lower rate of immigration, because it is more difficult for new animals and plants to reach them. The number of species present on an island is a function of isolation, size and the time that has passed since the start of colonisation. In the 1960s, Robert MacArthur and Edward Wilson developed the equilibrium theory of island biogeography. They proposed that the number of species present on an island was the result of a dynamic equilibrium between extinction and immigration.

After a mass extinction, such as caused by a flood or volcanic eruption, islands are recolonised by immigration. An example is the volcanic island of Krakatoa, which erupted in 1883 killing all plant and animal life. Observation over the past 100 years has confirmed the dynamic nature of island assemblages. Taxa with greater dispersal abilities are approaching an equilibrium abundance more quickly than species with poor dispersal abilities.

As human population grows, more and more wildlife exists in islands of remaining habitat, surrounded by seas of arable land, or urban or industrial development. The equilibrium theory of island biogeography has particular relevance to the planning of nature reserves and National Parks; the size and degree of isolation of a protected area will determine how effective it is as a long-term refuge for wild species.

Global Climate Change.

The problems associated with global climate change have been discussed earlier (*see* **L132**). The rate of warming due to the greenhouse effect is predicted to be an average of $2\cdot5°C$ in the next century. The poles will probably experience greater warming than the equator. It is likely that sea levels will rise due to the expansion of sea water as it warms and the melting of the polar ice caps. Low-lying land and many islands could be submerged. The ranges of many plants, animals and pathogens are likely to change.

One of the greatest challenges facing biogeographers today is to understand, predict, prevent and ameliorate the effects of global warming in the 21st century.

LITERARY
COMPANION

This section is arranged in three parts. The first provides a concise introduction to the history of the English Novel. The second contains a glossary of literary terms whilst the third section features special topics, including in this edition articles on the enduring genius of Shakespeare, post-war British theatre, children's literature and science fiction writing.

TABLE OF CONTENTS

LITERARY COMPANION

I. THE ENGLISH NOVEL

INTRODUCTION

Definition

A novel is a fictitious prose narrative, usually of more than 50,000 words in length. It often deals with characters and actions that give readers an illusion of reality, but it can also be fanciful or fantastic. Its elements conventionally include a plot or story, personages, dialogue and a setting. Some novels contain such poetic elements as symbol, metaphor and rhythmical construction. Just as the content and general approach of novels show many variations, so the techniques in their writing greatly differ: narratives told in the first or third persons, in the form of letters and from different points of view are amongst the devices of presentation that have been used.

Types

Certain types can be defined, although they cannot always be clearly distinguished from one another.

The *picaresque novel* has a *picaro* (Spanish: "rogue") at the centre of its action, but sometimes this main character is an innocent or foolish person. Many adventures, described comically, satirically or realistically, befall him and influence him. A famous example is Lesage's *Gil Blas* (1715, 1724, 1735). Fielding's *Tom Jones* (1749) and Dickens' *Pickwick Papers* (1836-7) are in this tradition, which has been widely followed in England.

The *Bildungsroman* (German: "formation novel") relates the upbringing and education of the hero, as in Goethe's *Wilhelm Meister's Apprenticeship* (1795-6) and Dickens' *David Copperfield* (1849-50).

Psychological novels, exploring character, motives and relationships, were first established in France, with Madame de La Fayette's *La Princesse de Clèves* (1678) and the Abbé Prévost's *Manon Lescaut* (1731). Richardson's *Pamela* (1740) belongs to this category of fiction, which is often considered the most significant of all the kinds, reaching great profundity in the work of Dostoevsky (1821-81), Tolstoy (1828-1910) and Henry James (1843-1916).

Social novels, with the aim of exposure and reform of abuses and injustice, were prominent in the nineteenth century. Examples are Mrs Gaskell's *Mary Barton* (1848) and Charles Kingsley's *Alton Locke* (1850). Balzac's numerous novels, collected as *La Comédie humaine* (1842-8), and many by Dickens (*e.g. Little Dorrit*, 1855-6) are social novels in a more comprehensive sense, depicting characteristics of French and English society respectively.

The *novel of manners* is a sophisticated presentation of social codes of behaviour, especially amongst the leisured classes. Meredith's *The Egoist* (1878) partly belongs to this type.

Naturalistic novels, like those in Emile Zola's series, *Les Rougon-Macquart* (1871-93), and many by George Gissing (1857-1903), emphasise the power of environment in moulding human character.

Regional novels, by Thomas Hardy (1840-1928) and Arnold Bennett (1867-1931), amongst others, place importance on the traditions and influences of particular areas of a country.

In *adventure* and *detective novels*, the story or plot is a principal feature, as in Wilkie Collins' *The Moonstone* (1868) and Robert Louis Stevenson's *Treasure Island* (1883). The thriller, a variation of this type, is marked by excitement and violence, as in the James Bond novels of Ian Fleming (1908-64).

The *historical novel* deals with the past, sometimes mixing fact and fiction, such as the novels of Sir Walter Scott (1771-1832), Flaubert's *Salammbô* (1862) and Tolstoy's *War and Peace* (1863-9).

Fantasy has become increasingly popular, especially in the form of *science fiction*; Jules Verne (1828-1905) was one of the earliest and most widely read writers of this genre. English writers who have used this kind of fiction include H. G. Wells (1866-1946) and John Wyndham (1903-69). J. R. R. Tolkien (1892-1973) created a new "legendary" world in *The Lord of the Rings* (1954-5).

Purpose

The purpose of a novel varies with its type. Anthony Trollope's statement, made in his study of Thackeray (1879), has a fundamental validity: "the object of a novel should be to instruct in morals while it amuses." At one extreme, some novels are expressly meant to teach, such as some Victorian children's novels and social novels (*e.g.* many written by Charles Kingsley). At the other, some novels are meant simply as entertainment, such as detective stories and much science fiction. Trollope's term, "morals", is difficult to define, but one can say that the aim of most novels is to reveal and stimulate thought about aspects of human behaviour both individually and in personal and social relationships. Apart from these generalisations, the specific purposes of some English novels are described separately in the following survey.

Rise and popularity of the novel

Though stories in verse and prose are as old as human life itself, the novel, as we know it today, became established in the late seventeenth and early eighteenth centuries. Its rise is related to changes in the climate of ideas during that period, with its increasing emphasis on the rational and the actual. Influenced by such thinkers as Sir Isaac Newton (1642-1727) and John Locke (1632-1704), philosophers investigated the ordinary, physical world rather than the world of metaphysical speculation. At the same time, the reading public had increased in numbers, especially amongst the middle classes. This public wanted to read about the behaviour of realistic people in credible surroundings. One result in England was the publication of novels by Defoe, Richardson, Fielding and Smollett in the first half of the eighteenth century.

THE EIGHTEENTH CENTURY

Daniel Defoe

Daniel Defoe (*c.*1661-1731) is regarded as the first notable English novelist. After many years as a political pamphleteer, he published *Robinson Crusoe* (1719), based on accounts of the actual adventures of the mariner, Alexander Selkirk. The book is written with convincing, detailed realism. Robinson Crusoe's practical approach to his predicament and his powerful individualism make him an admirable character who can be seen to have a universal significance. We are shown a man confronted by adversity and yet overcoming it by means of his resourcefulness and holding to his belief in a providential God. The basic idea of a person shipwrecked on an island had a wide appeal, which was reflected in many imitations, including *The Swiss Family Robinson* (1813) by Johann Rudolf Wyss. Defoe's other novels include *Captain Singleton* (1720), *Moll Flanders* (1722), *Colonel Jack* (1722) and *Roxana* (1724). He claimed that *Moll Flanders* had a moral purpose, in that from every part of it "something may be learned, and some just and religious inference is drawn." But it survives because of its lively and uninhibited representation of the personality and doings of its disreputable, resilient heroine, who (like Robinson Crusoe) tells her own story. Formally, Defoe is an unsophisticated writer, who relies mostly on his invention of incident to keep his narrative in motion. His strength lies in his powers of observation and in his rendering of particulars, conveyed in straightforward prose, so that readers feel that they are experiencing things that actually happened.

Richardson, Fielding, Smollett and Sterne

The first great period of the English novel is 1740-71, when four important novelists flourished: Samuel Richardson (1689-1761), Henry Fielding (1707-54), Laurence Sterne (1713-68) and Tobias Smollett (1721-71). George Saintsbury, in *The English Novel* (1913), aptly called them the "remarkable exponents of a new kind of Human Comedy."

Richardson was a printer who was compiling a

collection of model letters to suit various occasions when he thought of writing an epistolary novel. The outcome was *Pamela* (1740), in which the letters reveal the story of Pamela, a servant girl, who resists her master's attempts to seduce her but finally agrees to marry him. *Clarissa* (1747-8), also written in the form of letters, tells of the tragedy of its heroine, who dies after her rape by the libertine, Lovelace. Containing a million words, it is probably the longest novel in English. Richardson's third and last epistolary novel, *Sir Charles Grandison* (1754), centres upon the scrupulously gentlemanly conduct of its hero. These are not novels of external action but are explorations of human psychology, especially of the thoughts and emotions of the young women involved. Their main theme is sexual passion and the moral problems that arise from it. The novels are admired for their sensitive portrayals of emotional and mental processes, realistically presented by means of the letters written by the characters.

Henry Fielding's first novel, *Joseph Andrews* (1742), was conceived partly as a satire on *Pamela*, which he thought hypocritical and sentimental. In picaresque style, he relates the adventures of Joseph Andrews, who is supposedly Pamela's brother, and his companion, Parson Adams. His intention in this "comic epic in prose", as he called it, was to expose the ridiculous. He therefore displays and comments upon hypocritical and affected behaviour in several walks of life. Parson Adams is one of the great humorous characters of English literature and yet he epitomises a true Christian goodness. Fielding's ironic approach reached an extreme in *Jonathan Wild* (1743), in which he treats the villainous thief who is the hero as if he were a great man. *Tom Jones* (1749), his masterpiece, gives us in an ingenious plot the history of a young man of unknown birth: his boyhood in the country, his journey to London and his escapades when he gets there. The book is full of vivid characters and episodes and contains much moral comment from the author himself. *Amelia* (1751) is concerned with the misfortunes of the heroine and her husband and with her patience and virtue. An experienced playwright, Fielding uses dramatic devices and events, sometimes involving physical action. His comedy is occasionally coarse and boisterous but often drily ironical. The reader is frequently aware of his authorial presence and he intervenes directly in the narrative. Like many of his contemporaries, he acknowledges the influence of the classics of Greek and Latin literature and here and there writes in a mock-heroic style. He is the opposite of Richardson, as Dr Johnson said to Boswell: "there was as great a difference between them as between a man who knew how a watch was made (*i.e.* Richardson), and a man who could tell the hour by looking on the dial-plate (*i.e.* Fielding)."

Tobias Smollett is superficially reminiscent of Fielding in his novels: *Roderick Random* (1748), *Peregrine Pickle* (1751), *Ferdinand, Count Fathom* (1753), *Sir Lancelot Greaves* (1760-61) and *Humphry Clinker* (1771). All of them recount the wanderings and adventures of their heroes and can therefore be described as picaresque, although *Humphry Clinker* is an epistolary novel. Smollett depicts an often brutal world with a mixture of relish and repulsion and his novels have a remarkable vivacity of invention. The episodes on board ship in *Roderick Random*, for example, give an unforgettable picture of the cruelties and rigours of eighteenth-century seafaring life.

Laurence Sterne stands apart from the novelists of his time and indeed can still be regarded as unique. *Tristram Shandy* (1760-67) is an eccentric, digressive composition. Chronological order and the sequence of cause and effect do not apply to Sterne's handling of his subject-matter—the hero is not born till half way through the novel, for instance. The personages talk of this and that, the author intervenes at will, a chapter may break off suddenly or may be blank, and so on. Despite this whimsicality and the flux of ideas and impressions, characters, such as My Uncle Toby and the Widow Wadman, are fully realised and an atmosphere of gentle humanity prevails.

Although one cannot draw clear lines of influence, it is possible to see these four novelists—Richardson, Fielding, Smollett and Sterne—as representatives of kinds of approaches to fiction that were apparent in the next two centuries. Richardson displays the interest in psychological introspection characteristic of the work of many twentieth-century writers. The emphasis laid by Fielding and Smollett upon external action has its counterpart in the broad humour and simple characterisation of some nineteenth-century novels. Modern experiments in the form of the novel remind us of Sterne's rejection of the rational development of narrative.

Later Eighteenth-Century Novelists

After the middle of the century, no outstanding English novelist emerged until Scott and Jane Austen started to write fiction at its end. But a few memorable novels appeared, including Oliver Goldsmith's *The Vicar of Wakefield* (1766) and Fanny Burney's *Evelina* (1778). Horace Walpole's *The Castle of Otranto* (1765) is important as the first Gothic novel. This type contained mystery and terror, often associated with the supernatural and a medieval setting. Its famous exponents came later: Mrs Ann Radcliffe, who wrote *The Mysteries of Udolpho* (1794) and Matthew Gregory ("Monk") Lewis, who wrote *The Monk* (1796). The most celebrated is Mary Shelley's *Frankenstein* (1818).

THE EARLY NINETEENTH CENTURY

Sir Walter Scott

The Gothic novels just mentioned are typical of Romantic literature, of whom one of the principal representatives in Britain and Europe in the early years of the nineteenth century was Sir Walter Scott (1771-1832). In his own time and for long afterwards, Scott was regarded as akin to Shakespeare in his comprehensive renderings of human life and his powers of imagination. He was a prolific author, who wrote poems, dramas, short stories, biographies and histories as well as the following novels: *Waverley* (1814), *Guy Mannering* (1815), *The Antiquary* (1816), *The Black Dwarf* (1816), *Old Mortality* (1817), *Rob Roy* (1818), *The Heart of Midlothian* (1818), *The Bride of Lammermoor* (1819), *A Legend of Montrose* (1819), *Ivanhoe* (1820), *The Monastery* (1820), *The Abbot* (1820), *Kenilworth* (1821), *The Pirate* (1822), *The Fortunes of Nigel* (1822), *Peveril of the Peak* (1822), *Quentin Durward* (1823), *Saint Ronan's Well* (1824), *Redgauntlet* (1824), *The Betrothed* (1825), *The Talisman* (1825), *Woodstock* (1826), *The Fair Maid of Perth* (1828), *Anne of Geierstein* (1829), *Count Robert of Paris* (1832) and *Castle Dangerous* (1832). These are mostly historical novels, set in many places and periods. *Waverley* takes place in Scotland during the 1745 Jacobite Rebellion; *Ivanhoe* in the England of Richard I; and *Quentin Durward* in fifteenth-century France during the reign of Louis XI.

Scott presents a great range of characters, from the lowliest peasants to monarchs, and mingles actual and fictional personages convincingly together. He enables us to see in their adventures, attitudes and relationships the forces of history at work. Their private lives are affected by public events. He imaginatively recreates history in his novels, which also show his sympathy for—and understanding of—all kinds of people, whatever their religious and political beliefs. His narratives are vigorously inventive, with colourful and dramatic scenes, as adaptations for opera, films and television have demonstrated. Having once read them, the reader will recall such things as Waverley's journeyings in the Highlands of Scotland, the battles in *Rob Roy*, Jeanie Deans' interviews with the Duke of Argyll and Queen Caroline in *The Heart of Midlothian*, and Meg Merrilies' roadside curses upon the Laird of Ellangowan in *Guy Mannering*. His memorable characters are often Scots, such as Jeanie Deans, Meg Merrilies, Dominie Sampson (in *Guy Mannering*) and Jonathan Oldbuck (in *The Antiquary*), but also noteworthy are Caleb Balderstone (in *The Bride of Lammermoor*) and Diana Vernon (in *Rob Roy*). His portrait of King James I in *The Fortunes of Nigel* is a remarkably convincing representation of an historical personage. But some of his heroes and women characters tend to be colourless and commonplace. Scott was not greatly concerned with psychological probings or with profound moral or religious issues. He used a huge canvas on which he portrayed the actions of people of every kind and degree in specific places and historical periods. He rendered "the being of the age" (in George Lukács' phrase) and the richness and variety of human life within that age.

Jane Austen

No novelist could be more different from Scott than Jane Austen, as he himself recognised. In an admiring comment on her work, he wrote: "The big bow-bow strain I can do myself like any now going, but the exquisite touch which renders ordinary commonplace things and characters interesting from the truth of the description and sentiment, is denied to me." Jane Austen (1775–1817) wrote only six novels, which were published as follows: *Sense and Sensibility* (1811), *Pride and Prejudice* (1813), *Mansfield Park* (1814), *Emma* (1816), *Northanger Abbey* and *Persuasion* (both 1818). The dates of composition are sometimes different: for example, *Northanger Abbey*, which was published posthumously, was one of her earliest books, begun in 1798. She also wrote shorter stories and fragments, which are conveniently collected in one volume in the *Oxford Jane Austen*.

She based her novels on the people and places with which she was familiar: the upper middle-class society of southern England, particularly Hampshire, the county in which she was born and lived for most of her life. Her work, she modestly wrote, was "that little bit (two inches wide) of ivory, in which I work with so fine a brush as produces little effect after much labour." Her subject-matter is the relationships between men and women, especially those concerned with love and marriage, and she accepts the social code of her class and period. She uses no exciting or ingenious plots, no startlingly dramatic incidents. She ignores doings and people outside the small circle in which her characters move. Yet within these conventions of subject-matter and social code, she illuminates wider areas of human conduct. In *Persuasion*, for example, she tells the story of Anne Elliot, who had rejected the suit of Captain Wentworth, the man she truly loved, because she yielded to the well-meant advice of Lady Russell, a close friend of her family. Anne and Captain Wentworth, who have met again seven years afterwards, slowly but surely re-establish their loving relationship and eventually marry. Questions raised include the rights and wrongs of persuasion, the place of love and money in marriage, the pressures of family vanity, and motives of men and women respectively when they fall in love. Moral issues like these are treated by Jane Austen with irony and wit as well as sympathy.

Her dialogue and passages of description contain much that is subtle and drily amusing, revealing her as an author who views folly and pretension with amused disfavour and who values the qualities of prudence and tolerance. Elizabeth Bennett in *Pride and Prejudice* comes close to her ideal of what a person should be like and some words that she gives to her can represent the novelist's own approach: "I hope I never ridicule what is wise and good. Follies and nonsense, whims and inconsistencies do divert me, I own, and I laugh at them whenever I can."

Jane Austen's characters come alive through their dialogue and reflections and through the novelist's observations. She constructs her novels neatly and with a feeling of inevitability so that they have an effortless artistic unity. Although she wrote at the time of the Romantic Movement, she remained cool and rational; it is significant that Charlotte Brontë attacked her for lacking warmth and enthusiasm. But her clarity of style and form, her comedy and wit and, above all, her penetrating analyses of behaviour and motive have led to her justifiably being regarded today as one of the greatest of English novelists.

Minor Novelists of the 1820s and 1830s

Between the time of Scott and the time of Dickens, who shot to fame in 1836, there flourished many minor novelists. The most enduring of these is Thomas Love Peacock (1785–1866), who wrote *Headlong Hall* (1816), *Melincourt* (1817), *Nightmare Abbey* (1818), *Maid Marian* (1822), *The Misfortunes of Elphin* (1829), *Crotchet Castle* (1831) and *Gryll Grange* (1860). These were mostly comic, satirical novels of ideas, wittily satirising fashionable thinkers and intellectual tendencies of the age. Peacock's usual device is to place his characters round a dinner-table and to record their conversation. In this way, he could poke fun at the Gothic Novel, Byronic gloom and German romanticism (in *Nightmare Abbey*), modern trends in education and agriculture (in *Crotchet Castle*) and Rousseau's views on natural man (in *Melincourt*). Some of his characters are caricatures of living people: Scythrop is Shelley (in *Nightmare Abbey*) and Mr Fax is Malthus (in *Melincourt*). His is a rational voice, puncturing what he considered to be the pretensions and affectations of the Romantic Movement. The elegance and polish of his dialogues at the dinner-table make his novels a permanent delight.

Humour of a more obvious sort is present in the once-popular novels of Theodore Hook (1788–1841), such as *Sayings and Doings* (1826–9), but these are now forgotten. They are worth mentioning if only because some critics have seen Hook as a precursor of Dickens. "Fashionable" or "silver-fork" novels, relating the intrigues, customs and speech of high society, were also widely read at this time. Amongst the authors of these were Mrs Catherine Gore (1799–1861) and Edward Bulwer-Lytton (1803–73), whose *Pelham* (1828) still has a little amusing life in it. Bulwer-Lytton achieved fame, too, with his "Newgate Novels", such as *Paul Clifford* (1830) and *Eugene Aram* (1832), which depicted criminal life in a romanticised and even glamorous manner. Scott's prestige and influence led to the production of historical novels. Bulwer-Lytton's *The Last Days of Pompeii* (1834) and some by William Harrison Ainsworth (1805–82)—for example, *The Tower of London* (1840)—are readable, but those by G. P. R. James (1799–1860) have fallen into oblivion. These minor comic, "fashionable", "Newgate" and historical novels have little intrinsic interest for most readers today, although the student of the period will find them valuable for the insights they give, sometimes unwittingly, into the tastes and prejudices of the 1830s.

Undeserving of neglect, however, are the energetic novels of Captain Frederick Marryat (1792–1848). Like several naval officers of the period, he wrote seafaring fiction, beginning with *Frank Mildmay* (1829). *Peter Simple* (1834) and *Mr Midshipman Easy* (1836) were amongst the novels that followed. *Snarleyyow* (1837) is a macabre comedy about an apparently immortal dog. Towards the end of his writing career, Marryat turned to juvenile fiction, which included *Masterman Ready* (1841–2), *The Settlers in Canada* (1844) and *The Children of the New Forest* (1847). His novels are extrovert entertainments, full of vigour and knockabout comedy, written in an unpretentious prose style. Parts of them are reminiscent of Smollett and, more interestingly, of Dickens, who was one of his closest friends.

Some distinctively Scots novels were published at this time. John Galt (1779–1839) wrote *The Annals of the Parish* (1821), which chronicles the doings of a country parish in Scotland, and *The Entail* (1823), a tragicomedy of protracted disputes about an inheritance. Outstandingly original in form and content is *The Private Memoirs and Confessions of a Justified Sinner* (1824) by James Hogg (1770–1835). This story of evil and damnation, a narration followed by a confession, is centred upon the "sinner", who is encouraged in his wickedness by a friend, who—it becomes clear—is the Devil.

This period between Scott and Dickens was therefore productive of novels of great variety. If one had to choose amongst so many writers of fiction (and they have not all been named here), one could point to Peacock, Galt, Hogg and Marryat as novelists worth remembering and, with Bulwer-Lytton and Ainsworth not far behind them. All were suddenly outshone, however, in 1836 by the dazzling appearance of Dickens on the scene.

THE EARLY VICTORIAN NOVELISTS

Charles Dickens

Charles Dickens (1812–70), who first came to public notice with sketches and articles in periodicals (collected as *Sketches by Boz* in 1835–6), achieved fame with *Pickwick Papers* (1836–7). This was rapidly followed by *Oliver Twist* (1838), *Nicholas Nickleby* (1838–9), *The Old Curiosity Shop* (1840–41), *Barnaby Rudge* (1841), *A Christmas Carol* (1843) and *Martin Chuzzlewit* (1843–4). These early books were exuberant and original in invention of every kind: colourful characterisation, vivid episodes, extravagant humour, pathos and evocation of the macabre, and an unfailingly fluent, fresh prose style. Many of Dickens's fictional personages immediately became household words: Mr Squeers, Little Nell, Scrooge and Mrs Gamp, to name only four from the books just listed. Similarly, sayings and phrases entered the English language, such as Oliver Twist's asking for more and Mrs Gamp's remarks about her imaginary friend, Mrs Harris. Dickens's tragic powers, especially those displayed in *The Old Curiosity Shop*, were found deeply moving. His evident concern for children, the poor and the deprived appealed to the humanitarian instincts of many of his contemporaries. On the other hand, his comedy made a tremendous impact, as in the *Pickwick Papers*, where Mr Pickwick's adventures and Sam Weller's sayings gave great joy to thousands of readers.

Dombey and Son (1846–8) seems to mark a turning-point in Dickens's career. It is more carefully unified than its predecessors and it relies less on exaggeration of plot and feelings; its central theme of pride is all-important. Dickens's next novel, *David Copperfield* (1849–50), with its suggestions of autobiography, is written in a calmly flowing manner, although it contains characters and incidents as striking as anything he invented: Mr Micawber, Uriah Heep, the storm at Yarmouth. Its subject-matter, concerned chiefly with the private and domestic affections, is, we feel, the product of mature contemplation.

The later novels of Dickens are *Bleak House* (1852–3), *Hard Times* (1854), *Little Dorrit* (1855–7), *A Tale of Two Cities* (1859), *Great Expectations* (1860–61), *Our Mutual Friend* (1864–5) and *The Mystery of Edwin Drood* (unfinished, 1870). They are more sombre than the earlier books. They are constructed with some care and they often deal with specific themes and subjects: the intricacies and deceits of the law (*Bleak House*), the opposition of utilitarian and imaginative values (*Hard Times*), the inefficiencies, irresponsibilities and materialism of mid-Victorian society (*Little Dorrit* and *Our Mutual Friend*) and snobbery (*Great Expectations*).

As we read a Dickens novel, we enter a self-sufficient imaginative world. He has many of the characteristics of a poet. This impression of a fertile, comprehensive imagination is enhanced in his later books by his use of motifs and symbols, such as the fog in *Bleak House*, the prisons in *Little Dorrit* and the dust-heaps and the River Thames in *Our Mutual Friend*. Although he has often been said to draw caricatures rather than characters, the people he creates spring to life on the page. In any case, some of his characters have a convincing truth about them—for example, his self-tormented people, like Miss Wade in *Little Dorrit* and Bradley Headstone in *Our Mutual Friend*. He has an amazing ability to distinguish his numerous characters from one another by their idiosyncrasies of speech. His plots are over-complicated, in a melodramatic mode, but they help to increase the tensions and mysteries that are so important in his stories and also help to hold together the many elements of his complex narratives. It should be remembered that his novels were written and published as serials, which partly accounts for some of his repetitions and exaggerations.

Dickens has astonishing powers of observation, seeing people and things as no one had seen them before, especially their peculiarities and strange resemblances. Allied to these powers is his ability to animate everybody and everything, so that even the furniture in a room can seem to have an active life of its own. He conveys all of this in vital prose, which is capable of expressing a wide range of particulars and moods. His purpose in writing, apart from sheer entertainment, is to put forward a message of hope and love, which he trusts will triumph over evil and over the vices and narrow-mindedness of materialism and a mechanical, uncaring social system.

Dickens's strengths as a novelist include his striking characterisation, his versatile prose, his power to evoke laughter, tears and fears, and his fundamental, positive "message". In the force and extent of his imagination, he stands next to Shakespeare.

William Makepeace Thackeray

William Makepeace Thackeray (1811–63) wrote miscellaneous prose and verse in the 1830s. *Catherine* (1839–40) and *Barry Lyndon* (1844), his first novels, were written partly to satirise the contemporary vogue for "Newgate Novels". *Vanity Fair* (1847–8) established him as major novelist. This book, set mostly in the Regency period, tells the related stories of two contrasted women, Amelia Sedley and Becky Sharp. One of its principal purposes is to expose the shams and pretensions of high society, as is indicated by its title, which Thackeray took from Bunyan's *Pilgrim's Progress*. *Pendennis* (1848–50), like *David Copperfield*, is coloured by autobiographical reminiscence. Its eponymous hero encounters temptations during his youth in the country, at Oxbridge and in the London literary world. Thackeray turned to the eighteenth century, his favourite historical period, for the background of *Henry Esmond* (1852), whose melancholy, meditative hero is tormented by his love for Beatrix Esmond and is also active in military and political affairs, including an unsuccessful attempt to put the Old Pretender on the English throne. *The Newcomes* (1853–5) is a chronicle of the loves, intrigues, successes and disappointments of the Newcome family, centred upon Clive and his father, Colonel Newcome. Thackeray's last important novel was *The Virginians* (1857–9), which continues the story of the Esmond family into later generations, set mostly in America during the War of Independence. His career as a novelist ended with *Philip* (1861–2) and the unfinished *Denis Duval* (1864).

During his lifetime and for long afterwards, Thackeray was frequently contrasted with Dickens. Unlike the latter, he avoided complicated plots and caricatures. His narratives flow smoothly from one incident or tableau to another. Thackeray's aim was to be as truthful as possible in his portrayal of people. He disliked the falsities he detected in such novelists as Bulwer-Lytton. His characters, therefore, are often ambiguously conceived, since he refused to simplify what he saw as complexity. A good man like Dobbin in *Vanity Fair* can be ridiculous on occasions; a man as honourable as Henry Esmond can love a woman as fickle and hard-hearted as Beatrix; a schemer like Becky Sharp is sometimes sympathetically described by the author. Like Fielding, whom he admired, Thackeray sought to reveal and mock hypocrisy and cant, especially in the middle and aristocratic classes, from which his fictional personages invariably came. One topic that engaged his attention was snobbery, which he deplored. Yet gentlemanliness was all-important to him, as personified in Colonel Newcome.

Thackeray has been called both cynical and sentimental. On one hand, he shows that conduct is not always what it appears to be; on the other, he depicts some people, especially when they are female, with fulsome affection. In all his work he is a moralist, relating the behaviour, thoughts and motives of his characters to those of his readers and people in general. Commentary, description, dialogue and story-telling are blended in his novels. Furthermore, the novels connect with one another, since characters recur; *Pendennis*, for example, tells the story of the Newcomes. This fact increases that sense of an actual, fully realised world which many critics have found to be characteristic of Thackeray's fiction.

The Brontës

Charlotte Brontë (1816–55) wrote *Jane Eyre* in 1847. Its second edition, by the way, was dedicated to Thackeray. This novel, which has never lost its power to enthrall the reader, uses a melodramatic plot, coincidence and exaggeration. But these devices, poetically and imaginatively realised by the author, intensify the reality of the passion that informs the book: Jane's sufferings, anger, independent spirit and feelings of love. These are brought close to us by the first-person narration. Her two great temptations, first towards an illicit relationship with Rochester and secondly towards the loveless religious life that St John Rivers offers her, are necessary, we feel, so that she can deserve the final, hard-won happiness that she finds. It is therefore a convincing psychological and moral novel as well as one of dramatic impetus.

Charlotte Brontë's second published novel was *Shirley* (1849), set in the north of England during the Napoleonic Wars and Luddite Riots. In it, we read of the fortunes of Caroline Helstone and Shirley Keeldar. One of its themes is the independence of women, though the book ends conventionally with the happy marriage of each of the heroines. *Villette* (1853) is a strangely-constructed novel, to the point of clumsiness, although its mysterious opening and conclusion are remarkable. But more importantly, its love story of Lucy Snowe, the English teacher in Villette (*i.e.* Brussels), and Paul Emanuel, the

Belgian schoolmaster she meets there, is one of the most sincere and moving in English fiction. *The Professor*, Charlotte Brontë's first novel (written in 1846), was published posthumously in 1857. Basically, it has the same story as *Villette*, though roles and sexes are reversed: an English schoolmaster in Brussels falls in love with a Swiss pupil. It is a novel not to be underrated, since it has a calm air of truthfulness.

Charlotte Brontë was essentially a Romantic novelist, dealing with emotional issues. As already noted, she had a low opinion of Jane Austen's coolness. Her sister, Emily Brontë (1818–48), was even more intense in her treatment of passion. *Wuthering Heights* (1847), her only novel, concerns two generations of the Linton and Earnshaw families in Yorkshire and how they are tormented by the ferocity of Heathcliff, who was brought into their lives as a boy found in the streets of Liverpool. The love between him and Catherine Earnshaw is all-consuming, destructive and yet immortal. *Wuthering Heights*, which has been called a dramatic poem, is full of the most violent emotions, paradoxically made even more intense by the perspective in which they are placed by the various narrators of the story. The construction of the novel—its points of view and its time-shifts—is notable, as are its imagery and passages of poetic description. As in *Jane Eyre*, the settings are important: the interiors of the houses, the Yorkshire moors and the changing seasons.

Anne Brontë (1820–49) echoes some of the themes explored by her sisters. *Agnes Grey* (1847) is about a governess's life and *The Tenant of Wildfell Hall* (1848) is a tale of mystery, drunkenness and love (televised in 1996).

Anthony Trollope

Anthony Trollope (1815–82) wrote forty-seven novels, of which the best-known are contained in two "series". The Barsetshire Novels, dealing with the lives of the clergy and others in a fictional country district, are *The Warden* (1855), *Barchester Towers* (1857), *Doctor Thorne* (1858), *Framley Parsonage* (1860–61), *The Small House at Allington* (1862–4) and *The Last Chronicle of Barset* (1866–7). The Palliser Novels, which are mostly political, are *Can You Forgive Her?* (1864–5), *Phineas Finn* (1867–9), *The Eustace Diamonds* (1871–3), *Phineas Redux* (1873–4), *The Prime Minister* (1875–6) and *The Duke's Children* (1879–80). Other novels worth noting are *The Three Clerks* (1858), *Orley Farm* (1861–2), *The Vicar of Bullhampton* (1869–70) and *The Way We Live Now* (1875).

His novels are firmly constructed and written plainly and explicitly, without the poetic imagination of Dickens and the Brontës or the elegant subtlety of Thackeray (whom he admired above all contemporary novelists). Nathaniel Hawthorne, the American novelist, wrote that Trollope's novels were "solid and substantial, written on the strength of beef and the inspiration of ale, and just as real as if some giant had hewn a great lump out of the earth and put it under a glass case, with all its inhabitants going about their daily business, and not suspecting that they were being made a show of." If you want to have an accurate impression of what daily life was like amongst the upper middle-classes of England in the 1850s, then a reading of *Barchester Towers*, for example, will supply you with details of customs, dress, furniture and manner of speech. Apart from this characteristic, Trollope provides the reader with interesting and entertaining plots. The accusations of theft made against the Reverend Josiah Crawley and the ensuing complications make *The Last Chronicle of Barset* a fascinating novel. *The Eustace Diamonds* is another well-constructed tale of intrigue, about Lizzie Greystock's determination to retain an heirloom, a diamond necklace.

Trollope is especially skilful in working out the conflicts between public and private lives, in clerical and political matters above all: the disputes over the wardenship of Hiram's Hospital in *The Warden* and *Barchester Towers* and the jockeyings for power and influence in the Palliser novels. No other English novelist has so comprehensively treated this perpetually relevant subject, though C. P. Snow's *The Masters* (1951) is a modern example influenced by Trollope. He draws his characters with humour and sympathy but he occasionally disconcertingly interrupts his narration with authorial comments, as

Henry James noted disapprovingly. He unquestioningly accepts Victorian standards of morality and conduct and sees everything from the standpoint of an upper-middle class English gentleman. Trollope was proud of his craftsmanship and almost without exception his novels are carefully constructed. They remain reliably readable and amusing without being too demanding. The Prime Minister, John Major, unveiled a memorial tablet in Westminster Abbey in March 1993.

Benjamin Disraeli, Mrs Gaskell and Charles Kingsley

Three novelists who flourished in the mid-nineteenth century were Benjamin Disraeli (1804–81), Mrs Elizabeth Gaskell (1810–65) and Charles Kingsley (1819–75). Like many of their contemporaries, they were perturbed by the social conditions of England brought about by industrialisation. As a result, they wrote influential novels that highlighted the problems of capital and labour and the sufferings of the poor.

Disraeli's first novels (*e.g. Henrietta Temple*, 1837) were of the "fashionable" kind already discussed but in the 1840s he produced three that were concerned with politics and society: *Coningsby* (1844), *Sybil* (1845) and *Tancred* (1847). Disraeli, who at that time was already prominent as a politician, developed his theories of Conservatism in the first of these, using the education, career and ideas of its hero, Coningsby, as the basis of his story. The alternative title of *Sybil* is *The Two Nations*, by which Disraeli denotes the rich and the poor. He dramatises the issues by means of the love between Sybil, the daughter of a Chartist, and Charles Egremont, a member of the aristocracy. In *Tancred*, the hero, the son of a Duke, journeys to the Holy Land to seek guidance towards true belief and conduct.

Mrs Gaskell's social novels were *Mary Barton* (1848) and *North and South* (1854–5). The first, which is set in Manchester, vividly evokes the appalling conditions of the working class, which Mrs Gaskell knew at first hand. She sensationalises her problem by using a melodramatic plot, involving murder committed by the heroine's father, but there is no escaping the fact that it is a gripping novel that not surprisingly made a considerable impression upon readers in mid-Victorian England. *North and South* contrasts two regions of England, as its title implies, through the medium of its heroine, Margaret Hale, who leaves southern England to live in the industrial north. Mrs Gaskell sympathetically presents a balanced view of social problems, indicating some of the virtues as well as the shortcomings of the employers, personified in John Thornton, with whom Margaret falls in love. Mrs Gaskell's other novels include *Cranford* (1851–3), a quiet and charming account of life amongst genteel middle-class ladies in a northern village in the 1830s; *Ruth* (1853), a harrowing tale of seduction and desertion; *Sylvia's Lovers* (1863); and *Wives and Daughters* (1864–6, unfinished), about the characters and family relationships in a provincial town.

Charles Kingsley's interests as a clergyman and Christian Socialist inspired *Alton Locke* (1850), which is about working-class London and Chartism, and *Yeast* (1851), which is concerned with problems of rural England. As in all his books, Kingsley writes with enthusiasm and commitment, not hesitating to preach his social sermons when the occasion prompts. For the student of political and religious ideas of the period, these two novels are valuable sources. Kingsley also wrote historical novels: *Hypatia* (1853), *Westward Ho!* (1855) and *Hereward the Wake* (1866). *The Water Babies* (1863) is a lively, didactic story for children.

George Eliot

George Eliot (the pseudonym of Mary Ann Evans, 1819–80), wrote three long short stories, *Scenes of Clerical Life* (1857), and then the following novels: *Adam Bede* (1859), *The Mill on the Floss* (1860), *Silas Marner* (1861), *Romola* (1862–3), *Felix Holt, the Radical* (1866), *Middlemarch* (1871–2) and *Daniel Deronda* (1876). The first three novels are set in rural England, recalling the Warwickshire where she was born and brought up. *Adam Bede* is the tragic story of Hetty Sorrel, a village girl who is seduced, bears an illegitimate child and is convicted of infanticide. *The Mill on the Floss* is concerned mainly with the life, loves and emotional vicissitudes of Maggie Tulliver, who has some of the characteristics of the author herself. *Silas Marner* tells of an unhappy, miserly weaver, who regains his love of humanity after bringing up a child who has found her way to his cottage door. All, then, are about comparatively humble people and all sympathetically render the seasons, scenes, activities and speech of country life.

For her fourth novel, George Eliot turned to a completely different setting and period, as if to challenge her powers of invention: *Romola* is an historical novel, set in late fifteenth-century Florence, at the time of Machiavelli and Savonarola. It is a moving and exciting account of the conflicts of personal and public issues and of treachery and love. *Felix Holt* has the political events of 1832 as its background, although its principal interest lies in Esther's personal relationships and in the disputes over the ownership of an estate. By general agreement, *Middlemarch* is George Eliot's masterpiece. This long, complex novel has four interwoven plots revealing various themes: love and marriage, ambition, religious hypocrisy and the pressures exerted by a provincial environment. *Daniel Deronda* has two plots and themes, again interrelated: the character and unhappy marriage of Gwendolen Harleth and the revelation of Daniel's Jewish parentage.

George Eliot brought great seriousness of purpose to the novel. Like the other Victorian novelists, she made moral teaching an essential part of her fiction. Although she had lost her belief in orthodox Christianity, she held to the ideals of duty and personal responsibility. She explores these fundamental doctrines of hers through her characters and plots and through much authorial comment. In *Silas Marner*, for example, she shows how Godfrey Cass tries to ignore his past actions that have caused distress to himself and others and how instead he hopes that Chance will come to his aid. To make the point clear to her readers, she writes a long passage, almost like a sermon, on the error of not facing the consequences of one's actions and of trusting to Fortune. Nevertheless, she constantly shows sympathy and tolerance towards her characters. She can express her pity for such people as Casaubon, Rosamond Vincy and Bulstrode in *Middlemarch* whereas a novelist who saw personality in simpler terms would deplore or condemn their faults. Perhaps more than any previous novelist, she describes and analyses the sheer complexity of character, with the result that her portraits, especially of women, have great profundity—Maggie Tulliver in *The Mill on the Floss*, Mrs Transome in *Felix Holt*, Dorothea in *Middlemarch* and Gwendolen Harleth in *Daniel Deronda*. Some of her personages, especially rural folk in her earlier novels, are presented with humour—Mrs Poyser in *Adam Bede* and Maggie's aunts and uncles in *The Mill on the Floss*.

George Eliot was scrupulous in the construction of her novels, allowing few digressions or inessential characters. The villagers' "chorus" in *Silas Marner*, for example, is necessary for our understanding of their opinions of the main characters and of the kind of existence, past and present, amongst which those characters must live. By the standards of the time, she avoids exaggeration and highly coloured incidents. Because of her wise moral concern, her understanding of psychology, and her care over the structure of her novels, George Eliot is regarded nowadays as one of the greatest English novelists.

Charles Reade, Wilkie Collins, and Sensation Novels

From about 1860 onwards, "sensation novels" were enormously popular. Their ingredients could include crime, detection, and passionate and illicit love-affairs; they had, too, a highly emotional atmosphere. Two of the best-known were *Lady Audley's Secret* (1862) by Mary Elizabeth Braddon (1837–1915) and *Uncle Silas* (1864) by J. Sheridan Le Fanu (1814–73).

Dickens, Charles Reade and Wilkie Collins have sometimes been called "sensation novelists" although that is too limiting a description of them. Charles Reade (1814–84), an original and lively author, wrote two famous historical novels: *Peg Woffington* (1853), recounting an episode in the life of the eighteenth-century actress, and *The Cloister and the Hearth* (1861), a romance set in fifteenth-century Europe. His novels dealing with contemporary social abuses include *It is never too late to Mend* (1853), in which he exposes brutalities in the prisons, and *Hard Cash* (1863), in which he describes conditions in a lunatic asylum. Wilkie Collins (1824–89),

a friend and associate of Dickens, was a prolific writer. His most enduring novels, with ingenious plots, are *The Woman in White* (1859–60), *No Name* (1862) and *The Moonstone* (1868), which is often called the first English detective story.

THE LATE VICTORIAN PERIOD

George Meredith

George Meredith (1828–1908) was a substantial poet as well as a novelist. After writing an Oriental fantasy, *The Shaving of Shagpat* (1856), he wrote *The Ordeal of Richard Feverel* (1859), *Evan Harrington* (1860), *Emilia in England* (1864, retitled *Sandra Belloni*, 1886), *Rhoda Fleming* (1865), *Vittoria* (1867), *The Adventures of Harry Richmond* (1870–1), *Beauchamp's Career* (1874–5), *The Egoist* (1879), *The Tragic Comedians* (1880), *Diana of the Crossways* (1885), *One of our Conquerors* (1890–1), *Lord Ormont and his Aminta* (1894) and *The Amazing Marriage* (1895). Of these novels, *The Ordeal of Richard Feverel*, *The Egoist* and *Diana of the Crossways* are generally accounted the best.

Richard Feverel is brought up by his father, Sir Austin, according to a System, which should train him to be a perfect English gentleman, who would avoid making the kind of disastrous marriage that the baronet had suffered. The fine plans break down. Richard marries a girl of unsuitable birth and quickly becomes corrupted in London society. Not unexpectedly, there is a tragic end to everything. But the novel is remarkable for its disparate elements: its irony and satire, not only in situation but also in the wry comments of Adrian Harley; its passages of poetic description; the melodramatic turns of the plot; its humour and its pathos. *The Egoist*, in contrast, is perfectly organised, reminiscent of a comedy of manners in the theatre, especially in its denouement. Its comedy lies in the exposure of the egoism of the central character, Sir Willoughby Patterne, but the play of wit is modified by the sympathetic portrayal of Clara Middleton, to whom Sir Willoughby is engaged to be married, and the delightfully fresh portrayal of Crossjay Patterne, a twelve-year-old boy. *Diana of the Crossways* is about a witty, attractive young woman, involved in divorce proceedings and a love affair.

Like Fielding, Meredith set great store by the ability of comedy to reveal and rectify affectation. "Comedy is the foundation of good sense," he wrote in his *Essay on Comedy* (1877). Another relevant definition comes at the beginning of *The Egoist*: "Comedy is a game played to throw reflections upon social life, and it deals with human nature in the drawing-room of civilized men and women." His theory is brilliantly put into practice in the final chapters of *The Egoist*, when devices and revelations of different kinds bring about Sir Willoughby's humiliation.

His handling of his characters' psychology is occasionally elusive, but he has meaningful insights to offer and can be seen to be anticipating the "stream of consciousness" in parts of *The Egoist*, notably in "Clara's Meditations". Amongst his main themes are the tensions between appearance and reality (as in Evan Harrington's social position contrasted with his humble birth) and the independence of women (as shown in the fortunes of Clara and Diana).

Meredith was lionised towards the end of his life, but he is unjustly neglected today. At the least, he should be read for the new possibilities he found in the novel-form and for the risks he took. Apart from his importance in the history of the English novel, there is much in his writing that the modern reader will find intrinsically rewarding.

Thomas Hardy

The career of Thomas Hardy (1840–1928) divides into two parts. In the nineteenth century, up to 1896, he published novels. He then abandoned the writing of prose fiction and for the rest of his life concentrated wholly on poetry. He divided his novels into three groups. First, there are "Novels of Character and Environment", which comprise *Under the Greenwood Tree* (1872), *Far from the Madding Crowd* (1874), *The Return of the Native* (1878), *The Mayor of Casterbridge* (1886), *The Woodlanders* (1887), *Tess of the D'Urbervilles* (1891) and *Jude the Obscure* (1896). Secondly, there are the

"Romances and Fantasies": *A Pair of Blue Eyes* (1873), *The Trumpet-Major* (1880), *Two on a Tower* (1882) and *The Well-Beloved* (1892). Thirdly, there are the "Novels of Ingenuity": *Desperate Remedies* (1871), *The Hand of Ethelberta* (1876) and *A Laodicean* (1881). Hardy's major works are those in the first of these categories, with the possible additions of *A Pair of Blue Eyes*, *Desperate Remedies* and *The Trumpet-Major*. As well as these novels, Hardy wrote a considerable number of short stories.

His novels are set in Wessex, by which Hardy means Dorset and the adjacent counties of south-west England. This was the region where he was born and where he lived for most of his life. The scenery, occupations, customs, traditions and speech of Wessex all play vital parts in his narratives. One subject of his is the contrast between the rural world and the world outside, seen most dramatically when an outsider comes into the community or a former inhabitant returns. Fancy Day's coming to Mellstock in *Under the Greenwood Tree*, Sergeant Troy's arrival in *Far from the Madding Crowd* and the return of Clym Yeobright and Grace Melbury from the Continent to their native English villages in *The Return of the Native* and *The Woodlanders* respectively are examples of this kind of conflict. Hardy's great respect for traditional custom is evident in his loving rendering of typical country tasks and events: cider-making, tending sheep, felling trees, cutting furze, threshing wheat, lighting bonfires on 5 November, marriage ceremonies, and so on. Following George Eliot's practice, he uses conversation of village people as sources of commentary and local history. A setting can take on a symbolic function, as Egdon Heath does in *The Return of the Native* or the woods do in *The Woodlanders*. A character can become symbolically identified with his occupation and surroundings, like Diggory Venn in *The Return of the Native*.

Hardy's view of life was fatalistic, since he believed that the human situation was, in Lord David Cecil's words, "a struggle between man on the one hand and, on the other, an omnipotent and indifferent fate." One of his most forthright statements of this belief occurs at the end of *Tess of the D'Urbervilles* when he reports the execution of the heroine: " 'Justice' was done, and the President of Immortals, in Aeschylean phrase, had ended his sport with Tess." His novels therefore contain much that is pessimistic and melancholy. The last two, *Tess of the D'Urbervilles* and *Jude the Obscure*, are the most tragic of all. Jude and Sue Bridehead, the central characters of the last novel, find all their aspirations concerning love, marriage, education and religious belief confounded and defeated and their story ends with the death of Jude and the resignation of Sue to unhappiness.

As an aspect of Hardy's deterministic view of life, he believed in the importance of chance, accident and coincidence. A trivial or thoughtless action, such as Bathsheba Everdene's throwing up a hymn book to see whether it falls open or shut (in *Far from the Madding Crowd*), can have unforeseen, appalling consequences. "Life's Little Ironies" and "Satires of Circumstance", titles of collections of his short stories and verse respectively, can be appropriately applied to much that he wrote. His novels are full of strange, striking episodes, in line with his theory that the artist was justified in using exaggeration and distortion to make his points effectively. Readers of Hardy always remember such things as the slaughter of the pig in *Jude the Obscure*, the sale of Henchard's wife in *The Mayor of Casterbridge*, the death of Mrs Yeobright on the heath in *The Return of the Native* and Sergeant Troy's first encounter with Bathsheba in *Far from the Madding Crowd*. Such scenes and events are there for their emotional impact and for the illumination they shed on key motives and developments in the novels.

Hardy's stories are mostly about the tragedies and disappointments of love between men and women. A favourite plot of his depends on the relationship of a woman with two or three men (e.g. Fancy Day, Eustacia Vye, Anne Garland and Tess). Women play a dominant part in his novels. He draws them with sympathy and understanding and he is especially interested in the personalities and actions of strong-willed women or women striving for independence and a life of their own (Sue Bridehead is a famous example). Amongst his men characters, those who are tortured by misgivings, remorse and disappointment are dramatically presented, as witness Henchard, Boldwood and Jude.

Henry James

The importance of Henry James (1843–1916) in the history of the English and American novel is very great indeed. His practice and the theories he expounded in his essay, "The Art of Fiction" (1884), and in the Prefaces to his novels, have been widely influential in this century. An American by birth, James lived and worked in England for most of his life, writing short stories, travel books, essays and numerous novels.

It is convenient to divide the novels into three groups, corresponding to three stages in his career. A favourite theme of his early work is the mutual influences of European and American culture. Principal works of this period are *Roderick Hudson* (1875), *The American* (1877), *The Europeans* (1878), *Daisy Miller* (1879), *Washington Square* (1881), *The Portrait of a Lady* (1881), *The Bostonians* (1886) and *The Princess Casamassima* (1886). His middle period, in which his technique becomes more complex and his subject-matter frequently concerned with English topics, includes *The Tragic Muse* (1890), *The Spoils of Poynton* (1897), *What Maisie Knew* (1897), *The Turn of the Screw* (1898), *The Awkward Age* (1899) and *The Sacred Fount* (1901). James's most difficult novels, which show a return to his interest in the tensions between English and American values, are the final three: *The Wings of a Dove* (1902), *The Ambassadors* (1903) and *The Golden Bowl* (1904).

As a man who had experienced life in the United States and Europe, James was fascinated by the differences in culture between the Old and the New Worlds. On the one hand were the newness, potentiality and democracy of America (wonderfully evoked in the opening chapter of *The Europeans*) and on the other hand were the history and achievements of Europe. In his opinion, expressed in his study of Nathaniel Hawthorne, "it takes a great deal of history to produce a little literature" and "it needs a complex social machinery to set a writer in motion." His most famous treatment of the issues involved in this opposition of two ways of life is *The Portrait of a Lady*, which many critics think is his most fully accomplished work of fiction. Isabel Archer, an American girl, comes to England and Europe. She is attractive, frank and eager for adventure and experience. Having rejected two suitors and having inherited a fortune from her uncle, she makes a disastrously ill-judged marriage with an expatriate American but finally decides to endure the consequences of her error. The novel is rich in characterisation: apart from Isabel, the most intriguing personages are Ralph Touchett (her cousin, an invalid) and Madame Merle (a cosmopolitan woman, who arranges Isabel's marriage). James reveals, with understanding, tenderness and wit, the virtues and the weaknesses of Isabel. Moreover, he gives a wise and analytical picture of many aspects of human behaviour, relating them where appropriate to the society and culture of the United States, Europe and England. The theme of the young American woman who visits Europe with tragic consequences is repeated in *The Wings of a Dove*, with Milly Theale as the girl in question. *The Europeans*, one of James' earliest books, is a brief, elegant but searching presentation of the same basic subject; in that novel the scene is the United States, which the Europeans visit.

James was also interested in exploring the problems and corruptions of contemporary English society, as embodied in the contents of the house and the avarice for them displayed in *The Spoils of Poynton*. Or there are what the critic F. R. Leavis has called the "egotistic squalors" revealed in the comings and goings of the divorced people and spouses in *What Maisie Knew*. His fascination for observing the effects of corruption of a directly personal kind, irrespective of social pressures, is memorably realised in *The Turn of the Screw*.

He believed intensely in the importance of technique and form for the novelist, who held a "sacred office", in his view. The novelist had a duty, he maintained, to tell the truth and to impart to his fiction an "air of reality". In order to accomplish that aim, the writer had to ensure that the novel was an organic whole, with each of its parts contributing to the totality. James called some nineteenth-century novels "large, loose, baggy monsters" and sought in his own work to practise a strict control over his material. His novels are accordingly tautly constructed and written in the most meticulous prose style. This style in the later novels is difficult and subtle and some critics have thus accused him of sacrificing life and warmth for the sake of brilliant intellectual structures. Meredith and Hardy in their different ways broke with some of the conventions of the Victorian novel; but James departed radically from many of its features and can be regarded as the first of the modern novelists.

Robert Louis Stevenson and the Adventure Novel

Robert Louis Stevenson (1850–94), essayist, poet, travel-writer and novelist, achieved fame with *Treasure Island* (1883) and *Dr Jekyll and Mr Hyde* (1886). His subsequent novels include *Kidnapped* (1886), *The Black Arrow* (1888), *The Master of Ballantrae* (1889), *Catriona* (1893), *Weir of Hermiston* (unfinished, 1896) and *St. Ives* (completed by A. Quiller-Couch, 1898). With Lloyd Osbourne, his stepson, he wrote *The Wrong Box* (1889), *The Wrecker* (1892) and *The Ebb-Tide* (1894).

Stevenson was as scrupulous a writer as Henry James, one of his friends and correspondents. His novels are precisely and elegantly shaped and are expressed in clear, economical prose. He wrote that the artist's "one main and necessary resource" was his compulsion to "omit what is tedious or irrelevant, and suppress what is tedious and necessary." Action and the revelation of character through action form the main material of his novels. *Treasure Island*, written for boys, is a masterpiece of construction, beginning quietly but ominously, building up suspense with the discovery of Long John Silver's true nature and coming to a climax on the island with the battles between the pirates and Jim Hawkins and his friends. It has incidents and devices that stick in the mind (the black spot, the pirates' chorus) and colourful personages (Long John Silver, Ben Gunn). *Kidnapped* is admirable adventure fiction with an authentic feeling for place and period: Scotland in the years just after the '45 Jacobite Rebellion. Both books gain in immediacy through their first-person narration.

The Master of Ballantrae, set in post-1745 Scotland, is a remarkable tale of evil and persecution, personified in its leading character, the Master. It has a relentless urgency and a number of unforgettable scenes, such as the duel between the Master of Ballantrae and his brother by candlelight out-of-doors on a frosty night. Although Stevenson emphasised action rather than psychology, at least two of his characters have become household words: Long John Silver and Dr Jekyll, alias Mr Hyde.

The adventure novel or "romance" became popular towards the end of the nineteenth century. With Stevenson's successful *Treasure Island* in mind, Rider Haggard (1856–1925) wrote *King Solomon's Mines* (1885), followed by *She* (1887) and many other books of the same kind. G. A. Henty (1832–1902) wrote prolifically, producing some eighty novels for boys. Other adventures and romances were Conan Doyle's Sherlock Holmes stories (beginning in 1887 with *A Study in Scarlet*) and novels of exciting action, Stanley Weyman's historical novels from 1893 onwards, Anthony Hope Hawkins' *The Prisoner of Zenda*, George du Maurier's *Trilby* (1894), Bram Stoker's *Dracula* (1897) and E. W. Hornung's *Raffles* stories from 1899 onwards. The adventure novels of John Buchan (1875–1940) include *Prester John* (1910), *The Thirty-Nine Steps* (1915), *Greenmantle* (1916) and *Mr Standfast* (1919).

Naturalism: Gissing and Moore

Naturalism, which is sometimes used as a synonym for realism, was a literary movement associated mostly with the novels of Emile Zola (1840–1902). Writers who held the doctrine maintained that novels should be as physically detailed as possible, that novelists should use scientific methods of description and analysis and that they should emphasise the importance of environment. The subject-matter of naturalistic novels tended to be about the harsh realities of the lives of the poor and to concentrate on the least ideal aspects of human nature.

George Gissing (1857–1903) was one exponent of naturalism in England, writing about the poverty and miseries of working-class existence in novels such as *Workers in the Dawn* (1880), *The Unclassed* (1884), *Demos* (1886), *Thyrza* (1887), and *The Nether World* (1889). *New Grub Street* (1891) surveys writers' lives, contrasting the success of the unprincipled Jasper Milvain with the wretched life and

death of the uncompromising Edwin Reardon. *The Private Papers of Henry Ryecroft* (1903) is a series of semi-autobiographical reflections. George Moore (1852–1933), strongly influenced by Zola and Maupassant, wrote *Esther Waters* (1894), as well as a variety of other novels. In an objective and yet poignant manner, he relates the hardships suffered by Esther from the time she goes into domestic service as a seventeen-year-old girl. Samuel Butler (1835–1902), who wrote the fantasies, *Erewhon* (1872) and *Erewhon Revisited* (1901), achieved a high posthumous reputation with *The Way of All Flesh* (1903; written 1872–5), a satirical treatment of Victorian beliefs and values. Conventional moral ideas were also questioned by Oscar Wilde (1856–1900) in his "aesthetic" novel, *The Picture of Dorian Gray* (1891).

Naturalism: Arnold Bennett

Arnold Bennett (1867–1931) also modelled his novels on those of the French naturalists. Flaubert, the Goncourt brothers, Zola and Maupassant had established aesthetic ideals for him in their objectivity and precision of language. A writer of dogged productivity, he wrote over thirty novels, beginning with *A Man from the North* (1898). The first of importance was *Anna of the Five Towns* (1902), the title of which makes clear its setting in the Potteries, the midland region of England which is the environment of most of his best fiction. His reputation was established with *The Old Wives' Tale* (1908), a long, detailed study of Sophia and Constance Baines, two sisters, from youth to age. His achievement here is his skilful handling of Time, which E. M. Forster declared was the "real hero" of the book. *Clayhanger* (1910), *Hilda Lessways* (1911) and *These Twain* (1915) are collectively known as *The Clayhanger Family*. Set in the Five Towns, the first two deal respectively with the young lives of Edwin Clayhanger and Hilda Lessways and the third with their married life together. *The Card* (1911) is a lighter story about the agreeable rogue, Denry Machin. *Riceyman Steps* (1923) is a grim novel about a miserly second-hand bookseller in Clerkenwell; it is a tale of meanness, squalor, illness and death and is one of the most powerful of all Bennett's novels.

Bennett is meticulously realistic, supplying explicit details of the environment, thoughts and actions of his characters. He is a regional novelist, who shows us panoramic and close-up pictures of the places where his personages live. *The Old Wives' Tale* opens with a description of the county of Staffordshire, which surrounds his heroines, as he points out. The focus moves to the Five Towns, to St Luke's Square, to the Baines's shop and finally to the showroom. Bennett slowly completes his picture of the two girls, the shop and the town. Similarly, Edwin at the beginning of *Clayhanger* is shown standing on a canal bridge in a precisely depicted location in the Five Towns. Such accumulation of detail, leaving little to the imagination, was adversely criticised by later novelists, notably Virginia Woolf. But it gives a photographic verisimilitude to Bennett's stories. He is not an idealist or moralist; he is content to display to us his personages and their doings. He is not without sympathy and humour, he is inventive, he can give meaning to trivial and mundane happenings and he constructs his novels solidly.

THE TWENTIETH CENTURY

Rudyard Kipling

Rudyard Kipling (1865–1936) was another author sensitive to the aesthetic shaping of his work. He was primarily a poet and writer of short stories, but two novels of his are *The Light that Failed* (1890) and *Kim* (1901). The former, with its tragic account of the blindness that overcomes Dick Heldar, may be melodramatic and sentimental, but it has a compelling emotional drive that makes it hard to put down. *Kim* evokes the India of the Raj, which Kipling knew intimately as a child and young man. Its central character, the boy Kim, travels through India with a Tibetan lama and becomes involved in espionage organised by the British Secret Service. He is therefore torn between the demands of two ways of life: the contemplative and the active. The novel can be appreciated on several levels: as an adventure story, as an unrivalled description of the peoples, customs and scenes of India, as a glorification as well as a criticism of British imperialism, and as a presentation of conflicts of ideas and loyalties.

H. G. Wells

H. G. Wells (1866–1946) was a prolific and versatile writer whose abiding interests were science and socialist politics. He made his name with scientific romances, which include *The Time Machine* (1895), *The Island of Dr Moreau* (1896), *The Invisible Man* (1897), *The War of the Worlds* (1898) and *The First Men on the Moon* (1901). The "1896 Booker Prize" was awarded to *The Island of Dr Moreau* in 1996. Although Jules Verne's books were known in England, these were the first thoroughgoing examples of science fiction in English. Based on the sound scientific knowledge he had acquired as a London University student, his stories were daringly imaginative but convincing and still rank among the best of their kind. Their startling subject-matter includes travelling into the future, the coming of Martians to England and journeying to the moon, all realised in credible detail. Wells also wrote social comedies, typically featuring a "little man" of the lower middle class: *Love and Mr Lewisham* (1900), *Kipps* (1905) and *The History of Mr Polly* (1910). He explored social problems in a more serious manner in a third group of novels, including *Tono-Bungay* (1909), *Ann Veronica* (1909) and *The New Machiavelli* (1911). Apart from *Mr Britling Sees It Through* (1916), his later novels lack the vigour and imagination of his earlier novels.

Unlike James, Stevenson, Bennett and Kipling, Wells was impatient with the novel as an art-form, since for him its entertainment value and message were of prime importance. In his science fiction, he wanted to make his readers aware of the potentialities of technological discovery. His social novels had clear lessons to impart. *The History of Mr Polly* is an enjoyable story of the misfortunes and eventual happiness of its hero, with Dickensian humour in its characterisation (*e.g.* Uncle Pentstemon), Mr Polly's pathetically comic aspirations and actions (*e.g.* his conversation with the schoolgirl sitting on a wall and his attempted suicide) and his misuse of language. At the same time, Wells is making serious points about a system of society and education that can starve Mr Polly's imagination and stunt any possibilities of a fulfilled existence for him. The main purpose of *Ann Veronica* is an argument for women's liberation. *Tono-Bungay* is concerned with the world of commerce and *The New Machiavelli* with the world of politics, with relevance to the corruptions which Wells saw in Edwardian England.

Psychological subtlety and experiments with formal techniques have little part in Wells' novels, which succeed in their intention of giving much pleasure blended with instruction. His prose style is spontaneous and lively, sweeping the reader along. His instinctive skills and many-sidedness make him a novelist of considerable achievement.

Joseph Conrad

In contrast to the novels of Bennett and Wells, those by Joseph Conrad (1857–1924) are innovatory in a number of respects. Although he was Polish by birth, he served in the British Merchant Navy for many years and wrote all his novels in English. The principal ones are *Almayer's Folly* (1895), *An Outcast of the Islands* (1896), *The Nigger of the Narcissus* (1897), *Lord Jim* (1900), *The Heart of Darkness* (1902), *Typhoon* (1902), *Nostromo* (1904), *The Secret Agent* (1907), *Under Western Eyes* (1911), *Chance* (1913), *Victory* (1915) and *The Rover* (1923). Conrad also wrote short stories and some books in collaboration with Ford Madox Ford (1873–1939), who was a considerable novelist in his own right.

Conrad's experience as a seaman is reflected in the settings he uses: Malaysia and the Indian Ocean (as in *Lord Jim*), the Congo (*The Heart of Darkness*) and South America (*Nostromo*). London, however, is the setting of *The Secret Agent*. In such places a typical Conrad hero confronts dangers and is compelled to make immediate choices. Conrad concerns himself not so much with the relationships between people as the relationships between an individual person and circumstances. Questions of moral decision, heroism and cowardice, loyalty and treachery are therefore basic to his novels. In *Lord Jim*, Jim jumps overboard from the *Patna*, which

he mistakenly thinks is about to sink. Tormented by self-accusations of despicable conduct, he seeks to redeem himself. But after achieving a measure of redemption as the respected "Lord Jim", he makes another error of judgment, which brings about his death. Conrad may show us, too, how a sensitive man may be inferior at a moment of crisis to one of little imagination. A solid and stupid man like Captain MacWhirr in *Typhoon* triumphs over the terrible storm and brings his ship to safety.

To demonstrate the complexity of arriving at a true account of happenings and motives, Conrad disrupts chronology and uses various narrators. *Lord Jim* begins with Jim as a water clerk, recounts how the *Patna* hit something below the surface of the sea, and continues with the court of enquiry. At this point, Marlow (a narrator Conrad uses in several books) intervenes. Largely through him, we are given a vivid sense of the way Jim feels defeated and only then do we arrive at the crucial event: the desertion of the *Patna*. Thus chronological order is replaced by a dramatic, significant order. Perspective and shades of meaning are gained by Conrad's using the memories and prejudices of different story-tellers. In *Nostromo*, the events are narrated by the omniscient novelist and also by Captain Mitchell, Decoud (in a letter), Dr Monyghan (in his reflections) and Nostromo. Readers have to work hard at piecing together the mosaic of action and thought and are consequently made aware of the ambiguities and subtleties of human behaviour. Unity is derived from central themes: Jim's agonies of conscience in *Lord Jim*, the storm in *Typhoon* and the silver mine in *Nostromo*.

Conrad's use of English has its awkwardnesses, especially in colloquial speech, but these are outweighed by the scrupulous way in which he expresses shades of meaning and realises people and things in concrete detail. His novels have great depth and integrity, as well as sensibility.

Ford Madox Ford and Dorothy Richardson

The principal novels of Ford Madox Ford (1873–1939), who influenced Conrad and collaborated with him (*see above*), are *The Good Soldier* (1915), *Some Do Not* (1924), *No More Parades* (1925), *A Man Could Stand Up* (1926) and *The Last Post* (1928). The last four are known as the Tietjens tetralogy, after their principal character. In the interests of what he saw as truthful presentation, Ford used experimental techniques in his fiction, including time-shifts, different viewpoints and "*progression d'effet*" (*i.e.*, carrying on the story faster as it progresses). Together with authorial "invisibility" and irony, these methods give his narratives a sense of elusiveness and open up fascinating possibilities of interpretation. His psychological depictions (of Tietjens and Dowell, the protagonist of *The Good Soldier*, for example) are subtle and complex. Ford was concerned to explore such moral issues as honour and fidelity and also the codes and assumptions of society and class.

Dorothy Richardson (1873–1957) was one of the first English novelists fully to use the technique of the "stream of consciousness", which is associated particularly with the work of Virginia Woolf and James Joyce (*see below*). Her sequence of twelve novels, published between 1915 and 1938 and collectively known as *Pilgrimage*, have the "consciousness" of her heroine, Miriam, at their centre.

John Galsworthy, Hugh Walpole and Somerset Maugham

Three novelists who achieved immense popularity and yet who never rose high in critical esteem (at least in England) were John Galsworthy (1867–1933), Sir Hugh Walpole (1884–1941) and W. Somerset Maugham (1874–1965).

Galsworthy, who was also famous as a playwright, is remembered for *The Forsyte Saga* (1922), which consists of *The Man of Property* (1906), *In Chancery* (1920) and *To Let* (1921). The Forsyte story continues in two more trilogies: *A Modern Comedy* (1929) and *End of the Chapter* (1934). The substance of these novels is the relationships and intrigues of a wealthy upper-middle class family from the 1880s to the 1920s. The books have a comforting readability and a documentary value in their charting the outlook, habits and possessions of the family. Galsworthy was awarded the Nobel Prize for Literature in 1932.

Walpole's books have proved to be less durable. *Mr Perrin and Mr Traill* (1911), about the cruel rivalry of two schoolmasters, still has vitality. But once-favoured novels, such as *Jeremy* (1919), *The Cathedral* (1922) and the four known as *The Herries Chronicle* (1930–33) are little read today.

Somerset Maugham began in naturalistic style with *Liza of Lambeth* (1897). Equally successful as a playwright and a short-story writer, Maugham wrote *Of Human Bondage* (1915), *The Moon and Sixpence* (1919), *Cakes and Ale* (1930), *The Razor's Edge* (1944) and many other novels. His range is wide and he is always a supreme entertainer. His sardonic attitude may disturb some, but most readers find that this gives an edge to his clear, fluent narratives. Although he has been called superficial, no one can deny his sheer readability.

E. M. Forster

Besides Conrad, four novelists of the first half of the twentieth century extended the possibilities of the form: E. M. Forster, Virginia Woolf, James Joyce and D. H. Lawrence.

E. M. Forster (1879–1970) wrote *Where Angels Fear to Tread* (1905), *The Longest Journey* (1907), *A Room with a View* (1908), *Howards End* (1910) and *A Passage to India*. *Maurice* was written in 1914, but because of its homosexual theme was not published till 1971. After 1924, Forster wrote no more novels.

In all his writings, fiction and nonfiction, Forster is liberal and humanist in outlook. He always set great store by loving personal relationships and was suspicious of conceptions of duty, patriotism and imperialism. In a notorious statement in his essay, "What I Believe" (1939), he said: "I hate the idea of causes, and if I had to choose between betraying my country and betraying my friend, I hope I should have the guts to betray my country." Later in the same essay, he declared that he distrusted Great Men and believed in an aristocracy of the "sensitive, the considerate and the plucky".

His novels are elegant, drily humorous and witty, but at the same time they contain elements of the poetical and the mystical. The motto, "Only connect", which appears on the title page of *Howards End*, expresses one of his tenets. To bring out its implications, he will place two sets of ideas in opposition and show the tensions and connections between them. In *Where Angels Fear to Tread*, Lilia, an English girl from the conventional middle-classes, outrages her family when she marries Gino, an Italian dentist. After her death, they make attempts to "rescue" her baby. The comedy and the message of the novel, therefore, derive from the interactions between English and Mediterranean ways of life. The opposition in *Howards End* is that between the world of "telegrams and anger" and the world of culture and the finer feelings.

Forster's most ambitious novel, *A Passage to India*, is concerned with the mutual misunderstandings between the Indians and the ruling English in the India of 1910–20. The narrow-minded English community is angered by Dr Aziz' apparent assault on Adela Quested in the Marabar Caves. The principal characters are Fielding, the well-meaning and humane schoolmaster; Dr Aziz, impulsive and warm-hearted; Mrs Moore, the elderly, visionary Englishwoman; and Adela herself, who—like Fielding—has good intentions but is bewildered by her encounter with India. Forster carefully patterns his novel, writes amusing and lively description and dialogue and conveys a sense of the incomprehensibility and fascination of India felt by English people. As always, he seeks to inculcate the truth that love and understanding at the personal level are vital in all circumstances.

In *Aspects of the Novel* (1927), Forster deplored the need to tell a story in the novel. But his novels contain much that is amusing and thought-provoking: surprises in the plot, realistic dialogue, economical but convincing characterisation and unexpected authorial generalisations. Altogether, we get the impression of a sharp but tolerant perception of the virtues and frailties of mankind.

Virginia Woolf

E. M. Forster was associated with the Bloomsbury Group, although he was never a fully committed member of it. The relations and friends who formed the Group between 1905 and the 1930s (Lytton Strachey, Maynard Keynes, Virginia Woolf and her sister Vanessa Bell, Clive Bell, Duncan Grant, Roger Fry and others) saw themselves as rational, enlightened people who rejected the intolerance and narrow-minded morality of the Victorians. They valued love, friendship and the arts.

One of the central figures of the Bloomsbury Group was Virginia Woolf (1882–1941), whose career as a novelist began with two fairly conventional books: *The Voyage Out* (1915) and *Night and Day* (1919). She proceeded to experiment in both form and content and all her subsequent novels are works of originality, breaking with traditional approaches and methods: *Jacob's Room* (1922), *Mrs Dalloway* (1925), *To the Lighthouse* (1927), *Orlando* (1928), *The Waves* (1931), *The Years* (1937) and *Between the Acts* (1941).

Virginia Woolf was opposed to the technique of such Edwardian novelists as Bennett, Wells and Galsworthy. In her opinion, they were materialists, who were "concerned not with the spirit but with the body". Their painstaking renderings of a solid, exterior world meant, she argued, that the inner meaning of life escaped them. What she attempted to do, on the other hand, was to capture the transience and subtlety of experience and thought. In a famous statement, she said that "Life is not a series of gig lamps symmetrically arranged; life is a luminous halo, a semi-transparent envelope surrounding us from the beginning of consciousness to the end." Modern authors should therefore "record the atoms as they fall upon the mind in the order in which they fall" and "trace the pattern, however disconnected and incoherent in appearance, which each sight or incident scores upon the consciousness." To achieve these ends, she uses as a means the "stream of consciousness" technique. She takes us inside her characters' minds, revealing the flow of their thoughts and emotions, past, present and future. The trivial and the grand are fused; the exterior world impinges now and then; repetitions, allusions, memories blend together.

A typical example of this technique is the scene of the dinner-party in *To the Lighthouse*. Outwardly, Mrs Ramsay, the hostess, is serving the food and making unremarkable conversation with her guests. But we are witnesses of the interior lives of these people. The reflections of Mrs Ramsay, Lily Briscoe, Charles Tansley and William Bankes make a delicately woven texture of thoughts and emotions, adding to what we have already learned earlier in the novel.

Realising the difficulty of giving a clear shape to the intangible, Virginia Woolf uses repeated phrases and objects as focal points, such as the royal car in *Mrs Dalloway* and the lighthouse and Lily Briscoe's painting in *To the Lighthouse*. Her prose is supple and quietly rhythmical and contains memorable and beautiful imagery. Her novels have a refined artistry—too rarefied in the opinion of some, who have criticised her for narrowness of social range and for creating people who all share her own delicate sensitivity. But she is one of the most discerning and subtle of psychological novelists.

James Joyce

James Joyce (1882–1941), an exact contemporary of Virginia Woolf, was the most far-reaching innovator in the English novel of this century. His comparatively small output began with a collection of short stories, *Dubliners* (1914), economically realistic evocations of the frustrated lives of ordinary inhabitants of the Irish city. *A Portrait of the Artist as a Young Man* (1916) is an autobiographical novel. This was followed by his masterpiece, *Ulysses* (1922). His last book was *Finnegans Wake* (1939).

Joyce used the stream of consciousness technique, carrying it to greater lengths than Virginia Woolf. It can be seen in its purest form in Molly Bloom's soliloquy at the end of *Ulysses*, where her drifting mental processes as she lies half-asleep are rendered in unpunctuated prose that moves from one apparently disconnected thought to another. His most astonishing innovations were linguistic. *A Portrait of the Artist* begins with childish-sounding language mirroring the boy's immaturity. Throughout the book, his stages of development are recorded in appropriate levels of prose. *Ulysses* is written in widely varied styles of English, most obviously in the scene where Stephen and Bloom await the birth of a baby. The conception and growth of the child are reflected in Joyce's imitations of English prose from Anglo-Saxon times to the end of the nineteenth century. His most extreme linguistic experimentation is in *Finnegans Wake*, a book of such intensive verbal coinage and word-play that it can be said to be written in a new language, for which a key is necessary.

Joyce also employs allusions and symbols, which enrich his meaning once they are interpreted (which again can be a difficult process). *Ulysses* has indirect allegiances to Homer's epic poem, the *Odyssey*, but it is filled with the actuality of one day in Dublin: 16 June 1904. It contains numerous other emblems, references and echoes, making it a fascinatingly complex picture of human experience. His psychological explorations of character are associated with the life and traditions of Ireland, for although Joyce exiled himself from his native country as a young man its politics, religion and customs are inseparable from his work.

Stephen Daedalus, the hero of *A Portrait of the Artist as a Young Man*, is the fictional equivalent of Joyce. His education, temptations and artistic credo make the main subject-matter of the book. Stephen reappears as one of the central characters of *Ulysses*, in which his companion during the day's adventures is a middle-aged Jew, Leopold Bloom. Using their particular situations in early twentieth-century Ireland, Joyce creates a universal impression of the emotions and problems of humanity, by means of interior monologue, sensuous description, individualised dialogue and allusion. In *A Portrait of the Artist*, Stephen said that the highest form of literature is the dramatic. In that form, "the artist, like the God of creation, remains within or behind or beyond or above his handiwork, invisible, refined out of existence, indifferent, paring his fingernails." By fully and uncompromisingly presenting his characters' innermost thoughts and by withholding authorial moral judgement, Joyce aimed to achieve the ideal that Stephen desired.

D. H. Lawrence

D. H. Lawrence (1885–1930) differed in many remarkable aspects from James Joyce and Virginia Woolf in his approach to writing novels. He brought an urgency and spontaneity and, above all, a poetic sense to prose fiction. He was a prolific author, who produced numerous short stories, travel books, poems, plays and essays besides novels. His principal novels are *The White Peacock* (1911), *Sons and Lovers* (1913), *The Rainbow* (1915), *Women in Love* (1920), *The Lost Girl* (1921), *Aaron's Rod* (1922), *Kangaroo* (1923), *The Plumed Serpent* (1926) and *Lady Chatterley's Lover* (1928).

As a novelist, Lawrence considered himself "superior to the saint, the scientist, the philosopher, and the poet", since in his opinion the novel dealt with the complete human being instead of a particular aspect. "The novel," he declared, "is the one bright book of life." His main theme is the tensions, joys and sorrows that exist in personal relationships: those between parents and children, husbands and wives, and other people in love. *Sons and Lovers*, his most famous book, centres upon the semi-autobiographical hero, Paul Morel, whose attachment to his mother inhibits his love for Miriam. The novel is also deeply concerned with the opposition between Paul's sensual coal-mining father and his refined, sensitive mother. *The Rainbow*, to which *Women in Love* is a kind of sequel, shows three generations of the Brangwyn family: the conflict and mutual understanding inherent in passionate marriages and love-affairs and the disputes and reconciliations between parents and children are revealed as repeating themselves through a long period of time. But no summaries can convey the subtleties of Lawrence's handling of the psychological and moral issues involved.

For Lawrence, "blood" and instinct were the dominating forces of life, superior in strength to the dictates of reason, and he saw his task as a novelist to transmit these forces through the medium of words. The result is that his novels lack conventional form. What matters is the internal lives of his characters and not their external actions, except when these actions reveal significant behaviour. He therefore concentrates on episodes of intensity and he will, where necessary, ignore the reader's expectations of an even time-scale and the clear development of plot and character. "You mustn't look into my novel for the old stable *ego* of character," he wrote. "There is another *ego*, according to whose action the individual is unrecognisable, and passes through, as it were,

allotropic states which it needs a deeper sense than any we've been used to exercise, to discover and are states of the same single radically unchanged element." His writing consequently has a great emotional impact and gives the feeling of complete fidelity to life as it actually is, with its contradictions and uncertainties. But Lawrence's uncompromising frankness and refusal to conform to literary and social conventions led to the censorship and banning of some of his books, notably *Lady Chatterley's Lover*, which was too sexually explicit for contemporary English standards—it was not published in Britain in unexpurgated form until 1960.

Lawrence's descriptions of the physical appearance of his characters and their surroundings are direct and sensuous; his prose rhythms and choice of words remind us that he was a poet. Places he lived in inspired many of his settings: the Midlands countryside in *The White Peacock*, Australia in *Kangaroo*, Mexico in *The Plumed Serpent*. His imagery is rich in suggestion and is typically drawn from natural and religious sources. In *The Rainbow*, for example, the rainbow itself, doorways, archways and rural scenery and occupations evoke important aspects of the characters' lives and motives and give unity to the novel.

It has been argued that Lawrence was not always in touch with reality because the intense level at which his personages live lacks credibility. Some critics have deplored his preaching, his lack of humour and his repetitiveness. Some of these criticisms are justified only if the criterion of naturalism is rigorously applied. Most people will agree that his great novels—*Sons and Lovers*, *The Rainbow* and *Women in Love*—are masterpieces of psychological insight and moral profundity.

Other Novelists of the 1920s and 1930s

Although Ronald Firbank (1886–1926) began publishing his work in 1905, his slight, artificial novels seem to represent the frivolous side of the 1920s. Amongst them are *Vainglory* (1915), *Caprice* (1917), *Valmouth* (1919), *The Flower beneath the Foot* (1923), *Prancing Nigger* (1924) and *Concerning the Eccentricities of Cardinal Pirelli* (1926). The wit and fantasy of these books can also be related to the aestheticism of the 1890s.

One of the most influential writers of the two decades was Aldous Huxley (1894–1963). An intellectual and polymath, Huxley wrote satirical, comic novels of ideas, which have affinities with those of Peacock. They include *Crome Yellow* (1921), *Antic Hay* (1923) and *Those Barren Leaves* (1925). *Point Counterpoint* (1928) consists mainly of brilliant conversation pieces, in which the participants (e.g. Rampion, who is based on D. H. Lawrence) exchange ideas on philosophy, politics, religion, the arts and society. Of Huxley's later novels, the most important are *Brave New World* (1932), which is set six hundred years hence, *Eyeless in Gaza* (1936) and *Island* (1962).

Evelyn Waugh (1903–66) made his reputation with comic, witty, mocking novels: *Decline and Fall* (1928), *Vile Bodies* (1930), *Black Mischief* (1932), *A Handful of Dust* (1934), *Scoop* (1938) and *Put Out More Flags* (1942). Waugh's books of this period are characterised by an air of satirical detachment, black comedy and farce, the fertile invention of entertaining personages and episodes and a pointed prose style. They remain freshly amusing, though some readers dislike their apparent heartlessness. *Brideshead Revisited* (1945), with its nostalgic recollections of events centred upon a great country house, is, in contrast, a romantic and even sentimental novel. *The Loved One* (1948), a satire on American funeral customs, marked a return to his earlier manner. Waugh's last considerable work, which some consider to be his masterpiece, was a trilogy: *Men at Arms* (1952), *Officers and Gentlemen* (1955) and *Unconditional Surrender* (1961), later united as *Sword of Honour* (1965). Though this book contains much comedy, it is a sympathetic portrayal of the doubts and anxieties during the Second World War of its central figure, Guy Crouchback, a Roman Catholic and army officer.

The first novels of George Orwell (pseudonym of Eric Blair, 1903–50) reflect the period: *Burmese Days* (1934), *A Clergyman's Daughter* (1935), *Keep the Aspidistra Flying* (1936) and *Coming up for Air* (1939). His most celebrated were his last two: *Animal Farm* (1945), which is a short fable satirising revolution and dictatorship, and *Nineteen Eighty-*

Four (1949), which is a grim picture of a future authoritarian world.

Christopher Isherwood (1904–86) wrote *All the Conspirators* (1928), but made his reputation with the plays he wrote with W. H. Auden in the 1930s and with his two novels about Germany in the last days of the Weimar Republic: *Mr Norris Changes Trains* (1935) and *Goodbye to Berlin* (1939). The narrator of these says "I am a camera" and consequently records his experiences in a spare, objective manner, which nevertheless evokes the emotions of himself and the other characters. Isherwood's other novels, which are varied in content, include *Prater Violet* (1946) and *Down There On A Visit* (1962).

Other Novelists of the Period

Much of the fiction of Firbank, Huxley, Waugh, Orwell and Isherwood therefore reflects the spirit of the age. But other novelists of the time were free from contemporary preoccupations. The two most famous novels of John Cowper Powys (1872–1963) are *Wolf Solent* (1929) and *A Glastonbury Romance* (1932), which are conceived on a grand scale and are full of a metaphysical awareness of the forces of Nature. His brother, T. F. Powys (1875–1953), is best known for *Mr Weston's Good Wine* (1927). The novels of Ivy Compton-Burnett (1892–1969) are set at the end of the nineteenth century in a stylised world of middle-class families in country houses. Their titles, whose similarities denote the unchanging nature of the novels, include *Pastors and Masters* (1925), *Men and Wives* (1931), *A House and its Head* (1935), *A Family and a Fortune* (1939), *Manservant and Maidservant* (1947), *Two Worlds and their Ways* (1949), *A Father and his Fate* (1957), *The Mighty and their Fall* (1961) and *A God and his Gifts* (1963). Through the medium of mannered conversation, Ivy Compton-Burnett presents stories of wrongdoing, sin and crime. Aspects of evil are coolly exposed by means of her highly artificial narration.

J. B. Priestley (1894–1984) wrote *The Good Companions* (1929), which was a huge success, and followed this with numerous realistic, entertaining novels, including *Angel Pavement* (1930).

Graham Greene

Graham Greene (1904–91) was a writer of novels for over sixty years as well as short stories, plays, autobiography, essays and criticism. He began with *The Man Within* (1929) and his subsequent novels are *Stamboul Train* (1932), *It's a Battlefield* (1934), *England Made Me* (1935), *A Gun for Sale* (1936), *Brighton Rock* (1938), *The Confidential Agent* (1939), *The Power and the Glory* (1940), *The Ministry of Fear* (1943), *The Heart of the Matter* (1948), *The Third Man* (1950), *The End of the Affair* (1951), *Loser Takes All* (1955), *The Quiet American* (1955), *Our Man in Havana* (1958), *A Burnt-Out Case* (1961), *The Comedians* (1966), *Travels with my Aunt* (1969), *The Honorary Consul* (1973), *The Human Factor* (1978), *Doctor Fischer of Geneva* (1980), *Monsignor Quixote* (1982), *The Tenth Man* (1985; written 1944) and *The Captain and the Enemy* (1988).

Greene's novels are gripping and exciting, since they contain the basic features of such popular fiction as thrillers, adventure stories and spy stories. Their settings are dangerous or exotic places, such as Mexico (*The Power and the Glory*), West Africa (*The Heart of the Matter*), the Congo (*A Burnt-Out Case*), Haiti (*The Comedians*) and Argentina (*The Honorary Consul*). His vivid descriptions of places and people and his fast-moving pace are cinematic and many of his novels have been turned into successful films. Enmeshed in challenging circumstances, his characters are compelled to make moral choices and, in doing so, to face problems of loyalty and faith. As Greene was a Roman Catholic, these problems are generally related to religious belief. Pinkie, the young Roman Catholic criminal in *Brighton Rock*, is dedicated to evil but is opposed by the warm-hearted Ida, who has firm ideas of Right and Wrong, untroubled by theological considerations. Scobie in *The Heart of the Matter*, a self-tormented Catholic, chooses to commit the sin of suicide as a result of his entanglements in unhappy relationships with women. In his novella, *Doctor Fischer of Geneva*, Greene uses memorable, macabre events and strange—even grotesque—characterisation to stimulate thought about profound issues: greed, power, love, revenge and death.

Greene's settings, characters and themes, especi-

ally from *Brighton Rock* onwards, are fused into complete statements about the springs of human conduct. The environment, which has sometimes been called "Greeneland," can symbolise and emphasise the dangers experienced by the characters. Because of the quantity and quality of his achievement, Graham Greene is widely considered to be the outstanding English novelist of the past fifty years. He was appointed a Companion of Honour in 1966 and awarded the O.M. in 1986.

THE NOVEL SINCE 1940

Novelists of the 1940s

Some writers who began their literary careers in the 1930s became more prominent in the war and post-war years. Joyce Cary (1888–1957) began by writing novels set in Nigeria, where he had worked as a government official: *Aissa Saved* (1932), *An American Visitor* (1933), *The African Witch* (1936) and *Mister Johnson* (1939). He followed these with two books about childhood: *Charley is my Darling* (1940) and *A House of Children* (1941). Then there came a trilogy centred upon three characters, Gulley Jimson, Sara Monday and Wilcher: *Herself Surprised* (1941), *To Be a Pilgrim* (1942) and *The Horse's Mouth* (1944), which is generally accounted his best novel. Another trilogy, centred upon Chester Nimmo, was *Prisoner of Grace* (1952), *Except the Lord* (1953) and *Not Honour More* (1955). A further notable novel is *A Fearful Joy* (1949). Cary's most famous works, *Mister Johnson* and *The Horse's Mouth*, are exuberant, inventive and full of *joie de vivre*, largely owing to their central characters, Mister Johnson, an African clerk, and Gulley Jimson, a painter and rogue.

L. P. Hartley (1895–1972) wrote a trilogy dealing with the fortunes of a brother and sister in the early years of this century: *The Shrimp and the Anemone* (1944), *The Sixth Heaven* (1946) and *Eustace and Hilda* (1947). *The Go-Between* (1953) is a vivid, delicate evocation of a boy's being caught up in adult sexual intrigue and of Edwardian country house life.

The sensitive, psychologically penetrating novels of Elizabeth Bowen (1899–1973) include *The House in Paris* (1935), *The Death of the Heart* (1938), *The Heat of the Day* (1949)—usually said to be her greatest achievement, *A World of Love* (1955) and *Eva Trout* (1969).

Henry Green (pseudonym of Henry Yorke, 1905–73) wrote *Blindness* (1926), *Living* (1929), *Party Going* (1939), *Caught* (1943), *Loving* (1945), *Back* (1946), *Concluding* (1948), *Nothing* (1950) and *Doting* (1952). He explores personal relationships in rhythmical prose, much dialogue, imagery and symbols. His novels are some of the most imaginative works of the period. *Loving* was televised in 1996.

In contrast, the novels of C. P. Snow (1905–80) are heavily realistic, often dealing with people in the midst of public affairs (in, for example, government and university circles). His best-known novels form the *Strangers and Brothers* sequence: *Strangers and Brothers* (1940), *The Light and the Dark* (1947), *Time of Hope* (1949), *The Masters* (1951), *The New Men* (1954), *Homecomings* (1956), *The Conscience of the Rich* (1958), *The Affair* (1960), *Corridors of Power* (1964), *The Sleep of Reason* (1968) and *Last Things* (1970). The novels of Elizabeth Taylor (1912–75) include *At Mrs Lippincote's* (1945), *A View of the Harbour* (1947), *A Wreath of Roses* (1949), and *Mrs Palfrey at the Claremont* (1971). A selection of her short stories, *A Dangerous Calm*, came out in 1995.

Samuel Beckett

As a young man, Samuel Beckett (1906–89) was a friend and associate of James Joyce, whose stream-of-consciousness technique influenced his writing. He first came into prominence in England in 1955 when his English version of his play, *Waiting for Godot*, originally written in French, was performed in London. His first novel, *Dream of Fair to Middling Women* (1932), was published posthumously in 1992. *More Pricks than Kicks* (1934) was a collection of linked short stories. His novel, *Murphy* (1938), set in London, is written in a fairly traditional manner. *Watt*, completed *c.* 1944, was published in 1953. Three short novels, first written in French and in the form of monologues, comprise a trilogy: *Malone Dies* (1951; English version, 1956),

Molloy (1951; English version, 1955) and *The Unnamable* (1953; English version, 1958). Like much of Beckett's work, which includes plays, short prose pieces and poems, these three novels are characterised by moods of negation, despair and hopelessness but also by elements of grim humour. Beckett was awarded the Nobel Prize for Literature in 1969.

The 1950s: Anthony Powell, Lawrence Durrell, Sir Angus Wilson and Barbara Pym

Anthony Powell (b. 1905) wrote some amusing novels in the 1930s, rather like those of Evelyn Waugh: *Afternoon Men* (1931), *Venusberg* (1932), *From a View to a Death* (1933), *Agents and Patients* (1936) and *What's Become of Waring?* (1939). His major work, a sequence called *A Dance to the Music of Time*, began to appear in the 1950s: *A Question of Upbringing* (1951), *A Buyer's Market* (1952), *The Acceptance World* (1955), *At Lady Molly's* (1957), *Casanova's Chinese Restaurant* (1960), *The Kindly Ones* (1962), *The Valley of Bones* (1964), *The Soldier's Art* (1966), *The Military Philosophers* (1968), *Books Do Furnish A Room* (1971), *Temporary Kings* (1973) and *Hearing Secret Harmonies* (1975). Its subject is the relationships of a large circle of friends and acquaintances spanning a period of sixty years and including about three hundred characters. It is written with gentle irony and sharp observation of psychology, manners and social class. Powell has also written *O, How the Wheel Becomes It!* (1983) and *The Fisher King* (1986).

Lawrence Durrell (1912–90) published his best-known novels in this decade. The *Alexandria Quartet* consists of *Justine* (1957), *Balthazar* (1958), *Mountolive* (1958) and *Clea* (1960). These complex, erotic and exotic novels are notably experimental in their treatment of time. Durrell's other novels include *Tunc* (1968), *Nunquam* (1970), *Monsieur* (1974), *Livia* (1978), *Constance* (1982), *Sebastian* (1983) and *Quinx* (1985). The last five were later published as *The Avignon Quintet* (1992).

Sir Angus Wilson (1913–91) achieved success with two collections of short stories, *The Wrong Set* (1949) and *Such Darling Dodos* (1952). His novels are *Hemlock and After* (1952), *Anglo-Saxon Attitudes* (1956), *The Middle Age of Mrs Eliot* (1958), *The Old Men at the Zoo* (1961), *Late Call* (1964), *No Laughing Matter* (1967), *As If By Magic* (1973) and *Setting the World on Fire* (1980). An admirer of Dickens, Dostoevsky, Proust and Virginia Woolf, Angus Wilson writes in a realistic, detailed manner with convincing renderings of conversation, although this air of realism does not preclude him from using fantasy and symbolism, especially in his later work. The people and milieux he deals with are predominantly middle-class. His subject-matter is personal relationships, often amongst middle-aged men and women. Class is an important element in his varied work.

Barbara Pym (1913–80) wrote quiet fiction typically dealing with the lives of single, middle-class women in a sympathetic, observant manner, tinged with comedy. Her novels include *Some Tame Gazelle* (1950), *Excellent Women* (1952), *Jane and Prudence* (1953), *Less than Angels* (1955), *A Glass of Blessings* (1958), *No Fond Return of Love* (1961), *Quartet in Autumn* (1977), *The Sweet Dove Died* (1978), *A Few Green Leaves* (1980), *An Unsuitable Attachment* (1982; written 1961–63); *Crampton Hodnet* (1985; written 1939–40); *An Academic Question* (1986; written 1970–71) and *Civil to Strangers and Other Writings* (1987; written 1936, 1940–41).

Sir Kingsley Amis and John Wain

Other novelists of the 1950s took a disillusioned, ironical look at the postwar world, just as many of the new poets and playwrights of the period did. Distrusting anything grandiose and experimental, they wrote in wryly amusing and observant ways about people of no particular privileges, wealth or pretensions. William Cooper's *Scenes of Provincial Life* (1950), with its significant title, was a forerunner of the disrespectful, non-metropolitan stance which they adopted.

The most famous of these writers is Sir Kingsley Amis (1922–95), whose novels are *Lucky Jim* (1954), *That Uncertain Feeling* (1955), *I Like It Here* (1958), *Take a Girl Like You* (1960), *One Fat Englishman* (1963), *The Anti-Death League* (1966), *I Want It Now* (1968), *The Green Man* (1969), *Girl, 20* (1971), *The Riverside Villas Murder* (1973), *Ending Up* (1974), *The Alteration* (1976), *Jake's Thing*

(1978), *Russian Hide-and-Seek* (1980), *Stanley and the Women* (1984), *The Old Devils* (1986), *Difficulties with Girls* (1988), *The Folks That Live on the Hill* (1990), *We Are All Guilty* (1991), *The Russian Girl* (1992), *You Can't Do Both* (1994) and *The Biographer's Moustache* (1995). As a moral novelist, Amis writes with economy, precision, wit and cynical commonsense, constantly puncturing affectations and falsity. *Lucky Jim*, with its account of the fortunes and misfortunes of a provincial university teacher, has become one of the classic comic novels.

Another versatile novelist is John Wain (1925–94), whose *Hurry on Down* (1953) achieved the same kind of popularity as *Lucky Jim*. His other novels include *Living in the Present* (1955), *The Contenders* (1958), *A Travelling Woman* (1959), *Strike the Father Dead* (1962), *The Young Visitors* (1965), *A Winter in the Hills* (1974), *Young Shoulders* (1982) and the trilogy: *Where the Rivers Meet* (1988), *Comedies* (1990) and *Hungry Generations* (1994).

North of England Novelists

Novelists writing of life amongst the working classes, especially in the north of England, also came to the fore in the 1950s. John Braine (1922–86) wrote *Room at the Top* (1957) about a go-getting young man, Joe Lampton. His subsequent novels, which vary in theme, include *The Vodi* (1959), *Life at the Top* (1962), *The Crying Game* (1964), *Stay With Me Till Morning* (1970), *The Queen of a Distant Country* (1972), *Waiting for Sheila* (1976), *One and Last Love* (1981) *The Two of Us* (1984) and *These Golden Days* (1985). Alan Sillitoe (b. 1928) made his reputation with *Saturday Night and Sunday Morning* (1958) and went on to write novels of different kinds, including *The General* (1960), *Key to the Door* (1961), *The Death of William Posters* (1965), *A Start in Life* (1970), *Travels in Nihilon* (1971), *Raw Material* (1972), *A Flame of Life* (1974), *The Widower's Son* (1976), *The Storyteller* (1979), *The Second Chance* (1981), *Her Victory* (1982), *Down from the Hill* (1984), *Life Goes On* (1985), *Out of the Whirlpool* (1988), *The Open Door* (1989), *Last Loves* (1990), *Leonard's War* (1991), *Snowstop* (1993) and *The Broken Chariot* (1998). Stan Barstow (b. 1928) wrote *A Kind of Loving* (1960); the best-known of his other novels is *A Raging Calm* (1968); his latest are *Give Us This Day* (1989) and *Next of Kin* (1991). The first novel by David Storey (b. 1933) was *This Sporting Life* (1962), about Rugby League football. His other books include *Radcliffe* (1965), *Pasmore* (1972), *Saville* (1976), *A Prodigal Child* (1982), *Present Times* (1984) and *A Serious Man* (1998).

Room at the Top, *Saturday Night and Sunday Morning*, *A Kind of Loving* and *This Sporting Life*, are the most famous novels of northern working-class life of the 1950s.

Fantasy and Experiment

Amis, Wain, Braine, Sillitoe, Barstow and Storey are mainly realistic novelists writing without linguistic experimentation or poetic devices. Their subject-matter, point of view and style are down-to-earth. Others of their contemporaries and near-contemporaries used new fictional forms or explored more imaginative areas. J. R. R. Tolkien (1892–1973) wrote *The Lord of the Rings* (1954–5), a trilogy about an imaginary world that for many has the power and attraction of genuine mythology. In 1997, it was voted the Book of the Century in a survey carried out by Waterstone's and Channel 4. Mervyn Peake (1911–68) created a fantastic world in *The Gormenghast Trilogy*: *Titus Groan* (1946), *Gormenghast* (1950) and *Titus Alone* (1959).

Sir William Golding (1911–93) achieved great success with *Lord of the Flies* (1954), his story of shipwrecked boys who revert to a primitive, savage state. His other novels are *The Inheritors* (1955), *Pincher Martin* (1956), *Free Fall* (1959), *The Spire* (1964), *The Pyramid* (1967), *Darkness Visible* (1979) and *The Paper Men* (1984). *Rites of Passage* (1980), *Close Quarters* (1987) and *Fire Down Below* (1989) were later published in one volume as *To the Ends of the Earth: a Sea Trilogy* (1991). *The Double Tongue* was posthumously published in 1995. In complex, imaginative ways, Golding explores profound questions of morality, especially the nature of sin and evil. His novels are often difficult but original in technique and content. He was awarded the Nobel Prize in 1983.

Muriel Spark (b. 1918) has written *The Comforters* (1957), *Robinson* (1958), *Memento Mori* (1959), *The Bachelors* (1960), *The Ballad of Peckham Rye* (1960), *The Prime of Miss Jean Brodie* (1961), *The Girls of Slender Means* (1963), *The Mandelbaum Gate* (1965), *The Public Image* (1968), *The Driver's Seat* (1970), *Not to Disturb* (1971), *The Hothouse by the East River* (1973), *The Abbess of Crewe* (1974), *The Takeover* (1976), *Territorial Rights* (1979), *Loitering with Intent* (1981), *The Only Problem* (1984), *A Far Cry from Kensington* (1988), *Symposium* (1990) and *Reality and Dreams* (1996). Her novels are wittily written and sometimes fantastic. She presents the reader with provocative studies of moral and metaphysical issues. Her characterisation is vivid (*e.g.* Miss Brodie). There is occasionally an element of the fairy tale or myth (*e.g.* The Ballad of Peckham Rye). She was awarded the David Cohen British Literature Prize in 1997.

Doris Lessing (b. 1919), a novelist deeply concerned with psychological, political and social tensions (especially in Africa), has also experimented with techniques of fiction. Her novels include *The Grass is Singing* (1950), the *Children of Violence* series (1952–69), *The Golden Notebook* (1962), *The Good Terrorist* (1985), *The Fifth Child* (1988), *Love, Again* (1996) and *Mara and Dann* (1999).

Dame Iris Murdoch

One of the most prolific and inventive of postwar English novelists was Iris Murdoch (1919–99). Her novels are *Under the Net* (1954), *The Flight from the Enchanter* (1956), *The Sandcastle* (1957), *The Bell* (1958), *A Severed Head* (1961), *An Unofficial Rose* (1962), *The Unicorn* (1963), *The Italian Girl* (1964), *The Red and the Green* (1965), *The Time of the Angels* (1966), *The Nice and the Good* (1968), *Bruno's Dream* (1969), *A Fairly Honourable Defeat* (1970), *An Accidental Man* (1971), *The Black Prince* (1973), *The Sacred and Profane Love Machine* (1974), *A Word Child* (1975), *Henry and Cato* (1976), *The Sea, The Sea* (1978), *Nuns and Soldiers* (1980), *The Philosopher's Pupil* (1983), *The Good Apprentice* (1985) *The Book and the Brotherhood* (1987), *The Message to the Planet* (1989), *The Green Knight* (1993) and *Jackson's Dilemma* (1995). A professional philosopher as well as a novelist, Iris Murdoch raises philosophical issues in her fiction by implication, although she maintains that she writes primarily to entertain her readers. Her books contain numerous characters and incidents and often have complicated plots. Their surface attractions are considerable: narrative pace, lively descriptions of people and places, striking episodes and realistic, entertaining dialogue. She uses symbols (the bell and the sea in the appropriately titled novels, for example) and mysterious happenings and coincidences. She stimulates thought about such problems as intentions, appearance and reality, truth and falsity and the part played in life by contingency and chance.

The 1960s and 1970s

Anthony Burgess (1917–93) became well known in this period with *A Clockwork Orange* (1962). He was a productive, versatile and experimental novelist, whose many other works included *Inside Mr Enderby* (1963), *The Napoleon Symphony* (1974), *Earthly Powers* (1980), *The End of the World News* (1982), *Enderby's Dark Lady* (1984), *The Kingdom of the Wicked* (1985), *The Pianoplayers* (1986), *Any Old Iron* (1989), *A Dead Man in Deptford* (1993) and a novel in verse, *Byrne* (posthumous, 1995).

John Fowles (b. 1926) is an ingenious and innovatory novelist, whose books include *The Collector* (1963), *The Magus* (1966, revised 1977), *The French Lieutenant's Woman* (1969), *Daniel Martin* (1977), *Mantissa* (1982) and *A Maggot* (1985).

A number of African and West Indian novelists writing in English established themselves at this time. Chinua Achebe (b. 1930), a Nigerian, wrote *Things Fall Apart* (1958), followed by various novels and collections of short stories. V. S. Naipaul (b.1932), a Trinidadian, became acknowledged as one of the leading novelists of this period. His novels include *The Mystic Masseur* (1957), *A House for Mr Biswas* (1961), *Mr Stone and the Knights Companion* (1963), *The Mimic Men* (1967), *In a Free State* (1971), *Guerrillas* (1975), *A Bend in the River* (1979) and *The Enigma of Arrival* (1987). Knighted in 1990.

Some Women Novelists

Edna O'Brien (b. 1932) began her career with three novels that humorously and poignantly portrayed the lives and loves of young Irish women: *The Country Girls* (1960), *The Lonely Girl* (1962) and *Girls in their Married Bliss* (1964). Her other books include *August is a Wicked Month* (1965), *Johnny I Hardly Knew You* (1977), *The High Road* (1988), *Time and Tide* (1992), *House of Splendid Isolation* (1994) and *Down by the River* (1996). After the publication of *Wide Sargasso Sea* (1966), interest revived in the novels of Jean Rhys (1894–1979), including *Good Morning, Midnight* (1939). *Wide Sargasso Sea* is a sympathetic, brilliantly imaginative account of the early life in the West Indies of Mr Rochester's first wife, Charlotte Brontë's fictional character in *Jane Eyre*. The prevalent tone of Jean Rhys's novels is one of sadness and anguish, as experienced and expressed by a lonely suffering woman.

Margaret Drabble (b. 1939) has written novels that subtly explore human relationships, often with women at their centre. These are *A Summer Bird-Cage* (1963), *The Garrick Year* (1965), *The Millstone* (1965), *Jerusalem the Golden* (1967), *The Waterfall* (1969), *The Needle's Eye* (1972), *The Realms of Gold* (1975), *The Ice Age* (1977), *The Middle Ground* (1980), *The Radiant Way* (1987), *A Natural Curiosity* (1989), *The Gates of Ivory* (1991) and *The Witch of Exmoor* (1996).

Beryl Bainbridge (b. 1934) is a comically observant, ironical novelist who made her name with *The Bottle Factory Outing* (1974). Her other novels include *Harriet Said* (1972), *Sweet William* (1975), *A Quiet Life* (1976), *Injury Time* (1977), *Young Adolf* (1978), *Another Part of the Wood* (1979), *Winter Garden* (1980), *Watson's Apology* (1984), *Filthy Lucre* (1986), *An Awfully Big Adventure* (1989), *The Birthday Boys* (1991), *Every Man for Himself* (1996) and the widely acclaimed *Master Georgie* (1998).

The Campus Novel

Malcolm Bradbury (b. 1932) and David Lodge (b. 1935), both teachers and critics of literature, became well-known in the 1970s as novelists. They are associated particularly with "campus novels" dealing with the academic life. Bradbury's novels include *Eating People is Wrong* (1959), *Stepping Westward* (1965), *The History Man* (1975), *Rates of Exchange* (1983), *Cuts* (1987) and *Doctor Criminale* (1992). Lodge's include *The British Museum is Falling Down* (1965), *Changing Places* (1975), *How Far Can You Go?* (1980), *Small World* (1984), *Nice Work* (1988), *Paradise News* (1991) and *Therapy* (1995).

The 1980s and 1990s

Julian Barnes first came to notice with *Metroland* (1980). His subsequent novels include *Flaubert's Parrot* (1984), which is like a collection of reflective essays on the 19th century French novelist; *Staring at the Sun* (1986), *A History of the World in 10½ Chapters* (1989), *Talking It Over* (1991), *The Porcupine* (1992), *Cross Channel* (short stories, 1996) and *England, England* (1998). D. M. Thomas became famous with the publication of *The White Hotel* (1981), which combines the themes of psychoanalysis and the Holocaust in a dazzling display of styles and with some direct and vivid description. Other novels of his, also original in form, are *Ararat* (1983), *Swallow* (1984), *Sphinx* (1986), *Summit* (1987), *Lying Together* (1990), *Flying in to Love* (1992) *Pictures at an Exhibition* (1993) and *Eating Pavlova* (1994). Martin Amis, who achieved instant success with *The Rachel Papers* (1973), went on to write *Dead Babies* (1975), *Success* (1978), *Other People* (1981), *Money* (1984), *Einstein's Monsters* (1987), *London Fields* (1989), *Time's Arrow* (1991), *The Information* (1995), *Night Train* (1997) and *Heavy Water and Other Stories* (1998). The striking feature of his work is linguistic and structural virtuosity (*e.g.*, the reversal of time in *Time's Arrow*), revealing human behaviour and social attitudes in the contemporary world in startling prose.

Two writers of novels and short stories with the power to disturb readers with their perception of the darker and more macabre aspects of life are Angela Carter (1940–92) and Ian McEwen. One of Angela Carter's more remarkable books is *Nights at the Circus* (1984); others are *The Passion of New Eve*

(1977), *The Bloody Chamber* (1979), *Black Venus* (1985), *Wise Children* (1991) and *American Ghosts and Old World Wonders* (1993). Her collected short stories, *Burning Your Boats*, appeared in 1995. Ian McEwen's books include *The Cement Garden* (1978), *The Comfort of Strangers* (1981; filmed in 1990, with a screenplay by Harold Pinter), *The Child in Time* (1987), *The Innocent* (1990), *Black Dogs* (1992), *The Daydreamer* (children's stories; 1994), *Enduring Love* (1997) and *Amsterdam* (1998), which won the Booker Prize for Fiction. A. N. Wilson is a prolific writer of fiction, biography, criticism and miscellaneous journalism. His novels include *The Sweets of Pimlico* (1977), *Unguarded Hours* (1978), *Lead Kindly Light* (1979), *The Healing Art* (1980), *Who was Oswald Fish?* (1981), *Wise Virgin* (1982), *Scandal* (1983), *Gentlemen in England* (1985) and *The Vicar of Sorrows* (1993). *Incline Our Hearts* (1988), *A Bottle in the Smoke* (1990), *Daughters of Albion* (1991), *Hearing Voices* (1995) and *A Watch in the Night* (1996) are in The Lampitt Papers sequence. In contrast to many of the novelists surveyed so far, Wilson is traditional in approach, writing comic, entertaining novels, reminiscent of those by Evelyn Waugh.

William Boyd, Peter Ackroyd and others

Another novelist whose work has something of a conventional form is William Boyd: *A Good Man in Africa* (1981), his highly successful first novel, has been followed by *An Ice-Cream War* (1982), *Stars and Bars* (1984), *The New Confessions* (1987), *Brazzaville Beach* (1990), *The Blue Afternoon* (1993), *The Destiny of Nathalie X* (short stories, 1995) and *Armadillo* (1998). The innovative novels of Peter Ackroyd, characterised by literary pastiche and evocation of the past, include *The Great Fire of London* (1982), *The Last Testament of Oscar Wilde* (1983), *Hawksmoor* (1985), *First Light* (1989), *English Music* (1992) *The House of Doctor Dee* (1993), *Dan Leno and the Limehouse Golem* (1994), *Milton in America* (1996) and *The Plato Papers* (1999). Basing her story on her own experiences as a young married woman in Venezuela, Lisa St. Aubin di Teran wrote *Keepers of the House* (1982). Her subsequent novels include *The Tiger* (1984), *The Bay of Silence* (1986), *Black Idol* (1987), *Joanna* (1990), *Nocturne* (1992) and *The Palace* (1997). Fay Weldon, a versatile and combative author, writes entertainingly, putting the woman's point of view, at a time when feminist literary and cultural criticism has become influential. Thanks partly to a memorable television adaptation (and a 1989 film), *The Life and Loves of a She-Devil* (1984), a fantastic and disturbing serio-comedy, has enjoyed wide popularity. Her *Big Women* and *A Hard Time to be a Father* (short stories) appeared in 1998. Another feminist writer is Jeanette Winterson, whose first novel, *Oranges Are Not the Only Fruit* (1985), is a partly autobiographical account of her childhood in a strict, evangelical household. Her other novels are *Boating for Beginners* (1986), *The Passion* (1987), *Sexing the Cherry* (1989), *Written on the Body* (1992), *Art and Lies* (1994), *Gut Symmetries* (1997) and *The World and Other Places* (short stories, 1998). In quiet vein, Anita Brookner's *Hotel du Lac* (1984), which won the Booker Prize, sensitively conveys the feelings of a single woman involved in a disappointing love affair. Her other novels include *Visitors* (1997) and *Falling Slowly* (1998).

Lighter Fiction

We turn now to some authors who cannot easily be classified as either "popular" or "serious", to use these imprecise terms. Richard Adams' *Watership Down* (1972) made him a bestselling author on a huge scale; he subsequently wrote *Shardik* (1975), *The Plague Dogs* (1977), *The Girl on a Swing* (1980), *Maia* (1984) and *Traveller* (1989). One of the most subtle thriller writers, John Le Carré, who made his name with *The Spy Who Came in from the Cold* (1963), continues to produce his scrupulously crafted books. The most recent are *The Honourable Schoolboy* (1982), *The Little Drummer Girl* (1983), *A Perfect Spy* (1986), *The Russia House* (1989) *The Secret Pilgrim* (1991), *The Night Manager* (1993), *Our Game* (1995), *The Tailor of Panama* (1996) and *Single & Single* (1999).

Connoisseurs of the detective story admire the work of Colin Dexter (creator of Inspector Morse), Peter Dickinson, Dick Francis, P. D. James (who

was given a Life Peerage in the 1991 New Year's Honours List), H. R. F. Keating and Ruth Rendell (made a Life Peer, 1997).

Non-English Novelists

Many interesting novels come from writers writing in English but not of English descent. The most controversial example is Salman Rushdie's *The Satanic Verses* (1988), which provoked worldwide anger among Moslems, who considered it blasphemous. It was followed by *The Moor's Last Sigh* (1995). His most recent novel is *The Ground Beneath Her Feet* (1999). Rushdie made his reputation with *Midnight's Children*, which won the Booker Prize in 1981 and the "Booker of Bookers" in 1993. With Christoph Ransmayer (*see above*) and Thorkild Bjoernvig, Rushdie received the European Union Aristeion Literature Prize in 1996. Kazuo Ishiguro's novels include *An Artist of the Floating World* (which won the Whitbread Book of the Year award in 1986), *The Remains of the Day* (Booker Prize, 1989), and *The Unconsoled* (1995). Timothy Mo's *Sour Sweet* was awarded the Hawthornden Prize in 1982; *An Insular Possession* (1986) and *Brownout on Breadfruit Boulevard* (self-published, 1995) are his subsequent novels. Hanif Kureishi's first novel, *The Buddha of Suburbia* (1990; televised 1993) has been followed by *Black Album* (1995), *Love in a Blue Time* (1997) and *Intimacy* (1998). Ben Okri's *Astonishing the Gods* (1995), Vikram Seth's *A Suitable Boy* (1993), and *An Equal Music* (1999), Anita Desai's *Journey to Ithaca* (1995)and Arundhati Roy's *The God of Small Things* (Booker Prize, 1997) are other notable examples.

Other Novels

Notable novels of 1998, not mentioned above, included Paul Bailey's *Kitty and Virgil*, David Caute's *Fatima's Scarf*, Alan Hollinghurst's *The Spell*, Nick Hornby's *About a Boy*, Howard Jacobson's *No More Mr Nice Guy*, Will Self's *Tough Tough Toys for Tough Tough Boys* (short stories), Irvine Welsh's *Filth*, and Arnold Wesker's *The King's Daughters*. A novel by the playwright Joe Orton (1933–67), *Between Us Girls*, was published posthumously. Geoff Rymen's *253: The Journey of 253 Lifetimes* was claimed to be "the world's first fully interactive Internet novel". The novels on the short list for the Booker Prize in 1998 were Beryl Bainbridge's *Master Georgie*, Julian Barnes's *England, England*, Ian McEwan's *Amsterdam* (all three of which are included in this survey), Magnus Mills's *The Restraint of Beasts*, Martin Booth's *The Industry of Souls* and Patrick McCabe's *Breakfast on Pluto*.

PERSPECTIVES

Fiction today is probably more prolific and varied than it has ever been. In addition to the writers just considered, many more are worthy of inclusion—for example, Louis de Bernières, Penelope Fitzgerald, Margaret Forster, Penelope Lively, Brian Moore, P. H. Newby, V. S. Pritchett, Simon Raven, William Trevor, Joanna Trollope and Mary Wesley. But no particular English novelists seem to predominate in the current literary scene, though when we are so close to so many different books it is difficult to see things in proportion.

Over 8,000 new works of fiction are published annually in the United Kingdom. Among these are many bestsellers, which receive little or no critical attention. Literary historians and critics discuss "serious" novels; it is these works of fiction that receive literary awards and prizes and that eventually appear on school and college syllabuses. Meanwhile, the modern British and American authors who are read most widely include Jeffrey Archer, Maeve Binchy, Barbara Taylor Bradford, Agatha Christie, Jackie Collins, Catherine Cookson, Jilly Cooper, Frederick Forsyth, Dick Francis, John Grisham, Arthur Hailey, Jack Higgins, Stephen King, Robert Ludlum, Michael Moorcock, Rosamund Pilcher, Terry Pratchett, Sidney Sheldon, Wilbur Smith, and Sue Townsend. These popular novels, which make immense fortunes for their authors, are of various types: thrillers and detective stories, tales of adventure, espionage, sex and horror, historical romances, comedies, and science fiction. They are easy to read and they emphasise intrigue, suspense, action and immediacy of emotion rather than the complexities of psychology and morality that are traditionally the marks of the "serious" novel.

International Contexts

This survey has been confined to the British novel, which should be seen in the perspective of the great European and American novels of the past two or three centuries. Its qualities and its particular strengths and weaknesses can be truly judged only by considering it in relation to the work of such acknowledged masters as Cervantes; Stendhal, Balzac, Dumas, Flaubert, Zola and Proust; Tolstoy, Dostoevsky and Turgenev; Goethe and Thomas Mann; Hawthorne, Melville and Mark Twain; Manzoni and Svevo. Comparisons are especially important when we look at the work of modern novelists, since much of today's significant fiction comes from the United States (*e.g.*, John Barth, Saul Bellow, Joseph Heller, Norman Mailer, Thomas Pynchon, Philip Roth, John Updike and Gore Vidal have all published novels recently). It is necessary, therefore, to realise that this survey of the English novel deals with just one area of an extensive field.

Readers will find more details of some of the novelists mentioned here in **Section B**.

SOME LITERARY PRIZES

BOOKER PRIZE FOR FICTION

Awarded to the best full-length novel of the year written by a citizen of the UK, the Republic of Ireland, or the Commonwealth, and published in the UK between 1 October and 30 September. Prize: £20,000.

1990	A.S. Byatt, *Possession*
1991	Ben Okri, *The Famished Road*
1992	Michael Ondaatje, *The English Patient*
	Barry Unsworth, *Sacred Hunger*
1993	Roddy Doyle, *Paddy Clarke Ha Ha Ha*
1994	James Kelman, *How Late It Was, How Late*
1995	Pat Barker, *The Ghost Road*
1996	Graham Swift, *Last Orders*
1997	Arundhati Roy, *The God of Small Things*
1998	Ian McEwan, *Amsterdam*

WHITBREAD BOOK OF THE YEAR

The winner is chosen from the winners of four categories of books for adults: novels, first novel, biography and poetry. Separate prizes are given for children's books. Prize: £21,000.

1990	Nicholas Mosley, *Hopeful Monsters* (novel)
1991	John Richardson, *A Life of Picasso* (biography)
1992	Jeff Torrington, *Swing Hammer Swing!* (first novel)
1993	Joan Brady, *Theory of War* (novel)
1994	William Trevor, *Felicia's Journey* (novel)
1995	Kate Atkinson, *Behind the Scenes at the Museum* (first novel)
1996	Seamus Heaney, *Spirit Level* (poetry)
1997	Ted Hughes, *Tales from Ovid* (poetry)
1998	Ted Hughes, *Birthday Letters* (poetry)

II. GLOSSARY OF LITERARY TERMS

acatalectic. Having the complete number of syllables in a line of verse. See **catalectic** and **hyper-catalectic**.

accentual verse. Verse (like most English verse) which is measured by the number and pattern of stresses in a line and not by the number or quantitative value of syllables. See **metre** and **syllabic verse**.

act. Principal division of a dramatic work, some-times subdivided into scenes.

aestheticism. A movement that flourished in the 1880s and 1890s and that considered beauty, not morality, as the most important principle in literary and artistic work. Its key phrase was "Art for art's sake." Two of its chief exponents in England were Walter Pater and Oscar Wilde.

affective fallacy. A phrase coined by M. C. Beardsley and W. K. Wimsatt (1946), who contended that it was false to criticise a poem on the basis of its psychological effects on the reader because as a result "the poem itself, as an object of specifically critical judgement, tends to disap-pear." See **Intentional fallacy** and **New Critics**.

alexandrine. A line of verse containing six iambic feet. See **metre**.

alienation. The principle, propounded by Bertolt Brecht (1898–1956), that actors and audience should remain detached from a dramatic per-formance and not become identified with the rôles and action.

allegory. A narrative or description in prose or verse with a hidden meaning or moral message, e.g., Spenser's *Faerie Queene* and Bunyan's *Pilgrim's Progress*.

alliteration. The use of the same consonants in close proximity, often in verse, for the sake of euphony, memorability or emotional effect, e.g.,

"the *l*ow *l*ast edge of the *l*ong *l*one *l*and"
(Swinburne, "A Forsaken Garden").

See **assonance**.

ambiguity. Unclear or contradictory meaning. Positively, complexity of meaning and tone, as analysed in William Empson's *Seven Types of Ambiguity* (1930).

amphibrach. See **metre**.

anabasis. The progress of an action to a climax, especially in a drama.

anacoluthon. An inconsistency of construction in a sentence, so that the latter part does not gram-matically fit with the earlier part, e.g., "One of the prettiest touches was *when*, at the relation of the queen's death . . . *how* attentiveness wounded his daughter" (Shakespeare, *The Winter's Tale*, V, ii).

anacreontic. Applied to light-hearted poetry praising such pleasures as wine, women and song, e.g., Abraham Cowley's *Anacreontics*. (From Anacreon, Greek poet of the sixth century B.C.)

anacrusis. An additional syllable or half-foot at the beginning of a line of verse, e.g.,

"Cŏld/ănd cleár-/cŭt fáce/whў cŏme/yŏu šo crŭ-/ĕllў méek?"
(Tennyson, "Maud").

anagnorisis. The discovery or recognition, originally by the protagonist of a Greek tragedy, of a truth that leads to the resolution of the drama, e.g., Othello's discovery of Desdemona's innocence. (Term from Aristotle's *Poetics*.)

anapaest. See **metre**.

anaphora. The repetition of a word or phrase at the beginning of consecutive phrases or sentences, e.g.,

"*For gold* his sword the hireling ruffian draws,
For gold the hireling judge distorts the laws"
(Johnson, *The Vanity of Human Wishes*).

anti-hero. A principal character who has no traditional heroic qualities but who is diffident, cowardly, foolish and not particularly estimable, e.g., the eponymous hero of Kingsley Amis's *Lucky Jim*.

anti-novel. Loosely used for some twentieth century novels (by Beckett and Robbe-Grillet, for example) with minimal regard for such conventional features as plot and development of character. See **nouveau roman**.

antistrophe. In the Greek *chorus* (*q.v.*) and the *Pindaric Ode* (*q.v.*) the response to the *strophe* (*q.v.*), written in the same metrical form.

antithesis. The balanced juxtaposition of words or phrases for the sake of emphasis or contrast, widely used in eighteenth-century prose and verse, e.g.,

"But sometimes Virtue starves, while Vice is fed"
(Pope, *Essay on Man*).

apocope. The omission of the final letter, syllable or sound of a word, e.g., the poetic use of "th' " for "the."

aposiopesis. Breaking off a sentence, usually for dramatic effect, e.g.,

"I will have such revenges on you both
That all the world shall—I will do such things—
What they are yet I know not"
(Shakespeare, *King Lear*, II, iv).

apostrophe. Address to a person or a personified quality, place or thing, e.g., "Ye distant spires, ye antique towers" (Gray, "Ode on a Distant Prospect of Eton College"); "Stern Daughter of the Voice of God!" (Wordsworth, "Ode to Duty").

apron stage. A stage, like that in the Elizabethan theatre, which projects beyond the proscenium arch into the audience.

art for art's sake. See **aestheticism**.

assonance. The use of the same vowel-sounds in close proximity, often in verse, for the sake of euphony, memorability or emotional effect, e.g., "And deep-*asleep* he *seemed*" (Tennyson, "The Lotus-Eaters"). See **alliteration**.

asyndeton. The omission of a conjunction between words, phrases or clauses, .e.g.,

"And dreams of home,
Waving from window, spread of welcome,
Kissing of wife under single sheet"
(W. H. Auden, "The Wanderer").

See **ellipsis**.

Augustan. Referring to the reign of the Emperor Augustus (27 B.C.–14 A.D.), when Virgil, Horace and Ovid wrote, or to the neo-classical period in English literature between c. 1670 and 1790, when such writers as Dryden, Addison, Pope, Swift and Johnson conformed to the Augustan principles of reason, order and decorum. See **classical** and **neo-classicism**.

ballad. A narrative poem (often anonymous) telling of heroic or tragic deeds, typically written in quatrains of alternating four and three stresses and rhyming *abcb* or *abab*, e.g., "Sir Patrick Spens." See **quatrain**.

ballade. A poem of three eight-line stanzas (rhyming *ababbcbc*) and one four-line envoi (*bcbc*) with a refrain at the end of each of its four sections, e.g., those written by Hilaire Belloc. See **envoi**.

bathos. An anticlimax or sudden descent from the sublime to the commonplace, intentional or unintentional, e.g., the last two lines of Tennyson's "Enoch Arden":

"And when they buried him the little port
Had seldom seen a costlier funeral."

belles-lettres. Elegant, polished prose writing, especially essays, e.g., those written by Max Be-erbohm.

Bildungsroman. Literally, "formation novel" (German), i.e., one that relates the upbringing, education and development of its hero, e.g., Goethe's *Wilhelm Meister's Apprenticeship*. See **M4**.

black comedy. Comedy that finds amusement in what are conventionally regarded as tragic, sick or pessimistic people and situations, e.g., Joe Orton's *Loot*.

blank verse. Unrhymed iambic pentameter (see **metre**), as used in Shakespeare's plays, Milton's *Paradise Lost* and Wordsworth's *Prelude*.

bouts-rimés. Literally, "rhymed ends" (French), i.e., rhyming words supplied in advance to which lines must be fitted.

bowdlerise. To expurgate, from the Rev. Thomas Bowdler (1754–1825), who removed what he considered to be coarse expressions from the plays in his *Family Shakespeare*.

burlesque. A ludicrous, mocking imitation in prose or verse of a literary or dramatic work, *e.g.*, the Duke of Buckingham's *The Rehearsal*, a burlesque of seventeenth-century heroic plays. *See* **heroic tragedy**.

caesura. A break in a line of poetry, often towards the middle, sometimes used to emphasise an antithesis or comparison, *e.g.*,

> "Willing to wound, / and yet afraid to strike"
> (Pope, *Epistle to Arbuthnot*).

See **antithesis**.

canon. Authentic works of an author or standard works of literature (as studied on academic courses, for example).

canto. A division of a long poem, perhaps consisting of many **stanzas** (*q.v.*), as in Byron's *Don Juan*.

catachresis. A misuse or incorrect application of a word, *e.g.*, "chronic" to mean "severe".

catalectic. Describing a line of verse with one or more syllables missing in the final foot, *e.g.*,

> " Rúǐn / seize thěe, / rúthlěss / kǐng!"
> (Gray, "The Bard").

See **acatalectic**, **hypercatalectic** *and* **metre**.

catalyst. A substance that alters the rate of a chemical reaction but itself remains unchanged. T. S. Eliot used the term as an analogy in his theory of the poet's impersonality: "the more perfect the artist, the more completely separate in him will be the man who suffers and the mind which creates" ("Tradition and the Individual Talent," 1919).

catastrophe. The tragic climax of a drama or narrative.

catharsis. The purgation of pity and terror by means of the representation of those emotions in tragedy (Aristotle, *Poetics*). *See* **tragedy**.

character. A seventeenth-century genre of writing illustrating individual and social human types ("a modest man", "a shopkeeper", *etc.*), *e.g.*, John Earle's *Microcosmography*. More widely, a fictional personage, defined by E. M. Forster in *Aspects of the Novel* (1927) as either "flat" ("constructed round a single idea or quality") or "round" (with the "incalculability of life about it").

chiasmus. A "laying crosswise" of elements in a sentence, *i.e.*, the order of words in one of two parallel clauses or phrases is inverted in the other, *e.g.*,

> "Love without end, and without measure grace"
> (Milton, *Paradise Lost*).

chorus. A group of actors in Greek drama providing a commentary on the action; a device adapted, for example, by Shakespeare in *King Henry V* and T. S. Eliot in *Murder in the Cathedral*.

classical. Showing a regard for the values and forms of Ancient Greek and Latin literature and so having qualities of order, restraint, reason and precision. *See* **Augustan** *and* **neo-classical**.

clerihew. Comic biographical poem in the form of a *quatrain* (*q.v.*) with lines of various length, rhyming *aabb*, named after its inventor Eric Clerihew Bentley (1875–1956).

comedy. A literary or dramatic work, or aspect of it, that is amusing in various ways. More particularly, a work with a happy ending, *e.g.*, a comedy by Shakespeare. *See* **black comedy**.

comedy of ideas. A play (or novel) that is entertainingly and wittily concerned with ideas, problems and theories, *e.g.*, the novels of Thomas Love Peacock and the plays of Bernard Shaw.

comedy of manners. A play concerned with the behaviour and intrigues of elegant, sophisticated society, *e.g.*, Congreve's *The Way of the World* and Wilde's *The Importance of Being Earnest*.

conceit. An ingenious or highly fanciful example of imagery, perhaps using elaborate figures of speech and word-play, often associated with the *Metaphysical Poets* (*q.v.*), *e.g.*, Donne's comparison of two lovers' souls with a pair of compasses ("A Valediction: Forbidding Mourning").

couplet. Two successive rhyming lines. *See* **heroic couplet** *and* **rhyming couplet**.

dactyl. *See* **metre**.

decasyllable. A line of verse of ten syllables, often synonymous with the iambic pentameter. *See* **metre**.

deconstruction. A theory and method of textual analysis that emphasises the infinite number of

uncertainties and ambiguities that exist in any literary work. *See* **post-structuralism**.

defamiliarisation. A conception of artistic technique held by the Russian Formalist, Victor Shklovsky, who maintained that art enables us to experience the world afresh by means of making things unfamiliar and thus increasing "the difficulty and duration of perception". *See* **formalism**.

diaeresis. The separation of a diphthong into two sounds, sometimes indicated by a mark (˙) placed over the second vowel, *e.g.*, "Noël".

dialogue. Conversation between two or more people in a literary or dramatic work. Also, a separate genre often used for the discussion of ideas, *e.g.*, Landor's *Imaginary Conversations*.

didactic. Applied to a literary work in prose or verse that aims to instruct the reader lightly or seriously, *e.g.*, Pope's poem, *An Essay on Criticism*.

diegesis. The process of authorial explanations, commentaries and narrative in a fictional work as distinct from the direct display of characters and action by such means as dialogue. Sometimes used in criticism as the opposing term to **mimesis** (*q.v.*). (From Plato's *Republic*.)

dirge. A funeral song or poem, *e.g.*, Shelley's "Autumn: A Dirge". *See* **elegy** *and* **threnody**.

dissociation of sensibility. T. S. Eliot's term (in "The Metaphysical Poets," 1921) to explain the failure of post seventeenth-century poets to amalgamate "disparate experience" to form "new wholes". There was a separation of feeling from thought in their work.

distich. Two lines of verse expressing a complete idea.

dithyramb. A passionate, rapturous poem, *e.g.*, Dryden's "Alexander's Feast".

doggerel. Rough, technically incompetent verse, often comic, vulgar or abusive, *e.g.*, some of the street ballads of the nineteenth century.

donnée. A situation or idea given or suggested to an author, who then bases a literary work on it, *e.g.*, an anecdote at the dinner-table led to Henry James's *The Spoils of Poynton*.

dramatic irony. Words or a situation on the stage understood by the audience in a different way from the way the characters understand them, *e.g.*, Duncan's speech, "This castle hath a pleasant seat ...", spoken on the eve of his murder there (Shakespeare, *Macbeth*, I, vi).

dramatic monologue. Poem with one speaker addressing a listener or listeners and revealing, knowingly or unknowingly, important aspects of his character and situation, *e.g.*, Browning's "Fra Lippo Lippi".

eclogue. A fairly short pastoral poem often in the form of a dialogue, *e.g.*, the ten *Eclogues* of Virgil.

elegiac stanza. Quatrain of four iambic pentameters rhyming *abab*, as used in Gray's "Elegy in a Country Churchyard".

elegy. A poem of mourning or lament, *e.g.*, Milton's "Lycidas" and Shelley's "Adonais". *See* **dirge** *and* **threnody**.

elision. The suppression of a vowel or syllable in verse for the sake of metrical correctness, *e.g.*, "ta'en" for "taken".

ellipsis. The omission of words, especially in poetry, to achieve compression, complexity or surprise, *e.g.*, in passages of T. S. Eliot's *The Waste Land*. *See* **asyndeton**.

emblem. A symbolic picture with a motto and explanation, associated with allegorical and figurative writing in such seventeenth century works as Francis Quarles' *Emblems*, a collection of religious poems.

end-stopped. Describing a self-contained line of verse that ends with a punctuation mark, *e.g.*,

> "Black is the beauty of the brightest day!
> The golden ball of Heaven's eternal fire,
> That danced with glory on the silver waves,
> Now wants the glory that inflamed his beams"
> (Marlowe, *Tamburlaine*, 2nd Part, II, iv).

See **enjambment**.

enjambment. The running-on of one line of verse into another without a grammatical break, *e.g.*,

> "Nay, but this dotage of our general's
> O'er flows the measure ..."
> (Shakespeare, *Antony and Cleopatra*, I, i).

envoi. The short final stanza of a poem, especially a *ballade* (*q.v.*), addressed as parting words to a person or persons, emphasising the subject of the poem.

epic. A long narrative poem in an elevated style celebrating heroic personages and deeds, *e.g.*, Homer's *Iliad* and *Odyssey*.

epic simile. A long, elaborately developed comparison, as found in some epic poems. Sometimes termed *Homeric simile. See* **simile**.

epigram. A pointed, witty saying or verse that can be sarcastic, complimentary or amusing, *e.g.*,

> "Swans sing before they die; 'twere no bad thing
> Did certain persons die before they sing"
> (Coleridge).

epigraph. A quotation or motto at the beginning of a work or of a section of it, *e.g.*, "Mistah Kurtz—he dead" (quotation from Conrad's *Heart of Darkness* prefixed to T. S. Eliot's *The Hollow Men*).

epilogue. The final section of work, serving such purposes as pointing a moral or summarising, *e.g.*, Rosalind's concluding speech in Shakespeare's *As You Like it*.

epiphany. James Joyce's term for a significant moment of revelation that a writer should record: "a sudden spiritual manifestation, whether in the vulgarity of speech or of gesture or in a memorable phase of the mind itself " (Joyce, *Stephen Hero*).

epistolary novel. A novel written in the form of letters, *e.g.*, Samuel Richardson's *Clarissa* and Laclos' *Les Liaisons dangereuses*.

epode. In the Greek *chorus* (*q.v.*) and the *Pindaric Ode* (*q.v.*), the third and last section, coming after the *antistrophe* (*q.v.*).

essay. A fairly short discussion in prose (or, more rarely, in verse) of any topic, light-hearted or serious in tone and formal or informal in style, as written by Bacon, Addison and Lamb.

euphemism The use of a mild, pleasant term to express something disagreeable, harsh or vulgar, *e.g.*, "And lo, he had answered to his name, and stood in the presence of The Master" (Thackeray, *The Newcomes*), meaning "He had died"; "visually challenged" meaning "blind" or "partly blind".

euphony. Agreeable sound in verse or prose achieved by such means as metre, rhyme, alliteration and assonance, enhanced by the meanings and associations of the words chosen, frequently found, for example, in the poems of Tennyson.

euphuism. Highly elaborate prose style, as found in John Lyly's *Euphues* (1579–80).

eye-rhyme. A rhyme that is visually correct but orally incorrect, *e.g.*, "love" and "rove", though in considering older poetry changes in pronunciation must be borne in mind. Also, Spenser's practice of adjusting spelling to make a rhyme clear to both eye and ear.

fable. A short prose or verse narrative, often with animals as characters, intended to convey a moral lesson, as written, for example, by Aesop, La Fontaine and John Gay.

fabula. In Formalist criticism, a story as it would actually have happened chronologically and objectively, as distinct from its literary treatment in a specific text, which is termed the *sjuzet. See* **formalism**.

farce. A comedy of broad, absurd and slapstick humour, often of frantic pace and technical ingenuity, *e.g.*, Ben Travers' *Rookery Nook*.

fashionable novel. A novel about life in high society written in an inflated, sentimental style, popular in the 1820s and 1830s, *e.g.*, Disraeli's *The Young Duke. See* **M6**.

foot. *See* **metre**.

foregrounding. Emphasis and prominence achieved in literary work by such means as linguistic deviation from normal usage.

formalism. A critical theory and method developed by critics in Russia *c.* 1913–30 (*e.g.*, Shklovsky and Jakobson) that concentrated on the analysis of literary works as self-sufficient structures and paid little or no attention to biographical and social influences.

fourteener. A line of verse containing fourteen syllables arranged as seven iambic feet. *See* **metre**.

free verse. Verse with no regular metrical pattern or length of line but with its form sometimes determined by its meaning, *e.g.*, D. H. Lawrence's "Snake". Also known as *vers libre*.

genre. A kind or type of literary work defined by its form and/or its purpose, *e.g.*, comedy, satire, ode.

Georgian poetry. Poetry written between *c.* 1910 and 1925, during the reign of George V, in short, lyrical forms and of easy comprehensibility, typically dealing with English rural subjects in an affectionate and nostalgic manner. The principal poets included W. H. Davies, Walter de la Mare, James Stephens, Edward Thomas and Edmund Blunden.

Gothic novels. Melodramatic novels of the late eighteenth and early nineteenth centuries dealing with terror, mystery and the supernatural, often in medieval settings, *e.g.*, M. G. Lewis's *The Monk. See* **M5**.

grand style. A plain, natural and noble style of poetry, as found in Homer (termed thus by Matthew Arnold).

great tradition. Phrase used by the critic F. R. Leavis to denote certain novelists "significant in terms of that human awareness they promote", *i.e.*, Jane Austen, George Eliot, Henry James and Joseph Conrad (*The Great Tradition*, 1948). Leavis would later have added Dickens and D. H. Lawrence to the tradition.

haiku. Japanese verse form of seventeen syllables in three lines of five, seven and five syllables, conveying a single, sharp impression of an image or mood.

half-rhyme. Rhyme in which the consonants are the same but the vowels are different, *e.g.*, "leaves"/ "lives", "simmer"/"summer" (taken from Wilfred Owen's "Miners").

hamartia. The flaw or defect in a tragic hero that leads to his downfall (Aristotle, *Poetics*).

hemistich. Half a line of verse, divided at the *caesura* (*q.v.*).

hendecasyllabic. A line of verse of eleven syllables, as used by the Latin poet, Catullus, but rarely found in English.

hendiadys. Expression of a compound notion by two elements co-ordinated by "and" instead of by one element subordinated to the other, *e.g.*, "waving to him *white hands and courtesy*" (Tennyson, "Gareth and Lynette") for "courteous white hands."

heptameter. *See* **metre**.

heroic couplet. A pair of rhyming iambic pentameters, so called because the metre was used in seventeenth century "heroic" plays and poems by Dryden and others. (*See* **heroic tragedy**.) The prevalent metrical form in the eighteenth century. *See* **metre** and **rhyming couplet**.

heroic tragedy. Late seventeenth-century type of drama, dealing in an elevated manner with themes of love and honour, written in *heroic couplets* (*q.v.*), *e.g.*, John Dryden's *The Conquest of Granada*.

hexameter. *See* **metre**.

historical novel. A novel set in past times, sometimes mixing fictional and factual characters and events, *e.g.*, Sir Walter Scott's *Ivanhoe*. *See* **M4**.

Homeric simile. *See* **epic simile** *and* **simile**.

homonym. A word having the same sound and sometimes the same spelling as another but a different meaning, *e.g.*, "fast": "rapid"; "fast": "abstinence"; "fast": "fixed".

homophone. A word having the same pronunciation as another but a different meaning and spelling, *e.g.*, "son" and "sun".

hubris. In Greek tragedy, the arrogance of a hero or heroine who ignores divine commands and who is therefore brought to ruin, e.g., the behaviour of Creon in Sophocles' *Antigone*.

hypallage. Transference of epithet from the normal substantive to an unexpected one, *e.g.*, "Who sees his true love in her *naked bed* " (Shakespeare, *Venus and Adonis*).

hyperbaton. Transposition of words out of normal order or separation of words usually associated together, *e.g.*,

> "So much I hate a *breaking* cause to be
> *Of heavenly oaths*"
> (Shakespeare, *Love's Labour's Lost*, V, ii).

hyperbole. Exaggeration for the sake of emphasis or comedy, *e.g.*,

> "There emerged from scores of by-streets, lanes, and nameless turnings, innumerable people, carrying their dinners to the bakers' shops"
> (Dickens, *A Christmas Carol*).

hypercatalectic. Describing a line of verse with an extra syllable, *e.g.*,

> "Thĕ slíngs / ănd aŕ- / rŏws ŏf / oŭtrage- / oŭs
> fŏr- / tŭne"
> (Shakespeare, *Hamlet*, III, i).

See **acatalectic, catalectic** *and* **metre**.

hysteron proteron. Reversal of normal or temporal order, *e.g.*,

"Take, eat; this is my body"
(St. Matthew, ch. 26)

"Th'Antoniad, the Egyptian admiral,
With all their sixty, fly and turn the rudder"
(Shakespeare, Antony and Cleopatra, III, x).

idyll. A poem, pleasing and contented in tone, on an innocent, rural subject, of the type written by the Ancient Greek poet, Theocritus. More widely, a poem conveying a feeling of calm happiness.

imagery. Figures of speech and other devices of language used to convey sensuous and imaginative impressions to the reader.

Imagism. A poetic movement and theory, flourishing *c.* 1909–14, which emphasised direct treatment of subject-matter, concreteness, extreme economy of language and the rhythm of phrases rather than the rhythm of regular metres. The principal Imagist poets were Richard Aldington, H.D. (*i.e.*, Hilda Doolittle), F. S. Flint, Amy Lowell and Ezra Pound.

imitation. In particular, the practice, commended in the eighteenth century, of copying and adapting classical models (*e.g.*, Pope's *Imitations of Horace*). More generally, synonymous with *mimesis* (*q.v.*).

inscape. Gerard Manley Hopkins' term for the particular, unique, distinctive identity of a thing, an identity which the poet should capture in his work. *See* **instress**.

instress. Hopkins' term for the natural energy that determines an *inscape* (*q.v.*) and that maintains its existence: "the blue [of the sky] was charged with simple instress" (Hopkins' *Journal*, 1871).

intentional fallacy. A phrase coined by M. C. Beardsley and W. K. Wimsatt (1946), who argued that the "design or intention of the author is neither available nor desirable as a standard for judging the success of a work of literary art." *See* **affective fallacy** *and* **New Critics**.

interlude. In the sixteenth century a play performed in the midst of festivities. It could be farcical, romantic or religious and was sometimes indistinguishable from a *morality play* (*q.v.*). John Heywood's interludes are amongst the best-known.

internal rhyme. The rhyming of two or more words within one line of verse, *e.g.*,

"When you're lying *awake* with a dismal *headache*,
and repose is taboo'd by anxiety"
(Gilbert, Iolanthe).

See **rhyme**.

inversion. The reversal of normal syntax, usually by putting the verb before the subject, as in poetic language imitating Latin word-order, *e.g.*, the opening six lines of Milton's *Paradise Lost*: "Of Man's first disobedience . . . sing heavenly Muse". *See* **Latinism**.

irony. The use of words (verbal irony) or situations (situational irony) to convey the opposite of what is really meant or what might naturally be expected. It can be comic, tragic or satirical, *e.g.*, Fielding's description of Blifil as "this worthy young man" (*Tom Jones*), the remark made by Jane Austen's Mr Bennet about Mr Collins' "talent of flattering with delicacy" (*Pride and Prejudice*) and Thomas Hardy's portrayal of Jude's death in the midst of student festivities at Christminster (*Jude the Obscure*). *See* **dramatic irony**.

Johnsonian. In the literary style and manner of Dr Samuel Johnson (1709–84), *e.g.*, using weighty, well-balanced sentences and a Latinised vocabulary and expressing a pragmatic, common-sense attitude to life and literature.

Lake Poets. The English Romantic poets, Wordsworth, Coleridge and Southey, who lived in the Lake District.

lampoon. A personal satire, often malicious and coarse in tone, *e.g.*, Henry Carey's "Namby-Pamby" (a poem on the poet, Ambrose Philips). *See* **satire**.

langue. A language considered as a whole, abstract system, which all its speakers have in common. (Term used by the linguist, Ferdinand de Saussure.) *See* **parole**.

Latinism. Word, phrase, idiom or construction that imitates a Latin one. Characteristics can include sentence-inversion (*see* **inversion**), placing adjectives after and around substantives (see the first example below) and the use of many words (often learned and abstract) derived from Latin (see the second example), *e.g.*,

"I come to pluck your *berries harsh and crude*,
And with *forc'd fingers rude*
Shatter your leaves before the mellowing year"
(Milton, "Lycidas")

"A *doctrine* so *extraordinary* and so *sublime* must *inevitably* command the *veneration* of the people" (Gibbon, *Decline and Fall of the Roman Empire*).

lay. A narrative or lyrical poem recounting romantic or adventurous deeds, *e.g.*, Scott's *Lay of the Last Minstrel*.

Leavisite. Pertaining to the ideas and followers of F. R. Leavis (1895–1978), whose rigorous literary criticism was informed by a serious moral concern. *See* **great tradition**.

lexis. The vocabulary of a language, which therefore consists of lexical items (which can include words and brief phrases).

limerick. A comic five-line verse-form in anapaests (*see* **metre**), rhyming *aabba*, ideally with a surprising last line.

litotes. An understatement, particularly one that uses the negative, often made for the purposes of irony or emphasis, *e.g.*, "Mrs Blifil was not over and above pleased with the behaviour of her husband" (Fielding, *Tom Jones*); "No little band of yet remembered names" (Wordsworth, *The Prelude*, I). *See* **meiosis**.

loose sentence. A sentence with the main clause first, followed by subordinate clauses, *e.g.*, "There can be no doubt that this remarkable man owed the vast influence which he exercised over his contemporaries at least as much to his gloomy egotism as to the real power of his poetry" (Macaulay, *Byron*). *See* **periodic sentence**.

lyric. A short poem of a song-like nature, expressing a single—often personal—mood. For numerous examples, see Palgrave's *Golden Treasury*.

macaronic. Describing comic or burlesque verse written in mixed languages or languages adapted and distorted, *e.g.*, "Charmer virumque I sing, Jack plumigeramque Arabellam" (first line of "Narrative Macaronic Verses" by Frank Sidgwick).

malapropism. A word used in the wrong sense, sometimes for comic effect, *e.g.*, "I would have her instructed in *geometry*, that she might know something of the *contagious* countries" (Mrs Malaprop in Sheridan's *The Rivals*, I, ii).

masque. A courtly entertainment, popular in the late sixteenth and early seventeenth centuries, consisting of artificial, fantastic dramatic action, dancing, songs, and elaborate costumes and settings, *e.g.*, Ben Jonson's *Masque of Oberon*.

meiosis. An understatement, often used for purposes of comedy or emphasis, *e.g.*,

"A small accident had happened, which somewhat disconcerted them; and this was no other than the thief 's escape"
(Fielding, Joseph Andrews)

"But she is in her grave, and, oh,
The difference to me!"
(Wordsworth, "She dwelt among the untrodden ways").

See **litotes**.

melodrama. Extravagant drama of heightened emotions, characterised by sentimentality and sensationalism, *e.g.*, Leopold Lewis' *The Bells*, in which Henry Irving gave a famous performance.

metaphor. A figure of speech of comparison stating an identity rather than a likeness, *i.e.*, something is said to be that which it only resembles, *e.g.*, "I fall upon the thorns of life" (Shelley, "Ode to the West Wind"); "the very honey of earthly joy" (Cowley, "The Wish").

Metaphysical Poets. Seventeenth century poets, including John Donne, George Herbert, Henry Vaughan, Richard Crashaw and Andrew Marvell, whose subject-matter was usually love or religion. Their poems contain striking imagery, wit, intense passion and powers of argument and persuasion. (Term first used by Dr Johnson, who may have been influenced by a phrase of Dryden's.)

metonymy. The application of the name of an attribute to that of the thing meant, *e.g.*, "Dickens" for "the works of Dickens"; "the Bench" for "the magistrates".

metre. The measure of lines of verse, which in

English is basically **accentual** (*q.v.*). Each group of syllables (usually two or three) is a **foot**. These feet of stressed syllables (marked with ´) and unstressed syllables (marked with ˘) are often classified as follows: iambus (˘´); trochee (´˘); spondee (´´); pyrrhic (˘˘); anapaest (˘˘´); dactyl (´˘˘); amphibrach (˘´˘). The number of feet in a line is indicated as follows: monometer (1); dimeter (2); trimeter (3); tetrameter (4); pentameter (5); hexameter (6); heptameter (7). An *iambic pentameter*, for example, is therefore a line of five iambic feet, *e.g.*,

"Bĕlín- / dă smiled, / ănd áll / thĕ wórld / wăs gáy"
                (Pope, *The Rape of the Lock*).

Metrical variation, however, is a common feature of English verse.

Miltonic. Pertaining to the work of John Milton (1608–74), with reference to his Latinised syntax and vocabulary, his blank verse, his sonnets and his Protestant theology and outlook.

mimesis. Plato's term for artistic imitation or representation, which he thought necessarily false. Aristotle saw it as a basic function of art, stating that the "objects of imitation are the actions of men". The term can also denote more particularly the direct representation of speech and action in a literary work. *See* diegesis.

miracle plays. Fourteenth and fifteenth century plays, sometimes known as Mystery Plays, consisting of dramatised episodes from the Bible, from the Creation to the Day of Judgement, acted by members of trade guilds, usually on Corpus Christi day. Cycles survive from York, Coventry, Wakefield and Chester.

mock heroic. The satirical or comic application of heroic or epic styles, conventions, situations and characters to trivial or vulgar subjects, *e.g.*, Pope's *The Rape of the Lock*.

monodrama. A dramatic work for one character or performer, *e.g.*, Tennyson's poem, "Maud".

monologue. A prose or verse composition spoken by one character or performer, either as a separate work or as part of a work, *e.g.*, Beckett's *Krapp's Last Tape*. *See* **dramatic monologue, monodrama** *and* **soliloquy**.

morality plays. Allegorical dramas of the late fifteenth and early sixteenth centuries, in which personified virtues and vices contend for a man's soul, *e.g.*, *Everyman*.

morpheme. The smallest linguistic unit which has a grammatical function and an independent meaning, *e.g.*, sang, bread, -ing, -ed.

mystery plays. *See* miracle plays.

myth. Story of unknown origin expressing and explaining universal and religious experience (*e.g.*, fertility and seasonal change) often by means of the deeds of a hero or god. *See* **Section I Classical Mythology**.

Naturalism. Originating in nineteenth century France, a literary movement that aimed at presenting the reality of life, with an emphasis on environment, objectivity and amorality. Prominent naturalistic novelists included Zola, Gissing and Bennett. *See* **realism, J37** *and* **M11.**

negative capability. John Keats' phrase (in a letter, 1817) for the quality, found in such great poets as Shakespeare, "of being in uncertainties, mysteries, doubts, without any irritable reaching after fact and reason".

neo-classicism. The theory and application, particularly in the eighteenth century, of the classical values and rules of reason, order and decorum, as shown in the work of Dryden, Pope and Johnson, who emulated Homer, Virgil, Horace, Juvenal and other writers of Ancient Greece and Rome. *See* **Augustan** *and* **classical**.

neologism. A new word or phrase, or an old word used in a new sense, *e.g.*, "agnostic" (coined by T. H. Huxley) and "prestigious" (meaning "having prestige" instead of "juggling").

New Critics. American group of critics, including Cleanth Brooks, R. P. Blackmur, Robert Penn Warren, John Crowe Ransom and W. K. Wimsatt, who were active in the late 1930s and the 1940s and who advocated close textual analysis, free of biographical and contextual associations. *See* **affective fallacy** *and* **intentional fallacy**.

Newgate novels. Crime novels of the 1820s and 1830s that tended to romanticise criminals and highwaymen, *e.g.*, Bulwer Lytton's *Paul Clifford* and W. H. Ainsworth's *Rookwood*. *See* **M6**.

nouveau roman. Type of French novel that began

in the 1950s and that rejected conventional characterisation and plot, as written by Alain Robbe-Grillet. *See* **anti-novel**.

novel. *See* **M4–M19** for definitions, types and history.

novella. A short novel, *e.g.*, Conrad's *Typhoon* and D. H. Lawrence's *The Fox*.

objective correlative. T. S. Eliot's term (in his essay on *Hamlet*, 1919) for "a set of objects, a situation, a chain of events which shall be the formula" of a particular emotion expressed in art.

octave. *See* **sonnet**.

ode. A lyrical poem of elaborate structure and elevated diction written to celebrate or commemorate a noble, beautiful or admirable subject or theme, *e.g.*, Keats' "Ode to a Nightingale" and Tennyson's "Ode on the Death of the Duke of Wellington." *See* **Pindaric Ode**.

onomatopoeia. The use or invention of words to imitate sounds, *e.g.*, "buzz", "hiss", "swish", or the imitative effect of such word usage as Tennyson's "murmuring of innumerable bees" ("Come down, O maid").

ottava rima. Eight iambic pentameters (*see* **metre**) rhyming *abababcc*, as in Byron's *Don Juan*.

oxymoron. Combination of two contradictory terms in one expression, *e.g.*, "fearful joy" (Gray) and "sweet unrest" (Keats).

palindrome. A word, sentence or verse that reads the same backwards or forwards, *e.g.*, "level", "A man, a plan, a canal—Panama."

parable. A short, often realistic story told to exemplify a doctrine or moral, as told by Christ in the New Testament, *e.g.*, "The Sower" and "The Good Samaritan".

paradox. An apparent contradiction or absurdity often designed to upset conventional opinion and to indicate a truth, *e.g.*, G. K. Chesterton's "If we are to be international we must be national" and "The subtle man is always immeasurably easier to understand than the natural man."

parataxis. Arrangement of clauses without conjunctions, *e.g.*, "After a painful struggle I yielded to my fate: I sighed as a lover, I obeyed as a son; my wound was insensibly healed by time, absence, and the habits of a new life" (Gibbon, *Autobiography*).

parody. A comic or satirical imitation of an original work or of the characteristic style of a writer or literary movement, *e.g.*, Max Beerbohm's "Scruts" (a parody of Arnold Bennett) and Henry Reed's "Chard Whitlow" (a parody of T. S. Eliot's *Four Quartets*).

parole. An actual, individual utterance of language, as distinct from *langue* (*q.v.*). (Term used by the linguist, Ferdinand de Saussure.)

paronomasia. A play on words. *See* **pun**.

pastoral poetry. Poetry dealing in an idealised way with rustic life, especially the lives and emotions of shepherds and shepherdesses, *e.g.*, Spenser's *Shepherd's Calendar*.

pathetic fallacy. The false belief that human emotions exist in non-human things and phenomena. Such appearances are "entirely unconnected with any real power or character in the object, and only imputed to it by us", *e.g.*, "the cruel, crawling foam" (Ruskin, *Modern Painters*, where he coined, discussed and illustrated the term, 1856).

pentameter. *See* **metre**.

periodic sentence. A sentence that begins with subordinate clauses and ends with the main clause, *e.g.*, "Since then the imaginary right of vengeance must be at last remitted, because it is impossible to live in perpetual hostility, and equally impossible that of two enemies, either should first think himself obliged by justice to submission, *it is surely eligible to forgive early*" (Samuel Johnson, essay in *The Rambler*). *See* **loose sentence**.

peripeteia. In drama, a sudden change of fortune, "the reverse of what is expected from the circumstances of the action" (Aristotle, *Poetics*), as in Sophocles' *Oedipus Tyrannus*, where the messenger, meaning to make Oedipus happy, reveals the secret of his birth, with tragic consequences.

periphrasis. Roundabout speech or circumlocution, *e.g.*, Mr Micawber's speeches in Dickens' *David Copperfield*.

persona. A character or narrator who can in some cases be thought to be the author in disguise, *e.g.*, Stephen Daedalus in Joyce's *Portrait of the Artist as a Young Man*.

personification. Representation of a thing or quality

as a person, e.g., "There Honour comes, a pilgrim grey" (William Collins, "Ode").

Petrarchan sonnet. See sonnet.

phoneme. The minimum significant sound-unit in language, either consonant-type or vowel-type, e.g., "meat," "boy".

picaresque novel. A novel with a rogue as its hero, undergoing many adventures, e.g., Smollett's Peregrine Pickle. See **M4**.

Pindaric Ode. An ode modelled on the Greek odes of Pindar (518–438 B.C.) consisting of a strophe, antistrophe and epode (qq.v.) in complex stanzas, this three-part structure often being repeated at least once, e.g., Thomas Gray's "Progress of Poesy". See ode.

pleonasm. Using more words than are needed, either unconsciously or deliberately for emphasis, e.g., "at this moment of time" (for "now") and "most unkindest cut of all" (Shakespeare, Julius Caesar).

plot. The sequence or complex of connected events in a fictional narrative or drama, with (in Forster's definition in Aspects of the Novel, 1927) "a sense of causality" to distinguish it from story (q.v.).

poetic diction. Words, phrases and syntax pre-scribed specifically for poetic use, especially in the eighteenth century, and including periphrasis (q.v.) (e.g., "the finny tribe" for "fish"), personification and Latinised structures and expressions.

poetic prose. Prose using such devices as rhythm, elaborate imagery, figures of speech and symbols, conventionally associated with poetry, to be found, for example, in some of George Meredith's descriptive passages in his novels.

portmanteau word. One word formed by combining two or more words, e.g., "smog," a combination of "smoke" and "fog". (Term coined by Lewis Carroll in Through the Looking-Glass.)

poststructuralism. A development of structuralism (q.v.), which concentrates on the power of lang-uage as a creative force within itself and the indeterminate number of possibilities of meaning and interpretation. See deconstruction.

practical criticism. Exercises in the close analysis of texts, as advocated and practised by the critic and teacher I. A. Richards (in Practical Criticism, 1929).

prolegomenon. An introduction, sometimes of a learned nature, e.g., R. B. McKerrow's Prolegomena for the Oxford Shakespeare.

prolepsis. Anticipatory use of an epithet, e.g., "the two brothers and their murder'd man" (Keats, "Isabella") and " 'I'm killed, Sire!' " (Browning, "Incident in the French Camp").

prologue. The introductory section of a work with such functions as setting the scene, whetting the appetite of audience or reader and giving preliminary explanations, e.g., the opening Chorus of Shakespeare's Romeo and Juliet.

prosody. The study of versification, including rhythm, rhyme and stanza forms, as in George Saintsbury's History of English Prosody.

pun. A play on words, e.g.,

"I cannot say 'whore':
It does abhor me now I speak the word"
(Shakespeare, Othello, IV ii)

"They went and told the sexton, and
The sexton toll'd the bell"
(Thomas Hood, "Sally Brown").

pyrrhic. See metre.

quatrain. A four-lined stanza (q.v.).

realism. In the nineteenth century, the theory and practice of a belief that art (e.g., the novel) should be a precise, truthful representation of life, associated in France with Balzac and the Gon-court brothers, amongst others. Sometimes synonymous with naturalism (q.v.).

Revenge Tragedy. Popular seventeenth century type of drama, derived from Seneca's plays (1st century A.D.), in which revenge, ghosts and terror are prominent, e.g., Kyd's The Spanish Tragedy.

rhetorical question. A question which does not require an answer but which is put for purposes of emphasis, e.g., "Were they again to advance their money on pledges which had been forfeited over and over again?" (Macaulay, "Milton").

rhyme. Identity of sound from the last stressed vowel to the end, sometimes used in conventional patterns, such as rhyming couplets, sonnets and the Spenserian stanza (qq.v.).

rhyme royal. A stanza of seven iambic pentameters

rhyming ababbcc, used, for example, in Chaucer's Troilus and Criseyde. See metre.

rhyming couplet. The same as heroic couplet (q.v.), but rhyming couplets in iambic tetrameter (not known as heroic couplets) are also frequently used, e.g., in Swift's poems. See metre.

rhythm. Regular recurrence of stress or of long or short sounds, especially in poetry, analysed by the process of scansion. See metre. More widely, patterns of event or motif in various literary compositions, including novels.

roman à clef. A novel about actual people disguised as fictional personages, e.g., Aldous Huxley's Point Counterpoint.

roman-fleuve. A long series of inter-related novels, e.g., Proust's A la Recherche du temps perdu.

romance. A term of many meanings, including a medieval poetic or prose story of chivalry and love (e.g., Malory's Morte Darthur); later, a work dealing with adventures in a fanciful and un-realistic manner (e.g., Shakespeare's The Winter's Tale); in modern times, a glamorous, sentimental story of love (e.g., the "romantic novels" published by Mills and Boon).

Romanticism. In literature, the movement at the end of the eighteenth and the beginning of the nineteenth centuries identified with individual ex-pression, sensibility, imagination, emotion, the love of Nature and "simple" people (such as peasants and children) and a wide variety of literary forms. In part the movement was a reaction against neo-classicism (q.v.). Leading Romantic writers in English literature were Scott, Wordsworth, Coleridge, Byron, Shelley and Keats.

rondeau. A form of verse, originally French, in which lines are repeated at regular intervals. A typical pattern is aabba; aab and refrain; aabba and refrain, all octosyllabic. Written by some minor nineteenth century English poets, e.g., Austin Dobson.

run-on line. See enjambment.

saga. An ancient Icelandic or Scandinavian prose tale of heroes and great deeds, mostly oral in origin.

samizdat. Self-published, typescript, underground literature, in the former Soviet Union, expressing opinions unacceptable to the government.

sapphics. A classical, quantitative metre consisting of three longer lines and one shorter.

satire. Prose or verse composition ridiculing and criticising vice and folly by such means as irony (q.v.), sarcasm, the mock-heroic (q.v.), parody (q.v.) and invective. John Dryden said that "the true end of satire is the amendment of vices by correction" (Absalom and Achitophel, "To the Reader"). Famous examples include Swift's Modest Proposal and Pope's Dunciad.

scansion. The process of analysing metre (q.v.).

semiology. The science of studying signs, especially those used in systems of communication (including objects, gestures and clothes as well as language). See semiotics and **J47**.

semiotics. The study of patterns of behaviour in communication, particularly through the use of linguistics. More broadly, synonymous with semiology (q.v.).

sensation novel. Mid-nineteenth century English novels of crime, detection and passion, with an atmosphere of excitement, suffering and suspense, e.g., M. E. Braddon's Lady Audley's Secret. See **M9**.

sestet. See sonnet.

sestina. Elaborate verse-form of six six-line stanzas ending with a three-line envoi (q.v.).

Shakespearean sonnet. See sonnet.

signified and signifier. Saussure's terms for the concept and its oral or written verbal "sound image", indissolubly but arbitrarily connected to each other.

simile. A figure of speech in which two things or actions are likened to each other, usually by means of "as" or "like", e.g.,

"Your face, my Thane, is as a book where men
May read strange matters"
(Shakespeare, Macbeth, I, v)

"From the earth thou springest
Like a cloud of fire"
(Shelley, "To a Skylark").

sjuzet. See fabula.

soliloquy. A solo utterance often by a character in a

play talking to himself or thinking aloud, as if there were no audience, e.g., Hamlet's "To be or not to be . . .".

sonnet. Poem of fourteen iambic pentameters. The two main forms are the Petrarchan (after Petrarch, 1304–74), consisting of an **octave** (eight lines usually rhyming *abbaabba*) stating the theme and a **sestet** (six lines using different rhymes in various patterns) commenting on the theme or modifying it; the Shakespearean, consisting of three quatrains (usually rhyming *ababcdcdefef*) presenting the theme and a final **rhyming couplet** (*gg*) summarising or clinching the theme. *See* **metre**, **quatrain** *and* **rhyming couplet**.

Spenserian stanza. Eight iambic pentameters followed by one iambic hexameter (or **alexandrine**, *q.v.*) rhyming *ababbcbcc*, as used in Spenser's *Faerie Queene. See* **metre**.

spondee. *See* **metre**.

sprung rhythm. Gerard Manley Hopkins' metrical system, dependent on measuring stresses and not on regular numbers of feet and syllables; hence, like the rhythms of common speech, written prose, music and folk poetry.

stanza. A formal arrangement of a group of lines of poetry, usually in a rhyming pattern.

stichomythia. Interchange of short, one-line speeches in dramatic verse, e.g., some of the dialogue between King Richard and Queen Elizabeth in Shakespeare's *King Richard III*, IV, iv.

story. A tale, or the general, complete action of a narrative work, ranging more widely than the **plot** (*q.v.*).

stream of consciousness. Term coined by the philosopher William James (1890) to denote the unending, formless flow of human thoughts and emotions. Some novelists, e.g., James Joyce and Virginia Woolf, have conveyed this "stream" by various techniques (e.g., loose syntax and light punctuation) in order to explore the consciousness of their characters.

strophe. The first section of the Greek **chorus** or the **Pindaric Ode** (*q.v.*).

structuralism. As applied to literature, a complex form of textual analysis concentrating on formal linguistic and thematic patternings, as practised, for example, by Roland Barthes. *See* **J50**.

sub-plot. A plot of lesser importance but sometimes used as a parallel or foil to the main plot, e.g., the Falstaff-Prince Hal sub-plot in Shakespeare's *King Henry IV, Part 1. See* **plot**.

syllabic verse. Poetry written in metre measured by the number of syllables in each line, e.g., some of W. H. Auden's later verse.

syllepsis. A figure of speech in which one word has the same syntactical relationship to two or more other words but different meanings, e.g., The nymph may "lose her heart, or necklace, at a ball" (Pope, *The Rape of the Lock*). Sometimes synonymous with **zeugma** (*q.v.*).

symbolism. Artistic movement of the 1890s, mostly originating amongst French writers (e.g., Mallarmé and Valéry), using mystical, occult and magical images and musical, evocative language. More widely, the use of objects, actions, scenes and structures to represent or suggest significant themes and ideas in a literary work, e.g., the dust heaps and the Thames in Dickens' *Our Mutual Friend* and the rose, the tower, Troy and swans in Yeats' poetry.

synaesthesia. Combination of different sense impressions, as described in Baudelaire's sonnet, "Correspondances". They are often evoked in a single phrase, e.g., "dark music" (Isaac Rosenberg, "Louse Hunting") and "squealing light" (Edith Sitwell, "Gold Coast Customs").

syncope. The cutting short or contraction of a word, especially in poetic usage, e.g., "e'er" for "ever".

synecdoche. A figure of speech in which the part represents the whole or the whole represents the part, e.g., "the multitude of Coketown, generically called "the Hands' " (i.e., the factory-workers, Dickens, *Hard Times*) and "England" for "the English cricket team".

tercet. A three-lined stanza, particularly as used in **terza rima** (*q.v.*).

terza rima. Verse-form of three-lined stanzas rhyming *aba, bcb, cdc*, etc., as used in Dante's *Divina Commedia* and Shelley's "Ode to the West Wind".

tetrameter. *See* **metre**.

theme. The central idea or topic of a literary work.

threnody. A poem of lamentation. *See* **dirge** *and* **elegy**.

touchstones. Criteria of excellence in poetry provided by the "lines and expressions of the great masters", e.g., Homer, Dante, Shakespeare and Milton (Matthew Arnold's term and definition, "The Study of Poetry," 1880).

tragedy. "An imitation of some action that is important, entire, and of proper magnitude . . . effecting through pity and terror the correction and refinement of such passions" (Aristotle, *Poetics*). A drama that ends sadly, especially with the downfall of a flawed hero. *See* **catharsis**, **hamartia** *and* **peripeteia**.

tragi-comedy. A drama that mixes elements of tragedy and comedy, e.g., Shakespeare's *Measure for Measure*.

trimeter. *See* **metre**.

triolet. Verse-form of eight lines and two rhymes, in which the fourth line repeats the first and the eighth line repeats the second, popular with some late nineteenth century minor poets, including Austin Dobson.

triplet. Three rhyming lines, usually iambic pentameters, sometimes used for variation or emphasis in a poem of **rhyming** or **heroic couplets**.

trochee. *See* **metre**.

trope. A figure of speech in general.

unities. Theory partly deriving from Aristotle's *Poetics* and fully formulated by Castelvetro (1505–71) that a drama should conform to the three unities of Action (i.e., there must be no digressions), Time (i.e., the action in performance should correspond as nearly as possible to the duration of the action in real life) and Place (i.e., its scene should not change).

ut pictura poesis. "As a picture, so a poem", i.e., "a poem is like a picture", a much-discussed formulation by the Latin poet, Horace, in his *Art of Poetry*.

vers de société. Light, elegant verse dealing with people and behaviour in polite society, e.g., the poems of W. M. Praed.

vers libre. The same as **free verse** (*q.v.*).

verse. Originally a metrical line; more commonly, a stanza or versification and verse composition in general.

villanelle. Verse-form of five **tercets** (*q.v.*) and one **quatrain** (*q.v.*) with two rhymes. The first line ends the second and fourth tercet; the third line ends the first, third and fifth tercets; the first and third lines then end the final quatrain, e.g., William Empson's "Missing Dates."

zeugma. A figure of speech in which a single epithet or verb is applied to two substantives but is appropriate to only one of them, e.g., "See Pan with flocks, with fruits Pomona crowned" (Pope, *Windsor Forest*). Sometimes used to mean the same as **syllepsis** (*q.v.*).

III. SPECIAL TOPICS

THE PLAYS OF SHAKESPEARE

Shakespeare's plays are as alive and popular today as they have ever been with numerous productions by the Royal Shakespeare Company in Stratford-on-Avon and London, at the National Theatre, and at many theatres in all parts of the United Kingdom. One notable recent production at the National Theatre was *Antony and Cleopatra* with Alan Rickman and Helen Mirren in the title roles, directed by Sean Mathias (1998). Recent films include Franco Zeffirelli's *Hamlet* (1991), Kenneth Branagh's *King Henry V* (1989), *Much Ado About Nothing* (1993) and *Hamlet* (1997), Richard Loncraine's *King Richard III* (with Ian McKellen, 1995), Adrian Noble's *Midsummer Night's Dream* (1996), Trevor Nunn's *Twelfth Night* (1996), Baz Luhrmann's *Romeo and Juliet* (1996) and Al Pacino's *Looking for Richard* (1996). Recent BBC radio productions include *Twelfth Night* (1998) and *The Comedy of Errors* (1999). In 1998, listeners to the "Today" programme on Radio 4 voted Shakespeare the "Personality of the Millennium", and in 1999 Radio 3 ran a series on "Shakespeare 2000". The Prince of Wales published a personal selection from Shakespeare as a book, cassette and CD, entitled *The Prince's Choice* (1995). To celebrate the establishment of the International Globe Centre (planned by the late Sam Wanamaker and Theo Crosby) in Southwark, London, the Royal Mail issued a set of five postage stamps in 1995 depicting Elizabethan theatres. The film *Shakespeare in Love* won seven Oscars in 1999.

Many different, excellent editions are in print (the Oxford *Complete Works* (1988), for example, radically reconsidered textual matters), critical controversies are keenly pursued, and the discoveries in 1989 of remains of the Rose and Globe theatres in London added significantly to our knowledge of the Elizabethan theatre.

Life and Background

William Shakespeare, the third child and eldest son of John and Mary Shakespeare, was born in April 1564 in Stratford-on-Avon, where his father was a prominent citizen. He may have attended the grammar school in the town. In 1582, he married Ann Hathaway. They had three children: Susanna (b. 1583), and twins, Hamnet and Judith (b. 1585). Little is known about Shakespeare's youth, but in the early 1590s he established himself in London as an actor, poet and playwright. After about twenty years in the world of the London theatre, he seems to have retired to Stratford-on-Avon, where he died on 23 April 1616.

Shakespeare wrote and acted in a period of remarkable dramatic creativity. Among his contemporaries and near-contemporaries were Christopher Marlowe, Thomas Kyd, Ben Jonson, John Webster, John Ford, Francis Beaumont and John Fletcher. The London theatres at that time included the Rose, the Swan, the Globe and the Blackfriars, in which several actors' companies performed—Shakespeare was a member of the Lord Chamberlain's Men (later, the King's Men). The principal actors of the time were Richard Burbage (who acted the part of Hamlet, among many other Shakespearean roles), Will Kemp (a comedian, who acted Dogberry), Edward Alleyn (famous in Marlowe roles), and Richard Tarlton.

Publication and Chronology of the Plays

No authorial manuscripts of Shakespeare's plays exist although some scholars contend that part of the manuscript of *Sir Thomas More*, a late sixteenth-century play of unknown authorship, is in his hand. Eighteen of his plays were printed in separate Quarto volumes in his lifetime; a nineteenth, *Othello*, appeared in 1622. A few of these are called "Bad Quartos" because they print texts that are usually thought to be corrupt. *Romeo and Juliet* and *Hamlet* were printed in both "Bad" and "Good" quartos. In 1623, John Heminges and

Henry Condell, two of Shakespeare's fellow-actors, collected thirty-six of his plays in the so-called First Folio, "truly set forth, according to the first Original." They grouped the plays into three categories: Comedies, Histories and Tragedies. They omitted *Pericles* and *The Two Noble Kinsmen*, which were both partly written by Shakespeare. Some scholars now think that *Edward III* (1596) should be added to the canon. It has been included in *The New Cambridge Shakespeare* (1998). Editorial problems arise when discrepancies occur between the Quarto and Folio versions of a play (*e.g.*, *King Lear*) and when Shakespeare is thought to have collaborated with other playwrights (*e.g.*, in the two omitted plays and in *King Henry VI, Part 1* and *King Henry VIII*). Some editors and scholars have refined the three groups that Heminges and Condell made in the First Folio and have put some of the plays into more precise sub-groups. These are the "romantic comedies" (*The Merchant of Venice*, *Much Ado about Nothing*, *As You Like It*, and *Twelfth Night*); the "problem comedies" (*All's Well that Ends Well*, *Measure for Measure* and *Troilus and Cressida*); the "Roman Plays" (*Titus Andronicus*, *Julius Caesar*, *Antony and Cleopatra* and *Coriolanus*); and the "Romances" (*Pericles*, *The Winter's Tale*, *Cymbeline* and *The Tempest*).

The exact chronology of Shakespeare's plays cannot be determined but most scholars would agree that they could be roughly grouped as follows. The letters, C, H and T in brackets denote Comedy, History or Tragedy.

1592-4: *King Henry VI, Parts 1, 2, and 3* (H); *King Richard III* (H); *The Comedy of Errors* (C); *The Two Gentlemen of Verona* (C); *The Taming of the Shrew* (C); *Titus Andronicus* (T); *Love's Labour's Lost* (C).

1594-7: *Romeo and Juliet* (T); *King Richard II* (H); *A Midsummer Night's Dream* (C); *King John* (H); *The Merchant of Venice* (C).

1597-1600: *King Henry IV, Parts 1 and 2* (H); *King Henry V* (H); *Much Ado About Nothing* (C); *The Merry Wives of Windsor* (C); *As You Like It* (C); *Julius Caesar* (T); *Troilus and Cressida* (C/T).

1600-08: *Hamlet* (T); *Twelfth Night* (C); *Measure for Measure* (C); *All's Well That Ends Well* (C); *Othello* (T); *King Lear* (T); *Macbeth* (T); *Timon of Athens* (T); *Antony and Cleopatra* (T); *Coriolanus* (T).

After 1608: *Pericles* (C); *Cymbeline* (C); *The Winter's Tale* (C); *The Tempest* (C); *King Henry VIII* (H); *The Two Noble Kinsmen* (C).

It can be seen that up to 1600 Shakespeare wrote mostly comedies and histories (though *Romeo and Juliet* is one exception) and that his great tragedies appeared in the following eight years or so. As already noted, the first four plays in the post-1608 group are often called Romances. This term is used to denote their themes of loss, reunion and reconciliation and their use of "fantastic" elements. Some commentators have seen possible autobiographical significance in the different phases of Shakespeare's career but it is likely that changes in taste, literary fashion and theatrical conditions were also influential.

Form and Style

With the exception of *Much Ado about Nothing* and *The Merry Wives of Windsor*, Shakespeare's plays are written mainly in blank verse (*see* Glossary of Literary Terms **M20**). He also uses rhyme (especially to round off scenes, to convey axioms and moral advice and for songs). As time went on, he tended to use less rhyme and he developed more complex and varied blank verse. He generally uses prose for the speech of lower-class people (such as servants) and for reports of off-stage events, letters, and rapid exposition (*e.g.*, the three gentlemen's account of the identification of Perdita in *The Winter's Tale*, Act 5, Scene 2). His vocabulary of 20,000 words ranges from the learned to the vulgar and from the grand to the simple, often in juxtaposition (as in ". . . my hand will rather / The multitudinous seas incarnadine / Making the green one red" in *Macbeth*, Act 2, Scene 2). An outstanding feature of Shakespeare's language is his use of word-play and imagery, which can sometimes reveal important themes in the drama (as, for example, images of sickness and disease in *Hamlet*) (*see below*). Soliloquies are important (*see* **M25–26**) for the revelation of character and motive, especially in the tragedies (for example, those spoken by Brutus in *Julius Caesar*, Hamlet and Macbeth).

The plays vary in length, from *The Comedy of Errors* (which is the shortest, with 1,778 lines) to *Hamlet* (the longest, with 3,931 lines). Many of them are "mixed" in action, containing subplots (as in *King Henry IV, Parts 1 and 2* and *King Lear*) and both comic and tragic elements (*e.g.*, the porter in *Macbeth* and the melancholy expressed in *Twelfth Night*). They can also freely range in place and time (*e.g.*, Egypt and Rome in *Antony and Cleopatra* and the sixteen years that elapse in *The Winter's Tale*). The plays were often not divided into Acts and Scenes when they were first printed and stage-directions were minimal, and so the form in which we read the plays is largely the work of later editors. The convention is division into five Acts, with a climactic point reached at the end of Act 3. Most editors modernise the spelling and punctuation of the Quarto and Folio texts.

Shakespeare used various sources for his plays. Holinshed's *Chronicles* (1577), for example, supplied him with material for the Histories, *King Lear*, *Macbeth* and *Cymbeline* and he drew on Sir Thomas North's translation of Plutarch's *Lives* (1579) for the Roman plays. He sometimes combined sources, as in *A Midsummer Night's Dream*, where he seems to have used Plutarch, Ovid, Lucius Apuleius's *Golden Ass*, Chaucer, Spenser, Robert Greene and others. But he always transforms this material into his own imaginative creations.

The Globe Theatre: A Note

The Globe Theatre, in which several of Shakespeare's plays were performed, was built in 1599 on Bankside, London, where several other theatres existed at the time. It was jointly owned by the brothers Richard and Cuthbert Burbage and by other actors, including Shakespeare himself. It seems to have been a 20-sided polyhedron accommodating about 3,000 playgoers. It was accidentally burned down in 1613 but was rebuilt in 1614. Closed by the Puritans in 1642, it was pulled down in 1644. The foundations of the building were excavated in 1989 soon after the discovery nearby of the foundations of the Rose. In the 1970s and subsequent years, Sam Wanamaker (1919–93), the actor, and Theo Crosby (1925–94), the architect, conceived and designed a near-replica of the Globe. This new Globe was eventually built near the site of the original theatre using traditional materials (including oak, wooden pegs and thatch). Its completion was due to a grant of funds from the National Lottery. As with Elizabethan theatres, the reconstructed Globe, which can accommodate 1,400 playgoers, is open to the elements. It has a yard where members of the audience stand close to the stage and three galleries of seats. It is part of the International Shakespeare Globe Centre, which arranges exhibitions, lectures and other activities but which is as yet incomplete. Mark Rylance was appointed the Artistic Director of the Globe in 1995. It presents each summer highly successful productions of plays by Shakespeare and his contemporaries, which were first acted in theatres on Bankside.

Ten Favourite Plays

1. Romeo and Juliet

Written in 1594 or 1595, this tragedy was immediately popular, as shown by its appearance in Quarto editions in 1597, 1599 and 1609 (when two were published). The background to the play is the enmity between the Montague and Capulet families. Romeo, a Montague, falls in love with Juliet, a Capulet, and secretly marries her. Through a series of tragic happenings and misunderstandings,

Romeo, who thinks the drugged Juliet is dead, poisons himself. Consequently, she stabs herself. But the feuding families are reconciled over the dead bodies of the young lovers. A notable feature of the play is Shakespeare's use of a Chorus, who at the outset tells us that the "pair of star-crossed lovers" will meet their deaths and that this event, originating in the family feud, "is now the two-hours' traffic of our stage." The lyrical speeches of love and Mercutio's description of Queen Mab are celebrated passages of poetry. The Nurse is a vivid flesh-and-blood character who provides a down-to-earth contrast to the idealistic young lovers.

2. A Midsummer Night's Dream

This play was written at about the same time as *Romeo and Juliet* and printed as a Quarto in 1600. It is a comedy of love and misunderstanding set in a wood near Athens. Three plots are blended: the confusions experienced by four young lovers (Lysander, Hermia, Demetrius and Helena); the comic doings of Bottom, the weaver, and his fellow workmen; and the quarrel between Oberon and Titania, the Fairy King and Queen. These plots are framed by the nuptial ceremonies of Theseus and Hippolyta. Puck, the mischievous sprite, is an important agent in the action and speaks the Epilogue, which delicately indicates the dreamlike qualities of the play. As in *Romeo and Juliet*, musical, romantic poetry abounds (*e.g.*, Oberon's "I know a bank where the wild thyme blows" and the Fairies' song, "You spotted snakes with double tongue").

3. The Merchant of Venice

Probably written in 1596 or 1597, the play had "been divers times acted by the Lord Chamberlain his servants" before its publication as a Quarto in 1600. In order to lend money to his friend Bassanio, Antonio, the Merchant of Venice, borrows 3,000 ducats from Shylock, the Jew, agreeing to sacrifice a pound of his flesh if he cannot repay the loan. Bassanio needs the money to go to Belmont to try to win the hand of Portia. His mission is successful and subsequently Portia, disguised as a male lawyer, defeats Shylock's attempt to claim his "pound of flesh" from Antonio. Shakespeare's characterisation of Shylock is complex, since he is seen as both a cruel usurer and a man whose humanity transcends a racial stereotype ("If you prick us, do we not bleed?" as he himself asks). Portia has the independence and teasing wit that typify several Shakespearean heroines. The device of her man's disguise reminds us that only men and boys were allowed to act at that time (and also see the use of this device in *Twelfth Night*, **M29**).

4. King Henry IV, Parts 1 and 2

These plays were written in 1597 and 1598 and were published as Quartos in 1598 and 1600. In both, the King (who himself was seen leading a rebellion in *King Richard II*) is contending with rebellion from dissident noblemen and is ultimately successful through battle in maintaining his regal authority. His son, Prince Hal (later King Henry V), consorts with disreputable companions, the chief of whom is Sir John Falstaff, the fat and cowardly knight, who is one of the most famous of all Shakespeare's characters (he reappears in *The Merry Wives of Windsor*). The Prince has resolved, however, to reform and to renounce his friends. Loyalty (of subject to monarch and son to father) and honour, considered in various aspects, are underlying themes. The plays combine serious history, humorous and sardonic comments and events, and occasional poignancy. Besides Falstaff, the Prince and the King, the striking characters are Hotspur (in Part 1), Mistress Quickly (in Parts 1 and 2), and Justice Shallow (in Part 2).

5. Hamlet

Three versions exist of the play, which was probably written in 1600: Quartos of 1603 and 1604 and the Folio text. It is basically a "revenge tragedy," but its profundity and ambiguities arise from Hamlet's prolonged hesitations and reflections concerning the revenge he has been urged to take by the Ghost of his father, crystallised in his soliloquy, "To be or not to be". Fascinating interpretative problems include Hamlet's "madness", his not killing the King (his father's murderer) when at prayer, his treatment of Ophelia, and the scene of the "play within the play". These issues, along with Shakespeare's prolific invention of varied incidents, speeches and characters (*e.g.*, Claudius, the Queen, Ophelia, Polonius, Horatio and the First Gravedigger) have made the play perennially and universally popular. Above all, the character of Hamlet continues to intrigue us, perhaps because "it is *we* who are Hamlet," as William Hazlitt said.

6. Twelfth Night

It seems as if Shakespeare wrote the play in 1601, perhaps for a performance on Twelfth Night (6 January) that year. In this romantic comedy, which is tinged with sadness, Viola, disguised as a man, falls in love with her employer, Orsino, the Duke of Illyria, who is in love with Olivia. Malvolio, Olivia's Puritan steward, is tricked into believing that she is in love with him. Throughout these and other misunderstandings, runs a vein of deeply-felt love (as in Viola's self-description of a woman who "sat like Patience on a monument, / Smiling at grief " and in one of Feste's sad songs, "O mistress mine") and the tensions between appearance and reality. Broader humour is supplied by Sir Toby Belch and Sir Andrew Aguecheek.

7. Othello

Performed on 1 November 1604 before King James I in the Banqueting House at Whitehall, the play was probably written in the preceding twelve months. It is a tragedy based on the consuming power of jealousy and on the presence of apparently "motiveless malignity" (to use the words of Coleridge). Othello, a Moor, convinced by Iago that Desdemona, his wife, is guilty of infidelity with Cassio, smothers her in her bed. On discovering her innocence, he kills himself with a sword. Shakespeare's use of a compressed time-scheme, his portrayal of a black man as a noble and yet susceptible human being, and his disturbingly vivid personification of evil in Iago are among the technical and ethical problems raised by this unforgettable drama.

8. King Lear

This play, the most intense and overwhelming of Shakespeare's tragedies, was written in 1606 and printed in Quartos of 1608 and 1619. A different version appears in the First Folio. The aged King Lear, who impetuously disinherits his virtuous daughter, Cordelia, divides his kingdom between his other daughters, Goneril and Regan, who malevolently cast him out. Broken-hearted and accompanied by his Fool, he loses his reason on a storm-swept heath. Parallel to his evil treatment is that of the Duke of Gloucester, who is blinded by Cornwall, Regan's husband. By the end of the play, all the principal characters, except Edgar, Gloucester's son, have died. Lear's impassioned speeches, full of pity as well as bitterness, and Gloucester's expression of fatalism ("As flies to wanton boys are we to the gods; / They kill us for their sport") represent the profoundly tragic nature of *King Lear*.

9. Macbeth

The shortest of Shakespeare's tragedies, this is usually dated 1606. Influenced by the Three Witches' prophecies and urged on by his wife, Macbeth embarks on a course of murder in order to gain the crown of Scotland and then to establish his power. He is eventually killed by Macduff, and Malcolm, one of the murdered King Duncan's sons, succeeds to the kingdom. This is a play of relentless pace (sometimes acted without a break) that dramatises issues of ambition, kingly qualities, self-deception, the influence of the supernatural, and the nature of evil and conscience (revealed, for example, in Macbeth's soliloquies and in Lady Macbeth's sleepwalking scene).

10. The Tempest

Traditionally regarded as Shakespeare's farewell to the stage, the play was probably written in 1611. Unusually, it observes the unities of time and place. The exiled Prospero lives on an island with his daughter, Miranda, the airy spirit, Ariel, and the beast-like Caliban. Through his magical powers, he contrives the shipwreck of Alonso, the King of Naples, and others who belonged to his former courtly world and who were implicated in his banishment. After various complications and machinations, forgiveness and reconciliation ensue. Miranda will marry Ferdinand, the King's son, and Prospero renounces his magic. This is a romantic, supernatural and endlessly fascinating play, which blends coarse and delicate humour, resentment and love, and which finally instils feelings of satisfaction and happiness (as expressed in Miranda's exclamation, "O brave new world, / That has such people in it!")

Who's Who in Shakespeare

The following list is only a brief selection of the characters in the plays. Many of them are roles, however, that have much potential for varied interpretations by actors.

Angelo *(Measure for Measure)*. A "man of stricture and firm abstinence," whom the Duke, who is about to leave Vienna, has appointed his deputy. He condemns Claudio to death because of sexual immorality. But he tells Claudio's sister, Isabella, that he will reprieve him if she will yield to his desires: "Fit thy consent to my sharp appetite." Through the Duke's contrivance, Angelo sleeps with Mariana, thinking that she is Isabella. His misdeeds are exposed, but the Duke eventually pardons him.

Autolycus *(The Winter's Tale)*. A pedlar and pickpocket in Bohemia, who describes himself as "a snapper-up of unconsidered trifles." He sings two songs, "When daffodils begin to peer" and "Lawn as white as driven snow." Camillo, a Sicilian courtier, makes Autolycus exchange clothes with Florizel so that the latter can escape from Bohemia. In the guise of a gentleman, he frightens the Shepherd and his son into giving him gold, but after various turns in the plot he beseeches them to pardon his faults and to commend him to Florizel.

Beatrice *(Much Ado About Nothing)*. Leonato's niece, who is in love with Benedick, but continually teases and disparages him with witty raillery in many a "skirmish of wit." She tells Don Pedro: "there was a star danced, and under that was I born." In the end she agrees to marry Benedick: "I yield upon great persuasion."

Bottom *(A Midsummer Night's Dream)*. A weaver who with other workmen in the forest is preparing a performance of "Pyramus and Thisbe," an absurd and unintentionally comic production, which they act at the end of the play in front of Theseus and Hyppolita to celebrate their wedding. Although Bottom is given the part of Pyramus, he would have liked to be the lion, promising to roar "as gently as any sucking dove," if necessary. Through Puck's mischievous contrivance, his head is transformed into an ass's head and Titania, the Fairy Queen, falls in love with him, until Puck removes the spell.

Brutus *(Julius Caesar)*. One of the conspirators against Julius Caesar. Although he has no "personal cause" to oppose him and is tortured by anxiety, he thinks that Caesar must be killed before he becomes too powerful. He strikes the last blow when the conspirators stab Caesar to death, causing Caesar to exclaim, "Et tu, Brute?" When the conspirators are defeated by the forces of Antony and Octavius at the Battle of Philippi, Brutus kills himself upon his sword. Antony recognises Brutus's idealistic motives for his actions: "This was the noblest Roman of them all."

Cleopatra *(Antony and Cleopatra)*. The Queen of Egypt, no longer young, between whom and Mark

Antony there exists mutual passionate love. Enobarbus, one of Antony's friends, testifies to her attractions: "Age cannot wither her, nor custom stale / Her infinite variety." After Antony's forces are defeated, he accuses her of betraying him in battle. She sends word that she has committed suicide and he therefore attempts to kill himself. Badly wounded, he dies in her presence, leading her to declare that "The crown o' th' earth doth melt." Soon afterwards, Cleopatra commits suicide by applying two poisonous snakes to her body.

Cordelia *(King Lear).* The youngest daughter of King Lear, whom he disinherits when she is unable to make a public profession of her love for him. But unlike her two sisters, Goneril and Regan, Cordelia sincerely and deeply loves her father. She marries the King of France. After her father has been cast out and then brought to the French camp in England, she kisses him as he lies asleep and expresses her pity and distress. On waking, King Lear addresses her as "a soul in bliss." Cordelia and Lear are imprisoned, and Edmund orders her to be hanged. His reprieve comes too late. Lear appears with Cordelia dead in his arms, desperately hoping that she is still alive.

Coriolanus *(Coriolanus).* A Roman general, whose name is given to him in honour of his capture of Volscian town of Corioli. Always contemptuous of the plebeians of Rome, he is banished from the city by the Tribunes, who think that he seeks "tyrannical power." In revenge, he leads the Volscians against Rome, but spares the city after yielding to the pleas of his mother, Volumnia, and his wife, Virgilia. Aufidius, the Volscian leader, accuses him of treachery, and he is stabbed to death by conspirators. Just before his death, he proudly recalls that "like an eagle in a dove-cote, I / Fluttered your Volscians in Corioli."

Dogberry *(Much Ado About Nothing).* A constable, who has Verges as his second-in-command, both of whom are inept. Their arrest of Borachio and Conrade helps, however, to reveal Don John's plot against Claudio and Hero. Dogberry is notable for his comic verbosity, especially for the malapropism, "Comparisons are odorous."

Falstaff, Sir John *(King Henry IV, Parts 1 and 2; King Henry V; and The Merry Wives of Windsor).* A fat knight given to drinking and boasting, who is a close friend of Prince Hal, the heir to the throne. But when the latter becomes king (as Henry V), he casts Falstaff off. In *King Henry V*, Mistress Quickly movingly reports the death of Falstaff: "his nose was as sharp as a pen, and 'a babbled of green fields." Shakespeare makes Falstaff the hero of *The Merry Wives of Windsor*, in which he is the victim of a number of tricks and escapades.

Faulconbridge *(King John).* King Richard I's illegitimate son, who is known as the Bastard. He plays an active part in most of the principal events in the play, but at the same time is an ironical commentator on proceedings, with the function of a Chorus, as in his reflections on "Commodity, the bias of the world."

Fool *(King Lear).* King Lear's court jester, whose joking and witty remarks indicate the King's own foolishness in trusting Goneril and Regan. At the same time, the Fool expresses his pity and love for his master, as in his words when the King, on the heath, bitterly apostrophises the storm: "Good nuncle, in; ask thy daughters' blessing. Here's a night pities neither wise men nor fools." He abruptly leaves the action in Act 3, Scene 6, saying "And I'll go to bed at noon," and is heard of no more. King Lear's "And my poor fool is hanged!", which occurs in his final speech, may refer to him or to Cordelia.

Hal, Prince See *King Henry IV, Parts 1 and 2* in Ten Favourite Plays, above, and Henry V, below.

Hamlet. See *Hamlet* in Ten Favourite Plays, above.

Henry V *(King Henry V).* Having put off his "madcap" way of life on succeeding to the throne, the King is praised at the opening of the play by the Archbishop of Canterbury as someone "full of grace and fair regard." He leads his army against the French and on the eve of the Battle of Agincourt wanders in disguise among his men. His stirring speeches at the siege of Harfleur and at Agincourt are among the most famous in Shakespeare's works: "Once more unto the breach, dear friends" and "This day is called the feast of Crispian." In contrast, there is his courtship of the French Princess Katherine.

Hotspur *(King Richard II and King Henry IV, Part 1).* Henry Percy, a son of the Earl of Northumberland, is a fiery opponent of King Henry IV and hence also of his son, Prince Hal. To Hotspur, honour and fighting are all-important, an attitude mocked by Hal. But it is the Prince who kills him at the Battle of Shrewsbury and pays him tribute: "This earth that bears thee dead / Bears not alive so stout a gentleman."

Iago See *Othello* in Ten Favourite Plays, above.

Imogen *(Cymbeline).* The beautiful and virtuous daughter of King Cymbeline and the wife of Posthumus, who when he is banished for secretly marrying her boasts that Iachimo will be unable to seduce her. Although she remains virtuous, Iachimo convinces Posthumus that he was successful. Posthumus then plans to have her murdered, but after her various wanderings and ordeals all is happily resolved in a final scene of revelation and reconciliation.

Jaques *(As You Like It).* A lord attending the banished Duke in the Forest of Arden. He is called "the melancholy Jaques," and is given to moralising. He weeps over the death of a deer killed by hunters and (in his own words) "can suck melancholy out of a song, as a weasel sucks eggs." His best-known reflections are on the "seven ages" of man: "All the world's a stage, / And all the men and women merely players."

Katherina *(The Taming of the Shrew).* Baptista's eldest daughter, "renowned in Padua for her scolding tongue." But Petruchio, who is determined to marry her, eloquently woos her. After their marriage, he takes various actions to subdue her. In her final speech, she lengthily discourses on the need for women to "serve, love, and obey."

Lear See *King Lear* in Ten Favourite Plays, above.

Leontes *(The Winter's Tale).* The King of Sicilia, who irrationally and falsely accuses his wife, Hermione, of infidelity with his friend, Polixenes. When a baby daughter is born to her, he has the child (later named Perdita) cast into the wilderness and Hermione brought to trial for adultery. After the death of Mamilius, his son, and the reported death of Hermione, which seem to confirm the judgement of the oracle, Leontes is repentant. Sixteen years afterwards, Hermione and Perdita are both restored to him.

Macbeth See *Macbeth* in Ten Favourite Plays, above.

Malvolio *(Twelfth Night).* Olivia's puritanical steward, who (in her words) is "sick of self-love" and tastes "with a distempered appetite." He rebukes Sir Toby Belch, Sir Andrew Aguecheek and Feste, the clown, for their boisterous merrymaking. With Maria, the waiting woman, they trick him with a forged letter into believing that Olivia is in love with him and contrive to have him locked up for apparently mad behaviour. When he is released, he declares that he will be revenged on "the whole pack" of them.

Nurse *(Romeo and Juliet).* Juliet's garrulous and down-to-earth nurse, who fondly reminisces about the heroine's early childhood: "Thou wast the prettiest babe that e'er I nursed." She acts as a messenger between Romeo and Juliet, but when Romeo is banished she urges Juliet to marry Paris. When she finds Juliet unconscious after drinking Friar Laurence's potion, she is distraught and announces her apparent death to her parents.

Ophelia *(Hamlet).* The daughter of Polonius and sister of Laertes, both of whom warn her against Hamlet's professions of love. Hamlet frightens her with his strange actions and bitter words. After her father is killed by Hamlet, she becomes mad – "divided from herself and her fair judgement," in the words of Claudius. She sings strange, poignant songs and distributes flowers: "There's rosemary, that's for remembrance." She falls into "the weeping brook," where she drowns.

Pandarus *(Troilus and Cressida)*. Cressida's uncle, who is her and Troilus's go-between in their love-affair. He is a commentator on the action of the play. Troilus twice contemptuously calls him a "broker-lackey."

Polonius *(Hamlet)*. The Lord Chamberlain at the court of King Claudius and the father of Laertes and Ophelia. He gives sententious advice to Laertes when the latter is about to leave Denmark, including "Neither a borrower nor a lender be." He watches and reports on Hamlet's actions. When hidden in the Queen's closet in order to overhear Hamlet's conversation with his mother he is killed by Hamlet, who thrusts his sword through the arras.

Prospero See *The Tempest* in Ten Favourite Plays, above.

Richard II *(King Richard II)*. Because of the King's arbitrary and unjust actions, Henry Bolingbroke, whom he had banished from England, returns at the head of a rebellion against him. Richard is deposed and Bolingbroke becomes King Henry IV. He is imprisoned in Pomfret Castle, where he is killed by Sir Pierce of Exton and servants. Richard indulges in self-pity and imaginative soliloquies, as when he hears of the calamities that have befallen his cause: "For God's sake let us sit upon the ground / And tell sad stories of the death of kings."

Richard III *(King Richard III)*. As the Duke of Gloucester at the beginning of the play, he bitterly refers to his physical deformity and is "determined to prove a villain." He has the Duke of Clarence killed. He is declared King after the death of King Edward IV and arranges the murder of the two Princes in the Tower (one of whom is Edward V). On the eve of the Battle of Bosworth, the ghosts of the many he has had killed and of his wife, Anne, appear to him. In the battle, Richard desperately cries, "A horse! a horse! my kingdom for a horse!" He is killed by Richmond, who becomes King Henry VII.

Rosalind *(As You Like It)*. Having been ordered by Duke Frederick to leave the court, she goes, with Celia, to seek her banished father in the Forest of Arden. Both girls are disguised as men. Orlando, who is with the exiled Duke in the forest, is in love with Rosalind. Various misunderstandings and deceits occur because of her disguise, but all these are eventually resolved. She is high-spirited, witty and teasing: "men have died from time to time and worms have eaten them, but not for love."

Shylock See *The Merchant of Venice* in Ten Favourite Plays, above.

Timon *(Timon of Athens)*. An excessively generous citizen of Athens, surrounded by flatterers, who take advantage of him. When he loses his money, nobody will help him. He becomes a bitter misanthrope, railing upon all humanity and cursing the destructive power of gold. The epitaph on his gravestone describes him as one "who alive all living men did hate."

CLASSIC CHILDREN'S LITERATURE

Introduction

A number of events in the 1990s reminded us of the importance of children's literature. Ann Thwaite's biography of A. A. Milne was published (1990); the centenaries of the births of Richmal Crompton and Enid Blyton were commemorated in 1990 and 1997 respectively; the 125th anniversary of the publication of Lewis Carroll's *Alice in Wonderland* and the 50th anniversary of Puffin Books were

celebrated in 1991. 1998 saw the sixtieth year of publication of the *Beano*, one of the most popular of children's comics. The Post Office issued stamps depicting characters from favourite children's fiction (1993), scenes from Enid Blyton's books (1997), and characters from classic fantasy books for children (1998). But many famous children's authors died during the decade, including Roald Dahl (1990), Eve Garnett (1991), Dr Seuss (1991), Rosemary Sutcliff (1992), Janet Ahlberg (1994), Ian Serraillier (1994), Norman Hunter (1995), P. L. Travers (1996), the Reverend W. Awdry (1997) and Geoffrey Trease (1998).

Early Books

Nursery rhymes, fables, folk stories, and ballads have been familiar to countless generations of children, either orally or printed in chapbooks and broadsheets. In his *Children's Books in England* (1932; revised by Brian Alderson, 1982), F. J. Harvey Darton claims that the first book that set out to entertain children was *A Little Pretty Pocket Book* (1744), published by John Newberry. But until well into the nineteenth century it was assumed that children's books should be instructive and moralistic. Examples include Isaac Watts's *Divine and Moral Songs for Children* (1715), stories and periodicals by Mrs Sarah Trimmer in the late eighteenth century, John David Wyss's *Swiss Family Robinson* (1812–13, translated and adapted in various English versions), poems and stories by Jane and Ann Taylor in the early nineteenth century, Mrs Sherwood's *The Fairchild Family* (1818, and later), and Dean Farrer's *Eric; or, Little by Little* (1858). Some adult fiction was thought suitable for children: Bunyan's *Pilgrim's Progress* (1678, 1684), Defoe's *Robinson Crusoe* (1719; see **M4**) and Swift's *Gulliver's Travels* (1724). Shakespeare was available in Charles and Mary Lamb's *Tales from Shakespeare* (1807) and in the Reverend Thomas Bowdler's *Family Shakespeare* (1818).

With the advent of child-centred views of juvenile upbringing and education (influenced by Rousseau and Wordsworth, among others), children's literature increased in quantity and importance as the nineteenth century went on. Entertainment and the appeal to the imagination became prominent, although many authors still retained a moral purpose. Adventure, nonsense, fantasy, and school and family stories were all popular from the 1840s onwards.

Marryat and Ballantyne

Two of the first writers of adventure fiction were Frederick Marryat (*see* **M6**) and R. M. Ballantyne. Marryat completed four books for children: *Masterman Ready* (1841–42), *The Settlers in Canada* (1844), *The Mission* (1845), and *The Children of the New Forest* (1847). His unfinished book, *The Little Savage*, was completed by his son, Frank Marryat (1848–49). The most popular of these novels, *The Children of the New Forest*, is set at the end of the Civil War. It is realistically detailed and varied and exciting in its incidents, which concern the fortunes of an orphaned, Royalist family of four children. Ballantyne, who wrote over one hundred books, often set his stories in exotic and dangerous places, with boys as the heroes. *The Young Fur Traders* (1855), *The Coral Island* (1858), *Ungava* (1858), *Martin Rattler* (1858), and *The Gorilla Hunters* (1861), written in a vivid and exciting manner, have always been widely read. Other hugely successful writers in this *genre*, at different levels of sophistication, were G. A. Henty, R. L. Stevenson, and Rider Haggard (*see* **M11**), who were all active at the end of the nineteenth century.

Nonsense and Fantasy Stories

Nonsense and fantasy also appeared in different forms at about the middle of the century. The Grimms' *Fairy Tales* began to be published in English as early as 1823, and Hans Andersen's in the 1840s. Edward Lear's *Book of Nonsense* (1846), *Nonsense Songs* (1871), *More Nonsense* (1872), and *Laughable Lyrics* (1877), illustrated by himself, contained limericks and such comic verse as "The Owl and the Pussycat" and "The Jumblies". John Ruskin's short fantasy, *The King of the Golden River* (written 1841; published 1851), with illustrations by Richard Doyle, tells the story of two wicked brothers, Schwartz and Hans, and the triumph of a third, good brother, Gluck. William Makepeace Thackeray's *The Rose and the Ring* (1855), subtitled *A Fireside Pantomime for Great and Small Children*, is one of his Christmas stories; it is a humorous version of traditional pantomime stories, complete with Fairy Blackstick, a fairy godmother (*see* **M7**). Dickens wrote his light-hearted *Holiday Romance* (1868) for children. (In more serious vein he had written *A Child's History of England* in 1851–3) (*see* **M6–7**). Charles Kingsley's *The Water Babies* (1863), full of colourful, exuberant detail and containing moral and social comment, recounts the adventures of Tom, the little chimney-sweep, who is metamorphosed into a water baby. Kingsley had already written *The Heroes* (1856), a retelling of the Greek legends of Perseus, Jason and the Argonauts, and Theseus (*see* **M8**). Most famous of all were Lewis Carroll's *Alice's Adventures in Wonderland* (1865) and *Through the Looking Glass; and What Alice Found There* (1872), illustrated by John Tenniel. These two books owe their perennial freshness to their inventiveness, wit, and precise prose; they are free from solemnity, moralising, and didacticism. Alice is a remarkable young heroine for her time, charming and resourceful, with no sentimentality in Lewis Carroll's depiction of her. As well as the nonsense verse and parodies included in the Alice books, Lewis Carroll wrote other verse, notably *The Hunting of the Snark* (1876), illustrated by Henry Holiday. Other Victorian fantasies and fairy stories included Jean Ingelow's *Mopsa the Fairy* (1869), George MacDonald's *At the Back of the North Wind* (1871) and *The Princess and the Goblin* (1872)—both illustrated by Arthur Hughes, and Mrs Molesworth's *The Cuckoo Clock* (1877). At the end of the century, Andrew Lang published many volumes of collected fairy tales, beginning with *The Blue Fairy Book* (1889).

Stories of School and Family Life

As well as adventure and fantasy, realistic kinds of children's fiction were popular in the Victorian period. The most celebrated of all school stories appeared in 1856: Thomas Hughes's *Tom Brown's Schooldays*, which with memorably realised characterisation and events recounts its hero's life at Rugby school during Thomas Arnold's headmastership. At the same time, it sought to inculcate moral, manly virtues, although it was not so sentimental as *Eric; or, Little by Little*, mentioned on **M31**. Later, Talbot Baines Reed specialised in writing school stories, serialised in the *Boy's Own Paper* (founded in 1879). *The Fifth Form at St Dominic's* (1881) is the best-known, and innumerable books in the same vein by other writers have been subsequently produced. Between 1906 and 1946, Angela Brazil wrote over fifty set in girls' schools. Then there were the novels of family life, usually among middle-class households. One of the earliest of these was Catherine Sinclair's *Holiday House* (1839), a delightful story of mischievous children. But again we turn to the 1850s and after for their appearance in large numbers. Examples include Charlotte Mary Yonge's *The Daisy Chain* (1856), Mrs Ewing's *Jackanapes* (1833), and Mrs Molesworth's *Carrots— Just a Little Boy* (1876). Louisa May Alcott's novels of American family life just after the Civil War are still deservedly popular: *Little Women* (1868–69), *Good Wives* (1871), *Little Men* (1871), and *Jo's Boys* (1886). Contemporary with these were the equally popular American stories of Susan Coolidge (the pseudonym of Sarah Chauncy Woolsey), including *What Katy Did* (1872), *What Katy Did At School* (1873), and *What Katy Did Next* (1886). Mark Twain's *Tom Sawyer* (1876) and *Huckleberry Finn* (1884) had a wide readership in Britain.

The "Golden Age"

At the turn of the nineteenth and twentieth centuries, children's literature flourished so remarkably that some consider the period to have been a "golden age". Frances Hodgson Burnett, whose *Little Lord Fauntleroy* (1885) first appeared in the USA and was a sensational success, wrote a number of books for children, of which *The Secret Garden* (1911), illustrated by Charles Robinson, is regarded as her masterpiece. At the same time, E(dith) Nisbet's were appearing. Some were fantasies (*e.g. Five Children and It*, 1902) but others were realistic, including her stories of the Bastable family, such as

The Railway Children (1906), illustrated by C. E. Brock. This was the period, too, of J. M. Barrie's play, *Peter Pan* (1904), which he rewrote in book form as *Peter and Wendy* (1911), illustrated by F. D. Bedford. Rudyard Kipling (*see* **M11–12**) wrote *The Jungle Book* (1894), *The Second Jungle Book* (1895), *Stalky and Co* (1899), the *Just So Stories for Little Children* (1902), *Puck of Pook's Hill* (1906), and its sequel, *Rewards and Fairies* (1910), an astonishing variety of books, all of which have become classics of children's literature. Animals, in her delicately painted pictures and taut prose, were the characters in Beatrix Potter's books, which began with *The Tale of Peter Rabbit* (1901) and continued with such favourites as *The Tailor of Gloucester* (1903), *The Tale of Benjamin Bunny* (1904), and *The Tale of Jemima Puddle-Duck* (1908). Animal characters formed the cast of yet another classic of this period: Kenneth Grahame's *The Wind in the Willows* (1908), which featured Mole, Ratty, and Mr Toad. It was later illustrated by E. H. Shepard. Two dramatised versions have increased its fame: A. A. Milne's *Toad of Toad Hall* (1930) and Alan Bennett's *The Wind in the Willows*, first staged in 1990 at the National Theatre. Contemporary works from America were very popular: Frank Baum's *The Wonderful Wizard of Oz* (1900), Kate Douglas Wiggin's *Rebecca of Sunnybrook Farm* (1903), and L. M. Montgomery's *Anne of Green Gables* (1908).

Verse and Periodicals

Verse at this time included R. L. Stevenson's *A Child's Garden of Verses* (1885), the poems in Kipling's books, Belloc's various collections (such as *The Bad Child's Book of Beasts*, 1896), and Walter de la Mare's *Peacock Pie* (1913). Cheap periodicals were easily available—Billy Bunter appeared in *The Magnet* (founded in 1908) in stories by Frank Richards (the pseudonym of Charles Hamilton). In the field of non-fiction, Arthur Mee's *Children's Encyclopaedia* (first issued 1908–10) was a landmark. Covering a wide range of subjects, including science, literature, and history, and copiously illustrated, this work appeared in a number of subsequent editions until the 1950s. If we add to all these works in prose and verse the adventure stories by Henty, Haggard, Stevenson, and Conan Doyle (*see* **M11**) we can have some idea of the variety and quality of children's literature in the Edwardian period.

Twentieth-Century Children's Literature

In considering children's literature in the twentieth century, this survey has to be increasingly selective, so numerous and varied have become the publications. At the present time, over 8,000 titles, including reprints and new editions, are published annually, to say nothing of periodicals. Two of the most popular authors between the wars produced fantasies and realistic books respectively: Hugh Lofting, whose *Story of Doctor Dolittle* (1922) was followed by many others in the same series, and Arthur Ransome, whose *Swallows and Amazons* (1930) was also followed by stories of a similar kind, featuring children enjoying themselves in sailing.

The outstanding author of the period was A. A. Milne, creator of Winnie-the-Pooh and Christopher Robin. His four phenomenally successful books were two collections of verse, *When We Were Very Young* (1924) and *Now We Are Six* (1927), and two collections of stories, *Winnie-the-Pooh* (1926) and *The House at Pooh Corner* (1928). Despite occasional whimsicality, they are elegantly written and humorously inventive. E. H. Shepard's drawings complement Milne's text as inseparably as Tenniel's illustrations complement Lewis Carroll's *Alice* books. Richmal Crompton's *Just William* (1922), illustrated by Thomas Henry, was the first of a long series of books about her mischievous and subversive hero; the last appeared in 1970. Writers of adventure stories in the interwar period included Percy F. Westerman and Captain W. E. Johns, the creator of Biggles, though their outlook is sometimes considered jingoistic nowadays. Young children could enjoy Joyce Lankester Brisley's *Milly-Molly-Mandy* (1928), Alison Uttley's *Little Grey Rabbit* (1929), and Kathleen Hale's *Orlando the Marmalade Cat* (1938). Other notable books of the period, which retain their popularity, are Erich Kästner's *Emil and the Detectives* (1929; translated into English, 1931), P. L. Travers' *Mary Poppins*

(1934; illustrated by Mary Shepard: filmed in 1964 with Julie Andrews in the title role), Noel Streatfeild's *Ballet Shoes* (1936), Barbara Euphan Todd's *Worzel Gummidge* (1936), J. R. Tolkien's *The Hobbit* (1937), and Eve Garnett's *The Family from One End Street* (1937). As for poetry, children could read Walter de la Mare's anthology, *Come Hither* (1923), verse by Rose Fyleman and Eleanor Farjeon, and T. S. Eliot's *Old Possum's Book of Practical Cats* (1939).

Puffin Books, Enid Blyton and others

A significant event in the history of children's literature in Britain was the foundation of Puffin Books in 1941, which made available a wide variety of fiction, non-fiction and verse in the form of inexpensive, attractive paperbacks. Many of the works mentioned in this survey have been published in the series—the first Puffin was *Worzel Gummidge*.

Enid Blyton dominated the post-war world of children's books with her prolific production of school and adventure stories (*e.g., The Naughtiest Girl in the School*, 1940, and the "Famous Five" and "Secret Seven" series) and her Noddy stories, among much else. Her undemanding, innocuous fiction has been deplored by educationalists, but there is no gainsaying her popularity over the past fifty years. The 1940s also saw the debut of another author whose books have become a household word: the Reverend W. V. Awdry's *Thomas the Tank Engine* was published in 1946. Just over ten years later came the first appearance of another favourite: Michael Bond's *Paddington the Bear* (1958). Besides Enid Blyton, other writers continued to produce school stories, of which *Jennings Goes to School* (1950) by Anthony Buckeridge was one of the most notable.

In the middle years of the century a number of children's books achieved a high reputation for their qualities of imagination and literary style. These include the historical novels of Rosemary Sutcliff (*e.g., The Eagle of the North*, 1954) and the varied work, both fiction and non-fiction, of Geoffrey Trease (*e.g., Cue for Treason*, 1940). There were the fantasies conjured up in C. S. Lewis's Narnia books, beginning with *The Lion, the Witch and the Wardrobe* (1950); Mary Norton's *The Borrowers* (1952), and its successors; and Philippa Pearce's *Tom's Midnight Garden* (1958). William Mayne's *A Swarm in May* (1955), Maurice Sendak's *Where the Wild Things Are* (1963), and Alan Garner's *The Owl Service* (1967) are also admired by discerning critics. Dr Seuss's lively but carefully structured readers for young children began with *The Cat in the Hat* (1957); he wrote 47 books, which have sold more than 100 million copies in 18 languages.

Illustrated Books

Other international bestsellers are books containing the two serial strip cartoons from Belgium and France respectively: Hergé's *Tintin* and Goscinny and Underzo's *Asterix*. There is also the series of illustrated French books, which began in 1931, featuring Babar the elephant, created by Jean de Brunhoff and continued by Laurent, his son. Raymond Briggs's stories in pictures, such as *Fungus the Bogeyman* (1977), have a wide appeal.

Artists played a vital role in the production of children's books. Besides those mentioned in this survey, distinguished illustrators have included Randolph Caldecott (1846–86), Walter Crane (1846–1915), Kate Greenaway (1846–1901), Arthur Rackham (1867–1939), W. Heath Robinson (1872–1944), Mabel Lucie Attwell (1879–1964), and Edward Ardizzone (1890–1979). Present-day artists include Charles Keeping, Brian Wildsmith, John Burningham and Nicola Bayley.

Roald Dahl and others

The most popular children's author today is Roald Dahl, who published an amazing variety and quantity of fiction and verse, often illustrated by Quentin Blake. His first books included *James and the Giant Peach* (1961) and *Charlie and the Chocolate Factory* (1964); his last, posthumously published, was *The Minpins* (1991), illustrated by Patrick Penson. Prominent among authors for younger children are Allan and Janet Ahlberg. Salman Rushdie's *Haroun and the Sea of Stories* (1990),

written for his son, was adapted for the stage in 1998.

During the past forty years, some excellent anthologies of poetry have appeared: Janet Adam Smith's *Faber Book of Children's Verse* (1953), Eleanor Graham's *Puffin Book of Verse* (1953), Peter and Iona Opie's *Oxford Book of Children's Verse* (1973), Seamus Heaney and Ted Hughes's *The Rattle-Bag* (1982) and *The School Bag* (1997), Brian Patten's *Puffin Book of Twentieth-Century Children's Verse* (1991) and Neil Philip's *New Oxford Book of English Verse* (1996).

The Library Association's Carnegie Medal for children's fiction, first won in 1936 by Arthur Ransome, was awarded in 1998 to Tim Bowler, for his novel, *River Boy*. Best-selling authors in 1998 included Michael Rose, J.K. Rowling (for the Harry Potter stories), R.L. Stine (for the Goosebump stories) and Jacqueline Wilson.

SCIENCE FICTION WRITING

Introduction

Science fiction is a kind of popular fiction, which exists in written, visual and aural forms as books, films, and comics, or on television and radio. The term developed from 'scientifiction', a coinage of editor Hugo Gernsback in *Amazing Stories* (April 1926) to denote 'the Jules Verne, H. G. Wells and Edgar Allan Poe kind of story—a charming romance intermingled with scientific fact and prophetic vision'.

Whilst science fiction has roots in European literature, it has been predominantly produced by writers from the United States. These writers form a community which—in dialogue with their readers—produces fiction and criticism in a sort of on-going conversation, as ideas and plot devices are debated and recycled. Like most genres, the reader familiar with science fiction's particular set of conventions will find it easier to read than a novice will, each reader relating it back to her own history of reading. For much of this century science fiction has been dismissed as simple entertainment, but this is unfair. Science fiction poses the question 'what if?', and the answer tells us much about the world that we live in by depicting one in which we do not. At its best it is not about the future: it is in fact about the present.

Some Science Fiction Scenarios

Science fiction often enables the writer to explore human nature in extreme circumstances, by confronting it with the nonhuman. Disaster novels like John Wyndham's *The Day of the Triffids* (1951) in which carnivorous plants attack the mostly blinded population of Britain, show the instinct of humanity for survival. In the more adventurous novel, e.g. J. G. Ballard's *The Drowned World* (1962), such catastrophes are embraced. The encounter with aliens reveals human nature more clearly: humanity is either transformed utterly or faces annihilation. Arthur C. Clarke's *Childhood's End* (1953) remains the classic treatment of the idea; more recently it has been the basis for Carl Sagan's *Contact* (1985) and Mary Doria Russell's *The Sparrow* (1996).

But successful communication with living aliens seems so unlikely that some writers have examined the impact of the discovery of alien artifacts (so-called 'Big Dumb Objects') instead. Examples include the huge spaceships of Clarke's *Rendezvous with Rama* (1973), the vast hollow-earthlike Dyson Sphere *Orbitsville* (1975) by Bob Shaw, and structures scattered across the galaxy in Jack McDevitt's *The Engines of God* (1996).

The arbitrariness of reality is demonstrated by alternate histories—best exemplified by the Nazi-occupied America described in Philip K. Dick's *The Man in the High Castle* (1962). Alternate histories also include England without a Reformation (Keith Roberts, *Pavane*, published in 1968) and an Aztec-ruled England (Christopher Evans, *Aztec Century* published in 1995).

Science Fiction: A Brief History

The use of imaginary lands to comment upon contemporary events and mores can be traced back at least as far as Plato's Republic. Later examples include Thomas More's *Utopia* (1516 and 1551) and

Jonathan Swift's *Gulliver's Travels* (1726). It was only with the rise of the realist novel, around 1800, that science fiction became distinguishable from general literature: the fantastical fictional events drew verisimilitude from the ideas of science, whilst distorting reality.

It has been argued that the first science fiction novel was Mary Shelley's *Frankenstein, or The Modern Prometheus* (1818), where recent medical speculations upon the nature of life were used to update the ancient myth. The same author, in her unjustly neglected *The Last Man* (1826), drew upon her grief at the death of members of her circle to portray global genocide in the twenty-first century. In the 1890s, H. G. Wells produced a number of what he termed 'scientific romances', where science again replaced magic as the driving force behind his narratives. *The Time Machine* (1895) and *The War of the Worlds* (1898) both drew upon evolutionary theory, as well as astronomy and other sciences.

Wells was not alone, as many writers of the period wrote works of proto-science fiction: Robert Louis Stevenson, *Strange Case of Dr Jekyll and Mr Hyde* (1886), Joseph Conrad and Ford Madox Ford, *The Inheritors* (1901) and Jack London, *The Iron Heel* (1907) being only the best known.

The Golden Age

Whilst many writers produced the occasional science fiction novel—and still do so today—an increasing number of professional science fiction writers were published in magazines such as *Amazing* and *Astounding Stories*, the latter edited by science fiction writer John W. Campbell Jr. Thus Campbell published the first stories of Isaac Asimov and Robert A. Heinlein who were to shape science fiction writing. Most science fiction then took the form of short stories or novellas in magazines, which could later be linked together in book form; the most famous of these is Asimov's *Foundation* trilogy (1942–58). It tells the story of a predicted collapse of the galactic empire, and the establishment of foundations to bring about the inevitable new galactic order. Predictions—and their limitations—were at the heart of the sequence.

As science fiction was a fiction led by ideas, style and characterisation were often neglected. The sheer speed of production was a factor in this. During the 1950s, under the tutelage of editors such as Horace Gold (*Galaxy*) and Anthony Boucher (*Fantasy and Science Fiction*), this began to change. Theodore Sturgeon, Alfred Bester, Robert Sheckley and others brought a new wit and maturity to the form. The most important writer to emerge from this period was Philip K. Dick, whose paranoid fantasies form a commentary on the Cold War as well as on the nature of reality, and who has grown in critical stature since his early death in 1982. His best known novel, *Do Androids Dream of Electric Sheep?* (1968), features a bounty hunter tracking down escaped androids masquerading as humans. Its meditations on what it is to be authentically human have rarely been bettered.

The New Wave and after

By the 1960s, a literary revolution was looming. In the United States novels such as Robert A. Heinlein's *Stranger in a Strange Land* (1961) and Frank Herbert's *Dune* (1965) became first campus cults and then mainstream successes. Meanwhile, in Britain, a group of writers centred on *New Worlds* and its editor Michael Moorcock had become tired with the clichés of bug-eyed monsters and outer space; they wanted to explore the inner space landscapes of psychology and the media. Brian Aldiss, *Report on Probability A* (1968), Norman Spinrad, *Bug Jack Barron* (1969), Ballard, *The Atrocity Exhibition* (1970) and others did just that, with some financial backing from the Arts Council. Back in America, Harlan Ellison assembled an anthology *Dangerous Visions* (1967) in an attempt to shatter the taboos against dealing with sex, drugs and violence in science fiction.

The new wave of science fiction cleared the way for writers to deal head-on with real-world politics. *The Female Man* (1975), by Joanna Russ, was published half a decade after being written. Its exploration of the treatment of women made uncomfortable reading for some, but it rightly became a classic. Ursula Le Guin investigated sexual

politics in *The Left Hand of Darkness* (1969) by inventing a species who were only gendered at certain times of their year. Samuel R. Delany, one of the few black writers in the field, produced a best-seller, *Dhalgren* (1975), which combined explicit sex with modernist techniques. Yet, in retrospect, the 1970s marked a slow decline in the market. Even the spectacular box office success of filmed science fiction in the shape of *Star Wars* (1977) seemed to be a retrograde step, taking the naïve sensibility of fifty-year-old science fiction as a model.

Cyberpunk

The 1980s were dominated by cyberpunk, a subgenre of science fiction inspired by William Gibson's *Neuromancer* (1984). Whilst Gibson remains the supreme poet of the information age, much cyberpunk—including his—had a nostalgic air. It mixed sub-Hammett plots with computer technology, seasoned also with designer drugs and a noir sensibility. Some writers became labelled in contradistinction to cyberpunk: the mock-Victorian science fiction of K. W. Jeter's *Infernal Devices* (1987), along with the work of his friends Tim Powers and James Blaycock, found itself dubbed steampunk.

Cyberpunk-flavoured novels dominated the 1990s. Jack Womack used an alternative universe in *Elvissey* (1993) in much the same way as others used cyberspace to comment upon the dilemmas of their created near-future worlds. Australian Greg Egan has investigated computers and personal identity to great effect in *Permutation City* (1994). Personalities downloaded into Copies experience life in a mathematically-created universe. Meanwhile, Kim Stanley Robinson produced the Mars trilogy (1992–96), a fusion of utopian Marxism, structuralism and planet building. Stephen Baxter combined physics with an increasingly assured sense both of character and plotting in *Voyage* (1996) and *Titan* (1997), alternate versions of the largely abandoned space programme.

The Future of Science Fiction

A threat to the future of science fiction lies in the apparent success of novelisations of films and TV series. It might be argued that writing a *Doctor Who* or *Star Trek* novel is the apprenticeship that earlier generations served in producing short stories for magazines. But many medium successful writers are now using novelisations to pay the rent. The formulaic formats mean that the events of each novel cannot alter the characters: they must remain the same for the next in the series.

Meanwhile, the genre is still dominated by American white male writers. Neal Stephenson is a good place to start: his *Snow Crash* (1993) is within the cyberpunk tradition. Jonathan Lethem's first novel *Gun, With Occasional Music* (1994) pays homage to Chandler and Swanwick has recast Faustus as a parable about technology in *Jack Faust* (1997).

British science fiction, partly bolstered by magazines *Interzone* and *BBR*, is as healthy as it was back in the era of *New Worlds*. Jeff Noon, beginning with the award-winning *Vurt* (1993), has used a near-future Manchester setting for his version of cyberpunk. Manchester-born, Belfast-based Ian McDonald has pastiched the style of diverse writers in a remix version of science fiction, but this enables him to discuss Ulster politics in novels such as *Sacrifice of Fools* (1996). Beginning with *Consider Phlebas* (1987), Iain M. Banks has played with spaceships in a galaxy-wide setting, but with a left-wing, utopian rationale. Fellow Scot, Ken MacLeod, explores left-wing politics in both historical and future settings in *The Stone Canal* (1996). Other British names to watch include Michael Marshall Smith, *Spares* (1996), straddling genres of science fiction, crime and horror, Colin Greenland, *Take Back Plenty* (1990), with a strong female lead, Paul McAuley, *Fairyland* (1995), a thriller set firmly in Europe and Peter F. Hamilton (whose The Night's Dawn Trilogy is epic in every sense of the word).

Women Science Fiction Writers

A large number of women writers are now being published. Octavia Butler continues to explore issues of race in her works, the best known of which is *Kindred* (1979). Gwyneth Jones uses the politics of an alien invasion to consider gender roles in a trilogy begun by *White Queen* (1991). Pat Cadigan has been able to make virtual reality seem part of everyday life in her fiction. *Fools* (1992) melds this with a spectacularly fractured use of identity and viewpoint. Nicola Griffith combines biochemicals with a women-centred plot and a strong sense of place in *Slow River* (1995). N. Lee Wood pairs a sophisticated android with a female journalist disguised as a man in her thriller *Looking for the Mahdi* (1996). In *Glimmering* (1997) Elizabeth Hand examines AIDS and the coming millennium.

The Science Fiction Community

Science fiction fans keep in touch through magazines produced by and for fans (fanzines), or by joining conventions and societies. This community enables an informal sifting of what should be read and what can be ignored. At the annual world convention, fans vote on the Hugo Award in various categories of length and media—the professional equivalents to these are the Nebula Awards. British fandom's most important award is the BSFA Award.

These are essentially popularity contests, as opposed to a number of jury-based awards given by professional amateur experts. These include the Arthur C. Clarke (for best science fiction novel published in Britain), the Philip K. Dick (for paperback originals) and the James Tiptree (for gender-orientated science fiction). On occasions, these can generate as much controversy as the Booker Prize.

Reviews and articles may be found in magazines such as *Asimov's* and *Interzone* and the academic journals *Extrapolation, Science Fiction Studies* and *Foundation;* the latter often includes contributions from professional writers. One way to keep up with developments in short fiction is to read the Gardner Dozois annual collection, *The Year's Best SF.* To gain an overview of the field join the British Science Fiction Association. Its magazines provide news, reviews, articles and tips for writers. Details are available from Paul Billinger, 1 Long Row Close, Everdon, Daventry, NN11 3BE, UK.

POSTWAR BRITISH THEATRE

Introduction

Huge social changes have taken place in Britain since the Second World War and, in content and form, the theatre has reflected, responded to and occasionally led those changes. The country emerged from wartime austerity still clinging to the remnants of 1930s theatre: a mixture of 'drawing-room' comedies, classical revivals and the poetic drama of Christopher Fry played to largely middle class audiences. But major social transformations were under way. The number of white-collar workers increased, working class communities began to be eroded, the nuclear family was enshrined as the ideal (with women isolated at home), and there was a steady expansion in the supply of consumer goods. Mass culture arrived with the growth of the popular music industry, the cinema (*see* **Section W**) and, most significantly, television (commercial television started in 1955). Popular theatre competed with the new cultural attractions in the 1950s and 1960s with a succession of big American musicals (*see* **Section E, Special Topic**). Rogers and Hammerstein's ground-breaking *Oklahoma!* (1943) had extended the range of the form and paved the way for a series of shows, from Bernstein's *West Side Story* (1957, with lyrics by Sondheim) to Michael Bennett's *A Chorus Line* (1975).

Theatre of the 1950s

In the 'straight' theatre of the 1950s, dominated by the West End management of H. M. Tennant, Terence Rattigan's reputation was high and Agatha Christie's *The Mousetrap* (1952) ran and ran. The first event to shake the *status quo* was Peter Hall's revolutionary staging in 1955, in London's tiny Arts Theatre, of Samuel Beckett's *Waiting for Godot.* Young, home-grown dramatists were also beginning to react against prevailing social values to create plays about current issues. The role of the English Stage Company was seminal. The appointment of George Devine as artistic director in 1956 began a long commitment by the Company to new and often controversial young writers. In 1956 Devine had the vision to stage a play which was a milestone in the history of the British theatre, John Osborne's *Look Back in Anger*, from which the new writers gained the name 'Angry Young Men'.

Some Major Developments

A conscious political decision gave an impetus of another kind to theatre both classical and experimental with the establishment of the Arts Council in 1946. It was a clear commitment to the theatre by the state. Other public support came through cultural festivals. The first Edinburgh International Festival of Music and Drama, held in 1947, and the Festival of Britain in 1951 were both significant events for the theatrical world. Both festivals revived the York cycle of mystery plays, which engaged whole communities, something which was explored further in the more political community theatre of the 1960s and 1970s: Joan Littlewood's Theatre Workshop at Stratford in East London, and Ann Jellicoe's productions in Devon and Dorset involving whole communities in the later 1970s and early 1980s.

Public funding at last allowed the National Theatre to be established at the Old Vic under the directorship of Sir Laurence Olivier in 1963, while the Royal Shakespeare Company (RSC) at the Aldwych, under Peter Hall, expanded its repertory to include plays by new dramatists such as Peter Shaffer, and with experimental directors like Peter Brook whose radical productions included Peter Weiss's *The Marat/Sade* (1964) and the famous *Midsummer Night's Dream* (1970) with actors on trapezes and juggling.

Changing Social Attitudes

In the 1960s and 1970s the state's legislative responses to changes in the family and in attitudes towards sexuality and gender (abortion, divorce and homosexual reform acts) marked a break with the social conservatism of the 1950s. These were decades of protest in the arts against what came to be known as 'the Establishment'. The culture of protest focused on the archaic censorship powers of the Lord Chamberlain. These were abolished in 1968, allowing shows like *Hair* and Kenneth Tynan's deliberately provocative *Oh, Calcutta!* to parade nudity on stage the same year. The result for more serious drama was that plays could be written and produced about almost anything. Edward Bond's *Saved*, which had fallen foul of the censor in 1965 and included the stoning to death of a baby on stage, was given its first public performance in 1969. Bond was one of a number of young writers dealing with contemporary society who were promoted through the 1960s and 1970s at the Royal Court; they included David Storey, Arnold Wesker and Howard Brenton.

Regional Theatre

Theatre flourished in the regions. Glasgow's Citizens' Theatre (founded in 1943) was revitalised in 1970 under the artistic directorship of Giles Havergal, while Frank Dunlop's career – from director of the Bristol Old Vic in the 1950s, to the Nottingham Playhouse in the 1960s and Director of the Edinburgh Festival in the 1980s – provides an example of its continuing vitality. During the 1970s, 'fringe' or alternative theatre developed: the Joint Stock Company, founded by William Gaskill, Max Stafford-Clark, David Aukin and David Hare in 1975, and the Monstrous Regiment (consisting mainly of women) were among a number of community, women's and multi-cultural theatre groups which sprang up and flourished along with the classical companies. Under the directorship of Trevor Nunn and Terry Hands the RSC opened studio venues at The Place and later Donmar Warehouse in London, the Other Place at Stratford, as well as continuing with major projects such as the staging of the Roman plays in 1972 and *Henry VI* in 1977.

Developments in the 1980s

In 1979 Mrs Thatcher became Prime Minister and instigated a decade and a half of monetarist policies, privatisation and the notion that 'there is no such thing as society'. There was a sharp decline in state support for the arts and the theatre was faced with major funding problems. Inevitably there was also a decrease in the number of alternative theatre groups, although many excellent low-cost touring companies appeared: the Black Theatre Co-operative (1979), Cheek by Jowl (1981), Theatre de Complicité (1983). The larger classical companies, the National Theatre, now transferred from the Old Vic to Denys Lasdun's three-in-one building on the South Bank (1976), and the Royal Shakespeare Company in its two theatres at the Barbican (1982), also had to review their finances. Private sponsorship had to be sought to replace subsidy in many cases.

A New Commercialism

Thatcherism's effect on the commercial theatre was marked: 'safe' revivals and blockbuster musicals, most of them written by Andrew Lloyd Webber – *Evita* (1976), *Cats* (1981), *Starlight Express* (1984) and *Phantom of the Opera* (1986) – which could ensure the return of a sponsor's investment and pull in the tourists, predominated. Under directors such as Trevor Nunn and Richard Eyre the RSC and the National presented a decade of brilliant productions featuring performances by some of Britain's leading actors and actresses. Trevor Nunn's *Nicholas Nickleby* (1980) and Eyre's *Guys and Dolls* (1982) were both triumphantly popular as well as technical and imaginative *tours de force*. In spite of this, at the end of the 1980s there was anxiety about the future for new plays and experimental theatre.

Developments in the 1990s

Established dramatists have continued to provide fresh theatrical experiences in the 1990s – exemplified by David Hare's trilogy of plays about religion, the law and politics and Stoppard's *Arcadia* and *Indian Ink*. Various directorial ventures have challenged the big classical companies – Declan Donnellan's Cheek by Jowl touring company (founded 1981), Kenneth Branagh's actor-run Renaissance (founded 1987) and Peter Hall's experiment with a revival of repertory theatre at the Old Vic in the mid-1990s. The RSC, because of

financial problems, has had to limit its seasons at the Barbican but the National Theatre is undergoing a 'facelift' for the late 1990s. The international reputation of British theatre is still high. Sam Wanamaker's recreation of Shakespeare's Globe, which finally opened in 1996, was a major achievement. But the financial problems of the 1980s continue to haunt the theatre and Lottery funding, designed to support new projects, cannot help to maintain current ones. In November 1997, *The Independent* newspaper reported that 100 small performing arts companies had closed since 1992. British theatre is one of the best in the world but a question mark hangs over it as the millennium draws near.

Prospect and Retrospect

The picture of the theatre in Britain today is radically different from what it was in 1945. A wealth of new writers has appeared who have tackled a huge range of subjects. Here the contribution of non-native talent (Brian Friel from Ireland, Edward Albee and Tony Kushner from America, for example) should not be forgotten. The rise of the director as a potent force – from Peter Hall and Peter Brook to Sam Mendes and Deborah Warner – what Ronald Harwood called 'the dictator among the democrats' – has emerged. British acting has transcended the RADA/West End school to include working-class, ethnic and disabled actors and actresses.

The strength of the British theatre in the last 50 years can be seen in its ability to innovate within a traditional framework. Strong new writing, directing and acting talents have been displayed within a framework of companies and the continuity they provide – from major ones such as the RSC, the National Theatre, and the English Stage Company to Ayckbourn's Scarborough and Declan Donnellan's Cheek by Jowl.

The companies have been able to move out into the popular commercial arena as well – Trevor Nunn's production of *Les Miserables* is a long-running West End hit and the National Theatre has promoted Sondheim (marginalised in the United States, but appreciated in Britain). Television and the theatre have interacted fruitfully. Dennis Potter's innovative TV dramas depended on theatrical breakthroughs in subject and form in the 1950s and 1960s and Ayckbourn's plays have been able to explore more deeply domestic dramas made familiar by television. But popular success is tied to commercial interests – which are not necessarily conducive to new and experimental work. The theatre has achieved much in the last half-century: can it produce something new for the twenty-first century?

DICTIONARY
OF
ART

This new section provides a concise introduction to the key terms and movements in the history of art. Readers may also wish to refer to Section B for biographical details of prominent painters and artists.

DICTIONARY OF ART

This glossary has been compiled for readers of *Pears* by Dr. Shearer West.

A

abstract art designates paintings, prints or sculptures in which the subject-matter is simplified or schematised to a point that its representational qualities are subordinate to its form and colour. The term is sometimes used loosely to indicate non-objective (*q.v.*) painting.

Abstract Expressionism, a term embracing a diverse group of artists (including Jackson Pollock and Willem de Kooning) working in New York during the 1940s. Their work emphasised the precedence of the creative process over the finished product, giving rise to the name Action Painting (*q.v.*). Although not an organised movement, Abstract Expressionism was influential in Europe and America.

academy, an official institution concerned with the training of artists and/or the promotion of art. Academies were initially a means of raising the social status of the artist, and they were often under aristocratic or royal patronage. The first art academies in Florence (founded 1563) and Rome (founded 1593) influenced the foundation of other academies throughout Europe in the seventeenth and eighteenth centuries, including France (1648) and England (1768), and in America in the nineteenth century. Academies were increasingly governed by a rigid set of hierarchies and a stultifying training programme, but they nevertheless exerted great influence in Europe and America until the mid-nineteenth century, when excluded artists (such as the Impressionists, **L64**) actively rebelled against their authority.

Action Painting is often used synonymously with Abstract Expressionism (*q.v.*), but it refers primarily to a method employed by artists such as Jackson Pollock. It involves applying paint to a canvas in a spontaneous manner, by allowing it to drip or splash. The term suggests that the process of painting itself is the primary concern of the artist.

aerial perspective, or atmospheric perspective, refers to a sense of depth created by gradations of colour, rather than by the strictly mathematical formulas of perspective (*q.v.*). From the seventeenth century, much landscape painting, including that of Claude (**B15**) and Turner (**B61**) relies on this method.

Aesthetic Movement does not refer to an organised group of artists. It classifies a general cultural tendency in late nineteenth-century England and, to a lesser extent, America, which encompassed a fascination with morbidity, decadence and sexuality. This cultivation of amorality included the idea of "art for art's sake", which allowed art to exist apart from any moral or didactic purpose. Oscar Wilde (**B64**) was the movement's most famous exponent, and the artists James MacNeill Whistler (**B64**) and Aubrey Beardsley (**B6**) were also considered "Aesthetes".

aesthetics is a branch of philosophy concerned with concepts of art and beauty. The term was coined in the eighteenth century when the questions of how people perceive art and why they respond to it were considered by theorists such as Johann Joachim Winckelmann, Gotthold Ephraim Lessing (**B38**) and Immanuel Kant (**B35**).

alla prima, Italian for "at first", is a method of oil painting which involves applying paint in one session. By avoiding the contrivance of preliminary underdrawing or underpainting, the artist can achieve by this method a sense of spontaneity. This technique was favoured by the Impressionists (**L64**).

altarpiece, an object placed on or behind an altar, usually in a church. Altarpieces generally contain painting or sculpture and devotional or Biblical scenes, which are intended to enhance the spiritual experience of the worshipper. The subject-matter of altarpieces usually consists of images of the Madonna and Child with saints and/or donors (*q.v.*), or scenes from the life of the Virgin or Christ.

aquatint is a process of engraving which produces tonal effects similar to those of watercolour. It was especially common in England from the late eighteenth century for topographical views, and it has since been used to different effect by such artists as Goya (**B28**) and Picasso (**B48**).

Armory Show, an exhibition held in a Regimental Armory in New York in 1913. The presentation of over 1000 works included Impressionism (**L64**), Post-Impressionism (**L98**) and contemporary European and American painting. It had a radical impact on the development of American modern art.

Art Brut was the name given by Jean Dubuffet to the art of schizophrenics, prisoners and other individuals producing art outside the official and formal institutions and training traditions of the art establishment. Dubuffet believed that such "unsweetened" or untrained art was superior to the contrived and socially controlled productions of "fine artists".

Art Deco. *See* **L10.**

Art Nouveau. *See* **L10.**

Arte Povera literally translates "impoverished art", and it was a term invented by the Italian art critic Germano Celant in the 1960s. It refers to a disposable and Minimal (*q.v.*) art composed of perishable and easily accessible items such as sand and newspaper. Its premise was to detach art from market forces by stripping it of its consumer value, although ironically *Arte Povera* now fetches high prices. Its adherents include Michelangelo Pistoletto and Mario Ceroli.

Arts and Crafts Movement. *See* **L10.**

Ashcan School, a name given retrospectively to a group of American artists who explored similar themes of city life between *c.* 1908 and the First World War. The original group was dominated by Henri Bellows, but it was later extended to include artists such as Edward Hopper. The name "ashcan" referred to the city dust-bins and thus evocatively defined the group's interest in the ugly side of city life.

assemblage is a term often used to define a work of art which has been constructed from a variety of found (*q.v.*) materials. It is the three-dimensional equivalent of collage (*q.v.*).

atelier is the French word for studio, but it refers more specifically to nineteenth-century studios in which a nude model was provided for artists to paint. This type of informal setting was also called an *atelier libre* (free studio), because unlike official art schools, it was open to all. Somewhat confusingly, *ateliers* were also known as academies (*q.v.*), the most notable of which was the Académie Julian, where Matisse (**B41**) studied. Although professional artists usually provided tuition, *ateliers* often functioned without instructors.

attribution, a claim that a work is by a specific artist, based on stylistic and documentary evidence.

automatism is the process of producing a work of art or literature "automatically", or without the intervention of conscious thinking. It was favoured by Surrealist (**L116**) artists, who felt that they could use it to tap important subconscious thoughts. Joan Miró and André Masson used this technique most effectively, but only as a starting point for a work of art. The Abstract Expressionists (*q.v.*) embraced automatism more wholeheartedly, especially through the method of Action Painting (*q.v.*).

avant-garde is generally used in reference to art of the late nineteenth and early twentieth centuries, although it is employed loosely for other periods of art history as well. It indicates art which is perceived as "progressive" or which challenges conventions or traditions. The concept helped perpetuate the Romantic notion of the artist as an individual working in opposition to inherited tradition.

B

baldacchino (baldachin), a canopy placed over an altar or a holy place, such as the location of a saint's relics. Although it could sometimes be a moveable object in holy processions, it was usually a fixed part of a church, as in Bernini's elaborate *baldacchino* in St. Peters, Rome.

Barbizon School. *See* **L14.**

Baroque. *See* **L14–15.**

Bas-Relief. *See* **L15.**

Bauhaus. *See* **L15.**

Biedermeier refers to German, Austrian and Scandinavian art produced between the time of Napoleon's defeat (1815) and the period of European revolutions (1848). Its name derives from a conflation of two characters in a satirical Munich magazine, and it is therefore meant to be slightly mocking or pejorative. It signifies a sentimental Realist (**L103**) style favoured by the increasingly prosperous middle classes, and practised by such artists as Ferdinand Waldmüller and Carl Spitzweg, especially in landscape and genre (*q.v.*) scenes.

biomorphic forms are abstract shapes based on organic sources such as plants. In painting and sculpture, biomorphism became popular with Surrealist (**L116**) artists such as Yves Tanguy and Jean Arp, who exploited its sexually suggestive nature.

bitumen is a brown pigment commonly used by English artists in the eighteenth and early nineteenth centuries. It contributes to the richness of a painting's tone, but it darkens over time and causes chemical reactions which ultimately damage the paint surface. *See* **craquelure.**

Blaue Reiter, Der (the Blue Rider) was a group of artists based in Munich who banded together in 1912 to challenge the academic conventions of contemporary art. Among their membership were Wassily Kandinsky and Franz Marc, who invented the name to signify their belief in the spiritual significance of horses and the colour blue. An interest in the "Geist", or the inner nature of man, governed their paintings and the themes of their only publications, the *Blaue Reiter Almanac* (1912). They sponsored two travelling exhibitions in 1912 and 1913 which brought together progressive tendencies in European art. Their interest in the spiritual qualities of line and colour made their work an important contribution to Expressionism (**L42**).

Bloomsbury Group, a group of British writers and artists most influential between *c.* 1910 and *c.* 1940. One of the members, Roger Fry (**B25**), organised the so-called "Post-Impressionist" exhibitions in 1911 and 1912 in which many works by Cézanne (**B14**), Van Gogh (**B61**) and Gauguin received their first English showing. Fry's insistence on the importance of colour and "significant form" influenced the work of Duncan Grant and Vanessa Bell and fostered an interest in decorative art best seen today in Grant's former Sussex home, Charleston.

bodegón is Spanish for "tavern". In art, it refers to a type of genre painting (*q.v.*) set in a kitchen and including still-life detail. Velásquez (**B61**) produced several *bodegones* early in his career.

bozzetto, Italian for "sketch", but, more precisely, a model for sculpture made in clay or wax, rather than a sketch for painting.

Brücke, Die (the Bridge), a German Expressionist group formed in Dresden in *c.* 1905. The four original members, Ernst Ludwig Kirchner, Erich Heckel, Karl Schmidt-Rottluff and Fritz Bleyl, were not trained artists, and they cultivated a crude, untutored style as a means of perpetuating their interest in non-European art. They had a strong social consciousness and hoped to foster changes in society through their art, although these ideas were never clearly articulated. Their most notable contribution was a revival of the woodcut (*q.v.*) technique. In *c.* 1911 several members of the group moved to Berlin, and

Kirchner began painting scenes of city life which stressed claustrophobia and corruption. Internal dissension led to the dissolution of the group in 1913.

burin, a tool used in engraving to cut into a metal plate. It is also called a graver. As it must cut directly into the plate, more forceful pressure is applied than is needed with an etching needle, which scratches into a resinous ground.

burr. In engraving, a metal shaving remaining after a plate has been cut by a burin (*q.v.*). In line engravings (*q.v.*) the burr is scraped away, but in drypoint (*q.v.*) it is often left to create furry tonal effects in the print.

C

Cabaret Voltaire was the night club in Zürich in which the European Dada (**L32**) movement began. During the First World War, artists and intellectuals who were pacifists or dissenters gathered in neutral Switzerland. Among this group, Tristan Tzara, Jean Arp and Hugo Ball staged a series of events at the Cabaret Voltaire in 1916 which were intended to express their outrage at the pointlessness of modern life.

cabinet pictures, small paintings originally intended to be hung in the limited confines of seventeenth-century Dutch bourgeois interiors. These paintings consisted primarily of still-life, landscape or genre (*q.v.*), and their emergence in seventeenth-century northern Europe signalled the new importance of a wealthy art-buying middle-class.

Camden Town Group, an organisation of English artists who broke from the New English Art Club (*q.v.*) in *c.* 1911. Following the example of Sickert's (**B55**) works, Harold Gilman, Charles Ginner and Spencer Gore concentrated on painting the ordinary or even ugly aspects of London life. The group was characterised by a common enthusiasm for Post-Impressionism (**L98**), which they helped to popularise in England.

camera obscura, Latin for "dark chamber", is a dark box in which an image is projected through a lens to allow artists to copy it easily. A precursor of photography, the camera obscura was used by such artists as Vermeer (**B62**) and Canaletto (**B12**) to facilitate a sense of spatial illusion and accuracy in their works.

caricature, a portrait in which characteristic features are exaggerated or distorted to produce a comic effect. The first true caricatures were made in seventeenth-century Italy by Annibale Carracci. Caricature was popular in eighteenth- and nineteenth-century England, where it became a vehicle for political satire in the hands of James Gillray (**B27**) and George Cruikshank (**B17**). German artists such as George Grosz and Otto Dix produced a more vicious form of political and social caricature during the 1920s.

cartoon today signifies a comic strip or children's animation, but in the sixteenth century, it referred to a preparatory drawing which was the same size as the finished work and which was used to plan out the work itself. Raphael's (**B50**) cartoons for tapestry (now at the Victoria and Albert Museum, London) are the most famous extant example.

cassone, Italian for "coffer" or "chest". In fifteenth- and sixteenth-century Italy, cassoni were used for marriage chests, and they were richly, if sometimes crudely, painted, usually with a mythological scene containing a theme of love or marriage.

chiaroscuro. *See* **L25.**

chinoiserie, European decorative designs based on Chinese ornamentation. Chinoiserie was fashionable during the Rococo (**L105**) period, especially prevalent in decorative arts, landscape gardening and architecture.

chromolithography, a type of colour lithography (**L75**) in which a separate plate is used to print each colour.

classicism, like its derivatives "classic" and "classical", is a term often used loosely and inaccurately to refer to the best example of a period or style. In its strictest sense, it signifies an emulation of ancient Greek or Roman art, or the conscious attempt to recall the order and harmony associated with ancient sculpture and architecture. *See* **Neo-classical style.**

cloissonism is used to describe the style adopted by Gauguin in the 1880s. It refers to the use of large patches of colour surrounded by outlines, which recall the effects of stained glass windows. The term originally referred to enamel painting.

collage, objects such as newspaper, string or cloth which are pasted onto paper or canvas. Although it had long been an amateur pastime, this technique was first employed seriously by Picasso (**B48**) in *Still Life with Chair Caning* (1912), which signalled a move away from his Analytical Cubist works, towards the creation of Synthetic Cubism (*see* **L31**). Collage was later used satirically or humorously in the works of the German Dada (**L32**) artists, such as George Grosz and Kurt Schwitters, and for its startling juxtapositions in the works of Surrealists (**L116**) such as Max Ernst.

Colour Field Painting was a style prevalent in America during the 1950s and involving artists such as Barnett Newman, Mark Rothko and Clifford Still. Although included under the umbrella of Abstract Expressionism (*q.v.*), these artists were concerned more with large expanses of pure colour than with the Action Painting (*q.v.*) technique of other Abstract Expressionists such as Jackson Pollock.

complementary colours are green, blue and violet. They are produced when two primary colours (*q.v.*) are mixed together. Green is the complementary of red as it is produced by mixing blue and yellow; blue is the complementary of orange, and violet is the complementary of yellow.

Conceptual Art is a product of the late 1960s. Artists rejected traditional methods of producing and displaying art, and relied instead on photographs, videos and language to take the place of easel painting. In Conceptual Art, the idea is more important than the finished product.

Constructivism, a Russian art movement initiated by Vladimir Tatlin in *c.* 1913. After visiting Picasso (**B48**) in Paris, Tatlin returned to Russia with the idea that a "culture of materials" could result in an art which had social purpose. However, subsequent Constructivists were divided between the concept of art as utilitarian and the idea that art should be pure form. The Russian Revolution in 1917 gave the movement new impetus, but it was condemned by the Soviets in 1922.

contrapposto is usually used in relation to Italian Renaissance painting and sculpture, although it has been applied more widely. It refers to a twisted torso posture which creates an elegant S-curve. Used most effectively by Michelangelo (**B42**) in his *David*, contrapposto became more elaborate and virtuosic in the hands of Mannerist (*q.v.*) artists such as Giambologna.

conversation piece, an informal group portrait, usually of a family or friends. Its precedents are in Dutch seventeenth-century group portraiture, but it became more popular in eighteenth-century England through the work of such artists as William Hogarth (**B32**) and Johan Zoffany. Conversation pieces usually showed a family or friends in a domestic interior or standing before a country seat, and they gave the effect of cultivated informality.

craquelure, a pattern of cracks which appear on the surface of a canvas when the paint deteriorates.

Cubism. *See* **L31.**

D

Dada. *See* **L32.**

Degenerate Art (**Entartete Kunst**), the name given by Hitler (**B31–2**) to art which he felt was produced by Marxists or Jews and/or which had a negative subject-matter that did not glorify the German people. He contrasted "Degenerate Art" with his favoured brand of Nazi realism, which idealised German Aryan character and culture. The contrast between these two forms was highlighted in 1937, when a "Degenerate Art" exhibition and a "German Art Exhibition" were held simultaneously in Munich. After these exhibitions, the "degenerate" paintings were either sold to raise money for Germany or destroyed. This label encompassed the art of most modern movements, particularly Expressionism (*q.v.*).

diorama, a type of large painting invented by Daguerre in 1822. Like the panorama (*q.v.*), the diorama contained effects of atmosphere which were achieved by using translucent canvas, movement and special lighting. Three-dimensional elements, such as real plants or animals were also employed to make the effects of dioramas more convincing. Dioramas were an accessible form of public entertainment in the early nineteenth century.

diptych can refer to a type of altarpiece created when two panels are hinged together. Unlike triptychs (*q.v.*) and other polyptychs (*q.v.*), diptychs were often small and used for private devotional purposes in the Middle Ages. *See* **L34.**

Divisionism, the name given to the theory developed by Seurat and others, which suggests that colour placed on a canvas unmixed will give the optical effect of being mixed. The technique of Divisionism has also been called pointillism (*q.v.*) or Neo-Impressionism (*q.v.*). Divisionism also refers to an Italian art movement of the late nineteenth and early twentieth centuries in which such an application of colour is employed.

donor, a person who has given an altarpiece (*q.v.*) or other devotional image to a church as a means of securing God's grace. The term is most appropriately applied to late Medieval and early Renaissance art in Italy and the North. Artists such as Jan van Eyck (**B23**) and Hugo van der Goes included portraits of donors in their altarpieces.

drip painting, a technique used by Jackson Pollock and other Abstract Expressionists (*q.v.*) which involves applying paint not with a brush but through other methods such as dripping or splashing.

drypoint, an engraving (**L40**) technique used from the late fifteenth century which is similar to etching in its method. To make a drypoint, a copper plate is cut directly, producing a burr (*q.v.*), which softens the tonal effect. This technique is often used in combination with others, but it has the disadvantage of producing only a limited number of impressions, before the burr is worn away.

E

Earthwork (**Land Art**), a dispersed tendency in art of the late 1960s, which involved using large expanses of natural spaces. Earth art employs the landscape for artistic purposes and thus opposes the sophisticated industrialisation of city culture. Examples of this genre, such as Robert Smithson's *Spiral Jetty* (1970), need to be seen from aircraft or by means of photography.

encaustic, an ancient technique of painting in which pigments are submerged in soft hot wax. Examples of the encaustic process can be seen on Egyptian mummy cases. Despite the allure of the technique, there have been very few successful attempts to revive it through the centuries.

Engraving. *See* **L40.** *See also* aquatint, drypoint, etching and mezzotint (**L82**).

etching, a print technique in which an acid resistant ground is cut by a thin metal pencil. Parts of the plate are then "stopped out" or covered with a protective material, and the plate is dipped into acid which eats away at the exposed areas. The technique is simpler and more spontaneous than engraving (**L40**) and produces more convincing tonal gradations.

Euston Road School, a group of artists who studied together in the late 1930s at the School of Drawing and Painting on Euston Road in London. The group included William Coldstream, Lawrence Gowing and Victor Pasmore, and they rejected Modernist abstraction and Surrealism (**L116–17**) in favour of a return to an impressionistic rendering of everyday life.

Expressionism. *See* **L42.** *See also* **Blaue Reiter, Der** and **Brücke, Die.**

F

fancy picture is a vague term, usually used to define late eighteenth-century English paintings with fanciful subject matter. Gainsborough's (**B25**) idyllic evocations of rural life and portraits of winsome "peasant" children were given this name by his critics. Fancy pictures, unlike genre (*q.v.*) paintings, are not concerned with the mundane aspects of daily life.

Fauvism. *See* **L43–4**.

feminist art history, a movement in art-historical scholarship since *c.* 1970 which involves a reassessment of both women artists and of how women were and are perceived in art. Feminist art history challenges the canon of male "genius" artists by questioning the male dominance of art academies and art criticism. Such dominance has caused both the exclusion of women from professional art training and the relegation of women to the subject-matter of painting, or merely the object of male desire. Feminist art history has also been concerned with conflicting problems of gender and class, and with sexual theories, including those of Freud (**B25**).

fête galante, or "courtship party", was a name given to the paintings of the French artist Watteau (**B63**) in the early eighteenth century. It refers to a number of courtly paintings by him which show groups of men, women and characters from Italian theatre.

Fontainebleau, School of indicates two "schools" of sixteenth-century European art. The first of these originated in the 1530s, when the French king, Francis I, hired Italian artists to decorate his new palace at Fontainebleau. Artists such as Rosso Fiorentino and Niccolo dell'Abbate produced an elegant, mannered style which was much imitated in painting, sculpture and the decorative arts. The second school of Fontainebleau was a later development of the first.

foreshortening, a use of perspective related to individual figures or objects, rather than space. Foreshortening was used during the Renaissance (*q.v.*) by artists such as Mantegna to show their command of illusionism.

found object (objet trouvé) refers to a natural or man-made object which is displayed as a work of art. Found objects are not made by artists, but artists sometimes use them as a starting point for a creative idea.

fresco. *See* **L46**.

frottage, a technique employed by Surrealist (**L116**) artists such as Max Ernst, which involves placing a piece of paper over an object and rubbing the paper with chalk or charcoal. The impression left on the paper was used as a starting point for a work of art.

Futurism. *See* **L47**.

G

genre means literally "type" or "kind", and it signifies the painting of ordinary people or everyday life. Various genre details began appearing regularly in fifteenth and sixteenth-century Netherlandish painting, the most notable examples of which was Pieter Bruegel's peasant subjects. Genre painting became a distinctive class of painting in seventeenth-century Holland, when a prosperous middle-class preferred such accessible images to abstruse historical subjects.

gesso, an absorbant ground (*q.v.*) used in Medieval and Renaissance (*see* **J45–6**) panel painting. Several layers of gesso were laid onto a surface before the paint was applied. Its brilliant white colour added to the luminosity of these paintings.

Glasgow School refers both to the "Glasgow Boys" and to the followers of Charles Rennie Mackintosh's art nouveau (**L10**) style. The former was a group of Scottish painters influenced by Whistler (**B64**) and the French Impressionists (**L64**) and working in the 1880s and 1890s.

glaze, a thin transparent layer of paint put over the canvas surface to create a luminous effect. Because the glaze is transparent, it allows layers underneath to shine through.

Gothic. *See* **L52**.

gouache, a type of watercolour in which the paint is opaque, rather than transparent. It was used commonly in medieval manuscript illumination (**L63**), but was less popular for topographical watercolours produced in the eighteenth and nineteenth centuries. It is also known as body colour.

Grand Manner refers to the elevated style associated with history painting (*q.v.*). It was discussed by Joshua Reynolds (**B51**) in his Royal Academy discourses of the late eighteenth century. Reynolds described the Grand Manner as an art which stressed general concepts as opposed to particular details.

grisaille paintings are executed in grey or monochrome. They were often meant to imitate sculpture and were commonly used on the closed panels of altarpieces (*q.v.*) to create an austere image appropriate for Lent or fast days.

ground, the substance placed on the surface of a canvas or panel on which the colours are painted. The ground comes between the canvas itself and the paint, and serves both to preserve the painting and create a more satisfactory visual effect.

Group of Seven, a group of Canadian landscape painters who exhibited together in the early 1920s and 1930s. It included Lawren Harris and A. Y. Jackson. Their aim was to create a specifically Canadian brand of modern painting, using familiar Ontario landscapes and an Expressionist (*q.v.*) colourism.

H

Happening, a seemingly spontaneous event, which takes on qualities of both art and theatre, although it is more ephemeral than art and less coherent than theatre. The term is applied to art of the 1960s which involved performance and required the presence of an audience.

hatching, the use of parallel lines drawn or painted close together to create tonal effects. Cross-hatching refers to the use of crossed lines for the same purpose.

Hellenic Art. *See* **L57–8**.

Hellenistic Art. *See* **L58**.

Hieratic Art. *See* **L59**.

history painting represents scenes from the Bible, mythology, ancient history or classical literature which have an elevated or moralising theme. The idea that history painting was the highest form of art was cultivated by the French Academy in the seventeenth century and the Royal Academy of England in the eighteenth.

Hudson River School, a loosely linked group of American artists, including Thomas Cole and F. E. Church, who practised in the middle of the nineteenth century. They painted mostly landscapes, concentrating on the more remote parts of the north-eastern United States, and they were influenced by the Sublime (*q.v.*) paintings of the English artists Turner (**B61**) and John Martin. Their emphasis on a specifically American landscape had a nationalist flavour.

I

icon, in Byzantine culture, a sacred image of Christ or saints. The reverence for such images often bordered on idolatry and led to the Iconoclastic Controversy of the eighth century. Icons were common in Greek and Russian orthodox churches, and the image itself was interpreted as an intercessor between the worshipper and the holy person depicted.

iconography, the study of signs and symbols in art, or the interpretation of subject-matter. This practice often involves a reductive unpicking of complex symbolism, and it requires a detailed knowledge of diverse religious, literary and classical sources.

Illuminated MSS. *See* **L63**.

impasto, paint applied thickly to the surface of the canvas so that the brush strokes themselves are noticeable. This technique was commonly used by artists from the nineteenth century as a means of emphasising the paint surface and thus drawing attention away from the illusionistic qualities of painting.

Impressionism. See **L64**.

intaglio, a term used to describe types of printing such as etching and engraving in which the design on the plate is incised. This is opposed to relief printing, such as woodcuts (q.v.), in which the raised portion creates the design.

International Gothic, a style of art that existed throughout Europe in the late fourteenth and early fifteenth centuries. The style was characterized by an aristocratic elegance and a combination of Gothic (**L52**) mannerism with a new interest in realistic depiction. The style was spread by itinerant artists, and is best typified by Gentile da Fabriano in Italy and the Limbourg brothers in France.

Intimisme refers to the scenes of domestic interiors painted by Edouard Vuillard and Pierre Bonnard (**B9**) in the late nineteenth and early twentieth centuries.

intonaco, the final layer of plaster onto which frescos are painted. It serves as a protective ground between the other layers of plaster and the paint itself.

J

Junk Art, or Junk Sculpture, was popular in the late 1950s, when artists began using rubbish and other rejected items of consumer culture to create works of art. Generally, Junk Art refers to assemblages (q.v.), such as those produced by Robert Rauschenberg.

K

Kinetic Art. See **L70**.

Kit-Cat in the early eighteenth century was a name given to a club of Whigs who met in a tavern overseen by Christopher Cat. In artistic terms, the name refers to a series of portraits painted by Godfrey Kneller (**B36**) which represented the Kit-Cat Club members. Kneller's innovatory works were larger than half-length portraits but smaller than whole-lengths, and through the inclusion of at least one-hand, they allowed a greater variety of posing than previous small portraits. Kit-Cat later came to refer to a portrait of this size (136″ × 28″).

Kitchen Sink School was a group of artists, including John Bratby, who produced Social Realist (q.v.) paintings after the Second World War. The name "kitchen sink" referred originally to the concerns of the "Angry Young Man" movement initiated by the playwright John Osborne in 1956. This cultural tendency embraced a strong working-class consciousness as well as post-war disillusionment.

L

lay figure, a jointed doll or dummy used by portrait painters especially in the eighteenth century. Lay figures could be manipulated to provide a diversity of poses, and they could be dressed to allow a more detailed study of costume. Their use reflected the general artificiality of portrait painting in eighteenth-century England and the need for short cuts to produce speedy results.

linocut, a woodcut (q.v.) in which the plate is made from linoleum rather than wood. The soft flexibility of the linoleum allows for an easier process of cutting and larger, bolder effects.

lithography. See **L75**.

Luminism is not a movement as such, but a name given to works produced by American landscape painters in the nineteenth century. Artists such as George Caleb Bingham and the painters of the Hudson River School (q.v.) produced panoramic views dominated by sky. Luminism is also characterised by smooth canvases in which no obvious brush strokes or paint surface could be detected. These qualities distinguished it from the visible brush strokes of the impressionists (**L64**).

M

Macchiaioli, I, a group of Italian artists working mainly in Florence between 1855 and 1865. The name refers to the *macchia* or patches of colour that they used in their paintings. They were influenced by the Barbizon School (**L14**), and their technique in many ways prefigured that of the Impressionists (**L64**).

Magic Realism refers generally to a type of painting which combines a realistic technique with fanciful or dream-like subject matter, as in the paintings of René Magritte and other Surrealists (**L116–17**). In its strictest sense, Magic Realism was a type of German realist art produced in the 1920s; it is contrasted with Verism (q.v.), and both are considered aspects of *Neue Sachlichkeit* (q.v.).

Mannerism, a sixteenth-century art movement, chronologically positioned between the High Renaissance (q.v.) and the Baroque (**L14–15**). Unlike these movements, the characteristics of Mannerism are less defined. Generally, Mannerist paintings are distinguished by their sophistication, artificiality and anatomical distortion. They include unusual or brash colours and sometimes their treatment of subject-matter is disturbing. Parmigianino and Giulio Romano (**B27**) produced works considered Mannerist, but the term is also applied to artists such as Tintoretto (**B60**) and El Greco. It has been used equally to refer to sixteenth-century architecture in which playful satires on classical forms are apparent.

maquette, a clay or wax model for sculpture.

Marxist art history was a development in art-historical scholarship which sought to align art with the economic and political conditions behind its production. Although Marx himself did not tackle the subject of aesthetics, art historians have applied Marx's ideas of class struggle and bourgeois/proletarian conflict to pictures. With the collapse of communism following the fall of the Soviet Union the term is no longer in common usage.

medium, strictly speaking, is the liquid, whether oil or egg yolk, used with colour pigments to make paint. In a more general sense, it refers to painting, sculpture, charcoal drawing or any other method used by an artist.

Metaphysical Painting (Pittura Metafisica), a name given to the work of Georgio de Chirico (**B15**) and Carlo Carrà. These two artists met in a military hospital in Ferrara in 1917, where they gave this name to paintings which avoided the mechanical nature of modernist movements such as Cubism (**L31**) in favour of a dream-like evocation of more spiritual concerns. Their works contained unusual combinations of images which were painted in a realistic style, and they employed methods such as perspective (q.v.) drawn from Italian Renaissance (see **J45–6**) painting. The dream imagery of de Chirico was especially influential on the Surrealists (**L116–17**), particularly those who practised Magic Realism (q.v.).

mezzotint. See **L82**.

miniature, a small painting, usually a portrait. The term originally referred to medieval manuscript illumination (**L63**), but by the sixteenth century, it was used to signify small pictures painted on card. Miniatures became especially popular for keepsake portraits in the eighteenth century, and they often parroted the currently fashionable styles of oil painting.

Minimal Art was a movement which began in the United States in the 1960s. As its name implies it involves art, usually sculpture, which is reduced to its most essential form. Examples tend to be assemblages (q.v.) composed largely of limited abstract shapes.

mobile, a type of sculpture popularised by Alexander Calder in the 1930s. Mobiles are composed of flat geometric shapes hung on string and wire and allowed to move, or are moved by mechanical means. If mechanical means are used, mobiles can be considered Kinetic Art (**L70**).

modello, a small preliminary painting used as a "try out" for a larger painting. Unlike sketches, which are often unfinished or merely summary, modelli prefigure the final painting in great detail. In the Renaissance (*see* **Section J**) they were used as a sort of advertisement by artists trying to convince patrons of the worth of their work.

monotype, as the name suggests, refers to a printing process whereby only one impression can be made from each prepared plate. Monotypes are created by painting in oils directly onto a copper plate and then pressing the plate onto a piece of paper. This process was popular with twentieth-century artists such as Chagall (**B14**).

montage, like collage (*q.v.*) involves the arrangement of diverse images together on a sheet of paper. But montage refers specifically to components which are complete in themselves (*see* **photomontage**), rather than abstract forms.

N

Nabis, the, a group of French painters who followed the Symbolist (*q.v.*) concerns of Gauguin. Between 1889 and 1899, Pierre Bonnard (**B9**), Edouard Vuillard and Maurice Denis explored the symbolic possibilities of colour first examined by Gauguin in 1888. They were particularly interested in the use of large patches of colour to convey spiritual intensity. *See* **cloissonism**.

naive art results from either a real or seeming lack of technical skill. This produces child-like images which offer a very literal form of Realism (**L103**). Paradoxically, naive art became popular in the late nineteenth and twentieth centuries, with the work of artists such as Le Douanier Rousseau (**B52**). A revival of interest in the simple expression of children's art which characterised modern movements such as German Expressionism (**L42**) may be partly responsible for this.

narrative art. *See* **L85**.

naturalism. *See* **L86**.

Nazarenes, a group of German artists who worked in Rome in the early nineteenth century. In 1809 Friedrich Overbeck and Franz Pforr formed an artistic organisation called the Brotherhood of St. Luke in Vienna. They carried their interest in the revival of religious art to Rome in 1810, where they moved into an abandoned monastery and were joined by other artists. They hoped to capture the spirit of the Middle Ages through historical and religious subjects, and they were instrumental in the revival of fresco (**L46**) technique. Their large-scale murals and historical scenes for the German ruling class led them to be associated with the intensification of German nationalism in the nineteenth century.

Neo-classical style. *See* **L86**.

Neo-Expressionism, or Bad Art, refers to an international art movement of the late 1970s and 1980s involving the revival of Expressionist (**L42**) concerns. The prominent artists include George Baselitz and Francesco Clemente.

Neo-Impressionism. *See* **L86**.

Neo-Plasticism was a name used by Mondrian for a type of art which avoids representation in favour of abstraction. Mondrian's principles resulted in canvases which consisted solely of primary colours, black and white, and horizontal and vertical lines. His intention was to create an art which could have meaning for everyone, but paradoxically, his works usually puzzle the uninitiated.

Neo-Romanticism is a British art movement which began before the Second World War. Artists such as John Piper and Graham Sutherland (**B58**) initiated a revival of interest in the Romantic landscape painting of William Blake (**B8**) and Samuel Palmer (**B46**). This concern for evocative native landscapes was a manifestation of pre-war nationalism.

Neue Sachlichkeit, Die (The New Objectivity), a name given by the art dealer G. F. Hartlaub to describe a diverse group of German artists who rejected abstraction during the 1920s. These artists all attempted to represent reality, either through a precise, detailed Magic Realism (*q.v.*) or a satirical and scathing Verism (*q.v.*). The first *Neue Sachlichkeit* exhibition was in 1923.

New English Art Club, an organisation formed in 1886 in reaction against the stale practices and politics of the Royal Academy. The members of this group, including Walter Sickert (**B55**) and Philip Wilson Steer (**B57**) were trained in France, and they preferred the informal *atelier* (*q.v.*) system of education to the rigid strictures of the Royal Academy Schools. Their work was influenced by Whistler (**B64**) and Jules Bastien-Lepage.

Newlyn School, the name given to a group of artists who congregated in Cornwall during the 1880s and 1890s. The group included Laura Knight and Stanhope Forbes, and they were particularly concerned with *plein air* (*q.v.*) painting.

Non-Objective Art is the correct name for what is usually called Abstract Art (*q.v.*). Its name suggests that the representational object has been obliterated, whereas "abstract" implies that the work of art is a simplification or modification of some real object.

Novecento Italiano, an Italian art movement of the 1920s which encouraged a return to the principles of Italian Renaissance (*see* **Section J**) art. The interest in the Italian past was more than simply a stylistic phenomenon, as it was strongly connected with the nationalist spirit of Fascism. The artists of the group included Mario Sironi and Achille Funi, and they held their first exhibition in the Pesaro Gallery, Milan, in 1922.

Novembergruppe, a group of left-wing Berlin artists formed in 1918. The members, including Max Pechstein, were committed to socialist principles and wanted an art capable of appealing to the masses. The name of the group came from the November Communist uprising in Berlin of that year.

O

objet trouvé. *See* **found object.**

Omega Workshops, a cooperative founded by Roger Fry (**B25**) in 1913 aimed at producing quality decorative art. The artists of the Bloomsbury Group (*q.v.*), such as Duncan Grant and Vanessa Bell, were involved, and they decorated furniture for a small number of patrons. The impracticalities of their enterprise led to the organisation's demise in 1920.

Op Art, an art based solely on perceptual or optical effects, which was particularly popular in the 1960s. Its practitioners included Bridget Riley.

Orphism (Orphic Cubism). In response to the monochromatic coldness of Cubism (**L30**), the artists Robert and Sonia Delaunay began producing paintings in which colour was fragmented in the same way that the Cubists broke up form. This prismatic treatment of colour was called Orphism by the poet Apollinaire in 1912. Orphism differs further from Cubism in its emphasis on movement and city life, qualities more obviously characteristic of Futurism (**L47**). Orphist paintings eventually became totally abstract, but the movement did not last beyond the First World War.

P

panorama, a circular painting placed inside a large cylinder, in which people can sit or stand. Panoramas could be walked around, or they were moved mechanically to create a sense of total environment. They were invented in Scotland in 1787, and they quickly became a popular form of entertainment. Their subjects included exotic scenes and Picturesque (*q.v.*) landscapes, but they also depicted recent military campaigns during the Napoleonic wars. This latter quality gave panoramas the value of reportage and enhanced their accessibility to a wider public.

papier collé. French for "pasted paper", a type of collage (*q.v.*) popularised by Braque from 1913. This involved gluing bits of wallpaper or newspaper to a canvas. This process became an important aspect of Synthetic Cubism (**L31**), and it was used by Matisse (**B41**) for his paper cut-outs.

pastel, a chalk composed of powdered pigments which produces delicate but fragile images. The soft quality of pastel became especially popular in eighteenth-century European portraits.

pentimento, bits of painting which become visible when the top layer of paint wears away. Often pentimenti signal an artist's earlier rejected experiments, and they are therefore used both as authentication and as a means of studying the processes of work stages of an artist.

Performance Art is a general term referring to a pseudo-theatrical event which is considered art. The agitational demonstrations of the Futurists (**L47**), the nonsense recitations of the Dadaists (**L32**) and the Happenings (q.v.) of the 1960s are all examples of this type of art.

perspective, a space-creating device used most frequently by Italian Renaissance (see **Section J**) artists. Linear or one-point perspective involves mathematically calculating a vanishing point where a series of parallel lines converge. In Renaissance painting, these lines are often created by floor patterns or carefully placed bodies, which lead the eye back into the picture to give a sense of depth. The creation of three-dimensional effects on a two-dimensional surface was particularly important for the Renaissance idea of optical illusionism, although the effect produced by perspective is only approximate to true visual experience. One-point perspective was used less frequently after the fifteenth century, but aerial perspective (q.v.) was commonly employed for several centuries afterwards.

photomontage, a type of montage (q.v.) consisting wholly or partly of photographs. This technique was common among the Berlin Dada artists (**L32**), who used photographs from fashion magazines and other forms of popular culture to make satirical attacks on the superficiality of Weimar society.

Picturesque, with a capital "p", is an aesthetic term coined in the eighteenth century to describe landscapes which looked "like a picture". Like the Sublime (q.v.), the Picturesque was said to instill emotions in the observer, who associated the sight of rough beauty, ruins or irregular landscapes with various sentimental or melancholy moods. In the 1790s the term became the focus of a heated aesthetic debate which included such participants as Richard Payne Knight and Uvedale Price. The growing popularity of Picturesque ideas inspired artists and amateurs to take Picturesque tours, especially in the Lake District and Wales, in order to discover the possibilities in rugged or unusual landscapes.

pietà (Italian for "pity"), a devotional image of the Virgin Mary with the dead Christ on her lap.

plein air (French for "open air"), refers to painting out of doors. Before the nineteenth century, landscape painters commonly produced their works in a studio from sketches or studies. The French Barbizon (**L14**) painters cultivated the opposing practice of painting outside—a method that was wholeheartedly adopted by the Impressionists (**L64**).

polyptych, an altarpiece (q.v.) with more than one panel, such as a diptych (q.v.) or triptych (q.v.).

Pop Art, a phenomenon of the 1960s and 1970s which involved transforming objects of popular culture into works of art. The movement started in Britain, when a group of artists at the Institute of Contemporary Arts began using images from comic books and advertising in their art. Pop art either attacks modern consumer culture or it glorifies it nostalgically. Its main practitioners were Peter Blake and Richard Hamilton in England and Andy Warhol in America.

Post-Modernism is a cultural phenomenon. From the end of the Second World War, the failure of Modernism in all of its manifestations was evident, and artists, architects and writers began seeking other solutions to the problems of contemporary life. Post-Modernism is not one style but many styles, and it is often self-referential, playful or parodic. The exact meaning of the term, and those works of art which fall within its parameters, are a subject of continual debate, but a number of post-war developments, such as Happenings (q.v.) could be seen to be in its sphere.

Post-Painterly Abstraction was a term invented by the critic Clement Greenberg in 1964 to refer to non-objective (q.v.) artists who were not members of the Abstract Expressionist (q.v.) movement. The paintings of Kenneth Noland, Frank Stella and others were considered to fall within this definition, as they painted canvases with large patches of colour and which were carefully planned, rather than spontaneous, as in Action Painting (q.v.).

predella, the panel or panels running along the bottom of an Italian Renaissance (see **Section J**) painting, and usually containing a series of narrative scenes to complement the main devotional subject of the altarpiece itself.

Pre-Raphaelite Brotherhood. See **L98–9**.

provenance records the whole history of the ownership of a painting, from its first commission or sale to its present location. A confident provenance is often used to authenticate a work of art, but it can be equally revealing about patterns of taste and art purchase through the centuries.

Purism was a reaction against Cubism (**L31**) which drew upon some of Cubism's methods. The term was coined in 1918 when Amédée Ozenfant's book *Après le Cubisme* rejected the "decorative" qualities of Cubist painting, which he felt did not respond properly to the needs of modern industrial society. Purist painters such as Charles-Edouard Jeanneret (Le Corbusier, **B37**) and Ferdinand Léger embraced this "machine aesthetic", but it was most influential on architecture.

putto, a fat naked boy used as a decorative addition to painting and sculpture, especially in the Baroque (**L14–15**) period.

R

Rayonism was a short-lived Russian art movement including the work of Mikhail Larianov and Natalia Goncharova. The ideas behind it were consolidated in the 1913 Moscow Target exhibition. In the exhibition catalogue, Larianov described Rayonism as a combination of Cubism (**L31**), Futurism (**L47**) and Orphism (q.v.). It involved the use of intersecting rays of light, and partial or total abstraction.

ready-made was a word used by the twentieth-century artist Marcel Duchamp to signify an object selected by an artist to be displayed as a work of art. The artist does not actually produce the work but merely presents it, thus changing the significance of an otherwise ordinary object. A ready-made is similar to a found object (q.v.), but it is less concerned with aesthetic values. The presentation of a ready-made in some ways undermines the whole process of production and display of art and should be considered as a somewhat cynical statement.

Realism. See **L103**.

relief. See **L104**.

Renaissance. See **J45–6**.

repoussoir is French for "to push back". It signifies an object, usually a tree, which borders the foreground of a picture and draws the eye deeper into the space of a painting. It is especially used in landscape paintings by artists such as Claude (**B15**), where it serves a primarily compositional purpose.

Rococo. See **L105**.

Romanticism. See **L106**.

S

sacra conversazione, a type of altarpiece (q.v.) which originated in fifteenth-century Italy. It consists of the Madonna and Child with a group of saints standing around her. It departs from the Gothic (**L52**) tradition of separating the Madonna from saints in polyptychs (q.v.), and it allows a greater apparent ease of association among holy figures.

St. Ives painters, a group of artists who congregated in St. Ives, Cornwall, in 1939. The group included Adrian Stokes, Barbara Hepworth and Ben Nicholson (**B45**). Unlike other such artistic colonies, this group was diverse in both style and subject-matter.

salon, a French organisation that promoted art exhibitions. In 1667 the first salon was the exhibition of works by artists of the Académie

Royale, shown in the Salon d'Apollon of the Louvre. There academic artists exhibited occasionally until 1737, when exhibitions became a biennial event. Art exhibitions were consolidated into the academic structure in the eighteenth century through the introduction of juries, who rejected paintings they did not feel appropriate for the Salon. After the French Revolution, the Salon was held every year and became increasingly important in the French art world until the 1860s, when it was challenged by alternative salons (see **Salon des Refusés, Salon d'Automne** and **Salon des Indépendants**).

Salon d'Automne, one of the salons formed in competition to the official academy Salon (*q.v.*). It began holding exhibitions from 1903, the most famous of which was the 1905 exhibition. This included works by Matisse (**B41**), Dérain and Vlaminck which started the "Fauvist" (*q.v.*) movement.

Salon des Indépendants, one of the salons formed in competition to the official academy Salon (*q.v.*). It began in 1884 on the initiative of the *Société des Artistes Indépendants,* which included among its membership Seurat and Signac. This Salon rejected the jury system of the official Salon and became a major showplace for Post-Impressionist (**L98**) painting.

Salon des Refusés, an alternative salon set up in 1863 to house all the paintings rejected by the official Salon (*q.v.*). It resulted from an intensification of the anger and discouragement of French artists whose works had been consistently rejected by the Salon. To appease them, Napoleon III allowed all rejected works to be exhibited separately. The exhibition induced much derision and distaste in a conservative public, but it became the starting point for a more considered reaction against the French Academy and the hegemony of the official Salon. Manet's (**B40**) *Déjeuner sur l'herbe* was one of the works shown here.

scumbling, when an opaque colour is applied over an already existing colour but allows the other colour to show through. Scumbling creates a textured or broken effect on the surface of the canvas.

Secession (Sezession), the name given to a series of rebellions against the academic system in Germany and Austria during the 1890s. Throughout Europe at this time, the limitations of academies were becoming apparent to artists who wanted to experiment with new methods, ideas and techniques. The Munich Secession was the first to express this sense of rebellion by turning away from academic classicism towards an art nouveau (**L10**) style. Closely following this were the Vienna Secession (beginning 1897), which was also sympathetic to art nouveau, and the Berlin Secession (from 1899) which encouraged an Impressionist (**L64**) style.

secco, Italian for "dry", a term applied to fresco painting. Usually in a fresco, the plaster is painted while wet, but the *secco* method involves waiting for the plaster to dry before painting it. In the Middle Ages and the Renaissance (*see* **Section J**), this technique was usually used for touching up a finished fresco. If it was used exclusively, it caused more rapid deterioration in the painting.

sfumato, Italian for "smoke", is a term used in the sixteenth century to signify gradations of colour and tone which avoided stark outlines. It was applied especially to the soft tonal effects of Leonardo da Vinci's (**B38**) paintings.

silk screen printing is also called seriography. It is a technique invented in the early twentieth century which involves masking a silk screen with pieces of paper or cardboard and then pressing colour through the screen onto a piece of paper beneath it. Although a skilled designer is necessary for a successful silk screen print, the actual process of making the print can be carried out by anyone.

sinopia, an earthy red-brown colour used to make a preliminary drawing for a fresco in the Middle Ages and the Renaissance (*see* **J45–6**). The sinopia was applied first, then covered by intonaco (*q.v.*), which was then painted. It served as a preparatory sketch over which the final painting could be constructed.

Sistine Chapel. *See* **L111**.

Social Realism, a type of Realism (**L103**) concerned not just with style but with subject-matter. The term is applied to paintings of the nineteenth and twentieth centuries which have social or political subtexts, especially of a Leftist variety. Social Realism possibly began with Courbet, whose unapologetic, even heroic, paintings of peasants were especially subversive during a period of political unrest in Europe (*c.* 1848–9). The term has also been used to describe the work of the American Ashcan School (*q.v.*) and the British Kitchen Sink School (*q.v.*).

Socialist Realism, as opposed to Social Realism (*q.v.*), had a very specific propagandist purpose. In its strictest sense, it signified the official art of the Communist USSR. It used a Realist (**L103**) style with proletariat subject-matter as a form of instruction to the people. From 1934 until the period of *glasnost,* it was the only official art of the Soviet Union.

Stijl, De, a Dutch art magazine which perpetuated the Neo-Plasticism (*q.v.*) of Piet Mondrian and Theo van Doesburg. The magazine began in 1917, and its articles stressed pure abstract or non-objective (*q.v.*) form in painting, sculpture and architecture. Its subsequent influence was primarily in the realm of architecture, and the ideas of *De Stijl* were particularly influential in reforming the Bauhaus (**L15**) when Doesburg visited it in 1923.

still-life, a type of painting which precludes the depiction of human beings and concentrates on everyday objects such as fruit or flowers. It was popularised in Holland during the seventeenth century, when its immediate appeal was appreciated by the art-buying middle-class, and it continued to be popular throughout the eighteenth and nineteenth centuries, when its most notable practitioners were Chardin (**B14**) and Cézanne (**B14**). Still-lifes (the accepted plural form) often took on emblematic or moralistic meanings, reflecting the vanity or transience of human existence, but despite their potential depth of meaning, they were considered the lowest category of painting by European art academies (*q.v.*). This relegation of still-lifes also accentuated the repression of women artists, as they were excluded from official training institutions and often painted solely still-lifes.

Sublime, a term which has an ancient origin but was brought into the realm of aesthetics during the eighteenth century. Edmund Burke's (**B11**) *Enquiry Into the Origins of Our Idea of the Sublime and the Beautiful* (1757) postulated an aesthetic category which engaged the emotions. The sublime involved a feeling of awe or terror inspired by overwhelming natural forces. Burke's writings were influential on the growth of Gothic novels, and they were later used to good effect in landscape painting by artists such as Turner (**B61**) and John Martin.

Superrealism (Hyperrealism, Photorealism) describes paintings of the 1970s onwards which attempted to evoke a photographic illusion of reality. In some cases, the artist actually copies a photograph.

Suprematism, a term invented by the Russian artist Kasimir Malevich to describe his non-objective (*q.v.*) paintings, such as *White on White*. The theory behind Suprematism is complicated and involves an attempt to articulate in visual terms a "fourth dimension". Malevich's first exercises in Suprematism occurred in 1913, and he officially christened the movement in 1915.

Surrealism. *See* **L116–17**.

Symbolism began as a literary term referring to French poetry of the 1850s, but in the 1880s and 1890s it was applied to painting. Symbolist artists rejected the tenets of Impressionism (**L64**), which they saw as too involved with perceptual response. Instead they concentrated on the representation of spiritual and subjective feelings, which often manifested themselves in religious or erotic subject-matter. Its French exponents included Puvis de Chavannes, Odilon Redon and Gustav Moreau, but the ideas of Symbolism soon spread throughout Europe.

Synthetism refers to the work of Gauguin's followers who, in the 1890s, produced paintings which included large patches of concentrated colour surrounded by black lines, as in Gauguin's *cloisonnism* (*q.v.*). The root word "synthesis" refers to Gauguin's idea that painting should represent a concentrated synthesis of the artist's emotions. Synthetist artists painted from memory, rather than copied the world before them as the Impressionists (**L64**) had done.

T

Tachisme is sometimes used synonymously with Abstract Expressionism (*q.v.*), but it strictly refers to a French movement of the 1950s which consisted of paintings composed of large blobs or *taches* of colour.

tempera, a painting technique used commonly by medieval artists before it was superseded by oil painting in the fifteenth century. Tempera is made by mixing powdered colour with egg yolk, egg white or the whole egg to create an opaque paint.

tondo, Italian for "round", is a circular painting or sculpture. *Tondi* were popular in fifteenth-century Italy.

triptych, an altarpiece composed of three panels hinged together. This is one of the most common types of altarpieces, as the two outer panels can fold together over the inner panel. The outer panels were thus usually painted on the inside and the outside to allow two different visual effects.

trompe l'oeil literally means to "fool the eye". It refers to a considered attempt at illusionism that makes it difficult to tell whether or not a painted surface is real. *Trompe l'oeil* devices were commonly used in ceiling painting, and they were employed by the Cubists (**L31**) to create an amusing dissonance between optical space and the perspective distortions of Cubist space.

V

varnish is usually painted or sprayed over a finished painting in order to preserve it. Although varnish will help the paint to remain stable, it often darkens over time and paradoxically can cause extreme damage to a painting's surface.

Verism was a name given to German *Neue Sachlichkeit* (*q.v.*) artists such as George Grosz and Otto Dix, who produced scathing, and often disturbing, satires on Weimar society during the 1920s.

Vorticism, a British art movement which began in 1913 on the initiative of Wyndham Lewis, Ezra Pound (**B49**) and Edward Wadsworth. The movement brought both Cubism (**L31**) and Futurism (**L47**) into England, as its practitioners were concerned with modern life as well as with the abrogation of the stale stability of established art. From 1914 the artists produced a magazine called

BLAST, and they held their only exhibition in 1915. The First World War dissipated their momentum.

W

Wanderers, The, a group of nineteenth-century Russian artists who attempted to carry their ideas to the country peasantry. Reacting against the elitism of the Imperial Academy of Arts in St. Petersburg, artists such as Ilya Repin established itinerant exhibitions to show their Social Realist (*q.v.*) paintings of Russian peasant life and Russian history. Founded in 1870, the Wanderers continued to exist until the early twentieth century.

watercolour, a technique of painting involving water soluble colours. Watercolour creates a transparent effect, as opposed to the opaque effect of gouache, (*q.v.*), which is particularly useful for landscape painting. It was used by Dürer (**B21**) in the early sixteenth century for landscape sketches, but it only became popular at the end of the eighteenth century with the growth of Picturesque (*q.v.*) tourism. The ease of using watercolour made it a particularly appropriate technique for amateurs.

woodcut, a print technique which involves cutting into a block of wood, inking the block and then pressing it onto a piece of paper. The raised portions of the wood create the design, and the cut portions read as white spaces on the final print. It is one of the oldest printing techniques, and it was used from the fifteenth century. It was superseded by the more efficient method of engraving (**L40**), but it was revived in the early twentieth century by the German Expressionists.

World of Art (**Mir Iskusstva**), a Russian art magazine and art movement which began in St. Petersburg in 1896. A group of students including Leon Bakst (**B5**), Alexander Benois and Sergei Diaghilev (**B19**) intended their magazine to enlighten Russia about progressive European art movements. They reacted strongly against what they perceived as the parochialism of Russian art and attempted to instill the European values of "art for art's sake" in their native country. The movement was most influential in theatre design, particularly the productions in Paris of the *Ballet russe*, which involved innovations of set, costume and movement. The magazine continued to be published until 1905.

MEDICAL
MATTERS

Here we give a brief summary of up-to-date medical knowledge for a wide variety of the most common illnesses. The section includes new developments in areas such as the treatment of asthma and advances in transplant surgery. It must not be allowed to replace your doctor, who should be consulted immediately if you are worried. An index at the end of the section ensures easy reference.

TABLE OF CONTENTS

MEDICAL MATTERS

PART I. INTRODUCTION.

Background Note.

In earlier editions of *Pears* the Medical Section took the form of a dictionary. In recent years we have attempted something different: a small medical textbook for the layman. We have two reasons for this. Firstly, we feel that there are some readers who would like to have an overall picture of modern medicine and learn something of the progress in its various fields. They may like to read the section through as a continuous narrative. Secondly, there are always readers (probably the majority) who simply want to use the section as a ready-reference guide and to that end, rather than have an alphabetically arranged collection of snippets of information (which can be unsatisfying), we have grouped diseases under bodily "systems'. We have made no attempt to produce a *dictionary* of symptoms because self-diagnosis is foolish. However, we have retained an alphabetical index (Part IV) for easy reference.

Arrangement of the Section.

The plan in this section is to deal with diseases according to either (a) their cause (*e.g.*, the infections due to bacteria or viruses) or (b) the body system affected (*e.g.*, the nervous system, the heart and blood vessels, the lungs and so on). We cannot emphasise too strongly that this section is not intended as a substitute for seeking medical advice. It is one thing to satisfy curiosity or try and solve a puzzle about a disease, condition or collection of symptoms by "looking it up" but quite another to try and diagnose one's own disease, condition or collection of symptoms in the same way. In other words, this section is no substitute for a doctor and when you are ill, unless you know it to be a trivial, or relatively trivial, self-limiting condition, you must get medical advice. It is easy to listen to and believe unqualified opinions and to take and act on advice from unqualified persons. However, it is unwise to do so because although doctors are sometimes wrong (just as are lawyers, architects, judges and veterinary surgeons) the unqualified are much more likely to be wrong. So choose a doctor you can trust, and then believe what he or she tells you and carry out that advice. There is no use in complaining about the whole medical profession just because you are dissatisfied with your own GP. If you are, you should sign on with another.

Modern Medicine.

Much in medicine which is now taken for granted (that for the majority of diseases caused by identifiable organisms there is a specific drug treatment, for example) was undreamed of even as recently as 50 years ago. Progress in diagnosis, in preventive medicine and in treatment, both medical and surgical, has been so rapid as to be almost breathtaking. A doctor retiring from active practice in 1999 will have seen smallpox completely eradicated, poliomyelitis practically banished (at least from the UK), tuberculosis become curable, coronary artery disease relievable surgically and he will have witnessed the dramatic progress in the field of molecular biology and in the research by immunologists and geneticists into their efforts to control parasitic diseases like bilharzia, malaria and river blindness that affect millions of people in the Third World. One aspect of medicine and medical thinking still resistant to progress in understanding in spite of continued research is the effect of mind on body. Many of us still like to think that our bodies are just something we have got into, like cars, that ill-health is simply something that has "gone wrong" in one system or another and that therefore provided we find the appropriate expert (a chest physician, a gastro-enterologist or an ophthalmic surgeon, for example) to correct the fault, we will recover. Whereas that idea holds good for a broken leg, for instance, with many diseases the idea that mind can be totally separated from the "defective" part just isn't good enough. You cannot simply divorce your stomach, your bowels, your liver or your heart from your "self". They are all part of you and react, as you yourself react, to all the stresses and anxieties, fears and worries and the hundred and one other factors that are part and parcel of modern living. It is true that most of your stomach can be removed, your gall-bladder entirely so and with the aid of a dialysing machine or a transplant you can get by without your kidneys. As with your car, old or diseased parts can be repaired or totally replaced; even your heart, conventionally the very "seat" of the emotions.

Mens sana in corpore sano—a sound mind in a sound body. Your body and its many parts can be helped to normal function by modern medicines and surgery but, in general, it will only stay that way if you can rid yourself of all those emotional blemishes—anger, frustration, fear, worry and anxiety—which trouble you. Easier said than done, of course, but a good physician can help with good advice, with medicines if necessary—or simply with his ear. Emotional stress can not only inhibit healing of such things as duodenal or gastric ulcers but may even *cause* them. There are many diseases now recognised which are known to be associated with stress factors if not actually caused by them. Mainly these are diseases of the digestive tract or of the heart and blood vessels and you will find some of them discussed in the appropriate sections.

The state of the mind has more influence on bodily functions than you might think and recovery from many serious conditions can be slowed or hastened, depending on your state of mind. Every doctor has had experience of the patient who "loses the will to live", a situation which is unfortunately commoner than the reverse.

Preventive Medicine.

A word about preventive medicine—or helping yourself to health. A great deal of nonsense has been talked about the healthy life; at one time we were told to take eighteen chews to each bite, to do deep breathing, to take plenty of exercise, to get lots of fresh air, to eat regularly (or to indulge in peculiar diets). But more recently eminent doctors have cast doubt on most of these fancies. Moderate exercise is necessary to health, but athletes who indulge in violent exercise have not always been noted for longevity. Fresh air is pleasant and stimulating, but, where actual breathing is concerned, it is no better than the air in most rooms, though secondary smoking is now considered to be harmful. Certainly, one of the problems of our time is air pollution, but at present we are considering ordinary fresh air in comparison with the air indoors, and, in this case, the experts say there is little difference so far as health is concerned.

A balanced diet containing correct amounts of the basic food substances is essential, but there is no evidence that when, or at what intervals, you eat makes the slightest difference—unless you are a sufferer from stomach ulcer, in which case it is necessary that the intervals between meals should not be too long. The whole business of having meals at fixed intervals is nothing but a social convention, and in modern life obviously a matter of convenience. (*See* Diet, P39).

Sleep, too, is a necessity. But different people require different amounts of sleep. Some manage on as little as three hours, others need ten or more.

In a number of studies of men and women who lived to a ripe old age it was found that the only factors in common between them were that they had a good balanced diet of healthy food, that they had contented minds, and that they were interested in something which gave them an aim in life. They also came of long-lived families—for living a long and healthy life depends partly upon heredity.

So the main rules of health are:

(1) Don't abuse your body—*i.e.*, exercise it, feed it sensibly and in moderation and don't poison it with cigarette smoke (yours or anyone else's), with alcohol or with other drugs

(2) Think positively about health—make it a purpose for living

(3) Turn your thoughts away from those bodily functions (digestion, circulation, breathing and so on) which can look after themselves. Introspection leads to hypochondriasis, and

(4) Choose your parents for *their* longevity!

The Development of Medicines.

A great surgeon, the first of the moderns, was Ambrose Paré, who died in 1590, and one of his best known sayings was: "I apply the dressing, but God heals the wound." He was quite right; for until about sixty years ago, or even less, all the physician could do was to put the patient in as favourable a state as possible to enable his body to cure itself. That is to say, there were hardly any specific drugs—drugs that had a direct effect on the disease. There was quinine, discovered by the Spaniards in America, which was specific for malaria, and there were iron (specific for anaemia) and digitalis (specific for certain types of heart disease), but otherwise nothing until the nineteenth century, when Paul Ehrlich discovered salvarsan, which is specific for syphilis. Ehrlich died in 1914, having conceived the brilliant idea of drugs, which he described as "magic bullets"—*i.e.*, drugs which, like bullets, would be aimed at the real cause of the disease. They would, that is to say, be specific.

Discovery of New Drugs.

Since then a large number of such drugs have been discovered. For example, the antibiotics, such as penicillin, discovered in 1928 by Fleming at St. Mary's Hospital, Paddington. Later, Florey and Chain in Oxford, helped in the war years by the vast resources of the American pharmaceutical industry, were able to make penicillin available to the public in sufficient quantities by new techniques of production. Penicillin is practically non-poisonous (although it is possible to become allergic to it, sometimes with serious results). It can kill some germs in a dilution of one part of penicillin to one million parts of water; it is effective against streptococci, the cause of blood-poisoning, sepsis in wounds, and many other diseases; and also against the germs of anthrax, gonorrhoea, meningitis of some types, syphilis—penicillin is typically active at 1–10 ug/ml *i.e.* 1–10 parts per million. Blood-poisoning, whether from wounds or childbirth, used to be almost incurable—now the rate of cure is 80–90 per cent.; anthrax and gonorrhoea have an almost 100 per cent. rate of cure. In pneumonia the rate is 90 per cent., and early syphilis can be cured in a week, instead of the previous two to three years. But that was only the beginning. Other antibiotics—streptomycin, tetracycline, erythromycin, and many others—have greatly reduced the terrible scourges of the human race, in particular, in the case of streptomycin, tuberculosis. The sulpha group of drugs—sulphadiazine, sulphadimidine, etc.—have also proved a great boon. Then there are the new drugs which have created a revolution in

psychiatry—the tranquillisers which relieve anxiety, the drugs which clear up certain types of depression, and substances such as chlorpromazine which make it possible to nurse formerly violent patients in the wards of a general hospital. The antihistamine drugs help in allergies, anticoagulants are of value after heart attacks and levodopa mitigates some of the distressing features of Parkinson's Disease.

No drug, old or new, is completely safe—if we define "safe" as meaning having absolutely no potential for harm. The household aspirin, widely used in a variety of conditions for its analgesic (pain-relieving) and antipyretic (fever-reducing) qualities, can cause bleeding from the stomach and small intestine. Phenacetin, at one time a component of compound codeine tablets but now withdrawn, can—with prolonged use—damage the kidney. Chloramphenicol, a powerful antibiotic effective in typhoid fever, typhus and whooping cough, can damage the blood-forming cells of the bone marrow producing an agranulocytosis which can be fatal.

Clearly, in any one case, the doctor must weigh up the advantages and disadvantages of this or that drug before prescribing. Minor, self-limiting illnesses do not require potent, potentially toxic remedies. Chloramphenicol is rarely justified in whooping cough, but would never be withheld from a patient with typhoid fever.

Humans make up a unique species. A new chemical compound promising in animal experiments, for example, as an anti-inflammatory agent, apparently safe when given, say, to mice in a dose 100 times that required to produce that anti-inflammatory effect may, over a long period of time in us, not only have no effect but make his hair fall out or perhaps cause retention of urine. Nevertheless, some animal species do react like man, or vice versa, and it is possible to make reasonably accurate extrapolations from animals to man in terms of drug effect. It is also possible to estimate the toxicity of a drug on humans from its toxicity in certain animal species but the ultimate test, both of the effectiveness and the toxicity of a new drug, comes only when it is given to us.

Thalidomide was unique. In every animal test used throughout the drug industry at that time—it was introduced in the late 1950s—it had a clean bill of health. It was chemically related to other drugs which had been in use for a long time. Overdosage with other sedatives such as the barbiturates was common at that time, although less so now. Overdosage with thalidomide was unlikely to prove fatal. It was marketed in Europe and in Britain as a "safe sedative". The tragic results that followed its ingestion by women in the early weeks of pregnancy are now well known. Babies were born with severe deformities of limbs, internal organs or both. That effect could not have been foretold from any animal tests then in use. Since that date new drugs have been subjected to rigorous testing in various animal species to check the effect on foetal development as a statutory requirement, along with the older tests for toxicity which had always been undertaken by reputable drug companies.

The thalidomide disaster of the early 1960s led directly to the setting up of regulatory drug agencies in most countries of the world. In Britain the introduction and clinical testing of new compounds is controlled by the Medicines and Environmental Health Division of the Department of Health and Social Security, statutory machinery set up by the Medicines Act 1968, which followed the purely voluntary scheme of control under what was known as the Dunlop Committee after Sir Derrick Dunlop, its first chairman.

The development and introduction of new drugs is now very strictly controlled. No new drug can be marketed in Britain without the Medicines Commission being satisfied about its efficacy and its safety. We would need space in this edition almost the size of the complete Medical Section to describe fully the workings of the Commission and the limitations that the requirements of the Medicines Act inevitably place on the development and introduction of new remedies. The time from the initial synthesis of a novel compound likely to be of value to its eventual appearance in the pharmacy on prescription is now eight to 10 years. The cost is measured in millions of pounds because, for each successful drug, there will have been many thousands of unsuccessful ones.

The Control of New Drugs.

Briefly, no new drug or modification of an old one can be sold, whether or not on prescription, unless it has been granted a product licence by the Department of Health and Social Security through its Medicines and Environmental Health Division. Many stages have to be passed to acquire that licence, from the granting of certificates to allow the drug to be tested initially in a limited way in patients in a strictly controlled manner by investigators approved by the Commission, to permission for extension of those trials at a later date to include larger numbers of patients or more investigators, to perhaps a "monitored release"—that is, to enable its use in, say, hospitals only—to the final release on the granting of a full product licence. Thus, the Medicines Commission has control at all stages.

Furthermore, all the stages are dependent on production of evidence relating to the safety and efficacy of the drug, evidence which may take the drug company months, sometimes years, to produce and which, of course, must be acceptable to the Commission. Trials may be stopped at any time, for example, if evidence of side effects of an undesirable nature come to light during clinical testing, or when evidence from some other similar compound indicates a likely risk in the use of the drug in question. Of course, "acceptable" means that the strict criteria which have been laid down by the specialist committees appointed to deal with all the various aspects of drug development, such as toxicology, adverse reactions and so forth, have been met. Experts serve on these committees which meet regularly, but the day-to-day running of the Medicines Commission is in the hands of full-time medically qualified personnel as well as pharmacists, pharmacologists and toxicologists. In addition, outside consultant opinion can be sought.

As well as all these rigid controls on development and testing in the early stages, there is also a scheme of surveillance for untoward side effects. These are the action, or actions, of a drug apart from its main one. Take the well-known side effect of drowsiness which occurs with certain antihistamine drugs: the main action, the one for which the drug is prescribed, is the mitigation of the effects of allergy, such as urticaria. Drowsiness would be an unwanted effect if the patient is not incapacitated and is able to do his usual job. On the other hand, some antihistamines have an appetite-stimulating effect which could, of course, be a useful attribute in certain situations or even allow the drug to be used solely for that purpose, the anti-allergic effect then being incidental.

An adverse reaction is a type of side effect which by definition, is unwanted and potentially harmful. The intestinal bleeding associated with aspirin, or the depressive effects of some of the earlier drugs used to lower blood pressure, such as reserpine and methyldopa, are good examples. When new drugs first become licensed for marketing and are prescribed by doctors on a gradually increasing scale it is important that adverse reactions such as those are reported. Every doctor in the National Health Service, whether in general practice or in hospital, has access to a stock of special record cards on which he can record in a standard way the details of any untoward reaction occurring in his patient during the prescribing of a new or existing drug, and which he has good reason to believe is associated with the taking of that drug. These record cards are posted to the DHSS which has a special unit to deal with them. A doctor noticing, for example that one of his patients developed, say, double vision during treatment with a new antidepressant could not assume in the absence of other firm evidence that the two events were necessarily connected. However, if 100 cards are received by the DHSS reporting the same kind of event, there is good circumstantial evidence that those events are likely to be connected with drug administration. This adverse reaction reporting system, although voluntary, is working well and is an effective "early warning system" for drug toxicity

We have come a long way since thalidomide, but have had to steer between the Scylla of stifling innovation in drug research by excessive control of development and the Charybdis of the free-for-all, profit-motivated bonanzas of the pre-thalidomide era. No system can be perfect, and it is fair to say that had it been necessary, for example, for aspirin, penicillin and streptomycin to be put through the system as we have set it up now they would probably never have reached the market and thence the patient.

Mention must of course be made of the surgical advances and progress in anaesthesia. Hardly a week goes by without operations being undertaken which seemed inconceivable even as short a time as 40 years ago. Transplantation and re-plantation (the re-attachment of severed limbs) are regularly reported; haemodialysis (the 'cleansing' of blood in patients with irreversibe kidney disease) is now often undertaken in the patient's own home where, with appropriate adaptation and the modern kidney machine, he or she can run the procedure—singlehanded in many instances—and still keep his or her job; and the laser beam is used to deal with detached retinas or to obliterate tiny, microscopic blood vessel 'bubbles' (aneurysms) in the back of the eye while the patient is conscious and cooperative. The list grows daily.

Social Medicine.

Medicine has passed through many phases from the time when disease was regarded as a punishment from the gods or a sign of devil possession to the present era, when increasingly there is a tendency to look on society as the patient. Indeed, one commonly hears doctors and sociologists nowadays talking about "the sick society."

The early primitive stage came to an end—at least in one part of the world—when in Greece, five centuries before Christ, Hippocrates and others began to teach that all diseases were due to natural causes. But after the first ray of hope the outlook began to deteriorate when, during the Middle and Dark Ages (that is, from the fall of the Roman Empire right up to the fifteenth century), there was a return to the belief in devil possession and supernatural causes.

Eighteenth-century medicine in Europe was materialistic, regarding the body as a machine. It was founded upon a sort of pseudo-science—although, of course, there were always individual exceptions, physicians such as Sydenham in England, who, avoiding all theories, based their work on observation of the patient. This mechanistic approach persisted right through the nineteenth century, but medicine became more and more truly scientific, and the century saw the most rapid advances in the field ever known until our own times: the discovery of germs by Pasteur, of antiseptics to combat them by Lister, of vaccination by Jenner and anaesthetics by the American Wells and the Scot Simpson. The use of the microscope by Virchow, who was a German, brought great advances in the understanding of disease and Ehrlich, another German, conceived, as we have already seen, the idea of "magic bullets" which would attack the germs at the root of a disease without harming the patient. But one of the greatest of all these great men is perhaps the least known. His name was Edwin Chadwick.

From the earliest period of recorded history human communities had been constantly ravaged by great plagues which swept over their lands year after year, killing untold millions. The Black Death of 1348–9 wiped out almost half the population of Europe. But, even in the first quarter of the nineteenth century in London, tens of thousands died from typhus, typhoid, and small-pox.

In the face of these terrible visitations the individual physician was helpless. He could not treat each one of the many sick even had he known how, and Chadwick's claim to fame rests on the fact that he was the first man to think in terms of *social* control of diseases, by so dealing with their causes that they were prevented from arising at all. In order to wipe out typhoid and cholera, he argued, we must ensure clean water supplies; for these diseases are caused by germs carried in polluted water. In order to attack typhus and plague, one must get rid of the lice which carry the germs of typhus and the rat-fleas which carry the germs of plague (including, of course, the rats, which, in turn, carry the fleas).

Chadwick was born in a Lancashire farmhouse where the children were washed every day all over, and he ruthlessly drove an obsession with cleanliness into the heads of his countrymen. Thus one of the first public health measures was introduced by Chadwick and others when they brought in legislation to purify the water supply of London. Previously, the citizens had used water from the Thames (they still do, but only after it has been filtered and sterilised at the waterworks!), and from filthy, refuse-laden ponds and springs. Later, Chadwick helped to found the Poor Law Commission, and produced a Report in 1842, the principal suggestions of which were: a municipal water supply for all towns; scientific drainage both in town and country; and an independent health service with large powers for dealing with those who endangered the lives of others by polluting water or causing nuisances. He also proposed a national service for interment of the dead; for in those days bodies often remained for days in the overcrowded homes of the poor without burial.

What has the twentieth century contributed to the concept of social health? Well, of course, there has been a great deal of legislation along the lines initiated by Chadwick to control disease, and a great many other measures have been introduced concerned with the idea of positive health—not merely preventing bad health, but trying to bring about the highest possible state of good health. Orange juice, milk, and good meals for school-children brought about a transformation in child health which became apparent to the least observant. And the National Health service is in the direct line of descent from early nineteenth-century legislation.

But in future years it is probable that the main achievement of the twentieth century will prove to be its extension of the term "social health" to cover every aspect of community life, not only in such subjects as bodily health and its control of social means, but also such problems as mental illness, crime, delinquency, drug addiction, and so on. What we are now asking ourselves is: how far are these problems produced by society itself, and if this is the case, how far can we go in preventing them by social means?

Community medicine takes the view that these problems can never be dealt with solely by moralising and retribution, but only by dispassionately analysing causes and dealing with them. In this century we have developed a social conscience. Not always, it is true, a very well-informed social conscience, but at least this is a good beginning. There are organisations for dealing scientifically with delinquency, for dealing with problem children, for spreading knowledge about cancer in order to show people that it can be successfully treated if taken in time. We can well say with John Donne, who died in 1631, that "no man is an island . . . every man's death diminisheth me; for I am involved in mankind." This is the attitude of twentieth-century community medicine.

Summary. Perhaps we can sum up our progress in the past century and a half more dramatically in terms of hard facts.

Before that time a surgical operation was never undertaken except under the gravest circumstances. There were no anaesthetics and no antiseptics, and the operation was carried out by a surgeon in a filthy tail-coat, stained with the congealed blood of countless operations (indeed the surgeons of that time took pride in the dirty condition of their coats as showing how much experience they had previously had). Germs and the part they play in producing disease were unknown, and Paul Ehrlich had not yet been born, so there were no "magic bullets" to attack syphilis, or sera for diphtheria and other diseases. The mentally ill were simply locked up with little treatment and subjected to such indignities as the strait-jacket and the padded cell; now they are given treatment which becomes more effective each year, the padded cell and strait-jacket have gone, and in very few hospitals are the ward doors locked.

Earlier in the twentieth century you would very likely have died if you had developed pneumonia, "childbed fever" after the birth of a child, meningitis, dysentery, typhoid, or tuberculosis. With such infections as blood-poisoning you would have had practically no chance at all. Today, the sulpha drugs and the antibiotics have changed all that. Syphilis and gonorrhoea were lifelong tragedies both to the patient and his family, but now they, too, can be conquered. With scientific research and its application proceeding at a brisk pace many diseases are now being brought under control. However, other health threats are emerging. Cancer deaths are set to soar by 2025 (it has already overtaken heart disease). AIDS threatens millions world-wide. Older diseases, such as malaria, have yet to be eliminated.

The National Health Service has brought the possibility of good treatment equally to all, and it is up to us to see that all these facilities are used to the full by all who need them.

PART II. DISEASES ARRANGED BY CAUSE OR BODY SYSTEM AFFECTED

THE INFECTIOUS DISEASES.
INTRODUCTION.

Infectious diseases are those which are caused by an invasion of the human body by organisms from outside (the word "organism" simply means living things, and we are using this word because, as will be seen later, it is not only what are known as "germs" which can cause infection). We know, too, that what is generally typical about this group is: (a) that the disease can be passed on from one person to another, and (b) that it is usually accompanied by a raised temperature or fever. Now (a), of course, is always true, because the definition of an infectious disease is one that can be passed on to others, but (b) is not always true, because a few infections produce little or no temperature, and also because it is possible to have a raised temperature (again in only a few cases) without any infection. For example, certain types of brain injury, tumour, or haemorrhage can produce a raised—or lowered—temperature, and so can the injection of some foreign substance such as milk into the muscles. This is known as "protein shock," and was at one time used in the treatment of certain illnesses. Finally, solutions of dead germs, such as the antityphoid vaccine given to protect troops during the War, may lead when injected to very high temperatures. But, by and large, we are entitled to suppose that the patient with a raised temperature is probably suffering from an infection.

Types of Infection.

As we have seen, it is not only germs which cause infections—so from now on we shall give germs their proper name of "bacteria." Here is a list of the chief offenders which are liable to attack our bodies: bacteria, viruses, fungi, amoebae, worms and other parasites.

Bacteria are tiny living things which can be seen only under a fairly powerful microscope. Some are grouped like bunches of grapes (staphylococci) or in strings or chains (streptococci). They are given these names because "staphylos" is the Greek word for a bunch of grapes, and "streptos" means a chain. Yet others are comma-shaped (such as the cholera vibrio), or shaped like a drumstick—a rod with a small knob at the end (the tetanus bacillus, which causes lockjaw).

It would be a mistake to think that all bacteria are harmful; for without some species we could not survive for long. Bacteriologists divide them according to their behaviour in the human body into three groups: saprophytic, parasitic or pathogenic, and symbiotic. The *saprophytic* organisms are the bacteria normally found in the skin, mouth, and intestines; they do us neither harm nor good. The *parasitic*, or as they are more usually · called, pathogenic (*i.e.*, disease-producing) organisms, are the harmful ones with which we are naturally more concerned. Lastly, there are the *symbiotic* organisms, which, whilst taking something from the body, give something in return. For example, cattle would not be able to digest the cellulose of the grass they eat were it not for helpful bacteria in the lower parts of the intestines, and there are certain bacteria in the large intestine of man which produce vitamins.

Bacteria have two peculiar characteristics: each reproduces by splitting into two separate individuals as often as every twenty minutes in favourable circumstances like an open wound. If no bacterium were destroyed, one individual could produce a mass of bacteria larger than the whole world in a matter of a few weeks (since each of the offspring also divides into two, which in turn divide again—the progression goes: one gives birth to two, these two to four, the four to eight, eight to sixteen, sixteen to thirty-two, and so on—you will see, if you work it out, that in a short period the figure becomes astronomical). Fortunately, most bacteria do not find themselves in ideal conditions, so for the present the world is safe! The other curious thing about bacteria is that, barring accidents, they are potentially immortal. Under ideal conditions in which no bacteria were killed, none would die; for a bacterium there is no death from old age, no corpse except when it is actively destroyed. It simply goes on dividing, dividing, and subdividing for ever.

How, then, are bacteria destroyed? Briefly, the answer is that most are destroyed by the natural defences of the body of whatever host they are preying on; others are destroyed by antiseptics and the new drugs; and many are destroyed when they are excreted from the body in the sputum or through the bowels and land in places where they are dried up and cannot survive —although some bacteria in such circumstances can form what are called "spores," rather like the seeds of plants, so making it possible for them to survive in a state of suspended animation for months on end until picked up accidentally by

another unfortunate host. Finally, bacteria, in addition to all these possibilities, face another danger: they may themselves develop disease. This disease is caused by even more minute organisms known as bacteriophages (viruses which affect bacteria), discovered by F. W. Twort in 1915. Attack by bacteriophage causes whole groups of bacteria (known as "colonies") to disintegrate and become harmless.

Although bacteriophage have been used in the treatment of some diseases in human beings, this method has now been largely given up, since the new drugs are infinitely more effective.

Other Spirochaetes, like bacteria, are minute organisms, but differ in being shaped somewhat like a corkscrew and in being able to move. Their progress is produced by a sideways wriggling motion. The two main diseases caused by spirochaetes are syphilis and spirochaetal jaundice. Spirochaetal jaundice is carried by rats, and is common in those who work in mines. It is now rare in Britain, but still occurs in Japan, Egypt, and Malaysia; the infection is passed through the skin where the excreta of infected rats mingles with water on damp ground in the mine where miners kneel. Infection may also occur through eating infected food.

Viruses. Unlike bacteria, viruses are too small to be seen under an ordinary microscope. They can, however, be photographed in some cases under an electron microscope, which uses a magnetic field instead of a glass lens and a stream of electrons in place of a beam of light. Viruses cause such diseases as measles, mumps, poliomyelitis, smallpox, and chickenpox—not to mention such plant and animal diseases as tobacco mosaic disease and foot-and-mouth disease, which often have serious economic consequences. Other virus diseases are swine fever in pigs, influenza in Man, and myxomatosis in rabbits. They also cause the common cold.

The main characteristics of viruses are, first, that they can only grow in living cells—unlike bacteria, which readily grow in the laboratory on plates containing a jelly made from meat, broth, gelatin, milk, and other delicacies. The scientist, therefore, must keep them in portions of living tissue kept alive outside the body. Secondly, many are so small that they pass through the pores of the finest filter. Thirdly, a first attack usually produces immunity for life. Second attacks of the common virus diseases mentioned above are very rare; but unfortunately, this rule does not apply to influenza or the common cold. Fourthly, there is reason to believe that viruses represent an extraordinary intermediate stage between the living and non-living; they can, for instance, be produced in crystalline form and yet are just as dangerous when "thawed out." Lastly, the virus diseases have proved for the most part to be little affected by the new antibiotics and other drugs, although vaccination in smallpox and the injection of sera from infected patients in other infections may give immunity for longer or shorter periods, and progress has been made in developing drugs to combat some viruses, such as herpes viruses and the AIDS virus.

The two great practical problems that doctors face with viruses are: (i) many viruses are unknown because of the difficulty of growing them outside the body in suitable tissue culture. They cannot therefore be conveniently identified in specimens from the patient, as bacteria can; and (ii) most are unaffected by antibiotics like penicillin. It has been a great step forward to grow viruses artificially in tissue culture, in which they are identified indirectly by the effects they have on the cultured *cells*. But since we do not know exactly how to grow some viruses (like those of infective hepatitis) many have still not been seen.

When we recover from a viral illness like chickenpox, we probably do so by producing virus-killing substances such as interferon inside our own cells. Scientists are currently searching for these substances in case they can be used, like penicillin, to cure viral disease.

Fungi. Some infections are caused by fungi— that is to say organisms belonging to the same group as moulds, mushrooms, and toadstools. Penicillin and some other antibiotics are produced from moulds, so, as in the case of bacteria, some fungi are helpful; they even help to destroy each other, as bacteria do. For example actinomyces, which can cause infection of the jaw and other tissues, is destroyed by penicillin.

Most fungal infections are trivial and limited to the skin. But, although trivial, they can be unsightly and uncomfortable. Ringworm of the scalp, dhobie itch—an infection of the groin spread by infected underclothing—and so-called "athlete's foot" are caused by a fungus.

Amoebae. Amoebae are small, single-cell organisms, the largest of which (a harmless type found in stagnant ponds in Britain and elsewhere) is just visible to the naked eye. It is about the size of the head of a pin. Amoebae move, in the species which are capable of moving, by pushing forward a part of the cell in the appropriate direction and causing the rest to flow into the advancing portion. Like bacteria, they reproduce by dividing into halves, each of which becomes a new amoeba.

The main human disease caused by amoebae is amoebic dysentery (not to be confused with bacillary dysentery).

Parasites. These may live on the skin like lice (which can carry typhus) or fleas (carriers of plague) or the parasites of scabies which burrow into the skin, or they may live part of their time in the blood or other tissues, like malaria. They often have complicated life-cycles involving other hosts (like mosquitoes) at certain stages of development.

Worms. Worms are intestinal parasites, but the only common types found in Britain are threadworms, the tiny thread-like worms which cause irritability and itching in the skin of children, less often in adults; round-worms, somewhat resembling the ordinary garden earthworm, which seldom lead to symptoms; and tapeworms, which may reach a length of 3 or even 6 m. Many parasitic worms (like parasites elsewhere) lead a double life—they spend part of their life in the human intestine and the other part in the muscles of another animal. The tapeworm, for example, whilst in the human intestine, lays eggs which pass out of the body in the excreta, and are then swallowed by pigs, especially in those parts of the world where human excreta are used as manure in the fields. In the pig, the eggs form cysts in the muscles—meat infected in this way is known as "measly pork"—and when, in turn, the meat is eaten by man, the process in the intestine begins all over again.

Less common types, from our point of view, are the Russian tape-worm (which, as befits a Russian, grows to nearly 9 m!); this type is spread by caviare or undercooked infected fish. The small, leaf-shaped liver fluke lays eggs which are passed into canals or pools in tropical countries in the urine of infected people, hatch out and enter a water snail, and finally leave the snail in the form of small parasites which pierce the skin of bathers, whence they pass to the liver and subsequently the bladder and rectum. This is a serious condition, as is also filariasis (another tropical disease), for which, unlike bilharzia—caused by the liver fluke—no cure is known. The tropical disease known as loa-loa is caused by a variety of filaria.

How the Infection is Spread.

Infection is spread in many ways, some of which have already been mentioned. In the common fevers found in Europe and elsewhere one of the most frequent ways is by *droplet infection*—that is to say, by minute drops carrying the germs which are coughed or sneezed into the air by someone already suffering from the disease. Such droplets can be projected into the air for 3m or more, and when breathed in by someone within range infection may result. Next commonest mode of spread is perhaps by *infected food, water*, and the dirty hands of those who prepare food: cholera, dysentery, food-poisoning, and typhoid are spread in this way. Spread by *direct contact* is found in the venereal diseases (usually, but not

always, spread by sexual intercourse with someone who already has the disease), and, of course, lice, fleas, and other parasites, including the scabies mite, are spread by contact with the infested individual—or sometimes with his clothes or bed linen. Spread through an *intermediary host*, whether it be lice, fleas, or mosquitoes carrying infection, or the various means adopted by worms, has already been described above, so no more need be said. Lastly, the infection may result from *bacteria already within the body*; for example, Escherichia coli, which lives in the large intestine is harmless there, but if it gets into the bladder or the ureters (the tubes leading from kidney to bladder) a quite unpleasant result may follow in the form of cystitis or pyelitis.

How the Body Deals with Infection.

The body has many mechanisms of defence against intruders; these can generally be divided into two types. First, non-specific defence substances such as lysozyme, an enzyme that digests bacterial cell walls, are present in many body fluids, and a system of blood proteins known as the complement cascade punches holes in bacteria to kill them. Interferons and other so-called cytokines are produced when the body's cells are damaged by infection and help other cells to resist infection. A class of blood cell, known as macrophages, responds to infection and other damage by migrating to the affected part of the body and swallows bacteria and cell debris for destruction by the powerful enzymes that they contain. Secondly, specific defences are stimulated by infection: one class of lymphocytes produces antibodies, which recognise particular parts of bacteria and viruses, neutralising them and marking them out for destruction. Another class of lymphocytes hunts for foreign cells and kills them by a variety of methods, bursting them open and leaving debris for the macrophages to clear away.

Immunity can be induced by immunisation, which can be active or passive. In active immunisation, a vaccine is injected into the body to simulate the first time the body is infected with a disease-causing agent. Vaccines are made either from dead bacteria or viruses or from specially adapted strains which have lost their ability to cause disease. Passive immunisation is used when a person has already been exposed to a disease or when an effective vaccine is not available, and consists of injections of specific gamma-globulin obtained from the blood of a patient who has recently recovered from the disease concerned.

Immunology is one of the fastest-growing areas of medical research, as there are still many infectious diseases which are difficult to treat with antibodies, and manipulation of the immune system has great potential in the fight against cancer.

Antiseptics.

The earliest antiseptic was carbolic acid, used by Lister in his operating-theatre in the form of a fine spray directed throughout the operation on the wound, or sometimes in the form of steam from a kettle containing a solution of carbolic. But carbolic is dangerous, and since Lister's time many more useful antiseptics have been discovered. Acriflavine, thymol, and other old favourites have been discarded too. The various forms of carbolic are still used to disinfect drains, but, to tell the truth, the use of antiseptics nowadays is very limited. In surgery the *antiseptic* method has given way to the *aseptic* method—instead of fighting sepsis we see to it that no possibility of sepsis is present before operating; all instruments, the surgeons' and nurses' hands, the skin, are sterilised—the instruments by boiling, the dressings by dry heat, the hands by soap and water, and almost the only antiseptic used is to clean the patient's skin in the area to be operated on.

Antiseptics are used as first-aid treatment for cuts and wounds, but should be applied only once as a general rule—that is, when the wound is first received. The trouble with antiseptics is that as well as killing germs they also kill the surrounding tissues, which antibiotics never do.

Antiseptic sprays to purify the air of a room or to destroy germs lurking in the dust on the sick-room floor—or any other floor—are practically useless. To quote the *British Medical Journal*: "There is no good scientific evidence that any of the chemical air-disinfectants can control the spread of infection in places such as schools, offices, or cinemas. Nor is there good evidence that any substantial effect on the spread of illness can be obtained by disinfection of dust."

Neither is there any good reason to believe that mouth-washes and gargles have any effect other than making the mouth feel fresher and (temporarily) removing mouth odour—by covering it up with the scent of the antiseptic. Mouthwashes are in contact with the bacteria for far too short a time to have any damaging result, and, in the case of tonsillitis and other diseases, all the important bacteria are hidden far out of any danger from gargles.

Antibiotics.

Some antibiotics—penicillin, streptomycin, erythromycin and so on—have already been mentioned (*see* **P4**). In recent years many others have been introduced—ampicillin, gentamicin, cephalexin. Indiscriminate use of these drugs (*e.g.* for trivial complaints) has led to problems, the most important being the development of resistance by previously sensitive organisms. It is not always convenient or possible to be able to identify the particular germ responsible for an infection and determine to which drug it is sensitive, but if there is an initial clinical response, it can be assumed that the "right" drug has been used. It is important to have a full course of treatment—which usually means ten days minimum.

Other problems are hypersensitivity (allergic) reactions which can take many forms. Once hypersensitivity to one of the antibiotics has been identified (penicillin hypersensitivity is not rare) the patient must be made aware of this, and so protect himself from unwitting prescribing by another doctor. Hospital and GP records are clearly marked in such instances but it is very important that the patient himself knows.

Antibiotics are only available on prescription, at least in the U.K., but medicine cupboards are full of them, accumulated from unfinished courses. Self-prescribing is tempting but ill-advised; antibiotics must always be given under medical supervision. Side effects are common and some are dangerous. Repeated use may lead to rapid overgrowth of fungi *e.g.* thrush (Candida albicans) normally present in harmless numbers in the alimentary tract with serious, sometimes fatal results.

General Treatment of Fevers.

Fevers are ordinarily heralded in by a rise in temperature which is noticeable either by a flushed face or by alternate sensations of heat and cold. A patient with a high temperature may have shivering attacks known as "rigors." Tell the doctor.

A high temperature does not necessarily (especially in a child) mean that the trouble is serious but the lay person should always treat it as such and certainly call a doctor if the patient is a child or an elderly person. The majority of fevers are of a viral origin and usually self limiting. The patient tends to improve rapidly once the temperature is controlled.

Even the trained physician finds it difficult to tell one fever from another in the early days; for most of the common fevers begin in more or less the same way. It is only when a rash or some other more definite sign becomes evident that a certain diagnosis can be made, and these may not show themselves until the patient has been feeling "run-down" and fevered for some days. A clinical thermometer is a useful tool and inexpensive to buy. The more recent fever scans applied directly to the forehead also give an immediate and fairly accurate temperature reading. Control of temperature is important, especially in young children, where a high fever may produce a convulsion. A febrile convulsion is a frightening experience for any parent, particularly as their child may have seemed quite well a few minutes previously. High temperature, twitching, and increased irritation may herald the onset. Emergency management involves keeping the child on its side to avoid inhalation of vomit,

clearing debris around his mouth, removing his clothes and sponging him with lukewarm water. Get someone to summon medical help, but never leave an unconscious child alone. Above all, do not panic as the initial episode will usually soon pass.

Briefly, then, the way to treat a fever in the early stages before the doctor comes, and before one knows exactly what is wrong, is as follows:

(1) Put the patient to bed. The child is probably better on the living room sofa where he will feel less isolated and is more easily observed.

(2) Give plenty of clear fluids; water, water and fruit juice, weak tea or lemonade.

(3) Give small amounts of easily digested food but only if the patient requires it.

(4) Aspirin is no longer recommended for the treatment of feverish children, and should not be given to children under 12 years of age. This is because it has been linked to the development of "Reye's Syndrome", an acute encephalopathy or inflammation of the brain with delirium, convulsions and coma. Although very rare, "Reye's Syndrome" carries a high mortality.

Adults with a history of peptic ulcer or chronic indigestion should also avoid aspirin because of the possible risk of a gastrointestinal bleed.

Paracetamol is now the treatment of choice to reduce temperature and relieve headache and elixir preparations are available for children. The dose may be repeated 4/6 hourly and there are no gastro-intestinal side effects.

Medicines containing Paracetamol should be stored in a safe place as overdosage, accidental or otherwise, may cause liver damage without initial drowsiness or loss of consciousness. Symptoms may not be apparent for a number of days.

Other methods of cooling a feverish patient involve removing excess clothing, administering tepid baths or sponging with lukewarm water. Simply standing at an open door and allowing the cool outside air to waft around the feverish child, can have an immediate effect.

THE INFECTIOUS FEVERS.

The remarks made above apply to the management of *any* fever, and we are now going to discuss particular infectious diseases, beginning with the common childhood fevers, then passing on to less common ones, tropical diseases, and worm and parasitic infestations.

The common infectious fevers are caused by bacteria or viruses, and it is useful to know the meaning of the following terms: *incubation period* is the time which elapses between being infected and developing symptoms; *prodromal period* is the time which elapses between the end of the incubation period and the appearance of a rash; *quarantine period*, the maximum time during which a person who has been in contact with the infection may develop the disease—it is usually two days more than the incubation period; *isolation period* the time a patient is supposed to be isolated.

Virus Diseases.

First, we shall take the common virus diseases, measles, chickenpox, and rubella or German measles, then the other virus diseases, mumps, infective hepatitis, viral pneumonia, and some less common conditions which do not always produce a typical rash as in the case of the first three.

In nearly all of these fevers there is a long incubation period, and one infection gives immunity for life.

Measles. The incubation period is 10–11 days. The first sign is the appearance of symptoms rather like a severe cold. The eyes become red, and exposure to light is unpleasant, the nose runs, the throat becomes inflamed, and a dry, harsh cough develops. There may be headache and the temperature rises to 39°C or more. Usually the patient is a child, and especially typical is the development of so-called Koplik's spots, which are small, bluish-white, raised spots seen on the inside of the cheek at the back of the mouth. The rash begins on the fourth day of the prodromal period, *i.e.*, 14 days after the initial infection. It shows on the forehead and behind the ears, spreading within a day downwards over the whole body; in another two days it starts to disappear, but often leaves behind a sort of brownish staining which may last for one to two weeks.

Measles can be serious, especially in very young children because of its complications, such as bronchopneumonia and infection of the ear, which can now be treated with antibiotics. These drugs have no effect on the measles virus, but only on the secondarily invading bacteria which have invaded the lungs and ear during the illness. The illness can be attenuated or lessened by injection of antibodies (gamma globulin) from an immune adult, and this is often worth while in the very young. Effective vaccination is now available.

Rubella or German Measles. Incubation period 14–19 days. A mild fever, similar to measles except that the rash is usually the first sign that anything is wrong, and the temperature is rarely above 38°C. The eyes may be pink, and there are enlarged glands at the back of the neck. The rash disappears completely in thirty-six hours. There are no complications.

German measles, in itself, is harmless, but if a woman gets the disease in the early months of pregnancy malformations in the child may appear at birth. Vaccination is advised if a girl has not contracted the disease by the time she reaches puberty. There is no special treatment except the general rules for fevers given above.

Chickenpox. Incubation period 14–15 days, but may be more variable. In children chickenpox is a mild fever which begins with the appearance of tiny blisters on the chest and back. These later spread outwards to the legs, arms and face, and cause itching. Treatment is the general one for fevers already described. Calamine lotion or dusting powder will be helpful for the irritation, and the child's nails should be cut short to prevent scratching and infection of the spots. Whereas children are usually little bothered by chickenpox, young adults may be much more drastically affected—a temperature of 40°C is not uncommon, and then there may be severe headache. Shingles is a disease that sometimes follows chickenpox – usually by many years, and results from reactivation of the chicken pox virus, which 'hides' in the spinal cord after a childhood infection.

Mumps. Incubation period 17–18 days. The typical appearance of mumps is a swelling in the salivary glands in front of the ears which makes the face look full. This causes pain later on, and it may be difficult to open the mouth. Temperature is not usually high (about 38°C). Although uncomfortable, mumps is rarely dangerous, but orchitis—swelling of the testicles—is sometimes a complication, especially if the infection occurs beyond childhood. Fluid diet should be given if eating is painful, with mouth-washes, and rest in bed.

Infective Hepatitis. "Hepatitis" means inflammation of the liver, and infective hepatitis, which is much the commonest cause of jaundice in young adults, is a viral infection of the liver. The main symptoms are fever, followed by jaundice, which is first noticed in the whites of the eyes as yellow staining, then in the skin. The urine becomes coloured also, and this is most easily noticed if, on shaking in a bottle, the froth shows coloration. If the froth remains white, no jaundice is present. Treatment is a matter for the doctor, but great care should be taken, both by the patient and those in contact with him, to wash the hands thoroughly after urinating or defaecat-

ing, after handling utensils from the sickroom, and both before and after eating; for the disease is very infectious.

Viral Pneumonia. Pneumonia is usually caused by bacteria, and when we speak of pneumonia, that is the type we ordinarily refer to. Viral pneumonia can be caused by a variety of viruses. There is no specific treatment so far, and since diagnosis is a specialist matter little more need be said except that the symptoms in general resemble those of ordinary pneumonia. Although there is no specific treatment for virus infections of the lungs, it is always worth while trying antibiotics in view of the possibility that the lung condition may be caused by a secondary invasion of bacteria.

Influenza. While serious epidemics of influenza take the form of a very dramatic and often fatal disease—for example, the epidemic of "Spanish 'flu" which followed the First World War killed more people than the actual fighting—the milder type more usually seen is difficult to distinguish from the common cold. In fact, many people who complain of "a dose of the 'flu" are suffering from simple colds.

However, a sudden onset, aching in the muscles of the back and legs, and redness of the eyes, would suggest influenza, and especially typical is the depression and weakness which follow influenza but not a cold. The measures suggested above for the general treatment of fever should be applied; but the depression and weakness which follow influenza may need special treatment by the doctor. Effective vaccines are now available, and are particularly recommended for the elderly, though immunisation must be carried out each year to overcome the propensity of influenza viruses to change the proteins in their "coats."

Colds and Sinusitis. Although we all think we know what a "cold" is, the issue is not so simple; for the symptoms of fever, running nose, and a run-down, "headachy" feeling are found in many illnesses. They may be observed, as we have seen, in the early stages of measles before the arrival of the rash, or in a number of other fevers, such as whooping cough. Mild attacks of influenza (*see above*) may resemble the common cold, and blocking of the nose with discharge and fever may be due to *sinusitis*—although here there is usually pain above, between, or below the eyes. Colds can be caused by any one of more than 100 different viruses known as "rhinoviruses" This is why a single cold does not confer immunity on the sufferer. It is probable that you will not catch a cold from the same virus, at least for the rest of the year, but there are all those others waiting to infect you with other colds in buses, tubes, and other crowded places. Like all infections, do not forget that the best way to avoid them is to keep generally well, and in a good nutritional state. Do not spend money on injections or other vaccines. They do not work, probably because of the multiplicity of viruses involved. It is unlikely that adding vitamins or mineral supplements to normal diet will do any good at all provided you are eating sensibly. The vogue for prophylactic or therapeutic treatment of colds with massive doses of vitamin C has recently received much attention from scientists attempting, with little success, to prove the effect by controlled clinical trial and to find a rational basis for its use.

Poliomyelitis.

Polio, or infantile paralysis as it used to be known, is caused by a virus which has a particular affinity for the nerve cells of the spinal cord and which results in paralysis of those muscles under the control of the particular group of cells infected. Rarely, the infection is widespread in the nerve tissue causing paralysis of muscles of swallowing and respiration as well as those of the trunk and limbs. The usual pattern is for a single muscle group to be affected, for example, the muscles controlling the movements of the arm at the shoulder. Such paralysis may be transient with complete recovery, partial with some residual weakness, or total, leaving a "flail limb" which is wasted and powerless.

At one time in this country epidemics of polio-myelitis were common, mainly affecting children and young adults. There is no doubt that mild forms of the disease were always occurring in very young children, forms never diagnosed as such but conferring a natural immunity in later life.

In common with other infections, poliomyelitis begins with a mild or moderate fever, with a sore throat, headache, nausea and perhaps actual vomiting, some five to 10 days after contact with the virus. There may be rigidity of the neck muscles. Paralysis, if it occurs, will become apparent about the second or third day of illness. This stage may last two or three weeks, by which time the temperature will have subsided and the paralysis started to improve. There is no specific treatment and medical care is confined to sympto-matic relief. Difficulty with swallowing and breathing calls for special nursing measures. In severe cases, artificial means of maintaining respiration may have to be continued for months, or for the rest of the patient's life. Many severely paralysed polio victims of the post-war epidemics —the self-styled "responauts"—depend for their lives on artificial respirators ("iron lungs").

With the development of the oral vaccine early in the 1960s, and its introduction into the im-munisation schedule in this country, the disease has now virtually disappeared from Great Britain.

Smallpox. In previous editions we stated that "since the introduction of vaccination it (smallpox) is comparatively rare in industrialised countries." In the 88th edition we reported that smallpox (*variola major*) had now been eradicated throughout the world. The less serious form of the disease, *variola minor*, is still found in some parts of Africa, but all the signs are that it, too, will soon be eradicated. The last case of *variola major* occurred in Bangladesh in 1975, except for at least one accidental infection in England in the 1980s. With the disappearance of the disease vaccination will become unnecessary; however, the World Health Organisation is planning to store vaccine (which can be done almost indefinitely at a temperature of −20°C) in sufficient quantities to vaccinate many millions of people should the need ever arise again. We made no excuse therefore for leaving out of that edition of *Pears*, for the first time in its long history, the detailed description of the disease.

Glandular Fever. Sometimes called infectious mononucleosis, since one of its features is an in-crease in a certain type of white cell—the monocyte—and a change in its microscopic charac-teristics. It is caused by a virus (the Epstein-Barr), predominantly affects young children and adults and although often taking a protracted course, it is not in itself a serious infection. The main symptoms are fever, enlargement of lymph glands in the neck and a sore throat. A transient body rash may be seen occasionally, particularly during or after the treat-ment of the sore throat with penicillin or one of its synthetic cousins such as ampicillin. Diagnosis without laboratory tests on the blood (the Paul-Bunnel test) may not be easy although the com-bination of sore throat, swollen neck glands and a rash is highly suspicious. The disease is self-limiting and there is no treatment.

Rabies. Finally, we shall deal very briefly with a number of less common virus diseases, beginning, as is appropriate, with *hydrophobia* or *rabies*, since it was in this infection that the great French scientist Louis Pasteur (1822–95) showed the possibility of prevention by vaccination. Unlike Jenner, with his ready-made cowpox virus, which is probably the virus of smallpox weakened by natural passage through cows, Pasteur had to weaken the rabies virus by passing it through rabbits. The rabbits were infected, and after death the spinal cord was dried and powdered, and a solution passed through another rabbit, and so on until the virus was sufficiently weakened.

Rabies is spread by the bite of infected animals, usually dogs, cats, or wolves, who are driven mad

by the disease; in Trinidad, however, it has been spread by vampire bats. Those who are bitten usually show no symptoms for six weeks or more, but sooner or later convulsions and delirium arise, which within four to five days are fatal.

There is no cure once the symptoms have developed, but antirabies serum, followed by anti-rabies inoculation as soon as possible, prevents illness in the majority of cases. Dogs should be muzzled in areas where the disease is common, but quarantining imported dogs has made the infection almost unknown here. Effective immunisation is now available.

Sandfly Fever, or phlebotomus fever, *Dengue,* or breakbone fever, and *Trench Fever* are all somewhat similar conditions in that they resemble influenza and are rarely fatal. They are all due to viruses, spread in the first case by sandflies in tropical climates; in the second by mosquitoes in tropical climates; and in the third by lice in temperate climates. They are all typical "soldiers' diseases"; the first two were common in the Middle East and Far East during the last War, the third during the First World War in France.

Yellow Fever. Yellow fever is carried by a mosquito known as Aedes, common in South and Central America and in African ports. For its spread, it therefore needs: a hot climate, the Aedes mosquito, and an infected person.

In 1898 the United States was at war with Spain in Central America, where yellow fever was a serious problem. Following this war the United States, by this time acutely aware of this terrible disease, asked a Dr. G. E. Waring to deal with it in Havana, where it was rife. But Waring died of yellow fever, as had many millions before him, without knowing its cause, and it was left to Walter Reed, who died in 1902, to prove the con-nection between the mosquito and yellow fever. By a vigorous war on the mosquito, the disease has been eradicated from Havana and the West Indian islands, and Reed's discovery made possible the building of the Panama Canal.

In yellow fever there is a sudden high tempera-ture, aching of limbs and head, jaundice, and black vomit; the pulse-rate falls as the fever rises. Previous vaccination seems to be preventive if undertaken in time.

AIDS. AIDS stands for acquired immunodefi-ciency syndrome, and is caused by the human immunodeficiency virus (HIV). AIDS seems to be a new affliction for the human race, and was first described in 1981. In 1998, the number of persons contracting HIV in Britain was around 2,500 a year. Infection occurs by intercourse, the anal variety apparently being the more dangerous, by direct transmission through infected blood, and congenital transmission from mother to baby. Thus, the major risk factors for AIDS are male homosexuality, needle sharing by intravenous drug abusers, haemophilia, and having an infected mother. Heterosexual intercourse is also an important mode of spread, especially among prostitutes, who are the most promiscuous members of communities. AIDS can be avoided by restricting sexual relations to the one you trust, and by avoiding *any* contact with other people's blood.

HIV damages the T-lymphocytes that are respon-sible for protecting the body against infection. with the result that the sufferer becomes prey to a variety of otherwise rare infections such as *Pneumocystis carinii* pneumonia, as well as some rare tumours, particularly Kaposi's sarcoma and lymphomas. The incubation period can be very long, and the first signs are often lethargy, weight loss and swelling of the lymph glands. There is as yet no effective vaccine; treatment consists of taking a number of different anti-viral and enzyme inhibiting drugs. These have numerous side-effects and the treat-ment remains to be optimised. Long-term success rates are unclear.

Conclusion.

There is no specific cure for most viral diseases, though several can be prevented by immunisation or by social control of the creatures carrying the virus and by the use of common day-to-day hygiene, and drugs are beginning to be introduced against a few viruses. Incubation periods are generally of the order of days, though in the case of the AIDS virus can be measured in years. Where active immunisation is not available, passive protection with gamma globulin is often an effective alternative.

Bacterial Diseases.

Bacterial diseases differ from virus infections in a number of respects; their incubation period tends to be shorter: having the disease once does not often confer lifelong protection; and unlike virus diseases, most bacterial diseases respond to one of the antibiotics or sulphonamides. In some cases it is possible to inoculate against the disease to prevent it occurring, as is possible with some of the virus diseases.

Scarlet Fever and Other Streptococcal Infections. In the days, not so long ago, before the arrival of chemotherapy (sulphonamides and antibiotics), streptococci were very much feared and even caused a high mortality, particularly in such susceptible groups as chi'dren, and mothers and babies in maternity hospitals. They are still taken very seriously in the latter and rightly so, although one wonders how much of the mystique is simply a hangover from the days, fifty years ago, when many mothers died from "childbed fever." All signs of infection, such as fever, during the puerperium (the period following childbirth) must be promptly dealt with by a doctor, and only occasionally now is there real cause for anxiety provided treatment is prompt and rigorous.

Scarlet fever is much less common and very much less serious an illness than it used to be, partly because of the effective treatments available today, but also because of a definite but unexplained reduction in its severity. Perhaps the streptococcus has changed, and certainly the improved physical condition of people who are now much better fed and housed than they were, has helped to ward off the terrors of this disease as of so many other infections. The classical picture of signs and symptoms is now so rarely seen that it will not be further described. However, there is some evidence that streptococci are changing again, and becoming more pathogenic and difficult to treat.

The importance of streptococcal infections has shifted from the initial infection, such as a sore throat, to some serious conditions which occasionally arise as a result of some form of delayed sensitivity to the bacteria. Acute rheumatism or rheumatic fever (not to be confused with ordinary aches and pains nor with rheumatoid arthritis) occasionally arise in people who have had a sore throat a few weeks before. Since the streptococcus is not the direct cause of the damage which may consequently occur in the heart or kidney, the antibiotics are no answer except sometimes to keep off further streptococcal invasions.

Diphtheria. This used to be an extremely serious disease, but immunisation has made it almost unknown; it is important, therefore, that all children should be immunised. There are many modern and up-to-date doctors who have qualified since the war who have never seen a case because it has become so rare, and in spite of the propaganda of certain ill-informed people, this saving of children's lives is entirely the result of nationwide inoculation during the war and since. The following description is of historic interest only, and will remain so if a high level of inoculation is kept up by parents.

In a typical case of diphtheria the incubation period is about three days; the patient is a child who becomes ill and pale-looking (*i.e.*, the onset is not sudden, as in many fevers, but insidious); the temperature is only slightly raised to, perhaps, 37° or 38°C, and although there may be no complaint of sore throat, examination will reveal inflammation with—and this is typical of diphtheria —a grey membrane spread over the tonsils, the palate, and the back of the mouth generally. The diphtheria germ does not spread within the body. It stays at the place where it entered (in this case the throat) and sends its toxins throughout the body.

Even after the acute phase is over the patient must not be allowed to walk, because the diphtheria toxin is particularly poisonous to the heart. The ordinary rule is at least one or two months in bed.

Diphtheria also occurs in the larynx—in pre-inoculation days many children choked to death with this form of the infection; in the nose; and, although this is not generally known, wounds can be infected. The so-called "Desert sores" of the North African campaign seem to have been caused by diphtheria-like organisms.

Diphtheria may lead to paralysis of the throat, with difficulty in speaking or swallowing, and paralysis of the eyes or limbs; these are due to neuritis caused by the influence of the toxin on the nerves.

Whooping Cough. For many years whooping cough has been regarded merely as a bother to the patient and a nuisance to others, as, in fact, a trivial disease. Unfortunately, this is not so; because statistics show that it caused more deaths than polio, diphtheria, scarlet fever, and measles put together.

Whooping cough begins in a child as an ordinary cold with cough and slight fever, and this stage lasts for a week or ten days. Then the "paroxysmal stage" begins as a series of coughs following in rapid succession, during which time the patient is unable to breathe. The "whoop" is caused by the noisy indrawing of breath when the fit stops. The face may become blue and congested. Bronchitis is usually present, and bronchopneumonia may result as a complication, so inoculation of all children before the disease has a chance to strike them is most important.

Once whooping cough has begun, there is no specific treatment, although modern drugs can reduce the frequency of the fits of coughing. The antibiotic chloramphenicol has been used for this disease, but the general opinion is that it is ordinarily of little benefit. Chinese physicians once described whooping cough as the "hundred-days cough," and the cough may, indeed, continue for at least a hundred days. There is an effective vaccine.

Typhus. This disease used to be known as "jail fever," because it was frequent in prisons; but overcrowding, poverty, and bad hygienic surroundings anywhere are suitable conditions for epidemics of typhus. Improved conditions in industrialised countries have made it unusual, since typhus is carried from one person to another by infected body lice. It is due to the organism *Rickettsia prowazekii*, a very small type of bacterium.

Typhus comes on suddenly with a rise in temperature to about 39°C, but within four days it may be as high as 42°C. There may, or may not, be a rash at this time, and in the second week, when the temperature is at its highest, there is delirium, weakness, and a feeble pulse. The typical typhus rash appears about the fifth day as reddish blotches on the chest, abdomen, and wrists.

Typhus is, needless to say, very serious but responds to modern antibiotics. Preventive measures are directed towards eradicating lice.

Psittacosis. This disease which is of interest mainly in that it is spread by birds of the parrot group, such as parrots, lovebirds, macaws, and the rest is caused by chlamyclia, which are similar to bacteria. It occasionally occurs here in people who have been in contact with birds of this type, and is serious both to the bird and to its owner. Quarantine regulations greatly reduced the risk of infection in Britain. Concern over renewed outbreaks, not only of psittacosis but a number of economically important diseases such as fowl pest, led to their reintroduction in 1976.

The symptoms of psittacosis are fever, cough, and bronchitis. The disease is especially dangerous to old people, but it responds to the same antibiotics as typhus.

Tuberculosis. No disease causes more public concern, and no disease is more difficult to describe, than tuberculosis; for, like the Streptococcus or the Staphylococcus, the tubercle germ can attack many different parts of the body and manifest itself in many ways. Furthermore, it is a widely spread disease, infecting not only humans but also cattle, birds and reptiles. In Britain, in the 1990s, around 6,000 people are still diagnosed with T.B. each year. But here we shall be concerned with those types common to man—the human and bovine (*i.e.*, the type occurring in cattle which can be spread to man by infected milk).

The tubercle bacillus is particularly hardy, so that when coughed or spat out on the ground it continues to be infectious for a long time. Infection is therefore caused by: (*a*) drinking infected milk; (*b*) droplet infection from aerosols produced by coughing; (*c*) breathing in infected dust. In other words, tuberculosis is caused by absorption through either the lungs or the intestines; the former is common in adults, the latter in children.

But there is a good deal more to the problem than this; we know, for example, that over 90 per cent. of people in industrial countries have been infected with T.B. in early life and have conquered the infection. So the question arises: what conditions predispose to T.B.—why do some people get over the early infection and others not? There are two answers to this question: one is certain—that those who are impoverished and do not get enough food are liable to T.B.; the second is not so certain—that mental stress plays some part. Stress causes a general reduction in immunity, predisposing the body to several infections including T.B.

In children, lung tuberculosis is not common, |but tuberculosis of the bones and glands is, as is also infection in the abdomen, the kidney or spine, and, worst of all, tuberculous meningitis. These are often of the bovine type from infected milk. Ordinarily, T.B. in children is less serious than adult infections; but tuberculous meningitis used to be almost invariably fatal until streptomycin was discovered.

Adult tuberculosis usually occurs in the lungs or the pleura—the thin membrane surrounding the lungs. In younger people miliary tuberculosis, which is a form of T.B. blood-poisoning or septicaemia, is a very serious condition, and the infection spreads throughout the whole body in a few weeks.

Lung infection begins gradually in someone who has previously felt unwell. There may be cough, and later blood-stained sputum (although blood which is coughed up does not necessarily prove that T.B. is present). Whatever means of treatment is used, the struggle between disease and patient is likely to be fairly long, but the outlook is now good. The closure of the Swiss sanatoria is due partly to modern disbelief that air in one place is better than that in another, but mainly to improved treatment.

Prevention depends on legal action ensuring tuberculosis-free herds of cattle; on control of spread of the disease by those "open" cases who carry germs in their sputum; on the use of vaccination in childhood with B.C.G. vaccine (which you can ask your doctor about).

Many methods are used in treatment: drugs, such as streptomycin, isoniazid, and P.A.S., lung surgery, rest, and so on. T.B is now a fairly rare disease in developed countries, but there are worries that the emergence of antibiotic resistant strains will lead to an upsurge in its frequency. There are skin tests to show whether there is susceptibility to T.B.

Septicaemia. Commonly known as "blood-poisoning." This occurs generally by spread from some septic area such as a wound (or even a small prick), after childbirth, or any place where certain germs have got admission to the body. The most usual germ is the Streptococcus, although the pneumococcus—which ordinarily causes pneumonia—and the Staphylococcus may also cause septicaemia.

Fever comes on suddenly and rises rapidly with headaches, sweating, and shivering. The patient is obviously very ill, and later there is wasting and delirium. The white blood cells increase in number. Septicaemia sometimes occurs without any apparent local infection in those who are weak and debilitated.

Pyaemia is a type of septicaemia which leads to the formation of numerous abscesses throughout the body. Its symptoms are the same as described above, except that the causative germ is usually the Staphylococcus, and abscesses are found which may need surgical treatment.

However, in both conditions the state of affairs has been revolutionised by the use of the sulpha drugs and antibiotics; cure is now the rule rather than the exception.

Septicaemia should be suspected when any small wound or cut is followed by high temperature and the symptoms described above.

The word "*Toxaemia*" is used when the germs stay in their original position and produce symptoms by spreading their toxins throughout the body. Tetanus, diphtheria, and some kinds of childbirth infection come into this category; the symptoms may vary from mild disturbance to severe illness.

Meningitis means inflammation of the meninges, the covering which, like a layer of plastic, lies over the brain and spinal cord, just as the pleura covers the lungs and the peritoneum covers internal organs in the abdomen. (Hence inflammation of the pleura is known as pleurisy, and inflammation of the peritoneum as peritonitis.)

Various germs may cause meningitis, for example, some viruses, the bacillus of tuberculosis, the pneumococcus, which ordinarily causes pneumonia, and the Streptococcus or Staphylococcus, but ordinarily the word refers to *cerebrospinal meningitis* or "spotted fever" caused by the meningococcus and occurring at times as an epidemic. It is commonest in the years from infancy to the early twenties, and begins suddenly with headache, vomiting, and fever. The temperature rises quickly, and pain develops in the back and legs; on the second or third day a rash appears on the body, and particularly on the inside of the thighs. Later there is stiffness of the neck, the head may be drawn back, vomiting persists, and the headache can be so severe as to cause the patient to scream with pain.

Fortunately, this type of meningitis (and most of the others) respond to treatment with antibiotics or the sulpha drugs, so the risks are very much less than formerly. However, recent outbreaks (for example, among students) have reminded us of the need for vigilance.

Pneumococcal meningitis is an unusual complication of pneumonia, and the septic types (*streptococcal* or *staphylococcal*) arise either following an infected fracture of the skull or from infection of the ear or mastoid.

Tuberculous meningitis has already been mentioned; originally always fatal, it is now treatable with streptomycin.

All these diseases are very much a matter for specialist and hospital treatment, but it is worth while mentioning viral meningitis, in which, although all the symptoms of meningitis are present, recovery without specific treatment is invariable.

Tetanus is usually known as "lockjaw" because there may be difficulty in opening the mouth, although this is simply part of a spasm of all the muscles of the body. The tetanus bacillus is found in rich soil—hence the disease is less common in desert areas—and tetanus resembles rabies in that: (*a*) it enters at a wound; (*b*) it affects the nervous system; (*c*) it results in fits and ultimately death.

However, active immunisation with T.T. (tetanus toxoid) has resulted in the disease becoming uncommon, and even when developed, treatment with antitoxin, sedatives, muscle relaxants, and antibiotics may lead to cure.

The bacillus is anaerobic (*i.e.*, does not use oxygen) and is most likely to occur in such situations as when a man digging manure or working in his garden sticks a fork through his foot, or, in war-time, when he is wounded in soil contaminated with manure.

Undulant fever, also known as Malta fever, abortus fever or brucellosis, falls into two types: melitensis, which infects goats, and abortus, cattle and pigs. Man gets the disease by reason of close contact with or drinking the milk of infected animals. (The name abortus is given because abortion is produced in cattle and sows.)

In undulant fever, as one would suppose, the fever goes up and down for two to three weeks; it may then go down and rise again, persisting for many months. The disease may occur in Britain, but modern drugs are on the whole successful in dealing with it. A striking feature of the disease is the combination of a high temperature with an appearance of relative well-being.

Another disease carried by mammals is *Glanders* or *Farcy*, spread by horses. In glanders there is discharge from the nose and sometimes pneumonia. Occasionally the disease is fatal. In farcy abscesses form, usually along the lymph vessels. Both conditions are very contagious, and treatment is a matter for a specialist; infected horses should be destroyed.

Cholera. Cholera could be classified under the head of food-poisoning, because it is mainly spread by infected water (however, like typhoid, it can also be spread by flies, infected food, and carriers); it could also be classified as a tropical disease, since, although it used to be found in Europe, it is now mainly rife in India.

Cholera is caused by a vibrio, which is a spiral bacterium, and can be prevented by early inoculation and care over food supplies—boiling water and milk, washing uncooked foods in chlorinated water, and keeping flies away.

The fever begins in the usual way with a short incubation period, followed by abdominal pain, severe vomiting, and diarrhoea. Later with the loss of fluid from the body there may be cramps in the muscles, diarrhoea increases, and the motions become of the typical "rice-water" type —*i.e.*, there is no solid matter, and the appearance is that of water to which a little milk has been added. This stage is followed by collapse, with low pulse and cold hands and feet. Death, if adequate treatment is not available, results in about 70 per cent. of cases. Cholera can generally be survived simply by replacing the water and salts lost in the diarrhoea, along with antibiotic therapy.

Anthrax. The bacillus of anthrax, like that of tuberculosis, can exist outside the body for long periods, and, like that of tetanus, then takes the form of spores or seed-like bodies. It is spread by infected cattle and horses, which get the disease from eating grass containing spores.

In human beings the form the disease takes depends on where the germ alights; sometimes it comes from infected shaving-brushes, when it causes a large sore, like a boil, on the face, known as "malignant pustule"; sometimes it develops in those who inhale the dust from infected hides or wool (hence the name 'wool-sorters' disease," which is a form of bronchitis with blood-stained sputum); lastly it may arise through eating infected meat, when the result is intestinal anthrax.

In all cases the outlook was serious. Death was often common, preceded by a high temperature, skin symptoms in the first instance, lung symptoms in the second, and food-poisoning symptoms in the third. Penicillin or tetracycline is now increasingly effective.

Food Poisoning Diseases.

Strictly speaking there is no such thing as "food poisoning" if one is thinking of "poisoning" in terms of anything apart from germs. But not so long ago it used to be thought that decomposition of food in itself produced poisons known as "ptomaines" which were deadly to those who swallowed them. All food poisoning is caused by infection of food with bacteria and by no other cause—unless of course, we are thinking of the kind of poisoning which is the concern of the lawyer rather than the doctor!

Here we are considering those diseases which are commonly spread by contaminated food or drink. The classification is not scientific, but then no scientific classification has as yet been devised. First, we shall deal with typhoid, paratyphoid, and dysentery—uncommon here in Britain, although Sonné dysentery is fairly frequent. Then there is gastro-enteritis (which means irritation of the stomach and intestines), which is caused by staphylococci and the germs of the salmonella group, and lastly botulism, which is rare.

Typhoid and Paratyphoid. These diseases are spread by infected water, food, or hands— especially uncooked food, such as milk, salads, oysters, and shellfish. Flies, too, play some part in spreading the disease. Some people are "carriers" and carry and excrete the germs without being themselves affected; for example, "Typhoid Mary," a carrier in the United States in the early years of this century, spent a large part of her life in custody as a public danger, although she did not show any symptoms of typhoid. Nevertheless, this woman caused a great deal of illness in others in her chosen profession of cook.

The influence of Chadwick's propaganda for pure water supplies is shown by the fact that deaths from typhoid, still 332 per 1,000,000 in 1870, fell to 198 per 1,000,000 by 1900. In the 1920s the death-rate was only 25 per 1,000,000, and now it is even less.

Typhoid fever begins like most fevers with headache, raised temperature, and general feeling of unwellness. This stage lasts about a week, and then the rash appears in the form of rose-red spots on the front of the chest and abdomen and on the back. In the second week there is great weakness, sometimes diarrhoea, flatulence, and mental dullness, together with dry and cracked lips and tongue. The third week is the week, in hopeful cases, of gradual decrease in temperature and other symptoms, and the fourth week is the week of convalescence. Complications are perforation of the intestine (which needs surgical treatment), delirium, and bronchitis.

Paratyphoid fever is a milder form of typhoid (there are two forms, A and B); ordinarily it can be diagnosed only by scientific tests. The main thing is to inoculate contacts with T.A.B. vaccine and to protect food supplies; treatment is with chloramphenicol.

Dysentery. Dysentery may be caused either by a bacterium or an amoeba; the first type is known as bacillary dysentery, the latter as amoebic dysentery (which is dealt with under tropical diseases). Infection is spread in much the same way as in typhoid. There is high fever, abdominal pain, and diarrhoea, at first consisting of faecal matter, then blood and mucus. In severe cases the death-rate used to be over 20 per cent. Dysentry is caused by several species of bacteria of the genus *Shigella.*

However, in all these infections sulphaguanidine, ampicillin or tetracycline bring rapid relief, but care must be taken to avoid infection of other people.

Diarrhoea and Vomiting. Leaving out typhoid and paratyphoid fevers and dysentery, there is a group of infections known as "D. and V."— diarrhoea and vomiting. In Britain D. & V. is mostly due to:

(1) Salmonella infection.
(2) Staphylococcal infections.
(3) Other bacteria, ordinarily harmless, such as Escherichia coli, when present in sufficient numbers.
(4) Various viral infections, particularly rotavirus.

Salmonella Infections are the most serious of this group; they affect the small intestine and produce vomiting, severe abdominal pain, and diarrhoea. These symptoms occur about one day after eating infected food and usually clear up within about two weeks, but occasionally death results. Salmonella bacteria are most likely to be found in meat, egg powder, vegetables, and ducks' eggs. The number of cases has risen greatly in the 1980s and 1990s.

Staphylococcal Food Poisoning has greatly increased in recent years, so it is important to know what circumstances are likely to cause it. Staphylococci are liable to grow in milk products, such as ice-cream and cream buns. Food poisoning from staphylococci is seldom severe, and recovery takes place in about a week. Nevertheless, it is extremely infectious, and causes a great deal of lost time in industry and temporary illness in institutions; for it is in such situations that it is most likely to occur. The reason for the increase in staphylococcal food poisoning has nothing to do, as many people suppose, with greater use of canned foods, but it has much to do with the greater use of communal feeding and canteen meals. It is *possible* for bacterial toxins in infected food to bring about illness even when the canning process has killed the bacteria, but it is certainly extremely rare. Canned foods, in fact, are much safer than so-called "fresh" foods in this respect—except when they have been opened, left about, and then re-heated. The same applies to the re-heating of any kind of food.

The real enemy is the canteen worker with a boil, a discharging nose, dirty hands, or a septic finger. Occasionally food may be infected in the larder by rats or mice, but the sort of canteen or restaurant where this can happen has little to commend it. Frankly, these infections are caused by dirty or stupid people who do not realise that their sore finger or boil can become someone else's diarrhoea and vomiting. Where children are concerned, the outlook is potentially more serious, and in the early part of this century the Summer-time "procession of baby coffins" was all too familiar. Infection is much more common in artificially fed babies or in older children who eat infected ice-cream. However trivial the condition may seem, diarrhoea and vomiting with fever in a child should never be ignored. Those in charge of canteens or restaurants must ensure that staff is supervised, that anyone with a septic infection is put off duty, and that all know about washing after visiting the lavatory and absolute cleanliness.

Bacilli normally present in the intestine, such as Escherichia coli, can cause infections if absorbed in large amounts, or if of a different strain from those in the patient's intestine. They are not usually serious.

Botulism. Now uncommon, this is the disease which used to be known as "ptomaine poisoning" on the theory that it was caused by poisons produced by bad food apart from germs. In the 1920s a party of picnickers at Loch Maree in the Scottish Highlands developed botulism and a number died, with the result that the disease attracted much public attention. Botulism is caused by a germ, clostridium botulinum, which is peculiar in that, like tetanus, its poison attacks the nervous system rather than the intestines, resulting in fits, double vision, paralysis beginning in the face and spreading downwards, and difficulty in swallowing. It is found in tinned fruits or vegetables containing the toxin even when the germ has been killed, but, as we have already seen, the toxin comes from the bacilli, not from decomposition of food as such (in fact, food does not decompose in the absence of germs). Death is common in botulism, but an antitoxin is now available which, if used in time, can cure the disease.

Diseases Caused by Fungi.

Numerous fungi are pathogenic, and fungal diseases may be primary or secondary to other diseases; allergies to fungi are also important. The most common fungal disease is candidiasis, which is infection with the imperfect yeast-like fungus *Candida* albicans; this frequently infects the feet (athlete's foot), the mouth and the vagina, producing local itching as the main symptom. Ringworm or tinea, despite its name, is not caused by worms but fungi which cause ring-shaped pigmented patches on the skin, sometimes covered with vesicles or scales. Actinomycosis, a disease caused by bacteria which superficially resemble fungi, is a serious but treatable condition with inflamed lymph glands around the jaw or ulcerating sores on the skin; it can also affect the lungs, intestines and brain.

The Venereal Diseases.

The venereal diseases are those caused—or at least that is what the name means—by the goddess of love, Venus. Venus, of course, causes a great deal of trouble, but venereal disease is not necessarily the worst she can do. Sexually transmitted disease (Venereal Disease) is spread by sexual intercourse with an infected person.

Gonorrhoea is the result of an infection by the gonococcus (*Neisseria gonorrhoeae*) and ordinarily comes on after an incubation period of three to seven days. However, babies can get an infection of the eyes, known as ophthalmia neonatorum, from their mother if she is infected, and gonorrhoea in young children is often the result of being in contact with infected towels or clothes. The disease in adults is evident when there is a thick, creamy discharge from the sexual organs and sometimes pain on passing water; in infants ophthalmia is prevented by the use of silver nitrate eye-drops at birth. Gonorrhoea is fairly easily cured by the use of sulpha drugs or penicillin; but unfortunately venereal disease is increasing in recent years and drug-resistant forms are becoming more common.

Syphilis is a serious venereal disease caused by a spirochaete (*Treponema pallidum*). Stories about lavatory seats are simply stories, although it is occasionally possible to get syphilis by other than sexual means: for example, it has happened that a man playing football has been infected through his hand being grazed by the teeth of someone with syphilis. But this is very unusual, although kissing can spread the disease. Children, too, can be born with syphilis (the so-called congenital syphilis).

Adult syphilis begins with a sore, known as a hard chancre, at the point where the spirochete of syphilis has entered; this may be on the lips, through kissing; on the sexual organs, through intercourse; and very rarely, as explained above, elsewhere. In a short time the chancre disappears and all may seem to be well, but this primary stage is followed by a secondary stage with sore throat, a rash, headache, and enlargement of glands. This, if left alone, also clears up, but is followed by the tertiary stage, in which a chronic infection develops in some part of the body which, presumably, is most susceptible in the particular individual. Thus there may be chronic syphilis of the skin, the bones, the heart, liver, or nervous system.

In the nervous system, the commonest forms are the two diseases of *tabes dorsalis*, in which the spinal cord is infected, and G.P.I. (general paralysis of the insane), in which the brain and mind are affected. These will be discussed under Nervous Diseases.

In congenital syphilis the pregnant mother gives her child syphilis. Such infants are often still-born or premature, they look wizened, like little old men, and amongst other symptoms are eye disease, "snuffles," a flattened nose, and when the adult teeth appear the front ones may be notched at the biting surface.

The treatment, of course, is very much a matter for a specialist, but diagnosis is usually made through the Wassermann blood test. It was for syphilis that Ehrlich produced his "magic bullet"—an arsenical drug, known as salvarsan, which could attack the organism selectively without harming the body and was the first of the modern specific drugs. Present-day treatment is with penicillin. G.P.I. was once treated with malarial therapy with some success. Penicillin alone is often adequate.

It is important to understand that venereal disease can only be transmitted during sexual intercourse (or with intimate acts associated with it—*e.g.,* "oral sex"), that promiscuity therefore increases the risk, that not all lesions in, on or around the genitals are necessarily venereal disease and that *fear* of contracting it is widespread in many communities. If in doubt consult your own doctor or attend one of the many special clinics which can be found in most cities. Their location is usually advertised in conveniences and other public places. Delay is certainly dangerous.

Chancroid produces small septic ulcers around the sex organs, with swelling of the local glands in the groin, which may suppurate. It is caused by a bacillus, and can usually be cleared up by sulpha drugs within a week. Scabies and lice often pass from one body to another during sexual intercourse, but are not usually thought of as venereal in origin, although in many cases they are.

Tropical Diseases.

Nothing is more difficult than to define the term "tropical diseases." One might define them as the diseases which occur in tropical climates—but then measles occurs there too; and if they are defined as those diseases which are found *only* in the tropics, the solution is no easier, since leprosy, cholera, smallpox, and typhus are usually listed as tropical diseases, yet were found in this country until fairly recently—and the odd case still is.

But what a story could be told about the conquest of those infections which were—and many still are—the scourge of humanity! One day when generals and dictators are forgotten we shall remember that great international army of physicians and bacteriologists who have saved millions of lives and infinitely reduced human suffering: Koch and Ehrlich of Germany, Pasteur and Roux of France, Ross and Jenner of Britain, Reed of America, Noguchi of Japan, and many others. We shall remember how the Jesuit priests brought quinine from Peru to Europe in 1638, the first drug to save people from malaria; how in tropical heat Ronald Ross (1857–1932) peered for hours through his microscope to discover the connection between malaria and the mosquito until the sweat running from his brow rusted the instrument; how Major Walter Reed's work in Havana (1851–1902) made possible the building of the Panama Canal, and think, too, of the American soldiers who died in helping him to find the cause of yellow fever. In mentioning Jenner once more, we should recall Lady Mary Montagu (1689–1762), who brought the practice of vaccination to England from Turkey—or, rather, the practice of "variolation," which meant inoculating with the pus from smallpox cases. This was, of course, a dangerous practice, but the idea was there.

Relapsing Fever, common in India and Africa, may be louse- or tick-borne; the germ is a spirochaete, similar to that of syphilis, but the disease is non-venereal. Relapsing fever gets its name from the fact that the temperature remains high (39°–41°C) for about a week, returns to normal for a week, and rises again. There may be three to five relapses of this sort. Penicillin is effective; lice or ticks must be eradicated.

Epidemic Jaundice (also known as Weil's disease or—if you prefer it—ictero-haemorrhagica spirochaetosis), is also caused by a spirochaete, and spread by rats. Now it is rarely found in Europe, although it occurred in the trenches during the First World War, in men working in sewers, and in the women who worked in the fish market of Aberdeen, which at one time was rat-infested. It is rarely fatal, but leads to high fever and jaundice. Penicillin in high dosage or tetracycline may help.

Yaws is also a spirochaetal disease, common in the tropics and particularly in children. It is unpleasant, but not serious, and tends to clear up in a year or so. There are raspberry-like growths on the skin, which disappear with the drugs used in syphilis (although the condition is non-venereal). The Wassermann reaction, positive to syphilis, is also positive in yaws.

Leprosy. Whereas syphilis, relapsing fever, epidemic jaundice, and yaws are caused by spirochaetes, leprosy is caused by a bacillus resembling the bacillus of tuberculosis. Apart from the difficulty of classification, many popular beliefs about the disease are untrue. It is *not* the oldest disease afflicting man; *not* a disease confined to tropical countries; it is *not* very catching; *not* hereditary, *not* incurable; in leprosy the fingers and toes do *not* drop off; it is *not* a divine punishment for wrongdoing.

Leprosy is a serious disease not because of disfiguring light-coloured skin patches and lumps, but because it destroys peripheral nerves. Leprosy may disappear spontaneously, or it may progress until the face is lion-like and the hands and feet wasted and ulcerated. The disease rarely kills, but it is the world's greatest crippler.

Leprosy was once fairly common in colder Western countries, though its extent was exaggerated. The great majority of the millions of people who suffer from leprosy live in tropical countries, but it still exists in Iceland, Japan, Korea and some of the southern states of the United States. Prolonged and intimate contact with an "open" case is said to be the main mode of infection, but only one infected husband in twenty passes leprosy to his wife.

The cheap synthetic drug dapsone is highly effective in leprosy, but problems in delivery to third-world settings has resulted in the emergence of resistant strains, so that much more expensive drugs now have to be used. The WHO has launched an ambitious "multi-drug therapy" programme in an attempt to bring this disease under control. Established deformity (such as claw hand, drop foot, paralysed eyelids) can be mitigated by reconstructive surgery, although lost sensation cannot be restored.

In the past, only Christian missions were concerned with the plight of the leprosy sufferer. Now, non-sectarian voluntary agencies, Governments and the World Health Organisation have joined in the fight against the disease. Enough is known to control the disease, but not enough is being done, as only one victim in five is at present getting treatment.

Plague is another disease caused by bacteria, common in Europe at one time, but now largely restricted to Asia. Nevertheless, it caused millions of deaths in Europe during the years 1348–49 and 1665 and was the "Black Death," which, indeed, changed the course of history.

Plague is carried by the bite of the rat flea, but, once people become infected, spread may occur from one to the other by droplet infection—*i.e.*, by coughing and sneezing. After an incubation period of two to ten days, fever develops, rather like severe influenza, and in a day or two the glands in the groin begin to swell, followed perhaps by swelling of the glands elsewhere. This is the usual type of plague, but it is also possible to get disease of the lungs from droplet infection and blood-poisoning from infection of the blood-stream. Both the latter types are almost invariably fatal, and even the glandular type (bubonic plague) has a mortality of about 80 per cent. The vaccine has given place to streptomycin and sulpha drugs which are also used on contacts.

Although we have little space to discuss the subject of plagues and epidemics in general, it is worth noting that serious epidemics have almost always followed wars, revolutions, and economic and political collapse. Thus the Black Death followed the break-up of the Roman Empire, and, in the fourteenth century, accompanied the end of mediaeval civilisation. The Napoleonic wars were followed by other epidemics, and the wars of the 1830s in Europe were followed by influenza. In the most widespread outburst of influenza after the First World War, more people were killed by the disease than in all the fighting of four years. It is a reflection on the peculiar mentality of man that this devastating epidemic, which affected almost the whole world, occupies little space in his history books. Yet 20 million men, and women, and children died from influenza, and no cure has, as yet, been found!

Protozoal Diseases.

Nearly all the diseases caused by protozoa are tropical diseases, although one of the best-known protozoans is the harmless amoeba found in British ponds. Protozoal diseases are caused by these organisms, large in comparison with bacteria, which should really be thought of as one-celled animals. Viruses are neither animals nor plants, are much smaller than the other two groups, and have some distinctive characteristics described elsewhere.

Among the diseases caused by protozoa are sleeping sickness or trypanosomiasis, malaria, and amoebic dysentery (as contrasted with bacillary dysentery), another disease, leishmaniasis—also known by the numerous names of kala-azar, dum-dum fever, and, in milder form, Delhi boil, Oriental sore, or Baghdad sore—will also be mentioned briefly. More recently, humans have been affected by *cryptosporidosis*. This is an intestinal infection usually passed to humans from farm animals (*e.g.* by infected milk). Symptoms include severe diarrhoea. These infections are few, but important in their influence on man; for, as Dr. Clark-Kennedy has pointed out, malaria until recently was responsible for one-fifth of all human sickness, sleeping sickness not so long ago caused a large part of Central Africa to be uninhabitable, and in some areas of the tropics there are probably more people with, than without, amoebic dysentery.

Malaria. The word, of course, means "bad air," just as "influenza" means "influence"—in Italian *influenza di freddo*—the influence of cold. Human beings have a natural tendency to suppose that, when two events occur together, then one must be caused by the other. Yet, although malaria and "bad air" may often go together, and influenza and cold, it does not follow that bad air (whatever that may be) causes malaria nor that cold causes influenza. In fact, the Anopheles mosquito carries the amoeba of malaria, and the mosquito prefers climates which some people might describe as "bad," but it is the amoeba, not the air, which causes the disease. Anyhow, the unfortunate mosquito might well use the phrase honoured by many generations of schoolmasters: "It hurts me more than it hurts you!" For the mosquito, too, is sick, and passes on its sickness to the person it bites.

There are several types of Plasmodium—which is the scientific name for this amoeba—producing attacks of fever varying in severity and frequency: benign tertian, quartan, and malignant quartan. Entering the body from the mosquito bite, the parasites penetrate the blood cells, multiply there, and finally burst into the blood stream. When this happens the temperature rises, and then they return to the cells to carry out once more the same procedure. Depending on the type, the attacks of fever may be at intervals of three or four days, severe or milder. When someone with malaria is bitten by a mosquito the infection can be transmitted to the next person it meets, but malaria is not infectious from one person to another directly. Quinine, of course, is the time-honoured remedy, but many other drugs are now available: mepacrine, primaquine, chloroquine and some sulpha drugs. The drug must be taken long enough for the infection to die out, otherwise relapses can occur even after leaving a malarial country (but it is only fair to say that, just as some people continue to give themselves the title of "Major" when they have left the army, so others long in Britain continue to describe attacks of cold or 'flu as "my old malaria again," when, to say the least of it, they are exaggerating).

Important as are the drugs used in the treatment of malaria, even more so is the control of the parasite-bearing mosquito. The eggs of mosquitoes hatch in water, and there the young or larval forms can be attacked by pouring oil on the surface of pools so that they are unable to breathe, or by introducing small fish which have a partiality for them. Adult mosquitoes can be killed by insecticides or kept away by repellent creams or nets over beds. Prophylaxis with antimalaria before entering and while living in known malarial zones is important.

Blackwater Fever is a sequel to malaria in tropical Africa and some parts of India. Rather illogically, it is described as "Blackwater," although the urine is red and the skin is yellow but the result is due to breaking down of the red blood cells by some malarial toxin. Possibly too much quinine may help in producing the illness. Treatment is to give plenty of fluids and no quinine or any other anti-malarial drugs in the early stages. The death-rate is about 25 per cent.

Trypanosomiasis or sleeping sickness—not to be confused with *sleepy* sickness—is essentially an African disease (although also found in tropical America) spread by the tsetse fly. Its cause is the type of protozoan known as a trypanosome, almond-shaped with vibrating membranes at the sides which enable it to move through the blood-stream, rather like a flat fish in the water.

There are three stages of the disease: first, the stage of fever with enlarged glands and a rapid pulse; which may continue off and on for three years; secondly, the stage of trembling hands, legs, and tongue, vacant expression, and slow and stumbling speech; thirdly, and lastly, the stage of low temperature, apathy, wasting of the muscles, and possibly death.

Treatment is with pentamidine, suramin or melarsoprol—which give good results in early cases. Preventive measures in infected areas include the destruction of tsetse flies by insecticide, the cutting down of forests near rivers which are inhabited by tsetse flies, and some authorities have suggested the shooting of big game which may form a "reservoir" of the parasites, whence tsetse flies can carry them to human beings. For similar reasons infected people should not be allowed to move to noninfected areas.

Amoebic Dysentery, also known as *Amoebiasis*, is caused by the *Entamoeba histolytica*, an amoeba whose cysts are found in food and water, or spread by infected fingers or flies. There is mild fever and diarrhoea which contains blood. The disease may become chronic, and can cause abscesses, usually in the liver but sometimes in the lungs. Amoebiasis is treated with chloroquine or nitroimidazoles.

Leishmaniasis, kala-azar, or dum-dum fever, is another amoebic disease, probably spread in this instance by the bite of sandflies. It is also known as tropical splenomegaly—enlargement of the spleen in ordinary language—since infection results in enlargement of the spleen and liver, low, irregular fever, and death within a year or so. A milder form, affecting the skin, is known as Delhi boil, Oriental sore, or Baghdad sore, does not lead to kala-azar, and is fairly readily cured. The cure for both conditions is to give injections of antimony compounds which reduce the death-rate from kala-azar from 80 per cent, to about 5 per cent.

Diseases Caused by Parasitic Worms.

Many types of worms infest human beings and other animals. They are interesting for such reasons as their size (which may range from the almost invisible to 9 m or more), their life histories, and their serious or trivial consequences on their hosts. We shall mention only a few groups here, and mainly the ones likely to be met with in Europe—the tapeworms, the roundworms, and the threadworms—although some tropical types will be described briefly.

Tapeworms, as we have seen earlier, like many other types of intestinal worm, lead a double life. What usually happens is that the worm breeds in the human intestine, the eggs pass out in the faeces, and are then swallowed by animals eating contaminated material. In the animal the eggs hatch out into larvae—primitive forms which penetrate the muscle, forming cysts—and man is infected in turn by eating its meat. Thus *Taenia solium* gets into the flesh of pigs, which, if imperfectly cooked (measly pork), causes infestation of the intestine in man. It reaches a length of about 3 m. *Taenia saginata*, which reaches a length of about 6 m, is spread in imperfectly cooked beef, and in Baltic countries *Dibothriocephalus latus* gets into the human intestine, from caviare or undercooked fish. It reaches the awesome length of 9 m.

Now all the worms we have mentioned so far are found in the human intestine, and the cysts, which are much more dangerous and unpleasant, in the animal's muscles. But in some worms the reverse happens, with the adult in the animal's intestines and the cysts in man. Thus in Australia the dog tapeworm (*Taenia echinococcus*) produces cysts in both sheep and man. This is known as hydatid disease, and may remain unsuspected until cysts in the lungs, liver, or elsewhere become infected or rupture. *Trichinella spiralis* is similar in action, being found in the intestines of pigs and getting into the muscles or other organs of man. The main difference is that this worm migrates from the pig's intestines into its muscles, whence it reaches man in undercooked pork meat or sausages. The muscular cysts cause swellings and sometimes pain. There are changes in the blood, swelling of the face and leg in the early stages, and fever. A minor epidemic occurred in England in 1941. *Taenia echinococcus* and *Trichinella spiralis* are small—not more than 0·5 cm in length—but are more serious in their consequences than the large worms. Treatment is very difficult, and ordinarily all that can be done is to deal with individual cysts when they make themselves apparent.

The large tapeworms, *Taenia solium* and *saginata* and *Dibothriocephalus latus*, produce varying symptoms or none at all. Usually they are not discovered until some segments of the worm are excreted, but there may be mild indigestion, excessive hunger, and occasionally anaemia. However, when the worm is discovered the patient, not unnaturally, is likely to become anxious and uncomfortable at the thought of "having" a tapeworm; these symptoms are caused by the worry rather than the worm.

Treatment is, of course, a matter for a doctor, who now has a number of very effective drugs to choose from. One has to make sure that the head of the worm has been removed, otherwise it will continue to grow.

Roundworms are similar both in appearance and size to ordinary earth-worms, and the eggs reach man, not from an animal, but from the contaminated fingers of someone else who handles food. They give rise to no symptoms, and are noticed only when discharged in the faeces or occasionally vomited up. Piperazine is an effective treatment.

Threadworms, as the name suggests, are like small 0·5–1 cm long pieces of white thread. They are very common in children, and live mainly in the caecum—*i.e.*, the part of the large intestine near the appendix. The males, which are the smaller ones, remain there, but the females pass down towards the rectum at night-time and lay their eggs in the area around the anus. Infection is by contaminated hands handling food—especially uncooked food—and water. Threadworms are not serious, and cause few symptoms other than itching around the anus and between the legs, but heavily infected children may show symptoms of anaemia. The nervousness often shown by such children is usually the result of the irritation produced by the worms in the anal region. Infection is not common in adults, and in children tends to disappear at puberty.

Treatment is, in theory, simple; for the worms are easily destroyed by a number of drugs, such as piperazine and other, more modern drugs. Ointment is applied to the itching area, and the child should be prevented from scratching. However, since the eggs may lie about the house for some time, reinfection often happens, especially if there are several small children in the home who may pass the disease from one to another.

The idea that intestinal worms in general are likely to cause loss of weight by absorbing food eaten by the patient is largely mistaken; for although it is true that they do live on this food, the amount taken is certainly not enough to be significant.

Tropical Worms. Bilharzia has been mentioned before in connection with its frequency in Egypt, although it is also found in other parts of Africa, Arabia, and Iraq. There are two main types: one infecting the bladder (*Schistosoma haematobium*), the other the rectum (*Schistosoma mansoni*). Bilharzia is more correctly known as *schistosomiasis*.

The parasite's fantastic life-history begins when a man bathes in infected water, and the small swimming forms known as cercariae pierce and enter his skin—or they may enter the body by drinking infected water. From the skin they pass to the portal vein below the liver, remain there six weeks until they become adult and then swim against the blood-stream down to the pelvis, where the female lays eggs which have a sharp spine. The eggs penetrate into the bladder or rectum—depending on the type of fluke—and pass out in the faeces or urine. If they enter water they hatch out into small moving forms which seek out a water-snail, develop further in its body, and leave it in the form of cercariae ready to find a new human victim. The female fluke is slender and round, about 2·5 cm in length, the male, flat and leaf-shaped, is about 2 cm long, and, as we have seen, their grisly courting takes place in the portal vein, whence the impregnated female passes to the bladder (*haematobium*) or rectum (*mansoni*) to lay her eggs.

Infection results in raised temperature and, in the urinary type, blood in the urine; in the intestinal type blood is found in the faeces, and there are symptoms resembling dysentery—*e.g.*, diarrhoea. Treatment in both cases is with antimony tartrate or niridazole. Needless to say, attempts should be made at prevention by telling people to avoid infected canals (usually easier said than done), and by periodically cutting off the water supply to the canals to kill the snails.

Hookworm Disease, or ankylostomiasis, is found in many parts of the world, especially in miners who work on damp ground. The tiny worm enters the body usually through the feet, passes through the blood-stream to the lungs, eats through into one of the bronchial tubes, climbs the windpipe, and passes down the oesophagus into the stomach to end up in the duodenum. It causes anaemia, can be fairly readily cured, but is occasionally fatal.

Elephantiasis. Some types of parasitic worm are spread by insects. Thus in *Filiariasis* mosquitoes inject by their bites the infantile forms of a tiny worm which enters the lymphatic channels; there the blockade they cause leads to the swelling of the legs and the lower part of the body, known as elephantiasis.

PHYSICAL INJURIES AND FIRST AID.

This section which lists emergencies in alphabetical order is designed for rapid reference. Yet it would be wise to make sure now of knowing very thoroughly the parts dealing with bleeding, burns, resuscitation, shock and unconsciousness, situations which are immediately life threatening.

Nothing can teach first aid as effectively as attending one of the many courses organised by the three main organisations:

> St. John Ambulance Association, 1, Grosvenor Crescent, London, S.W.1.
> British Red Cross Society, 9, Grosvenor Crescent, London, S.W.1.
> St. Andrew's Ambulance Association, Milton Street, Glasgow, C.4.

Their local addresses are in the telephone directory; enquiry will get details of classes held at various hours of the day.

Purpose of First Aid.

First aid is not treatment proper (which is "Second Aid"). It aims to save life, to prevent further harm or suffering and to keep the victim in the best condition until taken over by a doctor or a nurse.

Under ordinary circumstances attempts to do more can be detrimental. If you limit your help to what is outlined here you cannot go wrong.

General Principles.

There are two priorities:

1. That the patient must breathe.
   (—*see* Choking, Resuscitation, Unconsciousness)
2. That severe bleeding is controlled.
   (—*see* Bleeding)

In any accident scene try to judge quickly which person most needs immediate attention. Treat a victim where he is; do not move him unless the surroundings suggest immediate danger (*e.g.*, fire, fumes, collapsing building).

Handle the patient with gentleness and sympathy yet achieve an atmosphere of reassurance and confidence by firm instructions and methodical actions.

Clear away a crowd (always demoralising to the victim) and use likely bystanders to telephone for an ambulance when necessary. Let your message be clear and written if possible. Let it clearly state the exact locality, the number of patients and the nature of their troubles. Always guard against shock (*q.v.*).

Asthma Attacks.

Breathing becomes very difficult, harsh and wheezing, fighting against air passages narrowed in spasm. Fear aggravates and relaxation relieves spasm. Show calm confidence.

1. Allow fresh air ventilation. Loosen tight clothes.
2. Help the mechanics of breathing by telling the patient
   to sit upright with a straight back but all the rest of the body relaxed;
   to direct breathing movements from the lower part of the chest.
3. Give him medicines he has prescribed for the emergency but avoid overdose.

Bleeding.

Treat mild bleeding as for wounds (*q.v.*).

For severe bleeding aim to let the blood clot by stopping or slowing the flow.

1. Immediately firmly press the edges of the wound together between fingers and thumb or press the palm of the hand hard down on it. (Maintain this at least ten minutes.)
2. Lie the patient down: elevate a bleeding limb (unless you suspect it to be fractured).
3. Slip a thick pad (handkerchief, gauze, wool) under your hand. Replace the hand pressure with a firmly bound bandage (stocking, belt, scarf).
4. If blood still leaks out add another pad and bandage.
5. Protect against shock (*q.v.*).

Nose Bleeding.

1. Have the patient sit up.
2. Get him to pinch between finger and thumb the whole lower half of the nose and maintain this for at least ten minutes. Repeat another ten minutes if necessary.
3. Tell him not to sniff or blow his nose.

Ear Bleeding.

1. Bandage or tape a loosely covering dressing (gauze, handkerchief) over the ear.
2. Lie the patient down towards the injured side.—*Nose or ear bleeding which follows a blow to the head may signify a fractured skull which needs immediate medical attention.*

Tooth Socket Bleeding.

This may follow after a dental extraction. Get the patient to bite hard on to a big pad (gauze, bunched-up handkerchief) placed over the bleeding area. He maintains pressure at least ten minutes sitting with a hand under his chin and the elbow on a table.

Blood Vomited.

This could appear black due to the effect of stomach acids.

1. Lie the patient down, on his side, with his head low.
2. Give him nothing to eat or drink.
3. Get a doctor or ambulance.
4. Guard against shock (*q.v.*).

Blood Coughed Up (*see also* Chest Injury).
Blood from the Back Passage.
Blood in the Urine.

However slight and brief the loss, always seek a doctor's opinion.

Blisters.

Leave them intact and protect them with a simple dressing. But if they are so big as to be in the way and need flattening:—

1. Boil a needle for ten minutes: leave it in the water until needed.
2. Wash the blister area with soap and water.
3. Holding the needle by one end pierce the blister at two opposite points. Press down with clean cloth to squeeze the fluid out.
4. Dress it like a wound (*q.v.*).

Burns (*see also* Chemical Burns).

1. Put out flames the quickest way: a douche of water; smothering with cloth (rug, coat, blanket).
2. Remove burnt clothes, but leave on what is adherent to the skin.
3. Cool the burnt part with cold water for at least ten minutes, longer if pain persists. Plunge a limb in a bucket or sink. Cover other parts with a thick cloth soaked in water; renew it if it dries.
4. Lie the patient down; keep a burnt limb elevated; remove possibly constricting things (rings, bracelets) from a burnt region before it swells.
5. Dress the burn as a wound (*q.v.*).
6. Guard against shock (*q.v.*)—in severe burns give to drink half a cupful of tepid water with a pinch of salt and sugar every ten or fifteen minutes.

Car Accidents.

1. Urgently stop severe bleeding (*q.v.*) or give resuscitation (*q.v.*) where this is needed; treat choking (*q.v.*). Unless they are at risk from fire or fumes leave the injured where they are. Look for victims thrown into ditches or over walls and hedges.
2. Minimise risks by forbidding smoking (petrol leak), by switching off the ignition and applying the brakes.
3. Set your own car off the road if possible; at night have its light shining on the scene.
4. Detail bystanders (wearing or carrying white objects at night) to stop approaching traffic some 200 yards on either side.
5. Send a message for help (written down) detailing the exact place, the number injured and the injuries.
6. Give other first aid to those in the cars without trying to move them: attempts to pull them out, especially from a distorted car, can do great harm. Leave to the rescue services.

Chemical Burns.

Rapidly wash away the chemical with copious free-flowing water. Remove any contaminated clothing. The contaminated eye, closed in painful spasm, may need gently forcing open; let the water flow on it without force and bend the patient towards the affected side so that the washings flow off at once.

Chest Injury.

Where there has been a severe blow or deep wound to the chest, possibly followed by blood being coughed up:

1. Clear the mouth of any obstruction (blood, vomit, dentures).
2. If there is an open wound at once close it with the palm of your hand firmly applied. While you keep it there, improvise a thick pad

(towel, cloth, handkerchief, sock) to replace your hand. Tape or bandage it securely to make an air-tight seal.

3. Loosen tight clothing.

4. Lie the patient down *towards* the injured side. If he has difficulty in breathing have him half propped up with head and shoulders raised.

5. Cover him loosely.

6. Get ambulance urgently.

Choking.

1. With your fingers try to clear any obstruction (food, toy, dentures) from the back of the throat.

2. If this tells the patient to relax, to bend well forward; give a hard slap between the shoulder blades. This may loosen the obstruction so that the patient can cough it out. A small child you place head down over your arm or your bent knee. Try up to four separate slaps.

If back slapping fails try to force the matter out by pressure:

1. Patient standing: stand behind him; put both your arms round his waist. Patient lying: turn him on his back; kneel astride him.

2. Place your fist (thumb side first) on his abdomen *between his navel and the lower end of his breast bone*; cover your fist with your other hand.

3. Make firm thrust inwards and upwards. This may propel the obstruction out of his windpipe. Try up to four separate thrusts. If these fail continue alternating four slaps and four thrusts. After each of these be ready to remove immediately any matter propelled into the mouth.

After receiving thrusts the patient must be checked by a doctor lest internal damage has occured.

If an obstruction is not cleared and the patient ceases breathing and collapses begin resuscitation (*q.v.*).

Always remember that in the unconscious the tongue may fall back and be an obstruction. *See* Unconsciousness.

Cold Effects. *See* Exposure and Hypothermia.

Cramp.

Cramps may follow severe loss of body fluid and minerals—as with severe repeated diarrhoea, vomiting or sweating. Slowly give tepid drinks containing a small pinch of table salt to each cupful or with diluted meat or yeast extracts.

Sudden cramp in a single muscle can be stopped by having the patient strongly stretch the muscle. In the front of the arm; straighten the elbow and swing the arm back. In the front of the thigh bend the knee and swing the leg back. In the back of the thigh: straighten the knee and swing the leg forward. In the calf: bend the foot up at the ankle while straightening the leg.

Diabetes.

Under certain circumstances a diabetic treated with insulin may suddenly collapse through sugar deficiency. Passing through phases of weakness, vagueness, sweating, tremor, uncoordinated actions and slurred speech he may go into a coma.

If he is conscious give him two teaspoonfuls (or lumps) of glucose or sugar in water. Failing this, give anything sweet; jam, honey, chocolate. This should clear him rapidly but repeat the dose after ten minutes.

If he is unconscious send for medical help urgently. Give nothing by mouth and put the patient in the recovery position (*q.v.*).

Ear—object in.

Do not try to poke it out.

A small object (*e.g.*, insect) can sometimes be floated out and out by lying the patient down with the ear uppermost and pouring in a little water or olive oil. But do not try this if the ear drum is possibly damaged or the ear is painful.

Electric Shock.

At once disconnect the current (at the switch or by pulling a plug out). If you cannot do this do not touch the patient but knock him away from his contact with dry non-conducting material; wooden stick, light furniture, folded thick garment.

He may need resuscitation (*q.v.*). He may have sustained a fracture (*q.v.*) or a burn. He may recover, only to collapse later; keep watch and send him to hospital.

Beware of very high voltage currents, as from wires of electric pylons: keep at least 20 feet away and do not try to rescue until the electricity authority has cut the current.

Epileptic Attack.

The patient may suddenly become unconscious, fall and soon begin convulsive jerkings, and sometimes frothing at the mouth.

1. Do not try to stop the jerking, but protect him from banging against furniture. Move the furniture or push cloth in position as buffer.

2. Clear froth from the mouth.

3. Once the convulsions stop put him in the recovery position (*q.v.*)—but beware lest he sustained a fracture (*q.v.*) in falling.

A succession of closely following attacks is dangerous: get medical aid at once.

Exposure.

A hill climber or a worker inadequately dressed against cold weather becomes slow, inefficient, clumsy, drowsy. Eventually he collapses and if not properly treated may die.

1. Put him to rest.

2. If you can, get him into a warm shelter. Otherwise protect him with screens of clothes or blankets and poles.

3. If he is conscious give warm drinks (cocoa, chocolate, tea). On no account give alcohol.

4. Get wet cold clothes off him if possible and put him in warm dry covers (sleeping bag, blankets). A plastic sheet over those helps to retain heat. Include the head, leaving only the face free. Well-prepared walkers will equip themselves with a special survival bag, now widely available.

See also Hypothermia.

Gradual rewarming is given when the patient has become cold gradually. When exposure has been sudden, as with falling in extremely cold water, you can warm up the patient fast in a bath at about 40° C. (103° F.).

Eye Injury.

Fix a loosely covering pad over the eye and get medical aid.—Do NOT use drops or ointments.—If the wound is severe and painful keep the patient on his back and cover both eyes (since movement of the good eye entails that of the injured one).

Eye—Object In.

Have the patient seated in a good light and stand behind him. If you can see the object on the white of the eye try to lift it off gently with the rolled-up and moistened twist of a handkerchief. If it does not come easily it may be embedded; leave it alone.

If it is within the coloured part of the eye leave it for a doctor to treat.

If you cannot see it look under the lids. The lower lid you pull down as he looks upwards. The upper lid you must evert as he looks down; lay a matchstick along the "hinge" of the lid; firmly grasp the edge of the lid and roll it up over the matchstick.

Fainting.

Lie the patient down with his legs higher than his head (if this is not possible, get him seated with his head bent low between his knees); loosen any tight clothes: tell him to breathe deeply and slowly. He should soon recover. A drink of water (provided he is conscious) will help. If he has fainted fully treat as for unconsciousness (*q.v.*).

Fractures.

Always suspect a broken bone where a blow or crush near a bone is followed by pain, swelling, deformity, weakened or restricted movement. Not all these features are always present: sometimes relatively slight pain is the only one.

Your task is to prevent movement which could worsen the condition by shifting a broken edge of bone into an important organ, or by making it pierce hitherto unbroken skin (with a risk of infection). No one will blame you for undue caution—but all will hold you responsible if you allow a fractured bone to do more damage by movement which could have been avoided.

When a fracture is suspected:—

1. Warn the patient not to move and bystanders not to try to lift him.
2. At once control any severe bleeding (*q.v.*). Dress any wound (*q.v.*) temporarily.
3. Now immobilise the fractured area including the joint at either end. The best splint is the patient's own body; *e.g.*, injured arm secured against chest, injured leg against good leg (move the good leg up to the injured one). Or a thin board or rolled-up newspaper, well buffered with cloths and towels tied round it can be slipped under a fore-arm and wrist. Between the injured part and the splinting surface fill any hollows with firm padding of wool, or bunched-up cloth, socks, handkerchiefs. Tie the whole firmly with bandages (or stocking, thin towels) making the knots over the splint (not the hurt part) and avoiding bandage directly over the level at which you suspect the fracture. Work gently; do not lift or move the injured part.
4. Help to reduce shock (*q.v.*).

These are the general principles. How best to apply them for individual fractures you can learn from first aid courses.

If you expect expert help (doctor, nurse, ambulance) to arrive soon, then omit step 3 above and keep the patient lying still.

The fractured spine. When a blow or fall gives a painful back or neck, the vertebral column may be fractured. Inexpert moving may possibly drive a bone fragment into the spinal cord of nerves, causing paralysis or loss of feeling. It is most important to let the patient lie still until experienced first aiders take over. Keep the patient warm with a loose covering of blanket or coat.

Frostbite.

Do not heat the area directly or put it in hot water. Do not rub it.

1. Remove any wet cover (*e.g.*, glove).
2. Remove any tight object (garter, ring, bracelet).
3. Cover the area loosely with dry material and let it warm up slowly. Fingers can be tucked under clothes into the opposite armpit. Nose, chin or ear can be covered with a dry hand.

Hanging.

Support the victim by his legs. Get the cord cut and be prepared to receive his weight as he falls. Loosen the cord round the neck. Act fast. Get medical help.

See also **Choking** *and* **Resuscitation**.

Head Injuries.

Blows to the head can cause fracture of the skull and also brain damage.

Fracture of the skull is not always obvious. Skin may swell over the site. Sometimes a fracture of the base of the skull (the body platform within the head at eye and ear level which supports the brain) may show up by bruising round an eye or by blood loss from ear or nose (*see* **Bleeding**).

Brain Damage may be of two kinds:—

Concussion, a temporary "shaking up" of brain tissue causing immediate "knock-out" unconsciousness. Recovery is in anything from a few seconds to several hours.

Compression of the brain develops from bleeding within the skull, from displacement of a fractured bone or from general swelling of the damaged brain tissues within the hard unyielding skull. The patient gradually (minutes or hours) becomes comatose and perhaps unconscious. This condition is dangerous.

The patient is unconscious—see unconsciousness.

The patient is dazed: put him in the recovery position (*q.v.*) and watch him closely while awaiting help.

The patient recovers after a knock-out (concussion). He may yet develop features of compression as well. However much he wants to carry on, keep him at rest, under observation and get medical advice.

In all cases remember that head injuries are often accompanied by injuries to other parts of the body.

Heart Attack.

Sudden heart attacks may produce:—

severe gripping pain in the centre of the chest, sometimes spreading to the neck, shoulder or arm; fast weak pulse; breathlessness; pallor and blueness; sweating.

or sudden painless breathlessness with slight cough and very wet bubbly breathing.

In either case send urgently for medical help. Get the patient to rest (in bed if possible). If he is very breathless it will be easier for him to be in a sitting position, against banked-up pillows. Otherwise have him laying down.

Loosen tight clothes. Keep him warmly but loosely covered. Mop any sweat from the face.

Heat Effects.

Heat Exhaustion. Anyone working in an unusually hot atmosphere is helped to remain cool by copious sweating which extracts heat from the body as it evaporates off the skin. But this loss of fluid also carries with it essential minerals from the body. The patient may collapse with his temperature normal or just a little raised; his skin is pale, moist and sunken, his pulse fast and weak. Muscles depleted of minerals go into cramp.

Let him rest in a cool place and give him (slowly) fruit juices or water with half a teaspoonful of salt added to each pint.

Heat Stroke happens in unusually hot and moist areas in rare industrial circumstances and in some tropical zones. Evaporation of sweat cannot take place in an atmosphere already saturated with water vapour. The patient becomes burning hot with a red dry skin and a fast forceful pulse. He may suddenly collapse and go into coma.

He must rest, have his clothes removed and be fanned or sponged down with cold (but not iced) water. The condition is dangerous and needs medical help.

Hypothermia.

Small babies and the elderly are specially susceptible to cold, *e.g.*, overnight in a poorly heated bedroom. They become lethargic, comatose and then unconscious. Extremely cold to touch, even under bedclothes, the skin is white (though in babies it may be deceptively pink). Death may follow.

Cover the patient well including the head, leaving the face free. Put him in the recovery position (*q.v.*). Warm him GRADUALLY by warming the whole room and by giving slowly warm (not hot) drinks. Do NOT give alcohol. Do NOT use electric blankets or hot-water bottles.

Insect Bites.

Cool with water or (better) smooth in anti-histamine cream.

If a bee sting has been left in the skin pull it out with fine tweezers: apply these well down near the skin so that they do not squeeze in any venom left at the free top of the sting.

Lightning.

As for electric shock (*q.v.*) except that the patient can be touched at once as he bears no electric charge. Put a dry dressing over any skin burns.

Nose Bleed. *See* Bleeding.

Nose—Object in.

Do not try to probe it. Unless GENTLE nose blowing gets it out consult a doctor.

Poisoning.

Do not try to administer antidotes. Do not give salt solutions.

If the patient is unconscious.

Treat as for unconsciousness (q.v.).

If he is conscious.

Give, slowly, soothing drinks to dilute the poison (water, barley water, milk and water).

Put him in the recovery position (q.v.) while awaiting the ambulance. He may lose consciousness.

In all cases.

Get the patient urgently to hospital.

Send with him any remaining poison or empty container and a sample of any vomit.

Keep a close watch on him all the time you are with him.

Poisoning by pesticides (weed or insect killers).

The patient must be at complete rest. If his clothes and skin are contaminated with the poison (splashes, spray droplets) remove clothes and wash the skin copiously with water (avoid contaminating yourself). If he is conscious give sweetened drinks.

Poisoning by gases.

Get the victim rapidly out of the contaminated atmosphere, but do not venture within this unless you have a lifeline and respirator, with others to safeguard you.

Recovery Position.

This safeguards the patient's comfort and breathing if he is unconscious, or comatose, or likely to lose consciousness. It consists in having him—

laying on his side;
with lower arm and leg stretched out straight behind him;
upper leg and arm bent forward at right angles at hip, knee, shoulder, elbow;
face tilted slightly downwards and head bent backwards (NO pillow).

This ensures a clear airway and lets any fluid in the mouth (saliva, blood, vomit) flow out and not choke the patient.

To get him in position:

1. Empty his pockets; remove items like bracelet or wrist watch. Put his belongings away safely. Loosen tight clothing.
2. Kneel alongside him.
3. Straighten his arms alongside his body; tuck the nearer hand below his hip.
4. Put one of your hands under his face to protect it as your other hand pulls him at the hip over towards you, on his side.
5. Adjust the limbs.
6. Cover him with a blanket or coat.

However, do not move the patient if circumstances suggest he received a heavy blow to the backbone. In that case ensure free breathing by keeping his head bent well back (never sideways). Be ready to clear immediately any vomit from his mouth.

Resuscitation.

This is the attempt to restore life to someone who has stopped breathing. NEVER try it unless this really is the case; you will do harm if the patient has collapsed but is still breathing. Do not try it if the problem is that of fighting against choking (q.v.).

In cases of drowning do not try to tip the patient up to drain out water; this wastes valuable time.

(It is best to have learnt the technique in organised first aid classes, practising only on a manikin.)

Artificial Respiration.

Act very quickly:—

1. Get the patient on his back.
2. Bend his head fully backwards and keep it thus all the time.
3. With fingers rapidly clear out any obstructing matter from mouth and throat.
4. Hold his mouth open (keep your fingers clear of his lips) and pinch his nose shut.
5. Take a deep breath in: open your mouth wide and seal your lips round his mouth: breathe firmly into his mouth. The air going in should make his chest rise. Do not blow more forcibly than is needed to achieve this.
6. Lift your mouth off. His chest will now sink as air comes out. Meantime you take another breath in.
7. Continue by repeating the breathing processes of steps 5 and 6.

The first four breaths you give quickly. Thereafter time yourself by the rise and the natural fall of the patient's chest.

With small children you need not pinch the nose, but let your mouth seal over both the nose and mouth of the patient. Much gentler blowing is needed, and quite small puffs are right for babies.

Keep on until medical authority takes over.

If patient vomits turn his head to one side and clear out the mouth. Then resume artificial respiration, with the first four breaths quick ones.

Successful artificial respiration should soon improve the patient's colour, and later you may find he begins to breathe for himself, even if only weakly. Watch this closely, for he may cease again.

Heart Compression.

If there is no improvement it may be necessary to add heart compression to artificial respiration. This, however, cannot be safely learnt except from first aid class teaching and demonstration. (See the Introduction to this section.)

Shock.

Failure of the heart and of the circulation of the blood may follow any serious injury (bleeding, wounds, burns, fractures). This can happen in minutes or hours according to the severity of the lesion.

In first aid terms this dangerous physical condition is called Shock. The patient is pale, cold, sweating, faint or comatose, with weak and fast pulse and breathing.

Try to prevent or to minimise the development of shock before it appears by applying the following simple but valuable measures to every badly hurt patient.

1. At once stop severe bleeding (q.v.).
2. Treat the patient where he is (unless you both are in an area of danger).
3. Lie him down: keep his head low and his legs raised (but avoid movement where a fracture is suspected).
4. Loosen tight clothing.
5. Keep him warm by covering below and loosely above him—but do not use hot-water bottles.
6. Gently dress any wounds—with the minimum of disturbance.
7. Guard his mental state. Be sympathetic but as optimistically reassuring as possible. Never whisper to others. Never assume that because the patient appears unconscious he cannot hear and understand what is said near him.

Do not give the badly injured patient anything to drink. This could worsen his condition and risk vomiting and choking, especially if he becomes unconscious or needs an anaesthetic. If he is very thirsty let him refresh himself by sucking a moistened handkerchief.

Snake Bite.

The adder is the only dangerous snake in Britain. Its bite can cause collapse and great pain, but only very rarely is it fatal.

1. Lie the patient down.
2. Wipe or wash the bite area. Put on a dry dressing.
3. Cover the area with a thick pad and bandage it in position so that it presses down very firmly.

4. Immobilise the bitten part as if it were a fracture (q.v.).
5. Get the patient rapidly to hospital.
6. Reassure him about his recovery. Give aspirin or paracetamol to minimise pain.

You NEVER cut or suck the bite, or apply chemicals. You NEVER use a tourniquet.

Sprains.

These are stretched and torn ligaments at a joint. Immediately after it happens you can reduce the swelling and pain which will follow by applying a cold compress—a cloth soaked in cold water and then wrung out to be just moist. Keep it in position half an hour, and renew it if it gets dry.

Otherwise support the joint firmly with layers of cotton wool interleaved between turns of crepe bandaging. Beware of making it so tight that it interferes with circulation in the limb.

A severe sprain may be difficult to distinguish from a fracture. If in doubt treat as for the latter.

Strains.

A strain is an overstretching of muscle fibres, and is very like a sprain except that it does not necessarily happen at a joint. Treat it as a sprain.

Strokes.

Some part of the brain has sudden damage of its blood supply. The results are as variable as are the functions of the brain: e.g., poor feeling or power in hand, arm or leg, altered speech, loss of bladder control, paralysis of one side, or unconsciousness.

A mild effect may be the forerunner of more serious damage. Get the patient to bed, if necessary in the recovery position (q.v.), and keep him under observation until the doctor arrives.

Unconsciousness.

In first aid finding the cause of unconsciousness is less important than protecting the patient's breathing. The unconscious patient lying on his back and with head straight or bent towards the chest is at risk of choking from his lax tongue, flopping against and obstructing his throat. Correct positioning prevents this. Act methodically:—

1. Has the patient stopped breathing? He will urgently need resuscitation (q.v.).
2. Is his airway blocked making breathing difficult? Clear any material from his mouth. Bend his head straight back at the neck (but do not twist or turn it), and keep it there (see Choking).
3. Arrest any severe bleeding (q.v.).
4. Dress any wounds (q.v.).
5. Consider the possibilities of fractures (q.v.). If you suspect they might be present do not move him (specially important if he might have injured the backbone); stay by his head to ensure its proper position and to clear out immediately any fluid (saliva, blood, vomit) which threatens to choke.

If he can be moved:—

6. Turn him into the recovery position (q.v.)

Two other important points are that you NEVER try to give anything by mouth to the unconscious or comatose, and that you realise how much you must guard your speech, since these patients may overhear and understand what is spoken near them.

Wounds.

The general treatment is simple, and should avoid the use of antiseptics or ointments.

1. At once control any severe bleeding (q.v.).

2. Sit or lay the patient down.
3. Put a clean temporary dressing on the wound.
4. Wash your hands. Prepare dressings and bandages.
5. Wash *around* the wound (but not the open wound itself) with swabs or clean material moistened with soap and water. Use a fresh swab or material area for each stroke.
6. Cover the wound with a large dry dressing. Over this place a thick soft pad. Bandage firmly.
7. Put the injured part at rest.
8. Take measures against shock (q.v.).

Dressings. Gauze from freshly opened pack. Or improvise from clean handkerchief or small towel, held by corners, allowed to fall open and then refolded so that inside surface comes to outside. A leg or arm can be slipped inside a pillowcase.

Padding. Cotton wool. Or improvise from bunched clean handkerchief, sock.

Bandages can be improvised from stockings, necktie, belt.

Object embedded in wound. Do not try to remove it. Cover it with a clean dressing and over this place a "frame" of padding to surround the side of the object and protect above it. You can now apply further padding and bandages without pressing on the object.

Tetanus (lockjaw) is a risk in wounds contaminated with soil or from animals or thorns. Get medical advice.

St. John Ambulance Brigade.

From its origins in 1887, the organisation now boasts some 62,000 volunteers who deal with over 300,000 casualties each year. These casualties can range from minor upsets such as nose bleeds to victims of heart attacks and broken limbs. The work of the St. John Ambulance is divided into two aspects: the Brigade, which provides volunteers to give first-aid at public meetings *etc.*, and the Association, which is engaged in the task of spreading first-aid education.

THE BLOOD.

Doctors who have made a special study of the blood are known as haematologists. Haematology itself is a complex subject because blood itself is complex and its many functions are not easy to describe and only a brief account is given here.

Blood consists of a fluid, called plasma, in which are suspended red and white blood cells and platelets and in which are dissolved many substances from the simple ones like glucose to the complex ones like hormones, proteins and fats. Total blood volume amounts to about five litres; the blood donor gives about half a litre at a session and feels no ill effects. Loss of a litre or more induces surgical shock (q.v. **Physical Injuries and First Aid**). Red cells are red because they carry a protein called haemoglobin which is capable of carrying oxygen. There are about five million red cells for each cubic millimetre of blood (that is an average sized drop), a total of 25 million million circulating in the body at any one time. The life of a red cell is about 120 days; new ones are constantly replacing old ones which are "buried" by the spleen.

The haemoglobin from dead cells is recycled; new cells are generated in the marrow of bones, including the breast bone, from which samples of marrow can be taken by a technique known as sternal puncture. Such samples are studied with a microscope to establish diagnoses of various blood disorders. White cells are of five basic types, the names of which need not concern us here. Each type has a specific function—some act as bacterial scavengers, some are concerned with antibodies (q.v.) and some with the general defence system of the body which is concerned with the development and maintenance of immunity to various diseases both bacterial and viral. There are also non-cell particles derived from large cells which the marrow produces. These are platelets, which are concerned with blood clotting. They have the capacity to "stick" to any gaps in blood vessels (such as may be caused by injury or, in the minutest of blood vessels, "wear and tear") and initiate blood clotting. All these types of cells can be studied in the test tube after taking a sample from the patient. This is known as venipuncture, a simple and virtually painless procedure, carried out by doctor or nurse or trained "phlebotomist", by inserting a needle on the end of a syringe into a dilated vein in the crook of the arm. Marrow samples can also be taken, as we have said, from the breast bone—but that is a very different procedure, requiring local anaesthetic and much more skill. For the patient it is not a comfortable procedure either.

The fluid part of the blood, plasma, is more the province of the biochemist than the haematologist. The immunologist is also interested in plasma and all three disciplines tend to overlap to some degree. Plasma can be studied in the same way as whole blood. A venipuncture is carried out, a chemical added to stop clotting and the cells can then be removed in a centrifuge. If blood is allowed to clot in the test tube, the cells are all caught up in the clot and the plasma remains liquid and can be poured off. It is then known as serum. Plasma contains substances which are either dissolved, that is, in solution, or are held "in suspension". By this is meant that the plasma forms an emulsion because fat particles and some proteins are not soluble and can only form suspensions in this way. The protein and fat particles are in suspension in a like manner. The substances both in solution and in suspension are much too numerous to be dealt with here.

The functions of blood are manifold, but essentially blood is a transport medium, concerned with moving gases (oxygen and carbon dioxide), moving food (protein, carbohydrate, fat, minerals and vitamins), eliminating waste products and protecting and repairing the body.

Red Cell Diseases.

These are of two main groups leading to a shortage of red cells (anaemia), or an excess (polycythaemia). The former is much the more common and there are many different kinds. In all of them the shortage of red cells results in a depletion of the capacity of the blood to carry oxygen. This means that the heart must work harder to send more blood than usual to the tissues, and even so the tissues will often go short. The patient will be persistently tired and listless, and if the anaemia is severe the action of the brain and heart will be seriously impeded, even leading to fainting, cardiac pain, and breathlessness on exertion. All these symptoms, however, can be caused by many other conditions. The only way to be sure they are due to anaemia is by a proper examination of the blood, and even this will not lead to the truth if the picture has been spoilt by the patient taking iron tonics and other remedies of his own accord. Therefore do not dose yourself with tonics, in case you really have anaemia. You may make it impossible to arrive at a proper diagnosis later.

Haemorrhagic Anaemia. Anaemia, a shortage of red cells, may be due to a variety of causes, singly or in combination. One very obvious cause is loss of blood or haemorrhage. Following the sudden loss of a half-litre of blood or more, the red-cell-producing bone marrow "factory" will step up its production; but even if it is adequately supplied with all the raw materials such as iron, it may well take many weeks to build up the numbers to normal. A very severe degree of haemorrhagic anaemia is usually treated by blood transfusion. Milder degrees can be treated by taking extra iron, often over a long period of time. The supply of iron for making new red-cell pigment is nearly always the bottle-neck which limits production. Haemorrhagic anaemia can commonly occur, however, without a sudden severe haemorrhage. From what has been said about the constant replacement of red cells as they wear out, it must be obvious that even if there is only a slight failure to keep pace with the numbers lost, several months of such a failure can eventually deplete the numbers to the level of very severe anaemia. This situation is common when small amounts of blood are being continuously or repeatedly lost, and here again it is a shortage of dietary iron which is the usual cause of the failure to replace the lost red cells. Normal menstrual loss in women and girls whose diet is on the border-line of iron deficiency is a common cause of progressive tiredness and lack of energy. Where the menstrual flow is heavier than usual, or where it is frankly excessive in older women due to the various common gynaecological disorders, serious anaemia is surprisingly common. During pregnancy a great deal of iron is lost by the mother to the baby, and this, together with the inevitable blood loss at delivery, often makes for a very tired mother indeed, just at the time when there is an enormous amount of work to be done to manufacture milk and attend to all the extra household tasks of baby care. For these reasons it is almost routinely advisable to build up stocks of iron throughout the pregnancy by remembering to take the pills provided. Men as well as women can lose small amounts of blood continuously in later life from gastro-intestinal conditions such as piles, ulcers, and tropical infestations such as hookworm; and here again the anaemia may be just as severe in the long run as that which inevitably follows a sudden, massive haemorrhage. One extra word of warning. Do not assume because you are pale that you are anaemic. Pallor is a very poor guide, because it is dependent on so many other things, like the blood vessels in your skin, and its thickness and translucency. Nothing but a blood test (which is so easy for your doctor to do) can really tell you if you are anaemic. And if your anaemia is due to a blood-losing condition, then that too must be treated. So do not be tempted to treat yourself, and never delay seeing your doctor about any unexplained bleeding.

Haemolytic Anaemia occurs when for any reason, there are more blood cells than usual being destroyed in the body. This may be because the cells are abnormally fragile, or because normal cells have been attacked by something to which you are allergic, or rarely because you have become sensitive to your own red cells. Sometimes unborn babies have severe haemolytic anaemia, due to an incompatability of blood group (Rh factor) between the mother and the baby, and the same sort of thing happens if incompatible blood is given by mistake in blood transfusion. Up to a point, in mild haemolytic anaemia, the bone marrow can keep pace with the increased loss of cells, but beyond this point anaemia develops. After incompatible blood transfusions a very dangerous situation results from the effects of the destruction of red cells and the liberation of their products into the blood. One form of jaundice is often produced in haemolytic anaemia, the patient becoming yellow because of the breakdown products of red cells circulating in excess as bile pigments. These latter are normally always present to a small extent due to the normal, comparatively small, rate of destruction of effete red cells.

Aplastic Anaemia is the term given to anaemia due to a virtually total failure of the bone marrow red-cell factory. Sometimes this occurs for no obvious reason. It is sometimes due to a heavy dose of radioactivity or X-rays knocking out the cells of the "factory." It may even be due to cancer cells growing in the bone marrow cavity and not leaving sufficient room for the red marrow cells. It is fortunate that aplastic anaemia is very rare, because it can only be treated by blood transfusions every few weeks for the rest of the patient's life. Very occasionally there have been exceptions to this rule, when the patient's marrow has re-awakened for no apparent reason and suddenly begins to make red cells again. Rapid progress has been made in the treatment òf marrow disease with bone marrow grafts.

Pernicious Anaemia. This is a fairly uncommon anaemia, which has a very interesting story. The processes by which red cells are manufactured are many and complex, and depend, like so many other bodily activities, on the supply of a vitamin containing cobalt, called vitamin B_{12}. This is nearly always present in more than adequate quantities in the diet, but in order for it to be absorbed from the intestine, there must also be a substance called "intrinsic factor" which is normally made by the lining of the stomach. People with pernicious anaemia have suffered a degeneration of the lining of their stomachs, probably because, for some reason, they have become "sensitive" to this part of their own tissue. This kind of civil war within the body is known as an "auto-immune" disease, and is comparable in type with some forms of haemolytic anaemia. In other words they destroy their own stomach lining, fail to produce "intrinsic factor," and as a result fail to absorb vitamin B_{12} into the body. Faced with a failure in the supply of this essential substance, the bone marrow produces too few red cells, and the few that are produced are deformed, much too large, and very fragile. In addition to its role in blood formation, vitamin B_{12} is essential to the normal functioning of the spinal cord, and in long-standing cases of untreated pernicious anaemia, there is often a neurological disability.

Nowadays pernicious anaemia is treated by small occasional injections of the vitamin, whose other name is cyanocobalamin. A similar molecule, without the cyanideion, is now used. This is called hydroxycobalamin.

Polycythaemia. Too many red cells per cubic millimetre of blood can be found without there being an increase of the total number of red cells in the body. This occurs in dehydration, when there is a loss of plasma without a comparable loss of cells, and is called haemo-concentration. Alternatively, the bone marrow can manufacture more cells than usual as a response to living for long periods at high altitudes. The beneficial result can be that the blood can carry normal amounts of oxygen, even though the supply (in the rarefied air) is reduced. Finally there is a red cell disease in which the bone marrow factory gets out of control and produces too many cells with no beneficial results. The number in the blood can be double the normal and the blood becomes so thick that the heart has difficulty pumping it round the body. This disease (*polycythaemia rubra vera*) used to be treated by repeatedly bleeding the patient to reduce the numbers of cells. It is now treated very successfully with carefully judged amounts of radioactive phosphorus or certain other "antimitotic" chemicals which reduce the rate of multiplication of bone marrow cells.

White Cell Diseases.

Diseases of the white cells are very much less common but are inevitably serious.

Agranulocytosis. In this condition the number of those white cells which are responsible for phagocytosis of bacteria falls precipitously. The result is that one of the main bodily defences against infection fails, and the patient may die from an overwhelming invasion of germs and the accompanying high fever. The usual cause is an abnormal sensitivity to a variety of drugs, often those which are in widespread use and only give trouble in the occasional case. One example among hundreds is the antibiotic chloramphenicol which specifically kills typhoid bacteria and is used for that purpose. It is believed that about one patient in 60,000 becomes sensitive to it and agranulocytosis often fatally follows, though appropriate treatment of infections has greatly reduced the likelihood of death. The fact that almost any drug *can* do this to some people and yet be quite safe for the majority, is one good reason not to dose yourself unnecessarily with over-the-counter medicines.

Leukaemia. Leukaemia comprises a spectrum of diseases which involve the abnormal production of white blood cells. Immature or blast cells are produced at an increased rate and tend to infiltrate various areas of the body, for example, bone marrow, lymph nodes and spleen. They are also found in the peripheral blood and cerebrospinal fluid. In spite of their large numbers these cells, because of their abnormality, are unable to deal effectively with infection and anaemia, sepsis and fever can result. The cause of this type of cancer is open to some speculation but we know there is an increased incidence in those with Down's Syndrome and other chromosomal abnormalities. Viral infections may also be implicated and there is almost certainly an association with ionising radiation. This latter fact was proved by the increased incidence of leukaemia in those who survived the atomic explosion in Japan at the end of the Second World War. Pregnant women should not be subject to X-Rays as this may cause an increased incidence of leukaemia in their children.

Cases of leukaemia are known to occur in clusters or small groups in certain areas. Sometimes this is thought to be associated with natural radiation arising from rock structures. However, it is also suspected that there is an increased incidence around atomic power stations and plants which reprocess nuclear waste. In particular, a great controversy has raged about the incidence of leukaemia around the Sellafield reprocessing plant with some authorities insisting that the rate of occurrence is no greater than normal. However, those working and living in the area have always felt this to be untrue and recent research has suggested that workers exposed to small amounts of radioactive material may suffer abnormal spermatic development so that the tendency to leukaemia may be passed on to their unborn children who may be prone to the disease later in life.

The outcome of the illness largely depends on the specific type. Chronic lymphatic leukaemia for example, which tends to affect older people, may have no clinical signs or symptoms. In fact, it can run a very indolent course, require no treatment and be compatible with a normal lifespan. On the other hand, acute myeloid leukaemia which tends to affect younger adults is a very serious disease with an acute onset and which if not treated can prove to be rapidly fatal.

Childhood Leukaemia.

In childhood, leukaemia is the most common form of malignant disease but nevertheless, it is quite rare with an incidence of approximately 25 per 1,000,000 children. Over 85% of all cases involve the type known as acute lymphoblastic leukaemia. With modern treatment, a remission (that is to say, a disease free period) can be induced in over 90% of children and cure rates are very high. Presenting features of acute leukaemia are tiredness, lethargy, abnormal susceptibility to infection, excessive bruising and occasionally bone or joint pain. A blood count usually helps in the diagnosis but this needs to be confirmed by examination of the bone marrow. Treatment involves repeated courses of cytotoxic drugs, sometimes combined with radiotherapy. For those with more resistant forms of the illness, bone marrow transplantation can often provide a cure. Treatment is best performed in specialist centres where the expertise is available to deal with the complicated drug regimes. With modern treatment the outlook for all forms of leukaemia has improved. For children, in particular, the outlook has been dramatically transformed and in a great many cases a cure can be successfully achieved. The address of the Leukaemia Care Society is 14 Kingfisher Court, Venny Bridge, Pinhoe, Exeter, Devon EX4 8JN.

Hodgkin's disease, Lymphosarcoma and Reticulosarcoma. These are diseases which are in some ways akin to *leukaemia*. Abnormal cells are found in the reticulo-edothelial system and proliferate in a disorganised manner, causing enlargement of lymph nodes (glands), spleen and sometimes the liver.

Hodgkin's disease, named after a 19th cent. Guy's physician, has been the subject of much research and therapeutic trial. The improvement in outlook for patients with Hodgkin's disease has been one of the success stories of the 1990s. In cases where the disease is caught early, it can be eradicated in over 95 per cent of sufferers (although progress has been less marked with non-Hodgkin's lymphoma).

Hæmorrhagic or Bleeding Diseases.

Whenever blood vessels are damaged by injury, there is a remarkable series of mechanisms which automatically come into operation to stem the flow of blood. There is a constriction of all the smaller vessels in the locality. Platelets stick together and release substances which help the vessels to stay constricted as well as others necessary to blood clotting, and yet others which help to bind the clot tightly together. Later, materials appear to prevent too much clotting, and eventually the clot is removed altogether as healing proceeds. There are some very complicated diseases of this blood-conserving mechanism which can lead to abnormal bleeding, sometimes beneath the skin to produce bruising or even smaller leaks; sometimes leading to a greater loss of blood, particularly following a wound. In some kinds of *purpura* (bleeding tendency) the blood vessels are the cause of the trouble, having become fragile and leaky for a number of reasons. This happens in old age (*senile purpura*), in scurvy, or vitamin C deficiency, as an occasional accompaniment to infective diseases, or as an immunological effect on the lining of blood vessels when the patient becomes sensitised to certain substances (*Schönlein-Henoch* or *anaphylactoid purpura*). The latter often follows a streptococcal sore throat, just as rheumatic fever and acute nephritis do; and as well as the purpura there may be joint pains and nephritis. Just as almost any drug or chemical will cause agranulocytosis in some people, so it can also cause anaphylactoid purpura.

Purpura may also be due to a lack of platelets, known as thrombocytopenia (a shortage of thrombocytes or platelets). This can happen if the bone marrow factory is depressed, since this is where platelets too are made. It is therefore a common accompaniment of leukaemia or aplastic anaemia. Or there can be increased destruction of platelets in some diseases of the spleen. Platelets normally last eight to ten days, but their lifespan can be shortened in heart failure, and following massive transfusions, or often for no apparent reason ("idiopathic" thrombocytopenia), when removal of the spleen can sometimes help.

Finally, defects of the *clotting mechanism* will lead to a bleeding tendency, and since the mechanism itself is very complex, so is the variety of things which can upset it. The liver provides the blood with many of the substances required for clotting, so it is not surprising that a clotting defect commonly accompanies liver disease. One necessary substance for blood clotting is called "anti-haemophilic factor" and is missing from people who have inherited the disease *haemophilia*. These people may die of haemorrhage from quite small cuts or minor surgical procedures.

THE HEART AND
BLOOD-VESSELS.

INTRODUCTION.

The heart consists of about 350g of muscle which makes up the walls of its four chambers. Anatomically the human heart closely resembles the sheeps' hearts to be found in a butcher's shop. Indeed it would be an instructive exercise to dissect one of these in the order described below, since there is no other way of properly appreciating what the chambers, valves, etc., are really like. There are two quite separate pumps in the heart—one on the owner's right (or on your *left* if you are looking at the front of someone else), and one on his left. The right heart collects spent, deoxygenated, "venous" blood which returns there from the whole of the body, and gives it the comparatively small push required to drive it through the adjacent lungs. The left heart collects the revitalised, oxygenated "arterial" blood as it leaves the lungs, and gives it the enormous push required to build up the arterial blood pressure, so that it can be forced through all the tissues of the body. As may be expected, the right heart chambers have much thinner walls than the left, since their muscle has less work to do. This will help you get your bearings with the sheep's heart. The tip, or apex, is the lowest part. The thick-feeling side is the left, the thin the right; and the great vessels are at the top.

The upper chamber on the right, or right atrium, has two large openings into it through which all the spent blood arrives from the upper and lower great veins (the superior and inferior venae cavae). Cut open the thin wall of the right atrium with scissors between these two holes to lay open the interior of the chamber, noting the "auricle" or "dog's ear" that forms a small cul-de-sac. The whole chamber is sometimes, inaccurately, called the auricle. You should be able to push a finger downwards into the lower chamber—the right ventricle—through a communicating hole guarded by the three thin cusps of the *tricuspid valve*. These will not obstruct your finger, since they are designed to permit blood flow in the same direction. When the atrium is full of blood, it squeezes its contents through the tricuspid valve into the right ventricle; and when, a split second later, the ventricle is full and contracts, the three cusps come together to prevent the blood from flowing backwards into the atrium again. Instead the spent blood is driven onwards through the *pulmonary valve* (in the upper part of the right ventricle), through the pulmonary artery, to be delivered to the lungs. The pulmonary valve has three very well-defined cusps which prevent blood from coming back into the ventricle as it relaxes to receive more blood from the atrium before the next contraction or beat. It is possible to pass a blade of the scissors from the opened-out right atrium, through the tricuspid valve towards the tip of the heart, and cut along the right border of the heart through the thickness of the ventricular muscle. Then cut upwards again, passing the scissors blade through the pulmonary valve and open up the *pulmonary artery*. If you have done this successfully you will have followed the path taken by the spent blood through the right heart to the lungs. Notice the thick round bands of muscle lining the ventricle, and notice too that you have not entered the left heart, which has no connection with the right except in some congenital malformations (see later). The same dissection can now be made of the left heart. Open up the *left atrium*, noting its "dog's ear" or "auricle," pass the scissors down into the *left ventricle* through the two rather flimsy cusps of the *mitral valve*. Notice how much thicker is the muscle of the left ventricle, and cut upwards through the three well-formed cusps of the *aortic valve* into the main artery of the body—the *aorta*. The aorta as it leaves the left heart is distinguishable from the pulmonary artery as it leaves the right, partly by the extreme toughness of the aortic wall (it has to withstand so much more blood-pressure); and partly by the entrances or orifices of the two small branches given off by the aorta, just beyond the valve cusps, which go to supply the heart muscle itself with blood. These are the *coronary arteries* which are so necessary for the heart's own survival.

The amount of blood pumped in unit time, or the *cardiac output*, can be varied a great deal, according to the needs of the moment. This is accomplished by altering both the heart rate and the stroke volume, the amount expelled per beat. Every minute, the healthy adult man at rest shifts about 5 litres of blood through the heart—an amount equivalent to all the blood he possesses. When exercise is taken, or in response to anxiety or fear, this is stepped up many times, so that the muscles can receive a greatly augmented supply of the materials required for action. The controlling mechanisms which allow these changes to be made automatically are partly organised in the brain by the so-called *cardiac centre*; and partly by local mechanical and chemical stimuli to the heart muscle itself. The cardiac centre is continuously receiving information through nerves about the physical and chemical state of the circulation, and also from the mind; which is partly how certain emotions make the heart beat faster. All the information is integrated, and a cardiac output continuously arranged which is appropriate for current demands.

Cardiac Neurosis. In ordinary circumstances at rest, most healthy people are not conscious of their heart-beat. However, there are many perfectly healthy people whose hearts slip in an extra beat occasionally. Sometimes their owners are aware of this and become unnecessarily alarmed. Their fear causes palpitations (a pounding of the heart) and the tension mounts. An undue anxiety about the tricks played by a healthy heart sometimes leads people to interpret minor pains in the chest, or even indigestion, as grave symptoms of heart disease, and the consequent anxiety leads to still worse symptoms. If you are one of these worried people, take your worries to your doctor, and let him decide for you whether there is anything wrong. A hundred to one there isn't, and then you will have to find something else to worry about, or better still give up the habit altogether. Many people secretly worry about heart disease and high blood-pressure for years, when very often they are worrying unnecessarily. Even if there is cause for worry, so much can be done for these conditions (as it can for cancer) provided medical advice is taken early in the course of the disease. Remember, too, that the slight feeling of giddiness when you get up suddenly from having been lying down, is often experienced by most normal people; but if you get frightened by it you will begin to breathe more quickly and deeply; and this in itself will make you feel even more faint—and so on.

Heart Failure. When the cardiac output of blood is too little for the requirements of the body, a state of *circulatory failure* has arisen, and when this is due primarily to the heart itself being at fault, it is more properly called *heart failure.* As will be seen, heart failure is not a disease, but the common result of a large number of different diseases. The signs and symptoms produced are caused by two sorts of process: (*a*) tissues of the body have too little blood flow through them and are therefore undersupplied; (*b*) blood accumulates and stagnates in tissues, causing congestion, since the failing heart cannot move forward the amount of blood presented to it in the great veins. Often the left or right side of the heart fails disproportionately. In *left heart failure* the lungs are congested because they are the territory from which the left heart is failing to move blood. The patient has great difficulty with his breathing, and in advanced cases may not be able to breathe when he lies down, because the lungs become so congested and waterlogged. In *right heart failure* the main veins are congested and the other parts of the body become swollen with excess tissue fluid, mainly in the lower parts such as the legs and ankles. This swelling with fluid is called oedema, and in heart failure is only partly due to the mechanics of the failing heart. It is mainly due to a poorly understood retention of sodium in the body, a situation in which excess water is also retained. Whatever the type of heart failure it is always likely to be a changing condition, since the amount of failure will depend as much on the demands being made as on the state of the heart. For instance, in mild cases at rest when the required cardiac output is small, there may be no signs or symptoms. These may only appear on exertion. Heart failure will be referred to again later under the various conditions which cause it.

Treatment of heart failure is quite logical. It aimed at correcting the imbalance between supply and demand of blood, and at the removal of the accumulated excess fluid. We can therefore (*a*) reduce the body's demand for blood; (*b*) increase the supply or cardiac output; and (*c*) promote the excretion of sodium and fluid. Demand for blood is reduced by rest, both physical and mental, and by reduction of weight, since obesity (being overweight) is an additional demand on the cardiovascular system. The cardiac output can be increased by administering a "tonic" to the heart muscle in the form of *digitalis*, which is a powerful heart stimulant derived from fox-

glove leaf. Fluid (and hence salt) accumulation can be helped by restricting the intake of salt and by giving drugs which promote its excretion by the kidneys (diuretics). Very occasionally, very large accumulations of fluid in the legs, abdomen, or thorax, are tapped and drained physically, with needles. These remarks on treatment, as elsewhere in the Medical Section, are of course very general and must not encourage anyone to treat himself for such a potentially serious condition as heart failure. Even such a simple measure as doing without salt can be practised quite unnecessarily by many people for years, simply as a result of reading a paragraph like the above. If you need to reduce salt intake you should be in your doctor's care, and so please let him decide.

Congenital Heart Disease. It has been estimated that of all the babies born who survive at least one month, there will be about one in every two hundred with some form of congenital heart disease; that is to say that the heart will have failed to develop properly in embryonic life. In some cases this is associated with a virus disease of the mother (commonly rubella, or German measles) or with certain drugs taken by the mother (e.g. thalidomide) at a time, very early in pregnancy, when organs are assuming their adult shape. Parents should see to it that their daughters get German measles(02sp)or the vaccine before they grow up; and drugs of all kinds should be avoided where possible during early pregnancy. In most cases of congenital heart disease, however, there is no known cause, and it seems that the manner of formation of the embryonic heart is so delicate that it can be thrown out of gear very easily, perhaps even by chance. Scores of different types of defect occur, singly and in combination. Any of the valves may be anatomically defective—either failing to close properly (*incompetence*) or being too tight (*stenosis*); the great vessels (pulmonary artery and aorta) may be switched round, or *transposed*, so that they emerge from the wrong ventricle; there may be defects in the wall (*septum*) which separates the atria or the ventricles on each side (*septal defect*, or "hole in the heart"); or there may be a persistence of the vessel which in the foetus normally by-passes the lungs by joining the pulmonary artery to the aorta (*patent ductus arteriosus*). This vessel normally closes at the time of birth when the first breaths are taken, and subsequently disappears, so that the whole output of the heart is then sent round the lungs. Detecting congenital heart disease early is one of the purposes of routine post-natal check-up examinations of the baby. Exact diagnosis requires very complicated techniques, and sometimes the structural defect can be corrected by surgery, with almost miraculous results.

Rheumatic Heart Disease. Acute rheumatic fever is not to be confused with other forms of rheumatism. Many tissues of the body (particularly the heart) are attacked, as well as the joints, and the trouble is due to a sensitivity which has developed to certain bacteria (*haemolytic streptococci*) which have probably caused a sore throat about three weeks before the onset of the disease. Why acute rheumatism only rarely follows streptococcal sore throat is poorly understood, but this is no consolation to the one per cent or so of the population whose hearts bear its scars. During the acute phase of the illness which usually occurs before the age of fifteen, inflammatory damage occurs to the valves, the heart muscle, and the sac in which the heart lives, the *pericardium*. So there is a *valvulitis* or *endocarditis*, a *myocarditis* and a *pericarditis*. There may be acute heart failure at this stage if the heart is severely affected. The better-known results of rheumatic heart disease, however, are caused in the ensuing years by scarring of the healed valves. The valves are thickened and deformed. They may have lost their elasticity and stretch, so that they do not close properly (*incompetence*); or they may contract and tighten (*stenosis*). In both cases the heart chamber situated next to the affected valve has to work progressively harder, either because it gets no rest in between beats (in *incompetence*); or it has to force the blood through too narrow a hole (in *stenosis*). The end result is some variety of heart failure (*q.v.*). Other causes of heart disease may be syphilis, congenital valvular anomaly, healed bacterial endocarditis, atherosclerosis, and mechanical injury.

The most commonly affected valve is the mitral, usually causing *mitral stenosis*, in which the opening between the left atrium and the left ventricle will sometimes only admit one finger-tip instead of three fingers as it should. In time the left atrium becomes much enlarged as it overworks to force blood through this narrow orifice. Later still a back pressure develops in the lungs causing congestion and breathlessness; and even later the right ventricle is strained as it tries to force blood into the already congested lung. This is a classic example of the march of trouble backwards from the site of the damaged valve involving first the chamber "behind" it (the left atrium), then the territory "behind" that (the lungs), then the pulmonary arteries taking blood to the lungs, and finally the right ventricle trying to send blood to the pulmonary artery. This steady march of events is usually very slow, and can commonly take twenty years or longer from the initial attack of acute rheumatism to the severer symptoms of advanced mitral stenosis. Treatment is both medical and surgical. The heart failure is treated medically as already described. These days surgical reopening of the valve is almost commonplace, either by inserting a finger through the left auricle and breaking down the constriction, or by opening up the heart and re-shaping the valve under direct vision. The latter involves the additional problem of by-passing the heart by the use of some sort of external pump and poses additional problems, even though from other points of view it is obviously more convenient. As always with major surgical procedures much of the problem is in selecting the patients who will benefit from the operation and in whom it is feasible. Quite often there are other valves involved, mainly the aortic or tricuspid or both, and the hydrostatic or "plumbing" problems can be extremely complex. With luck, however, combined with good judgement and good surgery, the lives of incapacitated patients can be transformed by mitral, and other valvular, surgery. Recently a great deal of progress has been made in designing new "ball-in-basket" valves of manmade materials to replace damaged natural valves. The *aortic valve* is stenosed or narrowed by other degenerative processes besides rheumatism. *Tricuspid stenosis* is nearly always rheumatic in origin.

Coronary Heart Disease. This is the term used whenever the blood supply to the heart muscle (through the coronary arteries) is reduced to such an extent that the heart muscle suffers from a lack of supplies. It has a number of causes, but the only really common one is partial obstruction of the coronary arteries by a condition known as *atheroma* or *atherosclerosis*, and sometimes inaccurately called *arteriosclerosis*. This arterial disease is described later (**P29**). It takes the form of swellings or lumps on the lining of the artery which, if they become large enough to interfere seriously with the flow of blood, produce a blood starvation or *ischaemia* of the tissue being supplied. Obviously, the smaller the artery, the more easily will a lump of given size impede the flow. Equally obviously the greater the demand for blood, as in exercise, the more blood "starvation" there will be. There are two degrees of coronary artery disease: one in which the blood flow is reduced to the point where the increased demands of hard work cannot be met, and this results in *angina pectoris* due to *coronary insufficiency*; the other is when the coronary artery becomes completely blocked, preventing the flow of blood altogether, usually by a *thrombus* or clot of blood, and this is *coronary thrombosis*, or heart attack.

Angina Pectoris. Whenever activity is increased in any muscle, the demands for oxygen and nutriments from the blood-stream increase, and as these are used up there is an increased production of waste products known as metabolites. To meet the demands for a greater supply and a more efficient waste-disposal, the blood flow through the exercising muscle must always be increased. If sufficient increase does not occur, not only will there be a shortage of supplies, but there will also be a pile-up of metabolites in the muscle which cannot be carried away. It is mainly because of these latter that pain is caused in ischaemic, or blood-starved muscle, and pain is one of the chief symptoms when heart muscle becomes ischaemic. One important mechanism for increasing blood flow normally to exercising muscle is by automatically dilating the vessels concerned. Diseased vessels, such as coronary arteries when they are affected by atheroma, are not so easily dilated, although certain drugs which are powerful dilators of arterioles can accomplish a great deal, albeit temporarily. The measures taken to relieve the pain and blood-starvation of angina are two-fold. The patient can reduce the demands of the heart by a few minutes' rest, and a drug (usually nitroglycerin) can be taken to dilate the coronary vessels of supply. Another obvious long-term way to reduce demands is for the overweight patient to eat less, and reduce the load of extra body weight on his circulation. It is very frustrating, to say the least, that such an incapacitating and often lethal condition should be caused by the narrowing or blockage of only 5 or 8 cm of narrow piping about 3.5 mm wide. Coronary bypass operations in which the blocked segment is replaced with a piece of blood vessel taken from another part of the body, are now fairly routine.

Heart Attack or *Coronary Thrombosis.* It should readily be understood from the above description that heart attacks will vary in their severity according to the amount of heart muscle deprived of blood; and this in turn will depend on where in the coronary artery the obstruction occurs. Most usually it is the left ventricular muscle which is cut off from supplies and dies, either in part or in all of its thickness. Since it is the left ventricle which does most of the work of pumping blood to the body, serious heart failure (**P27**) is to be expected. If too much muscle is killed, the heart will simply stop, and the patient will suddenly die. It is much more usual, however, for enough muscle to be left for survival, albeit with a greatly reduced cardiac efficiency. A heart attack is usually accompanied by severe pain, similar to the pain of angina but more severe, and unrelieved by rest or by the patient's usual drugs. Very occasionally the event occurs apparently without pain, or with so little that it is ignored. These so-called "silent" coronary attacks can make diagnosis extremely difficult. Since the doctor depends very considerably with heart attacks on an exact, spontaneous description of symptoms for his diagnosis, no description will be given here. There are many over-anxious people who will read these words and could be misled into an unspontaneous description of their own symptoms, and this could make the task of treating them such a problem that they could even be mis-diagnosed as a result. If you have the smallest worry that your chest pain is due to your heart, take your anxiety to your doctor without delay. He will almost certainly be able to reassure you; and if it happens to be your heart after all, you will have taken the first sensible step towards proper treatment. Dangerous as heart attacks are, they are by no means the death warrant that many lay people think, any more than cancer is. The treatment for a true heart attack is urgent and prolonged. Patients must be at complete rest and their pain relieved quickly. The area of heart muscle they have lost must be allowed to heal with a good, firm scar, and this can take three months of rest, often in hospital.

You can help to avoid a heart attack by not smoking, avoiding obesity and living a physically active life. Avoid sudden exercise, however, when you are not in training.

Blood pressure (Hypertension). The blood is under great pressure in the arterial system, since it is this which forces it into all the tissues of the body.

It is therefore no more meaningful to say you have "blood pressure" than to say you have a temperature. You would be very badly off without. Blood pressure which is too high (hypertension) can give rise to problems, though not always. It is another of those conditions like angina and cancer, which engender much anxiety among people even when they do not suffer from them. For this reason doctors are often unwilling to disclose a patient's blood pressure and because of this they unjustifiably earn a reputation for unreasonable secrecy. They are themselves to blame for the general public anxiety as the following true story shows. Some years ago a lady in her fifties wished to accompany her husband to a post abroad which was to last four years. All arrangements had been made—the husband resigned his previous job, sold the house, etc.—when it was discovered at a routine medical examination that she had a high blood pressure, and she was very solemnly advised by the rather elderly doctor not to go. There was great consternation and emotional upheaval, not least because of the inconvenience involved. Eventually she was allowed to go at her own risk. The husband's job lasted eight years instead of four, during which the lady was in no way inconvenienced by her blood pressure; except that she worried interminably about it. On returning home to retire she began to think she had angina, and elaborate hospital investigation revealed that, as might be expected, her arteries were not as young as they used to be. She was undoubtedly suffering from mild angina, but not as badly as she thought. The opportunity then arose, in her late sixties, to go abroad yet again, and this she did, living a quite strenuous life, and one which she enjoyed. She returned home again, twenty years after she had gone abroad for the first time, able to run a home and still with very little inconvenience from her blood pressure. There is no doubt that it had been very high all that time, and it is also certain that she will die one day, although it may well not be of her blood pressure. How much better it would have been for her not to have been told it was high in the first place and to have avoided all these years of anxiety. It is not being suggested here that high blood pressure is a trivial condition, but that it is for doctors to worry about rather than patients! If you ever find out your own blood pressure, never try to work out for yourself what the figures mean. It is much too complicated. Finally, it should be mentioned that high blood pressure may occasionally be associated with, or "secondary to," certain kidney diseases (*nephritis*) including a strange condition known as *toxaemia of pregnancy*, which lasts only as long as the pregnancy, provided great care is taken. Most high blood pressure is "primary", and without any known association or cause.

Low Blood pressure. Some people seem normally to have surprisingly low blood pressure all the time. There is nothing whatever wrong with this; indeed it may even be beneficial. At least they are unlikely ever to suffer the effects of high blood pressure. The sudden low blood pressure of circulatory failure or shock (**P27**) is another matter and must be urgently treated.

Irregularities of the Heart beat. How quickly or how slowly the heart beats is largely under the control of the cardiac centre in the brain and the level of certain hormones in the blood. The *regularity* of the beat, however, is controlled by the so-called pace-maker in the wall of the right atrium, and by the way impulses from the pacemaker travel through specialised conducting heart cells (the bundle of His and its branches) to the ventricles. When any part of this elaborate mechanism is upset, either by altering the biochemical or electrical conditions of these specialised tissues, or by killing some of them off by deprivation of blood supply in the course of a heart attack, disordered rhythm can result. Increase (*tachycardia*) or decrease (*bradycardia*) in rate is nearly always a normal response to exercise, or anxiety. Very occasional irregularity, such as the mis-timing of an occasional beat is also quite normal in some people, although many are alarmed by it. Persistent irregularity, however, is abnormal. Its true nature can usually be elucidated by making an electrical record of the heart beat—an electro cardiogram. The commonest causes are varieties of coronary artery diseases or rheumatic heart disease.

Pericarditis. The heart beats inside a bag or sac. At every beat its outer surface slides against the lining of the sac, lubricated by a small amount of fluid. This is the pericardial sac, the *pericardium* being strictly the lubricated membrane which lines the sac and which also covers the outer surface of the heart. Sometimes inflammation occurs—*pericarditis*—and the sliding surfaces become roughened and even separated by a fluid effusion. Very occasionally, so much fluid accumulates that the heart's action is seriously impeded. Pericarditis may be due to infection or to rheumatic fever, and it usually overlies the area of damaged muscle after a heart attack. This illustrates something which people rarely appreciate—that inflammation is not by any means always due to infection by bacteria. The last two varieties of pericarditis are quite free from germs (sterile).

Myocarditis. A term loosely applied to disorders affecting the heart muscle. There are lots of very rare causes. The really common ones are due to acute or chronic rheumatic causes or to coronary artery disease.

Endocarditis or inflammation of the lining of the heart is a term loosely applied to any disorder of the valves or heart lining. All varieties of rheumatic valvular disease (**P27**) are included. Bacterial endocarditis in its several forms usually involves valves already damaged by rheumatic disease. It is a complication which is still much to be feared, though somewhat less so now that antibiotic drugs are available.

Atheroma or *Atherosclerosis.* This is the condition referred to above in which lumps arise on the lining of arterial blood-vessels. Although it is therefore a disease of the arteries, its importance lies in the way blood flow is held up, either by the lumps themselves, or by thrombosis ultimately blocking the narrowed portion of the pipework. The effects on the body are therefore those of depriving the tissues of blood. It is an astonishing fact that in England and America, more people die of the consequences of atheroma than of any other single disease, including all forms of cancer put together. Furthermore, cancer is mainly a disease of old age, whereas many of the effects of atheroma on men occur in early middle age. If narrowing of the artery is going to do significant harm it is easy to see that it will be of more consequence in those parts of the body where small-bore vessels are supplying tissues whose functions are necessary for life. Exactly such a situation exists in the heart and in the brain. An additional factor is that the arrangement of the blood supply in these tissues is such that any particular area has only one vessel leading to it. This is unusual among the tissues generally, where several alternative, or "collateral" vessels usually supply an area, and where others can take over if one becomes obstructed. We have, therefore, a situation in which perhaps the most important tissues —the heart and the brain—run the greatest risk of deprivation, and this leads to angina and coronary thrombosis on the one hand, and cerebral thrombosis and haemorrhage ("stroke illness") on the other, accounting jointly for about one death in every five. In addition, the effects of atheromatous narrowing are often felt in the legs, where the blood supply to the muscles is inadequate for exercise, leading to intermittent pain comparable with that in the heart in similar circumstances. This is called *intermittent claudication*, or intermittent closing of the leg arteries. In its most severe forms, it leads to the need for amputation, although in most cases early treatment can avoid this. It is small wonder that there is intensive research into the causes of atheroma, as with cancer, but it is probably true to say that we still know rather more about cancer. A lot of attention has been given to the amounts of certain fats in the circulating blood, particularly cholesterol. This fat is found in larger amounts in the blood of sufferers from atheroma, and is also found in the arterial lumps themselves. Efforts have therefore been made to reduce blood cholesterol by modifications of the diet, but it has been extremely difficult to prove that this has done any good. Many other factors are known to contribute to atheroma, and hence to heart attacks and strokes, some of which can be reduced and others not. Such factors are age, obesity, high blood pressure, and smoking cigarettes. People who lead an active life, like bus conductors, seem to have less trouble than others who are less active, like bus drivers. Sudden severe exercise, however, is bad if you are not used to it. It is better, and life saving, to take regular, moderate exercise. Women have less atheroma than men, until the menopause when they begin to catch up, so that hormones have something to do with it. Serious starvation, such as occurred in the German-occupied territories of Holland and Scandinavia and in the concentration camps conferred one benefit—a freedom from atheroma, but obviously we cannot all starve, and the puzzle remains. Like many of the more important outstanding medical puzzles, there is no single factor responsible, and this is what makes it difficult to solve.

Aortic Disease. The aorta, the main artery of the body, running from the left ventricle down through the chest and abdomen, also suffers from atheroma, but is too wide (about 2·5 cm across) to become obstructed. However, weaknesses occur in the thickness of its wall, sometimes due to syphilis but nowadays much more usually due to atheroma, which results in a ballooning out of a part of the vessel, rather like you sometimes see in an old bicycle inner tube. In days gone by these *aneurysms,* as the dilations are called, reached an enormous size, and would wear away the breastbone and ribs, to appear as large pulsating masses on the chest. Now that advanced syphilis is less common, atheromatous aneurysm, with a predilection for the abdominal aorta, is the one most commonly seen; and these days it is treated by replacement of the diseased portion of vessel. *Dissecting aneurysms* of the aorta are another variety in which the blood, under high pressure, somehow finds its way in between the layers of the aortic wall and then suddenly rips up and down the whole length of the vessel, separating (or dissecting) one layer from another in its path. Sometimes it tracks back towards the heart and suddenly fills the pericardium with blood to stop the heart's action altogether.

Embolism. This term refers to any foreign object travelling in the circulation and becoming impacted when it reaches a vessel too small for it to pass through. It may be a thrombus (**P30**), a collection of cancer cells, a group of bacteria, a chunk of infected pus from an abscess, a collection of fat droplets or even a bubble of air. If it originates in a vein it travels to the right heart and to the lungs. If it comes from the left heart or an artery, it will impact in any part of the arterial tree. Reasonably enough an arterial embolus will commonly end up in those parts of the body with the richest blood supply, like the brain, the kidneys, the liver or the bone marrow. A thrombotic embolus will cause death of the tissue in the area previously supplied by the blocked vessel, a condition known as *infarction.* Perhaps the commonest source of thrombotic embolism is the lining of the heart chambers where a thrombus has occurred at the site of muscle damaged by a heart attack. Massive pulmonary (lung) embolism is usually the result of the thrombosis of the leg veins in people kept immobile following surgery or childbirth. That is why postoperative patients are got out of bed for a while as soon as the first day after the operation. The cells of a cancer embolus usually die; but if they survive, a new cancer deposit begins to grow where the embolus impacts, and this is one of the ways cancer may spread. An infected embolus may infect the vessel wall when it impacts, producing a weakness which may give way. Air embolism, if enough insoluble gas enters the circulation, can kill by making so much froth in the heart chambers as to impede the normal pumping action. If bubbles pass the lungs and enter the brain, all sorts of neurological disorders like scores of tiny strokes arise. The same sort of thing happens all over the body in the "*bends*" or "*caisson*" *disease,* in which nitrogen dissolved in the blood at high

pressure, usually in deep-sea diving, bubbles out of solution if decompression is too rapid. Fat embolism sometimes occurs after fractures, due to marrow fat entering damaged veins and being carried away to the lungs.

Thrombosis. This is not quite the same as clotting. It is the mass which arises when platelets adhere to the lining of blood-vessels or heart chambers. Blood clot accumulates among layers of deposited platelets and the thrombus therefore has structure, unlike pure blood clot. Thrombosis usually occurs when the lining of the vessel or chamber is damaged by atheroma or inflammation, or when the circulation becomes very stagnant. One danger is that it will become dislodged and travel as an embolus during the first week or ten days of its existence. Af·er this time it is usually firmly incorporated into the vessel walls by cells which migrate into it from the surrounding tissue. The other danger is, of course, that the tissue previously supplied by the blocked vessel will die before a collateral circulation can be established. As previously explained, this is called infarction. All the technical terms in this section are used elsewhere and can be looked up.

Varicose Veins. When veins become swollen they also often become tortuous (wriggly), and particularly on the surface of the leg look very unsightly. They are, however, a sign of a sluggish circulation, and are often due to disease in small valves within the veins which normally prevent the blood from pooling backwards, down towards the feet. They are often a normal maternal accompaniment of pregnancy and disappear after the child is born. If allowed to persist, the sluggish circulation allows the formation of unpleasant ulcers, mainly in elderly people. Treatment is according to severity. In the early stages they are helped by supportive stockings. Later, often as an out-patient, the sufferer may have to have them removed or obliterated by a surgeon.

Raynaud's Disease. This is a strange condition in which the finger tips and in severe cases all the fingers or the whole hand respond in an exaggerated way to cold. The vessels supplying the hand are constricted and the fingers go white as the blood drains from them. Then the capillaries dilate and become distended and filled with blood. But owing to stagnation it is venous and blue, and the fingers are therefore blue. Now we have all experienced this in very cold weather, but sufferers from Raynaud's disease, nearly always women, respond even to very slight cold, like putting their hands into cold water. Even emotional stress will start the process off. In very severe cases the fingers will be so deprived of blood for so long, that sores will develop and fingers can even be lost, but this is very rare, and can be avoided by an operation to cut the nerves which supply the circular muscle of the vessels concerned. In most cases it is sufficient to avoid getting the hands cold.

Frostbite. Strictly speaking, this is literally a freezing of the tissues and usually only occurs at temperatures below −13° C. The patient may feel a pricking feeling at first, and feel an area of firmer, pale skin on the cheeks, nose, ears, fingers, or toes. If these parts are numb with cold, the onset of frostbite may not be felt, and will often only be noticed by others. In countries where extreme cold is prevalent, it is usual for complete strangers to stop each other in the street and point it out when they see it. It is important not to rub the affected part nor to apply direct heat in any form. Rapid warming can be harmful; rewarming by close application of body temperature is good treatment, *e.g.,* fingers can be firmly held in the armpit or a warm hand closely applied to an ear or a nose.

THE RESPIRATORY SYSTEM.

INTRODUCTION.

When air is drawn in during the process of breathing, it is brought into very close contact with the blood passing through the lungs. In this way the air we breathe in, which contains 21 per cent oxygen, is confronted with "spent" blood returning from the tissues which contains much less, and oxygen therefore diffuses into the blood from the air. At the same time, the waste gas, carbon dioxide, passes by diffusion in the reverse direction from the blood into the air, because there is much more carbon dioxide in the returning "spent" blood than the tiny amount in the air we breathe. The blood is therefore continually circulating through the lungs and exchanging carbon dioxide for oxygen from the air we breathe in. When we breathe out, we disperse the carbon dioxide into the atmosphere.

When the air enters the nose or mouth, it passes into the windpipe or *trachea*, through the vocal cords in the pharynx. The trachea is held open all the time by rings of cartilage and is lined by a mucus-secreting membrane covered by millions of tiny "hairs" or cilia. These continuously waft a sheet of sticky mucus upwards, which traps any dust or other small particles we may have inhaled, until a collection of this material in the pharynx stimulates us to cough and expel the phlegm, usually to be swallowed. At its lower end, the trachea or windpipe divides into two, the right and left main *bronchus*. Each main bronchial tube enters a lung, one on each side, and proceeds to divide repeatedly within the lung until the air is being carried by more and more smaller and ever smaller tubes called *bronchioles*. There are many millions of these on each side, and each one ends in a collection of very small balloon-like structures —the air sacs or *alveoli*. If you were to cut across a lung and examine the cut surface in a good light, you would see that it is a spongy tissue, with many millions of tiny holes, each one just visible to the naked eye. These are the air sacs. In their walls run the blood capillaries, each one of which is a branch of the vessels carrying "spent" blood from the right side of the heart. At this stage, the blood is only separated from the air in the sacs by the walls of the capillaries and of the air sacs themselves. Both structures are extremely thin, making for easy diffusion of the gases between blood and air.

The action of breathing is accomplished by two muscular mechanisms. One is by the muscles which move the ribs, and the other by the diaphragm, a sheet of muscle which runs across the body, separating the chest cavity from the abdominal cavity. These muscles are all actuated by nerves, just as all other muscles are. Those running to the muscles of breathing are organised by a mechanism in the brain known as the *respiratory centre*. It is this centre—one of the so-called vital centres of the brain—which receives information from many different sources, and translates it into instructions for the breathing mechanism. Thus, when you run for a bus, you will automatically breathe more deeply and more quickly because the respiratory centre has been informed about all the extra carbon dioxide in your blood which has been produced by the exercising leg muscles. Even the conscious instructions involved when you blow a trumpet, inflate a balloon, or during speaking, all pass first to the respiratory centre. It is the death of the cells of this and other vital centres of the brain that is the ultimate cause of death in everyone who dies.

Bronchitis may be acute or chronic. It is an inflammation of the lining mucous membrane of the larger air passages or bronchi, and results in much more secretion than the amount normally produced, mixed with some pus. The acute form is often caused by viruses, with "secondary" infection from bacteria. It may sometimes be caused by irritant gases, like the sulphur dioxide in smog. The chronic, or long-standing form of bronchitis is often associated with *emphysema*, in which the small air sacs of the lung architecture are destroyed or distorted, leaving larger spaces than normal, often surrounded by fibrous scar tissue. Such an arrangement makes the normal gaseous exchange difficult between air and blood.

While the exact cause of chronic bronchitis is difficult to discover, because it is such a mixture of causes, it is mainly associated with older age groups, particularly men, in damp foggy climates like ours in Britain, with polluted town air and especially with smoking. Smoking also makes any existing bronchitis much worse. Bronchitis can cause even more trouble than lung cancer, since instead of dying in a short time, the bronchitic lives for many years in chronic sickness.

Each year over 6000 people die of bronchitis. It certainly isn't smart to smoke. Patients cough, and produce varying amounts of sputum, or phlegm. They often wheeze like asthmatics. This may go on for many years before the right side of the heart begins to fail (**P27**). Gradually, during this time, the chest tends to become barrel-shaped. Treatment consists of getting the patient to stop smoking or otherwise contaminating his lungs, preventing infection, particularly during winter months, with germ-killing antibiotics, and breathing exercises.

Bronchial Asthma is a condition in which the finer air passages become constricted due to an allergic response. In addition, an increased secretion tends to obstruct them and the patient wheezes. In many cases it can be shown that he is allergic to a particular component of dust, or, less commonly, a foodstuff. This is the same sort of thing as occurs in the upper respiratory passages in hay fever, but the effect is on a different, lower part of the respiratory system. Many other cases are due to respiratory infection of some sort, probably combined with an allergy to the bacteria causing it. A predisposition to asthma is often inherited. Once a patient has become asthmatic, his attacks will be triggered off by such additional things as emotional stress, changes in temperature (particularly sudden cold), irritating fumes or smoke, and physical exertion. These are secondary factors, and although much of the treatment is concerned with them, it is unlikely that any of them is a sole cause of the condition. Treatment is directed at the relief of the breathing difficulty and of the wheezing, as well as the control of the causative factors. Many useful drugs are available to dilate the contracted air passages and reduce the obstructing secretions. Asthma in children often gets better as the patient grows up. Asthma is another condition made much worse by smoking.

A tiny living mite about 0·3 millimetres long exists in large numbers in nearly all mattresses and floor dust. This is the cause of much asthma, and in such cases it is often very helpful to vacuum-clean mattresses and floors frequently.

The National Asthma Campaign has found that Britain has more asthma sufferers than any European country (and asthma is now our biggest childhood disease). For a further discussion of bronchial asthma, *see* **P61**.

Bronchiectasis. In this condition the bronchial air passages are abnormally and permanently dilated, and the normal structure of the walls destroyed. It is thought to be caused by obstructions of the tubes which lead to dilatation of the parts beyond. Secretions accumulate, and since they cannot easily drain away, they become infected. The infection helps to complete the process of destruction of structures in the bronchial wall. The patient has a chronic cough which often produces large quantities of purulent sputum, and there are often recurrent episodes of pneumonia. Diagnosis is made by a special X-ray examination—a bronchogram—in which a material, opaque to X-rays, is dropped into the air passages. MRI or CT scanning also shows the disease. In some cases, where the disease is localised to one part of the lung, it is often a good idea to cut out that portion, and this is particularly true in young people. Vigorous physiotherapy, involving drainage of the lungs by placing the patient in a suitable posture, together with antibiotic drugs for the infection, are other forms of treatment.

Cystic Fibrosis is an inborn disease which affects chiefly the lungs and the digestive system. It is sometimes called *Fibrocystic disease of the Pancreas*, and sometimes "mucoviscidosis". Until it was medically recognised forty years ago, children affected usually died from pneumonia in the first year of life. This, of course, was before antibiotics were available for the treatment of infections. Today, cystic fibrosis is known to be the commonest genetically determined disorder affecting children in Britain. One child in 2,000 receives one of the abnormal genes from each parent. Such a child therefore has a double dose of the harmful gene, and will have the disease from birth. One person in 25 of the general population carries only one of these abnormal genes, and such an individual will not have the disease, but will be a carrier of the abnormal gene. If such a seemingly normal carrier marries another carrier, there is a one in four chance of each of their children being affected. The children, therefore, who actually develop cystic fibrosis have inherited the disease *equally* from both parents, who are carriers, but are themselves unaffected by the disease. The disease is inherited recessively and involves a defect in pumping salt across cell membranes, particularly in glands. The prospects for survival into reasonably healthy adult life are steadily improving, but they depend upon early diagnosis and careful management through childhood. In cystic fibrosis most of the damage is caused by the excessive viscidity, or stickiness, of the mucus which is produced in the breathing tubes as a lubricant, and also in the ducts of the pancreatic gland which provides enzymes to help digestion. Being thick and sticky, instead of thin and slimy as in the normal, this mucus tends to block the passages instead of keeping them clear. The pancreatic cells are permanently destroyed. The gland cannot secrete pancreatic enzymes, and the food, especially protein and fat, is not properly absorbed. This deficiency can be compensated fairly well by giving pancreatic extract by mouth with every meal, and by dietary care.

The major clinical problem is in the lungs. The lung passages normally have a thin coating of mucus which is propelled steadily upwards, and is completely renewed in less than one hour. It moves more suddenly on coughing. In cystic fibrosis this upward movement is slowed down and interrupted. There is difficulty in keeping the passages clear, especially when infection with bacteria or viruses greatly increases the amount of mucus. This results in intermittent blocking of the air passages, difficulty in breathing, incomplete use of the lungs, and persistent local pockets of infection. If such infectious processes are not controlled, areas of lung will be destroyed, chronic infection will persist, and multiple lung cavities will develop. These predispose to further infection, interfering with the natural development of the lung—a process not normally complete until halfway through childhood—thus adding to the respiratory problems which the child will face in later life. Unless a correct diagnosis is made and proper treatment instituted before the first serious lung infection has occurred, the resulting lung damage may well be permanent.

Pneumonia. This is an infection of the lung tissue, rather than of the air passages. The lung is the only internal organ which is directly exposed to the air, and since there are germs of all kinds in the air, it is a source of surprise that pneumonia is not a much more common event in all of us. The answer lies, as with all infections, in the fact that it is not simply (or even mainly) bacteria which cause disease, but our own lack of resistance to them. If we allow germs to thrive and multiply by being unhealthy or run down or undernourished, infective disease will occur. If we are fit, the entry of those same harmful germs into the body causes us no inconvenience, unless we are very young, or very old, or unless the invasion of germs is abnormally overwhelming. This helps to explain why pneumonia is so often quoted as a cause of death. In most cases it is merely a terminal event occurring in the elderly sick, whose normal resistance is so far reduced by their illness that they succumb to an invasion which they would normally not notice. There are two main kinds of pneumonia, and in both the air sacs

become filled with inflammatory secretions, making the normally porous lung tissue as solid as liver. In *lobar pneumonia*, a whole segment (or lobe) of the lung becomes solid. In *bronchopneumonia*, areas of lung tissue surrounding the smaller bronchioles become consolidated, leaving normal porous lung tissue in between. Bronchopneumonia is the one which occurs in the rather stagnant lungs of people who are already ill or bedridden. Both forms respond to treatment with the appropriate antibiotics, provided any underlying debility does not interfere with the patient's own resistance. In the terminal bronchopneumonia of fatal illness, it is sometimes considered kinder not to treat the additional pneumonia. *Pleurisy* is a natural complication, and before the days of antibiotic drugs *lung abscess* was very much feared. For another form of pneumonia—*viral pneumonia*—*see* **P**9(2).

Pneumoconiosis. This is a term which refers to a large group of different diseases, all of which are caused by breathing in some form of dust over a very long period of time. It is therefore an occupational hazard of certain trades. We have already mentioned the mechanisms of mucus secretion in the air passages which normally trap small particles from the air, and prevent them reaching the lung. However, in some occupations there is so much dust breathed in over the months and years that these normal barriers are defeated. About a quarter of the earth's crust consists of silicon, in quartz, flint, or sand. *Silicosis* occurs in people who have worked for many years in trades like mining, stone crushing, sandblasting, or metal grinding, who are often breathing silicon dust in high concentration. When the particles arrive in the air sacs, they set up an irritant chemical reaction which produces nodules of scar tissue. Silicosis for some reason predisposes to tuberculosis. Emphysema also occurs and there is a general impairment of respiratory function. Coalminer's pneumoconiosis is similar to silicosis but not identical with it. It is more prevalent in some coalfields than others, owing to the different composition of the dust to which these unfortunate men are daily exposed. It is hoped that modern mining methods will help to reduce this dread disease. Asbestos is a complex silicate of magnesium, calcium, and iron. *Asbestosis* is caused by inhaling its fine fibres, and often leads to the appearance of a type of lung cancer called mesothelioma. *Berylliosis* is caused by compounds of beryllium, used in the manufacture of fluorescent lamps. *Farmer's lung* is a pneumoconiosis caused by inhaling hay and grain dust, and is similar to *bagassosis* and *byssinosis* caused by sugar cane and cotton dust respectively. The newest pneumoconiosis to be reported is *mushroom worker's lung*, caused by something in the compost in which mushrooms are commercially grown.

Pulmonary Embolism. This catastrophic, yet quite common condition has already been briefly referred to (**P**30(1)). It is a cause of tragic, sudden death in people who have had operations or have given birth to babies some days previously, or who have been bedridden for any other cause. The first event is that the blood in the veins of the legs becomes stagnant, due to the lack of exercise; and together with the tendency to clot which often follows surgery or childbirth, the whole length of a leg vein may be obstructed for twelve inches or more by an elongated clot of blood. This does little harm to the circulation of the leg, since there are plenty of other veins for returning blood to the heart. The danger is that the clot will become dislodged and be swept upwards towards the heart by the flow of returning blood. When this happens it is carried by way of the right atrium and ventricle into the pulmonary vessels which normally carry spent blood to the lungs. Here, for the first time, it enters vessels which are getting smaller as they divide, and it then impacts in the main pulmonary artery. The patient, who may have been recovering very well, suddenly collapses and not unusually dies there and then. At autopsy a long coiled-up mass of clot is found obstructing the pulmonary vessels. It often can be seen to form a cast of the leg vein and even bears the marks of the small venous valves which are present at its site of origin. With the dramatic advances being made in chest surgery, it is now sometimes possible in selected cases to operate to remove the clot. Thrombolysis, that is using injected drugs to dissolve clots, may also be used rather than pulmonary embolectomy. Three quarters of all cases of pulmonary embolism die within two hours, and therefore the best hope would be to prevent the occurrence altogether. This is not at present possible, but clotting in leg veins can be discouraged by early exercise following surgery and childbirth. Patients often resent having to get up the next day because it is so uncomfortable. Herein, however, lies their best hope of avoiding pulmonary embolism.

Haemoptysis. This means coughing up blood or blood-stained material. It must be distinguished from *haematemesis*, in which the blood is vomited from the stomach. It must always be taken seriously because of the underlying lung disease which may be present. No one who coughs up blood, in however small a quantity, should neglect to inform their doctor so that its source can be determined. Haemoptysis occurs in a variety of lung disease, some of which is not serious but much of which must be treated immediately if it is not to become so. This is a suitable place to repeat our general rule that you should see your doctor without delay if you have any unexplained bleeding from any part of the body, however well you feel. And this includes haemoptysis.

Fat Embolism. Liquid fat sometimes enters the bloodstream following extensive crush injuries to soft tissue and bone. It splits up into millions of small globules which are carried to the lungs, and impact in small blood vessels there, producing obstruction of the lung circulation and consequent difficulties in breathing.

Lung Cancer. This is one of the commonest and at present most incurable forms of cancer which can occur. It is also probably the easiest to prevent. Each year about 35,000 people die of lung cancer in Great Britain, all but 5,000 of them men. Every year the toll goes on. There has been no reasonable doubt for several years now that it is associated with cigarette smoking, and the evidence is overwhelming. However, in spite of this certain knowledge, smoking continues to increase, and every year there are more and more people dying unpleasantly of lung cancer (although it should be stressed not *all* lung cancer originates from smoking).

It seems that nothing the health authorities can do stops people smoking. Intensive campaigns of public advertising of the dangers, and well organised instruction in schools have so far made little impression whatever on the smoking habits even of people who accept the evidence. The only group of people who are known to have stopped smoking are British doctors, very many of whom have given it up, and it is easy to show that giving it up has saved them from the disease. Their colleagues who have not done so have continued to die. Undoubtedly a large factor contributing to the failure of anti-smoking propaganda is the enormous expenditure by the tobacco manufacturers on very clever advertising, amounting to many millions of pounds each year. Moreover they spend a pitiful fraction of this amount on their own research into the harmful effects of their own product, which has so far discovered nothing which was not already known by research doctors many years ago. Another problem is that it takes a number of years to get cancer. It is not like an infectious disease which is caught a few days after exposure to the bacteria concerned. It may be fifteen or twenty years before the cancer begins, and many smokers are apparently unwilling to look so far ahead. Furthermore, not everyone who smokes dies this way; and so a smoker can gamble with his life and hope it will not be him. The main encouragement to smoke probably comes from other people. Youngsters are easily impressed when their teachers and parents stop smoking.

In 1997 an EU report blamed *passive smoking* for causing the deaths of 20,000 persons annually across Europe.

Lung cancer grows in the wall of a main bronchial air passage. If it grows inwards it can obstruct the airway, choking that part of the lung it is supplying with air. This causes collapse and infection of the lung and may lead to *lung abscess*. The patient will then cough up blood-stained infected and purulent material. Such a case is comparatively lucky, since the disease declares itself early by producing symptoms. In others, the lump may grow outwards into the surrounding lung and produce no symptoms at all in the early stages. Indeed, it may spread to other parts of the body, like brain or bone or liver before causing any trouble to the patient. If this happens he may go to his doctor because of fits, changes of personality, or fracture, only to discover that the origin of the trouble is in the lung.

Cure rates are low, although much can be done to relieve the pain and suffering of the last stages of the illness. Survival rates vary from 16-53% at 5 years, depending on the type and severity of disease. Surgery, by removing the lung, and irradiation of the growth are the standard palliative treatment. It is not the practice of the Medical Section to alarm the reader unnecessarily, but if only a few are induced to stop giving themselves such a horrible disease, then writing in this way will have been justified.

Secondary Cancer of the Lung. In nearly all forms of cancer, the big problem is that it spreads to other parts of the body. If this were not so it could be eradicated by surgical removal more often than it is. One common way in which it spreads from any part of the body is by entering the bloodstream and being carried as clumps of living cancer cells to distant parts. When these come to rest in smaller blood vessels, they begin to grow and colonise the new environment. Such new colonies are called *secondary deposits* or *metastases*. It so happens that all veins (except portal veins of the liver) lead to the right heart and thence directly to the lungs, and for this reason the lungs are a very common site of *secondary* cancer, which may have begun in the bowel, or breast, or indeed anywhere else in the body. Other common sites of secondary, blood-borne cancer are the brain, liver, bone marrow, and kidney, since all of them have an abundant blood supply, and there is therefore a high chance of the travelling cells arriving there. Secondary cancer of the lung usually consists of several lumps scattered throughout the lung. Lung cancer itself is usually only one growth. One of the main reasons for the success of early diagnosis is that treatment may be possible before blood-borne and other means of spread have occurred. Unfortunately, in the case of primary cancer of the lung, even early diagnosis is of little avail, but in many other common cancers permanent cure is possible if treatment is begun early enough.

Pleurisy. The chest is lined by one layer of a thin membrane called the *pleura*. The lungs are covered and enclosed by a second, continuous layer of this same membrane. When the lungs move during respiration, the pleura covering the lungs rubs against the pleura lining the chest, lubricated by a very thin layer of pleural fluid separating the two pleura. Whenever the pleural surface becomes inflamed, this is known as *pleurisy*. It is nearly always due to inflammatory disease of the adjoining lung, and is therefore not strictly a disease in its own right. For example, pneumonia, tuberculosis, lung cancer, or a lung infarct will produce a pleurisy if the area of diseased lung adjoins the lung surface. Sometimes the area of inflamed inner pleura will tend to stick to its outer layer or rub painfully against it, producing a sharp pain when the patient breathes. Sometimes a large effusion of fluid is produced which separates the two layers and collapses the lung by occupying space in the chest which the lung should be occupying. This latter is more usual in tuberculosis or cancer.

The lung can be collapsed by the entry of anything between the normally adjacent layers of pleura. For example, air can be introduced, either deliberately to rest the lung in tuberculosis, or by accidental penetrating wounds of the chest wall, or by accidental rupture of the emphysematous lung (*q.v.*). This condition is called *pneumothorax* or "air in the chest." Bleeding into the cavity between the pleura is called *haemothorax.*

THE DIGESTIVE TRACT AND LARGE INTESTINE.

INTRODUCTION.

The digestive tract consists of the mouth, pharynx, oesophagus (or gullet), stomach, small intestine, large intestine (or colon), rectum, and anus. The small intestine is very long, and is subdivided into the duodenum, jejunum, and ileum. It ends at the junction of the ileum with the caecum, where there is a small blind side-tube, the appendix. The caecum leads into the colon. The whole tract has two main mechanical functions and two main biochemical ones. Mechanically, food has to be chewed in the mouth and further minced up by muscular squeezing, mainly by the stomach. It has also to be propelled along by an orderly series of squeezing movements known as *peristalsis.* While it is still in the digestive tract, food has to be digested. That is to say, it has to be broken down chemically into suitable materials for absorption into the system, and secondly, it has to be absorbed across the wall of the intestine into the blood stream, itself a highly complex biochemical process. The blood stream it now enters is a special part of the circulation, the "portal" system, which travels directly to the liver without first passing to the heart. In the liver the broken-down foods are processed and issued in their new form into the general, or "systemic" circulation, by which they are finally carried to all the tissues of the body.

As the food passes along the digestive tract (or, as it is sometimes called, the alimentary canal), it is mixed with various secretions which are either made in the wall of the tract, or by organs outside the wall connected to the main pathway by small tubes. Examples of the latter are bile, manufactured by the liver and sent into the duodenum through the bile ducts; and pancreatic juice, which comes from the pancreas down the pancreatic ducts, also into the duodenum. These secretions are either digestive juices concerned with splitting up the foodstuffs so that they can be absorbed, or they have a lubricant so that the gut contents slide along easily under the influence of peristalsis. Roughly speaking, it may be said that digestive juices give place to lubricant secretions at the junction between the small and large intestine.

The constituents of the diet are dealt with in a later section. The principal classes with whose digestion we are now concerned are carbohydrates, proteins, and fats.

Carbohydrates are sugars and starches. There are many sugars, which may exist alone, in pairs, or with lots of them stuck together. Alone they are such things as glucose or fructose. Common table sugar is a substance called sucrose, formed by sticking one glucose molecule to one fructose molecule. Starch is lots of glucose molecules all stuck together. Digestion of carbohydrates consists of splitting up sugars and starch into single sugars like glucose, since only single sugars can be absorbed into the system. The splitting is done by digestive *enzymes* which are found in the juices secreted into the digestive tract. Sugar-splitters are found in the saliva of the mouth, in the pancreatic juice of the duodenum, and in the duodenum's own juice from its own wall. On the face of it, you might think it would be better to eat glucose which needs no digestion and can be absorbed in

this form, than to eat starch which has first to be split; and so a lot of money has been made out of a gullible public by the sale of glucose drinks and powder. In fact digesting starch is no problem whatever, even for the sick, who can obtain their carbohydrate energy just as easily (and much more cheaply) from potatoes as from expensive glucose. The end result of eating both is the same. The starch-splitting enzyme in saliva is mixed with the food as it is chewed, and it is therefore probably a good idea to chew it well. However, even if the food is bolted it does not seem to matter very much. People without teeth (neither their own nor dentures) seem to digest their carbohydrate quite well, presumably by means of their pancreatic juice at a later stage.

Proteins, which are found in meat, cheese, and eggs, are very large molecules consisting of lots of small ones strung together. Unlike starch, in which all the component glucose molecules are identical, the amino acids of which proteins are composed come in many different types. They all contain nitrogen, and there are about twenty-seven varieties. One protein differs from another in the proportions of the mixture and the order in which they are stuck together. Only single amino acids can be absorbed from the food, and so protein digestion again consists of splitting the material down into its building bricks. There is a strong protein-splitting enzyme in the gastric (or stomach) juice called pepsin, whose job it is to split the long amino-acid chains into shorter chains. Several other protein-splitters in the duodenal and pancreatic juice contrive to break the smaller chains into individual amino acids which are then absorbed and sent to the liver for processing.

Fats mainly consist of glycerol to which are attached three fatty acid molecules for each molecule of glycerol. An enzyme in pancreatic juice splits the fatty acids off the glycerol, but would have some difficulty penetrating the globules of fat without the help of bile. One of the constituents of bile (bile salts) has detergent properties like washing-up powder and breaks the fat globules up into a very fine emulsion so that the enzyme can get at the fat. Some fat particles of this size can even be absorbed as such, without preliminary splitting.

The processes by which all these enzymic secretions are produced are very finely controlled. They are very expensive to make in terms of energy and raw materials, and so it would be very wasteful to produce them all the time, even when there was no food to digest. And so the body has some very well designed automatic arrangements for sampling the foods as they are eaten and passed on, which ensure that exactly the right kind of juice is waiting in every part of the digestive tract for whatever food arrives. As soon as the food is digested the supply of enzymes is automatically switched off, so that there is very little waste of precious materials. It is, of course, beyond the scope of this account to describe the control mechanisms. Suffice it to say that they are operated partly by nerve reflexes which signal the imminent arrival of food, and partly by special hormones produced in various parts of the gut wall. The best secretion is affected even by psychological factors, so that pleasant company and surroundings, attractive appearance of the food, and an eager anticipation of it all make for good digestion and good health. These psychological factors are all capable of proper scientific investigation and proof. The poor health of those who habitually and irregularly bolt unpalatable food is probably due to such factors as these. So is the failure of appetite in the depressed, the anxious adult, or the scolded child.

Nearly all the digestion which has been described occurs in the stomach and upper part of the small intestine (the duodenum, jejunum, and upper ileum). Almost all absorption of the products of digestion occurs in the small intestine which is long and intricately folded to give it a large surface area for this purpose. The colon, or large intestine, is adapted for conserving water, by removing it from the residual waste material. This has then to be eliminated, and being rather dry its passage has to be lubricated by suitable secretions of mucus.

Constipation. Here, perhaps we had better mention the morbid question of constipation, about which so many people are obsessed and hold such pronounced views. First of all, what is it? For some people it is entirely normal only to pass motions about once or twice a week. For others the normal frequency is once or twice a day. What is abnormal? The answer is that the only thing worth worrying about is only pronounced change of bowel habit, particularly in middle-aged and older people. By a change is meant a change from that individual person's normal routine. Such a pronounced change—either in the direction of constipation or diarrhoea—is worth consulting your doctor about if it persists for more than a week or two. Otherwise, forget your bowels and leave them to work naturally as they know best. Many believe that constipation is the root of all evil, that it causes a mysterious condition known to them (although, alas, not to doctors) as "auto-intoxication." Sedulously fostered by the manufacturers of patent medicines, their beliefs range from the notion that headaches, spotty skin, muddy skin, and tiredness are caused by constipation, to the more extreme idea that the whole system is being poisoned and that, if the bowels do not work, the individual will shortly die. Of course, all this is the merest rubbish; for, as Professor Samson Wright, whose *Applied Physiology* is one of the most famous of medical text-books, has pointed out, there is no such thing as absorption of poisonous products from the bowel. There is no such thing as "auto-intoxication." "The symptoms of constipation," he writes, "are largely due to distension and mechanical irritation of the rectum." It has been shown that an enema removes these symptoms *immediately*, which would not be the case if they were due to poisons in the blood, and exactly the same symptoms can be produced by packing the rectum with cotton-wool. Wright mentions the case of a man who went for just over a year without bowel motion, and at the end of that time, although his abdomen was distended and he felt some discomfort, he was not noticeably ill. Needless to say, telling these facts to the purgative addict will only make him annoyed, but it is as well to note that if no known diseases are due to constipation (although constipation may be a symptom of another disease), the regular use of purgatives *can* cause disease.

Constipation should be treated first by diet containing plenty of roughage—bran and oatmeal are excellent—plenty of stewed and fresh fruits, and at least 1½ litres of fluid should be taken daily. Failing that, one of the best things to take is a proprietary product prepared from senna pods. Never to be taken regularly are liquid paraffin, castor oil, preparations of aloes, Epsom salts, and all the other dreadful stuff that people swill down.

Oesophagus.

The oesophagus, or gullet, is more than a simple tube for taking the food from the mouth to the stomach. It is normally closed except when swallowing, and the act of swallowing is very complicated. When the material to be swallowed arrives in the back of the throat there is an automatic mechanism which opens the top end of the oesophagus to receive it, and from then onwards everything happens automatically. The next portion of the tube opens and the top closes strongly, so that the food (or drink) is propelled forcibly down the next segment. Then the part below this relaxes and the material is squeezed further downwards and so on until it arrives in the stomach. This squeezing (or milking) action is akin to the action known as peristalsis which propels contents in other parts of the gut. Thus when you see someone swallowing a glass of beer very quickly in warm weather, it is not going "down the hatch" under the influence of gravity, however much it may look like it. It is perfectly possible to swallow the same, or any other liquid, standing on your head. Getting into that position

is the only difficult part. Sometimes this complicated swallowing mechanism gets out of order, leading to difficulties of swallowing, or *dysphagia*. Another disorder known as *hiatus hernia* occurs at the lower end of the oesophagus as it meets the stomach. At this point the oesophagus has to pass through the diaphragm, the sheet of muscle which separates the chest from the abdomen. The muscular fibres of the diaphragm are normally arranged in a ring around the oesophagus. These help to keep the lower end shut, so that the acid contents of the stomach do not regurgitate upwards, causing inflammation (*oesophagitis*) or heartburn. A hiatus hernia is when muscle fibres get slack, and the upper end of the stomach can even slide upwards into the chest. People with hiatus hernia get heartburn after meals, and particularly when they bend down or lie down. Except for very severe forms, which need surgical repair, the treatment is to eat less at a time, reduce the acidity with a suitable antacid and reduce weight so that the weight of the abdomen does not press upwards so much. The other disease of the oesophagus, quite unrelated to the above, is *cancer of the oesophagus*, the cause of which is still unknown in most cases. When cancer occurs in the wall of any tube, it will often encircle the tube and gradually narrow the way through. This is what happens in the oesophagus, leading to difficulty in swallowing, particularly solids. It is a condition usually, of rather elderly men, although it is sometimes associated with a special form of severe anaemia in women. Treatment is in some way to keep the passage open, either by transplanting a new tube, or more usually, by removing the constricted piece and joining up the remainder.

The Stomach and Duodenum.

By far the commonest diseases of the stomach and duodenum are *gastric ulcer* and *duodenal ulcer*. They are actually the same condition in two different sites and are often classed together as *peptic ulcer* or *acid-peptic disease*. The ulcers, which are rather like sores on the lining of the stomach or duodenum, may be "acute" or "chronic." Acute ulcers tend to be small and there are often several of them. Chronic ulcers are usually single. They may be small, or they may be several centimetres across. Chronic ulcers smoulder for months and even years, like a sore which will not heal, and a great deal of scar tissue forms in their depths. Thus they may in time erode their way right through the wall of the stomach, destroying all its layers, and begin to eat into surrounding structures like the pancreas or liver. The fact that they do not perforate more frequently is due to all the fibrous scar tissue which is formed during the slow eroding process. Healing of such a destructive ulcer is nevertheless common, and the great problem is how to help the natural healing process to win against the ulcer's tendency to erode. Ulcers are very commonly associated with the bacterium Helicobacter pylori, which may be the cause of ulcers. Appropriate treatment to eradicate this organism is an important part of ulcer therapy. This extremely common affliction is confined to the human species and has been known since the earliest times. It does not vary very much with diet or with social class. Although occurring at all ages, it usually begins between the ages of twenty and forty, and is most commonly found in men between forty-five and fifty-five. Gastric ulcer is four times, and duodenal ulcer ten times more common in men than in women. It is always due to an inability of the lining to stand up to the normal digestive activity of the stomach contents. These are normally acid and contain a powerful enzyme for digesting proteins. Again it is perhaps more surprising that we all do not digest our own stomachs, rather than that some unfortunate people do digest small areas slowly. In certain abnormal conditions when the stomach stops making acid, ulcers always heal. However, some ulcers occur without excessive secretion of acid and many heal without the acid being neutralised with antacids. All this points to the main trouble being in the response of the lining to acid rather than to the acid itself. Nevertheless, the most effective treatment at present known involves regulating gastric secretion, and particularly its acidity. It is also known that peptic ulcers are more common in people whose occupations involve administrative and professional responsibility, competitive effort and nervous tension, long periods of anxiety or frustration Presumably the higher nervous system influences these events by the same nerves, which normally help to control secretion.

The main symptom of peptic ulcer is pain, and this usually responds well to proper doses of antacids. Many different varieties are available and a lot of money is made from selling them. When indigestion persists for longer than a few days it is always better to see your doctor so that a proper diagnosis can be made and the best remedies begun. Many other causes exist for similar pains, and you should not try to make the diagnosis yourself. It may be necessary to analyse your gastric secretions in the hospital laboratory. Almost certainly you will have a special X-ray examination, and since the stomach cannot easily be seen on a normal X-ray, they will have to show it up by making you drink a white material containing barium. This will be seen as a silhouette of the stomach and duodenal contents. Searching for an ulcer this way is a highly skilled matter and is performed by doctors specially trained in radiology.

Until recently, no drugs capable of influencing the course of peptic ulcer in any significant manner were available and the physician had to rely on general measures, such as rest, diet and the administration of antacids to relieve pain and discomfort: episodes of acute haemorrhage were not uncommon and required surgical intervention if life were threatened.

Most ulceration in the stomach and all in the duodenum is due to bacterial infection, *Helicobacter Pylori*. This damages the intestinal wall and makes damage from the stomach's own acid inevitable. Eradication cures the disease, although re-infection may occur. The gastro-enterologist can now pass a *flexible* instrument, the *gastroduodenal endoscope* (the gastroscope is a *rigid* tube), under mild sedation through the patient's gullet and into the stomach and duodenum and view the lesions directly. Once an ulcer is diagnosed, the time has come to stop treating yourself with antacids from the chemist's counter, and to take the ones your doctor decides are best. Smoking should be stopped by ulcer patients (as, indeed, by everyone else, but that is another matter) because it inhibits healing. Alcohol tends to increase acid secretion and should be avoided. It is also *extremely important* to avoid taking any form of aspirin, even in quite small amounts, since this can lead to very serious bleeding from the ulcer. The ulcer patient should be warned that hundreds of proprietary preparations contain aspirin and all of them are dangerous for him. Search for the formula in small print on the label before taking any remedy, looking particularly for acetylsalicylic acid—the systematic name for aspirin. Even some widely sold "hang-over" remedies which are sold for "upset stomach" contain large quantities of aspirin. Some of the patients with "upset stomach" are, of course, ulcer patients, and some even die of haemorrhage following the ingestion of aspirin.

The main complications of peptic ulcer are bleeding, perforation, and a narrowing of the pylorus, or lower part, known as *pyloric stenosis*. Bleeding is caused by the eroding ulcer eating away at one of the many blood vessels in the stomach or duodenal wall. It leads to the passing of "altered" blood in the stool (*melaena*), or to the vomiting of blood (*haematemesis*). When the initial bleeding occurs, the patient may feel suddenly faint, and a little later will notice the black, tarry colour of his stool. This is sometimes confused with a similiar colour when the patient is taking iron. Peptic ulcer is not the only cause of this very serious haemorrhage, which constitutes a hospital emergency whatever its cause. The treatment, like that of every large haemorrhage, is blood transfusion which must be continued until the bleeding stops, or until the patient is sufficiently fit for surgery, should that be deemed necessary. Perforation is perhaps the most serious complication of peptic ulcer, leading to the spilling of stomach contents within the abdominal cavity. Treatment is invariably surgical, either the closure of the perforation or the partial removal of the stomach.

Surgical removal of part of the stomach is often the only way to treat a peptic ulcer which has had its chance to heal in other ways. It is tempting for the patient to "have it out and done with," but the time for surgery is a matter of fine judgment. So many ulcers heal by medical means if you give them a chance, and operations are for those which persistently refuse, or which become complicated.

Stomach Cancer. The stomach is a fairly common site for primary cancer. There is no known reason for this, and it is particularly important to stress that we know of no connection whatever between the peptic ulcers which have just been discussed and cancer. Stomach cancer used to be the commonest cancer of men, but the current rise of lung cancer has pushed it into second place. There are some strange geographical differences in its distribution. For example, it is much commoner in Japan and Scandinavia than in England or the U.S.A. It is difficult to see any reason for this in dietary habits. In Wales it causes three times as many deaths as in South-East England. All this is very puzzling, as is so much of our information about cancer generally. One of the main problems with stomach cancer is that it often causes the patient no inconvenience and thus produces no symptoms of note until the disease is far advanced and it is difficult to do much. Treatment is by surgical removal of the growth, and even in the most advanced cases a great deal can often be done to make the patient more comfortable.

The Small Intestine.

The small intestine runs from the stomach to the caecum and comprises the duodenum, jejunum, and ileum in that order. On a more cheerful note it may be remarked that it is very rarely the site of cancer. Its main problems arise in connection with defects in absorption mechanisms, with obstructions, and with a strange inflammatory condition known as *regional enteritis*. Most obstructions are due not to blockages of the tube, but to failures of peristaltic propulsion, the process which is briefly described above under "oesophagus." Such a failure is called *ileus*. When peristalsis stops for any reason, the result is severe dehydration and loss of important chemicals like sodium and chloride from the body. This is because about 9 litres of fluid enter the small intestine each day in the form of digestive juices, and all of this has to be pushed onwards to be reabsorbed into the system at lower levels. If peristalsis fails, this bulk of fluid remains in the small intestine, or is vomited. In both cases it is lost to the body itself, leading to serious dehydration and illness. Treatment is by very careful replacement by transfusion of the fluid and the chemicals lost, and by removal of the trapped fluid within the intestine through a tube threaded down through the mouth.

Regional enteritis or *ileitis* is sometimes known as *Crohn's disease*. It is a very mysterious condition in which the normally supple wall of the small intestine becomes inflamed and gradually replaced by thick fibrous scar tissue, so that it looks and feels like a thick garden hose. Loops of inflamed gut stick together, and channels open between them, and if the disease progresses a mass of adherent, thickened intestine results to which everything in the neighbourhood also adheres. However, for some unknown reason some cases do not progress downhill in this way and get better spontaneously. Surgical treatment is necessary for the majority, however, particularly those with advanced disease leading to complications such as obstruction or perforation. Sometimes an early case can be resolved by cutting out the length of affected gut, although recurrences are unfortunately common.

Appendicitis. This must be one of the best-known surgical diseases of the intestinal tract.

The appendix is a narrow, blind-ended side tube attached to the caecum near the end of the small intestine. Appendicitis is when it becomes obstructed, or infected, or both. From its position it is almost predictable that it will get obstructed sooner or later by pieces of faecal matter which pass its entrance and which are normally infected. The surprising thing is that it does not happen more often. Once this has occurred, however, a closed abscess forms, and as the abscess distends the appendix, it first weakens its wall, making it gangrenous, and then bursts into the abdominal cavity causing *peritonitis* (see later). It would be useless and misleading to describe the symptoms of acute appendicitis in detail, since it is difficult even for experienced doctors to distinguish them from those of several other conditions. Suffice it to say that any severe, persisting pain in the abdomen, whether continuous or intermittent, whether associated with diarrhoea or not, should lead the sufferer to a doctor for a quick diagnosis. Germ-killing antibiotics are useless against appendicitis, and any laxative is extremely dangerous as it may cause an acutely inflamed appendix to perforate.

The Large Intestine or Colon.

The two main serious diseases of the colon are ulcerative colitis and cancer in its various forms. *Ulcerative colitis* is yet another mysterious disease in which severe ulceration of the lining of the colon gives rise most frequently to diarrhoea with the passage of blood and mucus. In fact it can be like dysentery, and it has often been considered to be due to some form of infection. Unfortunately no particular germ can routinely be found in these cases, and the situation is endlessly confused by the presence in the normal bowel of lots of different germs anyway. Nevertheless the ulcerated lining of the bowel certainly does get infected by the germs normally present, and this makes the disease worse. Therefore germ-killing antibiotics are often helpful in alleviating symptoms and can lead to an earlier settling down of the condition, although not to a cure. It has long been known that certain kinds of psychological upset are often associated, but here again the disease is so unpleasant for the sufferer that he is to be forgiven some despondency as a result of, rather than as a cause of, his troubles. It is also suspected that ulcerative colitis may be an auto-immune disease; that is it may represent rejection by the patient of his own colonic lining in a manner somewhat comparable to the tissue rejection which often follows organ transplantation. Some of the more alarming complications are perforation through the wall of the ulcerated bowel, and sometimes massive haemorrhage occurs. Treatment is with sulphasalazine or drugs derived from it, together with diet and the occasional use of other drugs to minimise symptoms. Surgery may be required to relieve obstruction, deal with perforation, remove chronically affected parts of the bowel, *etc.*

Cancer of the Colon and Rectum. This is another very common form of cancer, which can often be completely cured by surgical removal of the growth provided it is caught in the early stages before it has spread. The commonest symptom is a change in bowel habit, either towards constipation or, more often, towards diarrhoea, in the second half of life. There may be rectal bleeding, or the passage of mucus, and there may be abdominal pain. We cannot too often repeat that any such change of bowel habit, or any unexplained bleeding from any site should lead the patient promptly to his doctor.

Diverticulitis. Some people have small pockets or sacs in the wall of the colon known as diverticula. A minority of these sometimes get inflamed, and this is *diverticulitis.* Occasionally perforation occurs.

Hernia or Rupture. This is a condition in which abdominal contents, usually a loop of intestine, protrude forwards through the muscular wall of the abdomen. The wall consists of a sheet of muscle fibres running in several directions. They normally become tense when we cough, or strain, or in getting up from a recumbent position. There are places in the groin on each side where there is a way through the muscle for the spermatic cord in the male. In many men a weakness can arise at this point, and if it persists, the way through may enlarge and allow loops of bowel to emerge from behind the muscle sheet to appear as a lump under the skin of the groin. On relaxation the lump can be made to disappear by pushing the contents back the way they came; and they will re-emerge when the patient strains. This is an extremely common complaint in men, and it should be treated by an operation in which the muscle wall is repaired. Some men, however, neglect to have their rupture treated until one day it proceeds to "strangulate." This is the term used when the muscle tightens around the neck of the protruding loop of bowel, cutting off its blood supply. From then onwards the bowel becomes gangrenous and the intestine is obstructed by having a part of itself nipped outside the abdominal wall. The patient is in severe pain, vomits continuously, and quickly is liable to get into such a poor condition that surgical relief is difficult. It is therefore a surgical emergency, and it would have been better to have had the relatively simple repair operation earlier and at leisure. Hernia in the region of the groin is of two types: *inguinal hernia* and *femoral hernia*, the difference between them being technical and of no consequence to the patient. They nearly always occur in men. Other types of hernia less frequently occur in both sexes. *Incisional hernia* is when the muscle wall has been weakened at the site of an old abdominal operation and has failed to heal properly. *Umbilical hernia* occurs owing to the natural weakness of the abdominal wall at the navel, and is so common in babies as to be almost normal. When a baby cries and thereby puts a strain on his abdominal wall, a lump often appears in the region of the navel, and this can be very alarming for the parents. They should of course show it to their doctor who will nearly always be able to reassure them. It is self-healing without operation in the majority of cases.

Peritonitis. The cavity of the abdomen in which the intestines and other organs lie is called the peritoneal cavity, and it is lined by a thin membrane called the peritoneum. When this becomes inflamed the condition is a serious one and is called *peritonitis.* Inflammation may be bacterial, as occurs following a burst appendix and the spillage of bacteria and pus in the cavity. It may be a sterile peritonitis as often follows perforation of a peptic ulcer, when the inflammation is caused by the acid contents of the stomach. It is always very dangerous, probably because of the large surface area afforded by the peritoneum for the absorption of inflammatory toxins.

Haemorrhoids are simply varicose veins in the rectal and anal regions. They are very common, and are caused probably in about equal degrees by inherited weakness of the veins, strain such as heavy lifting, and constipation (this is one of the very few conditions in which constipation may do some damage, due to the mechanical pressure of hardened faeces in the rectum on the veins). Pregnant women are liable to develop haemorrhoids or "*piles*," as they are commonly called, owing to the pressure of the baby's head in the pelvis. Haemorrhoids may be external or internal, the former being in the anal region below the sphincter, the latter in the rectum; the two usually go together. There may be no symptoms, but the veins are liable to bleed, to get thrombosed (*i.e.*, a clot forms within) or to become infected. When clotting or infection occurs the piles enlarge and tend to be pushed out through the anus during defaecation, when they form extremely painful external swellings. Treatment in simple cases may be by the use of suppositories—cones of a firm grease containing suitable medicaments which are inserted in the rectum—in other cases the veins may be injected, as with varicose veins of the leg, in order to close them, but when there is much bleeding, thrombosis, infection, or interference with bowel movements they should be removed surgically.

THE LIVER.

The liver is a very large organ and has such a wide variety of known functions (to say nothing of the unknown) that it is also one of the most complicated. Nearly all of its functions are biochemical, and it is often called the laboratory of the body. Medical students, when asked to enumerate the functions of the liver, usually stick at about twenty-five, nearly all of them to do with general metabolism: that is the biochemical processing of substances taking part in structure or as body fuel. For example, the liver makes proteins from the amino-acids absorbed from the gut, and breaks down amino-acids and manufactures a waste product (urea) from them. It stores carbohydrates as glycogen, and conducts many of the processes necessary to turn carbohydrates into energy. It manufactures prothrombin with the help of vitamin K, and this is essential for blood clotting. It makes bile and secretes it into the gall bladder and bile ducts (see later). The three main constituents of bile (cholesterol, bile pigment or bilirubin, and bile acids) all have to be processed, or metabolised, in the liver during the production of bile. Vitamin B_{12} and iron are also stored and dealt with there, and these are involved in preventing various forms of anæmia (q.v.); and in addition to all these things the liver is the place where harmful substances, both from within the body and from outside it, are dealt with and rendered harmless. This last function of "detoxication" is often accomplished by making the offending molecules suitable for rapid excretion by the kidneys, or by altering their chemical shape to make them harmless.

Nearly all of these very different things are done by one single type of cell: the liver cell, and it is one of the remarkable features of the design that this cell can be so versatile. There also have to be some very efficient transport systems in the liver, in addition to the usual blood supply and venous drainage possessed by all other tissues.

One of these is the "portal venous system." Whenever a substance is absorbed across the gut wall from any part of the intestine into the interior of the body it enters the special draining blood vessels of the portal system, which are arranged throughout the length of the digestive tract. All these veins eventually unite in the main portal vein which enters the liver. Everything absorbed from the gut is therefore taken first to the liver to be processed. After this the products are carried away from the liver in the ordinary veins to the heart, and are distributed to the rest of the body by the arterial system. The liver has arteries of its own by which it receives oxygen and nutriment like any other tissue. The fourth transport system collects the bile as it is formed within the liver and delivers it to the gall bladder and bile ducts, which eventually drain it into the duodenum.

Portal Hypertension means high blood pressure in the portal venous system, and is the usual accompaniment to *cirrhosis* (see later). When the terminations of the portal veins in the liver are strangled and obstructed by cirrhotic disease, this tends to blow them up, or dilate them with blood. There is a natural escape route for the portal blood where the lower end of the oesophagus or gullet joins the upper end of the stomach. At this place some of the portal veins draining the stomach are connected with the ordinary veins draining the oesophagus so that when pressure rises in the portal system, blood tends to be diverted into these connecting veins, and they in turn become dilated, or varicose. Trouble begins when these dilated connecting veins, which bulge inwards into the oesophagus, are damaged by food particles passing across them and bleed severely into the stomach. The patient vomits large quantities of blood (*hæmatemesis*) or passes tarry altered blood in the stool

(*melaena*). The other main cause of these is the bleeding which occasionally accompanies peptic ulcer (q.v.).

A second complication of portal hypertension (and hence of cirrhosis) is *ascites*, in which large amounts of a lymph-like fluid accumulate in the abdominal cavity. The fluid contains a great deal of precious protein and salt which is lost to the body economy. Ascites also sometimes accompanies cancerous deposits in the abdomen.

Jaundice means being yellow because there is too much yellow bile pigment circulating in the blood, and there are three main possible causes for this. The term "yellow jaundice," like "gastric stomach" is therefore unnecessarily redundant: there is no other kind.

Bile pigment comes from broken-down red blood cells, which normally come to the end of their time after existing for about 120 days. The breakdown products of red cells can always be found in the blood of normal people, but there is normally insufficient colour to show. Abnormal amounts of colour build up quite logically in any of the following three circumstances:

(1) If too many red cells are being destroyed and even the normal liver cannot deal with the amount of bile pigment produced, it piles up in the blood, and *hæmolytic jaundice* is the result. The expression simply means jaundice due to (abnormally large) red-cell destruction.

(2) If the liver cells are themselves sick and unable to cope even with the normal amounts of pigment from normal red-cell destruction. Here too the pigment will pile up and cause *hepatocellular jaundice*, or liver-cell jaundice.

(3) If the bile ducts carrying bile away from the liver are blocked, then bile will pile up behind the blockage and re-enter the blood stream, causing *obstructive jaundice*. In this case the rate of red-cell breakdown is normal, and the liver cells are normal: at least for a time.

It is enormously important for the treatment of jaundice for the doctor to diagnose its type correctly, since the treatment varies from surgical relief of obstruction to the medical treatment of viral infection or of excess red-cell destruction. The so-called differential diagnosis of jaundice is often exceptionally difficult, and sometimes requires some very sophisticated laboratory tests and X-rays. At other times it is extremely easy and is obvious from a cursory glance at the urine and the stool. In any case all jaundice is a highly technical matter for the doctor who must be consulted early.

There is a special jaundice of newborn babies which resembles hæmolytic jaundice and can occasionally have serious consequences for the developing brain (*kernicterus*) if it is allowed to become too severe. When this is threatened, steps are taken to reduce the level of circulating bile pigment by replacement of the baby's blood or by other means.

The commonest cause of hepatocellular jaundice is infective or viral hepatitis. Obstructive jaundice is usually due either to blockage by gallstones (q.v.) or by a lump pressing on the bile ducts from an adjacent cancer. This can often be quite satisfactorily relieved by surgery.

Infective Hepatitis. There is a group of disorders affecting the liver which are caused by viruses. The incubation period is often very long, and the sickness and other debility caused is often quite severe and prolonged. One variety, known as serum sickness, is now much less common than a few years ago. It used to be transmitted by using the same needle for injections into several different people, or from transfusing contaminated blood. A greater awareness of the problem, and the use of disposable needles and syringes has cut down the incidence.

Cirrhosis. There are many different kinds of cirrhosis, the commonest of which has already been mentioned under *portal hypertension* above. In all cases, liver cells are slowly poisoned and are killed off over a long period of time. In response to this, the surviving liver cells undergo cell division, trying to make good the numbers lost, and at the same time fibrous scar tissue replaces the damaged tissue throughout the organ. The result is a hard, knobbly liver. The many "knobs" are spherical areas of regenerated new cells, and they are separated by thickened bands of scar tissue. All of this destroys the normal architecture and leads to the portal hypertension and ascites mentioned above. In some countries (*e.g.*, France and the United States) excessive alcohol is the main cause of the original liver damage which starts it all off. In others (*e.g.*, Bantu South Africa) it seems to be nutritional starvation of the liver. In England much less than half the cases are due to alcohol, and many are thought to be due to a previous episode of infective hepatitis (*q.v.*), but this is not certain. Infective hepatitis is quite common but cirrhosis is comparatively rare. So that the great majority of people do not progress from one to the other. One treatment for advanced cirrhosis is to replace the liver by transplantation, but there are still problems to overcome before this can become routine.

Cancer of the Liver. Cancer of the liver is quite common, but it is nearly always cancer which has spread in the blood stream from other parts of the body. The liver is a favourite site for such secondary deposits, since it has a large blood supply and will receive a generous helping of anything being carried. It is also a very "fertile soil" for the cancer seedlings to grow in. Primary cancer of the liver is uncommon, and only occurs in a few cases of pre-existing cirrhosis.

Gallstones. These are "stones" formed by some of the major constituents of bile coming out of solution and forming solid bodies. They are very common, and often cause no trouble at all. When they do, it is usually a colicky intermittent severe pain. This is due to the muscular walls of the bile passages contracting in an effort to expel an obstructing stone into the duodenum. The second common trouble arising from gallstones is obstructive jaundice, described above. It is small consolation to gallstone sufferers that the stones are often very pretty, often being composed of beautiful cholesterol crystals coloured by varying shades of bile. If they contain calcium they will be visible on an X-ray. Otherwise they are not seen. Stones often occur in conjunction with inflammation of the gall bladder, known as *cholecystitis*. The treatment for gallstones is to remove them surgically together with the gall bladder if they are causing persistent symptoms. Also, a flexible endoscope can be passed into the intestine and a tiny wire basket passed from it into the bile system to remove stones.

The Pancreas.

This is a soft, elongated gland lying behind the stomach; it is about 12·5 cm long and 5 cm wide. Within its tissues lies the duct, which, when it leaves the pancreas, passes into the duodenum near the point of entry of the bile-duct. This duct transmits the juices containing enzymes which aid in the digestion in the small intestine. The pancreas, however, has two main functions: not only does it manufacture these important digestive juices, but in certain specialised areas, known as the islets of Langerhans, it manufactures insulin, the hormone which makes it possible for the body to utilise sugar. *Diabetes mellitus* or ordinary diabetes is a chronic disorder usually caused by a deficient secretion of insulin. The unused sugar accumulates in the blood and acts as a poison, which, in extreme cases, sends the patient into coma and may—indeed, in former times, usually did—result in death. The treatment of diabetes was revolutionised by the discovery of the hormone insulin by Banting and Best in 1921. On the whole, diabetes is more severe in young people than in the elderly, but with correct treatment it is possible for all cases to lead a perfectly normal life except for dietary restrictions and insulin injections. Not to be confused with *Diabetes insipidus* (**P43**(1)). The main problem with diabetes mellitus now is that the wrong (albeit slightly) blood sugar levels that are found even with good therapy eventually damage small blood vessels, leading to problems with the eyes, peripheral nerves and kidneys.

DIET.

When considering diet, and the effect it has on our health and well-being, there is more to it than just the things we eat. We must also know about what our body does with the food, and it would be unscientific not to acknowledge the effects of our psychological make-up and our nutritional beliefs on what we eat, what we do with it, and how well (or ill) we feel as a result.

For example, a deep-rooted conviction that brown eggs or free-range poultry are better for us than white eggs or intensively reared birds is entirely unsupported by any evidence. However, if we believe such a thing sufficiently, we will not only eat the "better" ones, but we will feel happier and more secure afterwards, and this is likely to make us healthier. Food fads can occasionally be dangerous, as when extreme vegetarians become ill through lack of certain vitamins (*e.g.* B_{12}) which are present only in the foods they exclude. But this is so rare, even among strict vegetarians, that such danger can virtually be ignored. On the whole (and vegetarianism is probably a good example of this) food faddism often leads to a sense of health and well-being in the believer, and should not be attacked by the rest of us for that. It is an accepted fact that personal misfortune, even when it is severe, is more easily withstood by those with strong religious conviction than by others. In the same way, a firm attachment to a theory of what is good for you can produce a feeling of well-being and genuine good health, when another person on exactly the same food intake will not feel so fit. These factors—religious belief, food faddism, or the bedside manner of a kind or persuasive doctor —are commonly dismissed by free-thinking people because they are not "true" or "real." All three, however, can materially affect our health just as can a shock, a personal tragedy or being in love.

The basic constituents of any diet are protein, fats, carbohydrates, water, vitamins, minerals, salts, and indigestible roughage. All are chemicals whose structure and function are reasonably well understood. Even the mystical differences between fine table wines, so beloved of the connoisseur and gourmet, are reasonably well understood in chemical terms. Perhaps that is a pity.

Much nonsense is talked, especially by nutritionists, about minimal daily requirements. In general terms, however, requirements can be described in terms of how many calories there are in the total intake of proteins, fats, and carbohydrates per day, and how these are distributed between the three classes of food. The other substances mentioned above are only required in trace or small amounts except for water; and roughage is only required as a mechanical stimulus to bowel movement.

During the process of digestion (described earlier) all proteins are split into their constituent amino acids; all carbohydrates are split into their constituent simple sugars and most fats are converted into fatty acids and glycerol. At this stage, and not until this stage, all these simpler building bricks derived from the three classes of food are absorbed into the body proper, and taken to the liver and other tissues. Here they are "metabolised." That is to say they are either burned as fuel for the various processes of the body; or they are built up again into proteins, fats, and carbohydrates of the special kinds the body needs. They will either be used to rebuild structures suffering ordinary wear and tear or they will be stored. Many of them will be converted into a different class from the one they came from when they entered the body. For example, excess carbohydrate is converted into fat; or if there is a shortage of carbohydrate, some will be made out of the protein amino-acids which would normally have been used for tissue growth and repair. Thus it is only a generalisation to say that dietary carbohydrates are fuel and proteins are for building bodily structure. The body can convert one into the other, and spoil the calculation.

There is a great deal of confusion in people's minds about *energy*, and that is why the word *fuel* has been used above in connection with carbohydrates. The lay person uses energy as a term meaning something which allows us to leap about, running and jumping and skipping and dancing, and which keeps us from getting tired and run down. Thus, the food industry tells us, we need potatoes or breakfast cereals for these activities or for a hard day's work. This is a deliberate commercial confidence trick, and the scientist is largely to blame. He originally handed out the word energy to an eager food industry and an unsuspecting public, forgetting to explain that he meant it in the strictly scientific sense of fuel for bodily processes. It simply is not true that more potatoes, or more cornflakes will make you more active. Indeed the reverse is the case, and after a certain point they will only be converted into fat and reduce your activity. The nutritionist measures energy as calories, which are units of heat, and it is certainly true that you must eat enough of these each day if you wish to remain alive, let alone active.

All the three main classes of food provide calories, and in an ordinary well-balanced diet about 15 % are provided by protein. Carbohydrates produce most of the remainder. Each gram of fat contains about twice the calories of a similar quantity of carbohydrate. We simply eat less fat than carbohydrate, because fat has a "high satiety value." It takes away the appetite for more. Proteins are mostly found in meat, fish, eggs, cheese, and milk. However, there is quite a lot of protein in many predominantly starchy foods like bread, and such grains as wheat, rice, and corn. Carbohydrates are mainly found in bread, potatoes, sugar, pastry, sweets, and so forth. That is one of the words which fortunately seems to be used by both scientists and laymen in much the same sense.

Some substances are absolutely essential to the body if life is to continue, even if they are only needed in trace amounts. These are substances which the body's own factories (like the liver) cannot make for themselves, even if they are provided with the correct ingredients.

One group of such substances are the *vitamins*. Some of these are found in predominantly fatty foods (milk, butter, cheese and so on) and are known as the fat-soluble vitamins—Vitamins A, D, E and K; the others are water-soluble—the Vitamin B group and Vitamin C. All have now been chemically identified, are manufactured and can be bought over a pharmacist's counter. The myth has grown up that if a little is good for one then a lot more will be better and there are a great many vitamin enthusiasts who consume vast quantities of such manufactured products in the belief that by doing so they will induce extra vitality and energy. Unless your diet is unbalanced in some way (a vegetarian diet may be grossly deficient in Vitamin B_{12}) you will not need extra vitamins.

Fortunately, most people buy food because they like it, not because it does them good; and provided they have normal dietary tastes they will usually get a perfectly adequate selection of the things we have spoken of as necessary for good health. The main danger in England is to have a surfeit and become overweight. In addition there are certain times of life when conscious attention should be paid to what is necessary. For example babies and nursing mothers have special dietary needs and will hear about them from their Health Visitor or from their Welfare Clinic or Doctor. Elderly people living alone are also prone to dietary deficiencies for reasons ranging from poverty to loss of appetite or inability to look after themselves properly.

Recent surveys have revealed some interesting facts about people's attitude to food and their knowledge of it. For example, half the people asked knew that meat was a source of protein, a third mentioned eggs and a fifth cheese, fish, and milk. But practically no one knew there was protein in bread. Yet in England about a fifth of our daily protein intake comes from bread, and nearly a third from cereals as a whole. Fish is well known as a source of protein, but did you know that on average we only obtain 4 % of our daily protein from fish—less than we get from

potatoes (5 %)? No one seems to know that potatoes are an important source of vitamin C, although fruit and vegetables are well-known sources. Calcium is recognised in milk, but most people forget its presence in cheese. Most people are very confused about iron. Why does everyone think it is mainly in green vegetables, when these are really such a poor source? For our daily requirement of iron we would each have to eat 1 kg. spring greens or peas; or 2 kg. of sprouts! In fact meat provides one of our best sources, and one-fifth of our daily needs is contained in bread.

Since most of the people who read *Pears* live in Britain let us return finally to our commonest nutritional disease, or our commonest form of malnutrition in these islands: obesity. Call it "being overweight" if you like, but acknowledge that it means being fat. Being fat is not only unattractive and unsightly but it is dangerous to health and carries a high mortality. Ask any life insurance company how they view your chances if you are overweight and you will find they are as worried about it as if you had high blood pressure, or smoke heavily. It is a particularly important cause of heart disease. However, it is very important to know exactly what we mean by fatness. Many girls who are not at all fat think they are, and this leads them to diet unnecessarily. On the other hand there are people who do not appreciate they are overweight. Here is a table which shows what your weight should be according to your height.

DESIRABLE WEIGHTS FOR MEN AND
WOMEN ACCORDING TO HEIGHT AND
FRAME, AGES 25 AND OVER

Men Height (in shoes 2·5 cm heels)	Weight in kilograms (in indoor clothing)		
	Small frame	Medium frame	Large frame
157	51–54·5	53·5–59	57–64
160	52–56	55–60·5	59–65·5
162	53·5–57	56–62	60–67
165	55–59	58–63	61–69
167	56–60·5	59–65	63–71
170	58–62	61–67	64·5–73
172	60–64	63–69	67–75·5
175	62–66	64·5–71	68·5–77
177	63·5–68	66–72·5	70·5–79
180	65·5–70	68–75	72–81
183	67–72	70–77	74–83·5
185	69–73·5	72–79·5	76–86
188	71–76	73·5–82	78·5–88
190	72·5–77·5	76–84	81–90·5
193	74·5–79·5	78–86	82·5–93

Women Height (in shoes 5 cm heels)	Weight in kilograms (in indoor clothing)		
	Small frame	Medium frame	Large frame
147	42–44·5	43·5–48·5	47–54
150	43–46	44·5–50	48–55·5
152	43·5–47	46–51	49·5–57
155	45–48·5	47–53	51–58
157	46–50	48·5–54	52–59·5
160	48–51	50–55·5	53·5–61
162	49–53	51–57	55–63
165	50·5–54	53–59	57–64·5
167	52–56	54·5–61	59–66
170	53·5–58	56–63	60·5–68
172	55·5–59·5	58–65	62–70
175	57–61	60–67	64–72
177	59–63·5	62–68·5	66–74
180	61–65·5	63·5–70·5	68–76
183	63–67	65·5–72	69·5–78·5

If you are overweight according to these tables you need to slim, and the question is how? Answer: by will-power. There is no other satisfactory method than to decide to eat less. For the time being eat as much fruit, and green vegetables, as you like, but no sugar, starch, sweets, cakes, pastry, or biscuits, and no eating between meals. And cut down on beer and other alcoholic drinks. In case you are tempted to eat "slimming" foods, be aware that there is no such thing. There is nothing you can eat which will cause you to lose weight, in spite of what the advertisement says. In special cases doctors will prescribe tablets to suppress appetite, but they are too dangerous for general use without supervision, and they do not work as well as will-power. At the same time take more exercise. Walk to work. If you make a real and genuine effort for three months without success, you should ask your doctor for advice. Almost certainly you will have to admit you have not really tried. Good luck!

NUTRITIONAL DISORDERS.

Nutritional Deficiency and Malnutrition.—Until quite recently a consideration of malnutrition would have merely led to an account of how too little food, or a deficiency of certain articles in the diet, produced deficiency diseases at the time of the restriction. For example lack of vitamins of various kinds gives rise to such diseases as rickets, scurvy, beri-beri, and pellagra; and an overall shortage of food to general starvation. These may be considered the immediate or concurrent effects of a poor diet. Modern nutritionists, however, are beginning to be concerned with two more kinds of nutritional disorders; and although the study of both kinds is in its infancy, both will be introduced in this account.

The first deals with the effects of comparatively small amounts of harmful constituents in our diet, introduced either voluntarily or involuntarily, and consumed for a long period of time; and the second with the lasting effects on our adult well-being of nutritional deficiencies in early life even though they have long since been corrected.

When viewed in this light, one or other of these three kinds of nutritional disorder may at this moment be affecting almost every individual in every part of the world, "privileged" or "under-privileged." Let us first define some terms.

Undernutrition, strictly speaking, means a state of affairs in which the quality of the diet is perfectly good. There is the correct balance of the various dietary constituents and all the necessary components are present: but there is simply too little of it. Many hundreds of millions of people throughout the underprivileged world are suffering and dying from this kind of under-nutrition, and the simplicity of the problem must be appreciated: they simply need more food of the kind they are at present getting, and which can often be produced locally.

Malnutrition means an imbalance of the various constituents: a relative lack or excess of one or more of them. It usually leads to conditions which are, from the point of view of medical treatment, much more difficult to deal with. And therefore doctors often class them as "more serious."

The diseases of malnutrition range from the widespread protein deficiencies in other parts of the underprivileged world to *obesity* in our own better-off industrial countries, which is usually due to excess carbohydrate. Make no mistake about it: obesity (or being overweight) is a wide-spread disease of nutritional imbalance, and it kills. It is the commonest form of malnutrition in (for example) England and America today, and is a consequence of the sophistication of our diet in modern times. Between one-fifth and one-tenth of the population of the United States is more than 20% overweight, and to be 10% or 15% overweight is almost the rule nowadays in people over thirty. There are high authorities in the world of nutritional science who attribute all this overfed malnutrition to the consumption of refined sugar, or sucrose. They say it is not only the amount of refined sugar we put in our tea or on our breakfast cereals, but also the amount in sweet cakes, biscuits, drinks, chocolates and sweets, and so forth. For some people it adds up to a phenomenal quantity each day. According to this school of thought we are not so

much suffering from a surfeit of carbohydrates or starches, but from this single sugar, sucrose. It is interesting to reflect on the recent banning of the artificial sweetener, cyclamate, by many governments. This substance, having been used extensively throughout the world as an apparently harmless non-fattening substitute for sugar, was suddenly banned in America because in very large doses (equivalent to the amount taken in hundreds of cups of coffee per day for a long time) it was found to produce cancer in rats. It has never been shown to do humans any harm, whereas the effects of sugar in producing an overweight population, thereby indirectly kill tens of thousands of British people each year. This is a fascinating example of the difficulties confronting our legis-lators in making balanced judgments when decid-ing to ban a foodstuff, a drug, or an artificial fertiliser.

Much the most widespread form of malnutrition, however, is a variety protein-lack which is part of a collection of nutritional diseases known as *Protein-Calorie Deficiency*. In very large under-privileged areas of the world, the childhood popu-lation receives such an inadequate diet that children live continuously on the brink of nutri-tional disaster. It only requires a small extra restriction or stress to topple them over into one of the clinical conditions to be described. At this stage they cease to be merely hungry. They become nutritionally ill. Sometimes the force which produces the disaster is a community catastrophe like a famine, an earthquake, or a war. Sometimes it is a family catastrophe like the loss of a lactating mother or a parental delin-quency. Parents abandon young children as often in Africa as anywhere else. Sometimes the clini-cal nutritional disease is unmasked by a common childhood illness like measles, or gastro-enteritis which the well-fed child would have overcome. The starved child reveals his malnutrition instead and frequently dies. When the precipitating cause of the "epidemic" of malnutrition is a war or other national calamity, our newspapers and television screens carry distressing pictures of thin skeletal, pot-bellied children, and the conscience of a few is touched. It is insufficiently realised that these scenes can be witnessed anywhere in the continents of Africa and Asia, and in large parts of Central and South America any day of the week in normal times. The war has not been the cause, but is only the precipitating factor which has revealed the chronic malnutrition in more children than would normally exhibit it openly.

Protein-Calorie Deficiency is a collection of differ-ent kinds of childhood malnutrition. Some are due predominantly to deficiency of protein and are collectively called kwashiorkor, a West African word meaning "red-haired boy" (see below). Others are mainly due to a severe deficiency of overall foodstuffs and are called *marasmus*. But in any real-life situation the severe *mal*nutrition of kwashiorkor exists side-by-side with all grada-tions between itself and the severe *under*nutrition of marasmus, so that many intermediate forms of "marasmic kwashiorkor" are described. In kwashiorkor the child is typically listless, apathe-tic, whining, with a reddish discoloration of the hair, a peeling, scaly skin, and with much extra fluid in his tissues causing oedema. He is so listless as not even to be hungry. In marasmus the child is ravenously hungry. He is extremely thin and "starved" looking and is quite a different picture.

There is good reason to believe that even when protein-calorie deficiency is successfully treated, there will always be some lasting restriction of mental function, particularly if the malnutrition occurred as early as the first year of life. This is especially true in situations of appalling poverty in towns, where thousands of babies are not breast-fed because their mothers are at work. Many of them die. Some of them are no heavier than their birth weight at one year of age. Breast feeding in an underprivileged community is an essential insurance for childhood health and survival.

Two new avenues of nutritional inquiry were mentioned at the beginning of this section. The impact of very long continued intake of refined sugar over many years on our bodily health is an example of one of them. Scientists and others are also becoming alarmed at the effects of modern food additives when taken, even in small amounts, over a long period. These additives include colouring matter, decolorising chemicals, taste "enhancers," and so forth, which are present in everyone's diet in a "civilised community." We are as unable to avoid a constant dosage with them as if they had been added to our water supply. It is, however, difficult to strike a balanced attitude. It is one thing to suspect that these additives are harmful and quite another to prove it. Naturally if any of them are shown to produce harm in animals given reasonable quantities they are invariably withdrawn. But in practice it is extremely difficult for animal experiments to mimic the conditions of human intake, especially as the human life span involves eating the substance concerned in small quantities for several decades. Thus it is easy to postulate the harmful effects of monosodium glutamate (a very common taste enhancer) but practically impossible to prove the question either way. It is not sufficient to condemn "chemicals." All natural foods consist of chemicals, and so do we.

The other new topic in nutrition is more soundly based on animal experiment. It has been repeatedly found that if animals do not grow quickly enough at certain early periods of life, they not only become small, but they remain smaller than they should be even when they are subsequently given as much as they like to eat. This is true of all animals and birds so far studied. For example, if rats are suckled in large families it is found that they are smaller by the time they are weaned (3 weeks of age) than those suckled in small families. The interesting thing is that if they are then given as much as they want to eat for the rest of their lives, the small animals from the larger families never catch up to the others. Whereas if their growth is not restricted until later in their "childhood," full "catch-up" is possible soon after normal diet is resumed. In other words there is a critical time in early life when growth can be permanently affected. At the moment it is difficult to know whether the same is true of humans and, if so, when is our period of vulnerability. There is some suggestion that the corresponding critical period in humans is during the last part of gestation in the uterus, and the first year or so of postnatal life. This new idea may turn out to be very important for world nutrition. Since there will not be enough food for all the children all the time, it may become important to concentrate our aid to underprivileged countries on certain sections of the population only. It may be a good idea to see that pregnant mothers and small babies are specially fed. In this way we may be able to put off the periods of inevitable malnutrition until a time of life when it is recoverable. Such a plan would also go a long way to safeguarding the development of the brain which also occurs mostly at the same early time of life.

We shall now describe some of the better-known nutritional deficiencies, bearing in mind that vitamin deficiencies are virtually unknown in the better-off countries. No one in England need spend money buying vitamins, as has been emphasised in the preceding section. Vitamin deficiency can still occur, however, in elderly people living alone and not having a well-balanced diet. It also occurs for similar reasons in alcoholics, vagrants, *etc.*, and very occasionally in small children.

Beri-beri is a group of diseases usually confined to the Far East where a diet of polished rice results in a poor intake of vitamin B, (thiamine). In one form there is oedema (*q.v.*); in another the peripheral nerves are affected leading to tingling and numbness. A similar condition is occasionally seen in alcoholics and diabetics. Treatment is with thiamine, and with other vitamins too, since most sufferers are going short of more than one.

Pellagra is found among maize-eating populations and is due to a deficiency of several vitamins including niacin, another member of the B group of vitamins. There is dermatitis on exposed skin, and soreness of the mouth and tongue, with gastro enteritis.

Scurvy is due to vitamin C deficiency. In children bone growth is affected. At all ages there is bleeding into the skin (bruising), impaired wound healing, mental depression, and anaemia. Most fresh fruit and vegetables contain vitamin C and a diet containing these prevents the disease.

Vitamin A deficiency is commonly found in children in some underprivileged countries. It causes permanent blindness, with thickening opacity and dryness of the whites of the eyes leading to ulceration of the eye. Beyond a certain stage, therefore, a child's sight cannot be saved. The only real hope is prevention, with an adequate diet.

Rickets, another disease of early childhood, is caused by deficiency of vitamin D. Bones are not properly calcified, and their softness leads to deformities of the legs and many other bones. Vitamin D can either be eaten in the diet or produced under the skin under the influence of sunlight. Therefore rickets commonly occurs when both the diet and the sunlight are inadequate. It was once very common in industrial England, and is still to be seen very occasionally there and in impoverished urban communities in the United States.

THE ENDOCRINE GLANDS.

Glands are structures or organs which manufacture secretions (except for *lymph glands* which are not glands at all and should be called *lymph nodes*). The secretions are of two main kinds. The first are passed down tubes, or ducts, or are secreted directly into the hollow organs, and act locally. Good examples are the salivary glands which make saliva and pass it down ducts into the mouth for digestion of its contents and lubrication. These are *exocrine glands.* The second kind have no ducts, and secrete their product straight into the blood stream. This secretion is called a *hormone* and it is carried to all parts of the body by the blood where it acts at a distance on some remote part. These are the *endocrine glands* or *ductless glands*, and a number of them will be discussed in this section.

The first hormone, or "chemical messenger," was discovered by the British physiologist Starling in 1904, but the effects of removing some of the endocrine glands were known centuries before when removal of the male testes (castration) was practised to procure a form of manpower safe for the harem, to salvage a good male alto voice for the church choir, or to convert a rooster into a more eatable capon.

Anterior Pituitary.—Many of the endocrine glands do not act as separate autonomous organs in spite of their great differences. They are organised into a well-disciplined band by a "master-gland" called the anterior pituitary. Somebody once called it the "conductor of the endocrine orchestra" and the phrase is still repeated *ad nauseam* in students' examination papers. The pituitary, consisting of its two parts, anterior and posterior, is not much bigger than a pea and it sits right in the middle of the skull, centrally beneath the brain and joined to the brain by a short stalk. This astonishing tiny nodule of tissue produces at least eight important hormones.

One of these is *growth hormone*, which is necessary for normal growth, and also has an influence on insulin. An excess causes *gigantism* and *acromegaly*, often coinciding with diabetes, and too little results in a form of dwarfism. Three others, known as *gonadotrophic hormones* regulate the cyclical and other activities of the reproductive organs and lactating breast. Another, *thyrotrophic hormone*, regulates thyroid activity, *Adrenocorticotrophic hormone*, or *ACTH*, as its name implies, looks after the activities of another important endocrine gland, the adrenal cortex. And there are several others.

Hypopituitarism, including *Simmonds' disease* and *Sheehan's disease*, results from destruction of the anterior pituitary. It is extremely rare, and is usually associated with difficult childbirth involving very severe bleeding. There are disturbances of all the functions mentioned above, particularly thyroid and adrenal failure (q.v.) with upset sexual function. Treatment is by replacing the lost hormones.

Hyperpituitarism, including *gigantism* and *acromegaly*, results from over-activity of the anterior pituitary, and is usually due to a tumour or overgrowth of the gland. In acromegaly the growth hormone is produced in excess over a long period of time in an adult. This results in overgrowth of all the organs except the brain, and it is characteristic to find enlarged extremities— feet, hands, and jaw. In gigantism the same has occurred during childhood before the bones have stopped growing and the result is a person who may be 2 m tall or more.

Posterior Pituitary. The posterior part of the gland is really a quite separate gland. The main hormone it produces is concerned with the excretion of urine by the kidney (antidiuretic hormone). Deficiency of the hormone results in *diabetes insipidus*, not to be confused with *diabetes mellitus* or "sugar diabetes." In diabetes insipidus, the patient produces enormous quantities of dilute urine. He consequently has a prodigious thirst and consumes astonishing quantities of fluids. Treatment is by replacing the missing hormone.

Thyroid. The thyroid gland in the neck secretes an iodine containing hormone called thyroxine. Excess of it causes *hyperthyroidism, thyrotoxicosis*, or *Graves' disease*. Lack of it produces *cretinism* in the growing child or *myxodoema* in the adult. Thyroxine is concerned with the metabolic rate of cells throughout the body, or the rate at which they work, as well as with the proper growth of developing tissues, especially the brain. Too much thyroxine as in thyrotoxicosis leads to over-activity, warm sweatiness in an over-excitable patient whose pulse is rapid and who is eating ravenously to try to replace the wasted energy. In spite of his appetite he is very thin, and he often has bulging eyes for a reason not understood. Treatment is by drugs which neutralise the thyroxine or by cutting out some of the gland. A *cretin* is a child usually born with insufficient thyroid. He is destined to grow poorly, and to mental subnormality of a permanent and distressing kind. If the condition is diagnosed soon after birth treatment with thyroxine can avert most of the trouble. In myxoedema, thyroxine is deficient in an adult. They become slow in all their bodily processes, the hair thins and their flesh is puffy with a dry, wrinkled skin. Treatment is by thyroid replacement. *Goitre* simply means enlargement of the gland. It may be accompanied by overactivity or underactivity, or with little functional change. One variety (Derbyshire neck) occurs in areas short of iodine in the soil and drinking water.

Adrenal Cortex. The adrenal or suprarenal glands sit, as the name implies, one on top of each kidney. There are two distinct parts: the cortex or outside which secretes steroid hormones, and the *adrenal medulla*, or core, which secretes adrenalin. There are many different steroid hormones in the adrenale cortical secretion, which look after such diverse matters as sodium and potassium balance, sexual function, the reaction of the body to stress, and the regulation of sugar levels. *Addison's disease* (not to be confused with Addisonian anaemia) results from adrenal cortical insufficiency, and is often due to destruction of the gland by tuberculosis. There is weariness, malaise, pigmentation of skin creases and mucous membranes. They are short of sodium and have excess potassium. Treatment is with cortisone or synthetic steroids to replace the missing hormone. and by extra salt by mouth for the lack of sodium. *Cushing's* disease is due to excessive adrenal cortical function. and sometimes also occurs in patients treated with steroids for other purposes. They have a striking redistribution of fat in the face, neck, and trunk, with stretch marks similar to those acquired by most women during pregnancy. The facial obesity makes them "moon-faced," and female patients may suffer masculinisation with deepening of the voice and hirsutism.

Testis. The male testes, as well as producing sperm are also endocrine glands producing steroid hormones known as androgens. They are mainly concerned with maintaining secondary sex characteristics. At the time of puberty the controlling secretions from the anterior pituitary begin to appear and androgens are produced. There is a whole range of rare disorders, resulting in everything from precocious puberty to delayed puberty. It should be borne in mind that the normal time of puberty can vary by several years from one boy to another.

Ovary. The human ovary has two functions: to produce ova, or eggs; and to produce two hormones, oestrogen and progesterone. These functions begin at puberty, one of whose features in the female is the onset of menstruation, or menarche. Just as in boys, the timing of normal puberty is very variable, but on the average, girls achieve puberty before boys. As social conditions improve, the age of menarche is getting younger generation by generation. All the secondary sex characteristics are under the control of the ovarian hormones which are released in response to the appropriate anterior pituitary hormones. The changes which occur in the womb and elsewhere in the intervals between menstrual periods and the periods themselves are controlled by a cyclical or rhythmic secretion, first of oestrogen and then of progesterone, by the ovary. This cycle is upset by pregnancy to allow the development of the embryo. It can also be upset by taking certain combinations of the two hormones by mouth. These can prevent the formation of ova, and are a popular form of contraception. In late middle age, the ovaries lose their function, the menstrual cycles cease to occur, and reproductive life is at an end. This is called the *menopause* or "change of life," and is sometimes accompanied for a time by distressing symptoms due to a temporary imbalance between oestrogen and progesterone. Many sexual functions, however, continue well after the menopause into old age, and these can include a continuing libido or sexual desire.

Parathyroid. Four tiny parathyroid glands are buried behind the thyroid gland and are responsible for regulating the body calcium and phosphate. They are therefore particularly important for the building and maintenance of bones and teeth. Since a proper calcium level in the blood is necessary for muscle (including heart muscle) contraction, and for correct functioning of nerves, disorders of the parathyroids can give rise to muscular spasms as well as loss of bone calcium. The latter can result in fragility and fractures. Overactivity of the glands leads to too much calcium and the formation of stones especially in the kidney.

Pineal. We end this section with a mystery gland. Like the pituitary it is small—about the size of a pea—and sits well back at the base of the brain. It was endowed in ancient times with metaphysical properties all of which remain speculative. In fish and lizards and certain lower vertebrates it is a kind of third eye, and receives light. In higher mammals, like ourselves, it is so far from any source of light that it could scarcely do so. It can be removed without harm. Indeed it normally becomes calcified and inactive about the time of puberty, and its position seen on X-rays of the skull can be a good guide to whether the brain is being pushed to one side by an abnormal mass.

THE URINARY SYSTEM.

Everyone knows what kidneys look like—in fact, the term "kidney-shaped" is used to describe other objects. Within the kidneys the blood-vessels carrying waste materials subdivide and finally end up in little coils or glomeruli through which waste products are filtered into the other system, the system of tubes which, beginning as tiny cups around the glomerulus, become larger and larger until they join the ureter passing out at the foot of the kidney, the hilum, a point at which both the veins and tubes enter and leave. The kidneys, of course, lie one on each side in the loins, so that if one puts one's hands on the hips and then slides them farther back they will cover the area over the left and right kidney. The ureters pass down on each side to the bladder, which is the storage tank of the products excreted by the kidneys, and lies in the mid-line down low in the abdomen; it is somewhat pear-shaped, and at its base in men there lies the prostate gland—a gland which apparently has few functions but can be a nuisance. Its only known function is that it adds something to the semen from the testes without which the semen would be sterile. Then, from the base of the bladder a single tube, the urethra, passes to the outside. One can, in fact, visualise the urinary system as a capital Y, in which the two upper limbs are the ureters, the place where they meet is the bladder, and the single limb at the foot is the urethra. Clearly, then, there may be diseases of the kidneys, of the ureters, of the bladder, of the prostate gland, or of the urethra.

The amount of urine may be increased or diminished. It is *increased* in the following conditions: after drinking excess of fluids; after taking drugs (known as *diuretics*) which are given to increase the flow; in diabetes of both types—mellitus and insipidus; in some types of chronic kidney disease; and finally, in emotional states of excitement. It is *decreased* in the following conditions: acute nephritis; any disease in which fluid is being lost in other ways, such as diarrhoea or sweating in fevers; when the fluid intake is small; and when both ureters are blocked by stones. Passing a great deal of urine is known as *polyuria*, passing very little as *oliguria*, passing frequent small amounts is simply called *frequency*. Normally, the urine is acid, but in infections of the bladder it may become alkaline owing to decomposition by bacteria. Abnormal substances, or normal substances in abnormal quantities, may occur in the urine and give the doctor an indication of what is wrong. In fact, urine analysis is a very important part of medical diagnosis. Thus urea is a normal component of urine which is increased in fevers, wasting diseases, or diabetes; the amount of urea is to some extent a measure of the degree of tissue breakdown. Uric acid is found in small quantities in normal urine, but the amount is increased in fevers and after an attack of gout (uric acid is important in the causation of gout, but has nothing at all to do with rheumatism in general, so one may disregard the advertisements in the popular press showing unpleasant pictures of joints with sharp crystals of uric acid which are alleged to cause the pain of rheumatic disease). Oxalates are not ordinarily found in urine, but, since they occur in such foods as rhubarb and strawberries, and some people are unable to deal with them, such individuals may develop stones or have pain on passing urine after eating oxalate-containing fruits.

Albumin and Sugar.

Two very important substances which ought not to be in normal urine are albumin and sugar. Albumin is a protein, and its presence in the urine indicates that the filters of the kidney are leaking —they are allowing protein to pass out which ought to remain in the body. Albumin is easily tested for, and its presence may indicate kidney disease or nephritis as it is usually called by doctors. On the other hand, small amounts of albumin occur in fevers and in nervous conditions —*functional albuminuria*. Sugar, too, should not be present, but its presence does not necessarily indicate diabetes; for small amounts may occur in nervous conditions or in some people after taking large quantities of carbohydrate.

Blood in the urine may give it an appearance which varies from bright red to a dark, smoky colour. It is found in many diseases: acute nephritis, stone, tumours, poisoning by certain drugs, infec-

tions such as bilharzia or malaria, papilloma (*i.e.*, non-malignant tumour of the bladder), after injury, in high blood-pressure, scurvy, and blood diseases. Sometimes it occurs for no known reason at all.

It will be remembered that streptococcal infection of the throat may cause in some people disease of the valves in the heart or endocarditis. In such cases, although the germ is found in the throat, it is not found in the heart or indeed anywhere else in the body. *Acute nephritis* occurs in the same circumstances, with the sole difference that the kidneys instead of the heart are affected. The disease appears to be an allergic reaction to the toxins of the Streptococcus. The patient, often a child, has a sore throat (and even this may be absent or fail to be noticed) or sometimes the infection may arise in other sites: after scarlet fever, erysipelas, burns, and disease of the ear. A few days later there is headache, vomiting, pain in the loins, slight rise in temperature, and especially typical is *dropsy* or oedema. This begins in the face, first around the eyelids, and then affects the ankles; later it may become more 'general and affect the rest of the body. Blood and albumin are found in the urine, and the blood pressure is slightly raised. The outlook is usually good if the kidneys are rested by reducing the amount of protein taken in and also the amounts of salt and water. When this is done, the inflammation soon goes and no permanent harm results. In other cases, however, if treatment is inadequate or the condition severe, the symptoms may go, but the albumin found in the urine persists. This means that permanent damage has been done, and although there may be nothing else to show for many years, *chronic nephritis* develops. In this case, the blood pressure continues to rise, and since the filters of the kidneys no longer work efficiently, urea, the principal waste product of the body to be excreted in the urine, is retained in the blood and only small amounts escape from the system. Hence chronic nephritis sooner or later leads to heart failure or haemorrhage in the brain from the rising blood pressure, or to the form of poisoning known as *uraemia* which results from the retention of urea in the blood. Uraemia may come on suddenly or gradually, but ends in progressive coma, drowsiness, and unconsciousness. There may be convulsions similar to those of epilepsy, high fever, and difficulty in breathing to complicate the picture.

Another type of nephritis which seems to have nothing at all to do with streptococcal infections, and the cause of which is completely unknown, is *nephrosis*. Developing in early adult life, its onset is insidious, and the patient first shows signs of oedema in his white and puffy face and the swelling of his legs. (It should be said here that if you have swelling of the ankles or elsewhere, you would be foolish to jump to conclusions; for such swelling is common in many diseases—in heart disease, in allergic conditions, in neurotic illness, and even just from hot weather.) When the urine is examined in a case of nephrosis it is found to be full of albumin and, as in chronic nephritis, the blood urea starts to rise. The end results of nephrosis are the same as those of chronic nephritis and depend upon the original damage.

The modern diuretics of the thiazide group help to control the oedema and, provided enough healthy tissue remains, remove both the fluid and the waste-products.

In recent years there have been considerable advances in the development of the artificial kidney. Artificial kidneys or dialysers as they are known, can now be used in patients' own homes, thus obviating in some cases long journeys to hospital twice a week for treatment. Dialysis is a relatively temporary measure; renal transplants now offer real hope to many sufferers although there are far more suitable recipients than there are potential donors.

Pyelitis is an infection of the pelvis of the kidney, that is to say, of the part where the ureter leaves the kidney. It is usually caused by Escherichia coli, which is normally present in the body, or by the Streptococcus. These germs may reach the ureter through the blood-stream or may pass upwards from the bladder. Obstruction anywhere in the urinary tract which causes the urine to stagnate is liable to cause pyelitis. Symptoms come on suddenly, with high fever, pain in the loin (the infection is usually on one side only, and is commoner in women), and pain in the abdomen. When urine is passed there is a burning sensation, and it is passed frequently and in small amounts, On examination, the urine is found to be highly acid and full of Escherichia coli or whatever the causative germ may be. Pyelitis is fairly readily treated by the antibiotics or sulpha drugs. Plenty of fluids should be given and the urine made alkaline.

Cystitis means inflammation of the bladder, either acute or chronic, and its causes are much the same as in the case of pyelitis. There is pain over the lower abdomen, frequency, and sometimes slight fever. The treatment is as for pyelitis. *Urethritis* is an inflammation of the urethra, with burning pain on passing water and frequency. The most serious cause (although it can usually be easily dealt with now) is gonorrhoea. But nonspecific urethritis is common, especially in the newly wed and in this case various germs or none may bring about pain and frequency; there is often a large neurotic element. Urethritis should be regarded as probably due to gonorrhoea when there is a thick, creamy discharge from the penis or discharge in women following sexual intercourse with an infected person.

Kidney stones or Renal calculi sometimes form, and, as in the case of gall-stones, what causes them is not certain. They may be caused by disorders of metabolism—that is, in the inability of the body to deal with calcium, proteins, uric acid, and other products; or by vitamin deficiency, obstruction in the urinary tract, and urinary infections. But when a stone or stones are formed various events may occur: thus it may remain in the kidney and cause no symptoms; or it may cause repeated attacks of pain, infection, and blood in the urine (haematuria); or it may completely block the passage of urine from the kidney to such a degree that it degenerates and becomes useless; or, lastly, it may pass into the ureter, and when this occurs very severe pain, known as *renal colic*, will occur. A stone passing down the ureter into the bladder may become stuck in the urethra, although this is uncommon, since a stone small enough to get down the ureters is likely to be capable of manoeuvring through the rest of the tract. In fact, about 80–90 per cent. of stones are passed spontaneously. Stones not passed spontaneously may have to be removed by operation, but whether this is undertaken or not depends on various factors, such as the general health of the patient, the amount of trouble caused by the stone, and the health of the other kidney —for it is dangerous to operate on one kidney unless one is sure that the other is functioning efficiently. Lithotripters are also used to fragment stones without needing invasive surgery.

If a stone blocks the passage of urine on one side for any length of time *hydronephrosis* may result, in which the part where the ureter enters the kidney swells with the retained urine. Ultimately much of the kidney may be destroyed by the back-pressure. The same effect may be produced by kinking of the ureter or anything else which causes obstruction. Sometimes children are born with hydronephrosis, and when the dilation is due to kinking of the tube the condition may be intermittent, with attacks of renal colic during which only small amounts of urine are passed; this is followed with relief and the passage of large quantities.

Tumours and Cysts. The kidney may also be the site of tumours and cysts which produce pain in the loins, sometimes a lump over the kidney which can be felt, and blood in the urine. Cancer of the bladder is a serious condition in which the bladder may have to be removed, so the urinary flow has then to be directed elsewhere. Either the ureters are brought out on to the skin surface, a procedure known as *cutaneous ureterostomy*, or they are implanted in the large bowel, so that the urine flows out with the faeces. This is described as *uretero-colostomy*.

There may also be benign tumours of the bladder or *papillomas*, which are soft and bleed easily; a great deal of blood is passed, but there is usually little or no pain. In this, and similar, diseases of the bladder examination of the inside of the organ is carried out by means of a cystoscope, a thin tube which is passed up the urethra with fibre-optic light guides which enable the surgeon to see what is going on. Instruments may also be passed through the tube, and simple papillomas can be cauterised. Similar instruments are used in the examination of the stomach (gastroscope) and the bronchial tubes (bronchoscope). When some obstruction in the outlet of the bladder or in the urethra occurs the bladder, of course, fills with urine, which cannot be passed, and very painful dilation occurs. In this case an attempt may be made to pass a catheter, a thin rubber tube, into the bladder to relieve the tension, or if this fails a *suprapubic cystotomy* is performed—an incision is made in the abdomen over the bladder and a tube inserted into it, through which the urine escapes. This is ordinarily a temporary expedient, and later when the patient's health has improved an attempt will be made to remove the cause of obstruction. The most common cause of such obstruction is *enlargement of the prostate gland* at the base of the bladder, which surrounds this area and the beginning of the ureter. About 40 per cent. of men over sixty have some degree of obstruction due to this cause, and about 20 per cent. of these require operation. The gland is about the size of a walnut, and, as we have seen, its function is to supply part of the fluid which makes up the semen, the male sex secretion. Enlargement of the prostate may be benign or malignant, and, although nobody knows just why, such benign enlargement tends to occur in most men in later life. There may be no symptoms, but characteristically there is frequency during the day and the need to get up at night to pass water. The flow of urine being impeded by constriction of the urethra, the passage is less forceful than normal, and there is a tendency for dribbling to occur. If the obstruction is severe and not relieved the back-pressure may be transmitted to the ureters and kidneys, resulting finally in kidney failure and uraemia. The prostate, except in cases of very mild enlargement, has to be removed either through the abdomen or through the perineum (the part of the body lying between the sex organs and the anus). Sometimes, in less serious cases, it is possible without an incision to cut away the obstructing part by an electrocautery inserted, as is a cystoscope, through the urethra. Prostatectomy was once a serious operation, all the more so because the patient was usually elderly and not in good condition, but new techniques and the use of antibiotics have greatly improved the outlook.

Cancer of the Prostate is a potentially serious disease, but if diagnosed early and is localised, can often be cured by radiotherapy. If the disease spreads, or has spread at the time of diagnosis, it can often be controlled by various hormone treatments or by drugs, or by other forms of radiation. Even when the disease has spread, its progress can sometimes be slow. Cases of prostate cancer (currently the second biggest cancer killer after lung cancer) are rising fast as the population ages.

THE NERVOUS SYSTEM.

The nervous system consists of the central nervous system and the peripheral nervous system. The brain and spinal cord make up the former. The latter consists of the nerve fibres by which the central nervous system is connected to all parts of the body. Human beings have a more complicated brain than any other animal species, but it is only its complexity which makes it different from the brains of other mammals like rats and pigs and cows. We do not have the largest brains, since whales, for example, have much larger ones. Ours is not even the largest for the size of the body. Mice and dolphins and several other creatures have relatively larger brains when compared with body weight.

Before describing some of the diseases of the nervous system it will be helpful to say a little about how it is made and how it works. Each human brain probably contains about ten thousand million (10,000,000,000) nerve cells and perhaps four or five times this number of supporting "glial" cells. Each nerve cell has many long thin branching projections, called dendrites, rather like the branches of a tree, leading to many thousands of "twigs" for each single nerve cell. At the end of each "twig" there is a special structure called a *synapse* by which contact is made with other nerve cells. It is through these connections that very large numbers of nerve cells give information (or send impulses) to each other so that they can be co-ordinated. As well as these dendritic branches, each nerve cell gives off one large trunk called the *axon*, down which final messages are sent as the result of all the information it receives from its dendrites. Some axons are many feet long. Some end in another synapse, by which the outgoing message is passed to yet another nerve cell. Some axons, those of the peripheral nerves, end directly on organs like muscles or glands, instructing them and making them work.

Messages are passed along dendrites and axons as electrical impulses. These are generated in the nerve cell "body." They are modified according to information received from other nerve cells and propagated down the axon. It is this superficial resemblance to a series of electrical cables which has given rise to comparisons of the brain with a telephone system or a computer, and as long as it is realised how infinitely more complicated each brain is than any known computer, the comparison is not a bad one. However, the brain generates its own electric power from the fuel brought in its own blood supply; and no spare parts or spare cables are available if the originals should get damaged, except in peripheral nerves. Furthermore the contact of one nerve cell with another through a synapse is not an electrical contact, and neither is the contact between a nerve and the muscle or other organ it is controlling. In both cases the connection is chemical. Thus when an electrical impulse arrives at the end of the nerve fibre, a chemical is released into the gap between it and the next nerve or organ, and it is this chemical which carries the stimulus forward. There is also an arrangement to neutralise the chemical transmitter when the impulse has been transmitted. So the resemblance to a telephone exchange or computer can sometimes be misleading.

Many of the nerve axons which transmit electrical impulses are clothed in fatty *myelin sheaths*, a little like the plastic insulation around an electric wire. Here again the resemblance is only partial, since the myelin sheaths are interrupted at regular intervals and these gaps in the insulation play an important role in transmitting the impulse. One of the important functions of the non-nervous *glial* cells of the brain is to manufacture and maintain the myelin sheaths.

The Functions of the Brain.

Most of the functions of the brain are little known, and even the ones we know about are very poorly understood. It is the organ of higher mental function, of the mind and intellect, but much remains to be done on linking the different functions of the brain with the structures found within it. The brain is known to control all bodily functions by means of *motor* and other nerves which carry impulses from the brain outwards to all parts of the body. Sometimes these are under our voluntary control; mostly they are involuntary, reflex or automatic. Reflex actions are the result of impulses passed inwards from the body towards the brain by means of sensory nerves. Information arriving in the brain about the various sensations like heat, pain, touch, position, the need for saliva or gastric juice or even the thought or smell of food, are acted on in the various "centres" in the brain. These send out instructions down the "motor" or "secretary" nerves which instruct the muscles or glands to take appropriate action. Thus a *reflex* has a "sensory ending" which appreciates some sort of sensation. This is converted into an electrical impulse which is sent towards the brain or spinal cord along a sensory or "afferent" nerve. The impulse arrives at a "centre" in the central nervous system which co-ordinates all the relevant information and issues instructions. These travel as impulses outwards, along "efferent" nerves towards "effector" organs like muscles or glands,

and an appropriate action occurs automatically. The pathway from sensory ending to effector organ is called a *reflex arc*. Many reflex activities are partly under voluntary control, although mainly automatic. If you touch something hot you will automatically withdraw your hand. But if it is a hot china cup which has cost you a lot of money, you are capable of overriding the tendency to drop it, at least for a time. Breathing is automatic, but it can also be controlled, again at least for a time.

Clearly the brain is a very delicately organised piece of machinery, and its cells are extremely specialised for their job. Achieving this kind of specialised perfection brings many difficulties, however, and the brain cells have become highly dependent on the proper functioning of the other body systems, especially the blood circulation, the respiratory system, and the systems regulating the detailed nutrient composition of the blood. Failure of these systems, even for a very short time, can damage the nerve cells. Nearly all death is produced this way, by an ultimate interference with nerve cell function.

We have already mentioned that the brain and spinal cord are unable to repair or replace any components which get damaged. The vulnerability of the brain is even more obvious when it is realised how easily damage and destruction can occur. For example, unless a rich supply of oxygen and glucose is continuously arriving in the blood stream, brain cells will cease to function in a few seconds and will die in a few minutes, and they can never be replaced. This is in marked contrast to other tissues of the body. The leg, for example, may carry on for over half an hour without any blood at all because the muscle and other cells can find other ways of surviving. Thus the brain can be permanently damaged if the blood contains insufficient oxygen (through asphyxia), insufficient glucose, or if the blood supply is blocked or if the blood pressure falls. All these are likely to happen to any of us at any time, and so there are elaborate mechanisms trying to prevent them occurring. Much of the subject of physiology is concerned with the mechanisms designed to protect the brain, and most of us ultimately die because they eventually fail. One of the clever features of the body design is that all the mechanisms which protect the brain from a supply failure are controlled by the brain itself. Thus the brain has itself been made to control the heart beat and the breathing and the many other systems which are needed for its own survival.

In all that follows it will be seen that the effects of neurological disease on the patient are the direct result of something going wrong with one of the structures or mechanisms we have described.

Diagnostic Techniques in Neurology. The doctor has many ways of testing the nervous system, most of which test its various functions as outlined in the introduction. Thus tests of sensation, muscular movement and reflexes of all kinds as well as the special functions of taste, smell, vision, hearing, speech and intellect play a part. A great deal can be learned about the brain by *arteriography*. In this test a radio-opaque substance is put into the arteries supplying the brain, and an X-ray picture taken immediately afterwards shows up all the blood vessels. *Ventriculography* is an X-ray examination after gas has been introduced into the brain cavities or ventricles which are normally filled with *cerebrospinal fluid*; *myelography* is an X-ray of the spinal cord after a radio-opaque substance has been injected into the space between the spinal cord and the bony vertebral canal which houses it.

Computerised tomography (CT) scanning and Magnetic Resonance Imaging (MRI) have now made these "invasive" diagnostic tests less necessary.

In another development, *radioactive isotopes* can be put into the blood stream and carried into the brain where they can be detected from outside the skull by counters. *Electroencephalography* measures the electrical waves generated by the brain by placing electrodes on the scalp. *Electromyography* does the same for muscles.

Consciousness and Unconsciousness (Coma). Everyone knows what consciousness is until he tries to define it. Full consciousness is generally taken to imply not only wakefulness but the total complement of human mental faculties. In clinical medicine, however, something less than this is usually meant. For example a demented person, or one whose memory is lost (*amnesia*), or one whose powers of speech are lost (*aphasia*) may still be "conscious." There is really a continuous gradation between full consciousness and coma, passing through drowsiness and even "stupor" in which condition a patient can be aroused from coma but sinks back into it when left alone. Many different things can cause coma ranging from swelling of the brain, compressing it in its rigid box of bone, to disorders in other body systems resulting in a failure to provide for the brain's needs. Examples of the first are bleeding within the brain or *brain tumours*, both of which occupy space and can only do so by producing compression. In the second category are asphyxia preventing oxygen from reaching the brain, lack of glucose in the blood, circulatory failure in which there is insufficient blood, or insufficient blood pressure. Fainting is a comparatively minor example.

Sleep and Insomnia. Nobody knows what causes sleep, why it is necessary, and how it helps. It is quite different from coma or even stupor, since as much oxygen and glucose is necessary asleep as awake. Insomnia is experienced by everyone at some time, and for some reason is very distressing if it persists. There are three forms: failing to get to sleep, intermittent wakefulness, and awaking early. Nearly all insomniacs sleep more than they think. They should eat light evening meals and avoid stimulants like tea and coffee after mid-day. Elderly people should realise they need less sleep. Being cold or having a full bladder can be a cause. Or simply not being tired. Sedative drugs are a last resort, but they can be useful in "breaking the habit" of wakefulness. Obviously there may be psychological factors such as anxiety and excitement. *Narcolepsy,* or a true inability to keep awake is comparatively rare.

Headache is our most common pain. Here again we must distinguish between the very common varieties of comparatively trivial significance and the rare ones due to serious causes. Some headaches are due to continuous tightness in muscles of the scalp, and are often "nervous" or psychological in origin. Others result from nose blockage and congestion, sinus problems, eye strain, toothache, *etc.* Migraine is a special kind and will be described below. Very occasionally indeed headache is due to serious disease like brain tumour. Most headache results from "living it up" or being "run down," or both. The headache of alcoholic hangover is probably due to dehydration. It can often be avoided by consuming a great quantity of water (a half litre or so, before going to bed), but few people are prepared to do this in the circumstances. Be careful when using aspirin, which is a useful remedy for headache, since it is very dangerous for people with stomach complaints like gastritis or gastric or duodenal ulcer. Occasionally aspirin makes the stomach bleed, and this can be so severe as to kill. A safer pain killer is paracetamol. Be particularly careful in treating "hang-over" headaches by patent fizzy remedies. They are very effective, but often contain large quantities of aspirin described in small print by its proper name as acetyl salicylic acid.

Migraine. This is a very special variety of "sick headache" and requires special treatment under medical supervision. It has many different forms, but usually there is a definite sequence of events. An attack often starts with some alteration of vision. The patient has shimmering blind spots or other visual disorders. This is followed by a well localised severe headache which may end in nausea or vomiting. The whole thing is caused by a poorly understood disorder of the blood vessels. There are special drugs, mostly derivatives of ergot, which are effective, especially if used when the first signs of an attack appear. Although there is a direct physical cause for an attack, it is also certain that some of the trouble is psychological tenseness. People with migraine are often rather anxious, striving and perfectionist people. Also it has been noticed that attacks are much less frequent when the necessary pills are being carried available for use. However, as with all other conditions which are partly "psychological" in origin they are none the less distressing for the patient. It simply means that the treatment is also partly psychological in encouraging him to come to terms with his problems.

Menière's Disease is one of the conditions in which the organ of balance in the middle ear is affected, giving rise to *vertigo,* a form of giddiness. It usually begins in middle life in the same sort of person who sometimes has migraine. There is buzzing in the ears and some intermittent loss of hearing as well as vertigo. During an attack the patient may be unable to walk because of his loss of balance, and nausea and vomiting are common. Treatment is by special drugs, and occasionally an operation on the ear is necessary.

Epilepsy is a symptom, not a disease, which is common at all ages but especially children. It has been attributed to St. Paul, Julius Caesar, Napoleon, and (with more justice perhaps) to Dostoyevsky. Many varieties of attack occur often in the same patient, the commonest and best known being the *grand mal* or major seizure. In this the patient falls down unconscious and rigid and the jaw is clenched, so that there is danger of the tongue being bitten. This so-called tonic phase is followed, within a minute or so, by a clonic phase in which the limbs contract rhythmically. The attack ends with the patient going limp and gradually recovering consciousness, a process which may take up to an hour. Occasionally the patient has a brief warning, most often an indescribable feeling in the stomach. There are two common forms of minor seizure, one occurring mainly in children and the other more often in adults. The common minor attacks in children are often called *petit mal* or *absence,* which well describes the instantaneous and brief loss of consciousness often unaccompanied by any change in posture. Recovery is equally instantaneous. On the other hand, in the other forms of epilepsy which arise from various parts of the brain, but especially from the lobe under the temporal region, there is often a warning similar to that which may precede a major seizure. In these cases the patient shows only confusion, no definite loss of posture, but automatic activity such as fumbling with buttons, muttering, and grimacing. Following these attacks there may be a quite prolonged period of confusion in which the patient may wander away and occasionally may be violent. Criminal acts are very rarely carried out in this state.

A large number of people have had one or two fits in their lives, particularly at times of physical or psychological stress. "Fever" or "Febrile" convulsions (often called teething fits in the past) are extremely common in young children and are often thought of as something different from epilepsy since the attacks rarely continue in later years. This form of epilepsy and some cases of *petit mal* are the only forms in which hereditary factors are important in the causation, and these are the least serious forms of epilepsy. They are very rarely associated with serious physical or psychological disturbances. Most other forms of epilepsy are due to a scar or other area of brain damage. It is a proportion of these cases which develop the psychological disturbances that are occasionally very serious.

Not every patient who has had one or two fits need necessarily take regular anticonvulsant drugs; that is drugs which damp down the abnormal excessive activity of the brain that leads to the attacks. Many drugs are available of which the most important are phenobarbitone, phenytoin and clonazepam. The succinimides and troxidones are effective only against minor seizures. The choice is a matter of skilled medical judgment. Patients often find it difficult to get work because of the reluctance of employers to take on someone who may be more prone to accidents and whose fits may distress other workers. Obviously there are some jobs which epilepsy sufferers should not do because of the danger involved (from for example, moving machinery), and they should not drive a car. A few cases are so severe that work is almost impossible, but employers have a duty whenever possible to employ these people whose mental health may suffer greatly if they are made to feel outcasts and who ordinarily are as efficient, or even more so, as the next man. It is also hoped that employees will become less prejudiced about epilepsy as the general public become less ignorant about medical matters.

Congenital Malformations. The proper shape of the brain and spinal cord is achieved quite early in development by about the thirteenth week after conception. During this time very slight changes in the foetal environment can produce disastrous malformations. The drug thalidomide, for example, operated on other body systems while they were passing through this phase of construction. Some viruses can do the same thing. Most malformations are without known cause, but it is certain that something went wrong at this very early stage, and it only needs a very minor interference with the normal process to do the permanent damage. At about this time the bones of the spine are beginning to enclose, or form a roof over the developing spinal cord. Sometimes they fail to complete the process, resulting in *spina bifida*. If the coverings of the cord protrude through the defect, this is a *meningocoele*, and if the cord itself protrudes it is a *meningomyelocoele*. The whole protrusion may be covered with skin, but if it is not, the cord soon becomes infected. The effect on the patient is variable, according to the amount of damage to the nerve fibres in the cord, and there are varying degrees of paralysis and loss of sensation below the area involved together with loss of bowel and bladder control. Much help is often obtained from surgical repair, but many cases remain in a distressing condition always, and the only really useful attack on the problem is research to find the cause and prevent it happening. The same is true of the *malformations of the brain*. In one of these, hydrocephaly, the narrow channel is blocked which transmits the cerebrospinal fluid from the chambers within the brain where it is secreted to the outer coverings to be taken back into the blood stream. Blockage of the channel (or aqueduct) results in distension of the brain by fluid, enlargement of the head, and mental retardation. Sometimes a by-pass valve can be inserted to restore normal fluid circulation with very gratifying results.

Cerebral Palsy is a physically disabling condition of impaired muscle co-ordination caused before, during or shortly after birth by damage to or maldevelopment in the portion of the brain which controls movement. There are 3 main types: *spasticity*, *athetosis*, and *ataxia* depending on what area of the brain has been affected. Inherited defects do not play a large part in cerebral palsy. The general incidence of the disorder is thought to be 2.5 per 1,000 births. For further information and advice contact: SCOPE, 12 Park Crescent, London W1N 4EQ.

Motor Neurone Disease. This is a group of distressing diseases usually occurring in people over 40, in whom the parts of the brain and spinal cord which look after muscular movement degenerate. The group includes *amyotrophic lateral sclerosis*, *progressive muscular atrophy*, *progressive bulbar palsy*, and *primary lateral sclerosis*. The results are paralysis or weakness with wasting of the muscles of the body, including those concerned with arms, legs, breathing, speaking, *etc.* The Motor Neurone Disease Association, 61 Derngate, Northampton, NN1 1UE, provides help and advice to patients and their carers.

Parkinson's Disease, formerly known as the shaking palsy, derives its present name from the London physician James Parkinson (1755-1824) whose description established it as a clinical entity. It is one of the commonest illnesses to affect the human brain with more than one in 1,000 of the population as a whole (though one in 100 of those above 60 years of age) suffering from it. The average age of onset is about 55 though one in seven contract it in their thirties or forties. It has three classical features: shaking (or tremor), muscular rigidity and poverty of movement. A stooping, shuffling gait and a mask-like loss of facial expression are common. It is a progressive disease affecting patients in variable degrees of severity and different degrees of progression. A good deal can now be done to help these patients with drugs and since the condition results from a malfunctioning of brain cells which produce a chemical 'messenger' known as dopamine replacement of this substance by the drug levodopa (often accompanied by an additive in a combined preparation) is often the first line of treatment. Occasionally younger patients have benefited from surgical destruction of small areas of diseased brain. It is important to remember that many elderly people have some tremor of the head or hands called *senile tremor* and this is *not* Parkinson's Disease. It is merely one of the features of achieving advanced seniority as a citizen. The Parkinson's Disease Society of 215 Vauxhall Bridge Road, London SW1V 1EJ sponsors medical research and patient welfare.

Chorea. This is a group of diseases in which there is involuntary muscle movement, weakness, and emotional instability. There will be clumsiness, awkward gait, twitching of limbs, face, hands, trunk, or tongue. They include *acute chorea* or *St. Vitus' dance* occurring in children from 5 to 15, *hereditary* or *Huntington's chorea* occurring in a well-defined genetic pattern and beginning later, between 35 and 50. *Tics* or habit spasms are not part of these diseases but are often of psychological origin. They are usually eye blinking or head shaking.

Stroke Illness or Cerebrovascular Diseases. Strokes are due to diseases of the brain's blood vessels which either burst or get blocked. The same blood vessel disorders cause heart attacks by blocking the coronary arteries supplying the heart. Strokes and heart attacks together kill more people than any other single cause including cancer. They account for one death in every five. Perhaps less is known of the cause of this disease than is known about cancer, and much more research is needed to find out if it is to be prevented. The cause of the commonest cancer (of the lung) is now known and it can be prevented by stopping smoking. Perhaps the prevention of strokes and heart attacks will mean an equally difficult abstinence from all those foods which make us fat. At least it is known that being overweight leads to death from these causes, just as smoking may lead to death from lung cancer.

If any artery supplying blood to any part of the brain is blocked, the territory supplied will die; and the bodily functions for which that part of the brain is responsible will cease. The process is called *infarction* of the brain, the dead area being an *infarct*. The blockage is usually due to thrombosis (see **P30**) of the blood within a vessel, a *thrombus* being a rather complicated clot with a structure of its own. The underlying cause is the arterial disease, atheroma (see **P29**) together with stagnation of the circulation. About one blockage in ten is due to a small piece of a much larger thrombus in the heart chambers being flung into the blood stream and impacting in the distant vessel in the brain. This is *cerebral embolism* (see **P30**). If the area of dead or infarcted brain is not too large the patient will recover from his unconsciousness, but will be left with permanent loss of function (paralysis, etc.) related to that part of the brain.

When a blood vessel supplying the brain bursts, this causes *cerebral haemorrhage* or apoplexy. The vessel may be on the surface (*subarachnoid haemorrhage*) or in the depths of the tissue (*intracerebral haemorrhage*). Strokes tend to occur in older people, because the associated arterial disease is a product of age and high blood pressure. Occasionally a subarachnoid haemorrhage occurs in a younger person with an unsuspected malformation of the arteries of the base of the brain known as a *berry aneurysm*. This is a small berry-sized blown-out balloon due to a defect in the wall of the vessel. Berry aneurysms can often be treated surgically. Intracerebral haemorrhage carries a very poor outlook, however, since much brain tissue is often destroyed by the escaping blood, especially the deep tissues responsible for the vital functions. Haemorrhage within the brain cavity can also be caused by injury (see *concussion and compression*, **P21**).

Inflammatory Diseases of the Nervous System. The membranes covering the brain are called the meninges. Inflammation of these, nearly always by blood-borne infection or infection following injury, is called *meningitis.* Cerebrospinal or spotted fever which used to be common and very much feared was only one variety caused by a germ called "meningococcus." It is now rare. Almost any other germ may cause meningitis, and when the germ is susceptible to one of the antibiotics it is usually treatable. It will usually be necessary to identify the germ by taking a sample of cerebrospinal fluid from a convenient space around the spinal cord in the lower back. When the disease is caused by the tubercle bacillus (*tuberculous meningitis*) the problem is more difficult because the patient is often not so obviously ill until the later, less treatable stages. *Cerebral abscess,* or abscess of the brain is very serious because it occupies space in the closed box of the skull and compresses the brain, as well as being a destructive process. It may arise due to an infected piece of tissue or pus being carried to the brain in the blood stream from a distant site in the lungs or heart. When the brain or cord tissue is itself inflamed it is called *encephalitis* (brain) or *myelitis* (cord) or *encephalo-myelitis* (both).

Herpes zoster (Shingles) is a common viral infection of the nervous system which affects sensory nerve roots where they enter the spinal cord. The initial symptoms are of pain in the area supplied by the affected nerves—commonly one side of the trunk, the buttock or the face—followed by the appearance of blisters. Treatment is symptomatic, as there is no specific remedy. Soothing lotions may be applied to the blisters and analgesics given for the pain. The disease is fairly short-lived, but neuralgia may persist for weeks after the blisters have healed.

Shingles is interesting in that it is not a *primary* viral infection, but the result of reactivation of the varicella-zoster virus (so called because it causes *either* chicken pox or shingles) which has lain dormant in nerve root cells, probably since childhood. Primary infection with the virus at whatever age causes chicken pox, not shingles; if an adult who has never had chicken pox or shingles comes into contact with a child with chicken pox or an adult with shingles, he is likely to contract the former but not the latter.

Shingles is infectious from the time the blisters appear until they have crusted over and healed. However, it is not as infectious as chicken pox.

Multiple sclerosis is the most important of the *demyelinating diseases* in which the myelin or "fatty" sheaths which insulate nerve fibres appear to disintegrate. This occurs patchily and seemingly randomly throughout the central nervous system (*i.e.* the brain and spinal cord) and results in interference with the passage of impulses through the affected nerves. Changes in sensation, balance or muscular co-ordination occur at varying intervals of time and spaced out over months or years in such a way as to appear unconnected. There is at present no reliable, objective diagnostic test for multiple sclerosis and diagnosis has to be made from the history of such episodic symptoms. The cause is unknown, but from various pieces of evidence such as the odd distribution of the disease in the world one theory is that multiple sclerosis is the result of a recrudescence of a dormant viral infection which may be picked up during the teenage years. Others hold it to be an auto-immune disease. It is commonly held that once diagnosis of MS is made it means a sentence of years of increasingly severe disablement which will progress relentlessly and inexorably and reduce the patient to a helpless vegetable state in twenty or thirty years. That may be the case, but in fact such a gloomy picture is very uncommon. Much research has gone into the natural history of MS and it is clear that there are seven distinct patterns of the disease. These cover a wide range of symptom patterns from that characterised by a sudden onset of symptoms with relatively few relapses after the first year, to that manifested by sudden onset followed by unremitting relapses causing progressively greater degrees of physical impairment which may indeed lead to much distressing disability and relatively early death. But between these two extremes, of which the first is far the commonest form for the disease to take and the latter relatively infrequent, there lies a whole range of disease patterns and prediction is difficult.

The Multiple Sclerosis Society exists to sponsor research, to care for patients and to give advice and support to friends and relatives. For more information write to them at their offices at 25 Effie Road Fulham, London SW6 1EE. The Scottish office is at 27 Castle Street, Edinburgh, EH2 3DN.

Brain Tumours. The brain is no exception to the rule that any cell in any tissue of the body can suddenly begin to disobey the body's rules regarding its growth and multiplication. A largely unknown mechanism governs how many cells of a certain type there ought to be and calls a halt to cell multiplication when this number is reached. Every now and then one of them turns a blind eye and goes on dividing, and the result is a tumour, or lump, of anarchic cells which obey no rules. Tumours are commonest in cells which normally go on dividing throughout life, in order to replace those lost by wear and tear. Examples are the cells lining the air passages in the lung, or the alimentary tract in the stomach or large bowel. Fortunately for the brain there is little cell division once it has grown. Nerve cells cannot divide at all in an adult life, and the supporting glial cells only do so in response to injury. Therefore primary brain tumours are much less common than those elsewhere. Also many brain tumours like many of those elsewhere, are benign or "innocent" tumours. They are not cancerous, and need only be removed for the patient to be completely cured. The brain, however, is at two major disadvantages compared with other tissues when it comes to tumours. One is that all tumours as they grow take up space, and space in the skull is already fully occupied. Thus even an innocent tumour can compress the brain within its rigid box of bone and become most dangerous until it is removed. The second disadvantage is due to the very large blood supply of the brain. Cancer in other parts of the body spreads partly by sending small pieces of itself to other tissues by way of the blood stream, and those tissues like liver, lung, kidney, and brain which have a big blood supply naturally receive more than their share of other tissues' tumour. These secondary deposits, or *metastases,* cause compression and other trouble in the brain much more frequently than the brain's own primary tumours. Indeed convulsions or other signs of brain disorder may be the first indication that there is a primary tumour in the lung or breast or elsewhere.

Diseases of Peripheral Nerves. Compared with the nerves of the central nervous system (brain and spinal cord), the peripheral nerves are comparatively rarely affected by disease. They have some similarities of structure with central nerve fibres in that their fibres are often covered with myelin sheaths and are arranged in bundles. A special feature, however, is that they are enclosed by connective tissue sheaths and it is probably these which allow a peripheral nerve to grow again, or regenerate, after it has been cut or damaged. Central nerve fibres are unable to do this. After *injury of a peripheral nerve* the part away from the centre is cut off from its parent cell body and it dies. All function, whether motor or sensory, is lost. But in the course of many months the central surviving part grows into the connective tissue sheaths which act like tubes to guide the new nerve to its destination. Provided the cut ends are close enough together and correctly aligned, and provided enough fibres reach their correct destination, good functional recovery is possible.

A disorder of a peripheral nerve is called a *neuropathy* and means nothing more than that. There are many kinds. One of the most distressing is *trigeminal neuralgia,* again fortunately rare. The trigeminal or fifth cranial nerve has a motor and sensory territory on the face. In this condition there are paroxysmal episodes of extremely severe pain which may resist all treatment except destruction of the nerve itself with consequent facial paralysis and loss of sensation. At the other more trivial extreme are the occasions when a leg "goes to sleep" or gets "pins and needles" after crossing it and pressing on a nerve for too long. *Bell's Palsy* is sudden loss of function of the seventh cranial nerve and there is again paralysis on one side of the face which usually recovers in time. Some bacterial diseases, especially leprosy, invade the nerves themselves. Chronic alcoholism may affect the nerves, as may diabetes, probably by interfering with the nutrition of the nerve cell. So may exposure to arsenic or lead or an unpleasant nerve poison which may contaminate cooking oil known as TOCP, or triorthocresylphosphate.

Muscular Dystrophies. These are a series of diseases of muscle in which there is progressive wasting and weakness of muscle, the causes of which are entirely unknown. They are divided up according to the age of onset and the muscles involved. *Duchenne's muscular dystrophy* occurs in the first decade of life. It affects most of the muscles eventually, including the heart muscle and those concerned with breathing, and so the outlook is not good. Other forms are inherited. The Muscular Dystrophy Group (Nattrass House, 35 Macaulay Rd. London SW4 0QP) gives great assistance to sufferers.

Myasthenia Gravis. This is a strange disorder of the mechanism which transmits instructions from nerve to muscle at the "neuromuscular junction," leading to extreme weakness.

MENTAL ILLNESS

Conventionally mental illness is divided into two categories, psychosis (madness), and neurosis (exaggerated symptoms of commonly experienced states). The dividing line is not a clear one though, since even the acts of a madman are understandable if you accept his view of the world. Psychoses are themselves divided into: *organic*, implying that we can identify a physical cause, and *functional*, where the brain structure appears to be intact but its performance is abnormal. This division is now seen to be very blurred since there are physical diseases and drugs which can lower the threshold for response, or alter a person's perceptions so that he appears to be mad, albeit temporarily. The more research is done, the more organic causes are found for abnormal behaviour, and the more hope is raised for successful medical intervention.

Organic Psychoses.

The organic psychoses result from actual damage to the brain. This damage can be caused by disease, as in syphilis; by tumours; by dietary deficiencies, as in inadequate vitamin B12 absorption; by poisons such as alcohol and lead; by drugs such as LSD or amphetamine; by problems of blood circulation such as heart failure or atheroma; and by genetic inheritance. The onset of illness can be either an acute confusional state or a chronic reaction known as *dementia*. The acute episode is characterised by an impairment of consciousness which may vary from difficulty in holding on to the point of a story, to actual coma. The chronic reaction, on the other hand, does not affect consciousness but intellect, memory and personality. Characteristically, memory for recent events is lost, while that for remote ones is preserved. About one in ten men and women over the age of 65 is likely to be affected. Since it is the most commonly and voluntarily ingested poison, it is worth giving a special mention to alcohol. It is hard to define what is meant by the term 'alcoholic', but anyone whose daily intake of alcohol exceeds 5 units is generally agreed to qualify. (A unit of alcohol is a half pint of beer, or a single measure of spirits, or a glass of wine). Alcohol-related disabilities can be classed as social, psychological and physical. Social problems are often noticed first, and include failure to perform an expected role as parent or spouse or at work, or breaking social rules as in driving offences. Psychological difficulties include increased depression and personality deterioration. *Delerium tremens*, (DTs), is an acute confusional state involving intense fear and restlessness with hallucinations. Most alcoholics experience blackouts ranging from momentary lapses to memory loss involving several hours. Intellectual impairment can occur and may be permanent, even after alcohol is abandoned.

Other physical problems associated with alcoholism include a doubled death rate, liver damage, gastritis, anaemia, increased rates of cancer, and infections such as TB. Sexual incompetence is common. The children of alcoholic mothers are at increased risk of deformity and growth retardation.

Functional Psychoses.

Functional psychoses broadly fall into two categories: *schizophrenia* and *manic depressive psychosis*. Schizophrenia was a term introduced by Eugene Bleuler in 1911 to describe a group of illnesses in which there was a splitting of the psychic functioning so that the association between two ideas was bizarre, and mood seemed inappropriate to the circumstances. Nowadays schizophrenia is diagnosed on the presence of certain accepted symptoms such as a lack of insight, auditory hallucinations especially of voices discussing the patient in derogatory terms, the idea that radio and TV programmes refer to him directly, unreasonable suspicions, or a flatness of response. However, the concept has been challenged by workers such as Thomas Szasz, who regards it as a medical fiction, and Scheff, who believed that many of the symptoms arose from being labelled 'mad'. It seems that schizophrenia occurs in all societies, but in less developed countries appears to be more acute yet to offer better prospects for recovery. About one person in a hundred will develop the condition, and there is an increased risk where close relations are affected. There are many theories of causation though an inheritance factor is clear, but there is argument about what this factor might be, and the extent to which its influence is affected by life events. Theories invoking abnormalities in the substances responsible for the transmission of signals within the brain itself are supported by the fact that some symptoms of schizophrenia can be induced experimentally. But as yet the physical theories are not wholly proven. The concept of the 'schizophrenogenic' mother who causes illness in her child, and the theory that abnormal dominance patterns in the family are the cause have proved equally hard to verify. The 'double bind' hypothesis of Bateson, that an emotionally disturbed parent, who says one thing to a child but at the same time suggests a deeper, contradictory, message will eventually cause the child to withdraw into a fantasy world, is another explanation. The personal construct theory of Bannister and Fransella says that we build up constructs and relationships between them in order to understand our world. In this theory if the construct of generous-mean is linked with those of honest–dishonest and gentle–violent, then we expect someone we know to be generous to be also honest and gentle. If these associations are weak or inconsistent, then the world is a chaotic and fearful place. Whatever the role of early experience in the causation of schizophrenia it is clear that current stress brings on an attack.

The Treatment of Schizophrenia.

The treatment of schizophrenia was revolutionised by the introduction in the 1950s of phenothiazine drugs which not only tranquillise but also have specific anti-psychotic effects. The fact that schizophrenic patients are increasingly returned to their community, able to function, is due in large part to these pharmacological advances, and to the concept of 'milieu therapy' involving group activities, recreation and occupational therapies.

Manic depressive psychosis is characterised by swings of mood between depression and elation without apparent cause, and in this form is called the *bipolar* state. More frequently, the disease is *unipolar*, showing only periods of depression interspersed with periods of normality. The difficulty in defining depression as an illness is firstly to distinguish it from a symptom, and secondly to make a distinction between normal and morbid depression which is depression of greater severity and duration than would be expected in a given population from the apparent cause. This last is a very subjective rating and this makes depression a difficult subject for research. The expectancy that one will suffer a depressive illness in one's lifetime is about one to three per cent, with females more likely than males. Generally it is accepted as a phenomenon of later life, but can occur at any age.

In depression the major symptom is of a persisting sad, despairing mood, especially severe on waking up. Agitation or marked slowing down may be present, and hallucinations are not uncommon. Ideas of unworthiness, guilt and persecution are frequent, loss of appetite, loss of weight, loss of sexual drive and loss of menstruation are also common. The causation of depressive illness is another area where authorities are in dispute, and theories abound. Seligman points to learned helplessness as a cause. In his experiments animals exposed to repeated stresses beyond their control, exhibited apathy, difficulty in accepting that they could do anything to help themselves, loss of appetite, and reduced sociability. The idea that depression is the result of aggressive feelings which cannot be channelled out and so are turned in on oneself, is a simplified view of what Freud said. Some support is lent to this idea by the fact that depressive illness is less common in time of war. Certain biochemical changes have been found in the brains of depressed patients, and the anti-depressant drugs work in ways to correct these imbalances, but whether these intra-cellular changes are cause or effect, and how this comes about, is still not entirely clear. Treatment is by specific anti-depressant drugs of which there are now many, by psychotherapy of various kinds, and much more rarely now by electro-convulsive therapy (ECT) which can be life-saving in very severe cases. Treatment with lithium is often successful in reducing the severity of mood swings.

Mania is a state of elation, hurried speech, and physical overactivity. Irritability is common if the patient is frustrated. Grandiose plans are made and money can be lavishly spent. Gradually as the illness progresses the sufferer becomes confused, angry, hallucinated, incoherent and exhausted. Treatment is usually by tranquillising drugs.

Neurosis.

Neurosis as we now understand it is a concept we owe to Freud, and to him, too, we owe the distinction between the neurotic disorders of *hysteria*, *anxiety* and *obsessionality*, and the disorders of *personality*. Those in the latter category, while having no detectable disease, are treated by psychiatrists as if they had, and this is a decision of society as a whole since the alternative is to refer such people to the legal or social services. Because the category of neurosis is so vague, it is hard to put a figure on how many people may be affected, but researchers in general practice consultations estimate about one in ten women, and half that many men are at risk. The reason for this disparity is not clear, but may be due to factors such as the greater freedom for expression of frustration enjoyed by men in our society than women. The majority of neurotic illnesses clear up, and may do so spontaneously, although obsessional and hypochondriacal symptoms are more persistent.

Anxiety neurosis as a pathological state where anxiety is either unrelated to a recognisable threat, or the degree of anxiety is out of proportion to the threat. The mechanism of our response to a threat appears to depend on the level at which the threat is perceived, if at a conscious level, the response is fear, if at an unconscious level, the response is anxiety. Symptoms include weakness, dizziness, sweating and tiredness. The physical symptoms are themselves unpleasant and increase the feelings of being threatened. Treatment may be by reassurance and explanation, by psychotherapy aimed at bringing the threat into conscious appraisal, or by drugs which are now widely, and often inappropriately, prescribed. Phobic anxiety occurs when unreasonable fear is focused on a particular object or situation, and leads to avoidance. Agoraphobia, literally a fear of the market place, claustrophobia, fear of enclosed spaces, and animal phobias are well recognised. Social phobias, such as fear of eating in public or fear of vomiting are often harder for the sufferer to acknowledge. Phobic states are often associated with a traumatic event in the past, and avoidance through fear leads to a form of conditioning which reinforces the fear. Gradually the sufferer extends the range of feared and avoided stimuli. Behavioural therapy offers the chance to reverse this process.

Much is made of the manipulative nature of neurotics, and the idea of secondary gain, where the neurotic is perceived as getting the better of those around him by organising his, and other people's, lives to fit in with his symptoms. Certainly neurotic people can be very irritating in their demands and social failings, but their conscious experience is of personal suffering, their gains are at an unconscious level, and one cannot but be saddened by the waste their lives represent.

Suicide as a completed act is on the decline, but the rate of attempted suicide is rising. Most attempts are preceded by a warning of intention, often quite explicit. Men, especially alcoholic or physically ill men, are more likely to complete the attempt than are women.

Mental Illness in Childhood.

Mental illness in childhood can refer to illness specific to children such as autism (*see below*), to emotional disorders, and to disorders of conduct. Because children are dependent on their families, much interest has centred on relationships within the family and on maternal deprivation as factors in the creation of childhood difficulties. The work of Bowlby highlighted problems consequent on the infant's need for attachment being denied, and he expressed the view that poor early experiences led to failures in later life to develop social relationships. Autism is a state where the child displays abnormalities of language, indifference to people, and ritual behaviour. Autistic children do not grow into schizophrenics, they grow up into autistic adults, and most remain severely handicapped. Phobias and obsessional behaviour are common in children and usually appear and disappear rapidly, especially with prompt intervention. Depressive illness is rare before puberty and where depressive features are seen it is usually in response to environment.

Conduct disorders include persistent lying, stealing, disobeying, truanting, fighting or setting fires. The distinction from delinquency is important since the latter implies breaking the law which is quite common in adolescence. There is a high correlation between these behaviours and difficulty in reading, though whether this is because of a shared impairment or the result of educational frustration is not clear. Treatment is by careful assessment of the family situation, and by social and educational intervention. The future is not rosy though, since about half the antisocial boys in one long-term study went on to be antisocial men in later life.

Anorexia nervosa is usually a disorder of adolescent girls in which food avoidance, weight loss, failure of menstruation and overactivity predominate. Anorexics often display a distorted view of their own bodies, being unable to see how thin they have become. The underlying difficulty may be a need to control something in their life at a time of actual dependence on parents, or an attempt to avoid the challenge of puberty and the demands, particularly of sexuality, that adulthood makes. Treatment is by behaviour modification, supervised weight gain, and psychotherapy. Bulimia nervosa is a variant in which meals, often very large meals, are eaten and then vomiting is induced to get rid of them.

Autism.

Autism is a profound life-long handicap which is now believed to be caused by brain malfunction; often occurring with other disorders, including mental retardation, which affects three times as many boys as girls. The spectrum of the autistic condition encompasses dramatically different degrees of severity, varying from profound handicap through to subtle problems of social understanding in people of apparently normal or even superior intelligence. With the right therapy at an early age, continuing through to special education, autistic people can become less indifferent to others and can develop social responsiveness at a simple level.

There is no present cure for autism; most children who are born autistic will die autistic and it is essential that people with autism are cared for in a special community by dedicated staff.

THE SKIN

The skin in the course of development before birth is particularly closely associated with the nervous system. It is therefore not surprising that so many skin diseases are influenced by emotional states. Other causes of skin disease are infectious, glandular disorders, vitamin deficiencies, and the numerous conditions for which no cause has been discovered, but which presumably are due to metabolic disorders.

One of the commonest skin symptoms is *itching* or *pruritus*. It may accompany many different general diseases, for example diabetes and jaundice. It may also be troublesome during the menopause (the change of life in women), in old age, or in nervous conditions. Sedatives and sex hormones sometimes help the itching during the menopause, and there are ointments which may be useful.

Itching in the region of the anus and genital organs is relatively common. It may be caused by worms, by irritating vaginal discharge, or by sugar in the urine, as in diabetes. The alteration in the normal bacteria of the bowel which follows treatment with various antibiotics also often causes anal pruritus and soreness. In many cases however the itching has some psychological cause. In treatment it is important to avoid ointments and creams which contain a local anaesthetic, because these substances can cause severe allergic reactions if used for longer than a few days, and may thus make the condition much worse. Treatment with a local corticosteroid application is more effective and safer.

Parasites, such as the *scabies* mite or *lice* can cause severe and persistent itching. The scabies mite is very small, and since it burrows under the skin surface, is unlikely to be seen; it is the cause of itching most commonly between the fingers and on the front of the wrists. The itching is worst when the body becomes heated, as in bed. Treatment consists of painting the body from head to foot with benzyl benzoate application, followed the next day by a hot bath. Since scabies is contracted through close personal contact with an infested person it is often desirable for several or all members of a family to be treated at the same time, even though only one of them may be affected. Lice are specialists, one type of which affects the scalp, another the body, and a third the genital area. Head lice are destroyed by washing with shampoos containing organophosphorus insecticides such as malathion, body lice by insecticides and genital (pubic) lice by shaving off hair and washing. Obviously, the clothes, especially in the case of body lice, should be disinfested, by using a hot iron particularly over the seams, which lice (for some inexplicable reason) seem to favour. Apart from the discomfort they cause, lice are dangerous as potential carriers of typhus fever.

Baldness, or Alopecia, is a very common and often distressing condition, as is manifested by the number of preparations advertised as curing it. When many preparations are offered for the treatment of one condition it is a fair judgment to assume that none of them is likely to be effective. There are, in fact, two types of baldness; one, which is much the commoner, is hereditary, and cannot be influenced in the slightest by any treatment, the other, *alopecia areata,* is caused by nervous stress, and would recover in most cases by itself, whether one used a solution of soot and water or the most expensive "hair food." There is no such thing as a hair food, any more than there is such a thing as a nerve food, and although it is probable that hair hygiene may delay baldness, it certainly cannot prevent it. All hair tonics and "foods" are useless, and their uselessness is only equalled by their costliness. Those who have lost their hair and find it growing again after using some alleged tonic are people who have had *alopecia areata* and whose hair would have grown back anyhow. In women the hair often thins out soon after a pregnancy, but a few months later it usually returns to normal. Alopecia is a common side effect of many modern drugs used in treating cancer, because these drugs affect rapidly-growing cells, including those in hair follicles.

Seborrhoea is a condition in which there is overactivity of the sebaceous glands. The most usual form it takes is *dandruff.* However, it takes other forms, and those who have dandruff may also have rashes on the face, shoulders, and chest. In these areas there is a patchy, greasy, and often itchy, rash which does not clear up until the primary condition in the scalp is dealt with. The scalp should be washed with one of the modern sulphur-containing shampoos at least twice a week, and the affected parts on the face and chest can be dealt with by the use of a sulphur lotion (*not* on any account by greasy ointments). Seborrhoea is not in itself difficult to treat, but since the condition depends on over-secretion of sebum, the skin lubricant, treatment may have to be persisted in during the years of early adulthood, when it is most active.

Erythema Intertrigo is, quite simply, the sort of irritation which occurs usually from excessive sweating under the armpits, between the legs, and under the breasts in women. All that need be done is to wash frequently and to dust the affected areas after washing with powder. This is the condition which, in the tropics, is known as "prickly heat" and elsewhere as a "sweat rash." In some people *hyperhidrosis* or *excessive sweating* is a problem, especially when the sweating is accompanied with body odour—the sort of thing that, according to the advertisements, "even your best friends won't tell you." There is little need for anyone in these days to suffer in this way: for the cosmetic firms have produced many highly efficient deodorants which not only control odour but also control the amount of sweating. Chlorophyll, which has been much advertised as removing odours, is effective when applied directly to surfaces which give off an unpleasant smell. It is however ineffective when taken by mouth, and does not prevent body odours. Stale sweat smells bad because it is decomposed by bacteria, and this type of body odour can be largely prevented by preparations containing harmless antiseptic and anti-perspirants.

Erysipelas is an infection of the skin caused by the haemolytic streptococcus. It begins as a red, raised area anywhere on the body where the germs have been able to enter through a small crack or cut in the skin. The red area advances and spreads over the body until the disease is got under control. Erysipelas is very infectious, and those who look after the patient should wash their hands thoroughly after contact. At one time the disease used to spread as an epidemic throughout the hospital wards, but this is very rare nowadays. Treatment is, of course, a matter for the doctor.

Chilblains used to be common in cold weather, especially in those with poor circulation. Ordinarily they occur in the toes and fingers, but may appear on the nose and ears. The part affected becomes swollen, dusky, and there is pain and itching, sometimes leading to ulceration. Protection of the body, especially the hands and feet, from cold is the best and the only really effective way of preventing chilblains. Warm lined gloves and footwear, and arm stockings or trousers should be worn outdoors. Adequate heating of rooms is essential: a temperature between 18° and 21°C is recommended. Most tablets, medicines, ointment, or creams for chilblains are useless. A skin affection caused by heat is rather grandiosely described as *erythema ab igne,* and used frequently to be seen on the legs of ladies addicted to roasting their legs before the fire. It takes the form of red patches on the front of the legs and can be removed only by avoiding the cause.

Dermatitis means "inflammation of the skin," and therefore the word could be, strictly speaking, applied to any skin disease. In fact the term is used almost interchangeably with the term *eczema.* There are three main types of dermatitis or eczema. The first, *primary irritant dermatitis* results from injury of the skin by some powerful chemical, such as strong alkali or turpentine. The second, *contact dermatitis* is due to sensitisation of the skin to some substance which is normally liable to cause this type of allergic sensitivity; examples are nickel (in jewellery and suspender buckles), epoxy resins, rubber additives, primulas and chrysanthemums, and even ingredients of cosmetics. Contact dermatitis may continue for a long time, even after the patient is no longer in contact with the offending material. The third type is often called *constitutional eczema*. Although the skin is apt to react adversely to various irritants and sensitisers the major part is played by the personality, and there is often a history of eczema, hay fever or asthma in the family. Treatment is more difficult, but local corticosteroids and tar, sedatives and psychological treatment can be of great help. Infantile eczema also belongs in this category, but in most patients it disappears as the child grows up.

Impetigo is an infectious skin disease caused primarily by the Streptococcus, but later often infected with staphylococci. It usually occurs on the face, and takes the form of blisters filled with pus on a red base; when the blisters burst their place is taken by yellow crusts. Impetigo is very infectious and easily spread by the fingers, dirty towels, or cloths; therefore, one of the first necessities is to prevent infection of others or reinfection of oneself by avoiding scratching and using a different towel each day, which must on no account be used by anyone else. Treatment is simple with an antibacterial ointment, so the main issue is prevention of contamination.

Urticaria or *Nettlerash* is a familiar skin disease in which itching weals appear on the skin, usually for no obvious reason. It is not infectious, and can be caused by nervous stress, certain drugs, allergy to some foods, or even exposure of the skin to cold. In some people it is possible to write on the skin with a fingernail: the "writing" appears in the form of weals. This is known as *dermographism*; it occurs in many normal persons as well as in many patients with urticaria. The antihistamine drugs are the most useful in the treatment of urticaria. Urticarial swelling of the tongue or throat requires urgent medical attention.

Acne, or "*Blackheads*," is a condition found on the face and shoulders; its appearance is so familiar that no description is necessary. Acne is one of those conditions which is the end result of many factors. There is, first, a greasy skin, the result of glandular upset (which is why the disease usually occurs in adolescence); secondly, there is infection of the skin; and thirdly, there is blockage of the sebaceous ducts, which ordinarily allow the grease from the skin to pass out on to the surface. Since the condition starts with excess secretion of grease, ointments should never be used, and probably the best applications are drying lotions containing some sulphur preparation which inhibits secretion of grease. The face should be frequently washed, and it is possible now to obtain detergent solutions which are both antiseptic and prevent grease formation. In severe cases ultraviolet ray treatment may be necessary. Advances are presently being made in the case of vitamin A in treating acne, but great care must be taken to avoid overdosage with this poisonous substance.

Rosacea. As has already been implied elsewhere, although the wages of sin may be extremely unpleasant, the wages of extreme virtue may be no less troublesome. Thus *rosacea*, in which the nose and cheeks become red and greasy and the skin coarsened, occurs alike to chronic alcoholics and elderly ladies with no vices other than a preference for strong tea. Both cases are associated with indigestion, since, regrettable as it may seem, strong tea and alcohol are about equally liable to cause the gastritis which may be at the root of this complaint. However, in many patients the chronic flushing is caused in other ways and psychological factors are important.

Lichen Planus is one of the numerous skin diseases which seem to be due to nervous states of tension. It may occur on any part of the body, but is most common on the front of the forearms

and legs. The rash takes the form of nodules which are lilac in colour and have a dent on the top; when these disappear a stain is left behind. There is severe itching. Treatment is a matter for a doctor, as it also is in the case of *psoriasis*, a very common disease of largely unknown origin, which is extremely resistant to treatment. It tends to run in families. It takes the form of slightly raised papules, usually on the elbows and knees; typically the papules are covered with dry, silvery-looking scales. Apart from the rash, the patient is usually in perfectly good health and there is no itching. Many drugs have been used in psoriasis, notably chrysarobin, and while it is not difficult to cause the rash (which may occur anywhere on the body) to disappear in one area or even in all areas for a time it has a strong tendency to return.

Warts, or *Verrucae* are familiar enough. They are caused by a virus, and are, theoretically at least, contagious (although having removed many warts, the writer has never found them contagious). Most frequently they are found on the hands, but may occur elsewhere. Treatment is best carried out by a doctor, who will use a cautery, a caustic carbon dioxide frozen into "snow." A curious feature of the common wart is that it can sometimes be caused to disappear by suggestion, which is presumably why so many old wives charms are not necessarily without effect. Different altogether from the common wart is the *plantar wart*, which occurs on the soles of the feet and often causes a good deal of discomfort. It is best dealt with by a chiropodist or in bad cases by a skin specialist since it is highly infectious.

Ichthyosis is a disorder of skin formation with which some unfortunate people are born. The oil and sweat-producing glands do not function well and the skin is dry and scaly like the skin of a fish. It is, however, possible to help the condition, which does not affect the general health, by frequent alkaline baths to wash off the scales, and the subsequent use of lanolin to replace the lacking oil. Large doses of vitamin A seem to help in some cases, and there have been reports in the medical press of cases being helped by hypnosis; this, however, is very much a matter for speculation.

Cancer, Rodent Ulcer, and Cysts. Cancer of the skin occurs mostly in old people, and takes the form of what is described as an *epithelioma*. It is most common on the face or hands, and usually appears as a nodule which breaks down and produces an ulcer. The glands may later be affected, but such cancers can almost invariably be cured unless a considerable time has elapsed during which they have been neglected. Epitheliomas are much more common in persons over-exposed to the ultraviolet in sunlight, and there is great worry that their frequency will increase as the ozone layer of the atmosphere becomes more depleted. Great care should be taken in direct sunlight, especially when sunbathing. *Rodent ulcer* is a form of ulcer which appears on the inner corner of the eye or the side of the nose in old people. It does not spread over the body, but acts by eating into the tissues in the area where it has started. X-ray or operation is necessary, but the outlook is good. *Cysts* on the skin are due to blockage of the sebaceous glands. They may become very large, and are best removed, as they may become infected. They do not turn into cancer, and there is no such thing as "male" and "female" cysts. It does sometimes happen that *moles*, especially of the bluish-black type, may become malignant, forming a cancer called a malignant melanoma. This is a fast growing and extremely dangerous cancer, though cure rates after early treatment are good. Any change in size or shape of any mole must be shown to your doctor immediately.

Skin Grafts.

These are a very complex subject which can be only briefly discussed here. They are used basically for a number of conditions in which large areas of skin have been removed from the body, as in burns or serious accidents. In other cases, as in plastic surgery, grafts may be used to make a new nose, eyelids, and so on. The following are the main types:

Pinch Grafts are small, circular pieces of skin cut from some other part of the body. (The former method of using grafts from another person has been given up almost completely, since such grafts—except in the case of identical twins—never "take.") The small pieces are laid on the area without skin and gradually grow together. *Split-thickness grafts* are grafts removed from another part of the body by an instrument known as a dermatome, which cuts sections about 10 by 20 cm. containing part of the deep layers of the skin.

In *Full-thickness Grafts*, on the other hand, the whole thickness of skin is removed from elsewhere and applied to an area which has to bear friction or heavy weights, such as the hand or the foot. Lastly, and this is largely used in plastic surgery, there is the *pedicle graft*, which, unfortunately, although it is certainly the most exciting type, is rather difficult to describe. Briefly, if one, for example, wants to make a new nose, one cuts an area of skin and underlying fat about 5 cm wide and 12.5-15 cm long in the abdomen. One end, however, remains attached so that it gets adequate blood supply. The problem is how to get this tissue to the nose, and this is done by a complicated process of leap-frog. First, the free end of the graft is attached to the forearm, whilst its "root" remains in the original site, and when it begins to grow and get its blood supply from the arm, the original "root" is cut. So we now have a "sausage" of tissue attached to the arm. The arm is then lifted to the face and kept firmly in position there until the new free part becomes attached. It is then detached from the arm, modelled to the correct shape, and grows where the nose used to be!

THE JOINTS.

Rheumatism is a word most doctors wish did not exist. This is partly because they do not understand it, but mainly because it is a condition which strictly does not exist: which is small comfort to the many millions of people who are more or less totally incapacitated by it. The truth is it is used for a hotch-potch of very real diseases, in all of which there is pain and stiffness of what is called the musculo-skeletal system, *i.e.*, the muscles and the joints. It may mainly involve the joints, in which case it should be called arthritis; or it may involve other structures near the joints like tendons, muscles and fibrous tissue. Joints may either suffer from inflammation or degeneration or both, and the trouble may be acute or chronic or both; so it is easy to see what a mix-up the subject becomes, especially when we must include the joints of the spine as well as the limbs, feet and hands.

A good deal of arthritis used to be due to various germs, but these types are much less common now that the infections causing them have become rarer or better treated. They used to include gonorrhoea, tuberculosis, septic joints, syphilis, brucellosis, typhoid fever, dysentery and so on. The importance of *rheumatic fever*, which is a reaction to an infection (streptococcal sore throat) rather than being actually caused by the Streptococcus, is not because it involves the joints. This arthritis quickly clears up, but there may also be disease of the heart which may be serious and has been described on P27.

Rheumatoid arthritis is a completely different condition in which there is non-infective inflammation of connective tissues throughout the body. In the joints, the normally smooth, lubricated synovial membrane lining the joint cavity becomes scarred, leading to distortion, especially of smaller joints like those of the hand. Another characteristic feature is its capacity to vary in severity from time to time, with a strong tendency to unexplainable periods when it gets better or worse. This makes it extremely difficult to know whether any form of treatment is being useful, since any response may have occurred in any case. As in all diseases which behave like this, especially those in which medical men are also baffled, there are almost as many theories and treatments as there are doctors. It has never been satisfactorily shown to

be caused by infection, faulty nutrition, "glands," emotions or personality disturbance, nor is it convincingly inherited. The best current theory links it with an increased sensitivity reaction, perhaps to the body's own tissues, known as "autoimmunity." From the patient's point of view there is swelling and deformity of the joints with tenderness on pressure and pain on movement. Treatment involves a lengthy and complicated regime of rest, relief of pain with anti-inflammatory drugs such as aspirin, exercises and the application of heat, with attention to general physical and mental health. At some stage adrenal corticosteroids (cortisone and its derivatives) are often tried, but although these can give great relief they have to be very carefully used to avoid very unpleasant side-effects.

Osteoarthritis is another completely different condition closely related to the normal processes of ageing. Therefore it occurs in older people and tends to be in larger, weight-bearing joints of the spine, hips and knees rather than in the hand; although the end joint of the fingers is commonly affected. Hard wear and tear, especially that caused by overweight, or injury may be the beginning of it. It is *not* due to diet, and dieting has no part in treatment except in those who need to slim. Physiotherapy, including heat, is helpful. It is not such a relentless condition as rheumatoid arthritis and patients should be reassured about this. It is now known to be partly inherited.

Osteoporosis is a reduction in bone density without change in the chemical composition of bone, and has many causes including hormone imbalance, poor diet, age and long use of corticosteroid medicines. Hormone replacement therapy after the menopause is partly to prevent osteoporosis. Treatment is difficult, and it is better to avoid the condition by eating well and exercising regularly.

Fibrositis and other vague forms of "rheumatism" are very often manifestations of psychological problems. This does not make them any less real, but it directs treatment towards the mental state rather than to the joints and muscles.

EYES, EARS, NOSE AND THROAT.

Diseases of the *eyes* are very specialised and only very general information can be given here. The most common is inflammation of the conjunctiva causing redness and usually due to infection or some irritant substance or dust. If it persists and leads to hard crusts of yellow pus on waking in the morning, get it seen by a doctor for treatment probably with antibiotics. First-aiders are usually instructed how to remove small particles of grit from under the lids. It is important that these should not scratch the front of the eye—your window on the world—as this may lead to scarring and poor vision. So, above all, do not rub them in. Also, if you are fishing one out of someone else's eye, see it before removing it. Do not have a general sweep round in vague hopes of finding it. If in any doubts, obtain skilled help. Remember the eyes are part of the brain: the only visible part. Perhaps this is why people's eyes are so revealing.

Conditions such as glaucoma, cataract and disorders of vision are beyond the scope of this section.

Foreign bodies in the ears and nose are a constant minor problem with children. In these cases, whether they be peas, beads or peanuts, do *not* attempt to fish them out. They are doing no harm where they are, provided the child can be prevented from fiddling with them. Get him or her to a doctor who knows far better than you do about the delicate structures of the ear drum or the internal nose just behind the object.

Sore throats are a nuisance we all have to put up with from time to time. If they last more than a few days they should be treated professionally. Persistent or recurrent sore throats are often due to over-eager treatment with antibiotics not allowing the body to learn how to fight the germs itself. Never prescribe antibiotics for yourself, especially in lozenge form, and only expect your doctor to give them when other measures have failed.

Tonsils and their inflammation may be a problem. It is comparatively rarely that they should be removed, yet every year hundreds of thousands of innocent children are subjected to this ritual cruelty to satisfy the misconceptions of their parents and the greed (or ignorance) of some surgeons. Of course there are many children who benefit so much from having tonsils out that the operation (which has real dangers) is worth doing. But please allow your doctor to decide if it is necessary, and do not pressurise him into recommending it. (The same is true of *circumcision*, for which there are no hygienic, and few medical indications. If your reasons for inflicting this cruel assault on your little boy are religious or emotional, then please admit it: but do not pretend it is "necessary" or even medically helpful.)

DISEASES OF WOMEN.

The *internal sexual organs* of a woman, like the urinary system, can best be described as shaped like a capital Y. At the tips of the arms of the Y are the female sex glands, the ovaries: the two arms running downwards are the Fallopian tubes: the point where the arms meet is the womb or uterus: the single leg of the Y is the vagina. These are the *primary sexual organs* of a woman and they undergo regular cyclical changes in response to the control exercised over them by the pituitary gland, situated in the base of the skull. This control is mediated by chemical messengers (hormones) secreted into the circulation. The ovaries also secrete hormones, oestrogen, and progesterone, and a delicate hormonal balance is maintained between the pituitary gland and the ovaries. Each month an egg cell (ovum) matures and is released from the ovary, usually midway between two menstrual periods: the ovum is wafted along the Fallopian tubes by waves of contraction and if fertilised embeds in the lining of the uterus which has been conditioned to nourish it by the ovarian hormones. If it is not fertilised the ovum escapes from the uterus, altered hormone levels then cause the lining of the uterus to be shed (this is menstruation), usually about 14 days after ovulation. After menstruation a new cycle begins; another ovum matures and a fresh lining grows in the uterus. These cyclical changes recur from puberty to the menopause. Menstruation does not occur during pregnancy, of which a missed period is often the first sign. However, women do miss periods even though they are not pregnant, and this usually means that some minor and temporary change has occurred in the hormone balance. If three consecutive periods are missed it is wise to consult a doctor.

The *breasts* are called *secondary sexual organs* and are also under the influence of the ovarian hormones. Two conditions which need treatment are *mastitis* and *cancer of the breast*, both of which are characterised by lumps within the breast tissue. Mastitis may be uncomfortable but is not dangerous and can be treated medically, whereas cancer is more serious. The distinction between mastitis and cancer can only be made by a doctor and any woman who discovers a lump in her breast must seek medical aid *at once*.

Abscesses also occur in the breast, nearly always when the mother is feeding her child. Here again, a lump appears, the breast becomes red and very tender, and the woman may be feverish. Treatment with antibiotics is sometimes successful, especially if the mother consults her doctor quickly, otherwise treatment is by a small operation.

The Ovaries. The two commonest diseases of the ovaries are cysts and disorders arising from hormonal imbalance. The symptoms of ovarian disease are usually abdominal or low back pains, and heavy and painful loss during the periods, which may become irregular. These signs should be taken as a warning to consult a doctor.

The Fallopian Tubes. Infection of the Fallopian tubes is called salpingitis. The membrane lining the tubes is continuous with the lining of the uterus, hence an infection is rarely confined to a circumscribed area in either the tubes or the uterus, and pelvic inflammatory disease is a better name for this condition. Pelvic inflammatory disease often follows an abortion, or childbirth where part of the afterbirth (placenta) has been retained, or can spread from an infection in a nearby organ, for example the appendix. Infection is sometimes conveyed by the blood from another septic source in the body. The gonococcus is another cause of infection. The disease is characterised by pain and tenderness in the lower part of the abdomen, accompanied by fever, general malaise and frequently (but not invariably) a vaginal discharge. The treatment of pelvic inflammatory disease is usually medical and is the same irrespective of the primary site of infection. Before the introduction of antibiotics the disease often became chronic and the Fallopian tubes were frequently blocked by a cicatrising scar, a cause of subsequent sterility.

The Uterus. This is a hollow muscular organ and both its musculature and its lining membrane can be the site of disease. *Fibroids* are non-malignant muscular tumours which develop in many women. The main symptom is a heavy menstrual loss and surgical removal of the uterus (hysterectomy) is often necessary. This can be a major operation, but trans-vaginal hysterectomy, which does not involve opening the abdomen, has made this operation much less daunting. Hysterectomy does not impair sexual pleasure, but no more babies can be conceived. Infection of the lining of the uterus is usually part of a generalised pelvic inflammatory disease (*see* Fallopian tubes).

Cancer of the Uterus and Cervical Smears. The uterus is pear-shaped and consists of a body and neck. The wide end is uppermost (the body) and the narrow neck (cervix) projects into the top of the vagina. Cancer of the cervix is commonest in middle-aged women who have married young and have had a large family; cancer of the body of the uterus usually occurs after the menopause and is more common in nulliparous women. The symptoms are variable and it is sufficient to emphasise that any woman who has unexpected bleeding, especially after intercourse, whether her periods have stopped or not, *must* see her doctor at once. The treatment depends on individual circumstances, but is usually by operation. It is now possible to detect cancer of the cervix long before symptoms develop and at a stage when the disease can be eradicated by a relatively small operation. This early detection has been made possible by the development of exfoliative cytology. Cells taken from the cervix (without discomfort to the woman) are examined under a microscope. This test is popularly known as the "cancer test" or "cervical smear." A cervical smear is often taken as part of the routine gynaecological examination by consultants, general practitioners, and family planning doctors, and a nationwide screening programme is now in force. It is a big step forward in preventive medicine and may ultimately solve the problem of cancer of the cervix. Every woman between the ages of 25 and 60 should have the test done at least once every 5 years.

Prolapse means a sagging down of the uterus into the vagina and the cervix may even appear at the outside. It is a result of frequent childbirth and laxness of the ligaments which support the uterus: weakness of the vaginal walls often occurs at the same time. The symptoms of uterine prolapse are low back pain and a heavy dragging feeling in the lower abdomen: these are often overshadowed by the distressingly embarrassing incontinence which results from lax vaginal walls. The stress of only a sneeze, a cough, or a giggle often causes the involuntary escape of urine. The cure is operative and very rewarding.

Dysmenorrhoea or pain with the periods, is very common and most women experience this symptom at some time or another. Very often a girl's first periods are troublesome, but dysmenorrhoea develops after a year or two: this suggests that a psychological element is involved. Dysmenorrhoea is a symptom which has many varying causes, and the sensible thing to do, if pain is troublesome, is to see a doctor.

Amenorrhoea means stopping of the periods in a young woman. It may signify pregnancy or glandular disease or it can be purely psychological and generally occurs in girls with anorexia.

Abortion means the death and expulsion of a foetus before the 24th week of pregnancy. Abortion may happen spontaneously (*i.e.* naturally) or be deliberately induced. If deliberate, it may be legal or illegal (although a woman who aborts herself commits no offence) and the Abortion Act 1967 defines those conditions in which abortion is legal. The two main symptoms of abortion are bleeding and abdominal pain. Any bleeding occurring during pregnancy ought to be reported at once. Pain starts in the back and lower abdomen and is usually spasmodic in character, and like colic it works up to a peak and then temporarily passes off. Any pregnant woman with pain and bleeding should go to bed at once and send for her doctor. When doctors are convinced that a pregnancy should be terminated then an abortion by surgical means may be performed in hospital.

FAMILY PLANNING

In Britain a service of *free* family planning advice and supplies is in operation, that is, *free* to the consumer. The service is the responsibility of the Department of Health and Social Security which delegates its running mainly to Area Health Authorities and Family Doctors. The service is available to all men and women.

Sources of the Service.

1. *Area Health Authorities:* provide Family Planning Clinics in local Health Centres and sometimes in other buildings—*e.g.*, those taken over from the Family Planning Association. Some require an appointment but others provide a "walk-in" service at certain specified times.

2. *Family Doctors:* 90% of doctors in the Health Service primary care sector (GPs) have contracted to supply family planning to women *either* (a) just for their own patients *or* (b) for any woman who wishes to consult them. This service may be either (i) methods excluding the intra-uterine device ("IUCD" or "coil") or (ii) methods including the provison of IUCDs.

3. *Hospitals:* supply the service mainly
   (a) for the patients of that hospital referred from other departments and
   (b) for patients referred to their family planning clinics by the patients' own doctors (usually for IUCDs).

4. *Private Sector:*
   1. The Family Planning Association still provides clinics in some areas, including some special vasectomy clinics.
   2. Brook Advisory Centres operate in certain places and tend to specialise in advising the young.
   3. The Marie Stopes Clinic is in London (and advertises in the press).
   4. The British Pregnancy Advisory Service provides a pregnancy advisory service in some areas.
   5. Some Family Practitioners undertake vasectomies.
   6. Some hospital consultant surgeons do private vasectomies, female sterilisations and reversals of sterilisation operations.

How to find out about the Service.

Anyone wishing to use the service can obtain the address of a clinic or a family doctor from any one of a number of sources.

1. *The Citizens Advice Bureau:* the address is in the telephone directory.
2. *The telephone directory:* Area Health Authority clinics are usually under the heading Health and subheading Clinic for each Health Authority. Private clinics will be under their own names.
3. *Area Health Authorities:* (H.Q. telephone number usually in Directory) Health Centres; Health Visitors; Nurses; Midwives; Family Doctors;* Any clinic (baby, dental etc.)
4. *Family doctors' surgeries.*
5. *School nurses, school teachers, school counsellors.*
6. *Social workers.*

N.B. If a person goes to a family doctor she may be required to sign a form to the effect that the doctor has undertaken to provide her with contraception for the following 12 months. This is not binding on her and if for any reason she is unable to return to that doctor, or does not wish to, she may still obtain help elsewhere, *e.g.*, at a clinic or from another doctor. The patient has the choice.

    At most, but not all, family planning clinics an appointment system operates.

* The list of Family Doctors issued by the Family Practitioners Committees is available in Public Libraries and Post Offices. Doctors in the list who offer Family Planning Services have "C" or "C+" after their names.

METHODS OF FAMILY PLANNING

Methods Used by the Woman.

"The pill" ("combined oral contraceptive pill").

This consists of two female type hormones, oestrogen (usually pronounced as if the first "o" were another "e", that is eestrogen), and progestogen.

Preparations:

Many different combinations of these two hormones are marketed. Nowadays most formulae contain 30–50 units (micrograms) of oestrogen, whereas twelve years ago most contained 100 units. Even the amount of progestogen has been reduced to the bare minimum which is effective. Most pills have the same amount of hormone throughout the course but some recently produced pills have differing amounts of progestogen during the course, giving the lowest total amount of hormone per month.

Mode of action:

The pill works by stopping the egg cell from being shed from the ovary, and if no egg cell is shed, no fertilisation can take place. They are thus virtually 100% effective as a contraceptive, the tiny proportion of failure which occurs being almost invariably due to human error, *e.g.*, forgetting to take the pill.

The menstrual cycle.

Some people may like to have a more detailed description of the way in which the pill affects the normal menstrual cycle.

The menstrual cycle begins thus: A tiny part of the base of the brain (the *hypothalamus*) sends out a hormone called releasing factor (R.F.), which stimulates the pituitary gland to release a hormone called follicle stimulating hormone (F.S.H.). This in turn stimulates a group of folicles or egg sacs in the ovary. Each egg sac is a small fluid-filled bubble lined with special cells and containing an immature egg cell. The lining cells are stimulated to produce oestrogen and more and more of this accumulates in the blood stream. Eventually by "negative feedback" the oestrogen causes the pituitary gland to decrease the production of F.S.H. (*i.e.* high level of oestrogen o low level F.S.H.), and by "positive feedback" causes the pituitary gland to produce a sudden surge of another hormone called luteinising hormone, L.H. (*i.e.*, high level oestrogen → high level of L.H.). This L.H. causes the largest egg sac bubble to burst, releasing the egg cell, which is caught by the fringe at the free end of the uterine tube and wafted down the tube into the uterus, during which time it can be fertilised. Meanwhile the burst bubble in the ovary turns yellow and is called the "yellow body" (or *corpus luteum*). This produces both oestrogen and another hormone progesterone which are both vital for the continuation and promotion of any pregnancy. If no pregnancy occurs the yellow body collapses after 14 days, the lining of the uterus is shed in menstruation, the level of oestrogen (and progesterone) in the blood drops, and this causes the pituitary gland to step up the output of F.S.H. again.

The combined pill consists of oestrogen and progestogen, similar to those hormones produced by the "yellow body". These act on the pituitary gland as they would in a pregnancy and prevent the release of F.S.H. and L.H., so that egg cells are neither prepared nor released. Thus, taking the pill is in some ways like being constantly pregnant, which until the present century was probably the most natural and likely way for a woman in the fertile age group to be.

Method of taking the pill.

A woman starts to take the pill initially on the 1st day of a normal period, or on the 5th day of a normal period, depending on the particular pill. If she starts on the first day, she is protected from risk of pregnancy immediately. If she starts on the fifth day she is not protected until she has taken 14 pills. The pill is taken for 21 days followed by a rest interval of 7 days and this pattern is repeated indefinitely. The pills are provided in packets of 21. (There is one pill which is supplied in packs of 22 and a rest interval of only 6 days is required.) During the seven days without the pill the "pill period" comes. This is not a true period, but is simply due to stopping the pill, when such lining of the womb as has been allowed to form, is shed.

Protection from pregnancy is maintained unless:

she is more than 4–12 hours late in taking a pill (depending on the pill dosage)
she misses a pill
she has diarrhoea or vomiting so that the pill is lost before it can be absorbed.

If protection is lost she should continue to take the pills in the ordinary way but use other contraceptives, *e.g.*, the sheath, as well until the end of that packet of pills.

A few pills are put up in packets with 7 inactive tablets as well as 21 active tablets, so that a pill is taken every day. These are useful for people who find the "on–off" regime difficult to remember.

Other drugs and the pill.

A few drugs hasten the breakdown of the pill in the body and so make it less effective. Such drugs include some of those used to treat epilepsy and some, but not by any means all, antibiotics, some drugs for treating rheumatism and one or two other drugs more rarely used. Conversely, the pill is suspected of making some other drugs less effective, for example some drugs for treating depression. It is always advisable for a woman to remind any doctor who is prescribing for her that she is taking the pill.

The pill is the commonest method of birth control being used in Britain. 28% of the 11 million women in the fertile age group 15–44 use it, according to the Family Planning Association estimate 1979. In the under-30 age group, recent estimates are that about 70% are using it. In spite of the fact that the pill affects in some degree, usually slight or moderate, much body chemistry and therefore many body systems, rather as pregnancy does, most people feel no different on the pill.

Pill problems and side-effects

Connected with "pill period".

Occasionally slight bleeding happens during the days when pills are being taken, particularly when a woman first starts to take the pill. If it is very slight it is called "spotting", if rather heavier, *i.e.*, necessitating the wearing of some sort of protection, it is referred to as "breakthrough bleeding". If this is in the first month or two of pill-taking it usually settles down spontaneously. If later on, a change of pill may be indicated. It can be due to erratic pill-taking, *i.e.*, being late taking a pill, or forgetting to

take a pill, or it can be caused by having to take one of a very few other drugs which have the effect of hastening the breakdown of the pill in the body so that it does not have time to be effective. It is best to consult your doctor if bleeding happens, particularly if it happens when drug treatment is given. To be absolutely safe in those circumstances it is wise to use other contraceptives, *e.g.*, sheaths, as well until the end of that packet of pills.

Other side effects.

Occasionally, and usually in the early weeks of pill-taking, other side effects are experienced such as nausea, breast tenderness, headaches or weight gain. If these are troublesome and do not settle the pill may have to be changed or even, rarely, stopped. Some symptoms such as depression, general leg aches, and decreased interest in sex, are more doubtfully attributable to the pill and may have some quite other cause, but all these problems should be discussed with the doctor.

Headaches: Migraine headaches are usually one-sided, often associated with feeling sick or with actual vomiting and sometimes with disturbances of vision. Sometimes these headaches seem to improve when a woman takes the pill, but more often they seem to become more frequent. Sometimes they come only in the pill-free week. Often a change to a pill with a lower dose of oestrogen, or even to a progestogen-only pill, will eliminate such headaches.

It is advisable to stop taking the pill if

(a) *migraine occurs for the first time* when the pill is taken or
(b) migraine becomes "focal".

By "focal" is meant that other localised symptoms are experienced such as attacks of tingling or weakness on one side of the body, brief episodes of difficulty in speaking or visual disturbances such as transient loss of part of the field of vision. This might be a sign of a brief loss of blood supply to a part of the brain and a warning of the danger of stroke.

Headaches other than migraine: these are of course not uncommon in women who are not taking the pill. They are not uncommon in men. If they should increase when the pill is taken then changing the pill to one with a lower dose of oestrogen, or with a different progestogen (or even to one containing progestogen only) will help.

Blood pressure: In most women the blood pressure rises very slightly on the pill. In a few, it rises to above the normal level. Having a blood pressure higher than normal over a period of time renders a person more liable to diseases of the circulation. Fortunately the blood pressure is easy to monitor regularly.

Blood clotting: Blood clotting is a normal function of the body and is the body's way of sealing a cut or otherwise injured blood vessel. In women who take the pill various factors which influence blood clotting both in the blood itself and in the blood vessel wall, are altered, so that although the blood is slightly more liable to clot, the clot is more liable to be dissolved. The net result is still a slightly increased tendency to blood clotting (thrombosis).

Blood clotting or thrombosis can occur in a vein, or in an artery.

In a vein: It can extremely rarely occur in a normal vein in a person who is not taking the pill. It is only about four times more likely (or four times less unlikely) in a person taking the pill. If it occurs, it is usually in the deep veins of the leg, mainly because blood flow tends to be slowest there. It usually causes relatively little localised damage but very occasionally a piece of the blood clot can break off and be swept in the blood stream through the heart and into the lungs where it can block a blood vessel and even occasionally prove fatal.

N.B. Moderate varicose veins with no evidence of any past thrombosis are not reasons for not taking the pill.

In an artery (thrombosis) is due to the fact that "hardening of the arteries" (atherosclerosis) affects almost everyone and in the developed world has usually begun by the age of 20. Roughened patches on the artery wall allow blood clots to form on them and occasionally to block them. The pill slightly increases the risk of this happening, again by about 4–5 times. Other factors which more strongly increase the likelihood of this happening are smoking, which at less than 15 cigarettes/day increases the risk by 5 times and at more than 20 cigarettes/day increases the risk by 10 times,

increasing age, particularly the age of 35 years and older,

high blood pressure and

abnormal blood fats. A few people have these from birth, but this is a disorder which runs in families and can be detected by a blood test.

Clotting in an artery of the heart muscle is called coronary thrombosis. Clotting in an artery of the brain, and bleeding from an artery of the brain, which can result from a weak patch in a blood vessel and/or high blood pressure, are known as cerebral thrombosis or a stroke.

In October 1983 the results of one American and one British study of cancer among women using oral contraceptives were published in the medical press. The first of these appeared to suggest that long-term use of certain types of pill by younger women (under 25) may be associated with an increased risk of breast cancer; other previously published studies had shown no such connection. The British study showed that a group of women who had chosen to take a combined oral contraceptive had an increased incidence of cancer of the neck of the womb (cervical cancer) in comparison with a similar group of women who had elected to use intra-uterine contraceptive devices (*e.g.*, the coil). Both studies suggested that the progestogen content of mixed pills could be implicated. All the women in the pill group who had been found to have invasive cervical cancer were treated effectively.

The Committee on Safety of Medicines considered both these studies very carefully and concluded that women should be prescribed pills which had the lowest progestogen content but that there was no need for any woman to make an immediate change. Furthermore, the Committee endorsed the British study authors' recommendation that all long-term users of oral contraceptives should have regular cervical cytology examinations ("smears"). Of course, your family or clinic doctor will have all the Committee of Safety of Medicine's information and will know which pill to recommend.

Helpful side effects: the pill almost always prevents period pains. It also frequently reduces the unpleasant effects of "premenstrual tension" which some women experience, including feelings of depression, irritability and tenseness.

The Progestogen-only pill.

This pill, as its name implies, contains only one hormone, progestogen. It is sometimes called the mini-pill but as this name is also occasionally used for very low dose combined pills, it will be better to call it the progestogen-only pill, or P-O-P.

Until the past year or two this pill was used mainly by women who were breast feeding as it is 98 per cent effective as a contraceptive, but does not diminish the milk flow. A very small amount of the hormone does get into the milk; it is not known whether this can affect the baby but it is thought that it does not.

Recently the P-O-P is being more widely used, particularly by women over the age of 35, and also by younger women. It is probably the next most effective method of birth control to the combined pill, having a failure rate of rather less than 2 pregnancies among 100 women taking it for a year.

Mode of action: The P-O-P works mainly by making the secretion from the neck of the womb (the cervix) scanty and thick so that the sperms do not get through. The pill does not as a rule stop the egg cell from being shed, so that the periods which come are natural periods, though they may be lighter than usual because the pill does make the lining of the uterus thinner and less suitable for a fertilised egg cell to settle in. It also probably slows down the transporting of the egg cell in the uterine tubes by diminishing the waves of movement in them which normally help to get the egg cell into the uterus.

Side effects: There are two slight risks with the P-O-P. One is the slight risk of unwanted pregnancy. The other is the risk of the nuisance of irregular bleeding.

The irregular bleeding may take the form of more frequent, usually slight, bleeding or less frequent bleeding. Sometimes the periods cease altogether, or become extremely infrequent. This means that the very small amount of hormone in the pill is having a similar effect on the pituitary gland to that of the combined pill, so that it does not stimulate egg release in the ovaries. Provided it is ascertained that the pill-taker is not pregnant, the contraceptive effect is excellent in these people, and probably because the dose of hormone is so small the pituitary gland seems to recover its normal functions very rapidly when this pill is stopped. In general tests have shown that the P-O-P has far less effect on body chemistry than has the combined pill. Blood clotting and blood pressure seem to be little affected.

Method of taking the P-O-P.

The P-O-P is taken continuously and without breaks. Starting on the first day of a period it is taken every day. Because the effect on the secretion from the neck of the womb is greatest for the first six hours after taking it, it is advisable for it to be taken about six or seven o'clock in the evening, so that protection is high at bed time when intercourse is most likely. Because the effect rapidly declines after 24 hours it should be taken at the same time every day and not more than 2 hours late, otherwise the protection is broken. It takes about 2 weeks for the protection to build up initially, and the same after any break in protection due, for example, to being late taking a pill, missing a pill or pills or having a stomach upset.

The Coil or Intra Uterine Contraceptive Device (I.U.C.D.).

Coils are devices which are inserted into the uterus and remain there until a pregnancy is desired. All are made of plastic, some have very fine copper wire wound round them to increase their effectiveness. They are all highly effective, having a failure rate of about 2 pregnancies per 100 women using it for a year.

Various shapes of coils are used. The copper wire covered ones are the Copper 7, Gravgard, the Copper 1 and the Multiload. The plastic only ones are the Lippes loop and the Saf-T coil.

Each device has a thread attached to it which passes through the neck of the womb into the vagina. This can be pulled by the doctor when the coil is to be removed. A woman should never try to remove her coil herself.

The mode of action is not entirely clear, but the coil seems to prevent the fertilised egg cell from embedding in the uterus.

The method is generally considered to be more suitable for women who have had a baby than for those who have not, because in the latter the very slight risk of an infection ensuing is 7 times greater. An infection could occasionally, if untreated, proceed to involve the uterine tubes, even rarely sealing them. A woman fitted with a coil not infrequently has slightly longer and heavier and occasionally more painful periods than were usual for her.

The coil is used by about 5% of the 11 million women in the fertile age group 15–44.

The Cap or Diaphragm.

The cap or diaphragm is a circle of soft rubber with a firm rim which is inserted by the woman into the vagina so that it covers the neck of the womb (the cervix) and so physically prevents sperms from entering it. It is always used with a sperm-killing jelly or cream. There are a few different shapes of cap. Most are flat, but some are variations on a thimble shape and fit closely over the cervix. One of these is also made in plastic and can be used by a person who is allergic to rubber. The suitable cap size has to be estimated and the cap first fitted by a doctor (or nurse).

Method of use:

The cap can be put in anything up to 3 hours before intercourse, or longer if more sperm-killing preparation (spermicide) is inserted. The cap should be left in for 6–8 hours after intercourse, and if this happens again before 6 hours have elapsed, more spermicide is inserted and the cap is left in for a further 6 hours. It is then removed, washed with soft soap and water and stored in its box.

The cap has the advantage of being absolutely harmless to health. It does not affect the periods or the body systems or chemistry in any way.

It is slightly less effective than either pill or coil. The failure rate has been estimated variously as 2–8 per 100 women using it for a year, probably varying with the conscientiousness of the user.

It is used by about 3% of women in the fertile age group.

Method Used by the Man.

The sheath (or condom or French letter or "Durex"). The sheath is made of very fine rubber, nowadays almost always including a lubricant and usually including a spermicide. Most have a teat-shaped end to receive the semen.

Method of use: The air should be squeezed out of the teat end before the sheath is put on so that there is room for the semen and the sheath will not burst. The sheath should then be unrolled on to the erect penis before the penis makes any contact with the woman, as there can be a drop of fluid which contains sperms and is quite sufficient to make her pregnant. The man should hold the sheath in place when he withdraws. Unless the sheath contains spermicide the woman should always use a spermicidal pessary or foam in addition.

Advantages: Sheaths are completely harmless and in fact can give some protection against sexually transmitted diseases ("V.D.") They are readily available—*free* (when *prescribed* by the doctor) from all Area Health Authority Family Planning Clinics and on payment from chemists' shops and from slot machines which are found mainly in public houses, hotels, garages and service stations and sometimes in clubs, restaurants and holiday camps.

The failure rate is variously estimated at between 0·4 and 6 per 100 couples using it for a year and can be very low if the method is conscientiously used. The method is second only to the pill in the number of people using it—25 per cent of couples where the woman is in the fertile age-group.

Natural Methods of Birth Control.

Natural methods can have a high effectiveness rate. They are all based on the woman finding out when her egg cell is shed, *i.e.*, her "ovulation time", and avoiding intercourse around that time. Sperms can live in the vagina for up to 5 days and the egg cell lives for up to 24 hours after it is shed.

There are two methods of detecting ovulation time. The *calendar method* involves the woman in recording the length of her menstrual cycle for *at least* 6 months before it can any way be relied on. The woman must make a note of the first day of bleeding of each cycle. The last day of the cycle is the day before the next onset of bleeding. The calculation of the "safe period" is made by deducting 18 from the shortest cycle and 11 from the longest. For example, with a shortest cycle of 25 days and a longest of 31 days the safe period would be *before* day 7 and *after* day 20 (25−18=7; 31−11=20). If only the safe period around day 20 is used the method is considererably more reliable.

The *temperature method* is based on the fact that immediately after ovulation there is a distinct rise in body temperature which persists until the next period starts. The method involves taking the temperature first thing every morning before eating, drinking or smoking and plotting it on a chart each day. The safe period begins about four days *after* ovulation (as detected by the rise in temperature) and continues until the next menstrual period begins.

Other home-methods of finding the moment of ovulation continue to be explored, including tests on the mucus from the cervix, which becomes thin, clear and "stringy" at ovulation times; tests on vaginal enzymes; and even urine tests, but no simple test requiring no expertise is yet available.

Coitus interruptus, withdrawal or "being careful".

This should be mentioned in this section on "natural methods" because it is probably used at some time by many couples. It means that the man withdraws his penis before climax or ejaculation. This requires great will-power at the height of sexual excitation. Even if withdrawal is achieved, it may be too late. There are enough sperms in the drop of fluid which emerges from the penis in the early stages of sexual stimulation to cause a pregnancy. The method is therefore highly fallible, frustrating and often futile—akin to "shutting the stable door . . ." Although it cannot be recommended, it is a method requiring no expert help or artificial equipment, and is better than nothing. The failure rate is at least 17%.

Sterilisation.

Sterilisation of the woman. Tubal tie or tubal ligation.

This means cutting the tubes which carry the egg cells from the ovary to the uterus. Although this is not a major operation it may involve a general anaesthetic and an abdominal operation. It can now sometimes be done through a very small cut under a local anaesthetic with an instrument called a laparoscope, which can shine a light into the abdomen through a quite narrow tube. At operation the uterine tubes are cut and a piece taken out before each end is sealed. In addition the cut end nearest the uterus may also be embedded in the uterine wall to make doubly sure that the two ends do not rejoin. Sometimes the tubes are not cut but gold clips are put on to close the lumens of the tubes.

The operation must be regarded as irreversible as it is extremely rarely possible to reverse it.

Sterilisation of the man. Vasectomy.

Vasectomy means cutting the tubes which carry the sperms into the semen or seminal fluid, which is the fluid produced during intercourse.

The testicles have two functions. One is to produce sperms. The other is to produce the hormone testosterone which gives a man his maleness, for example his deep voice and his beard, and his sex drive. The hormone is carried in the blood stream. The sperms are carried in special tubes called the *vas deferens* which run under the skin of the scrotum. Thus the tubes are easily accessible to the surgeon. At operation the tube on each side is cut and a small piece is removed. This is to leave a gap to prevent the cut ends from re-uniting. The cut ends are sealed and the skin cut closed. The operation takes 15–20 minutes, can be done under general or local anaesthetic, and causes minimal discomfort afterwards. The result of the operation is that the sperms formed in the testicle do not get through to the penis. They go on being formed, but are gradually broken down again and reabsorbed by the blood stream. The sperms which are already in the *vas* beyond the cut end will still go into the seminal fluid, and it may be 3 months before they have all been ejected. A sample of fluid is usually checked about 2 months after the operation, and another 2 weeks later. There is no visible change in the fluid, only under the microscope it can be seen that there are no sperms in it. Nor is there any change in a man's virility, potency or sex drive. A man should have the operation only if he is sure he will not wish for further children. Although in some cases it may be possible to reverse the operation and give him back his fertility this can never be certain. He should be prepared to accept that it is irreversible.

DRUG ABUSE AND DRUG DEPENDENCE.

This section of earlier editions of *Pears* was simply called "Addiction." This word is still much used, but is gradually being replaced by the terms in the present title, because ideas about the nature of the problem and methods of dealing with it are changing.

Drug Abuse.

It is now realised by doctors, research scientists, social workers, and the police—if still not by society as a whole—that the truth is quite different. The *abuse* of drugs in this country is at present of large proportions, increasing rapidly and showing no signs of diminishing. It is responsible each year for thousands of deaths by suicide and by accidental overdosage; for an enormous but virtually unmeasurable amount of private suffering; and for the loss to society, in terms of reduced working efficiency, of millions of man-hours every year. It has nothing to do with opium smoking which was never in any case more than the eccentricity of the few. Opium is virtually unused in medicine these days, though serious problems are caused by the illegal importation and distribution of drugs such as heroin and cocaine. Nonetheless, the problems today arise chiefly from the misuse of drugs given by doctors for their effects on the central nervous system—the pain- killers, sleeping pills, "stimulants," and "tranquillisers."

Drugs and Medicines.

To the doctor, any substance is a drug that can be introduced into the body from outside, and that is capable of producing some detectable effect. Most such substances have a beneficial use. They are "medicines," and as such are given by doctors in suitable cases. Others, for example, nicotine (in cigarettes), alcohol (in beer, wine, or spirits), and carbon monoxide (in coal gas), are of doubtful benefit and of certain harm and are used by doctors, if at all, only under certain very special and usually experimental conditions.

Medicines may be classified under four main headings. First, there are those like quinine, or penicillin and other so-called antibiotics, that actually cure diseases by eradicating the organism (bacteria or other parasites) that cause disturbance of normal bodily function. Second, drugs such as insulin or the steroids overcome in the unhealthy the lack of some necessary substance a healthy body manufactures for itself: they must usually continue to be given for life. Third are the drugs which relieve the signs of disease—for example, there are many new drugs that lower the blood pressure or increase the output of urine—without being able to put right the disturbed basic situation which is the cause of the trouble. Fourth are drugs to relieve the patient's symptoms—which make him feel better, less breathless, take away his pain, help him to sleep, and so on—although we seldom know why they are able to do this. Indeed, in many cases we suspect that they are acting mainly as a token of help from doctor to patient, and so encouraging his body to fight a more successful battle on its own behalf.

There is no doubt that the genuine advances in beneficial drugs during the last forty years have been enormous; but the very successes of the penicillins, tetracyclines, antimalarials, hormones, and so on have bred in the public and in the medical profession itself an attitude of uncritical wonder. There have been relatively few drugs in the first and second categories mentioned above; and in the field of mental health, the importance of which is now so rightly emphasised, there are virtually none. Yet drugs which act upon the brain are often received as if they were curative although they may pose fresh problems rather than solve the old. Thus, although there are many drugs which act upon the mind, few do this in any fundamental sense; they relieve pain and anxiety, bring sleep and lessening of stress, and may allow the patient to recuperate himself during the relief they provide. But often this deeper change does not occur—sometimes because the doctor has not clearly seen his part in helping to bring it about—and then the symptomatic relief may come to be sought for its own sake.

Dangers of Long-term Medication with Drugs acting on the Brain.

1. *Toxic effects.* Drugs which act upon the nervous system, like any others, have characteristic toxic or unwanted effects of their own (incidentally, these may become apparent rapidly;

even, on rare occasions, after only a single dose). Such effects may have little or nothing to do with the desired effects for which they are being prescribed and taken. For example, it has only come to be realised quite recently that aspirin is liable to cause bleeding, which is occasionally serious, from the lining of the stomach in a large proportion of people who take aspirin regularly; or that phenacetin, another substance very frequently present in analgesics (*i.e.*, pain relievers) that can be bought from chemists without prescription, may lead (after prolonged use) to kidney damage. Some drugs may cause rashes and other allergic reactions in susceptible subjects; and jaundice, fainting, tremors, and motor disorders are known to occur in some patients taking a variety of other drugs.

2. *"Rebound."* The body works in such a way, over a variety of its activities, that it tends to return to a "neutral" position after it has departed from this for any reason. For example, over-eating tends to be followed by a lessening of appetite, at least for a time; the runner makes up for his air-deficit during the race by breathing more deeply thereafter; and if, at rest, you breathe for a time more rapidly and deeply than you need, this period will be followed by one in which you breathe *less* often than usual until the balance is restored. These illustrations—and there are others—have nothing to do with drugs; but in a similar way, it seems that if a continued pain, or an unpleasant emotional state such as anxiety or depression is changed into its opposite, or removed altogether by the use of a drug, the prior state may return with increased force when the drug is no longer taken. The "rebound" phenomenon, naturally, encourages the patient to take another dose, and so on.

3. *Habit formation.* This alternation of mood-changed-by-drug with the disturbed mood itself leads to the habit of taking the drug. The patient comes to rely upon it and to take it anyway, even before the unpleasant state has returned. At this stage he is said to be "habituated"; he has a psychological need for the drug, and later may become disturbed at the possibility that it will not be available when he needs it. This might not matter so greatly, if it were not that continued use of drugs in this way has physical consequences as well.

4. *Tolerance and habituation.* The body also tends to restore its own balance when drugs are given, too. It "learns" surprisingly quickly how to deal with substances with which it has never before been confronted, so that it eliminates subsequent doses more and more quickly and completely. Thus the effect of each successive dose is smaller and lasts for progressively shorter periods of time. To counter this, the patient tends to increase the dose: and the vicious circle continues. At this point he has become physically dependent upon the drug: and he may suffer physically—sometimes so severely that he dies—if supplies are not continued.

As he increases the dose in this way, so his tolerance of its effects increases, to such an extent that after prolonged use he may be taking doses of a drug that are five or ten times greater than those which will kill somebody not dependent upon them in this way. It sometimes happens that a patient develops a renewed craving at some point after a course of treatment, in which the dose of drug has been reduced without removing the underlying cause of his dependence. He may then obtain and use the dose he habitually took before treatment, not knowing that his body will have lost its tolerance of such doses. That dose is now as high for him as for any other person and so may be lethal. There has been a number of deaths for this reason.

Factors in the Causation of Dependence.

The risk of becoming dependent upon a drug is governed by three main factors; the drug itself, the personality of the individual who takes it, and the circumstances in which it is taken. Most adults have taken alcohol at one time or another, unless it is against their code to do so; yet *relatively* few are dependent upon it (relatively few, but many too many; more than half a million in the United Kingdom alone). Many of us have had morphine or some other strong analgesic for medical reasons, without becoming dependent upon it (whatever so-called addicts say, it is extremely rare for anyone to become dependent on an opiate because he was introduced to it in a medical setting). On the other hand, if we start to take such a drug "for kicks"—as more and more people, particularly teen-agers and young adults are doing—it is extremely probable that we shall become dependent upon it, and sooner rather than later at that. It is also probable that each one of us would become dependent, were he obliged to take it regularly, for long enough, and in sufficient dosage. Thus, although there are personalities—psychopathic, immature, or unstable—that are more prone than others to become dependent if they are exposed to the drug, there are also drugs that are more likely than others to cause such dependence no matter to whom they are given. The extent of the dependence will vary; with some, it is never physiological but remains psychological (but not the less real or disturbing for that). Also, the rate at which dependence develops may vary; and the picture presented by the dependent subject—the extent to which his normal life is impaired, or to which he becomes dangerous to himself or others—varies as well. In a very much oversimplified way, some of these relationships will now be summarised for certain substances.

Heroin, morphine and cocaine are usually injected. Barbiturates (sleeping pills) and amphetamines ("Benzedrine") are tablets or capsules, and marihuana ("reefer," hashish) is smoked in cigarettes. Heroin and cocaine are now usually taken together. Combinations of drugs often act differently from their individual constituents and patients dependent upon them are even more difficult to treat. Barbiturate and amphetamine, also, are often mixed (as in "purple hearts"). There is considerable *psychological* dependence on heroin, morphine, cocaine, and amphetamine, but much less with marihuana. *Physiological* dependence is great with heroin and morphine, less with barbiturates, alcohol, and amphetamine in that order, and virtually nil

with cocaine and marihuana. Personality plays a greater part in initiating dependence on alcohol, marihuana, and barbiturates than with the others. Heroin, cocaine, and morphine are the cause of more antisocial tendencies in dependent people than alcohol, barbiturates, and amphetamine. The chief danger of marihuana (mere possession of which is illegal) seems to be that the search for it will lead the searcher into localities where his risk of exposure to even more dangerous influences is greatly increased. It is thus sometimes argued that if it were legal to consume marihuana, the number of young people who yearly become dependent upon the other more dangerous drugs would in fact decrease. There is as yet no evidence for or against this proposition. The number of drug dependent people in the UK is rising fast for heroin and cocaine. This number is very large for alcohol, and is increasing in the case of barbiturates and marihuana. Very few people are dependent on morphine, and the number is not growing.

Treatment.

Exhortations, imprisonment, and other moralistic or legalistic approaches are useless. Treatment of any person dependent upon a drug is a matter for a qualified psychotherapist. It is liable to be time-consuming and frustrating for patient and doctor, and it is sometimes unsuccessful. At present, there are too few specialists or centres where treatment can be obtained, although it is to be hoped that this situation will change as the problem is increasingly seen by our society to be of exceptional gravity.

When there is little or no chance of cure, prevention is certainly the best treatment. Drugs should only be taken on the prescription of a doctor; and the patient should remind him from time to time, if this be necessary, that he would like to dispense with his drugs as soon as the doctor thinks it possible. It should also be remembered that there is often no need to reach for the aspirin (or any other drug that anyone can buy from the chemist without prescription) at the first sign of a headache—or to reach for it at all to help one sleep or relax, for which purpose such drugs are in any case pharmacologically useless. A wait for ten minutes is good discipline, and will frequently resolve the problem to an extent that makes a drug unnecessary.

PART III. SPECIAL TOPICS

ADVANCES IN BRONCHIAL ASTHMA

Bronchial asthma is a condition in which the smaller respiratory passages become narrowed by an allergic response and blocked with inflammatory exudate. This gives rise to symptoms of chest tightness, breathlessness and wheezing. In recent years the condition seems to have become more common and now it is estimated that up to 12% of children are affected and 5% of the adult population (childhood asthma is more common in Britain than almost anywhere else in the world). In addition, well over 50% of asthmatics are not diagnosed. In spite of a whole range of safe and effective therapy, more than 2,000 people die of this illness every year. This is largely due to a misunderstanding and under-estimation of the illness by both parents and doctors. The concept that asthma is largely emotional in origin is now very out-dated.

Asthmatics can be divided into two groups. In more than half, symptoms begin in childhood and are part of the Atopic Syndrome, that is to say, a triad of asthma, eczema and hayfever, which has a tendency to run in families. Attacks occur in episodes and may be triggered by infection, exertion or the presence of the house dust-mite. Sometimes the attacks can be seasonal, depending on the presence of grass pollen or fungal spores. Alcohol and tobacco smoke can also act as trigger factors.

Late Onset Asthma.

Not all asthmatics wheeze and one of the characteristic early features, particularly in children, is a persistent dry nocturnal cough. Asthma occurring in adult life is usually known as "Late Onset Asthma". There is no history of allergy or of similar problems in the family but it is often associated with nasal polyps. Late onset asthma is more resistant to treatment, but in both groups, the outlook is good and after a number of acute exacerbations, perhaps lasting several years, many people become symptom free or have only minor problems. Very few people become seriously incapacitated.

Treatment is directed at easing acute episodes and preventing their recurrence. Beta, receptor stimulants such as Salbutamol, and Terbutaline are now the most widely used drugs; they are usually given in inhaler form because their onset of action is immediate, whereas tablets take much longer to be absorbed and work. These help to dilate the respiratory airways and have a wide margin of safety; two puffs can be given every 4–6 hours. The need for increasing administration is a sign that the condition is becoming unstable and prophylactic therapy should be instigated. Many people, particularly the young and elderly, have difficulty in using pressurised aerosol inhalers, in that they are unable to co-ordinate their breathing with the administration of the drug. A wide variety of alternatives is available, for example, dry powder inhalers which are activated by inspiration—young children can usually manage these. Spacer devices which can be fitted on to ordinary inhalers are provided with a one-way valve so that the inhalant is not dissipated but can be taken into the lungs in the patient's own time. These devices are often bulky and some of the new inhalers are breath activated.

For those who suffer from more severe attacks, broncho-dilator drugs can be given by a nebuliser.

Nebulisers are electrically powered and give a high concentration of drug which is administered by placing a mask over the patient's nose and mouth. Unfortunately, they are not available on the National Health Service.

For young children, a plastic coffee cup can provide an inexpensive substitute. A small hole is cut in the base of the cup and the mouthpiece of an ordinary inhaler is inserted, the open end of the cup is placed over the child's nose and mouth and the usual dose of inhaler is given. The coffee cup acts as a reservoir so that most of the spray can be usefully inhaled without waste.

Preventive Therapy.

Patients who have frequent or severe attacks should be on some form of preventive therapy and again, this should be administered in an aerosol form. Intal or Disodium Cromoglycate is a very useful drug which helps to stabilise the lining of the cells in the bronchial tubes and so make them less susceptible to allergic stimuli. Small doses of inhaled steroid have a similar effect in dampening down the inflammatory response which is a major component of an asthmatic attack. For those who suffer from persistent episodes, this treatment should be taken on a regular basis. An acute attack which does not readily respond to broncho-dilator drugs can often be successfully treated by a short course of oral steroids. Patients often worry about the potential "side effects" of steroids but as these are only given in very short courses, any problems are likely to be minimal. Indeed, steroids can be life-saving and it is far better to start a course in the early stages of an attack, than wait until the condition is critical. Soluble preparations are available for children and can be dissolved in milk or juice. Parents should gain experience of handling these drugs themselves, so that severe attacks can be aborted in the early stages.

A peak flow meter is a very simple device which can often give early warning as to when a patient's condition is becoming less stable, and indicate when steroids might be used. Peak flow meters measure the rate at which air is exhaled from a forced expiration. Normal values vary depending on age and sex but the device is simple to use and can easily be handled by children.

Many asthmatics have only minor symptoms but for those who have frequent problems, the importance of using regular preventive medication cannot be overstressed. Studies have shown that, in the majority of fatal cases, no form of preventive medicine was being used. Although nebulisers are often extremely effective, they can induce a false sense of security and the necessity for their frequent use should be an indication that further treatment is necessary.

Emergency Problems.

Severe asthma, especially if it lasts for 24 hours, should be treated as an emergency and often requires hospitalisation. It is characterised by breathlessness, poorly relieved by broncho-dilator drugs, a fast pulse rate, irritability and exhaustion. Paradoxically, wheezing is not always present and the serious nature of the problem may be unrecognised. In such cases, oxygen and intravenous medication is essential. Such a situation is called Status Asthmaticus and requires urgent medical assessment. Appointment systems in general practice often work against asthmatics and if the patient or his relatives feel there is cause for concern, they should insist on being seen straight away.

TRANSPLANT SURGERY

The replacement of damaged organs and body parts is a continuing challenge to modern medicine. Failed organs can sometimes be replaced by transplantation of replacements from donors, though this is associated with a severe chronic shortage of donor organs as well as problems of rejection which require recipients to be maintained on long-term immunosuppressive therapy. Lost body parts – fingers, ears, noses, and so on – can sometimes be sewn back on if surgery is performed sufficiently quickly after an accident has occurred, but transplants are not generally carried out in these cases.

Materials technology and biotechnology have made dramatic advances in recent years in solving these problems. Straightforward replacements for damaged structures in the form of artificial joints have been with us for many years, and a new area of progress is currently being opened whereby replacement organs and parts are being made from patients' own tissues in the 'workshop'. Suitable types of cells are taken and, if necessary and possible, grown in a test tube, and are attached to a suitable carrier (scaffolding) ready for implantation back into the body. Depending on the needs of any particular situation, the carrier may remain permanently, or may slowly dissolve with time.

Organ Replacements.

The approach taken and the materials used depend on the organ concerned. The principle is generally that what needs to be replaced is the functional part of the organ, known as the *parenchyma*; parenchymal cells are collected together into a device which is implanted into the body in a site allowing the cells to respond to their normal controls and to fulfil their normal functions. Depending on the source of the cells, additional protection may need to be provided against the immune system, and additional structural organisation may also be needed for some parenchymal cells to work properly.

Artificial Livers.

Liver cells can be grown in the laboratory, and large numbers can be prepared from a small biopsy of the patient's own liver, using as normal a part as possible if the organ is diseased or a surviving part if extensive trauma or cancer has necessitated removal of liver tissue. However, cultured liver cells cannot simply be injected into the body; they depend on having a normal liver structure in order to function – that is, they need a supply of blood, and they need to be organised into lobules in which different cells have different positions and roles. Cultured liver cells are believed to be able to have all these potentials. An experimental route to making a new liver is to create a scaffold structure onto which the liver cells are seeded. The seeded structure is then incubated in the laboratory to allow the cells to generate the correct structure, and the device is then encapsulated in a suitable protective film and 'transplanted' into the body. Appropriate scaffolding polymers, which can be biodegradable or permanent, have been identified; these are produced as filaments which can be woven into a suitable support shape. In a number of studies, these matrices have been 'prevascularised' by seeding them with endothelial cells (which form the lining of blood vessels), and have then been seeded with liver cells. The result is an artificial liver which can be connected to the body's blood supply at some convenient point. Although these experiments are still in the very early stages, the results so far have been promising.

Bone Grafts.

Bone is another good example where tissue engineering is making important advances. Bone grafts are very commonly needed for repairing damage due to trauma, degeneration and cancer surgery. Small bone grafts are generally taken from other parts of the patient's body, while large ones come from bone banks, where supplies are very limited, and transplantation of bone produces all the problems of rejection. Additionally, pinning of bones with metal implants has a number of drawbacks, in that the result is generally weaker than natural bone, and the deprivation of surrounding bone by the pin can result in loss of strength here as well.

Mineral-based scaffolding materials, in the form of sea coral and hydroxyapatite (a form of calcium phosphate which occurs in bones) have been used with considerable success, though they are quite brittle. Degradable polymers, which encourage bone cells to colonise and grow into natural bone, and can be seeded with bone cells before implantation, have great potential for guiding the regeneration of new bone and replacing metal pins. Growth of the new organ in this case is after the scaffold has been implanted into the body.

Cosmetic Engineering.

This area of tissue engineering is more dramatic in that it will be used to provide replacements for lost appendages, such as ears and noses. These organs, particularly ears, have been the subject of study because they are anatomically relatively simple and can be generated using an easily available cell type.

Ears are composed of cartilage, which in turn is made by special cells called *chondrocytes*. Cartilage transplantation is a not uncommon technique, using cartilage from the ribs or cartilage from donors which has been treated with a variety of chemicals to reduce its likelihood of being rejected. The main problem with this method is that cartilage devitalised in this way lacks the chondrocytes which are needed to maintain the structure, and it is eventually reabsorbed by the body.

Making parts with artificial cartilage seems relatively straightforward because chondrocytes are quite easy to grow in laboratory conditions, and cartilage is a rather bloodless tissue with only limited requirements for arteries and veins. Filaments of appropriate polymers are woven into the shape of the part to be replaced, and are seeded with cultured chondrocytes and grown in the laboratory. In this situation, the cells proliferate on the matrix, attaching themselves to it and making the intercellular materials which make up cartilaginous tissue. The resulting tissue appears to follow the shape of the scaffolding material very precisely, and initial studies suggest that the shape is maintained even after dissolution of biodegradable scaffolds.

One group of scientists in the US has made a human-shaped ear by this method, using mouse chondrocytes, and maintenance of its structure was demonstrated by 'transplanting' it under the skin on the animal's back. Cartilage cells are also readily available from most patients, so rejection problems are easy to avoid.

The Natural Formation of Tissues.

The examples of organ and body part engineering mentioned above concern relatively simple tissues and structures. Preparation of artificial parts becomes increasingly difficult as anatomical and functional complexity increases, as specialised cell types require increasingly specialised environments. This leads to the question of how tissues form in natural conditions and how the process can be mimicked in the manufacture of artificial organs.

Knowledge in this area is continually increasing, and it is becoming apparent that normal organs form by migration and differentiation of cells in response to positional and functional stimuli. These stimuli can consist of contacts with adjacent cells and supporting materials (such as collagen fibres), and by chemicals, usually proteins, which are released by nearby cells to provide instructions to the new cells as to what kind of cells they are to become. These chemicals are termed growth factors, and there is considerable scope for attaching these to polymer scaffolds with the aim of attracting the right types of cell to colonise the scaffolds and then to differentiate into the appropriate final type of target cell. It should be possible to build up complicated structures in several stages to make the desired part; each stage would consist of adding the appropriate growth factor (quite possibly only to a part of the scaffold or partly formed structure), along with the relevant type of cell or precursor cell,

and waiting for differentiation into the desired cell type to occur.

Other Uses of Tissue Engineering.

Another potentially very valuable use of tissue engineering comes from its combination with genetic engineering. For example, a potential treatment for patients with a tendency to form atheromatous plaque in the cardiac arteries consists of inserting sections of artificial arteries lined with endothelial cells which have been genetically modified not to form plaques. Genetic diseases could be corrected by taking a patient's defective cells, correcting the deficiency, and reinserting them in the form of an artificial organ. For example, this method is likely to provide a useful treatment for an inherited inability of the liver to make a protein called low density lipoprotein receptor.

Artificial organs are also likely to be used in the future for delivery of drugs. This is based on the observation that more and more body substances are coming into use as drugs, and the concept is that a patient's cells will be given the ability to make these substances and then implanted as artificial organs to ensure long-term supplies of the substance.

The most pressing need in this area is in diabetes, resulting from a failure of a type of cell in the pancreas called the β cell; these occur in groups known as islets of Langerhans. The cells do not grow in the laboratory, and xenografts from animals are thus being investigated; the problem becomes one of keeping them away from the body's immune system, which would otherwise destroy them. Several attempts have been made to do this by coating groups of β cells in membranes which are permeable to the small molecules which provide nutrition to the cells and to the insulin which they produce, but not to the much larger destructive antibodies made by the immune system. The cells (experiments have used single cells, whole islets, and large collections of islets) are embedded in an alginate gel to provide structural support and are then coated in a polymeric material which provides the necessary permeability properties. The encapsulated cells are then inserted into devices in blood vessels or elsewhere into the body, where the β cells are exposed to the factors that regulate insulin production, the most important being the blood glucose concentration. It is possible that future research will reveal ways of growing β cells in the laboratory or to encourage them to grow on scaffolds to make an artificial insulin-secreting organ, though it is just as likely that the solution will lie in using a completely different cell type which has been genetically modified to make insulin, in quantities determined by the blood glucose level.

The Future.

Tissue engineering is a science on the edge of a number of enormous and dramatic advances. It is based on a range of disciplines, including anatomy, physiology, medicine, pharmacology, genetic engineering and materials science, and rapid progress continues to be made in all these areas; it seems very likely that we will all start to see the benefits within a few years.

PART IV. INDEX AND GLOSSARY

Change of life, 43 (2).

Chickenpox, 10 (1).

Chilblains, 52 (2).

Chill. This is not a proper medical word, but refers to the symptoms that occur when one first becomes infected with any germs which cause fever. When such germs enter the body, all the defending processes are mobilised and speeded up. The white cells in the blood increase in number, and the amount of energy used is greater than normal, causing the temperature to rise. This rise in temperature increases the ability of the body to fight back, and, in order to retain heat within the body, the blood-vessels in the skin contract so that less heat is lost by radiation. This makes the skin cold and pale. What is ordinarily called a chill is merely an infection by the germs causing cold and influenza. But a chill may be the preliminary to almost any infectious disease, such as measles, mumps, scarlet fever, pneumonia, and so on. The best treatment when the temperature is raised is to go to bed with as much warmth as possible. Hot drinks and hot-water bottles are helpful. *See* Colds, 10 (2).

Chlamydia, the most common sexually-transmitted infection in Britain.

Cholecystitis, 39 (1).

Cholera, 14 (1).

Cholesterol, 29 (2), 38 (1).

Chronic. A chronic disease is one which is prolonged and relatively mild, as opposed to an acute one which is short and severe.

Chronic nephritis, 44 (2).

Cilia, 31 (1).

Cirrhosis of the liver, 38 (2).

Claustrophobia. A physical symptom, which causes the individual to be afraid of enclosed spaces. *See under* Obsessional neurosis, 51 (1).

Cocaine, 61 (1).

Coccyx. The end of the spinal column.

Colds, 10 (2).

Colitis, 37 (1).

Coma, 47 (1).

Concussion, *see* Head injuries, 21 (1).

Congenital heart disease, 27 (2).

Conjunctivitis, 54 (2).

Consciousness and unconsciousness, 47 (1).

Constipation, 35 (1).

Contraception, *See* Family Planning, 56–59.

Coronary heart disease, 28 (1).

Coronary thrombosis, 28 (2).

Cortisone. A hormone produced by the suprarenal glands, 43 (1).

Cretin, 43 (1).

Cretinism, 43 (1).

C.S.F. (*i.e*, cerebrospinal fluid), 46 (2)

Cushing's disease, 43 (1).

Cutaneous ureterostomy, 45 (1).

Cystic fibrosis, 31 (2).

Cystitis, 45 (1).

Dandruff. *See* Seborrhoea, 52 (1).

Deficiency diseases, 41–2.

Dementia, 50 (1).

Demyelinating diseases, 49 (1).

Dengue, 11 (2).

Dermatitis, 52 (2).

Dhobie itch, 8 (1).

Diabetes insipidus, 43 (1).

Diabetes mellitus, 39 (1).

Diarrhoea, and vomiting, 14 (2).

Diet, 39–41.

Digestive tract, 34–38.

Diphtheria, 12 (1).

Diverticulitis, 37 (1).

Dropsy, 44 (2).

Drug abuse, 59–61

Duchenne's muscular dystrophy, 50 (1).

Ductless glands, 42 (2).

Duodenal ulcer, 35 (2).

Duodenum, 35 (2).

Dysentery, 14 (2).

Dyslexia, a specific learning disability that can affect reading, writing, memory etc. It is now known to be hereditary.

Dysmenorrhoea, 55 (2).

E.C.T. The abbreviated form of the name for a modern type of treatment for certain psychiatric disorders—electro-convulsive-therapy. *See under* Psychosis, 50 (1).

Eczema, 52(2).

Ehrlich, Paul (1854–1915). German bacteriologist, 4 (1), 5 (2).

Electrocardiogram, (E.C.G.), 29 (2).

Electroencephalography, (E.E.G.), 46 (2).

Electromyography, (E.M.G.), 46 (2).

Elephantiasis, 18 (2).

Embolism, 30 (1), 32 (2).

Emphysema, 31 (1).

Empyema. A collection of pus in the lung (usually a complication of other diseases).

Encephalitis, 49 (1).

Encephalo-myelitis, 49 (1).

Endemic. Referring to a disease, means prevalent in a particular area.

Endocarditis. Disease of the valves of the heart, 29 (2).

Endocrine glands, 42–3.

Enzymes, 34 (1).

Epidemic jaundice, 16 (1).

Epilepsy, 47 (2).

Epithelioma (cancer of the skin), 54 (1).

Erysipelas, 52 (2).

Exocrine glands, 42 (2).

Eye, disease of the, 54 (2).

Fallopian tubes, 55 (1).

Family Planning, 56–59.

Farcy, 14 (1).

Fat embolism, 33 (1).

Fats. *See* Diet.

Fevers, general treatment of, 9.

Fibroids, 55 (2).

Fibrositis, 54 (2).

First Aid, 18–23

Fits. *See* Epilepsy.

Fleming, Sir Alexander (1881–1955). Scottish bacteriologist, discoverer of penicillin, 4 (1).

Food poisoning diseases, 14–15.

Fractures, 20 (2).

Frostbite, 30 (2).

Fungi, diseases caused by, 7 (2), 15 (1).

Gall-bladder, 38 (1).

Gallstones, 39 (1).

Ganglion. A small cystic swelling, usually on the wrist, dealt with by simple surgical treatment.

Gastric ulcer, 35 (2).

Gastritis. Inflammation of the stomach.

Geriatrics. The medical study of old age.

German Measles, 10 (1).

Gigantism, 43 (1).

Gingivitis. Inflammation of the gums due to infection and requiring treatment by a dentist.

Glanders, 14 (1).

Glandular diseases, 42–3.

Glandular fever, 11 (1).

Glaucoma, 54 (2).

Glial cells of the brain, 46 (1).

Goitre, 43 (1).

Gonadotrophic hormones, 42 (2).

Gonorrhoea, 15 (2).

Gout, an excruciatingly painful inflammation of the joints (especially the toe) caused by crystals formed by uric acid.

Grand mal. See Epilepsy, 47 (2).

Graves' disease, 43 (1).

Growth hormone, 42 (2).

Gynaecology. 55–56.

Haematemesis. Vomiting of blood, 33 (1), 36 (1).

Haematuria. The passing of blood in the urine, 44 (1).

Haemoglobin. The red pigment in the blood.

Haemolytic anaemia, 24 (2).

Haemophilia, 26 (1).

Haemoptysis. The spitting-up of blood, 33 (1).

Haemorrhage anaemia, 24 (1).

Haemorrhagic diseases, 26 (1).

Haemorrhage of the brain, 48 (2).

Haemorrhoids, 37 (2).

Hair. See Alopecia, 52 (1).

Headache, 47 (1). See also Migraine.

Head injuries, 21 (1).

Health: general principles, 3 (2).

Heart: how it works, 26–7.

Heart attack, 28 (2).

Heart beat, 29 (1).

Heart failure, 27 (1).

Hepatic. Concerning the liver.

Hepatitis, infective, 10 (1), 38 (2).

Hereditary or Huntington's chorea, 48 (2).

Hernia, 37 (1).

Heroin, 61 (1).

Herpes zoster, 49 (1).

Hiatus hernia, 35 (2).

High blood-pressure, 28 (2).

Hodgkin's disease, 25 (2).

Hookworm disease, 18 (2).

Hormone replacement therapy, 61–2

Hormones. See Endocrine glands.

Huntington's chorea, a neurological disease which can cause paralysis in middle age.

Hydrocephaly, 48 (1).

Hydronephrosis, 45 (1).

Hyperpituitarism, 43 (1).

Hypertension, 28 (2), 62–3.

Hypochondriasis, the unfounded belief that one is suffering from a serious disease.

Hysteria, 51 (1).

IBD. Stands for inflammatory bowel disorder.

Ichthyosis, 53 (2).

Immunity, 8 (2).

Impetigo, 53 (1).

Incubation period. See Infectious Fevers, 9 (2).

Infantile paralysis. See Poliomyelitis, 10 (2).

Infarction, 30 (1), 48 (2).

Infection, how spread, 8 (1).

Infectious diseases, 6–18.

Infective hepatitis, 10 (1), 38 (2).

Inflammatory diseases of the nervous system, 49 (1).

Influenza, 10 (2).

Injuries, 18–23.

Insomnia, 47 (1).

Insulin. See Diabetes, 39 (1). For psychiatric use see Psychosis, 50 (2).

Intermittent claudication, 29 (2).

Itching, 52 (1).

Jaundice, 38 (2), 24 (2).

Jenner, Sir Edward (1749–1823). 16 (1).

Joints, Diseases of the, 54 (1).

Kala-azar, 17 (2).

Kidney diseases, 43–45.

Kidneys, function of, 43 (2).

Kidney stones, 45 (1).

Koch, Robert (1843–1910). bacteriologist, 16 (1).

Kwashiorkor, 41 (2).

Large intestine, diseases of the, 37 (1).

Legionnaire's Disease, caused by the Legionella bacterium. Very serious outbreaks (as at Stafford hospital in 1985 when 28 people died) can occur. Sometimes the bacterium is found in recirculating and hot-water systems.

Leishmaniasis (kala-azar or dum-dum fever), 17 (2).

Leprosy, 16 (1).

Leukaemia, 25 (2).

Lice. See Parasites, 8 (1), 52 (1).

Lichen planus, 53 (1).

Lister, Joseph (1827–1912). English surgeon who founded modern antiseptic surgery, 5 (2).

Liver, function of the, 38 (1).

Liver and gall-bladder, diseases of the, 38 (1).

Lockjaw. See Tetanus, 13 (2).

Lumbago. See Backache.

Lung cancer, 33 (1).

Lupus. Disease more prevalent in black people (especially women) which causes the patient's immune system to attack his or her own body tissues.

Lymph nodes, 25 (2), 42 (2).

Lymphosarcoma, 25 (2).

Malaria, 17 (1).

Malnutrition, 41 (1).

Malta fever (undulant fever), 13 (2).

Manic depression, 50 (2).

Marasmus, 41 (2).

ME (myalgic encephalomyelitis), illness with symptoms of extreme exhaustion and muscular pain. Sometimes dismissed as 'yuppie flu'.

Measles, 9 (2).

Medicines: classification, 22 (1).

Melancholia. See Manic-depressive insanity, 50 (2).

Menière's disease, 47 (2).

Meningitis, 13 (2), 49 (1).

Menopause, 43 (2).

Mental illnesses, 50.

Metastases or secondary deposits, 49 (2).

Migraine, 47 (1).

Minot, George Richards (1885–1950). American physician and pathologist, specialised in diseases of the blood, 25 (1).

Mitral stenosis, 28 (2).

Motor nerves, 46 (1).

Motor neurone disease, 48 (1).

MRSA (Methicillin Resistant Staphylococcus Aureus), a bacteria resistant to antibiotics which has been found in some hospitals.

Multiple sclerosis or disseminated sclerosis or "creeping paralysis", 49 (1).

Mumps, 10 (1).

Muscular dystrophies, 50 (1).

Myasthenia gravis, 50 (1).

Myelin sheaths, 46 (1).

Myelitis, 49 (1).

Myelography, 46 (2).

Myxoedema, 43 (1).

Narcolepsy, 47 (1).

Nephritis, acute and chronic, 44 (1).

Nephrosis, 44 (2).

Nerve cells, 45 (1).

Nervous system, diseases of, 45–50.

Nettlerash, 53 (1).

Neurology: diagnostic techniques, 46 (2).

Neurosis, 51 (1).

Nutritional disorders, 41–2.

SPORTING COMPANION

This section provides a wide-ranging variety of tables giving numerous winners of major popular sporting competitions, both in Britain and abroad. The sports included here range from long-established favourites such as bowls and cricket to newer contests such as American football and ice hockey.

SPORTING COMPANION

AMERICAN FOOTBALL

WORLD CHAMPIONSHIP SUPERBOWL WINNERS

I (1967)	Green Bay Packers	XVIII ((1984)	Los Angeles Raiders
II (1968)	Green Bay Packers	XIX (1985)	San Francisco 49ers
III (1969)	New York Jets	XX (1986)	Chicago Bears
IV (1970)	Kansas City Chiefs	XXI (1987)	New York Giants
V (1971)	Baltimore Colts	XXII (1988)	Washington Redskins
VI (1972)	Dallas Cowboys	XXIII (1989)	San Francisco 49ers
VII (1973)	Miami Dolphins	XXIV (1990)	San Francisco 49ers
VIII (1974)	Miami Dolphins	XXV (1991)	New York Giants
IX (1975)	Pittsburgh Steelers	XXVI (1992)	Washington Redskins
X (1976)	Pittsburgh Steelers	XXVII (1993)	Dallas Cowboys
XI (1977)	Oakland Raiders	XXVIII (1994)	Dallas Cowboys
XII (1978)	Dallas Cowboys	XXIX (1995)	San Francisco 49ers
XIII (1979)	Pittsburgh Steelers	XXX (1996)	Dallas Cowboys
XIV (1980)	Pittsburgh Steelers	XXXI (1997)	Green Bay Packers
XV (1981)	Oakland Raiders	XXXII (1998)	Denver Broncos
XVI (1982)	San Francisco 49ers	XXXIII (1999)	Denver Broncos
XVII (1983)	Washington Redskins		

ASSOCIATION FOOTBALL

WORLD CUP WINNERS

1930	(In Uruguay)	Uruguay	1970	(In Mexico)	Brazil
1934	(In Italy)	Italy	1974	(In West Germany)	West Germany
1938	(In France)	Italy	1978	(In Argentina)	Argentina
1950	(In Brazil)	Uruguay	1982	(In Spain)	Italy
1954	(In Switzerland)	West Germany	1986	(In Mexico)	Argentina
1958	(In Sweden)	Brazil	1990	(In Italy)	West Germany
1962	(In Chile)	Brazil	1994	(In the USA)	Brazil
1966	(In England)	England	1998	(In France)	France

The 2002 World Cup is to be co-hosted by Japan and South Korea

EUROPEAN CHAMPIONS

1960	(In France)	USSR	1980	(In Italy)	West Germany
1964	(In Spain)	Spain	1984	(In France)	France
1968	(In Italy)	Italy	1988	(In West Germany)	Holland
1972	(In Belgium)	West Germany	1992	(In Sweden)	Denmark
1976	(In Yugoslavia)	Czechoslovakia	1996	(In England)	Germany

EUROPEAN CHAMPIONS CUP WINNERS

1955–6	Real Madrid	1970–1	Ajax Amsterdam	1985–6	Steaua Bucharest
1956–7	Real Madrid	1971–2	Ajax Amsterdam	1986–7	FC Porto
1957–8	Real Madrid	1972–3	Ajax Amsterdam	1987–8	PSV Eindhoven
1958–9	Real Madrid	1973–4	Bayern Munich	1988–9	A C Milan
1959–60	Real Madrid	1974–5	Bayern Munich	1989–90	A C Milan
1960–1	Benfica	1975–6	Bayern Munich	1990–1	Red Star Belgrade
1961–2	Benfica	1976–7	Liverpool	1991–2	Barcelona
1962–3	A C Milan	1977–8	Liverpool	1992–3	Marseille
1963–4	Inter Milan	1978–9	Nottingham Forest	1993–4	A C Milan
1964–5	Inter Milan	1979–80	Nottingham Forest	1993–4	A C Milan
1965–6	Inter Milan	1980–1	Liverpool	1994–5	Ajax Amsterdam
1966–7	Glasgow Celtic	1981–2	Aston Villa	1995–6	Juventus
1967–8	Manchester United	1982–3	SV Hamburg	1996–7	Borussia Dortmund
1968–9	A C Milan	1983–4	Liverpool	1997–8	Real Madrid
1969–70	Feyenoord	1984–5	Juventus		

The 1998–9 finalists were Manchester United and Bayern Munich

EUROPEAN CUP–WINNERS' CUP WINNERS

1960–1	Fiorentina	1973–4	FC Magdeburg	1986–7	Ajax Amsterdam
1961–2	Atletico Madrid	1974–5	Dynamo Kiev	1987–8	Mechelen
1962–3	Tottenham Hotspur	1975–6	Anderlecht	1988–9	Barcelona
1963–4	Sporting Lisbon	1976–7	Hamburg SV	1989–90	Sampdoria
1964–5	West Ham United	1977–8	Anderlecht	1990–1	Manchester United
1965–6	Borussia Dortmund	1978–9	Barcelona	1991–2	Werder Bremen
1966–7	Bayern Munich	1979–80	Valencia	1992–3	Parma
1967–8	A C Milan	1980–1	Dynamo Tbilisi	1993–4	Arsenal
1968–9	Slovan Bratislava	1981–2	Barcelona	1994–5	Real Zaragoza
1969–70	Manchester City	1982–3	Aberdeen	1995–6	Paris St Germain
1970–1	Chelsea	1983–4	Juventus	1996–7	Barcelona
1971–2	Glasgow Rangers	1984–5	Everton	1997–8	Chelsea
1972–3	A C Milan	1985–6	Dynamo Kiev		

The 1998–9 finalists were Lazio and Real Mallorca (who defeated the holders, Chelsea, in the semi-final)

UEFA CUP WINNERS

1957–8	Barcelona	1972–3	Liverpool	1984–5	Real Madrid
1959–60	Barcelona	1973–4	Feyenoord	1985–6	Real Madrid
1960–1	A S Roma	1974–5	Borussia	1986–7	IFK Gothenburg
1961–2	Valencia		Moenchengladbach	1987–8	Bayer Leverkusen
1962–3	Valencia	1975–6	Liverpool	1988–9	Napoli
1963–4	Real Zaragoza	1976–7	Juventus	1989–90	Juventus
1964–5	Ferencvaros	1977–8	PSV Eindhoven	1990–1	Inter Milan
1965–6	Barcelona	1978–9	Borussia	1991–2	Ajax Amsterdam
1966–7	Dynamo Zagreb		Moenchengladbach	1992–3	Juventus
1967–8	Leeds United	1979–80	Eintracht Frankfurt	1993–4	Inter Milan
1968–9	Newcastle United	1980–1	Ipswich Town	1994–5	Parma
1969–70	Arsenal	1981–2	IFK Gothenburg	1995–6	Bayern Munich
1970–1	Leeds United	1982–3	Anderlecht	1996–7	Schalke
1971–2	Tottenham Hotspur	1983–4	Tottenham Hotspur	1997–8	Inter Milan

The 1998–9 UEFA finalists were Olympique Marseille and Parma.

ENGLISH FOOTBALL LEAGUE CHAMPIONS (POST WAR)

1946–7	Liverpool	1973–4	Leeds United
1947–8	Arsenal	1974–5	Derby County
1948–9	Portsmouth	1975–6	Liverpool
1949–50	Portsmouth	1976–7	Liverpool
1950–1	Tottenham Hotspur	1977–8	Nottingham Forest
1951–2	Manchester United	1978–9	Liverpool
1952–3	Arsenal	1979–80	Liverpool
1953–4	Wolverhampton Wanderers	1980–1	Aston Villa
1954–5	Chelsea	1981–2	Liverpool
1955–6	Manchester United	1982–3	Liverpool
1956–7	Manchester United	1983–4	Liverpool
1957–8	Wolverhampton Wanderers	1984–5	Everton
1958–9	Wolverhampton Wanderers	1985–6	Liverpool
1959–60	Burnley	1986–7	Everton
1960–1	Tottenham Hotspur	1987–8	Liverpool
1961–2	Ipswich Town	1988–9	Arsenal
1962–3	Everton	1989–90	Liverpool
1963–4	Liverpool	1990–1	Arsenal
1964–5	Manchester United	1991–2	Leeds United
1965–6	Liverpool	1992–3	Manchester United
1966–7	Manchester United	1993–4	Manchester United
1967–8	Manchester City	1994–5	Blackburn Rovers
1968–9	Leeds United	1995–6	Manchester United
1969–70	Everton	1996–7	Manchester United
1970–1	Arsenal	1997–8	Arsenal
1971–2	Derby County		
1972–3	Liverpool		

In 1998–9 the fight for the Premiership title developed into a three way battle between Manchester United, Arsenal and Chelsea. Prior to 1999 Manchester United had won the title 11 times and Arsenal also 11.

Titles won since Football League began in 1888

18	Liverpool	3	Blackburn Rovers, Huddersfield Town,
11	Arsenal, Manchester United		Leeds United, Wolverhampton Wanderers
9	Everton	2	Burnley, Derby County, Manchester City,
7	Aston Villa		Tottenham Hotspur, Portsmouth, Preston North End
6	Sunderland	1	Chelsea, Ipswich Town, Nottingham Forest,
4	Newcastle United, Sheffield Wednesday		Sheffield United, West Bromwich Albion

ENGLISH FOOTBALL ASSOCIATION CUP WINNERS (POST WAR)

1945–6	Derby County	1972–3	Sunderland
1946–7	Charlton Athletic	1973–4	Liverpool
1947–8	Manchester United	1974–5	West Ham United
1948–9	Wolverhampton Wanderers	1975–6	Southampton
1949–50	Arsenal	1976–7	Manchester United
1950–1	Newcastle United	1977–8	Ipswich Town
1951–2	Newcastle United	1978–9	Arsenal
1952–3	Blackpool	1979–80	West Ham United
1953–4	West Bromwich Albion	1980–1	Tottenham Hotspur
1954–5	Newcastle United	1981–2	Tottenham Hotspur
1955–6	Manchester City	1982–3	Manchester United
1956–7	Aston Villa	1983–4	Everton
1957–8	Bolton Wanderers	1984–5	Manchester United
1958–9	Nottingham Forest	1985–6	Liverpool
1959–60	Wolverhampton Wanderers	1986–7	Coventry City
1960–1	Tottenham Hotspur	1987–8	Wimbledon
1961–2	Tottenham Hotspur	1988–9	Liverpool
1962–3	Manchester United	1989–90	Manchester United
1963–4	West Ham United	1990–1	Tottenham Hotspur
1964–5	Liverpool	1991–2	Liverpool
1965–6	Everton	1992–3	Arsenal
1966–7	Tottenham Hotspur	1993–4	Manchester United
1967–8	West Bromwich Albion	1994–5	Everton
1968–9	Manchester City	1995–6	Manchester United
1969–70	Chelsea	1996–7	Chelsea
1970–1	Arsenal	1997–8	Arsenal
1971–2	Leeds United		

The 1999 Cup Final was between Manchester United and Newcastle United. Prior to the final, Manchester United had won the Cup 9 times, Newcastle United 6 times.

Wins since F.A. Cup began in 1872

9 Manchester United
8 Tottenham Hotspur
7 Arsenal, Aston Villa
6 Blackburn Rovers, Newcastle United
5 Everton, Liverpool, The Wanderers, West Bromwich Albion
4 Bolton Wanderers, Manchester City, Sheffield United, Wolverhampton Wanderers
3 Sheffield Wednesday, West Ham United
2 Bury, Chelsea, Nottingham Forest, Old Etonians, Preston North End, Sunderland
1 Barnsley, Blackburn Olympic, Blackpool, Bradford City, Burnley, Cardiff City, Charlton Athletic,
   Clapham Rovers, Coventry City, Derby County, Huddersfield Town, Ipswich Town, Leeds United,
   Notts County, Old Carthusians, Oxford University, Portsmouth, Royal Engineers, Southampton,
   Wimbledon

FOOTBALL LEAGUE & F.A. CUP 'DOUBLE' WINNERS

1888–9	Preston North End	1985–6	Liverpool
1896–7	Aston Villa	1993–4	Manchester United
1960–1	Tottenham Hotspur	1995–6	Manchester United
1970–1	Arsenal	1997–8	Arsenal

ENGLISH FOOTBALL LEAGUE CUP (WORTHINGTON CUP) WINNERS

1960–1	Aston Villa	1980–1	Liverpool
1961–2	Norwich City	1981–2	Liverpool
1962–3	Birmingham City	1982–3	Liverpool
1963–4	Leicester City	1983–4	Liverpool
1964–5	Chelsea	1984–5	Norwich City
1965–6	West Bromwich Albion	1985–6	Oxford United
1966–7	Queen's Park Rangers	1986–7	Arsenal
1967–8	Leeds United	1987–8	Luton Town
1968–9	Swindon Town	1988–9	Nottingham Forest
1969–70	Manchester City	1989–90	Nottingham Forest
1970–1	Tottenham Hotspur	1990–1	Sheffield Wednesday
1971–2	Stoke City	1991–2	Manchester United
1972–3	Tottenham Hotspur	1992–3	Arsenal
1973–4	Wolverhampton Wanderers	1993–4	Aston Villa
1974–5	Aston Villa	1994–5	Liverpool
1975–6	Manchester City	1995–6	Aston Villa
1976–7	Aston Villa	1996–7	Leicester City
1977–8	Nottingham Forest	1997–8	Chelsea
1978–9	Nottingham Forest	1998–9	Tottenham Hotspur
1979–80	Wolverhampton Wanderers		

SCOTTISH FOOTBALL LEAGUE CHAMPIONS (POST WAR)

1946–7	Rangers	1964–5	Kilmarnock	1982–3	Dundee United
1947–8	Hibernian	1965–6	Celtic	1983–4	Aberdeen
1948–9	Rangers	1966–7	Celtic	1984–5	Aberdeen
1949–50	Rangers	1967–8	Celtic	1985–6	Celtic
1950–1	Hibernian	1968–9	Celtic	1986–7	Rangers
1951–2	Hibernian	1969–70	Celtic	1987–8	Celtic
1952–3	Rangers	1970–1	Celtic	1988–9	Rangers
1953–4	Celtic	1971–2	Celtic	1989–90	Rangers
1954–5	Aberdeen	1972–3	Celtic	1990–1	Rangers
1955–6	Rangers	1973–4	Celtic	1991–2	Rangers
1956–7	Rangers	1974–5	Rangers	1992–3	Rangers
1957–8	Hearts	1975–6	Rangers	1993–4	Rangers
1958–9	Rangers	1976–7	Celtic	1994–5	Rangers
1959–60	Hearts	1977–8	Rangers	1995–6	Rangers
1960–1	Rangers	1978–9	Celtic	1996–7	Rangers
1961–2	Dundee	1979–80	Aberdeen	1997–8	Celtic
1962–3	Rangers	1980–1	Celtic	1998–9	Rangers
1963–4	Rangers	1981–2	Celtic		

Titles won since League began in 1890

48 Rangers
36 Celtic
 4 Aberdeen, Hearts, Hibernian

2 Dumbarton
1 Dundee, Dundee United, Kilmarnock,
   Motherwell, Third Lanark

SCOTTISH CUP WINNERS (POST WAR)

1946–7	Aberdeen	1964–5	Celtic	1981–2	Aberdeen
1947–8	Rangers	1965–6	Rangers	1982–3	Aberdeen
1948–9	Rangers	1966–7	Celtic	1983–4	Aberdeen
1949–50	Rangers	1967–8	Dunfermline Athletic	1984–5	Celtic
1950–1	Celtic	1968–9	Celtic	1985–6	Aberdeen
1951–2	Motherwell	1969–70	Aberdeen	1986–7	St Mirren
1952–3	Rangers	1970–1	Celtic	1987–8	Celtic
1953–4	Celtic	1971–2	Celtic	1988–9	Celtic
1954–5	Clyde	1972–3	Rangers	1989–90	Aberdeen
1955–6	Hearts	1973–4	Celtic	1990–1	Motherwell
1956–7	Falkirk	1974–5	Celtic	1991–2	Rangers
1957–8	Clyde	1975–6	Rangers	1992–3	Rangers
1958–9	St Mirren	1976–7	Celtic	1993–4	Dundee United
1959–60	Rangers	1977–8	Rangers	1994–5	Celtic
1960–1	Dunfermline Athletic	1978–9	Rangers	1995–6	Rangers
1961–2	Rangers	1979–80	Celtic	1996–7	Kilmarnock
1962–3	Rangers	1980–1	Rangers	1997–8	Hearts
1963–4	Rangers				

Wins since Scottish Cup began in 1873

30	Celtic	2	Dunfermline Athletic, Falkirk, Hibernian,
27	Rangers		Motherwell, Renton, Third Lanark
10	Queen's Park	1	Airdrieonians, Dumbarton, Dundee, Dundee
7	Aberdeen		United, East Fife, Morton, Partick Thistle, St
6	Hearts		Bernard's
3	Clyde, Kilmarnock, St Mirren, Vale of Leven		

SCOTTISH LEAGUE CUP WINNERS

1946–7	Rangers	1964–5	Rangers	1981–2	Rangers
1947–8	East Fife	1965–6	Celtic	1982–3	Celtic
1948–9	Rangers	1966–7	Celtic	1983–4	Rangers
1949–50	East Fife	1967–8	Celtic	1984–5	Rangers
1950–1	Motherwell	1968–9	Celtic	1985–6	Aberdeen
1951–2	Dundee	1969–70	Celtic	1986–7	Rangers
1952–3	Dundee	1970–1	Rangers	1987–8	Rangers
1953–4	East Fife	1971–2	Partick Thistle	1988–9	Rangers
1954–5	Hearts	1972–3	Hibernian	1989–90	Aberdeen
1955–6	Aberdeen	1973–4	Dundee	1990–1	Rangers
1956–7	Celtic	1974–5	Celtic	1991–2	Hibernian
1957–8	Celtic	1975–6	Rangers	1992–3	Rangers
1958–9	Hearts	1976–7	Aberdeen	1993–4	Rangers
1959–60	Hearts	1977–8	Rangers	1994–5	Raith Rovers
1960–1	Rangers	1978–9	Rangers	1995–6	Aberdeen
1961–2	Rangers	1979–80	Dundee United	1996–7	Rangers
1962–3	Hearts	1980–1	Dundee United	1997–8	Rangers
1963–4	Rangers				

SCOTTISH LEAGUE, SCOTTISH CUP AND LEAGUE CUP "TREBLE" WINNERS

1948–9	Rangers	1968–9	Celtic	1977–8	Rangers
1963–4	Rangers	1975–6	Rangers	1992–3	Rangers
1966–7	Celtic				

ATHLETICS

OLYMPIC CHAMPIONS (POST WAR)

Men's 100m
1948	Harrison Dillard (USA)
1952	Lindy Remigino (USA)
1956	Bobby Morrow (USA)
1960	Armin Hary (FRG)
1964	Robert Hayes (USA)
1968	James Hines (USA)
1972	Valeriy Borzov (USSR)
1976	Hasely Crawford (Tri)
1980	Allan Wells (UK)
1984	Carl Lewis (USA)
1988	Carl Lewis (USA)
1992	Linford Christie (UK)
1996	Donovan Bailey (Can)

Men's 200m
1948	Melvin Patton (USA)
1952	Andrew Stanfield (USA)
1956	Bobby Morrow (USA)
1960	Livio Berruti (Ita)
1964	Henry Carr (USA)
1968	Tommie Smith (USA)
1972	Valeriy Borzov (USSR)
1976	Donald Quarrie (Jam)
1980	Pietro Mennea (Ita)
1984	Carl Lewis (USA)
1988	Joe DeLoach (USA)
1992	Michael Marsh (USA)
1996	Michael Johnson (USA)

Men's 400m
1948	Arthur Wint (Jam)
1952	George Rhoden (Jam)
1956	Charles Jenkins (USA)
1960	Otis Davis (USA)
1964	Michael Larrabee (USA)
1968	Lee Evans (USA
1972	Vincent Matthews (USA)
1976	Alberto Juantorena (Cub)
1980	Viktor Markin (USSR)
1984	Alonzo Babers (USA)
1988	Steve Lewis (USA)
1992	Quincy Watts (USA)
1996	Michael Johnson (USA)

Men's 800m
1948	Malvin Whitfield (USA)
1952	Malvin Whitfield (USA)
1956	Thomas Courtney (USA)
1960	Peter Snell (NZ)
1964	Peter Snell (NZ)
1968	Ralph Doubell (Aus)
1972	David Wottle (USA)
1976	Alberto Juantorena (Cub)
1980	Steve Ovett (UK)
1984	Joaquim Cruz (Bra)
1988	Paul Ereng (Ken)
1992	William Tanui (Ken)
1996	Vebjorn Rodal (Nor)

Men's 1500m
1948	Henry Eriksson (Swe)
1952	Josef Barthel (Lux)
1956	Ron Delany (Ire)
1960	Herbert Elliott (Aus)
1964	Peter Snell (NZ)
1968	Kipchoge Keino (Ken)
1972	Pekka Vasala (Fin)
1976	John Walker (NZ)
1980	Sebastian Coe (UK)
1984	Sebastian Coe (UK)
1988	Peter Rono (Ken)
1992	Fermin Cacho (Spa)
1996	Noureddine Morceli (Alg)

Men's 5000m
1948	Gaston Reiff (Bel)
1952	Emil Zatopek (Cze)
1956	Vladimir Kuts (USSR)
1960	Murray Halberg (NZ)
1964	Robert Schul (USA)
1968	Mohamed Gammoudi (Tun)
1972	Lasse Viren (Fin)
1976	Lasse Viren (Fin)
1980	Miruts Yifter (Eth)
1984	Saïd Aouita (Mor)
1988	John Ngugi (Ken)
1992	Dieter Baumann (Ger)
1996	Venuste Nyongabo (Bur)

Men's 10,000m
1948	Emil Zátopek (Cze)
1952	Emil Zátopek (Cze)
1956	Vladimir Kuts (USSR)
1960	Pyotr Bolontikov (USSR)
1964	William Mills (USA)
1968	Naftali Temu (Ken)
1972	Lasse Viren (Fin)
1976	Lasse Viren (Fin)
1980	Miruts Yifter (Eth)
1984	Alberto Cova (Ita)
1988	Brahim Boutayeb (Mor)

1992   Khalid Skah (Mor)
1996   Haile Gebrsilassie (Eth)

Men's Marathon
1948   Delfo Cabrera (Arg)
1952   Emil Zátopek (Cze)
1956   Alain Mimoun (Fra)
1960   Abebe Bikila (Eth)
1980   Steve Ovett (UK)
1964   Abebe Bikila (Eth)
1968   Mamo Wolde (Eth)
1972   Frank Shorter (USA)
1976   Waldemar Cierpinski (GDR)
1980   Waldemar Cierpinski (GDR)
1984   Carlos Lopes (Por)
1988   Gelindo Bordin (Ita)
1992   Hwang Young-jo (SKo)
1996   Josiah Thugwane (SA)

Men's Steeplechase
1948   Tore Sjöstrand (Swe)
1952   Horace Ashenfelter (USA)
1956   Christopher Brasher (UK)
1960   Zdzislaw Kryszkowiak (Pol)
1964   Gaston Roelants (Bel)
1968   Amos Biwott (Ken)
1972   Kipchoge Keino (Ken)
1976   Anders Gärderud (Swe)
1980   Bronislaw Malinowski (Pol)
1984   Julius Korir (Ken)
1988   Julius Kariuki (Ken)
1992   Matthew Birir (Ken)
1996   Joseph Keter (Ken)

Men's 110m Hurdles
1948   William Porter (USA)
1952   Harrison Dillard (USA)
1956   Lee Calhoun (USA)
1960   Lee Calhoun (USA)
1964   Hayes Jones (USA)
1968   Willie Davenport (USA)
1972   Rodney Milburn (USA)
1976   Guy Drut (Fra)
1980   Thomas Munkelt (GDR)
1984   Roger Kingdom (USA)
1988   Roger Kingdom (USA)
1992   Mark McKoy (Can)
1996   Allen Johnson (USA)

Men's 400m Hurdles
1948   Roy Cochran (USA)
1952   Charles Moore (USA)
1956   Glenn Davis (USA)
1960   Glenn Davis (USA)
1964   Rex Cawley (USA)
1968   David Hemery (UK)
1972   John Akii-Bua (Uga)
1976   Edwin Moses (USA)
1980   Volker Beck (GDR)
1984   Edwin Moses (USA)
1988   Andre Phillips (USA)
1992   Kevin Young (USA)
1996   Derrick Adkins (USA)

Men's High Jump
1948   John Winter (Aus)
1952   Walter Davis (USA)
1956   Charles Dumas (USA)
1960   Robert Shavlakadze (USSR)
1964   Valeriy Brumel (USSR)
1968   Dick Fosbury (USA)
1972   Jüri Tarmak (USSR)
1976   Jacek Wszola (Pol)
1980   Gerd Wessig (GDR)
1984   Dietmar Mögenburg (FRG)
1988   Gennadiy Avdeyenko (USSR)
1992   Javier Sotomayor (Cub)
1996   Charles Austin (USA)

Men's Pole Vault
1948   Guinn Smith (USA)
1952   Robert Richards (USA)
1956   Robert Richards (USA)
1960   Donald Bragg (USA)
1964   Frederick Hansen (USA)
1968   Bob Seagren (USA)
1972   Wolfgang Nordwig (GDR)
1976   Tadeusz Slusarski (Pol)
1980   Wladyslaw Kozakiewicz (Pol)
1984   Pierre Quinon (Fra)
1988   Sergey Bubka (USSR)
1992   Maksim Tarasov (CIS/Rus)
1996   Jean Galfione (Fra)

Men's Triple Jump
1948   Arne Ahman (Swe)
1952   Adhemar Ferreira da Silva (Bra)
1956   Adhemar Ferreira da Silva (Bra)
1960   Jozef Schmidt (Pol)
1964   Jozef Schmidt (Pol)
1968   Viktor Saneyev (USSR)
1972   Viktor Saneyev (USSR)
1976   Viktor Saneyev (USSR)
1980   Jaak Uudmäe (USSR)
1984   Al Joyner (USA)
1988   Khristo Markov (Bul)
1992   Mike Conley (USA)
1996   Kenny Harrison (USA)

Men's Long Jump
1948   William Steele (USA)
1952   Jerome Biffle (USA)
1956   Gregory Bell (USA)
1960   Ralph Boston (USA)
1964   Lynn Davies (UK)
1968   Bob Beamon (USA)
1972   Randy Williams (USA)
1976   Arnie Robinson (USA)
1980   Lutz Dombrowski (GDR)
1984   Carl Lewis (USA)
1988   Carl Lewis (USA)
1992   Carl Lewis (USA)
1996   Carl Lewis (USA)

Men's Shot
1948   Wilbur Thompson (USA)
1952   Parry O'Brien (USA)
1956   Parry O'Brien (USA)
1960   William Nieder (USA)
1964   Dallas Long (USA)
1968   Randy Matson (USA)
1972   Wladyslaw Komar (Pol)
1976   Udo Beyer (GDR)
1980   Vladimir Kiselyov (USSR)
1984   Alessandro Andrei (Ita)
1988   Ulf Timmermann (GDR)
1992   Mike Stulce (USA)
1996   Randy Barnes (USA)

Men's Discus
1948   Adolfo Consolini (Ita)
1952   Sim Iness (USA)
1956   Al Oerter (USA)
1960   Al Oerter (USA)
1964   Al Oerter (USA)
1968   Al Oerter (USA)
1972   Ludvik Danek (Cze)
1976   Mac Wilkins (USA)
1980   Viktor Rashchupkin (USSR)
1984   Rolf Danneberg (FRG)
1988   Jürgen Schult (GDR)
1992   Romas Ubartas (Lit)
1996   Lars Riedel (Ger)

Men's Javelin
1948   Tapio Rautavaara (Fin)
1952   Cyrus Young (USA)
1956   Egil Danielsen (Nor)
1960   Viktor Tsibulenko (USSR)
1964   Pauli Nevala (Fin)
1968   Janis Lusis (USSR)
1972   Klaus Wolfermann (FRG)
1976   Miklós Németh (Hun)
1980   Dainis Kula (USSR)
1984   Arto Harkönen (Fin)
1988   Tapio Korjus (Fin)
1992   Jan Zelezny (Cze)
1996   Jan Zelezny (Cze. Rep)

Men's Hammer
1948   Imre Németh (Hun)
1952   József Csermak (Hun)
1956   Harold Connolly (USA)
1960   Vasiliy Rudenkov (USSR)
1964   Romuald Klim (USSR)
1968   Gyula Zsivótzky (Hun)
1972   Anatoliy Bondarchuk (USSR)
1976   Yuriy Sedykh (USSR)
1980   Yuriy Sedykh (USSR)
1984   Juha Tiainen (Fin)
1988   Sergey Litvinov (USSR)
1992   Andrey Abduvaliyev (CIS/Tjk)
1996   Balazs Kiss (Hun)

Men's Decathlon
1948   Robert Mathias (USA)
1952   Robert Mathias (USA)

1956 Milton Campbell (USA)
1960 Rafer Johnson (USA)
1964 Willi Holdorf (FRG)
1968 Bill Toomey (USA)
1972 Nikolay Avilov (USSR)
1976 Bruce Jenner (USA)
1980 Daley Thompson (UK)
1984 Daley Thompson (UK)
1988 Christian Schenk (GDR)
1992 Robert Zmelik (Cze)
1996 Dan O'Brien (USA)

Men's 20km Walk
1956 Leonid Spirin (USSR)
1960 Vladimir Golubnichiy (USSR)
1964 Kenneth Matthews (UK)
1968 Vladimir Golubnichiy (USSR)
1972 Peter Frenkel (GDR)
1976 Daniel Bautista (Mex)
1980 Maurizio Damilano (Ita)
1984 Ernesto Canto (Mex)
1988 Jozef Pribilinec (Cze)
1992 Daniel Plaza (Spa)
1996 Jefferson Perez (Ecu)

Men's 50km Walk
1948 John Ljunggren (Swe)
1952 Giuseppe Dordoni (Ita)
1956 Norman Read (NZ)
1960 Don Thompson (UK)
1964 Abdon Pamich (Ita)
1968 Christophe Höhne (GDR)
1972 Bernd Kannenberg (GDR)
1980 Hartwig Gauder (GDR)
1984 Raúl Gonzales (Mex)
1988 Vyacheslav Ivanenko (USSR)
1992 Andrey Perlov (CIS/Rus)
1996 Robert Korzeniowski (Pol)

Men's 4 × 100m Relay
1948 USA
1952 USA
1956 USA
1960 West Germany
1964 USA
1968 USA
1972 USA
1976 USA
1980 USSR
1984 USA
1988 USSR
1992 USA
1996 Canada

Men's 4 × 400m Relay
1948 USA
1952 Jamaica
1956 USA
1960 USA
1964 USA
1968 USA
1972 Kenya
1976 USA
1980 USSR
1984 USA
1988 USA
1992 USA
1996 USA

Women's 100m
1948 Fanny Blankers-Koen (Hol)
1952 Marjorie Jackson (Aus)
1956 Betty Cuthbert (Aus)
1960 Wilma Rudolph (USA)
1964 Wyomia Tyus (USA)
1968 Wyomia Tyus (USA)
1972 Renate Stecher (GDR)
1976 Annegret Richter (FRG)
1980 Lyudmila Kondratyeva (USSR)
1984 Evelyn Ashford (USA)
1988 Florence Griffith-Joyner (USA)
1992 Gail Devers (USA)
1996 Gail Devers (USA)

Women's 200m
1948 Fanny Blankers-Koen (Hol)
1952 Marjorie Jackson (Aus)
1956 Betty Cuthbert (Aus)
1960 Wilma Rudolph (USA)
1964 Edith Maguire (USA)
1968 Irena Szewinska (Pol)
1972 Renate Stecher (GDR)
1976 Bärbel Eckert (GDR)

1980 Bärbel Wöckel (née Eckert) (GDR)
1984 Valerie Brisco-Hooks (USA)
1988 Florence Griffith-Joyner (USA)
1992 Gwen Torrance (USA)
1996 Marie-Jose Perec (Fra)

Women's 400m
1964 Betty Cuthbert (Aus)
1968 Colette Besson (Fra)
1972 Monika Zehrt (GDR)
1976 Irena Szewinska (Pol)
1980 Marita Koch (GDR)
1984 Valerie Brisco-Hooks (USA)
1988 Olga Bryzgina (USSR)
1992 Marie-José Pérec (Fra)
1996 Marie-Jose Pérec (Fra)

Women's 800m
1960 Lyudmila Shevtsova (USSR)
1964 Ann Packer (UK)
1968 Madeline Manning (USA)
1972 Hildegard Falck (FRG)
1976 Tatyana Kazankina (USSR)
1980 Nadezhda Olizarenko (USSR)
1984 Doina Melinte (Rom)
1988 Sigrun Wodars (GDR)
1992 Ellen van Langren (Hol)
1996 Svetlana Masterkova (Rus)

Women's 1500m
1972 Lyudmila Bragina (USSR)
1976 Tatyana Kazankina (USSR)
1980 Tatyana Kazankina (USSR)
1984 Gabriella Doria (Ita)
1988 Paula Ivan (Rom)
1992 Hassiba Boulmerka (Alg)
1996 Svetlana Masterkova (Rus)

Women's 3000m
1984 Maricica Puica (Rom)
1988 Tatyana Samolenko (USSR)
1992 Yelena Romanova (CIS/Rus)
1996 Wang Junxia (Chn)

Women's 10,000m
1988 Olga Bondarenko (USSR)
1992 Derartu Tulu (Eth)
1996 Fernanda Ribeiro (Por)

Women's Marathon
1984 Joan Benoit (USA)
1988 Rosa Mota (Por)
1992 Valentina Yegorova (CIS/Rus)
1996 Fatuma Roba (Eth)

Women's 80m Hurdles
1948 Fanny Blankers-Koen (Hol)
1952 Shirley Strickland (Aus)
1956 Shirley Strickland (Aus)
1960 Irina Press (USSR)
1964 Karin Balzer (GDR)
1968 Maureen Caird (Aus)

Women's 100m Hurdles
1972 Annelie Ehrhardt (GDR)
1976 Johanna Schaller (GDR)
1980 Vera Komisova (USSR)
1984 Benita Fitzgerald-Brown (USA)
1988 Yordanka Donkova (Bul)
1992 Paraskevi Patoulidou (Gre)
1996 Lyudmila Engquist (Swe)

Women's 400m Hurdles
1984 Newal El Moutawakil (Mor)
1988 Debbie Flintoff-King (Aus)
1992 Sally Gunnell (UK)
1996 Deon Hemmings (Jam)

Women's High Jump
1948 Alice Coachman (USA)
1952 Esther Brand (SAf)
1956 Mildred McDaniel (USA)
1960 Iolanda Balas (Rom)
1964 Iolanda Balas (Rom)
1968 Miloslava Rezková (Cze)
1972 Ulrike Meyfarth (FRG)
1976 Rosemarie Ackermann (GDR)
1980 Sara Simeoni (Ita)
1984 Ulrike Meyfarth (FRG)
1988 Louise Ritter (USA)
1992 Heike Henkel (Ger)
1996 Stefka Kostadinova (Bul)

Women's Long Jump

1948	Olga Gyarmati (Hun)
1952	Yvette Williams (NZ)
1956	Elzbieta Krzesinska (Pol)
1960	Vyera Krepkina (USSR)
1964	Mary Rand (UK)
1968	Viorica Viscopoleanu (Rom)
1972	Heide Rosendahl (FRG)
1976	Angela Voigt (GDR)
1980	Tatyana Kolpakova (USSR)
1984	Anisoara Stanciu (Rom)
1988	Jackie Joyner-Kersee (USA)
1992	Heike Drechsler (Ger)
1996	Chioma Ajunwa (Nig)

Women's Shot

1948	Micheline Ostermeyer (Fra)
1952	Galina Zybina (USSR)
1956	Tamara Tishkyevich (USSR)
1960	Tamara Press (USSR)
1964	Tamara Press (USSR)
1968	Margitta Gummel (GDR)
1972	Nadezhda Chizhova (USSR)
1976	Ivanka Khristova (Bul)
1980	Ilona Slupianek (GDR)
1984	Claudia Losch (FRG)
1988	Natalya Lisovskaya (USSR)
1992	Svetlana Krivelyova (CIS/Rus)
1996	Astrid Kumbernuss (Ger)

Women's Discus

1948	Micheline Ostermeyer (Fra)
1952	Nina Ponomaryeva (USSR)
1956	Olga Fikotová (Cze)
1960	Nina Ponomaryeva (USSR)
1964	Tamara Press (USSR)
1968	Lia Manoliu (Rom)
1972	Faina Melnik (USSR)
1976	Evelin Schlaak (GDR)
1980	Evelin Jahl (née Schlaak) (GDR)
1984	Ria Stalmach (Hol)
1988	Martina Hellmann (GDR)
1992	Maritza Marten (Cub)
1996	Ilke Wyludda (Ger)

Women's Javelin

1948	Herma Bauma (Aut)
1952	Dana Zátopková (Cze)
1956	Inese Jaunzeme (USSR)
1960	Elvira Ozolina (USSR)
1964	Mihaela Penes (Rom)
1968	Angéla Németh (Hun)
1972	Ruth Fuchs (GDR)
1976	Ruth Fuchs (GDR)
1980	Maria C. Colón (Cub)
1984	Tessa Sanderson (UK)
1988	Petra Felke (GDR)
1992	Silke Renk (Ger)
1996	Heli Rantanen (Nor)

Women's Heptathlon

1984	Glynis Nunn (Aus)
1988	Jackie Joyner-Kersee (USA)
1992	Jackie Joyner-Kersee (USA)
1996	Ghada Shouaa (Syr)

Women's 10km Walk

1992	Chen Yueling (Chn)
1996	Yelena Nikolayeva (Rus)

Women's 4 × 100m Relay

1948	Holland
1952	USA
1956	Australia
1960	USA
1964	Poland
1968	USA
1972	West Germany
1976	East Germany
1980	East Germany
1984	USA
1988	USA
1992	USA
1996	USA

Women's 4 × 400m Relay

1972	East Germany
1976	East Germany
1980	USSR
1984	USA
1988	USSR
1992	CIS (united team)
1996	USA

Women's Triple Jump

1996	Inessa Kravets (Ukr)

BADMINTON

WORLD CHAMPIONS

	MEN	WOMEN
1977	Flemming Delfs (Denmark)	Lene Koppen (Denmark)
1980	Rudy Hartono (Indonesia)	Wiharjo Verawaty (Indonesia)
1983	Icuk Sugiarto (Indonesia)	Li Lingwei (China)
1985	Han Jian (China)	Han Aiping (China)
1987	Yang Yang (China)	Han Aiping (China)
1989	Yang Yang (China)	Li Lingwei (China)
1991	Zhao Jianhua (China)	Tang Jiuhong (China)
1993	Joko Suprianto (Indonesia)	Susi Susanti (Indonesia)
1995	Heryanto Arbi (Indonesia)	Ye Zhaoying (China)
1997	Peter Rasmussen (Denmark)	Ye Zhaoying (China)

ALL-ENGLAND CHAMPIONS (POST WAR)

	MEN	WOMEN
1947	Conny Jepsen (Sweden)	Marrie Ussing (Denmark)
1948	Jorn Skaarup (Denmark)	Kirsten Thorndahl (Denmark)
1949	Dave Freeman (USA)	Aase Jacobsen (Denmark)
1950	Wong Peng Soon (Malaya)	Tonny Olsen-Ahm (Denmark)
1951	Wong Peng Soon (Malaya)	Aase Jacobsen (Denmark)
1952	Wong Peng Soon (Malaya)	Tonny Olsen-Ahm (Denmark)
1953	Eddie Choong (Malaya)	Marie Ussing (Denmark)
1954	Eddie Choong (Malaya)	Judy Devlin (USA)
1955	Wong Peng Soon (Malaya)	Margaret Varner (USA)
1956	Eddie Choong (Malaya)	Margaret Varner (USA)
1957	Eddie Choong (Malaya)	Judy Devlin (USA)
1958	Erland Kops (Denmark)	Judy Devlin (USA)
1959	Tan Joe Hok (Indonesia)	Heather Ward (England)
1960	Erland Kops (Denmark)	Judy Devlin (USA)
1961	Erland Kops (Denmark)	Judy Hashman (née Devlin) (USA)
1962	Erland Kops (Denmark)	Judy Hashman (USA)
1963	Erland Kops (Denmark)	Judy Hashman (USA)
1964	Knud Nielsen (Denmark)	Judy Hashman (USA)
1965	Erland Kops (Denmark)	Ursula Smith (England)
1966	Tan Aik Huang (Malaya)	Judy Hashman (USA)
1967	Erland Kops (Denmark)	Judy Hashman (USA)
1968	Rudy Hartono (Indonesia)	Eva Twedberg (Sweden)
1969	Rudy Hartono (Indonesia)	Hiroe Yuki (Japan)
1970	Rudy Hartono (Indonesia)	Etsuko Takenaka (Japan)

1971	Rudy Hartono (Indonesia)	Eva Twedberg (Sweden)
1972	Rudy Hartono (Indonesia)	Noriko Nakayama (Japan)
1973	Rudy Hartono (Indonesia)	Margaret Beck (England)
1974	Rudy Hartono (Indonesia)	Hiroe Yuki (Japan)
1975	Sven Pri (Denmark)	Hiroe Yuki (Japan)
1976	Rudy Hartono (Indonesia)	Gillian Gilks (England)
1977	Flemming Delfs (Denmark)	Hiroe Yuki (Japan)
1978	Liem Swie King (Indonesia)	Gillian Gilks (England)
1979	Liem Swie King (Indonesia)	Lene Koppen (Denmark)
1980	Prakash Padukone (India)	Lene Koppen (Denmark)
1981	Liem Swie King (Indonesia)	Sun Ai Hwang (South Korea)
1982	Morten Frost (Denmark)	Zang Ailing (China)
1983	Luan Jin (China)	Zang Ailing (China)
1984	Morten Frost (Denmark)	Li Lingwei (China)
1985	Zhao Jianhua (China)	Han Aiping (China)
1986	Morten Frost (Denmark)	Kim Yun-Ja (South Korea)
1987	Morten Frost (Denmark)	Kirsten Larsen (Denmark)
1988	Ib Frederiksen (Denmark)	Gu Jiaming (China)
1989	Yang Yang (China)	Li Lingwei (China)
1990	Zhao Jianhua (China)	Susi Susanti (Indonesia)
1991	Ardy Wiranta (Indonesia)	Susi Susanti (Indonesia)
1992	Liu Jun (China)	Tang Jiuhong (China)
1993	Heryanto Arbi (Indonesia)	Susi Susanti (Indonesia)
1994	Heryanto Arbi (Indonesia)	Susi Susanti (Indonesia)
1995	Poul-Erik Hoyer Larsen (Denmark)	Lim Xiaoqing (Sweden)
1996	Poul-Erik Hoyer Larsen (Denmark)	Bang Soo-Hyun (South Korea)
1997	Dong Jiong (China)	Ye Zhaoying (China)
1998	Sun Jun (China)	Ye Zhaoying (China)

BASEBALL

WORLD SERIES WINNERS (POST WAR)

1946	St Louis Cardinals	1964	St Louis Cardinals	1982	St Louis Cardinals
1947	New York Yankees	1965	Los Angeles Dodgers	1983	Baltimore Orioles
1948	Cleveland Indians	1966	Baltimore Orioles	1984	Detroit Tigers
1949	New York Yankees	1967	St Louis Cardinals	1985	Kansas City Royals
1950	New York Yankees	1968	Detroit Tigers	1986	New York Mets
1951	New York Yankees	1969	New York Mets	1987	Minnesota Twins
1952	New York Yankees	1970	Baltimore Orioles	1988	Los Angeles Dodgers
1953	New York Yankees	1971	Pittsburgh Pirates	1989	Oakland Athletics
1954	New York Yankees	1972	Oakland Athletics	1990	Cincinnati Reds
1955	Brooklyn Dodgers	1973	Oakland Athletics	1991	Minnesota Twins
1956	New York Yankees	1974	Oakland Athletics	1992	Toronto Blue Jays
1957	Milwaukee Braves	1975	Cincinnati Reds	1993	Toronto Blue Jays
1958	New York Yankees	1976	Cincinnati Reds	1994	No Competition
1959	Los Angeles Dodgers	1977	New York Yankees	1995	Atlanta Braves
1960	Pittsburgh Pirates	1978	New York Yankees	1996	New York Yankees
1961	New York Yankees	1979	Pittsburgh Pirates	1997	Florida Marlins
1962	New York Yankees	1980	Philadelphia Phillies	1998	New York Yankees
1963	Los Angeles Dodgers	1981	Los Angeles Dodgers		

Wins since World Series began in 1903

24	New York Yankees
9	St Louis Cardinals
5	Boston Red Sox, Cincinnati Reds, Los Angeles Dodgers, New York Giants, Philadelphia Athletics, Pittsburgh Pirates
4	Detroit Tigers, Oakland Athletics
3	Baltimore Orioles
2	Atlanta Braves, Chicago Cubs, Chicago White Sox, Cleveland Indians, Minnesota Twins, New York Mets, Toronto Blue Jays
1	Brooklyn Dodgers, Florida Marlins, Kansas City Royals, Milwaukee Braves, Philadelphia Phillies, Washington Senators

BASKETBALL

WORLD CHAMPIONS

MEN

1950	Argentina	1978	Yugoslavia
1954	USA	1982	USSR
1959	Brazil	1986	USA
1963	Brazil	1990	Yugoslavia
1967	USSR	1994	USA
1970	Yugoslavia	1998	Yugoslavia
1974	USSR		

WOMEN

1953	USA	1979	USA
1957	USA	1983	USSR
1959	USSR	1987	USA
1964	USSR	1990	USA
1967	USSR	1994	Brazil
1971	USSR	1998	USA
1975	USSR		

NBA Champions (since 1980)

1980	Los Angeles Lakers	1987	Los Angeles Lakers	1993	Chicago Bulls
1981	Boston Celtics	1988	Los Angeles Lakers	1994	Houston Rockets
1982	Los Angeles Lakers	1989	Detroit Pistons	1995	Houston Rockets
1983	Philadelphia 76ers	1990	Detroit Pistons	1996	Chicago Bulls
1984	Boston Celtics	1991	Chicago Bulls	1997	Chicago Bulls
1985	Los Angeles Lakers	1992	Chicago Bulls	1998	Chicago Bulls
1986	Boston Celtics				

BOWLS

WORLD INDOOR CHAMPIONS

1980 David Bryant (Eng)	1990 John Price (Wal)
1981 David Bryant (Eng)	1991 Richard Corsie (Scot)
1982 John Watson (Scot)	1992 Ian Schuback (Aus)
1983 Bob Sutherland (Scot)	1993 Richard Corsie (Scot)
1984 Jim Baker (Ire)	1994 Richard Corsie (Scot)
1985 Terry Sullivan (Wal)	1995 Andy Thomson (Eng)
1986 Tony Allcock (Eng)	1996 David Gournlay Jnr (Scot)
1987 Tony Allcock (Eng)	1997 Hugh Duff (Scot)
1988 Hugh Duff (Scot)	1998 Paul Foster (Scot)
1989 Richard Corsie (Scot)	1999 Alex Marshall (Scot)

WORLD OUTDOOR CHAMPIONS

Men's Singles

1966 David Bryant (Eng)	1984 Peter Belliss (NZ)
1972 Malwyn Evans (Wal)	1988 David Bryant (Eng)
1976 Doug Watson (SAf)	1992 Tony Allcock (Eng)
1980 David Bryant (Eng)	1996 Tony Allcock (Eng)

Women's Singles

1969 Gladys Doyle (PNG)	1985 Merle Richardson (Aus)
1973 Elsie Wilkie (NZ)	1988 Janet Ackland (Wal)
1977 Elsie Wilkie (NZ)	1992 Margaret Johnston (Ire)
1981 Norma Shaw (Eng)	1996 Carmelita Anderson (NZ)

CRICKET

TEST MATCHES

England Test Record, 1993–April 1999

		W	L	D			W	L	D
1993–94	Away v W Indies	1	3	1	1996–97	Away v Zimbabwe	0	0	2
1994	Home v NZ	1	0	2	1996–97	Away v NZ	2	0	1
1994	Home v S Africa	1	1	1	1997	Home v Australia	2	3	1
1994–95	Away v Australia	1	3	1	1997–98	Away v W Indies	1	3	1*
1995	Home v W Indies	2	2	2	1998	Home v S Africa	2	1	2
1995–96	Away v S Africa	0	1	4	1998–99	Away v Australia	1	3	1
1996	Home v India	1	0	2					
1996	Home v Pakistan	0	2	1	*with a further Test abandoned				

WORLD CUP*

1975 West Indies	1987 Australia
1979 West Indies	1992 Pakistan
1983 India	1996 Sri Lanka

England were hosts to the 1999 World Cup

COUNTY CHAMPIONSHIP (POST WAR)

1946 Yorkshire	1963 Yorkshire	1981 Nottinghamshire
1947 Middlesex	1964 Worcestershire	1982 Middlesex
1948 Glamorgan	1965 Worcestershire	1983 Essex
1949 Middlesex	1966 Yorkshire	1984 Essex
Yorkshire	1967 Yorkshire	1985 Middlesex
1950 Lancashire	1968 Yorkshire	1986 Essex
Surrey	1969 Glamorgan	1987 Nottinghamshire
1951 Warwickshire	1970 Kent	1988 Worcestershire
1952 Surrey	1971 Surrey	1989 Worcestershire
1953 Surrey	1972 Warwickshire	1990 Middlesex
1954 Surrey	1973 Hampshire	1991 Essex
1955 Surrey	1974 Worcestershire	1992 Essex
1956 Surrey	1975 Leicestershire	1993 Middlesex
1957 Surrey	1976 Middlesex	1994 Warwickshire
1958 Surrey	1977 Kent	1995 Warwickshire
1959 Yorkshire	Middlesex	1996 Leicestershire
1960 Yorkshire	1978 Kent	1997 Glamorgan
1961 Hampshire	1979 Essex	1998 Leicestershire
1962 Yorkshire	1980 Middlesex	

Wins and shared wins since Championship began in 1864

33	Yorkshire	6	Essex
20	Surrey	5	Warwickshire, Worcestershire
19	Nottinghamshire	4	Gloucestershire
13	Middlesex	3	Glamorgan, Leicestershire
12	Lancashire	2	Hampshire
7	Kent	1	Derbyshire

NATWEST BANK TROPHY WINNERS

1963	Sussex	1975	Lancashire	1987	Nottinghamshire
1964	Sussex	1976	Northamptonshire	1988	Middlesex
1965	Yorkshire	1977	Middlesex	1989	Warwickshire
1966	Warwickshire	1978	Sussex	1990	Lancashire
1967	Kent	1979	Somerset	1991	Hampshire
1968	Warwickshire	1980	Middlesex	1992	Northamptonshire
1969	Yorkshire	1981	Derbyshire	1993	Warwickshire
1970	Lancashire	1982	Surrey	1994	Worcestershire
1971	Lancashire	1983	Somerset	1995	Warwickshire
1972	Lancashire	1984	Middlesex	1996	Lancashire
1973	Gloucestershire	1985	Essex	1997	Essex
1974	Kent	1986	Sussex	1998	Lancashire

SUNDAY LEAGUE WINNERS

1969	Lancashire	1979	Somerset	1989	Lancashire
1970	Lancashire	1980	Warwickshire	1990	Lancashire
1971	Worcestershire	1981	Essex	1991	Nottinghamshire
1972	Kent	1982	Sussex	1992	Middlesex
1973	Kent	1983	Yorkshire	1993	Glamorgan
1974	Leicestershire	1984	Essex	1994	Warwickshire
1975	Hampshire	1985	Essex	1995	Kent
1976	Kent	1986	Hampshire	1996	Surrey
1977	Leicestershire	1987	Worcestershire	1997	Warwickshire
1978	Hampshire	1988	Worcestershire	1998	Lancashire

BENSON & HEDGES CUP WINNERS

1972	Leicestershire	1981	Somerset	1990	Lancashire
1973	Kent	1982	Somerset	1991	Worcestershire
1974	Surrey	1983	Middlesex	1992	Hampshire
1975	Leicestershire	1984	Lancashire	1993	Derbyshire
1976	Kent	1985	Leicestershire	1994	Warwickshire
1977	Gloucestershire	1986	Middlesex	1995	Lancashire
1978	Kent	1987	Yorkshire	1996	Lancashire
1979	Essex	1988	Hampshire	1997	Surrey
1980	Northamptonshire	1989	Nottinghamshire	1998	Essex

CYCLING

TOUR DE FRANCE

1982	Bernard Hinault (Fra)	1991	Miguel Indurain (Spa)
1983	Laurent Fignon (Fra)	1992	Miguel Indurain (Spa)
1984	Laurent Fignon (Fra)	1993	Miguel Indurain (Spa)
1985	Bernard Hinault (Fra)	1994	Miguel Indurain (Spa)
1986	Greg Lemond (USA)	1995	Miguel Indurain (Spa)
1987	Stephen Roche (Ire)	1996	Bjarne Riis (Den)
1988	Pedro Delgado (Spa)	1997	Jan Ullrich (Ger)
1989	Greg Lemond (USA)	1998	Marco Pantani (Ita)*
1990	Greg Lemond (USA)		

*In the much-troubled race in 1998 Marco Pantani became the first Italian to win for 33 years.

WORLD ROAD RACE CHAMPIONS

1980	Bernard Hinault (Fra)	1990	Rudy Dhaenens (Bel)
1981	Freddie Maertans (Bel)	1991	Gianni Bugno (Ita)
1982	Giuseppe Saroni (Ita)	1992	Gianni Bugno (Ita)
1983	Greg Lemond (USA)	1993	Lance Armstrong (USA)
1984	Claude Criquielon (Bel)	1994	Luc Leblanc (Fra)
1985	Joop Zoetemelk (Hol)	1995	Abraham Olano (Spa)
1986	Moreno Argentin (Ita)	1996	Johan Museeuw (Bel)
1987	Stephen Roche (Ire)	1997	Laurent Brochard (Fra)
1988	Mauizio Fondriest (Ita)	1998	Oskar Camenzind (Swi)
1989	Greg Lemond (USA)		

GOLF

MAJOR TOURNAMENT WINNERS (POST WAR)

	UK Open	US Open	US Masters	PGA
1946	S Snead (USA)	L Mangrum (USA)	H Keiser (USA)	B Hogan (USA)
1947	F Daly (GBR)	L Worsham (USA)	J Demaret (USA)	J Ferrier (USA)
1948	H Cotton (GBR)	B Hogan (USA)	C Harmon (USA)	B Hogan (USA)
1949	B Locke (SAf)	C Middlecoff (USA)	S Snead (USA)	S Snead (USA)
1950	B Locke (SAf)	B Hogan (USA)	J Demaret (USA)	C Harper (USA)
1951	M Faulkner (GBR)	B Hogan (USA)	B Hogan (USA)	S Snead (USA)
1952	B Locke (SAf)	J Boros (USA)	S Snead (USA)	J Turnesa (USA)
1953	B Hogan (USA)	B Hogan (USA)	B Hogan (USA)	W Burkemo (USA)
1954	P Thomson (Aus)	E Furgol (USA)	S Snead (USA)	C Harbert (USA)
1955	P Thomson (Aus)	J Fleck (USA)	C Middlecoff (USA)	D Ford (USA)
1956	P Thomson (Aus)	C Middlecoff (USA)	J Burke (USA)	J Burke (USA)
1957	B Locke (SAf)	D Mayer (USA)	D Ford (USA)	L Herbert (USA)
1958	P Thomson (Aus)	T Bolt (USA)	A Palmer (USA)	D Finsterwald (USA)
1959	G Player (SAf)	B Caspar (USA)	A Wall (USA)	B Roseburg (USA)
1960	K Nagle (Aus)	A Palmer (USA)	A Palmer (USA)	J Hebert (USA)
1961	A Palmer (USA)	G Littler (USA)	G Player (SAf)	J Barber (USA)
1962	A Palmer (USA)	J Nicklaus (USA)	A Palmer (USA)	G Player (SAf)
1963	B Charles (NZL)	J Boros (USA)	J Nicklaus (USA)	J Nicklaus (USA)
1964	T Lema (USA)	K Venturi (USA)	A Palmer (USA)	B Nichols (USA)
1965	P Thomson (Aus)	G Player (SAf)	J Nicklaus (USA)	D Marr (USA)
1966	J Nicklaus (USA)	B Casper (USA)	J Nicklaus (USA)	A Geiberger (USA)
1967	R De Vicenzo (Arg)	J Nicklaus (USA)	G Brewer (USA)	D January (USA)
1968	G Player (SAf)	L Trevino (USA)	B Goalby (USA)	J Boros (USA)
1969	T Jacklin (GBR)	O Moody (USA)	G Archer (USA)	R Floyd (USA)
1970	J Nicklaus (USA)	T Jacklin (GBR)	B Casper (USA)	D Stockton (USA)
1971	L Trevino (USA)	L Trevino (USA)	C Coody (USA)	J Nicklaus (USA)
1972	L Trevino (USA)	J Nicklaus (USA)	J Nicklaus (USA)	G Player (SAf)
1973	T Weiskopf (USA)	J Miller (USA)	T Aaron (USA)	J Nicklaus (USA)
1974	G Player (SAf)	H Irwin (USA)	G Player (SAf)	L Trevino (USA)
1975	T Watson (USA)	L Graham (USA)	J Nicklaus (USA)	J Nicklaus (USA)
1976	J Miller (USA)	J Pate (USA)	R Floyd (USA)	D Stockton (USA)
1977	T Watson (USA)	H Green (USA)	T Watson (USA)	L Wadkins (USA)
1978	J Nicklaus (USA)	A North (USA)	G Player (SAf)	J Mahaffey (USA)
1979	S Ballesteros (Spa)	H Irwin (USA)	F Zoeller (USA)	D Graham (Aus)
1980	T Watson (USA)	J Nicklaus (USA)	S Ballesteros (Spa)	J Nicklaus (USA)
1981	B Rogers (USA)	D Graham (Aus)	T Watson (USA)	L Nelson (USA)
1982	T Watson (USA)	T Watson (USA)	C Stadler (USA)	R Floyd (USA)
1983	T Watson (USA)	L Nelson (USA)	S Ballesteros (Spa)	H Sutton (USA)
1984	S Ballesteros (Spa)	F Zoeller (USA)	B Crenshaw (USA)	L Trevino (USA)
1985	S Lyle (GBR)	A North (USA)	B Langer (WGR)	H Green (USA)
1986	G Norman (Aus)	R Floyd (USA)	J Nicklaus (USA)	B Tway (USA)
1987	N Faldo (GBR)	S Simpson (USA)	L Mize (USA)	L Nelson (USA)
1988	S Ballesteros (Spa)	C Strange (USA)	S Lyle (GBR)	J Sluman (USA)
1989	M Calcavecchia (USA)	C Strange (USA)	N Faldo (GBR)	P Stewart (USA)
1990	N Faldo (GBR)	H Irwin (USA)	N Faldo (GBR)	W Grady (Aus)
1991	I Baker-Finch (Aus)	P Stewart (USA)	I Woosnam (GBR)	J Daly (USA)
1992	N Faldo (GBR)	T Kite (USA)	F Couples (USA)	N Price (Zim)
1993	G Norman (Aus)	L Janzen (USA)	B Langer (GER)	P Azinger (USA)
1994	N Price (Zim)	E Els (SAf)	J M Olazabel (Spa)	N Price (Zim)
1995	J Daly (USA)	C Pavin (USA)	B Crenshaw (USA)	S Elkington (Aus)
1996	T Lehman (USA)	S Jones (USA)	N Faldo (GBR)	M Brooks (USA)
1997	J Leonard (USA)	E Els (SAf)	T Woods (USA)	D Love (USA)
1998	M O'Meara (USA)	L Janzen (USA)	M O'Meara (USA)	V Singh (Fij)

The 1999 US Masters was won by José Maria Olazabal.

RYDER CUP WINNERS (POST WAR)

USA v Great Britain

1947	Portland, Oregon	USA	1963	Atlanta, Georgia	USA
1949	Ganton, England	USA	1965	Southport, England	USA
1951	Pinehurst, North Carolina	USA	1967	Houston, Texas	USA
1953	Wentworth, England	USA	1969	Southport, England	Tied
1955	Thunderbird, California	USA	1971	St Louis, Missouri	USA
1957	Lindrick, England	Great Britain	1973	Muirfield, Scotland	USA
1959	Elorado, California	USA	1975	Laurel Valley, Pennsylvania	USA
1961	Royal Lytham, England	USA	1977	Royal Lytham, England	USA

USA v Europe

1979	Greenbrier, West Virginia	USA	1989	The Belfry, England	Tied
1981	Walton Heath, England	USA	1991	Kiawah Island, South Carolina	USA
1983	PGA Course, Florida	USA	1993	The Belfry, England	USA
1985	The Belfry, England	Europe	1995	Oak Hill, New York	Europe
1987	Columbus, Ohio	Europe	1997	Valderrama, Spain	Europe

Wins since competition began in 1927: USA 23; GB/Europe 7; Tied 2.

GREYHOUND RACING

THE DERBY WINNERS (POST WAR)

Year	Greyhound	Year	Greyhound
1945	Ballyhennessy Seal	1972	Patricia's Hope
1946	Monday's News	1973	Patricia's Hope
1947	Trev's Perfection	1974	Jimsun
1948	Priceless Border	1975	Tartan Khan
1949	Narrogar Ann	1976	Mutts Silver
1950	Ballymac Ball	1977	Balliniska Band
1951	Ballylanigan Tanist	1978	Lacca Champion
1952	Endless Gossip	1979	Sarah's Bunny
1953	Daws Dancer	1980	Indian Joe
1954	Paul's Fun	1981	Parkdown Jet
1955	Rushton Mack	1982	Laurie's Panther
1956	Dunmore King	1983	I'm Slippy
1957	Ford Spartan	1984	Whisper Wishes
1958	Pigalle Wonder	1985	Pagan Swallow
1959	Mile Bush Pride	1986	Tico
1960	Duleek Dandy	1987	Signal Spark
1961	Palm's Printer	1988	Hit-the-Lid
1962	The Grand Canal	1989	Lartigue Note
1963	Lucky Boy Boy	1990	Slippy Blue
1964	Hack Up Chieftain	1991	Ballinderry Ash
1965	Chittering Clapton	1992	Farloe Melody
1966	Faithful Hope	1993	Ringa Hustle
1967	Tric-Trac	1994	Moral Standards
1968	Camira Flash	1995	Moaning Lad
1969	Sand Star	1996	Shanless Slippy
1970	John Silver	1997	Some Picture
1971	Dolores Rocket	1998	Tom's the Best

HOCKEY

MEN'S WORLD CUP CHAMPIONS

Year	Country
1971	Pakistan
1973	Holland
1975	India
1978	Pakistan
1982	Pakistan
1986	Australia
1990	Holland
1994	Pakistan
1998	Holland

WOMEN'S WORLD CUP CHAMPIONS

Year	Country
1974	Holland
1976	West Germany
1978	Holland
1981	West Germany
1983	Holland
1986	Holland
1990	Holland
1994	Australia
1998	Australia

EUROPEAN CUP WINNERS

Year	Men	Women
1970	West Germany	–
1974	Spain	–
1978	West Germany	–
1983	Netherlands	Netherlands (1984)
1987	Netherlands	Netherlands
1991	Germany	England
1995	Germany	Netherlands

HORSE RACING

MAJOR RACE WINNERS (POST WAR)

Year	GRAND NATIONAL WINNERS	DERBY WINNERS
1946	Lovely Cottage	Airborne
1947	Caughoo	Pearl Diver
1948	Sheila's Cottage	My Love
1949	Russian Hero	Nimbus
1950	Freebooter	Galcador
1951	Nickel Coin	Arctic Prince
1952	Teal	Tulyar
1953	Early Mist	Pinza
1954	Royal Tan	Never Say Die
1955	Quare Times	Phil Drake
1956	ESB	Lavandin
1957	Sundew	Crepello
1958	Mr What	Hard Ridden
1959	Oxo	Parthia
1960	Merryman II	St Paddy
1961	Nicolaus Silver	Psidium
1962	Kilmore	Larkspur
1963	Ayala	Relko
1964	Team Spirit	Santa Claus
1965	Jay Trump	Sea Bird II
1966	Anglo	Charlottown

GRAND NATIONAL WINNERS

1967	Foinavon
1968	Red Alligator
1969	Highland Wedding
1970	Gay Trip
1971	Specify
1972	Well to Do
1973	Red Rum
1974	Red Rum
1975	L'Escargot
1976	Rag Trade
1977	Red Rum
1978	Lucius
1979	Rubstic
1980	Ben Nevis
1981	Aldaniti
1982	Grittar
1983	Corbiere
1984	Hallo Dandy
1985	Last Suspect
1986	West Tip
1987	Maori Venture
1988	Rhyme'n'Reason
1989	Little Polvier
1990	Mr Frisk
1991	Seagram
1992	Party Politics
1993	–
1994	Miinnehoma
1995	Royal Athlete
1996	Rough Quest
1997	Lord Gyllene
1998	Earth Summit

DERBY WINNERS

	Royal Palace
	Sir Ivor
	Blakeney
	Nijinsky
	Mill Reef
	Roberto
	Morston
	Snow Knight
	Grundy
	Empery
	The Minstrel
	Shirley Heights
	Troy
	Henbit
	Shergar
	Golden Fleece
	Teenoso
	Secreto
	Slip Anchor
	Shahrastani
	Reference Point
	Kahyasi
	Nashwan
	Quest for Fame
	Generous
	Dr Devious
	Commander in Chief
	Ehrhaab
	Lammtarra
	Shaamit
	Benny The Dip
	High-Rise

The 1999 Grand National was won by Bobbyjo

ICE HOCKEY

WORLD CHAMPIONS (POST WAR)

1947	Czechoslovakia	1965	USSR	1982	USSR
1948	Canada	1966	USSR	1983	USSR
1949	Czechoslovakia	1967	USSR	1984	USSR
1950	Canada	1968	USSR	1985	Czechoslovakia
1951	Canada	1969	USSR	1986	USSR
1952	Canada	1970	USSR	1987	Sweden
1953	Sweden	1971	USSR	1988	USSR
1954	USSR	1972	Czechoslovakia	1989	USSR
1955	Canada	1973	USSR	1990	USSR
1956	USSR	1974	USSR	1991	Sweden
1957	Sweden	1975	USSR	1992	Sweden
1958	Canada	1976	Czechoslovakia	1993	Russia
1959	Canada	1977	Czechoslovakia	1994	Canada
1960	USA	1978	USSR	1995	Finland
1961	Canada	1979	USSR	1996	Czech Republic
1962	Sweden	1980	USA	1997	Canada
1963	USSR	1981	USSR	1998	Sweden
1964	USSR				

Wins since competition began in 1920

24	USSR	7	Sweden	3	USA
12	Canada	6	Czechoslovakia	1	Czech Rep., Finland, Britain, Russia

NHL STANLEY CUP WINNERS

1982	New York Islanders	1990	Edmonton Oilers
1983	New York Islanders	1991	Pittsburgh Penguins
1984	Edmonton Oilers	1992	Pittsburgh Penguins
1985	Edmonton Oilers	1993	Montreal Canadiens
1986	Montreal Canadiens	1994	New York Rangers
1987	Edmonton Oilers	1995	New Jersey Devils
1988	Edmonton Oilers	1996	Colorado Avalanche
1989	Calgary Flames	1997	Detroit
		1998	Detroit

ICE SKATING

WORLD CHAMPIONS (since 1965)

Men		**Women**
1965	A Calmat (Fra)	P Burka (Can)
1966	E Danzer (Aut)	P Fleming (USA)
1967	E Danzer (Aut)	P Fleming (USA)
1968	E Danzer (Aut)	P Fleming (USA)

ICE SKATING

Men		Women
1969	T Wood (USA)	G Seyfert (GDR)
1970	T Wood (USA)	G Seyfert (GDR)
1971	O Nepela (Cze)	B Schuba (Aut)
1972	O Nepela (Cze)	B Schuba (Aut)
1973	O Nepela (Cze)	K Magnussen (Can)
1974	J Hoffmann (GDR)	C Errath (GDR)
1975	S Volkov (USSR)	D De Leeuw (Neth)
1976	J Curry (GBR)	D Hamill (USA)
1977	V Kovalyev (USSR)	L Fratianne (USA)
1978	C Tickner (USA)	A Potzsch (GDR)
1979	V Kovalyev (USSR)	L Fratianne (USA)
1980	J Hoffmann (GDR)	A Potzsch (GDR)
1981	S Hamilton (USA)	D Biellmann (Swi)
1982	S Hamilton (USA)	E Zayak (USA)
1983	S Hamilton (USA)	R Sumners (USA)
1984	S Hamilton (USA)	K Witt (GDR)
1985	A Fadeyev (USSR)	K Witt (GDR)
1986	B Boitano (USA)	D Thomas (USA)
1987	B Orser (Can)	K Witt (GDR)
1988	B Boitano (USA)	K Witt (GDR)
1989	K Browning (Can)	M Ito (Jap)
1990	K Browning (Can)	J Trenary (USA)
1991	K Browning (Can)	K Yamaguchi (Jap)
1992	V Petrenko (Ukr)	K Yamaguchi (Jap)
1993	K Browning (Can)	O Baiul (Ukr)
1994	E Stojko (Can)	Y Sato (Jap)
1995	E Stojko (Can)	L Chen (Chi)
1996	T Eldredge (USA)	M Kwan (USA)
1997	E Stojko (Can)	T Lipinski (USA)
1998	A Yagudin (Rus)	M Kwan (USA)

LAWN TENNIS

GRAND SLAM CHAMPIONSHIP WINNERS – MEN (POST WAR)

	Wimbledon	US Open	French Open	Australian Open
1946	Y Petra (Fra)	J Kramer (USA)	M Bernard (Fra)	J Bromwich (Aus)
1947	J Kramer (USA)	J Kramer (USA)	J Asboth (Hun)	D Pails (Aus)
1948	B Falkenberg (USA)	R Gonzales (USA)	F Parker (USA)	A Quist (Aus)
1949	T Schroeder (USA)	R Gonzales (USA)	F Parker (USA)	F Sedgman (Aus)
1950	B Patty (USA)	A Larsen (USA)	B Patty (USA)	F Sedgman (Aus)
1951	D Savitt (USA)	F Sedgman (Aus)	J Drobny (Egy)	D Savitt (USA)
1952	F Sedgman (Aus)	F Sedgman (Aus)	J Drobny (Egy)	K McGregor (Aus)
1953	V Seixas (USA)	T Trabert (USA)	K Rosewall (Aus)	K Rosewall (Aus)
1954	J Drobny (Egy)	V Seixas (USA)	T Trabert (USA)	M Rose (Aus)
1955	T Trabert (USA)	T Trabert (USA)	T Trabert (USA)	K Rosewall (Aus)
1956	L Hoad (Aus)	K Rosewall (Aus)	L Hoad (Aus)	L Hoad (Aus)
1957	L Hoad (Aus)	M Anderson (Aus)	S Davidson (Swe)	A Cooper (Aus)
1958	A Cooper (Aus)	A Cooper (Aus)	M Rose (Aus)	A Cooper (Aus)
1959	A Olmedo (USA)	N Fraser (Aus)	N Pietrangeli (Ita)	A Olmedo (USA)
1960	N Fraser (Aus)	N Fraser (Aus)	N Pietrangeli (Ita)	R Laver (Aus)
1961	R Laver (Aus)	R Emerson (Aus)	M Santana (Spa)	R Emerson (Aus)
1962	R Laver (Aus)	R Laver (Aus)	R Laver (Aus)	R Laver (Aus)
1963	C McKinley (USA)	R Osuna (Mex)	R Emerson (Aus)	R Emerson (Aus)
1964	R Emerson (Aus)	R Emerson (Aus)	M Santana (Spa)	R Emerson (Aus)
1965	R Emerson (Aus)	M Santana (Spa)	F Stolle (Aus)	R Emerson (Aus)
1966	M Santana (Spa)	F Stolle (Aus)	T Roche (Aus)	R Emerson (Aus)
1967	J Newcombe (Aus)	J Newcombe (Aus)	R Emerson (Aus)	R Emerson (Aus)
1968	R Laver (Aus)	A Ashe (USA)	K Rosewall (Aus)	B Bowrey (Aus)
1969	R Laver (Aus)	S Smith (USA)	R Laver (Aus)	R Laver (Aus)
1970	J Newcombe (Aus)	K Rosewall (Aus)	J Kodes (Cze)	A Ashe (USA)
1971	J Newcombe (Aus)	S Smith (USA)	J Kodes (Cze)	K Rosewall (Aus)
1972	S Smith (USA)	I Nastase (Rom)	A Gimeno (Spa)	K Rosewall (Aus)
1973	J Kodes (Cze)	J Newcombe (Aus)	I Nastase (Rom)	J Newcombe (Aus)
1974	J Connors (USA)	J Connors (USA)	B Borg (Swe)	J Connors (USA)
1975	A Ashe (USA)	M Orantes (Spa)	B Borg (Swe)	J Newcombe (Aus)
1976	B Borg (Swe)	J Connors (USA)	A Panatta (Ita)	M Edmondson (Aus)
1977	B Borg (Swe)	G Vilas (Arg)	G Vilas (Arg)	R Tanner (USA)
1978	B Borg (Swe)	J Connors (USA)	B Borg (Swe)	G Vilas (Arg)
1979	B Borg (Swe)	J McEnroe (USA)	B Borg (Swe)	G Vilas (Arg)
1980	B Borg (Swe)	J McEnroe (USA)	B Borg (Swe)	B Teacher (USA)
1981	J McEnroe (USA)	J McEnroe (USA)	B Borg (Swe)	J Kriek (SAf)
1982	J Connors (USA)	J Connors (USA)	M Wilander (Swe)	J Kriek (SAf)
1983	J McEnroe (USA)	J Connors (USA)	Y Noah (Fra)	M Wilander (Swe)
1984	J McEnroe (USA)	J McEnroe (USA)	I Lendl (Cze)	M Wilander (Swe)
1985	B Becker (WGR)	I Lendl (Cze)	M Wilander (Swe)	S Edberg (Swe)
1986	B Becker (WGR)	I Lendl (Cze)	I Lendl (Cze)	—
1987	P Cash (Aus)	I Lendl (Cze)	I Lendl (Cze)	S Edberg (Swe)
1988	S Edberg (Swe)	M Wilander (Swe)	M Wilander (Swe)	M Wilander (Swe)
1989	B Becker (WGR)	B Becker (WGR)	M Chang (USA)	I Lendl (Cze)
1990	S Edberg (Swe)	P Sampras (USA)	A Gomez (Ecu)	I Lendl (Cze)
1991	M Stich (Ger)	S Edberg (Swe)	J Courier (USA)	B Becker (Ger)

	Wimbledon	US Open	French Open	Australian Open
1992	A Agassi (USA)	S Edberg (Swe)	J Courier (USA)	J Courier (USA)
1993	P Sampras (USA)	P Sampras (USA)	S Brugera (Spa)	J Courier (USA)
1994	P Sampras (USA)	A Agassi (USA)	S Brugera (Spa)	P Sampras (USA)
1995	P Sampras (USA)	P Sampras (USA)	T Muster (Aut)	A Agassi (USA)
1996	R Krajicek (Hol)	P Sampras (USA)	Y Kafelnikov (Rus)	B Becker (Ger)
1997	P Sampras (USA)	P Rafter (Aus)	G Kuerten (Bra)	P Sampras (USA)
1998	P Sampras (USA)	P Rafter (Aus)	C Moya (Spa)	P Korda (Cze)

The 1999 season opened with Yevgeny Kafelnikov taking the Australian Open.

GRAND SLAM CHAMPIONSHIP WINNERS – WOMEN (POST WAR)

	Wimbledon	US Open	French Open	Australian Open
1946	P Betz (USA)	P Betz (USA)	M Osborne (USA)	N Bolton (Aus)
1947	M Osborne (USA)	L Brough (USA)	P Todd (USA)	N Bolton (Aus)
1948	L Brough (USA)	M Du Pont (USA)	N Landry (Fra)	N Bolton (Aus)
1949	L Brough (USA)	M Du Pont (USA)	M Du Pont (USA)	D Hart (USA)
1950	L Brough (USA)	M Du Pont (USA)	D Hart (USA)	L Brough (USA)
1951	D Hart (USA)	M Connolly (USA)	S Fry (USA)	N Bolton (Aus)
1952	M Connolly (USA)	M Connolly (USA)	D Hart (USA)	T Long (USA)
1953	M Connolly (USA)	M Connolly (USA)	M Connolly (USA)	M Connolly (USA)
1954	M Connolly (USA)	D Hart (USA)	M Connolly (USA)	T Long (USA)
1955	L Brough (USA)	D Hart (USA)	A Mortimer (GBR)	B Penrose (Aus)
1956	S Fry (USA)	S Fry (USA)	A Gibson (USA)	M Carter (Aus)
1957	A Gibson (USA)	A Gibson (USA)	S Bloomer (GBR)	S Fry (USA)
1958	A Gibson (USA)	A Gibson (USA)	Z Kormoczy (Hun)	A Mortimer (GBR)
1959	M Bueno (Bra)	M Bueno (Bra)	C Truman (GBR)	M Reitano (Aus)
1960	M Bueno (Bra)	D Hård (USA)	D Hard (USA)	M Smith (Aus)
1961	A Mortimer (GBR)	D Hard (USA)	A Haydon (GBR)	M Smith (Aus)
1962	K Susman (USA)	M Smith (Aus)	M Smith (Aus)	M Smith (Aus)
1963	M Smith (Aus)	M Bueno (Bra)	L Turner (Aus)	M Smith (Aus)
1964	M Bueno (Bra)	M Bueno (Bra)	M Smith (Aus)	M Smith (Aus)
1965	M Smith (Aus)	M Smith (Aus)	L Turner (Aus)	M Smith (Aus)
1966	B-J King (USA)	M Bueno (Bra)	A Jones (GBR)*	M Smith (Aus)
1967	B-J King (USA)	B-J King (USA)	F Durr (Fra)	N Richey (USA)
1968	B-J King (USA)	M Court (Aus)*	N Richey (USA)	B-J King (USA)
1969	A Jones (GBR)*	M Court (Aus)*	M Court (Aus)*	M Court (Aus)*
1970	M Court (Aus)*	M Court (Aus)*	M Court (Aus)*	M Court (Aus)*
1971	E Goolagong (Aus)	B-J King (USA)	E Goolagong (Aus)	E Goolagong (Aus)
1972	B-J King (USA)	B-J King (USA)	M Court (Aus)*	V Wade (GBR)
1973	B-J King (USA)	M Court (Aus)*	B-J King (USA)	M Court (Aus)*
1974	C Evert (USA)	B-J King (USA)	M Court (Aus)*	E Goolagong (Aus)
1975	B-J King (USA)	C Evert (USA)	C Evert (USA)	E Goolagong (Aus)
1976	C Evert (USA)	C Evert (USA)	S Barker (USA)	E Cawley (Aus)*
1977	V Wade (GBR)	C Evert (USA)	M Jauseovec (Yug)	K Reid (Aus)
1978	M Navratilova (Cze)	C Evert (USA)	V Ruzici (Rom)	C O'Neill (Aus)
1979	M Navratilova (Cze)	T Austin (USA)	C Evert (USA)	B Jordan (USA)
1980	E Cawley (Aus)*	C Evert (USA)	C Evert (USA)	H Mandlikova (Cze)
1981	C Evert (USA)	T Austin (USA)	H Mandlikova (Cze)	M Navratilova (USA)
1982	M Navratilova (USA)	C Evert (USA)	M Navratilova (USA)	C Evert (USA)
1983	M Navratilova (USA)	M Navratilova (USA)	C Evert (USA)	M Navratilova (USA)
1984	M Navratilova (USA)	M Navratilova (USA)	M Navratilova (USA)	C Evert (USA)
1985	M Navratilova (USA)	H Mandlikova (Cze)	C Evert (USA)	M Navratilova (USA)
1986	M Navratilova (USA)	M Navratilova (USA)	C Evert (USA)	—
1987	M Navratilova (USA)	M Navratilova (USA)	S Graf (WGR)	H Mandlikova (Cze)
1988	S Graf (WGR)	S Graf (WGR)	S Graf (WGR)	S Graf (WGR)
1989	S Graf (WGR)	S Graf (WGR)	A Sanchez (Spa)	S Graf (WGR)
1990	M Navratilova (USA)	G Sabatini (Arg)	M Seles (Yug)	S Graf (WGR)
1991	S Graf (Ger)	M Seles (Yug)	M Seles (Yug)	M Seles (Yug)
1992	S Graf (Ger)	M Seles (Yug)	M Seles (Yug)	M Seles (Yug)
1993	S Graf (Ger)	S Graf (Ger)	S Graf (Ger)	M Seles (Yug)
1994	C Martinez (Spa)	A Sanchez (Spa)	A Sanchez (Spa)	S Graf (Ger)
1995	S Graf (Ger)	S Graf (Ger)	S Graf (Ger)	M Pierce (Fra)
1996	S Graf (Ger)	S Graf (Ger)	S Graf (Ger)	M Seles (Yug)
1997	M Hingis (Swi)	M Hingis (Swi)	I Majoli (Cro)	M Hingis (Swi)
1998	J Novotna (Cze)	L Davenport (USA)	A Sanchez (Spa)	M Hingis (Swi)

* Players who have won before under maiden names:
A Jones as A Hayden, M Court as M Smith, E Cawley as E Goolagong

The 1999 season opened with Martina Hingis winning the Australian Open for the third year in succession.

DAVIS CUP WINNERS (POST WAR)

1946	USA	1957	Australia	1968	USA
1947	USA	1958	USA	1969	USA
1948	USA	1959	Australia	1970	USA
1949	USA	1960	Australia	1971	USA
1950	Australia	1961	Australia	1972	USA
1951	Australia	1962	Australia	1973	Australia
1952	Australia	1963	USA	1974	South Africa
1953	Australia	1964	Australia	1975	Sweden
1954	USA	1965	Australia	1976	Italy
1955	Australia	1966	Australia	1977	Australia
1956	Australia	1967	Australia	1978	USA

1979	USA	1986	Australia	1993	Germany
1980	Czechoslovakia	1987	Sweden	1994	Sweden
1981	USA	1988	West Germany	1995	USA
1982	USA	1989	West Germany	1996	France
1983	Australia	1990	USA	1997	Sweden
1984	Sweden	1991	France	1998	Sweden
1985	Sweden	1992	USA		

Wins since competition began in 1900

31	USA	7	Sweden
26	Australia or Australasia	3	Germany or West Germany
9	Great Britain or British Isles	1	Czechoslovakia, Italy, South Africa
8	France		

MOTOR RACING

FORMULA ONE WORLD CAR CHAMPIONSHIP

	Driver		Car	Constructors Cup
1950	Giuseppe Farina	Italy	Alfa Romeo	
1951	Juan Manuel Fangio	Argentina	Alfa Romeo	
1952	Alberto Ascari	Italy	Ferrari	
1953	Alberto Ascari	Italy	Ferrari	
1954	Juan Manuel Fangio	Argentina	Maserati/Mercedes	
1955	Juan Manuel Fangio	Argentina	Mercedes-Benz	
1956	Juan Manuel Fangio	Argentina	Lancia-Ferrari	
1957	Juan Manuel Fangio	Argentina	Maserati	
1958	Mike Hawthorn	Great Britain	Ferrari	Vanwall
1959	Jack Brabham	Australia	Cooper-Climax	Cooper-Climax
1960	Jack Brabham	Australia	Cooper-Climax	Cooper-Climax
1961	Phil Hill	USA	Ferrari	Ferrari
1962	Graham Hill	Great Britain	BRM	BRM
1963	Jim Clark	Great Britain	Lotus-Climax	Lotus-Climax
1964	John Surtees	Great Britain	Ferrari	Ferrari
1965	Jim Clark	Great Britain	Lotus-Climax	Lotus-Climax
1966	Jack Brabham	Australia	Brabham-Repco	Brabham-Repco
1967	Denny Hulme	New Zealand	Brabham-Repco	Brabham-Repco
1968	Graham Hill	Great Britain	Lotus-Ford	Lotus-Ford
1969	Jackie Stewart	Great Britain	Matra-Ford	Matra-Ford
1970	Jochen Rindt	Austria	Lotus-Ford	Lotus-Ford
1971	Jackie Stewart	Great Britain	Tyrell-Ford	Tyrell-Ford
1972	Emerson Fittipaldi	Brazil	Lotus-Ford	Lotus-Ford
1973	Jackie Stewart	Great Britain	Tyrell-Ford	Lotus-Ford
1974	Emerson Fittipaldi	Brazil	McLaren-Ford	McLaren-Ford
1975	Niki Lauda	Austria	Ferrari	Ferrari
1976	James Hunt	Great Britain	McLaren-Ford	Ferrari
1977	Niki Lauda	Austria	Ferrari	Ferrari
1978	Mario Andretti	USA	Lotus-Ford	Lotus-Ford
1979	Jody Scheckter	South Africa	Ferrari	Ferrari
1980	Alan Jones	Australia	Williams-Ford	Williams-Ford
1981	Nelson Piquet	Brazil	Brabham-Ford	Williams-Ford
1982	Keke Rosberg	Finland	Williams-Ford	Ferrari
1983	Nelson Piquet	Brazil	Brabham-BMW	Ferrari
1984	Niki Lauda	Austria	McLaren-TAG	McLaren-Porsche
1985	Alain Prost	France	McLaren-TAG	McLaren-TAG
1986	Alain Prost	France	McLaren-TAG	Williams-Honda
1987	Nelson Piquet	Brazil	Williams-Honda	Williams-Honda
1988	Ayrton Senna	Brazil	McLaren-Honda	McLaren-Honda
1989	Alain Prost	France	McLaren-Honda	McLaren-Honda
1990	Ayrton Senna	Brazil	McLaren-Honda	McLaren-Honda
1991	Ayrton Senna	Brazil	McLaren-Honda	McLaren-Honda
1992	Nigel Mansell	Great Britain	Williams-Renault	Williams-Renault
1993	Alain Prost	France	Williams-Renault	Williams-Renault
1994	Michael Schumacher	Germany	Benneton-Ford	Williams-Renault
1995	Michael Schumacher	Germany	Benneton-Renault	Benneton-Renault
1996	Damon Hill	Great Britain	Williams-Renault	Williams-Renault
1997	Jacques Villeneuve*	Canada	Williams-Renault	Williams-Renault
1998	Mika Hakkinen	Finland	McLaren-Mercedes	McLaren-Mercedes

ROWING

THE UNIVERSITY BOAT RACE

1946	Oxford	1965–7	Oxford
1947–51	Cambridge	1968–73	Cambridge
1952	Oxford	1974	Oxford
1953	Cambridge	1975	Cambridge
1954	Oxford	1976–85	Oxford
1955–8	Cambridge	1986	Cambridge
1959–60	Oxford	1987–92	Oxford
1961–2	Cambridge	1993–9	Cambridge
1963	Oxford		
1964	Cambridge		

Overall results since race began in 1829

Cambridge   76   Oxford 68   Dead Heat 1

Cambridge won the 1998 Boat Race in the record time of 16 min. 19 sec., shattering the course record held by Oxford since 1984.

RUGBY LEAGUE

LEAGUE CHAMPIONS (POST WAR)

1945–6	Wigan		1971–2	Leeds
1946–7	Wigan		1972–3	Dewsbury
1947–8	Warrington		1973–4	Salford
1948–9	Huddersfield		1974–5	St Helens
1949–50	Wigan		1975–6	Salford
1950–1	Workington Town		1976–7	Featherstone Rovers
1951–2	Wigan		1977–8	Widnes
1952–3	St Helens		1978–9	Hull Kingston Rovers
1953–4	Warrington		1979–80	Bradford Northern
1954–5	Warrington		1980–1	Bradford Northern
1955–6	Hull		1981–2	Leigh
1956–7	Oldham		1982–3	Hull
1957–8	Hull		1983–4	Hull Kingston Rovers
1958–9	St Helens		1984–5	Hull Kingston Rovers
1959–60	Wigan		1985–6	Halifax
1960–1	Leeds		1986–7	Wigan
1961–2	Huddersfield		1987–8	Widnes
1962–3	Swinton/Hunslet		1988–9	Widnes
1963–4	Swinton/Oldham		1989–90	Wigan
1964–5	Halifax		1990–1	Wigan
1965–6	St Helens		1991–2	Wigan
1966–7	Wakefield Trinity		1992–3	Wigan
1967–8	Wakefield Trinity		1993–4	Wigan
1968–9	Leeds		1994–5	Wigan
1969–70	St Helens		1995–6	Wigan
1970–1	St Helens			

Wins since competition began in 1906

17 Wigan
7 Huddersfield, St Helens
6 Hull, Salford
5 Hull Kingston Rovers
4 Swinton
3 Halifax, Leeds, Oldham, Warrington, Widnes
2 Bradford Northern, Hunslet, Leigh, Wakefield Trinity
1 Batley, Dewsbury, Featherstone Rovers, Workington Town

SUPER LEAGUE

1996	St Helens Saints	1997	Bradford Bulls	1998	Wigan

CHALLENGE CUP WINNERS (POST WAR)

1946	Wakefield Trinity		1973	Featherstone Rovers
1947	Bradford Northern		1974	Warrington
1948	Wigan		1975	Widnes
1949	Bradford Northern		1976	St Helens
1950	Warrington		1977	Leeds
1951	Wigan		1978	Leeds
1952	Workington Town		1979	Widnes
1953	Huddersfield		1980	Hull Kingston Rovers
1954	Warrington		1981	Widnes
1955	Barrow		1982	Hull
1956	St Helens		1983	Featherstone Rovers
1957	Leeds		1984	Widnes
1958	Wigan		1985	Wigan
1959	Wigan		1986	Castleford
1960	Wakefield Trinity		1987	Halifax
1961	St Helens		1988	Wigan
1962	Wakefield Trinity		1989	Wigan
1963	Wakefield Trinity		1990	Wigan
1964	Widnes		1991	Wigan
1965	Wigan		1992	Wigan
1966	St Helens		1993	Wigan
1967	Featherstone Rovers		1994	Wigan
1968	Leeds		1995	Wigan
1969	Castleford		1996	St Helens
1970	Castleford		1997	St Helens
1971	Leigh		1998	Sheffield Eagles
1972	St Helens		1999	Leeds Rhinos

The 1999 Challenge Cup Final was fought between London Broncos and Leeds Rhinos (who won by the record margin of 52 points to 16)

Wins since competition began in 1897

16 Wigan
11 Leeds
7 St Helens, Widnes
6 Huddersfield
5 Halifax, Wakefield Trinity, Warrington
4 Bradford Northern, Castleford

3 Batley, Featherstone Rovers, Oldham, Swinton
2 Broughton Rangers, Dewsbury, Hull, Hunslet, Leigh
1 Barrow, Hull Kingston Rovers, Rochdale Hornets, Salford, Sheffield Eagles, Workington Town

RUGBY UNION

WORLD CUP WINNERS

| 1987 | New Zealand | 1991 | Australia | 1995 | South Africa |

FIVE NATIONS CHAMPIONSHIP WINNERS (POST WAR)

1947	England	1965	Wales	1982	Ireland
	Wales	1966	Wales	1983	France
1948	Ireland	1967	France		Ireland
1949	Ireland	1968	France	1984	Scotland
1950	Wales	1969	Wales	1985	Ireland
1951	Ireland	1970	France	1986	France
1952	Wales		Wales		Scotland
1953	England	1971	Wales	1987	France
1954	England	1972	No competition	1988	France
	France	1973	England		Wales
	Wales		France	1989	France
1955	France		Ireland	1990	Scotland
	Wales		Scotland	1991	England
1956	Wales		Wales	1992	England
1957	England	1974	Ireland	1993	France
1958	England	1975	Wales	1994	Wales
1959	France	1976	Wales	1995	England
1960	England	1977	France	1996	England
	France	1978	Wales	1997	France
1961	France	1979	Wales	1998	France
1962	France	1980	England	1999	Scotland
1963	England	1981	France		
1964	Scotland				
	Wales				

Wins and shared wins since Championship began in 1883:

Wales 33   England 32   Scotland 22   France 20   Ireland 18

Grand Slam Winners:

England	11	Scotland	3
Wales	8	Ireland	1
France	6		

Triple Crown Winners:

England	21	Scotland	10
Wales	17	Ireland	6

HEINEKEN EUROPEAN CUP

| 1996 | Toulouse | 1997 | Brive | 1998 | Bath |

TETLEY BITTER CUP WINNERS

1972	Gloucester	1981	Leicester	1990	Bath
1973	Coventry	1982	Gloucester & Moseley	1991	Harlequins
1974	Coventry	1983	Bristol	1992	Bath
1975	Bedford	1984	Bath	1993	Leicester
1976	Gosforth	1985	Bath	1994	Bath
1977	Gosforth	1986	Bath	1995	Bath
1978	Gloucester	1987	Bath	1996	Bath
1979	Leicester	1988	Harlequins	1997	Leicester
1980	Leicester	1989	Bath	1998	Saracens

The 1999 Tetley Bitter Cup Final was between Newcastle and Wasps.

SWALEC CUP WINNERS

1972	Neath	1981	Cardiff	1990	Neath
1973	Llanelli	1982	Cardiff	1991	Llanelli
1974	Llanelli	1983	Pontypool	1992	Llanelli
1975	Llanelli	1984	Cardiff	1993	Llanelli
1976	Llanelli	1985	Cardiff	1994	Cardiff
1977	Newport	1986	Cardiff	1995	Swansea
1978	Swansea	1987	Cardiff	1996	Pontypridd
1979	Bridgend	1988	Llanelli	1997	Cardiff
1980	Bridgend	1989	Neath	1998	Llanelli

ALLIED DUNBAR ENGLISH LEAGUE CHAMPIONS

1987–8	Leicester	1991–2	Bath	1995–6	Bath
1988–9	Bath	1992–3	Bath	1996–7	Wasps
1989–90	Wasps	1993–4	Bath	1997–8	Newcastle
1990–1	Bath	1994–5	Leicester	1998–9	Leicester

HEINEKEN WELSH LEAGUE CHAMPIONS

1990–1	Neath	1993–4	Swansea	1996–7	Pontypridd
1991–2	Swansea	1994–5	Cardiff	1997–8	Swansea
1992–3	Llanelli	1995–6	Neath		

SNOOKER

EMBASSY WORLD PROFESSIONAL CHAMPIONS

1976 Ray Reardon (Wales)	1988 Steve Davis (England)
1977 John Spencer (England)	1989 Steve Davis (England)
1978 Ray Reardon (Wales)	1990 Stephen Hendry (Scotland)
1979 Terry Griffiths (Wales)	1991 John Parrott (England)
1980 Cliff Thorburn (Canada)	1992 Stephen Hendry (Scotland)
1981 Steve Davis (England)	1993 Stephen Hendry (Scotland)
1982 Alex Higgins (Northern Ireland)	1994 Stephen Hendry (Scotland)
1983 Steve Davis (England)	1995 Stephen Hendry (Scotland)
1984 Steve Davis (England)	1996 Stephen Hendry (Scotland)
1985 Dennis Taylor (Northern Ireland)	1997 Ken Doherty (Ireland)
1986 Joe Johnson (England)	1998 John Higgins (Scotland)
1987 Steve Davis (England)	1999 Stephen Hendry (Scotland)

In 1999 Stephen Hendry entered the record books by winning the Embassy World title for a seventh time, defeating Mark Williams 18–11.

SPEEDWAY

WORLD CHAMPIONS (since 1970)

1970 Ivan Mauger (New Zealand)	1985 Erik Gundersen (Denmark)
1971 Ole Olsen (Denmark)	1986 Hans Nielsen (Denmark)
1972 Ivan Mauger (New Zealand)	1987 Hans Nielsen (Denmark)
1973 Jerry Szczakiel (Poland)	1988 Erik Gundersen (Denmark)
1974 Anders Michanek (Sweden)	1989 Hans Nielsen (Denmark)
1975 Ole Olsen (Denmark)	1990 Per Jonsson (Sweden)
1976 Peter Collins (England)	1991 Jan Pedersen (Denmark)
1977 Ivan Mauger (New Zealand)	1992 Gary Havelock (England)
1978 Ole Olsen (Denmark)	1993 Sam Ermolenko (USA)
1979 Ivan Mauger (New Zealand)	1994 Tony Rickardsson (Sweden)
1980 Michael Lee (England)	1995 Hans Nielsen (Denmark)
1981 Bruce Penhall (USA)	1996 Billy Hamill (USA)
1982 Bruce Penhall (USA)	1997 Greg Hancock (USA)
1983 Egon Muller (West Germany)	1998 Tony Rickardsson (Sweden)
1984 Erik Gundersen (Denmark)	

SQUASH

BRITISH OPEN

Men

1990 Jahangir Khan (Pak)	1995 Jansher Khan (Pak)
1991 Jahangir Khan (Pak)	1996 Jansher Khan (Pak)
1992 Jansher Khan (Pak)	1997 Jansher Khan (Pak)
1993 Jansher Khan (Pak)	1998 Peter Nicol (Sco)
1994 Jansher Khan (Pak)	

Women

1990 Susan Devoy (NZ)	1995 Michelle Martin (Aus)
1991 Lisa Opie (Eng)	1996 Michelle Martin (Aus)
1992 Susan Devoy (NZ)	1997 Michelle Martin (Aus)
1993 Michelle Martin (Aus)	1998 Michelle Martin (Aus)
1994 Michelle Martin (Aus)	

SWIMMING

OLYMPIC CHAMPIONS (POST WAR)

Men's 50m Freestyle

	1972 Mark Spitz (USA)
	1976 Jim Montgomery (USA)
1988 Matt Biondi (USA)	1980 Jorg Woithe (GDR)
1992 Aleksandr Popov (CIS)	1984 Howdy Gaines (USA)
1996 Aleksandr Popov (Rus)	1988 Matt Biondi (USA)
	1992 Aleksandr Popov (CIS)
Men's 100m Freestyle	1996 Aleksandr Popov (Rus)

Men's 100m Freestyle

1948 Walter Ris (USA)	**Men's 200m Freestyle**
1952 Clarke Scholes (USA)	
1956 Jon Henricks (Aus)	1968 Mike Wenden (Aus)
1960 John Devitt (Aus)	1972 Mark Spitz (USA)
1964 Don Schollander (USA)	1976 Bruce Furniss (USA)
1968 Mike Wenden (Aus)	1980 Sergey Koplyakov (USSR)

1984 Michael Gross (FRG)
1988 Duncan Armstrong (Aus)
1996 Danyon Loader (NZ)

Men's 400m Freestyle

1948 William Smith (USA)
1952 Jean Boiteux (Fra)
1956 Murray Rose (Aus)
1960 Murray Rose (Aus)
1964 Don Schollander (USA)
1968 Mike Burton (USA)
1972 Brad Cooper (Aus)
1976 Brian Goodell (USA)
1980 Vladimir Salnikov (USSR)
1984 George DiCarlo (USA)
1988 Uwe Dassler (GDR)
1992 Yevgeniy Sadoviy (CIS)
1996 Danyon Loader (NZ)

Men's 1500m Freestyle

1948 James McLane (USA)
1952 Ford Konno (USA)
1956 Murray Rose (Aus)
1960 John Konrads (Aus)
1964 Bob Windle (Aus)
1968 Mike Burton (USA)
1972 Mike Burton (USA)
1976 Brian Goodell (USA)
1980 Vladimir Salnikov (USSR)
1984 Michael O'Brien (USA)
1988 Vladimir Salnikov (USSR)
1992 Kieren Perkins (Aus)
1996 Kieren Perkins (Aus)

Men's 100m Backstroke

1948 Allen Stack (USA)
1952 Yoshinobu Oyakawa (USA)
1956 David Theile (Aus)
1960 David Theile (Aus)
1968 Roland Matthes (GDR)
1972 Roland Matthes (GDR)
1976 John Naber (USA)
1980 Bengt Baron (Swe)
1984 Rick Carey (USA)
1988 Daichi Suzuki (Jap)
1992 Mark Tewksbury (Can)
1996 Jeff Rouse (USA)

Men's 200m Backstroke

1964 Jed Graef (USA)
1968 Roland Matthes (GDR)
1972 Roland Matthes (GDR)
1976 John Naber (USA)
1980 Sándor Wladár (Hun)
1984 Rick Carey (USA)
1988 Igor Polyanskiy (USSR)
1992 Martin López-Zubero (Spa)
1996 Brad Bridgewater (USA)

Men's 100m Breaststroke

1968 Don McKenzie (USA)
1972 Nobutaka Taguchi (Jap)
1976 John Hencken (USA)
1980 Duncan Goodhew (UK)
1984 Steve Lundquist (USA)
1988 Adrian Moorhouse (UK)
1992 Nelson Diebel (USA)
1996 Frederik Deburghgraeve (Bel)

Men's 200m Breaststroke

1948 Joseph Verdeur (USA)
1952 John Davies (Aus)
1956 Masaru Furukawa (Jap)
1960 William Mulliken (USA)
1964 Ian O'Brien (Aus)
1968 Felipe Munoz (Mex)
1972 John Hencken (USA)
1976 David Wilkie (UK)
1980 Robertas Zhulpa (USSR)
1984 Victor Davis (Can)
1988 József Szabó (Hun)

1992 Mike Barrowman (USA)
1996 Norbert Rozsa (Hun)

Men's 100m Butterfly

1968 Doug Russell (USA)
1972 Mark Spitz (USA)
1976 Matt Vogel (USA)
1980 Pär Arvidsson (Swe)
1984 Michael Gross (FRG)
1988 Anthony Nesty (Sur)
1992 Pablo Morales (USA)
1996 Denis Pankratov (Rus)

Men's 200m Butterfly

1956 William Yorzyk (USA)
1960 Mike Troy (USA)
1964 Kevin Berry (Aus)
1968 Carl Robie (USA)
1972 Mark Spitz (USA)
1976 Mike Bruner (USA)
1980 Sergey Fesenko (USSR)
1984 Jon Sieben (Aus)
1988 Michael Gross (FRG)
1992 Melvin Stewart (USA)
1996 Denis Pankratov (Rus)

Men's 200m Individual Medley

1968 Charles Hickcox (USA)
1972 Gunnar Larsson (Swe)
1984 Alex Baumann (Can)
1988 Tamás Darnyi (Hun)
1992 Tamás Darnyi (Hun)
1996 Attila Czene (Hun)

Men's 400m Individual Medley

1964 Richard Roth (USA)
1968 Charles Hickcox (USA)
1972 Gunnar Larsson (Swe)
1976 Rod Strachan (USA)
1980 Aleksandr Sidorenko (USSR)
1984 Alex Baumann (Can)
1988 Tamás Darnyi (Hun)
1992 Tamás Darnyi (Hun)
1996 Tom Dolan (USA)

Men's 4 × 100m Freestyle Relay

1964	USA	1988	USA
1968	USA	1992	USA
1972	USA	1996	USA
1984	USA		

Men's 4 × 200m Freestyle Relay

1948	USA	1976	USA
1952	USA	1980	USSR
1956	Australia	1984	USA
1960	USA	1988	USA
1964	USA	1992	CIS
1968	USA	1996	USA
1972	USA		

Men's 4 × 100m Medley Relay

1960	USA	1980	Australia
1964	USA	1984	USA
1968	USA	1988	USA
1972	USA	1992	USA
1976	USA	1996	USA

Men's Springboard Diving

1948 Bruce Harlan (USA)
1952 David Browning (USA)
1956 Robert Clotworthy (USA)
1960 Gary Tobian (USA)
1964 Kenneth Sitzberger (USA)
1968 Bernard Wrightson (USA)
1972 Vladimir Vasin (USSR)
1976 Philip Boggs (USA)
1980 Aleksandr Portnov (USSR)
1984 Greg Louganis (USA)

1988	Greg Louganis (USA)
1992	Mark Lenzi (USA)
1996	Ni Xiong (Chn)

Men's Highboard Platform Diving

1948	Samuel Lee (USA)
1952	Samuel Lee (USA)
1956	Joaquin Capilla (Mex)
1960	Robert Webster (USA)
1964	Robert Webster (USA)
1968	Klaus Dibiasi (Ita)
1972	Klaus Dibiasi (Ita)
1976	Klaus Dibiasi (Ita)
1980	Falk Hoffmann (GDR)
1984	Greg Louganis (USA)
1988	Greg Louganis (USA)
1992	Sun Shuwei (Chn)
1996	Dimitri Sautin (Rus)

Women's 50m Freestyle

1988	Kristin Otto (GDR)
1992	Yang Wenyi (Chn)
1996	Amy van Dyken (USA)

Women's 100m Freestyle

1948	Greta Andersen (Den)
1952	Katalin Szöke (Hun)
1956	Dawn Fraser (Aus)
1960	Dawn Fraser (Aus)
1964	Dawn Fraser (Aus)
1968	Jan Henne (USA)
1972	Sandra Neilson (USA)
1976	Kornelia Ender (GDR)
1980	Barbara Krause (GDR)
1984	Nancy Hogshead (USA) / Carrie Steinseifer (USA)
1988	Kristin Otto (GDR)
1992	Zhuang Yong (Chn)
1996	Le Jingyi (Chn)

Women's 200m Freestyle

1968	Debbie Meyer (USA)
1972	Shane Gould (Aus)
1976	Kornelia Ender (GDR)
1980	Barbara Krause (GDR)
1984	Mary Wayte (USA)
1988	Heike Friedrich (GDR)
1992	Nicole Haislett (USA)
1996	Claudia Poll (Costa Rica)

Women's 400m Freestyle

1948	Ann Curtis (USA)
1952	Valéria Gyenge (Hun)
1956	Lorraine Crapp (Aus)
1960	Chris Von Saltza (USA)
1964	Virginia Duenkel (USA)
1968	Debbie Meyer (USA)
1972	Shane Gould (Aus)
1976	Petra Thümer (GDR)
1980	Ines Diers (GDR)
1984	Tiffany Cohen (USA)
1988	Janet Evans (USA)
1992	Dagmar Hase (Ger)
1996	Michelle Smith (Ire)

Women's 800m Freestyle

1968	Debbie Meyer (USA)
1972	Keena Rothhammer (USA)
1976	Petra Thümer (GDR)
1980	Michelle Ford (Aus)
1984	Tiffany Cohen (USA)
1988	Janet Evans (USA)
1992	Janet Evans (USA)
1996	Brooke Bennett (USA)

Women's 100m Backstroke

1948	Karen Harup (Den)
1952	Joan Harrison (SAf)
1956	Judy Grinham (UK)
1960	Lynn Burke (USA)
1964	Cathy Ferguson (USA)
1968	Kaye Hall (USA)
1972	Melissa Belote (USA)
1976	Ulrike Richter (GDR)
1980	Rica Reinisch (GDR)
1984	Theresa Andrews (USA)
1988	Kristin Otto (GDR)
1992	Krisztina Egerszegi (Hun)
1996	Beth Botsford (USA)

Women's 200m Backstroke

1968	Pokey Watson (USA)
1972	Melissa Belote (USA)
1976	Ulrike Richter (GDR)
1980	Rica Reinisch (GDR)
1984	Jolanda de Rover (Hol)
1988	Krisztina Egerszegi (Hun)
1992	Krisztina Egerszegi (Hun)
1996	Krisztina Egerszegi (Hun)

Women's 100m Breaststroke

1968	Djurdjica Bjedov (Yug)
1972	Catherine Carr (USA)
1976	Hannelore Anke (GDR)
1980	Ute Geweniger (GDR)
1984	Petra Van Staveren (Hol)
1988	Tania Dangalakova (Bul)
1992	Yelena Rudkovskaya (CIS/Bls)
1996	Penelope Heyns (SA)

Women's 200m Breaststroke

1948	Petronella van Vliet (Hol)
1952	Eva Székely (Hun)
1956	Ursula Happe (FRG)
1960	Anita Lonsbrough (UK)
1964	Galina Prozumenshchikova (USSR)
1968	Sharon Wichman (USA)
1972	Beverley Whitfield (Aus)
1976	Marina Koshevaya (USSR)
1980	Lina Kachushite (USSR)
1984	Anne Ottenbrite (Can)
1988	Silke Hörner (GDR)
1992	Kyoko Iwasaki (Jap)
1996	Penelope Heyns (SA)

Women's 100m Butterfly

1956	Shelley Mann (USA)
1960	Carolyn Schuler (USA)
1964	Sharon Stouder (USA)
1968	Lynette McClements (Aus)
1972	Mayumi Aoki (Jap)
1976	Kornelia Ender (GDR)
1980	Caren Metschuck (GDR)
1984	Mary T. Meagher (USA)
1988	Kristin Otto (GDR)
1992	Qian Hong (Chn)
1996	Amy van Dyken (USA)

Women's 200m Butterfly

1968	Ada Kok (Hol)
1972	Karen Moe (USA)
1976	Andrea Pollack (GDR)
1980	Ines Geissler (GDR)
1984	Mary T. Meagher (USA)
1988	Kathleen Nord (GDR)
1992	Summer Sanders (USA)
1996	Susan O'Neil (Aus)

Women's 200m Individual Medley

1968	Claudia Kolb (USA)
1972	Shane Gould (Aus)
1984	Tracy Caulkins (USA)
1988	Daniela Hunger (GDR)
1992	Lin Li (Chn)
1996	Michelle Smith (Ire)

Women's 400m Individual Medley

1964	Donna De Varona (USA)
1968	Claudia Kolb (USA)
1972	Gail Neall (Aus)

1976 Ulrike Tauber (GDR)
1980 Petra Schneider (GDR)
1984 Tracy Caulkins (USA)
1988 Janet Evans (USA)
1992 Krisztina Egerszegi (Hun)
1996 Michelle Smith (Ire)

Women's 4 × 100m Freestyle Medley

1948 USA
1952 Hungary
1956 Australia
1960 USA
1964 USA
1968 USA
1972 USA
1976 USA
1980 East Germany
1984 USA
1988 East Germany
1992 USA
1996 USA

Women's 4 × 100m Medley Relay

1960 USA
1964 USA
1968 USA
1972 USA
1976 East Germany
1980 East Germany
1984 USA
1988 East Germany
1992 USA
1996 USA

Women's 4 × 200m Medley Relay

1996 USA

Women's Synchronized Swimming

Solo

1984 Tracie Ruiz (USA)

1988 Carolyn Waldo (Can)
1992 Kristen Babb-Sprague (USA)

Duet

1984 Candy Costie and Tracie Ruiz (USA)
1988 Michelle Cameron and Carolyn Waldo (Can)
1992 Karen and Sarah Josephson (USA)

Team

1996 USA

Women's Springboard Diving

1948 Victoria Draves (USA)
1952 Pat McCormick (USA)
1956 Pat McCormick (USA)
1960 Ingrid Krämer (GDR)
1964 Ingrid Engel (née Krämer) (GDR)
1968 Sue Gossick (USA)
1972 Micki King (USA)
1976 Jennifer Chandler (USA)
1980 Irina Kalinina (USSR)
1984 Sylvie Bernier (Can)
1988 Gao Min (Chn)
1992 Gao Min (Chn)
1996 Fu Mingxia (Chn)

Women's Highboard Platform Diving

1948 Victoria Draves (USA)
1952 Pat McCormick (USA)
1956 Pat McCormick (USA)
1960 Ingrid Krämer (GDR)
1964 Lesley Bush (USA)
1968 Milena Duchkova (Cze)
1972 Ulrika Knape (Swe)
1976 Elena Vaytsekhovskaya (USSR)
1980 Martina Jäschke (GDR)
1984 Zhou Jihong (Chn)
1988 Xu Yanmei (Chn)
1992 Fu Mingxia (Chn)
1996 Fu Mingxia (Chn)

WINTER OLYMPICS

MEDALS TABLE, 1998

(Games held at Nagano, Japan)

	Gold	Silver	Bronze	Total
Germany	12	9	8	29
Norway	10	10	5	25
Russia	9	6	3	18
Canada	6	5	4	15
USA	6	3	4	13
Netherlands	5	4	2	11
Japan	5	1	4	10
Austria	3	5	9	17
S Korea	3	1	2	6
Italy	2	6	2	10
Finland	2	4	6	12
Switzerland	2	2	3	7
France	2	1	5	8
Czech Rep	1	1	1	3
Bulgaria	1	0	0	1
China	0	6	2	8
Sweden	0	2	1	3
Denmark	0	1	0	1
Ukraine	0	1	0	1
Belarus	0	0	2	2
Kazakhstan	0	0	2	2
Australia	0	0	1	1
Belgium	0	0	1	1
Great Britain	0	0	1	1

YACHTING

AMERICA'S CUP

For the background to the America's Cup, *see* **L6**.

Winners (since 1960)

Year	Yacht	Skipper
1962	*Weatherly* (USA)	Emil Mosbacher Jr
1964	*Constellation* (USA)	Bob Bavier Jr
1967	*Intrepid* (USA)	Emil Mosbacher Jr
1970	*Intrepid* (USA)	Bill Ficker
1974	*Courageous* (USA)	Ted Hood
1977	*Courageous* (USA)	Ted Turner
1980	*Freedom* (USA)	Dennis Conner
1983	*Australia II* (Aus)	John Bertrand
1987	*Stars & Stripes* (USA)	Dennis Conner
1988	*Stars & Stripes* (USA)	Dennis Conner
1992	*America* (USA)	Bill Koch
1995	*Black Magic* (NZ)	Russell Coutts

ADMIRAL'S CUP (Since 1975)

Year	Country	Year	Country
1975	UK	1987	New Zealand
1977	UK	1989	UK
1979	Australia	1991	France
1981	UK	1993	Germany
1983	West Germany	1995	Italy
1985	West Germany	1997	USA

BIBLICAL GLOSSARY

This section provides an easy to use treasure-house of information about the biblical world. It presents a concise and valuable guide to the people, places and events which have had so much influence on the course of history.

THE LAND OF PALESTINE

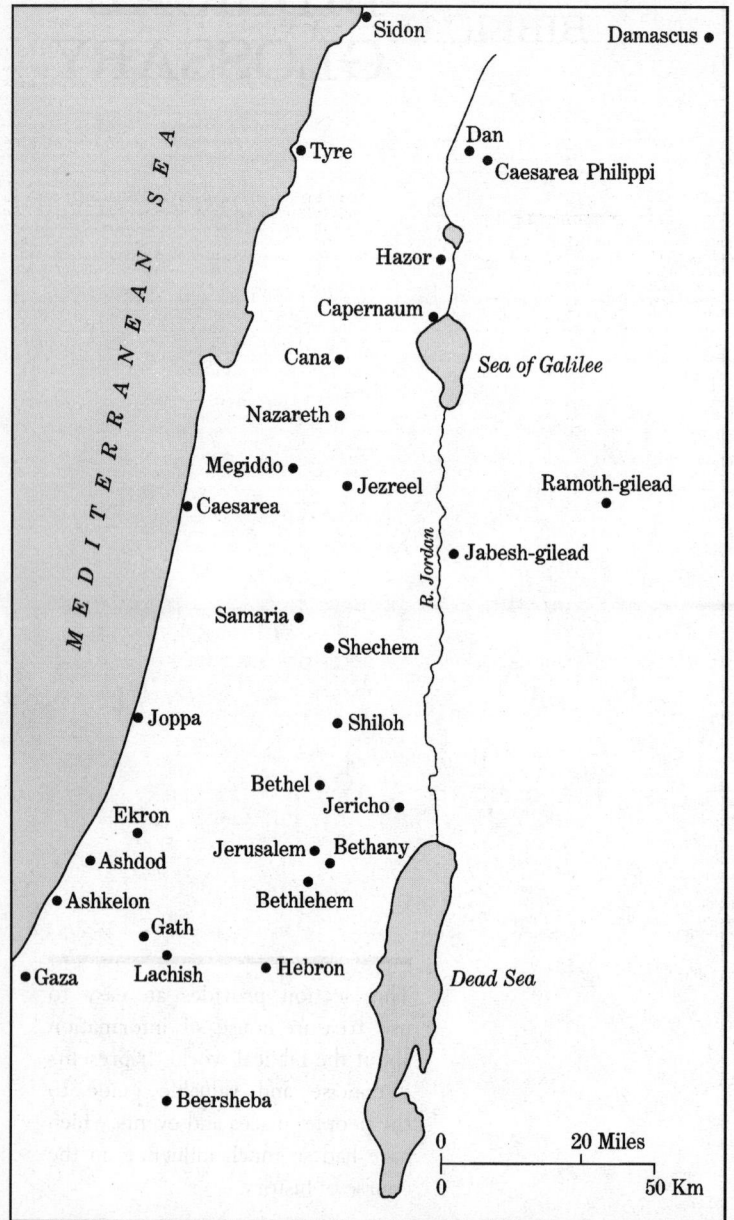

N.B. This map does not represent Palestine as it was at any one period of history. It shows most of the Palestinian locations mentioned in the text from whatever period.

BIBLICAL GLOSSARY

INTRODUCTION

There is a sense in which the Bible is part of every person's heritage. Though it is sometimes claimed that we are now living in a post-Christian era, the marks of a Christian culture are part of our everyday experience: the great cathedrals of our cities, the parish churches and village chapels of our countryside, the frequent allusions to biblical ideas or symbols in the works of many of our novelists, poets and playwrights, even the appearance of a Christian hymn, *Amazing Grace*, in the "pop" charts. At the root of this culture is the revelation of God offered by the Bible.

Even to those who do not accept the faith it proclaims, the Bible has much to commend it. It contains some fine poetry, vivid story-telling, deep insights into the human condition and moral guidance which has stood the test of time. It is also of enormous value simply as a historical resource. For Christians, of course, it is much more than this, a unique revelation of God.

It is not, however, an easy book. The modern reader has to bridge a major time-gap of at least 2,000 years (often much more) and enter into an alien culture if he is to become familiar with the biblical world. It is astonishing how many Christians have succeeded in making this transition with little or no help, and found that the Bible can still speak across the barriers of time and space. But today it should not be necessary for anyone to read the Bible unaided. Within the last century our understanding of the way the biblical writers worked, of the cultural background against which their lives were set, and of the wider historical and religious background of the surrounding nations have all increased enormously.

Much of this new knowledge is now available in large, definitive dictionaries of the Bible and in detailed commentaries on individual books. The reader who wishes seriously to improve his understanding of the Bible must consult such works. This section, however, is intended to offer assistance to those who do not possess more specialised works of reference, with information which is simply presented but does not gloss over the complexity of the issues, and which is based on the consensus of modern scholarly opinion.

ABBREVIATIONS USED IN GIVING BIBLICAL REFERENCES

Acts	Acts	Isaiah	Is	Nehemiah	Neh
Amos	Amos	James	Jas	Numbers	Num
Chronicles	Chr	Jeremiah	Jer	Obadiah	Obad
Colossians	Col	Job	Job	Peter	Pet
Corinthians	Cor	Joel	Joel	Philemon	Phlm
Daniel	Dan	John	Jn	Philippians	Phil
Deuteronomy	Deut	Jonah	Jon	Proverbs	Prov
Ecclesiastes	Ecc	Joshua	Josh	Psalms	Ps
Ephesians	Eph	Jude	Jude	Revelation	Rev
Esther	Esth	Judges	Judg	Romans	Rom
Exodus	Ex	Kings	Kgs	Ruth	Ruth
Ezekiel	Ezek	Lamentations	Lam	Samuel	Sam
Ezra	Ezra	Leviticus	Lev	Song of Songs	Song
Galatians	Gal	Luke	Lk	Thessalonians	Thes
Genesis	Gen	Malachi	Mal	Timothy	Tim
Habakkuk	Hab	Mark	Mk	Titus	Tit
Haggai	Hag	Matthew	Mt	Zechariah	Zech
Hebrews	Heb	Micah	Mic	Zephaniah	Zeph
Hosea	Hos	Nahum	Nah		

A

Aaron. The elder brother of Moses, he was appointed by God to be Moses' spokesman in the negotiations with the Egyptian Pharaoh for the release of the Jews (Ex 4:14). After the exodus, in Moses' absence, he made a golden calf for the people to worship (Ex 32:1-6). In spite of this lapse, tradition regards him as Israel's first High Priest (Ex 29:1-7).

Abednego. One of three young men who, according to the book of Daniel, survived being thrown into a blazing furnace for refusing to worship a gold statue set up by King Nebuchadnezzar (Dan 3:1-27).

Abel. The second son of Adam and Eve, he was killed by his elder brother Cain out of jealousy because God found Abel's offering of a lamb more acceptable than his offering of grain (Gen 4:1-8). The story probably reflects a feeling among traditionalists that the Jews had been corrupted by the agricultural civilisation of Canaan, and were less acceptable to God than when they had been shepherds.

Abiathar. When his father Ahimelech was killed by Saul for his unwitting involvement in David's escape, Abiathar fled to join David's outlaw band (1 Sam 22:16-23). He subsequently became David's High Priest, but was banished by Solomon because he supported Adonijah in the struggle for succession to the throne (1 Kgs 1:5-7, 26-27).

Abijah. King of Judah (915-913 B.C.).

Abner. Saul's commander-in-chief. After Saul's death he supported Ishbosheth, his only surviving son, as king of Israel, but soon became disenchanted with him. He was negotiating with David to transfer the allegiance of the northern tribes to him when he was murdered by David's commander, Joab, in pursuance of a family quarrel (2 Sam 3:6-27).

Abraham. Abraham, originally known as Abram, is regarded as the father of the Jewish people. While there are doubtless legendary elements in the stories told of him, there is no reason to question his historical existence, probably in the period 2000-1800 B.C. Through the stories of Abraham run two complementary themes: God's promises and Abraham's faith. God promises to Abraham that he will have numerous descendants, that they will occupy the land of Canaan and that they will be a source of blessing to all mankind (Gen 12:1-3). Abraham responds to these promises with faith, shown in his willingness to set out for the promised land not knowing where he is being led, and to sacrifice his son Isaac when he thinks that this is what God requires. Neighbouring peoples (e.g. the Moabites) still practised child sacrifice a thousand years later, and this story, as well as indicating Abraham's faith, reflects the early understanding of the Jews that God did not require human sacrifice.

Absalom. David's third son. After his sister Tamar had been raped by her elder half-brother Amnon, he plotted revenge and eventually had Amnon killed (2 Sam 13). As a result he had to flee to the small state of Geshur which his grandfather ruled. After three years he was permitted to return at the instigation of David's general, Joab, who probably felt that Amnon had only got his due punishment. He then proceeded to plot against his father, sowing seeds of discontent among the northern tribes especially (2 Sam 15:1-6) and finally raised an army to march on Jerusalem. David withdrew across the Jordan, gained time to organise loyal forces and crushed the rebels. In the decisive battle Absalom was killed by Joab, even though David had expressly instructed that he should not be harmed (2 Sam 18:6-15).

Acts of the Apostles. The book is clearly a sequel to Luke's gospel, being addressed to the same person, Theophilus, and referring to an earlier work which described "the things that Jesus did and taught from the time he began his work until the day when he was taken up to heaven." It is invaluable for the insight it gives into the first thirty years of the Christian church. Peter and Paul are the leading personalities in the book, yet the theme is not one of human heroes but of God at work among the community of believers through the gift of the Holy Spirit.

The somewhat surprising ending, with Paul under house arrest in Rome, has led many to wonder whether the work was unfinished or a third volume planned, yet in some ways this is a most fitting conclusion—Paul in spite of everything proclaiming the good news at the very heart of the Roman empire.

Adam. The name is simply the Hebrew for "man". Adam is therefore to be thought of not as the first man in a historical sense but as the symbolic prototype of all mankind.

Adonijah. The fourth son of David. As the eldest surviving son by the time his father reached old age, he expected to succeed to the throne and had himself declared king by Abiathar and Joab before David's death. David, however, nominated Solomon to succeed him and Solomon soon found occasion to accuse Adonijah of treachery and have him put to death (1 Kgs 1:5-53, 2:13-25).

Agrippa, *see* **Herod Family.**

Ahab. King of Israel (869-850 B.C.). The son of Omri, who arranged his marriage to Jezebel, daughter of the king of Tyre, as part of his policy of friendly relations with Phoenicia. His chief fault was his failure to curb the excesses of his wife, who was determined to supplant the worship of Yahweh with the worship of her own god, Baal Melkart. He ignored the advice of the prophet Micaiah to go to battle against the Syrians at Ramoth-Gilead, where he was fatally wounded by an arrow.

Ahaz. King of Judah (735-715 B.C.). Ahaz came to the throne at a moment of crisis. King Pekah of Israel and King Rezin of Damascus had formed an allegiance against the powerful Assyrians, and were threatening to attack Judah if she did not join them. In desperation, and against the advice of Isaiah, he appealed to the Assyrians for help. This he received, but at the cost of becoming an Assyrian vassal. He is criticised by the biblical historians for taking part in idolatrous practices, and is even said to have sacrificed his own son (2 Kgs 16:1-4).

Ahaziah. (1) King of Israel (850-849 B.C.). The son of Ahab, within two years of coming to the throne he fell from a balcony and never recovered from his injuries (2 Kgs 1:2).

(2) King of Judah (842 B.C.). The son of Jehoram, he had the misfortune to be visiting his father's namesake, Jehoram king of Israel, at the time of Jehu's rebellion in which he was killed (2 Kgs 9:27-28).

Ahijah. A prophet from Shiloh who predicted the division of the kingdom after Solomon's death by tearing his robe into twelve pieces and giving ten of them (representing ten tribes) to Jeroboam, later to be the first king of the breakaway state of Israel (1 Kgs 11:29-40).

Ahimelech. The priest at Nob who unwittingly assisted David's escape from Saul by giving him food and a sword. He was subsequently killed by Saul together with all the other priests at Nob (1 Sam 21:1-9).

Alexandria. Though only mentioned four times in the Bible (all the references being in Acts), Alexandria had a large Jewish community almost from its foundation in 332 B.C. by Alexander the Great, and it was here that the Septuagint, the Greek translation of the Old Testament, was made during the third and second centuries B.C.

Amalekites. A nomadic people who lived in the desert regions to the south of Israel. They attacked the Israelites during their march from Egypt to the promised land, and were later attacked and defeated by both Saul and David (1 Sam 15:1-9, 30:1-20).

Amaziah. King of Judah (800-783 B.C.). After succeeding in regaining territory earlier lost to the Edomites, Amaziah got into an unnecessary and disastrous quarrel with King Jehoash of Israel from which he emerged the clear loser. He was eventually assassinated at Lachish, where he had fled, having heard of a plot against his life (2 Kgs 14:1-19).

Ammonites. A trans-Jordanian tribe frequently at war with the Israelites. It was in action against the Ammonites that Saul proved his powers of leadership (1 Sam 11:1-15), and although David seems to have established good relations with King Nahash of Ammon, his son insulted David's envoys and bitter hostilities ensued. David ultimately took the Ammonite crown, but only after a long struggle (1 Sam 10:1–11:1, 13:26–31).

Amon. King of Judah (642–640 B.C.). The son of the hated Manasseh, he was soon assassinated because he continued in his father's idolatrous ways.

Amos. The first of the great reforming prophets of the eighth century B.C., we know relatively little about the man himself as opposed to what he taught. A herdsman and grower of figs from Tekoa in Judah, he prophesied in the cities of Israel to which he perhaps travelled to sell his produce. His prophetic career may have lasted as little as a few months sometime during the period 760–750 B.C.

Amos was appalled by a society in which an affluent minority exploited the poverty-stricken majority. Loans would be made to the poor, and when they were unable to repay them, their houses and land would be seized, or their children sold into slavery to pay off the debt. The use of false weights and measures by the merchants was commonplace, and bribery in the courts ensured that no case against them would ever succeed. Yet these same merchants made lavish sacrifices to God at the national shrines of Gilgal and Bethel.

Amos believed in a God of righteousness who demanded right living from his people. Furthermore, he was a God of limitless power who controlled the forces of the universe and directed the course of human history. If his people failed to see the evil of their ways he would use a foreign power as the instrument of his judgement upon them. The fact that they were a chosen people would not prevent this: indeed they, more than any other nation, should know what God required and their failure to meet his standards was all the more blameworthy.

The message of Amos is uncompromising, and needs to be balanced by the words of later prophets who saw the possibility of redemption as well as judgement. Nevertheless his importance is immense, as the man who proclaimed with a new clarity the incompatibility of worshipping God and exploiting one's fellow men.

Ananias. (1) A member of the early church who sold some property and gave part of the proceeds to the church, but claimed to have given all. Peter accused him of lying to God, and he fell down dead (Acts 5:1–6).

(2) A Christian in Damascus who, in response to a vision, went and baptised Saul following his conversion (Acts 9:10–19).

(3) The Jewish High Priest before whom Paul appeared after his arrest in the temple at Jerusalem (Acts 23:1–5).

Andrew. The brother of Simon Peter and one of the first disciples.

Annas. Though he had retired from the High Priesthood before the time of Jesus' trial, Annas continued to exercise influence through his son-in-law and successor, Caiaphas.

Antioch. (1) The capital of the Roman province of Syria and an important centre of early Christianity. It was here that disciples were first called Christians, and it was this church that sent Paul and Barnabas out on the first missionary journey (Acts 13:1–3).

(2) A city in Pisidia (part of Asia Minor) visited by Paul on his first missionary journey (Acts 13:13–52).

Apocalypse. Prophetic description of the end of the world from the Greek word meaning "revelation".

Apollos. A Jew from Alexandria who proclaimed the gospel in Ephesus but only knew about John's baptism as opposed to Christian baptism in the Holy Spirit. After Prisca and Aquila had explained Christianity more fully to him he went on to Corinth where, unfortunately, opposing factions developed according to whether they "followed" Apollos or other teachers (Acts 18:24–28, 1 Cor 1:12–13).

Aquila. A Jew who, with his wife Prisca, was expelled from Rome by an edict of Claudius and settled in Corinth. Here they welcomed Paul, and later worked with him in Ephesus (Acts 18:1–4, 24–26).

Aramaeans, see Syrians.

Areopagus. An open space in Athens, often used

for public debates, and where Paul addressed the Athenians (Acts 17:16–34).

Ark of the Covenant. An ornate wooden chest believed to contain the stone tablets on which the ten commandments were written. It accompanied the Israelites throughout their nomadic wanderings and was then kept at Shiloh during the early years of the occupation of Palestine. Brought by the Israelites to encourage them in battle against the Philistines at Aphek, it was in fact captured, but the Philistines soon returned it, attributing a series of disasters to its presence. David brought it to Jerusalem, where Solomon eventually enshrined it in the temple. It is presumed to have remained there until the temple was destroyed by the Babylonians in 586 B.C.

Artemis. A Greek goddess identified with the Roman Diana. Her temple at Ephesus was famous, though the worship there seems to have been based on an earlier fertility cult.

Asa. King of Judah (913–873 B.C.).

Ascension. Although this is the word normally used to describe Jesus' departure from the earth, its significance is metaphorical rather than literal. It signifies the return of Jesus to God, and the taking up again of the power and authority he voluntarily laid down in order to share the human experience (Acts 1:6–11).

Ashdod. One of the five Philistine city-states.

Asher. (1) The eighth son of Jacob, his second by Zilpah, Leah's slave-girl.

(2) The tribe of Asher which occupied fertile land along the coastal plain north of Mount Carmel.

Ashkelon. One of the five Philistine city-states.

Assyria. A major power to the north-east of Israel for over two centuries. As early as 853 B.C. Ahab had to meet the threat of an Assyrian invasion, though it was not until the accession of Tiglath-pileser III to the Assyrian throne in 745 B.C. that Assyria took a dominating role in the affairs of Palestine. By 721 B.C. the northern kingdom of Israel had become an Assyrian province and the southern kingdom of Judah was paying heavy tribute. An attempt by Hezekiah to become independent from Assyria in 705 B.C. was punished by an invasion in which all the fortified cities of Judah except for Jerusalem itself were taken and destroyed. Judah remained subservient to Assyria until the Assyrian empire began to break up under pressure from the Medes and the Babylonians about 630 B.C.

Athaliah. Queen of Judah (842–837 B.C.). The wife of Jehoram, king of Judah and mother of Ahaziah, who succeeded him. When Ahaziah lost his life in Jehu's rebellion, Athaliah seized the throne and put to death all male members of the royal family except for Joash, one of Ahaziah's sons who was hidden by his aunt. After six years in hiding he was proclaimed king by members of the forces acting on the instructions of Jehoiada the priest, and Athaliah was killed.

Athens. Visited by Paul on his second missionary journey. The sermon he preached there (Acts 17:16–34) is notable for its attempt to speak to Greek thinkers in terms they would find familiar, but his success appears to have been slight and Athens was never an important centre of Christianity.

Atonement, Day of. The most solemn day of fasting in the Jewish calendar. The High Priest went into the most sacred part of the temple (the only day of the year on which this was permitted) to make a special offering in expiation of the sins of the people. These sins were symbolically transferred to a goat (the "scape-goat") which was then driven out into the wilderness (Lev 16:20–34).

B

Baal. The Hebrew word means simply "master", "owner" or "husband", and it was used as a general term for foreign gods, but especially for the Canaanite fertility god. Although the debased sexual practices associated with the worship of this god were fiercely condemned by Hebrew writers, it was probably through contact with Canaanite religion that the people of Israel came to view their own God as creator and lord of the world of nature.

Baasha. King of Israel (900–877 B.C.), and involved in a border dispute with Asa, king of Judah.

Babel, Tower of. The significance of the story is mythological rather than historical. Partly it is an attempt to explain the variety of human languages, but it also reflects a view long held in certain sectors of Israelite society that man's close relationship with God was broken once he began to build cities and become, in his own eyes, self-sufficient. Like the story of Adam's disobedience it regards human greed and arrogance as the root causes of his estrangement from God.

Babylonians. When the Babylonians and Medes destroyed Assyria they divided her empire between them, with the Babylonians taking the southern portion. They therefore took over from the Assyrians the dominating role in Palestinian affairs from 605 B.C. Rebellions against Babylonian overlordship in 598 B.C. and 589 B.C. were disastrously unsuccessful, the latter resulting in the destruction of Jerusalem and its temple and the exile of many of its people in 586 B.C.

Baptism. The origins of baptism are obscure. John the Baptist baptised as a sign of repentance (Mk 1:4–5), and the Jews are known to have used a form of baptism as a means of entry to the Jewish faith for non-Jews, though it is uncertain whether or not this custom was established before John started baptising. There is no record of Jesus baptising anyone, yet it seems to have been established as the mode of entry into the Christian church from earliest times (Acts 1:38). Baptism was first administered to adult believers, or sometimes to whole families on the conversion of the head of household (Acts 16:33), and from this seems to have sprung the practice of baptising infants of Christian parents.

Barabbas. According to an established custom of releasing a prisoner at Passover time, Pilate set free Barabbas in preference to Jesus on the insistence of the crowd (Jn 18:38–40).

Barnabas. A prominent member of the early church, invariably exerting an influence for good at crucial moments. He was the first to befriend Paul in Jerusalem after his conversion (Acts 9:26–27). Sent by the Jerusalem church to report on work among the Gentiles which had begun in Syrian Antioch, he made a favourable recommendation, remained himself to continue the work and brought Paul to join him (Acts 11:19–26). He was Paul's companion on the first missionary journey (Acts 13:1–3), but did not accompany him on the second journey for characteristic reasons. Paul did not want to take John Mark, who had failed them on the first journey, while Barnabas wanted to give him a second chance. Significantly Paul was later to become reconciled to John Mark, thus confirming Barnabas' judgement (2 Tim 4:11).

Bartholomew. One of the twelve disciples, *See* **Nathaniel.**

Baruch. Acted as scribe to Jeremiah and read out a message from Jeremiah in the temple precincts at a time when Jeremiah himself had been banned from speaking there (Jer 36:1–8).

Bathsheba. The wife of Uriah, an officer in King David's army. Because she was expecting a child by David, he gave orders that Uriah be left in an exposed position during the fighting against the Ammonites, and he was killed. Bathsheba's child died in infancy, but she subsequently bore Solomon (2 Sam 11:2–12:25).

Beersheba. A town on the southernmost border of Judah: hence the expression "from Dan to Beersheba" to mean the whole of Israel.

Belshazzar. The last king of Babylon before its capture by the Persian monarch Cyrus in 539 B.C. Mentioned in the Bible only in the book of Daniel, particularly in the dramatic story of his downfall recorded in the fifth chapter.

Benjamin. (1) The twelfth son of Jacob, his second by Rachel, who died in giving birth to him (Gen 35:16–18).
(2) The tribe of Benjamin, occupying a relatively small area just north of Judah.

Bernice. The sister of Herod Agrippa II, she

heard with him Paul's defence of his conduct before the Roman governor Festus (Acts 25:13–26:31).

Bethany. A village just outside Jerusalem, the home of Lazarus, Martha and Mary. It was here that Jesus stayed on his final visit to Jerusalem.

Bethesda. A pool in Jerusalem believed to have healing properties, particularly when the waters were disturbed. The scene of one of Jesus' healing miracles in John 5:1–9.

Bethlehem. A town in Judaea some five miles south of Jerusalem and known from before King David's time. Chiefly famous as the birthplace of Jesus, although some scholars now believe it more likely he was born in or near Nazareth which was in Galilee.

Bildad. The second of Job's three "comforters" (Job 8).

Booths, *see* **Tabernacles.**

C

Caesarea. A city on the Palestinian coast built by Herod the Great and named after Caesar Augustus. The Roman governors of Palestine had their residence in Caesarea, and it was here that Paul was tried before Felix and Festus, spending the intervening two years under arrest (Acts 24:1–26:32).

Caiaphas. The High Priest during the time of Jesus' ministry, who presided at his examination before the Jewish Council.

Cain, *see* **Abel.**

Cana. A village in Galilee where Jesus attended a wedding celebration and, according to John 2:1–11, turned water into wine.

Canaanites. The people who occupied the territory subsequently taken over by the people of Israel. Their civilisation was materially more advanced than that of the people of Israel, but morally they lagged far behind and their cultic practices are condemned by biblical writers. Around 1800 B.C. they invented the alphabet.

Capernaum. A little frontier town by the Sea of Galilee which for a time was the centre of Jesus' ministry. It was here that he called Matthew (Mt 9:9) and performed a number of healings including that of the centurion's servant (Lk 7:1–9).

Carmel. The culmination of a spur branching westwards from the main north–south mountain range of Palestine and almost reaching the coast. It was the scene of Elijah's confrontation with the prophets of Baal (1 Kgs 18:19–40).

Chaldeans, *see* **Babylonians.**

Christ, *see* **Jesus** and **Messiah.**

Christian. A nickname, first used in Syrian Antioch (Acts 11:26), which gradually became the normal way of describing a follower of Christ. Elsewhere in the New Testament, Christians are referred to as followers of "the Way", Nazarenes or simply the saints.

Chronicles, Books of. These books give an account of the history of the Jews from the death of Saul to the return from the exile. They are therefore largely a retelling of events already recorded by earlier authors in the books of Samuel and Kings. The purpose of the chroniclers seems to have been to reassure their people of God's care for them in spite of the adversities recently suffered, and this leads them to present an unjustifiably rosy view of Israel's history (*e.g.* glorifying David's reign and glossing over his weaknesses). Consequently most scholars prefer to rely on the earlier and more sober accounts in Samuel and Kings, but, treated with caution, the information in Chronicles provides a useful supplement to the earlier records.

Colossians, Letter to the. As far as is known, Paul himself never visited Colossae, but the church there had been founded by Epaphras, a close associate of Paul (Col 1:7). Perhaps he felt some responsibility for the Colossian Christians because of this. The letter was probably written during Paul's imprisonment in Rome and appears to be a response to reports of false teachers in Colossae. These teachers suggest that there is a special kind of knowledge (over and above the knowledge of Christ) which is necessary for salvation, and they advocate an ascetic way of life. Paul's reply stresses that Christ alone is all-sufficient for the needs of his readers.

Commandments. There are, of course, many commandments in the Bible, but the ten commandments which God is said to have given to Moses on Mount Sinai have a special place. They are seen as the basis of God's agreement with the people of Israel and, significantly, combine religious and social obligations. In Israel's religion true worship and right living are not to be separated (Ex 20:1–17).

Corinth. Strategically situated at a major junction of trading routes, Corinth in New Testament times was a wealthy city which not even Athens could match in importance among the cities of Greece. It also had an evil reputation, however, because of its notoriously lax moral standards. Both its importance and its depravity may have commended it to Paul as a place to preach the Christian gospel. He spent 18 months there about A.D. 50 (Acts 18:1–18), and made at least one further visit, possibly two. His letters to the church at Corinth show that he was passionately concerned about its welfare.

Corinthians, Letters to the. Although Paul's correspondence with the Corinthians is collected into two letters in the New Testament, most scholars are agreed that they include parts of four separate communications summarised below:

(1) A letter of warning against pagan influences, a fragment of which appears in 2 Corinthians 6:14–7:1 and which is referred to in 1 Corinthians 5:9–13.

(2) The letter now known as 1 Corinthians.

(3) An extremely severe letter partly preserved in 2 Corinthians 10–13.

(4) A much more relaxed letter, perhaps showing relief that the severe letter had had the desired effect, and preserved in 2 Corinthians 1–9.

The letters afford valuable insights into the problems which faced a small Christian community set in a pagan environment, and into the relationship between Paul and a church which nearly drove him to distraction because of its waywardness and the depth of his concern for it.

Cornelius. A Roman centurion whose baptism by Peter represented an important step in the progress of the Christian church from a Jewish sect to a universal faith (Acts 10).

Covenant. The concept of the covenant—an agreement between God and man—is implicit throughout the Old Testament. The first explicit reference comes in the story of Noah where God makes a covenant to save Noah and his family from the impending flood and subsequently agrees never again to send such a flood upon the earth. God then makes a covenant with Abraham to establish his descendants as a chosen people, though it should be noted that they are chosen to bring God's blessing to all nations (Gen 12:3). It is however, the covenant made at Sinai after the exodus that is regarded as the most important. In this covenant God offers the people of Israel a special place in his plans if they will serve him alone and obey his commandments (Ex 19:5–6). Again it is noteworthy that the people of Israel are to serve God as priests, i.e. as people who mediate the knowledge of God to others.

Covenant, Book of the. In 622 B.C. during the course of repairs on the temple, a scroll was discovered which is described as the Book of the Covenant. When this was brought to King Josiah he realised that his people had failed to live up to God's demands, and set in motion the most far-reaching religious reforms ever known in Judah. These included the suppression of all pagan cults, an edict that in future sacrifice could only take place in the temple in Jerusalem, and the re-institution of the Passover which had apparently not been celebrated for many years (2 Kgs 22:3–23:23). The close similarities between these measures and instructions contained in the book of Deuteronomy suggest that the Book of the Covenant was in fact the first edition of Deuteronomy. It is thought to have been written by pious Jews during the long and evil reign of Manasseh

(687–642 B.C.) as a re-statement and amplification of the covenant with Moses. Not daring to publish it openly at the time, they hid it in the temple, hoping that it would later be discovered and acted upon.

Creation. There are two creation stories in the Old Testament, a primitive version which nevertheless has considerable charm starting at Genesis 2:4, and the more familiar version with which Genesis begins, but which is actually later in origin. *See also* **Genesis**.

Cross. The supreme symbol of the Christian faith because it represents the depths of suffering Jesus was prepared to embrace in order to save mankind by inaugurating God's Kingdom upon earth. Crucifixion was the normal method of execution for those who did not possess Roman citizenship, and because the wounds inflicted were not in themselves very serious, a strong man could take days to die. According to Mark 15:44, Pilate was surprised that Jesus had died within hours.

Cyrus (c. 559–530 B.C.). The Persian king who overthrew the Babylonian empire and allowed the exiled Jews to return to their homeland.

D

Damascus. An ancient city, the capital of Syria. In the Old Testament, in fact, Damascus and Syria are synonymous. It was on his way to Damascus to persecute the Christian community there that Paul had his conversion experience.

Dan. (1) The fifth son of Jacob, his first by Bilhah, Rachel's slave-girl.

(2) The tribe of Dan, occupying a small area north of Judah and west of Benjamin.

(3) The city of Dan in the far north of Israel; hence the expression "from Dan to Beersheba" meaning the whole of Israel.

Daniel. Almost certainly written between 167 and 164 B.C., Daniel is one of the last of the books of the Old Testament chronologically. At this time the Greek ruler Antiochus Epiphanes was attempting systematically to destroy the Jewish religion. The book was written to encourage the resistance movement with stories of Daniel and his friends, who refused to compromise in religious matters during the Babylonian captivity some four hundred years earlier. The second half of the book contains obscure visions which appear to predict the ultimate downfall of pagan empires and the triumph of the people of God.

David. King of Israel from about 1000 to about 960 B.C. It is not clear whether David first came to Saul's attention as a skilled musician able to soothe him in his depressions (1 Sam 16:17–23) or as the shepherd boy who killed the Philistine champion Goliath (1 Sam 17:12–51). In either case he soon showed his military skill, and before long was receiving adulation greater than Saul himself (1 Sam 18:7). Saul's insane jealousy forced David to flee from his court and become an outlaw, eventually offering his services, and those of the 600 men who had joined him, to the Philistines as a way of keeping out of Saul's clutches (1 Sam 27:1–4).

Whilst nominally a Philistine vassal, David attacked traditional enemies of Israel such as the Amalekites, and distributed his booty among the tribe of Judah, thus indicating that his change of allegiance was a temporary expedient (1 Sam 30:1–31). When Saul was killed in battle David was immediately accepted as king of Judah (2 Sam 2:4), but the northern tribes were ruled by Saul's son, Ishbosheth, until he was assassinated by two of his officers (2 Sam 4:5–8).

As king of all Israel David rapidly subdued the Philistines (2 Sam 5:17–25), and soon turned his attention to the Ammonites, who had insulted his ambassadors (2 Sam 10:1–5). During the Ammonite war he successfully beat off a Syrian attack and subsequently annexed much Syrian territory. He also conquered the Moabites and the Edomites east of the Jordan. In the end he ruled an empire stretching some 725 kilometres from north to south and 185 kilometres from east to west.

David was not just a brilliant military tactician however. He was a statesman who understood the need for national unity and the crucial part to be played by his people's religion in achieving this. He established his capital in Jerusalem because it was close to the boundary between Judah and the northern tribes, and did not actually belong to any of the tribes, being still in the hands of the Jebusites. This was presumably to avoid inter-tribal jealousy. Although he did not build a temple, he brought the ark of the covenant to Jerusalem, thus establishing it as a religious centre and not just an administrative capital.

David's later years were marred by struggles among his sons to gain the throne, and he seems to have been uncharacteristically weak and indecisive in dealing with them.

Deborah, Song of. If this hymn of triumph over the enemy commander, Sisera, was composed at the time of the events, as seems likely, it dates from before 1100 B.C. and is therefore one of the oldest fragments of literature in the Old Testament (Judg 5:2–31).

Dedication, Feast of. A feast to commemorate the rededication of the temple following its desecration by the Greek ruler Antiochus Epiphanes in 168 B.C.

Demetrius. A silversmith of Ephesus who stirred up trouble for the Christian community because the success of Christianity was affecting the trade of those who made silver models of the temple of Artemis (or Diana), the local goddess (Acts 19:23–41).

Deuteronomy, *see* **Covenant, Book of the.**

Devil. Contrary to popular opinion, the devil has a very minor role in the biblical writings. In the book of Job, Satan is counsel for the prosecution at the court of God, and therefore not a figure of evil as such. At the beginning of Jesus' ministry the devil appears in the role of tempter (Lk 4:1–13) and elsewhere as the adversary of God (1 Jn 3:8). Strictly, Jewish and Christian monotheism seems to offer no place for a devil except as a subordinate of God, and perhaps he is best regarded as a valuable, but mythological expression of the reality of evil.

Diana, *see* **Artemis.**

Dispersion (Greek Diaspora). Over a period of centuries many Jews left Palestine for a variety of reasons. Some left in times of famine to seek food elsewhere, some fled from invading armies or were forcibly exiled, others went voluntarily to set up business in the major centres of commerce. By New Testament times these Jews of the Dispersion outnumbered those in Palestine, and there were few cities round the eastern Mediterranean without a sizeable Jewish colony. It is no accident that some of the most important figures in the early church—Stephen, Philip, Barnabas and Paul, for example—were Jews of the Dispersion, for their circumstances made them less fettered by tradition and more open to new thinking.

Dorcas. A Christian woman who lived in Joppa and was renowned for her good deeds among the poor. According to Acts 9:36–42 Peter restored her to life after she had died.

E

Ecclesiastes. A strange book to find in the Bible because of its apparently unrelenting pessimism. The burden of the author's message seems to be that there is no fulfilment to be found in human existence. Man's life on earth is governed by the endless cycle of the seasons, all too soon to be ended by death, beyond which there is no certainty of anything. Some commentators suggest that the author was simply exposing the limitations of a purely rational approach and thereby demonstrating the need for a wider view of human life based on trust in God, but if this was the author's intention he fails to make it at all explicit.

Edomites. Recognised as relations of the Jews because of their alleged descent from Esau, the Edomites were nevertheless often in conflict with the people of Israel. Their territory extended from the southern end of the Dead Sea to the Gulf of Aqaba, and was of importance

because of its copper mines and because it afforded access to African trade routes via the Red Sea. David conquered the Edomites and Solomon made full use of the strategic advantages thus gained, but they gradually reasserted their independence and were never again completely subjugated by the people of Israel.

Egypt. Although the influence of Egypt on Palestinian affairs was less dramatic than that of the Mesopotamian empires of Assyria and Babylonia, it was far more persistent. From very early times the story of the Jews is linked with Egypt, and the great event of Jewish history is the escape from Egyptian captivity. During the period when Assyria and Babylon were at the height of their power, Egypt used the Palestinian states to foment trouble against them, promising assistance if they rebelled against their Mesopotamian overlords. The promised assistance did not always materialise, however, and when it did it was inadequate. After the destruction of the temple by the Babylonians in 586 B.C. a considerable number of Jews sought refuge in Egypt, and it was in Egypt during the third and second centuries B.C. that the Greek translation of the Old Testament was made. References to Egypt in the New Testament are far fewer, though Joseph and Mary are said to have fled there to protect their child from the wrath of Herod.

Ekron. One of the five Philistine city-states.

Elah. King of Israel (877–876 B.C.).

Eli. The priest who brought up Samuel (1 Sam 2:11).

Elihu. A young man who, after Job's three "comforters" had failed to persuade him of the error of his ways, made another attempt to do so (Job 32).

Elijah. A prophet from Tishbe in Gilead, Elijah is rightly considered one of the great figures of the Old Testament. He was the supreme champion of Israel's God at a time when Jezebel was trying to substitute the worship of her own god, Baal Melkart. This epic struggle is epitomised by the confrontation between Elijah and the prophets of Baal on Mount Carmel (1 Kgs 18:19–40). While many different interpretations of this story have been offered, ranging from the absolutely literal to the purely legendary, there can be no doubt whatever that the conflict it represents was real. Apart from this, however, the Elijah stories contain many pointers towards a more complete understanding of God. On Mount Horeb (Sinai) he realised that God was to be found in quiet reflection rather than in dramatic natural events, and the instructions he received there showed that God's power extended beyond Israel to the surrounding nations (1 Kgs 19:8–16). The encounter with King Ahab over Naboth's vineyard (1 Kgs 21:1–24), while not proclaiming anything new, is a forceful restatement of God's concern with social justice, and clearly anticipates the work of Amos.

Eliphaz. The first of Job's three "comforters" (Job 4).

Elisha. Though he is inevitably linked with his master and predecessor Elijah, Elisha is a very different character. More miraculous incidents are recorded about Elisha, yet many of them are trivial, e.g. recovering an axe-head from the river Jordan (2 Kgs 6:1–7), and the effect is to diminish rather than enhance his stature. Whereas Elijah was a largely solitary figure spending long periods in the wilderness, Elisha associated freely with the communities of prophets and lived in the capital city, Samaria, for at least part of his career. Though not always in sympathy with the kings of Israel, he advised them in military matters. He added little or nothing to the understanding of God achieved by Elijah, but some of the ways in which he exemplified that understanding are notable, e.g. the breadth of concern shown in the healing of Naaman, the commander of the Syrian army (2 Kgs 5:1–19).

Elizabeth. The mother of John the Baptist and a relative of Mary, mother of Jesus.

Emmanuel. The name, meaning "God with us", is in fact used in a prophecy of Isaiah to King Ahaz during a time of crisis. Isaiah says that a young woman will conceive and bring forth a son, whom she will name Emmanuel. He is saying, in effect, that in nine months' time the situation will have improved so much that parents will give their children a name expressive of God's care for his people. Though the immediate prophecy, therefore, refers to events in the immediate future, it is not surprising that Christians should have seen in these words the foreshadowing of God's presence with his people in Christ (Mt 1:22-23).

Epaphras. An associate of Paul who founded the church at Colossae (Col 1:7).

Epaphroditus. A Christian from Philippi who was sent by the Philippian church to render assistance to Paul during imprisonment, probably in Rome. While with Paul he had a serious illness and Paul thought it best to send him back home possibly taking the letter to the Philippians with him (Phil 2:25-30).

Ephesians, Letter to the. Although apparently written by Paul, there is considerable doubt as to the authorship of this letter. It was not uncommon in those times for a follower of a great teacher to write in the teacher's name and, far from being considered fraudulent, this was regarded as a mark of respect. The style of writing is not quite as in Paul's other letters, themes are introduced which appear nowhere else in his correspondence, and there is a remarkable absence of personal greetings considering that Paul had spent two years in Ephesus. If the author were not Paul, however, he was clearly well acquainted with Paul's writings, especially the letter to the Colossians, parts of which are quoted almost verbatim. The first part of the letter emphasises the unity of Christian believers, whose common life in Christ overrides all human distinctions, and the glory of the church which, whatever its human weaknesses, is Christ's body. The second part of the letter draws out the implications of this view of the church for practical living.

Ephesus (in Asia Minor). The capital of the Roman province of Asia and an important trading centre, Ephesus was famous for its temple of Artemis (Diana). It had a substantial Jewish population, and soon became an important centre of Christianity. Paul visited Ephesus as he returned from his second missionary journey (Acts 18:19-21) and subsequently spent two years there (Acts 19:1-10).

Ephraim. (1) Although he was Joseph's second son, he received from Jacob his grandfather the blessing normally due to the eldest, and established an important tribe (Gen 48:17-19).
(2) It appears that Joseph never had a tribe named after him, but he gave rise to two of the tribes of Israel, named after his sons Manasseh and Ephraim. The tribe of Ephraim occupied fertile land running down to the Mediterranean coast north of Dan and Benjamin and south of Manasseh. Its significance in the affairs of Israel was such that the northern kingdom was often referred to as Ephraim.

Epicureans. A school of Greek philosophers with whom Paul debated in Athens (Acts 17:18).

Esau. The first-born son of Isaac, he sold the birthright which was his by tradition to his younger brother, Jacob, for a bowl of soup (Gen 25:27-34). He is regarded as the ancestor of the Edomites.

Esther. Dated between 150 and 100 B.C., the book of Esther describes how a Jewish heroine of that name became queen to the Persian king, Xerxes, and was able to save her people from the evil plotting of one Haman. The book makes no mention of God at all, and it appears to have gained its place in the Old Testament purely as an expression of nationalist sentiments. The deliverance from Haman is still celebrated by Jews in the feast of Purim.

Eve. Adam's partner (Gen 2:21-24, 3:20). As Adam should be thought of as a symbolic prototype of mankind, so is Eve the typical woman rather than the first woman.

Exile. The term usually refers to the exile of the leading Jewish people in Babylon between 586 and 538 B.C., though there had been an earlier deportation in 597 B.C. This experience was of great importance to the Jews for a number of reasons. They had to learn how to worship God without the temple and without sacrifice, and so it was here that forms of worship developed which were based on the recollection of the way God had led them throughout their history. This in turn stimulated interest in writing down their history, and it was during the exile that much of the editorial work on the historical books of the Old Testament was done. On the negative side, the Jews became more exclusive during the exile because of fears that intermarriage would result in the loss of their religious and national identity. The Jews, therefore, emerged from the exile purified but also hardened in a way that was not entirely to the good.

Exodus. The name given to the escape of the people of Israel from Egypt, an escape always seen as the supreme symbol of God's concern for them and an event still celebrated annually by Jews in the feast of the Passover. While some allowance has to be made for exaggeration of the incidents leading up to the escape, there is no reason to doubt the essential historical truth of the account. It appears that, originally having gone to Egypt because of famine in Palestine, the Jews had become slave-labourers working on Egyptian building projects. They were freed from this oppression about 1250 B.C. under the leadership of Moses with the assistance of a remarkable sequence of events known as the plagues of Egypt (Ex 7:14-12:36). The pursuing Egyptian army fell into a panic as their chariots sank in the waters of a shallow swamp, successfully crossed on foot by the Israelites, in the area of the Suez canal today. Whatever our interpretation of these events, the people of Israel had no hesitation in ascribing them to God.

Exodus, Book of. As its name implies the book of Exodus tells the story of the Jews' escape from Egypt, but it contains much else of importance besides. It includes the account of God's covenant with the people of Israel at Sinai based on the ten commandments, and goes on to give instructions about the construction of the ark and of the tent in which it is to be housed, as well as directions concerning worship.

Ezekiel. Ezekiel is probably the most difficult of the major prophets for the modern reader to come to grips with. Among the Jews deported to Babylon in the first exile of 597 B.C., his call to be a prophet came in Babylon and the whole of his prophetic ministry was carried out there, though his prophecies are directed to his people in Jerusalem as well as to the exiles. Many of the messages of Ezekiel are in the form of symbolic visions of great complexity; in fact, Ezekiel has been called "the father of apocalyptic", a kind of visionary writing represented elsewhere in the Bible by the books of Daniel and Revelation. The Old Testament book stresses the responsibility of the individual before God, rather than the people as a corporate body (Ezek 18:1-4), looks forward to the restoration of his people (Ezek 37:1-14) and presents a vision of the future temple and its worship (chapter 40 onwards). This interest in ritual, the result of his priestly status (Ezek 1:1) is in sharp contrast to earlier prophets who tend to condemn ritual, or at least the insincerity of ritual without righteousness.

Ezra. A lawyer who led a party of exiles to Jerusalem from Babylon about 460 B.C. (Ezra 7:1-9) and played a major role in the re-establishment of the worship of the temple. Unfortunately he shows the hard-line tendencies some of the Jews developed in exile, to the extent of insisting that Jews who had married foreign wives should get rid of them and their children. The book of Ezra relates events from the first return of exiles in 538 B.C. up to those in which Ezra himself was involved. It is not clear how much of the book is the work of Ezra and how much the work of later editors.

F

Felix. The Roman governor of Judaea from about A.D. 52 to 58, he had a Jewish wife and was apparently well informed about the Christian way (Acts 24:22-25). He kept Paul in custody for two years, having no cause to condemn him but unwilling to release him for fear of opposition from the Jewish leaders (Acts 24:27).

Festivals, *see* separate entries under **Dedication, Feast of; New Year; Passover; Tabernacles, Feast of; Weeks, Feast of.**

Festus. The Roman governor of Judaea who succeeded Felix about A.D. 58. He seems to have behaved with absolute correctness in his dealings with Paul, and would probably have set him free had not Paul taken the matter out of his hands by appealing to Caesar (Acts 25:1–12, 26:30–32).

G

Gabriel. The literal meaning of the name is simply "man of God". In Jewish tradition one of seven archangels, he is said to have announced the birth of John the Baptist to Zechariah (Lk 1:5–20) and of Jesus to Mary (Lk 1:26–38).

Gad. (1) Jacob's seventh son, his first by Zilpah, Leah's slave-girl.

(2) The tribe of Gad, holding territory east of the Jordan to the north of that occupied by Reuben.

Galatia. The ancient kingdom of Galatia was in central Asia Minor, but the Roman province of the same name included a much larger area reaching down to the Mediterranean coast. Paul visited several towns within the Roman province on his first missionary journey.

Galatians, Letter to. One of the earliest of Paul's letters, probably written in *c.* A.D. 54, though some scholars would date it to A.D. 49, making it the first of all his surviving letters. It was written, almost certainly, to the churches Paul founded in the Roman province of Galatia on his first missionary journey, and is unusual in being addressed to a group of churches rather than a single church. The purpose in writing is very clear: Paul has been told that there are people going round the churches claiming that circumcision and the acceptance of the Jewish law is a necessary part of Christianity. Paul writes with the utmost urgency and vigour to refute these claims. He himself had been a Pharisee and knew that the attempt to satisfy God by perfect obedience to the law was impossible. It was faith in Christ which had liberated him from that futile pursuit, and the last thing he wanted was to see anyone persuaded into taking up something he had only discovered to be of no value. The letter gives some useful autobiographical information as Paul recounts the way in which he became an apostle, and lays the foundations for the more fully developed statement of his theology in the letter to the Romans some years later.

Galilee. The area west of the Sea of Galilee (actually an inland lake some 20 km long) where Jesus was brought up and spent the greater part of his ministry. In the time of Jesus it formed the northern part of the Roman province of Galilee and Peraea, governed by Herod Antipas.

Gallio. The proconsul of the Roman province of Achaia before whom Paul was accused during his eighteen-month stay at Corinth (Acts 18:12–17). An inscription from Delphi establishes that Gallio was in Corinth by A.D. 52, probably having been appointed the previous year. It is implied (though not definitely stated) in Acts that Paul's trial took place soon after Gallio's arrival, and if this is accepted it fixes Paul's ministry in Corinth within a year or so, providing a useful fixed point in the chronology of the early church.

Gamaliel. A well-known Jewish teacher who numbered Paul among his pupils (Acts 22:3), and who argued in the Jewish Council against trying to stamp out Christianity on the grounds that history would show whether it was a movement from God or a worthless novelty (Acts 5:34–40).

Gath. One of the five Philistine city-states.

Gaza. The southernmost of the five Philistine city-states.

Gedaliah. When Zedekiah, the last king of Judah, was taken in chains to Babylon in 586 B.C., the Babylonians appointed Gedaliah as governor. Though in his brief spell of office he seems to have acted with wisdom and humanity, he was soon assassinated by supporters of the royal house who regarded him as a traitor (2 Kgs 25:22–26).

Gehazi. Elisha's servant, condemned by Elisha for accepting gifts against his instructions from the healed Syrian commander, Naaman (2 Kgs 5:19–27).

Genesis. As the name implies, the first book of the Bible. Chapters 1–11 contain the acounts of the creation and the stories of Adam and Eve, Cain and Abel, Noah and the tower of Babel. These stories, though they may have some basis in historical fact, are important mainly for their mythological value. They are to be seen as parables, conveying in a vivid and often entertaining way, the convictions of their authors on immensely important matters—the nature of God, the nature of the universe and the nature of man. From chapter 12 onwards, with the entrance of Abraham into the story, the book is dealing with historical figures, however much allowance may have to be made for the inevitable legendary accretions acquired during centuries of handing down by word of mouth. Whatever their degree of historical accuracy, these stories of the early ancestors of the Jewish people are richly perceptive in their observations of human life and, above all, man's religious quest.

Gentiles. The word usually translated as Gentiles means literally "the peoples" or "the nations", i.e. the peoples other than the people of Israel. The Bible shows ambivalent attitudes among the Jews towards Gentiles. The covenants with Abraham and Moses both stress that the people of Israel are to be a blessing to "the nations", but during and following the exile the fear of religious and ethnic absorption made the Jews increasingly exclusive. Even in the early church there was a long and sometimes acrimonious debate before the mission to the Gentiles was accepted by all as an inevitable implication of Christian belief. It was this crucial decision which made Christianity a universal faith and no longer just a sect within Judaism.

Gethsemane. An olive grove on the western slopes of the Mount of Olives, facing Jerusalem across the Kidron valley, it was apparently Jesus' custom to go there with his disciples to avoid the crowds, and it was there that he was arrested (Mk 14:32–52).

Gibeah. A town some 7 km north of Jerusalem which was Saul's capital throughout his reign.

Gideon. Before the monarchy was established, the people of Israel relied on inspired leaders, known as judges, to raise armies and cope with enemy aggression as the need arose. Gideon was one such leader, renowned for his victory over the Midianites (Judg 7:1–22).

Gilgal. (1) A town on the west bank of the Jordan, just north of the Dead Sea, where the people of Israel first entered the "promised land" and Saul was later proclaimed king.

(2) A settlement north of Bethel where there was a community of prophets in the time of Elijah and Elisha (2 Kgs 2:1, 4:38).

God. The existence of God is never discussed in the Bible; it is simply assumed from start to finish. But if the biblical authors never question God's existence, they do question what sort of God he is and, as one would expect of a varied group of writers working over a period of many centuries, they do not all arrive at the same conclusion. Samuel believed that God demanded the total destruction of Israel's ancient enemy the Amalekites, severely criticised Saul because he had spared the life of Agag the Amalekite king, and himself cut him to pieces (1 Sam 15:1–33). The writer of 2 Kings 2:23–24 believed that God had punished some boys who had made fun of Elisha by causing them to be mauled by bears. Clearly these are primitive views of God.

In spite of these relics of an early religion, however, the Bible as a whole presents a remarkably unified view of God, with most of the key concepts established at quite an early date in

Israel's history. The "otherness" of God is expressed in the idea that no man could look upon the face of God and live (Ex 33:20) or that anyone who touched the ark, representing God's presence, would be struck dead (2 Sam 6:6-8). Later on these primitive attempts to express belief in a God whose ways are unsearchable, whose powers are unlimited, whose holiness is literally aweful, and who is as far removed from man as the heavens are from the earth, find nobler expression in such passages as the call vision of Isaiah (Is 6:1-8) and many of the Psalms. But the God of the Bible, though far removed from man in his wisdom, power and purity, is never remote. From the very earliest stories in the Bible he is a God who involves himself in the life of men, both making demands on them and caring for them. What he demands from men is justice in their dealings with each other. The ten . commandments (Ex 20:1-17) form the basis of the moral code by which men are to live, and it is significant that even the king is subject to these demands and open to criticism for failure (1 Kgs 21:17-19) unlike other monarchs of the day who were a law unto themselves. What he offers men is a constant concern for their welfare, seen at an early stage in the exodus and expressed more movingly among Old Testament writers by the prophet Hosea, who daringly compares God to a faithful husband whose love for his wife does not waver in spite of her infidelity. So the thinkers of the Old Testament prepared the way for one whose moral demands reached new and frightening heights in the commandment to "love your enemies and do good to those who hate you", but who offered men the means to reach these heights by their response to a God who "so loved the world that he sent his only begotten son".

Golgotha. The name of the place where Jesus was crucified, the word means "skull". Whether this is a reference to the shape of the hill or an indication that executions had long been carried out there is uncertain, as is the location.

Goliath. A Philistine warrior of enormous stature supposedly killed by David, though 2 Samuel 21:19 says that it was Elhaman who killed Goliath, and it seems possible that tradition transferred this exploit to the more famous David.

Gomorrah. One of five cities described in Genesis 14:3 as occupying the valley of Siddim. The location is not quite certain, but is thought to be covered now by the southern part of the Dead Sea. Notorious for its wickedness, the city was destroyed by burning sulphur according to Genesis 19:24-25.

Greeks. Apart from its literal meaning, the word is often used in the New Testament as a general word for non-Jews. Thus in Romans 1:16 Paul says that the gospel is the saving power of God for "the Jew first but the Greek also". Some modern versions use the translation "Gentile" when this is the sense intended.

H

Habakkuk. A prophet whose ministry coincided with the rise to power of the Babylonians in the closing years of the seventh century B.C. The Old Testament book views the ascendency of the Babylonians as an act of God, but nevertheless questions how God can countenance such ruthless people, and declares that they are doomed, whereas "the righteous shall live by faith" (Hab 2:4).

Hagar. The slave-girl of Abraham's wife Sarah. When it seemed that Sarah would never have a child, Hagar was given to him to bear his children, and gave birth to Ishmael (Gen 16:1-4, 15). After the birth of Sarah's own son, Isaac, she sent Hagar and Ishmael away, but God promised Abraham that Ishmael would become the father of a nation (Gen 21:9-20).

Haggai. A prophet who prophesied about 520 B.C. some twenty years after the first Jews had returned from the exile to Jerusalem. He said

that the reason for the poor harvests the people were getting was their failure to make a start on rebuilding the temple, and encouraged them to begin the rebuilding programme.

Haman. The villain of the book of Esther, an official at the Persian court who schemed to bring about the destruction of the Jews.

Hannah. The mother of Samuel, she was childless for many years and therefore considered to be out of favour with God. She made a promise that if God granted her a son she would dedicate him to the service of his sanctuary at Shiloh (1 Sam 1:1-28).

Hazael. An army officer who came to the Syrian throne shortly before 840 B.C. by suffocating the ruling monarch, Benhadad, in his bed. Elijah had been instructed to anoint Hazael king of Syria, but had not been able to do so before his death. Elisha is said to have told Hazael that he would become king, though he did not apparently anoint him (2 Kgs 8:7-15). Hazael was to be a scourge to Israel throughout his long reign, and it is significant that the people of Israel were prepared to see even an enemy who oppressed them as God's appointed agent.

Hazor. A large town in the far north of Israel, one of those which Solomon specially fortified and made into a garrison town for his chariot forces (1 Kgs 9:15-19).

Hebrew. The language in which the Old Testament was written. Over the last fifty years, archaeological work has brought to light a vast quantity of texts in Hebrew or closely related Semitic languages, and this has greatly increased our knowledge, making accurate translation possible where previously it was necessary to resort to conjecture.

Hebrews, Letter to the. Although traditionally ascribed to Paul, it has long been recognised that this is not one of Paul's letters, being quite unlike Paul's writing in both style and content. The main theme of the letter is an interpretation of the significance of Jesus' life and teaching based on the concept of priesthood—Jesus as the supreme mediator between God and man. It is most famous for its eleventh chapter on the nature of faith. The obviously Jewish outlook of the writer has led most commentators to assume that the letter was destined for a community of Jewish Christians, as the title implies, but even this has been questioned and it has to be said that authorship, destination and circumstances of writing remain conjectural.

Hebron. A city in the territory of Judah, it was David's capital for a time before the northern tribes accepted him as king and he established Jerusalem as the new religious and administrative centre. It had, however, been a city of importance for centuries before the Jews occupied Palestine.

Hermon. At over 2,800 m., Mt Hermon is the highest point in Palestine and also represents the far north-eastern frontier of Israel at the height of her power. It is considered by some to be the scene of the transfiguration because of its proximity to Caesarea Philippi.

Herod Family. Four Herods of four different generations are mentioned in the New Testament, in addition to Philip, who was also a member of the family. Herod the Great ruled the whole of the territory of the Jews (under Roman authority) from 40 to 4 B.C. He was the Herod ruling at the time of the birth of Jesus (which was incorrectly calculated when the Christian calendar was established: hence the anomaly of Jesus' birth taking place "before Christ"). Although suspicious and intolerant by nature, he kept his country free from conflict for 35 years, which was no mean achievement. On his death, his kingdom was divided between his three sons, Archelaus, Herod Antipas and Philip. Archelaus, however, was deposed in A.D. 6 and his territory came under the direct rule of a Roman governor. Herod Antipas, the Herod who had John the Baptist killed and before whom Jesus was tried, continued to rule Galilee and Peraea until his banishment in A.D. 39. Philip ruled Ituraea and Trachonitis until his death in A.D. 34. The territories of both Herod Antipas and Philip passed to Herod Agrippa I, who persecuted the Church and had James put to death (Acts 12:2). He himself died in A.D. 44 and was succeeded by

Herod Agrippa II, the king before whom Paul appeared in Acts 25.

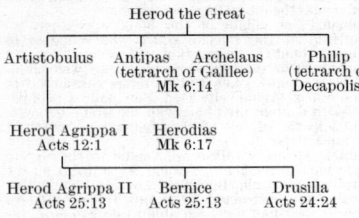

Herod the Great
- Artistobulus
- Antipas (tetrarch of Galilee) Mk 6:14
- Archelaus
- Philip (tetrarch of Decapolis)

- Herod Agrippa I Acts 12:1
- Herodias Mk 6:17

- Herod Agrippa II Acts 25:13
- Bernice Acts 25:13
- Drusilla Acts 24:24

Herodias. Originally the wife of Philip (not the tetrarch), she was subsequently married to his half-brother Antipas. It was John the Baptist's objection to this marriage which brought about his imprisonment and eventual death (Mk 6:14–29).

Hezekiah. King of Judah (715–687 B.C.). Hezekiah came to the throne as a vassal of Assyria as his father, Ahaz, had been. The Assyrian ruler, Sargon II, was having difficulties elsewhere in his empire, however, and Hezekiah soon removed Assyrian religious objects from the temple, a step he might have hesitated to take but for the temporary Assyrian weakness. He also attacked the old Canaanite places of worship which were still used, and broke a bronze serpent allegedly made by Moses before which incense was burned. The exact extent of his religious reforms is uncertain, but it is clear that they were far-reaching. In spite of his removal of Assyrian cult objects from the temple, Hezekiah did not join other small Palestinian states, led by the Philistine city of Ashdod, in rebellion against the Assyrians in 713 B.C., perhaps because Isaiah opposed the enterprise. In 705 B.C., however, when Sargon II died, Hezekiah did refuse tribute to Assyria. Facing troubles elsewhere, it was 701 B.C. before the new king Sennacherib was able to move against Judah. When he did, he devastated 46 of Judah's fortresses and, in the words of his own inscription, shut up Hezekiah in Jerusalem "like a bird in a cage". What happened at this point is not clear. 2 Kings 18:14–16 says that Sennacherib demanded vastly increased tribute and Hezekiah meekly agreed. 2 Kings 18:17–19:37, however, relates how Hezekiah defied Sennacherib and the Assyrian had to return home after his army had been struck down by some mysterious agency. No attempt to reconcile these conflicting statements is entirely satisfactory, and this has led some scholars to suggest that the account of Hezekiah's successful defiance relates to a second invasion about 688 B.C. There is no corroborative evidence for this however.

Hinnom. A deep valley south-west of Jerusalem where child sacrifice was carried out according to Jeremiah 7:30–34. It is not clear from Jeremiah when this occurred (at no time was it a normal feature of Jewish religion), but it may have been during the long and evil reign of Manasseh (687–642 B.C.).

Hittites. A people referred to many times in the early period of Old Testament history from the time of the patriarchs to the establishment of the monarchy. It is now known that they ruled a considerable empire, centred on Asia Minor and achieving its maximum influence between 1400 and 1200 B.C. They defeated Pharaoh Rameses II at the Battle of Kadesh, 1299 B.C.

Hosea. Hosea prophesied in the northern kingdom of Israel shortly after Amos (i.e. from about 750 B.C. onwards) during a period of political anarchy which was eventually to lead to the end of Israel as an independent kingdom in 721 B.C. His prophetic message is coloured throughout by his own experience of marriage, though the facts about his marriage are disputed, the evidence being ambiguous on many points. The most commonly accepted view is that his wife Gomer was unfaithful to him and eventually left him to become a prostitute. Falling upon hard times, she was sold into slavery, from which Hosea bought her back, attempting to reform her by keeping her in seclusion for a period of time. Such a view certainly accords well with Hosea's daring portrayal of God as the faithful and persistent lover who will not abandon his faithless wife Israel. Although Hosea's message is therefore supremely hopeful, being based on the constant love of God for his people, it is not lacking in stern warnings of judgement, for the concept of God's love does not exclude the possibility of corrective punishment and Hosea is utterly appalled by the idolatry and unrighteousness of his people. Yet even God's judgement is seen as something positive, as a necessary step towards the re-establishment of a relationship between God and his people which is based on faithfulness on both sides.

Hoshea. King of Israel (732–724 B.C.). The last king of Israel, Hoshea came to the throne by the assassination of his predecessor Pekah. It was a period of Assyrian domination and for a while Hoshea wisely remained subservient to his Assyrian masters. When the capable Assyrian ruler Tiglath-pileser III died in 727 B.C., however, Hoshea made an alliance with Egypt and withheld tribute. The new Assyrian king Shalmaneser V, attacked and overran Israel, taking Hoshea captive in 724 B.C., though the capital city, Samaria, held out against the Assyrians until 721 B.C. Thereafter Israel was an Assyrian province.

I

Iconium. A city in the Roman province of Galatia visited by Paul and Barnabas on Paul's first missionary journey (Acts 13:51–14:6).

Immanuel, see **Emmanuel.**

Isaac. The son of Abraham and Sarah, he was nearly sacrificed to God until God showed Abraham that he did not require child sacrifice (Gen 22:1–14). His wife Rebecca bore him twin sons, Esau and Jacob, whose descendants became the Edomites and the people of Israel respectively.

Isaiah. It has long been recognised that the book of Isaiah is the work of three major prophets, often known for convenience as first, second and third Isaiah.

First Isaiah, also sometimes called Isaiah of Jerusalem, prophesied from "the year that King Uzziah died" (i.e. 742 B.C.) until at least the end of the eighth century B.C., and his work occupies chapters 1–39 of the book which bears his name. It has been said that Isaiah was more of a statesman than a prophet because of the close interest he took in Judah's affairs, and especially his foreign policy. Thus, when King Ahaz was threatened by Pekah of Israel and Rezin of Syria, Isaiah advised against taking panic measures because he believed the threat would be short-lived. Ahaz, however, ignored his advice, appealed to Assyria for help and became an Assyrian vassal for the remainder of his reign. Later Isaiah warned King Hezekiah against becoming involved in rebellion against Assyria led by the Philistine city-state of Ashdod, and this time his advice was heeded. He also constantly spoke out against reliance on Egyptian help against the Assyrians. But to call Isaiah a statesman rather than a prophet is to ignore the religious foundations of his political advice. He believed in a God whose control of history was absolute. He also believed that his people's difficulties were the result of their failure to put their trust in God and to meet his moral demands in their social life. For him, therefore, the way to solve their problems was to put these things right. Political intrigues and alliances with foreign nations were not only worthless but diverted attention from the real issues. For much of his career Isaiah regarded the Assyrians as instruments of God's judgement, and consequently argued that resistance to them was futile, but towards the end of his life he encouraged King Hezekiah in defying them, perhaps feeling that his people had now received sufficient punishment and certainly believing that the arrogance of the

Assyrians must in its own time come under God's judgement.

Second Isaiah, the author of chapters 40–55 of the prophetic book, was a prophet of the exile. Like the earlier Isaiah he had a profound belief in the utter sovereignty of God, and expresses this in some of the most beautiful and exalted language in the Old Testament. His most important contribution to religious thought, however, comes in the sections which speak of a suffering servant of the Lord. These passages are enigmatic, and it is not clear whether Isaiah was speaking of a past, present or future figure. What is important is the insight—quite astonishing in his time—that a man who set himself to serve God faithfully might be despised, reviled and rejected and that God might somehow bring healing to his people through such a person. Whatever Isaiah himself intended, it is hardly surprising that Christians equate the suffering servant with Christ.

Third Isaiah, responsible for chapters 56–66, mostly addresses people back in Jerusalem after the exile, offering them encouragement through his belief in a God who keeps his promises. It may seem strange to us that the work of three different prophets, living at different times, should have been combined in this way in one book under one name, yet the book does show a fundamental unity of outlook, especially in its proclamation of God's sovereignty. It seems possible that the first Isaiah left behind a group of disciples which continued in existence long after his death, a group which included the two later authors and which was responsible for the editing of the book of Isaiah as we know it.

Ishbosheth. The only one of Saul's four sons to survive his final tragic battle against the Philistines, Ishbosheth was accepted as king by the northern tribes while Judah proclaimed David as its king (2 Sam 2:8–11). David carefully avoided open confrontation with Ishbosheth while constantly weakening his position by diplomatic pressure. Abner, Saul's general, soon defected and Ishbosheth was eventually murdered in his bed by two of his officers (2 Sam 4:5–7).

Ishmael. The son Abraham had by Hagar, Sarah's slave-girl, when it seemed that Sarah herself would have no children (Gen 16:1–4, 15). After Sarah had Isaac, Hagar and Ishmael were driven out (Gen 21:9–20).

Israel. In the first instance this is the name given to Jacob by his mysterious opponent in the wrestling match at Peniel (Gen 32:22–28). His descendants therefore became the children of Israel, or simply Israel. When, after Solomon's reign, the northern tribes rebelled against his son Rehoboam, the term was reserved for the northern kingdom as opposed to the southern kingdom of Judah. Sometimes the term "all Israel" is used of the undivided kingdom to distinguish this usage from the later use for the northern kingdom only.

Issachar. (1) The ninth son of Jacob, his fifth by Leah.

(2) The tribe of Issachar which occupied a fairly small area west of the Jordan and south of the Sea of Galilee.

J

Jabesh-Gilead. A town just east of the Jordan which Saul delivered from the Ammonites (1 Sam 11:1–11). In gratitude the men of Jabesh-Gilead rescued the bodies of Saul and his sons from the Philistines and took them back to give them a decent burial (1 Sam 31:11–13).

Jacob. One of twin brothers, Jacob nevertheless had no claim on his father's property or the special blessing reserved for the eldest son because he was the second from his mother's womb. However, he first got his brother, Esau, to agree to sell his birthright (Gen 25:29–33) and then tricked his blind father Isaac into giving him the blessing (Gen 27:1–29). He fled from his father's wrath to his uncle Laban, in whom he met someone almost as crafty as himself. He served Laban for seven years for his

younger daughter Rachel, only to find after his marriage that he had been given the elder daughter Leah (Gen 29:15–26). He then had to serve another seven years for Rachel. Nevertheless, Jacob prospered with Laban and returned a wealthy man to be reconciled with Esau (Gen 33:1–4). He ended his days in Egypt as the guest of his eleventh son, Joseph (Gen 47:11–12). The stories of Jacob which do not gloss over his failings, show a man who is often self-centred and careless about God in his early years, but who comes to see that God has plans for him and has in fact been caring for him throughout his life.

Jahweh, *see* **Yahweh.**

James. (1) One of the three disciples who were with Jesus on the mount of transfiguration (Mk 9:2–9). The brother of John and a son of Zebedee, he was later killed by Herod Agrippa I (Acts 12:1–2).

(2) Another disciple, the son of Alphaeus, of whom nothing more is known (Mk 4:18).

(3) The brother of Jesus who apparently became an apostle after a special resurrection appearance to him (1 Cor 15:7, Gal 1:19) and subsequently became leader of the Jerusalem church (Acts 15:13–21).

James, Letter of. Though some have identified the author as James the brother of Jesus, this can only be speculation, nor is there any clear indication to whom the letter was first addressed. It is a set of practical instructions on how to live the Christian life, and its emphasis on deeds (as opposed to Paul's emphasis on faith) led Luther to dismiss it as "a letter of straw". In reality, however, there is no conflict; for both James and Paul righteousness is a product of faith.

Jebusites. The original inhabitants of Jerusalem, they were not conquered by the people of Israel when they occupied Canaan but remained as an independent city-state. David took the city, however, by sending his men along a water tunnel, and established his capital there (2 Sam 5:6–10).

Jehoahaz. (1) King of Israel (815–801 B.C.). The son of Jehu, Jehoahaz was an ineffective ruler and spent the whole of his reign under Syrian domination.

(2) King of Judah (609 B.C.). The unfortunate Jehoahaz succeeded his father Josiah who had been killed in battle with the Egyptians. He was almost immediately deposed by the Egyptians in favour of his brother Eliakim, who took the throne-name Jehoiakim.

Jehoash. King of Israel (801–786 B.C.). A strong ruler who regained from Syria all the territory lost by his father Jehoahaz, and who also defeated King Amaziah of Judah after being provoked into a quarrel he did not seek.

Jehoiachin. King of Judah (598–597 B.C.). Jehoiachin came to the throne when a Babylonian army was already on the march against Jerusalem because of his father Jehoiakim's rebellion. Within three months he surrendered the city and was taken into exile where he spent the rest of his life.

Jehoiakim. King of Judah (609–598 B.C.). Placed on the throne by the Egyptians after they had killed his father Josiah in battle and deposed his elder brother Jehoahaz, Jehoiakim remained a vassal of Egypt until 605 B.C. when the Egyptians were routed by the Babylonians. He transferred his allegiance to Babylon, but in 601 B.C. another battle between the Egyptians and Babylonians on the Egyptian frontier resulted in the withdrawal of the Babylonian armies to reorganise. Interpreting this as weakness, Jehoiakim rebelled. In December 598 the Babylonians marched against him, and in the same month Jehoiakim died, possibly by assassination (this may be implied by Jeremiah 22:18, 36:30). Jeremiah, himself forced into hiding by Jehoiakim, is scathing in his criticism of the king as one who callously exploited the people and shed much innocent blood.

Jehoram. (1) King of Israel (849–842 B.C.). A son of Ahab, he actually succeeded his brother Ahaziah, who died after a short reign leaving no sons. During his reign the Moabites successfully rebelled against him, and the war against Syria, in which Ahab had lost his life, dragged on. It was while recovering from wounds received in the Syrian war that he was killed in Jehu's coup.

(2) King of Judah (849–842 B.C.). Like his contemporary and namesake in Israel, Jehoram of Judah lost territory to his enemies in Edom and also on the Philistine frontier. He was married to Ahab's sister (or possibly daughter) Athaliah, who was to seize the throne after the death of their son Ahaziah.

Jehoshphaphat. King of Judah (873–849 B.C.). A capable ruler who allied himself with Omri and Ahab, his contemporaries in Israel, to subjugate enemies across the Jordan and, with rather less success, keep the Syrians at bay. In 2 Chronicles 19:4–11 we are told of a reform of the judicial system he carried out, and it seems from 2 Kings 3:14 that Elisha held him in considerable respect.

Jehu. Jehu was anointed king while serving as commander of Jehoram's army by one of the prophets acting on Elisha's instructions (2 Kgs 9:1–10). He promptly killed Jehoram, who was recovering from wounds in Jezreel, King Ahaziah of Judah who had the misfortune to be visiting him at the time, and the evil Jezebel who, as queen mother, still exercised considerable influence. He went on to exterminate every surviving member of the royal family and the worshippers of Baal. In so doing he broke the alliance with Judah, on which Israel's defence against her enemies largely depended, and deprived the nation of many of its leading figures. In spite of the ferocity of his coup, he was unable to withstand the aggression of Hazael, king of Syria, and lost all his territory across the Jordan.

Jephthah. One of the inspired leaders of Israel known as judges, before the days of the monarchy. He defeated the Ammonites, having made a vow to sacrifice the first living thing he met on his return if God gave him victory. In consequence he was compelled to sacrifice his own daughter (Judg 11:1–39).

Jeremiah. Jeremiah was called to be a prophet as a young man about 630 B.C. and prophesied until after the fall of Jerusalem to the Babylonians in 586 B.C. His long prophetic ministry therefore spanned the last years of Judah as an independent kingdom. His early prophecies paint a terrifying picture of impending disaster (Jer 5:23–31) which, in the short term at least, never materialised and made Jeremiah feel that God had made a laughing stock of him (Jer 20:7). Among the many fascinations of the book of Jeremiah are the frankness of the prophet's conversations with God and his reflections on how to distinguish true prophecy from false. When Josiah carried out his great religious reforms in 622 B.C. Jeremiah supported them and thus aroused the anger of his family, who were priests at Anathoth just outside Jerusalem and probably objected to the ban on sacrificial worship except in the temple (Jer 11:1–8,21). Although a supporter of the reforms initially, Jeremiah soon saw their limitations or even dangers: because the external forms of Judah's religion had been regularised people might become complacent, failing to realise that what God really required was a change of heart. It was this that led Jeremiah to speak of a new covenant written in men's hearts (Jer 31:31–34). From Jehoiakim's time onwards Jeremiah became increasingly unpopular because of his insistence that the presence of the temple would not save the Jews from the Babylonians, contrary to the accepted doctrine that God would never permit his city to be taken or his temple destroyed (Jer 26:1–11). During the siege of Jerusalem he was imprisoned and nearly killed as a traitor because he constantly advocated surrender and was suspected of deserting to the Babylonians (Jer 37:11–38:13). When Jerusalem finally fell, Jeremiah was permitted to remain rather than being taken into exile on the express instructions of King Nebuchadnezzar (Jer 39:11–14). After the murder of the newly appointed governor, Gedaliah, Jeremiah was taken against his will to Egypt by the remaining officials who fled there. Here he ended his days. In spite of the almost unrelieved tragedy of his life, Jeremiah was not without hope. At the height of the siege of Jerusalem he bought a plot of land from a

kinsman as a symbol that people would one day have the confidence to engage in business again (Jer 32:1–15), and he wrote a letter to the first group of exiles, taken to Babylon in 597 B.C., declaring that the future of the nation was in their hands and that God had plans for their welfare (Jer 29:1–14).

Jericho. A very ancient city a few miles west of the Jordan, it was the first stronghold to be captured by Joshua after crossing the river. In Elijah's time it was the home of a company of prophets (2 Kgs 2:4–5), and in the gospels it is the setting for the healing of blind Bartimaeus and the rehabilitation of Zacchaeus (Lk 18:35–19:9).

Jeroboam I. King of Israel (922–901 B.C.). Jeroboam first appears as one of Solomon's officials in charge of forced labour. Told by the prophet Ahijah that he would receive ten of the twelve tribes of Israel, he became a marked man and had to flee to Egypt to escape Solomon's wrath (1 Kgs 11:26–40). After Solomon's death he returned to lead the northern tribes in their revolt against Rehoboam, and became the first king of the northern kingdom (1 Kgs 12:1–20). He established a capital at Shechem initially, but later moved to Tirzah, which remained the capital until the reign of Omri. Clearly he could not have his people going to the Jerusalem temple to worship, since the cult there celebrated amongst other things, God's eternal covenant with the house of David. He therefore established two rival centres at the ancient shrines of Dan and Bethel, and in each of them placed a golden calf. The significance of these animals is not in fact clear, but the biblical writers assume that they were idols and the name of Jeroboam is always associated with them with idolatry (1 Kgs 12:26–30).

Jeroboam II. King of Israel (786–746 B.C.). Long-lived and capable, in human terms Jeroboam II must be judged one of the most successful kings the northern kingdom ever had. The biblical record gives few details but states that he "restored the border of Israel from the entrance to Hamath as far as the Sea of Arabah" (2 Kgs 14:25). It appears from this that his north-eastern border stood where it had been in Solomon's time. The books of Amos and Hosea give a vivid picture of social conditions during Jeroboam's reign, a picture of great prosperity, but prosperity confined to a fortunate minority who cared little for the fate of the masses.

Jerusalem. An ancient city originally occupied by the Jebusites but captured from them by David. It made an ideal capital because of its military strength, because it was near the border between Judah and the northern tribes who were now being brought together again under David's rule, and because it did not actually belong to any of the tribes, having remained as an independent enclave until David took it. As time went on it acquired a mystical significance as the city of God, with the temple as his dwelling-place. This mystique was partly, though not entirely, destroyed by the experience of the exile, which showed that Israel's faith could survive without Jerusalem and its temple.

Jesse. The father of David (1 Sam 16:1).

Jesus. Without doubt more words have been written about Jesus than any other figure in history, and the debate still continues, not only about the historical facts but about their significance. It is impossible in a short article to do justice to the complexity of the issues arising from the life of this man, but the main facts of his public ministry may be stated with some certainty.

The existence of Jesus, as a religious leader put to death by the Romans at the instigation of the Jewish authorities, is attested by the contemporary Jewish historian Josephus. For the details of his life and teaching we have to rely mainly on the four gospels written some 35 to 65 years after his death. The earliest of these, Mark, does not record the birth of Jesus and the birth stories contained in Luke and Matthew are important more for their symbolic value than for their contribution to our historical knowledge. They do establish the date of Jesus' birth as about 4 B.C. (the obvious anomaly is due to the fact that when the

Christian calendar was established much later the date of Jesus' birth was miscalculated). Virtually nothing is known about his life until he was nearly thirty when he received baptism from John the Baptist and was confirmed in his conviction that God had entrusted him with a special mission and he retired to the wilderness to reflect upon it (Lk 3:21–22, 4:1–13). When he returned he declared his manifesto in the synagogue at Nazareth using some words of Isaiah, "to bring good news to the poor, to proclaim liberty to the captive and recovery of sight to the blind, to set free the oppressed, and to announce that the time has come when God will save his people". He proceeded to put this manifesto into practice in both words and actions. Jesus believed that the Kingdom of God foreshadowed in the Old Testament was about to be realised and his teaching was to prepare people for that Kingdom which he described in his parables. "Unless a man has been born again he cannot see the Kingdom of God" (Jn 3:3). Wherever he went he healed the sick. Whether these were miracles in the sense that normal physical laws were set aside is, of course, open to question, but they are such an integral part of the gospel records that they cannot be ignored. It seems clear that Jesus was able to heal people who could not otherwise be healed in his day, and drove himself to exhaustion in doing so, thus demonstrating in practice the love of God he preached. Inevitably this made him popular, in the end embarrassingly so, for the people came to have expectations of him which he had no intention of fulfilling (Jn 6:14–15). As it became clear that he was not going to lead his countrymen in throwing off the yoke of Roman rule, disillusionment set in. It had also become clear that alongside the tremendous assurance of God's unwavering love Jesus set demands far harder to meet than those of the Old Testament. What other teacher had ever required that they should love their enemies and do good to those who hated them (Mt 5:43–48)? The religious authorities had never shared the popular enthusiasm for Jesus, partly because of his disregard for sabbath rules (Mk 2:23–3:6) but even more so because the note of authority in his teaching put them to shame and seemed to imply a special relationship with God (Mk 2:1–12). Jesus, well aware that their net was closing in around him, set out for Jerusalem for the final confrontation (Lk 9:51). Here, having failed to trap him by any legal method the authorities arrested him by night with the connivance of Judas (Mk 14:43–46), condemned him in their own court on the charge of blasphemy (Mk 14:55–64) and rushed him before the Roman governor on charges of political subversion (Mk 15:1–5). Within hours he was dead, executed by crucifixion (Mk 15:24–37). Yet not long afterwards his followers, who had gone to ground after his arrest, were boldly proclaiming his message regardless of the risks and declaring that death had been unable to hold him fast (Acts 2:22–24). In all the inevitable questioning over the resurrection of Jesus one fact seems beyond dispute: that his disciples were prepared to stake their lives on its reality.

Jethro. A Midianite priest whose daughter Zipporah was married to Moses (Ex 2:16–22). He also advised Moses on the setting up of a judicial system after the exodus (Ex 18:13–26).

Jezebel. A Phoenician princess who was married to Ahab, probably as part of his father Omri's policy of friendly relations with the Phoenicians for trade purposes. She was a fanatical devotee of the Phoenician Baal Melkart and made strenuous efforts to introduce his worship to Israel, equally strenuously opposed by Elijah (1 Kgs 18:19–40). Her involvement in Naboth's unjust execution (1 Kgs 21:1–15) shows a completely despotic view of the king's rights. She outlived Ahab and continued to exercise an evil influence as queen mother during the reigns of his sons Ahaziah and Jehoram until killed in Jehu's rebellion.

Jezreel. A city which seems to have been used as a second capital by the kings of Israel about the time of Ahab. It was here that Jehoram

went to recover from his wounds received in the Syrian wars and where he was killed, together with Jezebel, in Jehu's coup (2 Kgs 9:14–35). Hosea named his first child Jezreel as a symbol of judgement on the house of Jehu for its unnecessary brutality (Hos 1:3–4).

Joab. David's commander-in-chief and a considerable influence upon him. It was he who persuaded David to accept Absalom back from exile (2 Sam 14:1–24), though after Absalom's death he took David to task for showing excessive grief over his rebellious son rather than gratitude to those who had been loyal to him (2 Sam 19:1–8). As David's life drew to a close Joab backed Adonijah as his successor, but David nominated Solomon, who subsequently had Joab killed (1 Kgs 1:5–6, 2:28–34).

Joash. King of Judah (837–800 B.C.). The only son of Ahaziah to escape Athaliah's slaughter, he was kept in hiding for six years and then proclaimed king at the age of seven on the instructions of Jehoiada the priest (2 Kgs 11:1–11). Under Jehoiada's influence he made repairs to the temple, but according to Chronicles 24:17–22 he showed a very different character once Jehoiada was dead. Certainly he must have aroused the hatred of his subjects, as he was eventually assassinated.

Job. The book of Job is a protest against the commonly accepted view that God rewards the good with prosperity and punishes the wicked with suffering. It postulates the case of a man who had led a blameless life (Job's personal code of conduct described in chapter 31 is astonishing in its closeness to the ideals later proclaimed by Jesus) who nevertheless suffers every conceivable disaster from the death of his children to painful and disfiguring illness. The major part of the book consists of dialogue between Job and three of his friends (later joined by a fourth). The friends try to convince Job that he must have done something to deserve his misfortunes, while Job continues to protest his innocence and cannot accept this explanation of his suffering. The book does not arrive at any specific answer to the problem of innocent suffering but rejects facile solutions, declaring in majestic poetry that God is far greater than human understanding can encompass.

Joel. The book of Joel tells us nothing about the author except his father's name, and there is no clear indication when he lived, though a date in the fifth or fourth century B.C. is likely. The prophet regards a severe infestation of locusts as a sign of God's judgement on his people, and calls them to repent. He looks forward to a time when God will pour out his spirit on everyone, men and women, young and old alike, a passage quoted by Peter on the first Whit Sunday.

John. (1) John the Baptist. A kinsman of Jesus, he was also his forerunner, preaching repentance to all who would listen and baptising them in the Jordan as a symbol of the new way of life to which they committed themselves (Lk 3:3–14). Jesus accepted baptism from John but then embarked on a very different kind of ministry. It is clear, however, that the two men regarded each other with the greatest respect (Lk 7:18–28). John was imprisoned by Herod Antipas for criticising his marriage to his half-brother's wife Herodias, and it was Herodias who eventually engineered his execution (Mk 6:17–28).

(2) The brother of James, a son of Zebedee and one of the inner group of disciples who were with Jesus on the mount of transfiguration. Though the identification between John and "the disciple whom Jesus loved" in John's gospel is not certain, it is widely assumed. In the early days of the Christian church he was a prominent leader with Peter (Acts 3:1–10, 4:1–21) but we hear relatively little of him afterwards. His connection with the writing of the fourth gospel is problematic (see next entry).

John, Gospel of. The fourth gospel is clearly different from the other three even to the casual reader. To name only the most obvious difference, whereas the teaching of Jesus in the first three gospels is in the form of short pithy sayings or vivid parables, in John it appears as long philosophical discourses. The gospel is not therefore so much an account of the life of Jesus as an interpretation of its significance. But although the author has deliberately and freely recast the teaching of Jesus into a more explicitly theological form, this does not mean that he is not concerned with the historical truth; indeed, the leading British New Testament scholar of recent times has argued that in some respects the historical information in the fourth gospel is superior to that in the other three. The author then was a man of great intellectual stature who had long reflected on the significance of Jesus, and was capable of expressing his conclusions in a form more akin to Greek philosophical writing than traditional Jewish teaching, but who was also in contact with a good historical source independent of the other three gospels. John the disciple of Jesus, with his humble background as a Galilean fisherman, seems an unlikely author, but may well have been the source of the author's historical information.

John, Letters of. The three letters of John show many similarities with the fourth gospel in their vocabulary, style and thematic content, but there are some difficulties in ascribing them to the same author. If they were not by the author of the fourth gospel they were certainly written by someone thoroughly steeped in his way of thinking. The first letter is concerned with a form of false teaching which claims that there is a special way of knowing God open only to the initiated, that Jesus was not truly a physical person and that morality, having nothing to do with actions in the physical world has nothing to do with religion. In opposing this heresy John insists on the physical reality of Jesus and declares that knowing God is inseparable from loving others. Whereas the first letter appears to be a "circular" for general dissemination among the churches, the second is addressed to "the dear lady and her children"—probably a local church. It is much shorter but deals with the same false teaching. The third letter is addressed to an individual, Gaius, encouraging him and warning him against one Diotrephes.

Jonadab. The son of Rechab, he seems to have been the real founder of the Rechabites who tried to maintain the way of life of their forefathers, living in tents rather than houses and not planting crops or vineyards or drinking wine. Apart from this the only information we have on Jonadab is that he helped Jehu in his seizure of the throne (2 Kgs 10:15–17).

Jonah. The book of Jonah is in effect a short story, making a very important point in a humorous way. The essence of the story is Jonah's reluctance to preach to the people of Nineveh, the Assyrian capital, in case they listen to him and consequently enjoy the benefits of God's favour! His attempt to flee to a distant place out of God's reach is foiled by a storm and the great fish which conveniently deposits him on the Palestinian shore once more. Realising that he has no option but to do as God has told him, he goes and preaches to the people of Nineveh, who, as he had feared, repent of their evil and turn to God. Jonah consequently sulks over God's failure to punish them for their previous sins until God shows him how unreasonable his attitude is. The book is thus a witty but serious appeal to the Jews to broaden their conception of God and to rejoice in his concern for other nations. In spirit it comes close to several of the parables of Jesus, e.g. the parable of the prodigal son and his elder brother who refuses to rejoice over the return of the lost one.

Jonathan. One of the four sons of Saul whose reckless daring was largely responsible for a victory over the Philistines at the pass of Michmash (1 Sam 14:1–23). He is best known, however, for his unwavering friendship with David which survived his father's intense jealousy and David's ultimate exile (1 Sam 19:1–7, 20:1–42). He was killed, together with his father and two other brothers, in battle against the Philistines (1 Sam 31:1–4).

Joppa. A port on the Palestinian coast where Peter was staying when he had his vision showing him that there was no distinction between Jew and Gentile in God's sight (Acts 10:9–23).

Joram, see Jehoram.

Jordan. The river Jordan runs north–south from the foot of Mount Hermon to the Dead Sea through a rift valley which is below sea level for the greater part of its length. It forms a natural division between the central highlands of Palestine to the west and the plateau of the Transjordanian desert to the east. As well as being a natural barrier it is also a psychological one, the crossing of the Jordan having the same sort of significance for the people of Israel as the crossing of the Rubicon for Julius Caesar—a decisive step on the road to conquest.

Joseph. (1) The eleventh son of Jacob, his first by Rachel. A precocious child who provoked the enmity of his brothers, he was taken and sold as a slave in Egypt by Ishmaelite or Midianite traders. Not only is the story confused on this point but also as to whether he was sold to the traders by his brothers or rescued by the traders from a pit where his brothers had left him (Gen 37:12–35). After various vicissitudes in Egypt he gained high office by his power to interpret dreams, and in this position he was able both to help and test his brothers incognito when they came seeking corn in time of famine (Gen 41:1–45:14). Eventually he brought his father and brothers to live in Egypt (Gen 47:11–12). While there is no reason to doubt that the Joseph stories have a historical basis, they may well have been embellished in order to drive home the theological point made in Joseph's words to his brothers when he revealed his identity: "so it was not really you who sent me here but God" (Gen 45:8). Joseph gave rise to two of the tribes of Israel named after his sons Ephraim and Manasseh.

(2) The husband of Mary. Information on Joseph is sparse. He was a descendant of David (Mt 1:20), and worked as a village carpenter in Nazareth (Mt 13:55). He is not mentioned after the visit to Jerusalem when Jesus was twelve (Lk 2:41–51), and it seems a reasonable supposition that he had died before Jesus began his public ministry. This has led to the tradition, not necessarily true, that he was much older than Mary.

(3) Joseph of Arimathea. A rich Jew who was a member of the Jewish Council but who sympathised with Jesus and his cause. After Jesus' execution he requested the body from Pilate and had it buried in his own rock-hewn tomb (Mk 15:42–46).

Joshua. The book of Joshua takes its name from Moses' successor and records the invasion and settlement of Canaan by the people of Israel under his leadership. While it includes some very early material, the book has been extensively edited and did not reach its final form until centuries after the events it describes. It is generally considered that the picture it presents is a simplified one, representing the invasion of Canaan as a single co-ordinated campaign with Joshua as commander-in-chief. In fact, the likelihood is that the occupation was far more haphazard, with some of the tribes at least acting independently and Joshua commanding only the most successful part of the invasion forces. In particular there are indications in Joshua 15:13–14 and Judges 1:11–21 that the southern tribes of Judah, Simeon and Benjamin may have operated in isolation from the main body with a man called Caleb as their leader. The most famous incident in the conquest is undoubtedly the battle of Jericho, and controversy still rages on what actually happened on this occasion (Josh 6:1–20). In spite of the unresolved historical questions, the character of Joshua emerges clearly—a man of simple faith who believed that God had given the land of Canaan to the people of Israel and would continue to support them if they remained true to him.

Josiah. King of Judah (640–609 B.C.). Josiah is chiefly remembered for the great religious reform he carried out in 622 B.C. following the discovery in the temple of a Book of the Covenant which made him realise how far short his people had fallen from the standards God demanded. He closed down all pagan altars and, in order to prevent irregularities, decreed that sacrifice could only be offered in the temple in Jerusalem. These measures were extended even to parts of the old northern kingdom of

Israel, indicating the degree of freedom Josiah enjoyed due to the preoccupation of the Assyrians with survival against the Medes and Babylonians. He also reinstated the celebration of the Passover which had apparently lapsed (2 Kgs 23:1–23). In 609 B.C. the Egyptians marched through Judah on their way to render assistance to the beleaguered Assyrians, preferring to maintain a weakened Assyria in power than to face a strong Babylon. Josiah tried to stop them and was killed in battle at Megiddo.

Jotham. King of Judah (742–735 B.C.). The son of Uzziah, Jotham ruled as co-regent with his father for some years as his father had contracted "leprosy" (*i.e.* a disfiguring skin disease, not necessarily leprosy as it is known today), and could not carry out public duties. Little is said about Jotham except that he continued the good work of his father, building the upper gate of the temple. At the end of his reign he was under pressure from Pekah of Israel and Rezin of Syria to join an anti-Assyrian coalition, but this problem was left to his successor Ahaz.

Judaea. Like many names which denote an area, the term Judaea is used differently at different times. Its most common usage, however, is to denote the Roman province of Judaea, the area of southern Palestine which from A.D. 6 onwards came under the rule of a Roman governor rather than a member of the Herod family. It was this province which was governed by Pontius Pilate and later by Felix and Festus.

Judah. (1) The fourth son of both Jacob and Leah.
(2) The tribe of Judah which occupied a large area to the west of the Dead Sea and as far as the Egyptian frontier.
(3) The name of the southern kingdom after the northern tribes had broken away under Jeroboam I. While its boundaries coincided roughly with the old tribal area of Judah, it also included most of the territory of Benjamin.

Judas. (1) Judas, son of James, a disciple of Jesus about whom nothing else is known.
(2) Judas Iscariot, the disciple of Jesus who betrayed him. John 12:4–6 states that he was in charge of the common purse used by the disciples and stole from it, but apart from that there is little information on him prior to his act of betrayal. After betraying Jesus for 30 pieces of silver (Mt 26:14–16) he returned the money and committed suicide (Mt 27:3–5). His motives will always remain a matter of speculation. The most charitable view is that he was trying to force Jesus into a position where he would have to perform a dramatic miracle to save himself, thus convincing the sceptics, and he never anticipated that Jesus would let himself be killed.

Jude, Letter of. A short letter warning of the dangers of false teaching and the judgement which will befall those who distort the Christian message. Though it has been suggested on the basis of Mark 6:3 that the author was one of the brothers of Jesus, this is by no means certain, nor is there any clear indication to whom the letter was addressed.

Judge. The term is used in several senses in the Old Testament, including the modern sense of one who arbitrates in a legal dispute or enforces the law. There is, however, an important special use of the term to describe men like Gideon, Jephthah and Samson who exercised leadership among the tribes of Israel, especially in times of danger, during the period between the settlement of Canaan and the establishment of the monarchy. Their authority was regarded as God-given and was entirely personal, *i.e.* it did not extend to their sons. In many ways they acted as kings, but for a long time the establishment of a recognised monarchy was resisted on the grounds that it would be a denial of God's sovereignty (Judg 8:22–23).

Judges, Book of. This book deals with the history of the people of Israel during the period of the Judges, *i.e.* from the death of Joshua until shortly before the anointing of Saul as Israel's first king. It contains some material (*e.g.* the song of Deborah in chapter five) which is contemporaneous with the events described, and therefore of enormous historical value, though

like all the historical books of the Old Testament it was not edited into its final form until centuries later. Much of the book is concerned with the battles for survival against hostile tribes, but as in all the writings of the Old Testament the uniting theme is a theological one, tracing in Israel's history a recurring cycle of disobedience, oppression, repentance, deliverance leading after a time to forgetfulness, further disobedience and so on.

K

Kenites. A tribe which lived in southern Palestine and, unlike many of the surrounding tribes enjoyed friendly relations with the people of Israel, perhaps because they had religious affinities with them. Moses' father-in-law, Jethro, was a Kenite (Judg 1:16) and the Rechabites who long persisted as an ascetic group among the people of Israel appear to have been closely connected with the Kenites (1 Chr 2:55).

Kidron. A stream running through a deep valley to the east of Jerusalem and separating the city from the Mount of Olives.

Kings, Books of. The two books of Kings are the major source for nearly 400 years of the history of the people of Israel, from the accession of Solomon around 960 B.C., through the division of the kingdom on Solomon's death and the end of the northern kingdom after the fall of Samaria in 721 B.C., to the destruction of Jerusalem and the exile of the leading people by the Babylonians in 586 B.C. Like all the historical books of the Old Testament, it is a composite work containing material of different ages and not reaching its final form until centuries after some of the incidents described. Many of the major events recorded, however, can be confirmed by archaeological evidence from other sources, *e.g.* the Moabite stone, an inscription of Mesha, king of Moab, which describes relations between his people and the northern kingdom of Israel about the time of Jehoram and, except in minor details, agrees with the biblical record. The interest of the authors of Kings was not in history as an academic exercise, however, but history as it revealed the hand of God, and the kings of Israel and Judah are therefore judged by their loyalty to Yahweh, and the fortunes of their people are related to this. On this criterion all the kings of Israel are judged to have failed, but among the kings of Judah, Uzziah, Hezekiah and Josiah especially are regarded as good kings.

L

Laban. Jacob's uncle and the father of Leah and Rachel.

Lachish. An important city and stronghold about 50 km south-west of Jerusalem. Against both the Assyrians in 701 B.C. and the Babylonians in 587 B.C. it proved its defensive strength, in the latter campaign holding out longer than any other city except Jerusalem itself. Important archaeological finds have been made there, including the Lachish letters written in the heat of the Babylonian invasion.

Lamentations, Book of. Traditionally known as the Lamentations of Jeremiah, there is in fact no evidence to connect them with the prophet. The book is a collection of fine poems mourning the devastation of Jerusalem in 586 B.C. The third chapter expressed hope for the future, however, and the fifth is a prayer for mercy.

Laodicea. A city of Asia Minor near Colossae. The church there is referred to in Revelation 3:14–22 and criticised for its lukewarmness. There is particular irony in the author's claim that the church is blind, for Laodicea was famed for an eye ointment made there. It appears from Colossians 4:16 that Paul wrote a letter to Laodicea, though he never visited it as far as is known.

Last Supper, *see* **Lord's Supper.**

Lazarus. (1) The brother of Martha and Mary whom, according to John 11:17–44, Jesus raised to life again.

(2) The poor beggar in Jesus' parable of the rich man and Lazarus (Lk 16:19-31).

Leah. The elder daughter of Laban and first wife of Jacob. She bore six of Jacob's twelve sons (Gen 29:31-30:20).

Levi. (1) The third son of both Jacob and Leah.
(2) *See* **Matthew**.

Levites. It appears that the descendants of Levi never possessed any tribal territory of their own but were dispersed among the other tribes. At an early stage, by a process which is far from clear, they were associated with the priesthood, and it became the custom that only Levites could be priests, although not all Levites were. Later the term was used for an order of temple assistants with lower status than priests, as in the parable of the good Samaritan.

Leviticus. As the name of the book implies it is almost entirely concerned with Levitical or priestly duties (*see* above), the offering of worship and sacrifice, the maintenance of ritual purity and the proper response to God's holiness. To the modern reader who does not accept the need for physical sacrifice as part of worship, much of it may appear irrelevant or even repugnant, yet it represents a real desire to give to God the respect properly due to him, and it is not completely taken up with obscure ritual instructions, for it includes the words quoted with approval by Jesus, "love your neighbour as you love yourself " (Lev 19:18).

Lord's Prayer. This brief prayer, given by Jesus in response to a request from his disciples (Lk 11:1), is highly characteristic of his thought. It first places God at the centre of the worshipper's life and only then concerns itself with human needs, asking only for the basic physical requirements of food from day to day and the spiritual necessities of forgiveness and strength under testing.

Lord's Supper. The name given both to the last meal Jesus had with his disciples and to its re-enactment by the Christian community subsequently. The earliest account of the meal occurs in 1 Corinthians 11:23-26, and it is clear from the fact that Paul was instructing the Corinthian church in the proper celebration of the Lord's Supper that it was an established part of Christian worship by the mid-fifties A.D. Accounts are also given in the first three gospels. While John does not describe the meal itself, his treatment of the feeding of the five thousand (Jn 6:25-58) which suggest strong sacramental overtones suggest a knowledge of the Lord's Supper. It is impossible to reconstruct with certainty the exact words of Jesus on this occasion, but it seems clear that he linked the breaking of bread and sharing of wine with his approaching sacrifice and ultimate triumph, and also with the new covenant (or new relationship) between God and man foreseen by Jeremiah (Mk 14:22-25).

Lot. A nephew of Abraham who journeyed with him to Canaan. Eventually they had to separate because their herds were too big to remain together, and Lot chose the plain of the Jordan near the Dead Sea as his territory. When escaping from the destruction of Sodom and Gomorrah his wife is said to have looked back and been turned into a pillar of salt (Gen 19:26).

Luke. Luke is referred to only three times in the New Testament, but is of special interest as being almost certainly the author of the third gospel and the book of Acts (*see* below). Only one of the references, that in Colossians 4:14, gives any information other than his name. Here he is spoken of as "our dear doctor", and since Paul has earlier named three people as the "only Jewish converts who work with me" it follows that Luke was a Gentile.

Luke, Gospel of. The question of the authorship of this gospel is closely linked to that of Acts, which is clearly a sequel to the gospel, being addressed to the same person Theophilus. The author of Acts sometimes uses the first person plural, showing that he was present himself for certain parts of the story, including Paul's crossing from Troas to Philippi on his second missionary journey and his voyage to Rome as a prisoner. It seems likely, therefore, that he would be among the people Paul names as his co-workers in his letters and, by a process of

elimination, Luke emerges as the strongest candidate. Since there is also a tradition going back to the second century that Luke was the author of the third gospel this seems a near certainty. About half the material in Luke's gospel comes from Mark (in those days copying another author's work, far from being considered unethical, was regarded a mark of respect), and some of the remainder comes from a collection of the sayings of Jesus which Matthew evidently used as well. Luke had other sources of his own, however, and it is to him that we owe the preservation of some of Jesus' best-loved parables including those of the good Samaritan and the prodigal son. He also gives us the delightful story of Zacchaeus and the account of the two disciples on the road to Emmaus. He lays special emphasis on Jesus' concern for Gentiles and outcasts, emphasises the role of women in his ministry and shows the importance of prayer in his life.

Lydia. A resident of Philippi and dealer in the purple-dyed cloth for which that area was famous, she was Paul's first convert there and opened her house to him and his companions (Acts 16:13-15).

Lystra. A city in the Roman province of Galatia visited by Paul during his first missionary journey (Acts 14:6-19).

M

Macedonia. A Roman province including parts of northern Greece, Albania and Yugoslavia with Philippi as its chief city. It was here that Paul first preached in Europe (as opposed to Asia Minor) in response to a vision of a man of Macedonia asking for his help (Acts 16:9-12).

Malachi. The book of Malachi clearly comes from some time after the reconstruction of the temple following the Babylonian exile. A probable date would be the first half of the fifth century B.C. The prophet takes his people to task for their laxity in the worship of God and their failure to obey the terms of God's covenant. He warns of God's judgement but also speaks of his saving power (Mal 4:2-3).

Malta. Paul was shipwrecked and spent the rest of the winter here on his journey to Rome (Acts 27:39-28:11).

Manasseh. (1) The elder of Joseph's two sons.
(2) The tribe of Manasseh, which occupied a large area on both banks of the Jordan to the north of Ephraim.
(3) King of Judah (687-642 B.C.). Regarded as the worst king in Judah's history, he actively promoted Assyrian and other pagan religious practices, sacrificed his own son and "killed so many innocent people that the streets of Jerusalem were flowing with blood" (2 Kgs 21:16).

Manna. The name of the food which God is said to have provided for the people of Israel during their wanderings in the wilderness (Ex 16:1-31). It is thought to have been a secretion formed by insects feeding on the scrublands of the desert.

Mark. The house of John Mark's mother, Mary, appears to have been the headquarters of the Jerusalem church (Acts 12:12). Paul and Barnabas took him to work with them in Antioch (Acts 12:25) and subsequently on the first missionary journey (Acts 13:5). He left them at Perga to return to Jerusalem, however, and this led to Paul refusing to take him on his second journey, with the consequence that Barnabas took him to Cyprus instead (Acts 15:36-40). It is clear from Colossians 4:10 and other references that Mark later became a close associate of Paul, and we are also told here that he was Barnabas' cousin. For his connection with the second gospel see below.

Mark, Gospel of. There is a tradition dating back to A.D. 135 that the second gospel was written by Mark on the basis of Peter's memories of the life and teaching of Jesus. It seems probable that Mark collected these reminiscences shortly before Peter's death in Nero's persecution of A.D. 64 and published his gospel in Rome soon afterwards. While the identification of this Mark with John Mark cannot be absolutely certain, it seems highly likely, since John Mark knew Peter from the early days in Jerusalem. The view that the gospel is based on the first-hand information of an eye-witness is borne out by the many vivid details it contains—details often omitted by Luke and Matthew when they later used Mark's work as a basis for their own. They had other material to include and economised on unnecessary detail. Mark's gospel is of special value, therefore, as the one with most direct links with the events described.

Martha. The sister of Mary and Lazarus, who gave Jesus hospitality at her home in Bethany just outside Jerusalem (Lk 10:38–41, Jn 11:1).

Mary. (1) The mother of Jesus. Our knowledge of Jesus' mother is very limited. The birth stories present her as a pious girl, open to God's bidding. Luke's account of the visit to Jerusalem when Jesus was twelve shows her anxious and somewhat uncomprehending at her unusual son (Lk 2:41–51), and it is later suggested (Mk 3:21) that she may have attempted to restrain Jesus in his public ministry. John records that she was present at the crucifixion, and that Jesus entrusted her to the "beloved disciple". By this time she must have been old by current standards and may well have died soon after.
(2) The sister of Martha and Lazarus, who was praised for her sense of priorities in listening to Jesus (Lk 10:38–41).
(3) Mary Magdalene. A woman whom Jesus cured of "seven demons" (Lk 8:2), and who became one of those who travelled with Jesus and his disciples ministering to their needs. She was present at the crucifixion, was among a group which discovered the empty tomb and was a witness of the resurrection (Mk 15:40, 16:1, Jn 20:11–18). The tradition which identifies her with the sinful woman of Luke 7:37 is wholly without foundation.
(4) The mother of James and Joseph. Another woman who followed Jesus to Jerusalem, witnessed his crucifixion and saw the empty tomb (Mk 15:40, 47, 16:1).
(5) The mother of John Mark (Acts 12:12).

Matthew. Also called Levi, Matthew was a tax collector before becoming one of the twelve disciples (Mt 9:9–13, cf. Mk 2:13–17).

Matthew, Gospel of. It is highly unlikely that the author of the gospel was the disciple Matthew, since he draws heavily on Mark for much of his material, and this would have been unnecessary for an eyewitness of the events. Like Luke, he also uses a collection of the sayings of Jesus in addition to some material of his own (e.g. the parable of the sheep and the goats). It is clear that the author was a Jewish Christian who was concerned among other things to stress the continuity between the Christian church and the old community of the people of Israel. Significantly, Matthew traces the ancestors of Jesus back to Abraham, whereas Luke traces them back to Adam, the symbolic father of the whole human race, and Matthew frequently states that events occurred in order to fulfil Old Testament prophecies. He arranges most of his material in five sections, possibly a conscious imitation of the Pentateuch (the five books of teaching which begin the Old Testament) and have a special status among the Old Testament writings for Jews). Each section begins with a narrative and continues with the teaching of Jesus. It is the teaching of the first main sections in chapters 5–7 which constitutes the so-called Sermon on the Mount.

Megiddo. A city of strategic importance controlling the pass through the Carmel ridge from the coastal plain on the south to the Plain of Esdraelon on the north side. It was fortified by Solomon, and it was here that King Josiah lost his life in battle against the Egyptians. It is an important archaeological site.

Melchizedek. A king and priest who gave hospitality to Abraham (Gen 14:18–20) and who is referred to by the author of Hebrews as a forerunner of Christ, himself a priest-king (Heb 7:1–8:2).

Menahem. King of Israel (745–738 B.C.). Menahem secured the throne by the murder of his predecessor Shallum and a bloody struggle against his opponents. He gave tribute to the Assyrian ruler Tiglath-pileser III, hoping both to forestall any Assyrian designs on his territory and gain support to keep him in power. He raised the money by taxation, for which he was not popular.

Mephibosheth. A crippled son of Jonathan who was befriended by David (2 Sam 9:1–13), though he later entertained hopes of gaining the throne as the only remaining descendant of Saul (2 Sam 16:3). Perhaps because this was by now a totally unrealistic hope, David chose to overlook the matter (Sam 19:24–30).

Mesha. The king of Moab during Jehoram's reign, he succeeded in regaining much territory from Israel, according to an ancient inscribed stone known as the Moabite stone. This is consistent with 2 Kings 3:27, which implies that after a highly successful campaign against Mesha, the Israelite forces were unnerved by Mesha's sacrifice of his son and withdrew, having failed to bring the rebel into subjection.

Meshach. One of the three young men who, according to the book of Daniel, survived being thrown into a blazing furnace for refusing to worship a gold statue set up by King Nebuchadnezzar (Dan 3:1–27).

Mesopotamia. The fertile area between the rivers Tigris and Euphrates. It was from this land that Abraham came, and it was also the land of the Assyrians and Babylonians who had such an influence on the history of the people of Israel.

Messiah. The Hebrew word means "anointed one" and therefore implies kingship. "Christ" is the Greek equivalent. The concept of a Messiah has a complex background, but essentially it was born out of Israel's calamitous history and a sense of disillusionment with her leaders. As a result of these factors the hope grew up of a future leader who would truly be God's representative and would consequently restore his people to the position of power and prosperity they enjoyed under David and Solomon. The balance between his spiritual and political functions seems to have been viewed differently by different groups, however, which may well explain why Jesus was apparently prepared to accept the title from his disciples (in a spiritual sense) while forbidding its general use for fear of misunderstanding (Mk 8:27–30).

Micah. A contemporary of Isaiah prophesying in the southern kingdom of Judah towards the end of the eighth century B.C., Micah pronounces God's judgement on his people for their failure to establish a just society and declares that not even the temple will be spared in the general destruction (Mic 3:12). His book is best known for its simple but searching statement of God's requirements: to do what is just, to show constant love and to walk in humble fellowship with God (Mic 6:8). Many scholars consider that the more hopeful elements in the book of Micah are later editorial insertions, and on this view Micah must be considered primarily as a prophet of judgement like Amos here him in the northern kingdom.

Micaiah. A prophet who, in contrast to the 400 court prophets, predicted disaster for King Ahab if he went to take Ramoth-Gilead from the Syrians (1 Kgs 22:1–35).

Miletus. A port near Ephesus. Paul called the leaders of the Ephesian church to meet him here on his last journey to Jerusalem, and warned them against false teachers (Acts 20:17–38).

Miriam. The elder sister of Moses, she is referred to as a prophetess when she leads the women of Israel in a song and dance of triumph after the crossing of the sea on the escape from Egypt (Ex 15:20–21).

Moabites. Occupying land east of the Dead Sea, the Moabites were generally hostile to the people of Israel. David conquered them, but they reasserted their independence in the period of weakness after the division of the kingdom, only to be subjugated again later by Omri. They were finally led to independence by Mesha while Jehoram was king of Israel.

Molech. A Canaanite god whose worship involved child-sacrifice. King Manasseh apparently worshipped him (2 Kgs 21:6), but Josiah desecrated the site of these sacrifices to prevent them happening again (2 Kgs 23:10).

Mordecai. The cousin and foster-father of Queen Esther (Esth 2:6–7).

Moses. If Abraham is the father of the Jewish race, Moses is the founder of Jewish religion. This does not mean, however, that the religion he established had no antecedents, but it was under Moses that it achieved its definitive form. While it is admittedly difficult to disentangle fact from legend in many of the stories of Moses, there is no reason to doubt their essential historical basis as recollections of the great leader who took the people of Israel from slavery in Egypt to the threshold of the promised land, and in the process firmly established their religious traditions. At the centre of Moses' religion is the concept of the covenant, an agreement between God and the people of Israel whereby God gives them a special position of responsibility in his plans and they pledge him their loyalty and obedience. This obedience is to be expressed not only in worship but also in behaviour towards others as laid down in the ten commandments. It is, in essence, a joyful religion because it springs from a sense of gratitude for what God has done, and in this respect as in many others, it is a precursor of Christianity.

N

Naaman. Commander of the Syrian army, cured of "leprosy" (*i.e.* a disfiguring skin disease) by Elisha (2 Kgs 5:1–19).

Naboth. Owner of a vineyard adjoining King Ahab's palace, he was put to death on false evidence at Jezebel's instigation so that Ahab could take the property in the absence of an heir (1 Kgs 21:1–16).

Nadab. King of Israel (901–900 B.C.). Assassinated within two years of his accession by Baasha whilst fighting the Philistines at Gibbethon (1 Kgs 15:27).

Nahum. The book is a poem exulting in the fall of the Assyrian capital Nineveh, which is seen as an example of God's judgement on a nation which had long taken for granted its dominant position and gave no thought to the suffering of its subject peoples. Nineveh fell in 612 B.C., and the poem appears to be contemporary with the event.

Naphtali. (1) The sixth son of Jacob, his second by Bilhah, Rachel's slave-girl.
(2) The tribe of Naphtali, occupying territory to the north and west of the Sea of Galilee.

Nathan. A prophet who advised David not to build a permanent temple in Jerusalem and rebuked him for his misconduct with Bathsheba. Nevertheless, he backed Bathsheba's son, Solomon, in the struggle for succession. It was largely through him that David was eventually persuaded to declare himself in Solomon's favour (1 Kgs 1:11–40).

Nathanael. Often identified with Bartholomew, since John omits all mention of Bartholomew but names Nathanael as one of the disciples. Brought to Jesus by Philip (who is linked with Bartholomew in the other gospels), Jesus referred to him as "a true Israelite in whom there is nothing false" (Jn 1:47).

Nazareth. The home of Joseph and Mary, and the place where Jesus lived until he began his itinerant ministry. Until then this small Galilean town was of no importance and is not even mentioned in the Old Testament.

Nazirite. A person dedicated to God's service and following an ascetic rule of life involving abstinence from alcohol and refusal to cut hair amongst other things. Samson was a Nazirite (Judg 13:2–24) and John the Baptist may have been (Lk 1:15).

Nebuchadnezzar. The Babylonian ruler (605–562 B.C.) under whose orders Jerusalem was taken and destroyed and the people exiled in 586 B.C. By the standards of his day he was not excessively ruthless, and it could be argued that only the intransigence of the Jews compelled him to treat them with severity.

Nehemiah. A Jewish exile who became cupbearer to the Persian king Artaxerxes and was allowed by him to go to Jerusalem as governor about 445 B.C. in order to accelerate reconstruction of the nation's life. The book of Nehemiah relates how he overcame opposition to get the walls of Jerusalem rebuilt. It also tells how Ezra read the law aloud to the people and got them to enter into an agreement to keep it. While it seems that the two men worked to-

gether on the re-establishment of the nation's religious and economic life, the relationship between them is not entirely clear.

New Year. Originally the Jewish New Year began in the autumn, but during the exile the Babylonian New Year starting in the spring was adopted. The autumn New Year was still maintained for cultic purposes, however, and there has been much speculation, based on strong but circumstantial evidence mainly from the Psalms, over the possibility that the autumn New Year was the occasion of a major religious festival celebrating and renewing the covenant.

Nicodemus. A member of the Jewish Council who sympathised with Jesus and came to see him by night—presumably fearful of associating with him openly (Jn 3:1–12). He objected to the Council condemning Jesus without giving him a chance to defend himself (Jn 7:50–51) and helped Joseph of Arimathea to give Jesus a decent burial (Jn 19:39–42).

Nineveh. The capital of Assyria until its destruction by the combined forces of the Medes and Babylonians in 612 B.C. Among the people of Israel it was legendary for its size and sinfulness (Jon 1:2).

Noah. While the story of Noah may have a historical basis, its primary value lies in what it says about God. It shows God as one who does not fully carry out the judgement which man's sinfulness deserves, but in his generosity makes a new start possible.

Numbers, Book of. The name of the book refers to two censuses of the people of Israel recorded in it, one just before they left Mount Sinai and the other about a generation later. The book covers the history of the people of Israel from the exodus until just before the crossing of the Jordan and lays down various rules for everyday life and worship.

O

Obadiah. (1) A high official under King Ahab who tried to protect loyal worshippers of Yahweh against the persecution of Queen Jezebel (1 Kgs 18:2–15).
(2) A prophet who wrote sometime after the fall of Jerusalem in 586 B.C., condemning the Edomites for taking advantage of Judah's plight to settle old scores, and predicting final victory for the people of Israel.

Omri. King of Israel (876–869 B.C.). Although Omri is only given six verses in the books of Kings (1 Kgs 16:23–28), and is condemned for leading his people into idolatry, he was a capable ruler who in a relatively short reign established good relations with both Judah and the Phoenician states, subjugated enemies east of the Jordan and built a new capital, Samaria.

Onesimus. A runaway slave who was converted by Paul and eventually sent back to his master Philemon, bearing with him the letter of that name.

P

Palestine. Derived from "Philistine", the name originally referred only to the southern part of the coastal plain around the Philistine cities, but it came to be used for the whole of the area bordering the eastern Mediterranean from the Lebanon southwards to the Egyptian frontier and across to the desert land of Transjordan.

Passover. A festival celebrated in spring by a special meal. Originally it probably derived from a custom of sacrificing the first lamb of the new season, but it became associated with the deliverance from slavery in Egypt, and it is as a way of remembering this that it has been celebrated ever since. It is followed by a week of eating unleavened bread, also in memory of the escape from Egypt.

Paul. We know more about Paul than about any other leader of the early church, our information coming both from Acts and his own letters. Born in Tarsus in Asia Minor, he was brought up in strictest Jewish tradition and studied under the renowned teacher, Gamaliel. He considered it his duty to persecute the Christian community, and was present at the stoning of Stephen, whose saintly behaviour towards his executioners almost certainly sowed the first seeds of doubt in his mind. These doubts culminated in a shattering conversion experience as he travelled to Damascus to continue his persecution of the Christians there. It was not until many years had elapsed, however, that Paul emerged as the leading figure in the mission to the Gentiles, and he did so at the instigation of Barnabas, who sent for him to help in the work at Antioch. Soon the church decided to send Paul and Barnabas on a missionary journey which took them first to Cyprus and then into the Roman province of Galatia. By this time some of the Jewish Christians were becoming alarmed at the large number of Gentile converts, and on their return they went to a gathering in Jerusalem to thrash out questions of policy with regard to the admission of Gentiles to the church. Here, Paul, more aware than anyone else of the futility of the Jewish law, strongly resisted the imposition of Jewish customs on Gentile converts, and appears to have won, though the argument was to rumble on for many years. Soon he undertook a second missionary journey with Silas, in the course of which he founded the first church in Europe at Philippi and stayed for eighteen months in Corinth. On a third journey he spent two years in Ephesus before revisiting the churches founded earlier during his second journey. On a visit to Jerusalem at the end of his third journey he was arrested by Roman guards during a disturbance in the temple courtyard when Jews alleged that he had taken Trophimus, a Gentile from Ephesus, into the temple. After two years' imprisonment during which he was neither condemned nor declared innocent, Paul appealed to Caesar and was duly sent to Rome. We are told in Acts 28:30 that he was there for two years, presumably waiting for his accusers to present a case against him, and this may imply that he was then released, since the rule was that a case must be presented within two years. However, this is not certain, and tradition has it that he died, together with Peter, in Nero's persecution of A.D. 64. From about A.D. 50 onwards Paul wrote numerous letters, mainly to churches he had founded, but occasionally to churches he had not visited himself, and some of these letters form a substantial part of the New Testament. Some have accused Paul of complicating the simple gospel preached by Jesus, yet the church today may owe its very existence to Paul's clear understanding that Christianity could not just remain an offshoot of Judaism, but must become a universal religion.

Pekah. King of Israel (737–732 B.C.). Seizing the throne by assassinating his predecessor, Pekah immediately entered an anti-Assyrian coalition with his Syrian neighbour Rezin. Together they made threats against Ahaz, king of Judah, who soon appealed to the Assyrians for help. In 733 B.C. Tiglath-pileser III attacked Israel, capturing many cities and deporting much of the population. It was possibly only Pekah's assassination by Hoshea, who promptly surrendered, which saved Israel from further destruction.

Pekahiah. King of Israel (738–737 B.C.). Assassinated after a short period by Pekah, probably because of discontent with his policy of submission to Assyria.

Pentateuch. The first five books of the Old Testament, having special significance for the Jews as the Torah, the basis of Jewish law.

Pentecost, see **Weeks, Feast of.**

Peter. The undisputed leader of the disciples, and of the Christian church during its earliest days. A Galilean fisherman, he was brought to Jesus by his brother Andrew and quickly became one of the inner group of disciples. He showed his leadership in his declaration of faith in Jesus as the Christ at Caesarea Philippi, and it was here that Jesus added the name Peter (the rock) to his original name Simon. After Jesus' arrest he denied all knowledge of him, but it could be argued that he was only exposed to this temptation because he had had the courage to follow Jesus to the High Priest's house. He was the first disciple to enter the empty tomb and preached the first Christian sermon on the day of Pentecost. He was also instrumental in paving the way for Gentiles to enter the church through the baptism of the Roman centurion Cornelius and his subsequent defence of this action (Acts 10:1–11:18). It is unfortunate, though understandable, that the emphasis in the second half of Acts on the work of Paul leave us in ignorance as to the subsequent development of Peter's ministry. Tradition has it that he founded the church in Rome, and died there in Nero's persecution of A.D. 64.

Peter, Letters of. There is considerable doubt whether either of these letters is by the disciple Peter, or indeed whether they are by the same author. The first letter is written to encourage Christians in Asia Minor who are suffering or are likely to suffer, for their Christian faith. If this were written during a specific period of persecution it would almost certainly have been that under the Roman emperor Domitian (A.D. 81–96), since Nero's persecution does not appear to have extended far beyond the capital, and this would rule out authorship by Peter if he had died in A.D. 64. The second letter, which shows a detailed knowledge of the letter of Jude, is a general warning against false teachers. Many scholars regard it as the latest document in the New Testament, with a date in the second century.

Pharaoh. The title of the kings of Egypt. The Pharaohs under whom the people of Israel served as forced labourers have not been identified with certainty, but the likelihood is that the Pharaoh at the time of the exodus was Rameses II (reigned 1304–1237 B.C.).

Pharisees. One of the chief sects within Judaism at the time of Jesus. The movement started as an attempt to bring everyday life more closely into conformity with the law of Judaism, so that religious observance became an integral part of daily living. Jesus would hardly have quarrelled with this aim, but the effect had been to emphasise trivial details and lose sight of basic principles. It was this, and the sense of self-righteousness so often engendered, that Jesus criticised in the Pharisees.

Philemon, Letter to. A short personal letter from Paul to a member of the church at Colossae. Onesimus, Philemon's slave, had run away to Rome, where he came into contact with Paul. Paul would have liked to keep him as he was proving so useful, but felt bound to return him to Philemon. begging Philemon to welcome him back not just as a slave but as a Christian brother.

Philip. (1) Ruler of Ituraea and Trachonitis (4 B.C.–A.D. 34), see **Herod family.**

(2) One of the twelve disciples about whom little is known, although John's gospel gives him slightly greater prominence than the other three (Jn 1:43–46, 12:20–22, 14:8–9).

(3) One of the seven deacons appointed to organise the distribution of resources in the system of sharing goods adopted by the early church in Jerusalem (Acts 6:1–6). In fact, he quickly became a notable evangelist, working among the Samaritans and also in southern Palestine, where he converted an Ethiopian official travelling home, before settling in Caesarea, where he still lived nearby thirty years later (Acts 8:4–40, 21:8).

Philippi. A city of Macedonia where Paul first preached in Europe (Acts 16:12).

Philippians, Letter to the. Unlike many of Paul's letters, the letter to the church at Philippi does not seem to have been written with any particular object in mind—to combat false teaching (Galatians) or pave the way for a possible future visit (Romans). It is simply keeping in touch with old friends, for the church at Philippi had apparently been the first to give Paul financial support so that he could be a full-time missionary without the necessity of plying a trade (Phil 4:15–16). Although he warns the Philippian Christians to be on their guard against any attempt to impose Jewish customs on them (Phil 3:2–7), he seems confident of their ability to maintain their Christian life against any opposition it encounters. The whole atmosphere of the letter is one of gratitude, joy and peace, all the more remarkable as Paul was in prison and possibly close to death as he wrote (Phil 1:20–24).

Philistines. A people who came from Crete or the Aegean islands to settle on the coastal plain of Palestine about the same time that the people of Israel were entering Canaan from the east. They were organised in five main city-states and were a serious threat to the Israelites because of their iron weapons (Israel being still in the Bronze Age), their use of chariots and their military form of government. After the period of acute antagonism which was brought to a close by David's unchallengeable superiority, they lived relatively peacefully apart from occasional incidents until, sometime after the exile, the Philistines disappeared as an independent entity. They were a more cultured people than previously thought.

Phoenicia. A term used to describe the coastal area north of Mount Carmel which is now the Lebanon. It was never a kingdom as such, but included a number of city-states, of which Tyre was the most important. The Phoenicians were seafarers and traders and times of prosperity in Israel often hinged upon good relations with Phoenicia, as in Solomon's reign.

Pilate, Pontius. The Roman governor of Judaea at the time of Jesus' execution, he does not seem to have handled the admittedly difficult task of governing the Jews particularly well. All the gospels represent him as resisting the death sentence on Jesus, however, and only passing it under Jewish pressure. John implies that the Jews had some kind of hold over Pilate: possibly because of previous blunders he could not afford to antagonise the Jews again. In fact, he was recalled to Rome c. A.D. 36, tried and imprisoned.

Priest. In the early period of Jewish religion there were no priests. The head of the family would perform any religious functions necessary. Samuel, however, is said to have condemned Saul for offering sacrifice, thereby usurping his proper function (1 Sam 13:8–14). This suggests that by now a specific priestly role was recognised. It was with the construction of the temple and the development of more elaborate rituals that a priesthood became essential, though it was the offering of sacrifice which remained the primary function.

Prisca, see Aquila.

Prophet. What marks a person out as a prophet has been much debated. The prophets of Baal on Mount Carmel present an extremely unedifying spectacle as they dance and cut themselves to invoke the power of their god (1 Kgs 18:26–29), yet there were prophets in Israel whose behaviour was not dissimilar (1 Sam: 10:10–13). There is clearly a vast gulf between such people and men of the calibre of Amos, Hosea or Jeremiah. The one thing they have in common is their enthusiasm for God. It is possible to trace the gradual transition from these primitive prophets who expressed themselves in emotional outbursts to the great religious thinkers of later times but to sum up the difference in terms of emotions against intellect (or any other pair of contrasting qualities) is an over-simplification. Possibly the best short definition of a prophet is "one who is convinced that God has something to say through him". Note that, although prophets were generally expected to have knowledge of future events, this is not an essential part of the Hebrew concept of prophecy.

Proselyte. One who was not a Jew by birth but who, by circumcision and a form of baptism, had become a Jew by faith. Acts 2:11 refers to the presence of proselytes in Jerusalem for the day of Pentecost.

Proverbs, Book of. This is basically a collection of short sayings offering advice on how to act in everyday situations, but, as with all the biblical writings, it emphasises an important theological belief—that all true wisdom comes from God and is based on respect for him. The sayings are traditionally ascribed to Solomon, who may indeed be responsible for some of them, but the compilation of the book certainly took place centuries after his death and incorporated much later material.

Psalms. It is a truism to say that the Psalms are the hymn book of the Old Testament, yet it is only recently that the implications of this obvious truth have been explored. If the Psalms were collected for use in corporate worship, we need to ask for each Psalm, "On what sort of occasion would these have been appropriate sentiments to express?" In recent years this approach has led to some interesting conclusions about the worship of the people of Israel, and greatly illuminated the Psalms themselves. For the ordinary reader, however, the attraction of these poems remains what it has always been—their expression of a very wide range of human emotions within an overall context of faith in God.

Publius. The chief official (his exact status is unclear) on Malta where Paul was shipwrecked. Paul cured his father of a fever (Acts 28:7–10).

Q

Qirinius. Described by Luke as the governor of Syria at the time of Jesus' birth, though if this took place in the reign of Herod the Great, Luke is wrong on this point. He later had two terms of office as governor of Syria, but at this time commanded the Roman army there.

R

Rabbah. The Ammonite capital, captured by David. It was during the siege of Rabbah that David arranged for Uriah to be left exposed to the enemy, in order to marry his wife Bathsheba (2 Sam 11:14–17).

Rabbi. Sometimes translated "teacher", but implying rather more than this. It is a respectful title, suggesting that the one who uses it accepts the authority of the one to whom it is used. In John's gospel Jesus is addressed in this manner several times.

Rachel. Laban's younger daughter and Jacob's second wife, though she was his first choice (Gen 29:18–28). She bore him Joseph and Benjamin.

Rahab. A prostitute of Jericho who concealed two spies sent by Joshua, and was subsequently spared when the other inhabitants were slaughtered (Josh 1:1–21, 6:22–25).

Rameses. An Egyptian city where Israelite slave labour was used, and from which the people of Israel started out on the exodus. It was on the eastern edge of the Nile delta, and is generally identified with a city earlier known as Avaris and later as Tanis.

Ramoth-Gilead. A town on the border between Israel and Syria which was the scene of bitter fighting between these traditional enemies. It was here that Ahab died, and that Jehoram received the wounds from which he was recovering at the time of Jehu's coup.

Rebecca. The sister of Laban, wife of Isaac, and mother of the twins Esau and Jacob.

Rechabites. The descendants of Rechab, about whom we know nothing except that he was the father of Jonadab, who laid down the rules of the Rechabite community. He insisted that they lived in tents and refrained from alcohol, thus trying to protect them against the corrupting influences of Canaanite civilisation. Jeremiah commends the Rechabites for their faithfulness to these principles, in contrast to the lack of faithfulness found elsewhere among the people of Israel (Jer 35:1–17).

Red Sea. The name translated as "Red Sea" in older versions of the Bible is not always to be equated with the Red Sea as known today. References in the exodus story may be to a shallow inland lake in the region now cut through by the Suez Canal, and in 1 Kings 9:26 the reference is to the Gulf of Aqaba, the eastern limb of the Red Sea, rather than the Red Sea itself.

Rehoboam. King of Judah (922–915 B.C.). The son of Solomon, Rehoboam refused to listen to the grievances of his people at the beginning of his reign and as a consequence was faced with rebellion by the ten northern tribes under Jeroboam's leadership. Rehoboam was unable to prevent the division and soon gave up any attempt to reassert his authority over Israel. He lost nearly all his foreign territory, was invaded by the Egyptians and had to ransack his treasury to pay the tribute demanded (1 Kgs 12:1-24, 14:25-26).

Resurrection. It is quite clear from the book of Acts that the resurrection of Jesus was the central theme of early Christian preaching. It is equally clear that those who proclaimed the resurrection in this way stood a considerable risk of sharing the fate of their leader. It follows that they must have been absolutely certain in their own minds of the truth and importance of their claims. Because these claims are admittedly extraordinary, it is natural that people should have sought explanations in terms of natural causes, but no such explanation has proved entirely satisfactory. In any case, an extraordinary event is needed to explain the transformation in the behaviour of the disciples. Among those who believe in the resurrection it is, of course, possible to find a wide variety of interpretations as to what exactly took place.

Reuben. (1) The first-born son of both Jacob and Leah.

(2) The tribe of Reuben, which occupied an area on the eastern shore of the Dead Sea between Ammonite and Moabite territory.

Revelation, Book of. Without doubt the most difficult book in the New Testament for modern readers because its thought-forms and imagery are so remote from those to which we are accustomed. Written during a time of persecution, probably that of the emperor Domitian in the last decade of the first century, it declares in highly metaphorical language that the stage of human history is set in the context of an eternal scheme of things, in which God reigns supreme. Whatever their present sufferings, ultimate victory is assured to those who put their trust in Jesus. The writer describes himself as John, and some scholars have identified him with the disciple John, but there is no solid evidence for this. There is no question of the writer being the author of John's gospel or the letters of John.

Rezin. King of Syria (about 740-732 B.C.). An ally of Pekah, king of Israel, against the Assyrians. Together they threatened to attack Judah if King Ahaz would not join their coalition. Rezin was killed by the Assyrians when they finally took his capital, Damascus.

Romans. The Roman empire provides the context in which the events of the New Testament took place. Many Jews hated the Romans, and there were frequent misguided attempts at rebellion which culminated in the revolt of A.D. 66 and the eventual destruction of Jerusalem by the Romans in A.D. 70. In spite of occasional persecution, Roman rule was generally helpful to the spread of Christianity through its maintenance of political stability and good communications.

Romans, Letters to the. Paul's letter to the Romans was written to an already flourishing church which he did not know personally. Its purpose was apparently to pave the way for further missionary work in the western Mediterranean, using Rome as a base. Paul seems to feel it necessary to lay before the Roman church the gospel that he preaches, and this letter provides the most coherent statement of his theology that we possess. Its great emphasis is on faith in Jesus as the sole necessity for reconciliation with God, and the inadequacy of legalistic forms of religion where the follower's relationship with God depends on his having met God's demands in every detail.

Rome. The capital of the Roman empire, a church seems to have been established there at an early but unknown date. Tradition says it was founded by Peter, but there is no biblical evidence for this. Paul spent two years there under arrest and, again according to tradition, died there with Peter in Nero's persecution.

Ruth. The book of Ruth is one of the gems of the Old Testament. It tells how Ruth, the Moabite widow of an Israelite husband, decides to accompany her widowed mother-in-law, Naomi, back to her home town of Bethlehem. In so doing Ruth accepts Israel's God as her own. Boaz, a kinsman of Naomi, notices Ruth gleaning the remains of his barley field and ultimately marries her, and they give birth to Obed, David's grandfather. The story is a parable (as is suggested by the names of the chief characters, all

of them symbolic), but may rest on a historical fact, for much of the point of the story depends on Ruth being David's great-grandmother, and if this were made up the point would be lost. The book is essentially a plea for tolerance of mixed marriages, and as such it shows a liberality of outlook matched in the Old Testament only by the book of Jonah. Attempts to date the book have proved very difficult, but the most likely period is shortly after the exile, when the Jewish community was becoming more exclusive.

S

Sabbath. The observance of the sabbath as a day of rest and worship goes back at least to the time of Moses, yet it was only during the exile that it came to assume the importance it has had ever since for Jews. Deprived of temple worship, and living among aliens, strict sabbath observance became the identifying characteristic of a good Jew. By Jesus' time the number of rules about the sabbath was enormous, and while Jesus clearly supported the principle of the sabbath, he would not let his work be hindered by such petty rules. This became one of the major sources of friction between him and the Pharisees.

Sacrifice. Although the Jews came to realise at an early stage that God did not require human sacrifice (Gen 22:9-14), animal sacrifice continued to be part of their worship until the destruction of Herod's temple by the Romans. Many of the prophets questioned the value of the practice, however, declaring that what God really wanted was justice and compassion in all men's dealings with their fellows.

Sadducees. A major party within Judaism at the time of Jesus. They were mainly of priestly background and, because many of them occupied positions which depended on the good will of the Romans, they generally favoured a conciliatory approach. Unlike the Pharisees, many of whom commanded respect by their conscientiousness, the Sadducees were liked by no one.

Salome. One of the women who had followed Jesus from Galilee to Jerusalem, watched the crucifixion and saw the empty tomb.

Samaria. Originally the name referred to the new capital city built by Omri, king of Israel. It was increasingly used, however, as another term for the northern kingdom as a whole. After the kingdom had ceased to exist it denoted an area corresponding to the central part of the old kingdom.

Samaritan. An inhabitant of Samaria. The Jews considered Samaritans to be excluded from their ranks because, following the deportation of many Samaritan citizens by the Assyrians in 721 B.C. and the establishment of people from other parts of the Assyrian empire on their soil, many mixed marriages had taken place. Since the northern kingdom had always been considered idolatrous by southern Jews, this put them both religiously and socially beyond the pale.

Samson. A Nazirite, and one of the most famous of the judges. He seems to have had more valour than discretion, however, and provoked the Philistines needlessly (Judg 15:1-6). He paid for this unnecessary bravado with his life (Judg 16:4-30).

Samuel. Samuel was the last great leader of Israel before the establishment of the monarchy, and a unique figure combining the functions of prophet, priest, judge and even ruler. Undoubtedly the most significant part of his work was the creation of the monarchy, but unfortunately the role he played in this is far from clear. There are two conflicting accounts interwoven in 1 Samuel. One represents Samuel privately anointing Saul as king on God's instructions, and later arranging for a public acclamation of his kingship when he has proved himself in battle. The other suggests that the people demanded a king against Samuel's advice and that only under protest did he arrange a system for choosing a king by lots. Whatever his initial attitude, his support for Saul was soon withdrawn when Saul offered sacrifice instead of waiting for Samuel to do it (1 Sam 13:8–14) and failed to destroy totally the Amalekites according to Samuel's instructions (1 Sam 15:13–23). It seems clear that Samuel came to regard Saul as one who was usurping God's position, and his hostility did much to break the man who, willingly or otherwise, he had created king.

Samuel, Books of. The two books of Samuel cover an epoch-making period in Israel's history. They trace the development of a loose confederation of tribes, without any established form of government, into a considerable empire under a dynastic ruler. Like all the historical books, they contain material from a variety of sources, some much closer to the events than others. We are fortunate, however, to have in 2 Samuel 9–20 (and continuing in 1 Kings 1–2) a continuous source which is widely recognised as the finest piece of history writing of its time from anywhere in the world. The author deals with the reign of David in such a way that he can only have been a close associate of the king himself. Not only does he describe in detail David's conversations with his advisers, but he does it so vividly that the characters of the major participants are laid open to scrutiny. He is quite remarkable in his absence of bias. He paints a sympathetic portrait of David but does not gloss over his failings, and neither condemns nor attempts to justify his more questionable activities. About no other king in the history of the monarchy is our information so reliable.

Sanhedrin. A council meeting under the High Priest at Jerusalem which had ultimate authority in religious and legal matters except for the power to pass the death penalty. This was why the Jews had to take Jesus before Pilate. The stoning of Stephen appears to have been a flagrant violation of this restriction. How and when the Sanhedrin was established is uncertain, but it came to an end with the destruction of Jerusalem in A.D. 70.

Sarah. Wife of Abraham and mother of Isaac. One of a number of women in the Bible whose child was seen as a special mark of God's favour because it came late in life.

Saul. (1) As the first king of Israel shortly before 1000 B.C., Saul faced a near impossible task, and his undoubted courage in battle was not an adequate qualification. The people of Israel wanted a king to defend them from their enemies, especially the Philistines, but they were not yet ready to give up their tribal independence, or support a permanent army as opposed to a constantly changing collection of volunteers. So he occupied an uncomfortable position in which more was expected of him than of the judges of old, but without any constitutional means of exercising his authority. When Samuel, a powerful influence on public opinion, withdrew his support, Saul clearly felt exposed and vulnerable, and the popularity of the young hero David increased his sense of insecurity. When David fled from his jealousy, helped unwittingly by the priest Ahimelech, Saul's slaughter of Ahimelech and his household was widely regarded as unjust, and must have alienated the priesthood. Thereafter much of his time and energy was diverted into hunting down David when it could have been more usefully employed in other ways. His final battle was an act of desperation, meeting the Philistines on level ground at the foot of Mount Gilboa, where their chariots gave them a decisive advantage. In the early years of his reign he seems to have enjoyed success, however, ejecting the Philistines from the central mountain range and, temporarily at least, being sufficiently free from the Philistine threat to strike at other enemies across the Jordan and far to the south. When he died there seems to have been no move to dispense with a king, so in spite of his ultimate failure, he seems to have achieved the acceptance of the monarchy by his people and thus paved the way for his successors.

(2) The Hebrew name by which Paul was known before his conversion. He may have taken the Roman form of his name to signify that he was "a new man in Christ", or possibly in order to identify himself with the Gentiles.

Scapegoat. A goat on which the sins of all the people were symbolically laid before driving it out into the wilderness. This happened annually on the Day of Atonement (Lev 16:20–22).

Scribes. The scribes were the professional interpreters of the law from the exile onwards. Many of them were also Pharisees, and the two are often linked in the New Testament.

Scripture. The term can be applied to any body of writings, but in the New Testament (where it is sometimes used in the plural) it invariably refers to the Old Testament. The use of the term by Christians to signify the Bible as a whole naturally came later.

Scrolls, Dead Sea. A collection of about 500 documents, the first of them discovered in 1947, from caves near the Dead Sea. Written between 170 B.C. and A.D. 70, some of them relate to the life of the ascetic community to which they belonged and others are parts of the Old Testament. Surprisingly the most ancient manuscripts of the Old Testament previously known were mediaeval, yet the differences in the text are mostly insignificant.

Sennacherib. The king of Assyria who invaded Judah in 701 B.C., destroyed 46 of its fortified cities and shut up Hezekiah "like a bird in a cage" (to use the words of his own inscription). He did not take Jerusalem, but it is not clear whether this was because of a disaster in the Assyrian camp or because Hezekiah accepted his punitive terms of surrender.

Septuagint. The Greek translation of the Old Testament, so called because of a tradition that it was made by 72 scribes. The latin septuaginta actually means 70, and hence the use of LXX as an abbreviation.

Shadrach. One of three young men, who according to the book of Daniel, survived being thrown into a blazing furnace for refusing to worship a gold statue set up by King Nebuchadnezzar (Dan 3:1–27).

Shallum. King of Israel (745 B.C.). He came to the throne by assassinating his predecessor and died in the same manner a month later.

Shaphan. The high official of King Josiah who took the Book of the Covenant from the temple and read it to him (2 Kgs 22:3–10). His family later protected Jeremiah, particularly during Jehoiakim's reign.

Sheba, Queen of. Sheba, in the Arabian peninsula, was a trading nation. The visit of the Queen of Sheba to Solomon (1 Kgs 10:1–10, 13) was probably what would now be called a trade mission, with Solomon offering copper in exchange for spices.

Shechem. A town with ancient religious connections, since Jacob is said to have built an altar there (Gen 33:18–20). Centrally situated on the borders of Ephraim and Manasseh, it became the first capital of the northern kingdom.

Shiloh. A town where the tabernacle was taken after the occupation of Canaan and which became the site for a permanent temple, the central sanctuary for the confederation of Israelite tribes before the monarchy (1 Sam 1:3). Jeremiah refers to the destruction of this temple, most probably by the Philistines (Jer 7:12).

Sidon. Next to Tyre, the most important city of Phoenicia and a good port. Jesus passed through its territory on at least one occasion (Mk 7:31).

Silas. Sent with Paul and Barnabas to present the findings of the Council of Jerusalem to the church at Antioch, he subsequently became Paul's companion on the second missionary journey (Acts 16:22–41). Probably to be identified with the Silvanus mentioned in some of Paul's letters.

Siloam. The name of a pool within the city walls of Jerusalem, fed from a spring outside by a tunnel some 620 m long. The tunnel was cut by Hezekiah (2 Chr 32:30) and can still be seen today.

Simeon. (1) The second son of Jacob and Leah.
(2) The tribe of Simeon which originally possessed territory south of Judah but was then absorbed into its neighbour.

Simon. (1) see Peter.
(2) **Simon the Zealot,** one of the twelve disciples, whose name suggests that he started at

least with very different political ideals from Jesus (Mk 3:18).

(3) **Simon the Pharisee.** The man with whom Jesus was eating when a sinful woman anointed him (Lk 7:36-47).

(4) **Simon of Cyrene.** The man who was compelled to carry Jesus' cross (Mk 15:21).

(5) **Simon Magus.** A miracle-worker in Samaria who, when he saw the effects of the Holy Spirit on a group of converts Peter and John had laid hands on, tried to buy this power from them (Acts 8:9-24).

Sinai. The peninsula between the Gulf of Suez and the Gulf of Aqaba which was the first objective on the exodus from Egypt. Mount Sinai (also called Horeb) has not been identified with certainty. If the giving of the law was accompanied by volcanic activity, as certain elements of the account suggest, a site on the eastern side of the Gulf of Aqaba (and therefore not on the Sinai peninsula at all) would be preferable on geological grounds.

Smyrna. An important city on the Aegean coastline of Asia Minor. The book of Revelation (Rev 2:8-11) refers sympathetically to the church there and its steadfastness under persecution, but we know little else about it.

Sodom. A city of evil reputation, probably to be located in an area now covered by the southern part of the Dead Sea. The city was destroyed by burning sulphur (presumably a volcanic disturbance) according to Genesis 19:24-25.

Solomon. King of Israel (c. 960-922 B.C.). Solomon is traditionally regarded as a wise king, yet by the end of his reign his subjects were seething with discontent, and it would have taken a man of exceptional ability to win back their loyalty. Rehoboam, his son, was not such a man, and so the great empire of Solomon was reduced almost overnight to two insignificant states. For this Solomon must take much of the blame. His reputation for wisdom is not without foundation, however. Inheriting a large and relatively peaceful empire from his father, David, he was never in serious danger from enemies, though he strengthened his defences and added chariots to his army just in case. He was thus able to concentrate on economic policy and proved a genius at exploiting his position across a number of major trade routes as well as developing the copper mines south of the Dead Sea. The wealth generated by this economic development went into building his own palace and its ancillary buildings and the first temple. He allowed himself to get carried away by the splendour of his own designs, however, and got into such debts that not even heavy taxation could pay them and he had to give away territory to his neighbour Hiram, king of Tyre, in payment for the supply of cedar wood (1 Kgs 9:10-11). These measures, together with the system of forced labour introduced to man the copper mines and the building projects, were exceedingly unpopular. So was his marriage to foreign wives (often in pursuance of trade agreements) and his tolerance of their pagan religions. Less obviously the reign of Solomon saw the beginnings of an insidious trend towards the concentration of power in the hands of a small number of people, which led ultimately to the kind of social injustice so fiercely condemned by the prophets. That Solomon was clever is beyond dispute; whether he was wise may be debated.

Sosthenes. The leader of the synagogue at Corinth who was beaten by the Jews (Acts 18:17). The reason for this is not stated. Possibly he had shown sympathy towards Christianity, since a Sosthenes is associated with Paul in the writing of 1 Corinthians (1 Cor 1:1).

Stephen. Appointed originally as one of the seven administrators of the charitable work of the Jerusalem church (Acts 6:1-6), Stephen soon showed himself a powerful advocate of the Christian faith. He was brought before the Jewish Council on charges of denigrating the temple and denying the necessity for the law of Moses, and was illegally executed by stoning, the traditional Jewish method (Acts 6:8-60).

Stoics. Members of a Greek school of philosophers who believed in the suppression of the emotions so as to remain unaffected by life's adversities. Paul debated with the Stoics in Athens (Acts 17:18).

Stoning. The method of execution among the Jews, and the prescribed penalty for 18 crimes. The accusers were required to throw the first stone (Deu 17:5-7, see John 8:7 for Jesus' reaction to this rule).

Sychar. According to John 4:5-6 the site of Jacob's well. Usually identified with Shechem.

Synagogue. The development of synagogue worship was a response to three things: the law forbidding sacrifice except in the Jerusalem temple, the destruction of the temple in 586 B.C. and the dispersion of the Jews. As a result, the offering of sacrifice could no longer be a regular way of worship and a non-sacrificial form of worship had to be developed. This was based on the reading and exposition of the Law, interspersed with psalms and prayers, and it set the pattern for later Christian worship.

Syrians. Also known as Aramaeans, these people were Israel's immediate north-eastern neighbours. At one time forming several small kingdoms, they gradually coalesced into a single state which was frequently at war with Israel. Syria became a province of Assyria following the destruction of Damascus, the capital, in 732 B.C.

T

Tabernacle. The name given to the "tent of meeting", the place where Moses met with God and which represented God's presence among his people. An elaborate structure, it was in effect a travelling temple.

Tabernacles, Feast of. Known also as the Feast of Booths, the festival was both a celebration of the grape harvest and a recollection of the wilderness wanderings, symbolised by people living in temporary shelters (booths) throughout the week.

Tarsus. A city in Asia Minor which was the home of Paul. It had a large Jewish population, but was also noted for its Greek philosophers, and it was this dual background that equipped Paul especially to be a missionary to the Gentiles.

Temple. There were three successive temples in Jerusalem. Solomon's temple, the first, was destroyed by the Babylonians in 586 B.C. After the exile a second temple was built, but due to the circumstances of the time this seems to have been a relatively poor affair. Then in 19 B.C. Herod the Great began work on the third temple, a large and imposing structure in every way. Though substantially complete by Jesus' time the finishing touches were not added until about A.D. 60. Ten years later it was destroyed by the Romans.

Ten Commandments, see **Commandments.**

Tertullus. A Roman or Romano-Jewish lawyer whom the Jewish Council employed to present the case against Paul before Felix (Acts 24:1-9).

Tetrarch. Both Herod Antipas and Philip were known as tetrarchs because they each received roughly a quarter of Herod the Great's kingdom (the other half going to Archelaus).

Thaddeus. One of the twelve disciples (Mk 3:18), known in Luke as Judas, son of James (Lk 6:16).

Thessalonians, Letters to the. The two letters of Paul to the Thessalonians are the earliest writings in the New Testament unless, as some scholars think, Galatians came earlier. They were written from Corinth, within a short time of each other, about A.D. 52. Amongst other things they show that the church at that time still expected the second coming of Christ in a literal form quite shortly, and that this expectation had led to undesirable behaviour such as refusal to work any more. Although Paul's correspondence with the Corinthians two to three years later shows that he still thought in terms of a second coming then, it is not a theme which occurs in his later letters.

Thessalonica. The capital of Macedonia in northern Greece, the city was visited by Paul during his second missionary journey (Acts 17:1-9) and presumably on the short tour he made of the Greek churches following his ministry in Ephesus (Acts 20:1-6).

Thomas. One of the twelve disciples well characterised in John's gospel, where he appears as loyal but slow to learn. His confession of Jesus as "My Lord and my God" after the resurrection identifies Jesus with God more clearly than any other statement in the gospels, however (Jn 20:28).

Tiglath-pileser III. King of Assyria (745–727 B.C.). It was Tiglath-pileser who established the Assyrian dominance of Palestine which was to last well over a century. It was to him that Ahaz of Judah appealed for help against Israel and Syria, both of which were invaded and devastated.

Timothy. Born of a Jewish mother and Greek father, Timothy was a native of Lystra. When Paul revisited the city at the start of his second missionary journey he asked Timothy to join him. From this time onwards he was constantly with Paul, or working elsewhere under Paul's oversight, and only three of the letters ascribed to Paul do not mention him.

Timothy, Letters to. There are difficulties in ascribing to Paul the two letters to Timothy. The style is not quite like Paul's, and the more formal organisation of the church suggests a later period. The most probable view is that they do contain fragments of personal notes written by Paul to Timothy, but that these have been used by a later author as the basis for general advice to church leaders. Similar considerations apply to the letter to Titus, which is often linked with the two letters to Timothy under the title of the Pastoral Letters.

Titus. A companion and co-worker of Paul, he seems to have been particularly involved in Paul's correspondence with Corinth, carrying his letters and acting as his representative (2 Cor 7:7, 8:16–17).

Titus, Letter to. *see* Timothy, Letters to.

Tongues, Speaking with. An outpouring of incomprehensible sounds which often accompanied a state of religious excitement in New Testament times, and still occurs in some churches today. The implication that the disciples actually spoke in foreign languages on the day of Pentecost is probably intended as a way of symbolising the universal relevance of the gospel. Paul warned against giving undue emphasis to this gift of the Spirit (1 Cor 14).

Tribes of Israel. Traditionally descended from the twelve sons of Jacob, the number remained twelve in spite of some changes. The descendants of Joseph in fact formed two tribes, named after his sons Ephraim and Manasseh, whereas Simeon fairly quickly became absorbed into Judah.

Tyre. The principal city of Phoenicia, and the centre of a city-state. The kings of Tyre were often on good terms with the kings of Israel, and the two nations traded to their mutual advantage (1 Kgs 5:1–11).

U

Unclean Foods. By long established tradition the Jews did not eat (and still do not eat) certain foods which were ritually unclean. This, and the fact that every meal was seen as a family religious occasion, meant that Jews rarely sat down at table with Gentiles. When Jewish and Gentile Christians began to associate with one another this was one of the difficulties they had to face (Rom 14:14–15).

Unleavened Bread, *see* Passover.

Ur. The home town of Abraham, sited in the southern part of the fertile flood-plain of the Tigris–Euphrates river system.

Urim and Thummim. Two objects used by a priest to determine God's will. It is not known how they were used, but the technique was probably to ask specific questions, to which the objects, on being thrown like dice, would then give a "yes" or "no" answer (1 Sam 14:41).

Uzziah. King of Judah (783–742 B.C.). Long-lived, capable and with the welfare of his people at heart, Uzziah was one of the better kings of Judah. He repaired and strengthened the defences of Jerusalem, re-equipped his army (with slings for hurling stones among other things), attacked the Philistine cities and recaptured from the Edomites the important port of Elath on the Gulf of Aqaba (2 Chr 26:1–15). Towards the end of his reign he was stricken by a skin disease and his public duties were taken over by his son Jotham.

W

Weeks, Feast of. Also known as Pentecost, the feast came at the end of the wheat harvest and later was associated with the giving of the Law on Sinai. It was during this feast that the apostles received the gift of the Holy Spirit (Acts 2:1–4).

Wisdom Literature. A name applied to books such as Proverbs, Job and Ecclesiastes which discuss philosophical issues or offer practical advice for living. There is a parallel literature from other middle-eastern civilisations, but the Hebrew literature is unique in its emphasis on the knowledge of God (and not merely academic knowledge but the knowing that comes from a relationship) as the basis of all wisdom.

Y

Yahweh. The proper name of the God of Israel was written as YHWH, there being no vowels in Hebrew. How it would have been pronounced (in fact it was considered too sacred ever to be spoken aloud) is a matter of speculation, but modern opinion favours Yahweh. Jehovah is an earlier and now outmoded attempt to render the same name.

Z

Zacchaeus. A tax collector of Jericho who became a follower of Jesus and generously compensated all those he had previously cheated (Lk 19:1–10).

Zadok. He appears to have been High Priest jointly with Abiathar during David's reign, but when Abiathar was banished by Solomon for supporting Adonijah in the struggle for succession, Zadok became the sole High Priest.

Zebulum. (1) The tenth son of Jacob, his sixth by Leah.
(2) The tribe of Zebulum which occupied a fairly small area of northern Israel surrounded by Manasseh, Issachar, Naphtali and Asher.

Zechariah. (1) King of Israel (746–745 B.C.). The son of Jeroboam II, he was assassinated by Shallum.
(2) A prophet who wrote chapters 1–8 of the book of Zechariah about 520 B.C. His prophecies look forward to the restoration of the temple and the new age about to dawn. Chapters 9–14 are from a later date.
(3) The father of John the Baptist.

Zedekiah. King of Judah (597–586 B.C.). The uncle of his predecessor Jehoiachin, he was placed on the throne by the Babylonians when Jehoiachin surrendered to them in 597 B.C. and was deported. In 589 B.C. Zedekiah himself rebelled and so precipitated the final crisis in the history of Judah. After Jerusalem fell in 586 B.C. he fled, but was captured, and after watching all his sons killed he was blinded and taken in chains to Babylon.

Zephaniah. A contemporary of Jeremiah, Zephaniah threatened a day of judgement against his people, primarily because of their unfaithfulness in worshipping other gods, but also he looked forward to repentance and restoration.

Zimri. King of Israel (876 B.C.). After assassinating his predecessor Elah, Zimri ruled for only seven days before committing suicide in order to avoid being murdered by Omri.

Zion. Originally just the name of one of the hills on which Jerusalem is built, it came to be a symbolic term indicating the dwelling-place of God and associated with the belief that he would always protect Jerusalem.

Zophar. The third of Job's "friends" (Job 11).

DICTIONARY OF COMPUTING

This new section in *Pears* provides a concise glossary of many of the key terms currently in use in the fast-changing world of computers and information technology in the late 1990s. A Special Topic takes a detailed look inside the Internet.

DICTIONARY OF COMPUTING

A

Access Time. In a disc drive or other mass storage device, this is the time taken to find and retrieve a particular piece of information, or block of data. For a disc drive it is the time taken up by the lateral motion of the head assembly (seek time) and waiting for the disc to rotate sufficiently for the area of interest to be under the head (rotational latency).

Ack. Abbreviation of Acknowledge. One of the characters transmitted for the purposes of hand-shaking in a data transfer. The character is sent back to the transmitting device by the receiving device to confirm that the last block of data has been received.

ActiveX. An adaptation of Microsoft's "Object Linking and Embedding" (OLE) technology which allows small programs, called "Controls" to be run from within HTML pages on the World Wide Web. The programs provide additional functionality beyond that contained within the HTML standard. Ideally the running of the Control is handled by the browser, requiring no additional action on the part of the user. It can provide similar functionality to **Java**.

ADC. *See* **Analogue to Digital Converter.**

AI. *See* **Artificial Intelligence.**

AIFF. Abbreviation of Audio Interchange File Format. A method for storing and distributing audio as computer data, developed by Apple Computers for their Macintosh range and adopted by other companies. Unlike the AU standard the Apple system uses linear encoding. It is also used for exchanging soundfiles over the Internet. *See also* **AU, WAV.**

Algorithm. In a computer, a sequential group of rules which, taken as a whole, will solve a specific problem. Each rule is sufficiently unambiguous that it can be executed by a machine. The algorithm can be considered as a symbolic representation of the problem. Generation of the algorithm is one of the stages of writing a computer program. The more accurately the algorithm models the problem, the more effective will be the program which results from it.

Algorithmic Composition. The use of, or a facility within, software to help music composition. Essentially computer generated music. Sometimes called Computer Aided Composition.

Aliasing. In digital video systems (especially computer screens) an effect that occurs to a greater or lesser extent when a curve is displayed on a video screen. On close inspection it is possible to see that the curve is approximated by jagged steps or "jaggies". The term is also used to describe a type of unwanted noise generated in digital audio systems if the sampling rate is less than twice the highest frequency found in the wanted signal.

Alpha Test. *See* **Bug.**

Analogue to Digital Converter. The encoding part of a digital device whose function is to sample an analogue signal such as sound or video and derive a numeric (binary) value from it at regular intervals.

Applets. *See* **Java.**

Artificial Intelligence. The concept (almost an article of faith for some) that computers will be able to, or can now, behave in a manner that resembles human intelligence, in that they will be able to learn to perform a task rather than require programming, be able to adapt to changing levels or types of input, perform deductively or reason and possibly even imagine. More strictly the branch of computer science which deals with such problems as pattern recognition and knowledge based or expert systems. Many new technologies are contributing to developments in this area including neural networks and bioelectronics.

ASCII. Acronym from American Standard Code for Information Interchange. One of a number of standard systems which determine how a specific character is represented by a specific binary numeric value in a computer. Thus the character "A" is represented by the number 65. ASCII is a seven bit code and thus allows 128 characters to be uniquely defined. The intention was to ensure that text data could be transmitted from one machine to another. There is a so called extended ASCII which is an eight bit version of ASCII used by IBM for its PCs. *See also* **UKASCII, EBCDIC.**

ASIC. Acronym from Application Specific Integrated Circuit. Essentially an integrated circuit (usually LSI) which has been manufactured to have a particular function, and which might replace an assembly of general purpose ICs which did the same job *e.g.* the image processing circuitry in a printer.

Asynchronous. A form of data transfer between two devices which have separate, free running clocks. In order to ensure that data are not missed, each byte is preceded by a start bit and succeeded by a stop bit. RS232C is asynchronous.

AU. Abbreviation of AUdio. A method for storing and distributing audio as computer data, developed by Sun Computers and adopted by other companies. It is also used for exchanging soundfiles over the Internet. Unlike the AIFF standard, the Sun AU system uses a logarithmic encoding scheme for its 8-bit formats; this is akin to audio compression and results in an apparently increased dynamic range equivalent to about 12-bit linear encoding at the expense of added noise. *See also* **AIFF, WAV.**

AV. Abbreviation of Audio Visual. Sometimes applied to computer systems which are optimised for processing sounds and images, for Multimedia work *etc.*

B

Back Up. (1) A copy of data which has been taken from a computer system and is stored separately from it. The intention is that the data can be restored to the computer in case of any accidental loss of the original. The back up can take the form of any type of memory such as floppy disc, RDAT *etc.* (2) A source of power such as a battery used when the main source of power has been removed. Normally encountered in devices such as synthesisers *etc.* whose memory contents are preserved by an internal battery when the device is switched off.

BASIC. Acronym from Beginner's All-purpose Symbolic Instruction Code. *See* **High Level Language.**

Baud Rate. The rate at which data are transmitted, and encountered with reference to MODEMs, Fax *etc.* If methods such as data compression and error correction are not being used then Baud Rate can be synonymous with bits per second (BPS), and related to the number of characters per second. In general it requires 10 bits to transmit a character such as a letter "A" (8 bits plus 1 start and 1 stop bits). So in these circumstances the character rate is one tenth the Baud Rate or BPS. However data compression can have the effect of representing more characters with the same or fewer bits, so the relationship between Baud Rate and character rate becomes less simple particularly at higher data rates.

Beta Test. *See* **Bug.**

Bidirectional. A form of data transfer which allows a device to receive and transmit data simultaneously. Also called Full-Duplex. The ability to receive only or transmit only at any given time is called Half Duplex.

Binary. A way of representing numbers using only two symbols "0" & "1". The system is described as a base 2 numbering system and follows the same rules as the more familiar base 10 or decimal system. In decimal each column is 10 times bigger than the one to its right (1000, 100, 10, 1). In Binary each column is 2 times bigger (8, 4, 2, 1). Any decimal number can be represented in binary although it may require more columns. In binary the columns are called Binary digITs or BITS for short. It is used by computers as it is easy to tell whether a voltage is present ("on" or "1") or not ("off" or "0"). Because of the relatively large number of columns or bits used to represent numbers, binary numbers are sometimes compressed by presenting them in hexadecimal (base 16) form, whereby one hexadecimal digit represents four binary digits.

bis. French for "again", a suffix added to come CCITT V-series standards to indicate derivation. For example V.32bis is a fast (14,400 BPS) derivative of the V.32 standard (9,600 BPS).

Block. In a mass storage device such as a disc drive, the smallest amount of data that can be accessed is called a block, it being more efficient to store a fixed minimum amount. A block is typically 512 or 1024 bytes. Also used in a general way to describe an amount of data which is being transmitted or processed.

BPS. Abbreviation of Bits Per Second. *See* **Data Rate.**

Browser. A computer application which displays and interprets HTML documents on the World Wide Web. The browser may provide additional facilities such as managing E-mail *etc.* While a few such applications are available the majority of users are served by two market leaders: Netscape Navigator and Microsoft Internet Explorer. In this rapidly developing technology there is considerable difference in ability between early and later versions of browsers and some incompatibility arises, with the result that HTML authors have something of a difficult job ensuring that features of their Web pages can be read correctly by the different browsers.

Bubble Printer. *See* **Printer.**

Buffer. An area of memory used for temporary storage of data, particularly as an intermediate stage between two devices which operate at different speeds. The presence of the buffer allows the data to be held until the slower device is ready to accept it.

Bug. A fault, defect or error in computer hardware or, more usually, software, which results in incorrect operation. To some extent bugs are inevitable. Indeed there is a body of mathematical thought which suggests that it is not possible to prove that a program is without error (this is an important issue for software controlled systems which are required to be 'intrinsically safe' such as flight automation and nuclear or chemical process control). For this reason most software houses can only rely on a two tier testing of their products. In-house or Alpha tests are designed to check that the program functions according to the design specification, and external Beta tests are intended to check that the program doesn't do anything which was not part of the design specification, like format the user's hard disk. Beta testers are usually trusted 'power users' who will put the program through its paces and report faults only to the authors of the software. A computer system which exhibits bugs is sometimes described as 'flaky'.

Bulletin Board. A computer fitted with a MODEM which allows similarly equipped people to make contact and to download information, software *etc.* from that computer to their own. The process of making the initial contact is usually called "Logging On". These often have a sort of club atmosphere as they tend to be aimed at people with a particular interest. Many universities *etc.* have them and they are a good source of the cheap software sometimes called shareware.

C

CAD. Acronym from Computer Aided Design. The D is also variously taken to stand for Drawing, Draughting and Dealing (stock markets). Other Computer Aided areas include CAEngineering, CAManufacture or Music and CAComposition.

Cancel. One of the characters transmitted for the purposes of handshaking in a data transfer. The character is sent back to the transmitting device by the receiving device to indicate that the receiver wants the transmission to cease.

Card. An alternative description for a printed circuit board.

Carrier. A signal which can be changed (modulated) in such a way that the changes in the signal can represent information. For example a continuous tone can be changed in pitch between a high and low pitch. These changes in pitch then effectively become binary data which can be used to represent text or images *etc.* Such a system could be described technically as a "frequency modulated carrier", and is the basic method whereby Modems and fax machines work.

CAV. Abbreviation of Constant Angular Velocity. In a mass storage device such as a disc drive, it refers to the fact that the disc rotates at a constant speed. This means that the data rate will increase for a track at the edge of a disc and decrease for a track in the centre of the disc, in much the same way as the outside pair of skaters in a line spinning around a central skater will be going much faster than the pair on either side of the central skater, although the speed of rotation of the line of skaters is constant. *See also* **CLV.**

CCITT. Abbreviation of Consultative Committee for International Telephone and Telegraph. A body which defines international standards for communication systems, such as fax machines, modems *etc.* Individual standards are often identified by V number prefix *e.g.* V.22, V.34bis, V.42 *etc.*

CD. Abbreviation of Compact Disc. A digital audio storage medium consisting of a 5 inch disc upon which digital audio data are recorded in a manner which allows them to be read by an optical laser for replay.

CD+MIDI. A type of CD ROM which includes both digital audio data and MIDI data. This means that a recording of the sound of a musical performance and the MIDI data which were used to generate the performance, are simultaneously available to the user, although in some cases the MIDI data might be for additional musical parts which do not appear in the sound recording. In any case this allows the user to "play with" the performance by choosing different sounds *etc.* on their MIDI network.

CD–I. Abbreviation of Compact Disc–Interactive. A system whereby images (maps, pictures *etc.*), text and sound are placed on a CD, along with a program which enables a computer to present all this information to a user in an interactive manner. A typical example might be a map disc, combining maps with pictures of locations on the map, text which describes the locations and the sounds which are heard at those locations *etc.* In principle anybody can access the information at will. In practise, there are often limitations on what is possible. *See also* **Interactive.**

Checksum. A simple means of error detection employed in data transfer between devices in a network. The checksum is a numeric value which is the result of some calculation performed on the data which are being transmitted. It might simply be the sum total of all the data, but other, more elegant methods tend to be used. The resulting value is then transmitted along with the block of data. The receiving device will then perform the same calculation on the data and compare its result with the checksum it has received. If there has been no error in the transmission (*i.e.* no data have been lost or changed) the checksum values will be identical. If the receiving device produces a different result, it will normally request that the data be sent again. In general the checksum can only tell a receiving device that a transmission error has occurred, it does not carry sufficient information to allow the error to be corrected. This limits the usefulness of checksums to data transfers which are non-real time *i.e.* it doesn't matter how long it takes the data to be transmitted. In situations where the data have to meet a deadline *e.g.* the digital to analogue converter in a CD player it is desirable to be able to detect and correct the error. *See also* **Error Correction.**

Chip. *See* **Integrated Circuit.**

CIRC. Acronym from Cross Interleaved Reed-Solomon Code. *See* **Error Correction.**

CISC. Acronym from Complex Instruction Set Computer (pronounced "sisk"). Essentially a microprocessor which has an elaborate and powerful instruction set which is ideal for implementing a general purpose microcomputer such as a PC. *See also* **RISC.**

Clipboard. In a computer, a temporary memory area which can be used to store sections of text or pictures, so that they can be moved within the current program, or transferred from one program to another. The clipboard generally holds only one thing at a time and this will usually not be preserved if the computer is switched off. *See also* **Copy, Cut** and **Paste.**

Clock. In a computer, a high frequency (typically 5 Mhz or more) oscillator which generates a pulse wave. This is used as a timing reference to ensure that each of the separate sections of the computer (memory, CPU *etc.*) operate in a synchronised manner. The clock rate can be a very crude indicator of the performance of the computer.

Clone. A term used to describe a device which offers the same facilities and compatibility as an established product made by a different manufacturer. Most commonly encountered to describe IBM-PC type computers made by companies other than IBM *etc.*

CLV. Abbreviation of Constant Linear Velocity. In contrast to CAV a mass storage system that has a disc whose speed varies, thus keeping the data rate at the head constant irrespective of the head's position on the disc. CD is an example of this method.

Coding. The process of altering the form of a signal or data. There are normally two complementary stages: encoding is the process which converts from the original to the new form, decoding is the process which converts back from the new to the original form. Coding methods are adopted for a number of reasons: to standardise data to make it easy to transfer between otherwise incompatible machines; to protect the data from errors which might occur during transfer (Error Correction); to reduce the size of the data file (Data Compression); or to make the data unreadable by the unauthorized (Encryption).

Compact Disc. *See* **CD.**

Compression Ratio. In data compression the ratio of uncompressed to compressed data. An indication of the saving in storage or increase in transmission speed which the data would otherwise require.

Computer. A device, usually electronic (the hardware), which processes data which are input, according to a set of instructions (the program or software) to produce data which are output. Almost all available computers conform to "von Neumann" architecture, which means, in essence, that they perform instructions one after the other and cannot do more than one thing at a time, although they may do serial operation so quickly that it appears parallel to our sluggish minds. Computers can be broadly classed according to speed or power in decreasing order: supercomputers, mainframes, minicomputers and microcomputers or personal computers (PCs). However the distinctions are not always clear cut; many personal computers are classed as micros, but are as powerful or fast as mainframes of a few years ago. For example the engine management systems of some cars have greater computing power and memory than the mainframes which ran the early Apollo space shots. The main computers found in UK homes, schools and businesses are the IBM PC and its "clones", and the Apple Macintosh. Acorn (especially in schools), Atari and Amiga also have some share of the computer market. Many pieces of technology available today, from cars to microwave ovens, also have considerable computer capability.

Computer Generations. Computers can be categorised according to power and type of technology into "generations" in the sense that each new generation is different from the last by virtue of some improvement in technology or design. Thus: first, *c.* 1951 using valve technology & magnetic or paper tape storage; second, *c.* 1961 using transistor technology and having separate systems to handle input & output thus freeing the CPU and programmable via a high level language; third, *c.* 1965 using SSI & MSI ICs and using hard disc storage, thus reducing physical size and improving reliability; fourth *c.* 1984, using LSI & VLSI technology and allowing networking and multitasking; Fifth, *c.* 199? using VLSI technology, parallel processing using RISCs or Transputers, for artificial intelligence (AI) and expert systems applications.

Contiguous. Literally meaning "alongside" from Latin *contigere*, to touch. In a mass storage device such as a hard disc, it refers to the practice of allocating blocks of data that are physically next to one another on the disc. This is advantageous as it means that once a track on the hard disc has been accessed, the head need not be stopped again until that track has been completely read.

Controls. *See* **ActiveX.**

Copy. In a computer, a command which places a previously selected section of text or picture in the clipboard so that it may be repeated elsewhere, either within the current program or another. *See also* **Cut, Paste.**

Copy Protection. A term most commonly used to describe any of various systems designed to prevent multiple copies being made of an original, or less commonly, a system such as the knock-out tabs on audio and video cassettes or the write-protect shutters on floppy disks and RDAT cassettes, which prevents inadvertent overwriting of an original. In the former sense with application to proprietary software it includes the use of hardware dongles, keys or registered user-passwords. *See also* **Encryption, Hacking.**

CPU. Abbreviation of Central Processor Unit. In a computer, the device or integrated circuit that actually carries out the computing processes.

CRC. Abbreviation of Cyclic Redundancy Checking. A method of error detection employed in data transfers such as FTP. The greater the number of bits used to define the CRC, the more reliable it is. ZMODEM uses a 32 bit CRC which is more reliable than the 16 bit CRC of XMODEM.

Cripple Ware. An ironic term which describes versions of computer software with some crucial features disabled (they might not load or save data, or they might quit after a short period of running). Often issued free to demonstrate the software to potential users.

CRT. Abbreviation of Cathode Ray Tube. A large valve used to display TV pictures or computer data.

CTS. *See* **RS232C.**

Cursor. The position on a computer monitor, usually indicated by a solid or flashing mark, where text *etc.* will appear or can be changed. On some systems the cursor can be moved with a mouse or trackball *etc.*

Cut. In a computer, a command which places a previously selected section of text or picture in the clipboard and simultaneously removes it from its current position, so that it may be moved elsewhere, either within the current program or another. *See also* **Copy, Paste.**

Cylinder. A term used by some manufacturers to refer to the entire surface of a data disk. The two sides of a floppy disk are considered by them to be like the surfaces of two separate cylinders. In a hard disk with several platters the cylinder is a set of tracks which coincide vertically on the platters.

D

DAC. *See* **Digital to Analogue Converter.**

Daisy Chain. A type of network whereby devices are connected one behind the other. In a network of seven devices a message generated by device 1 for device 7 is passed through (and ignored by) devices 2 to 6. SCSI is an example of this.

DAT. *See* **RDAT.**

Data. The information operated on by a computer as it executes a program. In general the data inside a computer are intended to be a representation of some aspect of the "real" world, that is, the data are symbolic. In digital audio the data represent sound. In digital video the data represent an image. Data is strictly a plural noun, the singular being datum.

Data Cartridge. Essentially a RAM or ROM integrated circuit packaged in a plastic box or thin card, which plugs into a computer or other device. This allows alternative versions of the device's internal memory to be stored, or new software *etc.* to be added to the device. PCMCIA is an example of this.

Data Compression. A process whereby the quantity of data required to represent some real world thing such as a sound or picture, is reduced by a variety of more or less successful means, so that the data occupy less space in a mass storage device, or can be transmitted in a shorter time. Most systems which do this operate with a compression ratio of between 2:1 and about 4:1. For data which represent text the process has little deleterious effect, but as you don't generally get something for nothing, you would be wise to expect some reduction in the quality of the sound or picture upon conversion from the data compressed form. Luckily humans are remarkably tolerant of "lossy" data compression.

Data Rate. The rate at which data are transferred from one place (*e.g.* a hard disc) to another (*e.g.* a computer). It is usually measured in Bits Per Second or kilobits per second (kb/S), but occasionally (and less meaningfully) in bytes per second. Sometimes called transfer rate.

Database. A category of computer software which allows a user to collect information or data about a number of different types of things, and keep it in a standard format. The user can then search through the information to find specific items of interest. The term is also used to refer to the collection of data itself. Properly speaking the total collection of information is called a datafile, the datafile is divided into records, where each record is a unique set of information *e.g.* an entry in the address book for s specific person. Each record is divided into fields, where each field is a particular unit of information *e.g.* a telephone number, a county, or a post code. Databases are useful for purposes other than address lists: stock control and statistical research are common uses.

DCD. *See* **RS232C.**

DCE. *See* **DTE.**

Decoding. *See* **Coding.**

Default. The condition adopted by a device when it is first powered up and has not yet received instructions which would cause any change to the condition. Most machines will simply be in whatever condition they were in prior to being powered down. Others will be completely blank, or in some more or less useful predetermined condition set by the manufacturers.

Desktop. A generic name for a type of personal computer system with separate components joined by cables, that is large enough to occupy part of your desk. Originally coined to distinguish between such devices and larger stand alone mainframes and minicomputers *etc.* The term is also used to refer to an abstract "desktop" environment represented on a computer screen by some user interfaces such as Windows or the Apple Desktop.

Desktop Publishing. Also called DTP. A category of computer software which allows a user to generate complex and finished documents such as magazines, books, display adverts, brochures *etc.* The user will be able to do such fancy things as "flow" the text around a picture so that it follows the boundary of the image, as well as the more mundane aspects of layout and style. Although superficially similar to a word processor, it is optimised to the creation and altering of layouts *i.e.* where text goes, rather than the initial keying of the text. It is not common to find a DTP software with a spelling checker, although this feature is common on word processors. Therefore the DTP software will normally be used to produce a layout or template into which the text, previously generated by a word processor, will be imported.

Digital Domain. An imaginary land where everything is described in terms of numbers. Thus when a signal is converted into digital form and then modified by the application of arithmetic so that the signal is altered in some way, for example, to reduce the amount of red in a colour picture, this is said to take place in the digital domain. If the digital data which represent a picture are transferred from one piece of equipment to another without conversion, the transfer is said to take place in the digital domain.

Digital Signal Processing. The modification of a signal which has first been converted into digital data, involving the application of arithmetic to the numbers which represent the signal. For example if a sound has been converted into digital form, making all the numbers 45% bigger will increase the amplitude of the sound, thus implementing a digital amplifier. In principle any process (tone control, *etc.*) can be applied to a sound in this way. The process can be also used to generate sounds from scratch, instead of relying on an existing set of data. This is the principle of most digital synthesisers. Similar processing can be applied to digital images, for example to reduce the amount of blue in a picture, or to increase contrast. Often shortened to DSP.

Digital to Analogue Converter. The decoding part of a digital device whose function is to sample binary values, at regular intervals and derive an analogue signal from them.

DIP Switch. An array of miniature (and fiddly to operate) switches, usually in groups of eight, which are sometimes fitted to devices to allow the user to preset certain functions for that device. DIP is an acronym from Dual In-line Package, a standard method of packaging components or circuits inside an oblong plastic or ceramic case with two rows of metal legs or pins, one on each of the long sides of the rectangle.

Direct to Disc Recording. The practice of recording digital audio data (or more recently video data) to a hard disc for later replay or editing.

Directory. In computer systems a term used to describe a collection of files in a mass storage device such as a hard disc. In its simplest form it may consist of a list of files. In more elaborate forms it may adopt a hierarchical structure with multiple directories being connected together like the branches of a tree. A directory may then have sub-directories in the same way as a branch has sub branches or twigs. From this metaphor the lowest level of a branched directory system is called the root or root directory.

Dither. (1) Dithered, Dithering *etc.* In digital video, a method of interpolating colour information between adjacent pixels, so that for example, an 8-bit imaging system with only 256 discrete colours can apparently represent the greater colour range of an image stored with more bits per pixel. (2) In digital audio, the principle of adding a small amount of random white noise to the signal with the intention of reducing the distortion which occurs when the signal level falls between resolution steps close to zero, *i.e.* those encoded by the LSB. *See also* **Quantisation Error.**

DMA. Abbreviation of Direct Memory Access. Many computers require that the CPU spend some of its precious time looking after the movement of data in and out of the memory. If a computer uses DMA the memory is controlled by a dedicated processor (MMU) which frees the processor from this tedious task. This has the effect of speeding up the task that the CPU is trying to carry out.

Dongle. A piece of hardware whose presence is required and verified by a piece of software before that software will run at all or, in some cases, become fully functional. It is one of a number of systems of copy protection. Usually it takes the form of a cartridge containing a ROM of some sort or a custom IC, which plugs into a socket on the computer. If the dongle is a ROM, it will probably contain a serial number which matches that of the software. If it contains a custom IC this will usually perform a mathematical function on a value generated by the software, the result of which is already known to the software. If the software gets the wrong answer (which includes no response) it may not load or it may start up in a 'demo mode' where it runs but with key features, such as the ability to load or save files, inhibited. *See also* **Hacking.**

DOS. Acronym from Disc Operating System. Often used as a short form of various operating systems for IBM PCs. *See also* **Operating System.**

Dot Matrix. *See* **Printer.**

Dot Pitch. *See* **DPI.**

DPI. Abbreviation of Dots Per Inch. An indication of the resolution of graphic imagers, such as computer monitors and printing systems. The higher the number, the greater the ability to show fine detail. Most laser printers operate at 300 DPI and this is quite adequate for most purposes, typesetting quality printers operate at 1200 or more DPI.

DSP. *See* **Digital Signal Processing.**

DSR. *See* **RS232C.**

DTE. Abbreviation of Data Terminal Equipment. A class of equipment, most commonly computers or printers, which can be directly connected via the RS232C interface to DCE (Data Communication Equipment) such as MODEMs.

DTP. *See* **Desktop Publishing.**

DTR. *See* **RS232C.**

Dynamic HTML. A rather nebulous term for technologies which add functionality to standard HTML such as JavaScript, Java, ActiveX *etc.*, as well as for features of the "official" HTML fourth generation. Such functionality can include altering a previously displayed image or playing a sound when the mouse pointer is passed over the image *etc.* The effect is to make the page more "interactive" with the user. *See also* **HTML.**

E

E-Mail. Abbreviation of Electronic-MAIL. The use of computers, as communication devices for sending text, graphics, or other data such as MIDI files or software *etc.* Particularly used with reference to computer communication over telephone lines using MODEMs. *See also* **Bulletin Boards.**

EBCDIC. Acronym from Extended Binary Coded Decimal Interchange Code (pronounced "ebsdick").

EIDE. *See* **IDE.**

Emulator. A system of software and/or hardware which allows a computer to run applications written for a different type of computer. In general, but not always, the application will run at a slower speed on the emulating computer than it would on its intended platform.

Encoding. *See* **Coding.**

Encryption. The alteration of a piece of information by some coding process so as to make it secure from unauthorised users, or to allow recovery from errors which might otherwise occur, when the information is transmitted from one place to another. *See also* **Error Correction, Hacking, Password Protection.**

EPROM. Acronym from Erasable Programmable Read Only Memory. A type of memory which can be written to once, read many times and subsequently erased, which distinguishes it from ROM and other types of WORM, (although erasure generally involves removing the EPROM from its circuit). The most common erasure method is exposure to strong ultra violet light for an hour or more. There is also EEPROM where the first E stands for electronic and specifies an electronic method of erasure.

EPS. Abbreviation of Encapsulated Postscript. An agreed standard file format for conveying text and graphic images from one system or software application to another. It consists of the list of Postscript commands required to print the page and a screen version of the image to allow positioning.

Erase. The removal of the recorded data from a data storage device, such as a floppy or hard disc. In practise the actual data are not erased, but the directory area of the storage device, which keeps a record of where data are, is erased. As it is no longer possible to find the data, they might just as well not be there. Systems that allow an unerase, are able to reconstruct the directory, and therefore find the data, as long as no new data have been recorded since the erasure was carried out. Also the removal of data from a memory device such as EPROM, although generally this cannot be undone.

Error Correction. A process whereby data which are being transferred from one computer to another, particularly via MODEM, can be protected against minor errors. The system is also used internally on some pieces of equipment such as CD and CD-ROM players. The data have extra pieces of information in the form of known "keywords" added to them. These extra pieces of data are interleaved or combined with the original data in such a way that if there is a problem in the data path (*e.g.* noise on the 'phone line or a scratch on the CD surface) which leads to the keyword becoming corrupted, the error can in most cases (but not always) be corrected. This is possible because of the interleaving method, the fact that the keyword is known, and therefore the precise way in which the data have been altered can be worked out and reversed. There are many methods, including Microcom Network Protocol (MNP) and Cross Interleaved Reed-Solomon Code (CIRC).

Executable. Said of any file which contains instructions or commands that can be carried out by a computer, *i.e.* the file contains some sort of computer program.

Expansion Slot. A socket provided on a piece of equipment, usually a computer, which allows additional hardware components to be added.

Export. In a computer, the act of placing data generated by the current program into a file which can be accessed by another program. This will be possible only if the data are formatted in a way the other program understands. This leads to a number of standardised file formats, such as TIFF and PICT for graphic images, AIFF and WAV for audio files and SYLK for database/spreadsheet files.

F

Fibre Optic. A method of data transmission in which a light beam (usually generated by a laser) is shone along a thin glass or plastic "cable". The light beam is turned on and off very rapidly in order to represent the bits of the digital word. The system can carry a much greater rate, and therefore amount of data, than most conventional electronic means, and is virtually immune to electromagnetic interference (EMI).

File. In a computer, a quantity of data which have been previously stored in such a way that they can be retrieved in the future. The storage will probably be a floppy disc or hard disc. In general the file is identified by a name which must be unique, unless it is the intention of the user to overwrite (and therefore destroy) the existing data with a new set. The act of creating such a file is called "saving" or "closing", while the act of retrieving the data in the file is called "opening".

Firmware. In a computer system the physical medium in which the software is contained *e.g.* a floppy disc, ROM or magnetic tape, as distinct from either the abstract form of the software itself, or the hardware which is controlled by it.

Flaky. *See* **Bug.**

Floppy Disc. A device for long term storage of computer data. The device is so called because of the floppy plastic disc surfaces which it uses rather than the hard metal surfaces used in hard discs. These plastic surfaces have a lower density of storage and slower speed of operation than hard discs. Floppy discs start at about 300 Kilobytes and currently go up to about 1.4 Megabytes.

FLOPS. Acronym from FLoating-point OPerations per Second. An indication of the numeric processing or "number crunching" speed of a computer. *See also* **MIPS.**

Flow Control. *See* **Handshaking.**

Font. A collection of symbols (usually letters, numbers *etc.*) of a given design, in a particular style and point size. Part of a typeface. *e.g.* "Times" is a typeface, whereas "12pt. Times Bold" is a font of the Times typeface.

Fragmentation. A condition of random access disc drives, particularly hard discs *etc.*, whereby long use and the pattern of erasure and writing will result in a file being discontiguous or fragmented, *i.e.* distributed over several areas of the disc instead of one contiguous file. The overhead of hunting around the disc and gathering up the various separate sections of the file will slow down its retrieval. Disc optimising software is available which can defragment a hard disc by shuffling the various file sections around into complete, contiguous files all at one "end" of the disc, with all the empty sections joined together at the other end.

FSK. Abbreviation of Frequency Shift Keying. A method of transmitting computer data via media which normally accommodate audio signals (*e.g.* telephone lines or audio tape), using two distinct frequencies to represent the binary states "on" & "off" of digital signals. It was quite commonly used in the early 1980s as the primary means of storing computer data, before disc drives became popular and is occasionally encountered as a system for "backing-up" disc drives.

FTP. Abbreviation of File Transfer Protocol. A system of data transfer which checks for errors in the data. If any are detected the receiver requests the data be present in the hope that the error will not occur again. The error checking method is Cyclic Redundancy Checking (CRC). Varieties of FTP include ZMODEM which uses a 32 bit CRC and flow control, and XMODEM, which uses a 16 bit CRC and does not require flow control. FTP is most commonly encountered on the Internet.

Full Duplex. *See* **Bidirectional.**

G

GEM. *See* **Operating System.**

GIF. Abbreviation of Graphic Image Format. A file format for transferring images as computer data. It indexes the colour information of the image according to a colour table with a range of 256 or fewer colours. It is perhaps less suitable for photographic type images which typically have many millions of colours but is perfectly suitable for artwork. It is one of a number of graphic formats used on the Internet. *See also* **JPEG.**

Gigabyte. 1,073,741,824 bytes. Not 1,000,000,000 as you might expect, but the nearest power of 2 which is close to a billion. This is a result of the influence of binary numbers on computer engineers.

GIPS. Acronym from Giga Instructions Per Second. *See also* **MIPS.**

Graphic User Interface. The ability of a device such as a computer (usually a function of the operating system) to symbolise and represent objects or concepts as pictures on a monitor which can be manipulated using a mouse or keyboard *etc.*, as opposed to the text based interfaces of older technologies such as

UNIX, or PC-DOS used on IBM PCs. It is considered more intuitive and easier to use, especially by computer novices.

Graphics. The use of pictures (as opposed to text) on a monitor by a computer. This very often has the advantage of making the computer more understandable or intuitive to use. Also the manipulation of pictures or video images by a computer.

GUI. *See* **Graphic User Interface.**

H

Hacking. Originally a term derived from 'hack', to describe an emergency or temporary modification of a computer system to fix a bug, but more recently used in the specific context of unauthorised modification of a computer system, and by extension any unauthorised access of such a system. Hacking became a cult underground activity in the late 1970s and early 1980s as many amateur (and professional) computer users found that they could access or 'hack into' systems which controlled billing of telephone and other utility services for their financial benefit, as well as cause general mayhem irrespective of benefit to themselves. A war of attrition has developed between hackers and their opponents who seek to ensure that distributed information systems (national and international telephone and data networks) remain secure, with each in turn leapfrogging the other. Hacking is also used to describe the practise of removing or bypassing copy-protection systems such as dongles from computer software to facilitate piracy. *See also* **Virus.**

Half Duplex. *See* **Bidirectional.**

Handshaking. In data transmission, the process of checking that a receiving device is ready to receive or that a transmitting device is ready to transmit. Or the method whereby such checking takes place. It is the principal means of stopping and starting the data transmission, a process otherwise known as "flow control". Two types are commonly described: Hardware handshaking where the data cable has conductors in addition to the normal receive and transmit wires, and which carry flow control signals in the form of changing voltage levels; and Software handshaking where particular codes called "X On" and "X Off" are sent in amongst the normal data stream. From this explanation it should be apparent that hardware handshaking is more expensive to implement as the data cable requires more connections. However it is essential for high speed data transfers or those which use error correction or data compression.

Hard Copy. Words or images printed on paper as opposed to soft-copy which has the same data but printed on a computer screen.

Hard Disc. A device for long term storage of computer data. The device is so called because of the hard metal disc surfaces which it uses rather than the floppy plastic surfaces used in floppy discs. These metal surfaces allow much greater density of storage and much higher speed of operation than floppy discs. Hard discs start at about 80 Megabytes and currently go up to about 9 Gigabytes (equivalent to about 10,000 floppies). Very large hard discs (above say 1 Gigabyte) are only usually encountered where large amounts of digital audio or video are being stored in "direct-to-disc recording".

Hardware. The electromechanical parts of a system, especially a computer system where the term is used to draw a distinction between the physical machine, the firmware and the abstract software that instructs it.

Header. Additional data which prefix a block of data either in a stored file or for the purposes of data transfer between devices. These data usually represent a description of the block of data which then follows. Postscript files which define the appearance of text and images for printers *etc.* use headers.

Hexadecimal. A numbering system using base 16. It is often used to represent equivalent binary values as the hexadecimal form is more convenient since one hexadecimal digit is equivalent to four binary digits. The system requires 16 different symbols and these are derived using the normal 0–9 supplemented by the letters A–F. *e.g.* the decimal number 1310 is represented by D16 in hexadecimal.

High Level Language. A computer programming language that is reasonably close to ordinary human language. Its significance is best understood by comparing it to low level language. This is the language the CPU understands, more specifically each program instruction corresponds to a machine code instruction executed in a single machine cycle. In a high level language, a single instruction that might read PRINT "so and so" would have to be compiled or interpreted by an interim process into a number (possibly hundreds) of machine code instructions, which are then executed. While it is possible, if laborious, to program in a low level language, a programmer will prefer to work with a high level language as it more closely resembles the language used in everyday thinking. Basic, Forth, Lisp and Pascal are high level languages.

HTML. Abbreviation of HyperText Mark-up Language. A system of "tags" which are embedded into the text of a document intended for the World Wide Web. The tags control the way the document is laid out and displayed, as well as allowing graphics and even sounds to be included in the pages. The most powerful feature of HTML as originally developed by Dr. Tim Berners-Lee at CERN, was the inclusion of tags which allow linking between HTML documents. The simplest of such links is the highlighting (perhaps by a different colour, or underlining) of a word or phrase. This marks the text as a referential "Link" to another document which can be activated by a mouse click. When activated the text of the linked document is called replacing the current document. Since its inception in 1990 HTML has evolved through a number of generations, each one providing new functionality to Web pages. Unfortunately these changes have occasionally been browser-led with the leading browser suppliers adding unofficial, idiosyncratic and competing features to HTML as implemented by their browser. In some cases these are adopted into the official HTML standard. Such leapfrogging can be confusing for HTML authors. The current fourth generation caters for so called Dynamic HTML with such features as cascading style sheets and support for objects implementing JavaScript, Java Applets or ActiveX Controls.

HTTP. Abbreviation of HyperText Transfer Protocol. An Internet protocol for specifying World Wide Web documents. It typically appears at the beginning of a web page URL.

Hypertext. A system available to a computer user which can store a large amount of data as a database and which has a user interface that allows so called "interactive" access to the data. In practise this might mean that the user does not have to approach the stored data in any sequential way, but can hop intuitively from one area to another. It might also mean that data is presented in a hierarchical manner, such that the most obvious bits are presented first and the user can then request that a particular section be expanded to provide more information about that specific area. The interface may present pictures as well as text. The WWW is a hypertext system.

I

Icon. A form of graphics where a picture is used by a computer to symbolise some sort of job carried out by the program. For example a picture of a wastebasket may be present on the monitor, any object placed in the wastebasket will be deleted. In general any picture which can be manipulated as a unit is an icon.

IDE. Abbreviation of Integrated Drive Electronics. A system for interfacing hard disc drives *etc.* which is used by IBM PCs and clones. The essential feature of IDE is the fact that the intelligent electronics are integrated on the disc drive as opposed to being carried on a separate card plugged into the PC's expansion slots. EIDE (Enhanced IDE) overcomes some limitations of speed and storage capacity of the earlier standard. It is effectively an alternative to SCSI.

Imagesetter. *See* **Printer.**

Import. In a computer, the act of placing data generated by another program into the current program. This will be possible only if the alien data are formatted in a way the current program understands.

Information Technology. *See* **IT.**

Inkjet. *See* **Printer.**

Instruction Set. A complete set of all possible instructions that a microprocessor can carry out. In the early years of microprocessor design the emphasis was on producing a wide variety of powerful and extended instructions, but it was found that programmers tended to use a small number of basic (forgive the pun) instructions to do almost every job. The recent fashion in certain applications has been to restrict the number of instructions to these basic functions, as the fewer instructions a microprocesor has, the faster it can execute any given instruction. This approach is particularly suited to microprocessors built into a product that has a specific purpose such as a printer and microprocessors using this approach are described as RISC. However if the microprocessor is going to live in a general purpose machine like a personal computer, where versatility takes precedence over speed of execution, it is convenient to have as elaborate an instruction set as possible and microprocessors using this approach are described as CISC.

Integrated Circuit. A method of compacting electronic circuits into a small space. This is achieved by manufacturing several tens, hundreds, thousands or even hundreds of thousands of diodes, transistors, *etc.*, more or less simultaneously onto one common semiconductor base called a substrate. There exist rough divisions of scale *i.e.* how many devices are present of SSI, MSI, LSI, VLSI. The components are joined by tiny tracks which are separated by distances comparable to wavelengths of light. This is the reason it is possible to see rainbow-like reflections off the surface of an IC. Connections to the outside world are made through tiny single strand wires much thinner than human hair. The complete assembly is typically only a millimetre or two square and is extremely fragile. In order to make the IC easy to handle and more robust it is generally packaged in some plastic material with the tiny wires welded to flat pins, which are then arranged in rows on the sides of the package. All manner of useful circuits from amplifiers to computers are available in this form.

Integrated Package. In a computer, a collection or suite of software, which combines the most common types of business software (usually database, word processor and spreadsheet). The package should be designed so that data from one program can be easily transferred to another within the package. This would allow a standard or form letter to be keyed in the word processor, but with blanks for personal names *etc.* The personal names would be held in the database software and would be added to the form letter during printing. This allows the user to send essentially the same letter, but personalised, to each customer, without the otherwise tedious task of manually filling in the name.

Interactive. In computing and media-speak, a two way communication process, with "mutual and simultaneous activity on the part of both participants" (Andrew B. Lippman) which has the following features: Interruptibility, one participant can interrupt the other without having to wait until the end of the current topic; infinite destination, the direction of the interaction can lead anywhere, not just to specific preprogrammed destinations. A lecture is not usually interactive, a conversation with a friend often is. Humans are very good at interaction, computers currently are not very good. Interactive is a vogue or hype word at the moment, however, few of the systems are properly interactive in the above sense. Some CD-I systems feature city maps which at first glance are very impressive. The user can "navigate" up a street and turn left (or right) into another street at will and see the correct buildings going past. Entering buildings is not however possible as the CD does not contain information about them. Such a system is interruptible, but has finite destinations, so it is not truly interactive. But it is a start. The projected major area for interactivity is computer aided learning. *See also* **Virtual.**

Interface. That which joins, or the point of connection of two joined things. Usually used to refer to electrical connections and their associated data structure such as MIDI, or more abstractly, in the sense of user interface the environment (graphic images on a monitor, front panel switches, keyboard *etc.*) in which a human communicates with a machine.

Interlaced Scan. A method of displaying an image on a video screen or monitor using two or more complete scans of alternate lines of the image area.

For example the system might scan (display) the even numbered lines and then return to the top of the image and scan the odd numbered lines. As there is a persistence effect both in the imaging system and the human eye then given a suitably fast refresh rate the image appears complete. Interlace is sometimes used as a synonym for "interleave" with reference to data systems.

Interleaving. A method of arranging, or rearranging, data according to some systematic rule, to increase the efficiency of a data storage device, or so that the data may be protected during transmission. *See also* **Error Correction.**

Internet. A global network of interconnected computers. Originally conceived as a "fault tolerant" method of connecting America's military computers, the system is now widely used and serviced by academic institutions, businesses and individuals. The system is a collection of computers connected by local national networks (including the telephone system) to Network Servers which are in turn connected internationally. It is hard to estimate the numbers of computers involved but currently it is probably at least 20 million and could be as many as 100 million. In any case it is set to increase in size. It is used for electronic mail (E-Mail); forums or newsgroups where particular interests or hobbies can be discussed; as well as publishing and broadcasting of information, software, audio and video. The World-Wide Web (WWW or W3) is a system for displaying information on the Internet in a graphic (as opposed to purely textual) manner, with intelligent or "hypertext" links between different areas of the Internet. *See* **V16–18.**

IO Device. *See* **Peripheral.**

ISDN. Abbreviation of Integrated Services Digital Network. A standard which allows high capacity direct data transfers through the telephone and other telecommunications networks obviating the need for MODEMs *etc.*

IT. Abbreviation of Information Technology. A generic term for all types of devices involved with information processing, storage, recovery *etc.* In general (especially educational) usage it simply means "computer-stuff".

J

Java. A programming language developed by Sun Microsystems which produces platform independent programs (in principle they can be made to run on any computer, called "Applets" which can be run from within HTML pages on the World Wide Web. Applets provide additional functionality beyond that contained within the HTML standard. Ideally the running of the Applet is handled by the browser, requiring no additional action on the part of the user. It can provide similar functionality to ActiveX.

JavaScript. In essence it can be considered a subset of Sun Microsystems Java programming language. It was developed by Netscape Communications Corp., to provide additional functionality to HTML pages on the World Wide Web beyond that contained within the HTML standard (so called "Dynamic HTML"). Unlike Java, a fully fledged programming language which produces stand alone applications (Applets) which are called and run by an HTML tag, JavaScript is a scripting language which is understood and implemented directly by the browser which is displaying the HTML page containing the script. In this way it can be seen as an extension of the HTML standard as it allows HTML authors to control how the browser responds to the user's interaction with the page, even, for example, generating web pages on the fly according to the user's requirements. It was standardised by the European Computer Manufacturers Association (ECMA) in June 1997.

Joystick. A hand operated stick-like control which has simultaneous movement in two axes (X and Y) and which allows the user (by waggling the stick) to define a unique position within the limits of movement of the control. Most commonly encountered on games computers, but sometimes used instead of a mouse or tracker ball, to position a cursor on the monitor.

JPEG. Abbreviation of Joint Photographic Expert Group. A committee of scientists, programmers, mathematicians *etc.*, which formed to specify the standard also known as JPEG, for a data-compression based graphic image file format, which would make it possible to transfer near photographic quality images as computer data. The system works by removing as much redundant information (large areas of the same shade on a balloon, for example) from the image as possible, thereby reducing the file size required to store the image and the bandwidth required to transmit it. It is "lossy" compression method in that some information about the image is thrown away. Usually when creating JPEG files the user has control over the compression ratio. Increasing the compression reduces the file size, and reduces the quality of the image. Some images will compress considerably with barely imperceptible loss of quality while other more complex images will not compress well at all. It is one of a number of graphic formats used on the Internet. *See also* **GIF, MPEG**.

K

kb/S. Abbreviation of Kilobits Per Second. *See* **Data Rate**.

Keyboard. A collection of keys in a staggered but broadly rectangular pattern, which are differentiated by symbols, and which forms a means of input of data into a computer. There are a number of stories which purport to explain the apparently irrational order of symbols in the keyboard layout (in America, Britain and much of Europe this layout is called QWERTY—from the top left row of keys). The most common of which suggests that they were laid out in this manner to slow enthusiastic operators so as to prevent jamming of the mechanism. This is fairly unlikely as even a slow typist can jam a manual machine. More likely is the explanation that one of the original manufacturers operated schools to train typists on their layout. As their layout was different from that of their rivals they increased sales by creating a work force of trained typists who would only work on one layout, forcing prospective employers to purchase machines of that type. Various attempts have been made to improve the efficiency and ergonomics (*see* **RSI**) of keyboards and these have produced quite startling devices such as the almost eponymous MOLD keyboard that looks just like a jelly mould. In general these have not been very successful due to the historic and universal establishment of the existing layout.

Keyboard Shortcuts. Combinations of particular keys on a computer keyboard which have the same effect as using a mouse to select a function or facility from a menu in a WIMP environment. Usually they will be mnemonic. For example, pressing the 'Control' key and the 'S' key simultaneously will have the same effect as selecting 'Save' from the 'File' menu. Likewise 'Command C' might be the same as selecting 'Cut' or 'Command P' might be the same as 'Print'.

Kilobyte. 1,024 bytes. Not 1,000 as you might expect, but the nearest power of 2 which is close to a thousand. This is a result of the influence of binary numbers on computer engineers.

L

Laptop. A generic name for a type of computer system that is allegedly easily portable, with all components (screen, computer, disc drive, keyboard and batteries) packaged in one box sufficiently small to sit on one's lap. The box will typically open up like a book to reveal the screen and keyboard which are otherwise covered up when not in use.

Laser Printer. *See* **Printer**.

LCD. Abbreviation of Liquid Crystal Display. A type of flat monitor, which is used on some computers (particularly those designed to be portable). Often monochrome, but more recently allowing colour display.

Least Significant. The rightmost value in any number system. In the decimal number 5,463, three is the least significant number as subtracting it would not make much difference to the value. *See also* **LSB**.

Line Printer. *See* **Printer**.

Long Word. *See* **Word**.

LSB. Abbreviation of Least Significant Bit. The rightmost bit or column of a binary number. So called because it has the least effect on the result of any sum involving the number. Occasionally in 16 bit or more (*i.e.* multi byte) systems it may be taken to stand for Least Significant Byte when referring to the rightmost byte for similar reasons. LSN is Least Significant Nibble.

LSI. Abbreviation of Large Scale Integration. An integrated circuit which contains about 1,000–90,000 active elements. *See also* **MSI, SSI, VLSI**.

M

Machine Code. In a computer, the numbers which represent individual instructions which can be executed by the CPU in a small number (1–4) of clock cycles. It is the lowest level at which a human programmer can work (inside a microprocessor there is a lower level called microcode, which the chip uses to perform the specific function, but this is built into the chip at the time of manufacture and is transparent to the programmer).

Magneto Optical. A method of mass storage in the form of a disc drive with removable discs held in cartridges. When writing information the system utilises a laser to heat the disc's surface thus altering its magnetic properties. The same laser or another can then scan the disc whose reflectivity is changed according to the pattern of magnetism laid down by the writing process. Once written the cartridges can be removed from the drive, which is advantageous in applications where data-portability is required.

Mainframe. A type of computer (strictly speaking of the third generation) which was first introduced in the mid-1960s and which took advantage of the (then) new SSI & MSI technologies. Machines of this type include the ICL 1900 series and IBM 300 series. More generally the term is used for a physically large computer which is located centrally to a network of users, each with their own terminal.

Mass Storage. A device or system for storing large amounts of data. There is a historical progression in the meaning of Mass in this context. Ten years ago a computer might have had "mass storage" of only 100 Kilobytes. "Mass" at the moment probably means more than 80 Megabytes, as the smallest hard disc that is worth making is about this size.

Master. In a system of devices, it is sometimes useful to have one device which governs the operation of the others (particularly as regards a timing reference, for example). This device is nominated the Master, the other devices become "slaves".

Megabyte. 1,024 Kbytes or 1,048,576 bytes. Not 1,000,000 as you might expect, but the nearest power of 2 which is close to a million. This is a result of the influence of binary numbers on computer engineers.

Memory. An area in a device such as a computer, where data are stored prior and subsequent to some manipulation determined by the program which the device executes. The memory can be in a variety of forms, such as semiconductor, magnetic tape, CD, floppy or hard disc. Memory is functionally classified according to whether data can only be read from memory (ROM) or can be both read and written (WORM, RAM), irrespective of the material form the memory takes.

Menu. In a computer system, the presentation to the user of a list of options, from which a choice may be made.

Microcomputer. A type of computer which is based on a microprocessor and which will probably include the keyboard and monitor in the same (or closely linked) package. The term is more or less synonymous with personal computer, or rather, a PC is a type of microcomputer.

Microprocessor. An integrated circuit (usually LSI) which has the function of the central processing unit (CPU) of a computer. It is the mass produced nature and comparative cheapness of these ICs which have contributed to the stupendous growth of information technology since the mid 1970s.

MIDI. Acronym from Musical Instrument Digital Interface. An internationally agreed standard of electronic hardware and language of commands, which allows musical (and increasingly non-musical such as lighting) equipment to be controlled and manipulated in a useful manner. It can also be defined as a system for encoding a musical performance digitally in such a way as it can be stored, manipulated and replayed on a computer. But it should be understood that it is only the instructions necessary to carry out the performance and related aspects which are encoded digitally and not the sound of the performance itself. Multimedia or "AV" (audio-visual) computers often implement MIDI.

MIDI Device. Any piece of equipment that can become part of a MIDI network. This includes computers, sequencers, drum machines, synthesisers, samplers, master keyboards, wind instrument type controllers, drum pads, effects units, even lighting units *etc.*

MIDI Message. A full instruction consisting of a digital signal with at least one status byte and frequently with one or more data bytes, which appears on a MIDI network and when received by an appropriate MIDI device causes it to perform some function described in the MIDI specification 1.0, such as turning on a note, or changing to a different sound. MIDI messages are divided into two broad categories: system messages and channel messages. System messages are further subdivided into system common, system real time and system exclusive. Channel messages are further subdivided into channel voice and channel mode (this latter subdivision is somewhat false as the messages concerned are types of channel voice message; specifically controller change messages).

MIDI Network. A term for a collection of MIDI devices connected together in such a way that MIDI messages can pass between them. The most common network is the daisy chain, although the MIDI specification does allow for a star network.

MIDI Socket. Multimedia computers which implement the MIDI standard will often have one or more MIDI connectors in the form of sockets mounted on a stand-alone box or a plug in card. The sockets have three functional types. MIDI In which allows a computer to receive MIDI messages from the network, MIDI Out which allows a computer to transmit MIDI messages to the network, and MIDI Thru which is simply a copy of everything received at the MIDI In socket and is there to facilitate daisy chain networks. A given MIDI device only needs to have those sockets which are appropriate to its function, for example a master keyboard might only have MIDI Out connectors, no MIDI In, as it is only required to generate messages. As it has no MIDI In there would also be no MIDI Thru on such a device. An effects unit such as a reverb, might only require a MIDI In socket to receive program changes *etc.* Whereas a computer should have at least a MIDI In and a MIDI Out, in practise most units have all three.

MIDI Specification. The internationally agreed document which defines the MIDI hardware and language standards. First described in October 1982 and formalised as version 1.0 in August 1983. Some other aspects have been added to it as MIDI devices have become more sophisticated. Such adjuncts include the MIDI sample dump standard and the standard MIDI file. Most multimedia computers utilise MIDI as the principal means of controlling electronic musical devices to provide sound effects and music to augment and accompany video presentations.

Minicomputer. *See* **Computer.**

MIPS. Acronym from Million Instructions Per Second. Invariably prefixed by a number *e.g.* 400 mips, and intended to give some indication of the performance of a computer (usually one in the supercomputer class). However the indication can be misleading, as it does not take account of factors such as access time to memory or storage devices. As a result some computer engineers wryly explain it as "Meaningless Indicator of Performance Speed". As technology improves GIPS is becoming more common (Giga is 1,000,000,000 or a billion).

MMU. Abbreviation of Memory Management Unit. *See* **DMA.**

MNP. Abbreviation of Microcom Network Protocol. Proprietary standards for Error Correction (MNP2–4), or Data Compression (MNP5) for use with communication devices such as modems and adopted into CCITT V.42 and V.42bis.

MODEM. Acronym from MOdulator/DEModulator. A device which allows digital data to be transmitted and received via a standard voice or telephone line.

It essentially uses FSK (*q.v.*) as a means of converting the digital data into an audio signal suitable for a voice line. Data rates for MODEMs vary from between 300 to 28,800 BPS, although by employing data compression equivalent transfer rates as high as 115,200 BPS can be achieved.

Most Significant. The leftmost value in any numbering system. In the decimal number 5,463, five is the most significant number as subtracting it would make a great difference to the value. *See also* **MSB.**

Mouse. A hand operated control which is free to travel across a horizontal surface. In its most common form, it consists of a ball in a frame which rolls over the surface when the mouse is moved. Movement of the ball in two dimensions is transmitted to sensors inside the mouse. The movement is interpreted and used to position a cursor on a computer monitor. It is usually fitted with one or more switches, the pressing of which will select or activate an area of the computer monitor currently under the cursor. Essentially it is an upside down tracker ball and is used instead of a tracker ball or joystick. Other forms have no ball but work optically by shining a pulsed LED at a semi-reflective surface. Lines printed on the surface decrease the intensity of the reflected light and this interference in the pulse rate is interpreted as movement.

MPEG. Abbreviation of Motion Picture Expert Group. A committee of scientists, programmers, mathematicians *etc.*, which formed to specify the standard also known as MPEG, for a data-compression based graphic image file format, which would make it possible to transfer moving images such as film or video as computer data. In some ways it is an extension of the still image JPEG standard. It is one of a number of moving-image formats used on the Internet. *See also* **JPEG, QuickTime.**

MSB. Abbreviation of Most Significant Bit. The leftmost bit or column of a binary number. So called because it has the most effect on the result of any sum involving the number. Occasionally in 16 bit or more (*i.e.* multi byte) systems it may be taken to stand for Most Significant Byte when referring to the left-most byte for similar reasons. MSN is Most Significant Nibble.

MSDOS. *See* **Operating System.**

MSI. Abbreviation of Medium Scale Integration. An integrated circuit which contains about 100–900 active elements. *See also* **LSI, SSI, VLSI.**

Multimedia. The mixed use of text, visual images and sound by a computer or other system, or the integration of music, picture and other effects during a presentation.

Multiplexer. A device which switches an input sequentially or in some other ordered fashion between a number of outputs or vice versa. This occurs in some computer communication systems as well as between components inside a computer.

Multisync. A term used to describe the facility of some computer monitors to display output from several different computer platforms without hardware modification.

Multitasking. A much abused phrase intended to suggest the ability of a computer to carry out more than one job simultaneously. In fact von Neumann architecture computers (which includes almost all currently in use) are serial operators and can only execute one instruction at a time. At best, all you can say is that the separate jobs are done sufficiently quickly that a human considers them to be almost simultaneous. In practice multi-tasking requires more memory and processor speed than is commonly found in domestic and even full scale business computers. Although these technologies are improving all the time, even research level computer workstations slow down noticeably when given more than one task to perform. The term is frequently used to describe a process whereby, once loaded, different software packages can coexist in a computer allowing the user to switch from one task to another. However in this case the previous task is generally suspended or at least given very low priority.

N

Nak. Abbreviation of Not Acknowledged. One of the characters transmitted for the purposes of handshaking in a data transfer. The character is sent back to the transmitting device by the receiving device to inform it that the last block of data has not been received without error and that it should be retransmitted. *See also* **Ack**.

Nibble. In computers and digital systems a group of four bits, *i.e.* half a byte (evidence that computer engineers do possess a rudimentary sense of humour!).

Non Volatile Memory. In a computer system, a type of memory whose contents will be retained during the time that the system is unpowered. This is either due to the presence of an alternative or back up source of power such as a battery (especially in the case of semiconductor memory), or because the memory is magnetic and does not require power to maintain the contents.

Non-executable. Said of any file which contains no instructions or commands that can be carried by a computer, *i.e.* the file contains data only.

Null Modem. A type of cable which can be used to connect equipment of the same type (such as two computers) together for data transfer. The cable is wired with "crossover" connections *i.e.* the transmit pins at each end are not connected together as is usual but instead are connected such that the transmit pin at one end is connected to the receive pin at the opposite end *etc.* The effect is to persuade each computer that it is connected to a MODEM.

O

Off Line. In a network of devices, the condition of any device which is unable to receive or transmit a signal.

On Line. In a network of devices, the condition of any device which is able to receive or transmit a signal.

Operating System. The part of a computer's software which looks after housekeeping tasks such as updating the monitor 75 times a second, opening and closing disc files, checking the keyboard for key presses *etc.*—the really mundane stuff. The OS is usually stored in a chip in the computer or has to be loaded from disc or some combination of these. Without an operating system the computer will not run any other software unless the author undertakes these chores as well as the main function of his software. Sometimes authors feel that they can speed up the operation of their software if they hijack these routine tasks and do them in a different way. This leads to incompatibility problems if the computer manufacturer improves their OS. This was the problem with some software when Microsoft recently introduced Windows '95 which had such improvements. GEM (Graphic Environment Manager), MS-DOS (Micro Soft Disc Operating System), TOS (Tramiel Operating System), PC-DOS, C/PM and the Apple Desktop are all operating systems of various levels of complexity.

Opto Isolator. A method of passing a signal via a light path thus avoiding a direct electrical connection between a transmitting device and a receiving device. This presents voltage spikes generated in one device finding their way into another, and stops earth loops forming. The unit consists of a light source (a LED) and a light detector (a phototransistor) enclosed in a sealed box (the whole package looks just like a normal IC). The incoming signal is used to turn the light source on and off. The light shines on the detector which has an output signal when it sees the light and changes the output when it doesn't. It is specified for use in MIDI connections and other types of "current loop" data connections between computers.

OS. *See* **Operating System**.

P

Parallel Data. A method of sending computer data whereby all bits of the digital word are sent simultaneously. This is generally more expensive as the connectors involved have to have a pin for each bit plus a few pins for ground, handshaking *etc.* However parallel data transfers are typically ten or more times faster than electrical serial methods. SCSI and Centronics are examples of parallel data standards.

Parity Bit. A bit added to a data word to provide a simple form of error checking. The bits of individual data words, when summed, will give either an odd or even value. The parity bit can be set to an odd or even value and added to the data word so that all words become, say, odd (or even). If the parity is even and the receiving device sees a data word which sums to an odd value, this must be because the data have become corrupted. In practice this may be merely ignored or a request may be made by the receiving device to instruct the transmitting device to resend the defective word.

Password Protection. A method of obtaining access to a computer system or file on a system, which requires the user to provide an input when requested in the form of a word which (in theory at least) is known only to authorised users. Often these are ludicrously easy to bypass. A major accounting software is shipped with the password "LETMEIN". This is rarely altered by users, with the result that many using this software have the same password. Most common passwords chosen by people are: dog, cat or goldfish's name, mother's maiden name, wife's maiden name, date of birth, social security number, user's first name and "Open Sesame". Needless to say this all makes the hacker's job rather trivial. *See* **Hacking**.

Paste. In a computer, a command which places a section of text or picture, previously placed in the clipboard, at the current cursor position. *See also* **Copy, Cut**.

PC. *See* **Microcomputer**.

PCMCIA. Abbreviation of Personal Computer Memory Card International Association. A formalised interface initially intended to provide a means of expanding the memory of computerised equipment with plug-in cards of RAM or ROM, now also used to provide additional facilities such as a MODEM *etc.*

Peripheral. In a computer system a device which either allows input to or output from the system or both apparently simultaneously. A printer or a monitor are output devices, a mouse or keyboard are input devices, while a disc drive is an input/output or IO device. Other peripherals include scanners, tape data storage devices, liquid crystal displays (LCD) *etc.*

Pixels. Derived from Picture Cells, the individual dots from which an image is produced on a computer monitor. Pixels can be categorised by bit depth which is another way of describing the number of light levels or colours the pixel can emit. 1-bit pixels are monochrome as they are either on or off. 4-bit pixels can display 16 shades of grey or colour. A 24-bit pixel can display in excess of 16.7 million shades of grey or more usually colour. This is arguably very many more than the average human can actually discriminate.

Platform. A term used instead of computer, when it is desirable to include all computers of a general type and their clones rather than specific models. For example an application will be described as running on the "Mac Platform", while an operating system like UNIX which can run on many different types of computer may be described as "Multi-Platform".

Port. An input or output socket on a device such as a computer.

Postscript. A high level computer language used to "program" the appearance of text or graphics on a printed page. Sometimes called a page description language. As it is standardised, any devices which adhere to the language structure can generate or process compatible files. It should be remembered that the quality of printed output is independent of the Postscript file which produced it, as the file is interpreted by the output device according to whatever resolution it can manage.

Printer. An output device used by a computer to render text and graphics onto paper or acetate *etc.* A number of technologies are available. Impact printers such as Dot Matrix form images using metal components which press an ink ribbon onto the page. These are generally low resolution <100 DPI. Other technologies which spray ink (inkjet) or explode ink bubbles (bubblejet) onto the paper can achieve higher resolutions, ≥300 DPI, and colour operation. Laser printers generate a negative image on a cylinder or drum using a variable electrostatic charge. This rotates past a dry powder ink or toner cartridge attracting the ink particles to the charged areas of the surface. The paper is passed over this drum where it picks up the particles. It is then heated causing the particles to fuse and coalesce into a permanent image. Laser printers range between 300 and 2400 DPI and can produce colour images. The highest resolution laser printers are sometimes called imagesetters.

Programmer. A person who writes software for computers.

PROM. A form of memory which can be programmed once only and not erased. See also **EPROM, ROM, WORM**.

Q

Quantisation Error. In computer systems and often with particular reference to digital audio, the number of bits a system uses to describe numbers (the word size) sets the limit to the maximum count or resolution of the system, and this consequently determines the maximum accuracy with which, for example, audio signals can be described digitally. With 4 bits it is possible to divide the amplitude of a signal into 16 quantisation steps. Thus a signal whose peak amplitude was 2 volts would be described in steps 125 mV apart. Signal levels which fall between these steps are not recorded (the quantisation error), and the signal is therefore distorted by the quantisation process. This distortion manifests itself as noise for large signals and as harmonic distortion at signal levels close to zero. In practice the resolution determines the signal to noise ratio and by extension the dynamic range of the encoded signal. In general the greater the number of bits the digital audio system uses to encode the signal, the greater the dynamic range.

QuickTime. A proprietary system of storing and distributing "moving-image with sound" or "Multimedia" files. It was developed by Apple Computers and is used on the Internet and CD-ROMs. The system supports replay of Standard MIDI Files conforming to the general MIDI (GM) format. Extensions to the system allow interactive "browsing" of 3D graphic environments. See also **MPEG**.

QWERTY. Acronym formed from the first six letters of the top letter row in a standard keyboard layout, used to describe a keyboard having that standard layout, as opposed to say the AZERTY layout used in some European countries.

R

RAM. Acronym from Random Access Memory. Essentially any form of memory which allows you to write new data into it at random, unrelated locations. Unlike say a tape recorder where things are stored sequentially. Generally used specifically to refer to semiconductor memory (chips), although strictly speaking disc drives are also RAM. See also **Virtual**.

RDAT. Acronym from Rotary head Digital Audio Tape. A standard for digital audio recording as well as a mass storage medium for backing up hard discs etc. The system employs a rotating head mechanism similar to that of video recorders, to record two channels of 16 bit digital audio information plus subcode and track information. The tape is housed in a case similar to a video cassette though much smaller. Maximum continuous record time for a cassette is 2 hours at standard play and four hours at long play with reduced quality. In data storage applications densities in excess of 4 Gigabytes can be achieved per tape.

Refresh Rate. The number of times per second that a complete screen image displayed on a monitor is "rewritten". It is expressed in Hz. Refresh rates of less than about 60 Hz are likely to "beat" with the mains line frequency and cause a low frequency flicker, which can be uncomfortable to look at for any length of time and may even precipitate epileptic fits in those prone to them.

Retrofit. The process of adding facilities to a device after it has been manufactured or even sold. The retrofit may be a software update in the form of an EPROM or ROM, but is more usually a complete circuit board. For example the fitting of memory or sound expansion boards etc.

RISC. Acronym from Reduced Instruction Set

Computer. Essentially a microprocessor which only implements a few instruction types. It is then able to execute these instructions much more quickly than a more general microprocessor, as there are fewer possibilities for it to look up each time an instruction is to be executed. The increased speed of operation is very desirable for processing digital audio and video data, and these ICs are often used in devices which are designed to perform a specific function. See also **Instruction Set, CISC**.

ROM. Acronym from Read Only Memory. Essentially any form of memory which allows you to read information or data from it, but not to write or add new information or data to it. Thus a prerecorded audio cassette (with its record tabs broken out) is a ROM. Generally used specifically to refer to semiconductor memory (chips). See also **EPROM, PROM**.

Root Directory. See **Directory**.

Rotational Latency. See **Access Time**.

RS232C. A serial data transfer or communications standard commonly adopted on personal computers. The standard defines cable connections for Transmit, Receive data lines and Signal ground. In addition, Request to Send (RTS) and Clear To Send (CTS) signals are used for "Handshaking", and Data Carrier Detect (DCD), Data Set Ready (DSR), Data Terminal Ready (DTR) for MODEM control. It has to be said that the standard is not straightforward or uniformly implemented with the result that DCD, DSR, and DTR are sometimes used by some manufacturers for Handshaking.

RSI. Abbreviation of Repetitive Strain Injury. A medical term used to describe the process of accumulating "insults" to an area of tissue, usually tendon, ligament or muscle, by overuse or awkward use to the extent that the tissue becomes injured through inflammation or rupture. It has previously been most commonly found in athletes etc. and some musical instrument performers, but is most recently associated with computer keyboard operators, especially those who make constant use of keyboard short cuts that require several keys to be depressed simultaneously. The achievement of this often requires operators to overflex tendons and other tissues in the hand and wrist. As the resulting injury can lead to loss of livelihood, RSI is increasingly cited in industrial injury compensation cases.

RTS. See **RS232C**.

S

Sample. In analogue to digital conversion, one instantaneous digital measurement of the analogue signal. As the sample value is expressed in binary there is a correlation between samples and bytes. However the precise relationship depends on a number of factors (the resolution of the converter and the number of simultaneously converted signal channels). For a 16 bit converter a sample is two bytes, for a 12 bit converter a sample is 1.5 bytes, for a 16 bit two channel converter a sample is 4 bytes etc.

Sampler. A device for making short term (say less than one minute) digital audio recordings specifically for musical effect (principally by altering the replay sample rate from a keyboard or MIDI message). Some computer soundcards offer this capability.

Sampling Rate. The rate at which samples of an analogue signal are encoded or decoded by a digital device. The higher the sampling rate is set during the encoding process the greater the bandwidth of signal it is possible to record without error.

Scanner. A computer input device which is the functional opposite of a printer. It "looks at" or scans an existing image and inputs the information in the image into a computer.

Scorewriter. A category of computer software which allows a user to create, edit and print notated music. Essentially it is to music what a word processor is to literature. Sequencers sometimes include this ability (in a rudimentary form), and scorewriters can often "play" (in a rudimentary manner) the score like a sequencer, but each is usually optimised to its own task. So it is sensible to record and edit a piece of music on a sequencer and then export the data to a scorewriter so that its appearance in notation can be edited separately.

Scroll. Originally a facility on a computer monitor that allowed the user to move a large text or image up or down to bring the previous or next section of it into view, rather like rolling the top part of a paper scroll while simultaneously unrolling the bottom part. Now extended to describe such movements in both dimensions (up/down, left/right). It is a common feature of graphic user interfaces such as Apple's Desktop or Microsoft's Windows.

SCSI. Acronym from Small Computer Systems Interface (pronounced "scuzzy" to rhyme with fuzzy). An agreed standard of hardware and command language, which allows data communication between components in a computer system. Primarily used for hard disc drives and other volume data storage devices, but also used for scanners and other types of devices. As the interface is a parallel type it is capable of high speed operation.

Sector. A subdivision of the surface of a data disc consisting of a number of blocks. In a hard disc with several platters the sector is a number of blocks in a vertical "slice" through the platters.

Seek Time. *See* Access Time.

Sequencer. A stand alone device, or a category of computer software, which allows a user to create, edit and (sometimes) print music by recording and playing back MIDI messages. While these are most commonly musical performance messages in theory any MIDI messages may be recorded. In practice they generally behave like tape recorders, in that they have a number of "tracks" and "transport controls" *etc*. Drum machines generally contain some sequencer capability. As regards printing of music or scorewriting, sequencers sometimes include this ability (in a rudimentary form), while scorewriters can often "play" (in a rudimentary manner) the score like a sequencer, but each is usually optimised to its own task. So it is sensible to record and edit a piece of music on a sequencer and then export the data to a scorewriter so that its appearance in notation can be edited separately.

Serial Data. This is a format for sending computer data whereby all bits of the digital word are sent one after the other. This is generally cheaper as the connectors involved only need one transmit pin and one receive pin plus ground. However serial data transfers are typically ten times slower than parallel methods. RS232C uses a serial data format. Fibre optic data transfers are also serial but can run at very much higher speeds than electrical serial methods and can surpass even parallel interfaces.

Shareware. Term used to describe software which is available in such a way that it can be tried without purchase, and only paid for if found to be useful. The cost of such software is often nominal, amounting to little more than a few pounds or dollars. Usually the application when run displays a page giving the address of the author and the nominal figure for payment. It is essentially an "honesty system" which relies on the good will of the author and potential users. Many people unfortunately abuse the system and use the software without payment. This is obviously a shame, and in fact counter productive as the author when contacted and paid will often forward an improved version of the software and register the user for similar upgrades at nominal cost. Shareware is not in the public domain.

Slave. In a system of devices, it is sometimes useful to have a number of devices which are subordinate in operation to one other device (particularly as regards a timing reference, for example). These devices are nominated slaves, the other device becomes the "master".

Software. The abstract form of the instructions which determine how the hardware of a computer system functions, *i.e.* a list of instructions that the computer will perform in sequence, so as to perform some useful task. The program is written by a programmer after analysing the problem to be solved, then identifying those instructions from the instruction set which will help solve the problem and assembling them into the right order. For any given task which it is desirable for a computer to carry out, there is probably an infinite number of methods resulting in a "correct" solution. Programming is something of an art. While apparently a scientific and logical process, the best and most elegant programs are often written by people with a good intuitive "feel" for the way problems work. Programs which do not work well probably result from a poor definition of the problem. There is some mathematical evidence to suggest that it is not possible to write a piece of software which contains no errors.

Soundcard. A printed circuit board which can be plugged into the expansion sockets of a personal computer and which considerably improves the ability of the computer to produce sound effects or music. These are often described by the prefix 8-bit, 16-bit *etc*. In general the higher the number the better the quality of sound. In a well designed 16-bit soundcard the quality should compare favourably with CD standard recordings. Soundcards occasionally add MIDI compatibility to the computer and many can act as samplers by making short term digital recordings of sounds for replay by the computer or from an external MIDI controller such as a master keyboard.

Spreadsheet. A category of computer software which allows a user to generate tables of arithmetic calculations. It will normally be used for such things as keeping track of income and expenditure. It consists of a grid of cells, in rows and columns, which may be independent or which may be related to one another by a mathematical formula or calculation. Cells may also be labelled. Thus the cell at the bottom of a column might be called "Total" and represent the sum of all cells above it, so that any numbers placed in a cell higher than Total will be added together automatically, the result appearing in the Total cell. Its usefulness lies in the fact that having established a set of mathematical relationships (which might represent the cash flow for a company) it is possible to alter specific values temporarily to see what the overall effect of that change is. Essentially a database optimised for number handling.

SSI. Abbreviation of Small Scale Integration. An integrated circuit which contains about 10–90 active elements. *See also* LSI, MSI, VLSI.

Start Bit. In serial data transmission (particularly asynchronous) the use of an extra bit which precedes the data bits and which serves to "wake up" the receiving device in readiness for the data which follow.

Stop Bit. In serial data transmission (particularly asynchronous) the use of an extra bit which succeeds the data bits and which serves to indicate to the receiving device that the data have stopped and that it may now rest.

Supercomputer. A computer whose speed of operation is close to the current maximum possible. Typically in 400–800 MIPS range. Some available technologies and the use of parallel processing will extend this above 1 GIPS in the immediate future. *See also* Computer.

SVGA. Abbreviation of Super Video Graphics Adaptor. An enhanced standard system for displaying text and images with higher quality (than VGA) on a computer monitor, widely used by IBM PCs *etc*.

Syquest. Proprietary system of mass storage which utilises removable magneto-optical (MO) storage on 5.25", 3.50" and 2.50" discs. Between about 40 and 100 megabyte storage is typical.

T

Tail. Additional data which suffix a block of data either in a stored file or for the purposes of data transfer between devices. These data usually serve the function of a "full stop" to the block of data which precedes them.

Terminal. In a computer system, particularly a mainframe type, a remote keyboard and monitor and sometimes printer, which allows a user of the system to communicate with the computer. It is an input/output or IO device.

TOS. *See* Operating System.

Tracker Ball. A hand operated control in the form of a captive but free rolling ball which allows simultaneous movement in two axes (X and Y) and which allows the user (who rolls the ball around in its frame) to define a unique position within the limits of movement of the control. Essentially it is a mouse mounted upside down. Sometimes used on computers instead of a mouse or joystick, to define the position of a cursor on the monitor. It is sometimes fitted with one or more switches, the pressing of which will select or activate an area of the computer monitor currently under the cursor.

Transfer Rate. *See* Data Rate.

Trojan Horse. A term used to describe a computer program which is concealed in some way and is unknowingly executed, sometimes with unpleasant results. It might take the form of a functionally useful and desirable application which contains a second program which operates as an unseen background activity of the first, or it may be a text file *etc.* which includes executable code. The latter situation is sometimes a problem on the Internet, where hackers might place a desirable file *e.g.* a picture, on the Internet, which when accessed by the unwary promptly returns the user's passwords, account details *etc.* to an address elsewhere on the Internet for the benefit of the hackers. They are not generally viruses. *See also* **Virus**.

U

UART. Acronym from Universal Asynchronous Receiver Transmitter. An integrated circuit that carries out the function of asynchronous, bidirectional communication between a microprocessor and a serial interface. It allows data to be transferred into or out of a microprocessor based equipment. It is commonly used on equipment which implements the RS232C and MIDI standards.

UKASCII. A variant of ASCII which takes account of (among other things) the fact that British people do not use the character "#" but do require the character "£" which is not normally part of ASCII. Thus the character represented by the decimal value 35 in an American computer is #, while the same value in a British computer produces £.

UPS. Abbreviation of Uninterruptible Power Supply. A type of power supply which can continue to provide power despite a momentary interruption or even complete failure of the mains supply to it. This is achieved by trickle charging batteries in the power supply while monitoring the mains supply for failures. If a failure is detected the batteries can be instantaneously connected to the load, through an "inverter" circuit that converts the DC of the batteries to the AC typical of mains supplies. The intention is not to replace a failed mains supply indefinitely, but simply for long enough that the connected equipment such as a computer can be "shut down" in a methodical and safe manner without loss of data *etc.*

URL. Abbreviation of Universal (or in some sources Uniform) Resource Locator. Essentially this is the unique address or identity of an Internet document. The URL specifies the Internet protocol used by the document; the name of the Internet server on which the document is stored; and the directory pathway and filename of the document. The protocol will be "http" for web pages, "ftp" for software, text, image or graphic documents, "wais" for database searches, "telnet" for remote operation of computers *etc.* The server will be named according to the international convention for such things and will include a domain name as well as various suffixes which on occasion help identify what sort of organisation is running the server *e.g.* a server name ending "ac.uk" is an academic establishment in the United Kingdom. The pathway and filename can be almost anything although there are a great many agreed file suffixes, *e.g.* myfile.htm almost certainly ought to be a web page while myfile.mid is likely to be a Standard MIDI File.

V

V.17, V.21, V.22, V.29, V.32bis, V.42 *etc.* Various communication standards recommended by the Consultative Committee for International Telephone and Telegraph (CCITT), V.17, V.21, V.29 are Facsimile standards, while V.22, V.32, V.32bis and V.34 are MODEM standards. V.42 and V.42bis are respectively Error Correction and Data Compression standards.

V.Fast Class. A proprietary standard for high speed (28,800 BPS) data transfer, mutually agreed by a number of MODEM manufacturers, who couldn't wait for the CCITT to finish their lunch break. It was subsequently adopted by CCITT as V.34.

V.FC. *See* **V. Fast Class**.

Vapourware. An ironic term to describe promised features in software or hardware which never actually get implemented.

VGA. Abbreviation of Video Graphics Adaptor. A standard system for displaying text and images on a computer monitor, widely used by IBM PCs *etc.*

Virtual. In computing, said of a facility or quality that appears to a user to exist and functions as if it did, but in fact does not. For example in Virtual Memory, a section of a mass storage device, such as a hard disc, is set aside and used by the computer's operating system as if it were the computer's main work memory or RAM. "Virtual Reality" is used to describe a system that simulates, and allows interaction with, an environment that is different to the one the user is in. This has obvious potential in the entertainments industry but has other applications. For example, in hazardous environments in the nuclear and chemical industries a real technician in a safe place with a VR system could control a robot remotely in a dangerous place.

Virus. A form of computer software which in operation has the ability to make copies of itself in new locations within a computer (in RAM, hard disc, or floppy discs inserted subsequently). This is occasionally harmless, but some viruses have pernicious effects which range from mere blanking of the computer screen to wholesale erasure of data. The problem can be acute if a virus is introduced to a computer which is part of a large network, as it can quickly spread throughout the network. It has to be said that there is considerable media hyperbole about viruses and some of the horror stories of viral incidents have not stood the test of a few minutes investigation. The origin of the first computer virus has likewise entered the realm of modern myths, but is generally attributed to a pair of brothers in Pakistan, involved in computer piracy of commercial software, who developed a virus to ensure that their illegal copies would not in turn be recopied. *See also* **Trojan Horse**.

VLSI. Abbreviation of Very Large Scale Integration. An integrated circuit which contains about 100,000 active elements. *See also* **LSI, MSI, SSI**.

W

W³. *See* **Internet**.

WAIS. Abbreviation of Wide Area Information Search. An Internet protocol for specifying remote database search criteria. This allows Internet users to search for keywords in one or more of the many useful databases available over the Internet.

Wait. One of the characters transmitted for the purposes of handshaking in a data transfer. The character is sent back to the transmitting device by the receiving device to indicate that the receiver wants the transmitter to pause. The transmission will then continue when the receiver sends an ack, or it will be stopped altogether if the receiver sends a cancel.

WAV. Derived from "Windows Wave". A standard (almost) with many variants for storing and distributing audio as computer data. It was developed by Microsoft and IBM. It is also used for exchanging soundfiles over the Internet. It allows data compression of the audio data resulting in smaller file sizes and reduced bandwidth requirement, albeit with arguably reduced sonic quality. Various data compression methods are used causing occasional problems in recognition of the files between different computers. *See also* **AIFF, AU**.

WIMP. Acronym from Windows, Icons, Mouse Pointer. A generic term used to describe any graphic user interface which employs these features in its operating system.

Window. In a computer, one of a number of areas of the monitor which can present information that is independent of and separate from another window or area on the same monitor. The dimensions of the window can generally be adjusted or "sized". This will result in more or less information being visible, or the information may be scaled to match the size of the window. A window may also be "opened" or "closed". Windows may present information about different parts of a single program, thus allowing the user to select the displays which are most relevant to their use of the program, or the windows may contain information from different programs, allowing information to be "copied" from one window and "pasted" into another.

Windows. The proprietary name used by Microsoft for their WIMP operating system for IBM-PC and compatible computers.

Word. In computers and digital systems the number of bits used by the system to define a single numerical value or sample. This indicates the resolution of number representations in the computer. An 8 bit word is 1 byte, a 12 bit word is 1.5 bytes, a 16 bit word is 2 bytes. However in general usage a word is considered to be 2 bytes unless otherwise qualified. 32 bits is often called a "long word".

Word Processor. Also called WP. A category of computer software which allows a user to generate and edit text documents, essentially a computerised pencil, paper and rubber. Initially used to create simple documents such as letters, but not complex documents such as newspapers or magazines, these programs are increasingly becoming more sophisticated and are now more likely to allow a user to place pictures within the text and format the text into a complex layout typical of a published magazine or book. To this extent there is no longer a clear cut line between WP software and desktop publishing software. However WP is normally optimised to the keying and altering of text, rather than to questions of layout (most WPs have spelling checkers, a feature which tends to be absent on desktop publishing software), so it is still common (and more sensible) to generate the text in the word processor and export it to the desktop publishing software.

Workstation. Describes a single device which contains a number of functions normally executed by a number of different devices, for example a powerful, self-contained system with adequate mass storage and graphics capability (as opposed to a terminal linked to a mainframe or file server).

World Wide Web. *See* **Internet**.

WORM. Write Once Read Many. Essentially any form of memory which allows information or data to be stored or saved once only, but the information can be read as many times as you like (until it wears out). Recordable CDs are an example of this. ROM also comes under this heading.

WP. *See* **Word Processor**.

WWW. *See* **Internet**.

X

X On/X Off. Abbreviation of transmitter on/transmitter off. The two codes used for software handshaking or flow control in computer communications or data transfers. It is used as an alternative to hardware handshaking, sometimes to reduce the cost of implementation as these cables can then be omitted. It is wise not to use X on/X off for high speed data transfers or those which use error correction or data compression.

XMODEM. *See* **FTP**.

Z

Zip Drive. Proprietary system of mass storage which utilises 100MB removable magneto-optical (MO) storage on 3·5″ cartridges.

ZMODEM. *See* **FTP**.

SPECIAL TOPIC

INSIDE THE INTERNET

Often regarded as the public face of the 'communications revolution', the Internet is a global infrastructure for several electronic communication services. Its roots lie in the ARPANET network, created in 1969 to link computers within the US Department of Defense, but the 1990s have seen it grow to become an everyday medium for many people, both at home and at work.

Physically, the Internet consists of host computers—in universities, government departments and companies around the world—permanently connected by cable or wireless links. The name derives from its origin as a collection of *inter*connected *networks*, including ARPANET, the UK Joint Academic Network (JANET) and the US National Science Foundation's NSFNET.

Standards.

Any form of communication requires an agreed language, and such standards for computer communication are known as protocols. Many are proprietary and controlled by software vendors, but the Internet adheres to open standards, which are freely available to anyone wishing to develop Internet technology. This openness, and the adoption of its standards by many public bodies, contributed to the Internet's wide reach, making it increasingly attractive for business use.

The key standard for the Internet is *Transmission Control Protocol/Internet Protocol* (TCP/IP). This establishes a channel of communication—given a physical connection—and provides the foundation for all its communication services. For practical purposes no knowledge of the protocol's operation is needed as this is managed by computer software.

Domain Names.

One important standard, to which users of the Internet are exposed, is the location of people or sources of information. Each is based around a *domain name* that identifies an organisation and follows the structure *name.type.country*, using standard abbreviations for the type and country portions. For example, UK domains take the *uk* suffix, Japanese *jp* or German *de*; commercial organisations are represented as *co*, educational as *ac* or non-profit organisations as *org*. Domain names in the US or international in scope differ slightly, often omitting a country suffix and using *.com* and *.edu* for commercial and academic bodies, respectively. A British company called Lo-Price might choose a domain name *lo-price.co.uk*; a company wishing to suggest a global presence would use the *.com* suffix *e.g. global-trade.com*.

A domain name must be registered with the appropriate national body (*e.g.* Nominet in the UK, InterNIC in the US), and can take any form within this standard structure. As the commercial benefits of the Internet become recognised, so the domain name becomes part of an organisation's public image.

Behind the scenes, host computers are identified by numeric Internet Protocol (IP) addresses of the form *123.45.67.89*. Domain names are converted into IP addresses by a Domain Naming System (DNS), provided by many Internet hosts. The process of looking up domain names is carried out by software and is invisible to the user unless seeking a domain name that does not exist in the DNS, which usually results in a message to this effect.

While the IP address identifies a specific computer, the domain name is conceptual in nature and identifies a location in Internet 'space'. A single Internet domain may span several host computers (*e.g.* a large company) or there may be several within one host (*e.g.* several companies sharing a computer).

Internet Service Providers.

The core of the Internet is made up of computers that are permanently connected, but these are usually available only in larger organisations. Individuals and small businesses can gain *ad hoc* access to the Internet via an *Internet Service Provider* (ISP). ISPs provide Internet hosts, into which a personal computer can dial, using a modem to connect to the telephone line, giving a temporary connection to the Internet for the duration of the telephone call. This form of access costs considerably less than a permanent Internet connection, usually as a fixed monthly fee or based on connection time. There is no additional fee for using different Internet facilities, though some sources may charge for the information they provide.

INTERNET SERVICES

The World Wide Web.

The *World Wide Web* ('Web' or WWW) was conceived in 1990 as a means for physicists to share information. Publicly available since 1993, it has grown extremely rapidly to become the best-known aspect of the Internet, and another key medium alongside print and broadcast.

The Web consists of millions of pages of information that can be viewed on request. A Web page comprises primarily text and graphics, but may also include sound or moving images. *Hypertext links* provide instant cross-references to other pages, typically by pointing and clicking with a mouse. Whereas printed material is organised in sequence, hypertext offers multiple routes through a collection of pages. Those from a single source are usually linked together to provide a coherent body of information known as a *Web site*. A link could equally point to a page held on the other side of the world and the name World Wide Web derives from this global set of links between pages.

Web pages are stored as files on host computers, and each page has a unique address, often called a *Uniform Resource Locator* (URL) (strictly, this term identifies the location of any Internet information service). At its simplest, a Web address might take the form *www.lo-price.co.uk* (*i.e.* based on the company's domain name), although a full URL takes the form *http://www.lo-price.co.uk/products/fruit.htm*, the latter portion identifying the location of the file *fruit.htm* within the *products* directory on the host computer. The prefix *http:* is common to all Web addresses and identifies the *HyperText Transport Protocol*, the means by which Web pages are retrieved. Although pages are transmitted across the Internet as basic text, comprising letters, numbers and certain symbols, they appear more attractively presented. This is achieved primarily by including *HyperText Mark-up Language* (HTML) codes in the document to describe how different text or graphic elements should be displayed.

Looking at information on the Web requires *browser* software. When given the address for a page (by either manual input or a link from another page), a browser retrieves a copy of the page, then interprets the HTML codes to create the page layout. Thus the browser through which they are viewed ultimately determines the precise appearance of Web pages.

Web publishing.

Since the distribution mechanism for Web pages (*i.e.* the Internet) is already in place, it is relatively easy to publish in this medium. Firstly, pages are created with one of many programs available for this purpose (similar to a word processor). Secondly, the pages are stored on host computer space where they are visible to Web users: this *Web space* can be rented from an ISP, while larger organisations might use their own hosts.

Finding information.

The ease of publication has given rise to the vast number of pages available around the world. Their sources vary widely and might include individual enthusiasts, academics or commercial information providers. Although the Web is frequently represented as a 'library', there is no overall selection process that ensures the quality of the material. Consequently, a key issue is how to find appropriate, authoritative information on a topic.

Directories and *search engines* both provide ways of narrowing down the vast body of Web pages, and are some of the most common starting points for using the Web. Directories offer a hierarchical arrangement of subjects, leading to a listing of references in the form of links. Some are based on human selection, offering quality control, but less choice. Search engines look for and list all pages containing given key words, although frequently there may be many thousand such pages. Most search engines offer advanced features that can help minimise irrelevant results, but choosing the most effective combination of key words—one that finds a manageable number of relevant pages—requires forethought and practice.

Publicly-funded sources aside, much of the 'free' information on the Web is paid for in more subtle ways, through advertising or in exchange for valuable market research. As demand builds, some may follow satellite television by moving to chargeable, pay-per-view services.

Electronic Mail.

Electronic mail (e-mail) provides fast, person-to-person written communication. E-mail systems exist on non-Internet computer networks, but follow different and incompatible standards, which limit them to internal communication within larger organisations. The Internet offers a common e-mail format, extending its reach outside such organisations to include individuals and smaller groups. Although it is possible to translate messages between different standards, the widespread use and increasing sophistication of Internet e-mail makes it an effective format for general use.

Delivery mechanism.

A message is sent immediately around the Internet until it reaches the recipient's electronic *mailbox*, held on a host computer and available to receive mail at any time. E-mail addresses identify an individual within a particular Internet domain, so *j.smith@lo-price.co.uk* identifies J.Smith's mailbox within Lo-Price (*i.e.* within Lo-Price's Internet domain). Mailbox space is part of the service offered by most ISPs, as well as in organisations with their own Internet hosts. No 'postage' is charged for an e-mail message, regardless of its destination, and the costs are covered by Internet subscription fees.

Software.

E-mail software manages the process of addressing, composing and sending messages. When running on a personal computer, it retrieves any new mail that has arrived in the host mailbox, while outgoing messages may be composed off-line and queued until ready for sending. Retrieving and sending mail is then carried out with a single, short connection to the Internet. Newer, Web-based e-mail services offer similar facilities, but with software running on the host computer, so that messages remain in the host's mailbox and are accessible from any location. This can be useful for those without regular access to the same personal computer. Because the format of messages is determined by the Internet e-mail standard, it is irrelevant which software the sender or recipient uses, as long as both cater for this standard.

Message content.

Messages must include the addresses of the sender and the recipient and normally include a brief subject heading followed by the body of the message. Unlike a word processor document, an e-mail message is limited to text alone, not appearance or layout. It is becoming possible to send and receive more visually attractive messages, based around HTML, but this requires both sender and recipient to have the facility available.

Although the appearance of messages themselves is limited, any computer file (which could contain a spreadsheet, picture or sound, for instance) can be attached to a message. Attachments are encoded in a standard form that can be sent through e-mail channels, and most software includes the facility for attaching files and extracting them from incoming messages.

Electronic mailing lists.

Any number of individuals can be included as addressees for a single message, making e-mail a powerful medium for circulars. Distributed automati-

cally, e-mail newsletters and mailing lists provide a regular flow of information on many topics to those who have chosen to receive them. This facility is increasingly being used as a promotional tool on the Internet but, unlike postal marketing, there is often no cost per recipient (for printing or postage), so little financial incentive to target only interested parties. This has the unfortunate result of many irrelevant messages being sent, causing inconvenience and using up Internet capacity.

Other Services.

The World Wide Web has superseded many of the Internet's older services. However, some continue to be useful, and newer services are emerging as the Internet grows. These include:

Internet *News* (also known as *Usenet*) allows ongoing group discussions, each with its own *newsgroup*. In a similar manner to e-mail, contributions are sent (or posted) as messages addressed to the group, and become visible to other participants. Newsgroup 'addresses' are formed from a hierarchy of topics, so *rec.arts.tv.uk.comedy* falls within the recreational category, arts sub-category and so forth. Newsgroup postings are sent around the Internet and copies kept on host computers that act as *news servers*. Individuals choose to subscribe to newsgroups, then receive (via the news server) copies of new messages posted to these groups.

Internet Relay Chat (IRC) provides access to live discussion groups. Unlike newsgroups, where messages may be composed and posted over a period of time, IRC discussions take the form of short, conversational exchanges.

File Transfer Protocol (FTP) retrieves (or downloads) files from another computer on the Internet. With many documents and programs held in archives across the Internet, this provides the means of accessing such files and is increasingly used by software companies for providing updates to customers.

Telnet provides a terminal for using another computer on the Internet. Typically this might be used for a mobile worker who needs to use software on the company's main computer.

Newer *conferencing* systems allow individuals to participate in on-line meetings with text, speech and video. Additionally, collaborative working may be included, so that all participants may be able to take turns in making changes to a word processor document. Although such systems have existed for many years, an Internet-based conferencing service allows easier and wider participation.

Integrated Internet Software.

Although the Internet's services are distinct from each other, access to the Internet allows the use of all such services. Consequently, software for the key services—Web, e-mail and newsgroups—is frequently bundled in a single package. Two of the most common are currently Netscape Communicator and Microsoft Internet Explorer.

INTERNET ISSUES

Business Use of the Internet.

Increasingly, businesses are viewing the Internet as an important commercial medium. Its services provide several means of internal communication to the extent that the term *intranet* describes the features and standards of the Internet made accessible only within an organisation. In many cases, this may enhance or replace existing internal communication, but the Internet—and the World Wide Web in particular—is also becoming widespread as a means of dealing with customers. Information that might previously have been provided by telephone or post can now be available electronically, allowing faster, cheaper and more comprehensive customer liaison.

In a more sophisticated manner, businesses are increasingly regarding the Web as providing a complete route from advertising through to sales, with some operating solely through the Internet. Advertisements (usually placed in popular Web locations such as search pages) link to the company's own site, which can provide further information and take credit card orders automatically. Where the product is in digital form, such as information, computer software or music, it can also be delivered via the Internet.

Democracy and Regulation.

The Internet is often promoted as a democratic medium, insofar as it allows easier access to government information and officials. However, this still relies on a policy of openness, which is independent of any means of communication and assumes access to the technology when many areas of the world still have only limited access to telephone communication. Where the Internet seems to offer greater potential is in the case of Web publication and newsgroup discussion, allowing wider expression and debate. However, the global reach of the Internet also highlights differences between national laws in areas such as official secrets, obscenity or copyright. Since information on the Internet is a collection of individual sources, no single 'publisher' can be held accountable. Most issues raised by the Internet about free speech and censorship are not new, even if its immediacy makes their significance seem greater than for other media.

Speed.

Much of the Internet's potential is limited by the speed at which it can operate as usage increases, in both the ability of host computers to handle demands for information and the rate at which connections can carry data. This may result in slow delivery of Web pages, for example, or, in extreme cases, total failure. As the Internet becomes used to deliver sound and video, speed limitations are even more evident. Because these time-based media require a high volume of data to be transmitted quickly, Internet speed severely limits the scope for higher quality.

The Future.

One trend of recent years has been the increasing convergence of three forms of communication: broadcast, telephone and computer. To date this has seen combined cable TV and telephone services being offered and telecommunications companies offering Internet services, as well as corporations in hitherto separate media growing or merging to span several. The emergence of digital broadcasting is likely to increase this convergence (though the wireless nature of broadcast currently limits its interactive use), while investment and technology developments may improve the speed and quality of Internet broadcasting.

Attempts have already been made to integrate television and computer as separate services in a single unit, but the point may come where the services themselves are indistinguishable and are necessarily combined. Precisely what form this could take remains to be explored, but it is certain to represent a major commercial opportunity. While the success of the Internet was built on public co-operation, it seems likely that the future will be determined by market forces.

THE
CINEMA

This section provides a brief but authoritative introduction to the world of the cinema. It includes sections on how the cinema has evolved, notes on the major directors, actors and actresses and a brief glossary of terms which anyone who enjoys the cinema will find of value. A Special Topic in this edition examines the magic of the films of Steven Spielberg.

TABLE OF CONTENTS

THE CINEMA

1. THE EVOLUTION OF THE CINEMA

The Background

It was in December 1895 that the Lumière brothers, Louis and Auguste, organised what is generally regarded as the first exhibition of "moving pictures" for admission money. The event was really the culmination of numerous photographic developments that had taken place over the preceeding decades. These included Eadweard Muybridge's famous photographs of horses in motion in 1871; Etienne Julius Marey's development of a so-called "photographic rifle" with which he could take ten pictures a second (the term "shooting" for a film is commonly thought to derive from this); George Eastman's launch in 1888 of the Kodak camera and his development of the celluloid roll film; and Thomas Edison's production in 1891 of the 35mm film and, with his brilliant assistant W.K.L. Dickson, the development of the Kinetoscope which showed photographic moving pictures in a peepshow.

The Lumière brothers owned a factory that manufactured cameras and photographic equipment and envisaged the motion picture primarily as an extension and promotion of this. Their work, mostly documentary with a number of comic or light dramatic set-pieces, is seen as a major precursor of realism in the cinema. Roughly contemporary with them was the stage magician, Georges Méliès who made the first trick films, using a variety of artificial devices and special effects to tell entertaining science and pseudo-historic tales. In some ways, the Lumières and Méliès exemplify the two major tendencies to which the cinema has been drawn throughout its history: film as magic carpet (the Méliès tradition) or film as window on the world (the Lumière tradition), film as dream or film as document.

Despite many short-lived innovations (such as three-dimensional cinema, which necessitated the wearing of a special pair of spectacles), the technical battery of cinema has remained in many respects remarkably moderate. Special effects, the development of sophisticated animation techniques, quadrophonic sound in certain large city-centre cinemas, and an increasingly sophisticated range of colour techniques are all quantitative rather than qualitative modifications, and plans to enlarge the sensory battery of cinema through pumping appropriate scents in the cinema (and even providing spectators with suitable tactile stimuli) have never developed in any sustained way. The major date in the history of the medium remains 1927, the year of the first sound film (*The Jazz Singer*, with Al Jolson). Sound was fiercely resisted (by Charlie Chaplin among others), but its possibilities were so rapidly recognised, not least by Rene Clair and Alfred Hitchcock who both made early innovatory use of it, that its survival was never long in jeopardy.

Introduction of Colour

As well as sound, another major technical development was in colour photography. Film prints had been tinted from the earliest days (a fact worth bearing in mind when it is sometimes assumed that all silent films were monochrome) but colour of a high technical standard did not become widely use until after the Second World War. Colour first tended to be used for fantasy or adventure genres or spectaculars such as *Gone With the Wind* (1939), and it was not until the mid 1960s that sales of film to television more or less demanded that every film be made in colour. Nevertheless, there are a number of films that continue to be filmed in black and white, not out of a hostility to colour, but for purposes of, for example, nostalgia (as in Woody Allen's *Manhattan*, 1979 or *Purple Rose of Cairo*, 1985), brutal realism (Scorsese's *Raging Bull*, 1980), pastiche and homage (Tim Burton's *Ed Wood*, 1994) and of dramatic newsreel evocation (as in Spielberg's

Schindler's List of 1993, with its momentary bursts of colour). Colour has also often been used expressively: for example, to evoke a mood (as in Antonioni's *Red Desert* of 1964) or as dramatic motif (the menacing use of red in Nicolas Roeg's *Don't Look Now* of 1973) or to suggest a process of ironic distancing from a set of stylistic conventions (as with the deliberately lurid colours in Douglas Sirk's melodramas). Although its use has sometimes been unimaginative and blandly naturalistic, colour has become a rich and important part of cinematic language and it has been shown that it can co-exist with black and white, sometimes even in the same film.

Another technical development was that of the big screen—in processes such as Cinerama, Cinemascope, Todd-AO—particularly associated with the fifties and sixties, when Hollywood's response to the threat of television was not necessarily to make movies better but at least to make them wider. Many directors hated this development, feeling that the new screen shape was only suitable for filming duck-shoots or dachshunds and not permitting the kind of concentrated detail a director had formerly required. "You can't get a close-up of a finger nail," commented Alfred Hitchcock disdainfully. Nevertheless, a director like Nicholas Ray (who had noted that every technical advance of the cinema had generally been greeted with dismay) demonstrated in a film like *Rebel Without a Cause* (1955) that it was possible to use colour and widescreen for eloquently expressive purposes. A recent film like Kenneth Branagh's *Hamlet* (1996) was made in 70mm in an attempt to emulate the visual splendour of epics of three decades ago, such as *Lawrence of Arabia* (1962).

In recent years, video technology had made it more possible for new film-makers to engage in comparatively inexpensive, independent and experimental work: experienced directors such as Antonioni, Godard and Chris Marker have also made use of this. But the major advances in the last decade have been in the area of special effects as generated by new technologies of computer animation. These have brought new virtuosity into the realm of the Disney cartoon; new visual wonders into spectaculars such as *Jurassic Park* (1993) and *Men in Black* (1997); and fresh tricks of illusion in their capacity seamlessly to blend live-action and animation or computer re-touching, as seen in the films of Robert Zemeckis such as *Who Framed Roger Rabbit* (1988) and *Forrest Gump* (1994). The downside of this is the danger that technology for its own sake might come to overwhelm narrative, characterisation, artistic creativity: precisely those qualities which have made cinema not simply one of the technological wonders of the twentieth century but its major new art form.

MAJOR DATES AND THEIR SIGNIFICANCE

1895

On 28 December, the Lumière brothers gave the first paying show of films, at the Grand Café in Paris—a programme of documentary and comedy shorts, "Our invention can be exploited for a certain time as a scientific curiosity," said Auguste Lumière, "but apart from that it has no commercial future whatsoever."

1896

2 February—the Lumière programme screened at the Regent Street Polytechnic in London, the first film-show in Britain. Later that year, the British film pioneer, R. W. Paul made a celebrated film of the Derby.

1903

Edwin S. Porter made the most famous of all early silent films, *The Great Train Robbery*, credited as being the first Western and the first film to tell a story. Porter was later to direct a film called *Rescued From an Eagle's Nest* (1907), the leading role being taken by a young actor called Lawrence Griffith who was later to change his initials to DW and his profession to director.

1909

The theatrical producers Klaw and Erlanger forbade their contracted actors to appear in films—a sign both of the way theatre looked down on the movies but also feared their competition.

1910

D. W. Griffith made a film in California, partly to avoid the prohibitive actions against independents by the New York based Motion Pictures Patent Company and partly because of the more favourable climate for filming. It marked the beginning of what was to become Hollywood.

1911

The first fan magazines, *Motion Picture Story Magazine* and *Photoplay* began publication in the USA. The era of the star was about to emerge, particularly when, in an elaborate publicity stunt, the independent producer Carl Laemmle revealed the identity of the 'Biograph girl' as Florence Lawrence.

1912

Adolph Zukor established the Famous Plays Film Company and had a big success with the distribution of *Queen Elizabeth* starring the legendary Sarah Bernhardt. "Mister Zukor," she told him, "you have put the best of me in pickle for all time."

1913

Mack Sennett made his first films from Keystone studios.

1914

The release of the first Chaplin film, *Making a Living*. His first appearance as the Tramp occurred shortly after in *Kid Auto Races at Venice*.

1917

Chaplin signed a million dollar contract making him the highest paid screen star up to this point.

1919

United Artists formed, with Chaplin, Mary Pickford, Douglas Fairbanks and D. W. Griffiths as partners.

1921

Roscoe "Fatty" Arbuckle was charged with the rape and murder of Virginia Rappe. Although later acquitted on all charges, his career never recovered and it was one of several scandals to rock Hollywood in the early 1920s—*e.g.* the unsolved murder of the director William Desmond Taylor in 1922, the death through morphine addiction of the actor Wallace Reid in 1923. The Arbuckle scandal "drew the lightning on us all," said Gloria Swanson: it reflected the sometimes morbid fascination of the public and the press with film stars that was later to become recognised as part of the price of fame and to have an impact on the development of some film careers (*e.g.* Chaplin, Ingrid Bergman, Marilyn Monroe).

1922

Lenin told the People's Commissar for Education: "Of all the arts, for us cinema is the most important."

1925

Director Mauritz Stiller and actress Greta Garbo left Sweden for Hollywood. The year of Eisenstein's film, *The Battleship Potemkin*, revolutionary in both theme and technique.

1927

The premiere of Abel Gance's *Napoleon* at the Paris Opera, with its fantastic climax on a triple screen that anticipated Cinerama by twenty-five years. "The day of the Image has arrived," declared Gance, but ironically it was not the day of the image but the dawn of sound. Al Jolson's "You ain't heard nothing yet" in *The Jazz Singer*, were the first words spoken on a film soundtrack.

1928

Mickey Mouse made his first appearance in *Plane Crazy*.

1929

The Great Depression hit the American stock market. Because of the recent advent of sound and the tendency for people to spend more on entertainment in periods of recession, the cinema was one of the few sectors of the economy not to feel its worst effects.

1932

Disney made *Flowers and Trees*, an innovative film in its use of Technicolor.

1933

Following Adolf Hitler's rise to power, Joseph Goebbels became Minister for Information in Germany and assumed total control over the national cinema. Acclaimed director of *Metropolis* (1926) and *M* (1931), Fritz Lang was invited to become head of the national film industry: instead he emigrated to America.

1934

The foundation of the Legion of Decency in America, to act as a self-appointed ethical police force for the cinema. It followed on from the Hays Code of twelve years earlier, which severely restricted controversial subject-matter, and inaugurated a period of extreme and sometimes risible prudery in Hollywood.

1936

When Mary Pickford divorced in order to marry Douglas Fairbanks in 1920, she had asked a friend: "Will my people ever forgive me?"—as if she were royalty contemplating abdication. But the American public would forgive her anything—even some of her films. They forgave her also when she divorced Fairbanks in 1936.

Hollywood's Anti-Nazi League was founded, foremost amongst its members being Dorothy Parker, Fritz Lang and Fredric March. (A decade later the League will be denounced by the newly constituted House of UnAmerican Activities Committee as a Communist front.)

1938

Former child star Jackie Coogan (immortalised in Chaplin's *The Kid* of 1921) sued his mother and stepfather for the recovery of earnings in his period of popularity. He won the case but the money was swallowed up in legal costs. (Fifty years on, star of *Home Alone* Macaulay Culkin would experience not dissimilar problems).

1939

The outbreak of the Second World War was marked by the banning of Renoir's *La Règle du Jeu* in France and the departure of many European directors for Hollywood. Fritz Lang had already left; Renoir left France in 1940.

1940

Tom and Jerry appeared in their first movie, *Puss gets the Boot* and Bugs Bunny asked "What's up, Doc?" in *A Wild Hare*. Meanwhile the British Ministry of Information took over the GPO Film Unit and proceeded to sponsor a major series of wartime documentaries.

1941

Germany invaded Russia, and the entire Soviet industry turned itself over to the war effort. In Hollywood there were two remarkable directing debuts: Orson Welles's *Citizen Kane* and John Huston's *The Maltese Falcon*.

1942

First use of the term "neo-realism" by the Italian critic Umberto Barbaro. Marcel Carné began work on *Les Enfants du Paradis* which took three years to make. One of the reasons for this was that it kept cast and production-team away from the fighting.

1946

The opening of the first Cannes Film Festival—originally planned for 1939 but postponed on account of the war. The peak year for box-office attendance in America (4,500 million entries)..

1947

The House of UnAmerican Activities (HUAC) began hearings in Los Angeles to root out "Communists" (i.e. liberals) in the industry. The investigation begun on October 18 wreaked enormous personal, financial, and artistic havoc. Cheryl Crawford, Elia Kazan and Lee Strasberg opened the Actors' Studio (home of 'The Method') in New York.

1948

French critic Alexandre Astruc predicted that the cinema would become "a means of writing just as flexible and subtle as written language", in an article that would have a tremendous impact on the French *Nouvelle Vague* directors.

1949

The release of Henry Cornelius's *Passport to Pimlico*, Alexander Mackendrick's *Whisky Galore* and Robert Hamer's *Kind Hearts and Coronets* highlighted a series of distinctive films emanating from Michael Balcon's Ealing Studios, whose humour and superb cast of character-actors ensured their success until the last of the great comedies (*The Ladykillers*) six years later.

1951

Akira Kurosawa's *Rashomon* won the Golden Lion at the Venice Film Festival, introducing the West to Japanese cinema.

1952

Charlie Chaplin, in England for his film *Limelight*, learned his re-entry permit to America had been rescinded, beginning a twenty year period of exile from that country. Twentieth Century Fox announced the imminent launching of their new wide screen system, Cinemascope. 3-D was invented, one of its few successes being *House of Wax*, directed by the one-eyed Andre De Toth.

1956

Satyajit Ray's *Pather Panchali* won a major award at the Cannes Festival, although a young French critic walked out of the screening declaring he was not interested in a film about Indian peasants: his name was Francois Truffaut.

1959

Francois Truffaut's *Les Quatre Cents Coups* and Godard's *Breathless* inaugurated what came to be known as the French "New Wave".

1960

Kirk Douglas (with *Spartacus*) and Otto Preminger (with *Exodus*) effectively ended the "anti-communist" blacklist when they employed as screenwriter the formerly blacklisted Dalton Trumbo. Antonioni's *L'Avventura* was noisily barracked at the Cannes Film Festival: within eighteen months, he was to be the most fashionable and esteemed director in Europe.

1961

Luis Buñuel was invited to return to Spain; he did so with *Viridiana*, which threw the Franco régime into a rage and survived only through a copy being smuggled out.

1962

In a poll of a hundred critics circulated by *Sight and Sound* magazine, *Citizen Kane* was voted the best film ever made, a position it has retained in each succeeding decade in which the poll was conducted.

1968

The year of the Russian invasion of Czechoslovakia, the intensification of protest against the American war in Vietnam, the "May events" in Paris had important repercussions for the cinema. The Cannes Film Festival ended abruptly when there were demonstrations in support of student protests. In America, the youth rebellion movie of the fifties took on a new lease of life, culminating in the success of Dennis Hopper's *Easy Rider* a year later.

1975

Steven Spielberg had a huge box-office success with *Jaws*, to be topped two years later by his friend and fellow "movie brat" George Lucas, with *Star Wars*. (Both films were to be immensely influential in future Hollywood thinking, particularly about the revenue to be made from merchandising spin-offs and the concept of the summer 'blockbuster'.) Nagisa Oshima's *Empire of the Senses*, surpassed even Bernardo Bertolucci's 1973 *Last Tango in Paris* for sexual frankness.

1980

A new version of Abel Gance's *Napoleon*, reconstructed by the film-maker and historian Kevin Brownlow, was shown to great acclaim in England, reviving an interest in silent film classics and their restoration for proper exhibition.

1987

Bernardo Bertolucci's *The Last Emperor* becomes the first Western film to be shot in Beijing (Peking). It coincided with a new Western interest in Chinese film, after recent festival successes by a new generation of film-makers (*e.g.* Chen Kaige, Zhang Yimou) emerging from the Beijing Film School.

1988

Krzysztof Kieslowski's *A Short Film About Killing* (U.S. title: *Thou Shalt Not Kill*) was voted best film at the first European Film Awards.

1993

The record breaking box-office success of Spielberg's *Jurassic Park* was unexpectedly followed by the same director's *Schindler's List*, a harrowing account of the Holocaust.

1995

Cinema celebrated its centenary since its first invention by the Lumière brothers.

1996

Mike Leigh's *Secrets and Lies* won the Golden Palm at the Cannes Film Festival and the director celebrated his victory as a comeback for the modestly priced film that deals with human values. By way of contrast, a Hollywood epic about alien invasion, *Independence Day*—a B-picture in all but inflated cost and special effects grandeur—became the box-office blockbuster of the summer. The death was announced of Krzysztof Kieslowski, arguably the greatest director of the last decade.

1997

The music magazine *Gramophone* gave an award to a recording by Joel McNeely and the Royal Scottish National Orchestra of Bernard Herrmann's complete score for Hitchcock's *Vertigo*—a sign of the new respect being accorded to film music of the popular era of the cinema, notably composers such as Herrmann, Miklos Rozsa, Nino Rota, Alex North, Elmer Bernstein, Franz Waxman and the astonishing

Viennese child prodigy Erich Wolfgang Korngold (whose centenary year this was).

1998

The death of director Akira Kurosawa, one of the giants of post-war cinema. Barry Levinson's *Wag the Dog* and Mike Nichols' *Primary Colors* offer prescient satires of the beleaguered Clinton administration. The success of Spielberg's *Saving Private Ryan* sparks a new interest in films about World War Two.

1999

Box office success of *Shakespeare in Love* which goes on to win 7 Oscars. Death of Japanese film-maker Keisuke Kinoshita, a prolific contemporary of Akira Kurosawa.

2. THE LEADING CINEMA DIRECTORS

Allen, Woody (b. 1935)

Woody Allen first achieved star status as an actor in movies he himself directed, playing a walking worry-bead who wore his urban anxiety like a red badge of courage. Films like *Take the Money and Run* (1969), *Bananas* (1971) and *Love and Death* (1975) seemed to align him with prior film farceurs like his favourite, Bob Hope. Since then he has become more ambitious and intellectual, with films such as *Annie Hall* (1977) and *Stardust Memories* (1980) being anguished as well as amusing self-portraits, *Interiors* (1978) being a study of family breakdown closer to Chekhov than Chaplin. Films such as *Zelig* (1983) and *The Purple Rose of Cairo* (1985) have shown him to be the technical equal of any contemporary American director, whilst *Hannah and her Sisters* (1986) and *Crimes and Misdemeanours* (1989) have the philosophical density of a Russian novel. He has become a rare phenomenon in modern cinema; prolific, unpredictable and artistically consistent, and someone whose films must be seen by anyone who cares for modern cinema and its development and modern civilisation and its discontents. However, after *Husbands and Wives* (1992) and a bitter and much publicised split with his partner Mia Farrow, he has returned to comedy, albeit spicing the humour with considerable formal adventurousness.

Altman, Robert (b. 1925)

Innovative, iconoclastic director who shot to prominence with the military comedy *M:A:S:H* (1970), and then proceeded to subvert some of America's major film genres, notably in his western *McCabe and Mrs. Miller* (1971), which was more about the rise of capitalism than the growth of civilisation, and in his private-eye movie, *The Long Goodbye* (1973), where he debunked Raymond Chandler's knight-errant hero, Philip Marlowe. His epic and ironic fresco on the American Dream, *Nashville* (1975) was a highpoint of his career. Since then he has become ever more esoteric and experimental. Nevertheless, in films like his imaginative realisation of the play, *Come Back to the Five and Dime, Jimmy Dean, Jimmy Dean* (1982), and the made-for-TV biopic of Van Gogh, *Vincent and Theo* (1990), he has shown he can still spring some surprises. His Hollywood satire, *The Player* (1992) was his most acclaimed film for a decade; and his ambitious adaptation of Raymond Carver short stories, *Short Cuts* (1994) was no less impressive.

Antonioni, Michelangelo (b. 1912)

Antonioni was the director who made alienation fashionable in the early 1960s with his trilogy *L'Avventura* (1960), *La Notte* (1961) and *The Eclipse* (1962), which explored the gap between his characters' material affluence and their spiritual

impoverishment. He also gave alienation a palpable visual form, each shot an eloquent comment on the tension between protagonist and environment. These films remain his greatest achievement, and in Monica Vitti he found a leading lady whose haunted performances greatly enhanced the emotional impact of his work. His other major films include *Le Amiche—The Girl Friends* (1955), *The Red Desert* (1964), *Blow-Up* (1966) and *The Passenger* (1975). Although disabled by a stroke he made a remarkable comeback with *Beyond the Clouds* (1996), a prize-winner at the Venice Festival.

Bergman, Ingmar (b. 1918)

The definitive example of the film artist, by virtue of the maturity and complexity of his themes and of the control he has had over all aspects of his films—writing, casting *etc*. Since he established his international reputation with a trio of masterly works in the 1950s—*Smiles of a Summer Night* (1955), *The Seventh Seal* (1956) and *Wild Strawberries* (1957)—he enjoyed almost complete creative freedom. Films like *The Seventh Seal*, *Through a Glass Darkly* (1960) and *Winter Light* (1962) test the validity of an individual's religious faith in a world of fearful cruelty, whilst a masterpiece like *Persona* (1966) is a revelatory study of character and creativity, superbly acted by Bibi Andersson and Liv Ullmann. There are those who criticise Bergman for the narrowness of his social range, his limited political vision, his spiritual masochism. But to Bergman the camera eye is the window of the soul and few have probed more deeply to the roots of human personality. And it is not all Scandinavian gloom. In *Fanny and Alexander* (1983), he created a wonderful reminder of his story-telling gifts, his rich visual sense, and his capacity to embrace life with all its pain, perils, and pleasures. Now retired, Bergman's autobiography, *The Magic Lantern* was published in 1988; and his screenplay about the early life of his parents, *Best Intentions* (1992) was memorably filmed by Bille August.

Bertolucci, Bernardo (b. 1940)

The Italian Communist Party evolved in the seventies the conception of the "historic compromise"—a tactical alliance on the part of a self-styled revolutionary party with progressive reformist forces. Bertolucci's aesthetic strategy can be seen as an (unconscious?) embodiment of this—a "message" of revolution often clothed in the glossy, star-studded forms of bourgeois Hollywood cinema (as in the two-part *1900* of 1976). Likewise, in *Last Tango in Paris* (1972), the brutal sexual frankness for which the film rapidly became notorious is cushioned by the reassuring Hollywood deep-orange glow in which the scenes are shot and the presence of attested Hollywood rebel Marlon Brando. He won an Oscar for the opulent epic, *The Last Emperor* (1987), but his best films to date are his early works—*Before the Revolution* (1964), *The Spider's Stratagem* (1970), *The Conformist* (1970)— which combine an incisive political and psychological analysis with a poetic and lyrical style.

Bresson, Robert (b. 1907)

The most reclusive and rigorous of French directors, expressing his religious themes through a style of pared-down purity. He rejects plot and for the most part uses non-professional actors, because acting is for the theatre, he believes, and what he is after is inner truth. His most famous film is *Diary of a Country Priest* (1950), but other works such as *A Man Escaped* (1956), *Pickpocket* (1959), *Balthazar* (1966) and *L'Argent* (1982) express his individuality equally strongly.

Brooks, Richard (1912–92)

Leading writer-director of the postwar American cinema. Author of the novel on which the film *Crossfire* (1947) was based and co-writer on Huston's powerful allegory *Key Largo* (1948), Brooks made his directing debut in 1950 and became a specialist in accessible, highly charged adaptations of literary classics. His best film is *Elmer Gantry* (1960), an incisive dissection of American evangelism that won Oscars for Brooks (as screenwriter) and its star, Burt Lancaster and features the characteristic Brooks protagonist: a dynamic, divided individualist treading a tightrope between redemption and damnation. Other key films: *Blackboard Jungle* (1955), *Cat on a Hot Tin Roof* (1958), *Sweet Bird of Youth* (1962), *Lord Jim* (1965), *The Professionals* (1966), *In Cold Blood* (1967).

Buñuel, Luis (1900–83)

Buñuel began his career by collaborating with Salvador Dali on a surrealist short, *Un Chien Andalou* (1928) and then scandalised audiences with *L'Age d'Or* (1930), which attacked the Church ("Thank God I'm an atheist", Buñuel declared) and bourgeois morality (which Buñuel always found deeply immoral). A powerful, hallucinatory film about violence and poverty in the slums, *Los Olvidados* (1950) launched a second phase of his career, and his religious assaults were continued in *El* (1953), which equated religious orthodoxy with emotional repression, and *Nazarin* (1959) and *Viridiana* (1961), which showed the impossibility of a modern Christ surviving in today's society. In his final years, he took pleasure not so much in savaging the bourgeoisie as in, metaphorically speaking, poisoning their food, serving them a dainty cultural dish with a sinister undertaste. *Belle de Jour* (1967), *Tristana* (1970) and *The Discreet Charm of the Bourgeoisie* (1972) are all slyly subversive, surreal works, dealing with the split between appearance and reality, decorum and desire. He believed man was unconsciously a slave to custom and to social orthodoxy and, with his enthusiasm for symbols and the world of dreams, which reveal the hidden fears and desires of modern man, Buñuel did everything in his power to shock man out of his complacency. His impish spirit was also revealed in his appropriately liberating autobiography, *My Last Breath*, published in 1983.

Campion, Jane (b. 1955)

A graduate of the Australian Film, TV and Radio School who made a stir with her short film *Peel* (1982). Her first features, *Sweetie* (1989) and *An Angel at my Table* (1990), an imaginative bio-pic of writer Janet Frame, were highly acclaimed, and she became the first ever woman director to win the Golden Palm at Cannes for her film *The Piano* (1993). She has since made an ambitious and visually striking adaptation of Henry James's *The Portrait of a Lady* (1996).

Capra, Frank (1897–1991)

The films of Sicilian-born Frank Capra embodied the American Dream. His major works were comedies with a strong moral lesson, and their message of optimism over adversity cheered up audiences during the Depression. His films were essentially variations on David and Goliath, with the common man victorious over seemingly insurmountable odds. His main characters, such as Gary Cooper's Mr. Deeds in *Mr. Deeds Goes To Town* (1936) or James Stewart's Mr. Smith in *Mr Smith Goes to Washington* (1939) were innocent idealists who vanquished the cynical, the crooked and the corrupt. After winning three directing Oscars in the 1930s, Capra never recovered his popularity after World War Two and retired after *A Pocketful of Miracles* in 1961. His testament is the aptly entitled *It's A Wonderful Life* (1946), a beautiful fantasy, with dark undertones, on the typical Capra theme that no man is born a failure.

Carné, Marcel (1909–96)

Carné occupied a role in the immediately pre-war cinema in many ways similar to that of Antonioni in the early sixties—the poet of an age's style of despair, whose fatalism receives tangible support and embodiment from the skilful use of decor and architecture. In Carné's case these were entirely studio-bound (his mature masterpieces eschewed location filming entirely), which may be one reason why his output has dated compared with, say, Renoir's. But *Quai des Brumes* (1938) and *Le Jour Se Leve* (1939) provide atmospheric frameworks for the acting of Jean Gabin, and *Les Enfants du Paradis* (1945), the three-and-a-half-hour tale of lost love and cynicism in the theatrical world of nineteenth-century Paris, remains exciting through its amalgam of "period" style and a tortured consciousness evocative of the time at which it was made. With Rene Clement (director of *Jeux Interdits*, 1952) and Henri-Georges Clouzot (maker of *Wages of Fear*, 1952 and *Les Diaboloques*, 1955) Carné fell out of fashion at the time of the less studio-and-script-bound films of the *Nouvelle Vague*, but in 1979, French critics voted *Les Enfants du Paradis* as the best French film ever made.

Cassavettes, John (1929–89)

Actor-director who, with associates such as his actress-wife Gena Rowlands and actor-friends such as Peter Falk and Ben Gazzara, made offbeat films that focused more on intimate relationships than exciting narrative. Improvisational and unashamedly indulgent, the films have been an inspiration to independent film-makers wishing to eschew the mainstream. Films include: *Shadows* (1960), *Faces* (1968), *Husbands* (1970), *A Woman Under the Influence* (1974), *Killing of a Chinese Bookie* (1976), *Love Streams* (1982).

Chabrol, Claude (b. 1930)

Like Godard and Truffaut, Chabrol first distinguished himself as an abrasive and articulate critic on the magazine *Cahiers du Cinema* before branching into direction. With Eric Rohmer (later also to become a director), he also wrote an influential book at this time on the films of Alfred Hitchcock. Hitchcock has been a strong influence on Chabrol's films, which are often cynical detective stories or psychological suspense thrillers set against carefully observed French provincial settings. He is a cool anatomist of the discreet charms and deadly passions of the bourgeoisie. His key films include *Les Cousins* (1958), *Les Bonnes Femmes* (1960), *Les Biches* (1968), *La Femme Infidele* (1969), *Killer!— Que la Bete meure* (1969), *Les Noces Rouges* (1973) and his best film, *Le Boucher* (1970). A recent work, *Judgment in Stone* (1994), adapted from a novel by Ruth Rendell, showed he had lost none of his venom and animosity towards the bourgeois nor his capacity to disturb.

Chen, Kaige (b. 1952)

With Zhang Yimou, the leading director of the so-called 'fifth generation' of film makers who graduated from the Beijing Film Academy in 1982, following its re-opening after Mao Tse-Tung's Cultural Revolution. His first film, *Yellow Earth* (1984) made an impact in the West comparable to that of *Rashomon* and *Pather Panchali* in its revelation of a new national cinema, and his international reputation was consolidated by *Farewell My Concubine* (1993), which shared the top prize at Cannes with *The Piano* and was nominated for an Oscar. Other key films: *The Big Parade* (1985),

King of the Children (1987), *Life on a string* (1991), *Temptress Moon* (1997).

Clair, Rene (1898–1981)

The first and still the greatest European musical director. His early interest in asynchronous sound (*i.e.* that which does not always correspond to what we see going on on the screen) led him to attach equal importance to natural noise and music and to dialogue in his early sound films (such as *Sous les Toits de Paris* of 1930). A delight in dance—the choreographed quality of fights, chases and crowd scenes—permeates his two most successful works, *Le Million* and the simplistic but vivacious satire on industrialisation, *A Nous la Liberté* (both 1931) which greatly influenced Chaplin's *Modern Times*.

Cocteau, Jean (1889–1963)

Cocteau was a poet who expressed himself variously in fiction, drama, painting and drawing as well as through the cinema. *Beauty and the Beast* (1946) was an imaginative telling of the familiar tale, with Jean Marais both frightening and poignant as the Beast. In *Orphée* of 1950 he produced one of the cinema's unquestioned fantastic masterpieces, using mirrors as links between the world of the living and that of the dead to great effect, and playing upon the connection between love and death in a way that must have influenced the makers of *Last Year in Marienbad* (Resnais and Robbe-Grillet) eleven years later.

Coen, Joel (b. 1958)

With his brother Ethan (who co-writes and produces), Joel Coen has fashioned some of the most original American films of the last decade, darkly comic, densely plotted dramas that artfully blend passion with pastiche. Key films: *Blood Simple* (1983), *Raising Arizona* (1987), *Miller's Crossing* (1990), *Barton Fink* (1991), *Fargo* (1996).

Coppola, Francis Ford (b. 1939)

The Godfather of modern American cinema, confidante and father-figure to the new generation of directors (such as George Lucas and Steven Spielberg) who emerged from film school to storm Hollywood in the early 1970s. Coppola's *The Godfather* (1972) and *The Godfather, Part II* (1974) combined the sweep of a dynastic family melodrama with a mature political analysis of corporate America. The former restored Marlon Brando to superstardom; the latter made stars of Al Pacino and Robert De Niro. Two other major films of the decade were *The Conversation* (1974), a tale of treacherous tapes and an atmosphere of paranoia that evoked Watergate; and *Apocalypse Now* (1979), in which America's incursion into Vietnam was interpreted as a mad, metaphysical journey into the heart of darkness. Since the trauma of *Apocalypse Now*, whose making was a nightmare that almost drove him mad, Coppola has seemed something of a lost soul in modern cinema, searching for inspiration, marking time and, with *Godfather III* (1990), revisiting old haunts. His version of *Dracula* (1992) showed his mastery of special effects and temporarily revived his career.

Costa Gavras, Constantin (b. 1933)

The cinema's specialist director of the political thriller, throwing up large social issues of corruption and responsibility under the guise of suspense melodrama. He achieved international prominence with *Z* (1969), an indictment of the repressive regime in Greece, and he has had equal success in the mainstream commercial cinema, particularly with *Missing* (1982) and *Music Box* (1989).

Cronenberg, David (b. 1943)

Canada's most controversial film export, whose early reputation was made with stomach-churning, mind-exploding horror films. Critical respectability came with *The Fly* (1986) and *Dead Ringers* (1988), which married the gore with intellect and compassion, but controversy flared again over his uninhibited adaptation of J. G. Ballard's notorious novel about eroticism and the automobile, *Crash* (1996).

Cukor, George (1899–1983)

Cukor came to Hollywood from directing on the New York stage, and this theatrical background was an important clue to his work. His films were often adaptations of plays, like *Gaslight* (1944); he was always intrigued by theatrical people indulging a flair for the dramatic, either on stage, like Ronald Colman in *A Double Life* (1947), or in a courtroom, like Spencer Tracy and Katherine Hepburn in *Adam's Rib* (1949); and his films are particularly remembered for their performances, *e.g.* Greta Garbo's in *Camille* (1937) or Judy Garland's in *A Star is Born* (1954). Cukor was one of the most civilised of Hollywood directors, versatile and visually stylish, but particularly revelling in the sex-war comedies of Tracy and Hepburn, such as *Adam's Rib* and *Pat and Mike* (1952), which debated feminist issues ahead of their time.

Curtiz, Michael (1888–1962)

Hungarian-born super-professional of Hollywood's heyday. He began his association with Warner Brothers in 1926, making over a hundred films there of every conceivable genre and with stars such as Errol Flynn, James Cagney and Humphrey Bogart. His most famous films include *Angels With Dirty Faces* (1938), *Yankee Doodle Dandy* (1942), *Mildred Pierce* (1945) and the immortal *Casablanca* (1943).

De Mille, Cecil B. (1881–1959)

An innovative director in the silent era, Cecil B. De Mille became indelibly associated in his later career with bigness in the movies. His gigantic epics include *The Sign of the Cross* with Charles Laughton in 1932, and two spectacularly tasteless versions of *The Ten Commandments* (1923 and 1956). The films themselves matter less nowadays than the reputation for scale and the consistently successful box-office returns. Joseph L. Mankiewicz's observation on de Mille is worth quoting: "He had his finger up the pulse of America."

De Sica, Vittorio (1902–74)

Although he began his screen career as an actor, Vittorio De Sica is remembered principally for a remarkable group of films he made immediately after World War II, collaborating with writer Cesare Zavattini on works which are regarded as key examples of Italian neo-realism; *Shoeshine* (1946), *Bicycle Thieves* (1948) and *Umberto D* (1952). These sympathetic studies of the poor were heavily criticised in their own country (for political simplemindedness by the Left and for unflattering and unpatriotic portraiture of Italy by the Right) but were widely acclaimed abroad. With the decline of neo-realism in the early 1950s, De Sica was never to scale the same heights, though he did direct Sophia Loren to an Oscar winning performance in *Two Women* (1961), and experienced a later flourish of critical acclaim for two of his final films, *The Garden of the Finzi Continis* (1971) and *A Brief Vacation* (1973).

Dreyer, Carl Theodor (1889–1968)

Dreyer is still regarded as the greatest artist in the history of Danish cinema, though it was in France that he directed his first masterpiece, *The Passion of Joan of Arc* (1928), with its remarkable leading performance by Renee Falconetti in her only screen role. The austerity and apparent severe Protestant guilt that pervade his work compare interestingly with Robert Bresson's Catholic severity. Dreyer's last film, *Gertrud* (1964) was disgracefully derided at its premiere, but it is now regarded as one of his finest works, both for its steady satire of the bourgeoisie and its sympathy with women and hatred of their oppression. The slowness of his work still causes difficulty, but the fantastical quality of *Vampyr* (1932), and the undercutting of fanaticism in *Days of Wrath* (1943) and *Ordet/The Word* (1955) are nowadays better appreciated than they were at the time of release.

Eisenstein, Sergei (1898–1948)

A prominent theorist as well as practitioner, Eisenstein's Marxist awareness of society as founded upon conflict rather than harmony led him to develop a theory of montage, or meaning built up by collision and clash of images. This theory found illustration in what are at the same time highly effective Socialist propaganda films: *The Battleship Potemkin* of 1925, whose massacre-sequence on the steps of the port of Odessa is among the most famous in cinematic history, *October* of 1927 (in which the Menshevik or moderate leader Kerensky is denigrated when his image is followed by that of a peacock—an example of the montage technique), and the more contorted and baroque *Ivan the Terrible* (Part one, 1942; Part two, 1945). This last caused Eisenstein to fall into disfavour with Stalin (who may have taken the portrait of the tyrant Ivan to be a reflection upon himself), and the financial difficulties and persecution because of his homosexuality led to his premature death of a heart attack. "Of all the arts", said Lenin, "for us the cinema is the most important". In Soviet Russia its most important voice was Eisenstein who, in finding filmic forms to express collectivism and brotherhood, gave substance to a national ideology.

Fassbinder, Rainer Werner (1946–82)

Phenomenally prolific hero of the new German cinema of the 1970s, Fassbinder's films at their best combined the political commitment of a Godard with the heady melodrama of a Hollywood director he much admired, Douglas Sirk. His best film is probably *The Marriage of Maria Braun* (1979), an extraordinary allegory of the history of post-war Germany with a magnetic leading performance from Hanna Schygulla. The best films in his melodramatic style are *The Merchant of Four Seasons* (1972), *The Bitter Tears of Petra von Kant* (1972), *Fear Eats the Soul* (1974) and *Veronika Voss* (1981).

Fellini, Federico (1920–93)

Fellini was an example of the director as star, delighting in treading a thin line between self-expression and self-indulgence. The films recall his early experience in the circus and as a cartoonist, being populated by grotesques and having a unique mixture of risk and spectacle, fantasy and fact. *I Vitelloni* (1953), a semi-autobiographical account of his wastrel adolescent days, established Fellini's reputation; it was enhanced by the international success of his next film, *La Strada* (1954), a parable of body and spirit, love and salvation. With *La Dolce Vita* (1960), a sensational view of contemporary Roman society, Fellini entered his decadent phase, which was to be continued in such films as *Fellini Satyricon* (1969) and Fellini's *Casanova* (1976). His most highly regarded films are his most autobiographical, *81/2* (1963), in which a film director encounters a creative crisis and ransacks his past for inspiration, and *Amarcord* (1973) which is a remembrance of his childhood.

Flaherty, Robert (1884–1951)

Often referred to as the "father of film documentary", Flaherty was actually as much a Romantic as a realist. He has been criticised for the political absences in his movies but he was not a polemicist but a poet, making films that were either hymns to a vanishing way of life or recorded elemental struggles between Man and Nature. His best films were his first, and last: respectively, *Nanook of the North* (1922) and *Louisiana Story* (1948).

Ford, John (1895–1973)

"My name's John Ford," he said. "I make Westerns." He not only made them: he transformed them into poetic statements of the American spirit. Particularly celebrated are those he made starring John Wayne: *Stagecoach* (1939), an odyssey of Western outcasts across hostile Indian territory: *The Searchers* (1956), in which Wayne's bitter racialism is eventually tamed; and *The Man Who Shot Liberty Valance* (1962) which pits Wayne against James Stewart. But he also excelled with Henry Fonda (*Drums Along the Mohawk* of 1939), and in non-Western films (*The Grapes of Wrath*, 1940). His greatest limitation is that he is preeminently a man's director, whose bourbon-soaked camaraderie and stress on tough, determined action in some of his less successful films palls rapidly.

His greatest strengths are as the unsurpassed chronicler of pioneering America and as the sympathetic observer of the endurance of the common people; and his insights into prejudice, injustice and the tragedy of destroyed families. "This is the West, sir", says the newspaper editor of *Liberty Valance*. "When the legend becomes fact, print the legend". Ford printed the legend better than anyone. Other key films: *The Informer* (1935), *My Darling Clementine* (1946), *Fort Apache* (1948), *The Quiet Man* (1952).

Forman, Milos (b. 1932)

Forman was one of a group of directors of the so-called Czech New Wave of the 1960s, whose comedies such as *A Blonde in Love* (1965) and *The Fireman's Ball* (1967) audaciously satirised authority, both parental and political. In Paris in 1968 when the Soviet tanks rolled into Prague and there was a clampdown on artistic expression, Forman eventually emigrated to America, where he has continued to score notable successes with offbeat films, most famously with *One Flew Over the Cuckoo's Nest* (1975) and *Amadeus* (1984). Other key films: *Taking Off* (1971), *The People vs Larry Flint* (1996).

Fuller, Samuel (1912–97)

A ferocious action director, castigated as neo-Fascist by his adversaries and lauded by his advocates for the tough, unsparing economy and desperate honesty of his work. Fuller worked across different genres, including the spy-thriller (*Pickup on South Street*, 1953) and the Western (*Run of the Arrow*, 1957). In *Shock Corridor* of 1963, his finest and most revelatory work, he combined the investigative-journalist picture with the drama of psychological horror to create an unnerving dissection of American prejudices and fears. His later films were few and far between, though *White Dog* (1983) showed that, given the opportunity, Fuller had lost none of his bite. His was tabloid cinema, done with tremendous verve, and admired by modern directors such as Scorsese and Tim Robbins.

Gance, Abel (1889–1981)

"The day of the Image has arrived", proclaimed Abel Gance at the triumphant premiere of his five-and-a-half-hour epic, *Napoleon* (1927), which deployed superimposition, slow-motion, split-screen, colour, and a triple-screen process, Polyvision, that anticipated Cinerama by nearly thirty years. Alas, Gance was mistaken: sound was round the corner and the visual innovations of *Napoleon* were rendered virtually obsolete before they had begun. Not until the film's restoration in 1980 was Gance's achievement appreciated and his own reputation restored as one of the great innovators of the silent screen.

Godard, Jean-Luc (b. 1930)

"We are the children of Marx and Coca-Cola", claimed Godard in the 1960s, when he seemed the most radical, innovative and controversial director in world cinema. Nowadays we are probably the children of McDonald's and market forces and his ideas and formal experiments seem correspondingly less urgent, more marginal. The turning-point was *Weekend* (1967), an apocalyptic black-comedy of chaos and cannibalism, of social and cultural breakdown. From his early films, which were often love letters to the Hollywood cinema, he had moved to an alternative political cinema that seemed to demand not audiences but disciples. Still, although his day as director is over, his influence on all spheres of alternative, independent, avant-garde film theory and practice continues to be immense. Other key films: *Breathless* (1959), *Vivre sa Vie* (1962), *Le Mepris-Contempt* (1963), *Une Femme Mariee* (1964), *Pierrot le Fou* (1965), *Tout Va Bien* (1972).

Griffith, D. W. (1875–1948)

Griffith more than any other individual was responsible for the cinema moving from short one and two-reelers to the grand epic scale. *The Birth of a Nation* (1915), despite overt racism, was the most exciting attempt the cinema had hitherto made to capture and reconstruct the course of historical events, and broke all box-office records as well as profoundly influencing Eisenstein. Its successor, *Intolerance* (1916), was even more grandiose and cost unimaginable sums by the standards of those days. Apart from *Broken Blossoms* (1919) and *Way Down East* (1920), Griffith's later films were undistinguished and his career ended in a prolonged, drink-sodden decline. Although sometimes criticised for his Victorian melodrama, Griffith is more properly remembered for his popularisation of feature-length narrative; his revelation of the creative possibilities of montage; and his encouragement of a new subtlety and realism in screen performance. He was the first figure in film history to give this new mass medium intellectual respectability.

Hamer, Robert (1911–63)

The problem child of Ealing studios, whose career was to decline due to alcoholism and what producer Michael Balcon was to call Hamer's "self-destructive streak", but who was responsible for at least three classics of British film: "The Haunted Mirror" episode from *Dead of Night* (1945); the neo-realist melodrama about the London underworld, *It Always Rains on Sunday* (1947); and, above all, the black comedy, *Kind Hearts and Coronets* (1949) in which Dennis Price purrs through some of the most suavely literate dialogue in British cinema as he attempts to kill off eight Alec Guinnesses on his way to a dukedom.

Hawks, Howard (1896–1977)

Hawks was the litmus-paper director for proponents of the auteur theory of criticism in the fifties and, even now that theory has been surpassed, one of the most versatile and consistent operators within the Hollywood studio system. Whatever genre he worked in, it was transmuted and made more ambiguous. Thus the Western *Rio Bravo* (1959) contains a minimum of big-scale outdoor action and a maximum of charged conversation; private-eye classic *The Big Sleep* (1946) is concerned with Bogart's process of ironic self-discovery rather than with who-dunnit (a question to which Hawks himself never worked out the answer); and the action in the civil-aviation drama *Only Angels Have Wings* (1939) takes place predominantly on the ground. His comedies, notably those with Cary Grant, hilariously subvert sex stereotypes, above all *Bringing Up Baby* (1938), whose plot vies in implausibility with W. C. Fields but whose thrusts at academic ossification, male chauvinism, and one-upmanship are masterfully worked into a framework of gag and slapstick.

Herzog, Werner (b. 1942)

One of the most exciting of the young wave of German directors, his treatment of madness is particularly penetrating. This is normally undertaken within the context of a part-historical, part-fictional society, as with the paranoia of the sixteenth-century Amazon conquistador in *Aguirre, Wrath of God* (1972), the scandalous insights of the supposed "savage" in *The Enigma of Kaspar Hauser* (1974), and the odd symbiosis between predator and victim in his Murnau remake *Nosferatu the Vampyre* (1978). "Dreams move mountains", says Herzog: it is his philosophy of film-making.

Hitchcock, Sir Alfred (1899–1980)

For half a century Hitchcock was the acknowledged master of mystery and suspense, whose coldly planned delight in playing on his audience's nerves has occasioned violent disagreement between those who see him as the medium's leading exponent of predestination and those for whom he is but a limited practical joker in bad taste. *Psycho* (1960) remains the most notorious film, less now perhaps for the murder of Janet Leigh in her shower than for the *coup de grace* when the murderer's "real identity" is revealed near the end. *North by North-West* of the previous year is among his least vicious and most accomplished works, a comic spy-thriller based (like so much that is funniest in Hollywood cinema) on a mistake involving the identity of Cary Grant. Sexually perverse or tabooed areas which

the conventional narrative cinema perforce ignored or treated as marginal assume central (though often implicit) places in his work, which is perhaps his greatest source of interest to students of film: *cf.* the latent homosexuality in *Strangers on a Train* (1951), the Grand Guignol parody of an Oedipus complex in *Psycho* and the treatment of repression and the traumatic return of what has been "forgotten" (*i.e.* repressed) in *Marnie* (1964). In recent years his early British films have been revalued and upgraded, and the sexual politics of his films have been earnestly analysed. He has also been the subject of a scandalous biography by Donald Spoto, *The Dark Side of Genius*. But he continues to fascinate because of the multi-sided personality of his work, which reveals at once the mask of a joker of genius, a nihilist, a Catholic moralist, a Freudian sexual psychologist and, in perhaps his greatest work, *Vertigo* (1958) an anguished romantic. He was more than the "master of suspense": he made murder into an art form. Other key films include: *Blackmail* (1929), *The Thirty-Nine Steps* (1935), *Sabotage* (1937), *The Lady Vanishes* (1938), *Rebecca* (1940), *Shadow of a Doubt* (1943), *Notorious* (1946), *Rope* (1948), *Rear Window* (1954) and *The Birds* (1963).

Huston, John (1906–87)

1941 marked two of the most sensationally successful debuts in directorial history—Orson Welles with *Citizen Kane* and Huston's *The Maltese Falcon*, an elegantly perverse private-eye tale in which double-crosses occur at a bewildering rate, thereby setting the mould for the *film noir* that was so prominent later in the decade. Huston's career intermittently maintained this initial impetus, though public and critical reception of his works was not always judicious: *Freud: The Secret Passion* (1962), a remarkable drama ahead of its time, was ill received, whereas *The African Queen*, for which Bogart won an Oscar in 1952, is an overrated, though entertaining, film. Huston was intrigued by over-reachers, people who pursue their dreams to the point of obsession. Even when their obsessions blow up in their faces, as they do in two of his best films, *The Treasure of the Sierra Madre* (1948) and *The Man who would be King* (1975), Huston is still impressed by the grandeur of human aspiration, by the ironies of courage and cowardice, by the stirring way humanity challenges its fate. His work was uneven but his career ended on a high note: a typically literate adaptation of a literary classic, *Under the Volcano* (1984); an impish Mafia black comedy, *Prizzi's Honor* (1985); and a serene rendering of James Joyce's elegiac short story, *The Dead* (1987). His direction also helped win Oscars for his family: for father Walter in *Sierra Madre*, and for daughter Anjelica in *Prizzi's Honor*. Other key films: *Key Largo* (1948), *Moby Dick* (1956), *The Misfits* (1961), *Reflections in a Golden Eye* (1967), *Fat City* (1972), *Wise Blood* (1979).

Kazan, Elia (b. 1909)

Dynamic director who founded the Actor's Studio with Lee Strasberg and is responsible for bringing the Method style of acting into the American cinema. His association on three films with Marlon Brando—*A Streetcar named Desire* (1951), *Viva Zapata* (1952) and *On the Waterfront* (1954)—was significant for its establishment of the prototype Kazan hero: a rebel, anguished and ambivalent about his personal situation and social responsibilities but with a tremendous drive to solve his problems. *On the Waterfront* was particularly controversial for its so-called "glorification of the informer" (an ex-Communist, Kazan had named names to the House UnAmerican Activities Committee in 1952). He also directed James Dean in *East of Eden* (1955), Montgomery Clift in *Wild River* (1960) and Robert De Niro in *The Last Tycoon* (1976), though in his later years he has occupied himself mainly in writing novels and a magnificent revelatory autobiography, *A Life*.

Kieslowski, Krzysztof (1941–96)

The greatest Polish directors, like Andrzej Wajda and Krzysztof Zanussi, see cinema as the nation's social conscience, the art-form that most courageously interrogates the country's moral and political values. Kieslowski was in that tradition and is best known abroad for his contemporary TV films on the theme of the Ten Commandments, two of which were expanded to feature-film length: *A Short Film About Killing* (1988) and *A Short Film About Love* (1989); and for his *Three Colours* trilogy, *Blue* (1993), *White* (1993) and *Red* (1994), which for some critics represents the finest achievement of European cinema in the 1990s. Other key films include: *Camera Buff* (1979), *No End* (1984), *The Double Life of Veronique* (1991).

Kubrick, Stanley (1928–99)

For Kubrick, the cinema is a laboratory for observation and experiment and his findings have revealed a mind of the highest intellect and provoked more critical debate than any American director since Orson Welles. Two films in the 1960s particularly confirmed his extraordinary gifts: the nuclear comedy, *Dr. Strangelove* (1964), which showed the tension between man and the machine; and his sci-fi epic, *2001: A Space Odyssey* (1968), a vast enigmatic meditation on evolution and the degree to which man has been mastered by the technology he has created. His following two films, *A Clockwork Orange* (1971) and *Barry Lyndon* (1975) were amongst the most controversial of the next decade, the former for its violence in depicting the issue of free-will, the latter for its sumptuousness in anatomising high society at the end of the eighteenth-century. Many were disappointed with his labyrinthine horror film, *The Shining* (1980) and his Vietnam movie *Full Metal Jacket* (1987), but he remains a key figure in modern film, analysing the tensions between the individual and history, man and science, language and social conditioning with a disturbingly clinical detachment. Other key films: *Paths of Glory* (1957), *Lolita* (1962).

Kurosawa, Akira (1910–98)

Kurosawa was the first Japanese director to make a major impact on Western audiences, with *Rashomon*, the recounting of a rape and murder from four separate perspectives, which was the great success of the Venice Film Festival in 1951. Compared to such as Mizoguchi and Ozu his work looks Westernised, but this can be of positive benefit, as in the Samurai "Westerns" he made with the actor Toshiro Mifune, where classic Western plot-schemes are translated into stylised Japanese settings (*The Seven Samurai*, 1954; *Sanjuro*, 1962). He has also made highly praised adaptations of Shakespeare, *Throne of Blood* (1957), a version of *Macbeth*, and *Ran* (1985), an interpretation of *King Lear*. Psychological extremes have always excited Kurosawa, and his pulsating visual style can be understood in terms of finding a powerful visual pattern to reflect the feverish inner intensity of his characters. But one should not overlook the strong humanist vein in Kurosawa, expressed most movingly in *Living* (1952). Other key films: *Drunken Angel* (1948), *The Idiot* (1951), *I Live in Fear* (1955), *The Lower Depths* (1957) and *Kagemusha* (1980).

Lang, Fritz (1890–1976)

Lang began as a leading exponent of German Expressionism, with the psychodrama *M* (1931), starring Peter Lorre as the self-hating child murderer, and *Metropolis* (1926), a science-fiction evocation of a nightmarish industrial city of the future. Goebbels was very taken with the latter film, and offered Lang the job of film-propaganda director to the Third Reich. Instead, he fled to America, and proceeded to provide auteurist critics with one of their juiciest test-cases by adapting his preoccupations with fate, revenge, and the social outcast to the turbulent American society of the pre-war and wartime years (*Fury*, 1936; *The Ministry of Fear*, 1944), and to genres such as the Western (*Rancho Notorious* in 1952) and the gangster film (*The Big Heat* in 1953). Two Edward G. Robinson performances—as a Professor implicated in murder in *The Woman in the Window* (1944) and as an artist infatuated with a prostitute in *Scarlet Street* (1945)—embody to perfection the typical Lang hero, trapped by personality, circumstance and environment. He is still arguably the most formidable pessimist in film history, and his presentation of fear and alienation in the modern metropolis has been profoundly influential on, among others, Godard, Hitchcock and Kubrick.

Lean, Sir David (1908–91)

The popular cinema's master story-teller. In *Brief Encounter* (1945), he made the British cinema's greatest love story; his Dickens' adaptations, *Great Expectations* (1946) and *Oliver Twist* (1948) have never been surpassed; and with *The Bridge on the River Kwai* (1957), *Lawrence of Arabia* (1962) and *Doctor Zhivago* (1965), he managed to align epic perspectives with intimate and intense characterisation. After the failure of *Ryan's Daughter* in 1970, his reputation slumped: "bourgeois impersonality" was the label on his films. But the success of *A Passage to India* (1984) helped to force a re-evaluation of his work and recognise its individual qualities: the emotional repression of his heroines; the visionary madness of his heroes; the spirit of place that pulses in his films; and his sensitivity to the erratic, exotic emotions that lurk beneath the surface of English propriety. Other key films include: *The Sound Barrier* (1952), *Hobson's Choice* (1954) and *Summer Madness* (1955).

Leigh, Mike (b. 1943)

English director of growing international reputation after his success with *Secrets and Lies* (1996), a tragi-comic study of family relationships that is Leigh's forte. He had made his first film as far back as 1971, but only in the last decade has he been able to develop some cinematic continuity. Cineastes cherish his quirky insight into character and his sharp, sometimes astringent, satire of middle-class mores. Key films: *Bleak Moments* (1971), *High Hopes* (1988), *Life is Sweet* (1990), *Naked* (1993), *Career Girls* (1997).

Leone, Sergio (1921–89)

Leone will always be remembered as the director who re-invigorated the western genre in the 1960s and made a star of Clint Eastwood. His spaghetti westerns—*A Fistful of Dollars* (1964), *For a Few Dollars More* (1965), *The Good, the Bad and the Ugly* (1966)—were an iconoclastic blend of parody and anti-heroism that appealed to a distrustful, anarchic age. His later films, *Once Upon a Time in the West* (1968) and *Once Upon a Time in America* (1989) were operatic meditations on the western and the gangster film respectively, both majestic and self-reflexive.

Loach, Ken (b. 1936)

Untamed radical film-maker who cut his teeth on social realist TV dramas, notably the massively influential *Cathy Come Home*, and then brought the same intensity to his feature films, most memorably *Kes* (1969), a work much admired for its social critique and documentary-style technique by directors such as Kieslowski. Like Mike Leigh, Loach has acquired a new lease of life in the 1990s, twice winning the European Film of the Year Award—for *Riff-Raff* (1990) and *Land and Freedom* (1995)—without compromising his vision, integrity or socialism.

Losey, Joseph (1909–84)

There were several Joseph Loseys: the American Losey renowned for cogent moral fables such as *The Prowler* (1951) before the McCarthyist blacklist forced him out of America; the British Losey in which, with collaborators like actors Stanley Baker and Dirk Bogarde and writer Harold Pinter, he analysed the sexual mores and class corruption of English society, as in *The Servant* (1963), *Accident* (1967) and *The Go-Between* (1970); and the European Losey of the final phase of his career, when he adapted classics such as *A Doll's House* (1973) or Mozart's *Don Giovanni* (1980) or offered trenchant insights into recent political history, as in *The Assassination of Trotsky* (1972) and *Mr. Klein* (1976). With a style often verging on the baroque, Losey tackled a variety of subject matter, but the themes were consistent: the hypocrisy and deceit of dominant social and sexual attitudes. He was the most Brechtian of directors and had one of the most lucid intellects in movies. Other key films include: *The Boy with Green Hair* (1948), *Blind Date* (1959), *The Criminal* (1960), *King and Country* (1964) and *Secret Ceremony* (1968).

Lubitsch, Ernst (1892–1947)

The master of sophisticated sex comedy who, in Billy Wilder's phrase, "could do more with a closed door than most modern directors can do with an entire bedroom". Born in Berlin, Lubitsch brought a European flavour to Hollywood farce, satirising the pretension and insensitivity that sometimes go with wealth and position. His best remembered films are *Ninotchka* (1939), in which Garbo laughs, and *To Be or Not to Be* (1942), in which Jack Benny plays Hamlet. They are not only comedies: they are fervent anti-Nazi satires made at a time when Lubitsch must have known that the Europe of his youth, so wittily and lovingly evoked on screen, was being destroyed forever. Other key films: *Trouble in Paradise* (1932) and *The Shop Around the Corner* (1940).

Lumet, Sidney (b. 1924)

The most enduring of the generation of directors (including John Frankenheimer, Martin Ritt and Franklin Schaffner) who graduated to the cinema in the 1950s after learning their craft on television. Lumet's first film, the jury-room drama, *12 Angry Men* (1957) was an instant classic, and his best films have often returned to the themes of justice, law and order, civic corruption and abuse of police power. A child actor on stage, he has developed a powerful rapport with actors and some of his films rival Kazan's in the skill and intensity of the performances. Arguably over-prolific, undeniably humourless, Lumet has nevertheless amassed a powerful body of work that testifies to his talent, professionalism and liberal values. Key films include: *Long Day's Journey into Night* (1962), *Fail Safe* (1964), *The Hill* (1965), *Dog Day Afternoon* (1975), *Prince of the City* (1981), *The Verdict* (1982), *Running on Empty* (1987).

Lynch, David (b. 1946)

One of the modern cinema's most unnerving directors. He achieved instant notoriety with the gruesome *Eraserhead* (1976); had a deserved success with the compassionate *The Elephant Man* (1980); but has since polarised critical opinion with such films as *Wild at Heart* (1990) and *Lost Highway* (1997), psychologically challenging or pretentiously incoherent, according to taste. His most fully achieved work to date is *Blue Velvet* (1987), a nightmarish investigation of the dark sexual secrets of 'typical' small-town America.

Mackendrick, Alexander (1912–93)

The most consistently brilliant of the Ealing directors, making four of its most successful and enduring comedies: *Whisky Galore* (1949), *The Man in the White Suit* (1951), *The Maggie* (1954) and *The Lady-Killers* (1955). His American debut—an exposé of yellow journalism—*Sweet Smell of Success* (1957) was also remarkable, but after a series of abortive projects in the 1960s, Mackendrick retired from directing to become Dean of the film department of the California Institute of the Arts. He left behind a fascinating body of work, notable for its extraordinary insights into the world of children, its fascination with the dangers of innocence, and its mordant observation of the intricate yet inevitable ways in which humans fail to communicate. Other key films: *Mandy* (1952), *Sammy Going South* (1963) and *A High Wind in Jamaica* (1965).

Malle, Louis (1932–95)

Formerly an assistant to Robert Bresson and Jacques Cousteau, Louis Malle developed into one of the most esteemed of international directors. He made films as dashing as *Zazie dans le Metro* (1960), as disturbing as *Lacombe Lucien* (1973), as atmospheric as *Atlantic City* (1980), and as moving as *Au Revoir les Enfants* (1987). Malle often challenged the norms of society and the boundaries of cinema, exploring such risky subjects as eroticism (in *Les Amants* in 1958), incest (in *Murmur of the Heart* in 1971) and child prostitution (in *Pretty Baby* in 1979) and yet still achieving popular success and critical acclaim. Isolation and social alienation were recurrent themes, fittingly so perhaps for one of the least predictable and most individualistic filmmakers of modern times. Other key films include:

Lift to the Scaffold (1957), *Le Feu Follet* (1963), *My Dinner With Andre* (1982) and *Damage* (1992).

Mankiewicz, Joseph L. (1909–93)

To those who find Mankiewicz's films too wordy, he replied: "There can never be an excess of *good* talk". Mankiewicz was one of the most eloquent of Hollywood's writer directors, who began by writing dialogue for W. C. Fields and, he claims, Rin-Rin-Tin (an unused screen-play about a dog that hates its master, a familiar Mankiewicz theme). His greatest period was during the ten years after the War, in which he won the writing and directing Oscars for two consecutive years (for *A Letter to Three Wives* in 1949 and *All About Eve* in 1950) and also made Hollywood's best Shakespearian film (*Julius Caesar* in 1952). His career never really picked up momentum after his labours on the mammothly expensive *Cleopatra* (1963), though he was proud to claim that his last film *Sleuth* (1972) is the only film ever to have its entire cast—*i.e.* Laurence Olivier and Michael Caine—nominated for Oscars. There are a lot of interesting recurrent motifs in Mankiewicz—generation conflict, ghosts from the past that will not stay dead—and nobody has made more haunting use of the flashback. Other key films: *The Ghost and Mrs. Muir* (1947), *Five Fingers* (1952), *The Barefoot Contessa* (1954) and *Suddenly Last Summer* (1959).

Mann, Anthony (1909–67)

Anthony Mann is best remembered for a series of Westerns he made with actor James Stewart, which were striking for their dramatic use of landscape and the psychological instability of their heroes. In *Winchester 73* (1950), *Bend of the River* (1952), *The Naked Spur* (1953), and *The Far Country* (1955), Stewart plays an ostensibly noble but actually neurotic hero who, whilst undertaking a perilous journey across a treacherous landscape, must also root out the evil in himself. Mann also made fine thrillers, a classic epic (*El Cid* in 1961) and even a stylish musical (*The Glenn Miller Story* in 1954) but it was the Mann of the Western that really showed his quality as a director. Other key films: *The Man from Laramie* (1955), *Man of the West* (1958) and *The Fall of the Roman Empire* (1964).

Melville, Jean-Pierre (1917–73)

Melville was something of a father figure of the *Nouvelle Vague* because of his economical and independent production methods. He made an exemplary adaptation of Jean Cocteau's novel *Les Enfants Terribles* (1950). However, he is most celebrated for a series of poetic, stylised existential gangster films, among them *Second Breath* (1966), *The Samurai* (1967), and *The Red Circle* (1970), which particularly took their inspiration from Melville's favourite director, John Huston. (Melville had chosen his pseudonym after his favourite author, Herman Melville: his actual surname was Grumbach). Perhaps his masterpiece, though, and certainly his most personal film, is *Army of the Shadows* (1969), a film about the French Resistance that drew on his own personal experience in the war.

Minnelli, Vincente (1910–86)

The name Vincente Minnelli is synonymous with the MGM musical—*Meet Me in St. Louis* (1944), *An American in Paris* (1951), *The Band Wagon* (1953), *Gigi* (1958) and others. Yet he was also adept at comedy, and did some remarkably intense melodramas, of which *Lust for Life* (1955), his bio-pic of Van Gogh, and *The Bad and the Beautiful* (1952), his glittering dissection of Hollywood ruthlessness, are particularly notable. He was interested in the plight of the artist in society, and the superiority of the world of imagination to that of reality. Hollywood's Dream Factory proved a most congenial environment for this most elegant of stylists. Other key films: *The Pirate* (1948), *Madame Bovary* (1949), *Father of the Bride* (1950). *Brigadoon* (1953), *The Cobweb* (1955) and *Some Came Running* (1958).

Mizoguchi, Kenji (1898–1956)

For many, Mizoguchi is the greatest of all Japanese directors, but his films are still not that well known in the West. The most famous is *Ugetsu*

Monogatari (1953), a ravishingly beautiful tale of two potters seduced by ghosts. Its articulation of history and fantasy, its lyrical style and its commitment to the treatment of women as equals are characteristic of the director. Other films include: *The Story of the Last Chrysanthemums* (1939), *The Life of Oharu* (1952), *Sansho the Bailiff* (1954).

Murnau, F. W. (1889–1931)

Murnau is renowned for three classics of silent film: *Nosferatu* (1922), the cinema's first version of the *Dracula* story and still the most frightening; *The Last Laugh* (1924), credited as being one of the few silent films to dispense with titles and remarkable for its fluid camera movement; and *Sunrise* (1927), his first American film. Tragically he was killed in a car crash in 1931.

Olmi, Ermanno (b. 1931)

An Italian director whose work is characterised by a sympathy for the working man and by a concern for human dignity. In films such as *Il Posto* (1961) and *The Tree of Wooden Clogs* (1979), he has kept the spirit of neo-realism alive.

Ophuls, Max (1902–57)

For a long time regarded as a talented minor director of exquisite trifles, Ophuls has been reinstated by recent—notably feminist—criticism to his rightful place as one of the greatest of forties and fifties directors. *Lola Montes* (1955) was his last film, about the beautiful "adventuress" who allows herself to be put on display in a circus ring at the end of her career. The swooping camera-movements and awareness of how feminine sexuality necessarily connotes being an object to be looked at are in evidence too in *Madame de . . .* (1953), as well as in the films he made in Austria, Germany and France before setting out to pursue his career in Hollywood. His best American film was the beautiful tragic romance, *Letter from an Unknown Woman* (1948); whilst both *Caught* (1949) and *The Reckless Moment* (1949) took conventional women's magazine material and, through intense visual style, transformed them into tense and subversive comments on romantic obsession and domestic imprisonment.

Oshima, Nagisa (b. 1932)

An acute awareness of the theatrical in its widest sense–the need to treat urgent social questions as dialectical dramas rather than as ready-made events for the camera to record—and a sense of the inter-relationship of the erotic and the political unmatched by any other living director have coexisted fruitfully in Oshima's work since *Death by Hanging*–about an execution that isn't—in 1968. But his name became familiar to most filmgoers only with *Ai No Corrida* (otherwise *Empire of the Senses*) in 1975. An innkeeper and his ex-servant make untiring love until she, at his behest, strangles him in the moment of orgasm. The much-touted erotic frankness–certainly far less surrogate than that in *Last Tango in Paris*—assumes its importance only when seen in conjunction with the film's critique of the position of women in Japanese society. In his first international film, *Merry Christmas, Mr. Lawrence* (1983), he explored the strange bond which grows between a Japanese captain and a British prisoner of war: a variation of his typical themes of forbidden passion, and his preoccupation with society's "enemies" whose psychology he seeks to understand. More recently he has completed a documentary for the BBC, *Kyoto, My Mother's Place* (1991), which gives a fascinating account of his background. Other key films: *Diary of A Shinjuku Thief* (1968), *Boy* (1969), *The Ceremony* (1971) and *Empire of Passion* (1978).

Ozu, Yasujiro (1903–63)

Like Mizoguchi, Ozu is a director long known to the Western public through only one work—*Tokyo Story* of 1953, about a visit paid by an elderly couple to their children in the capital. Ozu's style is slow, his narrative-lines not exactly eventful, his photography from a low level (the seated position traditional for social intercourse in Japan) perhaps difficult for Westerners to adjust to. But now he is accepted as one of the most important innovators in

film language, for the way in which his small-scale stories distil much that is important in Japanese life and history, and for the separating out of individual actions and gestures so that spectators have time fully to appreciate their implications. Key films include: *I Was Born But . . .* (1932), *Early Summer* (1951), *Good Morning* (1959) and *An Autumn Afternoon* (1962).

Pasolini, Pier Paolo (1922–76)

Pasolini's notorious death—murdered by a homosexual pick-up—could almost have been engineered as a publicity stunt to launch his final film, *Salo or the 120 Days of Sodom* (1976), in which the combination of intense and complex visual lucidity with a recoiling from the tyrannies of the twentieth century already evident in *Pigsty* (1969) reaches its zenith. Ideological revulsion from the present and an interest in the possibilities of film language motivate Pasolini's curious "Marxist-Freudian-Catholic" rewritings of classics for the screen— *Medea* (1969) and *The Decameron* (1971). His complex artistry is seen at its best in his first film, *Accatone!* (1961) and *The Gospel According to St. Matthew* (1964), an austere rendering of the Biblical story far removed from the Hollywood epic, and movingly attempting to reconcile Pasolini's Marxist political outlook with his religious mysticism.

Peckinpah, Sam (1925–84)

Peckinpah was a Hollywood maverick, associated with scenes of graphic violence photographed in loving slow motion. In fact, he had something of the visual lyricism and raucous male humour of John Ford, though whereas Ford disclosed the poetry behind America's pioneering past, Peckinpah explored its passions and perversions as well. He will always be remembered for *The Wild Bunch* (1969), his radical, revisionist Western that majestically dragged the genre, kicking and screaming, into the 20th century. Other key films: *Guns in the Afternoon* (1962), *Major Dundee* (1965), *Straw Dogs* (1971), *Pat Garrett and Billy the Kid* (1973) and *Cross of Iron* (1977).

Penn, Arthur (b. 1922)

An abrasive stylist, notable for his subversive way with popular film genres, his investigation of the reality behind legendary figures, and his insertion of counter-culture attitudes into mainstream movie-making. Key films: *The Left-Handed Gun* (1958), *The Miracle Worker* (1962), *Bonnie and Clyde* (1967), *Alice's Restaurant* (1969) and *Night Moves* (1975).

Polanski, Roman (b. 1933)

From early Surrealist shorts, Polanski moved into feature-length dramas of sexual tension with *Knife in the Water* (1962) and *Repulsion* (shot in England in 1965). The reputation for kinkiness he thereby gained was tragically highlighted when his wife, the actress Sharon Tate, was butchered by crazed followers of Charles Manson in 1969. His major box- office success has been the private-eye drama *Chinatown* (1974), in which Polanski himself slits open the nose of the character played by Jack Nicholson. He also breathed flesh and blood into the horror film with *Rosemary's Baby* (1968) and fresh life into the filmed literary classic with *Tess* (1979). His traumatic life has been recounted in his autobiography, *Roman*. Other key films: *Cul-de-Sac* (1966), *Macbeth* (1971) and *The Tenant* (1976).

Powell, Michael (1905–90) and Pressburger, Emeric (1902–88)

British cinema's most full-blooded fantasists, who peaked in the 1940s with such passionate and visually imaginative films as *The Life and Death of Colonel Blimp* (1943), *I Know Where I'm Going* (1945), *A Matter of Life and Death* (1946), *Black Narcissus* (1947) and their greatest success, *The Red Shoes* (1948). From the late 1950s, Powell went solo and created an enormous furore with *Peeping Tom* (1960), which was critically reviled at the time but has since attained classic status and is deeply admired by cineastes and fellow directors such as Martin Scorsese.

Preminger, Otto (1906–86)

Talented tyrant who thrived on controversy, whether it involved the use of "naughty" words in *The Moon is Blue* (1953) or the depiction of the world of the drug addict in *The Man with the Golden Arm* (1955). His best films are the detective thriller, *Laura* (1945), one of a number of Preminger's features about mysterious, irresistible women who lure men to their doom; and the courtroom drama *Anatomy of a Murder* (1959), a masterpiece of objectivity and ambiguity. Other key films: *Angel Face* (1953), *Carmen Jones* (1954), *Bonjour Tristesse* (1957), *Advise and Consent* (1962) and *The Cardinal* (1963).

Ray, Nicholas (1911–78)

Ray was one of the most inventive and consistent of Hollywood action directors, whose rhetorical question summed up his philosophy of cinema: "If it were all in the script, why make the film?" *Rebel Without A Cause* (1955) blazed the trail for a host of movies about rebellious youth, but the dignity of James Dean's performance and the symbolic richness of Ray's *mise-en-scene* have caused it to survive longer than most of its imitators. He enjoyed success also with Bogart, *In a Lonely Place* (1950) and Robert Mitchum, *The Lusty Men* (1952). The critics of *Cahiers du Cinema* particularly championed Ray's more extreme stylistic exercises, such as the feminist Western, *Johnny Guitar* (1954) and the baroque gangster film, *Party Girl* (1958). Alienated youth, the rebel, the outsider: these were the figures with whom Ray identified, sometimes melodramatically, often poetically. Other key films: *They Live By Night* (1948), *Knock on Any Door* (1949), *On Dangerous Ground* (1952), *Bigger Than Life* (1956) and *Bitter Victory* (1957).

Ray, Satyajit (1921–92)

Pather Panchali of 1955 introduced Indian cinema to a wider audience, and launched a highly successful trilogy, completed by *Aparajito* of 1957 and *The World of Apu* of 1959. The withdrawn, analytical style of Ray's output expanded with some of his work in the seventies (see *Company Limited*, 1972) to a greater awareness of the problems of Westernised India. His films were rooted in the tradition of the humanist documentary, influenced by the social concern of Italian neo-realists, and inspired by the natural lyricism of a director like Jean Renoir. Other key films: *The Music Room* (1958), *Charulata* (1964), *Days and Nights in the Forest* (1970), *The Middle Man* (1976), *The Chess Players* (1977) and *The Home and the World* (1984).

Reed, Sir Carol (1906–76)

Reed's reputation as one of the key directors of post-war British cinema rests on a small number of films: the Expressionist, *Odd Man Out* (1947), the last day-in-the-life of an IRA man on the run, and two adaptations of Graham Greene stories, *The Fallen Idol* (1948) and *The Third Man* (1949). Overall his films are notable for a self-effacing craftsmanship, a sympathy with the world of children, and a fascination with confrontations between innocence and experience. He won an Oscar for *Oliver!* (1968). Other key films include *Outcast of the Islands* (1951), one of the cinema's best adaptations of Conrad; and *The Man Between* (1953), using its post-war Berlin setting less evocatively than post-war Vienna in *The Third Man* but a gripping human drama nonetheless.

Renoir, Jean (1899–1979)

A career spanning nearly fifty years included one of the first great dramas to be shot entirely on location, *Toni*, made with a largely non-professional cast in the South of France in 1935; two magnificent performances from Michel Simon, in *La Chienne* (1931) and *Boudu Sauve Des Eaux* (1932); a period funded by the Left-wing Popular Front that produced the film about a workers' cooperative, *Le Crime de Monsieur Lange* (1935); and a forties and fifties output as an exile in Hollywood of considerable merit, including *The Southerner* of 1945. These would be enough to mark Renoir out as an all-time cinema great even were it not for his two pre-

Second-World-War masterpieces, *La Grande Illusion* (1937),a drama set in a POW camp, and the matchless *La Regle du Jeu* of 1939. This savage and frequently hilarious drama of love, class-antagonism, mixed identity, and the ambiguous corruption of aristocratic style so quickly achieved recognition as a masterpiece that it requires an effort now to remind outselves that it was banned on first release, so clearly was its scathing criticism of French society recognised.

Resnais, Alain (b. 1922)

Resnais began as a documentarist, and made his first feature film in 1959—*Hiroshima Mon Amour*, from a screenplay by the novelist Marguerite Duras. *Hiroshima*'s concern with the interaction of time, place and memory was taken up and amplified in *Last Year in Marienbad* (1961), where there is no reassuring continuity of character or coherence of time or space other than that imposed ambiguously, from moment to moment by the "eternal present" of the screen. Speculation about *Marienbad* reached quasi-metaphysical heights that have frequently tended to obscure the dazzling frozen eroticism of its *mise-en-scene*, its masterful exploitation of the dreamlike aspect of film-watching, and the performances of Georgio Albertazzi and Delphine Seyrig. Memory and imagination have continued to be important preoccupations in his work, and he remains one of the great "modernist" innovators of contemporary cinema, continually exploring new areas of expression. Key films: *Night and Fog* (1956), *Muriel* (1963), *Providence* (1977) and *L'Amour a Mort* (1984).

Rosi, Francesco (b. 1922)

Rosi began as an assistant to Luchino Visconti and is perhaps best known as the maker of the Placido Domingo film of *Carmen* (1984). But his natural home is the world of political corruption and paranoia, and no modern film-maker can match him for his trenchant critique of the institutions of power. His most important films in this vein are *Salvatore Giuliano* (1961), *Hands Over the City* (1963), *The Mattei Affair* (1972). *Illustrious Corpses* (1976), *Christ Stopped at Eboli* (1979) and *Three Brothers* (1981).

Rosselini, Roberto (1906–77)

A key figure in the Italian neo-realist movement, whose early films were made on shoestring budgets and in often difficult conditions (see *Rome, Open City*, 1945, about the anti-Fascist Resistance, shot when Mussolini's troops were still occupying Rome). *Voyage in Italy* (1953), in its open-endedness and preoccupation with George Sanders' and Ingrid Bergman's fluctuating senses of cultural alienation, foreshadowed the hesitant psychological explorations of Antonioni. Other key films: *Germany Year Zero* (1948), *Stromboli* (1949) and *The Rise of Louis XIV* (1966).

Rossen, Robert (1908–66)

One of the most socially aware of Hollywood directors who made his mark in the late 1940s with a hard-hitting boxing saga *Body and Soul* (1947), which was actually an allegory of capitalist corruption, and the Oscar-winning *All the King's Men* (1949), an indictment of creeping political Fascism. But then, hounded by the House UnAmerican Activities Committee for his Communist affiliations, he finally recanted and named names. He was able to work again but became, according to friends, a haunted, withdrawn individual. But his last two films were remarkable returns to form: a study of character and courage around the pool table, *The Hustler* (1961), and a study of madness, *Lilith* (1964), which was condemned on its first release but has gained an underground reputation as one of the most lyrical films of the American cinema.

Sautet, Claude (b. 1924)

Highly regarded French director who began as a screenwriter and who has belatedly secured recognition as a subtle anatomist of human behaviour through the international success of *Un Coeur en Hiver—A Heart in Winter* (1993) and *Nelly and M. Arnaud* (1995). Other key films: *Les Choses de la*

Vie—The Things of Life (1970), *Cesar et Rosalie* (1972), *Une Histoire Simple—A Simple Story* (1978).

Scorsese, Martin (b. 1942)

Arguably the most exciting of modern American film-makers. His movies are notable for their restless camera movement which reflects the inner tension of the characters. He has collaborated particularly closely with actor Robert De Niro, forging the most important actor-director partnership in American film since Brando and Kazan in the 1950s. Together they have made emotionally lacerating films about troubled masculinity and with a religious sense of redemption. Sometimes criticised for misogyny, Scorsese's films are nonetheless the most disturbing and challenging of contemporary mainstream cinema. Key films: *Mean Streets* (1973), *Taxi Driver* (1976), *Raging Bull* (1980), *The King of Comedy* (1983), *After Hours* (1985), *Goodfellas* (1990) *Cape Fear* (1991), *The Age of Innocence* (1993), *Casino* (1995) and *Kundun* (1997).

Siegel, Don (1912–91)

Siegel learnt his craft as head of montage at Warners before gaining a reputation on low budget thrillers such as *Riot in Cell Block 11* (1954), *Baby Face Nelson* (1957) and *The Line Up* (1958), that combined sharp observation of the social outsider with a real flair for staging violent action. The sci-fi classic *Invasion of the Body Snatchers* (1956) and a brilliant re-make of *The Killers* (1964) cemented his cult status, and his career achieved a decisive upturn through his association on five films with Clint Eastwood, notably on *Dirty Harry* (1971), where they created arguably the most controversial anti-hero of postwar cinema. Other key films: *Hell is for Heroes* (1962), *Madigan* (1968), *The Beguiled* (1971), *The Shootist* (1976), *Escape from Alcatraz* (1979).

Siodmak, Robert (1900–73)

Siodmak made his directing debut on the low budget German film, *Menschen am Sontag- People on Sunday* (1929), a work that has become famous for also launching the careers of directors Billy Wilder and Fred Zinnemann and cameraman Eugene Schufftan. Like them, Siodmak moved to Hollywood, and he did his best work during the 1940s, making a number of fatalistic, visually gloomy dramas that are acknowledged as classics of film noir or Grand Guignol suspense: *Phantom Lady* (1944), *The Spiral Staircase* (1945), *The Killers* (1946), *Cry of the City* (1948), *Criss Cross* (1949).

Sirk, Douglas (1900–87)

Long regarded as a curiosity, a Danish expatriate whose melodramas, richly shot and distinguished by narrative flamboyance, were treated with mild condescension. *Written on the Wind* (1956) was among the first to gain serious acceptance, with its dramatisation of the conflicts within a wealthy oil family whose problems (alcoholism, instability, sexual promiscuity) were sympathetically presented in a highly-coloured style that still managed to eschew portentousness or heavy realism. His other works, notably *All That Heaven Allows* (1955) and *Imitation of Life* (1959), also began to receive more serious and sympathetic treatment as ironic and subversive critiques of middle-class America: they had a profound influence on the work of Fassbinder. Other key films: *There's Always Tomorrow* (1956), *Tarnished Angels* (1957) and *A Time to Love and A Time to Die* (1958).

Spielberg, Steven (b. 1947)

The most successful director in the history of cinema, notably for four films: *Jaws* (1975), *Close Encounters of the Third Kind* (1977), *E.T.—the Extra-Terrestrial* (1982) and *Jurassic Park* (1993). His films are basically about ordinary people in extraordinary situations, and he directs these with a witty eye for the mores of American suburbia, a tremendous flair for suspense, and an unusually sympathetic presentation of the relationships between mothers and children. Recently a new maturity has come into his work with *The Color Purple* (1985), *Empire of the Sun* (1987) and *Schindler's List* (1993), his unexpected powerful film

of the holocaust. Other key films: *Duel* (1971), *The Sugarland Express* (1974), *Raiders of the Lost Ark* (1981), *Amistad* (1997) and *Saving Private Ryan* (1998). *See also* **W29**.

Stevens, George (1904–75)

Beginning his career as a cameraman on Laurel and Hardy shorts, Stevens' early reputation as a director was in comedy: *Woman of the Year* (1942) and *The More the Merrier* (1943). But his war experience, which included being part of the American force that liberated Dachau, changed his sensibility: comedy receded and his films became full of a feeling of tragic sacrifice. *The Diary of Anne Frank* (1959) is his memorial to the war dead. His own movie monument is probably a trio of films that encapsulates his sympathy for the outsider and constitutes his epic reassessment of the American Dream: *A Place in the Sun* (1951), *Shane* (1953), and *Giant* (1956). Other key films: *Alice Adams* (1935), *Gunga Din* (1939), *Talk of the Town* (1942), *I Remember Mama* (1948) and *The Greatest Story Ever Told* (1965).

Stone, Oliver (b. 1946)

Vietnam vet turned polemicist director. He turned his Army experience into compelling cinema in *Platoon* (1986) and *Born on the Fourth of July* (1989), for which he won directing Oscars, and his bio-pics of *JFK* (1991) and *Nixon* (1995) were powerfully paranoid assaults on the American political system. Often derided for the extreme views and excessive violence of his films, Stone is nonetheless a provocative presence in modern cinema. Other key films: *Salvador* (1985), *Wall Street* (1987), *Natural Born Killers* (1995).

Sturges, John (1911–92)

One of the finest directors of westerns during one of the genre's golden eras, the 1950s. His masterpiece is *Bad Day at Black Rock* (1955), which is both modern western and suspense thriller, and his other fine contributions to the genre include: *Escape from Fort Bravo* (1954), *Gunfight at the O.K. Corral* (1957), *The Law and Jake Wade* (1958), *Last Train from Gun Hill* (1959), and *The Magnificent Seven* (1960).

Sturges, Preston (1898–1959)

One of the first great writer-directors of the sound era in Hollywood, Sturges sold his screenplay *The Great McGinty* (1940) to Paramount for ten dollars on the condition he was allowed to direct. It was the first of eight comedies he wrote and directed within four years, each of which was interesting, some of which—*The Lady Eve* (1941), *Sullivan's Travels* (1942), *Palm Beach Story* (1942)—are classics. His comedies are distinguished by a frantic pace, tremendous ingenuity of dialogue and situation, and an air of shrill desperation. His characters comprise hapless millionaires, seductive gold-diggers and frustrated inventors, all whipped together in a sustained assault on what Sturges saw as all-American sacred cows—politics, motherhood, small-town life, the obsession with success. It is not surprising that his talent burnt out, but for a while his creative flame flared as brilliantly as anyone's.

Tarkovsky, Andrey (1932–86)

The greatest Soviet film-maker since Eisenstein— and the resemblance ends there. Tarkovsky found his inspiration not in the spirit of the Russian Revolution but in the spirituality of the classic Russian novel, and the questions his films posed were not about the nature of political power but about the possibilities of personal salvation. This inevitably brought him into conflict with the Soviet authorities, who disliked the unsocialist, surreal, avant-garde qualities in films such as *Andrei Rublev* (1966) and *Mirror* (1974). They also took exception to Tarkovsky's thinly concealed allegory of the struggles of the artist in a repressive society. His last films were made in exile, and his final film, *The Sacrifice* (1985), a typically hallucinatory drama about a dream of nuclear holocaust averted, was one of his most movingly accessible and affirmative. A dreamer, a poet, a prophet, Tarkovsky's provocative and challenging thoughts on cinema were published in his book, *Sculpting in Time* (1987). Other key films: *Ivan's Childhood* (1962), *Solaris* (1971), *Stalker* (1979) and *Nostalgia* (1982).

Truffaut, Francois (1932–84)

With Godard, one of the outstanding early names of the so-called French "New Wave". Truffaut's early work reveals a delight in the possibilities of the cinematic medium (notably in evoking situations of emotional fluidity and ambiguity) that is often exhilarating, as in *Shoot the Pianist* (with Charles Aznavour, 1960) and his masterpiece, *Jules et Jim* (1961). This deals with a menage a trois in the France of the beginning of the century, portrayed with tragic irony and a light yet serious treatment of historical and cultural influences on the relationship between Catherine (Jeanne Moreau) and her two lovers, the German Jules and the Frenchman Jim. His first feature film, *The 400 Blows* (1959) drew on his own difficult childhood and delinquent adolescence, and later films like *L'Enfant Sauvage* (1970) also deal sensitively with the world of childhood. He also made films like *Fahrenheit 451* (1965) and *The Bride Wore Black* (1968) in homage to Hitchcock. In the 1970s he made two of his most haunting films on his favourite theme of romantic obsession, *The Story of Adele H* (1975), and *The Green Room* (1978), but he also made one of the most affectionate of all films about film-making, *Day for Night* (1973). Truffaut loved movies and his death left cineastes feeling that they had lost a member of the family.

Vertov, Dziga (1896–1934)

The great documentary director, as Eisenstein was the great feature director, of the early Bolshevik Russian days. His principal work is *The Man with a Movie Camera* (1929), an exhilarating exploration of the relationship between the camera, the person holding it, and the subject-matter being filmed, and an illustration that documentary, propaganda, and artistic accomplishment, are far from incompatible.

Vidor, King (1984–1982)

A pioneer of the cinema, responsible for two of the masterpieces of American silent film, the World War One drama, *The Big Parade* (1925), and the urban realist classic, *The Crowd* (1928). His films of the sound era were less distinguished, curiously at their most impressive when he foresook realism in favour of melodrama. Key films include: *Hellelujah* (1929), *Our Daily Bread* (1934), *Stella Dallas* (1937), *The Citadel* (1938), *Duel in the Sun* (1947), *Ruby Gentry* (1952), *War and Peace* (1956).

Vigo, Jean (1905–34)

A great Surrealist director, whose early death from tuberculosis meant that he produced only two feature films, both masterpieces: *Zero de Conduite* (1933), an account of a rebellion in a repressive boys' school whose fragmentary, night-marish quality (partly a result of the tight conditions under which it was shot) is exceptional, and *L'Atalante* (1934), about a honeymoon on a barge, a haunting blend of lyricism and realism.

Visconti, Luchino (1906–77)

The most emotive and extravagant of the Italian neo-realists. Visconti came to attention with *La Terra Trema* (1948), about Sicilian fishermen; a mixture of tragic fatalism and concern for social change characteristic of Visconti pervades this, as it does the operatic *Rocco and his Brothers* of 1960 and his adaptation of the novel by Lampedusa, *The Leopard* (1963). Aristocrat yet communist, arthouse director who loved working with stars (like Dirk Bogarde and Burt Lancaster), Visconti was a strange mixture of extremes. His films dealt with forbidden passions; tormented heroes imprisoned by the standards of a society they despise; and superficially cultured ways of life in their death-throes. Nobody recreated the past more sumptuously on the screen than Visconti nor photographed doom more voluptuously. Other key films: *Ossessione* (1942), *Senso* (1954), *The Damned* (1969), *Death in Venice* (1971), *Ludwig* (1972) and *Conversation Piece* (1974).

Von Sternberg, Josef (1894–1969)

The supreme exponent of cinema as icon, of the image whose lavish and elaborate composition is its most immediately apparent justification. Yet his work escapes the arid aestheticism this statement might suggest, through its awareness of the central importance of woman as pursuer/pursued and of the symbiosis between man's desire for humiliation and woman's desire to castrate. This makes *The Blue Angel* (1930) the most harrowing of the films Sternberg made with Marlene Dietrich: most exotic is probably *The Devil is a Woman* (1935). Other key films: *Morocco* (1930), *Shanghai Express* (1932) and *The Scarlet Empress* (1934).

Von Stroheim, Erich (1885–1957)

"By God I told them the truth" said Stroheim of his classic film *Greed* (1923). Unfortunately for MGM, he told it at excessive length, and the film was cut from 42 to 10 reels in length. Stroheim's career as director never recovered from this. But John Grierson was to call him "the director of directors", for his unflinching realism and fanatical attention to detail. Billy Wilder thought he was ten years ahead of his time, though Stroheim contradicted him: "No—twenty". Key films: *Foolish Wives* (1922), *Merry-Go-Round* (1923) and *Queen Kelly* (1928).

Wajda, Andrzej (b. 1926)

Perhaps the most important film-maker Poland has ever produced. Wajda grew up in Poland during the Nazi occupation and his famous trilogy—*A Generation* (1955), *Kanal* (1956) and *Ashes and Diamonds* (1958)—records the wartime suffering and courage and the scramble for political power that followed the liberation. *Ashes and Diamonds*, in particular, with its charismatic performance by Zbigniew Cybulski, exemplifies Wajda's fascination with heroes who refuse to follow the tide of history and attempt to shape their own destinies through extreme action. For a time, history took second place to psychology and symbolism in his work. But in the mid 1970s, he returned head-on to contemporary issues, tackling the theme of censorship, political blackmail and the film-maker's responsibilities in *Man of Marble* (1976), and celebrating the rise of Solidarity in *Man of Iron* (1980) in a tone of prophetically precarious optimism. Wajda's films have often been set in transitional periods where one era has died and another is struggling to be born. His own career has also been subject to the turbulent tides of history, facing censorship, exile and rejection, but his achievements stand as an inspiring example of artistic talent surviving against difficult odds. Other key films: *Innocent Sorcerers* (1961), *Everything for Sale* (1968), *The Wedding* (1973), *The Conductor* (1980) and *Korczak* (1988).

Welles, Orson (1915–85)

Welles made his debut with *Citizen Kane* in 1941; over fifty years later, it is still a popular choice as the best film ever. Innovatory in film language (in its bold and extensive use of "deep-focus"—the camera plunging into the imaginary "depth" of the screen), suggestive in its plot (about a tycoon, modelled on William Randolph Hearst, whose public success is seen as a remedy for private unhappiness), electric in the quality of its camera-work and ensemble acting, and with its finale (the "secret" of Kane's life—the name of his confiscated childhood sledge, Rosebud) the most ironically well-kept secret in cinema history, the film succeeded on so many levels that hind-sight almost suggests Welles's subsequent career had to be an anti-climax. He has filmed Shakespeare (*Chimes at Midnight*, 1966), Kafka (*The Trial*, 1963) and a "documentary" about forgeries (*F. for Fake*, 1975), none to the effect of *Kane*. Nevertheless the qualities of his other films should not be overlooked: the tenderness of *The Magnificent Ambersons* (1942), the *film noir* virtuosity of *Lady from Shanghai* (1948), the magisterial study of police corruption in *Touch of Evil* (1958). It is tempting to see *Kane* as a prophetic study of promise unfulfilled, and Welles's career certainly had more than its share of disappointments and frustrations. But he still remains a giant of the cinema, probing themes of power and corruption with that virtuoso camera style that he said "describes that sense of vertigo, uncertainty, lack of stability, that melange of movement and tension that is our universe".

Wenders, Wim (b. 1945)

One of the major figures of the "New German Cinema" of the 1970s, cooler and less didactic than Fassbinder, more streetwise and less anti-American than Herzog. His ambivalent response to America's "Coca-colonisation" of Europe was explored in *The American Friend* (1977), which had guest roles for Nicholas Ray and Samuel Fuller; and films such as *The Goalkeeper's Fear of the Penalty* (1972) and *Kings of the Road* (1976) elaborated his interest in the alienation of the modern environment and the rootlessness of modern man. Wenders' films commonly start from place rather than plot and it is no surprise that his biggest international success to date is *Paris Texas* (1984), a film as remarkable for its disorienting landscape as its characters or story.

Wilder, Billy (b. 1906)

"It's not important that a director knows how to write," said Billy Wilder, "but it is important that he knows how to read." Fleeing from Nazi Europe and becoming a Hollywood screenwriter for, among others, Ernst Lubitsch, Wilder became a director in order to protect his own scripts. *Double Indemnity* (1944), *The Lost Weekend* (1945) and *Sunset Boulevard* (1950) were wonderfully macabre demonstrations of his talents, and films like *Some Like it Hot* (1959) and *The Apartment* (1960) consolidated his reputation as the sharpest satirist in Hollywood, with an unusually mordant view of human nature that did not, however, preclude the possibility of redemption. *Sabrina* (1954) and *Avanti!* (1972) show the melting of American materialism by European romanticism. His care for structure, his unceasing verbal wit and the intelligence of his character development make Wilder's overall achievement the equal of any Hollywood director's of the sound era. Other key films: *Ace in the Hole* (1951), *Stalag 17* (1953), *Witness for the Prosecution* (1957), *One, Two, Three* (1961), *The Fortune Cookie* (1966), *The Private Life of Sherlock Holmes* (1970) and *Fedora* (1978).

Wyler, William (1902–81)

One of the master craftsmen of Hollywood film. As well as winning three Oscars for himself (for *Mrs. Miniver*, 1942; *The Best Years of Our Lives*, 1946; and *Ben-Hur*, 1959), Wyler elicited more than a dozen Oscar-winning performances from his casts. Although he could handle the epic canvas as well as anyone, his forte was for drama in a confined setting and struggles for territorial advantage in a marriage or family. *The Little Foxes*, (1941), *The Heiress* (1949) and *Carrie* (1952) are all masterpieces of domestic claustrophobia. Whilst his heroes

tended to be withdrawn figures, needing to be convinced of the necessity for action (like the pacifist hero of *The Big Country*, (1958)), his heroines are more often dynamic creatures, kicking against the constraints of a masculine world. No wonder he was Bette Davis's favourite director and directed her in some of her best films: *Jezebel* (1938), *The Letter* (1940) and *The Little Foxes*. Although recurrent patterns and themes are discernible in his films (unrequited love, class confrontations between the complacent and the envious), he tended, like Huston, to subordinate his personality to the requirements of the story. For this reason, he has often been underestimated by *auteurist* critics. But if a great director is simply someone who has made a number of great films, Wyler was a great director. Other key films: *Dodsworth* (1936), *Wuthering Heights* (1939), *Roman Holiday* (1952) and *The Children's Hour* (1961).

Yimou, Zhang (b. 1950)

One of the key figures of modern Chinese cinema, an actor and cameraman (on Chen Kaige's *Yellow Earth* and *The Big Parade*) before turning to direction. Behind the sumptuous visual surfaces of his films lurk some telling observations on politics and patriarchy that have sometimes antagonised the Chinese authorities. His films have also made a major star of his leading actress Gong Li, whose characterisation often and excitingly subvert the stereotype of female submissiveness. Key films: *Red Sorghum* (1988), *Ju Dou* (1990), *Raise the Red Lantern* (1991), *The Story of Qui Ju* (1992), *Shanghai Triad* (1995).

Zinnemann, Fred (1907–97)

Born in Vienna, Zinnemann came to America in 1929, but his career did not really take off until *The Search* in 1948, a story of European children orphaned by the war and which presaged a number of his films about the impact and aftermath of war. But it was the western *High Noon* (1952) that established both Zinnemann's reputation and his fundamental theme: that of individual conscience. At considerable personal risk but on a point of principle, a character takes a stand against a community or institution that wishes him to compromise and conform: it is the theme also of *From Here to Eternity* (1953), *The Nun's Story* (1959) and *A Man for All Seasons* (1966). Unusually for Hollywood, these were dramas of reaction, not action, and with melancholy rather than happy endings. Their critical and commercial success testified to Zinnemann's skill at popularising complex themes without compromising his vision. Other key films: *The Seventh Cross* (1944), *Act of Violence* (1949), *Member of the Wedding* (1952), *Day of the Jackal* (1973) and *Julia* (1977). He published his autobiography in 1991.

3. FAMOUS SCREEN ACTORS AND ACTRESSES

Andrews, Julie (b. 1935)

The archetype of screen virtue who reached her peak of popularity in the mid-1960s with *Mary Poppins* (1964) and *The Sound of Music* (1965), in both of which her "English rose" image and pure singing voice enchanted audiences. She has since made a number of films for her second husband, director Blake Edwards, but without the same success.

Arbuckle, "Fatty" (1887–1933)

Superb silent comedian whose career was ruined when accused of the rape and murder of a starlet Virginia Rappe at a wild Hollywood party in 1921. Although completely cleared of all charges, Arbuckle was never allowed to appear on the screen again (the whole story is told in David Yallop's book, *The Day the Laughter Stopped*). Buster Keaton, who owed his start in movies to Arbuckle, said he learnt everything about film from him.

Astaire, Fred (1899–1987)

"Can't act, slightly bald, can dance a little", was the verdict of the screen test of Astaire, who, in partnership with Ginger Rogers, was to become the most stylish screen dancer in Hollywood history. He starred in such classic musicals as *Top Hat* (1935), *Swing Time* (1936), *Easter Parade* (1948) and *Funny Face* (1956). Turned to straight acting in his later career with such effect that Spencer Tracy felt threatened and sent the following wire to his friend: "You stop acting or I'll start dancing!"

Bacall, Lauren (b. 1924)

Bacall was one of the first examples of Hollywood's skill at playing on-and-off screen personas off against each other. Opposite Humphrey Bogart in *To Have and Have Not* (1944), she enchanted him on the screen as she did in real life while the film was being shot. (They were later to be married.) Her performance there is a remarkably knowing and ironic one (particularly in the famous scene where she tells Bogart how to whistle for her if he wants anything), and she was to play similar roles opposite him in *The Big Sleep* (1946), *Dark Passage* (Delmer Daves, 1947) and *Key Largo* (John Huston, 1948). Although she was never really able to repeat her success with Bogart, her persona in these films is interesting as a contrast to the submissive view of women often purveyed by Hollywood. She has been a great survivor and was only recently nominated for an Oscar for her performance in Barbra Streisand's *A Mirror has Two Faces* (1996).

Bardot, Brigitte (b. 1934)

"Created" by her then-husband Roger Vadim in *And God Created Woman* (1956), Bardot epitomised a certain popular view of French female sexuality—poutingly sensual, sporting a St. Tropez suntan and little else besides, as ardent and capricious in her off-screen romances as in those for the cameras. In Julien Duvivier's *La Femme et le Pantin* (1958) and Vadim's *Warrior's Rest* (1962) she exploited this role to perfection; but she did show that she had some acting ability in *Le Mepris*, made for Jean-Luc Godard in 1963, in *Viva Maria* (1965) for Louis Malle, and in *La Verité* (1960) for Henri-Georges Clouzot. Retired from the screen to devote herself to ecological issues.

Beatty, Warren (b. 1937)

Many people think of Beatty's career as beginning with *Bonnie and Clyde* (Arthur Penn, 1967), in which his performance as the debonair yet sexually insecure bandit Clyde steals the show. But he sprang to prominence as early as 1961 (Elia Kazan's *Splendour in the Grass*), and has appeared infrequently, but always to great effect, ever since, his best post-Bonnie performance perhaps being the gambler McCabe in Altman's *McCabe and Mrs. Miller* (1971). Directorial ambitions have preoccupied him more than acting recently, and he won an Oscar for the direction of *Reds* (1981).

Belmondo, Jean-Paul (b. 1933)

Belmondo sprang to fame with his performance as the confusedly amoral Michel Poiccard in Godard's *Breathless* (1959). This earned him recognition as one of the first "anti-heroes" of the European cinema, concerned with discovering himself through action and, in his second masterpiece for Godard, *Pierrot le Fou* (1965), contemplation as well. Both films featured Belmondo "betrayed", ostensibly by the women he chose (Jean Seberg and Anna Karina respectively), but as much by his own insecure openness. His later work (including *Borsalino* for Deray in 1970, and *Stavisky* for Resnais in 1974) tended to be glossier and more spectacular, to the detriment of the "anti-hero" persona, though he scored a big personal success in Claude Lelouch's recent updating of *Les Miserables* (1994).

Bergman, Ingrid (1915–82)

Enticed, like Greta Garbo, from Sweden to Hollywood at the end of the thirties, Bergman became one of Hollywood's star actresses, particularly in exotic "European" roles like that of Humphrey Bogart's lost *grand amour* in Michael Curtiz's *Casablanca* (1943) and in three films for Hitchcock, *Spellbound* (1945), *Notorious* (1946) and *Under Capricorn* (1949). She went on to freelance in Europe in the fifties, notably for Roberto Rosselini (whom she married), in neo-realist classics such as *Stromboli* (1950) and *Voyage in Italy* (1953). Made a triumphant comeback to Hollywood in *Anastasia* (1956), and in her later years had great success in *The Murder on the Orient Express* (1974) for which she won her third Oscar and in Ingmar Bergman's *Autumn Sonata* (1978).

Bogarde, Sir Dirk (1921–99)

It takes an effort to remind ourselves that the Bogarde destroyed by his death-wish passion for a young boy in Visconti's *Death in Venice* (1971) began his acting career in British comedy and melodrama and acquired real prominence as the accident-prone medical student in the "Doctor" films of the late fifties. His fine performance as a homosexual barrister in *Victim* (1960) marked a turning point

and Joseph Losey exploited his dramatic acting talent in *The Servant* (1963), which played off his British reserve against a highly-charged situation as Losey was also to do in *Accident* (1967). The association with Visconti confirmed him as one of the screen's subtlest and most accomplished actors. Semi-retired since his performance in Resnais's *Providence* (1977), he later made an effective comeback in Bertrand Tavernier's *These Foolish Things* (1990).

Bogart, Humphrey (1899–1957)

One of the all-time superstars. Bogart began as a stage actor and graduated to screen stardom with one of his theatre roles, the psychopathic gangster in Mayo's *The Petrified Forest* (1936). He became famous in the forties as an "outsider" figure, caught up in corrupt or devious situations from which he tried to stay aloof through a basic decency masquerading as hard-bitten cynicism. *Casablanca* (Michael Curtiz, 1943) revealed the persona to have a soft heart, in the scenes where he drinks to forget his love for Ingrid Bergman—or rather to remember it—and where he sacrifices it in the airport scene at the end with the immortal: "Here's looking at you, kid". For Howard Hawks he made *To Have and Have Not* in 1944 and *The Big Sleep* in 1946, both with Lauren Bacall and both exploiting the same persona. Small wonder that fifties anti-hero Belmondo elevated him to a god in *Breathless* (Godard, 1959), as did Woody Allen in a different way in *Play it Again, Sam* (1972). Closely associated with director John Huston, for whom he made six films, including *The Maltese Falcon* (1941), *The Treasure of the Sierra Madre* (1948) and the film for which he won his Oscar, *The African Queen* (1951).

Bow, Clara (1905–65)

Known as the "It" girl because of her enormously popular personal success in the film *It* (1927). Epitomised the "Roaring 20s" during the silent era but her career then foundered because of sound, scandals and mental illness. She was the Monroe of her time: a sad fate.

Brando, Marlon (b. 1924)

Brando came to the cinema from the stage, a leading proponent of the "Method" school of acting which relied upon naturalistic empathy with the part rather than careful professional stylisation. Laconic violence, often tending to the inarticulate, was his early stock-in-trade, exemplified in *A Streetcar Named Desire* (1951) and *On The Waterfront* (1954), both directed by Elia Kazan. Other rebels vied with Brando in the late fifties and sixties, and his career went into an eclipse from which it was rescued by two very different, but remarkable, performances as men aware that they have passed their personal peak—the *Mafioso* Don Corleone in Coppola's *The Godfather* (1972), and the self-loathing American in Bertolucci's *Last Tango in Paris* (1973). Has since tended to confine himself to expensive guest performances in movies like *Superman* (1980), though he gave a superb character performance as a Scottish liberal lawyer in the anti-apartheid drama, *A Dry White Season* (1989). Published a much publicised autobiography in 1994.

Brooks, Louise (1906–85)

Magnetic star whose film fame rests mainly on one charismatic performance: as Lulu in G. W. Pabst's *Pandora's Box* (1929). She retired from the screen in the early 1930s and led a reclusive life, though briefly surfaced to write a marvellous book of memoirs, *Lulu in Hollywood*.

Burton, Richard (1925–84)

Burton was initially a leading stage Shakespearian, but better-known to the film-going public for his flamboyant romance with Elizabeth Taylor and his resonant performances in costume-dramas (*Cleopatra* for Joseph L. Mankiewicz in 1963) and macho action-dramas (Hathaway's *Raid on Rommel*, 1971). His performance as the verbally aggressive college professor in Mike Nichols's *Who's Afraid of Virginia Woolf?* (1966) marked him out as a great screen actor, as did his performance in *The Spy who came in from the Cold* (1966). He was nominated seven times for the coveted Oscar without winning: his last performance was as the sinister interrogator O'Brien in the 1984 screen adaptation of George Orwell's *1984*.

Cagney, James (1899–1986)

Pugnacious leading man who started out as a dancer but whose energy and vitality made him ideal for the dynamic gangster movies of the 1930s, such as *Public Enemy* (1931), *Angels with Dirty Faces* (1938) and *The Roaring Twenties* (1939). Won an Oscar for *Yankee Doodle Dandy* (1942) but his most memorable characterisation was probably as the psychopathic, mother-fixated Cody Jarrett in Raoul Walsh's *White Heat* (1949).

Chaplin, Sir Charles (1889–1977)

Still the most famous film star and director in the history of movies. His creation of the "little man"—the wistful tramp figure who fantasises his way out of the hardships of life—achieved success on an unprecedented scale and effectively made the transition from silent shorts to feature-length films, the most famous being *The Gold Rush* (1925). He fought hard against the coming of sound, refusing to use any apart from music and sound effects in *City Lights* (1931), where the blend of slapstick and suspense was particularly well achieved. His later films, like *Modern Times* (1936), *The Great Dictator* (1940) and *Monsieur Verdoux* (1947) were infused with his socialist political sympathies which set him at odds with the American authorities and led to his exile in 1952. His reputation has plummeted since his death, but he remains the most significant and creative film comic of the century. A recent bio-pic *Chaplin* (1992) has been made by Sir Richard Attenborough, starring Robert Downey Jnr.

Christie, Julie (b. 1941)

Beautiful British actress who shot to international stardom with her performance in *Darling* (1965) and *Doctor Zhivago* (1965). Her best films include *Petulia* (1968), *The Go-Between* (1971), *McCabe and Mrs. Miller* (1971) and *Don't Look Now* (1973). In recent years, she has developed into a character actress of stature, particularly with her performances in *Hamlet* (1996) and *Afterglow* (1997).

Clift, Montgomery (1920–66)

Clift now enjoys a vogue as one of the great Hollywood victims, destroyed by drink, pills and inability to come to terms with his homosexuality. This litany should not obscure the fact that he was a tremendously gifted screen actor, as a tormented priest in *I Confess* (Hitchcock, 1952), as a cowboy opposite John Wayne in Hawk's *Red River* (1948), or with Clark Gable and Marilyn Monroe in that most macabre of pictures (it marked the end of virtually all its stars' careers), John Huston's *The Misfits* of 1960. Other key performances include *A Place in the Sun* (Stevens, 1951), *From Here to Eternity* (Zinnemann, 1953) and *Freud* (Huston, 1962). Speaking of his tormented personality, Marilyn Monroe once commented: "He's the only person I know who's in worse shape than I am."

Cooper, Gary (1901–61)

Cooper embodied quintessential American decency—not blustering like Wayne nor cynical like Bogart, the decent lad up from the country putting sophisticates to shame in *Mr. Deeds Goes to Town* (Frank Capra, 1936), the pacifist soldier in Hawks's *Sergeant York* (1941), or—his best-known role—the lone sheriff in Zinnemann's *High Noon* (1952).

Connery, Sean (b. 1930)

Connery achieved fame as the first and best of the screen James Bonds, but has been recognised as one of the best character-actor stars of modern cinema. Won an overdue Oscar for *The Untouchables* (1987) and has also given fine character performances in such films as Hitchcock's *Marnie* (1964), *The Hill* (1965), *The Man Who Would be King* (1975), *Robin and Marian* (1976) and *The Name of the Rose* (1987).

Costner, Kevin (b. 1955)

He had one line in *Frances* (1982) and his part in *The Big Chill* (1983) ended up on the cutting room floor. Yet within seven years, Kevin Costner had become one of Hollywood's biggest stars, shining in *The Untouchables* (1987), *Field of Dreams* (1989), and particularly the epic western *Dances with Wolves* (1990), a personal project that won him a directing Oscar. Since then his films have tended to be more grandiose than substantial.

Crawford, Joan (1906–77)

The leading unhappy-in-love female star of the thirties and early forties (as in Cukor's *The Women* of 1939), Crawford won an Oscar for *Mildred Pierce* (Michael Curtiz, 1945). In later life a successful and immensely wealthy businesswoman, she was better known perhaps as a star than for any individual performances, and as the subject of her daughter's sensational memoir, *Mommie Dearest*, filmed in 1981 with Faye Dunaway as Crawford. Played masochist to Bette Davis's sadist in the gleefully grotesque *Whatever Happened to Baby Jane?* (1962).

Cruise, Tom (b. 1962)

Of the group of young American actors who shot to fame in the 1980s and were known collectively as the "brat pack", Cruise has proved to be the most durable, combining good looks with career shrewdness. He has had his glossy hits like *Top Gun* (1986) and *Mission Impossible* (1995) but he has also, as learning experience, played unselfish supporting roles to two Oscar-winning performances—Paul Newman's in *The Color of Money* (1986) and Dustin Hoffman's in *Rain Man* (1988). The benefit of such experience can be seen in his own Oscar-nominated performances in *Born on the Fourth of July* (1989) and *Jerry Maguire* (1996).

Davis, Bette (1908–89)

"Nobody's as good as Bette when she's bad" was the slogan coined for Bette Davis, who excelled at playing dynamic or queen-bitch heroines. Among her major screen performances were three for William Wyler, *Jezebel* (1938), *The Letter* (1940) and *The Little Foxes* (1941), and when her career seemed destined for oblivion in the late 1940s, she returned with one of the classic characterisations of the screen, as the dominating actress Margot Channing in *All About Eve* (1950). Her autobiography *The Lonely Life* (1962) is one of the frankest and most intelligent of any screen star.

Day, Doris (b. 1924)

Pure, wholesome singing star who achieved her peak of popularity in the 1950s and early 1960s, particularly in a series of romantic comedies she made with Rock Hudson, including *Pillow Talk* (1959), *Lover Come Back* (1962) and *Send Me No Flowers* (1964). Recently appropriated by the feminists, who admire her screen persona for its career-woman independence and its healthy suspicion of male seductive strategies. Certainly someone who can upstage performers such as James Cagney (in *Love Me or Leave Me*, 1954), James Stewart (in *The Man Who Knew Too Much*, 1956) and Clark Gable (in *Teacher's Pet*, 1958) is no mean actress.

Dean, James (1931–55)

Dean made three starring feature roles before his death in a car crash in 1955. But those three, and particularly *Rebel Without a Cause* for Nicholas Ray in 1955, were enough to establish him as Hollywood's leading rebel (along with Brando—and how fascinating subsequent rivalry between their careers would have been). In *Rebel* Dean showed himself as a gentler, more idealistic figure than Brando, particularly in his "adoption" of the young runaway Sal Mineo. In *East of Eden* (Kazan, 1955), it is again his idealism that leads him to look out his mother, now running a whore-house, with disastrous results. In *Giant* (Stevens, 1956) he is an independent cowboy whose discovery of oil on his land will transform him into an isolated tycoon.

De Niro, Robert (b. 1943)

The finest American screen actor since Brando, noted for the dedication with which he immerses himself in his roles (for example, his gaining sixty pounds in weight to play the role of Jake LaMotta in decline in *Raging Bull*). He has had a particularly important collaboration with director Martin Scorsese, for whom he has turned in some of his finest studies of violent yet tortured masculinity: *Mean Streets* (1973), *Taxi Driver* (1976), *Raging Bull* (1980), *Cape Fear* (1991), *Casino* (1995). Other important films include: *The Godfather Part II* (1974), *The Deer Hunter* (1978).

Dietrich, Marlene (1902–92)

Overnight fame came Dietrich's way when Joseph von Sternberg cast her as the sensuous and manipulative night-club singer Lola in *The Blue Angel* (1930). She manipulates Emil Jannings's school teacher there as Sternberg's camera manipulates her (and us, the spectators), through a sequence of lushly masochistic masterpieces including *The Scarlet Empress* (1934). Her post-Sternberg career diversified into cabaret performance, and her subsequent movies, including *The Flame of New Orleans* for Rene Clair in 1941 and *Rancho Notorious* for Fritz Lang in 1952, did not attain the same heights as her work for Sternberg, though she gave striking performances in two Billy Wilder films, *A Foreign Affair* (1948) and *Witness for the Prosecution* (1957), and a memorable cameo in Welles's *Touch of Evil* (1958).

Douglas, Kirk (b. 1916)

Dimpled-chin he-man of the American screen, who excelled in roles of unscrupulous, ambitious anti-heroes, such as those in *Champion* (1949), *Ace in the Hole* (1951) and *The Bad and the Beautiful* (1952), though a more sensitive and tormented side to his persona is also seen in such films as *Lust for Life* (1955), in which he plays Van Gogh and *Paths of Glory* (1957). The father of successful screen actor and producer, Michael Douglas.

Eastwood, Clint (b. 1930)

Eastwood is in the great tradition of stars like John Wayne and Gary Cooper who projects pure Americanism and rectifies wrongs, though in a more ferocious manner than his predecessors. Became a star for his "Man With No Name" characterisation in Sergio Leone's violent, stylised "Dollars" westerns; and became a superstar after playing the tough cop in *Dirty Harry* (1971). Sometimes attacked for their Fascist overtones, Eastwood's films have also been praised for their strong female roles, Eastwood's willingness to examine his own screen persona, and their engagement with contemporary issues. Eastwood is also a talented director, sometimes starring in his own films (*e.g. The Outlaw Josey Wales*, 1976) and sometimes not (*Bird*, 1988). His revisionist Western *Unforgiven* (1992) was widely acclaimed as a classic and won him a directing "Oscar'.

Fairbanks, Douglas (1883–1939)

The supreme action man of silent cinema, excelling in such features as *The Three Musketeers* (1921), *Robin Hood* (1922) and *The Thief of Bagdad* (1924). Age and sound took their toll of his popularity as did his divorce from Mary Pickford in 1936, after a marriage of sixteen years. But during the silent era, nobody epitomised screen heroism more exuberantly.

Fields, W. C. (1879–1946)

Fields is the polar opposite of Chaplin as a screen comedian, in that, while the "little fellow" courts audience affection, Fields does everything in his drunken, misogynistic, mean, cynical, ill-tempered power to repel it. Through such titles as *Mrs. Wiggs of the Cabbage Patch* (Norman Taurog, 1934) and *Never Give a Sucker an Even Break* (Edward Cline, 1941), he paraded preposterous situations (usually of his own invention), and a battery of dislikes that included wives, children, domestic animals and authority figures. His best films were *It's A Gift* (1935) and *The Bank Dick* (1940). When discovered

on his death-bed reading the Bible, he explained that he was "looking for loopholes".

Finch, Peter (1916–77)

Rugged yet subtle screen performer, who won the British Academy Award four times for his performances in *A Town Like Alice* (1956), *The Trials of Oscar Wilde* (1960), *No Love for Johnnie* (1961) and *Sunday, Bloody Sunday* (1971). He won a posthumous Oscar for his performance in *Network* (1976).

Finney, Albert (b. 1936)

Finney made a big impression with his first screen performances in such films as *Saturday Night and Sunday Morning* (1961) and *Tom Jones* (1963), and was hailed as "a second Olivier". But, unlike Richard Burton, he preferred to eschew screen stardom in favour of theatrical work. The most powerful of his later film performances has been as the drunken Consul in Huston's adaptation of Malcolm Lowry's novel, *Under the Volcano* (1984).

Fonda, Henry (1905–82)

One of the major Hollywood leading men of the late thirties and forties, with distinguished starring roles for Fritz Lang (as the runaway in *You Only Live Once*, 1937) and John Ford (in *Young Mr. Lincoln* and *Drums Along the Mohawk*, both 1939, and *The Grapes of Wrath* (1940). His honest and conscientious stance was just right for the immediate pre- and post-war years. After a lull in his screen career, he made a successful comeback in such films as *Mister Roberts* (1955), *Twelve Angry Men* (1957) and *The Best Man* (1964), and won a long-awaited Oscar for his last film, *On Golden Pond* (1981), in which he co-starred with his daughter Jane.

Fonda, Jane (b. 1937)

Began her career in "sex-symbol" roles—in Hollywood and for her then husband Roger Vadim—that now appear incongruous in the light of her progressive political position (Edward Dmytryk's *Walk on the Wild Side*, 1962; Vadim's *Barbarella*, 1968). Her involvement with the women's movement and anti-Vietnam campaigns took her into such films as *Klute* (Pakula, 1971), where she plays a prostitute who regards herself as "the only truly liberated woman". She won an Oscar for *Klute* and won again later in the decade for *Coming Home* (1978), confirming herself as one of the most accomplished of modern screen actresses.

Ford, Harrison (b. 1942)

Recently voted the world's most popular film star, a well-earned reward for an actor whose career had begun with discouraging slowness. The turning point came with his role as Han Solo in *Star Wars* (1977) and his stardom was augmented when he became Steven Spielberg's Indiana Jones, a characterisation said to be much admired by Burt Lancaster for its difficult combination of athleticism and wit. An accomplished actor in both romantic comedy and complex character roles (*e.g.* in *Witness* and *The Mosquito Coast*), he is liked best by the public as a taciturn action man of the old school, even when, as in his recent film *Air Force One* (1997), he also happens to be President of the United States.

Foster, Jodie (b. 1962)

Child star who has developed into one of the foremost feminist talents of the cinema. Played a precocious moll in the child gangster spoof, *Bugsy Malone* (1976) and then created a furore with her role as an under-age prostitute in *Taxi Driver* (1976), fanned even further when an attempted assassination of President Reagan was said to have been inspired by the gunman's infatuation with Foster's role in that movie. She survived the attendant nororiety to develop into one of the modern screen's most adventurous actresses, winning Oscars for her performances as a rape victim in *The Accused* (1988) and a feisty female investigator in *Silence of the Lambs* (1991). She can direct too.

Gabin, Jean (1904–76)

In many ways Gabin was for the French cinema of the thirties and forties what Gary Cooper or Henry Fonda were for Hollywood—the stoically decent man of the people whose malediction sprang from his very ordinariness. He excelled for two directors in particular: Marcel Carné for whom he played a deserter in *Quai des Brumes* and a workman in *Le Jour se Leve* (1938 and 1939 respectively), both of whom meet violent deaths as a result of falling in love, and Jean Renoir, in whose *La Bete Humaine* (1938) he was an engine-driver vainly struggling against homicidal urges. A less doom-laden performance, but one that revealed his particular strength as an ensemble player as well as a "star", was also for Renoir, as one of the soldiers who escape from a POW camp in *La Grande Illusion* (1937).

Gable, Clark (1901–60)

Gable was Hollywood's number one heartthrob in the years immediately preceding the war. His open-handed cheerfulness and easy-going Americanism now might appear dated and unconvincing, but they bowled over a long list of leading ladies, including Claudette Colbert (in Frank Capra's *It Happened One Night*, 1934) and Vivien Leigh (in the Fleming/Cukor/Wood success *Gone with the Wind*, 1939). He is proof that Hollywood male chauvinism did not need the bullying qualities of a John Wayne to make its mark. He gave perhaps his greatest performance in his last film, *The Misfits* (1960).

Garbo, Greta (1905–90)

A career that lasted only seventeen years and a reclusive retirement combined to create the "Garbo myth", of world-weary, capricious and lonesome sensuality, which must be one of the most potent in cinema history. She moved from Sweden to Hollywood under the aegis of the director Mauritz Stiller in 1926, to become MGM's major star, whose every move was heralded by a barrage of studio publicity (thus, "Garbo talks!" before Clarence Brown's *Anna Christie* in 1930, and "Garbo laughs!" before *Ninotchka*, made for Ernst Lubitsch in 1939). Unlike her romantic co-star in the silent period, John Gilbert, Garbo triumphantly made the transition to talkies, her greatest successes being in *Queen Christina* (1934) and *Camille* (1937). But after the disaster of *Two-Faced Woman* (1941) she retired from the screen.

Garland, Judy (1922–69)

A prominent teenage star who became famous through her performance in *The Wizard of Oz* (Victor Fleming, 1939), where she first performed the song whose soaring yearning was to become her hallmark—"Over the Rainbow". She starred in musicals for her then-husband, Vincente Minnelli (including *Meet Me in St. Louis*, 1944), but the pattern of breakdown, emotional turmoil, and abuse of barbiturates had set in by the beginning of the fifties. Stage appearances and nervous breakdowns between them crowded out her mature film career, though her performance in *A Star is Born* (1954) was a tour-de-force.

Gibson, Mel (b. 1956)

'The most interesting young actor of his period,' said Franco Zeffirelli when casting Mel Gibson as Hamlet. An odd role ostensibly for the star of action extravaganzas like *Mad Max* (1979) and *Lethal Weapon* (1987) but then again, perhaps not: all are heroes unhinged by violent destruction of their family lives and who affect an antic disposition to cope with their torment. Gibson is good at character extremes, as well as being a competent director and a glamour film star of a kind rarely seen since the 1930s. Though actually born in New York, his first film successes were in Australia, but like director Peter Weir, for whom he starred in *Gallipoli* (1981) and *The Year of Living Dangerously* (1983), he moved to Hollywood in the early 1980s and has not looked back.

Gish, Lillian (1896–1993)

The longest career of movie actors—from D. W. Griffith's *An Unseen Enemy* (1912) through to Lindsay Anderson's *The Whales of August* (1987). She radiated innocence for Griffith in *The Birth of a Nation* (1915) and *Intolerance* (1916), before leaving his Biograph company to make more money, first for Inspiration and then for MGM. During the sound era, her screen appearances were intermittent, though she was particularly effective as the brave schoolma'am facing up to Robert Mitchum's demonic preacher in *The Night of the Hunter* (1955). Her performances in Griffith's *Broken Blossoms* (1919) and Victor Seastrom's *The Wind* (1928) are among the greatest of the silent film era.

Grant, Cary (1904–86)

His British origin shows in his debonair style and curious "mid-Atlantic" accent (imitated by Tony Curtis in Billy Wilder's *Some Like it Hot*, 1959). Beneath his gentlemanly urbanity, frenzy, even insanity, never seem far away, which accounts for the matchless ambiguity of his greatest performances—as the suspected wife-murderer in Hitchcock's *Suspicion* (1941), as baiting foil to Mae West in Wesley Ruggles's *I'm No Angel* (1933), as advertising man pursued across America by spies in *North by North-West* (Hitchcock, 1959), and above all the victim of the insecurity that stems from sex-stereotyping in the magnificent comedies he made opposite various leading ladies for Howard Hawks—*Bringing Up Baby* (with Katharine Hepburn, 1938), *His Girl Friday* (with Rosalind Russell, 1940), and *I Was a Male War Bride* (with Ann Sheridan, 1949). Small wonder that he won an Oscar in 1970 for "sheer brilliance".

Guinness, Sir Alec (b. 1914)

Guinness came to prominence as a screen actor in the great Ealing comedies, notably *Kind Hearts and Coronets* (1949), *The Man in the White Suit* (1951), *The Lavender Hill Mob* (1952), and *The Ladykillers* (1955). He also developed a close working relationship with David Lean, and won an Oscar for his superb performance in Lean's *The Bridge on the River Kwai* (1957). An actor of unobtrusive subtlety and infinite resource, he achieved his biggest popular success in *Star Wars* (1977) but more representative of his skills are his masterly characterisations in such films as *Tunes of Glory* (1960) and *Little Dorrit* (1987).

Hepburn, Audrey (1929–93)

Enchanting elfin actress who won an Oscar in her first starring role, *Roman Holiday* (Wyler, 1953). She then proceeded to bewitch some of Hollywood's most eminent senior citizens—Humphrey Bogart in *Sabrina* (1954), Gary Cooper in *Love in the Afternoon* (1957), Cary Grant in *Charade* (1963), Rex Harrison in *My Fair Lady* (1964). An adept comedienne, she also proved herself a formidable dramatic actress in *The Nun's Story* (1959), *The Children's Hour* (1961) and *Robin and Marian* (1976). She then virtually retired though Spielberg cast her appropriately as an angel in *Always* (1989).

Hepburn, Katharine (b. 1909)

The most intelligent and astringent of all screen comediennes—if not all screen actresses. She remained resolutely outside the mould of female stardom, regarded for years as box-office poison and relying on her mind rather than her body for impact. Her most celebrated films are those made with her long-time off-screen lover, Spencer Tracy—notably *Adam's Rib* and *Pat and Mike* for George Cukor (1949 and 1952 respectively), and *State of the Union* for Frank Capra in 1948. But her warm sharpness was equally in evidence with Cary Grant (*Bringing Up Baby* for Hawks in 1938) and Humphrey Bogart (*The African Queen* for John Huston in 1951). Winner of four best actress Oscars (more than any other recipient), she has recently published a set of autobiographical memoirs, *Me* (1991). Her greatest screen performances include *Alice Adams* (1935), *Summer Madness* (1955), *Suddenly Last Summer* (1959) and *Long Day's Journey into Night* (1962).

Heston, Charlton (b. 1923)

Heston's first starring role was in C. B. DeMille's circus epic, *The Greatest Show on Earth* (1952). He has since specialised in epic roles, bringing dignity and integrity to the genre, particularly in his title performances in *Ben Hur* (1959) and *El Cid* (1961). His historical roles range from Cardinal Richelieu to General Gordon, from Moses to Michelangelo; his best modern film role has probably been in Welles's *Touch of Evil* (1958). He has also excelled in westerns, notably in *The Big Country* (1958) and *Will Penny* (1968).

Hoffman, Dustin (b. 1937)

Earnest, intense method actor whose perfectionism has sometimes driven co-stars to distraction (Olivier: "Dustin is very talented—but why doesn't he just act?") but has certainly produced the goods—Oscars for his performances in *Kramer vs. Kramer* (1979) and *The Rain Man* (1988). Other important roles: *The Graduate* (1967), *Lenny* (1974), *All the President's Men* (1976), and *Tootsie* (1982).

Holden, William (1918–81)

Handsome leading man of the 1940s who was rescued from bland B-picture roles by Billy Wilder, who cast him as a screen writing gigolo in *Sunset Boulevard* (1950) and as a captive capitalist in *Stalag 17* (1953), for which Holden won an Oscar. After a lean spell in the 1960s, his career revived with his splendid leading performance in *The Wild Bunch* (1969), and before his death, he gave further thoughtful characterisations in *Network* (1976) and *Fedora* (1978). Other key roles: *Golden Boy* (1939), *Sabrina* (1954), *Picnic* (1955) and *The Bridge on the River Kwai* (1957).

Howard, Trevor (1916–87)

Leathery character actor of the British film, reputedly Graham Greene's favourite. Capable of acting just about anyone off the screen, which might be the reason that he only rarely got the parts (and therefore the recognition) that he deserved. Important films include: *Brief Encounter* (1945), *The Third Man* (1949), *Outcast Of The Islands* (1951), *The Key* (1958), *Sons and Lovers* (1960), *Mutiny on the Bounty* (1962) and *Ludwig* (1972).

Hudson, Rock (1925–85)

Solid Hollywood leading man who sprang back into the public eye in the 1980s because of his death from AIDS. This rather contradicted his screen image as the all-American romantic hero. An effective screen actor in dramas such as *Giant* (1956) or comedies such as *Send Me No Flowers* (1964), he had, in retrospect, his most resonant role in John Frankenheimer's sci-fi horror film, *Seconds* (1966), where a dissatisfied middle-aged man fakes his own death and, through plastic surgery, starts a new life looking like Rock Hudson—and finds that soul-destroying also.

Jannings, Emil (1884–1950)

A king of the German silent cinema, ruined by the coming of sound (which unkindly showed up his thick accent) and his collaboration with the Nazis. His massive self-sentimentalisation and Prussian obsession with lost status were triumphant in Murnau's *The Last Laugh* (1924), and even more so in his role as the puritanical schoolteacher Professor Rath, destroyed by his passion for Marlene Dietrich's Lola in Sternberg's *The Blue Angel* (1930). This performance remains the greatest monument of male sexual humiliation in cinema history. He epitomised silent film acting at its most Expressionist and expressive, though Luis Buñuel said he preferred Buster Keaton.

Karloff, Boris (1887–1969)

Here again on- and off-screen personas interacted intriguingly. Mild mannered English cricket-loving gentleman William Henry Pratt became the best-known horror star in Hollywood history with his performance as the blundering yet tender-hearted monster in James Whale's *Frankenstein* in 1931. Thenceforth his legendary status was secure, and augmented by his work for Karl Freund (*The Mummy* of 1932) and Charles Vidor (*The Mask of Fu Manchu*, 1932). As moving as his performance in *Frankenstein* in many ways is his valedictory

appearance in Peter Bogdanovich's *Targets* (shot in the year of his death) where he plays a retired Hollywood horror star whose essential kindness is appalled by the horror of American society.

Keaton, Buster (1895–1966)

Arguably the greatest director and the greatest actor of the American silent era. As an actor, Keaton's deadpan appearance, often almost suicidal insistence on choreographing and carrying out all his own stunts, and awareness of the element of fantasy identification in cinema have ensured that his performances remain consistently exciting and do not date. As a director, he masterfully exploited the relationship between man and machine—driver/train and actor/camera—in *The General* of 1926, and that between cinema and dream in *Sherlock Junior* of 1924. His career was undermined as much by the classic Hollywood afflictions—marital problems and heavy drinking—as by the coming of sound. But his reputation has soared since his death, and works such as *Our Hospitality* (1923), *Seven Chances* (1925), *The Navigator* (1927) and *Steamboat Bill Jr.* (1928), along with his aforementioned films, are now regarded as comedy classics. Appeared alongside Chaplin in an unforgettable routine in the latter's *Limelight* (1952).

Kelly, Gene (1912–96)

Arguably the most inventive and adventurous actor-choreographer of the American screen. Rival to Fred Astaire as Hollywood's dancing master, Kelly was even more creative in furthering the boundaries of the film musical, particularly in a trio of magnificent musicals he co-directed with Stanley Donen: *On the Town* (1949), *Singin' in the Rain* (1952) and *It's Always Fair Weather* (1955).

Kelly, Grace (1928–82)

Aloof but elegant leading lady who made her first major impression as Gary Cooper's Quaker wife in *High Noon* (1952) and then as the archetypal Hitchcockian ice-cool blonde in *Dial M for Murder* (1954), *Rear Window* (1954) and *To Catch a Thief* (1955). Her dramatic prowess was revealed in her Oscar-winning role in *The Country Girl* (1954) but she gave up stardom for royalty when she married Prince Rainier of Monaco in 1956.

Kerr, Deborah (b. 1921)

One of the most versatile and sensitive of British screen actresses, whose persona of "English rose" was changed when she played the nymphomaniac wife of an Army Captain in *From Here to Eternity* (1953). She has seemed at her best either when playing nuns with a hint of neurosis—*Black Narcissus* (1947), *Heaven Knows, Mr. Allison* (1957)—or prim teachers or governesses wrestling privately with emotional repression—*The King and I* (1955), *Tea and Sympathy* (1956), *The Innocents* (1961).

Lancaster, Burt (1913–94)

Acrobat turned actor, who revealed a sensitive interior behind his action-man mask. He won an Oscar for his role as a religious charlatan in *Elmer Gantry* (1960), and a Venice Festival award for a more introvert performance in *Bird Man of Alcatraz* (1962). "A deeply mysterious man" was the verdict on him of Luchino Visconti, who directed him to great effect in *The Leopard* (1963) and *Conversation Piece* (1974), and he triumphed also under Louis Malle in *Atlantic City* (1980). He had a career of fascinating contrasts, between swashbuckling and sensitive roles. Other key films include: *The Killers* (1946), *The Crimson Pirate* (1952), *From Here to Eternity* (1953), *Sweet Smell of Success* (1957), *1900* (1976) and *Twilight's Last Gleaming* (1977).

Laughton, Charles (1899–1962)

Bulky actor of phenomenal power and range, with the occasional tendency to ham but also capable of producing magical effects with a sympathetic director. It is sometimes thought that his heyday was in the thirties, when he excelled in *The Private Life of Henry VIII* (1933), *Ruggles of Red Gap* (1935), *Mutiny on the Bounty* (1935) and *The Hunchback of Notre Dame* (1939). But he was no less remarkable in later films such as *Hobson's Choice* (1954), *Witness for the Prosecution* (1957), *Spartacus* (1960) and *Advise and Consent* (1962). There is a sense of relish about his greatest acting, whether playing saint or sadist. One should not forget also his one and only film as director, an altogether remarkable, poetic thriller *The Night of the Hunter* (1955) that constitutes one of the most extraordinary directing debuts in the history of the cinema.

Laurel (1890–1965) and Hardy (1892–1957)

The first great comedy partnership in films, and never surpassed. Their films usually involve frantic attempts to gain social acceptance (*e.g.* as pianomovers or salesmen), that lead to the disasters ruefully described by Hardy as "another fine mess". Their features, including *Pack Up Your Troubles* (Marshall and Raymond McCarey, 1932) and *A Chump at Oxford* (Alfred Goulding, 1940), retain the personas—sly and skinny Stan and overweight Ollie trying to cling on to his dignity—almost intact. The comedy of failure in its purest, most unpretentious form. Key films include: *Big Business* (1929), *The Music Box* (1932), *Sons of the Desert* (1934), *Way Out West* (1937).

Leigh, Vivien (1913–67)

Fragile and exquisite English actress who remarkably scored her greatest film triumphs in two quintessentially American roles: as Scarlett O'Hara in *Gone With the Wind* (1939) and as Blanche DuBois in *A Streetcar Named Desire* (1951). Married to Laurence Olivier in 1940, her later career was blighted by physical and mental illness. She was divorced from Olivier in 1960, and her last major film roles were in *The Roman Spring of Mrs. Stone* (1961) and *Ship of Fools* [1965).

Lemmon, Jack (b. 1925)

Consummate film actor who is probably most associated in the public mind with a series of sublime comedy characterisations in films of Billy Wilder, such as *Some Like it Hot* (1959), *The Apartment* (1960) *The Fortune Cookie* (1966), and *Avanti!* (1972). But he is an equally forceful straight actor, as films such as *Days of Wine and Roses* (1962), *The China Syndrome* (1979), *Missing* (1982) and *Glengarry Glen Ross* (1992) demonstrate. The screen's best tragi-comedian since Chaplin.

Loren, Sophia (b. 1934)

Epitomises the stereotype of Latin female sexuality for the moviegoer, much as Marcello Mastroianni did for the male. She began for Hollywood in ripely sensual roles (e.g. *Desire under the Elms* for Delbert Mann in 1958), before moving on to more demanding dramatic parts, such as Vittorio de Sica's *Two Women* for which she won an Oscar in 1961.

Lorre, Peter (1904–64)

Among his best-known films there is only one in which he actually starred: *M* for Fritz Lang in 1931, where he portrayed a demented child-murderer, contorting his features as much as Lang's direction contorted the screen images. But he became one of Hollywood's most memorable supporting actors, as the crazed hitman in Huston's *The Maltese Falcon* (1941), and for Michael Curtiz (in *Casablanca* of 1943 and *Passage to Marseilles* of 1944) and Frank Capra (*Arsenic and Old Lace*, 1944). Like Karloff but in a very different way, he excelled at suggesting sensitivity beneath the contortions of horror and malice.

Maclaine, Shirley (b. 1934)

Prodigiously talented dancer-cum-comedienne-cum dramatic actress. Won an Oscar for *Terms of Endearment* (1983), but her best films are the early ones: *The Trouble With Harry* (1955), *Some Came Running* (1958), *The Apartment* (1960), *The Children's Hour* (1961) and *Sweet Charity* (1969).

March, Fredric (1897–1975)

One of Hollywood's finest character actors,

particularly when portraying ostensibly decent men with darker sides to their personalities. This was shown to particular effect in *Dr. Jekyll and Mr. Hyde* (1932) but was also a feature of some other of his major roles: *Les Miserables* (1935), *The Best Years of our Lives* (1946), *Death of a Salesman* (1952), *Executive Suite* (1954) and *The Desperate Hours* (1955).

Marx Brothers: Chico (1887–1961), Harpo (1888–1964), Groucho (1890–1978)

Hollywood's undisputed great comic family. Their films rely on the way in which the three brothers' fortés complement one another, so that as soon as a threat from one quarter is averted another one will appear. Groucho's undammable flow of insult and wisecrack, Chico's illogicalities and prevarications (delivered in a heavy mock-Italian accent), and Harpo's mute mime form an unbeatable trio, whether in the early Paramount features (such as *Duck Soup* for Leo McCarey in 1933) or in their later work for MGM, where musical and romantic interludes irksomely break up the stream of comedy (as in *A Day at the Races*—Sam Wood, 1937). Their most popular film, and Groucho's favourite, was *A Night at the Opera* (1935). (Another brother Zeppo appeared in some of their earlier films, either as an improbable romantic lead or even, in *Horse Feathers* of 1932, as Groucho's son.)

Mason, James (1909–84)

Mason's style migrated successfully from the British industry (as in *Odd Man Out*—Carol Reed, 1947) to Hollywood and the international circuit. He was an urbane villain for Hitchcock in *North by North-West* (1959), and a suitable articulate and obsessed lover for *Lolita* (Stanley Kubrick, 1962), somewhat removed from the persona of the romantic sadist with which he had first shot to fame (in *The Man in Grey*, 1943 and *The Wicked Lady*, 1945). One of those screen actors like Trevor Howard or David Niven who seemed incapable of giving a bad performance, however bad the film was around him. When the film was good—like, say, *Five Fingers* (1952), *A Star is Born* (1954), *The Verdict* (1982)—he could be quite exceptional.

Mastroianni, Marcello (1924–96)

The ultimate listless Latin lover, who seems wearied by the very thought of all the women to whom he is supposed to appeal. This quality in fact enables his screen persona to work quite subversively against the macho ideal of Hollywood, as in Fellini's *La Dolce Vita* (1959), where he plays a disillusioned journalist, or Antonioni's *La Notte* (1961), as the exhausted husband of Jeanne Moreau. His finest performance remains that in Fellini's *8½* (1963), as the film director (an obvious alter ego to Fellini), whose very prostration and inability to organise his neuroses into cinematic form at the end provide the mainspring that enables him to do so. The films with Fellini and Antonioni remain his best-known work. His most recent successes included *Macaroni* (1985), opposite Jack Lemmon; *Ginger and Fred* (1986), for Fellini; and a particularly intense performance in *The Beekeeper* (1986) for Greece's major contemporary director, Theo Angelopoulous.

McQueen, Steve (1930–80)

Supercool but smouldering anti-hero and loner, McQueen became a star after his POW antics on a motorbike in John Sturges' *The Great Escape* (1963), though the neurosis beneath the nonchalance had probably been better explored by director Don Siegel in *Hell is for Heroes* (1961). Best remembered for action roles like *The Magnificent Seven* (1960) or *Bullitt* (1968), McQueen was showing signs of greater artistic ambition towards the end of his life, producing as well as starring in an adaptation of Ibsen's *An Enemy of the People* (1979) and contributing a finely shaded, poignant performance in the elegiac Western, *Tom Horn* (1980).

Mifune, Toshiro (1920–97)

Japanese actor whose robust style, ironic as well as dramatic, was indelibly associated with the films he has made for Kurosawa, including *Seven Samurai*

W24

(1954), *Throne of Blood* (1957) and *Yojimbo* (1961). He also appeared in the occasional Hollywood film, most notably opposite Lee Marvin in *Hell in the Pacific* (1969).

Mitchum, Robert (1917–97)

A deceptively outstanding film actor whose lazy style concealed enormous range and prodigious depth. Directors as exacting as John Huston (*Heaven Knows Mr. Allison*, 1957) and Fred Zinnemann (*The Sundowners*, 1960) testified to Mitchum's exceptional abilities. Only once nominated for an Oscar (for *The Story of G.I. Joe*, 1945), his memorable performances are legion: *Pursued* (1947), *Build My Gallows High* (1947), *The Lusty Men* (1952), *The Night of the Hunter* (1955), *Cape Fear* (1962), *Ryan's Daughter* (1970), *The Friends of Eddie Coyle* (1973), *The Last Tycoon* (1976).

Monroe, Marilyn (1926–62)

Not the original cinematic sex symbol—that distinction belongs to Mary Pickford or Rudolph Valentino—but Monroe is certainly the best-known. Nowhere else have the on-and-off screen persona interacted to such devastating, and finally destructive, effect. She began as a "dumb blonde" in the early fifties before producers and directors recognised in her vulnerability and ambivalent attitude towards her own sexuality—pride tempered by the desire to be appreciated for something more—outstanding qualities. Her best films remain comedies in which her ambivalence was played upon to enrich the texture of the movies: *Bus Stop* for Joshua Logan in 1956, and for Billy Wilder, *The Seven-Year Itch* of 1955, and *Some Like It Hot* in 1959. She gave an extraordinary dramatic performance in Huston's *The Misfits* (1960), but was dismissed from her final project (Cukor's *Something's Got to Give*) for unreliability in 1960, and not long afterwards committed suicide. Revelations of her off-screen loneliness and the mysterious circumstances of her death went to fuel what is still Hollywood's most potent and macabre legend.

Moreau, Jeanne (b. 1928)

Described as the "thinking man's actress', and whose name was synonymous with some of the greatest and most controversial European art movies of the late fifties and early sixties: Malle's *The Lovers* (1958), Truffaut's *Jules et Jim* (1961), Antonioni's *La Notte* (1962) and Buñuel's *Diary of a Chambermaid* (1964).

Newman, Paul (b. 1925)

Blue-eyed boy of modern American film, exceptionally good looking and a considerable actor to boot. Early Oscar-nominated performances in *Cat on a Hot Tin Roof* (1958), *The Hustler* (1961), *Hud* (1963) and *Cool Hand Luke* (1967) testified to Newman's great skill in revealing an attractive, adventurous side to roles which, in other hands, could have seemed unsympathetic and morbid. He finally won his Oscar for *The Color of Money* (1987), Scorsese's sequel to *The Hustler*. He has also proved himself a sympathetic director, particularly of his actress-wife Joanne Woodward, in films such as *Rachel, Rachel* (1968) and *The Glass Menagerie* (1987).

Nicholson, Jack (b. 1937)

Nicholson broke into public prominence with his performance as the alcoholic ne'er-do-well in Hopper's *Easy Rider* (1969), and has remained at the top ever since with sardonic yet often tender performances. The versatility that often goes with understatement has enabled him to give outstanding performances as a drop-out classical musician (Bob Rafelson's *Five Easy Pieces* in 1970), a private eye (Polanski's *Chinatown* in 1974), a rebel in a mental hospital (Milos Forman's *One Flew Over The Cuckoo's Nest*, 1975) and a cynical writer (James L. Brooks' *As Good as it Gets*, 1997). Some later performances have bordered on self-parody, notably *Batman* (1989), and others (for example, *The Shining*, 1980) have been distinctly controversial. At least he is rarely dull.

Olivier, Sir Laurence (1907–89)

Perhaps the most exciting and respected actor of his generation, Olivier will first be remembered and revered for his achievement as actor and director in bringing Shakespeare to vivid life on screen with *Henry V* (1944), *Hamlet* (1948) and *Richard III* (1955). But his most subtle screen acting was to be found in two films he made for Wyler, *Wuthering Heights* (1939) and *Carrie* (1952), and one for Hitchcock, *Rebecca* (1940). His last major film role was in Mankiewicz's *Sleuth* (1972).

Pacino, Al (b. 1940)

Born in New York of Sicilian descent and an apostle of the great acting teacher Lee Strasberg, Pacino shot to prominence with his performance as Michael Corleone in *The Godfather* (1972), a role he was to repeat and refine in two sequels. An actor of great resource and range, he now rivals DeNiro as the most admired American screen actor since Marlon Brando. Key films include: *Godfather II* (1974), *Dog Day Afternoon* (1975), *Scarface* (1983), *Glengarry Glen Ross* (1992), *Heat* (1996), *Looking for Richard* (1996).

Peck, Gregory (b. 1916)

Archetypal screen symbol of liberal integrity, particularly embodied in his performance as the lawyer defending an unjustly accused Negro in *To Kill a Mockingbird* (1962), for which he justly won an Oscar. Other important films: *Gentleman's Agreement* (1947), *The Gunfighter* (1950), *Roman Holiday* (1953), *Moby Dick* (1956), *The Big Country* (1958), *The Stalking Moon* (1968) and *I Walk the Line* (1970).

Pickford, Mary (1893–1979)

The sentimentality of Pickford's early performances for D. W. Griffith between 1909 and 1912, and her peak period as "America's Sweetheart" when married to Douglas Fairbanks (*Daddy Long Legs* for Marshall Neilan in 1919, *Pollyanna* for Paul Powell in 1920) are considerably less interesting today than her ideological role as what Basil Wright has dubbed the "hearth goddess" of domesticity and her early status as one of the first multimillionaire film stars.

Poitier, Sidney (b. 1924)

Ground-breaking black actor, who was one of the first Negroes to attain Hollywood star status. Poitier won an Oscar for a now virtually forgotten movie, *Lilies of the Field* (1963), and is better remembered for such films as *The Defiant Ones* (1958), *In The Heat of the Night* (1967) and *Guess Who's Coming to Dinner* (1967). Also an accomplished director, though definitely in the commercial mainstream rather than in the radical alternative lane chosen by the new generation of black American directors such as Spike Lee and John Singleton.

Redford, Robert (b. 1937)

Redford is distinguished from his "peer-group" stars such as Beatty and Nicholson by a resolute rejection of the trappings of stardom. Athletically handsome (like John Wayne he went to university on a sports scholarship), he struck gold with *Butch Cassidy and the Sundance Kid* (George Roy Hill, 1969), and created perhaps his most successful dramatic role in the Scott Fitzgerald adaptation, *The Great Gatsby* for Jack Clayton in 1974. Increasingly his interest has turned to direction, understandably so since his directing debut, *Ordinary People* (1980) won him an Oscar.

Robinson, Edward G. (1893–1973)

Robinson made his name in gangster film roles such as *Little Ceasar* (1931) and as Johnny Rocco in Huston's *Key Largo* (1948). But he was actually a highly skilled actor in a variety of parts, at his best perhaps in two psychological dramas for Fritz Lang, *Woman in the Window* (1944) and *Scarlet Street* (1945); as the insurance investigator in Wilder's *Double Indemnity* (1944); and as a roguish diamond smuggler in Mackendrick's *Sammy Going South* (1963).

Signoret, Simone (1921–85)

Classy French actress who excelled at playing lovelorn women, most memorably in Jacques Becker's *Casque d'Or* (1952) and Jack Clayton's *Room at the Top* (1958). Among her other important films are *La Ronde* (1950), *Les Diaboliques* (1955), *The Army of the Shadows* (1969) and *Madame Rosa* (1977).

Stanwyck, Barbara (1907–90)

Vibrant, strong actress, much appreciated by directors such as Capra, DeMille, Lang, Sirk for her utter professionalism. Her stock-in-trade was as a hard-as-nails heroine who knew her own mind and was sometimes not to be trusted. Nominated for an Oscar four times without winning (for *Stella Dallas*, 1937; *Ball of Fire*, 1942; *Double Indemnity*, 1944; and *Sorry, Wrong Number*, 1948), she was finally given an honorary Oscar in 1982. Other key films: *The Bitter Tea of General Yen* (1933), *Annie Oakley* (1935), *The Lady Eve* (1941), *The Furies* (1950), *There's Always Tomorrow* (1956).

Stewart, James (1908–97)

Directors found complex uses for the slow drawl and shy demeanour of this adroit screen actor: all-American integrity, in his films for Capra (*Mr. Smith goes to Washington*, 1939; *It's A Wonderful Life*, 1946); seething inner intensity in his Anthony Mann westerns; and romantic vulnerability in his Alfred Hitchcock movies, most disturbingly and tragically so in *Vertigo* (1958). A versatile performer, who combined exceptional dramatic power, seen at its best in Preminger's *Anatomy of a Murder* (1959), with a flair for comedy: his performance in the latter vein in Cukor's *Philadelphia Story* (1940) won him an Oscar.

Streep, Meryl (b. 1951)

One of the leading ladies of the modern screen, who at one stage seemed to snatch all the big parts, whether they be English, Danish, Polish, or Australian, let alone American. She might not always move the heart, but the acting intelligence and technique are formidable. Her key films include: *The Deer Hunter* (1978), *Kramer Vs. Kramer* (1979), *The French Lieutenant's Woman* (1981), *Sophie's Choice* (1982), *Out of Africa* (1985), *The Bridges of Madison County* (1995).

Swanson, Gloria (1897–1983)

Perhaps the most glamorous of silent screen stars, particularly in her films for Cecil B. DeMille, like *Male and Female* (1919). She lost much of her wealth when producing *Queen Kelly* (1928), a film she stopped in mid-production owing to director Erich von Stroheim's extravagance: and talkies proved a problem. However, she made a triumphant return to the screen as Norma Desmond in Billy Wilder's *Sunset Boulevard* (1950), as the former silent star dreaming of a comeback. When the brash screenwriter says she used to be big, she snaps back imperiously: "I *am* big. It's the pictures that got small."

Tati, Jacques (1908–82)

Like Keaton, Tati's claim to fame is based on his direction as much as on his acting. Indeed it could be said that the two in a sense came into conflict in his later career, his directorial skill and concern with elaborate mechanised set-pieces causing his output to be irregular and often working against his lanky, absent-minded quality as a clown. *Mr. Hulot's Holiday* (1953) remains one of the greatest silent comedies in cinema history (sound was actually added after shooting, but its contribution to the comic impact is minimal), and Tati's greatest achievement in that film is perhaps the way in which he manages to render a specifically French social stereotype—the would-be sporting bourgeois on a seaside holiday—appealing to a much wider audience. Later films like *Mon Oncle* (1958), *Playtime* (1968) and *Traffic* (1971) have an almost mathematical precision in their comedy lay-out and a serious underlying theme: the decline of individuality in an age of mechanisation.

Taylor, Elizabeth (b. 1932)

Taylor started out as a child-star in Clarence Brown's *National Velvet* (1944) before becoming one of the major Hollywood sex symbols of the fifties, dark and sultry in Richard Brooks's *Cat on a Hot Tin Roof* (1958) and Mankiewicz's *Suddenly Last Summer* (1959). After her marriage to Richard Burton off-and-on screen persona were profitably played off against each other, this culminating in her Oscar-winning performance in Mike Nichols's *Who's Afraid of Virginia Woolf!* (1966). Directors like George Stevens and Joseph Losey have spoken glowingly of her skill as a screen actress, but it is as a star that she has excelled, and nobody has symbolised celluloid glamour more seductively. From being its loveliest child star, Elizabeth Taylor can now be fairly regarded as Hollywood's Queen Mother. Other important films: *Father of the Bride* (1950), *A Place in the Sun* (1951), *Butterfield 8* (1960), *Cleopatra* (1963), *Reflections in a Golden Eye* (1967) and *Secret Ceremony* (1968).

Temple, Shirley (b. 1928)

The most famous of all child stars, so precociously talented at singing, dancing and emoting that Graham Greene opined in print that she was a midget, leading to a libel suit and the eventual bankruptcy of the magazine he was writing for. The top box-office attraction of 1938, she was a has-been by 1940, and has spent her adult life engaged not in movies but in Republican politics. Main films include: *Little Miss Marker* (1934), *Wee Willie Winkie* (1937) and *Rebecca of Sunnybrook Farm* (1938).

Tracy, Spencer (1900–67)

Tracy successfully embodied in the thirties and forties certain "all-American" qualities—bluff decency, perceptive kind-heartedness, the "Honest Joe" syndrome—marked in such movies as Fritz Lang's *Fury* (1936) and Frank Borzage's *Big City* (1937). With Katharine Hepburn, he formed one of the archetypal American-movie couples. They strike sparks off each other in *Adam's Rib* and *Pat and Mike* for George Cukor (1949 and 1952 respectively), and in work for such directors as George Stevens and Frank Capra. An actor's actor, so natural that he seemed not to be acting at all, he was greatly admired by his peers, not least by Laurence Olivier, who commented: "I've learned more about acting from watching Tracy than in any other way. He has great truth in everything he does." His films included: *San Francisco* (1936), *Captains Courageous* (1937), *Boys' Town* (1938), *Woman of the Year* (1942), *Father of the Bride* (1950), *The Actress* (1953), *Bad Day at Black Rock* (1955), *Inherit the Wind* (1960) and *Judgment at Nuremberg* (1961).

Valentino, Rudolph (1895–1926)

Valentino was one of the first major Hollywood sex symbols whose funeral after a premature death from peritonitis was followed by thousands of sobbing fans. This now seems ironic due not only to changes in film fashions and sexual coding that make his savagely passionate oriental in *The Sheik* (George Melford, 1921) appear passé, but also to subsequent revelations about his unconsummated first marriage, homosexual tendencies and domination by his second wife, who took charge of his career and mismanaged it abominably. To women he symbolised exotic eroticism; to men, to quote an infamous *Chicago Tribune* editorial, a "painted pansy". His premature death (which is often a smart career move, as one cynical journalist remarked) only fanned the legend and the controversy. Other important films: *The Four Horsemen of the Apocalypse* (1921), *Blood and Sand* (1922) and *Son of the Sheik* (1926).

Wayne, John (1907–79)

Wayne remains perhaps Hollywood's greatest, most loved and most hated star. Loved, by Western fans the world over for performances that set the mould for the horseback hero—big physically and spiritually, charismatically dominating with men, awkward and latently sentimental with women, always coming out on top in a crisis. Hated, for his uncompromising right-wing political stance which led him to endorse the McCarthyite persecutions of the fifties and to give active support to the American invasion of Vietnam, even making a film—*The Green Berets* (1968)— in support of it. As an actor, Wayne revealed in his best parts more sensitivity than he often cared to off-screen—as the outlaw Ringo in Ford's *Stagecoach* (1939) who ends up with the prostitute Dallas, as the tamed Comanche-hater Ethan Edwards in Ford's *The Searchers* (1956), who walks off into the barren landscape at the end, and as the sheriff in Hawks's *Rio Bravo* (1959), holding a motley posse together by force of personality. He won an Oscar for *True Grit* (1969). Other important films: *Fort Apache* (1948), *Red River* (1949), *She Wore a Yellow Ribbon* (1949), *Sands of Iwo Jima* (1950), *The Quiet Man* (1952), *The Man Who Shot Liberty Valance* (1962) and *The Shootist* (1976).

West, Mae (1892–1980)

"I was Snow White—but I drifted." So said Mae West, whose raunchy style was seen at its best on film in *She Done Him Wrong* (1933) and *I'm No Angel* (1933). This blousy buxom blonde appealed to men because of her sex-appeal, and to women because of the way she seized the sexual initiative from the male and sent up his desires. Unfortunately the production code of 1934, which laid down strict guidelines on the treatment of sex on film, inhibited Miss West's screen career. Other key films: *Belle of the Nineties* (1934), *My Little Chickadee* (1940).

4. GLOSSARY OF TERMS

auteurism, a critical theory, popular in France in the fifties and sixties, that ascribed overall responsibility for the creation of a film to its director, and thereby provoked renewed critical analysis of much previously neglected Hollywood work. The "*politique des auteurs*" (auteur policy) was first stated by François Truffaut in the January 1954 issue of *Cahiers du Cinema*; the main exponent of the auteur "theory" in America was the critic Andrew Sarris.

back lighting, lighting directed at the camera from behind subject, which is therefore silhouetted.

back projection, background scene projected onto a screen behind the action so that they seem to be on location. A convention of classic Hollywood cinema that can now look somewhat dated, it became a source of great critical debate in Hitchcock's *Marnie* (1964), where its perceptible use was both attacked for technical sloppiness and defended as expressively meaningful.

bio-pic, a biographical film of a famous personality particularly popularised by Warner Brothers in the 1930s: *e.g. The Story of Louis Pasteur* (1936), *The Life of Emile Zola* (1937).

camera angle, looking up, looking down, tilted (the latter used particularly effectively in *The Third Man* to suggest a word out of joint).

chiaroscuro, a noticeable use of light and shade.

cinema verité, literally "cinema truth"; it signified a kind of documentary cinema that used lightweight equipment, minimal crews (camera and sound) and interview techniques.

crane shot, shot where the camera is mounted on a crane and rises above the ground to offer an aerial perspective. A famous example is the shot in *High Noon* (1952), where the crane shot of the Marshal in the empty street prior to his confrontation with the four gunmen emphasises his isolation, rejection and vulnerability.

cut, change from one shot to another.

    cross cutting: cutting back and forth from one action to another, giving the impression of parallel action and the two events happening simultaneously. Famous examples include the finale of D W Griffith's *Intolerance* (1916), where the chase to save the pardoned hero from execution in the modern story is crosscut with Christ's procession to Calvary; and the scene in *The Godfather* (1972), where the baptism of Michael Corleone's godson is crosscut with the violent elimination of Corleone's underworld rivals.

    jump cut: an ellipsis, sometimes surprising as when in the film *Don't Look Now* (1973), the director Nicolas Roeg cuts from the wife's scream on seeing her dead daughter to the drill her husband is using in his work on the church in Venice—a sound match and cut that, as Roeg said, fires the viewer like a bullet into the future.

    match cut: two shots linked by some aural or visual connection, like the moment in *2001: A Space Odyssey* (1968) where a bone tossed in the air by a primordial ape is visually displaced by a shot of a spinning spacecraft.

day for night, technique used for shooting night sequences during daytime with the use of special lens filters. Alluded to in Francois Truffaut's film about film-making, *La Nuit Americaine—Day for Night* (1973).

deep focus, a technique favoured by realists in which objects very near the camera as well as those far away are in focus at the same time: particularly associated with the cameraman Gregg Toland and the forties' films of Welles and Wyler.

dissolve, a visible transition where one scene fades out as another fades in.

documentary, a term first coined by John Grierson when describing Robert Flaherty's film about the daily life of a Polynesian youth, *Moana* (1926). It derived from *documentaire*, which the French used to describe travelogues, but it has come to be applied to all non-fiction films, albeit covering a wide variety of styles.

film noir, films with a grim, urban setting that deal mainly with dark and violent passions in a downbeat way. Especially associated with American thrillers of the forties and early fifties.

free cinema, a documentary movement in England in the 1950s that was a springboard for the careers in film of directors such as Lindsay Anderson, Karel Reisz and Tony Richardson.

genre, a type or class of film (*e.g.* the musical, the western).

German expressionism, a style of film common in Germany in the twenties, typified by dramatic lighting, distorted sets, symbolic action and characterisation as in, for example, *The Cabinet of Dr. Caligari* (Robert Wiene, 1920).

mise en scene, literally, "staging"—the way in which the elements and components in a film are arranged and encompassed by the camera, or the term usually used to denote that part of the cinematic process that takes place on the set, as opposed to montage, which takes place afterwards.

montage, the juxtaposition of material (successive shots, or items within a shot) to suggest meaning—as when Eisenstein in *Potemkin* evokes anger at the massacre by showing three successive shots of stone lions in various positions, shot to look as though they are one lion rising to its feet and roaring its fury.

movie brats, younger generation of Hollywood directors who exploded onto the scene in the early 1970s: *e.g.* Spielberg, George Lucas, Brian de Palma, Martin Scorsese.

narrative, structured series of events, linked by cause and effect, that provide the films' plots.

narration, the various means by which the events of the plot can be placed before the viewer. Also used of voice-over narration, a technique particularly associated with the fatalism of film noir, like that of the mortally wounded hero in *Double Indemnity* (1944) or that of the dead man in *Sunset Boulevard* (1950).

neo-realism, connected with movement out of the studio, shooting on real locations, sometimes the absence of a script and/or non-professional casts—all designed simultaneously to cut costs and increase the impression of spontaneity. In fact inaugurated by Renoir, but associated with Italian post-war directors (Rossellini, Visconti, De Sica).

new wave, a loose, heterogeneous group of young French critics (Chabrol, Rivette, Truffaut, Godard), who went into direction in the late fifties and sixties. Much influenced by Hollywood action cinema, they relied heavily on hand-held cameras, a laconic and non-moralistic style, a general sense of existential amoralism.

pan, camera looks around from a stationary position. Can be used for dramatic effect, as in John Ford's *Stagecoach* (1939) when a panning shot reveals the presence of Indians just when the stagecoach seems to be heading to safety.

point of view shot, shot where the action is seen through the eyes of a particular character, the shot generally preceded or followed by a shot of the character looking. Hitchcock's *Rear Window* (1954) structures its whole action around that principle; and Robert Montgomery's *The Lady in the Lake* (1948) also experimented with a subjective camera by showing us only what the leading character himself saw and only showing the character himself in mirror shots.

screwball comedy, type of comedy popular in thirties' Hollywood characterised by frantic action, verbal

wit, and a couple in a bizarre predicament, *e.g.* Capra's *It Happened One Night* (1934), Hawks's *Bringing Up Baby* (1938).

shot, single piece of film without cuts: long shot, medium shot, close shot or close up.

tracking shot: camera moves about in order to follow subject, a technique taken to its extreme in the continuous opening shot of Orson Welles' *Touch of Evil* (1958) or Robert Altman's *The Player* (1992) and in Hitchcock's use of ten-minute takes in *Rope* (1948).

zoom shot: a shot during which the focal length of the lens is adjusted and gives the impression of optical motion without moving the camera backwards or forwards. The zoom lens is a particularly favoured piece of apparatus of directors such as Robert Altman and Stanley Kubrick.

5. THE OSCAR WINNERS

Introduction

The film industry's most glittering prize remains the Hollywood Academy Award, or "Oscar'. The "Oscar' came about as a result of the formation of the Academy of Motion Picture Arts and Sciences in 1927. The Academy thought it would gain additional prestige and publicity if it gave out annual awards for artistic and technical merit. The first awards ceremony was in May 1929 and was a modest affair. Nowadays the ceremony is a lavish spectacle watched by countless millions on television worldwide.

The Oscar itself is a gold-plated statuette of a knight holding a crusader's sword and standing on a reel of film whose five spokes symbolise the original branches of the Academy (actors, directors, producers, technicians and writers). Legend has it that the name comes from a secretary Margaret Herrick, later an executive director of the Academy, who commented one day that the statuette "reminds me of my uncle Oscar".

Ben Hur (1959) and *Titanic* (1997) hold the record number of Oscars—11. *West Side Story* (1961) won 10; *Gone With the Wind* (1939), *Gigi* (1958), *The Last Emperor* (1987) and *The English Patient* (1996) each won nine. Katharine Hepburn has won more major acting Oscars than any other star (4). Bette Davis, Luise Rainer, Olivia de Havilland, Ingrid Bergman, Glenda Jackson, Jane Fonda, Sally Field and Jodie Foster have won Best Actress twice; Spencer Tracy, Fredric March, Gary Cooper, Marlon Brando, Dustin Hoffman, Jack Nicholson and Tom Hanks have done the same as Best Actor.

Best Actor

1927–28 Emil Jannings, *The Way of All Flesh*
1928–29 Warner Baxter, *In Old Arizona*
1929–30 George Arliss, *Disraeli*
1930–31 Lionel Barrymore, *A Free Soul*
1931–32 Fredric March, *Dr Jekyll and Mr Hyde*; Wallace Beery, *The Champ* (tie)
1932–33 Charles Laughton, *Private Life of Henry VIII*
1934   Clark Gable, *It Happened One Night*
1935   Victor McLaglen, *The Informer*
1936   Paul Muni, *Story of Louis Pasteur*
1937   Spencer Tracy, *Captains Courageous*
1938   Spencer Tracy, *Boys Town*
1939   Robert Donat, *Goodbye Mr Chips*
1940   James Stewart, *The Philadelphia Story*
1941   Gary Cooper, *Sergeant York*
1942   James Cagney, *Yankee Doodle Dandy*
1943   Paul Lukas, *Watch on the Rhine*
1944   Bing Crosby, *Going My Way*
1945   Ray Milland, *The Lost Weekend*
1946   Fredric March, *The Best Years of Our Lives*
1947   Ronald Colman, *A Double Life*
1948   Laurence Olivier, *Hamlet*

1949   Broderick Crawford, *All the King's Men*
1950   José Ferrer, *Cyrano de Bergerac*
1951   Humphrey Bogart, *The African Queen*
1952   Gary Cooper, *High Noon*
1953   William Holden, *Stalag 17*
1954   Marlon Brando, *On the Waterfront*
1955   Ernest Borgnine, *Marty*
1956   Yul Brynner, *The King and I*
1957   Alec Guinness, *The Bridge on the River Kwai*
1958   David Niven, *Separate Tables*
1959   Charlton Heston, *Ben Hur*
1960   Burt Lancaster, *Elmer Gantry*
1961   Maximilian Schell, *Judgment at Nuremberg*
1962   Gregory Peck, *To Kill a Mockingbird*
1963   Sidney Poitier, *Lilies of the Field*
1964   Rex Harrison, *My Fair Lady*
1965   Lee Marvin, *Cat Ballou*
1966   Paul Scofield, *A Man for All Seasons*
1967   Rod Steiger, *In the Heat of the Night*
1968   Cliff Robertson, *Charly*
1969   John Wayne, *True Grit*
1970   George C. Scott, *Patton* (refused)
1971   Gene Hackman, *The French Connection*
1972   Marlon Brando, *The Godfather* (refused)
1973   Jack Lemmon, *Save the Tiger*
1974   Art Carney, *Harry and Tonto*
1975   Jack Nicholson, *One Flew Over the Cuckoo's Nest*
1976   Peter Finch, *Network*
1977   Richard Dreyfuss, *The Goodbye Girl*
1978   Jon Voigt, *Coming Home*
1979   Dustin Hoffman, *Kramer vs. Kramer*
1980   Robert DeNiro, *Raging Bull*
1981   Henry Fonda, *On Golden Pond*
1982   Ben Kingsley, *Gandhi*
1983   Robert Duvall, *Tender Mercies*
1984   F. Murray Abraham, *Amadeus*
1985   William Hurt, *Kiss of the Spider Woman*
1986   Paul Newman, *The Color of Money*
1987   Michael Douglas, *Wall Street*
1988   Dustin Hoffman, *Rain Man*
1989   Daniel Day-Lewis, *My Left Foot*
1990   Jeremy Irons, *Reversal of Fortune*
1991   Anthony Hopkins, *The Silence of the Lambs*
1992   Al Pacino, *Scent of a Woman*
1993   Tom Hanks, *Philadelphia*
1994   Tom Hanks, *Forrest Gump*
1995   Nicolas Cage, *Leaving Las Vegas*
1996   Geoffrey Rush, *Shine*
1997   Jack Nicholson, *As Good As It Gets*
1998   Roberto Benigni, *Life is Beautiful*

Best Actress

1927–28 Janet Gaynor, *Seventh Heaven*
1928–29 Mary Pickford, *Coquette*
1929–30 Norma Shearer, *The Divorcee*
1930–31 Marie Dressler, *Min and Bill*
1931–32 Helen Hayes, *Sin of Madelon Claudet*
1932–33 Katharine Hepburn, *Morning Glory*
1934   Claudette Colbert, *It Happened One Night*

1935	Bette Davis, *Dangerous*	1944	*Going My Way*, Paramount
1936	Luise Rainer, *The Great Ziegfeld*	1945	*The Lost Weekend*, Paramount
1937	Luise Rainer, *The Good Earth*	1946	*The Best Years of Our Lives*, Goldwyn, RKO
1938	Bette Davis, *Jezebel*		
1939	Vivien Leigh, *Gone With the Wind*	1947	*Gentleman's Agreement*, 20th Century-Fox
1940	Ginger Rogers, *Kitty Foyle*	1948	*Hamlet*, Two Cities Film, Universal International
1941	Joan Fontaine, *Suspicion*		
1942	Greer Garson, *Mrs Miniver*	1949	*All the King's Men*, Columbia
1943	Jennifer Jones, *The Song of Bernadette*	1950	*All About Eve*, 20th Century-Fox
1944	Ingrid Bergman, *Gaslight*	1951	*An American in Paris*, MGM
1945	Joan Crawford, *Mildred Pierce*	1952	*Greatest Show on Earth*, Cecil B. De Mille, Paramount
1946	Olivia de Havilland, *To Each His Own*		
1947	Loretta Young, *The Farmer's Daughter*	1953	*From Here to Eternity*, Columbia
1948	Jane Wyman, *Johnny Belinda*	1954	*On the Waterfront*, Horizon-American Corp. Columbia
1949	Olivia de Havilland, *The Heiress*		
1950	Judy Holliday, *Born Yesterday*	1955	*Marty*, Hecht and Lancaster's Steven Productions UA
1951	Vivien Leigh, *A Streetcar Named Desire*		
1952	Shirley Booth, *Come Back, Little Sheba*	1956	*Around the World in 80 Days*, Michael Todd Co. UA
1953	Audrey Hepburn, *Roman Holiday*		
1954	Grace Kelly, *Country Girl*	1957	*The Bridge on the River Kwai*, Columbia
1955	Anna Magnani, *The Rose Tattoo*	1958	*Gigi*, Arthur Freed Production, MGM
1956	Ingrid Bergman, *Anastasia*	1959	*Ben-Hur*, MGM
1957	Joanne Woodward, *The Three Faces of Eve*	1960	*The Apartment*, Mirisch Co. UA
1958	Susan Hayward, *I Want to Live*	1961	*West Side Story*, United Artists
1959	Simone Signoret, *Room at the Top*	1962	*Lawrence of Arabia*, Columbia
1960	Elizabeth Taylor, *Butterfield 8*	1963	*Tom Jones*, Woodfall Prod. UA-Lopert Pictures
1961	Sophia Loren, *Two Women*		
1962	Anne Bancroft, *The Miracle Worker*	1964	*My Fair Lady*, Warner Bros.
1963	Patricia Neal, *Hud*	1965	*The Sound of Music*, 20th Century-Fox
1964	Julie Andrews, *Mary Poppins*	1966	*A Man for All Seasons*, Columbia
1965	Julie Christie, *Darling*	1967	*In the Heat of the Night*, United Artists
1966	Elizabeth Taylor, *Who's Afraid of Virginia Woolf?*	1968	*Oliver*, Columbia
		1969	*Midnight Cowboy*, United Artists
1967	Katharine Hepburn, *Guess Who's Coming to Dinner*	1970	*Patton*, 20th Century-Fox
		1971	*The French Connection*, 20th Century-Fox
1968	Katharine Hepburn, *The Lion in Winter*; Barbra Streisand, *Funny Girl* (tie)		
		1972	*The Godfather*, Paramount
1969	Maggie Smith, *The Prime of Miss Jean Brodie*	1973	*The Sting*, Universal
		1974	*The Godfather, Part II*, Paramount
1970	Glenda Jackson, *Women in Love*	1975	*One Flew Over the Cuckoo's Nest*, United Artists
1971	Jane Fonda, *Klute*		
1972	Liza Minnelli, *Cabaret*	1976	*Rocky*, United Artists
1973	Glenda Jackson, *A Touch of Class*	1977	*Annie Hall*, United Artists
1974	Ellen Burstyn, *Alice Doesn't Live Here Anymore*	1978	*The Deer Hunter*, EMI
		1979	*Kramer vs. Kramer*, Columbia
1975	Louise Fletcher, *One Flew Over the Cuckoo's Nest*	1980	*Ordinary People*, Paramount
		1981	*Chariots of Fire*, Fox
1976	Faye Dunaway, *Network*	1982	*Gandhi*, Columbia-Warner
1977	Diane Keaton, *Annie Hall*	1983	*Terms of Endearment*, Paramount
1978	Jane Fonda, *Coming Home*	1984	*Amadeus*, Columbia-Warner
1979	Sally Field, *Norma Rae*	1985	*Out of Africa*, Universal
1980	Sissy Spacek, *Coal Miner's Daughter*	1986	*Platoon*, Orion Pictures
1981	Katharine Hepburn, *On Golden Pond*	1987	*The Last Emperor*, Columbia
1982	Meryl Streep, *Sophie's Choice*	1988	*Rain Man*, United Artists
1983	Shirley MacLaine, *Terms of Endearment*	1989	*Driving Miss Daisy*, Warner Bros.
1984	Sally Field, *Places in the Heart*	1990	*Dances with Wolves*, Guild
1985	Geraldine Page, *The Trip to Bountiful*	1991	*The Silence of the Lambs*, Orion Pictures
1986	Marlee Matlin, *Children of a Lesser God*	1992	*Unforgiven*, Warner Bros.
1987	Cher, *Moonstruck*	1993	*Schindler's List*, Universal
1988	Jodie Foster, *The Accused*	1994	*Forrest Gump*, Paramount
1989	Jessica Tandy, *Driving Miss Daisy*	1995	*Braveheart*, Paramount/20th Century-Fox
1990	Kathy Bates, *Misery*		
1991	Jodie Foster, *The Silence of the Lambs*	1996	*The English Patient*, Miramax
1992	Emma Thompson, *Howards End*	1997	*Titanic*, 20th Century-Fox/Paramount
1993	Holly Hunter, *The Piano*	1998	*Shakespeare in Love*, Miramax Films/Universal Pictures
1994	Jessica Lange, *Blue Sky*		
1995	Susan Sarandon, *Dead Man Walking*		
1996	Frances McDormand, *Fargo*		
1997	Helen Hunt, *As Good As It Gets*		
1998	Gwyneth Paltrow, *Shakespeare in Love*		

Best Director

1927–28	Frank Borzage, *Seventh Heaven*
	Lewis Milestone, *Two Arabian Knights*
1928–29	Frank Lloyd, *The Divine Lady*
1929–30	Lewis Milestone, *All Quiet on the Western Front*

Best Film

1927–28	*Wings*, Paramount
1928–29	*Broadway Melody*, MGM
1929–30	*All Quiet on the Western Front*, Universal
1930–31	*Cimarron*, RKO
1931–32	*Grand Hotel*, MGM
	Special: Mickey Mouse, Walt Disney
1932–33	*Cavalcade*, 20th Century-Fox
1934	*It Happened One Night*, Columbia
1935	*Mutiny on the Bounty*, MGM
1936	*The Great Ziegfeld*, MGM
1937	*Life of Emile Zola*, Warner
1938	*You Can't Take It With You*, Columbia
1939	*Gone With the Wind*, Selznick International
1940	*Rebecca*, Selznick International
1941	*How Green Was My Valley*, 20th Century-Fox
1942	*Mrs Miniver*, MGM
1943	*Casablanca*, Warner

1930–31	Norman Taurog, *Skippy*
1931–32	Frank Borzage, *Bad Girl*
1932–33	Frank Lloyd, *Cavalcade*
1934	Frank Capra, *It Happened One Night*
1935	John Ford, *The Informer*
1936	Frank Capra, *Mr Deeds Goes to Town*
1937	Leo McCarey, *The Awful Truth*
1938	Frank Capra, *You Can't Take It With You*
1939	Victor Fleming, *Gone with the Wind*
1940	John Ford, *The Grapes of Wrath*
1941	John Ford, *How Green Was My Valley*
1942	William Wyler, *Mrs Miniver*
1943	Michael Curtiz, *Casablanca*
1944	Leo McCarey, *Going My Way*
1945	Billy Wilder, *The Lost Weekend*
1946	William Wyler, *The Best Years of Our Lives*

1947	Elia Kazan, *Gentleman's Agreement*	1973	George Roy Hill, *The Sting*
1948	John Huston, *Treasure of Sierra Madre*	1974	Francis Ford Coppola, *The Godfather*, Part
1949	Joseph L. Mankiewicz, *A Letter to Three*		*II*
	Wives	1975	Milos Forman, *One Flow Over the Cuckoo's*
1950	Joseph L. Mankiewicz, *All About Eve*		*Nest*
1951	George Stevens, *A Place in the Sun*	1976	John Avildsen, *Rocky*
1952	John Ford, *The Quiet Man*	1977	Woody Allen, *Annie Hall*
1953	Fred Zinnemann, *From Here to Eternity*	1978	Michael Cimino, *The Deer Hunter*
1954	Elia Kazan, *On the Waterfront*	1979	Robert Benton, *Kramer vs. Kramer*
1955	Delbert Mann, *Marty*	1980	Robert Redford, *Ordinary People*
1956	George Stevens, *Giant*	1981	Warren Beatty, *Reds*
1957	David Lean, *The Bridge on the River Kwai*	1982	Richard Attenborough, *Gandhi*
1958	Vincente Minnelli, *Gigi*	1983	James L. Brooks, *Terms of Endearment*
1959	William Wyler, *Ben Hur*	1984	Milos Foreman, *Amadeus*
1960	Billy Wilder, *The Apartment*	1985	Sydney Pollack, *Out of Africa*
1961	Jerome Robbins, Robert Wise, *West Side*	1986	Oliver Stone, *Platoon*
	Story	1987	Bernardo Bertolucci, *The Last Emperor*
1962	David Lean, *Lawrence of Arabia*	1988	Barry Levinson, *Rain Man*
1963	Tony Richardson, *Tom Jones*	1989	Oliver Stone, *Born on the Fourth of July*
1964	George Cukor, *My Fair Lady*	1990	Kevin Costner, *Dances with Wolves*
1965	Robert Wise, *The Sound of Music*	1991	Jonathan Demme, *The Silence of the Lambs*
1966	Fred Zinnemann, *A Man for All Seasons*	1992	Clint Eastwood, *Unforgiven*
1967	Mike Nichols, *The Graduate*	1993	Steven Spielberg, *Schindler's List*
1968	Sir Carol Reed, *Oliver*	1994	Robert Zemeckis, *Forrest Gump*
1969	John Schlesinger, *Midnight Cowboy*	1995	Mel Gibson, *Braveheart*
1970	Franklin J. Schaffner, *Patton*	1996	Anthony Minghella, *The English Patient*
1971	William Friedkin, *The French Connection*	1997	James Cameron, *Titanic*
1972	Bob Fosse, *Cabaret*	1998	Steven Spielberg, *Saving Private Ryan*

6. SPECIAL TOPIC

SPOTLIGHT ON SPIELBERG

Images of Spielberg

Tossing fish-bait into the sea, a Police Chief is startled out of his wits when a man-eating shark looms up out of the water and stares into his eyes in *Jaws* (1975). Seemingly checked by a police roadblock, a young cyclist with his alien companion suddenly becomes airborne and the shadow of a bicycle is later seen soaring across the moon in *E.T. The Extra Terrestrial* (1982). A girl look across in terror as a jelly wobbles ominously on a plate, the floor rocked by the resounding thud of an approaching rampaging dinosaur in *Jurassic Park* (1993).

These are some of the memorable images from the films of Steven Spielberg, the director who, it is claimed, has an instant hotline to the collective unconscious of the masses. If poetry is emotion recollected in tranquillity, cinema is emotion experienced in unanimity and, in the whole history of film, no director has tapped more effectively into mass emotion than Steven Spielberg. This has inevitably made him deeply suspicious in some eyes. He has been accused of gross sentimentality, Fascistic emotional manipulation, and of lowering the intelligence of popular cinema. Even the industry has been grudging with its rewards, withholding for twenty years the Oscar success he craved, seemingly out of envious recognition that they needed him more than he needed them. Yet the situation is changing and this director-superstar, creator of an unparalleled succession of record breaking movies that have made him a millionaire many times over, is now showing unmistakeable signs of becoming a major film artist.

Early Career

Born in December 1946, he had started making ambitious home movies as a teenager. Moving into television, he became the youngest ever director to be contracted by a major studio, Universal Pictures. Two early works, the horror film, *Something Evil* (1971) and the magnificent thriller-cum-road movie,

Duel (1972), in which a mild-mannered motorist is menaced on the highway by a truck whose driver we never see, can count among the finest TV movies ever made. His first feature film, *Sugarland Express* (1974) was described by the influential critic of the *New Yorker*, Pauline Kael as the most exciting American directing debut since *Citizen Kane*. By this time, Spielberg was being grouped with a new breed of Hollywood film makers, the so-called 'Movie Brats' (directors such as Francis Ford Coppola, Brian DePalma, George Lucas and John Milius) who were bringing a youthful fresh perspective to traditional film formulas. If there was something distinctive about Spielberg, it lay in his blend of innocence and precociousness. He combined the heart of a Peter Pan with the technique of an Alfred Hitchcock.

The Major Breakthrough

The big breakthrough came with *Jaws*, a monster hit that was also the most efficient manipulation of an audience's emotions since Hitchcock's *Psycho*. Disarmingly, Spielberg had no respect for the novel, feeling that the 'only likeable character was the shark who ate all the trashy characters'; and he had to overcome all kinds of technical problems when the mechanised monster obstinately refused to behave with the menace required. In response, Spielberg devised a cunning camera style that concealed sight of the shark for long periods, recognising that an unseen horror adds an extra dimension of terror; and he converted the narrative into an ingenious combination of Watergate (communal cover-up) and *Moby Dick* (the shark standing in for the whale). The result was a triumph of popular film-making. He followed it with a splendid science fiction spectacle, *Close Encounters Of The Third Kind* (1977). Five years later, he surpassed even these mega-hits with *E.T., The Extra Terrestrial*, a film that had no sex, no violence, no villains even, and an unsightly main character creature whom, Spielberg said, "only a mother could love". Yet somehow, in this story of an extra-terrestrial who is left behind on earth and is befriended by a lonely boy, Spielberg seemed to bring audiences of all ages into contact with the child within themselves, unleashing powerful, long-forgotten feelings of fantasy, longing and wonder. The cinema seemed to have discovered its new Walt Disney, its J.M. Barrie even.

The Magic of Spielberg

Yet even then, there seemed more to Spielberg than this picture might suggest. When asked to single out a key moment in his films, he would select that famous shot of the little boy in *Close Encounters* opening his door to the light of the UFO—'that beautiful but awful light just like fire coming through the doorway. And he's very small and it's a very large door, and there's a lot of promise or danger outside that door'. An awesome image, then, a daunting special effect of the kind for which he was celebrated; but an image also charged with a feeling of apprehension. For all their feelgood panache, Spielberg's films contained potent anxieties and darker shades. His main characters tended to be anxious, lonely figures; and his heroes were ordinary, flawed people contending precariously with forces larger than themselves. Even his modern matinee-style adventurer Indiana Jones had his phobias and was a scholar at heart. These were no macho supermen but characters uncertain of their masculinity: at this stage, the strongest relationships in his films were between mothers and children (perhaps reflecting his memory of his own childhood, his divorced parents, his absent father).

'The reason so many adults enjoy Steven Spielberg's films,' said the great Polish director, Andrzej Wajda, 'is that they appeal to what remains of a child in every adult. I love everything childish in these films. But it's only a film-maker of Spielberg's standing and intellectual independence who can carry it off.' But what happens to this childlike vision the further you move away from childhood? By the mid 1980s, Spielberg was getting a little old for a boy wonder. His controversial film of Alice Walker's *The Color Purple* (1985) might have prettified the book in some areas but it was still Spielberg's most unflinching portrait at that time of a sustained assault on childlike innocence. He surpassed it two years later in *Empire Of The Sun* (1987), a superb adaptation of J.G.Ballard's semi-autobiographical novel about a child interned in Shanghai during World War Two and so transformed and traumatised by the experience that, at the end, his parents barely recognise him.

New Forms, New Ideas

These were brave films but neither was successful with press or public. Spielberg acknowledged in an interview in 1988 that 'there are certain people in America who want to keep me young; that makes them feel safe ...' By contrast, he was looking to explore new forms, new ideas. When he finally got around to his long awaited version of Peter Pan, he seemed too old to believe it, and the resulting film, *Hook* (1991) was more about fatherhood than childhood and, for all the jolly piratical pranks, imbued less with childhood wonder than adult embitterment. His romantic fantasy, *Always* (1989) failed to connect with its audience, perhaps because Spielberg,

exceptionally deft with action, suspense, observational detail on childhood and suburban domesticity, seems embarrassed when dealing with a full-blown love story. Was he losing his touch?

1993 saw not only a return to box-office form but also a radically new departure. With *Jurassic Park*, he showed he was still unmatched in modern cinema for narrative suspense, astounding special effects and audience involvement. The theme might have contained a technological warning but the technique was a religious aura; the same story-telling gifts, the same unabashed emotionalism, augmented by the throbbing romanticism of the music of his regular composer, John Williams. But even more remarkable that year was *Schindler's List*, Spielberg's film of the Holocaust which, in its monochrome grimness and documentary-style honesty, revealed a maturity and toughness in the director of a kind few critics had ever expected to see.

Perceptions of Spielberg

Perceptions of Spielberg have had to change over recent years. There is still the recurrent theme of ordinary people pursued by large forces; still this distinctive thematic and stylistic mixture of populism and mysticism that sometimes clouds his films with a religious aura; the same story-telling gifts, the same unabashed emotionalism, augmented by the throbbing romanticism of the music of his regular composer, John Williams. But these ingredients are now all enriched by a new directness in the filming. The purging of the ghetto in *Schindler's List*, the drowning of the African slaves in *Amistad* (1997), the carnage of the D-Day landing that so shatteringly opens *Saving Private Ryan* (1998) offer three alternative visions of Spielberg's work to those with which this account opened, and are amongst the most harrowing yet brilliantly sustained sequences of modern cinema. Although these films are ultimately celebrations of human heroism, they do not shirk from showing the appalling behavioural extremes of which humanity in its darkest moments is also capable. At the time of *The Color Purple* he was still pulling his punches. Now there is no holding back.

Indeed, different concerns have now assumed greater prominence. In *Amistad*, he is not afraid of looking again at the vexed history of race relations in America and uncovering unpalatable truths. In *Schindler's List*, he tells a story that compels him in a stark and sombre way to confront his own Jewish identity and heritage. In *Saving Private Ryan*, he returns for the sixth time to the setting of World War Two but with a determination now to do justice to the reality, horror and sacrifice. There is a world of difference between the comic-strip Nazis of the Indiana Jones films and those depicted so chillingly in *Schindler's List*; and a further contrast of characterisation between the Nazis of *Schindler* and the German soldiers of *Saving Private Ryan* who are seen fighting for mere survival with the same frenzy of terror and desperation as their American counterparts. Spielberg has done more than mature: every decade has seen a quantum leap in his development. If the best is yet to come, we can anticipate something quite out of the ordinary.

THE WORLD OF WINE

This section provides a concise but authoritative introduction to a subject that has grown increasingly popular in recent years. There are sections on the history of wine, grape varieties and methods of wine production. There is also a helpful guide to the main wine-producing regions of the world. A Special Topic in this edition examines different types of sherry.

TABLE OF CONTENTS

THE WORLD OF WINE

INTRODUCTION

The Background.

Wine is simply an alcoholic beverage made by fermenting the sugars in grape juice, making alcohol. This simple definition belies the multifarious variables, both natural and man-made which affect the final taste. Different soils, grape varieties and climates, the decisions made by the grape farmer and the wine maker, and the vagaries of the weather mean that there is infinite variety in wine. This choice is what makes wine so fascinating. It is, however, too easy to forget that wine is, for many, one of the staples of life; as much part of the daily routine as bread. As such it is a simple and healthy beverage, something to be talked over, not talked about.

Most of the world's wine is produced in Europe. Italy and France are the biggest producers, followed by Spain. Wine consumption is similarly concentrated in the producing countries, with France, for example consuming over 60 litres per capita, compared with a quarter of this in the UK. Consumption is declining in the major producing countries, but increasing in many countries like the United Kingdom where production is limited. Total wine sales here have increased by nearly 300 per cent over the last twenty years.

History.

It is probable that the first wine was accidental. Perhaps wild grapes were left too long in a pot after being gathered. The weight of the grapes would cause those at the bottom to split, releasing juice which will ferment spontaneously as the necessary yeasts exist naturally on the grapes. The first recorded vineyard in the Judaic and Christian world appears in Genesis. Once the Ark landed after the great flood, Noah planted a vineyard, presumably on the slopes of Mount Ararat. Archaeological evidence too points to south-eastern Europe or the Middle East being wine's original home. Some of today's grape varieties bear witness to the middle eastern connection – the Syrah or Shiraz grape, originally from Syria, and the Muscat.

Wine was certainly known in ancient Egypt and Greece but it was Rome that spread viticulture far and wide. The histories of many of Europe's vineyard regions, from the Rhône to England start with "the vine was originally brought by the Romans". In only a few areas, such as Jerez in Southern Spain, were the Phoenicians responsible. Beyond Europe and the Mediterranean, the wine grape travelled with the European discoverers. Portuguese navigators and Spanish conquistadors were Catholics; they needed wine for the sacrament. Vineyards were established in South America in the 16th century, later spreading into California and the rest of North America. The Cape of Good Hope, established as a victualling station for the Dutch East India Company, was planted with fruit including vines, and the first grapes were pressed in 1652. Australasian vineyards were first planted with cuttings from the Cape.

The Taste of Wine.

A number of different factors influence the taste of wine. Climate, weather and soil are natural. Man can only make minor adjustments, or learn to use that which is given to the best advantage. The decision as to which grape variety to plant is that of the grower, but it is influenced heavily by the climate. Some grapes, such as Riesling, excel in cold areas, others can resist drought and excessive heat. Human influence is most important in grape grow-

ing (viticulture) and wine making (vinification) as at each stage of these processes decisions have to be made which will influence the character and quality of the wine.

Climate and Weather.

Since wine is made from grapes, it follows that it can be made anywhere that grapes can be made to ripen, from as far north as Britain to as far south as New Zealand. In practice there are two bands, one each side of the equator, within which the wine vine, *Vitis vinifera* produces well, situated approximately within the latitudes of 30° to 50° north and south of the equator. Within these zones the climate is suitable for vine cultivation. Other areas are either too cold for the grapes to ripen, or too warm, so the vine turns its energies to vegetative growth rather than fruit production. These bands cover large climatic variations. In the northern hemisphere the band stretches from Germany and southern Britain to North Africa. In the cooler climates, those nearer to the poles, the grapes are only just ripe and produce lighter wines, often with crisp, refreshing acidity. Most of these are white wines. The warmer climatic zones produce riper grapes with higher sugar content and lower acidity. This translates into higher alcohol and lower acidity in the wines, and the wines tend to have more body. The black grapes needed for red wine need more sun, so these areas produce more red wine.

Climate is affected by other geographical features such as proximity to or distance from large bodies of water, ocean currents, altitude and topography. Neighbouring vineyards can produce very different wines, particularly in the more marginal areas. In the Mosel in Germany the best wines are planted on steep south-facing slopes overlooking the river. The next plot of land, perhaps just around the next bend in the river, might be more shaded, to the detriment of the wines.

A region's climate is separate and distinct from its weather. The climate is a function of the geography. The topography and latitude do not vary, whereas weather patterns can alter from one year to the next. This is why one hears about good or bad vintages; a cold night in spring, or rain at the wrong time can adversely affect the crop. Annual weather conditions, sometimes philosophically referred to as the luck of the year, have more influence on wines from the traditional areas of western Europe, where the weather is variable, than "newer" areas such as Australia where the weather is more stable.

Soil.

Soil can have a profound influence on the taste of a wine, as can be seen from the subtle difference between wines from neighbouring vineyards. Vines assimilate trace elements through their roots which alter the chemical composition of the wine. The role of the soil is, however, generally more prosaic. Vines need good drainage, so chalk in Champagne and gravel in the Médoc are ideal. Other hotter areas, like the Sherry region in Spain, rely on the absorbent subsoil to retain water for the vine in the dry summers. Many vineyards are planted in soil which could not support any other agriculture because vines can stand poor soil.

Grape Variety.

As with other fruit, different grape varieties have different flavours, which show in the finished wine. Thousands of different grape varieties are used in wine production. Most are undistinguished, found only in certain areas where they make indifferent wine. However, other varieties have distinctive, recognizable flavours. These more noble grapes are often used unblended, sold under the varietal name. Grapes like Cabernet Sauvignon, Pinot Noir and Chardonnay have become popular internationally. They often flourish in their new homes to the extent that they have become better known there than in the original regions. New Zealand has adopted Sauvignon Blanc, and Australia Shiraz, developing their own particular and highly successful styles.

Grape Growing (Viticulture).

The vine needs careful tending if viticulture is to be profitable. Vines grow prolifically during the spring and summer, so in the winter they are severely pruned. A hedge of vines six or seven feet tall will be reduced to a series of small canes, or short spurs, as the pruners remove the dormant wood. Pruning not only allows access for other vineyard operations, it can also be used to control the quantity and quality of the fruit. Received wisdom is that these are inversely related, so a grower aiming for a high quality wine will prune even more severely to reduce the yield, whereas a bulk producer will maximize it. The main task for the viticulturalist during the rest of the year is controlling the pests and diseases that can attack the vine. Control of fungal and viral infection, and protection from birds and small animals and insect pests is vital. The most serious vineyard pest is *Phylloxera vastarix*, the vine louse accidentally imported to Europe from America during the 19th century. It devastated European vineyards, almost wiping out production until it was discovered that vines grafted onto rootstocks of American native vines were tolerant to it. Since then virtually all European vines have had to be grafted.

Once ripe, the grapes will be harvested, either by hand or machine, and taken to the winery to be made into wine.

Wine Making (Vinification).

Ripe grapes contain all the components required to make wine. The grape consists of a soft pulp gorged with sugar, water and acids, contained in a thin skin which contains colouring, additional flavouring matter and tannins. Tannins are an important preservative in red wines. On the surface of the grape there is a waxy bloom of yeast, required for fermentation. Wine making is thus a natural process; the wine maker's job is to control this.

White Wine Production.

White wine can be made from black or white grapes as all the colouring matter in black grapes is in the skins. The grapes will be pressed and the resulting clear juice (called *must*) transferred to a fermenting vessel where yeasts, either natural or added, convert the sugar into alcohol. For white wine the fermenters are usually kept cool to maintain the aromatic characters. After fermentation the young wine will be clarified and allowed to mature. Most white wines are matured for a short time only, some spending time in oak barrels to add flavour and complexity.

Many white wines are dry, *i.e.* with no detectable sweetness, but there are a number of medium-dry and sweet white wines. To make inexpensive medium-dry wines a quantity of unfermented sterile grape juice is added to the wine just before bottling. High quality classic dessert wines, Sauternes, Tokaji *etc.*, are made with grapes in which the sugars have been concentrated by the action of a fungus called *Botrytis cinerea*. This shrivels the grapes so they look like mouldy raisins. They may look unappealing, but the wines are stunning. It is also possible to make a sweet wine by removing the yeasts physically by using a filter.

This method is used in the production of wines such as Asti.

Red and Rosé Wine Production.

Black grapes are needed here. They are crushed, to break the skins and release the must, but fermented in contact with skins. As the alcohol is formed it extracts some of the colour and tannin, aided by stirring the wines up with pumps or paddles. For rosé wine the still fermenting must will be drained off after a day or two, when it has acquired some, but not much, colour. Red wines spend between five and fourteen days in contact with the skins, depending on the style required. Maturation will follow. For wines like Beaujolais this might only be a few weeks in large inert vats. Other wines, such as fine Claret or top Rioja might spend many months in oak barrels, followed by years, or even decades, in bottle, before reaching their peak.

Reading the Label.

A wine label is an advertisement, but also an identity card, giving all manner of information about the contents. It is a passport, permitting the wine to leave the producer's cellar and even reflects the character of the wine maker. Within the European Union (EU) wine legislation has codified regional, national and supranational regulations. Labels, like the wines themselves, must adhere to a host of rules, most of which consumers can ignore. Outside the EU the rules are less strict, but producers hoping to export must prove the integrity of their labels.

Wine Quality Grades.

All wine produced in the EU is officially categorised as either "Table Wine" or "Quality Wine". Table wine is required to reach certain minimum standards only, whereas quality wine which must come from a stated region must be made according to local regulations and should be typical of the area in which the grapes were grown. The use of the word "Quality" is potentially confusing. Quality wine must exhibit particular qualities, rather than necessarily being of intrinsically high quality. Quality wines are subject to controls on the area of production, type of grape varieties, minimum alcohol levels and methods of viticulture and vinification. Terms indicating Quality Wine include: *Vin Délimité de Qualité Supérieure* (VDQS) and *Appellation d'Origine Contrôlée* (AC) (France); *Qualitätswein bestimmte Anbaugebiete* (QbA) and *Qualitätswein mit Prädikat* (QmP) (Germany); *Denominazione di Origine Controllata* and *Denominazione di Origine Controllata e Garantita* (DOC and DOCG) (Italy); *Denominación de Origen* and *Denominación de Origen Calificada* (DO and DOC) (Spain) and *Denominação de Origem Controlada* in Portugal.

Table wines are usually labelled simply as table wine, but in the language of the producing country; *Vin de Table, Deutscher Tafelwein, Vinho de Mesa etc.* There is a higher grade of table wine which is usually well worth looking out for. These are the Country Wines, *Vins de Pays* in France, which often represent excellent value for money. Outside the EU, in particular in the New World, such rules do not apply. Here the producer's name is paramount and terms such as "Reserve", "Estate Wine", "Limited Release" *etc.* are used to denote the wines with the greatest character.

Other information on the label will include the country of origin, perhaps the region and maybe the grape variety. Each of these give some clue as to the taste of the wine. The year of vintage, when the grapes were picked and wine made, may also appear. This only indicates that all the wine in the bottle comes from the stated year. With the exception of Port and Champagne there is nothing inherently better about vintage wines; non-vintage wines can be as good.

II. WINES OF EUROPE

FRANCE.

France has long been the United Kingdom's most important supplier of wines. We have been buying her wines since long before Eleanor of Aquitaine married Henri d'Anjou, thus bringing Bordeaux and England under the same crown.

Although the totals vary from year to year, around forty per cent of all wine consumed in the UK comes from France; nearly five bottles out of every case (12 bottles) sold. The range of prices and qualities from France is probably greater than anywhere else in the world, from the basic *Vin Rouge* to the finest Bordeaux and Burgundies selling for thousands of pounds a case in the auction rooms of London and New York.

The main wine producing regions are:
*Bordeaux
*Burgundy
*Alsace
*Loire Valley
*Rhône Valley
*Languedoc-Roussillon

Bordeaux.

For 300 years, after 1154, Bordeaux and England shared a monarch. Trade was further aided by the accessibility of the city of Bordeaux, on the Garonne, for ships from London and Bristol. In spite of subsequent political upheavals and Anglo-French wars, claret, the red wine of Bordeaux, remained a popular wine, keeping the smugglers busy when trade with France was proscribed.

Bordeaux is the largest fine wine producing region of France, accounting for about ten per cent of France's total wine production. The range includes some of the finest red and sweet white wines produced anywhere in the world, but the majority of wines called "Bordeaux" are simply everyday wines, best drunk young. The city that gives the region its name lies on the river Garonne. This large river joins the Dordogne to form the Gironde, a wide navigable estuary which eventually flows into the Bay of Biscay. The rivers, the Gironde and the proximity of the Atlantic Ocean give Bordeaux a maritime climate; mild and free of extremes, but humid which can be a problem for the viticulturalist.

This is an area of blended wines; only few varietal wines are sold. The red wines are made principally from Cabernet Sauvignon and Cabernet Franc, related varieties which give high tannin and acidity to the wine with Merlot, which produces higher alcohol, having a softer taste and less tannin. Generally the higher the Cabernet content, the longer the ageing required because of the tannin. Basic Bordeaux Rouge will have a high Merlot content so as to be easy to drink when young.

The two Bordeaux districts that use the highest proportion of Cabernet are the Médoc and Graves. The best wines need time to mature and soften, both in cask and bottle. The best known Merlot-dominated areas are St Emilion and Pomerol. The white wines are made predominantly from a blend of Sauvignon Blanc, an aromatic grape giving high acidity, and Sémillon, a thin skinned grape, easily attacked by noble rot, the basis of the sweet wines such as Sauternes.

Bordeaux is divided into a number of districts, those with the highest reputation are covered below.

Médoc AC.

The Médoc, the most famous of the Bordeaux districts, is divided into two. The Haut-Médoc, the southern part, being the better. Within the Haut Médoc are the famous communes, or parishes, of St Estèphe, Pauillac, St Julien and Margaux. The wines, which are all red, are usually sold under the names of the châteaux, or estate, where the grapes were grown. In 1855, to coincide with an exhibition in Paris, the best wines of Bordeaux were classified. All but one of the red wines come from the Haut-Médoc. The exception, Château Haut Brion, is from Graves. Hundreds of châteaux were eligible, yet a mere 58 were classified as *Cru classé* ("classed growths"), or vineyard. Five levels were identified,

first to fifth growth. Originally only four châteaux, the greatest of all, were given the designation *premier cru classé* or first growth. Apart from the changes of ownership and occasional renaming of vineyards, the only change to the classification since its inception has been the promotion of Château Mouton Rothschild to First Growth in 1973.

Cru classé wines are thus inevitably expensive. *Cru Bourgeois*, a later classification, indicates above average, more affordable Bordeaux. Recent improvements have resulted in many of these having reached comparable quality to some *Cru Classé*.

Graves AC.

Graves is named for its gravel soil. Here red and white wines are produced, the latter in dry or off-dry styles. The northern part, around the city of Bordeaux, produces the best quality. Acknowledging this, the area was granted the AC Pessac-Léognan in 1987. Château Haut Brion is included in this appellation.

Sauternes AC.

Sauternes lies 30 miles south-east of Bordeaux, surrounded by Graves. Sauternes is always white and sweet, ideally made from grapes affected by *Botrytis cinerea*. The shrivelled grapes yield very concentrated juice which results in fine sweet wines. Like the Médoc, Sauternes was classified in 1855. Château d'Yquem became the only *Premier Grand Cru Classé*. There are also *Premier* and *Deuxième Cru Châteaux*.

Barsac is a commune within Sauternes. Its wines may be labelled Barsac or Sauternes, so all Barsac is Sauternes, but not all Sauternes is Barsac.

St Emilion AC.

On the right bank the soil is heavier, and the terrain hillier. The Merlot grown here gives wines rich in flavour, but which mature earlier than the wines of the Médoc. St Emilion is an Appellation for red wines only. Classification came later here, in 1955. In contrast to the Médoc it is revised every decade, so there is a variable number of classified Châteaux. The two most famous are Châteaux Ausone and Cheval Blanc.

Pomerol.

Pomerol is a small commune adjoining St Emilion making red wine only, again from the Merlot. No classification exists here but the two top wines, Châteaux Pétrus and Le Pin, regularly command prices higher than the first growths of the Médoc.

Burgundy.

Burgundy was probably the first of the French regions to establish a reputation beyond its frontiers, largely because of the interest taken by the Dukes of Burgundy. The first recorded edict to control wine quality was issued by Philip the Bold in 1395. Realising that the Gamay grape did not make good wine in northern Burgundy, he banished it from that area. Demand for fine Burgundy outstrips supply, largely because Burgundian production, excluding Beaujolais, is about 20% of that of Bordeaux. Fine Burgundy is never cheap. Burgundy is in central France, between Dijon and Lyon. It also includes Chablis, 60 miles to the north-west of Dijon, and Beaujolais. The climate here is more continental, characterised by extremes of temperature.

Only four grapes are important; in contrast to Bordeaux, they are largely used unblended. The red wines are made from Gamay in Beaujolais, giving soft, quaffable wines. More serious wines are made further north from Pinot Noir. From the best vineyards very fine wines result, medium in colour relying on high acidity rather than tannin to survive long ageing. Chardonnay makes all classic white Burgundy. Often fermented and aged in wood to add complexity and depth of flavour, Burgundy is the traditional home of that most international of jet-set grape varieties. Perhaps surprisingly, given the grape's international repute, Chardonnay almost never appears on Burgundian labels. Some wine is also made from Aligoté, a lesser white grape, usually sold under a varietal label, *e.g.* Bourgogne Aligoté.

The Appellations of Burgundy.

Most Burgundy is sold under a generic appellation, Bourgogne Rouge and Bourgogne Blanc. A higher appellation is the district one, such as Côte de Beaune or Haute Côte de Nuits. But it is the commune and vineyard appellations on which Burgundy's reputation rests. As in Bordeaux, the districts are divided into communes. Wines produced entirely from grapes grown in a particular commune take its name, *e.g.* Meursault. In the nineteenth century, at a time of poor sales in the area, communes added their name to that of their most famous vineyard, so the commune of Gevrey added the name of the vineyard of Chambertin becoming Gevrey-Chambertin. Nuits-St George and Puligny-Montrachet are other examples. The best vineyards are classified as *Premier Cru* or *Grand Cru*. In the past one has had to know the long list of these to recognise them from the label. Nowadays most producers are more explicit, clearly boasting of the higher grading.

There are five main districts in Burgundy. From the north the first is Chablis, producing white wine only from Chardonnay. Bone dry and almost flinty in character, Chablis rarely sees oak, so this is unadorned Chardonnay. The Côte d'Or, the golden slope between Dijon and Santenay is the heart of Burgundy. Here some of the most sought after red and white wines in the world are produced. It comprises the Côte de Nuits in the north, largely a red wine area, and the Côte de Beaune, where both Pinot Noir and Chardonnay are grown. Côte de Nuits includes such famous names as Gevrey-Chambertin, Nuits-St Georges and Chambolle-Musigny; the stars of the Côte de Beaune include Meursault and Puligny-Montrachet, Volnay and Pommard. Further south are the districts of Chalonnaise and Maconnais. Here more affordable Burgundies, both red and white are produced, an ideal introduction to the region. In red wine Macon forms the transition between the Côte d'Or and Beaujolais, being a blend of Pinot Noir and Gamay.

Beaujolais.

Beaujolais produces light fruity red wines from Gamay. Most are best drunk young, indeed most Beaujolais is drunk in the year of vintage, as Beaujolais Nouveau, released in November when the wine is two months old. The north of the district produces fuller wines, under the appellations of Beaujolais Villages or, better still, one of the ten communes, the best known being St Amour, Fleurie and Moulin-à-Vent.

Alsace.

Alsace, in north-eastern France, borders Germany. The border has moved at various times in history so Alsace has been German, and the Germanic influence is still visible in the architecture and vineyards of the area. Unusually for French wines, Alsace wines are usually varietally labelled, the most important being: Riesling, Gewurztraminer, Sylvaner, Pinot Gris and Pinot Blanc. A little red wine from Pinot Noir is also produced. Although made from Germanic grapes, and bottled in tall green flutes like Mosel bottles, Alsace wines are distinctly French, made to accompany the rich and diverse cuisine of the region. Unlike most German wine exported, the wines from here are generally dry with strong varietal character. They include the spicy, exotic Gewurztraminer, oily Pinot Gris and steely Riesling. Wines labelled "Reserve" or "Selection" or something similar, are blended from better vats, the pick of the crop. Vendange Tardive and Selection de Grains Nobles are rare and exquisite late picked wines, off-dry to sweet in taste.

Loire Valley.

The Loire is the longest river in France, rising in the Massif Central. Viticulturally only the lower half is considered "the Loire". Each of the four sub-

regions – Nantais, Anjou-Saumur, Touraine and the Central vineyards – has its own climate and wines. Most wines are made from one varietal, but here the name of the village or region is paramount. In this northerly part of France the climate is generally cool so white and rosé wines dominate.

Nantais is the home of Muscadet, one of the largest selling quality wines in the UK. Muscadet is the name of the grape as well as the wine, a dry, fairly neutral white wine usually drunk young and fresh to accompany lightly flavoured seafood.

Anjou-Saumur produces mostly dry white wines, from the Chenin Blanc under the Saumur appellation, and red, white and rosé as Anjou. The medium sweet Rosé d'Anjou has been the introductory wine for a generation of British wine lovers. The enclave of Côteaux du Layon produces sweet and medium sweet wine from the Chenin Blanc. This sheltered area, influenced by the river Layon, benefits from noble rot.

Farther up river in *Touraine* Chenin Blanc is joined by Sauvignon Blanc. Sauvignon is often used for the Touraine appellation, but Chenin makes the area's most famous appellation, Vouvray. From one grape a wide variety of styles are produced; dry, medium or sweet, still or sparkling. Confusingly the label does not always reveal the style of wine in the bottle, you need to trust your wine merchant.

The *Central Vineyards* are so-called because they are close to the centre of France. Here Sauvignon produces the famous Pouilly Fumé and Sancerre; appellations for what until recently was universally considered the world's best Sauvignon.

Some red wines are made in the Loire. As well as Anjou Rouge there are Chinon and Bourgueil, made from the Cabernet Franc, and red Sancerre from Pinot Noir.

Rhône Valley.

The Rhône Valley is one of the oldest wine producing regions of France. It is certain that wine existed there by *c.* 600 BC, and it is believed that the steep terraced vineyards of the northern Rhône were the earliest French vine plantations.

Historically Rhône wines were blended with lighter wines, including claret. Recently though their quality has begun to be appreciated, and finally the best are achieving prices comparable with Bordeaux and Burgundy. The region starts south of Lyons at Vienne and extends south to Avignon. It divides neatly in two with a gap around Montélimar, more famous for nougat. The northern and southern districts produce quite different styles of wine, a result of different topography, soils, grapes and climates. Basic Côtes du Rhône can be produced anywhere in the region, but in practice it is nearly always a southern Rhône wine. As with Beaujolais, there is a higher grade, labelled Côtes du Rhône Villages. This is more concentrated and fuller bodied.

The Northern Rhône.

The Northern Rhône comprises a steep hillside, facing east. Here the cliffs are so steep that terraces are required, and all the vineyard functions have to be done by hand. The grape here is Syrah, perhaps now better known by the Australian name Shiraz. Big, full flavoured wines with the structure to age result, sold under the names of the communes such as Côte Rôtie, Cornas and Hermitage. In the middle of the Northern Rhône lie two small, but very prestigious white wine vineyards, Condrieu and Chateau Grillet, producing the epitome of an unusual, flavoursome variety called Viognier.

The Southern Rhône.

The Southern Rhône is less uniform. The valley broadens out to a wide plain, the climate becomes very Mediterranean, with olives and oranges a frequent sight. The range of grapes here also broadens out. Over a dozen different varieties are permitted, but the Grenache is the most widely employed. Relatively pale coloured wines, with high alcohol and little staying power can result, but the majority of producers use judicious amounts of other grapes as improvers to their blends. In contrast to the north, this is the home of large volume average wines plus a few greats, including Châteauneuf-du-Pape, Gigondas and the dry rosé Tavel.

From 1309 to 1378, the Popes lived at Avignon. Pope John XXII built a new palace in the southern Rhône, hence Châteauneuf-du-Pape.

Languedoc-Roussillon.

This great swathe of vineyard extends from the Spanish border to the Rhône estuary and produces one third of all French wines. Once derided, the "Midi" is now a hotbed of innovation in viticulture and vinification. Once the source of much of the EU wine lake, today the emphasis is on quality.

A mix of local grapes goes into the area's appellations, which include Fitou, Côtes du Roussillon, Corbières and Minervois, but it is the international varieties used in the increasingly successful Vin de Pays d'Oc which are changing the area's reputation. Famous grapes, handled well, and marketed by variety offer the consumer a reliable and understandable product, at prices which offer excellent value.

GERMANY.

Germany maintains its ranking as one of the chief UK wine suppliers. For many, Germany is the introduction to wine drinking, but there is far more to Germany than Liebfraumilch. Germany's vineyards are in the south of the country, on the limit of vine cultivation. The climate is cool and damp, so the quality of the vintage depends heavily on the weather. The best vineyards are planted on steep south-facing hillsides, suntraps to collect every available solar ray. In such a marginal climate ripe grapes are at a premium, German wine legislation reflects this.

Deutscher Tafelwein and *Deutscher Landwein* are the two grades of table wine. Little is produced and even less exported. About 95 % of Germany's wine is quality wine, of which there are two grades. *Qualitätswein bestimmte Anbaugebiete* (QbA, or simply *Qualitätswein*) is the basic category. The wine will come from one of the thirteen *Anbaugebiete* (regions) which is stated on the label.

Each region is divided into districts, *Bereiche*, such as Bereich Bernkastel in the Mosel. Most individual wines come from single vineyards, *Einzellage*. For commercial reasons a group of vineyards producing similar wines may be grouped together into a *Grosslage*; examples include Niersteiner Gutes Domtal and Piesporter Michelsberg. Riper grapes than QbA can go to make *Qualitätswein mit Prädikat* (QmP). Again the wine must come only from the *Anbaugebiet* stated, but it is the level of ripeness, rather than the provenance which gains the wine its esteem. The categories, in ascending order of natural grape sugar at time of harvesting, are as follows:

Kabinett, from grapes harvested at the normal time but with higher natural grape sugar. These are amongst the lightest and most delicate of all wines.

Spätlese indicates late harvest; a more intense and concentrated style.

Auslese, where only extra ripe bunches are selected.

Beerenauslese wines are made from individually selected berries, a labour of love. These overripe individual grapes, normally affected by noble rot, produce wines with considerable residual sweetness.

Eiswein grapes have their sugar concentrated by freezing, on the vine. Frosts of −8 to −10°C are needed, for a minimum of about eight hours. This freezes the water in the grapes which are pressed when frozen. The resulting juice makes rare wines of great richness.

Trockenbeerenauslese is the highest grade, made from individually selected, heavily botrytised grapes which have shrivelled like raisins.

It is the sugar level of the grape, not the wine, which determines the quality level. *Kabinett*, *Spätlese*, and even occasionally *Auslese* wine are available in dry (trocken) styles, although medium sweet is more normal.

Germany has many grape varieties but three are

particularly important. Riesling is the finest German grape. Late ripening, but with fine flavours and acidity, it allows wine to mature almost indefinitely. Silvaner ripens earlier than Riesling, giving firm spicy wines. The productive Müller-Thurgau variety was developed because of the climate. It yields generously and is precocious, an insurance against the inclement autumns. Müller-Thurgau accounts for more vineyard area than any other variety.

There are thirteen vineyard regions in Germany, six are important for exports. All follow the routes of Germany's great rivers.

The Mosel.

Mosel-Saar-Ruwer produces pale, light in body yet intensely elegant wines. The steep, south facing slopes of the Mosel and its tributaries, with their slate soil, collect the warmth of the sun to ripen the grapes.

Rheinhessen and Pfalz.

These are the country's two largest regions. Their wines are fuller in style than Mosel. Generically these wines are referred to as "hock", from the village of Hocheim. Most Rheinhessen and Pfalz wines seen in export markets are Müller Thurgau based blends, sold as Liebfraumilch or Niersteiner Gutes Domtal. The vineyards around Nierstein, however, are capable of producing some stunning wines.

Rheingau.

Only here does the Rhine (in German, Rhein) flow east to west, giving the northern bank, the Rheingau, a perfect southerly exposure. Its aspect and topography make this the ideal area for Riesling, representing four-fifths of the regions' vineyards. Rheingau is home to some of Germany's greatest wine estates such as Vollrads, and Johannisberg, and famous villages such as Rüdesheim and Geisenheim.

Nahe.

This area marks the transition between the fuller Rhine styles and the delicate Mosel wines, in addition to producing some Liebfraumilch.

Baden.

Baden, opposite Alsace in the far south of Germany, is becoming important in export markets. The warmer climate permits fuller bodied wines, both red and white. They are mostly dry, and often appear more French, being bottled in shorter, wider bottles, like those used for Burgundy.

Liebfraumilch.

Liebfraumilch is not a region but a style of blended wine. The name originated from a vineyard at Worms in the Rheinhessen, but the wine can come from any one of the four Rhine regions, Rheinhessen, Pfalz, Rheingau or Nahe. The law requires it to be soft, fruity and easy to drink. It must be of QbA status.

ITALY.

So successful is the vine in Italy that the Greeks called the country Oenotria, the land of the vine. Fittingly, Italy is still the world's largest wine producer. Wine is integrally linked to the culture of the country. Wine is a staple part of the diet. A meal is not a meal without wine. As such the wines must match the local food, as diverse and individualistic as the Italian people.

Italy is made up of twenty regions, each individual and each intent on protecting its own identity. It is a long country, covering ten degrees of latitude; the climate, the people and the culture are very different from Piedmont to Sicily.

DOC (*Denominazione di Origine Controllata*) was introduced in 1963 with the rules designed along the same lines as *Appellation Controllée*. Very soon there were hundreds of DOC wines. To differentiate themselves, certain highly reputed areas were granted a higher grading, DOCG (*Denominazione di Origine*

Controllata e Garantita). DOCG imposes stricter controls, including mandatory regional bottling and organoleptic analysis. There are currently over a dozen DOCGs, a number which is growing steadily.

Table wine (*Vino da Tavola*) is normally simple, everyday, cheap wine, often sold in two litre bottles. Some producers, however, deliberately break the DOC rules by, for example, growing the "wrong" grape variety. The resulting wine is *Vino da Tavola*, but often more expensive than DOC.

An enormous number of grape varieties are cultivated in Italy. Some, like Nebbiolo, Lambrusco, Sangiovese and Verdiccio are natives, rarely grown elsewhere. There are also historical imports, now naturalised Italians. Pinot Grigio and Merlot, introduced at the time of Napoleon, are widely used in northern Italian wines. Additionally there are the inevitable internationals, Chardonnay and Cabernet Sauvignon.

DOC and DOCG wines always state the area of origin *e.g.* Barolo, Frascati. In some cases the region is prefixed with the grape as well: examples being Barbera d'Alba and Merlot di Pramaggiore. This latter method of labelling has an advantage where a number of different grapes are grown, used unblended.

Principal Wines.

Although Italy produces a vast range of wines, many are not exported in large volumes. The principal export wines are:

*Barolo DOCG – a Nebbilo based red wine from the village of Barolo in Piedmont, the foothills of the Alps. It must be at least three years old before sale, but then has great additional ageing potential. Barolo is a very full bodied wine with high alcohol, tannin and acidity.

*Barbaresco DOCG – is a red wine from the Nebbiolo grape in Piedmont. Similar to Barolo in style, though Barbaresco generally is a touch lighter.

*Valpolicella DOC – is normally a lighter red wine made from a mixture of grapes grown in vineyards near Verona, in the north east. Most Valpolicella should be drunk young.

*Soave DOC – a very dry but fruity white wine named after the commune of Soave near Verona.

*Lambrusco – a lightly sparkling and usually medium sweet Central Italian wine from the grape of the same name. Lambrusco is a black grape, so red, white and rosé wines can be made. Most is sold as table wine, but DOC Lambruscos are much finer.

*Pinot Grigio – dry white wine made from the Pinot Grigio grape in many parts of Italy, but particularly in the north east. It is a fresh, fruity wine with a crisp acidity.

*Chianti DOCG – a red wine produced in Tuscany and made from Sangiovese, and other grapes. It can vary in style from light red wines made for early drinking to well-aged wines with great depth of flavour. Chianti Classico, the centre of the area, produces some of the best Chiantis.

*Orvieto DOC – a white wine made in Umbria. Traditionally Orvieto was *abboccato*, or semi sweet, but today most Orvieto is made dry.

*Frascati DOC – is a white wine usually dry, although sweeter styles are permitted under the DOC. It is made just south of Rome. Like many Italian whites, it tends to be light in flavour.

SPAIN.

Spain has more land under vines than any other country, but because of the dry climate, ranks only third in production terms.

Spain's top quality black grape is Tempranillo. Found in both Spain and Portugal, under a whole host of synonyms, this gives the flavour, backbone and structure to all of Spain's top reds. Garnacha is also important, but more for volume. It is widely planted throughout Spain. For white wine the volume grape is Airén, the world's most widely planted variety, all in Spain. It produces refreshing neutral wines if well handled, but is not a high quality grape. Viura is the top white grape.

Spain too has both quality and table wines. Like Italy, there are two categories of Quality Wine, Denominacion de Origen (DO) and Denominacion

de Origen Calificada (DOC). There are over fifty DOs, and one DOC, Rioja. Little Spanish table wine, vino de mesa, is exported as many DO wines represent better value. The most important exports are:

Rioja.

Rioja is in northern Spain, along the banks of the river Ebro, and its tributary the Rio Oja, which gives the region its name. Divided into three (Alta Alavesa and Baja) the main centres are Logroño and Haro. Most Riojas are blended from the different districts and shipped by merchant houses in these two towns. Oak maturation, in American oak casks, gives the distinctive flavour to Reserva and Gran Reserva wines, both red and white. However, many Riojas are made without wood.

Navarra.

Navarra is north of Rioja. It enjoys a cool, temperate climate, enabling elegant red and white wines to be produced.

La Mancha.

This area is a vast arid plateau south of Madrid. The climate is extreme, scorching in the summer and very cold during the winter. The largest area of production in Spain, much of the wine goes to brandy production. The light wines, both red and white, are steadily improving.

Penedés DO.

Most Cava, Spain's quality sparkling wine, is produced here, west-south-west of Barcelona. This is also an area of innovation, with modern wine-makers using blends of traditional local varieties with international ones.

Other areas becoming more important through recent investment and improvement include Somontano, in the foothills of the Pyrenees and Ribera del Duero on the Duero river.

PORTUGAL.

Northern Portugal comprises a coastal littoral, rising steeply to mountainous inland regions. Further south the plains continue further inland. Atlantic winds bring rain during the winter months and the summers are hot.

Portuguese quality wine is categorised as Denominação de Origem Controlada or Indicação de Proveniencia Regulamentada. Often the label will simply give the catch-all initials of VQPRD. The regional wines, and some of the newer DOC wines from the south, Borba, Palmela, Arruda and Arrabida are gradually becoming more important than some of the classic DOC areas.

Portugal's most popular light wine export, selling in large quantities, is the medium dry rosé Mateus and a similar wine, Lancers. These are examples of excellent wine marketing; having no tradition or history, they were invented for export, and have been amongst the biggest selling brands of wine ever since.

Apart from Port, Vinho Verde and Mateus Rosé few other Portuguese light wines have had much export success until recently. The Salazar regime which came to an end in the early 1970s had imposed restrictive practices on the industry, limiting progress. Following the return of democracy and after joining the EU, Portugal has caught up. Traditional areas are improving, while new areas are now getting more international recognition. The main regions are listed below.

Vinho Verde.

"Vinho Verde" means "green wine" a reference to its youthful character. Fresh in acidity and moderate in alcohol, it is best consumed when young (or green). Vinho Verde is produced in northern Portugal. High trained vines give barely ripe grapes, while enabling other agriculture on the same land. More red wine than white wine is produced, but the red is only consumed in Portugal.

Dão.

Dão is south of the Douro valley in northern central Portugal, a wild and beautiful country with terraced vineyards on granite slopes. Until recently the wines tended to be dried out, aged for too long before sale. Investment since 1986 has rectified this.

Bairrada.

South of Oporto, between Dão and the Atlantic, Bairrada makes some excellent red wines, sometimes matured successfully for several years.

CENTRAL AND EASTERN EUROPE.

Eastern Europe has a long history of wine making, and a large collection of native grape varieties. The use of international varieties, however, has captured new export markets. The region's export successes started with Lutomer Laski Rizling. This medium dry white wine, from Slovenia, has been exported since the 1940s and is still amongst the biggest white wine brands on the UK market.

Apart from Bulgarian Cabernet Sauvignon, Romanian Pinot Noir and Hungarian Chardonnay, there are a couple of true Central European classics, both from Hungary.

Bulls Blood.

Bulls Blood of Eger, or *Egri Bikaver*, is made around the town of Eger in Hungary and takes its name from a 16th century legend in which the Turks besieged Eger. The soldiers manning the castle ramparts were kept supplied with wine. Inspired, or uninhibited by the wine, the soldiers fought so bravely that the Turks came to believe that their enemies had been drinking the blood of bulls.

Tokaji.

Tokaji Aszú has been famous since the time of the crusades. Made in north-east Hungary, near Slovakia, this is one of the world's great botrytis-affected dessert wines. Hot summers, long autumns and the proximity of the river Tisza, create ideal conditions for noble rot. Traditionally an oxidized style, the wine is orange brown in colour with a pungent honey and caramel character. Quality and sweetness grades are announced by the "*puttonyos*" level, marked on the label (usually between three and five, with six occasionally seen).

III. WINES OF THE NEW WORLD

THE NEW WORLD.

Introduction.

The New World is an arbitrary term in wine production. Officially the western hemisphere, the Americas, is has come to be a shorthand for all non-European wine producing countries which have been colonies of European powers, and retain a significant degree of European culture. Thus the Americas are included, alongside South Africa, Australia and New Zealand, but India is not. Rules here are less formal than in Europe. Unencumbered by the restrictions of *Appellation Contrôlée*, growers are freer to plant the grapes they chose, and winemakers can create blends that would horrify the European purist: all to the good of their markets.

The Earliest Vineyards.

The earliest New World vineyards were in Latin America, the vines having been brought by the Catholic Iberian sailors. Mexico can trace its viticultural history back to 1522, and vines are known to have been planted in Peru and Chile by the 1550s. South African vineyards were first planted in the middle of the seventeenth century by the Dutch East India Company. Cuttings were taken from the Cape to Australia, though unsuccessful, vineyard being planted in Sydney in 1788. New Zealand finally got its first vines in 1819.

North American viticulture started on two fronts. The missionary movement brought the vines successfully into California, but the settlers in Virginia, who started planting vines in the first half of the seventeenth-century, found their efforts were to no avail. Despite profuse growth of native vines their efforts failed. Only later was the nature of the pests and disease affecting their vines discovered, namely scourges of mildew and phylloxera which would later devastate European vineyards. High ambient temperatures and unsophisticated local markets meant many New World wines were historically high in alcohol (often fortified) and lacking finesse or character. Since the 1970s, however, there has been a sea change in attitudes. Nowadays the New World is the centre of innovation. A high degree of technical knowledge and an obsession with hygiene has made the wines of places such as Australia and California the envy of the rest of the world, while the lack of rigid rules has made it possible to follow wine fashion more easily than in the Old World.

NORTH AMERICA.

Vines are planted in most states of the USA, and in Canada, but California is by far the most important. The southerly latitude is compensated for by a cooling influence from the Pacific, making fine wine production possible. Initially vines were planted near Los Angeles, but the gold rush of 1849, a boom for the industry, moved the centre of gravity north to San Francisco. Prohibition from 1920 to 1933 devastated the winemaking industry but many major growers, such as Gallo, started then. Grape growing for home winemaking (for personal consumption) continued to be legal.

A massive proportion of the Californian grape harvest is controlled by E & J Gallo, whose main vineyards are in the hot Central Valley region. Smaller, more individual wineries, often called "boutique" are located in the finer areas such as Sonoma, Napa, Santa Barbera and Montery.

SOUTH AMERICA.

Argentina is one of the world's largest producers of wine, usually fourth in the league table. The vineyards are mostly in the west of the country, particularly around San Juan and Mendoza. Exports to the UK were growing in the 1970s but ceased at the time of the Falklands conflict in 1982, and have only recently started to recover.

Chile, the second largest South American producer is far more important in our market. The vineyards nestle between the peaks of the Andes in the east, and coastal ranges in the west. These, and the cooling influence of the Pacific, make for fine, varietal wines, with clear varietal definition. Bordeaux varieties in particular grow well here. Cabernet Sauvignon, Merlot and Sauvignon Blanc are widely used.

A number of other countries in South America

produce wine. Brazil is the third most important producer on the continent; Uruguay and Peru also produce significant volumes of wine, but these are rarely exported to the UK.

SOUTH AFRICA.

Introduction.

The South African wine industry's history is as long as that of the country itself. Records of successful winemaking date back to 1652, nine years after the founding of the Dutch colony at the Cape. The colony was founded to supply fresh food, in particular fruit, to Dutch trading ships rounding the Cape of Good Hope on their way to and from the East. Fortunately, Cape Town and the surrounding area enjoys a perfect climate for fruit production of all kinds; the grape is just one.

South Africa has a little over one per cent of the world's vineyards, ranking twentieth in area under vine, but yields are such that she produces enough wine to put her eighth in volume production. Until very recently South Africa produced more than twice as much wine as Australia, although over fifty per cent was used for non-wine purposes, such as brandy and grape spirit production.

South Africa's reputation as a wine producer has varied considerably during the last three hundred and fifty years. In the eighteenth century the great sweet Muscat based wines of Constantia, a vineyard on the Cape peninsula set up by the Governor Simon van der Stel in 1685, were considered amongst the best wines of the world, ranking alongside the legendary Tokaji and the finest Burgundies. The reputation fell over the subsequent century so that in 1918 the KWV, a farmers' co-operative with wide-ranging and highly restrictive powers was set up to bring supply and demand in the industry into balance. The KWV sets minimum prices and purchases surplus grapes for distillation. In addition, it controls the Wine of Origin certificates. Since the end of National Party rule and the increased acceptance of South African produce in world markets, export sales have increased dramatically, to the extent that the better producers do not have enough wine to sell.

Location.

Most of the best of South Africa's vineyards are within a radius of about sixty miles of Cape Town. Here, near the coast, the Benguela current from Antarctica cools the climate enough to produce elegant wines. Further away the vineyards are hotter and tend to produce base wines for fortified wines, or wines for distillation. The main vineyard region is mountainous but with wide valley-floors used for all forms of agriculture, including viticulture. Irrigation is necessary in some areas and most vineyards have the option to irrigate if needed. Soils vary widely.

Grapes.

Many different grapes are grown but the most important is Chenin Blanc, often vinified to a relatively neutral dry or just off-dry style. It is locally known as Steen. Sauvignon Blanc, Colombard, Crouchen (known as "Cape Riesling"), Clairette and Semillion are also important. Chardonnay got off to a late start here because of strict vine quarantine regulations. Additionally, vine cuttings smuggled in without going through quarantine turned out to be other varieties. It is now one of the most important varieties, but the vines themselves are still young.

Black varieties account for only fifteen per cent of the vineyard area, despite the warm climate. This is partly a function of the historical isolation of the industry here. Although black grapes ripen well, the market has been for white wine. Perhaps the opening-up of the export markets will change the balance and increase the planting of black varieties.

Most of the black varieties are from the Rhône. Cinsaut (spelt Cinsault in France), Syrah, Grenache and Carignan are important, as are Cabernet Sauvignon and, to a lesser extent, Pinot Noir. Pinotage is a variety developed locally by crossing Pinot Noir with Cinsaut. It produces big, strapping red wines with dark berry and banana skin aromas.

Labelling.

South Africa has had controls on its labelling for longer than most New World countries, and has been at the forefront of varietal, or cultivar, labelling. Unlike Australia and the USA where terms like Burgundy and Moselle have been overused, most South African wine is sold with its grape variety and region or district on the label. The Wine of Origin (WO) scheme was introduced in 1973. WO regulations are often compared to AC in France but the comparison is unfair. WO regulations do not control what grape is grown where, nor how the grapes are made into wine. WO guarantees the integrity of the label, so that if a grape variety, estate or vintage is claimed, it must be genuine (within the tolerances allowed). Each wine is certified, as indicated by a numbered seal on the capsule.

Wine Regions.

The three Cape wine districts most often seen on the export market are:

Constantia.

A small area in Cape Town's southern suburbs, and therefore cooled by the oceans on both sides of the peninsula. Klein Constantia is the most important producer here. Groot Constantia, once part of the same estate, was the home of the famed Constantia wine. It is now both a working wine farm and a popular tourist attraction.

Stellenbosch.

Stellenbosch is the university town where most South African wine makers take their degrees. The government research institute is based in Stellenbosch, and the district has the largest concentration of high rating estates.

Paarl.

Paarl has a number of leading estates, and is also the home of the KWV, the controlling body of the industry and producer of vast quantities of brandy and other spirits. The hotter climate here makes sherry-like fortified wines successful.

"Coastal Region" and "Western Cape" are terms for larger regions, allowing the blending of wines from two or more districts for commercial reasons.

AUSTRALIA.

Background Note.

It is not often realised that Australian wine has been on the UK market for many years. In the period immediately preceding World War II the UK imported more wine from Australia than from France, encouraged by Imperial Preference which reduced the tax payable. Sales dropped away after that however and by the time of their return to the market in the late 1980s Australian wine was seen by most in the UK as a novelty, sold in only a few outlets and hardly treated as serious wine. Now it is well established. Sales have increased every year and it now accounts for well over ten per cent of the growing wine market. This success can be traced to the reliable climate, simple, straightforward labelling and high technology.

History.

The first vines were brought to Australia from South Africa in 1788 and planted in the Governor's garden in Sydney. Vine cultivation soon grew. By the mid-nineteenth century South Australia, New South Wales and Victoria all had significant wine industries. Much of the wine was high-strength, often but not always, fortified. Modern Australian winemaking began in the 1950s when temperature control became feasible. Shortly after this the trend to light, and away from fortified, wines began, and in the 1970s varietal labelling became fashionable, one of the first parts of the world to take varietal labelling seriously.

Production.

All six mainland states and Tasmania make wine but it is the southern tips that dominate production. Here the climate is cooler (although no part of Australia has a climate ideal for ripening grapes.) South Australia is the most important wine producing state but Victoria, New South Wales and Western Australia also produce significant volumes. In contrast to France, brands are more important than regions here. Four big wine companies control four-fifths of the production, the remainder is made by hundreds of smaller producers. The major producers own vineyards but also supplement their needs by buying grapes from professional grape growers.

Free of the European paranoia about over production, irrigation is standard practice in many regions, particularly those high-volume workhorse regions producing less expensive wine. This is essential in areas with such a dry summer climate. In a country as vast as this, soils vary enormously. The generally held view has been that soils are not important but there is an increasing recognition of the importance of soil type and structure.

Even smaller wineries are well equipped. Hygiene is an obsession, so easy-to-clean stainless steel is standard. In such a warm area, temperature control is vital. Machine harvesting allows for night-time picking, so grapes arrive at the winery cool, and vast refrigeration plants within the winery are used to keep fermentation temperature down to preserve the fruit flavours.

Grapes.

Most exported Australian wine is made from internationally famed varieties. Shiraz, the Syrah of the northern Rhône, Cabernet Sauvignon, Grenache and Pinot Noir are the most important black grapes; Chardonnay, Sultana (better known as the table grape, Thomson Seedless) and Semillon the most important white ones.

Styles.

Australia has developed a distinctive wine style. Generally full flavoured, very modern and clean, they exhibit pronounced varietal characteristics. The use of new oak is widespread. Three wines made in Australia have no equivalents elsewhere and can be considered unique. These are the "Tokays" and Muscats of Victoria (in particular Rutherglen Muscats) and the unoaked, but often long aged Semillons of the Hunter Valley. These latter have often been likened to old dry Rieslings.

Regions.

The commonest Australian wine region seen in the UK is Southeast Australia. This term, which covers the states of South Australia, New South Wales and Victoria, permits blending from two or more regions within these states. Such inter-regional blending is an anathema in Europe but is used to add complexity or to ensure consistency of the wine.

The main areas for volume production are Riverland and Riverina. These irrigated areas, which are both within the Southeast Australia region, produce most of the inexpensive wine sold on the domestic market. Often this is sold in the bag-in-box format, rather than bottles.

South Australia.

The premium South Australian regions include Barossa and Coonawarra, renowned for their red wines, in particular Shiraz and Cabernet Sauvignon respectively. Clare Valley, north of Adelaide, and the Eden Valley in the Barossa ranges are famed for their Rieslings. Padthaway in the far south of the state is particularly noted for its Sauvignon and Chardonnay.

New South Wales.

New South Wales has the second largest production. Nearly two-thirds of the total comes from Riverina but the main premium area is the Hunter Valley. This has a very hot climate, moderated by the humidity. There are two distinct areas, the Upper and Lower Hunter. The Lower Hunter produces the famed Hunter Semillons whereas the Upper Hunter is noted in particular for Chardonnay.

Victoria.

Fittingly, in Victorian times, Victoria was the largest wine producing state. Stylistically a vast range of wines is made, from fortified wines in the northeast to cool climate sparkling wines. Some very high-quality areas such as the ultra-premium Yarra Valley, Mornington Peninsula and Geelong, surround Melbourne.

Western Australia.

Western Australia is isolated from the other three main production regions, the vineyards being mostly south of Perth. The hot Swan Valley was the most important district but higher quality wines are made in the cooler Margaret River, which although almost tropical is cooled by the Indian Ocean, and the much cooler Great Southern region.

Export of Expertise.

Not only is the export of finished wine a great success story for Australia, the Australian wine industry has had an enormous influence on the rest of the world. Modern vine pruning and training methods have been developed in Australia and exported, and the emphasis on varietal character has become the by-word for many traditional regions. The European vintage is six months later than in Australia, which enables graduates of Roseworthy to take their expertise and passion for clean, "fruit-driven" wines to the other side of the world, and make two vintages per year. Increasingly Australian-trained winemakers' names appear on bottles from all over the world.

NEW ZEALAND.

Apart from the relative youth of its wine industry, and the comparable concentration of technical expertise, Australia and New Zealand have little in common. New Zealand is relatively small and enjoys a maritime climate, cool and damp. As a result the country has become world famous for its care in viticulture, developing new ways to train vines that maximize the exposure of the grapes to sunlight, while reducing the humidity which can lead to rot. White wines predominate, with Chardonnay the most important variety. It is Sauvignon Blanc, however, that has really flourished in New Zealand, producing aromatic wines which have become the benchmarks for this variety.

SPECIAL TOPIC

SHERRY.

Introduction: The Fortified Wines.

Fortified wine, known in European legislative circles as "Liqueur Wine", is wine to which high strength grape spirit, or brandy, has been added. Originally a preservative, the practice has become a defining part of the style of these wines.

Fortified wines are made in many countries but it is from the Iberian Peninsula that the most important examples come, Port (and Madeira) from Portugal and Sherry from Spain. Other wines include Marsala from Sicily, the French Vin Doux Naturels and Rutherglen Muscats and "Tokays" (not to be confused with Hungarian Tokaji) from Australia. There are, too, many wines produced in the New World, sold on their domestic markets as Port or Sherry, usually pale imitations of the originals.

There are two fundamental types of fortified wine. Those, like Sherry, that are fortified after fermentation and those where the fermentation is arrested by the fortification. In the first case the wines are naturally dry, sweeter styles are produced by sweetening during the blending process. The second group are naturally sweet, the level of sweetness being dependent on the ripeness of the grapes and the timing of fortification.

Sherry: History and Varieties.

The viticultural history of Sherry goes back to Phoenician times, making it one of Europe's oldest vineyard regions. Over the centuries the capital has had many names, the current one being Jerez. Sherry is an Anglicisation of this. Sherry comes only from this part of Spain; a triangular-shaped region in Andalucia around the city of Jerez de la Fontera, bounded by rivers and the Atlantic. The climate here is hot and dry in the summer but the chalk-rich, water-retentive soil acts as a reservoir, soaking up the heavy winter rains, making viticulture viable. The main grape here is Palomino Fino, the local name for the Listan, a grape found in southern France. Here it produces a bland and frankly unexciting base wine of around 12% vol. From this inauspicious start one of the world's greatest and most historic wines is made. The only other grape used is Pedro Ximenez (PX), which is raisined before being turned into the sweetening wine for medium and cream Sherry.

Maturation.

It is the management of the wine, how it is matured and for how long, that gives Sherry its style. Two distinct forms of maturation are used, the biological ageing under "flor" and the physiochemical oxidative ageing. In each case the longer the ageing the more concentrated and better the wine, within the given natural limits.

Some four or five months after the vintage the wine will be classified by the bodega's expert. The lightest and finest wines will be classified as Fino, the fuller ones as Oloroso. Fortification follows. Finos are brought up to 15·5% vol., the ideal alcohol content for flor growth. Olorosos are fortified to 18% so that no flor can grow. Flor is a living blanket of yeast, omnipresent in the bodegas, which grows spontaneously, covering the surface of the wine, protecting it from oxidation. At the same time it feeds on various components in the wine and adds its distinctive yeasty flavour. Olorosos mature exposed to air, gradually oxidising to a deep brown colour while taking on a walnut and dried-fruit character.

These wines are the añada wines. They still have to be matured in the solera, a fractional blending system. The solera ensures a continual supply of consistent wine since no butt (cask) is ever emptied. When old wine is withdrawn for shipment a maximum of 25% is taken from each butt. This is topped up with slightly younger wine from the previous criadera, or level in the solera. This in turn is topped up with still younger wine until the youngest available is the añada. The young wine refreshes the old, particularly important for Finos where the flor needs to be fed, while taking on the character of its elders. Vintages are therefore of no significance in Sherry.

Amontillado.

If the flor on a Fino should die, the wine will start to oxidise. However, having once been a Fino it will not become Oloroso; instead it will take on a different character and become an Amontillado. These three, Fino, Oloroso and Amontillado, which are totally dry, are the basis for all commercial Sherries.

Fino is sold unblended and labelled Fino if matured in Jerez. Finos matured in the coastal towns of Sanlucar de Barrameda and Puerto de Santa Maria are lighter, more delicate and more yeasty, and are sold as Manzanilla and Puerto Fino respectively. Pale cream is a Fino sweetened with grape sugar.

True or classic old Amontillado (or Manzanilla amontillada if matured at Sanlucar) is a full flavoured dry wine, but most commercial blends exported are young wines blended with sweetening to be medium-dry.

Cream Sherry and the now almost extinct Brown Sherry are Olorosos blended with sweet wines made from Pedro Ximenez. The best Cream Sherries are made from old Oloroso blended with old Pedro Ximenez and then returned to a solera for further ageing.

One very unusual and rare type of Sherry is Palo Cortado. It starts life as a Fino on which the flor dies. Having developed into an Amontillado, the wine then takes on some Oloroso characteristics. The genuine article is a fluke of nature and is necessarily rare and expensive. Cheap Palo Cortado is likely to be a blend of Amontillado and Oloroso.

Advice on Serving.

The full-flavoured Olorosos and Amontillados are usually served at room temperature, but can benefit from being a little cooler in the summer. Once open they will keep for a few weeks, but not years. Fino and Manzanilla must always be served chilled and should then be treated like a light wine. Drink them up within a very few days to enjoy them at there freshest. As well as being the perfect aperitif, Fino is excellent with seafood and tapas. Dry Oloroso and Amontillado are confident, if unusual, partners for meat and game, while the sweeter styles can be served with pudding, cheese and nuts.

Sherry's Imitators.

Since January 1996, and following a protracted legal battle, the name Sherry has been protected within the European Union and can only be applied to true Sherry. Before this a number of other countries sold products with Sherry in the name. While some of these are acceptable drinks in their own right, they are not Sherry and should never be thought of as Sherry.

GENERAL COMPENDIUM

A collection of useful tables and data on a variety of unrelated subjects, such as Archbishops of Canterbury, the British monarchy, Prime Ministers since 1721, rulers of the Roman world, United States Presidents, phases of the moon, winners of the Nobel Prizes, eclipses, Roman numerals, foreign phrases, national currencies, the Beaufort wind scale and ranks in the armed forces.

TABLE OF CONTENTS

GENERAL COMPENDIUM

ENGLISH MONARCHS
(A.D. 827–1603)

Monarch	Accession	Died	Age	Reigned

I.—BEFORE THE CONQUEST.
SAXONS AND DANES

Monarch	Accession	Died	Age	Reigned
Egbert	827	839	—	12
Ethelwulf	839	858	—	19
Ethelbald	858	860	—	2
Ethelbert	858	865	—	7
Ethelred	865	871	—	6
Alfred the Great	871	899	50	28
Edward the Elder	899	924	54	25
Athelstan	924	939	45	15
Edmund	939	946	25	7
Eadred	946	955	32	9
Eadwig	955	959	18	3
Edgar	959	975	32	17
Edward the Martyr	975	978	17	3
Ethelred II ("the Unready")	978	1016	48	37
Edmund Ironside	1016	1016	27	Apr.–Nov.
Canute the Dane	1017	1035	40	18
Harold I	1035	1040	—	5
Hardicanute	1040	1042	24	2
Edward the Confessor	1042	1066	62	24
Harold II	1066	1066	44	Jan.–Oct.

II.—FROM THE CONQUEST TO THE PRESENT DAY.
NORMANS

Monarch	Accession	Died	Age	Reigned
William I	1066	1087	60	21
William II	1087	1100	43	13
Henry I	1100	1135	67	35
Stephen, Count of Blois	1135	1154	50	19

PLANTAGENETS

Monarch		Accession	Died	Age	Reigned
Henry II		1154	1189	56	35
Richard I		1189	1199	42	10
John		1199	1216	50	17
Henry III		1216	1272	65	56
Edward I		1272	1307	68	35
Edward II		1307	dep. 1327	43	20
Edward III		1327	1377	65	50
Richard II		1377	dep. 1399	34	22
Henry IV	Lancaster	1399	1413	47	13
Henry V		1413	1422	34	9
Henry VI		1422	dep. 1461	49	39
Edward IV	York	1461	1483	41	22
Edward V		1483	1483	13	Apr.–June
Richard III		1483	1485	32	2

TUDORS

Monarch	Accession	Died	Age	Reigned
Henry VII	1485	1509	53	24
Henry VIII	1509	1547	56	38
Edward VI	1547	1553	16	6
Jane	1553	1554	17	9 days
Mary I	1553	1558	43	5
Elizabeth I	1558	1603	69	44

THE BRITISH MONARCHY
(1603 to the present day)

Monarch	Accession	Died	Age	Reigned
STUARTS				
James I (VI of Scotland)	1603	1625	59	22
Charles I	1625	beh. 1649	48	24
COMMONWEALTH DECLARED, MAY 19, 1649				
Oliver Cromwell, Lord Protector . .	1653–8	—	—	—
Richard Cromwell, Lord Protector . .	1658–9	—	—	—
STUARTS (RESTORATION)				
Charles II	1660	1685	55	25
James II (VII of Scotland) .	1685	dep. 1688	68	3
Interregnum Dec. 11, 1688 to Feb. 13, 1689				
William III and Mary II	1689	1702	51	13
		1694	33	6
Anne	1702	1714	49	12
HOUSE OF HANOVER				
George I	1714	1727	67	13
George II	1727	1760	77	33
George III	1760	1820	81	59
George IV	1820	1830	67	10
William IV	1830	1837	71	7
Victoria	1837	1901	81	63
HOUSE OF SAXE-COBURG				
Edward VII	1901	1910	68	9
HOUSE OF WINDSOR				
George V	1910	1936	70	25
Edward VIII	1936	Abd. 1936	77	325 days
George VI	1936	1952	56	15
Elizabeth II	1952			

SCOTTISH MONARCHS
(1034–1603)

Monarch		Accession	Died
Duncan I	Son of Malcolm II	1034	1040
Macbeth	Slew Duncan in 1040	1040	1057
Malcolm III (Canmore)	Son of Duncan I	1058	1093
Donald Ban	Brother of Malcolm Canmore	1093	—
Duncan II	Son of Malcom Canmore, by first marriage	1094	1094
Donald Ban	Restored	1094	1097
Edgar	Son of Malcolm Canmore, by second marriage	1097	1107
Alexander I	Son of Malcolm Canmore	1107	1124
David I	Son of Malcolm Canmore	1124	1153
Malcolm IV (the Maiden)	Son of Henry, eldest son of David I	1153	1165
William I (the Lion)	Brother of Malcolm the Maiden	1165	1214
Alexander II	Son of William the Lion	1214	1249
Alexander III	Son of Alexander II, by second marriage	1249	1286
Margaret, Maid of Norway	Daughter of Eric II of Norway, granddaughter of Alexander III	1286	1290
John Baliol	Grandson of eldest daughter of David, Earl of Huntingdon, brother of William the Lion	1292	1296
Robert I (Bruce)	Great-grandson of 2nd daughter of David, Earl of Huntingdon, brother of William the Lion	1306	1329
David II	Son of Robert I, by second marriage	1329	1371
Robert II (Stewart)	Son of Marjorie, daughter of Robert I by first marriage, and Walter the Steward	1371	1390
Robert III	(John, Earl of Carrick) son of Robert II	1390	1406
James I	Son of Robert III	1406	1437
James II	Son of James I	1437	1460
James III	Eldest son of James II	1460	1488
James IV	Eldest son of James III	1488	1513
James V	Son of James IV	1513	1542
Mary	Daughter of James V, by second marriage	1542	1587
James VI (ascended the Throne of England 1603)	Son of Mary, by second marriage	1567	1625

BRITISH PRIME MINISTERS

	Party	Served
George II, 1727–60		
Sir Robert Walpole	Whig	1721–42
Earl of Wilmington	Whig	1742–3
Henry Pelham	Whig	1743–54
Duke of Newcastle	Whig	1754–6
Duke of Devonshire	Whig	1756–7
Duke of Newcastle	Whig	1757–60
George III, 1760–1820		
Duke of Newcastle	Whig	1760–2
Earl of Bute	Tory	1762–3
George Grenville	Whig	1763–5
Marquis of Rocking-ham	Whig	1766
Earl of Chatham	Tory	1766–8
Duke of Grafton	Whig	1766–9
Lord North	Tory	1770–82
Marquis of Rocking-ham	Whig	1782
Earl of Shelburne	Whig	1782–3
Duke of Portland	Coalition	1783
William Pitt	Tory	1783–1801
Viscount Sidmouth	Tory	1801–4
William Pitt	Tory	1804–6
Lord Grenville	Whig	1806–7
Duke of Portland	Tory	1807–9
Spencer Perceval	Tory	1809–12
George IV, 1820–30		
Earl of Liverpool	Tory	1812–27
George Canning	Tory	1827
Viscount Goderich	Tory	1827
Duke of Wellington	Tory	1827–30
William IV, 1830–7		
Earl Grey	Whig	1830–4
Viscount Melbourne	Whig	1834
Sir Robert Peel	Tory	1834–5
Viscount Melbourne	Whig	1835–7
Victoria, 1837–1901		
Viscount Melbourne	Whig	1837–41
Sir Robert Peel	Tory	1841–6
Lord John Russell	Whig	1846–52
Earl of Derby	Tory	1852
Earl of Aberdeen	Peelite	1852–5
Viscount Palmerston	Liberal	1855–8
Earl of Derby	Tory	1858–9
Viscount Palmerston	Liberal	1859–65
Earl Russell	Liberal	1865–6
Earl of Derby	Conservative	1866–8

	Party	Served
B. Disraeli	Conservative	1868
W. E. Gladstone	Liberal	1868–74
B. Disraeli	Conservative	1874–80
W. E. Gladstone	Liberal	1880–5
Marquis of Salisbury	Conservative	1885–6
W. E. Gladstone	Liberal	1886
Marquis of Salisbury	Conservative	1886–92
W. E. Gladstone	Liberal	1892–4
Earl of Rosebery	Liberal	1894–5
Marquis of Salisbury	Conservative	1895–1901
Edward VII, 1901–10		
Marquis of Salisbury	Conservative	1901–2
A. J. Balfour	Conservative	1902–5
Sir H. Campbell-Bannerman	Liberal	1905–8
H. H. Asquith	Liberal	1908–10
George V, 1910–36		
H. H. Asquith	Liberal	1910–15
H. H. Asquith	Coalition	1915–16
D. Lloyd George	Coalition	1916–22
A. Bonar Law	Conservative	1922–3
S. Baldwin	Conservative	1923–4
J. R. MacDonald	Labour	1924
S. Baldwin	Conservative	1924–9
J. R. MacDonald	Labour	1929–31
J. R. MacDonald	National	1931–5
S. Baldwin	National	1935–6
Edward VIII, 1936		
George VI, 1936–52		
S. Baldwin	National	1936–7
N. Chamberlain	National	1937–39
N. Chamberlain	War Cabinet	1939
W. S. Churchill	War Cabinet	1940–45
W. S. Churchill	Caretaker	1945
C. R. Attlee	Labour	1945–51
Sir W. S. Churchill	Conservative	1951–2
Elizabeth II, 1952–		
Sir W. S. Churchill	Conservative	1952–5
Sir A. Eden	Conservative	1955–7
H. Macmillan	Conservative	1957–63
Sir A. Douglas-Home	Conservative	1963–4
H. Wilson	Labour	1964–70
E. Heath	Conservative	1970–4
H. Wilson	Labour	1974–6
J. Callaghan	Labour	1976–9
Mrs. M. Thatcher	Conservative	1979–90
J. Major	Conservative	1990–97
A. Blair	Labour	1997–

PRESIDENTS OF THE UNITED STATES

The terms are for four years; only President F. D. Roosevelt has served more than two terms.

	Party	Served
1. George Washington	Fed.	1789–97
2. John Adams	Fed.	1797–1801
3. Thomas Jefferson	Rep.	1801–9
4. James Madison	Rep.	1809–17
5. James Monroe	Rep.	1817–25
6. John Quincey Adams	Rep.	1825–9
7. Andrew Jackson	Dem.	1829–37
8. Martin Van Buren	Dem.	1837–41
9. William H. Harrison (died in office)	Whig	1841
10. John Tyler	Whig	1841–5
11. James K. Polk	Dem.	1845–9
12. Zachary Taylor (died in office)	Whig	1849–50
13. Millard Fillmore	Whig	1850–3
14. Franklin Pierce	Dem.	1853–7
15. James Buchanan	Dem.	1857–61
16. Abraham Lincoln*	Rep.	1861–5
17. Andrew Johnson	Dem.	1865–9
18. Ulysses S. Grant	Rep.	1869–77
19. Rutherford B. Hayes	Rep.	1877–81
20. James A. Garfield*	Rep.	1881
21. Chester A. Arthur	Rep.	1881–5
22. Grover Cleveland	Dem.	1885–9
23. Benjamin Harrison	Rep.	1889–93
24. Grover Cleveland	Dem.	1893–7
25. William McKinley*	Rep.	1897–1901
26. Theodore Roosevelt	Rep.	1901–9
27. William Howard Taft	Rep.	1909–13
28. Woodrow Wilson	Dem.	1913–21
29. Warren G. Harding (died in office)	Rep.	1921–3
30. Calvin Coolidge	Rep.	1923–9
31. Herbert C. Hoover	Rep.	1929–33
32. Franklin D. Roosevelt (died in office)	Dem.	1933–45
33. Harry S. Truman	Dem.	1945–53
34. Dwight D. Eisenhower	Rep.	1953–61
35. John F. Kennedy*	Dem.	1961–3
36. Lyndon B. Johnson	Dem.	1963–9
37. Richard M. Nixon (resigned)	Rep.	1969–74
38. Gerald R. Ford	Rep.	1974–7
39. James Carter	Dem.	1977–81
40. Ronald Reagan	Rep.	1981–9
41. George Bush	Rep.	1989–93
42. William J. Clinton**	Dem.	1993–

*assassinated   **Re-elected November 1996

FOREIGN PHRASES

Fr., French.   Gr., Greek.   Ger., German.   It., Italian.   L., Latin.   Sp., Spanish

à bas (Fr.), down, down with.

ab extra (L.), from without.

ab incunabilis (L.), from the cradle.

ab initio (L.), from the beginning.

ab intra (L.), from within.

à bon chat, bon rat (Fr.), to be a good cat, a good rat; well attacked and defended; tit for tat; a Rowland for an Oliver.

à bon marché (Fr.), cheap, a good bargain.

à bras ouverts (Fr.), with open arms.

absente reo (L.), the accused being absent.

absit invidia (L.), let there be no ill-will; envy apart.

ab uno disce omnes (L.), from one specimen judge of all the rest; from a single instance infer the whole.

ab urbe conditâ (L.), from the building of the city; *i.e.*, Rome.

à capite ad calcem (L.) from head to heel.

à chaque saint sa chandelle (Fr.), to each saint his candle; honour where honour is due.

à cheval (Fr.), on horseback.

à compte (Fr.) on account; in part payment.

à corps perdu (Fr.), with might and main.

à couvert (Fr.), under cover; protected; sheltered.

ad astra (L.), to the stars.

ad calendas Græcas (L.), at the Greek calends; *i.e.*, never, as the Greeks had no calends in their mode of reckoning.

à demi (Fr.), by halves; half-way.

a Deo et rege (L.), from God and the king.

ad hoc (L.), arranged for this purpose; special.

ad hominem (L.), to the man; to an individual's interests or passions; personal.

adhuc sub judice lis est (L.), the case has not yet been decided.

a die (L.), from that day.

ad infinitum (L.), to infinity.

ad interim (L.), in the meantime.

ad libitum (L.), at pleasure.

ad modum (L.), after the manner of.

ad nauseam (L.), to disgust or satiety.

ad referendum (L.), for further consideration.

ad rem (L.), to the purpose; to the point.

ad valorem (L.), according to the value.

affaire d'amour (Fr.), a love affair.

affaire d'honneur (Fr.), an affair of honour; a duel.

affaire de cœur (Fr.), an affair of the heart.

a fortiori (L.), with stronger reason.

à gauche (Fr.), to the left.

à genoux (Fr.), on the knees.

à haute voix (Fr.), aloud.

à huis clos (Fr.), with closed doors; secretly.

à belle étoile (Fr.), under the stars; in the open air.

à la bonne heure (Fr.), well timed; all right; very well; as you please.

à l'abri (Fr.), under shelter.

à la mode (Fr.), according to the custom or fashion.

à la Tartuffe (Fr.), like Tartuffe, the hero of a celebrated comedy by Molière; hypocritically.

al fresco (It.), in the open air; out-of-doors.

al più (It.), at most.

alter ego (L.), another self.

à merveille (Fr.), to a wonder; marvellously.

amor patriæ (L.), love of country.

amour-propre (Fr.), self-love, vanity.

ancien régime (Fr.), the ancient or former order of things.

anguis in herba (L.), a snake in the grass.

anno Christi (L.), in the year of Christ.

anno Domini (L.), in the year of our Lord.

anno mundi (L.), in the year of the world.

annus mirabilis (L.), year of wonders; wonderful year.

ante bellum (L.), before the war.

ante lucem (L.), before light.

ante meridiem (L.), before noon.

à outrance (Fr.), to the utmost; to extremities; without sparing.

à pied (Fr.), on foot.

à point (Fr.), to a point, just in time, exactly right.

a posse ad esse (L.), from possibility to reality.

ariston metron (Gr.), the middle course is the best; the golden mean.

arrière-pensé (Fr.), hidden thought; mental reservation.

au courant (Fr.), fully acquainted with.

audi alteram partem (L.), hear the other side.

au fait (Fr.), well acquainted with; expert.

au fond (Fr.), at bottom.

auf Wiedersehen! (Ger.), till we meet again.

au pis aller (Fr.), at the worst.

au revoir (Fr.), adieu; till we meet again.

aut vincere aut mori (L.), either to conquer or to die; death or victory.

a verbis ad verbera (L.), from words to blows.

a vinculo matrimonii (L.), from the bond of matrimony.

à volonte (Fr.), at pleasure.

a vostra salute (It.) ⎫
à votre santé (Fr.) ⎬ to your health.
a vuestra salud (Sp.) ⎭

bas bleu (Fr.), a blue-stocking; a literary woman.

beau monde (Fr.), the world of fashion.

beaux esprits (Fr.), men of wit, gay spirits.

beaux yeux (Fr.), fine eyes; good looks.

ben trovato (It.), well or cleverly invented.

bête noire (Fr.), a black beast; a bugbear.

bon gré mal gré (Fr.), with good or ill grace; willing or unwilling.

bonhomie (Fr.), good-nature; artlessness.

bonne bouche (Fr.), a delicate or tasty morsel.

bon vivant (Fr.), a good liver; a gourmand.

brutum fulmen (L.), a harmless thunderbolt.

canaille (Fr.), rabble.

candida Pax (L.), white-robed Peace.

casus belli (L.), that which causes or justifies war.

causa sine qua non (L.), an indispensable cause or condition.

caveat emptor (L.), let the buyer beware (or look after his own interest).

cela va sans dire (Fr.), that goes without saying; needless to say.

ceteris paribus (L.), other things being equal.

chacun à son goût (Fr.), every one to his taste.

cogito, ergo sum (L.), I think, therefore I exist.

comme il faut (Fr.), as it should be.

compos mentis (L.), sound of mind; quite sane.

compte rendu (Fr.), an account rendered; a report or statement drawn up.

conditio sine qua non (L.), a necessary condition.

conseil de famille (Fr.), a family consultation.

consensus facit legem (L.), consent makes the law.

consilio et animis (L.), by wisdom and courage.

consilio et prudentia (L.), by wisdom and prudence.

constantia et virtute (L.), by constancy and virtue.

contra bonos mores (L.), against good manners.

contretemps (Fr.), an unlucky accident; a hitch.

cordon bleu (Fr.), blue ribbon; a cook of the highest class.

cordon sanitaire (Fr.), a line of guards to prevent the spreading of contagion or pestilence.

corpus delicti (L.), the body or substance of a crime or offence.

corrigenda (L.), things to be corrected.

coup de grâce (Fr.), a sudden decisive blow in politics; a stroke of policy.

coup de soleil (Fr.), sunstroke.

credat Judæus Apella (L.), let Apella, the superstitious Jew, believe it (I won't); tell that to the marines.

cucullus non facit monachum (L.), the cowl does not make the friar.

cui bono? (L.), For whose advantage is it? to what end?

culpam poena premit comes (L.), punishment follows hard upon crime.

cum grano salis (L.), with a grain of salt; with some allowance.

cum privilegio (L.), with privilege.

currente calamo (L.), with a fluent pen.

da locum melioribus (L.), give place to your betters.

damnant quod non intelligunt (L.), they condemn what they do not comprehend.

data et accepta (L.), expenditures and receipts.

de bon augure (Fr.), of good augury or omen.

de bonne grâce (Fr.), with good grace; willingly.

de die in diem (L.), from day to day.

de facto (L.), in point of fact; actual or actually.

dei gratia (L.), by God's grace.

de jure (L.), from the law; by right.

de mal en pis (Fr.), from bad to worse.

de novo (L.), anew.

deo volente (L.), God willing; by God's will.

de profundis (L.), out of the depths.

dernier ressort (Fr.), a last resource.

deus ex machina (L.), one who puts matters right at a critical moment; providential intervention.

dies non (L.), a day on which judges do not sit.

distingué (Fr.), distinguished; of genteel or elegant appearance.

dolce far niente (It.), a sweet doing-nothing; sweet idleness.

double entente (Fr.), a double meaning; a play on words.

dramatis personæ (L.), characters of the drama or play.

dum spiro, spero (L.), while I breathe, I hope.

ecce homo! (L.), behold the man!

eheu! fugaces labuntur anni (L.), alas! the fleeting years glide by.

einmal ist keinmal (Ger.), just once doesn't count.

en avant (Fr.), forward.

en badinant (Fr.), in sport; in jest.

en déshabillé (Fr.), in undress.

en famille (Fr.), with one's family; in a domestic state.

enfant terrible (Fr.), a terrible child, or one that makes disconcerting remarks.

enfin (Fr.), in short; at last; finally.

en passant (Fr.), in passing; by the way.

en plein jour (Fr.), in broad day.

en rapport (Fr.), in harmony; in agreement; in relation.

en règle (Fr.), according to rules; in order.

entente cordiale (Fr.), cordial understanding, especially between two states.

entre nous (Fr.), between ourselves.

en vérité (Fr.), in truth; verily.

e pluribus unum (L.), one out of many; one composed of many.

esprit de corps (Fr.), the animating spirit of a collective body, as a regiment, learned profession or the like.

et sequentes, et sequentia (L.), and those that follow.

et tu, Brute! (L.), and thou also, Brutus!

ex animo (L.), heartily; sincerely.

ex capite (L.), from the head; from memory.

ex cathedra (L.), from the chair or seat of authority, with high authority.

exceptio probat regulam (L.), the exception proves the rule.

ex curia (L.), out of court.

ex dono (L.), by the gift.

exeunt omnes (L.), all go out or retire.

exit (L.), he goes out.

ex mero motu (L.), from his own impulse, from his own free will.

ex nihilo nihil fit (L.), out of nothing, nothing comes; nothing produces nothing.

ex officio (L.), in virtue of his office.

ex post facto (L.), after the deed is done; retrospective.

face à face (Fr.), face to face.

façon de parler (Fr.), manner of speaking.

faire bonne mine (Fr.), to put a good face upon the matter.

fait accompli (Fr.), a thing already done.

fama clamosa (L.), a current scandal; a prevailing report.

faute de mieux (Fr.), for want of better.

faux pas (Fr.), a false step; a slip in behaviour.

festina lente (L.), hasten slowly.

fiat justitia, ruat cœlum (L.), let justice be done though the heavens should fall.

fiat lux (L.), let there be light.

fide et amore (L.), by faith and love.

fide et fiduciâ (L.), by fidelity and confidence.

fide et fortitudine (L.), with faith and fortitude.

fidei defensor (L.), defender of the faith.

fide non armis (L.), by faith, not by arms.

fide, sed cui vide (L.), trust, but see whom.

fides et justitia (L.), fidelity and justice.

fides Punica (L.), Punic faith; treachery.

filius nullius (L.), a son of nobody; a bastard.

finis coronat opus (L.), the end crowns the work.

flagrante bello (L.), during hostilities.

flagrante delicto (L.), in the commission of the crime.

floreat (L.), let it flourish.

fons et origo (L.), the source and origin.

force majeure (Fr.), irresistible compulsion; war, strike, Act of God, etc.

forensis strepitus (L.), the clamour of the forum.

fortuna favet fortibus (L.), fortune favours the bold.

functus officio (L.), having performed one's office or duty; hence, out of office.

gaudeamus igitur (L.), so let us be joyful!

genius loci (L.), the genius or guardian spirit of a place.

gradu diverso, via una (L.), the same road by different steps.

grande parure } (Fr.), full dress.
grande toilette }

guerra al cuchillo (Sp.), war to the knife.

Hannibal ante portas (L.), Hannibal before the gates; the enemy close at hand.

hiatus valde deflendus (L.), a chasm or deficiency much to be regretted.

hic et nunc (L.), here and now.

hic et ubique (L.), here and everywhere.

hic jacet (L.) here lies.

hic labor, hoc opus est (L.), this is a labour, this is a toil.

hic sepultus (L.), here buried.

hoc genus omne (L.), all of this sort or class.

hoi polloi (Gr.), the many; the vulgar; the rabble.

hominis est errare (L.), to err is human.

homme de robe (Fr.), a man in civil office.

homme d'affair (Fr.), a man of business.

homme d'esprit (Fr.), a man of wit or genius.

honi soit qui mal y pense (O. Fr.), evil to him who evil thinks.

honores mutant mores (L.), honours change men's manners or characters.

hors de combat (Fr.), out of condition to fight.

hors de propos (Fr.), not to the point or purpose.

hors d'œuvre (Fr.), out of course; out of order.

ich dien (Ger.), I serve.

idée fixe (Fr.), a fixed idea.

id est (L.), that is.

il a diable au corps (Fr.), the devil is in him.

Ilias malorum (L.), an Iliad of ills; a host of evils.

il penseroso (It.), the pensive man.

il sent le fagot (Fr.), he smells of the faggot; he is suspected of heresy.

imperium in imperio (L.), a state within a state; a government within another.

in actu (L.), in act or reality.

in articulo mortis (L.), at the point of death; in the last struggle.

in capite (L.), in chief.

in curia (L.), in court.

index expurgatorius } (L.), a list of books prohibited
index prohibitorius } to Roman Catholics.

in esse (L.), in being; in actuality.

in extenso (L.), at full length.

in extremis (L.), at the point of death.

in memoriam (L.), to the memory of; in memory.

in nubibus (L.), in the clouds.

in petto (It.), in (my) breast; to one's self.

in re (L.), in the matter of.

in sano sensu (L.), in a proper sense.

in situ (L.), in its original situation.

in vino veritas (L.), there is truth in wine; truth is told under the influence of intoxicants.

ipse dixit (L.), he himself said it; a dogmatic saying or assertion.

ipsissima verba (L.), the very words.

ipso facto (L.), in the fact itself.

ipso jure (L.), by the law itself.

jacta est alea (L.), the die is cast.

je ne sais quoi (Fr.), I know not what.

joci causa (L.), for the sake of a joke.

labor omnia vincit (L.), labour conquers everything.

l'allegro (It.), the merry man.

lapsus linguæ (L.), a slip of the tongue.

lares et penates (L.), household goods.

laus Deo (L.), praise to God.

le beau monde (Fr.), the fashionable world.

lector benevole (L.), kind or gentle reader.

le jeu n'en vaut pas la chandelle (Fr.), the game is not worth the candle; the object is not worth the trouble.

le mot de l'énigme (Fr.), the key to the mystery.

le point du jour (Fr.), daybreak.

lèse-majesté (Fr.), high-treason.

lettre de cachet (Fr.), a sealed letter containing private orders; a royal warrant.

lex loci (L.), the law or custom of the place.

lex non scripta (L.), unwritten law; common law.

lex scripta (L.), written law; statute law.

locum tenens (L.), a deputy.

lucri causa (L.), for the sake of gain.

magnum opus (L.), a great work.

mala fide (L.), with bad faith; treacherously.

mal à propos (Fr.), ill-timed; out of place.

malgré nous (Fr.), in spite of us.

malheur ne vient jamais seul (Fr.), misfortunes never come singly.

malum in se (L.), evil or an evil in itself.

mardi gras (Fr.), Shrove Tuesday.

mariage de convenance (Fr.), marriage from motives of interest rather than of love.

mauvais goût (Fr.), bad taste.

mauvaise honte (Fr.), false modesty.

mea culpa (L.), my fault; by my fault.

me judice (L.), I being judge; in my opinion.

mens agitat molem (L.), mind moves matter.

mens legis (L.), the spirit of the law.

mens sana in corpore sano (L.), a sound mind in a sound body.

meo periculo (L.), at my own risk.

meo voto (L.), according to my wish.

mise en scène (Fr.), the getting up for the stage, or the putting on the stage.

modus operandi (L.), manner of working.

more suo (L.), in his own way.

motu proprio (L.), of his own accord.

multum in parvo (L.), much in little.

mutatis mutandis (L.), with suitable or necessary alteration.

nervus probandi (L.), the sinews of the argument.

nihil ad rem (L.), irrelevant.

nil desperandum (L.), there is no reason to despair.

noblesse oblige (Fr.), rank imposes obligations; much is expected from one in good position.

nolens volens (L.), willing or unwilling.

nom de guerre (Fr.), a false or assumed name.

non compos mentis (L.), not of sound mind.

non sequitur (L.), it does not follow.

nosce te ipsum (L.), know thyself.

nota bene (L.), mark well.

nudis verbis (L.), in plain words.

obiter dictum (L.), a thing said by the way.

omnia vincit amor (L.), love conquers all things.

ora pro nobis (L.), pray for us.

O tempora! O mores! (L.), O the times! O the manners (or morals)!

ouï-dire (Fr.), hearsay.

padrone (It.), a master; a landlord.

par excellence (Fr.), by way of eminence.

pari passu (L.), at an equal pace or rate of progress.

particeps criminis (L.), an accomplice in a crime.

pas de quoi (Fr. abbrev. Il n'y a pas de quoi), don't mention it.

passim (L.), everywhere; in all parts of the book, chapter, etc.

pâté de foie gras (Fr.), goose-liver paté.

pater patriæ (L.), father of his country.

patres conscripti (L.), the conscript fathers; Roman senators.

pax vobiscum (L.), peace be with you.

per ardua ad astra (L.), through rough ways to the stars; through suffering to renown.

per capita (L.), by the head or poll.

per contra (It.), countrariwise.

per diem (L.), by the day; daily.

per se (L.), by itself; considered apart.

pied-à-terre (Fr.), a resting-place; a temporary lodging.

pis aller (Fr.), the worst or last shift.

plebs (L.), the common people.

poco a poco (It.), little by little.

poste restante (Fr.), to remain in the post-office till called for.

prima facie (L.), at first view or consideration.

primus inter pares (L.), first among equals.

pro forma (L.), for the sake of form.

pro patria (L.), for our country.

pro tanto (L.), for so much; for as far as it goes.

pro tempore (L.), for the time being.

quid pro quo (L.), one thing for another; tit for tat; an equivalent.

qui m'aime, aime mon chien (Fr.), love me, love my dog.

qui tacet consentit (L.), he who is silent gives consent.

quod erat demonstrandum (L.), which was to be proved or demonstrated.

quod erat faciendum (L.), which was to be done.

quod vide (L.), which see; refer to the word just mentioned.

quo jure? (L.), by what right?

raison d'être (Fr.), the reason for a thing's existence.

re (L.), in the matter or affair of.

reculer pour mieux sauter (Fr.), to draw back in order to make a better spring.

reductio ad adsurdum (L.), the reducing of a position to a logical absurdity.

requiescat in pace (L.), may he (or she) rest in peace.

respice finem (L.), look to the end.

respublica (L.), the commonwealth.

revenons à nos moutons (Fr.), let us return to our sheep; let us return to our subject.

re vera (L.) in truth.

sans peur et sans reproche (Fr.), without fear and without reproach.

sans rime ni raison (Fr.), without rhyme or reason.

sans souci (Fr.), without care.

sartor resartus (L.), the botcher repatched; the tailor patched or mended.

sauve qui peut (Fr.), let him save himself who can.

savoir-faire (Fr.), the knowing how to act; tact.

savoir-vivre (Fr.), good-breeding; refined manners.

semper idem (L.), always the same.

seriatim (L.), in a series; one by one.

sic passim (L.), so here and there throughout; so everywhere.

sicut ante (L.), as before.

sine die (L.), without a day being appointed.

sine mora (L.), without delay.

sine qua non (L.), without which, not; indispensable condition.

sotto voce (It.), in an undertone.

spirituel (Fr.), intellectual; witty.

stet (L.), let it stand; do not delete.

sub judice (L.), under consideration.

sub pœna (L.), under a penalty.

sub rosa (L.), under the rose; privately.

sub voce (L.), under such or such a word.

sui generis (L.), of its own or of a particular kind.

summum bonum (L.), the chief good.

tableau vivant (Fr.), a living picture; the representation of some scene by a group of persons.

tant mieux (Fr.), so much the better.

tant pis (Fr.), so much the worse.

tempora mutantur, nos et mutamur in illis (L.), the times are changing and we with them.

tempus fugit (L.), time flies.

tête-à-tête (Fr.), together in private.

tiers état (Fr.), the third estate; the commons.

to kalon (Gr.), the beautiful; the chief good.

to prepon (Gr.), the becoming or proper.

tour de force (Fr.), a feat of strength or skill.

tout à fait (Fr.), wholly; entirely.

tout à l'heure (Fr.), instantly.

toute de suite (Fr.), immediately.

tu quoque (L.), thou also.

ubique (L.), everywhere.

ubi supra (L.), where above mentioned.

ultra licitum (L.), beyond what is allowable.

ultra vires (L.), beyond powers or rights conferred by law.

urbi et orbi (L.), to the city (Rome), and the world.

utile dulci (L.), the useful with the pleasant.

ut infra (L.), as below.

ut supra (L.), as above stated.

vade in pace (L.), go in peace.

variæ lectiones (L.), various readings.

variorum notæ (L.), the notes of various commentators.

vede et crede (L.), see and believe.

veni, vidi, vici (L.), I came, I saw, I conquered.

verbatim et literatim (L.), word for word and letter for letter.

verbum sat sapienti (L.), a word is enough for a wise man.

ver non semper viret (L.), spring is not always green.

vexata quæstio (L.), a disputed question.

via media (L.), a middle course.

via trita, via tuta (L.), the beaten path is the safe path.

vice versa (L.), the terms of the case being reversed.

videlicet (L.), that is to say; namely.

vi et armis (L.), by force of arms; by main force; by violence.

vigilate et orate (L.), watch and pray.

vita brevis, ars longa (L.), life is short; art is long.

viva regina! (L.), long live the queen!

vivat rex! (L.), long live the king!

viva voce (L.), by the living voice; orally.

voilà (Fr.), behold; there is; there are.

voilà tout (Fr.), that's all.

volo, non valeo (L.), I am willing, but unable.

vox populi, vox Dei (L), the voice of the people is the voice of God.

MAJOR NATIONAL CURRENCIES

Country	Currency
Albania	Lek
Argentina	Austral
Australia	Dollar
Austria	Schilling*
Belgium/Lux.	Franc*
Belize	Dollar
Bolivia	Peso Boliviano
Brazil	Real
Bulgaria	Lev
Burma (Myanmar)	Kyat
Canada	Dollar
Chile	Peso
China	Renminbi
Colombia	Peso
Costa Rica	Colón
Cuba	Peso
Czech Republic	Koruna
Denmark	Krone
Ecuador	Sucre
Egypt	Pound
El Salvador	Colón
Ethiopia	Birr
Finland	Markka*
France	Franc*
Germany	D. Mark*
Greece	Drachma
Guatemala	Quetzal
Guyana	Dollar
Haiti	Gourde
Hungary	Forint
Iceland	Króna
India	Rupee
Indonesia	Rupiah
Iran	Rial
Iraq	Dinar
Israel	Shekel
Italy	New Lira*
Jamaica	Dollar
Japan	Yen
Jordan	Dinar
Kenya	K. Shilling
Lebanon	Pound
Malaysia	Ringgit
Mexico	Peso
Morocco	Dirham
Netherlands	Guilder*
New Zealand	Dollar
Nicaragua	Córdoba
Nigeria	Naira
Norway	Krone
Pakistan	Rupee
Panama	Balboa
Paraguay	Guaraní
Peru	Inti
Philippines	Peso
Poland	Zloty
Portugal	Escudo*
Romania	Leu
Russia	Rouble
Saudi Arabia	Rial
Slovakia	Koruna
South Africa	Rand
Spain	Peseta*
Sri Lanka	Rupee
Sweden	Krona
Switzerland	Franc
Syria	Pound
Tanzania	T. Shilling
Thailand	Baht
Trinidad and Tobago	T.T. Dollar
Tunisia	Dinar
Turkey	Lira
United Kingdom	Pound
USA	Dollar
Uruguay	Peso
Venezuela	Bolivar
Vietnam	Dong
Zambia	Kwacha
Zimbabwe	Dollar

*These currencies joined the Eurozone on 1 January 1999.

ROMAN NUMERALS

I 1	LX . . . 60
II 2	LXX . . 70
III 3	LXXX . . 80
IV 4	LXXXVIII . 88
V 5	XC . . . 90
VI 6	C . . . 100
VII 7	CX . . 110
VIII 8	CXI . . 111
IX 9	CXX . . 120
X 10	CC . . 200
XI 11	CCXX . . 220
XII 12	CCC . . 300
XIII 13	CCCXX . 320
XIV 14	CD . . 400
XV 15	D . . . 500
XVI 16	DC . . 600
XVII 17	DCC . . 700
XVIII 18	DCCC . 800
XIX 19	CM . . 900
XX 20	XM . . 990
XXX 30	M. . . 1000
XL 40	MD . . 1500
L. 50	MDCCC . 1800
LV 55	MM . . 2000

INTERNATIONAL TIME-TABLE (GMT)

Place	Time h	Place	Time h
Adelaide	21 30	Mauritius	16 00
Amsterdam	13 00	Melbourne	22 00
Ankara	14 00	Montreal	07 00
Athens	14 00	Moscow	15 00
Auckland (NZ)	24 00	Nairobi	15 00
Beijing	20 00	New York	07 00
Belgrade	13 00	Oslo	13 00
Berlin	13 00	Ottawa	07 00
Bombay (Mumbai)	17 30	Panama	07 00
		Paris	13 00
Brisbane	22 00	Perth (W.A.)	20 00
Brussels	13 00	Prague	13 00
Budapest	13 00	Quebec	07 00
Buenos Aires	09 00	Rangoon	18 30
Cairo	14 00	Rio de Janeiro	09 00
Calcutta	17 30	Rome	13 00
Cape Town	14 00	San Francisco	04 00
Chicago	06 00	St. John's (N.F.)	08 30
Copenhagen	13 00	Singapore	20 00
Gibraltar	13 00	Stockholm	13 00
Helsinki	14 00	Sydney	22 00
Hobart	22 00	Tehran	15 30
Hong Kong	20 00	Tokyo	21 00
Istanbul	14 00	Toronto	07 00
Jerusalem	14 00	Vancouver	04 00
London	12 00	Vienna	13 00
Madeira	12 00	Winnipeg	06 00
Madrid	13 00	Yokohama	21 00
Malta	13 00		

GREEK ALPHABET

A	α	Alpha	N	ν	nu
B	β	beta	Ξ	ξ	xi
Γ	γ	gamma	O	o	omicron
Δ	δ	delta	Π	π	pi
E	ε	epsilon	P	ρ	rho
Z	ζ	zeta	Σ	σ	sigma
H	η	eta	T	τ	tau
Θ	θ	theta	Y	υ	upsilon
I	ι	iota	Φ	φ	phi
K	κ	kappa	X	χ	chi
Λ	λ	lambda	Ψ	ψ	psi
M	μ	mu	Ω	ω	omega

BANK AND PUBLIC HOLIDAYS

The number of public holidays in England and Wales comprise at present six bank holidays (New Year's Day, Easter Monday, May Day, Spring and Late Summer Holidays at the end of May and August respectively, and Boxing Day), with also two common law holidays (Good Friday and Christmas Day); in Scotland (beginning in 1996) seven bank holidays (New Year's Day, Good Friday, Easter Monday, May Day, Spring and Late Summer Holidays at the end of May and August respectively, and Christmas Day); and in Northern Ireland seven bank holidays (New Year's Day, St. Patrick's Day,

Easter Monday, May Day, Spring Late Summer Holidays at the end of May and August respectively, plus two other public holidays (Easter Tuesday and the anniversary of the Battle of the Boyne).

To celebrate the millennium, a special Bank Holiday was declared for 31 December 1999.

Note: There are holidays in lieu of those public holidays which fall at weekends. In Scotland and Northern Ireland a general holiday is not necessarily observed on the same day as a bank holiday.

THE SEASONS

		1999			2000		
		d	h	m	d	h	m
Vernal Equinox—Spring begins	Mar	21	01	46	Mar 20	07	35
Summer Solstice—Summer begins	June	21	19	49	June 21	01	48
Autumnal Equinox—Autumn begins	Sept	23	11	31	Sept 22	17	27
Winter Solstice—Winter begins	Dec	22	07	44	Dec 21	13	37

THE COUNTRY CODE

GUARD AGAINST THE RISK OF FIRE. Great damage is done every year to crops, plantations, woodlands, and heaths. A match or cigarette thrown away or a pipe carelessly knocked out, picnic fires not properly put out or lighted near dry crops, can quickly start a blaze.

FASTEN ALL GATES. If animals get out of a field they stray. As a result they may do serious damage to crops, suffer injury on the roads, or eat food that is harmful.

KEEP DOGS UNDER CONTROL. Animals are easily frightened, even by small, playful dogs. Stillbirths may be the result.

KEEP TO THE PATHS ACROSS FARM LAND. Crops are damaged by treading; flattened crops are difficult to harvest. Grass is a valuable crop.

AVOID DAMAGING FENCING, HEDGES, AND WALLS. If these are damaged, gaps will be caused. Where a person goes, an animal may follow.

LEAVE NO LITTER. Litter is not just unsightly, but often a danger as well. Broken glass and tins may injure animals and harm machinery.

SAFEGUARD WATER SUPPLIES. Countrymen often depend on wells and streams for water for themselves and for their animals.

PROTECT WILD LIFE, PLANTS, AND TREES. Wild animals should not be disturbed, plants uprooted, or trees treated roughly.

GO CAREFULLY ON COUNTRY ROADS. If there is no footpath, walkers are generally safer on the right, facing on-coming traffic. Care and patience are needed by motorists when passing farm animals.

RESPECT THE LIFE OF THE COUNTRYSIDE. Many of the machines and much of the business stock of which the farmer depends for his livelihood have to be kept in the open. Take care not to damage them.

THE BEAUFORT SCALE OF WIND FORCE

Beau-fort number	Wind	Effect on land	Speed	
			mile/h	Knots
0	Calm	Smoke rises vertically	Less than 1	Less than 1
1	Light air	Direction shown by smoke but not by wind vanes	1–3	1–3
2	Light breeze	Wind felt on face; leaves rustle; wind vanes move	4–7	4–6
3	Gentle breeze	Leaves and twigs in motion; wind extends light flag	8–12	7–10
4	Moderate breeze	Raises dust, loose paper and moves small branches	13–18	11–16
5	Fresh breeze	Small trees in leaf begin to sway	19–24	17–21
6	Strong breeze	Large branches in motion; whistling in telegraph wires; difficulty with umbrellas	25–31	22–27
7	Moderate gale	Whole trees in motion; difficult to walk against wind	32–38	28–33
8	Fresh gale	Twigs break off trees; progress impeded	39–46	34–40
9	Strong gale	Slight structural damage occurs; chimney pots and slates blown off	47–54	41–47
10	Whole gale	Trees uprooted and considerable structural damage	55–63	48–56
11	Storm	Widespread damage, seldom experienced in England	64–75	57–65
12	Hurricane	Winds of this force rarely encountered outside tropical revolving storms[1]	Above 75	Above 65

[1]The most notable recent exception was the tremendous storm which devastated Southern England on the night of 15/16 October 1987. Storms of great severity also battered Britain in January and February 1990. Winds of great ferocity can be encountered regularly on a highly-elevated plateau (*e.g.* the Cairngorm Plateau in Scotland).

SUNRISE AND SUNSET FOR LONDON, 2000

		Rise	Set			Rise	Set			Rise	Set
		h m	h m			h m	h m			h m	h m
Jan	1	08 06	16 02	May	6	05 23	20 32	September	2	06 15	19 44
	8	08 05	16 10		13	05 12	20 43		9	06 26	19 28
	15	08 00	16 20		20	05 02	20 54		16	06 37	19 12
	22	07 53	16 31		27	04 53	21 03		23	06 49	18 56
	29	07 44	16 43						30	07 00	18 40
Feb	5	07 34	16 56	June	3	04 48	21 11	October	7	07 12	18 24
	12	07 22	17 09		10	04 44	21 17		14	07 23	18 09
	19	07 08	17 22		17	04 43	21 21		21	07 35	17 54
	26	06 54	17 34		24	04 44	21 22		28	06 48	16 41
March	4	06 39	17 47	July	1	04 48	21 21	November	4	07 00	16 28
	11	06 23	17 59		8	04 54	21 17		11	07 12	16 17
	18	06 07	18 11		15	05 01	21 11		18	07 24	16 07
	25	05 51	18 23		22	05 10	21 03		25	07 35	16 00
					29	05 20	20 53				
April	1	06 36	19 34					December	2	07 46	15 54
	8	06 20	19 46	August	5	05 31	20 41		9	07 54	15 52
	15	06 05	19 58		12	05 42	20 28		16	08 01	15 52
	22	05 50	20 09		19	05 53	20 14		23	08 05	15 56
	29	05 36	20 21		26	06 04	20 00		30	08 06	16 00

Note: These times are in GMT, except between 0100 on 26 Mar and 0100 on 29 Oct, when the times are in BST (1 hour in advance of GMT).

PHASES OF THE MOON, 2000

	New Moon				First Quarter				Full Moon				Last Quarter		
	d	h	m		d	h	m		d	h	m		d	h	m
Jan	6	18	14	Jan	14	13	34	Jan	21	04	40	Jan	28	07	57
Feb	5	13	03	Feb	12	23	21	Feb	19	16	27	Feb	27	03	53
Mar	6	05	17	Mar	13	06	59	Mar	20	04	44	Mar	28	00	21
Apr	4	18	12	Apr	11	13	30	Apr	18	17	41	Apr	26	19	30
May	4	04	12	May	10	20	00	May	18	07	34	May	26	11	55
June	2	12	14	June	9	03	29	June	16	22	27	June	25	01	00
July	1	19	20	July	8	12	53	July	16	13	55	July	24	11	02
July	31	02	25	Aug	7	01	02	Aug	15	05	13	Aug	22	18	51
Aug	29	10	19	Sept	5	16	27	Sept	13	19	37	Sept	21	01	28
Sept	27	19	53	Oct	5	10	59	Oct	13	08	53	Oct	20	07	59
Oct	27	07	58	Nov	4	07	27	Nov	11	21	15	Nov	18	15	24
Nov	25	23	11	Dec	4	03	55	Dec	11	09	03	Dec	18	00	41
Dec	25	17	22												

Note: All times are in GMT.

ECLIPSES, 2000

1. A total eclipse of the Moon on 21 January is visible from the northern part of Russia, Europe including the British Isles, north and west Africa, Atlantic Ocean, Greenland, Arctic regions, north, central and South America, western Antarctica and the east Pacific Ocean. The eclipse begins at 03h 03m and ends at 06h 25m. Totality lasts from 04h 06m to 05h 22m.

2. A partial eclipse of the Sun on 5 February is visible from Antarctica and central southern Indian Ocean. The eclipse begins at 10h 56m and ends at 14h 43m. The time of maximum eclipse is 12h 49m, when 0·58 of the Sun's diameter is obscured.

3. A partial eclipse of the Sun on 1 July is visible from central southern Pacific Ocean and the southern part of Chile and Argentina. The eclipse begins at 18h 07m and ends at 20h 58m. The time of maximum eclipse is 19h 33m, when 0·48 of the Sun's diameter is obscured.

4. A total eclipse of the Moon on 16 July is visible from Australasia, eastern Russia, Japan, China, south-east Asia, India, the Indian Ocean, Antarctica, Hawaiian Islands and east Pacific Ocean. The eclipse begins at 11h 58m and ends at 15h 54m. Totality lasts from 13h 03m to 14h 49m.

5. A partial eclipse of the Sun on 31 July is visible from west Russia, northern parts of Scandinavia and Greenland, north Russia, Arctic Ocean and north-west North America. The eclipse begins at 00h 38m and ends at 03h 49m. The time of maximum eclipse is 02h 13m, when 0·60 of the Sun's diameter is obscured.

6. A partial eclipse of the Sun on 25 December is visible from Mexico, West Indies, North America except Alaska and the extreme north of Canada, west Atlantic Ocean and the southern part of Greenland. The eclipse begins at 15h 27m and ends at 19h 43m. The time of maximum eclipse is 17h 35m, when 0·72 of the Sun's diameter is obscured.

Source: Reproduced, with permission, from data supplied by HM Nautical Almanac Office. © Copyright Particle Physics and Astronomy Research Council.

THE COMMONWEALTH

The Commonwealth of Nations is a free association of independent member nations and their dependencies. The political status of the member nations listed below is clarified and given legal substance in the *Statute of Westminster* drawn up in 1931, before the Commonwealth was founded, by the United Kingdom and the Dominions. The original Dominions were Australia, Canada, Irish Free State, Newfoundland, New Zealand and South Africa. On 1 June 1994, South Africa rejoined the Commonwealth, having left in 1961. In 1995 Cameroon and Mozambique joined the Commonwealth. There are currently (May 1999) 54 members. The Secretary-General is Emeka Anyaoku (Nigeria).

Country	Capital	Status	Joined	Population
1. Antigua and Barbuda	St. John's	M	1981	64,500 (1997)
2. Australia	Canberra	M	1931	18,500,000 (1997)
3. The Bahamas	Nassau	M	1973	287,000 (1997)
4. Bangladesh	Dhaka	R	1972	125,000,000 (1997)
5. Barbados	Bridgetown	M	1966	265,000 (1997)
6. Belize	Belmopen	M	1981	228,000 (1997)
7. Botswana	Gaborone	R	1966	1,500,000 (1996)
8. Brunei	Bandar Seri Begawan	M*	1984	300,000 (1996)
9. Cameroon	Yaoundé	R	1995	14,650,000 (1996)
10. Canada	Ottawa	M	1931	30,287,000 (1997)
11. Cyprus	Nicosia	R	1961	662,000 (1997)
12. Dominica	Roseau	R	1978	74,200 (1994)
13. Fiji	Suva	R	1970	783,800 (1995)
14. The Gambia	Banjul	R	1965	1,248,000 (1997)
15. Ghana	Accra	R	1957	18,000,000 (1996)
16. Grenada	St. George's	M	1974	95,950 (1993)
17. Guyana	Georgetown	R	1966	773,000 (1997)
18. India	New Delhi	R	1947	967,000,000 (1997)
19. Jamaica	Kingston	M	1962	2,500,000 (1996)
20. Kenya	Nairobi	R	1963	29,300,000 (1994)
21. Kiribati	Tarawa	R	1979	82,400 (1997)
22. Lesotho	Maseru	M*	1966	2,500,000 (1996)
23. Malawi	Lilongwe	R	1964	9,700,000 (1994)
24. Malaysia	Kuala Lumpur	M*	1957	21,000,000 (1997)
25. Maldives	Male	R	1982(S)	250,000 (1996)
26. Malta	Valletta	R	1964	367,000 (1994)
27. Mauritius	Port Louis	R	1968	1,110,000 (1993)
28. Mozambique	Maputo	R	1995	18,165,000 (1997)
29. Namibia	Windhoek	R	1990	1,727,000 (1997)
30. Nauru	Nauru	R	1968(S)	8,100 (1990)
31. New Zealand	Wellington	M	1931	3,653,000 (1997)
32. Nigeria	Abuja	R	1960†	99,000,000 (1995)
33. Pakistan	Islamabad	R	1947*	131,500,000 (1994)
34. Papua New Guinea	Port Moresby	M	1975	4,497,000 (1997)
35. St. Kitts and Nevis	Basseterre	M	1983	41,800 (1997)
36. St. Lucia	Castries	M	1979	148,000 (1997)
37. St. Vincent and the Grenadines	Kingstown	M	1979(S)	109,000 (1994)
38. Samoa	Apia	M*	1970	163,000 (1994)
39. Seychelles	Victoria	R	1976	77,300 (1997)
40. Sierra Leone	Freetown	R	1961	4,460,000 (1993)
41. Singapore	Singapore	R	1965	3,100,000 (1997)
42. Solomon Islands	Honiara	M	1978	411,000 (1997)
43. South Africa	Pretoria	R	1931**	40,440,000 (1997)
44. Sri Lanka	Colombo	R	1948	17,400,000 (1992)
45. Swaziland	Mbabane	M*	1968	1,030,000 (1997)
46. Tanzania	Dodoma	R	1961	28,000,000 (1996)
47. Tonga	Nuku'Alofa	M*	1970	102,000 (1998)
48. Trinidad and Tobago	Port of Spain	R	1962	1,276,000 (1997)
49. Tuvalu	Funafuti	M	1978(S)	10,090 (1994)
50. Uganda	Kampala	R	1962	20,000,000 (1997)
51. United Kingdom	London	M	1931	58,919,000 (1997)
52. Vanuatu	Port Vila	R	1980	176,000 (1997)
53. Zambia	Lusaka	R	1964	8,940,000 (1993)
54. Zimbabwe	Harare	R	1980	11,423,000 (1997)

M = Monarchy under Queen Elizabeth, represented by Governor-General in all countries except Britain.
M* = Country with its own monarchy. Brunei is a Sultanate.
R = Republic.
(S) = Special Member.
* = Pakistan left in 1972, rejoining in 1989.
** = South Africa left in 1961, rejoining in 1994.
† = Membership suspended in 1995. Nigeria was due to be re-admitted in 1999.

United Kingdom Overseas Territories

Anguilla
Bermuda
British Antarctic Territory
British Indian Ocean
  Territory
British Virgin Isles
Cayman Islands

Falkland Islands and Dependencies
  (South Georgia, South Sandwich Islands)
Gibraltar
Montserrat
Pitcairn Islands Group
St. Helena and Dependencies (Ascension,
  Tristan da Cunha)
Turks and Caicos Islands

Territories of Member Countries

Australia Norfolk Island, Heard Island, McDonald Island, Cocos (Keeling) Islands, Christmas Island, Asmore and Cartier Islands, Coral Sea Islands   *New Zealand* Cook Islands, Niue, Tokelau Islands

The Channel Islands and the Isle of Man are dependent territories of the crown and do not form part of the United Kingdom. They have their own legislative assemblies and legal and administrative systems.

POPES
(Since 1800)

Pius VII	1800	Benedict XV	1914
Leo XII	1823	Pius XI	1922
Pius VIII	1829	Pius XII	1939
Gregory XVI	1831	John XXIII	1958
Pius IX	1846	Paul VI	1963
Leo XIII	1878	John Paul I	1978
St. Pius X	1903	John Paul II	1978

ARCHBISHOPS OF CANTERBURY
(Since the Reformation)

1533	Thomas Cranmer	1768	Hon. Frederick Cornwallis
1556	Reginald Pole	1783	John Moore
1559	Matthew Parker	1805	Charles Manners Sutton
1576	Edmund Grindal	1828	William Howley
1583	John Whitgift	1848	John Bird Sumner
1604	Richard Bancroft	1862	Charles Thomas Longley
1611	George Abbot	1868	Archibald Campbell Tait
1633	William Laud	1883	Edward White Benson
1660	William Juxon	1896	Frederick Temple
1663	Gilbert Sheldon	1903	Randall Thomas Davidson
1678	William Sancroft	1928	Cosmo Gordon Lang
1691	John Tillotson	1942	William Temple
1695	Thomas Tenison	1945	Geoffrey Francis Fisher
1716	William Wake	1961	Arthur Michael Ramsey
1737	John Potter	1974	Frederick Donald Coggan
1747	Thomas Herring	1980	Robert Runcie
1757	Matthew Hutton	1991	George Carey
1758	Thomas Secker		

ARCHBISHOPS OF YORK
(Since 1900)

1891	William Maclagan	1961	Donald Coggan
1909	Cosmo Gordon Lang	1975	Stuart Blanch
1929	William Temple	1983	John Habgood
1942	Cyril Garbett	1995	David Hope
1956	Arthur Michael Ramsey		

ARMED FORCES: TRADITIONAL RANKS

The table below gives comparative rankings in the British armed forces. Radical plans to cut the number of ranks in the armed forces, put forward in a report by Sir Michael Bett in April 1995, were abandoned in 1996. The only proposal so far approved is to abolish the five star ranks – those of Admiral of the Fleet, Field Marshal and Marshal of the Royal Air Force.

Royal Navy	*Army*	*Royal Air Force*
1 Admiral of the Fleet	1 Field Marshal	1 Marshal of the RAF
2 Admiral	2 General	2 Air Chief Marshal
3 Vice-Admiral	3 Lieutenant-General	3 Air Marshal
4 Rear-Admiral	4 Major-General	4 Air Vice-Marshal
5 Commodore (1st & 2nd class)	5 Brigadier	5 Air Commodore
6 Captain	6 Colonel	6 Group Captain
7 Commander	7 Lieutenant-Colonel	7 Wing Commander
8 Lieutenant-Commander	8 Major	8 Squadron Leader
9 Lieutenant	9 Captain	9 Flight Lieutenant
10 Sub-Lieutenant	10 Lieutenant	10 Flying Officer
11 Acting Sub-Lieutenant	11 Second Lieutenant	11 Pilot Officer

RULERS OF THE ROMAN WORLD
(from 753 B.C. to 363 A.D.)

The Kingdom

753	Romulus (Quirinus)
716	Numa Pompilius
673	Tullus Hostilius
640	Ancus Marcius
616	L. Tarquinius Priscus
578	Servius Tullius
534	L. Tarquinius Superbus

The Republic

509	Consulate established
509	Quaestorship instituted
498	Dictatorship introduced
494	Plebeian Tribunate created
494	Plebeian Aedileship created
444	Consular Tribunate organized
435	Censorship instituted
366	Praetorship established
366	Curule Aedileship created
362	Military Tribunate elected
326	Proconsulate introduced
311	Naval Duumvirate elected
217	Dictatorship of Fabius Maximus
133	Tribunate of Tiberius Gracchus
123	Tribunate of Gaius Gracchus
82	Dictatorship of Sulla
60	First Triumvirate formed (Caesar, Pompeius, Crassus)
46	Dictatorship of Caesar
43	Second Triumvirate formed (Octavianus, Antonius, Lepidus)

The Empire

27	Augustus (Galus Julius Caesar Octavianus)
14	Tiberius I
37	Gaius Caesar (Caligula)
41	Claudius I
54	Nero
68	Galba
69	Galba; Otho, Vitellius
69	Vespasianus
79	Titus
81	Domitianus

96	Nerva
98	Trajanus
117	Hadrianus
138	Antoninus Pius
161	Marcus Aurelius and Lucius Verus
169	Marcus Aurelius (alone)
180	Commodus
193	Pertinax; Julianus I
193	Septimius Severus
211	Caracalla and Geta
212	Caracalla (alone)
217	Macrinus
218	Elagabalus (Heliogabalus)
222	Alexander Severus
235	Maximinus I (the Thracian)
238	Gordianus I and Gordianus II; Pupienus and Balbinus
238	Gordianus III
244	Philippus (the Arabian)
249	Decius
251	Gallus and Volusianus
253	Aemilianus
253	Valerianus and Gallienus
258	Gallienus (alone)
268	Claudius II (the Goth)
270	Quintillus
270	Aurelianus
275	Tacitus
276	Florianus
276	Probus
282	Carus
283	Carinus and Numerianus
284	Diocletianus
286	Diocletianus and Maximianus
305	Galerius and Constantius I
306	Galerius, Maximinus II, Severus I
307	Galerius, Maximinus II, Constantinus I, Licinius, Maxentius
311	Maximinus II, Constantinus I, Licinius, Maxentius
314	Maximinus II, Constantinus I, Licinius
314	Constantinus I and Licinius
324	Constantinus I (the Great)
337	Constantinus II, Constans I, Constantius II
340	Constantius II and Constans I
361	Julianus II (the Apostate)
363	Jovianus

Note: In 364 the Empire was divided between the brothers Valentinian (in the West) and Valens (East).

MAJOR PLACE NAMES OF ROMAN BRITAIN

Andover	Levcomagus	Gloucester	Glevum
Bath	Aquae Sulis	Ilchester	Lindinus
Cambridge	Durolipons	Leicester	Ratae Coritanorum
Caernarvon	Segontium	Lincoln	Lindum
Canterbury	Durovernum	London	Londinium
Carlisle	Luguvalium	Manchester	Mamucium
Carmarthen	Moridunum	Northwich	Condate
Catterick	Cataractonium	Pevensey	Anderita
Chelmsford	Caesaromagus	Richborough	Rutupiae
Chester	Deva	Rochester	Durobrivae
Chichester	Noviomagus Regnensium	St. Albans	Verulamium
Cirencester	Corinium Dobunnorum	Silchester	Calleva Atrebatum
Colchester	Camulodunum	South Shields	Caer Urfa
Doncaster	Danum	Towcester	Lactodorum
Dorchester	Durnovaria	Wight. I. of	Vectis
Dover	Portus Dubris	Winchester	Venta Belgarum
Dunstable	Durocobrivae	Wroxeter	Viroconium Cornoviorum
Exeter	Isca Dumnoniorum	York	Eboracum

THE NOBEL PRIZES

The Background

The Nobel Foundation was established at the beginning of the century to give effect to the wishes expressed by Alfred Nobel in his will. Alfred B Nobel (1833–96) was the inventor of dynamite and bequeathed $9,000,000 to the Foundation. The award of a Nobel Prize is accepted as the highest form of international recognition in the fields in which it is given: physics, chemistry, medicine, literature, peace and, since 1969, economics. The Royal Academy of Science in Sweden picks the prizewinners in physics, chemistry and economics. The medical faculty of Stockholm's Caroline Institute chooses the winner in the field of physiology or medicine. The Swedish Academy of Literature names the winner in the field of literature. The Norwegian parliament elects a committee of five persons to select the winner of the prize for peace. Currently the value of the prize is around £687,000.

CHEMISTRY

This was first awarded in 1901. The following Britons received the award prior to 1945:

1904	Sir William Ramsay
1908	Ernest Rutherford
1921	Frederick Soddy
1922	Francis W. Aston
1928	Arthur Harden (with Hans von Eulor-Chelpin (Swe, German-born)
1937	Walter N. Haworth (with Paul Karrer (Swi, Russian-born)

Winners since 1945 have been:

1945	Artturi I. Virtanen (Fin)
1946	James B. Sumner (USA)
	John H. Northrop (USA)
	Wendell M. Stanley (USA)
1947	Sir Robert Robinson (GB)
1948	Arne W. K. Tiselius (Swe)
1949	William F. Giauque (USA)
1950	Kurt Alder (Ger)
	Otto P. H. Diels (GDR)
1951	Edwin M. McMillan (USA)
	Glenn T. Seaborg (USA)
1952	Archer J. P. Martin (GB)
	Richard L. M. Synge (GB)
1953	Hermann Staudinger (GDR)
1954	Linus C. Pauling (USA)
1955	Vincent du Vigneaud (USA)
1956	Sir Cyril N. Hinshelwood (GB)
	Nikolai N. Semenov (USSR)
1957	Lord Todd (Alexander R. Todd) (GB)
1958	Frederick Sanger (GB)
1959	Jaroslav Heyrovsky (Cze)
1960	Willard F. Libby (USA)
1961	Melvin Calvin (USA)
1962	Sir John C. Kendrew (GB)
	Max F. Perutz (GB, Austrian-born)
1963	Giulio Natta (Ita)
	Karl Ziegler (GDR)
1964	Dorothy Crowfoot Hodgkin (GB)
1965	Robert B. Woodward (USA)
1966	Robert S. Mulliken (USA)
1967	Manfred Eigen (Ger)
	Ronald G. W. Norrish (GB)
	Sir George Porter (GB)
1968	Lars Onsager (USA, Norwegian-born)
1969	Derek H. R. Barton (GB)
	Odd Hassel (Nor)
1970	Luis F. Leloir (Arg, French-born)
1971	Gerhard Herzberg (Can, German-born)
1972	Christian B. Anfinsen (USA)
	Stanford Moore (USA)
	William H. Stein (USA)
1973	Ernest Otto Fischer (GDR)
	Geoffrey Wilkinson (GB)
1974	Paul J. Flory (USA)
1975	John W. Cornforth (GB)
	Vladimir Prelog (Swi, Yugoslavian-born)
1976	William N. Lipscomb Jr (USA)
1977	Ilya Prigogine (Bel, Russian-born)
1978	Peter Mitchell (GB)
1979	Herbert C. Brown (USA)
	Gerry Wittig (GDR)

1980	Frederick Sanger (GB)
	Paul Berg (USA)
	Walter Gilbert (USA)
1981	Roald Hoffman (USA)
	Kenichi Fukui (Jap)
1982	Aaron Klug (GB)
1983	Henry Taube (USA)
1984	R. Bruce Merrifield (USA)
1985	Herbert A. Hauptman (USA)
	Jerome Karle (USA)
1986	Dudley Herschbach (USA)
	Yuan T. Lee (USA)
	John C. Polanyi (Can)
1987	Donald J. Cram (USA)
	Charles J. Paderson (USA)
	Jean-Marie Lehn (Fra)
1988	Johan Deisenhofer (Ger)
	Robert Huber (Ger)
	Hartmut Michel (Ger)
1989	Thomas R. Cech (USA)
	Sidney Altman (USA)
1990	Elias J. Corey (USA)
1991	Richard R. Ernst (Swi)
1992	Rudolph Marcus (USA, Canadian-born)
1993	Michael Smith (Can, British-born)
	Kary Mullis (USA)
1994	George A. Olah (USA)
1995	Paul Crutzen (Hol)
	Mario Molina (USA)
	Sherwood Rowland (USA)
1996	Harold Croto (GB)
	Robert Curl (USA)
	Richard Smalley (USA)
1997	John Walker (GB)
	Paul Boyer (USA)
	Jens Skou (Den)
1998	John Pople (USA, UK born)
	Walter Kohn (USA)

ECONOMICS

The Nobel Prize for Economics is the most recent of the Nobel Prizes, having been established in 1969.

Winners have been:

1969	Ragnar Frisch (Nor)
	Jan Tinbergen (Hol)
1970	Paul A. Samuelson (USA)
1971	Simon Kuznets (USA)
1972	Kenneth J. Arrow (USA)
	Sir John R. Hicks (GB)
1973	Vassily Leontief (USA) (Russian-born)
1974	Gunnar Myrdal (Swe)
	Friedrich A. von Hayek (Aut)
1975	Leonid V. Kantorovich (USSR)
	Tjalling C. Koopmans (USA) (Dutch-born)
1976	Milton Friedman (USA)
1977	Bertil Ohlin (Swe)
	James Edward Meade (GB)
1978	Herbert Simon (USA)
1979	Sir Arthur Lewis (GB) (St Lucien-born)
	Theodore W. Schultz (USA)
1980	Lawrence Klein (USA)
1981	James Tobin (USA)
1982	George J. Stigler (USA)
1983	Gerard Debreu (USA)
1984	Sir Richard Stone (GB)
1985	Franco Modigliani (USA, Italian-born)
1986	James M. Buchanan (USA)
1987	Robert M. Solow (USA)
1988	Maurice Allais (Fra)
1989	Trygve Haavelmo (Nor)
1990	Harry M. Markowitz (USA)
	William F. Sharpe (USA)
	Merton H. Miller (USA)
1991	Ronald H. Coase (GB/USA)
1992	Gary Becker (USA)
1993	Robert W. Fogel (USA)
	Douglass C. North (USA)
1994	John Nash (USA)
	Reinhard Selter (Ger)
	John Harsanyi (USA)

1995	Robert E. Lucas (USA)
1996	James Mirrlees (GB) / William Vickrey (Can)
1997	Robert Merton (USA) / Myron Scholes (USA)
1998	Amartya Sen (Ind)

LITERATURE

Winners since 1945:

1945	Gabriela Mistral (Chi)
1946	Hermann Hesse (Swi) (German-born)
1947	André Gide (Fra)
1948	T. S. Eliot (GB) (USA-born)
1949	William Faulkner (USA)
1950	Bertrand Russell (GB)
1951	Par F. Lagerkvist (Swe)
1952	François Mauriac (Fra)
1953	Sir Winston Churchill (GB)
1954	Ernest Hemingway (USA)
1955	Halldor K. Laxness (Ice)
1956	Juan Ramon Jimenez (PR) (Spanish-born)
1957	Albert Camus (Fra)
1958	Boris L. Pasternak (USSR) Prize declined
1959	Salvatore Quasimodo (Ita)
1960	Saint-John Perse (Fra)
1961	Ivo Andric (Yug)
1962	John Steinbeck (USA)
1963	George Seferis (Gre)
1964	Jean-Paul Sartre (Fra) Prize declined
1965	Mikhail Sholokhov (USSR)
1966	Shmuel Yosef Agnon (Isr) (Austrian-born) / Nelly Sachs (Swe) (German-born)
1967	Miguel Angel Asturias (Gua)
1968	Yasunari Kawabata (Jap)
1969	Samuel Beckett (Ire)
1970	Aleksandr. I. Solzhenitsyn (USSR)
1971	Pablo Neruda (Chi)
1972	Heinrich Boll (Ger)
1973	Patrick White (Aus)
1974	Eyvind Johnson (Swe) / Harry Edmund Martinson (Swe)
1975	Eugenio Montale (Ita)
1976	Saul Bellow (USA)
1977	Vicente Aleixandre (Spa)
1978	Isaac Bashevis Singer (USA)
1979	Odysseus Elytis (Odysseus Alepoudelis) (Gre)
1980	Czeslaw Milosz (Pol)
1981	Elias Canetti (GB, Bulgarian-born)
1982	Gabriel Garcia Márquez (Mex, Colombian-born)
1983	William Golding (GB)
1984	Jaroslav Seifert (Cze)
1985	Claude Simon (Fra)
1986	Wole Soyinka (Nig)
1987	Joseph Brodsky (USA, USSR-born)
1988	Naguib Mahfouz (Egy)
1989	Camilo José Cela (Spa)
1990	Octavio Paz (Mex)
1991	Nadine Gordimer (SAf)
1992	Derek Walcott (StL)
1993	Toni Morrison (USA)
1994	Kenzaburo Oe (Jap)
1995	Seamus Heaney (Ire)
1996	Wislawa Szymborska (Pol)
1997	Dario Fo (Ita)
1998	José Saramago (Por)

MEDICINE

The Nobel Prize for Medicine dates from 1901. Up to 1945 the following British persons won the Nobel Prize:

1902	Sir Ronald Ross
1922	Archibald V. Hill
1929	Sir Frederick G. Hopkins (joint)
1932	Edgar D. Adrian / Sir Charles S. Sherrington
1936	Sir Henry H. Dale

Winners since 1945 have been:

1945	Sir Alexander Fleming (GB) / Ernst B. Chain (GB, German-born) / Sir Howard W. Florey (GB, Australian-born)
1946	Hermann J. Muller (USA)
1947	Carl F. Cori (USA, Czech-born) / Gerty T. Cori (USA, Czech-born) / Bernardo A. Houssay (Arg)
1948	Paul H. Müller (Swi)
1949	Walter R. Hess (Swi) / Antonio Moniz (Por)
1950	Philip S. Hench (USA) / Edward C. Kendall (USA) / Tadeus Reichstein (Swi, Polish-born)
1951	Max Theiler (USA, S. African-born)
1952	Selman A. Waksman (USA)
1953	Hans A. Krebs (GB, German-born) / Fritz A. Lipmann (USA, German-born)
1954	John F. Enders (USA) / Frederick C. Robbins (USA) / Thomas H. Weller (USA)
1955	Alex H. T. Theorell (Swe)
1956	André F. Cournand (USA, French-born) / Werner Forssmann (Ger) / Dickinson W. Richards Jr (USA)
1957	Daniel Bovet (Ita, Swiss-born)
1958	George W. Beadle (USA) / Edward L. Tatum (USA) / Joshua Lederberg (USA)
1959	Arthur Kornberg (USA) / Severo Ochoa (USA, Spanish-born)
1960	Sir F. Macfarlane Burnet (Aus) / Peter B. Medawar (GB, Brazilian-born)
1961	Georg von Békésy (USA, Hungarian-born)
1962	Francis H. C. Crick (GB) / James D. Watson (USA) / Maurice H. F. Wilkins (GB)
1963	Sir John C. Eccles (Aus) / Alan L. Hodgkin (GB) / Andrew F. Huxley (GB)
1964	Konrad E. Bloch (USA) / Feodor Lynen (Ger)
1965	François Jacob (Fra) / André Lwoff (Fra) / Jacques Monod (Fra)
1966	Charles B. Huggins (USA) / Francis Peyton Rous (USA)
1967	Ragnar Granit (Swe, Finnish-born) / Haldan Keffer Hartline (USA) / George Wald (USA)
1968	Robert W. Holley (USA) / Har Gobind Khorana (USA, Indian-born) / Marshall W. Nirenberg (USA)
1969	Max Delbrück (USA, German-born) / Alfred D. Hershey (USA) / Salvador D. Luria (USA. Italian-born)
1970	Julius Axelrod (USA) / Ulf von Euler (Swe) / Bernard Katz (GB)
1971	Earl W. Sutherland Jr (USA)
1972	Gerald M. Edelman (USA) / Rodney Porter (GB)
1973	Karl von Frisch (Aut) / Konrad Lorenz (Aut) / Nikolaas Tinbergen (GB, Dutch-born)
1974	Albert Claude (USA, Luxembourg-born) / Christian René de Duve (Bel) / George Emil Palade (USA, Romanian-born)
1975	David Baltimore (USA) / Howard Martin Temin (USA) / Renato Dulbecco (USA, Italian-born)
1976	Baruch S. Blumberg (USA) / D. Carleton Gajdusek (USA)
1977	Rosalyn S. Yalow (USA) / Roger C. L. Guillemin (USA, French-born) / Andrew V. Schally (USA)
1978	Werner Arber (Swi) / Daniel Nathans (USA) / Hamilton Smith (USA)
1979	Dr Hounsfield (GB) / Allan Cormack (USA)
1980	Baruy Benacerraf (Ven) / Jean Dausset (Fra) / George Snell (USA)
1981	Roger W. Sperry (USA) / David H. Hubel (USA) / Torsten N. Wiesel (Swe)
1982	Sune Bergstrom (Swe) / Bengt Samuelsson (Swe) / John R. Vane (GB)
1983	Barbara McClintock (USA)
1984	Cesar Milstein (GB, Argentinian-born) / Georges J. F. Kohler (Ger) / Niels K. Jerne (GB, Danish-born)
1985	Michael S. Brown (USA) / Joseph L. Goldstein (USA)
1986	Rita Levi-Montalcini (USA, Italian-born) / Stanley Cohen (USA)

1987	Susumu Tonegawa (Jap)
1988	Gertrude B. Elion (USA) George H. Hitchings (USA) Sir James Black (GB)
1989	J. Michael Bishop (USA) Harold E. Varmus (USA)
1990	Joseph E. Murray (USA) E. Donnall Thomas (USA)
1991	Edwin Neher (Ger) Bert Sakmann (Ger)
1992	Edwin Krebs (USA) Edmond Fischer (USA)
1993	Richard Roberts (GB) Phillip Sharp (USA)
1994	Alfred G. Gilman (USA) Martin Rodbell (USA)
1995	Edward B. Lewis (USA) Christiane Nüesslein-Volhard (Ger) Eric F. Wieschaus (USA)
1996	Peter Doherty (Aus) Rolf Zinkernagel (Swi)
1997	Stanley Prusiner (USA)
1998	Robert Furchgott (USA) Louis Ignarro (USA) Ferid Murad (USA)

PEACE

The first Nobel Prize was awarded in 1901, five years after the death of Alfred Nobel, to Jean Henri Dunant, the Swiss founder of the Red Cross, and Frederic Passy, a French advocate of international arbitration. The awards since 1945 have been as follows:

1945	Cordell Hull (USA)
1946	Emily G. Batch (USA) John R. Mott (USA)
1947	Friends Service Council (GB) American Friends Service Committee (USA)
1948	*no award*
1949	Lord John Boyd Orr (GB)
1950	Ralph J. Bunche (USA)
1951	Léon Jouhaux (Fra)
1952	Albert Schweitzer (Fra, German-born)
1953	George C. Marshall (USA)
1954	Office of the UN High Commission for Refugees
1955	*no award*
1956	*no award*
1957	Lester B. Pearson (Can)
1958	Georges Pire (Bel)
1959	Philip J. Noel-Baker (GB)
1960	Albert J. Luthuli (SAf)
1961	Dag Hammarskjöld (Swe) (posthumous)
1962	Linus C. Pauling (USA)
1963	International Committee of the Red Cross Red Cross Societies League
1964	Martin Luther King Jr (USA)
1965	United Nations Childrens Fund (UNICEF)
1966	*no award*
1967	*no award*
1968	René Cassin (Fra)
1969	International Labour Organization (ILO)
1970	Norman E. Borlaug (USA)
1971	Willy Brandt (FRG)
1972	*no award*
1973	Henry A. Kissinger (USA, German-born) Le Duc Tho (NViet)
1974	Eisaku Salo (Jap) Sean MacBride (Ire)
1975	Andrei D. Sakharov (USSR)
1976	Betty Williams (GB) Mairead Corrigan (GB)
1977	Amnesty International
1978	Anwar el Sadat (Egy) Menachem Begin (Isr)
1979	Mother Teresa of Calcutta (Alb)
1980	Adolfo Pérez Esquivel (Arg)
1981	Office of the UN High Commission for Refugees
1982	Alva Myrtal (Swe) Alfonso Garcia Robles (Mex)
1983	Lech Walesa (Pol)
1984	Archbishop Desmond Tutu (SAf)
1985	International Physicians for the Prevention of Nuclear War

1986	Elie Wiesel (USA, Romanian-born)
1987	President Oscar Arias Sanchez (CoR)
1988	UN Peacekeeping Forces
1989	Dalai Lama (Tib)
1990	Mikhail Gorbachev (USSR)
1991	Aung San Suu Kyi (Mya)
1992	Rigoberta Menchu (Gua)
1993	F. W. de Klerk (SAf) Nelson Mandela (SAf)
1994	Yitzak Rabin (Isr) Yasser Arafat (Pal) Shimon Peres (Isr)
1995	Joseph Rotblat (GB, Polish-born) Pugwash Conferences
1996	Carlos Felipe Belo (Timor) José Ramos-Horta (Timor)
1997	International Campaign to Ban Landmines Jody Williams (USA)
1998	John Hume (UK) David Trimble (UK)

PHYSICS

The first Nobel Prize for Physics was awarded in 1901 to Wilhelm C. Roentgen of Germany. Among the British recipients to be awarded the honour before 1945 were:

1904	Lord Rayleigh (John W. Strutt)
1906	Sir Joseph John Thomson
1915	Sir William H. Bragg
1917	Charles G. Barkla
1927	Charles T. R. Wilson (*joint award*)
1928	Owen W. Richardson
1933	Paul A. M. Dirac (*joint award*)
1935	Sir James Chadwick
1937	George P. Thomson (*joint award*)

The full list of winners since 1945 is:

1945	Wolfgang Pauli (USA)
1946	Percy Williams Bridgman (USA)
1947	Sir Edward V. Appleton (GB)
1948	Patrick M. S. Blackett (GB)
1949	Hideki Yukawa (Jap)
1950	Cecil F. Powell (GB)
1951	Sir John D. Cockcroft (GB) Ernest T. S. Walton (Ire)
1952	Felix Bloch (USA, Swiss-born) Edward Purcell (USA)
1953	Fritz Zernike (Hol)
1954	Max Born (GB, German-born) Walther Bothe (FRG)
1955	Polykarp Kusch (USA, German-born) Willis E. Lamb (USA)
1956	John Bardeen (USA) Walter H. Brattain (USA) William Shockley (USA)
1957	Tsung-Dao Lee (USA, Chinese-born) Chen Ning Yang (USA, Chinese-born)
1958	Paval A. Cherenkov (USSR) Ilya M. Frank (USSR) Igor J. Tamm (USSR)
1959	Owen Chamberlain (USA) Emilio G. Segrè (USA, Italian-born)
1960	Donald A. Glaser (USA)
1961	Robert Hofstadter (USA) Rudolf L. Mössbauer (FRG)
1962	Lev D. Landau (USSR)
1963	Maria Goeppert-Mayer (USA) J. Hans D. Jensen (FRG) Eugene P. Wigner (USA)
1964	Nikolai G. Basov (USSR) Aleksandr M. Prokhorov (USSR) Charles H. Townes (USA)
1965	Richard P. Feynman (USA) Julian S. Schwinger (USA) Sin-itiro Tomonaga (Jap)
1966	Alfred Kastler (Fra)
1967	Hans A. Bethe (USA, German-born)
1968	Luis W. Alvarez (USA)
1969	Murray Gell-Man (USA)
1970	Hannes O. G. Alfven (Swe) Louis E. F. Néel (Fra)
1971	Dennis Gabor (GB, Hungarian-born)

1972	John Bardeen (USA)	1985	Klaus von Klitzing (Ger)
	Leon N. Cooper (USA)		Erns Ruska (Ger)
	John R. Schrieffer (USA)	1986	Gerd Binnig (Ger)
1973	Ivar Giaever (USA, Norwegian-born)		Heinrich Rohrer (Swi)
	Leo Esaki (Jap)	1987	Georg Bednorz (Ger)
	Brian D. Josephson (GB)		Alex Müller (Swi)
1974	Antony Hewish (GB)	1988	Leon M. Lederman (USA)
	Sir Martin Ryle (GB)		Melvin Schwartz (USA)
1975	L. James Rainwater (USA)		Jack Steinberger (Ger)
	Aage Bohr (Den)	1989	Norman Ramsey (USA)
	Ben Roy Mottelson (Den, USA-born)		Hans Dehmelt (USA)
1976	Burton Richter (USA)		Wolfgang Paul (Ger)
	Samuel C. C. Ting (USA)	1990	Jerome Friedman (USA)
1977	John H. Van Vleck (USA)		Henry Kendall (USA)
	Philip W. Anderson (USA)		Richard Taylor (Can)
	Sir Nevill F. Mott (GB)	1991	Pierre-Giles de Gennes (Fra)
1978	Piotr Leontevich Kapitsa (USSR)	1992	Georges Charpak (Fra)
	Arno A. Penzias (USA, German-born)	1993	Russell Huise (USA)
	Robert W. Wilson (USA)		Joseph Taylor (USA)
1979	Abdus Salam (GB)	1994	Bertram N. Brockhouse (Can)
	Sheldon Glashow (USA)		Clifford G. Shull (USA)
	Steven Weinberg (USA)	1995	Frederick Reines (USA)
1980	James W. Cronin (USA)	1996	Douglas Osheroff (USA)
	Val Fitch (USA)		David Lee (USA)
1981	Nicolaas Bloemergern (USA)		Robert Richardson (USA)
	Arthur Schawlow (USA)	1997	Claude Cohen-Tannoudji (Fra)
1982	Kenneth Wilson (USA)		Steven Chu (USA)
1983	Subrahmanyan Chandrasekhar (USA)		William Phillips (USA)
	William Fowler (USA)	1998	Robert Laughlin (USA)
1984	Carlo Rubbia (Ita)		Daniel Tsui (USA)
	Simon van der Meer (Hol)		Horst Störmer (Ger)

CALENDAR 2000

RELIGIOUS CALENDARS

Epiphany	6 Jan	Low Sunday	30 Apr
Septuagesima Sunday	20 Feb	Rogation Sunday	28 May
Quinquagesima Sunday	5 Mar	Ascension Day—Holy Thursday	1 June
Ash Wednesday	8 Mar	Whit Sunday—Pentecost	11 June
Quadragesima Sunday	12 Mar	Trinity Sunday	18 June
Fourth Sunday in Lent—	2 Apr	Corpus Christi	22 June
Mothering Sunday			
Palm Sunday	16 April	First Sunday in Advent	3 Dec
Good Friday	21 Apr	Christmas Day (Monday)	25 Dec
Easter Day	23 Apr		
First Day of Passover (Pesach)	20 Apr	Day of Atonement (Yom Kippur)	9 Oct
Feast of Weeks (Shavuot)	9 June	First Day of Tabernacles (Succoth)	14 Oct
Jewish New Year	5761 30 Sept		
(Rosh Hashanah)			
Islamic New Year	1421 6 Apr	First day of Ramadân	28 Nov

All Jewish and Islamic dates above are tabular dates, which begin at sunset on the previous evening and end at sunset on the date tabulated. In practice, the dates of Islamic fasts and festivals are determined by an actual sighting of the appropriate new Moon.

CIVIL CALENDAR—UNITED KINGDOM

Accession of Queen Elizabeth II	6 Feb	Coronation Day	2 June
St David (Wales)	1 Mar	The Queen's Official Birthday	10 June
Commonwealth Day	13 Mar	Birthday of Prince Philip,	10 June
		Duke of Edinburgh	
St Patrick (Ireland)	17 Mar	Remembrance Sunday	12 Nov
Birthday of Queen Elizabeth II	21 Apr	Birthday of the Prince of Wales	14 Nov
St George (England)	23 Apr	St Andrew (Scotland)	30 Nov

INDEX

Each section has a letter and, where appropriate, the column is given in brackets after the page number, *e.g.*, F8(1), G25(2). Some of the sections are alphabetically arranged and index themselves. Their contents are not included here except where it is anticipated some special difficulty may arise. The sections "Medical Matters" and "The World of Music" have each a separate index and glossary.

C

D

E

F

U

V

W

X

Y

Z